Style and usage labels used in the dictionary

abbreviation	a shortened form of a word
approving	praising someone or something
Australian English	
child's word/expression	used by children
disapproving	used to express dislike or disagreement with someone or something
female	
figurative	used to express not the basic meaning of a word, but an imaginative one
formal	used in serious or official language or when trying to impress other people
humorous	used when you are trying to be funny
informal	used in ordinary speech (and writing) and not suitable for formal situations
Indian English	
Irish English	
legal	specialized language used in legal documents and in law courts
literary	formal and descriptive language used in literature
male	
Northern English	used in the north of England
not standard	commonly used but not following the rules of grammar
offensive	very rude and likely to offend people
old-fashioned	not used in modern English – you might find these words in books, used by older people, or used in order to be funny
old use	used a long time ago in other centuries
polite word/expression	a polite way of referring to something that has other ruder names
saying	a common phrase or sentence that gives advice, an opinion, etc.
Scottish English	
slang	extremely informal language, used mainly by a particular group
South African English	
specialized	used only by people in a particular subject such as doctors or scientists
trademark	the official name of a product
UK	British English
US	American English
written abbreviation	a shortened form of a word used in writing
A1 A2 B1 B2 C1 C2	These symbols show the *English Vocabulary Profile* level of a word, phrase, or meaning. A1 is the lowest level and C2 is the highest.

Parts of speech used in the dictionary

adj (adjective)
adv (adverb)
auxiliary verb
comparative
conjunction
determiner
exclamation
modal verb
noun
number
ordinal number
phrasal verb
predeterminer
prefix
preposition
pronoun
suffix
superlative
verb

Grammar labels used in the dictionary

[after noun]	adjective that only follows a noun
[after verb]	adjective that only follows a verb
[+ adv/prep]	verb that must be followed by an adverb or preposition
[as form of address]	word or phrase used when speaking or writing to someone
[before noun]	adjective that is placed only before a noun
[C]	countable noun
[I]	intransitive verb: does not take an object
[+ infinitive without to]	verb followed by an infinitive without **to**
[+ -ing verb]	followed by the **–ing** form of a verb
[L]	linking verb: followed by an adjective or noun
[not continuous]	verb not used in continuous tenses
[+ obj + to infinitive]	verb with an object followed by an infinitive with **to**
[+ obj + infinitive without to]	verb with an object followed by an infinitive without **to**
[+ obj + -ing verb]	verb with an object followed by the **–ing** form of another verb
[plural]	noun that can be used only in the plural
[+ question word]	verb with a question word
[S]	singular noun
[+ sing/pl verb]	noun that can be used with a singular or plural verb in British English
[+ speech]	verb used with direct speech
[T]	transitive verb: takes an object
[+ that]	verb used with **that**
[+ to infinitive]	followed by **to** and a verb in the infinitive
[+ two objects]	verb that has two objects
[U]	uncountable noun
[usually passive]	verb usually used in the passive

Cambridge Advanced Learner's Dictionary

Fourth Edition

Edited by
Colin McIntosh

CAMBRIDGE UNIVERSITY PRESS
Cambridge, New York, Melbourne, Madrid, Cape Town,
Singapore, São Paulo, Delhi, Mexico City

Cambridge University Press
The Edinburgh Building, Cambridge CB2 8RU, UK

www.cambridge.org
Information on this title: www.cambridge.org/9781107619500

First published 1995 as *Cambridge International Dictionary of English*
This edition first published 2013 as *Cambridge Advanced Learner's Dictionary*

Printed in India by Replika Press Pvt. Ltd

A catalogue record for this publication is available from the British Library

ISBN 978-1-107-035157 Hardback
ISBN 978-1-107-685499 Paperback
ISBN 978-1-107-674479 Hardback with CD-ROM
ISBN 978-1-107-619500 Paperback with CD-ROM

Contents

Acknowledgments

Editorial Team
Chief Editor
Colin McIntosh

Managing Editor
Sally Wehmeier

Project Manager
Anna Stevenson

Production Editor
Elizabeth Walter

Senior Development Editor
Helen Waterhouse

Editors
Rosalind Combley
Andrew Delahunty
Kate Mohideen
Lucy Hollingworth
Patrick Phillips
Miranda Steele
Laura Wedgeworth

Focus on Writing
Elizabeth Walter

Proofreading
Pat Bulhosen
Ann Kennedy Smith
Virginia Klein
Janice McNeillie
Glennis Pye
Helen Warren
Judith Willis
Kate Woodford

Global Publishing Manager
Paul Heacock

Advisers
Adviser for the print edition
Sally Wehmeier

Advisers for language pedagogy
Vânia Moraes
Francesca Moy

American English adviser
Wendalyn Nichols

Indian English adviser
Dr K. Narayana Chandran

South African English adviser
Joseph Seaton

English Vocabulary Profile
Chief Research Editor
Annette Capel

Project Manager
Julia Harrison

Research Editors
Carol-June Cassidy
Elizabeth Walter

Project Editor
Melissa Good

Cambridge International Corpus
Corpus Manager
Ann Fiddes

***Common Mistakes* notes**
Diane Nicholls

Systems
Reference systems manager
Dom Glennon

Database management
Daniel Perrett

Production and Design
Design
Boag Associates
Claire Parson

Typesetting
Data Standards Limited

Illustrations
Oxford Designers and Illustrators
Corinne Burrows
Ray Burrows
David Shenton

Photography
Trevor Clifford

Production
Andrew George

For the Third Edition
Senior Commissioning Editor
Elizabeth Walter

Commissioning Editor
Kate Woodford

Editor
Melissa Good

To the learner

In the few short years since the last edition of the *Cambridge Advanced Learner's Dictionary* was published, there has been a revolution in the way people communicate. The expansion of the internet, social media, electronic communication, and the integration of telecoms devices with the internet have all had an enormous impact on the way in which learners encounter English, as well as on the way dictionaries are used and what they are used for.

New words

The language has undergone change, particularly in the form of words and expressions related to new technologies and their uses. Hundreds of these new words have been added to the dictionary. (For example, try looking up these words: *autocomplete*, *cloudware*, *QR code*, *unfriend*.)

And of course new words have entered the language in fields other than technology. Just to mention a few, there have have been additions in the fields of media (*blogosphere*, *catch-up TV*, *pap*, *phone hacking*), fashion and lifestyle (*on-trend*, *spray tan*, *steampunk*), and society (*helicopter parent*, *megacity*, *Z-list*). Informal language changes rapidly; new arrivals include *eww*, *peeps*, and *zhuzh*.

New types of English

The growth of internet use has meant that distinctions between different varieties of English are far less watertight than they once were. When someone uses a search engine to access a website, the country of origin or type of English is not usually of high importance. Learners are therefore much more likely to experience different types of English from all over the world. For this reason, the fourth edition of the *Cambridge Advanced Learner's Dictionary* contains increased coverage of language from the US (*bump-start*, *double major*, *hydroplaning*), India (*crore*, *foreign-returned*), Australia (*hotel*, *lounge room*), and South Africa (*milliard*, *stoep*).

New ways of accessing the dictionary

At this moment you are reading a printed book, but it is likely that you also read English using other media, for example on the Web or using a mobile device or e-reader. The *Cambridge Advanced Learner's Dictionary* is available in a variety of different formats, to give you access to the dictionary in whichever situation you find yourself. These formats include online, CD-ROM, and mobile app.

Online

If you have an internet connection, the online dictionary, at *Cambridge Dictionaries Online*, is a convenient way to look up words when using your computer. You will also find extra help with your vocabulary learning here. You can find it at:

www.dictionary.cambridge.org

CD-ROM

Together with the printed dictionary you may have the CD-ROM. This offers you the maximum amount of information and ease of use, and without the need for an internet connection.

Extras on the CD include more entries and example sentences, spoken pronunciation, and a unique thesaurus feature, the *SMART-thesaurus*, which allows you to search for words that have a similar meaning or that belong to the same topic area.

Looking up a word is easy. You can find the word the you are looking for even if you do not know the correct spelling, and using the *QUICKfind* button you can find a word (and hear its pronunciation) simply by pointing at it using your mouse.

Mobile app

Using the mobile app, you can access the dictionary wherever you are in the world, hold a vast amount of information in one hand, and look up words and phrases in a fraction of a second.

You can find out more about the CALD mobile app by visiting *Cambridge Dictionaries Online*.

The dictionary for reference

Ease of access is not just for the electronic versions of the dictionary. With long entries it can be hard to find the exact information you are looking for. The new design of the printed dictionary will make it easier for you to find different parts of speech, idioms, and phrasal verbs, and the guidewords, printed in capital letters and in colour, will guide you towards the meaning you are looking for.

The dictionary for learning

Checking the dictionary for meanings and spellings may be what it is used for most, but you can get a lot more out of your dictionary.

In particular, the *Cambridge Advanced Learner's Dictionary* can help you to *learn* English.

English Vocabulary Profile

In the dictionary entries you will see the symbols A1, A2, B1, B2, etc. These symbols show you the words, meanings, and phrases that learners know at different levels, based on the Common European Framework of Reference (CEFR). A1 is the lowest level and C2 is the highest. You can use this information to decide which words you need to prioritize in your vocabulary learning.

Part of the English Profile Programme (a large research programme sponsored by the Council of Europe), the wordlists are based on extensive research using the *Cambridge Learner Corpus*, a collection of over 45 million words of English written by learners from all over the world. Combined with solid evidence of use in other sources, such as examination wordlists and classroom materials, this corpus confirms what learners can and cannot do at each level.

The dictionary for study

English is increasingly being used as a vehicle for the study of other subjects. You may be taking a business studies course in the US, or you may be in Sweden studying engineering – or planning to. In many cases, in English-speaking countries or not, you will need English for your studies.

For this edition of the dictionary we have added a new 30-page *Focus on Writing* section, which covers the essentials of writing for academic courses and for exams.

You will also find increased coverage of many fields of academic study, including applied linguistics and language teaching (*sociolect*, *fortis*, *CLIL*), bioscience and medicine (*genomics*, *circadian*, *norovirus*), economics and finance (*Keynesian*, *haircut*, *quantitative easing*), politics and international relations (*Tea Party*, *biosecurity*, *failed state*), and ecology and the environment (*carbon-zero*, *upcycling*, *vertical farming*).

As well as these specialized words, you will also find more high-level general academic vocabulary (*anonymized*, *societal*, *typology*), which are used in many different fields of study.

The dictionary for communicating

The *Cambridge Advanced Learner's Dictionary* helps you to communicate naturally, fluently, and correctly.

Natural English

One of the most important resources we have for getting information about how English works and what people actually say or write is the *Cambridge International Corpus*, a collection of over a billion and a half words of written and spoken language from a huge variety of sources. The corpus provides the evidence that the editors use when deciding what to say about words in the dictionary. It allows us to see which ways of saying things are more common, and helps us to write the example sentences which are such a useful model for learners to follow.

Fluent English

One of the best ways to sound fluent when speaking or writing is to use phrases to hang your ideas on. Ready-made phrases, such as *not as easy as it looks*, and collocations (words that go together), such as *a unique opportunity*, can be memorized and used when needed without having to construct your sentences word by word.

The example sentences in the entries are a good source of ready-made phrases. You will also notice that certain words in the examples are shown in bold type, for example, in the entry for **hurry**: *That's all right, there's no* ***great*** *hurry* and *Are you* ***in*** *a hurry?* These show common collocations that are worth learning as units.

The *Focus on Writing* section also provides a wealth of these phrases for you to use and adapt for your own writing.

Correct English

Cambridge also has an invaluable resource in the form of the *Cambridge Learner Corpus*, which contains over 45 million words of English written by learners. The CLC has been developed in partnership with Cambridge English Language Assessment, whose exams are taken by students all over the world. More than 23 million words of the CLC have been coded according to the mistakes learners make. We have looked at the most common mistakes made by advanced learners, and included 500 *Common Mistake* notes to help avoid them.

The Fourth Edition

This new edition of the *Cambridge Advanced Learner's* takes the dictionary to new places and new audiences. Getting there has involved hard work and dedication from the large team of specialists listed on page vii, to whom thanks are due. Thanks are also due to the community of millions of users around the world who use and love the dictionary, many of whom have given comments and advice that have informed the new edition.

Colin McIntosh

How to use the dictionary

1 Finding a word or phrase

Words at the beginning of entries are called **headwords**. Headwords are in alphabetical order.

A headword may have more than one part of speech. All parts of speech are listed at the beginning of the entry.

Idioms are shown at the end of the relevant part of speech. Idioms are listed at the first important word.

Phrasal verbs are shown after any ordinary verbs, or at the end of entries where there are no other verbs.

heap /hiːp/ noun; verb

▸noun [C] C2 an untidy pile or mass of things: *a heap of clothes/rubbish*

IDIOMS **the bottom of the heap** People who are at the bottom of the heap are poor and unsuccessful and have the lowest position in society. • **collapse/fall in a heap** to fall down heavily and lie on the ground without moving: *The woman staggered and collapsed in a heap.* • **a (whole) heap of sth** informal a lot of something: *I've got a whole heap of work to do.*

▸verb [T + adv/prep] to put things into a large untidy pile: *He heaped more food* ***onto*** *his plate.*

PHRASAL VERB **heap sth on sb** to give someone a lot of praise, criticism, etc.: *He deals well with all the criticism heaped on him.*

Words which are in the same **word family** as the headword, and which can easily be understood by knowing the headword, are shown at the end of entries.

harmless /ˈhɑːm.ləs/ US /ˈhɑːrm-/ adj B2 not able or not likely to cause harm: *Peter might look a bit fierce, but actually he's fairly harmless.* ◦ *There were those who found the joke offensive, but Johnson insisted it was just a bit of harmless* ***fun***. • **harmlessly** /-li/ adv • **harmlessness** /-nəs/ noun [U]

Compound words (two or more words used together as a single word) have their own entries, in alphabetical order.

ˈhair ˌgel noun [C or U] a thick liquid substance that is put in the hair to help the hair keep a particular shape or style

Sometimes a word in a compound has brackets around it. This shows that the meaning is the same if you use the word in brackets or not.

hansom (cab) /ˈhæn.səmˌkæb/ noun [C] a two-wheeled CARRIAGE pulled by a horse, used like a taxi in the past

If a word has more than one possible spelling, this is shown at the headword.

Halloween (also **Hallowe'en**) /ˌhæl.əʊˈiːn/ US /-oʊ-/ noun [C or U] the night of 31 October when children dress in special clothes and people try to frighten each other

Other alternative forms are shown in brackets.

ˌhome ˈrun noun [C] (informal **homer**) US a point scored in baseball by hitting the ball so far that you have time to run all the way round the four corners of the playing field before it is returned

Some words include *the* before the headword, to show that they are always used in this form. They are found in the alphabetical order of the second word.

the heebie-jeebies /ˌhiː.biˈdʒiː.biz/ noun [plural] informal strong feelings of fear or worry: *Don't start talking about ghosts – they* ***give*** *me the heebie-jeebies.*

2 Finding and understanding the right meaning

Numbers show the different meanings of a headword.

hallowed /ˈhæl.əʊd/ (US) /-oʊd/ **adj** **1** very respected and praised because of great importance or great age: *hallowed icons such as Marilyn Monroe and James Dean* **2** holy: *Can atheists be buried in hallowed ground?*

Where headwords have many meanings, or very different meanings, **guidewords** help you find the meaning you need. There can be more than one meaning belonging to a guideword. Entries in this dictionary are ordered by the frequency of the first meaning in each guideword group.

If a meaning of a word is always used in a particular **phrase**, but it is not an idiom, that phrase is shown at the beginning of the meaning.

highly /ˈhaɪ.li/ **adv** **ABOVE AVERAGE** ▷ **1** (B2) very, to a large degree, or at a high level: *a highly* ***paid*** *job* ◦ *a highly profitable line of products* ◦ *For our country to remain competitive, we need a highly skilled, highly educated workforce.* **2 think/speak highly of sb** (C2) to admire/say admiring things about someone: *He's very highly thought of within the company.* **IMPORTANT** ▷ **3** in an important or INFLUENTIAL (= having a lot of influence) position: *According to one highly* ***placed*** *source, the prime minister had threatened to resign over this issue.*

Definitions are written using words that learners of English are likely to know. If we have to use a word that is not on the list, it is in SMALL CAPITALS.

Where it is helpful, a short explanation is added after these words.

haploid /ˈhæp.lɔɪd/ **adj** having a single set of CHROMOSOMES (= structures containing chemical patterns that control what a plant or animal is like) that comes from one parent only: *a haploid cell* ◦ *Sex cells such as eggs and sperm are haploid.* → Compare **diploid**

3 Using words and phrases correctly

Labels in square brackets give you **grammar information**. These labels are explained inside the front cover of the dictionary.

When grammar information is shown before numbered meanings, it is true for all the meanings of the word.

Common grammar patterns are given next to examples that show their use.

When grammar information is shown after a sense number, it is only true for that sense.

haste /heɪst/ **noun** [U] disapproving (too much) speed: *Unfortunately the report was prepared* ***in*** *haste and contained several inaccuracies.* ◦ [+ to infinitive] ***In*** *her haste* ***to*** *get up from the table, she knocked over a cup.*

IDIOMS **make haste** old-fashioned hurry up: *Make haste!* • **more haste, less speed** UK saying said to mean that if you try to do things too quickly, it will take you longer in the end

hasten /ˈheɪ.sᵊn/ **verb** formal **1** [T] to make something happen sooner or more quickly: *There is little doubt that poor medical treatment hastened her death.* ◦ *These recent poor results have hastened the manager's departure.* **2** [+ to infinitive] If you hasten to do something, you quickly do it: *The president hastened to reassure his people that he was in perfect health.* **3** [+ to infinitive] If you hasten to say something, you want to make it clear: *It was an unfortunate decision and I hasten* ***to*** *say it had nothing to do with me.* ◦ *'People round here dress so badly – except you, Justin,' she hastened* ***to*** *add.*

Plural forms, verb forms, and comparatives and superlatives are shown if they are irregular. If you have the CD of this dictionary, you can see all the inflections of every verb.

halo /ˈheɪ.ləʊ/ (US) /-loʊ/ **noun** (plural **haloes** or **halos**) **1** [C] a ring of light around the head of a holy person in a religious drawing or painting **2** [C usually singular] a bright circle of light around something, or something that looks like this: *the halo around the moon* ◦ *a halo of blonde curls*

Thousands of **example sentences** adapted from the *Cambridge International Corpus* show you how to use words naturally.

heavily /ˈhev.ɪ.li/ adv TO A GREAT DEGREE ▷ **1** B1 to a great degree: *The terrorists are heavily armed.* ◦ *The compound is heavily guarded.* ◦ *She's heavily involved in the project.* WEIGHING A LOT ▷ **2** in a way which needs a lot of effort to move or lift: *The news she had received **weighed** heavily **on** her (= worried her).* SOLID ▷ **3** in a strong, thick, or solid way: *He's a heavily **built** (= large and strong) man.*

IDIOM **be heavily into sth** informal to be very interested in and involved with something: *When I was younger I was heavily into politics.*

Bold words in examples are 'word partners', also known as **collocations**. These are words that are used very often with words you are looking up. If you learn these word partners, your English will sound more natural.

Many common words have ***Word partners*** boxes, which show the most useful partners for that word.

Word partners for **heat noun**

feel/generate/give out/withstand heat • *great/ intense/searing* heat • a *high/low* heat

4 Other useful information

Labels tell you about how a word is used, for example if it is formal or informal. All these labels are explained inside the front cover of the dictionary.

heedless /ˈhiːd.ləs/ **adj** formal not giving attention to a risk or possible difficulty: *Heedless destruction of the rainforests is contributing to global warming.* ◦ *Journalists had insisted on getting to the front line of the battle, heedless **of** the risks.* • **heedlessly** /-li/ **adv**

If a word or meaning of a word is used only in British English or only in American English, this is shown with the labels UK or US.

ˈhot ˌbutton noun [C] US informal a subject that is important to people and about which they have strong opinions: *Gender issues have become something of a hot button.* ◦ *Immigration has become a hot button **issue**.*

If a word has a different spelling in American and British English, this is shown.

honourable UK (US **honorable**) /ˈɒn.ər.ə.bl/ US /ˈɑː.nɚ-/ **adj** honest and fair, or deserving praise and respect: *an honourable person* • **honourably** (US **honorably**) /-ə.bli/ **adv**

If the word you have looked up is used only in British English, and a different word is used in American English, this is shown.

ˈhair ˌslide noun [C] UK (US **barrette**) a small, decorative piece of plastic, metal, or wood that a woman or girl wears in her hair, often to stop it falling in front of her face

Common mistake boxes show you mistakes that learners of English often make, and help you avoid them. These notes are based on the *Cambridge Learner Corpus*.

! Common mistake: **home**

Warning: to talk about movement towards or away from someone's own home, you do not need a preposition.

Don't say 'go/come/arrive/leave to/at home', say **go/ come/arrive/leave home**:

~~*When I arrived to home, I realized my bag was missing.*~~

When I arrived home, I realized my bag was missing.

To talk about someone moving towards or away from a home that is not their own, it is usual to use a preposition:

You are welcome to come to my home.

Other ways of saying... boxes give more interesting words to use for very common words.

> **Other ways of saying hungry**
>
> The adjective **ravenous** can be used to describe someone who is very hungry:
>
> *I'm **ravenous**; when's dinner ready?*
>
> Informal words which mean 'very hungry' are **famished** or **starving**:
>
> *I'm **famished**! I haven't eaten anything since this morning.*
>
> *Is there anything to eat? I'm **starving**!*
>
> The phrase **have a good appetite** can be used for someone who is often hungry and eats a lot of food:
>
> *Both my children **have** very **good appetites**.*

Cross references help you learn more vocabulary connected with a word.

> **hardback** /ˈhɑːd.bæk/ (US) /ˈhɑːrd-/ noun [C or U] (US also **hardcover**) a book that has a stiff cover: *His latest novel will be published **in** hardback later this month.* → Compare **paperback, softback**

If you have the CD of this dictionary, you can use the *SMARTthesaurus* to look up synonyms and related words for every meaning of every word in this dictionary.

5 Pronunciation

British and American pronunciations of a word are shown after the headword. These are written using the International Phonetic Alphabet (IPA). See inside the back cover of the dictionary for full information about the phonetic symbols.

> **harbinger** /ˈhɑː.bɪn.dʒəʳ/ (US) /ˈhɑːr.bɪn.dʒɚ/ noun [C] literary a person or thing that shows that something is going to happen soon, especially something bad: *a harbinger **of doom***

At entries for compounds, stress marks show you which part or parts you should stress when you say it. The full pronunciation for each word in the compound is shown at the entry for that word.

> **ˈhair ˌspray** noun [C or U] (UK also **ˈhair ˌlacquer**) a sticky liquid that is SPRAYED (= forced out in small drops) onto someone's hair to keep it in a particular shape

6 *English Vocabulary Profile* levels

These symbols show you the words, meanings, and phrases that learners know at different levels, based on the Common European Framework of Reference (CEFR). A1 is the lowest level and C2 is the highest. If no level is shown, this means that it is above C2 level. You can use this information to decide which words you need to prioritize in your vocabulary learning.

> **happily** /ˈhæp.ɪ.li/ adv PLEASED ▷ **1** B1 in a happy way: *He was happily **married** with two young children.* ◦ *She munched happily on her chocolate bar.* **2** B2 willingly: *I'd happily offer to help him if I thought it would make any difference.* LUCKY ▷ **3** C1 having a good or lucky result: *Happily, the weather remained fine throughout the afternoon.*

Numbers that are used as words

You will sometimes find these numbers used like ordinary words in English, especially in newspapers or on the internet. This page tells you what they mean and how they are pronounced.

$64,000 question /ˌsɪk.sti.fɔːˌθaʊ.zənd.dɒ.ləˈkwes.tʃən/ Ⓤⓢ /-fɔːrˌθaʊ.zənd.dɑː.lɚ-/ **noun** [C usually singular] (also ˌ**million-dollar** ˈ**question**) an important or difficult question on which a lot depends: *The $64,000 question is, can we repeat last year's success?*

0800 number /ˌəʊ.eɪtˈhʌn.drədˌnʌm.bəʳ/ Ⓤⓢ /ˌoʊ.eɪtˈhʌn.drədˌnʌm.bɚ/ **noun** [C] in the UK, a free phone number that begins with 0800, provided by companies or other organizations offering advice or information

0898 number /ˌəʊ.eɪtˈnaɪn.eɪtˌnʌm.bəʳ/ Ⓤⓢ /ˌoʊ.eɪtˈnaɪn.eɪtˌnʌm.bɚ/ **noun** [C] in the UK, an expensive phone number that begins with 0898 that is provided by companies offering services such as CHATLINES

101 /wʌn.əʊˈwʌn/ Ⓤⓢ /-oʊ-/ **adj** mainly US humorous showing the most basic knowledge about a subject: *You should know how to boil an egg – that's cooking 101.* ◦ *Helping people get to the polls is a basic lesson of politics 101.*

112 /wʌn.wʌnˈtuː/ the phone number used in Europe to call the emergency services (sometimes used in addition to national numbers)

12A /ˌtwelvˈeɪ/ in the UK, a symbol that marks a film that cannot be legally watched alone by children who are under twelve years old

15 /ˌfɪfˈtiːn/ in the UK, a symbol used to mark a film that cannot be legally watched by children who are under 15 years old

18 /ˌeɪˈtiːn/ in the UK, a symbol used to mark a film that cannot be legally watched by children who are under 18 years old

180 /ˌwʌnˈeɪ.ti/ Ⓤⓢ /-t̬i/ **noun** [C usually singular] US informal a sudden change from a particular opinion, decision, or plan to an opposite one: *Jack's **done** a 180 and agreed to come on the trip.*

2:1 /ˌtuːˈwʌn/ **noun** [C] (also ˌ**upper** ˈ**second**) a degree qualification from a British university that is below a first and above a 2:2

2:2 /ˌtuːˈtuː/ **noun** [C] (also ˌ**lower** ˈ**second**) a degree qualification from a British university that is below a 2:1 and above a third

20/20 vision /ˌtwen.tiˌtwen.tiˈvɪʒ.ən/ Ⓤⓢ /-t̬iˌtwen.t̬i-/ **noun** [S] the ability to see perfectly, without needing to wear glasses or CONTACT LENSES: *You're so lucky to **have** 20/20 vision, Dom.*

.22 /ˌpɔɪnt.tuːˈtuː/ **noun** [C] a type of gun that fires small bullets, used especially for hunting small animals

24/7 /ˌtwen.ti.fɔːˈsev.ən/ Ⓤⓢ /-t̬i.fɔːʳ-/ **adv, adj** informal 24 hours a day, seven days a week: all the time: *We're open for business 24/7.* ◦ *We offer 24/7 internet access.*

24-hour clock /twen.tiˌfɔːr.aʊəˈklɒk/ Ⓤⓢ /-t̬iˌfɔːr.aʊrˈklɑːk/ **noun** [S] the system of using 24 numbers instead of twelve to refer to the hours in the day

3-D /ˌθriːˈdiː/ in a 3-D film or picture, the objects look real and solid instead of looking like a normal flat picture: *a 3-D effect* ◦ *These computer games rely on 3-D graphics.* ◦ *The picture looks great because it's **in** 3-D*

3Ws /θriːˈdʌb.l̩.juːz/ **noun** something you can say to represent 'www' at the beginning of a website address: *The dictionary website is 3Ws dot dictionary dot cambridge dot org.*

4G /ˌfɔːˈdʒiː/ Ⓤⓢ /ˌfɔːr-/ **adj** describes TECHNOLOGY that is new and improved, especially mobile phones on which you can use the internet, watch television, etc. 4G is short for 'fourth generation': *They invested heavily in 4G mobile phone networks.*

.45 /ˌfɔː.tiˈfaɪv/ Ⓤⓢ /ˌfɔːr.t̬i-/ **noun** [C] a large type of PISTOL (= small gun)

4WD **noun** [C or U] written abbreviation for **four-wheel drive**: a vehicle that has power supplied by the engine to all four wheels so that it can travel easily over difficult ground

4x4 /ˌfɔː.baɪˈfɔːʳ/ Ⓤⓢ /ˌfɔːr.baɪˈfɔːr/ **noun** [C or U] abbreviation for **four-wheel drive**: a vehicle that has power supplied by the engine to all four wheels so that it can travel easily over difficult ground

7/7 /ˌsev.ənˈsev.ən/ used in news reports to refer to 7 July, 2005, when four bombs killed many people in London

800 number /ˌeɪtˈhʌn.drədˌnʌm.bəʳ/ Ⓤⓢ /-bɚ/ **noun** [C] in the US, a free phone number that begins with 800, provided by companies or other organizations offering advice or information

900 number /ˌnaɪnˈhʌn.drədˌnʌm.bəʳ/ Ⓤⓢ /-bɚ/ **noun** [C] in the US, an expensive phone number that begins with 900, provided by companies offering services such as CHATLINES

9/11 /ˌnaɪn.ɪˈlev.ən/ mainly US September the eleventh, written in US style: the date of the attacks on the World Trade Center and the Pentagon in the US in 2001: *Since 9/11 there has been more cooperation between Russia and America.*

911 /ˌnaɪn.wʌnˈwʌn/ the phone number used in the US to call the emergency services

999 /ˌnaɪn.naɪnˈnaɪn/ the phone number used in the UK to call the emergency services: *a hoax 999 call* ◦ *There's been an accident – dial 999 and ask for an ambulance.*

A, a /eɪ/ **noun** (plural **As, A's** or **a's**) **LETTER** ▷ **1** [C or U] the first letter of the English alphabet **MUSIC** ▷ **2** [C or U] a note in Western music: *This concerto is in the key of A major.* **MARK** ▷ **3** [C or U] a mark in an exam or for a piece of work that shows that your work is considered excellent: *Sophie **got** (an) A for English.* ◦ *She got **straight** As (= all her marks were As) in her end-of-year exams.* **ELECTRICITY** ▷ **4** written abbreviation for **amp**

IDIOMS **from A to B** from one place to another: *Using this software, a driver can now work out the quickest route from A to B.* • **from A to Z** including everything: *This book tells the story of her life from A to Z.*

a weak /ə/ strong /eɪ/ **determiner** (also **an**) **NOT PARTICULAR** ▷ **1** A1 used before a noun to refer to a single thing or person that has not been mentioned before, especially when you are not referring to a particular thing or person: *I've bought a car.* ◦ *She's got a boyfriend.* ◦ *There was a sudden loud noise.* ◦ *Is he a friend **of** yours (= one of your friends)?* **2** A1 used to say what type of thing or person something or someone is: *She wants to be a doctor when she grows up.* ◦ *This is a very mild cheese.* ◦ *Experts think the painting may be a Picasso (= by Picasso).* **3** A1 used to mean any or every thing or person of the type you are referring to: *Can you ride a bike?* ◦ *A cheetah can run faster than a lion.* ◦ *A teacher needs to have a lot of patience.* **4** used before some UNCOUNTABLE nouns when you want to limit their meaning in some way, such as when describing them more completely or referring to one example of them: *I only have a limited knowledge of Spanish.* ◦ *He has a great love of music.* ◦ *There was a fierceness in her voice.* **5** A2 used before some nouns of action when referring to one example of the action: *Take a look at this, Jez.* ◦ *I'm just going to have a wash.* ◦ *There was a knocking at the door.* **6** A2 used when referring to a unit or container of something, especially something you eat or drink: *I'd love a coffee.* ◦ *All I had for lunch was a yogurt.* **7** A2 used before the first but not the second of two nouns that are referred to as one unit: *a cup and saucer* ◦ *a knife and fork* **8** A2 used before some words that express a number or amount: *a few days* ◦ *a bit of wool* ◦ *a lot of money* **9** used in front of a person's name when referring to someone who you do not know: *There's a Ms Evans to see you.* **10** used before the name of a day or month to refer to one example of it: *My birthday is on a Friday this year.* ◦ *It's been a very wet June.* **ONE** ▷ **11** A1 one: *a hundred* ◦ *a thousand* ◦ *a dozen* ◦ *There were three men and a woman.* **12** A2 used between a FRACTION and a unit of measurement: *half a mile* ◦ *a quarter of a kilo* ◦ *three quarters of an hour* ◦ *six tenths of a second* **13** A2 used when saying how often something happens in a certain period: *Take one tablet three times a day.* ◦ *I swim once a week.* **14** A2 used when saying how much someone earns or how much something costs in a certain period: *She earns $100,000 a year.* ◦ *My plumber charges £20 an hour.*

A2 /ˌeɪˈtuː/ **noun** [C] (plural **A2s**) a public exam taken in England and Wales by children aged 17 or 18. Students take AS LEVEL exams then A2s, usually a year later, which together make a full A LEVEL qualification. → See also **A level, AS level**

A3 /ˌeɪˈθriː/ **noun** [U] paper that is a standard size of 29.7 centimetres by 42 centimetres: *a sheet of A3* ◦ *A3 paper*

> **! Common mistake: a or an?**
>
> Use **an** in front of words that begin with a vowel sound: Don't say 'a animal' or 'a old building', say **an animal** or **an old building.**
>
> **Warning:** do not use **a** or **an** to refer to uncountable nouns:
>
> ~~*I have an exciting news for you.*~~
>
> *I have exciting news for you.*
>
> *I have some exciting news for you.*
>
> *I have an exciting piece of news for you.*

A4 /ˌeɪˈfɔːʳ/ (US) /-ˈfɔːr/ **noun** [U] paper that is a standard size of 21 centimetres by 29.7 centimetres: *a sheet of A4* ◦ *A4 paper*

AA /ˌeɪˈeɪ/ **noun DEGREE** ▷ **1** [C] abbreviation for Associate in Arts: a degree given by an American college to someone after they have finished a two-year course, or a person who has this degree **ALCOHOL** ▷ **2** abbreviation for Alcoholics Anonymous: an organization for people who drink too much alcohol and want to cure themselves of this habit: *an AA meeting* **CARS** ▷ **3 the AA** abbreviation for the Automobile Association: an organization in the UK that gives help and information to drivers who are members of it

AAA /ˌeɪ.eɪˈeɪ/ **noun** abbreviation for American Automobile Association: an organization in the US that gives help and information to drivers who are members of it

aah /ɑː/ **exclamation** another spelling of **ah**

A & E /ˌeɪ.əndˈiː/ **noun** [U or C] UK (US **eˈmergency room**) abbreviation for Accident and Emergency: the part of a hospital where people go when they are ill or injured and need treatment quickly

aardvark /ˈɑːd.vɑːk/ (US) /ˈɑːrd.vɑːrk/ **noun** [C] an African mammal with a long nose and large ears that lives underground and eats insects

AB /ˌeɪˈbiː/ **noun** [C] US for **BA**

aback /əˈbæk/ **adv be taken aback** to be very shocked or surprised: *I was rather taken aback **by** her honesty.*

abacus /ˈæb.ə.kəs/ **noun** [C] a square or rectangular frame holding an arrangement of small balls on metal rods or wires, used for counting or for doing calculations

abacus

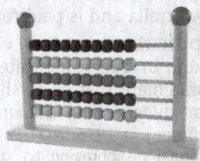

abalone /æb.əˈləʊ.ni/ (US) /-ˈloʊ.ni/ **noun** [C] a small sea creature that can be eaten. It lives inside a shell that is the shape of an ear and is white and shiny inside.

abandon /əˈbæn.dən/ **verb; noun**

▸**verb** [T] **LEAVE** ▷ **1** B2 to leave a place, thing, or person for ever: *We had to abandon the car.* ◦ *By the time the rebel troops arrived, the village had already been abandoned.* ◦ *As a baby he'd been abandoned by his mother.* ◦ *We were sinking fast, and the captain gave the order to abandon **ship**.* **STOP** ▷ **2** C1 to stop doing an activity before you have finished it: *The match was*

abandoned at half-time because of the poor weather conditions. ◦ *They had to abandon their attempt to climb the mountain.* ◦ *The party has now abandoned its policy of unilateral disarmament.* **3 abandon yourself to sth** to allow yourself to be controlled completely by a feeling or way of living: *He abandoned himself to his emotions.* • **abandoned** /əˈbæn.dənd/ **adj** B2 *An abandoned baby was found in a box on the hospital steps.* • **abandonment** /-mənt/ **noun** [U]

▸**noun** literary **with (gay/wild) abandon** in a completely uncontrolled way: *We danced with wild abandon.*

abase /əˈbeɪs/ **verb** formal **abase yourself** to make yourself seem to be less important or not to deserve respect • **abasement** /-mənt/ **noun** [U] *The pilgrims knelt in **self**-abasement.*

abashed /əˈbæʃt/ **adj** [after verb] embarrassed: *He said nothing but looked abashed.*

abate /əˈbeɪt/ **verb** [I] formal to become less strong: *The storm/wind/rain has started to abate.* ◦ *The fighting in the area shows no sign of abating.* → See also **unabated** • **abatement** /-mənt/ **noun** [U]

abattoir /ˈæb.ə.twɑːr/ (US) /-twɑːr/ **noun** [C] mainly UK (mainly US **slaughterhouse**) a place where animals are killed for their meat

abbess /ˈæb.es/ **noun** [C] a woman who is in charge of a CONVENT

abbey /ˈæb.i/ **noun** [C] a building where MONKS or NUNS live or used to live. Some abbeys are now used as churches: *Westminster Abbey*

abbot /ˈæb.ət/ **noun** [C] a man who is in charge of a MONASTERY

abbreviate /əˈbriː.vi.eɪt/ **verb** [T usually passive] to make a word or phrase shorter by using only the first letters of each word: *'Daniel' is often abbreviated **to** 'Dan'.* ◦ *'Chief Executive Officer' is abbreviated **as** 'CEO'.* • **abbreviated** /əˈbriː.vi.eɪ.tɪd/ (US) /-t̬ɪd/ **adj** *'Di' is the abbreviated **form** of 'Diane'.*

abbreviation /əˌbriː.viˈeɪ.ʃən/ **noun** [C] a short form of a word or phrase: *'ITV' is the abbreviation **for** 'Independent Television'.*

ABC /ˌeɪ.biːˈsiː/ **noun** ALPHABET ▷ **1** [S] (US usually **ABCs** [plural]) the alphabet: *He's learning his ABC at school.* **2** [S] (US usually **ABCs** [plural]) basic information about a subject: *What I need is a book that contains **the** ABC **of** carpentry.* TV ▷ **3** abbreviation for American Broadcasting Company: an organization that broadcasts on television in the US **4 the ABC** abbreviation for the Australian Broadcasting Corporation: an organization that broadcasts on radio and television in Australia and is paid for by the government

abdicate /ˈæb.dɪ.keɪt/ **verb** KING/QUEEN ▷ **1** [I or T] If a king or queen abdicates, he or she makes a formal statement that he or she no longer wants to be king or queen: *King Edward VIII abdicated (the British throne) in 1936.* NOT DO ▷ **2 abdicate responsibility** formal disapproving to stop controlling or managing something that you are in charge of: *She abdicated all responsibility for the project.* • **abdication** /ˌæb.dɪˈkeɪ.ʃən/ **noun** [U] *The council denied that their decision represented any abdication **of** responsibility.*

abdomen /ˈæb.də.mən/ **noun** [C] specialized the lower part of a person's or animal's body, containing the stomach, bowels, and other organs, or the end of an insect's body • **abdominal** /æbˈdɒm.ɪ.nəl/ (US) /-ˈdɑː.mə-/ **adj** *abdominal pains*

abdominals /æbˈdɒm.ɪ.nəlz/ (US) /-ˈdɑː.mə-/ **noun** [plural] (informal **abs**) muscles in the abdomen

abduct /æbˈdʌkt/ **verb** [T] to force someone to go somewhere with you, often using threats or violence: *The company director was abducted **from** his car by terrorists.* • **abductor** /æbˈdʌk.tər/ (US) /-tɚ/ **noun** [C] *She was tortured by her abductors.* • **abduction** /æbˈdʌk.ʃən/ **noun** [C or U] *There has been a series of abductions **of** young children **from** schools in the area.* ◦ *He was charged with abduction.*

aberrant /əˈber.ənt/, /ˈæb.ə.rənt/ **adj** formal different from what is typical or usual, especially in an unacceptable way: *aberrant behaviour/sexuality*

aberration /ˌæb.əˈreɪ.ʃən/ **noun** [C or U] formal a temporary change from the typical or usual way of behaving: ***In a moment of** aberration, she agreed to go with him.* ◦ *I'm sorry I'm late – I had a **mental** aberration and forgot we had a meeting today.*

abet /əˈbet/ **verb** [T] (-tt-) to help or encourage someone to do something wrong or illegal: *His accountant had **aided and** abetted him in the fraud.* • **abettor** /əˈbet.ər/ (US) /-ˈbet̬.ɚ/ **noun** [C]

abeyance /əˈbeɪ.əns/ **noun** [U] formal a state of not happening or being used at present: *Hostilities between the two groups have been **in** abeyance since last June.* ◦ *The project is being **held in** abeyance until agreement is reached on funding it.*

abhor /əˈbɔːr/ (US) /æbˈhɔːr/ **verb** [T not continuous] (-rr-) formal to hate a way of behaving or thinking, often because you think it is not moral: *I abhor all forms of racism.*

abhorrence /əˈbɒr.əns/ (US) /æbˈhɔːr-/ **noun** [S or U] formal a feeling of hating something or someone: *She looked at him **in/with** abhorrence.* ◦ *She has **an** abhorrence **of** change.*

abhorrent /əˈbɒr.ənt/ (US) /æbˈhɔːr-/ **adj** formal morally very bad: *an abhorrent crime* ◦ *Racism of any kind is abhorrent **to** me.*

abide /əˈbaɪd/ **verb** **1 can't abide sb/sth** If you can't abide someone or something, you dislike them very much: *I can't abide her.* ◦ *He couldn't abide laziness.* LIVE ▷ **2** [I usually + adv/prep] old use to live or stay somewhere

PHRASAL VERB **abide by sth** formal to accept or obey an agreement, decision, or rule: *Competitors must abide by the judge's decision.*

abiding /əˈbaɪ.dɪŋ/ **adj** [before noun] describes a feeling or memory that you have for a long time: *My abiding **memory** is of him in the garden.*

> **! Common mistake: ability**
>
> Remember that **ability** is never followed by 'of'.
> Don't say 'ability of doing something', say **ability to do something**:
>
> ~~*I admire people who have the ability of being positive.*~~
>
> *I admire people who have the ability to be positive.*

> **Word partners for ability**
>
> *demonstrate/have/possess* ability • *lack* ability • *lose* the ability to do sth • *affect/limit* sb's ability to do sth • *innate/instinctive/natural* ability • *amazing/remarkable/uncanny* ability • *proven* ability

ability /əˈbɪl.ɪ.ti/ (US) /-ə.t̬i/ **noun** [C or U] B1 the physical or mental power or skill needed to do something: *There's no doubting her ability.* ◦ [+ to infinitive] *She **had the** ability **to** explain things clearly and concisely.* ◦ *She's a woman of considerable abilities.* ◦ *I have children in my class of very **mixed** abilities*

(= *different levels of skill or intelligence*). ◦ *a mixed-ability class*

-ability /-ə.bɪl.ɪ.ti/ ⓤⓢ /-ə.t̬i/ **suffix** (also **-ibility**) used to form nouns from adjectives ending in '-able' or '-ible', to mean the quality of being the stated adjective: *suitability* ◦ *stability*

abject /ˈæb.dʒekt/ **adj** formal **EXTREME** ▷ **1 abject misery, poverty, failure, etc.** the state of being extremely unhappy, poor, unsuccessful, etc.: *They live in abject poverty.* ◦ *This policy has turned out to be an abject failure.* **NOT PROUD** ▷ **2** showing no PRIDE or respect for yourself: *an abject apology* ◦ *He is almost abject in his respect for his boss.* • **abjectly** /-li/ **adv**

abjure /əbˈdʒʊəʳ/ ⓤⓢ /-dʒʊr/ **verb** [T] formal to say formally or publicly that you no longer agree with a belief or way of behaving: *He abjured his religion/his life of dissipation.*

ablation /əˈbleɪ.ʃən/ ⓤⓢ /æbˈleɪ-/ **noun** [U] specialized the loss of ice or snow from a GLACIER or ICEBERG, or the loss of rock or similar material, caused by a process such as melting or EROSION

ablaze /əˈbleɪz/ **adj** [after verb] **1** burning very strongly: *The house was ablaze, and the flames and smoke could be seen for miles around.* **2** brightly lit or brightly coloured: *The ballroom was ablaze **with** lights.* ◦ *The field was ablaze **with** wild flowers.* **3** full of energy, interest, or emotion: *Her eyes were ablaze **with** excitement.*

able /ˈeɪ.bl̩/ **adj** **CAN DO** ▷ **1 be able to do sth** Ⓐ2 to have the necessary physical strength, mental power, skill, time, money, or opportunity to do something: *Will she be able to cope with the work?* ◦ *He's never been able to admit to his mistakes.* ◦ *I'm sorry that I wasn't able to phone you yesterday.* ◦ *It's so wonderful being able to see the sea from my window.* **2 be better able to do something** to find it easier to do something: *Get a good night's sleep and you'll feel better able to cope.*

> **! Common mistake: able**
>
> **Able** is followed by a verb in the infinitive with 'to'.
>
> Do not say 'able do something' or 'able doing something', say **able to do something**:
>
> ~~*I will be able start the job next week.*~~
>
> *I will be able to start the job next week.*

SKILFUL ▷ **3** Ⓒ2 clever or good at what you do: *an able child/student/secretary* ◦ *This problem is now being looked at by some of the ablest minds/scientists in the country.*

-able /-ə.bl̩/ **suffix** (also **-ible**) **CAN BE** ▷ **1** added to verbs to form adjectives which mean able to receive the action of the stated verb: *breakable* ◦ *washable* ◦ *movable* **WORTH BEING** ▷ **2** added to verbs to form adjectives which mean worth receiving the action of the stated verb: *an admirable person* ◦ *an acceptable answer*

ˌable-ˈbodied **adj** describes someone who is healthy and has no illness, injury, or condition that makes it difficult to do the things that other people do: *All able-bodied young men were forced to join the army.* • **the ˌable-ˈbodied** **noun** [plural]

ablution /əˈbluː.ʃən/ **noun** formal **1** [U] the act of washing yourself: *Ablution is part of some religious ceremonies.* **2 ablutions** [plural] humorous Your ablutions are the things you do when you wash yourself: *I must just **perform my** ablutions!*

ably /ˈeɪ.bli/ **adv** skilfully: *He performs his duties very ably.*

abnegate /ˈæb.nɪ.geɪt/ **verb** [T] formal **1** to not allow yourself to have something, especially something you like or want **2** to not accept something, or to say that you do not have something: *to abnegate responsibility/guilt* • **abnegation** /ˌæb.nɪˈgeɪ.ʃən/ **noun** [U]

abnormal /æbˈnɔː.məl/ ⓤⓢ /-ˈnɔːr-/ **adj** Ⓒ1 different from what is usual or average, especially in a way that is bad: *abnormal behaviour/weather/conditions* ◦ *Tests revealed some abnormal skin cells.* • **abnormally** /-i/ **adv** *The success rate was abnormally high.*

abnormality /ˌæb.nɔːˈmæl.ə.ti/ ⓤⓢ /-nɔːrˈmæl.ə.t̬i/ **noun** [C or U] something abnormal, usually in the body: *genetic/congenital abnormalities* ◦ *An increasing number of tests are available for detecting **foetal** abnormalities.* ◦ *The X-rays showed some slight abnormality.*

Abo /ˈæb.əʊ/ ⓤⓢ /-oʊ/ **noun** [C] (plural **Abos**) Australian English offensive word for an **Aborigine**

ABO /ˌeɪ.biːˈəʊ/ ⓤⓢ /-ˈoʊ-/ **noun** [S] specialized the system that divides human blood into four main BLOOD GROUPS (= types of blood), known as A, B, AB, and O: *the ABO blood group system*

aboard /əˈbɔːd/ ⓤⓢ /-ˈbɔːrd/ **adv, preposition** Ⓒ1 on or onto a ship, aircraft, bus, or train: *The flight attendant welcomed us aboard.* ◦ *Welcome aboard flight BA345 to Tokyo.* ◦ *The train's about to leave. All aboard!* ◦ *We spent two months **aboard ship** (= on the ship).*

abode /əˈbəʊd/ ⓤⓢ /-ˈboʊd/ **noun** [C usually singular] the place where someone lives: formal *The defendant is **of no fixed** abode (= has no permanent home).* ◦ humorous *Welcome to my **humble** abode!*

abolish /əˈbɒl.ɪʃ/ ⓤⓢ /-ˈbɑː.lɪʃ/ **verb** [T] Ⓑ2 to end an activity or custom officially: *National Service was abolished in the UK in 1962.* • **abolition** /ˌæb.əˈlɪʃ.ən/ **noun** [U] *the abolition of slavery*

abolitionist /ˌæb.əˈlɪʃ.ən.ɪst/ **noun** [C] a person who supports the abolition of something

abominable /əˈbɒm.ɪ.nə.bl̩/ ⓤⓢ /-ˈbɑː.mɪ-/ **adj** very bad or unpleasant: *The prisoners are forced to live in abominable conditions.* ◦ *The weather's been abominable all week.* • **abominably** /-bli/ **adv** *He behaved abominably towards her.*

Aˌbominable ˈSnowman **noun** [C] a **yeti**

abominate /əˈbɒm.ɪ.neɪt/ ⓤⓢ /-ˈbɑː.mɪ-/ **verb** [T not continuous] formal to hate something very much: *He abominates cruelty of all kinds.*

abomination /əˌbɒm.ɪˈneɪ.ʃən/ ⓤⓢ /-ˌbɑː.mɪ-/ **noun** [C] formal something that you dislike and disapprove of: *Cruelty to animals is an abomination.*

aboriginal /ˌæb.əˈrɪdʒ.ɪ.nəl/ **adj** describes a person or living thing that has existed in a country or continent since the earliest time known to people: *aboriginal forests* ◦ *aboriginal inhabitants*

Aboriginal /ˌæb.əˈrɪdʒ.ɪ.nəl/ **noun** [C] an Aborigine • **Aboriginal adj** *Aboriginal art/traditions*

Aborigine /ˌæb.əˈrɪdʒ.ən.i/ **noun** [C] a member of the race of people with dark skins who were the first people to live in Australia

abort /əˈbɔːt/ ⓤⓢ /-ˈbɔːrt/ **verb** **STOP** ▷ **1** [T] to cause something to stop or fail before it begins or before it is complete: *The plan/flight had to be aborted at the last minute.* **END PREGNANCY** ▷ **2** [T] to stop the development of a baby that has not been born, usually by having a medical operation: *Do you think it's wrong to use aborted **foetuses** for medical research?* **3** [I] another word for **miscarry (miscarriage)**

abortion /əˈbɔː.ʃən/ ⓤⓢ /-ˈbɔːr-/ **noun** **END OF PREGNANCY** ▷ **1** Ⓒ1 [C or U] the intentional ending of a

pregnancy: *She decided to* ***have/get*** *an abortion.* ◦ *Abortion is restricted in some American states.* → Compare **miscarriage, stillbirth** **FAILURE** ▷ **2** [C] slang a failure: *This project is a complete abortion.*

abortionist /ə'bɔː.ʃən.ɪst/ (US) /-'bɔːr-/ **noun** [C] a person who performs abortions to end unwanted pregnancies, often illegally and for money

abortive /ə'bɔː.tɪv/ (US) /-'bɔːr.t̬ɪv/ **adj** formal describes an attempt or plan that you have to give up because it has failed: *He made two abortive attempts on the French throne.*

abound /ə'baʊnd/ **verb** [I] to exist in large numbers: *Theories abound about how the Earth began.*

PHRASAL VERB **abound in/with sth** If something abounds in/with other things, it has a lot of them: *The coast here abounds with rare plants.*

about /ə'baʊt/ **preposition; adv; adj**

▸**preposition** **CONNECTED WITH** ▷ **1** A1 on the subject of, or connected with: *What's that book about?* ◦ *a film about the Spanish Civil War* ◦ *We were talking/laughing about Sophie.* ◦ *He's always* ***(going) on*** *about what a great job he's got.* ◦ *I'm worried about David.* ◦ *I really don't know what all the fuss is about.* ◦ *I wish you'd* ***do something*** *about (= take action to solve the problem of) your bedroom – it's a real mess.* ◦ UK informal *Could you make me a coffee too* ***while*** *you're about* ***it*** *(= while you are making one for yourself)?* ◦ *What didn't you like about the play?* ◦ ***There's something*** *about (= in the character of) her attitude that worries me.* ◦ ***There's something*** *special about him (= in his character).* ◦ *'Is that your car?' 'Yes,* ***what*** *about it?' (= Why are you asking me?)*

> **!** Common mistake: **about or regarding?**
>
> **Warning: about** is usually only used to introduce a topic in informal styles.
>
> In formal writing, don't use 'About ...', use **Regarding ...** or **With regard to ...**:
>
> ~~*About my wages, I kindly request that you review the situation.*~~

NO ORDER ▷ **2** mainly UK (US usually **around**) positioned around a place, often without a clear purpose or order: *Their belongings were flung about the room.* **POSITION** ▷ **3** UK formal in a particular place: *Do you have such a thing as a pen about* ***you/your person****? (= Have you got a pen?)*

IDIOM **how/what about...?** A2 used when suggesting or offering something to someone: *How about a trip to the zoo this afternoon?* ◦ *'Coffee, Sarah?' 'No, thanks.' 'What about you, Kate?'*

▸**adv** **APPROXIMATELY** ▷ **1** A1 a little more or less than the stated number or amount: *about six feet tall* ◦ *about two months ago* ◦ *'What time are you leaving work today?' 'About five.'* **ALMOST** ▷ **2** almost: *We're about ready to leave.* ◦ *Well, I think* ***that's*** *about* ***it*** *for now (= we have almost finished what we are doing for the present).* **ALL DIRECTIONS** ▷ **3** B2 mainly UK (US usually **around**) in many different directions: *They heard someone moving about outside.* ◦ *I've been running about all morning trying to find you.* **NO ORDER** ▷ **4** B2 mainly UK (US usually **around**) positioned around a place, often without a clear purpose or order: *She always leaves her clothes lying about on the floor.* **PLACE** ▷ **5** mainly UK (US usually **around**) in or near a place: *Is John about (= somewhere near)?* ◦ *There's a lot of flu about (= many people have it) at the moment.*

▸**adj** **INTENDING** ▷ **be about to do sth** B1 to be going to do something very soon: *I was about to leave when Mark arrived.* ◦ *She looked as if she was about to cry.*

> **+** Other ways of saying **about**
>
> Common alternatives to 'about' are **approximately** or **around**:
>
> *The job will take* ***approximately*** *three months.*
>
> *The accident happened* ***around*** *four o'clock.*
>
> When you are talking about an approximate number, you can use **roughly**:
>
> *There were* ***roughly*** *two hundred people at the meeting.*
>
> If you want to say 'about' and possibly more than a particular number, you can use the phrase **or so** or the suffix **-odd**:
>
> *They raised £200* ***or so*** *for charity.*
>
> *Her son must be 40-****odd*** *years old by now.*

a͵bout-'turn **noun** [C] UK (US **a͵bout-'face**) **1** a change of direction: *I'd only gone a little way down the street when I remembered I hadn't locked the door, so I* ***made/did*** *a quick about-turn.* **2** a complete change of opinion or behaviour: *This is the government's second about-turn* ***on*** *the issue.*

above /ə'bʌv/ **adv, preposition; adv, adj**

▸**adv, preposition** **HIGHER POSITION** ▷ **1** A1 in or to a higher position than something else: *There's a mirror above the washbasin.* ◦ *He waved the letter excitedly above his head.* ◦ *She's rented a room above a shop.* ◦ *Her name comes above mine on the list.* ◦ *The helicopter was hovering above the building.* ◦ *It's on the shelf just above your head.* **MORE** ▷ **2** A2 more than an amount or level: *It says on the box it's for children aged three and above.* ◦ *Rates of pay are above* ***average****.* ◦ *Temperatures rarely rise above zero in winter.* ◦ *She values her job above her family.* ◦ *They value their freedom above* ***(and beyond) all else****.* **3 above all** B1 most importantly: *Above all, I'd like to thank my family.* ◦ *Above all, I'd say I value kindness.* **RANK** ▷ **4** in a more important or advanced position than someone else: *Sally's a grade above me.* **TOO IMPORTANT** ▷ **5** C2 too good or important for something: *No one is above suspicion in this matter.* ◦ *He's not above* ***lying*** *(= he sometimes lies) to protect himself.*

▸**adv, adj** **ON PAGE** ▷ **1** B1 When used in a piece of writing, 'above' means higher on the page, or on a previous page: *Please send the articles to the address given above.* ◦ *The letter was sent to the above address.* **2 the above** all the people or things listed earlier: ***All of*** *the above should be invited.* ◦ *Once we've finished all of the above we can start on the next project.*

a͵bove-'mentioned **adj** formal refers to things or people in a document or book that have been mentioned earlier: *All of the above-mentioned films won Oscars.* → Compare **undermentioned**

abracadabra /͵æb.rə.kə'dæb.rə/ **exclamation** said by someone who is performing a magic trick, in order to help them perform it successfully

abrade /ə'breɪd/ **verb** [T] specialized to remove part of the surface of something by rubbing

abrasion /ə'breɪ.ʒən/ **noun** specialized **1** [U] the process of rubbing away the surface of something: *There seems to have been some abrasion of the surface.* **2** [C] a place where the surface of something, such as skin, has been rubbed away: *She had a small abrasion on her knee.*

abrasive /ə'breɪ.sɪv/ **adj; noun**

▸**adj** **PERSON** ▷ **1** rude and unfriendly: *She has a rather abrasive* ***manner****.* ◦ *He can sometimes be quite abrasive*

A

in meetings. **CLEANING SUBSTANCE ▷ 2** An abrasive substance is slightly rough, and often used for cleaning surfaces: *an abrasive cleaner/powder/liquid* • **abrasively** /-li/ **adv** • **abrasiveness** /-nəs/ **noun** [U]
▸**noun** [C] a substance used for rubbing away the surface of something, usually to clean it or make it shiny: *You'll need a strong abrasive for cleaning this sink.*

abreast /ə'brest/ **adv 1** describes two or more people who are next to each other and moving in the same direction: *We were running/cycling **two** abreast.* ◦ *The motorcyclist came abreast **of** her car and shouted abuse at her.* **2 keep abreast of sth** to make sure you know all the most recent facts about a subject or situation: *I try to keep abreast of any developments.*

abridge /ə'brɪdʒ/ **verb** [T] to make a book, play, or piece of writing shorter by removing details and information that is not important: *The book was abridged for children.* • **abridged** /ə'brɪdʒd/ **adj** *the abridged **edition/version** of her novel* • **abridgment** (also **abridgement**) /-mənt/ **noun** [C or U]

abroad /ə'brɔːd/ **adv** [after verb] **OTHER COUNTRY ▷ 1** B1 in or to a foreign country or countries: *He's currently abroad on business.* ◦ *We always **go** abroad in the summer.* **OUTSIDE ▷ 2** [after verb] literary or old use outside, or not at home: *Not a soul was abroad that morning.* **GOING AROUND ▷ 3** [after verb] formal describes ideas, feelings, and opinions that are shared by many people: *There's a rumour abroad that she intends to leave the company.*

abrogate /'æb.rə.geɪt/ **verb** [T] formal to end a law, agreement, or custom formally: *The treaty was abrogated in 1929.* • **abrogation** /ˌæb.rə'geɪ.ʃən/ **noun** [S or U]

abrupt /ə'brʌpt/ **adj SUDDEN ▷ 1** C2 describes something that is sudden and unexpected, and often unpleasant: *an abrupt change/movement* ◦ *Our conversation came to an abrupt **end** when George burst into the room.* ◦ *The road ended in an abrupt (= sudden and very steep) slope down to the sea.* **UNFRIENDLY ▷ 2** C2 using too few words when talking, in a way that seems rude and unfriendly: *an abrupt **manner/reply*** ◦ *He is sometimes very abrupt **with** clients.* • **abruptly** /-li/ **adv** *The talks ended abruptly when one of the delegations walked out in protest.* • **abruptness** /-nəs/ **noun** [U]

abs /æbz/ **noun** [plural] informal **abdominals**: *exercises to tone/build up your abs*

ABS /ˌeɪ.biː'es/ **noun** [S] abbreviation for anti-lock braking system: a BRAKE fitted to some road vehicles that prevents SKIDDING (= uncontrolled sliding) by reducing the effects of stopping suddenly

abscess /'æb.ses/ **noun** [C] a painful swollen area on or in the body, which contains PUS (= thick, yellow liquid): *She had an abscess **on** her gum.*

abscond /æb'skɒnd/ (US) /-'skɑːnd/ **verb** [I] **ESCAPE ▷ 1** to go away suddenly and secretly in order to escape from somewhere: *Two prisoners absconded last night.* ◦ *She absconded **from** boarding school **with** her boyfriend.* **STEAL ▷ 2** to go away suddenly and secretly because you have stolen something, usually money: *They absconded **with** £10,000 of the company's money.* • **absconder** /æb'skɒn.dər/ (US) /-'skɑːn.dɚ/ **noun** [C]

abseil /'æb.seɪl/ **verb** [I] UK (US **rappel**) to go down a very steep slope by holding on to a rope that is fastened to the top of the slope: *She abseiled **down** the rock face.* • **abseil** **noun** [C] UK (US **rappel**)

absence /'æb.səns/ **noun NOT BEING PRESENT ▷ 1** B2 [U or C] the fact of not being where you are usually expected to be: *A new manager was appointed **during/in** her absence.* ◦ *She has had repeated absences **from** work this year.* **NOT EXISTING ▷ 2** B2 [U] the fact of not existing: *He drew attention to the absence **of** concrete evidence against the defendant.* ◦ ***In the** absence **of** (= because there were not) more suitable candidates, we decided to offer the job to Mr Conway.*

abseil

IDIOM **absence makes the heart grow fonder** saying This means that when people we love are not with us, we love them even more.

absent adj; preposition; verb
▸**adj** /'æb.sənt/ **NOT PRESENT ▷ 1** B1 not in the place where you are expected to be, especially at school or work: *John has been absent **from** school/work for three days now.* ◦ *We drank a toast to absent **friends**.* **NOT EXISTING ▷ 2** not existing: *Any sign of remorse was completely absent **from** her face.* **NOT PAYING ATTENTION ▷ 3** describes a person or the expression on their face when they are thinking about other things and are not paying attention to what is happening near them
▸**preposition** /'æb.sənt/ US without: *Absent a detailed plan, the project was doomed from the start.*
▸**verb** /æb'sent/ **absent yourself** formal to not go to a place where you are expected to be, especially a school or place of work: *You cannot choose to absent yourself (**from** work/school) on a whim.*

absentee /ˌæb.sən'tiː/ **noun** [C] someone who is not at school or work when they should be: *There are several absentees in the school this week, because a lot of people have got flu.* • **absenteeism** /-ɪ.zəm/ **noun** [U] *The high rate of absenteeism is costing the company a lot of money.*

ˌabsentee 'ballot **noun** [C] US a piece of paper that a person who is unable to be present at an election can vote on and send in by post

ˌabsentee 'landlord **noun** [C] a person who rents out a house, apartment, or farm to someone, but never or almost never visits it

ˌabsentee 'vote **noun** [C] Australian English a piece of paper that a person who is unable to be present at an election can vote on and send in by post → Compare **absentee ballot**

absently /'æb.sənt.li/ **adv** as if you are not paying attention to what is happening near you, and are thinking about other things: *He stared absently at his food.*

ˌabsent-'minded **adj** describes someone who often forgets things or does not pay attention to what is happening near them because they are thinking about other things • **ˌabsent-'mindedly** **adv** *She absent-mindedly left her umbrella on the bus.* • **ˌabsent-'mindedness** **noun** [U]

absinthe (also **absinth**) /'æb.sæ̃θ/, /-sɪnθ/ **noun** [U] a strong alcoholic drink that is green and has a bitter taste

absolute /'æb.sə.luːt/ **adj VERY GREAT ▷ 1** B2 very great or to the largest degree possible: *a man of absolute integrity/discretion* ◦ *I have absolute faith in her judgment.* ◦ *There was no absolute proof of fraud.* **2** B2 [before noun] used when expressing a strong opinion: *He's an absolute idiot!* ◦ *That's absolute rubbish!* **NOT CHANGING ▷ 3** [before noun] true, right,

or the same in all situations and not depending on anything else: *an absolute law/principle/doctrine* ◦ *Do you think there's such a thing as absolute truth/beauty?* ◦ *Her contribution was better than most, but* ***in** absolute **terms*** (= *without comparing it with anything else*) *it was still rather poor.* **POWERFUL** ▷ **4** describes a ruler who has unlimited power: *an absolute monarch*

absolutely /ˌæb.səˈluːt.li/ **adv 1** B1 completely: *I believed/trusted him absolutely.* ◦ *You must be absolutely silent or the birds won't appear.* ◦ *We've achieved absolutely nothing today.* **2** B1 used for adding force to a strong adjective that is not usually used with 'very', or to a verb expressing strong emotion: *It's absolutely impossible to work with all this noise.* ◦ *The food was absolutely disgusting/delicious.* ◦ *I absolutely loathe/adore jazz.* **3** B2 used as a strong way of saying 'yes': *'It was an excellent film, though.' 'Absolutely!'* **4 absolutely not** C2 used as a strong way of saying 'no': *'Are you too tired to continue?' 'Absolutely not!'*

> **!** Common mistake: **absolutely**
>
> **Warning:** Common word-building error!
> If an adjective ends with 'te', just add 'ly' to make an adverb. Don't write 'absolutly' or 'absolutelly', write **absolutely**.

ˌabsolute maˈjority noun [C] a situation in which one person or political party wins more than half of the total votes in an election

ˌabsolute ˈzero noun [S] the lowest temperature possible (-273.15°C)

absolution /ˌæb.səˈluː.ʃən/ **noun** [U] formal the act of forgiving someone, especially in the Christian religion, for something bad that they have done or thought: *She was **granted/given** absolution.*

absolutism /ˈæb.sə.luː.tɪ.zəm/ US /-t̬ɪ-/ **noun** [U] a political system in which a single ruler, group, or political party has complete power over a country

absolve /əbˈzɒlv/ US /-ˈzɑːlv/ **verb** [T] formal (especially in religion or law) to free someone from GUILT, blame, or responsibility for something: *The report absolved her **from/of** all blame for the accident.* ◦ *The priest absolved him (**of** all his sins).*

absorb /əbˈzɔːb/ US /-ˈzɔːrb/ **verb** [T] **TAKE IN** ▷ **1** B2 to take something in, especially gradually: *Plants absorb carbon dioxide.* ◦ *In cold climates, houses need to have walls that will absorb heat.* ◦ *Towels absorb moisture.* ◦ *The drug is quickly absorbed **into** the bloodstream.* ◦ *Our countryside is increasingly being absorbed **by/into** the large cities.* **2** to reduce the effect of a physical force, shock, or change: *The barrier absorbed the main impact of the crash.* **UNDERSTAND** ▷ **3** C1 to understand facts or ideas completely and remember them: *It's hard to absorb so much information.* **INTEREST VERY MUCH** ▷ **4** B2 to take up someone's attention completely: *The project has absorbed her for several years.* → Synonym **engross PAY** ▷ **5** if a business absorbs the cost of something, it pays that cost easily: *The school has absorbed most of the expenses so far, but it may have to offer fewer places next year to reduce costs.* **TAKE CONTROL** ▷ **6** if one company absorbs another company, it takes control of it and they become one company: *Telecorp Holdings absorbed its Spanish subsidiary into its British headquarters.*

absorbed /əbˈzɔːbd/ US /-ˈzɔːrbd/ **adj** [after verb] **absorbed in sth** B2 very interested in something and not paying attention to anything else: *Simon was so absorbed **in** his book that he didn't even notice me come in.* → Synonym **engrossed** → See also **self-absorbed**

absorbent /əbˈzɔː.bənt/ US /-ˈzɔːr-/ **adj** able to take liquid in through the surface and to hold it: *absorbent paper* • **absorbency** /əbˈzɔː.bən.si/ US /-ˈzɔːr-/ **noun** [U] the ability to absorb liquid

absorbing /əbˈzɔː.bɪŋ/ US /-ˈzɔːr-/ **adj** describes something that is very interesting and keeps your attention: *I read her last novel and found it very absorbing.*

absorption /əbˈzɔːp.ʃən/ US /-ˈzɔːrp-/ **noun** [U] **TAKING IN** ▷ **1** the process of taking something into another substance: *Some poisonous gases can enter the body by absorption through the skin.* **INTEREST** ▷ **2** complete interest in something: *Her absorption **in** her work is so great that she thinks about nothing else.* → See also **ˌself-abˈsorption** (**ˌself-abˈsorbed**) **PAYING COSTS** ▷ **3** the situation in which a company pays the cost of something easily: *We can justify the company's absorption of higher manufacturing costs.* **TAKING CONTROL** ▷ **4** the situation in which one company takes control of another so that they become one company: *Reports confirmed the absorption **of** Kode's operations into DCM's offices.*

abstain /æbˈsteɪn/ **verb** [I] **NOT DO** ▷ **1** to not do something, especially something enjoyable that you think might be bad: *He took a vow to abstain **from** alcohol/smoking/sex.* **NOT VOTE** ▷ **2** to decide not to use your vote: *63 members voted in favour, 39 opposed, and 15 abstained.* **STAY AWAY** ▷ **3** Indian English to stay away from work: *During a recent general strike, employees of all major trade unions abstained.* • **abstainer** /æbˈsteɪ.nər/ US /-nɚ/ **noun** [C]

abstemious /æbˈstiː.mi.əs/ **adj** formal not doing things that give you pleasure, especially not eating good food or drinking alcohol • **abstemiously** /-li/ **adv**

abstention /æbˈsten.ʃən/ **noun NOT VOTING** ▷ **1** [C or U] the fact of not voting in favour of or against someone or something: *There were high levels of abstention (**from** voting) in the last elections.* ◦ *There were ten votes in favour, six against, and three abstentions.* **NOT DOING** ▷ **2** [U] formal not doing something, such as drinking alcohol or having sex: *Abstention **from** alcohol is essential while you are taking this medication.*

abstinence /ˈæb.stɪ.nəns/ **noun** [U] formal not doing something, such as drinking alcohol or having sex: *The best way to avoid pregnancy is total abstinence **from** sex.* • **abstinent** /-nənt/ **adj** *sexually abstinent*

abstract /ˈæb.strækt/ **adj; noun**

▸**adj GENERAL** ▷ **1** B2 existing as an idea, feeling, or quality, not as a material object: *Truth and beauty are abstract concepts.* **2** describes an argument or discussion that is general and not based on particular examples: *This debate is becoming too abstract – let's have some hard facts!* **3 the abstract** general ideas: *I have difficulty dealing with the abstract – let's discuss particular cases.* ◦ *So far we've only discussed the question **in** the abstract* (= *without referring to any real examples*). **ART** ▷ **4** B2 describes a type of painting, drawing, or SCULPTURE that uses shapes, lines, and colour in a way that does not try to represent the appearance of people or things: *abstract art* ◦ *an abstract painter*

▸**noun** [C] **SHORT DOCUMENT** ▷ **1** a short form of a speech, article, book, etc., giving only the most important facts or ideas: *There is a section at the end of the magazine that includes abstracts **of** recent articles/books.* **ART** ▷ **2** a painting that uses shapes, lines, and colour in a way that does not try to represent the appearance of people or things

abstracted /æbˈstræk.tɪd/ **adj** formal not giving attention to what is happening around you because you are thinking about something else: *He gave her an abstracted glance, then returned to his book.* • **abstractedly** /-li/ **adv**

abstraction /æbˈstræk.ʃən/ **noun** [U or C] formal the situation in which a subject is very general and not based on real situations: *She's always talking in abstractions.*

ˌabstract ˈnoun **noun** [C] a noun that refers to a thing that does not exist as a material object: *'Happiness', 'honesty', and 'liberty' are abstract nouns.* → Compare **concrete noun**

abstruse /æbˈstruːs/ **adj** formal difficult to understand: *an abstruse philosophical essay*

absurd /əbˈsɜːd/ (US) /-ˈsɝːd/ **adj** **1** (B2) stupid and unreasonable, or silly in a humorous way: *What an absurd thing to say! ◦ Don't be so absurd! Of course I want you to come. ◦ It's an absurd situation – neither of them will talk to the other. ◦ Do I look absurd in this hat?* **2 the absurd** things that happen that are stupid or unreasonable: *The whole situation **borders on** the absurd. ◦ She has a keen sense of the absurd.* • **absurdly** /-li/ **adv** *You're behaving absurdly. ◦ It was absurdly expensive.* • **absurdity** /əbˈzɜː.dɪ.ti/, /-ˈsɜː-/ (US) /-ˈzɝː.də.t̬i/ **noun** [U or C] *Standing there naked, I was suddenly struck by the absurdity **of** the situation. ◦ There are all sorts of absurdities in the proposal.*

ABTA /ˈæb.tə/ **noun** abbreviation for Association of British Travel Agents: a UK organization that protects travellers and people on holiday if a company that arranges travel fails to do something or goes out of business

abundance /əˈbʌn.dəns/ **noun** [S or U] formal the situation in which there is more than enough of something: *There was **an** abundance **of** food at the wedding. ◦ We had wine **in** abundance.*

abundant /əˈbʌn.dənt/ **adj** formal more than enough: *an abundant **supply** of food ◦ There is abundant **evidence** that cars have a harmful effect on the environment. ◦ Cheap consumer goods are abundant (= exist in large amounts) in this part of the world.* • **abundantly** /-li/ **adv** formal *The plant grows abundantly in woodland. ◦ You've made your feelings abundantly **clear** (= very clear).*

abuse **verb; noun**

▸**verb** [T] /əˈbjuːz/ **USE WRONGLY** ▷ **1** to use something for the wrong purpose in a way that is harmful or morally wrong: *She is continually abusing her position/authority by getting other people to do things for her. ◦ I never expected that he would abuse the **trust** I placed in him. ◦ to abuse alcohol* **TREAT CRUELLY** ▷ **2** to treat someone cruelly or violently: *Several of the children had been **sexually/physically/emotionally** abused.* **SPEAK RUDELY** ▷ **3** to speak to someone rudely or cruelly • **abuser** /əˈbjuː.zər/ (US) /-zɚ/ **noun** [C] *a child abuser ◦ a drug/solvent abuser*

▸**noun** /əˈbjuːs/ **WRONG USE** ▷ **1** (B2) [C or U] the use of something in a way that is harmful or morally wrong: *an abuse (= wrong use) of privilege/power/someone's kindness ◦ **Drug** and **alcohol** abuse (= using these substances in a bad way) contributed to his early death.* **CRUEL BEHAVIOUR** ▷ **2** (B2) cruel, violent, or unfair treatment of someone: *She claimed to have been a victim of **child** abuse. ◦ sexual/physical/mental abuse (= bad treatment)* **RUDE SPEECH** ▷ **3** (C2) [U] rude and offensive words said to another person: *He had apparently experienced a lot of **verbal** abuse from his co-workers. ◦ He **hurled** (**a stream/torrent of**) abuse at her (= he said a lot of rude and offensive things to her). ◦ 'Idiot!' is a **term of abuse** (= an insulting expression).*

abusive /əˈbjuː.sɪv/ **adj** (C2) using rude and offensive words: *an abusive letter/phone call ◦ He was apparently **abusive to** the flight attendants.*

abut /əˈbʌt/ **verb** [T never passive, I + prep] (-tt-) formal If a building or area of land abuts something or on something, it is next to it or touches it on one side: *Mexico abuts (**on**) some of the richest parts of the United States. ◦ Their house abutted (**onto**) the police station.*

abuzz /əˈbʌz/ **adj** [after verb] filled with noise and activity: *When we arrived, the party was in full swing and the room was abuzz. ◦ The air was abuzz **with** military helicopters.*

abysmal /əˈbɪz.məl/ **adj** very bad: *abysmal working conditions ◦ The food was abysmal. ◦ The standard of the students' work is abysmal.* • **abysmally** /-i/ **adv** *an abysmally poor book*

abyss /əˈbɪs/ **noun** [C usually singular] **HOLE** ▷ **1** literary a very deep hole that seems to have no bottom **BAD SITUATION** ▷ **2** a difficult situation that brings trouble or destruction: *The country is **sinking/plunging into** an abyss **of** violence and lawlessness. ◦ She found herself **on the edge of** an abyss.*

abyssal /əˈbɪs.əl/ **adj** specialized found in the deepest parts of the ocean or on the bottom of deep oceans: *abyssal marine life*

AC /ˌeɪˈsiː/ **noun** **ELECTRICITY** ▷ **1** [U] abbreviation for alternating current: electrical current that regularly changes the direction in which it flows → Compare **DC** **AIR** ▷ **2** [C or U] US abbreviation for **air conditioner** or **air conditioning**

acacia /əˈkeɪ.ʃə/ **noun** [C or U] a tree from warm parts of the world that has small leaves and yellow or white flowers

academe /ˈæk.ə.diːm/ **noun** [U] formal the part of society, especially universities, that is connected with study and thinking

academia /ˌæk.əˈdiː.mi.ə/ **noun** [U] the part of society, especially universities, that is connected with studying and thinking, or the activity or job of studying: *A graduate of law, he had spent his life **in** academia.*

academic /ˌæk.əˈdem.ɪk/ **adj; noun**

▸**adj** **STUDYING** ▷ **1** (B2) relating to schools, colleges, and universities, or connected with studying and thinking, not with practical skills: *academic subjects/qualifications/books ◦ an academic institution ◦ the academic year (= the time during which students go to school or college) ◦ academic standards* **2** (C2) describes someone who is clever and enjoys studying: *I was never a particularly academic child.* **IN THEORY** ▷ **3** based on ideas and theories and not related to practical effects in real life: *a purely academic argument/question* • **academically** /-ɪ.kəl.i/ **adv** *She's always done well academically.*

▸**noun** [C] (US or Indian English also **academician**) someone who teaches at a college, or who studies as part of their job

academician /əˌkæd.əˈmɪʃ.ən/ **noun** [C] **1** a member of an academy **2** US or Indian English for **academic**

academy /əˈkæd.ə.mi/ **noun** [C] an organization intended to protect and develop an art, science, language, etc., or a school that teaches a particular subject or trains people for a particular job: *a military/police academy ◦ the Royal Academy of Dramatic Art*

Aˌcademy Aˈward **noun** [C] (also **Oscar**) one of a set of American prizes given each year to the best film, the best male or female actor in any film, and to other people involved in the production of films

açaí /ˌæsaɪ'iː/ **noun** [U] a small, round, dark purple fruit from Brazil that people believe is good for their health: *The cocktails are made of tropical ingredients such as fresh passion fruit and açaí berries.*

a cappella /ˌæ.kə'pel.ə/ ⓤⓢ /ˌɑː-/ **adj** [before noun], **adv** specialized sung by a group of people without any musical instruments

accede /ək'siːd/ **verb**

PHRASAL VERB **accede to sth** formal **1** to agree to do what people have asked you to do: *He graciously acceded to our request.* ◦ *It is doubtful whether the government will ever accede to the nationalists' demands for independence.* **2 accede to the throne/accede to power** to become king or queen, or to take a position of power: *The diaries were written in 1837, when Queen Victoria acceded to the throne.*

accelerate /ək'sel.ə.reɪt/ ⓤⓢ /-ɚ.eɪt/ **verb 1** C2 [I] When a vehicle or its driver accelerates, the speed of the vehicle increases: *I accelerated to overtake the bus.* → Opposite **decelerate 2** C2 [I] If a person or object accelerates, he, she, or it goes faster. **3** C1 [I or T] to happen or make something happen sooner or faster: *Inflation is likely to accelerate this year, adding further upward pressure on interest rates.* ◦ *They use special chemicals to accelerate the growth of crops.*

acceleration /əkˌsel.ə'reɪ.ʃən/ **noun 1** [U] the increase in something's speed, or its ability to go faster: *An older car will have poor acceleration.* ◦ *High winds significantly hampered the plane's acceleration.* **2** [S or U] the increase in the speed at which something happens: *The acceleration **in** the decline of manufacturing industry began several years ago.*

accelerator /ək'sel.ə.reɪ.tər/ ⓤⓢ /-ɚ.eɪ.t̬ɚ/ **noun** [C] **1** the PEDAL (= a part that you push with your foot) in a vehicle that makes it go faster **2** specialized in physics, a machine that makes PARTICLES (= small pieces of matter) move very fast

accent noun; verb

▸**noun** [C] /'æk.sənt/ **PRONUNCIATION** ▷ **1** B1 the way in which people in a particular area, country, or social group pronounce words: *He's got a **strong** French/Scottish accent.* ◦ *She's French but she **speaks with** an impeccable English accent.* ◦ *He speaks with a **broad/heavy/strong/thick** Yorkshire accent.* ◦ *I thought I could detect a slight West Country accent.* **MARK** ▷ **2** B2 a mark written or printed over a letter to show you how to pronounce it: *a grave accent* ◦ *There's an acute accent **on** the e of 'café'.* **EMPHASIS** ▷ **3** specialized a special emphasis given to a particular syllable in a word, word in a sentence, or note in a set of musical notes: *The accent falls **on** the final syllable.* **4 the accent is on sth** great importance is given to a particular thing or quality: *This season the accent is definitely on long, flowing, romantic clothes.* • **accented** /'æk.sen.tɪd/ ⓤⓢ /'æk.sen.t̬ɪd/ **adj** *He spoke in **heavily** accented English.*

▸**verb** [T] /ək'sent/ ⓤⓢ /'æk.sent/ to emphasize something: *In any advertising campaign, you must accent the areas where your product is better than the competition.*

accentuate /ək'sen.tju.eɪt/ **verb** [T] to emphasize a particular feature of something or to make something more noticeable: *Her dress was tightly belted, accentuating the slimness of her waist.* ◦ *The new policy only serves to accentuate the inadequacy of provision for the homeless.* • **accentuation** /əkˌsen.tju'eɪ.ʃən/ **noun** [U]

accept /ək'sept/ **verb TAKE** ▷ **1** B1 [T] to agree to take something: *Do you accept credit cards?* ◦ *She was in London to accept an award for her latest novel.* ◦ *I offered her an apology, but she wouldn't accept it.* ◦ *I accept full responsibility for the failure of the plan.* ◦ *The new coffee machines will accept coins of any denomination.* **2** B1 [I or T] to say 'yes' to an offer or invitation: *We've offered her the job, but I don't know whether she'll accept it.* ◦ *I've just accepted an invitation to the opening-night party.* ◦ *I've been invited to their wedding but I haven't decided whether to accept.*

> **!** Common mistake: **accept or agree?**
>
> **Warning: accept** is not usually followed by another verb.
>
> Don't say someone 'accepts to do sth', say someone **agrees to do sth**:
>
> *My father agreed to pick me up from the airport.*

APPROVE ▷ **3** B2 [T] to consider something or someone as satisfactory: *The manuscript was accepted **for** publication last week.* ◦ *She was accepted **as** a full member of the society.* ◦ *His fellow workers refused to accept him (= to include him as one of their group).* **BELIEVE** ▷ **4** B2 [T] to believe that something is true: *The police refused to accept her version of the story.* ◦ *He still hasn't accepted the situation (= realized that he cannot change it).* ◦ [+ that] *I can't accept **that** there's nothing we can do.*

acceptable /ək'sept.ə.bl̩/ **adj 1** B1 satisfactory and able to be agreed to or approved of: *Clearly we need to come to an arrangement that is acceptable **to** both parties.* ◦ *This kind of attitude is simply not acceptable.* **2** B1 just good enough, but not very good: *Her performance was acceptable, but not stunning.* • **acceptability** /əkˌsep.tə'bɪl.ɪ.ti/ ⓤⓢ /-ə.t̬i/ **noun** [U]

acceptance /ək'sep.təns/ **noun** [U] **1** general agreement that something is satisfactory or right, or that someone should be included in a group: *The idea rapidly **gained** acceptance (= became approved of) in political circles.* ◦ *The party marked his acceptance into the community.* **2** C1 the act of agreeing to an offer, plan, or invitation: *Her acceptance of the award was very controversial.* ◦ *an acceptance speech* **3** the fact of accepting a difficult or unpleasant situation: *His attitude to his children's behaviour is one of resigned acceptance.*

accepted /ək'sep.tɪd/ **adj** C1 generally agreed to be satisfactory or right: *'Speed bump' now seems to be the generally accepted term for those ridges in the road that slow traffic down.*

access /'æk.ses/ **noun; verb**

▸**noun** [U] **GETTING NEAR** ▷ **1** B1 the method or possibility of getting near to a place or person: *The only access **to** the village is by boat.* ◦ *The main access **to** (= entrance to) the building is at the side.* ◦ *The children's father was **refused** access **to** them at any time (= refused official permission to see them).* **RIGHT** ▷ **2** B1 the right or opportunity to use or look at something: *The system has been designed to **give** the user quick and easy access **to** the required information.* ◦ *The tax inspector **had/gained** complete access **to** the company files.*

▸**verb** [T] B2 to open a computer FILE (= a collection of information stored on a computer) in order to look at or change information in it

'access ˌcourse **noun** [C] UK a set of classes that people take so they can get a qualification that can be used to get into university or college: *She didn't have any formal qualifications but took an access course to get into university.*

accessible /ək'ses.ə.bl̩/ **adj 1** B2 able to be reached or easily got: *The resort is easily accessible by road, rail, and air.* ◦ *The problem with some of these drugs is that* *they are so very accessible.* **2** ⓒ easy to understand: *Covent Garden has made some attempt to make opera accessible **to** a wider public.* • **accessibility** /əkˌses.əˈbɪl.ɪ.ti/ ⓤⓢ /-ə.t̬i/ **noun** [U] *Two new roads are being built to increase accessibility **to** the town centre.* ◦ *The accessibility of her plays means that she is able to reach a wide audience.*

accession /əkˈseʃ.ən/ **noun** [U] **1** formal the time when someone starts a position of authority, especially a king or queen: *1926 was the year of Emperor Hirohito's accession **to the throne**.* **2** the time when a country officially joins a group of countries or signs an agreement: *Poland's accession to the EU*

accessorize mainly US (UK usually **accessorise**) /əkˈses.ər.aɪz/ ⓤⓢ /-ɚ.aɪz/ **verb** [T] to add an accessory or accessories to something: *She was wearing a little black dress, accessorized simply with a silver necklace.*

accessory /əkˈses.ər.i/ ⓤⓢ /-ɚ-/ **noun** **EXTRA** ▷ **1** C1 [C usually plural] something added to a machine or to clothing that has a useful or decorative purpose: *She wore a green wool suit with **matching** accessories* (= shoes, hat, bag, etc.). ◦ *Sunglasses are much more than a **fashion** accessory.* ◦ *Accessories for the top-of-the-range car include leather upholstery, electric windows, and a sunroof.* **CRIMINAL** ▷ **2** [C] someone who helps another person to commit a crime but does not take part in it: *an accessory **to** murder* **3 accessory after the fact** legal someone who helps someone after they have committed a crime, for example by hiding them from the police **4 accessory before the fact** legal someone who helps in the preparation of a crime

ˈ**access proˌvider** **noun** [C] (also **ISP**) a company that allows you to use the internet and use email, and gives you space on the internet to put your documents: *the UK's largest **internet** access provider*

ˈ**access ˌroad** **noun** [C] (also ˈ**access ˌroute**) **1** a road leading from or to a particular place **2** UK a road leading to a main road

accha (also **achha**) /ˈætʃ.ɑː/ **exclamation** Indian English **1** used for showing that you agree with something or understand something: *Accha, that's good. Go ahead!* **2** used for showing surprise or happiness: *'I managed to buy it for half the price.' 'Accha!'*

accident /ˈæk.sɪ.dənt/ **noun** [C] **1** A2 something bad that happens that is not expected or intended and that often damages something or injures someone: *Josh **had** an accident and spilled water all over his work.* ◦ *She was injured **in** a car/road accident (= when one car hit another).* **2 by accident** B1 without intending to, or without being intended: *I deleted the file by accident.*

> **Word partners for accident**
>
> *have/be involved in* an accident • an accident *happens/occurs* • *cause* an accident • an accident *involving* sth • a *fatal/major/serious/tragic* accident • a *freak* accident • [killed/paralysed] *in* an accident

IDIOMS **accidents will happen** saying said after an accident in order to make it seem less bad • **an accident waiting to happen** a very dangerous situation in which an accident is very likely • **have an accident** to urinate or EXCRETE (= pass solid waste) when you do not intend to: *Even a six-year-old can have an accident at night sometimes.* • **more by accident than design** because of luck and not because of skill or organization: *The play was a success more by accident than design.*

accidental /ˌæk.sɪˈden.təl/ ⓤⓢ /-t̬əl/ **adj** B2 happening by chance: *Reports suggest that eleven soldiers were killed by accidental fire from their own side.*

ˌ**accidental** ˈ**death** **noun** [C] legal a VERDICT (= an opinion stated at the end of a trial) that is given when a death was the result of an accident and not of murder or SUICIDE

accidentally /ˌæk.sɪˈden.təl.i/ ⓤⓢ /-t̬əl-/ **adv** B1 by chance or by mistake: *I accidentally knocked a glass over.*

ˈ**accident-ˌprone** **adj** describes someone who often has accidents, usually because they are very awkward

acclaim /əˈkleɪm/ **noun; verb**

▸**noun** [U] public approval and praise: *Despite the **critical** acclaim, the novel did not sell well.* ◦ *Hamlet was played by Ion Caramitrou **to** rapturous acclaim.*

▸**verb** [T often passive] to give public approval and praise: *She was universally/widely/publicly acclaimed **for** her contribution to the discovery.* ◦ *She is being acclaimed (= publicly recognized) **as** the greatest dancer of her generation.* • **acclaimed** /əˈkleɪmd/ **adj** C1 *an acclaimed artist/writer/poet* ◦ *'Dinner Party', based on the **critically** acclaimed novel by Bill Davies, was made into a film last year.*

acclamation /ˌæk.ləˈmeɪ.ʃən/ **noun** [U] formal public approval and praise: *His speech was greeted with (shouts of) acclamation.*

acclimatize (UK usually **acclimatise**) /əˈklaɪ.mə.taɪz/ ⓤⓢ /-t̬aɪz/ **verb** [I or T] (US also **acclimate** /ˈæk.lə.meɪt/) to (cause to) change to suit different conditions of life, weather, etc.: *More time will be needed for the troops and equipment to become acclimatized **to** desert conditions.* ◦ *We found it impossible to acclimatize ourselves **to** the new working conditions.* ◦ *The defending champion has acclimatized **to** the 90°F sunshine by spending the past month in Florida.* • **acclimatization** (UK usually **acclimatisation**) /əˌklaɪ.mə.taɪˈzeɪ.ʃən/ ⓤⓢ /-t̬ɪ-/ **noun** [U]

accolade /ˈæk.ə.leɪd/ **noun** [C] formal praise and approval: *He's been granted the **ultimate** accolade – his face on a postage stamp.* ◦ *Her approval was the **highest** accolade he could receive.*

accommodate /əˈkɒm.ə.deɪt/ ⓤⓢ /-ˈkɑː.mə-/ **verb** [T] **FIND A PLACE FOR** ▷ **1** to provide with a place to live or to be stored in: *New students may be accommodated **in** halls of residence.* ◦ formal *There wasn't enough space to accommodate the files.* **SUIT** ▷ **2** to give what is needed to someone: *The new policies fail to accommodate the disabled.* ◦ *We always try to accommodate (= help) our clients **with** financial assistance if necessary.* **3 accommodate yourself** to change yourself or your behaviour to suit another person or new conditions: *Some find it hard to accommodate themselves to the new working conditions.*

accommodating /əˈkɒm.ə.deɪ.tɪŋ/ ⓤⓢ /-ˈkɑː.mə.deɪ.t̬ɪŋ/ **adj** describes a person who is eager or willing to help other people, for example by changing his or her plans: *I'm sure she'll help you – she's always very accommodating.*

> **Common mistake: accommodation**
>
> **Warning:** Check your spelling!
> **Accommodation** is one of the 50 words most often spelled wrongly by learners. Remember: the correct spelling has 'cc' and 'mm'.

accommodation /əˌkɒm.əˈdeɪ.ʃən/ ⓤⓢ /-ˌkɑː.mə-/ **noun** [U] mainly UK B1 a place to live, work, stay, etc. in: *There's a shortage of cheap accommodation (= places to live).*

! Common mistake: accommodation

In British English, **accommodation** does not have a plural form and cannot be used with **a** or **an**.

To talk about an amount of **accommodation**, do not say 'accommodations', just say **accommodation, some accommodation**, etc.:

~~*Would you like me to book overnight accommodations for you?*~~

Would you like me to book overnight accommodation for you?

To talk about **accommodation** in the singular, do not say 'an accommodation', just say **accommodation**:

~~*The college provides an excellent accommodation for students.*~~

The college provides excellent accommodation for students.

accommodations /əˌkɒm.əˈdeɪ.ʃənz/ US /-ˌkɑː.mə-/ noun [plural] US B2 a place to stay when you are travelling, especially a hotel room: *Sweepstakes winners will enjoy a week-long stay in luxury accommodations in Las Vegas.*

accompaniment /əˈkʌm.pən.ɪ.mənt/ noun **MUSIC ▷** **1** [C or U] music that is played with someone who is singing or playing the main tune: *a song with piano accompaniment* ◦ humorous *We worked* ***to the*** *accompaniment* ***of*** *(= while hearing the sound of) Mr French's drill.* **FOOD AND DRINK ▷** **2** [C] something that you eat or drink with something else: *A dry champagne makes the ideal accompaniment* ***for/to*** *this dish.*

accompanist /əˈkʌm.pə.nɪst/ noun [C] someone who plays an instrument such as the piano or guitar while someone else sings or plays the main tune: *The singer's accompanist* ***on*** *the piano was Charles Harman.*

accompany /əˈkʌm.pə.ni/ verb [T] **GO WITH ▷** **1** B1 to go with someone or to be provided or exist at the same time as something: *The course books are accompanied* ***by*** *four CDs.* ◦ *Depression is almost always accompanied* ***by*** *insomnia.* ◦ *The salmon was accompanied* ***by*** *(= served with) a fresh green salad.* **2** formal to show someone how to get to somewhere: *Would you like me to accompany you* ***to*** *your room?* **3** formal to go with someone to a social event or to an entertainment: *'May I accompany you* ***to*** *the ball?' he asked her.* ◦ *I have two tickets for the theatre on Saturday evening – would you like to accompany me?* **PLAY MUSIC ▷** **4** C2 to sing or play an instrument with another musician or singer: *Miss Jessop accompanied Mr Bentley* ***on*** *the piano.*

accompanying /əˈkʌm.pə.ni.ɪŋ/ adj appearing or going with someone or something else: *Front-page stories broke the news of the star leaving, and accompanying photographs showed her getting on the plane.* ◦ *Children under twelve require an accompanying parent or guardian to see this movie.*

accomplice /əˈkʌm.plɪs/ US /-ˈkɑːm-/ noun [C] a person who helps someone else to commit a crime or to do something morally wrong

accomplish /əˈkʌm.plɪʃ/ US /-ˈkɑːm-/ verb [T] C1 to finish something successfully or to achieve something: *The students accomplished the task in less than ten minutes.* ◦ *She accomplished such a lot during her visit.* ◦ *I feel as if I've accomplished nothing since I left my job.*

accomplished /əˈkʌm.plɪʃt/ US /-ˈkɑːm-/ adj skilled: *She's a very accomplished pianist/painter/horsewoman.* ◦ *He was accomplished* ***in*** *all the arts.*

accomplishment /əˈkʌm.plɪʃ.mənt/ US /-ˈkɑːm-/ noun **1** [C] something that is successful, or that is achieved after a lot of work or effort: *Getting the two leaders to sign a peace treaty was his* ***greatest*** *accomplishment.* **2** [U] the finishing of something: *We celebrated the successful accomplishment of our task.* **3** [C] a skill: *Cordon bleu cookery is just one of her many accomplishments.*

accord /əˈkɔːd/ US /-ˈkɔːrd/ noun; verb

▸noun [C or U] **1** (a formal) agreement: *On 31 May the two leaders signed a* ***peace*** *accord.* ◦ *The project is completely* ***in*** *accord* ***with*** *government policy.* **2 of your own accord** C2 If you do something of your own accord, you do it without being asked to do it: *She came of her own accord. No one asked her to come.* **3 with one accord** formal If people do something with one accord, they do it together and in complete agreement: *With one accord, the delegates walked out of the conference.*

▸verb [T] formal to treat someone specially, usually by showing respect: [+ two objects] *The massed crowds of supporters accorded him a hero's welcome.* ◦ *Certainly in our society teachers don't enjoy the respect that is accorded* ***to*** *doctors and lawyers.*

PHRASAL VERB **accord with sth** to be the same as something, or to agree with something: *His version of events does not accord with witnesses' statements.*

accordance /əˈkɔː.dəns/ US /-ˈkɔːr-/ noun formal **in accordance with a rule, law, wish, etc.** C1 following or obeying a rule, law, wish, etc.: *In accordance with her wishes, she was buried in France.*

accordingly /əˈkɔː.dɪŋ.li/ US /-ˈkɔːr-/ adv formal in a way that is suitable or right for the situation: *When we receive your instructions we shall* ***act*** *accordingly.* ◦ *She's an expert in her field, and is paid accordingly.*

acˈcording ˌto preposition **OPINION ▷** **1** B1 as stated by: *According to Sarah they're not getting on very well at the moment.* ◦ *According to our records you owe us $130.*

! Common mistake: according to

Warning: according to is used to introduce what another person said:

According to Rory, the training course was a waste of time.

To introduce your own opinion, don't say 'according to me', say **in my opinion** or **I think**:

~~*According to me, the training course was a waste of time.*~~

In my opinion, the training course was a waste of time.

METHOD ▷ **2** B2 in a way that agrees with: *Students are all put in different groups according to their ability.* **3 according to plan** Something that happens according to plan happens in the way it was intended to: *Did it all go according to plan?*

accordion /əˈkɔː.di.ən/ US /-ˈkɔːr-/ noun [C] a box-shaped musical instrument consisting of a folded central part with a keyboard, played by pushing the two ends towards each other

accordion

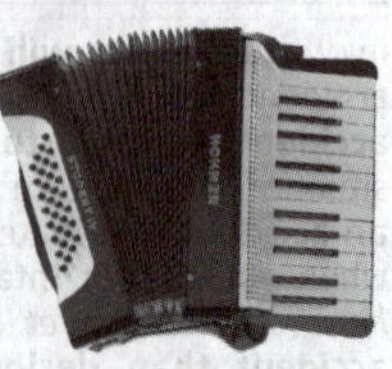

accost /əˈkɒst/ US /-ˈkɑːst/ verb [T often passive] formal to go up to or stop and speak to someone in a threatening way: *I'm usually accosted by beggars and drunks as I walk to the station.*

account /əˈkaʊnt/ noun; verb

▸noun **BANK** ▷ **1** B1 [C] (also ˈ**bank ac**ˌ**count**) an arrangement with a bank to keep your money there and to allow you to take it out when you need to: *I've **opened** an account **with** a building society.* ◦ *I paid the money into my account this morning.* ◦ UK *She **paid the cheque into** her account.* ◦ US *She **deposited the check in** her account.* ◦ *I need to **draw** some money **out of** my account.* **REPORT** ▷ **2** B2 [C] a written or spoken description of an event: *She **gave** a thrilling account **of** her life in the jungle.* ◦ *He **kept** a detailed account **of** the suspect's movements.* ◦ *Several eyewitnesses' accounts differed considerably from the official version of events.* **3 by/from all accounts** C1 as said by most people: *By all accounts, San Francisco is a city that's easy to fall in love with.* **4 by your own account** If something is true by your own account, what you say is true although you have not proved it: *By his own account, he's quite wealthy.* **REASON** ▷ **5 on account of sth** formal B2 because of something: *He doesn't drink alcohol on account of his health.* **BUSINESS** ▷ **6** [C] an agreement with a shop or business that allows you to buy things and pay for them later: *Could you **put** it **on/charge** it **to** my account (= can I pay for it later), please?* ◦ *Do you have an account **at** this store/**with** us, madam?* ◦ *Could you please **pay/settle** your account in full (= give us all the money you owe us)?* **7** [C] a customer who does business with a company: *If the advertising agency loses this account, it will make a big dent in their profits.* **IMPORTANCE** ▷ **8 be of no/little account** formal to not be important: *It's of no account to me whether he comes or not.* ◦ *His opinion is of little account to me.*

IDIOMS **be brought/called to account** mainly UK to be forced to explain something you did wrong, and usually to be punished: *We must ensure that the people responsible for the violence are brought to account.* • **on sb's account** If something is said to be on someone's or something's account, it is because of that person or thing: *I'm not very hungry, so please don't cook on my account (= don't cook just for me).* • **on no account** C2 If something must on no account/not on any account be done, it must not be done at any time or for any reason: *Employees must on no account make personal phone calls from the office.* ◦ *These records must not on any account be changed.* • **take sth into account** (also **take account of sth**) B2 to consider or remember something when judging a situation: *I hope my teacher will take into account **the fact that** I was ill just before the exams when she marks my paper.* ◦ *A good architect takes into account the building's surroundings.* ◦ *The UK's tax system takes no account of children.* ◦ *I think you have to take into account **that** he's a good deal younger than the rest of us.* • **turn/use sth to good account** UK formal to use your skills and abilities to produce good results: *I think we'd all agree that you turned your negotiating skills to very good account in this afternoon's meeting.*

▸verb [T + obj + noun/adj] formal **JUDGE** ▷ to think of someone or something in the stated way: *She was accounted a genius by all who knew her work.* → Synonym **judge**

IDIOM **there's no accounting for taste** saying said when it is difficult to explain why different people like different things, especially things that you do not like: *'I love working at weekends.' 'Well, there's no accounting for taste!'*

PHRASAL VERBS **account (to sb) for sth** C2 to explain the reason for something or the cause of something: *Can you account for your absence last Friday?* ◦ *She was unable to account for over $5,000 (= she could not explain where the money was).* ◦ *He has to account to his manager for (= tell his manager about and explain) all his movements.* • **account for sth** to form the total of something: *Students account for the vast majority of our customers.*

accountable /əˈkaʊn.tə.bl/ US /-t̬ə-/ **adj** C2 Someone who is accountable is completely responsible for what they do and must be able to give a satisfactory reason for it: *She is accountable only **to** the managing director.* ◦ *The recent tax reforms have made government more accountable **for** its spending.* ◦ *Politicians should be accountable **to** the public who elected them.* • **accountability** /əˌkaʊn.təˈbɪl.ɪ.ti/ US /-t̬əˈbɪl.ə.t̬i/ **noun** [U] *There were furious demands for greater police accountability.*

accountancy /əˈkaʊn.tᵊn.si/ US /-t̬ᵊn-/ **noun** [U] UK (US **accounting**) the job of being an accountant: *He works in accountancy.* ◦ *an accountancy firm*

accountant /əˈkaʊn.tᵊnt/ US /-t̬ᵊnt/ **noun** [C] B1 someone who keeps or examines the records of money received, paid, and owed by a company or person: *a firm of accountants*

accounting /əˈkaʊn.tɪŋ/ US /-t̬ɪŋ/ **noun** [U] **1** the skill or activity of keeping records of the money a person or organization earns and spends **2** US (UK **accountancy**) the job of being an accountant

accounts /əˈkaʊnts/ **noun** [plural] an official record of all the money a person or company has spent and received: *I **keep** my own accounts.*

accoutrements formal (US also **accouterments**) /əˈkuː.trə.mənts/ US /əˈkuː.t̬ə-/ **noun** [plural] the equipment needed for a particular activity or way of life

accredit /əˈkred.ɪt/ **verb** [T] to officially recognize, accept, or approve of someone or something: *The agency was not accredited by the Philippine Consulate to offer contracts to Filipinos abroad.* • **accreditation** /əˌkred.ɪˈteɪ.ʃᵊn/ US /-ə-/ **noun** [U] *The college received/was given full accreditation in 1965.*

accredited /əˈkred.ɪ.tɪd/ US /-t̬ɪd/ **adj** officially recognized or approved: *an accredited drama school* ◦ *accredited war correspondents*

accretion /əˈkriː.ʃᵊn/ **noun** [C or U] formal a gradual increase or growth by the addition of new layers or parts: *The fund was increased by the accretion of new shareholders.*

accrual /əˈkruː.əl/ **noun** [C or U] a gradual increase in an amount of money

accrue /əˈkruː/ **verb** [I] formal to increase in number or amount over a period of time: *Interest will accrue **on** the account at a rate of seven percent.* ◦ *Little benefit will accrue **to** London (= London will receive little benefit) from the new road scheme.*

acculturate /əˈkʌl.tʃᵊr.eɪt/ US /-tʃə.reɪt/ **verb** [I or T] to change so that you become more like people from a different culture, or to make someone change in this way: *How did Hispanics acculturate **to** life in America?* • **acculturation** /əˌkʌl.tʃᵊrˈeɪʃᵊn/ US /-tʃəˈreɪ-/ **noun** [U]

accumulate /əˈkjuː.mjʊ.leɪt/ **verb** **1** C2 [T] to collect a large number of things over a long period of time: *As people accumulate more wealth, they tend to spend a greater proportion of their incomes.* ◦ *We've accumulated so much rubbish over the years.* **2** C2 [I] to gradually increase in number or amount: *A thick layer of dust had accumulated in the room.* ◦ *If you don't sort out the papers on your desk on a regular basis, they just keep on accumulating.*

accumulation /əˌkjuː.mjʊˈleɪ.ʃᵊn/ **noun** [U or C] C2 an amount of something that has been collected:

Despite this accumulation of evidence, the government persisted in doing nothing.

accumulator /əˈkjuː.mjʊ.leɪ.təʳ/ (US) /-t̬ɚ/ **noun** [C] UK (US ˈ**storage** ˌ**battery**) a BATTERY that collects and stores electricity

accuracy /ˈæk.jʊ.rə.si/ **noun** [U] **1** B2 the fact of being exact or correct: *We can predict changes with **a** surprising **degree of** accuracy.* **2** the ability to do something without making mistakes

accurate /ˈæk.jʊ.rət/ **adj** B1 correct, exact, and without any mistakes: *an accurate machine* ◦ *an accurate description* ◦ *The figures they have used are just not accurate.* ◦ *Her novel is an accurate reflection of life in Spain.* ◦ *We hope to become more accurate **in** predicting earthquakes.* → Opposite **inaccurate** • **accurately** /-li/ **adv** B1 *The plans should be drawn as accurately as possible.*

accursed /əˈkɜː.sɪd/, /-ˈkɜːst/ (US) /-ˈkɝːst/ **adj** [before noun] old-fashioned very annoying

accusation /ˌæk.jʊˈzeɪ.ʃən/ **noun** [C or U] C1 a statement saying that someone has done something morally wrong, illegal, or unkind, or the fact of accusing someone: *You can't just make **wild** accusations like that!* ◦ *He glared at me **with an air of** accusation.* ◦ [+ that] *What do you say to the accusation **that** you are unfriendly and unhelpful?*

accusative /əˈkjuː.zə.tɪv/ (US) /-t̬ɪv/ **noun** [S] the form of a noun, PRONOUN, or adjective that is used in some languages to show that the word is the DIRECT OBJECT of a verb • **accusative adj** *the accusative ending*

accusatory /əˈkjuː.zə.tər.i/, /ˌæk.jʊˈzeɪ-/ (US) /-tɔːr.i/ **adj** formal suggesting that you think someone has done something bad: *When he spoke his tone was accusatory.* ◦ *She gave me an accusatory look.*

accuse /əˈkjuːz/ **verb** [T] **1** B2 to say that someone has done something morally wrong, illegal, or unkind: *'It wasn't my fault.' 'Don't worry, I'm not accusing you.'* ◦ *He's been accused **of** robbery/murder.* ◦ *Are you accusing me **of** lying?* ◦ *The surgeon was accused **of** negligence.* **2 stand accused of sth** formal If you stand accused of doing something wrong, people say that you have done it: *The government stands accused of eroding freedom of speech.* • **accuser** /əˈkjuː.zəʳ/ (US) /-zɚ/ **noun** [C] *She was given the chance to **face** her accusers.*

the acˈcused **noun** [C] (plural **the accused**) the person who is on trial in a law court: *The accused protested her innocence.* ◦ *The accused were all found guilty.*

accusing /əˈkjuː.zɪŋ/ **adj** suggesting that you think someone has done something bad: *an accusing glance/look* • **accusingly** /-li/ **adv** *'Has this dog been fed today?' she asked accusingly.*

accustom /əˈkʌs.təm/ **verb**

PHRASAL VERB **accustom yourself to sth** to make yourself familiar with new conditions: *It'll take time for me to accustom myself to the changes.*

accustomed /əˈkʌs.təmd/ **adj** **1** C1 familiar with something: *She quickly became accustomed **to** his messy ways.* ◦ *I'm not accustomed **to being** treated like this.* **2** formal usual: *She performed the task with her accustomed ease.*

ace /eɪs/ **noun; verb; adj**

▸**noun** [C] **PLAYING CARD** ▷ **1** one of the four playing cards with a single mark or spot, which have the highest or lowest value in many card games: *the ace of hearts/clubs/spades/diamonds* **SKILLED PERSON** ▷ **2** informal a person who is very skilled at something: *a tennis/flying ace* **TENNIS** ▷ **3** in tennis, a SERVE (= a hit of the ball that starts play) that is so strong and fast that the other player cannot return the ball: *That's the third ace Lawson has **served** this match.*

IDIOMS **an ace up your sleeve** (US also **an ace in the hole**) secret knowledge or a secret skill that will give you an advantage • **come within an ace of sth** UK to almost achieve something: *She came within an ace of winning the match.* • **have/hold all the aces** to be in a strong position when you are competing with someone else because you have all the advantages: *In a situation like this, it's the big companies who hold all the aces.*

▸**verb** [T] US informal to do very well in an exam: *I was up all night studying, but it was worth it – I aced my chemistry final.*

▸**adj** old-fashioned slang excellent: *He's an ace footballer.* ◦ *That's an ace bike you've got there.*

acerbic /əˈsɜː.bɪk/ (US) /-ˈsɝː-/ **adj** formal describes something that is spoken or written in a way that is direct, clever, and cruel: *The letters show the acerbic **wit** for which Parker was both admired and feared.* • **acerbity** /əˈsɜː.bə.ti/ (US) /-ˈsɝː.bə.t̬i/ **noun** [U]

acetaminophen /əˌsiː.təˈmɪn.ə.fen/ (US) /-t̬ə-/ **noun** [C or U] (plural **acetaminophens** or **acetaminophen**) US for **paracetamol**

acetate /ˈæs.ɪ.teɪt/ **noun** [U] a chemical substance made from acetic acid, or a smooth artificial cloth made from this

acetic acid /əˌsiː.tɪkˈæs.ɪd/ (US) /-t̬ɪk-/ **noun** [U] a clear ACID with a strong smell, found in VINEGAR

acetone /ˈæs.ɪ.təʊn/ (US) /-t̬oʊn/ **noun** [U] a strong-smelling, clear liquid that is used in the production of various chemicals and is sometimes added to paint to make it more liquid

acetylene /əˈset.ə.liːn/ (US) /-ˈset̬-/ **noun** [U] a gas with a strong smell that burns with a very hot, bright flame, used in cutting and joining metal

ache /eɪk/ **noun; verb**

▸**noun** [C] **1** B1 a continuous pain that is unpleasant but not very strong: *As you get older, you have all sorts of aches **and pains**.* ◦ *I've got a **dull** (= slight) ache **in** my lower back.* **2** B1 used in combinations with parts of the body to mean a continuous pain in the stated part: *earache/headache/toothache/backache* ◦ *I've had a stomach ache all morning.*

▸**verb** [I] B2 to have a continuous pain that is unpleasant but not very strong: *My head/tooth/back aches.* ◦ *I ache/I'm aching **all over**.* ◦ *I've got one or two aching muscles after yesterday's run.*

PHRASAL VERB **ache for sth** literary to want something very much: *He was lonely and aching for love.*

achha exclamation **accha**

achievable /əˈtʃiː.və.bl̩/ **adj** describes a task, ambition, etc. that is possible to achieve: *Before you set your targets, make sure that they are achievable.*

achieve /əˈtʃiːv/ **verb** [T] B1 to succeed in finishing something or reaching an aim, especially after a lot of work or effort: *The government's training policy, he claimed, was achieving its **objectives**.* ◦ *She finally achieved her **ambition** to visit South America.* → See also **underachieve**

achievement /əˈtʃiːv.mənt/ **noun** [C or U] B1 something very good and difficult that you have succeeded in doing: *An Olympic silver medal is a remarkable achievement for one so young.* ◦ *The Tale of Genji has been described as the greatest achievement of Japanese literature.* ◦ *It gives you a **sense of** achievement if you actually make it to the end of a very long book.*

Word partners for achievement

a *great/notable/remarkable/outstanding* achievement • sb's *crowning* achievement • a *record* of achievement • a *sense* of achievement • *belittle/detract from* sb's achievement • *celebrate* sb's achievement

achiever /əˈtʃiː.vər/ (US) /-vɚ/ noun **high/low achiever** a person who achieves more/less than the average: *Not enough attention is given to the low achievers in the class.*

Achilles heel /əˌkɪl.iːzˈhiːl/ noun [C usually singular] a small fault or weakness in a person or system that can result in failure: *A misbehaving minister is regarded as a government's Achilles heel and is expected to resign.*

Achilles tendon /əˌkɪl.iːzˈten.dən/ noun [C] the part of the body that connects the HEEL bone to the muscles in the lower part of the leg

achingly /ˈeɪ.kɪŋ.li/ adv literary extremely: *Sung by the world's greatest tenor, this aria is achingly beautiful.*

achkan /ˈætʃ.kən/ noun [C] a long coat that reaches to the knees and has buttons down the front, worn by men from South Asia

achoo /əˈtʃuː/ exclamation **atishoo**

achy /ˈeɪ.ki/ adj informal Someone who feels achy has continuous pains in their body that are unpleasant but not very strong: *I've been feeling tired and achy (= full of pains) all morning.*

acid /ˈæs.ɪd/ noun; adj

▸noun **CHEMICAL** ▷ **1** B2 [C or U] any of various usually liquid substances that can react with and sometimes dissolve other materials: *acetic/hydrochloric/lactic acid* ◦ *Vinegar is an acid.* **DRUG** ▷ **2** [U] slang for LSD (= an illegal drug that makes people see things that do not exist)

▸adj **CHEMICAL** ▷ **1** (also **acidic**) containing acid, or having similar qualities to an acid: *an acid taste/smell* ◦ *acid soil* **UNKIND** ▷ **2** describes a remark or way of speaking that is cruel or criticizes something in an unkind way: *her acid wit* ◦ *When she spoke her tone was acid.*

ˌacid-ˈfree adj Acid-free paper does not contain any harmful acid that can damage documents, paintings, etc.: *The books are printed on acid-free paper so they will last for generations.*

acidic /əˈsɪd.ɪk/ adj **1** containing acid: *acidic soil* **2** very sour: *a slightly acidic taste*

acidify /əˈsɪd.ɪ.faɪ/ verb [I or T] specialized to become an acid or to make something become an acid

acidity /əˈsɪd.ɪ.ti/ (US) /-ə.t̬i/ noun [U] the amount of acid in a substance or in your stomach: *This low pH level clearly shows the acidity of the soil here.*

ˌacid ˈjazz noun [U] a style of popular dance music that is a mix of FUNK, SOUL, and JAZZ

acidly /ˈæs.ɪd.li/ adv in a way that is cruel or criticizes: *'I suppose you expect me to thank you for coming,' he said acidly.*

acidophilus /ˌæs.ɪˈdɒf.ɪ.ləs/ (US) /-dɑːfə.ləs/ noun [U] specialized a type of bacterium used to make YOGURT or as a medicine to help people digest food if they have a stomach illness

ˌacid ˈrain noun [U] rain that contains large amounts of harmful chemicals as a result of burning substances such as coal and oil

the ˈacid ˌtest noun [S] the true test of the value of something: *It looks good, but will people buy it? That's the acid test.*

acknowledge /əkˈnɒl.ɪdʒ/ (US) /-ˈnɑː.lɪdʒ/ verb [T] **1** C1 to accept, admit, or recognize something, or the truth or existence of something: [+ -ing verb] *She acknowledged having been at fault.* ◦ [+ that] *She acknowledged **that** she had been at fault.* ◦ *You must acknowledge the truth of her argument.* ◦ *Historians generally acknowledge her **as** a genius in her field.* ◦ [+ obj + to infinitive] *She is usually acknowledged **to** be one of our best artists.* ◦ *They refused to acknowledge (= to recognize officially) the new government.* ◦ *He didn't even acknowledge my **presence** (= show that he had seen me).* ◦ *The government won't even acknowledge the existence of the problem.* **2** C1 to tell someone, usually in a letter or email, that you have received something they sent you: *Please acknowledge **receipt of** this letter.*

acknowledgment (also **acknowledgement**) /əkˈnɒl.ɪdʒ.mənt/ (US) /-ˈnɑː.lɪdʒ-/ noun **1** [C or U] the fact of accepting that something is true or right: *All I want is some acknowledgment that his behaviour is unreasonable.* **2** something given to thank someone for what they have done: *We sent her a copy of the book **in** acknowledgment **of** her part in its creation.* **3** a letter or email to say that something has been received: *I applied for four jobs, but I've only had one acknowledgment so far.* **4 acknowledgments** (also **acknowledgements**) [plural] a short text at the beginning or end of a book where the writer names people or other works that have helped in writing the book

the acme /ˈæk.mi/ noun [S] literary the best or most perfect thing that can exist or be achieved: *To act on this world-famous stage is surely the acme **of** any actor's career.*

acne /ˈæk.ni/ noun [U] a skin disease common in young people, in which small, red spots appear on the face and neck: *Acne is the curse of adolescence.*

acolyte /ˈæk.əl.aɪt/ noun [C] formal or specialized anyone who follows or helps another person, or someone who helps a priest in some religious ceremonies

acorn /ˈeɪ.kɔːn/ (US) /-kɔːrn/ noun [C] an oval nut that grows on an OAK tree and has an outer part shaped like a cup

acorn

acoustic /əˈkuː.stɪk/ adj; noun

▸adj **1** relating to sound or hearing: *The microphone converts acoustic waves to electrical signals for transmission.* **2** describes a musical instrument that is not made louder by electrical equipment: *an acoustic guitar*

▸noun [C usually plural] the way in which the structure of a building or room affects the qualities of musical or spoken sound: *The concert was recorded in a church that is famous for its acoustics.* • **acoustically** /-stɪ.kəl.i/ adv

acoustics /əˈkuː.stɪks/ noun [U] specialized the scientific study of sound

acquaint /əˈkweɪnt/ verb

PHRASAL VERB **acquaint sb/yourself with sth** formal to make someone or yourself familiar with something: *Take time to acquaint your**self** with the rules.* ◦ *The Broadcasting Museum offers workshops to acquaint children with the world of radio.*

acquaintance /əˈkweɪn.təns/ noun **1** C1 [C] a person that you have met but do not know well: *a business acquaintance* **2** [U] formal used in some expressions about knowing or meeting people: *It was at the Taylors' party that I first **made his** acquaintance (= first*

met him). ◦ *I wasn't sure about Darryl when I first met her, but* ***on further*** *acquaintance (= knowing her a little more) I rather like her.* **3** [U] formal knowledge of a subject: *Sadly, my acquaintance* ***with*** *Spanish literature is rather limited.* • **acquaintanceship** /-ʃɪp/ **noun** [C or U] formal *Ours was a strictly professional acquaintanceship (= relationship).*

IDIOM **have a passing/slight/nodding acquaintance with sth** formal to have very little knowledge or experience of a subject: *I'm afraid I have only a nodding acquaintance with his works.*

acquainted /əˈkweɪn.tɪd/ Ⓤⓢ /-t̬ɪd/ **adj** formal **1** [after verb] knowing or being familiar with a person: *I am not personally acquainted* ***with*** *the gentleman in question.* **2 be acquainted with sth** to know or be familiar with something, because you have studied it or have experienced it before: *Police said the thieves were obviously well acquainted with the alarm system at the department store.*

acquiesce /ˌæk.wiˈes/ **verb** [I] formal to accept or agree to something, often unwillingly: *Reluctantly, he acquiesced* ***to/in*** *the plans.*

acquiescent /ˌæk.wiˈes.ənt/ **adj** formal willing to do what other people want: *She has a very acquiescent nature.* • **acquiescence** /-əns/ **noun** [U] agreement: *I was surprised by her acquiescence* ***to/in*** *the scheme.*

acquire /əˈkwaɪər/ Ⓤⓢ /-ˈkwaɪɚ/ **verb** [T] B2 to get something: *He acquired the firm in 2008.* ◦ *I was wearing a* ***newly/recently*** *acquired jacket.* ◦ *During this period he acquired* ***a reputation*** *for being a womanizer.*

IDIOM **an acquired taste** something that you dislike at first, but that you start to like after you have tried it a few times: *Olives are an acquired taste.*

acquirer /əˈkwaɪ.rər/ Ⓤⓢ /-rɚ/ **noun** [C] mainly US a company that buys other companies, usually to sell them for a profit: *A business with so much growth is sure to generate interest among potential acquirers.*

acquisition /ˌæk.wɪˈzɪʃ.ən/ **noun** **1** [U] the process of getting something: *The acquisition of huge amounts of data has helped our research enormously.* ◦ ***Language*** *acquisition (= learning a language without being taught) starts at a very young age.* **2** [C] something that someone buys, often to add to a collection of things: *The museum's latest acquisition is a four-million-dollar sculpture.* ◦ *I like your earrings – are they a* ***recent*** *acquisition? (= Did you get them recently?)* **3** [C or U] something such as a building, another company, or a piece of land that is bought by a company, or the act of buying it

acquisitive /əˈkwɪz.ɪ.tɪv/ Ⓤⓢ /-ə.t̬ɪv/ **adj** formal WANTING THINGS ▷ **1** disapproving eager to own and collect things: *We live in an acquisitive society that views success primarily in terms of material possessions.* COMPANY ▷ **2** used to describe a company that buys other companies: *It has been one of the most acquisitive firms in recent times, buying over a dozen businesses in the last 18 months.*

acquit /əˈkwɪt/ **verb** (-tt-) **1** [T often passive] to decide officially in a law court that someone is not guilty of a particular crime: *She was acquitted* ***of*** *all the charges against her.* ◦ *Five months ago he was acquitted on a shoplifting charge.* → Compare **convict** **2 acquit yourself** formal to do better than expected in a difficult situation: *I thought that he acquitted himself admirably in today's meeting.*

acquittal /əˈkwɪt.əl/ Ⓤⓢ /-ˈkwɪt̬-/ **noun** [C or U] the decision of a court that someone is not guilty: *The first trial ended in a hung jury, the second in acquittal.* ◦ *Of the three cases that went to trial, two ended in acquittals.*

acre /ˈeɪ.kər/ Ⓤⓢ /-kɚ/ **noun** [C] C2 a unit for measuring area, equal to 4,047 square metres or 4,840 square YARDS: *He's got 400 acres of land in Wales.* • **acreage** /-ɪdʒ/ **noun** [C or U] *What acreage is (= how big is) her estate?*

acrid /ˈæk.rɪd/ **adj** describes a smell or taste that is strong and bitter and causes a burning feeling in the throat: *Clouds of acrid* ***smoke*** *issued from the building.*

acrimonious /ˌæk.rɪˈməʊ.ni.əs/ Ⓤⓢ /-ˈmoʊ-/ **adj** formal full of anger, arguments, and bad feeling: *an acrimonious dispute* ◦ *Their marriage ended eight years ago in an acrimonious* ***divorce.*** • **acrimoniously** /-li/ **adv** *In 2012 he separated acrimoniously from his wife.* • **acrimony** /ˈæk.rɪ.mə.ni/ Ⓤⓢ /ˈæk.rə.moʊ.ni/ **noun** [U] *The acrimony of the dispute has shocked a lot of people.*

acrobat /ˈæk.rə.bæt/ **noun** [C] a person who entertains people by doing difficult and skilful physical things, such as walking along a high wire

acrobatic /ˌæk.rəˈbæt.ɪk/ Ⓤⓢ /-ˈbæt̬-/ **adj** involving or able to perform difficult and attractive body movements: *an acrobatic leap into the air* ◦ *an acrobatic young dancer*

acrobatics /ˌæk.rəˈbæt.ɪks/ Ⓤⓢ /-ˈbæt̬-/ **noun** [U] the skills of an acrobat: *He had spent the last ten years in a Peking Opera school, studying martial arts and acrobatics.*

acronym /ˈæk.rə.nɪm/ **noun** [C] an abbreviation consisting of the first letters of each word in the name of something, pronounced as a word: *AIDS is an acronym for 'Acquired Immune Deficiency Syndrome'.*

across /əˈkrɒs/ Ⓤⓢ /-ˈkrɑːs/ **adv, preposition; preposition**

▸**adv, preposition** A2 from one side to the other of something with clear limits, such as an area of land, a road, or a river: *She walked across the field/road.* ◦ *They're building a new bridge across the river.* ◦ *When I reached the river, I simply swam across.*

▸**preposition** **1** A2 on the opposite side of: *The library is just across the road.* **2** in every part of a particular place or country: *Voting took place peacefully across most of the country.*

aˌcross-the-ˈboard **adj** [before noun] affecting everyone or everything within an organization, system, or society: *The proposed across-the-board cuts for all state agencies will total $84 million.*

acrostic /əˈkrɒs.tɪk/ Ⓤⓢ /-ˈkrɑː.stɪk/ **noun** [C] specialized a text, usually a poem, in which particular letters, such as the first letters of each line, spell a word or phrase

acrylic /əˈkrɪl.ɪk/ **noun; adj**

▸**noun** **1** [U] a type of cloth or plastic produced by chemical processes **2** [C usually plural] a type of paint

▸**adj** made of a substance or cloth produced by chemical processes from a type of ACID: *an acrylic scarf/sweater* ◦ *acrylic paint*

act /ækt/ **verb; noun**

▸**verb** BEHAVE ▷ **1** [I] to behave in the stated way: *Don't be so silly – you're acting* ***like*** *a child!* ◦ *He acted* ***as if*** *he'd never met me before.* DO SOMETHING ▷ **2** B2 [I] to do something for a particular purpose or to solve a problem: [+ to infinitive] *Engineers acted quickly* ***to*** *repair the damaged pipes.* ◦ *She acted without thinking.* ◦ *Who is acting* ***for/on behalf of*** *(= who is representing) the defendant?* ◦ *He never acts* ***on*** *other people's advice (= does what other people suggest).* ◦ *Acting* ***on impulse*** *(= without thinking first) can get you into a lot of trouble.* HAVE AN EFFECT ▷ **3** [I] to have an effect: *The* *anaesthetic acted quickly.* **PERFORM** ▷ **4** B1 [I or T] to perform a part in a film, play, etc.: *Ellis Pike was chosen to act the* ***part*** *of the lawyer in the film.* ◦ *Have you ever acted* ***in*** *a play before?* **5 act the fool, martyr, etc.** to behave in a particular, usually bad, way: *Why are you always acting the fool?*

PHRASAL VERBS **act as sth 1** B2 to do a particular job, especially one that you do not normally do: *He was asked to act as an adviser on the project.* **2** to have a particular effect: *Some people say that capital punishment acts as a deterrent.* • **act sth out 1** to perform the actions and say the words of a situation or story: *The children acted out their favourite poem.* **2** to express your thoughts, emotions, or ideas in your actions: *Children's negative feelings often get acted out in bad behaviour.* • **act up 1** If a person, especially a child, acts up, they behave badly: *Sophie got bored and started acting up.* **2** If a machine or part of the body acts up, it does not perform as well as it should: *My car always acts up in cold weather.* ◦ *Her shoulder was acting up (= hurting because of injury).*

▸noun **THING DONE** ▷ **1** B2 [C] something that you do: *an act* ***of*** *aggression/bravery/madness/terrorism* ◦ *a kind/thoughtless/selfish act* ◦ *The simple act of telling someone about a problem can help.* ◦ *Primitive people regarded storms as an act* ***of God****.* **PERFORMANCE** ▷ **2** C2 [S] behaviour that hides your real feelings or intentions: *Was she really upset or was that just an act?* **3** [C] a person or group that performs a short piece in a show, or the piece that they perform: *a comedy/juggling/trapeze act* ◦ *Our next act is a very talented young musician.* **4** B1 [C] a part of a play or OPERA: *The hero does not enter until the second act/Act Two.* **LAW** ▷ **5** [C] legal a law or formal decision made by a parliament or other group of people who make the laws for their country: *an Act of Parliament* ◦ *Almost two hundred suspects were detained in the UK last year* ***under*** *the Prevention of Terrorism Act.* ◦ *The state legislature* ***passed*** *an act banning the sale of automatic weapons.*

> Word partners for **act noun (THING DONE)**
>
> an act *of* sth • *commit* an act • a *barbaric/cowardly/despicable* act • a *criminal/terrorist/unlawful* act

IDIOMS **be a hard/tough act to follow** informal to be so good that it is not likely that anyone or anything that comes after will be as good: *His presidency was very successful – it'll be a hard act to follow.* • **do a disappearing/vanishing act** to go away, usually because you do not want to do something or meet someone: *Tim always does a vanishing act when my mother comes to stay.* • **get your act together** informal C2 to start to organize yourself so that you do things in an effective way: *She's so disorganized – I wish she'd get her act together.* • **get/muscle in on the act** informal to take advantage of something that someone else started: *We did all the hard work of setting up the company, and now everyone wants to get in on the act.* • **put on an act** informal to behave or speak in a false or artificial way: *He's just putting on an act for the boss's benefit.*

acting /ˈæk.tɪŋ/ noun; adj

▸noun [U] the job of performing in films or plays: *He wants to get into acting.*

▸adj **acting chairman, manager, etc.** someone who does a job for a short time while the person who usually does that job is not there: *He'll be the acting director until they can appoint a permanent one.*

action /ˈæk.ʃən/ noun; verb

▸noun **DOING SOMETHING** ▷ **1** B2 [U] the process of doing something, especially when dealing with a problem or difficulty: *This problem calls for* ***swift/prompt*** *action from the government.* ◦ [+ to infinitive] *Action* ***to*** *prevent the spread of the disease is high on the government's agenda.* ◦ *We must* ***take*** *action (= do something) to deal with the problem before it spreads to other areas.* ◦ *So what's the* ***plan of*** *action? (= What are we going to do?)* ◦ *The complaints system* ***swings into*** *action (= starts to work) as soon as a claim is made.* ◦ *The committee was* ***spurred into*** *action (= encouraged to do something) by the threat of government cuts.* **SOMETHING DONE** ▷ **2** B2 [C] something that you do: *She has to accept the consequences of her actions.* ◦ *I asked him to explain his actions.* **3** C2 [C] a physical movement: *I'll say the words and you can mime the actions.* ◦ *It only needs a small wrist action (= movement of the wrist) to start the process.* **ACTIVITY** ▷ **4** B1 [U] things that are happening, especially exciting or important things: *I like films with a lot of action.* ◦ *In her last novel, the action (= the main events) moves between Greece and southern Spain.* **5 where the action is** at the place where something important or interesting is happening: *A journalist has to be where the action is.* **EFFECT** ▷ **6** [S] the effect something has on another thing: *They recorded the action of the drug* ***on*** *the nervous system.* **WAR** ▷ **7** C2 [U] fighting in a war: *Her younger son was* ***killed in*** *action.* ◦ *He was reported* ***missing in*** *action.* ◦ *He* ***saw*** *action (= fought as a soldier) in the trenches.* **WAY THING WORKS** ▷ **8** C2 [U or C] the way something moves or works: *We studied the action of the digestive system.* ◦ *The car has a very smooth braking action.* **LEGAL PROCESS** ▷ **9** C1 [C or U] a legal process that is decided in a law court: *a libel action* ◦ *She* ***brought*** *an action (****for*** *negligence)* ***against*** *the hospital.* ◦ *A* ***criminal*** *action was* ***brought against*** *him.* ◦ *The book was halted in South Africa by a threat of* ***legal*** *action.*

> Word partners for **action**
>
> *take* action • *leap/spring/swing* into action • *galvanize/prod/spur* sb *into* action • *immediate/prompt/swift* action • *put* [a plan/an idea] *into* action • a *course/plan* of action • *in* action

IDIOMS **actions speak louder than words** saying said to emphasize that what you do is more important and shows your intentions and feelings more clearly than what you say • **out of action 1** C1 If a machine or vehicle is out of action, it is not working or cannot be used: *I'm afraid the TV's out of action.* **2** C1 If a person is out of action, they are injured or ill and cannot do things they usually do: *Jackson's torn ligaments will keep him out of action for the rest of the season.* • **a man of action** a man who prefers to do things rather than think about and discuss them • **a piece/slice of the action** informal involvement in something successful that someone else has started: *Now research has proved that the drug is effective, everyone wants a slice of the action.*

▸verb [T usually passive] to do something to deal with a particular problem or matter: *I'll just run through the minutes of the last meeting, raising those points that still have to be actioned.*

actionable /ˈæk.ʃən.ə.bl/ adj specialized If something is actionable, it gives someone a good reason for accusing someone in a law court: *She denies that her company has been involved in any actionable activity.*

ˈaction ˌfigure noun [C] a toy that is made to look like a soldier or a character from a film or television show

ˌaction-ˈpacked adj full of exciting events: *an action-packed thriller/weekend/finale*

ˌaction ˈreplay noun [C] UK (US **ˈinstant ˌreplay**) a repeat of an important moment from a sports event shown on television, often more slowly to show the action in detail: *They showed an action replay of the goal.*

ˈaction ˌstations noun [plural] UK informal **1** the situation in which you are as ready as possible to perform a task you have been preparing for: *The whole school was* ***at*** *action stations for the inspectors' visit.* **2 action stations!** used to tell people to get ready immediately to do the particular jobs that they have been given to do: *Right, everyone – action stations! We're starting in three minutes.*

activate /ˈæk.tɪ.veɪt/ verb [T] **1** to cause something to start: *The alarm is activated by the lightest pressure.* **2** specialized to make a chemical reaction happen more quickly, especially by heating • **activation** /ˌæk.tɪˈveɪ.ʃᵊn/ noun [U]

active /ˈæk.tɪv/ adj **BUSY** ▷ **1** B1 busy with a particular activity: *physically/mentally active* ◦ *You've got to try to* ***keep*** *active as you grow older.* **INVOLVED** ▷ **2** B2 involved in a particular activity: *Enemy forces remain active in the mountainous areas around the city.* ◦ *She's very active* ***in*** *(= involved in) local politics.* ◦ *It is important to educate children before they become* ***sexually*** *active.* **VOLCANO** ▷ **3** C1 describes a VOLCANO that might ERUPT (= throw out hot liquid rock or other matter) at any time **GRAMMAR** ▷ **4** B1 An active verb or sentence is one in which the subject is the person or thing that performs the stated action: *'Catrin told me' is an active sentence, and 'I was told by Catrin' is passive.* → Compare **passive**

actively /ˈæk.tɪv.li/ adv B2 in a way that involves positive action: *He's very actively* ***involved*** *in (= does a lot of work for) the local party.* ◦ *It's nice having a man who actively* ***encourages*** *me to spend money.* ◦ *I've been actively looking for a job for six months.*

activism /ˈæk.tɪ.vɪ.zᵊm/ noun [U] the use of direct and noticeable action to achieve a result, usually a political or social one: *black/student activism* ◦ *The levels of* ***political*** *activism in this country have greatly declined.*

activist /ˈæk.tɪ.vɪst/ noun [C] a person who believes strongly in political or social change and takes part in activities such as public protests to try to make this happen: *He's been a trade union/party activist for many years.* ◦ *an animal rights activist*

> **Word partners for activity (MOVEMENT)**
>
> *feverish/frantic/strenuous* activity • *business/economic/political* activity • a *flurry* of activity • the *level* of activity

> **Word partners for activity (ENJOYMENT)**
>
> *do/perform* an activity • *engage in/join in/participate in* an activity • an *outdoor/leisure* activity • a *(wide) range* of activities

activity /ækˈtɪv.ɪ.ti/ US /-ə.t̬i/ noun **MOVEMENT** ▷ **1** B2 [U] the situation in which a lot of things are happening or people are moving around: *There was a lot of activity in preparation for the Queen's visit.* ◦ *Economists are concerned by the low level of* ***economic*** *activity.* ◦ *There was a sudden* ***flurry of*** *activity when the director walked in.* **WORK** ▷ **2** B2 [C or U] the work of a group or organization to achieve an aim: *He was found guilty of* ***terrorist*** *activity.* ◦ *criminal activities* **ENJOYMENT** ▷ **3** A2 [C usually plural] something that is done for enjoyment, especially an organized event: *His spare-time activities include cooking, tennis, and windsurfing.* ◦ *We offer our guests a wide range of outdoor/sporting activities.*

acˈtivity ˌholiday noun [C] a holiday in which you can do a lot of sports and other activities

actor /ˈæk.təʳ/ US /-tɚ/ noun [C] (female also **actress**) A2 someone who pretends to be someone else while performing in a film, play, or television or radio programme: *'Who's your favourite actor?' 'Robert de Niro.'*

actress /ˈæk.trəs/ noun [C] a female actor

actual /ˈæk.tʃu.əl/, /-tju-/, /-tʃʊl/ adj [before noun] **1** B2 existing in fact: *We had estimated about 300 visitors, but the actual number was much higher.* ◦ *The exams are in July, but the actual results (= the results themselves) don't appear until September.* → Synonym **real 2 in actual fact** B2 really: *I thought she was Portuguese, but in actual fact she's Brazilian.*

> **! Common mistake: actual or current?**
>
> **Warning:** choose the right adjective!
>
> To describe something that exists now, don't say 'actual', say **current**:
>
> ~~*I am not at all happy in my actual job.*~~
>
> *I am not at all happy in my current job.*

actuality /ˌæk.tʃuˈæl.ə.ti/, /-tju-/ US /-ə.t̬i/ noun formal **1** [C usually plural] a fact: *He's out of touch with the actualities of life in Africa.* **2 in actuality** really: *In actuality, there were few job losses last year.*

actually /ˈæk.tʃu.ə.li/, /-tju-/, /-tʃʊ.li/ adv **IN FACT** ▷ **1** A2 in fact or really: *I didn't actually see her – I just heard her voice.* ◦ *So what actually happened?* **SURPRISE** ▷ **2** B1 used in sentences in which there is information that is in some way surprising or the opposite of what most people would expect: *I didn't like him at first, but in the end I actually got quite fond of him.* ◦ *I'm one of the few people who doesn't actually like champagne.* ◦ humorous *Don't tell me he actually paid for you!* **SAYING NO** ▷ **3** B2 used as a way of making a sentence slightly more polite, for example when you are expressing an opposing opinion, correcting what someone else has said, or refusing an offer: *'Alexander looks like he'd be good at sports.' 'Actually, he's not.'* ◦ *Actually, Gavin, it was Tuesday of last week, not Wednesday.* ◦ *'Do you mind if I smoke?' 'Well, actually, I'd rather you didn't.'*

actuarial /ˌæk.tjuˈeə.ri.əl/ US /-ˈer.i-/ adj relating to the work of an actuary, or to the job of being an actuary: *These figures are based on actuarial calculations of the risks involved.* ◦ *actuarial jobs*

actuary /ˈæk.tju.ə.ri/ US /-er.i/ noun [C] a person who calculates how likely accidents, such as fire, flood, or loss of property, are to happen, and tells INSURANCE companies how much they should charge their customers

actuate /ˈæk.tʃu.eɪt/, /-tju-/ verb [T] specialized or formal to make a machine work or be the reason a person acts in a certain way: *A detonator is actuated by heat, percussion, friction, or electricity.* ◦ *He was actuated almost entirely by altruism.*

acuity /əˈkjuː.ə.ti/ US /-ə.t̬i/ noun [U] formal the ability to hear, see, or think accurately and clearly: *Tiredness also affects visual acuity.* ◦ *He was a man of great political acuity.*

acumen /ˈæk.jʊ.mən/ US /əˈkjuː.mən/ noun [U] formal skill in making correct decisions and judgments in a particular subject, such as business or politics: *She has considerable* ***business/financial*** *acumen.*

acupressure /ˈæk.jʊ.preʃ.əʳ/ US /-ɚ/ noun [U] a

treatment for pain or illness in which certain parts of the body are pressed with the hands

acupuncture /ˈæk.jʊ.pʌŋk.tʃəʳ/ (US) /-tʃɚ/ **noun** [U] a treatment for pain or illness in which thin needles are positioned just under the surface of the skin at special points around the body

acute adj; noun

▸adj /əˈkjuːt/ **EXTREME** ▷ **1** If a bad situation is acute, it causes severe problems or damage: *She felt acute embarrassment/anxiety/concern at his behaviour.* ◦ *The problem of poverty is particularly acute in rural areas.* **2** An acute pain or illness is one that quickly becomes very severe: *acute abdominal pains* ◦ *an acute* ***attack*** *of appendicitis* **ACCURATE/CLEVER** ▷ **3** (of the senses, intelligence, etc.) very good, accurate, and able to notice very small differences: *acute eyesight/hearing* ◦ *an acute sense of smell* ◦ *a woman of acute intelligence/judgment* **ANGLE** ▷ **4** describes an angle that is less than 90 degrees → Compare **obtuse, reflex** • **acuteness** /-nəs/ **noun** [U]

▸noun [C] (also **aˌcute ˈaccent**) a sign that is written above a letter in some languages, showing you how to pronounce the letter: *There's an acute accent on the e in 'café'.*

acutely /əˈkjuːt.li/ **adv** **EXTREMELY** ▷ **1** completely or extremely: *Management is acutely* ***aware*** *of the resentment that their decision may cause.* ◦ *Another scandal would be acutely* ***embarrassing*** *for the government.* **ACCURATELY/CLEVERLY** ▷ **2** in a very clever or detailed way: *She acutely identified all the main problems.*

ad /æd/ **noun** [C] (A1) informal for an advertisement: *I often prefer the ads on TV to the actual programmes.*

AD /ˌeɪˈdiː/ **adv** abbreviation for Anno Domini: used in the Christian CALENDAR when referring to a year after Jesus Christ was born: *in 1215 AD/AD 1215* ◦ *during the seventh century AD* → Compare **BC, CE**

adage /ˈæd.ɪdʒ/ **noun** [C] a wise saying: *He remembered the* ***old*** *adage 'Look before you leap'.* → Synonym **proverb**

ˈad ˌagency **noun** [C] a company that produces advertisements

adagio /əˈdɑː.dʒi.əʊ/ (US) /-oʊ/ **noun** [usually sing] specialized a piece of music that should be played slowly: *Barber's Adagio for Strings* • **adagio adj, adv** *The adagio movement is beautiful.*

Adam /ˈæd.əm/ **noun** a character in the Bible who was the first man made by God

adamant /ˈæd.ə.mənt/ **adj** impossible to persuade, or unwilling to change an opinion or decision: [+ that] *I've told her she should stay at home and rest but she's adamant* ***that*** *she's coming.* • **adamantly** /-li/ **adv** *The mayor is adamantly opposed to any tax increase.*

ˌAdam's ˈapple **noun** [C] the part of your throat that sticks out, especially in men, and moves up and down when you speak or swallow

adapt /əˈdæpt/ **verb** **CHANGE** ▷ **1** (B2) [T] to change something to suit different conditions or uses: *Many software companies have adapted popular programs* ***to*** *the new operating system.* ◦ *The recipe here is a pork roast adapted* ***from*** *Caroline O'Neill's book 'Louisiana Kitchen'.* ◦ [+ to infinitive] *We had to adapt our plans* ***to*** *fit Jack's timetable.* ◦ *The play had been adapted* ***for*** *(= changed to make it suitable for) children.* **BECOME FAMILIAR** ▷ **2** (B2) [I] to become familiar with a new situation: *The good thing about children is that they adapt very easily* ***to*** *new environments.* ◦ *It took me a while to adapt* ***to*** *the new job.* • **adapted** /əˈdæp.tɪd/ **adj** *Both trees are* ***well*** *adapted* ***to*** *London's dry climate and dirty air.*

adaptable /əˈdæp.tə.bl/ **adj** able or willing to change in order to suit different conditions: *The survivors in this life seem to be those who are adaptable* ***to*** *change.* • **adaptability** /əˌdæp.təˈbɪl.ɪ.ti/ (US) /-ə.t̬i/ **noun** [U] *Adaptability is a necessary quality in an ever-changing work environment.*

adaptation /ˌæd.əpˈteɪ.ʃən/ **noun** **1** (C1) [U] the process of changing to suit different conditions: *Evolution occurs as a result of adaptation* ***to*** *new environments.* **2** [C] a film, book, play, etc. that has been made from another film, book, play, etc.: *Last year he starred in the film adaptation of Bill Cronshaw's best-selling novel.*

adapter (also **adaptor**) /əˈdæp.təʳ/ (US) /-tɚ/ **noun** [C] **DEVICE** ▷ **1** mainly UK a type of PLUG that makes it possible to connect two or more pieces of equipment to the same electrical supply **2** a device that is used to connect two pieces of equipment **WRITER** ▷ **3** a person who makes slight changes to a book, play, or other piece of text so that it can be performed

adaptive /əˈdæp.tɪv/ **adj** specialized having an ability to change to suit different conditions

ADC /ˌeɪ.diːˈsiː/ **noun** [C] abbreviation for **aide-de-camp**

add /æd/ **verb** [I or T] **1** (A2) to put two or more numbers or amounts together to get a total: *If you add (= calculate the total of) three and four you get seven.* ◦ *It's $45 – $50 if you add* ***in*** *(= include) the cost of postage.* ◦ *Don't forget to add* ***on*** *your travelling expenses/add your expenses* ***on***. **2** (A2) to put something with something else to increase the number or amount or to improve the whole: *Beat the butter and sugar together and slowly add the eggs.* ◦ *She's added a Picasso* ***to*** *her collection.* ◦ *Her colleagues' laughter only added* ***to*** *(= increased) her embarrassment.* **3** (B1) to say another thing: [+ that] *She was sad, she said, but added (= said also)* ***that*** *she felt she had made the right decision.* ◦ [+ speech] *'Oh, and thank you for all your help!' he added as he was leaving.*

IDIOMS **not add up** informal If a situation does not add up, there is no reasonable or likely explanation for it: *Why would she disappear the day before her holiday? It just doesn't add up.* • **to add insult to injury** (C2) said when you feel that someone has made a bad situation worse by doing something else to upset you: *They told me I was too old for the job, and then to add insult to injury, they refused to pay my expenses!*

PHRASAL VERBS **add (sth) up** (B1) to calculate the total of two or more numbers: *If you add those four figures up, it comes to over £500.* ◦ *She added the bill up.* ◦ *I'm not very good at adding up!* • **add up to sth** **AMOUNT** ▷ **1** to become a particular amount: *The various building programmes add up to several thousand new homes.* ◦ *We thought we'd bought lots of food, but it didn't add up to much when we'd spread it out on the table.* **RESULT** ▷ **2** to have a particular result or effect: *It all added up to a lot of hard work for all of us.* ◦ *Their proposals do not add up to any real help for the poor.*

ADD /ˌeɪ.diːˈdiː/ **noun** abbreviation for Attention Deficit Disorder: a condition in which someone, especially a child, is often in a state of activity or excitement and unable to direct their attention towards what they are doing

added /ˈæd.ɪd/ **adj** extra: *He had the added disadvantage of being the only man present.* ◦ *She lost her job last week, and now added* ***to that*** *she's pregnant again.*

ˌadded ˈvalue **noun** [U] an improvement or addition to something that makes it worth more: *The printer's added value makes it worth the extra cost.* • **ˌadded-ˈvalue adj** [before noun]

addendum /ə'den.dəm/ noun [C] (plural **addenda** /ə'den.də/) specialized something that has been added to a book, speech, or document

adder /'æd.əʳ/ (US) /-ɚ/ noun [C] a type of poisonous snake

addict /'æd.ɪkt/ noun [C] B2 a person who cannot stop doing or using something, especially something harmful: *a drug/heroin addict* ◦ *a gambling addict* ◦ humorous *I'm a chocolate/shopping addict.*

addicted /ə'dɪk.tɪd/ adj unable to stop taking drugs, or doing something as a habit: *By the age of 14 he was addicted **to** heroin.* ◦ *I'm addicted **to** (= I very often eat) chocolate.* ◦ *I know that if I start watching a soap opera I immediately become **hopelessly** addicted.* • **addiction** /ə'dɪk.ʃən/ B2 ***drug** addiction* ◦ *his addiction **to** alcohol*

addictive /ə'dɪk.tɪv/ adj **1** C1 An addictive drug is one that you cannot stop taking once you have started: *Tobacco is **highly** addictive.* **2** C1 describes an activity or food that you cannot stop doing or eating once you have started: *The problem with video games is that they're addictive.* ◦ *These nuts are addictive – I can't stop eating them.* **3 addictive personality** a set of characteristics that mean that you very quickly become addicted to drugs, food, alcohol, etc.: *He's got an addictive personality.* • **addictiveness** /-nəs/ noun [U]

addition /ə'dɪʃ.ən/ noun **1** B2 [U] the process of adding numbers or amounts together: *Twice a week the children are tested in basic mathematical skills such as addition (= calculating the total of different numbers put together) and subtraction.* **2 in addition (to)** B1 as well (as): *In addition to his flat in London, he has a villa in Italy and a castle in Scotland.* **3** B2 [C] something that has been added to something else: *A secretary would be **a welcome/useful** addition **to** our staff.* ◦ humorous *I hear you're expecting a small addition **to** the family (= you are going to have a baby)!* **4** [C] the act of adding a substance or thing to something else: *Most working environments are improved by **the** addition **of** (= by adding) a few plants and pictures.*

additional /ə'dɪʃ.ən.əl/ adj B2 extra: *additional costs/problems* • **additionally** /-i/ adv B2 *Additionally (= also), we request a deposit of $200 in advance.*

additive /'æd.ɪ.tɪv/ (US) /-ə.t̬ɪv/ noun [C] a substance that is added to food in order to improve its taste or appearance or to keep it fresh and stop it from decaying: *food additives* ◦ *This margarine is **full of** additives – just look at the label!*

addle /'æd.l̩/ verb [T] mainly humorous to make someone feel confused and unable to think clearly: *I think my brain's been addled by the heat!* • **addled** /'æd.l̩d/ adj mainly humorous *I'm afraid my sun-addled (= confused) brain couldn't make any sense of the instructions.*

'add-on noun [C] **1** a piece of equipment that can be connected to a computer to give it an extra use: *A printer is a useful add-on.* **2** an extra part that is added, especially to an officially organized plan, system, agreement, etc.: *Legal expenses cover is often sold as an add-on **to** household insurance policies.*

address noun; verb

▸noun [C] /ə'dres/ (US) /'æd.res/ **HOME DETAILS** ▷ **1** A1 the number of the house, name of the road, and town where a person lives or works and where letters can be sent: *her business/home address* ◦ *a change of address* **COMPUTERS** ▷ **2** A1 a series of letters and symbols that tell you where to find something on the internet or show where an email is sent to: *What's your email address?* ◦ *Do you have their Web address?* **3** specialized the place where a piece of information is stored in a computer's memory **SPEECH** ▷ **4** a formal speech: *She gave an address **to** the Royal Academy.*

> **! Common mistake: address**
>
> **Warning:** Check your spelling!
>
> **Address** is one of the 50 words most often spelled wrongly by learners. Remember: the correct spelling has 'dd' and 'ss'.

▸verb [T] /ə'dres/ **SPEAK TO** ▷ **1** C2 formal to speak or write to someone: *He addressed a few introductory remarks **to** the audience.* ◦ *He likes to be addressed **as** 'Sir' or 'Mr Partridge'.* **DEAL WITH** ▷ **2** C1 to give attention to or deal with a matter or problem: *The **issue** of funding has yet to be addressed.* **WRITE DETAILS** ▷ **3** C2 to write a name or address on an envelope or parcel: *The parcel was wrongly addressed.* ◦ *So why did you open a letter that was addressed **to** me?*

a'ddress ˌbook noun [C] (US **'address ˌbook**) **1** a computer document that keeps a list of names and email addresses **2** a book in which you write people's addresses

addressee /ˌæd.res'iː/ noun [C] a person whose name or address is written on a letter or parcel

adduce /ə'djuːs/ (US) /-'duːs/ verb [T often passive] formal to give reasons why you think something is true: *None of the evidence adduced in court was conclusive.*

adenoids /'æd.ən.ɔɪdz/ noun [plural] the soft mass of flesh between the back of the nose and the throat, which sometimes makes breathing difficult • **adenoidal** /ˌæd.ən'ɔɪ.dəl/ adj

adept /ə'dept/ adj having a natural ability to do something that needs skill: *She's very adept **at** dealing with the media.* ◦ *Tamsin Palmer gave a technically adept performance on the piano.* • **adeptly** /-li/ adv

adequate /'æd.ə.kwət/ adj B2 enough or satisfactory for a particular purpose: *Have we got adequate food for 20 guests?* ◦ *I didn't have adequate time to prepare.* ◦ *It's not a big salary but it's adequate **for** our needs.* ◦ *The council's provision for the elderly is **barely** adequate (= is not enough).* ◦ [+ to infinitive] *Will future oil supplies be adequate **to** meet world needs?* → Opposite **inadequate** • **adequacy** /'æd.ə.kwə.si/ noun [U] *The adequacy of public healthcare has been brought into question.* • **adequately** /-li/ adv B2 *While some patients can be adequately cared for at home, others are best served by care in a hospital.*

ADHD /ˌeɪ.diː.eɪtʃ'diː/ noun [U] mainly UK abbreviation for **attention deficit hyperactivity disorder**

adhere /əd'hɪəʳ/ (US) /-'hɪr/ verb [I] formal to stick firmly: *A smooth, dry surface helps the tiles adhere **to** the wall.*

PHRASAL VERB **adhere to sth** to continue to obey a rule or have a belief: *She adhered to her principles/ideals throughout her life.* ◦ *They failed to adhere to the terms of the agreement/treaty.* ◦ *The translator has obviously adhered very **strictly** to the original text.*

adherence /əd'hɪə.rəns/ (US) /-'hɪr.əns/ noun [U] formal the fact of someone behaving exactly according to rules, beliefs, etc.: *He was noted for his strict adherence **to** the rules.*

adherent /əd'hɪə.rənt/ (US) /-'hɪr.ənt/ adj; noun

▸adj formal sticky: *an adherent surface*

▸noun [C] formal a person who strongly supports a particular person, principle, or set of ideas: *She has long been an adherent of the Communist Party.*

adhesion /ədˈhiː.ʒən/ **noun** [U] the ability to stick: *At this stage a resin is used with a high level of adhesion.*

adhesive /ədˈhiː.sɪv/ **noun; adj**
▸**noun** [C or U] glue: *You'll need a/some strong adhesive to mend that chair.*
▸**adj** sticky: *adhesive tape/paper*

ad hoc /ˌædˈhɒk/ (US) /-ˈhɑːk/ **adj** [before noun] made or happening only for a particular purpose or need, not planned before it happens: *an ad hoc committee/meeting* ◦ *We deal with problems* ***on an*** *ad hoc* ***basis*** (= *as they happen*).

adieu /əˈdjuː/, /-ˈdjʊ/ (US) /-ˈduː/ **exclamation** literary or old use goodbye: *She* ***bade*** (= *said to*) *him adieu and left.*

ad infinitum /ˌæd.ɪn.fɪˈnaɪ.təm/ (US) /-t̬əm/ **adv** for ever, without ending: *'Why was she such a lousy boss?' 'Oh, because she was unreasonable, disrespectful, rude, inconsiderate – I could go on ad infinitum.'*

adios /ˌæd.iˈɒs/ (US) /-ˈoʊs/ **exclamation** mainly US informal goodbye

adipose /ˈæd.ɪ.pəʊs/, /-pəʊz/ (US) /-ə.poʊs/ **adj** [before noun] specialized relating to animal fat: *adipose* ***tissue*** (= *fat*)

adj **noun** written abbreviation for adjective

adjacent /əˈdʒeɪ.sənt/ **adj** formal C2 very near, next to, or touching: *They work in adjacent buildings.* ◦ *They lived in a house adjacent* ***to*** *the railway.*

adˌjacent ˈangle **noun** [C, usually plural] specialized one of the two angles on either side of a straight line that divides a larger angle into two

adjective /ˈædʒ.ek.tɪv/ **noun** [C] A2 a word that describes a noun or PRONOUN: *'Big', 'boring', 'purple', 'quick' and 'obvious' are all adjectives.* • **adjectival** /ˌædʒ.ekˈtaɪ.vəl/ **adj** *an adjectival phrase* • **adjectivally** /ˌædʒ.ekˈtaɪ.vəl.i/ **adv** *In 'kitchen table', the noun 'kitchen' is used adjectivally.*

adjoin /əˈdʒɔɪn/ **verb** [I or T] formal to be very near, next to, or touching: *The stables adjoin the west wing of the house.*

adjoining /əˈdʒɔɪ.nɪŋ/ **adj** [before noun] near, next to, or touching: *We asked for adjoining rooms.*

adjourn /əˈdʒɜːn/ (US) /-ˈdʒɝːn/ **verb** [I or T] formal to have a pause or rest during a formal meeting or trial: *The meeting was adjourned* ***until*** *Tuesday.* ◦ *Shall we adjourn* ***for*** *lunch?* • **adjournment** /-mənt/ **noun** [C or U] *The defence attorney requested an adjournment.* ◦ *The court's adjournment means that a decision will not be reached until December at the earliest.*

PHRASAL VERB **adjourn to somewhere** humorous to finish doing something and go somewhere, usually for a drink and some food: *Shall we adjourn to the sitting room for coffee?*

adjudge /əˈdʒʌdʒ/ **verb** [T often passive] formal to announce a decision or consider something, especially officially: [+ to infinitive] *Half an hour into the game Paterson was adjudged* ***to*** *have fouled Jackson and was sent off.* ◦ [+ noun/adj] *In October 1990, Mirchandani was adjudged bankrupt.* ◦ *Fairbanks was adjudged the winner.*

adjudicate /əˈdʒuː.dɪ.keɪt/ **verb** [I or T] to act as judge in a competition or argument, or to make a formal decision about something: *He was asked to adjudicate* ***on*** *the dispute.* ◦ *He was called in to adjudicate a local land dispute.* ◦ [+ two objects] *The game was adjudicated a win for Black.* • **adjudication** /əˌdʒuː.dɪˈkeɪ.ʃən/ **noun** [U or C] *The legality of the transaction is still* ***under*** *adjudication* (= *being decided*) *in the courts.* ◦ *His adjudication was later found to be faulty.*

adjudicator /əˈdʒuː.dɪ.keɪ.təʳ/ (US) /-t̬ɚ/ **noun** [C] a person or group that makes an official decision about something, especially about who is right in a disagreement: *She acted as adjudicator in the dispute.*

adjunct /ˈædʒ.ʌŋkt/ **noun** [C] **SOMETHING ADDED** ▷ **1** formal something added or connected to a larger or more important thing: *I hoped I would find the computer course a useful adjunct* ***to*** *my other studies.* **GRAMMAR** ▷ **2** specialized In grammar, an adjunct is an adverb or phrase that gives extra information in a sentence.

adjure /əˈdʒʊəʳ/ (US) /-ˈdʒʊr/ **verb** [T + to infinitive] formal to ask or order someone to do something: *The judge adjured him* ***to*** *answer truthfully.*

adjust /əˈdʒʌst/ **verb** **MAKE CHANGES** ▷ **1** B2 [T] to change something slightly, especially to make it more correct, effective, or suitable: *If the chair is too high you can adjust it to suit you.* ◦ *As a teacher you have to adjust your methods to suit the needs of slower children.* **2** [T] to arrange your clothing to make yourself look tidy: *She adjusted her skirt, took a deep breath, and walked into the room.* **BECOME FAMILIAR** ▷ **3** B2 [I] to become more familiar with a new situation: *I can't adjust* ***to*** *liv****ing*** *on my own.* ◦ *Her eyes slowly adjusted* ***to*** *the dark.* ◦ *The lifestyle is so very different – it takes a while to adjust.*

adjustable /əˈdʒʌs.tə.bl̩/ **adj** able to be changed to suit particular needs: *The height of the steering wheel is adjustable.* ◦ *Is the strap on this helmet adjustable?*

adjustment /əˈdʒʌst.mənt/ **noun** [C or U] **CHANGE** ▷ **1** B2 a small change: *She made a few* ***minor*** *adjustments* ***to*** *the focus of her camera.* **BECOMING FAMILIAR** ▷ **2** the ability to become more familiar with a new situation: *He has so far failed to make the adjustment* ***from*** *school* ***to*** *work.*

adjutant /ˈædʒ.ʊ.tənt/ **noun** [C] a military officer who does office work and who is responsible for rules and punishment among the lower ranks

ˌad ˈlib **adv** said without any preparation or practice: *I'd forgotten the notes for my speech so I had to* ***do*** *it ad lib.* • **ˌad-ˈlib** **adj** [before noun] *ad-lib comments*

ˌad-ˈlib **verb** [I or T] (**-bb-**) to speak in public without having planned what to say: *She ad-libbed her way through the entire speech.*

adman /ˈæd.mæn/ **noun** [C] (plural **-men** /-men/) informal a man who works in advertising

administer /ədˈmɪn.ɪ.stəʳ/ (US) /-stɚ/ **verb** **MANAGE** ▷ **1** [T often passive] to control the operation or arrangement of something: *The economy has been badly administered by the present government.* **2** [T often passive] to govern a country, region, etc.: *The economy has been badly administered by the present government.* **GIVE** ▷ **3** [T] formal to cause someone to receive something: *to administer medicine/punishment/relief* ◦ *Tests will be administered* ***to*** *schoolchildren at seven and twelve years.* **4** **administer an oath to sb** formal to be present while someone says an OATH (= a formal promise) officially

administration /ədˌmɪn.ɪˈstreɪ.ʃən/ **noun** **MANAGING** ▷ **1** C1 [U] (informal **admin** /ˈæd.mɪn/) the arrangements and tasks needed to control the operation of a plan or organization: *Teachers complain that more of their time is taken up with administration than with teaching.* ◦ *She has little experience in admin* (= *in organizing a business, etc.*). **MANAGEMENT** ▷ **2** C2 [C] the people in an organization who manage its business and operations: *The decision to cancel the trip was made by the school administration.* **GOVERNMENT** ▷ **3** C2 [C] a period of government, or the people who are in government: *the Obama*

administration/the last Republican administration **GIVING** ▷ **4** [U] the act of giving someone something: *There are strict controls on the administration of drugs.* **BUSINESS CLOSING** ▷ **5** [U] UK the process that takes place when a company cannot pay its debts and is allowed to make changes to its organization to try to avoid going into LIQUIDATION (= when a business is closed and the things it owns are sold): *The company has* ***gone into*** *administration, in order for money to be returned to creditors.*

administrative /əd'mɪn.ɪ.strə.tɪv/ (US) /-t̬ɪv/ **adj** C1 relating to the arrangements and work that is needed to control the operation of a plan or organization: *administrative work* ◦ *an administrative problem* ◦ *Your responsibilities will be mainly administrative.* • **administratively** /-li/ **adv**

administrator /əd'mɪn.ɪ.streɪ.tər/ (US) /-t̬ɚ/ **noun** [C] C1 someone whose job is to control the operation of a business, organization, or plan: *From 1969 to 1971, he was administrator of the Illinois state drug abuse program.* ◦ *She works as a school administrator.*

admirable /'æd.mɪ.rə.bl̩/ **adj** deserving respect or approval: *I think you showed admirable tact/restraint/self-control in your answer.* ◦ *The police did an admirable job in keeping the fans calm.* • **admirably** /-bli/ **adv** *I think she coped admirably (= very well) with a very difficult situation.*

admiral /'æd.mɪ.rəl/ **noun** [C] (also **Admiral**) an officer of very high rank in the navy: *Admiral Nelson/Horatio Nelson* ◦ [as form of address] *Yes, Admiral.*

the Admiralty /'æd.mɪ.rəl.ti/ (US) /-t̬i/ **noun** in the past in the UK, the government department in charge of the navy

admiration /ˌæd.mɪ'reɪ.ʃən/ **noun** [U] B2 the feeling of admiring someone or something: *My admiration* ***for*** *that woman grows daily.* ◦ *She gazed* ***in*** *admiration at his broad, muscular shoulders.*

> Word partners for **admiration**
>
> *express/feel/have* admiration • *earn/gain/win* (sb's) admiration • *genuine/great/profound* admiration • *grudging/sneaking* admiration • *mutual* admiration • admiration *for* sb/sth • [gaze/gasp/watch] *in/with* admiration

admire /əd'maɪər/ (US) /-'maɪr/ **verb** [T] **1** B1 to find someone or something attractive and pleasant to look at: *We stood for a few moments, admiring the view.* ◦ *I was just admiring your jacket, Delia.* **2** B2 to respect and approve of someone or their behaviour: *I admired him* ***for*** *his determination.* ◦ *I really admire people who can work in such difficult conditions.*

> Other ways of saying **admire**
>
> **Respect** is an alternative to 'admire':
>
> *I deeply* ***respect*** *David for what he has achieved.*
>
> **Revere** is a formal way of saying 'admire very much.':
>
> *Nelson Mandela is* ***revered*** *for his brave fight against apartheid.*
>
> **Look up to** or **think highly of** are phrases that can be used about someone you admire:
>
> *He'd always* ***looked up to*** *his uncle.*
>
> *She* ***thinks*** *very* ***highly of*** *her boss.*
>
> If a person admires someone very much or too much, you could use the verb **idolize**:
>
> *He* ***idolized*** *his mother.*

admirer /əd'maɪə.rər/ (US) /-'maɪr.ɚ/ **noun** [C] someone who finds someone else sexually attractive, or someone who admires someone or something: *She's got plenty of admirers.* ◦ *She's got a* ***secret*** *admirer who keeps sending her gifts.* ◦ *The policy has few admirers (= few people like it).*

admiring /əd'maɪə.rɪŋ/ (US) /-'maɪr.ɪŋ/ **adj** showing admiration: *Annette was getting lots of admiring* ***looks/glances*** *in her new red dress.* ◦ *She was surrounded by a group of admiring photographers.* • **admiringly** /-li/ **adv** *The women sitting opposite us were gazing admiringly (= with admiration) at baby Joe.*

admissible /əd'mɪs.ɪ.bl̩/ **adj** formal considered satisfactory and acceptable in a law court: *The judge ruled that new* ***evidence*** *was admissible.* → Opposite **inadmissible** • **admissibility** /ədˌmɪs.ə'bɪl.ɪ.ti/ (US) /-ə.t̬i/ **noun** [U]

admission /əd'mɪʃ.ən/ **noun** **ACCEPTING** ▷ **1** [C or U] the act of agreeing that something is true, especially unwillingly: *Her silence was taken as an admission* ***of*** *guilt/defeat.* ◦ [+ that] *I felt he would see my giving up now as an admission* ***that*** *I was wrong.* ◦ ***By/On*** *his* ***own*** *admission (= as he has said) he has achieved little since he took over the company.* **ALLOWING IN** ▷ **2** B1 [U or C] the money that you pay to enter a place: *How much do they* ***charge for*** *admission?* ◦ *The admission* ***charge/fee*** *is €5.* **3** B2 [U] permission to enter a place: *Admission* ***to*** *the exhibition will be by invitation only.* **4 admissions** [plural] the people allowed into a college, hospital, or other place, or the process of allowing people in: *Half of all* ***hospital*** *admissions are emergencies, and these are treated straight away.*

admit /əd'mɪt/ **verb** (-tt-) **ACCEPT** ▷ **1** B1 [T or I] to agree that something is true, especially unwillingly: *He admitted his guilt/mistake.* ◦ [+ (that)] *She admitted* ***(that)*** *she had made a mistake.* ◦ [+ -ing verb] *She admitted mak****ing*** *a mistake.* ◦ *At first he denied stealing the money but he later admitted* ***(to)*** *it.* ◦ *I wasn't entirely honest with him, I admit.* ◦ [+ to infinitive] *The new law was generally admitted* ***to*** *be difficult to enforce.* **2 admit defeat** to accept that you have failed and give up: *After several attempts to untie the knot, I admitted defeat and cut through it with a knife.* **ALLOW IN** ▷ **3** [T] to allow someone to enter a place: *Each ticket admits one member and one guest.* ◦ *Men will not be admitted* ***to*** *the restaurant without a tie.* **4** [T] to allow a person or country to join an organization: *Spain was admitted* ***to*** *the European Community in 1986.* **5** [T] to allow someone to enter a hospital because they need medical care: UK *She was admitted* ***to hospital*** (US ***to the hospital***) *suffering from shock.*

> Other ways of saying **admit**
>
> If a person admits that something is true, the verbs **accept** and **acknowledge** may be used:
>
> *I* ***accept*** *that things should have been done differently.*
>
> *He refuses to* ***acknowledge*** *the problem.*
>
> The verb **concede** is used if the person admits unwillingly that something is true:
>
> *She did eventually* ***concede*** *that the instructions were not very clear.*
>
> If a person admits to having done something bad or illegal, the verb **confess** is often used:
>
> *Rawlinson finally* ***confessed*** *to the robbery.*
>
> The phrasal verbs **own up** and (*informal*) **fess up**, and the expression **come clean** can also be used when a person admits to having done something:
>
> *I decided to* ***come clean*** *about the broken vase.*
>
> *Come on,* ***own up*** *– who's eaten the last sandwich?*

PHRASAL VERB **admit of sth** formal to allow something or make it possible: *The present schedule does not admit of modification (= it cannot be changed).* ◦ *The latest events admit of several interpretations.*

admittance /əd'mɪt.əns/ US /-'mɪţ-/ noun [U] formal permission to enter a place: *The sign read 'Private – no admittance'.* ◦ *The enquiry centred on how the assassin had **gained** admittance **to** (= succeeded in entering) the building.*

admittedly /əd'mɪt.ɪd.li/ US /-'mɪţ-/ adv B2 used when you are agreeing that something is true, especially unwillingly: *Admittedly, I could have tried harder but I still don't think all this criticism is fair.*

admixture /əd'mɪks.tʃər/ US /-tʃɚ/ noun [C usually singular] specialized something that is added to something else: *Platinum combines with phosphorus and arsenic and is seldom found without an admixture **of** related metals.*

admonish /əd'mɒn.ɪʃ/ US /-'mɑː.nɪʃ/ verb formal **1** [T] to tell someone that they have done something wrong: *His mother admonished him **for** eat**ing** too quickly.* **2** [T + to infinitive] to advise someone to do something: *Her teacher admonished her **to** work harder for her exams.*

admonition /ˌæd.mə'nɪʃ.ən/ noun [C] (also **admonishment** /əd'mɒn.ɪʃmənt/ US /-'mɑː.nɪʃ-/) a piece of advice that is also a warning to someone about their behaviour: *The most common parental admonition must surely be 'Don't stay out late'.* • **admonitory** /əd'mɒn.ɪ.tər.i/ US /-'mɑː.nə.tɔː.ri/ adj formal *an admonitory remark*

ad nauseam /ˌæd'nɔː.zi.æm/ US /-'nɑː-/ adv If someone discusses something ad nauseam, they talk about it so much that it becomes very boring: *He talks ad nauseam about how clever his children are.*

ado /ə'duː/ noun **without further/more ado** without wasting more time: *And so, without further ado, let me introduce tonight's speaker.*

adobe /ə'dəʊ.bi/ US /-'doʊ-/ noun [U] a mixture of earth and STRAW made into bricks and dried in the sun, used to build houses in some parts of the world: *an adobe house*

adolescence /ˌæd.ə'les.əns/ noun [U] the period of time in a person's life when they are developing into an adult: *She had a troubled adolescence.*

adolescent /ˌæd.ə'les.ənt/ noun; adj

▸noun [C] C2 a young person who is developing into an adult

▸adj **1** being or relating to an adolescent: *an adolescent boy* ◦ *adolescent concerns/traumas/problems* **2** describes an adult or an adult's behaviour that is silly and like a child's: *adolescent humour/behaviour*

Adonis /ə'dəʊ.nɪs/ US /-'dɑː.nɪs/ noun [C] a very beautiful or sexually attractive young man: *She walked in on the arm of some blond Adonis.*

adopt /ə'dɒpt/ US /-'dɑːpt/ verb TAKE CHILD ▷ **1** B2 [T or I] to take another person's child into your own family and legally take care of him or her as your own child: *They've adopted a baby girl.* ◦ *She had the child adopted (= she gave her baby to someone else to look after).* ◦ *They have no children of their own, but they're hoping to adopt.* → Compare **foster** START USING ▷ **2** B2 [T] to accept or start to use something new: *I think it's time to adopt a different strategy in my dealings with him.* ◦ *The new tax would force companies to adopt energy-saving measures.* ◦ *He's adopted a remarkably light-hearted attitude towards the situation.* CHOOSE ▷ **3** [T] to choose someone or something or take something as your own: *Dr Kennedy has been adopted **as** the party's candidate for South Cambridge.* **4** [T] to start behaving in a particular way, especially by choice: *Roz has adopted one or two funny mannerisms since she's been away.*

adopted /ə'dɒp.tɪd/ US /-'dɑːp-/ adj CHILD ▷ **1** B2 an adopted child has been legally taken by another family to be taken care of as their own child: *They've got two adopted children and one of their own.* COUNTRY ▷ **2** [before noun] An adopted country is one where someone chooses to live although they were not born there: *Spain is my adopted country.*

adoption /ə'dɒp.ʃən/ US /-'dɑːp-/ noun TAKING CHILD ▷ **1** B2 [C or U] the act of legally taking a child to be taken care of as your own: *She was homeless and had to **put** her child **up for** adoption (= ask for the child to be taken by someone else as their own).* ◦ *The last ten years have seen a dramatic fall in the number of adoptions.* STARTING TO USE ▷ **2** [U] accepting or starting to use something new: *Several suggestions have been offered for adoption by the panel.* CHOOSING ▷ **3** [U] choosing or taking something as your own: *The adoption of a woman candidate was seen as controversial.*

adoptive /ə'dɒp.tɪv/ US /-'dɑːp-/ adj [before noun] An adoptive parent is one who has adopted a child.

adorable /ə'dɔː.rə.bl̩/ US /-'dɔːr.ə-/ adj describes a person or animal that is easy to love because they are so attractive and often small: *She has the most adorable two-year-old girl.* ◦ *an adorable puppy*

adoration /ˌæd.ə'reɪ.ʃən/ noun [U] very strong love or worship for someone: *her complete adoration of her brother* ◦ *The painting depicts the Three Wise Men kneeling in adoration of the baby Jesus.*

adore /ə'dɔːr/ US /-'dɔːr/ verb [T not continuous] LOVE ▷ **1** to love someone very much, especially in a way that shows a lot of admiration or respect, or to like something very much: *She has one son and she adores him.* ◦ *I **absolutely** adore chocolate.* ◦ [+ -ing verb] *Don't you just adore ly**ing** in a hot bath?* RELIGION ▷ **2** formal to worship: *Let us adore God for all his works.*

adoring /ə'dɔː.rɪŋ/ adj showing very strong love for someone: *I refuse to play the part of the adoring wife.* • **adoringly** /-li/ adv *She gazed at her baby adoringly.*

adorn /ə'dɔːn/ US /-'dɔːrn/ verb [T] literary to add something decorative to a person or thing: *The bride's hair was adorned **with** white flowers.* • **adornment** /-mənt/ noun [C or U] something decorative, or the act of decorating something or someone

adrenal gland /ə'driː.nəlˌglænd/ noun [C] specialized one of a pair of GLANDS that produce adrenalin, found just above the KIDNEYS

adrenalin (also **adrenaline**) /ə'dren.əl.ɪn/ noun [U] a HORMONE produced by the body when you are frightened, angry, or excited, which makes the heart beat faster and prepares the body to react to danger: *These arguments always **get** my adrenalin **going** (= make me excited or angry).*

adrift /ə'drɪft/ adj [after verb] **1** If a boat is adrift, it is moving on the water but is not controlled by anyone because of a problem: *He spent three days adrift on his yacht.* **2** If a person is adrift, they do not have a clear purpose in life or know what they want to do: *Da Silva plays a bright, lonely student from New York, adrift in small-town Arizona.* **3 go/come adrift** informal to become loose: *The hem of my skirt's come adrift again.* **4 go adrift** informal If plans go adrift, they fail or do not produce the correct results: *Something seems to have gone adrift in our calculations.*

adroit /ə'drɔɪt/ adj very skilful and quick in the way you think or move: *an adroit reaction/answer/move-*

ment of the hand ◦ *She became adroit **at** deal**ing** with difficult questions.* • **adroitly** /-li/ adv *She adroitly avoided the question.* ◦ *He adroitly slipped the money into his pocket.* • **adroitness** /-nəs/ noun [U]

ADSL /ˌeɪ.diː.es'el/ noun [U] specialized abbreviation for asymmetric digital subscriber line: a system for providing a very fast internet connection that allows you to use a phone at the same time

aduki /ə'duː.ki/ noun [C] an **adzuki**

adulation /ˌæd.jʊ'leɪ.ʃən/ noun [U] very great admiration or praise for someone, especially when it is more than is deserved: *Minelli is a born performer – she loves the excitement and she loves the adulation.* • **adulatory** /ˌæd.jʊ'leɪ.tər.i/ US /'ædʒ.əl.ə.tɔː.ri/ adj formal *I found myself irritated by the adulatory tone (= showing too much admiration) of her biography.*

adult /'æd.ʌlt/, /ə'dʌlt/ **noun; adj**

▸noun [C] A1 a person or animal that has grown to full size and strength: *An adult under English law is someone over 18 years old.* ◦ *Adults pay an admission charge but children get in free.*

▸adj **1** A2 grown to full size and strength: *an adult male/elephant* ◦ *She spent most of her adult **life** in prison.* **2** typical of or suitable for adults: *Let's try to be adult about this.* **3** Adult films, magazines, and books show naked people and sexual acts and are not for children.

ˌadult eduˈcation noun [U] classes for people who have finished their school education

adulterate /ə'dʌl.tə.reɪt/ verb [T usually passive] to make food or drink weaker or to lower its quality, by adding something else: *There were complaints that the beer had been adulterated **with** water.* • **adulterated** /ə'dʌl.tə.reɪ.tɪd/ US /-t̬ɪd/ adj *adulterated drugs/food* • **adulteration** /əˌdʌl.tə'reɪ.ʃən/ noun [U]

adulterer /ə'dʌl.tə.rər/ US /-t̬ɚ.ɚ/ noun [C] formal a married person who has sex with someone who is not their wife or husband: *Her husband was a compulsive adulterer.*

adulteress /ə'dʌl.tə.rəs/ US /-t̬ɚ.əs/ noun [C] a female adulterer

adultery /ə'dʌl.tər.i/ US /-t̬ɚ.i/ noun [U] sex between a married man or woman and someone he or she is not married to: *Many people in public life have **committed** adultery.* • **adulterous** /ə'dʌl.tər.əs/ US /-t̬ɚ-/ adj *He had an adulterous relationship with his wife's best friend.*

adulthood /'æd.ʌlt.hʊd/, /ə'dʌlt-/ noun [U] the part of someone's life when they are an adult: *People in England legally **reach** adulthood at 18.*

adumbrate /'æd.əm.breɪt/ verb [T] formal to give only the main facts and not the details about something, especially something that will happen in the future: *The project's objectives were adumbrated in the report.* • **adumbration** /ˌæd.əm'breɪ.ʃən/ noun [U]

adv noun written abbreviation for adverb

advance /əd'vɑːns/ US /-'væns/ **verb; noun; adj**

▸verb **MOVE FORWARD** ▷ **1** [I or T] to go or move something forward, or to develop or improve something: *The fire advanced steadily through the forest.* ◦ *The troops advanced **on** the city (= approached it, ready to attack).* ◦ *We have advanced greatly in our knowledge of the universe.* ◦ *Her study has considerably advanced (= helped) the **cause** of equal rights.* ◦ *He's just trying to advance (= improve) his own **career**.* **PAY** ▷ **2** [T] to pay someone some money before the regular time: [+ two objects] *Could you advance me £50 until Tuesday?* **SUGGEST** ▷ **3** [T] formal to suggest an idea or theory: *the theory advanced in this article* **INCREASE** ▷ **4** [I] If something such as a SHARE price advances, it increases in value: *On the New York Stock Exchange 1,228 issues advanced and 1,157 declined.*

▸noun **MOVEMENT** ▷ **1** B2 [C or U] the forward movement of something, or an improvement or development in something: *Nothing could stop **the** advance **of** the floodwaters.* ◦ *Recent advances **in** medical science mean that this illness can now be cured.* **MONEY** ▷ **2** money paid to someone before the regular time: *She asked for a £300 advance **on** her salary.* **SEX** ▷ **3** [C usually plural] an attempt to start a sexual or romantic relationship with someone: *She rejected his unwelcome advances.* **PRICE** ▷ **4** [C] something such as a SHARE price that increases in value: *Declining stocks easily defeated advances 413 to 302.*

IDIOMS **in advance** B1 before a particular time, or before doing a particular thing: *If you're going to come, please let me know in advance.* • **in advance of sth/sb** formal before something or someone: *She arrived in advance of everyone else.*

▸adj [before noun] happening, done, or ready before an event: *advance payment/booking* ◦ *We got no advance **warning/notice** of the changes.*

advanced /əd'vɑːnst/ US /-'vænst/ adj **1** B1 modern and well developed: *This is the most advanced type of engine available.* **2** A2 at a higher, more difficult level: *an advanced English course* **3 advanced class/course** US a school class that is doing work of a higher standard than is usual for students at that stage in their education

adˌvance diˈrective noun [C] another term for **living will**

advancement /əd'vɑːns.mənt/ US /-'væns-/ noun [U] the development or improvement of something: *All she was interested in was the advancement of her own career.*

advancing /əd'vɑːn.sɪŋ/ US /-'væn-/ adj **advancing age/years** If you talk about someone's advancing age, you mean that they are getting older: *He only recently stopped working, due to his advancing years.*

advantage /əd'vɑːn.tɪdʒ/ US /-'væn.t̬ɪdʒ/ noun **1** B1 [C or U] a condition giving a greater chance of success: *The advantage **of** book**ing** tickets in advance is that you get better seats.* ◦ *Despite the twin advantages **of** wealth and beauty, she did not have a happy life.* ◦ [+ to infinitive] ***It** would be **to** your advantage (= it would improve the situation for you) **to** agree to his demands.* ◦ *For a goalkeeper, **it's** a great advantage **to** have big hands.* ◦ *His height and reach **give** him a big advantage **over** (= make him better than) other boxers.* **2 take advantage of sth** B1 to use the good things in a situation: *I thought I'd take advantage of the sports facilities while I'm here.* **3 take advantage of sb/sth** B2 disapproving to treat someone badly in order to get something good from them: *I think she takes advantage of his good nature.* ◦ *I know she's offered to babysit, but I don't want her to think we're taking advantage of her.* **4** [U] the word used in tennis when a player has won the point after DEUCE: *Advantage Miss Williams!*

> **Word partners for advantage**
>
> *a big/great/major/obvious* advantage • the *main* advantage • an *unfair* advantage • *have* an advantage • *give* sb an advantage • the advantage *of* sth • *put* sb/*be* at an advantage • *be/work* to sb's advantage

advantageous /ˌæd.væn'teɪ.dʒəs/ adj giving advantages or helping to make you more successful: *advantageous interest rates* ◦ *The lower tax rate is* *particularly advantageous* ***to*** *poorer families.* • **advantageously** /-li/ **adv**

advent /ˈæd.vent/, /-vənt/ **noun** [S] the fact of an event happening, an INVENTION being made, or a person arriving: *Life was transformed by* ***the*** *advent* ***of*** *the steam engine.*

Advent /ˈæd.vent/, /-vənt/ **noun** [U] the period of four weeks before Christmas

ˈAdvent ˌcalendar **noun** [C] a decorative piece of card, often hung on the wall, that has a small opening with a door for each of the days of the month before Christmas. Children open one of these doors each day, finding a picture under it.

Adventist /ˈæd.ven.tɪst/, /-vən-/ **noun** [C] → See **Seventh-Day Adventist**

adventitious /ˌæd.vᵊnˈtɪʃ.əs/, /-ven-/ **adj** formal not expected or planned: *an adventitious event/situation* • **adventitiously** /-li/ **adv**

adventure /ədˈven.tʃəʳ/ (US) /-tʃɚ/ **noun** [C or U] (A2) an unusual, exciting, and possibly dangerous activity, such as a trip or experience, or the excitement produced by such an activity: *She* ***had*** *some exciting adventures in Egypt.* ◦ *We got lost on the Metro – it was* ***quite an*** *adventure.* ◦ *Sam won't come – he's got no* ***sense of*** *adventure (= he does not enjoy dangerous or exciting situations).*

> **Word partners for adventure**
>
> *have* an adventure • a *big/exciting/great* adventure • be *looking for* adventure • *quite an* adventure • an adventure *story*

adˈventure ˌplayground **noun** [C] a public open space where children can play and climb on structures, usually made of wood, ropes, and old tyres

adventurer /ədˈven.tʃə.rəʳ/ (US) /-tʃɚ.ɚ/ **noun** [C] **1** someone who enjoys and looks for dangerous and exciting experiences: *He was something of an adventurer, living most of his life abroad.* **2** disapproving a person who takes risks, acts dishonestly, or uses the fact that they are sexually attractive to become rich or powerful: *He was portrayed in the press as a gold digger and adventurer.*

adventurous /ədˈven.tʃᵊr.əs/ (US) /-tʃɚ-/ **adj** **1** (B2) willing to try new or difficult things: *I'm trying to be more adventurous with my cooking.* ◦ *He's not very adventurous sexually.* **2** exciting and often dangerous: *She led an adventurous life.* • **adventurously** /-li/ **adv**

adverb /ˈæd.vɜːb/ (US) /-vɝːb/ **noun** [C] (A2) a word that describes or gives more information about a verb, adjective, adverb, or phrase: *In the phrase 'she smiled cheerfully', the word 'cheerfully' is an adverb.* • **adverbial** /ədˈvɜː.bi.əl/ (US) /-ˈvɝː-/ **adj** *an adverbial phrase*

adversarial /ˌæd.vəˈseə.ri.əl/ (US) /-vɚˈser.i-/ **adj** formal involving people opposing or disagreeing with each other: *In the old days of two-party adversarial politics, voting was easy.*

adversary /ˈæd.və.sᵊr.i/ (US) /ˈæd.vɚ.ser-/ **noun** [C] formal an enemy

adverse /ˈæd.vɜːs/, /ədˈvɜːs/ (US) /ædˈvɝːs/ **adj** [before noun] (C2) having a negative or harmful effect on something: *The match has been cancelled because of adverse* ***weather conditions.*** ◦ *They received a lot of adverse* ***publicity/criticism*** *about the changes.* ◦ *So far the drug is thought not to have any adverse* ***effects.*** • **adversely** /-li/ *A lot of companies have been adversely* ***affected*** *(= in a harmful way) by the recession.*

adversity /ədˈvɜː.sə.ti/ (US) /-ˈvɝː.sə.t̬i/ **noun** [U or C] a difficult or unlucky situation or event: *She was always cheerful* ***in*** *adversity.* ◦ *The road to happiness is paved with adversities.*

advert /ˈæd.vɜːt/ (US) /-vɝːt/ **noun** [C] UK (B1) an advertisement: *an advert* ***for*** *the local radio station*

advertise /ˈæd.və.taɪz/ (US) /-vɚ-/ **verb** [T or I] (B1) to make something known generally or in public, especially in order to sell it: *We advertised our car in the local newspaper.* ◦ *He advertises his services on the company notice board.* ◦ *I'm going to advertise* ***for*** *(= put a notice in the newspaper, local shop, etc., asking for) someone to clean my house.* ◦ *There's no harm in applying for other jobs, but if I were you, I wouldn't advertise* ***the fact*** *(= make it generally known) at work.* • **advertiser** /ˈæd.və.taɪ.zəʳ/ (US) /-vɚ.taɪ.zɚ/ **noun** [C] *Whilst claiming to promote positive images of women, advertisers are in fact doing the very opposite.*

advertisement /ədˈvɜː.tɪs.mənt/ (US) /ˈæd.vɝː.taɪz.mənt/ **noun** [C] **1** (A2) (informal **ad**, UK also informal **advert**) a picture, short film, song, etc. that tries to persuade people to buy a product or service: *a television/newspaper advertisement* ***for*** *a new car* ◦ *She scanned the job/property advertisements in the paper.* **2 be an advertisement for sth** If you are an advertisement for something, you show its good effects: *I'm afraid I'm not a very good advertisement for the diet since I've actually put on weight!*

> **Common mistake: advertisement**
>
> **Warning:** Check your spelling!
>
> **Advertisement** is one of the 50 words most often spelled wrongly by learners. Remember: the correct spelling has 'e' after the 's'.

> **Common mistake: advertisement or advertising?**
>
> **Warning:** Choose the right word!
>
> To talk about the business of trying to persuade people to buy products or services, don't say 'advertisement', say **advertising**:
>
> ~~*She works for a big advertisement agency.*~~

advertising /ˈæd.və.taɪ.zɪŋ/ (US) /-vɚ-/ **noun** [U] (B2) the business of trying to persuade people to buy products or services: *Fiona works* ***in*** *advertising.* ◦ *the advertising industry*

advertorial /ˌæd.vəˈtɔː.ri.ᵊl/ (US) /-ˈtɔːr.i-/ **noun** [C] an advertisement in a newspaper or magazine that is designed to look like an article by the writers of the magazine

> **Common mistake: advice**
>
> **Advice** does not have a plural form and cannot be used with **a** or **an**.
>
> To talk about an amount of **advice**, do not say 'advices', say **advice, some advice**, or **a lot of advice**:
>
> ~~*She listens to me and gives me a lot of useful advices.*~~
>
> *She listens to me and gives me a lot of useful advice.*
>
> To talk about **advice** in the singular, do not say 'an advice', say **a piece of advice**:
>
> ~~*She gave me a useful advice.*~~
>
> *She gave me a useful piece of advice.*

advice /ədˈvaɪs/ **noun** [U] (A2) an opinion that someone offers you about what you should do or how you should act in a particular situation: *Steven* ***gave*** *me some good advice.* ◦ *I think I'll* ***take*** *your advice (= do what you suggest) and get the green dress.* ◦ *Can I give*

you ***a piece of*** *advice?* ◦ *I need some advice* ***on*** *which computer to buy.* ◦ [+ to infinitive] *My advice is* ***to*** *go by train.* ◦ *We went to Paris* ***on*** *Sarah's advice.*

> **!** Common mistake: **advice or advise?**
>
> **Warning:** do not confuse the noun **advice** with the verb **advise**:
>
> ~~*I advice you to see a lawyer.*~~
>
> *I advise you to see a lawyer.*

> Word partners for **advice**
>
> *ask for/seek* advice • *give/offer/provide* advice • *follow/take* sb's advice • *good/helpful/sound* advice • *bad/conflicting* advice • *financial/legal/medical* advice • a *piece of* advice • advice *on/about* sth • *on* the advice *of* sb

advisable /əd'vaɪ.zə.bl̩/ **adj** [after verb] If something is advisable, it will avoid problems if you do it: [+ to infinitive] *It's advisable* ***to*** *book seats at least a week in advance.* ◦ *A certain amount of caution is advisable at this point.* • **advisability** /əd͵vaɪ.zə'bɪl.ɪ.ti/ Ⓤⓢ /-ə.t̬i/ **noun** [U] *They discussed the advisability of building so near to the airport.*

advise /əd'vaɪz/ **verb 1** Ⓑ① [I or T] to give someone advice: [+ to infinitive] *I think I'd advise him* ***to*** *leave the company.* ◦ *I'd strongly advise* ***against*** *making a sudden decision.* ◦ [+ that] *They're advising* ***that*** *children be kept at home.* ◦ [+ -ing verb] *I'd advise wait****ing*** *until tomorrow.* ◦ [+ question word] *She advised us* ***wh****en to come.* ◦ *She advises the president (= gives information and suggests types of action)* ***on*** *African policy.* ◦ *You* ***would be well*** *advised* ***to*** *(= it would be wise for you to) have the appropriate vaccinations before you go abroad.*

> **!** Note:
>
> Do not confuse with the noun, **advice**.

2 [T] formal to give someone official information about something: *They were advised* ***of*** *their rights.* ◦ [+ that] *Our solicitors have advised* ***that*** *the costs could be enormous.*

advisedly /əd'vaɪ.zɪd.li/ **adv** formal If you say you are using a word advisedly, you mean you are choosing it after thinking about it very carefully: *This action is barbaric – and I use the word advisedly.*

advisement /əd'vaɪz.mənt/ **noun** [U] US **1** the process or activity of advising someone about something: *a counseling and advisement center* ◦ *Contact Dr Gray about academic advisement.* ◦ *student/graduate/career advisement* **2 take sth under advisement** to consider something such as advice or information carefully: *Thank you for your input Mr Walters – I'll take what you've said under advisement.*

adviser /əd'vaɪ.zəʳ/ Ⓤⓢ /-zɚ/ **noun** [C] (also **advisor**) Ⓒ① someone whose job is to give advice about a subject: *She is the party's main economic adviser.* ◦ *a financial adviser*

advisory /əd'vaɪ.zəʳ.i/ Ⓤⓢ /-zɚ-/ **adj; noun**
▸**adj** giving advice: *She is employed by the president in an advisory capacity.*
▸**noun** [C usually plural] mainly US an official announcement that contains advice, information, or a warning: ***weather/travel*** *advisories*

advocate **verb; noun**
▸**verb** [T] /'æd.və.keɪt/ Ⓒ② to publicly support or suggest an idea, development, or way of doing something: [+ -ing verb] *She advocates tak****ing*** *a more long-term view.* ◦ *He advocates the return of capital punishment.* • **advocacy** /'æd.və.kə.si/ **noun** [U] *She is renowned for her advocacy* ***of*** *human rights.*
▸**noun** [C] /'æd.və.kət/ **LAWYER** ▷ **1** a lawyer who defends someone in a law court **SUPPORTER** ▷ **2** Ⓒ② someone who publicly supports something: *He's a strong advocate* ***of*** *state ownership of the railways.*

adze (US usually **adz**) /ædz/ **noun** [C] a tool like an AXE with the blade at an angle of approximately 90° to the handle, used for cutting and shaping wood

adzuki (also **aduki**, **azuki**) /æd'zuː.ki/ **noun** [C] a sweet, red bean used in Chinese and Japanese cooking

aegis /'iː.dʒɪs/ **noun** formal **under the aegis of sb/sth** with the protection or support of someone or something, especially an organization: *The project was set up under the aegis of the university.*

aeolian /iː'əʊ.li.ən/ Ⓤⓢ /-'oʊ-/ **adj** UK (US **eolian**) produced or carried by the wind: *aeolian landforms*

aeon /'iː.ɒn/ Ⓤⓢ /-ɑːn/ **noun** [C] mainly UK for **eon**

aerate /eə'reɪt/ Ⓤⓢ /er'eɪt/ **verb** [T] **1** to add a gas to liquid, especially a drink: *aerated water* **2** to allow air to act on something: *Earthworms help to aerate the soil.* ◦ *aerated soil* • **aeration** /eə'reɪ.ʃən/ Ⓤⓢ /er'eɪ-/ **noun** [U]

aerator /eə'reɪ.təʳ/ Ⓤⓢ /er'eɪ.t̬ɚ/ **noun** [C] a piece of equipment that adds air to water or soil

aerial /'eə.ri.əl/ Ⓤⓢ /'er.i-/ **noun; adj**
▸**noun** [C] (US also **antenna**) a structure made of metal rods or wires that receives or sends out radio or television signals
▸**adj** in or from the air, especially from an aircraft: *Meanwhile, the massive aerial* ***bombardment/bombing*** *of military targets continued unabated.* ◦ *aerial* ***photography***

'aerial ͵root **noun** [C] specialized a root that grows down to the ground from above the ground

aerie /'ɪə.ri/ Ⓤⓢ /'ɪr.i/ **noun** [C] mainly US for **eyrie**

aero- /eə.rəʊ-/, /eə.rə-/ Ⓤⓢ /er.oʊ-/ **prefix** of the air or of air travel: *aerodynamics* ◦ *aeronautics*

aerobatics /͵eə.rə'bæt.ɪks/ Ⓤⓢ /͵er.oʊ'bæt̬-/ **noun** [plural] skilful changes of position of an aircraft, such as flying upside down or in a circle: *The crowd was entertained with a display of aerobatics.* • **aerobatic** /͵eə.rə'bæt.ɪk/ Ⓤⓢ /͵er.oʊ'bæt̬-/ **adj** *an aerobatic display*

ae͵robic respi'ration **noun** [U] specialized a chemical process in which energy is produced in the body from food by using OXYGEN → Compare **anaerobic respiration**

aerobics /eə'rəʊ.bɪks/ Ⓤⓢ /er'oʊ-/ **noun** [U] energetic physical exercises, often performed with a group of people to music, that make the heart, lungs, and muscles stronger and increase the amount of OXYGEN in the blood: *She* ***does*** *aerobics.* ◦ *I go to aerobics (= to a class where we are taught such exercises) once a week.* ◦ *an aerobics instructor/teacher* • **aerobic** /eə'rəʊ.bɪk/ Ⓤⓢ /er'oʊ-/ **adj** *aerobic* ***exercise***

aerodrome /'eə.rə.drəʊm/ Ⓤⓢ /'er.ə.droʊm/ **noun** [C] UK old-fashioned for **airfield**

aerodynamic /͵eə.rəʊ.daɪ'næm.ɪk/ Ⓤⓢ /͵er.oʊ-/ **adj** relating to or using aerodynamics: *aerodynamic principles* ◦ *an aerodynamic design/car* • **aerodynamically** /-ɪ.kəl.i/ **adv** *aerodynamically designed/efficient*

aerodynamics /ˌeə.rəʊ.daɪˈnæm.ɪks/ US /ˌer.oʊ-/ **noun** [U] the science that studies the movement of gases and the way solid bodies, such as aircraft, move through them

aerogramme UK (US **aerogram**) /ˈeə.rə.græm/ US /ˈer.ə-/ **noun** [C] an **air letter**

aeronautics /ˌeə.rəˈnɔː.tɪks/ US /ˌer.əˈnɑː.t̬ɪks/ **noun** [U] the science of designing, building, and operating aircraft • **aeronautic** /ˌeə.rəˈnɔː.tɪk/ US /ˌer.əˈnɑː.t̬ɪk/ **adj** *aeronautic design/engineering* • **aeronautical** /ˌeə.rəˈnɔː.tɪ.kəl/ US /ˌer.əˈnɑː.t̬ɪ-/ **adj**

aeroplane /ˈeə.rə.pleɪn/ US /ˈer-/ **noun** [C] UK (US **airplane**) A2 a vehicle designed for air travel that has wings and one or more engines: *She has her own private aeroplane.*

aerosol /ˈeə.rə.sɒl/ US /ˈer.ə.sɑːl/ **noun** [C] a metal container in which liquids are kept under pressure and forced out in a SPRAY

aerosol

aerospace /ˈeə.rə.speɪs/ US /ˈer.oʊ-/ **adj** [before noun] producing or operating aircraft or spacecraft: *the aerospace industry* ◦ *an aerospace company*

aesthete (US also **esthete**) /ˈiːs.θiːt/ US /ˈes.θiːt/ **noun** [C] a person who understands and enjoys beauty: *The ugliness of the city would make an aesthete like you shudder.*

aesthetic (US also **esthetic**) /esˈθet.ɪk/ US /-ˈθet̬-/ **adj** **1** relating to the enjoyment or study of beauty: *The new building has little aesthetic value/appeal.* **2** describes an object or a work of art that shows great beauty: *furniture that is both aesthetic and functional* • **aesthetically** (US also **esthetically**) /-ɪ.kəl.i/ **adv** *I like objects to be both functional and aesthetically* ***pleasing***.

aesthetics (US also **esthetics**) /esˈθet.ɪks/ US /-ˈθet̬-/ **noun** [U] the formal study of art, especially in relation to the idea of beauty

aetiology UK specialized (US **etiology**) /ˌiː.tiˈɒl.ə.dʒi/ US /-t̬iˈɑː.lə-/ **noun** [U] the study of the causes of a disease

afaik written abbreviation for as far as I know: used when you believe that something is true, but you are not completely certain

afar /əˈfɑːr/ US /-ˈfɑːr/ **adv** from or at a great distance: *People came* ***from*** *afar to see the show.* ◦ humorous *I've never actually spoken to him – I've just admired him* ***from*** *afar.*

affable /ˈæf.ə.bl/ **adj** friendly and easy to talk to: *He struck me as an affable sort of a man.* ◦ *She was quite affable at the meeting.* • **affability** /ˌæf.əˈbɪl.ɪ.ti/ US /-ə.t̬i/ **noun** [U] • **affably** /-bli/ **adv** *He greeted us affably.*

affair /əˈfeər/ US /-ˈfer/ **noun** [C] **MATTER** ▷ **1** B2 a situation or subject that is being dealt with or considered: *She organizes her* ***financial*** *affairs very efficiently.* ◦ *He's always* ***meddling in*** *(= trying to influence) other people's affairs.* ◦ *What I do in my spare time is my affair (= only involves me).* **2** B2 a matter or situation that causes strong public feeling, usually of moral disapproval: *The arms-dealing affair has severely damaged the reputation of the government.* ◦ *The president's* ***handling*** *of the affair has been criticized.* **RELATIONSHIP** ▷ **3** B2 a sexual relationship, especially a secret one: *She's* ***having*** *an affair with a married man.* ◦ *The book doesn't make any mention of his* ***love*** *affairs.* ◦ *an* ***extramarital*** *affair* **EVENT** ▷ **4** an event: *The party turned out to be a quiet affair.* **THING** ▷ **5** old-fashioned an object of the type stated: *She wore a long black velvet affair.*

afˌfairs of ˈstate **noun** [plural] important government matters

affect /əˈfekt/ **verb** [T] **INFLUENCE** ▷ **1** B2 to have an influence on someone or something, or to cause a change in someone or something: *Both buildings were badly affected by the fire.* ◦ *The divorce affected every aspect of her life.* ◦ *It's a disease that affects mainly older people.* ◦ *I was deeply affected by the film (= it caused strong feelings in me).* **PRETEND** ▷ **2** formal to pretend to feel or think something: *To all his problems she affected indifference.* **3** formal mainly disapproving to start to wear or do something in order to make people admire or respect you: *At university he affected an upper-class accent.*

affectation /ˌæf.ekˈteɪ.ʃən/ **noun** [C or U] disapproving behaviour or speech that is not sincere: *She has so many little affectations.* ◦ *His manner reeks of affectation.* ◦ *'It doesn't concern me,' he said with* ***an*** *affectation* ***of*** *nonchalance.*

affected /əˈfek.tɪd/ **adj** disapproving artificial and not sincere: *an affected manner/style of writing* ◦ *I found her very affected.* • **affectedly** /-li/ **adv** *She laughed affectedly.*

affecting /əˈfek.tɪŋ/ **adj** formal causing a strong emotion, especially sadness: *It was an affecting sight.*

affection /əˈfek.ʃən/ **noun** **1** B2 [U or S] a feeling of liking for a person or place: *She* ***felt*** *no affection* ***for*** *the child.* ◦ *He* ***had*** *a* ***deep*** *affection for his aunt.* **2 affections** [plural] feelings of liking or love: *The former president still* ***holds a place in*** *the nation's affections.* ◦ *Sula seems to have* ***transferred*** *her affections from Jon to his brother.* **3 win sb's affections** to succeed in persuading someone to love you

affectionate /əˈfek.ʃən.ət/ **adj** C2 showing feelings of liking or love: *an affectionate kiss* ◦ *He's an affectionate little boy.* • **affectionately** /-li/ **adv** *She smiled affectionately at him.*

affective /əˈfek.tɪv/ **adj** specialized connected with the emotions: *He has no affective ties to his family.*

affidavit /ˌæf.əˈdeɪ.vɪt/ **noun** [C] a written statement that someone makes after they have promised officially to tell the truth, that might be used as proof in a law court

affiliate **verb**; **noun**

▸**verb** [T] /əˈfɪl.i.eɪt/ to cause a group to become part of or form a close relationship with another, usually larger, group, or organization: *a college affiliated* ***to*** *the University of London* ◦ *The school is affiliated* ***with*** *a national association of driving schools.*

▸**noun** [C] /əˈfɪl.i.ət/ an organization that is connected with or controlled by another, usually larger, organization: *Our college is an affiliate* ***of*** *the university.*

affiliation /əˌfɪl.iˈeɪ.ʃən/ **noun** [C or U] a connection with a political party or religion, or with a larger organization: *The group has affiliations* ***with*** *several organizations abroad.* ◦ *Their lack of affiliation* ***to*** *any particular bank allows them to give objective financial advice.* ◦ *political affiliations*

affinity /əˈfɪn.ɪ.ti/ US /-ə.t̬i/ **noun** **1** [S] a liking or sympathy for someone or something, especially because of shared characteristics: *She seems to have a natural affinity* ***for/with*** *water.* **2** [C or U] a close similarity between two things: *There are several close affinities* ***between*** *the two paintings.*

afˈfinity ˌcard **noun** [C] a CREDIT CARD that earns a small amount of money for a CHARITY each time something is bought with it

affirm /ə'fɜːm/ Ⓤⓢ /-'fɝːm/ **verb** [T] formal **1** to state something as true: [+ (that)] *The suspect affirmed (**that**) he had been at home all evening.* ◦ *She affirmed her intention to apply for the post.* **2** to publicly show your support for an opinion or idea: *The government has affirmed its commitment to equal rights.* • **affirmation** /ˌæf.ə'meɪ.ʃᵊn/ Ⓤⓢ /-ɚ-/ **noun** [C or U] *We welcome the government's affirmation of its intention to act.*

affirmative /ə'fɜː.mə.tɪv/ Ⓤⓢ /-'fɝː.mə.t̬ɪv/ **adj; noun**
▸**adj** relating to a statement that shows agreement or says 'yes': *an affirmative answer/response* → Opposite **negative** • **affirmatively** /-li/ **adv** *She answered affirmatively.*
▸**noun** [C or U] a word or statement that shows agreement or says 'yes': *She asked the question expecting an affirmative.* ◦ *He replied **in the** affirmative (= he said yes).* ◦ mainly US *'Were you in New York on 3 March?' 'Affirmative.' (= Yes.)*

afˌfirmative 'action **noun** [U] If a government or an organization takes affirmative action, it gives preference to women, black people, or other groups that are often treated unfairly, when it is choosing people for a job.

affix **verb; noun**
▸**verb** [T] /ə'fɪks/ formal to fix one thing to another: *She affixed a stamp **to** the envelope.*
▸**noun** [C] /'æf.ɪks/ a letter or group of letters added to the beginning or end of a word to make a new word: *The affixes un- and -less are often used to make negative words, such as 'unhappy' and 'careless'.*

afflict /ə'flɪkt/ **verb** [T] If a problem or illness afflicts a person or thing, they suffer from it: *It is an illness that afflicts women more than men.* ◦ *a country afflicted by civil war*

affliction /ə'flɪk.ʃᵊn/ **noun** [C or U] formal something that makes you suffer

affluent /'æf.lu.ənt/ **adj** Ⓒ1 having a lot of money or owning a lot of things: *affluent nations/neighbourhoods* → Synonym **rich, wealthy** • **affluence** /-əns/ **noun** [U] *What we are seeing increasingly is a society of private affluence and public squalor.* → Synonym **wealth**

afford /ə'fɔːd/ Ⓤⓢ /-'fɔːrd/ **verb** HAVE ENOUGH ▷ **1 can afford** Ⓑ1 to be able to buy or do something because you have enough money or time: *I don't know how he can afford a new car on his salary.* ◦ *Few people are able to afford cars like that.* ◦ *She couldn't afford the time off work to see him.* ◦ [+ to infinitive] *I can't afford **to** buy a house.*

> **!** Common mistake: **afford**
>
> When **afford** is followed by a verb, that verb cannot be in the **-ing** form.
>
> Do not say 'afford doing something', say **afford to do something**:
>
> ~~*I can't afford buying a new computer.*~~
>
> *I can't afford to buy a new computer.*

GIVE ▷ **2** [T] formal to allow someone to have something pleasant or necessary: *The hut afforded little protection from the elements.* ◦ [+ two objects] *Her seat afforded her an uninterrupted view of the stage.*

IDIOM **cannot afford** (formal **can ill afford**) Ⓒ2 If you cannot afford to do something, you must not do it because it would cause serious problems for you: *We can't afford to make any mistakes at this stage in the project.*

affordable /ə'fɔː.də.bl/ Ⓤⓢ /-'fɔːr-/ **adj** not expensive: *nice clothes at affordable prices*

afforest /ə'fɒr.ɪst/ Ⓤⓢ /-'fɔːr.əst/ **verb** [T] to plant trees on an area of land in order to make a forest • **afforestation** /æfˌɒr.ɪ'steɪ.ʃᵊn/ Ⓤⓢ /əˌfɔːr.ə-/ **noun** [U]

affray /ə'freɪ/ **noun** [C] legal a fight in a public place: *Wallace was **charged with** causing an affray at a Southampton nightclub.*

affricate /'æf.rɪ.kət/ **noun** [C] specialized a consonant sound that consists of a PLOSIVE and then a FRICATIVE made in the same place in the mouth: *The 'ch' sound at the beginning and end of 'church' is an affricate.*

affront /ə'frʌnt/ **noun; verb**
▸**noun** [C] a remark or action intended to insult or offend someone: *He regarded the comments as an affront **to** his dignity.*
▸**verb** [T usually passive] formal to insult or offend someone: *I was most affronted **by** his comments.* ◦ *an affronted look/glance*

Afghan hound /ˌæf.gæn'haʊnd/ **noun** [C] a tall, thin dog with long, smooth hair and a pointed nose

aficionado /əˌfɪʃ.i.ə'nɑː.dəʊ/ Ⓤⓢ /-doʊ/ **noun** [C] (plural **aficionados**) formal someone who is very interested in and enthusiastic about a particular subject: *a club for model railway aficionados* ◦ *an aficionado **of** French films*

afield /ə'fiːld/ **adv** **far/further afield** a long/longer distance away: *We export our products to countries as far afield as Japan and Canada.* ◦ *Our students come from Europe, Asia, and even further afield.*

afk written abbreviation for away from keyboard: used when you stop taking part in a discussion in a CHAT ROOM for a short time

aflame /ə'fleɪm/ **adj** [after verb] literary **1** burning: *The whole village was aflame.* **2** red or gold, as if burning: *It was autumn and the trees were aflame **with** colour.* ◦ *Her cheeks were aflame **with** embarrassment/anger.* **3** very excited: *Aflame **with** desire, he took her in his arms.*

afloat /ə'fləʊt/ Ⓤⓢ /-'floʊt/ **adj** [after verb] **1** floating on water: *She spent seven days afloat on a raft.* ◦ *He managed to **keep/stay** afloat by holding on to the side of the boat.* **2** having enough money to pay what you owe: *Many small businesses are struggling to **stay/keep** afloat.*

aflutter /ə'flʌt.əʳ/ Ⓤⓢ /-'flʌt̬.ɚ/ **adj** [after verb] humorous excited and nervous: *I'm **all** aflutter about meeting him after so long.* ◦ *Paul had walked into the room and set my **heart** aflutter.*

afoot /ə'fʊt/ **adj** [after verb] happening or being planned or prepared: *There are **plans** afoot to launch a new radio station.*

aforementioned /ə'fɔːˌmen.ʃᵊnd/ Ⓤⓢ /-'fɔːr-/ **adj; noun**
▸**adj** [before noun] (also **aforesaid** /ə'fɔː.sed/ Ⓤⓢ /-'fɔːr-/) mentioned earlier: *The aforementioned Mr Parkes then entered the cinema.*
▸**noun** (also **aforesaid**) **the aforementioned** the person or people mentioned earlier

afraid /ə'freɪd/ **adj** FEAR ▷ **1** Ⓐ2 [after verb] feeling fear, or feeling worry about the possible results of a particular situation: *He was/felt suddenly afraid.* ◦ *I've always been afraid **of** flying/heights/spiders.* ◦ *She was afraid **for** her children (= feared that they might be hurt).* ◦ [+ to infinitive] *Don't be afraid **to** say what you think.* ◦ [+ (that)] *She was afraid (**that**) he might be upset if she told him.* SORRY ▷ **2 I'm afraid...** Ⓐ2 used to politely introduce bad news or disagreement: *This is your room – it's rather small, I'm afraid.* ◦ *I don't agree at all, I'm afraid.* ◦ [+ (that)] *I'm afraid (**that**) we can't come this evening after all.* ◦ *'Was she impressed with our work?' 'I'm afraid not (= no).'* ◦ *'Does this mean I've got to leave?' 'I'm afraid so.' (= Yes.)*

A

Other ways of saying afraid

Other common ways of saying 'afraid' are **frightened** and **scared**. If someone is extremely afraid, then you can use adjectives such as **petrified**, **terrified**, **panic-stricken**, or the informal phrase **scared to death**:

*I'm **terrified** of flying.*

*She was **panic-stricken** when her little boy disappeared.*

*He's **scared to death** of having the operation.*

If someone is afraid because of worrying about something, then you can use adjectives such as **anxious**, **concerned**, **nervous**, or **worried**:

*I'm **worried** that something will go wrong.*

*All this waiting is making me feel **anxious**.*

If someone is afraid of something that might happen in the future, you can use the adjectives **apprehensive** or **uneasy**:

*He's a bit **apprehensive** about living away from home.*

To talk about something that is frightening in a shocking way, you could use the adjective **hair-raising**:

*The pilots are trained to do **hair-raising** stunts at low altitude.*

ˈA-frame noun [C] US a simple house shaped like an A, with two of its four walls sloping and meeting at the top to act as a roof: *an A-frame chalet*

A-frame

afresh /əˈfreʃ/ adv If you do something afresh, you deal with it again in a new way: *She tore up the letter and **started** afresh.*

Africa /ˈæf.rɪ.kə/ **noun** the continent that is to the south of the Mediterranean Sea, to the east of the Atlantic Ocean, and to the west of the Indian Ocean

African /ˈæf.rɪ.kən/ **adj; noun**

▸**adj** relating or belonging to Africa: *African history/music*

▸**noun** [C] someone from Africa

ˌAfrican Aˈmerican noun [C] a person who lives in the US and is a member of a race of people with dark skin that originally came from Africa • **ˌAfrican-Aˈmerican adj**

ˌAfrican ˈviolet noun [C] a small plant with purple, pink, or white flowers that is grown in a container in a house

Afrikaans /ˌæf.rɪˈkɑːns/ **noun** [U] a language that is related to Dutch and is spoken in South Africa

Afrikaner /ˌæf.rɪˈkɑː.nəʳ/ (US) /-nɚ/ **noun** [C] a South African person whose family was originally Dutch and whose first language is Afrikaans

Afro /ˈæf.rəʊ/, /-roʊ/ **noun** [C] (plural **Afros**) a way of arranging the hair so that it is very thick, curly, and has a rounded shape, especially like that of some black people

Afro- /æf.rəʊ-/ (US) /æf.roʊ-/ **prefix** of or connected with Africa: *Afro-Caribbean culture* ◦ *Afro-American literature*

aft /ɑːft/ (US) /æft/ **adj, adv** specialized in or towards the back part of a boat

after /ˈɑːf.təʳ/ (US) /ˈæf.tɚ/ **preposition; adv; conjunction**

▸**preposition 1** (A1) following in time, place, or order: *Shall we go for a walk after breakfast?* ◦ *Her name came after mine on the list.* ◦ *There's a good film on **the day after tomorrow**.* ◦ *She waited until **well** after midnight.* ◦ US *It's a quarter after four.* ◦ *She just keeps on working, **day** after **day**, **week** after **week** (= continuously).* ◦ *We've had meeting after meeting (= many meetings) to discuss this point.* ◦ *Jessie seemed very small after (= in comparison with) Michael's children.* ◦ *After (= despite) everything I've done for you, is this the way you treat me?* ◦ *After (= because of) what she did to me, I'll never trust her again.* ◦ *The children have to learn to tidy up after themselves (= after they have made things untidy).* ◦ *She slammed the door after (= behind) her.* ◦ *We ran after (= followed) him, but he escaped.* ◦ *Could you lock up after you (= when you leave), please?* **2 be after sb/sth** informal to be looking for someone or something or trying to find or get them: *The police are after him.* ◦ *I'm after a tie to go with this shirt.* ◦ *He's after Jane's job (= wants it for himself).* **3 after you a** used to say politely that someone can go in front of you or serve themselves with food before you: *'Can I pour you some coffee?' 'Oh no, after you.'* **b** UK informal used to ask another person to give you something which they are using when they have finished using it: *After you **with** the newspaper, Jack.* **4** typical of or similar to the style of: *a painting after Titian* ◦ *a concerto after Mozart* **5** (C2) used when giving someone or something the same name as another person or thing: *He was named Mark after his grandfather.*

IDIOM **after all 1** (C1) despite earlier problems or doubts: *The rain has stopped, so the game will go ahead after all.* **2** (B1) used to add information that shows that what you have just said is true: *I do like her – after all, she is my sister.*

▸**adv** (A2) later than someone or something else: *Hilary got here at midday and Nicholas arrived **soon** after.* ◦ *I can't go next week – how about the week after (= the following week)?* ◦ not standard *She got back at 4.30 and went to see Emilie after (= after she got back).*

▸**conjunction** (B1) at a time that is later than another event: *Three months after they moved out, the house was still empty.* ◦ ***Soon/shortly** after we set off, the car started to make a strange noise.* ◦ *I went to the post office **straight/immediately** after I left you.*

after- /ɑːf.tə-/ (US) /æf.tɚ-/ **prefix** coming after: *an after-dinner speech* ◦ *an after-hours club* ◦ *after-sales service*

afterbirth /ˈɑːf.tə.bɜːθ/ (US) /ˈæf.tɚ.bɝːθ/ **noun** [S] the material, including the PLACENTA, that is pushed out of a woman's or female animal's body soon after she has given birth

aftercare /ˈɑːf.tə.keəʳ/ (US) /ˈæf.tɚ.ker/ **noun** [U] the care of people after they have left a hospital or prison

aftereffects /ˈɑːf.tᵊr.ɪˌfekts/ (US) /ˈæf.tɚ-/ **noun** [plural] unpleasant effects that follow an event or accident, sometimes continuing for a long time or happening some time after it

afterglow /ˈɑːf.tə.gləʊ/ (US) /ˈæf.tɚ.gloʊ/ **noun** [C usually singular] a pleasant feeling produced after an experience, event, feeling, etc.: *The team were **basking in the** afterglow **of** winning the cup.*

afterlife /ˈɑːf.tə.laɪf/ (US) /ˈæf.tɚ-/ **noun** [S] the life, for example in heaven, that some people believe begins after death: *They'll be reunited **in the** afterlife.*

aftermath /ˈɑːf.tə.mæθ/, /-mɑːθ/ (US) /ˈæf.tɚ-/ **noun** [S] the period that follows an unpleasant event or accident, and the effects that it causes: *Many more people died **in the** aftermath **of** the explosion.*

afternoon /ˌɑːf.təˈnuːn/ (US) /ˌæf.tɚ-/ **noun; exclamation**

▸**noun** [C or U] (A1) the period that starts at about twelve

A

o'clock or after the meal in the middle of the day and ends at about six o'clock or when the sun goes down: *It was a sunny afternoon.* ◦ *She works three afternoons a week at the library.* ◦ *It was on a Saturday afternoon.* ◦ *My baby usually sleeps **in the** afternoon.* ◦ *Let's go to the park **this** afternoon.* ◦ *I spoke to her **yesterday** afternoon.* ◦ *I'll meet you **tomorrow** afternoon at about 3.30.* ◦ *She's coming round **on** Wednesday afternoon.* ◦ *He's been in a bad mood **all** afternoon.* ◦ *She likes to have an afternoon nap.* ◦ *We got an early-/mid-/late-afternoon flight.*
▸exclamation informal a friendly way of greeting someone when you meet them in the afternoon: *Afternoon, Bob! Lovely day, isn't it?* → Compare **good afternoon**

afternoons /ˌɑːf.təˈnuːnz/ US /ˌæf.tɚ-/ **adv** mainly US every afternoon or on many afternoons: *He works afternoons.*

ˌafternoon ˈtea **noun** [C or U] mainly UK a small meal eaten in the late afternoon, usually including cake and a cup of tea

afterparty /ˈɑːf.təˌpɑː.ti/ US /-tɚˌpɑːr.t̬i/ **noun** [C] a relaxed social event in which people sit and talk after they have been at a party or NIGHTCLUB

afters /ˈɑːf.təz/ US /ˈæf.tɚz/ **noun** [U] UK informal sweet food eaten at the end of a meal: *What's **for** afters, Dad?* → Synonym **dessert**

aftershave /ˈɑːf.tə.ʃeɪv/ US /ˈæf.tɚ.ʃeɪv/ **noun** [U] (also **ˈaftershave ˌlotion**) a liquid with a pleasant smell that a man puts on his face after SHAVING

aftershock /ˈɑːf.tə.ʃɒk/ US /ˈæf.tɚ.ʃɑːk/ **noun** [C] a sudden movement of the earth's surface that often follows an EARTHQUAKE and is less violent than the first main movement: *The initial earthquake was followed by **a series of** aftershocks.*

aftertaste /ˈɑːf.tə.teɪst/ US /ˈæf.tɚ-/ **noun** [C usually singular] the taste that a particular food or other substance leaves in your mouth when you have swallowed it: *The medicine **left** an unpleasant after-taste.*

afterthought /ˈɑːf.tə.θɔːt/ US /ˈæf.tɚ.θɑːt/ **noun** [C usually singular] an idea, thought, or plan that was not originally intended but is thought of at a later time: *She only asked me to her party **as an** afterthought.* ◦ *The pillars seem to have been **added** to the entrance **as an** afterthought.*

afterwards /ˈɑːf.tə.wədz/ US /ˈæf.tɚ.wɚdz/ **adv** (US also **afterward**) A2 after the time mentioned: *We had tea, and afterwards we sat in the garden for a while.* ◦ *They separated, and **soon/shortly** afterwards Jane left the country.*

again /əˈɡen/, /-ˈɡeɪn/ US /-ˈɡen/ **adv** ONE MORE TIME ▷ **1** A1 one more time: *Could you spell your name again, please?* ◦ *If he does it again I'll have to tell him.* ◦ *Deborah's late again.* ◦ *Throw it away and **start** again.* **2** A2 back to the original place or condition: *We went to Edinburgh and **back** again all in one day.* ◦ *Get some rest and you'll soon be well again.* **3 once again** B1 If something happens once again, it has already happened several times before: *You are reminded once again of the author's love of the sea.* **4 never again!** said after an unpleasant experience to show that you do not intend to do it again: *He drove me back home last night. Never again!* **5 yet again** B2 If something happens yet again, it has already happened many times before: *I'm afraid it's been delayed yet again.* **6 again and again** B1 repeatedly: *I've told you again and again not to do that.* **7 all over again** B2 If you do something all over again, you start again from the beginning: *It's already taken me two hours – I don't want to have to do it all over again.*

> **!** Common mistake: **again**
>
> **Warning: again** usually goes directly after the object in a sentence.
>
> Don't say 'do again something', say **do something again**:
>
> ~~*I hope you will again visit us.*~~
>
> *I hope you will visit us again.*
>
> If the sentence does not have an object, **again** usually goes at the end of the sentence:
>
> *It's raining again.*

IN ADDITION ▷ **8** in addition to the amount we know about or have mentioned already: *They are paid half **as much** again as we are.*

IDIOM **then again** (also **there again**) C2 used when you have had a new thought that is different from or the opposite of what you have just said: *I like to travel but, then again, I'm very fond of my home.*

against /əˈɡenst/, /-ˈɡeɪnst/ US /-ˈɡenst/ **preposition** OPPOSING ▷ **1** A2 disagreeing with a plan or activity: *She spoke against the decision to close the college.* ◦ *50 people voted against the new proposal.* ◦ *I'm very much against the idea that it is the woman's job to bring up the child.* ◦ *Germany are playing against Brazil in the cup final tonight.* ◦ *She's always rebelled against authority.* ◦ *She sold the house even though it was against his wishes.* ◦ *They called a demonstration to protest against proposed job cuts.* ◦ *Are you **for or** against my proposal?* ◦ *Stricter controls will help in the fight against inflation.* ◦ *They decided not to take legal action against him.* ◦ *They were **up** against a powerful pressure group.* ◦ *We **came up** against a lot of problems in the course of building our extension.* ◦ *The **chances/odds** against you winning such a competition are enormous.* ◦ *It's against **the law** (= illegal) to leave children under a certain age alone in the house.* ◦ *It's against my **beliefs/principles** to be nice to someone I dislike just because they're in a senior position.* ◦ *I wouldn't dare say anything against him (= criticize him) to his mother!* **2 have sth against sb** C1 If you have something against someone, you dislike them for a reason: *I've **nothing** against him – I just don't have much in common with him.* **3 count/go/work against sb** If something counts/goes/works against you, it gives you a disadvantage: *Lack of experience will generally count against you in an interview.* TOUCHING ▷ **4** A2 next to and touching or being supported by (something): *Why don't we put the bed against the wall?* ◦ *He loved the feel of her soft hair against his skin.* ◦ *The rain beat against her face as she struggled through the wind.* ◦ *She leaned against the door.* **5** in front of or compared to: *Paintings look best against a simple white wall.* IN OPPOSITE DIRECTION ▷ **6** B1 in the opposite direction to: *The last part of the course was hard because I was running against the wind.* ◦ *Commuting is not so bad when you are travelling against the traffic.* AS PROTECTION ▷ **7** as a protection or defence from the bad effects of: *We've insured the car against fire, theft, and accident.* ◦ *The police have to arm themselves against attack.*

IDIOMS **against time/the clock** If you do something against time/the clock, you do it as fast as possible and try to finish it before a certain time: *It was a real race against time to get all the costumes sewn for the play.* • **as against** compared to: *He earns $80,000 a year, as against my $40,000.* • **be up against it** informal to be having or likely to have serious problems or difficulties: *With seven members of the team missing, Hull are going to be up against it.* ◦ *Many families are up against it, unable to afford even basic items.*

agape /ə'geɪp/ **adj** with the mouth open, especially showing surprise or shock: *We watched, our mouths agape in excitement.*

agar /'eɪ.gɑːʳ/ (US) /-gɑːr/ **noun** [U] specialized a thick, clear substance that comes from SEAWEED, used for growing organisms such as bacteria in scientific work, and also for making liquids thicker

agarbatti /æg.ə'bʌt.i/ (US) /-ə'bʌt̬-/ **noun** [C] Indian English a thin wooden stick covered in a substance that is burned to produce a pleasant smell, especially as part of a religious ceremony → Compare **joss stick**

'Aga ˌsaga **noun** [C] UK humorous a story about the lives of people who have a good standard of living and live in the English countryside

agate /'æg.ət/ **noun** [C or U] a hard stone with strips of colour, used in jewellery

age /eɪdʒ/ **noun; verb**

▸**noun** **TIME SPENT ALIVE** ▷ **1** (A1) [C or U] the period of time someone has been alive or something has existed: *Do you know the age of that building?* ◦ *What age (= how old)* ***is*** *your brother?* ◦ *I'd guess she's about my age (= she is about as old as I am).* ◦ *She was 74* ***years of*** *age when she wrote her first novel.* ◦ *He left home* ***at the*** *age* ***of*** *16.* ◦ *I was married with four children* ***at*** *your age.* ◦ *She's starting to* ***show/look*** *her age (= to look as old as she is).* ◦ *I'm really beginning to* ***feel*** *my age (= feel old).* ◦ *His girlfriend's twice his age (= twice as old as he is).* **2 act your age!** said to someone to tell them to stop behaving like someone who is much younger **3 the age of consent** the age at which someone is considered by the law to be old enough to agree to have sex with someone **PERIOD** ▷ **4** (B1) [C] a particular period in time: *the Victorian age* ◦ *the modern age* ◦ *the nuclear age* **LONG TIME** ▷ **5 ages** (B1) [plural] (also **an age** [S]) mainly UK informal a very long time: *It* ***takes*** *ages to cook.* ◦ *I've been waiting* ***for*** *ages.* ◦ *It's been ages/an age since we last spoke.* **BEING OLD** ▷ **6** (C2) [U] the fact of being or getting older: *Her back was bent* ***with*** *age.* ◦ *This cheese/wine improves* ***with*** *age.*

> **Word partners for age noun**
>
> *live to/reach* the age of • *feel/look/show* your age • *at/by/from* the age *of* [20/30/55] • *at* [his/her/my] age • *between* the ages *of* [5 and 8, 40 and 55, etc.] • *at* an age [when/where] • [3/67] *years of* age

IDIOM **come of age 1** to reach the age when you are legally recognized as an adult **2** If something has come of age, it has reached its full successful development.

▸**verb** [I or T] (present tense UK **ageing** or US **aging**, past tense and past participle **aged**) **1** If someone ages or something ages them, they look older: *She's aged since the last time we met.* **2** to develop in flavour or leave something to do this: *The brandy is aged in oak for ten years.*

-age /-ɪdʒ/ **suffix** **ACTION** ▷ **1** used to form nouns that refer to the action or result of something: *blockage* ◦ *shrinkage* ◦ *wastage* ◦ *All breakages must be paid for.* **STATE** ▷ **2** used to form nouns that refer to a state or condition: *bondage* ◦ *marriage* ◦ *shortage* **PLACE** ▷ **3** used to form nouns that are names of places: *orphanage* ◦ *vicarage*

ˌage-ap'propriate **adj 1** suitable or right for people of a particular age: *age-appropriate clothing* ◦ *Is this movie age-appropriate for my child?* **2** of a suitable age: *The actors all look age-appropriate for their characters.*

'age-ˌbarred **adj** Indian English younger or older than the age at which a particular activity is legally or usually allowed: *If I wait another two years before I apply, I will become age-barred.*

aged **adj; noun**

▸**adj** **AGE** ▷ **1** (A2) /eɪdʒd/ [before noun] of the age of: *They've got one daughter, Isabel, aged three.* **OLD** ▷ **2** /'eɪ.dʒɪd/ old: *She has two rather aged aunts.*

▸**noun** [plural] /'eɪdʒɪd/ **the aged** old people when considered as a group: *The hospital was built to meet the needs of the aged.*

'age ˌgroup **noun** [C] (also **'age ˌrange**, **'age ˌbracket**) people of a similar age, considered as a group: *51 percent of enquiries were from those in the 25 to 40 age group.*

ageing (US usually **aging**) /'eɪ.dʒɪŋ/ **adj 1** relating to getting older: *the ageing process* **2** describes a person or thing that is getting old: *an ageing Hollywood actor* ◦ *ageing computers/machinery*

ageism (US also **agism**) /'eɪ.dʒɪ.zᵊm/ **noun** [U] unfair treatment of people because of their age • **ageist** (US also **agist**) /-dʒɪst/ **adj** *an ageist remark/job advertisement*

ageless /'eɪdʒ.ləs/ **adj** describes someone or something that never looks older: *She is beautiful and, at 43, somehow ageless.*

'age ˌlimit **noun** [C] the age at which a person is allowed or not allowed to do something: *the upper age limit* ◦ *The lower age limit for buying cigarettes in the UK is 16.*

agency /'eɪ.dʒᵊn.si/ **noun** **ORGANIZATION** ▷ **1** (B1) [C] a business that represents one group of people when dealing with another group: *an advertising/employment/estate/travel agency* **2** (C1) [C] a government organization: *an overseas aid agency* ◦ *the Central Intelligence Agency* **ACTIONS** ▷ **3 through the agency of sb** formal because of the actions of someone: *She was freed from prison through the agency of her doctor.*

agenda /ə'dʒen.də/ **noun** [C] **1** (C1) a list of matters to be discussed at a meeting: *There were several important items* ***on*** *the agenda.* ◦ *The question of security is* ***high on*** *the agenda for this afternoon's meeting.* **2** (C2) a list of aims or possible future achievements: *Women's rights have been put back* ***on*** *the agenda (= are being discussed publicly again).* ◦ *The subject of safety must be placed* ***high on/at the top of*** *the agenda (= must be discussed because it is very important).*

IDIOM **set the agenda** to decide what subjects other people should discuss and deal with

agent /'eɪ.dʒᵊnt/ **noun** [C] **REPRESENTATIVE** ▷ **1** (B2) a person who acts for or represents another: *Please contact our agent in Spain for further information.* **2** a person who represents an actor, artist, or writer **SPY** ▷ **3** (B2) someone who works secretly for the government or other organization: *a secret/foreign agent* **CAUSE** ▷ **4** a person or thing that produces a particular effect or change: *a powerful cleaning agent* ◦ *a raising agent for cakes* ◦ *a clotting agent* ◦ literary *He was the agent* ***of*** *their* ***destruction***.

agent provocateur /ˌæʒ.ɑ̃ː.prəˌvɒk.ə'tɜːʳ/ (US) /ˌɑːʒ.ɑ̃ː.proʊˌvɑː.kə'tɜː/ **noun** [C] (plural **agents provocateurs** /ˌæʒ.ɑ̃ː.prəˌvɒk.ə'tɜːʳ/ (US) /ˌɑːʒ.ɑ̃ː.proʊˌvɑː.kə'tɜː/) a person who intentionally encourages people to do something illegal so that they can be caught

ˌage-ˈold adj [before noun] literary very old: *an age-old story of love and betrayal*

agglomeration /əˌglɒm.əˈreɪ.ʃən/ (US) /-ˌglɑː.mə-/ noun [C] (also **agglomerate** /əˈglɒm.ər.ət/ (US) /-ˈglɑː.mə-/) a large group of many different things collected or brought together: *an agglomeration of various ethnic and religious groupings*

aggrandizement formal disapproving (UK usually **aggrandisement**) /əˈgræn.dɪz.mənt/ noun [U] an increase in power or importance: *He gives a lot of money to charity, but* ***personal*** *aggrandizement/****self-****aggrandizement is his motive.*

aggravate /ˈæg.rə.veɪt/ verb [T] **MAKE WORSE** ▷ **1** to make a bad situation worse: *Attempts to restrict parking in the city centre have further aggravated the problem of traffic congestion.* **2** to make a disease worse: *The treatment only aggravated the condition.* **ANNOY** ▷ **3** informal to annoy someone: *Stop aggravating me, will you!*

ˌaggravated asˈsault noun [U] legal a serious, violent attack on someone

ˌaggravated ˈburglary noun [U] UK legal a crime that involves using a weapon or committing another crime while illegally entering a person's house to steal something

aggravating /ˈæg.rə.veɪ.tɪŋ/ (US) /-t̬ɪŋ/ adj **ANNOYING** ▷ **1** informal annoying: *I find him really aggravating.* **MAKING WORSE** ▷ **2** formal or legal making something worse, such as a crime: *Aggravating* ***factors*** *can affect the sentence set by the court.*

aggravation /ˌæg.rəˈveɪ.ʃən/ noun **TROUBLE** ▷ **1** [C or U] (UK also informal **aggro** [U]) trouble or difficulty: *I've been getting a lot of aggravation at work recently.* ◦ *I don't need any more aggravation today.* **MAKE WORSE** ▷ **2** [U] formal the act of making something such as a problem or injury worse: *Rest the affected limb to avoid further aggravation of the condition.*

aggregate noun; adj; verb

▸**noun** [C or U] /ˈæg.rɪ.gət/ **TOTAL** ▷ **1** something formed by adding together several amounts or things: *They purchased an aggregate* ***of*** *3,000 shares in the company.* ◦ *Snowflakes are loose aggregates* ***of*** *ice crystals.* ◦ *Arsenal lost the second game, but got through to the final* ***on*** *aggregate (= adding together the goals in both matches).* **BUILDING STONES** ▷ **2** small stones used in building: *Volumes of aggregates, cement, and concrete used in the UK will rise this year.*

▸**adj** [before noun] /ˈæg.rɪ.gət/ total: *The seven companies have an aggregate turnover of £5.2 million.*

▸**verb** [T] /ˈæg.rɪ.geɪt/ to combine into a single group or total • **aggregation** /ˌæg.rɪˈgeɪ.ʃən/ noun [U]

aggregator /ˈæg.rɪ.geɪ.tər/ (US) /-t̬ɚ/ noun [C] (also **ˈcontent ˌaggregator**) a person or organization that collects information from the internet pages of other businesses and puts it on a single website

aggression /əˈgreʃ.ən/ noun [U] **1** (C1) spoken or physical behaviour that is threatening or involves harm to someone or something: *Some types of dog are bred for aggression.* ◦ *an* ***act of*** *aggression* **2** forceful playing in sport that is intended to win points

aggressive /əˈgres.ɪv/ adj **1** (B2) behaving in an angry and violent way towards another person: *Men tend to be more aggressive than women.* ◦ *If I criticize him, he gets aggressive and starts shouting.* **2** (C1) determined to win or succeed and using forceful action to win or to achieve success: *an aggressive election campaign* ◦ *aggressive marketing tactics* • **aggressively** /-li/ adv (B2) *Small children often behave aggressively.* ◦ *The company is aggressively pursuing new business opportunities.* ◦ *They played more aggressively in the second half.*

aggressor /əˈgres.ər/ (US) /-ɚ/ noun [C] a person or country that starts an argument, fight, or war by attacking first

aggrieved /əˈgriːvd/ adj unhappy and angry because of unfair treatment: *He felt aggrieved* ***at*** *not being chosen for the team.* ◦ *One aggrieved customer complained that he still hadn't received the book he had ordered several weeks ago.*

aggro /ˈæg.rəʊ/ (US) /-roʊ/ noun [U] UK informal **1** violent or threatening behaviour, especially between groups of young people: *There was some aggro between rival football fans at the station.* **2** trouble or difficulty: *Why are you being so uncooperative? I don't need this aggro.*

aghast /əˈgɑːst/ (US) /-ˈgæst/ adj [after verb] suddenly filled with strong feelings of shock and worry: *He looked at her aghast.*

agile /ˈædʒ.aɪl/ (US) /-əl/ adj **PHYSICALLY** ▷ **1** able to move your body quickly and easily: *Monkeys are very agile climbers.* ◦ *You need to have agile fingers to do this kind of work.* **MENTALLY** ▷ **2** able to think quickly and clearly: *For a man of 80, he has a remarkably agile* ***mind.*** • **agility** /əˈdʒɪl.ɪ.ti/ (US) /-ə.t̬i/ noun [U] *He's got the agility of a mountain goat.* ◦ *This job requires considerable* ***mental*** *agility.*

aging /ˈeɪ.dʒɪŋ/ mainly US present participle of **age**

agism /ˈeɪ.dʒɪ.zəm/ noun [U] mainly US for **ageism**

agitate /ˈædʒ.ɪ.teɪt/ verb **WORRY** ▷ **1** [T] to make someone feel worried or angry: *I didn't want to agitate her by telling her.* **ARGUE** ▷ **2** [I] to argue forcefully, especially in public, in order to achieve a particular type of change: *The unions continue to agitate* ***for*** *higher pay.* ◦ *As a young man, he had agitated* ***against*** *the Vietnam war.* **SHAKE** ▷ **3** [T] specialized to shake a liquid: *Pour the powder into the solution and agitate it until the powder has dissolved.* • **agitated** /ˈædʒ.ɪ.teɪ.tɪd/ (US) /-t̬ɪd/ adj *She became very agitated (= anxious) when her son failed to return home.*

agitation /ˌædʒ.ɪˈteɪ.ʃən/ noun [U] **WORRY** ▷ **1** worry and ANXIETY: *He arrived home in a* ***state of*** *agitation.* **PROTEST** ▷ **2** the situation in which people protest or argue, especially in public, in order to achieve a particular type of change: *The anti-war agitation is beginning to worry the government.*

agitator /ˈædʒ.ɪ.teɪ.tər/ (US) /-t̬ɚ/ noun [C] disapproving someone who tries to make people take part in protests and political activities, especially ones that cause trouble: *It is thought that the strike was the work of undercover political agitators.*

agitprop /ˈædʒ.ɪt.prɒp/ (US) /-prɑːp/ noun [U] (the spreading of) strongly political ideas or arguments expressed especially through plays, art, books, etc.

aglow /əˈgləʊ/ (US) /-ˈgloʊ/ adj [after verb] literary shining with light and colour: *a city at night, aglow* ***with*** *lights* ◦ *His face was* ***all*** *aglow* ***with*** *excitement.*

AGM /ˌeɪ.dʒiːˈem/ noun [C] UK abbreviation for **annual general meeting**

agnostic /ægˈnɒs.tɪk/ (US) /-ˈnɑː.stɪk/ noun; adj

▸**noun** [C] someone who does not know, or believes that it is impossible to know, if a god exists: *Although he was raised a Catholic, he was an agnostic for most of his adult life.* → Compare **atheist**

▸**adj** having the beliefs of an agnostic • **agnosticism** /ægˈnɒs.tɪ.sɪ.zəm/ (US) /-ˈnɑː.stə-/ noun [U]

ago /əˈgəʊ/ (US) /-ˈgoʊ/ adv (A2) back in time from the present: *He left the house over an hour ago.* ◦ *The dinosaurs died out 65 million years ago.* ◦ ***Long*** *ago/****A long time*** *ago, there lived a girl called Cinderella.*

agog /əˈɡɒɡ/ US /-ˈɡɑːɡ/ **adj** [after verb] excited and eager to know or see more: *We waited agog for news.*

agonize (UK usually **agonise**) /ˈæɡ.ə.naɪz/ **verb**

PHRASAL VERB **agonize over/about sth** If you agonize over/about something, you spend time worrying and trying to make a decision about it: *She agonized for days about whether she should take the job.*

agonized (UK usually **agonised**) /ˈæɡ.ə.naɪzd/ **adj** showing or feeling extreme physical or mental pain: *We heard an agonized cry.* ◦ *She gave him an agonized look.*

agonizing (UK usually **agonising**) /ˈæɡ.ə.naɪ.zɪŋ/ **adj** **1** causing extreme physical or mental pain: *an agonizing death* **2** causing extreme worry: *She went through an agonizing few weeks waiting for the test results.* ◦ *We are faced with an agonizing choice/decision/dilemma.* • **agonizingly** (UK usually **agonisingly**) /-li/ **adv**

agony /ˈæɡ.ə.ni/ **noun** [U or C] extreme physical or mental pain or suffering: *She lay there screaming* ***in*** *agony.* ◦ *I was* ***in*** *an agony* ***of*** *suspense.* ◦ *We've both* ***suffered*** *agonies* ***of*** *guilt over what happened.*

ˈagony ˌaunt **noun** [C usually singular] UK a person, usually a woman, who gives advice to people with personal problems, especially in a regular magazine or newspaper article

ˈagony ˌcolumn **noun** [C usually singular] UK the part of a magazine or newspaper where letters from readers about their personal problems are printed, together with advice about how to deal with them: *She wrote in to an agony column.*

agoraphobia /ˌæɡ.ə.rəˈfəʊ.bi.ə/ US /-ˈfoʊ-/ **noun** [U] specialized fear of going outside and being in open spaces or public places → Compare **claustrophobia**

agoraphobic **noun**; **adj**

▸**noun** [C] /ˌæɡ.ə.rəˈfəʊ.bɪk/ US /-ˈfoʊ-/ a person who suffers from agoraphobia

▸**adj** /ˌæɡ.rəˈfəʊ.bɪk/ US /-ˈfoʊ-/ relating to or suffering from agoraphobia: *She is agoraphobic and stays inside as much as she can.*

agrarian /əˈɡreə.ri.ən/ US /-ˈɡrer.i-/ **adj** specialized **1** related to the land, especially the use of land for farming: *This is prime agrarian land.* **2** describes a place or country that makes its money from farming rather than industry: *This part of the country is mainly agrarian.*

agree /əˈɡriː/ **verb** HAVE THE SAME OPINION ▷ **1** A2 [I or T] to have the same opinion: *Ann and I never seem to agree.* ◦ *I agree* ***with*** *you on this issue.* ◦ *My father and I don't agree* ***about/on*** *very much.* ◦ [+ that] *I agree* ***that*** *he should be invited.* ◦ [+ question word] *Experts seem unable to agree* ***wh****ether the drug is safe or not.* ◦ [+ speech] *'You're absolutely right,' agreed Jake.* SAY YES ▷ **2** B1 [I or T] UK to decide something together: *We finally agreed a deal.* ◦ *They agreed not to tell anyone about what had happened.* ◦ *We couldn't agree* ***on*** *what to buy.* **3** B2 [I or T] to accept a suggestion or idea: *I suggested that we should meet, and they agreed (= said yes).* ◦ [+ to infinitive] *The bank has agreed (= is willing)* ***to*** *lend me £5,000.* BE THE SAME ▷ **4** C2 [I] If two or more statements, ideas, sets of numbers, etc. agree, they are the same or very similar: *We've got five accounts of what happened and none of them agree.* GRAMMAR ▷ **5** [I] specialized When two words agree, or one word agrees with another word, they have the same grammatical form. For example, the words may both be singular or plural, MASCULINE or FEMININE, etc.

IDIOMS **agree to differ** If two people agree to differ, they accept that they have different opinions about something and stop trying to persuade each other that they are right. • **couldn't agree more/less** If you say you couldn't agree more/less, you mean you completely agree/disagree. • **not agree with sb** If a type of food or drink does not agree with you, it makes you feel slightly ill: *Those onions I ate didn't agree with me.*

PHRASAL VERBS **agree to sth** to accept something: *Both sides in the conflict have agreed to the terms of the peace treaty.* • **agree with sth** [usually in negatives] B2 to think that something is morally acceptable: *I don't agree with hunting.* • **agree with sb** If a situation or new conditions agree with you, they make you feel healthy and happy: *You look well – the mountain air must agree with you.*

agreeable /əˈɡriː.ə.bl̩/ **adj** PLEASANT ▷ **1** formal pleasant or pleasing: *We spent a most agreeable evening by the river.* AGREEING ▷ **2** able to be accepted by everyone: *The talks are aimed at finding a* ***mutually*** *agreeable solution.* ◦ *We must find a compromise that is agreeable* ***to*** *both sides of the party.* **3** formal willing to do or accept something: *If Bridget is agreeable* ***to*** *the proposal, we'll start the project in June.* • **agreeably** /-bli/ **adv** with enjoyment or pleasure: *We were agreeably* ***surprised*** *by the price.*

agreed /əˈɡriːd/ **adj** **1** accepted: *We have to stick to the agreed price.* ◦ *'So we'll meet at 5.30, shall we?' 'Agreed (= yes).'* **2 be agreed** If two or more people are agreed, they have the same opinion: *Are we all agreed (****on*** *that)?* ◦ [+ that] *The members are agreed* ***that*** *the proposal should be rejected.*

agreement /əˈɡriː.mənt/ **noun** SAME OPINION ▷ **1** B2 [U] the situation in which people have the same opinion, or in which they approve of or accept something: *The whole family was* ***in*** *agreement* ***with*** *her* ***about/on*** *what they should do.* ◦ *If the three parties cannot* ***reach*** *agreement now, there will be a civil war.* ◦ *I don't think you'll ever get Tony's agreement* ***to*** *these proposals.* ◦ [+ that] *There's widespread agreement* ***that*** *the law should be changed.* **2** B2 [C] a decision or arrangement, often formal and written, between two or more groups or people: *The dispute was settled by an agreement that satisfied both sides.* ◦ *The government has* ***entered into/signed*** *an international arms control agreement.* ◦ *They have* ***broken*** *(****the terms of****) the agreement* ***on*** *human rights.* ◦ *Finally the two sides have* ***reached*** *an agreement.* GRAMMAR ▷ **3** [U] the situation in which two words have the same grammatical form. For example, the words are both singular or plural, MASCULINE or FEMININE, etc.

> **Word partners for agreement**
>
> *reach* (an) agreement • *broad/general/widespread* agreement • be *in* agreement (*with* sb) • *with/without* sb's agreement • *nod in* agreement

agribusiness /ˈæɡ.riˌbɪz.nɪs/ **noun** [U] specialized the various businesses that are connected with producing, preparing, and selling farm products

agricultural /ˌæɡ.rɪˈkʌl.tʃər.əl/ US /-tʃɚ.əl/ **adj** used for farming or relating to farming: *The world's supply of agricultural land is shrinking fast.* ◦ *She's studying agricultural science.* ◦ *The country's economy is mainly agricultural (= based on farming).*

agriculture /ˈæɡ.rɪ.kʌl.tʃər/ US /-tʃɚ/ **noun** [U] B2 farming: *The area depends on agriculture for most of its income.* ◦ *70 percent of the country's population practises subsistence agriculture.* → Compare **horticulture**

agritourism /ˌæɡ.rɪˈtʊə.rɪ.zəm/ **noun** [U] the business of providing holidays for people on farms or in the countryside

agrochemical /ˌæg.rəʊˈkem.ɪ.kəl/ (US) /-roʊ-/ **noun** [C] a chemical that is used in farming to help grow crops or kill insects

aground /əˈgraʊnd/ **adj** [after verb] If a boat or ship is aground, it is unable to move because it is touching ground or in a place where there is very little water: *The ship is currently aground off the Brittany coast.* • **aground adv** *The oil tanker* ***ran/went*** *aground* ***on*** *a mud bank in thick fog.*

ah /ɑː/ **exclamation** (also **aah**) used to express understanding, pleasure, pain, surprise, or the fact that you have noticed something: *Ah, I see.* ◦ *Why has the train stopped? Ah, now we're off again.* ◦ *Ah, Jessica, how wonderful to see you!* ◦ *Ah, what a lovely baby!*

aha /ɑːˈhɑː/ **exclamation** used when you suddenly understand or find something: *Aha, now I see what you mean!* ◦ *Aha, that's where I put my keys!*

ahead /əˈhed/ **adv** **IN FRONT** ▷ **1** (B1) in front: *The road ahead is very busy.* ◦ *Turn left at the traffic lights, and you'll see the hospital* ***straight*** *ahead.* ◦ *Rick walked on ahead* ***of*** *us.* ◦ *You* ***go on*** *ahead* ***of*** *(= before) me, and I'll meet you there.* **2** (B2) having more points, votes, etc. than someone else in a competition, election, etc.: *Apparently, the latest opinion polls put the Democrats 15 percent ahead* ***of*** *the Republicans.* ◦ *Barcelona was ahead after ten minutes.* **3** (C2) making more progress than someone else: *Sophie is* ***way*** *(= far) ahead of the other children in her class.* **IN THE FUTURE** ▷ **4** (B1) in or into the future: *She has a difficult time ahead* ***of*** *her.* ◦ *He couldn't bear to think of the lonely year ahead.*

ahem /əˈhəm/ **exclamation** mainly humorous used to represent the little cough that someone makes to express slight embarrassment, enjoyment, doubt, or disapproval, or to attract attention

ahold /əˈhəʊld/ (US) /-ˈhoʊld/ **adv** US **1 get ahold of sth** to get something: *Drugs are too easy to get ahold of.* **2 get ahold of sb** to find or communicate with someone: *I'd like to get ahold of Debbie and talk to her about this.* **3 grab, take, etc. ahold of sth/sb** to take hold of something or someone: *I grabbed ahold of his legs and held on so he could not get away.* **4 get, grab, etc. ahold of sth/sb** to get power or control over someone or something: *Once the drugs get ahold of you, it just changes you completely.*

-aholic (also **-oholic**) /-ə.hɒl.ɪk/ (US) /-hɑː.lɪk/ **suffix** unable to stop doing, eating, or drinking something: *a workaholic* ◦ *an alcoholic* ◦ *a chocoholic*

ahoy /əˈhɔɪ/ **exclamation** **1** a shout used, especially by people in boats, to attract attention: *Ahoy there!* **2** used, especially on a boat, when you see something, usually something that is in the distance: *Land ahoy!* ◦ *Ship ahoy!*

AI /ˌeɪˈaɪ/ **noun** [U] abbreviation for **artificial intelligence** or **artificial insemination**

aid /eɪd/ **noun; verb**

▸**noun** **1** [U] help or support: *He gets about* ***with the*** *aid* ***of*** *a walking stick.* ◦ *She* ***went to the*** *aid* ***of*** *a man trapped in his car.* ◦ *A woman in the street saw that he was in trouble and* ***came to*** *his aid.* **2** (C1) [C] a piece of equipment that helps you to do something: *teaching aids, such as books and videos* ◦ *A thesaurus is a useful aid* ***to*** *writing.* **3** (C1) [U] help in the form of food, money, medical supplies, or weapons that is given by a richer country to a poorer country: *The Vatican has agreed to donate $80,000 in* ***humanitarian/emergency*** *aid to countries affected by the war.* ◦ *About a fifth of the country's income is in the form of* ***foreign/overseas*** *aid.* **4 in aid of sb/sth** (C1) UK in order to collect money for a group of people who need it: *a concert in aid of famine relief*

IDIOM **what's sth in aid of?** UK informal said when you want to know the reason for something: *What's all this shouting in aid of?*

▸**verb** [T] **1** (C1) to help: *Huge projects designed to aid poorer countries can sometimes do more harm than good.* ◦ *His excuse for drinking brandy is that it's said to aid digestion.* **2 aid and abet sb** legal or humorous to help someone to do something illegal or wrong: *Three tax inspectors were accused of aiding and abetting the men charged with fraud.*

aide /eɪd/ **noun** [C] a person whose job is to help someone important, such as a member of a government or a military officer of high rank: *a senior government aide* ◦ *an aide* ***to*** *the prime minister*

aide-de-camp /ˌeɪd.dəˈkɑ̃ː/ (US) /-ˈkæmp/ **noun** [C] (plural **aides-de-camp** /ˌeɪd.dəˈkɑ̃ː/ (US) /-ˈkæmp/) (abbreviation **ADC**) a military or NAVAL officer who helps an officer of higher rank

aide-mémoire /ˌeɪd.memˈwɑːʳ/ (US) /-ˈwɑːr/ **noun** [C] formal something, usually written, that helps you to remember something

AIDS (also **Aids**) /eɪdz/ **noun** [U] abbreviation for Acquired Immune Deficiency Syndrome: a serious disease caused by a virus that destroys the body's natural protection from infection: *Don had* ***full-blown*** *AIDS for over a year before he died.* ◦ *people living with AIDS* → Compare **HIV**

ˈaid ˌworker **noun** [C] someone who is working in a country where there is a war, no food, etc., in order to help people

ail /eɪl/ **verb** **CAUSE DIFFICULTY** ▷ **1** [T] formal to cause difficulty and problems for someone or something: *The government seems to have no understanding of* ***what*** *ails the country.* **BE/MAKE ILL** ▷ **2** [I or T] old-fashioned to be ill, or to cause to be ill: *She had been ailing for years before she died.*

aileron /ˈeɪ.lə.rɒn/ (US) /-rɑːn/ **noun** [C] specialized a part along the back edge of an aircraft's wing that can be moved to help the aircraft turn or to keep it level

ailing /ˈeɪ.lɪŋ/ **adj** **WITH DIFFICULTIES** ▷ **1** experiencing difficulty and problems: *the country's ailing economy* ◦ *Ted asked me if I could help him fix his ailing car.* **SICK** ▷ **2** weak and suffering from illness: *He's visiting his ailing father.*

ailment /ˈeɪl.mənt/ **noun** [C] an illness: *Treat* ***minor*** *ailments yourself.*

aim /eɪm/ **noun; verb**

▸**noun** **INTENTION** ▷ **1** (B1) [C] a result that your plans or actions are intended to achieve: *My* ***main*** *aim* ***in life*** *is to be a good husband and father.* ◦ *Our* ***short-term*** *aim is to deal with our current financial difficulties, but our* ***long-term*** *aim is to improve the company's profitability.* ◦ *The leaflet has been produced* ***with the*** *aim* ***of*** *increasing public awareness of the disease.* **POINTING** ▷ **2** [U] the act of pointing a weapon towards something: *He fired six shots at the target, but his aim was terrible, and he missed all of them.* ◦ *She raised her gun,* ***took*** *aim and fired.*

▸**verb** **INTEND** ▷ **1** (B1) [I] to intend: [+ to infinitive] *I aim* ***to*** *be a millionaire by the time I'm 35.* ◦ *We are aiming* ***for*** *(= planning to achieve) a 50 percent share of the German market.* **POINT** ▷ **2** [I or T] to point or direct a weapon towards someone or something that you want to hit: *Aim (the arrow) a little above the target.* ◦ *Aim* ***at*** *the yellow circle.* ◦ *There are hundreds of nuclear missiles aimed* ***at*** *the main cities.* ◦ *She aimed (= directed) a kick* ***at*** *my shins.* ◦ *Let's aim* ***for*** *(= go in* the direction of) Coventry first, and then we'll have a look at the map.

PHRASAL VERBS **aim at sth** C2 to plan, hope, or intend to achieve something: *The talks are aiming at a compromise.* ◦ [+ -ing verb] *The government's campaign is aimed at influencing public opinion.* • **aim sth at sb** [usually passive] B2 If information is aimed at a particular person or group of people, it is made known in a way that influences them or makes them interested in something: *These advertisements are specifically aimed at young people.*

aimless /ˈeɪm.ləs/ **adj** mainly disapproving without any clear intentions, purpose, or direction: *She said that her life seemed aimless after her children left home.* • **aimlessly** /-li/ **adv** *While she waited, she walked aimlessly around the car park.* • **aimlessness** /-nəs/ **noun** [U]

ain't /eɪnt/ **short form** not standard am not, is not, are not, has not, or have not: *He ain't going.* ◦ *'Can I have a fag?' 'I ain't got none left.'*

aioli /aɪˈəʊ.li/ US /-ˈoʊ-/ **noun** [U] a cold, thick sauce made from GARLIC, eggs, and OLIVE OIL

air /eəʳ/ US /er/ **noun; verb**

▸**noun** **GAS** ▷ **1** A2 [U] the mixture of gases that surrounds the earth and that we breathe: *I went outside to get some **fresh** air.* ◦ *You should put some air in your tyres – they look flat to me.* **2 the air** B2 [S] the space above the ground, especially high above the ground: *The air was filled with the scent of roses.* ◦ *Throw your gun down and put your hands **in** the air.* ◦ *The police fired **into** the air to clear the demonstrators from the streets.* **AIRCRAFT** ▷ **3** A2 [U] travel in an aircraft: *I don't travel much **by** air.* ◦ *an air crash/disaster* ◦ *air travel* **MANNER** ▷ **4** C2 [S] manner or appearance: *She has **an** air **of** confidence about her.* **BROADCAST** ▷ **5 be on/off (the) air** C1 If a programme or a person is on/off (the) air, they are/are not broadcasting on radio or television: *The radio station is on air from 6 a.m.* ◦ *As soon as the war started, any broadcasts with a military theme were **taken** off the air.* **TUNE** ▷ **6** [C] a simple tune: *Bach's Air on a G String*

IDIOMS **airs and graces** false ways of behaving that are intended to make other people feel that you are important and belong to a high social class: *He was always **putting on** airs and graces.* ◦ *She's got no reason to **give herself** airs and graces.* • **be walking/floating on air** to be very happy and excited because something very good has happened to you: *Ever since she met Mark, she's been walking on air.* • **in the air** If something is in the air, you feel that it is happening or about to happen: *Love/Change/Spring is in the air.* • **up in the air** If a matter is up in the air, it is uncertain, often because other matters have to be decided first: *The whole future of the project is still up in the air.*

▸**verb** **MAKE KNOWN** ▷ **1** [T] to make opinions or complaints known to other people: *Putting a complaint in the suggestions box is one way of airing your **grievances**.* ◦ *He'll air his **views** on the war whether people want to listen or not.* **DRY** ▷ **2** [I or T] to become dry and/or fresh, or to cause to become dry and/or fresh: *My mother always airs the sheets before she makes the beds.* ◦ *Leave the windows open to let the room air a bit.* **BROADCAST** ▷ **3** [I or T] US to broadcast something or be broadcast on radio or television: *The game will be aired **live on** CBS at 7.00 tonight.*

ˈair ˌambulance **noun** [C] a plane or HELICOPTER with all the equipment needed to fly sick or injured people to hospital

airbag /ˈeə.bæg/ US /ˈer-/ **noun** [C] a bag in a vehicle

that automatically fills with air if the vehicle is involved in an accident, in order to protect the driver or a passenger from injury: *In the event of a collision, the airbag stops the driver of the car from hitting his or her chest on the steering wheel.*

airbase /ˈeə.beɪs/ US /ˈer-/ **noun** [C] a military airport where aircraft are kept and can land and take off

airbed /ˈeə.bed/ US /ˈer-/ **noun** [C] UK (US **ˈair ˌmattress**) a large, rectangular rubber or plastic bag that you fill with air so that you can lie on it in water or use it as a bed

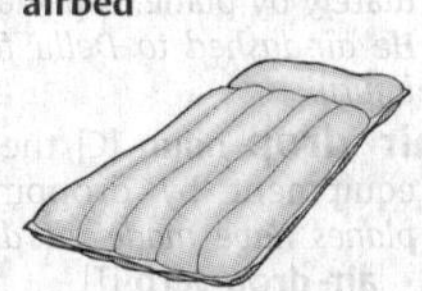
airbed

ˈair ˌbladder **noun** [C] specialized a small bag of air or gas inside a fish's body, that helps it to float or breathe

airborne /ˈeə.bɔːn/ US /ˈer.bɔːrn/ **adj** in the air, or carried by air or wind or by an aircraft: *The airborne radioactive particles have covered a huge area of Russia.* ◦ *Airborne troops were dropped by parachute behind enemy lines.* ◦ *The old plane had great difficulty **getting** airborne (= rising into the air).*

ˈair ˌbrake **noun** [C] a BRAKE operated by air pressure that is used on large vehicles such as buses and trains

airbrick /ˈeə.brɪk/ US /ˈer-/ **noun** [C] UK a special type of brick that has small holes in it that allow air to go through a wall

airbridge /ˈeə.brɪdʒ/ US /ˈer-/ **noun** [C] UK a covered passage by which passengers can go from an airport building to an aircraft

airbrush /ˈeə.brʌʃ/ US /ˈer-/ **noun; verb**

▸**noun** [C] a machine that spreads paint using air pressure, used for painting or for delicate improvement work on photographs

▸**verb** [T] **1** to use an airbrush to cover or improve the appearance of something: *pictures of airbrushed models* ◦ *It's so obvious in the photo that her wrinkles have been airbrushed **out** (= removed from the photograph with an airbrush).* **2** to represent something as being different from how it really is: *It's almost as if the revolutionary leaders have been airbrushed **out of history** (= ignored by the official version of history).*

ˈair ˌcon **noun** [U] UK abbreviation for **air conditioning**

ˈair-conˌditioned **adj** describes a building, room, or vehicle in which the air is kept cool: *an air-conditioned office*

ˈair conˌditioner **noun** [C] a machine that keeps the air in a building cool

ˈair conˌditioning **noun** [U] B1 the system used for keeping the air in a building or vehicle cool: *I wish my car had air conditioning.*

ˈair-cooled **adj** If an engine is air-cooled, it is kept cool by a flow of air. → Compare **water-cooled**

ˈair-ˌcooler **noun** [C] (also **cooler**) Indian English a machine for cooling the air in a room

aircraft /ˈeə.krɑːft/ US /ˈer.kræft/ **noun** [C] (plural **aircraft**) B2 any vehicle, with or without an engine, that can fly, such as a plane or HELICOPTER: *military aircraft*

> **Common mistake: aircraft**
>
> **Warning:** Irregular plural!
> If you want to form the plural of **aircraft**, don't write 'aircrafts', write **aircraft**.

ˈaircraft ˌcarrier **noun** [C] a large ship that carries

military aircraft and has a long, flat surface where they take off and land

aircrew /ˈeə.kruː/ (US) /ˈer-/ noun [C, + sing/pl verb] all the people, including the pilot, who work on an aircraft to fly it or to take care of the passengers

ˈair-ˌdash verb [I or T + adv/prep] Indian English to go somewhere, or transport someone, quickly or immediately by plane, especially because of an emergency: *He air-dashed to Delhi for specialist treatment for his injury.*

ˈair ˌdrop noun [C] the act of bringing supplies or equipment by dropping them from aircraft: *UN planes have made air drops to 300 flood-hit villages.* • **ˈair-ˌdrop** verb [T]

airfare /ˈeə.feəʳ/ (US) /ˈer.fer/ noun [C] the price of a journey by aircraft: *Transatlantic airfares are going up.*

airfield /ˈeə.fiːld/ (US) /ˈer-/ noun [C] (UK old-fashioned **aerodrome**) a level area where aircraft can take off and land, which has fewer buildings and services than an airport and is used by fewer passengers

ˈair ˌforce noun [C usually singular] (B1) the part of a country's military forces that uses aircraft and fights in the air: *the United States Air Force*

ˌAir Force ˈOne noun the plane that the US president uses for official journeys

ˈair ˌfreshener noun [C or U] a substance or device that makes a room or vehicle smell pleasant

airgun /ˈeə.gʌn/ (US) /ˈer-/ noun [C] a gun that uses air pressure to fire a PELLET (= small metal ball)

airhead /ˈeə.hed/ (US) /ˈer-/ noun [C] informal a stupid person

ˈair hostess noun [C] UK old-fashioned a woman who serves passengers on an aircraft

airing /ˈeə.rɪŋ/ (US) /ˈer.ɪŋ/ noun [S] **MAKING KNOWN** ▷ **1** an occasion when a subject is discussed in an open or public way: *The arguments for and against the proposals have been **given** a good airing.* **DRYING** ▷ **2** a period of time when you allow the air to make something dry and fresh: *The room was damp and smelly so we opened all the windows and **gave** it a good airing.*

ˈairing ˌcupboard noun [C] UK a heated cupboard where clothes, sheets, etc. that have been washed and are almost dry are put so that they can become completely dry

ˈair-kiss verb [I or T] to perform an action similar to kissing someone without touching them with your lips, especially in a way that is not sincere • **ˈair ˌkiss** noun [C]

airless /ˈeə.ləs/ (US) /ˈer-/ adj disapproving describes a place where it is difficult to breathe or the air is not fresh: *an airless office*

ˈair ˌletter noun [C] (also **aerogramme**) a letter that is sent by aircraft, usually consisting of a single very thin sheet of paper that is folded and then stuck at the edges to form its own envelope

airlift /ˈeə.lɪft/ (US) /ˈer-/ noun [C] an operation organized to move supplies or people by aircraft to or from a place that is difficult to reach because of war, a flood, etc. • **airlift** verb [T] *Over 10,000 refugees were airlifted **out of** the region.*

airline /ˈeə.laɪn/ (US) /ˈer-/ noun [C] (B1) a business that operates regular services for carrying passengers and/or goods by aircraft: *What airline did you fly with?*

airliner /ˈeəˌlaɪ.nəʳ/ (US) /ˈerˌlaɪ.nɚ/ noun [C] a large passenger aircraft

airlock /ˈeə.lɒk/ (US) /ˈer.lɑːk/ noun [C] **ROOM** ▷ **1** a room between two areas that have different air pressure, allowing you to go from one area to the other: *Airlocks are commonly found on submarines and manned spacecraft.* **BUBBLE** ▷ **2** a bubble in a pipe that prevents liquid from flowing along it

airmail /ˈeə.meɪl/ (US) /ˈer-/ noun [U] a system of sending letters and parcels by aircraft: *If you send it (**by**) airmail, it'll be very expensive.*

airman /ˈeə.mən/ (US) /ˈer-/ noun [C] (plural **-men** /-mən/) a member of the British or US air force with a low rank

ˈair ˌmattress noun [C] US for **airbed**

ˈAir ˌMiles noun [plural] trademark points worth part of a plane journey that are given free when you buy products or services from particular companies

airplane /ˈeə.pleɪn/ (US) /ˈer-/ noun [C] US for **aeroplane**

airplay /ˈeə.pleɪ/ (US) /ˈer-/ noun [U] (the amount of) broadcasting time that someone or something, such as a piece of recorded music, has on the radio: *Unless a song **gets** lots of airplay, it won't sell in the shops.* → Compare **airtime**

ˈair ˌpocket noun [C] an area in the sky where the air is flowing differently from the way it is in the surrounding parts, which sometimes causes aircraft to go up or down suddenly

airport /ˈeə.pɔːt/ (US) /ˈer.pɔːrt/ noun [C] (A2) a place where aircraft regularly take off and land, with buildings for passengers to wait in: *an international airport* ◦ *a military airport* ◦ *Gatwick Airport* ◦ *an airport terminal/runway*

ˈair ˌpower noun [U] the force of a country's military aircraft and the ability of these aircraft to be used for defending the country and attacking other countries

ˈair ˌquotes noun [plural] imaginary QUOTATION MARKS that you make in the air with your fingers, to show that you are using a word or phrase in an unusual way or repeating exactly what someone has said

ˈair ˌrage noun [U] sudden angry and violent behaviour by a passenger on an aircraft during a flight: *an increase in air rage incidents*

ˈair ˌraid noun [C] an attack by enemy aircraft, usually dropping bombs: *an air raid **shelter/siren***

ˈair rifle noun [C] a gun with a long BARREL (= part shaped like a tube) that is fired from the shoulder and uses air pressure to fire a PELLET (= small metal ball) → Compare **airgun**

ˈair ˌsac noun [C] specialized **1** a space filled with air that continues from a bird's lungs into one of its bones or another body area, used in breathing **2** a wide part like a bag in the tubes an insect uses for breathing **3** an ALVEOLUS (= a very small air bag in the lungs)

ˌair-sea ˈrescue noun [C or U] (an act of) using aircraft, including HELICOPTERS, and boats to try to save people in danger at sea

airship /ˈeə.ʃɪp/ (US) /ˈer-/ noun [C] mainly UK (mainly US **blimp**) a large aircraft without wings, used especially in the past, consisting of a large bag filled with gas that is lighter than air and driven by engines. Passengers were carried in a structure hanging below.

airshow /ˈeə.ʃəʊ/ (US) /ˈer.ʃoʊ/ noun [C] a public show of flying skills and special aircraft, often performed at an AIRBASE (= military airport) specially opened to visitors

airsick /ˈeə.sɪk/ (US) /ˈer-/ adj having the feeling that you will vomit because of the movement of an aircraft you are travelling in • **airsickness** /-nəs/ noun [U]

airspace /ˈeə.speɪs/ (US) /ˈer-/ **noun** [U] the air or sky above a country that is considered to belong to that country: *The government claimed that the plane had illegally entered its airspace.*

airspeed /ˈeə.spiːd/ (US) /ˈer-/ **noun** [U] the speed of an aircraft, measured against the speed of the air through which it is moving

airstream /ˈeə.striːm/ (US) /ˈer-/ **noun** [C] a current of air: *a strong southwesterly airstream*

airstrike /ˈeə.straɪk/ (US) /ˈer-/ **noun** [C] an attack by military aircraft on a city, enemy soldiers, or their supplies, either by bombing or by firing guns

airstrip /ˈeə.strɪp/ (US) /ˈer-/ **noun** [C] (also ˈ**landing** ˌ**strip**) a long, flat piece of land from which trees, rocks, etc. have been removed so that aircraft can take off and land: *We landed at a tiny airstrip in the middle of the jungle.*

ˈ**air** ˌ**terminal noun** [C] a building in an airport or in a place near an airport where aircraft passengers go before their flight leaves or from which they leave after their flight has arrived

airtight /ˈeə.taɪt/ (US) /ˈer-/ **adj** completely closed so that no air can get in or out: *Biscuits will stay crisp if you keep them in an airtight container.*

airtime /ˈeə.taɪm/ (US) /ˈer-/ **noun** [U] (the amount of) broadcasting time that someone or something has on television or radio: *The smaller political parties are campaigning to be allowed free airtime before general elections.* → Compare **airplay**

ˌ**air-to-**ˈ**air adj** [before noun] involving a weapon that is shot from an aircraft at another aircraft: *an air-to-air missile*

ˌ**air-to-**ˈ**ground adj** [before noun] (also ˌ**air-to-**ˈ**surface**) involving a weapon that is shot from an aircraft at a place on the ground: *an air-to-ground attack*

ˌ**air traffic con**ˈ**trol noun** [U, + sing/pl verb] the activity of managing aircraft from the ground as they take off, fly, and land, or the people who do this: *Air traffic control at Heathrow have given us clearance to land in 20 minutes.* • ˌ**air traffic con**ˈ**troller noun** [C] *an air traffic controllers' strike*

airwaves /ˈeə.weɪvz/ (US) /ˈer-/ **noun** [plural] the radio waves used for broadcasting radio and television programmes, or, more generally, radio or television broadcasting time: *The new series will be* ***on the*** *airwaves at 6 p.m. every Tuesday.*

airway /ˈeə.weɪ/ (US) /ˈer-/ **noun** [C] specialized the passage through the mouth and throat that carries air to the lungs

airworthy /ˈeəˌwɜː.ði/ (US) /ˈerˌwɜː-/ **adj** describes an aircraft that is in safe working condition and safe to fly • **airworthiness** /-nəs/ **noun** [U]

airy /ˈeə.ri/ (US) /ˈer.i/ **adj** LIGHT ▷ **1** approving with a lot of light and space: *The new offices are light and airy.* DELICATE ▷ **2** delicate, as if full of air: *a light, airy fabric* NOT SERIOUS ▷ **3** showing no worry or serious thought: *'I don't care – you choose,' he said, with an airy wave of the hand.* • **airily** /ˈeə.rɪ.li/ (US) /ˈer-/ **adv** *'He can do what he likes – it doesn't bother me,' she said airily.* • **airiness** /-nəs/ **noun** [U] approving

ˌ**airy-**ˈ**fairy adj** UK informal not practical or not based on the situation as it really is: *She's talking about buying an old castle in Ireland. It all sounds a bit airy-fairy to me.*

aisle /aɪl/ **noun** [C] **1** a long, narrow space between rows of seats in an aircraft, cinema, or church: *Would you like an aisle* ***seat*** *or would you prefer to be by the window?* **2** a long, narrow space between the rows of shelves in a large shop: *You'll find the shampoo and the soap in the fourth aisle along from the entrance.*

IDIOM **go/walk down the aisle** informal to get married

aitch /eɪtʃ/ **noun** [C] the letter 'h' written as a word

IDIOM **drop your aitches** UK to not pronounce the 'h' at the beginning of words

ajar /əˈdʒɑːʳ/ (US) /-ˈdʒɑːr/ **adj** [after verb] describes a door that is slightly open: *We* ***left*** *the door ajar so that we could hear what they were saying.*

aka /ˌeɪ.keɪˈeɪ/ abbreviation for also known as: used when someone has another name: *James Brown, aka the 'Godfather of Soul'*

akimbo /əˈkɪm.bəʊ/ (US) /-boʊ/ **adj** [after noun] If a person's arms are akimbo, they are bent at the ELBOWS (= the middle part of the arms where they bend) with the hands on the hips: *He stood,* ***arms*** *akimbo, refusing to move.*

akin /əˈkɪn/ **adj** [after verb] having some of the same qualities: *They speak a language akin* ***to*** *French.*

-al /-əl/ **suffix** used to add the meaning 'connected with' to adjectives, or 'the action of' to nouns: *medical (= connected with medicine)* ◦ *approval (= the act of approving)*

à la /ˈæl.ə/ **preposition** in the style of: *She has her hair blonde and curly, à la Marilyn Monroe.*

alabaster /ˌæl.əˈbæs.təʳ/ (US) /ˈæl.ə.bæs.tɚ/ **noun** [U] an almost transparent, white stone, often used for making decorative objects

à la carte /ˌæl.əˈkɑːt/ (US) /-ˈkɑːrt/ **adj** [before noun], **adv** If you eat à la carte, you choose each dish from a separate list instead of eating a fixed combination of dishes at a fixed price: *You get more choice if you eat à la carte/from the à la carte* ***menu***. → Compare **table d'hôte**

alack /əˈlæk/ humorous **alas and alack** an expression of sadness

alacrity /əˈlæk.rə.ti/ (US) /-t̬i/ **noun** [U] formal speed and eagerness: *She accepted the money* ***with*** *alacrity.*

Aladdin's cave /əˌlæd.ɪnzˈkeɪv/ **noun** [S] UK a store of very many interesting or unusual objects: *His shop, a veritable Aladdin's cave of antiques, is for sale.*

à la mode /ˌæl.əˈməʊd/ (US) /-ˈmoʊd/ **adj; adv**
▸**adj 1** [after verb] old-fashioned in the most modern style or fashion **2** [after noun] US served with ice cream: *apple pie à la mode*
▸**adv** old-fashioned in the most modern style or fashion

alarm /əˈlɑːm/ (US) /-lɑːrm/ **noun; verb**
▸**noun** WARNING ▷ **1** [C] a warning of danger, usually a loud noise or flashing light: *If there's any trouble,* ***raise/sound the*** *alarm by pulling the emergency cord.* ◦ *The first two bomb alerts were* ***false*** *alarms, but the third was for real.* **2** (B1) [C] a device that makes a loud noise to warn of danger: *a burglar/car/fire/smoke alarm* **3** (A2) [C] an **alarm clock** **4** (B1) [C] If an electronic device such as a watch or computer has an alarm, it can be set to make a noise at a particular time. WORRY ▷ **5** (C2) [U] sudden worry and fear, especially that something dangerous or unpleasant might happen: *I didn't tell her that he was late because I didn't want to* ***cause*** *her any alarm.* ◦ *Villagers have reacted with alarm to news of a proposed new road.*

IDIOMS **raise the alarm** (C2) to make people understand the danger of something: *A local doctor was the first to raise the alarm about this latest virus.* • **ring/sound alarm bells** If something rings/sounds alarm bells, it makes you start to worry because it is a sign that there may be a problem: *The name rang alarm bells in her mind.*

▸verb [T] C1 to make someone worried or frightened: *I didn't want to alarm him by telling him that she was ill.*

aˈlarm ˌcall noun [C] a phone call to wake you up at a particular time, for example in a hotel

aˈlarm ˌclock noun [C] (also **alarm**) A2 a clock that you can set to wake you up at a particular time with a loud noise: *My alarm clock **went off** at 7.30.* ◦ *I've **set** the alarm **for** 7.30.*

alarmed /əˈlɑːmd/ US /-lɑːrmd/ adj **PERSON** ▷ **1** [after verb] worried or frightened by something: *I was a bit alarmed **at/by** how much weight she'd lost.* ◦ [+ to infinitive] *I was alarmed **to** hear that she was coming.* ◦ [+ that] *I'm rather alarmed **that** we haven't heard anything.* **VEHICLE** ▷ **2** An alarmed vehicle or place has an ALARM in it that, when active, will make a loud noise if anyone enters or touches it: *Warning: this building is alarmed.*

alarming /əˈlɑː.mɪŋ/ US /-ˈlɑːr-/ adj C1 causing worry or fear: *alarming news* ◦ *There has been an alarming rise in the rate of inflation.* • **alarmingly** /-li/ adv *Alarmingly, the hole in the ozone layer has doubled in size this year.*

alarmist /əˈlɑː.mɪst/ US /-ˈlɑːr-/ adj; noun

▸adj disapproving intentionally showing only the bad and dangerous things in a situation, and so worrying people: *The government has dismissed newspaper reports of 200 dead as being alarmist.*

▸noun [C] disapproving someone who makes people worried by telling them about bad or dangerous things when it is not necessary or helpful

alas /əˈlæs/ adv formal or humorous used to express sadness or feeling sorry about something: *I love football but, alas, I have no talent as a player.* ◦ *'Will you be able to come tomorrow?' 'Alas, no.'*

IDIOM **alas and alack** humorous an expression of sadness

albatross /ˈæl.bə.trɒs/ US /-trɑːs/ noun **BIRD** ▷ **1** [C] a large white bird with long, strong wings that lives near the sea, found especially in the areas of the Pacific and South Atlantic oceans **PROBLEM** ▷ **2** [S] something or someone you want to be free from because they are causing you problems: *Her own supporters see her as an albatross who could lose them the election.*

albeit /ɔːlˈbiː.ɪt/ US /ɑːl-/ conjunction formal C2 although: *The evening was very pleasant, albeit a little quiet.*

albino /ælˈbiː.nəʊ/ US /-ˈbaɪ.noʊ/ noun [C] (plural **albinos**) a person or animal with white skin and hair and pink eyes • **albino** adj *an albino rabbit*

album /ˈæl.bəm/ noun [C] **MUSIC** ▷ **1** A2 a collection of several pieces of music, made available as a single item on a CD, the internet, etc.: *Have you heard their new album?* **BOOK** ▷ **2** A2 a book with plain pages, used for collecting together and protecting stamps, photographs, etc.: *a stamp/photograph album*

albumen /ˈæl.bjʊ.mən/ US /ælˈbjuː-/ noun [U] specialized the clear part inside an egg that is white when cooked

alchemy /ˈæl.kə.mi/ noun [U] **1** a type of chemistry, especially in the Middle Ages, that dealt with trying to find a way to change ordinary metals into gold and with trying to find a medicine that would cure any disease **2** literary a process that is so effective that it seems like magic: *She manages, **by** some extraordinary alchemy, to turn the most ordinary of ingredients into the most delicious of dishes.* • **alchemist** /ˈæl.kə.mɪst/ noun [C]

alcohol /ˈæl.kə.hɒl/ US /-hɑːl/ noun [U] A2 a clear liquid that can make you drunk, also used as a SOLVENT (= a substance that dissolves another) and in fuel and medicines: *Most wines contain around twelve percent alcohol.* ◦ *an alcohol-**free** lager*

alcoholic /ˌæl.kəˈhɒl.ɪk/ US /-ˈhɑː.lɪk/ adj; noun

▸adj B1 containing alcohol: *alcoholic drinks* ◦ *Could I have something non-alcoholic, like orange juice, please?*

▸noun [C] (slang **alky, alkie**) C2 a person who is unable to give up the habit of drinking alcohol very often and in large amounts

alcoholism /ˈæl.kə.hɒl.ɪ.zᵊm/ US /-hɑː.lɪ-/ noun [U] the condition of being an alcoholic: *Alcoholism cost me my job, my health, and finally my family.*

alcopop /ˈæl.kəʊ.pɒp/ US /ˈæl.koʊ.pɑːp/ noun [C] a sweet FIZZY alcoholic drink (= one with bubbles)

alcove /ˈæl.kəʊv/ US /-koʊv/ noun [C] a small space in a room, formed by one part of a wall being further back than the parts on each side: *We've put some bookshelves in the alcove.*

al dente /ˌælˈden.teɪ/ adj, adv approving describes cooked PASTA or other food that is still firm when bitten

alderman /ˈɔːl.də.mən/ US /ˈɑːl.dɚ-/ noun [C] (plural **-men** /-mən/) **1** in the UK , in the past, a member of a local government chosen by the other members **2** in the US, Australia, and Canada, an elected member of a city government

ale /eɪl/ noun [C or U] any of various types of beer, usually one that is dark and bitter: *brown ale*

alert /əˈlɜːt/ US /-ˈlɝːt/ adj; noun; verb

▸adj C1 quick to see, understand, and act in a particular situation: *I'm not feeling very alert today – not enough sleep last night!* ◦ *A couple of alert readers posted comments on the website pointing out the mistake.* ◦ *Parents should be alert **to** sudden changes in children's behaviour.* • **alertness** /-nəs/ noun [U]

▸noun [C or U] C1 a warning to people to be prepared to deal with something dangerous: *a **bomb** alert* ◦ *The army was **put on** (**full**) alert as the peace talks began to fail.* ◦ *The public were warned to be **on the** alert **for** (= watching carefully for) suspicious packages.*

▸verb [T] C2 to warn someone of a possibly dangerous situation: *An anonymous letter alerted police **to** the possibility of a terrorist attack at the airport.*

ˈA ˌlevel noun [C or U] (formal **Adˈvanced ˌlevel**) a public exam taken in England and Wales by children aged 17 or 18. Students take AS LEVEL exams then A2S, usually a year later, which together make a full A level qualification: *You usually need three A levels to get into university.* ◦ *I failed my History A level.* ◦ *Have you got an A level **in** maths?* ◦ *This problem should be easy enough for someone who's done physics **at** A level.* → See also **A2, AS level** → Compare **GCSE**

alfalfa /ˌælˈfæl.fə/ noun [U] a plant grown as food, especially for farm animals, or used in salads before it is completely developed

al fresco /ˌælˈfres.kəʊ/ US /-koʊ/ adj, adv (especially of food and eating) outside: *an al fresco lunch on the patio* ◦ *Most summer evenings we eat al fresco.*

algae /ˈæl.giː/ noun [plural] very simple, usually small plants that grow in or near water and do not have ordinary leaves or roots

algebra /ˈæl.dʒə.brə/ noun [U] a part of mathematics in which signs and letters represent numbers • **algebraic** /ˌæl.dʒəˈbreɪ.ɪk/ adj

algorithm /ˈæl.gə.rɪ.ðᵊm/ noun [C] specialized a set of mathematical instructions that must be followed in a fixed order, and that, especially if given to a computer, will help to calculate an answer to a mathematical problem

alias /ˈeɪ.li.əs/ **preposition; noun**
▸**preposition** used when giving the name that a person is generally known by, after giving their real name: *Malcolm Little, alias Malcolm X*
▸**noun** [C] a false name, especially one used by a criminal: *He travels* ***under*** *(= using) an alias.*

alibi /ˈæl.ɪ.baɪ/ **noun** [C] **1** proof that someone who is thought to have committed a crime could not have done it, especially the fact or statement that they were in another place at the time it happened: *He has a* ***cast-iron*** *(= very strong) alibi – he was in hospital the week of the murder.* **2** an excuse for something bad or for a failure: *After eight years in power, the government can no longer use the previous government's policy as an alibi* ***for*** *its own failure.*

Alice band /ˈæl.ɪs.bænd/ **noun** [C] UK for **hairband**

alien /ˈeɪ.li.ən/ **adj; noun**
▸**adj 1** coming from a different country, race, or group: *an alien culture* → Synonym **foreign 2** strange and not familiar: *When I first went to New York, it all felt very alien* ***to*** *me.* **3** [before noun] relating to creatures from another planet: *an alien spacecraft*
▸**noun** [C] **1** legal someone who lives in a country of which they are not a legal CITIZEN: *When war broke out the government rounded up thousands of aliens and put them in temporary camps.* **2** a creature from a different planet

alienate /ˈeɪ.li.ə.neɪt/ **verb** [T] **LOSE SUPPORT** ▷ **1** to cause someone or a group of people to stop supporting and agreeing with you: *All these changes to the newspaper have alienated its traditional readers.* **MAKE UNWELCOME** ▷ **2** to make someone feel that they are different and do not belong to a group: *Disagreements can alienate teenagers* ***from*** *their families.*

alienation /ˌeɪ.li.əˈneɪ.ʃən/ **noun** [U] **SEPARATION** ▷ **1** the feeling that you have no connection with the people around you: *Depressed people frequently feel a sense of alienation* ***from*** *those around them.* **LOSS OF SUPPORT** ▷ **2** the act of making someone stop supporting and agreeing with you: *This short-sighted alienation of their own supporters may lose them the election.*

alight /əˈlaɪt/ **adj; verb**
▸**adj** [after verb] **BURNING** ▷ **1** burning: *I had to use a bit of petrol to* ***get*** *the fire alight.* ◦ *The rioters overturned several cars and* ***set*** *them alight.* ◦ *He was smoking in bed and his blankets* ***caught*** *alight.* **SHINING BRIGHTLY** ▷ **2** brightly lit up: *The sky was alight* ***with*** *hundreds of fireworks.* **3** literary showing excitement and happiness: *Her eyes were alight* ***with*** *mischief.*
▸**verb** old-fashioned **GET OUT OF** ▷ **1** [I] formal to get out of a vehicle, especially a train or bus: *The suspect alighted* ***from*** *the train at Euston and proceeded to Heathrow.* **LAND ON** ▷ **2** [I + adv/prep] formal to land on something: *A butterfly alighted gently* ***on*** *the flower.* **3** [I + adv/prep] literary to find or unexpectedly see something: *As she glanced round the room her eyes alighted* ***upon*** *a small child.* ◦ *I spent an hour in the bookshop before alighting* ***on*** *the perfect present.*

align /əˈlaɪn/ **verb** [T] to put two or more things into a straight line: *When you've aligned the notch on the gun* ***with*** *the target, fire!* ◦ *Align the ruler* ***and*** *the middle of the paper and then cut it straight.*

PHRASAL VERB **align yourself with sth/sb** If you align yourself with an organization or person, you agree with and support their aims: *The major unions are aligned with the government on this issue.*

alignment /əˈlaɪn.mənt/ **noun POSITION** ▷ **1** [U] an arrangement in which two or more things are positioned in a straight line or parallel to each other: *The problem is happening because the wheels are* ***out of*** *alignment* ***with*** *each other.* **SUPPORT** ▷ **2** [C] an agreement between a group of countries, political parties, or people who want to work together because of shared interests or aims: *New alignments are being formed within the business community.*

alike /əˈlaɪk/ **adj; adv**
▸**adj** [after verb] (B1) similar to each other: *The children all* ***look*** *very alike.*
▸**adv 1** (B2) in a similar way: *The twins even dress alike.* ◦ *My father treated us all alike.* **2** (B2) used after referring to two groups of people or things to show that both groups are included: *Friends and family alike were devastated by the news of her death.*

alimentary canal /æl.ɪˌmen.tᵊr.i.kəˈnæl/ (US) /-t̬ɚ-/ **noun** [C] the parts of the body that food goes through as it is eaten and digested

alimony /ˈæl.ɪ.mə.ni/ (US) /-moʊ-/ **noun** [U] a regular amount of money that a law court orders a person to pay to his or her partner after a DIVORCE (= the legal ending of a marriage)

ˈA-line adj An A-line skirt or dress is narrow at the top and wider at the bottom: *An A-line skirt disguises fuller hips.*

ˈA-list adj [usually before noun] used for describing people who are the most famous: *A-list* ***celebrities*** • **ˈA-lister noun** [C]

alive /əˈlaɪv/ **adj 1** (B1) [after verb] living, not dead: *He must be 90 if he's* ***still*** *alive.* ◦ *Doctors* ***kept*** *him alive on a life-support machine.* ◦ *She's alive* ***and well*** *and living in New Zealand.* **2** (C2) If something is alive, it continues to exist: *Relatives of the missing sailors are struggling to* ***keep*** *their hopes alive.*

IDIOMS **alive to sth** UK If you are alive to something, you are thinking about it or familiar with it: *I ski for the excitement, but I'm also always alive to the risks.* • **alive with sth** full of things that are living and moving: *The pond was alive with frogs.* • **be alive and well/kicking 1** (C2) to continue to live or exist and be full of energy: *She said she'd seen him last week and he was alive and kicking.* **2** (C2) to continue to be popular or successful: *Despite rumours to the contrary, feminism is alive and well.* ◦ *Traditional jazz is still alive and kicking in New Orleans.* • **come alive 1** If a place comes alive, it becomes filled with activity: *The city centre really comes alive at the weekend.* **2** If you make something come alive, you make it seem real and interesting: *She's a writer who really knows how to make her characters come alive.*

alkali /ˈæl.kᵊl.aɪ/ **noun** [C or U] (plural **alkalis**) specialized a substance that has the opposite effect or chemical behaviour to an ACID • **alkaline** /ˈæl.kᵊl.aɪn/ **adj** *Some plants will not grow in very alkaline soils.*

alkaloid /ˈæl.kə.lɔɪd/ **noun** [C] specialized a type of chemical found in plants that often acts as a drug or poison, or is used in medicines: *Morphine and cocaine are powerful alkaloids.*

alkane /ˈæl.keɪn/ **noun** [C] specialized any gas in a group that contains only carbon and HYDROGEN atoms, with the carbon atoms joined together in a simple chain: *Alkanes, such as butane and methane, are very flammable.*

alkene /ˈæl.kiːn/ **noun** [C] specialized any gas in a group that contains carbon and HYDROGEN atoms, with the carbon atoms joined together in a DOUBLE BOND: *Ethene and propene are alkenes.*

alky (also **alkie**) /ˈæl.ki/ noun [C] slang an **alcoholic**

all /ɔːl/ (US) /ɑːl/ determiner, predeterminer, pronoun; adv

▸**determiner, predeterminer, pronoun 1** (A1) every one (of), or the complete amount or number (of), or the whole (of): *All animals have to eat in order to live.* ◦ *She's got four children, all under the age of five.* ◦ *The cast all lined up on stage to take their bow.* ◦ *Have you drunk all (**of**) the milk?* ◦ *Have you drunk it all?* ◦ *All the eggs got broken.* ◦ *Now the money's all mine!* ◦ *All my friends agree.* ◦ *I've been trying all day/week to contact you.* ◦ *She had £2,000 under the bed and the thieves took it all.* ◦ *I had to use all my powers of persuasion to get her to agree.* ◦ *Remember all that trouble we had with the police last year?* ◦ *So long as he's happy – that's all that matters (= the most important thing).* ◦ *All (= the only thing) I need is a roof over my head and a decent meal.* ◦ *The judge cleared the court of all **but** (= everyone except) herself and the witness.* ◦ *Why do you get so angry with me all **the time** (= very often)?* ◦ *It's very kind of you to come all **the way** to meet me.* **2 all in all** considering all the different parts of the situation together: *All in all, I think you've done very well.* **3 all the… you have** the only and small amount or number of something you have: *Her parents died when she was a baby, so I was all the family she ever had.*

> **! Common mistake: all**
>
> **Warning:** check your word order!
>
> **All** usually goes directly before the main verb in a sentence.
>
> Don't say 'do all something', say **all do something**:
>
> ~~*The students need all to do more exercise.*~~
>
> *The students all need to do more exercise.*
>
> **All** can also go before the subject of the sentence:
>
> *All the students need to do more exercise.*
>
> But if the main verb is **am/is/are/was/were**, **all** usually goes directly after it:
>
> ~~*The students all are too lazy.*~~
>
> *The students are all too lazy.*

> **! Common mistake: all or everything?**
>
> **Warning:** choose the correct pronoun!
>
> **All** is usually used to mean 'everything' only before a relative clause:
>
> *I told him all that I could remember.*
>
> When using a pronoun to refer to all things, don't say 'all', say **everything**:
>
> ~~*My English is good but I don't understand all.*~~
>
> *My English is good but I don't understand everything.*

IDIOMS **all good things (must) come to an end** saying said when you accept that even enjoyable experiences cannot last for ever: *It's been a fantastic couple of weeks but all good things must come to an end.* • **all of sth** used to emphasize the amount or number of something, usually when something is small in a disappointing or unusual way: *In the last two years the book has sold all of 200 copies.* • **be all (that) you can do** informal If it is all (that) you can do to do something, you are trying very hard to do it and it is difficult: *This is so boring, it's all I can do to stay awake.* • **that's all I/you/we need!** used when something bad has happened to make a situation that is already difficult worse: *And now it's raining – that's all I need!*

▸**adv 1** (A2) completely: *The cake was all eaten last night.* ◦ *The downstairs rooms were painted all in greens and blues.* ◦ *The baby got food all **over** her dress.* ◦ *Don't let her get you all upset.* ◦ *She's been all over town looking for you.* ◦ *I've been hearing all about your weekend!* ◦ *We had a difficult time but it's all **over** now.* ◦ *The princess lived all **alone/by** her**self** in the middle of the forest.* **2** (B1) used after a number to mean that both teams or players in a game have equal points: *The score at half-time was still four all.* **3 all but** (C2) almost: *The game was all but over by the time we arrived.* ◦ *I'd all but given up on you.* **4 all round** UK (US **all around**) in every way: *It was a ghastly business all round.* ◦ *It's been a good day all around.* **5 all the better, stronger, more exciting, etc.** (C2) even or much better, stronger, more exciting, etc.: *She felt all the better **for** the drink.*

IDIOMS **be all in** If you say that you are all in, you mean that you are very tired and unable to do anything more: *I'm going home now – I'm all in.* • **be sb all over** informal to be the typical behaviour of a particular person: *She's always talking – that's Claire all over.* • **be all go** UK If a situation or place is all go, it is extremely busy: *It was all go in town today.* • **be not all there** informal to be slightly stupid or strange • **go all out** to put all your energy or enthusiasm into what you are doing: *The team went all out **for** a win.*

all- /ɔːl-/ (US) /ɑːl-/ prefix **1** used in front of many nouns to form adjectives meaning 'every', 'every type of', or 'the whole of' that particular thing: *an all-night bar (= a bar that is open for the whole night)* **2** used in front of many adjectives and present participles to mean 'everything' or 'everyone': *an all-inclusive price* ◦ *all-conquering armies* **3** used in front of many nouns and adjectives to mean 'completely': *all-cotton socks (= socks that are made completely of cotton)* ◦ *Do you believe in an all-**powerful** god (= one with unlimited power)?*

Allah /ˈæl.ə/ noun the name of God for Muslims and Arab Christians

ˌall-Aˈmerican adj; noun

▸**adj** TYPICALLY AMERICAN ▷ **1** considered to be typical of the US, and respected and approved of by Americans: *He was the perfect image of a clean-cut, all-American boy.* WHOLE COUNTRY ▷ **2** involving people or things from everywhere in the US: *an all-American talent contest/business consortium* SPORT ▷ **3** US describes an AMATEUR sports person from the US who is considered to be one of the best in their sport: *an all-American football player*

▸**noun** [C] US an AMATEUR sports person from the US who is considered to be one of the best AMATEURS in their sport: *The team was led by an all-American from Yale.*

ˌall-aˈround adj US for **all-round**

allay /əˈleɪ/ verb [T] formal If you allay a strong emotion felt by someone, such as fear or worry, you cause them to feel it less or to feel calm again: *The government is trying to allay public **fears/concern** about the spread of the disease.*

the ˌall-ˈclear noun [S] a signal that tells you that a dangerous or difficult situation has ended: *The police **gave** us the all-clear and we drove on.*

ˈall-ˌcomers noun [plural] any people who want to take part in a particular competition or activity

allegation /ˌæl.əˈgeɪ.ʃən/ noun [C] formal (C1) a statement that has not been proved to be true which says that someone has done something wrong or illegal: *Several of her patients have **made** allegations **of** professional misconduct **about/against** her.* ◦ [+ that] *Allegations **that** Mr Dwight was receiving money from known criminals have caused a scandal.*

A

allege /ə'ledʒ/ verb [T] formal ⓒ2 to say that someone has done something illegal or wrong without giving proof: [+ (that)] *The two men allege* (***that***) *the police forced them to make false confessions.* ◦ [+ to infinitive] *She is alleged* ***to*** *have been at the centre of an international drugs ring.* ◦ [+ that] ***It*** *was alleged* ***that*** *Johnson had struck Mr Rahim on the head.*

alleged /ə'ledʒd/ adj formal ⓒ1 said or thought by some people to be the stated bad or illegal thing, although you have no proof: *It took 15 years for the alleged criminals (= people thought to be criminals) to prove their innocence.* • **allegedly** /ə'ledʒ.ɪd.li/ adv ⓒ2 *That's where he allegedly killed his wife.*

allegiance /ə'liː.dʒəns/ noun [C or U] formal loyalty and support for a ruler, country, group, or belief: *Soldiers must* ***swear*** *allegiance* ***to*** *the Crown/the King.* ◦ *In many American schools, the students* ***pledge*** *allegiance* (***to the flag***) *at the beginning of the school day.* ◦ *As an Englishman who'd lived for a long time in France, he felt a certain conflict of allegiances when the two countries played soccer.*

allegory /'æl.ə.gə.ri/ Ⓤⓢ /-gɔːr.i/ noun [C or U] a story, play, poem, picture, or other work in which the characters and events represent particular qualities or ideas, related to morals, religion, or politics: *The play can be read as allegory.* ◦ *Augustine's 'City of God' is an allegory* ***of*** *the triumph of Good over Evil.* • **allegorical** /ˌæl.ə'gɒr.ɪ.kəl/ Ⓤⓢ /-'gɔːr-/ adj • **allegorically** /ˌæl.ɪ'gɒr.ɪ.kəl.i/ Ⓤⓢ /-'gɔːr-/ adv

allegro /ə'leg.rəʊ/ Ⓤⓢ /-roʊ/ noun; adj, adv
▸noun [C] (plural **allegros**) specialized a piece of music that is played in a fast and energetic way
▸adj, adv specialized (played) in a fast and energetic way: *the allegro movement*

allele /ə'liːl/ noun [C] specialized a GENE that is found in one of two or more different forms in the same position in a CHROMOSOME, and so produces a particular characteristic that can be different for different people, such as eye colour

alleluia /ˌæl.ɪ'luː.jə/ exclamation, noun [C] **hallelujah**

Allen key /'æl.ənˌkiː/ noun [C] (also **Allen ˌwrench**) trademark an L-shaped metal tool with six sides that is used to turn a SCREW with a six-sided hole in the top

allergen /'æl.ə.dʒən/ Ⓤⓢ /-ɚ-/ noun [C] specialized a substance that can cause an allergy (= condition of the body reacting badly to something) but is not harmful to most people

allergic /ə'lɜː.dʒɪk/ Ⓤⓢ /-lɝː-/ adj **1** [after verb] having an allergy: *I'm allergic* ***to*** *cats.* **2** [before noun] caused by an allergy: *an allergic* ***reaction*** **3** humorous having a strong dislike of something: *My dad's allergic* ***to*** *pop music.*

allergy /'æl.ə.dʒi/ Ⓤⓢ /-ɚ-/ noun [C] a condition that makes a person become sick or develop skin or breathing problems because they have eaten certain foods or been near certain substances: *an allergy* ***to*** *wheat* ◦ *a wheat allergy*

alleviate /ə'liː.vi.eɪt/ verb [T] formal to make something bad such as pain or problems less severe: *The drugs did nothing to alleviate her pain/suffering.* • **alleviation** /əˌliː.vi'eɪ.ʃən/ noun [U] *the alleviation of poverty*

alley /'æl.i/ noun [C] (also **alleyway** /'æl.i.weɪ/) **1** a narrow road or path between buildings **2** a path in a park or garden, especially with trees or bushes on both sides

IDIOM **up/down your alley** US and Australian English to be the type of thing that you are interested in or that you enjoy doing: *Kate loves dancing, so salsa lessons would be* ***right*** *up her alley.*

alliance /ə'laɪ.əns/ noun [C] **1** ⓒ2 a group of countries, political parties, or people who have agreed to work together because of shared interests or aims: *a* ***military*** *alliance* **2** ⓒ2 an agreement to work with someone else to try to achieve the same thing: *The three smaller parties have* ***forged/formed*** *an alliance* ***against*** *the government.* ◦ *Some of us feel that the union is* ***in alliance with*** *management against us.*

allied /'æl.aɪd/, /ə'laɪd/ adj **1** ⓒ2 [before noun] connected by a political or military agreement: *an allied offensive* ◦ *allied bombers/forces* **2** formal similar or related in some way: *Computer science and allied subjects are not taught here.* **3** combined: *It takes a lot of enthusiasm, allied* ***with/to*** *a love of children, to make a good teacher.*

Allied /'æl.aɪd/ adj [before noun] relating to the Allies: *Allied forces* ◦ *the Allied landings in Normandy*

the 'Allies noun [plural] the countries, including the US, the UK, the USSR, and France, that fought against the AXIS countries in the Second World War

alligator /'æl.ɪ.geɪ.təʳ/ Ⓤⓢ /-t̬ɚ/ noun [C] (US informal **gator**) a large reptile with a hard skin that lives in and near rivers and lakes in the hot, wet parts of America and China. It has a long nose that is slightly wider and shorter than that of a CROCODILE.

ˌall-im'portant adj extremely important: *It was Johansson who scored the all-important goal shortly before half-time.*

ˌall-in'clusive adj including everything: *a seven-night all-inclusive package* ◦ *an all-inclusive resort*

ˌall-in-'one adj; noun
▸adj UK doing the work of two or more usually separate parts: *an all-in-one cleaner and polish*
▸noun [C] UK a piece of clothing that covers the whole body rather than being divided into a separate top and bottom part: *She wears a pink Lycra all-in-one for her aerobics class.*

ˌall-in 'wrestling noun [U] a type of WRESTLING (= sport in which people fight) in which there are very few rules

alliteration /əˌlɪt.ə'reɪ.ʃən/ Ⓤⓢ /əˌlɪt̬-/ noun [U] specialized the use, especially in poetry, of the same sound or sounds, especially CONSONANTS, at the beginning of several words that are close together: *'Round the rugged rocks the ragged rascal ran' uses alliteration.* → Compare **assonance**

allium /'æl.i.əm/ noun [C] a type of plant that belongs to the group that includes ONIONS and GARLIC, with a circular mass of flowers on a long stem

ˌall-'night adj [before noun] continuing all night: *I haven't been to an all-night* ***party*** *since my college days.*

ˌall-'nighter noun [C] **1** informal an event that lasts all night **2** US informal a time when you spend all night studying, especially for an exam: *I* ***pulled*** *an all-nighter last night.*

allocate /'æl.ə.keɪt/ verb [T] ⓒ1 to give something to someone as their share of a total amount, for them to use in a particular way: *The government is allocating £10 million* ***for*** *health education.* ◦ [+ two objects] *As project leader, you will have to allocate people jobs/allocate jobs* ***to*** *people.* ◦ *It is not the job of the investigating committee to allocate blame* ***for*** *the disaster/to allocate blame* ***to*** *individuals.* • **allocation** /ˌæl.ə'keɪ.ʃən/ noun [U] ⓒ2 *the allocation of resources/funds/time*

allopathy /ə'lɒp.ə.θi/ Ⓤⓢ /ə'lɑː.pə-/ noun [U] a name for CONVENTIONAL (= traditional and ordinary) medicine

used by some followers of ALTERNATIVE MEDICINE • **allopathic** /ˌæl.əˈpæθ.ɪk/ **adj** *Allopathic medicine is what most of us encounter when we go to the doctor.*

allophone /ˈæl.ə.fəʊn/ (US) /-foʊn/ **noun** [C] specialized one of the ways in which a particular PHONEME (= speech sound) can be pronounced

allot /əˈlɒt/ (US) /-ˈlɑːt/ **verb** [T] **(-tt-)** to give something, especially a share of something available, for a particular purpose: [+ two objects] *They allotted everyone a separate desk.* ◦ *They allotted a separate desk **to** everyone.* ◦ *The ministry of culture will be allotted about $6 million less this year.* ◦ *Three hours have been allotted **to/for** this task.* ◦ *The museum is planning to increase the amount of **space** allotted to modern art.* • **allotted** /əˈlɒt.ɪd/ (US) /-ˈlɑː.t̬ɪd/ **adj** *Did you finish your essay in the allotted **time** (= the time available)?*

allotment /əˈlɒt.mənt/ (US) /-ˈlɑːt-/ **noun** **GROUND** ▷ **1** [C] UK a small piece of ground in or just outside a town that a person rents for growing vegetables, fruits, or flowers **SHARE** ▷ **2** [U or C] the process of sharing something, or the amount that you get: *The allotment of the company's shares to its employees is still to be decided.* ◦ *We have used up this year's allotment of funds.*

allotropy /æˈlɒt.rə.piː/ (US) /əˈlɑː.trə-/ **noun** [U] specialized the existence of the same chemical substance in more than one form, each with different physical qualities • **allotropic** /ˌæl.əˈtrɒp.ɪk/ (US) /-ˈtrɑː.pɪk/ **adj** *Diamond and graphite are allotropic forms of carbon.*

ˌall-ˈout **adj** [before noun] complete and with as much effort as possible: *We made an all-out **effort** to get the project finished on time.*

> **Other ways of saying allow**
>
> A common alternative to the verb 'allow' is **let**:
>
> *She wanted to go but her parents wouldn't **let** her.*
>
> A more formal word for 'allow' is **permit**:
>
> *Eating is not **permitted** in any part of the building.*
>
> If someone in authority allows something, you can use the verb **authorize**:
>
> *Who **authorized** this expenditure?*
>
> You can use **go-ahead** or **green light** to say that someone in an official job allows a plan to happen:
>
> *The city council has given the **green light** to the new shopping mall.*
>
> *The government has given the **go-ahead** for a multibillion-dollar highway project.*

allow /əˈlaʊ/ **verb** **GIVE PERMISSION** ▷ **1** (B1) [T] to give permission for someone to do something, or to not prevent something from happening: [+ to infinitive] *Do you think Dad will allow you **to** go to Jamie's party?* ◦ *You're not allowed **to** talk during the exam.* ◦ *Her proposals **would** allow (= make it possible for) more people **to** stay in full-time education.* ◦ *The loophole has allowed hundreds of drink-drivers **to** avoid prosecution.* ◦ *The government has **refused to** allow foreign journalists into the area for several weeks.* ◦ *Prisoners have been moved to allow the demolition of part of the prison.* ◦ *Pets aren't allowed in this hotel.* ◦ [+ -ing verb] *Smok**ing** is not allowed in this restaurant.* ◦ [+ two objects] *He didn't allow us enough time to finish the test.* ◦ *Red Cross officials were allowed **access** to the prison for the first time a few days ago.* ◦ UK *The referee decided to allow (= officially accept) the goal.* ◦ *At the weekend I allow myself (= I give myself the special pleasure of having) a box of chocolates.* ◦ *How much time do you allow yourself (= make available to yourself) to get ready in the morning?* **2 allow me** old-fashioned a polite expression used when offering to help in some way: *You can't carry all those bags yourself – please, allow me.* **ADMIT** ▷ **3** [+ that] formal to admit or agree that something is true: *She allowed **that** she might have been too suspicious.*

PHRASAL VERBS **allow for sth** (C1) to consider something when you are planning something: *We allowed for living expenses of £20 a day.* ◦ [+ -ing verb] *You should allow for the plane be**ing** delayed.* ◦ *We have to allow for the **possibility** that we might not finish on schedule.* • **allow of sth** formal If a rule or situation allows of something, it makes it possible: *This rule allows of no exceptions.* ◦ *The evidence allows of only one interpretation – he was murdered by his wife.*

allowable /əˈlaʊ.ə.bl̩/ **adj** allowed according to the rules or laws that control a particular area of activity: *A certain level of error is allowable (= permitted to happen).* ◦ UK *allowable expenses (= expenses on which no taxes are paid)*

allowance /əˈlaʊ.ənts/ **noun** **AMOUNT GIVEN** ▷ **1** (C1) [C] money that you are given regularly, especially to pay for a particular thing: *The perks of the job include a company pension and a generous **travel** allowance.* ◦ *I couldn't have managed at college if I hadn't had an allowance from my parents.* **2** [C] an amount of something that you are allowed: *The **baggage/luggage** allowance for most flights is 20 kilos.* **3** [C] mainly US for **pocket money** **PREPARATION** ▷ **4 make allowance for** to prepare for the possibility of: *We should make allowance for bad weather and have plenty of umbrellas available.* **ACCEPTING** ▷ **5 make allowances for** (C2) To make allowances for someone is to think about their characteristics and not judge them too severely: *You should make allowances for him – he's been quite ill recently.* ◦ *'This is a poor piece of work.' 'Yes, but you should make allowances for the fact that she's only seven.'*

alloy **noun; verb**

▸**noun** [C or U] /ˈæl.ɔɪ/ a metal that is made by mixing two or more metals, or a metal and another substance: *Brass is an alloy **of** copper and zinc.* ◦ *alloy wheels*

▸**verb** [T] /əˈlɔɪ/ literary to spoil something or reduce it in value: *My pleasure in receiving the letter was somewhat alloyed by its contents.*

ˌall-points ˈbulletin **noun** [C] (abbreviation **APB**) US a radio message about a person or vehicle that the police are looking for, sent to all the police officers who work in a particular area: *The Palm Springs police most likely have an all-points bulletin out on her right now.*

all-ˈpurpose **adj** [before noun] able to be used in many different ways or situations: *an all-purpose household cleaner*

ˌall-purpose ˈflour **noun** [U] US for **plain flour**

ˌall ˈright **adj, adv; exclamation**

▸**adj** [after verb], **adv** (also not standard **alright**) **GOOD/SATISFACTORY** ▷ **1** (A1) (in a way that is) satisfactory or reasonably good: *I wouldn't say she's rich, but she's **doing** all right (= being reasonably successful).* ◦ *Is **everything** all right, madam?* **2** (B1) only just good enough: *'What did you think of the film?' 'It was all right. Nothing special.'* ◦ *The food was all right, I suppose, but I've had better.* **3** not unpleasant or bad: *This wine's all right, isn't it?* ◦ *Her Mum's really strict, but her Dad's all right.* **4** very good: *You can work at home? That's all right, isn't it?* **5 it's all right for sb** used to show that you think someone is lucky or has an easy life when the same is not true for you: *It's all right for Helen – her Mum looks after the children* whenever she wants. ◦ He has a live-in housekeeper? It's ***all right for some***, isn't it? **SAFE** ▷ **6** Ⓐ2 safe, well, or not harmed: *She was very ill for a while but she's all right now.* ◦ *Did you get home all right (= safely) last night?* **ABLE TO MANAGE** ▷ **7** able to manage: *Are you managing all right in your new job?* ◦ *Are you sure you'll be all right on your own?* ◦ *Are you all right with those cases?* **8 I'm all right** informal used to refuse the offer of food or drink: *'Can I get you a drink?' 'No, I'm all right, thanks.'* **AGREED** ▷ **9** Ⓐ1 used to show that something is agreed, understood, or acceptable: *All right, I'll lend you the money.* ◦ *All right, that's enough noise!* ◦ *Tell me if you start to feel sick, all right?* ◦ *'Are you sure you won't come with us?' 'All right then. If you insist.'* ◦ *All right, so I made a mistake (= I accept that I was wrong).* ◦ *I'd rather not go to Tricia's party if that's all right* ***with*** *you.* ◦ *Would it be all right* ***if*** *I came?* ◦ [+ to infinitive] *Chris wants to know if* ***it'll*** *be all right* ***to*** *come over to see us this evening.* ◦ *She seems to think that* ***it's perfectly*** *all right* ***to*** *break the law.* **10 it's all right** Ⓐ2 (also **that's all right**) an answer to someone who has just thanked you for something or just said they are sorry for something they have done: *'Thank you for the flowers.' 'It's all right (= there's no need to thank me). I thought they might cheer you up.'* ◦ *'I'm sorry I broke the vase.' 'Oh, that's all right (= it's not important). It wasn't very expensive.'* **CERTAINLY** ▷ **11** certainly or without any doubt: *'Are you sure it was Gillian with him?' 'Oh, it was her all right.'*

▸**exclamation** (also **alright**) **GREETING** ▷ **1** UK informal used to greet someone at the same time as asking if they are well: *'All right, John?' 'Not bad thanks, and you?'* **APPROVAL** ▷ **2** slang said with the main emphasis on 'right', expressing approval of what has been said or done: *'Did you hear I hit that creep who'd been pestering me?' 'All right!'*

ˌall-ˈround adj [before noun] (US **ˌall-aˈround**) describes a person who has many different types of skills and abilities: *She's a fantastic all-round sportswoman.*

ˌall-ˈrounder noun [C] UK a person who has many different types of skills and abilities

ˌall-ˈsinging adj **all-singing, all-dancing** humorous An all-singing, all-dancing piece of equipment or system has a lot of advanced technical features, and therefore is able to do many things: *She showed us the new all-singing, all-dancing graphics software she'd bought for her computer.*

allspice /ˈɔːl.spaɪs/ ⓤⓢ /ˈɑːl-/ noun [U] a powder made from a small fruit grown in hot countries, used as a spice in cooking

ˈall-star adj [before noun] having or including famous actors or players: *His latest film featured an all-star* ***cast***. ◦ *an all-star baseball team*

ˌall-terrain ˈvehicle noun [C] (abbreviation **ATV**) a small vehicle with a seat and HANDLEBARS like a motorcycle but with three or four wheels, that can travel over very rough ground

ˌall-ˈtime adj [before noun] An all-time high, low, best, etc. is the highest, lowest, best, etc. level that has ever been: *After three years of drought, the water in the lake had reached an all-time low.*

allude /əˈluːd/ verb

PHRASAL VERB **allude to sb/sth** formal to mention someone or something without talking about them directly: *She mentioned some trouble that she'd had at home and I guessed she was alluding to her son.*

allure /əˈljʊəʳ/, /-ˈlʊəʳ/ ⓤⓢ /-ˈlʊr/ noun [U] the quality of being attractive, interesting, or exciting: *the allure* ***of*** *work****ing*** *in television* ◦ ***sexual*** *allure*

alluring /əˈljʊə.rɪŋ/, /-ˈlʊə-/ ⓤⓢ /-ˈlʊr-/ adj attractive or exciting: *I didn't find the prospect of a house with no electricity very alluring.* ◦ *She was wearing a most alluring dress at Sam's dinner party.* • **alluringly** /-li/ adv

allusion /əˈluː.ʒᵊn/ noun [C] something that is said or written that is intended to make you think of a particular thing or person: *The film is full of allusions* ***to*** *Hitchcock.* ◦ *Her novels are packed with* ***literary*** *allusions.*

allusive /əˈluː.sɪv/ adj formal containing a lot of allusions • **allusiveness** /-nəs/ noun [U]

alluvium /əˈluː.vi.əm/ noun [U] specialized earth and sand that has been left by rivers, floods, etc. • **alluvial** /-əl/ adj *an alluvial plain* ◦ *Some alluvial* ***deposits*** *are a rich source of diamonds.*

ˌall-wheel ˈdrive noun [C or U] US a system in which a vehicle's engine supplies power to all its wheels instead of just to two, so that the vehicle can travel over very rough ground, or a vehicle that uses this system → Compare **four-wheel drive**

ally noun; verb

▸**noun** [C] /ˈæl.aɪ/ **1** Ⓒ2 a country that has agreed officially to give help and support to another one, especially during a war: *The US is one of Britain's* ***staunchest*** *allies.* ◦ *During the First World War, Turkey and Germany were allies/Turkey was an ally of Germany.* → See also **the Allies 2** Ⓒ1 someone who helps and supports someone else: *He is generally considered to be the prime minister's* ***closest*** *political ally.*

▸**verb** /əˈlaɪ/

PHRASAL VERB **ally yourself to/with sb** to join someone and support them: *He allied himself with the left of the party.*

ˌall-you-can-ˈeat adj [before noun] **1** used to describe a meal at a restaurant where people can serve themselves as much food as they want: *The bar has an all-you-can-eat buffet lunch for $10.* **2** used to describe an arrangement in which a company allows customers to use a service as much as they like or to DOWNLOAD as much as they like from the internet for a fixed amount of money: *all-you-can-eat packages of voice, video, and internet services*

alma mater /ˌæl.məˈmɑː.təʳ/, /-ˈmeɪ.təʳ/ ⓤⓢ /-ˈmɑː.t̬ɚ/, /ˌɑːl-/ noun [S] **1 your alma mater** formal the school, college, or university where you studied **2** US the official song of a school, college, or university

almanac (also **almanack**) /ˈɔːl.mə.næk/, /ˈæl-/ ⓤⓢ /ˈɑːl-/, /ˈæl-/ noun [C] **1** a book published every year that includes information for that year such as important days, times of the sun rising and going down, or changes in the moon **2** a book published every year that contains facts and information about a particular subject or activity

almighty /ɔːlˈmaɪ.ti/ ⓤⓢ /ɑːlˈmaɪ.t̬i/ adj **GOD** ▷ **1** (of God) having the power to do everything: *Almighty* ***God*** **BIG** ▷ **2** [before noun] informal very big, loud, or serious: *All of a sudden we heard an almighty crash from the kitchen.* ◦ *There was an almighty* ***row*** *when I asked them to leave.*

IDIOM **God/Christ almighty!** informal an expression of anger or surprise. Some people consider this offensive.

the Alˈmighty noun [S] God: *We must pray to the Almighty for forgiveness.*

almirah /ælˈmaɪ.rə/ noun [C] Indian English a cupboard or WARDROBE that is not fixed to a wall

almond /ˈɑː.mənd/ US /ˈɑːl-/ **noun** [C] an oval nut with a hard shell that can be eaten, or the tree that it grows on: *ground/toasted almonds*

ˌalmond ˈpaste **noun** [U] UK **marzipan**

almost /ˈɔːl.məʊst/ US /ˈɑːl.moʊst/ **adv** A2 nearly: *She's almost 30.* ◦ *It was almost six o'clock when he left.* ◦ *I almost wish I hadn't invited him.* ◦ *It'll cost almost as much to repair it as it would to buy a new one.* ◦ *Almost* ***all*** *the passengers on the ferry were French.* ◦ *They'll almost* ***certainly*** *forget to do it.* ◦ *The town was almost entirely destroyed during the war.* ◦ *We were bitten by mosquitoes almost* ***every*** *night.* ◦ *The boat sank almost* ***immediately*** *after it had struck the rock.* ◦ *Most artists find it almost* ***impossible*** *to make a living from art alone.*

> **!** Common mistake: **almost**
>
> **Warning:** check your word order!:
>
> **Almost** usually goes directly before the main verb in a sentence.
>
> Don't say 'do almost something', say **almost do something**:
>
> ~~*I failed almost the exam.*~~
>
> *I almost failed the exam.*
>
> But if the main verb is **am/is/are/was/were**, **almost** usually goes directly after it:
>
> ~~*I almost am as tall as my brother.*~~
>
> *I am almost as tall as my brother.*
>
> **Remember: almost** does not usually come before a preposition:
>
> ~~*There is a pub almost in every village.*~~
>
> *There is a pub in almost every village.*

alms /ɑːmz/ **noun** [plural] old use clothing, food, or money that is given to poor people: *In the past, people thought it was their religious duty to* ***give*** *alms to the poor.*

almshouse /ˈɑːmz.haʊs/ **noun** [C] a private house built in the past where old or poor people could live without having to pay rent

aloe /ˈæl.əʊ/ US /-oʊ/ **noun** [C] an EVERGREEN plant (= one that never loses its leaves) with thick, pointed leaves

aloe vera /ˌæl.əʊˈvɪə.rə/ US /-oʊˈvɪr.ə/ **noun** [C or U] a type of plant with thick pointed leaves, or the thick liquid found in the leaves that is used to treat damaged skin

aloft /əˈlɒft/ US /-ˈlɑːft/ **adv** formal in the air or in a higher position: *We* ***held*** *our glasses aloft.*

alone /əˈləʊn/ US /-ˈloʊn/ **adj, adv; adj**

▸**adj** [after verb], **adv** A2 without other people: *He likes being alone in the house.* ◦ *She decided to climb the mountain alone.* ◦ *Do you like living alone?* ◦ *At last, we're alone together (= there are just the two of us here).* ◦ *The Swedes are* ***not*** *alone* ***in*** *finding their language under pressure from the spread of English.* ◦ *I don't like the man and I'm* ***not*** *alone* ***in that*** *(= other people agree).*

▸**adj** [after noun] C2 without any others: *She alone must decide what to do (= no one else can do it for her).* ◦ *These facts alone (= even if nothing else is considered) show that he's not to be trusted.* ◦ *He won't get the job through charm alone (= he will need something else).* ◦ *The airfare alone would use up all my money, never mind the hotel bills.*

> **+** Other ways of saying **alone**
>
> The phrase **on your own** is often used instead of 'alone':
>
> *I like living* ***on my own****.*
>
> If you do something without the help of anyone else, you could use **(all) by yourself, single-handed**, or **unaided**:
>
> *She had made the meal* ***by herself/unaided****.*
>
> *He has raced sailboats both as part of a crew and* ***single-handed****.*
>
> **Unaccompanied** can be used when someone goes somewhere alone:
>
> *To everyone's great surprise, she arrived at the ball* ***unaccompanied****.*
>
> If someone feels very sad because of being alone, you could use the words **lonely** or **isolated**:
>
> *She felt very* ***lonely*** *without him.*
>
> *Older people can often feel very* ***isolated****.*
>
> Someone who lives alone and does not like going out or talking to people can be described as a **recluse**:
>
> *He is a millionaire* ***recluse*** *who refuses to give interviews.*

along /əˈlɒŋ/ US /-ˈlɑːŋ/ **preposition; adv**

▸**preposition** FROM ONE END TO ANOTHER ▷ **1** A2 from one part of a road, river, etc. to another: *a romantic walk along the beach/river* NEXT TO ▷ **2** B1 in a line next to something long: *a row of houses along the river* ◦ *Cars were parked all along the road.* AT A PARTICULAR PLACE ▷ **3** B2 at a particular place on a road, river, etc.: *Somewhere along this road there's a garage.*

IDIOM **along the way** during the time that something is happening or that you are doing something: *I've been in this job for 30 years, and I've picked up a good deal of expertise along the way.*

▸**adv** FORWARD ▷ **1** B1 moving forward: *We were just walking along, chatting.* WITH YOU ▷ **2** B1 with you: *Why don't you* ***take*** *him along* ***with*** *you when you go?* ◦ *I'll* ***bring*** *some food along and we can have a picnic.* **3 along with sb/sth** B2 in addition to someone or something else: *California, along with Florida and Hawaii, is among the most popular US tourist destinations.*

IDIOMS **all along** B2 from the very beginning: *Do you think he's been cheating us all along?* • **come/go/be along for the ride** informal to join in an activity without playing an important part in it: *My wife is speaking at the dinner and I'm* ***just*** *going along for the ride.*

alongside /əˌlɒŋˈsaɪd/ US /əˈlɑːŋ.saɪd/ **preposition, adv** C1 next to, or together with: *A car pulled up alongside (ours).* ◦ *The new pill will be used alongside existing medicines.* ◦ *Most of the staff refused to* ***work*** *alongside the new team.* ◦ *The UK* ***fought*** *alongside France, Turkey, and Sardinia during the Crimean War.*

aloo (also **alu**) /ˈɑː.luː/ **noun** [U] Indian English for **potato**

aloof /əˈluːf/ **adj** **1** not friendly or willing to take part in things: *She seemed rather aloof when in fact she was just shy.* **2** not interested or involved, usually because you do not approve of what is happening: *Whatever is happening in the office, she always* ***remains*** *aloof.* ◦ *She* ***kept*** *herself aloof* ***from*** *her husband's business.* • **aloofness** /-nəs/ **noun** [U]

alopecia /ˌæl.əˈpiː.ʃə/ /-əʊˈ-/ US /-oʊˈ-/ **noun** [U] specialized loss of hair, especially from the head, that either happens naturally or is caused by disease

aloud /əˈlaʊd/ **adv** B1 in a voice loud enough to be heard: *He* ***read*** *her letter aloud to the rest of the family.* ◦ *People are starting to* ***wonder*** *aloud (= question* publicly) whether the economic reforms have gone too far.

alpaca /ælˈpæk.ə/ **noun** [U] **1** a South American animal with a long neck and long hair that looks like a LLAMA **2** a type of wool made from the hair of the alpaca, used for making expensive clothes

alpha /ˈæl.fə/ **noun; adj**
▸**noun** [C or U] (symbol α) the first letter of the Greek alphabet → Compare **beta, gamma, delta**
▸**adj** [before noun] Alpha software is at the first stage of development: *an alpha version of the program*

alphabet /ˈæl.fə.bet/ **noun** [C] **B1** a set of letters arranged in a fixed order, used for writing a language: *the Roman/Cyrillic alphabet*

alphabetical /ˌæl.fəˈbet.ɪ.kəl/ US /-ˈbet̬-/ **adj** (also **alphabetic** /ˌæl.fəˈbet.ɪk/) **B2** arranged in the same order as the letters of the alphabet: *an alphabetical list* ◦ *The names are published **in** alphabetical **order**.* • **alphabetically** /-ɪ.kəl.i/ **adv**

ˌ**alpha** ˈ**male** **noun** [C usually singular] **1** specialized the most successful and powerful male in any group **2** a strong and successful man who likes to be in charge of others

alphanumeric /ˌæl.fə.njuːˈmer.ɪk/ US /-nuː-/ **adj** specialized containing or using letters of the alphabet and also numbers: *alphanumeric characters*

ˈ**alpha** ˌ**particle** **noun** [C] specialized an extremely small piece of matter with a positive electrical CHARGE, produced when a RADIOACTIVE atom is broken down, usually in a nuclear reaction

alpine /ˈæl.paɪn/ **adj; noun**
▸**adj** **1 Alpine** relating to the Alps: *Alpine ski resorts* **2** relating to high mountain areas: *Our window looked out on a beautiful alpine scene.*
▸**noun** [C] (also ˌ**alpine** ˈ**plant**) a plant that grows naturally in high mountain areas where trees are unable to grow

already /ɔːlˈred.i/ US /ɑːl-/ **adv** **1** **A2** before the present time: *I asked him to come to the exhibition but he'd already seen it.* ◦ *The concert had already begun by the time we arrived.* ◦ *I've already told him.* ◦ *As I have already mentioned, I doubt that we will be able to raise all the money we need.* **2** **B1** earlier than the time expected: *Are you buying Christmas cards already? It's only September!* ◦ *I've only eaten one course and I'm already full.*

> **! Common mistake: already**
> **Warning:** check your word order!
> **Already** usually goes directly before the main verb in a sentence:
> ~~*We have already enough supermarkets in this town.*~~
> *We already have enough supermarkets in this town.*
> But if the main verb is **am/is/are/was/were**, **already** usually goes directly after it:
> *There are already enough supermarkets here.*

alright /ɔːlˈraɪt/ US /ɑːl-/ **adj, adv, exclamation** non-standard form of **all right**

Alsatian /ælˈseɪ.ʃən/ **noun** [C] (also ˌ**German** ˈ**shepherd**) a large, brown and black dog, often used for guarding buildings and in police work

also /ˈɔːl.səʊ/ US /ˈɑːl.soʊ/ **adv** **A1** in addition: *She's a photographer and also writes books.* ◦ *I'm cold, and I'm also hungry and tired.*

> **! Common mistake: also**
> **Warning:** check your word order!
> **Also** usually goes directly before the main verb in a sentence.
> Don't say 'do also something', say **also do something**:
> ~~*I like dogs, but I like also cats.*~~
> *I like dogs, but I also like cats.*
> But if the main verb is **am/is/are/was/were, also** usually goes directly after it:
> ~~*I like dogs, but I am fond also of cats.*~~
> *I like dogs, but I am also fond of cats.*

ˈ**also-ran** **noun** [C] someone in a competition who is unlikely to do well or who has failed

Alt (key) /ˈælt.kiː/ **noun** [C] a key on a computer keyboard that you press at the same time as another key to produce a particular result: *Press Alt and F1 to move the cursor to the next field.*

altar /ˈɔːl.təʳ/, /ˈɒl-/ US /ˈɑːl.t̬ɚ/ **noun** [C] a type of table used in ceremonies in a Christian church or in other religious buildings

alter /ˈɒl.təʳ/ US /ˈɑːl.t̬ɚ/ **verb** **CHANGE** ▷ **1** **B2** [I or T] to change something, usually slightly, or to cause the characteristics of something to change: *We've had to alter some of our plans.* ◦ *Although the cost of making phone calls is going up, the charge for connecting to the internet will not alter.* ◦ *Giving up our car has radically altered our lifestyle.* **2** [T] to change the size of clothes so that they fit better: *I took the coat back to the shop to **have** it **altered**.* **REMOVE ORGANS** ▷ **3** [T] US polite word for **castrate** or **spay**

alteration /ˌɒl.təˈreɪ.ʃən/ US /ˌɑːl.t̬ə-/ **noun** **1** **C1** [C] a change, usually a slight change, in the appearance, character, or structure of something: *Several police officers are being questioned about the alteration of the documents.* ◦ *The house needed extensive alterations when we moved in.* ◦ *Some alterations **to** our original plans might be necessary.* **2** [C or U] a change or changes made to the size or shape of a piece of clothing so that it fits better: *She's getting some alterations done to her dress.* **3** **C1** [U] the process of changing something: *The landscape has undergone considerable alteration.*

altercation /ˌɒl.təˈkeɪ.ʃən/ US /ˌɑːl.t̬ɚ-/ **noun** [C] formal a loud argument or disagreement: *According to witnesses, the altercation **between** the two men started inside the restaurant.*

ˌ**alter** ˈ**ego** **noun** [C] (plural **alter egos**) the part of someone's personality that is not usually seen by other people: *Superman is Clark Kent's alter ego.*

alternate **verb; adj**
▸**verb** /ˈɒl.tə.neɪt/ US /ˈɑːl.t̬ɚ-/ **1** **C1** [I usually + adv/prep] to happen or exist one after the other repeatedly: *She alternated **between** cheerfulness and deep despair.* **2** [T usually + adv/prep] to make something happen or exist one after the other repeatedly: *He alternated working in the office **with** long tours overseas.* • **alternately** /ɒlˈtɜː.nət.li/ US /ɑːlˈtɝː-/ **adv** *The film is alternately depressing and amusing.*
▸**adj** [before noun] /ɒlˈtɜː.nət/ US /ɑːlˈtɝː-/ **1** with first one thing, then another thing, and then the first thing again: *a dessert with alternate layers of chocolate and cream* **2** **C1** If something happens on alternate days, it happens every second day: *Private cars are banned from the city on alternate days.* **3** US (UK **alternative**) An alternate plan or method is one that you can use if you do not want to use another one. • **alternating** /ˈɒl.tə.neɪ.tɪŋ/ US /ˈɑːl.t̬ɚ.neɪ.t̬ɪŋ/ **adj** *alternating moods of anger and sadness*

alˌ**ternate** ˈ**angle** **noun** [C, usually plural] UK (US

ˈalternate ˌangle) one of two equal angles on opposite sides of a line that crosses two usually PARALLEL (= always the same distance apart) lines, and on opposite sides of those lines → Compare **corresponding angle**

ˈalternating ˌcurrent noun [U] (abbreviation **AC**) an electrical current that regularly changes the direction in which it moves → Compare **direct current**

alternation /ˌɒl.təˈneɪ.ʃən/ (US) /ˌɑːl.tɚ-/ **noun** [S or U] a situation in which one thing repeatedly happens or exists after another: *Flowers and trees are planted to produce a lovely alternation of light and shade in the garden.*

alternative /ɒlˈtɜː.nə.tɪv/ (US) /ɑːlˈtɝː.nə.t̬ɪv/ **adj; noun**

▸**adj 1** B2 (US also **alternate**) An alternative plan or method is one that you can use if you do not want to use another one: *The opposition parties have so far failed to set out an alternative strategy.* ◦ *An alternative venue for the concert is being sought.* **2** B2 describes things that are considered to be unusual and often have a small but enthusiastic group of people who support them: *alternative comedy*

▸**noun** [C] B2 something that is different from something else, especially from what is usual, and offering the possibility of choice: *an alternative **to** coffee* ◦ *There must be an alternative **to** people sleeping on the streets.* ◦ *I'm afraid I have **no** alternative **but to** ask you to leave (= that is what I have to do).*

> Word partners for **alternative noun**
>
> *find/look for/seek* an alternative • *come up with/offer/provide/suggest* an alternative • *have* [little/no] alternative • an *affordable/feasible/sensible/viable* alternative • the *only* alternative • an alternative *to* sth • *as* an alternative

alˌternative ˈlifestyle noun [C usually singular] a way of living that is unusual, especially when you choose not to have the type of home and job that is considered normal in modern society: *to pursue/seek an alternative lifestyle*

alternatively /ɒlˈtɜː.nə.tɪv.li/ (US) /ɑːlˈtɝː.nə.t̬ɪv-/ **adv** B2 used to suggest another possibility: *We could go to the Indian restaurant, **or** alternatively, we could try that new Italian place.*

alˌternative ˈmedicine noun [U] a range of treatments for medical conditions that people use instead of or with western medicine: *Alternative medicine includes treatments such as acupuncture, homeopathy, and hypnotherapy.*

alternator /ˈɒl.tə.neɪ.təʳ/ (US) /ˈɑːl.tɚ.neɪ.t̬ɚ/ **noun** [C] specialized a device that produces AC electricity

although /ɔːlˈðəʊ/ (US) /ɑːlˈðoʊ/ **conjunction 1** B1 despite the fact that: *She walked home by herself, although she knew that it was dangerous.* ◦ *He decided to go, although I begged him not to.* **2** B1 but: *He's rather shy, although he's not as bad as he used to be.* ◦ *She'll be coming tonight, although I don't know exactly when.*

> ! Common mistake: **although**
>
> **Warning:** Check your spelling!
>
> **Although** is one of the 50 words most often spelled wrongly by learners.

altimeter /ˈæl.tɪ.miː.təʳ/ (US) /ælˈtɪm.ə.t̬ɚ/ **noun** [C] a device used in an aircraft to measure how high it is from the ground

altitude /ˈæl.tɪ.tjuːd/ (US) /-t̬ə.tuːd/ **noun** [C] height above sea level: *We are currently flying **at** an altitude of 15,000 metres.* ◦ *Mountain climbers use oxygen when they reach **higher** altitudes.*

alto /ˈæl.təʊ/ (US) /-toʊ/ **noun; adj**

▸**noun** [C] (plural **altos**) (a woman with) a low adult female singing voice or (a boy with) the lowest boys' singing voice or (a man with) the highest adult male singing voice: *She began by singing soprano, then changed to alto.*

▸**adj** describes a musical instrument that is of a size and range between SOPRANO and TENOR: *an alto saxophone/flute*

altocumulus /ˌæl.təʊˈkjuː.mjə.ləs/ (US) /-toʊˈ-/ **noun** [U] specialized a type of CUMULUS (= a tall, rounded, white cloud with a flat base) found at medium height, above the level of cumulus → Compare **cirrocumulus, stratocumulus**

altogether /ˌɔːl.təˈgeð.əʳ/ (US) /ˌɑːl.təˈgeð.ɚ/ **adv; noun**

▸**adv 1** B1 in total: *That'll be £52.50 altogether, please.* **2** B2 completely: *The government ought to abolish the tax altogether.* ◦ *She wrote less and less often, and eventually she stopped altogether.* ◦ *It's all right working with him, but living with him would be a different matter altogether.* ◦ *I'm not altogether sure I want that (= I have doubts about it).* ◦ *I think Graham will agree, but convincing Mary will be altogether more (= much more) difficult.* **3** B2 considering everything: *He's bad-tempered, selfish, and altogether an unpleasant man.*

▸**noun** [S] **be in the altogether** old-fashioned to be naked

altostratus /ˌæl.təʊˈstrɑː.təs/ (US) /-toʊˈstreɪ.t̬əs/, /-ˈstrɑː-/ **noun** [U] specialized a type of STRATUS (= a flat, grey cloud) formed in thin layers and found at medium height, above the level of stratus → Compare **cirrostratus, nimbostratus**

altruism /ˈæl.tru.ɪ.zəm/ **noun** [U] willingness to do things which bring advantages to others, even if it results in disadvantage for yourself: *She's not known for her altruism.* • **altruist** /-ɪst/ **noun** [C]

altruistic /ˌæl.truˈɪs.tɪk/ **adj** showing a wish to help or bring advantages to others, even if it results in disadvantage for yourself: *I doubt whether her **motives** for donating the money are altruistic – she's probably looking for publicity.* • **altruistically** /-tɪ.kəl.i/ **adv**

alu noun [U] → **aloo**

alum /ˈæl.əm/ **noun** [U] specialized a chemical substance containing aluminium used in DYEING (= changing the colour of something) and as an ASTRINGENT (= substance that causes skin to tighten)

aluminium /ˌæl.jəˈmɪn.i.əm/ **noun** [U] UK (US **aluminum** /əˈluː.mɪ.nəm/) B2 (symbol **Al**) a chemical element that is a light, silver-coloured metal, used especially for making cooking equipment and aircraft parts: *an aluminium saucepan* ◦ *Cover the fish with aluminium **foil** and cook over a low heat.*

alumna /əˈlʌm.nə/ **noun** [C] (plural **alumnae** /-niː/) mainly US a female alumnus

alumnus /əˈlʌm.nəs/ noun [C] (plural **alumni** /-naɪ/) mainly US someone who has left a school, college, or university after finishing their studies there: *the alumni of St MacNissi's College* ◦ *Several **famous** alumni have agreed to help raise money for the school's restoration fund.*

alveolar /ˌæl.viˈəʊ.ləʳ/ (US) /ælˈviː.ə.lɚ/ **adj** specialized (of a speech sound) made by putting your tongue against the hard place behind your top front teeth: */t/, /z/, and /n/ are alveolar sounds in English.*

ˌalveolar ˈridge noun [C] specialized the hard area behind your top front teeth

alveolus /ˌæl.viˈəʊ.ləs/ (US) /ælˈviː.ə-/ noun [C] (plural **alveoli** /-laɪ/) specialized one of the many very small air bags in the lungs, with thin walls that allow OXYGEN to enter the blood

always /ˈɔːl.weɪz/ (US) /ˈɑːl-/ adv **EVERY TIME** ▷ **1** (A1) every time or all the time: *It's always cold in this room.* ◦ *She always spells my name wrong.* **FOR EVER** ▷ **2** (A2) for ever: *I'll always remember you.* **UNTIL NOW** ▷ **3** (A2) at all times in the past: *I've always liked him.* ◦ *I always thought I'd have children eventually.* **POSSIBILITY** ▷ **4** (B1) used with 'can' or 'could' to suggest another possibility: *If you miss this train you can always catch the next one.* **MANY TIMES** ▷ **5** (B2) again and again, usually in an annoying way: [+ -ing verb] disapproving *You're always complaining.*

> **! Common mistake: always**
>
> **Warning:** Check your spelling!
>
> **Always** is one of the 50 words most often spelled wrongly by learners. Remember: the correct spelling has only one 'l'.

> **! Common mistake: always**
>
> **Warning:** check your word order!
>
> **Always** usually goes directly before the main verb in a sentence.
>
> Don't say 'do always something', say **always do something**:
>
> ~~*I forget always my mobile phone number.*~~
>
> *I always forget my mobile phone number.*
>
> But if the main verb is **am/is/are/was/were**, **always** usually goes directly after it:
>
> ~~*She always is late for meetings.*~~
>
> *She is always late for meetings.*

> **+ Other ways of saying always**
>
> If you use **always** to mean 'again and again', then you could also use **constantly**, **continually**, **forever**, or the fixed expressions **time after time** or **all the time**:
>
> *He's **constantly/forever** losing his keys.*
>
> *I'm fed up with you making excuses **all the time**.*
>
> The word **invariably** is a more formal way of saying **always**, especially when talking about something you wish did not happen:
>
> *The train is **invariably** late.*
>
> **Consistently** is used when something happens or someone does something in the same way again and again:
>
> *He received **consistently** high marks throughout his school years.*
>
> The fixed expression **without fail** can be used to show that someone always does something, even when it is difficult:
>
> *He visited her every Sunday **without fail**.*

ˌalways-ˈon adj [before noun] available or operating at all times: *always-on IT support*

Alzheimer's /ˈælts.haɪ.məz/ (US) /ˈɑːlts.haɪ.mɚz/ noun [U] (also **ˈAlzheimer's diˌsease**) a disease of the brain that affects especially old people and results in the gradual loss of memory, speech, movement, and the ability to think clearly: *an Alzheimer's patient*

a.m. /ˌeɪˈem/ adv (A1) used when referring to a time between twelve o'clock at night and twelve o'clock in the middle of the day: *The first election results are expected around 1 a.m.* → Compare **p.m.**

am strong /æm/ weak /əm/ verb i form of **be**: *Am I included?*

AM /ˌeɪˈem/ noun **RADIO** ▷ **1** [U] abbreviation for amplitude modulation: a type of radio broadcasting in which the strength of the signal changes, producing sound of a lower quality than FM: *You're listening to Radio Gold, broadcasting 24 hours a day on 909 AM.* **POLITICIAN** ▷ **2** [C] UK abbreviation for Assembly Member: a person who has been elected to the Welsh Assembly

amalgam /əˈmæl.gəm/ noun **OF METALS** ▷ **1** [U] specialized a mixture of MERCURY and another metal, especially one used by dentists to repair teeth: *an amalgam filling* **OF PARTS** ▷ **2** [S] a combination of parts that create a complete whole: *The show was a wonderful amalgam **of** dance, music, and drama.*

amalgamate /əˈmæl.gə.meɪt/ verb [I or T] to join or unite to form a larger organization or group, or to make separate organizations do this: *The electricians' union is planning to amalgamate **with** the technicians' union.* ◦ *The different offices will be amalgamated **as/into** employment advice centres.*

amalgamation /əˌmæl.gəˈmeɪ.ʃən/ noun [U or C] the process in which separate organizations unite to form a larger organization or group, or an organization or group formed in this way: *The association was **formed by** the amalgamation of several regional environmental organizations.* ◦ *The company began as an amalgamation of small family firms.*

amanuensis /əˌmæn.juˈen.sɪs/ noun [C] (plural **amanuenses** /-siːz/) formal a person whose job is to write down what another person says or to copy what another person has written

amaretto /ˌæm.əˈret.əʊ/ (US) /ˈret̬.oʊ/ noun **DRINK** ▷ **1** [U] a sweet alcoholic drink made from ALMONDS (= a type of nut) **BISCUIT** ▷ **2** [C] (plural **amaretti** /-i/) an Italian biscuit made from ALMONDS (= a type of nut)

amass /əˈmæs/ verb [T] to get a large amount of something, especially money or information, by collecting it over a long period: *She has amassed a huge **fortune** from her novels.* ◦ *Some of his colleagues envy the enormous **wealth** that he has amassed.*

amateur adj; noun

▸adj /ˈæm.ə.təʳ/ (US) /-tʃɚ/ **1** (C1) taking part in an activity for pleasure, not as a job: *an amateur astronomer/boxer/historian* ◦ *He was an amateur singer until the age of 40, when he turned professional.* → Compare **professional 2** relating to an activity, especially a sport, where the people taking part do not receive money: *amateur athletics*

▸noun [C] /ˈæm.ə.təʳ/ (US) /-tʃɚ/ **1** (C1) a person who takes part in an activity for pleasure, not as a job: *This tennis tournament is open to both amateurs and professionals.* → Compare **professional 2** (C1) disapproving someone who does not have much skill in what they do: *I won't be giving them any more work – they're a bunch of amateurs.*

ˌamateur draˈmatics noun [plural] theatre performances in which the people involved are not paid but take part for their own enjoyment

amateurish /ˈæm.ə.tᵊr.ɪʃ/ (US) /ˌæm.əˈtʊr.ɪʃ/ adj disapproving having no skill, or showing no skill: *Their website looks amateurish.* • **amateurishly** /-li/ adv • **amateurishness** /-nəs/ noun [U]

amatory /ˈæm.ə.tᵊr.i/ (US) /-tɔːr-/ adj formal relating to sexual love: *amatory adventures*

amaze /əˈmeɪz/ verb [T] to cause someone to be extremely surprised: [+ question word] *I was amazed **by how** well he looked.* ◦ *You've done all your homework*

A

in an hour? You amaze me. ◦ [+ that] ***It** amazes me **that** she's got the energy for all those parties.* ◦ [+ to infinitive] ***It** amazes me **to** think that Anna is now in charge of the company.* ◦ ***It** amazes me **how** you can put up with living in such a dirty house.* ◦ ***It never ceases to** amaze me **how** he can talk for so long without ever saying anything interesting.*

amazed /əˈmeɪzd/ **adj** B1 extremely surprised: *She was amazed **at** how calm she felt after the accident.* ◦ *I was **absolutely** amazed when I heard he'd been promoted.* ◦ [+ to infinitive] *Mr Graham was amazed **to** find 46 ancient gold coins inside the pot.* ◦ *I was amazed **to hear** that Chris had won first prize.* ◦ *We were amazed **to discover** that we'd been at school together.* ◦ [+ (that)] *I'm amazed **(that)** she didn't complain.*

amazement /əˈmeɪz.mənt/ **noun** [U] B2 extreme surprise: *She stared **in** amazement.* ◦ ***To my** amazement, he ate the whole lot.*

amazing /əˈmeɪ.zɪŋ/ **adj** **1** B1 extremely surprising: *This stain remover really works – it's amazing!* ◦ *The new theatre is going to cost an amazing (= very large) **amount** of money.* ◦ ***It's** amazing **to** think that the managing director is only 23.* ◦ ***It's** amazing **that** no one else has applied for the job.* ◦ *The amazing **thing** is that it was kept secret for so long.* ◦ *What an amazing **coincidence**!* **2** A2 informal approving very good: *This wine is really amazing.* • **amazingly** /-li/ **adv** B1 *Amazingly **enough**, no one else has applied for the job.* ◦ *The food was amazingly **good**.*

amazon /ˈæm.ə.zən/ US /-zɑːn/ **noun** [C] humorous a tall, strong, or forceful woman • **amazonian** /ˌæm.əˈzəʊ.ni.ən/ US /-ˈzoʊ-/ **adj**

Amazonian /ˌæm.əˈzəʊ.ni.ən/ US /-ˈzoʊ-/ **adj** relating to the area around the Amazon river in South America: *the Amazonian **rainforest***

ambassador /æmˈbæs.ə.dər/ US /-dɚ/ **noun** [C] B2 an important official who works in a foreign country representing his or her own country there, and who is officially accepted in this position by that country: *The UK's ambassador **in** Moscow has refused to comment.* ◦ *She's a former ambassador **to** the United States.* ◦ *Late last night, the French ambassador was summoned to the Foreign Office to discuss the crisis.*

ambassadorial /æmˌbæs.əˈdɔː.ri.əl/ US /-ˈdɔːr.i-/ **adj** belonging or relating to an ambassador: *the ambassadorial car/residence* ◦ *He achieved ambassadorial rank in 1958.*

amber /ˈæm.bər/ US /-bɚ/ **noun** [U] **1** a hard, transparent, yellowish-brown substance that was formed in ancient times from RESIN (= a substance produced by trees) and is used in jewellery: *He has a collection of prehistoric insects **preserved in** amber.* **2** UK (US also **yellow**) the yellowish-orange traffic light that shows between the green and the red to warn drivers that the lights are about to change: *The lights turned to amber.* • **amber** **adj** *an amber **light*** ◦ *an amber necklace (= made of amber)*

ambidextrous /ˌæm.bɪˈdek.strəs/ **adj** able to use both hands equally well

ambience (also **ambiance**) /ˈæm.bi.əns/ US /ˌɑːm.biˈɑːns/ **noun** [S] the character of a place or the quality it seems to have: *Despite being a busy city, Dublin has the ambience **of** a country town.*

ambient /ˈæm.bi.ənt/ **adj** [before noun] specialized (especially of environmental conditions) existing in the surrounding area: *ambient conditions/lighting/noise/temperature*

ˌambient ˈmusic **noun** [U] a type of music, often without a tune or beat, that is intended to make people relax or create a particular mood

ambiguity /ˌæm.bɪˈgjuː.ɪ.ti/ US /-ə.t̬i/ **noun** [C or U] C2 (an example of) the fact of something having more than one possible meaning and therefore possibly causing confusion: *We wish to remove any ambiguity concerning our demands.* ◦ *There are some ambiguities in the legislation.*

ambiguous /æmˈbɪg.ju.əs/ **adj** C2 having or expressing more than one possible meaning, sometimes intentionally: *His reply to my question was somewhat ambiguous.* ◦ *The wording of the agreement is ambiguous.* ◦ *The government has been ambiguous on this issue.* • **ambiguously** /-li/ **adv** *Some questions were badly or ambiguously worded.*

ambit /ˈæm.bɪt/ **noun** [U] formal the range or limits of the influence of something: *They believe that all the outstanding issues should **fall within the** ambit **of** the talks.*

ambition /æmˈbɪʃ.ən/ **noun** **1** B1 [C] a strong wish to achieve something: [+ to infinitive] *His ambition is ultimately **to** run his own business.* ◦ *He has already **achieved** his main ambition in life – to become wealthy.* ◦ *political ambitions* ◦ *She doubts whether she'll ever be able to **fulfil** her ambition.* ◦ *I've always had a **burning** (= very great) ambition to be a film director.* ◦ *After his heart attack, he abandoned his ambition **to become** prime minister.* **2** B2 [U] a strong wish to be successful, powerful, rich, etc.: *She's got a lot of ambition.*

> **Word partners for ambition**
>
> a ***burning/great/lifelong*** ambition • a ***secret*** ambition • ***achieve/fulfil/realize*** your ambition • ***cherish/harbour/have*** an ambition • ***pursue*** an ambition • ***lack*** of ambition

ambitious /æmˈbɪʃ.əs/ **adj** **1** B2 having a strong wish to be successful, powerful, or rich: *an ambitious **young** lawyer* ◦ *He's very ambitious **for** his children (= he wants them to be successful).* **2** B2 If a plan or idea is ambitious, it needs a great amount of skill and effort to be successful or be achieved: *She has some ambitious **plans** for her business.* ◦ *The government has announced an ambitious plan to modernize the railway network.* ◦ *The original completion date was **over**-ambitious, so we have had to delay the opening.* • **ambitiously** /-li/ **adv**

ambivalent /æmˈbɪv.ə.lənt/ **adj** having two opposing feelings at the same time, or being uncertain about how you feel: *I **felt** very ambivalent **about** leaving home.* ◦ *He has fairly ambivalent **feelings** towards his father.* ◦ *an ambivalent **attitude** to exercise* • **ambivalently** /-li/ **adv** • **ambivalence** /-ləns/ **noun** [U] the state of feeling or being ambivalent: *her ambivalence **towards** men*

amble /ˈæm.bl̩/ **verb; noun**

▸**verb** [I usually + adv/prep] to walk in a slow and relaxed way: *He was ambling **along** the beach.* ◦ *She ambled **down** the street, stopping occasionally to look in the shop windows.*

▸**noun** [S] a slow, relaxed walk

ambrosia /æmˈbrəʊ.zi.ə/, /-ʒə/ US /-ˈbroʊ.ʒə/ **noun** [U] literary **1** the food eaten by Greek and Roman gods **2** a very pleasant food: *The chocolate mousse she makes is sheer ambrosia (= tastes extremely good).*

ambulance /ˈæm.bjʊ.ləns/ **noun** [C] A2 a special vehicle used to take sick or injured people to hospital: *I **called** an ambulance.* ◦ *We were woken in the night by the wail of ambulance **sirens**.* ◦ *an ambulance **driver*** ◦ *An ambulance **crew** was called to his home, but he was dead by the time they arrived.*

ˈambulance ˌchaser noun [C] informal disapproving a lawyer who tries to get work by persuading someone who has been in an accident to claim money from the person or company responsible for the accident: *An ambulance chaser contacted her the day she was injured and persuaded her to sue the city council for negligence.* • **ˈambulance-ˌchasing** adj [before noun] informal

ambulanceman /ˈæm.bjʊ.ləns.mən/ noun [C] (plural **-men** /-mən/) UK a man whose job is to drive an ambulance and to help or give treatment to the people carried in it

ambulancewoman /ˈæm.bjʊ.ləns ˌwʊm.ən/ noun [C] (plural **-women** /-wɪmɪn/) UK a female ambulance-man

ambulatory /ˌæm.bjəˈleɪ.tᵊr.i/ (US) /ˈæm.bjə.lə.tɔːr-/ adj specialized relating to or describing people being treated for an injury or illness who are able to walk, and who, when treated in a hospital, are usually not staying for the night: *an ambulatory surgery*

ambush /ˈæm.bʊʃ/ verb; noun

▸verb [T] to suddenly attack a person or a group of people after hiding and waiting for them: *Five soldiers died after their bus was ambushed on a country road.* ◦ *He was ambushed **by gunmen** on his way to work.*

▸noun [C or U] **1** an occasion when a person or group of people are ambushed: *Several passers-by were killed **in** the ambush.* ◦ *Fear of ambush prevents the police from going to high-risk areas.* **2 lie/wait in ambush** to hide and wait for someone in order to attack them.

ameba /əˈmiː.bə/ noun [C] mainly US for **amoeba**

amebic /əˈmiː.bɪk/ adj mainly US for **amoebic (amoeba)**

ameliorate /əˈmiː.l.jə.reɪt/ verb [T] formal to make a bad or unpleasant situation better: *Foreign aid is badly needed to ameliorate the effects of the drought.* • **amelioration** /əˌmiː.li.əˈreɪ.ʃᵊn/ noun [U]

amen /ˌɑːˈmen/, /ˌeɪ-/ exclamation formal said or sung at the end of a prayer or a religious song to express agreement with what has been said

IDIOM **amen to that** said to show that you agree strongly with something that someone has just said: *'Thank goodness we didn't go.' 'Amen to that!'*

amenable /əˈmiː.nə.bl̩/ adj willing to accept or be influenced by a suggestion: *She might be more amenable **to** the idea if you explained how much money it would save.* ◦ *Do you think the new manager will **prove** more amenable **to** our proposals?*

amend /əˈmend/ verb [T] (C2) to change the words of a text, especially a law or a legal document: *MPs were urged to amend the law to prevent another oil tanker disaster.* ◦ *In line 20, 'men' should be amended (= changed) **to** 'people'.* ◦ *Until the constitution is amended, the power to appoint ministers will remain with the president.*

amendment /əˈmend.mənt/ noun **1** (C2) [U or C] a change or changes made to the words of a text: *He insisted that the book did not need amendment.* ◦ *I've **made** a few last-minute amendments **to** the article.* ◦ *Presidential power was reduced by a **constitutional** amendment in 1991.* **2** [C] a change to a law that is not yet in operation and is still being discussed: *An amendment to the **bill** was agreed without a vote.*

amends /əˈmendz/ noun [plural] **make amends** to do something good to show that you are sorry about something you have done: *She tried to make amends **by** inviting him out to dinner.* ◦ *I wanted to make amends **for** the worry I've caused you.*

amenity /əˈmiː.nɪ.ti/ (US) /əˈmen.ə.t̬i/ noun [C usually plural] **1** something, such as a swimming pool or shopping centre, that is intended to make life more pleasant or comfortable for the people in a town, hotel, or other place: *The council has some spare cash, which it proposes to spend on **public** amenities.* **2 basic amenities** things considered to be necessary to live comfortably, such as hot water: *The 200-year-old jail is overcrowded, understaffed, and **lacking in** basic amenities.*

America /əˈmer.ɪ.kə/ noun **1** the US **2** North or South America

American /əˈmer.ɪ.kən/ adj; noun

▸adj **1** of or relating to the US: *They drive a big American car.* **2** of or relating to North or South America

IDIOM **as American as apple pie** typical of the way of life in the US: *Leather jackets are as American as apple pie and Harley-Davidsons.*

▸noun [C] someone from the US: *He said he was proud to be an American.*

the Aˌmerican ˈdream noun [S] the belief that everyone in the US has the chance to be successful, rich, and happy if they work hard

Aˌmerican ˈfootball noun [U] UK (US **football**) a game for two teams of eleven players in which an oval ball is moved along the field by running with it or throwing it

Aˌmerican ˈIndian noun [C] a **Native American**

Americanism /əˈmer.ɪ.kə.nɪ.zᵊm/ noun [C] a word or expression that was first used in the US but is now used by people in other countries, especially those where English is spoken

Americanize (UK usually **Americanise**) /əˈmer.ɪ.kᵊn.aɪz/ verb [T] to become or make something typical of the US or US culture: *Linda Chan was born in Hong Kong but grew up in New York and quickly became Americanized.* ◦ disapproving *Many European cities have been Americanized with burger bars and diners.* • **Americanization** (UK usually **Americanisation**) /əˌmer.ɪ.kᵊn.aɪˈzeɪ.ʃᵊn/ (US) /-ɪˈ-/ noun [U]

Aˈmerican ˌplan noun [U] US for **full board**

Amerindian /ˌæm.əˈrɪn.di.ən/ noun [C], adj **American Indian**

amethyst /ˈæm.ə.θɪst/ noun **1** [C or U] a transparent purple stone used in jewellery **2** [U] a purple colour • **amethyst** adj *amethyst eyes*

amiable /ˈeɪ.mi.ə.bl̩/ adj pleasant and friendly: *He seemed an amiable young man.* ◦ *So amiable was the mood of the meeting that a decision was soon reached.* • **amiably** /-bli/ adv *They were chatting quite amiably on the phone last night so I assumed everything was okay.* • **amiability** /ˌeɪ.mi.əˈbɪl.ɪ.ti/ (US) /-ə.t̬i/ noun [U] *I hate all that false amiability that goes on at parties.*

amicable /ˈæm.ɪ.kə.bl̩/ adj **1** relating to behaviour between people that is pleasant and friendly, often despite a difficult situation: *His manner was perfectly amicable but I felt uncomfortable.* **2** relating to an agreement or decision that is achieved without people arguing or being unpleasant: *Few people have amicable **divorces**.* ◦ *Eventually we reached an amicable **settlement**.* • **amicably** /-bli/ adv *I hope we can **settle** this amicably.*

amid /əˈmɪd/ preposition (also **amidst** /əˈmɪdst/) (C1) in the middle of or surrounded by: *On the floor, amid mounds of books, were two small envelopes.* ◦ *The new perfume was launched amidst a fanfare of publicity.* → Synonym **among**

amidships /əˈmɪd.ʃɪps/ adv in the middle part of a ship

amino acid /əˌmiː.nəʊˈæs.ɪd/ (US) /-noʊ-/ noun [C]

specialized any of the chemical substances found in plants and animals that combine to make PROTEIN (= a substance necessary for the body to grow)

amiss /əˈmɪs/ adj [after verb] **1** wrong, not suitable, or not as expected: *I could see by the look on their faces that **something was** amiss.* **2 not go amiss** informal If something might/would not go amiss, it would be useful and might help to improve a situation: *A word of apology might not go amiss.* ◦ *A sense of proportion would not go amiss in all of this.* **3 take sth amiss** to be offended by something that someone has said to you: *I was worried that he might take my remark amiss.*

amity /ˈæm.ɪ.ti/ US /-ə.t̬i/ noun [U] formal a good relationship: *The two groups had lived **in** perfect amity for many years before the recent troubles.* → Synonym **friendship**

ammeter /ˈæm.iː.təʳ/ US /-t̬ɚ/ noun [C] a device for measuring the strength of an electric current in units called AMPS

ammonia /əˈməʊ.ni.ə/ US /-ˈmoʊ-/ noun [U] a gas with a strong, unpleasant smell used in making explosives, FERTILIZERS (= substances that help plants grow), and some cleaning products

ammonite /ˈæm.ə.naɪt/ noun [C] specialized an EXTINCT sea creature (= one that no longer exists) often found as a FOSSIL (= an animal turned into rock), with a flat, SPIRAL shell

ammonium /əˈməʊ.ni.əm/ US /-ˈmoʊ-/ noun [U] specialized a type of ION that is DERIVED from ammonia and is contained in chemical COMPOUNDS of it: *ammonium chloride* ◦ *ammonium nitrate*

amˌmonium hyˈdroxide noun [U] specialized a chemical consisting of water and ammonia, used as a BLEACH and a strong cleaning solution

ammunition /ˌæm.jʊˈnɪʃ.ən/ noun [U] **1** (informal **ammo** /ˈæm.əʊ/ US /-oʊ/) objects that can be shot from a weapon, such as bullets or bombs: *a good supply of ammunition* ◦ *a shortage of ammunition* **2** facts that can be used to support an argument: *His bad behaviour **provided plenty of** ammunition for his opponents.*

amnesia /æmˈniː.zi.ə/, /-ʒə/ noun [U] a medical condition that makes you unable to remember things: *After the accident he suffered periods of amnesia.*

amnesty /ˈæm.nɪ.sti/ noun **1** [C or U] a decision by a government that allows political prisoners to go free: *Most political prisoners were freed under the terms of the amnesty.* **2** [C usually singular] a fixed period of time during which people are not punished for committing a particular crime: *People who hand in illegal weapons will not be prosecuted during the amnesty.* ◦ *The government refused to declare an amnesty **for** people who had not paid the disputed tax.*

amniocentesis /ˌæm.ni.əʊ.senˈtiː.sɪs/ US /-oʊ-/ noun [U or S] a medical test in which a needle is used to remove a small amount of the liquid that surrounds a baby in the mother's WOMB in order to examine the baby's condition

amnion /ˈæm.ni.ən/ noun [C] (plural **amnions** or **amnia** /-ə/) specialized a bag made of thin skin that contains amniotic fluid and surrounds the EMBRYO of a mammal, bird, or reptile inside its mother • **amniotic** /ˌæm.niˈɒt.ɪk/ US /-ˈɑː.t̬ɪk/ adj

ˌamniotic ˈfluid noun [U] specialized the liquid that surrounds the EMBRYO of a mammal, bird, or reptile

amoeba (plural **amoebae** /-biː/ or **amoebas**) (US also **ameba** (plural **amebae** or **amebas**)) /əˈmiː.bə/ noun [C] a very small, simple organism consisting of only one cell • **amoebic** (mainly US **amebic**) /-bɪk/ adj

aˌmoebic ˈdysentery noun [U] UK (US **amebic dysentery**) an illness of the bowels caused by an amoeba

amok (also **amuck**) /əˈmɒk/ US /-ˈmʌk/ adv **run amok** to be out of control and act in a wild or dangerous manner: *The soldiers ran amok after one of their senior officers was killed.* ◦ *The two dogs ran amok in a school playground.*

among /əˈmʌŋ/ preposition (also **amongst** /əˈmʌŋst/) **1** B1 in the middle of or surrounded by other things: *I saw a few familiar faces among the crowd.* ◦ *Rescue teams searched among the wreckage for survivors.* **2** A2 happening or being included as part of a group of people or things: *a decision that has caused a lot of anger among women* ◦ *Relax, you're amongst friends.* ◦ *Talk about it among yourselves (= talk to each other about it without me) for a while.* ◦ *She has worked as an estate agent among **other things** (= as well as other things).* **3** C1 to each one in a group of three or more people or things: *He divided the country among his sons.* ◦ *The cost should be shared equally among the three of you.*

amoral /ˌeɪˈmɒr.əl/ US /ˌeɪˈmɔːr-/ adj without moral principles: *Humans, he argues, are amoral and what guides them is not any sense of morality but an instinct for survival.* → Compare **immoral, moral** • **amorality** /ˌeɪ.mɒrˈæl.ɪ.ti/ US /-mɔːrˈæl.ə.t̬i/ noun [U]

amorous /ˈæm.ə.rəs/ US /-ɚ.əs/ adj of or expressing sexual DESIRE: *The opera centres around the amorous **adventures/exploits** of its handsome hero.* ◦ *Amanda had rejected his amorous advances.*

amorphous /əˈmɔː.fəs/ US /-ˈmɔːr-/ /eɪ-/ adj having no fixed form or shape: *an amorphous **mass** of jelly*

amortize formal (UK usually **amortise**) /əˈmɔː.taɪz/ US /ˈæm.ɔːr-/ verb [T] to reduce a debt by paying small regular amounts: *The value of the machinery is amortized over its estimated useful life.* • **amortizable** (UK usually **amortisable**) /əˈmɔː.taɪ.zə.bl̩/ US /ˌæm.ɔːrˈtaɪ-/ adj • **amortization** (UK usually **amortisation**) /əˌmɔː.tɪˈzeɪ.ʃən/ US /ˌæm.ɔːr.t̬ə-/ noun [U]

amount /əˈmaʊnt/ noun; verb

▸noun [C] B1 a collection or mass, especially of something that cannot be counted: *They didn't deliver the right amount **of** sand.* ◦ *Small amounts **of** land were used for keeping animals.* ◦ *He paid regular amounts **of** money to a charity.* ◦ *I didn't expect the bill to come to this amount (= of money).* ◦ *The new tax caused a huge amount **of** public anger.* ◦ *I had **a certain** amount **of** (= some) difficulty finding the house.* ◦ *You wouldn't believe **the** amount **of** trouble (= what a lot of trouble) I've had with this car.*

> **!** Common mistake: **amount of or number of?**
>
> **Remember: amount of** is usually used with uncountable nouns.
>
> With countable nouns, don't say 'amount of', say **number of**:
>
> ~~*They received a large amount of complaints.*~~
>
> *They received a large number of complaints.*

IDIOM **any amount of** a very large amount of: *We had any amount of people applying for the job.*

▸verb

PHRASAL VERB **amount to sth** [not continuous] **ADD UP TO** ▷ **1** to become a particular amount: *The annual cost of income support to single parents amounted to £700 million in that year.* **BE** ▷ **2** to be the same as something, or to have the same effect as something:

His behaviour amounted to serious professional misconduct. ◦ *He gave what amounted to an apology on behalf of his company.*

amour propre /ˌæ.muəˈprɒ.prə/ ⓤⓢ /ˌɑː.mʊrˈproʊ-/ noun [U] literary a belief and confidence in your own ability and value

amp /æmp/ noun [C] **ELECTRICITY** ▷ **1** (formal **ampere** /ˈæm.peəʳ/ ⓤⓢ /-pɪr/) the standard unit of measurement for the strength of an electrical current: *a 30-amp fuse* **SOUND** ▷ **2** informal an **amplifier**

amperage /ˈæm.pə.rɪdʒ/ ⓤⓢ /-prɪdʒ/ noun [U] the strength of electrical current needed to make a piece of electrical equipment work

ampersand /ˈæm.pə.sænd/ ⓤⓢ /-pɚ-/ noun [C] the sign (&) used for 'and'

amphetamine /æmˈfet.ə.miːn/, /-mɪn/ ⓤⓢ /-fet̬-/ noun [C or U] any of several types of drug used as a STIMULANT (= a substance that makes the mind or body more active): *Floyd was banned from racing after a drug test revealed traces of amphetamine in his urine.*

amphibian /æmˈfɪb.i.ən/ noun [C] an animal, such as a FROG, that lives both on land and in water but must produce its eggs in water

amphibious /æmˈfɪb.i.əs/ adj **1** of or relating to a type of animal that lives both on land and in water: *amphibious animals* **2** relating to vehicles that operate both on land and in water: *amphibious vehicles/aircraft* ◦ *an amphibious landing/attack* (= *from the sea onto the land*)

amphitheatre

amphitheatre mainly UK (US usually **amphitheater**) /ˈæm.fɪˌθɪə.təʳ/ ⓤⓢ /-fəˌθiː.ə.t̬ɚ/ noun [C] **1** a circular or oval area of ground around which rows of seats are arranged on a steep slope, for watching plays, sports, etc. outside **2** a large hall for LECTURES in which the rows of seats are arranged on a slope

amphora /ˈæm.fᵊr.ə/ ⓤⓢ /-fɚ.ə/ noun [C] (plural **amphorae** /-iː/ or **amphoras**) a long, narrow clay container, wider at the top than at the base, that has two handles and was used in ancient times especially for storing oil or wine

ample /ˈæm.pl/ adj **ENOUGH** ▷ **1** Ⓒ1 more than enough: *You'll have ample* ***opportunity*** *to ask questions after the talk.* ◦ *There's ample* ***evidence*** *that the lawyer knew exactly what she was doing.* ◦ *They had ample warning of the factory closure.* **FAT** ▷ **2** humorous If the shape of someone's body or part of their body is ample, it is large: *her ample* ***bosom*** • **amply** /-pli/ adv *They face a hard task, as yesterday's discussions amply (= clearly) demonstrated.*

amplification /ˌæm.plɪ.fɪˈkeɪ.ʃᵊn/ noun [U] **1** Amplification makes music or other sounds louder: *electronic amplification* **2** formal added detail: *The horror lies in the violence itself, which needs no amplification.*

amplifier /ˈæm.plɪ.faɪ.əʳ/ ⓤⓢ /-ɚ/ noun [C] (informal **amp**) an electrical device that makes sounds louder

amplify /ˈæm.plɪ.faɪ/ verb [T] **1** to make something louder: *amplified music/guitar* **2** formal to increase the size or effect of something: *A funeral can amplify the feelings of regret and loss for the relatives.*

amplitude /ˈæm.plɪ.tjuːd/ ⓤⓢ /-tuːd/ noun **LARGE** ▷ **AMOUNT** ▷ **1** [U] formal a large amount or wide range: *The sheer amplitude of the novel invites comparisons with Tolstoy.* **CURVE** ▷ **2** [C usually singular] specialized the distance between the top and the bottom of a wave

ampoule /ˈæm.puːl/ noun [C] (US also **ampule** /ˈæm.pjuːl/) a small, usually glass, container for a single measured amount of medicine, especially for an INJECTION

amputate /ˈæm.pjʊ.teɪt/ verb [T or I] to cut off a part of the body: *They had to amputate his foot to free him from the wreckage.* ◦ *In these cases there is no choice but to amputate.* • **amputation** /ˌæm.pjʊˈteɪ.ʃᵊn/ noun [U or C] *Amputation of the limb is really a last resort.* ◦ *Most amputations in this region are the result of accidents with land mines.*

amputee /ˌæm.pjʊˈtiː/ noun [C] a person who has had an arm or leg cut off

amuck /əˈmʌk/ adv **amok**

amulet /ˈæm.jʊ.lət/ ⓤⓢ /-jə-/ noun [C] an object worn because it is believed to protect against evil, disease, or unhappiness

amuse /əˈmjuːz/ verb [I or T] **1** Ⓑ2 to entertain someone, especially by humorous speech or action or by making them laugh or smile: *I've brought an article from yesterday's paper that I thought might amuse you.* ◦ [+ obj + to infinitive] *I think* ***it*** *amuses him* ***to*** *see people make fools of themselves.* ◦ *Apparently these stories are meant to amuse.* **2** Ⓑ2 to keep someone happy, especially for a short time: *We amused our****selves*** *by watching the passers-by.* ◦ *Shall I put on a video to amuse the kids?*

amused /əˈmjuːzd/ adj **1** Ⓑ2 showing that you think something is funny: *an amused smile* ◦ *She was very amused* ***by/at*** *your comments.* **2 keep sb amused** Ⓑ2 to keep someone interested and help them to have an enjoyable time: *Toddlers don't need expensive toys and games to keep them amused.*

IDIOM **be not amused** to be annoyed: *I told Helena about what had happened and she was not amused.*

amusement /əˈmjuːz.mənt/ noun **1** Ⓑ2 [U] the feeling of being entertained or made to laugh: *She looked at him* ***with*** *amusement.* ◦ *I looked on* ***in*** *amusement as they started to argue.* ◦ *Carl came last in the race,* ***(much) to*** *my amusement.* ◦ *I play the piano just* ***for*** *my* ***own*** *amusement (= to entertain myself, not other people).* **2** Ⓑ2 [C] an activity that you can take part in for entertainment: *There was a range of* ***fairground*** *amusements, including rides, stalls, and competitions.*

aˈmusement arˌcade noun [C] a place in which you can pay to play games on machines

aˈmusement ˌpark noun [C] a **funfair** or **theme park**

amusing /əˈmjuː.zɪŋ/ adj Ⓑ1 entertaining: *an amusing story/person/situation* • **amusingly** /-li/ adv

amylase /ˈæm.ɪ.leɪz/ noun [U] specialized an ENZYME (= a chemical substance made by living cells) in SALIVA, plants, and in the PANCREAS that helps change STARCH into sugar

amyl nitrite /ˌæm.ᵊlˈnaɪ.traɪt/, /ˌeɪ.mᵊlˈ-/ noun [U] (also **ˌamyl ˈnitrate**) a drug that can be used for increasing pleasure during sex and was originally used for treating ANGINA

an weak /ən/ strong /æn/ determiner Ⓐ1 used instead of 'a' when the following word begins with a vowel sound: *an orange* ◦ *an honour* ◦ *an easy question* ◦ *an interesting story*

A

! Common mistake: an or and?

Warning: Choose the right word!
These two words look similar, but they are spelled differently and have completely different meanings.

-an /-ən/ **suffix** (also **-ean**, **-ian**) connected with or belonging to the stated place, group, or type: *an American* ◦ *a Canadian* ◦ *a Korean* ◦ *a Christian* ◦ *Russian literature* ◦ *Italian opera*

anabolic steroid /ˌæn.ə.bɒl.ɪkˈster.ɔɪd/, /-ˈstɪə.rɔɪd/ (US) /-bɑː.lɪkˈster.ɔɪd/, /-ˈstɪr.ɔɪd/ **noun** [C] a HORMONE (= a chemical made by living cells) that causes muscle and bone growth. Anabolic steroids are sometimes used illegally by ATHLETES competing in sports competitions: *He was disqualified after testing positive for anabolic steroids.*

anachronism /əˈnæk.rə.nɪ.zəm/ **noun** [C] a person, thing, or idea that exists out of its time in history, especially one that happened or existed later than the period being shown, discussed, etc.: *For some people, marriage is an anachronism from the days when women needed to be protected.* • **anachronistic** /əˌnæk.rəˈnɪs.tɪk/ **adj** *He described the law as anachronistic (= more suitable for an earlier time) and ridiculous.* • **anachronistically** /əˌnæk.rəˈnɪs.tɪ.kəl.i/ **adv**

anaconda /ˌæn.əˈkɒn.də/ (US) /-ˈkɑːn-/ **noun** [C] a large South American snake that curls around a live animal and crushes it to kill it for food

anaemia (mainly US **anemia**) /əˈniː.mi.ə/ **noun** [U] a medical condition in which there are not enough red blood cells in the blood: *The main symptoms of anaemia are tiredness and pallor.*

anaemic (mainly US **anemic**) /əˈniː.mɪk/ **adj 1** suffering from anaemia: *Lack of iron in your diet can make you anaemic.* **2** without any energy and effort: *Both actors gave fairly anaemic performances.*

anaerobic /ˌæn.əˈrəʊ.bɪk/ (US) /-ˈroʊ-/ **adj** specialized not needing or without OXYGEN: *Some bacteria can only live in anaerobic* ***conditions***. ◦ *anaerobic exercise* → Compare **aerobic (aerobics)**

anaesthesia (mainly US **anesthesia**) /ˌæn.əsˈθiː.zi.ə/, /-ʒə/ **noun** [U] **1** a state in which someone does not feel pain, usually because of drugs they have been given **2** specialized the quality of being unable to feel heat, cold, pain, touch, etc.

anaesthetic (mainly US **anesthetic**) /ˌæn.əsˈθet.ɪk/ (US) /-ˈθet̬-/ **noun** [C or U] a substance that makes you unable to feel pain: *The operation is performed* ***under*** *anaesthetic.* ◦ *The procedure is carried out under* ***local*** *anaesthetic (= a substance that makes you unable to feel pain in part of your body).* ◦ *I've never had a* ***general*** *anaesthetic (= a substance that makes you unconscious so you do not feel pain).*

anaesthetist (mainly US **anesthetist**) /əˈniːs.θə.tɪst/ (US) /-ˈnes.θə.t̬ɪst/ **noun** [C] a doctor who gives anaesthetic to people in hospital • **anaesthetize** (UK usually **anaesthetise**, mainly US **anesthetize**) /-taɪz/ **verb** [T]

anagram /ˈæn.ə.græm/ **noun** [C] a word or phrase made by using the letters of another word or phrase in a different order: *'Neat' is an anagram* ***of*** *'a net'.*

anal /ˈeɪ.nəl/ **adj** **BODY PART** ▷ **1** relating to the ANUS (= the opening at end of the INTESTINES through which solid waste leaves the body): *the anal passage/sphincter* ◦ *anal sex* **MENTAL STATE** ▷ **2** informal **anally retentive**: *his anal fondness for filing* • **anally** /-i/ **adv**

analgesic /ˌæn.əlˈdʒiː.zɪk/ **noun** [C] a type of drug that stops you from feeling pain: *This cream contains a mild analgesic to soothe stings and bites.* • **analgesic adj** *analgesic properties*

ˌanally reˈtentive **adj** (also **ˌanal-reˈtentive**) describes someone who is too worried about being organized and tidy

analogue /ˈæn.ə.lɒg/ (US) /-lɑːg/ **adj; noun**
▸**adj** (US also **analog**) **SOUND** ▷ **1** describes a recording that is made by changing the sound waves into electrical signals of the same type → Compare **digital** **WATCH** ▷ **2 analogue clock/watch** a clock/watch that shows the time using numbers around the edge and HANDS that point to the numbers → Compare **digital**
▸**noun** [C] formal (US also **analog**) something that is similar to or can be used instead of something else: *He has been studying the European analogues* ***of*** *the British Parliament.*

analogy /əˈnæl.ə.dʒi/ **noun** [C or U] (C2) a comparison between things that have similar features, often used to help explain a principle or idea: *He* ***drew*** *an analogy* ***between*** *the brain and a vast computer.* ◦ *It is sometimes easier to illustrate an abstract concept* ***by*** *analogy* ***with*** *(= by comparing it with) something concrete.* • **analogous** /əˈnæl.ə.gəs/ **adj** (C2) *The experience of mystic trance is in a sense analogous* ***to*** *sleep or drunkenness.*

analyse UK (US **analyze**) /ˈæn.əl.aɪz/ **verb** [T] (B2) to study or examine something in detail, in order to discover more about it: *Researchers analysed the purchases of 6,300 households.* ◦ *Water samples taken from streams were analysed* ***for*** *contamination by chemicals.*

analysis /əˈnæl.ə.sɪs/ **noun** [C or U] (plural **analyses** /-siːz/) (B2) the act of analysing something: *Chemical analysis revealed a high content of copper.* ◦ *I was interested in Clare's analysis* ***of*** *(= examination of and judgment about) the situation.*

IDIOM **in the last/final analysis** something you say when you are talking about what is most important or true in a situation: *In the final analysis, the only people who will benefit are property owners.*

analyst /ˈæn.ə.lɪst/ **noun** [C] **1** (B2) someone whose job is to study or examine something in detail: *a financial/food/political/systems analyst* **2 psychoanalyst (psychoanalyse)**

analytical /ˌæn.əˈlɪt.ɪ.kəl/ (US) /-ˈlɪt̬-/ **adj** (formal **analytic** /ˌæn.əlˈɪt.ɪk/ (US) /-əˈlɪt̬-/) (C1) examining or liking to examine things very carefully: *He has a very analytical* ***mind***. ◦ *Some students have a more analytical* ***approach*** *to learning.* • **analytically** /-ɪ.kəl.i/ **adv**

anarchic /əˈnɑː.kɪk/ (US) /-ˈnɑːr-/ **adj 1** not showing respect for official or accepted rules, behaviour, organizations, leaders, etc.: *Milligan's anarchic humour has always had the power to offend as well as entertain.* **2** without organization or control, especially describing a society with no government or a very weak government

anarchism /ˈæn.ə.kɪ.zəm/ (US) /-ɚ-/ **noun** [U] the political belief that there should be little or no formal or official organization to society but that people should work freely together

anarchist /ˈæn.ə.kɪst/ (US) /-ɚ-/ **noun** [C] **1** a person who believes in anarchism: *an anarchist group/slogan/bookshop* **2** disapproving someone who wishes to destroy the existing government and laws • **anarchistic** /ˌæn.əˈkɪs.tɪk/ (US) /-ɚ-/ **adj**

anarchy /ˈæn.ə.ki/ (US) /-ɚ-/ **noun** [U] a situation in which there is no organization and control, especially in society, because there is no effective government: *What we are witnessing is the country's slow slide into*

A

anarchy. ◦ *The country has been in* ***a state of*** *anarchy since the inconclusive election.* ◦ *If the pay deal isn't settled amicably there'll be anarchy in the factories.*

anathema /əˈnæθ.ə.mə/ **noun** [C usually singular, U] something that is strongly disliked or disapproved of: *Credit controls are anathema* ***to*** *the government.*

anaˌtomically corˈrect **adj** showing the body of a person or animal accurately, including the sexual organs: *an anatomically correct doll*

anatomy /əˈnæt.ə.mi/ (US) /-ˈnæt̬-/ **noun** **1** [U] the scientific study of the body and how its parts are arranged: *An understanding of human anatomy is important to a dancer.* ◦ *He later became professor of anatomy at Kiel.* **2** [C or U] the structure of an animal or plant: *the female anatomy* ◦ *the anatomy of a leaf* **3** [C] humorous a person's body: *On which part of her anatomy is she tattooed?* **4** [C] formal a detailed examination of a subject: *The whole play reads like an anatomy* ***of*** *evil.* • **anatomical** /ˌæn.əˈtɒm.ɪ.kəl/ (US) /-ˈtɑː.mɪ-/ **adj** *anatomical drawings* • **anatomically** /ˌæn.əˈtɒm.ɪ.kəl.i/ (US) /-ˈtɑː.mɪ-/ **adv**

-ance /-əns/ **suffix** **-ence**

ancestor /ˈæn.ses.tər/ (US) /-tɚ/ **noun** [C] **1** (B2) a person related to you who lived a long time ago: *There were portraits of his ancestors on the walls of the room.* → Compare **descendant** **2** a plant, animal, or object that is related to one existing at a later point in time: *This wooden instrument is the ancestor of the modern metal flute.* • **ancestral** /ænˈses.trəl/ **adj** [before noun] *an ancestral home* ◦ *ancestral rights*

ancestry /ˈæn.ses.tri/ **noun** [U or C] your ancestors who lived a long time ago, or the origin of your family: *He was proud of his Native American ancestry.* ◦ *His wife was* ***of*** *royal ancestry.* ◦ *The family has* ***traced*** *its ancestry* ***back to*** *the Norman invaders.*

anchor /ˈæŋ.kər/ (US) /-kɚ/ **noun**; **verb**

anchor

▸**noun** [C] **ON A BOAT** ▷ **1** (C2) a heavy metal object, usually shaped like a cross with curved arms, on a strong rope or chain, that is dropped from a boat into the water to prevent the boat from moving away: *We* ***dropped*** *anchor (= lowered the anchor into the water) and stopped.* ◦ *It was time to* ***weigh*** *anchor (= pull up the anchor and sail away).* **SUPPORT** ▷ **2** (C2) someone or something that gives support when needed: *She was my anchor when things were difficult for me.* ◦ *This treaty has been called the anchor (= strongest part) of their foreign policy.* **BROADCASTER** ▷ **3** mainly US an **anchorman** or **anchorwoman**

▸**verb** **FASTEN** ▷ **1** (C2) [I or T] to lower an anchor into the water in order to stop a boat from moving away **2** (C2) [T] to make something or someone stay in one position by fastening them firmly: *We anchored ourselves* ***to*** *the rocks with a rope.* **BROADCAST** ▷ **3** [T] mainly US to act as the ANCHORMAN or ANCHORWOMAN of a programme: *She will anchor the new morning news show.*

anchorage /ˈæŋ.kər.ɪdʒ/ (US) /-kɚ-/ **noun** [C or U] **1** a place where a boat is or can be anchored: *The bay is well known as a safe anchorage.* **2** a place where something is fastened firmly: *The anchorage* ***point*** *(= fixing point) for the seat belt is not adjustable.*

anchorite /ˈæŋ.kər.aɪt/ (US) /-kɚ-/ **noun** [C] someone who lives alone away from other people for religious reasons → Synonym **hermit**

anchorman /ˈæŋ.kə.mæn/ (US) /-kɚ-/ **noun** [C] (plural **-men** /-men/) US a man who is the main news reader on a television or radio news programme: *The late-night current affairs show has a new anchorman.*

anchorwoman /ˈæŋ.kəˌwʊm.ən/ (US) /-kɚ-/ **noun** [C] (plural **-women** /-ˌwɪmɪn/) US a female anchorman

anchovy /ˈæn.tʃə.vi/ (US) /ˈæn.tʃoʊ-/ **noun** [C or U] (plural **anchovies**) a small fish with a strong, salty taste: *Decorate the top of the pizza with anchovies/strips of anchovy.*

ancien régime /ɒn.sjæn.reɪˈʒiːm/ (US) /ˌɑːn.si.æn.rə-/ **noun** [U] formal an old system, especially a political or social one, that has been replaced by a more modern system

ancient /ˈeɪn.ʃənt/ **adj** **1** (B1) of or from a long time ago, having lasted for a very long time: *ancient civilizations/rights/laws* ◦ *ancient monuments/ruins/woodlands* ◦ *the ancient kingdoms of Mexico* ◦ *People have lived in this valley since ancient* ***times.*** ◦ *History, ancient* ***and modern,*** *has taught these people an intense distrust of their neighbours.* **2** informal very old: *He's got an ancient computer.* **3** (B1) describes the period in European history from the earliest known societies to the end of the Roman EMPIRE: *the ancient Egyptians/Greeks/Romans* ◦ *The ancient Britons inhabited these parts of England before the Roman invasion.*

ancillary /ænˈsɪl.ər.i/ (US) /ˈæn.sə.ler.i/ **adj** providing support or help: *ancillary staff/workers* ◦ *an ancillary role* ◦ *Campaigning to change government policy is ancillary* ***to*** *the charity's direct relief work.*

-ancy /-ən.si/ **suffix** → **-ency**

and strong /ænd/ weak /ənd/ /ən/ **conjunction** **ALSO** ▷ **1** (A1) used to join two words, phrases, parts of sentences, or related statements together: *Ann and Jim* ◦ *boys and girls* ◦ *knives and forks* ◦ *We were wet and tired.* ◦ *We kissed and hugged each other.* ◦ *Tidy up your room. And don't forget to make your bed!* **2 and so on** (A2) (also **and so forth**) together with other similar things: *schools, colleges, and so on* **3 and all** **a** and everything else: *She bought the whole lot – house, farm, horses, and all.* **b** UK slang too: *I'd like some and all.* **4 and all that** informal and everything related to the subject mentioned: *She likes grammar and all that.* **5 and/or** used to mean that either one of two things or both of them is possible: *Many pupils have extra classes in the evenings and/or at weekends.* **THEN** ▷ **6** (A1) used to join two parts of a sentence, one part happening after the other part: *I got dressed and had my breakfast.* **7** as a result: *Bring the flowers into a warm room and they'll soon open.* ◦ *Stand over there and you'll be able to see it better.* **8** (A2) With certain verbs, 'and' can mean 'in order to': *I asked him to* ***go*** *and find my glasses.* ◦ *Come and see me tomorrow.* ◦ ***Wait*** *and* ***see*** *(= wait in order to see) what happens.* ◦ informal ***Try*** *and get (= try to get) some tickets for tonight's performance.* **FOR EMPHASIS** ▷ **9** (B1) If 'and' is used to join two words that are the same, it makes their meaning stronger: *She spends hours and hours (= a very long time) on the phone.* ◦ *The sound grew louder and louder (= very loud).* ◦ *We laughed and laughed (= laughed a lot).* **BUT** ▷ **10** used to express surprise: *You're a vegetarian and you eat fish?*

andante /ænˈdæn.teɪ/ (US) /ɑːnˈdɑːn.teɪ/ **noun**; **adj**, **adv**

▸**noun** [C usually singular] specialized a piece of music that should be played quite slowly: *Andante in A minor*

▸**adj**, **adv** specialized (played) quite slowly: *the andante movement* ◦ *The second movement of the symphony should be played andante.*

androgynous /æn'drɒdʒ.ɪ.nəs/ (US) /-'drɑː.dʒɪ-/ **adj** **1** not clearly male or female: *With her lean frame and cropped hair, Lennox had a fashionably androgynous look.* **2** specialized having both male and female features • **androgyny** /-ni/ **noun** [U] *One or two of the earlier photos reveal an intriguing androgyny not normally associated with the actress.*

android /'æn.drɔɪd/ **noun** [C] a ROBOT (= machine controlled by computer) that is made to look like a human

anecdotal /ˌæn.ɪk'dəʊ.təl/ (US) /-'doʊ.ţəl/ **adj** describes information that is not based on facts or careful study: *anecdotal* ***evidence***

anecdote /'æn.ɪk.dəʊt/ (US) /-doʊt/ **noun** [C] a short, often funny story, especially about something someone has done: *He told one or two amusing anecdotes about his years as a policeman.*

anemia /ə'niː.mi.ə/ **noun** [U] mainly US for **anaemia**

anemometer /ˌæn.ɪ'mɒm.ɪ.tər/ (US) /-mɑː.mə.ţɚ/ **noun** [C] specialized a device that measures the speed and force of wind

anemone /ə'nem.ə.ni/ **noun** [C] any of several types of small plant, wild or grown in gardens, with red, blue, or white flowers

anesthesia /ˌæn.əs'θiː.zi.ə/, /-ʒə/ **noun** [U] mainly US for **anaesthesia**

anesthesiologist /ˌæn.əsˌθiː.zi'ɒl.ə.dʒɪst/ (US) /-'ɑːl.ə-/ **noun** [C] US specialized **anesthetist**

anesthetic /ˌæn.əs'θet.ɪk/ (US) /-'θeţ-/ **noun** [C] mainly US for **anaesthetic**

anesthetist /ə'niːs.θə.tɪst/ (US) /-'nes.θə.ţɪst/ **noun** [C] US for **anaesthetist**

anew /ə'njuː/ (US) /-'nuː/ **adv** formal again or one more time, especially in a different way: *The film tells anew the story of his rise to fame and power.*

angel /'eɪn.dʒəl/ **noun** [C] **1** (B1) a spiritual being in some religions who is believed to be a messenger of God, usually represented as having a human form with wings **2** someone who is very good, helpful, or kind: ***Be an*** *angel and help me with this.* **3** [as form of address] used when speaking to someone you like very much and know very well: *What's the matter, angel?* ◦ *Come along, my angels, time for bed.*

IDIOMS **be no angel** to sometimes behave badly: *He's no angel but he can't be blamed for everything that has happened.* • **be on the side of the angels** UK to be doing something good or kind: *He was, in this matter at least, firmly on the side of the angels.*

ˈangel ˌhair **noun** [U] a type of PASTA in the shape of very thin threads

angelic /æn'dʒel.ɪk/ **adj** very beautiful and very good: *an angelic voice/face/smile* • **angelically** /-ɪ.kəl.i/ **adv**

angelica /æn'dʒel.ɪ.kə/ **noun** [U] the green stem of a plant, boiled in sugar and used for decorating cakes and other sweet food, or the plant itself: *strips of angelica*

the Angelus /'æn.dʒəl.əs/ **noun** [S] **1** prayers said in the morning, in the middle of the day and in the evening in the Roman Catholic Church **2** the ringing of bells to show that it is time for these prayers

anger /'æŋ.gər/ (US) /-gɚ/ **noun; verb**

▸**noun** [U] (B2) a strong feeling that makes you want to hurt someone or be unpleasant because of something unfair or unkind that has happened: *I think he feels a lot of anger* ***towards*** *his father, who treated him very badly as a child.* ◦ *There is a danger that anger* ***at*** *the new law may turn into anti-government feeling.*

> **Word partners for anger noun**
>
> *express/show/voice* your anger • *arouse/provoke/spark* anger • *growing/mounting/widespread* anger • *pent-up/simmering/suppressed* anger • *public* anger • do sth *in* anger • anger *at/over/towards* sb/sth

▸**verb** [T] to make someone angry: *The remark angered him.* ◦ *It always angers me to see so much waste.*

angina pectoris /ænˌdʒaɪ.nə'pek.tə.rɪs/ (US) /-tɚ-/ **noun** [U] (also **angina**) a disease that repeatedly causes sudden strong pains in the chest because blood containing OXYGEN is prevented from reaching the heart muscle by blocked ARTERIES (= thick tubes carrying blood from the heart)

angioplasty /'æn.dʒi.əʊˌplæs.ti/ (US) /-oʊ-/ **noun** [C or U] specialized a medical operation to remove something blocking an ARTERY (= thick tube carrying blood from the heart) in a person who has angina

angle /'æŋ.gl/ **noun; verb**

▸**noun** [C] **SPACE BETWEEN LINES** ▷ **1** (C1) the space between two lines or surfaces at the point at which they touch each other, measured in degrees: *The interior angles of a square are* ***right*** *angles or angles* ***of*** *90* ***degrees.*** ◦ *The boat settled into the mud* ***at*** *a 35° angle/at an angle* ***of*** *35°.* **2 at an angle** (C1) not horizontal or vertical, but sloping in one direction: *The picture was hanging at an angle.* ◦ *He wore his hat at a* ***jaunty*** *angle.* **3** the corner of a building, table, or anything with straight sides **POSITION** ▷ **4** (C1) a position from which something is looked at: *The tower is visible* ***from*** *every angle/all angles.* ◦ *I realized I was looking at it* ***from*** *the wrong angle.* **WAY OF THINKING** ▷ **5** (C1) a way of considering, judging, or dealing with something: *Try looking at the problem* ***from*** *another angle/****from*** *my angle.* ◦ *The press was looking for a* ***new/fresh*** *angle* ***on*** *the situation.*

▸**verb** [T] **SLOPE** ▷ **1** to aim, turn, or position something in a direction that is not horizontal or vertical: *The stage had been steeply angled (= was sloping very noticeably).* **DIRECT** ▷ **2** to direct information at a particular group of people: *The magazine is angled* ***at*** *the 20 to 35-year-old women's market.* • **angled** /'æŋ.gld/ **adj** *His angled shot (= from the side, not from straight in front) beat the goalkeeper from 20 yards.*

PHRASAL VERB **angle for sth** disapproving If someone is angling for something, they are trying to get something without asking for it directly: *He's clearly angling for a job/an invitation.*

ˈangle ˌbracket **noun** [C] the symbol < or >, found on a computer keyboard and used, for example, around TAGS (= codes for marking particular types of information)

angler /'æŋ.glər/ (US) /-glɚ/ **noun** [C] a person whose hobby is catching fish

Anglican /'æŋ.glɪ.kən/ **adj; noun**

▸**adj** relating to the Church of England, or an international Church connected with it: *an Anglican priest*

▸**noun** [C] a member of the Anglican church: *He's an Anglican.* • **Anglicanism** /'æŋ.glɪ.kə.nɪ.zəm/ **noun** [U]

Anglicism /'æŋ.glɪ.sɪ.zəm/ **noun** [C] an English word or phrase that is used in another language: *'Le weekend' is an Anglicism used by the French.*

anglicize (UK usually **anglicise**) /'æŋ.glɪ.saɪz/ **verb** [T] to make or become English in sound, appearance, or character: *She married Norwegian immigrant Niels Larsen, who later anglicized his name.*

A

angling /ˈæŋ.glɪŋ/ noun [U] the sport of trying to catch fish with a rod, LINE (= plastic thread), and HOOK (= curved piece of wire)

Anglo- /ˈæŋ.gləʊ-/ US /-gloʊ-/ prefix relating to England or the UK: *an Anglophile (= someone who loves England)*

ˌAnglo-Aˈmerican adj describes something involving the UK and US: *an Anglo-American agreement*

ˌAnglo-ˈCatholic adj refers to the group in the Anglican Church whose religious practice is similar to that of the Roman Catholic Church

ˌAnglo-ˈIndian noun [C] **1** a person with British and Indian parents or grandparents **2** old-fashioned an English person born or living in India • **ˌAnglo-ˈIndian** adj

anglophile /ˈæŋ.glə.faɪl/ noun [C] a person who is not English but is interested in, likes, or supports England or the UK

anglophone /ˈæŋ.glə.fəʊn/ US /-foʊn/ noun [C] specialized a person who speaks English, especially in countries where other languages are also spoken • **anglophone** adj *The anglophone countries of Africa include Kenya and Zimbabwe.*

ˌAnglo-ˈSaxon adj; noun
▸adj **1** describes the people who lived in England from about 600 AD and their language and customs **2** describes modern societies that are based on or influenced by English customs
▸noun **PERSON** ▷ **1** [C] one of the Anglo-Saxon people → See also **WASP** **LANGUAGE** ▷ **2** [U] the language of the Anglo-Saxon people

angora /æŋˈgɔː.rə/ US /-ˈgɔːr.ə/ noun [U] the wool or material made from the long, soft hair of a type of RABBIT or GOAT: *an angora sweater*

Angostura /ˌæŋ.gəˈstjʊə.rə/ US /-ˈstʊr.ə/ noun [U] (also **ˌAngostura ˈbitters**) trademark a bitter liquid that can be used to flavour alcoholic drinks

angrez /ʌŋˈreɪz/ noun; adj
▸noun [C] (plural **angrez**) Indian English an English person
▸adj Indian English English

angry /ˈæŋ.gri/ adj **EMOTIONAL** ▷ **1** A2 having a strong feeling against someone who has behaved badly, making you want to shout at them or hurt them: *He's really angry **at/with** me for upsetting Sophie.* ◦ *I don't understand what he's angry **about**.* ◦ [+ that] *They feel angry **that** their complaints were ignored.* ◦ *I **got** really angry **with** her.* ◦ *It made me really angry.* **STORMY** ▷ **2** literary An angry sea or sky is one where there is a storm, or where it looks as if there will be a storm soon. **PAINFUL** ▷ **3** If an infected area of the body is angry, it is red and painful: *On her leg was an angry sore.* • **angrily** /-grɪ.li/ adv B1 *'Don't do that!' she shouted angrily.* ◦ *The prime minister **reacted** angrily to claims that he had lied to the House of Commons.*

angst /æŋst/ US /ɑːŋst/ noun [U] strong worry and unhappiness, especially about personal problems: *All my children went through a period of late-adolescent angst.*

anguish /ˈæŋ.gwɪʃ/ noun [U] extreme unhappiness caused by physical or mental suffering: *His anguish **at** the outcome of the court case was very clear.* ◦ ***In** her anguish she forgot to leave a message.* • **anguished** /ˈæŋ.gwɪʃt/ adj *an anguished cry*

angular /ˈæŋ.gjʊ.ləʳ/ US /-lɚ/ adj **1** having or relating to one or more angles **2** having a clear shape with sharp points: *Her features were too angular, her face a little too long for beauty.* • **angularity** /ˌæŋ.gjʊˈlær.ɪ.ti/ US /-ˈler.ə.ti/ noun [U]

> **Other ways of saying angry**
>
> See also: **annoy, bad-tempered**
>
> If someone is angry about something that has happened, you can say that this person is **annoyed** or **irritated**:
>
> *He was a bit **annoyed** with her for being late.*
> *I was **irritated** that he didn't thank me.*
>
> If someone is extremely angry, you can use adjectives such as **furious, irate**, or **livid**:
>
> *My boss was **furious** with me.*
> *Hundreds of **irate** passengers have complained to the airline.*
>
> If you are angry with a child, you might describe yourself as **cross**:
>
> *I'm **cross** with you for not telling me where you were going.*
>
> The expression **up in arms** is sometimes used when people are angry about something they think is unfair:
>
> *Local people are **up in arms** over plans to close the local swimming pool.*
>
> If someone suddenly becomes very angry, you can use the informal expression **go crazy** or the idiom **hit the roof**:
>
> *Dad **went crazy** when he found out we'd broken the window.*
>
> An angry argument can be described as **heated** or **acrimonious**:
>
> *He was involved in an **acrimonious** dispute with his neighbour.*

animal /ˈæn.ɪ.məl/ noun; adj
▸noun [C] **CREATURE** ▷ **1** A1 something that lives and moves but is not a human, bird, fish, or insect: *wild/domestic animals* ◦ *Both children are real animal **lovers**.* ◦ *Surveys show that animal **welfare** has recently become a major concern for many schoolchildren.* **2** B2 anything that lives and moves, including people, birds, etc.: *Humans, insects, reptiles, birds, and mammals are all animals.* **BAD PERSON** ▷ **3** informal an unpleasant, cruel person or someone who behaves badly: *He's a real animal when he's had too much to drink.* **TYPE** ▷ **4** used to describe what type of person or thing someone or something is: *At heart she is a political animal.* ◦ *She is that **rare** animal (= she is very unusual), a brilliant scientist who can communicate her ideas to ordinary people.* ◦ *Feminism in France and England are rather different animals (= are different).*
▸adj **FROM ANIMALS** ▷ **1** made or obtained from an animal or animals: *animal products* ◦ *animal fat/skins* **2** relating to, or taking the form of, an animal or animals rather than a plant or human being: *The island was devoid of all animal life (= there were no animals on the island).* **PHYSICAL** ▷ **3** [before noun] relating to physical DESIRES or needs, and not spiritual or mental ones: *As an actor, he has a sort of animal **magnetism**.* ◦ *She knew that Dave wasn't the right man for her but she couldn't deny the animal **attraction** between them.*

the ˈanimal ˌkingdom noun [S] the group of all living creatures that are animals

animate adj; verb
▸adj /ˈæn.ɪ.mət/ having life: *animate beings*
▸verb [T] /ˈæn.ɪ.meɪt/ to make someone seem more happy or active: *A sparkle in his eyes animated his face whenever he smiled.*

A

animated /ˈæn.ɪ.meɪ.tɪd/ (US) /-t̬ɪd/ **adj** ENERGETIC ▷ **1** C2 full of interest and energy: *There was an extremely animated discussion on the subject.* ◦ *They must have been having an interesting conversation – they both looked very animated.* IMAGE ▷ **2** describes films, drawings, models, etc. that are photographed and shown in a way that makes them move and appear to be alive • **animatedly** /-li/ **adv** *They were talking animatedly.*

animation /ˌæn.ɪˈmeɪ.ʃən/ **noun** ENERGY ▷ **1** [U] enthusiasm and energy: *She spoke with great animation about her latest discoveries.* IMAGE ▷ **2** [C or U] moving pictures: *Encyclopedias on CD-ROM include sound, illustrations, and simple animations.* ◦ *Thanks to* ***computer*** *animation, it is now possible to make cartoon films much more quickly than in the past.*

animator /ˈæn.ɪ.meɪ.təʳ/ (US) /-t̬ɚ/ **noun** [C] someone who makes ANIMATED films, drawings, models, etc.: *Walt Disney is the most famous animator of feature-length films.*

animatronics /ˌæn.ɪ.məˈtrɒn.ɪks/ (US) /-ˈtrɑː.nɪks/ **noun** [U] specialized the use of machines controlled by computers to make PUPPETS and models move in a natural way in films and other types of entertainment • **animatronic** /ˌæn.ɪ.məˈtrɒn.ɪk/ (US) /ˌæn.ɪ.məˈtrɑː.nɪk/ **adj** *The most popular exhibit in the museum was a giant animatronic dinosaur.*

anime /ˈæn.ɪ.meɪ/, /ˈæn.ɪ.mə/ **noun** [U or C] Japanese films made using characters and images that are drawn rather than real, or one of these films: *Until recently, anime had little more than a cult following outside Japan.* ◦ *an anime that blurs the line between man and machine*

animism /ˈæn.ɪ.mɪ.zəm/ **noun** [U] specialized the belief that all natural things, such as plants, animals, rocks, and thunder, have spirits and can influence human events • **animist** /-mɪst/ **noun** [C], **adj**

animosity /ˌæn.ɪˈmɒs.ɪ.ti/ (US) /-ˈmɑː.sə.t̬i/ **noun** [C or U] strong dislike, opposition, or anger: *Of course we're competitive, but there's no personal animosity* ***between*** *us.* ◦ *In spite of his injuries, he* ***bears no*** *animosity* ***towards*** *his attackers.*

anion /ˈæn.aɪən/ **noun** [C] specialized an ION with a negative electrical charge

anise /ˈæn.ɪs/, /ænˈiːs/ **noun** [U] a Mediterranean plant with small, yellowish-white flowers and seeds that taste of LIQUORICE, used to give this flavour to food and drink

aniseed /ˈæn.ɪ.siːd/ **noun** [U] the seeds of the anise plant, used to flavour sweet food and alcoholic drinks: *aniseed balls*

ankle /ˈæŋ.kl/ **noun** [C] B1 the JOINT (= place where two bones are connected) between the foot and the leg, or the thin part of the leg just above the foot: *I fell over and* ***sprained/twisted*** *my ankle.*

ˈankle ˌboot **noun** [C] a short boot that covers only the foot and ankle

ˈankle ˌsock **noun** [C] (US also **anklet**) a short sock that covers only the foot and ankle

anklet /ˈæŋ.klət/ **noun** [C] JEWELLERY ▷ **1** a chain or ring worn as jewellery around the ankle SOCK ▷ **2** US for **ankle sock**

annals /ˈæn.əlz/ **noun** [plural] formal historical records of the activities of a country or organization, or history in general: *The signing of the Treaty of Rome was the greatest event in the annals* ***of*** *European integration.* ◦ *Quite whether he will* ***go down in*** *the annals* ***of*** *American history (= be considered) as a great leader remains to be seen.*

anneal /əˈniːl/ **verb** [T] specialized to make metal or glass soft by heating and then cooling it slowly

annex /ænˈeks/ **verb** [T] to take possession of an area of land or a country, usually by force or without permission: *The UK annexed this small island west of Scotland in 1955.* • **annexation** /ˌæn.ekˈseɪ.ʃən/ **noun** [C or U]

annexe UK (US **annex**) /ˈæn.ɪks/ **noun** [C] an extra building added to a larger building: *Delicate and valuable books are kept in an air-conditioned annexe* ***to*** *the main library.*

annihilate /əˈnaɪ.ə.leɪt/ **verb** [T] **1** to destroy something completely so that nothing is left: *a city annihilated by an atomic bomb* **2** informal to defeat completely: *He was annihilated in the finals of the competition.* • **annihilation** /əˌnaɪ.əˈleɪ.ʃən/ **noun** [U] *During the Cold War the threat of nuclear annihilation was always on people's minds.* ◦ informal *The opposition party's candidate suffered annihilation (= complete defeat) at the polls.*

anniversary /ˌæn.ɪˈvɜː.sər.i/ (US) /-ˈvɝː.sɚ-/ **noun** [C] B1 the day on which an important event happened in a previous year: *We always celebrate our* ***wedding*** *anniversary with dinner in an expensive restaurant.* ◦ *Tomorrow is the 30th anniversary* ***of*** *the revolution.*

annotate /ˈæn.ə.teɪt/ **verb** [T] formal to add a short explanation or opinion to a text or drawing: *Annotated editions of Shakespeare's plays help readers to understand old words.* • **annotation** /ˌæn.əˈteɪ.ʃən/ **noun** [C or U] *The annotation of literary texts makes them more accessible.* ◦ *The revised edition of the book includes many useful annotations.*

announce /əˈnaʊns/ **verb** [T] **1** B1 to make something known or tell people about something officially: *They announced the death of their mother in the local paper.* ◦ *She announced the winner of the competition* ***to*** *an excited audience.* ◦ [+ that] *The prime minister has announced* ***that*** *public spending will be increased next year.* **2** to show that something is going to happen: *The first few leaves in the gutter announced the beginning of autumn.*

announcement /əˈnaʊns.mənt/ **noun** [C or U] **1** B1 something that someone says officially, giving information about something: *The president* ***made*** *an unexpected announcement this morning.* **2** the act of announcing something: *The announcement* ***of*** *the changes has been delayed.*

announcer /əˈnaʊn.səʳ/ (US) /-sɚ/ **noun** [C] someone who introduces programmes or reads the news on the television or radio: *a radio/TV announcer*

annoy /əˈnɔɪ/ **verb** [T] B1 to make someone angry: *Tim really annoyed me in the meeting this morning.* ◦ *I'm sorry – is my cough annoying you?* ◦ [+ that] ***It*** *annoys me* ***that*** *she just expects us to help.* ◦ ***It*** *really annoys me when people expect me to tip as well as pay a service charge in a restaurant.*

annoyance /əˈnɔɪ.əns/ **noun** **1** C1 [U] the feeling or state of being annoyed: *I can understand your annoyance – I'd be furious if she ever treated me like that.* ◦ ***(Much) to*** *our annoyance, (= we were very annoyed that) we couldn't see anything from the back row of the theatre.* **2** [C] something that makes you annoyed: *One of the greatest annoyances was being bitten by mosquitoes every night.*

annoyed /əˈnɔɪd/ **adj** B1 angry: *I was so annoyed* ***with*** *him for turning up late.* ◦ *He was annoyed* ***at*** *the way she tried to take over the whole meeting.* ◦ *My parents were rather annoyed* ***(that)*** *I hadn't told them*

A

Other ways of saying annoy

See also: **angry**

Irritate or **peeve** are alternatives to 'annoy':

*After a while her behaviour really began to **irritate** me.*

*What **peeved** her most was that he hadn't even called her.*

Bug or **aggravate** are informal ways of saying 'annoy':

*He's been **bugging** me all morning.*

*It really **aggravates** me the way he never thanks me for what I've done.*

A more formal way of saying 'annoy' would be to use the verb **irk**:

*The negative reply to my complaint really **irked** me.*

If something annoys you, especially because you can do nothing to change a situation, you could use the verb **exasperate**:

*Being dependent on other people **exasperated** her.*

If noise or behaviour annoys you, you could say that it **grates on** you:

*After a while, her voice really started to **grate on** me.*

about the accident. ◦ *She was annoyed **to** discover that her husband had taken her car keys.*

annoying /əˈnɔɪ.ɪŋ/ **adj** B1 making you feel annoyed: *It's really annoying when a train is late and there's no explanation.* ◦ *He's got a really annoying laugh.* • **annoyingly** /-li/ **adv** *Rather annoyingly, I'd just bought the hardback when the paperback edition came out.*

annual /ˈæn.ju.əl/, /-jʊl/ **adj**; **noun**

▸**adj** [before noun] **1** B1 happening once every year: *an annual event/visit/holiday* ◦ *Companies publish annual **reports** to inform the public about the previous year's activities.* **2** B1 relating to a period of one year: *annual income/salary/profit*

▸**noun** [C] **BOOK** ▷ **1** a book or magazine published once a year, especially for children, with the same title and style but different contents **2** US for **yearbook**: *a high school annual* **PLANT** ▷ **3** a plant that grows, produces seeds, and dies within one year → Compare **biennial, perennial**

ˌannual ˌgeneral ˈmeeting **noun** [C] UK (abbreviation **AGM**, US **ˌannual ˈmeeting**) a meeting that happens once every year in which a company or other organization discusses the past year's activities and elects new officers

annualized specialized (UK usually **annualised**) /ˈæn.ju.ə.laɪzd/, /-jʊ.laɪzd/ **adj** (of an amount or number) calculated over a year: *Exports fell at an annualized rate of 12.3 percent, while imports rose at a 7.5 percent pace.*

annually /ˈæn.ju.ə.li/, /-jʊ.li/ **adv** B2 once every year: *Your starting salary is £23,000 per annum and will be reviewed annually.*

annuity /əˈnjuː.ə.ti/ US /-t̬i/ **noun** [C] a fixed amount of money paid to someone every year, usually until their death, or the INSURANCE agreement or INVESTMENT that provides the money that is paid: *an annuity policy* ◦ *annuity income* ◦ *She receives a small annuity.*

annul /əˈnʌl/ **verb** [T] (**-ll-**) legal to officially announce that something such as a law, agreement, or marriage no longer exists: *His second marriage was annulled because he never divorced his first wife.* • **annulment** /-mənt/ **noun** [C or U] *Judges only **grant** marriage annulments in exceptional circumstances.*

annus horribilis /ˌæn.əs.həˈrɪ.bɪ.lɪs/ **noun** [S] formal a year of extremely bad events

annus mirabilis /ˌæn.əs.mɪˈrɑː.bɪ.lɪs/ **noun** [S] formal a year of extremely good events: *1969 was the annus mirabilis in which man first landed on the moon.*

anode /ˈæn.əʊd/ US /-oʊd/ **noun** [C] specialized one of the ELECTRODES (= objects that electricity moves through) in a piece of electrical equipment. The anode is the negative electrode in a BATTERY and the positive electrode in an ELECTROLYTIC cell. → Compare **cathode**

anodize specialized (UK usually **anodise**) /ˈæn.ə.daɪz/ US /-oʊ-/ **verb** [T] to cover a metal with a layer of OXIDE by using an electric current

anodyne /ˈæn.ə.daɪn/ US /-oʊ-/ **adj** formal mainly disapproving intended to avoid causing offence or disagreement, especially by not expressing strong feelings or opinions: *This is daytime television at its most anodyne.* ◦ *Somehow this avoids being just another silly pop song with anodyne lyrics about love and happiness.*

anoint /əˈnɔɪnt/ **verb** [T] **IN A CEREMONY** ▷ **1** to make someone holy in a religious ceremony by putting holy water or oil on them **2** to make someone king or queen, especially as part of a religious ceremony: [+ obj + noun] *In 751 Pepin was anointed king.* **FOR A JOB** ▷ **3** formal to choose someone to do a particular job, usually by a person in authority: [+ as + noun] *It remains to be seen whom the chairman will anoint **as** his successor.* • **anointed** /əˈnɔɪn.tɪd/ US /-t̬ɪd/ **adj** formal *He's generally believed to be the anointed **heir/successor** to (= the one who will be chosen for) the presidency.* • **anointment** /-mənt/ **noun** [U]

anomaly /əˈnɒm.ə.li/ US /-ˈnɑː.mə-/ **noun** [C or U] formal a person or thing that is different from what is usual, or not in agreement with something else and therefore not satisfactory: *Statistical anomalies can make it difficult to compare economic data from one year to the next.* ◦ *The anomaly of the social security system is that you sometimes have more money without a job.* • **anomalous** /-ləs/ **adj** *In a multicultural society is it not anomalous to have a blasphemy law that only protects one religious faith?* • **anomalously** /-ləs.li/ **adv**

anomie /ˈæn.əm.i/ **noun** [U] formal a state of no moral or social principles in a person or in society

anon. /əˈnɒn/ US /-ˈnɑːn/ abbreviation for ANONYMOUS (= a writer whose name is not known), usually written at the end of a piece of writing

anon /əˈnɒn/ US /-ˈnɑːn/ **adv** old use or humorous soon or in the near future: ***See you** anon.*

anonymity /ˌæn.ɒnˈɪm.ɪ.ti/ US /-əˈnɪm.ə.t̬i/ **noun** [U] the situation in which someone's name is not given or known: *The police have reassured witnesses that they will be guaranteed anonymity.*

anonymize /əˈnɒn.ɪ.maɪz/ US /-ˈnɑː.nə-/ **verb** [T] to remove any information that shows which particular person something relates to: *We anonymize the data so researchers cannot identify any individual subjects.* ◦ *anonymized medical records*

anonymous /əˈnɒn.ɪ.məs/ US /-ˈnɑː.nə-/ **adj** **1** C2 made or done by someone whose name is not known or not made public: *The money was donated by an anonymous **benefactor**.* ◦ *He received an anonymous **letter** threatening to disclose details of his affair if he didn't pay the money.* ◦ *For reasons of personal safety, the informant wishes to **remain** anonymous.* **2** having no unusual or interesting features: *He has a rather anonymous face.* • **anonymously** /-li/ **adv** *The donation was made anonymously.*

A

anopheles /əˈnɒf.ɪ.liːz/ (US) /-ˈnɑː.fə-/ **noun** [C] (plural **anopheles**) specialized a type of MOSQUITO (= small flying insect), especially one that spreads MALARIA to humans

anorak /ˈæn.ə.ræk/ **noun** [C] COAT ▷ **1** mainly UK (US usually **parka**) a short coat that protects the wearer against wind, rain, and cold weather, usually with a part for covering the head PERSON ▷ **2** UK disapproving a boring person who is too interested in the details of a hobby and finds it difficult to meet and spend time with other people: *There are enough facts and figures in this book to keep even the most obsessive anorak fascinated for hours.*

anorak

anorexia nervosa /æn.əˌrek.si.ə.nəˈvəʊ.sə/ (US) /-nɚ-ˈvoʊ-/ **noun** [U] (informal **anorexia**) a serious illness often resulting in dangerous weight loss, in which a person does not eat, or eats too little, for psychological reasons: *Reports of anorexia and other eating disorders are on the increase.* → Compare **bulimia**

anorexic /ˌæn.əˈrek.sɪk/ **adj; noun**
▸**adj** (also **anorectic** /ˌæn.ərˈek.tɪk/ (US) /-əˈrek-/) suffering from or relating to anorexia: *She looks anorexic to me.*
▸**noun** [C] (also **anorectic**) a person who suffers from anorexia: *Anorexics tend to be obsessional and perfectionist.*

another /əˈnʌð.əʳ/ (US) /-ɚ/ **determiner, pronoun** ADDITIONAL ▷ **1** A2 one more person or thing or an extra amount: *I'm going to have another piece of cake.* ◦ *'Would you get me a bar of chocolate from the kitchen?' 'Another one?'* ◦ *We can fit another person in my car.* ◦ *Danny's had* **yet** *another car accident.* ◦ ***For*** *another £30 (= for £30 more) you can buy the model with a touchscreen.* ◦ *Just think,* **in** *another three months (= three months from now) it'll be summer again.* **2 one… after another** a lot of things, one after the other: *I'm not surprised he's feeling ill – he was eating one ice cream after another!* DIFFERENT ▷ **3** A2 a different person or thing: *She's finished with that boyfriend and found herself another (**one**).* ◦ *Do you want to exchange this toaster for another (**one**) or do you want your money back?* **4 one another** B1 each other: *They gave one another presents when they met at the airport.* **5 one way or another** in some way that is not known yet: *We'll get out of this mess one way or another.*

> **!** Common mistake: **another**
>
> Remember that **another** is written as one word.
> Don't write 'an other', write **another**:
> ~~*Would you like an other cup of coffee?*~~
> *Would you like another cup of coffee?*

IDIOMS **be another matter/thing 1** to be a different situation that is likely to be judged differently: *Cars are useful, but their impact on the environment is another matter altogether.* **2** to be very different and likely to involve more problems or difficulties: *Wanting to help the homeless is one thing, finding cheap secure accommodation for them is quite another (thing).* • **be another story** to be something that you do not want to say more about at this particular time: *When we finally got home, we found that we'd been burgled – but that's another story.*

A.N. Other /ˌeɪ.enˈʌð.əʳ/ (US) /-ɚ/ **noun** UK used at the end of a list of people to refer to someone whose name is not yet known: *The conference will be attended by Ian Taylor, Joe Sellars, and A.N. Other.*

answer /ˈɑːn.səʳ/ (US) /ˈæn.sɚ/ **noun; verb**
▸**noun** [C] REACTION ▷ **1** A1 a reaction to a question, letter, phone call, etc.: *The minister promised to give a written answer* **to** *the MP's detailed question.* ◦ *We've emailed him asking him if he's free on that date but we haven't had an answer yet.* ◦ *I've just rung him but there was no answer.* ◦ *I didn't realize we had to write each answer on a new sheet of paper.* ◦ *I got eight correct answers and two wrong ones in last week's exam.* ◦ ***In answer to*** *your letter of 30 May, I am writing to accept your offer of £3,575 in compensation.* SOLUTION ▷ **2** B1 a solution to a problem: *It's a difficult situation and I don't know what the answer is.* ◦ *There's no* ***easy*** *answer* ***to the problem.***

> Word partners for **answer noun (REACTION)**
>
> *get/receive* an answer • *give/provide* an answer • *guess/know* the answer • a *correct/wrong* answer • the *short/simple* answer is • an *honest/straight* answer • the answer *to* sth • *in* answer (*to* sth)

IDIOM **sb's answer to sb/sth** If something or someone is the answer to another thing or person, it is or they are considered to be similar or as good: *She's Lithuania's answer to Madonna.*

▸**verb** REACT ▷ **1** A1 [I or T] to say, write, or do something as a reaction to a question, letter, etc.: *I can't answer (you) without more detailed information.* ◦ *You haven't answered my* ***question.*** ◦ *I texted asking whether he'd be coming to the party but he hasn't answered yet.* ◦ [+ speech] *'I'd love to have dinner with you, but I won't be able to get there before nine o'clock,' she answered.* ◦ [+ that] *She answered* ***that*** *she wouldn't be able to come before nine o'clock.* ◦ formal *Does anyone here answer* ***to the name of*** *(= is anyone here called) Wallis?* **2** A2 [I or T] to open the door to someone or pick up the phone: *Someone's at the door – would you answer it, please?* ◦ *I phoned last night but nobody answered.* BE SUITABLE FOR ▷ **3** [T] to be suitable for and satisfy someone's needs: *I've got a bit of furniture round the back that I think might answer your needs.* MATCH ▷ **4** [I or T] (also **answer to**) to match a description: *A woman who answers to the suspect's description was seen in the area on the night of the crime.*

PHRASAL VERBS **answer (sb) back** to speak rudely when answering someone in authority: *Don't you dare answer me back, young lady!* • **answer back** to react to criticism by arguing or explaining: *The company criticized in the documentary was given the opportunity to answer back.* • **answer for sth** to be responsible for something bad, or to be punished for something: *I expect parents to answer for their children's behaviour.* ◦ *'Why do you think there's so much violence nowadays?' 'Well, violence on television has* ***a lot to*** *answer for (= is the cause of much of it).'* • **answer for sb/sth** If you say that you can answer for someone or for a quality that they have, you mean that you know from experience that they can be trusted, or that they have that quality: *I can certainly answer for her professionalism, and whole-heartedly recommend her to any employer.* • **answer to sb** to take orders from, obey, and explain your actions to someone: *The great thing about working for yourself is that you don't have to answer to anyone.*

answerable /ˈɑːn.sᵊr.ə.bl/ (US) /ˈæn.sɚ-/ **adj 1 be answerable for sth** to be responsible for something that happens: *Soldiers who obey orders to commit* *atrocities should be answerable for their crimes.* **2 be answerable to sb** If you are answerable to someone, you have to explain your actions to them because they have the main control and responsibility: *Any European central bank should be directly answerable to the European Parliament.*

ˈanswering maˌchine noun [C] mainly US for **answerphone**

ˈanswering ˌservice noun [C usually singular] a company that receives and answers phone calls for its customers

answerphone /ˈɑːn.sə.fəʊn/ (US) /ˈæn.sɚ.foʊn/ noun [C] mainly UK (US usually **ˈanswering ˌmachine**) a device connected to a phone that answers calls automatically and records messages from the person calling: *She wasn't in so I **left a message on** her answerphone.* ◦ *I rang several times last week, but I kept **getting** his answerphone.*

ant /ænt/ noun [C] B1 a very small insect that lives under the ground in large and well-organized social groups

IDIOM **have ants in your pants** old-fashioned humorous to not be able to keep still because you are very excited or worried about something

-ant /-ənt/ suffix (also **-ent**) (a person or thing) performing or causing the stated action: *assistant* ◦ *participant* ◦ *disinfectant* ◦ *an expectant look* ◦ *a defiant child*

antacid /ˌænˈtæs.ɪd/ noun [C or U] a substance used to reduce or prevent ACID collecting in the body, especially in the stomach

antagonism /ænˈtæg.ə.nɪ.zᵊm/ noun [U or C] hate, extreme unfriendliness, or active opposition to someone: *There's a history of antagonism **between** the two teams.* ◦ *the antagonism **towards** neighbouring states* ◦ *the historic antagonisms **between** the countries of western Europe*

antagonist /ænˈtæg.ə.nɪst/ noun [C] formal a person who is strongly opposed to something or someone: *The antagonists in this dispute are quite unwilling to compromise.* → Compare **protagonist**

antagonistic /ænˌtæg.əˈnɪs.tɪk/ adj actively opposing or showing unfriendliness towards something or someone: *He's extremely antagonistic **towards** all critics.*

antagonize (UK usually **antagonise**) /ænˈtæg.ə.naɪz/ verb [T] to make someone dislike you or feel opposed to you: *It's a very delicate situation and I've no wish to antagonize him.*

Antarctic /ænˈtɑːk.tɪk/ (US) /-ˈtɑːrk-/ noun; adj

▸noun **the Antarctic** the very cold area around the South Pole that includes Antarctica and the surrounding seas

▸adj relating to the very cold area around the South Pole: *the Antarctic Ocean/Circle/Zone*

ante /ˈæn.ti/ (US) /-t̬i/ noun; verb

▸noun [C] an amount of money that each person must risk in order to be part of a game that involves GAMBLING: *a $30 ante*

IDIOM **up the ante** If you up the ante, you increase your demands or the risks in a situation in order to achieve a better result: *The government has upped the ante by refusing to negotiate until a ceasefire has been agreed.*

▸verb (past tense and past participle **anteing**)

PHRASAL VERB **ante up (sth)** US informal to give money, often unwillingly: *At least 200 people have been persuaded to ante up big money for the charity event.*

ante- /æn.ti-/ (US) /-t̬i-/ prefix before or in front of: *antedate* ◦ *antenatal* ◦ *anteroom* → Compare **pre-**

anteater /ˈæntˌiː.təʳ/ (US) /-t̬ɚ/ noun [C] a mammal that eats ANTS OT TERMITES and has a long nose and tongue and no teeth

antebellum /ˌæn.tiˈbel.əm/ (US) /-t̬ə-/ adj [before noun] mainly US relating to the time before a war, especially the American Civil War: *Many homes and churches of the antebellum South can still be visited today.*

antecedent /ˌæn.tiˈsiː.dᵊnt/ (US) /-t̬ə-/ noun; adj

▸noun [C] **1** formal someone or something existing or happening before, especially as the cause or origin of something existing or happening later: *Charles Babbage's mechanical calculating engines were the antecedents of the modern computer.* **2** specialized a word or phrase that a PRONOUN refers back to: *In the sentence 'He picked a book off the shelf and handed it to Sally', 'book' is the antecedent of 'it'.*

▸adj formal previous: *When the college was established in 1546, it inherited a hall from each of three antecedent institutions.*

antechamber /ˈæn.tiˌtʃeɪm.bəʳ/ (US) /-t̬iˌtʃeɪm.bɚ/ noun [C] an **anteroom**

antedate /ˌæn.tiˈdeɪt/ (US) /ˈæn.t̬i.deɪt/ verb [T] formal for **predate**

antediluvian /ˌæn.ti.dɪˈluː.vi.ən/ (US) /-t̬i-/ adj humorous extremely old-fashioned: *My mother has some hopelessly antediluvian ideas about the role of women.*

antelope /ˈæn.tɪ.ləʊp/ (US) /-tᵊl.oʊp/ noun [C] (plural **antelope** or **antelopes**) a mammal like a DEER with horns and long, thin legs that allow it to run very fast: *a **herd of** antelope*

antenatal /ˌæn.tiˈneɪ.tᵊl/ (US) /-ˈneɪ.t̬ᵊl/ adj [before noun] UK (US **prenatal**) relating to the medical care given to pregnant women before their babies are born: *antenatal **care/classes*** ◦ *the antenatal **clinic*** → Compare **postnatal** • **antenatally** /-i/ adv *Some foetal abnormalities can now be detected antenatally.*

antenna /ænˈten.ə/ noun **ORGAN** ▷ **1** [C] (plural **antennae** /-iː/) either of a pair of long, thin organs that are found on the heads of insects and CRUSTACEANS (= animals with hard outer shells) and are used to feel with **NOTICING** ▷ **2** [C usually plural] (plural **antennae** or **antennas**) the natural ability to notice things and understand their importance: *Her finely-tuned political antennae helped her to sense problems that less experienced politicians might not detect.* **PART OF RADIO** ▷ **3** [C] (plural **antennas**) mainly US for **aerial**

antepenultimate /ˌæn.ti.pəˈnʌl.tɪ.mət/ (US) /-t̬i-/ adj formal third from last: *X is the antepenultimate letter of the alphabet.* → Compare **penultimate**

anterior /ænˈtɪə.ri.əʳ/ (US) /-ˈtɪr.i.ɚ/ adj [before noun] specialized positioned at or towards the front: *Specimens for examination were taken from the anterior side of the left ventricle from each heart.* → Compare **posterior**

anteroom /ˈæn.ti.rʊm/, /-ruːm/ (US) /-t̬i-/ noun [C] (also **antechamber**) a small room, especially a waiting room, that leads into a larger, more important room: *The ministers waited for their meeting in the Cabinet anteroom.*

anthem /ˈæn.θəm/ noun [C] **1** a song that has special importance for a particular group of people, an organization, or a country, often sung on a special occasion: *The **national** anthems of the teams are played at the beginning of international football matches.* ◦ *John Lennon's 'Imagine' has become the anthem of peace-lovers all over the world.* **2** a religious song sung by a CHOIR with organ music

anthemic /æn'θem.ɪk/ **adj** formal describes music that has qualities that are suitable for an anthem, such as a strong tune and seriousness

anther /'æn.θəʳ/ US /-θɚ/ **noun** [C] the part of a flower that contains POLLEN

anthill /'ænt.hɪl/ **noun** [C] a pile of soil created by ANTS when they are making their nests underground

anthology /æn'θɒl.ə.dʒi/ US /-'θɑː.lə-/ **noun** [C] a collection of artistic works that have a similar form or subject, often those considered to be the best: *an anthology of modern quotations/American verse* → Compare **omnibus** • **anthologist** /-dʒɪst/ **noun** [C]

anthracite /'æn.θrə.saɪt/ **noun** [U] (also ˌ**hard** '**coal**) a very hard type of coal that burns slowly and produces a lot of heat with very little smoke and a small flame

anthrax /'æn.θræks/ **noun** [U] a disease that causes fever, swelling, and often death in animals, especially sheep and CATTLE (= male and female cows), and can be passed on to humans

anthropo- /æn.θrə.pəʊ-/ US /-θrə.pə-/ **prefix** (also **anthrop-**) relating to humans: *anthropomorphism*

the Anthropocene /'æn.θrə.pəˌsiːn/ **noun** [S] the time from the 18th century until now, in which it is possible to see the effect that people have had on the environment and CLIMATE (= weather conditions)

anthropocentric /ˌæn.θrə.pə'sen.trɪk/ **adj** formal considering humans and their existence as the most important and central fact in the universe • **anthropocentrism** /ˌæn.θrə.pə'sen.trɪ.zᵊm/ **noun** [U]

anthropoid /'æn.θrə.pɔɪd/ **adj** [before noun] like a human being or an APE: *Gorillas, chimpanzees, and gibbons are all anthropoid apes, having long arms, no tails, and highly developed brains.* • **anthropoid noun** [C] *Monkeys, apes, and humans are all anthropoids.*

anthropologist /ˌæn.θrə'pɒl.ə.dʒɪst/ US /-'pɑː.lə-/ **noun** [C] someone who scientifically studies humans and their customs, beliefs, and relationships

anthropology /ˌæn.θrə'pɒl.ə.dʒi/ US /-'pɑː.lə-/ **noun** [U] the study of the human race, its culture and society, and its physical development • **anthropological** /ˌæn.θrə.pə'lɒdʒ.ɪ.kᵊl/ US /-'lɑː.dʒɪ-/ **adj** *anthropological research/fieldwork* • **anthropologically** /ˌæn.θrə.pə'lɒdʒ.ɪ.kᵊl.i/ US /-'lɑː.dʒɪ-/ **adv**

anthropomorphism /ˌæn.θrə.pə'mɔː.fɪ.zᵊm/ US /-pə'mɔːr-/ **noun** [U] the showing or treating of animals, gods, and objects as if they are human in appearance, character, or behaviour: *The books 'Alice in Wonderland', 'Peter Rabbit', and 'Winnie-the-Pooh' are classic examples of anthropomorphism.* • **anthropomorphic** /-fɪk/ **adj**

anti /'æn.ti/ US /-t̬i/ **adj, preposition; noun**

▸**adj, preposition** informal opposed to or against a particular thing or person: *We've received a lot of anti letters about that newspaper article.* ◦ *Just because I won't join you, it doesn't mean that I'm anti you.*

▸**noun** [C] (plural **antis**) informal a person who is opposed to something or someone: *So what do you think about smoking in public places – are you a pro or an anti? (= do you support or oppose it?)*

anti- /æn.ti-/ US /-t̬i-/, /-taɪ-/ **prefix 1** opposed to or against → Compare **pro- 2** opposite of **3** preventing

ˌ**anti-**'**ageing** **adj** [before noun] describes substances that are intended to prevent or limit the process of becoming old: *anti-ageing creams*

ˌ**anti-**'**aircraft** **adj** describes weapons, equipment, or activities that are intended to destroy or defend against enemy aircraft: *an anti-aircraft missile/gun/weapon* ◦ *anti-aircraft defences/fire*

antibacterial /ˌæn.ti.bæk'tɪə.ri.əl/ US /-t̬i.bæk'tɪr.i-/ **adj** intended to kill or reduce the harmful effects of bacteria especially when used on the skin: *an antibacterial facial wash*

antibiotic /ˌæn.ti.baɪ'ɒt.ɪk/ US /-t̬i.baɪ'ɑː.t̬ɪk/ **noun** [C] (C2) a medicine or chemical that can destroy harmful bacteria in the body or limit their growth: *I'm **taking** antibiotics for a throat infection.* ◦ *a one-month **course of** antibiotics* ◦ *Some types of antibiotic are used to promote growth in farm animals.* ◦ *He's **on** antibiotics for an ear infection.*

antibody /'æn.tiˌbɒd.i/ US /-t̬iˌbɑː.di/ **noun** [C] a PROTEIN produced in the blood that fights diseases by attacking and killing harmful bacteria: *Antibodies found in breast milk protect newborn babies against infection.*

ˌ**anti-**'**choice** **adj** disapproving opposing the idea that a pregnant woman should have the freedom to choose an ABORTION (= the intentional ending of pregnancy): *the anti-choice lobby*

Antichrist /'æn.ti.kraɪst/ US /-t̬i-/ **noun** [S] originally the main enemy of Jesus Christ, who was expected to rule the world until Jesus Christ's Second Coming, now any enemy of Jesus Christ or the Christian religion

anticipate /æn'tɪs.ɪ.peɪt/ **verb** [T] **EXPECT** ▷ **1** (C1) to imagine or expect that something will happen: *We don't anticipate any trouble.* ◦ *We had one or two difficulties along the way that we didn't anticipate.* ◦ *Are you anticipating a lot of people at the party tonight?* ◦ [+ -ing verb] *They anticipate hav**ing** several applicants for the job.* ◦ [+ that] *They anticipate **that** they will have several applicants for the job* ◦ [+ question word] *At this stage we can't really anticipate **what** will happen.* ◦ *The anticipated inflation figure is lower than last month's.* **TAKE ACTION** ▷ **2** (C1) to take action in preparation for something that you think will happen: *It's always best to anticipate a problem before it arises.* ◦ *The army anticipated (= took action in preparation for) the explosion by evacuating the town.*

anticipation /ænˌtɪs.ɪ'peɪ.ʃᵊn/ **noun** [U] **1** (C2) a feeling of excitement about something that is going to happen in the near future: *As with most pleasures, it's not so much the experience itself as the anticipation that is enjoyable.* ◦ *The postponement of the film's sequel has held cinemagoers **in eager** anticipation for several months.* **2 in anticipation (of)** (C2) in preparation for something happening: *She's even decorated the spare room in anticipation of your visit.*

anticlerical /ˌæn.ti'kler.ɪ.kᵊl/ US /-t̬i-/ **adj** opposed to organized religion having influence in politics and public life: *an anticlerical law/constitution* • **anticlericalism** /-ɪ.zᵊm/ **noun** [U]

anticlimax /ˌæn.ti'klaɪ.mæks/ US /-t̬i-/ **noun** [C or U] an event or experience that causes disappointment because it is less exciting than was expected or because it happens immediately after a much more interesting or exciting event: *When you really look forward to something it's often an anticlimax when it actually happens.* ◦ *Coming home after a trip somewhere is always **a bit of an** anticlimax.* ◦ *Even when you win a match there's often a sense of anticlimax – you always feel you could have played better.* • **anticlimactic** /ˌæn.ti.klaɪ'mæk.tɪk/ US /-t̬ɪk/ **adj** *There was so much publicity and hype beforehand that the performance itself was a touch anticlimactic.*

anticline /'æn.ti.klaɪn/ US /-t̬i-/ **noun** [C] specialized an upward, curved fold in the layers of rock in the Earth's surface → Compare **syncline**

anticlockwise /ˌæn.ti'klɒk.waɪz/ US /-t̬i'klɑːk-/ **adj, adv** UK (US **counterclockwise**) in the opposite

A

direction to the movement of the hands of a clock: *'How do I get the top off this bottle?' 'Push it down and twist it anticlockwise.'*

anticoagulant /ˌæn.ti.kəʊ'æg.jʊ.lənt/ (US) /-t̬i.koʊ-/ noun [C] a drug that prevents or slows down the process of blood forming a CLOT (= a solid mass) • **anticoagulant adj** *an anticoagulant drug*

antics /'æn.tɪks/ (US) /-t̬ɪks/ **noun** [plural] funny, silly, or strange behaviour: *But the rock star, whose stage antics used to include smashing guitars, is older and wiser now.* ◦ *The crowds were once again entertained by the number-one tennis player's antics on and off the court.*

anticyclone /ˌæn.ti'saɪ.kləʊn/ (US) /-t̬i'saɪ.kloʊn/ **noun** [C] an area of high ATMOSPHERIC pressure that causes calm weather

antidepressant /ˌæn.ti.dɪ'pres.ənt/ (US) /-t̬i-/ **noun; adj**

▸**noun** [C] a drug used to reduce feelings of sadness and worry: *She's been* **on** *antidepressants ever since her husband died.*

▸**adj** [before noun] describes a drug that is used to reduce feelings of sadness and worry: *antidepressant drugs*

antidote /'æn.ti.dəʊt/ (US) /-t̬i.doʊt/ **noun** [C] **1** a chemical, especially a drug, that limits the effects of a poison: *Sales of nerve gas antidotes increased dramatically before the war.* **2** a way of preventing or acting against something bad: *Regular exercise is the best antidote* **to** *tiredness and depression.*

antifreeze /'æn.ti.friːz/ (US) /-t̬i-/ **noun** [U] a liquid that is added to water in order to lower the temperature at which it freezes, used especially in car RADIATORS (= cooling systems) in very cold weather

antigen /'æn.tɪ.dʒən/, /-dʒen/ (US) /-t̬i-/ **noun** [C] specialized a substance that causes the production of ANTIBODIES in the body

antihero /'æn.tiˌhɪə.rəʊ/ (US) /-t̬iˌhɪr.oʊ/ **noun** [C usually singular] (plural **antiheroes**) the central character in a play, book, or film who does not have traditionally HEROIC qualities, such as courage, and is admired instead for what society generally considers to be a weakness of their character: *He plays the classic antihero who drops out of society.*

antihistamine /ˌæn.ti'hɪs.tə.mɪn/, /-miːn/ (US) /-t̬i-/ **noun** [C or U] a type of drug that is used to treat medical conditions caused by an extreme reaction to particular substances: *Antihistamine is often used to treat hay fever and insect bites.*

ˌanti-inˈflammatory adj; noun

▸**adj** describes a drug that is used to reduce pain and swelling: *anti-inflammatory drugs for arthritis*

▸**noun** [C] an anti-inflammatory drug: *Aspirin is an anti-inflammatory.*

antiknock /ˌæn.ti'nɒk/ (US) /ˌæn.t̬i'nɑːk/ **noun** [U] a chemical that is added to the fuel of a car engine in order to make the fuel burn more effectively, so that the engine stops making a regular knocking sound • **antiknocking** /-ɪŋ/ **adj** [before noun]

ˌanti-ˈlife adj disapproving supporting the idea that a pregnant woman should have the freedom to choose an ABORTION (= the intentional ending of pregnancy): *the anti-life lobby*

ˌanti-ˈlock adj [before noun] used to describe a type of BRAKE that prevents the uncontrolled sliding of a vehicle by reducing the effects of braking suddenly

antilogarithm /ˌæn.ti'lɒg.ə.rɪ.ðəm/ (US) /–t̬i'lɑː.gə.ɪ-/ **noun** [C] (informal **antilog** /ˌæn.ti'lɒg/ (US) /'æn.t̬i.lɑːg/) specialized the number to which a LOGARITHM belongs

antimacassar /ˌæn.ti.mə'kæs.ər/ (US) /-t̬i.mə'kæs.ɚ/ **noun** [C] a cloth, used mainly in the past, for putting over the back of a chair in order to keep it clean or to decorate it

antimony /'æn.tɪ.mə.ni, æn'tɪm.ə-/ (US) /'æn.t̬ə.moʊ-/ **noun** [U] (symbol **Sb**) a chemical element that is a silver-white, poisonous metal. It is hard but easily broken and is used to make other metals harder and stronger and to make SEMICONDUCTORS for computers.

ˈanti-noise noun [U] sound that is produced in such a way that it matches exactly and removes the effect of loud and possibly harmful noises, such as those produced by large engines in factories

ˌanti-ˈnuclear adj opposed to the production and use of nuclear weapons, or to the production of electricity from nuclear power: *the anti-nuclear lobby/movement* ◦ *Some environmentalists are vehemently anti-nuclear.*

antioxidant /ˌæn.ti'ɒk.sɪ.dənt/ (US) /-t̬i-/ **noun** [C] a substance that slows down the rate at which something decays because of OXIDIZATION (= combining with oxygen)

antipasto /ˌæn.ti'pæs.təʊ/ (US) /-t̬i'pɑː.stoʊ/ **noun** [C] (plural **antipasti** /-ti/ (US) /-sti/) a small amount of food eaten at the beginning of an Italian meal

antipathy /æn'tɪp.ə.θi/ **noun** [C or U] a feeling of strong dislike, opposition, or anger: *Despite the deep antipathies* **between** *them, the two sides have managed to negotiate an agreement.* ◦ *He is a private man with a deep antipathy* **to/towards** *the press.* • **antipathetic** /ˌæn.ti.pə'θet.ɪk/ (US) /-t̬i.pə'θet̬-/ **adj** formal *antipathetic attitudes towards smokers*

ˌanti-personˈnel adj [before noun] describes weapons intended to kill or injure people rather than damage weapons or buildings: *anti-personnel mines*

antiperspirant /ˌæn.ti'pɜː.spər.ənt/ (US) /-t̬i'pɝː.spɚ-/ **noun; adj**

▸**noun** [C or U] a substance that is put on the skin, especially under the arms, in order to prevent or reduce SWEATING

▸**adj** acting to prevent or reduce SWEATING: *an antiperspirant deodorant*

the Antipodes /æn'tɪp.ə.diːz/ **noun** [plural] mainly humorous a way of referring to Australia and New Zealand by people living in the northern HEMISPHERE (= half of the Earth): *I rather fancy the Antipodes for a holiday this summer.* • **Antipodean** /ænˌtɪp.ə'diː.ən/ **noun** [C], **adj** *an Antipodean accent* ◦ *Of course for Antipodeans it's now winter.*

antiquarian /ˌæn.tɪ'kweə.ri.ən/ (US) /-t̬ɪ'kwer.i-/ **adj; noun**

▸**adj** connected with the trade, collection, or study of old and valuable or rare objects: *an antiquarian bookshop/bookseller*

▸**noun** [C] a person who studies or collects old and valuable or rare objects • **antiquarianism** /ˌæn.tɪ'kweə.ri.ə.nɪ.zəm/ (US) /-t̬ɪ'kwer.i-/ **noun** [U]

antiquary /'æn.tɪ.kwə.ri/ (US) /-t̬ə.kwer.i/ **noun** [C] old use for **antiquarian**

antiquated /'æn.tɪ.kweɪ.tɪd/ (US) /-t̬ə.kweɪ.t̬ɪd/ **adj** old-fashioned or unsuitable for modern society: *It will take many years to modernize these antiquated industries.* ◦ *Compared with modern satellite dishes, ordinary TV aerials look positively antiquated.* ◦ *antiquated ideas/attitudes/values* ◦ *antiquated laws/machinery/technology*

antique /æn'tiːk/ **noun; adj**

▸**noun** [C] **B1** something made in an earlier period that is collected and considered to have value because it is beautiful, rare, old, or of high quality: *You can't give* *away Granny's old bookcase – it's a valuable antique.* ◦ *My mother* ***collects*** *antiques.*

▸**adj 1** B1 made in an earlier period and considered to have value because of being beautiful, rare, old, or of high quality: *antique silver/jewellery/lace/furniture* **2** trading or relating to antiques: *an antique* ***dealer*** ◦ *antique shops/markets/fairs/auctions*

antiquity /æn'tɪk.wɪ.ti/ (US) /-wə.t̬i/ **noun 1** [U] the DISTANT past (= a long time ago), especially before the sixth century: *Cannabis has been used for medicinal purposes since antiquity.* ◦ *Before creating this sculpture, she studied all the masterpieces of* ***classical*** *antiquity.* **2** [C] an object that was created a very long time ago: *Under Greek law, all antiquities that are discovered in Greece belong to the government.*

ˌanti-ˈracist adj; noun

▸**adj** opposed to the unfair treatment of people who belong to other races: *anti-racist legislation*

▸**noun** [C] an anti-racist person

antiretroviral /æn.tiˌret.rəʊ'vaɪə.rəl/ (US) /-t̬iˌret.roʊ-'vaɪ.rəl/ **adj** used to treat AIDS (= the virus that causes a serious disease that destroys the body's ability to fight infection): *antiretroviral drugs*

antirrhinum /ˌæn.tɪ'raɪ.nəm/ (US) /-t̬ɪ-/ **noun** [C] formal for **snapdragon**

ˌanti-Seˈmitic adj having or showing a strong dislike of Jewish people, or treating them in a cruel and unfair way: *anti-Semitic propaganda* ◦ *anti-Semitic remarks* • **ˌanti-ˈSemite noun** [C] an anti-Semitic person: *He was a virulent anti-Semite.*

ˌanti-ˈSemitism noun [U] the strong dislike or cruel and unfair treatment of Jewish people: *Nazi anti-Semitism forced him to emigrate to the US.*

antiseptic /ˌæn.ti'sep.tɪk/ (US) /-t̬i-/ **noun; adj**

▸**noun** [C or U] a chemical used for preventing infection in an injury, especially by killing bacteria: *Antiseptic is used to sterilize the skin before giving an injection.* ◦ *Many of the ingredients for antiseptics come from the rainforests.*

▸**adj 1** completely free from infection **2** disapproving too clean and showing no imagination and character: *There's an antiseptic feeling to the new town centre, with its covered shopping mall.*

antisocial /ˌæn.ti'səʊ.ʃəl/ (US) /-t̬i'soʊ-/ **adj 1** C1 harmful to society: *antisocial* ***behaviour*** ◦ *Increasingly, smoking is regarded as an antisocial habit.* **2** C1 often avoiding spending time with other people: *I hope they won't think I'm antisocial if I don't join them in the bar.* • **antisocially** /-i/ **adv**

ˌanti-ˈspam adj [before noun] produced and used to prevent people sending and receiving unwanted emails, especially advertisements: *anti-spam legislation/policies/resources/tools*

ˌanti-ˈstatic adj relating to devices or methods for preventing damage when electricity collects on the surface of objects

ˌanti-ˈtank adj [before noun] describes weapons that destroy or damage enemy TANKS (= large military fighting vehicles): *anti-tank missiles/rockets*

ˌanti-ˈterrorist adj Anti-terrorist laws or activities are intended to prevent or reduce TERRORISM (= violent acts for political purposes): *Several governments have adopted tough new anti-terrorist legislation in the wake of the attacks.*

antithesis /æn'tɪθ.ə.sɪs/ **noun** [C] (plural **antitheses** /-siːz/) **1** the exact opposite: *She is slim and shy – the very antithesis* ***of*** *her sister.* **2** a contrast between two things: *Thanks to the collapse of communism the political antithesis* ***between*** *Left and Right is less important.* • **antithetical** /ˌæn.tɪ'θet.ɪ.kəl/ (US) /-t̬ɪ'θet̬-/ **adj** (also **antithetic**) *antithetical views*

antitoxin /ˌæn.ti'tɒk.sɪn/ (US) /-t̬i'tɑːk-/ **noun** [C] specialized a substance that stops or reduces the effect of a TOXIN (= poisonous substance) in your body

antitrust /ˌæn.ti'trʌst/ (US) /-t̬i-/ **adj** [before noun] specialized relating to efforts to prevent companies from working together to control prices unfairly or to create a MONOPOLY (= a single company or group of companies that is the only supplier of something)

antiviral /ˌæn.ti'vaɪ.rəl/ (US) /-t̬i-/ **adj; noun**

▸**adj** describes a drug or treatment that is used to cure an infection or disease caused by a virus: *an antiviral agent/drug*

▸**noun** [C] an antiviral drug

ˌanti-ˈvirus adj [before noun] produced and used to protect the main memory of a computer against infection by a virus: *anti-virus* ***software/programs*** ◦ *an anti-virus company/product/package*

ˌanti-ˈwar adj opposed to a particular war or to all wars: *anti-war protestors* ◦ *an anti-war demonstration*

antler /'ænt.lər/ (US) /-lɚ/ **noun** [C] a horn with parts like branches that grows on the head of a DEER: *a pair of antlers*

antonym /'æn.tə.nɪm/ (US) /-t̬ən.ɪm/ **noun** [C] specialized a word that means the opposite of another word: *Two antonyms of 'light' are 'dark' and 'heavy'.* → Compare **synonym** • **antonymous** /æn'tɒn.ɪ.məs/ (US) /-'tɑː.nɪ-/ **adj** *'Long' and 'short' are antonymous (words).*

antsy /'ænt.si/ **adj** US informal very nervous, worried, or unpleasantly excited: *It was a long drive and the children started to* ***get*** *antsy.* ◦ *I always get antsy* ***about*** *meeting my husband's boss.*

anus /'eɪ.nəs/ **noun** [C] the opening at the end of the ALIMENTARY CANAL through which solid waste leaves the body

anvil /'æn.vɪl/ **noun** [C] **EQUIPMENT** ▷ **1** a heavy block of iron on which heated pieces of metal are made into a particular shape with a hammer **BONE** ▷ **2** specialized one of the small bones of the ear

anvil

anxiety /æŋ'zaɪ.ə.ti/ (US) /-t̬i/ **noun WORRY** ▷ **1** B2 [U] an uncomfortable feeling of nervousness or worry about something that is happening or might happen in the future: *Children normally feel a lot of anxiety* ***about*** *their first day at school.* ◦ *That explains his anxiety* ***over*** *his health.* ◦ *Her son is a source of considerable anxiety.* **2** [C] something that causes a feeling of fear and worry: *job anxieties* **EAGERNESS** ▷ **3** [U + to infinitive] eagerness to do something: *Peter's leaving at the end of this week – hence his anxiety* ***to*** *get his work finished.* **MEDICAL CONDITION** ▷ **4** [U] a medical condition in which you always feel frightened and worried: *He has helped patients suffering from anxiety, depression, and eating disorders.* ◦ *an anxiety disorder/****attack***

anxious /'æŋk.ʃəs/ **adj WORRIED** ▷ **1** B1 worried and nervous: *My mother always gets a bit anxious if we don't arrive when we say we will.* ◦ *The drought has made farmers anxious* ***about*** *the harvest.* **EAGER** ▷ **2** B2 eager to do something: *Developing countries that are anxious* ***for*** *hard currency can rarely afford to protect the environment.* ◦ [+ to infinitive] *I'm anxious* ***to*** *get home to open my presents.* ◦ [+ that] *I'm anxious* ***that*** *we get there on time because I don't think there'll be many seats left.* • **anxiously** /-li/ **adv** B2 *We waited* *anxiously by the phone.* ◦ *Tomorrow the children will receive their anxiously (= eagerly)* ***awaited*** *presents.*

any /ˈen.i/ **determiner, pronoun; adv**

▸**determiner, pronoun** SOME ▷ **1** A1 some, or even the smallest amount or number of: *Is there any of that lemon cake left?* ◦ *There was hardly any food left by the time we got there.* ◦ *'Is there some butter I could use?' 'No, there's some margarine but there isn't any butter.'* ◦ *'Is there any* ***more*** *soup?' 'No, I'm afraid there isn't any left.'* ◦ *I haven't seen any of his films.* ◦ *I don't expect we'll have any* ***more*** *trouble from him.* ◦ *I go to church for weddings but not for any* ***other*** *reason.* ◦ *Are you sure there isn't any way of solving this problem?* NOT IMPORTANT WHICH ▷ **2** A1 one of or each of a particular type of person or thing when it is not important which: *Any food would be better than nothing at all.* ◦ *The offer was that you could have any three items of clothing you liked for £30.* ◦ informal *On Sundays I just wear any* ***old*** *thing (= anything) that I happen to find lying around.* ◦ *Any of you should be able to answer this question.* ◦ *Any idiot with a basic knowledge of French should be able to book a hotel room in Paris.* ◦ *Any advice (= whatever advice) that you can give me would be greatly appreciated.* ◦ *Any* ***minute/day/time now*** *(= very soon) there's going to be a massive quarrel between those two.* ◦ *There were a lot of computers at the exhibition, any (one) of which would have suited me perfectly.*

▸**adv** B1 at all or in the least: *Can't you run any faster?* ◦ *Those trousers don't look any different from the others.* ◦ *Are you feeling any better after your illness?* ◦ *Houses in this area used to be a real bargain, but they're not cheap any* ***more*** *(= now).* ◦ *This radio is****n't*** *any* ***good*** *(= it's useless) – I'll have to buy another.* ◦ *I used to walk to work every day, but* ***not*** *any* ***longer*** *(= not now).* ◦ US informal *I tried talking him out of it, but that didn't help any – he still left home.*

anybody /ˈen.iˌbɒd.i/ US /-ˌbɑː.di/ **pronoun** **anyone**

anyhow /ˈen.i.haʊ/ **adv** ANYWAY ▷ **1** B2 **anyway** WITHOUT CARE ▷ **2** (informal also ˈ**any old** ˌ**how**) without care or interest or in an untidy way: *He looked a complete mess – dressed anyhow with his hair sticking up.*

anymore /ˌen.iˈmɔːʳ/ US /-ˈmɔːr/ **adv** A2 US for **any more**, see at **more**

anyone /ˈen.i.wʌn/ **pronoun** (also **anybody**) **1** A2 used in questions and negatives to mean 'a person or people': *I haven't spoken to anyone all day.* ◦ *I haven't told anyone.* ◦ *Was there anyone you knew at the meeting?* ◦ *Has anyone seen my glasses anywhere?* **2** B1 any person or any people: *Anyone can go – you don't have to be invited.* ◦ *Anyone could dress well with all that money.*

IDIOM **anyone who is/was anyone** all the most famous and important people: *In those days anyone who was anyone dined in this exclusive little restaurant.*

anyplace /ˈen.i.pleɪs/ **adv** US for anywhere: *Oh just put it anyplace – it doesn't matter where.*

anyroad /ˈen.i.rəʊd/ US /-roʊd/ **adv** Northern for **anyway**

anything /ˈen.i.θɪŋ/ **pronoun** SOMETHING ▷ **1** A1 used in questions and negatives to mean 'something': *Is there anything I can do to help?* ◦ *Was there anything* ***else*** *you wanted to say or is that it?* ◦ *Have you got anything less expensive?* ◦ *Let me know if anything happens, won't you.* ◦ *I didn't know anything about computers till I started this job.* ◦ *I was looking for a birthday present for my mother but I didn't find anything suitable.* ◦ *Did you notice anything strange about him?* ◦ *Spending Christmas with him and his brother – I can't imagine anything worse!* ◦ *If he eats anything with wheat in it he's very sick.* ANY OBJECT/SITUATION ▷ **2** A1 any event, act, object, or situation: *He said I could order anything on the menu.* ◦ *She could be anything (= any age)* ***between*** *30* ***and*** *40.*

IDIOMS **anything but** used to mean the opposite of the stated quality: *She's meant to be really nice but she was anything but nice when I met her.* • **as... as anything** mainly UK informal used to add emphasis to an adjective or adverb: *He's as fat as anything (= very fat).* • **for anything (in the world)** informal If you say that you would not do a particular thing for anything (in the world), it means that you certainly would not do it: *I wouldn't have missed your party for anything.*

anytime (UK also **any time**) /ˈen.i.taɪm/ **adv** at a time that is not or does not need to be decided or agreed: *Call round to see me anytime.* ◦ *We don't expect the economic situation to change anytime* ***soon****.*

anyway /ˈen.i.weɪ/ **adv** (also **anyhow**) **1** A2 whatever else is happening, without considering other things: *Of course I don't mind taking you home – I'm going that way anyway.* ◦ *'I thought you said everyone had left.' 'Well, some of them have anyway.'* ◦ *Her parents were opposed to her giving up her course, but she did it anyway.* **2** A2 In conversation, anyway is also used to change the subject, return to an earlier subject, or get to the most interesting point: *Anyway, as I said, I'll be away next week.* ◦ *What was he doing with so much of the company's money in his personal account anyway?* **3** B1 used to give a more important reason for something that you are saying: *I don't have time to go, and anyway it's too expensive.*

anywhere /ˈen.i.weəʳ/ US /-wer/ **adv** (US also **anyplace**) **1** A2 in, to, or at any place: *You won't find a better plumber anywhere in England.* ◦ *Go anywhere in the world and you'll find some sort of hamburger restaurant.* ◦ *I was wondering if there was anywhere I could go to get this mended.* ◦ *There are quite a few words that they use in that part of the country that you don't hear anywhere* ***else****.* ◦ *As a teacher you could expect to be paid anywhere (= any amount)* ***between*** *£15* ***and*** *£50 per hour.* ◦ *He charges anywhere* ***from*** *$20* ***to*** *$50 for a haircut.* ◦ *They live in some tiny little village* ***miles from*** *anywhere (= a very long way from any towns).* **2** used in questions or negatives to mean 'a place': *I can't find my keys anywhere.* ◦ *Is there anywhere in particular you wanted to go to eat tonight?* ◦ *Did you go anywhere interesting this summer?* ◦ *Is there anywhere to eat around here?*

IDIOMS **anywhere near** informal C1 close in time, quality, distance, or amount: *Are we anywhere near finishing yet or is there still some way to go?* • **not anywhere near** very much less: *He isn't anywhere near* ***as*** *popular as he used to be.* • **not anywhere to be found** impossible to see or find: *We searched the house, but it wasn't anywhere to be found.* • **not get/go anywhere** informal B2 If you are not getting/going anywhere, you are not improving or advancing a particular situation: *I've been sorting out my study all day, but it's such a mess I don't feel I'm getting anywhere.*

AOB /ˌeɪ.əʊˈbiː/ UK **abbreviation for** any other business: used at the end of the list of subjects to be discussed at a meeting

A-OˈK **adj** [after verb] US informal completely right or acceptable: *The doctor says I'm A-OK now, that there's absolutely nothing wrong with me.*

aorta /eɪˈɔː.tə/ US /-ˈɔːr.t̬ə/ **noun** [C] the main ARTERY

(= thick tube carrying blood from the heart) that takes blood to the other parts of the body • **aortic** /eɪˈɔː.tɪk/ (US) /-ˈɔːr.t̬ɪk/ **adj** *the aortic valve*

apace /əˈpeɪs/ **adv** formal or literary quickly: *The project is **coming on** apace (= advancing quickly).*

apart /əˈpɑːt/ (US) /-ˈpɑːrt/ **adv; adj**

▸**adv** SEPARATED ▷ **1** B1 separated by a distance or by time: *Stand with your feet wide apart.* ◦ *How far apart should the speakers be?* ◦ *We were asked to stand in two lines three metres apart.* ◦ *The two lines of children moved slowly apart.* ◦ *The garage, large enough for two cars, is set apart **from** (= not joined to) the house.* ◦ *I forget the exact age difference between Mark and his brother – they're two or three years apart.* **2** B2 into smaller pieces: *My jacket is so old it's **falling** apart.* ◦ *I **took** the motor apart (= separated it into pieces) to see how it worked.* EXCEPT ▷ **3 apart from** B1 except for or not considering: *He works until nine o'clock every evening, and that's **quite** apart from the work he does over the weekend.* ◦ *Apart from the salary/Salary apart, it's not a bad job.* ◦ *Apart from you and me/You and me apart, I don't think there was anyone there under 30.*

▸**adj** [after verb] B2 living or staying in a different place from the person that you are married to or have a close relationship with: *When you're apart you rely so heavily on the phone.*

apartheid /əˈpɑː.taɪt/, /-teɪt/ (US) /-ˈpɑːr.taɪt/ **noun** [U] (in the past in South Africa) a political system in which people of different races were separated: *the long-awaited dismantling (= end) of apartheid*

apartment /əˈpɑːt.mənt/ (US) /-ˈpɑːrt-/ **noun 1** A2 [C] mainly US (UK usually **flat**) a set of rooms for living in, especially on one floor of a building: *I'll give you the keys to my apartment.* ◦ *They have six holiday/luxury apartments for sale.* **2 apartments** [plural] a set of large rooms with expensive furniture and decoration in, for example, a public building or castle

aˈpartment ˌbuilding **noun** [C] US A2 a large building that is divided into apartments

apathetic /ˌæp.əˈθet.ɪk/ (US) /-ˈθet̬-/ **adj** showing no interest or energy and unwilling to take action, especially over something important: *Young people today are so apathetic **about** politics.* ◦ *Don't be so apathetic – how are you going to get a job if you don't even start looking?*

apathy /ˈæp.ə.θi/ **noun** [U] behaviour that shows no interest or energy and shows that someone is unwilling to take action, especially over something important: ***widespread** apathy among students* ◦ *voter apathy*

APB /ˌeɪ.piˈbiː/ **noun** [C] abbreviation for **all-points bulletin**

ape /eɪp/ **noun; verb**

▸**noun** [C] an animal like a large monkey that has no tail and uses its arms to move through trees: *Chimpanzees and gorillas are both apes.*

IDIOM **go ape** (offensive **go apeshit**) to become extremely angry: *She went ape because I was half an hour late.*

ape

▸**verb** [T] disapproving to copy something or someone badly and unsuccessfully: *He called the new building unoriginal and said that it merely aped the classical traditions.*

aperitif /əˌper.ɪˈtiːf/ **noun** [C] an alcoholic drink, especially one that is drunk before a meal: *Would you like an aperitif before dinner?*

aperture /ˈæp.ə.tʃəʳ/ (US) /-ɚ.tʃɚ/ **noun** [C] a small and often narrow opening, especially one that allows light into a camera

apex /ˈeɪ.peks/ **noun** [C] (plural **apexes** or **apices** /ˈeɪ.pɪ.siːz/) **1** specialized the highest point or top of a shape or object: *the apex of a triangle/pyramid* **2** figurative the highest point or most successful part of something: *He reached **the** apex **of** his career during that period.* • **apical** /ˈeɪ.pɪ.kəl/ **adj**

aphasia /əˈfeɪ.ʒə/ **noun** [U] specialized a medical condition that makes a person unable to speak, write, or understand speech or writing because of damage to the brain • **aphasic** /-zɪk/ **adj** *The girl was aphasic because of brain damage suffered during a difficult birth.*

aphid /ˈeɪ.fɪd/ **noun** [C] any of various small insects, such as the GREENFLY, that suck the juices of plants for food

aphorism /ˈæf.ə.rɪ.zəm/ (US) /-ɚ.ɪ-/ **noun** [C] a short clever saying that is intended to express a general truth: *Oscar Wilde was famous for such aphorisms as 'Experience is the name everyone gives to their mistakes'.*

aphrodisiac /ˌæf.rəˈdɪz.i.æk/ (US) /-ˈdiː.ʒæk/ **noun; adj**

▸**noun** [C] something, usually a drug or food, that is believed to cause sexual DESIRE in people: *Are oysters really an aphrodisiac?* ◦ *They say that power is an aphrodisiac.*

▸**adj** belonging or relating to an aphrodisiac: *the aphrodisiac properties of champagne*

API /ˌeɪ.piˈaɪ/ **noun** [C] abbreviation for application programming interface: a way of communicating with a particular computer program or internet service

apiary /ˈeɪ.pi.ə.ri/ (US) /-er.i/ **noun** [C] a place where people keep BEES, especially a collection of HIVES kept to provide HONEY

apices plural of **apex**

apiece /əˈpiːs/ **adv** each: *In good condition, dolls from this period sell for £500 apiece.*

aplenty /əˈplen.ti/ (US) /-t̬i/ **adj** [after noun] formal available in large amounts: *If that's not enough, there are shows, movies, and amusements aplenty.*

aplomb /əˈplɒm/ (US) /-ˈplɑːm/ **noun** [U] confidence and style: *Rosalind conducted the meeting **with** characteristic aplomb/**with** her usual aplomb.*

apnoea (US **apnea**) /ˈæp.ni.ə/ **noun** [U] a medical condition that makes someone stop breathing for a short time, especially when they are sleeping: *sleep apnoea*

apocalypse /əˈpɒk.ə.lɪps/ (US) /-ˈpɑː.kə-/ **noun 1** [S or U] a very serious event resulting in great destruction and change: *The book offers a vision of the future in which there is a great nuclear apocalypse.* **2 the Apocalypse** [S] in the Bible, the total destruction and end of the world

apocalyptic /əˌpɒk.əˈlɪp.tɪk/ (US) /-ˌpɑː.kə-/ **adj** showing or describing the total destruction and end of the world, or extremely bad future events: *apocalyptic **visions** of a nuclear confrontation*

apocryphal /əˈpɒk.rɪ.fəl/ (US) /-ˈpɑː.krɪ-/ **adj** formal describes a story that is probably not true although often told and believed by some people to have happened: *an apocryphal **story*** ◦ *It's a good story but I dare say it's apocryphal.*

apogee /ˈæp.ə.dʒiː/ **noun** [S] formal the most successful, popular, or powerful point: *At their apogee, the novels of Spillane claimed worldwide sales of over $180 million.*

apolitical /ˌeɪ.pəˈlɪt.ɪ.kəl/ US /-ˈlɪţ-/ **adj** not interested in or connected with politics, or not connected to any political party: *The organization insists that it is apolitical and does not identify with any one particular party.*

apologetic /əˌpɒl.əˈdʒet.ɪk/ US /-ˌpɑː.ləˈdʒeţ.ɪk/ **adj** C2 showing that you feel sorry about having caused someone problems or unhappiness: *She was so apologetic* ***about*** *forgetting my birthday it was almost embarrassing.* ◦ *I hope he was suitably apologetic* ***for*** *breaking your glasses.* • **apologetically** /-ɪ.kəl.i/ **adv** *She smiled apologetically.*

apologist /əˈpɒl.ə.dʒɪst/ US /-ˈpɑː.lə-/ **noun** [C] formal a person who supports a particular belief or political system, especially an unpopular one, and speaks or writes in defence of it: *communism and its apologists* ◦ *There are few apologists* ***for*** *the old system.*

apologize (UK usually **apologise**) /əˈpɒl.ə.dʒaɪz/ US /-ˈpɑː.lə-/ **verb** [I] B1 to tell someone that you are sorry for having done something that has caused them problems or unhappiness: *I must apologize* ***to*** *Isobel for my lateness.* ◦ *Trains may be subject to delay – we apologize* ***for*** *any inconvenience caused.* ◦ *She apologized* ***profusely for*** *having to leave at 3.30 p.m.*

> **!** Common mistake: **apologize or apology?**
>
> **Warning:** do not confuse the verb **apologize** with the noun **apology**:
>
> ~~*I must insist on an apologize.*~~
>
> *I must insist on an apology.*

apology /əˈpɒl.ə.dʒi/ US /-ˈpɑː.lə-/ **noun** **SAYING SORRY** ▷ **1** B1 [C or U] an act of saying sorry: *I have an apology to* ***make*** *to you – I'm afraid I opened your letter by mistake.* ◦ *He's demanding a* ***full*** *apology* ***from*** *the newspaper for making untrue allegations about his personal life.* ◦ *'Was he at all sorry for what he'd done?' 'Oh he was* ***full of*** *apologies (= extremely sorry).'* ◦ *She complained to the company and they sent her a* ***written*** *apology.* ◦ *I* ***owe*** *you an apology – I'm afraid I forgot to send that report.* ◦ *a letter of apology* **MESSAGE** ▷ **2 (your) apologies** B1 [plural] formal a message politely telling someone that you cannot be present at their meeting or party: *The vice chair has* ***sent*** *his apologies – he's abroad at present.* ◦ *Apologies were received from Phil Baker.* **EXPLANATION** ▷ **3** [C] formal a formal explanation or defence of a belief or system, especially one that is unpopular

IDIOM **be an apology for sth** UK informal to be an extremely bad example of something: *You're not coming out because you're tired? That's an apology for an excuse!*

apoplectic /ˌæp.əˈplek.tɪk/ **adj** extremely and obviously angry: *He was apoplectic* ***with*** *rage/fury.*

apoplexy /ˈæp.ə.plek.si/ **noun** [U] **ANGER** ▷ **1** very great anger: *In a* ***fit of*** *apoplexy, he thumped the table with both hands.* **ILLNESS** ▷ **2** old use a **stroke** resulting from a brain HAEMORRHAGE

apostasy /əˈpɒs.tə.si/ US /-ˈpɑː.stə-/ **noun** [U] formal the act of giving up your religious or political beliefs and leaving a religion or a political party: *In those days apostasy was punishable by death.*

apostate /əˈpɒs.teɪt/ US /-ˈpɑː.steɪt/ **noun** [C] formal someone who has given up their religion or left a political party

apostle /əˈpɒs.l/ US /-ˈpɑː.sl/ **noun** **1** [C] formal someone who strongly supports a particular belief or political movement: *an apostle* ***of*** *world peace/liberty* **2 the Apostles** [plural] the group of early Christians who travelled to different places telling people about Jesus Christ → See also **disciple** • **apostolic** /ˌæp.əˈstɒl.ɪk/ US /-ˈstɑː.lɪk/ **adj** formal

apostrophe /əˈpɒs.trə.fi/ US /-ˈpɑː.strə-/ **noun** [C] **1** B2 the symbol ' used in writing to show when a letter or a number has been left out, as in I'm (= I am) or '85 (= 1985), or that is used before or after s to show possession, as in Helen's house or babies' hands: *'It's' with an apostrophe means 'it is' or 'it has'.* **2** sometimes used before s to show the plural of a number or a letter: *There are two p's in 'supper'.*

apothecary /əˈpɒθ.ə.kər.i/ US /-ˈpɑː.θəˌker.i/ **noun** [C] a person who in the past made and sold medicines

apotheosis /əˌpɒθ.iˈəʊ.sɪs/ US /-ˌpɑː.θiˈoʊ-/ **noun** [C usually singular] (plural **apotheoses** /-siːz/) formal **1** the best or most extreme example of something: *Most people agree that her acting career* ***achieved*** *its apotheosis in this movie.* ◦ *Bad taste in clothes* ***reached*** *its apotheosis in the 1970s.* **2 the apotheosis of sb** the act of making someone into a god: *the apotheosis of the Emperor Trajan*

app /æp/ **noun** [C] **1** abbreviation for application: a computer program that is designed for a particular purpose: *You can run an app on your PC that will find the files and burn them to a CD.* **2** abbreviation for application: a computer program or piece of software designed for a particular purpose that you can DOWNLOAD onto a mobile phone or other mobile device: *There are apps for everything, from learning a language to booking movie tickets.*

appal (-ll-) (US usually **appall**) /əˈpɔːl/ US /-ˈpɑːl/ **verb** [T] to make someone have strong feelings of shock or of disapproval: *I was appalled* ***at/by*** *the lack of staff in the hospital.* ◦ *The state of the kitchen appalled her.* • **appalled** /əˈpɔːld/ US /-ˈpɑːld/ **adj** *an appalled silence/fascination*

appalling /əˈpɔː.lɪŋ/ US /-ˈpɑː-/ **adj** **1** C1 very bad: *appalling weather* ◦ *The journey home was appalling.* **2** C2 shocking and very bad: *appalling injuries* ◦ *Prisoners were kept in the most appalling conditions.* • **appallingly** /-li/ **adv** *The number of casualties was appallingly high in both wars.* ◦ *The whole play was appallingly (= very badly) acted.*

apparatus /ˌæp.əˈreɪ.təs/ US /-ˈræţ.əs/ **noun** (plural **apparatuses**) **EQUIPMENT** ▷ **1** [U or C] a set of equipment or tools or a machine that is used for a particular purpose: *a* ***piece of*** *apparatus* ◦ *The divers checked their breathing apparatus.* **ORGANIZATION** ▷ **2** [C usually singular] an organization or system, especially a political one: *The whole apparatus of communism was already falling apart.*

apparel /əˈpær.əl/ **noun** [U] **1** mainly US clothes of a particular type when they are being sold in a shop: *sports apparel* **2** old use or formal clothes

apparent /əˈpær.ənt/ US /-ˈper-/ **adj** **1** B2 able to be seen or understood: *Her unhappiness was apparent* ***to*** *everyone.* ◦ [+ that] ***It*** *was becoming increasingly apparent* ***that*** *he could no longer look after himself.* ◦ *I was on the metro this morning when* ***for no*** *apparent* ***reason*** *the man opposite suddenly screamed.* **2** C1 [before noun] seeming to exist or be true: *There are one or two apparent discrepancies between the two reports.*

apparently /əˈpær.ənt.li/ US /-ˈper-/ **adv** **1** B2 used to say you have read or been told something although you are not certain it is true: *Apparently it's going to rain today.* ◦ *Apparently he's had enough of England*

and is going back to Australia. **2** B2 used when the real situation is different from what you thought it was: *You know I told you Alice's party was on the 13th? Well I saw her last night and apparently it's on the 14th.* ◦ *She looks about ten but apparently she's 14.* ◦ *I thought they were married but apparently* ***not*** *(= they are not married).* **3** B2 used to say that something seems to be true, although it is not certain: *An 80-year-old woman was badly hurt in what the police describe as an apparently motiveless attack (= an attack with no obvious purpose).*

apparition /ˌæp.əˈrɪʃ.ən/ noun [C] the spirit of a dead person appearing in a form that can be seen

appeal /əˈpiːl/ noun; verb

▸noun **REQUEST** ▷ **1** C1 [C] a request to the public for money, information, or help: *They're* ***launching*** *(= starting) an appeal to raise money for famine victims.* ◦ [+ to infinitive] *The police have issued an appeal* ***to*** *the public* ***to*** *stay away from the area at the weekend.* **LEGAL** ▷ **2** [C or U] a request made to a law court or to someone in authority to change a previous decision: *The case went to the* ***court of*** *appeal/the appeal* ***court.*** ◦ *He won his appeal and the sentence was halved.* ◦ *She has* ***lodged*** *(= made) an appeal* ***against*** *the severity of the fine.* **QUALITY** ▷ **3** B2 [U] the quality in someone or something that makes them attractive or interesting: ***sex*** *appeal* ◦ *Spielberg films have a* ***wide*** *appeal.* ◦ *This used to be a marvellous hotel but it has* ***lost*** *its appeal in recent years.*

▸verb **REQUEST** ▷ **1** C1 [I] to make a serious or formal request, especially to the public, for money, information, or help: *They're appealing* ***for*** *clothes and blankets to send to the devastated region.* ◦ *The police are appealing* ***to*** *the public* ***for*** *any information about the missing girl.* ◦ *I tried to appeal* ***to*** *(= ask for support based on) his sense of loyalty, stressing how good the company had been to him.* ◦ [+ to infinitive] *Church leaders have appealed* ***to*** *the government* ***to*** *halt the war.* **LEGAL** ▷ **2** [I] to request a higher law court to consider again a decision made by a lower court, especially in order to reduce or prevent a punishment: *The teenager has been given leave (= allowed) by the High Court to appeal* ***against*** *her two-year sentence.* ◦ *They're appealing* ***to*** *the High Court to reduce the sentence to a fine.* **3** [I] to formally request that a legal or official decision be changed: *The parents appealed* ***against*** *the school's decision not to admit the child.* ◦ *The footballer appealed* ***to*** *the referee* ***for*** *a free kick.* **ATTRACT** ▷ **4** B2 [I not continuous] to interest or attract someone: *I haven't been skiing – it's never really appealed.* ◦ *It's a programme designed to appeal mainly* ***to*** *16 to 25-year-olds.* ◦ *I think what appeals* ***to*** *me about his painting is his use of colour.*

appealing /əˈpiː.lɪŋ/ adj **1** attractive or interesting: *The idea of not having to get up early every morning is rather appealing (***to*** *me).* ◦ *He had a nice smile and an appealing personality.* → Opposite **unappealing** **2** showing that you want people to help or protect you: *a little dog with appealing big brown eyes* • **appealingly** /-li/ adv

appear /əˈpɪər/ US /-ˈpɪr/ verb **BE PRESENT** ▷ **1** B1 [I] to start to be seen or to be present: *He suddenly appeared in the doorway.* ◦ *We'd been in the house a month when dark stains started appearing on the wall.* ◦ *His name appears in the film credits for lighting.* **2** [I] If you appear in court, you are there officially because you are involved in a trial: *Both women will be appearing* ***before*** *magistrates later this week.* **SEEM** ▷ **3** B1 [L or I, not continuous] to seem: *You've got to appear (***to be***) calm in an interview even if you're terrified underneath.* ◦ *To people who don't know him he probably appears (***to be***) rather unfriendly.* ◦ *Things aren't always* ***what they*** *appear* ***to be.*** ◦ [+ to infinitive] *She appears* ***to*** *actually like the man, which I find incredible.* ◦ ***There*** *appears* ***to*** *be some mistake.* ◦ [+ (that)] ***It*** *appears (***that***) she left the party alone.* ◦ ***It*** *appears to me (***that***) (= I think that) we need to make some changes.* ◦ formal ***It would*** *appear (***that***) (= it seems that) nobody on board the aircraft actually had a licence to fly it.* ◦ [+ adv/prep] ***It*** *appears* ***as if/as though*** *I was wrong.* ◦ *Everything was not* ***as*** *it appeared – secret deals had been done.* ◦ *I know* ***how*** *it must appear, but it's not really as bad as it looks.* ◦ *'Has he left?'* ***'It*** *appears* ***not/so.****'* ◦ [after so] *'I think we're late.'* ***'So it*** *appears.'* **PERFORM** ▷ **4** B1 [I usually + adv/prep] to perform publicly in a play, film, or show: *She will be appearing in the latest adaptation of 'Bleak House'.* ◦ *She appears briefly in the new Bond film.* **BECOME AVAILABLE** ▷ **5** B2 [I] to start to exist or become available: *I've noticed that smaller cars are starting to appear (= be produced or sold) again.* ◦ *The film, currently showing in the States, will be appearing on our screens (= we will be able to see it) later this year.* **ARRIVE** ▷ **6** [I] to arrive: *If she hasn't appeared by ten o'clock I'm going without her.*

PHRASAL VERB **appear for sb** If a lawyer appears for someone, he or she acts for and represents the person: *Ms Hawley was appearing for the defence.*

appearance /əˈpɪə.rəns/ US /-ˈpɪr.əns/ noun **BEING PRESENT** ▷ **1** B2 [C] an occasion when someone appears in public: *It was his first appearance on television/television appearance* ***as*** *president.* ◦ *She will be making a* ***public*** *appearance, signing copies of her latest novel.* **2** [C] an occasion when someone goes to court to be officially involved in a trial: *This was the defendant's third* ***court*** *appearance for the same offence.* **3** B2 [C] a public performance by an ENTERTAINER: *He made his first* ***stage/TV*** *appearance at the age of six.* **4 put in an appearance** to be present somewhere for a short time: *I didn't really want to go to the party, but I thought I'd better put in an appearance.* **WAY YOU LOOK** ▷ **5** B1 [C or U] the way a person or thing looks to other people: *a middle-aged man* ***of*** *smart appearance* ◦ *You can* ***alter/change*** *the whole appearance* ***of*** *a room just by lighting it in a certain way.* ◦ *There was nothing unusual about/in her physical appearance.* ◦ *The large car outside the house gave the appearance* ***of*** *wealth (= suggested wealthy people lived there).* ◦ *Appearances can be deceptive.* **6 to/from all appearances** judging from what can be seen: *To all appearances their marriage is fine, but I think she gives him a bad time in private.*

> Word partners for **appearance** (**BEING PRESENT**)
>
> a ***brief/fleeting/sudden*** appearance • a ***rare/recent/ regular*** appearance • sb's ***farewell/final/first*** appearance • a ***personal/public*** appearance • ***make/put in*** an appearance • sb's appearance ***as*** sth • sb's appearance ***in*** sth

> Word partners for **appearance** (**WAY YOU LOOK**)
>
> the ***external/outward*** appearance • sb's ***personal/ physical*** appearance • a ***dishevelled/scruffy/ unkempt*** appearance • a ***striking*** appearance • ***improve*** your/sth's appearance

appease /əˈpiːz/ verb [T] formal disapproving to prevent further disagreement in arguments or war by giving to the other side an advantage that they have demanded: *She claimed that the government had only* changed the law in order to appease their critics. • **appeasement** /-mənt/ **noun** [U]

appellation /ˌæp.əˈleɪ.ʃən/ **noun** [C] formal a name or title: *As a child, he received the appellation 'Mouse'.*

append /əˈpend/ **verb** [T] formal to add something to the end of a piece of writing: *The author appends a short footnote* ***to*** *the text explaining the point.*

appendage /əˈpen.dɪdʒ/ **noun** [C] formal **1** something that exists as a smaller and less important part of something larger: *The committee is a* ***mere*** *appendage* ***of*** *the council and has no power of its own.* ◦ *The organism has small leaf-like appendages.* **2** an arm, leg, or other body part: *He had a tattoo on every visible appendage.*

appendectomy /ˌæp.enˈdek.tə.mi/, /-ən-/ **noun** [C] specialized a medical operation to remove the appendix

appendicitis /əˌpen.dɪˈsaɪ.tɪs/ (US) /-t̬ɪs/ **noun** [U] an illness in which the appendix is infected and painful and usually needs to be removed in an operation

appendix /əˈpen.dɪks/ **noun** [C] **BODY PART** ▷ **1** (plural **appendixes**) a small tube-shaped part that is joined to the INTESTINES on the right side of the body and has no use in humans: *She* ***had*** *her appendix* ***out*** *(= medically removed) last summer.* **BOOK PART** ▷ **2** (plural **appendixes** or **appendices** /-dɪ.siːz/) a separate part at the end of a book or magazine that gives extra information: *There's an appendix at the end of the book with a list of dates.*

appertain /ˌæp.əˈteɪn/ (US) /-ɚ-/ **verb**

PHRASAL VERB **appertain to sth** formal to be connected to or belong to: *She enjoyed the privileges appertaining to the office of chairman.*

appetite /ˈæp.ɪ.taɪt/ **noun** **FOOD** ▷ **1** C1 [C or U] the feeling that you want to eat food: *All that walking has* ***given*** *me an appetite.* ◦ *I won't have any chocolate, thanks. It will* ***spoil*** *(= reduce) my appetite.* ◦ *I haven't* ***got much of*** *an appetite (= I am not hungry).* ◦ *The children all* ***have healthy/good*** *appetites (= they eat a lot).* ◦ *Both viruses cause fever and* ***loss of*** *appetite.* **NEED** ▷ **2** C2 [C] the feeling of wanting or needing something: *her appetite* ***for*** *adventure* ◦ *his* ***insatiable*** *sexual appetite* ◦ *I've read an excerpt of the book on the Web and it's* ***whetted*** *my appetite (= increased my interest in it).*

appetizer (UK usually **appetiser**) /ˈæp.ɪ.taɪ.zəʳ/ (US) /-zɚ/ **noun** [C] **1** a small amount of food eaten before a meal: *At 6.30 everyone gathered for drinks and appetizers in the lounge.* **2** mainly US the first part of a meal: *The average cost of a full three-course meal – appetizer, main course, and dessert – is about $45.*

appetizing (UK usually **appetising**) /ˈæp.ɪ.taɪ.zɪŋ/ **adj** describes food or smells that make you want to eat: *appetizing smells from the kitchen*

applaud /əˈplɔːd/ (US) /-ˈplɑːd/ **verb** **CLAP** ▷ **1** C1 [I or T] to show enjoyment or approval of something such as a performance or speech by clapping the hands repeatedly to make a noise: *You should have heard the audience applaud – the noise was fantastic.* ◦ *She was applauded for a full five minutes after her speech.* **PRAISE** ▷ **2** C2 [T] formal to say that you admire and agree with a person's action or decision: *We applaud the family's decision to remain silent over the issue.*

applause /əˈplɔːz/ (US) /-ˈplɑːz/ **noun** [U] C1 the sound of people clapping their hands repeatedly to show enjoyment or approval of something such as a performance or speech: *His speech* ***met with*** *(= received) loud applause.* ◦ *So let's have a* ***round of*** *applause, please,* ***for*** *(= please applaud) a very lovely and talented young lady who is going to sing for us.*

apple /ˈæp.l̩/ **noun** [C or U] A1 a round fruit with firm, white flesh and a green, red, or yellow skin: *to peel an apple* ◦ *apple* ***pie/sauce*** ◦ *an apple* ***tree***

IDIOMS **an apple a day keeps the doctor away** saying This means that eating an apple each day can help to keep you healthy. • **the apple of sb's eye** old-fashioned the person who someone loves most and is very proud of: *His youngest daughter was the apple of his eye.* • **be in apple-pie order** UK old-fashioned to be perfectly arranged and tidy: *Their house is always in apple-pie order.*

applejack /ˈæp.l̩.dʒæk/ **noun** [U] mainly US a type of BRANDY (= alcoholic drink) made from apples

ˈapple ˌjuice **noun** [U] juice from crushed apples, used for a drink or to make VINEGAR

applet /ˈæp.lət/ **noun** [C] specialized a small computer program, often used on websites, that performs one particular task and works from within a larger program

appliance /əˈplaɪ.əns/ **noun** [C] C1 a device, machine, or piece of equipment, especially an electrical one that is used in the house, such as a cooker or washing machine: *electric/domestic/household appliances*

applicable /əˈplɪk.ə.bl̩/ **adj** affecting or relating to a person or thing: *This part of the law is only applicable* ***to*** *companies employing more than five people.* ◦ *The new qualifications are applicable* ***to*** *all European countries.*

applicant /ˈæp.lɪ.kənt/ **noun** [C] a person who formally requests something, especially a job, or a place at college or university: *How many applicants did you have* ***for*** *the job?*

application /ˌæp.lɪˈkeɪ.ʃən/ **noun** **REQUEST** ▷ **1** B1 [C or U] an official request for something, usually in writing: *a* ***letter of*** *application* ◦ *Free information will be sent out* ***on*** *application* ***to*** *(= if you ask) the central office.* ◦ *I've sent off applications* ***for*** *four different jobs.* ◦ *Have you filled in the application* ***form*** *for your passport yet?* ◦ [+ to infinitive] *Argentina has submitted an application* ***to*** *host the World Cup.* **COMPUTER** ▷ **2** B2 [C] a computer program that is designed for a particular purpose: *spreadsheet applications* **USE** ▷ **3** C2 [C or U] a way in which something can be used for a particular purpose: *The design has many applications.* ◦ *the application of this research in the treatment of cancer* **HARD WORK** ▷ **4** [U] the determination to work hard over a period of time in order to succeed at something: *Joshua clearly has ability in this subject but lacks application.* **PUTTING ON** ▷ **5** [C or U] the act of spreading or rubbing a substance such as cream or paint on a surface, or a layer of cream or paint: *Leave the paint to dry between applications.* ◦ *Regular application of the cream should reduce swelling within 24 hours.* **RELATION TO** ▷ **6** [C or U] a way in which a rule or law, etc. relates to or is important for someone or something: *The new laws have (a) particular application* ***to*** *the self-employed.*

applicator /ˈæp.lɪ.keɪ.təʳ/ (US) /-t̬ɚ/ **noun** [C] a device used to put something on or into a particular place

applied /əˈplaɪd/ **adj** [before noun] relating to a subject of study, especially a science, that has a practical use: ***pure and*** *applied mathematics/science*

apˌplied linˈguistics **noun** [U] the study of language as it affects situations in real life, for example in education or technology

appliqué /əˈpliː.keɪ/ **noun** [U] decorative work in which one piece of cloth is sewn or fixed onto another, or the activity of decorating cloth in this way • **appliqué** verb [T]

apply /əˈplaɪ/ verb **REQUEST** ▷ **1** B1 [I] to request something, usually officially, especially by writing or sending in a form: *I've applied for a new job with the local newspaper.* ◦ *Please apply in writing **to** the address below.* ◦ *We've applied **to** a charitable organization **for** a grant for the project.* ◦ [+ to infinitive] *Tim's applied **to** join the police.* **RELATE TO** ▷ **2** B2 [I] (especially of rules or laws) to have a connection or be important: *That bit of the form is for UK citizens – it doesn't apply **to** you.* ◦ *Those were old regulations – they don't apply any more.* **USE** ▷ **3** C1 [T] to make use of something or use it for a practical purpose: *He wants a job in which he can apply his foreign languages.* ◦ *The court heard how the driver had failed to apply his brakes in time.* ◦ *If you apply pressure to a cut it's meant to stop the bleeding.* **PUT ON** ▷ **4** [T] to spread or rub a substance such as cream or paint on a surface: *Apply the cream liberally **to** exposed areas every three hours and after swimming.* ◦ *The paint should be applied thinly and evenly.* **WORK HARD** ▷ **5 apply yourself** C2 If you apply yourself to something, you work hard at it, directing your abilities and efforts in a determined way so that you succeed.

appoint /əˈpɔɪnt/ verb **PERSON** ▷ **1** C1 [T] to choose someone officially for a job or responsibility: *We've appointed three new teachers this year.* ◦ *He's just been appointed (**as**) director of the publishing division.* ◦ [+ to infinitive] *A commission has just been appointed **to** investigate fraud claims.* **DATE** ▷ **2** [T usually passive] formal to arrange a date or time when a meeting or other event will happen: *A date has been appointed for the election.*

appointed /əˈpɔɪn.tɪd/ US /-t̬ɪd/ adj **PERSON** ▷ **1** officially chosen for a job or responsibility: *I'd like to introduce our newly appointed members of staff.* → See also **self-appointed** **DATE** ▷ **2** (of a day or time) arranged for a meeting, etc. to happen: *Ten minutes before the appointed **time**, he sat nervously outside her office.* **ROOM** ▷ **3** formal If buildings or rooms are appointed in a particular way, they have furniture and equipment of the stated standard: *It says in the ad that the bathroom is spacious and **well** appointed.* → See also **well appointed**

appointee /əˌpɔɪnˈtiː/ noun [C] someone who has been chosen officially for a job or responsibility: *a government appointee* ◦ *The new appointee will be working closely with both departments.*

appointment /əˈpɔɪnt.mənt/ noun **ARRANGEMENT** ▷ **1** A2 [C] a formal arrangement to meet or visit someone at a particular time and place: *I'd like to **make** an appointment **with** Dr Evans, please.* ◦ *She had to **cancel** her **dental** appointment.* ◦ [+ to infinitive] *I've got an appointment **to** see Ms Edwards at two o'clock.* ◦ *I've got a two o'clock appointment **with** Ms Edwards.* ◦ *If he didn't have a secretary to remind him, he wouldn't **keep** (= remember to be present at) any of his appointments.* ◦ *That's the second appointment he's **missed**.* **2 by appointment** at a previously arranged time: *House for sale, two bedrooms. Viewing by appointment only.* **JOB** ▷ **3** C2 [C or U] the act of officially choosing someone for a job, or the job itself: *his appointment **as** senior lecturer* ◦ *We would like to announce **the** appointment **of** Julia Lewis **as** head of sales.* ◦ *Our department expects to **make** five new appointments (= appoint five new people) this year alone.* **4 by appointment** in the UK, used by businesses to show that their goods and services are sold to the Queen: *Carter's Ltd, confectioners by appointment **to** the Queen*

apportion /əˈpɔː.ʃən/ US /-ˈpɔːr-/ verb [T] formal to give or share out, especially blame or money among several people or things: *When we know how much is profit, then we can apportion the money **among/between** us.* ◦ *The investigation into the air crash would inevitably apportion **blame to** certain members of the crew.*

apposite /ˈæp.ə.zɪt/, /-zaɪt/ adj formal suitable and right for the occasion: *an apposite phrase/quotation/remark*

apposition /ˌæp.əˈzɪʃ.ən/ noun [U] specialized in grammar, a situation in which two nouns or noun phrases are used to refer to the same person or thing: *In the expression 'my brother Joe', 'my brother' and 'Joe' are **in** apposition.*

appraisal /əˈpreɪ.zəl/ noun [C or U] **1** the act of examining someone or something in order to judge their qualities, success, or needs: *The newspaper gave an editorial appraisal **of** the government's achievements of the past year.* **2** (also **ˈjob/perˈformance apˌpraisal**) a meeting in which an employee discusses his or her progress, aims, and needs at work with his or her manager or employer: *Many companies operate regular job appraisals, often on an annual basis.*

appraise /əˈpreɪz/ verb [T] **1** to examine someone or something in order to judge their qualities, success, or needs: *At the end of each teaching practice, trainee teachers are asked to appraise their own **performance**.* ◦ *In cooperation with other professionals, social workers will appraise the individual's needs.* ◦ *He coolly appraised the **situation**, deciding which person would be most likely to succeed.* **2** US for **value**: *The ring was appraised **at $40,000**.* • **appraisee** /ə.preɪˈziː/ noun [C] a person who is being appraised • **appraiser** /əˈpreɪ.zər/ US /-zɚ/ noun [C] a person who appraises someone or something

appreciable /əˈpriː.ʃə.bl̩/ adj If an amount or change is appreciable, it is large or noticeable enough to have an important effect: *There has been an appreciable drop in the number of unemployed since the new government came to power.* • **appreciably** /-bli/ adv *Her health has improved appreciably since she changed her treatment.*

> **!** Common mistake: **would appreciate**
>
> **Remember: would appreciate** is usually followed by **it**.
>
> Don't say 'I would appreciate if …', say **I would appreciate it if …**:
>
> ~~*I would appreciate if you could pick me up from the airport.*~~

appreciate /əˈpriː.ʃi.eɪt/ verb **VALUE** ▷ **1** B2 to recognize how good someone or something is and to value them: *There's no point buying him expensive wines – he doesn't appreciate them.* **2** C2 [T] to understand a situation and realize that it is important: *We appreciate the need for immediate action.* ◦ [+ that] *I appreciate **that** it's a difficult decision for you to make.* ◦ [+ question word] *I don't think you appreciate **how** much time I spent preparing this meal.* **3 I/we appreciate...** B2 used when you are thanking someone or showing that you are grateful: *We really appreciate all the help you gave us last weekend.* ◦ [+ -ing verb] *I appreciate your mak**ing** the effort to come.* **4 would appreciate** B2 used when you are politely asking for something: *I would appreciate **it** if you could let me know (= please let me know) in advance whether or not you will be coming.* **INCREASE** ▷ **5** [I] to increase in value: *Our house has* appreciated (**in value**) **by** 50 percent in the last two years. → Opposite **depreciate**

! Common mistake: **appreciate**

Warning: Check your spelling!

Appreciate is one of the 50 words most often spelled wrongly by learners.

appreciation /əˌpriː.ʃiˈeɪ.ʃən/ noun [U] VALUE ▷ **1** B2 the act of recognizing or understanding that something is valuable, important, or as described: *Max has no appreciation **of** the finer things in life.* ◦ *The crowd cheered **in** appreciation.* ◦ *Children rarely show any appreciation **of/for** what their parents do for them.* ◦ *These flowers are a token of my appreciation **of/for** all your help.* INCREASE ▷ **2** increase in price, value, etc.: *There has been little appreciation in the value of property recently.*

appreciative /əˈpriː.ʃə.tɪv/ US /-t̬ɪv/ adj showing that you understand how good something is, or are grateful for something: *It's nice to have an appreciative audience.* ◦ *I'm very appreciative **of** all the support you've given me.* • **appreciatively** /-li/ adv *She smiled appreciatively at him.*

apprehend /ˌæp.rɪˈhend/ verb [T] formal CATCH ▷ **1** to catch and arrest someone who has not obeyed the law: *The police have finally apprehended the killer.* UNDERSTAND ▷ **2** to understand something

apprehension /ˌæp.rɪˈhen.ʃən/ noun [U] WORRY ▷ **1** worry about the future, or a fear that something unpleasant is going to happen: *It's normal to feel a little apprehension before starting a new job.* ◦ *There is some apprehension in the office **about** who the new director will be.* CATCHING ▷ **2** formal the situation in which the police catch and arrest someone who has not obeyed the law: *Both the army and the police were involved in the apprehension of the terrorists.* UNDERSTANDING ▷ **3** formal the act of understanding something

apprehensive /ˌæp.rɪˈhen.sɪv/ adj feeling worried about something that you are going to do or that is going to happen: *I'm a bit apprehensive **about** tomorrow's meeting.* ◦ *I've invited a lot of people to the party, but I'm a bit apprehensive **that** no one will come.* • **apprehensively** /-li/ adv *They looked at each other apprehensively.*

apprentice /əˈpren.tɪs/ US /-t̬ɪs/ noun; verb

▸noun [C] someone who has agreed to work for a skilled person for a particular period of time and often for low payment, in order to learn that person's skills: *Most of the work was done by apprentices.* ◦ *an apprentice carpenter*

▸verb [T usually passive] old-fashioned to make someone an apprentice: *Michelangelo was apprenticed **to** Ghirlandaio in Florence for three years.*

apprenticeship /əˈpren.tɪs.ʃɪp/ US /-t̬ɪs-/ noun [C or U] a period of time working as an apprentice

apprise /əˈpraɪz/ verb [T] formal to tell someone about something: *The president has been apprised **of** the situation.*

approach /əˈprəʊtʃ/ US /-ˈproʊtʃ/ verb; noun

▸verb COME NEAR ▷ **1** B1 [I or T] to come near or nearer to something or someone in space, time, quality, or amount: *We could just see the train approaching in the distance.* ◦ *If you look out of the window on the left of the bus, you'll see that we're now approaching the Tower of London.* ◦ *I see it's approaching lunchtime, so let's take a break.* ◦ *In my opinion, no other composers even begin to approach (= come near in quality to) Mozart.* ◦ *The total amount raised so far is approaching (= almost) $1,000.* ◦ *He's very active for a man approaching 80 (= who is almost 80 years old).* DEAL WITH ▷ **2** B2 [T] to deal with something: *I'm not sure how to approach the problem.* COMMUNICATE ▷ **3** [T] to speak to, write to, or visit someone in order to do something such as make a request or business agreement: *We've just approached the bank **for/about** a loan.* ◦ *She's been approached by a modelling agency.*

▸noun DEALING WITH ▷ **1** B2 [C] a way of considering or doing something: *Since our research so far has not produced any answers to this problem, we need to **adopt** a different approach **to** it.* ◦ *Michael is always very logical **in** his approach.* COMING NEAR ▷ **2** B2 [C or U] the fact of getting nearer in distance or time: *The siren signalled the approach **of** an ambulance.* ◦ *Many kinds of birds fly south **at** the approach of winter.* ◦ *Please fasten your seat belts, the plane is now making its final approach (**in**)**to** (= is coming near to and preparing to land at) Heathrow.* **3** a route that leads to a place: *There is a very steep approach to the house.* ◦ *We got stuck in a traffic jam on the approach **road**.* **4 the closest/nearest approach to sth** mainly UK the most similar thing to something else that is mentioned: *That's the nearest approach to an apology you're going to get from Paula.* COMMUNICATION ▷ **5** [C] an act of communicating with another person or group in order to ask for something: *The hospital is **making** approaches **to** local businesses (= asking them to help) in their bid to raise money.* ◦ *I hear that Everton have **made** an approach **to** (= an attempt to make a business arrangement with) Arsenal to buy one of their players.*

approachable /əˈprəʊ.tʃə.bl̩/ US /-ˈproʊ-/ adj CHARACTER ▷ **1** friendly and easy to talk to: *Graham's always very approachable – why don't you talk the problem over with him?* PLACE ▷ **2** If a place is approachable, you can reach it or get near to it: *It's one of the few lakeside villages approachable by car.*

approbation /ˌæp.rəˈbeɪ.ʃən/ noun [U] formal approval or agreement, often given by an official group: *The council has finally indicated its approbation of the plans.*

appropriate adj; verb

▸adj /əˈprəʊ.pri.ət/ US /-ˈproʊ-/ B2 suitable or right for a particular situation or occasion: *appropriate footwear for the country* ◦ *Is this film appropriate **for** small children?* ◦ *I didn't think his comments were very appropriate at the time.* ◦ *Is this an appropriate occasion to discuss finance?* ◦ *Please complete the appropriate parts of this form (= the parts that are right or necessary for your particular situation) and return it as soon as possible.* → Opposite **inappropriate** • **appropriately** /-li/ adv B2 *She didn't think we were appropriately dressed for a wedding.* • **appropriateness** /-nəs/ noun [U]

▸verb [T] /əˈprəʊ.pri.eɪt/ US /-ˈproʊ-/ formal TAKE ▷ **1** to take something for your own use, usually without permission: *He lost his job when he was found to have appropriated some of the company's money.* KEEP MONEY ▷ **2** to keep an amount of money to use for a particular purpose: *The government have appropriated millions of pounds **for** the project.*

appropriation /əˌprəʊ.priˈeɪ.ʃən/ US /-ˌproʊ-/ noun [C or U] TAKING ▷ **1** the act of taking something for your own use, usually without permission: *The author objected to the appropriation of his story by an amateur film maker.* SUM OF MONEY ▷ **2** formal an amount of money to be used for a particular purpose: *The committee approved an appropriation of £10,000.* ◦ [often plural] *The foundation was promised a*

seven percent increase to bring its appropriations to $2.07 billion.

approval /ə'pruː.vəl/ **noun** [U] **GOOD OPINION** ▷ **1** B2 the feeling of having a positive opinion of someone or something: *He showed his approval by smiling broadly.* ◦ *Alan is someone who always needs the approval of other people.* ◦ *Sam always tried hard to* ***win*** *his father's approval.* ◦ formal *Does the wine* ***meet with your*** *approval? (= Do you like the wine?)* **2 on approval** If you buy something on approval, you can return it without payment if it is not satisfactory. **PERMISSION** ▷ **3** B2 official permission: *The project has now* ***received*** *approval from the government.* ◦ *The teacher gave the student* ***a nod of*** *approval.*

approve /ə'pruːv/ **verb** **HAVE A GOOD OPINION** ▷ **1** B2 [I] to have a positive opinion of someone or something: *She doesn't approve* ***of*** *my friends.* ◦ *He doesn't approve* ***of*** *smok****ing****.* ◦ *I thoroughly approve* ***of*** *what the government is doing.* → Opposite **disapprove** **AGREE** ▷ **2** B1 [T] to accept, allow, or officially agree to something: *We had to wait months for the council to approve our plans to extend the house.* ◦ *The court approved the sale of the property.*

approved /ə'pruːvd/ **adj** describes something that is generally or officially accepted as being correct or satisfactory: *What's the approved way of dealing with this?* ◦ *This school only offers approved language courses.*

ap,proved 'school **noun** [C] UK old-fashioned for **young offenders' institution** (= a prison for young people)

approving /ə'pruː.vɪŋ/ **adj** showing that you have a positive opinion about something or someone: *She gave him an approving smile.* • **approvingly** /-li/ **adv** *She smiled at him approvingly.*

approx. /ə'prɒks/ US /-'prɑːks/ **adv** abbreviation for **approximately**

approximant /ə'prɒk.sɪ.mənt/ US /-'prɑːk-/ **noun** [C] specialized a consonant sound in which air is able to flow almost completely freely: *The sounds /w/, /l/, and /r/ are examples of approximants in English.*

approximate **adj; verb**

▸**adj** /ə'prɒk.sɪ.mət/ US /-'prɑːk/ B2 not completely accurate but close: *The train's approximate time of arrival is 10.30.* ◦ *The approximate* ***cost*** *will be about $600.* ◦ *Can you give me an approximate* ***idea*** *of the numbers involved?*

▸**verb** [I + adv/prep, T] /ə'prɒk.sɪ.meɪt/ US /-'prɑːk-/ formal to be almost the same as: *The newspaper reports of the discussion only* ***roughly*** *approximated* ***to*** *(= were not exactly the same as) what was actually said.* ◦ *Student numbers this year are expected to approximate 5,000 (= to be about 5,000).*

approximately /ə'prɒk.sɪ.mət.li/ US /-'prɑːk-/ **adv** B1 close to a particular number or time although not exactly that number or time: *The job will take approximately three weeks, and cost approximately £1,000.*

approximation /ə,prɒk.sɪ'meɪ.ʃən/ US /-,prɑːk-/ **noun** [C] formal a guess of a number that is not exact but that is close: *Could you give me a* ***rough*** *approximation* ***of*** *how many people will be coming?* ◦ *What he said bore no approximation whatsoever* ***to*** *the truth (= was not at all like the truth).*

appurtenance /ə'pɜː.tɪ.nəns/ US /-'pɝː.t̬ɪ-/ **noun** [C usually plural] formal a possession or piece of property that is considered to be a typical feature of a particular way of living

APR /,eɪ.piː'ɑːr/ US /-'ɑːr/ **noun** [S] abbreviation for Annual Percentage Rate: the rate at which someone who borrows money is charged, calculated over a period of twelve months: *The interest rate on my credit card is currently 25.5 percent APR.*

après-ski /,æp.reɪ'skiː/ **noun** [U] social activities that take place in the evening at hotels and restaurants in places where people go to ski: *après-ski entertainment*

apricot /'eɪ.prɪ.kɒt/ US /-kɑːt/ **noun** **FRUIT** ▷ **1** [C] a small, round, soft fruit with a pale orange, FURRY skin **COLOUR** ▷ **2** [U] a pale orange colour • **apricot adj**

April /'eɪ.prəl/ **noun** [C or U] (written abbreviation **Apr.**) A1 the fourth month of the year, after March and before May: *We came back* ***in*** *April.* ◦ *The meeting is* ***on*** *4 April.* ◦ *I haven't seen her since* ***last*** *April.*

,April 'fool **noun; exclamation**

▸**noun** [C usually singular] a trick played on someone on April Fool's Day, or the person who is tricked

▸**exclamation** UK (US **April fools!**) said on April Fool's Day when you have tricked someone

,April 'Fool's ,Day (UK also **,All 'Fools' ,Day**) 1 April, a day when people play tricks on people

a priori /,eɪ.praɪ'ɔː.raɪ/, /-priː'ɔː.ri/ US /-'ɔːr.aɪ/ **adj** [before noun] formal relating to an argument that suggests the probable effects of a known cause, or using general principles to suggest likely effects: *'It's freezing outside, you must be cold' is an example of a priori reasoning.* • **a priori adv**

apron /'eɪ.prən/ **noun** [C] **CLOTHING** ▷ **1** a piece of clothing that you wear over the front of other clothes to keep the clothes clean while you are doing something dirty, such as cooking or cleaning **AIRPORT** ▷ **2** the part of an airport in which aircraft are turned around or goods are put onto them **THEATRE** ▷ **3** (also **'apron ,stage**) part of a stage in a theatre that is in front of the curtain

apron

apropos /,æp.rə'pəʊ/ US /-'poʊ/ **adv, preposition; adj**

▸**adv, preposition** formal used to introduce something that is related to or connected with something that has just been said: *I had an email from Sally yesterday – apropos* ***(of)*** *which, did you send her that article?* ◦ *Apropos what you said yesterday, I think you made the right decision.*

▸**adj** [after verb] formal suitable in a particular situation or at a particular time: *clothes that are apropos* ***to*** *the occasion*

apse /æps/ **noun** [C] specialized an area with curved walls at the end of a building, usually at the the east end of a church

apt /æpt/ **adj** **SUITABLE** ▷ **1** suitable or right for a particular situation: *an apt* ***comment/description*** **LIKELY** ▷ **2 be apt to do sth/be apt to be sth** to be likely to do something or to often do something: *The kitchen roof is apt to (= likely to) leak when it rains.* ◦ *She's in her eighties now and apt to be a bit forgetful.* **CLEVER** ▷ **3** formal having a natural ability or skill: *We have some particularly apt students in the class this year.* • **aptly** /'æptli/ **adv** *We spent a week at the aptly* ***named*** *Grand View Hotel.* • **aptness** /-nəs/ **noun** [U] *the aptness of his comment* ◦ old-fashioned formal *an aptness* ***for/at*** *drawing*

aptitude /'æp.tɪ.tjuːd/ US /-tuːd/ **noun** [C or U] a natural ability or skill: *My son has no/little aptitude* ***for*** *sport.* ◦ *We will take your* ***personal*** *aptitudes and abilities into account.*

A

ˈaptitude ˌtest noun [C] a test to find out if someone has a natural ability for a particular type of work: *I had to take an aptitude test before I began training as a nurse.*

aqua /ˈæk.wə/ noun [U] **WATER** ▷ **1** UK specialized water, when it is used in make-up and beauty products **COLOUR** ▷ **2** a greenish-blue colour • **aqua** adj of a greenish-blue colour

ˌaqua-aeˈrobics noun [U] exercises performed to music in a swimming pool, usually in an organized group: *an aqua-aerobics class*

ˈAqua-Lung noun [C] trademark a container of air that someone carries on their back while swimming under the surface of the water, which has a tube taking air to their mouth or nose to allow them to breathe

aquamarine /ˌæk.wə.məˈriːn/ noun **STONE** ▷ **1** [C or U] a greenish-blue stone used in jewellery **COLOUR** ▷ **2** [U] a greenish-blue colour • **aquamarine** adj of a greenish-blue colour

aquaplane /ˈæk.wə.pleɪn/ verb [I] UK (US **hydroplane**) If a motor vehicle aquaplanes, it slides out of control on a wet road.

aquaplaning /ˈæk.wə.pleɪn.ɪŋ/ noun [U] UK (US **hydroplaning**) a situation in which a vehicle slides out of control on a wet road

aquarium /əˈkweə.ri.əm/ (US) /-ˈkwer.i-/ noun [C] (plural **aquariums** or **aquaria** /-ə/) **1** a glass container in which fish and other water creatures can be kept **2** a building, usually open to the public, that holds many aquariums

Aquarius /əˈkweə.ri.əs/ (US) /-ˈkwer.i-/ noun [C or U] the eleventh sign of the ZODIAC, relating to the period 21 January to 19 February, or a person born during this period • **Aquarian** /-ən/ noun [C], adj

aquatic /əˈkwæt.ɪk/ (US) /-ˈkwæṭ-/ adj living or growing in, happening in, or connected with water: *aquatic* ***plants*** ◦ *aquatic sports* • **aquatically** /-ɪ.kəl.i/ adv

aquatics /əˈkwæt.ɪks/ (US) /-ˈkwæṭ-/ noun [U] a group of Olympic sports including swimming, DIVING, and WATER POLO

aquatint /ˈæk.wə.tɪnt/ noun [C] a picture produced by cutting it into a COPPER sheet with ACID and then printing it: *an aquatint by Picasso*

aqueduct /ˈæk.wɪ.dʌkt/ noun [C] a structure for carrying water across land, especially one like a high bridge with many ARCHES that carries pipes or a CANAL across a valley

aqueous /ˈeɪ.kwi.əs/ adj specialized like or containing water: *an aqueous solution*

ˌaqueous ˈhumour noun [U] specialized a clear liquid that fills the space inside your eye between the CORNEA (= outer covering) and the LENS

aquifer /ˈæk.wɪ.fəʳ/ (US) /ˈɑː.kwə.fɚ/ noun [C] specialized a layer of rock, sand, or earth that contains water or allows water to pass through it

aquiline /ˈæk.wɪ.laɪn/ adj literary of or like an EAGLE (= large bird): *an aquiline nose (= a nose curved like an eagle's beak)* ◦ *aquiline features (= a face with this type of nose)*

Arab /ˈær.əb/ (US) /ˈer-/ noun [C] a person from the Middle East or North Africa who speaks Arabic as a first language • **Arab** adj *The Arab countries include Iraq, Saudi Arabia, Syria, and Egypt.* • **Arabian** /əˈreɪ.bi.ən/ adj *the Arabian peninsula*

arabesque /ˌær.əˈbesk/ (US) /ˌer-/ noun **DANCE** ▷ **1** [C] a position in BALLET in which the dancer stands on one leg with the other leg held out straight behind **ART** ▷ **2** [C or U] a type of design based on flowers, leaves, and branches twisted together, found especially in Islamic art

Arabic /ˈær.ə.bɪk/ (US) /ˈer-/ noun [U] a Semitic language spoken in the Middle East and North Africa • **Arabic** adj *Arabic literature*

ˌArabic ˈnumeral noun [C usually plural] a symbol used for writing a number in many parts of the world: *1 and 2 are Arabic numerals.* → Compare **Roman numeral**

arable /ˈær.ə.bl/ (US) /ˈer-/ adj describes farming land that is used for, or is suitable for, growing crops: *arable farming/farmers/farms/land*

arachnid /əˈræk.nɪd/ noun [C] specialized any of a group of small animals, similar to insects but with four pairs of legs, that include SPIDERS, SCORPIONS, TICKS, and MITES

arachnophobia /əˈræk.nəˌfəʊ.bi.ə/ (US) /-ˌfoʊ-/ noun [U] specialized a very strong fear of SPIDERS

arbiter /ˈɑː.bɪ.təʳ/ (US) /ˈɑːr.bɪ.ṭɚ/ noun [C] someone who makes a judgment, solves an argument, or decides what will be done: *the arbiters* ***of fashion/taste*** ◦ *The government will be the* ***final*** *arbiter in the dispute.*

arbitrage /ˌɑː.bɪˈtrɑːʒ/ (US) /ˈɑːr.bɪ.trɑːʒ/ noun [U] specialized the method on the STOCK EXCHANGE of buying something in one place and selling it in another place at the same time, in order to make a profit from the difference in price in the two places

arbitrageur /ˌɑː.bɪ.trɑːˈʒɜːʳ/ (US) /ˈɑːr.bɪ.trɑː.ʒɚ/ noun [C] specialized a person who makes money from arbitrage

arbitrary /ˈɑː.bɪ.trər.i/ (US) /ˈɑːr.bə.trer-/ adj **CHANCE** ▷ **1** (C2) based on chance rather than being planned or based on reason: *arbitrary decision-making* ◦ *Did you have a reason for choosing your destination or was it arbitrary?* **UNFAIR** ▷ **2** disapproving using unlimited personal power without considering other people's wishes: *an arbitrary ruler* ◦ *The company has been the subject of an arbitrary take-over.* • **arbitrarily** /ˌɑː.bɪˈtreə.rɪ.li/ (US) /ˌɑːr.bɪˈtrer.ɪ-/ adv *We made the decision to go to Italy quite arbitrarily.* • **arbitrariness** /-nəs/ noun [U]

arbitrate /ˈɑː.bɪ.treɪt/ (US) /ˈɑːr-/ verb [I or T] to make a judgment in an argument, usually because asked to do so by those involved: *I've been asked to arbitrate* ***between*** *the opposing sides.* ◦ *An outside adviser has been brought in to arbitrate the dispute between the management and the union.*

arbitration /ˌɑː.bɪˈtreɪ.ʃən/ (US) /ˌɑːr-/ noun [U] the process of solving an argument between people by helping them to agree to an acceptable solution: *Both sides in the dispute have agreed to* ***go to*** *arbitration (= to have the disagreement solved by an arbitrator).*

arbitrator /ˈɑː.bɪ.treɪ.təʳ/ (US) /ˈɑːr.bɪ.treɪ.ṭɚ/ noun [C] a person who has been officially chosen to make a decision between two people or groups who do not agree

arboreal /ɑːˈbɔː.ri.əl/ (US) /ɑːrˈbɔːr.i-/ adj specialized of or living in trees: *arboreal animals*

arborio /ɑːˈbɔː.ri.əʊ/ (US) /ɑːrˈbɔːr.i.oʊ/ noun [U] (also **arˌborio ˈrice**) a type of Italian rice with short, fat grains

arbour UK (US **arbor**) /ˈɑː.bəʳ/ (US) /ˈɑːr.bɚ/ noun [C] a sheltered place in a garden formed by trees and bushes that are grown to partly surround it: *a rose arbour*

arc /ɑːk/ (US) /ɑːrk/ noun; verb

▸noun [C] **CURVE** ▷ **1** the shape of part of a circle, or

other curved line: *The ball rose* ***in*** *a high arc and fell behind the boundary line.* **ELECTRICITY** ▷ **2** a powerful flow of electricity that goes across a space between two points

▸verb **CURVE** ▷ **1** [I] to move in the shape of an arc: *The rocket arced gracefully into the sky.* **ELECTRICITY** ▷ **2** [I usually + adv/prep] to make an electric arc

arcade /ɑːˈkeɪd/ Ⓤⓢ /ɑːr-/ **noun** [C] **1** a covered area or passage in which there are shops: *a* ***shopping*** *arcade* **2** a covered passage joined to a building on one side and with columns and ARCHES along the other side

Arcadia /ɑːˈkeɪ.di.ə/ Ⓤⓢ /ɑːr-/ **noun** [S] literary an image or idea of life in the countryside that is believed to be perfect • **Arcadian** /-ən/ **adj**

arcane /ɑːˈkeɪn/ Ⓤⓢ /ɑːr-/ **adj** formal mysterious and known only by a few people: *He was the only person who understood all the arcane details of the agreement.*

arch /ɑːtʃ/ Ⓤⓢ /ɑːrtʃ/ **noun; verb; adj**

▸**noun** [C] **1** Ⓑ2 a structure, consisting of a curved top on two supports, that holds the weight of something above it: *In many churches the side aisles are separated from the central aisle by a row of arches.* ◦ *Passing through the arch, you enter an open courtyard.* → See also **archway** **2** something that has the shape of an arch, often used for decoration **3** the raised curve on the bottom of your foot: *She's got very* ***high*** *arches.*

▸**verb** [I or T] Ⓒ2 to make the shape of an arch: *Trees arch* ***over*** *the river.* ◦ *Her eyebrows arched in contempt.* ◦ *She watched the cat arch its* ***back***.

▸**adj** showing that you think it is funny that you know more about something than someone else does: *an arch tone of voice* • **archly** /ˈɑːtʃli/ Ⓤⓢ /ˈɑːrtʃli/ **adv** *She smiled archly at him.* ◦ *'I fail to understand what you're suggesting,' said Claire archly.*

arch- /ɑːtʃ-/ Ⓤⓢ /ɑːrtʃ-/ **prefix** **MAIN** ▷ **1** most important: *an archbishop* ◦ *an archduke* **EXTREME** ▷ **2** greater or especially worse than others of the same type: *an arch-criminal* ◦ *his arch-enemy* ◦ *He's always been an arch-opponent of the scheme.*

archaeological (US also **archeological**) /ˌɑː.ki.əˈlɒdʒ.ɪ.kəl/ Ⓤⓢ /ˌɑːr.ki.əˈlɑː.dʒɪ-/ **adj** involving or relating to archaeology: *an archaeological dig/excavation* ◦ *an area/site of archaeological interest* • **archaeologically** (US also **archeologically**) /-ɪ.kəl.i/ **adv**

archaeologist (mainly US **archeologist**) /ˌɑː.kiˈɒl.ə.dʒɪst/ Ⓤⓢ /ˌɑːr.kiˈɑː.lə-/ **noun** Ⓒ1 someone who studies the buildings, GRAVES, tools, and other objects of people who lived in the past

archaeology (US also **archeology**) /ˌɑː.kiˈɒl.ə.dʒi/ Ⓤⓢ /ˌɑːr.kiˈɑː.lə-/ **noun** [U] Ⓒ1 the study of the buildings, GRAVES, tools, and other objects which belonged to people who lived in the past, in order to learn about their culture and society

archaic /ɑːˈkeɪ.ɪk/ Ⓤⓢ /ɑːr-/ **adj** of or belonging to an ancient period in history: *an archaic system of government* ◦ *an archaic law/rule/language* • **archaically** /-ɪ.kəl.i/ **adv**

archaism /ɑːˈkeɪ.ɪ.zəm/ Ⓤⓢ /ɑːr-/ **noun** [C] specialized a word or expression that is not generally used any more

archangel /ˈɑːˌkeɪn.dʒəl/ Ⓤⓢ /ˈɑːr-/ **noun** [C] an ANGEL of high rank: *the Archangel Gabriel*

archbishop /ˌɑːtʃˈbɪʃ.əp/ Ⓤⓢ /ˌɑːrtʃ-/ **noun** [C] a BISHOP of the highest rank who is in charge of churches and other bishops in a particular large area: *The Archbishop of Canterbury holds the highest position in the Church of England.*

archbishopric /ˌɑːtʃˈbɪʃ.ə.prɪk/ Ⓤⓢ /ˌɑːrtʃ-/ **noun** [C] **1** the period of time during which a person serves as an archbishop **2** the area of which an archbishop is in charge

archdeacon /ˌɑːtʃˈdiː.kən/ Ⓤⓢ /ˌɑːrtʃ-/ **noun** [C] in the Anglican Church, a priest next in rank below a BISHOP

archdiocese /ˌɑːtʃˈdaɪə.sɪs/ Ⓤⓢ /ˌɑːrtʃ-/ **noun** [C] the area of which an ARCHBISHOP in some Christian Churches is in charge

archduke /ˌɑːtʃˈdjuːk/ Ⓤⓢ /ˌɑːrtʃˈduːk/ **noun** [C] a man of very high rank, especially in the past in the Austrian royal family: *The assassination of the Archduke Ferdinand started off the First World War.*

arched /ɑːtʃt/ Ⓤⓢ /ɑːrtʃt/ **adj** having a shape or structure with an curve at the top, like an arch: *The entrance to the cathedral is through an arched door.*

ˌarch-ˈenemy **noun** [C] an especially bad enemy

archeology /ˌɑː.kiˈɒl.ə.dʒi/ Ⓤⓢ /ˌɑːr.kiˈɑː.lə-/ **noun** [U] mainly US for **archaeology**

archer /ˈɑː.tʃər/ Ⓤⓢ /ˈɑːr.tʃɚ/ **noun** [C] a person who shoots arrows from a BOW for sport or as a weapon

archery /ˈɑː.tʃə.ri/ Ⓤⓢ /ˈɑːr.tʃɚ.i/ **noun** [U] the art or sport of shooting arrows

archetype /ˈɑː.kɪ.taɪp/ Ⓤⓢ /ˈɑːr-/ **noun** [C] a typical example of something, or the original model of something from which others are copied: *The United States is* ***the*** *archetype* ***of*** *a federal society.* • **archetypal** /ˌɑː.kɪˈtaɪ.pəl/, /ˈɑː.kɪ-/ Ⓤⓢ /ˌɑːr-/ **adj** (also **archetypical**) *an archetypal English gentleman* • **archetypically** /ˌɑː.kɪˈtɪp.ɪ.kəl.i/ Ⓤⓢ /ˌɑːr-/ **adv**

archipelago /ˌɑː.kɪˈpel.ə.ɡəʊ/ Ⓤⓢ /ˌɑːr.kɪˈpel.ə.ɡoʊ/ **noun** [C] (plural **archipelagos** or **archipelagoes**) a group of small islands or an area of sea in which there are many small islands: *the Hawaiian archipelago*

architect /ˈɑː.kɪ.tekt/ Ⓤⓢ /ˈɑːr-/ **noun** [C] **1** Ⓑ1 a person whose job is to design new buildings and make certain that they are built correctly **2** a person responsible for achieving a particular plan or aim: *Bevan was the architect of the British National Health Service.*

architectural /ˌɑː.kɪˈtek.tʃər.əl/ Ⓤⓢ /ˌɑːr.kɪˈtek.tʃɚ-/ **adj** relating to architecture: *architectural drawings/plans* ◦ *a building of architectural interest* • **architecturally** /-i/ **adv**

architecture /ˈɑː.kɪ.tek.tʃər/ Ⓤⓢ /ˈɑːr.kɪ.tek.tʃɚ/ **noun** [U] **1** Ⓑ1 the art and practice of designing and making buildings: *to study architecture* **2** Ⓑ1 the style in which buildings are made: *Roman architecture*

archive /ˈɑː.kaɪv/ Ⓤⓢ /ˈɑːr-/ **noun; verb**

▸**noun** [C] **1** (also **archives** [plural]) a collection of historical records relating to a place, organization, or family: *archive* ***film/footage****/material* ◦ *These old photographs should go in the family archives.* **2** (also **archives** [plural]) a place where historical records are kept: *I've been studying village records in the local archive.* **3** a computer file used to store electronic information or documents that you no longer need to use regularly

▸**verb** [T] **1** to store historical records or documents in an archive **2** in computer technology, to store electronic information that you no longer need to use regularly: *This software helps firms archive and retrieve emails.* • **archival** /ˌɑːˈkaɪ.vəl/ Ⓤⓢ /ˌɑːr-/ **adj**

A

archivist /ˈɑː.kɪ.vɪst/ US /ˈɑːr-/ noun [C] a person whose job is to take care of archives

archway /ˈɑːtʃ.weɪ/ US /ˈɑːrtʃ-/ noun [C] an entrance or passage formed by an ARCH

ˈarc ˌlamp noun [C] (also **ˈarc ˌlight**) a device that gives light produced by an electric ARC

Arctic /ˈɑːk.tɪk/ US /ˈɑːrk-/ noun; adj

▸noun **the Arctic** the very cold area around the North Pole: *Polar bears live in the Arctic.*

▸adj **1** belonging or relating to the Arctic: *No trees grow in the Arctic regions.* **2** figurative very cold: *The North of England has been experiencing Arctic **conditions** these past few days.*

the ˌArctic ˈCircle noun [S] an imaginary line around the Earth at approximately 70° North

ˈarc ˌwelding noun [U] the joining together of pieces of metal using an electric ARC

ardent /ˈɑː.dənt/ US /ˈɑːr-/ adj [before noun] showing strong feelings: *an ardent **supporter** of Manchester United ◦ an ardent feminist* • **ardently** /-li/ adv

ardour UK (US **ardor**) /ˈɑː.dəʳ/ US /ˈɑːr.dɚ/ noun [U] great enthusiasm or love: *His ardour **for** her cooled after only a few weeks.*

arduous /ˈɑː.dju.əs/ US /ˈɑːr.dʒu-/ adj difficult, needing a lot of effort and energy: *an arduous climb/task/journey* • **arduously** /-li/ adv • **arduousness** /-nəs/ noun [U]

are strong /ɑːʳ/ US /ɑːr/ weak /əʳ/ US /ɚ/ verb we/you/they form of **be**: *Are you hungry? ◦ They're (= they are) very late.*

area /ˈeə.ri.ə/ US /ˈer.i-/ noun **PLACE** ▷ **1** B1 [C] a particular part of a place, piece of land, or country: *All areas **of** the country will have some rain tonight. ◦ The area **of** New York to the south of Houston Street is known as Soho. ◦ Houses in **the** London area (= in and around London) are very expensive. ◦ He's an area manager (= is responsible for business in a particular area) for a computer company. ◦ This is a very poor area. ◦ Dogs are not allowed in the children's play area.* **SUBJECT** ▷ **2** B2 [C] a subject or activity, or a part of it: *Marketing is Paul's area. ◦ Software is not really my area **of expertise**.* **MEASURE** ▷ **3** [C or U] the size of a flat surface calculated by multiplying its length by its width: *the area of a rectangle ◦ Meadow Farm is 50 square kilometres **in** area.*

IDIOM **in the area of** approximately: *The repair work will cost in the area of £200.*

ˈarea ˌcode noun [C] **dialling code**

arena /əˈriː.nə/ noun [C] **PLACE** ▷ **1** a large, flat area surrounded by seats used for sports or entertainment: *an Olympic/a sports arena* **ACTIVITY** ▷ **2** an activity that involves argument and discussion: *After 30 years in the **political** arena, our local member of parliament is retiring next year.*

aren't /ɑːnt/ US /ɑːrnt/ short form of **1** are not: *The boys aren't going to the party.* **2** am not, used in questions: *I'm late again, aren't I?*

argan oil /ˈɑː.gən.ɔɪl/ US /ˈɑːr-/ noun [U] a type of oil from the argan tree, originally from Morocco, that is used to treat dry skin and hair or that can be used in cooking

argon /ˈɑː.gɒn/ US /ˈɑːr.gɑːn/ noun [U] (symbol **Ar**) a chemical element that is a gas found in air. Argon does not react with other elements and is sometimes used to make electric lights.

argot /ˈɑː.gəʊ/ US /ˈɑːr.goʊ/ noun [C or U] words and expressions that are used by small groups of people and that are not easily understood by other people: *thieves' argot*

arguable /ˈɑː.gju.ə.bl̩/ US /ˈɑːrg-/ adj **1** If something is arguable, there could be some disagreement about it: *It is arguable which way is quicker.* **2 it is arguable that...** it is possibly true that: *It is arguable that the government has failed in this respect.*

arguably /ˈɑː.gju.ə.bli/ US /ˈɑːrg-/ adv used when stating an opinion or belief that you think can be shown to be true: *He is arguably the world's best football player. ◦ Arguably, the drug should not have been made available.*

argue /ˈɑː.gjuː/ US /ˈɑːrg-/ verb **DISAGREE** ▷ **1** B1 [I] to speak angrily to someone, telling them that you disagree with them: *The children are always arguing. ◦ Kids, will you stop arguing **with** each other? ◦ They were arguing **over/about** which film to go and see.* **GIVE REASONS** ▷ **2** B2 [I or T] to give the reasons for your opinion, idea, belief, etc.: *The minister argued **for/in favour of/against** making cuts in military spending. ◦* [+ that] *The minister argued **that** cuts in military spending were needed. ◦ You can argue the **case** either way.* → See also **well argued** **SHOW** ▷ **3** [T] to show that something is true or exists: *The evidence argues a change in policy.*

IDIOM **argue the toss** UK informal disapproving to disagree with a decision or statement: *It doesn't matter what you say, he'll always argue the toss!*

> **Other ways of saying argument**
>
> The word **disagreement** can be used as an alternative to 'argument':
>
> *There was a **disagreement** over who should pay the bill.*
>
> If an argument involves a lot of angry feelings, you can use the word **quarrel**:
>
> *There were bitter **quarrels** between the two neighbours.*
>
> An argument about something that is not important can be described as a **squabble**:
>
> *I'm always dealing with **squabbles** between the children.*
>
> A **tiff** is an informal word for a slight argument between two people:
>
> *A **tiff** with a teammate had something to do with his leaving the game early.*
>
> If you want to suggest that an argument is polite and not very serious, you can use the phrase **a difference of opinion**:
>
> *There was a slight **difference of opinion** over whose turn it was to do the dishes.*
>
> An official argument can be described as a **dispute**:
>
> *He was involved in a bitter **dispute** with his employer.*
>
> If a lot of people are arguing about a subject that affects many people, you can use the word **controversy**:
>
> *There was a big **controversy** over the issue of a school dress code.*
>
> An angry argument that lasts for a long time can be described as a **feud**:
>
> *Relatives can't remember how the **feud** between the brothers began.*

argument /ˈɑː.gjʊ.mənt/ US /ˈɑːrg-/ noun [C or U] **DISAGREEMENT** ▷ **1** B1 a disagreement, or the process of disagreeing: *The children **had** an argument **about/over** what game to play. ◦ He **got into an** argument **with** Jeff in the pub last night. ◦ A decision was finally made after some **heated** argument.* **REASON** ▷ **2** B2 a

reason or reasons why you support or oppose an idea or suggestion, or the process of explaining them: *Now that we've heard all the arguments **for** and **against** the proposal, shall we vote on it?* ◦ [+ that] *Her husband was not convinced by her argument **that** they needed a bigger house.* ◦ *I don't think that's a very **strong/convincing/powerful** argument.* ◦ *The central argument (= main point) **of** the book is that some of the plays were not written by Shakespeare.*

> Word partners for **argument** (**DISAGREEMENT**)
>
> *have* an argument • *cause/provoke/start* an argument • *be drawn into/get into/be involved in* an argument • *lose/win* an argument • an *angry/big/fierce/heated* argument • an argument *about/over* sth • an argument *with* sb • an argument *between* [two people]

> Word partners for **argument** (**REASON**)
>
> *make/put forward* an argument • *refute/reject* an argument • *accept* an argument • a *convincing/good/powerful/strong* argument • the argument *against/for/in favour of* sth • a *line* of argument

argumentation /ˌɑː.ɡjʊ.menˈteɪ.ʃən/ (US) /ˌɑːrɡ-/ **noun** [U] a set of arguments used to explain something or to persuade people: *He produced very clever argumentation in support of the proposal.*

argumentative /ˌɑː.ɡjʊˈmen.tə.tɪv/ (US) /ˌɑːr.ɡjʊˈmen.t̬ə.t̬ɪv/ **adj** disapproving often arguing or wanting to argue: *Don't be so argumentative.* • **argumentatively** /-li/ **adv**

argy-bargy /ˌɑː.dʒiˈbɑː.dʒi/ (US) /ˌɑːr.dʒiˈbɑːr-/ **noun** [U] UK informal loud argument or disagreement that is not usually serious: *Did you hear all that argy-bargy last night?*

aria /ˈɑː.ri.ə/ (US) /ˈɑːr.i-/ **noun** [C] a piece of music sung by one person in an OPERA

-arian /-eə.ri.ən/ (US) /-er.i-/ **suffix** (a person who has) a connection with or belief in the stated subject: *a librarian (= person who works in a library)* ◦ *humanitarian aid (= help for injured, ill, or hungry people)*

arid /ˈær.ɪd/ (US) /ˈer-/ **adj 1** (C2) very dry and without enough rain for plants: *The desert is so arid that nothing can grow there.* **2** formal unsuccessful: *After several arid years, the company has started to become successful.* **3** formal not interesting and showing no imagination: *I found his writing extremely arid.*

Aries /ˈeə.riːz/ (US) /ˈer.iːz/ **noun** [C or U] the first sign of the ZODIAC, relating to the period 21 March to 20 April, represented by a RAM, or a person born during this period • **Arian** /ˈeə.ri.ən/ (US) /ˈer.i.ən/ **noun** [C], **adj**

aright /əˈraɪt/ **adv** old use or literary correctly: *Did I **hear/understand** you aright?*

arise /əˈraɪz/ **verb** [I] (**arose, arisen**) **HAPPEN** ▷ **1** (C1) formal to happen: *Should the **opportunity** arise, I'd love to go to China.* ◦ *Could you work on Saturday, should the **need** arise (= if it were to be necessary)?* ◦ *Are there any **matters** arising **from** (= caused by) the last meeting?* **GET UP** ▷ **2** literary to get out of bed: *We arose early on Christmas morning.*

the aristocracy /ˌær.ɪˈstɒk.rə.si/ (US) /ˌer.ɪˈstɑː.krə-/ **noun** [C, + sing/pl verb] a class of people who hold high social rank: *members of the aristocracy*

aristocrat /ˈær.ɪ.stə.kræt/ (US) /ˈer-/ **noun** [C] a person of high social rank who belongs to the aristocracy: *Many aristocrats were killed in the French Revolution.* • **aristocratic** /ˌær.ɪ.stəˈkræt.ɪk/ (US) /ˌer.ɪ.stəˈkræt̬-/ **adj** *an aristocratic family*

arithmetic /əˈrɪθ.mə.tɪk/ (US) /-t̬ɪk/ **noun** [U] **1** the part of mathematics that involves the adding and multiplying, etc. of numbers: *I've never been very good at arithmetic.* ◦ *an arithmetic test* **2** calculations involving adding and multiplying, etc. numbers: *I did some quick **mental** arithmetic and decided it was going to cost too much.* ◦ *I can't work out which of these is cheaper – could you **do the** arithmetic?* • **arithmetical** /ˌær.ɪθˈmet.ɪ.kəl/ (US) /ˌer.ɪθˈmet̬-/ **adj** (also **arithmetic** /ˌær.ɪθˈmet.ɪk/) *arithmetical problems* • **arithmetically** /ˌær.ɪθˈmet.ɪ.kəl.i/ (US) /ˌer.ɪθˈmet̬-/ **adv**

arithˌmetical/arithˌmetic proˈgression **noun** [C] a SEQUENCE (= ordered series of numbers) in which the numbers get bigger or smaller by the same amount, such as 3, 6, 9…, or 9, 6, 3

the ark /ɑːk/ (US) /ɑːrk/ **noun** [S] **SHIP** ▷ **1** (also **ˌNoah's ˈark**) (in the Bible) a large wooden ship built by Noah in order to save his family and a male and female of every type of animal when the world was covered by a flood **BOX** ▷ **2 the Ark of the Covenant** (also **the Ark**) (in the Bible) a wooden box that contained the writings of Jewish law, and that represented to the people of Israel the idea of God being present and leading them

IDIOMS **be/come out of the ark** UK to be very old-fashioned: *Her hat was straight out of the ark.* • **went out with the ark** If an object or method went out with the ark, it has not been used for a long time.

arm /ɑːm/ (US) /ɑːrm/ **noun; verb**

▸**noun BODY PART** ▷ **1** (A1) [C] either of the two long parts of the upper body that are fixed to the shoulders and have the hands at the end: *My arms ache from carrying this bag.* ◦ *She **put/threw** her arms **round** me and gave me a hug.* ◦ *He **took/held** her **in** his arms (= held her closely).* **2** (C2) [C] The arm of a piece of clothing or furniture is a part of it that you put your arm in or on: *the arm of a jacket* ◦ *the arm of a chair* **3 arm in arm** (C2) When two people are arm in arm, they both have one arm bent at the ELBOW and passing around and supporting, or being supported by, the arm of the other person: *We walked arm in arm along the river bank.* **WEAPONS** ▷ **4 arms** [plural] weapons and equipment used to kill and injure people: *They have been charged with supplying arms to the guerrillas.* ◦ *An arms **cache** was discovered in South Wales.* ◦ *The minister has called on the terrorists to **lay down** their arms (= stop fighting).* ◦ *They are willing to **take up** arms (= prepare to fight) (**against** the government) if they have to.* **OF LAND/WATER** ▷ **5** [C] An arm of land or water is a long, thin part of it that is joined to a larger area. **OF ORGANIZATION** ▷ **6** [C] An arm of an organization is a part of it that is responsible for a particular activity or place: *The British company is one arm of a large multinational.*

IDIOMS **an arm and a leg** informal a lot of money: *These shoes **cost** me an arm and a leg.* • **keep sb at arm's length** (C2) to not allow someone to become too friendly with you: *I always had the feeling she was keeping me at arm's length.* • **under arms** provided with weapons and willing to fight: *The rebels now have thousands of people under arms.* • **be up in arms** informal to be very angry: *They're up in arms **about/over** the new management scheme.*

▸**verb 1** [I or T] to provide yourself or others with a weapon or weapons: *Nobody knows who is arming the terrorists.* ◦ *I armed my**self with** a baseball bat and went to investigate the noise.* ◦ *They are currently arming for war.* → Opposite **disarm 2** (C2) [T] to provide yourself or others with equipment or knowledge in order to complete a particular task: *She armed her**self for** the interview by finding out all she could* *about the company in advance.* ◦ *I went to the meeting armed* ***with*** *the relevant facts and figures.*

armada /ɑːˈmɑː.də/ Ⓤⓢ /ɑːr-/ **noun** [C] a large group of armed ships that fight wars at sea

armadillo /ˌɑː.məˈdɪl.əʊ/ Ⓤⓢ /ˌɑːr.məˈdɪl.oʊ/ **noun** [C] (plural **armadillos**) a small animal whose body is covered in hard strips that allow it to roll into a ball when attacked

Armageddon /ˌɑː.məˈged.ən/ Ⓤⓢ /ˌɑːr-/ **noun** [S or U] **1** a final war between good and evil at the end of the world, as described in the Bible **2** an event of great destruction: *an environmental Armageddon*

armament /ˈɑː.mə.mənt/ Ⓤⓢ /ˈɑːr-/ **noun 1** [U] the process of increasing the number and strength of a country's weapons: *As the country prepares for war, more and more money is being spent on armament.* **2 armaments** [plural] weapons or military equipment: *the country's armaments programme*

armband /ˈɑːm.bænd/ Ⓤⓢ /ˈɑːrm-/ **noun 1** [C] a piece of material that a person wears around the arm as a sign of something, for example an official position: *All the stewards at the racetrack were wearing armbands.* ◦ ***black*** *armbands for a funeral* **2** [C usually plural] UK (US **waterwings**) a hollow ring-shaped piece of plastic filled with air, which people who are learning to swim wear on their arms in water to help them float

ˈarm ˌcandy noun [U] informal a very attractive person who goes to social events with someone in order to impress other people

armchair /ˈɑːm.tʃeəʳ/ Ⓤⓢ /ˈɑːrm.tʃer/ **noun; adj**

▸**noun** [C] **A2** a comfortable chair with sides that support your arms: *She sat in an armchair by the fire, reading a newspaper.*

▸**adj** [before noun] describes a person who knows, or says they know, a lot about a subject without having direct experience of it: *an armchair* ***critic****/gardener/traveller*

armed /ɑːmd/ Ⓤⓢ /ɑːrmd/ **adj B2** using or carrying weapons: *an armed* ***robbery*** ◦ *armed* ***conflict*** ◦ *These men are armed* ***and dangerous****, and should not be approached.* → Opposite **unarmed**

-armed /-ɑːmd/ Ⓤⓢ /-ɑːrmd/ **suffix** having the stated number or type of arms: *a one-armed person*

the ˌarmed ˈforces noun [plural] a country's military forces, usually an army, navy, and air force

armful /ˈɑːm.fʊl/ Ⓤⓢ /ˈɑːrm-/ **noun** [C] the amount that a person can carry in one or both arms: *She struggled along with an armful* ***of*** *clothes.*

armhole /ˈɑːm.həʊl/ Ⓤⓢ /ˈɑːrm.hoʊl/ **noun** [C] an opening in a shirt, coat, etc. through which you put your arm

armistice /ˈɑː.mɪ.stɪs/ Ⓤⓢ /ˈɑːr-/ **noun** [C] an agreement between two countries or groups at war to stop fighting for a particular time, especially to talk about possible peace: *A two-week armistice has been* ***declared*** *between the rival factions.*

suit of armour

armour UK (US **armor**) /ˈɑː.məʳ/ Ⓤⓢ /ˈɑːr.mɚ/ **noun** [U] **1** strong covering that protects something, especially the body: *Police put on* ***body*** *armour before confronting the rioters.* ◦ *In the past, knights used to wear* ***suits of*** *armour (= protective covering made of metal) in battle.* ◦ *These grenades are able to pierce the armour of tanks.* **2** military vehicles that are covered in strong metal to protect them from attack: *The troops were backed by tanks, artillery, and other heavy armour.*

armoured UK (US **armored**) /ˈɑː.məd/ Ⓤⓢ /ˈɑːr.mɚd/ **adj** protected by a strong covering, or using military vehicles protected by strong covering: *an armoured tank* ◦ *armoured troops*

ˌarmoured personˈnel ˌcarrier (US **ˌarmored personˈnel ˌcarrier**) noun [C] a special vehicle covered with strong metal that is used for carrying soldiers

armourer UK (US **armorer**) /ˈɑː.mə.rəʳ/ Ⓤⓢ /ˈɑːr.mɚ.ɚ/ **noun** [C] a person who makes, repairs, and supplies weapons

ˌarmour-ˈplated (US **ˌarmor-ˈplated**) **adj** describes something that has been covered with special metal to give protection

armoury UK (US **armory**) /ˈɑː.mə.ri/ Ⓤⓢ /ˈɑːr.mɚ.i/ **noun 1** [C] all the weapons and military equipment that a country owns: *The two countries signed an agreement to reduce their nuclear armouries.* **2** [C] a place where weapons and other military equipment are stored: *Fighter planes have successfully bombed the enemy's main armoury.* **3** [C usually singular] things or qualities that can be used to achieve a particular aim: *The only weapon left in his armoury was indifference.*

armpit /ˈɑːm.pɪt/ Ⓤⓢ /ˈɑːrm-/ **noun** [C] the hollow place under your arm where your arm joins your body: *sweaty/hairy armpits*

armrest /ˈɑːm.rest/ Ⓤⓢ /ˈɑːrm-/ **noun** [C] (also **arm**) the part of a chair that supports the arm

ˈarms conˌtrol noun [U] the action of setting a limit on the number of weapons a country is allowed to own, usually in agreement with another country

ˈarms ˌrace noun [S] the situation in which two or more countries try to have more and stronger weapons than each other

ˈarm-ˌtwisting noun [U] behaviour in which you try to make someone do something by persuading them forcefully or by threatening them: *The vote was won only as the result of much arm-twisting by the government.*

ˈarm-ˌwrestling noun [U] a game played by two people who place the ELBOWS (= the middle part of the arm where it bends) of one of their arms on a table, hold hands, and then try to push the other person's hand down onto the table

army /ˈɑː.mi/ Ⓤⓢ /ˈɑːr-/ **noun 1 the army** [+ sing/pl verb] **B1** a particular country's fighting force: *When did you join the army?* ◦ *He has decided on a career* ***in*** *the British Army.* ◦ *The army was/were called out to enforce the curfew.* **2 B1** [C] a military force that has the training and equipment to fight on land: *Both the armies suffered heavy losses in the battle.* **3 C2** [C usually singular] a large group of people who are involved in a particular activity: *She brought an army* ***of*** *supporters with her.*

ˌarmy disˈposals ˌstore noun [C] Australian English a shop where ARMY SURPLUS is sold → Compare **army surplus store**

ˌarmy-ˈnavy ˌstore noun [C] US for **army surplus store**

ˌarmy ˈsurplus noun [U] clothes and equipment that are not needed by the army, and are made available for sale to the public

ˌarmy ˈsurplus ˌstore noun [C] (US usually **ˌarmy-ˈnavy ˌstore**) a shop where army surplus is sold

aroma /əˈrəʊ.mə/ Ⓤⓢ /-ˈroʊ-/ **noun** [C] a strong,

pleasant smell, usually from food or drink: *the aroma **of** freshly baked bread* ◦ *a wine with a light, fruity aroma*

aromatherapy /əˌrəʊ.məˈθer.ə.pi/ (US) /-ˌroʊ-/ noun [U] the treatment of worry or nervousness, or medical conditions that are not serious, by rubbing pleasant-smelling natural oils into the skin or breathing in their smell: *aromatherapy massage* ◦ *aromatherapy oils* • **aromatherapist** /-pɪst/ noun [C] *a trained aromatherapist*

aromatic /ˌær.əˈmæt.ɪk/ (US) /ˌer.əˈmæt̬-/ adj having a pleasant smell: *aromatic herbs*

arose /əˈrəʊz/ (US) /-ˈroʊz/ verb past simple of **arise**

around /əˈraʊnd/ preposition, adv; adv

▸**preposition, adv** (mainly UK **round**) IN THIS DIRECTION ▷ **1** (A2) in a position or direction surrounding, or in a direction going along the edge of or from one part to another (of): *We sat around the table.* ◦ *He put his arm around her.* ◦ *A crowd had gathered around the scene of the accident.* ◦ *She had a woollen scarf around her neck.* ◦ *The moon goes around the Earth.* ◦ *I walked around the side of the building.* ◦ *As the bus left, she turned around (= so that she was facing in the opposite direction) and waved goodbye to us.* ◦ *He put the wheel on the **right/wrong way** around (= facing the right/wrong way).* ◦ *The children were dancing around the room.* ◦ *I spent a year travelling around Africa and the Middle East.* ◦ *The museum's collection includes works of art from all around the world.* ◦ *She passed a plate of biscuits around (= from one person to another).* ◦ *This virus has been going around (= from one person to another).* IN THIS PLACE ▷ **2** (A2) positioned or moving in or near a place, often without a clear direction, purpose, or order: *He always leaves his clothes lying around (on the floor).* ◦ *She went into town and spent two hours just walking around.* ◦ *I used to live around (= near) here.* ◦ *She's never around (= near here) when you need her.* ◦ *Will you be around next week?* ◦ *There's a lot of flu around (= a lot of people have it) at the moment.* ◦ *Smartphones **have been** around (= existed) for quite a while.*

▸**adv** APPROXIMATELY ▷ (A2) approximately: *around six feet tall* ◦ *around two months ago* ◦ *around four o'clock* ◦ *She earns around $40,000 a year.*

aˌround-the-ˈclock adj **round-the-clock**

arouse /əˈraʊz/ verb [T] **1** (C) to cause someone to have a particular feeling: *It's a subject that has aroused a lot of **interest**.* ◦ *Our **suspicions** were first aroused when we heard a muffled scream.* → See also **rouse 2** to cause someone to feel sexual excitement • **arousal** /əˈraʊ.zəl/ noun [U] *a state of (**sexual**) arousal (= being sexually excited)* • **aroused** /əˈraʊzd/ sexually excited

arpeggio /ɑːˈpedʒ.i.əʊ/ (US) /ɑːrˈpedʒ.i.oʊ/ noun [C] (plural **arpeggios**) the notes of a musical CHORD played quickly one after the other instead of together

arr. 1 written abbreviation for **arrive** or **arrival**: used in TIMETABLES to show the time at which a bus, train, or aircraft reaches a place: *Flight 226: dep. 10.25, arr. 13.45.* **2** written abbreviation for arranged by: used before the name of the person who has arranged a piece of music

arraign /əˈreɪn/ verb [T] legal to formally accuse someone in a law court of a particular crime and ask them to say if they are guilty or not: *He was arraigned **on** charges of aiding and abetting terrorists.* • **arraignment** /-mənt/ noun [C or U]

arrange /əˈreɪndʒ/ verb PLAN ▷ **1** (B1) [I or T] to plan, prepare for, or organize something: *I'm trying to arrange my work so that I can have a couple of days off next week.* ◦ *The meeting has been arranged **for** Wednesday.* ◦ [+ to infinitive] *They arranged **to** have dinner the following month.* ◦ *I've already arranged **with** him **to** meet at the cinema.* ◦ *She's arranged **for** her son **to** have swimming lessons.* ◦ [+ that] *I'd deliberately arranged **that** they should arrive at the same time.* ◦ [+ question word] *We haven't yet arranged **when** to meet.* PUT IN POSITION ▷ **2** (B2) [T] to put a group of objects in a particular order: *She arranged her birthday cards along the shelf.* ◦ *Who arranged these flowers so beautifully?* ◦ *His books are **neatly** arranged in alphabetical order.* MUSIC ▷ **3** [T] to make changes to a piece of music so that it can be played in a different way, for example by a particular instrument: *Beethoven's fifth symphony has been arranged **for** the piano.* • **arranger** /əˈreɪn.dʒəʳ/ (US) /-dʒɚ/ noun [C] *a flower arranger*

arˌranged ˈmarriage noun [C] a marriage in which the parents choose who their son or daughter will marry

arrangement /əˈreɪndʒ.mənt/ noun PLAN ▷ **1** (B1) [C usually plural] a plan for how something will happen: *They'd **made** all the arrangements **for** the party.* ◦ [+ to infinitive] *Arrangements were made **to** move the prisoners to another jail.* ◦ *What are your current childcare arrangements?* **2** (B2) [C or U] an agreement between two people or groups about how something happens or will happen: [+ that] *We **had** an arrangement **that** he would clean the house and I would cook.* ◦ *I'm sure we can **come to** an arrangement (= reach an agreement).* ◦ *You can only withdraw money from this account by (**prior**) arrangement (= after making plans to do so) **with** the bank.* POSITION ▷ **3** (B2) [C] a group of objects that have been put in a particular order or position: *There was a striking arrangement of dried flowers on the table.* MUSIC ▷ **4** [C] a piece of music that has had changes made to it so that it can be played in a different way, especially by different instruments: *This new arrangement of the piece is for saxophone and piano.*

> Word partners for **arrangement** (PLAN)
>
> *make* arrangements • *come to/have* an arrangement • by *prior* arrangement • arrangements *for* sth • *alternative/the necessary/special* arrangements

arrant /ˈær.ənt/ (US) /ˈer-/ adj old-fashioned **arrant nonsense** used to say how bad something is: ◦ *He dismissed the rumours as 'arrant nonsense'.*

array /əˈreɪ/ noun; verb

▸**noun** [C usually singular] a large group of things or people, especially one that is attractive or causes admiration or has been positioned in a particular way: *There was a splendid array **of** food on the table.* ◦ *They sat before an array **of** microphones and cameras.*

▸**verb** [T usually passive] **1** to arrange a group of things in a particular way: *A large number of magazines were arrayed on the stand.* ◦ *Arrayed (= standing in a group) before him were 40 schoolchildren in purple and green.* **2** to arrange a group of soldiers in a position for fighting

arrayed /əˈreɪd/ adj [after verb] formal dressed in a particular way, especially in beautiful clothes: *She was arrayed **in** purple velvet.*

arrears /əˈrɪəz/ (US) /-ˈrɪrz/ noun [plural] money that is owed and should already have been paid: *rent arrears*

IDIOM **in arrears 1** owing money that should have been paid already: *My account is badly in arrears.* ◦ *They are in arrears **on/with** their mortgage payments.* **2** If someone is paid in arrears, they are paid at the end of the period of time during which the money was earned: *I'm paid a week in arrears.*

arrest /əˈrest/ verb; noun
▸verb [T] CATCH ▷ **1** B1 If the police arrest someone, they take them away to ask them about a crime that they might have committed: *He was arrested when customs officers found drugs in his bag.* ◦ *The police arrested her* ***for*** *drinking and driving.* STOP ▷ **2** formal to stop or interrupt the development of something: *The treatment has so far done little to arrest the spread of the cancer.* MAKE NOTICE ▷ **3** formal to attract or catch someone's attention: *A photo of a small boy arrested my* ***attention****.*
▸noun [C or U] B2 the act of arresting someone: *Two arrests were made, but the men were later released without charge.* ◦ *She was stopped outside the shop and placed/put* ***under*** *arrest.*

arresting /əˈres.tɪŋ/ adj very attractive in a way that attracts a lot of attention: *an arresting-looking woman*

arrival /əˈraɪ.vəl/ noun **1** B1 [C or U] the fact of arriving somewhere: *Hundreds gathered to await the boxer's arrival* ***at*** *the airport.* ◦ ***On*** *arrival* ***at*** *the police station, they were taken to an interview room.* ◦ *We regret the late arrival* ***of*** *Flight 237.* ◦ *New arrivals (= people who have just come to a place) were being housed in refugee camps.* ◦ *Sue and Michael are delighted to announce the arrival (= birth)* ***of*** *Emily, born on 21 August.* ◦ *The arrival (= introduction) of satellite television changed the face of broadcasting.* **2** [C] informal a baby that has recently been born: *Their* ***new*** *arrival was keeping them busy.*

> **Other ways of saying arrive**
>
> You can use **get** instead of arrive when you arrive at a particular place:
>
> *What time did you* ***get*** *there?*
>
> *We* ***got to*** *the airport at six o'clock.*
>
> If you arrive somewhere after a lot of travelling, you could use the verb **reach**:
>
> *We won't* ***reach*** *Miami until evening.*
>
> If you successfully arrive somewhere when it has been difficult, in informal English, you could say **make**:
>
> *We* ***made*** *it to the airport just in time for our flight.*
>
> If you arrive by plane or train, or a plane or train you are travelling on arrives, you can say that you or it **gets in**:
>
> *The train* ***gets in*** *at 6.40 p.m.*
>
> **Turn up** and **show up** are informal phrasal verbs that can be used when someone arrives at a place, especially when that person is late or was not expected:
>
> *She* ***turned up*** *at my house late one night.*
>
> *He finally* ***showed up****, three hours late.*

arrive /əˈraɪv/ verb [I] REACH ▷ **1** A2 to reach a place, especially at the end of a journey: *What time will your train arrive?* ◦ *It was dark by the time we arrived* ***at*** *the station.* ◦ *We arrived* ***in*** *Prague later that day.* ◦ *I arrived back to find that my room had been burgled.* ◦ *I ordered some CDs over a month ago, but they still haven't arrived (= I have not received them).* BEGIN ▷ **2** to happen or start to exist: *The leaves starting to turn brown is a sign that autumn has arrived.* **3** If a baby arrives, it is born: *Their baby Olivia arrived on the date she was expected.*

IDIOM **to have arrived** to have achieved success and become famous: *He felt he had truly arrived when he got his first part in a Broadway play.*

PHRASAL VERB **arrive at sth** C2 to reach an agreement about something: *We all argued about it for hours and eventually arrived at a decision.*

> **Common mistake: arrive**
>
> **Remember:** the most usual prepositions to use after **arrive** are **in** and **at.**
>
> Don't say 'arrive to' a country, city, town, etc., say **arrive in a country, city, town, etc.**:
>
> *~~I arrived to England in May.~~*
>
> *I arrived in England in May.*
>
> Don't say 'arrive to' a building, say **arrive at**:
>
> *~~Call me when you arrive to the airport.~~*
>
> *Call me when you arrive at the airport.*

arriviste /ˌær.iːˈviːst/ noun [C] disapproving a person who is trying to move into a higher class in society

arrogant /ˈær.ə.gənt/ US /ˈer-/ adj B2 unpleasantly proud and behaving as if you are more important than, or know more than, other people: *I found him arrogant and rude.* • **arrogance** /ˈær.ə.gəns/ US /ˈer-/ noun [U] *He has a self-confidence that is sometimes seen as arrogance.* • **arrogantly** /-li/ adv *The authorities had behaved arrogantly, she said.*

arrogate /ˈær.ə.geɪt/ US /ˈer.ə-/ verb [T] formal to take something without having the right to do so: *They arrogate* ***to*** *themselves the power to punish people.*

arrow /ˈær.əʊ/ US /ˈer.oʊ/ noun [C] **1** B2 a weapon that is like a long, thin stick with a sharp point at one end and often feathers at the other, shot from a BOW (= a long, thin piece of wood bent into a curve by a piece of string): *Robin Hood asked to be buried where his arrow landed.* → Compare **dart 2** B2 a sign consisting of a straight line with an upside down V shape at one end of it, which points in a particular direction, and is used to show where something is: *I followed the arrows to the car park.*

arrowhead /ˈær.əʊ.hed/ US /ˈer.oʊ-/ noun [C] the sharp point at the end of an arrow

arrowroot /ˈær.əʊ.ruːt/ US /ˈer.oʊ-/ noun [U] a powder made from a Caribbean plant, used in cooking to make sauces thicker

arse /ɑːs/ US /ɑːrs/ noun; exclamation; verb
▸noun [C] UK (US **ass**) **1** the part of your body that you sit on: *She's got a huge arse.* **2** a stupid person

IDIOMS **get off your arse** (also **get your arse in gear**) to force yourself to start doing something or to make yourself hurry: *Tell him to get off his arse and do some work for once.* ◦ *If she doesn't get her arse in gear, she's going to be late.* • **go arse over tit/tip** UK (US **go ass over (tea)kettle**) to lose your balance suddenly and fall over: *I fell off my bike and went arse over tit.* • **move/shift your arse!** offensive used to rudely tell someone to hurry up or to get out of your way • **my arse!** offensive said when you do not believe what someone has just said: *'She says she's got food poisoning.' 'Food poisoning, my arse! She just drank too much last night.'* • **not know your arse from your elbow** offensive to be stupid and unable to understand very simple things

▸exclamation UK offensive used when you feel annoyed
▸verb

PHRASAL VERB **arse about/around** UK offensive to act in a silly way or waste time: *I wish he'd stop arsing around and actually do some work.*

arsed /ɑːst/ US /ɑːrst/ adj UK informal **not be arsed** If you cannot be arsed to do something, you do not

want to make the effort to do it: [+ to infinitive] *I can't be arsed to go shopping this afternoon.*

arsehole /ˈɑːs.həʊl/ (US) /ˈɑːrs.hoʊl/ noun [C] UK offensive (US **asshole**) **UNPLEASANT PERSON** ▷ **1** an unpleasant or stupid person: *Some arsehole had parked so I couldn't get out.* **BODY PART** ▷ **2** the **anus**

arse-licker /ˈɑːsˌlɪk.əʳ/ (US) /ˈɑːrsˌlɪk.ɚ/ noun [C] UK offensive (US **ass-licker** /ˈæs-/) a person who tries to get an advantage from other people by being extremely pleasant to them in a way that is not sincere

arsenal /ˈɑː.sən.əl/ (US) /ˈɑːr-/ noun [C] **1** a building where weapons and military equipment are stored **2** a collection of weapons: *The country has agreed to reduce its nuclear arsenal.*

arsenic /ˈɑː.sən.ɪk/ (US) /ˈɑːr-/ noun [U] (symbol **As**) a chemical element that is very poisonous, often used to kill RATS

arson /ˈɑː.sən/ (US) /ˈɑːr-/ noun [U] the crime of intentionally starting a fire in order to damage or destroy something, especially a building: *A cinema was burned out in north London last night. Police suspect arson.* • **arsonist** /-ɪst/ noun [C] *Police are blaming arsonists for the spate of fires in the Greenfields housing estate.*

art /ɑːt/ (US) /ɑːrt/ noun **EXPRESSION** ▷ **1** (A2) [U] the making of objects, images, music, etc. that are beautiful or that express feelings: *Can television and pop music really be considered art?* ◦ *I enjoyed the ballet, but it wasn't really great art.* **2** (A2) [U] the activity of painting, drawing, and making SCULPTURE: *Art and English were my best subjects at school.* ◦ *an art teacher* **3** (A2) [U] paintings, drawings, and SCULPTURES: *The gallery has an excellent collection of modern art.* ◦ *an exhibition of Native American art* ◦ *The Frick is an art* ***gallery*** *in New York.* **4** (B2) [C] an activity through which people express particular ideas: *Drama is an art that is traditionally performed in a theatre.* ◦ *Do you regard film as entertainment or as an art?* ◦ *She is doing a course in the performing arts.* **5 the arts** the making or showing or performance of painting, acting, dancing, and music: *More government money is needed for the arts.* ◦ *public interest in the arts* **NOT SCIENCE** ▷ **6 arts** (C1) [plural] subjects, such as history, languages, and literature, that are not scientific subjects: *Children should be given a well-balanced education in both the arts and the sciences.* ◦ *arts graduates/degrees* **SKILL** ▷ **7** (C1) [C] a skill or special ability: *the art of conversation* ◦ *Getting him to go out is* ***quite*** *an art (= needs special skill).*

art deco /ˌɑːtˈdek.əʊ/ (US) /ˌɑːrtˈdeɪ.koʊ/ noun [U] a style of decoration that was especially popular in the 1930s and uses simple shapes and lines and strong colours

artefact /ˈɑː.tɪ.fækt/ (US) /ˈɑr.t̬ɪ-/ noun [C] mainly UK (US usually **artifact**) an object that is made by a person, such as a tool or a decoration, especially one that is of historical interest: *The museum's collection includes artefacts dating back to prehistoric times.*

artery /ˈɑː.tər.i/ (US) /ˈɑː.r.t̬ɚ-/ noun [C] **IN BODY** ▷ **1** one of the thick tubes that carry blood from the heart to other parts of the body: *Hardening of the coronary arteries can lead to a heart attack.* **ROUTE** ▷ **2** an important road or railway line: *the main arteries leading into London* • **arterial** /ɑːˈtɪə.ri.əl/ (US) /ɑːrˈtɪr.i-/ adj *the arterial walls* ◦ *arterial roads*

artesian well /ɑːˌtiː.zi.ənˈwel/ (US) /ɑːrˌti.ʒən-/ noun [C] a hole in the ground from which water is forced to the surface by natural pressure

artful /ˈɑːt.fəl/ (US) /ˈɑːrt-/ adj clever and skilful, especially in getting what you want: *He has shown himself to be an artful politician.* ◦ *The prime minister dealt with the interviewer's questions in a very artful way.* • **artfully** /-i/ adv *His clothes were artfully arranged to look stylishly casual.* • **artfulness** /-nəs/ noun [U]

ˈart-house adj (also **arthouse**) used to describe films from other countries or the type of films that small film companies make: *an art-house* ***cinema*** • **ˈart ˌhouse** noun [C]

arthritic /ɑːˈθrɪt.ɪk/ (US) /ɑːrˈθrɪt̬-/ adj; noun

▸adj suffering from or affected by arthritis: *Her hands were swollen and arthritic.* ◦ *arthritic* ***joints***

▸noun [C] a person who suffers from arthritis: *Many arthritics find it difficult to climb stairs.*

arthritis /ɑːˈθraɪ.tɪs/ (US) /ɑːrˈθraɪ.t̬əs/ noun [U] a serious condition in which a person's JOINTS (= places where two bones are connected) become painful, swollen, and stiff: *In later life she was crippled with arthritis.*

arthropod /ˈɑː.θrə.pɒd/ (US) /ˈɑːr.θrə.pɑːd/ noun [C] specialized a type of animal with no SPINE, a hard outer skin, legs with bones joined together, and a body divided into different parts, for example a SPIDER, CRAB, or ANT

artichoke /ˈɑː.tɪ.tʃəʊk/ (US) /ˈɑːr.t̬ɪ.tʃoʊk/ noun [C] a **globe artichoke** or **Jerusalem artichoke**

article /ˈɑː.tɪ.kl̩/ (US) /ˈɑːr.t̬ɪ-/ noun [C] **NEWSPAPER** ▷ **1** (B1) a piece of writing on a particular subject in a newspaper or magazine, or on the internet: *There was an interesting article* ***on*** *vegetarianism in the paper yesterday.* **GRAMMAR** ▷ **2** (B1) any of the English words 'a', 'an', and 'the' or words in other languages that do the same job as these → See also **definite article, indefinite article** **OBJECT** ▷ **3** a particular thing, especially one that is one of several things of a similar type or in the same place: *Guests are advised not to leave any articles of value in their hotel rooms.* ◦ *An article* ***of clothing*** *was found near the river.* **LAW** ▷ **4** a separate part in a written document such as a legal agreement: *East and West Germany united under article 23 of the Bonn constitution.* **5 be doing/in articles** UK to be working in a law office while training to be a lawyer

articled /ˈɑː.tɪ.kl̩d/ (US) /ˈɑːr.t̬ɪ-/ adj UK training to be a lawyer: *She is articled* ***to*** *a big law firm (= she is working there as part of her training) in the City of London.* ◦ *an articled* ***clerk***

ˌarticle of ˈfaith noun [C] something that you believe in very strongly: *Socialism was an article of faith with his parents.*

articulate adj; verb

▸adj /ɑːˈtɪk.jʊ.lət/ (US) /ɑːr-/ able to express thoughts and feelings easily and clearly, or showing this quality: *an intelligent and highly articulate young woman* ◦ *She gave a witty, entertaining, and articulate speech.* • **articulately** /-li/ adv • **articulateness** /-nəs/ noun [U] (also **articulacy** /-lə.si/)

▸verb [T] /ɑːˈtɪk.jʊ.leɪt/ (US) /ɑːr-/ formal **1** to express in words: *I found myself unable to articulate my feelings.* ◦ *Many people are opposed to the new law, but have had no opportunity to articulate their opposition.* **2** to pronounce: *When children first learn to talk, there are some sounds that they find difficult to articulate.*

articulated /ɑːˈtɪk.jʊ.leɪ.tɪd/ (US) /ɑːrˈtɪk.jʊ.leɪ.t̬ɪd/ adj describes a vehicle that consists of two or more parts that bend where they are joined, in order to help the vehicle turn corners: *an articulated vehicle* ◦ UK *An articulated* ***lorry*** *has overturned on the southbound carriageway, shedding its load.*

articulation /ɑːˌtɪk.jʊˈleɪ.ʃən/ (US) /ɑːr-/ noun [U]

SAYING ▷ **1** the way in which you pronounce words or produce sounds: *A good singer needs to have good articulation (= a clear way of pronouncing words).* **2** the way in which you express your feelings and ideas, etc. JOINING ▷ **3** in something that consists of two or more parts, the way in which the parts are joined and able to move in relation to each other

artifact /ˈɑː.tɪ.fækt/ (US) /ˈɑːr.t̬ɪ-/ **noun** [C] an **artefact**

artifice /ˈɑː.tɪ.fɪs/ (US) /ˈɑːr.t̬ɪ-/ **noun** [C or U] formal (the use of) a clever trick or something intended to deceive: *Amazingly for Hollywood, she seems almost entirely without artifice.*

artificial /ˌɑː.tɪˈfɪʃ.əl/ (US) /ˌɑːr.t̬ɪ-/ **adj 1** B2 made by people, often as a copy of something natural: *clothes made of artificial fibres ◦ an artificial heart ◦ an artificial lake ◦ artificial fur/sweeteners/flowers* **2** C2 disapproving not sincere: *Their cheerfulness seemed rather strained and artificial.* • **artificiality** /ˌɑː.tɪ.fɪʃ.iˈæl.ɪ.ti/ (US) /ˌɑːr.t̬ɪ.fɪʃ.iˈæl.ə.t̬i/ **noun** [U] • **artificially** /-i/ **adv** B2 *Most mushrooms sold in supermarkets have been grown artificially (= not in natural conditions) in manure.*

> **Other ways of saying artificial**
>
> Something that is artificial because it is made of substances that are not natural can be described as **man-made** or **synthetic**:
>
> *Nylon is a **man-made** fibre.*
>
> **Fake**, **false**, and **imitation** mean the same as artificial when something is made to look exactly like something real:
>
> ***fake** fur jackets*
>
> ***false** eyelashes*
>
> **Bogus** can be used when something is made to look like something in order to be dishonest:
>
> *If you get a call from a **bogus** charity asking for money, report it to the police.*

ˌartificial insemiˈnation noun [U] (abbreviation **AI**) the process of putting SPERM into a female using methods that do not involve sexual activity between a male and female

ˌartificial inˈtelligence noun [U] (abbreviation **AI**) C2 the study of how to produce machines that have some of the qualities that the human mind has, such as the ability to understand language, recognize pictures, solve problems, and learn

ˌartificial respiˈration noun [U] the act of forcing air in and out of the lungs of a person who has stopped breathing, especially by blowing into their mouth and pressing their chest to help them start breathing again: *Rescuers pulled the child from the river, and she was **given** artificial respiration.*

artillery /ɑːˈtɪl.ər.i/ (US) /ɑːrˈtɪl.ɚ-/ **noun** [U] very large guns that are moved on wheels or metal tracks, or the part of the army that uses these: *Naval gunfire and ground-based artillery are generally less accurate than many aircraft-borne weapons.*

artisan /ˈɑː.tɪ.zæn/ (US) /ˈɑːr.t̬ɪ-/ **noun** [C] someone who does skilled work with their hands

artist /ˈɑː.tɪst/ (US) /ˈɑːr.t̬ɪst/ **noun** [C] **1** A2 someone who paints, draws, or makes SCULPTURES: *Monet is one of my favourite artists.* **2** someone who creates things with great skill and imagination: *He described her as one of the greatest film artists of the 20th century.*

artiste /ɑːˈtiːst/ (US) /ɑːr-/ **noun** [C] a skilled performer, especially a dancer, singer, or actor: *a popular 19th-century music hall artiste ◦ circus artistes*

artistic /ɑːˈtɪs.tɪk/ (US) /ɑːr-/ **adj 1** B2 [before noun] relating to art: *the artistic director of the theatre ◦ artistic endeavours ◦ a work of artistic merit* **2** B2 able to create or enjoy art: *His friends are all artistic – they're painters, musicians, and writers.* **3** skilfully and attractively made: *That's a very artistic flower arrangement you have there.* • **artistically** /-tɪ.kəl.i/ **adv**

artistry /ˈɑː.tɪ.stri/ (US) /ˈɑːr.t̬ɪ-/ **noun** [U] great skill in creating or performing something, such as in writing, music, sport, etc.: *You have to admire the artistry of her novels.*

artless /ˈɑːt.ləs/ (US) /ˈɑːrt-/ **adj** simple and not wanting to deceive: *'Why did you take the money?' she asked the child. 'Because I wanted it,' came the artless reply.* • **artlessly** /-li/ **adv** • **artlessness** /-nəs/ **noun** [U]

art nouveau /ˌɑːt.nuːˈvəʊ/ (US) /ˌɑːrt.nuːˈvoʊ/ **noun** [U] a style of art and decoration that uses curling lines and plant and flower shapes

ˌarts and ˈcrafts noun [plural] the skills of making objects, such as decorations, furniture, and POTTERY (= objects made from clay) by hand

artsy (US) /ˈɑːrt.si/ **adj** US for **arty**

artwork /ˈɑːt.wɜːk/ (US) /ˈɑːrt.wɝːk/ **noun** [U] the pieces of art, such as drawings and photographs, that are used in books, newspapers, and magazines: *All the artwork in the book has been done by the author.*

arty /ˈɑː.ti/ (US) /ˈɑːr.t̬i/ **adj** (US **artsy**) informal usually disapproving being or wishing to seem very interested in everything connected with art and artists: *She hangs out with a lot of arty types.*

ˌarty-ˈcrafty adj UK (US **artsy-craftsy** /ˌɑːt.siˈkrɑːft.si/ (US) /ˌɑːrt.siˈkræft.si/) interested or involved in making decorative objects: *an arty-crafty market/gift shop*

arty-farty /ˌɑː.tiˈfɑː.ti/ **adj** UK informal disapproving (US **artsy-fartsy** /ˌɑːt.siˈfɑːrt.si/ /ˌɑːrt.siˈfarft.si/) describes someone who tries too hard to make other people admire their artistic knowledge and ability

arugula /əˈruː.gə.lə/ **noun** [U] US (UK **rocket**) a plant whose long, green leaves are used in salads

Aryan /ˈeə.ri.ən/ (US) /ˈe.ri.ən/ **adj** relating to white people from northern Europe, especially those with pale hair and blue eyes, who were believed by the NAZIS to be better than members of all other races • **Aryan noun**

as weak /əz/ strong /æz/ **adv; preposition; conjunction**

▸**adv** A2 used in comparisons to refer to the degree of something: *She'll soon be as tall **as** her mother. ◦ I can't run as fast **as** you. ◦ skin as soft **as** a baby's ◦ It's not as good **as** it used to be.*

▸**preposition** A1 used to describe the purpose or quality of someone or something: *She **works** as a waitress. ◦ It could be **used** as evidence against him. ◦ The news came as quite a shock to us. ◦ I meant it as a joke.*

▸**conjunction** BECAUSE ▷ **1** A2 because: *As it was getting late, I decided to book into a hotel. ◦ You can go first as you're the oldest.* WHILE ▷ **2** B1 during the time that: *I saw him as I was coming into the building. ◦ He gets more attractive as he gets older.* LIKE ▷ **3** B1 in the same way: *He got divorced, (**just**) as his parents had done years before. ◦ This year, as in previous years, tickets sold very quickly. ◦ As **with** his earlier movies, the special effects in his latest film are brilliant. ◦ As **is** often the case with children, Amy was completely better by the time the doctor arrived. ◦ As I was just saying, I think the proposal needs further consideration. ◦ Knowing him as I do, I can't believe he would do such a thing.*

Common mistake: as or like?

Warning: as is not usually used before a noun or noun phrase to make comparisons.

Before a noun or noun phrase, don't say 'as', say **like**:

~~*He hopes to become a teacher as his father.*~~

He hopes to become a teacher like his father.

Remember: as only goes directly before a noun or noun phrase in the expression **as… as…**:

He is as tall as his father.

Common mistake: as

Warning: when **as** is used before a verb and has the meaning 'in the same way', it is not usually followed by 'it'.

Don't say 'as it is/happened', say **as is/happened etc.**:

~~*She was late, as it is often the case.*~~

She was late, as is often the case.

ALTHOUGH ▷ **4** although: *Angry as he was, he couldn't help smiling.*

IDIOMS **as and when** UK (US **if and when**) at the time that something happens: *We don't own a car – we just rent one as and when we need it.* • **as for sb/sth** B2 used to talk about how another person or thing is affected by something: *As for Louise, well, who cares what she thinks.* • **as if!** informal said to show that you do not believe something is possible: *'Did you get a pay rise?' 'As if!'* • **as if/though** B2 used to describe how a situation seems to be: *She looked as if she'd had some bad news.* ◦ *I felt as though I'd been lying in the sun for hours.* ◦ *They stared at me as if I was crazy.* • **as is** in the state that something is in at the present time: *Will you wait till it's finished or take it home as is?* • **as it is** already: *I'm not buying the children anything else today – I've spent far too much money as it is.* • **as it were** sometimes said after a FIGURATIVE (= not meaning exactly what it appears to mean) or unusual expression: *If he still refuses we could always apply a little pressure, as it were.* • **as of/from** starting from a particular time or date: *As of next month, all the airline's fares will be going up.* • **as to** formal about: *He was uncertain as to which road to take.* ◦ *There's no decision as to when the work might start.* • **as to/for** changing the subject to: *As to where we'll get the money from, we'll talk about that later.* • **as you wish/like** formal used to agree to a request, especially when you do not approve: *'I think we should leave now.' 'Very well. As you wish.'*

ASAP /ˌeɪ.es.eɪˈpiː/ abbreviation for as soon as possible: *Please reply ASAP.*

asbestos /æsˈbes.tɒs/ US /-tɑːs/ **noun** [U] a soft, greyish-white material that does not burn, used especially in the past in buildings, clothing, etc. as a protection against fire and as a form of INSULATION (= a way of stopping heat from escaping)

asbestosis /ˌæs.besˈtəʊ.sɪs/ US /-ˈtoʊ-/ **noun** [U] a serious medical condition caused by breathing threads of asbestos into the lungs

ASBO /ˈæz.bəʊ/ US /-boʊ/ **noun** [C] UK abbreviation for anti-social behaviour order: an official order that a person must stop behaving in a way that annoys or harms other people

ascend /əˈsend/ **verb** formal GO UP ▷ **1** [I or T] to move up or climb something: *They slowly ascended the steep path up the mountain.* ◦ *There's a long flight of steps ascending (= leading up)* ***to*** *the cathedral doors.* HIGHER POSITION ▷ **2** [I] to rise to a position of higher rank: *He eventually ascended* ***to*** *the position of chief executive.*

IDIOM **ascend the throne** to become queen or king

ascendancy (also **ascendency**) /əˈsen.dᵊn.si/ **noun** [U] formal a position of power, strength, or success: *They are in danger of losing their political ascendancy (= controlling power).* ◦ *Supporters of the proposal are currently* ***in the*** *ascendancy* ***over*** *its opponents (= are more powerful than them).*

ascendant /əˈsen.dᵊnt/ **noun** formal **in the ascendant** increasingly successful or powerful: *He's very much in the ascendant in Hollywood.*

ascending /əˈsen.dɪŋ/ **adj** increasing in size or value: *I shall list my objections to the plan in ascending* ***order*** *of importance.*

Ascension Day /əˈsen.ʃᵊnˌdeɪ/ **noun** [C or U] the sixth Thursday after Easter, when Christians celebrate Christ's journey from earth to heaven

ascent /əˈsent/ **noun** CLIMB ▷ **1** [C usually singular] the act of climbing or moving upwards: *She made her first successful ascent of Everest last year.* ◦ *As the plane made its ascent, we saw thick smoke coming from one engine.* SLOPE ▷ **2** [C] a slope, path, or road that goes up something: *We struggled up the slippery ascent.* TO HIGHER POSITION ▷ **3** [S] formal the fact of starting to become successful: *His ascent* ***to*** *power was rapid and unexpected.*

ascertain /ˌæs.əˈteɪn/ US /-ɚ-/ **verb** [T] formal **1** to discover something: *The police have so far been unable to ascertain* ***the cause*** *of the explosion.* ◦ [+ question word] *Have you ascertained* ***whether*** *she's coming or not?* **2** to make certain of something: [+ that] *I ascertained* ***that*** *no one could overhear us before I told Otto the news.*

ascetic /əˈset.ɪk/ US /-ˈset̬-/ **adj; noun**

▸**adj** avoiding physical pleasures and living a simple life, often for religious reasons: *They live a very ascetic life.* • **ascetically** /-ɪ.kᵊl.i/ **adv** • **asceticism** /əˈset.ɪ.sɪ.zᵊm/ US /-ˈset̬-/ **noun** [U]

▸**noun** [C] someone who lives an ascetic life, often for religious reasons: *He lived as an ascetic.*

ASCII /ˈæs.ki/ **noun** [U] abbreviation for American Standard Code for Information Interchange: a way of storing numbers, letters, or symbols for exchanging information between computer systems: *a document in ASCII format*

ascorbic acid /əˌskɔː.bɪkˈæs.ɪd/ US /-ˌskɔːr-/ **noun** [U] specialized **vitamin C**

ascot /ˈæs.kɒt/ US /-kɑːt/ **noun** [C] US (UK **cravat**) a wide, straight piece of material worn like a tie in the open neck of a shirt

ascribe /əˈskraɪb/ **verb**

PHRASAL VERBS **ascribe sth to sth** formal to believe or say that something is caused by something else: *To what do you ascribe your phenomenal success?* • **ascribe sth to sb** formal to believe that something was said, written, or created by a particular person: *After years of research, scholars have finally ascribed this anonymous play to Christopher Marlowe.* • **ascribe sth to sb/sth** formal to believe that someone or something has a particular quality: *People like to ascribe human feelings to animals.*

ASEAN /əˈziː.ən/ **noun** abbreviation for Association of Southeast Asian Nations

aseptic /ˌeɪˈsep.tɪk/ **adj** medically clean or without infection: *an aseptic wound/dressing/bandage*

asexual /ˌeɪˈsek.sju.əl/ **adj** **1** without sex or sexual organs **2** having no interest in sexual relationships: *I must say I've always found him rather asexual.* • **asexuality** /ˌeɪ.sek.sjuˈæl.ɪ.ti/ (US) /-ə.t̬i/ noun [U] • **asexually** /-i/ adv

aˌsexual reproˌduction noun [U] specialized a method of producing new young plants or animals from a single plant or animal and without separate male and female cells joining together

ash /æʃ/ noun **POWDER** ▷ **1** [U] the soft grey or black powder that is left after a substance, especially tobacco, coal, or wood, has burned: *cigarette ash* **2 ashes** [plural] what is left of something after it has been destroyed by fire, especially what is left of a human body after it has been burned: *Her ashes were* ***scattered*** *at sea.* ◦ *Allied bombing left Dresden in ashes in 1945.* **TREE** ▷ **3** [C] a forest tree that has a smooth, grey BARK (= outer covering), small greenish flowers, and seeds shaped like wings **4** [U] the wood from an ash tree

ASH /æʃ/ noun abbreviation for Action on Smoking and Health: an organization in Australia, the UK, and the US that tries to stop the sale and use of tobacco products

ashamed /əˈʃeɪmd/ adj [after verb] (B1) feeling guilty or embarrassed about something you have done or a quality in your character: *You've got nothing to be ashamed* ***of.*** ◦ *She ought to be thoroughly ashamed* ***of herself*** *– talking to her mother like that!* ◦ [+ to infinitive] *He was ashamed* ***to*** *admit to his mistake.* ◦ [+ that] *I was ashamed* ***that*** *I'd made so little effort.* ◦ *I'm ashamed* ***to*** *be seen with you when you behave so badly!* ◦ *I* ***felt*** *so ashamed of myself for making such a fuss.* ◦ *I'm so ashamed* ***of*** *you (= embarrassed to be connected with you)!*

> **Other ways of saying ashamed**
>
> **Embarrassed** is often used instead of 'ashamed':
>
> *I was too* ***embarrassed*** *to admit I was wrong.*
>
> If someone feels very ashamed, you could say that person is **mortified:**
>
> *She'd be* ***mortified*** *if she knew she'd upset her family.*
>
> If you feel ashamed because you know you have done something wrong, you could use the word **guilty:**
>
> *I feel so* ***guilty*** *about forgetting her birthday.*
>
> You could use the word **humiliated** when people are so ashamed that they lose respect for themselves:
>
> *Feeling betrayed and* ***humiliated****, she considered quitting her job.*

ˌash ˈblonde adj; noun
▸adj describes hair that is very pale yellow, almost white
▸noun [C] someone with ash blonde hair: *She's an ash blonde.*

ashcan /ˈæʃ.kæn/ noun [C] US old-fashioned for **dustbin**

ashen /ˈæʃ.ᵊn/ adj without colour, or pale grey in colour: *Julie walked in, ashen-****faced*** *with shock.* ◦ *She was thin and her face was ashen.*

ashore /əˈʃɔːʳ/ (US) /-ˈʃɔːr/ adv towards or onto land from an area of water: *We swam ashore.* ◦ *A few pieces of wood had washed ashore.* ◦ *Strong winds blew the ship ashore.*

ashram /ˈæʃ.rəm/ noun [C] a place where a group of Hindus live together away from the rest of society, or a place where Hindus can go in order to pray

ashtray /ˈæʃ.treɪ/ noun [C] a small dish or container, sometimes decorative, in which people can leave cigarette ASH and cigarette ends

ˌAsh ˈWednesday noun [C or U] the first day of Lent in the Christian religion

Asia /ˈeɪ.ʒə/ noun the continent that is to the east of Europe, the west of the Pacific Ocean, and the north of the Indian Ocean

Asian /ˈeɪ.ʒᵊn/ noun; adj
▸noun [C] **1** someone who comes from the continent of Asia, or a member of a race originally from Asia **2** in the US, Canada, Australia, and New Zealand, someone from China, Japan, or countries near them **3** in the UK, someone from India, Pakistan, or countries near them
▸adj of or related to Asia

Asiatic /ˌeɪ.ziˈæt.ɪk/ (US) /-ˈæt̬-/ adj specialized relating to Asia, especially when considering its GEOGRAPHY or its plants and animals, rather than social or cultural matters

aside /əˈsaɪd/ adv; noun
▸adv **TO ONE SIDE** ▷ **1** (B2) on or to one side: ***Stand*** *aside, please, and let these people pass.* ◦ *He* ***pulled*** *the curtain aside.* ◦ *I gave her a plate of food but she pushed it aside.* ◦ *I've forgotten my wallet, so could you* ***put*** *this book aside (= keep this book) for me and I'll come back later on.* ◦ *She* ***took*** *me aside (= took me away from the other people) to tell me the news.* **2 put/set sth aside** (B2) If you put/set aside money, you save it for a particular purpose: *Every week I put aside some money for a new TV.* **3 leave/put sth aside** If you leave or put a problem or request aside, you ignore it until you are able to solve it: *Let's leave that matter aside for now and talk about the more urgent problem facing us.* **EXCEPT** ▷ **4 aside from** (B2) except for: *Money continues to be a problem but aside from that we're all well.* ◦ *I hardly watch any television, aside from news and current affairs.*
▸noun [C] **1** a remark that someone makes in a quiet voice because they do not want everyone to hear it: *a whispered aside* **2** a remark or story in a speech or text that is not part of the main subject

asinine /ˈæs.ɪ.naɪn/ adj formal extremely stupid: *an asinine comment*

> **Common mistake: ask for** *sth*
>
> **Warning:** when the object of **ask** is the thing that is wanted, remember to use the preposition **for:**
>
> Don't say 'ask something', say **ask for something**:
>
> ~~*I think you should ask more information about the course.*~~
>
> **Remember:** you **ask** a question, but you **ask for** an answer.

ask /ɑːsk/ (US) /æsk/ verb **QUESTION** ▷ **1** (B1) [I or T] to put a question to someone, or to request an answer from someone: [+ two objects] *She asked me a question.* ◦ *Can I ask you a favour?*/formal *Can I ask a favour* ***of*** *you?* ◦ *She asked a question* ***about*** *Welsh history.* ◦ *She asked me* ***about*** *Welsh history.* ◦ *She asked* ***about*** *Welsh history.* ◦ [+ question word] *I've no idea what time the train leaves. Ask the guard* ***wh****ether he knows.* ◦ *I asked the guard the time of the train's departure.* ◦ *I asked* ***wh****en the train would leave.* ◦ [+ speech] *'What time does the train leave?' I asked.* ◦ *If you need any help, please don't hesitate to ask.* ◦ *You should ask (your accountant)* ***for*** *some financial advice.* ◦ [+ to infinitive] *You should ask your accountant* ***to*** *give you some financial advice.* ◦ *I asked* ***to*** *see my accountant.* ◦ *I'd like to ask your* ***advice/opinion*** *on a financial matter.* ◦ *You have to ask* ***permission*** *to leave.* ◦ [+ that] formal

*The solicitor asked **that** her client be allowed to make a phone call.* ◦ formal *We ask **that** any faulty goods be returned in their original packaging.* **2 ask yourself sth** C2 to consider something carefully: *She needs to ask herself why nobody seems to like her.* **INVITE** ▷ **3** A2 [T] to request or invite someone to go somewhere with you or to come to your home: UK *I've asked David **to** the party.* ◦ [+ to infinitive] US *I've asked David **to come to** the party.* ◦ *'Are you going to Muriel's party?' 'No, I haven't been asked.'* ◦ *Ian's asked us **over for** dinner next Friday.* ◦ UK *Ian's asked us **round to/for** dinner next Friday.* ◦ *In fact they've asked us **to** stay for the whole weekend.* **EXPECT** ▷ **4** [T] to expect or demand something: *Greg's asking (= expecting to be paid) £250,000 **for** his house.* ◦ *He asks too much **of** me – I can't always be there to help him.* ◦ ***It's asking a lot** when your boss wants you to work weekends as well as evenings.*

> **Other ways of saying ask**
>
> If someone is asking for information, the word **inquire** can be used:
>
> *She called to **inquire** when her car would be ready.*
>
> The verb **consult** is often used when you are asking for advice or information from someone who knows a lot because it is their job:
>
> ***Consult** your doctor if your symptoms don't improve.*
>
> If someone asks a lot of people in order to get information or help, you can use the phrasal verb **ask around**:
>
> *I'll **ask around** and see if anyone knows of a good carpenter.*
>
> The verb **question** is used in serious or official situations:
>
> *The police are **questioning** him about the robbery.*
>
> If someone asks a person questions for a television programme or newspaper article, the verb **interview** is often used:
>
> *After the race, she was **interviewed** by journalists.*

IDIOMS **be sb's for the asking** If something is yours for the asking, you only have to ask for it in order to be given it: *With three years' experience behind her, the promotion was Kate's for the asking.* • **be asking for it/trouble** to be behaving stupidly in a way that is likely to cause problems for you: *Drinking alcohol before driving is really asking for trouble.* ◦ *I'm not surprised she lost her job – she was really asking for it.* • **don't ask me** informal B2 said when you do not know the answer to a question: *Don't ask me where you've left your glasses!* • **I ask you!** informal something that you say in order to show your surprise or anger at something someone has done: *They stayed for a month and left without even saying thank you! Well, I ask you!* • **if you ask me** C2 said when giving your opinion on something: *If you ask me, people should go on a training course before they become parents.* • **you may well ask** (also **well may you ask**) it would be very interesting to know: *How could Jonathan afford to buy a new car? You may well ask.*

PHRASAL VERBS **ask after sb** UK (US **ask about**, Scottish English **ask for**) to ask for information about someone, especially about their health: *Tell your father I was asking after him.* • **ask around** to ask a lot of different people in order to get information or help: *Our babysitter's just moved away, so we're asking around **for** a replacement.* • **ask for sb** to say that you would like to see or speak to someone: *A young man was here asking for you this morning.* • **ask for sth** If you say you couldn't ask for someone or something better, you mean that that person or thing is the best of their type: *She's great to work for – I really couldn't ask for a better boss.* • **ask sb in** to invite someone to come into a building or room, especially your home: *I'd ask you in **for** a coffee but I have to get up early for work in the morning.* • **ask sb out** to invite someone to come with you to a place such as the cinema or a restaurant, especially as a way of starting a romantic relationship: *She's asked Steve out to the cinema this evening.* ◦ *You should ask her out sometime.*

askance /ə'skɑːns/ US /-'skæns/ **adv look askance** to look at or think about someone or something with doubt, disapproval, or no trust: *They looked askance **at** our scruffy clothes.*

askew /ə'skjuː/ **adj** [after verb] not straight or level: *Isn't that picture slightly askew?* • **askew adv**

'asking ˌprice noun [S] the amount of money someone wants when they sell something, especially a building or a piece of land: *The asking price for the flat was £89,500.*

asleep /ə'sliːp/ **adj** [after verb] **1** B1 sleeping or not awake: *I **fell** asleep (= I started to sleep) as soon as my head hit the pillow.* ◦ *I'm surprised to see you awake – ten minutes ago you were **fast/sound** (= completely) asleep.* ◦ *I've only just got up and I'm still **half** asleep (= not completely awake).* **2** If your arm or leg is asleep, it cannot feel anything because it has been in the same position for so long.

> **Other ways of saying asleep**
>
> The verbs **doze** and **snooze** and the expression **have/take a nap** all mean 'to sleep a short time':
>
> *She's always **dozing** in front of the TV.*
>
> *Grandad was **snoozing** in his chair.*
>
> *Owen is tired so he's just **taking a nap**.*
>
> The phrasal verbs **doze off** and (*informal*) **nod off** mean to start to sleep, especially during the day:
>
> *I must have **dozed off** after lunch.*
>
> *She **nodded off** during the lecture.*
>
> If you have slept for longer than you intended, you can use the verb **oversleep**:
>
> *I **overslept** and was late for work.*

A'S ˌlevel noun [C] (formal **Adˌvanced Sub'sidiary ˌlevel**) an exam of a standard between GCSE and A LEVEL taken in England and Wales, which allows more subjects to be studied than is possible at A level because less information needs to be learned for it. Students then take A2 exams, usually a year later, which together make a full A LEVEL qualification: *I'm doing (= studying) five AS levels.* ◦ *AS level French* → See also **A2, A level**

asp /æsp/ **noun** [C] a small poisonous snake found especially in North Africa, which was a symbol of ROYALTY in ancient Egypt

asparagus /ə'spær.ə.gəs/ US /-'sper-/ **noun** [U] a plant with pale green, JUICY stems that are cooked and eaten as a vegetable: *asparagus **spears***

aspartame /'æs.pə.teɪm/ US /-pɚ-/ **noun** [U] a very sweet substance that contains very little energy and is used instead of sugar to make drinks and foods sweet

aspect /'æs.pekt/ **noun FEATURE** ▷ **1** B2 [C] one part of a situation, problem, subject, etc.: *Which aspects **of** the job do you most enjoy?* ◦ *His illness affects almost every aspect **of** his life.* ◦ *That's the most worrying aspect **of** the situation.* ◦ *Lighting is a vitally important aspect **of** filmmaking.* ◦ *Have you thought about the problem from every aspect?* **DIRECTION** ▷ **2** [C] the direction in which a building, window, room, or sloping field faces, or the view that can be seen because of this direction: *The dining room has a southern aspect, which allows us to make the most of the sun.* **APPEARANCE ▷ 3** [S] formal the appearance of a place, or the expression on a person's face: *The glasses and the beard lend him a rather scholarly aspect.* **GRAMMAR ▷ 4** [C or U] specialized the form of a verb that shows how the meaning of that verb is considered in relation to time, typically expressing if an action is complete, repeated, or continuous **TV ▷ 5** [C] (also ˌ**aspect ˈratio**) specialized a measurement of the width compared to the height of the picture on a TV or computer screen: *A widescreen picture has an aspect ratio of 16:9.*

Asperger's syndrome /ˈæs.pɜː.dʒəzˌsɪn.drəʊm/ US /-pɝː.dʒɚzˌsɪn.droʊm/ **noun** [U] a type of AUTISM in which someone does not develop normal social abilities, and is often very interested in one particular subject

asperity /əˈsper.ɪ.ti/ US /-ə.t̬i/ **noun** [U] formal the quality of being severe in the way that you speak and behave

aspersions /əˈspɜː.ʃənz/ US /-ˈspɝː.ʒənz/ **noun** [plural] formal → See **cast aspersions on sb/sth** at **cast**

asphalt /ˈæs.fɔːlt/ US /-fɑːlt/ **noun; verb**

▸**noun** [U] a black, sticky substance mixed with small stones or sand, which forms a strong surface when it becomes hard

▸**verb** [T] to cover something, typically a roof or road, with asphalt: *an asphalted road/pitch/court*

asphyxiate /əsˈfɪk.si.eɪt/ **verb** [T often passive] formal to cause someone to be unable to breathe, usually resulting in that person's death: *The murder inquiry found that the children had been asphyxiated.* • **asphyxiation** /əsˌfɪk.siˈeɪ.ʃən/ **noun** [U]

aspic /ˈæs.pɪk/ **noun** [U] a transparent JELLY made from animal bones that is used in cold SAVOURY foods

aspidistra /ˌæs.pɪˈdɪs.trə/ **noun** [C] a large EVERGREEN plant (= one that never loses its leaves), usually grown inside, that has purple flowers shaped like bells and long, strong leaves

aspirant /ˈæs.pɪ.rənt/, /əˈspaɪ-/ US /ˈæs.pɚ.ənt/ **noun** [C] formal someone who very much wants to achieve something: *an aspirant **to** the throne*

aspirate **noun; verb**

▸**noun** [C] /ˈæs.pɪ.rət/ US /-pɚ.ət/ specialized the sound represented in English by the letter 'h', in words such as 'house'

▸**verb** /ˈæs.pɪ.reɪt/ **1** [T] to breathe out air when pronouncing a PLOSIVE consonant sound **2** [I or T] US specialized to breathe in, or to breathe a substance into your lungs by accident

aspiration /ˌæs.pɪˈreɪ.ʃən/ US /-pəˈeɪ-/ **noun** **HOPE ▷ 1** C2 [C usually plural, U] something that you hope to achieve: *I've never **had** any political aspirations.* **PHONETICS ▷ 2** [U] the noise that is made when air escapes after a PLOSIVE consonant sound: *In English, aspiration is an important feature in whether we hear a sound as /p/ or /b/ at the beginning of a word.*

aspirational /ˌæs.pɪˈreɪ.ʃən.əl/ US /-pəˈeɪ-/ **adj** UK showing that you want to have more money and a higher social position than you now have: *High-end smartphones have become aspirational status symbols, especially among the young.*

aspire /əˈspaɪər/ US /-ˈspaɪr/ **verb**

PHRASAL VERB **aspire to sth** C2 to have a strong wish or hope to do or have something: *Few people who aspire to fame ever achieve it.* ◦ [+ to infinitive] *As a child, he aspired to be a great writer.*

aspirin /ˈæs.pɪ.rɪn/ **noun** [C or U] (plural **aspirin** or **aspirins**) B1 a common drug that reduces pain, fever, and swelling: *I always **take** a couple of aspirins when I feel a cold starting.* ◦ *Aspirin should not be **given** to young children.*

aspiring /əˈspaɪə.rɪŋ/ US /-ˈspaɪr.ɪŋ/ **adj** **an aspiring actor, politician, writer, etc.** C2 someone who is trying to become a successful actor, politician, writer, etc.

ass /æs/ **noun** **ANIMAL ▷ 1** [C] old use a **donkey** **STUPID PERSON ▷ 2** [C] informal a stupid person: *a pompous ass* **BOTTOM ▷ 3** [C] mainly US offensive (UK **arse**) the part of the body that you sit on **4** [U] US offensive used by men to refer to sexual activity, or to women considered only as possible sexual partners: *I've never seen so much gorgeous ass.* **5 your ass** mainly US offensive yourself: *Get your ass in my office now!*

IDIOMS **be on sb's ass** mainly US offensive to annoy someone by refusing to leave them alone: *The police have been on my ass ever since I got out of jail.* • **be up sb's ass** mainly US offensive to be driving too close to the car in front of you: *I had a sports car up my ass for the first 50 miles.* • **bore the ass off sb** mainly US offensive to bore someone a lot: *Jamie? He bores the ass off me!* • **make an ass of yourself** informal to behave stupidly and look silly: *Simon always makes a **complete** ass of himself when he's had too much to drink.* • **the law is an ass** UK saying said about a law that is so stupid that it should be changed or ended • **shove/stick sth up your ass!** mainly US offensive used to tell someone angrily that you do not want or need something that they are offering you or telling you to do: *If she asks me to work over the weekend, I'll tell her to shove it up her ass!* • **talk sb's ass off** mainly US offensive to talk to someone too much • **work sb's ass off** mainly US offensive to make someone work very hard: *They work your ass off but they pay you well.* • **work your ass off** mainly US offensive to work very hard: *I worked my ass off for that man.*

assail /əˈseɪl/ **verb** formal **1** [T] to attack someone violently or criticize someone strongly: *The victim had been assailed **with** repeated blows to the head and body.* ◦ *He was assailed **with** insults and abuse as he left the court.* **2** [T often passive] to cause someone to experience a lot of unpleasant things: *to be assailed **by** doubts/fears/problems*

assailant /əˈseɪ.lənt/ **noun** [C] formal a person who attacks another person: *Can you describe your assailant?*

assassin /əˈsæs.ɪn/ **noun** [C] someone who kills a famous or important person, usually for political reasons or in exchange for money: *John Lennon's assassin was Mark Chapman.* ◦ *She **hired** an assassin to eliminate her rival.*

assassinate /əˈsæs.ɪ.neɪt/ **verb** [T] to kill someone famous or important: *a **plot to** assassinate the president*

assassination /əˌsæs.ɪˈneɪ.ʃən/ **noun** [C or U] the murder of someone famous or important: *an assassination **attempt*** ◦ *the assassination **of** the opposition leader*

assault /əˈsɒlt/ US /-ˈsɑːlt/ **noun; verb**

▸**noun** **1** C2 [C or U] a violent attack: *He was charged with **sexual** assault.* ◦ UK *The number of **indecent** assaults has increased alarmingly over the past year.* ◦ *an assault **on** a police officer* ◦ *They **launched** an assault **on** the capital yesterday.* **2** [C] a determined or serious attempt to do something difficult: *Women's groups have demanded a nationwide assault **on** sexism in the workplace.* ◦ *She died heroically during an*

A

assault ***on*** *the world's second-highest mountain.* **3 assault and battery** [U] legal a threat to injure someone followed by a violent attack on them
▸**verb** [T] C2 to attack someone violently: *A woman and a man have been convicted of assaulting a police officer.* ◦ *He had attempted to* ***sexually*** *assault the woman.*

as'sault ˌcourse noun [C] UK (US **'obstacle ˌcourse**) an area of land on which soldiers have to run between and climb over or cross various objects, designed to test their strength and physical condition: figurative *Meetings with tax inspectors are often bureaucratic assault courses.*

assay /ə'seɪ/, /æs'eɪ/ **verb** [T] specialized to perform an examination on a chemical in order to test how pure it is • **assay noun** [C]

assemblage /ə'sem.blɪdʒ/ **noun 1** [C] formal a collection of things or a group of people or animals: *A varied assemblage of birds was probing the mud for food.* **2** [U] the process of joining or putting things together

assemble /ə'sem.bl̩/ **verb GATHER** ▷ **1** C2 [I or T] to come together in a single place or bring parts together in a single group: *We assembled in the meeting room after lunch.* ◦ *to assemble data* ◦ *At the staff meeting, the manager told the assembled* ***company*** *(= everyone there) that no one would lose their job.* **JOIN** ▷ **2** C2 [T] to make something by joining separate parts: *furniture that is easy to assemble*

assembly /ə'sem.bli/ **noun MEETING** ▷ **1** C2 [C] a group of people, especially one that meets regularly for a particular purpose, such as government, or, more generally, the process of coming together, or the state of being together: *the United Nations General Assembly* ◦ *She has been tipped as a future member of the Welsh Assembly.* **2 Assembly** US one of the two parts of the government that makes laws in many US States: *the New York Assembly* ◦ *The Senate and the Assembly put aside political differences to pass the aid package.* **3** [C or U] a meeting in a school of several classes, usually at the beginning of the school day, to give information or to say prayers together: *All pupils are expected to attend school assembly.* ◦ *There's a religious assembly every morning.* **JOINING** ▷ **4** C2 [U] the process of putting together the parts of a machine or structure **5** [C] specialized the structure produced by this process: *The frame needs to be strong enough to support the engine assembly.*

as'sembly ˌline noun [C usually singular] a line of machines and workers in a factory that a product moves along while it is being built or produced. Each machine or worker performs a particular job, which must be finished before the product moves to the next position in the line: *assembly-line workers*

assemblyman /ə'sem.bli.mæn/, /-mən/ **noun** [C] (plural **-men** /-mən/) US a man who belongs to a part of the official law-making body in many US states

assemblywoman /ə'sem.bliˌwʊm.ən/ **noun** [C] (plural **-women** /-wɪmɪn/) US a female assemblyman

assent /ə'sent/ **noun; verb**
▸**noun** [U] formal official agreement to or approval of an idea, plan, or request: *Once the directors have* ***given*** *their assent* ***to*** *the proposal we can begin.* ◦ *She nodded her assent* ***to*** *the proposal.* ◦ UK *Before an Act of Parliament can become law, it needs to receive* ***Royal*** *Assent (= an official signature) from the monarch.* → Compare **dissent**
▸**verb** [I] formal to agree to or give official approval to something: *Have they assented* ***to*** *the terms of the contract?*

assert /ə'sɜːt/ US /-'sɝːt/ **verb** [T] **1 assert yourself** C2 to behave in a way that expresses your confidence, importance, or power and earns you respect from others: *I really must assert myself more in meetings.* **2** C1 formal to say that something is certainly true: [+ that] *He asserts* ***that*** *she stole money from him.* **3** C2 to do something to show that you have power: *Throughout the Cold War, the Allies asserted their* ***right*** *to move freely between the two Berlins.* ◦ *She very rarely asserts her* ***authority*** *over the children.*

assertion /ə'sɜː.ʃən/ US /-'sɝː-/ **noun** [C + that] a statement that you strongly believe is true: *I certainly don't agree with his assertion* ***that*** *men are better drivers than women.*

assertive /ə'sɜː.tɪv/ US /-'sɝː.t̬ɪv/ **adj** C2 describes someone who behaves confidently and is not frightened to say what they want or believe: *If you really want the promotion, you'll have to be more assertive.* • **assertively** /-li/ **adv** • **assertiveness** /-nəs/ **noun** [U]

assess /ə'ses/ **verb** [T] B2 to judge or decide the amount, value, quality, or importance of something: *The insurers will need to assess the flood damage.* ◦ *They assessed the cost of the flood damage* ***at*** *£1,500.* ◦ *Exams are not the only means of assessing a student's ability.* ◦ *It's too early to assess the long-term consequences of the two countries' union.* ◦ [+ question word] *We need to assess* ***wh****ether the project is worth doing.*

asˌsessable 'income noun [U] UK specialized the amount of money that is considered when calculating tax payments

assessment /ə'ses.mənt/ **noun** [C or U] B2 the act of judging or deciding the amount, value, quality, or importance of something, or the judgment or decision that is made: *Would you say that is a* ***fair*** *assessment of the situation?* ◦ *Both their assessments of production costs were hopelessly inaccurate.*

assessor /ə'ses.əʳ/ US /-ɚ/ **noun** [C] someone whose job is to judge or decide the amount, value, quality, or importance of something: *The assessor stated that the fire damage was not as severe as the hotel's owner had claimed.*

asset /'æs.et/, /-ɪt/ **noun 1** C1 [C] a useful or valuable quality, skill, or person: *He'll be a great asset* ***to*** *the team.* ◦ *Her eyes are her* ***best*** *asset (= most attractive feature).* ◦ *Knowledge of languages is a real asset in this sort of work.* **2** C1 [C usually plural] something valuable belonging to a person or organization that can be used for the payment of debts: *A company's assets can consist of cash, investments, specialist knowledge, or copyright material.* ◦ ***liquid*** *assets (= money or things that can easily be changed into money)* → Compare **liabilities (liability)**

'asset ˌmanager noun [C] a person or company that manages someone else's money, STOCKS, and SHARES, etc. • **'asset ˌmanagement noun** [U]

'asset-ˌstripping noun [U] disapproving the activity in which a company buys an unsuccessful company cheaply and sells its assets separately at a profit • **'asset-ˌstripper noun** [C]

asshole /'æs.həʊl/ US /-hoʊl/ **noun** [C] mainly US **arsehole**

assiduous /ə'sɪd.ju.əs/ **adj** formal showing hard work, care, and attention to detail: *assiduous research/efforts* ◦ *an assiduous student* ◦ *The government has been assiduous* ***in*** *the fight against inflation.* • **assiduously** /-li/ **adv** • **assiduousness** /-nəs/ **noun** [U]

assign /əˈsaɪn/ verb [T] **CHOOSE** ▷ **1** C1 [often passive] to give a particular job or piece of work to someone: [+ two objects] *UN troops were assigned the task of rebuilding the hospital.* ◦ *The case has been assigned **to** our most senior officer.* **2** If you assign a time for a job or activity, you decide it will be done during that time: *Have you assigned a day **for** the interviews yet?* **3** If you assign a characteristic to something, you say that it has it: *Each visitor to the site chooses an online alter ego, which is assigned a name.* **4** to decide a reason for something: *Detectives have been unable to assign a motive **for** the murder.* ◦ *The report assigned the **blame** for the accident **to** inadequate safety regulations.* **SEND** ▷ **5** C2 to send someone somewhere to do a job: *She was assigned **to** the newspaper's Berlin office.* **COMPUTING** ▷ **6** specialized to put a value in a particular position in the memory of a computer **GIVE LEGALLY** ▷ **7** legal to give property, money, or rights using a legal process: *Her property was assigned **to** her grandchildren.*

PHRASAL VERB **assign sb to sth** [often passive] C2 to choose someone to do a particular job: *Which police officer has been assigned to this case?*

assignation /ˌæs.ɪɡˈneɪ.ʃən/ noun [C] formal a meeting, especially one between two people having a romantic relationship, that is secret or not allowed

assignment /əˈsaɪn.mənt/ noun **1** B1 [C] a piece of work given to someone, typically as part of their studies or job: *a freelance/photo assignment* ◦ *I have a lot of reading assignments to complete before the end of term.* **2** [C] a job that someone is sent somewhere to do: *a foreign/diplomatic assignment* **3 on assignment** Someone who is on assignment is doing a particular job or piece of work, usually in a particular place where they have been sent for a period of time: *Both journalists were killed by terrorists whilst on assignment in Colombia.* **4** [U] the process of giving a particular job or piece of work to someone, or of sending someone to a chosen place to do a job: *assignment **of** the various tasks*

assimilate /əˈsɪm.ɪ.leɪt/ verb [I or T] **JOIN** ▷ **1** to become part of a group, country, society, etc., or to make someone or something become part of a group, country, society, etc.: *The European Union should remain flexible enough to assimilate more countries quickly.* ◦ *You shouldn't expect immigrants to assimilate **into** an alien culture immediately.* **LEARN** ▷ **2** to understand and remember new information and make it part of your basic knowledge so that you can use it as your own: *It's hard to assimilate so much information.* **ABSORB** ▷ **3** to absorb food into the tissue of a living organism: *In this form vitamins can be easily assimilated by the body.* • **assimilable** /-lə.bl/ adj *A textbook needs to be assimilable (= able to be understood) to sell a lot of copies.*

assimilation /əˌsɪm.ɪˈleɪ.ʃən/ noun [U] **TAKING IN** ▷ **1** the process of becoming a part, or making someone become a part, of a group, country, society, etc.: *The assimilation of ethnic Germans in the US was accelerated by the two world wars.* **2** the process of absorbing food into the tissue of a living organism: *Poor assimilation of vitamins and nutrients can cause health problems.* **PHONETICS** ▷ **3** the fact of a speech sound being influenced by the sound that comes before or after it

assist /əˈsɪst/ verb [I or T] formal **1** B2 to help: *The army arrived to assist **in** the search.* ◦ *You will be expected to assist the editor **with** the selection of illustrations for the book.* **2 assist the police with/in their inquiries** UK If someone is assisting the police with their inquiries, it usually means they have been taken to the police station to be asked questions about a crime.

assistance /əˈsɪs.tənts/ noun [U] **1** B2 help: *The company needs more **financial** assistance from the government.* ◦ *A £1 billion investment would be **of** considerable assistance to the railways.* ◦ *Can I be **of any** assistance (= can I help), madam?* ◦ *Teachers can't **give** pupils any assistance in exams.* **2 come to sb's assistance** to help someone

assistant /əˈsɪs.tənt/ noun [C] **1** B1 someone who helps someone else to do a job: *an administrative/office assistant* ◦ *an assistant editor/manager* **2** A2 UK someone who works in a shop, selling goods to customers and giving advice about the goods sold in the shop: *a **sales/shop** assistant*

asˌsisted ˈsuicide noun [U or C] the act of helping someone who wants to die to kill themselves when they are too ill to do it alone, or an occasion when this happens

assizes /əˈsaɪ.zɪz/ noun [plural] (in Wales and England until 1971) one or more of the meetings of the most important court in each COUNTY, usually held four times a year by a travelling judge

Assn noun [C] written abbreviation for **association**

Assoc. written abbreviation for **association** or **associate**

associate verb; noun; adj

▸verb [T] /əˈsəʊ.si.eɪt/ US /-ˈsoʊ-/ C1 to connect someone or something in your mind with someone or something else: *Most people associate this brand **with** good quality.*

PHRASAL VERBS **be associated with sth** B2 If problems or dangers are associated with a particular thing or action, they are caused by it: *The cancer risks associated with smoking have been well documented.* • **associate with sb** C2 to spend time with a group of people, especially people who are disapproved of: *I don't want my children associating with drug addicts and alcoholics.*

▸noun [C] /əˈsəʊ.si.ət/ US /-ˈsoʊ-/ **FRIEND** ▷ **1** someone who is closely connected to another person as a COMPANION, friend, or business partner: *A close associate of the author denied reports that she had cancer.* ◦ *a **business** associate* **QUALIFICATION** ▷ **2** US someone who holds an ASSOCIATE'S DEGREE: *an associate of arts*

▸adj [before noun] /əˈsəʊ.si.ət/ US /-ˈsoʊ-/ used in the title of a person whose rank is slightly lower or less complete than the full official position described: *an associate member of an organization* ◦ *associate director/producer*

associated /əˈsəʊ.si.eɪ.tɪd/ US /-ˈsoʊ.si.eɪ.t̬ɪd/ adj connected: *She was prepared to take on the job, with all its associated risks.*

asˌsociate proˈfessor noun [C] US a teacher of high rank in a college or university who has a lower rank than a PROFESSOR

asˌsociate's deˈgree noun [C] US the qualification given to a student by a JUNIOR COLLEGE after successfully finishing two years of study

association /əˌsəʊ.siˈeɪ.ʃən/ US /-ˌsoʊ-/ noun **GROUP** ▷ **1** B2 [C, + sing/pl verb] a group of people who work together in a single organization for a particular purpose: *The Football Association* ◦ *The British Medical Association is/are campaigning for a complete ban on tobacco advertising.* **INVOLVEMENT** ▷ **2** C1 [U] the fact of being involved with or connected to someone or something: *her association **with** the*

university ◦ *This event was organized* ***in*** *association* ***with*** *a local school.* **3** [C or U] a feeling or thought that relates to someone or something: *The south of France has positive associations for me as I used to holiday there as a child.*

As,sociation 'football noun [U] UK formal **soccer**

assonance /'æs.ən.əns/ noun [U] specialized the similarity in sound between two syllables that are close together, created by the same vowels but different consonants (e.g. 'back' and 'hat'), or by the same consonants and different vowels (e.g. 'hit' and 'heart') → Compare **alliteration**

assorted /ə'sɔː.tɪd/ (US) /-'sɔːr.t̬ɪd/ **adj** consisting of various types mixed together: *a case of assorted wines*

assortment /ə'sɔːt.mənt/ (US) /-'sɔːrt-/ noun [C usually singular] a group of different types of something: *an assortment* ***of*** *vegetables* ◦ *An unlikely assortment* ***of*** *rock stars and politicians attended the charity concert.*

Asst adj written abbreviation for **assistant**

assuage /ə'sweɪdʒ/ **verb** [T] formal to make unpleasant feelings less strong: *The government has tried to assuage the public's fears.*

assume /ə'sjuːm/ (US) /-'suːm/ **verb** [T] **ACCEPT** ▷ **1** (B2) to accept something to be true without question or proof: [+ (that)] *I assumed (****that****) you knew each other because you went to the same school.* ◦ ***Let's*** *assume (****that****) they're coming and make plans on that basis.* ◦ [+ to infinitive] *We can't assume the suspects* ***to*** *be guilty simply because they've decided to remain silent.* ◦ *We mustn't assume the suspects' guilt.* **PRETEND TO HAVE** ▷ **2** to pretend to have a different name or be someone you are not, or to express a feeling falsely: *Moving to a different town, he assumed a false name.* ◦ *During the investigation, two detectives assumed the* ***identities*** *of antiques dealers.* ◦ *He assumed a look of indifference but I knew how he felt.* **TAKE CONTROL** ▷ **3** (C2) to take or begin to have responsibility or control, sometimes without the right to do so, or to begin to have a characteristic: *The new president assumes office at midnight tonight.* ◦ *The issue has assumed considerable political proportions (= has become a big political problem).*

as'suming (that) **conjunction** accepting as true without question or proof: *Even assuming that smokers do see the health warnings, I doubt they'll take any notice.*

assumption /ə'sʌmp.ʃən/ noun **1** (C1) [C] something that you accept as true without question or proof: *People tend to* ***make*** *assumptions* ***about*** *you when you have a disability.* ◦ *These calculations are* ***based on*** *the assumption that prices will continue to rise.* **2 assumption of power, responsibility, etc.** [U] the act of taking a position of power, responsibility, etc.: *The revolutionaries' assumption of power took the army by surprise.*

assurance /ə'ʃɔː.rəns/ (US) /-'ʃʊr.əns/ noun **PROMISE** ▷ **1** (C1) [C] a promise: [+ (that)] *She gave me her assurance (****that****) she would sign the contract immediately.* ◦ *Despite the government's repeated assurances* ***to the contrary****, taxation has risen over the past decade.* **CONFIDENCE** ▷ **2** (C2) [U] confidence: *He spoke with calm assurance.* **INSURANCE** ▷ **3** [U] UK a type of INSURANCE against events that will certainly happen, such as death, not those that may happen, such as illness, fire, or having your property stolen

assure /ə'ʃɔːr/ (US) /-'ʃʊr/ **verb** [T] **SAY WITH CERTAINTY** ▷ **1** (B2) to tell someone confidently that something is true, especially so that they do not worry: *The unions assured the new owners* ***of*** *the workers' loyalty to the company.* ◦ [+ speech] *'Don't worry, your car will be ready tomorrow,' the mechanic assured him.* ◦ [+ (that)] *She assured him (****that****) the car would be ready the next day.* ◦ *The prime minister assured the electorate (****that****) taxes would not be increased after the election.* ◦ *You can* ***rest*** *assured (= feel confident) that I shall be there as promised.* **MAKE CERTAIN** ▷ **2** (C1) to cause something to be certain: *The play's popularity has been assured by the critics' rave reviews.* **PROTECT** ▷ **3** UK (of an organization) to promise to pay an amount of money to a person or their family if they become ill, get injured, or die, in return for small regular payments

assured /ə'ʃɔːd/ (US) /-'ʃʊrd/ **adj** **CONFIDENT** ▷ **1** (also **,self-as'sured**) showing skill and confidence: *an assured* ***performance*** **CERTAIN** ▷ **2** certain to be achieved or obtained: *Now that the finance has been secured, the production of the film is assured.*

assuredly /ə'ʃɔː.rɪd.li/ (US) /-'ʃʊr.ɪd-/ **adv** **CONFIDENTLY** ▷ **1** confidently: *After a disappointing first set, Nadal played assuredly and went on to win the match.* **CERTAINLY** ▷ **2** certainly: *These problems might not be solved by money alone, but they will assuredly not be solved without it.*

asterisk /'æs.tər.ɪsk/ (US) /-tə-/ **noun; verb**

▸**noun** [C] the symbol *, used to refer readers to a note at the bottom of a page of text, or to show that a letter is missing from a word: *Sometimes taboo words are written with asterisks to avoid causing offence.*

▸**verb** [T] to write an asterisk next to something

astern /ə'stɜːn/ (US) /-'stɝːn/ **adv** behind a ship, or going backwards when in a ship

asteroid /'æs.tər.ɔɪd/ (US) /-tə.rɔɪd/ **noun** [C] one of many large rocks that circle the sun

asthma /'æs.mə/ (US) /'æz-/ **noun** [U] a medical condition that makes breathing difficult by causing the air passages to become narrow or blocked: *an asthma sufferer* ◦ *an asthma* ***attack***

asthmatic /æs'mæt.ɪk/ (US) /æz'mæt̬-/ **adj; noun**

▸**adj** of, relating to, or suffering from asthma: *an asthmatic attack*

▸**noun** [C] an asthmatic person: *She's been an asthmatic since her childhood.*

astigmatism /ə'stɪg.mə.tɪ.zəm/ **noun** [U] a fault in the LENS of the eye that reduces the quality of sight, especially a fault that stops the eye from FOCUSING • **astigmatic** /,æs.tɪg'mæt.ɪk/ (US) /-'mæt̬-/ **adj**

astonish /ə'stɒn.ɪʃ/ (US) /-'stɑː.nɪʃ/ **verb** [T] to surprise someone very much: *I was astonished* ***by*** *how much she'd grown.* ◦ *What astonished me was that he didn't seem to mind.*

astonished /ə'stɒn.ɪʃt/ (US) /-'stɑː.nɪʃt/ **adj** (B2) very surprised: [+ to infinitive] *I was astonished* ***to*** *see Miriam there.* ◦ *They looked astonished when I announced I was pregnant.* ◦ *The doctors were astonished* ***at*** *the speed of her recovery.*

astonishing /ə'stɒn.ɪ.ʃɪŋ/ (US) /-'stɑː.nɪ-/ **adj** (B2) very surprising: *Her first novel enjoyed an astonishing success.* ◦ [+ to infinitive] *It's astonishing* ***to*** *think that only a few years ago he was a completely unknown actor.* • **astonishingly** /-li/ **adv** *Astonishingly, I've never visited the British Museum in all the years I've lived here.* ◦ *She did astonishingly well in her exams.*

astonishment /ə'stɒn.ɪʃ.mənt/ (US) /-'stɑː.nɪʃ-/ **noun** [U] (B2) very great surprise: ***To the*** *astonishment* ***of*** *her colleagues, she resigned.* ◦ *She gasped* ***in*** *astonishment.*

astound /ə'staʊnd/ **verb** [T] to surprise or shock someone very much: *The news astounded me.*

astounded /ə'staʊn.dɪd/ **adj** very surprised or

shocked: [+ to infinitive] *I was astounded* ***to*** *hear that Tim had left.*

astounding /əˈstaʊn.dɪŋ/ **adj** very surprising or shocking: *an astounding fact/decision/revelation* ◦ *an astounding (= very great) victory/achievement/success* • **astoundingly** /-li/ **adv**

astrakhan /ˈæs.trə.kæn/ **noun** [U] the skin of very young sheep from Astrakhan in southern Russia that is covered in grey or black wool that is tightly curled and looks like fur, or a type of cloth that looks like this skin

astral /ˈæs.trəl/ **adj** **STARS** ▷ **1** relating to the stars or outer space **FORCES** ▷ **2** [before noun] relating to forces that are not known or understood

astray /əˈstreɪ/ **adv** away from the correct path or correct way of doing something: *The letter must have* ***gone*** *astray in the post.* ◦ *I was* ***led*** *astray by an out-of-date map.* ◦ *Her parents worried that she might be* ***led*** *astray (= encouraged to behave badly) by her unsuitable friends.*

astride /əˈstraɪd/ **preposition; adv**
▸**preposition** with a leg on each side of something: *She sat proudly astride her new motorbike.* ◦ figurative *The town lies astride (= on either side of) the River Havel.*
▸**adv** with legs wide apart: *He stood there, legs astride.*

astringent /əˈstrɪn.dʒənt/ **noun; adj**
▸**noun** [C] a drug or cream that causes the skin or other tissue to tighten: *You can use an astringent to make your skin less oily.*
▸**adj** **MEDICINE** ▷ **1** describes a substance that acts as an astringent: *an astringent cream* **SEVERE** ▷ **2** describes remarks that are clever but unkind or criticize someone: *astringent criticism* ◦ *her astringent wit* • **astringently** /-li/ **adv** • **astringency** /-dʒən.si/ **noun** [U]

astro- /æs.trəʊ-/ (US) /-troʊ-/ **prefix** relating to space, the planets, stars, or other objects in space, or to a structure in the shape of a star: *astrology* ◦ *astronaut* ◦ *astrophysics*

astrologer /əˈstrɒl.ə.dʒər/ (US) /-ˈstrɑː.lə.dʒɚ/ **noun** [C] someone who studies astrology

astrology /əˈstrɒl.ə.dʒi/ (US) /-ˈstrɑː.lə-/ **noun** [U] the study of the movements and positions of the sun, moon, planets, and stars, and the skill of describing the expected effect that some people believe these have on the character and lives of people • **astrological** /ˌæs.trəˈlɒdʒ.ɪ.kəl/ (US) /-ˈlɑː.dʒɪ-/ **adj**

astronaut /ˈæs.trə.nɔːt/ (US) /-nɑːt/ **noun** [C] a person who has been trained for travelling in space

astronautics /ˌæs.trəˈnɔː.tɪks/ (US) /-trəˈnɑː.t̬ɪks/ **noun** [U] the technology related to space travel

astronomer /əˈstrɒn.ə.mər/ (US) /-ˈstrɑː.nə.mɚ/ **noun** [C] someone who studies astronomy

astronomical /ˌæs.trəˈnɒm.ɪ.kəl/ (US) /-ˈnɑː.mɪ-/ **adj** **SCIENTIFIC** ▷ **1** [before noun] connected with astronomy: *the Royal Astronomical Society* ◦ *astronomical observations/instruments* **LARGE** ▷ **2** (also **astronomic**) informal describes an amount that is extremely large: *an astronomical rent/bill/price/fee*

astronomically /ˌæs.trəˈnɒm.ɪ.kəl.i/ (US) /-ˈnɑː.mɪ-/ **adv** **LARGE** ▷ informal by a very large amount: *Oil prices have risen astronomically since the early 70s.*

astronomy /əˈstrɒn.ə.mi/ (US) /-ˈstrɑː.nə-/ **noun** [U] (C2) the scientific study of the universe and of objects that exist naturally in space, such as the moon, the sun, planets, and stars

astrophysics /ˌæs.trəʊˈfɪz.ɪks/ (US) /-troʊ-/ **noun** [U] the type of astronomy that uses physical laws and ideas to explain the behaviour of the stars and other objects in space • **astrophysical** /-ɪ.kəl/ (US) /-troʊ-/ **adj** • **astrophysicist** /-ɪ.sɪst/ (US) /-troʊ-/ **noun** [C] someone who studies astrophysics

AstroTurf /ˈæs.trə.tɜːf/ (US) /-troʊ.tɝːf/ **noun** [U] trademark a type of artificial grass surface, used especially for sports fields

astute /əˈstjuːt/ (US) /-ˈstuːt/ **adj** clever and quick to see how to take advantage of a situation: *an astute investor/businesswoman* ◦ *his astute handling of the situation* • **astutely** /-li/ **adv** • **astuteness** /-nəs/ **noun** [U]

asunder /əˈsʌn.dər/ (US) /-dɚ/ **adv** literary into forcefully separated pieces: *Their lives were* ***torn*** *asunder by the tragedy.* → Synonym **apart**

asylum /əˈsaɪ.ləm/ **noun** **PROTECTION** ▷ **1** [U] protection or safety, especially that given by a government to people who have been forced to leave their own countries for their safety or because of war: *to* ***seek/apply for political*** *asylum* **HOSPITAL** ▷ **2** [C] old use a hospital for people with mental illnesses: *a lunatic asylum*

aˈsylum ˌseeker **noun** [C] someone who leaves their own country for their safety, often for political reasons or because of war, and who travels to another country hoping that the government will protect them and allow them to live there: *genuine/bogus asylum seekers* ◦ *A record number of asylum seekers arrived in the UK last month.*

asymmetric /ˌeɪ.sɪˈmet.rɪk/ **adj** (also **asymmetrical** /-əl/) with two halves, sides, or parts that are not exactly the same in shape and size: *Lisette came back from New York with a trendy asymmetric haircut.* • **asymmetrically** /-rɪ.kəl.i/ **adv** • **asymmetry** /eɪˈsɪm.ə.tri/ **noun** [C or U]

ˌasymmetric ˈbars **noun** [plural] UK (US **unˌeven ˈbars**) two horizontal bars of different height that are used in an event in women's GYMNASTICS, or the event itself

asynchronous /eɪˈsɪŋ.krə.nəs/ **adj** formal not happening or done at the same time or speed: *an asynchronous online course that can be followed from anywhere in the world* → Opposite **synchronous**

at weak /ət/ strong /æt/ **preposition** **PLACE** ▷ **1** (A1) used to show an exact position or particular place: *We'll meet you at the entrance.* ◦ *That bit at the beginning of the film was brilliant.* ◦ *She's sitting at the table in the corner.* ◦ *She was standing at the top of the stairs.* ◦ *The dog came and lay down at (= next to) my feet.* ◦ *There's someone at the door (= someone is outside and wants to come in).* ◦ *We spent the afternoon at a football match.* ◦ *I enjoyed my three years at university.* ◦ *I rang her but she was at lunch (= away, eating her lunch).* **TIME** ▷ **2** (A1) used to show an exact or a particular time: *There's a meeting at 2.30 this afternoon.* ◦ *Are you free at lunchtime?* ◦ *In theory, women can still have children at the age of 50.* ◦ *The bells ring at regular intervals through the day.* ◦ *At no* ***time/point*** *did the company do anything illegal.* ◦ *I'm busy at* ***the moment*** *(= now) – can you call back later?* ◦ *It's a shame I wasn't here to meet you – I was in London at* ***the time*** *(= then).* **DIRECTION** ▷ **3** (A1) in the direction of: *She smiled at me.* ◦ *They waved at us as we drove by.* ◦ *She aimed at the target.* ◦ *He's always shouting at the children.* **CAUSE** ▷ **4** (A2) used to show the cause of something, especially a feeling: *We were surprised at the news.* ◦ *I was quite excited at the prospect.* ◦ *Why does no one ever laugh at my jokes?* **ACTIVITY** ▷ **5** (B1) used to show the activity in which someone's ability is being judged: *I was never very good at sports.* ◦ *He's very good at getting on with people.* ◦ *She's hopeless at*

A

organizing things. **EMAIL ADDRESS** ▷ **6** A1 the @ symbol that joins the name of a person or a department in an organization to a DOMAIN NAME to make an email address: *'What's your email address?' 'It's dictionary at cambridge dot org.'* **AMOUNT** ▷ **7** B2 used to show a price, temperature, rate, speed, etc.: *I'm not going to buy those shoes at $150!* ◦ *Inflation is running at 5 percent.* ◦ *He was driving at 120 mph when the police spotted him.* **8** (usually @) used in financial records to show the price, rate, etc. of a particular thing or of each of a number of things on a list: *50 units @ £4.75* **CONDITION** ▷ **9** used to show a state, condition, or continuous activity: *a country at war* ◦ *children at play*

ˌat ˈall adv (used to make negatives and questions stronger) in any way or of any type: *He's had no food at all.* ◦ *I haven't been at all well recently.* ◦ *I'm afraid I've got **nothing** at all to say.* ◦ *Is there any uncertainty at all about the way she died?* ◦ *Why bother getting up at all when you don't have a job to go to?*

atavistic /ˌæt.əˈvɪs.tɪk/ (US) /ˌæţ-/ **adj** formal happening because of a very old habit from a long time ago in human history, not because of a conscious decision or because it is necessary now: *an atavistic fear of the dark* • **atavism** /ˈæt.ə.vɪ.zᵊm/ (US) /ˈæţ-/ **noun** [U]

ate /et/, /eɪt/ **verb** past simple of **eat**

atelier /əˈtel.i.eɪ/ **noun** [C] literary a room or building in which an artist works

atheist /ˈeɪ.θi.ɪst/ **noun** [C] someone who believes that God does not exist → Compare **agnostic** • **atheism** /-ɪ.zᵊm/ **noun** [U] • **atheist adj** (also **atheistic** /ˌeɪ.θiˈɪs.tɪk/)

athlete /ˈæθ.liːt/ **noun** [C] B1 a person who is very good at sports or physical exercise, especially one who competes in organized events: *He became a **professional** athlete at the age of 16.* ◦ *She has the build of an athlete.*

ˌathlete's ˈfoot **noun** [U] a disease in which the skin between the toes CRACKS (= breaks open) and feels sore

athletic /æθˈlet.ɪk/ (US) /-ˈleţ-/ **adj 1** B2 strong, healthy, and good at sports: *She looks very athletic.* **2** [before noun] relating to athletes or the sport of athletics: *This college has a long tradition of athletic excellence.*

athleticism /æθˈlet.ɪ.sɪ.zᵊm/ (US) /-ˈleţ-/ **noun** [U] skill in running, jumping, throwing, and similar sports: *The team's superb athleticism compensated for their lack of international experience.*

athletics /æθˈlet.ɪks/ (US) /-ˈleţ-/ **noun** [U] **1** B1 UK (US **ˌtrack and ˈfield**) the general name for a particular group of sports in which people compete, including running, jumping, and throwing: *an athletics team/club/meeting* **2** US sports and physical activities of any type: *Girls who participate in high school athletics are more likely to graduate than those who don't.*

athˌletic supˈporter **noun** [C] US formal for **jockstrap**

-athon /-ə.θɒn/ (US) /-θɑːn/ **suffix** added to the end of words referring to an activity or event, especially one that has been organized to raise money for CHARITY, to show that it continues for a long time: *a 24-hour dance-athon* ◦ *a walkathon*

-ation /-eɪ.ʃᵊn/ **suffix -ion**

atishoo /əˈtɪʃ.uː/ **exclamation** (also **achoo**) UK used, especially in writing, to represent the sound of a SNEEZE

-ative /-ə.tɪv/ (US) /-ə.ţɪv/ **suffix** (also **-itive**) added to verbs to form adjectives meaning showing the ability to perform the activity represented by the verb

Atkins diet /ˈæt.kɪnzˌdaɪət/ **noun** [S] trademark an eating plan in which someone eats PROTEIN (= foods such as meat, cheese, eggs, etc.), but no or few CARBOHYDRATES such as bread, potatoes, or fruit, in order to lose body weight

atlas /ˈæt.ləs/ **noun** [C] a book containing maps: *a **road** atlas* ◦ *an atlas of the world*

ATM /ˌeɪ.tiːˈem/ **noun** [C] abbreviation for automated teller machine: a machine, usually in a wall outside a bank, shop, etc. from which you can take money out of your bank account using a special card: *Is there an ATM on this street? I need to get some money out.*

atmosphere /ˈæt.mə.sfɪəʳ/ (US) /-sfɪr/ **noun** **AIR** ▷ **1 the atmosphere** B2 [S] the mixture of gases around the Earth: *These factories are releasing toxic gases into the atmosphere.* **2** [C] a mixture of gases that surrounds any planet: *the search for planets with a breathable atmosphere* **3** B2 [S] the air that you breathe in a place: *The atmosphere in the room was so stuffy I could hardly breathe.* ◦ *A few plants in an office will improve the atmosphere.* **MOOD** ▷ **4** B1 [S] the character, feeling, or mood of a place or situation: *There's a very relaxed atmosphere in our office.* ◦ *There has been **an** atmosphere **of** gloom in the factory since it was announced that it would be closing.* **5** [U] approving a feeling that a place has of being pleasant and interesting or exciting: *He put on some soft music and turned the lights down in order to give the room a bit more atmosphere.*

> **Word partners for atmosphere (AIR)**
>
> *contaminate/poison/pollute* the atmosphere • the atmosphere *contains* sth • a *smoky/steamy/stuffy* atmosphere • *from/in/into* the atmosphere

> **Word partners for atmosphere (MOOD)**
>
> a *friendly/good/homely/relaxed* atmosphere • a *bad/oppressive/poisonous/tense* atmosphere • the *general* atmosphere • an (emotionally/highly/politically) *charged* atmosphere • *create* an atmosphere (**of** sth) • *enjoy/experience/soak up* the atmosphere • an atmosphere *of* sth

atmospheric /ˌæt.məsˈfer.ɪk/ **adj** **AIR** ▷ **1** [before noun] relating to the air or to the atmosphere: *Plants are the main source of atmospheric oxygen.* ◦ *If atmospheric **conditions** are right, it may be possible to see this group of stars tonight.* **MOOD** ▷ **2** approving creating a special feeling, especially a mysterious or romantic feeling: *atmospheric lighting/music*

atmosˌpheric ˈpressure **noun** [U] specialized the force with which the atmosphere presses down on the surface of the Earth

atmospherics /ˌæt.məsˈfer.ɪks/ **noun** [plural] specialized unusual conditions in the atmosphere, such as those caused by LIGHTNING, or the continuous short, sharp noises produced by a radio during these conditions

atoll /ˈæt.ɒl/ (US) /-ɑːl/ **noun** [C] a ring-shaped island formed of CORAL (= rock-like natural substance) that surrounds a LAGOON (= area of sea water): *the Bikini Atoll*

atom /ˈæt.əm/ (US) /ˈæţ-/ **noun** [C] B2 the smallest unit of any chemical element, consisting of a positive NUCLEUS surrounded by negative ELECTRONS. Atoms can combine to form a MOLECULE: *A molecule of carbon dioxide (CO_2) has one carbon atom and two oxygen atoms.* ◦ figurative *He hasn't an atom **of** sense (= he has no sense), that boy.*

ˈatom ˌbomb noun [C] (also **aˌtomic ˈbomb**) old-fashioned an extremely powerful bomb that uses the explosive power resulting from SPLITTING the atom

atomic /əˈtɒm.ɪk/ (US) /-ˈtɑː.mɪk/ adj **1** relating to atoms: *atomic structure/nuclei* → See also **nuclear 2** (B2) using the energy that is created when an atom is divided: *atomic* ***energy/power*** ◦ *atomic scientists* • **atomically** /-ɪ.kəl.i/ adv

aˌtomic ˈmass noun [C or U] specialized the mass of a specific ISOTOPE of a particular chemical element, usually expressed in atomic mass units → Compare **relative atomic mass**

aˌtomic ˈmass ˌunit noun [C] (abbreviation **u**) a unit used for measuring atomic mass, equal to one twelfth of the mass of an atom of carbon in its commonest form, carbon-12

aˌtomic ˈnumber noun [C] specialized the number of PROTONS found in the NUCLEUS of an atom of a particular chemical, used as a way of listing the chemical elements in order in the PERIODIC TABLE

aˌtomic ˈweight noun [C or U] specialized another term for **relative atomic mass**

atomizer (UK usually **atomiser**) /ˈæt.ə.maɪ.zər/ (US) /ˈæt̬.ə.maɪ.zɚ/ noun [C] a device that changes a liquid into small drops by forcing it out through a very small hole: *This perfume is available in both a normal bottle and an atomizer.*

atonal /ˌeɪˈtəʊ.nəl/ (US) /-ˈtoʊ-/ adj specialized Atonal music is written in a way that is not based on any particular KEY. → Compare **tonal**

atone /əˈtəʊn/ (US) /-ˈtoʊn/ verb

PHRASAL VERB **atone for sth** formal to do something that shows that you are sorry for something bad that you did: *The country's leader has expressed a wish to atone for his actions in the past.*

atonement /əˈtəʊn.mənt/ (US) /-ˈtoʊn-/ noun [U] formal something that you do to show that you are sorry for something bad that you did: *He said that young hooligans should do community service as atonement* ***for*** *their crimes.*

atop /əˈtɒp/ (US) /-ˈtɑːp/ preposition mainly US on or at the top of: *She sat atop a two-metre wall.*

at-ˈrisk adj [before noun] **IN DANGER** ▷ **1** in danger of being harmed or damaged, or of dying: *at-risk* ***children/patients*** ◦ *Many residents in at-risk areas move their cars to higher ground when floods threaten.* **FAILING** ▷ **2** in danger of closing or failing: *at-risk* ***schools/students***

atrium /ˈeɪ.tri.əm/ noun [C] (plural **atriums**) **ROOM** ▷ **1** a very large room, often with glass walls or roof, especially in the middle of a large shop or office building **HEART** ▷ **2** (also **auricle**) one of the two spaces at the top part of the heart that receive blood from the VEINS and push it down into the VENTRICLES (= lower spaces)

atrocious /əˈtrəʊ.ʃəs/ (US) /-ˈtroʊ-/ adj **VERY BAD** ▷ **1** of very bad quality: *an atrocious film/piece of acting* ◦ *The weather has been atrocious all week.* ◦ *Conditions in the prison were atrocious.* **CRUEL** ▷ **2** violent and shocking: *an atrocious crime* • **atrociously** /-li/ adv *The children have been behaving absolutely atrociously.*

atrocity /əˈtrɒs.ɪ.ti/ (US) /-ˈtrɑː.sɪ.t̬i/ noun [C or U] an extremely violent and shocking act: *They're on trial for* ***committing*** *atrocities* ***against*** *the civilian population.*

atrophy /ˈæt.rə.fi/ verb [I] (of a part of the body) to be reduced in size and therefore strength, or, more generally, to become weaker: *After several months in a hospital bed, my leg muscles had atrophied.* ◦ *In the 1980s, their political power gradually atrophied (= became weaker).* • **atrophy** noun [U]

attach /əˈtætʃ/ verb [T] **CONNECT** ▷ **1** (B1) to fasten, join, or connect something: *I attached a photo* ***to*** *my application form.* ◦ *Use this cable to attach the printer* ***to*** *the computer.* ◦ *In the UK , packets of cigarettes come with a government health warning attached* ***to*** *them (= on them).* → Compare **detach** **COMPUTING** ▷ **2** (B1) to join a file such as a document, picture, or computer program, to an email **TAKE GOODS** ▷ **3** UK legal to officially take someone's money or the things that they own, or to arrest them, usually because they have failed to pay money that they owe

PHRASAL VERBS **attach sth to sth** formal (C2) To attach a particular quality to something is to consider it to have that quality: *I don't attach any importance/significance to these rumours.* • **attach to sb/sth** mainly UK formal If you say that a particular quality attaches to someone or something, you mean that they have that quality: *Don't worry – it was an accident and no blame attaches to either of you.* ◦ [+ -ing verb] *Great honour attaches to winning this award.* • **attach yourself to sb/sth** If you attach yourself to a person or group, you join them or it, usually for a limited period of time: *Being on his own, he attached himself to a noisy group at the bar.*

attaché /əˈtæʃ.eɪ/ noun [C] a person who works in an EMBASSY and has a particular area of responsibility in which they have special knowledge: *a naval/military/press/cultural attaché*

atˈtaché ˌcase noun [C] a rectangular case with hard sides, used especially for carrying business documents → Compare **briefcase**

attaché case

attached /əˈtætʃt/ adj **be attached to sb/sth** to like someone or something very much: *The children are very attached to their grandparents.* ◦ *I'm very attached to my old guitar.*

attachment /əˈtætʃ.mənt/ noun **PART** ▷ **1** (B2) [C] an extra piece of equipment that can be added to a machine: *This food processor has a special attachment for grinding coffee.* **COMPUTING** ▷ **2** (B2) [C] a computer file that is sent together with an email message: *I'll email my report to you* ***as an*** *attachment.* ◦ *I wasn't able to* ***open*** *that attachment.* **FEELING OF LOVE** ▷ **3** (C2) [C or U] a feeling of love or strong connection to someone or something: *At university I* ***formed*** *a strong attachment* ***to*** *one of my tutors.* ◦ *She is unlikely to give up her lifelong attachment* ***to*** *feminist ideas.* **TAKING GOODS** ▷ **4** [C or U] UK legal the act of arresting a person for failing to obey the order of a court, or of officially taking their property because they have failed to pay money that they owe

attack /əˈtæk/ verb; noun

▸verb **HURT** ▷ **1** B1 [I or T] to try to hurt or defeat using violence: *He was attacked and seriously injured by a gang of youths.* ◦ *Army forces have been attacking the town since dawn.* ◦ *Most wild animals won't attack unless they are provoked.* → Compare **defend** **CRITICIZE** ▷ **2** C1 [T] to criticize someone strongly: *She wrote an article attacking the judges and their conduct of the trial.* ◦ *The report attacks the idea of exams for seven and eight-year-olds.* **DAMAGE** ▷ **3** C2 [T] If something, such as a disease or a chemical, attacks something, it damages it: *AIDS attacks the body's immune system.* **SPORT** ▷ **4** [I or T] If players in a team attack, they move forward to try to score points, goals, etc. **DEAL WITH** ▷ **5** [T] to deal with something quickly and in an effective way: *We have to attack these problems now and find some solutions.* ◦ *The children rushed in and eagerly attacked the food (= quickly started to eat it).*

> **Other ways of saying attack**
>
> See also: **criticize**
>
> **Assault** is a word that can be used instead of attack when a person is attacked. It is often used in legal contexts:
>
> *The player was suspended for **assaulting** a referee.*
>
> The phrasal verb **go for** is a less formal way of saying 'attack':
>
> *She suddenly lost her temper and **went for** me.*
>
> If someone moves towards another person in order to attack, you could use the phrase **come at**:
>
> *He **came at** me with a baseball bat.*
>
> **Mug** is often used when someone is attacked in the street and the attacker steals something:
>
> *She was **mugged** in broad daylight.*
>
> If someone is attacked by someone who has been hiding and waiting, you could use the verb **ambush**:
>
> *He was **ambushed** by three men on his way to work.*
>
> **Invade** or **storm** are used when a large group of people such as an army attack a place:
>
> *Troops **invaded** the capital.*
>
> *Soldiers **stormed** the building.*

> **Word partners for attack noun (VIOLENT ACT)**
>
> *carry out/launch/make/mount* an attack (on sb/sth) • *be under/come under* attack (from sb/sth) • an attack *happens/occurs* • a *brutal/frenzied/savage/violent* attack • an *unprovoked* attack • a *personal/scathing* attack • an attack *against/on* sb/sth • a *series/spate/string/wave* of attacks

▸noun **VIOLENT ACT** ▷ **1** B1 [C or U] a violent act intended to hurt or damage someone or something: *a racist attack* ◦ *Enemy forces have **made** an attack **on** the city.* ◦ *These bomb blasts suggest that the terrorists are **(going) on the** attack (= trying to defeat or hurt other people) again.* ◦ *The town was once again **under** attack (= being attacked).* **CRITICISM** ▷ **2** C2 [C or U] a strong criticism of someone or something: *a **scathing** attack on the president* ◦ *The government has **come under** attack **from all sides** for cutting education spending.* **ILLNESS** ▷ **3** [C] a sudden and short period of illness: *an attack of asthma/flu/malaria* ◦ figurative *an attack of the giggles* **SPORT** ▷ **4** B1 [C or U] the part of a team in some sports that tries to score points: *The team has a strong attack, but its defence is weak.* ◦ *The team is strong **in** (US **on**) attack but useless in defence.* **5** [U] determination in the way you play a sport, trying hard to score points: *The team needs to put some more attack into its game.*

attacker /əˈtæk.əʳ/ US /-ɚ/ noun [C] a person who uses violence to hurt someone: *The police think she must have known her attacker.*

attain /əˈteɪn/ verb [T] formal C1 to reach or succeed in getting something: *He has attained the highest grade in his music exams.* ◦ *We need to identify the best ways of attaining our **objectives/goals**.* ◦ *India attained independence in 1947, after decades of struggle.* → Synonym **achieve**

attainable /əˈteɪ.nə.bl̩/ adj formal C2 possible to achieve: *We must ensure that we do not set ourselves goals that are not attainable.* → Opposite **unattainable**

attainment /əˈteɪn.mənt/ noun **1** [U] formal the act of achieving something: *the attainment of a goal* ◦ *attainment **targets*** **2** [C usually plural] UK formal Someone's attainments are the things they have done and the skills they have learned.

attempt /əˈtempt/ verb; noun

▸verb [T] B1 to try to do something, especially something difficult: [+ to infinitive] *He attempted **to** escape through a window.* ◦ *He attempted a joke, but no one laughed.* ◦ *There's no point in even attempting an explanation – he'll never listen.*

▸noun [C] **1** B2 the act of trying to do something, especially something difficult: [+ to infinitive] *She **made** a few half-hearted attempts **to** join in their conversation.* ◦ *He **made no** attempt to be sociable.* ◦ *This is my second attempt **at** the exam.* ◦ *None of our attempts **at** contacting Dr James was successful.* ◦ *They closed the road **in an** attempt (= to try to) to reduce traffic in the city.* **2 an attempt on sb's life** an act of trying to kill someone: *This is the third attempt on the president's life.*

> **Word partners for attempt noun**
>
> *make* an attempt • an *abortive/failed/unsuccessful* attempt • a *successful* attempt • *(in)* a *desperate/frantic/vain* attempt • a *final/first/last/previous* attempt • a *conscious/deliberate* attempt • an attempt *at* sth • *in* an attempt to do sth

attempted /əˈtemp.tɪd/ adj [before noun] legal (of a crime) that someone has tried to commit without success: *A man is being questioned in relation to the attempted **murder/robbery** last night.*

attend /əˈtend/ verb **BE PRESENT** ▷ **1** B1 [I or T] to go to an event, place, etc.: *Over two hundred people attended the funeral.* ◦ *The meeting is on the fifth and we're hoping everyone will attend.* → See also **well attended** **2** B1 [T] to go officially and usually regularly to a place: *Which school do your children attend?* ◦ *I attended the classes/seminars/lectures for a month or two.*

> **Common mistake: attend**
>
> Remember that when **attend** means 'to go to an event, place, etc.' it is never followed by 'to'.
>
> Don't say 'attend to an event, place, etc.', say **attend an event, place, etc.**:
>
> ~~*All staff will attend to the training course.*~~
>
> *All staff will attend the training course.*

NOTICE ▷ **3** [I] formal to give attention to what someone is saying: *I'm afraid I wasn't attending **to** what was being said.* **PROVIDE HELP** ▷ **4** [T] to provide a service to someone, especially as part of your job: *The queen was attended by her ladies-in-waiting.* **RESULT FROM** ▷ **5** [T] formal to happen as a result of, and at the same time as: *the publicity that attends a career in television*

Other ways of saying attend

Instead of the verb 'attend' people usually say **come/go to**:

*How many people **came to** the meeting?*

*He **goes to** the gym regularly.*

The verb **make** is sometimes used when people are talking about whether or not they are able to attend an event:

*I'm afraid I can't **make** the meeting this afternoon (= I will not be able to attend).*

The expression **make it** is also used, meaning 'to get to a place, even when there are problems':

*The traffic was so bad we only just **made it** in time for the start of the movie.*

PHRASAL VERB **attend to sb/sth** to deal with something or help someone: *Doctors tried to attend to the worst injured soldiers first.* ◦ *I always have so many things to attend to when I come into the office after a trip abroad.*

attendance /əˈten.dᵊns/ noun **BEING PRESENT** ▷ **1** C1 [U or C] the fact of going somewhere such as a church, school, etc. regularly: *Attendance **at** lectures is compulsory.* **2** C1 [C or U] the number of people who go to an event, meeting, etc.: *Attendances **at** church are falling.* **PROVIDING HELP** ▷ **3 in attendance** C2 present with someone and helping or taking care of them: *He never goes out without his security men **in** attendance.*

attendant /əˈten.dᵊnt/ **noun; adj**

▸**noun** [C] **1** someone whose job is to be in a place and help visitors or customers: *a cloakroom/museum attendant* **2** someone whose job is to travel or live with an important person and help them: *The Prince was followed by his attendants.*

▸**adj** formal **1** coming with a stated thing or resulting from it: *debt and its attendant problems* ◦ *There are too many risks attendant **on** such a large investment of money.* **2** present with someone to help them, or present at an event, place, etc.: *attendant staff* ◦ *the attendant crowd/fans*

attendee /ə.tenˈdiː/ noun [C] someone who goes to a place, event, etc.

Common mistake: attention

Remember that when **attention** is used with a verb such as **attract** or **pay**, the correct preposition to use is **to**.

Don't say 'attention on sth', say **attention to sth**:

~~*I would like to draw your attention on a number of issues.*~~

attention /əˈten.ʃᵊn/ noun [U] **NOTICE** ▷ **1** B1 notice, thought, or interest: *Ladies and gentlemen, could I **have your** attention, please?* ◦ *They're organizing a campaign to **draw** people's attention **to** the environmentally harmful effects of using their cars.* ◦ *Wait a moment and I'll **give** you my **full/undivided** attention (= I'll listen to and think about only you).* ◦ *After an hour, my attention started to **wander** (= I stopped taking notice).* **2 get/attract/catch sb's attention** B2 to make someone notice you: *I knocked on the window to get her attention.* **3 pay attention (to sth/sb)** B1 to watch, listen to, or think about something or someone carefully or with interest: *If you don't pay attention now, you'll get it all wrong later.* ◦ *Don't pay any attention to Nina – she doesn't know what she's talking about.* ◦ *He wasn't paying attention to the safety instructions.* **4 the centre of attention** the thing or person that a lot of people notice: *He likes telling jokes and being the centre attention at parties.* **5 turn your attention(s) to sth/sb** to start to think about or consider a particular thing or person: *Many countries are starting to turn their attention to new forms of energy.* **CARE** ▷ **6** special care or treatment: *The paintwork will **need** a little attention.* ◦ *If symptoms persist, seek **medical** attention.* **WAY OF STANDING** ▷ **7** (especially in the armed forces) a way of standing, with the feet together, arms by your sides, head up, and shoulders back, and not moving: *soldiers standing **at/to** attention*

Word partners for attention (NOTICE)

devote/pay attention (*to* sth/sb) • *give* sth your attention • *attract/catch/get/hold/keep* sb's attention • *call/draw* (sb's) attention *to* sth • *turn* your attention *to* sth • sb's attention *wanders* • sb's *full/undivided* attention • *careful/close/special* attention • attention *to detail*

atˌtention ˌdeficit hyperacˈtivity disˌorder noun [U] (abbreviation **ADHD**) UK a condition in which someone, especially a child, is often in a state of activity or excitement and unable to direct their attention towards what they are doing

Note:

This condition is usually called '**attention deficit disorder**' in the US.

atˈtention ˌspan noun [C] the length of time that someone can keep their thoughts and interest fixed on something: *Young children have quite short attention spans.*

attentive /əˈten.tɪv/ US /-t̬ɪv/ adj **LISTENING** ▷ **1** listening carefully: *an attentive audience* **HELPING** ▷ **2** If someone is attentive, they are very helpful and take care of you: *He was very attentive **to** her when she was ill.* ◦ *A good teacher is always attentive **to** their students' **needs**.* • **attentively** /-li/ adv *The children sat **listening** attentively to the story.* • **attentiveness** /-nəs/ noun [U]

attenuate /əˈten.ju.eɪt/ verb [T] formal to make something smaller, thinner, or weaker: *Radiation from the sun is attenuated by the Earth's atmosphere.* • **attenuated** /əˈten.ju.eɪ.tɪd/ US /-t̬ɪd/ adj • **attenuation** /əˌten.juˈeɪ.ʃᵊn/ noun [U]

attest /əˈtest/ verb [I or T] formal to show something or to say or prove that something is true: *Thousands of people came out onto the streets to attest their support for the democratic opposition party.* ◦ *The number of old German cars still on the road attests **(to)** the excellence of their manufacture.* ◦ *As his career attests, he is a cricketer of world-class standard.* ◦ specialized *The will needs to be attested (= officially marked to show that the signature of the person who made the will is correct) by three witnesses.*

attestation /ˌæt.esˈteɪ.ʃᵊn/ US /ˌæt̬-/ noun [C] specialized a formal statement that you make and officially say is true

attic /ˈæt.ɪk/ US /ˈæt̬-/ noun [C] B2 the space or room at the top of a building, under the roof, often used for storing things: *I've got boxes of old clothes in the attic.* ◦ *an attic bedroom at the top of the house*

attire /əˈtaɪəʳ/ US /-ˈtaɪr/ noun [U] formal clothes, especially of a particular or formal type: *I hardly think jeans are appropriate attire for a wedding.* • **attired** /əˈtaɪəd/ US /-ˈtaɪrd/ adj [after verb] *She was attired from head to foot in black.*

attitude /ˈæt.ɪ.tjuːd/ US /ˈæt̬.ɪ.tuːd/ noun **OPINION** ▷ **1** B1 [C or U] a feeling or opinion about something or

someone, or a way of behaving that is caused by this: *It's often very difficult to change people's attitudes.* ◦ [+ that] *She **takes** the attitude **that** children should be allowed to learn at their own pace.* ◦ *He has a very bad attitude **to/towards** work.* ◦ *He seems to have undergone a change **in/of** attitude recently, and has become much more cooperative.* ◦ *I don't like your attitude (= the way you are behaving).* ◦ *That boy has a real attitude **problem** (= behaves in a way that makes it difficult for other people to have a relationship with him or work with him).* **CONFIDENCE** ▷ **2** [U] If you say that someone has attitude, you mean that they are very confident and want people to notice them. **POSITION** ▷ **3** [C] literary a position of the body: *She lay sprawled across the sofa, in an attitude **of** complete abandon.*

Word partners for attitude (OPINION)

have/take a [positive/relaxed, etc.] attitude • a ***negative/positive/relaxed*** attitude • sb's attitude ***to/towards*** sb/sth • attitudes ***among*** [a group of people] • a ***change in/of*** attitude • an attitude ***problem***

IDIOM **strike an attitude** formal to hold your body in a way that suggests a particular quality or feeling: *He struck an attitude **of** offended dignity and marched out of the room.*

attorney /ə'tɜː.ni/ (US) /-'tɝː-/ **noun** [C] C1 US for lawyer: *a defense attorney* ◦ *an attorney for the plaintiff* ◦ *a civil/criminal attorney*

at,torney 'general **noun** [C] (plural **attorneys general**) the top legal officer in some countries, who advises the leader of the government

Other ways of saying attract

The verb **draw** can be used when a place or event attracts a lot of people:

*The game **drew** a crowd of 30,000.*

If someone is attracted to something by the offer of something pleasant or exciting, the verbs **entice** or **lure** can be used:

*The smell of coffee **enticed** people to enter the shop.*

*I was **lured** into the store by the smell of fresh bread.*

If something **tempts** you, you are attracted to it even though you know you do not need it or should not have it:

*I was **tempted** by the offer of a free phone.*

You can use the verb **seduce** when something attracts you so much that you do something you would not usually do:

*I wouldn't normally have bought this but I was **seduced** by the low price.*

When something attracts a particular person or group, you can use the verb **appeal**:

*The scheme is designed to **appeal** to 18-year-olds.*

attract /ə'trækt/ **verb** **1** B1 [T] (of people, things, places, etc.) to pull or draw someone or something towards them, by the qualities they have, especially good ones: *These flowers are brightly coloured in order to attract butterflies.* ◦ *The circus is attracting huge **crowds/audiences**.* ◦ *Magnets attract iron filings.* ◦ *The government is trying to attract industry **to** the area (= to persuade people to place their industry there).* ◦ *Her ideas have attracted a lot of **attention/criticism** in the scientific community.* **2** B2 [T usually passive] If you are attracted by or to someone, you like them, often finding them sexually interesting: *I'm not **physically/sexually** attracted to him.*

attraction /ə'træk.ʃən/ **noun** **1** B1 [C or U] something that makes people want to go to a place or do a particular thing: *Life in London has so many attractions – nightclubs, good restaurants, and so on.* ◦ ***tourist** attractions* ◦ *The opportunity to travel is one of the **main** attractions of this job.* ◦ *Skiing **holds** no attraction **for** me.* **2** C2 [U] the feeling of liking someone, especially sexually, because of the way they look or behave: *She felt an immediate **physical** attraction **to** him.*

attractive /ə'træk.tɪv/ **adj** **1** A2 very pleasing in appearance or sound: *a very attractive young woman* ◦ *I **find** him very attractive (= he attracts me sexually).* ◦ *attractive countryside* ◦ *an attractive colour scheme* **2** B2 causing interest or pleasure: *Spending twelve hours on a plane isn't a very attractive (= pleasant) prospect.* ◦ *an attractive **offer** (= an offer with benefits for me)* ◦ *We need to make the club attractive **to** a wider range of people.* • **attractively** /-li/ **adv** *She always dresses very attractively.* • **attractiveness** /-nəs/ **noun** [U] *her attractiveness to men* ◦ *High mortgage rates have decreased the attractiveness of home-owning.*

Other ways of saying attractive

The adjectives **beautiful** and **lovely** are often used instead of 'attractive', and are used to describe both people and things:

*His wife is very **beautiful**.*

*We drove through some really **beautiful/lovely** countryside.*

*You look **lovely**!*

If a person is attractive, we can say that the person is **good-looking**. The adjective **handsome** is also sometimes used for men, and **pretty** for women:

*He's certainly very **good-looking**.*

*Your daughter is very **pretty**.*

If *someone*, especially a woman, is extremely attractive, you can say that the person is **gorgeous** or **stunning**:

*You look **gorgeous** in that dress!*

*The bride is absolutely **stunning**.*

If *something* is extremely attractive, you can say that it is **breathtaking**, **exquisite**, **stunning**, or **gorgeous**:

*The views from the window were **breathtaking**.*

*These handmade decorations are **exquisite**.*

If something is so attractive that you notice it immediately, you can say that it **catches** *your* **eye**:

*The design on these plates really **caught my eye**.*

If *someone* or *something* is attractive because of being small, you can say that the person or thing is **cute** or **sweet**:

*He's got a really **cute** baby brother.*

*Look at that kitten; isn't she **sweet**?*

Adjectives such as **stylish** and **chic** can be used to describe something that has been made to look attractive and fashionable:

*He took me to a very **chic** restaurant.*

*Their house is very **stylish**.*

attributable /ə'trɪb.jʊ.tə.bl̩/ (US) /-t̬ə-/ **adj** [after verb] caused by: *Do you think that these higher-than-average temperatures are attributable **to** global warming?*

attribute **noun**; **verb**

▸**noun** [C] /'æt.rɪ.bjuːt/ C2 a quality or characteristic that someone or something has: *Organizational ability is an essential attribute for a good manager.*

A

▸verb /əˈtrɪb.juːt/, /-juːt/

PHRASAL VERBS **attribute sth to sb** to think that someone or something has a particular quality or feature: *I wouldn't dream of attributing such a lack of judgment to you.* • **attribute sth to sb/sth** C2 to say or think that something is the result or work of something or someone else: *The doctors have attributed the cause of the illness to an unknown virus.* ◦ *To what do you attribute this delay?* ◦ *Most experts have attributed the drawing to Michelangelo.*

attribution /ˌæt.rɪˈbjuː.ʃən/ **noun** [U] the act of saying or thinking that something is the result or work of a particular person or thing: *The usual attribution **of** the work **to** Leonardo is now disputed by several experts.*

attributive /əˈtrɪb.jʊ.tɪv/ US /-t̬ɪv/ **adj** specialized (of the position or use of an adjective, noun, or phrase) before a noun: *In 'a sudden movement', 'sudden' is an adjective in the attributive position.* • **attributively** /-li/ **adv**

attrition /əˈtrɪʃ.ən/ **noun** [U] **1** formal gradually making something weaker and destroying it, especially the strength or confidence of an enemy by repeatedly attacking it: *Terrorist groups and the government have been engaged in a costly **war of** attrition since 2008.* **2** US for **natural wastage**

attuned to /əˈtjuːnd/ US /-ˈtuːnd/ **adj** [after verb] **1** able to understand, or being very familiar with: *A good nurse has to be attuned to the needs of his or her patients.* **2** If your ears are attuned to a particular sound, they are able to recognize it very easily: *A mother's ears are attuned to even the slightest variation in her baby's breathing.*

ATV /ˌeɪ.tiːˈviː/ **noun** [C] US abbreviation for **all-terrain vehicle**

atypical /ˌeɪˈtɪp.ɪ.kəl/ **adj** different from all others of the same type: *The sociable behaviour of lions is considered atypical **of** the cat family.*

aubergine /ˈəʊ.bə.ʒiːn/ US /ˈoʊ.bɚ-/ **noun** [C or U] UK (US **eggplant**) B2 an oval, purple vegetable that is white inside and is usually eaten cooked

auburn /ˈɔː.bən/ US /ˈɑː.bɚn/ **adj** (of hair) reddish-brown in colour: *auburn-haired* • **auburn noun** [U]

auction /ˈɔːk.ʃən/ US /ˈɑːk-/ **noun; verb**

▸**noun** [C or U] C1 a usually public sale of goods or property, where people make higher and higher BIDS (= offers of money) for each thing, until the thing is sold to the person who will pay most: *a furniture auction* ◦ *They're **holding** an auction **of** jewellery on Thursday.* ◦ *The painting will be sold **at** (UK also **by**) auction next week.* ◦ *The house and its contents are being **put up for** auction.*

▸**verb** [T] to sell something in a public auction: *The stamps will be auctioned tomorrow.* ◦ *The family is auctioning (**off**) its art collection.*

auctioneer /ˌɔːk.ʃəˈnɪəʳ/ US /ˌɑːk.ʃəˈnɪr/ **noun** [C] a person in charge of an auction who calls out the prices that people offer

ˈauction ˌhouse **noun** [C] a company whose business is selling things by auction

ˌauction of ˈpromises **noun** [C] an occasion when people BID (= offer money and compete against other people) for something that someone has offered to do, for example cook a meal, wash a car, etc. It is usually done in order to get money for a CHARITY.

audacious /ɔːˈdeɪ.ʃəs/ US /ɑː-/ **adj** showing a willingness to take risks or offend people: *He described the plan as ambitious and audacious.* ◦ *an audacious remark/suggestion* • **audaciously** /-li/ **adv** • **audaciousness** /-nəs/ **noun** [U]

audacity /ɔːˈdæs.ə.ti/ US /ɑːˈdæs.ə.t̬i/ **noun** [U] courage or confidence of a kind that other people find shocking or rude: [+ to infinitive] *It took a lot of audacity to stand up and criticize the chairman.* ◦ disapproving *He **had the** audacity **to** blame me for his mistake!*

audible /ˈɔː.dɪ.bl̩/ US /ˈɑː-/ **adj** able to be heard: *The lecturer spoke so quietly that he was scarcely audible at the back of the hall.* ◦ *She gave an audible sigh of relief.* • **audibly** /-bli/ **adv**

audience /ˈɔː.di.əns/ US /ˈɑː-/ **noun** [C] **GROUP OF PEOPLE** ▷ **1** B1 [+ sing/pl verb] the group of people together in one place to watch or listen to a play, film, someone speaking, etc.: *She lectures to audiences all over the world.* ◦ *The secret to public speaking is to get the audience on your side.* ◦ *The audience was/were clearly delighted with the performance.* ◦ *The magic show had a lot of audience **participation**, with people shouting things to the performers and going up on stage.* **2** B2 [+ sing/pl verb] the (number of) people watching or listening to a particular television or radio programme, reading a particular book, or visiting a particular website: *The television company has **lost** a large part of its audience since it changed its programming.* ◦ *Her latest book should appeal to a large audience (= many people will want to read it).* **FORMAL MEETING** ▷ **3** a formal meeting that you have with an important person: *She had a private audience **with** the king.*

audio /ˈɔː.di.əʊ/ US /ˈɑː.di.oʊ/ **adj** connected with sound and the recording and broadcasting of sound: *an audio signal*

audio- /ɔː.di.əʊ/ US /ɑː.di.oʊ/ **prefix** relating to hearing or sound: *audiotape*

ˌaudio-ˈvisual **adj** [before noun] (abbreviation **AV**) describes something that involves seeing and hearing: *audio-visual equipment/aids/software*

audit /ˈɔː.dɪt/ US /ˈɑː-/ **verb; noun**

▸**verb** [T] **FINANCE** ▷ **1** specialized to make an official examination of the ACCOUNTS of a business and produce a report **EDUCATION** ▷ **2** US to go to a class or educational course for pleasure or interest, without being tested or receiving a qualification at the end: *As a senior citizen, he is allowed to audit university classes.*

▸**noun** [C] an official examination of the ACCOUNTS of a business: *The company has an audit at the end of each financial year.*

audition /ɔːˈdɪʃ.ən/ US /ɑː-/ **noun; verb**

▸**noun** [C] C1 a short performance that an actor, musician, dancer, etc. gives in order to show they are suitable for a particular play, film, show, etc.: *His audition went well and he's fairly hopeful about getting the part.* ◦ *The director is **holding** auditions next week **for** the major parts.*

▸**verb** [I or T] to give a short performance in order to show that you are suitable for a part in a film, play, show, etc., or to make someone do this: *I'm auditioning **for** the part of Lady Macbeth.* ◦ *We're auditioning local rock bands **for** the music festival.*

auditor /ˈɔː.dɪt.əʳ/ US /ˈɑː.dɪ.t̬ɚ/ **noun** [C] someone whose job is to carry out an official examination of the ACCOUNTS of a business and to produce a report: *The **external** auditors (= from outside the company) come in once a year.*

auditorium /ˌɔː.dɪˈtɔː.ri.əm/ US /ˌɑː.dɪˈtɔːr.i-/ **noun** [C] (plural **auditoriums** or **auditoria** /-ə/) **1** the part of a theatre, or similar building, where the people who are watching and listening sit: *No smoking in the*

auditorium. **2** mainly US a large public building where meetings, concerts, etc. are held

auditory /ˈɔː.dɪ.tᵊr.i/ (US) /ˈɑː.də.tɔːr.i/ adj specialized of or about hearing

ˈauditory ˌnerve noun [C] specialized a nerve in the ear that carries electrical signals from the INNER EAR to the brain

au fait /ˌəʊˈfeɪ/ (US) /ˌoʊ-/ adj **be au fait with sth** to be familiar with or know about something: *Are you au fait with the rules of the game?*

auger /ˈɔː.gəʳ/ (US) /ˈɑː.gɚ/ noun [C] a tool consisting of a twisted rod of metal fixed to a handle, used for making large holes in wood or in the ground

aught /ɔːt/ (US) /ɑːt/ pronoun old use anything

augment /ɔːgˈment/ (US) /ɑːg-/ verb [T] formal to increase the size or value of something by adding something to it: *He would have to find work to augment his income.* • **augmentation** /ˌɔːg.menˈteɪ.ʃᵊn/ (US) /ˌɑːg-/ noun [C or U]

augˌmented reˈality noun [U] images produced by a computer and used together with a view of the real world

au gratin /ˌəʊˈgræt.æn/ (US) /oʊˈgrɑː.tᵊn/ adj [after noun] cooked with a covering of cheese or BREADCRUMBS mixed with butter: *potatoes au gratin*

augur /ˈɔː.gəʳ/ (US) /ˈɑː.gɚ/ verb [I + adv/prep, T] formal to be a sign of especially good or bad things in the future: *The company's sales figures for the first six months augur **well** for the rest of the year.* ◦ *Do you think that this recent ministerial announcement augurs (= is a sign of) a shift in government policy?*

augury /ˈɔː.gjʊ.ri/ (US) /ˈɑː.gjɚ.i/ noun formal [C] a sign of what might happen in the future: *These sales figures are a good augury **for** another profitable year.*

august /ɔːˈgʌst/ (US) /ɑː-/ adj formal having great importance and especially of the highest social class: *the society's august patron, the Duke of Norfolk*

August /ˈɔː.gəst/ (US) /ˈɑː-/ noun [C or U] (written abbreviation **Aug.**) (A1) the eighth month of the year, after July and before September: *They usually go to their holiday home **in** August.* ◦ *We're going to Australia **on** 1 August.* ◦ *They got married **last** August.*

aunt /ɑːnt/ (US) /ænt/ noun [C] (informal **auntie**, **aunty**) (A2) the sister of someone's father or mother, or the wife of someone's uncle or aunt: *I have an aunt in Australia.* ◦ *This is my Aunt Camille.* ◦ [as form of address] *Do you want some tea, Aunt Alice?*

auntie /ˈɑːn.ti/ (US) /ˈæn.t̬i/ noun [C] (also **aunty**) informal **1** an **aunt**: *My auntie and uncle are coming to visit.* ◦ [as form of address] *Thank you for the present, Auntie Louise.* **2** Indian English any female adult that you know who is older than you

au pair /ˌəʊˈpeəʳ/ (US) /ˌoʊˈpeər/ noun [C] a foreign person, usually a young woman, who lives with a family in order to learn their language and who takes care of the children or cleans the house in return for meals, a room, and a small payment

aura /ˈɔː.rə/ (US) /ˈɔːr.ə/ noun [C] **1** a feeling or character that a person or place seems to have: *The woods **have** an aura **of** mystery.* ◦ *There's an aura **of** sadness **about** him.* **2** a type of light that some people say they can see around people and animals

aural /ˈɔː.rəl/ (US) /ˈɔːr.ᵊl/ adj relating to hearing: *aural teaching aids, such as CDs*

aureole /ˈɔː.ri.əʊl/ (US) /ˈɔːr.i.oʊl/ noun [C] literary a bright circle of light, especially around the head → Synonym **halo**

auricle /ˈɔː.rɪ.kᵊl/ noun [C] specialized one of the two spaces in the top part of the heart that receive blood from the VEINS and push it down into the VENTRICLES (= lower spaces)

the aurora australis /əˌrɔː.rə.ɒsˈtreɪ.lɪs/ (US) /-ˌrɔːr.ə.ɔːˈstreɪ-/ noun [S] (also **the ˌSouthern ˈLights**) a pattern of differently coloured lights that are sometimes seen in the night sky in the most southern parts of the world → Compare **the aurora borealis**

the aurora borealis /əˌrɔː.rə.bɒr.iˈeɪ.lɪs/ (US) /-ˌrɔːr.ə.bɔːr.iˈæl.ɪs/ noun [S] (also **the ˌNorthern ˈLights**) a pattern of differently coloured lights that are sometimes seen in the night sky in the most northern parts of the world → Compare **the aurora australis**

auspices /ˈɔː.spɪ.sɪz/ (US) /ˈɑː-/ noun [plural] formal **under the auspices of sb/sth** with the protection or support of someone or something, especially an organization: *Financial aid is being provided to the country under the auspices of the International Monetary Fund.*

auspicious /ɔːˈspɪʃ.əs/ (US) /ɑː-/ adj formal suggesting a positive and successful future: *They won their first match of the season 5–1 which was an auspicious **start/beginning**.* ◦ *Our first meeting was not auspicious – we had a huge argument.* • **auspiciously** /-li/ adv

Aussie /ˈɒz.i/ (US) /ˈɑː.zi/ adj, noun [C] informal Australian, or an Australian person

austere /ɔːˈstɪəʳ/ (US) /ɑːˈstɪr/ adj **1** very simple and without comfort or unnecessary things, especially because of severe limits on money or goods: *an austere childhood during the war* **2** plain and without decoration: *The courtroom was a large, dark chamber, an austere place.* **3** very severe and unfriendly in manner • **austerely** /-li/ adv *Her dress was simple and austerely elegant.*

austerity /ɔːˈster.ɪ.ti/ (US) /ˈɑː.ster.ɪ.t̬i/ noun **1** [C or U] the condition or practice of living without things that are not necessary and without comfort, with limited money or goods, or a practice, habit, or experience that is typical of this: *The wartime austerity of my early years prepared me for later hardships.* ◦ *The austerities of life in a small rural community were not what I was used to.* **2** [U] the quality of being austere in appearance or manner

Australasia /ˌɒs.trəˈleɪ.ʒə/ (US) /ˌɑː.strə-/ noun the continent and islands to the east of the Indian Ocean, the west of the Pacific Ocean, and the south of Asia

Australasian /ˌɒs.trəˈleɪ.ʒən/ (US) /ˌɑː.strə-/ noun; adj
▸noun [C] a person from Australasia
▸adj of or from Australasia

authentic /ɔːˈθen.tɪk/ (US) /ɑːˈθen.t̬ɪk/ adj (C1) If something is authentic, it is real, true, or what people say it is: *an authentic 1920s dress* ◦ *authentic Italian food* ◦ *He was there and saw what happened, so his is the only authentic account.* • **authentically** /-tɪkᵊl.i/ (US) /-t̬ɪkᵊl.i/ adv

authenticate /ɔːˈθen.tɪ.keɪt/ (US) /ɑːˈθen.t̬ɪ-/ verb [T] to prove that something is real, true, or what people say it is: *They used carbon dating tests to authenticate the claim that the skeleton was two million years old.* • **authentication** /ɔːˌθen.tɪˈkeɪ.ʃᵊn/ (US) /ɑːˌθen.t̬ɪ-/ noun [U]

authenticity /ˌɔː.θenˈtɪs.ɪ.ti/ (US) /ˌɑː.θenˈtɪs.ə.t̬i/ noun [U] the quality of being real or true: *The authenticity of her story is beyond doubt.*

author /ˈɔː.θəʳ/ (US) /ˈɑː.θɚ/ noun; verb
▸noun [C] **1** (B1) the writer of a book, article, play, etc.: *He is the author **of** two books on French history.* **2** formal a person who begins or creates something: *She's the author **of** the company's recent success/**of** all our troubles.*

A

►**verb** [T] **1** formal to write a book, article, etc.: *He has authored more than 30 books.* **2** mainly US to create something: *The deal is being authored by a Greek diplomat.*

authorial /ɔːˈθɔː.ri.əl/ US /ɑːˈθɔːr.i-/ **adj** [before noun] formal relating to the author of a book, article, play, etc.

authoring /ˈɔː.θə.rɪŋ/ US /ˈɑː.θɚ.ɪŋ/ **noun** [U] the design and production of computer programs and websites, using special SOFTWARE: *authoring **tools**/software* ◦ *web authoring*

authoritarian /ˌɔː.θɒr.ɪˈteə.ri.ən/ US /əˌθɔːr.ɪˈter.i-/ **adj** disapproving demanding that people obey completely and refusing to allow them freedom to act as they wish: *an authoritarian **regime**/government/ruler* ◦ *His manner is extremely authoritarian.* • **authoritarian noun** [C] an authoritarian person: *My father was a real authoritarian so we were brought up very strictly.* • **authoritarianism** /-ə.nɪ.zəm/ **noun** [U]

authoritative /ɔːˈθɒr.ɪ.tə.tɪv/ US /əˈθɔːr.ɪ.t̬ə.t̬ɪv/ **adj** **1** showing that you are confident, in control, and expect to be respected and obeyed: *She has an authoritative **manner** that at times is almost arrogant.* **2** containing complete and accurate information, and therefore respected: *The book is an authoritative **account** of the Second World War.* • **authoritatively** /-li/ **adv**

authority /ɔːˈθɒr.ɪ.ti/ US /əˈθɔːr.ɪ.t̬i/ **noun** **POWER** ▷ **1** B2 [U] the moral or legal right or ability to control: *The United Nations has **used/exerted/exercised** its authority **to** restore peace in the area.* ◦ *We need to get the support of someone **in** authority (= an important or high-ranking person).* ◦ *They've been acting illegally and without authority (= permission) from the council.* ◦ [+ to infinitive] *I'll give my lawyers authority (= permission) **to** act on my behalf.* ◦ *He's got no authority **over** (= ability to control) his students.* ◦ *She spoke **with** authority (= as if she was in control or had special knowledge).* **2** C1 [C] a group of people with official responsibility for a particular area of activity: *the health authority* ◦ *the local housing authority* **3 the authorities** [plural] the group of people with official legal power to make decisions or make people obey the laws in a particular area, such as the police or a local government department: *I'm going to report these holes in the road to the authorities.* **EXPERT** ▷ **4** C2 [C] an expert on a subject: *She's a world authority **on** 19th-century Irish history.*

> Word partners for **authority**
>
> *give* sb (the) authority (to do sth) • *have* (no) authority (to do sth) • *assert/exercise/exert/use* your authority • *challenge/question/undermine* sb's authority • be *in* authority • authority *over* sb/sth • a *position* of authority • an authority *figure*

IDIOM **have something on good authority** to be able to believe a piece of information because you trust the person who told you it: *I have it on good authority **that** she's getting married.*

authorization (UK usually **authorisation**) /ˌɔː.θər.aɪˈzeɪ.ʃən/ US /ˌɑː.θɚ-/ **noun** [C or U] official permission for something to happen, or the act of giving someone official permission to do something: *This information cannot be disclosed without authorization **from** a minister.* ◦ [+ to infinitive] *The authorization **to** sell the shares arrived too late.*

authorize (UK usually **authorise**) /ˈɔː.θər.aɪz/ US /ˈɑː.θɚ-/ **verb** [T] C1 to give official permission for something to happen, or to give someone official permission to do something: *Who authorized this expenditure?* ◦ [+ to infinitive] *I authorized my bank **to** pay her £3,000.* • **authorized** (UK usually **authorised**) /ˈɔː.θər.aɪzd/ US /ˈɑː.θɚ-/ C1 *This is a restricted area, open to authorized (= permitted) personnel only.*

authorship /ˈɔː.θə.ʃɪp/ US /ˈɑː.θɚ-/ **noun** [U] the state or fact of being the person who wrote a particular book, article, play, etc.: *The article is of unknown authorship (= it is not known who wrote it).* ◦ *She is being attacked for her authorship **of** the policy document.*

autism /ˈɔː.tɪ.zəm/ US /ˈɑː.t̬ɪ-/ **noun** [U] a failure to develop social abilities, language, and other communication skills to the usual level: *Autism is four times more common in boys than in girls.* • **autistic** /ɔːˈtɪs.tɪk/ US /ɑː-/ **adj** *One child in 5,000 is autistic.*

auto /ˈɔː.təʊ/ US /ˈɑː.t̬oʊ/ **adj; noun**
►**adj** [before noun] relating to cars: *auto insurance/mechanics/engineers* ◦ *the auto industry/market/business*
►**noun** [C] (plural **autos**) US old-fashioned a car

auto- /ˌɔː.təʊ-/ US /ɑː.t̬oʊ-/ **prefix** of or by yourself, or operating independently and without needing help: *an autofocus camera* ◦ *an auto-immune disease*

autobiography /ˌɔː.tə.baɪˈɒg.rə.fi/ US /ˌɑː.t̬ə.baɪˈɑː.grə-/ **noun** **1** [C] a book about a person's life, written by that person: *Tony Blair's autobiography was a bestseller.* → Compare **biography** **2** [U] the area of literature relating to such books: *His life story is recounted in two fascinating volumes of autobiography.* • **autobiographer** /-fər/ US /-fɚ/ **noun** [C] someone who writes (an) autobiography: *Biographers tend to be more accurate and objective than autobiographers.* • **autobiographical** /ˌɔː.təˌbaɪ.əˈgræf.ɪ.kəl/ US /ˌɑː.t̬ə-/ **adj** *an autobiographical story/novel/poem*

autoclave /ˈɔː.təʊ.kleɪv/ US /ˈɑː.t̬oʊ-/ **noun** [C] a piece of equipment that uses steam at high pressure to STERILIZE (= clean) objects used in medical operations • **autoclave verb** [T]

autocomplete /ˈɔː.təʊ.kəmˌpliːt/ US /ˈɑː.t̬oʊ-/ **noun** [U] a computer program that automatically finishes a word that someone has started to TYPE (= write on a keyboard)

autocracy /ɔːˈtɒk.rə.si/ US /ɑːˈtɑː.krə-/ **noun** **1** [U] government by a single person or small group that has unlimited power or authority, or the power or authority of such a person or group **2** [C] a country or society that has this form of government

autocrat /ˈɔː.tə.kræt/ US /ˈɑː.t̬ə-/ **noun** [C] a ruler with unlimited power, or someone who demands that people completely obey them

autocratic /ˌɔː.təˈkræt.ɪk/ US /ˌɑː.t̬əˈkræt̬-/ **adj** relating to an autocrat: *an autocratic **ruler/regime*** ◦ *an autocratic style of government/leadership/management* ◦ *The president resigned after 30 years of autocratic rule.* • **autocratically** /-ɪ.kəl.i/ **adv**

autocross /ˈɔː.tə.krɒs/ US /ˈɑː.t̬oʊ.krɑːs/ **noun** [U] UK the sport of racing cars around a rough grass track

Autocue /ˈɔː.təʊ.kjuː/ US /ˈɑː.t̬oʊ-/ **noun** [C or U] UK trademark (US **teleprompter**) an electronic device used by people speaking on a television programme that shows the words they have to say while they look directly at the television camera

autoeroticism /ˌɔː.təʊ.ɪˈrɒt.ɪ.sɪ.zəm/ US /ˌɑː.t̬oʊ.ɪˈrɑː.t̬ɪ-/ **noun** [U] the use of your own body and imagination to get sexual pleasure • **autoerotic** /ˌɔː.təʊ.ɪˈrɒt.ɪk/ US /ˌɑː.t̬oʊ.ɪˈrɑː.t̬ɪk/ **adj**

autograph /ˈɔː.tə.grɑːf/ US /ˈɑː.t̬ə.græf/ **noun; verb**
►**noun** [C] a SIGNATURE (= your name written by

yourself), especially of a famous person: *Did you get his autograph?*
▸verb [T] to write your SIGNATURE (= your name written by yourself) on something for someone else to keep: *I got her to autograph my T-shirt.* ◦ *She gave me an autographed photograph of herself.*

autoimmune /ˌɔː.təʊ.ɪˈmjuːn/ (US) /ˌɑː.t̬oʊ-/ **adj** [before noun] specialized relating to a condition in which someone's ANTIBODIES attack substances that are naturally found in the body: *One type of diabetes is an autoimmune* ***disease/disorder*** *that may be triggered by a virus.*

automate /ˈɔː.tə.meɪt/ (US) /ˈɑː.t̬ə-/ **verb** [T] to make a process in a factory or office operate by machines or computers, in order to reduce the amount of work done by humans and the time taken to do the work: *Massive investment is needed to automate the production process.* • **automated** /ˈɔː.tə.meɪ.tɪd/ (US) /ˈɑː.t̬ə.meɪ.t̬ɪd/ **adj** *a fully automated system* • **automation** /ˌɔː.təˈmeɪ.ʃᵊn/ (US) /ˌɑː.t̬ə-/ **noun** [U] *office/factory automation*

ˌautomated ˈteller maˌchine noun [C] (abbreviation **ATM**) a **cash machine**

automatic /ˌɔː.təˈmæt.ɪk/ (US) /ˌɑː.t̬əˈmæt̬-/ **adj; noun**
▸adj **INDEPENDENT** ▷ **1** (B2) An automatic machine or device is able to operate independently of human control: *automatic doors* ◦ *an automatic rifle* ◦ *automatic focus on a camera* **NOT CONSCIOUS** ▷ **2** (C2) done without thinking about it: *Over time, driving just becomes automatic.* ◦ *My automatic response was to pull my hand away.* **CERTAIN** ▷ **3** (C2) certain to happen as part of the normal process or system: *Citizenship is automatic for children born in this country.* ◦ *You get an automatic promotion after two years.*
▸noun [C] a vehicle in which you do not have to change the GEARS: *Kate drives an automatic.*

automatically /ˌɔː.təˈmæt.ɪ.kᵊl.i/ (US) /ˌɑː.t̬əˈmæt̬-/ **adv** **INDEPENDENTLY** ▷ **1** (B2) If a machine or device does something automatically, it does it independently, without human control: *The camera adjusts the shutter speed automatically.* **NOT CONSCIOUSLY** ▷ **2** (B2) If you do something automatically, you do it without thinking about it: *I automatically put my hand out to catch it.* **CERTAINLY** ▷ **3** If something happens automatically, it happens as part of the normal process or system: *Employees who steal are dismissed automatically.*

ˌautomatic ˈpilot noun [C or U] **autopilot**

ˌautomatic ˈteller machine noun [C] Australian English a machine, usually in a wall outside a bank, from which you can take money out of your bank account using a special card → Compare **cash machine**

ˌautomatic transˈmission noun [U] a system that allows a vehicle to change GEAR without being controlled by the driver → Compare **manual transmission**

automaton /ɔːˈtɒm.ə.tᵊn/ (US) /ɑːˈtɑː.mə.t̬ᵊn/ **noun** [C] (plural **automatons** or **automata** /-tə/) a machine that operates on its own without the need for human control, or a person who acts like a machine, without thinking or feeling: *I do the same route to work every day, like some sort of automaton.*

automobile /ˈɔː.tə.mə.biːl/ (US) /ˈɑː.t̬ə.moʊ-/ **noun** [C] US a car: *the automobile industry*

automotive /ˌɔː.təˈməʊ.tɪv/ (US) /ˌɑː.t̬əˈmoʊ.t̬ɪv/ **adj** [before noun] relating to road vehicles: *the automotive industry* ◦ *automotive manufacturing/engineers*

autonomous /ɔːˈtɒn.ə.məs/ (US) /ɑːˈtɑː.nə-/ **adj** **1** independent and having the power to make your own decisions **2** an autonomous organization, country, or region is independent and has the freedom to govern itself: *an autonomous region/province/republic/council*

autonomy /ɔːˈtɒn.ə.mi/ (US) /ɑːˈtɑː.nə-/ **noun** [U] **1** the right of an organization, country, or region to be independent and govern itself: *Demonstrators demanded immediate autonomy* ***for*** *their region.* ◦ *The universities want to preserve their autonomy* ***from*** *central government.* **2** the ability to make your own decisions without being controlled by anyone else

autopilot /ˈɔː.təʊˌpaɪ.lət/ (US) /ˈɑː.t̬oʊ-/ **noun** [C or U] a device that keeps aircraft, spacecraft, and ships moving in a particular direction without human involvement: *The plane was* ***on*** *autopilot when it crashed.*

IDIOM **on autopilot** doing something without thinking about it or without making an effort: *I worked the last hour of my shift on autopilot.*

autopsy /ˈɔː.tɒp.si/ (US) /ˈɑː.tɑːp-/ **noun** [C or U] the cutting open and examination of a dead body in order to discover the cause of death: *They* ***carried out/performed*** *an autopsy.* ◦ *The body arrived for autopsy at the Dallas hospital.*

autorickshaw /ˈɔː.təʊ.rɪk.ʃɔː/ (US) /ˈɑː.t̬oʊ.rɪk.ʃɑː/ **noun** [C] (in South Asia) a small motor vehicle with three wheels that is used as a taxi. There is a seat for the driver at the front and a seat for passengers at the back.

autosuggestion /ˌɔː.təʊ.səˈdʒes.tʃᵊn/ (US) /ˌɑː.t̬oʊ-/ **noun** [U] the influencing of your physical or mental state by thoughts and ideas that come from yourself rather than from other people: *Autosuggestion is the power of mind over matter – if you convince yourself that you are cured, you will be.* • **autosuggestive** /-tɪv/ **adj**

autumn /ˈɔː.təm/ (US) /ˈɑː.t̬ᵊm/ **noun** [C or U] (US usually **fall**) (A2) the season of the year between summer and winter, lasting from September to November north of the EQUATOR and from March to May south of the equator, when fruits and crops become ready to eat and are picked, and leaves fall: *We like to travel* ***in*** ***(the)*** *autumn when there are fewer tourists.* ◦ ***Last*** *autumn we went to Germany.* ◦ *It's been a very mild autumn.* ◦ *autumn colours/leaves* ◦ *an autumn day/evening*

IDIOM **autumn years** literary Someone's autumn years are the later years of their life, especially after they have stopped working.

autumnal /ɔːˈtʌm.nəl/ (US) /ɑː-/ **adj** typical of autumn: *autumnal colours/sunshine/days*

auxiliary /ɔːɡˈzɪl.i.ᵊr.i/ (US) /ɑːɡˈzɪl.i.er-/ **adj; noun**
▸adj giving help or support, especially to a more important person or thing: *auxiliary* ***staff****/nurses*
▸noun **PERSON** ▷ **1** [C] a person whose job is to give help or support to other workers: *semi-skilled auxiliaries* **2** [C usually plural] a soldier of one country who fights for another country **VERB** ▷ **3** [C] (also **auˌxiliary ˈverb**) a verb that gives grammatical information not given by the main verb of a sentence: *In the sentence 'she has finished her book', 'has' is an auxiliary.*

auˌxiliary ˈnurse noun [C] UK (US **ˌnurse's ˈaide**) someone whose job is to help nurses to take care of people

auxin /ˈɔːk.sɪn/ (US) /ˈɑːk-/ **noun** [C] specialized a chemical substance that controls growth in plants

AV /ˌeɪˈviː/ **adj** [before noun] abbreviation for **audiovisual**: *Our teacher sent us to the AV room for a projector.*

avail /əˈveɪl/ noun; verb

▸**noun** [U] use, purpose, advantage, or profit: *We tried to persuade her not to resign, but **to no** avail (= did not succeed).* ◦ *My attempts to improve the situation were **of little/no** avail.*

▸**verb** [T] **1** old use to help or be useful to someone or something: *Our efforts availed us **nothing** (= did not help).* **2** Indian English to make use of something: *Over a thousand learners have already availed the **opportunity** to study at our college.* ◦ *To avail this **offer**, please click here.*

PHRASAL VERB **avail yourself of sth** formal to make use of something: *Employees should avail themselves of the opportunity to buy cheap shares in the company.*

availability /əˌveɪ.ləˈbɪl.ɪ.ti/ ⓤⓢ /-ə.t̬i/ noun [U] **1** B2 the fact that something can be bought, used, or reached, or how much it can be: *The ready availability **of** guns has contributed to the escalating violence.* ◦ *Abortion rates are high because the availability of contraceptives is limited.* **2** B2 the fact of someone being free to speak on the phone, work, etc.: *I shall check the availability of my staff for that date.*

available /əˈveɪ.lə.bl̩/ adj **1** A2 able to be bought or used: *Is this dress available in a larger size?* ◦ *Our autumn catalogue is now available **from** our usual stockists.* ◦ *There's no money available **for** an office party this year.* ◦ *It is vital that food is **made** available **to** the famine areas.* ◦ *Do you have any double rooms available this weekend?* **2** If someone is available, they are not busy and so are able to do something: [+ to infinitive] *I'm afraid I'm not available **to** help with the show on the 19th.* ◦ *Every available officer will be assigned to the investigation.*

> **!** Common mistake: **available**
>
> **Warning:** Check your spelling!
> **Available** is one of the 50 words most often spelled wrongly by learners.

avalanche /ˈæv.əl.ɑːnʃ/ ⓤⓢ /-æntʃ/ noun [C] **1** a large amount of ice, snow, and rock falling quickly down the side of a mountain **2** too many things that arrive or happen at the same time: *We were swamped by an avalanche **of** letters/phone calls/complaints.*

avant-garde /ˌæv.ɑ̃ːˈɡɑːd/ ⓤⓢ /-ˈɡɑːrd/ adj describes ideas, styles, and methods that are very original or modern in comparison to the period in which they happen: *avant-garde art/cinema/painting*

the ˌavant-ˈgarde noun [S, + sing/pl verb] (the work of) the painters, writers, musicians, and other artists whose ideas, styles, and methods are very original or modern in comparison to the period in which they live: *New York is the international capital of the musical avant-garde.*

avarice /ˈæv.ər.ɪs/ ⓤⓢ /-ɚ-/ noun [U] formal an extremely strong wish to get or keep money or possessions → Synonym **greed** • **avaricious** /ˌæv.əˈrɪʃ.əs/ adj • **avariciously** /ˌæv.əˈrɪʃ.əs.li/ adv

avatar /ˈæv.ə.tɑːʳ/ ⓤⓢ /-tɑːr/ noun [C] **1** an image that represents you in ONLINE games, CHAT ROOMS, etc. and that you can move around the screen: *You can talk to other avatars with your words displayed in a cartoon bubble.* **2** especially in Hinduism, a god who appears on earth as a person

Ave noun [U] written abbreviation for **avenue**: *13 Victoria Ave*

avenge /əˈvendʒ/ verb [T] formal to do harm to or punish the person responsible for something bad done to you or your family or friends in order to achieve a fair situation: *He swore he would avenge his brother's death.* ◦ *She determined to avenge her**self on** the killer.* • **avenger** /əˈven.dʒəʳ/ ⓤⓢ /-dʒɚ/ noun [C] *Russell Crowe stars as a grief-stricken avenger on the trail of his family's killers.*

avenue /ˈæv.ə.njuː/ ⓤⓢ /-nuː/ noun [C] **ROAD** ▷ **1** C1 a wide road with trees or tall buildings on both sides, or a wide countryside path or road with trees on both sides: *Fremont Avenue* **2** UK a road that leads to a large house **POSSIBILITY** ▷ **3** C2 a method or way of doing something: *We should **explore/pursue** every avenue in the search for an answer to this problem.* ◦ *Only two avenues are **open** to us – either we accept his offer or we give up the fight completely.* → Synonym **possibility**

aver /əˈvɜːʳ/ ⓤⓢ /-ˈvɝː/ verb [T] (-rr-) formal to say that something is certainly true: *The lawyer averred her client's innocence.* ◦ [+ speech] *'He's guilty, I tell you,' she averred.* ◦ [+ that] *She averred **that** he was guilty.*

average /ˈæv.ər.ɪdʒ/ ⓤⓢ /-ɚ-/ noun; verb; adj

▸**noun AMOUNT** ▷ **1** B1 [C or U] the result you get by adding two or more amounts together and dividing the total by the number of amounts: *The average of the three numbers 7, 12, and 20 is 13, because the total of 7, 12, and 20 is 39, and 39 divided by 3 is 13.* ◦ *Prices have risen by an average **of** four percent over the past year.* ◦ *My income's rather variable, but I earn £73 a day **on** average.* **USUAL STANDARD** ▷ **2** B1 [S or U] a standard or level that is considered to be typical or usual: *The audience figures were lower than average for this sort of film.* ◦ *In western Europe, a seven to eight-hour working day is about **the** average.* ◦ ***On** average, people who don't smoke are healthier than people who do.* ◦ *The quality of candidates was **(well) below/above** average.* ◦ *I expect to spend **an** average **of** $50 to $60 on a meal in a restaurant.*

> Word partners for **average** (**AMOUNT**)
>
> *annual/monthly/weekly/yearly* average • *charge/cost/pay/spend* an average *of* sth • *earn/make/receive* an average *of* sth • an average *drops/falls/rises* • *on* average • *about/above/below* (the) average • the average *for* sth

> Word partners for **average** (**USUAL STANDARD**)
>
> *about/above/below* (the) average • *on* average • *better/worse* than (the) average • *higher/lower* than (the) average

▸**verb** [T] to reach a particular amount as an average: *Enquiries to our office average 1,000 calls a month.* ◦ *Many doctors average (= work an average of) 70 hours a week.* ◦ *Trainee accountants average (= earn an average of) £12,000 per year.*

PHRASAL VERBS **average sth out** to calculate the average of a set of numbers or amounts: *If I average out what I earn a month, it's about £1,500.* • **average out** to be or become equal in amount or number: *The highs and lows of life tend to average out in the end.* • **average out at sth** to have a particular number or amount as the average: *My annual holiday varies, but it averages out at five weeks a year.*

▸**adj AMOUNT** ▷ **1** B1 [before noun] An average number is the number you get by adding two or more amounts together and dividing the total by the number of amounts: *average **earnings/income/rainfall*** ◦ *The average **age** of the US soldiers who fought in the Vietnam War was 19.* **USUAL** ▷ **2** A2 typical and usual: *The average person in the street is a lot better off than they were 40 years ago.* ◦ *a student of average ability* ◦ *The food was fairly average (= not excellent, although not bad).* • **averagely** /-li/ adv *He's an averagely attractive man.*

A

averse /əˈvɜːs/ (US) /-ˈvɝːs/ **adj** [after verb] strongly disliking or opposed to: *Few people are averse* ***to*** *the idea of a free holiday.* ◦ *I'm* ***not*** *averse* ***to*** *(= I like) the occasional glass of champagne myself.*

aversion /əˈvɜː.ʃən/, /-ʒən/ (US) /-ˈvɝː.ʒən/ **noun** [C usually singular] (a person or thing that causes) a feeling of strong dislike or of not wishing to do something: *I felt an instant aversion* ***to*** *his parents.* ◦ *She has a deep aversion* ***to*** *getting up in the morning.* ◦ *Greed is my* ***pet*** *aversion (= the thing I dislike most of all).*

aˈversion ˌtherapy **noun** [U] a method of treating habits or types of behaviour that are not wanted or not acceptable, by causing the patient to connect them with bad feelings: *Despite what many people think, aversion therapy is no longer used by professional psychologists in this country.*

avert /əˈvɜːt/ (US) /-ˈvɝːt/ **verb** [T] **PREVENT** ▷ **1** to prevent something bad from happening: *to avert a* ***crisis****/conflict/strike/famine* ◦ *to avert* ***disaster****/economic collapse* → Synonym **avoid** **TURN** ▷ **2** to turn away your eyes or thoughts: *I averted my* ***gaze/eyes*** *while he dressed.* ◦ *We tried to avert our thoughts* ***from*** *our massive financial problems.*

avian /ˈeɪ.vi.ən/ **adj** of or relating to birds

ˌavian ˈflu **noun** [U] (also **ˈbird ˌflu**) an illness that kills birds and can sometimes pass from birds to people

aviary /ˈeɪ.vi.ə.ri/ (US) /-er.i/ **noun** [C] a large CAGE (= area surrounded by wire or bars) or closed space in which birds are kept as pets

aviation /ˌeɪ.viˈeɪ.ʃən/ **noun** [U] the activity of flying aircraft, or of designing, producing, and keeping them in good condition: *the British Civil Aviation Authority* ◦ *the US Federal Aviation Administration* ◦ *aviation fuel*

aviator /ˈeɪ.vi.eɪ.tər/ (US) /-t̬ɚ/ **noun** [C] old-fashioned an aircraft pilot: *Amy Johnson was a pioneering aviator who made record-breaking flights to Australia and South Africa in the 1930s.*

avid /ˈæv.ɪd/ **adj** extremely eager or interested: *an avid football* ***fan*** ◦ *an avid* ***supporter*** *of the arts* ◦ *He took an avid* ***interest*** *in the project.* ◦ formal *She hadn't seen him for six months and was avid* ***for*** *news.* • **avidity** /əˈvɪd.ɪ.ti/ (US) /-ə.t̬i/ **noun** [U] formal • **avidly** /-li/ **adv** *She* ***reads*** *avidly.* ◦ *We avidly awaited news of him.*

avionics /ˌeɪ.viˈɒn.ɪks/ (US) /-ˈɑː.nɪks/ **noun** **1** [U] the science and TECHNOLOGY of the electronic devices used in AERONAUTICS and ASTRONAUTICS **2** [plural] the electronic devices of an aircraft or spacecraft • **avionic** /ˌeɪ.viˈɒn.ɪk/ (US) /-ˈɑː.nɪk/ **adj**

avocado /ˌæv.əˈkɑː.dəʊ/ (US) /-doʊ/ **noun** [C] (plural **avocados**) (UK also **ˌavocado ˈpear**) a tropical fruit with thick, green, or purple skin, a large, round seed, and green flesh that can be eaten

avoid /əˈvɔɪd/ **verb** [T] **1** B1 to stay away from someone or something: *I try to avoid supermarkets on Saturdays – they're always so busy.* ◦ *I'm* ***anxious to*** *avoid the motorway at rush hour.* ◦ *Do you think Tim's avoiding me? I haven't seen him all day.* **2** B2 to prevent something from happening or to not allow yourself to do something: [+ -ing verb] *I try to avoid going shopping on Saturdays.* ◦ *The report studiously avoided any mention of the controversial plan.* ◦ *The plane* ***narrowly*** *avoided disaster when one of the engines cut out on take-off.* ◦ *I left the pub to avoid a fight (= prevent a fight from happening).* ◦ *Unnecessary paperwork should be avoided (= prevented)* ***at all costs.***

> **!** Common mistake: **avoid or prevent?**
> **Warning:** choose the correct verb!
> To talk about not allowing someone else to do something, don't say 'avoid', say **prevent**:
> ~~*My parents tried to avoid me seeing him.*~~
> *My parents tried to prevent me seeing him.*

IDIOM **avoid sth like the plague** to be determined to avoid something completely: *I'm not a fan of parties – in fact I avoid them like the plague.*

avoidable /əˈvɔɪ.də.bl/ **adj** possible to avoid: *A number of illnesses are entirely avoidable.* ◦ *In spite of these latest threats, war may still be avoidable.*

avoidance /əˈvɔɪ.dəns/ **noun** [U] the act of avoiding something or someone: *The avoidance of injury is critical to a professional athlete.*

avow /əˈvaʊ/ **verb** [T] formal to admit something or say something publicly: [+ that] *He avowed* ***that*** *he regretted what he had done.* ◦ *It is a society in which homosexuality is rarely avowed.*

avowal /əˈvaʊ.əl/ **noun** [C or U] formal a statement in which you say or admit something that you believe, support, or intend to do: *They were imprisoned for their avowal* ***of*** *anti-government beliefs.* ◦ *Her public avowals* ***to*** *reduce crime have yet to be put into effect.*

avowed /əˈvaʊd/ **adj** [before noun] formal stated: *The government's avowed intent/purpose/aim is to reduce tax.* ◦ *An avowed traditionalist, he is against reform of any kind.* • **avowedly** /əˈvaʊ.ɪd.li/ **adv** *an avowedly feminist author*

avuncular /əˈvʌŋ.kjʊ.lər/ (US) /-lɚ/ **adj** formal friendly, kind, or helpful, like the expected behaviour of an uncle: *an avuncular, quietly spoken man*

aw /ɔː/ **exclamation** mainly US used to express disapproval or sympathy

await /əˈweɪt/ **verb** [T] formal to wait for or be waiting for something: *He's anxiously awaiting his test results.* ◦ *A marvellous reception awaited me on my first day at work.* ◦ *The* ***long/eagerly*** *awaited sequel is now available on video.*

awake /əˈweɪk/ **adj**; **verb**

▸**adj** [after verb] **1** B1 not sleeping: *'Is Oliver awake yet?' 'Yes, he's* ***wide*** *(= completely) awake and running around his bedroom.'* ◦ *I find it so difficult to* ***stay*** *awake during history lessons.* ◦ *I drink a lot of coffee to* ***keep*** *me awake.* ◦ *She used to* ***lie*** *awake at night worrying about how to pay the bills.* **2 be awake to sth** mainly UK If you are awake to something, you know about it: *Businesses need to be awake to the advantages of European integration.*

▸**verb** [I or T] (**awoke** or US also **awaked**, **awoken**) **1** literary to stop sleeping or to make someone stop sleeping: *I awoke at seven o'clock.* ◦ *She awoke me at seven.* **2** to start to understand or feel something or to make someone start to understand or feel something: *The chance meeting awoke the old passion between them.* ◦ *Young people need to awake* ***to*** *the risks involved in casual sex.*

awaken /əˈweɪ.kən/ **verb** [I or T] literary to stop sleeping or to make someone stop sleeping: *They were awakened by the sound of gunfire.* ◦ *I awakened at dawn to find him beside me.*

PHRASAL VERBS **awaken (sth) in sb** If a wish, interest, or emotion awakens or is awakened in you, you notice it for the first time: *My holiday in Paris awakened a passion for French food in me.* • **awaken sb to sth** If you awaken someone to something, you make them notice it or make them remember it: *I awakened him to his responsibilities for his children.*

awakening /əˈweɪ.kən.ɪŋ/ **noun** [S] the act of starting to understand something or feel something: *a religious awakening* ◦ *the awakening of public concern about the environment* ◦ *He's in for a* ***rude*** *awakening (= will be shocked) when he starts work!*

award /əˈwɔːd/ (US) /-ˈwɔːrd/ **verb; noun**

▸**verb** [T] (B2) to give money or a prize following an official decision: *Carlos was awarded first prize in the essay competition.* ◦ *The jury awarded libel damages of £100,000.* ◦ [+ two objects] *The university has awarded her a $500 travel grant.*

▸**noun** [C] (B2) a prize or an amount of money that is given to someone following an official decision: *They have authorized awards of £900* ***to*** *each of the victims.* ◦ *the Academy Award for Best Director*

awardee /ə.wɔːˈdiː/ (US) /-wɔːr-/ **noun** [C] a person who is given money, a prize, etc. by an official organization: *Click on the link below to see a list of this year's research grant awardees.*

aˈward-ˌwinning **adj** [before noun] having won a prize or prizes for being of high quality or very skilled: *an award-winning author/TV series/design*

aware /əˈweəʳ/ (US) /-ˈwer/ **adj** [after verb] **1** (B2) knowing that something exists, or having knowledge or experience of a particular thing: [+ that] *I wasn't even aware* ***that*** *he was ill.* ◦ *Were you aware* ***of*** *the risks at the time?* ◦ *She was* ***well*** *(= very) aware that he was married.* ◦ *'Has Claude paid the phone bill?' 'Not* ***as far as I'm*** *aware.' (= I don't think so)* ◦ *I suddenly became aware* ***of*** *(= started to notice) him looking at me.* **2** having special interest in or experience of something and so knowing what is happening in that subject at the present time: *to be ecologically/politically aware* ◦ *sexually aware*

awareness /əˈweə.nəs/ (US) /-ˈwer-/ **noun** [U] (C1) knowledge that something exists, or understanding of a situation or subject at the present time based on information or experience: *Public awareness* ***of*** *the problem will make politicians take it seriously.* ◦ *Environmental awareness has increased dramatically over the past decade.*

awash /əˈwɒʃ/ (US) /-ˈwɑːʃ/ **adj** [after verb] **1** covered with a liquid, especially water: *By the time I discovered the problem, the floor was awash.* **2** having an amount of something that is very large or larger than necessary or wanted: *The city is awash* ***with*** *drugs and the police are powerless to do anything about it.*

away /əˈweɪ/ **adv; adj**

▸**adv** SOMEWHERE ELSE ▷ **1** (A2) somewhere else, or to or in a different place, position, or situation: *Ms Watson is away on holiday until the end of the week.* ◦ *Keep/Stay away* ***from*** *him.* ◦ *Just* ***go*** *away and leave me alone!* ◦ *The sight was so horrible that I had to look/turn away.* ◦ *The recent flood has swept away the footbridge.* ◦ *I've given away all my old clothes to charity.* ◦ UK *Would you like your burger to eat in or take away?* DISTANT ▷ **2** (A2) at a distance (of or from here): *How far away is the station?* ◦ *The office is a half-hour drive away.* ◦ *We live five kilometres away* ***from*** *each other.* ◦ *Life's so much quieter away* ***from*** *the city.* ◦ informal *Oh, it's* ***miles*** *away (= a long distance from here).* INTO PLACE ▷ **3** (B1) in or into the usual or a suitable place, especially one that can be closed: *Would you put the ice cream away in the freezer?* ◦ *My grandparents had £800 hidden away in an old shoe box.* GONE ▷ **4** (B2) gradually until mostly or completely gone: *All the snow had melted away.* ◦ *The music faded away as the procession moved slowly up the street.* ◦ *We used to while away (= spend time at) the weekends at my aunt's cottage in the country.* ◦ *We danced the night away (= until the night was over).* IN THE FUTURE ▷ **5** (B1) in the future: *My English exam's only a week away and I haven't even started to prepare.* CONTINUOUSLY ▷ **6** (C2) continuously or repeatedly, or in a busy way: *I was still writing away when the exam finished.* ◦ *Chris has been working away in the garden all day.* ◦ *We were chatting away at the back and didn't hear what he said.*

▸**adj** (C1) An away match or game is played at an opposing team's sports ground: *We lost the away* ***game*** *but won both the home games.*

awe /ɔː/ (US) /ɑː/ **noun; verb**

▸**noun** [U] (C2) a feeling of great respect sometimes mixed with fear or surprise: *I've always* ***held*** *musicians* ***in*** *awe.* ◦ *As children we were rather* ***in*** *awe* ***of*** *our grandfather.* ◦ *You can't help but* ***stand in*** *awe* ***of*** *(= respect greatly and fear slightly) powerful people.*

▸**verb** [T] (past tense and past participle UK **aweing** or US **awing**) to cause someone to feel awe: *I was awed but not frightened by the huge gorilla.* ◦ *Her paintings have awed and amazed the public for half a century.* ◦ *The audience was awed* ***into*** *silence by her stunning performance.* • **awed** /ɔːd/ (US) /ɑːd/ **adj** *We stood there in awed* ***silence.*** ◦ *'How does she manage to run so fast at her age?' he asked in awed* ***tones.***

ˈawe-inˌspiring **adj** causing you to feel great respect or admiration: *Niagara Falls really is an awe-inspiring sight.*

awesome /ˈɔː.səm/ (US) /ˈɑː-/ **adj** **1** (C2) causing feelings of great admiration, respect, or fear: *An awesome challenge/task lies ahead of them.* ◦ *awesome scenery* **2** (A2) US informal extremely good: *You look totally awesome in that dress.*

awestruck /ˈɔː.strʌk/ (US) /ˈɑː-/ **adj** (also **awestricken**) filled with feelings of admiration or respect: *an awestruck admirer/fan/visitor/tourist* ◦ *I could tell she was impressed from the awestruck expression on her face.*

awful /ˈɔː.fəl/ (US) /ˈɑː-/ **adj** BAD ▷ **1** (A2) extremely bad or unpleasant: *He suffered awful injuries in the crash.* ◦ *We had awful weather.* ◦ *She's got an awful boss.* ◦ *What an awful thing to say!* ◦ *Would life be so awful without a car?* ◦ *The food was awful.* ◦ *She'd been ill and she* ***looked*** *awful.* VERY GREAT ▷ **2** (B2) [before noun] very great: *I don't know* ***an*** *awful* ***lot*** *(= very much)* ***about*** *art, but I'm learning.* ◦ *Fortunately it won't make* ***an*** *awful* ***lot of*** *difference if I don't pass the test.* ◦ *It was an awful risk to take.* • **awfulness** /-nəs/ **noun** [U] *You can't appreciate the true/sheer awfulness of war until you've actually experienced it.*

awfully /ˈɔː.fəl.i/ (US) /ˈɑː-/ **adv** GREATLY ▷ **1** (US informal also **awful**) very or extremely, when used before an adjective or adverb: *It's an awfully long time since we last saw each other.* ◦ *I'm awfully sorry, but we've forgotten to reserve you a table.* BADLY ▷ **2** extremely badly: *England played awfully throughout the game.*

awhile /əˈwaɪl/ **adv** literary for a short time: *Stay awhile and rest.* ◦ *I read awhile, then slept.*

awkward /ˈɔː.kwəd/ (US) /ˈɑː.kwəd/ **adj** DIFFICULT ▷ **1** (B2) difficult to use, do, or deal with: *It's an awkward corner, so take it slowly.* ◦ *Some of the questions were rather awkward.* ◦ *It was an awkward ascent, but we reached the top eventually.* ◦ [+ to infinitive] *My car's quite awkward* ***to*** *drive.* ◦ *He's an awkward* ***customer*** *(= a difficult person to deal with).* EMBARRASSING ▷ **2** (B2) causing problems, worry, or embarrassment: *an awkward position/situation* ◦ *There followed an awkward silence while we all tried to think of something to say.* ◦ *They'd chosen an awkward time to call as I'd*

A

just got into the bath. ◦ *The police asked some awkward questions about where the money had come from.* **3** Ⓒ embarrassed or nervous: *I always **feel** awkward when I'm with Chris – he's so difficult to talk to.* ◦ *He seemed a little awkward when I first met him.* **NOT HELPFUL** ▷ **4** mainly UK intentionally not helpful: *Just stop being so awkward and help me push the car, will you!* → Synonym **uncooperative** **MOVEMENT** ▷ **5** moving in a way that is not natural, relaxed, or attractive: *His movements were slow and awkward.* • **awkwardness** /-nəs/ **noun** [U] *In spite of the divorce, there was no awkwardness between them – in fact they seemed very much at ease.*

awkwardly /ˈɔː.kwəd.li/ Ⓤⓢ /ˈɑː.kwɚd-/ **adv** **WITH EMBARRASSMENT** ▷ **1** in a worried or embarrassed way: *He shifted awkwardly from one foot to the other.* **2** in an embarrassing or worrying way, or a way that causes problems: *The publication of the economic statistics was awkwardly timed for the government.* **MOVE** ▷ **3** moving in a way that is not natural, relaxed, or attractive: *She fell awkwardly when she was skiing and twisted her ankle.* **WITH DIFFICULTY** ▷ **4** in a way that is difficult to deal with, use, or do: *The car was parked awkwardly across the pavement.* **NOT HELPFULLY** ▷ **5** in an intentionally unhelpful way

awl /ɔːl/ Ⓤⓢ /ɑːl/ **noun** [C] a pointed tool for making small holes in wood or leather

awning /ˈɔː.nɪŋ/ Ⓤⓢ /ˈɑː-/ **noun** [C] (US also **sunshade**) a cloth or plastic cover fastened to a building or structure and supported by a frame that is used to protect someone or something from the sun or rain: *The gaily striped awnings of the market stalls made an attractive scene.*

awoke /əˈwəʊk/ Ⓤⓢ /-ˈwoʊk/ **verb** past simple of **awake**

awoken /əˈwəʊ.k^{ə}n/ Ⓤⓢ /-ˈwoʊ-/ **verb** past participle of **awake**

AWOL /ˈeɪ.wɒl/ Ⓤⓢ /-wɑːl/ **adj** [after verb] abbreviation for absent without leave: describes a member of the armed forces who is away without permission: *The pilot is serving 22 days' detention for **going** AWOL.*

IDIOM **go AWOL** informal If something has gone AWOL, it is not in its usual place or has been stolen: *Two computers have gone AWOL from the office.*

awry /əˈraɪ/ **adj** [after verb], **adv** **1** not in the intended way: *Anything that **goes** awry (= goes wrong) in the office is blamed on Pete.* ◦ *The strike has sent the plans for investment seriously awry.* **2** in the wrong position: *She rushed in, her face red and sweaty and her hat awry.*

ˌaw ˈshucks **exclamation** US humorous or old-fashioned used to show that you feel embarrassed or shy → See also **shucks** • **ˌaw-ˈshucks** showing a shy or a MODEST character or way of behaving: *He shrugged and gave us one of his aw-shucks smiles.*

axe /æks/ **noun; verb**

▸**noun** [C] (US also **ax**) **1** a tool that has a heavy iron or STEEL blade at the end of a long wooden handle, used for cutting wood: *Julian used an axe to chop down the old apple tree.* **2 the axe** UK (US also **the ax**) the situation in which someone loses their job: *Over 500 staff are facing the axe.* **3 get the axe** UK When a service, plan, etc. gets the axe, it is stopped or prevented from happening: *Religious programmes will be the first to get the axe if she's put in charge of the station.*

IDIOM **have an axe to grind** to have a strong personal opinion about something that you want people to accept and that is the reason why you do something: *Environmentalists have no political axe to grind – they just want to save the planet.*

▸**verb** [T] (US also **ax**) to reduce services, jobs, payments, etc. a lot or completely without warning or in a single action: *Because of the recession the company is to axe 350 jobs.* ◦ *The TV series will be axed owing to a decline in popularity.*

axes **noun** **1** plural of **axis** **2** plural of **axe**

axil /ˈæk.sɪl/ **noun** [C] specialized on a plant, the angle between the top of a leaf or stem and the stem or branch that it grows from

axiom /ˈæk.si.^{ə}m/ **noun** [C] **1** formal a statement or principle that is generally accepted to be true, but need not be so: *It is a widely held axiom that governments should not negotiate with terrorists.* **2** specialized a formal statement or principle in mathematics, science, etc., from which other statements can be obtained

axiomatic /ˌæk.si.əˈmæt.ɪk/ Ⓤⓢ /-ˈmæt̬-/ **adj** formal obviously true and therefore not needing to be proved: *It is an axiomatic fact that governments rise and fall on the state of the economy.* ◦ *It seems axiomatic that everyone would benefit from a better scientific education.* • **axiomatically** /-ɪ.k^{ə}l.i/ **adv**

axis /ˈæk.sɪs/ **noun** [C] (plural **axes** /ˈæk.siːz/) **IN MATHEMATICS** ▷ **1** a real or imaginary straight line going through the centre of a object that is spinning, or a line that divides a SYMMETRICAL shape into two equal halves: *The Earth revolves around the axis that joins the North and South Poles.* ◦ *The diameter of a circle is also an axis.* **2** a fixed line on a GRAPH used to show the position of a point: *Plot distance on the vertical y-axis against time on the horizontal x-axis.* **POLITICAL AGREEMENT** ▷ **3** an agreement between governments or politicians to work together to achieve a particular aim: *the Franco-German axis*

the ˈAxis **noun** [+ sing/pl verb] the countries, including Germany, Italy, and Japan, that fought against the ALLIES in the Second World War: *the Axis **powers/nations***

axle /ˈæk.sl̩/ **noun** [C] a bar connected to the centre of a circular object such as a wheel that allows or causes it to turn, especially one connecting two wheels of a vehicle

ayatollah /ˌaɪ.əˈtɒl.ə/ Ⓤⓢ /-ˈtoʊ.lə/ **noun** [C] an important religious leader of Shiite Muslims in Iran

aye /aɪ/ **adv; noun**

▸**adv** mainly UK another word for 'yes': *'Would you prefer not to work?' 'Oh aye, I'd stop tomorrow if I could.'* ◦ *All those who support this proposal say 'Aye'.*

▸**noun** [C] a vote to support a suggestion, idea, law, etc., or a person who votes 'yes': ***The ayes have it*** (= *the people who voted 'yes' have won*).

Ayurvedic medicine /aɪ.ʊəˌveɪ.dɪkˈmed.sən/ Ⓤⓢ /-ʊr-/ **noun** [U] a traditional system of medicine from India in which illnesses are treated with a combination of certain foods, herbs, massage, and special physical exercise

azuki /əˈzuː.ki/ **noun** [C] an **adzuki**

azure /ˈæʒ.ə^{r}/, /ˈæz.jʊə^{r}/ Ⓤⓢ /-ɚ/ **adj** having the bright blue colour of the sky on a clear day: *The once azure skies of Athens have been ruined by atmospheric pollution.* • **azure** **noun** [U]

B

B

B, b /biː/ noun (plural **Bs, B's** or **b's**) **LETTER** ▷ **1** [C or U] the second letter of the English alphabet **MUSIC** ▷ **2** [C or U] a note in Western music: *Bach's Mass in B minor* **MARK** ▷ **3** [C or U] a mark in an exam or for a piece of work that shows that your work is good but not excellent: *I was a bit disappointed just to be given a B, as I was hoping for an A.* ◦ *I **got** B for physics last term.*

b US (UK **bn**) written abbreviation for **billion**

b. written abbreviation for **born**: *John Winston Lennon (b. 9 October 1940, Liverpool, d. 8 December 1980, New York).*

B2B /ˌbiː.təˈbiː/ US /-t̬ə-/ abbreviation for business-to-business: describing or involving business arrangements or trade between different businesses, rather than between businesses and the general public: *a B2B **exchange/company***

B2C /ˌbiː.təˈsiː/ US /-t̬ə-/ abbreviation for business-to-consumer: describing or involving the sale of goods or services directly to customers for their own use, rather than to businesses: *B2C **companies/e-commerce***

BA /ˌbiːˈeɪ/ noun [C] (US also **AB**) abbreviation for Bachelor of Arts: a first university degree (= qualification) in the arts or SOCIAL SCIENCES, or someone who has this degree: *Farida **has** a BA **in** History from the University of Sussex.*

baa /bɑː/ US /bæ/ noun [C] the sound that a sheep makes • **baa verb** [I] (**baaing, baaed, baaed**)

baba /ˈbæ.bə/ noun [C] Indian English **1** father: used by some South Asians to show respect to an older man **2** used by some South Asians when talking to a friend or a child, especially a man or boy

babble /ˈbæb.l̩/ verb; noun

▸verb **TALK** ▷ **1** [I or T] to talk or say something in a quick, confused, excited, or silly way: *She was babbling something **about** her ring being stolen.* **WATER NOISE** ▷ **2** [I] literary (of a stream) to make the low, continuous noise of water flowing over stones: *They rested a while by a babbling **brook**.*

▸noun [U] a continuous low or confused sound, especially the sound of several people talking: *I could hear the babble **of** voices in the next room.*

babe /beɪb/ noun [C] **1** literary a small baby: *a newborn babe* **2** informal a word you can use when you are talking to someone you love such as your wife, husband, partner, etc.: *It's up to you, babe. I'll do whatever you say.* **3** informal a sexually attractive young person: *He's a **total** babe.*

ˌbabe in ˈarms noun [C] (plural **babes in arms**) mainly UK a very young baby

babel /ˈbeɪ.bəl/ noun [S] formal a state of confusion caused by many people talking at the same time or using different languages: *a babel **of** voices*

baboon

baboon /bəˈbuːn/ noun [C] a type of large monkey found in Africa and Asia, which has a long, pointed face like a dog and large teeth

baby /ˈbeɪ.bi/ noun; verb

▸noun [C] **1** A1 a very young child, especially one that has not yet begun to walk or talk: *a newborn baby* ◦ *a six-week-old baby* ◦ *a baby boy* ◦ *baby clothes* ◦ *baby food* ◦ *Sandra **had** a baby (= gave birth to it) on 29 May.* ◦ *Owen is the baby (= the youngest person) of the family.* **2** A2 a very young animal: *a baby elephant/monkey* **3** disapproving an adult or especially an older child who is crying or behaving like a child: *It didn't hurt that much – don't be such a baby!* **4** mainly US a word you can use when you are talking to someone you love such as your wife, husband, partner, etc.: *Oh baby, I love you.* **5 baby carrot, sweetcorn, etc.** a type of vegetable that is specially grown to stay small **6** informal Someone's baby is something that they have a special interest in and responsibility for: *I don't know much about the project – it's Philip's baby.*

▸verb [T] informal to treat an older child as if he or she were a much younger child: *The boys were now ten and twelve and didn't want their mother to baby them.*

ˈbaby ˌblues noun [plural] a feeling of sadness that some women experience after they have given birth to a baby: *According to this article, as many as 60 percent of women suffer from the baby blues.*

ˈbaby ˌboom noun [C usually singular] a large increase in the number of babies born among a particular group of people during a particular time: *There was a baby boom in the UK and the US after the Second World War.*

ˈbaby-ˌboomer noun [C] (US informal **boomer**) a person who was born during a baby boom, especially the one that happened in the UK and the US following the Second World War

ˈbaby ˌcarriage noun [C] (also **ˈbaby ˌbuggy**) US for **pram**

Babygro /ˈbeɪ.bi.grəʊ/ US /-oʊ/ noun [C] UK trademark a piece of clothing for a baby that covers the whole body

babyhood /ˈbeɪ.bi.hʊd/ noun [U] the period of time when you are a baby

babyish /ˈbeɪ.bi.ɪʃ/ adj disapproving only suitable for a baby: *The older children found the toys too babyish.*

ˈbaby ˌmilk noun [U] artificial milk that can be given to babies instead of milk from their mother

babysit /ˈbeɪ.bi.sɪt/ verb [I or T] (present tense **babysitting**, past tense and past participle **babysat**) (US also **sit**) B1 to take care of someone's baby or child while that person is out, usually by going to their home: *I babysit **for** Jane on Tuesday evenings while she goes to her yoga class.* • **babysitting** /ˈbeɪ.biˌsɪt.ɪŋ/ US /-ˌsɪt̬.ɪŋ/ noun [U] *He earns a bit of extra pocket money by doing babysitting.*

babysitter /ˈbeɪ.biˌsɪt.əʳ/ US /-ˌsɪt̬.ɚ/ noun [C] (mainly US **sitter**) B1 someone who takes care of your baby or child while you are out, usually by coming to your home, especially someone you pay to do this: *I promised the babysitter that we'd be home by midnight.*

ˈbaby ˌtalk noun [U] the words that a very young child uses, or the words used by adults when they talk to babies

ˈbaby ˌtooth noun [C] (also **ˈmilk ˌtooth**) one of the teeth of young children and some other young mammals that fall out and are replaced by permanent teeth

baccalaureate /ˌbæk.əˈlɔː.ri.ət/ US /-ˈlɔːr.i.ət/ noun [C] an exam in several subjects taken in the last year of school around the age of 18 in France and some other countries → See also **the International Baccalaureate**

B

bacchanalian /ˌbæk.əˈneɪ.li.ən/ **adj** literary (especially of a party) involving a lot of drinking of alcohol, uncontrolled behaviour, and possibly sexual activity: *a bacchanalian orgy*

baccy /ˈbæk.i/ **noun** [U] UK slang for **tobacco**

bachelor /ˈbætʃ.əl.əʳ/ ⓤⓢ /-ɚ/ **noun** [C] a man who has never married: *He remained a bachelor until he was well into his 40s.* ◦ *Simon is a* ***confirmed*** *bachelor (= he is unlikely ever to want to get married).*

bachelorette /ˌbætʃ.əl.əˈret/ **noun** [C] mainly US a woman, especially a young woman, who has never married • **bachelorette adj** [before noun] *a bachelorette apartment*

bacheloˈrette ˌparty **noun** [C] US a party for a woman who is going to get married, to which only her female friends are invited → Compare **bachelor party, hen night**

ˈbachelor ˌparty **noun** [C] US a party for a man who is going to get married, to which only his male friends are invited → Compare **stag night/party**

ˌbachelor's deˈgree **noun** [C] a first degree at college or university

bacillus /bəˈsɪl.əs/ **noun** [C] (plural **bacilli** /-aɪ/) specialized a BACTERIUM (= an extremely small organism) that is shaped like a rod. There are various types of bacillus, some of which can cause disease.

back /bæk/ **adv; noun; verb; adj**

▸**adv** **RETURN** ▷ **1** B2 in, into, or towards a previous place or condition, or an earlier time: *When you take the scissors, remember to put them back.* ◦ *He left a note saying 'Gone out. Back soon.'* ◦ *She went to America for two years, but now she's back (= has returned).* ◦ *He looked back (= looked behind him) and saw they were following him.* ◦ *Looking at her old photographs* ***brought*** *back (= made her remember) a lot of memories.* ◦ *I was woken by a thunderstorm, and I couldn't* ***get*** *back* ***to*** *sleep (= could not sleep again).* ◦ *The last time we saw Lowell was back (= at an earlier time) in January.* ◦ *This tradition dates back to (= to the earlier time of) the 16th century.* **2** A2 in return: *If he hits me, I'll hit him back.* **3** A2 in reply: *I'm busy at the moment – can I call you back?* ◦ *I wrote to Donna several months ago, but she hasn't written back yet.* **FURTHER AWAY** ▷ **4** B2 further away in distance: *If we push the table back against the wall, we'll have more room.* ◦ *'Keep back!' he shouted, 'Don't come any closer!'* ◦ *He sat back on the sofa.* ◦ *She threw back her head and laughed uproariously.* ◦ *The house is set back* ***from*** *the road.*

IDIOMS **back and forth** C2 moving first in one direction and then in the opposite one: *She swayed gently back and forth to the music.* • **back in the day** used for talking about a time in the past, usually when you are remembering nice things about that time: *Back in the day, we had an apartment with a swimming pool.* • **back to square one** If you are back to square one, you have to start working on a plan from the beginning because your previous attempt failed completely: *If this doesn't work we're back to square one.*

▸**noun** [C] **FURTHEST PART** ▷ **1** A2 the inside or outside part of an object, vehicle, building, etc. that is furthest from the front: *He jotted her name down on the back* ***of*** *an envelope.* ◦ *I found my tennis racket at the back* ***of*** *the cupboard.* ◦ *We sat at the back* ***of*** *the bus.* ◦ *Our seats were right at the back* ***of*** *the hall.* ◦ *Ted was* ***out/round*** *the back (US* ***out*** *back) (= in the area behind the house).'* ◦ *There is a beautiful garden* ***at*** *the back* ***of*** (US also ***in*** *back* ***of***) *(= behind) the house.* ◦ *If there's no reply at the front door, come* ***round*** *the back.* ◦ *He put his jacket on the back* ***of*** *his chair (= the part of the chair that you put your back against when you sit on it).* **2** **back to back a** close together and facing in opposite directions: *The office was full of computers, and we had to sit back to back in long rows.* **b** happening one after another, without interruption → See also **back-to-back** **3** **back to front** C2 UK (US **backwards**) with the back part of something where the front should be: *You've put your jumper on back to front.* **4** **the back of your hand** the side of your hand that has hair growing on it **BODY PART** ▷ **5** A2 the part of your body that is opposite to the front, from your shoulders to your bottom: *I've got a bad back.* ◦ *Sleeping on a bed that is too soft can be bad for your back.* ◦ *He lay* ***on*** *his back, staring at the ceiling.* ◦ *I* ***turned*** *my back (= turned round so that I could not see) while she dressed.* **SPORT** ▷ **6** (in some sports, such as football) one of the players in a team who try to stop players from the other team from scoring goals, rather than trying to score goals themselves → Compare **forward**

IDIOMS **at/in the back of your mind** If something is at/in the back of your mind, you intend to do it, but are not actively thinking about it: *It's been at the back of my mind to call José for several days now, but I haven't got round to it yet.* • **the back of beyond** UK informal a place far away from any big town: *They live in some village* ***in*** *the back of beyond.* • **be on sb's back** informal to criticize someone several times in an annoying way: *She's on my back again about those sales figures – I just haven't had a moment to do them.* • **behind sb's back** C2 If you do something behind someone's back, you do it without them knowing, in a way that is unfair: *I dread to think what they say about me behind my back.* • **sb could do sth with one arm/hand tied behind their back** informal If someone could do something with one arm/hand tied behind their back, they can do it very easily: *Her part in the film wasn't very demanding – she could have played it with one hand tied behind her back.* • **get off sb's back** informal used to tell someone to stop criticizing you: *Why don't you get off my back! I'm doing my best.* • **have your back to/against the wall** to have very serious problems that limit the ways in which you can act: *He owes money to everyone – he's really got his back to the wall now.* • **on the back of sth** soon after an earlier success, and as a result of it: *The advertising agency secured the contract on the back of its previous successful campaigns.* • **on the back of sb/sth** by using or taking advantage of someone or something else: *They have carried on their business operations by* ***riding*** *on the back of established firms.* • **put/get sb's back up** informal to annoy someone: *Just ignore him – he's only trying to put your back up.*

▸**verb** **SUPPORT** ▷ **1** C2 [T] to give support to someone or something with money or words: *The management has refused to back our proposals.* **RISK MONEY** ▷ **2** to risk money by saying that you think a horse, team, etc. will win a race, game, or competition in order to win more money if they do: *The horse I backed came in last.* **MOVE AWAY** ▷ **3** C2 [I or T, + adv/prep] to (cause to) move backwards: *Ann gave up driving when she backed the car* ***into*** *the garage door.* ◦ *Please could you back your car* ***up*** *a few feet so that I can get mine out of the driveway?* **COVER** ▷ **4** [T] to cover the back of something with a material, often to make it stronger or thicker: *The material is backed* ***with*** *a heavy lining.*

IDIOM **back the wrong horse** to make the wrong decision and support a person or action that is later unsuccessful: *In all his years as a book publisher, he rarely backed the wrong horse.*

PHRASAL VERBS **back away 1** to move backwards away from something or someone, usually because you are frightened: *She saw that he had a gun and backed away.* **2** to show that you do not support a plan or idea any longer and do not want to be involved with it: *The government has backed away **from** plans to increase taxes.* • **back down** to admit that you were wrong or that you have been defeated: *Eventually, Roberto backed down and apologized.* ◦ *Local residents have forced the local council to back down **from/on** its plans to build a nightclub on their street.* • **back off** informal **1** to stop being involved in a situation, usually in order to allow other people to deal with it themselves: *She started to criticize me, then she suddenly backed off.* ◦ *Just back off and let us do this on our own, will you?* **2** B2 to move backwards away from someone, usually because you are frightened: *I saw the knife and backed off.* • **back onto sth** If a building backs onto something, its back faces that thing: *The house backs onto a narrow alley.* • **back out** B2 to decide not to do something that you had said you would do: *You agreed to come. You can't back out now!* ◦ *They backed out **of** the deal the day before they were due to sign the contract.* • **back sb up 1** B2 to support or help someone: *My family backed me up throughout the court case.* **2** C2 to say that someone is telling the truth: *Honestly, that's exactly what happened – Claire will back me up.* ◦ *Will you back me up if I say that I never saw him?* • **back sth up** [M often passive] **1** C2 to prove something is true: *His claims are backed up by recent research.* **2** B2 to make an extra copy of computer information: *Make sure you back up your files.* → See also **backup** • **back (sth) up** to drive backwards • **back up** If traffic backs up, the vehicles have to wait in a long line because there are too many of them: *The traffic is starting to back up on the M25.*

►**adj** [before noun] **POSITION** ▷ **1** at or near the back of something: *She left the house by the back **door**.* ◦ *The back **seat** of the car folds down.* **PAID LATER** ▷ **2** paid after the end of a period of time when it should have been paid: *They owe the staff several thousand in back **pay**.* ◦ *back **rent/taxes***

IDIOMS **on the back burner** If something is on the back burner, it is temporarily not being dealt with or considered, especially because it is not urgent or important: *We've all had to **put** our plans on the back burner for a while.* • **take a back seat** to choose not to be in a position of responsibility in an organization or activity

backache /ˈbæk.eɪk/ **noun** [C or U] B1 a pain in your back: *Gardening gives me such backache.*

backbench /ˌbækˈbentʃ/ **noun** [C usually plural] (the seats used by) members of the British Parliament who do not have official positions in the government or in an opposing political party: *The prime minister expects strong support from **the** Labour backbenches.* ◦ *a backbench revolt* → Compare **front bench**

backbencher /ˌbækˈben.tʃəʳ/ US /-tʃɚ/ **noun** [C] **1** a member of the British parliament who does not have any official position in the government or in one of the opposing parties: *The advantage of being a backbencher is that you can speak your mind.* → Compare **frontbencher 2** (also **back-bencher**) Indian English a student who does not work hard or is not successful

backbiting /ˈbækˌbaɪ.tɪŋ/ US /-t̬ɪŋ/ **noun** [U] unpleasant and unkind words that are said about someone who is not there: *A lot of backbiting goes on in our office.*

backboard /ˈbæk.bɔːd/ US /-bɔːrd/ **noun** [C] the board behind the BASKET in a game of BASKETBALL

backbone /ˈbæk.bəʊn/ US /-boʊn/ **noun** **BONES** ▷ **1** [C] the line of bones down the centre of the back that provides support for the body: *She stood with her backbone rigid.* → Synonym **spine** **STRENGTH** ▷ **2 the backbone of sth** the most important part of something, providing support for everything else: *Farming is the backbone of the country's economy.* **3** [U] courage and strength of character: [+ to infinitive] *Will he **have** the backbone **to** tell them what he thinks?*

backbreaking /ˈbækˌbreɪ.kɪŋ/ **adj** needing a lot of hard, physical effort and making you feel extremely tired: *Digging the garden was backbreaking **work**.*

backchat /ˈbæk.tʃæt/ **noun** [U] (US usually ˈ**back** ˌ**talk**) rude remarks made when answering someone in authority: *That's enough backchat! You do as you're told.*

backcomb /ˈbæk.kəʊm/ US /-koʊm/ **verb** [T] UK (US **tease**) to hold your hair away from your head and brush it towards your head with a COMB, in order to make it look thicker

ˈ**back** ˌ**copy** **noun** [C] (also ˈ**back** ˌ**issue**/ˌ**number**) a newspaper or magazine of an earlier date than the one now on sale

backdate /ˌbækˈdeɪt/ US /ˈbæk.deɪt/ **verb** [T] to make something, especially a pay increase, effective from an earlier time: *They got a pay rise in March that was backdated **to** January.* → Compare **predate, postdate**

ˌ**back-**ˈ**door** **adj** [before noun] disapproving relating to something that is done secretly or in a way that is not direct or honest: *The prime minister's proposal was immediately dismissed as a back-door tax increase.*

backdrop /ˈbæk.drɒp/ US /-drɑːp/ **noun** **1** [C] (mainly UK **backcloth** /ˈbæk.klɒθ/ US /-klɑːθ/) a large piece of cloth with buildings, countryside, etc. painted on it, hung at the back of a stage during a performance **2** [S] the view behind something: *The mountains form a dramatic backdrop **to** the little village.* **3** [S] the general situation in which particular events happen: *Their love affair began **against** a backdrop of war.*

-backed /-bækt/ **suffix** **SUPPORTED** ▷ **1** used to form adjectives that describe who is providing support, especially financial support: *government-backed contracts* ◦ *US-backed intervention* **BACK PART** ▷ **2** used to form adjectives that describe what substance or material is at the back of something, or what the back of something is like: *foam-backed carpet* ◦ *high-backed dining chairs*

ˌ**backed** ˈ**up** **adj** [after verb] If traffic is backed up, the vehicles have to wait in a long line because there are too many of them: *The traffic is backed up for six miles on the road to the coast.*

backer /ˈbæk.əʳ/ US /-ɚ/ **noun** [C] someone who gives financial support to something: *We need financial backers **for** the project.*

backfire /ˌbækˈfaɪəʳ/ US /-ˈfaɪr/ **verb** [I] **BAD RESULT** ▷ **1** (of a plan) to have the opposite result from the one you intended: *Her plans to make him jealous backfired **on** her when he went off with her best friend.* **ENGINE** ▷ **2** (of an engine) to make a loud noise as a result of fuel burning too early: *I was woken by the sound of a truck backfiring.*

backgammon /ˈbæk.gæm.ᵊn/ **noun** [U] a game for two people in which you throw DICE and move circular pieces around a special board with a pattern of narrow triangles

background /ˈbæk.graʊnd/ **noun; adj**
▸**noun PICTURE** ▷ **1** B2 [C] the things that can be seen behind the main things or people in a picture: *The artist himself did not paint the backgrounds* ***to*** *his pictures – they were done by his pupils.* ◦ *He has photographed her* ***against*** *lots of different backgrounds.* ◦ *They were filmed* ***against*** *a background* ***of*** *dark fir trees.* ◦ *The book's cover has white lettering* ***on*** *a blue background.* ◦ *The little figure that you can just see* ***in the*** *background* ***of*** *the photograph is me.* → Compare **foreground SOUND** ▷ **2** B2 [S] sounds that can be heard behind other sounds that are louder: *If you listen carefully to this piece of music, you can hear a flute* ***in the*** *background.* ◦ *We couldn't hear what they were saying on the tape – there was too much background* ***noise****.* **SITUATION** ▷ **3** B2 [S or U] the conditions that existed before a particular event happened, and that help to explain why it happened: *These decisions have had to be taken* ***against a*** *background of high unemployment.* ◦ *Can you give me some background* ***on*** *(= information about the conditions that existed before) the situation?* **4 the background** C2 If someone or something is in the background, they are not the main point of attention: *Her worries about her job have* ***faded into*** *the background since she learned about her father's illness.* **FAMILY EXPERIENCE** ▷ **5** B1 [C] your family and your experience of education, living conditions, money, etc.: *The school has pupils* ***from*** *many different ethnic/cultural/religious backgrounds.* ◦ *They* ***come from*** *a privileged/wealthy background.* ◦ *a background* ***in*** *publishing*
▸**adj** [before noun] describes something that is done before, and in preparation for, something else: *Students are expected to do some background reading before the course starts.* ◦ *The book provides background* ***information*** *on the history of the region.*

ˌbackground radiˈation noun [C] specialized RADIATION found naturally on Earth that comes from some soil and rocks, etc. and from outer space

backhand /ˈbæk.hænd/ **noun** [C] (in sports such as tennis) a hit in which the arm is brought across the body with the back of the hand facing the same direction as the hit itself, or the player's ability to perform this hit: *What a wonderful backhand* ***return****!* ◦ *Nadal has one of the finest backhands in the game.* → Compare **forehand**

backhanded /ˌbækˈhæn.dɪd/ **adj** A backhanded remark seems pleasant but may really be a criticism or mean something unkind: *a backhanded* ***compliment***

backhander /ˌbækˈhæn.dəʳ/ (US) /-dɚ/ **noun** [C] informal for **bribe**

backing /ˈbæk.ɪŋ/ **noun SUPPORT** ▷ **1** C2 [U] support, especially money, that someone gives to a person or plan: *If I go ahead with the plan, can I count on your backing?* **MUSIC** ▷ **2** [U] music or singing that is played or performed to support a song or tune, especially a popular one: *a backing* ***track*** ◦ *She sang as part of an all-women backing* (US usually *backup*) ***group****.* **MATERIAL** ▷ **3** [C or U] something put on the back of something else in order to make it stronger or protect it: *It's strong cloth – it might be useful as (a) backing.*

backlash /ˈbæk.læʃ/ **noun** [C] a strong feeling among a group of people in reaction to a change or recent events in society or politics: *the 60s backlash* ***against*** *bourgeois materialism* ◦ *the backlash* ***against*** *feminism*

backless /ˈbæk.ləs/ **adj** (of a dress) not covering most of your back

backlist /ˈbæk.lɪst/ **noun** [C] (a list of) all the books a particular publisher has produced in the past that are still available: *a publisher's backlist*

backlit /ˈbæk.lɪt/ **adj** lit up from behind, especially in order to create a special effect: *His trophies were proudly displayed in a backlit cabinet.*

backlog /ˈbæk.lɒg/ (US) /-lɑːg/ **noun** [C usually singular] a large number of things that you should have done before and must do now: *I've got a huge backlog* ***of*** *work to do.*

backpack /ˈbæk.pæk/ **noun; verb**
▸**noun** [C] (also **rucksack**) a large bag used to carry things on your back, used especially by people who go walking or climbing
▸**verb** [I] to visit places, usually far from your home, carrying your clothes and other things that you need in a backpack: *We backpacked around Thailand.*

backpack

backpacker /ˈbækˌpæk.əʳ/ (US) /-ɚ/ **noun** [C] B1 a person who travels with a backpack

backpacking /ˈbækˌpæk.ɪŋ/ **noun** [U] B1 the activity of visiting places, usually far from your home, carrying your clothes and other things that you need in a backpack: *to go backpacking* ◦ *a backpacking trip/holiday*

ˌback ˈpassage noun [C] UK polite expression for **rectum**

backpedal /ˈbækˌped.əl/, /ˌbækˈped-/ **verb** [I] **(-ll-** or US usually **-l-) BICYCLE** ▷ **1** to move the PEDALS (= parts you operate with your feet) backwards on a bicycle: *Some types of bike have brakes that you operate by backpedalling.* **CHANGE OPINION** ▷ **2** to change an opinion that you had expressed before, or do something different from what you had said you would do: *As soon as I said I thought she was wrong, she started backpedalling.*

ˈback ˌroad noun [C] C1 a small road that does not have much traffic on it

backroom /ˌbækˈruːm/, /-rʊm/ **noun** [C] a room in which work or other activities are done out of public view or secretly: *backroom staff* ◦ *backroom negotiations*

ˈbackroom ˌboys noun [plural] people in an organization whose work is not seen by the public

ˈback ˌsaw noun [C] US for **tenon saw**

ˌback-seat ˈdriver noun [C] a passenger in a car who keeps giving the driver advice that he or she has not asked for: figurative *It is expected that the former prime minister will be a back-seat driver (= have a controlling influence on what happens) in the new government.*

backside /ˈbæk.saɪd/ **noun** [C] informal **BODY** ▷ **1** the part of the body that you sit on: *After cycling for the whole day, my backside was very sore.* → Synonym **bottom BACK PART** ▷ **2** Indian English the back part of something: *On the backside of this building you will find a door.* ◦ *Do not write anything on the backside of your answer book.*

IDIOMS **a boot/kick up the/your backside** slang the act of telling someone forcefully to start doing something more quickly or actively: *She's so lazy – she needs a good boot up the backside.* • **get off your backside** slang to stop being lazy: *Get off your backside and do some work!* • **sit (around) on your backside** slang disapproving to do nothing: *I do all the work, while all you do is sit around on your backside all day.*

backslapping /ˈbækˌslæp.ɪŋ/ **noun** [U] a noisy expression of happiness and positive feelings, usually showing admiration for a shared success: *There was a party after the ceremony where much drinking and backslapping went on.*

backslash /ˈbæk.slæʃ/ **noun** [C] the symbol \ used for separating words or numbers in the names of computer files

backslide /ˈbæk.slaɪd/ **verb** [I] (**backslid**) to go back to doing something bad when you have been doing something good, especially to stop working hard or to fail to do something that you had agreed to do: *My diet was going well but I'm afraid I've been backsliding a bit recently.*

backspace /ˈbæk.speɪs/ **noun** [S] the key that you press on a computer keyboard to move the CURSOR (= symbol showing your place on the screen) to an earlier point • **backspace verb** [I] to use the backspace key: *It's ok – just backspace and type it again.*

backstabber /ˈbækˌstæb.əʳ/ (US) /-ɚ/ **noun** [C] someone who says harmful things about you when you are not there to defend yourself

backstage /bækˈsteɪdʒ/ **adj, adv 1** in the area behind the stage in a theatre, especially the rooms in which actors change their clothes or where equipment is kept: *We went backstage after the show to meet the actors.* ◦ *backstage workers* **2** If something happens backstage, it is not generally known about: *The organizers say it's a fair contest but who knows what goes on backstage?*

backstop /ˈbæk.stɒp/ (US) /-stɑːp/ **noun** [C] **PLAYER** ▷ **1** (in ROUNDERS) a player who stands directly behind the player from the opposing team who is trying to hit the ball, and attempts to catch the ball after it has been thrown if the person does not hit it **2** US informal for **catcher FENCE** ▷ **3** (in baseball) a high fence behind the player hitting the ball, which prevents balls from leaving the playing area if they are not hit or caught

ˈback ˌstory noun [C] the things that have happened to someone before you first see or read about them in a film or story

ˌbackstreet aˈbortion noun [C] UK (US **ˌback-ˌalley aˈbortion**) an illegal and usually dangerous operation to end a pregnancy done by someone who is not medically trained

backstreets /ˈbæk.striːts/ **noun** [plural] the older and poorer areas of a town or city: *She grew up in the backstreets of Bolton.* • **backstreet** /ˈbæk.striːt/ **adj** [before noun]

backstroke /ˈbæk.strəʊk/ (US) /-stroʊk/ **noun** [S or U] a way of swimming in which you lie on your back and move one arm and then the other straight behind you so that they pass the sides of your head, while kicking with your legs: *Can you **do** backstroke?*

ˈback ˌtalk noun [U] US for **backchat**

backtick /ˈbæk.tɪk/ **noun** [C] the symbol ` on a keyboard, used mainly in writing computer programs

ˌback-to-ˈback adj [before noun] **CLOSE TOGETHER** ▷ **1** close together and facing in opposite directions: UK *back-to-back terraced houses* **CONTINUOUS** ▷ **2** happening one after another, without interruption: *Hamilton is celebrating back-to-back victories in the German and British Grands Prix.* → See also **back to back**

backtrack /ˈbæk.træk/ **verb** [I] **GO BACK** ▷ **1** to go back along a path that you have just followed: *We went the wrong way and had to backtrack till we got to the right turning.* **CHANGE OPINION** ▷ **2** to say that you did not mean something you said earlier or say that you have changed your opinion: [+ speech] *'All right,' he backtracked, 'It's possible that I was mistaken.'* ◦ *The officers were forced to backtrack **on** their statements.* ◦ *She refused to backtrack **from** her criticisms of the proposal.*

backup /ˈbæk.ʌp/ **noun 1** (B2) [C or U] (someone or something that provides) support or help, or something that you have arranged in case your main plans, equipment, etc. go wrong: *We're going to need some professional backup for this project.* ◦ *The party is going to be outdoors, so we'll need to organize somewhere as a backup in case it rains.* ◦ *Remember, your colleagues are your backup **system** when things go wrong.* **2** (B2) [C] a copy of information held on a computer that is stored separately from the computer: *Before we leave work each day, we **make** a backup **of** all the records we have entered into the computer that day.* ◦ *The department's backup **disks** are all stored in a different building.* **3** [C] US a player who plays when the person who usually plays is not available: *He's a backup for the Dallas Cowboys.*

ˈbackup ˌsoftware noun [U] computer programs that automatically create copies of the information on a computer system so that it can be stored separately and used to replace the original information if it is damaged or lost

backward /ˈbæk.wəd/ (US) /-wɚd/ **adj; adv**

▸**adj NOT CLEVER/MODERN** ▷ **1** (C2) not advanced: *When he was a child, his teachers thought he was backward (= unable to learn as much as most children).* ◦ *People still think of it as a backward country/region/area (= one without industry or modern machines).* **OPPOSITE DIRECTION** ▷ **2** towards the direction that is the opposite to the one in which you are facing: *She left without a backward **glance**.* • **backwardness** /-nəs/ **noun** [U] *They were accused of backwardness (= very old-fashioned ways) because they had no washing machine.*

IDIOMS **be backward in coming forward** to be shy and not often express wishes or opinions: *I'm sure Matt will tell you what he thinks of the idea – he's not usually backward in coming forward.* • **without (so much as) a backward glance** If you leave without a backward glance, you are completely happy to leave and have no sad feelings about it: *She left the city where she had lived all her life without a backward glance.*

▸**adv** US for **backwards**

ˈbackward-ˌlooking adj disapproving opposed to change or new ideas

backwards /ˈbæk.wədz/ (US) /-wɚdz/ **adv 1** (B1) (US also **backward**) towards the direction that is opposite to the one in which you are facing or opposite to the usual direction: *I walked backwards towards the door.* ◦ *He took **a step** backwards to allow her to pass.* ◦ *He began counting backwards: 'Ten, nine, eight...'* → Compare **forwards 2** returning to older and less effective ways: *The breakdown in negotiations will be seen as **a step** backwards.* **3 backwards and forwards** first in one direction and then in the opposite one: *Paul paced anxiously backwards and forwards.*

IDIOM **bend/lean over backwards** (C1) to try very hard to do something: *I've been bending over backwards trying **to** help you, and this is all the thanks I get!*

backwash /ˈbæk.wɒʃ/ (US) /-wɑːʃ/ **noun WATER** ▷ **1** [U] the backward movement of waves, or the backward movement of water caused by something, such as a boat, passing through it: *The waterskier was caught in the backwash from a motorboat.* **EFFECT** ▷ **2** [S] an effect that is not the direct result of something: *The economic and political backwash **of** the war is still being felt.*

backwater /ˈbæk.wɔː.təʳ/ (US) /-wɑː.t̬ɚ/ **noun** [C] **1** a part of a river where the water does not flow: *We tied the boat up in a quiet backwater overnight.* **2** disapproving a place that is not influenced by new ideas or events that happen in other places and does not change: *He grew up in a rural backwater.* → Compare **jerkwater**

the backwoods /ˈbæk.wʊdz/ **noun** [plural] a place in the countryside that is a long way from any town and in which not many people live: *They spent their childhood **in** the backwoods.*

backyard /ˌbækˈjɑːd/ (US) /-ˈjɑːrd/ **noun** [C] **1** UK a small space surrounded by walls at the back of a house, usually with a hard surface: *The house has a small backyard, surrounded by a high brick wall.* **2** B1 US a space at the back of a house, usually surrounded by a fence, and covered with grass

IDIOM **in your backyard** informal in the area where you live, or in the area of interest or activity which you are involved in or responsible for: *How would you feel about them building a nuclear power station in your backyard?* ◦ *We should take a look at what is happening in our **own** backyard before criticizing what is taking place in other countries.*

bacon /ˈbeɪ.kᵊn/ **noun** [U] B1 meat from the back or sides of a pig, often eaten fried in thin slices: *a bacon sandwich* ◦ *a slice/rasher of bacon* ◦ *bacon and eggs*

bacteria /bækˈtɪə.ri.ə/ (US) /-ˈtɪr.i-/ **noun** plural of **bacterium**

bacterial /bækˈtɪə.ri.ᵊl/ (US) /-ˈtɪr.i-/ **adj** caused by, made from, or relating to bacteria: *a bacterial infection* ◦ *bacterial contamination/growth*

bacteriology /bækˌtɪə.riˈɒl.ə.dʒi/ (US) /-ˌtɪr.iˈɑː.lə-/ **noun** [U] the scientific study of bacteria, especially those that cause disease • **bacteriological** /bækˌtɪə.ri.əˈlɒdʒ.ɪ.kᵊl/ (US) /-ˌtɪr.i.əˈlɑː.dʒɪ-/ **adj** • **bacteriologist** /-dʒɪst/ **noun** [C]

bacterium /bækˈtɪə.ri.əm/ (US) /-ˈtɪr.i-/ **noun** [C usually plural] (plural **bacteria**) C1 a type of very small organism that lives in air, earth, water, plants, and animals, often one that causes disease: *an illness caused by bacteria in drinking water* ◦ *The bacterium Streptococcus pneumoniae causes about a third of some 3,000 annual meningitis cases.*

bad /bæd/ **adj**; **adv**; **noun**

▸**adj** **UNPLEASANT** ▷ **1** A1 (**worse**, **worst**) unpleasant and causing difficulties or harm: *Our holiday was spoiled by bad **weather**.* ◦ *We've just had some very bad **news**.* ◦ *I had a very bad **night** (= did not sleep well) last night.* ◦ *Watch out – he's **in a** bad **mood** (= being unpleasant to everyone).* ◦ *She's just a bad **loser** (= she is unpleasant when she loses).* ◦ *The company has been getting a lot of bad **publicity** (= negative things have been written or said about it) recently.* ◦ *The company's financial situation is **looking** rather bad at the moment.* ◦ *The damage caused by the storm was **nothing like as/nowhere near as** bad (= not as serious) **as** we'd feared it might be.* ◦ *Breathing in other people's cigarette smoke is bad **for** you (= has a harmful effect on your health).* ◦ *This is rather a bad (= not convenient or suitable) time for me to talk. Can I call you back later?* **2 not (too) bad** A2 informal quite good or satisfactory: *'How are things?' 'Not too bad, thanks.'* **3 not bad** informal very good: *He was best in his age group – not bad, eh?* **4 feel bad** B1 to feel ashamed and sorry: *Knowing that I hurt her makes me feel really bad.* ◦ *I feel bad **about** letting them down.* **5 go from bad to worse** If a situation goes from bad to worse, it was difficult and unpleasant, and is becoming even more so: *Things have gone from bad to worse.*

> **!** Common mistake: **bad or badly?**
>
> **Warning:** do not confuse the adjective **bad** with the adverb **badly**:
>
> ~~*The concert was bad organized.*~~
>
> *The concert was badly organized.*
>
> **Bad** is sometimes used in informal US English to mean 'very much':
>
> *I miss him real bad.*

LOW QUALITY ▷ **6** A2 (**worse**, **worst**) of low quality, or not acceptable: *The plumber did a bad job on the repairs.* ◦ *Are the company's current difficulties a result of bad (= harmful) **luck** or bad (= of low quality) judgment?* ◦ *He has some very bad **habits**.* ◦ *In some parts of the world, it is considered bad **manners** to pick up food or cutlery with the left hand.* ◦ *He was sent home from school for bad **behaviour**.* ◦ *That remark was in (rather) bad **taste**, wasn't it?* ◦ *I'm very bad **at** cooking (= cannot do it very well).* **EVIL** ▷ **7** B1 (**worse**, **worst**) (of people or actions) evil or morally unacceptable: *There are a lot of bad people in the world.* ◦ *He's got his faults but he's not a bad person.* **PAINFUL** ▷ **8** C1 (**worse**, **worst**) causing or experiencing pain: *She can't walk up all those steps, not with her bad leg!* ◦ *a bad cough* **DECAYED** ▷ **9** B2 harmful to eat because of being decayed: *We'd better eat this chicken before it **goes** bad.* • **badness** /ˈbæd.nəs/ **noun** [U] the quality of being evil or morally unacceptable: *There is goodness and badness in everyone.*

IDIOMS **be in a bad way** UK to be ill, unhappy, or in a bad state: *She was thin and tired-looking and generally in a bad way.* ◦ *After five years of war, the country was in a bad way.* • **give sth up as a bad job** UK to stop doing something because you do not feel it is worth continuing: *After three attempts to mend it, I gave it up as a bad job.*

▸**adv** US informal for badly (= very much): *He needs the money real bad.* ◦ *My arm hurts so bad.*

IDIOM **have got it bad** informal to be very much in love

▸**noun** [U] things or events that are not good or that are morally wrong: *She only ever sees the bad in people.*

IDIOMS **go to the bad** to become a morally bad person: *She thought her children would go to the bad unless they were strictly brought up.* • **my bad** US informal used for saying that you accept that you are wrong or that something is your fault: *'You brought the wrong book.' 'Okay, my bad. I'll go get it.'* • **take the bad with the good** to accept all the features or parts of something, good and bad: *You have to take the bad with the good in any career.* • **to the bad** UK having lost or spent a particular amount of money as a result of something: *He ended the day £50 to the bad.*

ˌbad ˈblood **noun** [U] feelings of hate between people because of arguments in the past: *There has been bad blood **between** the two families for years.*

ˌbad ˈbreath **noun** [U] breath that smells unpleasant

ˌbad ˈdebt **noun** [C or U] (a) debt that is not likely to be paid

baddy /ˈbæd.i/ **noun** [C] (also **baddie**) mainly UK informal a bad person in a film, book, etc.: *In the old cowboy films, the baddies always get beaten in the end.*

bade /bæd/ **verb** past simple of **bid**

ˌbad ˈfaith noun [U] dishonest or unacceptable behaviour: *They **acted in** bad faith by selling her a car that they knew to be faulty.*

ˌbad-ˈfaith adj [before noun] mainly US done in a dishonest way with the intention of tricking someone: *There are laws prohibiting bad-faith conduct by insurers.* → Compare **good-faith**

ˌbad ˈfeeling noun [U] **bad blood**

badge /bædʒ/ noun [C] B2 a small piece of metal, plastic, cloth, etc., with words or a picture on it, that is fastened or sewn to your clothing, often to show your support for a political organization or belief, or your rank, or that you are a member of a group, etc.: *Everyone at the conference wore a badge with their name on.*

IDIOM **be a badge of sth** to be something that shows that you have achieved a particular thing: *For Tony, owning a big car was a badge of **success**.*

badger /ˈbædʒ.əʳ/ US /-ɚ/ noun; verb

badger

▸noun [C] an animal with greyish-brown fur, a black and white head and a pointed face, that lives underground and comes out to feed at night
▸verb [T] to persuade someone by telling them repeatedly to do something, or to question someone repeatedly: *Stop badgering me – I'll do it when I'm ready.* ◦ [+ into + -ing verb] *She's been badgering me **into doing** some exercise.* ◦ [+ to infinitive] *Every time we go into a shop, the kids badger me **to** buy them sweets.*

ˌbad ˈhair ˌday noun [C] informal a day when you feel that you do not look attractive, especially because of your hair, and everything seems to go wrong: *I'm **having** a bad hair day.*

badinage /ˈbæd.ɪ.nɑːʒ/ noun [U] literary conversation or remarks that are joking and not serious → Synonym **banter**

badlands /ˈbæd.lændz/ noun [plural] a dry area without plants and with large rocks that the weather has worn into strange shapes, especially the area like this in Dakota and Nebraska in the US

ˌbad ˈlanguage noun [U] words that are considered offensive by most people: *There's far too much bad language on television.*

ˌbad ˈlot noun [C usually singular] UK old-fashioned a bad and unpleasant person: *He's not a bad lot – just a bit wild.*

badly /ˈbæd.li/ adv (**worse, worst**) **UNPLEASANTLY** ▷ **1** A2 in a severe and harmful way: *She was badly affected by the events in her childhood.* ◦ *Fortunately, none of the passengers was badly **hurt/injured** in the crash.* ◦ *I thought he was **treated** very badly.* **IN A BAD WAY** ▷ **2** A2 in a way that is not acceptable or of good quality: *The event was very badly organized.* ◦ *I thought he behaved very badly.* ◦ *Their children are extremely badly **behaved**.* **VERY MUCH** ▷ **3** A2 very much: *He needs the money really badly.* ◦ *They are badly **in need of** help.*

ˌbadly ˈoff adj (**worse off, worst off**) having little money and few of the things you need to live: *They're not badly off but they don't have much money to spare.*

badminton /ˈbæd.mɪn.tᵊn/ noun [U] A2 a sport in which two or four people hit a SHUTTLECOCK (= a light object with feathers) over a high net

ˈbad-mouth verb [T] informal to criticize someone or something in a very unpleasant manner: *Stop bad-mouthing him all the time.*

ˌbad-ˈtempered adj B2 describes a person who becomes angry and annoyed easily: *She's very bad-tempered in the mornings!*

> **Other ways of saying bad-tempered**
>
> See also: **angry**
>
> **Irritable** is an alternative way of saying 'bad-tempered':
>
> *Be careful what you say; he's very **irritable** today.*
>
> **Grumpy** and **cranky** (US) are informal ways of saying 'bad-tempered':
>
> *I'm just a little tired and **grumpy** today.*
>
> *She's very **cranky** because she has a toothache.*
>
> **Short-tempered** is a more formal way of saying 'bad-tempered':
>
> *I found her to be rather **short-tempered**.*
>
> People who are bad-tempered because they argue and complain a lot could be described as **cantankerous**:
>
> *He's getting a bit **cantankerous** in his old age.*
>
> **Petulant** can be used when someone is bad-tempered and complains in a childish and rude way:
>
> *She can be very **petulant** at times.*
>
> If someone is bad-tempered and seems rude and unfriendly, you could use the word **surly**:
>
> *We were served by a very **surly** waiter.*

baffle /ˈbæf.l/ verb [T] to cause someone to be completely unable to understand or explain something: *She was **completely** baffled **by** his strange behaviour.* • **bafflement** /-mənt/ noun [U] • **baffling** /ˈbæf.lɪŋ/ adj *I found what he was saying completely baffling.*

bag /bæg/ noun; verb

▸noun [C] **CONTAINER** ▷ **1** A1 a soft container made out of paper or thin plastic, or a stronger container made of leather, plastic, or other material, usually with a handle, in which you carry personal things or clothes or other things that you need for travelling: *a paper/plastic bag* ◦ *a shopping bag (= a bag in which shopping is carried)* ◦ *a bag **of** apples/nuts* ◦ *Don't eat that whole bag **of** (= the amount the bag contains) sweets at once.* ◦ *I hadn't even **packed** my bags (= put the things I need in cases/bags).* **2 bags under your eyes** dark, loose, or swollen skin under your eyes because of tiredness or old age **WOMAN** ▷ **3** slang a rude and insulting name for a woman, especially an older one: *Silly **old** bag!* **TROUSERS** ▷ **4 bags** UK old-fashioned trousers with a wide and loose style: *Oxford bags*

IDIOMS **bags of sth** mainly UK informal a lot of something: *Come and stay with us – we've got bags of room.* ◦ *Don't panic, there's bags of time yet.* • **be sb's bag** old-fashioned slang If something is your bag, you are interested in it and do it for pleasure: *Tennis isn't really my bag, I'm afraid.* • **be in the bag** informal If something is in the bag, you are certain to get it or to achieve it: *Once we'd scored the third goal, the match was pretty much in the bag.*

▸verb (**-gg-**) **GET** ▷ **1** [T] informal to get something before other people have a chance to take it: [+ two objects] *Bag us some decent seats/Bag some decent seats **for** us if you get there first, won't you?* → See also **bagsy** **WIN PRIZE** ▷ **2** [T] UK informal to win sth, especially a prize: *He's the bookies' favourite to bag an Oscar.* ◦ *He is eager to bag his fifth victory of the season.* **KILL** ▷ **3** [T] to hunt and kill an animal or bird **CRITICIZE** ▷ **4** [T] Australian

English informal to criticize or laugh at someone or something in an unkind way: *Stop bagging her (**out**) – she's doing her best.* **PUT IN CONTAINER** ▷ **5** [T] to put something in a bag: *Shall I bag (**up**) those tomatoes for you?* **HANG LOOSELY** ▷ **6** [I] to hang loosely like a bag: *I hate these trousers – they bag (**out**) at the back.*

IDIOM **bags I...** UK informal used when you claim the right to have something or do something: *Bags I sit in the front seat! (= I said I wanted to do it first, so I should do it, not you.)*

bagatelle /ˌbæg.əˈtel/ noun **SMALL AMOUNT** ▷ **1** [C usually singular] literary something, especially an amount of money, that is small and not important: *A thousand pounds is **a mere** bagatelle **to** him.* **GAME** ▷ **2** [U] a game in which small balls are hit, usually by a small rod on a spring that the player pulls, towards holes that have numbers on a board with a rounded end

bagel /ˈbeɪ.gəl/ noun [C] a type of bread that is small, hard, and in the shape of a ring: *an onion bagel*

bagful /ˈbæg.fʊl/ noun [C] the amount that a bag contains: *a bagful of shoes/socks/shirts*

baggage /ˈbæg.ɪdʒ/ noun [U] **BAGS** ▷ **1** B1 all the cases and bags that you take with you when you travel: *How many **pieces of** baggage do you have?* ◦ *We had to pay extra for our **excess** baggage (= our bags and cases that weighed more than was allowed).* → Synonym **luggage** **FEELINGS** ▷ **2** C2 the beliefs and feelings that influence how you think and behave: *We all **carry** a lot of **emotional** baggage around with us.*

ˈbaggage alˌlowance noun [C usually singular] the weight or number of cases and bags that you are allowed to take onto an aircraft without paying extra

ˈbaggage ˌcar noun [C] US for **luggage van**

ˈbaggage ˌhandler noun [C] a person who takes passengers' bags and cases and puts them onto or removes them from an aircraft

ˈbaggage ˌroom noun [C usually singular] US for **left-luggage office**

baggy /ˈbæg.i/ adj (of clothes) hanging loosely because of being too big or having been stretched: *baggy trousers*

ˈbag ˌlady noun [C] a woman who has no home and carries everything that she owns around with her in bags

bagpipes /ˈbæg.paɪps/ noun [plural] (also **pipes**) a type of musical instrument, played especially in Scotland and Ireland, from which you produce sound by blowing air into a leather bag and forcing it out through pipes • **bagpipe** /-paɪp/ adj [before noun] *bagpipe music*

bagsy /bæg.zi/ verb [T] UK child's word to claim the right to have or do something because you said you wanted it first: *I bagsied the best seat before anyone else arrived.*

baguette /bægˈet/ noun [C] (UK also ˌ**French** ˈ**stick**) **1** a long, thin stick of white bread, of a type that originally came from France **2** a baguette, or part of a baguette, that is filled with cold food such as meat, cheese, or salad, and eaten as a SANDWICH: *a ham and cheese baguette*

bah /bɑː/ exclamation old-fashioned an expression of anger or disapproval

baht /bɑːt/ noun [C] (plural **baht**) the standard unit of money used in Thailand

bail /beɪl/ noun; verb

▸noun **MONEY** ▷ **1** [U] an amount of money that a person who has been accused of a crime pays to a law court so that they can be released until their trial. The payment is a way of making certain that the person will return to court for trial: *He was **released/remanded on** bail (**of** $100,000).* ◦ *Because of a previous conviction, the judge refused to **grant** bail (= allow the accused person to be released).* ◦ *Her parents have agreed to **put up/stand** (US **post**) (= pay) bail **for** her.* **CRICKET** ▷ **2 bails** [plural] the two small pieces of wood on top of the STUMPS in a game of cricket, that can be knocked off with the ball to make the player who is BATTING (= hitting the ball) out

▸verb **REMOVE WATER** ▷ **1** (UK also **bale**) [I] to remove water from a boat using a container: *The boat's sinking! Start bailing quickly!* **MONEY** ▷ **2** [T] If someone accused of a crime is bailed, they are released until their trial after paying bail to the court: *She was yesterday bailed for three weeks on drink-driving offences.* ◦ [+ to infinitive] *He was bailed **to** appear at the Magistrates' Court next month.*

PHRASAL VERBS **bail out** (UK also **bale out**) **JUMP** ▷ **1** to jump out of an aircraft with a PARACHUTE because the aircraft is going to have an accident: *The plane's engine failed and the pilot was forced to bail out.* **STOP** ▷ **2** mainly US to stop doing or being involved with something: *The actor has bailed out **of** the film after only three weeks' shooting.* • **bail sb out** to pay money to a court so that someone can be released from prison until their trial • **bail sb/sth out** (UK also **bale sb/sth out**) to help a person or organization that is in difficulty, usually by giving or lending them money: *She keeps running up huge debts and asking friends to bail her out.* • **bail sth out** (UK also **bale sth out**) to remove water from the bottom of a boat

bailiff /ˈbeɪ.lɪf/ noun [C] **1** (in the UK) an official who takes away someone's possessions when they owe money: *They didn't pay their rent, so the landlord **called/sent in** the bailiffs.* **2** (in the US) an official who is responsible for prisoners who are appearing in court **3** (in the UK) a person whose job is to take care of someone else's land or property

bailout /ˈbeɪl.aʊt/ noun [C usually singular] the act of helping a person or organization that is in difficulty, usually by giving or lending them or it money: *Three years of huge losses forced the bank to seek a **government** bailout.* ◦ *The administration assembled the $50 billion emergency bailout **package** to ease a financial crisis in Mexico.*

bairn /beən/ US /bern/ noun [C] Scottish English or Northern English a child

bait /beɪt/ noun; verb

▸noun **FISH/ANIMAL** ▷ **1** [U] a small amount of food on a HOOK (= curved piece of wire) or in a special device used to attract and catch a fish or animal: *They were digging up worms to use for bait.* ◦ *We put down some poisoned bait to kill the rats.* **OFFER** ▷ **2** [C or U] something that is said or offered to people in order to make them react in a particular way: *Free holidays were **offered as** (**a**) bait **to** customers.* ◦ *I told my sister I'd lend her my new shirt if she let me borrow her jacket, but she didn't **take** the bait.*

▸verb [T] **MAKE ANGRY** ▷ **1** to intentionally make a person angry by saying or doing things to annoy them: *Ignore him – he's just baiting you.* **DOG** ▷ **2** to make dogs attack an animal for cruel entertainment: *In the past, **bear**-baiting was a common form of entertainment in the UK .* **FISH/ANIMAL** ▷ **3** to put food on a HOOK (= curved piece of wire) or in a special device to attract and catch a fish or animal: *Have you got any stale cheese that I can bait the mousetrap **with**?*

baize /beɪz/ noun [U] thick, usually green material

made from wool and used to cover the special tables on which SNOOKER, BILLIARDS, and card games are played

bak written abbreviation for back at the keyboard: used when you return to a discussion in an internet CHAT ROOM after you have left it for a short time

bake /beɪk/ verb **1** A2 [I or T] to cook inside a cooker, without using added liquid or fat: *I made the icing while the cake was baking.* ◦ *a baked potato* ◦ *freshly baked bread* ◦ *Bake* ***at*** *180°C for about 20 minutes.* ◦ *Bake* ***for*** *5–7 minutes in a preheated oven.* ◦ *a baking dish/tin/tray* **2** [I or T] to make something such as earth or clay hard by heating it, usually in order to make bricks **3** [I] informal to be or become very hot: ***It's*** *baking outside.* ◦ *You'll bake in that fleece jacket!*

ˌbaked ˈbeans noun [plural] beans that have been cooked in tomato sauce, sugar, and spices, usually sold in TINS

ˌbaked poˈtato noun [C] (UK also **ˌjacket poˈtato**) a potato baked whole with its skin

Bakelite /ˈbeɪ.kə.laɪt/ noun [U] trademark a type of hard plastic used especially in the past: *a 1940s Bakelite radio*

baker /ˈbeɪ.kəʳ/ US /-kɚ/ noun [C] **1** B1 a person whose job is to make bread and cakes for sale, or to sell bread and cakes **2** (UK also **baker's**) a shop where bread and cakes are sold and sometimes made

ˌbaker's ˈdozen noun [S] old-fashioned 13

bakery /ˈbeɪ.kᵊr.i/ US /-kɚ.i/ noun [C] B2 a place where bread and cakes are made and sometimes sold

ˈbaking ˌpowder noun [U] a mixture of powders used to make cakes rise and become light when they are baked

ˈbaking ˌsheet noun [C] a flat metal dish used to cook things in an oven

ˈbaking ˌsoda noun [U] **1** a mixture of powders used to make cakes rise and become light when they are baked **2** mainly US for **bicarbonate of soda**

bakkie /ˈbæk.i/ noun [C] South African English a small vehicle with an open part at the back in which goods can be carried → See also **pickup truck**

baksheesh /bækˈʃiːʃ/ noun [U] informal (especially in some Asian countries) a small amount of money or a present that is given to someone as a BRIBE, to persuade them to do something, sometimes something dishonest

balaclava /ˌbæl.əˈklɑː.və/ noun [C] a closely fitting covering for the head and neck, usually made from wool

balalaika /ˌbæl.əˈlaɪ.kə/ noun [C] a type of musical instrument with a three-sided body and three strings, played especially in Russia

balance /ˈbæl.ᵊns/ noun; verb

▸noun **EQUAL STATE** ▷ **1** B2 [S or U] a state where things are of equal weight or force: *The toddler wobbled and* ***lost*** *his balance (= started to fall sideways).* ◦ *She had to hold onto the railings to* ***keep*** *her balance (= to stop herself from falling).* ◦ *New tax measures are designed to* ***redress*** *the balance (= make the situation more equal) between rich and poor.* ◦ *We must* ***strike a*** *balance* ***between*** *reckless spending* ***and*** *penny-pinching (= try to have something between these two things).* → Synonym **equilibrium** **2** [U] The balance on a piece of electronic equipment for playing music is the particular mixture of different sounds, or the device that controls this. **3 on balance** B2 after thinking about all the different facts or opinions: *I would say that, on balance, it hasn't been a bad year.* **WEIGHING MACHINE** ▷ **4** [C] a device used for weighing things, consisting of two dishes hanging on a bar that shows when the contents of both dishes weigh the same **MONEY** ▷ **5** B2 [C usually singular] the amount of money you have in a bank account, or the amount of something that you have left after you have spent or used up the rest: *Once we know how much money we'll need, let's spend the balance (= the amount left).* ◦ *The company's success is reflected in its healthy* ***bank*** *balance.* **6** [U] Indian English the money that is returned to someone who has paid for something that costs less than the amount that they gave → See also **change**

> **Word partners for balance noun (EQUAL)**
> *keep/redress/restore* the balance • *find/get/maintain/strike* a balance (between sth and sth) • *alter/change/shift/upset* the balance • *keep/lose* your balance • *knock/push/throw* sb/sth off balance • a *careful/delicate/fine* balance • *in/out of* balance

IDIOM **in the balance** C2 If a situation is in the balance, it has reached a stage where it will soon be decided one way or another: *The game* ***hung*** *in the balance until the last minute when an exciting point decided it.*

▸verb **1** B2 [I or T] to be in a position where you will stand without falling to either side, or to put something in this position: *The flamingos balanced gracefully* ***on*** *one leg.* ◦ *She balanced a huge pot effortlessly* ***on*** *her head and walked down to the river.* **2** B2 [T] to give several things equal amounts of importance, time, or money so that a situation is successful: *I struggle to balance work and family commitments.* **3** [T] to arrange a system that relates to money so that the amount of money spent is not more than the amount received: *Stringent measures were introduced so that the government could balance its* ***budget/the economy.*** **4 balance the books** to make certain that the amount of money spent is not more than the amount of money received: *If the business loses any more money, we won't be able to balance the books this year.*

PHRASAL VERBS **balance sth against sth** to compare the advantages and disadvantages of something: *The ecological effects of the factory need to be balanced against the employment it generates.* • **balance (sth) out/up** to be equal in amount or value, or to make things equal in amount or value: *I spend a lot one month and not so much the next and in the end it balances out.* ◦ *We'd better ask a few men to the party to balance up the numbers.*

balanced /ˈbæl.ᵊnst/ adj **1** B2 considering all sides or opinions equally: *The news programme prided itself on its balanced reporting.* **2** containing an equal amount or number of similar things or people: *The committee is* ***evenly*** *balanced, with six members from each party.* → See also **well balanced**

ˌbalanced ˈdiet noun [C] a combination of the correct types and amounts of food: *If you have a balanced diet, you are getting all the vitamins you need.*

ˌbalance of ˈpayments noun [S] (also **ˌbalance of ˈtrade**) the difference between the money that a country receives from EXPORTS and the money that it spends on IMPORTS

ˌbalance of ˈpower noun [S] a position in which both or all of the groups or people involved, usually in a political situation, have equal power: *Both*

*countries have a vested interest in **maintaining** the balance of power.*

IDIOM **hold the balance of power** to be able to support either opposing side in a competition, etc. and therefore be able to decide who will win: *If the independents do end up holding the balance of power, then they decide whether Labor or the Liberals govern the state for the next four years.*

ˈbalance ˌsheet noun [C] a statement that shows the value of a company's ASSETS (= things of positive value) and its debts

ˈbalancing ˌact noun [C usually singular] a situation in which a person tries to give care and attention to two or more activities at the same time: *I found myself having to do a balancing act **between** work and family.*

balcony /ˈbæl.kə.ni/ noun [C] **ON BUILDING** ▷ **1** B1 an area with a wall or bars around it that is joined to the outside wall of a building on an upper level: *We had drinks on the hotel balcony.* **IN THEATRE** ▷ **2** C2 an area of seats at an upper level in a theatre: *Our seats are in row F of the balcony.*

bald /bɔːld/ US /bɑːld/ adj **NO HAIR** ▷ **1** B1 with little or no hair on the head: *At 20 he was already **going** bald.* **2 as bald as a coot** UK informal (US **as bald as a cue ball**) completely bald **PLAIN** ▷ **3** basic and with no unnecessary words or detail: *There was just this bald **statement** of resignation – no explanation or anything.* **SMOOTH** ▷ **4** a bald tyre is one that has worn away to become very smooth and is therefore dangerous: *The tyre was completely bald.* • **baldness** /ˈbɔːld.nəs/ US /ˈbɑːld-/ noun [U] *He suffered from premature baldness, losing his hair in his twenties.* ◦ *The baldness of her question shocked him.*

bald

ˌbald ˈeagle noun [C] a large North American EAGLE with a white head, used as a symbol of the US

balderdash /ˈbɔːl.də.dæʃ/ US /ˈbɑːl.də-/ noun [U], exclamation old-fashioned something that is stupid or not true: *'Balderdash!' he spluttered indignantly.* → Synonym **nonsense**

ˈbald-faced adj [before noun] mainly US (US also **ˈboldfaced**) showing no shame or embarrassment about doing something bad: *a bald-faced **lie***

balding /ˈbɔːl.dɪŋ/ US /ˈbɑːl-/ adj becoming BALD: *Eammon was plump and balding.*

baldly /ˈbɔːld.li/ US /ˈbɑːld-/ adv in plain or basic language, without unnecessary words or details: *To put it baldly, I can't afford to take the risk.*

ˈbald ˌpatch noun [C] UK (US **ˈbald ˌspot**) an area of a person's head that has no hair: *He tries to hide his bald patch by brushing his hair across it.*

baldy (also **baldie**) /ˈbɔːl.di/ US /ˈbɑːl-/ noun [C] humorous an unkind name for someone who has lost or is losing the hair on their head: *'Hey, baldy!'*

bale /beɪl/ noun; verb
▸noun [C] a large amount of something such as HAY, paper, wool, or cloth that has been tied tightly together
▸verb **REMOVE WATER** ▷ **1** mainly UK to **bail TIE UP** ▷ **2** [I or T] to tie up something tightly into bales: *We were baling (**up**) the hay all day.*

PHRASAL VERB **bale out** UK for **bail sb/sth out**

baleful /ˈbeɪl.fəl/ adj literary threatening to do something bad or to hurt someone: *He gave me a baleful look.* ◦ *his baleful influence* • **balefully** /-i/ adv *She glared balefully at me.*

balk /bɔːk/ US /bɑːlk/ verb; noun
▸verb [I] (UK also **baulk**) to be unwilling to do something or to allow something to happen: *I balked **at** the prospect of spending four hours on a train with him.*
▸noun [C] (UK also **baulk**) a rough, thick piece of wood

the ˈBalkans noun [plural] a region in southeast Europe between the Mediterranean Sea and the Black Sea

ball /bɔːl/ US /bɑːl/ noun [C] **ROUND OBJECT** ▷ **1** A1 any object in the shape of a SPHERE, especially one used as a toy by children or in various sports such as tennis and football: *a beach/golf/tennis ball* ◦ *Just try to concentrate on **hitting** the ball.* ◦ *The kitten **curled** itself **into a** ball (= the shape of a ball).* **2** A1 a long piece of thread that has been rolled into a ball: *a ball of string/wool* **3** the rounded part of your foot or thumb where the toes join the foot and the thumb joins the hand **DANCE** ▷ **4** a large formal occasion where people dance: *Did you go to the Summer Ball last year?*

IDIOMS **the ball is in sb's court** If the ball is in someone's court, they have to do something before any progress can be made in a situation: *It's up to you what to do – the ball is in your court now.* • **be on the ball** C1 to be quick to understand and react to things: *I didn't sleep well last night and I'm not really on the ball today.* • **have a ball** informal to enjoy yourself very much: *'So how was the party last night?' 'Oh, it was brilliant, – we had a ball!'* • **start/set/get the ball rolling** C2 to do something that starts an activity, or to start doing something in order to encourage other people to do the same: *I decided to set the ball rolling and got up to dance.*

ballad /ˈbæl.əd/ noun [C] a song or poem that tells a story, or (in popular music) a slow love song

ˌball-and-ˈsocket joint noun [C] specialized a JOINT (= place where two bones are connected) consisting of a round end and a hollow SOCKET that fit together and move easily: *The hip joint is a ball-and-socket joint.*

ballast /ˈbæl.əst/ noun [U] heavy matter such as sand or stone that is used at the bottom of a ship or a HOT-AIR BALLOON to make it heavier, or the small stones on which railways and roads are made

ˌball ˈbearing noun [C] a small metal ball or several of these arranged in a ring to make particular parts of a machine move more easily

ˈball ˌboy/ˌgirl noun [C] a boy/girl who picks up balls during a tennis competition and gives them back to the players

ballcock /ˈbɔːl.kɒk/ US /ˈbɑːl.kɑːk/ noun [C] a device in a water TANK that controls the level of water, consisting of a floating ball fixed to a rod

ballerina /ˌbæl.əˈriː.nə/ noun [C] a female ballet dancer

ballet /ˈbæl.eɪ/ US /bælˈeɪ/ noun [C or U] B1 a type of dancing where carefully organized movements tell a story or express an idea, or a theatre work that uses this type of dancing: *a ballet **dancer*** ◦ *By the age of 15 he had already composed his first ballet (= music for a ballet).* • **balletic** /bəˈlet.ɪk/ US /-ˈlet̬-/ adj *balletic movements*

ˈballet ˌshoe noun [C] (also **ˈballet ˌpump**) a type of soft, flat shoe worn by ballet dancers

B

ballgame /ˈbɔːl.geɪm/ (US) /bɑːl-/ **noun** [C] mainly US a baseball match

IDIOM **a whole new ballgame** a completely different situation, often one that is difficult or that you know little about: *We'd done a lot of climbing in Scotland but the Himalayas were a whole new ballgame.*

ballgown /ˈbɔːl.gaʊn/ (US) /ˈbɑːl-/ **noun** [C] a formal dress that is often made from an expensive material and usually has a long skirt

ballistic /bəˈlɪs.tɪk/ **adj** informal **1 go ballistic** to become extremely angry: *If your dad finds out you've been skipping school, he'll go ballistic.* **2** connected with ballistics

balˌlistic ˈmissile **noun** [C] a MISSILE (= flying weapon) that has power in order to direct it on its flight, but that continues and falls towards its target without power

ballistics /bəˈlɪs.tɪks/ **noun** [U] the study of objects that are shot or thrown through the air, such as a bullet from a gun

balloon /bəˈluːn/ **noun; verb**

▸**noun** [C] **1** A2 a small, very thin rubber bag that you blow air into or fill with a light gas until it is round in shape, used for decoration at parties or as a children's toy **2** (also **hot-ˈair balˌloon**) a very large balloon that is filled with hot air or gas and can carry people in a BASKET (= open container) hanging under it **3** a **speech bubble**

IDIOM **the balloon goes up** If the balloon goes up, a situation suddenly becomes very serious or unpleasant: *The balloon went up last Friday when the scandal became public.*

▸**verb** [I] **1** to get bigger and rounder: *I ballooned when I was pregnant with my second baby.* **2** to quickly increase in size, weight, or importance: *The rumours soon ballooned **into** a full-blown scandal.*

balloonist /bəˈluː.nɪst/ **noun** [C] a person who takes part in the sport of travelling by balloon: *He's a keen balloonist.*

ballot /ˈbæl.ət/ **noun; verb**

▸**noun** **1** [C or U] a system or occasion of secret voting: *Representatives were elected **by** ballot.* ◦ *They decided to **hold a** ballot.* **2** [C] (also **ˈballot ˌpaper**) a piece of paper on which you write your vote **3 put sth to the ballot** to vote secretly on a particular matter: *OK, this seems to be an area of disagreement, so let's put it to the ballot.*

▸**verb** [T] to organize a secret vote by a group of people in order to find out their views: *The union decided to ballot its members on the issue.*

ˈballot ˌrigging **noun** [U] the practice of using illegal methods to obtain a particular result in an election: *Rumours of ballot rigging discouraged many from voting.*

ballpark /ˈbɔːl.pɑːk/ (US) /ˈbɑːl.pɑːrk/ **noun; adj**

▸**noun** [C] US a place where ball games, especially baseball games, are played

IDIOMS **be in the same ballpark** to be of a similar amount or cost: *Jamie makes over two hundred thousand dollars and I don't know how much Tom makes, but I guess it's in the same ballpark.* • **be in the (right) ballpark** to be close to the right amount: *'And do you think the projected sales figures are realistic?' 'They're in the right ballpark.'*

▸**adj** [before noun] US A ballpark estimate or FIGURE is a number that is a guess, but one that you believe is near the correct number: *We'll have to go away and cost this carefully, but as a ballpark **figure** I'd say that it'll be about two million dollars.*

ballpoint /ˈbɔːl.pɔɪnt/ (US) /ˈbɑːl-/ **noun** [C] (also **ˌballpoint ˈpen**) a pen with a small metal ball at the end that puts ink on the paper: *We aren't allowed to write **in** ballpoint at school.*

ballroom /ˈbɔːl.rʊm/, /-ruːm/ (US) /ˈbɑːl-/ **noun** [C] a large room that is used for dancing

ˌballroom ˈdancing **noun** [U] a type of dancing where two people dance together using steps and movements to special music, such as the WALTZ or TANGO

balls /bɔːlz/ (US) /bɑːlz/ **noun; verb**

▸**noun** [plural] offensive **BODY** ▷ **1 testicle**: *She fought off her attacker by kicking him in the balls.* **NONSENSE** ▷ **2** complete nonsense: *What he said was **a load of** balls.* ◦ *'All men are pigs.' 'Balls! (= I completely disagree!)'* **COURAGE** ▷ **3** courage and confidence: *You have to admit it – the woman's **got** balls!*

IDIOM **have sb by the balls** offensive to have someone in a situation where you have complete power over them

▸**verb**

PHRASAL VERB **balls (sth) up** UK offensive to spoil something by making a mistake or doing something stupid: *Trust me to balls up the interview!*

ˈballs-up **noun** [C usually singular] UK offensive something that is done wrong or badly: *The whole trip was a complete balls-up.*

ballsy /ˈbɔːl.zi/ (US) /ˈbɑːl-/ **adj** US informal brave and determined: *She's one ballsy lady!*

ballyhoo /ˌbæl.ɪˈhuː/ (US) /ˈbæl.ɪ.hu/ **noun** [U] old-fashioned slang a lot of noise and activity, often with no real purpose: *I can't see what all this ballyhoo is about.*

balm /bɑːm/ **noun** [C or U] **OIL** ▷ **1** an oil that comes from particular tropical trees and is used especially to treat injuries or reduce pain: *a new skin balm* → See also **lip balm** **COMFORT** ▷ **2** something that gives comfort: *Her gentle words were a balm **to** me.*

balmy /ˈbɑː.mi/ **adj** (of weather) pleasantly warm: *a balmy summer **evening***

baloney /bəˈləʊ.ni/ (US) /-ˈloʊ-/ **noun** **NONSENSE** ▷ **1** [U] informal nonsense: *That's **a load of** baloney if you ask me.* **SAUSAGE** ▷ **2** [C or U] US a smoked sausage, sliced and eaten cold

balsa (wood) /ˈbɒl.səˌwʊd/ (US) /ˈbɑːl-/ **noun** [U] very light wood that is soft and easily cut, sometimes used in making models of aircraft, etc.

balsam /ˈbɒl.səm/ (US) /ˈbɑːl-/ **noun** [C or U] a pleasant-smelling substance used as the base for medical or beauty treatments: *a balsam shampoo*

balsamic vinegar /bɔːlˌsæm.ɪkˈvɪn.ɪ.gər/ (US) /-gə/ **noun** [U] a type of sweet, dark Italian VINEGAR made from GRAPES in a traditional way

balti /ˈbɒl.ti/ (US) /ˈboʊl-/ **noun** [C or U] spicy food from South Asia that is cooked and served in a metal dish and eaten with bread

balustrade /ˌbæl.əˈstreɪd/ (US) /ˈbæl.ə.streɪd/ **noun** [C] a RAILING or wall to prevent people from falling over the edge of stairs, a BALCONY, etc.

bamboo /bæmˈbuː/ **noun** [U or C] a tall tropical grass with hard, hollow stems, or the stems of this plant: *Use bamboo **canes** to support tomato plants.*

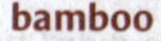

bamboozle /bæmˈbuː.zl/ verb [T] informal to trick or deceive someone, often by confusing them: *She was bamboozled* ***into*** *tell****ing*** *them her credit card number.*

ban /bæn/ verb; noun

▸verb [T usually passive] (**-nn-**) B2 to FORBID (= refuse to allow) something, especially officially: *The film was banned (= the government prevented it from being shown) in several countries.* ◦ [+ from + -ing verb] *She was banned* ***from*** *driv****ing*** *for two years.*

▸noun [C] B2 an official order that prevents something from happening: *There should be a ban* ***on*** *talk****ing*** *loudly in cinemas.*

banal /bəˈnɑːl/ adj boring, ordinary, and not original: *He just sat there making banal remarks all evening.* ◦ *banal pop songs* • **banality** /-ə.ti/ US /-ə.ţi/ noun [C or U] formal

banana /bəˈnɑː.nə/ US /-ˈnæn.ə/ noun [C or U] A1 a long, curved fruit with a yellow skin and soft, sweet, white flesh inside: *a bunch of bananas* ◦ *banana milkshake*

baˌnana reˈpublic noun [C] disapproving offensive a small country, especially in South and Central America, that is poor, CORRUPT, and badly ruled

bananas /bəˈnɑː.nəz/ US /-ˈnæn.əz/ adj [after verb] informal **1** very silly: *You're going out in this weather? You must be bananas!* **2 go bananas** to become extremely angry or excited: *She'll go bananas when you tell her the news.*

baˈnana ˌskin noun [C] UK informal a sudden unexpected situation that makes a person appear silly or causes them difficulty: *The new tax has proved to be a banana skin for the government.*

baˌnana ˈsplit noun [C] a sweet dish made of a banana cut in half with ice cream and cream on top

band /bænd/ noun; verb

▸noun **MUSICIANS** ▷ **1** A1 [C, + sing/pl verb] a group of musicians who play modern music together: *a jazz/rock band* ◦ *The Beatles were probably the most famous band in the world.* **2 boy/girl band** a group of young men or women who perform popular songs together and dance as a group **STRIP** ▷ **3** C2 [C] a thin, flat piece of cloth, ELASTIC, metal, or other material put around something to fasten it or make it stronger, or a long, narrow piece of colour, light, etc. that is different from what surrounds it: *a wrist band* ◦ *a red silk band* ◦ *A narrow band of grass separated the greenhouse from the vegetable garden.* **RANGE** ▷ **4** [C] a particular range of values, numbers, etc.: *The scheme is devised for young people in the 15–20* ***age*** *band.* **GROUP** ▷ **5** [C, + sing/pl verb] a group of people who share the same interests or beliefs, or who have joined together for a special purpose: *The former president still has a small band of supporters.*

▸verb

PHRASAL VERB **band together** to join together as a group in order to be able to do something better: *We decided to band together and organize a protest.*

bandage /ˈbæn.dɪdʒ/ noun; verb

▸noun [C or U] (US also **gauze**) A2 a long, narrow piece of cloth that is tied around an injury or a part of someone's body that has been hurt

▸verb [T] to tie a bandage around an injury or part of someone's body, or put bandages on someone or something: *You ought to bandage* (***up***) *that cut.*

ˈBand-Aid noun [C] US trademark (UK **plaster**, **ˈsticking ˌplaster**) a small piece of sticky cloth or plastic that you use to cover and protect a cut in the skin

ˌband-aid soˈlution noun [C] mainly US a temporary solution that does not deal with the cause of a problem: *Tax credits given to students are merely a band-aid solution to the rising cost of getting an education.*

bandana mainly UK (US usually **bandanna**) /bænˈdæn.ə/ noun [C] a brightly coloured piece of cloth that is worn around the neck or head

ˌB and ˈB (also **ˌB & ˈB**) noun [C] abbreviation for **bed and breakfast**

bandh /bʌnd/ noun [C] Indian English an occasion when offices, businesses, schools, etc. close for a day and people stop working in order to show that they disagree with something or to show respect; a STRIKE

bandicoot /ˈbæn.dɪ.kuːt/ noun [C] a type of MARSUPIAL (= an animal that lives in a bag on its mother's body after birth) that lives in Australia

bandit /ˈbæn.dɪt/ noun [C] a thief with a weapon, especially one belonging to a group that attacks people travelling through the countryside

bandleader /ˈbændˌliː.dəʳ/ US /-dɚ/ noun [C] old-fashioned a person who leads a large group of musicians while they play, and who often plays an instrument at the same time

bandmaster /ˈbændˌmɑː.stəʳ/ US /-ˌmæs.tɚ/ noun [C] a person who leads the music of a military BAND or a BRASS BAND

bandobast /ˈbʌn.də.bʌst/ noun Indian English **1** [U] protection of a person, building, or organization against crime or attack: *Poor bandobast has been cited as reason for the assassinations.* **2** [C] the group of people responsible for protecting a person, building, or organization: *Elaborate arrangements for the bandobast were made during the president's visit to our town.*

bandsman /ˈbændz.mən/ noun [C] (plural **-men** /-mən/) a person who plays a musical instrument in a military BAND or a BRASS BAND

bandstand /ˈbænd.stænd/ noun [C] a covered place where musical groups can play outside

bandwagon /ˈbændˌwæg.ən/ noun [C usually singular] an activity, group, movement, etc. that has become successful or fashionable and so attracts many new people: *a bandwagon effect*

IDIOM **jump/climb/get on the bandwagon** C2 to become involved in an activity that is successful so that you can get the advantages of it yourself: *The success of the product led many firms to try to jump on the bandwagon.*

bandwidth /ˈbænd.wɪtθ/ noun [C usually singular] **1** a measurement of the amount of information that can be sent between computers, through a phone line, etc.: *The system will handle signals that need* ***high*** *bandwidth, for instance those that encode TV pictures.* ◦ *high-bandwidth* ***services/applications*** **2** the range of FREQUENCIES used to send information over a distance using phone wires **3** in radio, the width of a particular WAVEBAND

bandy /ˈbæn.di/ adj; verb

▸adj (of legs) bending out at the knees: *I couldn't help laughing at his bandy* ***legs***.

▸verb

IDIOM **bandy words** old-fashioned to argue: *I haven't come here to bandy words* ***with*** *you.*

PHRASAL VERB **bandy sth about/around** to mention something often, without considering it carefully: *Large figures were bandied about, but no money was ever paid.*

bane /beɪn/ noun **the bane of sth** a cause of continuous trouble or unhappiness: *Keeping noise levels low is the bane of airport administration.* ◦ *That cat is the bane of* ***my life!***

bang /bæŋ/ verb; noun; exclamation; adv
▸verb NOISE ▷ **1** B2 [I or T] to (cause something to) make a sudden very loud noise or noises: *She banged her fist angrily on the table.* ◦ *Outside a door was banging in the wind.* ◦ *He could hear someone banging* ***at*** *the door.* ◦ *I could hear her in the kitchen banging* ***about*** (= doing things noisily). HIT ▷ **2** [T] to hit a part of the body against something by accident: *I banged my head* ***against/on*** *the shelf as I stood up.* SEX ▷ **3** [T] offensive to have sex with someone

PHRASAL VERBS **bang on** informal disapproving to talk about something for a long time, especially in a way that is boring to other people: *My parents are always banging on* ***about*** *how much better life was 20 years ago.* • **bang sb up** slang to lock someone up, especially in prison

▸noun [C] NOISE ▷ **1** B2 a sudden very loud noise: *The window slammed shut with a loud bang.* HIT ▷ **2** an act of hitting someone or something: *I think she must have got a bang* ***on*** *the head.*

IDIOMS **go with a bang** UK (US **go over with a bang**) If a party or event goes with a bang, it is very exciting and successful. • **more bang for your buck(s)** informal If you get more bang for your buck(s), you get a better result for the amount of effort or money that you have put into something

▸exclamation **1** used to suggest the sound of a sudden loud noise, such as a GUNSHOT or an explosion: *'Bang! Bang! You're dead!' said the child, pointing a plastic gun at me.* **2 go bang** to make a sudden loud noise: *The balloon* ***went*** *bang when it landed on the bush.*

IDIOM **bang goes sth** informal said when you have just lost the opportunity to do something: *He says I have to work late tonight – so bang goes my trip to the cinema.*

▸adv informal exactly or directly: *The car came to a halt bang* ***in the middle of*** *the road.* ◦ *I live bang* ***opposite*** *the cinema.* ◦ *I turned the corner and walked* ***slap*** *bang* ***into*** *him.* ◦ *software that is bang (= completely)* ***up to date***

IDIOM **be bang on** to be exactly right: *What was your answer? 76? That's absolutely bang on!*

banger /ˈbæŋ.əʳ/ US /-ɚ/ noun [C] UK CAR ▷ **1** a very old car in bad condition FIREWORK ▷ **2** a small, noisy FIREWORK (= small container of explosives that makes a loud noise when it explodes) FOOD ▷ **3** informal for sausage: *bangers* ***and mash*** (= potatoes)

banging /ˈbæŋ.ɪŋ/ adj slang very good or enjoyable: *a banging party*

bangle /ˈbæŋ.ɡl/ noun [C] a ring of stiff plastic, metal, etc. worn around the wrist or arm as jewellery

bangs /bæŋz/ noun [plural] US for **fringe**

banish /ˈbæn.ɪʃ/ verb [T] **1** to send someone away, especially from their country, and not allow them to come back: *He was banished* ***to*** *an uninhabited island for a year.* ◦ *They were banished (= sent out)* ***from*** *the library for making a noise.* **2** to get rid of something completely: *You must try to banish all thoughts of revenge* ***from*** *your mind.* • **banishment** /-mənt/ noun [U]

banister /ˈbæn.ɪ.stəʳ/ US /-stɚ/ noun [C] (also **banisters** [plural]) the row of posts at the side of stairs and the wooden or metal bar on top of them

banjo /ˈbæn.dʒəʊ/ US /-dʒoʊ/ noun [C] (plural **banjos** or **banjoes**) a STRINGED musical instrument with a long neck and a hollow circular body

bank /bæŋk/ noun; verb
▸noun [C] MONEY ▷ **1** A1 an organization where people and businesses can INVEST or borrow money, change it to foreign money, etc., or a building where these services are offered: *I need to go to the bank at lunch time.* ◦ *I had to take out a bank* ***loan*** *to start my own business.* **2** In GAMBLING, the bank is money that belongs to the owner and can be won by the players. RIVER ▷ **3** B2 sloping raised land, especially along the sides of a river: *By the time we reached the opposite bank, the boat was sinking fast.* ◦ *These flowers generally grow on* ***river*** *banks and near streams.* MASS ▷ **4** a pile or mass of earth, clouds, etc.: *A dark bank* ***of*** *cloud loomed on the horizon.* ROWS ▷ **5** a row of similar things, especially machines or parts of machines: *a bank of switches* STORE ▷ **6** A bank of something, such as blood or human organs for medical use, is a place that stores these things for later use: *a blood bank* ◦ *a sperm bank*
▸verb MONEY ▷ **1** [I or T] to keep your money in a particular bank, or to put money into a bank: *I used to bank* ***with*** *Lloyd's.* **2** [T] informal to win or earn a particular amount of money: *She banked £500 in tips that day!* TURN ▷ **3** [I] (of an aircraft) to fly with one wing higher than the other when turning: *We felt the plane bank steeply as it changed direction.* MASS ▷ **4** [I or T] to collect in or form into a mass, or to make something do this: *The snow had banked* ***up*** *in the corner of the garden.* ◦ *We banked* ***up*** *the fire (= put more coal on it) to keep it burning all night.*

PHRASAL VERB **bank on sb/sth** to expect something or depend on something happening: *Can I bank on your support?* ◦ [+ -ing verb] *I wouldn't bank on him being there.* ◦ *'Do you think she'll come?' 'I wouldn't bank on it.'* ◦ *I'd banked on* ***getting*** *a pay rise this year.*

bankable /ˈbæŋ.kə.bl̩/ adj informal likely to make money: *She is currently Hollywood's most bankable actress (= her films make large profits).* • **bankability** /bæŋ.kəˈbɪl.ɪ.ti/ US /-ə.t̬i/ noun [U] an ability to make money: *His bankability as a pop star decreased as he got older.*

ˈbank acˌcount noun [C] B1 an arrangement with a bank in which the customer puts in and removes money and the bank keeps a record of it

ˈbank ˌbalance noun [C] the amount of money in a bank account: *I'd like to* ***check*** *my bank balance, please.*

ˈbank ˌcharges noun [plural] amounts of money paid by a customer for a bank's services: *You'll pay some hefty bank charges if you go overdrawn without permission.*

banker /ˈbæŋ.kəʳ/ US /-kɚ/ noun [C] **1** B2 someone with an important position in a bank: *She was a successful banker by the time she was 40.* **2** the person in GAMBLING games who is responsible for dealing with the money

ˈbanker's ˌcard noun [C] (also **ˈbank ˌcard**) a **cheque guarantee card**

ˌbanker's ˈorder noun [C] a **standing order**

ˌbank ˈholiday noun [C] UK an official holiday when banks and most businesses are closed for a day

banking /ˈbæŋ.kɪŋ/ **noun** [U] B2 the business of operating a bank: *international banking*

ˈbank ˌmanager **noun** [C] the person in charge of a local bank

banknote /ˈbæŋk.nəʊt/ US /-noʊt/ **noun** [C] a piece of printed paper that has a particular value as money: *a £20 banknote*

the ˌBank of ˈEngland **noun** the CENTRAL BANK of the UK

ˈbank ˌrate **noun** [C] **1** the rate of interest set by a central bank in a country that is the lowest rate at which it lends money to other banks. This rate affects the interest rates that are then charged to customers by the banks. **2** the amount of interest that a bank charges when it lends money

bankroll /ˈbæŋk.rəʊl/ US /-roʊl/ **verb** [T] informal to support a person or activity financially: *a joint project bankrolled by the US space agency*

bankrupt /ˈbæŋ.krʌpt/ **adj; noun; verb**

▸**adj** **1** C1 legal unable to pay what you owe, and having had control of your financial matters given, by a law court, to a person who sells your property to pay your debts: *He **went** bankrupt after only a year in business.* ◦ *The recession has led to many small businesses **going** bankrupt.* **2** informal having no money: *I shall go bankrupt if you children keep on asking for more pocket money!* **3** disapproving not having any good qualities: *He believes that modern society is **morally** bankrupt.*

▸**noun** [C] legal a person who is officially bankrupt: *He was **declared** a bankrupt in 2011.*

▸**verb** [T] legal to cause someone to become bankrupt: *They feared that the loss would bankrupt them.*

bankruptcy /ˈbæŋ.krəpt.si/ **noun** legal **1** [C or U] a situation in which a business or a person becomes bankrupt: *The company was forced into bankruptcy.* ◦ *The toll of bankruptcies was rising daily.* **2** [U] the fact of good qualities being completely absent: ***moral** bankruptcy*

ˈbank ˌstatement **noun** [C] a printed record of the money put into and removed from a bank account

banner /ˈbæn.əʳ/ US /-ɚ/ **noun** **1** [C] a long piece of cloth, often stretched between two poles, with a sign written on it, usually carried by people taking part in a march: *The demonstrators walked along the street, carrying banners and shouting angrily.* **2** [C] a **banner advertisement** **3** [S] an idea, principle, or belief that is strongly supported by someone: *They won the election **under** the banner **of** lower taxes.*

ˈbanner adˌvertisement **noun** [C] (also **ˈbanner ˌad**) an advertisement that appears across the top of a page on the internet or in a newspaper

ˌbanner ˈheadline **noun** [C] a large title of a story in a newspaper that stretches across the top of the front page

banns /bænz/ **noun** [plural] a public announcement, made in a church, that two people are going to get married: *The banns were **published** in their local parish church.*

banoffee pie (also **baˌnoffi ˈpie**) /bəˌnɒ.fiˈpaɪ/ **noun** [C or U] a sweet dish made from BANANAS, cream, and TOFFEE on pastry

banquet /ˈbæŋ.kwɪt/ **noun** [C] a large formal meal for many people, often followed by speeches in honour of someone: *Medieval banquets are held in the castle once a month.* • **banqueting** /ˈbæŋ.kwɪ.tɪŋ/ US /-t̬ɪŋ/ **noun** [U] *The dinner is to be held in the banqueting hall/suite.*

banshee /ˈbæn.ʃiː/ **noun** [C] a female spirit in traditional Irish stories whose crying sound tells you that someone in your family is going to die

bantam /ˈbæn.təm/ US /-t̬əm/ **noun** [C] a small breed of chicken

bantamweight /ˈbæn.təm.weɪt/ US /-t̬əm-/ **noun** [C] a BOXER weighing between 51 and 53.5 kilograms

banter /ˈbæn.təʳ/ US /-t̬ɚ/ **noun; verb**

▸**noun** [U] conversation that is funny and not serious

▸**verb** [I] to talk to someone in a friendly and humorous way: *He stood around bantering **with** his colleagues.* • **bantering** /-ɪŋ/ **adj**

banyan /ˈbæn.jæn/ **noun** [C] a South Asian fruit tree with branches that produce roots that grow down into the ground to form extra TRUNKS

bap /bæp/ **noun** [C] UK a round, soft form of bread that is usually smaller than a LOAF: *a soft white bap*

baptism /ˈbæp.tɪ.zəm/ **noun** [C or U] a Christian ceremony in which a person has water poured on their head, or is covered for a very short time in water, in order to show that they have become a member of the Christian Church: *infant baptism*

IDIOM **a baptism of/by fire** a very difficult first experience of something: *I was given a million-dollar project to manage in my first month – it was a real baptism of fire.*

Baptist /ˈbæp.tɪst/ **noun** [C] a member of a Christian group that believes that baptism should not happen until a person is old enough to ask for it and to understand its meaning

baptize (UK usually **baptise**) /bæpˈtaɪz/ **verb** [T usually passive] to make someone officially a member of the Christian Church in a service of baptism: [+ obj + noun] *Were you baptized a Catholic?* → Compare **christen**

bar /bɑːʳ/ US /bɑːr/ **noun; verb; preposition**

▸**noun** [C] DRINKING PLACE ▷ **1** A1 a place where drinks, especially alcoholic drinks, are sold and drunk, or the area in such a place where the [illegible] person serving the drinks stands: *They noticed him going into the hotel bar.* ◦ *There weren't any free tables, so I sat **at the** bar.* ◦ *Why don't you ask the guy **behind** the bar (= serving drinks there)?* LONG PIECE ▷ **2** B2 a long, thin, straight piece of metal or wood: *The gorilla rattled the bars of its cage.* **3** B1 a substance that has been made into a solid rectangular shape: *a bar of soap* ◦ *a chocolate bar* **4** The bar of an ELECTRIC HEATER is a long, thin wire in the shape of a SPRING that is wrapped tightly around a tube. When electricity passes through it, it produces heat and red light. MUSIC ▷ **5** (US also **measure**) one of the small equal parts into which a piece of music is divided, containing a fixed number of BEATS: *Waltzes have three beats **in/to the** bar (= in each bar).* ON UNIFORM ▷ **6** US for **stripe** PREVENTING ▷ **7** C2 [usually singular] something that prevents a particular event or development from happening: *A lack of formal education is no bar **to** becoming rich.*

IDIOM **behind bars** B2 in prison: *He's spent most of his life behind bars.*

▸**verb** [T] (-rr-) PREVENT ▷ **1** to prevent something or someone from doing something or going somewhere, or to not allow something: *The centre of the town was barred **to** (US usually barred **off to**) football supporters.* ◦ *The incident led to him being barred **from** the country/barred **from** playing for England.* ◦ *I tried to push past her but she barred my **way/path** (= stood in front of me and prevented me from getting past).* CLOSE ▷ **2** to put bars across something, especially to keep it closed: *We barred the door to stop anyone getting into the room.*

▸**preposition** formal except: *Everyone is leaving the village, bar the very old and ill.* ◦ *They're the best*

songwriters of this century, bar ***none*** *(= no one else is better).*

IDIOM **be (all) over bar the shouting** UK If an activity is all over bar the shouting, the result of it is known, but it has not been officially finished or announced, so people can still say that a different result is possible: *With practically all the results declared, the Nationalist Party has 68 percent of the vote, so it's all over bar the shouting.*

the ˈBar noun [S, + sing/pl verb] **1** UK lawyers who are allowed to argue a case in a higher court **2** US all lawyers thought of as a group **3 be called to the Bar** UK to gain a qualification as a lawyer who can argue a case in a higher court **4 be admitted to the Bar** US to gain a qualification as a lawyer

barb /bɑːb/ (US) /bɑːrb/ noun [C] **POINT** ▷ **1** the sharp part that points backwards from a fish HOOK (= curved piece of wire) or arrow, making it hard to remove it from something **REMARK** ▷ **2** a remark that is clever but cruel and unkind: *I tried to ignore their barbs about my new jacket.*

barbarian /bɑːˈbeə.ri.ən/ (US) /bɑːrˈber.i-/ noun [C] **1** a member of a group of people from a very different country or culture that is considered to be less socially advanced and more violent than your own: *The walled city was attacked by barbarian hordes.* **2** disapproving a person with little education who has no interest in art and culture

barbaric /bɑːˈbær.ɪk/ (US) /bɑːr-/ adj extremely cruel and unpleasant: *She found the idea of killing animals for pleasure barbaric.* ◦ *barbaric acts of violence* • **barbarically** /-ɪ.kəl.i/ adv

barbarism /ˈbɑː.bə.rɪ.zəm/ (US) /ˈbɑːr.bɚ.ɪ-/ noun [U] extremely cruel and unpleasant behaviour: *He witnessed some appalling acts of barbarism during the war.*

barbarity /bɑːˈbær.ə.ti/ (US) /bɑːrˈbær.ə.t̬i/ noun [C or U] behaviour that is very cruel, or a very cruel act: *This barbarity must cease!* ◦ *The dictatorship has been responsible for countless barbarities.*

barbarous /ˈbɑː.bər.əs/ (US) /ˈbɑːr.bɚ-/ adj formal extremely cruel or unpleasant, or failing to reach acceptable social standards: *His murder was an outrageous and barbarous* ***act.*** ◦ *How can they forgive such barbarous* ***behaviour?***

barbecue /ˈbɑː.bɪ.kjuː/ (US) /ˈbɑːr-/ noun [C] (UK or Australian English informal **barbie**, written abbreviation **BBQ**) **1** (A2) a metal frame on which meat, fish, or vegetables are cooked outside over a fire **2** (A2) a meal prepared using such a frame that is eaten outside, often during a party • **barbecue** verb [T] (B1) to cook food on a barbecue: *Their traditional sausages are delicious grilled or barbecued.*

ˌbarbecue ˈsauce noun [C or U] a spicy sauce that is used to flavour food cooked on a barbecue

barbed /bɑːbd/ (US) /bɑːrbd/ adj **WITH SHARP POINT** ▷ **1** having a sharp point that curves backwards **CRITICIZING** ▷ **2** unkind and criticizing: *She made some rather barbed* ***comments*** *about my lifestyle.*

ˌbarbed ˈwire noun [U] a type of strong wire with sharp points on it, used to prevent people or animals from entering or leaving a place, especially a field: *a barbed wire fence*

barbed wire

barbell /ˈbɑː.bel/ (US) /ˈbɑːr.bel/ noun [C] a long bar with a weight on each end that you lift up and down to make your arm and shoulder muscles stronger → Compare **dumbbell**

barber /ˈbɑː.bər/ (US) /ˈbɑːr.bɚ/ noun [C] (B1) a man whose job is cutting men's hair

barber's /ˈbɑː.bəz/ (US) /ˈbɑːr.bɚz/ noun [C] (plural **barbers**) (US also **barbershop**) a shop where a barber works

barbershop /ˈbɑː.bə.ʃɒp/ (US) /ˈbɑːr.bɚ.ʃɑːp/ noun **SINGING** ▷ **1** [U] a type of singing in which four, usually male, voices in close combination perform popular romantic songs, especially from the 1920s and 1930s: *a barbershop* ***quartet*** **HAIR** ▷ **2** (B1) [C] US for **barber's**

ˈbarber's pole noun [C] a pole with red and white stripes that traditionally is put on the front of a barber's shop

barbiturate /bɑːˈbɪt.jʊ.rət/ (US) /bɑːr-/ noun [C] a strong drug that makes people calm or helps them to sleep: *He died from an overdose of alcohol and barbiturates.*

ˈbar ˌchart/ˌgraph noun [C] a mathematical picture in which different amounts are represented by thin vertical or horizontal rectangles that have the same width but different heights or lengths

ˈbar ˌcode noun [C] a small rectangular pattern of thick and thin black lines printed on a product, or on its container, so that the details of the product can be read by and recorded on a computer system → Compare **QR code**

bard /bɑːd/ (US) /bɑːrd/ noun [C] **1** literary a poet **2 the Bard** William Shakespeare

bare /beər/ (US) /ber/ adj; verb

▸adj **NO CLOTHES** ▷ **1** (B2) without any clothes or not covered by anything: *Don't walk around outside* ***in*** *your bare* ***feet.*** ◦ *There's no carpet in the room, just bare floorboards.* → See also **barefoot** **BASIC** ▷ **2** (C2) only the most basic or important: *I just packed the bare* ***essentials*** *(= the most basic and necessary things).* ◦ *There isn't much time, so I'll just give you the bare* ***facts/details.*** **3 the bare minimum** the least possible amount: *She eats only the bare* ***minimum*** *to stay alive.* **EMPTY** ▷ **4** (C2) literary If a cupboard or room is bare, there is nothing in it.

IDIOM **with your bare hands** (C2) without using any type of tool or weapon: *He wrestled the lion to the ground with his bare hands.*

▸verb [T] to take away the thing that is covering something so that it can be seen: *The men bared their* ***heads*** *(= took their hats off as a sign of respect) as they entered the church.* ◦ *He became nervous when the dog growled and bared its* ***teeth*** *at him (= showed its teeth to him).*

IDIOM **bare your heart/soul** to tell someone your secret thoughts and feelings: *We don't know each other that well. I certainly wouldn't bare my soul* ***to*** *her.*

bareback /ˈbeə.bæk/ (US) /ˈber-/ adj, adv without a SADDLE on the back of a horse that is being ridden: *a bareback rider* ◦ *Is it difficult* ***riding*** *bareback?*

the ˌbare ˈbones noun [plural] the most important facts about something, to which more detail might be added later: *the bare bones* ***of*** *the story* ◦ *I don't need all the details – just give me the bare bones.*

barefaced /ˈbeə.feɪst/ (US) /ˈber-/ adj disapproving not trying to hide your bad behaviour: *That's a barefaced lie!*

barefoot /ˈbeə.fʊt/ (US) /ˈber-/ adj, adv not wearing any shoes or socks: *We took off our shoes and socks and* ***walked*** *barefoot along the beach.*

bareheaded /ˌbeəˈhed.ɪd/ (US) /ˈber-/ adj, adv without any covering on your head

B

ˌbare inˈfinitive noun [C] specialized in grammar, the INFINITIVE form of a verb without the word 'to': *In the sentence 'Let her go!', the bare infinitive is the word 'go'.*

barely /ˈbeə.li/ (US) /ˈber-/ **adv** B2 by the smallest amount: *They have barely enough (= no more than what is needed) to pay the rent this month.* ◦ *She was barely (= only just) 15 when she won her first championship.*

barf /bɑːf/ (US) /bɑːrf/ verb [I] slang to vomit • **barf** noun [U]

ˈbarf ˌbag noun [C] US slang a WATERPROOF paper bag provided for each passenger on an aircraft in case they need to vomit

bargain /ˈbɑː.gɪn/ (US) /ˈbɑːr-/ **noun; verb**

▸noun [C] **LOW PRICE** ▷ **1** B1 something on sale at a lower price than its true value: *This coat was half-price – a real bargain.* ◦ *The airline regularly offers last-minute bookings at bargain* ***prices****.* ◦ *The sales had started and the bargain* ***hunters*** *(= people looking for things at a low price) were out in force.* **AGREEMENT** ▷ **2** an agreement between two people or groups in which each promises to do something in exchange for something else: *'I'll tidy the kitchen if you clean the car.' 'OK, it's a bargain.'* ◦ *The management and employees eventually* ***struck/made*** *a bargain (= reached an agreement).*

IDIOM **into the bargain** (US also **in the bargain**) C2 in addition to other facts previously mentioned: *He's intelligent, witty, a loving husband, and an excellent cook into the bargain.*

▸verb [I or T] to try to make someone agree to give you something that is better for you, such as a better price or better working conditions: *Unions bargain* ***with*** *employers for better rates of pay each year.*

PHRASAL VERBS **bargain sth away** to exchange something good for something of less value: *I realized that by trying to gain security I had bargained* ***away*** *my freedom.* • **bargain for/on sth** to expect or be prepared for something: *We hadn't bargained on such a long wait.* ◦ *The strength of the opposition was rather* ***more than*** *she'd bargained* ***for****.*

ˌbargain ˈbasement noun [C usually singular] an underground room in a shop where things are sold at reduced prices: [before noun] *Jonathan manages to buy all his clothes at bargain-basement prices (= very cheaply).*

ˈbargaining ˌchip noun [C] (UK also **ˈbargaining ˌcounter**) something that someone else wants that you are willing to lose in order to reach an agreement: *Missiles were used as a bargaining chip in negotiations for economic aid.*

ˈbargaining ˌpower noun [U] the ability of a person or group to get what they want: *Rising unemployment has diminished the bargaining power of people with jobs.*

barge /bɑːdʒ/ (US) /bɑːrdʒ/ **verb; noun**

▸verb [I or T, usually + adv/prep] to hurry somewhere or through a place in a rude and forceful way: *They barged* ***through*** *the crowds.* ◦ *When the doors opened she barged her* ***way*** *to the front of the queue.* ◦ *The man barged (= pushed)* ***into*** *her and ran on without stopping.*

PHRASAL VERBS **barge in** informal to interrupt rudely: *Sorry to barge in, but I couldn't help overhearing what you were saying.* • **barge in/into sth** informal to walk into a room quickly, without being invited: *I wish he'd knock instead of just barging in.*

▸noun [C] a long boat with a flat bottom, used for carrying heavy objects on rivers or CANALS

barista /bɑːrˈiːs.tə/ **noun** [C] a person who serves customers in a COFFEE SHOP (= small restaurant that serves coffee)

baritone /ˈbær.ɪ.təʊn/ (US) /-toʊn/ **noun** [C] a man with a singing voice that is lower than a TENOR but not as low as a BASS, or a musical instrument with this range

barium /ˈbeə.ri.əm/ (US) /ˈber.i-/ **noun** [U] (symbol **Ba**) a chemical element that is a soft, silver-white metal, is ALKALINE, and combines with OXYGEN very easily

ˌbarium ˈmeal noun [C or U] UK (US **ˌbarium ˈsulphate** [U]) a chemical that is swallowed by a person just before an X-RAY is taken of their stomach and bowels, so that these organs can be seen clearly

bark /bɑːk/ (US) /bɑːrk/ **noun; verb**

▸noun **TREE** ▷ **1** [U] the hard outer covering of a tree **DOG** ▷ **2** [C] the loud, rough noise that a dog and some other animals make

IDIOM **sb's bark is worse than their bite** If someone's bark is worse than their bite, they are not as unpleasant as they seem, and will not carry out all of their threats: *Don't let her frighten you – her bark is worse than her bite.*

▸verb **1** B2 [I] (of a dog) to make a loud, rough noise: *They heard a dog barking outside.* **2** C2 [T] to shout at someone in a forceful manner: *The sergeant barked (****out****) a succession of orders to the new recruits.*

IDIOM **be barking up the wrong tree** informal to be wrong about the reason for something or the way to achieve something: *She thinks it'll solve the problem, but I reckon she's barking up the wrong tree.*

barkeeper /ˈbɑːˌkiː.pəʳ/ (US) /ˈbɑːrˌkiː.pɚ/ **noun** [C] (also **barkeep** /ˈbɑː.kiːp/ (US) /ˈbɑːr-/) US a person who serves drinks in a bar, or the owner or manager of a bar: *She spent the summer working as a barkeeper at the resort.*

barker /ˈbɑː.kəʳ/ (US) /ˈbɑːr.kɚ/ **noun** [C] old-fashioned a person who advertises an activity at a public event by calling out to people who are walking past

ˌbarking (ˈmad) adj [after verb] UK old-fashioned informal crazy or extremely silly: *She must have been barking mad to lend him so much money.*

barley /ˈbɑː.li/ (US) /ˈbɑːr-/ **noun** [U] a tall plant like grass with long, straight hairs growing from the head of each stem, or the grain from this plant, used for food and for making beer and WHISKY

ˈbarley ˌsugar noun [C or U] a hard sweet made from boiled sugar

ˈbarley ˌwater noun [U] **1** UK a drink made from barley and fruit juice **2** US a drink made from barley and water boiled together and given to someone who is sick to make them feel better

ˈbar ˌline noun [C] UK (US **bar**) a vertical line that divides one BAR from another in a written piece of music

barmaid /ˈbɑː.meɪd/ (US) /ˈbɑːr-/ **noun** [C] UK a woman who serves drinks in a bar → Compare **bartender**

barman /ˈbɑː.mən/ (US) /ˈbɑːr-/ **noun** [C] (plural **-men** /-mən/) mainly UK B1 a man who serves drinks in a bar → Compare **bartender**

bar mitzvah /bɑːˈmɪts.və/ (US) /bɑːr-/ **noun** [C usually singular] a Jewish ceremony held to celebrate a boy reaching the age of 13, in which he is given the religious responsibilities and duties of an adult man → Compare **bat mitzvah**

barmy /ˈbɑː.mi/ (US) /ˈbɑːr-/ **adj** mainly UK informal behaving strangely, or very silly: *Not another one of her barmy ideas!*

barn /bɑːn/ ⓤⓢ /bɑːrn/ **noun** [C] C2 a large building on a farm in which animals or HAY (= dried grass) and grain are kept

barnacle /ˈbɑː.nə.kl̩/ ⓤⓢ /ˈbɑːr-/ **noun** [C] a small sea creature with a shell, that sticks very tightly and in large numbers to rocks and the bottom of boats

ˈbarn ˌdance **noun** [C] an informal dance in which people do traditional dancing in rows and circles, changing partners regularly

barnet /ˈbɑː.nɪt/ ⓤⓢ /ˈbɑːr-/ **noun** [C] UK slang a person's hair and the style it is worn in

barney /ˈbɑː.ni/ ⓤⓢ /ˈbɑːr-/ **noun** [C] mainly UK informal a loud argument

barnstorm /ˈbɑːn.stɔːm/ ⓤⓢ /ˈbɑːrn.stɔːrm/ **verb** [I or T] mainly US **1** to travel to a lot of small towns and make political speeches to try to get people's votes or support: *He plans to barnstorm across the state to generate public support.* **2** In the past, to barnstorm was to travel to a lot of small towns and perform flying tricks in aircraft.

barnstorming /ˈbɑːnˌstɔː.mɪŋ/ ⓤⓢ /ˈbɑːrnˌstɔːr.mɪŋ/ **adj** exciting and energetic: *It was a barnstorming* ***performance***.

barnyard /ˈbɑːn.jɑːd/ ⓤⓢ /ˈbɑːrn.jɑːrd/ **noun** [C] mainly US for **farmyard**

barometer /bəˈrɒm.ɪ.tər/ ⓤⓢ /-ˈrɑː.mɪ.t̬ɚ/ **noun** [C] **1** a device that measures air pressure and shows when the weather is likely to change **2** something that can show how a particular situation is developing, or how people's opinions on a particular matter are changing: *This survey is considered to be a reliable barometer* ***of*** *public opinion.*

baron /ˈbær.ən/ **noun** [C] **1** a British man who has a low rank in the highest social class **2** an extremely powerful person in a particular area of business: ***media/press*** *barons* ◦ *a* ***drug*** *baron*

baroness /ˈbær.ən.es/ **noun** [C] a British woman who has a low rank in the highest social class, or who is the wife of a baron

baronet /ˈbær.ən.et/ **noun** [C] a man who has the lowest title of honour that can be given in the UK, below a baron but above a KNIGHT, and given from father to son

baronetcy /ˈbær.ən.et.si/ **noun** [C] the rank of baronet: *Robert's grandfather was given the baronetcy after the war.*

baronial /bəˈrəʊ.ni.əl/ ⓤⓢ /-ˈroʊ-/ **adj** **1** very large, grand, and impressive: *baronial splendour* ◦ *a baronial mansion/hall* **2** belonging or relating to a BARON: *a baronial coat of arms*

barony /ˈbær.ən.i/ **noun** [C] the rank of a BARON, or the land owned by a BARON

baroque /bəˈrɒk/ ⓤⓢ /-ˈrɑːk/ **adj** relating to the heavily decorated style in buildings, art, and music that was popular in Europe in the 17th century and the early part of the 18th century: *baroque architecture/painters*

barrack /ˈbær.ək/ **verb** [T] UK to shout loudly in order to interrupt someone that you disagree with: *Every time the minister got up to speak he was barracked mercilessly.*

PHRASAL VERB **barrack for sb** Australian English to shout encouragement to the players in a team → Compare **support**

barracking /ˈbær.ə.kɪŋ/ **noun** [U] UK loud shouting by someone who disagrees with a person who is speaking: *She could not make herself heard above the constant barracking.*

barracks /ˈbær.əks/ **noun** [C, + sing/pl verb] (plural barracks) a building or group of buildings where soldiers live: *The barracks was/were surrounded by a high wall.*

barracuda /ˌbær.əˈkuː.də/ **noun** [C] **1** a large tropical sea fish with sharp teeth, that eats other fish and can attack people **2** US disapproving a person who does business in a way that shows they only think about their own advantage, even if this harms others

barrage /ˈbær.ɑːʒ/ ⓤⓢ /bəˈrɑːʒ/ **noun** ATTACK ▷ **1** [C usually singular] the action of continuously firing large guns to protect soldiers advancing on an enemy: *an artillery barrage* **2 a barrage of sth** a great number of complaints, criticisms, or questions suddenly directed at someone: *The TV station has received a barrage of complaints about the amount of violence in the series.* STRUCTURE ▷ **3** [C] a structure that is built across a river to provide water for farming, to produce electricity, or to allow boats to travel more easily

ˈbarrage balˌloon **noun** [C] a large BALLOON, especially one of a group that is tied to the ground with metal ropes in order to stop enemy aircraft that are flying low

barre /bɑːr/ ⓤⓢ /bɑːr/ **noun** [C] a horizontal bar fixed at a convenient height for dancers to hold on to, in order to help them balance while exercising

barred /bɑːd/ ⓤⓢ /bɑːrd/ **adj** If a door is barred, a bar of wood or metal has been put across it so that it cannot be opened: *They arrived at the house to find the door locked and barred.*

barrel /ˈbær.əl/ **noun**; **verb**

barrel

▸**noun** [C] CONTAINER ▷ **1** a large container, made of wood, metal, or plastic, with a flat top and bottom and curved sides that make it fatter in the middle: *They drank a whole barrel of beer (= the contents of a barrel) at the party.* **2** In the oil industry, a barrel of oil is equal to 159 litres. GUN PART ▷ **3** the long part of a gun that is shaped like a tube

IDIOMS **be a barrel of laughs/fun** informal to be funny or enjoyable: *'He's a bit serious, isn't he?' 'Yeah,* ***not exactly*** *a barrel of laughs.'* • **have sb over a barrel** informal to put someone in a very difficult situation in which they have no choice about what they do: *She knows I need the work so she's got me over a barrel in terms of what she pays me.*

▸**verb** [I, + adv/prep] (**-ll-** or US usually **-l-**) informal to travel somewhere very quickly: *We were barrelling along the autobahn at 180 kph.*

ˈbarrel ˌorgan **noun** [C] a large musical instrument that plays music when you turn a handle on the side. In the past, barrel organs were played outside to entertain people.

ˈbarrel ˌroll **noun** [C] a movement of an aircraft in which it turns over and then back up again

barren /ˈbær.ən/ **adj** **1** unable to produce plants or fruit: *We drove through a barren, rocky* ***landscape***. **2** formal unable to have children or young animals **3** not creating or producing anything new: *She became very depressed during the barren years when she was unable to paint.* → Compare **fertile** • **barrenness** /-nəs/ **noun** [U]

barrette /bəˈret/ **noun** [C] US for **hair slide**

barricade /ˈbær.ɪ.keɪd/, /bær.ɪˈkeɪd/ **noun**; **verb**

▸**noun** [C] a line or pile of objects put together, often quickly, to stop people from going where they want to

go: *Inmates **erected** a barricade between themselves and the prison officers.*
►verb [T] to build a barricade across, around, or in front of something: *Barricade the doors!* ◦ [+ adv/prep] *Terrified villagers have barricaded them**selves into** their houses.*

barrier /ˈbær.i.əʳ/ US /-ɚ/ **noun** [C] FENCE ▷ **1** B2 a long pole, fence, wall, or natural feature, such as a mountain or sea, that stops people from going somewhere: *Barriers have been erected all along the route the Pope will take.* ◦ *The mountains acted as a natural barrier **to** the spread of the disease.* → See also **crash barrier** **2** a gate in some railway stations through which you must go to get on a train: *Passengers are requested to show their tickets at the barrier.* OBSTACLE ▷ **3** B2 anything that prevents people from being together or understanding each other: *Despite the **language** barrier (= not speaking the same language), they soon became good friends.* ◦ *Shyness is one of the biggest barriers **to** mak**ing** friends (= something that makes this difficult).*

ˈ**barrier** ˌ**cream** noun [C] UK a cream that stops dirt or chemicals from getting through to the skin

barring /ˈbɑː.rɪŋ/ US /ˈbɑːr.ɪŋ/ **preposition** except if a particular thing happens: *We should arrive at ten o'clock, barring any (= if there are no) unexpected delays.*

barrio /ˈbær.i.əʊ/ US /ˈbɑːr.i.oʊ/ **noun** [C] **1** in the US, a part of a city where poor, mainly Spanish-speaking people live **2** in Spain and other Spanish-speaking countries, one of the areas into which a city is divided

barrister /ˈbær.ɪ.stəʳ/ US /-stɚ/ **noun** [C] a type of lawyer in the UK , Australia, and some other countries who can give specialized legal advice and can argue a case in both higher and lower courts

barrow /ˈbær.əʊ/ US /-oʊ/ **noun** [C] **1** a **wheelbarrow** **2** UK a vehicle moved by a person from which fruit and vegetables, etc. are sold at the side of a road

ˈ**barrow** ˌ**boy** noun [C] UK in the past, a man or boy who sold fruit and vegetables, etc. from a barrow

ˈ**bar** ˌ**stool** noun [C] a tall seat with no support for the back or arms, for sitting on while drinking or eating at a bar

bartender /ˈbɑːˌten.dəʳ/ US /ˈbɑːrˌten.dɚ/ **noun** [C] mainly US B2 someone who makes and serves drinks in a bar → Compare **barmaid, barman**

barter /ˈbɑː.təʳ/ US /ˈbɑːr.t̬ɚ/ **verb; noun**
►verb [I or T] to exchange goods for other things rather than for money: *He bartered his stamp collection **for** her comics.* ◦ *We spent a whole hour bartering **with** stallholders for souvenirs.*
►noun [U] the act or system of bartering goods: *The currency has lost so much of its value that barter has become the preferred way of doing business.*

basalt /ˈbæs.ɒlt/ US /-ɑːlt/ **noun** [U] a type of black rock that comes from a VOLCANO

base /beɪs/ **noun; adj; verb**
►noun BOTTOM ▷ **1** B2 [C] the bottom part of an object, on which it rests, or the lowest part of something: *a crystal glass with a heavy base* ◦ *At the base of the cliff was a rocky beach.* ◦ *This cream provides an excellent base for your make-up (= a good bottom layer on which other layers can be put).* MAIN PLACE ▷ **2** B2 [C] the main place where a person lives and works, or a place that a company does business from: *I spend a lot of time in Brussels, but London is still my base.* ◦ *Nice is an excellent base **for** (= place to stay when) exploring the French Riviera.* MILITARY ▷ **3** a place where there are military buildings and weapons and where members of the armed forces live: *an old naval/military base* IN BASEBALL ▷ **4** [C] one of the four positions on a square that a player must reach to score a point in the game of baseball NECESSARY PART ▷ **5** [C] the activity or people from which someone or something gets most of their support, money, etc.: *A strong economy depends on a healthy **manufacturing** base.* ◦ *We're aiming to expand our **customer** base.* MAIN PART ▷ **6** C2 [C usually singular] the main part of something: *a cocktail with a whisky base* IN MATHEMATICS ▷ **7** [C usually singular] specialized the number on which a counting system is built: *A binary number is a number written **in** base 2, using the two numbers 0 and 1.* IN CHEMISTRY ▷ **8** [C] specialized a chemical that dissolves in water and combines with an ACID to create a SALT
►adj literary not showing any honour and having no morals: *I accused him of having base **motives**.* • **basely** /ˈbeɪs.li/ adv • **baseness** /ˈbeɪs.nəs/ noun [U]
►verb [T usually + adv/prep] B2 to have a particular town or area, etc. as the main place that you live and work in, or where you do business from: *Where is your firm based?* ◦ *He was based in (= he lived in or was at a military establishment in) Birmingham during the war.*

PHRASAL VERB **base sth on sth** B1 If you base something on facts or ideas, you use those facts or ideas to develop it: *The film is based on a short story by Thomas Mann.*

baseball /ˈbeɪs.bɔːl/ US /-bɑːl/ **noun** [C or U] A1 (the ball used in) a game played especially in North America by two teams of nine players, in which a player hits a ball with a BAT (= stick) and tries to run around four BASES on a large field before the other team returns the ball: *Jake never **played** baseball like the other kids.* ◦ *He had a baseball and a couple of bats in his sports bag.*

ˈ**baseball** ˌ**cap** noun [C] a tightly fitting hat, originally worn by baseball players, with a long flat piece at the front to protect the eyes from the sun

ˈ**baseball** ˌ**jacket** noun [C] a jacket made of a shiny material that fits tightly round the waist and fastens with a ZIP

baseboard /ˈbeɪs.bɔːd/ US /-bɔːrd/ **noun** [C or U] US for **skirting board**

ˈ**base** ˌ**camp** noun [C usually singular] a place where food and general supplies are kept, especially for people climbing a mountain

-based /-beɪst/ **suffix** MAIN PLACE ▷ **1** used to form adjectives showing the main place or area in which something or someone works, lives, or does business: *a Manchester-based company* MAIN PART ▷ **2** used to form adjectives describing the main thing from which a particular substance or object is made: *This is a cream-based sauce.*

ˈ**base** ˌ**form** noun [C] specialized in grammar, the simplest form of a verb, without a special ending: *The base form of 'calling' is 'call'.*

ˈ**base** ˌ**jumping** noun [U] (also **BASE jumping**) the sport of jumping from a high building, bridge, etc. with a PARACHUTE • ˈ**base** ˌ**jumper** noun [C]

baseless /ˈbeɪs.ləs/ **adj** formal not based on facts: *baseless **accusations/allegations/rumours***

baseline /ˈbeɪs.laɪn/ **noun** [C usually singular] **1** a line on a sports field, such as the one in tennis, that marks the end of the playing area, or the one in baseball that marks the path along which players run **2** an imaginary line used as a starting point for making comparisons: *a baseline assessment*

basement /ˈbeɪs.mənt/ **noun** [C] B2 a part of a building consisting of rooms that are partly or completely below the level of the ground: *Our kitchenware department is in the basement.* ◦ *a basement flat/apartment*

ˌbase ˈmetal noun [C] specialized a common metal, such as LEAD, TIN, or COPPER, that reacts easily with other chemicals and is not a precious metal

ˈbase ˌrate noun [C] UK specialized a RATE (= level of interest) decided by the Bank of England that banks use when deciding how much to charge for lending money: *Your mortgage interest payments are two percent below the base rate.*

bases 1 plural of **base 2** plural of **basis**

bash /bæʃ/ verb; noun

▸verb **HIT** ▷ **1** [I or T] informal to hit hard: *He bashed his arm* ***against*** *a shelf.* **CRITICIZE** ▷ **2** [T] to criticize someone severely: *He kept bashing local government officials.*

PHRASAL VERB **bash on** UK informal to continue doing something that is difficult, boring, or takes a long time: *Oh well, that's enough chatting. I suppose I'd better bash on* ***with*** *this essay.*

▸noun **HIT** ▷ **1** [C usually singular] informal a hit: *a bash* ***on*** *the head* **PARTY** ▷ **2** [C] informal a party: *He had a big bash for his 18th birthday.* **ATTEMPT** ▷ **3 have a bash** UK informal to try to do something you have not done before: *I've never been skiing before, but I'm prepared to have a bash (****at*** *it).* • **basher** /ˈbæʃ.əʳ/ Ⓤⓢ /-ɚ/ noun

-basher /-bæʃ.əʳ/ Ⓤⓢ /-ɚ/ suffix slang **HIT** ▷ **1** used in nouns meaning someone who hits or attacks a particular type of person: *gay/queer-basher* **CRITICIZE** ▷ **2** used in nouns meaning someone who strongly criticizes a particular type of person or thing: *union-basher*

bashful /ˈbæʃ.fəl/ adj often feeling uncomfortable with other people and easily embarrassed: *She gave a bashful* ***smile*** *as he complimented her on her work.* → Synonym **shy** • **bashfully** /-i/ adv • **bashfulness** /-nəs/ noun [U]

-bashing /-bæʃ.ɪŋ/ suffix slang **HIT** ▷ **1** used in nouns meaning the practice of attacking a particular type of person violently: *gay/queer-bashing* **CRITICIZE** ▷ **2** used in nouns meaning strong criticism of a particular type of person or thing: *union-bashing*

basic /ˈbeɪ.sɪk/ adj **1** (B1) simple and not complicated, so able to provide the base or starting point from which something can develop: *I really need to get some basic financial advice.* ◦ *He only has a basic command of English (= he only knows the most important and simple words and expressions).* ◦ *The basic (= most important) problem is that they don't talk to each other enough.* ◦ *It's the most basic model (= it only has the most simple features).* ◦ *The crisis has led to price rises in basic foodstuffs, such as meat, cheese, and sugar.* **2 basic pay, salary, wage, etc.** what a person earns before other amounts of money, such as payments for working extra hours, are added: *She earns a basic salary of £450K per annum.*

BASIC /ˈbeɪ.sɪk/ noun [U] a common language for writing computer programs in that uses instructions that are similar to English

basically /ˈbeɪ.sɪ.kəl.i/ adv (B2) used when referring to the main or most important characteristic or feature of something: *Basically, (= the most important thing is that) they want a lot more information about the project before they'll put any money into it.* ◦ *'So what's the difference between these two TVs?' 'Well, they're basically* ***the same****, but the more expensive one has 3D.'* ◦ *The car's basically sound (= in good condition), but the paintwork needs a bit of attention.*

basics /ˈbeɪ.sɪks/ noun [plural] **1** (B2) the simplest and most important facts, ideas, or things connected with something: *I really must learn* ***the*** *basics* ***of*** *first aid.* ◦ *The college can't even afford basics such as books and paper.* **2 back to basics** If you get back to basics, you start to give your attention to the simplest and most important matters after ignoring them for a while: *This is all part of a new back-to-basics campaign to raise standards.*

basil /ˈbæz.əl/ Ⓤⓢ /ˈbeɪ.zəl/ noun [U] a herb with a sweet smell that is used to add flavour in cooking

basilica /bəˈsɪl.ɪ.kə/, /-ˈzɪl-/ noun [C] a public building in ancient Rome that was round at one end and had two rows of columns supporting the roof, or a large church with a similar design

basin /ˈbeɪ.sən/ noun [C] **CONTAINER** ▷ **1** (B1) mainly UK an open, round container shaped like a bowl with sloping sides, used for holding food or liquid: *a pudding basin* **2** mainly UK the amount of something that a basin can hold: *a basin* ***of*** *water* **3** mainly UK a **washbasin**: *I've cleaned the basin and scrubbed the bath.* **AREA** ▷ **4** the area of land from which streams run into a river, lake, or sea **5** a sheltered area of deep water where boats are kept

basis /ˈbeɪ.sɪs/ noun [C] (plural **bases** /-siːz/) **IMPORTANT FACTS** ▷ **1** (C1) the most important facts, ideas, etc. from which something is developed: *This document will* ***form*** *the basis* ***for*** *our discussion.* ◦ *Their proposals have no proven scientific basis.* ◦ *Decisions were often made* ***on the*** *basis* ***of*** *(= using) incorrect information.* **METHOD** ▷ **2** (B2) a way or method of doing something: *Most of our staff work for us* ***on a voluntary*** *basis (= they work without being paid).*

bask /bɑːsk/ Ⓤⓢ /bæsk/ verb [I usually + adv/prep] to lie or sit enjoying the warmth especially of the sun: *We could see seals on the rocks, basking* ***in*** *the sun.*

PHRASAL VERB **bask in sth** to take pleasure from something that makes you feel good: *He basked in his moment of glory, holding the trophy up to the crowd.*

basket /ˈbɑː.skɪt/ Ⓤⓢ /ˈbæs.kɪt/ noun [C] **CONTAINER** ▷ **1** (B1) a light container, often with a handle, that is made of thin strips of wood, metal, or plastic twisted together, used for carrying or storing things: *a shopping/picnic basket* ◦ *a wicker basket* ◦ *a laundry/clothes basket* **2** the contents of a basket: *We picked lots of strawberries, but we'd eaten half the basket by the time we got home.* **INTERNET** ▷ **3** a place on a website where you collect things you plan to buy from the website: *There are four items in your basket.* **BASKETBALL** ▷ **4** In the game of basketball, a basket is an open net hanging from a metal ring through which the players try to throw the ball to score points for their team, or the successful throwing of the ball through the ring. **GROUP** ▷ **5** a group of related things: *the value of the pound against a basket* ***of*** *world currencies*

basket

basketball /ˈbɑː.skɪt.bɔːl/ Ⓤⓢ /ˈbæs.kɪt.bɑːl/ noun [C or U] (A1) (a ball used in) a game played by two teams of five players who score points by throwing a large ball through an open net hanging from a metal ring

ˈbasket ˌcase noun [C] **PERSON** ▷ **1** informal someone who is extremely nervous or ANXIOUS and is therefore

B

unable to organize their life: *By the end of the course I was a complete basket case.* COUNTRY/COMPANY ▷ **2** a country or company that is very unsuccessful financially: *20 years ago the country was an **economic** basket case.*

basketful /ˈbɑː.skɪt.fʊl/ US /ˈbæs.kɪt-/ noun [C] the amount of something that a basket can hold: *a basketful of apples*

basketwork /ˈbɑː.skɪt.wɜːk/ US /ˈbæs.kɪt.wɝːk/ noun [U] (also **basketry** /ˈbɑː.skɪ.tri/ US /ˈbæs.kə-/) the making of baskets and other objects by twisting together thin strips of wood, plastic, etc.

basmati /bæsˈmɑː.ti/ US /bæsˈmæ.t̬i/ noun [U] a type of South Asian rice with long grains

basque /bæsk/, /bɑːsk/ US /bæsk/ noun [C] tight-fitting underwear for women that covers the top part of the body and provides support for the breasts

Basque /bæsk/, /bɑːsk/ US /bæsk/ adj; noun
▸adj connected with a people living in the area around the Pyrenees in Spain and France, or connected with the language of this people
▸noun [C or U] the language of the Basque area, or a person from the Basque people

bas-relief /ˌbæs.rɪˈliːf/ noun [C or U] a type of art in which shapes are cut from the surrounding stone so that they stand out slightly against a flat surface, or a work of art done in this way

bass[1] /beɪs/ noun; adj
▸noun (plural **basses**) **1** [C or U] the lowest range of musical notes, or a man with a singing voice in this range: *He **sings** bass.* ◦ *Italy's leading bass* **2** [U] the set of low musical sounds on a radio, music system, etc.: *Turn down the bass.* **3** [C] a **double bass** **4** [C] (also ˌ**bass guiˈtar**) an electric guitar with four strings that plays very low notes: *He plays bass guitar.*
▸adj [before noun] playing, singing, or producing the lowest range of musical notes: *a bass drum/guitar/trombone*

bass[2] /bæs/ noun [C] (plural **bass**) a type of fish found in rivers or the sea

ˈ**bass** ˌ**clef** noun [C usually singular] a sign on a STAVE (= the five lines on which music is written) that shows that the notes are below MIDDLE C (= the C near the middle of a piano keyboard)

ˌ**bass** ˈ**drum** noun [C] a large drum that produces a low sound

basset (hound) /ˈbæs.ɪtˌhaʊnd/ noun [C] a type of dog with smooth hair, a long body, short legs, and long ears

bassinet /bæs.ɪˈnet/ noun [C] US a small bed for a very young baby

bassist /ˈbeɪ.sɪst/ noun [C] someone who plays either the BASS GUITAR or the DOUBLE BASS

bassoon /bəˈsuːn/ noun [C] a large musical instrument that is played by blowing into a long, curved tube

bastard /ˈbɑː.stəd/ US /ˈbæs.tɚd/ noun [C] UNPLEASANT ▷ **1** offensive an unpleasant person: *He was a bastard **to** his wife.* ◦ *You lied to me, **you** bastard!* ◦ humorous *You won again? You **lucky** bastard!* (= I don't think you deserve it) ◦ *This crossword's a bastard* (= very difficult). CHILD ▷ **2** old use a person born to parents who are not married to each other: *He was born in 1798, the bastard son of a country squire and his mistress.* → Compare **illegitimate**

bastardize (UK usually **bastardise**) /ˈbɑː.stə.daɪz/ US /ˈbæs.tɚ-/ verb [T] to change something in a way that makes it fail to represent the values and qualities that it is intended to represent • **bastardized** (UK usually **bastardised**) /ˈbɑː.stə.daɪzd/ US /ˈbæs.tɚ-/ adj *a bastardized **form** of the word/language*

baste /beɪst/ verb [T] POUR ▷ **1** to pour hot fat and liquid over meat while it is cooking: *Baste the turkey at regular intervals.* SEW ▷ **2** mainly US for **tack**: *Baste the seams.*

bastion /ˈbæs.ti.ən/ noun [C] **1** something that keeps or defends a belief or a way of life that is disappearing or threatened: *British public schools are regarded as one of the **last** bastions **of** upper-class privilege.* **2** a part of the wall of a castle that sticks out from it in order to protect it

bat /bæt/ noun; verb
▸noun [C] STICK ▷ **1** A1 a specially shaped piece of wood used for hitting the ball in many games: *a baseball/cricket/rounders/table tennis bat* → See also **batsman** ANIMAL ▷ **2** B1 a small animal like a mouse with wings that flies at night

IDIOMS **do sth off your own bat** UK informal to do something without anyone else telling you or asking you to do it: *I didn't ask her to buy them a present – she did it off her own bat.* • **have bats in the belfry** old-fashioned disapproving to be silly and slightly crazy and behave in a confused way • **off the bat** US immediately: *You can't expect to be accepted in a new town **right/straight** off the bat.*

▸verb (-tt-) EYELASHES ▷ **1** [T] (especially of women) to open and close your eyes quickly several times, especially to attract attention or admiration: *She smiled and batted her **eyelashes** at him.* BALL ▷ **2** [I or T] to try to hit a ball with a bat: *He batted the ball high into the air.* ◦ *Jones will be the first to bat.*

IDIOM **not bat an eyelid** to show no sign of surprise or worry when something unexpected happens: *She told him she'd spent all her savings but he didn't bat an eyelid.*

batch /bætʃ/ noun [C] **1** a group of things or people dealt with at the same time or considered similar in type: *The cook brought in a fresh batch **of** homemade cakes.* ◦ *We looked at the job applications **in** two batches.* **2** Indian English a group of students who are taught together at school, college, or university

batchmate /ˈbætʃ.meɪt/ noun [C] Indian English someone who is in the same year as you at school, college, or university

bated /ˈbeɪ.tɪd/ US /-t̬ɪd/ adj **with bated breath** C2 in an ANXIOUS (= worried and nervous) or excited way: *I waited for the results with bated breath.*

bath /bɑːθ/ US /bæθ/ noun; verb
▸noun **1** A1 [C] UK (US **bathtub**) a long plastic, metal, or CERAMIC container that is filled with water so that a person can sit or lie in it to wash their whole body **2** A1 [C usually singular] the activity of washing yourself or someone else in a bath: mainly UK *Susannah **has** a long hot bath every evening.* ◦ mainly US *I **took** a bath this morning.* ◦ *bath oil* **3 run a bath** UK (US **fill the tub**) to fill a bath with water for washing: *I'll run you a bath while you take off those wet clothes.* **4** [C] US used to refer to a bathroom when describing a home: *a four-bedroom two-bath house* **5** [C] UK a health treatment: *mud/thermal baths* **6** [C] UK any container holding liquid: *a bird bath* **7 baths** [C, + sing/pl verb] (plural **baths**) **a** UK old-fashioned **swimming baths** **b** a public place where people went in the past to have a hot bath
▸verb [I or T] UK (US usually **bathe**) to wash in a bath or to wash someone in a bath: old-fashioned *She baths every morning.* ◦ *I usually bath the kids in the evening.*

bathe /beɪð/ verb; noun
▸verb **SWIM** ▷ **1** [I] to swim, especially in the sea, a river, or a lake: *Children suffering from the illness had bathed* ***in*** *sea water contaminated by sewage.* **COVER** ▷ **2** [T] to cover something with a liquid, especially in order to make part of the body feel better: *I bathed my feet* ***in*** *salt water.* **3** [T] to cover something with something that causes a pleasant feeling or appearance: *In the afternoon the sun bathes the city* ***in*** *shades of pink and gold.* **WASH** ▷ **4** [T] US for bath (= to wash)
▸noun [S] UK formal an occasion when you swim or spend time in water: *I went for a bathe every evening.*

bather /ˈbeɪ.ðər/ US /-ðɚ/ noun [C] a person who is swimming in the sea, a river, etc.

bathhouse /ˈbɑːθ.haʊs/ US /ˈbæθ-/ noun [C] a public building where people can have a bath

bathing /ˈbeɪ.ðɪŋ/ noun [U] the activity of going for a swim: *At midnight they all decided to* ***go*** *bathing.*

ˈbathing ˌcostume noun [C] UK old-fashioned a piece of clothing that you wear for swimming

ˈbathing ˌsuit noun [C] old-fashioned or US A2 a piece of clothing that you wear for swimming

ˈbathing ˌtrunks noun [plural] UK old-fashioned **swimming trunks**

ˈbath ˌmat noun [C] a piece of material that you stand on after getting out of a bath or shower to stop the floor from getting wet, or a piece of rubber that is put inside the bath or shower to prevent you sliding and falling

bathos /ˈbeɪ.θɒs/ US /-θɑːs/ noun [U] literary a sudden change from a beautiful or important subject to a silly or very ordinary one, especially when this is not intended

bathrobe /ˈbɑːθ.rəʊb/ US /ˈbæθ.roʊb/ noun [C] **1** a loose piece of clothing like a coat worn before or after a bath **2** a **dressing gown**

bathroom /ˈbɑːθ.rʊm/, /-ruːm/ US /ˈbæθ-/ noun [C] **1** A1 a room with a bath and/or shower and often a toilet: *an en suite bathroom (= a bathroom joined to a bedroom)* **2** US a room with a toilet in it: *Where's the bathroom?*

IDIOM **go to the bathroom** US to use the toilet: *Wait a moment – I just need to go to the bathroom.*

ˈbathroom ˌsuite noun [C] the set of fixed objects in a bathroom that includes a bath and/or shower, a toilet, and a sink

ˈbath ˌsalts noun [plural] grains of a substance that you dissolve in bath water to make it smell pleasant or to make your skin soft

bathtime /ˈbɑːθ.taɪm/ US /ˈbæθ-/ noun [C or U] the time at which a child has a bath, or the activity of having a bath

ˈbath ˌtowel noun [C] a large TOWEL with which you dry yourself after a bath or shower

bathtub /ˈbɑːθ.tʌb/ US /ˈbæθ-/ noun [C] (also **tub**) B1 mainly US for **bath**

bathwater /ˈbɑːθ.wɔː.tər/ US /ˈbæθ.wɑː.t̬ɚ/ noun [U] water in a bath

batik /bætˈiːk/ noun [U] a method of printing patterns on cloth, in which WAX is put on the cloth before it is put in the DYE (= substance for changing the colour of cloth) or the cloth itself

batman /ˈbæt.mən/ noun [C] (plural **-men** /-mən/) the personal servant of an officer especially in the British armed forces

bat mitzvah /ˌbætˈmɪts.və/ noun [C usually singular] a Jewish ceremony held to celebrate a girl reaching the age of twelve, in which she is given the religious responsibilities and duties of an adult woman → Compare **bar mitzvah**

baton /ˈbæt.ɒn/ US /bəˈtɑːn/ noun [C] **MUSIC** ▷ **1** a stick used by a CONDUCTOR (= person who controls the performance of a group of musicians) to show the speed of the music **SPORT** ▷ **2** a stick that is passed from one runner to another in a RELAY RACE **MARCHING** ▷ **3** a hollow metal stick that a MAJORETTE or DRUM MAJOR turns and throws while marching **WEAPON** ▷ **4** (UK also **truncheon**, US also **nightstick**) a thick, heavy stick used as a weapon by police officers

ˈbaton ˌcharge noun [C] UK an attacking movement by a large group of police who run forward carrying their batons

batsman /ˈbæt.smən/ noun [C] (plural **-men** /-mən/) in cricket, a person who hits the ball: *a former England batsman*

battalion /bəˈtæl.i.ən/ noun [C] a military unit consisting of three or more COMPANIES

batten /ˈbæt.ən/ US /ˈbæt̬-/ noun; verb
▸noun [C] a long piece of wood, often fixed to something to make that thing stronger
▸verb [T] to fasten something by fixing pieces of wood onto it: *The boxes were securely battened before the journey.*

IDIOM **batten down the hatches 1** to fasten the entrances to the lower part of a ship using wooden boards **2** to prepare for a difficult situation: *When you're coming down with flu all you can do is batten down the hatches and wait for it to pass.*

batter /ˈbæt.ər/ US /ˈbæt̬.ɚ/ verb; noun
▸verb [T, I + adv/prep] to hit and behave violently towards a person, especially a woman or child, repeatedly over a long period of time, or to hit something with force many times: *He was battered* ***to death*** *with a rifle butt.* ◦ *He was battering* ***(at/on)*** *the door with his fists and howling.* ◦ *The waves battered* ***against*** *the rocks at the bottom of the cliff.* ◦ *The burglars had battered* ***down*** *the door of the house (= hit it so hard that it broke and fell down).*
▸noun **FOOD** ▷ **1** [U] a mixture of flour, eggs, and milk, used to make PANCAKES or to cover food before frying it: *fish* ***in*** *batter* **PLAYER** ▷ **2** [C] (also **hitter**) the person in baseball or ROUNDERS who hits the ball

battered /ˈbæt.əd/ US /ˈbæt̬.ɚd/ adj **HIT** ▷ **1** hurt by being repeatedly hit: *She set up a sanctuary for battered* ***wives***. **2** damaged, especially by being used a lot: *battered furniture/toys* **COOKED** ▷ **3** covered with a mixture of flour, eggs, and milk before being cooked: *battered cod* **DRUNK** ▷ **4** slang UK very drunk

battering /ˈbæt.ər.ɪŋ/ US /ˈbæt̬.ɚ.ɪŋ/ noun [C or U] an act of hitting someone: *baby/wife battering*

IDIOM **take a battering** to be defeated heavily: *Once again, our team took a battering on Saturday.*

ˈbattering ˌram noun [C] a long, heavy pole that was used by armies in the past to break down castle doors, etc., now used by police and fire officers to break down house doors

battery /ˈbæt.ər.i/ US /ˈbæt̬.ɚ.i/ noun; adj
▸noun **ELECTRICAL DEVICE** ▷ **1** A2 [C] a device that produces electricity to provide power for radios, cars, etc.: *a rechargeable battery* ◦ *a battery-operated hairdryer* ◦ *This alarm clock takes two medium-sized batteries.* ◦ *I think the battery is* ***dead/gone*** (UK also ***flat***) (= has lost its power). **LARGE NUMBER** ▷ **2 a battery of sth** a number of things of a similar type: *In the kitchen an impressive battery of stainless steel utensils hangs on the wall.* **GUNS** ▷ **3** [C] a number of large guns and similar weapons operating together in

B

the same place: *The shore battery opened fire.* **ATTACK** ▷ **4** [U] **assault and battery**
►adj [before noun] using a system of producing a large number of eggs cheaply by keeping a lot of chickens in rows of small CAGES (= boxes made of wire): *battery farming* ◦ *battery* ***hens/eggs***

batting /ˈbæ.tɪŋ/ (US) /ˈbæ.t̬ɪŋ/ **noun** [U] (the part of the game) when you BAT (= it is your team's turn to hit the ball) in cricket: *The England captain* ***opened the batting*** *(= batted first).*

battle /ˈbæt.l̩/ (US) /ˈbæt̬-/ **noun; verb**
►noun [C] **FIGHT** ▷ **1** (B1) a fight between armed forces: *the Battle of the Somme* ◦ *Her only brother was killed* ***in*** *battle (= while fighting).* **ARGUMENT** ▷ **2** (B2) an argument between two groups or against a situation that a group wants to change: *The aid agency continues the battle* ***against*** *ignorance and superstition.* ◦ *The battle* ***for*** *women's rights still goes on.* **EFFORT** ▷ **3** (B2) a determined effort to achieve something in a difficult situation or to change a bad situation: *a long battle against cancer*

IDIOMS **battle of wits** the situation in which two people or two groups use their intelligence and ability to think quickly to try to defeat each other • **do battle** to fight or argue in a serious way: *No agreement was reached and both sides prepared to do battle.*

►verb [I] **1** to fight: *Police battled* ***with*** *residents in this inner-city area for three days.* ◦ *For years the two nations battled* ***over*** *territory.* **2** (C2) to try hard to achieve something in a difficult situation: *He had to battle* ***against*** *prejudice to get a job.* ◦ *The parents battled* ***for*** *the right to be involved in the decision-making.* ◦ *We battled* ***with*** *the elements* ***to*** *get the roof fixed.*

battleaxe UK (US ˈ**battle**-ˌ**ax**) /ˈbæt.l̩.æks/ (US) /ˈbæt̬-/ **noun** [C] **WEAPON** ▷ **1** a large AXE used as a weapon in the past **WOMAN** ▷ **2** a frightening and unpleasant older woman with strong opinions: *Our headmistress was a real* ***old*** *battleaxe.*

ˈ**battle** ˌ**cry** **noun** [C] **1** a shout given by soldiers as they run towards the enemy **2** a phrase used by people supporting a particular cause: *'Reclaim the night' was the battle cry of women fighting for the right to walk safely at night.*

battledress /ˈbæt.l̩.dres/ (US) /ˈbæt̬-/ **noun** [U] uniform worn by soldiers and other military groups especially when they go to fight

battlefield /ˈbæt.l̩.fiːld/ (US) /ˈbæt̬-/ **noun** [C] **PLACE** ▷ **1** a place where a BATTLE is being fought or has been fought in the past: *They carried the wounded from the battlefield.* **SUBJECT** ▷ **2** a subject on which people strongly disagree: *The issue has become a political battlefield in recent years.*

battleground /ˈbæt.l̩.graʊnd/ (US) /ˈbæt̬-/ **noun** [C] a **battlefield**

battlements /ˈbæt.l̩.mənts/ (US) /ˈbæt̬-/ **noun** [plural] a wall around the top of a castle, with regular spaces in it through which the people inside the castle can shoot

battleship /ˈbæt.l̩.ʃɪp/ (US) /ˈbæt̬-/ **noun** [C] a very large military ship with big guns

batty /ˈbæt.i/ (US) /ˈbæt̬-/ **adj** informal disapproving silly and slightly crazy and behaving in a confused way: *my batty old aunt*

bauble /ˈbɔː.bl̩/ (US) /ˈbɑː-/ **noun** [C] **1** a piece of bright but cheap jewellery **2** UK a ball-shaped Christmas decoration for hanging on a tree

baulk /bɔːk/ (US) /bɑːlk/ **verb** [I], **noun** [C] UK for **balk**

bauxite /ˈbɔːk.saɪt/ (US) /ˈbɑːk-/ **noun** [U] a type of rock from which ALUMINIUM is obtained

bawdy /ˈbɔː.di/ (US) /ˈbɑː-/ **adj** containing humorous remarks about sex: *bawdy humour/songs* • **bawdily** /-dɪ.li/ **adv** • **bawdiness** /-nəs/ **noun** [U]

bawl /bɔːl/ (US) /bɑːl/ **verb** [I or T] **SHOUT** ▷ **1** to shout in a very loud voice: *She bawled* ***at*** *me to sit down.* **CRY** ▷ **2** to cry loudly: *He was bawling his eyes out.*

PHRASAL VERB **bawl sb out** US informal to tell someone angrily that something they have done is wrong: *He's always bawling people out in meetings.*

bay /beɪ/ **noun; verb**
►noun [C] **COAST** ▷ **1** (B1) a part of the coast where the land curves in so that the sea is surrounded by land on three sides: *We sailed into a beautiful, secluded bay.* ◦ *Dublin Bay* ◦ *the Bay* ***of*** *Naples* **SPACE** ▷ **2** a partly surrounded or marked space: *Visitors must park their cars in the marked bays.* → See also **sickbay** **TREE** ▷ **3** (also ˈ**bay** ˌ**tree**) a small EVERGREEN TREE (= one that never loses its leaves) that has leaves that are used to add flavour to cooking **HORSE** ▷ **4** a brown horse

IDIOMS **hold/keep sb/sth at bay** (C2) to prevent someone or something unpleasant from harming you: *Exercise can help keep fat at bay.* • **at bay** If an animal is at bay, it is about to be caught or attacked.

►verb [I] (of dogs and WOLVES) to make a long, deep cry repeatedly

IDIOM **bay for blood** disapproving If a group of people are baying for blood, they want someone to be hurt or punished: *By now the crowd was baying for blood.*

ˈ**bay** ˌ**leaf** **noun** [C] a leaf from a bay tree, often dried and used in cooking to add flavour

bayonet /ˈbeɪ.ə.nət/ **noun** [C] a long, sharp blade fixed on to a RIFLE (= gun) • **bayonet verb** [T] (plural **-t-** or **-tt-**) *He viciously bayoneted the straw dummy.*

bayou /ˈbaɪ.uː/ **noun** [C] (in the southern US) an area of slowly moving water at the side of the main river

ˌ**bay** ˈ**window** **noun** [C] a window that sticks out from the outer wall of a house and usually has three sides

bazaar /bəˈzɑːʳ/ (US) /-ˈzɑːr/ **noun** [C] **1** an area of small shops and people selling things, especially in the Middle East and South Asia, or any group of small shops or people selling goods of the same type **2** an event where people sell things to raise money, especially for an organization that helps other people: *a Christmas bazaar*

bazooka /bəˈzuː.kə/ **noun** [C] a long, tube-shaped gun, fired from the shoulder, that is used to shoot MISSILES at military vehicles

the BBC /ˌbiː.biːˈsiː/ **noun** (UK informal **the Beeb**) abbreviation for the British Broadcasting Corporation: a British organization that broadcasts on television, radio, and the internet → Compare **ITV**

ˌ**BBC** ˈ**English** **noun** [U] the standard pronunciation of southern British English that is often used by ANNOUNCERS on the BBC

BBQ written abbreviation for **barbecue**

BC /ˌbiːˈsiː/ **adv** abbreviation for Before Christ: used in the Christian CALENDAR when referring to a year before Jesus Christ was born: *The Battle of Actium took place in 31 BC.* → Compare **AD, BCE**

bcc /ˌbiːsiːˈsiː/ abbreviation for blind carbon copy: a copy of a letter or email that is sent to someone without the knowledge of the other person or people it is sent to

BCE /ˌbiː.siːˈiː/ **adv** abbreviation for Before Common Era or Before Current Era or Before Christian Era: used when referring to a year before the birth of Jesus

Christ when the Christian CALENDAR starts counting years: *Celtic remains were found dating from as early as 1200 BCE.* → Compare **BC, CE**

bcnu written abbreviation for be seeing you: a way of saying goodbye at the end of an email or when leaving a discussion in an internet CHAT ROOM

be strong /biː/ weak /bi/ /bɪ/ **verb; auxiliary verb**
▸**verb (being, was, were, been)** **DESCRIPTION** ▷ **1** A1 [L] used to say something about a person, thing, or state, to show a permanent or temporary quality, state, job, etc.: *He is rich.* ◦ *It's cold today.* ◦ *I'm Andy.* ◦ *That's all for now.* ◦ *What do you want to be (= what job do you want to do) when you grow up?* ◦ *These books are (= cost) £3 each.* ◦ *Being afraid of the dark, she always slept with the light on.* ◦ *Never having been ill himself, he wasn't a sympathetic listener.* ◦ *Be quiet!* ◦ *Do be quiet!* ◦ [+ -ing verb] *The problem is deciding what to do.* ◦ [+ to infinitive] *The hardest part will be **to** find a replacement.* ◦ [+ that] *The general feeling is **that** she should be asked to leave.* ◦ ***It's** not **that** I don't like her – **it's** just **that** we rarely agree on anything!* **2** A1 [I usually + adv/prep] used to show the position of a person or thing in space or time: *The food was already on the table.* ◦ *Is anyone there?* ◦ *The meeting is now (= will happen) next Tuesday.* ◦ ***There's** a hair in my soup.* **3** [L] used to show what something is made of: *Is this plate pure gold?* **ALLOW** ▷ **4** [+ to infinitive] used to say that someone should or must do something: *You're **to** sit in the corner and keep quiet.* ◦ *Their mother said they were **not to** (= not allowed to) play near the river.* ◦ *There's no money left – what are we **to** do?* **FUTURE** ▷ **5** [+ to infinitive] formal used to show that something will happen in the future: *We are **to** (= we are going to) visit Australia in the spring.* ◦ *She was **never to** see (= she never saw) her brother again.* **6** [+ to infinitive] used in CONDITIONAL sentences to say what might happen: *If I were **to** refuse they'd be very annoyed.* ◦ formal *Were I **to** refuse they'd be very annoyed.* **CAN** ▷ **7** [+ to infinitive] used to say what can happen: *The exhibition of modern prints is currently **to** be seen at the City Gallery.* **EXIST** ▷ **8** [I] to exist or live: formal *Such terrible suffering should never be.* ◦ old use or literary *By the time the letter reached them their sister had ceased to be (= had died).*

> **! Common mistake: be**
> **Warning:** Check your verb endings!
> Many learners make mistakes when using **be** in the **-ing** form. Don't write 'beeing', write **being**.

PHRASAL VERB **be in for sth** C2 to be going to experience something unpleasant very soon: *The weather forecast says we're in for heavy rain this evening.* ◦ *You'll be in for **it** (= she will be very angry) if you don't do what she tells you.*

▸**auxiliary verb (being, was, were, been)** **CONTINUE** ▷ **1** A2 [+ -ing verb] used with the present participle of other verbs to describe actions that are or were still continuing: *I'm still eat**ing**.* ◦ *She's study**ing** to be a lawyer.* ◦ *The audience clearly wasn't enjoy**ing** the show.* ◦ *You're always complain**ing**.* ◦ *I'll be com**ing** back (= I plan to come back) on Tuesday.* **PASSIVE** ▷ **2** A2 [+ past participle] used with the past participle of other verbs to form the PASSIVE: *I'd like to go but I haven't been ask**ed**.* ◦ *Troublemakers are encourag**ed** to leave.* ◦ *A body has been discover**ed** by the police.*

beach /biːtʃ/ **noun; verb**
▸**noun** [C] A1 an area of sand or small stones near the sea or another area of water such as a lake: *We spent the day **on** the beach.* ◦ *a beach café*
▸**verb** [T] to pull or force a boat, etc. out of the water onto the land: *The boat had been beached near the rocks.*

> **! Common mistake: beach**
> **Warning:** use the correct preposition!
> Don't say 'in the beach', say **on the beach**:
> ~~*We spent the whole day playing in the beach.*~~

ˈbeach ˌball **noun** [C] a large, light, brightly coloured ball filled with air that people play with, especially on the beach

ˈbeach ˌbuggy **noun** [C] a small car with large wheels and open sides that is designed to be driven on areas covered in sand

ˈbeach ˌbum **noun** [C] informal someone who spends most of their time enjoying themselves on the beach

beachcomber /ˈbiːtʃˌkəʊ.məʳ/ US /-ˌkoʊ.mɚ/ **noun** [C] a person who walks along beaches looking for objects of value or interest

beached /biːtʃt/ **adj** [before noun] describes a WHALE, DOLPHIN, etc. that has swum onto a beach and cannot get back into the water

beachfront /ˈbiːtʃ.frʌnt/ **noun** [C] mainly US a strip of land along a beach: *a house on the beachfront*

beachhead /ˈbiːtʃ.hed/ **noun** [C] an area of land near the sea or a river that an attacking army has taken control of and from where it can move forward into enemy country: *The troops quickly **established** a beachhead and were preparing to advance.* → Compare **bridgehead**

ˌbeach ˈvolleyball **noun** [U] a form of VOLLEYBALL played on sand by two teams of two players

beachwear /ˈbiːtʃ.weəʳ/ US /-wer/ **noun** [U] clothes that you wear on a beach

beacon /ˈbiː.kən/ **noun** [C] a light or fire on the top of a hill that acts as a warning or signal: *As part of the centenary celebrations a chain of beacons was **lit** across the region.* ◦ figurative *She was a beacon **of** hope in troubled times.*

bead /biːd/ **noun** [C] **JEWELLERY** ▷ **1** a small, coloured, often round piece of plastic, wood, glass, etc. with a hole through it. It is usually put on a string with a lot of others to make jewellery: *She wore a necklace of brightly coloured wooden beads.* **LIQUID** ▷ **2** a very small amount of liquid: *Beads **of** sweat stood out on his forehead.*

beaded /ˈbiː.dɪd/ **adj** **JEWELLERY** ▷ **1** decorated with beads: *She wore an elaborately beaded 20s-style dress.* **LIQUID** ▷ **2** **beaded with sweat, perspiration, etc.** covered with small drops of SWEAT or a similar liquid: *After an hour of aerobics your face will be beaded with sweat.*

beading /ˈbiː.dɪŋ/ **noun** [C or U] a long, thin piece of wood stuck to the edge of, or used to decorate, wooden furniture, picture frames, etc.

beady /ˈbiː.di/ **adj** disapproving (of eyes) small and bright, especially like a bird's eyes: *His beady little **eyes** were fixed on the money I held out.* ◦ *She's always got her beady eyes on what I'm doing (= she watches me closely).*

beagle /ˈbiː.gl/ **noun** [C] a dog with short hair, a black, brown, and white coat, short legs, and long ears: *Snoopy is the world's most famous beagle.*

beak /biːk/ **noun** [C] **BIRD'S MOUTH** ▷ **1** C1 the hard, pointed part of a bird's mouth: *Birds use their beaks to pick up food.* **NOSE** ▷ **2** informal a large nose: *He'd be* *quite handsome if it wasn't for that great beak of his.* **JUDGE** ▷ **3** UK old-fashioned slang a judge

B

beaker /ˈbiː.kəʳ/ (US) /-kɚ/ noun [C] **1** UK a cup, usually with no handles, used for drinking: *She gave the children beakers **of** juice.* **2** a glass or plastic container used in chemistry

ˈbe-all noun **the be-all and end-all** the most important thing: *We all agreed that winning was not the be-all and end-all.*

beam /biːm/ noun; verb

▸noun [C] **LINE** ▷ **1** (B2) a line of light that shines from a bright object: *The rabbit stopped, mesmerized by the beam **of** the car's headlights.* → See also **moonbeam, sunbeam** **2** a line of RADIATION or PARTICLES flowing in one direction: *a **laser** beam* ◦ *an **electron** beam* **WOOD** ▷ **3** a long, thick piece of wood, metal, or concrete, especially used to support weight in a building or other structure: *The sitting room had exposed **wooden** beams.* **4 the beam** in the sport of women's GYMNASTICS, a wooden bar on which the competitors balance and perform movements

▸verb **SMILE** ▷ **1** [I] to smile with obvious pleasure: *She beamed **with** delight/pleasure at his remarks.* ◦ *The child beamed **at** his teacher as he received the award.* ◦ [+ speech] *'I'm so pleased to see you,' he beamed (= said as he smiled).* **SEND OUT** ▷ **2** [I or T] to send out a beam of light, an electrical or radio signal, etc.: *The midday sun beamed (= shone brightly) **down on** the boat as it drifted along.* ◦ *The concert was beamed (= broadcast) by satellite all over the world.*

ˈbeam ˌbalance noun [C] specialized a device for measuring the weight of something by putting it into a small dish that hangs from one end of a straight bar and balancing it with weights at the other end

beaming /ˈbiː.mɪŋ/ adj describes a smile that is very wide and happy, or someone who is smiling in this way: *a beaming smile*

bean /biːn/ noun [C] (A1) a seed, or the POD containing seeds, of various climbing plants, eaten as a vegetable: *green beans* ◦ *kidney beans* ◦ *baked beans* ◦ *Coffee beans are the bean-like seeds of the coffee tree.*

IDIOM **not have a bean** informal to have no money

beanbag /ˈbiːn.bæg/ noun [C] **SEAT** ▷ **1** (also ˌ**beanbag ˈchair**) a soft seat consisting of a large cloth bag filled with dried beans or something similar **TOY** ▷ **2** a small bag filled with dried beans or similar objects, used as a children's toy

ˈbean ˌcounter noun [C] mainly US informal disapproving an ACCOUNTANT (= someone who takes care of a company's financial affairs), especially one who works for a large company and does not like to allow employees to spend money: *It looked like the project was going to be approved, but the bean counters said it wasn't cost-effective.*

ˈbean ˌcurd noun [U] **tofu**

beanfeast /ˈbiːn.fiːst/ noun [C usually singular] UK old-fashioned informal a party or social occasion

beanie /ˈbiː.ni/ noun [C] **1** a small hat that fits closely to the head: *a beanie hat/cap* **2** Australian English a hat made from wool with a small round wool ball on top → Compare **bobble hat**

beano /ˈbiː.nəʊ/ (US) /-noʊ/ noun [C] (plural **beanos**) old-fashioned informal a party

beanpole /ˈbiːn.pəʊl/ (US) /-poʊl/ noun [C] informal humorous a very tall, thin person

ˈbean ˌsprout noun [C] a bean that has just started to grow and is eaten as a vegetable

bear /beəʳ/ (US) /ber/ verb; noun

▸verb (**bore, borne** or US also **born**) **ACCEPT** ▷ **1** (B2) [T] to accept, TOLERATE, or ENDURE something, especially something unpleasant: *The strain must have been enormous but she bore it well.* ◦ *Tell me now! I can't bear **the suspense**!* ◦ *It's your decision – you must bear **the responsibility** if things go wrong.* ◦ [+ to infinitive] *He couldn't bear **to** see the dog in pain.* ◦ [+ -ing verb] *I can't bear be**ing** bored.* **2 not bear thinking about** to be too unpleasant or frightening to think about: *'What if she'd been travelling any faster?' 'It doesn't bear thinking about.'* **HAVE** ▷ **3** (C1) [T] to have or continue to have something: *Their baby bears **a** strong **resemblance/an uncanny likeness to** its grandfather.* ◦ *The stone plaque bearing his name was smashed to pieces.* ◦ *On display were boxing gloves that bore Rocky Marciano's signature.* ◦ [+ two objects] *I don't bear them any ill feeling (= I do not continue to be angry with or dislike them).* **SUPPORT** ▷ **4** [T] to hold or support something: *The chair, too fragile to bear her **weight**, collapsed.* **PRODUCE** ▷ **5** (C2) [T] formal to give birth to young, or (of a tree or plant) to give or produce fruit or flowers: *She had borne six children by the time she was 30.* ◦ [+ two objects] *When his wife bore him **a child** he could not hide his delight.* ◦ *The pear tree they planted has never borne **fruit**.* **BRING** ▷ **6** [T] formal to carry and move something to a place: *At Christmas the family descend on the house bearing **gifts**.* ◦ *Countless waiters bore trays of drinks into the room.* ◦ *The sound of the ice cream van was borne into the office on the wind.* **CHANGE DIRECTION** ▷ **7** (C1) [I usually + adv/prep] to change direction slightly so that you are going in a particular direction: *After you go past the church keep bearing **left/right**.* **SAY** ▷ **8 bear testimony/witness** formal **a** to say you know from your own experience that something happened or is true: *She bore witness **to** his patience and diligence.* **b** If something bears testimony to a fact, it proves that it is true: *The iron bridge bears testimony **to** the skills developed in that era.* **9 bear false witness** old use to lie

IDIOMS **bear fruit** formal (C2) If something that someone does bears fruit, it produces successful results: *Eventually her efforts bore fruit and she got the job she wanted.* • **bear the scars** to still suffer emotional pain from something unpleasant that happened in the past

PHRASAL VERBS **bear down on sb/sth** to move in a threatening way towards someone or something: *I looked up to see the car bearing down on me* • **bear on sth** formal to be connected or related to something: *I don't see how that information bears on this case.* • **bear sb/sth out** to support the truth of something: *His version of events just isn't borne out by the facts.* ◦ *If you tell them what happened I will bear you out (**on** it).* • **bear up** to deal with a very sad or difficult situation in a brave and determined way: *'How has she been since the funeral?' 'Oh, she's bearing up.'* • **bear with sb** to be patient and wait while someone does something: *If you'll just bear with me **for a moment**, I'll find you a copy of the drawings.*

▸noun [C] **ANIMAL** ▷ **1** (A2) a large, strong wild mammal with a thick fur coat that lives especially in colder parts of Europe, Asia, and North America: *a brown/black bear* ◦ *a bear cub (= young bear)* → See also **grizzly bear, polar bear, teddy** **FINANCE** ▷ **2** specialized a person who sells SHARES when prices are expected to fall, in order to make a profit by buying them back again at a lower price → Compare **bull**

IDIOMS **be like a bear with a sore head** (US also **like a (real) bear**) to be in a bad mood that causes you to treat other people badly and complain a lot: *You're like a bear with a sore head this morning. What's wrong* *with you?* • **do bears shit in the woods?** humorous or offensive saying used to say that the answer to a question you have just been asked is obviously 'yes'

bearable /ˈbeə.rə.bl/ (US) /ˈber.ə-/ **adj** If an unpleasant situation is bearable, you can accept or deal with it: *As far as she was concerned, only the weekends **made** life bearable.*

beard /bɪəd/ (US) /bɪrd/ **noun; verb**

▸**noun** [C] **1** A1 the hair that some men allow to grow on the lower part of their face: *a flowing white beard* ◦ *He's **growing** a beard.* ◦ *He **shaved off** his beard but kept his moustache.* **2** the long hair that grows under a GOAT's mouth

▸**verb** [T] literary to face, meet, or deal with an unpleasant or frightening person in a brave or determined way: *With a nervous swallow he bearded the formidable-looking librarian behind the desk.*

IDIOM **beard the lion (in his/her den)** to visit an important person in order to tell or ask them something unpleasant

bearded /ˈbɪə.dɪd/ (US) /ˈbɪr.dɪd/ **adj** with a beard: *A thin, bearded man sat opposite me on the train.*

beardless /ˈbɪəd.ləs/ (US) /ˈbɪrd-/ **adj** without a beard

bearer /ˈbeə.rəʳ/ (US) /ˈber.ɚ/ **noun** [C] **1** a person whose job is to carry something, or a person who brings a message: *He was a **coffin** bearer at his father's funeral.* ◦ *I'm sorry to be the bearer **of bad news**.* **2** specialized the person who owns an official document or banknote

ˈbear ˌhug noun [C] the action of putting your arms around someone very tightly and quite roughly

bearing /ˈbeə.rɪŋ/ (US) /ˈber.ɪŋ/ **noun** **MACHINE PART** ▷ **1** [C] a part of a machine that supports another part that turns round: *a wheel bearing* ◦ *a roller bearing* **POSITION** ▷ **2 get/find your bearings a** to discover your exact position: *The road system was so complicated that we had to stop to get our bearings several times.* **b** to succeed in becoming familiar with a new situation: *It takes a while to get your bearings when you start a new job.* **3 lose your bearings** If you lose your bearings, you do not know where you are: *They lost their bearings in the dark.* **4** [C] specialized an exact position, measured CLOCKWISE (= to the right) from north. Bearings are given as three numbers: *Nottingham is 70 km from Birmingham **on a** bearing **of** 045 degrees.* ◦ *The yachtsman **took** a bearing **on** (= found his position by using) the lighthouse.* **INFLUENCE** ▷ **5 have a bearing on sth** to have an influence on something or a relationship to something: *What you decide now could have a considerable bearing on your future.* **MANNER** ▷ **6** [U] formal someone's way of moving and behaving: *She had a proud, distinguished bearing.*

-bearing /-beə.rɪŋ/ (US) /-ber.ɪŋ/ **suffix** supporting or holding the stated thing: *a **load**-bearing wall* ◦ *ore-bearing rocks*

bearish /ˈbeə.rɪʃ/ (US) /ˈber.ɪʃ/ **adj** **ANIMAL** ▷ **1** looking or behaving like a BEAR **FINANCE** ▷ **2** specialized expecting a fall in prices: *The overall oil price outlook is expected to remain bearish.*

ˈbear ˌmarket noun [C] specialized a time when the price of SHARES is falling and a lot of people are selling them

béarnaise /ˌbeəˈneɪz/ (US) /ˌber-/ **noun** [U] (also **ˌbéarnaise ˈsauce**) a sauce made with eggs and TARRAGON (= a herb) that is eaten with meat or fish

bearskin /ˈbeə.skɪn/ (US) /ˈber-/ **noun** **SKIN** ▷ **1** [C or U] the skin of a BEAR, with its fur, especially when it has been removed from its body: *An old bearskin **rug** lay on the floor.* **HAT** ▷ **2** [C] a tall, black fur hat that is worn by particular soldiers, especially for formal ceremonies

beast /biːst/ **noun** [C] **1** formal an animal, especially a large or wild one: *a wild beast* ◦ *The room wasn't fit for man or beast.* **2** old-fashioned an unpleasant, annoying, or cruel person: *He was a beast to her throughout their marriage.*

IDIOM **beast of burden** literary an animal such as a DONKEY or an ox that is used to carry or pull things

beastie /ˈbiː.sti/ **noun** [C] **INSECT** ▷ **1** informal an insect: *Keep still, you've got a beastie in your hair.* **ANIMAL** ▷ **2** Scottish English or humorous an animal: *A lot of beasties live in the forest.*

beastly /ˈbiːst.li/ **adj** old-fashioned unkind or unpleasant: *Why are you being so beastly **to** me?* ◦ *We've had beastly weather all summer.*

beat /biːt/ **verb; adj; noun**

▸**verb** (**beat**, **beaten** or US also **beat**) **DEFEAT** ▷ **1** B1 [T] to defeat or do better than: *Simon always beats me **at** tennis.* ◦ *Holland beat Belgium **(by)** 3–1.* ◦ *Our team was comfortably/easily/soundly beaten in the first round of the competition.* ◦ *The Nationalists were **narrowly** beaten in the local election.* ◦ *He beat me **fair and square** (= without cheating).* ◦ *They were beaten **hands down** (= completely) by their opponents.* ◦ *She has beaten her own **record** of three minutes ten seconds.* ◦ US *He beat **out** all the top competitors in his sport.* **2** C2 informal to be more enjoyable than another activity or experience: [+ -ing verb] *Taking the bus sure beats walk**ing**.* ◦ slang *Taking the bus beats **the hell out of** (= is much better than) walking all the way there.* ◦ *You can't beat (= there is nothing more enjoyable than) a cold beer on a hot afternoon.* **3** [T] To beat something that is going to happen is to take action before the thing happens: *I always do my shopping early to beat **the rush**.* **4 beat sb to it** to do something before someone else does it: *I was just going to tidy up the kitchen, but you've beaten me to it.* **HIT** ▷ **5** B2 [I or T, usually + adv/prep] to hit repeatedly: *They saw him beating his dog with a stick.* ◦ *The child had been brutally/savagely beaten.* ◦ *She was beaten **to death**.* ◦ [+ obj + adj] *He was beaten **senseless**.* ◦ *Beat the **drum**.* ◦ *The rain was beating **down** incessantly **on** the tin roof.* **6 beat a path through sth** to form a path in an area where long grass or bushes grow closely together, by hitting the plants with your hands or an object, or by stepping on them: *We beat a path through the undergrowth.* **MIX** ▷ **7** C1 to mix something repeatedly using a UTENSIL such as a spoon or WHISK: *To make an omelette you must first beat the eggs.* **MOVEMENT** ▷ **8** B1 [I or T] to (cause to) make a regular movement or sound: *Her heart started to beat faster.* ◦ *The hummingbird beats its wings at great speed.* **9 beat time** to make a regular sound or movement to music

IDIOMS **beat sb at their own game** to use to your own advantage the methods by which someone else has tried to defeat you • **beat sb hollow** UK to defeat someone easily and by a large amount: *We played my brother's school at football and beat them hollow.* • **beat sb's brains out** informal to hit someone repeatedly with great force • **beat your breast/chest** to show how sad or guilty you feel in an obvious or public way: *There's no point in beating your breast about losing the money – you won't get it back.* • **beat a path to sb's door** to be eager to buy or get something from someone: *She was a successful lawyer and had clients beating a path to her door.* • **beat a retreat** (also **beat**

your retreat) to run away from a dangerous or unpleasant situation: *When we saw the police arriving we beat a **hasty** retreat.* • **beat around the bush** (UK also **beat about the bush**) C1 to avoid talking about what is important: *Don't beat around the bush – get to the point!* • **beat it!** slang go away! • **beat the rap** US to escape or avoid blame or punishment • **if you can't beat 'em, join 'em** informal saying said when you accept that you cannot be as successful as someone else without doing what they do, although you do not approve of or agree with it • **it beats me** (also **what beats me**) said when you do not understand a situation or someone's behaviour: *It beats me how she got the job.* ◦ *What beats me is why she stays with him.* • **take some beating** If something takes some beating, it is so good that it is hard to improve on it: *His new world record will take some beating.* • **that beats everything** (US also **that beats all**) used to express great surprise: *You mean she just left her job without telling anyone she was going? Well, that beats everything!*

PHRASAL VERBS **beat sb/sth back** If you beat back someone or something, you use force to move them away from you: *Riot police beat back the crowds of demonstrators.* • **beat down** If the sun beats down, it shines very strongly and makes the air very hot: *The tropical sun beat down **on** them mercilessly.* • **beat sb down** informal to persuade someone to accept a lower amount of money for something: *He wanted £50 for the bike, but I managed to beat him down **to** £35.* • **beat sb off** to manage to defeat someone who is attacking you: *She beat off her attacker by hitting him with her handbag.* ◦ figurative *The company managed to beat off the competition and secure the contract.* • **beat off** US offensive to MASTURBATE • **beat sth out** **MUSIC** ▷ **1** to make sounds that have a particular rhythm by hitting something such as a drum: *The drummer beat out a steady rhythm while we marched.* **FIRE** ▷ **2** to make a fire go out by hitting it repeatedly with an object, such as a large piece of cloth: *She beat the flames out with her bare hands.* • **beat sb out** mainly US to defeat someone or do better than them in a competition, sport, or business: *They beat out several other rivals for the contract.* • **beat sth out of sb** to make someone say things they do not want to by hitting them: *The men claimed that the police had beaten the confession out of them.* • **beat sb up** informal B2 to hurt someone badly by hitting or kicking them repeatedly: *He claims he was beaten up by the police.*

▸**adj** [after verb] informal extremely tired: *I'm beat – I'm going to bed.* ◦ UK *You've been working too hard, you look **dead** beat.* → See also **deadbeat**

▸**noun** **MOVEMENT** ▷ **1** B2 [C or U] a regular movement or sound, especially that made by your heart: *I put my head on his chest but I could feel no **heart** beat.* ◦ *My heart missed a beat (= I felt very excited) when she said, 'Yes, I'll marry you'.* **MUSIC** ▷ **2** B2 [C or U] in music, a regular emphasis, or a place in the music where such an emphasis is expected: *The guitar comes in **on** the third beat.* ◦ *He tapped his foot to the beat (= rhythm) of the music.* **AREA** ▷ **3** [C usually singular] an area for which someone, such as a police officer, has responsibility as part of their job: *Bob has worked as an officer **on** this particular beat for 20 years.* **4 be on/walking the beat** A police officer who is on/walking the beat is on duty, walking around rather than driving in a police car.

beaten /ˈbiː.tᵊn/ US /-t̬ᵊn/ **adj** **1** [before noun] describes gold or another metal that has been made flat by having been hit repeatedly with a hard object: *She was wearing a necklace of beaten gold.* **2** [before noun] describes a path or track that people walk along regularly so that the ground has become hard and the path is clear

IDIOM **off the beaten track** (US also **off the beaten path**) C2 in a place where few people go, far from any main roads and towns

beater /ˈbiː.təʳ/ US /-t̬ɚ/ **noun** [C] **DEVICE** ▷ **1** a device that is used for repeatedly hitting something, especially in order to clean it, or for mixing foods. Beater is often used as a combining form: *an electric beater* ◦ *a carpet beater* ◦ *an egg beater* **PERSON** ▷ **2** used as a combining form to refer to a person who repeatedly hits people, especially members of their family: *a wife-beater* **3** a person paid by people hunting to force birds and animals into a place where they can be seen and therefore shot

beatific /ˌbiː.əˈtɪf.ɪk/ **adj** literary appearing happy and calm, especially in a holy way: *The angels in the painting have beatific **smiles**.* • **beatifically** /-fɪ.kᵊl.i/ **adv**

beatify /biˈæt.ɪ.faɪ/ US /-ˈæt̬-/ **verb** [T] to announce formally in the Roman Catholic Church that someone who is dead has lived a holy life, usually as the first stage in making that person a SAINT • **beatification** /biˌæt.ɪ.fɪˈkeɪ.ʃᵊn/ US /-ˌæt̬-/ **noun** [C or U]

beating /ˈbiː.tɪŋ/ US /-t̬ɪŋ/ **noun** [C] **DEFEAT** ▷ **1** a defeat: *We **took** a beating (= we were defeated) in our last match.* **HIT** ▷ **2** an act of hitting someone repeatedly and hard: *She **gave** her son a severe beating.*

beatnik /ˈbiːt.nɪk/ **noun** [C] (especially in the 1950s and 1960s) a young person who did not accept society's customs and principles, and showed this by the way they dressed and behaved

ˌbeat ˈup **adj** (also **ˌbeaten ˈup**) (of things) in bad condition: [before noun] *a beat-up old car*

beau /bəʊ/ US /boʊ/ **noun** [C] (plural **beaux** /bəʊz/ US /boʊz/ or **beaus**) old-fashioned a BOYFRIEND

the Beaufort scale /ˈbəʊ.fətˌskeɪl/ US /ˈboʊ.fɚt-/ **noun** [S] specialized a fixed set of numbers used for measuring and comparing wind speeds, from 0 (for calm) to 12 (for HURRICANE)

beaut /bjuːt/ **noun** [C] old-fashioned informal something that, or someone who, is very good or noticeable: *Let me have a look at that bruise. Oh, that's a beaut!* • **beaut** **adj** Australian English informal *That was a beaut dinner.*

beauteous /ˈbjuː.ti.əs/ US /-t̬i-/ **adj** literary very attractive to look at → Synonym **beautiful**

beautician /bjuːˈtɪʃ.ᵊn/ **noun** [C] a trained person whose job it is to improve the appearance of a customer's face, body, and hair, using creams, make-up, and other types of treatment, often in a BEAUTY SALON

! Common mistake: beautiful

Warning: Check your spelling!
Beautiful is one of the 50 words most often spelled wrongly by learners. Remember: the correct spelling has 'eau' and only one 'l'.

! Common mistake: beautiful

Warning: Common word-building error!
Adjectives that end in the suffix **-ful** have only one 'l'. Don't write 'beautifull', write **beautiful**.

beautiful /ˈbjuː.tɪ.fᵊl/ US /-t̬ɪ-/ **adj** **1** A1 very attractive: *a beautiful woman* ◦ *breathtakingly beautiful scenery* ◦ *She was wearing a beautiful dress.* **2** A1 very pleasant: *a beautiful piece of music* ◦ *beautiful* *weather* **3** mainly US very kind: *You did a beautiful thing in helping those poor children.* • **beautifully** /-i/ **adv** B1 *She dresses beautifully.* ◦ *Their house is beautifully decorated.*

Other ways of saying beautiful

If someone (a man or woman) is beautiful, we can say that the person is **attractive** or **good-looking**. The adjective **handsome** is also used for men, and **pretty** for women:

*Her husband is really **good-looking**.*

*Your daughter is very **pretty**.*

If someone, especially a woman, is extremely beautiful, you can say that the person is **gorgeous** or **stunning**:

*You look **gorgeous** in that dress!*

*I think she's **stunning**.*

The adjectives **breathtaking, lovely,** and **gorgeous** are often used to describe scenery that is very beautiful:

*The view from the window is **breathtaking**.*

*We drove through some **gorgeous** countryside.*

The adjective **exquisite** is sometimes used to describe objects that are very beautiful and often delicate:

*They make **exquisite** lace.*

IDIOMS **the beautiful game** UK football • **the beautiful people** fashionable, rich people: *This café is a favourite haunt of the beautiful people.*

beautify /ˈbjuː.tɪ.faɪ/ US /-t̬ɪ-/ **verb** [T] mainly humorous to improve the appearance of someone or something • **beautification** /ˌbjuː.tɪ.fɪˈkeɪ.ʃən/ US /-t̬ɪ-/ **noun** [U]

beauty /ˈbjuː.ti/ US /-t̬i/ **noun** BEING BEAUTIFUL ▷ **1** B1 [C or U] the quality of being pleasing, especially to look at, or someone or something that gives great pleasure, especially when you look at it: *This is an area of outstanding **natural** beauty.* ◦ *The piece of music he played had **a** haunting beauty.* ◦ *beauty products/treatments* ◦ *She was a great beauty (= a beautiful woman) when she was young.* EXCELLENT THING ▷ **2** [C] informal something that is an excellent example of its type: *She showed me her car – it's a beauty.* ◦ *Your roses are beauties this year.* ADVANTAGE ▷ **3** a quality that makes something especially good or attractive: *The beauty **of** this plan (= what makes it good) is that it won't cost too much.*

Word partners for beauty

natural/physical beauty • *great/outstanding/sheer/stunning* beauty • beauty *products/treatments* • beauty *secrets/tips* • *a thing* of beauty • the beauty *of* sth

IDIOMS **beauty is in the eye of the beholder** saying used to express the fact that not all people have the same opinions about what is attractive • **beauty is only skin deep** saying used to say that a person's character is more important than how they look • **your beauty sleep** humorous the sleep that you need in order to feel and look healthy and attractive

ˈbeauty ˌcontest noun [C] UK (US **ˈbeauty ˌpageant**) a competition in which women are judged on how physically attractive they are

ˈbeauty ˌqueen noun [C] a woman who wins a beauty contest

ˈbeauty ˌsalon/ˌparlour noun [C] (US also **ˈbeauty ˌshop**) a place where your hair, face, and body can be given special treatments to improve their appearance

ˈbeauty ˌspot noun [C] COUNTRYSIDE ▷ **1** a place in the countryside that is very attractive SKIN ▷ **2** a small, dark mark on a woman's face that is considered to make her look more attractive

beaux noun plural of **beau**

beaver /ˈbiː.vəʳ/ US /-vɚ/ noun; verb

beaver

▸**noun** [C] (plural **beavers** or **beaver**) ANIMAL ▷ **1** an animal with smooth fur, sharp teeth, and a large, flat tail, that lives in a DAM (= a wall of sticks and earth) that it builds across a river PERSON ▷ **2** informal a person who works very hard: *a busy beaver* → See also **eager beaver**

▸**verb**

PHRASAL VERB **beaver away** informal to work hard for a long time: *She has been beavering away **at** that essay for hours.*

bebop /ˈbiː.bɒp/ US /-bɑːp/ **noun** [U] (also **bop**) a type of JAZZ music

becalmed /bɪˈkɑːmd/ **adj** If a ship with sails is becalmed, it cannot move because there is no wind.

became /bɪˈkeɪm/ **verb** past simple of **become**

because /bɪˈkəz/, /-ˈkɒz/ US /-ˈkɑːz/ **conjunction** A1 for the reason that: *'Why did you do it?' 'Because Carlos told me to'.* ◦ *We can't go to Julia's party because we're going away that weekend.* ◦ ***Just** because I'm lending you my dress for tonight doesn't mean you can borrow it whenever you want to.* ◦ informal *Have you been away, because (= the reason I am asking is that) we haven't seen you recently?*

Common mistake: because

Warning: Check your spelling!

Because is one of the 50 words most often spelled wrongly by learners. Remember: don't write 'ou', write **au**.

Common mistake: because or because of?

Because is a conjunction and is used before a clause with a verb. It is never followed by 'of':

~~*I was late because of there was heavy traffic.*~~

I was late because there was heavy traffic.

Because of is a preposition and is always used before a noun or noun phrase:

~~*I was late because heavy traffic.*~~

I was late because of heavy traffic.

beˈcause ˌof preposition B1 as a result of: *The train was delayed because of bad weather.*

béchamel /ˈbeɪ.ʃə.mel/ **noun** [C or U] (also **ˌbéchamel ˈsauce**) a white sauce, made with butter, flour, and milk

beck /bek/ **noun** [C] UK Northern English a small river → Synonym **stream**

IDIOM **at sb's beck and call** always willing and able to do whatever someone asks: *Go and get it yourself! I'm not at your beck and call, you know.*

beckon /ˈbek.ən/ **verb** **1** [I or T] to move your hand or head in a way that tells someone to come nearer: *The customs official beckoned the woman **to** his counter.* ◦ *'Hey you!' she called, beckoning me **over** with her finger.* ◦ *He beckoned **to** me, as if he wanted to speak to me.* **2** [I] If something beckons, it attracts people: *For*

B

many young people, the bright lights of London beckon, though a lot of them end up sleeping on the streets. **3** [I] If an event or achievement beckons, it is likely to happen: *She's an excellent student, **for** whom a wonderful future beckons.*

become /bɪˈkʌm/ verb (**became**, **become**) **BE** ▷ **1** A2 [L] to start to be: *I was becoming increasingly suspicious of his motives.* ◦ *It was becoming cold, so we lit the fire.* ◦ *Margaret Thatcher became the UK's first woman prime minister in 1979.* ◦ *He has just become a father.* **SUIT** ▷ **2** [T] old-fashioned to cause someone to look attractive, or to be suitable for someone: *That colour really becomes you.*

PHRASAL VERB **become of sb/sth** [not continuous] C2 If you ask what became of someone or something, you want to know where they are and what happened to them: *Whatever became of that parcel you sent?*

becoming /bɪˈkʌm.ɪŋ/ adj old-fashioned describes something attractive that suits the person wearing or doing it: *That's a most becoming dress, my dear.*

becquerel /ˌbek.əˈrel/ noun [C] specialized a unit of measurement for RADIOACTIVITY

bed /bed/ noun; verb

▸noun **FURNITURE** ▷ **1** A1 [C or U] a large, rectangular piece of furniture, often with four legs, used for sleeping on: *He lived in a room with only two chairs, a bed, and a table.* ◦ *He likes to have breakfast **in** bed on a Saturday morning.* ◦ *She didn't get **out of** bed till lunchtime today.* ◦ *I'm exhausted – I'm **going to** bed (= going to get into a bed in order to sleep).* ◦ *I always **put** the children **to** bed (= make certain that they get into a bed and are comfortable there ready for going to sleep) at 7.30 p.m.* **2 make the bed** B2 to make a bed tidy after you have slept in it **BOTTOM** ▷ **3** C2 [C] the bottom of something or something that serves as a base: *Many strange plants and fish live on the sea bed.* ◦ *The railway was built on a bed **of** solid rock.* **4 a bed of sth** a pile of one type of food on which other food is arranged as a meal: *roasted vegetables on a bed of rice* **AREA OF GROUND** ▷ **5** C2 [C] a piece of ground used for growing plants in a garden: *They've got some beautiful **flower** beds in their garden.*

IDIOMS **be in bed with** informal to work with a person or organization, or to be involved with them, in a way that causes other people not to trust you: *The newspaper editor is obviously in bed with the president.* • **bed of nails** a difficult situation or way of life • **bed of roses** an easy and happy existence • **get out of bed (on) the wrong side** (US **get up on the wrong side of the bed**) to be in a bad mood and to be easily annoyed all day • **go to bed with sb** informal to have sex with someone • **in bed** having sex: *She found her boyfriend in bed with another woman.* • **put sth to bed** informal to start printing something • **you've made your bed and now you must lie in it** saying said to someone who must accept the unpleasant results of something they have done

▸verb [T] (**-dd-**) old-fashioned to have sex with someone

PHRASAL VERBS **bed down** **SLEEP** ▷ **1** to lie down somewhere, usually somewhere different from where you usually sleep, in order to go to sleep: *I bedded down **on** the couch for the night.* **WORK WELL** ▷ **2** If a new process or organization beds down, it starts to operate well because it has existed for long enough: *It did not take the procedure long to bed down.* • **bed sth out** to move young or delicate plants from inside and plant them outside: *May is the time to bed out the geraniums.*

BEd /biːˈed/ noun [C] abbreviation for Bachelor of Education: a degree taken by some teachers, or a person who has this degree

ˌ**bed and** ˈ**board** noun [U] UK for **board and lodging**

ˌ**bed and** ˈ**breakfast** noun [C or U] (abbreviation **B and B**, **B & B**) a room to sleep in for the night and a morning meal, or a private house or small hotel offering this: *There are several bed and breakfast **places** near the station.* ◦ *We're staying at a farm that **does** bed and breakfast.* ◦ *Can you recommend a good bed and breakfast near Brighton?*

bedaub /bɪˈdɔːb/ US /-ˈdɑːb/ verb [T] formal to cover something very roughly with something sticky or dirty: *The child's face was bedaubed **with** chocolate.*

ˈ**bed** ˌ**bath** noun [C usually singular] UK (US ˈ**sponge** ˌ**bath**) a wash that you give to someone who cannot leave their bed

bedbug /ˈbed.bʌg/ noun [C] a very small insect that lives mainly in beds and feeds by sucking people's blood

bedclothes /ˈbed.kləʊðz/ US /-kloʊðz/ noun [plural] the sheets and covers that you put on a bed

bedding /ˈbed.ɪŋ/ noun [U] the covers on a bed, or the dry grass, etc., that an animal sleeps on

ˈ**bedding** ˌ**plant** noun [C] a type of plant that is planted outside in the earth when its flowers are beginning to open, and dug up when the flowers have gone

bedeck /bɪˈdek/ verb [T usually passive] literary to decorate or cover: *The hall was bedecked **with** flowers.*

bedevil /bɪˈdev.əl/ verb [T] (**-ll-** or US usually **-l-**) to confuse, annoy, or cause problems or difficulties for someone or something: *Ever since I started playing tennis, I've been bedevilled **by** back pains.*

bedfellow /ˈbedˌfel.əʊ/ US /-oʊ/ noun [C] a person connected with another in a particular activity: *The priest and the politician made **strange/odd/unlikely** bedfellows in their campaign for peace.*

bedlam /ˈbed.ləm/ noun [U] a noisy situation with no order

ˈ**bed** ˌ**linen** noun [U] the sheets and covers that you put on a bed

bedmate /ˈbed.meɪt/ noun [C] someone who you share your bed with

Bedouin /ˈbed.u.ɪn/ noun [C] (plural **Bedouin** or **Bedouins**) a member of an Arab people living in or near the desert

bedpan /ˈbed.pæn/ noun [C] a flat dish used as a toilet by people who are too ill to get out of bed

bedpost /ˈbed.pəʊst/ US /-poʊst/ noun [C] one of the four corner poles that support a bed

bedraggled /bɪˈdræg.l̩d/ adj wet, dirty, and untidy

bedridden /ˈbed.rɪ.dən/ adj having to stay in bed because of illness or injury: *His aunt was 93 and bedridden.*

bedrock /ˈbed.rɒk/ US /-rɑːk/ noun **ROCK** ▷ **1** [U] the hard area of rock in the ground that holds up the loose soil above **BASE** ▷ **2** [S] the main principles on which something is based: *Some people believe that the family is **the** bedrock **of** society.*

bedroom /ˈbed.rʊm/, /-ruːm/ noun; adj

▸noun [C] A1 a room used for sleeping in: *Our home has three bedrooms.* ◦ *the master bedroom (= the main bedroom in a house)* ◦ *You can stay in the spare bedroom.* ◦ *We've just bought some new bedroom furniture.*

▸adj [before noun] relating to sexual activity: *My dad was embarrassed by the bedroom **scenes** in the play.*

ˌ**bedroom comˌmunity** noun [C] US for a **dormitory town**

-bedroomed /-bed.rʊmd/, /-ruːmd/ **suffix** having the stated number of bedrooms: *a two-bedroomed house*

ˈ**bed sheet** noun [C] mainly Indian English a sheet that you sleep on

bedside /ˈbed.saɪd/ **noun** [C usually singular] the area at the side of a bed: *I like to have my phone **at** my bedside.*

ˌ**bedside** ˈ**manner** noun [S] the way in which a doctor treats people who are ill, especially in relation to kind, friendly, and understanding behaviour: *He has a lovely bedside manner.*

ˌ**bedside** ˈ**table** noun [C] UK (US **nightstand**, ˈ**night** ˌ**table**) a small table that is kept at the side of a bed

bedsit /ˈbed.sɪt/ **noun** [C] (also **bedsitter**, formal ˌ**bed**ˈ**sitting room**) UK a rented room that has a bed, table, chairs, and somewhere to cook in it: *He lives in a tiny student bedsit.*

bedsore /ˈbed.sɔːʳ/ (US) /-sɔːr/ **noun** [C] a painful place on the body, caused by having to lie in bed for a long time

bedspread /ˈbed.spred/ **noun** [C] a decorative cover put on a bed, on top of sheets and other covers

bedstead /ˈbed.sted/ **noun** [C] the wooden or metal frame of an old-fashioned bed

ˈ**bed-tea** noun [U] Indian English tea that is served to you in bed early in the morning

bedtime /ˈbed.taɪm/ **noun** [U or C] the time at which you usually get into your bed in order to sleep: *Put your toys away now, it's bedtime.* ◦ *Eleven o'clock is **past my** bedtime.* ◦ *I like to have a hot drink **at** bedtime.*

ˈ**bed-ˌwetting** noun [U] the habit, often found among young children, of urinating while sleeping

bee /biː/ **noun** [C] **INSECT** ▷ **1** B1 a yellow and black flying insect that makes HONEY and can STING you: *A **swarm of** bees flew into the garden.* ◦ *My arm swelled up where I was **stung** by a bee.* → See also **bumblebee** **GROUP** ▷ **2** US a group of people who come together in order to take part in a particular activity: *a sewing bee* ◦ *a spelling bee*

IDIOMS **be (as) busy as a bee** to be moving about quickly doing many things • **be the bee's knees** UK informal to be excellent or of an extremely high standard: *Have you tried this ice cream? It's the bee's knees, it really is.* • **have a bee in your bonnet** informal to keep talking about something again and again because you think it is very important

the Beeb /biːb/ noun UK informal for **the BBC**

beech /biːtʃ/ **noun** [C or U] a tree with a smooth, grey TRUNK and small nuts, or the wood from this tree: *a row of beeches* ◦ *a chair made of beech* ◦ *a beech floor/hedge*

beef /biːf/ noun; verb

▸noun **MEAT** ▷ **1** B1 [U] the flesh of CATTLE (= cows), eaten as food: *The spaghetti sauce is made with **minced** (US **ground**) beef.* ◦ *People in England often have **roast** beef **and Yorkshire pudding** for lunch on Sundays.* **COMPLAINT** ▷ **2** [C] informal a complaint: *My main beef **about** the job is that I have to work on Saturdays.*

▸verb [I] informal to complain: *He was beefing **about** having to do the shopping.*

PHRASAL VERB **beef sth up** to make something stronger or more important: *We need to find some new players to beef up the team.* ◦ *The company has plans to beef up its production.* ◦ *Your report on the new car park is fine, but why don't you beef it up a bit **with** some figures?*

beefburger /ˈbiːfˌbɜː.gəʳ/ (US) /-ˌbɝː.gɚ/ **noun** [C] UK for **hamburger** (= meat from a cow pressed into a circle, fried, and eaten between round pieces of bread)

beefcake /ˈbiːf.keɪk/ **noun** [U] informal an attractive man with big muscles, or men with such bodies as shown in pictures or in shows → Compare **cheesecake**

beefeater /ˈbiːˌfiː.təʳ/ (US) /-t̬ɚ/ **noun** [C] a guard at the Tower of London

ˌ**beef to**ˈ**mato** noun [C] UK (US ˌ**beefsteak to**ˈ**mato**) a type of very large tomato

beefy /ˈbiː.fi/ **adj** informal **1** describes someone who looks strong, heavy, and powerful: *a beefy footballer* **2** powerful and effective: *I want to buy myself a beefier computer.*

beehive /ˈbiː.haɪv/ **noun** [C] **CONTAINER** ▷ **1** a container shaped like a box in which BEES are kept so that their HONEY can be collected **HAIR** ▷ **2** a woman's hairstyle in which the hair is arranged in a pile high on the head

beehive

beekeeper /ˈbiːˌkiː.pəʳ/ (US) /-pɚ/ **noun** [C] someone who keeps BEES in order to produce HONEY • **beekeeping** /-pɪŋ/ **noun** [U]

beeline /ˈbiː.laɪn/ **noun** **make a beeline for sb/sth** informal to go directly and quickly towards someone or something: *At parties he always makes a beeline for the prettiest woman in the room.*

been /biːn/, /bɪn/ **verb** **1** past participle of **be** **2** used to mean 'visited', 'travelled', or 'arrived': *I've never been **to** Kenya, but I hope to visit it next year.* ◦ *The postman hasn't been yet.* ◦ *The doctor's just been (= has arrived and left).* **3** used as the past participle of 'go' when the action referred to is finished: *She's been to the hairdresser's (= and now she has returned).*

beep /biːp/ **verb** **1** [I or T] (to cause) to make a short, loud sound: *The taxi-driver beeped (his horn) impatiently **at** the cyclist.* ◦ *I don't like those watches that keep beeping every hour.* **2** [T] US (UK **bleep**) to call someone, for example a doctor, by sending a signal to a beeper that they carry • **beep noun** [C] a short, loud sound: *The voice on the answering machine said 'Please leave any message after the beep'.*

beeper /ˈbiː.pəʳ/ (US) /-pɚ/ **noun** [C] US (UK **bleeper**) a **pager**

beer /bɪəʳ/ (US) /bɪr/ **noun** **1** A1 [U or C] an alcoholic drink made from grain and HOPS (= a type of plant): *He asked for a pint of beer.* ◦ *This beer is **brewed** in Mexico.* **2** A1 [C] a glass or container of this drink: *After a hard day's work I enjoy a beer or two.*

ˈ**beer** ˌ**belly** noun [C usually singular] (also ˈ**beer** ˌ**gut**) the fat stomach that a man develops when he has drunk a lot of beer over a long period

ˈ**beer** ˌ**garden** noun [C] an area of land belonging to a pub where people can sit outside and have a drink

ˈ**beer** ˌ**mat** noun [C] a small piece of cardboard that you put under a glass to protect a table surface in a pub or bar

beery /ˈbɪə.ri/ (US) /ˈbɪr.i/ **adj** smelling of beer: *beery **breath*** ◦ *a beery kiss*

beeswax /ˈbiːz.wæks/ **noun** [U] the substance containing a lot of fat that BEES produce, used for making candles and POLISH for wood

beet /biːt/ noun [C or U] **1** a plant with a thick root, often fed to animals or used to make sugar → See also **sugar beet 2** mainly US for **beetroot**

beetle /ˈbiː.tl/ ⓤⓢ /-t̬l/ **noun; verb**
▸**noun** [C] an insect with a hard shell-like back: *a black beetle* ◦ *a deathwatch beetle* ◦ *a dung beetle*
▸**verb** [I] UK informal to go somewhere quickly: *Hoping to miss the traffic jams, she beetled* ***off*** *home at four o'clock.*

Beetle /ˈbiː.tl/ ⓤⓢ /-t̬l/ **noun** [C] trademark a small car with a rounded front, top, and back, made by the company Volkswagen

beetroot /ˈbiːt.ruːt/ noun [C or U] UK (US usually **beet**) the small, round, dark red root of a plant, eaten cooked as a vegetable, especially cold in salads

befall /bɪˈfɔːl/ ⓤⓢ /-ˈfɑːl/ verb [T or I] (**befell**, **befallen**) literary If something bad or dangerous befalls you, it happens to you: *Should any harm befall me on my journey, you may open this letter.*

befit /bɪˈfɪt/ verb [T] (**-tt-**) formal to be suitable or right for someone or something: *She was buried in the cathedral, as befits someone of her position.* • **befitting** /bɪˈfɪt.ɪŋ/ ⓤⓢ /-ˈfɪt̬-/ adj

before /bɪˈfɔːʳ/ ⓤⓢ /-ˈfɔːr/ **preposition, adv, conjunction; preposition**
▸**preposition, adv, conjunction 1** (A1) at or during a time earlier than (the thing mentioned): *You should always wash your hands before meals.* ◦ *Before leav**ing** he said goodbye to each of them.* ◦ *She's always up before dawn.* ◦ *Before he could reach the door, she quickly closed it.* ◦ *Before we make a decision, does anyone want to say anything else?* ◦ *She had to give the doorman a tip before he would help her with her suitcases (= he would not do it until she had given him a tip).* **2** (B1) until (the event mentioned): *It was an hour before the police arrived.* **3** (A2) in the past: *He said he had never seen her before.* ◦ *I feel as though I've been here before.*
▸**preposition 1** (B1) in front of: *The letter K comes before L in the English alphabet.* ◦ *Many mothers put their children's needs before their own.* ◦ *We have the whole weekend before us – what shall we do?* ◦ *He stood up before a whole roomful of people, and asked her to marry him.* **2** (A2) If a place is before another place, you will arrive at it first when you are travelling towards the second place: *The bus stop is just before the school.* **3** To be before someone or a group of people, is to be formally considered or examined by that person or group: *The proposal before the committee is that we try and reduce our spending by ten percent.* ◦ *The men* ***appeared*** *before the judge yesterday.*

beforehand /bɪˈfɔː.hænd/ ⓤⓢ /-ˈfɔːr-/ adv earlier (than a particular time): *I knew she was coming that afternoon because she had phoned beforehand to say so.*

befriend /bɪˈfrend/ verb [T] to be friendly towards someone: *He was befriended by an old lady.*

befuddled /bɪˈfʌd.ld/ adj confused: *I'm so tired, my poor befuddled brain can't absorb any more.*

beg /beg/ verb (**-gg-**) **1** (B2) [I or T] to make a very strong and urgent request: *They begged* ***for*** *mercy.* ◦ [+ speech] *'Please, please forgive me!' she begged (him).* ◦ [+ obj + to infinitive] *He begged her* ***to*** *stay, but she simply laughed and put her bags in the car.* **2** (B2) [I or T] to ask for food or money because you are poor: *There are more and more homeless people begging* ***on the streets*** *these days.* ◦ *She had to beg* ***for*** *money and food for her children.* ◦ *He begged a loan from his boss.* **3** [I] If a dog begs, it sits with its front legs in the air as if to ask for something: *They have trained their dog to* ***sit up and*** *beg.* **4 I beg your pardon a** a polite way of saying 'I am sorry' or 'Could you repeat what you just said?' **b** a way of showing that you are angry about something that someone has just said: *I beg your pardon? I hope you're not implying that I lied!*

IDIOMS **beg the question 1** If a statement or situation begs the question, it causes you to ask a particular question: *Spending the summer travelling round India is a great idea, but it does rather beg the question of how we can afford it.* ◦ *To discuss the company's future begs the question whether it has a future.* **2** to talk about something as if it were true, even though it may not be • **beg, borrow, or steal** to do whatever is necessary to get something: *I'm going to get a dress for the ball, whether I have to beg, borrow, or steal one.* • **go begging** UK informal If something is going begging, it is available to be taken because no one else wants it: *If that bottle of wine is going begging, I'll have it.* • **I beg to differ/disagree** a polite way of saying 'I do not agree'

PHRASAL VERB **beg off** to ask to be allowed not to do something that you are expected to do: *She begged off early* ***from*** *the party because she was so tired.*

began /bɪˈgæn/ verb past simple of **begin**

beget /bɪˈget/ verb [T] (present participle **begetting**, past tense **begot** or **begat**, past participle **begotten** or **begot**) **1** old use to be the father of: *In the Bible it says that Adam begat Cain and Abel.* **2** formal to cause: *Poverty begets hunger, and hunger begets crime.*

beggar /ˈbeg.əʳ/ ⓤⓢ /-ɚ/ **noun; verb**
▸**noun** [C] **1** a poor person who lives by asking others for money or food **2** UK informal a person, especially when you are expressing an opinion about something that they have done, or that has happened to them: *You've won again, you lucky beggar.* ◦ *Those children have been running about in my rose garden again, the little beggars (= annoying people)!*

IDIOM **beggars can't be choosers** saying said when you recognize that you must accept an offer or a situation because it is the only one available to you

▸**verb** [T] literary to make a person or organization, etc. extremely poor

IDIOM **beggar belief/description** to be impossible to believe or describe: *His cruelty beggared belief/description.*

begin /bɪˈgɪn/ verb [I or T] (present participle **beginning**, past tense **began**, past participle **begun**) **START TO HAPPEN** ▷ **1** (A1) to start to happen or exist: *What time does the concert begin?* ◦ *The bridge was begun five years ago and the estimated cost has already doubled.* ◦ *The film they want to watch begins* ***at*** *seven.* ◦ *The meeting began* ***promisingly****, but then things started to go wrong.* **START TO DO** ▷ **2** (A2) to start to do something: *I began the book six months ago, but I can't seem to finish it.* ◦ [+ -ing verb] *Jane has just begun learn**ing** to drive.* ◦ *If you want to learn to play a musical instrument, it might be a good idea to begin* ***on*** *something simple.* ◦ [+ to infinitive] *After waiting for half an hour she was beginning* ***to*** *get angry.* ◦ *I have so much to tell you, I don't know where to begin.* **3 to begin with a** (B1) at the start of a process, event, or situation: *There were six of us to begin with, then two people left.* **b** (B2) used to give the first important reason for something: *The hotel was awful! To begin with, our room was far too small.* **START SPEAKING** ▷ **4** to start speaking: [+ speech] *'Well,' he began. 'I don't quite know how to tell you this.'* **FIRST PART** ▷ **5** to have

B

something as the first part: *The word 'cat' begins* ***with*** *the letter 'c'.*

! Common mistake: begin

Warning: Check your verb endings!

Many learners make mistakes when using **begin** in the past tense.

The past simple of **begin** is **began**:

~~*He closed his eyes and begun to sing.*~~

He closed his eyes and began to sing.

Begun is the past participle of **begin**:

The town has begun to flourish.

IDIOM **can't (even) begin** If you can't (even) begin to do something, it is very difficult for you to do it: *As a wealthy businessman, he couldn't even begin to imagine real poverty.*

beginner /bɪˈɡɪn.əʳ/ (US) /-ɚ/ **noun** [C] A2 a person who is starting to do something or learn something for the first time: *This judo class is for beginners only.*

beˌginner's ˈluck noun [U] unexpected success experienced by a person who is just starting a particular activity: *When I won the first contest I entered, he put it down to beginner's luck.*

beginning /bɪˈɡɪn.ɪŋ/ **noun 1** A2 [C usually singular, U] the first part of something or the start of something: *Notes on how to use this dictionary can be found* ***at*** *the beginning* ***of*** *the book.* ◦ *She sat down and read the book straight through* ***from*** *beginning* ***to end****.* ◦ *I enjoyed my job* ***at/in*** *the beginning (= when I started it), but I'm bored with it now.* **2** [C often plural] the origin of something, or the place, time, or way in which something started: *The city had its beginnings in Roman times.*

! Common mistake: beginning

Warning: Check your spelling!

Beginning is one of the 50 words most often spelled wrongly by learners. Remember: the correct spelling has 'nn' in the middle.

IDIOM **the beginning of the end** the point where something starts to get gradually worse, until it fails or ends completely: *It was the beginning of the end* ***for*** *their marriage when he started drinking.*

begone /bɪˈɡɒn/ (US) /-ˈɡɑːn/ **exclamation** old use or literary go away: *'Begone!' he shouted. 'And never show your face again!'*

begonia /bɪˈɡəʊ.ni.ə/ (US) /-ˈɡoʊ-/ **noun** [C] a garden plant with brightly coloured flowers

begrudge /bɪˈɡrʌdʒ/ **verb** [T] **1** to feel unhappy because someone has something that you think they do not deserve: [+ two objects] *I don't begrudge him his freedom.* **2** to feel unhappy about spending money on something or spending time doing something: *They begrudged every day they had to stay with their father.* ◦ [+ -ing verb] *She begrudged pay****ing*** *so much for an ice cream cone.*

beguile /bɪˈɡaɪl/ **verb** [T] literary to persuade, attract, or interest someone, sometimes in order to deceive them: *He was completely beguiled by her beauty.* ◦ *The salesman beguiled him* ***into*** *buying a car he didn't want.*

beguiling /bɪˈɡaɪ.lɪŋ/ **adj** interesting or attractive, but perhaps not to be trusted: *That's a beguiling argument, but I'm not convinced by it.* • **beguilingly** /-li/ **adv** *She smiled beguilingly at him.*

begun /bɪˈɡʌn/ **verb** past participle of **begin**

behalf /bɪˈhɑːf/ (US) /-ˈhæf/ **noun on behalf of sb** (also **on sb's behalf**) **a** B2 representing: *On behalf of the entire company, I would like to thank you for all your work.* ◦ *Unfortunately, George cannot be with us today so I am pleased to accept this award on his behalf.* **b** for the good of or because of: *Please don't leave on my behalf.*

behave /bɪˈheɪv/ **verb** [I or T] **1** B1 to act in a particular way: *She always behaves* ***well/badly*** *when her aunts come to visit.* ◦ *Whenever there was a full moon he would start behaving strangely.* ◦ *They behaved as if nothing had happened.* **2** B1 to be good by acting in a way that has society's approval: *Did the children behave (them****selves****)?*

-behaved /-bɪ.heɪvd/ **suffix** used after a word describing how someone behaves: *well/badly/perfectly-behaved children*

behaviour UK (US **behavior**) /bɪˈheɪ.vjəʳ/ (US) /-vjɚ/ **noun** [U] B1 the way that someone behaves: *Her behaviour is often appalling.* ◦ *He was notorious for his violent and threatening behaviour.*

! Common mistake: behaviour

Behaviour does not have a plural form except in specialized use.

Do not say 'behaviours', say **behaviour**:

~~*There can be many reasons for children's bad behaviours.*~~

There can be many reasons for children's bad behaviour.

Word partners for behaviour

exemplary/good/normal behaviour • ***aggressive/ anti-social/bad/violent*** behaviour • a ***pattern*** of behaviour • ***standards*** of behaviour • the behaviour ***of*** sb/sth • sb's behaviour ***toward(s)*** sb • ***change/influence*** sb's behaviour

behavioural UK (US **behavioral**) /bɪˈheɪ.vjə.rəl/ (US) /-vjɚ.əl/ **adj** relating to behaviour: *She studied behavioural* ***psychology*** *at college.*

behaviourism UK (US **behaviorism**) /bɪˈheɪ.vjə.rɪ.zᵊm/ (US) /-vjɚ.ɪ-/ **noun** [U] specialized the theory that the study of the human mind should be based on people's actions and behaviour, and not on what they say that they think or feel • **behaviourist** (US **behaviorist**) /bɪˈheɪ.vjə.rɪst/ (US) /-vjɚ.ɪst/ **adj, noun** [C]

beˈhaviour ˌtherapy noun [U] (also **beˈhavioural ˌtherapy**) in PSYCHOLOGY (= the study of the human mind), a form of treatment that tries to change someone's behaviour rather than treat the cause of it

behead /bɪˈhed/ **verb** [T often passive] to cut off someone's head, especially as a punishment

beheld /bɪˈheld/ **verb** past simple and past participle of **behold**

behemoth /bɪˈhiː.mɒθ/ (US) /-mɑːθ/ **noun** [C] formal something that is extremely large and often extremely powerful: *a grocery chain behemoth*

behest /bɪˈhest/ **noun** formal **at sb's behest/at the behest of sb** because someone has asked or ordered you to do something: *The budget proposal was adopted at the president's behest.*

behind /bɪˈhaɪnd/ **preposition, adv; adv; preposition; noun**

▸**preposition, adv** A1 at the back (of): *Look behind you!* ◦ *I hung my coat behind the door.* ◦ *Alex led, and I followed along behind.* ◦ mainly UK *As hard as she tried, she always* ***fell*** *behind the other swimmers in the races.* ◦ figurative *I knew that behind (= hidden by) her smile was sadness.*

B

IDIOMS **be behind sb (all the way)** B1 to support someone (completely) in what they are doing • **be behind sb** C2 If a bad experience or your own bad behaviour is behind you, it does not exist or affect your life now: *Those dark days are behind me now, I'm glad to say.* • **behind the wheel** driving a motor vehicle: *I'm a different person when I'm behind the wheel.* • **put sth behind you** If you put a bad experience or your own bad behaviour behind you, you do not let it affect your life now: *It's over. You need to put it behind you now, and make plans for the future.*

▸adv PLACE ▷ **1** B1 in the place where someone or something was before: *I was annoyed to discover that I'd **left** my bag behind.* ◦ *After the party a few people **stayed** behind to help clear up.* SLOWER ▷ **2** C1 slower or later than someone else, or than you should be: *The old woman was behind **with** (= late paying) the rent.*

▸preposition C1 responsible for or the cause of: *He wondered what was behind his neighbour's sudden friendliness.* ◦ *Marie Curie was the woman behind enormous changes in the science of chemistry.*

▸noun [C] informal the part of the body on which a person sits: *He tripped and fell on his behind.* ◦ *Why don't you **get off** your behind (= stand up) and do something!* → Synonym **bottom**

behindhand /bɪˈhaɪnd.hænd/ adv, adj UK formal late in doing something or slower doing something than expected: *I worked late last night because I was behindhand **with** my accounts.*

behold /bɪˈhəʊld/ US /-ˈhoʊld/ verb [T] (**beheld**, **beheld**) old use or literary to see or look at someone or something: *The new bridge is an incredible sight to behold.* • **beholder** /bɪˈhəʊl.dəʳ/ US /-ˈhoʊl.dɚ/ noun [C]

beholden /bɪˈhəʊl.dən/ US /-ˈhoʊl-/ adj [after verb] formal feeling you have a duty to someone because they have done something for you: *She wanted to be independent and beholden **to** no one.*

behove /bɪˈhəʊv/ US /-ˈhoʊv/ verb UK old-fashioned formal (US **behoove** /bɪˈhuːv/) **it behoves sb to** it is right for someone to do something: *It **ill** behoves you to (= you should not) speak so rudely of your parents.*

beige /beɪʒ/ noun [U] a pale brown colour • **beige** adj

being /ˈbiː.ɪŋ/ noun [C or U] **1** C2 a person or thing that exists: *A nuclear war would kill millions of living beings.* ◦ *Strange beings from outer space are still a popular subject for sci-fi films.* **2** the state of existing: *We do not know exactly how life first **came into** being (= began to exist.)*

bejewelled /bɪˈdʒuː.əld/ adj literary (US usually **bejeweled**) wearing a lot of jewellery or decorated with PRECIOUS STONES: *a bejewelled woman* ◦ *a bejewelled crown*

belabour UK formal (US **belabor**) /bɪˈleɪ.bəʳ/ US /-bɚ/ verb [T] EXPLAIN ▷ **1** to explain something more than necessary: *There's no need to belabour the **point**.* HIT ▷ **2** old-fashioned to hit someone or something hard and repeatedly: *She belaboured him with her walking stick.*

belated /bɪˈleɪ.tɪd/ US /-t̬ɪd/ adj coming later than expected: *a belated apology* ◦ *They did make a belated **attempt** to reduce the noise.* ◦ *Belated birthday greetings!* • **belatedly** /-li/ adv

belch /beltʃ/ verb [I or T] to allow air from the stomach to come out noisily through the mouth: *He belched noisily.* ◦ figurative *The exhaust pipe belched **out** (= produced) dense black smoke.* • **belch** noun [C] *The baby let out a loud, satisfied belch.*

beleaguered /bɪˈliː.gəd/ US /-gɚd/ adj formal **1** having a lot of problems or difficulties: *The arrival of the fresh medical supplies was a welcome sight for the beleaguered doctors working in the refugee camps.* **2** surrounded by an army: *The occupants of the beleaguered city had no means of escape.*

belfry /ˈbel.fri/ noun [C] the tower of a church where bells are hung

belie /bɪˈlaɪ/ verb [T] (present tense **belying**, past tense and past participle **belied**) to show something to be false, or to hide something such as an emotion: *Her calm face belied the terror she was feeling.*

belief /bɪˈliːf/ noun [C or S or U] **1** B2 the feeling of being certain that something exists or is true; something that you believe: *All religious and political beliefs should be respected equally.* ◦ [+ that] *It is my (firm) belief that nuclear weapons are immoral.* ◦ *His belief **in** God gave him hope during difficult times.* ◦ *Recent scandals have **shaken** many people's belief **in** (= caused people to have doubts about) politicians.* ◦ *He called at her house **in the** belief **that** (= confident that) she would lend him the money.* **2 beyond belief** C2 too bad, good, difficult, etc. to be imagined: *The brutality of the murders was beyond belief.*

> **Word partners for belief**
>
> a *firm/strong* belief • a *false/misguided/mistaken* belief • a *common/popular/widely held/widespread* belief • *have/hold* a belief • sth *beggars/defies* belief • a belief *in* sth • beliefs *about* sth • *in* the belief that

believable /bɪˈliː.və.bl̩/ adj If something is believable, it seems possible, real, or true: *I didn't find any of the characters in the film believable.*

believe /bɪˈliːv/ verb [T] **1** A2 to think that something is true, correct, or real: *Strangely, no one believed us when we told them we'd been visited by a creature from Mars.* ◦ [+ that] *He believes **that** all children are born with equal intelligence.* ◦ *She's arriving tomorrow, I believe.* ◦ *'Is she coming alone?' 'We believe **not/so** (= we think she is not/is).'* ◦ [+ obj + to infinitive] *I believe her **to** be the finest violinist in the world.* ◦ [+ obj + adj] *All the crew are missing, believed dead.* **2 not believe a word of it** to not believe that something is true: *He told me she was just a friend, but I don't believe a word of it!* **3 believe it or not** B1 (also **would you believe it?**) said when telling someone about something that is true, although it seems unlikely: *He's upstairs doing his homework, believe it or not.* **4 if you believe that, you'll believe anything!** informal something that you say to emphasize that something is obviously not true: *He said the car in front backed into him, and if you believe that, you'll believe anything!* **5 make believe** to pretend or imagine: *Let's make believe (**that**) we're pirates.* → See also **make-believe**

> **Common mistake: believe**
>
> **Warning:** Check your spelling!
>
> **Believe** is one of the 50 words most often spelled wrongly by learners. Remember: the correct spelling has 'ie'.

IDIOMS **believe sth when you see it** If you say you will believe something when you see it, you mean you think it will not happen: *'Hetty says she'll be here on time.' 'I'll believe that when I see it.'* • **not believe your eyes/ears** B1 to be so surprised by what you see or hear that you think you are imagining it: *I couldn't believe my ears **when** she said they were getting divorced.* • **not believe your luck** to be very surprised and very pleased

PHRASAL VERBS **believe in sth 1** (B1) to be certain that something exists: *Do you believe in ghosts?* **2** (B2) to be confident that something is effective and right: *They don't believe in living together before marriage.* ◦ *He believes in saying what he thinks.* • **believe in sb** to trust someone because you think that they can do something well or that they are a good person: *Gradually, since her divorce, she's beginning to believe in **herself** again.*

believer /bɪˈliː.vəʳ/ (US) /-vɚ/ noun [C] a person who has a religious belief or who strongly believes that something is right or good: *She's been a believer since she survived a terrible car accident.* ◦ *Harvey's a **great** believer **in** health food.* ◦ *I'm a great believer **in** allow**ing** people to make their own mistakes.*

Belisha beacon /bəˌliː.ʃəˈbiː.kᵊn/ noun [C] in the UK, a post with a flashing orange light on top that shows where cars must stop to allow people to walk across a road

belittle /bɪˈlɪt.l̩/ (US) /-ˈlɪţ-/ verb [T] to make a person or an action seem as if it or they are not important: *Though she had spent hours fixing the computer, he belittled her efforts.*

bell /bel/ noun [C] **1** (B1) an electrical device that makes a ringing sound when you press a button: *I stood at the front door and **rang** the bell several times.* **2** (B2) a hollow metal object shaped like a cup that makes a ringing sound when hit by something hard, especially a CLAPPER: *The church bells **rang out** to welcome in the New Year.*

IDIOMS **bells and whistles** extra features that make something more attractive, useful, etc.: *That software has all the usual functions plus the latest bells and whistles.* • **give sb a bell** UK informal to phone someone: *Give me a bell sometime next week, won't you?* • **warning/alarm bells start to ring/sound** used to describe an occasion when you realize that something is wrong: *When Frank suggested coming to stay for a couple of days, alarm bells started to ring **in my head**.* • **with bells on** US informal To do something or go somewhere with bells on is to do it or go there eagerly: *'Are you coming to Paul's tonight.' 'Sure, I'll be there – with bells on.'*

belladonna /ˌbel.əˈdɒn.ə/ (US) /-ˈdɑː.nə/ noun [U] **deadly nightshade**

ˈ**bell-bottoms** noun [plural] trousers that are very wide below the knee

bellboy /ˈbel.bɔɪ/ noun [C] (US also **bellhop**) a person in a hotel employed to carry cases, open doors, etc.

belle /bel/ noun [C] old-fashioned a beautiful and attractive woman or one who is beautifully dressed

IDIOM **be the belle of the ball** to be the most attractive woman at a party or similar event

belles-lettres /ˌbelˈlet.rə/ noun [plural] specialized works of literature that are beautiful and pleasing in an artistic way, rather than being very serious or full of information

bellicose /ˈbel.ɪ.kəʊs/ (US) /-koʊs/ adj formal wishing to fight or start a war

-bellied /-bel.ɪd/, /-id/ suffix having a BELLY (= stomach) of the type mentioned: *pot-bellied* ◦ *big-bellied*

belligerent /bəˈlɪdʒ.ᵊr.ᵊnt/ (US) /-ɚ-/ adj **1** disapproving wishing to fight or argue: *a belligerent person* ◦ *a belligerent gesture* ◦ *Watch out! Lee's in a belligerent mood.* **2** specialized fighting a war: *The belligerent countries are having difficulties funding the war.* • **belligerence** /-ᵊns/ noun [U] (also **belligerency** /-ᵊnsi/) *I can't stand his belligerence (= his wish to argue with people all the time).* • **belligerently** /-li/ adv

ˈ**bell ˌjar** noun [C] a large glass cover shaped like a bell used to cover chemical equipment, especially to prevent any gas from escaping

bellow /ˈbel.əʊ/ (US) /-oʊ/ verb [I or T] to shout in a loud voice, or (of a cow or large animal) to make a loud, deep sound: [+ speech] *'Keep quiet!' the headmaster bellowed across the room.* ◦ *We could hear the sergeant bellowing commands to his troops.* ◦ *The bull bellowed in pain.* • **bellow** noun [C] *He gave a bellow **of** rage.*

bellows /ˈbel.əʊz/ (US) /-oʊz/ noun [plural] a tool used to blow air, especially into a fire to make it burn better: *a **pair of** bellows*

ˈ**bell ˌpepper** noun [C] US for a **pepper**

ˈ**bell pull** noun [C] UK a rope or handle that is pulled to ring a bell

ˈ**bell push** noun [C] UK a button, usually by the front door of a house, that makes a bell ring inside

ˈ**bell-ˌringer** noun [C] a **campanologist (campanology)**

bellwether /ˈbelˌweð.əʳ/ (US) /-ðɚ/ noun [C] someone or something that shows how a situation will develop or change: *The report is viewed as a bellwether for economic trends.*

belly /ˈbel.i/ noun [C] **1** informal the stomach or the front part of the body between your chest and your legs: *He fell asleep with a full belly and a happy heart.* ◦ *Now six months pregnant, Gina's belly had begun to swell.* **2** the rounded or curved part of an object: *The belly of the aircraft was painted red.*

IDIOM **go/turn belly up** informal If a company or plan goes/turns belly up, it fails: *The business went belly up after only six months.*

bellyache /ˈbel.i.eɪk/ noun; verb
▸noun [C] informal a pain in the stomach
▸verb [I] informal to complain: *I wish you'd stop bellyaching and just get on with the job.* • **bellyaching** noun [U]

ˈ**belly ˌbutton** noun [C] informal or child's word **navel**

ˈ**belly ˌdance** noun [C] a dance originally from the Middle East in which a woman moves her hips and stomach • ˈ**belly ˌdancer** noun [C]

bellyflop /ˈbel.iˌflɒp/ (US) /-ˌflɑːp/ noun [C] informal an awkward jump into water in which a person's stomach hits the water

bellyful /ˈbel.i.fʊl/ noun informal **have had a bellyful of sb/sth** to have had more than you can deal with of someone or something bad or annoying: *I've had a bellyful of their lies.*

ˈ**belly ˌlaugh** noun [C] a loud, uncontrolled laugh: *I've never heard Robin laugh like that – it was a real belly laugh.*

belong /bɪˈlɒŋ/ (US) /-ˈlɑːŋ/ verb **1** (B2) [I + adv/prep] to be in the right place or a suitable place: *This table belongs **in** the sitting room.* ◦ *Where do these spoons belong?* ◦ *These papers belong **with** the others.* **2** (B2) [I] to feel happy or comfortable in a situation: *After three years in Cambridge, I finally feel as if I belong here.*

PHRASAL VERBS **belong to sb** (A2) to be someone's property: *This book belongs to Sarah.* ◦ *You shouldn't take what doesn't belong to you.* • **belong to sth** (B1) to be a member of a group or organization: *They belong to the same chess club.*

B

belongings /bɪˈlɒŋ.ɪŋz/ (US) /-ˈlɑːŋ-/ noun [plural] B2 the things that a person owns, especially those that can be carried: *I put a few **personal** belongings in a bag and left the house for the last time.*

beloved /bɪˈlʌv.ɪd/, /-ˈlʌvd/ adj; noun
▸adj formal loved very much: *Her beloved husband died last year.* ◦ *Eric was a gifted teacher beloved **by** all those he taught over the years.*
▸noun formal **your beloved** someone that you love and who you have a romantic relationship with: *He's sending some flowers to his beloved.*

below /bɪˈləʊ/ (US) /-ˈloʊ/ adv, preposition POSITION ▷ **1** A1 in a lower position (than), under: *From the top of the skyscraper the cars below us looked like insects.* ◦ *The author's name was printed below the title.* ◦ *For further information on this subject, **see** below (= lower on the page or later in the book).* ◦ *The ship's captain went below (= to the lower, covered part of the ship).* ◦ *Do you usually wear your skirts above or below the knee?* ◦ *She has three people **working** below her (= people to whom she gives orders).* LESS ▷ **2** B1 less than a particular amount or level: *They have three children below **the age of** (= younger than) four.* ◦ *His marks in English have been below average for some time now.* ◦ *The temperature has fallen below zero/freezing (= cooled to less than zero) recently.* ◦ *Last night it was eight degrees below (= eight degrees less than zero).*

IDIOM **below the belt** informal If a remark is below the belt, it is very insulting and unfair.

belt /belt/ noun; verb
▸noun CLOTHING ▷ **1** A2 [C] a strip of leather or material worn around the waist to support clothes or for decoration: *She **fastened** her belt tightly around her waist.* ◦ *He had eaten so much that he had to **undo** his belt a couple of notches.* MOVING STRIP ▷ **2** [C] a flat strip of material in a machine that moves along continuously to keep another part turning, or to keep objects on it moving along: *a fan belt* ◦ *a conveyor belt* AREA ▷ **3** [C usually singular] an area, usually just outside a city, where a particular group of people live, such as the COMMUTER belt and the STOCKBROKER belt, or an area that is known for a particular characteristic, such as the cotton belt (= an area where cotton is grown) HIT ▷ **4** [C usually singular] informal a hard hit or PUNCH: *a belt **on** the jaw*

IDIOMS **belt and braces** UK informal the use of two or more actions in order to be extra careful about something, although only one is really necessary: *I wrote to them and phoned as well – belt and braces, I admit.* • **have sth under your belt** to have learned or succeeded in something which might be an advantage in the future: *Basic computer skills are a good thing to have under your belt.*

▸verb MOVE FAST ▷ **1** [I + adv/prep] UK informal (especially of a vehicle) to travel with great speed: *The car was belting **along/down** the road.* HIT ▷ **2** [T] informal to hit someone or something hard, especially with violence: *He belted him **in** the face.* CLOTHING ▷ **3** [T] to tie something with a belt: *I belted my coat tightly.*

PHRASAL VERBS **belt sth out** informal to sing or play a musical instrument very loudly: *The band was belting out all the old favourites.* • **belt up** UK BE QUIET ▷ **1** very informal used to tell someone to stop talking or making a noise: *Just belt up, will you! I'm trying to concentrate.* FASTEN ▷ **2** (US **buckle up**) to fasten the belt that keeps you in your seat in a car or a plane: *Don't forget, belt up before you drive off.*

beltway /ˈbelt.weɪ/ noun [C] US for **ring road**

belying /bɪˈlaɪ.ɪŋ/ verb present participle of **belie**

bemoan /bɪˈməʊn/ (US) /-ˈmoʊn/ verb [T] formal to complain or express sadness about something: *Researchers at universities are always bemoaning their lack of funds.*

bemuse /bɪˈmjuːz/ verb [T] to slightly confuse someone: *Her answer bemused us all.*

bemused /bɪˈmjuːzd/ adj slightly confused: *I must admit that I was rather bemused at his sudden anger.*

bench /bentʃ/ noun **1** B2 [C] a long, usually hard seat for two or more people, often found in public places, or a long table for working on: *a **park** bench (= a seat in a public garden)* ◦ *a **work** bench (= a table for working at)* **2 the bench a** a seat or area of seats where players sit during a game when they are not playing: *He was injured, and spent the last few weeks of the season **on** the bench.* **b** the judge or MAGISTRATE in a law court, or the place where he or she sits: *Kindly address your remarks to the bench, Mr Smith.* **3 serve/sit/be on the bench** to work as a judge or MAGISTRATE **4 take the bench** US **a** to become a judge or MAGISTRATE **b** If a judge takes the bench, he or she begins a formal meeting of a law court. **5 the benches** in the UK parliament building, the seats used by the members: *There was jeering from the Labour benches.*

bench

benchmark /ˈbentʃ.mɑːk/ (US) /-mɑːrk/ noun; verb
▸noun [C] a level of quality that can be used as a standard when comparing other things: *Her outstanding performances **set** a **new** benchmark for singers throughout the world.* • **benchmark** adj *a benchmark **case***
▸verb [T] to measure the quality of something by comparing it with something else of an accepted standard: *His reports said that all schools should be benchmarked **against** the best.* • **benchmarking** /ˈbentʃˌmɑː.kɪŋ/ (US) /-ˌmɑːr-/ noun [U] *rigorous benchmarking of research performance*

benchtop /ˈbentʃ.tɒp/ (US) /-tɑːp/ noun [C] Australian English a flat surface in a kitchen, especially on top of low furniture, on which food can be prepared → Compare **worktop**

bend /bend/ verb; noun
▸verb (**bent, bent**) CURVE ▷ **1** B2 [I or T] to (cause to) curve: *The road bends to the left after the first set of traffic lights.* **2** B2 to move your body or part of your body so that it is not straight: *I bent **down** and picked up the coins lying on the road.* ◦ *Now, bend **forward/over** and touch your toes!* ◦ *Make sure you bend your knees when you're picking up heavy objects.* ◦ *After her fall she complained that she couldn't bend her leg properly.* **3 on bended knee** in a position in which the knee of one leg is touching the floor: *He **went down** on bended knee to ask her to marry him.*

IDIOMS **bend sb's ear** informal to talk to someone for a long time, especially about a problem, or to ask for something • **bend the law/rules** to change the rules in a way that is considered to be not important or not harmful: *Can't you bend the rules a little? I was only a few minutes late.*

PHRASAL VERB **bend to sth** to unwillingly accept the opinions or decisions of other people: *The local council was forced to bend **to** public pressure.*

▸noun **CURVE** ▷ **1** B2 [C] a curved part of something: *There's a bend in the pipe so you can't see from one end to the other.* ◦ *The car came **round the** bend on the wrong side of the road.* **ILLNESS** ▷ **2 the bends** [plural] a serious medical condition that DIVERS (= people who swim underwater) get when they come up to the surface of the water too quickly

IDIOMS **drive/send sb round the bend** UK informal C2 to make someone very bored or very angry: *My mother's been driving me round the bend.* ◦ *Staying at home all day was driving her round the bend.* • **round the bend** UK informal To be/go round the bend is to be/ become mentally confused or unable to act in a reasonable way: *If I'd stayed there any longer I'd have gone round the bend.*

bendable /ˈben.də.bl̩/ **adj** that can be bent: *bendable copper pipe*

bender /ˈben.dər/ US /-dɚ/ **noun** [C] informal a period during which a large amount of alcohol is drunk: *They **went on a** bender for two days after they won the championship.*

bendy /ˈben.di/ **adj** UK informal describes something that has many bends in it or that can be easily bent: *a bendy road* ◦ *a bendy toy*

beneath /bɪˈniːθ/ **preposition; adv**

▸preposition **BELOW** ▷ **1** B2 in or to a lower position than someone or something, under someone or something: *Jeremy hid the letter beneath a pile of papers.* ◦ *We huddled together for warmth beneath the blankets.* ◦ *After weeks at sea, it was wonderful to feel firm ground beneath our feet once more.* ◦ *Emma was so tired and hungry that her legs were beginning to **give way** beneath her (= she was about to fall over).* **NOT GOOD ENOUGH** ▷ **2 be beneath sb** C2 to not be good enough for someone: *Office work of any description he felt was beneath him.*

▸adv below: *She looked out of the window at the children playing beneath.*

benedictine /ˌben.ɪˈdɪk.tiːn/ **noun** [U] a type of alcoholic drink

Benedictine /ˌben.ɪˈdɪk.tiːn/ **noun** [C] a MONK OR a NUN who is a member of a Christian group that follows the rules of St Benedict

benediction /ˌben.ɪˈdɪk.ʃən/ **noun** [C] a prayer asking God for help and protection for someone

benefactor /ˈben.ɪ.fæk.tər/ US /-t̬ɚ/ **noun** [C] (female also **benefactress**) someone who gives money to help an organization, society, or person

beneficent /bɪˈnef.ɪ.sənt/ **adj** formal helping people and doing good acts: *a beneficent aunt*

beneficial /ˌben.ɪˈfɪʃ.əl/ **adj** B2 helpful, useful, or good: *The improvement in sales figures had a beneficial **effect**/influence on the company as a whole.* ◦ *A stay in the country will be beneficial **to** his health.*

beneficiary /ˌben.ɪˈfɪʃ.ər.i/ US /-i.er.i/ **noun** [C] a person or group who receives money, advantages, etc. as a result of something else: *Her husband was the chief beneficiary **of** her will.*

benefit /ˈben.ɪ.fɪt/ **noun; verb**

▸noun **ADVANTAGE** ▷ **1** B1 [C or U] a helpful or good effect, or something intended to help: *The discovery of oil brought many benefits to the town.* ◦ *One of the many benefits **of** foreign travel is learning how to cope with the unexpected.* ◦ *He's had **the** benefit **of** an expensive education and yet he continues to work as a waiter.* ◦ *I didn't **get/derive** (**much**) benefit **from** school.* ◦ *With the benefit **of hindsight** (= helped by the knowledge learned later) it is easy for us to see where we went wrong.* ◦ formal *She drinks a lot less now, **to the** benefit **of** her health as a whole.* **2** [C, usually plural] an advantage such as medical insurance, life insurance, and sick pay, that employees receive from their employer in addition to money **MONEY FROM GOVERNMENT** ▷ **3** [C or U] the money given by the government to people who need financial help, for example because they cannot find a job: mainly UK ***unemployment*** *benefit* ◦ *I'm **on** benefit at the moment.* **EVENT** ▷ **4** [C] an event such as a concert, performance, etc. that is organized in order to raise money for people in need: *benefit **concert***

> Word partners for **benefit noun**
>
> ***derive/gain/get*** benefit (from sth) • ***enjoy/have*** the benefit of sth • [the drawbacks/risks, etc.] ***outweigh*** the benefits • ***considerable/enormous/great/ maximum*** benefit • ***limited/marginal*** benefit • be ***of*** benefit ***to*** sb • be ***for/to*** sb's benefit

IDIOM **give sb the benefit of the doubt** to believe something good about someone, rather than something bad, when you have the possibility of doing either: *I didn't know whether his story was true or not, but I decided to give him the benefit of the doubt.*

▸verb [I or T] (**-t-**) B2 to be helped by something or to help someone: *I feel that I have benefited greatly **from** her wisdom.* ◦ *How can we benefit those who most need our help?*

benevolent /bɪˈnev.əl.ənt/ **adj** kind and helpful: *He was a benevolent old man and wouldn't hurt a fly.* • **benevolence** /-əns/ **noun** [U] • **benevolently** /-li/ **adv** *She smiled benevolently at me.*

beˈnevolent soˌciety **noun** [C] an organization that gives money to and helps a particular group of people in need: *a benevolent society for sailors' widows*

benighted /bɪˈnaɪ.tɪd/ US /-t̬ɪd/ **adj** literary without knowledge or morals: *Some of the early explorers thought of the local people as benighted savages who could be exploited.*

benign /bɪˈnaɪn/ **adj** **PERSON** ▷ **1** pleasant and kind: *a benign old lady* **DISEASE** ▷ **2** describes a TUMOUR that is not likely to cause death: *a benign tumour* → Compare **malignant** • **benignly** /-li/ **adv**

benny /ˈben.i/ **noun** [C] informal a sudden period of uncontrolled anger → Synonym **tantrum**

bent /bent/ **verb; adj; noun**

▸verb past simple and past participle of **bend**

▸adj **NOT STRAIGHT** ▷ **1** curved and not straight or flat: *The metal bars were bent and twisted.* **DISHONEST** ▷ **2** mainly UK slang (especially of a person in a position of authority) dishonest: *a bent copper* **GAY** ▷ **3** UK old-fashioned offensive (especially of men) gay

IDIOMS **be bent on sth/doing sth** to be determined to do or have something: *He was bent on getting married as soon as possible.* • **get bent out of shape** US informal to become very angry or upset: *I'm not getting bent out of shape because people don't respect my opinion. I'm used to that.*

▸noun [S] a natural skill: *She has **a** scientific bent/**a** bent **for** science.*

ˌbent ˈdouble **adj** describes a person who is standing with their upper body curved forwards and down towards the ground, often as a result of strong emotion or pain: *He was bent double **with laughter/pain**.*

B

benumbed /bɪˈnʌmd/ **adj** formal unable to feel because of cold, shock, etc.: *a face benumbed with cold*

benzene /ˈben.ziːn/ **noun** [U] a clear liquid made from PETROLEUM, from which plastics and many chemical products can be made

benzoic acid /benˌzəʊ.ɪkˈæs.ɪd/ US /-ˌzoʊ-/ **noun** [U] specialized a clear substance found in various RESINS and BERRIES, used in food PRESERVATIVES, medical and COSMETIC products, etc.

bequeath /bɪˈkwiːð/ **verb** [T + two objects] formal to arrange for money or property to be given to somebody after your death: *Her father bequeathed her the family fortune in his will.* ◦ *Picasso bequeathed most of his paintings and sculptures* ***to*** *Spain and France.*

bequest /bɪˈkwest/ **noun** [C] the money or property belonging to someone that they say that, after their death, they wish to be given to other people: *Her will included small bequests* ***to*** *her family, while most of her fortune went to charity.*

berate /bɪˈreɪt/ **verb** [T] formal to criticize or speak in an angry manner to someone: *As he left the meeting, he was berated by angry demonstrators.* ◦ *Doctors are often berated* ***for*** *being poor communicators, particularly when they have to give patients bad news.*

bereave /bɪˈriːv/ **verb** [T] **be bereaved** to have a close relation or friend who has died: *Everyone who has been bereaved has to find his or her own way of coping.*

bereaved /bɪˈriːvd/ **adj; noun**

►**adj** having a close relation or friend who has recently died: *a bereaved widow*

►**noun** [C] **the bereaved** (plural **the bereaved**) a person whose close relation or friend has recently died: *It is generally accepted that the bereaved benefit from counselling.*

bereavement /bɪˈriːv.mənt/ **noun** [C or U] the death of a close relation or friend: *She has recently* ***suffered*** *a bereavement.*

bereft /bɪˈreft/ **adj** [after verb] formal not having something or feeling great loss: *Alone now and almost penniless, he was bereft* ***of*** *hope.* ◦ *After the last of their children had left home the couple* ***felt*** *utterly bereft.*

beret /ˈber.eɪ/ US /bəˈreɪ/ **noun** [C] a round, flat hat made of soft material

bergamot /ˈbɜː.gə.mɒt/ US /ˈbɝː.gə.mɑːt/ **noun** [U] an oil from the skin of a type of small orange

bergschrund /ˈbɜːg.ʃrʊnd/ US /ˈbɝg-/ **noun** [C] specialized a deep CRACK near or at the top of a GLACIER, separating moving ice from ice that is not moving

berk (also **burk**) /bɜːk/ US /bɝːk/ **noun** [C] UK slang a stupid person: *I felt a* ***right*** *berk when I couldn't remember where I'd parked the car.*

berry /ˈber.i/ **noun** [C] B2 a small, round fruit on particular plants and trees

berserk /bəˈzɜːk/ US /bɚˈzɝːk/ **adj** very angry or out of control: *My mother will* ***go*** *berserk (= be extremely angry) when she finds out I've ruined her favourite dress.*

berth /bɜːθ/ US /bɝːθ/ **noun; verb**

►**noun** [C] a bed in a boat, train, etc., or a place for a ship or boat to stay in a port: *She booked a berth on the ferry from Palermo to Naples.*

►**verb** [I or T] If a ship or boat berths or if you berth it somewhere, it is tied up and stays in that place: *The ship berthed* ***at*** *Sydney.*

beryllium /bəˈrɪl.i.əm/ **noun** [U] (symbol **Be**) a chemical element that is a hard, light, silver-grey metal, used to make strong ALLOYS (= mixtures of metals)

beseech /bɪˈsiːtʃ/ **verb** [T] (past tense and past participle **beseeched** or **besought**) old use or literary to ask for something in a way that shows you need it very much: *Stay a little longer, I beseech you!* → Synonym **beg**

beset /bɪˈset/ **adj** [after verb] having a lot of trouble with something, or having to deal with a lot of something that causes problems: *With the amount of traffic nowadays, even a trip across town is beset* ***by/with*** *dangers.*

beside /bɪˈsaɪd/ **preposition** **1** A2 at the side of, next to: *Come and sit here beside me.* ◦ *Our school was built right beside a river.* **2** compared to another person or thing: *Those books seem rather dull beside this one.* **3 be beside the point** C2 to be in no way connected to the subject that is being discussed: *Let's stick to discussing whether the road should be built at all. The exact cost is beside the point.*

IDIOM **be beside yourself** C2 If you are beside yourself with a particular feeling or emotion, it is so strong that it makes you almost out of control: *He was beside himself with grief when she died.*

besides /bɪˈsaɪdz/ **adv, preposition** B1 in addition to; also: *She won't mind your being late – besides, it's hardly your fault.* ◦ *Do you play any other sports besides football and basketball?*

> **!** Common mistake: **besides or also?**
>
> **Warning:** choose the correct adverb!
>
> Use **besides** at the beginning of a clause to add a fact or reason that is stronger than what you have already said:
>
> *I'm too tired to go to the supermarket. Besides, it's closed on Sunday.*
>
> To just add extra information, don't say 'besides' say **in addition** or **also:**
>
> ~~*I speak French fluently. Besides, I speak some Italian.*~~
>
> *I speak French fluently. Also, I speak some Italian.*

besiege /bɪˈsiːdʒ/ **verb** [T often passive] **1** to surround a place, especially with an army, to prevent people or supplies getting in or out: *The town had been besieged for two months but still resisted the aggressors.* **2** When someone is besieged, a lot of people surround them: *When the pop star tried to leave her hotel she was besieged* ***by*** *waiting journalists and fans.* **3** to make many requests or complaints about something: *After showing the controversial film, the channel was besieged with phone calls from angry viewers.*

besmeared /bɪˈsmɪəd/ US /-ˈsmɪrd/ **adj** [after verb] formal covered with marks from dirt, oil, etc.: *His face was besmeared* ***with*** *chocolate.*

besmirch /bɪˈsmɜːtʃ/ US /-ˈsmɝːtʃ/ **verb** [T] literary to say bad things about someone to influence other people's opinion of them: *His accusations were false, but they served to besmirch her* ***reputation****.*

besotted /bɪˈsɒt.ɪd/ US /-ˈsɑː.t̬ɪd/ **adj** completely in love with someone and always thinking of them: *He was so completely besotted* ***with*** *her that he couldn't see how badly she treated him.*

besought /bɪˈsɔːt/ US /-sɑːt/ **verb** past simple and past participle of **beseech**

bespattered /bɪˈspæt.əd/ US /-ˈspæt̬.ɚd/ **adj** [after verb] formal covered with spots of liquid: *The backs of my legs were bespattered* ***with*** *mud after walking home in the rain.*

bespeak /bɪˈspiːk/ **verb** [T] (**bespoke**, **bespoken**) formal to suggest or show: *His letter bespeaks his willingness to help.*

bespectacled /bɪˈspek.tɪ.kl̩d/ **adj** formal wearing glasses: *a small, bespectacled man in a drab suit*

bespoke /bɪˈspəʊk/ (US) /-ˈspoʊk/ **adj** UK formal (US ˌ**custom-ˈmade**) specially made for a particular person: *a bespoke suit* ◦ *bespoke furniture*

beˌspoke ˈtailor **noun** [C] UK formal a person who makes or sells clothing that is specially made for the customer

best /best/ **adj; adv; noun; verb**

▸**adj** A1 of the highest quality, or being the most suitable, pleasing, or effective type of thing or person: *This is the best meal I've ever had.* ◦ *He's one of our best students.* ◦ *Are you sure this is the best way of doing it?* ◦ *What's the best (= shortest or quickest) way to get to the station?* ◦ *Your parents only want what is best* ***for*** *you.* ◦ *She was my best* ***friend*** *(= the friend I liked most).* ◦ ***It's*** *best (= it is wise)* ***to*** *get to the supermarket early.*

IDIOMS **be on your best behaviour** to behave extremely well and be very polite on a particular occasion: *I'd just met his parents for the first time so I was on my best behaviour.* • **best bet** informal Your best bet is the action that is most likely to be successful: *If you want to get to the station before ten o'clock, your best bet would be to take a taxi.* • **be the best thing since sliced bread** informal to be an excellent person or thing • **may the best man/person win!** said before a race or competition, meaning that you want the person who is the fastest, strongest, or most skilled to win or succeed • **put your best foot forward** to try as hard as you can • **with the best will in the world** UK used to mean 'I would like to if I possibly could', in a situation where you cannot do something: *With the best will in the world, I can't employ him in the shop unless I can trust him.*

▸**adv** **1** B1 in the most suitable, pleasing, or satisfactory way, or to the greatest degree: *Which evening would suit you best for the party?* ◦ *The Grand Canyon is best seen at sunset.* ◦ *He couldn't decide which one he* ***liked*** *best (= preferred).* **2** to the greatest degree when used as the SUPERLATIVE of adjectives beginning with 'good' or 'well': *They were the best-dressed couple at the party.* ◦ *He was voted the best-looking (= most attractive) actor in Hollywood.* **3** **as best you can** mainly UK as well as you can: *It is a difficult passage, but just translate it as best you can.*

IDIOMS **do as you think best** to choose the action that you judge to be most suitable: *'Do you think I should take this job or try for another?' 'You should do as you think best.'* • **had best/better** mainly UK used to suggest an action or to show that it is necessary: *You had best tell her (= it would be wise if you told her) that you won't be able to come to her party.* ◦ *We'd best be going now (= we should go now).*

▸**noun** [S] **1** B1 the most excellent in a group of things or people: *My tastes are simple – I only like* ***the*** *best.* ◦ *He wanted* ***the*** *best for his children – good schools, a nice house, and trips abroad.* ◦ *I like all of Hitchcock's films, but I think 'Notorious' is* ***the*** *best.* ◦ *Chris and I are* ***the*** *best* ***of*** *friends (= we are very close friends).* **2** **all the best!** A2 mainly UK informal used to say goodbye or to end a letter to someone you know well **3** **at best** C2 even when considered in the most positive way: *The food was bland at best, and at worst completely inedible.* **4** **at its best** B1 at the highest standard that can be achieved: *The documentary was an example of investigative journalism at its best.* **5** **be at your best** to be as active or intelligent as you can be: *I'm not at my best in the morning.* **6** **best of all** B2 this is the most pleasing thing: *There was wonderful food, good company, and, best of all, a jazz band.* **7** **best of luck** used to wish someone success before an exam or a difficult activity: *Best of luck* ***with*** *your exams!* ◦ *We would like to wish you* ***the*** *(very) best of luck* ***with*** *your move to the States.* **8** **the best of** In a sport such as tennis, if you play the best of a particular number of games, you play that number of games and the winner is the player who wins the greatest number of those games. **9** **do/try your best** B1 to make the greatest effort possible: *It doesn't matter if you fail, just do your best.* **10** **have had the best of** If you have had the best of something, you have enjoyed the most pleasant part of it, and everything that is left is worse: *I think we've already had the best of the hot weather this summer.* **11** **to the best of your ability** as well as you can: *Just do the job to the best of your ability.* **12** **to the best of my knowledge/belief** B2 from what I know and understand from the information that I have: *To the best of my knowledge, the chemicals which were found are not dangerous.* **13** **for the best** C2 If an action is for the best, it is done to improve a situation or produce a good result, although it might seem unpleasant at the time: *Ending a relationship is always hard but in this case it's for the best.* **14** **make the best of** B2 to make an unsatisfactory situation as pleasant as possible: *We'll have to spend the night here, so we might as well make the best of it.*

IDIOMS **at the best of times** C2 when everything is going well: *Our car is slow* ***even*** *at the best of times.* • **the best of a bad bunch/lot** informal the person or thing of a group that is not as bad as the others, although none of the group is good • **the best of both worlds** C1 a situation in which you can enjoy the advantages of two very different things at the same time: *She works in the city and lives in the country, so she* ***gets*** *the best of both worlds.* • **the best of British (luck)** UK informal used to wish someone luck, especially when you do not think they have much chance of success or happiness: *You're going to ask her father for money? Best of British, mate!* • **with the best of them** informal as well as anyone: *He can dance with the best of them.*

▸**verb** [T] formal to defeat someone in a fight or competition: *He bested his opponent in just two rounds.*

ˌ**best-beˈfore** ˌ**date** **noun** [C] UK the day or month before which food or drink should be eaten or drunk

ˌ**best ˈboy** **noun** [C] specialized the person who helps the GAFFER (= the person responsible for the electrical work) when a film or television programme is being made

bestial /ˈbes.ti.əl/ **adj** formal disapproving cruel or like an animal: *The soldiers were accused of bestial acts against unarmed civilians.*

bestiality /ˌbes.tiˈæl.ə.ti/ (US) /-t̬i/ **noun** [U] SEX ▷ **1** sex between a person and an animal CRUELTY ▷ **2** disapproving behaviour that is very cruel or like that of an animal: *the bestiality of war*

bestiary /ˈbes.ti.ə.ri/ (US) /-er.i/ **noun** [C] a book written in the Middle Ages containing descriptions of real and imaginary animals, intended to teach morals and to entertain

bestir /bɪˈstɜːʳ/ (US) /-ˈstɝː/ **verb** formal or humorous **bestir yourself** to become active after a period of rest: *I'd better bestir myself – there's work to be done.*

ˌ**best ˈman** **noun** [S] a male friend or relation of the

B

BRIDEGROOM who stands with him and helps him during a marriage ceremony

bestow /bɪˈstəʊ/ (US) /-ˈstoʊ/ verb [T often passive] formal to give something as an honour or present: *The Chancellorship of the University was bestowed **upon** her in 2010.* ◦ *The George Cross is a decoration that is bestowed **on** British civilians for acts of great bravery.* • **bestowal** /-əl/ noun [U or S] *Her father's blessing represented a bestowal of consent **upon** her marriage.*

ˌbest ˈpractice noun [C or U] a working method or set of working methods that is officially accepted as being the best to use in a particular business or industry, usually described formally and in detail: *a model for best practice in the treatment of diabetes* ◦ *a best-practice policy/programme*

bestrew /bɪˈstruː/ verb [T usually passive] (**bestrewed, bestrewn** or **bestrewed**) literary to lie covering a surface, or to cover a surface with things that are far apart and in no particular arrangement: *During the festival, the city streets are bestrewn **with** flowers.*

bestride /bɪˈstraɪd/ verb [T] (**bestrode, bestridden**) formal to sit or stand with a leg on either side of an object or animal: *He bestrode the chair as though it were a horse.*

bestseller /ˌbestˈsel.əʳ/ (US) /-ɚ/ noun [C] (B2) a product that is extremely popular and has sold in very large numbers: *The 'Harry Potter' novels were all bestsellers.* ◦ *His latest book has gone to number two in the bestseller **list*** (= *the list of the most popular books*). • **ˌbest-ˈselling** adj [before noun] *She's a best-selling **author*** (= *an author whose books are very popular*).

bet /bet/ verb; noun

▸verb (present tense **betting**, past tense and past participle **bet**) **1** (C1) [I or T] to risk money on the result of an event or a competition, such as a horse race, in the hope of winning more money: *He regularly goes to the races and bets heavily.* ◦ *She bet £500,000 **on** the horse that came in second.* ◦ [+ two objects, + that)] *I bet you $25 (**that**) I'll get there before you.* **2** (B1) [T] informal If you say you bet (someone) that something is true or will happen, you mean you are certain that it is true or will happen: [+ (that)] *I bet you (**that**) she's missed the bus.* ◦ *I bet (**that**) he won't come.*

IDIOMS **(how much) do you want to bet?** informal said in answer to something that someone has said, meaning that you are certain that they are wrong: *'Surely she won't be late this time.' 'How much do you want to bet?'* • **don't bet on it** (also **I wouldn't bet on it**) used to tell someone that you think something is unlikely to be true or to happen: *'Do you think they'll give me back the money they owe me?' 'I wouldn't bet on it.'* • **I bet** (also **I'll bet**) said to show that you understand why someone has a particular opinion or feels a particular way: *'I'm so annoyed with her.' 'I'll bet.'* ◦ *'I was so relieved I didn't have to clean up after the party.' 'I bet you were.'* • **what do you bet?** used to say that it is very likely that something is true or will happen • **you bet** informal used to emphasize a statement or to mean 'certainly': *'Are you coming to the party?' 'You bet!'* • **you can bet your life** (also **you can bet your bottom dollar**) used to say that you are completely certain that something is true or will happen: *You can bet your bottom dollar **that** he'll be the next president.*

▸noun [C] **1** (C2) an amount of money that you risk on the result of an event or a competition, such as a horse race: *He **placed/put** a bet **on** the grey horse.* **2** informal a guess or opinion: [+ (that)] *My bet is (**that**) their baby will be a girl.*

IDIOMS **be a fair bet** UK to be something that is likely to happen: *It's a fair bet (**that**) the government will increase taxes in the coming term.* • **be a good bet** to be something that would be useful, clever, or enjoyable to do: *Putting your savings in a high-interest account is a good bet.* • **be a safe bet** (C2) to be something that you are certain will happen: *It's a safe bet (**that**) Martin will be the last to arrive.* • **be your best bet** (C2) to be the best decision or choice: *Your best bet would be to take a bus to the airport.* • **do sth for a bet** (US usually **do sth on a bet**) to do something dangerous or take a risk because someone says that they do not think you will: *She jumped in the fountain for a bet.*

beta /ˈbiː.tə/ (US) /ˈbeɪ.t̬ə/ noun; adj

▸noun [C or U] (symbol β) the second letter of the Greek alphabet → Compare **alpha, gamma, delta**

▸adj [before noun] Beta software is at the second stage of development: *You can download the beta **version** from the website.*

ˌbeta-ˈcarotene noun [U] a form of CAROTENE that the body is able to change into VITAMIN A, found especially in green, red, and orange vegetables

ˈbeta deˌcay noun [U] specialized the process in which a NEUTRON breaks up into a PROTON and an ELECTRON

ˈbeta ˌmale noun [C] a man who is not as successful or powerful as other men → Compare **alpha male**

ˈbeta ˌparticle noun [C] specialized an extremely small piece of matter with a positive or negative electric charge, produced when a RADIOACTIVE atom is broken down

betel /ˈbiː.təl/ (US) /-t̬əl/ noun [U] an Asian plant that has leaves and red nuts that act as a drug when CHEWED

bête noire /betˈnwɑːʳ/ (US) /-ˈnwɑːr/ noun [C] (plural **bêtes noires**) a person or thing that you dislike very much or that annoys you

betide /bɪˈtaɪd/ verb [I or T] literary to happen (to someone) → See **woe betide sb**

betoken /bɪˈtəʊ.kən/ (US) /-ˈtoʊ-/ verb [T] old use to be a sign of something

betray /bɪˈtreɪ/ verb [T] NOT LOYAL ▷ **1** (B2) to not be loyal to your country or a person, often by doing something harmful such as helping their enemies: *He was accused of betraying his country during the war.* ◦ *She felt betrayed by her mother's lack of support.* ◦ *For years they betrayed the UK's secrets **to** Russia.* ◦ formal *He promised never to betray his wife* (= *never to leave her for another person*). **2** formal If someone betrays something such as a promise, they do not do what they promised: *The government has been accused of betraying its election promises.* ◦ *By staying out so late, they have betrayed my trust* (= *disappointed me because I had trusted them not to*). SHOW ▷ **3** to show feelings, thoughts, or a particular characteristic without intending to: *If he is nervous on stage, he does not betray it.*

betrayal /bɪˈtreɪ.əl/ noun [C or U] an act of betraying someone or something, or the fact of someone or something being betrayed: *This was the first in a series of betrayals.* ◦ *I felt a sense of betrayal when my friends refused to support me.*

betroth /bɪˈtrəʊð/ (US) /-ˈtroʊð/ verb [T] old use to cause someone to promise formally to marry someone: *She was betrothed **to** her cousin at an early age.* • **betrothal** /bɪˈtrəʊ.ðəl/ (US) /-ˈtroʊ-/ noun [C] *The play revolves round the betrothal of a duke **to** a doctor's daughter.*

betrothed /bɪˈtrəʊðd/ (US) /-ˈtroʊðd/ noun [S] formal or old use a person someone has promised to marry or has been promised to as a marriage partner: *He sent a dozen roses to his betrothed.* → Synonym **fiancé, fiancée**

better /ˈbet.əʳ/ (US) /ˈbeţ.ɚ/ **adj; adv; noun; verb**

▸**adj 1** (A1) comparative of **good**: of a higher standard, or more suitable, pleasing, or effective than other things or people: *He stood near the front to get a better view.* ◦ *Relations between the two countries have never been better.* ◦ *It's much better to have a small, cosy room* ***than*** *a big, cold one.* ◦ *The film was better* ***than*** *I expected.* ◦ *She is much better* ***at*** *tennis than I am.* ◦ *It is* ***far*** *(= much) better to save some of your money than to spend it all at once.* ◦ *Fresh vegetables are better* ***for*** *you (= more beneficial to you) than canned ones.* ◦ *The longer you keep this wine,* ***the*** *better it tastes (= it has a better flavour if you keep it for a long time).* ◦ *The bed was hard, but it was better* ***than nothing*** *(= than not having a bed).* **2** (A1) If you are or get better after an illness or injury, you are healthy and no longer ill: *I hope you get better soon.* **3 get better** to improve: *After the ceasefire, the situation in the capital got better.* ◦ *She's getting much better* ***at*** *pronouncing English words.*

IDIOMS **better late than never** saying said when you think that it is better for someone or something to be late than never to arrive or to happen • **better luck next time** said to tell someone that you hope they will succeed when they try again: *I'm sorry to hear that you failed your driving test. Better luck next time, eh!* • **better safe than sorry** saying said when you think it is best not to take risks even when it seems boring or difficult to be careful • **better the devil you know (than the devil you don't)** UK saying said when you think it is wiser to deal with someone or something familiar, although you do not like them, than to deal with someone or something that you do not know, that might be worse • **go one better** to do something that is more advanced or more generous than someone else: *I gave her a card, but my brother went one better and bought her a present.* • **be no better than (a) sth** If you say that someone is no better than a person who is unpleasant or unkind, you mean that they have behaved in a similar way to this type of person: *People who don't pay their bus fares are no better than common criminals.*

▸**adv 1** (A2) in a more suitable, pleasing, or satisfactory way, or to a greater degree: *The next time he took the test, he was better prepared.* ◦ *She did much better (= was more successful) in the second half of the match.* ◦ *I* ***like*** *this jacket much better than (= I prefer it to) the other one.* ◦ *She knows her way around the college better* ***than*** *I do.* **2** to a greater degree, when used as the COMPARATIVE of adjectives beginning with 'good' or 'well': *She is better-looking (= more attractive) than her brother.* ◦ *He is much better known for his poetry than his songwriting.* **3 better still** (also **even better**) used to say that a particular choice would be more satisfactory: *Why don't you give her a call or, better still, go and see her?* **4 sb would do better** UK it would be wiser: *You would do better* ***to*** *bring the plants inside when the weather gets colder.* **5 sb had better do sth** (A2) used to give advice or to make a threat: *You'd better (= you should) go home now before the rain starts.* ◦ *He'd better pay me back that money he owes me soon,* ***or else.***

▸**noun 1** [U] something that is of a higher standard than something else: *He ran the 100 metres in 9.91 seconds, and I have not seen better (= a faster result) this year.* **2** [U] behaviour, work, or treatment that is more suitable, pleasing, or satisfactory: *You shouldn't have been so mean to your mother – she* ***deserves*** *better.* ◦ *I didn't think he would go out without telling me – I expected better* ***of*** *him.* **3 betters** [plural] old-fashioned people of a higher rank or social position than you: *As children, we were taught not to argue with our* ***elders and*** *betters.*

> **! Common mistake: better**
>
> **Warning:** check your word order!
>
> **Better** does not usually come between the verb and its object.
>
> Don't say 'do better something', say **do something better**:
>
> ~~*Since my visit to England I understand better English.*~~
>
> *Since my visit to England I understand English better.*

IDIOMS **for better or (for) worse** If you do something for better or (for) worse, you accept the bad results of the action as well as the good ones: *Anyway, for better or for worse, I followed her advice.* • **for the better** If something changes for the better, it improves: *Most people think that things have changed for the better since the new government came to power.* • **get the better of sb 1** to defeat someone in a competition: *He fought fiercely, but his opponent easily got the better of him.* **2** If a feeling gets the better of you, you cannot stop yourself from allowing that feeling to make you do something, despite knowing that what you are doing is wrong: *Her curiosity got the better of her and she opened the door and peeped inside.* • **so much the better** (also **all the better**) used to say that a particular action or situation would be even more successful: *If you can go there this afternoon, so much the better.*

▸**verb** [T] **1** to improve a situation: *The organization was established to better conditions for the disabled.* **2 better yourself** to improve your social position, often by getting a better job or education: *He tried to better himself by taking evening classes.*

ˌbetter ˈhalf noun [C usually singular] (plural **better halves**) humorous A person's better half is their husband, wife, or usual sexual partner.

betterment /ˈbet.ə.mənt/ (US) /ˈbeţ.ɚ-/ **noun** [U] formal improvement: *Several changes have been made for the betterment of the sport.*

ˌbetter ˈnature noun [C usually singular] A person's better nature is the more HONOURABLE or moral side of their character.

ˈbetter ˌoff adj; noun

▸**adj be better off a** to have more money than you had in the past or more money than most other people: *Obviously we're better off now we're both working.* ◦ *When his parents died, he found himself $100,000 better off (= he had $100,000 more than before).* **b** to be in a better situation, if or after something happens: *He'd be better off working for a bigger company.*

▸**noun** [plural] **the better off** people who have more money than most others: *The tax on fuel will not have a serious impact on the better off.*

betting /ˈbet.ɪŋ/ (US) /ˈbeţ-/ **noun** [U] the habit of risking money on horse races, sports events, etc.: *Betting can be as addictive as drinking or smoking.*

IDIOM **what's the betting?** (also **the betting is**) informal used to say that it is very likely that something is true or will happen: *What's the betting Dan forgets to bring the tickets?*

B

ˈbetting ˌshop noun [C] UK a place where people go to risk money on horse races or other sports events

between /bɪˈtwiːn/ **preposition, adv; preposition**

▸**preposition, adv** **SPACE** ▷ **1** A1 in or into the space that separates two places, people, or objects: *The town lies halfway between Rome and Florence.* ◦ *Standing between the two adults was a small child.* ◦ *She squeezed between the parked cars and ran out into the road.* ◦ *There were two houses with a narrow path* ***in*** *between.* **AMOUNT** ▷ **2** A2 If something is between two amounts, it is greater than the first amount but smaller than the second: *She weighs between 55 and 60 kilograms.* ◦ *The competition is open to children between six and twelve years of age.* ◦ *The room was either extremely cold or hot, never anything* ***in*** *between* (= in the middle). **TIME** ▷ **3** A1 (also **in between**) in the period of time that separates two different times or events: *You shouldn't eat between meals.* ◦ *There is a break of ten minutes between classes.* ◦ *The shop is closed for lunch between 12.30 and 1.30.* ◦ *In between sobs, he managed to tell them what had happened.* ◦ *He visits his parents every month and sometimes* ***in*** *between.*

IDIOM **between times** during the periods between the separate events mentioned: *If you only go to the supermarket once a month, what do you do between times?*

▸**preposition** **SHARED** ▷ **1** B1 among two or more people or things: *The money was divided equally between several worthy causes.* ◦ *We drank two bottles of wine between four of us.* ◦ *Trade between the two countries (= their trade with each other) has increased sharply in the past year.* ◦ *There is a great deal of similarity between Caroline and her mother (= they are very similar).* **OPPOSING** ▷ **2** A1 A discussion, argument, or game between two or more people or groups of people involves both people or groups: *The negotiations between the union and management have broken down.* ◦ *There has always been a fierce rivalry between the two clubs.* ◦ *Tonight's game is between the New Orleans Saints and the Los Angeles Rams.* **CHOICE** ▷ **3** If you choose between two things, you choose one thing or the other: *You'll have to* ***choose*** *between a holiday or a new washing machine.* ◦ *She was* ***torn*** *between loyalty to her father and love for her husband (= she could not decide which one to support).* **CONNECTING** ▷ **4** A2 connecting two or more places, things, or people: *There is a regular train service between Glasgow and Edinburgh.* ◦ *The survey shows a link between asthma and air pollution.* **5** from one place to another: *He commutes daily between Leeds and Manchester.* **SEPARATING** ▷ **6** A2 separating two places or things: *The wall between East and West Berlin came down in 1989.* ◦ *The report states that the gap between the rich and the poor has increased dramatically over the past decade.*

IDIOM **between you and me** (US also **between us**) used to tell someone that what you are about to say should be kept secret: *Between you and me, I don't think she'll stay in this job very long.*

betwixt /bɪˈtwɪkst/ old use **betwixt and between** between two positions, choices, or ideas; not really one thing or the other

bevel /ˈbev.əl/ **noun; verb**

▸**noun** [C] **1** a sloping edge **2** a tool used to make a sloping edge

▸**verb** [T] (**-ll-** or US usually **-l-**) to give something, such as a piece of wood or metal, a sloping edge: *He bevelled the edges of the bookcase.*

bevelled UK (US usually **beveled**) /ˈbev.əld/ **adj** having a sloping edge or surface: *A picture frame often has bevelled* ***edges****.*

beverage /ˈbev.ər.ɪdʒ/ US /-ɚ-/ **noun** [C] formal a drink of any type: ***Hot*** *beverages include tea, coffee, and hot chocolate.* ◦ *We do not sell* ***alcoholic*** *beverages.*

bevvy /ˈbev.i/ **noun** [C] UK slang an alcoholic drink: *Are you coming down the pub for a bevvy?*

bevy /ˈbev.i/ **noun** [C] a large group of people, especially women or girls, or a large group of similar things: *Victorian postcards often featured bevies* ***of*** *bathing beauties.*

bewail /bɪˈweɪl/ **verb** [T] literary to express great sadness or disappointment about something: *He bewailed his misfortune and the loss of his most treasured possessions.*

beware /bɪˈweər/ US /-ˈwer/ **verb** [only in infinitive and imperative] **1** C1 [I or T] used to warn someone to be very careful about something or someone: *Beware salespeople who promise offers that seem too good to be true.* ◦ *You should beware* ***of*** *undercooked food when staying in hot countries.* ◦ *Beware* ***of*** *falling asleep while sunbathing.* **2** [I] used on signs to warn people of something dangerous: *Beware* ***of*** *the dog.*

bewigged /bɪˈwɪgd/ **adj** literary wearing a WIG (= a covering of artificial hair on the head)

bewilder /bɪˈwɪl.dər/ US /-dɚ/ **verb** [T] to confuse someone: *The instructions completely bewildered me.* • **bewildered** /-dəd/ US /-dɚd/ **adj** *Arriving in a strange city at night, I felt alone and bewildered.*

bewildering /bɪˈwɪl.dər.ɪŋ/ US /-dɚ.ɪŋ/ **adj** **1** confusing and difficult to understand: *He gave me directions to his house, but I found them utterly bewildering.* **2** making you feel confused because you cannot decide what you want: *The college offers a bewildering* ***range*** *of courses.*

bewilderment /bɪˈwɪl.də.mənt/ US /-dɚ-/ **noun** [U] confusion: *a state of bewilderment* ◦ *As he walked through the door, she stared at him* ***in*** *utter bewilderment.*

bewitch /bɪˈwɪtʃ/ **verb** [T] **1** [often passive] to attract or interest someone a lot so that you have the power to influence them: *He was bewitched by her beauty.* **2** to put a magic spell on someone or something in order to control them

bewitching /bɪˈwɪtʃ.ɪŋ/ **adj** so beautiful or attractive that you cannot think about anything else: *He was mesmerized by her bewitching green eyes.*

beyond /biˈjɒnd/ US /-ˈjɑːnd/ **preposition, adv** **FURTHER AWAY** ▷ **1** B1 further away in the distance (than something): *In the distance, beyond the river, was a small town.* **OUTSIDE A LIMIT** ▷ **2** B1 outside or after (a stated limit): *Few people live beyond the age of a hundred.* ◦ *We cannot allow the work to continue beyond the end of the year.* ◦ *I've got nothing to tell you beyond (= in addition to) what I told you earlier.* ◦ *The repercussions will be felt throughout the industry and beyond (= in other areas).* ◦ *Tonight's performance has been cancelled due to* ***circumstances*** *beyond* ***our control*** *(= events that we are unable to deal with).* ◦ *She has always lived beyond her* ***means*** *(= spent more than she has earned).* **3 beyond belief, repair, recognition, etc.** C2 too great or bad for anyone to believe, repair, recognize, etc.: *His thoughtlessness is beyond* ***belief****.* ◦ *He survived the accident, but his car was damaged beyond* ***repair****.* **4 beyond reasonable doubt** UK (US **beyond a reasonable doubt**) If a legal case or a person's GUILT is proved beyond reasonable doubt, there is enough proof for the person accused of a crime to be judged guilty: *Her guilt was* *established beyond reasonable doubt.* **NOT UNDERSTAND** ▷ **5 be beyond sb** C1 informal If something is beyond you, you are unable to understand it: *I'm afraid physics is completely beyond me.*

IDIOMS **beyond compare** literary C2 Something that is beyond compare is so good that nothing can be compared to it: *Her beauty is beyond compare.* • **beyond a joke** If something is beyond a joke, it has stopped being funny and is now a serious matter: *I used to think he was funny, but his behaviour has now gone way beyond a joke.* • **beyond a shadow of a doubt** C2 If you know or believe something beyond a shadow of a doubt, you are certain that it is true: *He is responsible beyond a shadow of a doubt.* • **beyond the pale** If someone's behaviour is beyond the pale, it is unacceptable: *Her recent conduct is beyond the pale.* • **from beyond the grave** after a person has died

bf written abbreviation for **boyfriend**

bhaji /ˈbɑː.dʒi/ noun [C] a spicy South Asian cake made of vegetables, flour, egg, and water, fried in oil: *an* ***onion*** *bhaji*

bhangra /ˈbæŋ.grə/ noun [U] a type of pop music based on traditional music from North India and Pakistan

bhindi /ˈbɪn.di/ noun [C or U] Indian English for **okra**

bi- /baɪ-/ prefix **TWICE** ▷ **1** twice, or once every two: *We meet bi-monthly (= twice every month or once every two months).* **TWO** ▷ **2** having two: *a biped (= an animal that walks on two legs)* ◦ *a biplane (= an old-fashioned aircraft with two wings)*

biannual /baɪˈæn.ju.əl/ adj [before noun] happening twice a year: *The committee has just published its biannual report.* → Compare **annual, biennial**

bias /ˈbaɪ.əs/ noun; verb

▸noun **PREFERENCE** ▷ **1** C2 [C usually singular, U] the action of supporting or opposing a particular person or thing in an unfair way, because of allowing personal opinions to influence your judgment: *The government has accused the media of bias.* ◦ *Reporters must be impartial and not show* ***political*** *bias.* ◦ *There was clear evidence of a strong bias* ***against*** *her.* ◦ *There has always been a slight bias* ***in favour of/towards*** *employing arts graduates in the company.* **2** [C usually singular] the fact of preferring a particular subject or thing: *She showed a scientific bias at an early age.* **CLOTHING** ▷ **3** [U] specialized a direction at an angle across the threads of WOVEN material: *The dresses in his new winter collection are all cut* ***on the*** *bias (= in a diagonal direction across the cloth).*

▸verb [T] (-s- or UK also -ss-) to cause someone or something to have a bias: *The judge ruled that the information should be withheld on the grounds that it would bias the jury* ***against*** *the accused.*

biased /ˈbaɪ.əst/ adj C1 showing an unreasonable like or dislike for a person based on personal opinions: *The newspapers gave a very biased report of the meeting.* ◦ *I think she's beautiful but then I'm biased since she's my daughter.* → Opposite **unbiased**

biathlon /baɪˈæθ.lən/ US /-lɑːn/ noun [C] a sports competition that combines skiing and shooting a RIFLE (= gun) → Compare **decathlon, heptathlon, pentathlon**

bib /bɪb/ noun [C] a cover made of cloth or plastic that is worn by young children when eating to protect their clothes

IDIOM **your best bib and tucker** UK old-fashioned your best clothes that you wear on special occasions

bible /ˈbaɪ.bl̩/ noun [C or S] **1** (usually **Bible**, also ˌ**Holy** ˈ**Bible**) (a copy of) the holy book of the Christian religion consisting of the Old and New Testaments, or the holy book of the Jewish religion consisting of the Law, the Prophets and the Writings: *In* ***the Bible*** *it says that Adam and Eve were the first human beings.* ◦ *Her parents gave her a bible when she was a young child.* ◦ *Bible-****reading*** *classes are held in the church hall every Thursday evening.* **2** a book, magazine, etc. that gives important advice and information about a particular subject: *Vogue magazine quickly became the bible* ***of*** *fashionable women.*

ˈ**Bible-ˌbasher** noun [C] informal disapproving (mainly US **Bible-thumper** /ˈbaɪ.bl̩ˌθʌmp.əʳ/ US /-ɚ/) someone who tries in a forceful or enthusiastic way to persuade other people to believe in the Christian religion and the Bible • ˈ**Bible-ˌbashing** adj [before noun] (mainly US ˈ**Bible-ˌthumping**)

the ˈ**Bible** ˌ**Belt** noun [S] the southern and central regions of the US where many people have traditional Christian beliefs

biblical /ˈbɪb.lɪ.kəl/ adj in or relating to the Bible

bibliography /ˌbɪb.liˈɒg.rə.fi/ US /-ˈɑː.grə-/ noun [C] a list of the books and articles that have been used by someone when writing a particular book or article: *Other sources of information are found in the bibliography at the end of this article.* • **bibliographical** /ˌbɪb.li.əˈgræf.ɪ.kəl/ adj *bibliographical information*

bibliophile /ˈbɪb.li.ə.faɪl/ noun [C] formal a person who loves or collects books

bicameral /ˌbaɪˈkæm.ər.əl/ US /-ɚ.əl/ adj specialized (of a parliament) having two parts, such as the Senate and the House of Representatives in the US: *a bicameral legislature*

bicarb /ˈbaɪ.kɑːb/ US /-kɑːrb/ noun [U] informal **bicarbonate of soda**

bicarbonate of soda /baɪˌkɑː.bən.ət.əvˈsəʊ.də/ US /-ˌkɑːr.bən.ət.əvˈsoʊ-/ noun [U] mainly UK (mainly US ˈ**baking** ˌ**soda**) a white powder used to make foods rise in baking

bicentenary /ˌbaɪ.senˈtiː.nər.i/ US /-ˈten.ɚ-/ noun [C] (US **bicentennial**) the day or year that is 200 years after a particular event, especially an important one: *A statue was erected to mark the bicentenary* ***of*** *the composer's birth.* ◦ *bicentenary celebrations*

bicentennial /ˌbaɪ.senˈten.i.əl/, /-sən-/ noun US for **bicentenary**: *bicentennial celebrations*

biceps /ˈbaɪ.seps/ noun [C] (plural **biceps**) the large muscle at the front of the upper arm → Compare **triceps**

bicker /ˈbɪk.əʳ/ US /-ɚ/ verb [I] disapproving to argue about things that are not important: *Will you two stop bickering!* ◦ *They're always bickering* ***with*** *each other* ***about/over*** *their personal problems.* • **bickering** /-ɪŋ/ noun [U] *The council finally elected a leader after several days of bickering.*

bickie /ˈbɪk.i/ noun [C] UK (Australian English also **bikkie**) informal for **biscuit**: *I've bought a packet of choccy (= chocolate) bickies for tea.*

ˌ**bi-**ˈ**curious** adj A bi-curious person is sexually interested in both men and women but may not be completely BISEXUAL. → Compare **bisexual**

> **!** Common mistake: **bicycle**
>
> **Warning:** Check your spelling!
>
> **Bicycle** is one of the 50 words most often spelled wrongly by learners.

bicycle /ˈbaɪ.sɪ.kl/ noun [C] A2 a two-wheeled vehicle that you sit on and move by turning the two PEDALS (= flat parts you press with your feet): *I go to work* ***by***

bicycle. ◦ *He* ***got on*** *his bicycle and rode off.* ◦ *You should never* ***ride*** *your bicycle without lights at night.*

B

ˈbicycle ˌlane noun [C] US for **cycle lane/path**

bid /bɪd/ verb; noun

▸verb **OFFER** ▷ **1** (B2) [I or T] (present participle **bidding**, past tense **bid**, past participle **bid**) to offer a particular amount of money for something that is for sale and compete against other people to buy it, especially at a public sale of goods or property: *She knew she couldn't afford it, so she didn't bid.* ◦ *The communications group has shown an interest in bidding* ***for*** *the company.* ◦ *A foreign collector has bid £500,000* ***for*** *the portrait.* ◦ [+ two objects] *What am I bid* ***for*** *this fine vase?* **2** [I] (present participle **bidding**, past tense **bid**, past participle **bid**) If two or more people bid for a job, they compete with each other to do the work by offering to do it for a particular amount of money: *The department is trying to ensure fairer competition among firms bidding* ***for*** *government contracts.* **3** [T + to infinitive] (present participle **bidding**, past tense **bid**, past participle **bid**) If someone bids to do something, they compete with other people to do it: *Paris is bidding* ***to*** *host the next Olympics.* **TELL** ▷ **4** [T] (present participle **bidding**, past tense **bid** or **bade**, past participle **bidden**) old-fashioned to give a greeting to someone, or to ask someone to do something: [+ two objects] *They bade her good morning.* ◦ *I must now bid you* ***farewell*** *(= say goodbye to you).* ◦ [+ object + (to) infinitive] *He bade (= asked) them (****to****) leave at once.*

▸noun [C] **OFFER** ▷ **1** (B2) an offer of a particular amount of money for something that is for sale: *I* ***made*** *a bid of $150* ***for*** *the painting.* ◦ *She* ***made/put in*** *a bid of £69,000 for the flat, which was accepted.* **2** (C1) an offer to do something when you are competing with other people to do it: [+ to infinitive] *Sydney* ***made*** *a successful bid* ***to*** *host the Olympic Games.* ◦ *I gave the job to the contractors who* ***made/gave*** *the lowest bid (= who offered to do the work for the lowest amount of money).* **ATTEMPT** ▷ **3** (B2) an attempt to achieve or get something: *Her bid* ***for*** *re-election was unsuccessful.* ◦ *The company has managed to fight off a hostile* ***takeover*** *bid (= an attempt by another company to take control of it).* ◦ *The government has reduced the cost of borrowing in a bid* ***to*** *get the economy moving again.*

bidder /ˈbɪd.əʳ/ (US) /-ɚ/ noun [C] someone who offers to pay a particular amount of money for something: *In an auction, goods or property are sold to the* ***highest*** *bidder (= the person who offers the most money).*

bidding /ˈbɪd.ɪŋ/ noun [U] **OFFER** ▷ **1** the act of offering to pay a particular amount of money for something, by different people: *Most of the bidding was done by phone.* **2 open the bidding** to make the first offer of money for an object at a public sale of goods **TELL** ▷ **3 at sb's bidding** old-fashioned You do something at someone's bidding if they have asked or told you to do it: *At my grandmother's bidding, I wore my best dress.*

ˈbidding ˌwar noun [C usually singular] the situation in which two or more companies or people compete against each other in order to buy something: *British distributors are currently involved in a bidding war* ***for*** *the movie.*

biddy /ˈbɪd.i/ noun [C] informal disapproving an old woman: *an* ***old*** *biddy*

bide /baɪd/ verb **bide your time** to wait calmly for a good opportunity to do something: *She was biding her time until she could get her revenge.*

bidet /ˈbiː.deɪ/ (US) /bɪˈdeɪ/ noun [C] a small, low bath in which a person washes the lower part of their body

biennial /baɪˈen.i.əl/ adj; noun

▸adj happening once every two years → Compare **annual, biannual**

▸noun [C] a plant that lives for two years, producing seeds and flowers in its second year → Compare **annual, biannual, perennial**

bier /bɪəʳ/ (US) /bɪr/ noun [C] a frame on which a dead body or a COFFIN is carried before a FUNERAL

biff /bɪf/ verb; noun

▸verb [T] informal to hit someone, especially with the FIST (= closed hand)

▸noun [C] informal a hit or PUNCH: *a biff on the nose*

bifocals /ˌbaɪˈfəʊ.kəlz/ (US) /-ˈfoʊ-/ noun [plural] glasses with LENSES that are divided into two parts. The upper half is for looking at things far away and the lower half is for reading or for looking at things that are near. • **bifocal** /-kəl/ adj *bifocal lenses*

bifurcate /ˈbaɪ.fə.keɪt/ (US) /-fɚ-/ verb [I] formal (of roads, rivers, branches, etc.) to divide into two parts: *A sample of water was taken from the point where the river bifurcates.*

bifurcation /ˌbaɪ.fəˈkeɪ.ʃən/ (US) /-fɚˈ-/ noun formal **1** [U] the fact that something is divided into two parts or the act of dividing something into two parts **2** [C] either of the two parts into which something divides

big /bɪg/ adj; verb

▸adj (**bigger, biggest**) **LARGE** ▷ **1** (A1) large in size or amount: *He's a big man.* ◦ *Could I try these shoes in a bigger size?* ◦ *They've got a big house in the country.* ◦ *She has blonde hair and big blue eyes.* ◦ *She's had a big pay rise.* ◦ *I had a* ***great*** *big slice of chocolate cake for tea.* ◦ *A thousand people took part in the region's biggest* ***ever*** *cycle race.* ◦ informal *She's always been a big* ***spender*** *(= she has always spent a lot of money).* ◦ informal *You're not a very big* ***eater****, are you? (= You do not eat a lot.)* **2** (A2) informal older or more like an adult: *Her big (= older)* ***sister/brother*** *told her to go away.* ◦ *I'm ashamed of you. You're big enough to know better (= at an age where you should know that your behaviour is not acceptable).* **3** (B2) [before noun] informal used to add emphasis: *You're a big bully!* ◦ *He fell for her* ***in a*** *big* ***way*** *(= was greatly attracted to her).* **IMPORTANT** ▷ **4** (A2) important, because of being powerful, or having a lot of influence or a serious effect: *He had a big decision to make.* ◦ *There's a big difference between starting up a business and just talking about it.* ◦ *The big story in the news this week is the minister's resignation.* ◦ *The four biggest banks are all planning to cut their service charges.* **5 be big somewhere/in sth** informal to be important or famous in a particular place or type of work: *They're big in Japan, but no one's heard of them here.* **6** (C1) informal If a product or activity is big, it is extremely popular: *Hip-hop is still big today.*

> **!** Common mistake: **big or great?**
>
> **Remember:** you do not usually use 'big' before uncountable nouns.
>
> Don't say 'big progress/fun/shame/admiration', say **great progress/fun/shame/admiration:**
>
> ~~*My work is of big importance to me.*~~
>
> *My work is of great importance to me.*

IDIOMS **a big ask** informal something you ask someone to do that will be difficult for them: *It's a big ask I know, but we need the project finished by June.* • **be big of sb** informal disapproving If an action is big of someone, it is kind, good, or helpful. This phrase is usually used humorously or angrily to mean the opposite: *You can spare me an hour next week? That's really big of you!* • **be big on sth** informal to like something very much: *I'm not very big on classical music.* • **be no big deal** informal to not be a serious problem: *We'll have to pay a little more – it's no big deal.* • **big deal!** informal said when you do not think that what someone has said or done is important or special: *'I ran five miles this morning.' 'Big deal! I ran ten.'* • **big fish/gun/noise/shot** (US also **big wheel**) a person who has an important or powerful position in a group or organization: *She's a big gun in city politics.* ◦ *He's a big shot in advertising.* • **the big/bigger picture** the most important facts about a situation and the effects of that situation on other things: *In my political work I try to concentrate on the big picture and not be distracted by details.* • **the bigger the better** how much you value or want something is decided by how big it is: *He likes getting big presents – the bigger the better as far as he's concerned.* • **the big I am** informal disapproving If someone is acting the big I am, or giving it the big I am, they are behaving as if they are very important: *He was always **giving it the big I am** with his little gang.* • **have big ideas** informal to have plans that need great effort, skill, and luck to achieve: *She's got big ideas **about** starting up her own company.* • **make it big** informal to become famous or successful • **too big for your boots** UK (US **too big for your britches**) behaving as if you are more important than you really are: *He's been getting a bit too big for his boots since he got that promotion.* • **what's the big idea?** informal used to ask someone why they have done something annoying: *What's the big idea? I was watching that programme!*

▸verb informal

PHRASAL VERB **big sb/sth up** to talk a lot about how excellent someone or something is, sometimes praising them or it more than is deserved

bigamy /ˈbɪg.ə.mi/ noun [U] the crime of marrying a person while already legally married to someone else: *In court, he admitted that he had **committed** bigamy.* → Compare **monogamy, polygamy** • **bigamist** /-mɪst/ noun [C] *He was accused of being a bigamist.* • **bigamous** /-məs/ adj *a bigamous marriage* • **bigamously** /-məs.li/ adv *She has been married four times, once bigamously.*

the ˌBig ˈApple noun [S] informal New York City: *She's planning a trip to the Big Apple.*

ˈbig ˌband noun [C] a large group of musicians who play JAZZ and dance music: *Big band **music** was very popular during the 1930s and 40s.*

the ˌBig ˈBang noun [S] the large explosion that many scientists believe created the universe

ˌbig ˈbeast noun [C] **1** a large wild animal: *Prehistoric fires may have killed off the big beasts that once roamed Australia.* **2** a large and powerful organization, or a powerful person: *They are the big beasts among TV networks.*

the ˈbig ˌboys noun [plural] informal the most important people in an activity or organization, or the most powerful businesses with the most influence in a particular area: *We're only a small business and don't have the capital to compete with the big boys.*

ˌBig ˈBrother noun [S] a way of referring to a government, ruler, or person in authority that has complete power and tries to control people's behaviour and thoughts and limit their freedom

ˌbig ˈbucks noun [plural] mainly US for **big money**

ˌbig ˈbusiness noun [U] **BUSINESS** ▷ **1** powerful and INFLUENTIAL businesses and financial organizations (= ones with a lot of influence) when considered as a group: *The party receives most of its financial support from big business.* **POPULAR** ▷ **2** something that makes a lot of money: *Health clubs are big business these days.*

ˌbig ˈcat noun [C] a lion, TIGER, or other large wild animal from the cat family: *Tigers are among the rarest of the big cats.*

the ˌbig ˈday noun [S] informal the day when you get married: *When's the big day, then?*

ˌbig ˈdipper noun [C] UK old-fashioned a small railway in an AMUSEMENT PARK that travels very quickly along a narrow track that slopes and bends suddenly

the ˌBig ˈDipper noun [S] US for **the Plough**

Bigfoot /ˈbɪg.fʊt/ noun [S] (also **Sasquatch**) a large creature like a human covered in hair that some people believe exists in the northwest of the US and western Canada

ˌbig ˈgame noun [U] large wild animals that are hunted and shot for sport

biggie /ˈbɪg.i/ noun [C] informal something that is very important or successful: *His new movie will be the Hollywood biggie this summer.*

ˌbig ˈhair noun [U] informal hair that forms a large shape all around the head: *At that time big hair was fashionable.*

bighead /ˈbɪg.hed/ noun [C] disapproving someone who thinks that they are more important or cleverer than they really are: *He's always boasting. He's such a bighead!*

bigheaded /ˌbɪgˈhed.ɪd/ adj disapproving thinking that you are more important or cleverer than you really are: *She's so bigheaded!* → Compare **swollen head**

big-ˈhearted adj kind and generous

ˌbig ˈhitter noun [C] an important and INFLUENTIAL person or thing (= one with a lot of influence), especially of their particular type: *The big hitters in the cast include Michael Caine and Ewan McGregor.*

ˌbig ˈmoney noun [U] informal a large amount of money: *Tournament organizers need to offer big money to attract the top players.*

ˈbig ˌmouth noun [C usually singular] informal disapproving If someone is or has a big mouth, they often say things that are meant to be kept secret: *He **is/has** such a big mouth.* ◦ *He went and **opened** his big mouth and told them the whole story.*

ˌbig ˈname noun [C] informal a famous or important person: *Are there any big names in the movie?* ◦ *She's a big name **in** politics.*

bigot /ˈbɪg.ət/ noun [C] disapproving a person who has strong, unreasonable beliefs and who thinks that anyone who does not have the same beliefs is wrong: *a religious bigot* ◦ *He was known to be a loud-mouthed, opinionated bigot.* • **bigoted** /ˈbɪg.ə.tɪd/ (US) /-t̬ɪd/ adj *She's so bigoted that she refuses to accept anyone who doesn't think like her.* • **bigotry** /ˈbɪg.ə.tri/ noun [U]

the ˌbig ˈscreen noun [S] films that are shown in cinemas: *He will soon be returning to the big screen for his first movie since 1990.* • **ˌbig-ˈscreen** adj [before noun] *Her first big-screen success was in the movie 'Rosemary's Baby'.*

the ˌBig ˈSmoke noun [S] informal a large city, especially London: *I wouldn't like to live in the Big Smoke.*

big-ˈticket adj [before noun] mainly US Big-ticket things are things that are expensive to buy, such as cars or furniture.

ˈbig ˌtime adv; noun

▸adv informal If you do something big time, you do it to a great degree: *'How was the interview?' 'Terrible, I messed up big time.'* ◦ *Chrissy's into skiing big time (= likes skiing a lot).*

B

▸noun informal **the big time** the state of being famous or successful: *She finally **hit** the big time (= became famous or successful) with her latest novel.* ◦ *You've really **made** the big time now (= become famous or successful).* • **ˈbig-ˌtime** adj highest or most successful: *Steve Largent was regarded as Seattle's first big-time football star.*

ˌbig ˈtoe noun [C] the largest toe on your foot

ˌbig ˈtop noun [C usually singular] the main tent in a CIRCUS

ˌbig ˈwheel noun [C] UK (US **ˈFerris ˌwheel**) a large, vertical wheel in an AMUSEMENT PARK with seats that stay horizontal as the wheel turns round

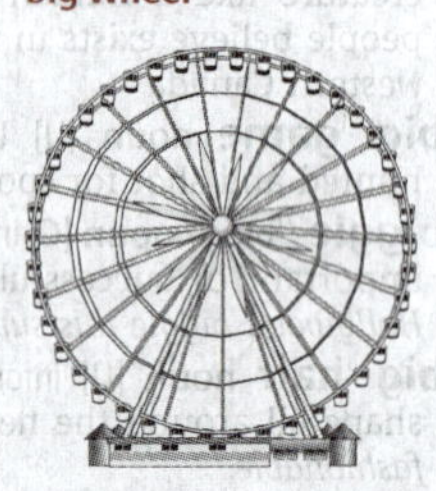

big wheel

bigwig /ˈbɪg.wɪg/ noun [C] informal a person who has an important or powerful position: *We were invited to a lunch with **local** bigwigs.*

ˌbig ˈword noun [C] informal a long, difficult word, or a word that expresses a serious or important idea: *He tried to impress his teachers by using big words in all his essays.*

bijou /ˈbiː.ʒuː/ adj [before noun] UK (especially of a building) small but attractive: *The harbour front is lined with bijou cafés and bars.* ◦ *The estate agent described the flat as a bijou **residence**.*

bike /baɪk/ noun; verb

▸noun [C] **1** A1 a bicycle: *It would be better for the environment if more people used bikes rather than cars.* ◦ *My youngest child is learning to **ride** a bike.* **2** B1 informal a motorcycle

IDIOM **on your bike!** UK slang a rude way of telling someone to go away: *'Can you lend me some money?' 'On your bike, mate!'*

▸verb **1** [I] informal to go somewhere by bicycle: *Should we bike to the park, or walk?* **2** [T] to use a motorcycle to take something to someone: *We biked a copy **over** to Greg at the BBC.*

ˈbike ˌlane noun [C] US for **cycle lane/path**

biker /ˈbaɪ.kəʳ/ US /-kɚ/ noun [C] **1** a member of a group of people riding motorcycles **2** someone who rides a bicycle, especially a MOUNTAIN BIKE

ˈbike ˌrack noun [C] US for **cycle rack**

ˈbike ˌshed noun [C] UK a small building in which bicycles are stored: *Your bike will be safer if you leave it in the bike shed.*

bikie /ˈbaɪk.i/ noun [C] Australian English a member of a group of people riding motorcycles → Compare **biker**

bikini /bɪˈkiː.ni/ noun [C] B2 a two-piece SWIMMING COSTUME for women: *a bikini top* ◦ *bikini bottoms/briefs*

bikkie /ˈbɪk.i/ noun [C] Australian informal for **biscuit**

bilabial /ˌbaɪˈleɪ.bi.əl/ adj specialized (of a sound) made using both lips: *'P' is a bilabial consonant.*

bilateral /ˌbaɪˈlæt.ər.əl/ US /-ˈlæt̬.ɚ-/ adj involving two groups or countries: *France and Germany have signed a bilateral **agreement** to help prevent drug smuggling.* → Compare **multilateral, unilateral** • **bilaterally** /-i/ adv

bilberry /ˈbɪl.bər.i/ US /-ber-/ noun [C] the dark blue fruit of a small bush that grows wild in northern Europe, similar to a BLUEBERRY

bile /baɪl/ noun [U] **1** the bitter, yellow liquid produced by the LIVER that helps to digest fat **2** very angry feelings, words, or behaviour: *His article was full of loathing and bile.*

ˈbile ˌduct noun [C] specialized the tube from the LIVER and GALL BLADDER through which bile passes into the SMALL INTESTINE

bilge /bɪldʒ/ noun TALK ▷ **1** [U] old-fashioned slang nonsense: *Don't talk such bilge!* SHIP ▷ **2** [C usually plural] the bottom inside part of a ship where dirty water collects: *The bilges had been pumped and the ship was ready to set sail once again.*

ˈbilge ˌwater noun [U] the dirty water that collects in the bottom inside part of a ship

bilharzia /bɪlˈhɑː.zi.ə/ US /-ˈhɑːr.zi-/ noun [U] a serious disease that is caused by a type of small worm getting into the blood. It is common in parts of Africa and South America.

bilingual /baɪˈlɪŋ.gwəl/ adj C1 (of a person) able to use two languages equally well, or (of a thing) using or involving two languages: *She works as a bilingual secretary for an insurance company.* ◦ *a bilingual dictionary* → Compare **monolingual, multilingual, trilingual**

bilious /ˈbɪl.i.əs/ adj **1** relating to an illness caused by too much BILE, which can cause vomiting: *She suffered from bilious **attacks**.* **2** formal If someone is bilious, they are always in a bad mood: *a bilious old man* **3** extremely unpleasant: *His shirt was a bilious shade of green.*

bill /bɪl/ noun; verb

▸noun REQUEST FOR PAYMENT ▷ **1** A2 [C or S] a request for payment of money owed, or the piece of paper on which it is written: *an electricity/gas/phone bill* ◦ *They sent us a bill **for** the work they had done.* ◦ *She **ran up** (= caused herself to have) a huge phone bill.* ◦ *They asked the waitress for the bill.* ◦ *Could we have the bill, please?* ◦ *Her mother agreed to **foot** (= pay) the bill.* LAW ▷ **2** [C] a formal statement of a planned new law that is discussed before being voted on: *The bill was **amended** (= changed).* ◦ *When a bill is **passed** in Parliament it becomes law.* ◦ informal *The bill was **thrown out** (= did not go past the first stage of discussion and will not become law).* MONEY ▷ **3** B1 [C] mainly US (UK usually **note**) a piece of paper money: *a dollar/one-dollar bill* ◦ *a ten-dollar bill* → See also **billfold** BIRD ▷ **4** [C] the beak of a bird NOTICE ▷ **5** [C] a notice giving information about something, especially an event or performance **6 be on the bill** to be performing in a show: *There were lots of big names (= famous people) on the bill.* **7 head/top the bill** to be the most important actor in a show

IDIOM **fill/fit the bill** to be exactly what is needed in a particular situation: *That box will fill the bill nicely.*

▸verb REQUEST PAYMENT ▷ **1** [T] to give or send someone a bill asking for money that they owe for a product or service: *Please bill me for any expenses you incur.* ADVERTISE ▷ **2** [T usually passive] to advertise something with a particular description: *The film was billed **as** a romantic comedy.*

PHRASAL VERB **bill sb as sth** [usually passive] to describe someone in a particular way in order to advertise them: *The young author was billed as 'the new Beckett'.*

the ˈBill noun [S, + sing/pl verb] (also **the ˌOld ˈBill**) UK slang the police

billabong /ˈbɪl.ə.bɒŋ/ US /-bɑːŋ/ noun [C] In Australia, a low area of ground that was part of a river in the past and that only fills up with water from the river during a flood.

billboard /ˈbɪl.bɔːd/ US /-bɔːrd/ noun [C] US for **hoarding**

billet /ˈbɪl.ɪt/ **noun** [C] a place for soldiers to stay in for a short time: *Our billets were about a mile out of town.* • **billet verb** [T] *The soldiers were billeted in the town hall.*

billfold /ˈbɪl.fəʊld/ (US) /-foʊld/ **noun** [C] US (UK **wallet**) a small folding case for carrying money

billhook /ˈbɪl.hʊk/ **noun** [C] a tool with a wide blade on a handle used for cutting branches off trees

billiards /ˈbɪl.i.ədz/ (US) /ˈbɪl.jɚdz/ **noun** [U] a game played by two people on a table covered in green cloth, in which a CUE (= a long stick) is used to hit balls against each other and into pockets around the table • **billiard** /ˈbɪl.i.əd/ (US) /ˈbɪl.jɚd/ **adj** [before noun] *a billiard ball*

billing /ˈbɪl.ɪŋ/ **noun** [U] **REQUEST FOR PAYMENT** ▷ **1** the process of sending people BILLS asking them to pay money owed: *itemized (= detailed) billing* **INFORMATION** ▷ **2** information, especially about a performance: *Unfortunately, the show never **lived up to** (= was not as good as) its billing.* **3 star/top billing** the top position that someone is advertised as having in a show

billion /ˈbɪl.jən/ **noun** [C] **1** (B2) the number 1,000,000,000: *The population of China is over a/one billion.* ◦ *Cosmetics is a billion-dollar industry.* ◦ *The government has invested billions **of** dollars in the project.* **2** UK old-fashioned 1,000,000,000,000

> **! Note:**
>
> This number is now called a **trillion**.

3 billions of sth informal a very large number: *There were billions of flies everywhere.*

> **! Common mistake: billions (of sth) or billion?**
>
> When **billion** is used after a particular number, it is used in the singular form and without 'of'.
>
> Don't say 'five/ten/fifteen billions of sth', say five/ten/fifteen **billion** sth:
>
> ~~*The palace cost at least 3 billions of dollars.*~~
>
> *The palace cost at least 3 billion dollars.*
>
> When **billion** is used without a particular number, it is used in the plural form and is sometimes followed by 'of':
>
> *The palace must have cost billions (of dollars).*

billionaire /ˌbɪl.jəˈneəʳ/ (US) /-ˈner/ **noun** [C] a person who has money, property, etc. that is worth at least 1,000,000,000 dollars, pounds, euros, etc.

billionth /ˈbɪl.i.ənθ/ (US) /-jənθ/ **ordinal number; noun**

▸**ordinal number** 1,000,000,000th written as a word

▸**noun** [C] one of a billion equal parts of something: *a/one billionth **of** a second*

ˌbill of ˈfare noun [C usually singular] old-fashioned a MENU (= list of food) in a restaurant

ˌbill of ˈrights noun [S] a statement of the basic laws to protect the rights of a country's CITIZENS to have JUSTICE and fairness

billow /ˈbɪl.əʊ/ (US) /-oʊ/ **verb** [I] to spread over a large area, or (especially of things made of cloth) to become filled with air and appear to be larger: ***Smoke** billowed (**out**) from the burning building.* ◦ *The sheets/shirts hanging on the line billowed in the breeze.* • **billow noun** [C usually plural] *billows **of** smoke*

billy /ˈbɪl.i/ **noun** [C] (also **billycan**) UK a metal container used for cooking outside over a fire

ˈbilly ˌclub noun [C] US for **truncheon**

ˈbilly ˌgoat noun [C] a male GOAT

ˈbilly-o adv UK old-fashioned informal **like billy-o** a lot or very quickly, strongly, etc.: *We worked like billy-o to get it finished.*

biltong /ˈbɪl.tɒŋ/ (US) /-tɑːŋ/ **noun** [U] South African English meat that has been cut into long pieces, FLAVOURED with spices, and dried

bimbo /ˈbɪm.bəʊ/ (US) /-boʊ/ **noun** [C] (plural **bimbos**) slang disapproving a young woman considered to be attractive but not intelligent: *He went out with a succession of **blonde** bimbos.*

bimetallic strip /ˌbaɪ.met.æl.ɪkˈstrɪp/ **noun** [C] specialized a strip, used in a THERMOSTAT, made from two different metals that grow larger by different amounts when heated, causing the strip to bend and switch a device on or off

bimonthly /ˌbaɪˈmʌnθ.li/ **adj, adv** happening or appearing every two months or twice a month: *a bimonthly publication/report* ◦ *The magazine is published bimonthly, with six issues a year.*

bin /bɪn/ **noun; verb**

▸**noun** [C] **WASTE** ▷ **1** (B1) UK a container for waste: *a **litter** bin* ◦ *a **rubbish** bin* ◦ *The supermarket has installed **recycling** bins for old newspapers, bottles, and cans.* ◦ *Do you want this or shall I **throw** it **in** the bin?* **2** (B1) UK a **dustbin** **STORAGE** ▷ **3** a large container used for storing things: *a bread bin*

▸**verb** [T] (**-nn-**) UK to throw something away: *Shall I bin these old shoes?*

binary /ˈbaɪ.nᵊr.i/ (US) /-nɚ-/ **adj** specialized consisting of two parts

ˌbinary ˈnumber noun [C] specialized a number that is expressed using 1 and 0: *Computers operate using binary numbers.*

ˈbin ˌbag noun [C] (also **ˈbin ˌliner**) UK a plastic bag that you put inside a container for holding waste

bind /baɪnd/ **verb; noun**

▸**verb** (**bound, bound**) **1** (C2) [T] to tie something tightly or to fasten something: *They bound the packages **with** brightly coloured ribbon.* ◦ *Bind **together** the two broken ends.* ◦ *The prisoner was bound **hand and foot**.* **2** (C2) [T] to unite people: *The things that bind them **together** are greater than their differences.* **3** [T] (also **bind up**) To bind a part of the body, especially a part that is damaged, is to tie something round it: *He had already bound the child's arm when I arrived.* **4** [T] to sew or stick material along the edges of something such as a jacket, in order to make it stronger or to decorate it **5** [T] to make separate pieces of paper into a book: *There are several different ways to bind a book, for example you can stitch or stick the pages together.* → See also **bookbinding (bookbinder)** **6** [I or T] When an egg or water is used, especially in cooking, to bind something it provides a way of making everything stick together in a solid mass: *The mixture wouldn't bind (**together**).*

PHRASAL VERB **bind sb to sth** [usually passive] to force someone to keep a promise: *His sister had been bound **to secrecy**.* ◦ *We are bound to the original contract.*

▸**noun** [S] informal a difficult or annoying situation in which you are prevented from acting as you might like: *Having to visit her every week is **a** terrible bind.* ◦ *Borrowing money may **put** you **in a** real bind.*

binder /ˈbaɪn.dəʳ/ (US) /-dɚ/ **noun** [C] **1** a hard cover in which paper documents or magazines are stored: *a leather/plastic binder* **2** a **bookbinder**

bindi /ˈbɪn.di/ **noun** [C] a small coloured mark or JEWEL (= precious stone) that is worn between the EYEBROWS, especially by Hindu women to show that they are married

binding /ˈbaɪn.dɪŋ/ **adj; noun**
▸**adj** (especially of an agreement) that cannot be legally avoided or stopped: *a binding* ***agreement*** ◦ *The contract wasn't* ***legally*** *binding.*
▸**noun 1** [C or U] the type of cover that a book has **2** [U] a thin strip of material that can be sewn along the edges of clothes or other objects

bindweed /ˈbaɪnd.wiːd/ **noun** [U] a wild plant with white and pink flowers that twists itself around other plants as it grows

binge /bɪndʒ/ **noun; verb**
▸**noun** [C] informal an occasion when an activity is done in an extreme way, especially eating, drinking, or spending money: *a drinking/eating/spending binge* ◦ *The annual office binge (= party) is in December.* ◦ *He* ***went on*** *a five day drinking binge.*
▸**verb** [I] (past tense and past participle **bingeing** or **binging**) informal to eat too much of something: *I tend to binge* ***on*** *chocolate when I'm watching TV.*

ˈ**binge** ˌ**drinking** **noun** [U] the activity of drinking too much alcohol on one occasion • ˈ**binge** ˌ**drinker** **noun** [C]

ˈ**binge** ˌ**eating** **noun** [U] eating a lot of food, especially without being able to control yourself

bingo /ˈbɪŋ.gəʊ/ Ⓤⓢ /-goʊ/ **noun; exclamation**
▸**noun** [U] a game in which prizes can be won by matching numbers on a card with those chosen by chance
▸**exclamation** informal an expression of surprise and, usually, pleasure: *I was just about to give up waiting when bingo! – he turned up.*

binman /ˈbɪn.mæn/ **noun** [C] (plural **-men** /-men/) UK informal for **dustman**

binoculars /bɪˈnɒk.jʊ.ləz/ Ⓤⓢ /-ˈnɑː.kjʊ.lɚz/ **noun** [plural] a pair of tubes with glass LENSES at either end that you look through to see things far away more clearly: *a pair of binoculars*

binoculars

bint /bɪnt/ **noun** [C] UK slang an offensive word for a woman

bio- /baɪ.əʊ-/ Ⓤⓢ /-oʊ-/ **prefix** connected with life and living things: *bioethics* ◦ *biodiversity*

biochemical /ˌbaɪ.əʊˈkem.ɪ.kəl/ Ⓤⓢ /-oʊ-/ **adj** connected with the chemistry of living things • **biochemically** /-i/ **adv**

biochemistry /ˌbaɪ.əʊˈkem.ɪ.stri/ Ⓤⓢ /-oʊ-/ **noun** [U] the scientific study of the chemistry of living things • **biochemist** /-ɪst/ **noun** [C]

biodata /ˈbaɪ.əʊˌdeɪ.tə/ Ⓤⓢ /-oʊˌdeɪ.t̬ə/ **noun** [U] details about someone's life, job, and achievements

biodefence (US **biodefense**) /ˌbaɪ.əʊ.dɪˈfens/ Ⓤⓢ /-oʊ-/ **noun** [U] the development and use of equipment and systems that protect against BIOTERRORISM (= violent action using living matter, such as bacteria, to harm or kill people for political reasons): *They have a store of biodefence drugs and vaccines that can be flown anywhere in the nation within twelve hours.*

biodegradable /ˌbaɪ.əʊ.dɪˈgreɪ.dɪ.bl/ Ⓤⓢ /-oʊ-/ **adj** able to decay naturally and in a way that is not harmful: *Biodegradable packaging helps to limit the amount of harmful chemicals released into the atmosphere.*

biodegrade /ˌbaɪ.əʊ.dɪˈgreɪd/ Ⓤⓢ /-oʊ-/ **verb** [I] *Some plastics are designed to biodegrade when their useful life is over.*

biodiesel /ˈbaɪ.əʊˌdiː.zəl/ Ⓤⓢ /-oʊ-/ **noun** [U] fuel made from vegetable oils or animal fat

biodiversity /ˌbaɪ.əʊ.daɪˈvɜː.sɪ.ti/ Ⓤⓢ /-oʊ.dɪˈvɝː.sə.t̬i/ **noun** [U] the number and types of plants and animals that exist in a particular area or in the world generally, or the problem of protecting this

bioenergy /ˌbaɪ.əʊˈen.ə.dʒi/ Ⓤⓢ /-oʊˈen.ɚ.dʒi/ **noun** [U] energy that is produced from a BIOFUEL (= a fuel that is made from living things or their waste): *Bioenergy crops have replaced food as the most profitable crop in several European countries.*

bioethanol /ˌbaɪ.əʊˈeθ.ə.nɒl/ Ⓤⓢ /-oʊˈeθ.ə.nɑːl/ **noun** [U] a type of fuel that is made from plants, and can be mixed with PETROL as a fuel for cars

bioethics /ˈbaɪ.əʊˌeθ.ɪks/ Ⓤⓢ /-oʊ-/ **noun** [U] the study of what is right and wrong in new discoveries and techniques in biology, such as GENETIC ENGINEERING and the TRANSPLANTATION of organs: *The uproar led to the establishment of bioethics committees to oversee research.*

biofeedback /ˌbaɪ.əʊˈfiːd.bæk/ Ⓤⓢ /-oʊ-/ **noun** [U] a method by which a person learns to control their heart rate or other physical or mental processes by using information from recordings of those processes

bioflavonoid /ˌbaɪ.əʊˈflæv.ə.nɔɪd/ Ⓤⓢ /-oʊˈ-/ **noun** [C] a **flavonoid**

biofuel /ˈbaɪ.əʊˌfjuː.əl/ Ⓤⓢ /-oʊˈ-/ **noun** [C or U] a fuel that is made from living things or their waste • **biofuelled** /-ˌfjuː.əld/ **adj** *a biofuelled car*

biogas /ˈbaɪ.əʊˌgæs/ Ⓤⓢ /-oʊ-/ **noun** [U] specialized a gas containing METHANE that can be burned as a fuel, produced by dead plants and animals as they decay

biographer /baɪˈɒg.rə.fər/ Ⓤⓢ /-ˈɑː.grə.fɚ/ **noun** [C] someone who writes the story of a particular person's life: *Boswell was Dr Johnson's biographer.*

biographical /ˌbaɪ.əˈgræf.ɪ.kəl/ Ⓤⓢ /-oʊ-/ **adj** about someone's life: *There was a biographical note about the author on the back of the book.*

biography /baɪˈɒg.rə.fi/ Ⓤⓢ /-ˈɑː.grə-/ **noun** [C or U] **B1** the life story of a person written by someone else: *He wrote a biography* ***of*** *Winston Churchill.* → Compare **autobiography**

biohazard /ˌbaɪ.əʊˈhæz.əd/ Ⓤⓢ /-oʊˈhæz.ɚd/ **noun** [C] something, such as a disease or a chemical, that may harm people, animals, or the environment

biological /ˌbaɪ.əˈlɒdʒ.ɪ.kəl/ Ⓤⓢ /-ˈlɑː.dʒɪ-/ **adj 1** **B2** connected with the natural processes of living things: *the biological sciences* ◦ *Eating is a biological* ***necessity!*** **2** [before noun] related by birth: *She decided to search for her biological* ***mother*** *after her adoptive parents died.* **3** UK describes a substance used for cleaning that uses ENZYMES to remove dirt: *biological washing powder* → Compare **non-bio 4** using living matter, such as bacteria, to seriously harm and kill people and animals, and to damage crops: *biological* ***weapons/warfare*** • **biologically** /-i/ **adv** *biologically active/stable chemicals*

bioˌlogical ˈclock **noun** [C] your body's natural habit of sleeping, eating, growing, etc. at particular times: *Long-haul flights can seriously disrupt your biological clock.*

IDIOM **sb's biological clock is ticking (away)** informal When a woman says her biological clock is ticking (away), she means that she is worried that she is getting too old to have a baby.

bioˌlogical conˈtrol **noun** [U] the use of one plant

or animal to control another, especially to prevent disease or damage

biologist /baɪˈɒl.ə.dʒɪst/ US /-ˈɑː.lə-/ **noun** [C] a scientist who studies biology

biology /baɪˈɒl.ə.dʒi/ US /-ˈɑː.lə-/ **noun** [U] A2 the scientific study of the natural processes of living things: *human biology ◦ marine biology ◦ molecular biology ◦ The book deals with the reproductive biology* ***of*** *the buffalo.*

biomass /ˈbaɪ.əʊˌmæs/ US /-oʊ-/ **noun** [U] specialized **1** dead plant and animal material suitable for using as fuel: *biomass* ***fuel/energy*** **2** the total MASS of living things in a particular area

biome /ˈbaɪ.əʊm/ US /-oʊm/ **noun** [C] specialized a region of the earth's surface and the particular combination of CLIMATE (= general type of weather), plants, and animals that are found in it: *Tropical rainforest is a very complex biome.*

biometric /ˌbaɪ.əʊˈmet.rɪk/ US /-oʊ-/ **adj** referring to detailed information about someone's body, such as the patterns of colour in their eyes, that can be used to prove who they are: *biometric* ***data*** *◦ a biometric passport*

bionic /baɪˈɒn.ɪk/ US /-ˈɑː.nɪk/ **adj 1** using artificial materials and methods to produce activity or movement in a person or animal: *a bionic arm/leg* **2** humorous used to refer to a person who has greater powers of strength, speed, etc. than seem to be possible for a human: *a bionic man/woman*

biophysics /ˌbaɪ.əʊˈfɪz.ɪks/ US /-oʊ-/ **noun** [U] the science that uses the laws and methods of physics to explain biology

biopic /ˈbaɪ.əʊ.pɪk/ US /-oʊ-/ **noun** [C] informal a film about the life of a real person

biopsy /ˈbaɪ.ɒp.si/ US /-ɑːp-/ **noun** [C] the process of removing and examining a small amount of tissue from a sick person, in order to discover more about their illness: *a tissue biopsy*

biorhythm /ˈbaɪ.əʊ.rɪ.ðəm/ US /-oʊ-/ **noun** [C] a regular pattern of physical processes in an organism

bioscience /ˈbaɪ.əʊˌsaɪəns/ US /-oʊ-/ **noun** [C or U] any of the areas of scientific study that relate to living things: *Kansas City University of Medicine and Biosciences*

biosecurity /ˌbaɪ.əʊ.sɪˈkjʊə.rɪ.ti/ US /-oʊ.sɪˈkjʊr.ə.t̬i/ **noun** [U] the methods that are used to stop a disease or infection from spreading from one person, animal, or place to others

biosphere /ˈbaɪ.əʊ.sfɪəʳ/ US /-oʊ.sfɪr/ **noun** [U] specialized the part of the earth's environment where life exists

biotechnology /ˌbaɪ.əʊ.tekˈnɒl.ə.dʒi/ US /-oʊ.tek-ˈnɑː.lə-/ **noun** [U] (informal **biotech** /ˈbaɪ.əʊ.tek/ US /-oʊ-/) the use of living things, especially cells and bacteria, in industrial processes: *a biotech company/firm*

bioterrorism /ˌbaɪ.əʊˈter.ə.rɪ.zəm/ US /-oʊˈter.ɚ-/ **noun** [U] violent action using living matter, such as bacteria, to harm or kill people for political reasons • **bioterrorist** /-ˈter.ə.rɪst/ US /-ˈter.ɚ.ɪst/ **noun** [C]

biotic /baɪˈɒt.ɪk/ US /-ˈɑː.t̬ɪk/ **adj** specialized involving, caused by, or relating to living things in the environment: *Climate can also be affected by biotic factors.*

bipartisan /ˌbaɪˈpɑː.tɪ.zæn/ US /-ˈpɑːr.t̬ɪ-/ **adj** supported by or consisting of two political parties: *a bipartisan committee*

biped /ˈbaɪ.ped/ **noun** [C] specialized an animal that walks on two legs → Compare **quadruped** • **bipedal** /baɪˈpiː.dəl/ US /-ˈped.əl/ **adj** *bipedal motion*

biplane /ˈbaɪ.pleɪn/ **noun** [C] an old type of aircraft with two sets of wings, one above the other → Compare **monoplane**

bipolar /ˌbaɪˈpəʊ.ləʳ/ US /-ˈpoʊ.lɚ/ **adj** suffering from bipolar disorder

biˈpolar disˌorder **noun** [U] a mental illness causing someone to change often from being extremely excited to being very DEPRESSED

biracial /ˌbaɪˈreɪ.ʃəl/ **adj** concerning or containing members of two different races: *biracial children*

birch /bɜːtʃ/ US /bɝːtʃ/ **noun TREE** ▷ **1** [C] a tree with a smooth, often white BARK (= outer covering) and thin branches **PUNISHMENT** ▷ **2 the birch** [S] UK an official punishment in the past, that involved hitting a person across the bottom with thin sticks. The thin sticks are also called the birch. • **birch verb** [T] to punish someone with the birch

bird /bɜːd/ US /bɝːd/ **noun** [C] **CREATURE** ▷ **1** A1 a creature with feathers and wings, usually able to fly: *caged/wild birds ◦ wading birds ◦ Most birds lay eggs in the spring. ◦ Penguins and ostriches are* ***flightless*** *birds (= they cannot fly). ◦ We watched a* ***flock of*** *birds fly over the field.* → See also **dicky bird, hummingbird, songbird PERSON** ▷ **2** old-fashioned a particular type of person: *He's a rare bird, is Nick.* **3** UK slang a young woman: *Is that Lee's new bird?* **4 old bird** informal an older woman: disapproving *This old bird was lecturing the shop assistant about her manners.* ◦ approving *She's a* ***game*** *old bird (= one who is energetic and willing to do risky things).*

IDIOMS **be (strictly) for the birds** informal to be stupid or not important • **the bird has flown** UK saying said when the person you are looking for has gone away or escaped • **a bird in the hand (is worth two in the bush)** saying said when you recognize that you should not risk losing something you already have by trying to get something you think might be better • **the birds and the bees** humorous the basic facts about sex and how babies are produced: *She's only six, but she already knows about the birds and the bees.* • **a bird's eye view** a view from a very high place that allows you to see a large area: *Climb to the top of the Eiffel Tower if you want a bird's eye view of Paris.* • **birds of a feather** often disapproving people who are similar in character: *He'll get on well with Anthony – they're birds of a feather.* • **birds of a feather flock together** saying said about people who have similar characters or interests, especially ones of which you disapprove, and who often spend time with each other • **do bird** UK old-fashioned slang to spend time in prison • **(as) free as a bird** completely free to do as you want

birdbath /ˈbɜːd.bɑːθ/ US /ˈbɝːd.bæθ/ **noun** [C] a bowl filled with water for birds to drink and BATHE (= cover themselves in water) in

birdbrain /ˈbɜːd.breɪn/ US /ˈbɝːd-/ **noun** [C usually singular] mainly US informal a stupid person • **birdbrained** /-breɪnd/ **adj** mainly US informal stupid

birdcage /ˈbɜːd.keɪdʒ/ US /ˈbɝːd-/ **noun** [C] a CAGE (= container with wire bars) in which birds are kept so that people can look at them

ˈbird ˌdog **noun** [C] US for **gun dog**

ˈbird ˌfeeder **noun** [C] a device containing nuts or seeds for wild birds to eat

ˈbird ˌflu **noun** [U] (also **ˈavian ˌflu**) an illness that kills birds and can sometimes pass from birds to people

birdhouse /ˈbɜːd.haʊs/ ⓤⓢ /ˈbɝːd-/ noun [C] US for **nesting box**

birdie /ˈbɜː.di/ ⓤⓢ /ˈbɝː-/ noun; verb

▸noun [C] **BIRD** ▷ **1** child's word a small bird **GOLF** ▷ **2** in GOLF, an act of getting the ball into the hole in one SHOT (= hit) less than PAR (= the expected number) for that hole **NET GAME** ▷ **3** US for **shuttlecock**

▸verb [I or T] (in golf) to get a birdie for a particular hole: *He birdied the fifth and the 18th and finished two strokes under par.*

birdlike /ˈbɜːd.laɪk/ ⓤⓢ /ˈbɝːd-/ adj looking or behaving similar to a bird: *He was a little birdlike man with a pointed nose and darting eyes.*

ˌbird of ˈparadise noun [C] a bird found in New Guinea, the male of which has brightly coloured feathers

ˌbird of ˈpassage noun [C] (plural **birds of passage**) **1** UK a bird that MIGRATES (= moves from one area to another when the season changes) **2** a person who stays for only a short period of time in one place, job, etc.

ˌbird of ˈprey noun [C] (plural **birds of prey**) a bird, such as an EAGLE or a HAWK, that kills and eats small birds and animals

birdseed /ˈbɜːd.siːd/ ⓤⓢ /ˈbɝːd-/ noun [U] seeds for feeding birds

birdsong /ˈbɜːd.sɒŋ/ ⓤⓢ /ˈbɝːd.sɑːŋ/ noun [U] the musical calls of a bird or birds

ˈbird ˌtable noun [C] a small raised structure outside a building on which food for wild birds is put

birdwatching /ˈbɜːdˌwɒtʃ.ɪŋ/ ⓤⓢ /ˈbɝːdˌwɑː.tʃɪŋ/ noun [U] the hobby of studying wild birds in their natural environment • **birdwatcher** /-ˌwɒtʃ.əʳ/ ⓤⓢ /-ˌwɑː.tʃɚ/ noun [C]

Biro /ˈbaɪ.rəʊ/ ⓤⓢ /-roʊ/ noun [C] (plural **Biros**) UK trademark a type of **ballpoint**

birth /bɜːθ/ ⓤⓢ /bɝːθ/ noun **1** Ⓐ2 [C or U] the time when a baby or young animal comes out of its mother's body: *It was a difficult birth.* ◦ *He weighed eight pounds **at** birth.* ◦ *More men are present **at the** births of their children these days.* ◦ *The application form will ask for your **country/place of** birth (= where you were born).* **2** [C] a child that is born: *The percentage of **live** births (= children who are born alive and continue to live) continues to increase.* ◦ *Registration of births **and deaths** became compulsory in 1871.* **3** [U] the position of the family into which you are born, especially its social position: *He had received all the advantages of birth (= having been born into a family of a high social class) and an expensive education.* **4** **American, Italian, etc. by birth** Ⓑ2 born in a particular place or having parents of a particular nationality: *Oscar Wilde was Irish by birth.* **5** Ⓒ1 the beginning of something: *These asteroids were formed **at the** birth of the solar system.*

IDIOM **give birth** Ⓑ2 When a woman or female animal gives birth, she produces a baby or young animal from her body: *She gave birth **to** twins.* ◦ *Our cat gave birth last night.* ◦ figurative *This extraordinary experience gave birth **to** (= gave him the idea for) his latest novel.*

ˈbirth caˌnal noun [C] specialized the part of the female body, starting from the UTERUS, that a baby travels through in order to be born naturally

ˈbirth cerˌtificate noun [C] a document recording a baby's birth including such information as name, time, place, and parents

ˈbirth conˌtrol noun [U] the various methods or types of equipment that allow people to have sex without having children: [before noun] *a new type of birth-control pill*

birthday /ˈbɜːθ.deɪ/ ⓤⓢ /ˈbɝːθ-/ noun [C] Ⓐ1 the day that is exactly a year or number of years after a person was born: ***Happy** birthday, Flavio!* ◦ *Are you going to Ellen's birthday **party** next week?* ◦ *It's her 21st birthday.*

IDIOM **in your birthday suit** humorous not wearing any clothes

ˌBirthday of ˌMartin ˌLuther ˌKing, ˈJr. noun a US holiday on the third Monday in January, when people remember the CIVIL RIGHTS leader, Martin Luther King, Jr.

ˈbirth ˌdefect noun [C] a physical problem with a body part or process that is present at birth

birthmark /ˈbɜːθ.mɑːk/ ⓤⓢ /ˈbɝːθ.mɑːrk/ noun [C] a brownish or reddish mark that is on a person's skin from when they are born

ˈbirth ˌmother noun [C] the woman who gave birth to a child, although she may not now be the child's legal mother

ˈbirth ˌparent noun [C] the woman who gave birth to a child or the man who helped to CONCEIVE a child (= cause a baby to begin to form), although she or he may not now be the child's legal parent

birthplace /ˈbɜːθ.pleɪs/ ⓤⓢ /ˈbɝːθ-/ noun [C usually singular] the house, town, etc. where a person was born

ˈbirth ˌrate noun [C usually singular] the number of births that happen during a period of time in a particular place

birthright /ˈbɜːθ.raɪt/ ⓤⓢ /ˈbɝːθ-/ noun [C usually singular] something that you believe you deserve to have because of your family situation or social class, or because you believe it is your right as a human being: *Some men see well-paid, powerful jobs as their birthright.*

biscuit /ˈbɪs.kɪt/ noun [C] **FLAT CAKE** ▷ **1** Ⓐ1 UK (US **cookie**) a small, flat cake that is dry and usually sweet: *chocolate/ginger biscuits* ◦ *a **packet of** biscuits* ◦ *We had **tea and** biscuits at half past three.* **BREAD** ▷ **2** US a type of bread usually baked in small, round pieces: *baking-powder biscuits* ◦ *biscuits and gravy*

IDIOM **(really) take the biscuit** UK (US **(really) take the cake**) You say that something or someone (really) takes the biscuit when it or they have done something that you find extremely annoying or surprising: *And you say she's opening your letters now? Oh, that really takes the biscuit!*

bisect /baɪˈsekt/ verb [T] to divide something into two, usually equal, parts: *The new road will bisect the town.*

bisector /baɪˈsek.təʳ/ ⓤⓢ /-tɚ/ noun [C] specialized a straight line that divides an angle or line into two equal parts

bisexual /baɪˈsek.sju.əl/ noun [C] a person who is attracted to both men and women → Compare **heterosexual, homosexual** • **bisexual** adj

bishop /ˈbɪʃ.əp/ noun [C] **PRIEST** ▷ **1** a priest of high rank who is in charge of the priests of lower rank in a particular area: *the Bishop **of** Durham* ◦ *Bishop Desmond Tutu* **CHESS** ▷ **2** a piece that moves from corner to corner along squares of the same colour

bishopric /ˈbɪʃ.ə.prɪk/ noun [C] **1** the period of time during which a person serves as a bishop **2** an area of a country for which a bishop is responsible

bison /ˈbaɪ.sən/ noun [C] (plural **bison**) a large wild animal, similar to a cow but having a larger head and shoulders covered in hair, found in North America and Europe. The North American bison is also called BUFFALO.

bisque /biːsk/, /bɪsk/ **noun** [U] a thick soup, especially one that is made from SHELLFISH (= sea creatures that live in shells)

bistro /ˈbiː.strəʊ/ Ⓤⓢ /-stroʊ/ **noun** [C] (plural **bistros**) a small informal restaurant or bar, especially one in France or one in a French style

bit /bɪt/ **noun; verb**

▸**noun** [C] **AMOUNT** ▷ **1** A2 informal a small piece or amount of something: *Would you like a bit of chocolate?* ◦ *The glass smashed into* ***little*** *bits.* ◦ *There were bits* ***of*** *paper all over the floor.* ◦ *She tries to do a bit* ***of*** *exercise every day.* **2 a bit** informal B2 a short distance or period of time: *I'm just going out* ***for*** *a bit. See you later.* ◦ *Can you move up a bit?* **3 a bit of sth** C1 a slight but not serious amount or type of something: *Maria's put on a bit of weight, hasn't she?* ◦ *It's a bit of a nuisance.* ◦ *He's a bit of a prat.* **4 a bit... a** A2 slightly: *The dress is a bit* ***too*** *big for me.* ◦ *That was a bit silly, wasn't it?* ◦ *I'm a bit nervous.* ◦ *Would you like a bit* ***more*** *cake?* ◦ *It's a bit* ***like*** *a Swiss chalet.* **b** UK very: *Blimey, it's a bit cold!* ◦ *And she didn't invite him? That was a bit mean!* **5 bit by bit** C1 gradually: *I saved up the money bit by bit.* **6 not a bit** not in any way: *She wasn't a bit worried about her exams.* ◦ *My parents were not a bit happy (= were very unhappy) about my choice.* ◦ *'Are you getting tired?' 'Not a bit.'* **7 quite a bit** B1 a lot: *She's got quite a bit of money.* **8 to bits a** into small pieces: *The car was* ***blown*** *to bits.* ◦ *It just* ***fell*** *to bits in my hands.* **b** very much: *I love my son to bits.* **HORSE** ▷ **9** a piece of metal put in a horse's mouth to allow the person riding it to control its movements **COMPUTER** ▷ **10** specialized a unit of information in a computer that must be either 0 or 1: *a 32-bit computer (= a computer that processes 32 bits of information at a time)* **COIN** ▷ **11** UK old use a small coin: *a threepenny/sixpenny bit* → Compare **two bits** **TOOL** ▷ **12** the part of a tool used for cutting or DRILLING (= making holes)

IDIOMS **be a bit much** informal to be a situation, request, or behaviour that is unfair, unreasonable, or more than you can deal with: *I thought being asked to miss my lunch was a bit much.* • **be a bit of all right** UK slang to be an attractive person • **a bit of fluff/stuff/skirt** UK slang old-fashioned a sexually attractive woman: *Have you seen his latest bit of skirt?* • **a bit of rough** UK humorous informal someone, usually a man, from a lower social class than their sexual partner • **a bit on the side** mainly UK humorous informal a sexual relationship with someone who is not married to you, or the person you have the relationship with: *We've thought for a while that he was* ***having*** *a bit on the side.* • **get the bit between your teeth** (US also **take the bit between your teeth**) to do what you have decided to do in a forceful and energetic way: *She wasn't keen at first, but she loved it once she got the bit between her teeth.* • **not a bit of it** UK informal said when a situation or event is very different from what you expected: *I thought he would be sorry, but not a bit of it.* • **be in bits** UK informal to be very upset: *He was in bits after her death.* • **bits and pieces** C2 informal (UK also **bits and bobs**) small things or jobs of different types

▸**verb** past simple of **bite**

bitch /bɪtʃ/ **noun; verb**

▸**noun** **ANIMAL** ▷ **1** [C] a female dog **UNPLEASANT PERSON** ▷ **2** [C] offensive an unkind or unpleasant woman: *She can be a real bitch.* **PROBLEM** ▷ **3** [S] informal something that causes difficulties or problems, or that is unpleasant: *I've had* ***a*** *bitch* ***of a*** *week at work.* **COMPLAINT** ▷ **4** [S] informal the act of complaining or talking unkindly about people: *Most of us enjoy* ***having a (good)*** *bitch from time to time.* **CONTROLLED PERSON** ▷ **5** [C] offensive slang someone who will do everything you tell them to do because you have complete control over them

IDIOM **life's a bitch (and then you die)** saying said when you find a situation difficult or have had a bad experience

▸**verb** [I] informal to complain and make unkind remarks about someone or something: *She's always bitching* ***about*** *Tanya.*

bitchy /ˈbɪtʃ.i/ **adj** informal often talking unkindly about other people: *She's so bitchy!* ◦ *a bitchy remark* • **bitchiness** /-nəs/ **noun** [U]

bite /baɪt/ **verb; noun**

▸**verb** (**bit, bitten**) **USE TEETH** ▷ **1** B1 [I or T] to use your teeth to cut into something or someone: *He bit* ***into*** *the apple.* ◦ *He bites his fingernails.* **2** [I] When a fish bites, it swallows the food on the HOOK (= curved piece of wire) at the end of a fishing line: *The fish aren't biting today.* **SNAKE/INSECT** ▷ **3** If an insect or snake bites you, it injures you by making a small hole in your skin: *An insect bit me on the arm.* **AFFECT BADLY** ▷ **4** [I] to have a bad or unpleasant effect: *Higher mortgage rates are beginning to bite.* **SHOW INTEREST** ▷ **5** [I] to show interest in buying something: *The new service is now available but clients don't seem to be biting.*

IDIOMS **bite sb's head off** informal to speak to someone in a quick, angry way, for no good reason: *I only asked if I could help – there's no need to bite my head off!* • **bite your lip** to prevent yourself from showing your reaction to something by speaking or laughing: *I really wanted to laugh – I had to bite my lip.* • **bite your tongue** to stop yourself from saying something that you would really like to say: *I wanted to tell him exactly what I thought of him, but I had to bite my tongue.* • **bite me!** US offensive used to say to someone that they have made you feel angry or embarrassed • **bite off more than you can chew** informal to try to do something that is too difficult for you: *We bit off more than we could chew in our original reform proposals.* • **bite the bullet** to force yourself to do something unpleasant or difficult, or to be brave in a difficult situation • **bite the dust 1** to fall so that your body hits the ground heavily: *As they came round the bend several riders bit the dust.* **2** to end in failure: *His career bit the dust when he lost his job.* • **bite the hand that feeds you** to act badly towards the person who is helping or has helped you • **come back to bite sb** If something will come back to bite you, it will become a bigger problem in the future because you have not dealt with it. • **sb/sth won't bite** humorous used to say that someone does not need to be frightened of a particular person or thing: *Just go and ask her – she won't bite.*

PHRASAL VERBS **bite back (at sb/sth)** to react angrily, especially to someone who has done something unpleasant to you: *A cricket club has bitten back at vandals by covering its roof with razor-sharp security wire.* • **bite sth back** UK to stop yourself from saying something or from expressing an emotion: *bite back tears/laughter* • **bite into sth** to reduce something valuable: *People are worried about inflation biting into their savings and investments.*

▸**noun** **USING TEETH** ▷ **1** B2 [C] the act of biting something: *He* ***took a*** *bite (= bit a piece)* ***out of*** *the apple.* **INJURY** ▷ **2** B2 [C] a sore place or injury where a person, an animal, or an insect has bitten you **FISH** ▷

3 [S] the act of a fish biting the HOOK (= curved piece of wire) on the end of a fishing line so that it is caught **FOOD** ▷ **4 have a bite to eat** C2 (also **have a quick bite**) to eat a small amount of food or a small meal **STRONG TASTE** ▷ **5** [U] If food has bite, it has a sharp or strong taste: *I like mustard with a bit of bite.* **STRONG EFFECT** ▷ **6** [U] a powerful effect: *This satire has (real) bite.*

IDIOM **another/a second bite of the cherry** another opportunity to do something: *He missed a medal in the 100 metres, but will **get** a second bite of the cherry in the 400 metres.*

ˈbite-sized adj (also **biteˈbite-size)** describes something that is small enough to put in your mouth whole: *Cut the cheese into bite-sized **pieces**.*

biting /ˈbaɪ.tɪŋ/ (US) /-t̬ɪŋ/ adj **COLD** ▷ **1** describes weather that is extremely cold, especially when it causes you physical pain: *a biting **wind** ◦ biting **cold*** **CRITICAL** ▷ **2** disapproving describes words or people that criticize someone or something, usually in a clever but unkind way: *He made some biting remarks about the whole occasion. ◦ a biting wit*

bitmap /ˈbɪt.mæp/ noun [C] a computer image formed from PIXELS that are each stored as a value of one or more BITS (= units of information)

ˈbit ˌpart noun [C] a small and unimportant part in a film or a play

bitten /ˈbɪt.ən/ verb past participle of **bite**

bitter /ˈbɪt.əʳ/ (US) /ˈbɪt̬.ɚ/ adj; noun

▸adj **ANGRY** ▷ **1** B2 describes a person who is angry and unhappy because they cannot forget bad things that happened in the past: *I feel very bitter **about** my childhood and all that I went through. ◦ She'd suffered terribly over the years but it hadn't made her bitter.* **2** B2 describes an experience that causes deep pain or anger: *Failing the final exams was a bitter **disappointment** for me. ◦ She learned through bitter **experience** that he was not to be trusted.* **3** B2 expressing a lot of hate and anger: *a bitter fight/row ◦ bitter recriminations ◦ He gave me a bitter look.* **TASTE** ▷ **4** B1 with an unpleasantly sharp taste: *a bitter flavour/taste/liquid* **COLD** ▷ **5** B2 describes weather that is extremely cold, especially in a way that causes physical pain: *a bitter wind ◦ Wrap up warmly – it's bitter outside.*

IDIOMS **a bitter pill (to swallow)** something that is very unpleasant but must be accepted: *Losing to a younger player was a bitter pill to swallow.* • **to the bitter end** C2 until something is finished

▸noun [U] **1** UK a type of dark brown beer with a bitter taste: *a pint of bitter* → Compare **mild 2 bitters** a strong, bitter alcoholic drink made from spices and plant products that is mixed with other alcoholic drinks

ˌbitter ˈlemon noun [C or U] a FIZZY drink (= one with bubbles) with a slight taste of lemon, that is not alcoholic but is sometimes mixed with alcoholic drinks

bitterly /ˈbɪt.ə.li/ (US) /ˈbɪt̬.ɚ-/ adv **STRONG EMOTION** ▷ **1** in a way that shows strong negative emotion such as anger or disappointment: *She **wept** bitterly at the news. ◦ He was bitterly **disappointed** not to get the job.* **COLD** ▷ **2 bitterly cold** extremely and unpleasantly cold

bittern /ˈbɪt.ən/ (US) /ˈbɪt̬.ən/ noun [C] a type of European water bird that has long legs and is related to the HERON

bitterness /ˈbɪt.ə.nəs/ (US) /ˈbɪt̬.ɚ-/ noun [U] **TASTE** ▷ **1** an unpleasantly sharp taste **ANGER** ▷ **2** a feeling of anger and unhappiness: *He was full of bitterness after he lost his job.*

bittersweet /ˈbɪt.ə.swiːt/ (US) /ˈbɪt̬.ɚ-/ adj **EMOTION** ▷ **1** containing a mixture of sadness and happiness **TASTE** ▷ **2** tasting both bitter and sweet

ˌbittersweet ˈchocolate noun [U] US for **dark chocolate**

bitty /ˈbɪt.i/ (US) /ˈbɪt̬-/ adj UK informal made up of a lot of different things that do not fit together well: *I enjoyed the film but I found it quite bitty, jumping from one family's story to another.*

bitumen /ˈbɪtʃ.ʊ.mən/ (US) /bɪˈtuː-/ noun [U] a black, sticky substance such as TAR or ASPHALT, used for making roads and roofs

bivalve /ˈbaɪ.vælv/ noun [C] specialized a type of MOLLUSC, such as an OYSTER, that has its body inside two connected shells • **bivalve** adj *a bivalve mollusc*

bivouac /ˈbɪv.u.æk/ noun; verb

▸noun [C] **1** a temporary shelter or CAMP for sleeping in outside, that is not a tent **2** (also **ˌbivouac ˈtent**) a small, light tent that is just big enough for one or two people to lie in

▸verb [I usually + adv/prep] (present tense **bivouacking**, past tense and past participle **bivouacked**) to CAMP (= sleep) in a bivouac: *The soldiers bivouacked in the mountains for two nights.*

bivvy (US **bivy**) /ˈbɪv.i/ noun [C] **1** informal for **bivouac 2** informal for **bivvy sack**

ˈbivvy ˌsack noun [C] UK (informal **bivvy**, US **bivy sack**) a thin, light cover that fits over a SLEEPING BAG for extra protection, often used by climbers

biweekly /baɪˈwiːk.li/ adj, adv happening or appearing every two weeks or twice a week: *a biweekly magazine*

biz /bɪz/ noun [S] informal a particular type of business: *the **entertainment/movie/music** biz ◦ She is one of the top amateur riders **in the** biz.*

IDIOM **be the biz** UK informal to be extremely good or skilful: *This skin cream really is the biz.*

bizarre /bɪˈzɑːʳ/ (US) /-ˈzɑːr/ adj B2 very strange and unusual: *a bizarre situation ◦ bizarre behaviour* • **bizarrely** /-li/ adv • **bizarreness** /-nəs/ noun [U]

BL /ˌbiːˈel/ noun [C] (also **LLB**) US abbreviation for Bachelor of Laws: a degree in law

blab /blæb/ verb [I or T] (**-bb-**) informal to talk carelessly or too much, often telling others something you should keep secret: *Someone blabbed **to** the press.*

blabber /ˈblæb.əʳ/ (US) /-ɚ/ verb [I] informal to talk a lot, especially in a way that people find annoying or embarrassing: *He's always blabbering **on about** computers.*

blabbermouth /ˈblæb.ə.maʊθ/ (US) /-ɚ-/ noun [C] informal disapproving a person who talks carelessly, often telling secrets to other people

black /blæk/ adj; noun; verb

▸adj **COLOUR** ▷ **1** A1 having the darkest colour there is, like the colour of coal or of a very dark night: *black shoes* **PEOPLE** ▷ **2 Black** A2 relating or belonging to people with black or dark brown skin, especially people who live in Africa or whose family originally came from Africa: *Black culture ◦ Black Americans* **COFFEE/TEA** ▷ **3** without any milk or cream added: *a cup of strong black coffee ◦ I like my tea black, with sugar.* **BAD** ▷ **4** without hope: *The future looked black.*

IDIOMS **black and blue** with dark marks on your skin caused by being hit or having an accident: *His arm was black and blue.* • **not be as black as you are painted** not to be as bad as people say you are

• **paint a black picture of sth/sb** to describe a situation or person as extremely bad

▸noun COLOUR ▷ **1** A2 [U] the colour of coal or of the sky on a very dark night: *She often dresses* ***in*** *black (= in black clothes).* **2 black and white** describes photography that has no colours except black, white, and grey: *The old newsreels were filmed* ***in*** *black and white.* ◦ *a black and white photo* PEOPLE ▷ **3 Black** a black person

IDIOMS **be (down) in black and white** to be written down: *I couldn't believe it was true, but there it was, in black and white.* • **be in the black** If a bank account is in the black, it contains some money, and if a person or business is in the black, they have money in the bank and are not in debt. → Compare **be in the red** • **black-and-white** describes a subject or situation in which it is easy to understand what is right and wrong: *Disarmament isn't a black-and-white issue for me.* • **brown, green, etc. is the new black** used to say that something is the most popular or fashionable colour or thing at the moment: *Designers say that brown is the new black.* • **see things in black and white** to have a simple view of what is right and wrong, or good and bad

▸verb [T] MAKE DARK ▷ **1** to put a black substance on something or to make something black: *The commandos blacked their faces.* AVOID ▷ **2** If a TRADE UNION blacks goods or people, it refuses to handle or work with them.

PHRASAL VERBS **black sth out** COVER ▷ **1** to cover a face or a name so that it cannot be seen: *In the TV interview, they blacked out the victim's face.* NO LIGHT ▷ **2** to make a place dark, especially by covering or switching off all the lights: *The entire city was blacked out overnight.* • **black out** to become unconscious suddenly but for a short period

ˌblack ˈAfrica noun the part of Africa south of the Sahara Desert

blackball /ˈblæk.bɔːl/ (US) /-bɑːl/ verb [T] to vote against allowing someone to be a member of an organization or group

ˌblack ˈbelt noun [C] **1** the symbol of a very high standard in the sport of JUDO or KARATE **2** someone who has received a black belt as a symbol of achieving a very high standard in JUDO or KARATE: *He's a black belt at karate.*

blackberry /ˈblæk.bᵊr.i/ (US) /-ber-/ noun; verb
▸noun [C] a small dark purple fruit that grows wild in Europe and is usually cooked before being eaten: *blackberry and apple pie*
▸verb **go blackberrying** to pick wild blackberries

blackbird /ˈblæk.bɜːd/ (US) /-bɝːd/ noun [C] a European bird, the male of which has black feathers and a bright yellow beak

blackboard /ˈblæk.bɔːd/ (US) /-bɔːrd/ noun [C] A2 a dark surface on a wall or frame that a teacher writes on with CHALK (= white substance)

ˌblack ˈbox noun [C] a small machine that records information about an aircraft during its flight, used to discover the cause of an accident

ˌblack ˈcomedy noun [C or U] a film, play, etc. that looks at the funny side of things that we usually consider to be very serious, like death and illness

blackcurrant /ˌblækˈkʌr.ᵊnt/ (US) /ˈblæk.kɝː-/ noun [C or U] a small, round, dark purple fruit that grows on a bush and is usually cooked before being eaten: *blackcurrant jam*

the ˌBlack ˈDeath noun [S] a disease that killed an extremely large number of people in Europe and Asia in the 14th century

ˌblack eˈconomy noun [C usually singular] business activity and income that people do not record in order to avoid paying tax on it

blacken /ˈblæk.ᵊn/ verb MAKE DARK ▷ **1** [I or T] to become black or to make something become black: *The folds of the curtains were blackened* ***with*** *dirt.* SPOIL ▷ **2 blacken sb's name, image, reputation, etc.** to spoil someone's reputation: *The financial crash blackened the image of bankers.*

ˌblack ˈeye noun [C] an area of skin around the eye that has gone dark because it has been hit: *He had a fight at school and came home with a black eye.*

ˌblack-eyed ˈbean noun [C] UK (US **ˌblack-eyed ˈpea**) a small bean that is a pale colour and has a black spot

blackfly /ˈblæk.flaɪ/ noun [C or U] a small black insect with two wings that feeds on the juices of plants: *Do your broad beans suffer from blackfly (= are they attacked by blackfly)?*

blackguard /ˈblæg.ɑːd/, /-əd/ (US) /-ɑːrd/ noun [C] old-fashioned a person, usually a man, who is not honest or fair and has no moral principles

blackhead /ˈblæk.hed/ noun [C] a very small, dark spot on the skin caused by a blocked PORE (= small hole in the skin's surface)

ˌblack ˈhole noun [C] **1** specialized a region in space where GRAVITY is so strong that nothing, not even light, can escape **2** an imaginary place in which things are lost

ˌblack ˈhumour noun [U] a humorous way of looking at or treating something that is serious or sad

ˌblack ˈice noun [U] a dangerous type of ice on roads that is so thin that it cannot be seen by a driver

blackjack /ˈblæk.dʒæk/ noun CARD GAME ▷ **1** [U] (also **pontoon**) a type of card game played for money WEAPON ▷ **2** [C] US a short, thick metal stick covered in rubber or leather, used to hit people with

blackleg /ˈblæk.leg/ noun [C] UK disapproving a person who works while others that they work with are on STRIKE → Synonym **scab**

blacklist /ˈblæk.lɪst/ noun; verb
▸noun [C] a list of people, countries, etc. who are considered by a particular authority or group to be unacceptable and who should be avoided and not trusted
▸verb [T often passive] to put someone's name on a blacklist: *They were blacklisted because of their extreme right-wing views.*

ˌblack ˈlook noun [C] an expression on your face that is full of anger and hate: *She* ***gave*** *me a black look.*

ˌblack ˈmagic noun [U] a type of magic that is believed to use evil SPIRITS (= people who cannot be seen) to do harmful things

blackmail /ˈblæk.meɪl/ noun; verb
▸noun [U] C2 the act of getting money from people or forcing them to do something by threatening to tell a secret of theirs or to harm them: *In a position of authority, any weakness leaves you* ***open*** *to blackmail.*
▸verb [T] C2 to get money from someone by blackmail: *They used the photographs to blackmail her* ***into*** *spying for them.* • **blackmailer** /-ˌmeɪ.ləʳ/ (US) /-ˌmeɪ.lɚ/ noun [C]

ˌblack ˈmark noun [C usually singular] informal the fact of people noticing and remembering something that you have done wrong or failed to do: *If I'm late for work again, it will be another black mark* ***against*** *me.*

ˌblack ˈmarket noun [C usually singular] illegal trading of goods that are not allowed to be bought and sold, or that there are not enough of for everyone who wants them: *During the war, they bought food **on the** black market.* • ˌ**black marketˈeer** noun [C]

ˌ**black ˈmass** noun [C usually singular] a ceremony in which the Devil is worshipped instead of the Christian God

ˌ**black ˈmoney** noun [U] money that is earned illegally, or on which the necessary tax is not paid → Compare **white money**

ˌ**black ˈmood** noun [C] a very unhappy feeling: *She was **in** one of her black moods today.*

blackness /ˈblæk.nəs/ noun [U] the quality of being very dark or an area of darkness

black ˈops noun [plural or U] secret military activities, especially illegal ones, that are ordered by a government or organization but that they will not admit to having ordered: *a black ops agent/team*

blackout /ˈblæk.aʊt/ noun [C] **HIDING** ▷ **1** a time when all lights must be hidden by law, or when there is no light or power because of an electricity failure: *wartime blackouts* ◦ *Power lines were blown down and we had a blackout of several hours.* **2** the action taken to make certain that information about something is not reported to the public: *a **news** blackout* **UNCONSCIOUSNESS** ▷ **3** a short period when someone suddenly becomes unconscious: *He can't drive because he suffers from blackouts.*

ˌ**black ˈpepper** noun [U] a powder made by crushing whole black PEPPERCORNS, used to give food a hot spicy taste

ˌ**black ˈpudding** noun [C or U] mainly UK a type of sausage, usually very dark in colour, that is made from pig's blood, fat, and grain

ˌ**black ˈsheep** noun [S] a person who has done something bad that brings embarrassment or shame to his or her family: *He's **the** black sheep **of the family**.*

blacksmith /ˈblæk.smɪθ/ noun [C] a person who makes and repairs iron objects and HORSESHOES

ˈ**black ˌspot** noun [C usually singular] UK **1** a place on a road that is considered to be dangerous because several accidents have happened there: *This corner is an **accident** black spot.* **2** a place where something is very bad: *an **unemployment** black spot*

ˌ**black ˈtie** noun [U] clothes, including for men a black BOW TIE, worn for very formal social occasions: *Do we need to wear black tie?* • ˌ**black-ˈtie** adj *a black-tie event*

ˌ**black ˈwidow** noun [C] a very poisonous SPIDER that lives in warm areas

bladder /ˈblæd.əʳ/ ⓤⓢ /-ɚ/ noun [C] an organ like a bag inside the body of a person or animal, where urine is stored before it leaves the body: *to **empty** your bladder (= urinate)*

blade /bleɪd/ noun [C] **FLAT PART** ▷ **1** B2 the flat part on a knife or similar tool or weapon, with a very thin edge used for cutting: *a sword with a steel blade* ◦ *a packet of razor blades* **2** a wide, flat part on a tool or machine, used to push back water or air: *a propeller blade* ◦ *windscreen wiper blades* **3** used in the names of other objects that are flat, thin, and sometimes long, like a blade **4** a long, narrow leaf of grass or a similar plant: *a blade of grass* **5** the metal part on the bottom of an ICE SKATE → See also **shoulder blade**

blag /blæg/ verb [T] (-gg-) UK informal to persuade someone in a clever or slightly dishonest way to allow you to do something or to give you something: *Somehow they managed to blag their **way in**.* ◦ *There are often people heading my way so it's easy to blag a lift.* • **blagger** /ˈblæg.əʳ/ ⓤⓢ /-ɚ/ noun [C]

blah blah (blah) /ˌblɑː.blɑːˈblɑː/ exclamation informal a phrase used to represent boring speech: *Oh blah blah blah – I've heard it all before!*

blame /bleɪm/ verb; noun

▸**verb** [T] **1** B1 to say or think that someone or something did something wrong or is responsible for something bad happening: *Don't blame me (= it is not my fault) if you miss the bus!* ◦ *Hugh blames his mother **for** his lack of confidence.* ◦ *Hugh blames his lack of confidence **on** his mother.* ◦ *You can't really blame Helen **for** not wanting to get involved.* **2 I don't blame sb** C2 said in order to tell someone that you understand why they are doing something and that you agree with their reason for doing it: *I don't blame him **for** getting angry – she's behaving dreadfully.* ◦ *'I decided to leave.' 'I don't blame you!'* **3 be to blame** C1 to be the reason for something that happens: *The hot weather is partly to blame **for** the water shortage.*

IDIOM **a bad workman blames his tools** UK saying said when someone has blamed a mistake or failure on the things that they use for their work

▸**noun** [U] **1** B2 the situation in which people say or think that someone or something did something wrong or is responsible for something bad happening: *Health officials **put** the blame **for** the disease **on** (= say that the reason for the disease is) poor housing conditions.* ◦ *They tried to **pin** (= put) the blame **for** the killing **on** an innocent army officer.* ◦ *We want to find out what happened, not to **apportion** blame (= to say someone or something was wrong).* **2 take the blame** If you take the blame for something, you say that you did it or that it is your fault: *If anything goes wrong, I'll **take** the blame.*

> Word partners for **blame noun**
>
> *accept/shoulder/take* (the) blame • *get the* blame (for sth) • *apportion* blame • *lay/place/pin* the blame on sb • *share* the blame • *deflect/shift* (the) blame • blame *lies with/rests with* sb/sth • blame *for* sth

ˈ**blame ˌgame** noun [C] informal a situation in which people try to blame each other for something bad that has happened: *Police and the government are **playing the blame game** over the mistaken shooting of a suspected terrorist.*

blameless /ˈbleɪm.ləs/ adj not responsible for anything bad: *It was mainly my fault, but she wasn't entirely blameless.*

blameworthy /ˈbleɪmˌwɜː.ði/ ⓤⓢ /-ˌwɝː-/ adj formal having done something wrong

blanch /blɑːntʃ/ ⓤⓢ /blæntʃ/ verb **PALE** ▷ **1** [I] to turn pale, for example because you are shocked: *While most people would blanch at the prospect of so much work, Daniels seems to enjoy it.* **2** [T] to make a plant pale by covering it up so that the light does not reach it as it grows **BOIL** ▷ **3** [T] to put vegetables or similar foods into boiling water for a few minutes to make them white, remove the skins, get rid of strong flavours, or prepare them for freezing: *blanched almonds*

blancmange /bləˈmɒ̃ʒ/ ⓤⓢ /-ˈmɑːnʒ/ noun [U] UK a cold, sweet food made from milk, sugar, and CORNFLOUR

bland /blænd/ adj usually disapproving C2 not having a strong taste or character or not showing any interest or energy: *I find chicken a little bland.* ◦ *Pop music these days is so bland.* • **blandly** /ˈblænd.li/ adv • **blandness** /ˈblænd.nəs/ noun [U]

B

blandishments /ˈblæn.dɪʃ.mənts/ noun [plural] formal pleasant words or actions used in order to persuade someone to do something: *She was impervious to his blandishments.*

blank /blæŋk/ adj; verb; noun
▸adj **EMPTY** ▷ **1** B1 empty or clear, or containing no information or mark: *a blank sheet of paper* ◦ *a blank computer screen* ◦ *Sign your name in the blank space at the bottom of the form.* **NOT REACTING** ▷ **2** C2 showing no understanding or no emotion in the expression on your face: *a blank **stare/expression*** • **blankly** /ˈblæŋk.li/ adv *He just **stared** blankly at me.*
▸verb

PHRASAL VERB **blank sth out** **COVER** ▷ **1** to intentionally cover over something that is written so that it cannot be read: *Some of the names in the report have been blanked out.* **FORGET** ▷ **2** to stop yourself thinking about a memory because it is unpleasant and you would prefer not to remember it

▸noun [C] **1** a space in a piece of writing or on a form, left empty for information to be added: ***Fill in** the blanks in this form.* **2** something not yet drawn or finished, such as a key not yet cut into a finished shape **3** (also ˌ**blank** ˈ**cartridge**) a small tube containing explosive but no bullet, used in a gun in order to make a loud noise without causing harm: *The starter's pistol **fires** blanks.*

ˌ**blank** ˈ**cheque** UK (US ˌ**blank** ˈ**check**) noun [C] a CHEQUE that has been signed but does not yet have the amount of money written on it

blanket /ˈblæŋ.kɪt/ noun; adj; verb
▸noun [C] A2 a flat cover made of wool or similar warm material, usually used on a bed

IDIOM **a blanket of sth** C2 a thick covering of something: *The ground was covered by a thick blanket of snow.*

▸adj [before noun] including or affecting everything, everyone, or all cases, in a large group or area: *a blanket **ban***
▸verb [T often passive] literary to cover something completely with a thick layer: *Outside the fields were blanketed **in** fog.*

ˈ**blanket** ˌ**bombing** noun [U] the act of dropping a lot of bombs over a large area such as a city, without aiming for any particular buildings

ˌ**blank** ˈ**verse** noun [U] a type of poetry that does not RHYME, usually with ten syllables in each line

blare /bleəʳ/ US /bler/ verb [I or T] to make an unpleasantly loud noise: *The loudspeakers blared across the square.* ◦ *The radio was blaring **(out)** martial music.* • **blare** noun [S] *the blare of trumpets*

blarney /ˈblɑː.ni/ US /ˈblɑːr-/ noun [U] a friendly and pleasant way of talking that makes someone good at persuading people to do things: *Don't listen to any of his blarney!*

blasé /ˌblɑːˈzeɪ/ adj bored or not excited, or wishing to seem so: *He flies first class so often, he's become blasé **about** it.*

blaspheme /ˌblæsˈfiːm/ verb [I] to use offensive words or make statements that show no respect for God or religion

blasphemous /ˈblæs.fə.məs/ adj considered offensive to God or religion: *a blasphemous remark* • **blasphemously** /-li/ adv

blasphemy /ˈblæs.fə.mi/ noun [C or U] something that you say or do that shows you do not respect God or a religion: *to be accused of blasphemy* ◦ figurative humorous *Madonna fans think that any criticism of her is blasphemy.*

blast /blɑːst/ US /blæst/ verb; noun; exclamation
▸verb **EXPLODE** ▷ **1** [I or T] to explode or destroy something or someone with explosives, or to break through or hit something with a similar, very strong force: *A tunnel was to be blasted through the mountains.* ◦ *They heard the guns blasting **away** all night.* ◦ figurative *Their latest album blasted (its way) up the charts (= moved very quickly because of its popularity).* → See also **sandblast** **NOISE** ▷ **2** [I or T] to make a very loud and unpleasant noise: *guns/music blasting **(away/out)*** **CRITICIZE** ▷ **3** [T] informal to criticize someone or something severely: *The government was blasted by the opposition for failing to create jobs.*

PHRASAL VERB **blast off** If a rocket blasts off, it leaves the ground to go into space.

▸noun [C] **EXPLOSION** ▷ **1** an explosion: *Three people were injured **in** the blast.* **AIR** ▷ **2** a sudden strong blow of air: *A blast **of** cold air hit him as he opened the window.* **NOISE** ▷ **3** a sudden loud noise: *a blast **of** music* ◦ *The headteacher blew three blasts **on** a whistle.* **EVENT** ▷ **4** [usually singular] US informal an exciting or enjoyable experience or event, often a party: *You should have come with us last night – we had a real blast!*

IDIOM **a blast from the past** humorous something or someone that surprises you because you had almost forgotten about it

▸exclamation (also **blast it**) old-fashioned informal an expression of anger: *Oh blast! I've left my keys at home!*

blasted /ˈblɑː.stɪd/ US /ˈblæs-/ adj **ANGRY** ▷ **1** [before noun] old-fashioned informal used in phrases to express anger: *I've forgotten my blasted keys!* **DRUNK** ▷ **2** [after verb] informal drunk: *Patrick got absolutely blasted last night.*

ˈ**blast** ˌ**furnace** noun [C] a container in which iron is produced by blowing extremely hot air through a mixture of iron ORE, COKE, and LIMESTONE

ˈ**blast-off** noun [U] the moment when a spacecraft leaves the ground: *Five seconds to blast-off!*

blatant /ˈbleɪ.tᵊnt/ adj describes something bad that is very obvious or intentional: *a blatant **lie*** ◦ *The whole episode was a blatant **attempt** to gain publicity.* • **blatantly** /-li/ adv *It was blatantly **obvious** that she was telling a lie.*

blather /ˈblæð.əʳ/ US /-ɚ/ verb [I] (also **blether**) to talk for a long time in a silly or annoying way: *What on earth are you blathering **on** about?* ◦ *Stop blethering, woman!* • **blather** (also **blether**) noun [U]

blaze /bleɪz/ verb; noun
▸verb [I] **1** to burn brightly and strongly: *The sun was blazing **down** that afternoon.* **2** literary to be brightly lit or full of colour: *Isaac's eyes suddenly blazed **with** anger.*

IDIOM **blaze a trail** to do something that has never been done before: *Le Corbusier blazed a trail in architecture.*

▸noun [C] **FIRE** ▷ **1** a large, strong fire: *Firefighters took two hours to **control** the blaze.* **STRONG EFFECT** ▷ **2** **a blaze of sth** something that has a very powerful or noticeable effect: *The garden is a blaze **of colour** in autumn.* ◦ *His book was launched in a blaze **of publicity**.* **MARK** ▷ **3** a white mark on the face of a horse or other animal

IDIOM **what the blazes...?** old-fashioned informal used to give force to something you feel angry about: *What the blazes did he do that for?*

B

blazer /ˈbleɪ.zəʳ/ (US) /-zɚ/ **noun** [C] a type of formal jacket, often with the symbol of a school or organization sewn on the front pocket and worn as part of a uniform: *my new/old **school** blazer*

blazing /ˈbleɪ.zɪŋ/ **adj 1** very bright and hot or powerful: *We quickly grew tired in the blazing **sunshine**.* **2** [before noun] violent and frightening: *They used to have some blazing **rows** over money.*

blazingly /ˈbleɪ.zɪŋ.li/ **adv** extremely: *blazingly hot* ◦ *blazingly fast speeds*

blazon /ˈbleɪ.zᵊn/ **verb** [T] **emblazon**

bleach /bliːtʃ/ **noun; verb**

▸**noun** [U] a strong chemical used for cleaning things or removing colour from things

▸**verb** [T] to remove the colour from something or make it lighter using chemicals: *Gary's had his hair bleached.*

bleachers /ˈbliː.tʃəz/ (US) /-tʃɚz/ **noun** [plural] US a sloping area of seats at a sports ground that are not covered and are therefore not expensive to sit in

bleak /bliːk/ **adj 1** (C2) If a place is bleak, it is empty, and not welcoming or attractive: *The house stands on a bleak, windswept moor.* **2** bleak weather is cold and unpleasant **3** (C2) If a situation is bleak, there is little or no hope for the future: *The economic **outlook** is bleak.* • **bleakness** /ˈbliːk.nəs/ **noun** [U]

bleary /ˈblɪə.ri/ (US) /ˈblɪr.i/ **adj** If you have bleary eyes, your eyes are red or have tears in them and you cannot see clearly, because you are tired or have just woken up: *to be bleary-**eyed*** • **blearily** /ˈblɪə.rɪ.li/ (US) /ˈblɪr.ɪ-/ **adv** *Carl stared blearily (= in a very tired way) at the newspaper.*

bleat /bliːt/ **verb** [I] **1** When a sheep or GOAT bleats, it makes the typical sound of these animals. **2** informal to complain in an annoying way: *She's always bleating (**on**) about how badly she's been treated.* • **bleat noun** [C]

bleed /bliːd/ **verb** (**bled**, **bled**) **1** (B1) [I] to lose blood: *Your arm is bleeding.* ◦ *He was bleeding heavily.* **2** [T] (in the past) to make someone lose blood, as a cure for an illness **3** [T] If you bleed a closed system such as a RADIATOR or a BRAKE, you remove air or liquid from it to make it work correctly.

IDIOM **bleed sb dry** informal to take a lot of money from someone over a period of time: *The West is bleeding poorer countries dry through interest payments on their debts.*

bleeder /ˈbliː.dəʳ/ (US) /-dɚ/ **noun** [C] UK old-fashioned informal a person you feel annoyed with or sorry for: *Children? I can't stand the little bleeders!*

bleeding /ˈbliː.dɪŋ/ **adj** [before noun] UK slang used when you are annoyed with something: *I can't get the bleeding car to start!*

ˌbleeding-ˈedge adj [before noun] relating to or describing systems, devices, or ideas that are so modern that they are still being developed: *bleeding-edge technology*

ˌbleeding ˈheart noun [C] disapproving someone who shows too much sympathy for everyone: [before noun] *I'm sick of bleeding-heart liberal politicians.*

bleep /bliːp/ **noun; verb**

▸**noun** [C] a short, high sound made by a machine, especially if it is repeated

▸**verb 1** [I] (of a machine) to make a short, high sound: *I heard his alarm clock bleeping this morning.* **2** [T] UK (US **beep**) to call someone, for example a doctor, by sending a signal to a bleeper that they carry: *Bleep me if his condition worsens.*

bleeper /ˈbliː.pəʳ/ (US) /-pɚ/ **noun** [C] UK (US **beeper**) a small device that you carry or wear, which moves or makes a noise to tell you that someone wants you to phone them

blemish /ˈblem.ɪʃ/ **noun; verb**

▸**noun MARK** ▷ **1** [C] a mark on something that spoils its appearance: *freckles, scars, and other minor **skin** blemishes* **FAULT** ▷ **2** [C or U] a fault in a person's character: *Is any politician's record **without** blemish on this issue?*

▸**verb** [T] to spoil something: *This latest revelation has seriously blemished the governor's **reputation**.*

blench /blentʃ/ **verb** [I] **1** to move back or away suddenly or react physically because something frightens, DISGUSTS (= shocks), or upsets you: *At the sight of the dead animal, Diana blenched.* **2** humorous to be very unwilling to do something: *My sister blenches **at** the very thought of changing a baby's nappy.*

blend /blend/ **noun; verb**

▸**noun** [C] (C2) a mixture of different things or styles: *a rich blend of the finest coffee beans* ◦ *Their music is a blend of jazz and African rhythms.*

▸**verb** [I or T] to mix or combine together: *Blend the ingredients into a smooth paste.* ◦ *The cushions blend well **with** the colour of the carpet.*

PHRASAL VERB **blend in/blend into sth** to look or seem the same as surrounding people or things and therefore not be easily noticeable: *We tried to blend into the crowd.* ◦ *They have adopted local customs and tried to blend in **with** the community.*

blended /ˈblen.dɪd/ **adj** describes a drink that contains two or more different types of the same product: *blended whisky*

blender /ˈblen.dəʳ/ (US) /-dɚ/ **noun** [C] an electric machine used in the kitchen for breaking down foods or making smooth liquid substances from soft foods and liquids

bless /bles/ **verb** [T] (**blessed**, **blessed** or literary **blest**) to ask for God's help and protection for someone or something, or to call or make someone or something holy

IDIOMS **bless my soul!** (also **bless me!**, also **well I'm blessed!**) an expression of surprise • **bless you!** something you say to a person who has just SNEEZED • **bless you** (also **bless your heart**) something you say to tell someone you are grateful to them when they have been kind to you: *'Here, let me help you with your shopping.' 'Oh, bless you, dear.'*

blessed adj 1 /ˈbles.ɪd/, /blest/ formal holy: *Blessed are the meek for they shall inherit the Earth.* **2** /ˈbles.ɪd/ literary bringing you happiness, luck, or something you need: *blessed peace/rain/silence* ◦ *a blessed relief* **3 be blessed with sth** /blest/ formal to be lucky in having a particular thing: *Fortunately we were blessed with fine weather.* ◦ *She is blessed with both beauty and brains.* **4** /ˈbles.ɪd/ [before noun] informal an expression of anger: *Take that blessed cat out!*

the ˌBlessed ˈVirgin noun [S] a name for the mother of Jesus

blessing /ˈbles.ɪŋ/ **noun RELIGIOUS WORDS** ▷ **1** [C or U] a request by a priest for God to take care of a particular person or a group of people, or God's act of doing this: *The mass always ends with a blessing.* ◦ *We ask God's blessing **on** Joan at this difficult time.* **LUCKY SITUATION** ▷ **2** [C] something that is extremely lucky or makes you happy: *It was a blessing* ***that*** *no one was killed in the accident.* **APPROVAL ▷ 3 sb's blessing** approval that someone gives to a plan or action: *The government has* ***given*** *its blessing* ***to*** *the plan.* ◦ *Eventually they got married with her father's blessing.*

IDIOM **a blessing in disguise** something that seems bad or unlucky at first, but results in something good happening later: *Losing that job was a blessing in disguise really.*

blether /ˈbleð.əʳ/ ⓤⓢ /-ɚ/ noun, verb → **blather**

blew /bluː/ verb past simple of **blow**

blight /blaɪt/ noun; verb

▸noun **1** [U] a disease that damages and kills plants **2** [S or U] something which spoils or has a very bad effect on something, often for a long time: *His arrival* ***cast a*** *blight* ***on*** *the wedding day.*

▸verb [T] to spoil something: *A broken leg blighted her* ***chances*** *of winning the championship.*

blighter /ˈblaɪ.təʳ/ ⓤⓢ /-t̬ɚ/ noun [C] UK old-fashioned informal a man or child, especially an annoying one: *The little blighters next door have trampled all over my flowers again.*

Blighty /ˈblaɪ.ti/ noun UK informal old-fashioned or humorous a way of referring to the UK or England, used especially by soldiers during the First World War

blimey /ˈblaɪ.mi/ exclamation UK old-fashioned informal an expression of surprise: *Blimey, what a lot of food!*

blimp /blɪmp/ noun [C] mainly US an **airship**

blind /blaɪnd/ adj; verb; noun

▸adj **SIGHT ▷ 1** B1 unable to see: *She's been blind since birth.* ◦ *He started to* ***go*** *(= become) blind in his sixties.* **EXTREME ▷ 2** describes an extreme feeling that happens without thought or reason: *blind anger/faith/prejudice* **NOT CONSCIOUS ▷ 3** describes an extreme feeling that happens without thought or reason: *blind anger/faith/prejudice* **4 be blind to sth** C2 to not be conscious of something or to refuse to notice something that is obvious to others: *She seems blind to his faults.* • **blindness** /ˈblaɪnd.nəs/ noun [U]

IDIOMS **(as) blind as a bat** informal humorous unable to see well: *I'm as blind as a bat without my glasses.* • **not take a blind bit of notice** UK informal to pay no attention to something: *He didn't take a blind bit of notice* ***of*** *what I said.*

▸verb [T] **DAMAGE SIGHT ▷ 1** to make someone unable to see, permanently or for a short time: *She was blinded in an accident at an early age.* ◦ *Turning the corner the sun blinded me, so I didn't see the other car.* **CAUSE TO IGNORE ▷ 2** to make someone unable to notice or understand something: *We mustn't let our prejudices blind us* ***to*** *the facts of the situation.*

IDIOM **blind sb with science** UK to confuse someone by using difficult or technical words to describe something

▸noun **WINDOW ▷ 1** [C] (US **shade**) a cover for a window made of a single piece or strips of cloth, paper, or plastic that is pulled up or down by a string: *a roller blind* ◦ *a Venetian blind* **SIGHT ▷ 2 the blind** C1 [plural] people who are unable to see: *She trains guide dogs for the blind.*

IDIOM **the blind leading the blind** used to describe a situation where a person who knows nothing is getting advice and help from another person who knows almost nothing

ˌblind ˈalley noun [C] a situation or method that is not effective or will not produce results: *This sort of thinking just seems to be* ***leading*** *us* ***up/down*** *a blind alley.*

ˌblind ˈdate noun [C] **1** a romantic social meeting between two people who have never met each other: *Elaine arranged for me to* ***go on*** *a blind date with a guy from her office.* **2** either of the people who meet for a blind date

ˌblind ˈdrunk adj informal extremely drunk

blinder /ˈblaɪn.dəʳ/ ⓤⓢ /-dɚ/ noun **GOOD PERFORMANCE ▷ 1** [S] UK informal an excellent performance at some activity, especially in sport: *Weir* ***played a*** *blinder in yesterday's semifinal.* **HORSE EQUIPMENT ▷ 2 blinders** [plural] US for **blinker**

blindfold /ˈblaɪnd.fəʊld/ ⓤⓢ /-foʊld/ noun; verb

▸noun [C] a strip of cloth which covers someone's eyes and stops them from seeing

▸verb [T] to cover someone's eyes with a blindfold: *She was blindfolded and taken somewhere in the back of a van.* • **blindfold** adv humorous *I've been there so often I could probably drive there blindfold.*

blinding /ˈblaɪn.dɪŋ/ adj extremely bright: *There was loud bang and a sudden blinding* ***light.***

IDIOM **a blinding flash** an idea or answer that suddenly becomes obvious: *The answer came to her* ***in*** *a blinding flash.*

blindingly /ˈblaɪn.dɪŋ.li/ adv extremely: *It's blindingly* ***obvious*** *that she's not happy at school.*

blindly /ˈblaɪnd.li/ adv **NOT SEEING ▷ 1** not able to see or not noticing what is around you: *The room was completely dark and I fumbled blindly for the door.* **NOT AWARE ▷ 2** not thinking about or understanding what you are doing: *They just blindly followed orders.*

ˌblind man's ˈbuff noun [U] a children's game in which one person has a cloth tied over their eyes and tries to catch the others

blindside /ˈblaɪnd.saɪd/ verb [T] US to surprise someone, usually with harmful results: *The recession blindsided a lot of lawyers who had previously taken for granted their comfortable income.*

ˈblind ˌside noun [S] the area behind and slightly to one side of you which you cannot see, for example when you are driving

ˈblind ˌspot noun [C usually singular] **1** an area that you are not able to see, especially the part of a road you cannot see when you are driving, behind and slightly to one side of the car: *It can be very dangerous if there's a vehicle* ***in*** *your blind spot.* **2** a subject that you find very difficult to understand at all, sometimes because you are not willing to try: *I am quite good at English, but I* ***have*** *a bit of* ***a*** *blind spot where spelling is concerned.*

bling /blɪŋ/ adj informal describes jewellery which attracts attention because it is big and expensive • **bling** noun [U] informal jewellery of this type

blini /ˈbliː.ni/ noun [plural] small PANCAKES

blink /blɪŋk/ verb; noun

▸verb **1** B2 [I or T] When you blink, you close and then open your eyes quickly once or several times, and when an eye blinks, it does this: *You've got something in your eye – try blinking a few times.* **2** [I] literary If a light blinks, it flashes on and off.

IDIOM **not blink** informal to not show any shock or surprise: *When he was told I was expecting twins, Harry didn't even blink.*

▸noun [C usually singular] the act of blinking

IDIOMS **in the blink of an eye** C2 extremely quickly: *In the blink of an eye, he was gone.* • **on the blink** informal

When a machine is on the blink, it is not working correctly.

B

blinker /ˈblɪŋ.kəʳ/ ⓤⓢ /-kɚ/ noun **LIGHT** ▷ **1** [C] US a light on the outside of a vehicle which turns on and off quickly to show other people you are going to turn in that direction **HORSE EQUIPMENT** ▷ **2 blinkers** [plural] UK (US **blinders**) two pieces of leather that are put at the side of a horse's eyes so that it can only see forward

blinkered /ˈblɪŋ.kəd/ ⓤⓢ /-kɚd/ adj A blinkered person is unable or unwilling to understand other people's beliefs, and blinkered opinions or ways of behaving show someone is unable or unwilling to understand other people: *He's very blinkered in his outlook.*

blinking /ˈblɪŋ.kɪŋ/ adj [before noun] UK old-fashioned informal an expression of anger: *I wish they'd turn down that blinking music!*

blip /blɪp/ noun [C] **1** a small spot of light, sometimes with a short sharp sound, that appears on a computer screen **2** a temporary change that does not have any special meaning: *Last month's rise in inflation was described by the chancellor as only a blip.*

bliss /blɪs/ noun; verb

▸noun [U] perfect happiness: *Lying on a sunny beach is my idea of* ***sheer*** *bliss.* ◦ ***wedded/domestic*** *bliss*

▸verb

PHRASAL VERB **bliss (sb) out** informal to become, or to make someone, completely happy and relaxed: *to bliss out* ***on*** *music/LSD* ◦ *I like to go off on my own – to sit back and bliss out in a darkened movie theater.*

ˌblissed ˈout adj informal completely happy and relaxed: *They sat hand in hand, blissed out in the sunshine.*

blissful /ˈblɪs.fᵊl/ adj extremely or completely happy: *a blissful childhood/holiday* ◦ *We spent a blissful year together before things started to go wrong.* • **blissfully** /-i/ adv *They seemed blissfully* ***happy.*** ◦ *All this time I was blissfully* ***unaware*** *of the situation.*

IDIOM **in blissful ignorance** not knowing any of the unpleasant facts about something: *All the time his business was failing, he kept his wife and family in blissful ignorance.*

ˈB-list adj [usually before noun] used for describing people who are quite famous but not as famous as the A-LIST people: *He's just a B-list actor.* • **ˈB-lister** noun [C]

blister /ˈblɪs.təʳ/ ⓤⓢ /-tɚ/ noun; verb

▸noun [C] **1** ⓒ a painful swelling on the skin that contains liquid, caused usually by continuous rubbing, especially on your foot, or by burning: *New shoes always give me blisters.* **2** a hollow rounded swelling that appears on a surface

▸verb [I or T] to get blisters or cause blisters: *The sun blistered the paintwork.* • **blistered** /-təd/ ⓤⓢ /-tɚd/ adj

blistering /ˈblɪs.tᵊr.ɪŋ/ ⓤⓢ /-tɚ-/ adj **HOT** ▷ **1** extremely hot: *We went out in the blistering* ***heat.*** **FAST** ▷ **2** extremely fast: *The runners set off at a blistering* ***pace.*** **ANGRY** ▷ **3** extremely angry and unkind: *blistering remarks/sarcasm*

blithe /blaɪð/ adj old-fashioned happy and without worry: *She shows a blithe disregard for danger.* • **blithely** /-li/ adv

blithering idiot /ˌblɪð.ᵊr.ɪŋˈɪd.i.ət/ ⓤⓢ /-ɚ-/ noun [C] old-fashioned informal an extremely stupid person

blitz /blɪts/ noun [C] **ATTACK** ▷ **1** a fast, violent attack on a town, city, etc., usually with bombs dropped from aircraft **ACTIVITY** ▷ **2** a lot of energetic activity: *The car was launched with a massive* ***media/advertising blitz,*** *involving newspapers, magazines, television, and radio.* **3** specialized the situation in which both players have to make a lot of moves in a very short period at the end of a game of CHESS, before the time allowed is past • **blitz** verb [T]

IDIOM **a blitz on sth** informal a great effort to improve something or do something that needs to be done: *We* ***had*** *a blitz on the house at the weekend and cleaned it completely.*

the ˈBlitz noun [S] the big attacks on British towns made by German aircraft in 1940–1: *She was killed* ***in/during*** *the Blitz.*

blitzkrieg /ˈblɪts.kriːg/ noun [C] a sudden attack that is intended to surprise and quickly defeat the enemy, involving aircraft and forces on the ground

blizzard /ˈblɪz.əd/ ⓤⓢ /-ɚd/ noun **SNOW** ▷ **1** [C] a severe snow storm with strong winds: *We once got* ***stuck in*** *a blizzard for six hours.* ◦ *In Sussex, blizzard* ***conditions*** *made the main roads almost impassable.* **LARGE AMOUNT** ▷ **2** [S] informal a large amount of something which arrives or is produced together in a confusing or badly organized way: *a blizzard* ***of*** *statistics/handouts*

bloat /bləʊt/ ⓤⓢ /bloʊt/ verb [I or T] to swell up, or to make someone or something swollen: *If I eat it, my stomach bloats* ***up.*** • **bloating** /ˈbləʊ.tɪŋ/ ⓤⓢ /ˈbloʊ.t̬ɪŋ/ noun [U]

bloated /ˈbləʊ.tɪd/ ⓤⓢ /ˈbloʊ.t̬ɪd/ adj **SWOLLEN** ▷ **1** swollen and rounded because of containing too much air, liquid, or food: *a bloated* ***stomach*** ◦ *a bloated (= uncomfortably full)* ***feeling*** **VERY RICH** ▷ **2** disapproving larger or richer than necessary: *a bloated bureaucracy* ◦ *a bloated capitalist*

bloater /ˈbləʊ.təʳ/ ⓤⓢ /ˈbloʊ.t̬ɚ/ noun [C] a HERRING or MACKEREL that has been kept in salt water and then lightly smoked

blob /blɒb/ ⓤⓢ /blɑːb/ noun [C] **DROP** ▷ a fat, round drop, usually of something sticky or thick: *a blob* ***of*** *glue/paint*

bloc /blɒk/ ⓤⓢ /blɑːk/ noun [C] a group of countries or people that have similar political interests: *The European Union is a powerful* ***trading/trade*** *bloc.* ◦ *the former* ***Eastern/Communist*** *bloc countries*

block /blɒk/ ⓤⓢ /blɑːk/ noun; verb

▸noun **AREA** ▷ **1** Ⓐ2 [C] mainly US the distance along a street from where one road crosses it to the place where the next road crosses it, or one part of a street like this, especially in a town or city: *The museum is just six blocks away.* ◦ *My friend and I live* ***on the*** *same block.* **2** Ⓐ2 [C] a square group of buildings or houses with roads on each side: *I took a walk around the block.* **3 round/around the block** on the next street which crosses this street: *He lives just round the block.* **PIECE** ▷ **4** Ⓑ2 [C] a solid, straight-sided piece of hard material: *a block of wood/ice* **5 the block** [S] (in the past) a large piece of wood on which criminals had their head cut off: *Anne Boleyn* ***went to*** *(= was killed on) the block.* **BUILDING** ▷ **6** Ⓑ1 [C] a large, usually tall building divided into separate parts for use as offices or homes by several different organizations or people: *an* ***office*** *block* ◦ UK *a* ***tower*** *block* ◦ UK *a block* ***of flats*** **GROUP** ▷ **7** [C] a group of things bought, dealt with, or considered together: *a block of tickets/seats/shares* ◦ *Corporate hospitality firms make block* ***bookings*** *(= buy large numbers of seats) at big sporting events.* **OBJECT BLOCKING** ▷ **8** ⓒ [C usually singular] something that blocks a tube or opening: *A block* ***in***

(= *an object blocking*) *the pipe was preventing the water from coming through.* → Synonym **blockage**

IDIOM **have/put your head on the block** to risk a bad thing happening to you by doing something or helping someone: *I'm not going to put my head on the block* ***for*** *you.*

▸verb [T] **1** B2 to prevent movement through something: *A fallen tree is blocking the road.* ◦ *As she left the court, an angry crowd tried to block her way.* **2** C1 to be between someone and the thing they are looking at, so that they cannot see: *My view was blocked by a tall man in front of me.* **3** C2 to stop something from happening or succeeding: *She was very talented and I felt her parents were blocking her* ***progress****.* ◦ *A group of politicians blocked the* ***proposal****.* • **blocked** /blɒkt/ US /blɑːkt/ **adj** *The road is blocked – you'll have to go round the other way.* ◦ *I've got a blocked* (***up***) ***nose****.*

PHRASAL VERBS **block sth/sb in** to put a vehicle so close to another vehicle that it cannot drive away: *Another car had parked behind me and blocked me in.* • **block sth off** to close a road, path, or entrance so that people cannot use it: *All the roads out of the town had been blocked off by the police.* • **block sth out** STOP FROM PASSING ▷ **1** to stop light or noise from passing through something: *The tree outside the window blocks out the sun.* STOP FROM THINKING ▷ **2** to stop yourself from thinking about an unpleasant memory because it upsets you: *He's trying to block out memories of the accident.* • **block sth up** to fill a narrow space with something so that nothing can pass through: *In autumn, leaves block the drains up.*

blockade /blɒkˈeɪd/ US /blɑːˈkeɪd/ **noun** [C] the situation in which a country or place is surrounded by soldiers or ships to stop people or goods from going in or out: *an air and sea blockade* ◦ *The Soviet blockade* ***of*** *Berlin was* ***lifted*** *in May 1949.* ◦ *There is still some hope that the* ***economic*** *blockade will work and make military intervention unnecessary.* • **blockade verb** [T] *The Estonian port of Tallinn was blockaded for a time by Soviet warships.*

blockage /ˈblɒk.ɪdʒ/ US /ˈblɑː.kɪdʒ/ **noun** [C or U] something that stops something else passing through, or the act of stopping something passing through: *His death was caused by a blockage in one of his arteries.*

ˌblock and ˈtackle noun [U] a device for raising objects off the ground, consisting of one or more small wheels with a rope or chain going around them, connected to a high part of a building

blockbuster /ˈblɒkˌbʌs.təʳ/ US /ˈblɑːkˌbʌs.tɚ/ **noun** [C] informal a book or film that is very successful: *a blockbuster* ***movie****/novel*

ˌblock ˈcapitals noun [plural] (also **ˌblock ˈletters**) a style of writing in which each letter of a word is written separately and clearly using the capital letters of the alphabet: *Please print your name and address in block capitals.*

ˈblock ˌgraph noun [C] specialized a type of GRAPH that shows different amounts or numbers as rectangular blocks of different sizes

blockhead /ˈblɒk.hed/ US /ˈblɑːk-/ **noun** [C] old-fashioned informal a stupid person

ˌblock of ˈflats noun [C] UK (US **aˈpartment ˌbuilding**) a large building that is divided into apartments

ˌblock ˈvote noun [C] (also **ˈcard ˌvote**) UK a large number of votes that are made in the same way by one person who represents a large group of people

blog /blɒg/ US /blɑːg/ **noun; verb**

▸noun [C] (also **weblog**) B1 a regular record of your thoughts, opinions, or experiences that you put on the internet for other people to read

▸verb [I] (-gg-) B1 to write or add material to a blog • **blogger** /ˈblɒg.əʳ/ US /ˈblɑː.gɚ/ **noun** [C] B1 someone who writes a blog

the blogosphere /ˈblɒg.əs.fɪəʳ/ /blɑːg.əs.fɪɚ/ **noun** [S] informal all the blogs on the internet, and the people who write or read them: *The blogosphere has been very excited about the story.*

bloke /bləʊk/ US /bloʊk/ **noun** [C] UK informal a man, often one who is considered to be ordinary: *Paul's a really good bloke* (= *I like him a lot*). ◦ *He's a funny* (*sort of*) *bloke* (= *slightly strange*).

blokeish (also **blokish**) /ˈbləʊ.kɪʃ/ US /ˈbloʊ-/ **adj** UK informal describes a man who behaves in the way people traditionally think ordinary men behave when they are together: *He's too blokeish for me – always talking about football and cars.*

blonde /blɒnd/ US /blɑːnd/ **adj; noun**

▸adj (also **blond**) A2 with pale yellow or gold hair: *blonde hair/highlights* ◦ *a blonde woman/a blond man*

IDIOM **have a blonde moment** informal to forget something or do something silly, in a way that is sometimes thought to be typical of women with blonde hair

▸noun [C] a woman with pale yellow or gold hair: *Who's the blonde talking to Bob?*

IDIOM **blondes have more fun** saying said to express the common belief that men are more attracted to women with blonde hair and give them more attention

blood /blʌd/ **noun; verb**

▸noun [U] LIQUID ▷ **1** A2 the red liquid that is sent around the body by the heart, and carries OXYGEN and important substances to organs and tissue, and removes waste products: *He* ***lost*** *a lot of blood in the accident.* **2 give/donate blood** to allow a trained person to take some blood from your body so that it can be stored and is ready to be given to people who have lost a lot of blood in an accident or operation FAMILY ▷ **3** C2 family relationship by birth rather than marriage: *They are related* ***by*** *blood.* ◦ *She has Russian blood* (= *one or more of her relatives was Russian*).

IDIOMS **be after sb's blood** informal to be very angry with someone and threatening to harm them: *You'd better stay out of her way – she's after your blood.* • **be in the/sb's blood** If an ability or skill is in someone's blood, they have it naturally, usually because it already exists in their family: *His father and grandmother were painters too, so it's obviously in the blood.* • **blood and guts** informal extreme violence: *There was a bit too much blood and guts in the film for my liking.* • **blood is thicker than water** saying said to emphasize that you believe that family connections are always more important than other types of relationship • **get blood out of/from a stone** to make someone give or tell you something, when it is extremely difficult because of the character or mood of the person or organization you are dealing with: *Persuading Chris to buy a round of drinks is like getting blood out of a stone.* • **have (sb's) blood on your hands** to be responsible for someone's death: *The leaders of this war have the blood of many thousands of people on their hands.* • **make sb's blood boil** C2 to make someone extremely angry: *The way they have treated those people makes my blood boil.* • **make sb's blood run cold** C2 A sound, sight, or thought that makes your blood run cold frightens you very much: *I heard a tapping on the window which made my blood run cold.* • **new/fresh blood** C1 people who join an organization and who can provide new ideas and energy: *The company has brought in some new blood in an effort to revive its fortunes.*

▸verb [T] to give someone their first experience of something: *They decided to blood him in the international team at the age of only 18.*

ˈblood ˌbank noun [C] a cool place where blood is stored before it is used in hospitals

bloodbath /ˈblʌd.bɑːθ/ US /-bæθ/ noun [S] an extremely violent event in which a great number of people are killed: *Is there nothing that the outside world can do to* ***prevent a*** *bloodbath?*

ˌblood ˈbrother noun [C] a man who has promised to treat another man as his brother in a ceremony in which they cut themselves and mix their blood together

ˈblood ˌcount noun [C usually singular] the number of red and white blood cells in a person's blood, or a medical test to discover this

bloodcurdling /ˈblʌdˌkɜː.dl̩.ɪŋ/ US /-ˌkɝː-/ adj causing a feeling of extreme fear: *a bloodcurdling story/****scream***

ˈblood ˌdonor noun [C] someone who regularly gives some of their blood for people who need it because they are sick

-blooded /-blʌd.ɪd/ suffix having the type of blood mentioned: *warm-blooded*

ˈblood ˌgroup UK for **blood type**

bloodhound /ˈblʌd.haʊnd/ noun [C] a large dog that has a very good ability to smell things, and is used for hunting animals or finding people who are lost

bloodless /ˈblʌd.ləs/ adj **NOT VIOLENT** ▷ **1** describes a military operation involving no deaths: *The rebel soldiers seized power in a bloodless* ***coup.*** **PALE** ▷ **2** describes a face or skin that is extremely pale: *His face was thin and bloodless.* **NO EMOTION** ▷ **3** without emotion

bloodletting /ˈblʌdˌlet.ɪŋ/ US /-ˌlet̬-/ noun **1** [U] formal killing and violence, especially between enemy groups involved in an argument that has existed for a long time: *ethnic bloodletting* **2** [S or U] the situation in which a company reduces the number of people working for it: *EWS carried out further bloodletting by sacking some senior employees.* **3** [U] in the past, a medical treatment in which blood was taken from a person who was ill

bloodline /ˈblʌd.laɪn/ noun [C] all the members of a family group of people or animals over a period of time, especially when considering their shared family characteristics: *Ismailis believe that a bloodline joins the Aga Khan to Mohammed.* ◦ *This is a pedigree poodle – her bloodline is pure.*

ˈblood ˌlust noun [U] enjoyment of being violent or watching other people being violent

ˈblood ˌmoney noun [U] **1** disapproving money paid to the family of a murdered person **2** money paid to someone for killing someone else, or for giving information about a person who has killed someone

ˈblood ˌorange noun [C] a type of ORANGE (= fruit) that has red flesh

ˈblood ˌpoisoning noun [U] **septicaemia** or **toxaemia**

ˈblood ˌpressure noun [U] a measure of the pressure at which the blood flows through the body: *The nurse will* ***take*** *your blood pressure in a moment.* ◦ *to have/suffer from* ***high/low*** *blood pressure*

ˌblood reˈlation noun [C] (also **blood ˈrelative**) someone who is related to you by birth rather than through marriage

bloodshed /ˈblʌd.ʃed/ noun [U] killing and violence: *The army was brought in to try to prevent further bloodshed.*

bloodshot /ˈblʌd.ʃɒt/ US /-ʃɑːt/ adj When your eyes are bloodshot, they are red or pink on the white parts.

ˈblood ˌsport noun [C usually plural] any sport that involves animals being killed or hurt to make the people watching or taking part feel excitement

bloodstain /ˈblʌd.steɪn/ noun [C] a mark made by blood, often as a result of a violent event

bloodstained /ˈblʌd.steɪnd/ adj with marks of blood on it: *Bloodstained* ***clothing*** *was found near the scene.*

bloodstream /ˈblʌd.striːm/ noun [S] the flow of blood around the body: *The drug works more quickly if it is injected directly into the bloodstream.*

bloodsucker /ˈblʌd.sʌk.əʳ/ US /-ɚ/ noun [C] an animal or insect that sucks blood from other animals: *Leeches and mosquitoes are bloodsuckers.*

ˈblood ˌtest noun [C] a scientific examination of a person's blood to find out if they have any diseases or lack any important substances

bloodthirsty /ˈblʌdˌθɜː.sti/ US /-ˌθɝː-/ adj eager to see or take part in violence and killing: *a bloodthirsty killer*

ˈblood ˌties noun [plural] the relationships that exist by birth rather than through marriage

ˈblood transˌfusion noun [C] a process in which blood that has been taken from one person is put into another person's body, especially after an accident or during an operation

ˈblood ˌtype noun [C] (UK also **ˈblood ˌgroup**) one of the groups that human blood is divided into: *a* ***rare/common*** *blood type*

ˈblood ˌvessel noun [C] any of the tubes through which blood flows in the body

IDIOM **(almost) burst a blood vessel** humorous to become very angry about something: *Mum almost burst a blood vessel when I told her what happened.*

bloody /ˈblʌd.i/ adj, adv; adj; verb

▸adj [before noun], adv mainly UK very informal **ANGER** ▷ **1** C2 used to express anger or to emphasize what you are saying in a slightly rude way: *I've had a bloody* ***awful*** *week.* ◦ *It's a bloody* ***disgrace*** *that some war widows don't get a decent pension.* ◦ *Don't be a bloody* ***idiot!*** ◦ *This computer's bloody* ***useless!*** *It's always going wrong.* ◦ *Don't you tell me what to do! I'll do what I bloody* ***well*** *like in my own house.* **EMPHASIS** ▷ **2** C2 used to emphasize an adjective, adverb, or noun in a slightly rude way: *Life would be bloody* ***boring*** *if nothing ever went wrong.* ◦ *Don't be so bloody* ***stupid.*** ◦ *She's done bloody* ***well*** *to reach the semifinal.* ◦ *You must think I'm a bloody* ***fool.*** ◦ *I had a bloody* ***good*** *time last night.* ◦ *I'm afraid there's* ***not a*** *bloody* ***thing*** *(= nothing) you can do about it.* ◦ *I can't see* ***a*** *bloody* ***thing*** *(= anything) in here.*

IDIOM **bloody hell** very informal a rude way of expressing great anger: *Bloody hell! I've lost my wallet.* ◦ *What the bloody hell did you do that for?*

▸adj **1** B2 covered with or full of blood: *a bloody nose* **2** C1 extremely violent and involving a lot of blood and injuries: *It was a long and bloody battle and many men were killed.*

B

▸verb [T] to make something bloody: *The first punch bloodied his nose.* • **bloodied** /-id/ **adj** literary covered in blood

Bloody Mary /ˌblʌd.iˈmeə.ri/ (US) /-ˈmer.i/ **noun** [C] an alcoholic drink made of VODKA and tomato juice

ˌ**bloody-ˈminded** **adj** informal describes someone who makes things difficult for others and opposes their views for no good reason: *He's just **being** bloody-minded.* • ˌ**bloody-ˈmindedness** **noun** [U]

bloom /bluːm/ **verb; noun**

▸**verb** [I] **PRODUCE FLOWERS** ▷ **1** When a flower blooms, it opens or is open, and when a plant or tree blooms it produces flowers: *These flowers will bloom all through the summer.* **DEVELOP** ▷ **2** to grow or develop successfully: *Rimbaud's poetic genius bloomed early.*

▸**noun** **FLOWER** ▷ **1** [C] a flower on a plant **2 be in bloom** to be producing flowers: *The apple trees are in **full** bloom (= completely covered in flowers).* **3 come into bloom** to start to produce flowers: *The roses are just coming into bloom.* **GOOD HEALTH** ▷ **4** [S or U] literary health, energy, and good looks: *He was 19, in the **full** bloom of youth.*

bloomer /ˈbluː.məʳ/ (US) /-mɚ/ **noun** **MISTAKE** ▷ **1** [C] UK old-fashioned slang a silly or embarrassing mistake that does not have serious results **BREAD** ▷ **2** [C] UK a type of large LOAF of bread that has sloping cuts on the top **CLOTHING** ▷ **3 bloomers** [plural] **a** in the past, large loose underwear worn below the waist by women **b** in the past, long loose trousers made to fit tightly around the ANKLES, worn by women under a skirt or for sport

blooming /ˈbluː.mɪŋ/ **adj, adv; adj**

▸**adj** [before noun], **adv** mainly UK old-fashioned informal used to emphasize a noun, adverb, or adjective, or to express anger: *It's a blooming disgrace!* ◦ *I'm not going to bloomin' well apologize to him!*

▸**adj** A person who is blooming has a healthy, energetic, and attractive appearance: *Jo looked really well, positively blooming.*

blooper /ˈbluː.pəʳ/ (US) /-pɚ/ **noun** [C] US informal a funny mistake made by an actor during the making of a film or television programme and usually removed before the film or programme is shown

blossom /ˈblɒs.əm/ (US) /ˈblɑː.səm/ **verb; noun**

▸**verb** [I] **1** When a tree or plant blossoms, it produces flowers before producing fruit that can be eaten: *The cherry tree is beginning to blossom.* **2** When people blossom, they become more attractive, successful, or confident, and when good feelings or relationships blossom, they develop and become stronger: *She has really blossomed recently.* ◦ *She is suddenly blossoming **into** a very attractive woman.* ◦ *Sean and Sarah's friendship blossomed **into** love.*

▸**noun** [C or U] a small flower, or the small flowers on a tree or plant: *apple/cherry blossom*

IDIOM **be in blossom** to have flowers growing

blot /blɒt/ (US) /blɑːt/ **noun; verb**

▸**noun** [C] a small area of ink made by mistake: *an ink blot*

IDIOMS **a blot on sb's character** a fault that spoils someone's reputation • **a blot on the landscape** something such as an ugly building that spoils a pleasant view

▸**verb** [T] (**-tt-**) **DRY** ▷ **1** to dry a wet surface, or writing done in ink, by pressing something soft against it: *I signed my name and blotted the paper.* ◦ *She put on her lipstick and then carefully blotted her lips **with** a tissue.* **SPOIL** ▷ **2** to make a blot or blots on something

IDIOM **blot your copybook** UK to do something that makes other people respect or trust you less: *I really blotted my copybook by missing the meeting.*

PHRASAL VERB **blot sth out** **SUN** ▷ **1** to hide or block the light from something, especially the sun: *A dark cloud suddenly blotted out the sun.* **MEMORY** ▷ **2** to stop yourself thinking about something unpleasant: *Perhaps there are some memories so bad that you have to blot them out.*

blotch /blɒtʃ/ (US) /blɑːtʃ/ **noun** [C usually plural] a mark that is not regular in shape, for example on a person's skin: *Her face was covered in purple blotches.* • **blotchy** /ˈblɒtʃ.i/ (US) /ˈblɑː.tʃi/ **adj** *He'd been crying and his face was all blotchy.*

blotter /ˈblɒt.əʳ/ (US) /ˈblɑː.t̬ɚ/ **noun** [C] a large piece of blotting paper with a stiff back that is used to absorb ink, and is often put on the top of a desk to protect it when writing

ˈ**blotting** ˌ**paper** **noun** [U] thick, soft paper for pressing onto a piece of paper you have just written on in ink, in order to dry it

blotto /ˈblɒt.əʊ/ (US) /ˈblɑː.t̬oʊ/ **adj** old-fashioned slang extremely drunk

blouse /blaʊz/ (US) /blaʊs/ **noun** [C] (A1) a shirt for a woman or girl: *a white silk blouse*

blouse

blouson /ˈbluː.zɒn/ (US) /-sɑːn/ **noun** [C] a loose, short jacket that is worn on the upper body and fits tightly around the waist: *She was wearing a silk blouson (**jacket**).*

blow /bləʊ/ (US) /bloʊ/ **verb; noun**

▸**verb** (**blew, blown**) **SEND OUT AIR** ▷ **1** (B1) [I or T] to move and make currents of air, or to be moved or make something move on a current of air: *The wind was blowing **harder** every minute.* ◦ *The letter blew **away** and I had to run after it.* ◦ *A gale-force wind had blown the fence **down**.* ◦ *I blew the dust **off** the books.* ◦ *I wish you wouldn't blow smoke **in** my face.* **2** (C2) [I or T] to make a sound by forcing air out of your mouth and through an instrument, or to make a sound when someone does this: *Ann blew a few notes on the trumpet.* ◦ *He scored the winning goal just before the whistle blew.* **3** [T] to shape glass that has been heated until it is soft into an object by blowing air into it down a tube: *a beautiful blown glass vase* **4 blow your nose** (B1) to force air from your lungs and through your nose to clear it **5 blow sb a kiss** (also **blow a kiss to/at sb**) to kiss your hand and blow on it in the direction of someone **DESTROY** ▷ **6** [T] to cause something to be destroyed by a bomb, technical failure, etc.: *His car had been blown **to** pieces.* **7** [I or T] If an electrical FUSE (= a short, thin piece of wire) blows, or if something electrical blows a fuse, the device it is fitted to stops working because it is receiving too much electricity. **8** [I] informal If a tyre blows, it suddenly gets a hole in it and goes flat. **9 blow sth sky-high** to seriously damage something by making it explode: *The explosion blew the building sky-high.* **SPEND** ▷ **10** [T] informal to spend a large amount of money, especially on things that are not really necessary: *When I got paid I blew it all **on** a night out.*

B

IDIOMS **be blowed if...** old-fashioned informal If someone says that they are blowed if they will do something, they are determined not to do it: *I'm blowed if I'm going to pay for his taxi home.* • **blow (it)!** old-fashioned informal an expression of anger: *Oh, blow it! I've forgotten to invite Paul to the party.* • **blow sb's brains out** slang to kill someone by shooting them in the head • **blow sb's cover** to make known secret information about who someone is or what they are doing • **blow sth/sb out of the water** to destroy or defeat something or someone completely: *They came to court with fresh evidence that would, they said, blow the prosecution's case completely out of the water.* • **blow sb's mind** informal C2 If something blows your mind, you find it very exciting and unusual: *There was one scene in the film that really blew my mind.* → See also **mind-blowing** • **blow your own trumpet/horn** to tell everyone proudly about your achievements • **blow a fuse/gasket** old-fashioned informal to become very angry: *When he told her how much it cost, she blew a gasket.* • **blow hot and cold** to sometimes like or be interested in something or someone and sometimes not, so people are confused about how you really feel: *He's been blowing hot and cold **about** the trip to Holland.* • **blow it** (also **blow your chance**) C2 to fail to take advantage of an opportunity by doing or saying something wrong: *I really blew it when I turned down that job offer, didn't I?* • **blow the cobwebs away** UK to get rid of feelings of tiredness, usually with fresh air or exercise: *We went for a five-mile jog to blow the cobwebs away.* • **blow the gaff** UK old-fashioned to make known a secret: *He's a good bloke – he wouldn't blow the gaff **on** us.* • **blow the whistle on sb/sth** informal to tell people publicly about something bad that someone is doing • **I'll be blowed!** (also **blow me!**) old-fashioned informal an expression of great surprise: *'Kate's getting married.' 'Well, I'll be blowed!'*

PHRASAL VERBS **blow sb away** PLEASE ▷ **1** informal to surprise or please someone very much: *The ending will blow you away.* KILL ▷ **2** US informal to kill a person by shooting them • **blow sb/sth away** US informal to defeat someone or something completely, especially in a sports competition: *They blew the other team away in the second half of the game.* • **blow sth/sb off** US to treat something or someone as if they are not important: *Just blow off his comments, he's only joking.* • **blow (sth) out** B1 If a flame blows out or you blow it out, it stops burning when a person or the wind blows on it: *After dinner she blew out the candles.* ◦ *The sudden breeze made the candles blow out.* • **blow sb out** informal to disappoint someone by not meeting them or not doing something that you had arranged to do with them: *She was supposed to go to that party with me, but she blew me out.* • **blow over** SITUATION ▷ **1** When an argument blows over, it becomes gradually less important until it ends and is forgotten: *I thought that after a few days the argument would blow over.* STORM ▷ **2** When a storm blows over, it becomes gradually less strong until it ends: *The storm raged all night but by morning it had blown over.* • **blow (sb/sth) up** B1 to destroy something or kill someone with a bomb, or to be destroyed or killed by a bomb: *They threatened to blow up the plane if their demands were not met.* ◦ *He drove over a landmine and his Jeep blew up.* • **blow sth up** FILL WITH AIR ▷ **1** B1 to fill something with air: *Would you help me blow up these balloons?* PHOTO ▷ **2** to print a photograph or picture in a larger size • **blow up** STORM ▷ **1** When a storm blows up, it begins. ANGER ▷ **2** informal to suddenly become very angry: *My dad blew up (**at** me) when he saw the bill.*

▸noun HIT ▷ **1** C2 [C] a hard hit with a hand or a weapon: *a sharp blow **to** the stomach* BAD EVENT ▷ **2** C2 [C] an unexpected event that has a damaging effect on someone or something: *Losing his job was a severe blow **to** his confidence.* ◦ *Her death came as a terrible blow **to** her parents.* AIR ▷ **3** [C usually singular] the act of blowing something, such as your nose or an instrument: *Have a good blow (= blow your nose well).* DRUG ▷ **4** [U] UK slang **cannabis** **5** [U] US slang **cocaine**

IDIOM **come to blows** to have a physical fight or a serious argument with someone: *Demonstrators nearly came to blows **with** the police during the march.* ◦ *Do you think the two countries will come to blows **over** this?*

ˌblow-by-ˌblow adj [before noun] informal A blow-by-blow description contains every detail and action of an event.

ˈblow-dry verb [T] to dry your hair using an electric HAIRDRYER • **ˈblow-dry** noun [C] *She had a cut and blow-dry.*

the blower /ˈbləʊəʳ/ noun [S] UK old-fashioned informal the phone: *Get **on** the blower and invite him round.*

blowfly /ˈbləʊ.flaɪ/ US /ˈbloʊ-/ noun [C] a fly that leaves its eggs in decaying meat, solid animal waste, and injuries in which the skin is broken

blowgun /ˈbləʊ.gʌn/ US /ˈbloʊ-/ noun [C] US for **blowpipe**

blowhard /ˈbləʊ.hɑːd/ US /ˈbloʊ.hɑːrd/ noun [C] US informal disapproving a person who likes to talk about how important they are

blowhole /ˈbləʊ.həʊl/ US /ˈbloʊ.hoʊl/ noun [C] an opening in the top of the head of a WHALE (= very large sea mammal), through which it breathes

ˈblow ˌjob noun [C usually singular] offensive the activity of giving sexual pleasure to a man by using the mouth on his PENIS

blowlamp /ˈbləʊ.læmp/ US /ˈbloʊ-/ noun [C] UK a **blowtorch**

blown /bləʊn/ US /bloʊn/ verb past participle of **blow**

blowout /ˈbləʊ.aʊt/ US /ˈbloʊ-/ noun [C] EXPLOSION ▷ **1** mainly US a sudden explosion of a tyre on a road vehicle while it is moving quickly MEAL ▷ **2** UK informal a very large meal PARTY ▷ **3** US informal a large party or social occasion

blowpipe /ˈbləʊ.paɪp/ US /ˈbloʊ-/ noun [C] UK (US **blowgun**) a weapon in the shape of a tube with which arrows are shot by blowing through it

blowsy (also **blowzy**) /ˈblaʊ.zi/ adj describes a woman who is quite fat and untidy looking, often with badly fitting clothes

blowtorch /ˈbləʊ.tɔːtʃ/ US /ˈbloʊ.tɔːrtʃ/ noun [C] (UK also **blowlamp**) a tool used to heat metal or remove paint from a surface by producing an extremely hot flame

blowtorch

ˈblow-up adj; noun

▸adj needing to be filled with air in order to be used: *a blow-up **mattress/pillow***

▸noun [C] informal ARGUMENT ▷ **1** a sudden argument: *The expected blow-up among the students never happened.* PHOTOGRAPH ▷ **2** a photograph, document, or picture that has been made bigger: *a five-foot-high blow-up of the magazine's cover*

blowy /ˈbləʊ.i/ (US) /ˈbloʊ-/ adj informal with a lot of wind: *a blowy day* → Synonym **windy**

BLT /biː.elˈtiː/ noun [C] abbreviation for bacon, lettuce, and tomato: a sandwich with bacon, LETTUCE (= a green salad vegetable), and tomato in it

blubber /ˈblʌb.əʳ/ (US) /-ɚ/

▸verb [I] (-rr-) informal disapproving (UK informal **blub**) to cry in a noisy way like a child: *There he sat, cowering against the wall, blubbering like a child.*

▸noun [U] **1** the thick layer of fat under the skin of sea mammals such as WHALES, which keeps them warm **2** informal too much body fat on a human: *Take some exercise and get rid of some of that blubber!*

bludgeon /ˈblʌdʒ.ən/ verb [T] **1** to hit someone hard and repeatedly with a heavy weapon: *The two boys had been mercilessly bludgeoned **to death**.* **2** to force someone to do something: *The children bludgeoned their parents **into** tak**ing** them to the zoo.*

blue /bluː/ adj; noun

▸adj **COLOUR** ▷ **1** (A1) of the colour of the sky without clouds on a bright day, or a darker or lighter type of this: *a faded blue shirt* ◦ *pale blue eyes* ◦ *Her hands were blue **with cold*** (= slightly blue because of the cold). **SEXUAL** ▷ **2** showing or mentioning sexual activity in a way that offends many people: *a blue joke* ◦ *a blue movie/film* ◦ *His humour is a bit too blue for my tastes.* **SAD** ▷ **3** (C2) [after verb] informal feeling or showing sadness: *He's been a bit blue since he failed his exams.* → See also **have the blues** **MEAT** ▷ **4** (also ˌ**extra-ˈrare**) (of meat) cooked so that it is still very red

IDIOMS **once in a blue moon** not very often: *My sister lives in Alaska, so I only see her once in a blue moon.* • **scream/shout blue murder** informal to show your anger about something, especially by shouting or complaining very loudly: *He'll scream blue murder if he doesn't get his way.* • **until you are blue in the face** If you say or shout something until you are blue in the face, you are wasting your efforts because you will get no results: *You can tell her to tidy her room until you are blue in the face, but she won't do it.*

▸noun **COLOUR** ▷ **1** (A2) [C or U] a blue colour **SPORTS** ▷ **2** [C] UK a person who has played a sport for Oxford University against Cambridge University or for Cambridge University against Oxford University, or the title given to them for this

IDIOM **out of the blue** (C1) If something happens out of the blue, it is completely unexpected: *One day, out of the blue, she announced that she was leaving.*

ˈ**blue** ˌ**baby** noun [C] a baby born with slightly blue skin, usually because it has something wrong with its heart

bluebell /ˈbluː.bel/ noun [C] **1** a small European plant that usually grows in woods and has blue flowers shaped like bells **2** Scottish English for **harebell**

blueberry /ˈbluː.bər.i/, /-ˌber-/ noun [C] the dark blue fruit of a bush that is grown in North America, similar to a BILBERRY

bluebird /ˈbluː.bɜːd/ (US) /-bɝːd/ noun [C] a small blue singing bird found in North America

ˌ**blue** ˈ**blood** noun [C] the fact of someone having been born into a family which belongs to the highest social class

ˌ**blue-ˈblooded** adj describes someone who has been born into a family that belongs to the highest social class

bluebottle /ˈbluːˌbɒt.l̩/ (US) /-ˌbɑː.t̬l̩/ noun [C] a big fly with a dark blue shiny body

ˌ**blue** ˈ**cheese** noun [U] a cheese with a strong flavour that has thin blue lines of bacteria going through it

ˌ**blue-ˈchip** adj [before noun] A blue-chip company or INVESTMENT is one that can be trusted and is not likely to fail.

ˌ**blue-ˈcollar** adj [before noun] describes people who do work needing strength or physical skill rather than office work

ˌ**blue-eyed** ˈ**boy** noun [C usually singular] UK informal disapproving (US ˌ**fair-haired** ˈ**boy**) a boy or man who is liked very much and is treated well by someone, especially someone in authority

bluegrass /ˈbluː.grɑːs/ (US) /-græs/ noun [U] a type of COUNTRY music from the southern US played on STRINGED instruments such as guitars, BANJOS, and VIOLINS

bluejay /ˈbluː.dʒeɪ/ noun [C] a small North American bird with a bright blue back, a grey front, and feathers that stand up on the top of its head

ˈ**blue** ˌ**jeans** noun [plural] US old-fashioned JEANS (= trousers made of strong blue cotton cloth)

ˈ**blue** ˌ**law** noun [C] US old-fashioned informal a law that limits activities that are considered not to be moral for religious reasons, such as shopping or working on Sundays

blueprint /ˈbluː.prɪnt/ noun [C] **1** a photographic copy of an early plan for a building or machine **2** an early plan or design which explains how something might be achieved: *their blueprint **for** economic reform*

ˌ**blue** ˈ**ribbon** noun [C] **1** (UK also ˌ**blue** ˈ**riband**) the highest prize in a competition or event: *He won the men's blue-ribbon **event**, the 100 metres freestyle.* **2** a decoration made of strips of blue cloth that is given to the winner of a competition

blues /bluːz/ noun [U] a type of slow, sad music, originally from the southern US, in which the singer typically sings about their difficult life or bad luck in love: *a famous blues singer* → See also **blue**

IDIOM **have the blues** informal to feel sad

ˌ**blue-ˈsky** adj [before noun] using the imagination to think of ideas that do not yet have practical uses or make money: *blue-sky **research*** ◦ *blue-sky **thinking***

bluestocking /ˈbluːˌstɒk.ɪŋ/ (US) /-ˌstɑː.kɪŋ/ noun [C] old-fashioned an intelligent and well-educated woman who spends most of her time studying and is therefore not approved of by some men

ˈ**blue** ˌ**tit** noun [C] a small European bird with a blue head and wings and a yellow front

bluetongue /ˈbluː.tʌŋ/ noun [U] (also ˈ**bluetongue di**ˌ**sease**) a disease that affects some farm animals, especially sheep and cows, in which the mouth and tongue of the affected animals turns blue

Bluetooth /ˈbluː.tuːθ/ noun [U] trademark a system for connecting electronic equipment such as mobile phones, computers, and electronic organizers to each other and to the internet using radio signals

bluff /blʌf/ verb; noun; adj

▸verb [I or T] **1** to deceive someone by making them think either that you are going to do something when you really have no intention of doing it, or that you have knowledge that you do not really have, or that you are someone else: *Is he going to jump or is he only bluffing?* ◦ *Tony seems to know a lot about music, but sometimes I think he's only bluffing.* ◦ *She bluffed the doorman **into** think**ing** that she was a reporter.* **2 bluff**

B

your way into/out of sth If you bluff your way into or out of a situation, you get yourself into or out of it by deceiving people: *However did Mina manage to bluff her way into that job?* ◦ *He's one of those people who is very good at bluffing their way out of trouble.*
▸noun **PRETEND** ▷ **1** [C or U] an attempt to bluff: *When she said she was leaving him, he thought it was* ***only*** *a bluff.* **CLIFF** ▷ **2** [C] a CLIFF or very steep bank
▸adj direct or too honest, often in a way that people find rude: *Despite her bluff* ***manner****, she's actually a very kind woman.*

bluish (also **blueish**) /ˈbluː.ɪʃ/ adj slightly blue: *bluish-grey eyes*

blunder /ˈblʌn.dəʳ/ (US) /-dɚ/ noun; verb
▸noun [C] a serious mistake, usually caused by not taking care or thinking: *He said that the tax was a major political blunder.* ◦ *I* ***made*** *a bit of a blunder by getting his name wrong.*
▸verb **MOVE** ▷ **1** [I usually + adv/prep] to move in an awkward way: *I could hear him blundering* ***around*** *in the darkness.* **MISTAKE** ▷ **2** [I] to make a serious mistake, usually because of not taking care or thinking: *Police blundered by not releasing more details about the case to focus public interest.* • **blunderer** /-əʳ/ (US) /-ɚ/ noun [C] • **blundering** /-ɪŋ/ adj [before noun] *You blundering idiot! What do you think you're doing?*

blunderbuss /ˈblʌn.də.bʌs/ (US) /-dɚ-/ noun [C] an old-fashioned gun with a wide mouth that shoots a lot of small metal balls

blunt /blʌnt/ adj; verb
▸adj **NOT SHARP** ▷ **1** (C2) describes a pencil, knife, etc. that is not sharp, and therefore not able to write, cut, etc. well **RUDE** ▷ **2** (C2) saying what you think without trying to be polite or considering other people's feelings: *I'll be blunt – that last piece of work you did was terrible.* • **bluntness** /ˈblʌnt.nəs/ noun [U]
▸verb [T] **1** to make something less sharp **2** to make a feeling less strong: *My recent bad experience has rather blunted my* ***enthusiasm*** *for travel.*

bluntly /ˈblʌnt.li/ adv If you speak bluntly, you speak without trying to be polite or considering other people's feelings: ***To put it*** *bluntly, I can't afford it.*

blur /blɜːʳ/ (US) /blɝː/ noun; verb
▸noun [S] **1** something that you cannot see clearly: *If I don't wear my glasses, everything is* ***just a*** *blur.* **2** something that you cannot remember or understand clearly: *It all happened so long ago that it's* ***just a*** *blur to me now.* ◦ *The last few days seem to have gone by* ***in a*** *blur.*
▸verb [I or T] (-rr-) **1** to (make something or someone) become difficult to see clearly: *As she drifted into sleep, the doctor's face began to blur and fade.* **2** to make the difference between two things less clear, or to make it difficult to see the exact truth about something: *This film blurs the* ***line/distinction/boundary*** *between reality and fantasy.*

blurb /blɜːb/ (US) /blɝːb/ noun [C] a short description of a book, film, etc., written by the people who have produced it, and intended to make people want to buy it or see it: *The blurb on the back of the book says that it 'will touch your heart'.*

blurred /blɜːd/ (US) /blɝːd/ adj **1** (also **blurry** /ˈblɜː.ri/ (US) /ˈblɝː.i/) difficult to see: *The photograph was very blurred.* ◦ *The picture on the TV went all blurry.* **2** difficult to understand or separate clearly: *Do you agree that male and female roles are becoming blurred?* **3** unable to see clearly: *My eyes were blurred* ***with*** *tears.*

blurt /blɜːt/ (US) /blɝːt/ verb
PHRASAL VERB **blurt sth out** to say something suddenly and without thinking, usually because you are excited or nervous: *He blurted everything out about the baby, though we'd agreed to keep it a secret for a while.* ◦ [+ speech] *She suddenly blurted out, 'I can't do it!'* ◦ [+ that] *Late one evening, Gianni blurted out* ***that*** *he loved her.*

blush /blʌʃ/ verb [I] (B2) to become pink in the face, usually from embarrassment: *I always blush when I speak in public.* ◦ *I blush* ***to think*** *of what a fool I made of myself.* • **blush** noun [C] *A blush of shame crept up his face.*

blusher /ˈblʌʃ.əʳ/ (US) /-ɚ/ noun [C or U] (US also **blush**) a powder or cream that is put on the cheeks to make them look pink

bluster /ˈblʌs.təʳ/ (US) /-tɚ/ verb [I] to speak in a loud, angry, or offended way, usually with little effect: [+ speech] *'You had no right to do it, no right at all,' he blustered.* • **bluster** noun [U] *I knew that it was all bluster and he wasn't really angry with me.*

blustery /ˈblʌs.tᵊr.i/ (US) /-t̬ɚ-/ adj with strong winds: *a blustery day* ◦ *blustery weather*

Blu-Tack /ˈbluː.tæk/ noun [U] trademark a soft, sticky substance that can be used more than once to temporarily fix light things to a wall or similar surface: *Helga stuck her posters up with Blu-Tack.*

Blvd noun written abbreviation for **boulevard**

BM /ˌbiːˈem/ noun [C] US **DEGREE** ▷ (UK **MB**) abbreviation for Bachelor of Medicine: a degree in medicine, or a person who has this

BMI /ˌbiː.emˈaɪ/ noun [S] abbreviation for body mass index: a measurement of someone's weight in relation to their height: *Adults who have a BMI of 30 or higher are defined as obese.*

ˈB-ˌmovie noun [C] a cheaply made film, often of poor quality, that in the past was shown before the main film in a cinema

bn UK (US **b**) written abbreviation for **billion**

BO /ˌbiːˈəʊ/ (US) /-ˈoʊ/ noun [U] abbreviation for **body odour**

boa /ˈbəʊ.ə/ (US) /ˈboʊ-/ noun [C] **CLOTHING** ▷ **1** a long, thin piece of clothing made of feathers, worn around the neck especially by women: *a feather boa* **SNAKE** ▷ **2** (also ˈ**boa conˌstrictor**) a large, strong snake, found in South and Central America, that kills animals and birds by wrapping itself around them and crushing them

boar /bɔːʳ/ (US) /bɔːr/ noun [C] a male pig kept for breeding on a farm, or a type of wild pig → Compare **hog, sow**

board /bɔːd/ (US) /bɔːrd/ noun; verb
▸noun **WOOD** ▷ **1** (B2) [C] a thin, flat piece of cut wood or other hard material used for a particular purpose: *Cut the vegetables on a* ***chopping*** *(US* ***cutting****) board.* ◦ *There was a 'For Sale' board outside the house.* → See also **breadboard, soundboard 2** (A2) [C] a flat piece of wood or other hard material with a special pattern on it, used for playing games: *a chess board* **3** (A1) [C] a **blackboard** or **whiteboard**: *The teacher wrote her name up on* ***the*** *board.* **4** (A2) [C] a **noticeboard**: *I stuck the notice (up) on* ***the*** *board.* **5** [C] a **diving board**: *I dived off the top board today, Dad.* **6 the boards** [plural] **a** the wooden fence surrounding the ice surface in ICE HOCKEY **b** old-fashioned the stage in a theatre **PEOPLE** ▷ **7** (C1) [C usually singular, + sing/pl verb] the group of people who are responsible for controlling and organizing a company or organization: *Every decision has to be passed by* ***the*** *board* ***(of directors)****.* ◦ *She started in the*

firm by making the tea and now she's **on the** board/a board **member**. ◦ **The** board **of governors** meet/meets once a month to discuss school policy. **EXAM** ▷ **8 boards** [plural] US informal an official examination given by some medical and business organizations in the US: *This is my last chance to pass the boards.* **TRANSPORT** ▷ **9 on board** B1 on a boat, train, or aircraft: *As soon as I was on board, I began to have second thoughts about leaving.* **MEALS** ▷ **10** B2 [U] meals provided when you are staying somewhere, usually for money

IDIOMS **above board** describes a plan or business agreement that is honest and not trying to deceive anyone: *The deal was completely* ***open and*** *above board.* • **across the board** C2 happening or having an effect on people at every level and in every area: *The improvement has been across the board, with all divisions either increasing profits or reducing losses.* → See also **across-the-board** • **go by the board** to be forgotten or not used: *Does this mean our holiday plans will have to go by the board?* • **on board** as part of a group or team, especially for a special purpose: *Let's* ***bring*** *Rob on board for the Saudi deal – he's the expert.* • **take sth on board** C1 to understand or accept an idea or a piece of information: *Banks need to take on board the views of their customers.*

▸verb **GET ON** ▷ **1** B1 [I or T] to get onto or allow people to get onto a boat, train, or aircraft: *At London airport she boarded a plane to Australia.* ◦ *Will passengers waiting to board please go to the ticket counter?* **STAY** ▷ **2** [I] to pay to sleep and eat meals in someone's house: *During his stay in England he boarded* ***with*** *a family in Bath.* **3** [I] to sleep and eat at school during the school TERM: *When you went to school were you a day student or did you board?* **4** [T] to arrange for a pet animal to be temporarily taken care of at a place other than its home: *He boards the dog* ***out*** *when he goes on business trips.*

PHRASAL VERB **board sth up** to cover a door or window with wooden boards

ˌboard and ˈlodging noun [U] UK (US **ˌroom and ˈboard**) the meals and room that are provided when someone pays to stay somewhere, for example when working or studying away from home

boarder /ˈbɔː.dəʳ/ US /ˈbɔːr.dɚ/ **noun** [C] a student at a school who sleeps and eats there and only goes home during school holidays → Compare **day pupil**

ˈboard ˌgame noun [C] A2 any of many games, for example CHESS, in which small pieces are moved around on a board with a pattern on it

boarding /ˈbɔː.dɪŋ/ US /ˈbɔːr-/ **noun** [U] boards that have been fastened side by side to each other

ˌboarding and ˈlodging noun [U] (also **ˌfooding and ˈlodging**) Indian English food and a place to stay: *Hotel Swagat: Boarding and Lodging* → See also **board and lodging**

ˈboarding ˌcard noun [C] UK (mainly US **ˈboarding ˌpass**) a card that a passenger must have to be allowed to get on an aircraft or a ship

ˈboarding ˌhouse noun [C] a private house where you can pay to stay and receive meals

ˈboarding ˌschool noun [C] a school where students live and study

boardroom /ˈbɔːd.rʊm/, /-ruːm/ US /ˈbɔːrd-/ **noun** [C] a room where the people who control a company or organization meet

ˈboard ˌshorts noun [plural] Australian a piece of men's clothing that is worn when swimming → See also **swimming trunks**

boardwalk /ˈbɔːd.wɔːk/ US /ˈbɔːrd.wɑːk/ **noun** [C] US a path made of wooden boards built along a beach

boast /bəʊst/ US /boʊst/ **verb; noun**

▸verb **SPEAK PROUDLY** ▷ **1** B2 [I or T] disapproving to speak too proudly or happily about what you have done or what you own: *He didn't talk about his exam results in case people thought he was boasting.* ◦ *Parents enjoy boasting* ***about*** *their children's achievements.* ◦ [+ that] *They boasted* ***that*** *they had never lost a single game.* **HAVE** ▷ **2** C2 [T not continuous] to have or own something to be proud of: *Ireland boasts beautiful beaches, great restaurants, and friendly locals.*

> **Other ways of saying boast**
>
> An alternative to 'boast' is **brag**:
>
> *She likes to* ***brag*** *about how much money she earns.*
>
> The verb **trumpet** can be used when someone boasts about how successful he or she has been:
>
> *He's always* ***trumpeting*** *his latest triumph.*
>
> If someone often boasts, you can describe that person as **boastful**:
>
> *He was* ***boastful*** *and arrogant.*

▸noun [C] disapproving something you are proud of and like to tell people about: [+ that] ***It*** *is her proud boast* ***that*** *she has never missed a single episode of the soap opera.*

boastful /ˈbəʊst.fəl/ US /ˈboʊst-/ **adj** disapproving praising yourself and what you have done • **boastfully** /-i/ **adv** • **boastfulness** /-nəs/ **noun** [U]

boat /bəʊt/ US /boʊt/ **noun** [C] **1** A1 a small vehicle for travelling on water: *a rowing/sailing boat* ◦ *a fishing boat* ◦ *We took turns to* ***row*** *the boat up the river.* **2** informal a ship: *Are you travelling* ***by*** *boat or by air?* ◦ *I'm* ***taking the*** *boat from Dover to Calais.*

boater /ˈbəʊ.təʳ/ US /ˈboʊ.t̬ɚ/ **noun** [C] a stiff hat made of STRAW with a flat top

boathook /ˈbəʊt.hʊk/ US /ˈboʊt-/ **noun** [C] a long pole with an iron HOOK on the end, used to pull a boat towards you, to push a boat away, etc.

boathouse /ˈbəʊt.haʊs/ US /ˈboʊt-/ **noun** [C] a small building at the side of a river or lake, in which boats are kept

boating /ˈbəʊ.tɪŋ/ US /ˈboʊ.t̬ɪŋ/ **noun** [U] the activity of travelling on water in a boat for pleasure: *We decided to* ***go*** *boating.*

boatload /ˈbəʊt.ləʊd/ US /ˈboʊt.loʊd/ **noun** [C] **1** the number of people or the amount of something that can be transported by a boat: *a boatload of refugees/tourists* **2** informal a large amount: *They made boatloads of money from that project.*

ˈboat ˌpeople noun [plural] people who have left their country by boat, usually hoping to finding safety in another place

boatswain (also **bosun**) /ˈbəʊ.sən/ US /ˈboʊ-/ **noun** [C] the officer on a ship who is responsible for taking care of the ship's equipment

ˈboat ˌtrain noun [C] a train that is planned to reach or leave a port at the right time for passengers who are leaving or arriving on a ship

boatyard /ˈbəʊt.jɑːd/ US /ˈboʊt.jɑːrd/ **noun** [C] a place where boats are made, kept, or repaired

bob /bɒb/ US /bɑːb/ **verb; noun**

▸verb (-bb-) **1** [I] to move up and down quickly and gently, especially on the surface of water: *In the harbour, the boats bobbed gently* ***up and down*** *on the water.* **2** [I usually + adv/prep, T] to move quickly in a

particular direction: *I dropped the bottle into the sea and watched it bob **up** to the surface a moment later.* ◦ *Suddenly a head bobbed **up** from behind the hedge.* ◦ *She bobbed **a curtsy** (= bent down from the knees briefly as a sign of respect) **to** the Queen.*
▸noun **HAIRSTYLE** ▷ **1** [C] (plural **bobs**) a women's hairstyle with the hair cut to neck length all around the head: *I've had/worn my hair **in a** bob for ages.* **MONEY** ▷ **2** [C] (plural **bob**) UK old-fashioned informal a **shilling**: a British coin used in the past: *That coat cost me ten bob in 1956.* **MOVEMENT** ▷ **3** [C] (plural **bobs**) a quick movement up and down: *She acknowledged me with a quick bob **of** her **head**.* **SMALL THINGS** ▷ **4 bits and bobs** [plural] UK informal small things or jobs of different types

Bob /bɒb/ (US) /bɑːb/ noun UK old-fashioned informal **Bob's your uncle** used to mean that something will happen very quickly and simply: *Just tell them you're a friend of mine and, Bob's your uncle, you'll get the job.*

bobbed /bɒbd/ (US) /bɑːbd/ adj (of a style of women's hair) cut to neck length all around the head: *short, bobbed hair*

bobbin /ˈbɒb.ɪn/ (US) /ˈbɑː.bɪn/ noun [C] a small round or tube-shaped object around which thread is put, often to go in a sewing machine

bobble /ˈbɒb.l̩/ (US) /ˈbɑː.bl̩/ noun [C] mainly UK (US **pompom**) a small, round ball of soft material used as decoration

ˈbobble ˌhat noun [C] UK a hat made from wool with a small, round wool ball on top

bobby /ˈbɒb.i/ (US) /ˈbɑː.bi/ noun [C] UK old-fashioned informal a police officer: *People liked seeing their friendly **local/neighbourhood** bobby on his beat.*

ˈbobby ˌpin noun [C] US for **hairgrip**

bobotie /bəˈbuː.ti/ (US) /-t̬i/ noun [U] South African English a dish made with MINCED (= very finely cut) meat, spices, and dried fruit, baked with a mixture containing eggs on top

bobsleigh /ˈbɒb.sleɪ/ (US) /ˈbɑːb-/ noun [C] UK (US **bobsled**) a small vehicle with long metal blades under it, built for racing down tracks covered with ice

bobsleigh

bod /bɒd/ (US) /bɑːd/ noun [C] **BODY** ▷ **1** informal for **body**: *That guy has a great bod!* **PERSON** ▷ **2** UK informal old-fashioned a person: *She's a bit of an **odd** bod.*

bode /bəʊd/ (US) /boʊd/ verb [I or T] formal to be a sign of something that will happen in the future, usually something very good or bad: *These recently published figures bode **ill**/do not bode **well** for the company's future.* ◦ *The hurricane bodes disaster **for** those areas in its path.*

bodge /bɒdʒ/ (US) /bɑːdʒ/ noun [C], verb [T] UK for **botch**

bodice /ˈbɒd.ɪs/ (US) /ˈbɑː.dɪs/ noun [C] **1** the upper part of a woman's dress: *She was wearing a ballgown with a **fitted** bodice.* **2** a piece of women's underwear that fits tightly to the body above the waist, worn in the past

bodice-ripper /ˈbɒd.ɪsˌrɪp.əʳ/ (US) /ˈbɑː.dɪsˌrɪp.ɚ/ noun [C] humorous a romantic story, set in the past, in which there is a lot of sex

-bodied /-bɒd.id/ (US) /-bɑː.did/ suffix **PHYSICAL STRUCTURE** ▷ **1** having a particular type of body: *a long-bodied insect* ◦ *a soft-bodied doll* **QUALITY** ▷ **2** having a particular quality or strength of flavour: *a medium-bodied wine*

bodily /ˈbɒd.ɪ.li/ (US) /ˈbɑː.dɪ-/ adj; adv
▸adj relating to the human body: *bodily **fluids*** (= blood, SALIVA, etc.) ◦ *They didn't cause him any bodily **harm**.* ◦ *to lose control of your bodily **functions***
▸adv If you lift or carry someone bodily, you lift or carry them in your arms: *He carried her bodily up the stairs.*

bodkin /ˈbɒd.kɪn/ (US) /ˈbɑːd-/ noun [C] a large needle that does not have a sharp point, used especially for pulling a strip of material through cloth

body /ˈbɒd.i/ (US) /ˈbɑː.di/ noun **PHYSICAL STRUCTURE** ▷ **1** (A1) [C] the whole physical structure that forms a person or animal: *A good diet and plenty of exercise will help you to keep your body healthy.* ◦ *She rubbed sun lotion over her entire body.* **2** (B1) [C] the main part of a person's or animal's body, without the head, or without the head, arms, and legs: *He had a fat body but rather thin legs and arms.* **3** (A2) [C] a dead person: *A body was washed up on the beach last week.* **4** [C] the painted metal shell of a vehicle, such as a car or an aircraft → See also **bodywork** **5** [C] UK (US **bodysuit**) a piece of tight-fitting women's clothing that covers the top half of the body and fastens between the legs **GROUP OF PEOPLE** ▷ **6** (C2) [C, + sing/pl verb] a group of people who have joined together for a particular reason: *a governing body* ◦ *an advisory body* ◦ *There is a large body **of** people who are unaware of their basic rights.* **7 in a body** formal If people do something in a body, they do it together as a group, in an official way: *The cleaning staff went in a body to the manager to complain.* **AMOUNT** ▷ **8** [C] a large amount of something: *There is a growing body **of** evidence to support their claim.* ◦ *She collected a huge body **of** information on the subject.* ◦ *A substantial body **of opinion*** (= a large group of people with the same opinion) *is opposed to any change.* **9** [C] formal A body of water is a large area of water, such as a lake. **MAIN PART** ▷ **10 the body** [S] **a** the main part of a book, article, etc.: *I thought the most interesting details in the book were not in the body **of** the text, but in the notes at the end.* **b** the main part of a large building: *to enter the body of the cathedral* **OBJECT** ▷ **11** [C] specialized a separate object or mass: *The distance between the two bodies in space was measured daily.* **QUALITY** ▷ **12** [U] a strong or thick quality: *This Bordeaux **has** a flowery bouquet and plenty of body* (= strong flavour). ◦ *Conditioner can give your hair more body.*

IDIOM **keep body and soul together** (C2) to be able to pay for your food, clothing, and somewhere to live: *His wages are barely enough to keep body and soul together.*

ˈbody ˌarmour UK (US **ˈbody ˌarmor**) noun [U] special clothes worn by a soldier or police officer for protection

ˈbody ˌbag noun [C] a heavy plastic bag used to transport a dead person, especially a soldier who has been killed in a war

ˈbody ˌblow noun [C] **1** something that causes serious problems and disappointment for a person trying to do something: *Having all her research notes stolen was a real body blow for her.* **2** a hit to the main part of your body

bodyboard /ˈbɒd.i.bɔːd/ (US) /ˈbɑː.di.bɔːrd/ noun [C] a short, light board that you lie on and ride over waves on the sea • **bodyboarding** /-ɪŋ/ noun [U] a sport you do using a bodyboard

bodybuilding /ˈbɒd.iˌbɪl.dɪŋ/ (US) /ˈbɑː.di-/ noun [U]

B

special exercises that you do regularly to make your muscles bigger • **bodybuilder** /-dəʳ/ (US) /-dɚ/ **noun** [C]

ˈbody ˌclock **noun** [C] informal your body's natural need to sleep, eat, etc. at particular times

bodyguard /ˈbɒd.i.ɡɑːd/ (US) /ˈbɑː.di.ɡɑːrd/ **noun** [C, + sing/pl verb] a person or group of people whose job is to protect someone from attack: *The prince is always accompanied by his bodyguards.*

ˈbody ˌlanguage **noun** [U] the movements or positions of your body that show other people how you are feeling, without using words: *I could tell from her body language that she was very embarrassed.*

ˈbody ˌmass ˌindex **noun** [C] (abbreviation **BMI**) a measurement of a person's weight in relation to their height, used to find out if they are too fat: *Obesity for adults was defined as a body mass index of 30 or greater.*

ˈbody ˌodour **noun** [U] (abbreviation **BO**) an unpleasant smell on a person's body that is caused by SWEAT

ˈbody ˌstocking **noun** [C] a piece of clothing made of thin material that tightly covers the whole body except for the head, often worn by dancers

bodysuit /ˈbɒd.i.suːt/ (US) /ˈbɑː.di-/ **noun** [C] US (UK **body**) a piece of tight-fitting women's clothing that covers the top half of the body and fastens between the legs

bodysurf /ˈbɒd.i.sɜːf/ (US) /ˈbɑː.di.sɝːf/ **verb** [I] to SURF (= ride on waves) without a board to lie on, but using your body like a board on the water

bodywarmer /ˈbɒd.iˌwɔː.məʳ/ (US) /ˈbɑː.diˌwɔːr.mɚ/ **noun** [C] UK (US **vest**) a short jacket, without sleeves and made of thick material, that fits closely to your body

bodywork /ˈbɒd.i.wɜːk/ (US) /ˈbɑː.di.wɝːk/ **noun** [U] **1** the painted metal outer structure of a car, aircraft, etc.: *My car's bodywork is in terrible condition.* **2** US the process of making or repairing the outer structure of a vehicle

Boer /bɔːʳ/ (US) /bɔːr/ **noun** [C] a white person in South Africa who is related to the Dutch people who went to live there in the 17th century

boerewors /ˈbuː.rə.vɔːz/ (US) /-vɔːrz/ **noun** [C or U] South African English a sausage containing spices, usually made of BEEF and PORK

boffin /ˈbɒf.ɪn/ (US) /ˈbɑː.fɪn/ **noun** [C] mainly UK informal a scientist who is considered to know a lot about science and not to be interested in other things

bog /bɒɡ/ (US) /bɑːɡ/ **noun; verb**

▸**noun** **WET AREA** ▷ **1** [C or U] soft, wet ground, or an area of this **TOILET** ▷ **2** [C] UK slang a toilet: *I'm just going to nip to the bog.* ◦ *We've run out of bog **paper/roll**.*

▸**verb** (**-gg-**)

PHRASAL VERBS **be/get bogged down** to be/become so involved in something difficult or complicated that you cannot do anything else: *Let's not get bogged down **with** individual complaints* ◦ UK *Try not to get too bogged down **in** the details.* • **bog off** UK slang used to tell someone to go away: *Bog off and leave me alone.*

bogan /ˈbəʊ.ɡən/ (US) /ˈboʊ-/ **noun** [C] Australian English informal an insulting word for a person whose way of dressing, speaking, and behaving is thought to show their lack of education and low social class

bogey /ˈbəʊ.ɡi/ (US) /ˈboʊ-/ **noun; verb**

▸**noun** **NOSE** ▷ **1** [C] UK (US **booger**) a piece of dried MUCUS from inside the nose **FEAR** ▷ **2** [C usually singular] (also **bogie**, **bogy**) something that causes fear among a lot of people, often without reason: *the bogey of unemployment* **GOLF** ▷ **3** [C] in GOLF, the act of getting the ball into the hole in one SHOT (= hit) more than PAR (= the expected number) for that hole

▸**verb** [T] (in golf) to score a bogey for a particular hole: *He bogeyed the sixth, but birdied the seventh.*

bogeyman /ˈbəʊ.ɡi.mæn/ (US) /ˈboʊ.ɡi.mæn/ **noun** [C] (plural **-men** /-mən/) (also **bogyman**, US also **boogeyman**) an imaginary evil person who harms children: *Be good, or the bogeyman will come and get you!*

boggle /ˈbɒɡ.l̩/ (US) /ˈbɑː.ɡl̩/ **verb** **1** [I or T] to (cause something or someone to) have difficulty imagining or understanding something: *My **mind** boggles **at** the amount of money they spend on food.* ◦ *It boggles the **imagination**, doesn't it?* → See also **mind-boggling** **2** [I] to be very surprised and uncertain about how to deal with something: *He boggled **at** the suggestion.*

boggy /ˈbɒɡ.i/ (US) /ˈbɑː.ɡi/ **adj** describes ground that is soft and wet

bogie /ˈbəʊ.ɡi/ (US) /ˈboʊ-/ **noun** [C] Indian English a CARRIAGE on a train (= one of the separate parts in which passengers sit)

BOGOF /bɒɡˈɒf/ (US) /bɑːɡˈɑːf/ abbreviation for buy one get one free: an offer used in shops, in which if you buy one thing, you get another of the same thing for no extra cost

ˌbog-ˈstandard **adj** UK informal disapproving completely ordinary, without anything special added: *My last car was just a bog-standard model.*

bogus /ˈbəʊ.ɡəs/ (US) /ˈboʊ-/ **adj** false, not real, or not legal: *On investigation, his claim was found to be bogus.*

bohemian /bəʊˈhiː.mi.ən/, /bə-/ (US) /boʊ-/ **noun** [C] (informal **boho**) a person who is interested in art, music, and/or literature, and lives in a very informal way, ignoring the usually accepted ways of behaving • **bohemian** **adj**

boil /bɔɪl/ **verb; noun**

▸**verb** **HEAT LIQUID** ▷ **1** (A2) [I or T] to reach, or cause something to reach, the temperature at which a liquid starts to turn into a gas: *Liquid nitrogen boils at a very low temperature.* ◦ *She scalded herself on some boiling **water**.* ◦ *If you give water to a small baby to drink, you have to boil it first.* **2** (B1) [I or T] to heat a container, especially one used for cooking, until the liquid in it starts to turn into a gas: *Could you boil the **kettle** for me?* ◦ *The pan's boiling.* **3** (B1) [T] to cook food by putting it in water that is boiling: *I've boiled some potatoes for dinner.* ◦ *boiled carrots* **4** **boil dry** If a container or food boils dry, all the liquid in the container in which the food was cooking turns to gas. **5** [T] to wash clothes in a container of very hot water **BE ANGRY** ▷ **6** [I usually continuous] informal to be extremely angry: *He was boiling **with** rage.*

IDIOM **can't boil an egg** humorous Someone who can't boil an egg, is unable to cook even the simplest meal.

PHRASAL VERBS **boil away** When a liquid boils away, it all turns into a gas so that none of it is left in liquid form. • **boil (sth) down** to heat a liquid or food so that part of it is turned into gas and its amount is reduced • **boil sth down** to reduce information, usually so that it contains only its most important parts: *He had boiled down a lengthy report **to** just a few paragraphs.* • **boil down to sth** If a situation or problem boils down to something, that is the main reason for it: *The problem boils down to one thing – lack of money.* • **boil over** **PERSON** ▷ **1** If a difficult situation or negative emotion boils over, it cannot be controlled any more and people start to argue or fight. **LIQUID** ▷ **2** If a liquid that is being heated boils over, it rises up and flows over the edge of the pan: *Take the milk off the heat before it boils over.* **3** If a pan

B

boils over, the liquid in it rises up and flows over the edge: *That saucepan is boiling over.* • **boil up** If a bad emotion boils up, it becomes very strong and difficult to control: ***Anger** suddenly boiled up in him.* • **boil sth up** to heat up liquid or food in a pan until it boils: *Could you boil some water up for me?*

▸noun **SWELLING** ▷ **1** [C] a painful swelling on the skin that is filled with PUS (= thick, yellow liquid) **HEAT** ▷ **2** [S] the act of washing or cooking something in very hot water **3 the boil** the state of boiling: ***Bring** the water **to** the boil, then add the pasta.* ◦ *Let the liquid **come to** the boil and then reduce the heat.*

IDIOM **go off the boil** UK to lose interest or become less urgent: *They were really excited about the project, but now they seem to have gone off the boil.*

boiled /bɔɪld/ **adj** A2 (of food) cooked in water that is boiling: *boiled eggs/bacon* ◦ *a hard-boiled/soft-boiled egg (= one boiled for a long/short time)*

ˌboiled ˈsweet noun [C] UK (US **ˌhard ˈcandy**) a hard, often brightly coloured sweet

boiler /ˈbɔɪ.ləʳ/ (US) /-lɚ/ **noun** [C] **1** a device that heats water, especially to provide heating and hot water in a house **2** the part of a steam engine where water is heated to provide power

boilerplate /ˈbɔɪ.lə.pleɪt/ (US) /-lɚ-/ **noun** [U] US **STANDARD** ▷ **1** text that can be copied and used in legal documents, agreements, etc. with only very small changes **ORDINARY** ▷ **2** a way of writing or thinking that is not special and does not show any imagination: *The lyrics are boilerplate and uninspiring.*

ˈboiler ˌroom noun [C] **HEAT** ▷ **1** a room in a building or on a ship where the boiler is **SALES** ▷ **2** a room in which people work very hard to sell products by phone

ˈboiler ˌsuit noun [C] UK (US usually **coveralls**) a suit made in one piece, worn when doing dirty work

boiler suit

ˌboiling (ˈhot) adj informal B2 very hot: *I wish I'd worn something cooler – I'm boiling.* ◦ *We don't usually have such boiling hot weather.*

ˈboiling ˌpoint noun **LIQUID** ▷ **1** [S or C] The boiling point of a liquid is the temperature at which it becomes a gas: *The boiling point of water is 100°C.* **OUT OF CONTROL** ▷ **2** [S] the point when a situation is about to get out of control and become violent: *The situation in the inner city was **reaching/at** boiling point, so the police were out in force.* **3** [S] the stage at which someone is about to become very angry

boisterous /ˈbɔɪ.stᵊr.əs/ (US) /-stɚ-/ **adj** noisy, energetic, and rough: *boisterous children* ◦ *a boisterous game* • **boisterously** /-li/ **adv**

bold /bəʊld/ (US) /boʊld/ **adj** **BRAVE** ▷ **1** B2 not frightened of danger: *She was a bold and fearless climber.* ◦ *The newspaper made the bold **move**/took the bold **step** of publishing the names of the men involved.* → Synonym **brave** **NOTICEABLE** ▷ **2** B1 strong in colour or shape, and very noticeable to the eye: *They painted the kitchen in bold **colours*** **3 in bold (type/print)** printed in thick dark letters: ***This sentence is printed in bold.*** **NOT SHY** ▷ **4** not shy, especially in a way that shows no respect: *He was a bold and defiant little boy.*

• **boldly** /ˈbəʊld.li/ (US) /ˈboʊld-/ **adv** • **boldness** /ˈbəʊld.nəs/ (US) /ˈboʊld-/ **noun** [U] *He is famous for the boldness of his business methods.*

IDIOM **(as) bold as brass** with extreme confidence or without the respect or politeness people usually show: *She marched into the shop, as bold as brass, and demanded her money back.*

boldfaced /ˈbəʊld.feɪst/ (US) /ˈboʊld-/ **adj** [before noun] US **bald-faced**

bolero /bəˈleə.rəʊ/ (US) /-ˈler.oʊ/ **noun** [C] (plural **boleros**) **PIECE OF CLOTHING** ▷ **1** a woman's short jacket that stops just above the waist and has no buttons **DANCE** ▷ **2** a Spanish dance, or the music it is danced to: *Ravel's Bolero*

boll /bəʊl/ (US) /boʊl/ **noun** [C] the part of the cotton plant that contains the seeds

bollard /ˈbɒl.ɑːd/ (US) /ˈbɑː.lɚd/ **noun** [C] **1** a short, thick post that boats can be tied to **2** mainly UK a post that is put in the middle or at the end of a road to keep vehicles off or out of a particular area

bollocking /ˈbɒl.ə.kɪŋ/ (US) /ˈbɑː.lə-/ **noun** [C] UK offensive angry words spoken to someone who has done something wrong: *She **gave** me a right bollocking for being late.*

bollocks /ˈbɒl.əks/ (US) /ˈbɑː.ləks/ **noun** **1** [plural] UK offensive for **testicle** **2** [U] UK offensive nonsense: *That's **a load of** bollocks.* ◦ *Bollocks **to** that (= that's nonsense)!*

Bollywood /ˈbɒl.i.wʊd/ (US) /ˈbɑː.li-/ **noun** the centre of the Hindi film industry, based mainly in the Indian city of Mumbai

bologna /bəˈləʊ.ni/ (US) /-ˈloʊ-/ **noun** [U] (also **baloney**) US a cooked smoked sausage that is sliced and eaten cold

bolognese /ˌbɒl.əˈneɪz/ (US) /ˌboʊ.ləˈniːz/ **noun** [C or U] (also **ˌbolognese ˈsauce**) a type of sauce made with minced meat (= meat cut up into very small pieces) and tomatoes, usually eaten with PASTA: *spaghetti bolognese*

boloney /bəˈləʊ.ni/ (US) /-ˈloʊ-/ **noun** [U] **baloney**

Bolshevik /ˈbɒl.ʃə.vɪk/ (US) /ˈboʊl-/ **noun** [C] a supporter of the group led by Lenin that took power in Russia in 1917 • **Bolshevism** /-vɪ.zᵊm/ **noun** [U]

bolshy (also **bolshie**) /ˈbɒl.ʃi/ (US) /ˈboʊl-/ **adj** UK informal describes someone who often argues and makes difficulties: *He's a bit bolshy these days.*

bolster /ˈbəʊl.stəʳ/ (US) /ˈboʊl.stɚ/ **verb; noun**

▸verb [T] to support or improve something or make it stronger: *More money is needed to bolster the industry.* ◦ *She tried to bolster my **confidence/morale** (= encourage me and make me feel stronger) by telling me that I had a special talent.* ◦ *They need to do something to bolster their **image**.*

▸noun [C] a long firm cylinder-shaped PILLOW

bolt /bəʊlt/ (US) /boʊlt/ **noun; verb**

bolt

▸noun [C] **LOCK** ▷ **1** a metal bar on a door or window that slides across to lock it closed: *I closed the window and **drew the** bolt (= slid the bolt across).* **SCREW** ▷ **2** a SCREW-like metal object without a point, used with a NUT to fasten things together **LIGHTNING** ▷ **3** a flash of LIGHTNING that looks like a white line against the sky: *The house next to ours was struck by a bolt **of lightning**.* → See also **thunderbolt** **ROLL** ▷ **4** a length or roll of cloth or WALLPAPER **WEAPON** ▷ **5** a type of short arrow shot

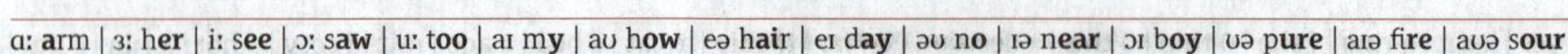

from a CROSSBOW (= a type of weapon) **QUICK MOVEMENT** ▷ **6 make a bolt for somewhere** to try to escape by running towards something: *The thief tried to make a bolt for the exit.*

IDIOM **a bolt from/out of the blue** something completely unexpected that surprises you very much: *The news of his marriage was a bolt from the blue.*

▸verb **MOVE QUICKLY** ▷ **1** [I] to move very fast, especially as a result of being frightened: *Frightened by the car horn, the horse bolted.* **EAT** ▷ **2** [T] (also **bolt down**) to eat food very quickly: *Don't bolt your food like that – you'll get indigestion.* **LOCK** ▷ **3** [I or T] to lock a door or window by sliding a bolt across: *Have you locked and bolted the door?* ◦ *The door bolts on the inside.* **SCREW** ▷ **4** [T usually + adv/prep] to fasten something in position with a bolt: *On a ship the furniture is often bolted **to** the deck.*

PHRASAL VERB **bolt sth on** to add an extra part or feature: *Other insurers will allow you to bolt on critical illness cover to standard life cover.*

ˈbolt-hole noun [C] mainly UK a place where you can hide, especially to escape from other people

ˈbolt-on adj [before noun] added to a main product, service, or plan as a smaller, extra part or feature, especially in business: *Davidow said the business would continue to make bolt-on **acquisitions**.*

ˌbolt ˈupright adv vertical and very straight: *Suddenly she **sat** bolt upright as if something had startled her.*

bomb /bɒm/ (US) /bɑːm/ noun; verb

▸noun **WEAPON** ▷ **1** (B1) [C] a weapon that explodes and is used to kill or hurt people or to damage buildings: *A 100-pound bomb **exploded/went off** today, injuring three people.* ◦ *The terrorists had **planted** a bomb near the police station.* ◦ *During the Second World War, the British **dropped** a huge number of bombs on Dresden.* **2 the bomb** one or more ATOM BOMBS: *The US was the first country to have the bomb.* **FAILURE** ▷ **3** [S] US informal something that has failed: *The play was a real bomb.* **MONEY** ▷ **4 a bomb** UK informal a lot of money: *That coat must have cost a bomb.*

IDIOMS **go (like/down) a bomb** UK informal to be very successful or popular: *The party's really going a bomb, isn't it?* ◦ *Your fruit punch went down a bomb.* • **go like a bomb** to move very quickly: *His new car goes like a bomb.*

▸verb **USE WEAPON** ▷ **1** (B1) [T] to drop bombs on something: *Planes bombed the city every night.* **2** (B1) [T] to destroy something by exploding a bomb inside it: *This pub was bombed a few years ago.* ◦ *The building was completely bombed **out** (= completely destroyed by a bomb).* **GO FAST** ▷ **3** [I + adv/prep] informal to travel very fast in a vehicle: *He was bombing along on his motorbike.* **FAIL** ▷ **4** [I] mainly US informal to fail: *Her last book really bombed.*

bombard /bɒmˈbɑːd/ (US) /bɑːmˈbɑːrd/ verb [T] to attack a place with continuous shooting or bombs: *The troops bombarded the city, killing and injuring hundreds.* • **bombardment** /-mənt/ noun [C or U] ***aerial** bombardment*

PHRASAL VERB **bombard sb with sth** to direct so many things at someone, especially to ask them so many questions, that they find it difficult to deal with them: *The children bombarded her with questions.*

bombardier /bɒm.bəˈdɪəʳ/ (US) /ˌbɑːm.bəˈdɪr/ noun [C] **1** a soldier with a low rank in the ARTILLERY of some armies **2** a military person who aims and often releases bombs from an aircraft

bombast /ˈbɒm.bæst/ (US) /ˈbɑːm-/ noun [U] language that is intentionally difficult, usually to make something sound more important than it is

bombastic /bɒmˈbæs.tɪk/ (US) /bɑːm-/ adj using long and difficult words, usually to make people think you know more than you do: *a bombastic preacher* ◦ *a bombastic statement*

ˈbomb disˌposal ˌunit noun [C] UK (US **ˈbomb ˌsquad**) a group of people whose job is to examine and remove bombs that are found, and to prevent them from exploding

bombed /bɒmd/ (US) /bɑːmd/ adj informal experiencing the strong effect of alcohol or illegal drugs

bomber /ˈbɒm.əʳ/ (US) /ˈbɑː.mɚ/ noun [C] **PERSON** ▷ **1** (B2) a person who uses bombs: *Rajiv Gandhi is believed to have been killed by a **suicide** bomber (= a person who carries a bomb on their body).* **AIRCRAFT** ▷ **2** (C2) an aircraft that drops bombs

ˈbomber jacket noun [C] a short jacket that fits tightly at the waist, often made of leather

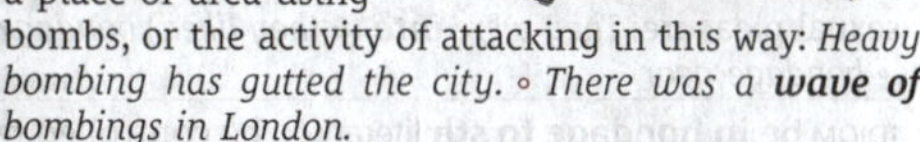
bomber jacket

bombing /ˈbɒm.ɪŋ/ (US) /ˈbɑː.mɪŋ/ noun [C or U] (B2) an attack or attacks on a place or area using bombs, or the activity of attacking in this way: *Heavy bombing has gutted the city.* ◦ *There was a **wave of** bombings in London.*

bomblet /ˈbɒm.lət/ (US) /ˈbɑːm-/ noun [C] one of several small bombs that are released when a larger explosive device such as a CLUSTER BOMB explodes

ˈbomb ˌscare noun [C] a situation in which people are warned that a bomb has been left somewhere and people are told to leave the area or building

bombshell /ˈbɒm.ʃel/ (US) /ˈbɑːm-/ noun **NEWS** ▷ **1** [C usually singular] a sudden and often unpleasant piece of news: *My sister **dropped** a bombshell by announcing she was leaving her job.* **WOMAN** ▷ **2** [C] a very attractive woman: *a **blonde** bombshell*

bombsite /ˈbɒm.saɪt/ (US) /ˈbɑːm-/ noun [C] an empty area in a town where all the buildings have been destroyed by a bomb

bona fide /ˌbəʊ.nəˈfaɪ.di/ (US) /ˌboʊ-/ adj real, not false: *Make sure you are dealing with a bona fide company.* • **bona ˈfides** noun [plural] legal good or sincere intentions

bonanza /bəˈnæn.zə/ noun [C] **1** a situation from which large profits are made: *The rise in house prices meant that those who were selling enjoyed a bonanza.* ◦ *April was a bonanza month for car sales.* **2** a large amount of something good: *The magazine will hold another fashion bonanza in the spring.*

bonbon /ˈbɒn.bɒn/ (US) /ˈbɑːn.bɑːn/ noun [C] US Australian a tube of brightly coloured paper given at CHRISTMAS parties, which makes a noise when pulled apart by two people and contains a small present, a paper hat, and a joke → See also **Christmas cracker**

bond /bɒnd/ (US) /bɑːnd/ noun; verb

▸noun **CONNECTION** ▷ **1** (B2) [C] a close connection joining two or more people: *the bond(s) of friendship/love* ◦ *There has been a close bond **between** them ever since she saved him from drowning.* ◦ *In societies with strong **family** bonds (= relationships), people tend to live longer.* **FINANCIAL DOCUMENT** ▷ **2** [C] an official paper given by the government or a company to show that you have lent them money that they will pay back to you at a particular INTEREST RATE: *I invested*

B

some money in savings bonds. **PROMISE** ▷ **3** [C] a written agreement or promise: *They have entered into a solemn bond.* **4** [C] US legal an amount of money that is paid to formally promise that someone accused of a crime and being kept in prison will appear for trial if released: *The judge ordered that he* ***post*** *a $10,000 bond pending his appeal of the verdict.* **JOIN** ▷ **5** [C usually singular] a place where single parts of something are joined together, especially with glue, or the type of JOINT made: *When the glue has set, the bond formed is watertight.* ◦ *a strong/weak/permanent bond* **ROPES** ▷ **6 bonds** [plural] literary the ropes or chains that hold prisoners and prevent them moving around or escaping: *Loose his bonds and set him free.*

▸verb [I or T] **JOIN** ▷ **1** to stick materials together, especially using glue: *This new adhesive can bond metal* ***to*** *glass.* **MAKE CONNECTION** ▷ **2** C2 to develop a close connection or strong relationship with someone: *The aim was to bond the group into a closely knit team.* ◦ *The hospital gives mothers no quiet private time in which to bond* ***with*** *their babies.*

bondage /ˈbɒn.dɪdʒ/ US /ˈbɑːn-/ **noun** [U] **SERVANT** ▷ **1** literary the state of being another person's SLAVE (= a person who is owned by them and has to work for them): *The slaves were kept* ***in*** *bondage until their death.* **SEX** ▷ **2** the activity of tying parts of a person's body so that they cannot move in order to get or give sexual pleasure: *They were* ***into*** *(= they liked) bondage.* ◦ *bondage gear*

IDIOM **be in bondage to sth** literary to be controlled by something

bondholder /ˈbɒnd.həʊl.dəʳ/ US /ˈbɑːnd.hoʊl.dɚ/ **noun** [C] a person or organization that holds a bond

bonding /ˈbɒn.dɪŋ/ US /ˈbɑːn-/ **noun** [U] the process by which a close emotional relationship is developed: *Much of the bonding between mother and child takes place in those early weeks.*

bone /bəʊn/ US /boʊn/ **noun; verb**

▸noun [C or U] **1** B1 any of the hard parts inside a human or animal that make up its frame: *human/animal bones* **2** B1 the bone in meat or fish: *There's still a lot of meat left on the bone – shall I slice some off for you?*

IDIOMS **bone dry** completely dry • **bone idle** UK extremely lazy: *He never does any exercise – he's bone idle.* • **a bone of contention** something that two or more people argue about strongly over a long period of time • **have a bone to pick with sb** C2 to want to talk to someone about something annoying they have done: *I've got a bone to pick with you – you've been using my shaver again.* • **make no bones about sth** not to try to hide your feelings: *He made no bones about his dissatisfaction with the service.* • **to the bone** all the way through, or very badly: *I was* ***frozen/chilled*** *to the bone after waiting so long for the bus.*

▸verb **SEX** ▷ **1** [I or T] offensive to have sex with someone **FOOD** ▷ **2** [T] to take the bones out of something: *Ask the fishmonger to bone the fish for you.*

PHRASAL VERB **bone up** informal to learn as much as you can about something for a special reason: *She boned up* ***on*** *economics before applying for the job.*

ˌbone ˈchina **noun** [U] a delicate and expensive type of CHINA made using animal bone powder

-boned /-bəʊnd/ US /-boʊnd/ **suffix** having bones of the type mentioned: *She is* ***big****-boned, but she's not fat.*

bonehead /ˈbəʊn.hed/ US /ˈboʊn-/ **noun** [C] slang a stupid person

boneless /ˈbəʊn.ləs/ US /ˈboʊn-/ **adj** (US also **boned**) without a bone: *a boneless breast of chicken*

ˈbone ˌmarrow **noun** [U] **marrow**

bonemeal /ˈbəʊn.miːl/ US /ˈboʊn-/ **noun** [U] a substance made from crushed dried bones that is used to improve the earth to make plants grow better

boner /ˈbəʊ.nəʳ/ US /ˈboʊ.nɚ/ **noun** [C] **PENIS** ▷ **1** mainly US offensive an ERECTION (= when a man's PENIS is hard) **MISTAKE** ▷ **2** US informal a mistake which causes embarrassment to the person who makes it

bonfire /ˈbɒn.faɪəʳ/ US /ˈbɑːn.faɪr/ **noun** [C] a large fire that is made outside to burn unwanted things, or for pleasure

ˈBonfire ˌNight **noun** [C or U] UK another name for GUY FAWKES NIGHT, the night of 5 November, when many people in the UK light bonfires and watch FIREWORKS

bong /bɒŋ/ US /bɑːŋ/ **noun** [C] a musical noise made especially by a large clock: *I heard the bong of the grandfather clock.*

bongo (drum) /ˈbɒŋ.gəʊˌdrʌm/ US /ˈbɑːŋ.goʊ-/ **noun** [C] one of a pair of small drums that are played with the hands

bonhomie /ˌbɒn.əˈmiː/ US /ˌbɑː.nəˈmiː/ **noun** [U] formal friendliness and happiness: *There was a lot of cheerful bonhomie amongst the people on the trip.*

bonk /bɒŋk/ US /bɑːŋk/ **verb** **HIT** ▷ **1** [T] informal humorous to hit someone or something, not very hard: *He bonked me on the head with his newspaper.* **HAVE SEX** ▷ **2** [I or T] UK humorous slang to have sex with someone: *'I bonked the prince, says sexy Sarah' declared the newspaper headline.* • **bonk** **noun** [C] *a bonk on the head*

bonkbuster /ˈbɒŋk.bʌs.təʳ/ US /ˈbɑːŋk.bʌs.tɚ/ **noun** [C] UK informal humorous a type of popular book with a story in which the characters have a lot of sex

bonkers /ˈbɒŋ.kəz/ US /ˈbɑːŋ.kɚz/ **adj** [after verb] informal humorous silly or stupid: *She must be bonkers to do that.*

bon mot /ˌbɒnˈməʊ/ US /ˌbɑːnˈmoʊ/ **noun** [C] (plural **bons mots**) formal a clever remark

bonnet /ˈbɒn.ɪt/ US /ˈbɑː.nɪt/ **noun** [C] **HAT** ▷ **1** a type of hat that covers the ears and is tied under the chin, worn by babies or, especially in the past, by women **METAL COVER** ▷ **2** UK (US **hood**) the metal cover over the part of a car where the engine is: *I looked under the bonnet and clouds of smoke poured out.*

bonny /ˈbɒn.i/ US /ˈbɑː.ni/ **adj** mainly Scottish English beautiful and healthy: *a bonny* ***baby*** ◦ *a bonny lass*

bonsai /ˈbɒn.saɪ/ US /ˌbɑːnˈsaɪ/ **noun** [C] (also **ˈbonsai ˌtree**) a very small tree that is grown in a small container and is stopped from growing bigger by repeatedly cutting

bonus /ˈbəʊ.nəs/ US /ˈboʊ-/ **noun** [C] **1** B2 an extra amount of money that is given to you as a present or a reward for good work as well as the money you were expecting: *a productivity bonus* ◦ *a Christmas bonus* **2** B2 a pleasant extra thing: *I love the job, and it's an* ***added*** *bonus* ***that*** *it's so close to home.*

bon vivant /ˌbɔ̃ːŋ.viːˈvɑ̃ːŋ/ US /ˌbɑːn.viːˈvɑːnt/ **noun** [C] (plural **bons vivants**) (UK also **bon viveur** /ˌbɔ̃ːŋ.viːˈvɜːʳ/ US /ˌbɑːn.viːˈvɝː/ (plural **bons viveurs**)) a person who enjoys good food and wines and likes going to restaurants and parties

bon voyage /ˌbon.vɔɪˈɑːʒ/ US /ˌbɑːn.vwaɪ-/ **exclamation** a phrase said to people who are going away, meaning 'I hope you have a safe and enjoyable journey'

bony /ˈbəʊ.ni/ US /ˈboʊ-/ **adj** very thin: *long bony fingers*

bonzer /ˈbɒn.zəʳ/ (US) /ˈbɑːn.zɚ/ **adj** Australian old-fashioned informal very good or pleasant

boo /buː/ **verb; noun; exclamation**

▸**verb** [I or T] (present tense **booing**, past tense and past participle **booed**) to make an expression of strong disapproval or disagreement: *People at the back started booing loudly.* ◦ *Her singing was so bad that she was booed **off** the stage.*

▸**noun** [C] (plural **boos**) the act of booing

▸**exclamation** an expression, usually shouted, used to surprise and frighten someone who does not know you are near them: *She jumped out of the cupboard and shouted 'Boo!'.*

boob /buːb/ **noun; verb**

▸**noun** [C] **MISTAKE** ▷ **1** UK informal a silly mistake: *Forgetting the president's name was a bit of a boob.* **BREAST** ▷ **2** very informal a woman's breast: *You know her – blonde hair and big boobs.*

▸**verb** [I] to make a silly mistake: *He boobed rather badly **by** getting her name wrong.*

ˈboob ˌjob noun informal **have a boob job** to have an operation to change the shape of the breasts, usually to make them larger: *So do you think she's had a boob job?*

ˈboo-boo noun [C] (plural **boo-boos**) **1** informal a mistake: *Oops, I think I **made** a boo-boo there – I hope she's not too upset.* **2** US child's word a slight injury: *Tess fell down and got a boo-boo on her hand.*

ˈboob ˌtube noun [C] **CLOTHING** ▷ **1** informal a piece of women's clothing that is made of a material that stretches and covers the top half of the body very tightly **TV** ▷ **2** US informal for television

booby /ˈbuː.bi/ noun [C] (US also **boob**) a stupid person

ˈbooby ˌprize noun [C] a prize given as a joke to the person who finishes last in a competition

ˈbooby ˌtrap noun [C] something dangerous, especially a bomb, that is hidden inside somewhere that looks safe: *a booby-trap bomb* ◦ *They put a bucket of water on top of his door as a booby trap.* • **ˈbooby-ˌtrap** verb [T] *The police discovered that the car was booby-trapped.*

booger /ˈbuː.gəʳ/ (US) /-gɚ/ noun [C] US for **bogey**

boogeyman /ˈbuː.gi.mæn/ noun [C] (plural **-men** /-mən/) US for **bogeyman**

boogie /ˈbuː.gi/ verb [I] (present tense **boogieing**, past tense and past participle **boogied**) informal to dance to pop music: *We boogied away all night long.* • **boogie** noun [S] *I like a good boogie.*

boohoo /ˌbuːˈhuː/ **exclamation** the sound of noisy crying like a child's: *'Boohoo!' she wailed 'I'm lost.'*

book /bʊk/ **noun; verb**

▸**noun** **TEXT** ▷ **1** (A1) [C] a written text that can be published in printed or electronic form: *Have you read any good books recently?* ◦ *He's got a new book out (= published).* ◦ *She wrote a book **on** car maintenance.* **2** (A1) [C] a set of pages that have been fastened together inside a cover to be read or written in: *a **hardback/paperback** book* ◦ *I took a book with me to read on the train.* ◦ *He writes all his expenses in a little book he carries with him.* **3** [C] one of the parts that a very long book, such as the BIBLE, is divided into: *the book of Job* **4** (C2) [C] a number of one type of thing fastened together flat inside a cover: *a book **of** stamps/tickets/matches* **MONEY RECORD** ▷ **5 books** [plural] the written records of money that a business has spent or received: *At the end of the year, the accountant goes over (= checks) **the** books.* ◦ *Running a school is much more of a business than it used to be, – by law we have to **balance** our books.* **6** [S] the situation in which a BOOKMAKER accepts and pays out amounts of money that are risked on a particular result: *They've already **opened/started** a book **on** the result of the next World Cup.*

IDIOMS **be in sb's good/bad books** (C2) If you are in someone's good/bad books, they are pleased/not pleased with you: *He's in Melanie's bad books because he arrived two hours late.* ◦ *I cleaned the bathroom yesterday so I'm in Mum's good books.* • **be on the books** to be employed by a company, or (pay to) belong to a organization, society, sports team, etc.: *There are 256 people on the books at the cement works.* ◦ *The nursery has 30 babies on the books and 13 on the waiting list.* • **go by the book/do sth by the book** (C2) to do something exactly as the rules tell you: *My lawyer always goes strictly by the book.* ◦ *This is a private deal – we don't have to do everything by the book.* • **in my book** in my opinion: *She's never lied to me, and in my book that counts for a lot.*

▸**verb** **ARRANGE** ▷ **1** (A2) [T or I] to arrange to have a seat, room, performer, etc. at a particular time in the future: [+ two objects] *I've booked us two tickets to see 'Carmen'/I've booked two tickets **for** us to see 'Carmen'.* ◦ *She'd booked a table **for** four at their favourite restaurant.* ◦ *Will booked a seat on the evening flight to Edinburgh.* ◦ *We were advised to book early if we wanted to get a room.* ◦ *They booked a jazz band for their wedding.* ◦ *The hotel/restaurant/theatre is **fully** booked (**up**) (= all the rooms/tables/tickets have been taken).* ◦ *I'd like to go but I'm afraid I'm booked **up** (= I have arranged to do other things) until the weekend.* **MAKE A RECORD** ▷ **2** [T] If a police officer, REFEREE, etc. books someone, they write down the person's name in an official record because they have done something wrong: *A player in a football match who is booked twice in a game is sent off the field.* ◦ *My grandmother was booked **for** speeding last week.*

PHRASAL VERBS **book in/book into somewhere** UK to say that you have arrived and sign an official book when you get to a hotel: *After booking into our hotel, we went straight down to the beach.* ◦ *As soon as she arrived in Tokyo, she booked in at her hotel.* • **book sb in/book sb into sth** mainly UK (B1) to arrange for someone to stay at a hotel: *They've booked us into the hotel in the main square.* ◦ *I've booked you in at the Savoy.*

bookable /ˈbʊk.ə.bl̩/ adj **ARRANGE** ▷ **1** A bookable seat, room, performer, etc. can be booked for a particular time in the future. **RECORD** ▷ **2** A bookable OFFENCE (= something you do wrong) is one that a police officer, REFEREE, etc. can book you for, by writing down your name in an official record.

bookbinder /ˈbʊkˌbaɪn.dəʳ/ (US) /-dɚ/ noun [C] **1** someone whose work or skill involves fastening loose pages together inside a cover to make a book **2 bookbinder's** (plural **bookbinders**) a place where bookbinders work • **bookbinding** /-dɪŋ/ noun [U]

bookcase /ˈbʊk.keɪs/ noun [C] (A1) a piece of furniture with shelves to put books on

ˈbook ˌclub noun [C] **GROUP** ▷ **1** a group of people who meet regularly to talk about a book which they have all read **ORGANIZATION** ▷ **2** an organization in which members can buy books more cheaply than in the shops

bookend /ˈbʊk.end/ noun [C] an object used, especially in pairs, to keep a row of books standing vertically

bookie /ˈbʊk.i/ noun [C] informal for **bookmaker**

B

booking /ˈbʊk.ɪŋ/ noun [C] B1 an arrangement you make to have a hotel room, tickets, etc. at a particular time in the future: *We **made** the booking three months ago.* ◦ *Julian was ill so we had to **cancel** the booking.* ◦ *The show had already taken £4 million in **advance** bookings.* ◦ *I filled in the booking **form** and sent it off.*

ˈbooking ˌoffice noun [C] UK a place, usually in a theatre, where tickets can be bought before a performance

bookish /ˈbʊk.ɪʃ/ adj mainly disapproving describes someone who enjoys reading books, especially serious books

bookkeeping /ˈbʊkˌkiː.pɪŋ/ noun [U] the job or activity of keeping an exact record of the money that has been spent or received by a business or other organization • **bookkeeper** /-pəʳ/ US /-pɚ/ noun [C]

booklet /ˈbʊk.lət/ noun [C] B2 a very thin book with a small number of pages and a paper cover, giving information about something

bookmaker /ˈbʊkˌmeɪ.kəʳ/ US /-kɚ/ noun [C] (informal **bookie**) **1** a person who accepts and pays out amounts of money risked on a particular result, especially of horse races **2 bookmaker's** (plural **bookmakers**) a place where bookmakers work

bookmark /ˈbʊk.mɑːk/ US /-mɑːrk/ noun; verb

▸noun [C] **PLACE IN BOOK** ▷ **1** (also **bookmarker**) a piece of card, leather, or plastic that you put between the pages of a book so that you can find a page again quickly **COMPUTING** ▷ **2** B2 the address of a web page that is kept on your computer so that you can find it again easily: *Keep this site as a bookmark.*

▸verb [T] B2 to make a record of the address of a web page on your computer so that you can find it again easily: *Don't forget to bookmark this page.*

bookmobile /ˈbʊkˌmə.biːl/ US /-ˌmoʊ-/ noun [C] US for **mobile library**

bookplate /ˈbʊk.pleɪt/ noun [C] a decorative piece of paper stuck inside the front cover of a book to show who owns it

bookseller /ˈbʊkˌsel.əʳ/ US /-ɚ/ noun [C] a person or company that sells books: *an online bookseller*

bookshelf /ˈbʊk.ʃelf/ noun [C] (plural **bookshelves**) A2 a shelf in a BOOKCASE

bookshop /ˈbʊk.ʃɒp/ US /-ʃɑːp/ noun [C] mainly UK (US usually **bookstore**) A2 a shop or website where books are sold

bookstall /ˈbʊk.stɔːl/ US /-stɑːl/ noun [C] mainly UK a table or a very small shop with an open front where books, magazines, etc. are sold

ˈbook ˌtoken noun [C] UK a card worth a particular amount of money that is given as a present and can only be used to buy a book: *a £10 book token*

bookworm /ˈbʊk.wɜːm/ US /-wɝːm/ noun [C] informal a person who reads a lot

Boolean search /ˌbuː.liənˈsɜːtʃ/ US /-ˈsɝːtʃ/ noun [C] specialized in computer science, a method of searching using words such as 'and', 'not', and 'or'

boom /buːm/ noun; verb

▸noun **SOUND** ▷ **1** [C] a deep and loud hollow sound **PERIOD OF GROWTH** ▷ **2** [C or U] a period of sudden economic growth, especially one that results in a lot of money being made: *This year has seen a boom **in** book sales.* ◦ *The insurance business suffered from a vicious cycle of boom **and bust**.* ◦ *the **property** boom* **BOAT** ▷ **3** [C] specialized (on a boat) a long pole that moves and that has a sail fastened to it **FILMING** ▷ **4** [C] a long pole with a MICROPHONE on one end that is held above the actors so that it records their voices but cannot be seen by the people watching, used in television and film-making

▸verb **MAKE A SOUND** ▷ **1** [I or T] to make a very deep and loud hollow sound: *The cannons boomed (**out**) in the night.* ◦ *He boomed (**out**) an order to the soldiers.* **GROW** ▷ **2** [I] to increase or become successful and produce a lot of money very quickly: often in continuous tenses *The leisure industry is booming.* • **booming** /ˈbuː.mɪŋ/ adj *a booming **voice***

ˈboom ˌbox noun [C] mainly US informal a large radio and CD player you can carry with you

boomer /buː.məʳ/ US /-ɚ/ noun [C] **PERSON** ▷ **1** a baby-boomer **KANGAROO** ▷ **2** a large male KANGAROO

boomerang /ˈbuː.mə.ræŋ/ noun; verb

boomerang

▸noun [C] a curved stick that, when thrown in a particular way, comes back to the person who threw it

▸verb [I] If a plan boomerangs, it brings a harmful result instead of the intended good one: *Our plan to take over the business could boomerang **on** us if we're not careful.*

ˈboom ˌtown noun [C] a town that experiences sudden economic growth

boon /buːn/ noun [C usually singular] something that is very helpful and improves the quality of life: *Guide dogs are a great boon **to** the partially sighted.*

ˌboon comˈpanion noun [C usually singular] literary a very close friend

the boondocks /ˈbuːn.dɒks/ US /-dɑːks/ noun [plural] US disapproving any area in the country that is quiet, has few people living in it, and is a long way away from a town or city

boondoggle /ˈbuːnˌdɒg.l̩/ US /-ˌdɑː.gl̩/ noun [C] US informal an unnecessary and expensive piece of work, especially one that is paid for by the public

boor /bʊəʳ/ US /bʊr/ noun [C] a person who is rude and does not consider other people's feelings • **boorish** /ˈbʊər.ɪʃ/ US /ˈbɔː.rɪʃ/ adj

boost /buːst/ verb; noun

▸verb [T] B2 to improve or increase something: *The theatre managed to boost its audiences by cutting ticket prices.* ◦ *Share prices were boosted by reports of the president's recovery.* ◦ *I tried to boost his **ego** (= make him feel more confident) by praising his cooking.*

▸noun [C usually singular] B2 the act of boosting something: *The lowering of interest rates will give a much-needed boost **to** the economy.* ◦ *Passing my driving test was such a boost **to** my **confidence**.*

booster /ˈbuː.stəʳ/ US /-stɚ/ noun [C] **IMPROVEMENT** ▷ **1** something which improves or increases something: *a **confidence/morale** booster* **ENGINE** ▷ **2** an engine on a spacecraft that gives extra power for the first part of a flight: *a rocket booster* **DRUG** ▷ **3** an extra small amount of a drug given to increase the effect of the same drug given some time before, to protect a person from illness: *a polio booster*

ˈbooster ˌseat noun [C] (also **ˈbooster ˌcushion**) mainly UK a seat for a young child, usually used in a car, that raises him or her to a higher level

boot /buːt/ noun; verb

▸noun **SHOE** ▷ **1** A1 [C] a type of shoe that covers the whole foot and the lower part of the leg: *wellington boots* ◦ *walking boots* ◦ *riding boots* **CAR** ▷ **2** B1 [C] UK (US **trunk**) a covered space at the back of a car, for storing things in **END** ▷ **3 the boot** [S] UK informal the situation in which your job is taken away from you, usually because you have done something wrong or badly: *She* ***got*** *the boot for stealing money from the till.* ◦ *Williams has been* ***given*** *the boot* ***from*** *the team.* **KICK** ▷ **4** [C] informal a kick with the foot: *He* ***gave*** *the ball a good boot.* **WHEEL** ▷ **5** [C] (also **Denver boot**) US a **wheel clamp**

IDIOMS **put the boot in** informal **1** to kick someone when they are already on the ground **2** to make a bad situation worse, by criticizing or being unkind: *After he lost his job, his wife put the boot in by announcing she was leaving him.* • **the boot/shoe is on the other foot** the situation is now the opposite of what it was, especially because someone who was weak now has power • **to boot** old-fashioned in addition: *He's kind, handsome, and wealthy to boot.*

▸verb **KICK** ▷ **1** [T usually + adv/prep] informal to kick someone or something hard with the foot: *They booted him* ***in*** *the head.* **COMPUTER** ▷ **2** [I or T] (also **boot up**) When a computer boots (up), it becomes ready for use by getting the necessary information into its memory, and when you boot (up) a computer, you cause it to do this.

ˈboot ˌcamp noun [C] **1** US a place for training soldiers **2** a place for young criminals that is used instead of prison, and is similar to a place where soldiers are trained

bootcut /ˈbuːt.kʌt/ adj **bootleg**

bootee (US also **bootie**) /ˈbuː.tiː/ ⓤⓢ /-t̬iː/ noun [C] a baby's soft boot that is often made of wool

booth /buːð/ ⓤⓢ /buːθ/ noun [C] **1** a small space like a box that a person can go into: *a* ***phone*** *booth* ◦ *a* ***polling*** *booth* **2** a partly closed area, table, or small tent at a fair, EXHIBITION, or similar event

bootlace /ˈbuːt.leɪs/ noun [C] a long, thin string or strip of leather used to fasten boots

bootleg /ˈbuːt.leg/ adj; verb

▸adj **ILLEGAL** ▷ **1** illegally made, copied, or sold: *bootleg CDs/liquor* **TROUSERS** ▷ **2** (also **bootcut**) describes trousers that are slightly wider at the ANKLE than at the knee: *bootleg jeans* • **bootlegs** /-legz/ noun [plural] bootleg trousers: *a pair of bootlegs*

▸verb [I or T] (-gg-) to illegally make, copy, or sell something • **bootlegger** /-əʳ/ ⓤⓢ /-ɚ/ noun [C]

bootstrap /ˈbuːt.stræp/ noun [C] a piece of leather or other strong material at the back of a boot that you use to help you pull the boot on

IDIOM **pull/haul yourself up by the/your (own) bootstraps** to improve your situation without any help from other people: *He left school at 15 and pulled himself up by his bootstraps to ultimately earn a degree in politics.*

booty /ˈbuː.ti/ ⓤⓢ /-t̬i/ noun **STOLEN GOODS** ▷ **1** [U] any valuable things or money stolen by an army at war or by thieves **BODY PART** ▷ **2** [C] US slang the part of the body that you sit on → Synonym **bottom**

bootylicious /ˌbuː.tiˈlɪʃ.əs/ ⓤⓢ /-t̬i-/ adj US slang sexually attractive

booze /buːz/ noun; verb

▸noun [U] informal alcohol: *The party's at Kate's on Friday night – bring some booze.*

IDIOM **on the booze** UK informal drinking a lot of alcohol: *Every Friday night Rick would* ***go*** *out on the booze.*

▸verb [I] informal to drink alcohol: *Have you been out boozing again?*

boozer /ˈbuː.zəʳ/ ⓤⓢ /-zɚ/ noun [C] **1** informal a person who drinks a lot **2** UK informal a pub: *the* ***local*** *boozer*

ˈbooze-up noun [C] informal a party or similar occasion where people drink a lot of alcohol

boozy /ˈbuː.zi/ adj informal drinking or containing a lot of alcohol: *a boozy night out*

bop /bɒp/ ⓤⓢ /bɑːp/ verb; noun

▸verb (-pp-) **DANCE** ▷ **1** [I] informal to dance to pop music: *They were all bopping* ***to*** *the music.* **HIT** ▷ **2** [T usually + adv/prep] humorous to hit someone or something, especially in a friendly way: *to bop someone* ***on*** *the head*

▸noun **MUSIC** ▷ **1** [U] (also **bebop**) a type of JAZZ music first played by small groups in the 1940s **DANCE** ▷ **2** [C usually singular] a dance to pop music: *There are a couple of decent clubs where you can go for a bop.* • **boppy** /ˈbɒp.i/ ⓤⓢ /ˈbɑː.pi/ adj informal describes music that is good for dancing to

borage /ˈbɒr.ɪdʒ/ ⓤⓢ /ˈbɔːr-/ noun [U] a plant whose leaves can be used in cooking and whose oil can be used in medicines

borax /ˈbɔː.ræks/ ⓤⓢ /ˈbɔːr.æks/ noun [U] a white powder used to make glass and cleaning products

Bordeaux /bɔːˈdəʊ/ ⓤⓢ /bɔːrˈdoʊ/ noun [C or U] (plural **Bordeaux**) (a type of) red or white wine from the Bordeaux area of France: *They've got several nice Bordeaux in stock.*

bordello /bɔːˈdel.əʊ/ ⓤⓢ /bɔːrˈdel.oʊ/ noun [C] (plural **bordellos**) literary a **brothel**

border /ˈbɔː.dəʳ/ ⓤⓢ /ˈbɔːr.dɚ/ noun; verb

▸noun [C] **DIVISION** ▷ **1** B1 the line that divides one country from another: *Were you stopped at the border?* ◦ *The train crosses the border* ***between*** *France and Spain.* ◦ *The two countries have had frequent border disputes.* **EDGE** ▷ **2** a strip that goes around or along the edge of something, often as decoration: *The dress was white with a delicate lace border.* ◦ *a picture with a decorative/plain border* **3** a narrow strip of ground around a garden, usually planted with flowers: *to weed/plant the borders*

▸verb **FORM EDGE** ▷ **1** [T usually passive] to form a line around the edge of something: *The fields are bordered by tall trees.* **BE NEXT TO** ▷ **2** [T] to be next to and have a border with another country: *Swaziland borders South Africa and Mozambique.* • **bordering** /-ɪŋ/ adj *bordering countries/counties*

PHRASAL VERB **border on sth** If behaviour, a quality, or a feeling borders on something more extreme, it is almost that thing: *His suggestion borders on the ridiculous.*

borderline /ˈbɔː.də.laɪn/ ⓤⓢ /ˈbɔːr.dɚ-/ adj; noun

▸adj between two different conditions, with the possibility of belonging to either one of them: *Only in borderline* ***cases*** *(= cases where students might succeed or fail) will pupils have an oral exam.* ◦ *She was a borderline candidate.*

▸noun [S] something that separates two different qualities: *The borderline* ***between*** *friendship and intimacy is often hard to define.*

bore /bɔːʳ/ ⓤⓢ /bɔːr/ verb; noun

▸verb **FAIL TO INTEREST** ▷ **1** [T] to talk or act in a way that makes someone lose interest: *'Am I boring you?' she asked anxiously.* **2 bore sb silly** to make someone feel very bored: *We were all bored silly by the play.* **MAKE A HOLE** ▷ **3** [I or T, usually + adv/prep] to make a hole in something using a tool: *He used a drill to bore a hole in the wall.* ◦ *The workmen bored* ***through*** *the rock.* **BEAR** ▷ **4** past simple of **bear**

B

PHRASAL VERB **bore into sb** If someone's eyes bore into you, they look at you very hard and make you feel nervous.

▸noun **NOT INTERESTING** ▷ **1** [C] disapproving someone who talks too much about boring subjects: *I had to sit next to Michael at dinner – he's such a bore.* **2** [S] informal an activity or situation that is annoying or unpleasant: *Ironing is such a bore.* ◦ [+ -ing verb] *It's an awful bore cook**ing** a meal every night.* ◦ [+ to infinitive] *It's such a bore **to** have to write this out all over again.* **HOLE** ▷ **3** [C] (US usually **gauge**) the space inside a pipe or tube, or the DIAMETER (= measurement across the widest part) of this space: *a narrow bore* ◦ *a bore of 16 millimetres*

-bore /-bɔːʳ/ (US) /-bɔːr/ **suffix** mainly UK (US usually **-gauge**) used in adjectives to express the width of the space inside a cylinder, especially the inside of a gun BARREL (= part shaped like a tube): *a twelve-bore shotgun*

bored /bɔːd/ (US) /bɔːrd/ **adj** A1 feeling unhappy because something is not interesting or because you have nothing to do: *It was a cold, wet day and the children were bored.* ◦ *He was getting bored **with/of** doing the same thing every day.*

IDIOM **bored stiff** (also **bored to death/tears**) extremely unhappy because something is not interesting or because you have nothing to do

boredom /ˈbɔː.dəm/ (US) /ˈbɔːr-/ **noun** [U] the state of being bored: *They started quarrelling **out of** sheer boredom.*

borehole /ˈbɔː.həʊl/ (US) /ˈbɔːr.hoʊl/ **noun** [C] a deep hole made in the ground when looking for oil, gas, or water: *We must **sink** a borehole so that people will have water.* ◦ *They obtained information about the rock by **drilling** boreholes.*

boring /ˈbɔː.rɪŋ/ (US) /ˈbɔːr.ɪŋ/ **adj** A1 not interesting or exciting: *She finds opera boring.* ◦ *It's boring to sit on the plane with nothing to read.* ◦ *a boring lecture* ◦ *The film was so boring I fell asleep.* • **boringly** /-li/ **adv** *The film has a boringly predictable ending.*

> **Other ways of saying boring**
>
> We often use **bland** instead of boring when describing food:
>
> *This sauce is really **bland.** It doesn't taste of anything.*
>
> If a piece of writing, a performance, or a person is boring, you can say that the person, performance, or writing is **dull**:
>
> *I find her writing a bit **dull**.*
>
> **Monotonous** is often used about something that you listen to:
>
> *The teacher had a really **monotonous** voice and I almost fell asleep.*
>
> When describing an activity, **tedious** is sometimes used:
>
> *You have to fill in various forms, which is **tedious**.*
>
> If something is boring because it is too long, you can describe it as **drawn out** or **interminable**:
>
> *He gave a **long-drawn-out** explanation of why he'd changed his mind.*
>
> *Her delay seemed **interminable.***
>
> You can say that a person who is boring because he or she talks too much is a **bore**:
>
> *He's a real **bore** when he starts talking about computers.*

borlotti bean /bɔːˌlɒt.iˈbiːn/ (US) /bɔːrˌlɑː.t̬i-/ **noun** [C] a large, round, pink bean, which becomes brown when cooked

born /bɔːn/ (US) /bɔːrn/ **verb; adj**

▸verb **1 be born** A2 to come out of a mother's body, and start to exist: *She was born in 1950.* ◦ *We saw a lamb being born.* ◦ *Diana was born **into** an aristocratic family.* ◦ *Ann was born **and brought up** in Ealing.* **2** having started life in a particular way: *The toll of babies born **with** AIDS is rising.* ◦ *Stevie Wonder was born blind.* **3** C2 formal or literary If an idea is born, it starts to exist. **4 born of sth** formal existing as the result of something: *With a courage born of necessity, she seized the gun and ran at him.*

IDIOMS **born and bred** describes someone who was born and grew up in a particular place, and has the typical character of someone who lives there: *He's a Parisian born and bred.* • **born with a silver spoon in your mouth** to have a high social position and be rich from birth • **not be born yesterday** to not be stupid or easy to deceive: *You don't fool me – I wasn't born yesterday.* • **wish you had never been born** to be extremely unhappy: *When I've finished with you you're going to wish you'd never been born!*

▸adj having a natural ability or liking: *a born writer/athlete* ◦ [+ to infinitive] *I felt born **to** look after animals.*

-born /-bɔːn/ (US) /-bɔːrn/ **suffix** born in the way, place, or order mentioned: *newborn* ◦ *Ben Okri is a Nigerian-born poet and novelist.* ◦ *the first-born son*

ˌborn-aˈgain adj 1 describes someone who has decided to accept a particular type of EVANGELICAL Christianity, especially after a deep spiritual experience: *Cliff Richard is a born-again Christian.* **2** [before noun] describes someone who is extremely enthusiastic about a new interest or hobby: *She's a born-again health freak.*

borne /bɔːn/ (US) /bɔːrn/ **verb** past participle of **bear**

-borne /-bɔːn/ (US) /-bɔːrn/ **suffix** carried or moved by a particular thing: *airborne* ◦ *waterborne*

boron /ˈbɔː.rɒn/ (US) /ˈbɔːr.ɑːn/ **noun** [U] (symbol **B**) a hard, yellow-brown chemical element used in NUCLEAR REACTORS to absorb NEUTRONS and in various COMPOUNDS that are important in MANUFACTURING

borough /ˈbʌr.ə/ (US) /ˈbɝː.oʊ/ **noun** [C] a town, or a division of a large town

borrow /ˈbɒr.əʊ/ (US) /ˈbɑːr.oʊ/ **verb** **RECEIVE** ▷ **1** A2 [T] to get or receive something from someone with the intention of giving it back after a period of time: *Could I borrow your bike **from** (non-standard **off**) you until next week?* ◦ *She used to borrow money and not bother to pay it back.* ◦ *He borrowed a novel from the library.* **2** C1 [I or T] to take money from a bank or other financial organization and pay it back over a period of time: *Like so many companies at that time, we had to borrow **heavily** to survive.* ◦ *We could always borrow some money from the bank.* **3** [T] to take and use a word or idea from another language or piece of work: *English has borrowed many words **from** French.* **MATHEMATICS** ▷ **4** [T] to put a number into a different column when doing SUBTRACTION • **borrower** /-əʳ/ (US) /-ɚ/ **noun** [C] a person, organization, etc. that borrows • **borrowing** /-ɪŋ/ **noun** [C or U] *Public borrowing has increased in recent years.*

IDIOM **live on borrowed time 1** to continue living after a point at which you might easily have died: *Since his cancer was diagnosed, he feels as if he's living on borrowed time.* **2** to continue to exist longer than expected: *It is unlikely that serious decisions will be taken by a minority government living on borrowed time.*

borscht (also **borsch**) /bɔːʃt/ (US) /bɔːrʃt/ **noun** [U] a

B

type of soup made from BEETROOT (= a small, dark red vegetable)

borstal /ˈbɔː.stəl/ ⓤⓢ /ˈbɔːr-/ noun [C or U] UK (in the past) a prison for boys who were too young to be sent to an ordinary prison

bosom /ˈbʊz.əm/ noun [C usually singular] **1** a woman's breasts: *a large/ample bosom* **2** literary the front of a person's chest, especially when thought of as the centre of human feelings: *She **held** him tightly **to** her bosom.* ◦ *A dark jealousy stirred **in** his bosom.*

IDIOM **in the bosom of sth** formal If you are in the bosom of a group of people, especially your family, you are with them and protected and loved by them.

ˌbosom ˈfriend/ˈbuddy/ˈpal noun [C] a friend that you like a lot and have a very close relationship with

boss /bɒs/ ⓤⓢ /bɑːs/ noun; verb

▸noun [C] **MANAGER** ▷ **1** A2 the person who is in charge of an organization and who tells others what to do: *She was the boss of a large international company.* ◦ *I started up my own business and now I'm my **own** boss* (= I work for myself and no one tells me what to do). ◦ informal *Who's the boss* (= the person who makes all the important decisions) *in your house?* **DECORATION** ▷ **2** a raised rounded decoration, such as on a SHIELD or a ceiling

▸verb [T usually + adv/prep] informal disapproving to tell someone what to do all the time: *I wish he'd stop bossing me **around/about**.*

ˈbossa ˌnova noun [C or U] a type of Brazilian popular music, or a dance to this music

ˈboss-eyed adj UK slang having eyes that look in towards the nose → Synonym **cross-eyed**

bossy /ˈbɒs.i/ ⓤⓢ /ˈbɑː.si/ adj disapproving B2 describes someone who is always telling people what to do • **bossily** /ˈbɒs.ɪ.li/ ⓤⓢ /ˈbɑː.sɪ.li/ adv • **bossiness** /-nəs/ noun [U]

bossyboots /ˈbɒs.iˌbuːts/ ⓤⓢ /ˈbɑː.s.iˌbuːts/ noun [S] child's word someone who is very bossy

bosun /ˈbəʊ.sən/ ⓤⓢ /ˈboʊ-/ noun [C] a **boatswain**

bot /bɒt/ ⓤⓢ /bɑːt/ noun [C] **ROBOT** ▷ **1** informal a **robot** **COMPUTING** ▷ **2** specialized a computer program that works automatically, especially one that searches for and finds information on the internet: *Criminals are more sophisticated these days, creating networks of bots that roam the internet infecting PCs with malware.* **BODY PART** ▷ **3** UK informal a person's bottom

botanical /bəˈtæn.ɪ.kəl/ adj (also **botanic** /bəˈtæn.ɪk/) involving or relating to plants or the study of plants: *a botanical print* ◦ *Several new botanical species have been discovered in the last year.*

boˌtanic ˈgarden noun [C often plural] (also **boˌtanical ˈgarden**) a garden, usually open to the public, where a wide range of plants are grown for scientific and educational purposes

botanist /ˈbɒt.ən.ɪst/ ⓤⓢ /ˈbɑː.t̬ən-/ noun [C] a scientist who studies plants

botany /ˈbɒt.ən.i/ ⓤⓢ /ˈbɑː.t̬ən-/ noun [U] the scientific study of plants

botch /bɒtʃ/ ⓤⓢ /bɑːtʃ/ verb; noun

▸verb [T] (UK also **bodge**) to spoil something by doing it badly: *We botched **(up)** our first attempt at wallpapering the bathroom.*

▸noun [C] (UK also **bodge**, also **ˈbotch-up**, UK also **bodge**, **ˈbodge-up**) something that is spoiled by being done badly: *The concert was very badly organized. In fact, the whole thing was a real botch-up.*

botched /bɒtʃt/ ⓤⓢ /bɑːtʃt/ adj (UK also **bodged**) describes something, usually a job, that is done badly: *Our landlord redecorated the bedroom, but it was such a botched **job** that we decided to redo it.* ◦ *Thousands of women are infertile as a result of botched **abortions**.*

both /bəʊθ/ ⓤⓢ /boʊθ/ **predeterminer, determiner, pronoun** A1 (referring to) two people or things together: *Both my parents are teachers.* ◦ *They have two grown children, both **of whom** live abroad.* ◦ *She has written two novels, both **of which** have been made into television series.* ◦ *Both Mike and Jim have red hair/ Mike and Jim both have red hair.* ◦ *I loved them both/I loved both **of** them.* ◦ *The problem with both **of these** proposals is that they are hopelessly impractical.* ◦ *Are both **of us** invited, or just you?* ◦ *Would you like milk or sugar or both?* ◦ *Both men **and** women have complained about the advertisement.* ◦ *I felt both happy and sad at the same time.* ◦ *I think it's important to listen to both **sides** of the argument.* ◦ *Improved childcare facilities would benefit both sexes, not just women.* ◦ *I failed my driving test because I didn't keep both hands on the steering wheel.*

> **!** Common mistake: **both**
>
> **Warning:** check your word order!
>
> **Both** usually goes directly before the main verb in a sentence.
>
> Don't say 'do both something', say **both do something**:
>
> ~~*My brothers live both in London.*~~
>
> *My brothers both live in London.*
>
> **Both** can also go before the subject of the sentence:
>
> *Both my brothers live in London.*
>
> But if the main verb is **am/is/are/was/were**, **both** usually goes directly after it:
>
> ~~*My brothers both are shop assistants.*~~
>
> *My brothers are both shop assistants.*

bother /ˈbɒð.ər/ ⓤⓢ /ˈbɑː.ðɚ/ verb; noun; exclamation

▸verb **MAKE AN EFFORT** ▷ **1** B2 [I or T] to make the effort to do something: [+ to infinitive] *He hasn't even bothered **to** write.* ◦ *You could have phoned us but you just didn't bother.* ◦ [+ -ing verb] *Don't bother mak**ing** the bed – I'll do it later.* ◦ [+ -ing verb or + to infinitive] *You'd have found it if you'd bothered look**ing/to** look.* ◦ *You won't get any credit for doing it, **so why** bother?* **2 can't be bothered** B2 UK informal If you can't be bothered doing/to do something, you are too lazy or tired to do it: *I can't be bothered to iron my clothes.* ◦ *Most evenings I can't be bothered cooking.* **WORRY** ▷ **3** B2 [T] to make someone feel worried or upset: *Does it bother you that he's out so much of the time?* ◦ *Living on my own has never bothered me.* ◦ *I don't care if he doesn't come – it doesn't bother me.* ◦ [+ that] *It bothers me **that** he doesn't seem to notice.* **ANNOY** ▷ **4** A2 [T] to annoy or cause problems for someone: *Don't bother your father when he's working.* ◦ *I'm **sorry to** bother **you**, but could you direct me to the station?* ◦ *I didn't want to bother her **with** work matters on her day off.* ◦ *The noise was beginning to bother us, so we left.* ◦ *She threatened to call the police if he didn't stop bothering her.*

▸noun **EFFORT** ▷ **1** [U] trouble or problems: *I can take you – it's really no bother.* ◦ *Some people don't get married because they don't want **the** bother* (= they don't want to make the effort that is necessary). ◦ *Please **don't go to any** bother on my account* (= don't make any special effort for me). ◦ *It hardly seems **worth** the bother to go all that way just for two nights.* ◦ UK *I had **a bit of** bother getting hold of his phone number.* **ANNOYING** ▷ **2** [S] UK an annoying person or

situation: *I'm sorry to be a bother, but could I have that number again?*
▸exclamation UK old-fashioned used to express anger: *Oh bother! It's raining and I left my umbrella at home.*

botheration /ˌbɒð.əˈreɪ.ʃən/ (US) /ˌbɑː.ðə-/ exclamation UK old-fashioned an expression of anger: *Oh botheration! I can't find my keys.*

bothered /ˈbɒð.əd/ (US) /ˈbɑː.ðɚd/ **adj** [after verb] **1** B2 If you are bothered about something, it is important to you and you are worried about it: *He's very bothered **about** what people think of him.* ◦ *They were an hour late and she didn't seem at all bothered.* ◦ *The bright sunshine made him feel **hot and** bothered (= hot and uncomfortable).* **2 not bothered** UK informal If you are not bothered about something, it is not important to you or does not worry you: *'Tea or coffee?' 'Either – I'm not bothered.'* ◦ *I'm not bothered whether I go or not.*

bothersome /ˈbɒð.ə.səm/ (US) /ˈbɑː.ðɚ-/ **adj** old-fashioned annoying or causing trouble: *a bothersome little man* ◦ *bothersome noise*

botnet /ˈbɒt.net/ (US) /ˈbɑːt-/ **noun** specialized a group of computers that are by controlled by software containing harmful programs, without their users' knowledge

Botox /ˈbəʊ.tɒks/ (US) /ˈboʊ.t̬ɑːks/ **noun** [U] trademark a substance that is INJECTED (= put in through a needle) into the skin in order to make it look smooth and young • **botox verb** [T]

bottle /ˈbɒt.l̩/ (US) /ˈbɑː.t̬l̩/ **noun; verb**

▸**noun CONTAINER** ▷ **1** A2 [C] a container for liquids, usually made of glass or plastic, with a narrow neck: *a milk bottle* ◦ *a wine bottle* ◦ *a bottle **of** beer/whisky* ◦ ***Plastic** bottles are lighter than glass ones.* **2** [C] a special container with a rubber top for giving milk and other drinks to a baby: *Give the baby her bottle when she wakes up.* ◦ *Most medical experts believe that breastfeeding is better than bottle-**feeding**.* **COURAGE** ▷ **3** [U] UK slang approving courage or willingness to take risks: *It took **a lot of** bottle to do what she did.*

IDIOM **the bottle** informal the habit of regularly drinking a lot of alcohol: *She started to **hit** the bottle (= drink too much alcohol) after her divorce.*

▸**verb** [T] to put something into bottles or jars: passive *The wine is bottled at the vineyard.* ◦ *To bottle fruit you put fresh fruit into special containers.*

PHRASAL VERBS **bottle out** UK slang to suddenly decide not to do something because you feel frightened and lose your confidence: *I was going to enter a belly-dancing contest, but I bottled out at the last minute.* • **bottle sth up** When a person bottles things up, they refuse to talk about things that make them angry or worried.

ˈbottle ˌbank noun [C] UK a large container into which people put empty bottles and other glass objects so that the glass can be used again

bottled /ˈbɒt.l̩d/ (US) /ˈbɑː.t̬l̩d/ **adj** contained, stored, or sold in bottles: *bottled **water*** ◦ *bottled gas*

ˌbottled ˈwater noun [U] water that has been treated in order to make it very clean or that has come from a special place, sold in bottles

ˈbottle-feed verb [I or T] to feed a baby with milk from a bottle: *She bottle-fed both of her babies.* → Compare **breastfeed** • **ˈbottle-feeding noun** [U]

ˌbottle ˈgreen noun [U] a very dark green colour • **ˌbottle-ˈgreen adj**

bottleneck /ˈbɒt.l̩.nek/ (US) /ˈbɑː.t̬l̩-/ **noun** [C] **1** a place where a road becomes narrow, or a place where there is often a lot of traffic, causing the traffic to slow down or stop: *Roadworks are causing bottlenecks in the city centre.* **2** a problem that delays progress: *Is there any way of getting round this bureaucratic bottleneck?*

ˈbottle ˌopener noun [C] a device for removing the metal top from a bottle → Compare **corkscrew**

ˈbottle ˌtop noun [C] (US also **ˈbottle ˌcap**) a circular piece of metal used to close a bottle of beer or a FIZZY drink (= one with bubbles)

bottom noun; verb

▸**noun** /ˈbɒt.əm/ (US) /ˈbɑː.t̬əm/ **LOWEST PLACE** ▷ **1** A1 [C usually singular] the lowest part of something: *He stood at the bottom **of** the stairs and called up to me.* ◦ *Extra information will be found at the bottom of the page.* ◦ *The ship had sunk to the bottom of the sea/the sea bottom.* ◦ *At school, Einstein was (at the) bottom of (= the least successful student in) his class.* ◦ *The manager of the hotel started **at the** bottom (= in one of the least important jobs) 30 years ago, as a porter.* ◦ *The rich usually get richer, while the people **at the** bottom (= at the lowest position in society) stay there.* **2 bottoms** [plural] the lower part of a piece of clothing that consists of two parts: *I've found my bikini bottoms but not my top.* ◦ *Have you seen my pyjama/tracksuit bottoms anywhere?* **FARTHEST PART** ▷ **3** B1 [C usually singular] the farthest part of something: UK *They live at the bottom of our street (= the other end of the street from us).* ◦ UK *The apple tree at the bottom (= end) of the garden is beginning to blossom.* **BODY PART** ▷ **4** B1 [C] the part of your body that you sit on: *She slipped and fell on her bottom.*

IDIOMS **at bottom** UK formal in a basic way: *Jealousy is, at bottom, a lack of self-confidence.* • **be at the bottom of sth** to be the real reason for or the cause of something: *The desire for money is at the bottom of much of the world's violence.* • **bottoms up!** informal humorous sometimes said by people in a friendly way just before drinking an alcoholic drink together • **from the bottom of your heart** very sincerely: *When I said I loved you, I **meant** it from the bottom of my heart.* • **get to the bottom of sth** to discover the truth about a situation: *I'm not sure what is causing the problem, but I'm determined to get to the bottom of it.* • **the bottom drops/falls out of the market** If the bottom drops out of the market of a product, people stop buying it: *The bottom has fallen out of the fur coat market.*

▸**verb** /ˌbɒt.əm/ (US) /ˌbɑː.t̬əm/

PHRASAL VERB **bottom out** to have reached the lowest point in a continuously changing situation and to be about to improve: *The government claims that the recession is bottoming out.*

ˌbottom ˈdrawer noun [C usually singular] UK old-fashioned (US **ˈhope ˌchest**) clothes, sheets, etc. that a young woman traditionally collects for use after she is married

bottomless /ˈbɒt.əm.ləs/ (US) /ˈbɑː.t̬əm-/ **adj** without a limit or end: *The generosity of the local people is bottomless.*

ˌbottomless ˈpit noun [C usually singular] something that seems to have no limits, or a situation that will never end: *We'll be pouring money into a bottomless pit if we try to keep that factory open.*

ˌbottom ˈline noun [S] **MONEY** ▷ **1** the final line in the accounts of a company or organization, which states the total profit or loss that has been made: *How will the rise in interest rates affect our bottom line?* **IMPORTANT FACT** ▷ **2 the bottom line** C2 the most important fact in a situation: *The bottom line is that we need another ten thousand dollars to complete the project.*

B

ˌbottom-ˈup adj considering the smaller or less important parts or details of a plan, organization, etc. first: *a bottom-up* ***approach*** *to building a successful company*

botulism /ˈbɒt.jʊ.lɪ.zᵊm/ (US) /ˈbɑː.tʃə-/ noun [U] a serious type of FOOD POISONING caused by bacteria in badly preserved food

boudoir /ˈbuː.dwɑːʳ/ (US) /-wɑːr/ noun [C] a beautifully decorated room used in the past by a woman for sleeping, dressing, relaxing, and entertaining

bouffant /ˈbuː.fɒ̃/ (US) /-fɑːnt/ adj describes a hairstyle in which the hair is arranged in a high rounded shape

bougainvillea /ˌbuː.gᵊnˈvɪl.i.ə/ noun [C or U] a climbing plant, common in hot countries, that has red or purple flowers

bough /baʊ/ noun [C] literary a large branch of a tree

bought /bɔːt/ (US) /bɑːt/ verb past simple and past participle of **buy**

bouillabaisse /ˌbuː.jəˈbes/ noun [C or U] a thick soup made from fish, vegetables, and spices

bouillon /ˈbuː.jɒ̃/ (US) /ˈbʊl.jɑːn/ noun [C or U] a thin, clear soup made by boiling meat and vegetables in water

ˈbouillon ˌcube noun [C] US for **stock cube**

boulder /ˈbəʊl.dəʳ/ (US) /ˈboʊl.dɚ/ noun [C] a very large rock

boules /buːl/ noun [U] a game played especially in France, in which metal balls are thrown so that they land as close as possible to a smaller ball

boulevard /ˈbuː.lə.vɑːd/ (US) /ˈbʊl.ə.vɑːrd/ noun [C] (written abbreviation **Blvd**) a wide road in a city, usually with trees on each side or along the centre

bounce /baʊns/ verb; noun

▸verb **JUMP** ▷ **1** (B1) [I or T] to (cause to) move up or away after hitting a surface: *The ball bounced* ***off*** *the post and into the net.* ◦ *She bounced the ball quickly.* ◦ *Her bag bounced (= moved up and down) against her side as she walked.* ◦ *The children had broken the bed by bouncing (= jumping up and down) on it.* ◦ *He bounced the baby (= lifted it up and down) on his knee.* ◦ figurative *Television pictures from all over the world are bounced* ***off*** *satellites (= are sent to and returned from them).* **2** (B2) [I usually + adv/prep] to move in an energetic and enthusiastic manner: *Tom bounced* ***in****, smiling broadly.* **NOT PAY** ▷ **3** [I or T] informal to (cause a CHEQUE to) not be paid or accepted by a bank because there is no money in the account: *I had to pay a penalty fee when my cheque bounced.* **EMAIL** ▷ **4** (C2) [I or T] If an email that you send bounces or is bounced, it comes back to you because the address is wrong or there is a computer problem.

PHRASAL VERBS **bounce back** (C1) to start to be successful again after a difficult period, for example after experiencing failure, loss of confidence, illness, or unhappiness: *Stock prices bounced back after a steep plunge earlier this week.* ◦ *Children often seem to bounce back* ***from*** *illness more quickly than adults do.* • **bounce sb into sth** UK to force someone to do something that they do not want to do, usually relating to politics: [+ -ing verb] *The opposition hopes to bounce the prime minister into call****ing*** *an early election.* • **bounce sth off sb** If you bounce something off someone, you tell someone about an idea or plan in order to find out what they think of it: *Can I bounce a couple of ideas off you?*

▸noun [C or U] the act of bouncing, or the quality that makes something able to bounce: *In tennis you must hit the ball before its second bounce.* ◦ figurative *This shampoo will give your hair bounce (= make it look attractively thick) and shine.*

IDIOM **on the bounce** informal one after another with nothing else between: *The team has had five wins on the bounce.*

bouncer /ˈbaʊn.səʳ/ (US) /-sɚ/ noun [C] someone whose job is to stand outside a bar, party, etc. and either stop people who cause trouble from coming in or force them to leave

bouncing /ˈbaʊn.sɪŋ/ adj [before noun] (especially of a baby) healthy and energetic: *We've got two grandchildren – a three-year-old girl and a bouncing* ***baby*** *boy.*

bouncy /ˈbaʊn.si/ adj **1** able to bounce: *This ball's not very bouncy.* **2** happy and energetic: *He's always bouncy in the morning.*

bound /baʊnd/ adj; verb; noun

▸adj **CERTAIN** ▷ **1** (B2) [after verb] certain or extremely likely to happen: [+ to infinitive] *You're bound* ***to*** *forget people's names occasionally.* ◦ *You're bound* ***to*** *feel nervous about your interview.* ◦ *These two young musicians are bound* ***for*** *international success (= are certain to be successful).* **2 be bound and determined** US to be seriously intending to do something: *They are bound and determined to build their own house someday.* **3 I'll be bound** UK old-fashioned I am certain: *He's in the pub, I'll be bound.* **FORCED** ▷ **4** [after verb, + to infinitive] having a moral or legal duty to do something: *The company is bound by a special agreement* ***to*** *involve the union in important decisions.* ◦ *She* ***feels*** *(****duty****)-bound* ***to*** *tell him everything.* **FASTENED** ▷ **5** tied with rope, CORD, string, etc.: *We found the girl bound* ***and gagged****.* **6** (of a book) having a cover made of paper, leather, or other material: *The book was bound in shiny green leather.* **DIRECTION** ▷ **7** (C1) [after verb] going to: *She was on a plane bound* ***for*** *Moscow when she became ill.*

▸verb **JUMP** ▷ **1** [I usually + adv/prep] to move quickly with large jumping movements **BORDER** ▷ **2** [T usually passive] to mark or form the limits of: *The village is bounded on one side* ***by*** *a river.* **TIE** ▷ **3** past simple and past participle of **bind**

▸noun **JUMP** ▷ **1** [C] a quick, large jump: *With one bound the dog was over the fence.* **LIMIT** ▷ **2 bounds** [plural] legal or social limits: *The committee felt that newspaper coverage of the murder* ***went beyond*** *reasonable bounds.* ◦ *What you did was* ***beyond/outside the*** *bounds* ***of*** *acceptable behaviour.* ◦ *His desire for political power apparently* ***knows no*** *bounds (= seems to be unlimited).* **3 be out of bounds** If an area is out of bounds, people are not allowed to go there.

-bound /-baʊnd/ suffix **DIRECTION** ▷ **1** travelling in the stated direction: *Northbound traffic is moving very slowly because of the accident.* ◦ US *The line did not close completely, but inbound and outbound trains (= trains which were arriving and leaving) had to share one of the two tracks near the station.* **PREVENTING LEAVING** ▷ **2** (causing people to be) unable to leave a place because of an unwanted condition: *During his long illness he was completely housebound (= he could not leave the house).* ◦ *She has been wheelchair-bound for several years.* ◦ *The airport was completely fogbound (= covered by fog).* **COVERED** ▷ **3** used to describe a book that is covered or held together in the stated way: *a leather-bound book* ◦ *a spiral-bound notebook* **4** used to describe clothes or other objects that have edges covered in the stated way: *leather-bound cuffs*

boundary /ˈbaʊn.dᵊr.i/, /-dri/ (US) /-dɚ-/ noun [C] **1** (C1) a real or imagined line that marks the edge or limit of

B

something: *The Ural mountains mark the boundary **between** Europe and Asia.* ◦ *Residents are opposed to the prison being built **within** the city boundary.* **2** C1 the limit of a subject or principle: *Electronic publishing is **blurring** the boundaries between dictionaries and encyclopedias.*

bounden duty /ˌbaʊn.dᵊnˈdjuː.ti/ US /-ˈduː.t̬i/ **noun** [U] old-fashioned or humorous something that you feel you must do: *She felt that it was her bounden duty to tell the police about the incident.*

bounder /ˈbaʊn.dəʳ/ US /-dɚ/ **noun** [C] old-fashioned a man who behaves badly or in a way that is not moral, especially in his relationships with women

boundless /ˈbaʊnd.ləs/ **adj** having no limit: *boundless optimism* ◦ *She has boundless **energy** and **enthusiasm**.*

ˌbound ˈup **adj** [after verb] C2 closely connected or involved: *The survival of whales is intimately bound up **with** the health of the ocean.*

bountiful /ˈbaʊn.tɪ.fᵊl/ US /-t̬ɪ-/ **adj** literary **1** large in amount: *We found a bountiful **supply** of coconuts on the island.* **2** generous in giving to others: *our bountiful benefactor*

bounty /ˈbaʊn.ti/ US /-t̬i/ **noun** **REWARD** ▷ **1** [C] money paid as a reward: *A bounty of $10,000 has been offered for the capture of his murderer.* **KINDNESS** ▷ **2** [U] literary great kindness or willingness to give: *The charity is totally dependent on the Church's bounty.* **PLENTY** ▷ **3** [C usually singular] a large amount: *a bounty of food*

ˈbounty ˌhunter **noun** [C] someone who searches for criminals or hunts animals in exchange for a reward

bouquet /buˈkeɪ/, /bəʊ-/ US /boʊ-/ **noun** **FLOWERS** ▷ **1** [C] a group of flowers that have been fastened together and attractively arranged so that they can be given as a present or carried on formal occasions: *a bouquet **of** flowers* **SMELL** ▷ **2** [C or U] specialized the characteristic smell of a wine or LIQUEUR: *This wine has a rich, oaky bouquet.*

bouquet

bourbon /ˈbɜː.bᵊn/ US /ˈbɝː-/ **noun** [C or U] a type of American WHISKY

bourgeois /ˈbɔː.ʒwɑː/ US /ˈbʊrʒ-/ **adj** disapproving belonging to or typical of the MIDDLE CLASS (= a social group between the rich and the poor) especially in supporting existing customs and values, or in having a strong interest in money and possessions

the bourgeoisie /ˌbɔː.ʒwɑːˈziː/ US /ˌbʊrʒ-/ **noun** [S, + sing/pl verb] (in Marxism) the part of society, including employers and people who run large companies, that has most of the money and takes advantage of ordinary workers

bourse /bɔːs/ US /bɔːrs/ **noun** [C] specialized a STOCK MARKET, especially one in Europe, not including the UK: *In Brussels, the bourse closed little changed.*

bout /baʊt/ **noun** [C] **SHORT PERIOD** ▷ **1** a short period of illness or involvement in an activity: UK *She had a bout **of** flu over Christmas.* ◦ US *She had a bout **with the** flu recently.* ◦ *He suffered from periodic bouts of insanity.* ◦ *a **drinking** bout (= short period of drinking a lot of alcohol)* **SPORT** ▷ **2** a BOXING or WRESTLING match: *He's a former heavyweight champion and is expected to win the bout easily.*

boutique /buːˈtiːk/ **noun** [C] a small shop that sells fashionable clothes, shoes, jewellery, etc.

bovine /ˈbəʊ.vaɪn/ US /ˈboʊ-/ **adj** **1** specialized connected with cows: *a bovine virus* → See also **BSE** **2** slow or stupid in a way that a cow is thought to be: *He had a gentle, rather bovine expression.*

bovver /ˈbɒv.əʳ/ US /ˈbɑː.vɚ/ **noun** [U] UK informal violent or threatening behaviour

bow¹ /baʊ/ **verb; noun**

▸**verb** [I or T] to bend your head or body forward, especially as a way of showing someone respect or expressing thanks to people who have watched you perform: *They bowed **to** the Queen.* ◦ *We bowed our **heads** in prayer.* ◦ *He bowed **down** (= very low) before (= in front of) the king and begged for mercy.* → Compare **curtsy**

IDIOM **bow and scrape** disapproving to show too much politeness or attention to someone: *It's embarrassing to see staff bowing and scraping to the new director.*

PHRASAL VERBS **bow down to sb** mainly UK to agree to obey someone: *He expects me to bow down to him and do everything he tells me.* • **bow out** to leave a job or stop doing an activity, usually after a long time: *She'll be bowing out at the end of the month, after presenting the programme for eight years.* • **bow to sb/sth** to do what someone else wants you to do, usually unwillingly: *Eventually the government was forced to bow to public **pressure** and reform the tax.*

▸**noun** [C] **BEND** ▷ **1** the movement of bending your head or body forward, especially as a way of showing someone respect or expressing thanks to people who have watched you perform: *The audience applauded enthusiastically, and she came back on stage to **take** another bow.* **FRONT PART** ▷ **2** (also **bows**) the front part of a ship → Compare **stern**

IDIOM **fire a (warning) shot across sb's bow** formal to do something in order to warn someone that you will take strong action if they do not change their behaviour: *Airline staff have fired a warning shot across the company's bows by threatening to strike if higher pay increases are not offered.*

bow² /bəʊ/ US /boʊ/ **noun** [C] **KNOT** ▷ **1** B2 a knot with two curved parts and two loose ends, used as a decoration or to tie shoes: *I tied the ribbon around the parcel in a pretty bow.* **WEAPON** ▷ **2** B2 a weapon for shooting arrows, made of a long, thin piece of wood bent into a curve by a tightly stretched string: *bow **and arrows*** → See also **crossbow** **MUSIC** ▷ **3** C2 a long, thin piece of wood with hair from the tail of a horse stretched along it, used to play musical instruments that have strings: *Violins are played with bows.*

bowdlerize disapproving (UK usually **bowdlerise**) /ˈbaʊd.lə.raɪz/ **verb** [T] to remove words or parts from a book, play, or film that are considered to be unsuitable or offensive

bowed **adj** **1** /bəʊd/ US /boʊd/ curved: *The table had delicate bowed legs.* **2** /baʊd/ bent over: *He struggled along the path, bowed **under** the weight of the heavy bags he was carrying.*

bowel /ˈbaʊ.ᵊl/, /baʊəl/ **noun** [C usually plural] **1** the long tube that carries solid waste from the stomach out of the body: *He has trouble with his bowels.* ◦ *bowel cancer/cancer of the bowel* **2** **move your bowels** (said especially by doctors and nurses) to EXCRETE (= pass from the body) the solid waste that is contained in the bowels

IDIOM **the bowels of sth** the parts of something that are furthest away from the outside: *The fire started deep in the bowels of the ship.*

ˈbowel ˌmovement **noun** [C] (abbreviation **BM**) (used especially by doctors and nurses) the act of emptying the contents of the bowels, or the material that is emptied

bower /ˈbaʊ.əʳ/ (US) /-ɚ/ **noun** [C] literary a pleasant place under the branches of a tree in a wood or garden

bowl /bəʊl/ (US) /boʊl/ **noun; verb**

▸**noun** DISH ▷ **1** (A2) [C] a round container that is open at the top and is deep enough to hold fruit, sugar, etc.: *a soup/cereal/salad/sugar bowl* ◦ *a bowl of soup/ rice/porridge* ◦ *She eats a bowl (= the contents of a bowl)* ***of*** *cereal every morning.* ◦ *Sift the flour and baking powder into a* ***mixing*** *bowl.* ◦ UK *Just put the dirty dishes in the* ***washing-up*** *bowl, and I'll do them later.* **2** [C] the rounded inside part of something: *The* ***toilet*** *bowl was cracked and stained, and the walls were covered in mould.* **3** [C] mainly US a large bowl-shaped building or structure, used for important sports events or musical performances: *the Hollywood Bowl* GAME ▷ **4 bowls** [U] a game played either outside on smooth grass or inside on an artificial surface, in which the players roll a large black or brown ball as close as possible to a smaller white ball: *Bowls is one of the most popular sports in the UK.* **5** [C] a large ball used in the game of bowls

▸**verb** [I or T] CRICKET ▷ **1** to throw a ball towards a BATSMAN (= the player who hits the ball) using a vertical circular movement of the arm while running: *Pringle was tired after bowling for an hour.* ROLL ▷ **2** to roll a ball along a smooth grass or artificial surface during a game of bowls

PHRASAL VERBS **bowl down/along sth** to go quickly: *They bowled down the street on their new bicycles.* • **bowl sb out** in the game of cricket, to make someone have to leave the cricket field by hitting the WICKET (= three vertical sticks) behind them with the ball • **bowl sb over** [usually passive] KNOCK DOWN ▷ **1** to knock someone to the ground by running into them: *She was almost bowled over by a huge dog.* PLEASE ▷ **2** to surprise and please someone a lot: *She was bowled over when she heard she'd won the competition.*

bow-legged /ˈbəʊ.legd/, /-legɪd/ (US) /ˈboʊ-/ **adj** A bow-legged person has legs that curve out at the knees.

bowler /ˈbəʊ.ləʳ/ (US) /ˈboʊ.lɚ/ **noun** [C] PERSON ▷ **1** someone who bowls (= throws the ball), especially in cricket **2 fast/pace bowler** a bowler who bowls the ball fast: *It isn't easy to score runs against pace bowlers.* **3 spin bowler** a bowler who spins the ball so that when it hits the ground it BOUNCES in an unexpected way, making it difficult to hit HAT ▷ **4** a **bowler hat**

ˌbowler ˈhat noun (also **bowler**, US also **derby**) a man's hat that is black and has a round, hard top • **ˌbowler-ˈhatted adj** [before noun] UK describes a person wearing a bowler hat: *The bowler-hatted British businessman is not a common sight any more.*

bowling /ˈbəʊ.lɪŋ/ (US) /ˈboʊ-/ **noun** [U] CRICKET ▷ **1** (the part of the game) when you bowl the ball in cricket: *The England captain* ***opened the*** *bowling (= bowled first).* ROLL ▷ **2** (UK also **tenpin bowling**) a game played inside, in which you roll a heavy ball down a track to try to knock down a group of PINS (= tall, thin wooden objects)

ˈbowling ˌalley noun [C] a building in which you can go bowling, or the narrow track along which balls are rolled during a bowling game

ˈbowling ˌball noun [C] a large, heavy ball with three holes for your fingers, used in the sport of bowling

ˈbowling ˌgreen noun [C] an area of very short, smooth grass where you can play BOWLS

bow tie /ˌbəʊˈtaɪ/ (US) /ˌboʊ-/ **noun** [C] a special type of TIE (= a strip of cloth put around a collar) in the shape of a BOW, worn especially by men on formal occasions

bow window /ˌbəʊˈwɪn.dəʊ/ (US) /ˌboʊˈwɪn.doʊ/ **noun** [C] a curved window that sticks out from the wall of a house

bow-wow noun; exclamation

▸**noun** [C] /ˈbaʊ.waʊ/ child's word a dog

▸**exclamation** /ˌbaʊˈwaʊ/ child's word the sound that a dog makes

box /bɒks/ (US) /bɑːks/ **noun; verb**

▸**noun** CONTAINER ▷ **1** (A1) [C] a square or rectangular container with stiff sides and sometimes a lid: *a cardboard box* ◦ *a cigar box* ◦ *a matchbox* **2** (A1) [C] a box and its contents, or just the contents of a box: *a box of matches* ◦ *He ate a whole box of chocolates.* **3** [C] UK (US **cup**) a piece of hard plastic worn by men to protect their sex organs when playing sport SQUARE SPACE ▷ **4** (A2) [C] any square or rectangular space on a form, sports field, road, etc., separated from the main area by lines: *If you would like more information, mark this box.* **5** [C] US for **box junction** **6** [C] a small space with walls: *a jury/phone box* ◦ *Their new house is just a box (= very small).* **7** [C] a small area with seats that is separate from the other seats in a theatre or at the side of a sports field: *Can you see Prince Charles in the* ***royal*** *box?* TELEVISION ▷ **8 the box** [S] UK informal television: *There's nothing worth watching* ***on*** *the box tonight.* ADDRESS ▷ **9** [C] (also **ˈbox ˌnumber**) a number that you can give instead of your address, especially in newspaper advertisements: *Please reply to Box 307, The Times, London.* TREE ▷ **10** [U] a small EVERGREEN tree (= one that never loses its leaves) with small, shiny leaves → See also **boxwood**

▸**verb** SPORT ▷ **1** [I or T] to fight someone in the sport of BOXING: *He used to box every weekend.* ◦ *I've boxed (****against****) some of the best.* PUT IN CONTAINER ▷ **2** [T] (also **box up**) to put something in a box: *Should I box these shoes up for you, or would you like to wear them now?*

IDIOM **box sb's ears** (UK also **give sb a box on the ears**) to hit someone on the ears, usually as a punishment

PHRASAL VERBS **box sb/sth in** [M often passive] to move so close to someone or something that they cannot move away: *When I got back to my car, I found it had been boxed in by a lorry.* • **box sb in** [M often passive] to prevent someone from doing what they want to do: *She did not want to send her son to a school where he would be boxed in by so many rules and regulations.*

boxcar /ˈbɒks.kɑːʳ/ (US) /ˈbɑːks.kɑːr/ **noun** [C] US a railway CARRIAGE with a roof, used for carrying goods

boxer /ˈbɒk.səʳ/ (US) /ˈbɑːk.sɚ/ **noun** [C] SPORTSPERSON ▷ **1** someone who takes part in the sport of BOXING: *He was a* ***heavyweight*** *boxer before he became an actor.* DOG ▷ **2** a dog of medium size with short, light brown hair and a short, flat nose

ˈboxer ˌshorts noun [plural] (also **boxers**) men's underwear that fits loosely and is similar to short trousers

boxing /ˈbɒk.sɪŋ/ (US) /ˈbɑːk-/ **noun** [U] (B1) a sport in which two competitors fight by hitting each other with their hands: *He's a former world heavyweight boxing champion.*

ˈBoxing ˌDay noun [C or U] in the UK, the day after Christmas Day

ˈboxing ˌgloves noun [plural] a pair of large, thick

hand coverings that are worn for protection when boxing

ˈboxing ˌring noun [C usually singular] a limited area where boxing takes place

ˈbox ˌjunction noun [C] UK (US **box**) a place where two roads cross with a square of yellow lines painted in the centre, which you can drive over only when the road in front is clear

ˈbox ˌlunch noun [C] (also ˈ**bag** ˌ**lunch**) US for **packed lunch**

ˈbox ˌoffice noun **1** [C] the place in a theatre or cinema where tickets are sold: *The box office opens at ten.* **2** [S or U] a measure of how popular and financially successful a film or actor is: *Her last film was a surprise box-office* ***hit***.

boxroom /ˈbɒks.ruːm/, /-rʊm/ (US) /bɑːks-/ noun [C] UK a small room in a house used for storing large objects such as cases and furniture

ˈbox ˌspanner noun [C] UK (US ˈ**box** ˌ**wrench**) a metal tool with a six-sided end that is used for tightening NUTS

ˈbox ˌspring noun [C] a spring or set of springs fastened to a frame and covered in cloth, for supporting a bed

boxwood /ˈbɒks.wʊd/ (US) /ˈbɑːks-/ noun [U] a hard wood which comes from a BOX tree: *Boxwood is used for making small carved objects and tool handles.*

boxy /ˈbɒk.si/ (US) /ˈbɑːk-/ adj disapproving shaped like a box: *The trouble with many small houses is that they tend to be boxy.*

boy /bɔɪ/ noun; exclamation

▸noun [C] **1** (A1) a male child or, more generally, a male of any age: *a teenage/adolescent boy* ◦ *As a young boy, my father used to walk three miles to school.* ◦ *You've been a very naughty boy!* ◦ *Their little boy (= their young son) is very sick.* ◦ *All right, boys* ***and girls***, *quiet down!* **2 the boys** (B2) [plural] **a** a group of male friends: *He used to like spending Friday nights with the boys.* **b** (also **our boys**) an approving way of speaking about your country's soldiers: *We must not forget our boys serving far from home.* **3 one of the boys** a typical male: *He plays football, drinks a lot of beer and generally acts like one of the boys.*

IDIOMS **boys will be boys** saying said to emphasize that people should not be surprised when boys or men act in a rough or noisy way because this is part of the male character • **my (dear) boy** UK old-fashioned a friendly way of talking to a man: *Look here, my boy, this simply won't do.* • **the boys in blue** informal a humorous name for the police

▸exclamation (also **oh boy**) mainly US informal used to express excitement or to emphasize something: *Boy, that was good!*

ˈboy ˌband noun [C] a pop music group made up of young men who sing and dance

boycott /ˈbɔɪ.kɒt/ (US) /-kɑːt/ verb [T] to refuse to buy a product or take part in an activity as a way of expressing strong disapproval: *People were urged to boycott the country's products.* ◦ *The union called on its members to boycott the meeting.* • **boycott** noun [C] *A boycott* ***of/against*** *goods from the EU began in June.*

boyfriend /ˈbɔɪ.frend/ noun [C] (A2) a man or boy who a person is having a romantic or sexual relationship with: *He's not my boyfriend – we're just good friends!* ◦ *Cathy's* ***ex-****boyfriend was a really nice guy.* → Compare **girlfriend**

boyhood /ˈbɔɪ.hʊd/ noun [C or U] the period when a person is a boy, and not yet a man, or the state of being a boy: *I had a very happy boyhood.* ◦ *The transition from boyhood to manhood can be a confusing period.* ◦ *It was his boyhood ambition/dream to become a film director.* ◦ *James Bond was a boyhood hero of mine.* → See also **childhood, girlhood**

boyish /ˈbɔɪ.ɪʃ/ adj describes behaviour or characteristics that are like those of a boy: *a boyish grin* ◦ *She had her hair cut in a boyish style.* ◦ *Even as an old man he retained his boyish* ***charm***. ◦ *She found his boyish* ***good looks*** *very attractive.* • **boyishly** /-li/ adv *He is still boyishly handsome at the age of 45.*

ˌboy-meets-ˈgirl adj [before noun] relating to a story, book, or film whose main subject is romantic relationships: *It was the usual boy-meets-girl sort of film.*

ˌBoy ˈScout noun [C] old-fashioned or US for a member of the SCOUTS

ˈboy ˌtoy noun [C] US informal an attractive young man, especially one who has relationships with older, powerful, or successful people → See also **toy boy**

ˌboy ˈwonder noun [C] a young man who has achieved more than what is expected for his age

bozo /ˈbəʊ.zəʊ/ (US) /ˈboʊ.zoʊ/ noun [C] (plural **bozos**) mainly US slang a stupid person

bra /brɑː/ noun [C] (formal **brassiere**) (B2) a piece of women's underwear that supports the breasts

braai /braɪ/ noun [C] South African English a meal prepared on a BARBECUE (= a metal frame for cooking over a fire) and eaten outside → Compare **barbecue**

brace /breɪs/ noun; verb

▸noun SUPPORT ▷ **1** [C] (plural **braces**) something that connects, fastens, makes stronger, or supports: *I had to wear a brace (US usually* ***braces****) for my crooked teeth when I was a teenager.* ◦ *He was recently fitted with a brace for his bad back.* **2 braces** [plural] **a** UK (US **suspenders**) a pair of narrow straps which stretch from the front of the trousers over your shoulders to the back to hold them up: *a pair of braces* **b** US **calipers** PAIR ▷ **3** [C] (plural **brace**) two things of the same type, especially two wild birds that have been killed for sport or food: *a brace* ***of*** *pheasants*

▸verb [T] SUPPORT ▷ **1** to support an object in order to stop it from falling down: *The side wall of the old house was braced* ***with*** *a wooden support.* PREPARE ▷ **2 brace yourself** to prepare yourself physically or mentally for something unpleasant: *The passengers were told to brace themselves (= to press their bodies hard against something or hold them very stiff)* ***for*** *a crash landing.* ◦ *She told me she had some bad news for me and I braced myself* ***for*** *a shock.*

bracelet /ˈbreɪ.slət/ noun [C] (A2) a piece of jewellery that is worn around the wrist or arm: *a gold/silver/diamond bracelet* ◦ *a chain bracelet*

bracing /ˈbreɪ.sɪŋ/ adj (especially of air or an activity) healthy and fresh: *We enjoyed a bracing walk on the beach.*

bracken /ˈbræk.ən/ noun [U] a large FERN (= a type of plant) that grows thickly in open areas of countryside, especially on hills, and in woods

bracket /ˈbræk.ɪt/ noun; verb

▸noun SYMBOL ▷ **1** (B2) [C usually plural] either of two symbols put around a word, phrase, or sentence in a piece of writing to show that what is between them should be considered as separate from the main part: *Biographical information is included* ***in*** *brackets.* GROUP ▷ **2** (C1) [C] a set group with fixed upper and lower limits: *They were both surgeons in a high* ***income*** *bracket.* ◦ *Most British university students are in the 18–22* ***age*** *bracket.* SUPPORT ▷ **3** [C] a piece of metal, wood, or plastic, usually L-shaped, that is fastened to a wall and used to support something such as a shelf

B

▸verb [T] USE SYMBOL ▷ **1** to put brackets around words, phrases, numbers, etc.: *I've bracketed the bits of text that could be omitted.* PUT IN GROUP ▷ **2** If you bracket two or more things or people, you consider them to be similar or connected to each other: *He's often bracketed **with** the romantic poets of this period although this does not reflect the range of his work.*

brackish /ˈbræk.ɪʃ/ adj Brackish water is salty, dirty, and unpleasant.

bract /brækt/ noun [C] specialized a type of leaf that grows from the area just below a flower and is sometimes different in shape or colour from the main leaves: *Poinsettias are popular for their attractive red bracts.*

bradawl /ˈbræd.ɔːl/ (US) /-ɑːl/ noun [C] a small, sharp tool used for making holes

brag /bræɡ/ verb [I] (-gg-) informal disapproving to speak too proudly about what you have done or what you own: *She's always bragging **about** how much money she earns.* ◦ [+ that] *They bragged **that** their team had never been beaten.*

braggart /ˈbræɡ.ət/ (US) /-ɚt/ noun [C] old-fashioned disapproving someone who proudly talks a lot about themselves and their achievements or possessions

Brahman (also **Brahmin**) /ˈbrɑː.mən/ noun [C] a member of the highest Hindu CASTE (= social group): *Brahmans traditionally become priests in the Hindu religion.*

braid /breɪd/ noun; verb

▸noun CLOTH ▷ **1** [U] (also **braiding**) a thin strip of cloth or twisted threads that is fixed onto clothes, uniforms, or other things made of cloth, as a decoration: *The captain of the ship wore a peaked cap decorated with **gold** braid (= twisted gold threads).* HAIR ▷ **2** [C] US for **plait**

▸verb [I or T] US for **plait**

Braille /breɪl/ noun [U] a system of printing for blind people, in which each letter is represented as a raised pattern that can be read by touching it with the fingers: *The book has been printed in six languages and in Braille.*

brain /breɪn/ noun; verb

▸noun **1** A2 [C] the organ inside the head that controls thought, memory, feelings, and activity: *Doctors tried desperately to reduce the swelling in her brain.* ◦ *The accident left him with permanent brain **damage**.* ◦ *His wife died from a brain **tumour**.* **2** C1 [C] used to refer to intelligence: *Marie has an amazing brain (= is very intelligent).* ◦ *That can't possibly be the right way to do it – **use** your brain!* ◦ *The poor child inherited his mother's brains and his father's looks.* ◦ *He's got brains but he's too lazy to use them (= he is clever but lazy).* **3** [C usually plural] informal a very intelligent person, especially one who has spent a lot of time studying: *We've got the best brains in the land working on this problem.* **4 the brains** [S] the cleverest person of a group, especially the person who plans what the group will do: *My little brother's the brains **of** the family.*

IDIOM **have sth on the brain** informal disapproving to not be able to stop thinking or talking about one particular thing: *You've got cars on the brain. Can't we talk about something else for a change?*

▸verb [T] informal to hit someone on the head: *I'll brain you if you don't keep quiet.*

brainchild /ˈbreɪn.tʃaɪld/ noun [S] a clever and original idea, plan, or INVENTION: *The project was the brainchild of one of the students.*

ˈbrain-dead adj **1** If someone is brain-dead, they have serious and permanent damage to their brain, and need machines in order to stay alive. **2** humorous If someone is brain-dead, their mind is not working effectively, usually because they are very tired or very bored: *By the time I leave work I'm completely brain-dead.*

ˈbrain ˌdeath noun [U] the situation in which a person's brain stops working and they need machines in order to stay alive

ˈbrain ˌdrain noun [S] the situation in which large numbers of educated and very skilled people leave their own country to live and work in another one where pay and conditions are better: *Britain has suffered a huge brain drain in recent years.*

-brained /-breɪnd/ suffix **1** having a particular type of brain: *These dinosaurs were large-brained and more intelligent than most.* **2** disapproving used in various phrases to describe someone as stupid or badly organized: *bird-brained* ◦ *harebrained* ◦ *scatterbrained*

brainless /ˈbreɪn.ləs/ adj informal stupid: *What sort of brainless idiot would do that?*

brainpower /ˈbreɪnpaʊəʳ/ (US) /ˈbreɪnpaʊɚ/ noun [U] informal your intelligence or your ability to think

brainstorm /ˈbreɪn.stɔːm/ (US) /-stɔːrm/ verb; noun

▸verb [I or T] (of a group of people) to suggest a lot of ideas for a future activity very quickly before considering some of them more carefully: *The team got together to brainstorm (the project).*

▸noun [C] **1** UK informal a sudden state of being unable to think clearly: *I must have **had** a brainstorm – I went shopping and forgot to take any money.* **2** US for **brainwave**

brainstorming /ˈbreɪnˌstɔː.mɪŋ/ (US) /-ˌstɔːr-/ noun [U] an activity or business method in which a group of people meet to suggest a lot of new ideas for possible development: *We need to do some brainstorming before we get down to detailed planning.* ◦ *We're having a brainstorming **session** on Friday.*

brainteaser /ˈbreɪnˌtiː.zəʳ/ (US) /-zɚ/ noun [C] (also **teaser**) a problem for which it is hard to find the answer, especially one which people enjoy trying to solve as a game: *The paper publishes two brainteasers every Saturday.*

ˈbrain ˌtrust noun [C] US (UK **ˈbrains ˌtrust**) a group of people who advise a leader: *The candidate's brain trust is gathering this weekend to plan strategy for the primary election.*

brainwash /ˈbreɪn.wɒʃ/ (US) /-wɑːʃ/ verb [T] disapproving to make someone believe something by repeatedly telling them that it is true and preventing any other information from reaching them: *The government is trying to brainwash them **into** think**ing** that war is necessary.* • **brainwashing** /-ɪŋ/ noun [U] *Many people thought the sect was guilty of brainwashing.*

brainwave /ˈbreɪn.weɪv/ noun [C] UK informal IDEA ▷ **1** (US **brainstorm**) a sudden clever idea: *I couldn't see how I could get home from the station – then I **had a** brainwave.* PATTERN ▷ **2** any of several patterns of electrical activity in the brain

brainy /ˈbreɪ.ni/ adj informal clever

braise /breɪz/ verb [T] to cook food slowly in a covered dish in a little fat and liquid: *braised celery*

ˈbraising ˌsteak noun [U] UK meat from CATTLE that is usually cut into small pieces and cooked slowly in liquid

brake /breɪk/ noun; verb

▸noun [C] **1** B1 a device that makes a vehicle go slower or stop, or a PEDAL, bar, or handle which makes this device work: *She had no brakes on her bicycle.* ◦ *The* *driver suddenly* ***applied*** *(US* ***put on****) his brakes.* ◦ informal *I* ***slammed on*** *(= quickly used) the brake, but it was too late.* ◦ *All our new models have* ***anti-lock*** *brakes.* **2 screech/squeal of brakes** the loud, unpleasant noise of a car suddenly stopping: *Suddenly we heard a screech of brakes and saw the car swerve to miss the cyclist.*

B

IDIOM **put a brake on** (also **put the brakes on**) to slow down or stop an activity: *The government has put a brake on further spending.*

▸**verb** [I] B2 to make a vehicle go slower or stop, using its brake: *When it's icy, brake* ***gently****.* ◦ *He would zoom up to junctions and brake hard/sharply at the last minute.*

ˈbrake ˌblock noun [C] UK (US **ˈbrake ˌpad**) one of the two rectangular pieces of rubber that press against the wheels of a bicycle to reduce their speed when the brakes are used

ˈbrake ˌcable noun [C] one of the wires on a bicycle which connect the part of the brake that you operate with your hand to the part that stops the wheel

ˈbrake ˌlight noun [C] one of the red lights at the back of a motor vehicle, that light up when the brakes are used

ˈbrake ˌpedal noun [C] the PEDAL which you push down with your foot to make a vehicle slow down or stop

bramble /ˈbræm.bl̩/ **noun 1** [C or U] a wild bush with THORNS, that produces BLACKBERRIES: *We carefully pushed our way through the low brambles.* **2** [C] UK a **blackberry**: *We stopped to pick brambles by the side of the road.* ◦ *bramble jam* **3** [C] US any wild bush with THORNS

bran /bræn/ **noun** [U] the outer covering of grain that is separated when making white flour. Bran is added to other foods because it contains a lot of the FIBRE needed for a healthy body: *wheat/oat bran* ◦ *Both these breakfast cereals have added bran.*

branch /brɑːntʃ/ US /bræntʃ/ **noun; verb**

▸**noun** [C] **PART** ▷ **1** B2 a part of something larger: *Immunology is a branch* ***of*** *biological science.* ◦ *One branch* ***of*** *their family (= one group of relatives) emigrated to Brazil.* ◦ *In the US, the president is part of the executive branch of the government.* **2** B1 one of the offices or groups that form part of a large business organization: *I used to work in the* ***local*** *branch* ***of*** *a large bank.* ◦ *She's a branch* ***manager****.* ◦ *Take the forms into your local branch* ***office****.* **TREE PART** ▷ **3** B1 one of the parts of a tree that grows out from the main TRUNK and has leaves, flowers, or fruit on it: *bare/leafy/flowering branches* ◦ *The fruit on the lower branches was protected from the sun.* ◦ *Watch out for* ***overhanging*** *branches.* **RIVER/ROAD** ▷ **4** a part of a river or road that leaves the main part: *This branch of the river eventually empties into the Atlantic.*

▸**verb** [I] **TREE** ▷ **1** to produce branches: *The top of the tree had been cut off to encourage it to branch (****out****) lower down.* **SPLIT** ▷ **2** to divide into two: *The road branches at the bottom of the hill.*

PHRASAL VERBS **branch off** If a road or path branches off, it goes in another direction: *We drove down a narrow track that branched off* ***from*** *the main road.* • **branch off sth** to leave a main road by turning into a smaller road: *We branched off the main route and went through the countryside.* • **branch out** to start to do something different from what you usually do, especially in your job: *This designer has recently branched out* ***into*** *children's wear.* ◦ *After a couple of years working for other people, she branched out* ***on*** *her* ***own*** *(= started her own business).*

ˈbranch ˌline noun [C] a railway that goes from the main railway to small towns and countryside areas

brand /brænd/ **noun; verb**

▸**noun** [C] **PRODUCT** ▷ **1** B2 a type of product made by a particular company: *This isn't my usual brand* ***of*** *deodorant.* ◦ *When I go to a supermarket I usually buy* ***own*** *(US* ***store****) brands (= the cheaper products with the shop's own name on them).* **2 brand of sth** a particular type of something, or way of doing something: *a team that plays a distinctive brand of football* ◦ *Do you like his brand of humour?* **FLAME** ▷ **3** literary a piece of burning wood used to give light **MARK** ▷ **4** a mark that is burned or frozen into the skin of an animal such as a cow to show who owns it: *The brand was still visible on the animal's hide.*

▸**verb JUDGE** ▷ **1** [T + obj + noun/adj] to say that you think someone is as stated: *Because of one minor offence he was branded (****as****) a common criminal.* ◦ *The newspapers have branded the rebel MP disloyal.* **MARK** ▷ **2** [T] to mark an animal such as a cow by burning or freezing its skin to show you own it: *The cattle were rounded up and branded.*

branding /ˈbræn.dɪŋ/ **noun** [U] the act of giving a company a particular design or symbol in order to advertise its products and services

ˈbranding ˌiron noun [C] a long piece of metal with a special design at one end, used to burn an owner's mark on the skin of animals such as cows and horses

brandish /ˈbræn.dɪʃ/ **verb** [T] to wave something in the air in a threatening or excited way: *She brandished a saucepan* ***at*** *me so I ran out of the kitchen.*

ˈbrand ˌname noun [C] the name given to a particular product by the company that makes it

ˌbrand ˈnew adj B1 completely new, especially not yet used: *How can he afford to buy himself a brand new car?* ◦ *His coat looked as if it was brand new.*

brandy /ˈbræn.di/ **noun** [C or U] a strong alcoholic drink made from wine and sometimes flavoured with fruits

ˌbrandy ˈbutter noun [U] a sweet food made of sugar, butter, and brandy, served especially at Christmas in the UK and Ireland on CHRISTMAS PUDDING and MINCE PIES

ˈbrandy ˌsnap noun [C] mainly UK a thin, hard biscuit that is rolled into a tube

brash /bræʃ/ **adj** disapproving **1** (of people) showing too much confidence and too little respect: *a brash young banker* **2** (of clothes) too bright and colourful: *Don't you think that suit's a bit brash for a funeral?* • **brashness** /ˈbræʃ.nəs/ **noun** [U]

brass /brɑːs/ US /bræs/ **noun; adj**

▸**noun METAL** ▷ **1** C1 [U] a bright yellow metal made from COPPER and ZINC: *The door handles were made of brass.* **2** [C] a thin piece of brass on the floor or wall in a church, with a picture or writing cut into it: *The church has several beautiful medieval brasses.* **3 the brass** C2 [S] the group of brass instruments or players in a BAND or ORCHESTRA: *The brass seems to me too loud in this recording.* **CONFIDENCE** ▷ **4** [U] UK informal complete confidence and lack of fear: *I don't know how she* ***has the*** *brass* ***to*** *do it.* **MONEY** ▷ **5** [U] UK old-fashioned informal money

IDIOMS **brass monkey weather** UK informal extremely cold weather • **get down to brass tacks** to start talking about the most important or basic facts of a situation: *Let's get down to brass tacks. Who's paying for all this?*

▸adj [before noun] (of a musical instrument) made of metal and played by blowing: *The trumpet and trombone are brass* ***instruments***. ◦ *He plays in the brass* ***section*** *of the orchestra.* → Compare **percussion, woodwind**

ˌbrass ˈband noun [C] a BAND (= group of musicians) in which most of the musical instruments are made of brass

ˌbrassed ˈoff adj [after verb] UK informal annoyed and bored: *I'm getting a bit brassed off* ***with*** *his attitude.*

brasserie /ˈbræs.ə.ri/ (US) /ˌbræs.əˈriː/ noun [C] a French-style restaurant that serves cheap and simple food

brassiere /ˈbræz.i.eəʳ/ (US) /brəˈzɪr/ noun [C] formal for **bra**

ˌbrass ˈknuckles noun [plural] US for **knuckleduster**

ˌbrass ˈneck noun [S or U] UK informal disapproving If someone has (a) brass neck, they are extremely confident about themselves and are unable to understand that their behaviour is unacceptable to others: *She's got* ***a*** *brass neck* ***to*** *ask for a day off when we're so busy.*

ˈbrass ˌrubbing noun [C or U] the activity of putting a sheet of paper on top of a BRASS in a church, and rubbing it with a special pencil to make a picture, or a picture that is made in this way

brassy /ˈbrɑː.si/ (US) /ˈbræs.i/ adj **METAL** ▷ **1** like BRASS in colour, or too bright: *a brassy yellow* **SOUND** ▷ **2** disapproving loud and unpleasant: *Her brassy voice rang out from the next room.* **CONFIDENT** ▷ **3** disapproving describes a woman who speaks and laughs too loudly and who dresses in bright, cheap clothes, often wearing too much make-up: *She was your typical brassy blonde.*

brat /bræt/ noun [C] informal disapproving a child, especially one who behaves badly: *She's behaving like a* ***spoilt*** *(US* ***spoiled****) brat.*

bravado /brəˈvɑː.dəʊ/ (US) /-doʊ/ noun [U] a show of courage, especially when unnecessary and dangerous, to make people admire you: *It was an* ***act of*** *bravado that made him ask his boss to resign.*

brave /breɪv/ adj; verb; noun

▸adj (B1) showing no fear of dangerous or difficult things: *a brave soldier* ◦ *It was a brave decision to quit her job and start her own business.* ◦ *She was very brave* ***to*** *learn to ski at 50.* ◦ *Of the three organizations criticized, only one was brave* ***enough to*** *face the press.* ◦ *Richards has made a brave* ***attempt*** *to answer his critics.* ◦ *This action will cause problems, despite the bank's brave* ***talk/words*** *about carrying on as if nothing had happened.* • **bravely** /ˈbreɪv.li/ adv (B1) *She faced the consequences bravely.*

IDIOM **put on a brave face** (also **put a brave face on it**) to behave as if a problem is not important or does not worry you: *She seems all right but I suspect she's just putting on a brave face.*

▸verb [T] to deal with an unpleasant or difficult situation: *Shall we brave the snow and go for a walk (= go for a walk although it is snowing)?* ◦ literary *She braved the wrath of her parents by refusing to marry the man they had chosen.*

▸noun [C] old-fashioned a young Native American WARRIOR (= fighting man). This word is usually considered offensive.

bravery /ˈbreɪ.vᵊr.i/ (US) /-vɚ-/ noun [U] (B2) brave behaviour or actions: *They were awarded medals for their bravery.* ◦ *acts of exceptional bravery*

bravo /ˌbrɑːˈvəʊ/ (US) /ˈbrɑː.voʊ/ exclamation used to express your pleasure when someone, especially a performer, has done something well

Other ways of saying brave

A common alternative to 'brave' is the word **courageous**:

She was a ***courageous*** *woman who never complained about her illness.*

It was a ***courageous*** *decision to leave and start a new life in Australia.*

If someone is brave because he or she is not afraid of taking risks, you can use the adjectives **daring** or **bold**:

He made a ***daring*** *escape from his kidnappers.*

I wasn't ***bold*** *enough to leave my job.*

Someone who is brave because he or she is willing to try things that might be dangerous can be described as **adventurous**:

She's a very ***adventurous*** *person and enjoys mountain climbing.*

If someone is so brave that people admire what he or she has done, the adjective **heroic** can be used:

He made a ***heroic*** *attempt to rescue his neighbour from the fire.*

The word **valiant** can be used when someone does something that is brave when there is not much hope of succeeding:

He made a ***valiant*** *attempt to finish the race but the pain was too much.*

The adjectives **gutsy**, **plucky**, or the phrase **have guts** can be used in informal situations to describe someone who is brave:

In the movie she plays a ***gutsy*** *mother of six.*

She's a ***plucky*** *little girl who refuses to let her disability ruin her life.*

I didn't ***have the guts*** *to go on my own.*

bravura /brəˈvjʊə.rə/ (US) /-ˈvjʊr.ə/ noun [U] impressive technical skill that is shown in an artistic performance or work: *He gave a bravura* ***performance.***

brawl /brɔːl/ (US) /brɑːl/ noun; verb

▸noun [C] a noisy, rough, uncontrolled fight: *a* ***drunken*** *brawl*

▸verb [I] to fight in a rough, noisy, uncontrolled way: *The young men had nothing better to do than brawl in the streets.*

brawn /brɔːn/ (US) /brɑːn/ noun [U] **STRENGTH** ▷ **1** physical strength and big muscles: *She said she preferred brawn to brains (= a man who is physically attractive rather than a clever one).* **FOOD** ▷ **2** UK meat from the head of a pig, cooked, and pressed into a block • **brawny** /ˈbrɔː.ni/ (US) /ˈbrɑː-/ adj

bray /breɪ/ verb [I] to make a loud, unpleasant noise: *The mules suddenly started braying.* ◦ *She had a loud, braying laugh.*

brazen /ˈbreɪ.zᵊn/ adj; verb

▸adj obvious, without any attempt to be hidden: *There were instances of brazen cheating in the exams.* ◦ *He told me a brazen* ***lie.*** • **brazenly** /-li/ adv

▸verb

PHRASAL VERB **brazen sth out** to act confidently and not admit that a problem exists: *I decided to brazen* ***it*** *out and hoped they wouldn't notice the scratch on the car.*

brazier /ˈbreɪ.zi.əʳ/ (US) /-ʒ.ɚ/ noun [C] a metal container for burning coal, wood, etc., used outside, to give warmth or to cook on

Brazil nut /brəˈzɪl ˌnʌt/ noun **1** [C] a large curved nut, which grows in a hard three-sided shell **2** [C or U] (also **Brazil nut tree**) a South American tree that produces a large, dry fruit filled with large three-sided nuts

B

brb written abbreviation for be right back: used when you stop taking part in a discussion in an internet CHAT ROOM for a short time

breach /briːtʃ/ noun; verb

▸noun [C] **BROKEN PROMISE/RULE** ▷ **1** an act of breaking a law, promise, agreement, or relationship: *They felt that our discussions with other companies constituted a breach **of/in** our agreement.* ◦ *He was sued for breach **of contract**.* ◦ *There have been serious **security** breaches (= breaks in our security system).* **2 (a) breach of the peace** legal (an example of) illegal noisy or violent behaviour in a public place **3 be in breach of sth** formal to be breaking a particular law or rule: *The cinema was in breach of the Health and Safety Act for having no fire doors.* **OPENING** ▷ **4** formal a hole that is made in a wall or another structure used for protection during an attack: *A cannon ball had made a breach in their castle walls.*

▸verb [T] formal **BREAK PROMISE/RULE** ▷ **1** to break a law, promise, agreement, or relationship: *They breached the agreement they had made with their employer.* **MAKE OPENING** ▷ **2** to make an opening in a wall or fence, especially in order to attack someone or something behind it: *Their defences were easily breached.*

bread /bred/ noun [U] **A1** a food made from flour, water, and usually YEAST, mixed together and baked: *a **slice of** bread* ◦ *a **loaf of** bread* ◦ ***white/brown** bread* ◦ ***wholemeal** (US **whole wheat**) bread* ◦ ***sliced** bread* ◦ *This bread is **fresh/stale**.* ◦ *Do you **bake** your own bread?*

IDIOMS **(your) (daily) bread** the money that you need so that you can pay for food, clothes, and other ordinary needs: *He **earns** his daily bread as a tourist guide.* • **bread and circuses** literary activities or official plans that are intended to keep people happy and to stop them from noticing or complaining about problems • **man cannot live by bread alone** saying used to say that people need not just food, but also poetry, art, music, etc. to live happily

ˌbread and ˈbutter noun [U] **your bread and butter** a job or activity that provides you with the money you need to live: *Gardening is my bread and butter at the moment.* • **ˌbread-and-ˈbutter** adj [before noun] Bread-and-butter ideas or problems are the basic things that directly relate to most people: *Health and education are the sort of bread-and-butter **issues** that people vote on.*

ˈbread ˌbasket noun **CONTAINER** ▷ **1** [C] an open container in which bread is put on a table during a meal **FARMING** ▷ **2** [S] a large farming area which provides other areas with food: *The Eastern Province is the country's bread basket.*

ˈbread ˌbin noun [C] UK (US **breadbox** /ˈbred.bɒks/ (US) /-bɑːks/) a container in which bread is stored

breadboard /ˈbred.bɔːd/ (US) /-bɔːrd/ noun [C] a wooden board that is used to cut bread on

breadcrumbs /ˈbred.krʌmz/ noun [plural] very small pieces of dried bread, especially used in cooking: *Sprinkle the breadcrumbs over the mixture before baking.*

breaded /ˈbred.ɪd/ adj covered in breadcrumbs before being cooked: *breaded chicken breasts*

breadfruit /ˈbred.fruːt/ noun [C] (plural **breadfruit**) a large, round tropical fruit which looks and feels like bread after it has been baked

ˈbread ˌknife noun [C] a long, sharp knife that has a row of sharp points along one edge, and is used to cut bread

breadline /ˈbred.laɪn/ noun **INCOME** ▷ **1 the breadline** [S] UK the level of income someone has when they are extremely poor: *Most students are **on/close to/below** the breadline.* **GROUP** ▷ **2** [C] US a group of people waiting outside a particular building to be given food: *You'll see breadlines outside many New York churches at lunchtime.*

breadstick /ˈbred.stɪk/ noun [C] a long, thin stick of bread that is CRISP (= hard enough to break) like a biscuit

breadth /bredθ/, /bretθ/ noun **1** [C or U] the distance from one side to another: *The length of this box is twice its breadth.* **2** **C2** [S] the fact of including many different things, features, subjects, or qualities: *The breadth of her knowledge is amazing.*

breadwinner /ˈbredˌwɪn.əʳ/ (US) /-ɚ/ noun [C] the member of a family who earns the money that the family needs: *Men are often expected to be the breadwinner in a family.*

break /breɪk/ verb; noun

▸verb (**broke, broken**) **DAMAGE** ▷ **1** **A2** [I or T] to (cause something to) separate suddenly or violently into two or more pieces, or to (cause something to) stop working by being damaged: *The dish fell to the floor and broke.* ◦ *Charles is always breaking things.* ◦ *She fell and broke her arm (= broke the bone in her arm).* ◦ *I dropped the vase and it broke **into pieces**.* ◦ *I think I've broken your phone.* ◦ *I picked it up and the handle broke **off**.* ◦ *We heard the sound of breaking glass.* **END** ▷ **2** **B2** [I or T] to destroy or end something, or to come to an end: *Eventually someone spoke, breaking the silence.* ◦ *She laughed and that broke the tension.* ◦ *The enemy were unable to break the **code** (= understand it and so make it useless).* ◦ *Outside workers were brought in in an attempt to break (= end) the **strike**.* **3 break a/the record** **B2** to do something better than the best known speed, time, number, etc. previously achieved: *She broke the record for the 5,000 metres.* **NOT OBEY** ▷ **4** **B2** [T] to fail to keep a law, rule, or promise: *He didn't know he was breaking **the law** (= doing something illegal).* ◦ *She broke her **promise/word** to me (= did not do what she promised she would).* **DIVIDE** ▷ **5** [I or T, + adv/prep] to (cause something to) divide into two or more parts or groups: *These enzymes break **down** food in the stomach (= cause food to separate into smaller pieces).* ◦ *I asked her to break her expenses **down into** travel and personal costs.* **INTERRUPT** ▷ **6** **B1** [T] to interrupt or to stop something for a short period: *We usually break for lunch at 12.30.* ◦ *I needed something to break **the monotony** of my typing job.* ◦ *The phone rang, breaking my **concentration**.* ◦ UK *They decided to break their **journey** in Singapore.* **USE FORCE** ▷ **7** **C2** [I or T, usually + adv/prep] to go somewhere or do something by force: *He threatened to break the door **down** (= enter using force).* ◦ *The horse tried to break **free** from its stable.* ◦ *In the storm the boat broke **loose** from its moorings.* ◦ *The thieves broke the safe **open** and stole the diamonds.* ◦ *The police broke **up** the fight (= ended it forcefully).* **EMOTION** ▷ **8** [I or T] to lose your confidence, determination, or ability to control yourself, or to make someone do this: *He thought she would break under the strain.* ◦ *They tried to break his **will** (= make him lose his control) but he resisted.* **BECOME KNOWN** ▷ **9** **C2** [I or T] to become known or to make something become known: *When the **scandal** broke (= came to the public's attention), the company* director committed suicide. ◦ *It was the local newspaper which first broke the* ***story*** *(= told the public).* **WAVES ▷ 10** [I usually + adv/prep] (of waves) to reach and move over the beach, hit a CLIFF or wall, etc.: *A huge wave broke* ***on/against*** *the shore/****over*** *the boat.* **WEATHER ▷ 11** C2 [I] (of the weather) to change suddenly and usually become worse: *The forecast is for the hot weather to break today.* **STORM ▷ 12** C2 [I] (of a storm) to start suddenly: *We arrived just as a storm was breaking.* **DAY ▷ 13 dawn/day breaks** When DAWN or day breaks, the sun starts to appear in the sky early in the morning: *Dawn broke* ***over*** *the city.* **VOICE ▷ 14** [I] When a boy's voice breaks it begins to sound like a man's: *His voice broke when he was 13.* **15** [I] If someone's voice breaks, it changes because of strong emotions: *Her voice was breaking* ***with*** *emotion as she pleaded for her child's return.* **SPORT ▷ 16 break serve** (in tennis) to win a game in which another player is SERVING (= hitting the ball first): *Sampras broke Ivanisevic's serve in the second set.*

+ Other ways of saying break

See also: **broken**

An informal word that means the same as 'break' is **bust**:

One of the children has ***busted*** *the DVD player.*

If something such as glass breaks into many small pieces, you can use the verbs **shatter** or **smash**:

The baseball hit the window and ***shattered*** *it.*

I dropped the vase and it ***smashed***.

The verb **snap** is used for something that is thin and breaks suddenly into two pieces with a cracking sound:

She bent the ruler and it ***snapped***.

If someone breaks a small piece off the edge of something, the verb **chip** can be used:

I ***chipped*** *the cup when I was putting it away.*

You can use the verb **crack** when something does not separate into pieces but has lines on its surface:

A stone hit the window and ***cracked*** *it.*

When something has very deep lines in it, or breaks into two pieces in a straight line, you can use the verb **split**:

The wood had ***split***.

If parts break off something because it is in bad condition, the phrasal verb **fall apart** can be used:

I've only had these shoes for a week and they're already ***falling apart***.

IDIOMS **break your back** informal to work extremely hard: *He broke his back to get the project done on time.* • **break sb's heart 1** B2 to make someone who loves you very sad, usually by telling them you have stopped loving them: *He's broken a lot of girls' hearts.* **2** B2 If an event or situation breaks your heart, it makes you feel very sad: *She really broke her mother's heart when she left home.* • **break bread 1** old use to eat a meal **2** to take HOLY COMMUNION • **break cover** When an animal or person breaks cover, they run out of their hiding place. • **break down barriers** to improve understanding and communication between people who have different opinions: *The talks were meant to break down barriers between the two groups.* • **break even** C1 to have no profit or loss at the end of a business activity: *After paying for our travel costs, we* ***barely*** *(= only just) broke even.* • **break fresh/new ground** C2 to do or discover something new: *This recovery technique breaks new ground.* • **break it up** informal said to stop people fighting: *Break it up, you two!* • **break it/the news to sb** C2 to tell someone about something unpleasant which will affect or upset them: *Come on, what happened? Break it to me* ***gently*** *(= in a kind way).* ◦ *I didn't want to be the one to break the news to him.* • **break ranks** to publicly show disagreement or criticism of the group that you belong to: *His medical colleagues advised him not to break ranks by talking about the hospital's problems to the newspapers.* • **break the back of sth** UK to get most or the worst part of a particular task done: *We've broken the back of it now and we should be finished by Friday.* • **break the bank** humorous to cost too much: *It only costs £2. That's not going to break the bank.* • **break the ice** informal B2 to make people who have not met before feel more relaxed with each other: *Someone suggested that we play a party game to break the ice.* → See also **icebreaker** • **break the mould** UK (US **break the mold**) to be new and different: *Their approach to sports teaching broke the mould.* • **break wind** to release gas from the bowels through the bottom • **breaking and entering** illegally forcing your way into a house, especially to steal something

PHRASAL VERBS **break away** **ESCAPE ▷ 1** to leave or to escape from someone who is holding you: *He grabbed her, but she managed to break away.* ◦ figurative *One or two of the tourists broke away* ***from*** *the tour group.* **NOT AGREE ▷ 2** to stop being part of a group because you begin to disagree with them: *In the early 1980s some members of the British Labour Party broke away to form the Social Democratic Party.* • **break down** **MACHINE ▷ 1** B2 If a machine or vehicle breaks down, it stops working: *Our car broke down and we had to push it off the road.* **COMMUNICATION ▷ 2** If a system, relationship, or discussion breaks down, it fails because there is a problem or disagreement. **CRY ▷ 3** to be unable to control your feelings and to start to cry: *When we gave her the bad news, she broke down and cried.* • **break sb in** If you break someone in, you train them to do a new job or activity: *The boss did not believe in breaking his staff in* ***gently***. • **break sth in 1** to wear new shoes or use new equipment for short periods to make them more comfortable: *My new hiking boots will be great once I've broken them in.* **2** US for **run sth in** • **break in/break into sth** B1 to get into a building or car using force, usually to steal something: *The burglars broke in through the kitchen window.* ◦ *My car's been broken into twice this month.* • **break in** to interrupt when someone else is talking: *As she was talking, he suddenly broke in, saying, 'That's a lie.'* • **break into sth** to suddenly begin to do something: *He felt so happy that he broke into* ***song*** *(= suddenly began to sing).* ◦ *She walked quickly, occasionally breaking into a* ***run*** *(= starting to run).* • **break sth off** **SEPARATE ▷ 1** to separate a part from a larger piece, or to become separate: *He broke off a piece of chocolate.* **RELATIONSHIP ▷ 2** B2 to end a relationship: *They've broken off their engagement.* ◦ *The governments have broken off diplomatic relations.* • **break (sth) off** B2 to suddenly stop speaking or doing something: *She broke off in the middle of a sentence.* • **break out** **START ▷ 1** B2 If something dangerous or unpleasant breaks out, it suddenly starts: *War broke out* ***in*** *1914.* ◦ *Fighting has broken out all over the city.* **2 break out in a rash/spots/sweat** to suddenly have spots or SWEAT appear on your skin: *She broke out in a rash after eating some strawberries.* ◦ *It didn't take much exercise to make him break out in (a) sweat.* ◦ *When I heard the noise I broke out in a* ***cold*** *sweat.* **ESCAPE ▷ 3** to escape from prison: *They broke out* ***of*** *prison and fled the country.* • **break through sth** B2 to force yourself through something that is holding you back: *Protesters broke through the barriers.* • **break sth**

B

up to divide into many pieces, or to divide something into many pieces: *The company has been broken up and sold off.* • **break (sth) up** If an occasion when people meet breaks up or someone breaks it up, it ends and people start to leave: *The meeting broke up at ten to three.* ◦ *I don't want to break up* ***the party*** *but I have to go now.* • **break up** END RELATIONSHIP ▷ **1** B1 If a marriage breaks up or two people in a romantic relationship break up, their marriage or their relationship ends: *Jenny and George have broken up.* ◦ *She's just broken up* ***with*** *her boyfriend.* STOP CLASSES ▷ **2** B1 UK When schools and colleges, or the teachers and students who go to them break up, their classes stop and the holidays start: *We broke up* ***for*** *the holidays in June.* STOP BEING HEARD ▷ **3** If someone who is talking on a mobile phone is breaking up, their voice can no longer be heard clearly. • **break with sth** to intentionally not continue doing something that is normal, expected, or traditional: *We decided to break with* ***tradition*** *and not spend Christmas with our family.*

▸noun INTERRUPTION ▷ **1** [C] an interruption: *Finally there was a break* ***in*** *the rain and we went out.* **2** [C] mainly UK the short period of advertisements between television programmes: *I'll make us a cup of tea in the next break.* **3** A2 [C] a short period of rest, when food or drink is sometimes eaten: *a coffee break* ◦ UK *a tea break* ◦ *a lunch/dinner break* ◦ *We'll* ***take*** *another break at 3.30.* ◦ *They worked through the night without a break.* ◦ *Do you usually* ***take*** *a* ***morning/afternoon*** *break?* **4** [U] (also **break time**) mainly UK the regular time in the middle of the morning or afternoon, for school students to talk or play, and sometimes have food or drink: *We were talking about it at break.* **5** B1 [C] a time away from work or your regular activity, or a holiday: *Take a couple of weeks off – you need a break.* ◦ *How long is the Christmas break this year?* ◦ *We decided to have a* ***short/spring/winter/weekend*** *break in Paris.* ◦ *I'll read your report* ***over*** *(= during) the Easter break.* ◦ *I need a break* ***from typing.*** **6 give sb a break a** to allow someone some time away from their work or regular activities: *I babysit every Friday to give her* ***a bit of*** *a (= small) break.* **b** informal to stop criticizing or annoying someone, or behaving in an unpleasant way: *Give her a break – she's only a child and she didn't mean any harm.* OPPORTUNITY ▷ **7** C2 [C] an opportunity for improving a situation, especially one which happens unexpectedly: *Her* ***big*** *break came when she was offered a role in a Spielberg film.* DAMAGE ▷ **8** C1 [C] a place where something has broken: *There's a break in the pipe.* END ▷ **9** [C] the end of a relationship, connection, or way of doing something: *Their decision to not name their daughter Jane was a break* ***with*** *family* ***tradition.*** **10 make a break** (also **make the break**) to stop having a close relationship with someone, especially stop living with them, or to change a course of action that you have had for a long time: *You've been in your job for years – it's time you made a break.* ◦ *When a relationship ends, it's often best to make a* ***clean/complete*** *break (= suddenly and completely stop seeing each other).* SPORT ▷ **11** [C] in tennis, a game won by the player who was not serving (= hitting the ball first): *Rafter must get another break (****of serve****) to win.* **12** [C] in SNOOKER and BILLIARDS, the number of points that a player gets during one turn at hitting the balls ESCAPE ▷ **13 make a break (from/for)** to escape from/towards somewhere or something, often by force: *A group of prisoners made a break from the jail some years back.* ◦ *The cat made a break for the door.* ◦ *When he let go, I made a break* ***for it*** *(= escaped quickly).* → See also **breakout** MORNING ▷ **14 break of day** [U] literary the time when the sun rises in the morning: *We set out* ***at*** *break of day.* → See also **daybreak**

breakable /ˈbreɪ.kə.bl/ adj B2 describes something that might easily break: *Have you got anything breakable in your bag?*

breakage /ˈbreɪ.kɪdʒ/ noun [C or U] something that has been broken: *Any breakages must be paid for.*

breakaway /ˈbreɪ.kə.weɪ/ noun [C] an act of separating from a group, especially because of disagreement: *The sports association accepted the inevitability of a breakaway by the elite clubs.* ◦ *The breakaway group formed a new political party.*

breakdancing /ˈbreɪkˌdɑːn.sɪŋ/ US /-ˌdæn-/ noun [U] a form of dance with very energetic movements

breakdown /ˈbreɪk.daʊn/ noun FAILURE ▷ **1** B2 [C] a failure to work or be successful: *I had a breakdown (= my car stopped working) in the middle of the road.* ◦ *Both sides blamed each other for the breakdown* ***of*** *talks.* → See also **break down** DIVISION ▷ **2** C2 [C or U] a division of something into smaller parts: *We asked for a breakdown* ***of*** *the accident figures* ***into*** *day time and night time.* ◦ *The rate of breakdown of muscle protein was assessed.* ILLNESS ▷ **3** B2 [C] a **nervous breakdown**

ˈ**breakdown** ˌ**truck** noun [C] UK for **tow truck**

breaker /ˈbreɪ.kəʳ/ US /-kɚ/ noun [C] a wave moving towards the coast: *We swam out beyond the breakers.*

-breaker /-breɪ.kəʳ/ US /-kɚ/ suffix USE FORCE ▷ **1** someone who uses force to go into or open the stated thing: *a house-breaker* NOT OBEY ▷ **2** someone who does not obey a law or rule, etc.: *a lawbreaker*

ˈ**breaker's yard** noun [C] UK a place where old cars are taken apart and the parts are sold

breakfast /ˈbrek.fəst/ noun; verb

▸noun [C or U] A1 a meal eaten in the morning as the first meal of the day: *What do you want* ***for*** *breakfast?* ◦ *Jane never eats breakfast.* ◦ *She arrived shortly after breakfast.* ◦ *Breakfast is served in the dining room from 8.30 till 10.00.* ◦ *I love to eat breakfast* ***in bed*** *on Saturdays.*

▸verb [I] formal to eat breakfast: *She usually breakfasts alone.* ◦ *They breakfasted hurriedly* ***on*** *tea and toast (= ate tea and toast for breakfast).*

ˌ**breakfast** ˈ**television** noun [U] television shows consisting of many short parts that people can watch while they are getting up in the morning and eating breakfast

ˈ**break-in** noun [C] an occasion when a building is entered illegally by a criminal or criminals, usually by damaging a window or door, especially in order to steal something

ˈ**breaking** ˌ**point** noun [S] the stage at which your control over yourself or a situation is lost: *The situation* ***reached*** *breaking point when his son crashed the family car.* ◦ *Her nerves were* ***at*** *breaking point.*

ˈ**break-**ˌ**journey** adj [after noun] Indian English refers to an occasion when you interrupt your journey for a period of time: *You cannot buy a break-journey ticket on certain long-distance trains*

breakneck /ˈbreɪk.nek/ adj [before noun] carelessly fast and dangerous: *They were cycling along* ***at*** *breakneck* ***speed/at a*** *breakneck* ***pace.***

breakout /ˈbreɪk.aʊt/ noun; adj

▸noun [C] a violent escape, especially by a group, from prison: *There has been a mass breakout* ***from*** *one of Germany's top security jails.*

▸adj [before noun] used in connection with smaller groups that separate from a meeting to discuss a particular issue, before returning to the main meeting: *a breakout **session/meeting/room***

ˈbreak ˌpoint noun [C] In tennis if you win a break point, you have broken (= won a game against) the opposing player's SERVE.

breakthrough /ˈbreɪk.θruː/ noun [C] B2 an important discovery or event that helps to improve a situation or provide an answer to a problem: *Scientists are hoping for a breakthrough **in** the search for a cure for cancer.* ◦ *A **major** breakthrough **in** negotiations has been achieved.*

ˌbreak-up noun **DIVISION** ▷ **1** [S] a gradual division into smaller pieces: *It was feared that the break-up **of** the oil tanker would result in further pollution.* **END** ▷ **2** [C] the coming to an end of a business or personal relationship, caused by the separation of those involved: *Long separations had contributed to their **marriage** break-up.* ◦ *The break-up **of** the pop group came as no surprise.*

breakwater /ˈbreɪkˌwɔː.təʳ/ US /-ˌwɑː.t̬ɚ/ noun [C] a very large wall that is built from the coast out into the sea to protect a beach or HARBOUR from big waves

bream /briːm/ noun [C or U] (plural **bream** or **breams**) **1** a type of fish found especially in lakes and rivers which can be eaten **2 sea bream** a fish like a bream that lives in the sea

breast /brest/ noun **WOMAN** ▷ **1** B1 [C] either of the two soft, rounded parts of a woman's chest that produce milk after she has a baby: *When a woman becomes pregnant her breasts tend to grow larger.* ◦ *breast **cancer*** ◦ *Do you think she's had breast **implants**?* **BIRD/ANIMAL** ▷ **2** [C] the front part of a bird's body: *A robin is easy to identify because of its red breast.* **3** [U or C] the meat from the front part of the body of a bird or other animal: *I had a cold **chicken** breast and salad for lunch.* ◦ *breast of turkey/lamb/veal* **CLOTHING** ▷ **4** [C] the part of a piece of clothing that covers a person's chest: *He put a silk hanky in his breast **pocket** (= a pocket on the top front part of a shirt or coat).* **CHEST** ▷ **5** [C] literary a person's chest: *The dagger entered his breast.* **6** [C] literary the centre of a person's feelings: *A feeling of love surged **in** his breast.*

breastbone /ˈbrest.bəʊn/ US /-boʊn/ noun [C] the long, flat vertical bone in the centre of your chest

-breasted /brest.ɪd/ US /-t̬ɪd/ suffix **CLOTHING** ▷ **1** (of a coat or jacket, etc.) designed with the stated arrangement of buttons at the front: *double-breasted* ◦ *single-breasted* **WOMAN** ▷ **2** having the stated type of breasts: *a big/small-breasted woman*

breastfeed /ˈbrest.fiːd/ verb [I or T] (**breastfed**) When a mother breastfeeds her baby, she feeds it with milk directly from her breasts rather than with artificial or cow's milk from a bottle. • **breastfeeding** /-ɪŋ/ noun [U]

breastplate /ˈbrest.pleɪt/ noun [C] a piece of ARMOUR (= metal military clothing worn in the past) that protects the chest

breaststroke /ˈbrest.strəʊk/ US /-stroʊk/ noun [S or U] a way of swimming in which the arms make a circular movement in front of the body while the knees are brought up towards the body and then kicked out and back: *I can only **do** breaststroke.*

breath /breθ/ noun **1** B1 [U] the air that goes into and out of your lungs: *Her breath smelled of garlic.* ◦ *She was dizzy and **short of** breath (= unable to breathe in enough air).* ◦ *He burst into the room, red-faced and **out of** breath (= unable to breathe comfortably because of tiredness or excitement).* **2 catch your breath** (UK also **get your breath back**) C1 to pause or rest for a short time until you can breathe comfortably or regularly again: *I had to stop running to catch my breath.* **3 draw breath a** to breathe: *Without pausing to **draw** breath she told me everything.* **b** to pause for a short time between doing one thing and the next: *Give me a moment to draw breath, won't you?* **4 hold your breath a** B2 to keep air in your lungs and not release it so that you need more: *How long can you hold your breath under water?* **b** C2 to wait for something to happen, often feeling anxious: *Fans held their breath waiting for the final whistle.* **5** [C] a single action of breathing air into your lungs **6 take a breath** B2 to breathe air into your lungs (as a single action): *The doctor told me to take a **deep** breath (= breathe in a lot of air).* **7 a breath of air a** the smallest amount of wind: *There wasn't a breath of air in the room.* **b** a short period of time spent outside: *I'm just going out for a breath of (fresh) air – I won't be long.*

> **!** Common mistake: **breath or breathe?**
>
> **Warning:** do not confuse the noun **breath** with the verb **breathe**:
>
> ~~*Pollution is damaging the air that we breath.*~~
>
> *Pollution is damaging the air that we breathe.*

IDIOMS **a breath of fresh air** C2 someone or something that is new and different and makes everything seem more exciting: *Angela's so cheerful and lively – she's **like** a breath of fresh air when she visits.* • **don't hold your breath** humorous said in order to tell someone that an event is not likely to happen: *She said she might have finished by this afternoon but don't hold your breath.* • **in the same breath** If you say two things in the same breath, you say two things that are so different that if one is true, the other must be false: *You say you're bored and frustrated but in the same breath say you're resigned to staying in the same job.* • **take sb's breath away** B2 to be extremely beautiful or surprising: *The beauty of the Taj Mahal took my breath away.* • **under your breath** C2 quietly so that other people cannot hear exactly what you are saying: *He muttered something under his breath.* • **with your last/dying breath** literary just before you die: *She asked him with her dying breath to look after her child.*

breathable /ˈbriː.ðə.bl̩/ adj A breathable ATMOSPHERE is one that is suitable for humans to breathe.

breathalyse UK (US **breathalyze**) /ˈbreθ.əl.aɪz/ verb [T] to test a driver's breath to see how much alcohol they have drunk

breathalyser UK trademark (US **breathalyzer**) /ˈbreθ.əl.aɪz.əʳ/ US /-ɚ/ noun [C] a device like a small bag with a tube at one end, which the police can ask a driver to blow into to see how much alcohol the driver has drunk

breathe /briːð/ verb **AIR** ▷ **1** B1 [I or T] to move air into and out of the lungs: *It's so airless in here – I can hardly breathe.* ◦ *The instructor told us to breathe **in** deeply and then breathe **out** slowly.* ◦ *I'm sorry if I'm breathing (= blowing out air containing) garlic fumes all **over** you!* **WORDS** ▷ **2** [I, + speech] literary to say something very quietly: *'Here they come,' he breathed.* **WINE** ▷ **3** [I] specialized If you allow wine to breathe, you open the bottle for a short time before you drink from it, in order to improve the wine's flavour.

IDIOMS **breathe your last** literary to die: *Her eyes fluttered open for a moment and then she breathed her last.* • **breathe down sb's neck** disapproving to stay close to someone, watching everything that they do:

It's awful having a boss who breathes down your neck all the time. • **breathe (new) life into** to bring new ideas and energy to: *We need some new people to breathe life into this project.*

breather /ˈbriː.ðəʳ/ (US) /-ðɚ/ noun [C] informal a short rest: *He'd been working hard and felt he needed (to **have/take**) a breather.*

ˈbreath ˌfreshener noun [C or U] something you eat to make your breath smell pleasant: *People often suck a peppermint as a breath freshener.*

breathing /ˈbriː.ðɪŋ/ noun [U] the act or process of taking air into your lungs and releasing it: *She lay awake listening to her sister's steady breathing.* ◦ *I could hear the sound of **heavy** breathing as he slowly climbed the stairs.*

ˈbreathing ˌspace noun [C or U] (US also **ˈbreathing ˌroom**) a period of rest in order to increase strength or give you more time to think about what to do next: *I wanted a little breathing space between jobs.* ◦ *The court's decision gave us some breathing space.*

breathless /ˈbreθ.ləs/ adj not able to breathe easily: *I was breathless after climbing the stairs.* ◦ *That one kiss had left her breathless **with** excitement.* • **breathlessly** /-li/ adv

breathtaking /ˈbreθˌteɪ.kɪŋ/ adj (B2) extremely exciting, beautiful, or surprising: *The view from the top of the mountain is breathtaking.* ◦ *His performance is described in the paper as 'a breathtaking display of physical agility'.* • **breathtakingly** /-li/ adv *The scenery was breathtakingly **beautiful**.*

ˈbreath ˌtest noun [C] a test in which the police ask a driver to blow into a BREATHALYSER (= a device shaped like a bag) to show if they have drunk too much alcohol to be allowed to drive

breathy /ˈbreθ.i/ adj describes a voice or way of speaking in which the breath can be heard: *Marilyn Monroe was famous for her breathy voice.*

breech /briːtʃ/ adj If a baby in the WOMB is in a breech position, it is lying so that the lower part of its body will come out first: *a breech **birth/delivery***

breeches /ˈbrɪtʃ.ɪz/, /ˈbriː.tʃɪz/ noun [plural] (US **britches**) trousers that do not cover the whole of the leg: *riding breeches* ◦ *a pair of breeches*

breed /briːd/ verb; noun

▸verb (**bred**, **bred**) **REPRODUCE** ▷ **1** (B2) [T] to keep animals for the purpose of producing young animals in a controlled way: *Terriers are bred **for** their fighting instincts.* ◦ *His main income comes from breeding cattle.* → See also **inbred**, **purebred**, **thoroughbred**, **well bred** **2** [I] (of animals) to have sex and produce young animals: *The blackbird, like most birds, breeds in the spring.* **CAUSE** ▷ **3** (C2) [T] to cause something to happen, usually something bad: *Favouritism breeds **resentment**.*

▸noun [C] **1** (B2) a particular type of animal or plant: *a breed of dog/cat/horse/sheep/cattle* **2** informal a type of person: *Arletty was that **rare** breed **of** actress – beautiful, sexy and funny.* ◦ *A **new** breed **of** film-maker has taken over Hollywood.* ◦ *Authentic blues singers are a **dying** breed* (= becoming rare) *these days.*

breeder /ˈbriː.dəʳ/ (US) /-dɚ/ noun [C] someone who breeds animals: *She was one of the country's top sheep breeders.*

breeding /ˈbriː.dɪŋ/ noun [U] **ANIMALS** ▷ **1** the keeping of animals or plants in order to breed from them: *The family's business was horse-breeding.* **2** the process in which animals have sex and produce young animals: *The penguins' breeding **season** has begun.* **BEHAVIOUR** ▷ **3** (also **good breeding**) polite and socially correct behaviour that someone has because they were taught it when they were a child

ˈbreeding ˌground noun [C] **1** a place where animals breed and produce their babies: *These animals always return to the same breeding ground.* **2** a place where something develops easily, especially something unpleasant: *Poor housing conditions are breeding grounds **for** crime.*

breeze /briːz/ noun; verb

▸noun **WIND** ▷ **1** (B1) [C] a light and pleasant wind: *a warm/cool breeze* ◦ *She let the gentle breeze cool her face.* **SOMETHING EASY** ▷ **2** [S] informal something that is easy to achieve, often unexpectedly: *You won't have any problems with the entrance test – it's an absolute breeze.*

▸verb [I usually + adv/prep] **WALK** ▷ **1** to walk somewhere quickly and confidently, without worry or embarrassment: *She just breezed **in** as if she'd only been away a day instead of a year.* **DO EASILY** ▷ **2** informal to easily complete or win something: *She breezed **through** the song as though she'd been singing it for years.* ◦ mainly US *In 1985 he breezed **to** victory with 78 percent of the vote.*

breezy /ˈbriː.zi/ adj **WINDY** ▷ **1** with wind that is quite strong but pleasant: *It was a breezy day, just right for sailing.* **HAPPY** ▷ **2** happy, confident, and enthusiastic: *He had the breezy **manner** of a salesman.* • **breezily** /-zɪ.li/ adv

brethren /ˈbreð.rən/ noun [plural] old-fashioned (used as a form of address to members of an organization or religious group) brothers

breve /briːv/ noun [C] specialized a musical note with a time value equal to two SEMIBREVES or four MINIMS

brevity /ˈbrev.ɪ.ti/ (US) /-ə.t̬i/ noun [U] using only a few words or lasting only a short time: *His essays are models of clarity and brevity.*

brew /bruː/ verb; noun

▸verb **DRINK** ▷ **1** [T] to make beer **2** [I or T] If you brew tea or coffee, you add boiling water to it to make a hot drink, and if it brews, it gradually develops flavour in the container in which it was made: [+ two objects] *He brewed us some coffee./He brewed some coffee **for** us.* **BAD SITUATION** ▷ **3** [I] If an unpleasant situation or a storm is brewing, you feel that it is about to happen: *It was too quiet – I felt that trouble was brewing.* ◦ *A storm was brewing in the distance.*

▸noun **DRINK** ▷ **1** [C] a type of beer, especially one made in a particular place or at a particular time **2** [C usually singular] UK informal a drink of tea or a drink of beer: *Make us a brew, Bren.* **MIX** ▷ **3** [C] a mixture of several things: *They gave her a strange brew to drink.* ◦ *War, with its fear, its deprivation, its excitement and violence makes for a very **heady** brew* (= powerful combination).

brewer /ˈbruː.əʳ/ (US) /-ɚ/ noun [C] a person or company that makes beer

brewery /ˈbrʊə.ri/ (US) /ˈbrʊr.i/ noun [C] a company that makes beer or a place where beer is made

brewpub /ˈbruː.pʌb/ noun [C] US a pub which makes and sells beer

briar (also **brier**) /ˈbraɪəʳ/ (US) /braɪr/ noun [C or U] a wild bush, especially a rose bush with long stems and sharp THORNS

bribe /braɪb/ verb; noun

▸verb [T] (C1) to try to make someone do something for you by giving them money, presents, or something else that they want: *He bribed immigration officials and entered the country illegally.* ◦ [+ to infinitive] *They bribed the waiter **to** find them a better table.*

▸noun [C] C1 money or a present that you give to someone so that they will do something for you, usually something dishonest: *He was accused of **accepting/taking** bribes from wealthy businessmen.* • **bribery** /ˈbraɪ.bᵊr.i/ US /-bɚ-/ **noun** [U] C2 *The organization was rife with bribery **and corruption**.*

bric-a-brac /ˈbrɪk.ə.bræk/ **noun** [U] small decorative objects of various types and of no great value: *It's one of those shops that sells antiques and bric-a-brac.*

brick /brɪk/ **noun; verb**

▸noun BUILDING BLOCK ▷ **1** B2 [C] a rectangular block of hard material used for building walls and houses: *The chimney was made of bricks.* ◦ *We lived in a Victorian terrace of **red**-brick houses.* ◦ *He was so embarrassed – his face went brick-**red** (= a dark red).* → See also **airbrick, red-brick** GOOD PERSON ▷ **2** [C usually singular] old-fashioned or humorous a very helpful and kind person who can be trusted: *Thanks for bringing all that food along to the party, Tony. **You're a** brick!*

IDIOMS **bricks and clicks** (also **clicks and bricks**) business in which a company uses both shops and the internet to sell products: *Traditional stores are now pursuing a bricks and clicks strategy.* • **be/come up against a brick wall** to be unable to make more progress with a plan or discussion because someone is stopping you • **bricks and mortar** property in the form of buildings usually when considered as an INVESTMENT: *I was nearly 40 when I finally invested in bricks and mortar.*

▸verb

PHRASAL VERB **brick up sth** to build a wall of bricks around something, or to fill something with bricks: *The doors and windows had been bricked up to prevent squatters from getting in.*

brickbat /ˈbrɪk.bæt/ **noun** [C] a spoken attack: *The members of parliament **hurled** brickbats at the minister.* → Synonym **insult**

bricklayer /ˈbrɪkˌleɪ.əʳ/ US /-ɚ/ **noun** [C] (UK informal **brickie**) a person who builds walls or buildings using bricks, especially as a job • **bricklaying** /-ɪŋ/ **noun** [U] *Bricklaying is a skilled job.*

brickwork /ˈbrɪk.wɜːk/ US /-wɝːk/ **noun** [U] the bricks in a wall or building

bridal /ˈbraɪ.dᵊl/ **adj** [before noun] of a woman about to be married, or of a marriage ceremony: *The magazine had a section on bridal wear (= the clothes that a woman wears at her marriage).* ◦ *We stayed in the hotel's bridal **suite** (= the rooms for recently married people).*

bride /braɪd/ **noun** [C] B1 a woman who is about to get married or has just got married: *He returned from New York with his lovely **new** bride.* ◦ *The bride **and groom** posed for pictures outside the church.*

bridegroom /ˈbraɪd.grʊm/, /-gruːm/ **noun** [C] (also **groom**) a man who is about to get married or has just got married: *The bridegroom was late for the ceremony.*

bridesmaid /ˈbraɪdz.meɪd/ **noun** [C] a girl or woman who during the marriage ceremony helps the woman who is getting married

ˌbride-to-ˈbe **noun** [C] (plural **brides-to-be**) a woman who is going to be married soon

bridge /brɪdʒ/ **noun; verb**

▸noun LARGE STRUCTURE ▷ **1** A2 [C] a structure that is built over a river, road, or railway to allow people and vehicles to cross from one side to the other: *We drove **across/over** the bridge.* ◦ *the Brooklyn Bridge* **2** C2 [C usually singular] something that makes it easier to make a change from one situation to another: *Voluntary work can provide a bridge **between** staying at home **and** working full-time.* PART OF A SHIP ▷ **3** [C] the raised part of a ship on which the CAPTAIN and other officers stand and from where they control the movement of the ship NOSE ▷ **4** [C usually singular] the top part of the nose, between the eyes, or (on a pair of glasses) the piece that is supported by the top part of the nose: *The blow caught him right on the bridge of his nose.* GAME ▷ **5** [U] a card game for four players who play in pairs TEETH ▷ **6** [C] (also **bridgework** [U]) a piece of material that contains one or more artificial teeth and is kept in place by being fastened to the natural teeth MUSICAL INSTRUMENT ▷ **7** [C] a small piece of wood over which the strings are stretched on a musical instrument such as a guitar or VIOLIN

▸verb [T] BRING TOGETHER ▷ **1** to make the difference or division between two things smaller or less severe: *We must bridge **the gap** between labour and management.* BUILD ▷ **2** to build a bridge over or across something: *The river had been bridged at its narrowest point.*

bridgehead /ˈbrɪdʒ.hed/ **noun** [C] a good position that an army has taken in enemy land, from which it can attack the enemy more effectively: *The advance troops **established a** bridgehead early in the fighting.* → Compare **beachhead**

ˈbridging ˌloan **noun** [C] UK (US **ˈbridge ˌloan**) an arrangement by which a bank lends a person some money for a short time until that person can get the money from somewhere else, often so that they can buy another house before they sell their own

bridle /ˈbraɪ.dl/ **noun; verb**

bridle

▸noun [C] a set of leather straps that are put around a horse's head to allow its rider to control it

▸verb SHOW ANGER ▷ **1** [I] to show sudden anger: *She bridled **at** the suggestion that she had been dishonest.* CONTROL ANIMAL ▷ **2** [T] to put a bridle on a horse or similar animal: *Polly saddled and bridled her favourite horse.*

ˈbridle ˌpath **noun** [C] (UK also **bridleway**) a track in the countryside that you ride horses on

Brie /briː/ **noun** [U] a soft French cheese

brief /briːf/ **adj; verb; noun**

▸adj SHORT IN TIME ▷ **1** B1 lasting only a short time or containing few words: *His acceptance speech was mercifully brief.* ◦ *I had a brief **look** at her report before the meeting.* ◦ *It'll only be a brief **visit** because we really haven't much time.* ◦ *After a brief **spell/stint** in the army, he started working as a teacher.* ◦ *The company issued a brief **statement** about yesterday's accident.* **2** used to express how quickly time goes past: *For a few brief weeks we were very happy.* SHORT IN LENGTH ▷ **3** (of clothes) very short

▸verb [T] formal to give someone instructions or information about what they should do or say: *We had already been briefed **about/on** what the job would entail.* → Compare **debrief**

▸noun SHORT FORM ▷ **1 in brief** B2 If something is said in brief, it is said in a very short form, with very few details: *'So you didn't enjoy the party then.' 'In brief, no.'* UNDERWEAR ▷ **2 briefs** [plural] a piece of underwear worn by men or women, covering the area

B

between the waist and the tops of the legs: *cotton briefs* **INSTRUCTIONS** ▷ **3** [C] UK a set of instructions or information: [+ to infinitive] *It was my brief **to** make sure that the facts were set down accurately.* **4** [C] legal a document or set of documents containing the details about a court case

briefcase /ˈbriːf.keɪs/ **noun** [C] a rectangular case, used especially for carrying business documents

briefing /ˈbriː.fɪŋ/ **noun** [C or U] information that is given to someone just before they do something, or a meeting where this happens: *They received (a) thorough briefing before they left the country.* ◦ *We had to attend a briefing once a month.*

briefly /ˈbriːf.li/ **adv** **SHORT TIME** ▷ **1** B1 for a short time: *We chatted briefly about the weather.* **FEW WORDS** ▷ **2** using few words or without giving a lot of details: *Briefly, the company needs to cut its expenditure.*

brier /ˈbraɪəʳ/ US /braɪr/ **noun** [C] a **briar**

brig /brɪɡ/ **noun** [C] US a military prison, especially one on a US navy ship

brigade /brɪˈɡeɪd/ **noun** **1** [C] a large group of soldiers in an army **2** [C usually singular] informal a group of people who have something in common, especially an enthusiasm for a particular belief or subject: *Since she gave up smoking she's joined the anti-smoking brigade.*

brigadier /ˌbrɪɡ.əˈdɪəʳ/ US /-ˈdɪr/ **noun** [C] (also **Brigadier**) an officer in the British army whose rank is above a COLONEL and below a MAJOR GENERAL, and who is in charge of a brigade: *Brigadier Jones/David Jones* ◦ [as form of address] *Thank you, Brigadier.*

ˌbrigadier ˈgeneral **noun** [C] an officer of the US Army of the same rank as a brigadier

brigand /ˈbrɪɡ.ənd/ **noun** [C] literary a thief with a weapon, especially one of a group living in the countryside and stealing from people travelling through the area

bright /braɪt/ **adj; noun**

▸**adj** **LIGHT** ▷ **1** B1 full of light, shining: *bright sunshine* ◦ *The rooms were bright and airy.* ◦ *The lights are too bright in here – they're hurting my eyes.* ◦ *A bright star was shining in the East.* ◦ *When she looked up her eyes were bright **with** tears.* ◦ *In 2009 I moved to London, attracted by the bright **lights** (= the promise of excitement) of the city.* **COLOUR** ▷ **2** A2 strong in colour: *Leslie always wears bright **colours**.* ◦ *He said hello and I felt my face turn bright red.* ◦ *a bright **shade** of green* **INTELLIGENT** ▷ **3** B2 (of a person) clever and quick to learn: *They were bright children, always asking questions.* ◦ *She was enthusiastic and full of bright **ideas** (= clever ideas) and suggestions.* **HAPPY** ▷ **4** B2 full of hope for success or happiness: *You're very bright **and cheerful** this morning.* ◦ *Things are starting to look brighter **for** British businesses.* ◦ *She's an excellent student with a bright **future**.* • **brightness** /ˈbraɪt.nəs/ **noun** [U] *The brightness of the snow made him blink.* • **brightly** /ˈbraɪt.li/ **adv** B2 *a brightly lit room* ◦ *Clowns often wear brightly coloured clothing.* ◦ *Despite her fear, she spoke brightly to the group.*

IDIOM **bright-eyed and bushy-tailed** eager and happy: *He always leaps out of bed bright-eyed and bushy-tailed.*

▸**noun** **brights** [plural] US informal A car's brights are its HEADLIGHTS (= the powerful lights at the front) on full power.

brighten /ˈbraɪ.tən/ US /-t̬ən/ **verb** [I or T] **LIGHTER** ▷ **1** to (cause to) become lighter: *The room was small and dark, without so much as a ray of light to brighten the gloom.* ◦ *It was rainy this morning, but **it** brightened **up** (= the sun started shining) after lunch.* **HAPPIER** ▷ **2** to (cause to) become happy or full of hope: *Her **eyes** brightened when she saw him enter the room.* ◦ *There are, however, one or two items of good news to brighten the economic picture a bit.*

ˌbright ˈspark **noun** [C] **1** UK a person who is intelligent, and full of energy and enthusiasm **2** humorous a stupid person: ***Some** bright spark left the door open overnight.*

brill /brɪl/ **adj, exclamation** UK informal for **brilliant**: *You should buy this CD – it's brill!*

brilliance /ˈbrɪl.i.əns/ **noun** [U] **CLEVERNESS** ▷ **1** great skill or intelligence: *Her first novel showed signs of brilliance.* **SHINE** ▷ **2** great brightness of light or colour: *I had never seen diamonds shine with such brilliance before.*

brilliant /ˈbrɪl.i.ənt/ **adj** **VERY GOOD** ▷ **1** A2 UK informal very good: *'Did you like the film?' 'I thought it was brilliant.'* ◦ *She's got a brilliant sense of humour.* ◦ *Oh, brilliant! My parcel's arrived.* **CLEVER** ▷ **2** B1 extremely clever or skilled: *Her mother was a brilliant scientist.* ◦ *He gave a brilliant performance.* ◦ *The idea was quite brilliant.* ◦ *She seemed to have a brilliant career ahead of her (= was likely to be extremely successful).* **SHINING** ▷ **3** B1 full of light, shining, or bright in colour: *The sky was a brilliant, cloudless blue.* ◦ *I was dazzled by a brilliant light.* • **brilliantly** /-li/ **adv**

brilliantine /ˈbrɪl.i.ən.tiːn/ **noun** [U] a type of oil used to make men's hair smooth and shiny

brim /brɪm/ **noun; verb**

▸**noun** **PART OF HAT** ▷ **1** [C usually singular] the bottom part of a hat that sticks out all round → Compare **crown** **TOP** ▷ **2** [C] the very top edge of a container: *She poured the cream until it reached the brim.* ◦ *He **filled** the jug **to the** brim.* ◦ *She passed him the mug, **filled/full to the** brim **with** hot black coffee.* • **-brimmed** /-d/ **suffix** *She wore a **wide**-brimmed hat.*

▸**verb** [I] **(-mm-)** to become full of something, especially a liquid: *Her eyes brimmed **with tears** when she heard that he was alive.* ◦ figurative *His recent triumphs have left the tennis ace brimming (**over**) **with** (= full of) confidence and energy.*

brimful /brɪmˈfʊl/ **adj** **brimful of sth** full of something good

brimstone /ˈbrɪm.stəʊn/ US /-stoʊn/ **noun** [U] old use the chemical SULPHUR

brine /braɪn/ **noun** [U] water with salt in it, especially when used to preserve food: *tuna/olives **in** brine*

bring /brɪŋ/ **verb** [T] (**brought**, **brought**) **TOWARDS PLACE** ▷ **1** A2 to take or carry someone or something to a place or a person, or in the direction of the person speaking: *'Shall I bring anything **to** the party?' 'Oh, just a bottle.'* ◦ [+ two objects] *Bring me that knife/Bring that knife **to** me.* ◦ *Can you help me bring **in** the shopping (= take it into the house)?* ◦ *The police brought several men **in for questioning** (= took them to the police station because they might have been involved in a crime).* ◦ *When they visit us they always bring their dog **with** them.* **CAUSE** ▷ **2** B1 to cause, result in, or produce a state or condition: [+ two objects] *She's brought us so much happiness over the years.* ◦ [+ -ing verb] *The explosion brought the whole building crash**ing** to the ground.* ◦ *Several trees were brought **down** (= made to fall) by the storm.* ◦ *The closure of the factory brought poverty **to** the town (= resulted in it becoming poor).* ◦ *Bring the water **to the boil** (US **to a boil**) (= make it start boiling).* ◦ *She suddenly brought the interview **to an end**.* ◦ *Her tragic story brought*

***tears to** my **eyes** (= made me cry). ◦ What **will the future** bring for these refugees?* **3 bring sb to sth** to cause someone to come to a particular place or thing: *This subject brings me to the second part of the discussion. ◦ What brings you (= why have you come) **to** London?* LAW ▷ **4** to make or begin as part of an official legal process: *He was arrested for fighting, but police have decided not to bring **charges**.*

IDIOMS **bring sb to book** UK to punish someone and make them explain their behaviour • **bring sb up short** mainly UK to make someone suddenly stop doing something or talking, usually because they are surprised: *Her rudeness brought me up short.* • **bring home the bacon** informal to earn money for a family to live on: *I can't sit around all day – someone's got to bring home the bacon.* • **bring the house down** If someone or something brings the house down during a play or show, they make the people watching it laugh or clap very loudly: *The clown sang a duet with the talking horse, which brought the house down every night.* • **bring up the rear** to be at the back of a group that is going somewhere: *You two go ahead – Sam and I'll bring up the rear.* • **not bring yourself to do something** to not be able to force yourself to do something that you think is unpleasant: *I just couldn't bring myself to speak to him about it.*

PHRASAL VERBS **bring sth about** to cause something to happen: *He brought about his company's collapse by his reckless spending.* • **bring sb/sth along** mainly UK to take someone or something with you: *Can I bring a friend along to the party?* • **bring sb around** mainly US for **bring sb round** • **bring sth back** RETURN ▷ **1** (A2) to return from somewhere with something: [+ two objects] *Can you bring me back some milk?* REMEMBER ▷ **2** to make someone think about something from the past: *The photos brought back some wonderful memories.* DO AGAIN ▷ **3** to start to do or use something that was done or used in the past: *Few politicians are in favour of bringing back the death penalty.* • **bring sb down** to cause someone in a position of power to lose their job: *This scandal could bring down the government.* • **bring sth down** to reduce the level of something: *They've really brought down the price of DVD players.* • **bring sth forward** mainly UK to change the date or time of an event so that it happens earlier than planned: *The elections were brought forward by three months.* • **bring sth in** INTRODUCE ▷ **1** to introduce something new such as a product or a law: *New safety regulations have been brought in.* MONEY ▷ **2** to make money: *Their chain of pubs and restaurants brings in millions of pounds a year.* • **bring sb in** to ask someone to do a particular job: *We need to bring in an expert to deal with this problem.* • **bring sth off** to succeed in doing something difficult: *It was an important event, and she's managed to bring it off brilliantly.* • **bring sth on 1** to make something happen, usually something bad: *The loud music brought on another one of his headaches.* **2 bring it on!** informal said to show that you are prepared and willing to compete in a competition or to do something difficult: *England versus Brazil – bring it on!* • **bring sb out** UK to make a shy person happier and more confident: *Paulo's very shy – he needs bringing out.* • **bring sth out** PRODUCE ▷ **1** (B2) to produce something to sell to the public: *They keep bringing out smaller phones.* MAKE NOTICEABLE ▷ **2** to make a particular quality or detail noticeable: *A crisis can bring out **the best** and **the worst** in people. ◦ The seasoning really brings out **the flavour** of the meat.* • **bring sb out in sth** UK If something brings you out in spots, a RASH, etc., it causes them to appear on your skin: *Seafood always brings me out in huge spots.*

• **bring sb round** (US usually **bring sb around**) MAKE CONSCIOUS ▷ **1** to make someone become conscious again after being unconscious PERSUADE ▷ **2** to persuade someone to have the same opinion as you have: *At first they refused but I managed to bring them round (**to** my way of thinking).* • **bring sb to** to make someone become conscious again after being unconscious • **bring sb/sth together** to cause people to be friendly with each other: *The disaster brought the community together.* • **bring sb up** (B1) to care for a child until it is an adult, often giving it particular beliefs: *She was brought up by her grandmother. ◦ They brought her up (**as/to be**) a Catholic.* ◦ [+ to infinitive] *David was brought up **to** respect authority.* • **bring sth up** TALK ▷ **1** (B2) to start to talk about a particular subject: *She's always bringing up her health problems.* VOMIT ▷ **2** UK informal to vomit something: *She was crying so much I thought she'd bring up her breakfast.*

ˌbring-and-ˈbuy ˌsale noun [C] UK a sale, usually to collect money for a CHARITY, where people bring things to be sold and buy things brought by other people

brinjal /ˈbrɪn.dʒəl/ noun [C or U] Indian English or South African English **aubergine**

brink /brɪŋk/ noun [S] **1** (C2) the point where a new or different situation is about to begin: *Extreme stress had driven him to **the** brink **of** a nervous breakdown. ◦ Scientists are **on the** brink **of** (= extremely close to) a major new discovery.* **2** literary the edge of a CLIFF or other high area: *She was standing right **on the** brink **of** the gorge.*

brinkmanship /ˈbrɪŋk.mən.ʃɪp/ noun [U] the activity, especially in politics, of trying to get what you want by saying that if you do not get it, you will do something dangerous: *The talks have collapsed and both sides have resorted to brinkmanship.*

briny /ˈbraɪ.ni/ adj; noun

▸adj describes water that contains a lot of salt

▸noun [S] **the briny** UK old-fashioned humorous the sea: *Do you fancy a dip in the briny?*

brioche /ˈbri.ɒʃ/ (US) /-ɑːʃ/ noun [C or U] soft, slightly sweet bread made with eggs and butter

briquette (also **briquet**) /brɪˈket/ noun [C] a small block made from coal dust or PEAT, used as fuel in a fire

brisk /brɪsk/ adj quick, energetic, and active: *a brisk **walk** ◦ He set a brisk **pace** and we struggled to keep up. ◦ Her tone on the phone was brisk (= she spoke quickly and used few words) **and businesslike**.* • **briskly** /ˈbrɪsk.li/ adv *She walked briskly into town. ◦ Beat the eggs whites briskly until soft peaks form. ◦ 'Let's get it over with,' he said briskly.* • **briskness** /ˈbrɪsk.nəs/ noun [U]

brisket /ˈbrɪs.kɪt/ noun [U] meat from the chest of a cow

bristle /ˈbrɪs.l̩/ noun; verb

▸noun **1** [C] a short, stiff hair, usually one of many: *The old woman had a few grey bristles sprouting from her chin.* **2** [C or U] The bristles of a brush are the stiff hairs or pieces of plastic that are connected to it • **bristly** /ˈbrɪs.li/ adj *He had furry eyebrows and bristly (= short, sticking up) hair.*

▸verb HAIR ▷ **1** [I] (of hair) to stand up: *The cat's fur bristled and it arched its back.* REACT ANGRILY ▷ **2** to react angrily: *She bristled **at** the suggestion that she had in any way neglected the child.*

PHRASAL VERB **bristle with sth** to have a large amount of something, or to be full of something: *The* *helicopter hovered above them bristling with machine guns.*

Brit /brɪt/ noun [C] informal a British person: *You could tell by their clothes that they were Brits.*

Britain /ˈbrɪt.ᵊn/ noun England, Scotland, and Wales

britches /ˈbrɪtʃ.ɪz/ noun [plural] US for **breeches**

British /ˈbrɪt.ɪʃ/ (US) /ˈbrɪţ-/ **adj; noun**

▸adj of the United Kingdom of Great Britain and Northern Ireland: *He's got a British passport.*

▸noun [plural] **the British** people from Britain

ˌBritish ˈSummer ˌTime noun [U] (abbreviation **BST**) the time used in the UK from late March to late October, that is one hour ahead of GREENWICH MEAN TIME

Briton /ˈbrɪt.ᵊn/ (US) /ˈbrɪţ-/ noun [C] a British person: *Six Britons are believed to have been involved in the accident.*

brittle /ˈbrɪt.l̩/ (US) /ˈbrɪţ-/ **adj** **EASILY BROKEN** ▷ **1** delicate and easily broken: *As you get older your bones become increasingly brittle.* ◦ *The pond was covered in a brittle layer of ice.* **UNKIND** ▷ **2** unkind and unpleasant: *She gave a brittle laugh and turned away.*

bro /brəʊ/ (US) /broʊ/ noun [C] (plural **bros**) **1** informal a brother **2** mainly US informal used when talking to a male friend: [as form of address] *Hey, bro, what's up?*

broach /brəʊtʃ/ (US) /broʊtʃ/ **verb; noun**

▸verb [T] **BEGIN** ▷ to begin a discussion of something difficult: *At some point we've got to discuss money but I don't know quite how to broach the* ***subject*** *with him.*

▸noun [C] US for **brooch**

broad /brɔːd/ (US) /brɑːd/ **adj; noun**

▸adj **WIDE** ▷ **1** (B1) very wide: *We walked down a broad avenue lined with trees.* ◦ *He flashed a broad* ***grin*** *at us.* ◦ *My brother is very broad-****shouldered****.* → Compare **narrow 2** (B1) If something is a particular distance broad, it measures this distance from side to side: *This river is over 500 metres broad at its widest point.* **GENERAL** ▷ **3** (B1) including a wide range of things; general: *The politician gave a broad* ***outline*** *of his proposals.* ◦ *The magazine covers a broad* ***range*** *of subjects, from sewing to psychology.* **STRONG** ▷ **4** If someone has a broad ACCENT (= way of speaking), it is strong and noticeable, showing where they come from: *He spoke with a broad Australian accent.* **INFORMATION** ▷ **5 broad hint** a HINT (= when you tell someone something without saying it directly) that is easy to understand • **broadly** /ˈbrɔːd.li/ (US) /ˈbrɑːd-/ **adv** (C1) *Broadly* ***speaking****, don't you think women make better drivers than men?* • **broadness** /ˈbrɔːd.nəs/ (US) /ˈbrɑːd-/ noun [U] *She was struck by the broadness of his back.*

IDIOMS **broad in the beam** old-fashioned humorous having wide hips and a large bottom: *Her mother was fairly broad in the beam.* • **in broad daylight** If a crime is committed in broad daylight, it happens during the day, when it could have been seen and prevented: *Thieves had broken into the house in broad daylight.*

▸noun [C] US offensive a woman

broadband /ˈbrɔːd.bænd/ (US) /ˈbrɑːd-/ noun [U] (B2) a system that makes it possible for many messages or large amounts of information to be sent at the same time and very quickly between computers or other electronic devices: *Internet connection via broadband offers many advantages.* ◦ *broadband services/networks/technology/transmission*

ˌbroad ˈbean noun [C] a large, pale green bean that can be eaten

broadcast /ˈbrɔːd.kɑːst/ (US) /ˈbrɑːd.kæst/ **verb; noun**

▸verb [I or T] (**broadcast**, **broadcast** or US also **broadcasted**, **broadcasted**) (B2) to send out a programme on television or radio: *Radio Caroline used to broadcast* ***from*** *a boat in the North Sea.* ◦ *The tennis championship is broadcast live* ***to*** *several different countries.* ◦ figurative *I'm leaving but please don't broadcast (= tell everyone) the fact.* • **broadcasting** /-ˌkɑː.stɪŋ/ (US) /-ˌkæs.tɪŋ/ noun [U] *Huge amounts of money are spent on sports broadcasting.*

▸noun [C] a television or radio programme: *a* ***radio/television*** *broadcast* ◦ *We watched a* ***live*** *broadcast of the concert.*

broadcaster /ˈbrɔːdˌkɑː.stəʳ/ (US) /ˈbrɑːdˌkæs.tɚ/ noun [C] someone whose job is to speak on radio or television programmes: *He was a famous broadcaster in the 1930s.*

ˌbroad ˈchurch noun [S] UK a group, organization, or set of beliefs which includes a wide range of different opinions or ideas: *The Conservative Party is a broad church.*

broaden /ˈbrɔː.dᵊn/ (US) /ˈbrɑː-/ **verb** **WIDER** ▷ **1** [I or T] to become wider, or to cause something to become wider: *The track broadens and becomes a road at this point.* ◦ *They are broadening the bridge to speed up the flow of traffic.* **MORE GENERAL** ▷ **2** (C1) [T] to increase the range of something: *They've introduced all sorts of new elements to that programme in order to broaden its* ***appeal****.* ◦ *I hoped that going to university might broaden my* ***horizons*** *(= increase the range of my knowledge and experience).*

PHRASAL VERB **broaden out** to become wider: *The river broadens out around the next bend.*

the ˈbroad ˌjump noun [S] US for **the long jump**

ˌbroad-ˈminded adj approving (C2) willing to accept other people's behaviour and beliefs, especially sexual behaviour: *At 70 she was surprisingly broad-minded.* → Compare **narrow-minded** • **ˌbroad-ˈmindedness** noun [U] *My parents always prided themselves on their broad-mindedness.*

broadsheet /ˈbrɔːd.ʃiːt/ (US) /ˈbrɑːd-/ noun [C] UK a newspaper that is printed on large sheets of paper, or an advertisement printed on a large sheet of paper: *In Britain, the broadsheets are generally believed to be more serious than the tabloids.*

broadside /ˈbrɔːd.saɪd/ (US) /ˈbrɑːd-/ noun [C] **1** a strong written or spoken attack (on someone): *The opposition* ***fired/launched*** *yet another broadside* ***at*** *the prime minister.* **2** specialized the action of firing all the guns on one side of a navy ship at the same time

brocade /brəˈkeɪd/ noun [U] heavy cloth with a raised design often of gold or silver threads: *curtains of rich brocade*

broccoli /ˈbrɒk.ᵊl.i/ (US) /ˈbrɑː.kᵊl-/ noun [U] (B1) a vegetable with a thick green stem and a dark green top

brochette /brɒʃˈet/ (US) /broʊˈʃet/ noun [C or U] a long, thin metal pin that is pushed through small pieces of meat or vegetables to hold them in place while they are cooked, or a dish of food cooked this way: *brochettes of lamb*

brochure /ˈbrəʊ.ʃəʳ/ (US) /broʊˈʃʊr/ noun [C] (B1) a type of small magazine that contains pictures and information on a product or a company

brogue /brəʊg/ (US) /broʊg/ noun **WAY OF SPEAKING** ▷ **1** [C usually singular] an Irish or sometimes Scottish way of speaking English: *She spoke in her soft lilting brogue.* **SHOES** ▷ **2 brogues** [plural] strong leather shoes, usually worn by men, often with a pattern in the leather

B

broil /brɔɪl/ verb [T] US for **grill**

broiler /ˈbrɔɪ.ləʳ/ US /-lɚ/ noun [C] a young chicken suitable for ROASTING or GRILLING

ˈbroiler ˌpan noun [C] US for **grill pan**

broiling /ˈbrɔɪ.lɪŋ/ adj US informal very hot: *It was already broiling (= very hot weather) by breakfast time.*

broke /brəʊk/ US /broʊk/ verb; adj

▸verb past simple of **break**

▸adj [after verb] informal without money: *I can't afford to go on holiday this year – I'm (**flat**) broke.* ◦ *Many small businesses **went** broke (= lost all their money) during the recession.*

IDIOM **go for broke** to risk everything in the hope of having great success

broken /ˈbrəʊ.kən/ US /ˈbroʊ-/ verb; adj

▸verb past participle of **break**

▸adj **DAMAGED** ▷ **1** A2 damaged, no longer able to work: *He attacked the man with a broken bottle.* ◦ *My watch is broken.* ◦ *Careful – there's broken **glass** on the floor.* **2** [before noun] suffering emotional pain so great that it changes the way you live, usually as a result of an unpleasant event: *He was **a** broken **man** after his wife died.* **INTERRUPTED** ▷ **3** C1 interrupted or not continuous: *He tried to explain what had happened in broken English (= not spoken easily and stopping a lot).* **ENDED** ▷ **4** C2 destroyed or ended: *a broken engagement* ◦ *She comes from a broken **home** (= one where the parents have separated).* **NOT KEPT** ▷ **5** (of a law, rule, or promise) not obeyed or not kept: *a broken promise*

> **Other ways of saying broken**
>
> If a piece of equipment is broken (not working properly), you can use adjectives such as **dead**, **defunct**, or, informally, **bust** (UK):
>
> *You won't be able to watch the game, the TV's **bust**.*
>
> *The phone's **dead**; there must be a problem with the line.*
>
> If a piece of equipment or machinery in a public place is broken, you can say that it is **out of order**:
>
> *The coffee machine was **out of order**.*
>
> If a piece of equipment has broken, in informal situations you can use the expression **have had it**:
>
> *The kettle's **had it**.*

ˌbroken-ˈdown adj [before noun] describes something that does not now work: *a broken-down washing machine*

ˌbroken-ˈhearted adj extremely unhappy: *She was broken-hearted when her boyfriend left her.* • **broken ˈheart noun** [C] a feeling of great sadness, especially when someone you love dies or does not love you: *They say he **died of a** broken heart.*

broker /ˈbrəʊ.kəʳ/ US /ˈbroʊ.kɚ/ noun; verb

▸noun [C] **1** a person who buys and sells foreign money, SHARES in companies, etc., for other people: *a commodity/insurance/mortgage broker* ◦ *I called my broker for advice about investing in the stock market.* **2** a person who talks to opposing sides, especially governments, making arrangements for them or bringing disagreements to an end: *During the war Wallas became a power broker in governmental circles.*

▸verb [T] to arrange something such as a deal, agreement, etc. between two or more groups or countries: *The foreign ministers have failed in their attempts to broker a ceasefire.*

brokerage /ˈbrəʊ.kər.ɪdʒ/ US /ˈbroʊ-/ noun (also **ˈbrokerage ˌhouse**) specialized **1** [C] an organization that buys and sells foreign money, SHARES in companies, etc. for other people: *an online brokerage* **2** [U] the activity of buying and selling foreign money, SHARES in companies, etc. for other people, or the money that is charged for doing this: *The company's main activity is insurance brokerage.*

brolly /ˈbrɒl.i/ US /ˈbrɑː.li/ noun [C] UK informal for **umbrella**

bromide /ˈbrəʊ.maɪd/ US /ˈbroʊ-/ noun **DRUG** ▷ **1** [C or U] old-fashioned a drug used to calm people who are very unhappy or worried **COMMENT** ▷ **2** [C] formal a remark or statement which, although it might be true, is boring and has no meaning because it has been said so many times before

bromine /ˈbrəʊ.miːn/ US /ˈbroʊ-/ noun [U] (symbol **Br**) a chemical element that exists as a strong-smelling, dark red liquid that changes easily into a gas, used in photographic materials and other industries

bronchial /ˈbrɒŋ.ki.əl/ US /ˈbrɑːŋ-/ adj of the pipes that carry air from the WINDPIPE (= tube in the throat) to the lungs: *bronchial **tubes***

bronchiole /ˈbrɒŋ.ki.əʊl/ US /ˈbrɑːŋ.ki.oʊl/ noun [C] specialized in the lungs, one of the very small tubes that branch out from the bronchi and connect to the ALVEOLI (= little air bags)

bronchitis /brɒŋˈkaɪ.tɪs/ US /brɑːŋˈkaɪ.t̬ɪs/ noun [U] an illness in which the bronchial tubes become infected and swollen, resulting in coughing and difficulty in breathing

bronchus /ˈbrɒŋ.kəs/ US /ˈbrɑːŋ-/ noun [C] (plural **bronchi** /-kaɪ/) specialized one of the two tubes that branch from the TRACHEA (= tube that carries air from the throat to the lungs) and carry air into the lungs

bronco /ˈbrɒŋ.kəʊ/ US /ˈbrɑːŋ.koʊ/ noun [C] (plural **broncos**) a wild horse of the western US

brontosaurus /ˌbrɒn.təˈsɔː.rəs/ US /ˌbrɑːn.t̬əˈsɔːr.əs/ noun [C] (plural **brontosauruses** or **brontosauri**) a large DINOSAUR that ate plants and had four legs, a very long neck and tail and a small head

Bronx cheer /ˌbrɒŋksˈtʃɪəʳ/ US /ˌbrɑːŋksˈtʃɪr/ noun [C] US slang a rude sound made by sticking the tongue out and blowing

bronze /brɒnz/ US /brɑːnz/ noun; adj

▸noun **1** C2 [U] a brown metal made of COPPER and TIN: *The church bells are made of bronze.* **2** [U] a dark orange-brown colour, like the metal bronze **3** [C] a STATUE (= large artistic object) made of bronze **4** C1 [C] (also **bronze ˈmedal**) a small, round piece of bronze given to a person who finishes third in a competition: *He **got** a bronze in the high jump.*

▸adj C2 being dark orange-brown in colour, like the metal bronze

the ˈBronze ˌAge noun [S] the time in the past when tools and weapons were made of bronze, before iron was discovered → Compare **the Iron Age, the Stone Age**

bronzed /brɒnzd/ US /brɑːnzd/ adj If someone is bronzed, their skin is attractively brown because they have been in the sun.

bronzer /ˈbrɒn.zəʳ/ US /ˈbrɑːn.zɚ/ noun [C or U] a cream or powder that you put on your face and body to make your skin look brown from being in the sun

brooch (US also **broach**) /brəʊtʃ/ US /broʊtʃ/ noun [C] a small piece of jewellery with a pin at the back that is fastened to a woman's clothes: *She wore a small silver brooch.*

brood /bruːd/ noun; verb

▸noun [C] **1** a group of young birds all born at the same time: *The blackbird flew back and forth to its*

B

brood. **2** humorous a person's young children: *Ann was at the party with her brood.*

▸**verb** [I] to think for a long time about things that make you sad, worried, or angry: *I wish she wouldn't sit brooding in her room all day.*

brooding /ˈbruː.dɪŋ/ **adj** **1** making you feel uncomfortable or worried, as if something bad is going to happen: *He stood there in the corner of the room, a dark, brooding* ***presence****.* **2** feeling sad, worried, or angry for a long time

ˈbrood ˌmare noun [C] a female horse kept especially for breeding

broody /ˈbruː.di/ **adj** WANTING YOUNG ▷ **1** If a HEN (= female chicken) is broody, she is ready to produce eggs and sit on them. **2** informal describes someone, especially a woman, who feels as if they would like to have a baby: *Much to her surprise, Ruth started feeling broody in her late twenties.* WORRIED ▷ **3** always thinking unhappy thoughts • **broodiness** /-nəs/ **noun** [U]

brook /brʊk/ **noun; verb**

▸**noun** [C] a small stream: *I could hear the sound of a* ***babbling*** *brook.*

▸**verb** formal **brook no sth/not brook sth** to not allow or accept something, especially a difference of opinion or intention: *She won't brook any criticism of her work.*

broom /bruːm/ **noun** BRUSH ▷ **1** /brʊm/ [C] a brush with a long handle, used for cleaning the floor PLANT ▷ **2** [U] a bush with small yellow flowers

broomstick /ˈbruːm.stɪk/, /ˈbrʊm-/ **noun** [C] **1** a broom made of sticks: *In children's books, witches are often shown riding broomsticks.* **2** the long handle of a broom

Bros. /brɒs/ US /brɑːs/ **noun** [plural] abbreviation for brothers (when used in a company's name): *He hired a suit from Moss Bros.*

broth /brɒθ/ US /brɑːθ/ **noun** [U] a thin soup, often with vegetables or rice in it: *chicken/turkey/beef broth*

brothel /ˈbrɒθ.əl/ US /ˈbrɑː.θəl/ **noun** [C] a place where men go and pay to have sex with PROSTITUTES

brother /ˈbrʌð.əʳ/ US /-ɚ/ **noun** [C] **1** A1 a man or boy with the same parents as another person: *Do you have any brothers and sisters?* ◦ *I have three brothers and a sister.* ◦ *Johnny is my younger/older/big/baby/little brother.* ◦ *My brother lives in Washington.* **2** a man who is a member of the same group as you or who shares an interest with you or has a similar way of thinking to you: [as form of address] *'Let us unite, brothers and fight this unjust law!'* **3** US informal sometimes used by a black man to address or refer to another black man **4** used as the title of a man, such as a MONK, who belongs to a religious organization: *Brother Michael and Brother John were deep in conversation.* ◦ [as form of address] *Bless you, Brother.*

IDIOM **I am not my brother's keeper** saying used as a way of saying that you are not responsible for what someone else does or for what happens to them

brotherhood /ˈbrʌð.ə.hʊd/ US /-ɚ-/ **noun** [C, + sing/pl verb] **1** (the members of) a particular organization: *The various groups eventually fused into a single brotherhood.* **2** friendship and loyalty: *The ideal of the brotherhood* ***of man*** *(= where everyone loves each other) is still far from reality.*

ˈbrother-in-law noun [C] (plural **brothers-in-law**) B2 the husband of your sister or brother, or the brother of your husband or wife, or the man who is married to the sister or brother of your wife or husband

brotherly /ˈbrʌð.əl.i/ US /-ɚ.li/ **adj** showing the kindness, interest, or love that you would expect a brother to show: *Can I give you some brotherly advice?*

brougham /bruːm/ **noun** [C] a light CARRIAGE with four wheels and a roof

brought /brɔːt/ US /brɑːt/ **verb** past simple and past participle of **bring**

brouhaha /ˈbruː.hɑː.hɑː/ **noun** [U] old-fashioned informal a lot of noise or angry complaining about something: *the brouhaha* ***over*** *his latest film*

brow /braʊ/ **noun** FACE ▷ **1** [C usually singular] literary the FOREHEAD (= part of the face above the eyes): *She* ***wrinkled*** *her brow as she thought.* ◦ *He paused at the top of the hill and* ***mopped*** *his brow (= rubbed the sweat away).* HILL ▷ **2** [S] the top part of a hill or the edge of something high such as a CLIFF or rock: ***the brow of the*** *hill*

browbeat /ˈbraʊ.biːt/ **verb** [T] (**browbeat**, **browbeaten**) to try to force someone to do something by threatening them or persuading them forcefully and unfairly: *Don't be browbeaten* ***into*** *working more hours than you want.*

brown /braʊn/ **noun; verb**

▸**noun** [C or U] A1 the colour of chocolate or soil: ***dark/light*** *brown* • **brown adj** A1 *Both my parents have curly brown hair.*

▸**verb** [I or T] to make food brown by cooking it: ***Lightly*** *brown the onion before adding the tomatoes.*

ˌbrown-ˈbag adj; verb

▸**adj** [before noun] **brown-bag lunch** food that you take to work with you to eat for your meal in the middle of the day: *There are as many brown-bag lunches eaten today as lunches in restaurants.*

▸**verb** [I or T] US to take your own food to eat during the day, usually in a brown paper bag: *The park has become a place where office workers brown-bag* ***it*** *and take leisurely strolls.*

ˌbrown ˈbread noun [U] mainly UK bread that is light brown in colour, often still containing all the natural qualities of the grain in it

ˌbrowned ˈoff adj [after verb] UK old-fashioned informal annoyed: *I think she gets a bit browned off with him borrowing the car all the time.*

brownfield /ˈbraʊn.fiːld/ **adj** [before noun] UK describes an area of land in a town or city that was previously used for industry and where new buildings can be built

brownie /ˈbraʊ.ni/ **noun** [C] a small, square chocolate cake, often with nuts in it

Brownie /ˈbraʊ.ni/ **noun** [C] (UK also **ˈBrownie ˌGuide**) a girl aged between seven and ten who is a member of the international organization for young women called the Guides, or the Girl Scouts in the US: *The girls wanted to join a Brownie* ***pack*** *(= group).*

IDIOM **earn/get/score brownie points** humorous to get praise or approval for something you have done: *I thought I could score some brownie points with my mother-in-law by offering to cook dinner.*

brownish /ˈbraʊ.nɪʃ/ **adj** slightly brown: *She's got brownish-green eyes.*

ˈbrown-nose verb [I] informal to try too hard to please someone, especially someone in a position of authority, in a way that other people find unpleasant: *The rest of the class were sick of watching him brown-nose.*

ˌbrown ˈpaper noun [U] a strong type of brown paper that is often used for wrapping things in when they are to be sent through the post

brown ˈrice noun [U] rice that still has its outer covering

brownstone /ˈbraʊn.stəʊn/ (US) /-stoʊn/ noun [C] mainly US a house with its front built of a reddish-brown stone, especially common in New York City

brown ˈsugar noun [U] sugar that has only been partly REFINED

browse /braʊz/ verb; noun

▸verb **LOOK** ▷ **1** B2 [I] to look through a book or magazine without reading everything, or to walk around a shop looking at several things without intending to buy any of them: *I was browsing **through** fashion magazines to find a new hairstyle.* **COMPUTING** ▷ **2** B2 [I or T] to look at information on the internet: *to browse the Web* **FEED** ▷ **3** [I] (of animals) to feed on grass, leaves, etc. in a relaxed way: *Deer were browsing (**on** grass) under the trees.*

▸noun [S] mainly UK an act of browsing or period of time spent browsing: *I **had** a browse **through** the books on his desk.*

browser /ˈbraʊ.zəʳ/ (US) /ˈbraʊ.zɚ/ noun [C] **PROGRAM** ▷ **1** B2 a computer program that makes it possible for you to read information on the internet: *a Web browser* **PERSON** ▷ **2** someone who browses, for example through books or goods for sale

bruise /bruːz/ noun; verb

▸noun [C] B2 an injury or mark where the skin has not been broken but is darker in colour, often as a result of being hit by something: *His arms and back were **covered in** bruises.* ◦ *She had a few **cuts and** bruises but nothing serious.* ◦ *One or two of the peaches had bruises on them.*

▸verb [I or T] to develop a bruise or to cause someone or something to have a bruise: *How did you bruise your arm?* ◦ *Bananas and other soft fruits bruise easily.*

bruised /bruːzd/ adj **1** having bruises: *a bruised shoulder/knee/elbow* ◦ *She was **badly** bruised but otherwise unhurt.* **2** emotionally hurt as a result of a bad experience: *Divorce generally leaves both partners feeling rather bruised.*

bruiser /ˈbruː.zəʳ/ (US) /-zɚ/ noun [C] informal disapproving a big, strong, rough man: *He's an ugly bruiser – I wouldn't like to meet him down a dark alley!*

bruising /ˈbruː.zɪŋ/ adj; noun

▸adj A bruising experience is one in which someone defeats you or is very rude to you: *I had a bruising **encounter** with my ex-husband last week.*

▸noun [U] bruises: *The bruising should soon become less painful.*

bruit /bruːt/ verb [T] formal to tell everyone a piece of news: *It's been bruited **abroad/around** that he's going to leave the company.*

Brummie /ˈbrʌm.i/ noun; adj

▸noun [C] UK informal a person who comes from the Birmingham area, in central England

▸adj UK informal from or relating to the Birmingham area: *a Brummie accent*

brunch /brʌntʃ/ noun [C] a meal eaten in the late morning that is a combination of breakfast and LUNCH

brunette /bruˈnet/ noun [C] a white woman or girl with dark hair: *a tall brunette*

brunt /brʌnt/ noun [S] **the brunt of sth** the main force of something unpleasant: *The infantry have **taken/borne** the brunt of the missile attacks.* ◦ *Small companies are **feeling** the **full** brunt of the recession.*

bruschetta /brʊˈsket.ə/ (US) /-ˈsket̬-/ noun [U] a food consisting of a piece of bread that has been TOASTED (= made warm and brown) with tomato, cheese, cold meat, vegetables, etc. on top, often served at the start of a meal

brush /brʌʃ/ noun; verb

▸noun **TOOL** ▷ **1** A2 [C] an object with short pieces of stiff hair, plastic, or wire fixed into a base or handle, used for cleaning, tidying the hair, or painting: *I can't find my brush, but I still have my comb.* ◦ *You'll need a stiff brush to scrape off the rust.* ◦ *a clothes brush* ◦ *a scrubbing (US scrub) brush* ◦ *a pastry brush* **2** A2 [C] used as a combining form: *a hairbrush* ◦ *a toothbrush* ◦ *a paintbrush* **3** B2 [S] mainly UK an act of cleaning with a brush: *These shoes need **a good** brush.* ◦ *Don't forget to **give your hair a** brush before you go out.* **TOUCH** ▷ **4** [C usually singular] a quick, light touch: *He felt the brush **of** her hand on his.* **5 a brush with sth** a situation in which you experience something, or almost experience something, especially something unpleasant: *Jim **had** a brush with death (= was nearly killed) on the motorway.* ◦ *Was that your first brush with **the law** (= experience of being in trouble with the police)?* **BUSHES** ▷ **6** [U] US small, low bushes or the rough land they grow on: *We spotted a jackrabbit hidden in the brush.* ◦ *The dry weather has increased the risk of brush **fires**.* **7** [U] US **brushwood** **TAIL** ▷ **8** [C] the tail of a FOX

▸verb **TOUCH** ▷ **1** B2 [I + adv/prep, T] to touch (something) quickly and lightly or carelessly: *Charlotte brushed **against** him (= touched him quickly and lightly with her arm or body) as she left the room.* ◦ *His lips gently brushed her cheek and he was gone.* **2** C1 [T + adv/prep] to move something somewhere using a brush or your hand: *Jackie brushed the hair out of her eyes.* ◦ *He brushed **away** a tear.* ◦ *She stood up and brushed the wrinkles from her dress.* **CLEAN** ▷ **3** A2 [T] to clean something or make something smooth with a brush: *When did he last brush his **teeth**, she wondered.* ◦ *She brushed her **hair** with long, regular strokes.* ◦ [+ obj + adj] *My trousers got covered in mud, but luckily I was able to brush them clean.*

PHRASAL VERBS **brush sb/sth aside** to refuse to consider something seriously because you feel that it is not important: *She brushed their objections aside, saying 'Leave it to me.'* • **brush sb/sth off** C1 to remove dust or dirt from someone or something by using your hands or a brush: *He brushed the snow off his coat.* • **brush sth off** to refuse to listen to what someone says, or to refuse to think about something seriously: *He just brushed off all their criticisms.* • **brush past sb** to walk quickly past someone, usually because you do not want to speak to them: *Ignoring their protests, Newman brushed past waiting journalists.* • **brush up (on) sth** C1 to improve your knowledge of something already learned but partly forgotten: *I thought I'd brush up (on) my French before going to Paris.*

brushed /brʌʃt/ adj [before noun] describes material that has been treated to make it soft and like fur: *Her nightdress was made of brushed **nylon/cotton**.*

the ˈbrush-off noun [S] informal **give sb the brush-off** to refuse to talk or be pleasant to someone: *So she's given you the brush-off, has she?*

brushstroke /ˈbrʌʃ.strəʊk/ (US) /-stroʊk/ noun [C usually plural] **1** the way in which something, especially paint, is put on to a surface with a brush: *The artist painted this picture using tiny/vigorous/swirling brushstrokes (= movements of the brush).* **2** the way in which a plan or idea is explained: *She described the project in very **broad** brushstrokes (= without any details).*

brushwood /ˈbrʌʃ.wʊd/ noun [U] (also **brush**) small branches that have broken off from trees and bushes

brushwork /ˈbrʌʃ.wɜːk/ (US) /-wɝːk/ noun [U] the

particular style that an artist has of putting paint onto the painting with a brush

B

brusque /bruːsk/ ⓊⓈ /brʌsk/ **adj** quick and rude in manner or speech: *His secretary was rather brusque **with** me.* • **brusquely** /-li/ **adv** *'I haven't got time to deal with it today,' she said brusquely.* • **brusqueness** /-nəs/ **noun** [U]

Brussels sprout /ˌbrʌs.əlz ˈspraʊt/ **noun** [C] (UK also **sprout**) a green vegetable like a very small CABBAGE that is boiled and eaten

brutal /ˈbruː.təl/ ⓊⓈ /-t̬əl/ **adj** **1** C1 cruel, violent, and completely without feelings: *a brutal dictator* ◦ *He had presided over a brutal regime in which thousands of people had 'disappeared'.* ◦ *He was imprisoned in 1945 for the brutal **murder** of a twelve-year-old girl.* **2** not considering someone's feelings: *She spoke with brutal **honesty** – I was too old for the job.* • **brutally** /-i/ **adv** *The old man had been brutally **attacked/murdered**.* ◦ *To be brutally **honest/frank**, you look fat in that dress.*

brutality /bruːˈtæl.ə.ti/ ⓊⓈ /-t̬i/ **noun** [U or C] behaviour that is very cruel or violent and showing no feelings for others, or an act of this type: *the brutalities of war* ◦ *Seeing so much brutality towards prisoners had not hardened them to it.*

brutalize (UK usually **brutalise**) /ˈbruː.təl.aɪz/ ⓊⓈ /-t̬əl-/ **verb** [T] to treat someone in a cruel and violent way: *The police in that country routinely brutalize prisoners.*

brute /bruːt/ **noun; adj**

▸**noun** [C] **1** disapproving a rough and sometimes violent man: [as form of address] *Take your hands off me, you brute!* **2** an animal, especially a large one: *Your dog's an ugly brute, isn't it?* ◦ *The oldest elephant was lame, poor brute.*

▸**adj** [before noun] **brute force** great physical force or strength: *In the end she used brute force to push him out.*

brutish /ˈbruː.tɪʃ/ ⓊⓈ /-t̬ɪʃ/ **adj** rough, unpleasant, and often violent: *It has been said that life is often 'nasty, brutish, and short'.*

bruv /brʌv/ **noun** [C usually singular] UK informal humorous a brother: *So he's a bit of an idiot, but he's still my bruv, ain't he?*

BS /ˌbiːˈes/ **noun** US informal abbreviation for **bullshit**

BSc /ˌbiː.esˈsiː/ **noun** [C] UK (US **BS**) abbreviation for Bachelor of Science: a first-level university degree in science: *C.G. Smith, BSc* ◦ *a BSc **in** geology/chemistry/ biology*

BSE /ˌbiː.esˈiː/ **noun** [U] abbreviation for bovine spongiform encephalopathy: a brain disease in CATTLE (= male and female cows) that causes the death of the animal

BST /ˌbiː.esˈtiː/ **noun** [U] abbreviation for **British Summer Time**

btw written abbreviation for by the way: used, for example in emails, when you are writing something that relates to the subject you are discussing, but is not the main point of the discussion

bub /bʌb/ **noun** [C] US old-fashioned informal a form of address used to a man, sometimes in a slightly angry way: *That may be what you do at home, but listen, bub, you don't do it here!*

bubble /ˈbʌb.l/ **noun; verb**

▸**noun** **AIR BALL** ▷ C1 [C] a ball of gas that appears in a liquid, or a ball formed of air surrounded by liquid that floats in the air: *As water begins to boil, bubbles rise to the surface.*

IDIOM **the bubble bursts** If the bubble bursts, a very happy, pleasant, or successful time suddenly ends: *He made millions before the dotcom bubble burst.*

▸**verb** [I] C2 to produce bubbles: *We could hear the porridge bubbling **away** (= bubbling strongly) in the pot.*

PHRASAL VERB **bubble over** C1 to be very excited and enthusiastic: *She was bubbling over **with** excitement/ enthusiasm.*

ˌbubble and ˈsqueak **noun** [U] UK a food made by mixing together and heating cooked potato and CABBAGE

ˈbubble ˌbath **noun** [C or U] a special liquid soap with a pleasant smell, that you put in a bath to make a lot of bubbles

ˈbubble ˌgum **noun** [U] CHEWING GUM that you can blow into the shape of a bubble

bubblejet /ˈbʌb.l̩.dʒet/ **adj** [before noun] specialized describes a very fast and quiet method of printing, in which the ink is directed electronically onto the paper: *a bubblejet printer*

ˈbubble ˌwrap **noun** [U] trademark a sheet of plastic bubbles that is used for wrapping things in order to protect them, for example, when they are being posted or taken somewhere

bubbly /ˈbʌb.li/ **adj; noun**

▸**adj** informal (especially of a woman or girl) attractively full of energy and enthusiasm: *She's a very bubbly character.*

▸**noun** [U] informal CHAMPAGNE (= expensive white or pink alcoholic drink with bubbles): *Let's crack open a bottle of bubbly to celebrate.*

bubonic plague /bjuːˌbɒn.ɪkˈpleɪɡ/ ⓊⓈ /-ˌbɑː.nɪk-/ **noun** [U] a very infectious disease spread by RATS, causing swelling, fever, and usually death. In the 14th century it killed half the people living in Europe.

buccaneer /ˌbʌk.əˈnɪəʳ/ ⓊⓈ /-ˈnɪr/ **noun** [C] a person who attacked and stole from ships at sea, especially in the 17th and 18th centuries → Synonym **pirate**

buck /bʌk/ **noun; verb**

▸**noun** [C] **MONEY** ▷ **1** (plural **bucks**) US Australian English, informal a dollar: *Can I borrow a couple of bucks?* ◦ *He charged me 20 bucks for a new hubcap.* **2** (plural **bucks**) Indian English, informal a **rupee** **3** (plural **bucks**) South African English, informal a **rand** **4** (plural **bucks**) informal used in a number of expressions about money, usually expressions referring to a lot of money: *He earns **mega**bucks (= a lot of money) working for an American bank.* ◦ *So what's the best way to **make a fast** buck (= earn money easily and quickly)?* **ANIMAL** ▷ **5** (plural **buck** or **bucks**) the male of some animals such as DEER and RABBITS, or (in South Africa) a male or female ANTELOPE → Compare **doe**

IDIOMS **pass the buck** to blame someone or make them responsible for a problem that you should deal with: *She's always trying to pass the buck and I'm sick of it!* • **the buck stops here** saying said by someone who is responsible for making decisions and who will be blamed if things go wrong

▸**verb** [I] (of a horse) to jump into the air and kick out with the back legs

IDIOMS **buck the system** to refuse to follow the rules of an organization • **buck the trend** to be obviously different from the way that a situation is developing generally, especially in connection with financial matters: *This company is the only one to have bucked the trend of a declining industry.*

PHRASAL VERB **buck (sb/sth) up** UK informal to become happier or more positive or to make someone happier or more positive: *Oh, buck up for heaven's sake, Anthony! I'm sick of looking at your miserable face.* ◦ *She was told that if she didn't buck her* ***ideas*** *up* (= start working in a more positive way)*, she'd be out of a job.* ◦ *A holiday will buck her up.*

bucket /ˈbʌk.ɪt/ noun; verb
▸noun [C] B1 a container with an open top and a handle, often used for carrying liquids: *Armed with a bucket and a mop, I started washing the floor.* ◦ *I took my two-year-old nephew down to the beach with his bucket* ***and spade****.*

IDIOMS **in buckets** informal in great amounts: *The rain came down in buckets.* • **sweat buckets** informal to SWEAT a lot: *It was my first interview and I was sweating buckets.* • **weep buckets** UK (US **cry buckets**) to cry a lot: *That was such a sad film – I wept buckets at the end of it.*

▸verb

PHRASAL VERB **bucket down** UK informal to rain heavily: *It's absolutely bucketing down.*

bucketload /ˈbʌk.ɪt.ləʊd/ US /-loʊd/ noun [C usually plural] UK informal a large amount of something: *He has bucketloads* ***of*** *charm.*

ˈ**bucket** ˌ**seat** noun [C] a rounded seat with high sides for one person, especially in a car

ˈ**bucket** ˌ**shop** noun [C] UK informal a travel company that sells aircraft tickets at a low price

buckle /ˈbʌk.l̩/ noun; verb
▸noun [C] a piece of metal at one end of a belt or strap, used to fasten the two ends together
▸verb FASTEN ▷ **1** [T or I] to fasten or be fastened with a buckle BEND ▷ **2** [T or I] to bend something or become bent, often as a result of force, heat, or weakness: *The intense heat from the fire had caused the factory roof to buckle.* ◦ *Both* ***wheels*** *on the bicycle had been badly buckled.* ◦ *I felt faint and my* ***knees*** *began to buckle.* BE DEFEATED ▷ **3 buckle under sth** to be defeated by a difficult situation: *But these were difficult times and a lesser man would have buckled under the strain.* • **buckled** /-l̩d/ adj *a tightly buckled belt*

PHRASAL VERB **buckle down** to start working hard: *He'll have to buckle down* (***to*** *his work) soon if he wants to pass these exams.*

ˌ**buck** ˈ**naked** adj US informal completely naked

ˌ**Buck's** ˈ**Fizz** noun [C or U] UK (US **mimosa**) an alcoholic drink made from CHAMPAGNE and orange juice

buckshot /ˈbʌk.ʃɒt/ US /-ʃɑːt/ noun [U] many small balls of metal shot from a SHOTGUN

buckskin /ˈbʌk.skɪn/ noun [U] soft, strong leather made from the skin of a DEER or a sheep

ˈ**bucks** ˌ**party** noun [C] Australian a party for a man who is going to get married, to which only his male friends are invited → See also **stag night/party**

ˌ**buck** ˈ**teeth** noun [plural] informal upper front teeth that stick out • ˌ**buck-**ˈ**toothed** adj

buckwheat /ˈbʌk.wiːt/ noun [U] small, dark grain used for feeding animals and for making flour

bucolic /bjuˈkɒl.ɪk/ US /-ˈkɑː.lɪk/ adj literary relating to the countryside: *The painting shows a typically bucolic scene with peasants.*

bud /bʌd/ noun; verb
▸noun [C] PLANT PART ▷ **1** a small part of a plant, that develops into a flower or leaf **2 in bud** covered with buds: *It was springtime and the fruit trees were in bud.* MAN ▷ **3** US informal **buddy**
▸verb [I] (**-dd-**) to produce buds: *The unusually cold winter has caused many plants to bud late this year.*

Buddha /ˈbʊd.ə/ noun **1** the holy man (563–483 BC) on whose life and teachings Buddhism is based **2** [C] an image or STATUE (= large model) of Buddha

Buddhism /ˈbʊd.ɪ.zəm/ noun [U] a religion that originally comes from South Asia, and teaches that personal spiritual improvement will lead to escape from human suffering

Buddhist /ˈbʊd.ɪst/ noun [C] someone who believes in Buddhism • **Buddhist** adj *a Buddhist temple*

budding /ˈbʌd.ɪŋ/ adj [before noun] beginning to develop or show signs of future success in a particular area: *While still at school she was clearly a budding* ***genius****.*

buddy /ˈbʌd.i/ noun; verb
▸noun [C] informal **1** a friend: *Bob and I have been great buddies for years.* **2** [as form of address] (also **bud**) US used when talking to a man, sometimes in a friendly way but often when you are annoyed **3** someone who provides friendly help to someone with an illness or a problem: *We run a buddy system to support recovering alcoholics.*
▸verb

PHRASAL VERB **buddy up** informal to become friends with someone: *He quickly buddied up with Jan's husband.*

budge /bʌdʒ/ verb [I or T] MOVE ▷ **1** If something will not budge or you cannot budge it, it will not move: *I've tried moving the desk but it won't budge/I can't budge it.* CHANGE ▷ **2** to change your opinion or to make someone change their opinion: *I've tried persuading her, but she* ***won't*** *budge.*

PHRASAL VERB **budge up** UK informal said to someone in order to ask them to move so that there is room for you

budget /ˈbʌdʒ.ɪt/ noun; verb; adj
▸noun **1** B2 [C or U] a plan to show how much money a person or organization will earn and how much they will need or be able to spend: *The firm has* ***drawn up*** *a budget for the coming financial year.* ◦ *Libraries are finding it increasingly difficult to remain* ***within*** (their) *budget.* **2** B2 [C] the amount of money you have available to spend: *an annual budget of £40 million*
▸verb [I or T] to plan how much money you will spend on something: *An extra £20 million has been budgeted* ***for*** *schools this year.* • **budgetary** /ˈbʌdʒ.ɪ.tər.i/ US /-ter.i/ adj *budgetary constraints*
▸adj [before noun] B2 very cheap: *a budget holiday/hotel/price*

ˌ**the** ˈ**Budget** noun [C] in the UK, the official statement that the government makes about how much it will collect in taxes and spend on public services in the future

budgie /ˈbʌdʒ.i/ noun [C] (formal **budgerigar**) a small, brightly coloured bird, often kept as a pet

ˈ**budgie** ˌ**smugglers** noun [plural] UK informal humorous small, tight SWIMMING TRUNKS for men

buff /bʌf/ noun; adj; verb
▸noun [C] informal a person who knows a lot about and is very interested in a particular subject: *a computer/opera/film buff*

IDIOM **in the buff** informal naked

▸adj COLOUR ▷ **1** (of) a pale, yellowish-brown colour: *a buff envelope* HEALTHY ▷ **2** If a man is buff, he has a body that is a good shape, and looks as if he has done a lot of exercise: *He was spotted on the beach looking extremely buff.*

▸verb [T] to rub an object made of metal, wood, or leather in order to make it shine, using a soft, dry cloth

buffalo /ˈbʌf.ə.ləʊ/ (US) /-loʊ/ **noun** [C] (plural **buffaloes** or **buffalo**) a large animal of the CATTLE family, with long, curved horns

buffer /ˈbʌf.əʳ/ (US) /-ɚ/ **noun; verb**

▸noun **PROTECTION** ▷ **1** [C] something or someone that helps protect from harm: *I bought a house as a buffer **against** inflation.* **2** [C] the metal parts at the front and back of a train or at the end of a track, that help protect the train and reduce damage if the train hits something **EXTRA SUPPLY** ▷ **3** [C] an extra supply of materials that a company keeps in order to prevent a situation where none are available: *'Just-in-time production' means that no buffer **stocks** are held in the factory.* **MAN** ▷ **4** [C] UK old-fashioned a silly old man: *Silly old buffer!*

▸verb [T] **PROVIDE PROTECTION** ▷ **1** to provide protection against harm **STORE INFORMATION** ▷ **2** specialized When a computer buffers information, it stores it temporarily in its memory, for example while you are sending it from one place to another.

ˈbuffer ˌstate noun [C] a peaceful country between two larger countries, that reduces the chances of war between them

ˈbuffer ˌzone noun [C] an area intended to separate two armies that are fighting

buffet noun; verb

▸noun [C] /ˈbʊf.eɪ/ (US) /bəˈfeɪ/ **1** a meal where people serve themselves different types of usually cold food: *Are you having a sit-down meal or a buffet at the wedding?* **2** UK a restaurant in a station, where food and drinks can be bought and eaten

▸verb [T] /ˈbʌf.ɪt/ (of wind, rain, etc.) to hit something repeatedly and with great force: *The little boat was buffeted mercilessly by the waves.*

ˈbuffet ˌcar noun [C] mainly UK a CARRIAGE on a train where food and drinks can be bought

buffoon /bəˈfuːn/ **noun** [C] a person who does silly things, usually to make other people laugh: *Doesn't he get tired of **playing the** buffoon in class?* • **buffoonery** /bəˈfuː.nəʳr.i/ (US) /-nɚ-/ **noun** [U]

bug /bʌɡ/ **noun; verb**

▸noun **INSECT** ▷ **1** (B1) [C] a very small insect **ILLNESS** ▷ **2** (B2) [C] informal a bacteria or a virus causing an illness that is usually not serious: *I had a **tummy/stomach** bug last week.* ◦ *There's a bug **going around*** (= *an illness that many people are getting*). **COMPUTER PROBLEM** ▷ **3** (B2) [C] a mistake or problem in a computer program: *A bug caused the company's computer system to crash.* **DEVICE** ▷ **4** [C] a very small device fixed on to a phone or hidden in a room, that allows you to listen to what people are saying without them knowing **ENTHUSIASM** ▷ **5** [S] informal a very strong enthusiasm for something: *He's **been bitten by** the sailing bug.*

▸verb [T] (-gg-) **ANNOY** ▷ **1** informal to annoy or worry someone: *He's been bugging me all morning.* **HIDE DEVICE** ▷ **2** to place or hide a listening device inside something: often passive *She suspected that her phone had been bugged.*

bugbear /ˈbʌɡ.beəʳ/ (US) /-ber/ **noun** [C] a particular thing that annoys or upsets you: *Smoking is a particular bugbear **of** his.*

ˈbug-eyed adj having eyes that stick out

bugger /ˈbʌɡ.əʳ/ (US) /-ɚ/ **noun; exclamation; verb**

▸noun [C] **1** UK offensive a silly or annoying person: *Well you shouldn't have drunk so much, should you, you daft bugger!* ◦ *The stupid bugger's given me the wrong ticket!* **2** informal used to or about someone that you feel sympathy for: *The **poor** bugger has nowhere else to sleep.* **3** US informal a person or animal, especially a young one that you like very much: *He's a cute little bugger, isn't he?* **4** UK offensive something that is very difficult or annoying: *This tin is a bugger to open.*

IDIOM **bugger all** UK offensive very little or nothing: *'How much do you know about marketing?' 'Bugger all.'*

▸exclamation UK offensive **1** used to express anger: *Oh bugger, it's raining!* **2 bugger it!** used to express great anger: *Bugger it! I'm going to miss my train.* **3 bugger me!** used to express great surprise: *Bugger me! Did you see the speed that motorbike was going?*

▸verb [T] **DAMAGE** ▷ **1** UK offensive to break or spoil something: *You've just buggered your **chances** of promotion!* **HAVE SEX** ▷ **2** offensive or legal to have sex by putting the PENIS in another person's ANUS • **buggery** /-i/ **noun** [U] offensive or legal ANAL sex

IDIOM **I'm buggered if...** UK offensive used to show that you certainly will not or cannot do something: *I'm buggered if I'm going to lend him any more money.*

PHRASAL VERBS **bugger about** UK offensive to waste time doing silly or unimportant things • **bugger sb about** UK offensive to treat someone badly by wasting their time or causing them problems: *Stop buggering me about and tell me the truth!* • **bugger off** UK offensive to leave or go away, used especially as a rude way of telling someone to go away: *By the time I got there you two had already buggered off!* ◦ *Bugger off, will you?* • **bugger sth up** UK offensive to damage something or cause problems by doing something stupid: *Mike's buggered up the video again.*

buggered /ˈbʌɡ.əd/ (US) /-ɚd/ **adj** UK offensive broken, or very tired: *The television's buggered, but I can't afford to get it repaired.* ◦ *I walked over 20 miles – I was buggered the next day.*

buggy /ˈbʌɡ.i/ **noun** [C] **BABY CHAIR** ▷ **1** UK a **pushchair** **CAR** ▷ **2** a small car, usually with no roof, designed for driving on rough ground: *a golf/dune buggy* **CARRIAGE** ▷ **3** old-fashioned a light CARRIAGE pulled by one horse

bugle /ˈbjuː.ɡl/ **noun** [C] a musical instrument like a simple TRUMPET, used especially in the army

build /bɪld/ **verb; noun**

▸verb (**built, built**) **1** (A2) [T or I] to make something by putting bricks or other materials together: *They're building new **houses** by the river.* ◦ *The birds built their nest in the tree.* ◦ *These old houses are built* (= *made*) ***of** stone.* ◦ *Contractors have started building on waste land near the town.* **2** [T] to create and develop something over a long period of time: *We want to build a better **future** for our children.*

IDIOMS **build bridges** to improve relationships between people who are very different or do not like each other: *A local charity is working to build bridges **between** different ethnic groups in the area.* • **Rome wasn't built in a day** saying said to emphasize that you cannot expect to do important things in a short period of time

PHRASAL VERBS **build around sth** [usually passive] to base something on an idea or principle: *The independence movement sought to unify the country with a national identity built around a common language.* • **build sth in/into sth** to include something as part of a plan, system, or agreement: *When drawing up a contract it is vital to build in safety measures.* ◦ figurative *Inequalities are often built into* (= *cannot be separated from*) *society.*

• **build on sth** to use a success or achievement as a base from which to achieve more success: *We must build on our reputation to expand the business.* ◦ *A good relationship is built on trust.* • **build (sb/sth) up** C1 to increase or become larger or stronger, or to cause someone or something to do this: *Tension is building up **between** the two communities.* ◦ *They gave him soup to build up his **strength**/build him up.* ◦ *It took her ten years to build up her publishing business.* • **build sth/sb up** to praise something or someone in a way that will influence people's opinions

▸**noun** [C or U] the size and shape of a person's body: *She was of **slim** build with short, dark hair.*

builder /ˈbɪl.dər/ US /-dɚ/ noun [C] B1 a person whose job it is to make buildings

building /ˈbɪl.dɪŋ/ noun **1** A2 [C] a structure with walls and a roof, such as a house or factory: *The once-empty site was now covered with buildings.* **2** A2 [U] the process or business of making structures such as houses or factories: *He started off in the building **trade** before opening his own restaurant.*

ˈbuilding ˌblock noun **1** [C] a piece of wood or plastic used by children to build things with **2 building blocks** [plural] the basic things that are put together to make something exist: *Science and the arts are the building blocks **of** a good education.*

ˈbuilding ˌsite noun [C] a piece of land on which a house or other building is being built

ˈbuilding soˌciety noun [C] UK (US **ˌsavings and ˈloan associˌation**) a business that lends you money if you want to buy a house, or pays you interest on money you INVEST there

ˈbuild-up noun [C usually singular] **INCREASE** ▷ **1** an increase, especially one that is gradual: *The build-up of troops in the region makes war seem more likely.* **PRAISE** ▷ **2** a situation in which someone or something is praised, advertised, or talked about on the internet, in newspapers, etc.: *The group got a big build-up before their tour, being touted by many as the next Beatles.* **PREPARATION** ▷ **3** UK the period of preparation before something happens: *There was a lot of excitement in **the** build-up **to** the Olympics.*

ˌbuilt-ˈin adj [before noun] If a place or piece of equipment has built-in objects, they are permanently connected and cannot be easily removed: *All the rooms have built-in **cupboards/wardrobes**.*

ˌbuilt-ˈup adj [before noun] A built-up area is one where there are a lot of buildings.

bulb /bʌlb/ noun [C] **PLANT** ▷ **1** a round root of some plants from which the plant grows: *tulip bulbs* **LIGHT** ▷ **2** B1 a **light bulb**

bulbous /ˈbʌl.bəs/ adj If a part of the body is bulbous, it is fat and round: *He had a huge, bulbous nose.*

bulgar (also **bulgur**) /ˈbʌl.gər/ US /-gɚ/ noun [U] (also **ˌbulgar ˈwheat**) grains of WHEAT that are boiled, dried, and used in cooking

bulge /bʌldʒ/ verb; noun

▸**verb** [I] to stick out in a round shape: *Her bags were bulging **with** shopping.* • **bulging** /ˈbʌl.dʒɪŋ/ adj *She dragged her bulging (= very full) suitcase up the stairs.* ◦ *big, bulging (= sticking out) eyes*

▸**noun** [C] **1** a curved shape sticking out from the surface of something: *I wondered what the bulge in her coat pocket was.* **2** a sudden increase that soon returns to the usual level: *There was a bulge **in** spending in the early part of the year.*

bulgur /ˈbʌl.gər/ US /-gɚ/ noun [U] **bulgar**

bulimia /buˈlɪm.i.ə/, /-ˈliː.mi-/ noun [U] a mental illness in which someone eats in an uncontrolled way and in large amounts, then vomits intentionally → Compare **anorexia nervosa** • **bulimic** /buˈlɪm.ɪk/, /-ˈliː.mɪk/ noun [C], adj

bulk /bʌlk/ noun; verb

▸**noun 1** [C usually singular] something or someone that is very large: *She eased her large bulk out of the chair.* **2** [U] large size or mass: *It was a document of surprising bulk.* **3 in bulk** C1 in large amounts: *The office **buys** paper in bulk to keep down costs.* **4 the bulk of sth** C1 most of something: *In fact, the bulk of the book is taken up with criticizing other works.*

▸**verb**

IDIOM **bulk large** literary to be present and important: *Fears of his death bulked large in her thoughts.*

PHRASAL VERB **bulk sth out** to make something bigger or thicker by adding something: *I added some potatoes to the stew to bulk it out.*

ˌbulk-ˈbuy verb [T or I] to buy something in large amounts: *Because we're such a large family, we find it cheaper to bulk-buy foods we eat a lot of.*

bulkhead /ˈbʌlk.hed/ noun [C] specialized a wall that divides the inside of a ship or aircraft

bulky /ˈbʌl.ki/ adj C1 too big and taking up too much space: *bulky equipment*

bull /bʊl/ noun **ANIMAL** ▷ **1** B1 [C] a male cow, or the male of particular animals such as the ELEPHANT or the WHALE: *They did not see the sign by the gate saying 'Beware of the bull'.* **FINANCE** ▷ **2** [C] specialized a person who buys SHARES in companies hoping the price will rise, so that they can be sold later at a profit → Compare **bear NONSENSE** ▷ **3** [U] informal complete nonsense or something that is not true: *Don't **give** me **that** bull **about** not knowing the time.*

IDIOMS **like a bull in a china shop** If someone is like a bull in a china shop, they are very careless in the way that they move or behave: *We told her it was a delicate situation but she went into the meeting like a bull in a china shop.* • **take the bull by the horns** to do something difficult in a brave and determined way: *Why don't you take the bull by the horns and tell him to leave?*

ˈbull ˌbar noun [C usually plural] a metal frame fixed in front of the front lights of a vehicle to prevent serious damage if the vehicle hits an animal

bulldog /ˈbʊl.dɒg/ US /-dɑːg/ noun [C] a small dog that can be frightening and has a strong body, short legs, and a large, square-shaped face

ˈbulldog ˌclip noun [C] UK trademark (US **clip**) a metal device used for holding pieces of paper together

bulldoze /ˈbʊl.dəʊz/ US /-doʊz/ verb [T] **1** to destroy buildings and make an area flat with a bulldozer **2** to force someone to do something, although they might not want to: *She bulldozed her daughter **into** buying a new dress.*

bulldozer /ˈbʊlˌdəʊ.zər/ US /-ˌdoʊ.zɚ/ noun [C] a heavy vehicle with a large blade in front, used for pushing earth and stones along and for making areas of ground flat at the same time

bulldozer

bulldyke /ˈbʊl.daɪk/ noun [C] offensive a LESBIAN (= a woman who is sexually attracted to other women) who is very like a man in appearance and behaviour

bullet /ˈbʊl.ɪt/ noun [C] **1** B2 a small, metal object that is shot from a gun: *A bullet had lodged in the boy's leg.* **2** a **bullet point**

B

bulletin /ˈbʊl.ə.tɪn/ (US) /-t̬ɪn/ noun [C] a short news programme on television or radio, often about something that has just happened, or a short newspaper printed by an organization: *an hourly news bulletin* ◦ *The company publishes a fortnightly bulletin for its staff.*

ˈbulletin ˌboard noun [C] **1** a place on a computer system where users can read messages and add their own **2** B1 US for **noticeboard**

ˈbullet ˌpoint noun [C] (also **bullet**) a symbol, often a small, black circle, used in text to show separate things in a list

bulletproof /ˈbʊl.ɪt.pruːf/ adj Something that is bulletproof prevents bullets from going through it: *bulletproof **glass*** ◦ *a bulletproof **vest***

bullfight /ˈbʊl.faɪt/ noun [C] a traditional public entertainment, especially in Spain, in which a person fights and sometimes kills a BULL (= male cow) • **bullfighter** /-ˌfaɪ.təʳ/ (US) /-ˌfaɪ.t̬ɚ/ noun [C] • **bullfighting** /-ˌfaɪ.tɪŋ/ (US) /-ˌfaɪ.t̬ɪŋ/ noun [U]

bullfinch /ˈbʊl.fɪntʃ/ noun [C] a small European bird with a black head and a pink chest

bullfrog /ˈbʊl.frɒg/ (US) /-frɑːg/ noun [C] a large North American FROG that makes a loud, deep, rough noise

bullheaded /ˌbʊlˈhed.ɪd/ adj disapproving very determined to do what you want to do, especially without considering other people's feelings

bullhorn /ˈbʊl.hɔːn/ (US) /-hɔːrn/ noun [C] US old-fashioned for **megaphone**

bullion /ˈbʊl.i.ən/ noun [U] gold or silver in the form of bars: *gold bullion*

bullish /ˈbʊl.ɪʃ/ adj **ATTITUDE** ▷ **1** giving your opinions in a powerful and confident way: *She's being very bullish about the firm's future.* **FINANCIAL MARKET** ▷ **2** describes a financial market in which SHARE prices are rising

ˈbull ˌmarket noun [C] a time when the prices of most SHARES are rising

bullock /ˈbʊl.ək/ noun [C] a young male cow that has had its TESTICLES removed

bullpen /ˈbʊl.pen/ noun [C] US in baseball, a place near the playing area where PITCHERS (= people throwing the ball) can throw the ball to get ready to play in the game

bullring /ˈbʊl.rɪŋ/ noun [C] a circular area surrounded by seats, used for BULLFIGHTS

bullseye /ˈbʊl.zaɪ/ noun **CENTRE** ▷ [C usually singular] the circular centre of the object aimed at in games such as DARTS, or the shot or throw that hits this

bullshit /ˈbʊl.ʃɪt/ exclamation, noun; verb

▸exclamation, noun [U] offensive complete nonsense or something that is not true: *Bullshit! He never said that!* ◦ *He gave me some excuse but it was **a load of** bullshit.*

▸verb [I or T] (**-tt-**) offensive to try to persuade someone or make them admire you by saying things that are not true: *You're bullshitting me!* ◦ *Quit bullshitting, will you!* • **bullshitter** /-ˌʃɪt.əʳ/ (US) /-ˌʃɪt̬.ɚ/ noun [C]

ˌbull ˈterrier noun [C] a strong-looking type of dog with short hair

bully /ˈbʊl.i/ noun; verb

▸noun [C] C1 someone who hurts or frightens someone who is smaller or less powerful than them, often forcing them to do something they do not want to do: *You're just a **big** bully!* ◦ *Teachers usually know who the bullies are in a class.*

IDIOM **bully for sb** old-fashioned used to show that you do not think what someone has done or said is very exciting or interesting: *'He's started ironing his own shirts.' 'Well, bully for him!'*

▸verb [T] C1 to hurt or frighten someone who is smaller or less powerful than you, often forcing them to do something they do not want to do: *Our survey indicates that one in four children is bullied at school.* ◦ *Don't let anyone bully you **into** doing something you don't want to do.* • **bullying** /-ɪŋ/ noun [U] *Bullying is a problem in many schools.*

ˈbully ˌboy noun [C] informal a rough and threatening man, especially one paid by someone to hurt or frighten other people: [before noun] *bully-boy tactics*

bulrush /ˈbʊl.rʌʃ/ noun [C] a plant with tall stems that grows near rivers and lakes

bulwark /ˈbʊl.wək/ (US) /-wɚk/ noun [C] formal something that protects you from dangerous or unpleasant situations: *My savings were to be a bulwark **against** unemployment.*

bum /bʌm/ noun; adj; verb

▸noun [C] **BODY PART** ▷ **1** mainly UK informal the part of the body that you sit on → Synonym **bottom** **PERSON** ▷ **2** US informal someone who has no home or job and lives by asking other people for money

▸adj [before noun] slang bad in quality or not useful: *He gave us bum directions, but we eventually found the place.*

▸verb [T] (**-mm-**) slang to ask someone for something without intending to pay for it: *Could I bum a cigarette **off** you?*

PHRASAL VERBS **bum around** informal to spend time being lazy and doing very little: *I wish you'd stop bumming around and start looking for a job.* • **bum around/about (somewhere)** informal to travel around in different places or in a particular area, with no plans, no job, and little money: *After college she spent a year bumming around the States.*

bumbag /ˈbʌm.bæg/ noun [C] UK (US **ˈfanny ˌpack**) a small bag fixed to a long strap that you fasten around your waist, used for carrying money, keys, etc.

bumble /ˈbʌm.bl̩/ verb [I + adv/prep] to speak or move in a confused way

bumblebee /ˈbʌm.bl̩.biː/ noun [C] a large BEE that is covered with short hairs and makes a loud noise when it flies

bumbling /ˈbʌm.blɪŋ/ adj confused and showing no skill: *I've never seen such bumbling incompetence!*

bumf (also **bumph**) /bʌmf/ noun [U] mainly UK informal printed information, such as an advertisement or official document, that is usually unwanted and not interesting: *I got a load of bumf from my bank in the post today.*

bummer /ˈbʌm.əʳ/ (US) /-ɚ/ noun [S] offensive something that is very annoying or not convenient: *'I've left my wallet at home.' 'What a bummer!'* ◦ US *I locked my keys in the car – bummer!*

bump /bʌmp/ verb; noun

▸verb **HIT** ▷ **1** B2 [I + adv/prep] to hit something with force: *She bumped **into** his tray, knocking the food onto his lap.* **2** B2 [T usually + adv/prep] to hurt part of your body by hitting it against something hard: *I bumped my head **on** the shelf as I stood up.* **TRAVEL** ▷ **3** [I + adv/prep] to travel, usually in a vehicle, in an uncomfortable way because the surface you are moving over is rough: *We bumped **along** the track in our car holding on to our seats.*

PHRASAL VERBS **bump into sb** C1 to meet someone you know when you have not planned to meet them: *We bumped into Alison when we were in London last week.* • **bump sb off** slang to murder someone • **bump sth up** informal to increase the amount or size of something: *The distributors will probably bump up the **price** of the software when the next version is released.*

▸noun [C] **RAISED AREA** ▷ **1** C1 a round, raised area on a surface or on the body: *Her bicycle hit a bump in the road and threw her off.* ◦ *Tim had a nasty bump on his head from when he'd fallen over.* **HIT** ▷ **2** the sound of something falling to the ground: *We heard a bump from the next room.* **3** an accident involving a car, especially one that is not serious: *A van drove into their car but luckily it was just a bump.*

bumper /ˈbʌm.pəʳ/ US /-pɚ/ noun; adj
▸noun [C] B2 a horizontal bar along the lower front and lower back part of a motor vehicle to help protect it if there is an accident

IDIOM **bumper to bumper** with so many cars that are so close that they are almost touching each other: *By eight o'clock the traffic was bumper to bumper.*

▸adj [before noun] larger in amount than usual: *Farmers have reported a bumper **crop** this year.*

ˈ**bumper** ˌ**car** noun [C usually plural] (UK also **dodgem**) a small electric car driven for entertainment in a special closed space where the aim is to try to hit other cars

ˈ**bumper** ˌ**sticker** noun [C] a sign that you stick on a car, often with a funny message on it

bumph /bʌmf/ noun [U] another spelling of **bumf**

bumpkin /ˈbʌmp.kɪn/ noun [C] (also ˌ**country** ˈ**bumpkin**) informal disapproving a person from the countryside who is considered to be awkward and stupid

ˈ**bump-start** verb [T] **push-start**

bumptious /ˈbʌmp.ʃəs/ adj disapproving unpleasantly confident: *a bumptious young man* • **bumptiously** /-li/ adj • **bumptiousness** /-nəs/ noun [U]

bumpy /ˈbʌm.pi/ adj not smooth: *We drove along a narrow, bumpy **road**.* ◦ *It might be a bumpy **flight** (= an uncomfortable and rough flight) because there's a lot of air turbulence ahead.*

IDIOM **have a bumpy ride** informal C2 to have a difficult time: *She's had a bumpy ride at work over the last few months.*

ˌ**bum** ˈ**steer** noun [S] US informal a piece of bad advice: *He gave us a bum steer about that restaurant – it was terrible!*

bun /bʌn/ noun **FOOD** ▷ **1** B2 [C] a small, sweet, usually round cake: *a currant bun* **2** B2 [C] mainly US a small, round piece of bread, especially one that is cut horizontally and holds a BURGER: *a hamburger bun* **HAIRSTYLE** ▷ **3** [C] a woman's hairstyle where the hair is brought together into a round shape at the back of the head: *She wore her hair **in a bun**.* **BOTTOM** ▷ **4** [C usually plural] mainly US informal a BUTTOCK (= one side of a person's bottom)

IDIOM **have a bun in the oven** old-fashioned humorous to be pregnant

bunch /bʌntʃ/ noun; verb
▸noun **GROUP** ▷ **1** B1 [C] a number of things of the same type fastened together or in a close group: *a bunch of flowers/grapes/bananas/keys* ◦ mainly US informal *The reorganization will give us **a whole bunch** (= a lot) **of** problems.* **2** B1 [S] a group of people: *They're a bunch **of** hooligans.* ◦ *Your friends are a nice bunch.* **3 the best/pick of the bunch** the best person or thing from a group of similar people or things **HAIRSTYLE** ▷ **4 bunches** [plural] UK If a girl has her hair in bunches, it is tied together in two parts with one at each side of her head.
▸verb

PHRASAL VERBS **bunch (sth) up/together** to move close together to form a tight group: *The monkeys bunched together in their cage.* • **bunch (sth) up** If material bunches up, or if someone bunches it up, it moves into tight folds: *Your shirt's all bunched up at the back.*

bundle /ˈbʌn.dl̩/ noun; verb
▸noun [C] C2 a number of things that have been fastened or are held together: *a bundle **of** clothes/newspapers/books* ◦ *a bundle **of** sticks*

IDIOMS **bundle of joy** a baby: *Three days after the birth, Paul and Sandra took their precious bundle of joy home.* • **a bundle of laughs** informal a funny, entertaining person or situation: *He's not exactly a bundle of laughs, is he?* • **a bundle of nerves** informal C2 someone who is extremely nervous and worried: *Sorry for shouting – I'm a bundle of nerves these days.* • **go a bundle on sth** UK informal to like something very much: usually in negative *I don't go a bundle on his taste in clothes.*

▸verb **PUSH** ▷ **1** [I or T, + adv/prep] to push or put someone or something somewhere quickly and roughly: *He bundled his clothes **into** the washing machine.* ◦ *She was bundled **into** the back of the car.* ◦ *The children were bundled **off** to school early that morning.* **SELL TOGETHER** ▷ **2** [T] to include an extra computer program or other product with something that you sell: *The system came bundled **with** a word processor, spreadsheet, and graphics program.* • **bundling** /ˈbʌnd.lɪŋ/ noun [U] the act of selling several products or services together: *the bundling of services/software/products*

PHRASAL VERBS **bundle (sb) up** to put warm clothes on yourself or someone else: *The kids were bundled up in coats and scarves.* • **bundle sth up** to tie a number of things together

bung /bʌŋ/ noun; verb
▸noun [C] UK informal **CLOSING DEVICE** ▷ **1** (usually US **stopper**) a round piece of rubber, wood, etc. that is used to close the hole in a container **MONEY** ▷ **2** a payment made to someone to persuade them to do something, usually something dishonest: *Of course both the politicians denied taking bungs.*
▸verb [T + adv/prep] mainly UK informal to put something somewhere in a careless way: *'Where shall I put my coat?' 'Oh, bung it anywhere.'*

PHRASAL VERB **bung sth up** UK informal to cause something to be blocked so that it does not work in the way it should: *The toilet was bunged up with paper.*

bungalow /ˈbʌŋ.ɡəl.əʊ/ US /-oʊ/ noun [C] a house that has only one STOREY (= level): *It was a seaside town filled with small, white bungalows.*

ˌ**bunged** ˈ**up** adj UK informal If your nose is bunged up, you find it difficult to breathe because you have a cold.

bungee (cord) /ˈbʌn.dʒiˌkɔːd/ US /-ˌkɔːrd/ noun [C] mainly US a CORD that stretches with a HOOK at each end, used to hold things in place, especially on a bicycle or car

ˈ**bungee** ˌ**jumping** noun [U] the sport of jumping off a very high bridge or similar structure, with a long

ELASTIC rope tied to your legs, so that the rope pulls you back before you hit the ground

B

bungle /ˈbʌŋ.gl/ verb [T] to do something wrong, in a careless or stupid way • **bungled** /-gld/ adj *a bungled robbery* • **bungler** /-gləʳ/ (US) /-glɚ/ noun [C] *He's an incompetent bungler.* • **bungling** /-glɪŋ/ adj *What bungling* ***idiot*** *did this?*

bunion /ˈbʌn.jən/ noun [C] a painful swelling on the first JOINT of the big toe

bunk /bʌŋk/ noun; verb

▸noun **BED** ▷ **1** [C] a narrow bed that is fixed to a wall, especially in a boat or a train **2** [C often plural] (also **bunk bed**) one of two beds fixed together, one on top of the other: *The twins sleep in bunk beds.* ◦ *Can I sleep in the top bunk?* **NONSENSE** ▷ **3** [U] (also **bunkum** /ˈbʌŋ.kəm/) old-fashioned informal complete nonsense or something that is not true: *Most economists think his theories are sheer bunk.* **FOR FUEL** ▷ **4** [C] Indian English **petrol bunk** **LEAVE** ▷ **5 do a bunk** UK old-fashioned slang to leave suddenly and unexpectedly: *They'd done a bunk without paying the rent.*

▸verb

PHRASAL VERBS **bunk down** informal to sleep: *We were able to bunk down in the spare room for the night.* • **bunk off (sth)** UK informal to stay away from school or work or to leave early, especially without permission: *A lot of people bunk off early on Friday.* ◦ *It was a sunny day so they decided to bunk off* ***school.***

bunker /ˈbʌŋ.kəʳ/ (US) /-kɚ/ noun [C] **SHELTER** ▷ **1** a shelter, usually underground, that has strong walls to protect the people inside it from bullets or bombs **GOLF** ▷ **2** (US also **sand trap**) in GOLF, a hollow area of ground filled with sand, that is difficult to hit a ball out of

bunny /ˈbʌn.i/ noun [C] (also **bunny rabbit**) child's word a **rabbit**

ˈ**bunny** ˌ**slope** noun [C] US for **nursery slope**

Bunsen burner /ˈbʌn.sənˌbɜː.nəʳ/ (US) /-ˌbɝː.nɚ/ noun [C] a small device that burns gas to produce a flame, used to heat things in scientific work and EXPERIMENTS

bunting /ˈbʌn.tɪŋ/ (US) /-t̬ɪŋ/ noun [U] rows of brightly coloured little flags that are hung across roads or above a stage as decoration for special occasions

buoy /bɔɪ/ (US) /ˈbuː.i/ noun; verb

▸noun [C] a floating object on the top of the sea, used for directing ships and warning them of possible danger

▸verb **FLOAT** ▷ **1** [T] to prevent someone or something from sinking: *The very salty water buoyed her* ***(up)*** *as she swam.* **MAKE HAPPIER** ▷ **2** [T usually passive] to make someone feel happier or more confident about a situation: *She was buoyed* ***(up)*** *by the warm reception her audience gave her.* **MAKE SUCCESSFUL** ▷ **3** [T usually passive] to support something and make it more successful: *House prices have been buoyed* ***(up)*** *in the area by the possibility of a new factory opening.*

buoyant /ˈbɔɪ.ənt/ adj **FLOATING** ▷ **1** able to float: *Cork is light and buoyant.* **HAPPY** ▷ **2** happy and confident: *After reading the letter he was in a buoyant* ***mood.*** **SUCCESSFUL** ▷ **3** successful or making a profit: *The housing market remains buoyant.* • **buoyancy** /ˈbɔɪ.ən.si/ noun [U] *We tested the boat for buoyancy.* ◦ *He was a man of remarkable buoyancy (= able to stay positive despite problems).* • **buoyantly** /-li/ adv

bur /bɜːʳ/ (US) /bɝː/ noun [C] another spelling of **burr**

burble /ˈbɜː.bl/ (US) /ˈbɝː-/ verb **MAKE SOUND** ▷ **1** [I] to make a low, continuous bubbling sound, like water moving over stones **TALK** ▷ **2** [I or T] to talk about something continuously and in a way that is not very clear: *She was burbling* **(on) about** *what she'd do if she won the lottery.*

burden /ˈbɜː.dən/ (US) /ˈbɝː-/ noun; verb

▸noun [C] **1** a heavy LOAD that you carry: *The little donkey struggled under its* ***heavy*** *burden.* **2** (C1) something difficult or unpleasant that you have to deal with or worry about: *the burden of responsibility* ◦ *My elderly mother worries that she's* ***a*** *burden* ***to*** *me.* ◦ *Buying a house often places a large* ***financial*** *burden* ***on*** *young couples.*

IDIOM **the burden of proof** legal the responsibility for proving something

▸verb [T] to trouble someone with something difficult or unpleasant: *I don't want to burden you* ***with*** *my problems.*

burdensome /ˈbɜː.dən.səm/ (US) /ˈbɝː-/ adj formal causing difficulties or work: *a burdensome task*

bureau /ˈbjʊə.rəʊ/ (US) /ˈbjʊr.oʊ/ noun [C] (plural **bureaux** or US usually **bureaus**) **ORGANIZATION** ▷ **1** an organization or a business that collects or provides information: *Her disappearance was reported to the police department's Missing Persons Bureau.* **2** mainly US a government organization: *the Federal Bureau of Investigation* **FURNITURE** ▷ **3** UK a piece of furniture with a lid that opens to form a writing surface **4** US for **chest of drawers**

bureaucracy /bjʊəˈrɒk.rə.si/ (US) /bjʊˈrɑː.krə-/ noun [U or C] mainly disapproving (C2) a system for controlling or managing a country, company, or organization that is operated by a large number of officials employed to follow rules carefully

bureaucrat /ˈbjʊə.rə.kræt/ (US) /ˈbjʊr.ə-/ noun [C] mainly disapproving someone working in a bureaucracy: *It turned out she was one of those* ***faceless*** *bureaucrats who control our lives.*

bureaucratic /ˌbjʊə.rəˈkræt.ɪk/ (US) /ˌbjʊr.əˈkræt̬-/ adj mainly disapproving **1** relating to a system of controlling or managing a country, company, or organization that is operated by a large number of officials **2** involving complicated rules and processes that make something slow and difficult: *I had a lot of bureaucratic hassle trying to get the information I needed.*

bureau de change /ˌbjʊə.rəʊ.dəˈʃɑ̃ːʒ/ (US) /ˌbjʊr.oʊ-/ noun [C] (plural **bureaux de change** /ˌbjʊə.rəʊ.dəˈʃɑ̃ːʒ/, (US) /ˌbjʊr.oʊ-/ an office where you can change the money of one country for that of another

burette /bjʊˈret/ noun [C] specialized a glass tube with measurements printed on it and with a small TAP at the base, used for adding a measured quantity of liquid into something

burgeon /ˈbɜː.dʒən/ (US) /ˈbɝː-/ verb [I] literary to develop or grow quickly: *Love burgeoned between them.*

burgeoning /ˈbɜː.dʒən.ɪŋ/ (US) /ˈbɝː-/ adj developing quickly: *The company hoped to profit from the burgeoning communications industry.*

burger /ˈbɜː.gəʳ/ (US) /ˈbɝː.gɚ/ noun [C] (A2) meat or other food pressed into a round, flat shape and fried: *a burger and chips* ◦ *a hamburger* ◦ *a veggie burger*

burgher /ˈbɜː.gəʳ/ (US) /ˈbɝː.gɚ/ noun [C] old-fashioned or humorous a person who lives in a city

burglar /ˈbɜː.ɡləʳ/ US /ˈbɝː.ɡlɚ/ **noun** [C] B2 a person who illegally enters buildings and steals things

ˈburglar aˌlarm **noun** [C] a device on a building that gives a warning such as making a loud noise or flashing a light, or tells the police, if someone tries to enter the building illegally

burglary /ˈbɜː.ɡlᵊr.i/ US /ˈbɝː.ɡlɚ-/ **noun** [C or U] B2 the crime of illegally entering a building and stealing things

burgle /ˈbɜː.ɡl/ US /ˈbɝː-/ **verb** [T] mainly UK (US usually **burglarize** /ˈbɜː.ɡlər.aɪz/) B2 to enter a building illegally and steal things: *When they got back from their holiday they found that their home had been burgled.*

burgundy /ˈbɜː.ɡᵊn.di/ US /ˈbɝː-/ a dark reddish-purple colour, like the colour of red wine • **burgundy** adj

burial /ˈber.i.əl/ **noun** [C or U] C2 the act of putting a dead body into the ground, or the ceremony connected with this: *We went back to Ireland for my uncle's burial.* → See also **bury**

ˈburial ˌground **noun** [C] an area of land where dead bodies are buried, especially a long time ago

burk /bɜːk/ US /bɝːk/ **noun** [C] another spelling of **berk**

burka (also **burqa**) /ˈbɜː.kə/ US /ˈbɝː.r-/ **noun** [C] a piece of clothing that covers the whole head and body, with a hole for the eyes, worn by some Muslim women

burkini /bɜːˈkiː.ni/ US /bɝːr-/ **noun** [C] trademark a piece of women's clothing for swimming that is in two pieces and that covers the whole body except the face, hands, and feet

burlap /ˈbɜː.læp/ US /ˈbɝː-/ **noun** [U] US for **hessian**

burlesque /bɜːˈlesk/ US /bɝː-/ **noun** **1** [C or U] a type of writing or acting that tries to make something serious seem stupid **2** [U] US a type of theatre entertainment in the US in the late 19th and early 20th centuries that had funny acts and a STRIPTEASE (= a performance in which someone removes their clothes)

burly /ˈbɜː.li/ US /ˈbɝː-/ **adj** describes a man who is large and strong: *a burly policeman*

burn /bɜːn/ US /bɝːn/ **verb; noun**

▸**verb** (**burnt** or **burned**, **burnt** or **burned**) **DAMAGE** ▷ **1** B1 [I or T] to be hurt, damaged, or destroyed by fire or extreme heat, or to cause this to happen: *He was badly burned in the blaze.* ◦ *She burned his old love letters.* ◦ *The brandy burned (= felt too hot on) my throat.* ◦ *On her first day in the Caribbean Josie was badly burned (= her skin became red and painful from too much sun).* ◦ *Fair-skinned people burn easily in the sun.* ◦ *Unable to escape, six people were burned **alive**/burned **to death** (= died by burning) in the building.* ◦ *The vegetables were burned **to a crisp** (= badly burned).* **2** [T always passive] to cause emotional pain or damage to someone **3 burn sb at the stake** to kill someone by tying them to a post and burning them **4 burn sth to the ground** to completely destroy a building by fire: *The building was burned to the ground ten years ago.* **PRODUCE FLAMES** ▷ **5** B1 [I] to be on fire, or to produce flames: *The wood was wet and would not burn.* ◦ *Helplessly we watched our house burning.* ◦ *A fire was burning brightly in the fireplace.* **PRODUCE LIGHT** ▷ **6** [I] to produce light: *I saw a light burning in her window.* **FEEL HOT** ▷ **7** [I] If your face burns, it feels very hot: *His face burned **with** embarrassment/shame/anger.* **WANT** ▷ **8** [+ to infinitive] to want to do something very much: *She was burning to tell us her news.* **COPY** ▷ **9** B2 [T] to copy information, recorded music, images, etc. onto a CD: *Burn your favourite songs or your important files **onto** CDs.*

IDIOMS **burn your boats/bridges** If you are in a situation and you burn your boats/bridges, you destroy all possible ways of going back to that situation. • **burn a hole in sb's pocket** If money is burning a hole in your pocket, you are very eager to spend it. • **burn the candle at both ends** to work or do other things from early in the morning until late at night and so get very little rest • **burn the midnight oil** C2 to work late into the night • **get/have your fingers burned** (also **burn your fingers**) to suffer unpleasant results of an action, especially loss of money, so you do not want to do the same thing again: *She'd invested extensively in stocks and got her fingers burned when the market collapsed.*

PHRASAL VERBS **burn (sth) down** B2 to destroy something, especially a building, by fire, or to be destroyed by fire: *He tried to burn down the school by setting fire to papers on a noticeboard.* • **burn sth off/up** B2 to use or get rid of energy or fat by doing a lot of physical exercise: *Running is an excellent way to burn off excess calories.* • **burn out FIRE** ▷ **1** If a fire burns out, it stops producing flames because nothing remains that can burn. **BREAK** ▷ **2** B2 If something such as a motor burns out, it stops working because of damage from heat: *It looks like the starter motor on the car has burned out.* • **burn yourself out** to be forced to stop working because you have become ill or very tired from working too hard: *Stop working so hard – you'll burn yourself out.* → See also **burn-out** • **burn (sth) up** B2 to destroy something completely with fire or heat, or to be destroyed completely by fire or heat: *Meteorites often burn up in the atmosphere before they reach the ground.* • **burn up** informal to have a bad fever: *'You're burning up!' she said, touching his forehead.* • **burn up with sth** If you burn up with an emotion, you feel that emotion so strongly that you cannot act in a reasonable way: *He was burned up with jealousy and suspicion.* • **burn with sth** If you burn with an emotion, you feel that emotion very strongly: *They were both burning with desire.*

▸**noun** [C] **DAMAGE** ▷ **1** a place where fire or heat has hurt or damaged something: *One rescue worker caught in the explosion sustained severe burns.* ◦ *I noticed a cigarette burn in the carpet.* → See also **heartburn, sunburn** **STREAM** ▷ **2** Scottish English a small stream

burner /ˈbɜː.nəʳ/ US /ˈbɝː.nɚ/ **noun** [C] the part of a cooker, light, etc. that produces flame or heat

burning /ˈbɜː.nɪŋ/ US /ˈbɝː-/ **adj** **ON FIRE** ▷ **1** B1 producing flames: *A man staggered from the burning car.* **HOT** ▷ **2** very hot: *burning sand* ◦ *Suddenly she felt a burning (**sensation**) (= feeling of heat) in her throat.* **STRONG** ▷ **3** C1 A burning DESIRE, need, etc., is one that is very strong: *a burning ambition* ◦ *He spoke of his burning desire to play for England.* **4 burning issue/question** C1 a subject or question that must be dealt with or answered quickly

ˌburning ˈghat **noun** [C] → **ghat**

burnish /ˈbɜː.nɪʃ/ US /ˈbɝː-/ **verb** [T] **1** literary to rub metal until it is smooth and shiny **2** If you burnish something such as your public image, you take action to improve it and make it more attractive. • **burnished** /-nɪʃt/ **adj** literary smooth and shiny

ˈburn-out **noun** [U] extreme tiredness usually caused by working too much: *employees complaining of/suffering burn-out*

burnt /bɜːnt/ US /bɝːnt/ **verb; adj**

▸**verb** past simple and past participle of **burn**

B

▸adj destroyed or made black by fire or heat

ˌburnt ˈoffering noun [C] **1** something, often an animal, that is burned in honour of a god **2** UK humorous a meal that has been spoiled by burning

ˌburnt ˈout adj FIRE ▷ **1** describes a building or vehicle that has been badly damaged by fire: *After the fire the factory was completely burnt out.* ◦ [before noun] *a burnt-out shell* TIRED ▷ **2** ill or very tired from working too hard

ˌburnt siˈenna noun [U] a reddish-brown colour • **ˌburnt siˈenna** adj

burp /bɜːp/ (US) /bɝːp/ verb **1** [I] to allow air from the stomach to come out through the mouth in a noisy way **2** [T] to gently rub a baby's back to help air to come out of its stomach • **burp** noun [C]

burqa /ˈbɜː.kə/ (US) /ˈbɝː-/ noun [C] a **burka**

burr /bɜːʳ/ (US) /bɝː/ noun SOUND ▷ **1** [C usually singular] a way of speaking English in which the 'r' sound is more noticeable than usual: *He spoke in a soft West Country burr.* SEED ▷ **2** [C] (also **bur**) a very small, round seed container that sticks to clothes and to animals' fur because it is covered in little HOOKS

burrito /bəˈriː.təʊ/ (US) /-ˈriː.t̬oʊ/ noun [C] (plural **burritos**) a type of Mexican food made by folding a TORTILLA (= thin, round bread) and putting meat, beans, and cheese inside it

burrow /ˈbʌr.əʊ/ (US) /ˈbɝː.oʊ/ noun; verb

▸noun [C] a hole in the ground dug by an animal such as a RABBIT, especially to live in

▸verb **1** [I usually + adv/prep] to dig a hole in the ground, especially to live in: *Rats had burrowed **into** the bank of the river.* **2** [T + adv/prep] to move yourself into a position where you can feel warm, comfortable, or safe: *Suddenly shy, our young daughter burrowed her head **into** my shoulder.* **3** [I + adv/prep] to search for something, as if by digging: *I burrowed **through** the clothes in the drawer looking for a clean pair of socks.*

bursar /ˈbɜː.səʳ/ (US) /ˈbɝː.sɚ/ noun [C] the person in a college, school, or university who is responsible for controlling its money

bursary /ˈbɜː.sᵊr.i/ (US) /ˈbɝː.sɚ-/ noun [C] UK an amount of money given to a person by an organization, such as a university, to pay for them to study

burst /bɜːst/ (US) /bɝːst/ verb; noun

▸verb (**burst, burst**) **1** (B2) [I or T] to break open or apart suddenly, or to make something do this: *I hate it when balloons burst.* ◦ *Suddenly the door burst **open** (= opened suddenly and forcefully) and police officers rushed in.* ◦ *The river was threatening to burst its **banks**.* ◦ figurative humorous *If I eat any more cake I'll burst (= I cannot eat anything else)!* **2** (C2) [I] to feel a strong emotion, or strong wish to do something: *I knew they were bursting **with** curiosity but I said nothing.* ◦ [+ to infinitive] informal *I'm bursting **to** go to the loo!* ◦ *Tom was bursting **to** tell everyone the news.* **3 burst into flames** (C2) to suddenly burn strongly, producing a lot of flames: *Smoke started pouring out from underneath, then the truck burst into flames.*

IDIOMS **burst at the seams** informal to be completely full: *When all the family come home the house is bursting at the seams.* • **burst into song/tears/laughter** (B2) to suddenly begin to sing/cry/laugh: *Much to my surprise, Ben suddenly burst into song.* • **burst out laughing/crying** (B2) to suddenly start laughing/crying: *I walked in and everyone burst out laughing.*

PHRASAL VERBS **burst in/into (somewhere)** (B2) to enter a room or building suddenly and without warning: *The side door of the pub flew open and three men burst in.* • **burst in on sb/sth** to enter a room suddenly and without warning, interrupting the people or activity inside: *Katya burst in on him without warning.* • **burst out** (C2) to suddenly say something loudly: *'Don't go!' he burst out.*

▸noun [C] BREAK ▷ **1** the act of breaking open so that what is inside comes out: *a burst in the water pipe* INCREASE ▷ **2** a sudden increase in something, especially for a short period: *a burst **of speed/applause/laughter***

burton /ˈbɜː.tᵊn/ (US) /ˈbɝː.t̬ᵊn/ noun UK old-fashioned informal **gone for a burton** spoiled or lost: *That's our quiet evening in gone for a burton.*

bury /ˈber.i/ verb [T] **1** (B1) to put a dead body into the ground: *His father is buried **in** the cemetery on the hill.* → See also **burial 2** (B2) to put something into a hole in the ground and cover it: *The dog trotted off to bury its bone.* ◦ *buried **treasure*** **3** usually passive to cover something or someone completely with a large quantity of something: *If an avalanche strikes, skiers can be buried **alive** by snow.* **4** (C2) to put something in a place where it is difficult or impossible to find or see: *I found the article buried (**away**) in the business section of the newspaper.* ◦ *She buried her face **in** her hands and began to sob.* **5** to intentionally forget an unpleasant experience: *He'd had to bury his pain over the years.* **6** old-fashioned If someone says they buried someone, usually a close relation, they mean that the person died: *She buried both her parents last year.*

IDIOM **bury the hatchet** to stop an argument and become friends again: *Can't you two just bury the hatchet?*

PHRASAL VERB **bury yourself in sth** (C2) to give all your attention to something: *Since her marriage ended, she has buried herself in her work.*

bus /bʌs/ noun; verb

▸noun [C] (plural **buses** or US also **busses**) VEHICLE ▷ **1** (A1) a large vehicle in which people are driven from one place to another: *You should **take the bus/go by bus** (= travel by bus) if you want to see the sights.* → See also **minibus, omnibus, trolleybus** COMPUTER ▷ **2** a set of wires in a computer along which information can be sent to and from other parts of the computer

▸verb [T] (**-ss-** or US usually **-s-**) **1** to take people somewhere by bus: *Demonstrators were bussed in from all parts of the country to attend the protest rally.* **2** US to take children by bus to school in another area every day

busboy /ˈbʌs.bɔɪ/ noun [C] US a person who works in a restaurant removing dirty dishes and bringing clean ones

busby /ˈbʌz.bi/ noun [C] a fur hat worn by some British soldiers for formal ceremonies

ˈbus conˌductor noun [C] the person on some buses whose job is to take your money and give you a ticket

bush /bʊʃ/ noun PLANT ▷ **1** (B2) [C] a plant with many small branches growing either directly from the ground or from a hard stem, giving the plant a rounded shape: *a rose bush* AREA OF LAND ▷ **2 the bush** (C2) [S] (especially in Australia and Africa) an area of land covered with bushes and trees that has never been used for growing crops and where there are very few people

bushed /bʊʃt/ adj [after verb] informal very tired

bushel /ˈbʊʃ.ᵊl/ noun [C] a unit of measurement equal to approximately 36.4 litres in Britain or 35.2 litres in the US: *a bushel of wheat*

ˈbush ˌfire noun [C] a fire burning in the bush (= a

wild area of land) that is difficult to control and sometimes spreads quickly

bushman /ˈbʊʃ.mən/ noun [C] (plural **-men** /-mən/) mainly Australian a person who lives in the bush (= a wild area of land)

bushranger /ˈbʊʃˌreɪn.dʒəʳ/ (US) /-dʒɚ/ noun [C] Australian old-fashioned a criminal or thief who lived in bush (= a wild area of land)

ˌbush ˈtelegraph noun [S] UK old-fashioned humorous the informal way in which information quickly spreads from person to person

bushy /ˈbʊʃ.i/ adj describes hair or fur that is very thick: *a squirrel's bushy **tail** ◦ bushy **eyebrows***

busily /ˈbɪz.ɪ.li/ adv in a busy, active way: *I was busily preparing for their arrival.*

business /ˈbɪz.nɪs/ noun **SELLING** ▷ **1** (A1) [U] the activity of buying and selling goods and services: *My brother's **in** business. ◦ He's **in the** frozen food business. ◦ Our firm **does** a lot of business **with** overseas customers. ◦ Eventually they found a consultant they felt they could **do** business **with** (= with whom they could work well). ◦ Currently, there are fewer firms **in** business (= operating) in the area than ever before. ◦ This new tax will put a lot of small firms **out of** business (= they will stop operating). ◦ She **set up in** business (= started her own company) as a management consultant.*

> **! Common mistake: business**
>
> **Warning:** Choose the right verb!
>
> Don't say 'make business', say **do business**:
>
> ~~*We have been making business with this company for five years.*~~
>
> *We have been doing business with this company for five years.*

COMPANY ▷ **2** (A2) [C] a particular company that buys and sells goods and services: *The two brothers established/set up/started up a clothes retailing business. ◦ She runs her own printing business. ◦ They put a lot of money into the family business.* **WORK** ▷ **3** (B1) [U] work that you do to earn money: *I'm in Baltimore **on** business. ◦ a business appointment* **4** [U] the amount of work done or the number of goods or services sold by a company or organization: *◦ Business is good/brisk/booming/flourishing (= I'm selling a lot). ◦ Business is bad/slack/quiet (= I'm not selling much). ◦ How is business (= are you selling much) at the moment?* **MATTER** ▷ **5** [S or U] a situation or activity, often one that you are giving your opinion about: *Arranging a trip abroad is **a** time-consuming business. ◦ These killings are **a** dreadful business. ◦ I **make it** my business (= I feel it is my particular duty) to check the monthly accounts. ◦ We've got some **unfinished** business to discuss (= we still have something important to discuss).* **THINGS YOU DO** ▷ **6** [U] the things that you do or the matters that relate only to you: *I got on with **the** business **of** filling in the form. ◦ What she does with her life is her business.*

> **! Common mistake: business**
>
> **Warning:** Check your spelling!
>
> **Business** is one of the 50 words most often spelled wrongly by learners. Remember: the correct spelling has 's' in the middle and 'ss' at the end.

IDIOMS **be in business** informal to be ready and able to start doing something that you planned: *Once we get the computer installed we'll be in business.* • **be none of sb's business** (B2) If something is none of someone's business, they do not need to know about it: *Stop pestering me; it's none of your business!* • **be the**

> **Word partners for business (SELLING)**
>
> *run* a business • *set up/start* a business • *conduct/do* business (*with* sb) • *go out of* business • a business *collapses/folds/goes under* • *in* business • *on* business

business UK slang to be extremely good or skilful: *That new defender is the business!* • **(it's) business as usual** saying said when things are continuing as they always do, despite a difficult situation • **do the business 1** informal to do what is wanted or needed in a situation: *As long as he does the business on the football field, the club is happy with him.* **2** UK slang to have sex • **get down to business** to start talking about the subject to be discussed: *If the introductions are over I'd like to get down to business.* • **have no business doing sth** to have no right to do something: *You had no business reading my private letters.* • **like nobody's business** very quickly or very much: *He was scribbling away like nobody's business.* • **not be in the business of sth** If a person or organization is not in the business of doing something considered wrong, they do not normally do it: *The intelligence service is not in the business of routinely monitoring the activities of law-abiding citizens.* • **what a business!** old-fashioned used to mean that something was annoying and caused a lot of trouble for you: *It took ages to sort out the documentation needed to get into the country – what a business!*

ˈbusiness ˌcard noun [C] (also **card**) a small card that has your name, company name, and the job you do printed on it

ˈbusiness ˌclass noun [S], adv travelling conditions on an aircraft that are better than the conditions you get when you travel more cheaply: *Do you usually travel business class?*

ˌbusiness-ˈcritical adj specialized necessary for a business to be successful: *We want people who understand that e-commerce is business-critical – it's got to work.*

ˈbusiness ˌend noun [S] informal The business end of something, such as a knife or a gun, is the end that does the work or damage rather than the handle.

businesslike /ˈbɪz.nɪs.laɪk/ adj getting things done in a quick and practical way: *The meeting was brief and businesslike.*

businessman /ˈbɪz.nɪs.mən/ noun [C] (plural **-men** /-mən/) (A2) a man who works in business, especially one who has a high position in a company

> **! Common mistake: businessman**
>
> **Remember: businessman** is written as one word.
>
> Don't write 'business man', write **businessman**:
>
> ~~*A lot of business men suffer from stress.*~~

ˈbusiness ˌpark noun [C] an area that is specially designed to have business offices, small factories, etc.

ˈbusiness ˌplan noun [C] a detailed plan describing the future plans of a business

ˈbusiness ˌschool noun [C] a college, or part of a college or university, where students are taught subjects related to business: *Harvard Business School*

ˌbusiness-to-ˈbusiness adj [before noun] (abbreviation **B2B**) describing or involving arrangements or trade between different businesses, rather than between businesses and the general public

ˌbusiness-to-conˈsumer adj [before noun] (abbreviation **B2C**) describing or involving the sale of goods or services to single customers for their own use, rather than to businesses

businesswoman /ˈbɪz.nɪsˌwʊm.ən/ **noun** [C] (plural **-women** /-wɪmɪn/) A2 a woman who works in business, especially one who has a high position in a company: *She's a good/shrewd businesswoman.*

busk /bʌsk/ **verb** [I] UK to play music or sing in a public place so that the people who are there will give money • **busker** /ˈbʌs.kəʳ/ US /ˈbʌs.kɚ/ **noun** [C] a musician or performer who busks for money

ˈbus ˌlane **noun** [C] a special wide strip on a road, on which only buses are allowed to travel

busman's holiday /ˌbʌs.mənzˈhɒl.ɪ.deɪ/ US /-ˈhɑː.lɪ-/ **noun** [S] humorous a holiday where you do something similar to your usual work instead of having a rest from it

ˈbus shelter **noun** [C] a place to wait for buses that has a roof

ˈbus ˌstation **noun** [C] A2 a place where buses start and end their journeys

ˈbus ˌstop **noun** [C] A2 a place, usually with a pole with a sign, where a bus stops to allow passengers to get on and off

bust /bʌst/ **noun; verb; adj**

▸**noun** [C] **BREASTS** ▷ **1** a woman's breasts, or the measurement around a woman's breasts and back: *I couldn't find anything in the shop in my bust size.* **HEAD** ▷ **2** a model of the head and shoulders of a person **ARREST** ▷ **3** slang an occasion when police arrest people who are thought to have broken the law: *In their latest **drugs** bust police entered a warehouse where cocaine dealers were meeting.*

▸**verb** [T] (**bust**, **bust** or US **busted**, **busted**) **BREAK** ▷ **1** US informal to break something: *Oh no! I've bust his MP3 player.* **ARREST** ▷ **2** US slang When the police bust a person, they arrest them, or when they bust a building or a place, they arrest people in it who they believe are breaking the law: *The police busted him because they think he's involved with a terrorist group.*

IDIOM **bust a gut** informal to work very hard or make a big effort to achieve something: *I really bust a gut to get that report finished on time.*

PHRASAL VERB **bust up** mainly US informal to end a relationship after an angry argument: *She's bust up with Carlo.* → See also **bust-up**

▸**adj** [after verb] (US also **busted**) **BROKEN** ▷ **1** broken: *I think my watch is bust.* **BUSINESS** ▷ **2 go bust** If a company goes bust, it is forced to close because it is financially unsuccessful.

buster /ˈbʌs.təʳ/ US /-tɚ/ **noun** [as form of address] US informal used to address a man or a boy you do not like: *Cut it out, buster!*

-buster /-bʌs.təʳ/ US /-tɚ/ **suffix** a person or thing intended to destroy the stated thing: *crime-busters*

bustle /ˈbʌs.l̩/ **verb; noun**

▸**verb** [I + adv/prep] to do things in a hurried and busy way: *Thora bustled **about** the flat, getting everything ready.*

▸**noun** **ACTIVITY** ▷ **1** [U] busy activity: *I sat in a café, watching the (**hustle and**) bustle of the street outside.* **DRESS** ▷ **2** [C] a frame worn under a dress or skirt by women in the late 19th century to make the skirt stick out

bustling /ˈbʌs.lɪŋ/ **adj** If a place is bustling, it is full of busy activity: *This used to be a bustling town but a lot of people have moved away over recent years.* ◦ *The house, usually bustling **with** activity, was strangely silent.*

ˈbust-up **noun** [C] UK informal a serious argument, especially one that ends a relationship: *She **had** a big bust-up **with** her brother-in-law.*

busty /ˈbʌs.ti/ **adj** informal A busty woman has large breasts.

busy /ˈbɪz.i/ **adj; verb**

▸**adj** **DOING THINGS** ▷ **1** A2 If you are busy, you are working hard, or giving your attention to a particular thing: *Mum was busy in the kitchen.* ◦ *The kids are busy **with** their homework.* ◦ *She's busy writ**ing** out the wedding invitations.* ◦ *I've got plenty of jobs to **keep** you busy.* ◦ *He was **too** busy talking **to** notice us come in.* **2** A1 A busy place is full of activity or people: *a busy restaurant* ◦ *Their house is near a very busy road.* **3** A2 In a busy period, you have a lot of things to do: *I've got a busy week ahead of me.* ◦ *Have a rest – you've had a busy day.* **4** (UK also **engaged**) If a phone line is busy, someone is using it: *I tried calling you but the line was busy.* **WITH PATTERNS** ▷ **5** disapproving having too much decoration or too many colours: *The jacket was a bit busy for my tastes – I'd prefer something a bit plainer.*

▸**verb** **busy yourself** to make the time pass by doing something: *I busied myself with tidying up my desk.*

busybody /ˈbɪz.iˌbɒd.i/ US /-ˌbɑː.di/ **noun** [C] informal a person who is too interested in things that do not involve them: *Some interfering busybody had rung the police.*

but strong /bʌt/ weak /bət/ **conjunction; preposition, conjunction; adv; noun**

▸**conjunction** A1 used to introduce an added statement, usually something that is different from what you have said before: *She's very hard-working but not very imaginative.* ◦ *This is not caused by evil, but by simple ignorance.* ◦ *The play's good, but not that good – I've seen better.* ◦ *I'm sorry, but I think you're wrong when you say she did it deliberately.* ◦ *Call me old-fashioned, but I like handwritten letters.* ◦ *I can understand his unhappiness. But to attempt suicide!* ◦ *'She said she's leaving.' 'But why?'* ◦ *You can invite Keith to the party, but please don't ask that friend of his.* ◦ *We must not complain about the problem, but (= instead we must) help to put it right.* ◦ *She's not a painter but a writer (= she is a writer, not a painter).* ◦ *She's **not only** a painter but **also** a writer (= she is both).* ◦ *He said he hadn't been there, but **then** (= it is not surprising that) he would say that.* ◦ *I think it's true, but **then** (= it should be understood that), I'm no expert.*

▸**preposition, conjunction** B1 except: *Eventually, **all** but **one** of them promised to come to his leaving party.* ◦ *He's **anything** but violent (= not violent in any way).* ◦ *I'd have crashed the car but **for** your warning.* ◦ *This is the **last** episode but **one** (= one before the last) of this drama serial.* ◦ *She's one of those guests who does **nothing** but complain.* ◦ *This car has been **nothing** but trouble – it's always breaking down!*

▸**adv** **FOR EMPHASIS** ▷ **1** used to give force to a statement: *Everyone, but everyone, will be there.* **ONLY** ▷ **2** formal only; just: *She's but a young girl!*

▸**noun** **no buts (about it)** used to emphasize that something will happen even if the person you are talking to does not want it to

butane /ˈbjuː.teɪn/ **noun** [U] a gas obtained from PETROLEUM, used in its liquid form as a fuel

butch /bʊtʃ/ **adj** (of a woman) looking or behaving like a man, or (of a man) being very strong with big muscles, and behaving in a traditionally male way

butcher /ˈbʊtʃ.əʳ/ US /-ɚ/ **noun; verb**

▸**noun** [C] **SHOP** ▷ **1** B1 a person who sells meat in a shop **2** (UK also **butcher's**) a shop where butchers work **MURDER** ▷ **3** someone who murders a lot of people, especially in a cruel way

IDIOM **have a butcher's** UK old-fashioned slang to look at something: *Let's have a butcher's* ***at*** *your present, then.*

▸verb [T] **1** to cut an animal into pieces of meat **2** to kill someone in a very violent way

butchery /ˈbʊtʃ.ər.i/ (US) /-ɚ-/ noun [U] **1** the preparation of meat for sale **2** cruel killing

butler /ˈbʌt.ləʳ/ (US) /-lɚ/ noun [C] the most important male servant in a house, usually responsible for organizing the other servants

butt /bʌt/ noun; verb

▸noun **CIGARETTE** ▷ **1** [C] the part of a finished cigarette that has not been smoked **BOTTOM** ▷ **2** (C1) [C] US slang for bottom: *She told him to* ***get off*** *his butt and do something useful.* **GUN** ▷ **3** [C] the thick end of a RIFLE (= gun) handle: *They struck him with their rifle butts.* **PERSON** ▷ **4 be the butt of sb's jokes** to be a person who is joked about or laughed at: *He was fed up with being the butt of their jokes.* **CONTAINER** ▷ **5** [C] a large container used to store liquids: *a rain/water butt*

▸verb [I or T] to hit something or someone hard with the head or the horns

PHRASAL VERB **butt in** informal (C2) to interrupt a conversation or discussion or someone who is talking: *He kept on butting in with silly comments.*

butter /ˈbʌt.əʳ/ (US) /ˈbʌt̬.ɚ/ noun; verb

▸noun [U] (A1) a pale yellow solid food containing a lot of fat that is made from cream and is spread on bread or used in cooking: *We were served scones with butter and jam.* ◦ *Have some* ***bread and*** *butter (= bread spread with butter).* ◦ *a butter* ***dish***

IDIOM **butter wouldn't melt in sb's mouth** used when someone looks as if they would never do anything wrong, although you feel they might: *Tommy looked as if butter wouldn't melt in his mouth.*

▸verb [T] to spread butter on something • **buttered** /ˈbʌt.əd/ (US) /ˈbʌt̬.ɚd/ adj *buttered* ***toast***

PHRASAL VERB **butter sb up** informal to be very kind or friendly to someone or try to please them, so that they will do what you want them to do: *You'll have to butter them up a bit before they'll agree.*

ˈ**butter** ˌ**bean** noun [C usually plural] UK (US **lima** ˌ**bean**) a large, flat, yellow bean

buttercream /ˈbʌt.ə.kriːm/ (US) /ˈbʌt̬.ɚ-/ noun [U] a soft mixture of butter and sugar that is put on top or in the middle of a cake

buttercup /ˈbʌt.ə.kʌp/ (US) /ˈbʌt̬.ɚ-/ noun [C] a small, bright yellow wild flower

butterfingers /ˈbʌt.əˌfɪŋ.gəz/ (US) /ˈbʌt̬.ɚˌfɪŋ.gɚz/ noun [S] humorous a person who drops things they are carrying or trying to catch: [as form of address] *'Butterfingers!' she called as I dropped the hot plates.*

butterfly /ˈbʌt.ə.flaɪ/ (US) /ˈbʌt̬.ɚ-/ noun [C] **INSECT** ▷ **1** (B1) a type of insect with large, often brightly coloured wings **PERSON** ▷ **2** disapproving a person who is not responsible or serious, and who is likely to change activities easily or only be interested in pleasure: *She's such a* ***social*** *butterfly.* **JEWELLERY** ▷ **3** the small metal part put on the back of a STUD (= piece of jewellery worn in the ear) that keeps it in place **SWIMMING** ▷ **4** [S or U] the **butterfly stroke**

IDIOM **have butterflies (in your stomach)** informal to feel very nervous, usually about something you are going to do: *I had terrible butterflies before I gave that talk in Venice.*

ˈ**butterfly** ˌ**stroke** noun [S or U] (also **the butterfly**) a way of swimming on your front by kicking with your legs while raising your arms together out of the water and then bringing them down in front of you

buttermilk /ˈbʌt.ə.mɪlk/ (US) /ˈbʌt̬.ɚ-/ noun [U] the liquid that is left after taking the fat from cream to make butter

butternut squash /ˌbʌt.ə.nʌtˈskwɒʃ/ (US) /ˌbʌt̬.ɚ.nʌtˈskwɑːʃ/ noun [C or U] a type of **squash** that is typically fat and round at one end, with pale brown skin and orange flesh

butterscotch /ˈbʌt.ə.skɒtʃ/ (US) /ˈbʌt̬.ɚ.skɑːtʃ/ noun [C or U] a hard, light-brown coloured, sweet food made by boiling butter and sugar together

buttery /ˈbʌt.ər.i/ (US) /ˈbʌt̬.ɚ-/ adj mainly UK containing or spread with a lot of butter, or tasting of butter: *buttery potatoes*

ˌ**butt** ˈ**naked** adj US slang completely naked

buttock /ˈbʌt.ək/ (US) /ˈbʌt̬-/ noun [C usually plural] either side of a person's bottom

button /ˈbʌt.ən/ (US) /ˈbʌt̬-/ noun; verb

▸noun [C] **ON CLOTHING** ▷ **1** (B1) a small, usually circular object used to fasten something, for example a shirt or coat: *I* ***did up/undid*** *(= fastened/unfastened) the buttons on my blouse.* **ON MACHINE** ▷ **2** (B1) a small, sometimes circular object that you press to operate a device or a machine, or an area on a computer screen that looks and acts like one of these: *He inserted the disk and pressed the 'play' button.*

IDIOMS **at the push of a button** very easily: *You can't expect to get everything you need at the push of a button.* • **right on the button** exactly correct: *She was right on the button when she said I'd regret moving out.*

▸verb [I or T] to fasten something, usually a piece of clothing, using buttons: *Button* ***(up)*** *your coat, it's cold outside.*

IDIOM **button it** informal a rude way of telling someone to stop talking: *Button it, OK! I'm trying to think.*

ˈ**button** ˌ**day** noun [C] Australian a day when money is collected in public places for a CHARITY → See also **flag day**

ˌ**button-down** ˈ**collar** noun [C] a collar on a shirt that has the pointed ends fastened to the shirt by buttons

ˌ**buttoned-**ˈ**down** adj [before noun] (also ˌ**button-**ˈ**down**) US formal and old-fashioned or boring: *a buttoned-down accountant/lawyer*

ˌ**button** ˈ**fly** noun [C] an opening at the front of a pair of trousers that fastens with buttons

buttonhole /ˈbʌt.ən.həʊl/ (US) /ˈbʌt̬.ən.hoʊl/ noun; verb

▸noun [C] **1** a hole that a button is pushed through to fasten a shirt, coat, etc. **2** mainly UK a flower that a man wears in the buttonhole of, or fastened to, his jacket on a special occasion such as a WEDDING

▸verb [T] to stop someone and make them listen to you: *Greg buttonholed me about sales figures when I came out of the meeting.*

ˌ**button** ˈ**mushroom** noun [C] a very small MUSHROOM

ˌ**button-through** adj [before noun] describes a dress or skirt fastened with buttons from the top to the bottom

buttress /ˈbʌt.rəs/ noun; verb

▸noun [C] a structure made of stone or brick that sticks out from and supports a wall of a building

▸verb [T] **1** to build buttresses to support a building or structure: *It was decided to buttress the crumbling walls.* **2** to make support for an idea or argument stronger by providing a good reason for it: *The arguments for change are buttressed by events elsewhere.*

butty /ˈbʌt.i/ ⓤⓢ /ˈbʌt̬-/ noun [C] Northern informal for a sandwich

buxom /ˈbʌk.səm/ adj (of a woman) healthy-looking and slightly fat, with large breasts

> **Other ways of saying buy**
>
> **Get** is a common word that can be used instead of 'buy':
>
> *I need to go to the supermarket and **get** some bread.*
>
> **Purchase** is a formal word that means the same as 'buy':
>
> *Tickets must be **purchased** two weeks in advance.*
>
> If a country buys products from another country, you could use the verb **import**:
>
> *We **import** a large number of cars from Japan.*
>
> The phrasal verb **buy up** can be used when someone buys everything that is available:
>
> *He **bought up** all the land in the area.*
>
> If someone buys something quickly and enthusiastically because it is cheap or exactly what is wanted, you could use **snap up**:
>
> *The tickets for the concert were all **snapped up** within two hours of going on sale.*
>
> **Stock up on** is often used when people buy large amounts of something so that they have it when they need it:
>
> *People are **stocking up on** supplies in anticipation of the hurricane.*
>
> If you **pick** something **up**, you buy it very cheaply:
>
> *I **picked up** lots of bargains during the sales.*
>
> **Invest in** could be used when you buy something that you think will be useful even if it is expensive:
>
> *We've decided it's time to **invest in** a new computer.*
>
> If you offer to buy something for another person, you could use the verb **treat**:
>
> *I'll **treat** you to a cup of coffee.*

buy /baɪ/ verb; noun

▸verb (**bought, bought**) **PAY FOR** ▷ **1** A1 [I or T] to get something by paying money for it: *Eventually she had saved enough money to buy a small car.* ◦ [+ two objects] *He bought his mother some flowers/He bought some flowers **for** his mother.* ◦ *There are more people buying at this time of the year so prices are high.* ◦ *The company was set up to buy and sell shares on behalf of investors.* ◦ *I bought my camera **from** a friend of mine.* **2 buy sb's silence** to pay someone or do something for someone, so that they do not tell anyone something that they know about and that you want to remain secret: *What will we have to do to buy her silence?* **BELIEVE** ▷ **3** [T] informal to believe that something is true: *She'll never buy that story about you getting lost!*

IDIOMS **buy time** to do something in order to be allowed more time: *He tried to buy time by saying he hadn't been well.* • **sb has bought it** slang used to say that someone has been killed: *'Marvin's bought it!' screamed the sergeant.*

PHRASAL VERBS **buy sth in** UK to buy something for future use and not because you need it now: *We bought in lots of tinned food in case of heavy snow.* • **buy into sth BELIEVE** ▷ **1** disapproving to completely believe in a set of ideas: *I don't buy into all that New Age stuff.* **BUSINESS** ▷ **2** to buy a part of a business in order to have some control over it: *McDowell was trying to buy into the newspaper business.* • **buy sb off** to pay someone so that they do not cause you any trouble: *They tried to buy the guard at the bank off but he told the police and the gang was arrested.* • **buy sb out** to buy a part of a company or building from someone else so that you own all of it: *Allied Chemicals have been trying to buy out their competitor's share in the target company.* • **buy yourself out** UK If you buy yourself out of the armed forces, you pay an amount of money so that you can leave earlier than you had previously agreed to. • **buy sth up** To buy something up is to buy large amounts of it, or all that is available: *He bought up all the land in the surrounding area.*

▸noun **a good/bad buy** to be worth/not be worth the price: *This jacket is a really good buy, at £20.*

buyback /ˈbaɪ.bæk/ noun [C or U] an arrangement in which a business or person sells something, especially SHARES in companies, and then buys them again according to a fixed agreement: *His company have just announced a $1 billion stock buyback.*

buyer /ˈbaɪ.ər/ ⓤⓢ /-ɚ/ noun [C] **1** B1 someone who buys something expensive such as a house: *He's still looking for a buyer **for** his house.* **2** someone whose job it is to decide what will be bought by a company: *She's the buyer for a stylish boutique in Dublin.*

buyer's ˈmarket noun [S] a time when there are more goods for sale than there are people to buy them, so prices are usually low

ˈbuy-in noun **1** [C] a situation in which a person or group buys enough shares in a company to get control of it: *She led a buy-in of the group and is now its director.* **2** [C] a situation in which a company buys its own shares from SHAREHOLDERS **3** [U] the fact of agreeing with and accepting something that someone suggests: *If you want to go ahead with these plans, you'll need buy-in from the staff.*

buyout /ˈbaɪ.aʊt/ noun [C] (in business) a situation in which a person or group buys all the SHARES belonging to a company and so gets control of it: *a **management** buyout*

buzz /bʌz/ verb; noun

▸verb **MAKE SOUND** ▷ **1** C2 [I] to make a continuous, low sound such as the one a BEE makes: *I can hear something buzzing.* **2** [I or T] to press a BUZZER in order to get someone's attention: *I buzzed him but there was no answer.* **BE VERY ACTIVE** ▷ **3** C2 [I usually + adv/prep] to be busy and full of energy: *The place was buzzing (**with** excitement).* ◦ *Reporters were buzzing **around**, trying to get the full story.* **4 your head/mind is buzzing** If your head/mind is buzzing, you are thinking about many different things at the same time. **FLY LOW** ▷ **5** [T] informal If an aircraft buzzes a place or people, it flies over it or them very low and fast. **CUT HAIR** ▷ **6** [T] informal to cut someone's hair very short using a special machine

PHRASAL VERB **buzz off** informal **1** to go away: *I've got some stuff to do at home, so I'm going to buzz off now.* **2** used to tell someone to go away in a rude way: *Buzz off, I'm busy!*

▸noun [S] **SOUND** ▷ **1** C2 a continuous, low sound: *I heard a buzz and then saw the plane in the distance.* **FEELING** ▷ **2** C2 informal a feeling of excitement, energy, and pleasure: *I love cycling fast – it **gives** me **a** real buzz.* ◦ *I **get a** buzz **out of** public speaking.*

IDIOM **give sb a buzz** informal to phone someone: *I'll give you a buzz next week.*

B

buzzard /ˈbʌz.əd/ (US) /-ɚd/ **noun** [C] a large European bird that is a type of HAWK, or a type of North American VULTURE that feeds on the flesh of dead animals

ˈ**buzz** ˌ**cut** **noun** [C] US a **crew cut**

buzzed ˈ**up** **adj** informal **1** very excited: *He's so buzzed up about his wedding.* **2** Someone who is buzzed up has drunk so much alcohol or taken so many drugs that they do not behave normally.

buzzer /ˈbʌz.əʳ/ (US) /-ɚ/ **noun** [C] an electronic device that makes a buzzing sound: *I* ***pressed*** *the buzzer and after a while someone came to the door.*

buzzword /ˈbʌz.wɜːd/ (US) /-wɜːd/ **noun** [C] a word or expression from a particular subject area that has become fashionable by being used a lot, especially on television and in the newspapers: *'Diversity' is the new buzzword in education.*

buzzy /ˈbʌz.i/ **adj** informal exciting, especially because a lot of people are present and a lot of things are happening: *There's always a buzzy atmosphere in the restaurant.*

by /baɪ/ **preposition; preposition, adv**

▸**preposition AGENT** ▷ **1** (A2) used to show the person or thing that does something: *The motorcycle was driven by a tiny bald man.* ◦ *We were amazed by what she told us.* ◦ *I'm reading some short stories (written) by Chekhov.* ◦ *The book was translated by a well-known author.* ◦ *I felt frightened by the anger in his voice.* **METHOD** ▷ **2** (A2) used to show how something is done: *They travelled across Europe by train/car.* ◦ *She did the decorating (****all****) by herself (= alone, without help from anyone).* ◦ *We went in by (= through) the front door.* ◦ *Do you wish to be paid in cash or by cheque?* ◦ *He learned English by listen****ing*** *to the radio.* ◦ *Suddenly, she grabbed him by the arm (= took hold of this part of his body).* ◦ *I refuse to live by (= following) their rules.* **NOT LATER THAN** ▷ **3** (A2) not later than; at or before: *She had promised to be back by five o'clock.* ◦ *The application must be in by the 31st to be accepted.* ◦ *By the time I got to the station the train had already gone.* **MEASUREMENT** ▷ **4** (B2) used to show measurements or amounts: *Our office floor space measured twelve metres by ten (= was twelve metres in one direction and ten in the other).* ◦ *Their wages were increased by 15 percent.* ◦ *Freelance workers are paid by the hour (= for every hour they work).* ◦ *These phones have sold by the thousand.* **DURING** ▷ **5** during: *We travelled by night and rested by day.* **6 by nature, profession, trade, etc.** used when describing someone's character, job, etc.: *She is, by nature, a sunny, positive sort of a person.* ◦ *He's a plumber by trade.* **7 be all right/fine by sb** If something is all right/fine by someone, they agree that it can happen: *'I'd prefer to go later.' 'That's fine by me.'* ◦ *If it's all right by you, I'd like to leave now.*

IDIOM **by and by** old-fashioned after a short period: *By and by a man appeared.*

▸**preposition, adv** (B1) near, at the side of or (in distance or time) past: *A small child stood sullenly by her side.* ◦ *He wanted to keep her close by him always.* ◦ *The policewoman walked by (= past) them without saying a word.* ◦ *The years flew by.*

bye /baɪ/ **exclamation; noun**

▸**exclamation** (also **bye-**ˈ**bye**) (A1) informal goodbye: *Bye! See you next week!*

▸**noun** [C] If someone is given a bye, they are allowed to miss out part of a competition and continue to the next stage without having to win anything: *European teams were granted a bye into the third round of the Cup.*

ˈ**bye-byes** **noun** **go (to) bye-byes** mainly UK informal an expression used by or to young children, meaning 'go to sleep': *It's getting late – it's time for you to go to bye-byes.*

ˈ**by-e**ˌ**lection** **noun** [C] in the UK, an election that happens at a different time from a main election, to choose a Member of Parliament to replace one who has died or left his or her job

ˈ**bye** ˌ**week** **noun** [C] in sports, especially American football, a week during the playing SEASON in which a team does not play a game

bygone /ˈbaɪ.gɒn/ (US) /-gɑːn/ **adj; noun**

▸**adj** [before noun] belonging to or happening in a past time: *a bygone* ***era***

▸**noun** [plural] **let bygones be bygones** used to tell someone they should forget about unpleasant things that happened in the past, and especially to forgive and forget something bad that someone has done to them: *Just let bygones be bygones and be friends again.*

by-ˈ**heart** **verb** [T] Indian English to learn something in such a way that you can say it from memory

bylaw (also ˈ**bye-law**) /ˈbaɪ.lɔː/ (US) /-lɑː/ **noun** [C] **1** a law made by local government that only relates to its particular region **2** US a rule that governs the members of an organization

byline /ˈbaɪ.laɪn/ **noun** [C] specialized a line at the top of a newspaper or magazine article giving the writer's name

BYOB written abbreviation for bring your own bottle: used on a party invitation to request that guests bring their own alcoholic drinks

bypass /ˈbaɪ.pɑːs/ (US) /-pæs/ **verb; noun**

▸**verb** [T] **1** to avoid something by going around it: *We were in a hurry so we decided to bypass Canterbury because we knew there'd be a lot of traffic.* **2** to ignore a rule or official authority: *They bypassed the committee and went straight to senior management.*

▸**noun** [C] **ROAD** ▷ **1** a road built around a town or village so that traffic does not need to travel through it **OPERATION** ▷ **2** (also **heart bypass**) a medical operation in which the flow of a person's blood is changed to avoid a DISEASED part of their heart: *a triple bypass operation*

byplay /ˈbaɪ.pleɪ/ **noun** [U] things that happen, especially in a play, at the same time as the main action but that are less important than it

ˈ**by-**ˌ**product** **noun** [C] something that is produced as a result of making something else, or something unexpected that happens as a result of something: *Buttermilk is a by-product* ***of*** *making butter.* ◦ *Illness is one of the by-products* ***of*** *overcrowded housing.*

byre /baɪəʳ/ (US) /baɪr/ **noun** [C] UK old-fashioned a building in which cows are kept → Synonym **cowshed**

bystander /ˈbaɪˌstæn.dəʳ/ (US) /-dɚ/ **noun** [C] a person who is standing near and watching something that is happening but is not taking part in it: *Many* ***innocent*** *bystanders were injured by the explosion.*

byte /baɪt/ **noun** [C] specialized a unit of computer information, consisting of a group of (usually eight) BITS → See also **gigabyte, kilobyte, megabyte, terabyte**

byway /ˈbaɪ.weɪ/ **noun** [C] a small road that not many cars or people travel on

byword /ˈbaɪ.wɜːd/ (US) /-wɜːd/ **noun** [C] a person or thing that is very closely connected with a particular quality: *Their shops are a byword* ***for*** *good value.*

byzantine /bɪˈzæn.taɪn/, /ˈbɪz.ən.tiːn/ **adj** formal disapproving complicated and difficult to understand: *rules of byzantine complexity*

C

C, c /siː/ noun (plural **Cs**, **C's** or **c's**) LETTER ▷ **1** [C or U] the third letter of the English alphabet MUSIC ▷ **2** [C or U] a note in Western music: *This song is in (**the key of**) C.* MARK ▷ **3** [C or U] a mark in an exam or for a piece of work that shows that your work is average: *Rachel got (a) C for her French exam.* NUMBER ▷ **4** (also **c**) [C] the sign used in the Roman system for the number 100 TEMPERATURE ▷ **5** [after noun] abbreviation for **Celsius**: *The temperature today reached 25°C.* COMPUTER LANGUAGE ▷ **6** a computer programming language

c. preposition (also **ca**) written abbreviation for **circa**

C++ /ˌsiː.plʌsˈplʌs/ noun an OBJECT-ORIENTED version of C (= a computer programming language)

cab /kæb/ noun [C] PART OF VEHICLE ▷ **1** the separate front part of a large vehicle, such as a truck, bus, or train, in which the driver sits VEHICLE ▷ **2** B1 a taxi: *It'll save time if we go **by** cab.* → See also **minicab** **3** in the past, a vehicle pulled by a horse, used as a taxi

cabal /kəˈbæl/, /-ˈbɑːl/ noun [C] disapproving a small group of people who plan secretly to take action, especially political action

cabaret /ˈkæb.ə.reɪ/ US /-ə.eɪ/ noun [C or U] a performance of popular music, singing, or dancing, especially in a restaurant or bar: *a cabaret **act***

cabbage /ˈkæb.ɪdʒ/ noun **1** B1 [C or U] a large round vegetable with large green, white, or purple leaves, which can be eaten cooked or uncooked: *a savoy cabbage* ◦ *red/white cabbage* **2** [C] UK offensive a person who has lost all their powers of thought or speech usually as the result of a serious accident or illness

cabbie (also **cabby**) /ˈkæb.i/ noun [C] informal a driver of a taxi

caber /ˈkeɪ.bər/ US /-bɚ/ noun [C] a long, heavy wooden pole that is thrown as a test of strength in traditional sports competitions in Scotland: ***tossing** (= throwing) the caber*

cabin /ˈkæb.ɪn/ noun [C] HOUSE ▷ **1** B1 a small, simple house made of wood: *a log cabin* ON SHIP ▷ **2** C2 a small room where you sleep in a ship IN AIRCRAFT ▷ **3** B1 the area where passengers sit in an aircraft OFFICE ▷ **4** Indian English a small separate space for someone to work in, inside a larger office

ˈcabin ˌboy noun [C] old-fashioned a boy who is a servant on a ship

ˈcabin ˌcrew noun [C, + sing/pl verb] (also **ˈcabin ˌstaff**) in an aircraft, the people whose job it is to take care of the passengers

ˈcabin ˌcruiser noun [C] a boat with a motor and one or more small rooms for sleeping in

cabinet /ˈkæb.ɪ.nət/ noun GOVERNMENT ▷ **1** (usually **Cabinet**) [C usually singular, + sing/pl verb] a small group of the most important people elected to government, who make the main decisions about what should happen: *The Cabinet meet/meets every Thursday.* ◦ *a cabinet **minister*** ◦ *The prime minister has announced a cabinet **reshuffle** (= changes in the Cabinet).* FURNITURE ▷ **2** A2 [C] a piece of furniture with shelves, cupboards, or drawers, used for storing or showing things: *Valuable pieces of china were on display in a glass-fronted cabinet.* ◦ *a **bathroom/filing** cabinet*

cabinetmaker /ˈkæb.ɪ.nətˌmeɪ.kər/ noun [C] a person who makes or repairs good quality furniture

ˈcabin ˌfever noun [U] the feeling of being angry and bored because you have been inside for too long: *The rain had kept me indoors all weekend and I was beginning to get cabin fever.*

cable /ˈkeɪ.bl/ noun; verb

▸noun WIRE ▷ **1** B2 [C or U] a set of wires, covered by plastic, that carries electricity, phone signals, etc.: *a length of cable* ◦ *The road has been dug up in order to **lay** cables.* ◦ *overhead power cables* SYSTEM ▷ **2** B1 [U] the system of sending television programmes or phone signals along wires under the ground: *The office has gone over to cable.* ◦ *cable TV* ◦ *This channel is only available **on** cable.*

▸verb [T usually passive] (also **cable up**) to put cables under the ground in an area so that television or phone signals can be sent along them: *Many rural areas have not yet been cabled.* ◦ *You will have to buy a satellite dish or get cabled up.*

ˈcable ˌcar noun [C] **1** a vehicle which hangs from and is moved by a cable and transports people up steep slopes **2** US a vehicle on a cable railway

ˈcable ˌrailway noun [C] US a transport system that uses cables under the road to pull passenger vehicles up steep slopes

ˈcable ˌstitch noun [U] a pattern of wool used in KNITTING, which looks like twisted cables

caboodle /kəˈbuː.dl/ noun informal **the whole (kit and) caboodle** the whole of something, including everything that is connected to it: *I like everything about summer – the light, the warmth, the clothes – the whole caboodle.*

caboose /kəˈbuːs/ noun [C] US for **guard's van**

cabstand /ˈkæb.stænd/ noun [C] US for **taxi rank**

cacao /kəˈkaʊ/ noun [U] the seeds of a tropical tree, from which chocolate and COCOA are made: *cacao beans*

cachaça /kəˈʃæ.sə/ US /-ʃɑː-/ noun [U] a strong alcoholic drink similar to RUM, made in Brazil from the juice of the SUGAR CANE plant

cache /kæʃ/ noun **1** [C] a hidden store of things, or the place where they are kept: *an arms cache* **2** (also **cache memory**) [C or U] an area or type of computer MEMORY in which information that is often in use can be stored temporarily and got to especially quickly: *256 Kb secondary cache*

cachet /ˈkæʃ.eɪ/ US /kæʃˈeɪ/ noun [S or U] formal a quality which marks someone or something as special and worth respect and admiration: *This type of jacket used to have **a certain** cachet.*

cack-handed /ˌkækˈhæn.dɪd/ adj UK slang disapproving describes someone who often drops or breaks things or does things badly: *That's a cack-handed way of going about it!*

cackle /ˈkæk.l̩/ verb [I] **1** to make the loud, unpleasant sound of a chicken: *The hens cackled in alarm.* **2** disapproving to laugh in a loud, high voice: *A group of women were cackling in a corner.* ◦ *a cackling witch* • **cackle** noun [C]

cacophony /kəˈkɒf.ə.ni/ US /-ˈkɑː.fə-/ noun [S] an unpleasant mixture of loud sounds: *What a cacophony!* ◦ *As we entered the farmyard we were met with **a** cacophony **of** animal sounds.* • **cacophonous** /-nəs/ adj

cactus /ˈkæk.təs/ noun [C] (plural **cacti** /ˈkæk.taɪ/ or **cactuses**) any of many types of desert plant usually with sharp SPINES and thick stems for storing water

cactus

cad /kæd/ noun [C] old-fashioned a man who behaves badly or dishonestly, especially to women

CAD /kæd/ noun [U] abbreviation for computer aided design: the use of computers to design objects

cadaver /kəˈdæv.əʳ/ ⓤⓢ /-ɚ/ noun [C] specialized a dead human body

cadaverous /kəˈdæv.ᵊr.əs/ ⓤⓢ /-ɚ-/ adj looking pale, thin, and ill: *cadaverous features*

caddie /ˈkæd.i/ noun; verb

▸**noun** [C] (also **caddy**) a person who carries the equipment for someone who is playing GOLF

▸**verb** [I] (present tense **caddying**, past tense and past participle **caddied**) (also **caddy**) to be a caddie for someone

caddy /ˈkæd.i/ noun [C] **1** a small container, especially one for storing tea leaves: *tea caddy* **2** **caddie**

cadence /ˈkeɪ.dᵊns/ noun [C] **VOICE** ▷ **1** the regular rise and fall of the voice **MUSIC** ▷ **2** specialized a set of CHORDS (= different notes played together) at the end of a piece of music

cadet /kəˈdet/ noun [C] a student in the armed forces or the police

cadge /kædʒ/ verb [T] informal often disapproving to (try to) get something from someone else without paying for it: *He's always cadging free meals and free trips* ***from/off*** *his clients.* ◦ *Can I cadge a lift home?* • **cadger** /ˈkædʒ.əʳ/ ⓤⓢ /-ɚ/ noun [C]

cadmium /ˈkæd.mi.əm/ noun [U] (symbol **Cd**) a chemical element that is a soft bluish-white metal

cadre /ˈkɑː.dəʳ/ ⓤⓢ /-dɚ/ noun **1** [C, + sing/pl verb] a small group of trained people who form the basic unit of a military, political, or business organization **2** [C] a member of such a group

caecum (plural **caeca** /-ə/) UK specialized (US **cecum** (plural **ceca**)) /ˈsiː.kəm/ noun [C] the bag-shaped part at the beginning of the LARGE INTESTINE (= lower part of the bowels) where it joins onto the ILEUM

caesarean (section) (US usually **cesarean**) /sɪˌzeə.ri.ənˈsek.ʃᵊn/ ⓤⓢ /-ˌzer.i-/ noun [C or U] an operation in which a woman's WOMB is cut open to allow a baby to be born: *I had to have a caesarean.* ◦ *The baby was born* ***by*** *caesarean.* ◦ *a caesarean* ***birth/delivery***

caesium (US **cesium**) /ˈsiː.zi.əm/ noun [U] (symbol **Cs**) a chemical element that is a soft silver-white ALKALINE metal, that reacts strongly with other chemicals and is used in PHOTOCELLS

café (also **cafe**) /ˈkæf.eɪ/ noun [C] (UK informal **caff**) **1** Ⓐ1 a restaurant where simple and usually quite cheap meals are served: *There's a little café on the corner that serves very good coffee.* **2** South African English a small shop

cafeteria /ˌkæf.əˈtɪə.ri.ə/ ⓤⓢ /-ˈtɪr.i-/ noun [C] Ⓐ2 a restaurant (often in a factory, a college, or an office building) where people collect food and drink from a serving area and take it to a table themselves after paying for it

cafetière /ˌkæf.əˈtjeəʳ/ ⓤⓢ /-ˈtjer/ noun [C] a glass container for making coffee, in which hot water is poured onto coffee and then a FILTER (= net) is pushed down into the container to keep the solids at the bottom

caff /kæf/ noun [C] UK informal for **café**

caffeinated /ˈkæf.ɪ.neɪ.tɪd/ ⓤⓢ /-ə.neɪ.t̬ɪd/ adj containing caffeine: *caffeinated drinks/beverages* → Compare **decaffeinated**

caffeine /ˈkæf.iːn/ noun [U] a chemical, found for example in tea and coffee, that is a STIMULANT (= something that makes people more active)

caftan /ˈkæf.tæn/ noun [C] a **kaftan**

cage /keɪdʒ/ noun; verb

▸**noun** [C] Ⓑ1 a space surrounded on all sides by bars or wire, in which animals or birds are kept

▸**verb** [T usually passive] to put or keep birds or animals in a cage: *caged birds/animals* ◦ *Sam's been prowling about* ***like a*** *caged* ***animal*** *all morning.*

ˈcage diving noun [U] an activity in which people are taken underwater in a cage so that they can see SHARKS (= very large fish with sharp teeth) swimming near them

cagey /ˈkeɪ.dʒi/ adj (**cagier**, **cagiest**) informal unwilling to give information: *He was very cagey* ***about*** *what happened at the meeting.* • **cagily** /-dʒɪ.li/ adv • **caginess** /-nəs/ noun [U]

cagoule (also **kagoul**) /kəˈguːl/ noun [C] UK a light jacket with a HOOD (= head cover) that protects you against wind and rain

cahoots /kəˈhuːts/ noun [plural] informal **in cahoots (with)** acting together with others for an illegal or dishonest purpose: *A banker and a government minister were in cahoots over a property deal.*

caiman /ˈkeɪ.mən/ noun [C] another spelling of **cayman**

caipirinha /ˌkaɪ.pɪˈriːn.jə/ noun [C or U] a Brazilian alcoholic drink made with Brazilian RUM, LIME juice, sugar, and ice

cairn /keən/ ⓤⓢ /kern/ noun [C] a small pile of stones made, especially on mountains, to mark a place or as a MEMORIAL (= an object to make people remember someone or something)

cajole /kəˈdʒəʊl/ ⓤⓢ /-ˈdʒoʊl/ verb [I or T] to persuade someone to do something they might not want to do, by pleasant talk and (sometimes false) promises: *He really knows how to cajole people* ***into*** *doing what he wants.* ◦ *I managed to cajole her* ***out of*** *leaving too early.* ◦ *The most effective technique is to cajole rather than to threaten.*

Cajun /ˈkeɪ.dʒᵊn/ noun; adj

▸**noun** [C] a person who lives in the US state of Louisiana and whose relations in the past were French-speaking Canadians

▸**adj** belonging to or relating to Cajuns: *Cajun cooking/food*

cake /keɪk/ noun; verb

▸**noun** **FOOD** ▷ **1** Ⓐ1 [C or U] a sweet food made with a mixture of flour, eggs, fat, and sugar: *Would you like a piece of/a slice of/some cake?* ◦ *chocolate/sponge cake* ◦ *a birthday/Christmas cake* ◦ *cream cakes* ◦ *He* ***made/baked*** *a delicious cake.* → See also **oatcake**, **pancake** **SHAPE** ▷ **2** [C] a small flat object made by pressing together a soft substance: *fish/potato cakes* ◦ *a cake* ***of*** *soap*

IDIOMS **have your cake and eat it** to have or do two good things at the same time that are impossible to have or do at the same time: *You can't have your cake and eat it – if you want more local services, you can't expect to pay less tax.* • **the slice/share of the cake** the amount of money, goods, etc., available: *Everyone should have a fair slice of the cake.*

▸**verb** [T usually passive] to cover something or someone thickly with a substance that then dries out: *The men were caked* ***in*** *layers of filth and grime.* ◦ *boots caked* ***with*** *mud*

C

cakewalk /ˈkeik.wɔːk/ US /-wɑːk/ **noun** [S] US informal something that is very easy to achieve: *The Superbowl was a cakewalk* ***for*** *the Forty-Niners.*

CAL /kæl/ specialized abbreviation for computer-aided learning: the use of computers and computer software for teaching and training

calabash /ˈkæl.ə.bæʃ/ **noun** [C] (a tropical plant which produces) a large fruit, the outside of which becomes hard when dried and can be used as a container

calamine (lotion) /ˌkæl.ə.maɪnˈləʊ.ʃən/ US /-ˈloʊ-/ **noun** [U] a pink liquid used to reduce pain on sore skin

calamity /kəˈlæm.ɪ.ti/ US /-ə.t̬i/ **noun** [C] a serious accident or bad event causing damage or suffering: *A series of calamities ruined them – floods, a failed harvest, and the death of a son.* • **calamitous** /kəˈlæm.ɪ.təs/ US /-t̬əs/ **adj** • **calamitously** /-təs.li/ US /-t̬əs.li-/ **adv**

calcify /ˈkæl.sɪ.faɪ/ **verb** [I or T] to become hard or make something hard, especially by the addition of substances containing calcium

calcium /ˈkæl.si.əm/ **noun** [U] a chemical element that is present in teeth, bones, and CHALK

ˌcalcium ˈcarbonate noun [U] specialized a common, white chemical COMPOUND found naturally as CHALK, MARBLE, and LIMESTONE, and in bones and shells, etc.

carbonate /ˈkɑː.bən.eɪt/ US /-ˈkɑːr-/ **noun** [C] specialized a salt containing carbon and OXYGEN together with another chemical

ˌcalcium hyˈdroxide noun [U] specialized a white ALKALINE chemical compound used to make CEMENT and PLASTER and to reduce ACIDITY in soil

ˌcalcium ˈsulphate UK specialized (US **ˌcalcium ˈsulfate**) **noun** [U] **1** a white chemical substance used to make CEMENT and PLASTER OF PARIS and to make other substances dry **2 gypsum**

calculate /ˈkæl.kjʊ.leɪt/ **verb** [T] B2 to judge the number or amount of something by using the information that you already have, and adding, taking away, multiplying, or dividing numbers: *The cost of the damage caused by the recent storms has been calculated* ***as/at*** *over £5 million.* ◦ *The new tax system would be calculated* ***on*** *the value of property owned by an individual.* ◦ [+ question word] *At some stage we need to calculate* ***when*** *the project will be finished.* ◦ [+ that] *He's calculated* ***that*** *it would take him two years to save up enough for a car.*

PHRASAL VERB **calculate on sth** to expect or depend on a particular amount or time: *We're calculating on about 30 guests.*

calculated /ˈkæl.kjʊ.leɪ.tɪd/ US /-t̬ɪd/ **adj** C2 planned or arranged in order to produce a particular effect: *It was a cruel, calculated crime with absolutely no justification.* ◦ [+ to infinitive] *It's a policy that was hardly calculated to (= will not) win votes.*

ˌcalculated ˈrisk noun [C] a risk which you consider worth taking because the result, if it is successful, will be so good: *The director took a calculated risk in giving the film's main role to an unknown actor.*

calculating /ˈkæl.kjʊ.leɪ.tɪŋ/ US /-t̬ɪŋ/ **adj** often controlling situations for your own advantage in a way that is slightly unpleasant and causes people not to trust you: *In the film she's depicted as a very* ***cold and*** *calculating character.*

calculation /ˌkæl.kjʊˈleɪ.ʃən/ **noun** NUMBERS ▷ **1** B2 [C or U] the process of using information you already have and adding, taking away, multiplying, or dividing numbers to judge the number or amount of something: *The calculations that you* ***did/made*** *contained a few inaccuracies.* PERSON ▷ **2** [U] careful planning to control a situation for your own advantage in a way that is slightly unpleasant and causes people not to trust you: *There's an element of calculation in his behaviour that makes me distrust him.*

> **Word partners for calculation**
>
> *do/make/perform* a calculation • *base* your calculations *on* sth • calculations *indicate/show/suggest* sth • a *rough/quick* calculation • a *detailed/precise* calculation • a *simple/complex* calculation

calculator /ˈkæl.kjʊ.leɪ.təʳ/ US /-t̬ɚ/ **noun** [C] B1 a small electronic device that is used for doing calculations: *a* ***pocket*** *calculator*

calculus /ˈkæl.kjʊ.ləs/ **noun** [U] specialized an area of advanced mathematics in which continuously changing values are studied

caldera /kælˈdeə.rə/ /-ˈder-/ **noun** [C] specialized a very large circular hollow that remains when the central part of a VOLCANO falls in after an ERUPTION

caldron /ˈkɔːl.drən/ US /ˈkɑːl-/ **noun** [C] US for **cauldron**

calendar /ˈkæl.ɪn.dəʳ/ US /-dɚ/ **noun** [C] **1** A2 a printed table showing all the days, weeks, and months of the year: *An old calendar for 2012 was still hanging on the wall of her office.* **2** US a book with a separate space or page for each day, in which you write down your future arrangements, meetings, etc.: *He wrote the date of the meeting in his calendar.* **3** the system used to measure and arrange the days, weeks, months, and special events of the year according to a belief system or tradition: *the Christian/Jewish/Chinese calendar* **4** a list of events and dates within a particular year that are important for an organization or for the people involved in a particular activity: *the political/school calendar*

ˈcalendar ˌmonth noun [C] one of the twelve named months that the year is divided into: *Your salary will be paid on the third week of each calendar month.*

ˈcalendar ˌyear noun [C] a period of 365 or 366 days, starting on 1 January and ending on 31 December

calendula /kəˈlen.djə.lə/ US /-dʒə-/ **noun** [C or U] a plant that is used for making a substance that you rub into your skin to make it less sore

calf /kɑːf/ US /kæf/ **noun** [C] (plural **calves**) ANIMAL ▷ **1** B1 a young cow, or the young of various other large mammals such as ELEPHANTS and WHALES → See also **calve 2 in calf** If a cow is in calf, it is pregnant. LEG ▷ **3** C2 the thick curved part at the back of the human leg between the knee and the foot: *She's been unable to play since January because of a torn calf* ***muscle.***

ˈcalf-length adj describes clothing or boots that end at the middle point between the foot and the knee: *a calf-length skirt*

calfskin /ˈkɑːf.skɪn/ US /ˈkæf-/ **noun** [U] leather made from the skin of a young cow: *calfskin boots*

calibrate /ˈkæl.ɪ.breɪt/ **verb** [T] specialized **1** to mark units of measurement on an instrument such so that it can measure accurately: *a calibrated stick for measuring the amount of oil in an engine* **2** to check a measuring instrument to see if it is accurate • **calibration** /ˌkæl.ɪˈbreɪ.ʃən/ **noun** [C or U]

calibre UK (US **caliber**) /ˈkæl.ɪ.bəʳ/ (US) /-bɚ/ noun **QUALITY** ▷ **1** [U] the quality of someone or something, especially someone's ability: *If teaching paid more it might attract people **of** (a) **higher** calibre.* ◦ *The competition entries were **of** such (a) **high** calibre that judging them was very difficult.* **MEASUREMENT** ▷ **2** [C or U] the width of the inside of a pipe, especially of the long cylinder-shaped part of a gun, or the width of a bullet

calico /ˈkæl.ɪ.kəʊ/ (US) /-koʊ/ noun [U] a heavy plain cloth made from cotton

calipers /ˈkæl.ɪ.pəz/ (US) /-pɚz/ noun [plural] **TOOL** ▷ **1** (UK also **callipers**) a device for measuring widths or distances, consisting of two long, thin pieces of metal fixed together at one end **LEG SUPPORT** ▷ **2** (US **braces**) metal supports that are fastened to the legs of people who have difficulties with walking

caliph /ˈkeɪ.lɪf/ noun [C] a Muslim ruler

calisthenics /ˌkæl.ɪsˈθen.ɪks/ noun [U, + sing/pl verb] US for **callisthenics**

call /kɔːl/ (US) /kɑːl/ verb; noun

▸verb **NAME** ▷ **1** (B1) [T + obj + noun] to give someone or something a name, or to know or address someone by a particular name: *They've called the twins Edward and Thomas.* ◦ *What's that actor called that we saw in the film last night?* ◦ *His real name is Jonathan, but they've always called him 'Johnny'.* ◦ *What's her new novel called?* **2 call sb names** (C2) If a person, especially a child, calls someone names, he or she addresses that person with a name that is intended to be offensive: *Tom's worried that if he wears glasses at school the other children will call him names.* **PHONE** ▷ **3** (A2) [I or T] to phone someone: *He called (you) last night when you were out.* ◦ *She called (me) this morning at the office and we had a brief chat.* ◦ *I've been calling all morning but I can't get through.* ◦ *Do you think we should call the police?* **4 call collect** US (US also and UK **reverse (the) charges**) to make a phone call that is paid for by the person who receives it

> **! Common mistake: call**
>
> Remember that when **call** means 'to telephone', it is not usually followed by 'to'.
>
> Don't say 'call to someone', say **call someone**:
>
> ~~*Call to me if you have any more questions.*~~
>
> *Call me if you have any more questions.*

CONSIDER ▷ **5** [T + obj + noun] to consider someone or something to be: *He knows a lot of people, but only one or two that he'd call close friends.* ◦ *One sandwich and a lettuce leaf – I don't call that a meal!* ◦ *I'm not calling you a liar – I'm just suggesting that you misunderstood the facts of the situation.* **6 call sth your own** to consider something as belonging to you: *I don't aspire to anything very grand – I just want a place I can call my own.* **SHOUT/CRY** ▷ **7** (B1) [I or T] to say something in a loud voice, especially in order to attract someone's attention, or (of animals) to make a loud, high sound, especially to another animal: *Someone in the crowd called (**out**) his name.* ◦ *Did you call?* ◦ [+ speech] *'Hey, you! Come over here!' she called.* ◦ *The blackbird called **to** its mate.* **8 call for order** (also **call sth to order**) to ask people in a meeting to stop talking so that the meeting can continue: *She called for order/called the meeting to order.* **ASK TO COME** ▷ **9** (C1) [I or T] to ask someone to come to you: *She called me **over** to where she was sitting.* ◦ *I keep the bedroom door open in case the children call (**for**) me in the night.* ◦ *I was called **to** an emergency meeting this morning.* ◦ *At school she was always being called **into** the headteacher's office.* **VISIT** ▷ **10** [I] to visit someone, especially for a short time: *The electrician must have called (**round**) this morning when we were out – there's a note on the door mat.* **DECIDE ON** ▷ **11** (C1) [T] to decide officially to have a particular event or take particular action: *The managing director has called **a meeting** to discuss pay levels.* ◦ *The papers are predicting that the prime minister will call **an election** in the spring.* ◦ *It's reckoned that the unions will call **a strike** if management will not agree to their demands.* ◦ *They had to call **a halt to** (= end) the match because of the heavy rain.*

IDIOMS **call sb's bluff** to make someone prove that what they are saying is true, or to make someone prove that they will really do what they say they will do, because you do not believe them • **call your shot** US to say clearly what your intentions are • **call a spade a spade** informal to say the truth about something, even if it is not polite or pleasant • **call into question** formal to cause doubts about something: *The fact that a party can be voted into power by a minority of the electorate calls into question the country's electoral system.* • **call it a day** informal (C2) to stop the work you are doing: *I'm getting a bit tired now – shall we call it a day?* • **call it quits** informal **1** to stop doing something **2** to agree with someone that a debt has been paid and that no one owes anything more: *I paid for last week's shopping and you paid for this week's, so let's call it quits.* • **call the shots** (also **call the tune**) to be in the position of being able to make the decisions that will influence a situation • **sth is calling you** If something is calling you, you have a strong feeling that you must do it, have it, go there, etc.: *That last piece of chocolate cake is calling me.*

PHRASAL VERBS **call back** (B2) to return to a place in order to see someone or collect something: *She said she'd call back later to pick up that report.* • **call sb back** (A2) to phone someone again, or to phone someone who called you earlier: *I'm a bit busy – can I call you back later?* • **call by** to visit somewhere for a short while on your way to somewhere else: *I just thought I'd call by on my way into town.* • **call for sb** (B1) to go to a place in order to collect someone: *I'll call for you at eight.* • **call for sth 1** to need or deserve a particular action, remark, or quality: *This calls for a celebration!* ◦ *It's the sort of work that calls for a high level of concentration.* ◦ *He told you that you were an idiot? Well, I don't think that was called for (= I think it was rude and not deserved)!* **2** (C2) to demand that something happens: *Members have called for his resignation.* • **call forth sth** formal to cause something to exist: *The proposed shopping centre has called forth an angry response from local residents.* • **call sb in** to ask someone to come to help in a difficult situation: *A new team of detectives were called in to conduct a fresh inquiry.* • **call sth in** If a bank calls in money, it demands that you pay back the money it has lent to you: *He needs to make the business work before the bank calls in the loan.* • **call sb/sth off** to order a dog, or sometimes a person, to stop attacking someone or something: *I shouted to him to call his dog off, but he just laughed at me.* ◦ *Call off your thugs, and I'll show you where the money is.* • **call sth off** (B2) to decide that a planned event, especially a sports event, will not happen, or to end an activity because it is no longer useful or possible: *Tomorrow's match has been called off because of the icy weather.* ◦ *The police have called off the search for the missing child until dawn tomorrow.* • **call (in) on sb** to visit someone for a short time: *I thought we might call in on your mother on our way – I've got some magazines for her.* • **call on sb** [+ to infinitive] (C1) to ask someone in a formal way to do something: *They're calling on all men and boys over the age of 14 to join the army.* ◦ formal *I now call on everyone to raise a glass to the happy couple.* • **call on sth** formal to use something, especially a quality that you have, in order to achieve something: *She would have to call on all her strength if she was to survive the next few months.* • **call (sth) out** to say something in a loud voice: *He used to call out in his sleep.* ◦ *Don't just call the answers out – raise your hand.* • **call sb out** ASK TO COME ▷ **1** to ask someone to come in order to do a job, especially when it is an emergency: *We had to call out a doctor.* ◦ *The government called the army out to deal with violent disorder on the streets.* CRITICIZE ▷ **2** informal to criticize someone or ask them to explain their actions: *If he did anything wrong, I'd be the first to call him out **on** it.* • **call sb up** PHONE ▷ **1** mainly US to phone someone: *My dad called me up to tell me the good news.* MILITARY ▷ **2** C2 [M usually passive] to order someone to join a military organization or to ask someone to join an official, especially national, team: *He was called up when the war began.* ◦ *Lucie Saint was called up for the final against Brazil.* • **call sth up** C2 to find and show information on a computer screen: *You can use the search facility to call up all the occurrences of a particular word in a document.*

▸noun PHONE ▷ **1** A2 [C] the act of using the phone: *I got a call **from** an old college friend last night.* ◦ *If there are any calls **for** me, could you write them down next to the phone?* ◦ *I've just got a couple of calls to **make**.* ◦ *That decorator you called about painting the house – did he ever **return** your call?* ◦ *The radio station **received** a lot of calls complaining about the show's bad language.* ◦ *Before six o'clock, calls are charged at peak rate.* ANIMAL ▷ **2** B1 [C] the sound an animal makes or the sound of someone shouting something: *The whale has a very distinctive call.* ◦ *She could hear calls **for help** from inside the burning building.* ◦ *I'll be in the next room, so **give** me a call if you need any help.* DEMAND ▷ **3** [U] the fact of people wanting or needing a particular thing: *There's **not much** call **for** fur coats these days.* ◦ formal *I certainly don't think there's any call **for** that sort of language, young lady!* **4** C1 [C] a demand for something to happen: *Management have so far ignored the union's calls **for** stricter safety regulations.* VISIT ▷ **5** C1 [C] a short visit, especially an official one made by someone whose job is connected with health: *Doctor Seward is out **on a** call this morning.* ◦ *The nurse has got a few calls to **make** this afternoon.* ◦ old-fashioned *I thought I'd **pay** a call **on** (= visit) an old friend of mine this weekend.* DECISION ▷ **6** [C] informal a decision: *It was a **tough call**, but eventually I decided to give up my job.* ◦ *More investment? That's got to be your call – you're the one that's paying!*

IDIOMS **call of nature** humorous the need to use the toilet • **on call** If a worker such as a doctor is on call, he or she is available to work or make official visits at any time when needed: *She's a doctor, so she's often on call at the weekend.* → See also **on-call**

Callanetics /kæl.əˈnet.ɪks/ US /-ˈneṱ-/ noun [U] UK trademark a system of physical exercise that involves repeating small movements of the muscles and is intended to make the body firmer and more attractively shaped

ˈcall ˌbox noun [C] **1** UK a **phone box** **2** US a small box next to a main road containing a phone to use after an accident or other emergency

ˈcall ˌcentre noun [C] UK a large office in which a company's employees provide information to its customers, or sell or advertise its goods or services by phone

caller /ˈkɔː.ləʳ/ US /ˈkɑː.lɚ/ noun [C] PHONE ▷ **1** someone who makes a phone call, especially a member of the public who calls a radio or television programme while it is being broadcast VISIT ▷ **2** a visitor

ˌcaller IˈD noun [U] a service that allows you to see the phone number of the person who is calling you

ˈcall ˌgirl noun [C] a female PROSTITUTE (= woman who has sex for money) who arranges her meetings with men over the phone

calligraphy /kəˈlɪg.rə.fi/ noun [U] (the art of producing) beautiful writing, often created with a special pen or brush: *There's some wonderful calligraphy in these old manuscripts.*

ˈcall-in noun [C] US for **phone-in**

calling /ˈkɔː.lɪŋ/ US /ˈkɑː-/ noun [C] formal a strong wish to do a job, usually one that is socially valuable

callipers noun [plural] UK for **calipers**

callisthenics UK (US **calisthenics**) /ˌkæl.ɪsˈθen.ɪks/ noun [U, + sing/pl verb] (a system of) simple physical exercises that are done to make the body firm, able to stretch easily, and more attractive

callous /ˈkæl.əs/ adj unkind, cruel, and without sympathy or feeling for other people: *It might sound callous, but I don't care if he's homeless. He's not living with me!* • **callously** /-li/ adv • **callousness** /-nəs/ noun [U]

ˈcall-out (also **callout**) noun [C] an occasion when someone is asked to come to a person's home or to a particular place in order to do a job, help someone, etc.: *Many plumbers charge double for an emergency call-out over the weekend.* ◦ *call-out **fees/charges/service*** ◦ *The mountain rescue service had several call-outs last week.*

callow /ˈkæl.əʊ/ US /-oʊ/ adj literary disapproving describes someone, especially a young person, who behaves in a way that shows they have little experience, confidence, or judgment: *Mark was just a callow **youth** of 16 when he arrived in Paris.*

ˈcall-up noun [C usually singular] **1** (US also **draft**) an order to join a military organization: *She was very upset when her boyfriend received his call-up (**papers**).* **2** an invitation to play in an official, especially national, team: *Le Tissier was delighted when he received his England call-up.*

callus /ˈkæl.əs/ noun [C] an area of hard skin, especially on the feet or hands: *He had workman's hands which were rough and covered with calluses.*

calm /kɑːm/ adj; verb; noun

▸adj **1** B1 peaceful, quiet, and without worry: *He has a very calm manner.* ◦ *Now **keep** calm everyone, the police are on their way.* **2** without hurried movement or noise: *After a night of fighting, the streets are now calm.* **3** B1 describes weather when there is no wind, or the sea or a lake when it is still and has no waves • **calmly** /ˈkɑː.m.li/ adv B2 in a quiet or relaxed way: *She reacted surprisingly calmly to the news of his death.* • **calmness** /ˈkɑː.m.nəs/ noun [U]

▸verb [T] **1** to stop someone feeling upset, angry, or excited: *He tried to calm the screaming baby by rocking it back and forth.* **2** **calm sb's fears** to make someone feel less worried about something

PHRASAL VERB **calm (sb) down** B2 to stop feeling upset, angry, or excited, or to stop someone feeling this way: *She sat down and took a few deep breaths to calm herself down.* ◦ *Calm down, for goodness sake. It's nothing to get excited about!*

Other ways of saying calm

If someone is calm in a difficult situation, you can use the words **cool** or **unruffled**:

*He was very **cool** about the problem and didn't shout or lose his temper.*

*He seemed remarkably **unruffled** for a man who was about to lose his job.*

The idiom **not lose your head** can also be used when someone stays calm in a difficult situation:

She doesn't lose her head under pressure.

If someone is very calm and in control of his or her emotions, the word **composed** can be used:

*After being so **composed** throughout this series, the team suddenly became shaky.*

The word **level-headed** can be used for people who are usually calm in difficult situations:

*She's very **level-headed** and unlikely to get upset by what has happened.*

Someone who is usually calm because it is part of his or her nature can be described as **placid**:

*She was a very **placid** baby who hardly ever cried.*

When someone becomes calm again after being angry, you can use the phrasal verb **calm down**:

*Dad was furious and it was a long time before he **calmed down**.*

▸**noun 1** a quiet or peaceful period or situation: *It was the calm of the countryside that he loved so much.* **2** a quiet and relaxed manner

IDIOM **the calm before the storm** a quiet or peaceful period before a period during which there is great activity, argument, or difficulty

Calor gas /ˈkæ.lə͵gæs/ (US) /-lɚ-/ **noun** [U] UK trademark a type of gas that is sold in metal containers and can be taken to places where there is no gas supply, used for heating and cooking: *We took a Calor gas **stove** for cooking on when we went camping.*

calorie /ˈkæl.ər.i/ (US) /-ɚ-/ **noun** [C] **FOOD** ▷ **1** a unit of energy, often used as a measurement of the amount of energy that food provides: *There are about 50 calories in an apple.* ◦ *He found calorie-**counting** the best way of losing weight.* **HEAT** ▷ **2** specialized a unit of heat energy

͵calorie-conˈtrolled adj If someone is on a calorie-controlled diet, they count all the calories that they eat in order not to eat too much.

calorific /͵kæl.əˈrɪf.ɪk/ **adj** containing calories (= units of energy provided by food): *Fatty foods have a high calorific **value**.* ◦ *Although it's only a quick snack, a hamburger is very calorific (= it contains a lot of calories).*

calumny /ˈkæl.əm.ni/ **noun** [C or U] formal (the act of making) a statement about someone that is not true and is intended to damage the reputation of that person: *He was subjected to the most vicious calumny, but he never complained and never sued.*

Calvados /ˈkæl.və.dɒs/ (US) /-doʊs/ **noun** [U] a strong alcoholic drink made from apples, produced in northern France

calve /kɑːv/ (US) /kæv/ **verb** [I] When a cow calves, it gives birth to a CALF (= a young cow): *Four cows calved overnight.*

calves /kɑːvz/ (US) /kævz/ plural of **calf**

Calvinist /ˈkæl.vɪ.nɪst/ **adj** (also **Calvinistic** /͵kæl.vɪˈnɪs.tɪk/) **1** relating to the Christian teachings of John Calvin, especially the belief that God controls what happens on earth: *Calvinist doctrine* **2** having severe moral standards and considering pleasure to be wrong or not necessary: *Her parents have very Calvinist attitudes.* • **Calvinism** /-nɪ.zəm/ **noun** [U] • **Calvinist noun** [C]

calypso /kəˈlɪp.səʊ/ (US) /-soʊ/ **noun** [C] (plural **calypsos**) a type of popular Caribbean song whose words, often invented as the song is sung, deal with a subject of interest at the present time

calyx /ˈkeɪ.lɪks/ **noun** [C] (plural **calyces** /ˈkeɪ.lɪ.siːz/ or **calyxes**) specialized the outer part of a flower formed by the SEPALS (= separate outer parts), which covers and protects the PETALS, etc. as they develop

camaraderie /͵kæm.əˈrɑː.dər.i/ (US) /-dɚ-/ **noun** [S or U] a feeling of friendliness towards people that you work or share an experience with: *When you've been climbing alone for hours, there's a tremendous sense of camaraderie when you meet another climber.*

camber /ˈkæm.bər/ (US) /-bɚ/ **noun** [C or U] a gradual slope down from the middle of a road to each edge, which helps water to flow off it

Cambrian /ˈkæm.bri.ən/ **adj** from or referring to the period of time between about 543 and 490 million years ago, in which many different types of INVERTEBRATES (= animals with no SPINE) first appeared: *the Cambrian era/period* ◦ *Cambrian rocks* • **the Cambrian noun** the Cambrian period

camcorder /ˈkæm͵kɔː.dər/ (US) /-͵kɔːr.dɚ/ **noun** [C] a small VIDEO CAMERA that can be held easily in one hand → Compare **video camera**

came /keɪm/ **verb** past simple of **come**

camel /ˈkæm.əl/ **noun** **ANIMAL** ▷ **1** (B1) [C] a large animal with a long neck, that lives in the desert and has one or two HUMPS (= large raised areas of flesh) on its back → See also **dromedary** **CLOTH** ▷ **2** [U] (also **camel hair**) a soft, pale brown cloth made from wool and used to make coats

camel

camellia /kəˈmiː.li.ə/ **noun** [C] a bush with dark shiny leaves and large white, pink, or red flowers that are similar to ROSES

Camembert /ˈkæm.əm.beər/ (US) /-ber/ **noun** [C or U] a soft French cheese with a white outside and a yellow inside

cameo /ˈkæm.i.əʊ/ (US) /-oʊ/ **noun** [C] (plural **cameos**) **PERFORMANCE** ▷ **1** a small but noticeable part in a film or play, performed by a famous actor: *He appears briefly towards the end of the film in a cameo **role** as a priest.* **JEWELLERY** ▷ **2** a piece of usually oval jewellery on which there is a head or other shape of one colour on a surface of a different colour: *a cameo **brooch***

camera /ˈkæm.rə/ **noun** [C] **1** (A1) a device for taking photographs or making films or television programmes: *I forgot to take my camera with me to Portugal, so I couldn't take any photos.* ◦ *Television camera **crews** broadcast the event all round the world.* ◦ *It was said of Marilyn Monroe that the camera loved her (= that she looked very attractive on film and in photographs).* **2 on camera** appearing on a piece of film: *They were caught on camera as they brutally attacked a man.*

cameraman /ˈkæm.rə.mæn/, /-mən/ **noun** [C] (plural **-men** /-men/, /-mən/) a person who operates a camera when films or television programmes are being made

C

ˈcamera-shy adj [after verb] If someone is camera-shy, they dislike having their photograph taken.

camerawork /ˈkæm.rə.wɜːk/ (US) /ˈkæm.rə.wɝːk/ noun [U] the way in which cameras are used in films: *The camerawork in some of these animal documentaries is fantastic.*

camiknickers /ˈkæm.iˌnɪk.əz/ (US) /-ɚz/ noun [plural] UK a piece of women's underwear consisting of a light part to cover the top half of the body, connected to a pair of KNICKERS

camisole /ˈkæm.ɪ.səʊl/ (US) /-soʊl/ noun [C] a light piece of women's underwear for the top half of the body, with thin straps that go over the shoulders

camomile (also **chamomile**) /ˈkæm.ə.maɪl/ noun [U] a sweet-smelling plant whose white and yellow flowers have uses in medicine and are also used to make tea: *camomile* ***tea***

camouflage /ˈkæm.ə.flɑːʒ/ noun **1** [U] the use of leaves, branches, paints, and clothes for hiding soldiers or military equipment so that they cannot be seen against their surroundings: *a camouflage jacket* **2** [S or U] the way that the colour or shape of an animal or plant appears to mix with its natural environment to prevent it from being seen by ATTACKERS: *The lizard's light brown skin acts as (****a****) camouflage in the desert sand.* **3** [S or U] something that is meant to hide something, or behaviour that is intended to hide the truth: *Using smoke as (****a****) camouflage, the army advanced up the hill.* ◦ *He believed that her kindness was merely a camouflage for her real intentions.* • **camouflage verb** [T] *The troops had camouflaged them****selves*** *so effectively that the enemy didn't notice them approaching.*

camp /kæmp/ noun; verb; adj

▸noun **TENTS/BUILDINGS** ▷ **1** (B1) [C or U] a place where people stay in tents or other temporary structures: *We* ***pitched/set up*** *camp (= put up our tents) by the lakeside.* **2** (B2) [C] an area where people are kept temporarily for a particular reason: *a* ***labour/prison/refugee*** *camp* **3** (B2) [C or U] a place where soldiers stay when they are training or fighting a war: *an army camp* **OPINION** ▷ **4** [C, + sing/pl verb] a group of people who share an opinion, especially a political one: *The pro-abortion camp are fighting to decriminalize abortion.*

▸verb [I] (A2) to put up a tent and stay in it for a short while, for example while on holiday: *We camped on one of the lower slopes of the mountain.*

PHRASAL VERBS **camp it up** informal to behave in a camp manner • **camp out** to sleep outside in a tent

▸adj informal **1** (of a man) behaving and dressing in a way that some people think is typical of a gay man: *What's the name of that amazingly camp actor with the high voice and a funny walk?* **2** using bright colours, loud sounds, unusual behaviour, etc. in a humorous way: *Their shows are always incredibly camp and flamboyant.*

campaign /kæmˈpeɪn/ noun; verb

▸noun [C] **1** (C1) a planned group of especially political, business, or military activities that are intended to achieve a particular aim: *The protests were part of their campaign* ***against*** *the proposed building development in the area.* ◦ *This is the latest act of terrorism in a long-standing and bloody campaign* ***of violence***. ◦ *The endless public appearances are an inevitable part of an* ***election*** *campaign.* ◦ *She's the campaign* ***organizer*** *for the Labour Party.* ◦ *The government have just* ***launched*** *(= begun) their annual Christmas campaign* ***to*** *stop drunken driving.* ◦ *a controversial new* ***advertising*** *campaign* **2** (C1) a group of connected actions or movements that forms part of a war: *a bombing campaign*

▸verb [I] (C1) to organize a series of activities to try to achieve something: [+ to infinitive] *They've been campaigning for years* ***to*** *get him out of prison.* ◦ *He's spending a lot of his time at the moment campaigning* ***for/on behalf of*** *the Conservative Party.* ◦ *They're busy campaigning* ***against*** *the building of a new motorway near here.*

campaigner /ˌkæmˈpeɪ.nəʳ/ (US) /-nɚ/ noun [C] a person who takes part in organized activities that are intended to change something in society: *an animal rights campaigner*

camˈpaign ˌtrail noun [C usually singular] a series of planned events in different places taken part in or given by a politician who is trying to be elected: *She went* ***on the*** *campaign trail around the Southern states.*

campanology /ˌkæm.pəˈnɒl.ə.dʒi/ (US) /-ˈnɑː.lə-/ noun [U] specialized the art or skill of ringing church bells • **campanologist** /-dʒɪst/ noun [C]

ˈcamp ˌbed noun [C] UK (US **cot**) a light bed that can be folded so that it can be easily carried and stored

camper /ˈkæm.pəʳ/ (US) /-pɚ/ noun [C] **1** a person who stays in a tent or in a HOLIDAY CAMP on holiday **2** (UK also **camper van**) a **motor home 3** (also **trailer**) US for **caravan**

ˈcamper ˌvan noun [C] UK a **motor home**

campfire /ˈkæmp.faɪəʳ/ (US) /-faɪr/ noun [C] an outside fire, made and used by people who are staying outside or in tents

ˈcamp ˌfollower noun [C] a person who is interested in and supports a particular political party or other organization but is not a member of it

campground /ˈkæmp.graʊnd/ noun [C] US a piece of land where people on holiday can CAMP, usually with toilets and places for washing

camphor /ˈkæm.fəʳ/ (US) /-fɚ/ noun [U] a whitish substance with a strong smell, sometimes used in medicine

camping /ˈkæm.pɪŋ/ noun [U] (A2) the activity of staying in a tent on holiday: *We used to* ***go*** *camping in Spain when I was a child.* ◦ *camping* ***equipment***

ˈcamping ˌground noun [C] Australian English a piece of land where people on holiday can CAMP, usually with toilets and places for washing → Compare **campsite**

campsite /ˈkæmp.saɪt/ noun [C] **1** (B1) (US also **campground**) a piece of land where people on holiday can CAMP, usually with toilets and places for washing: *The campsite is in a beautiful location next to the beach.* **2** US a place for one tent at a place where people stay in tents: *Our tent was so large that they charged us for two campsites.*

campus /ˈkæm.pəs/ noun [C or U] (B2) the buildings of a college or university and the land that surrounds them: *There's accommodation for about five hundred students* ***on*** *campus.*

campy /ˈkæm.pi/ adj mainly US describes an activity, or someone's behaviour or appearance, that is funny because it is obviously intended to be strange or shocking

camshaft /ˈkæm.ʃɑːft/ (US) /-ʃæft/ noun [C] a device which causes the VALVES of an engine to open or close at the correct time

can[1] strong /kæn/ weak /kən/ modal verb **ABILITY** ▷ **1** (A1) to be able to: *Can you drive?* ◦ *She can speak four languages.* ◦ *Can you read that sign from this distance?* ◦ *The doctors are doing all that they can, but she's still not breathing properly.* ◦ *Do the best you can – I realize* the circumstances are not ideal. ◦ *If the party is awful, we can **always** leave (= that would be one possible solution to our problem).* ◦ *'She's really furious about it.' 'Can you blame her (= I'm not surprised)?'* **2 can do** US informal used to say that you can and will do something: *'Will you mail this letter for me, please?' 'Can do.'* ◦ *'I need you to pick up the kids today.' 'Sorry, no can do (= no I can't).'* **PERMISSION** ▷ **3** A1 to be allowed to: *Can I use your bike, John?* ◦ *You can park over there.* ◦ *You can have a piece of cake after you've eaten your vegetables!* **4** informal sometimes used to tell someone angrily to do something: *If you carry on being horrible to your sister, Sophie, you can just go to bed!*

> **!** Usage: **can, could or may?**
>
> **Can** is used in standard spoken English when asking for permission. **Could** is slightly more formal. Both of these are acceptable in most forms of written English, although in very formal writing, such as official instructions, **may** is usually used instead:
>
> *Persons under 14 unaccompanied by an adult may not enter.*

REQUEST ▷ **5** A1 used to request something: *If you see Adrian, can you tell him I'm in London next weekend?* ◦ *Can you make a little less noise, please? I'm trying to work.* **POSSIBILITY** ▷ **6** A2 used to express possibility: *You can get stamps from the local newsagents.* ◦ *You can get very nasty skin diseases from bathing in dirty water.* ◦ *Smoking can cause cancer.* ◦ *Noise can be quite a problem when you're living in a flat.* ◦ *He can be really annoying at times (= he is sometimes very annoying).* **OFFER** ▷ **7** A1 used in polite offers of help: *Can I help you with those bags?* ◦ *I'm afraid Ms Ferguson has already left the office. Can I be of any help?*

> **!** Common mistake: **can**
>
> **Can** is followed by an infinitive verb without 'to'.
>
> Don't say 'can to do something', say **can do something**:
>
> ~~*I'm glad you can to come to my cousin's wedding.*~~
>
> *I'm glad you can come to my cousin's wedding.*

can² /kæn/ noun; verb

▸**noun** **CONTAINER** ▷ **1** A2 [C] (UK also **tin**) a closed metal container, especially cylinder-shaped, in which some types of drink and food are sold: *a can of soup/beans* **2** [C] (UK also **tin**) the amount of food or drink that is contained in a can: *You'll need a can of tuna for this recipe.* **3** [C] a metal container, especially one with a lid, handle, and shaped opening for pouring: *an **oil** can* ◦ *a can of paint* **PRISON** ▷ **4 the can** [S] US informal for prison: *He spent ten years **in** the can for armed robbery.* **TOILET** ▷ **5 the can** US informal for toilet

IDIOMS **can of worms** informal a situation which causes a lot of problems for you when you start to deal with it: *Corruption is a serious problem, but nobody has yet been willing to **open** up that can of worms.* • **in the can** informal If a film is in the can, filming has finished and it is ready to be prepared for showing to the public.

▸**verb** [T] (**-nn-**) **FOOD** ▷ **1** to put food and drink into a closed metal container without air: *He works in a factory where they can fruit.* **STOP** ▷ **2** mainly US informal to stop doing something or making noise: *Hey, can **it**, would you? I'm trying to sleep.*

canal /kəˈnæl/ noun [C] B1 a long, thin stretch of water that is artificially made either for boats to travel along or for taking water from one area to another: *The Panama Canal provides a crucial shipping link between the Atlantic and Pacific oceans.* → See also **alimentary canal**

caˈnal ˌboat noun [C] (also **narrowboat**) a long, narrow boat that is used on a canal

canapé /ˈkæn.ə.peɪ/ noun [C usually plural] a small, thin, salty biscuit or small piece of bread with food such as cheese, fish, or meat on top, that is served with drinks, especially at a party

canard /ˈkæn.ɑːd/ US /kəˈnɑːrd/ noun [C] literary a false report or piece of information that is intended to deceive people

canary /kəˈneə.ri/ US /-ˈner.i/ noun [C] a small, yellow bird that is well known for its singing, sometimes kept as a pet

canasta /kəˈnæs.tə/ noun [U] a card game for two to six people that is played with two sets of cards

cancan /ˈkæn.kæn/ noun [C] a fast dance, originally performed in France in the 19th century, in which a row of women on a stage kick their legs high and lift their skirts

cancel /ˈkæn.səl/ verb (**-ll-** or US usually **-l-**) **1** B1 [I or T] to decide that an organized event will not happen, or to stop an order for goods or services that you no longer want: *They've had to cancel tomorrow's football match because of the bad weather.* ◦ *The 7.10 train to London has been cancelled.* ◦ *to cancel a magazine subscription* **2** [T] to mark a stamp to show that it has been used and cannot be used again

> **+** Other ways of saying **cancel**
>
> **Call off** is an alternative to 'cancel' when talking about events:
>
> *The game has been **called off** because of the weather.*
>
> If something has been cancelled, you can say that it is **off**:
>
> *The meeting's **off** because James is ill.*
>
> **Scrap** can be used when you cancel a plan:
>
> *We've **scrapped** our plans for a trip to France.*
>
> **Suspend** can be used when something is cancelled either temporarily or permanently:
>
> *The ferry service has been **suspended** for the day because of bad weather.*
>
> **Postpone** can be used when someone cancels something but plans to do it later:
>
> *We've **postponed** the wedding until next year.*
>
> If you cancel something before you have finished it, you could use the words **abandon** or **curtail**:
>
> *They had to **abandon** their attempt to climb the mountain.*
>
> *We **curtailed** our trip when John became ill.*

PHRASAL VERB **cancel sth out** to remove the effect of one thing by doing another thing that has the opposite effect: *This month's pay cheque will cancel out his debt, but it won't give him any extra money.*

cancellation /ˌkæn.səlˈeɪ.ʃən/ noun [C or U] C1 the act of deciding that an organized event will not happen or of stopping an order for something: *Many trains are subject to cancellation because of the flooding.* ◦ *The theatre tickets were sold out, so we waited to see if there were any cancellations (= unwanted returned tickets).*

cancer /ˈkæn.səʳ/ US /-sɚ/ noun **1** B1 [C or U] a serious disease that is caused when cells in the body grow in a way that is uncontrolled and not normal, killing normal cells and often causing death: *He died of liver cancer.* ◦ *cancer **of** the cervix/stomach* ◦ *breast/bowel/lung cancer* ◦ *cancer cells* ◦ *a cancer patient* ◦ *It was a* *secondary cancer.* → See also **carcinogen** **2** [C] a harmful activity that spreads quickly: *Drug abuse is a cancer which is destroying our society.* • **cancerous** /-əs/ **adj** *a cancerous growth/tumour*

Cancer /ˈkæn.səʳ/ (US) /-sɚ/ **noun** [C or U] the fourth sign of the ZODIAC, relating to the period from 22 June to 22 July and represented by a CRAB, or a person born during this period

candelabra /ˌkæn.dəˈlɑː.brə/ **noun** [C] (plural **candelabra** or **candelabras**) a decorative object that holds several candles or lights

candelabra

candid /ˈkæn.dɪd/ **adj** approving honest and telling the truth, especially about something difficult or painful: *The two presidents have had candid talks about the current crisis.* ◦ ***To be candid with you, I think you're making a dreadful mistake.*** → See also **candour** • **candidly** /-li/ **adv**

candida /ˈkæn.dɪ.də/ **noun** [U] specialized a type of FUNGUS that can cause an infection, especially in the VAGINA or mouth

candidacy /ˈkæn.dɪ.də.si/ **noun** [C usually singular, U] (UK also **candidature** /ˈkæn.dɪ.də.tʃəʳ/) the fact of being a candidate in an election: *She is expected to **announce** officially her candidacy for president early next week.*

candidate /ˈkæn.dɪ.dət/, /-deɪt/ **noun** [C] **1** (B2) a person who is competing to get a job or elected position: *There are three candidates standing in the election.* **2** a person or thing considered likely to receive or experience something: *The English Department is a likely candidate **for** staff cuts.* **3** (B1) UK someone who is taking an exam: *Candidates must write their names on the top page of the exam paper.*

candied /ˈkæn.did/ **adj** preserved by boiling in sugar: *candied fruit*

ˌcandied ˈpeel **noun** [U] the skin of lemons and oranges, preserved with sugar and used for making cakes

candle /ˈkæn.dl̩/ **noun** [C] (B1) a stick-shaped piece of WAX with a WICK (= piece of string) in the middle of it that produces light as it slowly burns: *Shall I **light** a candle?*

candlelight /ˈkæn.dl̩.laɪt/ **noun** [U] the light that a candle produces when it is burning • **candlelit** /-lɪt/ **adj** [before noun] *a candlelit **dinner***

candlestick /ˈkæn.dl̩.stɪk/ **noun** [C] an object that holds a candle

ˌcan-ˈdo **adj** [before noun] US If someone has a can-do character or way of dealing with a problem, they are very positive about their ability to achieve success: *Her can-do **attitude** is what made her our choice for the job.*

candour UK (US **candor**) /ˈkæn.dəʳ/ (US) /-dɚ/ **noun** [U] the quality of being honest and telling the truth, especially about a difficult or embarrassing subject: *'We really don't know what to do about it,' she said with surprising candour.* → See also **candid**

candy /ˈkæn.di/ **noun** [C or U] US (A2) a sweet food made from sugar or chocolate, or a piece of this: *a candy **bar***

ˈcandy-ass **noun** [C] US offensive a person who is not brave

candyfloss /ˈkæn.di.flɒs/ (US) /-flɑːs/ **noun** [U] UK (US **ˌcotton ˈcandy**) a large soft ball of white or pink sugar in the form of thin threads, usually sold on a stick and eaten at FAIRS and AMUSEMENT PARKS

ˈcandy-striped **adj** Something that is candy-striped has narrow stripes of white and a bright colour such as pink: *a candy-striped shirt*

cane /keɪn/ **noun; verb**

▸**noun** **1** [C or U] the long, hard, hollow stem of particular plants such as BAMBOO, sometimes used to make furniture or support other plants in the garden **2** [C] a long stick used especially by old, ill, or blind people to help them walk **3** [S] a long, thin stick used in the past as a school punishment

▸**verb** [T] to hit a child at school with a stick as a punishment

caned /keɪnd/ **adj** slang UK drunk

canine /ˈkeɪ.naɪn/ **adj; noun**

▸**adj** of or relating to dogs: *The city's canine population (= the number of dogs in the city) has grown dramatically over recent years.*

▸**noun** [C] **TOOTH** ▷ **1** (also **canine tooth**) one of four pointed teeth in the human mouth → Compare **incisor, molar** **DOG** ▷ **2** specialized a dog

canister /ˈkæn.ɪ.stəʳ/ (US) /-stɚ/ **noun** [C] a metal container, usually cylinder-shaped, for gases or dry things: *The police fired **tear gas** canisters into the crowd.*

canker /ˈkæŋ.kəʳ/ (US) /-kɚ/ **noun** **TREES** ▷ **1** [C or U] specialized a disease which attacks the wood of trees **ANIMALS** ▷ **2** [U] specialized a disease affecting the ears and mouth of animals and humans **EVIL** ▷ **3** [C usually singular] formal something evil that spreads through a person's mind, an organization, or a society: *Poverty is a canker eating away at the heart of society.*

cannabis /ˈkæn.ə.bɪs/ **noun** [U] a usually illegal drug made from the dried leaves and flowers of the HEMP plant, which produces a pleasant feeling of being relaxed when smoked or eaten

canned /kænd/ **adj** (UK also **tinned**) (B2) preserved and sold in a metal container: *canned fruit/tomatoes*

ˌcanned ˈlaughter **noun** [U] recordings of laughter that have been added to a humorous radio or television programme when something funny has been said or done

ˌcanned ˈmusic **noun** [U] disapproving **Muzak**

cannelloni /ˌkæn.əlˈəʊ.ni/ (US) /-ˈoʊ-/ **noun** [U] tubes of PASTA, usually filled with cheese or meat and covered with sauce

cannery /ˈkæn.ər.i/ (US) /ˈ-ɚ-/ **noun** [C] a factory where food is put into metal containers

cannibal /ˈkæn.ɪ.bəl/ **noun** [C] a person who eats human flesh, or an animal which eats the flesh of animals of its own type • **cannibalism** /-ɪ.zəm/ **noun** [U] • **cannibalistic** /-ˈɪs.tɪk/ **adj**

cannibalize (UK usually **cannibalise**) /ˈkæn.ɪ.bəl.aɪz/ **verb** [T] to take parts from a machine or vehicle in order to make or repair another machine or vehicle: *He bought an old engine and cannibalized it for spare parts.*

cannon /ˈkæn.ən/ **noun; verb**

▸**noun** [C] (plural **cannon** or **cannons**) **1** a large, powerful gun fixed to two or four wheels, that was used in the past to fire heavy stone or metal balls **2** a gun fastened to an aircraft

▸**verb** [I usually + adv/prep] UK to knock or hit against someone or something suddenly and forcefully as you are running: *I was rushing along with my head* *down when I cannoned **into** an old lady walking the other way.*

cannonade /ˌkæn.əˈneɪd/ **noun** [C] a period of continuous heavy firing of large guns, especially as part of an attack

cannonball /ˈkæn.ən.bɔːl/ **noun** [C] a heavy metal or stone ball shot from a cannon

ˈcannon ˌfodder **noun** [U] If you describe soldiers as cannon fodder, you mean that they are not considered important by their officers and are sent into war without their leaders worrying if they die.

cannot /ˈkæn.ɒt/ Ⓤ /-ɑːt/ **modal verb** **1** A1 the negative form of the verb 'can': *I cannot predict what will happen next year.* **2 cannot but** formal used to say that something will certainly happen: *If we persevere, we cannot but succeed.*

> **! Common mistake: cannot**
>
> **Cannot** is always written as a single word.
>
> Don't write 'can not', write 'cannot':
>
> ~~*I can not imagine life without my computer.*~~
>
> *I cannot imagine life without my computer.*

canny /ˈkæn.i/ **adj** **CLEVER** ▷ **1** thinking quickly and cleverly, especially in business or financial matters: *These salesmen are a canny lot.* **PLEASANT** ▷ **2** Northern English good or pleasant: *a canny lad* • **cannily** /-ɪ.li/ **adv**

canoe /kəˈnuː/ **noun; verb**

▸**noun** [C] **1** a small light narrow boat, pointed at both ends and moved using a PADDLE (= a short pole with a flat blade) **2** UK for **kayak**

▸**verb** [I usually + adv/prep] (present tense **canoeing**, past tense and past participle **canoed**) to travel in a canoe • **canoeing** /-ɪŋ/ **noun** [U] *They died in a canoeing accident.* • **canoeist** /-ɪst/ **noun** [C] a person travelling in a canoe

canon /ˈkæn.ən/ **noun** **PRIEST** ▷ **1** [C] a Christian priest with special duties in a CATHEDRAL **STANDARD** ▷ **2** [C usually plural] formal or specialized a rule, principle, or law, especially in the Christian Church **WRITINGS** ▷ **3** [C usually singular] specialized all the writings or other works known to be by a particular person: *the Shakespearean canon* • **canonical** /kəˈnɒn.ɪ.kəl/ Ⓤ /-ˈnɑː.nɪ-/ **adj**

canonize (UK usually **canonise**) /ˈkæn.ə.naɪz/ **verb** [T] (in the Roman Catholic Church) to announce officially that a dead person is a SAINT

canoodle /kəˈnuː.dl/ **verb** [I] old-fashioned informal If two people canoodle, they kiss and hold each other in a sexual way.

ˈcan ˌopener **noun** [C] (UK also **ˈtin ˌopener**) a tool for opening metal containers of food

canopy /ˈkæn.ə.pi/ **noun** [C] **COVER** ▷ **1** a cover fixed over a seat or bed, etc. for shelter or decoration **OF TREES** ▷ **2** the branches and leaves that spread out at the top of a group of trees forming a type of roof **OF AIRCRAFT** ▷ **3** the transparent part in a military aircraft which covers the place where the pilot sits **OF PARACHUTE** ▷ **4** the large circular piece of cloth that is the main part of a PARACHUTE

can't /kɑːnt/ Ⓤ /kænt/ **short form** **1** cannot: *Speak up! I can't hear you.* **2** often used to suggest that someone should do a particular thing, especially when it seems the obvious thing to do: *Can't you just take the dress back to the shop if it doesn't fit?*

cant /kænt/ **noun** [U] **1** statements, especially on religious or moral subjects, that are not sincerely believed by the person making them **2** special words used by a particular group of people such as thieves, lawyers, or priests, often in order to keep things secret

Cantabrigian /ˌkæn.təˈbrɪdʒ.i.ən/ **adj** relating to the town or university of Cambridge in England, or to the university of Harvard in Cambridge, Massachusetts • **Cantabrigian noun** [C]

cantaloupe /ˈkæn.tə.luːp/ Ⓤ /-t̬ə.loʊp/ **noun** [C or U] a type of MELON (= large fruit with a thick skin) that is round and has yellow or green skin and sweet orange flesh

cantankerous /ˌkænˈtæŋ.kər.əs/ Ⓤ /-kɚ-/ **adj** arguing and complaining a lot: *He's getting a bit cantankerous in his old age.*

cantata /kænˈtɑː.tə/ Ⓤ /kənˈtɑː.t̬ə/ **noun** [C] a short musical work, with words usually based on a religious subject → Compare **oratorio**

canteen /kænˈtiːn/ **noun** [C] **RESTAURANT** ▷ **1** B1 a place in a factory, office, etc. where food and meals are sold, often at a lower than usual price **KITCHEN EQUIPMENT** ▷ **2** UK (a small flat case containing) a complete set of knives, forks, and spoons: *We're giving them a canteen **of cutlery** as a wedding present.* **CONTAINER** ▷ **3** a small container for carrying water or another drink, used especially by soldiers or travellers

canter /ˈkæn.təʳ/ Ⓤ /-t̬ɚ/ **verb** [I] If a horse canters, it moves at quite a fast but easy and comfortable speed. • **canter noun** [C usually singular] *The horses set off **at** a canter.*

cantilever /ˈkæn.tɪ.liː.vəʳ/ Ⓤ /-t̬ɪ.liː.vɚ/ **noun** [C] specialized a long bar that is fixed at only one end to a vertical support and is used to hold a structure such as an ARCH, bridge, or shelf in position: *a cantilever bridge*

canton /ˈkæn.tɒn/ Ⓤ /-tɑːn/ **noun** [C] a political region or local government area in some countries, especially one of the 23 political regions into which Switzerland is divided

Cantonese /kæn.təˈniːz/ **noun** [U] a Chinese language spoken in the south of China and used as an official language in Hong Kong

cantor /ˈkæn.tɔːʳ/ Ⓤ /-tɔːr/ **noun** [C] **1** an official of a Jewish SYNAGOGUE (= religious building) who sings and leads prayers **2** someone who formally leads the singing in a Christian church CHOIR

Canuck /kəˈnʌk/ **noun** [C] informal a person from Canada • **Canuck adj**

canvas /ˈkæn.vəs/ **noun** **1** [U] strong, rough cloth used for making tents, sails, bags, strong clothes, etc. **2** [C] a piece of this cloth used by artists for painting on, usually with oil paints, or the painting itself: *These two canvases by Hockney would sell for £500,000.* **3 under canvas** in a tent: *I love sleeping under canvas.*

canvass /ˈkæn.vəs/ **verb** **GET SUPPORT** ▷ **1** [I or T] to try to get political support or votes, especially by visiting all the houses in an area: *I've been out canvassing **for** the Labour Party every evening this week.* **ASK** ▷ **2** [T] to try to discover information or opinions by asking people: *The council has been canvassing local **opinion**/local people to get their thoughts on the proposed housing development.* **SUGGEST** ▷ **3** [T] UK formal to suggest an idea or plan to be considered: *Wind and wave power are now being seriously canvassed as the solution to our energy problems.* • **canvass noun** [C] • **canvasser** /ˈkæn.və.səʳ/ Ⓤ /-sɚ/ **noun** [C]

canyon /ˈkæn.jən/ **noun** [C] a large valley with very

steep sides and usually a river flowing along the bottom

canyoning /ˈkæn.jə.nɪŋ/ **noun** [U] a sport that involves jumping into a mountain stream that is flowing very fast and being carried down the stream while you float on your back

cap /kæp/ **noun; verb**

▸**noun** [C] **HAT** ▷ **1** A2 a soft flat hat that has a curved part sticking out at the front, often worn as part of a uniform **2** a thin hat that stops your hair getting wet when swimming or taking a shower: *a **shower/swimming** cap* **3** UK a hat given to someone who plays for their national team in a particular sport, or a player who receives this: *Davis has 17 Scottish caps (= has played for Scotland 17 times).* ◦ *The team contains five international caps.* **COVER** ▷ **4** a small lid or cover: *The camera has a **lens** cap to protect the lens surface.* **5** an artificial covering on a tooth that protects it **BIRTH CONTROL** ▷ **6** UK **diaphragm** **EXPLOSIVE** ▷ **7** a very small amount of explosive powder in a paper container, used especially in toy guns to produce a loud noise **LIMIT** ▷ **8** a limit on the amount of money that can be charged or spent in connection with a particular activity: *Central government has imposed a cap **on** local tax increases.*

IDIOM **go cap in hand to sb** to ask someone in a polite and sincere way for something, especially money or to be forgiven

▸**verb** (-pp-) **LIMIT** ▷ **1** C1 [T often passive] to put a limit on the amount of money that can be charged or spent in connection with a particular activity: *High spending councils have all been (rate/charge) capped.* ◦ *Our mortgage is capped at 8.75 percent for five years.* **SPORT** ▷ **2 be capped** to play for your national team in a particular sport: *She's been capped **for** Scotland nine times.* **COVER** ▷ **3** [T] to cover the top of something: *The mountain was capped **with** snow.* ◦ *have your teeth capped (= protected with an artificial covering)*

IDIOM **to cap it all** C1 used when you mention something in addition to all the other (bad) things that have happened: *It's been a terrible week and now, to cap it all, I've got a cold.*

capability /ˌkeɪ.pəˈbɪl.ɪ.ti/ US /-ə.t̬i/ **noun** [C or U] **ABILITY** ▷ **1** C1 the ability to do something: *These tests are beyond the capability of an average twelve-year-old.* ◦ [+ to infinitive] *With the new machines we finally have the capability (= power) **to** do the job properly.* **WEAPONS** ▷ **2** the number of weapons, soldiers, etc. a country has to fight a war: *Several countries are trying to develop a **nuclear** capability.*

> **!** Common mistake: **capable**
>
> Don't say 'capable to do something', say **capable of doing something**:
>
> ~~The new receptionist must be capable to deal with customers.~~
>
> *The new receptionist must be capable of dealing with customers.*

capable /ˈkeɪ.pə.bl̩/ **adj** **1** B2 able to do things effectively and skilfully, and to achieve results: *She's a very capable woman/worker/judge.* ◦ *We need to get an assistant who's capable and efficient.* **2 capable of sth/doing sth** B2 having the ability, power, or qualities to be able to do something: *Only the Democratic Party is capable of running the country.* ◦ *A force ten wind is capable of blowing the roofs off houses.* ◦ *When she's drunk she's capable of saying (= likely to say) awful, rude things.* ◦ *I think your plan is capable of being (= could be) improved.* → Opposite **incapable** • **capably** /-bli/ **adv** *She drove very capably.*

IDIOM **in sb's capable hands** humorous being dealt with by the person mentioned: *I'm going away next week, so I'll be **leaving** everything in your capable hands.*

-capable /-keɪ.pə.bl̩/ **suffix** added to nouns to form adjectives which mean able to use the stated thing: *These are nuclear-capable aircraft (= they can carry nuclear weapons).*

capacious /kəˈpeɪ.ʃəs/ **adj** formal having a lot of space and able to contain a lot: *a capacious pocket/handbag*

capacitor /kəˈpæs.ɪ.təʳ/ US /-t̬ɚ/ **noun** [C] specialized a device which collects and stores electricity, and is an important part of electronic equipment such as televisions and radios

capacity /kəˈpæs.ə.ti/ US /-t̬i/ **noun** **AMOUNT** ▷ **1** B2 [C or S or U] the total amount that can be contained or produced, or (especially of a person or organization) the ability to do a particular thing: *The stadium has a **seating** capacity of 50,000.* ◦ *The game was watched by a capacity **crowd/audience** of 50,000 (= the place was completely full).* ◦ *She has a great capacity **for** hard work.* ◦ *The purchase of 500 tanks is part of a strategy to increase military capacity by 25 percent over the next five years.* ◦ [+ to infinitive] *It seems to be **beyond** his capacity **to** (= he seems to be unable to) follow simple instructions.* ◦ *Do you think it's **within** his capacity **to** (= do you think he'll be able to) do the job without making a mess of it?* ◦ *The generators each have a capacity **of** (= can produce) 1,000 kilowatts.* ◦ *The larger cars have bigger capacity engines (= the engines are bigger and more powerful).* ◦ *All our factories are working **at** (**full**) capacity (= are producing goods as fast as possible).* ◦ *We are running **below** capacity (= not producing as many goods as we are able to) because of cancelled orders.* ◦ *He suffered a stroke in 2008, which left him unable to speak, but his **mental** capacity (= his ability to think and remember) wasn't affected.* **POSITION** ▷ **2** C1 [S] formal a particular position or job: *She was speaking in her capacity **as** a novelist, rather than as a television presenter.*

cape /keɪp/ **noun** [C] **LAND** ▷ **1** a very large piece of land sticking out into the sea: *the Cape of Good Hope* **COAT** ▷ **2** a type of loose coat without sleeves that is fastened at the neck and hangs from the shoulders

caper /ˈkeɪ.pəʳ/ US /-pɚ/ **verb; noun**

▸**verb** [I + adv/prep] to run and jump about in an energetic, happy way

▸**noun** **ACTIVITY** ▷ **1** [C] an illegal, unusual, or entertaining activity: *The whole incident started as an innocent caper.* **FOOD** ▷ **2** [C usually plural] a small, dark green flower BUD that is used in sauces to give a slightly sour taste to food

capillary /kəˈpɪl.ᵊr.i/ US /-ɚ-/ **noun** [C] specialized a very thin tube, especially one of the smaller tubes that carry blood around the body

capital /ˈkæp.ɪ.tᵊl/ US /-t̬ᵊl/ **noun; adj**

▸**noun** **CITY** ▷ **1** A2 [C] a city that is the centre of government of a country or smaller political area: *Australia's capital city is Canberra.* **2** [C] the most important place for a particular business or activity: *London used to be the financial capital of the world.* **LETTER** ▷ **3** A2 [C] (also **capital letter**) a letter of the alphabet in the form and larger size that is used at the beginning of sentences and names: *print in capitals* **MONEY** ▷ **4** [U] money and possessions, especially a large amount of money used for producing more WEALTH or for starting a new business: *She leaves her capital untouched in the bank and lives off the interest.* ◦ *We've* **put** *£20,000 capital* **into** *the business, but we're unlikely to see any return for a few years.* **COLUMN** ▷ **5** [C] specialized the top part of a column

IDIOM **make capital out of sth** to use a situation to get an advantage for yourself: *The Opposition is making a lot of* ***political*** *capital out of the government's failure to invest in education.*

▸**adj** **LETTER** ▷ **1** (of a letter of the alphabet) in the form and larger size that is used at the beginning of sentences and names: *Do you write 'calvinist' with a capital 'C'?* **DEATH** ▷ **2** **capital crime/offence** a crime that can be punished by death: *In some countries, importing drugs is a capital offence.* **EXCELLENT** ▷ **3** UK old-fashioned very good or excellent: *That's a capital* ***idea!***

IDIOM **with a capital A, B, etc.** said after the name of a particular quality to say that it is very strong, using its first letter: *He's trouble with a capital T!*

ˌcapital ˈassets noun [plural] the buildings and machines owned by a business or other organization

ˌcapital ˈgains noun [plural] profits made by selling property or an INVESTMENT

ˌcapital ˈgains ˌtax noun [U] (also **CGT**) tax on the profits made from selling something you own

ˌcapital inˈtensive adj describes an industry, business, or process that needs a lot of money to buy buildings and equipment in order to start operating: *As agriculture became more capital intensive, many farm labourers moved to the towns and cities to look for work.*

ˌcapital inˈvestment noun [U] (also **capital exˈpenditure**) money that is spent on buildings and equipment to increase the effectiveness of a business

capitalism /ˈkæp.ɪ.təl.ɪ.zəm/ (US) /-t̬əl-/ noun [U] (C2) an economic, political, and social system in which property, business, and industry are privately owned, directed towards making the greatest possible profits for successful organizations and people → Compare **communism, socialism**

capitalist /ˈkæp.ɪ.təl.ɪst/ (US) /-t̬əl-/ noun; adj

▸**noun** [C] **1** someone who supports capitalism **2** someone who has a large amount of money INVESTED (= given hoping to get more back) in a business

▸**adj** (also **capitalistic**) (C2) based on the system of capitalism: *a capitalist economy/country*

capitalization (UK usually **capitalisation**) /ˌkæp.ɪ.təl.aɪˈzeɪ.ʃən/ (US) /-t̬əl-/ noun **MONEY** ▷ **1** [S or U] the total value of a company's SHARES on a STOCK EXCHANGE **LETTER** ▷ **2** [U] the use of capital letters

capitalize (UK usually **capitalise**) /ˈkæp.ɪ.təl.aɪz/ (US) /-t̬əl-/ verb **LETTER** ▷ **1** [T] to write a letter of the alphabet as a capital, or to write the first letter of a word as a capital: *The names of political parties are always capitalized, e.g. the Green Party.* **MONEY** ▷ **2** [T often passive] to supply money to a business so that it can develop or operate as it should

PHRASAL VERB **capitalize on sth** to use a situation to your own advantage: *She capitalized on her knowledge and experience to get a new and better paid job.*

ˌcapital ˈpunishment noun [U] punishment by death, as ordered by a legal system → Compare **the death penalty**

capitation /ˌkæp.ɪˈteɪ.ʃən/ noun [C or U] specialized a tax, charge, or amount that is fixed at the same level for everyone: *Doctors receive capitation of £13.85 per patient.*

Capitol /ˈkæp.ɪ.təl/ (US) /-t̬əl/ noun **1 the Capitol** the building in which the US Congress meets **2** [C usually singular] a building in which a US state government meets

capitulate /kəˈpɪt.jʊ.leɪt/ verb [I] **1** to accept military defeat: *Their forces capitulated five hours after the bombardment of the city began.* **2** to accept something or agree to do something unwillingly: *The sports minister today capitulated* ***to*** *calls for his resignation.* • **capitulation** /kəˌpɪt.jʊˈleɪ.ʃən/ noun [C or U]

capoeira /ˌkæp.əʊˈeɪ.rə/ (US) /ˌkɑː.poʊˈeɪ.rə/ noun [U] an activity from Brazil that combines music and movements from dance with MARTIAL ARTS

capon /ˈkeɪ.pɒn/ (US) /-pɑːn/ noun [C] a male chicken that has had part of its sex organs removed to improve the taste of its flesh for food

-capped /-kæpt/ suffix with a top covered in the way mentioned: *a snow-capped mountain*

cappuccino /ˌkæp.ʊˈtʃiː.nəʊ/ (US) /-noʊ/ noun [C or U] (plural **cappuccinos**) a coffee made with heated milk with a thick mass of bubbles

caprice /kəˈpriːs/ noun [C or U] literary (the quality of often having) a sudden and usually silly wish to have or do something, or a sudden and silly change of mind or behaviour: *The $300 million palace was built to satisfy the caprice of one man.* → Synonym **whim**

capricious /kəˈprɪʃ.əs/ adj literary changing mood or behaviour suddenly and unexpectedly: *a capricious child* ◦ *He was a cruel and capricious tyrant.* • **capriciously** /-li/ adv • **capriciousness** /-nəs/ noun [U]

Capricorn /ˈkæp.rɪ.kɔːn/ (US) /-kɔːrn/ noun [C or U] the tenth sign of the ZODIAC, relating to the period from 23 December to 20 January and represented by a GOAT, or a person born during this period

capsicum /ˈkæp.sɪ.kəm/ noun [C or U] specialized a **pepper**

capsize /kæpˈsaɪz/ verb [I or T] to (cause a boat or ship to) turn upside down by accident while on water: *A huge wave capsized the yacht.* ◦ *When the boat capsized we were trapped underneath it.*

ˈcaps lock (ˌkey) noun [C or U] a key on a computer keyboard that you press to make any letters you type appear as capital letters until you press it again

capstan /ˈkæp.stən/ noun [C] **1** a machine with a spinning vertical cylinder that is used, especially on ships, for pulling heavy objects with a rope **2** a thin spinning cylinder in a TAPE RECORDER (= a machine that records and plays back sound) which pulls the TAPE through the machine

capsule /ˈkæp.sjuːl/ (US) /-səl/ noun [C] **MEDICINE** ▷ **1** a small container with medicine inside which you swallow **SPACECRAFT** ▷ **2** the part of a spacecraft in which the people on it live

captain /ˈkæp.tɪn/ (US) /-tən/ noun; verb

▸**noun** **1** (B1) [C] the leader of a sports team: *It's unusual to have a goalkeeper as (the) captain of a football team.* **2** (B2) [C] the person in charge of a ship or an aircraft: *This is your captain speaking. We expect to be landing at London Heathrow in an hour's time.* **3** [C] (also **Captain**) an officer's rank in the army or navy, or in the US air force, or in the US police and fire departments: *The captain gave him his orders.* ◦ *Captain Lane/Alex Lane* ◦ [as form of address] *Yes, Captain.*

▸**verb** [T] to lead and be the captain of a team, military group, ship, or aircraft: *He captained the England* *cricket team for five years.* • **captaincy** /-si/ **noun** [C or U]

ˌ**captain of ˈindustry** noun [C] a person who has an important job in industry and who can influence company and national planning: *In a speech to captains of industry, she predicted economic growth of 3.5 percent next year.*

caption /ˈkæp.ʃən/ **noun** [C] a short piece of text under a picture in a book, magazine, or newspaper which describes the picture or explains what the people in it are doing or saying

captious /ˈkæp.ʃəs/ **adj** formal often expressing criticisms about matters that are not important

captivate /ˈkæp.tɪ.veɪt/ **verb** [T] to hold the attention of someone by being extremely interesting, exciting, pleasant, or attractive: *With her beauty and charm, she captivated film audiences everywhere.* • **captivating** /-veɪ.tɪŋ/ US /-veɪ.t̬ɪŋ/ **adj** *a captivating performance*

captive /ˈkæp.tɪv/ **noun** [C] **1** a person or animal whose ability to move or act freely is limited by being closed in a space; a prisoner, especially a person held by the enemy during a war: *When the town was recaptured, we found soldiers who had been captives for several years.* **2 hold/take sb captive** to keep someone as a prisoner or make someone a prisoner: *The terrorists were holding several diplomats captive.* • **captive adj** *captive soldiers*

ˌ**captive ˈaudience** noun [C] a group of people who listen to or watch someone or something because they cannot leave

captivity /kæpˈtɪv.ɪ.ti/ US /-ə.t̬i/ **noun** [U] the situation in which a person or animal is kept somewhere and is not allowed to leave: *All the hostages, when released **from** captivity, looked remarkably fit and well.* ◦ *Animals bred **in** captivity would probably not survive if they were released into the wild.*

captor /ˈkæp.təʳ/ US /-tɚ/ **noun** [C] a person who has captured a person or animal and refuses to release them

capture /ˈkæp.tʃəʳ/ US /-tʃɚ/ **verb** [T] **CATCH** ▷ **1** B2 to take someone as a prisoner, or to take something into your possession, especially by force: *Two of the soldiers were killed and the rest were captured.* ◦ *Rebel forces captured the city after a week-long battle.* **2** to succeed in getting something when you are competing with other people: *The Democratic Party captured 70 percent of the vote.* **RECORD** ▷ **3** B2 to represent or describe something very accurately using words or images: *It would be impossible to capture her beauty in a painting.* **4** B2 to record or take a picture of something using a camera: *A passer-by captured the whole incident **on film**.* **5** specialized If a computer or similar machine captures information, it takes it in and stores it. **INTEREST** ▷ **6** C1 If something captures your imagination or attention, you feel very interested and excited by it: *The American drive to land a man on the Moon captured the **imagination/attention** of the whole world.* • **capture noun** [S or U] C1 *They witnessed **the** capture **of** the city by rebel troops.*

car /kɑːʳ/ US /kɑːr/ **noun** [C] **1** A1 a road vehicle with an engine, four wheels, and seats for a small number of people: *They don't have a car.* ◦ *Where did you park your car?* ◦ *It's quicker **by** car.* ◦ *a car chase/accident/factory* **2** a part of a train used for a special purpose: *a **restaurant/sleeping** car*

carafe /kəˈræf/ **noun** [C] a tall glass container with a wide round bottom for serving wine or water in a restaurant, or the amount contained in this

carambola /ˌkær.əmˈbəʊ.lə/ US /ˌker.əmˈboʊ-/ **noun** [C] a **starfruit**

carafe

caramel /ˈkær.ə.məl/ US /ˈkɑːr.məl, ˈker.ə-/ **noun** **1** [U] burnt sugar used to give flavour and a brown colour to food **2** [C or U] a sticky brown sweet made from sugar that has been heated with milk, butter, or cream in hot water: *chocolates with caramel centres*

caramelize (UK usually **caramelise**) /ˈkær.ə.məl.aɪz/ US /ˈkɑːr.məl-/ /ˈker.ə-/ **verb** **1** [I] If sugar caramelizes, it turns into caramel. **2** [T] to cook a food with sugar so that the food becomes sweet and often brown: *caramelized onions/nuts*

carapace /ˈkær.ə.peɪs/ US /ˈker-/ **noun** [C] specialized a hard shell that covers and protects animals such as CRABS and TURTLES

carat /ˈkær.ət/ US /ˈker-/ **noun** [C] **1** a unit for measuring the weight of JEWELS (= precious stones) **2** UK (US **karat**) a unit for measuring how pure gold is: *24-carat gold is the purest.*

caravan /ˈkær.ə.væn/ US /ˈker-/ **noun** [C] **VEHICLE** ▷ **1** UK (US **trailer**) a wheeled vehicle for living or travelling in, especially for holidays, which contains beds and cooking equipment and can be pulled by a car **2** UK a painted wooden vehicle that is pulled by a horse and in which people live: *a gypsy caravan* **GROUP** ▷ **3** a group of people with vehicles or animals who travel together for safety through a dangerous area, especially across a desert on CAMELS

caravanning /ˈkær.ə.væn.ɪŋ/ US /ˈker-/ **noun** [U] UK (US ˈ**trailer** ˌ**camping**) the activity of going on holiday in a caravan

ˈ**caravan** ˌ**park** noun [C] Australian English an area of ground where caravans can be parked, especially by people spending their holidays in them → Compare **caravan site**

ˈ**caravan** ˌ**site** noun [C] UK (US ˈ**trailer** ˌ**park**) an area of ground where caravans can be parked, especially by people spending their holidays in them

caraway /ˈkær.ə.weɪ/ US /ˈker-/ **noun** [U] a short plant or its small seed-like fruits that have a flavour similar to but weaker than ANISEED and are used in food, especially for making bread or cake: *caraway **seeds***

carb /kɑːb/ US /kɑːrb/ **noun** [C or U] informal for **carbohydrate**: *Studies have indicated a low-carb diet can pose heart and kidney risks.*

carbine /ˈkɑː.baɪn/ US /ˈkɑːr-/ **noun** [C] specialized a short light RIFLE (= gun) originally used by soldiers on horses

carbohydrase /ˌkɑː.bəʊˈhaɪ.dreɪz/ US /ˌkɑːr.boʊ-/ **noun** [C] specialized any ENZYME (= chemical substance made by living cells) that causes a chemical reaction that helps the body to digest carbohydrate

carbohydrate /ˌkɑː.bəʊˈhaɪ.dreɪt/ US /ˌkɑːr.boʊ-/ **noun** [C or U] one of several substances, such as sugar or STARCH, that provide the body with energy, or foods containing these substances such as bread, potatoes, PASTA, and rice

carbolic acid /kɑːˌbɒl.ɪkˈæs.ɪd/ US /kɑːrˌbɑː.lɪk-/ **noun** [U] a liquid which destroys bacteria, and is used for cleaning injuries or surfaces to prevent disease

carbolic soap /kɑːˌbɒl.ɪkˈsəʊp/ US /kɑːrˌbɑː.lɪkˈsoʊp/ **noun** [U] a strong soap made from COAL TAR

ˈ**car** ˌ**bomb** noun [C] a bomb put inside a car and left to explode in a public place

C

carbon /ˈkɑː.bᵊn/ (US) /ˈkɑːr-/ noun **SUBSTANCE** ▷ **1** (B2) [U] (symbol **C**) a chemical element that exists in its pure form as DIAMOND or GRAPHITE, and is an important part of other substances such as coal and oil, as well as being contained in all plants and animals **DOCUMENT** ▷ **2** [C] a **carbon copy** • **carbonic** adj specialized containing carbon

carbonara /ˌkɑː.bᵊˈnɑː.rə/ (US) /ˌkɑːr.bᵊˈnɑːr.ə/ adj [after noun] used to describe a sauce made with eggs and BACON: *spaghetti carbonara* • **carbonara** noun [C or U]

carbonated /ˈkɑː.bᵊn.eɪ.tɪd/ (US) /ˈkɑːr.bᵊn.eɪ.t̬ɪd/ adj A carbonated drink is FIZZY because it contains bubbles of CARBON DIOXIDE: *carbonated drinks/water*

ˈcarbon ˌcapture noun [U] (also **ˌcarbon ˌcapture and ˈstorage**, abbreviation **CCS**) specialized a way of catching the carbon produced by machines so that it is not released into the air: *We will never be able to combat climate change without carbon capture.*

ˈcarbon ˌchain noun [C] specialized in chemistry, a line of connected carbon atoms

ˌcarbon ˈcopy noun [C] **DOCUMENT** ▷ **1** (also **carbon**) a copy of a document, made with CARBON PAPER **SAME APPEARANCE** ▷ **2** a person or thing that is very similar to or exactly like another person or thing: *She's a carbon copy* ***of*** *her mother.*

the ˈcarbon ˌcycle noun [S] specialized the continuous movement of carbon between different living organisms on Earth and between living organisms and the environment, through natural processes like PHOTOSYNTHESIS, RESPIRATION, and DECOMPOSITION in the soil, and also the burning of FOSSIL FUELS

ˌcarbon ˈdating noun [U] a method of calculating the age of extremely old objects by measuring the amount of a particular type of carbon in them

ˌcarbon diˈoxide noun [U] (symbol **CO²**) (B2) the gas formed when carbon is burned, or when people or animals breathe out: *carbon dioxide emissions*

ˈcarbon eˌmissions noun [plural] carbon dioxide that planes, cars, factories, etc. produce, thought to be harmful to the environment: *We all need to do more to reduce carbon emissions.*

ˌcarbon ˈfootprint noun [C] (B2) Someone's carbon footprint is a measurement of the amount of carbon dioxide that their activities produce.

carˌbonic ˈacid noun [U] specialized a weak ACID made of carbon dioxide dissolved in water

carboniferous /ˌkɑː.bəˈnɪf.ᵊr.əs/ (US) /ˌkɑːr.bəˈnɪf.ɚ-/ adj specialized containing or producing carbon: *carboniferous rocks*

Carboniferous /ˌkɑː.bəˈnɪf.ᵊr.əs/ (US) /ˌkɑːr.bəˈnɪf.ɚ-/ adj specialized from or referring to the period of time, between around 363 and 290 million years ago, when the first REPTILES appeared and there were forests covering large areas which later formed Earth's coal layers: *Carboniferous rocks*

carbonize specialized (UK usually **carbonise**) /ˈkɑː.bᵊn.aɪz/ (US) /ˈkɑːr-/ verb [I or T] to change or be changed to carbon by burning

carbon monoxide /ˌkɑː.bᵊn.məˈnɒk.saɪd/ (US) /ˌkɑːr.bᵊn.məˈnɑː-/ noun [U] (symbol **CO**) (B2) the poisonous gas formed by the burning of carbon, especially in the form of car fuel

ˌcarbon-ˈneutral adj If a person, organization, event, etc. is carbon-neutral, it does things such as planting trees to reduce CARBON DIOXIDE by the same amount as it produces it.

ˌcarbon ˈoffset noun [U] (also **ˌcarbon ˈoffsetting**) the activity of trying to stop the damage caused by activities that produce carbon by doing other things to reduce it, such as planting trees

ˈcarbon ˌpaper noun [U] thin paper with a covering of carbon or other dark substance on one side, used between sheets of writing to make copies

ˈcarbon ˌsink noun [C] specialized an area of forest that is large enough to absorb large amounts of CARBON DIOXIDE from the Earth's ATMOSPHERE and therefore to reduce the effect of GLOBAL WARMING

ˈcarbon ˌtax noun [C] specialized a tax on the use of fuels that produce GREENHOUSE GASES which harm the ATMOSPHERE (= mixture of gases around the Earth)

ˈcarbon ˌtrading noun [U] a system for controlling POLLUTION. Companies and governments can buy or sell LICENCES to produce CARBON DIOXIDE.

ˌcarbon-ˈzero adj specialized If a company or an organization is carbon-zero, it does not release any CARBON DIOXIDE into the environment or it removes the same amount of carbon dioxide from the environment as it puts into it. → See also **carbon-neutral**

ˌcar ˈboot ˌsale noun [C] UK (US **ˈswap ˌmeet**) an event in a public place where people sell their unwanted possessions, often from the backs of their cars

carbuncle /ˈkɑː.bʌŋ.kl/ (US) /ˈkɑːr-/ noun [C] **SWELLING** ▷ **1** specialized a large painful swelling under the skin **JEWEL** ▷ **2** a dark red PRECIOUS STONE

carburettor UK (US **carburetor**) /ˌkɑː.bəˈret.əʳ/ (US) /ˌkɑːr.bəˈret̬.ɚ/ noun [C] the part of an engine that mixes fuel and air, producing the gas that is burned to provide the power needed to operate the vehicle or machine

carcass (UK also **carcase**) /ˈkɑː.kəs/ (US) /ˈkɑːr-/ noun [C] **1** the body of a dead animal, especially a large one that is soon to be cut up as meat or eaten by wild animals: *Vultures flew around in the sky waiting to pick at the rotting carcass* ***of*** *the deer.* ◦ slang *Move your great carcass (= your body) out of that chair!* **2** the frame of an old or broken object, car, ship, etc.: *Carcasses of burned-out vehicles lined the roads near the scene of the worst fighting.*

carcinogen /kɑːˈsɪn.ə.dʒᵊn/ (US) /kɑːr-/ noun [C] a substance which causes CANCER

carcinogenic /ˌkɑː.sᵊn.əˈdʒen.ɪk/ (US) /ˌkɑːr.sᵊn.oʊ-/ adj describes a substance which causes CANCER

carcinoma /kɑː.sɪˈnəʊ.mə/ (US) /kɑːr.sɪˈnoʊ-/ noun [C] specialized a CANCEROUS growth that forms on or inside the body → Compare **tumour**

ˈcar-crash adj [before noun] **car-crash TV/telly** informal television programmes about real people that are shocking or embarrassing but very interesting to watch

card /kɑːd/ (US) /kɑːrd/ noun; verb

▸noun **PERMISSION** ▷ **1** (B1) [C] a small, rectangular piece of card or plastic, often with your SIGNATURE, photograph, or other information proving who you are, which allows you to do something, such as make a payment, get money from a bank, or enter a particular place: *I don't have any cash – can I* ***put*** *this* ***on*** *(= pay using) my* ***(credit/charge)*** *card?* ◦ *The bank's closed now, but I can get some money out with my* ***(cash)*** *card.* ◦ *You usually have to show your (membership) card at the door.* → See also **phone card, railcard, scorecard** **GAME** ▷ **2** (A2) [C] (also **playing card**) one of a set of 52 small rectangular pieces of stiff paper each with a number and one of four signs printed on it, used in games: *After dinner, Ted got out a* ***pack*** *(US also* ***deck****) of cards* ◦ *John* ***shuffled*** *(= mixed* up) *the cards before he* ***dealt*** *them* (***out***) (= *gave them to the players*). ◦ *Whist is my favourite card* ***game***. ◦ *a card table* **3 cards** A2 [plural] any of a range of games played with cards, such as POKER, WHIST, and BRIDGE: *I've never been much good at cards.* ◦ *Shall we* ***have a game of/play*** *cards?* **GREETINGS** ▷ **4** A2 [C] a rectangular piece of stiff paper, folded in half, with a picture on the front and often a message printed inside, sent on a special occasion: *anniversary/get-well cards* ◦ *It's Steve's birthday on Thursday – I must* ***send*** *him a card.* **5** [C] a **postcard** **INFORMATION** ▷ **6** B1 [C] a small, rectangular piece of stiff paper with information printed on it, especially a person's job title, business address, and phone number: *Here, let me give you my* (***business***) *card.* **STIFF PAPER** ▷ **7** [C or U] (a piece of) thick stiff paper **COMPUTER** ▷ **8** B1 [C] a thin plate inside a computer that contains very small electronic CIRCUITS and controls certain operations of the computer: *a graphics/sound card* **PERSON** ▷ **9** [C] old-fashioned informal a funny or strange person: *You're such a card, Patrick!*

IDIOMS **be on the cards** UK (US **be in the cards**) C2 to be likely to happen: *'So you think there'll be an election next year.' 'I think it's on the cards.'* • **your best/strongest/trump card** your main advantage over other people • **have a card up your sleeve** to have an advantage that other people do not know about: *England have definitely been the weaker side, but I think they've still got one or two cards up their sleeve.* • **keep/hold your cards close to your chest** to keep your intended actions secret: *You never quite know what Barry's going to do next – he keeps his cards very close to his chest.* • **put/lay your cards on the table** to be honest about your feelings and intentions: *I thought it was time I laid my cards on the table, so I told him that I had no intention of marrying him.*

▸verb [T] US to ask someone to show you a document, especially an IDENTITY CARD, in order to prove how old they are

cardamom /ˈkɑː.də.məm/ US /ˈkɑːr-/ (also **cardamon**) noun [C or U] a South Asian plant, the seeds of which are used as a spice: *cardamom seeds*

cardboard /ˈkɑːd.bɔːd/ US /ˈkɑːrd.bɔːrd/ **noun; adj**
▸noun [U] B2 material like very thick stiff paper, usually pale brown in colour, used especially for making boxes: *a cardboard* ***box***
▸adj disapproving relating to something, usually a character in a film or play, that does not seem to be real or interesting: *I've never enjoyed his plays – somehow all his characters are cardboard.*

ˌcard-carrying ˈmember noun [C] A card-carrying member of an organization is an active and involved member: *My brother's a card-carrying member of the Communist Party.*

cardholder /ˈkɑːdˌhəʊl.dəʳ/ US /ˈkɑːrdˌhoʊl.dɚ/ **noun** [C] someone who has been given permission to use a card which allows them to do something, especially a CHEQUE CARD or a CREDIT CARD

cardi- /kɑː.di-/ US /kɑːr-/ **prefix** specialized **cardio-**

cardiac /ˈkɑː.di.æk/ US /ˈkɑːr-/ **adj** of the heart or heart disease: *cardiac* ***arrest*** (= *a condition in which the heart stops beating*)

cardigan

cardigan /ˈkɑː.dɪ.gən/ US /ˈkɑːr-/ **noun** [C] (UK informal **cardy**, also **cardie**) B2 a piece of clothing made from wool, which covers the upper part of the body and the arms, fastening at the front with buttons, and usually worn over other clothes

cardinal /ˈkɑː.dɪ.nəl/ US /ˈkɑːr-/ **noun; adj**
▸noun [C] **PRIEST** ▷ **1** a priest of very high rank in the Roman Catholic Church: *Cardinals elect and advise the Pope.* **NUMBER** ▷ **2** (also **cardinal number**) a number that represents amount, such as 1, 2, 3, rather than order, such as 1st, 2nd, 3rd → Compare **ordinal** **BIRD** ▷ **3** a North American bird, the male of which has bright red feathers
▸adj [before noun] of great importance: *a cardinal rule/error/sin*

ˌcardinal ˈpoint noun [C] one of the four main points of the COMPASS: north, south, east, and west

ˌcardinal ˈvowel noun [C] specialized one of the vowels in the system for describing vowels to which other vowels can be compared and referred

ˈcard ˌindex noun [C] a box for storing cards in a particular order

cardio /ˈkɑː.di.əʊ/ US /ˈkɑːr.di.oʊ/ **noun** [U] informal physical exercise that increases the rate at which your heart works: *My workout usually includes 15 to 20 minutes of cardio.* ◦ *cardio exercises/training/workouts*

cardio- /kɑː.di.əʊ-/ US /kɑːr.di.oʊ-/ **prefix** (also **cardi-**) of the heart: *cardiovascular*

cardiogram /ˈkɑː.di.ə.græm/ US /ˈkɑːr-/ **noun** [C] specialized the picture drawn by a cardiograph, which shows a record of the heart's activity

cardiograph /ˈkɑː.di.ə.græf/, /-grɑːf/ US /ˈkɑːr.di.ə.græf/ **noun** [C] specialized a machine for recording the beating of the heart

cardiography /ˌkɑː.diˈɒg.rə.fi/ US /ˌkɑːr.diˈɑː.grə-/ **noun** [U] specialized the use of a machine to record the beating of the heart

cardiologist /ˌkɑː.diˈɒl.ə.dʒɪst/ US /ˌkɑːr.diˈɑː.lə-/ **noun** [C] specialized a doctor who specializes in treating diseases of the heart

cardiology /ˌkɑː.diˈɒl.ə.gi/ US /ˌkɑːr.diˈɑː.lə-/ **noun** [U] specialized the study and treatment of medical conditions of the heart

cardiovascular /ˌkɑː.di.əʊˈvæs.kjʊ.ləʳ/ US /ˌkɑːr.di.oʊˈvæs.kjə.lɚ/ **adj** specialized relating to the heart and blood VESSELS (= tubes that carry blood around the body): *cardiovascular disease*

ˈcard sharp noun [C] a person who earns money by playing cards dishonestly

ˈcard ˌvote noun [C] (also **ˈblock ˌvote**) UK a way of voting in which your vote represents other members of your organization, especially at TRADE UNION meetings

cardy (also **cardie**) /ˈkɑː.di/ US /ˈkɑːr-/ **noun** [C] UK informal for **cardigan**

care /keəʳ/ US /ker/ **noun; verb**
▸noun **PROTECTION** ▷ **1** B2 [U] the process of protecting someone or something and providing what they need: *The standard of care at our local hospital is excellent.* ◦ *Nurseries are responsible for the children* ***in*** *their care.* **2** [U] used as a combining form: *skincare/healthcare/childcare* **3 take care of sb/sth** B1 to protect someone or something and provide the things that they need: *Take* ***good*** *care of that girl of yours, Patrick – she's very special.* ◦ *Don't worry about me, I can take care of myself* (= *I do not need anyone else to protect me*). **4 in care** (also **take/put into care**) UK Children who are in care or who have been taken/put into care are not living with their natural parents but instead with a national or local government organization or another family: *Both children were taken into care when their parents died.* **5 care in the community** UK a system in which people with mental

illness or reduced mental ability are allowed to continue living in their own homes, with treatment and help, and are not kept in hospital

! Common mistake: take care

The correct preposition to use after **take care** is **of**.

Don't say 'take care about/for something', say **take care of something:**

~~*Please take care about my plants while I am on holiday.*~~

Please take care of my plants while I am on holiday.

ATTENTION ▷ **6** B1 [U] serious attention, especially to the details of a situation or something: *She painted the window frames* ***with*** *great care so that no paint got onto the glass.* ◦ *You need to* ***take*** *a bit more care* ***with*** *your spelling.* ◦ *The roads are icy, so drive* ***with*** *care.* ◦ ***Take*** *care on these busy roads (= drive with attention so that you do not have an accident).* ◦ [+ to infinitive] ***Take*** *care not* ***to*** *(= make certain that you do not) spill your coffee.* ◦ [+ that] ***Take*** *care (= make certain)* ***that*** *you don't fall.* ◦ *The parcel had a label on it saying '****Handle with*** *care'.* **DEAL WITH** ▷ **7 take care of sth** C1 to deal with something: *If you can sort out the drink for the party, I'll take care of the food.* ◦ *All the travel arrangements have been taken care of.* ◦ *No, you paid for dinner last time, let me take care of (= pay for) it.* **WORRY** ▷ **8** C2 [C or U] a feeling of worry or ANXIETY: *She seemed weighed down by all her cares.*

Word partners for care noun

take care *of* sb • *provide* care • *in/under* sb's care • *constant/long-term/round-the-clock* care • care *facilities/services/workers*

IDIOMS **have all the cares of the world on your shoulders** to be very worried by many different problems: *You look as if you have all the cares of the world on your shoulders.* • **take care (of yourself)** A2 used when saying goodbye to someone: *'Bye, Melissa.' 'Goodbye Rozzie, take care.'* • **without a care in the world** (also **not a care in the world**) without worrying about anything: *Look at her, not a care in the world!*

▸**verb** [I] **WORRY** ▷ **1** B1 to think that something is important and to feel interested in it or upset about it: *She's never cared very much* ***about*** *her appearance.* ◦ [+ question word] *I really don't care* ***wh****ether we go out or not.* ◦ *I don't care* ***how*** *much it costs, just buy it.* ◦ *'Was Lorna happy about the arrangements?' 'I* ***don't know and*** *I don't care.'* ◦ *Your parents are only doing this because they care* ***about*** *(= love) you.* **2 I couldn't care less** C1 informal used to emphasize rudely that you are not interested in or worried about something or someone: *'Mike's really fed up about it.' 'I couldn't care less.'* **3 for all I care** informal used to say that you are not interested in or worried about what someone else is doing: *You can go to the match with Paula, for all I care.* **4 as if I care** informal used to say that you are not interested in or worried about something that has happened or that someone has said: *He said he didn't approve of what I'd done, as if I cared.* **5 who cares?** B2 informal used to emphasize rudely that you do not think something is important: *'It looks as if we are going to lose.' 'Who cares?'.* **WANT** ▷ **6** formal used in polite offers and suggestions: ***Would*** *you care* ***for*** *a drink?* ◦ [+ to infinitive] ***Would*** *you care* ***to*** *join us for dinner?*

PHRASAL VERBS **care for sb** **PROTECT/PROVIDE FOR** ▷ **1** B1 to protect someone or something and provide the things they need, especially someone who is young, old, or ill: *The children are being cared for by a relative.* ◦ *She can't go out to work because she has to stay at home to care for her elderly mother.* ◦ *It's good to know that the dogs will be well cared for while we're away.* **LIKE** ▷ **2** formal to love someone and feel romantic towards them: *You know I care for you, Peter.* • **not care for sb/sth** to not like something or someone: *I have to say I don't much care for modern music.* ◦ *Your father thought she was nice but Camille and I didn't care for her.*

careen /kəˈriːn/ **verb** [I + adv/prep] mainly US to go forward quickly while moving from side to side: *The driver lost control of his car when the brakes failed, and it went careening* ***down*** *the hill.*

career /kəˈrɪəʳ/ (US) /-ˈrɪr/ **noun; verb**

▸**noun** [C] B1 the job or series of jobs that you do during your working life, especially if you continue to get better jobs and earn more money: *He's hoping for a career* ***in*** *the police force/****as*** *a police officer.* ◦ *When he retires he will be able to look back over a* ***brilliant*** *career (= a working life which has been very successful).* ◦ *It helps if you can move a few rungs up the career* ***ladder*** *before taking time off to have a baby.* ◦ *I took this new job because I felt that the career* ***prospects*** *were much better.* ◦ *Elaine has become a real career* ***woman/girl*** *(= is interested in and spends most of her time on her job).* ◦ *Judith is very career-****minded/-oriented*** *(= gives a lot of attention to her job).*

! Common mistake: career

Warning: Check your spelling!

Career is one of the 50 words most often spelled wrongly by learners.

▸**verb** [I usually + adv/prep] (especially of a vehicle) to move fast and in a way that is out of control: *The coach careered* ***down*** *a slope and collided with a bank.*

caˈreer ˌbreak **noun** [C] a period of time when you choose not to have a job, for example because you want to travel or take care of your children: *I* ***took*** *a career break for a year and travelled around the world.*

careerist /kəˈrɪə.rɪst/ (US) /-ˈrɪr.ɪst/ **noun** [C] often disapproving someone who thinks that their career is more important than anything else, and who will do anything to be successful in it

caˈreer-ˌlimiting **adj** A career-limiting action or fault is one that damages your chances of being successful in your job: *Career-limiting habits you should avoid include unreliability and resistance to change.*

careers /kəˈrɪəz/ (US) /-ˈrɪrz/ **adj** [before noun] UK (US **career**) relating to advice about jobs and training: *a careers adviser/officer*

caˈreer ˌwoman **noun** [C] a woman whose job is more important to her than having children

carefree /ˈkeə.friː/ (US) /ˈker-/ **adj** C2 having no problems or not being worried about anything: *I remember my carefree student days.*

careful /ˈkeə.fəl/ (US) /ˈker-/ **adj** A2 giving a lot of attention to what you are doing so that you do not have an accident, make a mistake, or damage something: ***Be*** *careful* ***with*** *the glasses.* ◦ ***Be*** *careful* ***wh****ere you put that hot pan.* ◦ ***Be*** *careful* ***to*** *look both ways when you cross the road.* ◦ *Michael is a very careful worker.* ◦ *After careful consideration of your proposal, I regret to say that we are unable to accept it.* ◦ *He's in a really foul temper so be careful* ***(about/of)*** *what you say to him.*

! Common mistake: careful

Warning: Common word-building error!

Adjectives which end in the suffix **-ful** have only one 'l'. Don't write 'carefull', write **careful**.

C

+ Other ways of saying careful

If someone is careful to avoid risks or danger, you can describe them as **cautious:**

*She's a very **cautious** driver.*

The idiom **play it safe** also means 'to be careful to avoid risks':

*I think I'll **play it safe** and take the earlier train.*

If someone does something in a very careful way, paying great attention to detail, you can use adjectives such as **meticulous**, **methodical**, and **painstaking**:

*This book is the result of years of **meticulous/ painstaking** research.*

carefully /ˈkeə.fᵊl.i/ (US) /ˈker-/ **adv** (A2) with great attention: *She carefully folded the letter and put it in her pocket.* ◦ *Drive carefully on those icy roads.*

caregiver /ˈkeəˌɡɪv.əʳ/ (US) /ˈkerˌɡɪv.ɚ/ **noun** [C] mainly US or specialized **carer**

ˈ**care** ˌ**home** **noun** [C] a place where someone who is old or ill lives when they cannot live at home any more

careless /ˈkeə.ləs/ (US) /ˈker-/ **adj** **NO ATTENTION** ▷ **1** (B1) not taking or showing enough care and attention: *My son's teacher says that his work is often rather careless.* ◦ *He made a careless remark (= one made without thinking) about her appearance that really upset her.* **NO WORRY** ▷ **2** literary relaxed, natural, and free from worry → See also **carefree** • **carelessly** /-li/ **adv** (B2) *He told me off for driving carelessly.* • **carelessness** /-nəs/ **noun** [U]

+ Other ways of saying careless

Sloppy is an alternative to the word 'careless':

*Spelling mistakes always look **sloppy** in a formal letter.*

The informal adjective **slapdash** can be used when work is careless because it is done too quickly without enough thought:

*His work is always hurried and **slapdash**.*

If someone does something without thinking about the results, the adjective **rash** is often used:

*That was a **rash** decision – you didn't think about the costs involved.*

If someone carelessly says something that could upset someone, you can use the word **thoughtless**:

*The senator made a **thoughtless** remark about the environment.*

Someone who does not do something properly and causes a serious mistake to be made can be described as **negligent**:

*If a doctor is **negligent** in treating a patient, he or she can be sued in court.*

The adjectives **reckless** and **irresponsible** can be used when people are careless and do not think about the dangers of what they are doing:

*He was found guilty of **reckless** driving.*

*Some dog owners are **irresponsible** and do not keep dangerous dogs under control.*

carer /ˈkeə.rəʳ/ (US) /ˈker.ɚ/ **noun** [C] UK (US **caregiver**, **caretaker**) someone who takes care of a person who is young, old, or sick

caress /kəˈres/ **verb** [I or T] to touch or kiss someone in a gentle and loving way: *Gently he caressed her cheek.* • **caress noun** [C]

caret /ˈkær.ət/ (US) /ˈker-/ **noun** [C] **1** the symbol ^, found on a keyboard and used in marking text **2** a CURSOR on a screen that shows where text should be entered

caretaker /ˈkeəˌteɪ.kəʳ/ (US) /ˈkerˌteɪ.kɚ/ **noun** [C] **IN A BUILDING** ▷ **1** UK (US or Scottish English **janitor**, US also **custodian**) a person employed to take care of a large building, such as a school, and who deals with the cleaning, repairs, etc. **GIVES CARE** ▷ **2** US for **carer** • **caretaking** /-kɪŋ/ **noun** [U] *caretaking staff/duties*

ˌ**caretaker** ˈ**government** **noun** [C] UK a government that has power for a short period of time until a new one is chosen

careworn /ˈkeə.wɔːn/ (US) /ˈker.wɔːrn/ **adj** appearing tired, worried, and unhappy: *Her mother, who couldn't have been much more than 30, looked old and careworn.*

carfare /ˈkɑː.feəʳ/ (US) /ˈkɑːr.fer/ **noun** [U] mainly US the money paid by a passenger for travelling in a bus, taxi, etc.: *You'll need a couple of dollars for carfare.*

ˈ**car** ˌ**ferry** **noun** [C] a ship designed for carrying vehicles and passengers

cargo /ˈkɑː.ɡəʊ/ (US) /ˈkɑːr.ɡoʊ/ **noun** [C or U] (plural **cargoes** or **cargos**) (C2) the goods carried by a ship, aircraft, or other large vehicle: *a cargo ship/ plane* ◦ *The ship was carrying a cargo **of** wood.*

ˈ**cargo** ˌ**pants** **noun** [plural] loose trousers with large pockets on the outside of the legs

Caribbean /ˌkær.ɪˈbiː.ᵊn/, /kəˈrɪb.i-/ (US) /ˌker.ɪˈbiː-/ **adj, noun; noun**

▸**adj, noun** [C] → See table of **Geographical names**: *Caribbean food*

▸**noun** [S] **the Caribbean** the islands and countries that border the Caribbean Sea: *They're holidaying somewhere in the Caribbean.*

caribou /ˈkær.ɪ.buː/ (US) /ˈker-/ **noun** [C] (plural **caribous** or **caribou**) a large North American REINDEER

caricature /ˈkær.ɪ.kə.tʃʊəʳ/ (US) /ˈker.ɪ.kə.tʃʊr/ **noun; verb**

▸**noun** [C or U] (the art of making) a drawing or written or spoken description of someone that usually makes them look silly by making part of their appearance or character more noticeable than it really is: figurative *Over the years he's become a grotesque caricature **of** himself.*

▸**verb** [T] to create a caricature: *Charles Dickens caricatured lawyers (= represented them in a way which made them look silly) in several of his novels.* • **caricaturist** /ˌkær.ɪ.kəˈtʃʊə.rɪst/ (US) /ˌker.ɪ.kəˈtʃʊr.ɪst/ **noun** [C] a person who creates caricatures

caries /ˈkeə.riːz/ (US) /ˈker.iːz/ **noun** [U] specialized decay in the teeth or bones

carillon /kəˈrɪl.jən/ (US) /ˈkær.ə.lɑːn/ **noun** [C] (a tune played on) a set of bells, usually hung in a tower

caring /ˈkeə.rɪŋ/ (US) /ˈker.ɪŋ/ **adj** (B2) describes someone who is kind and gives emotional support to others: *I've always thought of Jo as a very caring person.*

ˈ**caring** **pro**ˌ**fession** **noun** [C] UK a job such as NURSING that involves taking care of people

carjacking /ˈkɑːˌdʒæk.ɪŋ/ (US) /ˈkɑːr-/ **noun** [C or U] the crime of stealing someone's car while they are in it by using physical force or threats • **carjacker** /-əʳ/ (US) /-ɚ/ **noun** [C]

carmine /ˈkɑː.maɪn/ (US) /ˈkɑːr-/ **noun** [U] a deep bright red colour • **carmine adj**

carnage /ˈkɑː.nɪdʒ/ (US) /ˈkɑːr-/ **noun** [U] the violent killing of large numbers of people, especially in war: *The Battle of the Somme was a scene of dreadful carnage.*

carnal /ˈkɑː.nəl/ (US) /ˈkɑːr-/ adj formal relating to the physical feelings and wants of the body: *carnal desires* → Compare **sexual** • **carnality** /kɑːˈnæl.ɪ.ti/ (US) /kɑːrˈnæl.ə.t̬i/ noun [U]

ˌcarnal ˈknowledge noun [U] formal sex

carnation /kɑːˈneɪ.ʃən/ (US) /kɑːr-/ noun [C] (a plant with) a small flower with a sweet smell, usually white, pink, or red in colour

carnival /ˈkɑː.nɪ.vəl/ (US) /ˈkɑːr-/ noun **1** B2 [C or U] (a special occasion or period of) public enjoyment and entertainment involving wearing unusual clothes, dancing, and eating and drinking, usually held in the roads of a city: *There's a real carnival atmosphere in the streets.* **2** [C] US for **funfair** and **fete**

carnivore /ˈkɑː.nɪ.vɔːʳ/ (US) /ˈkɑːr.nɪ.vɔːr/ noun [C] an animal that eats meat: *Lions and tigers are carnivores.* ◦ humorous *I did mostly vegetarian food but put a couple of meat dishes out for the carnivores (= people who eat meat).* → Compare **herbivore** • **carnivorous** /kɑːˈnɪv.ər.əs/ (US) /kɑːrˈnɪv.ɚ-/ adj *carnivorous plants*

carob /ˈkær.əb/ (US) /ˈker-/ noun [C or U] (the dark brown seeds that are like beans of) a Mediterranean tree: *Carob is sometimes used in sweet foods as a healthier alternative to chocolate.*

carol /ˈkær.əl/ (US) /ˈker-/ noun; verb

▸noun [C] a happy or religious song, usually one sung at Christmas: *a carol concert* ◦ *'Silent Night' is my favourite (**Christmas**) carol.*

▸verb [I] (-ll- or US usually -l-) to sing songs, especially carols, in a loud and happy way

ˈcarol ˌsinger noun [C] UK (US **caroler**) a member of a group of people who go from house to house singing carols at Christmas • **ˈcarol ˌsinging** noun [U] (US **caroling**)

caron /ˈkær.ən/ (US) /ˈker-/ noun [C] the symbol ˇ, used over some letters in some languages to change the pronunciation

carotene /ˈkær.ə.tiːn/ (US) /ˈker-/ noun [U] an orange-yellow or red PIGMENT (= a substance which gives colour) contained in some foods

carotid (artery) /kəˌrɒt.ɪd'ɑː.tər.i/ (US) /-ˈɑːr.t̬ɚ-/ noun [C] specialized one of two ARTERIES (= thick tubes carrying blood from the heart) that pass up through your neck and take blood to your brain

carouse /kəˈraʊz/ verb [I] literary or humorous to enjoy yourself by drinking alcohol and speaking and laughing loudly in a group of people: *We'd been up carousing till the early hours and were exhausted.*

carousel /ˌkær.ʊˈsel/ (US) /ˌker.ə-/ noun [C] **AMUSEMENT** ▷ **1** mainly US for **merry-go-round** **AIRPORT** ▷ **2** a continuous moving strip on which passengers' bags are put for collection in an airport

carp /kɑːp/ (US) /kɑːrp/ noun; verb

▸noun [C or U] (plural **carp**) a large fish that lives in lakes and rivers and can be eaten

▸verb [I] to complain all the time about matters that are not important: *I can't stand the way he's always carping.*

carpal tunnel syndrome /ˌkɑː.pəlˈtʌn.əlˌsɪn.drəʊm/ (US) /ˌkɑːr.pəlˈtʌn.əlˌsɪndroʊm/ noun [U] specialized a medical condition of pain and weakness in the hand, caused by repeated pressure on a nerve in the wrist

ˈcar ˌpark noun [C] UK **AREA** ▷ **1** A2 (US **parking lot**) an area of ground for parking cars **BUILDING** ▷ **2** (US **parking garage**) a building for parking cars

carpel /ˈkɑː.pel/ (US) /ˈkɑːr-/ noun [C] specialized the female part in a flower, made of the OVARY, the STIGMA, and the STYLE

carpenter /ˈkɑː.pɪn.təʳ/ (US) /ˈkɑːr.pɪn.t̬ɚ/ noun [C] a person whose job is making and repairing wooden objects and structures → Compare **joiner**

carpentry /ˈkɑː.pɪn.tri/ (US) /ˈkɑːr-/ noun [U] the skill of making and repairing wooden objects

carpet /ˈkɑː.pɪt/ (US) /ˈkɑːr-/ noun; verb

▸noun **1** A2 [C or U] (a shaped piece of) thick material used for covering floors: *We've just had a new carpet **fitted/laid** in our bedroom.* ◦ UK *We've got **fitted** (= cut to fit exactly) carpets in the bedrooms.* **2** [S] a layer of something that covers the ground: *a carpet of snow* ◦ *Our lawn is **a** carpet **of** daisies.*

IDIOM **be on the carpet** mainly US to be in trouble with someone in authority

▸verb [T] **COVER** ▷ **1** to cover something with carpet: *We need to carpet the stairs.* **2 be carpeted with sth** to be covered with something: *In spring this area is carpeted with bluebells.* **CRITICIZE** ▷ **3** UK informal to severely criticize someone who has made a mistake

carpetbagger /ˈkɑː.pɪtˌbæg.əʳ/ (US) /ˈkɑːr.pɪtˌbæg.ɚ/ noun [C] **POLITICS** ▷ **1** mainly US disapproving someone who tries to be elected as a politician in a place away from their home because they think there is a greater chance of succeeding there **MONEY** ▷ **2** UK disapproving someone who INVESTS in a financial organization that is owned by its members, in order to make a profit if it is sold

ˈcarpet-ˌbombing noun [U] the act of dropping a lot of bombs all over a particular area so that it will be destroyed

carpeted /ˈkɑː.pə.tɪd/ (US) /ˈkɑːr.pə.t̬ɪd/ adj covered with carpet

carpeting /ˈkɑː.pɪ.tɪŋ/ (US) /ˈkɑː.pɪ.t̬ɪŋ/ noun [U] material for making carpets

ˈcarpet ˌslipper noun [C usually plural] old-fashioned UK for **slipper**

ˈcarpet ˌsweeper noun [C] a machine with a brush fixed to the bottom of it for cleaning carpets

ˈcar ˌphone noun [C] a phone that is kept and used in a car and is connected to the NETWORK by radio

carpool /ˈkɑː.puːl/ noun [C, + sing/pl verb] **PEOPLE** ▷ **1** a group of people who travel together, especially to work or school, usually in a different member's car each day **CARS** ▷ **2** a group of cars owned by a company or other organization that can be used by any of its employees • **carpooling** /-puː.lɪŋ/ noun [U]

carport /ˈkɑː.pɔːt/ (US) /ˈkɑːr.pɔːrt/ noun [C] a shelter for cars with a roof and one or more open sides that can be built against the side of a house

carriage /ˈkær.ɪdʒ/ (US) /ˈker-/ noun **VEHICLE** ▷ **1** C2 [C] a vehicle with four wheels that is usually pulled by horses and was used mainly in the past: *a **horse-drawn** carriage* **2** C1 [C] UK any of the separate parts of a train in which the passengers sit: *a **railway** carriage* **TRANSPORTING** ▷ **3** [U] UK (the cost of) transporting goods: *That will be £150, carriage included.* **BODY MOVEMENT** ▷ **4** [U] formal the way in which a person moves or keeps their body when they are standing, sitting, or walking

carriage ˌclock noun [C] a small, rectangular, decorative clock with a metal handle on top

carriageway /ˈkær.ɪdʒ.weɪ/ (US) /ˈker-/ noun [C] UK one of the two halves of a main road

carrier /ˈkær.i.əʳ/ (US) /ˈker.i.ɚ/ noun [C] **TRANSPORT** ▷ **1** a person or thing that carries something **2** a company which operates aircraft **3** used as a combining form, especially in phrases which refer to military vehicles of a type which carry other vehicles or groups of soldiers: *an armoured troop-carrier* ◦ *a freight carrier* **4** informal for **aircraft carrier** **BAG** ▷ **5** (also **carrier bag**) UK (US **shopping bag**) a large plastic or paper bag with handles, used to put your shopping in **SPREAD** ▷ **6** someone who does not suffer from a disease but has the infection or GENETIC fault that causes it and can give the disease to someone else: *There are an estimated 1.5 million HIV carriers in the country.*

ˈcarrier ˌpigeon noun [C] a PIGEON that is trained to carry messages

carrion /ˈkær.i.ən/ (US) /ˈker-/ **noun** [U] dead or decaying flesh

carrot /ˈkær.ət/ (US) /ˈker-/ noun **VEGETABLE** ▷ **1** A2 [C or U] a long pointed orange root eaten as a vegetable **REWARD** ▷ **2** C2 [C] informal something that is offered to someone in order to encourage them to do something

IDIOM **carrot and stick** a system in which you are rewarded for some actions and threatened with punishment for others: *Sometimes I just have to resort to the carrot and stick approach with my children.*

carroty /ˈkær.ə.ti/ (US) /ˈker.ə.t̬i/ **adj** the orange colour of carrots: *Leo has bright carroty* ***hair.***

carry /ˈkær.i/ (US) /ˈker-/ verb **TRANSPORT** ▷ **1** A1 [I or T] to hold something or someone with your hands, arms, or on your back and transport it or them from one place to another: *Would you like me to carry your bag for you?* ◦ *She carried her tired child upstairs* ***to*** *bed.* ◦ *These books are too heavy for me to carry.* ◦ *We only had a small suitcase, so we were able to carry it* ***onto*** *the plane.* ◦ *Robson injured his leg in the second half of the match and had to be carried* ***off.*** ◦ *Thieves broke the shop window and carried* ***off*** *(= removed) jewellery worth thousands of pounds.* **2** B2 [I or T] to move someone or something from one place to another: *The bus that was involved in the accident was carrying children* ***to*** *school.* ◦ *The Brooklyn Bridge carries traffic across the East River* ***from*** *Brooklyn* ***to*** *Manhattan.* ◦ *Police think that the body was carried* ***down*** *the river (= was transported by the flow of the river).* ◦ *Underground cables carry electricity* ***to*** *all parts of the city.* ◦ *Rubbish left on the beach during the day is carried* ***away*** *(= removed) at night by the tide.* **HAVE WITH YOU** ▷ **3** B1 [T] to have something with you all the time: *Police officers in Britain do not usually carry guns.* ◦ figurative *He will carry the* ***memory*** *of the accident with him (= will remember the accident) for ever.* **HAVE** ▷ **4** C2 [T] to have something as a part, quality, or result: *All cigarette packets carry a government health warning.* ◦ *Our cars carry a twelve-month guarantee.* ◦ *His speech carried so much* ***conviction*** *that I had to agree with him.* ◦ *In some countries, murder carries the death penalty.* ◦ *I'm afraid my opinion doesn't carry any* ***weight*** *with (= influence) my boss.* ◦ US *The salesclerk said they didn't carry (= have a supply of) sportswear.* **SPREAD** ▷ **5** C1 [T] to take something from one person or thing and give it to another person or thing: *Malaria is a disease carried by mosquitoes.* **SUPPORT WEIGHT** ▷ **6** C2 [T] to support the weight of something without moving or breaking: *The weight of the cathedral roof is carried by two rows of pillars.* **KEEP IN OPERATION** ▷ **7** [T] to support, keep in operation, or make a success: *We can no longer afford to carry people who don't work as hard as they should.* ◦ *Luckily they had a very strong actor in the main part and he managed to carry the whole play (= make a success of it through his own performance).* **WIN** ▷ **8** [T] to win the support, agreement, or sympathy of a group of people: *The management's plans to reorganize the company won't succeed unless they can carry the workforce with them.* **APPROVE** ▷ **9** [T usually passive] to give approval, especially by voting: *The* ***motion/proposal/resolution/bill*** *was carried* ***by*** *210 votes to 160.* **BROADCAST** ▷ **10** [T] (of a newspaper or radio or television broadcast) to contain particular information: *This morning's newspapers all carry the same story on their front page.* **REACH** ▷ **11** [I] to be able to reach or travel a particular distance: *The sound of the explosion carried for miles.* ◦ *The ball carried high into the air and landed the other side of the fence.* **DEVELOP** ▷ **12** [T usually + adv/prep] to develop or continue something: *Lenin carried Marx's ideas a stage further by putting them into practice.* ◦ *If we carry this argument* ***to*** *its logical conclusion, we realize that further investment is not a good idea.* ◦ *She carries tidiness* ***to*** *extremes/****to*** *its limits (= she is too tidy).* ◦ *We must end here, but we can carry today's discussion* ***forward*** *at our next meeting.* ◦ *He always carries his jokes too far (= he continues making jokes when he should have stopped).* **MOVE BODY** ▷ **13 carry yourself** to move your body in a particular way: *You can tell she's a dancer from the way that she carries herself.* **MATHEMATICS** ▷ **14** [T] to put a number into another column when doing addition **BE PREGNANT WITH** ▷ **15** [T] to be pregnant with a child: *It was quite a shock to learn that she was carrying twins.*

IDIOMS **carry a torch for sb** informal to be in love with someone: *Terry has been carrying a torch for Liz for years, but she seems not to notice.* • **carry the can** UK informal to take the blame or responsibility for something that is wrong or has not succeeded: *As usual, I was left to carry the can.*

PHRASAL VERBS **carry sb away 1 be/get carried away** B2 to become so excited about something that you do not control what you say or do: *There's far too much food – I'm afraid I got a bit carried away.* ◦ *The manager warned his young players not to get carried away by the emotion of the occasion.* **2** to cause someone to become very excited and to lose control: *The crowd were carried away by his passionate speech.* • **carry sth forward/over** to include an amount of money in a later set of calculations: *The balance in our account for June includes £5,000 carried over from May.* • **carry sth off** to succeed in doing or achieving something difficult: *I thought he carried off the part of Hamlet with great skill.* ◦ *She was nervous about giving a talk to her colleagues, but she carried* ***it*** *off very well.* • **carry (sth) on** B1 to continue doing something, or to cause something to continue: *Let's carry on this discussion at some other time.* ◦ *Carry on* ***the good work!*** ◦ *Sorry to interrupt, do carry on (****with*** *what you were saying).* ◦ *You just have to carry on as if nothing's happened.* ◦ [+ -ing verb] *Steve just carried on play****ing*** *on his computer.* ◦ *Daphne is carrying on the family tradition by becoming a lawyer.* • **carry on BEHAVE** ▷ **1** informal to behave in an uncontrolled, excited, or ANXIOUS (= worried and nervous) way: *The children have been carrying on all day.* **HAVE SEX** ▷ **2** old-fashioned informal to have a sexual relationship: *Is it true that Rachel and Marcus have been carrying on (****with*** *each other)?* • **carry sth out** B1 to do or complete something, especially that you have said you would do or that you have been told to do: *Nigel is carrying out research on early Christian art.* ◦ *The hospital is carrying out tests to find out what's wrong with her.* ◦ *Our soldiers carried out a successful attack last night.* ◦ *It is hoped that the kidnappers will not* *carry out their threat to kill the hostages.* ◦ *Don't blame me, I'm only carrying out my orders/instructions.* • **carry sth over** to use or do something at a later time than planned: *The performance has had to be carried over* ***to/till*** *next week because the repairs to the theatre aren't finished yet.* • **carry (sth) over** If something from one situation carries over or is carried over into another situation, it is allowed to affect the other situation: *I try not to let my problems at work carry over* ***into*** *my private life.* • **carry sb through (sth)** to help someone be able to deal with a difficult situation: *The soldiers' courage carried them through.* • **carry sth through** to complete something successfully: *It is doubtful whether it will be possible to carry through the education reforms.*

carryall /ˈkær.i.ɔːl/ (US) /ˈker.i.ɑːl/ noun [C] US for **holdall**

carrycot /ˈkær.i.kɒt/ (US) /ˈker.i.kɑːt/ noun [C] UK a container shaped like a rectangular box with two handles, in which a baby can be carried

ˈcarrying ˌcharge noun [C usually singular] US an extra charge added when you buy goods by making regular small payments for them until the full amount owed has been paid

ˌcarrying-ˈon noun [C or U] (plural **carryings-on**) activity that is not honest or moral: *The company seems to have been involved in some rather dishonest carrying-on.*

ˈcarry-on noun; adj

▸noun **BEHAVIOUR** ▷ **1** [S] UK informal behaviour that shows you are annoyed, worried, not satisfied, or excited, usually more than the situation deserves: *There was a real carry-on when Pat was found kissing Ashley.* **LUGGAGE** ▷ **2** [C] (plural **carry-ons**) mainly US a small case or bag that you take onto a plane with you

▸adj [before noun] mainly US relating to things that you take onto a plane with you: *All carry-on* ***luggage*** *must be stored under your seat or in the overhead compartments.*

carryout /ˈkær.i.aʊt/ (US) /ˈker-/ noun [C or U], **adj** US or Scottish English for **takeaway**

carsick /ˈkɑː.sɪk/ (US) /ˈkɑːr-/ adj feeling that you want to vomit because of the movement of a car • **carsickness** /ˈkɑːˌsɪk.nəs/ (US) /ˈkɑːr-/ noun [U]

cart /kɑːt/ (US) /kɑːrt/ noun; verb

▸noun [C] **1** a vehicle with either two or four wheels, pulled by a horse and used for carrying goods: *a* ***horse and*** *cart.* **2** (B2) US for **trolley**

IDIOM **put the cart before the horse** to do things in the wrong order: *Aren't you putting the cart before the horse by deciding what to wear for the wedding before you've even been invited to it?*

▸verb [T + adv/prep] to take something or someone somewhere, especially using a lot of effort: *We carted all the rubbish to the bottom of the garden and burned it.* ◦ *Council workers have carted* ***away*** *all the dead leaves that had collected at the side of the road.* ◦ informal *I've been carting (= carrying) these letters* ***around*** *with me all week, and I still haven't posted them.* ◦ informal *The drunks who had been sleeping in the park were carted* ***off*** *(= taken by force) to the police station.*

carte blanche /ˌkɑːtˈblɑ̃ːʃ/ (US) /ˌkɑːrtˈblɑːnʃ/ noun [S or U] complete freedom to do something: [+ to infinitive] *The landlord has* ***given*** *her carte blanche* ***to*** *redecorate the living room.*

cartel /kɑːˈtel/ (US) /kɑːr-/ noun [C] a group of similar independent companies who join together to control prices and limit competition: *an oil cartel*

carter /ˈkɑː.təʳ/ (US) /ˈkɑːr.t̬ɚ/ noun [C] old use a person who drives a cart

Cartesian /kɑːˈtiː.zi.ən/ (US) /kɑːrˈtiː.ʒən/ adj [before noun] specialized of or connected with the ideas and theories of the MATHEMATICIAN René Descartes: *Cartesian doubt/dualism* ◦ *Cartesian geometry/coordinates*

carthorse /ˈkɑːt.hɔːs/ (US) /ˈkɑːrt.hɔːrs/ noun [C] a large strong horse used for pulling CARTS

cartilage /ˈkɑː.təl.ɪdʒ/ (US) /ˈkɑːr.t̬əl/ noun [C or U] (a piece of) a type of strong tissue found in humans in the JOINTS (= places where two bones are connected) and other places such as the nose, throat, and ears: *He has a* ***torn*** *cartilage in his knee.*

cartload /ˈkɑːt.ləʊd/ (US) /ˈkɑːrt.loʊd/ noun [C] **1** the amount that a CART holds **2** informal a large amount of something

cartographer /kɑːˈtɒg.rə.fəʳ/ (US) /kɑːrˈtɑː.grə.fɚ/ noun [C] someone who makes or draws maps

cartography /kɑːˈtɒg.rə.fi/ (US) /kɑːrˈtɑː.grə-/ noun [U] the science or art of making or drawing maps

carton /ˈkɑː.tən/ (US) /ˈkɑːr.t̬ən/ noun [C] a box made from thick cardboard, for storing goods, or a container made from cardboard or plastic, in which milk or fruit juice, etc. is sold: *a carton* ***of*** *orange juice*

cartoon /kɑːˈtuːn/ (US) /kɑːr-/ noun [C] **DRAWING** ▷ **1** (A2) a drawing, especially in a newspaper or magazine, that tells a joke or makes a humorous political criticism **2** specialized in art, a drawing made especially in preparation for a painting **FILM** ▷ **3** (A2) a film, usually a funny one, made using characters and images that are drawn rather than real

cartoonist /kɑːˈtuː.nɪst/ (US) /kɑːr-/ noun [C] a person who draws cartoons

cartouche /kɑːˈtuːʃ/ (US) /kɑːr-/ noun [C] **1** a drawing or piece of stone that looks like a SCROLL (= a long roll of paper) with the ends rolled up, often with writing on it and used as a decoration **2** a decorative frame around a piece of writing

cartridge /ˈkɑː.trɪdʒ/ (US) /ˈkɑːr-/ noun [C] **1** a small part with a particular purpose, used in a larger piece of equipment, which can be easily replaced with another similar part: *an ink/printer cartridge* **2** a small tube containing an explosive substance and a bullet for use in a gun

ˈcartridge ˌpaper noun [U] thick strong paper for drawing or writing on

ˈcartridge ˌpen noun [C] a pen in which there is a plastic cartridge filled with ink, which can be replaced when it is empty

ˈcart ˌtrack noun [C] UK a narrow road with a rough surface that is usually made of soil

cartwheel /ˈkɑːt.wiːl/ (US) /ˈkɑːrt-/ noun [C] a fast skilful movement like a wheel turning, in which you throw yourself sideways onto one hand, then onto both hands with your legs and arms straight and your legs pointing up, before landing on your feet again • **cartwheel** verb [I]

carve /kɑːv/ (US) /kɑːrv/ verb [I or T] **1** (C2) to make something by cutting into especially wood or stone, or to cut into the surface of stone, wood, etc.: *This totem pole is carved* ***from/out of*** *a single tree trunk.* ◦ *He carved her name* ***on*** *a tree.* ◦ *Some of the tunnels in the cliff are natural, some were carved* ***out*** *(= cut into the rock) by soldiers for defensive purposes.* **2** to cut thin pieces from a large piece of cooked meat: *Would you like me to carve (the chicken)?*

IDIOM **carved in stone** informal If a suggestion, plan, rule, etc. is carved in stone, it cannot be changed:

C

These proposals are for discussion, they're not carved in stone.

PHRASAL VERBS **carve sth out (for yourself)** to successfully create or get something, especially a work position, by working for it: *He hopes to carve out **a niche** for himself as a leading researcher in his field of study.* ◦ *She carved out a reputation for herself as an aggressive manager.* • **carve sb up** UK informal to drive past someone in a car and then suddenly drive in front of them • **carve sth up** disapproving to divide something into smaller parts: *The Nazi-Soviet pact carved up the Baltic states in 1939.*

C

carver /ˈkɑː.vəʳ/ (US) /ˈkɑːr.vɚ/ **noun** [C] a knife with a blade that is moved very quickly by electricity, used for cutting cooked meat

carvery /ˈkɑː.vəʳr.i/ (US) /ˈkɑːr.vɚ-/ **noun** [C] a restaurant where you eat meat that is cut for you at a special table

carving /ˈkɑː.vɪŋ/ (US) /ˈkɑːr-/ **noun** [C or U] a shape or pattern cut into wood or stone or the skill of doing this: *wooden/stone carvings*

ˈcarving ˌknife **noun** [C] a large knife used for cutting cooked meat

ˈcar ˌwash **noun** [C] a machine which you can drive through to have your car cleaned automatically

Casanova /ˌkæs.əˈnəʊ.və/ (US) /ˌkæs.əˈnoʊ-/ **noun** [C] informal disapproving a man who has had a lot of sexual relationships

cascade /kæsˈkeɪd/ **noun; verb**

▸noun [C] **1** a small WATERFALL, often one of a group **2** a large amount of something which hangs down: *A cascade **of** golden hair fell down his back.*

▸verb [I usually + adv/prep] to fall quickly and in large amounts: *Coins cascaded **from/out of** the fruit machine.*

case /keɪs/ **noun; verb**

▸noun **SITUATION** ▷ **1** (B1) [C] a particular situation or example of something: *Over a hundred people were injured, in several cases seriously.* ◦ *Jobs are hard to find but **in** his case that's not the problem because he has so much experience.* ◦ *I wouldn't normally agree but I'll make an exception **in this** case.* ◦ *The number of new cases **of** the illness appears to be declining.* ◦ *We have lots of applications from people who want to study here and in **each** case we consider the candidate very carefully.* ◦ *She was suffering from an **extreme** case of sunburn.* **2 in that case** (B2) because of the mentioned situation: *There's no coffee left? In that case I'll have tea.* **3 (not) the case** (B1) (not) true: *If that is the case then I will be very disappointed.* **4 in any case** (B2) also: *I don't want to go and in any case, I haven't been invited.* **5 (just) in case** (B1) because of a possibility of something happening, being needed, etc.: *I don't think I'll need any money but I'll bring some just in case.* ◦ *Bring a map in case you get lost.* **6 in the case of sth/sb** in connection with someone or something, or in the situation of something: *The law will apply equally to men and women except in the case of maternity leave.* **7 a case of sth** used when a situation is of a particular type: *She doesn't want to work full-time, it's a case of having to.* **8 a case in point** an example that shows that what you are saying is true or helps to explain why you are saying it: *Lack of communication causes serious problems and their marriage is a case in point.* **9 as the case might be** (also **whatever the case might be**) one of the stated possibilities that is true: *When the election is called in April, or June, as the case might be, we shall be ready for it.* **PROBLEM** ▷ **10** (B2) [C] a problem, a series of events or a person being dealt with by police, doctors, lawyers, etc.: *Several social workers have looked into the child's case.* ◦ *The detective **on** the case (= responsible for solving it) has been suspended from duty.* ◦ *When he first went for treatment at the hospital he seemed to be a **hopeless** case (= a person who could not be cured).* **11** (B2) [C] legal a matter to be decided by a judge in a law court: *a murder case* ◦ *The case will go before the European Court next month.* ◦ *She accused her employer of unlawful dismissal and **won/lost** her case.* **CONTAINER** ▷ **12** (A2) [C] a container or box for storing things in → See also **bookcase, briefcase, pillowcase** **13 a case of wine, etc.** a box holding twelve bottles of wine or another type of alcoholic drink, or the twelve bottles and their contents **ARGUMENT** ▷ **14** (C2) [S] arguments, facts, and reasons in support of or against something: *There's a good case **for/against** bringing in new regulations.* ◦ *The case **against** cigarette advertising is becoming stronger all the time.* ◦ *She's very busy so don't **overstate** the case – just give her the facts.* **GRAMMAR** ▷ **15** [C or U] specialized any of the various types to which a noun can belong, according to the work it does in a sentence, shown in some languages by a special word ending: *the accusative/dative case*

IDIOMS **be on the case** informal to be doing what needs to be done in a particular situation: *'We need to book a flight before it's too late.' 'Don't worry, I'm on the case.'* • **get off sb's case** informal to stop continuously criticizing someone for something they have done: *I told him the problem had already been dealt with and he could get off my case.* • **get on sb's case** informal to criticize someone in an annoying way for something they have done: *I just don't want him getting on my case for being late for work.* • **make a case for sth** (UK also **make out a case for sth**) to argue that something is the best thing to do, giving your reasons: *We will only publish a new edition if you can make a convincing case for it.*

▸verb slang **case the joint** to look at a place with the intention of stealing from it later

cased /keɪst/ **adj** covered in a tight case (= container or covering)

ˌcase ˈhistory **noun** [C] a record of a person's health, development, or behaviour, kept by an official such as a doctor: *The report was written after analysing data from the case histories of thousands of patients.*

ˈcase ˌlaw **noun** [U] legal law based on decisions that have been made by judges in the past

caseload /ˈkeɪs.ləʊd/ (US) /-loʊd/ **noun** [C] the amount of work which someone, especially a doctor or lawyer, has to do in a period of time: *a heavy caseload*

casement (window) /ˌkeɪ.smənt ˈwɪn.dəʊ/ (US) /-doʊ/ **noun** [C] a type of window that is fixed on one side and opens like a door

ˌcase-ˈsensitive **adj** If a computer program is case-sensitive, it can recognize if a letter is a capital or a small letter.

ˈcase ˌstudy **noun** [C] a detailed account giving information about the development of a person, group, or thing, especially in order to show general principles: *This is an interesting psychiatric case study of a child with extreme behavioural difficulties.*

cash /kæʃ/ **noun; verb**

▸noun [U] (A2) money in the form of notes and coins, rather than CHEQUES or CREDIT CARDS: *Do you have any cash on you?* ◦ *Will you pay by credit card or **in** cash?* ◦ *He says he wants cash **in advance** before he'll do the job.* ◦ informal *I'm a bit **short of/strapped for** cash (= I do not have much money) at the moment.* → See also **COD**

C

▸verb [T] to exchange a CHEQUE, etc. for cash: *Would you cash a cheque for me?*

PHRASAL VERBS **cash in on sth** to get money or another advantage from an event or situation, often in an unfair way: *Her family have been accused of cashing in on her death.* • **cash up** to count all the money taken by a shop or business at the end of each day: *When she had cashed up, she realized there was £10 missing from the till.*

ˌcash-and-ˈcarry noun [C] a large shop where people, usually from another business, can buy large amounts of goods cheaply and take them away immediately

cashback /ˈkæʃ.bæk/ noun [U] UK **PAYMENT** ▷ **1** a system in which banks or businesses encourage people to buy something by giving them money after they have bought it: *The major banks are offering cashback deals of up to £5,000 on their mortgages.* **MONEY** ▷ **2** an amount of money that a shop, usually a SUPERMARKET, allows you to take from your bank account when you pay for something with a bank card: *£20 cashback*

ˈcash ˌcard noun [C] UK (US **ATˈM card**) a special plastic card given to you by a bank that allows you to take money out of your bank account using a CASH MACHINE

ˈcash ˌcrop noun [C] a crop that is grown mainly to be sold, rather than used by the people who grew it or those living in the area it is grown in → Compare **subsistence crop**

ˈcash ˌdesk noun [C] UK the place in a shop where you can pay for the things that you buy

ˈcash disˌpenser noun [C] UK a **cash machine**

cashew /ˈkæʃ.uː/, /kəˈʃuː/ noun [C] (also **ˈcashew ˌnut**, **caˈshew nut**) a small nut from a tropical American tree that can be eaten

ˈcash ˌflow noun [U] the amount of money moving into and out of a business: *strong/improved cash flow* ◦ [before noun] *Small traders often have short-term cash-flow problems.*

cashier /kæʃˈɪəʳ/ (US) /-ˈɪr/ noun; verb

▸noun [C] a person whose job is to receive and pay out money in a shop, bank, restaurant, etc.

▸verb [T] to officially DISMISS (= remove from a job) a person from a military organization, especially making them lose their honour at the same time

cashless /ˈkæʃ.ləs/ adj using or operating with CREDIT and DEBIT cards and electronic systems, not money in the form of coins or notes: *a cashless society*

ˈcash maˌchine noun [C] mainly UK (US usually **ATM**) (B1) a machine, usually in a wall outside a bank, from which you can take money out of your bank account using a special card

cashmere /ˈkæʃ.mɪəʳ/ (US) /-mɪr/ noun [U] very soft, expensive wool material that is made from the hair of goats from Kashmir

cashpoint /ˈkæʃ.pɔɪnt/ noun [C] UK (B1) a **cash machine**

ˈcash ˌregister noun [C] a machine in a shop or other business that records sales and into which money received is put

ˈcash-strapped adj not having enough money: *cash-strapped universities*

casing /ˈkeɪ.sɪŋ/ noun [C or U] a covering that protects something

casino /kəˈsiː.nəʊ/ (US) /-noʊ/ noun [C] (plural **casinos**) a building where games, especially ROULETTE and card games are played for money

cask /kɑːsk/ (US) /kæsk/ noun [C] a strong, round, wooden container used for storing liquid: *a cask of water/wine*

casket /ˈkɑː.skɪt/ (US) /ˈkæs.kɪt/ noun [C] **1** a small decorative box, especially one used to keep jewellery in **2** US for **coffin**

cassava /kəˈsɑː.və/ noun [U] (also **manioc**) a South American plant with large roots, or a type of flour made from these roots

casserole /ˈkæs.ᵊr.əʊl/ (US) /-ə.roʊl/ noun [C or U] (C2) a dish made by cooking meat, vegetables, or other foods in liquid inside a heavy container at low heat, or the heavy, deep container with a lid used in cooking such dishes: *lamb casserole*

cassette /kəˈset/ noun [C] a flat rectangular device containing a very long strip of MAGNETIC material that is used to record sound and/or pictures, or a machine that uses such devices: *a video cassette* ◦ *an audio cassette*

cassock /ˈkæs.ək/ noun [C] a long, loose, usually black piece of clothing worn especially by priests

cast /kɑːst/ (US) /kæst/ noun; verb

▸noun **ACTORS** ▷ **1** (B2) [C, + sing/pl verb] the actors in a film, play, or show: *After the final performance the director threw a party for the cast.* ◦ *Part of the film's success lies in the strength of the **supporting** cast (= the actors who were not playing the main parts).* **SHAPE** ▷ **2** [C] an object made by pouring hot liquid into a container and leaving it to become solid **3** [C] a **plaster cast**

▸verb (**cast, cast**) **ACTORS** ▷ **1** (C2) [T] to choose actors to play particular parts in a play, film, or show: *He was often cast **as** the villain.* ◦ *In her latest film she was cast **against type** (= played a different character than the one she usually played or might be expected to play).* ◦ figurative *They like to cast the opposing political party **as** (= to say that they are) the party of high taxes.* → See also **typecast** **LIGHT** ▷ **2** (C2) [T usually + adv/prep] to send light or SHADOW (= an area of darkness) in a particular direction: *The moon cast a white light into the room.* ◦ *The tree cast a shadow **over/on** his face.* ◦ figurative *Her arrival cast a shadow **over/on** the party (= made it less pleasant).* **3 cast light on sth** to provide an explanation for a situation or problem, or information that makes it easier to understand: *The discovery of the dinosaur skeleton has cast light on why they became extinct.* **LOOK** ▷ **4 cast a look, glance, smile, etc.** to look, smile, etc. in a particular direction: *She cast a quick look in the rear mirror.* **5 cast an/your eye over sth** to look quickly at something: *Could you cast an eye over this report for me?* **THROW** ▷ **6** [T + adv/prep] literary to throw something: *The knight cast the sword far out into the lake.* **7** [I or T] (in fishing) to throw something, such as a line, into the water to catch fish with: *He cast the line to the middle of the river.* **DOUBT** ▷ **8 cast doubt/suspicion on sb/sth** (C2) to make people feel less sure about or have less trust in something or someone: *New evidence has cast doubt on the guilty verdict.* **9 cast aspersions on sb/sth** formal to criticize or make damaging remarks or judgments about someone or something: *His opponents cast aspersions on his patriotism.* **REMEMBER** ▷ **10 cast your mind back** (C2) to try to remember: *If you cast your mind back, you might recall that I never promised to go.* **VOTE** ▷ **11 cast a/your vote** (C2) to vote: *All the votes in the election have now been cast and the counting has begun.* **SHAPE** ▷ **12** [T] to make an object by pouring hot liquid, such as melted metal, into a shaped container where it becomes hard **MAGIC** ▷ **13 cast a spell** (C2) to use words thought to be magic, especially in order to have an effect on someone: *The old woman cast a spell **on** the prince and he turned into a frog.* ◦ figurative *When I was 17, jazz cast its spell **on** me (= I started to like it very much).* **SKIN** ▷ **14** [T] If a snake casts its skin, the outer layer of old skin comes off its body.

IDIOMS **be cast in the same mould** to be very similar in character to someone else • **cast your net wide** to include many people or things when you are looking for something • **cast pearls before swine** to offer something valuable or good to someone who does not know its value: *I'm afraid you're casting pearls before swine with your good advice – he won't listen.*

PHRASAL VERBS **cast around/about** to look around for something: *Fashion editors are always casting around **for** words to describe colours.* • **cast sb/sth aside/off** formal to get rid of someone or something: *You must cast aside all thoughts of revenge.* • **cast off LEAVE** ▷ **1** If a boat casts off, it leaves the SHORE: *The ship was scheduled to cast off at 8 p.m.* **FINISH** ▷ **2** specialized in KNITTING, to use special STITCHES to finish the thing you are making • **cast on** specialized in KNITTING, to make special STITCHES to start the thing you are making • **cast sb/sth out** literary to get rid of someone or something, especially forcefully: *Cast out by his family, he was forced to fend for himself.*

castanets /ˌkæs.təˈnets/ noun [plural] a musical instrument consisting of two small pieces of wood tied together by string and knocked against each other in the hand to make a noise

castaway /ˈkɑː.stə.weɪ/ ⓤⓢ /ˈkæs.tə-/ noun [C] a person who has escaped from a ship that has sunk, and managed to get to an island or country where there are few or no other people

caste /kɑːst/ ⓤⓢ /kæst/ noun [C or U] a system of dividing Hindu society into classes, or any of these classes: *the caste **system***

castellated /ˈkæs.tɪ.leɪ.tɪd/ ⓤⓢ /-t̬ɪd/ adj specialized describes a building that is made to look like a castle by having towers and BATTLEMENTS (= a wall with regular spaces in it)

caster /ˈkɑː.stəʳ/ ⓤⓢ /ˈkæs.tɚ/ noun [C] US for **castor**

ˈcaster ˌsugar noun [U] UK white sugar with very small grains, often used in cooking

castigate /ˈkæs.tɪ.ɡeɪt/ verb [T] formal to criticize someone or something severely: *Health inspectors castigated the kitchen staff **for** poor standards of cleanliness.*

ˈcasting ˌcouch noun [C usually singular] humorous If you say that someone has got a good part in a film or play by using the casting couch, you mean that they had sex with the person who was choosing the actors in order to get the part.

ˌcasting ˈvote noun [S] a single vote, given by the person in charge of a meeting if the number of votes about something is equal, that decides the matter

ˌcast ˈiron noun [U] a type of hard iron that will not bend easily and is made into shapes by being poured into a MOULD when melted

ˌcast-ˈiron adj **1 cast-iron guarantee, alibi, etc.** a guarantee, alibi, etc. that can be trusted completely: *Can you give me a cast-iron guarantee that the work will be completed on time?* **2** [before noun] very strong: *He has a cast-iron stomach – he can eat anything.*

castle /ˈkɑː.sl/ ⓤⓢ /ˈkæs.l̩/ noun; verb

▸noun [C] **1** Ⓐ2 a large strong building, built in the past by a ruler or important person to protect the people inside from attack **2** informal for **rook**

IDIOM **castles in the air** plans that have very little chance of happening

▸verb [I] specialized in CHESS, to make a special move which puts your king in a more protected place at the side of the board

ˈcast-ˌoffs noun [plural] things, usually clothes, that you no longer want: *I always had to wear my sister's cast-offs as a child.* • **ˈcast-ˌoff** adj [before noun] *cast-off clothes*

castor UK (US **caster**) /ˈkɑː.stəʳ/ ⓤⓢ /ˈkæs.tɚ/ noun [C] a small wheel, usually one of a set, that is fixed to the bottom of a piece of furniture so that it can be moved easily

ˌcastor ˈoil noun [U] a thick usually yellow oil, used especially as a medicine to help people pass the solid waste in their bowels out of the body

castrate /kæsˈtreɪt/ verb [T] to remove the TESTICLES of a male animal or human • **castration** /kæsˈtreɪ.ʃᵊn/ noun [U]

casual /ˈkæʒ.ju.əl/ adj **INFORMAL** ▷ **1** Ⓑ1 describes clothes that are not formal or not suitable for special occasions: *casual **clothes*** **NOT INTERESTED** ▷ **2** not taking or not seeming to take much interest: *The psychologist's **attitude** seemed far too casual, even brutal.* ◦ *Security around the conference hotel seemed almost casual.* ◦ *Although close to tears, she tried to make her voice sound casual.* **TEMPORARY** ▷ **3** Ⓒ2 [before noun] not regular or fixed: *casual **labour/labourers/workers*** ◦ *casual **sex*** **CHANCE** ▷ **4** Ⓑ2 [before noun] not serious or considered, or done by chance: *It was just a casual **comment**, I didn't mean it to be taken so seriously.* ◦ *To a casual **observer**, everything might appear normal.* • **casually** /-i/ adv Ⓑ2 *She was dressed casually in shorts and a T-shirt.*

casualty /ˈkæʒ.ju.əl.ti/ noun **INJURED** ▷ **1** Ⓒ2 [C] a person injured or killed in a serious accident or war: *The train was derailed but there were no casualties, police said.* ◦ *The rebels **suffered heavy** casualties.* **BADLY AFFECTED** ▷ **2** [C] a person or thing that suffers as a result of something else happening: *She lost her job in 2011, a casualty **of** the recession.* **HOSPITAL** ▷ **3** Ⓒ2 [U] UK (US **emergency room**) the part of a hospital where people who are hurt in accidents or suddenly become ill are taken for urgent treatment: *She had to be rushed **to** casualty.*

casuistry /ˈkæz.ju.ɪ.stri/ noun [U] formal the use of clever arguments to trick people

cat /kæt/ noun [C] Ⓐ1 a small animal with fur, four legs, a tail, and CLAWS, usually kept as a pet or for catching mice, or any member of the group of similar animals such as the lion

IDIOMS **be the cat's whiskers** UK old-fashioned to be better than everyone else • **fight like cat and dog** informal to argue violently all the time: *As kids we used to fight like cat and dog.* • **has the cat got your tongue?** informal something you say to someone when you are annoyed because they will not speak: *What's the matter? Has the cat got your tongue?* • **let the cat out of the bag** to allow a secret to be known, usually without intending to: *I was trying to keep the party a secret, but Mel went and let the cat out of the bag.* • **like a cat on a hot tin roof** (UK old-fashioned **like a cat on hot bricks**) describes someone who is in a state of extreme nervous worry • **look like something the cat brought/dragged in** informal to look very untidy and dirty • **not have a cat in hell's chance** (mainly US **not have a snowball's chance in hell**) to be completely unable to achieve something:

*They haven't a cat in hell's chance **of** getting over the mountain in weather like this.* • **play cat and mouse** to try to defeat someone by tricking them into making a mistake so that you have an advantage over them • **put/set the cat among the pigeons** UK to say or do something that causes trouble or makes a lot of people very angry • **while the cat's away, the mice will play** saying said when the person who is in charge of a place is not there, and the people there behave badly

cataclysm /ˈkæt.ə.klɪ.zᵊm/ (US) /ˈkæṭ-/ **noun** [C] literary an event that causes a lot of destruction, or a sudden violent change • **cataclysmic** /ˌkæt.əˈklɪz.mɪk/ (US) /ˌkæṭ-/ **adj** *These countries are on the brink of cataclysmic famine.*

catacomb /ˈkæt.ə.kuːm/ (US) /ˈkæṭ-/ **noun** [C usually plural] a series of underground passages and rooms where bodies were buried in the past: *They went down into catacombs beneath the church.*

Catalan /ˈkæt.ə.læn/ (US) /ˈkæṭ-/ **noun** [U] a language spoken in Catalonia in Spain

catalepsy /ˈkæt.ə.lep.si/ (US) /ˈkæṭ-/ **noun** [U] a medical condition in which a person's body becomes stiff and stops moving, as if they were dead • **cataleptic** /ˌkæt.əˈlep.tɪk/ (US) /ˌkæṭ-/ **adj**

catalogue /ˈkæt.ᵊl.ɒg/ (US) /ˈkæṭ.ᵊl.ɑːg/ **noun; verb**

▸**noun** (US usually **catalog**) **LIST** ▷ **1** (B2) [C] a book with a list of all the goods that you can buy from a shop: *a **mail-order** catalogue* **2** [C] a list of all the books, paintings, etc. that exist in a place **BAD EVENTS** ▷ **3** [S] A catalogue of unwanted events is a series of them: *The whole holiday was **a catalogue of** disasters.* ◦ *a catalogue of errors/crimes/complaints*

▸**verb** [T] to record something, especially in a list: *Many plants become extinct before they have even been catalogued.*

catalysis /kəˈtæl.ə.sɪs/ **noun** [U] specialized the process of making a chemical reaction happen more quickly by using a catalyst • **catalytic** /kæt.əˈlɪ.tɪk/ (US) /kæṭ.əˈlɪ.ṭɪk/ **adj**

catalyst /ˈkæt.ᵊl.ɪst/ (US) /ˈkæṭ-/ **noun** [C] **1** specialized something that makes a chemical reaction happen more quickly without itself being changed **2** an event or person that causes great change: *The high suicide rate **acted as** a catalyst **for** change in the prison system.*

ˌcatalytic conˈverter **noun** [C] specialized a device on a car that reduces the amount of poisonous gas that is released from the EXHAUST

catamaran /ˈkæt.ə.mə.ræn/ (US) /ˈkæṭ-/ **noun** [C] a sailing boat that has two parallel HULLS (= floating parts) held together by a single DECK (= flat surface)

catapult /ˈkæt.ə.pʌlt/ (US) /ˈkæṭ-/ **noun; verb**

▸**noun** [C] **1** a device that can throw objects at a high speed: *In the past, armies used catapults to hurl heavy stones at enemy fortifications.* ◦ *On that type of aircraft carrier, a catapult was used to help launch aircraft.* **2** UK (US **slingshot**) a Y-shaped stick or piece of metal with a piece of ELASTIC (= material that stretches) fixed to the top parts, used especially by children for shooting small stones

▸**verb** [T usually + adv/prep] **1** to throw someone or something with great force: *When the two vehicles collided, he was catapulted **forwards**.* **2 be catapulted into sth** to suddenly experience a particular state, such as being famous: *The award for best actress meant that almost overnight she was catapulted **into** the limelight.*

cataract /ˈkæt.ə.rækt/ (US) /ˈkæṭ-/ **noun** [C] **DISEASE** ▷ **1** a disease in which an area of someone's eye becomes less clear so that they cannot see clearly, or the area affected in this way **WATER FEATURE** ▷ **2** literary a large WATERFALL

catarrh /kəˈtɑːʳ/ (US) /-ˈtɑːr/ **noun** [U] a condition in which a lot of MUCUS is produced in the nose and throat, especially when a person has an infection, or the MUCUS produced

catastrophe /kəˈtæs.trə.fi/ **noun** [C] **1** (C2) a sudden event that causes very great trouble or destruction: *They were warned of the ecological catastrophe to come.* **2** a bad situation: *The emigration of scientists is a catastrophe for the country.* • **catastrophic** /ˌkæt.əˈstrɒf.ɪk/ (US) /ˌkæṭ.əˈstrɑː.fɪk/ **adj** *An unchecked increase in the use of fossil fuels could have catastrophic results for the planet.*

catatonic /ˌkæt.əˈtɒn.ɪk/ (US) /ˌkæṭ.əˈtɑː.nɪk/ **adj** describes someone who is stiff and not moving or reacting, as if they were dead

ˈcat ˌburglar **noun** [C] a thief who enters and leaves a building by climbing up walls to an upper window, door, etc.

catcall /ˈkæt.kɔːl/ (US) /-kɑːl/ **noun** [C] a loud shout or WHISTLE (= high sound) expressing disapproval, especially made by people in a crowd

catch /kætʃ/ **verb; noun**

▸**verb** (**caught**, **caught**) **TAKE HOLD** ▷ **1** (A1) [I or T] to take hold of something, especially something that is moving through the air: *I managed to catch the glass before it hit the ground.* ◦ *We saw the eagle swoop from the sky to catch its prey.* ◦ *Our dog ran past me and out of the house before I could catch it.* ◦ *He caught **hold of** my arm.* ◦ *We placed saucepans on the floor to catch (= collect) the drops of water coming through the roof.* ◦ UK specialized *The batsman was caught (**out**) (= someone in the other team caught the ball when he hit it).* **STOP ESCAPING** ▷ **2** (B1) [T] to find and stop a person or animal that is trying to escape: *Great pressure was put on the police to catch the terrorists as soon as possible.* ◦ [+ -ing verb] *Two armed men were caught try**ing** to cross the frontier at night.* ◦ *They were happy because they had caught a lot of fish that day.* ◦ figurative *I can see you're busy right now, so I'll catch you (= speak to you) later.* **NOTICE** ▷ **3** (B2) [T] to discover, see, or realize something, especially someone doing something wrong: [+ -ing verb] *He caught her read**ing** his old love letters.* ◦ *If the virus is caught (= discovered) in time, most patients can be successfully treated.* ◦ *I caught **sight of**/caught **a glimpse of** (= saw for a moment) a red coat in the crowd.* **4 catch sb's attention, imagination, interest, etc.** (B2) to make someone notice something and feel interested: *A ship out at sea caught his attention.* ◦ *Her pictures caught my imagination.* **5 be caught without sth** to not have something, especially when it is needed: *He doesn't like to be caught without any biscuits in the house.* **6 you won't catch sb doing sth** said to mean that you will certainly not see someone doing a particular thing or in a particular place: *You won't catch me at work after four o'clock.* **TRAVEL** ▷ **7** (A1) [T] to travel or be able to travel on an aircraft, train, bus, etc.: *He always catches the 10.30 a.m. train to work.* ◦ *She was worried that she'd arrive too late to catch the last bus home.* **BECOME INFECTED** ▷ **8** (A2) [T] to get an illness, especially one caused by bacteria or a virus: *He caught **a cold** on holiday.* **STICK** ▷ **9** (C2) [I or T] to stick somewhere, or to make something stick somewhere: *The sleeve of my jacket (got) caught **on** the door handle and ripped.* ◦ *Her hair got caught (**up**) **in** her hair dryer.* **BE IN TIME** ▷ **10** [T] to manage to be in time to see or do something: *I went home a bit early to catch the beginning of the programme.* ◦ *You'll have to* *run if you want to catch* ***the post*** *(= send a letter before the post has been collected).* **HEAR/SEE ▷ 11** [T] to manage to hear something: *I couldn't catch what the announcer said, with all the other noise going on.* **HIT ▷ 12** [T] to hit something, especially without intending to: *His head caught the edge of the table as he fell.* ◦ *Medical teams were caught* ***in the crossfire*** *of the opposing armies.* **INVOLVE ▷ 13 get caught up in sth** C2 to become involved in something, often without wanting to: *They were having an argument and somehow I got caught up in it.* **BREATHE ▷ 14 catch your breath** to stop breathing for a moment, or to begin to breathe correctly again after running or other exercise: *I had to sit down and catch my breath.* **BE TOUCHED BY ▷ 15 catch the sun** UK If you have caught the sun, the sun has made your skin a slightly darker brown or red colour: *You've caught the sun on the back of your neck.* **16 catch a few rays** (also **catch some rays**) to stay outside in the sun for a period of time: *I'm going out to catch a few rays before lunch.* **17 catch the light** If something catches the light, a light shines on it and makes it look shiny. **BURN ▷ 18 catch fire** B1 to start burning: *For reasons which are not yet known, the factory caught fire late yesterday evening.* **19** [I] to begin to burn: *This wood's too wet, the fire won't catch.*

IDIOMS **catch sb's eye 1** to get someone's attention: *A sudden movement caught my eye.* **2** C2 to get someone's attention, especially by looking at them: *I tried to catch the waiter's eye, so we could order.* **3** C2 to be attractive or different enough to be noticed by someone: *It was the unusual colour of his jacket that caught my eye.* • **catch sb napping** informal If someone is caught napping, something happens to them that they are not prepared for: *The goalkeeper was caught napping and the ball went straight in.* • **catch sb red-handed** to discover someone while they are doing something bad or illegal: *He was caught red-handed tak****ing*** *money from the till.* • **catch sb with their pants/trousers down 1** to discover someone doing something that they want to keep secret, usually something sexual **2** to ask someone unexpectedly to do or say something that they are not prepared for

PHRASAL VERBS **catch on BECOME POPULAR ▷ 1** C1 to become fashionable or popular: *I wonder if the game will ever catch on with young people?* **UNDERSTAND ▷ 2** C2 informal to understand, especially after a long time: *He doesn't take hints very easily, but he'll catch on (****to*** *what you're saying) eventually.* • **catch sb out** informal **SHOW WRONG ▷ 1** to show that someone is doing wrong: *I suspected he wasn't telling me the truth, and one day I caught him out when I found some letters he'd written.* **TRICK ▷ 2** to trick someone into making a mistake: *The examiner will try to catch you out, so stay calm and think carefully before you speak.* **CAUSE DIFFICULTY ▷ 3** to put someone in a difficult situation: *A lot of people were caught out* ***by*** *the sudden change in the weather.* • **catch (sb) up** B2 to reach someone in front of you by going faster than them: *I ran after her and managed to catch up* ***with*** *her.* ◦ UK *Go on to the shops without me, I'll catch you up.* • **catch up REACH SAME STANDARD ▷ 1** C1 to reach the same quality or standard as someone or something else: *Will Western industry ever catch up* ***with*** *Japanese innovations?* ◦ *He was off school for a while and is finding it hard to catch up.* **DO SOMETHING ▷ 2** B2 to do something you did not have time to do earlier: *She's staying late at the office to catch up* ***with/on*** *some reports.* **DISCUSS ▷ 3** B2 to learn or discuss the latest news: *Let's go for a coffee – I need to catch up* ***on*** *all the gossip.* • **catch up with sb CAUSE PROBLEMS ▷ 1** C2 If something bad that you have done or that has been happening to you catches up with you, it begins to cause problems for you: *His lies will catch up with him one day.* **PUNISH ▷ 2** If someone in authority catches up with you, they discover that you have been doing something wrong and often punish you for it: *They had been selling stolen cars for years before the police caught up with them.*

▸**noun PROBLEM ▷ 1** [S] a hidden problem or disadvantage: *Free food? It sounds too good to be true.* ***What's the catch?*** **SOMETHING CAUGHT ▷ 2** [C] an amount of fish caught: *The fishermen were disappointed with their catch that day.* **3** [S] informal a person who is considered to be very suitable for a relationship: *Her new boyfriend's not much of a catch really, is he?* **FASTENING DEVICE ▷ 4** [C] a small device on a door, window, bag, etc. that keeps it fastened **STIFFNESS ▷ 5** [C or U] Indian English a feeling of stiffness in part of your body: *She would complain of catch in the joints during winter.*

catch-22 /ˌkætʃ.twen.tiˈtuː/ **noun** [S or U] an impossible situation where you are prevented from doing one thing until you have done another thing that you cannot do until you have done the first thing: *a catch-22* ***situation***

ˈcatch-all adj; noun
▸**adj** [before noun] general and intended to include everything: *'South London' is a catch-all* ***phrase/term*** *for anywhere south of the river.*
▸**noun** [C] a very general description

catcher /ˈkætʃ.əʳ/ US /ˈketʃ.ɚ/ **noun** [C] in baseball, the player who catches the ball if the BATTER fails to hit it

catching /ˈkætʃ.ɪŋ/ **adj** [after verb] informal If an illness is catching, it can easily be passed from one person to another: *Flu is catching, so stay away from work.*

catchment area /ˈkætʃ.məntˌeə.ri.ə/ US /-ˌer.i-/ **noun** [C] the area served by a school or hospital

catchphrase /ˈkætʃ.freɪz/ **noun** [C] a phrase that is often repeated by and therefore becomes connected with a particular organization or person, especially someone famous such as a television ENTERTAINER

ˈcatch-up noun; adj
▸**noun** [C] **1** UK a meeting at which people discuss what has happened since the last time that they met: *I'm seeing my boss for a catch-up next week.* **2 play catch-up** to try to reach the same standard, stage, or level as others after you have fallen behind them: *They raced ahead into new markets, leaving other companies to play catch-up.*
▸**adj** [before noun] used to describe something that helps you reach the same standard or stage as others, usually after you have missed something such as lessons or opportunities to practise: *catch-up* ***exercises/sessions***

ˌcatch-up TˈV noun [U] UK a system for watching TV programmes after they have been broadcast using a computer, phone, etc. that is connected to the internet: *We offer catch-up TV, so that people who miss a programme will be able to view it on demand.*

catchword /ˈkætʃ.wɜːd/ US /-wɝːd/ **noun** [C] a word or phrase that is often repeated by, or becomes connected with a particular organization, especially a political group

catchy /ˈkætʃ.i/ **adj** (especially of a tune or song) pleasing and easy to remember: *a catchy tune* ◦ *a song with catchy lyrics* ◦ *a catchy name/slogan*

catechism /ˈkæt.ə.kɪ.zᵊm/ US /ˈkæţ-/ **noun** [C usually singular] a group of questions and answers, especially about a set of Christian beliefs

categorical /ˌkæt.əˈgɒr.ɪ.kəl/ US /ˌkæţ.əˈgɑːr-/ **adj** without any doubt or possibility of being changed: *a categorical statement/reply/assurance* • **categorically** /-kəl.i/ **adv** *He categorically* ***refused*** *to take part in the project.*

categorize (UK usually **categorise**) /ˈkæt.ə.gər.aɪz/ US /ˈkæţ.ə.gə.raɪz/ **verb** [T] to put people or things into groups with the same features: *The books are categorized* ***into*** *beginner and advanced.* ◦ *I would categorize this* ***as*** *a very early example of Tudor art.* • **categorization** (UK usually **categorisation**) /ˌkæt.ə.gər.aɪˈzeɪ.ʃən/ US /ˌkæţ.ə.gə.raɪ-/ **noun** [U]

category /ˈkæt.ə.gri/ US /ˈkæţ-/ **noun** [C] B2 (in a system for dividing things according to appearance, quality, etc.) a type, or a group of things having some features that are the same: *There are three categories of accommodation – standard, executive, and deluxe.*

> Word partners for **category**
>
> *divide into/group into/organize into/put into* categories • *belong to/fall into/fit into* categories • *create/define* a category • *broad/general/main* categories • *distinct/separate/specific* categories • categories *of* sth

cater /ˈkeɪ.tər/ US /-ţɚ/ **verb** [I or T] C1 to provide, and sometimes serve, food: *I'm catering* ***for*** *twelve on Sunday, all the family are coming.* ◦ *Which firm will be catering at the wedding reception?* ◦ US *Who catered your party?*

PHRASAL VERBS **cater for sb/sth** mainly UK C1 to provide what is wanted or needed by someone or something: *The club caters for children between the ages of four and twelve.* • **cater to sb/sth** C1 to try to satisfy a need, especially one that is not popular or not generally acceptable: *This legislation simply caters to racism.*

catering /ˈkeɪ.tər.ɪŋ/ US /-ţɚ-/ **noun** [U] B2 *I've always wanted to work* ***in catering.*** ◦ *Who is going to* ***do the catering*** *for the wedding?* ◦ *a high-class* ***catering company*** • **caterer** /-ər/ US /-ɚ/ **noun** [C]

caterpillar /ˈkæt.ə.pɪl.ər/ US /ˈkæţ.ɚ.pɪl.ɚ/ **noun** [C] a small, long animal with many legs, which feeds on the leaves of plants, and develops into a BUTTERFLY or MOTH

caterpillar

ˈCaterpillar ˌtrack noun [C] trademark a belt of metal plates around the sets of wheels on each side of a vehicle that help it to move over rough ground

ˈCaterpillar ˌtractor noun [C] a heavy vehicle fitted with a Caterpillar track

caterwaul /ˈkæt.ə.wɔːl/ US /ˈkæţ.ɚ.wɑːl/ **verb** [I] (of a person or animal) to make a high unpleasant noise like a cat

catfish /ˈkæt.fɪʃ/ **noun** [C] (plural **catfish**) a fish with a flat head and long hairs around its mouth, which lives in rivers or lakes

catgut /ˈkæt.gʌt/ **noun** [U] strong CORD made from the dried INTESTINES of animals, especially sheep, used for the strings of musical instruments

catharsis /kəˈθɑː.sɪs/ US /-ˈθɑːr-/ **noun** [C or U] (plural **catharses** /-siːz/) the process of releasing strong emotions through a particular activity or experience, such as writing or theatre, which helps you to understand those emotions • **cathartic** /-tɪk/ **adj** *a cathartic* ***experience***

cathedral /kəˈθiː.drəl/ **noun** [C] A2 a very large, usually stone, building for Christian worship. It is the largest and most important church of a DIOCESE.

catherine wheel /ˈkæθ.rɪn ˌwiːl/, /-ər.ɪn-/ US /ˈkeθ.ɚ.ɪn-/ **noun** [C] a round FIREWORK that is fixed to a stick and that SPINS around

catheter /ˈkæθ.ɪ.tər/ US /-ţɚ/ **noun** [C] specialized a long, very thin tube used to take liquids out of the body

cathode /ˈkæθ.əʊd/ US /-oʊd/ **noun** [C] specialized one of the ELECTRODES (= object that electricity moves through) in a piece of electrical equipment. The cathode is the positive electrode in a BATTERY and the negative electrode in an ELECTROLYTIC cell. → Compare **anode**

ˌcathode ˈray tube noun [C] (abbreviation **CRT**) a tube-shaped part in a television or computer screen, inside which a continuous flow of ELECTRONS is produced to create the images or text

catholic /ˈkæθ.əl.ɪk/ **adj** formal including many different types of thing: *As a young person he had more catholic* ***tastes*** *than he does now.*

Catholic /ˈkæθ.əl.ɪk/ **noun** [C], **adj** (a) ROMAN CATHOLIC: *Is he (a) Catholic?* ◦ *a Catholic school/church* → See also **the Roman Catholic Church** • **Catholicism** /kəˈθɒl.ɪ.sɪ.zəm/ US /-θɑː.lɪ-/ **noun** [U]

cation /ˈkæt.aɪən/ **noun** [C] specialized in chemistry, an ION (= type of atom) that has a positive electric charge and therefore moves towards the CATHODE (= negative part of electric cell) during ELECTROLYSIS

catkin /ˈkæt.kɪn/ **noun** [C] a group of small flowers hanging like short pieces of string from the branches of particular trees in the spring: *birch/willow/hazel catkins*

catnap /ˈkæt.næp/ **noun** [C] a short sleep • **catnap verb** [I] (plural **-pp-**)

cat-o'-nine-tails /ˌkæt.əˈnaɪn.teɪlz/ US /ˌkæţ-/ **noun** [S] (informal **cat**) a WHIP (= long thin device for hitting) made from rope that has nine ends, that was used especially in the past for hitting people to punish them

CAT scan /ˈkæt.skæn/ **noun** [C] abbreviation for computerized axial tomography scan: a medical test that involves using X-RAYS to create a THREE-DIMENSIONAL image of the inside of the body: *The doctor arranged for me to have a CAT scan.* → See also **CT scan**

ˌcat's ˈcradle noun [C or U] in children's games, a special pattern or series of patterns made by wrapping string around the fingers of both hands

ˈcat's eyes noun [plural] UK (US **reflectors**) small pieces of glass or plastic that are put along the middle and sometimes the sides of a road, to reflect the lights of a car, in order to show the driver where to drive when it is dark

catsuit /ˈkæt.suːt/ **noun** [C] UK a piece of women's clothing that fits tightly and covers the body, arms, and legs

catsup /ˈkæt.səp/ **noun** [C or U] US for **ketchup**

cattery /ˈkæt.ər.i/ US /ˈkæţ.ɚ-/ **noun** [C] a place where cats are taken care of while their owners are away or where cats are bred for sale

cattle /ˈkæt.l/ US /ˈkæţ-/ **noun** [plural] B1 cows and BULLS that are kept for their milk or meat: ***beef/dairy*** *cattle*

ˈcattle ˌcake noun [U] a type of dried food for cattle

ˈcattle ˌgrid noun [C] a set of bars over a hole in the road which allows vehicles to cross, but not animals such as cows and sheep

catty /ˈkæt.i/ US /ˈkæţ-/ **adj** describes words, especially speech, that are unkind because they are intended to hurt someone: *She's always making catty* ***remarks*** *about her sister.* • **cattily** /ˈkæt.ɪ.li/ US /ˈkæţ.ə-/ **adv** • **cattiness** /-nəs/ **noun** [U]

catwalk /ˈkæt.wɔːk/ US /-wɑːk/ **noun** [C] **1** the long, narrow stage that MODELS walk along in a FASHION SHOW **2** a narrow path, raised above the ground, often built for workers to walk on outside a building that is being built or repaired

Caucasian /kɔːˈkeɪ.ʒən/ US /kɑː-/ **adj** belonging to the races of people who have skin that is of a pale colour: *The chief suspect for the robbery is a Caucasian male.* • **Caucasian noun** [C]

caucus /ˈkɔː.kəs/ US /ˈkɑː-/ **noun** [C] **1** (a meeting of) a small group of people in a political party or organization who have a lot of influence, or who have similar interests **2** in the US, a meeting held to decide which CANDIDATE a political group will support in an election

caught /kɔːt/ US /kɑːt/ **verb** past simple and past participle of **catch**

cauldron (mainly US **caldron**) /ˈkɔːl.drən/ US /ˈkɑːl-/ **noun** [C] a large round container for cooking in, usually supported over a fire, and used especially in the past

cauliflower /ˈkɒl.ɪˌflaʊ.əʳ/ US /ˈkɑː.lɪˌflaʊr/ **noun** [C or U] (UK informal **cauli**) a large, round, white vegetable that is eaten cooked or uncooked

ˌcauliflower ˈcheese noun [U] UK a dish of cooked cauliflower in a cheese sauce

ˌcauliflower ˈear noun [C] a swollen, badly shaped ear caused by repeated hitting

causal /ˈkɔː.zəl/ US /ˈkɑː-/ **adj** formal **causal relationship, link, etc.** a relationship, link, etc. between two things in which one causes the other: *Is there a causal relationship between violence on television and violent behaviour?*

causality /kɔːˈzæl.ɪ.ti/ US /kɑːˈzæl.ə.ţi/ **noun** [U] formal the principle that there is a cause for everything that happens

causation /kɔːˈzeɪ.ʃən/ US /kɑː-/ **noun** [U] formal the process of causing something to happen or exist

causative /ˈkɔː.zə.tɪv/ US /ˈkɑː.zə.ţɪv/ **adj** formal acting as the cause of something: *Smoking is a causative* ***factor*** *in the development of several serious diseases, including lung cancer.*

> **Word partners for cause noun**
>
> the cause *of* sth • the *main* cause • a *common/major/primary* cause • the *root/underlying* cause • *determine/discover/establish* the cause

cause[1] /kɔːz/ US /kɑːz/ **noun; verb**

▸**noun** **REASON** ▷ **1** B2 [C or U] the reason why something, especially something bad, happens: *The police are still trying to establish the cause* ***of*** *the fire.* ◦ *She had died of natural causes.* ◦ *I wouldn't tell you* ***without*** (***good***) *cause* (= *if there was not a (good) reason*). ◦ *I believe we have/there is* ***just*** *cause* (= *a fair reason*) ***for*** *taking this action.* **2** C2 [U] a reason to feel something or to behave in a particular way: *He's never given me any cause* ***for*** *concern.* **PRINCIPLE** ▷ **3** C1 [C] a socially valuable principle that is strongly supported by some people: *They are fighting for a cause – the liberation of their people.* ◦ *I'll sponsor you for £10 – it's all in a* ***good*** *cause.*

> **Other ways of saying cause**
>
> An alternative to 'cause' is the phrasal verb **bring about**:
>
> *Many illnesses are* ***brought about*** *by poor diet and lack of exercise.*
>
> When something causes something to happen or exist, you can use the verbs **result in** or **lead to**:
>
> *The fire* ***resulted in*** *damage to their house.*
>
> *Reducing speed limits has* ***led to*** *fewer deaths on the motorways.*
>
> If something causes someone or something to be in a particular state, the verb **make** is often used:
>
> *The heat is* ***making*** *me tired.*
>
> The verb **arouse** is sometimes used when something causes a strong feeling or emotion:
>
> *It's a subject that has* ***aroused*** *a lot of interest.*
>
> If the feeling it causes is negative, you can use the verb **breed**:
>
> *Favouritism* ***breeds*** *resentment.*
>
> The verbs **trigger** or **spark** are sometimes used to talk about something causing something else to happen:
>
> *Some people find that certain foods* ***trigger*** *their headaches.*
>
> *Her theories have* ***sparked*** *a great deal of debate.*
>
> For talking about the person or thing who causes something to happen, you can use the phrase **responsible for**:
>
> *Last month's bad weather was* ***responsible for*** *the crop failure.*

▸**verb** [T] B2 to make something happen, especially something bad: *The difficult driving conditions caused several accidents.* ◦ [+ obj + to infinitive] *The bright light caused her* ***to*** *blink.* ◦ *Most heart attacks are caused* ***by*** *blood clots.* ◦ [+ two objects] *I hope the children haven't caused you too much trouble.*

cause[2] /kɒz/ US /kɑːz/ **conjunction** informal because: *I'll host the party cause I've got plenty of room at my house.* ◦ *I try to practise my French every day, cause I'm not very good at it.*

cause célèbre /ˌkɔːz.selˈeb.rə/ US /ˌkɑːz-/ **noun** [C] (plural **causes célèbres**) an event, such as a famous legal trial, that attracts a lot of public attention

causeway /ˈkɔːz.weɪ/ US /ˈkɑːz-/ **noun** [C] a raised path, especially across a wet area

caustic /ˈkɔː.stɪk/ US /ˈkɑː-/ **adj** **CHEMICAL** ▷ **1** describes a chemical that burns or destroys things, especially anything made of living cells: *a caustic substance* **WORDS** ▷ **2** describes a remark or way of speaking that is HURTFUL, CRITICAL, or intentionally unkind: *caustic comments* ◦ *She's famous in the office for her caustic wit.* • **caustically** /ˈkɔː.stɪ.kəl.i/ US /ˈkɑː-/ **adv**

ˌcaustic ˈsoda noun [U] a caustic chemical used in industrial processes such as soap and paper production, and in powerful cleaning substances

cauterize specialized (UK usually **cauterise**) /ˈkɔː.tər.aɪz/ US /ˈkɑː.ţɚ-/ **verb** [T] to burn an injury to stop BLEEDING and prevent infection

caution /ˈkɔː.ʃən/ US /ˈkɑː-/ **noun; verb**

▸**noun** **CARE** ▷ **1** C1 [U] great care and attention: *We need to* ***proceed with/exercise*** *caution* (= *be careful in taking action, making decisions, etc.*) ◦ *They* ***treated*** *the story of his escape* ***with*** (*some/great/extreme*) *caution* (= *thought that it might not be true*). **WARNING** ▷ **2** [C] UK a spoken warning given by a police officer or official to someone who has broken the law: *As it was her first offence, she was only given a caution.* **3** [C or U] advice or a warning: *Just a* ***word of*** *caution – the cheaper models probably aren't worth buying.*

▸verb [T] **1** If the police caution someone, they give them an official warning. **2** C2 formal to warn someone: *The newspaper cautioned its readers* ***against*** *buying shares without getting good advice first.*

cautionary /ˈkɔː.ʃən.ər.i/, /-ri/ US /ˈkɑː.ʃən.er.i/ **adj** formal giving a warning

ˌcautionary ˈtale noun [C] a story which gives a warning: *Her story is a cautionary tale for women travelling alone.*

cautious /ˈkɔː.ʃəs/ US /ˈkɑː-/ **adj 1** B2 Someone who is cautious avoids risks: *He's a cautious driver.* **2** B2 A cautious action is careful, well considered, and sometimes slow or uncertain: *a cautious approach* **3 cautious optimism** a feeling that there are some reasons to hope for a good result, even if you do not expect complete success or improvement • **cautiously** /-li/ **adv** in a cautious way • **cautiousness** /-nəs/ **noun** [U]

cava /ˈkɑː.və/ **noun** [U] a white FIZZY (= with bubbles) wine, produced in Spain

cavalcade /ˌkæv.əlˈkeɪd/ **noun** [C] a line of people, vehicles, horses, etc. following a particular route as part of a ceremony

cavalier /ˌkæv.əlˈɪər/ US /-ˈɪr/ **adj** disapproving not considering other people's feelings or safety: *That's a rather cavalier* ***attitude****.*

Cavalier /ˌkæv.əlˈɪər/ US /-ˈɪr/ **noun** [C] a supporter of the king in the English Civil War in the 1640s

cavalry /ˈkæv.əl.ri/ **noun** [U, + sing/pl verb] the group of soldiers in an army who fight in TANKS, or (especially in the past) on horses → Compare **infantry** • **cavalryman** /-mən, -mæn/ **noun** [C] (plural **-men** /-mən, -men/)

cave /keɪv/ **noun; verb**

▸noun [C] B1 a large hole in the side of a hill, CLIFF or mountain, or one that is underground

▸verb

PHRASAL VERB **cave in FALL** ▷ **1** If a ceiling, roof, or other structure caves in, it breaks and falls into the space below: *Because of the explosion, the roof of the building caved in, trapping several people.* **AGREE** ▷ **2** informal to agree to something that you were against before, after someone has persuaded you or threatened you: *At first, they refused to sign the agreement, but they caved in when they heard another firm was being approached.*

caveat /ˈkæv.i.æt/ **noun** [C] formal a warning to consider something before acting further, or a statement that limits a more general statement: *He agreed to the interview, with the caveat that he could approve the final article.* → Synonym **proviso**

caveat emptor /ˌkæv.i.ætˈemp.tɔːr/ US /-ɔːr/ formal used for saying that the person who buys something must take responsibility for the quality of goods that he or she is buying

caveman /ˈkeɪv.mæn/ **noun** [C] (plural **-men** /-men/) **1** someone who lived in a cave in the early stages of the development of human society **2** informal a modern man who is very rude or violent towards other people, especially women

caver /ˈkeɪ.vər/ US /-vɚ/ **noun** [C] UK (US **spelunker**) a person who walks and climbs in caves as a sport

cavern /ˈkæv.ən/ US /-ɚn/ **noun** [C] a large cave

cavernous /ˈkæv.ən.əs/ US /-ɚn-/ **adj** If something is cavernous, there is a very large open space inside it: *a cavernous 4,000-seat theatre*

caviar (also **caviare**) /ˈkæv.i.ɑːr/ US /-ɑːr/ **noun** [U] the eggs of various large fish, especially the STURGEON, eaten as food. Caviar is usually very expensive.

cavil /ˈkæv.əl/ **verb** [I] (**-ll-** or US usually **-l-**) formal to make unreasonable complaints, especially about things that are not important

caving /ˈkeɪ.vɪŋ/ **noun** [U] UK (US **spelunking**) the sport of walking and climbing in caves → See also **potholing**

cavity /ˈkæv.ɪ.ti/ US /-ə.t̬i/ **noun** [C] **1** a hole, or an empty space between two surfaces: *The gold was hidden in a secret cavity.* **2** a hole in a tooth

ˌcavity ˈwall noun [C] a wall of a building formed from two walls with a space, usually for air, between them. It is made in this way to keep out water and cold air.

cavort /kəˈvɔːt/ US /-ˈvɔːrt/ **verb** [I] to jump or move around in a PLAYFUL way, sometimes noisily, and often in a sexual way

caw /kɔː/ US /kɑː/ **noun** [C] the loud, rough cry of a bird such as a CROW • **caw verb** [I]

cayenne pepper /ˌkeɪ.enˈpep.ər/ US /-ɚ/ **noun** [U] a red powder made from a type of PEPPER and used to give a hot taste to food

cayman (also **caiman**) /ˈkeɪ.mən/ **noun** [C] an animal similar to an ALLIGATOR

CB /ˌsiːˈbiː/ **noun** [U] abbreviation for **Citizens' Band**

CBA /ˌsiː.biːˈeɪ/ humorous abbreviation for can't be arsed: used when you do not want to do something because you feel lazy: *'Do you want to go out?' 'CBA.'*

CBS /ˌsiː.biːˈes/ **noun** abbreviation for Columbia Broadcasting System: an organization that broadcasts on television in the US

CBT /ˌsiː.biːˈtiː/ **noun** [U] specialized abbreviation for cognitive behavioural therapy: a treatment which helps people to feel better by changing the way they think about their problems

cc /ˌsiːˈsiː/ **noun; verb**

▸noun **MEASURE** ▷ **1** abbreviation for cubic centimetre: *a 750cc motorcycle* **COPIES** ▷ **2** abbreviation for **carbon copy**: written at the end of a business letter or in an email before the names of the people who will receive a copy

▸verb [T] to send a copy of a business letter or an email to someone: *I hate it when people cc me on emails that have nothing to do with me.*

CCTV /ˌsiː.siː.tiːˈviː/ abbreviation for **closed-circuit television**: a system which sends television signals to a limited number of screens, and is often used in shops and public places to prevent crime: *CCTV cameras*

CD /ˌsiːˈdiː/ **noun** [C] A1 abbreviation for **compact disc**: a small plastic disc with a shiny surface on which information, especially high quality sound, is recorded

ˌCˈD ˌburner noun [C] (also **ˌCˈD ˌwriter**) the part of a computer that you use for putting information onto a CD

C. difficile /ˌsiːdɪˈfɪsɪliː/ **noun** [U] (also **C. diff** /ˌsiːˈdɪf/) specialized abbreviation for Clostridium difficile: a type of BACTERIUM (= an extremely small organism) that can cause serious illness and that is very difficult to treat: *The elderly are at increased risk from C. diff.*

ˌCˈD ˌplayer noun [C] A1 a machine that is used for playing music CDs

C

CD-ROM /ˌsiː.diːˈrɒm/ (US) /-ˈrɑːm/ **noun** [C or U] B1 abbreviation for compact disc read-only memory: a COMPACT DISC that holds large amounts of information that can be read by a computer but cannot be changed: *Cambridge dictionaries are available* ***on*** *CD-ROM.*

CD-RW /ˌsiː.diː.ɑːˈdʌb.l̩.juː/ (US) /-ɑːr-/ **noun** [C] abbreviation for compact disc re-writable: an empty COMPACT DISC which you can use to record information on and read information from, using a special type of DRIVE (= computer device)

ˌCˈD ˌwriter noun [C] (also **ˌCˈD ˌburner**) the part of a computer that you use for putting information onto a CD

CE /ˌsiːˈiː/ **adv** abbreviation for Common Era or Christian era: used when referring to a year after the birth of Jesus Christ when the Christian CALENDAR starts counting years: *The Scandinavian countries became Christian between 900 and 1100 CE.* → Compare **BCE, AD**

cease /siːs/ **verb; noun**

▸**verb** [I or T] formal B2 to stop something: *Whether the protests will cease remains to be seen.* ◦ *The company has decided to cease all UK operations after this year.* ◦ [+ to infinitive] *Workplace nurseries will cease* ***to*** *be liable for tax.*

▸**noun** formal **without cease** without stopping → See also **cessation**

ceasefire /ˈsiːs.faɪəʳ/ (US) /-faɪr/ **noun** [C usually singular] an agreement, usually between two armies, to stop fighting in order to allow discussions about peace: *declare a ceasefire*

ceaseless /ˈsiːs.ləs/ **adj** formal without stopping, or seeming to have no end • **ceaselessly** /-li/ **adv**

cecum noun [C] US for **caecum**

cedar /ˈsiː.dəʳ/ (US) /-dɚ/ **noun 1** [C] a tall, wide EVERGREEN tree (= one that never loses its leaves) **2** [U] (also **cedarwood**) the wood of this tree

cede /siːd/ **verb** [T] formal to allow someone else to have or own something, especially unwillingly or because you are forced to do so: *Hong Kong was ceded* ***to*** *Britain after the Opium War.*

cedilla /sɪˈdɪl.ə/ **noun** [C] (used when writing some languages) a mark made under a letter, especially c, then written as ç, to show that the letter has a special sound

Ceefax /ˈsiː.fæks/ **noun** [U] UK trademark in Britain, a system of giving written information on television, provided by the BBC

ceilidh /ˈkeɪ.li/ **noun** [C] a special event at which people dance to traditional music, especially in Scotland and Ireland

ceiling /ˈsiː.lɪŋ/ **noun** TOP OF A ROOM ▷ **1** A2 [C] the inside surface of a room which you can see when you look above you LIMIT ▷ **2** C2 [C usually singular] an upper limit, usually relating to money: *They have* ***imposed/set*** *a ceiling on pay rises.* → See also **glass ceiling**

celeb /sɪˈleb/ **noun** [C] informal short form of **celebrity**: *A number of celebs attended the party.*

celebrant /ˈsel.ɪ.brənt/ **noun** [C] a person who takes part in or the priest who leads a religious ceremony

celebrate /ˈsel.ɪ.breɪt/ **verb** ENJOY AN OCCASION ▷ **1** B1 [I or T] to take part in special enjoyable activities in order to show that a particular occasion is important: *We always celebrate our wedding anniversary* ***by*** *going out to dinner.* ◦ *If this plan works, we'll celebrate* ***in style*** *(= in a special way).* PRAISE ▷ **2** [T] formal to express admiration and approval for something or someone: *His work celebrates the energy and enthusiasm of the young.* LEAD A CEREMONY ▷ **3** [T] to lead or take part in a religious ceremony: *to celebrate Mass*

celebrated /ˈsel.ɪ.breɪ.tɪd/ (US) /-t̬ɪd/ **adj** famous for some special quality or ability: *a celebrated opera singer/city/novel* → Compare **notorious**

celebration /ˌsel.ɪˈbreɪ.ʃən/ **noun 1** B1 [C] a special social event, such as a party, when you celebrate something: *There were lively New Year celebrations all over town.* ◦ *Such good news* ***calls for*** *(= deserves) a celebration!* **2** [U] the act of celebrating something: *Let's buy some champagne* ***in*** *celebration* ***of*** *her safe arrival.*

celebratory /ˌsel.ɪˈbreɪ.tər.i/ (US) /-t̬ɚ-/ **adj** celebrating an important event or a special occasion: *When we heard she'd got the job, we all went off for a celebratory drink.*

celebrity /sɪˈleb.rɪ.ti/ (US) /-t̬i/ **noun 1** B1 [C] someone who is famous, especially in the entertainment business **2** [U] the state of being famous

celeriac /səˈler.i.æk/ **noun** [U] a type of celery with a large, round, white root, eaten as a vegetable

celerity /səˈler.ɪ.ti/ (US) /-t̬i/ **noun** [U] formal speed

celery /ˈsel.ər.i/ (US) /-ɚ-/ **noun** [U] a vegetable with long thin whitish or pale green stems that can be eaten uncooked or cooked: *a stick of celery*

celestial /sɪˈles.ti.əl/ (US) /-tʃəl/ **adj** formal of or from the sky or outside this world: *The moon is a celestial body.*

celibate /ˈsel.ɪ.bət/ **adj; noun**

▸**adj** not having sexual activity, especially because you have made a religious promise not to • **celibacy** /-bə.si/ **noun** [U]

▸**noun** [C] formal a person who does not have sex

cell /sel/ **noun** [C] ORGANISM ▷ **1** B2 the smallest basic unit of a plant or animal ROOM ▷ **2** B2 a small room with not much furniture, especially in a prison or a MONASTERY or CONVENT ELECTRICAL DEVICE ▷ **3** a device for producing electrical energy from chemical energy PART ▷ **4** a small part of something: *the cells of a honeycomb*

cellar /ˈsel.əʳ/ (US) /-ɚ/ **noun** [C] B2 a room under the ground floor of a building, usually used for storing things

-celled /-seld/ **suffix** (of a plant or an animal) containing the stated number of cells: *a single-celled life form*

cellist /ˈtʃel.ɪst/ **noun** [C] a musician who plays the cello

cellmate /ˈsel.meɪt/ **noun** [C] the person who a prisoner shares a prison cell with

cello /ˈtʃel.əʊ/ (US) /-oʊ/ **noun** [C] (plural **cellos**) (formal **violoncello**) B2 a wooden musical instrument with four strings, that is held vertically between the legs and is played by moving a BOW across the strings

Cellophane /ˈsel.ə.feɪn/ **noun** [U] trademark thin, quite stiff, transparent material used for covering goods, especially flowers and food

ˈcell phone noun [C] mainly US (also **ˌcellular ˈphone**, UK usually **ˌmobile ˈphone**) A1 a phone that is connected to the phone system by radio instead of by a wire, and can be used anywhere where its signals can be received

cellular /ˈsel.jʊ.ləʳ/ (US) /-lɚ/ **adj** ORGANISM ▷ **1** connected with the cells of a plant or animal PART ▷ **2** made of small parts: *The organization has a cellular structure (= is made of many small groups that work independently).*

cellulite /ˈsel.jʊ.laɪt/ **noun** [U] fat in the human body, especially in the upper legs, which makes the surface of the skin appear LUMPY (= not smooth)

celluloid /ˈsel.jʊ.lɔɪd/ **noun** [U] **1** old-fashioned films or the cinema generally **2** a type of plastic used to make many things, especially, in the past, photographic film

cellulose /ˈsel.jʊ.ləʊs/ (US) /-loʊs/ **noun** [U] the main substance in the cell walls of plants, also used in making paper, artificial threads and cloth, and plastics

Celsius /ˈsel.si.əs/ **noun** [U], **adj** (also **centigrade**, written abbreviation **C**) (of) a measurement of temperature on a standard in which 0° is the temperature at which water freezes, and 100° the temperature at which it boils: *Are the temperatures given **in** Celsius or Fahrenheit?* ∘ *The sample was heated to (a temperature of) 80°C.* → Compare **Fahrenheit**

Celtic /ˈkel.tɪk/, /ˈsel-/ **adj** of an ancient European people who are related to the Irish, Scots, Welsh, and Bretons, or of their language or culture: *Celtic art*

cement /sɪˈment/ **noun; verb**

▸**noun** [U] **BUILDING MATERIAL** ▷ **1** a grey powder that is mixed with water and sand to make MORTAR or with water, sand, and small stones to make concrete: *a bag of cement* ∘ *a cement factory* **GLUE** ▷ **2** a substance that sticks things together: *Dentists use cement to hold crowns and bridges in place.*

▸**verb** [T] **STICK TOGETHER** ▷ **1** to put cement on a surface or stick things together using cement **MAKE STRONGER** ▷ **2** to make something such as an agreement or friendship stronger: *The university's exchange scheme has cemented its links with many other academic institutions.*

ceˈment ˌmixer **noun** [C] a machine that has a large container that turns round and round, in which cement, water, and small stones are mixed to make concrete

cemetery /ˈsem.ə.tri/ (US) /-ter.i/ **noun** [C] (B2) an area of ground in which dead bodies are buried, especially one that is not next to a church

cenotaph /ˈsen.ə.tɑːf/, /-tæf/ **noun** [C] a public MONUMENT (= special STATUE or building) built in memory of particular people who died in war, often with their names written on it

censor /ˈsen.səʳ/ (US) /-sɚ/ **noun; verb**

▸**noun** [C] a person whose job is to read books, watch films, etc. in order to remove anything offensive from them, or who reads private letters, especially ones sent during war or from prison, to remove parts considered unsuitable

▸**verb** [T] to remove anything offensive from books, films, etc., or to remove parts considered unsuitable from private letters, especially ones sent during war or from a prison: *The book was heavily censored when first published.*

censorship /ˈsen.sə.ʃɪp/ (US) /-sɚ-/ **noun** [U] the act of censoring books, films, etc.: *censorship of the press*

censure /ˈsen.ʃəʳ/ (US) /-ʃɚ/ **noun** [U] formal strong criticism or disapproval: *His dishonest behaviour came under severe censure.* • **censure** **verb** [T] *Ministers were censured **for** their lack of decisiveness during the crisis.*

census /ˈsen.səs/ **noun** [C] a count for official purposes, especially one to count the number of people living in a country and to collect information about them: *We have a census in this country every ten years.* ∘ *She was stopped in her car for a traffic census.*

cent /sent/ **noun** [C] **1** (A2) a unit of money worth 0.01 of a dollar, or a coin with this value: *A call will cost you around 25 cents.* ∘ *On the foreign exchanges the pound rose two cents against the dollar.* **2** a unit of money worth 0.01 of a euro

centaur /ˈsen.tɔːʳ/ (US) /-tɔːr/ **noun** [C] a creature in ancient Greek stories that has a human's upper body and the lower body and legs of a horse

centenarian /ˌsen.təˈneə.ri.ən/ (US) /-ţəˈner.i-/ **noun** [C] someone who is a 100 years old or more

centenary /senˈtiː.nᵊr.i/, /-ˈten.ᵊr-/ (US) /-ˈten.ɚ-/ **noun** [C] (US usually **centennial**) (the day or year that is) 100 years after an important event: *centenary celebrations* ∘ *Next year is the centenary **of** her death.* → See also **bicentenary, tercentenary**

center /ˈsen.təʳ/ (US) /-ţɚ/ **noun, verb** US for centre

centerfold /ˈsen.tə.fəʊld/ (US) /-ţɚ.foʊld/ **noun** [C] US for **centrefold**

centerpiece /ˈsen.tə.piːs/ (US) /-ţɚ-/ **noun** [C] US for **centrepiece**

centi- /sen.ti-/ (US) /-ţi-/ **prefix** 0.01 of the stated unit: *a centimetre* ∘ *a centilitre*

centigrade /ˈsen.tɪ.greɪd/ (US) /-ţɪ-/ **noun** [U], **adj** **Celsius**

centigram /ˈsen.tɪ.græm/ (US) /-ţɪ-/ **noun** [C] (UK also **centigramme**) a unit of mass equal to 0.01 of a gram

centilitre UK (US **centiliter**) /ˈsen.tiˌliː.təʳ/ (US) /-ţiˌliː.ţɚ/ **noun** [C] (written abbreviation **cl**) a unit of measurement of liquid equal to 0.01 of a litre

centimetre UK (US **centimeter**) /ˈsen.tɪˌmiː.təʳ/ (US) /-ţɪˌmiː.ţɚ/ **noun** [C] (written abbreviation **cm**) (A2) a unit of length equal to 0.01 of a metre

centipede /ˈsen.tɪ.piːd/ (US) /-ţɪ-/ **noun** [C] a small, long, thin animal with many legs

centipede

central /ˈsen.trəl/ **adj** **NEAR THE MIDDLE** ▷ **1** (B1) in, at, from, or near the centre or most important part of something: *central Europe/London* ∘ *Of course, you pay more for premises with a central location (= in or near the centre of a town).* **IMPORTANT** ▷ **2** (C2) main or important: *a central role* ∘ *Community involvement is central **to** our plan.* **ORGANIZATION** ▷ **3** (C1) [before noun] controlled or organized in one main place: *central authorities* ∘ *the US central bank* ∘ *central planning*

ˌcentral ˈbank **noun** [C] a bank that provides services to a national government, puts the official financial plans of that government into operation, and controls the amount of money in the economy

ˌcentral ˈgovernment **noun** [U] national government from a single important city rather than local government

ˌcentral ˈheating **noun** [U] (B1) a system of heating buildings by warming air or water at one place and then sending it to different rooms in pipes

centralism /ˈsen.trə.lɪ.zᵊm/ **noun** [U] the principle or action of putting something under the control of one central place

centralize (UK also **centralise**) /ˈsen.trə.laɪz/ **verb** [T] to remove authority in a system, company, country, etc. from local places to one central place so that the whole system, etc. is under central control: *Payment of bills is now centralized (= organized at one place instead of several).* • **centralization** (UK also **centralisation**) /ˌsen.trəˈlaɪzeɪ.ʃᵊn/ **noun** [U]

centrally /ˈsen.trə.li/ **adv** **NEAR THE MIDDLE** ▷ **1** in, at, from, or near the centre or most important part of something: *centrally located* **ORGANIZATION** ▷ **2** from one main place: *centrally managed*

ˌcentral ˈnervous ˌsystem noun [U] the main system of nerve control in a living thing, consisting of the brain and the main nerves connected to it

ˌcentral reserˈvation noun [C usually singular] UK (US or Australian English **ˈmedian ˌstrip**) the narrow piece of land between the two halves of a large road

centre /ˈsen.təʳ/ (US) /-t̬ɚ/ noun; noun, adj; verb

►noun [C] UK (US **center**) **MIDDLE** ▷ **1** (A2) the middle point or part: *There was a large table in the centre of the room.* ◦ *the* ***town*** *centre* **2 centre of attention** (C2) the person or thing that everyone is most interested in and pays most attention to: *She's the centre of attention everywhere she goes.* **3 be at the centre of sth** to be most involved in a situation: *Mark was at the centre of the argument.* ◦ *A social worker was at the centre of the scandal.* **PLACE** ▷ **4** (A2) a place or building, especially one where a particular activity happens: *a sports/leisure/health centre* ◦ *a garden/shopping centre* ◦ *Grants will be given to establish centres* ***of excellence*** *(= places where a particular activity is done extremely well) in this field of research.*

►noun [S, + sing/pl verb], adj UK (US **center**) (C2) in politics, the people in a group who hold opinions that are not extreme but are between two opposites: *His political views are known to be* ***left of/right of*** *centre.* ◦ *a centre left party*

►verb [T] UK (US **center**) to put something in the middle of an area: *Centre (= put at equal distances from the left and right sides of the page) all the headings in this document.*

PHRASAL VERB **centre around/on sth** to have something as the main subject of discussion or interest: *The discussion centred around reducing waste.*

centrefold UK (US **centerfold**) /ˈsen.tə.fəʊld/ (US) /-t̬ɚ.foʊld/ noun [C] a large photograph that covers the two pages opposite each other in the middle of a magazine, usually of a young woman with few or no clothes on, or the person who appears in such a picture

ˌcentre ˈforward noun [C] in some team sports, the person who is in the middle of the front row of players who try to score goals

ˌcentre of ˈgravity noun [C usually singular] (plural **centres of gravity**) the point in an object where its weight is balanced

centrepiece UK (US **centerpiece**) /ˈsen.tə.piːs/ (US) /-t̬ɚ-/ noun [C] **IMPORTANT PART** ▷ **1** the most important or attractive part or feature of something: *The reduction of crime levels is the centrepiece* ***of*** *the president's domestic policies.* ◦ *The centrepiece* ***of*** *the shopping centre is a giant fountain.* **DECORATION** ▷ **2** a decorative object put in the centre of a table, especially for a formal meal

ˌcentre ˈspread noun [C] the two pages opposite each other in the middle of a newspaper or magazine, which deal only with one particular subject and include many pictures

ˌcentre ˈstage noun [U] **1** the middle of a theatre stage **2** a situation in which someone or something receives a lot of attention: *He* ***took*** *centre stage in his party's struggle with the unions.*

-centric /-sen.trɪk/ **suffix** having the stated thing as your main interest: *Eurocentric* • **-centrism** /-trɪ.zᵊm/ **suffix**

centrifugal /ˌsen.trɪˈfjuː.gᵊl/ adj (of a turning object) moving away from the point around which it is turning: *centrifugal* ***force***

centrifuge /ˈsen.trɪ.fjuːdʒ/ noun [C] a machine which turns a container round very quickly, causing the solids and liquids inside it to separate by centrifugal action

centripetal /ˌsen.trɪˈpiː.tᵊl/ (US) /-t̬ᵊl/ adj specialized (of a turning object) moving towards the point around which it is turning: *centripetal* ***force***

centrist /ˈsen.trɪst/ adj supporting the centre of the range of political opinions • **centrist noun** [C]

centurion /senˈtjʊə.ri.ən/ (US) /-ˈtʊr.i-/ noun [C] an officer in the army of ancient Rome who was responsible for 100 soldiers

century /ˈsen.tʃᵊr.i/ noun [C] **1** (A2) a period of 100 years: *The city centre has scarcely changed in over a century.* ◦ *This sculpture must be centuries old.* ◦ *Her medical career spanned half a century.* → Compare **millennium 2** a period of 100 years counted from what is believed to be the year of the birth of Jesus Christ: *Rome was founded in the eighth century BC (= before Christ).* ◦ *He's an expert on 15th-century Italian art.* **3** a score of 100 RUNS in cricket **4 the turn of the century** the time when one century ends and another begins: *The museum reopened at the turn of the century.*

CEO /ˌsiː.iːˈəʊ/ (US) /-ˈoʊ/ noun [C] abbreviation for **chief executive officer**: the person with the most important position in a company

cephalopod /ˈsef.ᵊl.əʊ.pɒd/ (US) /-ə.pɑːd/ noun [C] specialized an animal such as an OCTOPUS or SQUID, that has TENTACLES (= long parts like arms) around the head

ceramics /sɪˈræm.ɪks/ noun **1** [U] the art of making objects by shaping pieces of clay and then baking them until they are hard **2** [plural] the objects produced by shaping and baking clay, especially when considered as art • **ceramic** /-ɪk/ adj *ceramic tiles*

cereal /ˈsɪə.ri.əl/ (US) /ˈsɪr.i-/ noun [C or U] **1** (C1) a plant that is grown to produce grain: *cereal crops* **2** (A2) a food that is made from grain and eaten with milk, especially in the morning: *breakfast cereals*

cerebellum /ˌser.əˈbel.əm/ noun [C] (plural **cerebella** or **cerebellums**) specialized a large part at the back of the brain that controls your muscles, movement, and balance

cerebral /ˈser.ɪ.brᵊl/ adj **1** specialized relating to the brain or the cerebrum **2** formal demanding or involving careful thinking and mental effort rather than feelings: *She makes cerebral films that deal with important social issues.*

ˌcerebral ˈcortex noun [C, C] specialized the grey outer layer of the cerebrum, responsible for language, thinking, creating new ideas, etc.

ˌcerebral ˈhemisphere noun [C] specialized one of the two halves of the cerebrum, each of which controls the opposite side of the body

cerebral palsy /ˌser.ə.brᵊlˈpɔːl.zi/ noun [U] a physical condition involving permanent tightening of the muscles that is caused by damage to the brain around or before the time of birth

cerebrum /sɪˈriː.brəm/ noun [C] (plural **cerebra** /-brə/ or **cerebrums**) specialized the front part of the brain, which is involved with thought, decision, emotion, and character

ceremonious /ˌser.ɪˈməʊ.ni.əs/ (US) /-ˈmoʊ-/ adj describes behaviour that is very or too formal or polite • **ceremoniously** /-li/ adv

ceremony /ˈser.ɪ.mə.ni/ noun **FORMAL ACTS** ▷ **1** (B1) [C or U] (formal **ceremonial**) (a set of) formal acts, often fixed and traditional, performed on important social or religious occasions: *a wedding/graduation ceremony* **FORMAL BEHAVIOUR** ▷ **2** [U] very formal and polite behaviour: *She arrived at the airport without the* ***pomp and*** *ceremony that usually accompanies important politicians.* ◦ *I handed her my letter of resignation* ***without*** *ceremony (= in an informal way).* • **ceremonial** /ˌser.ɪˈməʊ.ni.əl/ (US) /-ˈmoʊ-/ **adj** *ceremonial occasions/duties* • **ceremonially** /ˌser.ɪˈməʊ.ni.ə.li/ (US) /-ˈmoʊ-/ **adv**

cerise /səˈriːs/ **noun** [U] a dark reddish-pink colour • **cerise adj**

cert. noun [C] written abbreviation for **certificate**

cert /sɜːt/ (US) /sɝːt/ **noun** [C usually singular] UK informal something or someone that is thought to be certain to happen or be successful: *With all her experience she's a* ***dead*** *cert* ***for*** *(= is certain to get) the job.* ◦ [+ to infinitive] *The Russian team is a cert* ***to*** *win the gold medal.*

certain /ˈsɜː.tən/ (US) /ˈsɝː-/ **adj; determiner; pronoun**

▸**adj** **WITHOUT DOUBT** ▷ **1** B1 having no doubt or knowing exactly that something is true, or known to be true, correct, exact, or effective: [+ (that)] *Are you absolutely certain* ***(that)*** *you gave them the right number?* ◦ *I* ***feel*** *certain* ***(that)*** *you're doing the right thing.* ◦ *You should* ***make*** *certain* ***(that)*** *everyone understands the instructions.* ◦ *The police* ***seem*** *certain* ***(that)*** *they will find the people responsible for the attack.* ◦ [+ question word] *I'm not certain* ***how*** *much it will cost.* ◦ *He was quite certain* ***about/of*** *his attacker's identity.* ◦ *One thing is certain – she won't resign willingly.* **2 know/say for certain** C1 to know or say something without doubt: *I don't know for certain if she's coming.* ◦ *I can't say for certain how long I'll be there.* **EXTREMELY LIKELY** ▷ **3** B1 impossible to avoid or extremely likely: [+ to infinitive] *The population explosion is certain* ***to*** *cause widespread famine.* ◦ *Oil prices are certain* ***to*** *rise following the agreement to limit production.* ◦ *After all his hard work, he's certain* ***to*** *pass his exams.* ◦ *The team looks* ***almost*** *certain* ***to*** *win the match.* ◦ [+ (that)] ***It*** *is virtually certain* ***(that)*** *she will win the gold medal.* ◦ *Even if a ceasefire can be agreed, how can they* ***make*** *certain* ***(that)*** *neither side breaks it?* ◦ *Cancer sufferers no longer face certain death as they once did.* ◦ *This scandal will mean certain defeat for the party in the election.* **NAMED** ▷ **4** [before noun] formal named but neither famous nor known well: *I had lunch today with a certain George Michael – not* ***the*** *George Michael, I should explain.* **LIMITED** ▷ **5** [before noun] limited: *I like modern art to a certain* ***extent/degree****, but I don't like the really experimental stuff.*

▸**determiner** **1** B1 particular but not named or described: *We have certain reasons for our decision, which have to remain confidential.* ◦ *Do you think war is justifiable in certain circumstances?* ◦ *Certain members of the audience may disagree with what I'm about to say.* **2 a certain** B2 used before a noun when it is difficult to describe something exactly or give its exact amount: *The song has a certain appeal, but I'm not sure what it is.*

▸**pronoun** formal some: *Certain* ***of*** *the candidates were well below the usual standard, but others were very good indeed.*

certainly /ˈsɜː.tən.li/ (US) /ˈsɝː-/ **adv** **IN NO DOUBT** ▷ **1** A2 used to reply completely or to emphasize something and show that there is no doubt about it: *She certainly had a friend called Mark, but I don't know whether he was her boyfriend.* ◦ *'This is rather a difficult question.' 'Yes, it's certainly not easy.'* ◦ *'Do you think more money should be given to education?' 'Certainly!'* ◦ *'Had you forgotten about our anniversary?' 'Certainly not! I've reserved a table at Michel's*

restaurant for this evening.' **2** A2 used when agreeing or disagreeing strongly to a request: *'Could you lend me £10?' 'Certainly.'* ◦ *'Did you take any money out of my purse?' 'Certainly not!'* **EXTREMELY LIKELY** ▷ **3** very likely to happen: *She will certainly win the election if the opinion polls are accurate.*

certainty /ˈsɜː.tən.ti/ (US) /ˈsɝː-/ **noun** **IN NO DOUBT** ▷ **1** [C] something that cannot be doubted: *There are few absolute certainties in life.* **2** B2 [U] the state of being completely confident or having no doubt about something: *I'm unable to answer that question* ***with*** *any certainty.* **EXTREMELY LIKELY** ▷ **3** C2 [C] something that is very likely to happen: *Joan will win – that's a certainty.* ◦ [+ to infinitive] *Joan is a certainty* ***to*** *win.*

certifiable /ˈsɜː.tɪ.faɪ.ə.bl̩/ (US) /ˈsɝː.t̬ə-/ **adj** **1** mentally ill **2** informal behaving in a silly or stupid way: *Simon's washing his car again – that man's certifiable!*

certificate /səˈtɪf.ɪ.kət/ (US) /sɚ-/ **noun** [C] **1** B1 an official document which states that the information on it is true: *a birth/marriage/death certificate* ◦ *a doctor's/medical certificate* **2** B1 the qualification that you receive when you are successful in an exam: *She has a Certificate in Drama Education.*

certified /ˈsɜː.tɪ.faɪd/ (US) /ˈsɝː.t̬ə-/ **adj** [before noun] having a document that proves that you have successfully finished a course of training: *a certified teacher/nurse*

ˌcertified ˈmail **noun** [U] US for **recorded delivery**

ˌcertified ˌpublic acˈcountant **noun** [C] (abbreviation **CPA**) US for **chartered** accountant (= an accountant who has received special training)

certify /ˈsɜː.tɪ.faɪ/ (US) /ˈsɝː.t̬ə-/ **verb** **1** [I or T] to say in a formal or official way, usually in writing, that something is true or correct: [+ (that)] *I hereby certify* ***(that)*** *the above information is true and accurate.* ◦ [+ noun/adj] *The driver was certified* ***(as)*** *dead on arrival at the hospital.* ◦ *The meat has been certified* ***(as)*** *fit for human consumption.* **2** [T] to say officially that someone is mentally ill: *As a young man, he had been certified and sent to a hospital for the mentally ill.* • **certification** /ˌsɜː.tɪ.fɪˈkeɪ.ʃən/ (US) /ˌsɝː.t̬ə-/ **noun** [U]

certitude /ˈsɜː.tɪ.tjuːd/ (US) /ˈsɝː.t̬ə.tuːd/ **noun** [U] formal the state of being certain or confident: *It is impossible to predict the outcome of the negotiations with any degree of certitude.*

cerulean /səˈruː.li.ən/ **adj** literary deep blue in colour

ˌcervical ˈsmear **noun** [C] a medical test in which some cells are taken from a woman's cervix (= the opening of her WOMB) and then tested to discover if she has CANCER

cervix /ˈsɜː.vɪks/ (US) /ˈsɝː-/ **noun** [C] (plural **cervices** /-vɪs.iːz/) specialized the narrow lower part of the WOMB that leads into the VAGINA • **cervical** /səˈvaɪ.kəl/, /ˈsɜː.vɪ-/ (US) /ˈsɝː.vɪ-/ **adj** *cervical cancer/screening*

cesarean /sɪˈzeə.ri.ən/ (US) /-zer.i-/ **noun** [C], **adj** US for **caesarean (section)**

cesium /ˈsiː.zi.əm/ **noun** [U] US for **caesium**

cessation /sesˈeɪ.ʃən/ **noun** [C or U] formal ending or stopping: *Religious leaders have called for a total cessation* ***of*** *the bombing campaign.* → See also **cease**

cesspit /ˈses.pɪt/ **noun** [C] **1** (also **cesspool**) a large underground hole or container that is used for collecting and storing solid waste, urine, and dirty water **2** disapproving a situation that causes strong shock, disapproval, and dislike

c'est la vie /ˌseɪ.læˈviː/ **exclamation** used to say that situations of that type happen in life, and you cannot do anything about them: *I can't go to the football on Saturday – I've got to work. Oh well, c'est la vie.*

cetacean /sɪˈteɪ.ʃən/ noun [C] specialized any of various types of mammal, such as the WHALE, that live in the sea like fish • **cetacean adj**

C

cf. /siːˈef/ formal used in writing when you want the reader to make a comparison between the subject being discussed and something else

CFC /ˌsiː.efˈsiː/ noun [C] abbreviation for chlorofluorocarbon: a gas used in fridges and, in the past, in AEROSOLS (= a metal container in which liquids are kept under pressure and forced out in drops): *CFCs cause damage to the ozone layer.*

CGI /siː.dʒiːˈaɪ/ noun [U] abbreviation for **computer-generated imagery**

cha-cha(-cha) /ˈtʃɑː.tʃɑː, ˌtʃɑː.tʃɑːˈtʃɑː/ noun [C] (a piece of music written for) an energetic modern dance, originally from South America, involving small fast steps and movement of the bottom from side to side

chad /tʃæd/ noun [C] the piece that you remove when you make a hole in a piece of paper or card

chador /ˈtʃɑː.dəʳ/ (US) /-ɚ/ noun [C] (also **chadar**) a large, usually black cloth worn by some Muslim women to cover their heads and bodies

chafe /tʃeɪf/ verb **RUB** ▷ **1** [I or T] to make or become damaged or sore by rubbing: *The bracelet was so tight that it started to chafe (my wrist).* **BE ANNOYED** ▷ **2** [I usually + adv/prep] to be or become annoyed or lose patience because of rules or limits: *We have been chafing **under** petty regulations for too long.*

chaff /tʃɑːf/ (US) /tʃæf/ noun [U] **1** the outer layer that is separated from grains such as WHEAT before they are used as food **2** dried grass and stems when used to feed CATTLE

chaffinch /ˈtʃæf.ɪntʃ/ noun [C] a common small European bird

chagrin /ˈʃæg.rɪn/ noun [U] formal disappointment or anger, especially when caused by a failure or mistake: *My children have never shown an interest in music, much **to** my chagrin.* • **chagrined** /-rɪnd/ adj

chai /tʃaɪ/ noun [U] Indian English tea, with milk and sugar added

chain /tʃeɪn/ noun; verb

▸noun **CONNECTED THINGS** ▷ **1** (B2) [C] a set of connected or related things: *She has built up a chain of 180 bookshops across the country.* ◦ *His resignation was followed by a remarkable chain **of events**.* **RINGS** ▷ **2** (A2) [C or U] (a length of) rings usually made of metal that are connected together and used for fastening, pulling, supporting, or limiting freedom, or as jewellery: *The gates were locked with a padlock and a heavy steel chain.* ◦ *Put the chain on the door if you are alone in the house.* ◦ *Mary was wearing a beautiful silver chain around her neck.* **3 in chains** tied with chains: *The hostages were kept in chains for 23 hours a day.* **4** [plural] a fact or situation that limits a person's freedom: *At last the country has freed itself from the chains **of** the authoritarian regime.* **HOUSE SALE** ▷ **5** [C] UK a situation in which someone selling their house cannot complete the sale because the person who wants to buy it needs to sell their house first: *Some sellers refuse to exchange contracts with buyers who are in a chain.*

▸verb [T usually + adv/prep] to fasten someone or something using a chain: *It's so cruel to keep a pony chained **up** like that all the time.* ◦ *They chained themselves **to** lampposts in protest at the judge's decision.* ◦ figurative *I don't want a job where I'm chained **to** a desk for eight hours a day.*

ˈchain ˌletter noun [C] a letter sent to several people, who are each asked to send copies to several others, that sometimes threatens that bad things will happen if they do not send these copies

ˌchain-link ˈfence noun [C] US a fence made of strong wire net

ˈchain ˌmail noun [U] (also **mail**) small metal rings that have been joined together to look like cloth. It was used in the past to protect the body of a soldier from injury when fighting.

ˌchain reˈaction noun [C] a set of related events in which each event causes the next one, or a chemical reaction in which each change causes another

chainsaw /ˈtʃeɪn.sɔː/ noun [C] a large SAW with a motor, used especially for cutting trees, that has teeth-like parts fitted onto a continuous chain

ˈchain-smoke verb [I] to smoke cigarettes one after another: *Joan's under a lot of pressure these days – she's been chain-smoking ever since her divorce.* • **ˈchain-smoker noun [C]**

ˈchain ˌstitch noun [U] a decorative sewing style in which each STITCH is connected to the next so that they form a chain

ˈchain ˌstore noun [C] (one of) a group of shops that belong to a single company, have the same appearance, and sell similar goods

chair /tʃeəʳ/ (US) /tʃer/ noun; verb

▸noun [C] **FURNITURE** ▷ **1** (A1) a seat for one person, which has a back, usually four legs, and sometimes two arms → See also **armchair, deckchair, pushchair, wheelchair 2 the chair** informal for **the electric chair** **TITLE** ▷ **3** (the official position of) a person in charge of a meeting or organization, or a position in an official group, or the person in charge of or having an important position in a college or university department: *All questions should be addressed to the chair.*

▸verb [T] to be the person in charge of a meeting, etc.: *Would you like to chair tomorrow's meeting?*

chairlift /ˈtʃeə.lɪft/ (US) /ˈtʃer-/ noun [C] a set of chairs, hanging from a moving wire driven by a motor, that carries people, especially people who are going skiing, up and down mountains

chairman (plural **-men** /-mən/) (also **chair, chairperson**) /ˈtʃeə.mən/ noun [C] a person in charge of a meeting or organization

chairmanship /ˈtʃeə.mən.ʃɪp/ (US) /ˈtʃer-/ noun [C usually singular] the position of being a chairman or the period during which someone is a chairman: *His chairmanship lasted a year.*

chairwoman /ˈtʃeəˌwʊm.ən/ (US) /ˈtʃer-/ noun [C] (plural **-women** /-ˌwɪmɪn/) a woman in charge of a meeting or organization

chaise longue /ˌʃezˈlɔ̃ːŋ/ noun [C] (plural **chaises longues**) a long, low seat, with an arm at one side and usually a low back along half of its length, that a person can stretch out his or her legs on

chakra /ˈtʃæk.rə/ noun [C] specialized in YOGA and traditional South Asian medicine, one of the seven centres of energy in the human body

chalet /ˈʃæl.eɪ/ noun [C] a small wooden house found in mountain areas, especially in Switzerland, or a house built in a similar style, especially one used by people on holiday

chalice /ˈtʃæl.ɪs/ noun [C] **1** in Christian ceremonies, a large, decorative gold or silver cup from which wine is drunk **2** in magic, a cup representing the element of water

chalk /tʃɔːk/ (US) /tʃɑːk/ **noun; verb**
▸**noun** [C or U] a type of soft white rock, or (a stick of) this rock or a similar substance used for writing or drawing • **chalky** /ˈtʃɔː.ki/ (US) /ˈtʃɑː-/ **adj** *The soil in this area is very chalky (= contains chalk).* • **chalkiness** /ˈtʃɔː.ki.nəs/ (US) /ˈtʃɑː-/ **noun** [U]

IDIOM **be like chalk and cheese** UK If two people are like chalk and cheese, they are completely different from each other: *My brother and I are like chalk and cheese.*

▸**verb** [I or T] to write something with a piece of chalk

IDIOM **chalk sth up to experience** to accept failure and learn from a particular experience: *'So your new job didn't work out very well?' 'No, it didn't, but never mind – chalk **it** up to experience.'*

PHRASAL VERB **chalk sth up** to achieve something, such as a VICTORY, or to score points in a game: *Today's victory is the fifth that the Irish team has chalked up this year.* ◦ *It was doubtful whether the Conservatives could chalk up a fourth successive election victory, but they did.*

chalkboard /ˈtʃɔːk.bɔːd/ (US) /ˈtʃɑːk.bɔːrd/ **noun** [C] US for **blackboard**

challah (also **hallah**) /ˈhɒ.lə/ **noun** [C or U] a type of bread that Jewish people eat on special religious days

challenge /ˈtʃæl.ɪndʒ/ **noun; verb**
▸**noun DIFFICULT JOB** ▷ **1** (B1) [C or U] (the situation of being faced with) something that needs great mental or physical effort in order to be done successfully and therefore tests a person's ability: *Finding a solution to this problem is one of the greatest challenges **faced** by scientists today.* ◦ *You know me – I like a challenge.* ◦ *It's going to be a difficult job but I'm sure she'll **rise to** the challenge.* **INVITATION** ▷ **2** [C] an invitation to compete or take part, especially in a game or argument: *'I bet you can't eat all that food on your plate.' 'Is that a challenge?'* ◦ [+ to infinitive] *She **issued** a challenge **to** her rival candidates to take part in a public debate.* **QUESTION** ▷ **3** (C2) [C or U] asking if something is true or legal: *The result of the vote **poses** a serious challenge **to** the government's credibility.* ◦ *Because of the way this research was conducted, its findings are open to challenge.* **INSTRUCTION** ▷ **4** [C] an instruction given by a soldier or guard at a border or gate, telling someone to stand still and say their name and reasons for being there **REFUSAL** ▷ **5** [C] legal the act of refusing to accept someone as a member of a JURY: *A challenge **to** a member of the jury should be made before the trial begins.*

> Word partners for **challenge** (**DIFFICULT JOB**)
> *a big/exciting/major/serious* challenge • *pose/present* a challenge • *accept/face* a challenge • *relish* a challenge • *rise to* the challenge

> Word partners for **challenge** (**INVITATION**)
> *issue/throw down* a challenge (to sb) • *accept/take up* a challenge

> Word partners for **challenge** (**QUESTION**)
> *pose/present* a challenge (to sb) • a *credible/direct/serious/strong* challenge • a challenge *to* sb/sth

▸**verb** [T] **INVITE** ▷ **1** to invite someone to compete or take part, especially in a game or argument: *Tina has challenged me **to** a game of poker* **DOUBT** ▷ **2** (B2) to question if something is true or legal: *Children challenge their parents' authority far more nowadays than they did in the past.* **TEST** ▷ **3** to test someone's ability or determination **STOP** ▷ **4** to tell someone at a border or gate to stand still and say their name and reasons for being there **REFUSE TO ACCEPT** ▷ **5** legal to refuse to accept someone as a member of a JURY

challenger /ˈtʃæl.ɪn.dʒəʳ/ (US) /-dʒɚ/ **noun** [C] someone who tries to win a competition, fight, or sports event from someone who has previously won it

challenging /ˈtʃæl.ɪn.dʒɪŋ/ **adj** (B1) difficult, in a way that tests your ability or determination: *This has been a challenging time for us all.*

chamber /ˈtʃeɪm.bəʳ/ (US) /-bɚ/ **noun ROOM** ▷ **1** [C] formal a room used for a special or official purpose, or a group of people who form (part of) a parliament: *Meetings of the council are held in the council chamber.* ◦ *a **torture** chamber* ◦ *There are two chambers in the British parliament – the House of Commons is the lower chamber, and the House of Lords is the upper chamber.* **2** [plural] a judge's private office. A judge may have legal discussions with lawyers in private in his or her chambers. **3** [C] Indian English an office, especially of a person in an important position **4 in chambers** formal UK legal If a trial is in chambers, it happens in a court room without the public, newspaper REPORTERS, etc. being there. **BEDROOM** ▷ **5** [C] old use a room in a house, especially a bedroom **SPACE** ▷ **6** [C] specialized a closed space in a machine, plant, or body: *The human heart has four chambers.*

chambermaid /ˈtʃeɪm.bə.meɪd/ (US) /-bɚ-/ **noun** [C] a woman employed in a hotel to clean and tidy bedrooms

ˈchamber ˌmusic **noun** [U] music written for a small group of musicians so that it can be performed easily in a small room, or, in the past, in a private home

ˌchamber of ˈcommerce **noun** [C] (plural **chambers of commerce**) an organization consisting of people in business, who work together to improve business in their town or local area

ˈchamber ˌorchestra **noun** [C] a small ORCHESTRA

ˈchamber ˌpot **noun** [C] a large, round, bowl-shaped container, which in the past was kept under a bed and used as a toilet at night or during an illness

chameleon /kəˈmiː.li.ən/ **noun** [C] **ANIMAL** ▷ **1** a LIZARD that changes skin colour to match what surrounds it so that it cannot be seen **PERSON** ▷ **2** a person who changes their opinions or behaviour to please other people

chamois /ˈʃæm.wɑː/ **noun** (plural **chamois**) **ANIMAL** ▷ **1** [C] a small animal like a GOAT that lives in the mountains of Europe and southwest Asia **LEATHER** ▷ **2** (also ˌ**chamois ˈleather**, ˌ**shammy** (ˈ**leather**)) [C or U] (a piece of) soft leather used for cleaning and making things shine, or (a piece of) cotton cloth made to feel like leather

champ /tʃæmp/ **verb; noun**
▸**verb** [I or T] to **chomp**

IDIOM **champ at the bit** (US also **chomp at the bit**) to be eager and not willing to wait to do something

▸**noun** [C] informal for **champion**

champagne /ʃæmˈpeɪn/ **noun** [U] (UK old-fashioned informal **champers**) (A2) an expensive white or pink FIZZY (= with bubbles) wine made in the Champagne area of Eastern France, or, more generally, any similar wine. Champagne is often drunk to celebrate something: *We always celebrate our wedding anniversary with a bottle of champagne.*

chamˈpagne ˌflute **noun** [C] (also **flute**) a tall, narrow glass with a long stem, used for drinking champagne

ˌchampagne ˈsocialist **noun** [C] disapproving a rich

person who says he or she supports a fair society in which everyone has equal rights and the rich help the poor, but who may not behave in this way

champion /ˈtʃæm.pi.ən/ noun; verb; adj, exclamation

C

▸noun [C] **WINNER** ▷ **1** B1 (informal **champ**) someone or something, especially a person or animal, that has beaten all other competitors in a competition: *an Olympic champion* ◦ *She is the world champion for the third year in succession.* ◦ *The defending champion will play his first match of the tournament tomorrow.* ◦ *Who are the reigning European football champions?* **SUPPORTER** ▷ **2** C2 a person who enthusiastically supports, defends, or fights for a person, belief, right, or principle: *She has long been a champion* ***of*** *prisoners' rights/the disabled/free speech.*

▸verb [T] to support, defend, or fight for a person, belief, right, or principle enthusiastically: *He has championed constitutional reform for many years.*

▸adj, exclamation Northern English informal excellent

championship /ˈtʃæm.pi.ən.ʃɪp/ noun **COMPETITION** ▷ **1** B1 [C] a high-level competition to decide who is the best, especially in a sport: *the British Diving Championship* ◦ *The world championships will be held in Scotland next year.* ◦ *He has been playing championship tennis for three years now.* **2** [C] the position of being a champion: *She has held the championship for the past three years.* **SUPPORT** ▷ **3** [U] the support someone gives to a person, belief, right, or principle

chance /tʃɑːns/ US /tʃæns/ noun; verb

▸noun **OPPORTUNITY** ▷ **1** B1 [C] an occasion which allows something to be done: *I didn't* ***get/have*** *a chance to speak to her.* ◦ [+ to infinitive] *If you* ***give*** *me a chance* ***to*** *speak, I'll explain.* ◦ *Society has to* ***give*** *prisoners a* ***second*** *chance when they come out of jail.* ◦ *He left and I* ***missed*** *my chance to say goodbye to him.* ◦ *I'd go now* ***given half a*** *chance (= if I had the slightest opportunity).* → Synonym **opportunity** **POSSIBILITY** ▷ **2** B1 [S or plural] the level of possibility that something will happen: *You'd have* ***a*** *better chance/more chance* ***of*** *passing your exams if you worked a bit harder.* ◦ [+ (that)] *There's* ***a good*** *chance* ***(that)*** *I'll have this essay finished by tomorrow.* ◦ *There's* ***a slim/slight*** *chance* ***(that)*** *I might have to go to Manchester next week.* ◦ *If we hurry, there's still* ***an outside*** *(= very small) chance* ***of*** *catch****ing*** *the plane.* ◦ *'Is there any chance* ***of*** *speak****ing*** *to him?'* ***'Not a/No*** *chance, I'm afraid.'* ◦ *I don't think I* ***stand/have a*** *chance* ***of*** *winning.* ◦ UK *John thinks they're* ***in with a*** *chance (= they have a possibility of doing or getting what they want).* ◦ *Her resignation has improved my chances* ***of*** *promotion.* ◦ *What are her chances* ***of*** *survival?* ◦ [+ that] *What are the chances* ***that*** *they'll win?* → Synonym **likelihood** **RISK** ▷ **3** B2 [C] a possibility that something negative will happen: *I'm delivering my work by hand – I'm not* ***taking*** *any chances.* ◦ *There's a chance* ***of*** *injury in almost any sport.* → Synonym **risk** **LUCK** ▷ **4** B1 [U] the force that causes things to happen without any known cause or reason for doing so: *Roulette is a game of chance.* ◦ *I got this job completely* ***by*** *chance.* ◦ [+ (that)] ***It*** *was* ***pure/sheer*** *chance* ***(that)*** *we met.* ◦ *We must double-check everything and* ***leave nothing to*** *chance.* **5 by any chance** C2 used to ask a question or request in a polite way: *Are you Hungarian, by any chance?* ◦ *Could you lend me a couple of pounds, by any chance?*

IDIOMS **chance would be a fine thing** UK informal said when you would very much like something to happen but there is no possibility that it will: *'You should relax a bit more.' 'Chance would be a fine thing.'*

> **Word partners for chance (OPPORTUNITY)**
> *give/offer* sb a chance • *get/have* a chance • *miss/pass up* a chance • *jump at/leap at/seize* a chance • a *second* chance • a *last* chance • a *rare* chance • a chance *of* doing sth

> **Word partners for chance (POSSIBILITY)**
> an *outside/slight/slim/small* chance • a *fair/fighting/good/realistic* chance • *be in with/have/stand* a chance • *lessen/minimize/reduce* the chances of sth • *improve* the chances of sth • *fancy* sb's chances

• **(the) chances are** informal C2 it is likely: *Chances are* ***(that)*** *they'll be late anyway.* • **not give much for sb's chances** to not believe someone will succeed: *I wouldn't give much for his chances in the next race.*

▸verb **RISK** ▷ **1** [T] to risk something: *You'd be a fool to chance your life savings* ***on*** *a single investment.* **LUCK** ▷ **2** [I] old-fashioned or literary to happen or do something by chance: [+ to infinitive] *They chanced* ***to*** *be in the restaurant when I arrived.* ◦ *I chanced* ***on/upon*** *(= found unexpectedly) some old love letters in a drawer.* ◦ *Ten years after leaving school, we chanced* ***on/upon*** *(= unexpectedly met) each other in Regent Street.*

IDIOM **chance your arm** to take a risk in order to get something that you want: *Aren't you chancing your arm a bit giving up a secure job to start up a business?*

chancel /ˈtʃɑːn.səl/ US /ˈtʃæn-/ noun [C] the part of a church containing the ALTAR, where the priests and CHOIR sit

chancellery /ˈtʃɑːn.səl.ər.i/ US /ˈtʃæn.səl.ɚ-/ noun [C] a building or room where a chancellor works or lives, or the people who work in a chancellor's offices

chancellor /ˈtʃɑːn.səl.əʳ/ US /ˈtʃæn.səl.ɚ/ noun [C] C2 a person in a position of the highest or high rank, especially in a government or university: *Helmut Kohl became the first Chancellor of a united Germany in 1990.* ◦ *A former politician has been appointed Chancellor of the university.* • **chancellorship** /-ʃɪp/ noun [S]

ˌChancellor of the Exˈchequer noun the person in the UK government who is responsible for deciding tax levels and how much money the government can spend

chancy /ˈtʃɑːn.si/ US /ˈtʃæn-/ adj informal involving the possibility of something bad happening: *Investing in the stock market is a chancy business.*

chandelier /ˌʃæn.dəˈlɪəʳ/ US /-ˈlɪr/ noun [C] a decorative light which hangs from the ceiling and has several parts like branches for holding BULBS or, especially in the past, candles

chandelier

chandler /ˈtʃɑːnd.ləʳ/ US /ˈtʃænd.lɚ/ noun [C] a person who trades in supplies for ships

change /tʃeɪndʒ/ verb; noun

▸verb **BECOME DIFFERENT** ▷ **1** A1 [T] to exchange one thing for another thing, especially of a similar type: *She's just changed* ***jobs.*** ◦ *Let's change* ***the subject*** *(= talk about something different).* **2** A2 [I or T] to make or become different: *I almost didn't recognize her – she'd changed so much.* ◦ *That was 20 years ago and things have changed since then.* ◦ *Nothing changes, does it – I've been away two*

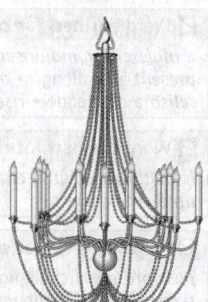

C

years and the office still looks exactly the same. ◦ *People have changed their diets a lot over the past few years.* ◦ *I'm going to change my hairstyle.* **3** B1 [I or T] to take something you have bought back to a shop and exchange it for something else: *I had to change those trousers I bought* ***for*** *(= take them back to the shop in order to get) a bigger pair.* **4 change your mind** B1 to form a new opinion or make a new decision about something that is different from your old one: *If you change your mind about coming tonight, just give me a call.* ◦ *When I first met him I didn't like him but I've changed my mind.* **5 change for the better** to improve: *Her attitude has definitely changed for the better since she started this new job.* **6 change places** to be in someone else's situation: *I wouldn't change places with him for the world!* **7 change your ways** to improve the bad parts of your behaviour: *If he wants to carry on living here, he's going to have to change his ways and learn to be a bit more tidy.* **TRANSPORT** ▷ **8** A2 [I or T] to get off a train, bus, etc. and catch another in order to continue a journey: *I had to change (trains) twice to get there.* ◦ *Change at Peterborough for York.* **MONEY** ▷ **9** A2 [T] to get or give money in exchange for money, either because you want it in smaller units, or because you want the same value in foreign money: *Could you change a £10 note (****for*** *two fives), please?* ◦ *Could you change a £5 note* ***for*** *me?* ◦ *I need to change my dollars* ***for/into*** *English money.* **CLOTHES/BEDS** ▷ **10** A2 [I or T] to remove one set of clothes and put a different set on yourself or a young child, especially a baby, or to remove dirty sheets from a bed and put clean ones on it: *You don't need to change – you look great as you are.* ◦ *I'll just change* ***into*** *(= get dressed in) something a bit smarter.* ◦ *Give me five minutes to change* ***out of*** *(= remove) my work clothes and I'll come out with you.* ◦ *How often do you think he changes his shirt?* ◦ *Could you change the* ***baby*** *(= the baby's* NAPPY*)?* ◦ *I've changed the* ***sheets****/the* ***bed*** *(= the sheets on the bed) in the guest room.* **WIND/SEA** ▷ **11** [I] When the wind or the TIDE (= the rise and fall of the sea) changes, it starts to move in a different direction: *The tide is starting to change.* **SPEED** ▷ **12** [I or T] (US usually **shift**) to put a vehicle into a different GEAR, usually in order to change the speed at which it is moving: *to change* ***gear*** ◦ *I changed* ***into*** *fourth (gear).* ◦ UK *Change* ***down*** *to go round the corner.*

IDIOMS **change (your) tack** to try a different method to deal with the same problem: *I've written twice and received no reply, so I might change tack and call her.* • **change your tune** disapproving to change your opinion completely, especially because you know it will bring you an advantage: *He was against the idea to start with, but he soon changed his tune when he realized how much money he'd get.* • **change hands** to go from one owner to another: *That Italian restaurant is nowhere near as good since it changed hands.*

PHRASAL VERBS **change over** to stop using or having one thing and to start using or having something else: *We've just changed over* ***from*** *gas central heating* ***to*** *electric.* • **change sth round/around** to move objects such as furniture into different positions: *The room looks very different since you've changed the furniture round.*

►noun **BECOMING DIFFERENT** ▷ **1** A2 [C or U] the act of becoming different, or the result of something becoming different: *Let me know if there's any change* ***in*** *the situation.* ◦ *We're living in a time of great change.* ◦ *We need a change* ***of*** *government.* ◦ *a change* ***in*** *lifestyle* ◦ *They've* ***made*** *a lot of changes* ***to*** *the house.* ◦ *The new management will* ***make fundamental/radical/sweeping*** *changes (= do things in a very different way).* **2** B1 [S] something that is pleasant or interesting because it is unusual or new: *It's nice to see her smile* ***for a*** *change.* ◦ *'Shall we eat in the garden?' 'Why not – it'll* ***make a*** *change.'* ◦ *We've always had a red car – it's time we* ***had a*** *change!* **3 change of scene** a new situation: *She'd been with the same company for too many years and felt she needed a change of scene, so she applied for a job as a stage manager.*

> **Other ways of saying change**
>
> The verb **alter** is a common alternative to 'change':
>
> *We've had to* ***alter*** *our plans.*
>
> If you often change something that you do, you can use the verb **vary**:
>
> *Try to* ***vary*** *the children's diet a little.*
>
> If someone changes the purpose or appearance of something, you can use the verb **convert**, or the phrasal verb **turn into**:
>
> *We're going to* ***convert*** *the spare bedroom into an office.*
>
> *There are plans to* ***turn*** *his latest book* ***into*** *a movie.*
>
> If you change something completely and improve it, the verb **transform** is sometimes used:
>
> *The riverside area has been* ***transformed*** *into a shopping and sports complex.*
>
> If you change something slightly in order to improve it, you can use the verb **modify**:
>
> *The engine was* ***modified*** *to improve its performance.*
>
> If someone changes from doing or using one thing to doing or using another, the verb **switch** is sometimes used:
>
> *We've* ***switched*** *over to low-fat milk.*
>
> *Jack has just* ***switched*** *jobs.*

> **Common mistake: change**
>
> **Warning:** Choose the right verb!
>
> Don't say 'do changes', say **make changes**, or in slightly more formal English **implement changes**:
>
> ~~*I suggest you do some changes to the programme.*~~
>
> *I suggest you make some changes to the programme.*

> **Word partners for change noun**
>
> a ***fundamental/major/significant*** change • a ***dramatic/radical/sweeping*** change • ***implement/make*** a change • ***undergo*** a change • ***bring about/cause*** a change • a change ***in/to*** sth • a change ***of*** sth

MONEY ▷ **4** A2 [U] money in the form of coins rather than notes: *She gave me £5* ***in*** *change.* ◦ *My dad always used to carry a lot of* ***loose/small*** *change (= coins) in his pocket.* **5** [U] smaller units of money given in exchange for larger units of the same amount: *Have you got change for a 20-dollar bill?* **6** A2 [U] the money that is returned to someone who has paid for something that costs less than the amount that they gave: *I think you've given me the* ***wrong*** *change.* **CLOTHES** ▷ **7** [C] the action of putting on different clothes: *She did a quick change before going on TV.* **8 a change of clothes** A2 a set of clothes as well as the ones that you are wearing: *You'll need a change of clothes if you're staying overnight.* **TRANSPORT** ▷ **9** [C] the action of getting off a train, bus, etc.

and catching another in order to continue a journey: *I hate journeys where you've got a lot of changes.*

IDIOMS **the change (of life)** old-fashioned for the **menopause**: *She's* ***going through*** *the change.* • **a change is as good as a rest** UK saying You can get as much good from changing the work you do as from having a rest. • **change of heart** C2 If someone has a change of heart, they change their opinion or the way they feel about something: *She was going to sell her house but had a change of heart at the last minute.*

changeable /ˈtʃeɪn.dʒə.bl̩/ adj C1 describes something that often changes: *The weather in Britain is notoriously changeable.* ◦ *His moods are very changeable.*

changed /tʃeɪndʒd/ adj **a changed man/woman** someone whose behaviour and character has changed a lot, especially improved: *He's a changed man since he met Debbie.*

changeless /ˈtʃeɪndʒ.ləs/ adj literary describes something that never seems to change: *Surrounded by this changeless landscape, one can imagine the world as it was many thousands of years ago.*

changeling /ˈtʃeɪndʒ.lɪŋ/ noun [C] (especially in stories) a baby who is secretly used to take the place of another baby

changeover /ˈtʃeɪndʒˌəʊ.vəʳ/ US /-ˌoʊ.vɚ/ noun [C usually singular] a complete change from one system or method to another: *The changeover* ***to*** *the new taxation system has created a lot of problems.*

changing /ˈtʃeɪn.dʒɪŋ/ adj in a state of becoming different: *the rapidly changing world of politics* ◦ *changing attitudes towards childcare* ◦ *changing circumstances*

ˈchanging ˌroom noun [C] a room where people can change their clothes, for example before and after sports or, in a shop, where people can try on clothes before buying them

channel /ˈtʃæn.əl/ noun; verb

▸noun [C] **TELEVISION** ▷ **1** A2 a television station: *a cable/terrestrial channel* ◦ *a music/movie/news/shopping/sports channel* ◦ *the news* ***on*** *Channel 4* ◦ *She* ***switched/turned to*** *another channel to watch the football.* **PASSAGE** ▷ **2** a passage for water or other liquids to flow along, or a part of a river or other area of water that is deep and wide enough to provide a route for ships to travel along: *There are* ***drainage/irrigation*** *channels all over this flat agricultural land.* ◦ *The boats all have to pass through this narrow channel.* **3 the (English) Channel** the area of sea that separates England from France: *We're going to have a day-trip across the Channel.* ◦ *We took the car to France overnight on a* ***(cross-)****channel ferry.* **AIRPORT/PORT** ▷ **4** a route or way out of an airport or port where travellers' bags are examined: *If you have nothing to declare, go through the* ***green*** *channel.* ◦ *Goods to declare – use the* ***red*** *channel.* **COMMUNICATING** ▷ **5** C2 a way of communicating with people or getting something done: *We must open the channels* ***of communication*** *between the two countries.* ◦ *The government pursued every* ***diplomatic/official*** *channel to free the hostages.* ◦ *Complaints should be made through the* ***proper/usual*** *channels.* **MAKING AVAILABLE** ▷ **6** a way of making a product, information, etc. available: *The insurer sells its products through a variety of* ***distribution*** *channels, including banks.*

▸verb [T] (**-ll-** or US usually **-l-**) **DIRECT** ▷ **1** C2 to direct something into a particular place or situation: *Ditches were constructed to channel* ***water*** *away from the buildings.* ◦ *If she could only channel all that* ***energy into*** *something useful.* ◦ *A lot of* ***money*** *has been channelled* ***into*** *research in that particular field.* **ACT LIKE** ▷ **2** to behave like or copy another person, so that you almost seem to be that other person: *The band were dressed in 1960s outfits and seemed to be channelling the Beatles.*

ˈchannel-ˌhopping noun [U] quickly changing from one TV channel to another to find something you want to watch

chant /tʃɑːnt/ US /tʃænt/ verb; noun

▸verb [I or T] **1** to repeat or sing a word or phrase continuously: *The crowd were chanting the name of their football team.* ◦ *Demonstrators chanted anti-government slogans in the square.* **2** to sing a religious prayer or song to a simple tune: *We could hear the monks chanting.*

▸noun [C] a word or phrase that is repeated many times: *The fans started to sing the familiar* ***football*** *chant, 'Here we go, here we go, here we go!'.*

chanterelle /ˌʃɑ̃ː.n.təˈrel/ noun [C] a type of small, yellow MUSHROOM that grows in forests and is used in cooking

chanteuse /ˌʃɑ̃ːnˈtɜːz/ noun [C] literary a female singer, especially one who sings on the stage in a bar

chantey (also **chanty**) /ˈʃæn.ti/ noun [C] US a **shanty**

Chanukah /ˈhɑː.nə.kə/ noun [C or U] **Hanukkah**

chaos /ˈkeɪ.ɒs/ US /-ɑːs/ noun [U] B2 a state of total confusion with no order: *Snow and ice have caused chaos on the roads.* ◦ *Ever since our secretary walked out, the office has been* ***in*** *a state of total/utter chaos.* ◦ *We muddled up the name labels and chaos ensued (= resulted).*

ˈchaos ˌtheory noun [U] a scientific theory about situations that obey particular laws but appear to have little or no order: *A frequent metaphor for one aspect of chaos theory is called the Butterfly Effect – butterflies flapping their wings in the Amazon affect the weather in Chicago.*

chaotic /keɪˈɒt.ɪk/ US /-ˈɑː.t̬ɪk/ adj C1 in a state of chaos: *The house is a bit chaotic at the moment – we've got all these extra people staying and we're still decorating.* ◦ *He's a chaotic sort of a person – always trying to do twenty things at once.* • **chaotically** /-kəl.i/ adv

chap /tʃæp/ noun [C or] (also **chappie**, **chappy**) UK informal old-fashioned a man: *He's a friendly sort of a chap.*

chap. noun [C] written abbreviation for **chapter**: *Chap. 21*

chapatti (plural **chapattis**) (also **chapati** (plural **chapatis**)) /tʃəˈpæ.ti/ US /-t̬i/ noun [C] a type of flat, round South Asian bread made without YEAST

chapel /ˈtʃæp.əl/ noun [C] **1** C2 a room that is part of a larger building and is used for Christian worship: *The college/hospital/prison has its own chapel.* ◦ *the Chapel of St Paul* **2** C2 mainly UK a building used for Christian worship by Christians who do not belong to the Church of England or the Roman Catholic Church

chaperone /ˈʃæp.ə.rəʊn/ US /-ə.oʊn/ noun; verb

▸noun [C] (also **chaperon**) **1** (especially in the past) an older person, especially a woman, who goes with and takes care of a younger woman who is not married when she is in public: humorous *She's asked me to go to the cinema with her and Andrew, I think as a sort of chaperone.* **2** a female nurse who is in the same room when a female patient is examined by a male doctor, or a police officer who protects a person injured by a criminal when they are in public **3** US an older person who is present at a social event for young people to encourage correct behaviour: *Several parents acted as chaperones for the school disco.*

▸verb [T] (also **chaperon**) **1** (especially in the past) to go with and take care of a young woman who is not married when she is in public: *Do you trust him on your own or do you want me to chaperone you?* **2** US to be present as an adult at a social event for young people to encourage correct behaviour: *Several parents volunteered to chaperone class bus trips.*

chaplain /ˈtʃæp.lɪn/ noun [C] a Christian official who is responsible for the religious needs of an organization: *the college/hospital/prison chaplain*

chaplaincy /ˈtʃæp.lɪn.si/ noun [C] the job of a chaplain, or a building or office where a chaplain works

chapped /tʃæpt/ adj describes skin that is sore, rough, and broken, especially caused by cold weather: *chapped lips* ◦ *She'd been working outside all winter and her hands were red and chapped.* • **chap** /tʃæp/ verb [I or T] (-pp-) *The cold wind had chapped her lips.*

chappie /ˈtʃæp.i/ noun [C] UK old-fashioned informal a **chap**

chaps /tʃæps/ noun [plural] leather clothing worn over trousers by COWBOYS to protect their legs when riding a horse

chapter /ˈtʃæp.təʳ/ (US) /-tɚ/ noun [C] **BOOK** ▷ **1** (B1) (written abbreviation **chap.**) any of the separate parts into which a book or other piece of text is divided, usually given a number or title: *Read Chapter 10 before class tomorrow.* **PERIOD** ▷ **2** a period that is part of a larger amount of time during which something happens: *The period before the revolution is an interesting chapter **in** British history.* ◦ *That chapter **of** my life closed when I had a serious riding accident.* **SOCIETY** ▷ **3** US or formal a local division of a larger organization: *The local chapter of the League of Women Voters meets at the library.*

IDIOMS **be a chapter of accidents** UK to be a series of unpleasant events: *The whole trip was a chapter of accidents.* • **give /quote sth/sb chapter and verse** to give exact information about something, especially something in a book: *I can't quote you chapter and verse but I think it's a line from 'Macbeth'.*

char /tʃɑːʳ/ (US) /tʃɑːr/ verb; noun

▸verb (-rr-) **BURN** ▷ **1** [I or T] to burn and become black or to burn something so that it becomes black **CLEAN** ▷ **2** [I] UK old-fashioned to clean and tidy a house or office for payment

▸noun [C] UK old-fashioned informal **charwoman**

character /ˈkær.ɪk.təʳ/ (US) /ˈker.ɪk.tɚ/ noun **QUALITY** ▷ **1** (B1) [C or U] the particular combination of qualities in a person or place that makes them different from others: *Politeness is traditionally part of the British character.* ◦ *It would be very **out of** character (= not typical) of her to lie.* ◦ *One of the joys of being a parent is watching the child's character develop.* ◦ *The idea was to modernize various aspects of the house without changing its essential character.* ◦ *It's not **in his** character to be (= he is not usually) jealous.* **2** (B2) [U] qualities that are interesting and unusual: *a hotel **of** character* ◦ *I'd prefer an old place with a bit of character.* ◦ *Old books are said to give a room character.* ◦ *As people grow older, their faces acquire more character.* **3** [U] the quality of being determined and able to deal with difficult situations: *She has such **strength of** character.* **IN A STORY** ▷ **4** (B1) [C] a person represented in a film, play, or story: *The film revolves around three main characters.* ◦ *She had Mickey Mouse or some other cartoon/Disney character on her sweater.* ◦ *He made his name as a character **actor** (= an actor who plays unusual and often humorous people).* **PERSON** ▷ **5** (C2) [C] a person, especially when you are describing a particular quality that they have: *She's a curious character – I don't really know what to think of her.* ◦ *There were one or two strange-looking characters hanging around the bar.* **6** (C1) [C] informal someone whose behaviour is different from most people's, especially in a way that is interesting or funny: *He's **quite a** character/**a real** character, is Ted – he's 70 now and still riding that motorbike.* **MARK** ▷ **7** (C1) [C] a letter, number, or other mark or sign used in writing or printing, or the space one of these takes: ***a string of** characters (= a line of marks)* ◦ *The address was written in **Chinese/Japanese** characters (= systems of writing).* ◦ *The computer screen on this laptop is 66 characters (= spaces) wide.*

> **Word partners for character (QUALITY)**
>
> a *distinct/distinctive* character • *change* the character of sth • *in* sb's character • *out of* character

> **Word partners for character (IN A STORY)**
>
> the *central/leading/main* character • a *minor* character • *play* a character • *depict/portray* a character • a character *based on* sb

ˈcharacter assassinˌation noun [C or U] an intentional attempt to spoil the reputation of a person by criticizing them severely, especially unfairly, in the newspapers or on television

characteristic /ˌkær.ɪk.təˈrɪs.tɪk/ (US) /ˌker-/ noun; adj

▸noun [C] (B2) a typical or noticeable quality of someone or something: *Unfortunately a big nose is a **family** characteristic.* ◦ *Sentimentality seems a characteristic **of** all the writers of that period.* ◦ *The male bird **displays** (= has) several characteristics which distinguish him from the female.*

▸adj (C2) typical of a person or thing: *With the hospitality so characteristic **of** these people, they opened their house to over 50 guests.* ◦ *She behaved with characteristic dignity.* ◦ *The creamy richness is characteristic **of** the cheese from this region.* • **characteristically** /-tɪ.kəl.i/ adv *She gave a characteristically skilful performance.*

characterization (UK usually **characterisation**) /ˌkær.ɪk.tə.raɪˈzeɪ.ʃən/ (US) /ˌker.ɪk.tə.rɪ-/ noun **IN A STORY** ▷ **1** [U] the way that people are represented in a film, play, or book so that they seem real and natural: *The plots in her books are very strong but there's almost no characterization.* ◦ *The film's characterization of the artist **as** a complete drunk has annoyed a lot of people.* **QUALITY** ▷ **2** [C] the way in which something is described by stating its main qualities

characterize (UK usually **characterise**) /ˈkær.ɪk.tə.raɪz/ (US) /ˈker.ɪk.tɚ.aɪz/ verb [T] **1** Something which characterizes another thing is typical of it: *Bright colours and bold strokes characterize his early paintings.* **2** to describe something by stating its main qualities: *In her essay, she characterizes the whole era **as** a period of radical change.*

characterless /ˈkær.ɪk.tə.ləs/ (US) /ˈker.ɪk.tɚ-/ adj a characterless person or thing is not interesting or has no style or unusual qualities: *It's just one of those characterless modern cities.* ◦ *a perfect but characterless face*

ˌcharacter recogˈnition noun [U] the ability of an electronic device to recognize printed or written letters or numbers → See also **optical character recognition**

ˈcharacter ˌreference noun [C] a statement of a person's good qualities, written by someone who knows the person well, that is sent to a future employer

charade /ʃəˈrɑːd/ (US) /-ˈreɪd/ noun **FALSE SITUATION** ▷ **1** [C] an act or event that is clearly false: *Everyone knew who was going to get the job from the start – the interviews were just a charade.* **GAME** ▷ **2 charades** [U] a team game in which each member tries to communicate to the others a particular word or phrase that they have been given, by expressing each syllable or word using silent actions

charcoal /ˈtʃɑː.kəʊl/ (US) /ˈtʃɑːr.koʊl/ noun [U] a hard black substance similar to coal which can be used as fuel or, in the form of sticks, as something to draw with: *charcoal for the barbecue* ◦ *I prefer sketching* ***in*** *charcoal to pencil.* ◦ *a charcoal* ***drawing*** ◦ *The uniform is charcoal* ***(grey)*** *(= dark grey) and red.*

chard /tʃɑːd/ (US) /tʃɑːrd/ noun [U] (also **ˌSwiss ˈchard**) a vegetable with large dark green leaves and white stems, which can be cooked and eaten

Chardonnay /ˈʃɑː.də.neɪ/ noun [C or U] a type of white wine, or the type of GRAPE from which the wine is made

charge /tʃɑːdʒ/ (US) /tʃɑːrdʒ/ verb; noun

▸verb **MONEY** ▷ **1** (B1) [T or I] to ask an amount of money for something, especially a service or activity: ***How much/What*** *do you charge* ***for*** *a haircut and blow-dry?* ◦ *The bank charged* ***commission*** *to change my traveller's cheques.* ◦ [+ two objects] *They charge you $20 just to get in the nightclub.* ◦ *The local museum doesn't charge for admission.* **2 charge sth to your account** If you charge something you have bought to your account, the amount you have spent is recorded and you pay for it at a later time: *Charge the bill to my account, please.* ◦ *Shall we charge the flowers to your account?* **ACCUSE FORMALLY** ▷ **3** (B2) [T] (of the police) to make a formal statement saying that someone is accused of a crime: *She's been charged* ***with*** *murder.* ◦ *She is charged* ***with*** *murder****ing*** *her husband.* **4** formal to publicly accuse someone of doing something bad: *The paper charged her* ***with*** *us****ing*** *the company's money for her own purposes.* **MOVE FORWARD** ▷ **5** (B2) [I or T] to move forward quickly and violently, especially towards something that has caused difficulty or anger: *The violence began when the police charged* ***(at)*** *a crowd of demonstrators.* **6** [I + adv/prep] informal to hurry from one place to another: *I've been charging* ***about/around*** *all day and I'm exhausted.* ◦ *He came charging* ***up*** *the stairs to tell me the good news.* **EXPLOSIVE** ▷ **7** [T] to put enough explosive into a gun to fire it once **ORDER** ▷ **8** [T often passive] formal to order someone to do something: *He was charged* ***with*** *tak****ing*** *care of the premises.* **9** [T] US legal When a JUDGE charges a JURY, he or she explains the details of the law to them. **SUPPLY ENERGY** ▷ **10** (B2) [I or T] specialized to put electricity into an electrical device such as a BATTERY: *She drove the car round the block to charge* ***(up)*** *its batteries.* ◦ *It's not working – I don't think the battery is charging.*

▸noun **MONEY** ▷ **1** (B1) [C or U] the amount of money that you have to pay for something, especially for an activity or service: *Is there a charge* ***for*** *children or do they go free?* ◦ *There's an* ***admission*** *charge of £5.* ◦ *They fixed my watch* ***free of*** *charge.* **FORMAL ACCUSATION** ▷ **2** (C1) [C] legal a formal police statement saying that someone is accused of a crime: *The 19-year-old will be appearing in court on Thursday where she will face* ***criminal*** *charges.* ◦ *He has been arrested* ***on*** *a charge* ***of*** *murder.* ◦ *The police* ***brought a*** *charge of theft* ***against*** *him.* ◦ *The police have had to* ***drop*** *(= stop) charges* ***against*** *her because they couldn't find any evidence.* ◦ *He claimed he had been arrested on a* ***trumped-up*** *(= false) charge.* **3** [C] formal the act of accusing someone of something bad: [+ that] *The president responded angrily to the charge* ***that*** *she had lost touch with her country's people.* ◦ *Her refusal to condemn the violence* ***laid/left*** *her* ***open to the*** *charge* ***of*** *positive support for the campaign (= allowed people to say that she supported it).* **CONTROL** ▷ **4 in charge** (B1) being the person who has control of or is responsible for someone or something: *Who will be in charge* ***of*** *the department when Sophie leaves?* ◦ *I* ***left*** *Jack in charge of the suitcases while I went to get the tickets.* **5** (B2) [U] responsibility for controlling or caring for something: *Her ex-husband* ***has*** *charge* ***of*** *the children during the week and she has them at the weekend.* ◦ *His boss asked him to* ***take*** *charge* ***of*** *the office for a few days while she was away.* **6** [C] old-fashioned a person, especially a child, who is in your care and who you are responsible for **EXPLOSIVE** ▷ **7** [C] the amount of explosive to be fired at one time, or the bullet or other explosive object shot from a gun **MOVE FORWARD** ▷ **8** [C] an attack in which people or animals suddenly run forwards: *a charge* ***of*** *buffalo/elephants* ◦ *a police charge* **ORDER** ▷ **9** [C] formal an order to do something **SUPPLY ENERGY** ▷ **10** [C usually singular] specialized the amount of electricity that an electrical device stores or that a substance carries **11 on charge** UK If something is on charge, you are putting an amount of electricity into it.

chargé (d'affaires) /ˌʃɑː.ʒeɪ.dæfˈeəʳ/ (US) /ˌʃɑːr.ʒeɪ.dæfˈer/ noun [C] (plural **chargés (d'affaires)**) a person who represents the leader of his or her government, either temporarily while the AMBASSADOR is away, or permanently in a country where there is no ambassador: *the Belgian chargé d'affaires/the chargé d'affaires* ***for*** *Belgium*

chargeable /ˈtʃɑː.dʒə.bl̩/ (US) /ˈtʃɑːr-/ adj Something is chargeable if you have to pay tax on it: *chargeable earnings/income* ◦ *earnings/income chargeable* ***to*** *tax*

ˈcharge acˌcount noun [C] US for **credit account**

ˈcharge ˌcard noun [C] a small, plastic card that you get from a particular shop and use to buy goods from it that you can pay for later

charged /tʃɑːdʒd/ (US) /tʃɑːrdʒd/ adj **EMOTIONS** ▷ **1** (of arguments or subjects) causing strong feelings and differences of opinion or, more generally, filled with emotion or excitement: *Abortion is a* ***highly*** *charged issue.* ◦ *He spoke in a voice charged* ***with*** *emotion.* **ENERGY** ▷ **2** containing a particular type of energy, especially electrical energy: *electrically charged particles/ions*

ˈcharge ˌnurse noun [C] UK a male nurse who is responsible for a particular part of a hospital. He is the male equal of a SISTER.

charger /ˈtʃɑː.dʒəʳ/ (US) /ˈtʃɑːr.dʒɚ/ noun [C] **DEVICE** ▷ **1** a device that is used to RECHARGE a BATTERY (= fill it with electricity), for example in a mobile phone **HORSE** ▷ **2** old use or literary a soldier's horse

chargesheet /ˈtʃɑːdʒ.ʃiːt/ (US) /ˈtʃɑːrdʒ-/ verb [T] Indian English (of the police) to make a formal statement telling someone that they are accused of a crime: *Even ministers are chargesheeted before a trial.*

ˈcharge ˌsheet noun [C] UK an official document on which a police officer records the details of the crime a person is accused of → Compare **rap sheet**

chargrill /ˈtʃɑː.grɪl/ (US) /ˈtʃɑːr-/ verb [T] to cook food over or under direct heat so that its surface burns slightly and becomes dark: *chargrilled steak*

chargrilled /ˈtʃɑː.grɪld/ (US) /ˈtʃɑːr-/ **adj** describes food that is cooked over or under direct heat so that its surface becomes slightly black: *chargrilled tuna steaks*

chariot /ˈtʃær.i.ət/ (US) /ˈtʃer-/ **noun** [C] a two-wheeled vehicle that was used in ancient times for racing and fighting and was pulled by a horse or horses

charioteer /ˌtʃær.i.əˈtɪəʳ/ (US) /ˌtʃer.i.əˈtɪr/ **noun** [C] a person who drives a chariot

charisma /kəˈrɪz.mə/ **noun** [U] C2 a special power which some people have naturally which makes them able to influence other people and attract their attention and admiration: *On screen Garbo had this great charisma so that you couldn't take your eyes off her.* ◦ *How did a man **of** so little personal charisma get to be prime minister?*

charismatic /ˌkær.ɪzˈmæt.ɪk/ (US) /-ˈmæţ-/ **adj** **CHARACTER** ▷ **1** C2 describes a person who has charisma: *Few were able to resist this charismatic and persuasive leader.* **CHURCH** ▷ **2** belonging or relating to various groups within the Christian Church who believe that God gives people special powers, such as the ability to make others well again and to speak to him in a special language: *the charismatic movement*

charitable /ˈtʃær.ɪ.tə.bl̩/ (US) /ˈtʃer.ɪ.ţə-/ **adj** **GIVING** ▷ **1** [before noun] giving money, food, or help free to those who are in need because they are ill, poor, or have no home: *a charitable **foundation/organization/trust*** ◦ *The entire organization is funded by charitable donations.* ◦ *The school has charitable **status** (= it is officially a charity).* **KIND** ▷ **2** kind, and not judging other people in a severe way: *Some critics said the show was good in parts – those less charitable said the whole thing was a disaster.*

charitably /ˈtʃær.ɪ.tə.bli/ (US) /ˈtʃer.ɪ.ţə-/ **adv** in a kind way, not judging other people in a severe way: *She described him, rather charitably, as quiet whereas I would have said he was boring.*

charity /ˈtʃær.ɪ.ti/ (US) /ˈtʃer.ɪ.ţi/ **noun** **GIVING** ▷ **1** B1 [C or U] a system of giving money, food, or help free to those who are in need because they are ill, poor, or have no home, or any organization that has the purpose of providing money or helping in this way: *She does a lot of work **for** charity.* ◦ *People tend to **give to** (= give money to) charity at Christmas time.* ◦ *Proceeds from the sale of these cards will **go to** (= be given to) local charities.* ◦ *UNICEF is an international charity.* ◦ *They did a charity **performance** on the first night, to raise money for AIDS research.* **KIND** ▷ **2** C2 [U] formal the quality of being kind to people and not judging them in a severe way

IDIOM **charity begins at home** saying You should take care of your family and other people who live close to you before helping people who are living further away or in another country.

ˈ**charity** ˌ**shop** **noun** [C] a shop in which a charity sells all types of used goods that are given by the public, or in which they sell new goods, to make money for the work of the charity

charlady /ˈtʃɑːˌleɪ.di/ (US) /ˈtʃɑːr-/ **noun** [C] UK old-fashioned a **charwoman**

charlatan /ˈʃɑː.lə.tən/ (US) /ˈʃɑːr.lə.ţən/ **noun** [C] disapproving a person who pretends to have skills or knowledge that they do not have, especially in medicine

Charleston /ˈtʃɑːl.stən/ (US) /ˈtʃɑːrl-/ **noun** [C or U] a fast energetic dance that was popular in the 1920s

charley horse /ˈtʃɑː.liˌhɔːs/ (US) /ˈtʃɑːr.liˌhɔːrs/ **noun** [C] (plural **charley horses**) US informal a CRAMP (= a sudden painful tightening of a muscle) in your arm or leg

charlie /ˈtʃɑː.li/ (US) /ˈtʃɑːr-/ **noun** [C] UK old-fashioned informal a silly person: *He **looked a right** charlie in that hat!*

charm /tʃɑːm/ (US) /tʃɑːrm/ **noun; verb**

►**noun** **ATTRACTION** ▷ **1** B2 [C or U] a quality that makes you like or feel attracted to someone or something: *a woman **of** great charm* ◦ *It's a town with a lot of **old-world** charm.* ◦ *Even as a young boy he knew how to **turn on the** charm (= be pleasant intentionally) when he wanted something.* ◦ *I had to use all my charms to get them to lend us the hall.* **LUCKY OBJECT** ▷ **2** C2 [C] an object or saying that is thought to have magical powers, such as the ability to bring good luck: *He keeps a rabbit's paw as a **lucky/good luck** charm.* **JEWELLERY** ▷ **3** [C] a small, especially gold or silver, object worn on a chain as jewellery

►**verb** [T often passive] C2 to attract someone or persuade someone to do something because of your charm: *We were charmed by his boyish manner.*

IDIOM **charm the pants off sb** slang to make someone like you very much, especially when they meet you for the first time: *'How did your sister's boyfriend get on with your mum?' 'Oh, he charmed the pants off her.'*

ˈ**charm** ˌ**bracelet** **noun** [C] a chain that is worn round the wrist and to which small, especially gold or silver, objects are fixed

charmed /tʃɑːmd/ (US) /tʃɑːrmd/ **adj** **1** very pleased or attracted by someone's charm: *He said he would be charmed if a woman gave him flowers.* **2 lead/live a charmed life** to be very lucky in life, often escaping dangerous situations without being hurt

charmer /ˈtʃɑː.məʳ/ (US) /ˈtʃɑːr.mɚ/ **noun** [C] **1** a person who has good qualities that make you like them: *Bella's a little charmer – you'll never meet a more likeable child.* **2** a person who uses CHARM to influence other people, usually for their own purposes: *He's a real charmer is Paul – you want to be careful with him!*

charming /ˈtʃɑː.mɪŋ/ (US) /ˈtʃɑːr-/ **adj** **1** B1 pleasant and attractive: *We had dinner with our director and his charming wife.* ◦ *What a charming street this is.* **2** disapproving describes people who use their ATTRACTIVENESS to influence people or to make other people like them: *He's very charming but I wouldn't trust him.* **3** disapproving often humorous used to show that you do not approve of what someone has said or done: *'Shut up, will you, I'm trying to watch TV!' 'Oh, charming!'* • **charmingly** /-li/ **adv** approving

charmless /ˈtʃɑːm.ləs/ (US) /ˈtʃɑːrm-/ **adj** disapproving unpleasant and without CHARM or interest: *I've always found him a most charmless individual.*

ˈ**charm** **of**ˌ**fensive** **noun** [C usually singular] an intentional attempt to achieve something by using CHARM: *to **launch** (= start) a charm offensive*

charnel house /ˈtʃɑː.nəlˌhaʊs/ (US) /ˈtʃɑːr-/ **noun** [C] old use a building where the bodies of dead people are kept

charred /tʃɑːd/ (US) /tʃɑːrd/ **adj** burned and black: *charred meat* ◦ *The charred body of a man was found by police in a burned-out car last night.*

chart /tʃɑːt/ (US) /tʃɑːrt/ **noun; verb**

►**noun** [C] **DRAWING** ▷ **1** B2 a drawing which shows information in a simple way, often using lines and curves to show amounts: *There is a chart on the classroom wall showing the relative heights of all the children.* ◦ *The sales chart shows a distinct decline in the past few months.* ◦ *the TV **weather** chart* **2** a detailed map of an area of water: *a naval chart* **MUSIC** ▷ **3 the charts** B2 [plural] the lists produced each week of the records with the highest sales: *the dance charts* ◦ *It's been number one **in** the charts for six weeks.*

IDIOM **off the charts** informal **1** at a very high level: *His blood pressure was off the charts* **2** mainly US extremely popular or successful: *The new restaurant is totally off the charts.*

C

▸verb **SHOW/FOLLOW** ▷ **1** [T] to show something on a chart: *We need some sort of graph on which we can chart our **progress**.* ◦ *The map charts the course of the river where it splits into two.* **2** [T] to watch something with careful attention or to record something in detail: *A global study has just been started to chart the effects of climate change.* **3** [T] mainly US to arrange a plan of action: *The local branch of the party is meeting to chart their election campaign.* **MUSIC** ▷ **4** [I] informal to enter the music charts: *Their first record didn't even chart.*

charter /ˈtʃɑː.təʳ/ (US) /ˈtʃɑːr.t̬ɚ/ noun; verb

▸noun **OFFICIAL PAPER** ▷ **1** [C] a formal statement of the rights of a country's people, or of an organization or a particular social group, that is agreed by or demanded from a ruler or government: *a charter of rights* ◦ *Education is one of the basic human rights written into the United Nations Charter.* ◦ *The government have produced a Citizen's/Parents'/Patients' Charter.* **RENT** ▷ **2** [U] the renting of a vehicle: *boats **for** charter* ◦ *a charter **flight*** ◦ *a major charter **operator***

▸verb [T] **RENT** ▷ **1** to rent a vehicle, especially an aircraft, for a special use and not as part of a regular service: *They've chartered a plane to take delegates to the conference.* **OFFICIAL START** ▷ **2** to officially start a new organization by giving it a charter: *Cambridge University Press was chartered in 1534.*

chartered /ˈtʃɑː.təd/ (US) /ˈtʃɑːr.t̬ɚd/ adj **JOB** ▷ **1** UK (of people who do particular jobs) having successfully finished the necessary training and exams: *He's a chartered **surveyor/accountant**.* **RENTED** ▷ **2** [before noun] rented for a particular purpose: *a small chartered plane* ◦ *They spent their annual holiday on a chartered yacht in the Caribbean.*

Chartreuse /ʃɑːˈtrɜːz/ (US) /ʃɑːrˈtruːz/ noun [U] trademark a strong French alcoholic drink that is green or yellow

charwoman /ˈtʃɑːˌwʊ.mən/ (US) /ˈtʃɑːr-/ noun [C] (plural **-women** /-wɪmɪn/) (also **charlady**, informal **char**) UK old-fashioned a woman whose job is to clean and tidy an office or private house

chary /ˈtʃeə.ri/ (US) /ˈtʃer.i/ adj uncertain and frightened to take risks, or unwilling to take action: *I'm a bit chary **of** using a travel agency that doesn't have official registration.*

chase /tʃeɪs/ verb; noun

▸verb **FOLLOW** ▷ **1** (B2) [I or T] to hurry after someone or something in order to catch them: *The police car was going so fast, it must have been chasing someone.* ◦ *She was chasing (**after**) a man who had snatched her bag.* **MOVE FAST** ▷ **2** [I usually + adv/prep] to hurry or run in various directions: *She couldn't study with the children chasing **around** the house.* **TRY TO GET** ▷ **3** (C2) [T] to try to get something that is difficult to get or achieve: *It's depressing how many people there are chasing so few jobs.* ◦ *After years of chasing her **dreams**, she finally got a part in a film.* **4** [I or T] to try very hard to persuade someone to have a relationship with you: *She's always chasing (**after**) men.* **GET RID OF** ▷ **5** (B2) [T + adv/prep] to run after a person or an animal in a threatening way in order to make them leave: *He used to chase the children **away** from his apple trees.* ◦ *She's always chasing cats **out** of the garden to protect her precious birds.*

IDIOMS **be chasing your tail** to be busy doing a lot of things but achieving very little • **chase the dragon** slang to take the drug HEROIN, by smoking it

PHRASAL VERB **chase sb up** informal to ask someone to do something that they have said they would do but that they have not yet done: *If you don't hear from the builders this week, make sure you chase them up.*

▸noun [C] **1** the act of going after someone or something very quickly in order to catch them: *a tedious movie with endless **car/police** chases* **2 the chase** the sport of hunting animals: *Asked why he went fox-hunting, he replied that he loved **the thrill of** the chase.*

IDIOM **give chase** to go after a criminal quickly in order to catch them

chaser /ˈtʃeɪ.səʳ/ (US) /-sɚ/ noun [C] **1** UK a small alcoholic drink that is drunk after a weaker alcoholic drink: *beer with a **whisky** chaser* **2** US a drink with little or no alcohol in it that is drunk after a small strong alcoholic drink: *whisky with a beer chaser*

chasm /ˈkæz.ᵊm/ noun [C] **1** a very deep, narrow opening in rock, ice, or the ground: *They leaned over the rails and peered down into the dizzying chasm below.* **2** formal a very large difference between two opinions or groups of people: *There is still a vast economic chasm **between** developed and developing countries.*

chassis /ˈʃæs.i/ (US) /ˈtʃæs.i/ noun [C] (plural **chassis** /ˈʃæs.iz/ (US) /ˈtʃæs.iz/) the frame of a vehicle, usually including the wheels and engine, onto which the metal covering is fixed: *The car's lightweight chassis is made from aluminium sheets.*

chaste /tʃeɪst/ adj formal **1** not having had sex, or only having a sexual relationship with the person you are married to: *In the past, a woman needed to be chaste to make a good marriage.* ◦ *They exchanged a few chaste kisses (= not expressing sexual desire).* **2** describes decoration or style that is very simple and smooth: *I like the simple, chaste lines of their architecture.*

chasten /ˈtʃeɪ.sᵊn/ verb [T usually passive] formal to make someone understand that they have failed or done something wrong and make them want to improve: *He was chastened by the defeat and determined to work harder.*

chastise /tʃæsˈtaɪz/ verb [T] formal to criticize someone severely: *Charity organizations have chastised the government **for** not doing enough to prevent the latest famine in Africa.* • **chastisement** /-mənt/ noun [U]

chastity /ˈtʃæs.tə.ti/ (US) /-t̬i/ noun [U] the state of not having sexual relationships or never having had sex: *As a monk, he took vows of chastity, poverty, and obedience.*

ˈchastity ˌbelt noun [C] a device that some women were forced to wear in the past to prevent them from having sex. It had a part that went between the woman's legs and a lock so that it could not be removed.

chat /tʃæt/ verb; noun

▸verb [I] (-tt-) **1** (A2) to talk to someone in a friendly informal way: *She spends hours on the phone chatting **to** her friends.* ◦ *We were just chatting **about** what we did last weekend.* ◦ *Whenever I walk in, I always find the two of them chatting **away** (= talking eagerly).* **2** (A2) to take part in a discussion with someone on the internet

PHRASAL VERB **chat sb up** UK informal B2 to talk to someone in a way that shows them that you are sexually attracted to them: *He spent all evening chatting her up and buying her drinks.*

▸**noun** [C or U] A2 a friendly, informal conversation: *Why don't you give me a call and we'll* ***have*** *a chat?* ◦ *I had a chat* ***with*** *my boss today* ***about*** *a possible salary increase.* ◦ *It was the usual* ***idle*** *chat (= conversation about unimportant things).* → See also **chit-chat**

chateau /ˈʃæt.əʊ/ US /ʃætˈoʊ/ **noun** [C] (plural **chateaux**) a large house or castle in France

chatline /ˈtʃæt.laɪn/ **noun** [C] UK a phone service where people can speak to other people for enjoyment: *He ran up an enormous phone bill by ringing up chatlines all the time.*

ˈchat ˌroom noun [C] a part of the internet where you can use email to discuss a subject with other people

ˈchat ˌshow noun [C] UK (mainly US **ˈtalk ˌshow**) B1 an informal television or radio programme on which famous people are asked questions about themselves and their work

chattel /ˈtʃæt.əl/ US /ˈtʃæţ-/ **noun** [C] old use or formal a personal possession: *He treated his wife as little more than a chattel.* ◦ ***goods and*** *chattels*

chatter /ˈtʃæt.əʳ/ US /ˈtʃæţ.ɚ/ **verb; noun**

▸**verb** [I] TALK/NOISE ▷ **1** to talk for a long time about things that are not important: *She spent the morning chattering* ***away*** *to her friends.* ◦ *He chattered* ***on*** *about nothing in particular.* **2** If animals chatter, they make quick repeated noises: *The gun shot made the monkeys chatter in alarm.* TEETH ▷ **3** If your teeth chatter, they knock together repeatedly because you are very cold or frightened: *I could hardly talk, my teeth were chattering so much.*

▸**noun** [U] **1** conversation about things that are not important: *I can't concentrate with Ann's constant chatter.* **2** the quick repeated noises that some animals make: *He could hear the chatter of birds in the trees overhead.*

chatterbox /ˈtʃæt.ə.bɒks/ US /ˈtʃæţ.ɚ.bɑːks/ **noun** [C] informal a person, especially a child, who talks a lot: *Your sister's a real chatterbox!*

the ˈchattering ˌclasses noun [plural] UK informal disapproving well-educated middle-class people who enjoy discussing political, cultural, and social matters and who express opinions on a lot of subjects

chatty /ˈtʃæt.i/ US /ˈtʃæţ-/ **adj** informal **1** C1 liking to talk a lot in a friendly, informal way **2** C1 If a piece of writing is chatty, it is informal: *a chatty letter/style*

ˈchat-up ˌline noun [C] UK (US **ˈcome-on ˌline**) a remark which someone makes to a person who they are sexually attracted to in order to make their sexual interest known to them and start a conversation with them: *'Have you been here before?' 'That's one of the oldest chat-up lines I've ever heard!'*

chauffeur /ˈʃəʊ.fəʳ/ US /ʃoʊˈfɝː/ **noun; verb**

▸**noun** [C] someone whose job is to drive a car for a rich or important person: *a chauffeur-driven limousine*

▸**verb** [T] to drive someone somewhere: *His mother spoils him terribly and chauffeurs him* ***(around/about)*** *everywhere.*

chauvinism /ˈʃəʊ.vɪ.nɪ.zəm/ US /ˈʃoʊ-/ **noun** [U] disapproving **1** the strong and unreasonable belief that your own country or race is the best or most important: *The war stimulated an intense national chauvinism.* **2** (also **male chauvinism**) the belief that women are naturally less important, intelligent, or able than men

chauvinist /ˈʃəʊ.vɪ.nɪst/ US /ˈʃoʊ-/ **adj** (also **chauvinistic** /ˌʃəʊ.vɪˈnɪs.tɪk/ US /ˌʃoʊ-/) **1** believing or showing an unreasonable belief that your own country or race is the best or most important **2** believing or behaving as if women are naturally less important, intelligent, or able than men: *It is a deeply chauvinist community where the few women who have jobs are ridiculed.* • **chauvinist noun** [C] *She called him a* ***(male)*** *chauvinist because of his insistence on calling all women 'girls'.* • **chauvinistically** /ˌʃəʊ.vɪˈnɪs.tɪ.kəl.i/ US /ˌʃoʊ-/ **adv**

chav /tʃæv/ **noun** [C] UK informal an insulting word for someone, usually a young person, whose way of dressing, speaking, and behaving is thought to show their lack of education and low social class • **chavvy** /tʃæv.i/ **adj** *chavvy jewellery*

cheap /tʃiːp/ **adj; adv**

▸**adj** LOW PRICE ▷ **1** A1 costing little money or less than is usual or expected: *I got a cheap flight at the last minute.* ◦ *Food is usually cheaper in supermarkets.* ◦ *Children and the elderly are entitled to cheap train tickets.* ◦ *The scheme is simple and cheap* ***to*** *operate.* ◦ *During times of mass unemployment, there's a pool of cheap* ***labour*** *for employers to draw from.* ◦ figurative *In a war, human life becomes very cheap (= seems to be of little value).* **2** If a shop or restaurant is cheap, it charges low prices: *I go to the cheapest hairdresser's in town.* **3 cheap and cheerful** UK cheap but good or enjoyable: *There's a restaurant round the corner that serves cheap and cheerful food.* **4 on the cheap** informal If you get goods on the cheap, you get them for a low price, often from someone you know who works in the company or business that produces them. LOW QUALITY ▷ **5** C1 disapproving describes goods that are both low in quality and low in price: *I bought some cheap wine for cooking with.* ◦ *He bought some cheap shoes that fell apart after a couple of months.* **6 cheap and nasty** UK costing little and of very bad quality MEAN ▷ **7** US (UK **mean**) unwilling to spend money: *He's so cheap he didn't even buy me a card for my birthday.* DRESSED SEXILY ▷ **8** disapproving If you describe the way a person is dressed as cheap, you mean that it is very obvious that they are trying to sexually attract other people. UNKIND ▷ **9** disapproving unpleasant and unkind: *I wish you'd stop making cheap jokes about my friends.*

> **Other ways of saying cheap**
>
> If something is cheap enough for most people to be able to buy, you can say that it is **affordable**, **inexpensive**, or **reasonable**:
>
> *There's very little* ***affordable*** *housing around here.*
>
> *They sell* ***inexpensive*** *children's clothes.*
>
> *I thought the food was very* ***reasonable****.*
>
> If something is very cheap, in informal English you can say that it is **dirt cheap**:
>
> *Most of the books they sell are* ***dirt cheap****.*
>
> The adjective **cut-rate** is sometimes used to describe something that is cheaper than usual:
>
> *We managed to get* ***cut-rate*** *tickets the day before the show.*
>
> A piece of equipment that is cheap to use is often described as **economical**:
>
> *I need a car that's reliable and* ***economical****.*

IDIOMS **cheap at half the price** humorous very expensive • **a cheap shot** a criticism of someone that is unfair: *She dismissed his comments as a cheap shot, saying that he was only concerned to defend himself.*

▸**adv** for little money or for less than is usual: *I got* some shoes cheap in the sale. ◦ There were some chairs in the market **going** cheap (= they were not expensive).

IDIOM **not come cheap** If you say that something does not come cheap, you mean that it is of good quality and is therefore expensive: *If you want a qualified accountant, their services don't come cheap.*

cheapen /ˈtʃiː.pᵊn/ verb [T] **COST LESS** ▷ **1** to reduce the price: *This has had the effect of cheapening UK exports.* **RESPECT LESS** ▷ **2** disapproving to make someone or something seem less valuable or important so that people respect them less: *She felt that the photos were exploitative and cheapened her.*

cheaply /ˈtʃiː.p.li/ adv for a low price: *The shop round the corner does shoe repairs very cheaply.*

cheapness /ˈtʃiːp.nəs/ noun [U] the low price: *The relative cheapness of foreign travel means that more people are going abroad than ever before.*

cheapo /ˈtʃiː.pəʊ/ US /-poʊ/ adj [before noun] informal low in price and often low in quality: *We stayed in a cheapo hotel to save money.*

ˈcheap ˌrate noun [C] the amount charged for a service that is lower than usual because there is not so much demand for the service at that time: *Cheap rate for overseas phone calls is from 8 p.m. to 8 a.m.* • **ˈcheap-ˌrate** adj *cheap-rate calls*

cheapskate /ˈtʃiː.p.skeɪt/ noun [C] informal disapproving a person who is unwilling to spend money: *My dad's such a cheapskate that he cuts his hair himself.*

cheat /tʃiːt/ verb; noun

▸verb [I or T] **B2** to behave in a dishonest way in order to get what you want: *Anyone caught cheating will be immediately disqualified from the exam.* ◦ *He cheats **at** cards?* ◦ *She cheated **in** the test by copying from the boy in front.* ◦ *I suspect he cheats the taxman (= avoids paying taxes by using illegal methods).*

IDIOM **cheat death** literary to succeed in staying alive in an extremely dangerous situation: *As a racing driver, he was involved in many serious crashes and had cheated death on several occasions.*

PHRASAL VERBS **cheat on sb** informal **B2** If you cheat on your husband, wife, or usual sexual partner, you secretly have a sexual relationship with someone else: *She found out that he'd been cheating on her.* • **cheat sb out of sth** to unfairly prevent someone from getting or achieving something that they should have: *She claimed that her cousin had cheated her out of her inheritance.*

▸noun **1** [C] a person who behaves in a dishonest way: *Trouble broke out in the match when one of the players called a member of the other team a cheat.* **2** [S] something dishonest which makes people believe that something is true when it is not: *You can use cocoa powder to make the cake rather than chocolate – it's a bit of a cheat, but nobody notices the difference.* **3** [C] a collection of instructions or special information which someone can use to help them play a computer game more successfully: *the latest game cheats* ◦ *cheat **codes***

check /tʃek/ verb; noun; exclamation

▸verb **EXAMINE** ▷ **1** **A2** [I or T] to make certain that something or someone is correct, safe, or suitable by examining it or them quickly: *You should always check your oil, water, and tyres before taking your car on a long trip.* ◦ *Customs stopped us and checked (= searched) our bags **for** alcohol and cigarettes.* ◦ *After I'd finished the exam, I checked my answers **for** mistakes.* ◦ *The doctor will call next week to check **on** your progress.* ◦ *My wife checks **on** (= visits) our elderly neighbour every few days to make sure that he's alright.* ◦ [+ (that)] *I always check (**that**) I've shut the windows before I leave the house.* ◦ *He **double**-checked all the doors (= checked them all twice) before leaving the house.* → See also **crosscheck** **2** **B1** [I or T] to find out about something: [+ question word] *I rang them yesterday to check **wh**en they were arriving.* ◦ [+ to infinitive] *If you're near the garage, could you check **to** see (= ask) if the car's ready?* ◦ *If you're unsure of your legal rights, I would check **with** (= ask) a lawyer.* **STOP** ▷ **3** [T] to stop someone from doing or saying something, or to prevent something from increasing or continuing: *They have begun to vaccinate children in an attempt to check the spread of the disease.* **LEAVE** ▷ **4** [T] US to leave something with someone at a particular place, so that they can take care of it for a short time: *It was hot so we checked our coats before going round the gallery.* **AGREE** ▷ **5** [I] mainly US If information checks, it agrees with other information: *Her statement checks **with** most of the eye-witness reports.* **MARK** ▷ **6** **A1** [I or T] US for **tick**

PHRASAL VERBS **check in** **B1** to show your ticket at an airport so that you can be told where you will be sitting and so that your bags can be put on the aircraft: *Passengers are requested to check in two hours before the flight.* • **check in/check into sth** **B1** to say who you are when you arrive at a hotel so that you can be given a key for your room: *Please would you check in **at** the reception desk and sign your name in the book.* • **check sth off** US to mark names or things on a list as correct or as having been dealt with: *He checked off their names on the list as they got on the coach.* • **check out** **B1** to leave a hotel after paying and returning your room key: *We checked out (**of/from** our hotel) at 5 a.m. to catch a 7 a.m. flight.* • **check sth out** **EXAMINE** ▷ **1** **C1** informal to examine something or get more information about it in order to be certain that it is true, safe, or suitable: *We'll need to check out his story.* **GO TO SEE** ▷ **2** **C1** informal to go to a place in order to see what it is like: *I'm going to check out that new club.* **BORROW** ▷ **3** mainly US to borrow books from a library • **check up on sb** **C1** to try to discover what someone is doing in order to be certain that they are doing what they should be doing: *My mum checks up on me most evenings to see that I've done my homework.*

▸noun **MONEY** ▷ **1** [C] US for **cheque** **EXAMINATION** ▷ **2** **B1** [C] an examination of something in order to make certain that it is correct or the way it should be: *The soldiers gave their equipment a final check before setting off.* ◦ *'I can't find my keys.' 'Have another check **in/through** your jacket pockets.'* ◦ ***Security** checks have become really strict at the airport.* ◦ *The police are carrying out **spot** checks on (= quick examinations of a limited number of) drivers over the Christmas period to test for alcohol levels.* ◦ *It's my job to **keep** a check **on** stock levels.* ◦ *I'll just **run** a check **on** (= find information about) that name for you in the computer.* **PATTERN** ▷ **3** [C or U] a pattern of squares formed by lines of different colours crossing each other: *a shirt with a pattern of blue and yellow checks* ◦ *a grey check suit* **RESTAURANT** ▷ **4** **A2** [C] US for **bill**: *Can I have the check, please?* **LIMIT** ▷ **5** **hold/keep sth in check** to limit something: *We must find ways of keeping our expenditure in check.* **6** **checks and balances** rules intended to prevent one person or group from having too much power within an organization: *A **system of** checks and balances exists to ensure that our government is truly democratic.* **MARK** ▷ **7** **A2** [C] US for **tick**

▸exclamation US used to say yes to someone who is making certain that all the things on a list have been dealt with or included: *'Did you bring your sleeping bag?' 'Check.' 'Pillow?' 'Check.'*

checkbook /ˈtʃek.bʊk/ noun [C] US for **chequebook**

checked /tʃekt/ adj (also UK **chequered**, US **checkered**) with a pattern of squares formed by lines of different colours crossing each other: *a red and white checked tablecloth*

checker /ˈtʃek.əʳ/ (US) /-ɚ/ noun [C] US a **cashier**

checkered /ˈtʃek.əd/ (US) /-ɚd/ adj US for **chequered**

checkers /ˈtʃek.əz/ (US) /-ɚz/ noun [U] US for **draught**

ˈ**check-in (desk)** noun [C] B1 the place at an airport where you show your ticket so that you can be told where you will be sitting: *A representative from the tour company will meet you at the check-in.* ◦ *I'll meet you at the check-in desk.*

ˈ**checking acˌcount** noun [C] US for **current account**

checklist /ˈtʃek.lɪst/ noun [C] a list of things that you must think about, or that you must remember to do: *I have a checklist of things that I must do today.*

checkmate /ˈtʃek.meɪt/ noun [U] **1** a winning position in CHESS in which you have put the other player's king under a direct attack from which it cannot escape **2** a situation in which someone has been defeated or a plan cannot develop or continue → Compare **stalemate** • **checkmate verb** [T] *My Dad can always checkmate me within 20 moves.*

checkout /ˈtʃek.aʊt/ noun [C] **1** B1 the place in a shop, especially a large food shop, where you pay for your goods: *Your fruit and vegetables will be weighed at the checkout.* ◦ *She works **on** the checkout at the local supermarket.* **2** B1 the place on a website where you order and pay for goods: *Choose your CD-ROMs and proceed to checkout.*

checkpoint /ˈtʃek.pɔɪnt/ noun [C] a place where people are stopped and asked questions and vehicles are examined, especially at a border between two countries

checkroom /ˈtʃek.ruːm/, /-rʊm/ noun [C] US for **cloakroom** (= a room in a public building where you can leave your coat, bag, etc. while you are in the building)

ˈ**check-up** noun [C] a medical examination to test your general state of health: *She goes to her doctor for regular check-ups.* ◦ *a dental check-up*

cheddar /ˈtʃed.əʳ/ (US) /-ɚ/ noun [U] a hard British cheese: *Do you prefer **mild** or **mature** cheddar?*

cheek /tʃiːk/ noun; verb

▸noun **FACE** ▷ **1** B1 [C] the soft part of your face that is below your eye and between your mouth and ear: *The tears ran down her cheeks.* ◦ *rosy cheeks* ◦ *He embraced her, kissing her on both cheeks.* **BEHAVIOUR** ▷ **2** [S or U] UK behaviour or talk that is rude and shows no respect: *He told me off for being late when he arrived half an hour after me. What **a** cheek!* ◦ [+ to infinitive] *She's got some cheek **to** take your car without asking.* ◦ *He **had the** cheek **to** ask me to pay for her!* ◦ *She's always getting into trouble for **giving** her teachers cheek (= being rude to them).* **BOTTOM** ▷ **3** [C] informal either of the two halves of your bottom

IDIOM **cheek by jowl** very close together: *The poor lived cheek by jowl in industrial mining towns in Victorian England.*

▸verb [T] UK informal to be rude to someone: *He's always getting into trouble for cheeking his teachers.*

cheekbone /ˈtʃiːk.bəʊn/ (US) /-boʊn/ noun [C usually plural] one of the two bones at the top of your cheeks, just below your eye and towards your ear: *She has the **high** cheekbones of a supermodel.*

-cheeked /-tʃiːkt/ suffix **red-/rosy-cheeked** having red cheeks

cheeky /ˈtʃiː.ki/ adj UK B2 slightly rude or showing no respect, but often in a funny way: *She's got such a cheeky grin.* ◦ *Don't be so cheeky!* • **cheekily** /-kɪ.li/ adv • **cheekiness** /-nəs/ noun [U]

cheep /tʃiːp/ noun [C] the high weak cry made by a young bird • **cheep verb** [I]

cheer /tʃɪəʳ/ (US) /tʃɪr/ verb; noun

▸verb [I] B2 to give a loud shout of approval or encouragement: *Everyone cheered as the winners received their medals.* ◦ *He was cheering **for** the other side.*

PHRASAL VERBS **cheer sb on** C2 to shout loudly in order to encourage someone in a competition: *As the runners went by, we cheered them on.* • **cheer (sb) up** B2 If someone cheers up, or something cheers them up, they start to feel happier: *She was ill so I sent her some flowers to cheer her up.* ◦ *He cheered up **at** the prospect of a meal.* ◦ *Cheer up! It's not that bad!* ◦ *She went shopping to cheer her**self** up.* • **cheer sth up** to make a place look brighter or more attractive: *A coat of paint and new curtains would really cheer the kitchen up.*

▸noun **SHOUT** ▷ **1** C2 [C] a loud shout of approval or encouragement: *Her speech was received with cheers and a standing ovation.* ◦ *His victory in the 400 metres earned him the biggest cheer of the afternoon.* ◦ ***Three** cheers for the winning team!!* **HAPPINESS** ▷ **2** [U] formal or old-fashioned a feeling of happiness: *The victory in the by-election has brought great cheer to the Liberal Democrats.* **3 be of good cheer** old use to be happy

cheerful /ˈtʃɪə.fəl/ (US) /ˈtʃɪr-/ adj **1** B1 happy and positive: *He's usually fairly cheerful.* ◦ *You're in a cheerful mood this morning.* ◦ *She manages to stay cheerful (= happy and positive) despite everything.* **2** B2 describes a place or thing that is bright and pleasant and makes you feel positive and happy: *The doctor's waiting room was bright and cheerful with yellow walls and curtains.* ◦ *Turn that dreadful wailing music off and put on something cheerful.* • **cheerfully** /-i/ adv B2 *She walked down the road, whistling cheerfully.* ◦ humorous *By the end of the evening I could cheerfully have (= I would like to have) punched him.* • **cheerfulness** /ˈtʃɪə.fəl.nəs/ (US) /ˈtʃɪr-/ noun [U]

cheering /ˈtʃɪə.rɪŋ/ (US) /ˈtʃɪr-/ adj; noun

▸adj describes something that encourages you and makes you feel happier: *We received some cheering news.*

▸noun [U] shouts of encouragement and approval

cheerio /ˌtʃɪə.riˈəʊ/ (US) /ˌtʃɪr.iˈoʊ/ exclamation UK old-fashioned goodbye: *Cheerio! Have a good trip!*

cheerleader /ˈtʃɪəˌliː.dəʳ/ (US) /ˈtʃɪrˌliː.dɚ/ noun [C] (especially in America) a person, usually a woman or girl, who leads the crowd in shouting encouragement and supporting a team at a sports event: *She was a cheerleader **for** the Dallas Cowboys.*

cheerless /ˈtʃɪə.ləs/ (US) /ˈtʃɪr-/ adj not bright or pleasant and making you feel sad: *a cold and cheerless winter afternoon* ◦ *a bare, cheerless apartment* • **cheerlessness** /-nəs/ noun [U]

cheers! /tʃɪəz/ (US) /tʃɪrz/ exclamation **1** B1 a friendly expression said just before you drink an alcoholic drink: *Cheers! Your good health.* **2** B2 UK informal used to mean 'thank you': *'I've bought you a drink.' 'Cheers, mate.'* **3** B1 UK informal used to mean 'goodbye': *'Bye.' 'Cheers, see you next week.'*

cheery /ˈtʃɪə.ri/ (US) /ˈtʃɪr.i/ adj bright and happy: *She* walked in with a cheery 'Good morning!' ◦ He gave us a cheery wave as we drove past. • **cheerily** /ˈtʃɪə.rɪ.li/ (US) /ˈtʃɪr.ɪ-/ **adv** He waved cheerily. • **cheeriness** /-nəs/ **noun** [U]

cheese /tʃiːz/ **noun; verb**

▸**noun** [C or U] (A1) a food made from milk, that can be either firm or soft and is usually yellow or white in colour: *Would you like a slice/piece of cheese with your bread?* ◦ ***goat's** cheese* ◦ *You need 250 grams of **grated** cheese for this recipe.* ◦ *I like **soft** French cheeses such as Brie and Camembert.* ◦ *I prefer **hard** cheeses, like cheddar.* ◦ *cheese and biscuits*

IDIOMS **hard/tough cheese!** UK (US **stiff cheese!**) something that you say to or about someone who has had something bad happen to them in order to show that you have no sympathy for them: *So he's fed up because he's got to get up early one morning in seven, is he? Well hard cheese!* • **say cheese** something that someone who is taking a photograph of you tells you to say so that your mouth makes the shape of a smile

▸**verb**

PHRASAL VERB **cheese sb off** UK informal to annoy someone: *Her attitude to the whole thing really cheeses me off!*

ˌcheese ˈbiscuit noun [C] UK (US **cracker**) a SAVOURY biscuit that is eaten with cheese or contains cheese

cheeseboard /ˈtʃiːz.bɔːd/ (US) /-bɔːrd/ **noun** [C] a board on which several different types of cheese are arranged for you to choose from at the end of a meal, or cheese served in this way

cheeseburger /ˈtʃiːzˌbɜː.gəʳ/ (US) /-ˌbɝː.gɚ/ **noun** [C] a HAMBURGER (= round, flat shape made of meat, eaten between bread) with a slice of melted cheese

cheesecake /ˈtʃiːz.keɪk/ **noun** **FOOD** ▷ **1** [C or U] a cake made from a layer of biscuit, or a sweet pastry base, covered with soft cheese, eggs, sugar, and sometimes fruit: *lemon/almond cheesecake* **WOMEN** ▷ **2** [U] mainly US old-fashioned slang photographs of sexually attractive young women wearing very few clothes, or the women who appear in such photographs → Compare **beefcake**

cheesecloth /ˈtʃiːz.klɒθ/ (US) /-klɑːθ/ **noun** [U] thin, loose cotton cloth

ˌcheesed ˈoff adj [after verb] UK informal annoyed and disappointed with something or someone: *She's a bit cheesed off **with** her job.*

ˈcheese ˌknife noun [C] a small knife with a curved blade ending in two sharp points, used to cut and pick up pieces of cheese

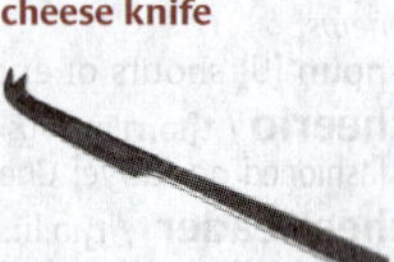
cheese knife

cheeseparing /ˈtʃiːzˌpeə.rɪŋ/ (US) /-ˌper.ɪŋ/ **noun** [U] disapproving unwillingness to spend money

cheesy /ˈtʃiː.zi/ **adj** **BAD STYLE** ▷ **1** informal clearly of cheap quality or in bad style: *cheesy hotel music* ◦ *cheesy adverts* **2** UK informal describes a wide smile that is not sincere: *She gave a cheesy **grin** to the cameras.* **LIKE CHEESE** ▷ **3** tasting like or of cheese: *cheesy snacks* **4** UK informal If someone's feet, shoes, or socks are cheesy, they smell unpleasant: *Someone here's got cheesy feet!*

cheetah /ˈtʃiː.tə/ (US) /-t̬ə/ **noun** [C] a wild animal of the cat family, with yellowish-brown fur and black spots, that can run faster than any other animal: *Cheetahs are mainly found in Africa.*

chef /ʃef/ **noun** [C] (A2) a skilled and trained cook who works in a hotel or restaurant, especially the most important cook: *He is one of the top chefs in Britain.* ◦ *She is **head** chef at the Waldorf Astoria.*

chef-d'oeuvre /ˌʃeɪˈdɜː.vrə/ (US) /-ˈɝː-/ **noun** [C] (plural **chefs-d'oeuvre**) formal an artist or writer's greatest piece of work

chemical /ˈkem.ɪ.kəl/ **noun; adj**

▸**noun** [C] (B2) any basic substance that is used in or produced by a reaction involving changes to atoms or MOLECULES: *The government has pledged to reduce the amount of chemicals used in food production.* ◦ *Each year, factories release millions of tonnes of **toxic** (= poisonous) chemicals into the atmosphere.*

▸**adj** (B2) relating to chemicals: *The chemical **industry** produces such things as petrochemicals, drugs, and rubber.* • **chemically** /-i/ **adv** *The fund provides money to clean up chemically polluted industrial sites.*

ˌchemical ˈelement noun [C] specialized a substance that cannot be broken down into any simpler chemical substances and is made of atoms all of the same type

ˌchemical engiˈneering noun [U] the design and operation of machinery used in industrial chemical processes

ˌchemical eˈquation noun [C] a statement containing chemical symbols, used to show the changes that happen during a particular chemical reaction

ˌchemical ˈformula noun [C] the way of representing a substance using the symbols of its elements: *H_2O is the chemical formula for water.*

ˌchemical reˈaction noun [C] a process in which the structure of atoms or MOLECULES that make up a substance are changed

ˌchemical ˈwarfare noun [U] the use of poisonous gases and other harmful chemicals against enemy forces

ˌchemical ˈweapon noun [C] a substance, such as a poisonous gas rather than an explosive, which can be used to kill or injure people

chemise /ʃəˈmiːz/ **noun** [C] a loose piece of clothing for women that covers the top part of the body and is worn under other clothes

chemist /ˈkem.ɪst/ **noun** [C] **SCIENCE** ▷ **1** (B1) a person who studies chemistry, or a scientist who works with chemicals or studies their reactions **MEDICINE** ▷ **2** UK (US **druggist**, also **pharmacist**) a person whose job is to prepare and sell medicines in a shop **3** (A2) UK (UK also **chemist's**, US **drugstore**, also **pharmacy**) a shop where you can buy medicines, make-up, and products used for washing yourself

chemistry /ˈkem.ɪ.stri/ **noun** [U] **SCIENCE** ▷ **1** (A2) (the part of science which studies) the basic characteristics of substances and the different ways in which they react or combine with other substances: *She studied chemistry and physics at college.* ◦ *A team of scientists has been studying the chemistry **of** the ozone layer.* ◦ *a chemistry department/laboratory* **RELATIONSHIP** ▷ **2** informal a quality that exists when two people understand and are attracted to each other: *The **sexual** chemistry **between** them was obvious.*

chemotherapy /ˌkiː.məʊˈθer.ə.pi/ (US) /-moʊ-/ **noun** [U] the treatment of diseases using chemicals: *Chemotherapy is often used in the treatment of cancer.*

chenille /ʃəˈniːl/ **noun** [U] a thick, soft thread used for decorating cloth, or the material that is made from this: *a chenille jumper/bedspread*

cheque UK (US **check**) /tʃek/ **noun** [C] (A2) a printed form, used instead of money, to make payments from your bank account: *I **wrote** him a cheque **for** £50.* ◦ *I* don't have any cash on me, so could I pay ***with a/by*** *cheque?* ◦ *Who should I **make out** this cheque **to**? (= Whose name should I write on it?)* ◦ *Please make your cheques **payable to** The Brighter Toyshop Ltd (= write this name on them).*

chequebook /ˈtʃek.bʊk/ **noun** [C] UK (US **checkbook**) **1** a book of cheques with your name printed on them that is given to you by your bank to make payments with **2 chequebook journalism** UK (US **checkbook journalism**) the activity in which a newspaper persuades someone involved in a news story to give their report of events by paying them a lot of money

ˌcheque guaranˈtee ˌcard **noun** [C] UK (UK also **ˈcheque ˌcard**, US **ˌcheck guaranˈtee ˌcard**) a small plastic card that you sometimes show when you pay for something by cheque as proof that your bank will pay the money you owe

chequered /ˈtʃek.əd/ (US) /-ɚd/ **adj** UK (US **checkered**) GOOD AND BAD ▷ **1** having had both successful and unsuccessful periods in your past: *He's had a chequered business **career**.* PATTERN ▷ **2** (also **checked**) having a pattern of squares in two or more colours: *red and white chequered tablecloths*

the ˌchequered ˈflag **noun** [S] (US **the ˌcheckered ˈflag**) the black and white flag that is waved to show that a car has won a race: *Three minutes from the chequered flag, Hamilton was in the lead by 2.25 seconds.*

cherish /ˈtʃer.ɪʃ/ **verb** [T] **1** to love, protect, and care for someone or something that is important to you: *Although I cherish my children, I do allow them their independence.* ◦ *Her most cherished possession is a 1926 letter from F. Scott Fitzgerald.* ◦ *Freedom of speech is a cherished (= carefully protected) right in this country.* **2** to keep hopes, memories, or ideas in your mind because they are important to you and bring you pleasure: *I cherish the memories of the time we spent together.*

cheroot /ʃəˈruːt/ **noun** [C] a short, thin CIGAR with both ends cut flat

cherry /ˈtʃer.i/ **noun; adj**
▸**noun** [C] (B2) a small, round, soft red or black fruit with a single hard seed in the middle, or the tree on which the fruit grows
▸**adj** (also **ˌcherry-ˈred**) bright red: *cherry-red lips*

cherub /ˈtʃer.əb/ **noun** [C] (plural **cherubs** or formal **cherubim** /-ə.bɪm/) **1** an ANGEL that is represented in art as a beautiful, fat, naked child with small wings **2** informal approving a beautiful and well-behaved child

cherub

cherubic /tʃəˈruː.bɪk/ **adj** having a round, attractive face like that of a child: *a blonde-haired girl with a cherubic face*

chervil /ˈtʃɜː.vɪl/ (US) /ˈtʃɝː-/ **noun** [U] a herb used in cooking that has delicate leaves like feathers and a flavour like LIQUORICE

chess /tʃes/ **noun** [U] (A2) a game played by two people on a square board, in which each player has 16 pieces that can be moved on the board in different ways

chessboard /ˈtʃes.bɔːd/ (US) /-bɔːrd/ **noun** [C] a square board divided into 64 smaller squares, half of which are light and half dark in colour, used for playing the game of chess or DRAUGHTS

ˈchess ˌset **noun** [C] the pieces used to play chess and the board on which the game is played

chessboard

chest /tʃest/ **noun** [C] BODY PART ▷ **1** (B2) the upper front part of the body of humans and some animals, between the stomach and the neck, containing the heart and lungs: *He was shot in the chest at point blank range.* ◦ *He folded his arms **across** his chest.* ◦ *His shirt was open to the waist revealing a very **hairy** chest.* ◦ *She went to the doctor complaining of chest **pains**.* BOX ▷ **2** (C2) a large strong box, usually made of wood, used for storing goods or for moving possessions from one place to another: *Her books and clothes were packed into chests and shipped across to Canada.*

IDIOM **get sth off your chest** informal (C2) to tell someone about something that has been worrying you or making you feel guilty for a long time: *I had spent two months worrying about it and I was glad to get **it** off my chest.*

-chested /-tʃes.tɪd/ **suffix** with a chest (= top half of the body) of the stated type: *He was **bare**-chested.* ◦ *She is rather **flat**-chested (= she has small breasts).*

chestnut /ˈtʃes.nʌt/ **noun; adj**
▸**noun 1** [C] a large, shiny, reddish-brown nut, or the tree on which the nuts grow: *A man in the street was selling bags of **roast** chestnuts.* ◦ *a 200-year-old chestnut **tree*** → See also **horse chestnut 2** [C] a reddish-brown horse **3** [U] a reddish-brown colour

IDIOM **old chestnut** informal a subject, idea, or joke that has been discussed or repeated so often that it is not funny any more

▸**adj** reddish-brown in colour

ˌchest of ˈdrawers **noun** [C] (US also **bureau**) (B1) a piece of furniture with drawers in which you keep things such as clothes

chesty /ˈtʃes.ti/ **adj** mainly UK having or relating to a lot of MUCUS (= thick liquid) in the lungs: *a chesty cough*

chevron /ˈʃev.rᵊn/, /-rɒn/ **noun** [C] a shape like a V or an upside down V, used especially on the sleeve of a police or military uniform to show the wearer's rank, or on road signs in Britain to show a severe bend in the road

chew /tʃuː/ **verb; noun**
▸**verb** [I or T] **1** (B2) to crush food into smaller, softer pieces with the teeth so that it can be swallowed: *This meat is difficult to chew.* ◦ *You don't chew your food enough – that's why you get indigestion.* **2** (B2) to bite something with your teeth, usually in order to taste its flavour: *Would you like some gum to chew?* ◦ *She gave the children some sweets to chew (**on**) during the long car journey.* ◦ *She sat in the dentist's waiting room, nervously chewing (**at**) (= biting) her nails.*

IDIOM **chew the fat** informal to talk with someone in an informal and friendly way: *We sat in a bar most of the evening just chewing the fat.*

PHRASAL VERBS **chew sb out** US informal to tell someone angrily that they have done something wrong: *The coach chewed his team out for playing so badly.* • **chew sth over** informal to think about or discuss something carefully for a long time: *I've been chewing the problem over since last week.* • **chew sth up** If a machine chews up something that you have put inside it, it damages or destroys it: *The cash machine chewed up my card!*

▸**noun** [C] **1** an act of chewing something **2** a hard sweet that gets softer the more you chew it

C

ˈchewing ˌgum noun [U] B1 a sweet that you keep in your mouth and chew to get its flavour, but do not swallow: *Would you like a* ***piece/stick*** *of chewing gum?*

chewy /ˈtʃuː.i/ **adj** describes food that needs to be chewed a lot before it is swallowed: *The meat was tasteless and chewy.*

chi /tʃiː/ noun [U] (or **qi**) in some systems of Chinese medicine and exercise, the most important energy that a person has

chiaroscuro /kiˌɑː.rəˈskʊə.rəʊ/ US /-ˌɑːr.əˈskjʊr.oʊ/ **noun** [U] specialized the use of areas of light and darkness in a painting: *Caravaggio is famous for his use of chiaroscuro.*

chic /ʃiːk/ **adj** stylish and fashionable: *I like your haircut – it's very chic.* ◦ *a chic restaurant* • **chic noun** [U] *British politicians are not renowned for their chic.*

chicane /ʃɪˈkeɪn/ noun [C] specialized a piece of road with severe bends like an 'S', which forces drivers to go more slowly, especially in motor racing

chicanery /ʃɪˈkeɪ.nər.i/ US /-nɚ-/ **noun** [U] formal clever, dishonest talk or behaviour that is used to deceive people: *The investigation revealed political chicanery and corruption at the highest levels.*

Chicano /tʃɪˈkɑː.nəʊ/ US /-noʊ/ **noun** [C] (plural **Chicanos**) informal someone living in the US who was born in Mexico or whose parents came from Mexico

chichi /ˈʃiː.ʃi/ **adj** informal disapproving trying too hard to be decorated in a stylish or attractive way and therefore having no real style or beauty: *They live in a rather chichi part of town.*

chick /tʃɪk/ noun [C] **BIRD** ▷ **1** a baby bird, especially a young chicken **WOMAN** ▷ **2** slang a young woman. This word is considered offensive by many women.

chicken /ˈtʃɪk.ɪn/ **noun; adj; verb**

▸**noun BIRD** ▷ **1** A2 [C or U] a type of bird kept on a farm for its eggs or its meat, or the meat of this bird that is cooked and eaten: *A male chicken is called a cock and a female chicken is called a hen.* ◦ *We're having* ***roast/fried*** *chicken for dinner.* **PERSON** ▷ **2** [C] informal a person who is not brave: *Jump, you chicken!* → Synonym **coward**

IDIOMS **a chicken and egg situation** informal a situation in which it is impossible to say which of two things existed first and which caused the other one • **play chicken** slang to play dangerous games in order to discover who is the bravest

▸**adj** [after verb] child's word not brave: *Why won't you jump? Are you chicken?* → Compare **cowardly**

▸**verb**

PHRASAL VERB **chicken out** slang disapproving to decide not to do something because you are too frightened: *I was going to go bungee jumping, but I chickened out.*

chickenfeed /ˈtʃɪk.ɪn.fiːd/ **noun** [U] informal a small and not important amount of money: *They're losing $200,000 on this deal, but that's chickenfeed* ***to/for*** *a company with yearly profits of $25 million.*

chickenpox /ˈtʃɪk.ɪn.pɒks/ US /-pɑːks/ **noun** [U] an infectious disease that causes a slight fever and red spots on the skin: *Chickenpox is common among children.*

chickenshit /ˈtʃɪk.ɪn.ʃɪt/ **noun** [C], **adj** US slang disapproving for **chicken** (= a person who is not brave): *C'mon, don't be such a chickenshit – just go up and ask her to dance.*

ˈchicken ˌwire noun [U] NETTING (= material in the form of a net) made of metal wire, which was originally used to make closed areas for chickens

ˈchick ˌflick noun [C] informal humorous a film about relationships, love, etc. that attracts mainly women

ˈchick ˌlit noun [U] informal humorous stories written by women, about women, for women to read

chickpea /ˈtʃɪk.piː/ noun [C] UK (US **garˈbanzo ˌbean**) a hard, pale brown, round bean that can be cooked and eaten

chicory /ˈtʃɪk.ər.i/ US /-ɚ-/ **noun** [U] **1** (US also **endive**) a vegetable with white leaves that taste bitter and are eaten uncooked in salads **2** a powder made from the root of this plant and added to or used instead of coffee

chide /tʃaɪd/ **verb** [T] formal to speak to someone severely because they have behaved badly: *She chided him* ***for*** *his bad manners.*

chief /tʃiːf/ **adj; noun**

▸**adj** [before noun] **MOST IMPORTANT** ▷ **1** B2 most important or main: *The chief problem we have in the area now is the spread of disease.* ◦ *The weather was our chief reason for coming here.* **PERSON IN CHARGE** ▷ **2** B2 highest in rank: *the chief fire officer/accountant*

▸**noun** [C] B2 the person in charge of a group or organization, or the ruler of a TRIBE: *a police chief* ◦ *A new chief* ***of*** *the security forces has just been appointed.* ◦ [as form of address] UK humorous *Can you sign this form for me, chief?*

IDIOM **too many chiefs and not enough Indians** informal too many managers and not enough people to do the work

ˌchief ˈconstable noun [C usually singular] in Britain, the police officer in charge of the police in a particular area

ˌchief exˈecutive noun [C usually singular] the person with the most important position in a company or organization: *She's the chief executive of one of the country's largest charities.*

the ˌChief Eˈxecutive noun [S] US the president of the US

ˌchief eˌxecutive ˈofficer noun [C] (abbreviation **CEO**) the person with the most important position in a company

ˌchief ˈjustice noun [C usually singular] the most important judge of a law court, especially a very important court in a country

chiefly /ˈtʃiːf.li/ **adv** mainly: *The island chiefly attracts upmarket tourists.* ◦ *magazines intended chiefly for teenagers*

ˌchief of ˈstaff noun [C] (plural **chiefs of staff**) an officer of very high rank in the armed forces

chieftain /ˈtʃiːf.tən/ noun [C] the leader of a TRIBE

chiffon /ˈʃɪf.ɒn/ US /ʃɪˈfɑːn/ **noun; adj**

▸**noun** [U] a very thin, almost transparent cloth of SILK or NYLON

▸**adj** [before noun] US describes food that is made light by adding the clear part of eggs that have been beaten: *lemon chiffon pie*

chignon /ˈʃiː.njɒ/ US /-njɑːn/ **noun** [C] a woman's hairstyle where the hair is arranged in a knot or roll at the back of her head

chihuahua /tʃɪˈwɑː.wə/ **noun** [C] a very small dog with large eyes and smooth hair

chilblain /ˈtʃɪl.bleɪn/ noun [C] a painful red swelling on the toes or fingers, caused by cold weather

child /tʃaɪld/ noun [C] (plural **children**) **1** A1 a boy or girl from the time of birth until he or she is an adult, or a son or daughter of any age: *an eight-year-old child* ◦ *As a child I didn't eat vegetables.* ◦ *A small group of children waited outside the door.* ◦ *Both her children are now married with children of their own.* ◦ *Jan is married with three **young** children.* ◦ *They campaign for the rights of the **unborn** child.* → See also **brainchild 2** disapproving an adult who behaves badly, like a badly behaved child: *He's such a child if he doesn't get his own way.* **3 a child of sth** someone who has been very influenced by a particular period or situation: *Me, I'm a child of the 60s.*

> **!** Common mistake: **child**
>
> **Warning:** Irregular plural!
>
> If you want to form the plural of **child**, don't write 'childs', write **children**.

IDIOMS **be child's play** informal to be very easy: *Using computers nowadays is child's play.* • **(great) with child** old use (very) pregnant

ˌchild aˈbuse noun [U] behaviour in which adults intentionally treat children in a cruel or violent way

childbearing /ˈtʃaɪldˌbeə.rɪŋ/ US /-ˌber.ɪŋ/ noun [U] the process of having babies: *The survey is only concerned with women of childbearing **age**.*

ˌchild ˈbenefit noun [U] UK money received regularly by families from the government to help pay for the costs of taking care of children

childbirth /ˈtʃaɪld.bɜːθ/ US /-bɝːθ/ noun [U] the act of giving birth to a baby: *A great number of women used to die **in** childbirth.*

childcare /ˈtʃaɪld.keəʳ/ US /-ker/ noun [U] care for children provided by either the government, an organization, or a person, while parents are at work or are absent for another reason: *What childcare facilities does your company offer?* ◦ *Without the adequate provision of childcare, many women who wish to work are unable to do so.*

ˌchild-ˈfriendly adj **1** (also **ˌfamily-ˈfriendly**) A child-friendly place has special features that parents and children like: *The hotel is very child-friendly and offers a babysitting service.* **2** suitable for children: *The book provides child-friendly definitions of mathematical words.*

childhood /ˈtʃaɪld.hʊd/ noun [C or U] B1 the time when someone is a child: *She had an unhappy childhood.* → Compare **boyhood, girlhood**

childish /ˈtʃaɪl.dɪʃ/ adj **1** B2 typical of a child: *childish handwriting* **2** B2 disapproving If an adult is childish, they behave badly in a way that would be expected of a child: *He wasn't enjoying the occasion so he thought he'd spoil it for everyone else – it was very childish of him.* → Compare **childlike** • **childishly** /-li/ adv disapproving • **childishness** /-nəs/ noun [U] disapproving

childless /ˈtʃaɪld.ləs/ adj without children: *Couples who are childless can feel excluded from the rest of society.* • **childlessness** /-nəs/ noun [U]

childlike /ˈtʃaɪld.laɪk/ adj (of adults) showing the good qualities that children have, such as trusting people, being honest and enthusiastic: *a childlike innocence/quality* ◦ *All her life she had a childlike trust in other people.* → Compare **childish**

childminder /ˈtʃaɪldˌmaɪn.dəʳ/ US /-dɚ/ noun [C] UK (US **babysitter**) a person, usually a woman, whose job is to take care of other people's children in her own home: *a registered childminder* • **childmind** /-maɪnd/ verb [I or T] (US **babysit**) • **childminding** /-dɪŋ/ noun [U] (US **babysitting**)

ˈchild moˌlester noun [C] a person who tries to have sex with children

ˌchild ˈprodigy noun [C] a young child who has very great ability in something: *A child prodigy, he made his first professional tour as a pianist at the age of six.*

childproof /ˈtʃaɪld.pruːf/ adj describes containers and locks that cannot be opened or operated by a child: *Most bottles of bleach have childproof lids.*

ˈchild-ˌrearing noun [U] the work of taking care of children until they are old enough to look after themselves: *Why shouldn't a woman have a job after years of child-rearing?*

children /ˈtʃɪl.drən/ noun plural of child

ˈchildren's ˌhome noun [C] a place where children are cared for if their parents are dead or unable to take care of them

ˈchild supˌport noun [U] money that someone gives the mother or father of their children when they do not live with them → See also **maintenance**

chill /tʃɪl/ verb; noun; adj

▸verb [I or T] to (cause to) become cold but not freeze: *I've put the beer in the fridge to chill.* ◦ *Chill the wine before serving.*

IDIOM **chill sb to the bone/marrow** to frighten someone very much: *This is a film that will chill you to the marrow.*

PHRASAL VERB **chill out** (also **chill**) B2 to relax completely, or not allow things to upset you: *I'm just chilling out in front of the TV.* ◦ *Chill out, Dad. The train doesn't leave for another hour!*

▸noun COLD ▷ **1** C2 [S] a feeling of cold: *There was a chill in the air this morning.* ILLNESS ▷ **2** [C] a slight fever: *Don't go out with wet hair, you might **catch** a chill.* BAD FEELING ▷ **3** C2 [S] a sudden unpleasant feeling, especially of fear: *I suddenly realized, with a chill of apprehension, the danger ahead.*

IDIOMS **send chills down/up sb's spine** to make someone feel very frightened: *His words sent a chill down her spine.* • **take the chill off sth** to make something slightly less cold: *We lit the fire to take the chill off the room.*

▸adj literary **chilly** (= cold)

IDIOM **the chill wind of sth** literary the problems caused by something: *Many more businesses are feeling the chill wind of the recession.*

chillax /tʃɪˈlæks/ verb [I] informal to become calm and relax: *Just chillax, Dan, they'll be here soon.*

chilled /tʃɪld/ adj informal relaxed, not worrying about anything: *Me, I'm feeling pretty chilled.*

chilli (plural **chillies**) UK (US **chili** (plural **chilies**)) /ˈtʃɪl.i/ noun [C or U] A2 the small, red or green seed case from particular types of PEPPER plant that is used to make some foods very hot and spicy

chilli con carne /ˌtʃɪl.i.kɒnˈkɑː.ni/ US /-kɑːnˈkɑːr-/ noun [U] a spicy dish of meat, onions, chillies or chilli powder, and usually beans

chilling /ˈtʃɪl.ɪŋ/ adj frightening: *a chilling tale* ◦ *The monument stands as a chilling reminder of man's inhumanity to man.* • **chillingly** /-li/ adv

ˈchilli ˌpowder noun [U] a dark red powder made from dried chillies and other spices, used to give flavour to particular foods

ˈchill ˌroom noun [C] RELAXING AREA ▷ **1** (also **ˈchill-out ˌroom**) a room that people can use to relax in, for example at a dance CLUB or office: *The club has three rooms, a chill room and two dance floors.* **COLD STORE** ▷ **2** a room used for storing things that is kept cold, usually used for keeping food fresh

chilly /ˈtʃɪl.i/ adj **COLD** ▷ **1** C1 (literary **chill**) (of weather, conditions in a room, or parts of the body) cold: *The bathroom* ***gets*** *chilly in the winter.* ◦ *I felt a bit chilly so I put on a jacket.* ◦ *a chilly October day* **UNFRIENDLY** ▷ **2** unfriendly: *I went to see the sales manager but got a rather chilly reception.*

chime /tʃaɪm/ verb; noun

▸verb [I or T] (of bells) to make a clear ringing sound: *In the square the church bells chimed.*

PHRASAL VERB **chime in** informal to interrupt or speak in a conversation, usually to agree with what has been said: *'It's very difficult,' I said. 'Impossible,' she chimed in.* ◦ *Andy chimed in* ***with*** *his view of the situation.*

▸noun **1** [C] a ringing sound: *I was woken up by the chimes of the cathedral bells.* **2** [plural] a set of small bells, or objects that make ringing sounds: *wind chimes*

chimera /kaɪˈmɪə.rə/ US /-ˈmɪr.ə/ noun [C] formal a hope or dream that is extremely unlikely ever to come true • **chimerical** /kaɪˈmer.ɪ.kəl/ adj

chimney /ˈtʃɪm.ni/ noun [C] **PIPE** ▷ **1** B2 a hollow structure that allows the smoke from a fire inside a building to escape to the air outside: *Factory chimneys belched dense white smoke into the sky.* **PASSAGE** ▷ **2** specialized a narrow vertical passage in the rock of a CLIFF or mountain, through which a person can climb

chimney

ˈ**chimney** ˌ**breast** noun [C] the part of a wall in a room that is built around a chimney and into which a FIREPLACE is built

ˈ**chimney pot** noun [C] a short pipe, often made of clay, fixed to the top of a chimney

ˈ**chimney stack** noun [C] UK the part of a chimney that sticks out above a roof

ˈ**chimney** ˌ**sweep** noun [C] (informal **sweep**) a person whose job is to clean inside chimneys, usually using a set of brushes with a very long handle

chimpanzee /ˌtʃɪm.pænˈziː/ noun [C] (informal **chimp**) a small, very intelligent African APE with black or brown fur

chin /tʃɪn/ noun [C] B1 the part of a person's face below their mouth: *To keep the helmet in position, fasten the strap beneath the chin.* ◦ *She sat behind the table, her chin resting in her hands.*

IDIOMS **chin up!** informal something you say to someone in a difficult situation in order to encourage them to be brave and try not to be sad: *Chin up! It'll soon be the weekend.* • **take it on the chin** informal to accept unpleasant events bravely and without complaining

china /ˈtʃaɪ.nə/ noun [U] clay of a high quality that is shaped and then heated to make it permanently hard, or objects made from this, such as cups and plates: *china plates*

Chinatown /ˈtʃaɪ.nə.taʊn/ noun [C or U] an area of a city outside China where many Chinese people live and there are a lot of Chinese restaurants and shops

chinchilla /tʃɪnˈtʃɪl.ə/ noun [C] a small South American animal with very soft, pale grey fur that is used to make expensive coats, etc.

ˌ**Chinese** ˈ**chequers** UK (US ˌ**Chinese** ˈ**checkers**) noun [U] a game played on a star-shaped board where small balls are moved from hole to hole

ˌ**Chinese** ˈ**gooseberry** noun [C] a **kiwi**

ˌ**Chinese** ˈ**lantern** noun [C] a folding decoration made from thin coloured paper

ˌ**Chinese** ˈ**puzzle** noun [C] **1** a game where you have to solve the problem of fitting many different pieces together, especially boxes inside other boxes **2** a situation that is complicated and difficult to understand

chink /tʃɪŋk/ noun; verb

▸noun **CRACK** ▷ **1** [C] a small narrow CRACK or opening: *I peered through a chink in the curtains and saw them all inside.* **SOUND** ▷ **2** [C usually singular] a light ringing sound: *On a hot day it's lovely to hear the chink of ice in a glass.* → Synonym **clink**

IDIOM **chink in sb's armour** a fault in someone's character or argument that may cause problems for them: *A single chink in our armour at the negotiating table means we could lose out badly.*

▸verb [I] to make a light ringing sound: *The coins chinked lightly in his pocket as he walked along.* → Synonym **clink**

Chink /tʃɪŋk/ noun [C] (UK also **Chinky**) an offensive word for a Chinese person

Chinky /ˈtʃɪŋ.ki/ noun [C] UK slang an offensive word for a restaurant serving Chinese food

chinless /ˈtʃɪn.ləs/ adj mainly UK (US usually ˌ**weak**ˈ**chinned**) having a very small chin, sometimes thought of as a sign of a weak character

ˌ**chinless** ˈ**wonder** noun [C] UK informal a silly man, typically of high social class

-chinned /-tʃɪnd/ suffix having a particular type of chin: *square-chinned*

chinos /ˈtʃiː.nəʊz/ US /-noʊz/ noun [plural] loose cotton trousers, usually of a light brown colour

ˈ**chin** ˌ**rest** noun [C] the part of an instrument, such as a VIOLIN, on which a person puts their chin for support while playing

chinstrap /ˈtʃɪn.stræp/ noun [C] a strap that goes around the lower part of a person's head to keep a hat, especially a HELMET, in place

chintz /tʃɪnts/ noun [U] cotton cloth, usually with patterns of flowers, that has a slightly shiny appearance

chintzy /ˈtʃɪnt.si/ adj **DECORATION** ▷ **1** decorated with a lot of chintz: *I find their house a bit too chintzy.* **CHEAP** ▷ **2** US (of things) cheap and of low quality, or (of people) not willing to spend money: *It's a chintzy hat, you can't expect it to last for long.* ◦ *Don't be so chintzy, the whole evening will only cost you ten bucks.*

chinwag /ˈtʃɪn.wæg/ noun [C] informal a long and pleasant conversation between friends: *We had a* ***good*** *chinwag over a bottle of wine.*

chip /tʃɪp/ noun; verb

▸noun **FRIED FOOD** ▷ **1** A1 [C usually plural] UK (US **French fry**) a long thin piece of potato that is fried and usually eaten hot: *fish and chips* ◦ *beans/egg/sausage and chips* ◦ *oven chips (= chips that are baked in a cooker)* **2** A2 [C usually plural] US for **crisp**: *a bag of chips* **3** [C usually plural] a thin slice of fried MAIZE, BANANA, or other food that is eaten cold: *banana chips* **COMPUTER PART** ▷ **4** B2 [C] (also **microchip**) a very small piece of SEMICONDUCTOR, especially in a computer, that contains extremely small electronic CIRCUITS and devices, and can perform particular operations: *a silicon chip* **PIECE** ▷ **5** [C] a small piece that has been broken off a larger object, or the mark left on an object such as a cup, plate, etc. where a small piece has been broken off it: *wood chips* ◦ *Polly fell and knocked a chip **out of** her front tooth.* ◦ *This mug's got a chip **in it/out of** it.* **PLASTIC COIN** ▷ **6** [C] a small plastic disc used to represent a particular amount of money in GAMBLING: figurative *The hostages are being held as a **bargaining** chip by terrorist organizations.*

IDIOMS **a chip off the old block** informal someone who is very similar in character to their father or mother • **have a chip on your shoulder** informal to seem angry all the time because you think you have been treated unfairly or feel you are not as good as other people: *He's got a chip on his shoulder about not having been to university.* • **have had your chips** UK informal to have lost your position, importance, or power • **when the chips are down** informal when you are in a very difficult or dangerous situation, especially one that makes you understand the true value of people or things: *One day when the chips are down, you will know who your true friends are.*

▸verb [I or T] (-pp-) to break a small piece off something by accident: *I wish my nail polish wouldn't keep chipping.* ◦ *He's chipped a bone in his wrist.*

PHRASAL VERBS **chip (sth) in** informal to give some money when several people are giving money to pay for something together: *They all chipped in £100 and bought their mother a trip to Greece.* • **chip in** mainly UK informal to interrupt a conversation in order to say something: *I'll start and you can all chip in **with** your comments.*

ˌchip and ˈPIN noun [U] a way of paying for goods and services using a CREDIT CARD and a secret number instead of a SIGNATURE

chipboard /ˈtʃɪp.bɔːd/ (US) /-bɔːrd/ noun [U] hard material made from small pieces of wood mixed with glue, often used instead of wood in making furniture because it is cheaper: *veneered chipboard*

chipmunk /ˈtʃɪp.mʌŋk/ noun [C] a small North American animal with fur and dark strips along its back

chipolata (also **chippolata**) /ˌtʃɪp.əˈlɑː.tə/ (US) /-t̬ə/ noun [C] UK a small thin sausage

chipped /tʃɪpt/ adj with a small piece or pieces broken off: *a chipped glass* ◦ *All the plates were old and chipped.*

chipper /ˈtʃɪp.əʳ/ (US) /-ɚ/ adj informal very happy: *You seem mighty chipper this morning – what's up?*

chipping /ˈtʃɪp.ɪŋ/ noun [C usually plural] UK a small piece of stone, put in road surfaces or under railway tracks

chippy /ˈtʃɪp.i/ adj; noun
▸adj UK easily offended or annoyed
▸noun [C] UK informal for **chip shop**

ˈchip ˌshop noun [C] (informal **chippy**) UK a shop that sells fried fish, potatoes, and other foods, to take away to eat

chiropodist /kɪˈrɒp.ə.dɪst/, /ʃɪ-/ (US) /-ˈrɑː.pə-/ noun [C] a person whose job is to treat problems and diseases of people's feet • **chiropody** /-di/ noun [U]

chiropractor /ˈkaɪ.rəʊ.præk.təʳ/ (US) /-roʊ.præk.tɚ/ noun [C] a person whose job is to treat diseases by pressing a person's JOINTS (= places where two bones are connected), especially those in the back

• **chiropractic** /ˌkaɪᵊ.rəʊˈpræk.tɪk/ (US) /-roʊ-/ noun [U] the system of treatment used by a chiropractor

chirp /tʃɜːp/ (US) /tʃɝːp/ verb **1** [I] (also **chirrup**) (especially of a bird) to make a short high sound or sounds **2** [+ speech] to say something with a high, happy voice: *'Morning!' she chirped.*

chirpy /ˈtʃɜː.pi/ (US) /ˈtʃɝː-/ adj happy and active: *She seemed quite chirpy this morning.* • **chirpily** /-pɪ.li/ adv • **chirpiness** /-nəs/ noun [U]

chisel /ˈtʃɪz.ᵊl/ noun; verb
▸noun [C] a tool with a long metal blade that has a sharp edge for cutting wood, stone, etc.
▸verb [T] (-ll- or US usually -l-) to use a chisel: *She chiselled a figure **out of** the marble.*

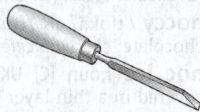

chisel

chiselled (US usually **chiseled**) /ˈtʃɪz.ᵊld/ adj (of a man's face or features) strong and sharp, in an attractive way: *She brought with her a young man with finely chiselled **features**.*

chit /tʃɪt/ noun [C] **NOTE** ▷ **1** UK old-fashioned an official note giving information or showing an amount of money that is owed or has been paid: *a chit for the dry cleaner's* **GIRL** ▷ **2** old-fashioned disapproving a young and silly girl: *just a chit **of a girl***

ˈchit-chat noun [U] informal informal conversation about matters that are not important: *'What did you talk about?' 'Oh, just chit-chat.'* • **ˈchit-chat** verb [I] (-tt-) *We were just chit-chatting about this and that.*

chitin /ˈkaɪ.tɪn/ (US) /-tᵊn/ noun [U] specialized a hard substance in the outer shell of insects and animals such as SHRIMP and LOBSTER, and in the cell walls of some FUNGI

chivalrous /ˈʃɪv.ᵊl.rəs/ adj A chivalrous man is polite, honest, fair, and kind towards women. • **chivalrously** /-li/ adv

chivalry /ˈʃɪv.ᵊl.ri/ noun [U] **1** very polite, honest, and kind behaviour, especially by men towards women **2** the system of behaviour followed by KNIGHTS in the MEDIEVAL period of history, that put a high value on honour, kindness, and courage: *the age of chivalry*

chives /tʃaɪvz/ noun [plural] a plant with long thin leaves and purple flowers, or its leaves when cut into small pieces and used in cooking to give a flavour similar to onions

chivvy /ˈtʃɪv.i/ verb [T usually + adv/prep] UK informal to encourage someone to do something they do not want to do: *He kept putting off writing the report so I had to chivvy him **along**.* ◦ *I had to chivvy him **into** writing the report.*

chloride /ˈklɔː.raɪd/ (US) /ˈklɔːr.aɪd/ noun [C or U] specialized a chemical COMPOUND that is a mixture of chlorine and another substance: *Sodium chloride is the chemical name for common salt.*

chlorinate /ˈklɔː.rɪ.neɪt/ (US) /ˈklɔːr.ɪ-/ verb [T] to add chlorine to water in order to kill organisms that might cause infection • **chlorinated** /-neɪ.tɪd/ (US) /-neɪ.t̬ɪd/ adj *chlorinated swimming pools*

chlorine /ˈklɔː.riːn/ (US) /ˈklɔːr.iːn/ noun [U] (symbol **Cl**) a chemical element that is a greenish-yellow gas with a strong smell, added to water in order to kill organisms that might cause infection: *The chlorine in the pool makes my eyes sore.*

chlorofluorocarbon /ˌklɔː.rəʊˌflɔː.rəˈkɑː.bᵊn/ (US) /ˌklɔːr.oʊˌflɔːr.oʊˈkɑːr-/ noun [C or U] specialized **CFC**

chloroform /ˈklɒr.ə.fɔːm/ (US) /ˈklɔːr.ə.fɔːrm/ noun [U] a clear liquid with a sweet smell that makes you unconscious if you breathe it in

chlorophyll /ˈklɒr.ə.fɪl/ (US) /ˈklɔːr.ə-/ **noun** [U] the green substance in plants, that allows them to use the energy from the sun

C

chloroplast /ˈklɒr.ə.plɑːst/ (US) /ˈklɔːr.ə.plæst/ **noun** [C] specialized one of the parts in a plant cell that contain chlorophyll and where energy provided by light from the sun is turned into food by PHOTOSYNTHESIS

chocaholic /ˌtʃɒk.əˈhɒl.ɪk/ (US) /ˌtʃɑː.kəˈhɑː.lɪk/ **noun** [C] another spelling of **chocoholic**

choccy /ˈtʃɒk.i/ (US) /ˈtʃɑːk-/ **noun** [C or U] UK informal chocolate: *choccy bickies*

ˈchoc ice **noun** [C] UK a small block of ICE CREAM covered in a thin layer of chocolate

chock /tʃɒk/ (US) /tʃɑːk/ **noun** [C] a block of wood that can be put under a wheel or a heavy object to prevent it from moving

chocka /ˈtʃɒk.ə/ (US) /ˈtʃɑːk-/ **adj** [after verb] UK slang for **chock-a-block**

ˌchock-a-ˈblock **adj** [after verb] informal describes a place that is very full of people or things: *The streets were chock-a-block (**with** cars).*

chocker /ˈtʃɒk.ə/ (US) /ˈtʃɑːk-/ **adj** (also **chockers**) UK slang for **chock-a-block**

ˌchock-ˈfull **adj** [after verb] informal completely full: *The whole room was chock-full **of** books.*

chocoholic /ˌtʃɒk.əˈhɒl.ɪk/ (US) /ˌtʃɑː.kəˈhɑː.lɪk/ **noun** [C] (also **chocaholic**) informal humorous a person who loves chocolate and eats a lot of it

chocolate /ˈtʃɒk.lət/ (US) /ˈtʃɑːk-/ **noun** **1** A1 [C or U] a sweet, usually brown, food made from CACAO seeds, that is usually sold in a block, or a small sweet made from this: *a bar of chocolate* ◦ *chocolate biscuits/mousse* ◦ *milk/dark/white chocolate* ◦ *I took her a **box of** chocolates.* **2** [C or U] UK for **hot chocolate** **3** [U] a dark brown colour • **chocolate adj** of a dark brown colour

ˈchocolate-box **adj** [before noun] UK describes something that looks very attractive, but is traditional and boring: *a chocolate-box village*

chocolatey /ˈtʃɒk.lət.i/ (US) /ˈtʃɑːk.lət̬-/ **adj** like chocolate in smell, taste, or colour: *The sauce itself was like chocolatey toffee.*

chocolatier /ˈtʃɒk.lət.ɪəʳ/ (US) /ˈtʃɑːk.lət̬.ɪr/ **noun** [C] a person or company that makes or sells chocolate

choice /tʃɔɪs/ **noun; adj**

▸**noun** **ACT** ▷ **1** B1 [C or U] an act or the possibility of choosing: *If the product doesn't work, you are given the choice of a refund or a replacement.* ◦ *It's a difficult choice to **make**.* ◦ *It's your choice/The choice is yours (= only you can decide).* ◦ *It was a choice **between** pain now or pain later, so I chose pain later.* ◦ *Now you know all the facts, you can make an **informed** choice.* ◦ *I'd prefer not to work but I do**n't have much** choice (= this is not possible).* ◦ *He **had no** choice **but to** accept (= he had to accept).* ◦ *Is she single **by** choice?* ◦ *Champagne is their drink **of** choice (= the one they most often drink).* **VARIETY** ▷ **2** B1 [S or U] the range of different things from which you can choose: *There wasn't much choice on the menu.* ◦ *The evening menu offers a **wide** choice of dishes.* ◦ *The dress is available **in a** choice **of** colours.* **PERSON/THING** ▷ **3** B1 [C] a person or thing that has been chosen or that can be chosen: *Harvard was not his **first** choice.* ◦ *He wouldn't be my choice **as** a friend.* ◦ *This type of nursery care may well be the best choice **for** your child.*

> **Common mistake: choice or choose?**
>
> **Warning:** do not confuse the noun **choice** with the verb **choose**:
>
> ~~*There are a wide range of dishes to choice from.*~~
>
> *There are a wide range of dishes to choose from.*

> **Word partners for choice (ACT)**
>
> *have* a choice • *make* a choice • *give/offer* sb a choice • be *faced with* a choice • an *informed* choice • a choice *between* [two things or people] • a choice *of* sth • *by/from* choice

> **Word partners for choice (VARIETY)**
>
> a *bewildering/excellent/wide* choice • *offer* a choice of sth • a choice *of* sth

> **Word partners for choice (PERSON/THING)**
>
> a *good/obvious/popular/wise* choice • an *odd/unfortunate* choice • sb's choice *of* sth • sb's *first/second* choice

▸**adj** of high quality: *I had the the most expensive dish on the menu – a choice fillet of fish.*

choir /kwaɪəʳ/ (US) /kwaɪr/ **noun** [C, + sing/pl verb] B2 a group of people who sing together, especially in a church: *He sings **in** the church choir.* ◦ *choir **practice***
→ See also **choral, chorister**

choirboy /ˈkwaɪə.bɔɪ/ (US) /ˈkwaɪr-/ **noun** [C] a boy who sings in a church choir

choirmaster /ˈkwaɪəˌmɑː.stəʳ/ (US) /ˈkwaɪrˌmæs.tɚ/ **noun** [C] a person who trains a choir and is in control of their singing when they perform

choke /tʃəʊk/ (US) /tʃoʊk/ **verb; noun**

▸**verb** **STOP BREATHING** ▷ **1** [I or T] If you choke, or if something chokes you, you stop breathing because something is blocking your throat: *She choked **to death** on a fish bone.* ◦ *Children can choke **on** peanuts.* ◦ *Peanuts can choke a small child.* **2** [T] to make someone stop breathing by pressing their throat with the hands **FILL** ▷ **3** [T usually passive] (also **choke up**) to fill something such as a road or pipe, so that nothing can pass through: *At lunchtime the streets were choked with traffic.* **FAIL** ▷ **4** [I] (also **choke it**) (usually in sports) to fail to do something at a time when it is urgent, usually because you suddenly lose confidence: *He could score points at will during the qualifying matches, but in the final he completely choked.*

PHRASAL VERB **choke sth back** If you choke back feelings or tears, you force yourself not to show how angry or upset you are: *Choking back my anger, I tried to speak calmly.* ◦ *'John has had an accident,' she said, choking back **the tears**.*

▸**noun** [C or U] a device in a motor vehicle that changes the amount of air going into the engine, allowing more fuel compared to air to go in and therefore making the engine easier to start

choked /tʃəʊkt/ (US) /tʃoʊkt/ **adj** [after verb] unable to speak because you are upset: *She tried to say a few words but found herself choked.*

choker /ˈtʃəʊ.kəʳ/ (US) /ˈtʃoʊ.kɚ/ **noun** [C] a narrow strip of cloth or a NECKLACE that fits very closely around a woman's neck: *a pearl choker*

cholera /ˈkɒl.ᵊr.ə/ (US) /ˈkɑː.lɚ-/ **noun** [U] a serious infection of the bowels caused by drinking infected water or eating infected food, causing DIARRHOEA, vomiting, and often death

choleric /kɒlˈer.ɪk/ (US) /kəˈler-/ **adj** formal very angry or easily annoyed

cholesterol /kəˈles.tᵊr.ɒl/ (US) /-tə.rɑːl/ noun [U] C1 a substance containing a lot of fat that is found in the body tissue and blood of all animals, thought to be part of the cause of heart disease if there is too much of it: *an oil which is high in polyunsaturates and low in cholesterol*

chomp /tʃɒmp/ (US) /tʃɑːmp/ verb [I or T] (also **champ**) to CHEW food noisily: *He was chomping **away** on a bar of chocolate.*

choo-choo /ˈtʃuː.tʃuː/ noun [C] (plural **choo-choos**) child's word a train

chook /tʃʊk/ noun [C] Australian English informal a chicken

choose /tʃuːz/ verb [I or T] (**chose**, **chosen**) **1** A1 to decide what you want from two or more things or possibilities: *She had to choose **between** the two men in her life.* ◦ *Danny, come here and choose your ice cream.* ◦ *He chose a shirt **from** the many in his wardrobe.* ◦ [+ question word] *It's difficult choosing **wh**ere to live.* ◦ [+ two objects] *I've chosen Luis a present/I've chosen a present **for** Luis.* ◦ *Yesterday the selectors chose Dales **as** the team's new captain.* ◦ [+ obj + to infinitive] *The firm's directors chose Emma **to** be the new production manager.* **2 choose to do sth** B1 to decide to do something: *Katie chose (= decided) **to** stay away from work that day.* **3 little/not much to choose between** When there is little to choose between two or more things, they are (all) very similar.

> **Common mistake: choose**
>
> **Warning:** Check your verb endings!
>
> Many learners make mistakes when using **choose** in the past tense. In the past simple, don't say 'choosed' or 'chosed', say **chose**. The past participle is **chosen**.

> **Other ways of saying choose**
>
> The verbs **pick** and **select** are often used when someone chooses someone or something after thinking carefully:
>
> *He's been **picked** for the school football team.*
>
> *We've **selected** three candidates.*
>
> In more informal situations **go for**, **opt for**, or **decide on** are sometimes used:
>
> *I've **decided on** blue walls for the bathroom.*
>
> *I think I'll **go for** the chocolate cake.*
>
> *Mike's **opted for** early retirement.*
>
> The verbs **opt** and **decide** can also be used when someone chooses to do something:
>
> *Most people **opt** to have the operation.*
>
> *I've **decided** to take the job.*

choosy /ˈtʃuː.zi/ adj informal difficult to please because you are very exact about what you like: *She's very choosy **about** what she eats and drinks.*

chop /tʃɒp/ (US) /tʃɑːp/ verb; noun

▸verb [T] (-pp-) **1** B2 to cut something into pieces with an AXE, knife, or other sharp instrument: *He was chopping wood in the yard.* ◦ *Add some fresh parsley, finely chopped.* ◦ *Chop (**up**) the onions and carrots roughly.* ◦ informal *Laura had her hair chopped (= cut) yesterday.* **2** If something is chopped in business, it is stopped or reduced: *Because of lack of funding many long-term research projects are being chopped.*

IDIOM **chop and change** UK to keep changing your ideas, opinions, activities, or job: *After six months of chopping and changing, we've decided to go back to our old system.*

PHRASAL VERBS **chop sth down** C2 to cut through something to make it fall down: *Most of the diseased trees were chopped down last year.* • **chop sth off** to cut off part of something with a sharp tool: *Two of his fingers were chopped off in the accident.*

▸noun [C] **MEAT** ▷ **1** a small piece of meat with a bone still in it: *a lamb/pork chop* **CUT** ▷ **2** an act of cutting something with an AXE, knife, or other sharp instrument **3 the chop a** mainly UK (US usually **the axe**) the situation in which your job is taken away from you, either because you have done something wrong or as a way of saving money: *If you're late for work again, you'll be **for** the chop.* ◦ *Anyone stepping out of line is liable to **get** the chop.* ◦ *Hundreds of workers at the factory have already been **given** the chop.* **b** the ending of a factory, school, etc. or plan: *When the reorganization occurs, the smaller departments will be the first **for** the chop.* **MOUTH** ▷ **4 chops** [plural] informal the area of the face surrounding the mouth of a person or an animal: *a dog **licking** its chops* ◦ *I'll give him a smack in the chops if he doesn't shut up.*

ˌchop-ˈchop exclamation informal used to tell someone to hurry: *Come on, chop-chop, we're late!*

chophouse /ˈtʃɒp.haʊs/ (US) /ˈtʃɑːp-/ noun [C] a restaurant that mainly serves thick slices of meat such as chops and STEAKS

chopper /ˈtʃɒp.əʳ/ (US) /ˈtʃɑː.pɚ/ noun **AIRCRAFT** ▷ **1** [C] informal for **helicopter** **TOOL** ▷ **2** [C] a small AXE held in one hand **TEETH** ▷ **3 choppers** [plural] slang teeth, especially a set of artificial teeth **PENIS** ▷ **4** [C] UK slang for PENIS

choppy /ˈtʃɒp.i/ (US) /ˈtʃɑː.pi/ adj (of sea, lakes, or rivers) with a lot of small, rough waves caused by the wind

chopstick /ˈtʃɒp.stɪk/ (US) /ˈtʃɑːp-/ noun [C usually plural] one of a pair of narrow sticks that are used for eating East Asian food

chop suey /ˌtʃɒpˈsuː.i/ (US) /ˌtʃɑːp-/ noun [U] a Chinese dish made from small pieces of meat and vegetables, especially BEAN SPROUTS, cooked together

choral /ˈkɔː.rᵊl/ (US) /ˈkɔːr.ᵊl/ adj of (music sung by) a CHOIR or a CHORUS: *choral music* ◦ *a choral society*

chorale /kɒrˈɑːl/, /kəˈrɑːl/ noun [C] a formal song written to be sung by a CHOIR, especially in a church

chord /kɔːd/ (US) /kɔːrd/ noun [C] three or more musical notes played at the same time

chore /tʃɔːʳ/ (US) /tʃɔːr/ noun [C] C1 a job or piece of work that is often boring or unpleasant but needs to be done regularly: *I'll go shopping when I've **done my** chores (= done the jobs in or around the house).* ◦ *I find writing reports a real chore (= very boring).*

choreography /ˌkɒr.iˈɒg.rə.fi/ (US) /ˌkɔːr.iˈɑː.grə-/ noun [U] the skill of combining movements into dances to be performed: *a flamboyant style of choreography* • **choreograph** /ˈkɒr.i.ə.grɑːf/ (US) /ˈkɔːr.i.ə.græf/ verb [T] *The ballet was choreographed by Ashton.* • **choreographer** /-fəʳ/ (US) /-fɚ/ noun [C]

chorister /ˈkɒr.ɪ.stəʳ/ (US) /ˈkɔːr.ɪ.stɚ/ noun [C] one of a group of people who sing together in a CHOIR, either in a CATHEDRAL or in a special school connected to a university

chorizo /tʃəˈriː.zəʊ/ (US) /-zoʊ/ noun [C or U] (plural **chorizos**) a spicy sausage from Spain or Latin America

choroid /ˈkɔː.rɔɪd/ (US) /ˈkɔːr.ɔɪd/ noun [C] specialized the layer between the RETINA and the outer white covering of the eye, which contains BLOOD VESSELS and PIGMENT (= substance giving colour)

chortle /ˈtʃɔː.tl/ (US) /ˈtʃɔːr.t̬l/ verb [I] to laugh, showing pleasure and satisfaction, often at someone else's bad luck: *She chortled* ***with*** *glee at the news.* • **chortle** noun [C] *I thought I heard a chortle at the back of the room.*

chorus /ˈkɔː.rəs/ (US) /ˈkɔːr.əs/ **noun; verb**

▸**noun** SONG PART ▷ **1** [C] part of a song that is repeated several times, usually after each VERSE (= set of lines) or a piece of music written to be sung by a CHOIR (= group of singers): *I'll sing the verses and I'd like you all to* ***join in*** *the chorus.* ◦ *The choir will be performing the Hallelujah Chorus at the concert.* ◦ *They burst into* ***a*** *chorus* ***of*** *(= they sang the song) Happy Birthday.* SINGING GROUP ▷ **2** [C, + sing/pl verb] a group of people who are trained to sing together: *He sings with the Los Angeles Gay Men's Chorus.* THEATRE GROUP ▷ **3** [C, + sing/pl verb] a group of performers who, as a team, sing or dance in a show: *She quickly left the chorus for a starring role.* ◦ *a chorus* ***girl*** **4** [S, + sing/pl verb] specialized a group of actors in ancient Greek plays who explained or gave opinions on what was happening in the play using music, poetry, and dance SPEAKING TOGETHER ▷ **5** [C usually singular] many people speaking together or saying a similar thing at the same time: *The newcomers added their voices to the chorus expressing delight at the result.* ◦ *There was* ***a*** *chorus* ***of*** *disapproval/complaint/condemnation at his words (= everyone complained together).*

▸**verb** [T + speech] literary (of a group of people) to say similar things at the same time: *'Not now,' the children chorused* ***in unison****, 'we're watching TV.'*

ˈ**chorus** ˌ**line** noun [C usually singular, + sing/pl verb] a row of people dancing and sometimes singing in an entertainment

chose /tʃəʊz/ (US) /tʃoʊz/ verb past simple of **choose**

chosen /ˈtʃəʊ.zən/ (US) /ˈtʃoʊ-/ verb past participle of **choose**

IDIOM **the chosen few** a small group of people who are treated better than other people, often when they do not deserve it: *There's a staff canteen for everyone and there's a smarter restaurant for the chosen few.*

choux pastry /ʃuːˈpeɪ.stri/ noun [U] a type of pastry made with eggs, which when cooked forms a hollow case for filling with cream or other thick liquids

chow /tʃaʊ/ noun [U] old-fashioned slang food

chowder /ˈtʃaʊ.dər/ (US) /-dɚ/ noun [U] mainly US a type of thick soup usually made from fish or other sea creatures: *clam chowder*

chow mein /ˌtʃaʊˈmeɪn/ noun [C or U] a Chinese dish consisting of vegetables, meat, and long, thin NOODLES, all fried together

christen /ˈkrɪs.ən/ verb [T] GIVE NAME ▷ **1** to give a baby a name at a Christian ceremony and make him or her a member of the Christian Church: *She's being christened in June.* ◦ [+ noun] *She was christened Maria.* **2** to give a person a name based on a characteristic that they have: *We christened him 'Slowcoach' because he took so long to do anything.* USE FIRST ▷ **3** informal to use something for the first time: *I'm going to christen my new walking boots on Saturday.*

Christendom /ˈkrɪs.ən.dəm/ noun [U] old use Christian people or countries as a whole: *All Christendom responded to the call.*

christening /ˈkrɪs.ən.ɪŋ/ noun [C] a Christian ceremony at which a baby is given a name and made a member of the Christian Church

Christian /ˈkrɪs.tʃən/, /-ti.ən/ **adj; noun**

▸**adj** **1** of or belonging to the religion based on the teachings of Jesus Christ: *a Christian charity/organization* ◦ *the Christian faith* **2** describes a person or action that is good, kind, helpful, etc.

▸**noun** [C] someone who believes in and follows the teachings of Jesus Christ

the ˈ**Christian** ˌ**era** noun [S] the period of time that begins with the birth of Jesus Christ

Christianity /ˌkrɪs.tiˈæn.ɪ.ti/ (US) /-tʃiˈæn.ə.t̬i/ noun [U] a religion based on belief in God and the life and teachings of Jesus Christ, and on the Bible

ˈ**Christian** ˌ**name** noun [C] in Western countries, the first name and not the family name → Compare **first name**

ˌ**Christian** ˈ**Science** noun [U] a religion which considers that illness can be cured by religious belief, making medicine unnecessary

Christmas /ˈkrɪs.məs/ noun [C or U] (the period just before and after) 25 December, a Christian holy day which celebrates the birth of Jesus Christ: *We're going to my mother's for Christmas.* ◦ *Happy Christmas!* ◦ *We had a lovely Christmas.* ◦ *the Christmas holidays*

ˈ**Christmas** ˌ**cake** noun [C or U] UK a cake containing a lot of dried fruit and nuts and covered with ICING, eaten at Christmas

ˈ**Christmas** ˌ**card** noun [C] a decorated card that you send to someone at Christmas

ˌ**Christmas** ˈ**carol** noun [C] a traditional or religious song that people sing at Christmas

ˌ**Christmas** ˈ**cracker** noun [C] UK (US **bonbon**) a tube of brightly coloured paper, usually given at Christmas parties, that makes a noise when pulled apart by two people and contains small presents

Christmas cracker

ˌ**Christmas** ˈ**Day** noun [C or U] 25 December: *We spent Christmas Day with Ben's parents.*

ˌ**Christmas** ˈ**Eve** noun [C or U] 24 December, the day before Christmas Day

ˌ**Christmas** ˈ**pudding** noun [C or U] UK a sweet, dark food containing dried fruit, eaten at the end of the meal in some countries at Christmas

ˌ**Christmas** ˈ**stocking** noun [C] a large sock that children leave out when they go to bed the night before Christmas so that it can be filled with presents

Christmassy /ˈkrɪs.mə.si/ adj informal typical of Christmas, or happy because it is Christmas: *It looks very Christmassy in here with the tree and all the decorations.* ◦ *I'd feel more Christmassy if it snowed.*

ˈ**Christmas time** noun [U] (old use **Christmastide** /ˈkrɪs.məs.taɪd/) the period around Christmas Day

ˈ**Christmas** ˌ**tree** noun [C] a real or artificial FIR tree that is decorated and kept in the home at Christmas

chromatic /krəˈmæt.ɪk/ (US) /kroʊˈmæt̬-/ adj specialized COLOUR ▷ **1** [before noun] relating to colours: *a chromatic range/combination* MUSIC ▷ **2** belonging or relating to a musical SCALE in which the notes follow each other in SEMITONES: *the chromatic* ***scale***

chromatography /ˌkrəʊ.məˈtɒg.rə.fi/ (US) /ˌkroʊ.məˈtɑː.grə-/ noun [U] specialized a scientific method of finding what separate substances are in a mixture by making it flow, as a liquid or gas, through a material such as paper which different substances pass through at different speeds

chrome /krəʊm/ (US) /kroʊm/ noun [U] a hard, shiny metal that is an ALLOY of chromium and other metals: *office furnishings in glass and chrome*

ˌ**chrome** ˈ**yellow** noun [U] a bright yellow colour • ˌ**chrome-**ˈ**yellow** adj

chromium /ˈkrəʊ.mi.əm/ (US) /ˈkroʊ-/ **noun** [U] (symbol **Cr**) a chemical element that is a hard, blue-grey metal, used in combination with other metals to make chrome

chromosome /ˈkrəʊ.mə.səʊm/ (US) /ˈkroʊ.mə.soʊm/ **noun** [C] any of the rod-like structures found in all living cells, containing the chemical patterns which control what an animal or plant is like: *X and Y chromosomes* ◦ *sex chromosomes* • **chromosomal** /ˌkrəʊ.məˈsəʊ.məl/ (US) /ˌkroʊ.məˈsoʊ-/ **adj** *chromosomal abnormalities/defects*

chronic /ˈkrɒn.ɪk/ (US) /ˈkrɑː.nɪk/ **adj** LONG-LASTING ▷ **1** (C2) (especially of a disease or something bad) continuing for a long time: *chronic diseases/conditions* ◦ *chronic arthritis/pain* ◦ *a chronic invalid* ◦ *There is a chronic* ***shortage*** *of teachers.* **BAD** ▷ **2** UK informal very bad: *The acting was chronic.* • **chronically** /ˈkrɒn.ɪ.kəl.i/ (US) /ˈkrɑː.nɪ-/ **adv** *care for the chronically ill*

ˌchronic faˈtigue ˌsyndrome **noun** [U] (UK also **ME**) an illness, sometimes lasting for several years, in which a person's muscles and JOINTS (= places where two bones are connected) hurt and they are generally very tired

chronicle /ˈkrɒn.ɪ.kl̩/ (US) /ˈkrɑː.nɪ-/ **noun; verb**
▸**noun** [C] **1** a written record of historical events: *the Anglo-Saxon Chronicle* ◦ *a chronicle* ***of*** *the French Revolution* **2** part of the name of a newspaper: *the Hampshire Chronicle*
▸**verb** [T] to make a record or give details of something: *The book chronicles the writer's coming to terms with his illness.* • **chronicler** /-kləʳ/ (US) /-klɚ/ **noun** [C]

chronograph /ˈkrɒn.ə.grɑːf/ (US) /ˈkrɑː.nə.græf/ **noun** [C] specialized a piece of equipment which measures and records periods of time

chronology /krəˈnɒl.ə.dʒi/ (US) /-ˈnɑː.lə-/ **noun** [C or U] the order in which a series of events happened, or a list or explanation of these events in the order in which they happened: *I'm not sure of the chronology of events.* • **chronological** /ˌkrɒn.əˈlɒdʒ.ɪ.kəl/ (US) /-ˈlɑː.dʒɪ-/ **adj** *Give me the dates* ***in*** *chronological* ***order.*** • **chronologically** /ˌkrɒn.əˈlɒdʒ.ɪ.kəl.i/ (US) /-ˈlɑː.dʒɪ-/ **adv**

chronometer /krəˈnɒm.ɪ.təʳ/ (US) /-ˈnɑː.mɪ.t̬ɚ/ **noun** [C] specialized a piece of equipment which measures time very accurately

chrysalis /ˈkrɪs.əl.ɪs/ **noun** [C] (plural **chrysalises** /-ɪz/) an insect covered by a hard case at the stage of development before it becomes a MOTH or BUTTERFLY with wings, or the case itself

chrysanthemum /krɪˈsænθ.ə.məm/ **noun** [C] any of several types of garden plant, including some with many small flowers and some with few but very large flowers

chubby /ˈtʃʌb.i/ **adj** (especially of children) fat in a pleasant and attractive way: *chubby legs* ◦ *chubby cheeks* • **chubbiness** /-nəs/ **noun** [U]

chuck /tʃʌk/ **verb; noun**
▸**verb** **THROW** ▷ **1** [T often + adv/prep] informal to throw something carelessly: *Chuck it over there/into the corner.* ◦ [+ two objects] *Chuck me the keys.* **END** ▷ **2** [T] UK old-fashioned informal to end a romantic relationship with someone: *He's just chucked his girlfriend.*

PHRASAL VERBS **chuck sth away/out** informal to throw something away: *I've chucked out all my old clothes.* • **chuck sth in** informal to stop doing something which was a regular job or activity: *I've decided to chuck in my job.* • **chuck sb out** informal to force someone to leave a place: *He'd been chucked out* ***of*** *a club for fighting.*

▸**noun** **PERSON** ▷ **1** (also **chuckie**) Northern informal a friendly form of address: *'All right, then, chuck?'* **MACHINE** ▷ **2** [C] specialized a device for holding an object firmly in a machine

chuckle /ˈtʃʌk.l̩/ **verb** [I] to laugh quietly: *She was chuckling as she read the letter.* • **chuckle** **noun** [C] *He gave a chuckle in response to her question.*

ˌchuck ˈsteak **noun** [C] a piece of meat cut from the shoulder area of a cow

chuffed /tʃʌft/ **adj** [after verb] UK informal pleased or happy: *He was really chuffed with his present.*

chug /tʃʌg/ **verb** [I usually + adv/prep] (**-gg-**) to make the sound of an engine or motor, or to move making this sound: *The lorry chugged up the hill.* • **chug** **noun** [C often singular] *We heard the chug of the boat's engine in the distance.*

chugger /ˈtʃʌg.əʳ/ (US) /-ɚ/ **noun** [C] informal disapproving someone who stands on the street and asks people who are walking past to give money regularly to a CHARITY • **chugging** /-ɪŋ/ **noun** [U] the job or activity of being a chugger

chum /tʃʌm/ **noun; verb**
▸**noun** [C] old-fashioned informal a friend: *They were old school/college chums.* ◦ [as form of address] *That's all right by me, chum.*
▸**verb** (**-mm-**)

PHRASAL VERB **chum up** UK old-fashioned informal to become friends: *She chummed up* ***with*** *some girls from Bristol on holiday.*

chummy /ˈtʃʌm.i/ **adj** informal friendly: *They're very chummy* ***with*** *their neighbours.*

chump /tʃʌmp/ **noun** [C] old-fashioned informal a silly or stupid person: [as form of address] *You chump! Why did you tell her that?*

IDIOM **be off your chump** UK old-fashioned informal to be extremely silly or stupid

chunder /ˈtʃʌn.dəʳ/ (US) /-dɚ/ **verb** [I] mainly Australian English informal to vomit • **chunder** **noun** [U] *I nearly stepped in* ***a pool of*** *chunder.*

chunk /tʃʌŋk/ **noun** [C] **1** a roughly cut piece: *a chunk* ***of*** *cheese/meat* ◦ *pineapple/tuna chunks* **2** informal a part of something, especially a large part: *a chunk* ***of*** *text* ◦ *a substantial chunk of our profits* ◦ *Three hours is quite a chunk out of my working day.*

chunky /ˈtʃʌŋ.ki/ **adj** **1** describes clothes that are thick and heavy, or jewellery made of large pieces: *a chunky sweater* ◦ *a chunky necklace* **2** approving describes a person who is short and heavy

the Chunnel /ˈtʃʌn.əl/ **noun** [S] informal for **the Channel Tunnel**

chunni /ˈtʃʊn.i/ **noun** [C] a long SCARF that some South Asian women wear around their head and shoulders

chunter /ˈtʃʌn.təʳ/ (US) /-t̬ɚ/ **verb** [I] UK informal to complain, especially in a low voice: *Al was chuntering (****on****)* ***about*** *being the last to know what was happening.*

chupatti /tʃəˈpæ.ti/ (US) /-t̬i/ **noun** [C] a **chapatti**

church /tʃɜːtʃ/ (US) /tʃɝːtʃ/ **noun** **BUILDING** ▷ **1** (A2) [C] a building for Christian religious activities: *The town has four churches.* ◦ *a church hall (= a building belonging to a church, with a large room for meetings)* **ORGANIZATION** ▷ **2** [C or U] an official Christian religious organization: *All the local churches were represented at the memorial service.* ◦ *He went on a walking trip with some of his friends from church.* **3** [U] an occasion when this organization meets as a group of people: *I'll see her after church.* ◦ *They* ***go to*** *church every Sunday.* ◦ *church* ***services*** **4 the Church** [S] Christian religious organizations: *Some people think the Church shouldn't interfere in politics.*

IDIOM **go into/enter the church** to become a priest: *He was in his thirties when he decided to enter the church.*

churchgoer /ˈtʃɜːtʃˌɡəʊ.əʳ/ (US) /ˈtʃɝːtʃˌɡoʊ.ɚ/ noun [C] a person who goes regularly to church: *He's never been a regular churchgoer.* • **churchgoing** /-ɪŋ/ noun [U] *Churchgoing in this country is declining.*

churchman /ˈtʃɜːtʃ.mən/, /-mæn/ (US) /ˈtʃɝːtʃ-/ noun [C] (plural **-men** /-mən/) a man who is actively involved in the Church, especially as a priest or other official

the ˌChurch of ˈEngland noun (abbreviation **ˌC of ˈE**) the official Church in England: *a Church of England bishop/vicar* ◦ *The Queen is the head of the Church of England.*

churchwoman /ˈtʃɜːtʃˌwʊm.ən/ (US) /ˈtʃɝːtʃ-/ noun [C] (plural **-women** /-wɪmɪn/) a woman who is actively involved in the Church or who is a priest or official in the Church

churchy /ˈtʃɜː.tʃi/ (US) /ˈtʃɝː-/ adj informal disapproving looking like or suitable for a church: *churchy music*

churchyard /ˈtʃɜːtʃ.jɑːd/ (US) /ˈtʃɝːtʃ.jɑːrd/ noun [C] an area of land around a church, where dead bodies are buried

churidars /ˈtʃʊ.rɪ.dɑːz/ (US) /-dɑːrz/ noun [plural] a type of trousers worn by people from South Asia

churlish /ˈtʃɜː.lɪʃ/ (US) /ˈtʃɝː-/ adj rude, unfriendly, and unpleasant: *They invited me to dinner and I thought* ***it would be*** *churlish* ***to*** *refuse.* • **churlishly** /-li/ adv • **churlishness** /-nəs/ noun [U]

churn /tʃɜːn/ (US) /tʃɝːn/ verb; noun

▸verb **MOVE/MIX** ▷ **1** [T] (also **churn up**) to mix something, especially a liquid, with great force: *The sea was churned up by heavy winds.* **2** [T] to mix milk until it becomes butter **3** [I] If your stomach is churning, you feel ill, usually because you are nervous: *I had my driving test that morning and my stomach was churning.*

PHRASAL VERB **churn sth out** informal to produce large amounts of something quickly, usually something of low quality: *The factory churns out thousands of pairs of these shoes every week.* ◦ *She churns out a new best-selling novel every year.*

▸noun **CONTAINER** ▷ **1** [C] a large container for transporting milk or for making milk into butter: *a milk churn* ◦ *a butter churn* **CUSTOMERS** ▷ **2** [S or U] (also **churn rate**) the number of customers who decide to stop using a service offered by one company and to use another company, usually because it offers a better service or price: *Internet and cable television companies suffer from a high churn rate.*

chute /ʃuːt/ noun [C] **SLIDE** ▷ **1** a narrow, steep slope down which objects or people can slide: *a water chute* ◦ *a laundry chute* ◦ *a garbage/rubbish chute* ◦ *an emergency chute* **CLOTH DEVICE** ▷ **2** informal for **parachute**

ˌchutes and ˈladders noun [plural] US trademark **snakes and ladders**

chutney /ˈtʃʌt.ni/ noun [C or U] a mixture containing fruit, spices, sugar, and VINEGAR, eaten cold with especially meat or cheese: *tomato and apple chutney*

chutzpah /ˈhʊt.spə/ noun [U] approving unusual and shocking behaviour, involving taking risks but not feeling guilty

the CIA /ˌsiː.aɪˈeɪ/ noun [+ sing/pl verb] abbreviation for the Central Intelligence Agency: a US government organization that secretly collects information about other countries

ciabatta /tʃəˈbæt.ə/ noun [C or U] a type of Italian bread in a long flat shape

ciao /tʃaʊ/ exclamation informal used for saying 'goodbye' and less often 'hello'

cicada /sɪˈkɑː.də/ noun [C] (plural **cicadas**) a large insect found in warm countries, which produces a high continuous sound

CID /ˌsiː.aɪˈdiː/ noun [+ sing/pl verb] abbreviation for Criminal Investigation Department: the part of a UK police force which does not wear uniform and is responsible for discovering who has committed crimes

cider /ˈsaɪ.dəʳ/ (US) /-dɚ/ noun [U] **1** UK (US **hard cider**, Australian English **rough cider**) an alcoholic drink made from apples **2** US (UK **apple juice**) juice from crushed apples, used as a drink or to make VINEGAR

cig /sɪɡ/ noun [C] informal a cigarette

cigar /sɪˈɡɑːʳ/ (US) /-ɡɑːr/ noun [C] a tube made from dried and rolled tobacco leaves, which people smoke: *an after-dinner cigar and brandy*

cigarette /ˌsɪɡ.əʳˈret/ (US) /ˈsɪɡ.ə.ret/ noun [C] (A2) a small paper tube filled with cut pieces of tobacco, which people smoke: *a packet of cigarettes* ◦ *She* ***lit*** *a cigarette.*

cigaˈrette ˌend noun [C] (also **cigaˈrette ˌbutt**) the part of a cigarette that is left after it has been smoked: *The floor was littered with cigarette ends.*

cigarˈette ˌholder noun [C] a tube that someone uses for holding a cigarette while they are smoking it

cigarˈette ˌlighter noun [C] a device which produces a small flame

cigarˈette ˌpaper noun [C] a thin piece of paper used in making a cigarette, especially by someone who makes their own

ciggie (also **ciggy**) /ˈsɪ.ɡi/ noun [C] informal a cigarette

cilantro /sɪˈlæn.trəʊ/ (US) /-troʊ/ noun [U] US the leaves of the CORIANDER plant, used to add flavour to food

ciliary muscle /ˈsɪl.i.əʳr.iˌmʌs.l/ (US) /-er-/ noun [C] specialized one of the muscles around the LENS of the eye that can change the shape of the LENS in order to produce a clear image

cilium /ˈsɪl.i.əm/ noun [C] (plural **cilia** /-ə/) specialized one of the very small parts like hairs on the surface of a cell which move regularly and keep the surrounding liquid moving around it or help an organism with only one cell to move

ˌC.-in-ˈC. noun [C] abbreviation for **commander-in-chief**

cinch /sɪntʃ/ noun [S] informal something that is very easy and is therefore certain to be a success: *The exam was a cinch.*

cinder /ˈsɪn.dəʳ/ (US) /-dɚ/ noun [C] a small piece of partly burned coal or wood: *The cake was* ***burned to a*** *cinder (= burned black).*

ˈcinder ˌblock noun [C] US a small, light block made of concrete mixed with burnt coal, used in building

Cinderella /ˌsɪn.dəʳˈrel.ə/ (US) /-dəˈrel-/ noun [S] **1** someone or something that is given little attention or care, especially less than they deserve: *Mental health has long been considered the Cinderella of the health service.* **2** a girl in a traditional story who was badly treated by her sisters but who met and married a PRINCE

cinema /ˈsɪn.ə.mə/ **noun** **1** A2 [C] mainly UK (US usually **movie theater**) a theatre where people pay to watch films: *The town no longer has a cinema.* ◦ *a cinema ticket* **2 the cinema** C1 mainly UK (US usually **the movies**) the business of making films: *He was well known for his work in the cinema.* **3 go to the cinema** (US also **go to the movies**) to go to watch a film

cinemagoer /ˈsɪ.nə.məˌɡəʊ.əʳ/ US /-ˌɡoʊ.ɚ/ **noun** [C] UK (US **moviegoer**) a person who regularly goes to watch films at the cinema • **cinemagoing** /-ɪŋ/ **noun** [U], **adj** UK (US **moviegoing**) *Cinemagoing is still popular with the young.*

ˈ**cinema** ˌ**hall** noun [C] Indian English a cinema

cinematic /sɪ.nəˈmæt.ɪk/ US /-ˈmæţ-/ **adj** specialized relating to the cinema: *The cinematic effects in her films are clearly borrowed from the great film-makers of the past.*

cinematography /ˌsɪn.ə.məˈtɒɡ.rə.fi/ US /-ˈtɑː.ɡrə-/ **noun** [U] specialized the art and methods of film photography • **cinematographer** /-fəʳ/ US /-fɚ/ **noun** [C]

cinnamon /ˈsɪn.ə.mən/ **noun** [U] the BARK (= hard outer covering) of a tropical tree, or a brown powder made from this, used as a spice to give a particular taste to food, especially sweet food: *a cinnamon* ***stick***

cipher /ˈsaɪ.fəʳ/ US /-fɚ/ **noun** **SECRET LANGUAGE** ▷ **1** (also **cypher**) [C or U] a system of writing that prevents most people from understanding the message: *The message was written* ***in*** *cipher.* → Synonym **code** **PERSON** ▷ **2** [C] formal disapproving a person or group of people without power, but used by others for their own purposes, or someone who is not important: *The interim government is a* ***mere*** *cipher for military rule.* **NUMBER** ▷ **3** [C] US a zero: *If you have no children, enter a cipher in the space on the form.*

circa /ˈsɜː.kə/ US /ˈsɝː-/ **preposition** (written abbreviation **c, ca**) (used especially with years) approximately: *He was born circa 1600.*

circadian /sɜːˈkeɪ.di.ən/ US /sɝː-/ **adj** specialized used to describe the processes in animals and plants that happen naturally during a 24-hour period: *Our circadian* ***clock*** *makes it difficult to sleep during the day.*

circle /ˈsɜː.kl̩/ US /ˈsɝː-/ **noun; verb**

▸**noun** **SHAPE** ▷ **1** A2 [C] a continuous curved line, the points of which are always the same distance away from a fixed central point, or the area inside such a line: *Coloured paper was cut into circles.* ◦ *We sat in a circle.* **GROUP** ▷ **2** B2 [C] a group of people with family, work, or social connections: *The subject was never discussed outside the* ***family*** *circle.* ◦ *She's not one of my close circle* ***of friends****.* ◦ *We never meet these days – we* ***move in*** *different circles (= do not have the same group of friends).* **UPPER FLOOR** ▷ **3 the circle** [S] UK an upper floor in a theatre or cinema where people sit to watch the performance: *Shall I get seats in the circle or in the stalls?* → Compare **gallery, stall**

IDIOM **go/run round in circles** to keep doing or talking about the same thing without achieving anything: *The discussion kept going round in circles.* ◦ *I've been running round in circles trying to get all the reports finished before the meeting.*

▸**verb** **1** C2 [I or T] to move in a circle, often around something: *The plane circled for an hour before receiving permission to land.* ◦ *Security staff circled the grounds of the house with guard dogs every hour.* **2** B1 [T] to draw a circle around something: *Circle the answer you think is correct.* → See also **encircle**

circuit /ˈsɜː.kɪt/ US /ˈsɝː-/ **noun** **VISITS** ▷ **1** C2 [C] a regular pattern of visits or the places visited: *They first met each other* ***on the*** *tennis circuit (= while at different tennis competitions).* ◦ *He was a familiar figure* ***on the*** *lecture circuit.* **2** [C] legal a particular area containing different courts which a judge visits: *The judge had served for many years* ***on the*** *northeastern Circuit.* ◦ *a circuit* ***judge*** **TRACK** ▷ **3** C2 [C] something shaped approximately like a circle, especially a route, path, or sports track that starts and ends in the same place: *They test the car tyres on a motor racing circuit.* ◦ *We* ***made a*** *leisurely circuit* ***of*** *the city walls.* **CLOSED SYSTEM** ▷ **4** C2 [C] a closed system of wires or pipes through which electricity or liquid can flow: *A defect was found in the water-cooling/electrical circuit.*

ˈ**circuit** ˌ**board** noun [C] specialized a set of electrical connections made by thin lines of metal fixed onto a surface

ˈ**circuit** ˌ**breaker** noun [C] a safety device which stops the flow of current in an electrical circuit when there is a fault → Compare **fuse**

ˈ**circuit** ˌ**diagram** noun [C] a plan of an electrical or electronic circuit

circuitous /sɜːˈkjuː.ɪ.təs/ US /sɝːˈkjuː.ɪ.ţəs/ **adj** formal not straight or direct: *a circuitous route/path* ◦ *a circuitous (= long and indirect) explanation* • **circuitously** /-li/ **adv**

circuitry /ˈsɜː.kɪ.tri/ US /ˈsɝː-/ **noun** [U] the CIRCUITS that an electrical or electronic device contains, considered as a single system

ˈ**circuit** ˌ**training** noun [U] a type of sports training which involves sets of different exercises done in order one after the other

circular /ˈsɜː.kjʊ.ləʳ/ US /ˈsɝː.kjʊ.lɚ/ **adj; noun**

▸**adj** **1** B2 shaped like a circle: *a circular flowerbed/tablecloth* **2** C2 describes an argument which keeps returning to the same points and is not effective • **circularity** /ˌsɜː.kjʊˈlær.ɪ.ti/ US /ˌsɝː.kjʊˈler.ɪ.ţi/ **noun** [U] *the circularity of political arguments*

▸**noun** [C] a letter or notice sent to a large number of people: *Circulars and other junk mail go straight in the bin.*

circulate /ˈsɜː.kjʊ.leɪt/ US /ˈsɝː-/ **verb** [I or T] to move around or through something, or to make something move around or through something: *Hot water circulates through the heating system.* ◦ *I try to circulate (= move around and talk to a lot of people) at a party and not just stay with the friends I came with.* ◦ *I've circulated a good luck card for everyone to sign.*

circulation /ˌsɜː.kjʊˈleɪ.ʃən/ US /ˌsɝː-/ **noun** **1** [U] the process in which something such as information, money, or goods passes from one person to another: *Police have warned that there are a lot of fake £50 notes* ***in*** *circulation.* ◦ *Add her name to the circulation* ***list*** *for this report (= the people who will be given it to read).* ◦ figurative *I hear she's* ***out of*** *circulation/back* ***in*** *circulation (= taking part/not taking part in social activities) after her accident.* **2** C2 [C usually singular] the number of people that a newspaper or magazine is regularly sold to: *The paper has a circulation of 150,000.* **3** C2 [U] the movement of blood around the body: *Exercise helps to improve circulation.*

circumcise /ˈsɜː.kəm.saɪz/ US /ˈsɝː-/ **verb** [T] to cut the protecting loose skin off a boy's PENIS, or to cut away a girl's CLITORIS and the skin around it, for medical, traditional, or religious reasons • **circumcision** /ˌsɜː.kəmˈsɪʒ.ən/ US /ˌsɝː-/ **noun** [C or U]

circumference /səˈkʌm.fər.əns/ US /sɚˈkʌm.fɚ-/ **noun** [C or U] **1** the line surrounding a circular space, or the length of this line: *the circumference of a circle* **2** the outside edge of an area or object that is round or curved, or the length of this edge: *the circumference of an orange*

circumflex /ˈsɜː.kəm.fleks/ (US) /ˈsɝː-/ noun [C] a sign (^) over a letter, especially a vowel, which shows that it has a different pronunciation from the letter without a sign over it

circumlocution /ˌsɜː.kəm.ləˈkjuː.ʃən/ (US) /ˌsɝː-/ noun [C or U] formal (an example of) an INDIRECT way of saying something, especially something unpleasant: *'Economical with the truth' is a circumlocution for 'lying'.* ◦ *Politicians are experts in circumlocution.* • **circumlocutory** /-tᵊr.i/ (US) /-t̬ɚ.i/ adj

circumnavigate /ˌsɜː.kəmˈnæv.ɪ.geɪt/ (US) /ˌsɝː-/ verb [T] **SAIL AROUND** ▷ formal to sail all the way around something: *They circumnavigated Cape Horn Island in canoes.* • **circumnavigation** /sɜː.kəmˌnæv.ɪˈgeɪ.ʃən/ (US) /ˌsɝː-/ noun [C or U] formal *a circumnavigation of the globe from west to east*

circumscribe /ˈsɜː.kəm.skraɪb/ (US) /ˈsɝː-/ verb **1** [T often passive] formal to limit something: *Their movements have been severely circumscribed since the laws came into effect.* ◦ *There followed a series of tightly circumscribed visits to military installations.* **2** [T] specialized If you circumscribe a triangle, square, etc., you draw a circle that surrounds it and touches each of its corners.

circumspect /ˈsɜː.kəm.spekt/ (US) /ˈsɝː-/ adj formal careful not to take risks: *Officials were circumspect* ***about*** *what the talks had achieved.* • **circumspection** /ˌsɜː.kəmˈspek.ʃən/ (US) /ˌsɝː-/ noun [U] *This is a very sensitive case requiring extreme circumspection.* • **circumspectly** /-li/ adv

circumstance /ˈsɜː.kəm.stɑːns/ (US) /ˈsɝː.kəm.stæns/ noun **1** (B2) [C usually plural] a fact or event that makes a situation the way it is: *I think she coped very well* ***under the*** *circumstances.* ◦ *Obviously we can't deal with the problem until we know all the circumstances.* ◦ *She died* ***in suspicious*** *circumstances.* ◦ *We oppose capital punishment* ***in/under any*** *circumstances.* ◦ ***Under no*** *circumstances should you (= you should not) approach the man.* ◦ *The meeting has been cancelled* ***due to*** *circumstances* ***beyond our control.*** **2** [U] formal events that change your life, over which you have no control: *They were victims of circumstance.* ◦ *We were obliged to go by force of circumstance.* **3 circumstances** how much money someone has: *Grants are available depending on your circumstances.* ◦ *By now she was alone and living* ***in*** *reduced circumstances (= with little money).*

circumstantial /ˌsɜː.kəmˈstæn.ʃəl/ (US) /ˌsɝː.kəmˈ-/ adj containing information, especially about a crime, which makes you think something is true but does not completely prove it: *circumstantial evidence* ◦ *The case against her was circumstantial.*

circumvent /ˌsɜː.kəmˈvent/ (US) /ˌsɝː-/ verb [T] formal to avoid something, especially cleverly or illegally: *Ships were registered abroad to circumvent employment and safety regulations.* • **circumvention** /-ˈven.ʃən/ noun [U]

circus /ˈsɜː.kəs/ (US) /ˈsɝː-/ noun **ENTERTAINMENT** ▷ **1** (B1) [C or S] a group of travelling performers including ACROBATS (= people skilled in difficult physical movements) or those who work with trained animals, or a performance by such people usually in a large tent: *She ran away to join the circus.* ◦ *The horses trotted into the circus* ***ring*** *(= the large circle, with seats all round, in which a circus performs).* ◦ *The children loved being taken to the circus.* **ATTENTION** ▷ **2** [S] disapproving a lot of activity and interest caused by an event or situation: *the media circus surrounding the case* **ROAD** ▷ **3** [C] UK an open circular area where several roads join: *Piccadilly Circus*

cirrhosis /sɪˈrəʊ.sɪs/ (US) /-ˈroʊ-/ noun [U] a serious disease of the LIVER which usually causes death: *The commonest cause of cirrhosis is alcohol consumption.* ◦ *cirrhosis of the liver*

cirrocumulus /ˌsɪr.əʊˈkjuː.mjə.ləs/ (US) /-oʊ-/ noun [U] specialized a type of CUMULUS (= tall rounded white cloud with a flat base) formed in a very thin layer and often in a regular pattern → Compare **altocumulus, stratocumulus**

cirrostratus /ˌsɪr.əʊˈstrɑː.təs/ (US) /-oʊˈstreɪ.t̬əs/ noun [U] specialized a type of flat whitish cloud formed in a very thin layer and seen high in the sky → Compare **altostratus, nimbostratus**

cirrus /ˈsɪr.əs/ noun [U] specialized a type of light FEATHERY cloud that is seen high in the sky → Compare **cumulus, nimbus, stratus**

cissy /ˈsɪs.i/ noun [C], adj **sissy**

cistern /ˈsɪs.tən/ (US) /-tɚn/ noun [C] a container in which water is stored, especially one connected to a toilet or in the roof of a house

citadel /ˈsɪt.ə.del/ (US) /ˈsɪt̬-/ noun [C] **BUILDING** ▷ **1** a strong castle in or near a city, where people can shelter from danger, especially during a war: *The town has a 14th century citadel overlooking the river.* **ORGANIZATION** ▷ **2** literary a powerful organization in which finding a job is difficult for someone who does not know people who work there: *At the age of 32, she managed to enter one of the citadels of high fashion.*

citation /saɪˈteɪ.ʃən/ noun [C] **EXAMPLE** ▷ **1** a word or piece of writing taken from a written work: *All citations are taken from the 2007 edition of the text.* **NAME** ▷ **2** legal an official request for someone to appear in a law court: *The court issued a contempt citation against city council members who refused to comply with a court order.* **PRAISE** ▷ **3** official praise for a person in the armed forces for brave actions: *The four soldiers are to receive citations from the president* ***for*** *their brave actions.*

cite /saɪt/ verb [T] formal **GIVE EXAMPLE** ▷ **1** to mention something as proof for a theory or as a reason why something has happened: *She cited three reasons why people get into debt.* ◦ *The company cited a 13 percent decline in new orders* ***as*** *evidence that overall demand for its products was falling.* **2** to speak or write words taken from a particular writer or written work: *She cites both T.S. Eliot and Virginia Woolf in her article.* **NAME** ▷ **3** legal to officially name or mention someone or something in a law court, or to officially request someone to appear in a court of law: *The lawyer cited two similar cases.* ◦ *He has been cited* ***as*** *the co-respondent in the divorce case.* **PRAISE** ▷ **4** to praise someone in the armed forces publicly because of their brave actions: *He was cited* ***for*** *bravery.*

citizen /ˈsɪt.ɪ.zən/ (US) /ˈsɪt̬-/ noun [C] (B2) a person who is a member of a particular country and who has rights because of being born there or because of being given rights, or a person who lives in a particular town or city: *The interests of British citizens living abroad are protected by the British Embassy.* ◦ *He applied to* ***become*** *an American citizen.* ◦ *The citizens of Moscow woke up this morning to find they had a new government.* ◦ *Old people are just treated like* ***second-class*** *citizens (= unimportant people).* ◦ *He reassured people that* ***law-abiding*** *citizens (= people who do not break the law) would have nothing to fear from the enquiries.*

the citizenry /ˈsɪt.ɪ.zən.ri/ (US) /-ˈsɪt̬-/ noun [S, + sing/pl verb] formal the group of people who live in a particular city, town, area, or country: *The country's citizenry is/are more politically aware than in the past.*

ˌCitizens Adˈvice noun an organization in the UK that gives people free advice about their problems

ˌCitizens' ˈBand noun [C or U] (also **ˌCitizens' Band ˈradio**, also **CB**) trademark a radio communication system for members of the public: *Long-distance truck drivers often use CB radio to talk to each other.*

citizenship /ˈsɪt.ɪ.zən.ʃɪp/ (US) /ˈsɪţ-/ noun [U] **1** the state of being a member of a particular country and having rights because of it: *He was granted Canadian citizenship.* ◦ *He holds joint citizenship in Sweden and Peru.* **2** the state of living in a particular area or town and behaving in a way that other people who live there expect of you

ˌcitric ˈacid noun [U] a weak ACID found in many types of fruit, especially oranges and lemons

citronella /ˌsɪt.rənˈel.ə/ noun [U] a natural substance, found in a type of grass also called citronella, that smells of lemons and is used to keep insects away and in making PERFUMES

citrus /ˈsɪt.rəs/ noun [C] (plural **citrus** or **citruses**) any of a group of plants which produce ACIDIC fruits with a lot of juice: *The field was planted with citrus **trees**.* ◦ *Oranges, lemons, and grapefruit are types of citrus **fruit**.* • **citric** /-rɪk/ adj *a wine with a sharp, citric flavour*

city /ˈsɪt.i/ (US) /ˈsɪţ.i/ noun [C] **TOWN** ▷ **1** (A1) a large town: *Many of the world's cities have populations of more than five million.* ◦ *Wellington is the **capital** city (= centre of government) of New Zealand.* **2** any town in the UK that has a CATHEDRAL (= large, important church): *The city of Ely has about 15,000 inhabitants.* **FINANCIAL CENTRE** ▷ **3 the City** [S] UK **a** the business centre of London where the large financial organizations are, such as the Bank of England: *He works in the City.* ◦ *a City analyst* **b** the financial organizations as a group and the people who work for them: *The City acted swiftly to the news of a fall in the value of sterling.*

ˌcity ˈcentre noun [C] UK the central part of a city: *It's impossible to park in the city centre.* → Compare **downtown**

ˌcity ˈcouncil noun [C] the local government of a city • **ˌcity ˈcouncillor** noun [C] *City councillors have voted to pedestrianize the city centre.*

ˈcity ˌdesk noun [C usually singular] **1** UK the department of a newspaper that deals with financial and business news **2** US the department of a newspaper that deals with local news

ˌcity ˈfathers noun [plural] old-fashioned members of the governing group of a city

ˌcity ˈhall noun [C] mainly US a building used as offices by people working for a city government → Compare **town hall**

ˌCity ˈHall noun [U] mainly US the government of a city: *You will have to apply to City Hall for a building permit.*

ˌcity ˈslicker noun [C] informal disapproving a person who knows how to deal with the problems of living in a city, and who pretends to know more about fashion and culture than people who live in the countryside

ˌcity ˈstate noun [C] in the ancient world, a city and the area around it with an independent government: *Rome and Athens were some of the great city states of the ancient world.*

citywide /ˌsɪt.iˈwaɪd/ (US) /ˈsɪţ-/ adj, adv mainly US existing or happening in all parts of the city: *a citywide outbreak of crimes against vehicles* ◦ *This office is one of 46 citywide.*

civet /ˈsɪv.ɪt/ noun **1** [C] a small animal like a cat from Africa and southern Asia **2** [U] a strong-smelling substance from this animal, used for making PERFUME

C

civic /ˈsɪv.ɪk/ adj [before noun] of a town or city or the people who live in it: *The prime minister met many civic **leaders**, including the mayor and the leaders of the immigrant communities.* ◦ *She felt it was her civic **duty** (= her duty as a person living in the town) to tell the police.* ◦ *The opera house is a great source of civic **pride**.*

civics /ˈsɪv.ɪks/ noun [U] mainly US the study of the way in which a local government works and of the rights and duties of the people who live in the city

civil /ˈsɪv.əl/ adj **ORDINARY** ▷ **1** (C1) [before noun] not military or religious, or relating to the ordinary people of a country: *Helicopters are mainly used for military rather than civil use.* ◦ *After ten years of military dictatorship, the country now has a civil **government**.* ◦ *We weren't married in church, but we had a civil **ceremony** in a registry office.* **LAW** ▷ **2** [before noun] legal relating to private arguments between people or organizations rather than criminal matters: *The matter would be better dealt with in the civil **court** rather than by an expensive criminal proceeding.* **POLITE** ▷ **3** polite and formal: *His manner was civil, though not particularly friendly.*

IDIOMS **keep a civil tongue in your head** old-fashioned used to tell someone to stop being rude • **not have a civil word to say about sb** to not be able to think of anything good to say about someone

ˌcivil ˈaction noun [C] an official complaint, made by a person or company in a law court against someone who is said to have done something to harm them, that is dealt with by a JUDGE: *She **brought** a civil action **against** her former employer.*

ˌcivil deˈfence noun [U] the organizing and training of ordinary people to protect themselves or their property from an enemy attack during a war

ˌcivil disoˈbedience noun [U] the act by a group of people of refusing to obey laws or pay taxes, as a peaceful way of expressing their disapproval of those laws or taxes and in order to persuade the government to change them

ˌcivil enginˈeering noun [U] the planning and building of things not used for religious or military purposes, such as roads, bridges, and public buildings • **ˌcivil enginˈeer** noun [C] someone whose job is to plan and build public buildings, roads, bridges, etc.

civilian /sɪˈvɪl.i.ən/ noun [C] (C2) a person who is not a member of the police or the armed forces: *The bomb killed four soldiers and three civilians.* • **civilian** adj *The army has been criticized for attacking the unarmed civilian **population**.*

civility /sɪˈvɪl.ɪ.ti/ (US) /-ţi/ noun [C or U] politeness or a polite remark: *She greeted them **with** civility, but not much warmth.* ◦ *After a few civilities, they got down to business.*

civilization (UK usually **civilisation**) /ˌsɪv.əl.aɪˈzeɪ.ʃən/ noun **DEVELOPED SOCIETY** ▷ **1** (B2) [C or U] human society with its well developed social organizations, or the culture and way of life of a society or country at a particular period in time: *Some people think that nuclear war would mean the end of civilization.* ◦ *Cuzco was the centre of one of the world's most famous civilizations, that of the Incas.* **2** (C1) [U] mainly humorous a place that has comfortable living conditions: *How* *does it feel to be back in civilization after all those weeks in a tent?* **PROCESS** ▷ **3** [U] the process of educating a society so that its culture becomes more developed: *The civilization of Britain by the Romans took years to complete.*

C

civilize (UK usually **civilise**) /ˈsɪv.ɪ.laɪz/ verb [T] **1** to educate a society so that its culture becomes more developed: *The Romans set out to civilize the Ancient Britons.* **2** to improve someone's behaviour: *I like to think I had a civilizing effect on my younger brothers.*

civilized (UK usually **civilised**) /ˈsɪv.ɪ.laɪzd/ adj **DEVELOPED** ▷ **1** describes a society or country that has a well developed system of government, culture, and way of life and that treats the people who live there fairly: *A fair justice system is a fundamental part of a civilized society.* ◦ *The terrorist attack on the UN building has shocked the civilized world.* **POLITE** ▷ **2** If a person or their behaviour is civilized, they are polite and behave in a calm and reasonable way: *Let's discuss this like civilized people (= politely and calmly).* **COMFORTABLE** ▷ **3** describes a pleasant or comfortable place or thing: *'This is all very civilized,' he said, settling himself down in a chair by the fire.*

ˌcivil ˈlaw noun [U] the part of the legal system which relates to personal matters, such as marriage and property, rather than crime

ˌcivil ˈliberties noun [plural] the rights of a person to do, think, and say what they want if this does not harm other people: *The introduction of identity cards has been opposed by the campaign for civil liberties.*

ˈcivil ˌlist noun [C usually singular] UK the amount of money allowed by Parliament for what is spent by the king or queen and royal family in doing their duties

civilly /ˈsɪv.ɪl.li/ adv in a polite way: *He greeted us civilly.*

ˌcivil ˈpartnership noun [C or U] in the UK, a legal relationship between two people of the same sex that gives them the same rights as people who are married

ˌcivil ˈrights noun [plural] the rights that each person has in a society, whatever their race, sex, or religion: *Civil rights include freedom, equality in law and in employment, and the right to vote.*

ˌcivil ˈservant noun [C] a person who works in the Civil Service

the ˌcivil ˈservice noun the government departments responsible for putting central government plans into action: *The British civil service is supposed to be non-political.*

ˌcivil ˈwar noun [C] a war fought by different groups of people living in the same country: *The Spanish Civil War lasted from 1936 to 1939.*

civvies /ˈsɪv.iz/ noun [plural] old-fashioned informal ordinary clothes that are not part of a uniform: *I didn't realize he was a soldier because he was **in** civvies.*

civvy street /ˈsɪv.iˌstriːt/ noun [U] UK old-fashioned informal ordinary life that is not connected with the armed forces: *How does it feel to be back **in** civvy street?*

CJD /ˌsiː.dʒeɪˈdiː/ noun [U] abbreviation for **Creutzfeldt-Jakob disease**: a disease that damages the brain and the main nerves connected to it and usually causes death: *When it was first realized that BSE could lead to **new variant** CJD, the European Commission banned the sale of all British beef.*

cl written abbreviation for **centilitre**: *a 75 cl bottle*

clack /klæk/ noun [C usually singular] a short sharp noise made by two hard objects being hit together: *He could hear the clack of high heels walking past in the corridor.* • **clack** verb [I] *Their heels clacked on the bare concrete.*

clad /klæd/ adj literary (of people) dressed, or (of things) covered: *A strange figure appeared in the doorway, clad **in** white.* ◦ *an ivy-clad wall* ◦ *an armour-clad vehicle*

cladding /ˈklæd.ɪŋ/ noun [U] material which covers the surface of something and protects it: *The pipes froze because the cladding had fallen off.*

clag /klæg/ noun [U] Australian English a type of glue

claim /kleɪm/ verb; noun

▸verb **SAY** ▷ **1** B2 [T] to say that something is true or is a fact, although you cannot prove it and other people might not believe it: [+ (that)] *The company claims (**that**) it is not responsible for the pollution in the river.* ◦ [+ to infinitive] *He claims **to** have met the president, but I don't believe him.* ◦ *All parties have claimed **success** in yesterday's elections.* ◦ *An unknown terrorist group has claimed **responsibility** for this morning's bomb attack.* **2** [T] If an organization or group claims a particular number of members, that number of people are believed to belong to it. **DEMAND** ▷ **3** B2 [T] to ask for something of value because you think it belongs to you or because you think you have a right to it: *The police said that if no one claims the watch, you can keep it.* ◦ *When King Richard III died, Henry VII claimed the English throne.* **4** B2 [I or T] to make a written demand for money from a government or organization because you think you have a right to it: *The number of people claiming unemployment **benefit** has risen sharply this month.* ◦ *Don't forget to claim (**for**) your travelling expenses after the interview.* ◦ *When my bike was stolen, I claimed **on** the insurance and got £150 back.* ◦ UK *If the shop won't give me a replacement TV, I'll claim my money back.* **5 claim damages** to make an official request for money after an accident, from the person who caused your injuries

IDIOMS **claim sb's life** If a violent event, fighting, or a disease claims someone's life, it kills them: *The war has claimed thousands of lives.* • **claim the moral high ground** to say that you are morally better than someone else

▸noun [C] **STATEMENT** ▷ **1** C1 a statement that something is true or is a fact, although other people might not believe it: *He said the police assaulted him while he was in custody, a claim which the police deny.* ◦ [+ that] *The government's claim **that** it would reduce taxes proved false.* ◦ *Can you give any evidence to **support** your claim?* ◦ *He **made** wild claims **about** being able to cure cancer.* **DEMAND** ▷ **2** B2 a written request asking an organization to pay you an amount of money which you believe they owe you: *After her house was burgled, she **made** a claim **on** her insurance.* ◦ *Please **submit** your claim **for** travelling expenses to the accounts department.* **3** a right to have something or get something from someone: *She has no **rightful** claim **to** the title.* ◦ *Our neighbours have no claim to (= cannot say that they own) that strip of land between our houses.* ◦ *My ex-wife has **no** claims **on** me (= has no right to any of my money).*

IDIOMS **sb's/sth's claim to fame** a reason why someone or something is famous: *This little town's only claim to fame is that the president was born here.* • **make no claim to be sth** to not be trying to make people believe that you are a particular thing: *I make no claim to be a brilliant pianist, but I can play a few tunes.*

Word partners for claim noun (STATEMENT)

make a claim • *support* a claim • *challenge/deny/dispute/investigate* a claim • a *false/unsubstantiated* claim • *competing/conflicting* claims • claims *of* sth

Word partners for claim noun (DEMAND)

make/put in/submit a claim • *stake* a claim • *lay* claim *to* sth • *pay/settle* a claim • *bogus/false/fraudulent* claims • a *legitimate/rightful/valid* claim • a claim *for* sth • a claim *against* sb/sth

claimant /ˈkleɪ.mənt/ noun [C] a person who asks for something which they believe belongs to them or which they have a right to

ˈclaim ˌform noun [C] an official document that you use to request an amount of money from an organization, when you think you are owed it

clairvoyant /ˌkleəˈvɔɪ.ənt/ ⓤⓢ /ˌkler-/ noun [C] a person who says they have powers to see the future or see things which other people cannot see: *She went to see a clairvoyant who said he could communicate with her dead husband.* • **clairvoyance** /-əns/ noun [U] • **clairvoyant** adj

clam /klæm/ noun; verb

▸noun [C] a type of sea creature with a shell in two parts that can close together tightly, and a soft body that can be eaten

▸verb (-mm-)

PHRASAL VERB **clam up** (also **shut up like a clam**) to become silent suddenly, usually because you are embarrassed or nervous, or do not want to talk about a particular subject: *He just clams up if you ask him about his childhood.*

clambake /ˈklæm.beɪk/ noun [C] US an event in which SEAFOOD is cooked and eaten outside, usually near the sea

clamber /ˈklæm.bəʳ/ ⓤⓢ /-bɚ/ verb [I usually + adv/prep] to climb up, across, or into somewhere with difficulty, using the hands and the feet: *They clambered* ***over/up*** *the rocks.* ◦ *I clambered* ***into/onto*** *the bus.* ◦ *She clambered* ***into*** *bed.* • **clamber** noun [C usually singular] *I was worn out after my clamber up the hillside.*

clammy /ˈklæm.i/ adj sticky and slightly wet in an unpleasant way: *My hands felt all clammy.* ◦ *It was a hot, clammy day.* • **clamminess** /-nəs/ noun [U]

clamorous /ˈklæm.ᵊr.əs/ ⓤⓢ /-ɚ-/ adj literary **1** making loud demands or complaints **2** making a lot of noise: *clamorous, excited* ***voices***

clamour /ˈklæm.əʳ/ ⓤⓢ /-ɚ/ verb; noun

▸verb [I] UK (US **clamor**) to make a loud complaint or demand: *The children were all clamouring* ***for*** *attention.* ◦ [+ to infinitive] *She clamours* ***to*** *go home as soon as she gets to school.*

▸noun [S or U] UK (US **clamor**) **1** a loud complaint about something or a demand for something: *After the bombing, there was* ***a*** *public clamour* ***for*** *vengeance.* **2** formal loud noise, especially made by people's voices: *the clamour* ***of*** *the city* ◦ *a clamour* ***of*** *voices*

clamp /klæmp/ noun; verb

▸noun [C] a device made of wood or metal that is used to hold two things together tightly: *Carefully* ***tighten*** *the clamp until it firmly supports the pipette in a vertical position.*

▸verb **FASTEN** ▷ **1** [T usually + adv/prep] to fasten two things together, using a clamp: *Clamp the two pieces of wood* (***together***) *for 15 minutes.* **2** [T] mainly UK If the police or another person in authority clamps a vehicle, they fix a metal device to one of its wheels, usually because it is parked illegally. The device is usually only removed when the owner pays an amount of money: *When I finally got back, I found my car had been clamped.* → See also **wheel clamp** **HOLD TIGHTLY** ▷ **3** [T + adv/prep] If you clamp something in a particular place, you hold it there tightly: *He clamped his hand* ***over*** *her mouth.* ◦ *A heavy iron chain was clamped* ***around*** *his wrists.*

PHRASAL VERB **clamp down on sth** to take strong action to stop or limit a harmful or unwanted activity: *The government is clamping down on teenage drinking.*

clampdown /ˈklæmp.daʊn/ noun [C] a sudden action taken by a government or people in authority to stop or limit a particular activity: *Following the military coup, there has been a clampdown* ***on*** *press reporting in the capital.*

clan /klæn/ noun [C, + sing/pl verb] **1** a group of families, especially in Scotland, who originally came from the same family and have the same name **2** informal a large family, or a group of people who share the same interest: *Is/Are the whole clan coming to visit you for Christmas?*

clandestine /klænˈdes.tɪn/ adj formal planned or done in secret, especially describing something that is not officially allowed: *He has been having a clandestine affair with his secretary for three years.* ◦ *She undertook several clandestine operations for the CIA.* • **clandestinely** /-li/ adv

clang /klæŋ/ verb [I or T] to make a loud deep ringing sound like that of metal being hit, or to cause something to make this sound: *He woke up to hear the sound of bells clanging in the distance.* ◦ [+ obj + adj] *She clanged the metal gate shut behind her.* • **clang** noun [C usually singular] *The bell made a resounding clang.*

clanger /ˈklæŋ.əʳ/ ⓤⓢ /-ɚ/ noun [C] mainly UK informal something that you say by accident that embarrasses or upsets someone: *Claire* ***dropped*** *(= said) a clanger by joking about his dog that's been dead for three months.*

clank /klæŋk/ verb [I or T] to make a short loud sound like that of metal objects hitting each other, or to cause something to make this sound: *My bike chain was clanking in an alarming way as I pedalled along.* • **clank** noun [C usually singular] *I heard the clank of buckets as they went to milk the cows.*

clannish /ˈklæn.ɪʃ/ adj disapproving describes members of a group of people or society who are friendly to each other, but not to people outside the group • **clannishness** /-nəs/ noun [U] disapproving

clansman /ˈklænz.mən/ noun [C] (plural **-men** /-mən/) a member of a Scottish CLAN

clanswoman /ˈklænzˌwʊm.ən/ noun [C] (plural **-women** /-wɪmɪn/) a female member of a Scottish CLAN

clap /klæp/ verb; noun

▸verb (-pp-) **MAKE NOISE** ▷ **1** B1 [I or T] to make a short loud noise by hitting your hands together: *'When I clap my hands, you must stand still,' said the teacher.* ◦ *The band played a familiar tune which had everyone clapping* ***along***. ◦ *The audience clapped* ***in time to*** *the music.* **2** B1 [I or T] to clap your hands repeatedly to show that you like or admire someone or have enjoyed a performance: *The audience clapped and cheered when she stood up to speak.* ◦ *We all clapped his performance enthusiastically.* **PUT QUICKLY** ▷ **3** [T + adv/prep] to put a person or thing somewhere quickly or suddenly: *She clapped her hand* ***over*** *her*

C

mouth to try to stop herself from laughing. ◦ *The police clapped him **into/in** prison for possession of drugs.* **HIT** ▷ **4** [T + adv/prep] to hit someone lightly on the shoulder or back in a friendly way, especially to express pleasure at what they have done: *He clapped his daughter **on** the back and told her how proud of her he was.*

▸noun **NOISE** ▷ **1** [S] the act of clapping your hands continuously to show that you like or admire someone or something: *Let's give **a** big clap **to/for** our winning contestant!* **2** (C2) [C] a sudden loud noise made by thunder: *There was **a** clap **of** thunder and then it started to pour with rain.* **HIT** ▷ **3** [C] the act of hitting someone lightly on the shoulder or back in a friendly way, especially to express pleasure at what they have done: *He gave me a friendly clap **on** the shoulder and said, 'Well done!'* **DISEASE** ▷ **4 the clap** [S] slang for **gonorrhoea**: *a nasty dose of the clap*

clapboard /ˈklæp.bɔːd/ (US) /-bɔːrd/ **noun** **1** [U] US a series of boards fixed horizontally to the outside of a building, with each board partly covering the one below, to protect the building from the weather **2** [C] US for **clapperboard**

ˌclapped ˈout adj mainly UK informal **1** describes machines that are old and no longer work well: [before noun] *She drives a clapped-out old Mini.* **2** describes people who are very tired or unhealthy

clapper /ˈklæp.əʳ/ (US) /-ɚ/ **noun** [C] a piece of metal which hangs inside a bell and makes the bell ring when it hits the sides

IDIOM **like the clappers** UK old-fashioned informal extremely fast: *You'll have to **run** like the clappers if you want to catch your train.*

clapperboard /ˈklæp.ə.bɔːd/ (US) /-ɚ.bɔːrd/ **noun** [C] (US usually **clapboard**) a device, used by people making films, that consists of a board with two parts that are hit together at the start of filming

clapperboard

claptrap /ˈklæp.træp/ **noun** [U] informal disapproving silly talk that means nothing and should not be believed: *Don't believe a word of what he says. It's just **a load of** claptrap.*

claret /ˈklær.ət/ (US) /ˈkler-/ **noun** **1** [C or U] red wine made in the region near Bordeaux in France **2** [U] a colour that is between dark red and purple

clarification /ˌklær.ɪ.fɪˈkeɪ.ʃᵊn/ (US) /ˌkler-/ **noun** [C or U] (C1) an explanation or more details which makes something clear or easier to understand: *Some further clarification of your position is needed.*

clarified /ˈklær.ɪ.faɪd/ (US) /ˈkler-/ **adj** specialized (of fat) with water and unwanted substances removed by heating: *You often use clarified **butter** when making curry.*

clarify /ˈklær.ɪ.faɪ/ (US) /ˈkler-/ **verb** [T] **EXPLAIN** ▷ **1** (C1) to make something clear or easier to understand by giving more details or a simpler explanation: *Could you clarify the first point please? I don't understand it completely.* ◦ *The **position** of all shareholders will be clarified next month when we finalize our proposals.* **COOKING** ▷ **2** specialized to remove water and unwanted substances from fat, such as butter, by heating it

clarinet /ˌklær.ɪˈnet/ (US) /ˌkler-/ **noun** [C] a tube-shaped musical instrument that is played by blowing through a single REED • **clarinettist** (US **clarinetist**) /-ˈnet.ɪst/ (US) /-ˈneṭ.ɪst/ **noun** [C] a person who plays the clarinet

clarion call /ˈklær.i.ənˌkɔːl/ (US) /ˈkler.i.ənˌkɑːl/ **noun** [C usually singular] literary a very clear message or instruction about what action is needed: *to issue/sound a clarion call **for** change*

clarity /ˈklær.ɪ.ti/ (US) /ˈkler.ɪ.ṭi/ **noun** [U] **EASY TO UNDERSTAND** ▷ **1** (C2) the quality of being clear and easy to understand: *There has been a call for greater clarity in this area of the law.* **EASY TO HEAR/SEE** ▷ **2** the quality of being easy to see or hear: *She was phoning from Australia, but I was amazed at the clarity of her voice.* **THINKING CLEARLY** ▷ **3** the ability to think clearly and not be confused: *He has shown great clarity **of mind**.* ◦ *mental clarity*

clash /klæʃ/ **verb; noun**

▸verb **FIGHT** ▷ **1** (C2) [I usually + adv/prep] to fight or argue: *Students clashed **with** police after demonstrations at five universities.* ◦ *The government and the opposition parties have clashed **over** the cuts in defence spending.* **2** [I] If two opinions, statements, or qualities clash, they are very different from each other: *This latest statement from the White House clashes **with** important aspects of US foreign policy.* **COMPETE** ▷ **3** [I] If two people or teams clash in a sports competition or race, they compete seriously against each other. **NOT ATTRACTIVE** ▷ **4** (C2) [I not continuous] If colours or styles clash, they look ugly or wrong together: *I like red and orange together, though lots of people think they clash.* **HAPPEN TOGETHER** ▷ **5** (C2) [I not continuous] UK If two events clash, they happen at the same time in a way that is not convenient: *Her party clashes **with** my brother's wedding, so I won't be able to go.* **LOUD NOISE** ▷ **6** [I or T] to make a loud noise like metal hitting metal, or to cause something to make this noise: *The saucepans clashed as he piled them into the sink.* ◦ *She clashed the cymbals together.*

▸noun **FIGHT** ▷ **1** (C2) [C] a fight or argument between people: *Rioters hurled rocks and petrol bombs in clashes **with** police at the weekend.* ◦ *There were violent clashes **between** the police and demonstrators in the city centre.* **2** (C2) [C usually singular] a situation in which people's opinions or qualities are very different from and opposed to each other: *a clash of opinions/loyalties/personalities* **COMPETITION** ▷ **3** [C] a sports competition or race between two people or teams **NOT ATTRACTIVE** ▷ **4** [C] the fact of colours or styles looking ugly or wrong together **HAPPENING TOGETHER** ▷ **5** [C] UK the situation when two events happen at the same time in a way that is not convenient: *In the new timetable, there's a clash **between** history and physics.* **LOUD NOISE** ▷ **6** [C] a loud noise that sounds like metal hitting metal: *a clash of cymbals*

clasp /klɑːsp/ (US) /klæsp/ **verb; noun**

▸verb [T] to hold someone or something firmly in your hands or arms: *He was clasping the vase tightly, terrified of dropping it.* ◦ *Lie on your back, clasp your knees and pull them down towards your chest.* ◦ *She clasped her son **in** her arms.*

▸noun **1** [S] a tight hold with your hand or arms: *She held the child's hand in a **firm** clasp as they crossed the road.* **2** [C] a small metal device that is used to fasten a belt, bag, or a piece of jewellery

ˈclasp ˌknife **noun** [C] (US usually **pocketknife**) a knife with one or more folding blades

class /klɑːs/ (US) /klæs/ **noun; verb; adj**

▸noun **TEACHING GROUP** ▷ **1** (A1) [C, + sing/pl verb] a group of students who are taught together at school, college, or university: *Which class are you in this year?* ◦ *She gave the whole class extra homework for a week.*

◦ *My class (= the people in my class) was/were rather noisy this morning.* ◦ [as form of address] *Okay, class, settle down and open your books.* **2** A1 [C, + sing/pl verb] a period of time in which students are taught something: *My last class ends at four o'clock.* ◦ *I was told off for talking* ***in*** *class.* ◦ *Who* ***takes/teaches*** *your environmental studies class?* ◦ *I missed my aerobics class yesterday.* ◦ *Classes have been cancelled today because of a staff meeting.* **3 the class of 2012, 2013, etc.** mainly US a group of students who successfully finished their studies in a particular year

> **!** Common mistake: **class or classroom?**
> **Warning:** choose the right word!
> To talk about a room where students are taught, don't say 'class', say **classroom**:
> ~~The classes had central heating and big windows.~~
> *The classrooms had central heating and big windows.*

ECONOMIC GROUP ▷ **4** B2 [C or U] a group of people within society who have the same economic and social position: *The Labour Party has lost a lot of support among the* ***working*** *class.* ◦ *She belongs to the rich American* ***upper*** *class.* ◦ *We live in a* ***middle*** *class neighbourhood.* ◦ *She comes from an* ***upper middle*** *class background.* ◦ *He was a member of the* ***ruling*** *classes.* ◦ *She's studying the class* ***structure*** *of Japan.* → See also **underclass** **RANK** ▷ **5** A2 [C] a group into which goods, services, or people are put according to their standard: *Whenever I travel by train, I always travel* ***first*** *class.* ◦ ***first/second*** *class mail* ◦ *a* ***business/economy*** *class ticket* ◦ *All the vegetables we sell are Class A.* ◦ *When it comes to mathematics, he's in* ***a different*** *class* ***to*** *his peers.* **6** [C] UK in Britain, the standard which someone has reached in their university degree: *What class of degree did you get?* ◦ *He graduated with a second-class honours degree in physics.* **7 be in a class of your own** to be the best at a particular activity: *As a long-distance runner, she's in a class of her own.* **8 be in a class by itself/of its own** to be something of such a high quality that nothing can be compared to it **9 be out of your class** to be much better at doing something than you: *I can't play chess with him. He's completely out of my class!* **STYLE** ▷ **10** [U] the quality of being stylish or fashionable: *She's got real class.* **BIOLOGY** ▷ **11** [C] specialized a group of related plants or animals, in the general CLASSIFICATION of plants and animals

> Word partners for **class** (**TEACHING GROUP**)
> *attend* classes • *take/teach* a class • *join* a class • *in* class

> Word partners for **class** (**ECONOMIC GROUP**)
> *middle/upper/working* class • class *barriers/conflict* • the class *system*

▸**verb** [T] C1 to consider someone or something to belong to a particular group because of their qualities: *I'm 17, but I'm still classed* ***as*** *a child when I travel by bus.* ◦ *I would class her* ***among/with*** *the top ten American novelists.*

▸**adj** informal very good: *a class act* ◦ *He's a class golfer.*

ˌclass ˈaction noun [C] specialized a legal ACTION (= case that is decided in a law court) that is organized by a group of people who all have the same legal problem: *Plaintiffs' lawyers have tried to get the courts to combine all the potential suits into a single class action.* ◦ [before noun] *a class-action lawsuit*

ˈclass-conscious adj clearly understanding the differences between the various social classes or that you belong to a particular social class

classic /ˈklæs.ɪk/ **adj; noun**

▸**adj** **HIGH QUALITY** ▷ **1** B2 having a high quality or standard against which other things are judged: *Have you ever read Fielding's classic* ***novel*** *'Tom Jones'?* ◦ *Another classic goal there from Corley!* **EXTREMELY FUNNY/BAD** ▷ **2** informal extremely or UNUSUALLY funny, bad, or annoying: *Then she fell over backwards into the flowerbed – it was absolutely classic!* ◦ *That was classic! That van-driver signalled right, and then turned left.* **TYPICAL** ▷ **3** having all the characteristics or qualities that you expect: *He's a classic* ***example*** *of a kid who's clever but lazy.* ◦ *He had all the classic* ***symptoms*** *of the disease.* **4** informal disapproving bad or unpleasant, but not very surprising or unexpected: *It's classic – you arrive at the station on time and find that the train's left early.* **TRADITIONAL** ▷ **5** having a simple, traditional style that is always fashionable: *She wore a classic navy suit.*

▸**noun** **HIGH QUALITY** ▷ **1** B2 [C] a piece of writing, a musical recording, or a film that is well known and of a high standard and lasting value: *Jane Austen's 'Pride and Prejudice' is a classic* ***of*** *English literature.* ◦ *Many of the Rolling Stones' records have become rock classics.* **2 the classics** [plural] the most famous works of literature: *I spent my childhood* ***reading*** *the classics.* **STUDY** ▷ **3 classics** [U] the study of ancient Greek and Roman culture, especially their languages and literature: *She* ***studied/read*** *classics at Cambridge.* ◦ *a classics scholar.* **TRADITIONAL** ▷ **4** [C] a piece of clothing that is always fashionable: *A long wool coat is a classic no wardrobe should be without.*

classical /ˈklæs.ɪ.kəl/ adj **MUSIC** ▷ **1** A2 describes music that is considered to be part of a long especially formal tradition and to be of lasting value: *Do you prefer classical music like Mozart and Mahler, or pop?* **2** specialized describes a style of music written in Europe between about 1750 and 1830: *The works of Haydn and Mozart belong to the classical period.* **TRADITIONAL** ▷ **3** C2 traditional in style or form, or based on methods developed over a long period of time: *Does she study classical ballet or modern ballet?* **4** describes something that is attractive because it has a simple, traditional style: *I love the classical lines of his dress designs.* **CULTURE** ▷ **5** belonging to or relating to the culture of ancient Rome and Greece: *the classical world* ◦ *classical literature* → See also **neoclassical** • **classically** /-i/ adv *She is a classically trained dancer.* ◦ *The dress combines stylish lines with an attractive floral print for a classically feminine look.* ◦ *a classically beautiful face*

ˌclassic ˈcar noun [C] a car produced since 1930 that is no longer in production: *The Triumph Spitfire is a classic car.* → Compare **veteran car, vintage car**

classicism /ˈklæs.ɪ.sɪ.zəm/ noun [U] specialized a style in painting, SCULPTURE, and building, based on particular standards in Greek and Roman art: *Poussin was a famous exponent of classicism.* → See also **neoclassicism (neoclassical)**

classicist /ˈklæs.ɪ.sɪst/ noun [C] a person who studies ancient Greek or Roman culture

classification /ˌklæs.ɪ.fɪˈkeɪ.ʃən/ noun **1** C2 [U] the act or process of dividing things into groups according to their type: *Do you understand the system of classification used in ornithology?* **2** C2 [C] a group that something is divided into

classified /ˈklæs.ɪ.faɪd/ adj describes information that is officially stated to be secret: *These documents contain classified* ***material****.*

ˌclassified ˈad noun [C] (also **classified**) a small advertisement that you put in a newspaper or a magazine, usually because you want to sell or buy something or to find or offer a job

classify /ˈklæs.ɪ.faɪ/ verb [T] C1 to divide things into groups according to their type: *The books in the library are classified* ***by/according to*** *subject.* ◦ *Biologists classify animals and plants* ***into*** *different groups.* • **classifiable** /-ə.bl̩/ adj

C

classless /ˈklɑːs.ləs/ US /ˈklæs.ləs/ adj **1** not belonging to a particular social class: *Her accent is classless.* **2** having no different social classes: *The prime minister claims that he wants to create a classless* ***society****.*

classmate /ˈklɑːs.meɪt/ US /ˈklæs-/ noun [C] A2 someone who is in the same class as you at school

classroom /ˈklɑːs.ruːm/, /-rʊm/ US /ˈklæs-/ noun [C] **1** A1 a room in a school or college where groups of students are taught **2 in the classroom a** being taught by a teacher: *Students learning computer studies spend two days each week in a computer lab and four days in the classroom.* **b** teaching classes of students in school or college: *There are also no promotions within the school, so that teachers remain in the classroom throughout their careers.*

ˈ**class** ˌ**struggle** noun [S or U] in MARXISM, a continuing fight between the CAPITALIST class and the working class for political and economic power

classware /ˈklɑːs.weəʳ/ US /ˈklæs.wer/ noun [U] specialized software that is used for teaching students in a class

classy /ˈklɑː.si/ US /ˈklæs.i/ adj stylish or fashionable

clatter /ˈklæt.əʳ/ US /ˈklæt̬.ɚ/ verb [I or T] to make continuous loud noises by hitting hard objects against each other, or to cause objects to do this: *Don't clatter the dishes – you'll wake the baby up.* ◦ *He was clattering* ***away*** *at his keyboard.* • **clatter** noun [S] *the clatter of dishes in the kitchen*

clause /klɔːz/ US /klɑːz/ noun [C] specialized **LEGAL DOCUMENT** ▷ **1** a particular part of a written legal document, for example a law passed by Parliament or a CONTRACT (= an agreement): *They have* ***added/deleted/amended*** *a clause in the contract which says the company can make people redundant for economic reasons.* **GRAMMAR** ▷ **2** B2 a group of words, consisting of a subject and a FINITE form of a verb: *In the sentence 'I can't cook very well but I make quite good omelettes', both 'I can't cook very well' and 'I make quite good omelettes' are* ***main/independent*** *clauses (= they are of equal importance and could each exist as a separate sentence).* ◦ *In the sentence 'I'll get you some stamps if I go to town', 'if I go to town' is a* ***subordinate/dependent*** *clause (= it is not as important as the main part of the sentence and could not exist as a separate sentence).*

claustrophobia /ˌklɒs.trəˈfəʊ.bi.ə/ US /ˌklɑː.strəˈfoʊ-/ noun [U] fear of being in closed spaces: *He* ***suffers from*** *claustrophobia so he never travels on underground trains.* → Compare **agoraphobia**

claustrophobic /ˌklɒs.trəˈfəʊ.bɪk/ US /ˌklɑː.strəˈfoʊ-/ adj; noun

▸adj **1** describes a place that is small and closed, and makes you feel uncomfortable when you are in it: *My room's a bit claustrophobic.* **2** specialized describes a person suffering from a fear of being in closed spaces

▸noun [C] specialized a claustrophobic person

clavichord /ˈklæv.ɪ.kɔːd/ US /-kɔːrd/ noun [C] an early keyboard instrument in which the strings are hit by pieces of metal when the keys are pressed

clavicle /ˈklæv.ɪ.kl̩/ noun [C] specialized for **collarbone**

claw /klɔː/ US /klɑː/ noun; verb

claws

▸noun [C] **1** one of the sharp curved nails at the end of each of the toes of some animals and birds: *Our cat likes to* ***sharpen*** *her claws on the legs of the dining table.* **2** one of the two pointed parts, used for holding things, at the end of the legs of some insects and sea creatures

IDIOM **get your claws into sb** informal disapproving **1** to find a way of influencing or controlling someone: *If the loan company gets its claws into you, you'll still be paying off this debt when you're 50.* **2** If a woman gets her claws into a man, she manages to start a relationship with him, often because she wants to control him or get something from him: *If she gets her claws into that young man, she'll ruin his political career.*

▸verb [I or T] to use claws to tear something or someone: *He was seriously injured when one of the lions clawed his back.* ◦ *When our cat is hungry, she starts clawing* ***at*** *my legs.*

IDIOM **claw your way (somewhere)** to move forwards with difficulty, especially by using stiff curved fingers to remove the things that are in your way: *The rescuers could hear the sound of the trapped people desperately trying to claw their way* ***through*** *the rubble.* ◦ figurative *Sidney ruthlessly clawed his way (****up****)* ***from*** *the position of junior clerk* ***to*** *chairman of the company (= he achieved success with effort and by hurting other people).*

PHRASAL VERB **claw sth back 1** to get possession of something again with difficulty: *The airline is beginning to claw back some of the business it lost after the bomb explosion.* **2** mainly UK If the government, for example, claws back money, it takes money back in one way that it has already given in another way: *We got a government grant for setting up our business, but they clawed it all back again in taxes.*

clay /kleɪ/ noun [U] thick, heavy soil that is soft when wet, and hard when dry or baked, used for making bricks and containers • **clayey** /ˈkleɪ.i/ adj containing a lot of clay: *clayey soil*

ˌ**clay** ˈ**pigeon** noun [C] a disc made of clay that is shot into the air to be shot at for sport: *clay pigeon shooting*

clean /kliːn/ adj; verb; noun; adv

▸adj **NOT DIRTY** ▷ **1** A1 not dirty: *a clean white shirt* ◦ *clean air/water* ◦ *Make sure your hands are clean before you have your dinner.* ◦ *Hospitals need to be kept* ***spotlessly*** *(= extremely) clean.* **HONEST** ▷ **2** C2 honest or fair, or showing that you have not done anything illegal: *a good clean* ***fight/contest*** ◦ *The judge took the defendant's clean* ***record*** *(= the absence of previous involvement in crime) into account when passing sentence.* ◦ *I've always had a clean* ***driving licence****.* **3** slang not doing anything illegal, or not having or carrying illegal drugs or stolen goods: *The police busted Pete last night, but he was clean.* **MORAL** ▷ **4** morally acceptable: *It's all* ***good*** *clean* ***fun****.* ◦ *clean* ***living*** **5** not about sex: *Can't you think of any clean* ***jokes****?* **NOT ROUGH** ▷ **6** having no rough edges, and smooth, straight, or equally balanced: *I've broken my leg, but the doctor says that it's a clean* ***break****, so it should heal easily.* ◦ *A good clean hit from Pietersen sent the ball straight out to the boundary.* ◦ *What he liked about the car was its clean* ***lines****.* ◦ *I* tried to make a clean **cut**, but the knife wasn't sharp enough. **COMPLETE** ▷ **7** [before noun] complete: *It's better for both of us if we* ***make a*** *clean* ***break*** *(****of it****) (= end our relationship completely).* ◦ *Sara says she needs a clean* ***break with*** *the past.* ◦ *The new prime minister is expected to* ***make a*** *clean* ***sweep*** *(= a complete change)* ***of*** *the government.* **NOTHING ON** ▷ **8** [before noun] When something you write on is clean, there is nothing on it or it is not yet used: *Take a clean sheet of paper.*

Other ways of saying clean

To emphasize that something is very clean, you could use the adjectives **immaculate** or **spotless**:

The whole house was ***immaculate****.*

He was wearing a ***spotless*** *white shirt.*

An informal phrase you can use for a place that is clean and neat is **spick and span**:

Their house is always ***spick and span****.*

If air or water is clean and has no harmful substances in it, the word **pure** can be used:

I love the ***pure*** *mountain air.*

If an object is clean and has no bacteria on it, you can use the adjective **sterile**:

All equipment used in medical operations must be ***sterile****.*

IDIOMS **(as) clean as a (new) pin** (also **(as) clean as a whistle**) extremely clean • **a clean bill of health** informal **1** a decision by a doctor that someone is healthy: *He's been* ***given*** *a clean bill of health by the doctor.* **2** a decision by someone in authority that a particular thing is in good condition: *Of 30 countries inspected for airline safety, only 17 received a clean bill of health.* • **a clean sheet/slate** informal the situation in which people decide to forget your past behaviour, usually because it was not good: *You were very lazy last term, but we'll* ***start*** *again with a clean sheet this term.* • **come clean** to tell the truth about something that you have been keeping secret: *I thought it was time to come clean (****with*** *everybody)* ***about*** *what I'd been doing.* • **make a clean breast of it** to tell the truth about something: *Julia finally made a clean breast of it and admitted that she had stolen the money.*

▸**verb 1** (A1) [T] to remove dirt from something: *I'm going to clean the windows this morning.* ◦ *You should always clean your teeth after meals.* ◦ *Would you clean the fingermarks* ***from/off*** *the door?* ◦ *He asked her to help him clean* ***out*** *the stables.* **2** [I usually + adv/prep] to become clean: *This carpet doesn't clean very well.* ◦ *I hope these bloodstains will clean* ***off*** *my shirt.* **3** [T] to prepare a fish or an animal killed for food by removing the inside parts of it that are not eaten

IDIOM **clean up your act** to start to obey certain laws or generally accepted standards of behaviour: *You're going to have to clean up your act if you're serious about keeping your job.*

PHRASAL VERBS **clean sth out** (C2) to take everything out of a room, car, container, etc. and clean the inside of it: *I found these photos while I was cleaning out my cupboards.* • **clean sb/sth out** informal to use or steal all of someone's money or goods: *Buying our new house has completely cleaned us out.* ◦ *Richard came home for the weekend and completely cleaned us out* ***of*** *food.* ◦ *The burglars cleaned out the shop.* • **clean (sb/sth) up** (C1) to make a person or place clean and tidy: *We'll go out as soon as I've cleaned up the kitchen.* ◦ *I need to clean up (= clean myself or the place where I am) before we go out.* ◦ *Clean your****self*** *up a bit before dinner.* • **clean (sth) up** slang to win a lot of money: *We cleaned up at the poker table last night.* • **clean sth up** **CRIME** ▷ **1** to stop illegal or dishonest activity in a place or organization: *We need a mayor who is tough enough to clean up this town.* **BAD BEHAVIOUR** ▷ **2** to stop or limit the violence, sex, or bad behaviour shown or contained in programmes or books, magazines, etc., to make them more acceptable: *Some people think that television should be cleaned up.* • **clean up after sb** to remove dirt or problems that someone has made: *I'm fed up with cleaning up after you all the time.*

▸**noun** [S] when something is cleaned: *These windows need a really thorough clean.*

▸**adv** completely: *I clean* ***forgot*** *that I was supposed to be meeting Lucy last night.* ◦ *He's been cheating his customers for years, and* ***getting*** *clean* ***away*** *with it.* ◦ *The bullet went clean* ***through*** *his shoulder.*

ˌclean-ˈcut adj **MAN** ▷ approving describes a man who is tidy in appearance and behaves well: *Julie's fiancé is a nice clean-cut young man.*

cleaner /ˈkliː.nəʳ/ (US) /-nɚ/ noun **1** (A2) [C] a person whose job is to clean houses, offices, public places, etc.: *Chris has an evening job as an office cleaner.* **2** [C or U] a substance used for cleaning things: *We've run out of floor cleaner.* **3 cleaner's** (C1) [C] a shop where clothes that cannot be washed in an ordinary washing machine are cleaned: *Could you pick up my suit from the cleaner's for me, please?* → See also **dry-cleaner's**

IDIOM **take sb to the cleaner's** informal **1** to get a lot of money from someone, usually by cheating them: *Paul was really taken to the cleaner's* ***on*** *that deal.* **2** to defeat someone by a very large amount: *In the second half, United were really taken to the cleaner's, and they finally lost the match 6–1.*

cleaning /ˈkliː.nɪŋ/ noun [U] the activity of removing the dirt from things and places, especially in a house: *It's your turn to* ***do the*** *cleaning.* ◦ *Joan has a cleaning job.*

ˌclean-ˈlimbed adj approving healthy-looking and active: *The school sports field swarmed with clean-limbed young people eager for the day's events.*

cleanliness /ˈklen.li.nəs/ noun [U] the state of being clean, or the act of keeping things clean

cleanly /ˈkliːn.li/ adv **HONESTLY** ▷ **1** fairly and honestly: *The election campaign was not conducted very cleanly.* **NOT ROUGHLY** ▷ **2** with smooth straight edges: *The plate* ***broke*** *cleanly in half.* **EQUALLY** ▷ **3** equally: *Opinions were* ***split*** *cleanly between men and women.*

cleanness /ˈkliːn.nəs/ noun [U] how clean something is → See also **cleanliness**

cleanse /klenz/ verb [T] **1** to make something completely clean: *Cleanse the* ***cut/wound*** *thoroughly before you bandage it.* **2** to make someone or something morally clean or pure: *to cleanse the thoughts of our hearts* ◦ figurative *The mayor has promised to cleanse the city* ***of*** *drug dealers (= to remove them from the city).*

cleanser /ˈklen.zəʳ/ (US) /-zɚ/ noun [C or U] a substance used for cleaning, especially your face: *I use cleanser on my face every night.* ◦ *Kitchen cleansers are all more or less the same.*

ˌclean-ˈshaven adj describes a man who has no hair on the lower part of his face

cleansing /ˈklen.zɪŋ/ adj [before noun] describes something that cleans or is used for cleaning: *a cleansing cream*

ˈclean-up noun [S] the act of making a place clean

and tidy: *It's time you gave your bedroom* ***a*** *good clean-up.* ◦ *Residents have called for a clean-up campaign to keep their streets free from rubbish.*

clear /klɪəʳ/ (US) /klɪr/ **adj; verb; adv; noun**

▸adj **ABLE TO BE UNDERSTOOD** ▷ **1** (A2) easy to understand, hear, read, or see: *clear instructions/directions* ◦ *Can we make the sound any clearer?* ◦ *These books have lovely clear print.* ◦ *Our new television has a very clear picture.* **2 do I make myself clear?** (also **is that clear?**) something you say in order to emphasize what you have just said, or to express your authority: *I will not tolerate this behaviour any longer. Do I make myself clear?* **CERTAIN** ▷ **3** (B1) certain, having no doubt, or obvious: *He isn't at all clear* ***about*** *what he wants to do with his life.* ◦ [+ (that)] *It is rapidly becoming clear (****to*** *me) (****that****) I'm not suited to being a teacher.* ◦ [+ question word] *It isn't clear* ***how*** *long the strike will go on for.* ◦ *It's a clear* ***case*** *of corruption.* ◦ *You've* ***made*** *your* ***position*** *quite clear (= there is no doubt about what you think).* **PURE** ▷ **4** (B1) pure or easy to see through, with no marks or areas that are less transparent: *clear glass* ◦ *The* ***water*** *in the lake is so clear that you can see the bottom.* ◦ *We could see hundreds of stars in the clear desert* ***sky****.* ◦ *She has a beautifully clear* ***skin/complexion*** *(= with no marks or spots).* ◦ *The* ***weather*** *is expected to remain clear for the next few days.* ◦ *You can see the mountains from here on a clear* ***day****.* **5** describes a pleasant, pure sound: *the clear sound of the flute* **6** describes something that you remember easily: *I have clear* ***memories*** *of visiting my grandfather's farm as a child.* **NOT BLOCKED** ▷ **7** (C1) not covered or blocked by anything: *We have a clear* ***view*** *of the ocean from our hotel window.* ◦ *The journey was quite quick because the* ***road*** *was clear (= there was not much traffic on it).* ◦ *I always like to leave my* ***desk*** *clear (= with no work on it) at the end of the day.* **8** not busy or filled by any planned activity: *The only time I have clear next week is Tuesday afternoon.* ◦ *We've got two clear (= whole) weeks in which to finish the decorating.* **NOT GUILTY** ▷ **9** without being or feeling guilty: *to have a clear* ***conscience*** **NOT CONFUSED** ▷ **10** free from confusion; able to think quickly and well: *Marie is good at making decisions because she's a very clear* ***thinker****.* **WITHOUT PROBLEMS** ▷ **11** [after verb] without problems or difficulties: *This is the first time in his life that he's been clear* ***of*** *(= without) debt.* **LEFT** ▷ **12** describes an amount of money that is left after all necessary payments have been made: *The school summer fair made a clear* ***profit*** *of £500.* ◦ *Bill earns a clear $400 a week/earns $400 a week clear.* **NOT TOUCHING** ▷ **13** not touching something, or away from something: *Only one competitor made a clear jump of the highest fence (= jumped over it without touching it).* ◦ *When we're clear* ***of*** *the main road, we'll stop for our picnic.*

IDIOMS **(as) clear as a bell** very easy to hear: *Clear as a bell, from the back of the theatre came a child's voice saying, 'I want to go home'.* • **(as) clear as day 1** very easy to understand: *The instructions were as clear as day.* **2** certain: *It's as clear as day that the government is going to win the election.* • **(as) clear as mud** humorous very difficult to understand: *His instructions were as clear as mud.*

▸verb **REMOVE BLOCK** ▷ **1** (B1) [I or T] to remove or get rid of whatever is blocking or filling something, or to stop being blocked or full: *It took several hours to clear the road after the accident.* ◦ *I'll make the coffee if you'll clear the* ***table****.* ◦ *If you use this nasal spray, your nose should clear a bit.* ◦ *After my aunt died, we arranged for her house to be cleared (= for the furniture to be removed from it).* ◦ *If you press this key, the computer screen will clear (= the text and pictures will be removed from it).* ◦ *Shops are currently holding sales to clear their summer stock (= get rid of goods by selling them cheaply).* ◦ *Paul helped his elderly neighbour by clearing her path* ***of*** *snow/clearing snow* ***from*** *her path.* ◦ *Could you clear your things* ***off/from*** *the sofa?* ◦ *I never leave work until I've cleared my in-tray (= have finished the work that needs to be done).* **2 clear your throat** to give a small cough: *She cleared her throat nervously before she began to speak.* **PROVE INNOCENCE** ▷ **3** [T] to prove that someone is not guilty of something that they were accused of: *After many years in prison, the men were finally cleared* ***of*** *the bombings.* **GIVE PERMISSION** ▷ **4** [T] to give official permission for something: *Despite local opposition, the plans for the new supermarket have been cleared by the council.* ◦ *Ladies and gentlemen, air-traffic control has now cleared the plane* ***for*** *take-off.* ◦ *I don't know if I can get the car tonight – I'll have to clear it* ***with*** *Mum.* **5** [T] to satisfy the official conditions of something: *Before you can enter the country, you have to clear* ***customs****.* **MAKE PURE** ▷ **6** [I or T] to become or make something pure or easy to see through: *The children enjoyed stirring the mud at the bottom of the pond, then watching the water slowly clear again.* ◦ *Your skin would clear (= become free of spots) if you had a healthier diet.* ◦ *After the thunderstorm, the sky cleared (= stopped being cloudy).* ◦ *The fog is expected to have cleared (****away****) (= gone) by midday.* **NOT CONFUSED** ▷ **7** [T] to make your mind free from confusion so that you can think quickly and well: *I need to get some fresh air to clear my* ***head*** *(= to make me able to think well).* **GET RID OF** ▷ **8 clear your debts/clear yourself of debts** to pay back all the money that you owe **HAVE LEFT** ▷ **9** [T] to have an amount of money left from your earnings after any necessary payments, charges, taxes, etc.: *Bill clears $200 a week.* **CHEQUE** ▷ **10** [I or T] to (cause a CHEQUE to) go from one bank to another through a central organization, so that money can be paid to the person it is owed to: *It usually takes four to five working days for a cheque to clear.* **NOT TOUCH** ▷ **11** [T] to jump or go over something without touching it: *The horse cleared the fence with inches to spare.*

IDIOMS **clear the air 1** to make the air cooler, fresher, and more comfortable: *The rain has helped clear the air.* **2** (C2) to remove the bad feelings between people: *I had a massive argument with Sue, but at least it has cleared the air.* • **clear the decks** informal to remove unnecessary things so that you are ready for action: *Let's clear the decks and then we can start cooking dinner.* • **clear the way** to make it possible for something to happen: *We've got a loan from the bank which has cleared the way* ***for*** *us to buy a house.*

PHRASAL VERBS **clear sth away** (C1) to make a place tidy by removing things from it or putting them where they should be: *I want you to clear all these toys away before bedtime.* • **clear sb off sth** to make someone go away from somewhere: *The police used dogs to clear the campers off the village green.* • **clear off** used to tell someone to go away in a rude way: *'Clear off or I'll call the police!'* • **clear sth out** to tidy a place by getting rid of things that you do not want: *If we clear out the spare room, you can use it as a study.* • **clear out** informal to leave a place: *I hear Daphne's finally told her husband to clear out (= to leave home).* ◦ *My landlord's given me a week to clear out* ***of*** *my flat.* • **clear (sth) up** **TIDY** ▷ **1** (B2) mainly UK to make a place tidy by removing things from it or putting them where they should be: *Dad was clearing up in the kitchen.* ◦ *I'm* tired of always having to clear up **after** you (= tidy your things). **ILLNESS** ▷ **2** If an illness clears up, or if medicine clears an illness up, the illness goes away: *You won't be able to go swimming tomorrow if your cold hasn't cleared up.* ◦ *These pills should clear your rash up.* • **clear sth up** B2 to give or find an explanation for something, or to deal with a problem or argument: *They never cleared up the* ***mystery*** *of the missing money.* ◦ *After 20 years the case has finally been cleared up.* • **clear up** informal B2 If the weather clears up, the cloud and rain disappear: *I hope it clears up in time for the picnic.*

▸adv **1** not touching, or away from: *Stand clear* ***of*** *the doors, please.* ◦ *Make sure you park clear* ***of*** *the kerb.* ◦ *The children were saved from the fire only because a neighbour pulled them clear.* **2 steer/stay/keep clear** C2 to avoid something or someone: *His parents warned him to steer clear* ***of*** *trouble.*

▸noun

IDIOM **be in the clear 1** to not be guilty of a crime: *The police breathalysed Andy last night, but he was in the clear.* **2** C2 to have no problems after being in a difficult situation: *The X-rays showed that she's in the clear.*

clearance /ˈklɪə.rəns/ US /ˈklɪr.əns/ noun **REMOVE** ▷ **1** [S or U] the process of removing waste or things you do not want from a place: *house/slum clearance* **CHEAP SALE** ▷ **2** [U] an occasion when goods are offered for sale cheaply so that people will be encouraged to buy them and there will be space for new goods: *We bought our new carpet at a clearance* ***sale***. **NOT TOUCHING** ▷ **3** [C or U] the distance or space that is needed for one thing to avoid touching another thing: *It was difficult getting the piano through the doorway because we only had a clearance* ***of*** *a few centimetres.* ◦ *High vehicles must take an alternative route because of* ***low*** *clearance under the bridge.* **OFFICIAL PERMISSION** ▷ **4** [U] official permission for something or the state of having satisfied the official conditions of something: *The plane will be taking off as soon as it gets clearance.* ◦ *To visit the prison, you'll need* ***security*** *clearance.* **CHEQUE** ▷ **5** [U] the process of a cheque going from one bank to another through a central organization, so that money can be paid to the person it is owed to: *Clearance (of a cheque) can take up to a week.*

ˌclear-ˈcut adj clear or obvious without needing any proof: *She has clear-cut evidence that the company cheated her.*

clearing /ˈklɪə.rɪŋ/ US /ˈklɪr.ɪŋ/ noun [C] an area in a wood or forest from which trees and bushes have been removed

ˈclearing ˌbank noun [C] a bank which exchanges CHEQUES with other banks through a central organization called a clearing house

ˈclearing ˌhouse noun [C] a central office used by banks to collect and send out money and CHEQUES

ˌclear ˈl noun [C] specialized a way of saying an /l/ sound, in which air escapes past the sides of the tongue: *A clear l usually only occurs before vowels.*

clearly /ˈklɪə.li/ US /ˈklɪr-/ adv **EASY TO UNDERSTAND** ▷ **1** A2 in a way that is easy to see, hear, read, or understand **CERTAIN** ▷ **2** B1 used to show that you think something is obvious or certain: *The accident was clearly the lorry driver's fault.* ◦ *Clearly, you should tell her the truth.* **NOT CONFUSED** ▷ **3** A2 When you think clearly, you are not confused.

ˈclear-out noun [C usually singular] mainly UK an occasion when you tidy a place by getting rid of things that you do not want: *We need to give the garage a* ***good*** *clear-out.*

ˌclear-ˈsighted adj having a good understanding of a particular subject and the ability to make good judgments about it: *Simon has a clear-sighted vision of the company's future.*

clearway /ˈklɪə.weɪ/ US /ˈklɪr-/ noun [C] UK a road on which you are only allowed to stop if your car stops working

cleat /kliːt/ noun [C] **1** US for **stud 2** US a boot that is worn for playing football, baseball, etc.

cleavage /ˈkliː.vɪdʒ/ noun [C or U] **BODY AREA** ▷ **1** the narrow space between a woman's breasts, that is seen when she wears a piece of clothing which does not cover the top of them: *Clare was wearing a low-cut dress which showed off her cleavage.* **DISAGREEMENT** ▷ **2** formal (a) division or disagreement

cleave /kliːv/ verb [I] (**cleaved** or US also **clove**, **cleaved** or US also **cloven**) literary or old use to separate or divide, or cause something to separate or divide, often violently: *With one blow of the knight's axe, he clove the rock* ***in twain*** *(= into two pieces).*

PHRASAL VERB **cleave to sth** literary **1** to stick or hold firmly onto something: *The ancient ivy cleaved to the ruined castle walls.* **2** to continue to believe firmly in something: *People in the remote mountain villages still cleave to their old traditions.*

cleaver /ˈkliː.vəʳ/ US /-vɚ/ noun [C] a heavy knife with a large square blade: *a meat cleaver*

clef /klef/ noun [C] a sign put at the beginning of a line of music to show how high or low the notes are: *the bass/treble/alto clef*

cleft /kleft/ noun [C] an opening or CRACK, especially in a rock or the ground: *Eagles often nest in a cleft* ***in*** *the rocks.*

ˌcleft ˈlip noun [C] an upper lip which does not join in the middle because it did not develop normally before birth: *Bobby was born with a cleft lip.*

ˌcleft ˈpalate noun [C] an opening in the top of the mouth caused when a baby does not develop normally before it is born

ˌcleft ˈstick noun UK **be in a cleft stick** to be in a situation where it is very difficult to decide what to do, usually because both of your two choices of action would cause problems

clematis /ˈklem.ə.tɪs/ US /-t̬əs/ noun [C or U] (plural **clematis**) a climbing plant with flat white, pink, or purple flowers

clemency /ˈklem.ən.si/ noun [U] formal **KINDNESS** ▷ **1** kindness when giving a punishment: *The jury passed a verdict of guilty, with an appeal to the judge for clemency.* **WEATHER** ▷ **2** (of weather) the quality of being pleasant or not severe

clement /ˈklem.ənt/ adj formal describes weather that is pleasant or not severe: *It's very clement for the time of year.*

clementine /ˈklem.ən.tiːn/ noun [C] a fruit like a small orange

clench /klentʃ/ verb [T] to close or hold something very tightly, often in a determined or angry way: *The old man clenched his* ***fist*** *and waved it angrily at us.* ◦ *With a knife clenched* ***in/between*** *his teeth, he climbed up the tree to cut some coconuts.* ◦ *'Get out of here,' she said through clenched* ***teeth***.

clergy /ˈklɜː.dʒi/ US /ˈklɝː-/ noun [plural] priests, especially in the Christian Church: *We were surprised* when he announced he wanted to **join the** clergy (= become a priest).

clergyman /ˈklɜː.dʒɪ.mən/ (US) /ˈklɝː-/ **noun** [C] (plural **-men** /-mən/) a man who is a member of the clergy

clergywoman /ˈklɜː.dʒɪˌwʊm.ən/ (US) /ˈklɝː-/ **noun** [C] (plural **-women** /-wɪmɪn/) a woman who is a member of the clergy

cleric /ˈkler.ɪk/ **noun** [C] a priest: *a Buddhist/Catholic/Muslim cleric*

clerical /ˈkler.ɪ.kəl/ **adj** OFFICE WORK ▷ **1** relating to work done in an office: *a clerical* ***job*** *(= a job performing general office duties).* ◦ *a clerical* ***error*** *(= a mistake made in the office)* PRIEST ▷ **2** relating to a priest or priests: *clerical ministry*

ˌclerical ˈcollar **noun** [C] a stiff white piece of material that is worn round the neck as part of a priest's clothing

clerk /klɑːk/ (US) /klɝːk/ **noun; verb**

▸**noun** [C] **1** a person who works in an office, dealing with records or performing general office duties: *a* ***filing*** *clerk* ◦ *a junior* ***office*** *clerk* **2** US a hotel employee who welcomes guests when they arrive: *The* ***(desk)*** *clerk checked us in and gave us our key.* **3** US someone who sells things in a shop: *Take your purchases to the* ***(sales)*** *clerk, and he will wrap them for you.*

▸**verb** [I] to work as a clerk: *Debbie has a summer job clerking in an office.*

clever /ˈklev.əʳ/ (US) /-ɚ/ **adj** **1** (A1) having or showing the ability to learn and understand things quickly and easily: *Judy has never been very clever, but she tries hard.* ◦ *Fiona is very clever* ***at*** *physics.* ◦ *Charlie has a clever* ***idea/plan*** *for getting us out of our present difficulties.* **2** skilful: *My mother is very clever* ***with*** *her hands.* **3** (B1) well-designed: *I've got a clever little gadget for opening jars.*

IDIOMS **be too clever by half** to be too confident of your own intelligence in a way that annoys other people: *She was too clever by half – always correcting the teacher or coming back with a smart answer.* • **clever dick/clogs** UK informal disapproving someone who shows that they are clever, in a way which annoys other people: *If you're such a clever dick, you finish the crossword puzzle.*

ˈclever-ˌclever **adj** UK informal disapproving trying too hard to seem clever: *I wish Jon would make some constructive proposals instead of just making clever-clever remarks.*

cleverly /ˈklev.əl.i/ (US) /-ɚ.li/ **adv** in a clever or skilful way: *I thought you handled the situation very cleverly.*

cleverness /ˈklev.ə.nəs/ (US) /-ɚ-/ **noun** [U] ability to understand and learn quickly and easily

cliché /ˈkliː.ʃeɪ/ (US) /kliːˈʃeɪ/ **noun** [C or U] (C2) a saying or remark that is very often made and is therefore not original and not interesting: *My wedding day – and I know it's a cliché – was just the happiest day of my life.* • **clichéd** /ˈkliː.ʃeɪd/ (US) /kliːˈʃeɪd/ **adj** (C2) *He made some clichéd remark.*

ˈcliché-ˌridden **adj** containing a lot of clichés: *a cliché-ridden speech*

click /klɪk/ **verb; noun**

▸**verb** OPERATE COMPUTER ▷ **1** (A2) [I or T] specialized to carry out a computer operation by pressing a button on the mouse: *If you want to open a file, click twice* ***on*** *the icon for it.* ◦ *When you have selected the file you want, click the 'Open' box.* MAKE SOUND ▷ **2** (C2) [I or T] to make a short, sharp sound, or to make something do this: *The door clicked shut behind her.* ◦ *Can you hear that strange clicking noise?* ◦ *Paul clicked his* ***fingers*** *(= moved his thumb against his middle finger to make a short sharp sound) to attract the waiter's attention.* ◦ *Soldiers click their* ***heels*** *(= bring them sharply together) when they stand to attention.* BECOME FRIENDLY ▷ **3** (C2) [I] informal to become friendly or popular: *Liz and I really clicked the first time we met.* ◦ *The new daytime soap opera has yet to show signs that it's clicking* ***with*** *the television audience.* BECOME CLEAR ▷ **4** (C2) [I] informal to be understood, or become clear suddenly: *Suddenly everything clicked and I realized where I'd met him.* ◦ [+ question word] *As he talked about his schooldays,* ***it*** *suddenly clicked* ***where*** *I had met him before.* ◦ [+ that] *So it's finally clicked* ***that*** *you're going to have to get yourself a job, has it?* ◦ *In the last act of the play, everything clicks* ***into place****.*

▸**noun** [C] SOUND ▷ **1** a short, sharp sound: *The soldier gave a click* ***of*** *his heels as he saluted.* COMPUTER OPERATION ▷ **2** (A2) the act of pressing a button on the MOUSE (= small control device) of a computer to operate it

IDIOM **clicks and mortar** (also **clicks and bricks**, or **bricks and clicks**) used for talking about businesses that involve selling things in stores as well as on the internet: *Retailing is set to be very much clicks and mortar.* ◦ *the development of a clicks-and-mortar strategy*

clickable /ˈklɪk.ə.bl/ **adj** describes a word or image on a computer screen which you can click on to make further information appear or a new process begin: *To find your nearest UK school, we have a clickable map dividing the UK into regions.*

clickstream /ˈklɪk.striːm/ **noun** [C] (also **clickpath** /-pɑːθ/ (US) /-pæθ/) specialized a record of a person's activities on the internet, such as the websites they visit, and how long they spend on each one

client /ˈklaɪ.ənt/ **noun** [C] CUSTOMER ▷ **1** (B2) a customer or someone who receives services: *Mr Black has been a client* ***of*** *this firm for many years.* ◦ *We always aim to give our clients personal attention.* COMPUTER ▷ **2** a computer that is connected to a SERVER (= large central computer) from which it gets information

clientele /ˌkliː.ɒnˈtel/ (US) /-ɑːn-/ **noun** [S, + sing/pl verb] all the customers of a business when they are considered as a group: *The nightclub has a very fashionable clientele.*

ˌclient-ˈserver **adj** [before noun] using or consisting of several computers that are connected to a SERVER (= a large central computer) from which they get information: *client-server* ***systems/applications***

ˌclient ˈstate **noun** [C] a country which gets support and protection from another larger and more powerful country

cliff /klɪf/ **noun** [C] (B1) a high area of rock with a very steep side, often on a coast: *Keep away from the edge of the cliff – you might fall.* ◦ *the cliff edge*

cliffhanger /ˈklɪfˌhæŋ.əʳ/ (US) /-ɚ/ **noun** [C] a story or a situation that is exciting because its ending or result is uncertain until it happens: *It looks as if the election is going to be a cliffhanger.*

clifftop /ˈklɪf.tɒp/ (US) /-tɑːp/ **noun** [C] an area of ground at the top of a cliff: *We stayed in a marvellous clifftop hotel.*

CLIL /klɪl/ noun [U] abbreviation for content and language integrated learning: (in some countries) a teaching method that involves teaching students about a subject in a foreign language

climate /ˈklaɪ.mət/ noun **WEATHER** ▷ **1** B1 [C or U] the general weather conditions usually found in a particular place: *a hot/dry/harsh climate* ◦ *The Mediterranean climate is good for growing citrus fruits and grapes.* ◦ *When we retire, we're going to move to a warmer climate.* **SITUATION** ▷ **2** C2 [C] the general development of a situation, or the situation, feelings, and opinions that exist at a particular time: *the political/social climate* ◦ *I don't think we should expand our business in the current* ***economic*** *climate.* ◦ *Terrorism* ***creates*** *a climate* ***of*** *fear.*

ˈclimate ˌchange noun [U] B2 the way the world's weather is changing

climatic /klaɪˈmæt.ɪk/ US /-ˈmæţ-/ adj relating to general weather conditions: *Some parts of the world seem to be experiencing climatic changes.*

climatology /ˌklaɪ.məˈtɒl.ə.dʒi/ US /-ˈtɑː.lə-/ noun [U] the scientific study of general weather conditions

climax /ˈklaɪ.mæks/ noun; verb

▸noun [C] **1** the most important or exciting point in a story or situation, which usually happens near the end: *The climax* ***of*** *the air show was a daring flying display.* ◦ *The election campaign* ***reaches*** *its climax next week.* → See also **anticlimax** **2** the highest point of sexual pleasure • **climactic** /klaɪˈmæk.tɪk/ adj *The third movement of the symphony ends in a climactic crescendo (= has a loud and exciting ending).*

▸verb [I] **1** to reach the most important or exciting part: *The show climaxed* ***with*** *all the performers singing on stage together.* ◦ *The Olympics climaxed* ***in*** *a spectacular closing ceremony.* **2** to reach the highest point of sexual pleasure

climb /klaɪm/ verb; noun

▸verb **RISE** ▷ **1** B2 [I] to go up, or to go towards the top of something: *The plane climbed quickly* ***to*** *a height of 30,000 feet.* ◦ *As it leaves the village, the road climbs steeply* ***up*** *the mountain.* ◦ *The sun climbed higher in the sky.* **2** A2 [I or T] to use your legs, or your legs and hands, to go up or onto the top of something: *to climb the stairs/mountain* ◦ *I hate climbing ladders.* ◦ *We're going climbing (= climbing mountains as a sport) in Scotland next weekend.* **3** [I] If a price, number, or amount climbs, it increases: *Our costs have climbed rapidly in the last few years.* **4** [I] to move into a higher social position, or to improve your position at work: *He quickly climbed to the top of his profession.* **MOVE** ▷ **5** B2 [I usually + adv/prep] to move into or out of a small space awkwardly or with difficulty or effort: *They climbed* ***into*** *the truck and drove away.* ◦ *We can't stop Tom climbing* ***out of*** *his cot.* **GROW** ▷ **6** [I] to grow upwards: *There's masses of ivy climbing* ***up/over*** *the walls of our house.*

IDIOM **be climbing the walls** to suffer unpleasant feelings, such as worry, in an extreme way: *to be climbing the walls* ***with*** *boredom/anger/frustration.*

PHRASAL VERB **climb down** UK to change your opinion or admit that you were wrong: *The government has been forced to climb down* ***over*** *the issue of increased taxes.*

▸noun [C] **1** an act or process of climbing: *We were very tired after our climb.* ◦ *The climb* ***down*** *the mountain took longer than the climb* ***up.*** ◦ *I've* ***made*** *three climbs so far this year.* ◦ *Her climb* ***to*** *power has been very rapid.* **2** a place or object to be climbed: *The north face of the Eiger is a very difficult climb.*

climbdown /ˈklaɪm.daʊn/ noun [C] UK an occasion when you change your opinion or admit that you were wrong: *Saying she was wrong was a difficult climbdown for Sarah.*

climber /ˈklaɪ.məʳ/ US /-mɚ/ noun [C] **PERSON** ▷ **1** someone who climbs mountains for sport **PLANT** ▷ **2** a plant which grows up a supporting surface

climbing /ˈklaɪ.mɪŋ/ noun; adj

▸noun [U] A2 rock climbing: the sport of climbing mountains: *Chris has just taken up climbing.*

▸adj [before noun] **PLANT** ▷ **1** describes a plant which grows up a supporting surface: *I need some climbing* ***plants*** *that will grow on a north-facing wall.* **SPORT** ▷ **2** relating to the sport of climbing mountains: *He needs some climbing boots.*

ˈclimbing ˌframe noun [C] UK (US **ˈjungle ˌgym**) a large frame made of bars that children can climb on

climes /klaɪmz/ noun [plural] literary a place where the weather is different in a particular way: *We're off to* ***sunnier*** *climes next week.*

clinch /klɪntʃ/ verb; noun

▸verb informal **WIN** ▷ **1** [T] to finally get or win something: *I hear he finally clinched the* ***deal*** *to buy the land he wanted.* **DECIDE** ▷ **2 clinch it** to make someone decide what to do after a lot of thought or discussion: *When they said the job would involve travelling to Paris, that clinched it (****for*** *her) (= that made her certain that she wanted the job).*

▸noun [C] the position two people are in when they are holding each other tightly in their arms, when fighting or showing love

clincher /ˈklɪn.tʃəʳ/ US /-tʃɚ/ noun [C usually singular] something which helps someone make a decision: *It was the offer of a large discount on the TV that was the real clincher.*

cling /klɪŋ/ verb (**clung, clung**) **HOLD** ▷ **1** C2 [I + adv/prep] to stick onto or hold something or someone tightly, or to refuse to stop holding them: *We got so wet that our clothes clung* ***to*** *us.* ◦ *They clung* ***together*** *in terror as the screams grew louder.* ◦ *One little girl was clinging* ***onto*** *a cuddly toy.* ◦ *She clung* ***to*** *the handrail as she walked down the slippery steps.* **STAY CLOSE** ▷ **2** [I usually + adv/prep] to stay close or near: *The road clings* ***to*** *(= closely follows) the coastline for several miles, then it turns inland.* **3** [I] disapproving to stay close to someone who is taking care of you, because you need their support: *Jenny is the kind of child who always clings whenever she's taken to a new place.* • **clinging** /ˈklɪŋ.ɪŋ/ adj (also **clingy**)

PHRASAL VERBS **cling (on) to sth** C2 to try very hard to keep something: *He clung on to power for another ten years.* • **cling to sth** to refuse to stop believing or hoping for something: *She clings to the hope that her husband will come back to her.*

ˈcling film noun [U] UK (US **ˈplastic wrap**) thin, transparent, plastic material, used for wrapping food to keep it fresh: *I've put some cling film over the salad.*

clingy /ˈklɪŋ.i/ adj **STICKING** ▷ **1** describes something that sticks onto someone or something tightly: *clingy material* **STAYING CLOSE** ▷ **2** disapproving describes someone who stays close to someone who is taking care of them and depends on them: *Jimmy is a very clingy child.*

clinic /ˈklɪn.ɪk/ noun [C] B1 a building, often part of a hospital, to which people can go for medical care or advice relating to a particular condition: *Bring your baby to the clinic and we'll take a look at her.* ◦ *Antenatal clinics provide care for pregnant women.*

IDIOM **hold a clinic 1** to be available at a particular place to provide medical care to members of the public: *Dr Clark holds a clinic on Tuesday mornings.* **2** UK to be available at a particular place to provide advice to members of the public: *Our MP holds a clinic every Friday evening.*

clinical /ˈklɪn.ɪ.kəl/ adj **MEDICAL** ▷ **1** Ⓒ1 describes medical work or teaching that relates to the examination and treatment of ill people: *clinical tests/training* ◦ *the Department of Clinical Medicine* ◦ *Clinical **trials** of the new drug may take five years.* **WITHOUT EMOTION** ▷ **2** Ⓒ2 disapproving expressing no emotion or feelings: *She seems to have a very clinical attitude towards her children.* **3** showing no character and warmth: *We were going to paint our kitchen white, but we decided that would look too clinical.* • **clinically** /-i/ adv *This toothpaste has been clinically proven (= shown in experiments) to protect your teeth.* ◦ *Doctors pronounced him clinically **dead** (= judged him to be dead by examining his body).* ◦ disapproving *Should doctors always remain clinically detached from (= express no emotion towards) their patients?*

ˌclinical deˈpression noun [U] a mental illness that causes feelings of sadness and loss of hope, changes in sleeping and eating habits, loss of interest in your usual activities, and pains which have no physical explanation • **ˌclinically deˈpressed** adj

ˌclinical therˈmometer noun [C] a device used for measuring the body temperature of a person or animal

clinician /klɪˈnɪʃ.ən/ noun [C] specialized someone, such as a doctor, who has qualifications in an area of very skilled health work

clink /klɪŋk/ verb; noun

▸verb [I or T] to (cause something to) make a short ringing sound like pieces of glass or metal knocking lightly together: *The ice clinked as she dropped it into the glass.* ◦ *We all clinked our **glasses** together and drank to a happy new year.* • **clinking** /ˈklɪŋ.kɪŋ/ noun [S] *the clinking of glasses*

▸noun **SOUND** ▷ **1** [S] a short ringing sound like pieces of glass or metal knocking lightly together: *I could hear **the** clink **of** coins in his pocket.* **PRISON** ▷ **2** [S or U] informal prison: *Everyone always said Joe would end up **in** (the) clink.*

clinker /ˈklɪŋ.kər/ ⓤⓢ /-kɚ/ noun **POWDER** ▷ **1** [C or U] the ASH (= powder) and rough hard pieces that remain after coal has been burned **MISTAKE** ▷ **2** [C] US old-fashioned slang a mistake, especially a wrong musical note

clip /klɪp/ noun; verb

▸noun **FASTENER** ▷ **1** [C] a small object usually made of metal or plastic, used for fastening things together or holding them in position: *a paper/hair/tie clip* ◦ *The wires were fastened together with a plastic clip.* **FILM** ▷ **2** [C] a short part of a film or television programme: *I've seen a clip **from** the film.* **SPEED** ▷ **3 at a fast/good clip** US informal fast: *We set off at a good clip, but we gradually slowed down.* **GUN PART** ▷ **4** [C] a container that is fastened to a gun, from which bullets go into the gun to be fired **CUT** ▷ **5** [S] the act of cutting something in order to make it tidy: *That hedge needs a clip.* **HIT** ▷ **6 a clip round/on the ear** [C usually singular] UK old-fashioned a quick hit on the side of someone's head: *You do that once more and you'll **get** a clip round the ear, my lad.*

▸verb (-pp-) **CUT** ▷ **1** [T] to cut something with SCISSORS or a similar sharp tool, especially to make it tidier: *I'm going to clip the hedge this weekend.* ◦ *When the guard came to clip my train ticket (= make a hole in it to show that it had been used), I couldn't find it.* ◦ *I'm always clipping recipes **out of** magazines.* **2** [T] to reduce something by the stated amount: *Christie has clipped a tenth of a second **off** the record.* **HIT** ▷ **3** [T] to hit something or someone with a short sharp movement: *He clipped the edge of the kerb with his front tyre.* **FASTEN** ▷ **4** [I or T, usually + adv/prep] to fasten something with a clip: *You can always tell a real bow tie from one that clips **on**.* ◦ *When you've finished your worksheets, clip them **together** and hand them in to me.*

IDIOM **clip sb's wings** to limit someone's freedom

ˈclip ˌart noun [U] small pictures that are stored on your computer and can be easily added to a document: *The site links to about 24 other sites offering clip art.* ◦ *a clip art collection/library*

clipboard /ˈklɪp.bɔːd/ ⓤⓢ /-bɔːrd/ noun **WRITING SURFACE** ▷ **1** [C] a board with a clip at the top that holds sheets of paper in position and provides a surface for writing on: *A woman with a clipboard stopped us in the street to ask us some questions.* **COMPUTING** ▷ **2** [C usually singular] an area for storing information temporarily in a computer when you are moving it from one position or document to another: *You draw the shape somewhere on your worksheet, click on it and copy it to the clipboard.*

clip-clop /ˈklɪp.klɒp/ ⓤⓢ /-klɑːp/ noun [C usually singular] a sound like that of horses' HOOFS on a hard surface: *the clip-clop **of** horses coming up the road* • **clip-clop** verb [I] (plural **-pp-**) *We heard horses clip-clopping (= making a sound with their feet) along the road.*

ˈclip ˌjoint noun [C] informal disapproving a bar or NIGHTCLUB where customers are charged too much for food and drink of low quality

ˈclip-on adj [before noun] describes something that is fastened with a CLIP: *clip-on earrings/sunglasses* • **ˈclip-on** noun [C usually plural] *They only had earrings for pierced ears, but I wanted clip-ons.*

clipped /klɪpt/ adj **SPEAKING** ▷ **1** with words pronounced quickly and clearly, sometimes with parts missing, or in a very short and unfriendly way: *I heard the clipped **tones** of his secretary saying 'I have Mr Watson for you.'* **TIDY** ▷ **2** cut short and tidy: *a clipped beard/moustache*

clippers /ˈklɪp.əz/ ⓤⓢ /-ɚz/ noun [plural] a device for cutting especially nails, hair, wire, or bushes

clipping /ˈklɪp.ɪŋ/ noun **1** [C usually plural] a piece that has been cut off something: *grass/nail clippings* **2** [C] an article cut from a newspaper: *A friend sent me a **newspaper** clipping about someone we were at school with.*

clique /kliːk/ ⓤⓢ /klɪk/ noun [C, + sing/pl verb] disapproving a small group of people who spend their time together and do not welcome other people into that group: *Our golf club is run by a very unfriendly clique (**of** people).* ◦ *There's a clique at work that never talks/who never talk to anyone else.*

cliquey /ˈkliː.ki/ adj (**cliquier**, **cliquiest**) (also **cliquish**) behaving like a clique, not making other people feel welcome: *I decided not to join the tennis club because I found it very cliquey.*

clitoris /ˈklɪt.ər.ɪs/ ⓤⓢ /ˈklɪţ.ɚ-/ noun [C] a sexual organ above the VAGINA that can give a woman sexual pleasure when it is touched • **clitoral** /ˈklɪt.ər.əl/ ⓤⓢ /ˈklɪţ.ɚ-/ adj

cloak /kləʊk/ (US) /kloʊk/ **noun; verb**
▸**noun** PIECE OF CLOTHING ▷ **1** [C] a loose outer piece of clothing without sleeves, which fastens at the neck, and is worn instead of a coat HIDE ▷ **2** [S or U] something which hides, covers, or keeps something else secret: *The restaurant he owned was just a cloak* ***for*** *(= hid) his drug-dealing activities.* ◦ *They left the house under cloak* ***of*** *darkness.*
▸**verb** [T] to cover or hide something: *He has always kept his love affairs cloaked* ***in*** *secrecy (= kept them secret).* ◦ *The river is often cloaked* ***in*** *mist in the early morning.*

ˌcloak-and-ˈdagger **adj** describes an exciting story involving secrets and mystery, often about SPIES, or something which makes you think of this: *I'm tired of all these cloak-and-dagger (= secretive) meetings – let's discuss the issues openly.*

cloakroom /ˈkləʊk.rʊm/, /-ruːm/ (US) /ˈkloʊk-/ **noun** [C] **1** (US also **checkroom**) a room in a public building such as a restaurant, theatre, etc. where coats, bags, and other personal things can be left while their owners are in the building **2** UK polite word for toilet, especially one in a public building

clobber /ˈklɒb.əʳ/ (US) /ˈklɑː.bɚ/ **verb; noun**
▸**verb** [T] informal HIT ▷ **1** to hit someone or something hard and repeatedly: *If you do that again, I'll clobber you* ***(one)****.* **2** to punish someone: *The government is proposing new measures to clobber tax dodgers.* **3** to harm someone financially: *The new supermarket is really going to clobber the small local shops.* DEFEAT ▷ **4** to defeat completely: *The government clobbered the opposition's proposals.*
▸**noun** [U] UK informal possessions, especially those that you carry around with you, or clothes: *I've got far too much clobber in my handbag.* ◦ *Did you bring all your tennis clobber?*

cloche /klɒʃ/ (US) /kloʊʃ/ **noun** [C] COVER ▷ **1** (also **cold frame**) a piece of clear material, sometimes on a frame, used to cover plants for a short time, usually to protect them from cold weather or to help them grow faster HAT ▷ **2** a woman's hat, shaped like a bell and fitting closely around the head, that was popular in the 1920s

clock /klɒk/ (US) /klɑːk/ **noun; verb**
▸**noun** TIME ▷ **1** (A1) [C] a device for measuring and showing time, usually found in or on a building and not worn by a person: *We have an antique clock on our mantelpiece.* ◦ *The town-hall clock* ***says*** *(= shows that the time is) nine o'clock.* ◦ *I think the kitchen clock is* ***fast/slow*** *(= is showing a later/earlier time than it should).* ◦ *The clock began to* ***strike*** *twelve.* ◦ *She* ***set*** *her clock (= put it to the right time) by the time signal on the radio.* **2 put/turn the clocks back** UK (US **set/turn the clocks back**) to change the time on your clocks to an hour earlier, at an officially chosen time of year **3 put/turn the clocks forward** (US also **set the clocks ahead**) to change the time on your clocks to an hour later, at an officially chosen time of year SPEED ▷ **4 the clock** [S] **a** a SPEEDOMETER (= a device that measures speed): *I was only doing 30 mph* ***on*** *the clock.* **b** a MILOMETER (= a device for recording distance travelled): *My car's only got 10,000 miles* ***on*** *the clock.*

IDIOMS **against the clock 1** If you do something against the clock, you do it as fast as possible and try to finish it before a certain time. **2** When people do something against the clock, the time they take to do it is recorded, in order to find which person or attempt is the fastest. • **be watching the clock** (also **have/keep your eye on the clock**) to be looking to see what the time is, usually because you are bored or eager to leave: *I had a train to catch, so I was watching the clock all through the meeting.* • **put/turn the clock back** to make things the same as they were at an earlier time: *The court's decision on this case will turn the clock back 50 years.* ◦ *If I could turn the clock back and do things differently, I would.* • **round/around the clock** (C1) all day and all night: *Doctors and nurses* ***worked*** *round the clock to help those injured in the train crash.* ◦ *She needed round-the-clock nursing.* • **turn back the clock** to remember or imagine times in the past: *Now we're going to turn back the clock with some rock 'n' roll from the 1950s.*

▸**verb** [T] TIME ▷ **1** to take a particular time exactly to do or complete something: *He clocked ten seconds in the 100 metres (= he ran it in ten seconds).* SPEED ▷ **2** to show or reach a particular speed or distance on a measuring device: [+ -ing verb] *The police clocked him doing 80 mph in a 50 mph area.* ◦ *Jim's car has clocked* ***(up)*** *(= travelled) 40,000 miles in less than two years.* HIT ▷ **3** UK informal to hit someone, especially on the head or face: *Then the other guy turned round and clocked him* ***one*** *(= hit him).*

PHRASAL VERBS **clock in** (UK also **clock on**) to record the time you arrive at work on a special machine: *What time did you clock in this morning?* ◦ *Clocking-in time is 9.00 a.m.* • **clock out** (UK also **clock off**) to leave work, especially by recording the time you leave on a special machine • **clock sth up** mainly UK informal to win or achieve a large number of similar things: *The Australians have clocked up three gold medals and two silvers in the swimming events.*

ˌclock ˈradio **noun** [C] a **radio alarm clock**

ˈclock ˌtower **noun** [C] a tower that has a clock at the top of it

ˈclock-ˌwatching **noun** [U] disapproving the act of repeatedly looking to see what time it is in order to see how much longer you have to work • **ˈclock-ˌwatcher noun** [C]

clockwise /ˈklɒk.waɪz/ (US) /ˈklɑːk-/ **adj, adv** in the direction in which the HANDS (= thin parts that point) of a clock move: *Turn the knob clockwise/in a clockwise direction.* → Opposite **anticlockwise, counterclockwise**

clockwork /ˈklɒk.wɜːk/ (US) /ˈklɑːk.wɝːk/ **noun** [U] a system of springs and wheels that you WIND (= turn) with a key or handle to make some clocks, toys, and other devices operate: *a clockwork train/mouse*

IDIOMS **like clockwork** (also **(as) regular as clockwork**) very regularly, or at exactly the planned times: *Since the recent improvements to the service, the buses are running like clockwork.* ◦ *My daughter always calls me every Friday evening, (as) regular as clockwork.* • **run/go like clockwork** to happen exactly as planned, without any trouble: *The party went like clockwork.*

clod /klɒd/ (US) /klɑːd/ **noun** [C] SOIL ▷ **1** a piece of soil or clay: *Their hoofs threw up clods* ***of*** *earth as they galloped across the field.* PERSON ▷ **2** old-fashioned a stupid person: *Don't be such a clod!*

clodhopper /ˈklɒdˌhɒp.əʳ/ (US) /ˈklɑːdˌhɑː.pɚ/ **noun** [C] informal PERSON ▷ **1** a person who moves in an awkward way: *Look where you're going, you* ***great*** *clodhopper.* SHOE ▷ **2** a heavy shoe: *You're not coming in the house in those* ***great*** *clodhoppers.* • **clodhopping** /-ˌhɒp.ɪŋ/ (US) /-ˌhɑː.pɪŋ/ **adj** [before noun] *You clodhopping idiot!* ◦ *big, clodhopping shoes*

clog /klɒg/ (US) /klɑːg/ **verb; noun**
▸**verb** [I or T] (**-gg-**) to (cause something to) become blocked or filled so that movement or activity is difficult: *The roads are clogged* ***with*** *holiday traffic.* ◦ *Eating too much fat causes your arteries to clog* ***(up)****.*

◦ *Leaves are clogging (***up***) the drain.* • **clogged** /klɒgd/ Ⓤⓢ /klɑːgd/ **adj** blocked: *clogged pipes*
▸**noun** [C usually plural] a type of shoe made of wood, or with the top part made of leather and the bottom part of wood

C

cloister /ˈklɔɪ.stər/ Ⓤⓢ /-stɚ/ **noun** [C usually plural] a covered stone passage around the four sides of a COURTYARD (= a square or rectangular space) especially in a religious building such as a church or MONASTERY

cloistered /ˈklɔɪ.stəd/ Ⓤⓢ /-stɚd/ **adj 1** separated from and communicating little with the outside world: *These academics lead such a cloistered* ***life/existence****.* **2** surrounded by covered passages: *a cloistered courtyard*

clone /kləʊn/ Ⓤⓢ /kloʊn/ **noun; verb**
▸**noun** [C] **1** a plant or animal that has the same GENES as the original from which it was produced **2** informal disapproving someone or something that looks very much like someone or something else: *Most people saw her as just another blond-haired, red-lipped Marilyn Monroe clone.* **3** specialized a computer that operates in a very similar way to the one that it was copied from
▸**verb** [T] to create a clone of a plant or animal: *Scientists have already cloned a sheep.* • **cloning** /ˈkləʊ.nɪŋ/ Ⓤⓢ /ˈkloʊ-/ **noun** [U] *animal/human cloning*

close **verb; noun; adj; adj, adv**
▸**verb** /kləʊz/ Ⓤⓢ /kloʊz/ **NOT OPEN** ▷ **1** A1 [I or T] to (cause something to) change from being open to not being open: *Could you close the* ***door/window*** *please?* ◦ *Close your* ***eyes*** *– I've got a surprise for you.* **2** A2 [I] When a shop, restaurant, or public place closes, people cannot go into it: *The banks had closed (***to*** customers) so I couldn't get any money out.* ◦ *The museum closes* ***at*** *5.30.* ◦ *We can't get a drink! It's after (***pub***) closing* ***time****.* **END** ▷ **3** C2 [I or T] to (cause something to) end: *The play closed* ***with*** *the tragic death of both hero and heroine.* ◦ *She closed the meeting with a short speech.* ◦ *The pound closed* ***at*** *(= was worth) $1.47 at the end of the day's trading.* **4** B2 [I or T] to (cause a business, organization, or business arrangement to) stop operating: *I closed that bank* ***account*** *when I came to London.* ◦ *The* ***factory*** *closed over ten years ago.* **5** **close a deal** to make a successful business arrangement with someone: *We closed a deal* ***with*** *a major supermarket.*

IDIOMS **close your eyes to sth** to ignore something bad and pretend it is not happening: *She closed her eyes to* ***the fact*** *that her son was stealing.* • **close ranks** When the members of a group or organization close ranks, they make an effort to stay united, especially in order to defend themselves from severe criticism: *In the past, the party would have closed ranks around its leader and defended him loyally.*

PHRASAL VERBS **close (sth) down** B2 If a business or organization closes down or someone closes it down, it stops operating: *All the mines in this area were closed down in the 1980s.* ◦ *Our local butcher is closing down.* • **close in** C2 to gradually get nearer to someone, usually in order to attack them: *The advancing soldiers closed in* ***on*** *the town.* ◦ *The hunt chased the fox until it was too tired and weak to run and then closed in* ***for the kill****.* • **close sth off** C1 to put something across the entrance of a place to stop people from entering: *Police quickly closed off the area.*

▸**noun** **END** ▷ **1** /kləʊz/ Ⓤⓢ /kloʊz/ [S] the end of something, or the time when you end it: *I tried to* ***bring*** *the conversation* ***to a*** *close.* ◦ *'Let's* ***draw*** *this meeting* ***to a*** *close, gentlemen,' said the chairman.* **ROAD** ▷ **2** /kləʊs/ Ⓤⓢ /kloʊs/ [C] UK a road, usually with private houses, which vehicles can only enter from one end: *He lives at 83 Barker Close.*
▸**adj** /kləʊs/ Ⓤⓢ /kloʊs/ **RELATIONSHIP** ▷ **1** B1 having direct family connections or shared beliefs, support, and sympathy: *There weren't many people at the funeral – just close* ***family/relatives****.* ◦ *They're a worrying political party because of their close* ***links/ties*** *with terrorist groups.* ◦ *In those early months, there's a very close* ***bond*** *between mother and child.* ◦ *a close community* **2** A2 describes people who know each other very well and like each other a lot, or who see and talk to each other a lot: *Mira is one of my closest* ***friends****.* ◦ *Her relationship isn't good with her father, but she's very close* ***to*** *her mother.* ◦ *My brother and I have become much closer over the years.* **CAREFUL** ▷ **3** C2 looking at or listening to someone or something very carefully: *Police are paying close* ***attention*** *to the situation.* ◦ *Take a closer* ***look*** *at this photograph.* **SECRETIVE** ▷ **4** unwilling to talk about things to other people: *He's so close* ***about*** *his past – it seems like he's hiding something.* **LACKING AIR** ▷ **5** describes weather or air conditions in which it is difficult to breathe and it is uncomfortably warm: *Can I open the window? It's very close in here.*
▸**adj, adv** /kləʊs/ Ⓤⓢ /kloʊs/ **NEAR** ▷ **1** A1 not far in position or time: *Don't get too close* ***to*** *that dog, Rosie.* ◦ *I hate people standing too close* ***to*** *me.* ◦ *As Christmas gets closer, the shops get more and more crowded.* ◦ *Emma looked close* ***to*** *tears (= almost going to cry).* **2** **close by** near: *Shall we call in on Miranda? You know she lives quite close by.* **SIMILAR** ▷ **3** C1 having only a small difference: *The election results were so close they had to vote again.* ◦ *He came second in the race, but it was very close.* ◦ *The youngest boys are so close* ***in*** *age they look like twins.* ◦ *Both children bear a very close* ***resemblance*** *to their father.* **4** **close on/to** almost: *I think there are close on three million unemployed at present.*

IDIOMS **at close quarters/range** (from) a short distance away: *When you see famous people at close quarters, they always appear much smaller than you imagined them.* ◦ *He was shot at close range.* • **be close to the bone** If something you say or write is close to the bone, it is close to the truth in a way that might offend some people. • **be too close for comfort** humorous to be so close to you that you feel worried or frightened: *His mother lives in the next street to us, which is a little too close for comfort.*

ˌclose ˈcall **noun** [C] a **close shave**

ˌclose-ˈcropped **adj** describes hair or grass that has been cut very short

> **! Common mistake: closed or close?**
> **Warning:** choose the correct adjective!
> To talk about something not being distant in position or time, don't say 'closed', say **close**:
> ~~*Our house is very closed to the airport.*~~
> *Our house is very close to the airport.*

> **! Common mistake: closed or close?**
> To talk about people who know each other well and like each other a lot, don't say 'closed', say **close**:
> ~~*I am very closed to her although I don't see her often.*~~
> *I am very close to her although I don't see her often.*

closed /kləʊzd/ Ⓤⓢ /kloʊzd/ **adj** **NOT OPEN** ▷ **1** A1 not open: *It might be less draughty if the door were closed.* **2** A1 not open for business: *All the shops were closed,* so we couldn't buy any food. **ENDED** ▷ **3** finished and therefore not able to be discussed further: *'The matter is closed,' said the health minister.* **NOT ACCEPTING IDEAS** ▷ **4** C2 not wanting to accept new ideas, people, customs, etc.: *You have such a closed mind.* ◦ *The setting of the novel is the closed world of banking.*

IDIOM **behind closed doors** C2 If something happens behind closed doors, it is hidden or kept secret from public view: *The deal was negotiated behind closed doors.*

ˌclosed ˈbook noun [S] informal a subject about which you know or understand nothing: *I'm afraid physics will always be a closed book **to** me.*

ˌclosed-ˈcasket adj US used to describe a funeral at which the COFFIN is closed and people cannot see the dead person's body: *a closed-casket **funeral/service***
→ Compare **open-casket**

ˌclosed-circuit ˈtelevision noun [U] (abbreviation **CCTV**) a system which sends television signals to a limited number of screens and is often used in shops as protection against thieves

ˈclosed ˌseason noun [S] US for **close season**

ˌclosed ˈshop noun [C usually singular] a place of work where you have to belong to a particular TRADE UNION (= organization of workers)

ˌclose-ˈfitting adj describes clothing that fits very tightly

ˌclose-ˈgrained adj describes wood that has a pattern of narrow rings or lines

ˌclose-ˈknit adj describes a group of people in which everyone helps and supports each other: *a close-knit family/community*

closely /ˈkləʊs.li/ US /ˈkloʊs-/ adv **RELATIONSHIP** ▷ **1** B2 in a way that is directly connected or has a strong relationship: *English and German are closely **related**.* ◦ *Both politicians have been closely **associated** with the movement for some time.* ◦ *We are **working** closely with the police.* **CAREFULLY** ▷ **2** C1 carefully and paying attention to details: *Pollution levels are closely **monitored**.* ◦ *He looked again more closely at the marks.* **SIMILAR** ▷ **3** without a big difference between two people, groups, or things: *The two teams are closely matched.* ◦ *It was a closely fought election.* **SECRETIVE** ▷ **4** in a way that tries hard to keep something secret: *a closely **guarded** secret* **NEAR** ▷ **5** C1 not far in time or position: *The Swiss boat is in the lead, followed closely by the French.*

closeness /ˈkləʊs.nəs/ US /ˈkloʊs-/ noun [U] **NEAR** ▷ **1** C1 being close in position or time **RELATIONSHIP** ▷ **2** C1 the quality of knowing someone very well, liking them a lot, and spending a lot of time with them: *A special closeness is supposed to exist between twins.* **LACKING AIR** ▷ **3** the quality of weather or air conditions in which it is difficult to breathe and is uncomfortably warm

closeout /ˈkləʊz.aʊt/ US /ˈkloʊz-/ noun [C] US an occasion when the price of goods in a shop or factory is reduced so they can be sold quickly

ˌclose-ˈrun adj UK won or decided by a very small distance, or number of points, votes, etc.: *a close-run competition/contest/decision/race* ◦ *It was a close-run **thing** and Millar had to endure a five-minute wait before the judges decided that he had won.*

ˈclose ˌseason noun [S] UK (mainly US **ˈclosed ˌseason**) a period of the year in which the hunting of a particular type of animal, for example birds or fish, is not allowed: *This is the close season **for** salmon.*
→ Compare **open season**

ˌclose-ˈset adj describes eyes or teeth that are very close to each other

ˌclose ˈshave noun [C] (also **ˌclose ˈcall**) a situation in which you come extremely close to a dangerous or unpleasant situation or only just manage to avoid it: *I had a close shave this morning, – some idiot almost knocked me off my bike.*

closet /ˈklɒz.ɪt/ US /ˈklɑː.zɪt/ noun; verb; adj

▸noun [C] mainly US A2 a cupboard or a small room with a door, used for storing things, especially clothes: *a bedroom/linen/storage closet*

IDIOM **come out of the closet** to tell your family, friends, or the public that you are gay, after previously keeping this secret

▸verb [T usually passive] to put yourself in a place, especially a closed space, and stay there: *Two weeks before my exams I closeted my**self** (**away**) **in** my room with my books and I didn't speak to anyone.* ◦ *The president is closeted **with** (= having a private meeting with) his advisers.*

▸adj [before noun] describes a belief, activity, or feeling that is kept secret from the public, usually because you are frightened of the results of it becoming known: *a closet alcoholic/homosexual*

ˈclose-up noun [C] a photograph taken from a short distance that gives a very detailed picture: *She **took** a stunning close-up **of** him.*

closing /ˈkləʊ.zɪŋ/ US /ˈkloʊz-/ adj [before noun] describes something which comes near the end of a speech, event, activity, etc.: *In his closing remarks, the chairman thanked everyone who had helped.* ◦ *the closing ceremony of the Olympic Games*

closure /ˈkləʊ.ʒəʳ/ US /ˈkloʊ.ʒɚ/ noun **1** C2 [C] the fact of a business, organization, etc. stopping operating: *factory/branch closures* ◦ *Many elderly people will be affected by the library closures.* **2** [U] the feeling or act of bringing an unpleasant situation, time, or experience to an end, so that you are able to start new activities: *a sense of closure* ◦ *to **achieve/reach** closure*

clot /klɒt/ US /klɑːt/ noun; verb

▸noun [C] **PIECE** ▷ **1** an almost solid piece of something: *He had a **blood** clot removed from his brain.* **PERSON** ▷ **2** UK old-fashioned informal a stupid person: *Look what you've done, you clot!*

▸verb [I] (-tt-) to form clots: *He was rushed into hospital because his blood wasn't clotting properly.* ◦ *an anti-clotting agent*

cloth /klɒθ/ US /klɑːθ/ noun **1** B2 [U] (a type of) WOVEN material: *a piece/length of cloth* **2** B2 [C] a small piece of material, used in cleaning to remove dirt, dust, or liquid: *a washing-up cloth*

> **!** Common mistake: **cloth or clothes?**
>
> **Warning:** Choose the right word!
>
> To talk about things that you wear, don't say 'cloth' or 'cloths', say **clothes**:
>
> ~~Bring summer cloths with you as the weather will be warm.~~
>
> **Remember: clothes** is always plural. To talk about one particular thing that you wear, say **a piece/item of clothing.**

clothe /kləʊð/ US /kloʊð/ verb [T] to provide someone with clothes: *It costs a lot to **feed and** clothe five children.*

clothed /kləʊðd/ US /kloʊðd/ adj wearing clothes: *Bathers must be **fully** clothed before entering the restaurant.*

clothes /kləʊðz/ US /kloʊðz/ noun [plural] A1 things

such as dresses and trousers that you wear to cover, protect, or decorate your body: *She usually* ***wears*** *smart/casual clothes.* ◦ *I'm just* ***putting*** *my clothes* ***on.*** ◦ ***Take*** *your clothes* ***off*** *and get in the bath.* ◦ ***designer*** *clothes* ◦ *a clothes shop*

> **Word partners for clothes**
>
> *wear* clothes • *pull on/put on/throw on* clothes • *pull off/take off/tear off* clothes • *change* your clothes • *designer/expensive/trendy* clothes • *clean/fresh* clothes • a *change* of clothes

ˈclothes ˌbasket noun [C] a container that you put clothes in when they need washing

ˈclothes ˌbrush noun [C] a brush for removing dust and dirt from clothes

ˈclothes ˌhanger noun [C] a **hanger**

ˈclothes ˌhorse noun [C] **FRAME** ▷ **1** a frame on which wet clothes can be hung to dry, usually used inside the house **PERSON** ▷ **2** disapproving a person, especially a woman, who is employed to wear expensive and fashionable clothes

clothesline /ˈkləʊðz.laɪn/ (US) /ˈkloʊðz-/ noun [C] a length of rope or string from which wet clothes are hung, usually outside, to dry

ˈclothes ˌpeg noun [C] UK (US **clothespin**) a device used for holding clothes onto a clothes line while they dry

clothing /ˈkləʊ.ðɪŋ/ (US) /ˈkloʊ-/ noun [U] formal (B2) clothes, especially of a type made to protect the wearer against heat, water, or machinery: ***Protective*** *clothing must be worn.* ◦ *You can only take three* ***articles/items of*** *clothing into the changing room.*

ˌclotted ˈcream noun [U] a thick cream with soft LUMPS in it, made especially in southwest England

cloud /klaʊd/ noun; verb

▸noun **IN SKY** ▷ **1** (A2) [C or U] a grey or white mass in the sky, made up of very small floating drops of water: *Do you think those are* ***rain*** *clouds on the horizon?* ◦ *The sky was a perfect blue – not a cloud in sight.* ◦ *There was so much cloud, we couldn't see anything.* ◦ *Dark clouds massed on the horizon.* **MASS** ▷ **2** (B2) [C] a mass of something such as dust or smoke that looks like a cloud: *On the eastern horizon, a huge cloud* ***of*** *smoke from burning oil tanks stretched across the sky.* ◦ *The initial cloud* ***of*** *tear gas had hardly cleared before shots were fired.* **COMPUTING** ▷ **3 the cloud** [S] a computer network where files and programs can be stored, especially the internet: *All the photographs are kept on the cloud rather than on hard drives.*

IDIOMS **be on cloud nine** informal (C2) to be extremely happy and excited: *'Was Helen pleased about getting that job?' 'Pleased? She was on cloud nine!'* • **be under a cloud** to not be trusted or popular because people think you have done something bad: *The cabinet minister left office under a cloud after a fraud scandal.* • **a cloud on the horizon** something that threatens to cause problems or unhappiness in the future: *The only cloud on the horizon is the physics exam in June.* • **every cloud has a silver lining** saying said to emphasize that every difficult or unpleasant situation has some advantage

▸verb **1** [I or T] If something transparent clouds, or if something clouds it, it becomes difficult to see through. **2** (C2) [T] to make someone confused, or make something more difficult to understand: *When it came to explaining the lipstick on his collar, he found that drink had clouded (= confused) his* ***memory.***

PHRASAL VERB **cloud over SKY** ▷ **1** If the sky clouds over, it becomes covered with clouds. **FACE** ▷ **2** If a person's face clouds over, they suddenly look unhappy or worried: *At the mention of her dead husband, her face clouded over.*

ˈcloud ˌbank noun [C] a big low mass of cloud

cloudburst /ˈklaʊd.bɜːst/ (US) /-bɝːst/ noun [C] a sudden heavy fall of rain

ˌcloud comˈputing noun [U] the use of services, computer programs, etc. that are on the internet rather than ones that you buy and put on your computer

ˌcloud ˈcuckoo land disapproving **live/be in cloud cuckoo land** to think that things that are completely impossible might happen, rather than understanding how things really are: *When referees make contentious decisions players are going to be upset, and anyone who thinks otherwise is living in cloud cuckoo land.*

cloudless /ˈklaʊd.ləs/ adj with no clouds: *a cloudless sky/night*

cloudware /ˈklaʊd.weəʳ/ (US) /-wer/ noun [U] services, computer programs, etc. that are available to use on the internet rather than ones that you buy and put on your computer

cloudy /ˈklaʊ.di/ adj **1** (A2) with clouds: *a cloudy sky/day* ◦ *Scotland will be cloudy with wintry showers.* **2** not transparent: *The beer was cloudy and dark.*

clout /klaʊt/ verb; noun

▸verb [T] informal to hit someone or something with the hand or with a heavy object: *Quigley clouted me smartly across the side of the head.*

▸noun **POWER** ▷ **1** [U] power and influence over other people or events: *The Queen may have privilege but she* ***has*** *no real* ***political*** *clout.* **HIT** ▷ **2** [C] informal the act of hitting someone or something with your hand or with a heavy object: *If the photocopier stops working, just* ***give*** *it* ***a*** *clout.*

clove /kləʊv/ (US) /kloʊv/ noun; verb

▸noun **PLANT PART** ▷ **1** [C] a small separate part of a BULB of GARLIC (= a plant used in cooking): *This recipe takes four cloves of garlic.* **SPICE** ▷ **2** [C or U] a small, dark brown dried flower of an EVERGREEN tree (= one that never loses its leaves), used as a spice: *sweet spices such as ginger and clove*

▸verb past simple of **cleave**

cloven /ˈkləʊ.vᵊn/ (US) /ˈkloʊ-/ adj; verb

▸adj describes something, especially an animal's HOOF, that is divided into two parts: *The devil was painted with horns and cloven* ***hoofs.***

▸verb past participle of **cleave**

clover /ˈkləʊ.vəʳ/ (US) /ˈkloʊ.vɚ/ noun [U] a small plant with three round leaves on each stem, often fed to cows

IDIOM **live/be in clover** to enjoy a life of money and comfort: *With the income from the family estate, she's in clover.*

clown /klaʊn/ noun; verb

▸noun [C] **1** (A2) an ENTERTAINER who wears funny clothes, has a painted face, and makes people laugh by performing tricks and behaving in a silly way **2** someone who behaves in a silly way, often intentionally

▸verb [I usually + adv/prep] to act stupidly, often to make other people laugh: *Left alone, the class threw books, pulled faces, and generally clowned* ***around.***

cloying /ˈklɔɪ.ɪŋ/ adj **TOO SWEET** ▷ **1** literary disapproving too sweet and therefore unpleasant: *This is a* *wonderful wine – honeyed and rich without being remotely cloying.* **TOO EMOTIONAL** ▷ **2** disapproving too good or kind, or expressing feelings of love in a way that is not sincere: *She criticized the cloying sentimentality of the film.* • **cloyingly** /-li/ adv *cloyingly sweet*

club /klʌb/ noun; verb

▸noun **GROUP** ▷ **1** A2 [C, + sing/pl verb] an organization of people with a common purpose or interest, who meet regularly and take part in shared activities: *I've just* ***joined*** *the local golf/squash/tennis club.* ◦ *Visitors must be accompanied by club* ***members.*** **2** B1 [C, + sing/pl verb] a team: *The Orioles are an exciting club this year.* ◦ *Stockport County Football Club* **3** [C] a building in which a club meets **DANCE** ▷ **4** B1 [C] a place that people go to in order to dance and drink in the evening → Synonym **nightclub** **GOLF** ▷ **5** [C] a long, thin stick used in GOLF to hit the ball: *a set of* ***golf*** *clubs* **WEAPON** ▷ **6** [C] a heavy stick used as a weapon **CARD** ▷ **7 clubs** [plural or U] one of the four SUITS in playing cards, which has one or more black symbols with three round leaves: *the three/King* ***of*** *clubs* **8** [C] a playing card from the SUIT of clubs: *Now you have to play a club if you have one.*

IDIOM **in the club** UK old-fashioned slang pregnant

▸verb [T] (-bb-) to beat a person or an animal, usually repeatedly, with a heavy stick or object: *He was clubbed over the head.* ◦ *The alligators are then clubbed* ***to death.***

PHRASAL VERB **club together** If a group of people club together, they share the cost of something between them: *If we club together, we'll be able to get her the complete dinner set.*

clubber /ˈklʌb.əʳ/ (US) /-ɚ/ noun [C] someone who goes clubbing

clubbing /ˈklʌb.ɪŋ/ noun **go clubbing** to go out dancing in clubs: *Roz and I went clubbing last weekend.*

clubhouse /ˈklʌb.haʊs/ noun [C] a building where members of a club meet and have social events

clubland /ˈklʌb.lænd/ noun [U] the places where people go to drink and dance at night, or the people who work and spend time there: *London clubland*

ˌclub ˈsandwich noun [C] a sandwich made from three pieces of bread with meat, egg, cheese, salad, or other cold food between them

ˌclub ˈsoda noun [C or U] US for **soda**

cluck /klʌk/ verb **1** [I] to make the low interrupted noise that a chicken makes **2** [I or T] informal to express disapproval or other emotion by making a short sharp sound with your tongue: *to cluck* ***in*** *disapproval/amazement* ◦ *She shakes her head, smiles, and clucks her tongue.* **3** [I] informal to express an unnecessary amount of sympathy, worry, or approval towards someone: *The attendants clucked and fussed* ***over*** *passengers.*

clue /kluː/ noun; verb

▸noun [C] B2 a sign or some information which helps you to find the answer to a problem, question, or mystery: *Police are still* ***looking for*** *clues in their search for the missing girl.* ◦ *I'm never going to guess the answer if you don't* ***give*** *me a clue.*

> **Word partners for clue**
>
> *give/offer/provide* a clue • *look for/search for* clues • an *important/useful/vital* clue • a clue *about/as to/to* sth

IDIOM **not have a clue** informal B2 to be completely unable to guess, understand, or deal with something: *'Who invented algebra?' 'I haven't a clue.'* ◦ *Don't ask your father which key to press – he hasn't got a clue* ***about*** *computers.*

▸verb (present participle **clueing**, past tense and past participle **clued**)

PHRASAL VERB **clue sb in** US (UK **clue sb up**) to give someone information that is necessary or new: *He'd been out of the country for weeks, so I clued him in* ***on*** *all that's been happening.*

ˌclued ˈup adj [after verb] UK having a special and detailed knowledge of something: *Ben's more clued up* ***on/about*** *movies than I am.*

clueless /ˈkluː.ləs/ adj informal having no knowledge of something, or of things in general: *Most people are completely clueless* ***about*** *tide directions and weather conditions.*

clump /klʌmp/ noun; verb

▸noun **GROUP** ▷ **1** [C] a group, especially of trees or flowers: *a clump of grass/daffodils* **LUMP** ▷ **2** [C] a solid mass of something such as soil: *There were big clumps* ***of*** *soil on his boots.* **NOISY STEPS** ▷ **3** [C usually singular] the loud sound of slow, heavy steps: *We could hear the clump of his feet on the wooden floor.*

▸verb **WALK NOISILY** ▷ **1** [I + adv/prep] to walk noisily with slow, heavy steps: *She clumped* ***around*** *the room/* ***up*** *the stairs in her boots.* **FORM GROUP** ▷ **2** [I or T] to form a group, or to put things into a group: *As it started to rain, everyone clumped* ***together*** *in doorways.*

clumsy /ˈklʌm.zi/ adj **1** awkward in movement or manner: *The first mobile phones were heavy and clumsy to use, but nowadays they are much easier to handle.* ◦ *My attempts to apologize were very clumsy (= not said well).* **2** B2 describes someone who often has accidents because they do not behave in a careful, controlled way: *That's the third glass you've smashed this week – you're so clumsy!* • **clumsily** /-zɪ.li/ adv • **clumsiness** /-nəs/ noun [U]

clung /klʌŋ/ verb past simple and past participle of **cling**

clunk /klʌŋk/ noun [C usually singular] a deep low sound made by two heavy objects hitting each other: *He shut the van door with a clunk.*

clunky /ˈklʌŋ.ki/ adj disapproving **SOLID** ▷ **1** heavy and solid in an ugly way: *The clunky handsets looked old-fashioned as soon as they were launched.* ◦ *He wore a clunky gold ring.* **AWKWARD** ▷ **2** awkward or badly done: *The writing is clunky in places and full of clichés.* **SLOW** ▷ **3** old-fashioned or slow: *It was the slow, clunky technology it used that was responsible for the firm's failure.*

cluster /ˈklʌs.təʳ/ (US) /-tɚ/ noun [C] **1** [+ sing/pl verb] a group of similar things that are close together, sometimes surrounding something: *Have a look at the cluster* ***of*** *galaxies in this photograph.* ◦ *There was a cluster* ***of*** *fans around him, asking for autographs.* **2** specialized a group of two or more consonant sounds that are together and have no vowel sound between them: *The /str/ at the beginning of 'stray' is a cluster.* • **cluster** verb [I] *People clustered* ***around*** *the notice-board to read the exam results.*

ˈcluster ˌbomb noun [C] an explosive device which throws out smaller bombs when it explodes

clutch /klʌtʃ/ verb; noun

▸verb [I or T] C2 to take or try to take hold of something tightly, usually in fear, worry, or pain: *Silent and pale, she clutched (****onto****) her mother's hand.* ◦ *Clutching the money* ***to*** *his chest, he hurried to the bank.* ◦ *He collapsed, clutching his stomach.*

PHRASAL VERB **clutch at sth** to try very hard to hold something: *Feeling herself fall, she clutched at a branch.*

▸noun **MACHINE PART** ▷ **1** [C usually singular] a device that allows turning movement to be sent from one part of a machine to another: *I've booked the car into the garage because the clutch is **slipping**.* **2** C1 [C usually singular] the PEDAL or handle in a vehicle that is used to operate the engine's clutch: ***Push the** clutch **in**, put the car into gear, rev the engine, and then gently **let the** clutch **out**.* **GROUP** ▷ **3** [C] a small group of eggs produced by the same bird, especially in a nest **4** [S] a small group of people or things: *a fresh clutch **of** students* **CONTROL** ▷ **5 sb's clutches** C2 [plural] humorous the control of someone: *He **is in/has fallen into** the clutches **of** that woman.*

ˈ**clutch** ˌ**bag** noun [C] a small flat bag without a handle, carried by women, especially on formal occasions

clutter /ˈklʌt.əʳ/ US /ˈklʌṭ.ɚ/ **noun; verb**

▸noun [U] (a lot of objects in) a state of being untidy: *Sorry about the clutter in the kitchen.* ◦ *My desk is covered in/full of clutter.*

▸verb [T] to fill something in an untidy or badly organized way: *The kids always clutter the hall (**up**) **with** school bags and coats and stuff.* ◦ *Every shelf is cluttered **with** ornaments.* ◦ figurative *I try not to clutter (**up**) my mind with useless information.* • **cluttered** /ˈklʌt.əd/ US /ˈklʌṭ.ɚd/ **adj** *a cluttered desk/room*

cm noun written abbreviation for **centimetre**: *a piece of glass 22 cm by 35 cm*

c'mon /kəˈmɒn/ US /-mɑːn/ informal short form of come on: *Oh c'mon, you don't really mean that!*

CMYK /ˌsiː.em.waɪˈkeɪ/ **noun** [U] abbreviation for cyan, magenta, yellow, black: the system of colour printing that uses four colours of ink

CND /ˌsiː.enˈdiː/ **noun** abbreviation for Campaign for Nuclear Disarmament: a British organization which opposes the development and use of nuclear weapons

CNN /ˌsiː.enˈen/ **noun** abbreviation for Cable News Network: a US organization that broadcasts news on television internationally

ˈ**C-note** noun [C] US slang a piece of paper money with the value of 100 dollars

CO /ˌsiːˈəʊ/ US /-ˈoʊ/ **noun** [C] abbreviation for Commanding Officer: a person in charge of a military unit

c/o /ˌsiːˈəʊ/ US /-ˈoʊ/ abbreviation for care of: used in addresses when the person you are writing to is staying at someone else's home: *Sylvia Mendez, c/o Ann Smith, 12 Glastonbury Lane, Bickerton*

co- /kəʊ-/ US /koʊ-/ **prefix** together; with: *co-ownership* ◦ *a co-writer/co-author* ◦ *Appalling poverty and great wealth coexist in the city.*

Co. /kəʊ/ US /koʊ/ **noun** [U] **BUSINESS** ▷ **1** abbreviation for company (= business): *Peters, Stynes & Co.* **AREA** ▷ **2** written abbreviation for **county**, when used in names: *Co. Durham*

IDIOM **and co.** informal and other people: *K. Branagh and co. achieved great success in a very short time.*

coach /kəʊtʃ/ US /koʊtʃ/ **noun; verb; noun, adv**

▸noun **TEACHER** ▷ **1** B1 [C] someone whose job is to teach people to improve at a sport, skill, or school subject: *a tennis/maths coach* **VEHICLE** ▷ **2** A2 [C] (US usually **bus**) a long motor vehicle with comfortable seats, used to take groups of people on journeys: *We're going to the airport **by** coach.* ◦ *a coach trip* **3** [C] an old-fashioned CARRIAGE pulled by horses, now used mainly in official or royal ceremonies **4** [C] UK (US **car**) a CARRIAGE in a train **5** [U] US **coach class**

▸verb [I or T] B2 to give special classes in sports or a school subject, especially privately, to one person or a small group: *She coaches students **in** French, usually for exams.* • **coaching** /ˈkəʊ.tʃɪŋ/ US /ˈkoʊ-/ **noun** [U] B2 *You're very behind in your English – why don't you get some extra coaching?*

▸noun [U], adv US the cheapest type of seats on a plane or train: *Even the company's director **flies** coach most of the time.*

ˈ**coach** ˌ**class** noun [U], adv US (also **coach**, UK **e**ˈ**conomy** ˌ**class**) (using) the cheapest type of seats on a plane or train: *Traveling in coach class is not a great way to spend your time.* → Compare **first class**

ˈ**coach** ˌ**station** noun [C] UK A2 a place where coaches (= vehicles) arrive and leave from

coachwork /ˈkəʊtʃ.wɜːk/ US /ˈkoʊtʃ.wɝːk/ **noun** [U] UK the body of a car or other vehicle, especially the outside painted surface

coagulate /kəʊˈæg.jʊ.leɪt/ US /koʊ-/ **verb** [I or T] to change from liquid to a more solid state, or to cause something to do this: *The venom of this snake coagulates the blood.*

coal /kəʊl/ US /koʊl/ **noun** [C or U] C1 a hard, black substance that is dug from the earth in pieces, and can be burned to produce heat or power, or a single piece of this: *How much coal was **mined** here?* ◦ *a burning/red hot coal*

IDIOMS **carry/take coals to Newcastle** UK to supply something to a place or person that already has a lot of that particular thing: *Exporting pine to Scandinavia seems a bit like carrying coals to Newcastle.* • **haul/drag sb over the coals** to speak angrily to someone because they have done something you disapprove of: *He was hauled over the coals **for** coming in late for work.*

ˌ**coal** ˈ**black** noun [U] a pure black colour • ˌ**coal**-ˈ**black** adj

ˈ**coal** ˌ**bunker** noun [C] a large container, especially outside a house, for storing coal

coalesce /kəʊ.əˈles/ US /koʊ-/ **verb** [I] formal If two or more things coalesce, they come or grow together to form one thing or system.

coalescence /kəʊ.əˈles.ᵊns/ US /koʊ-/ **noun** [U] **1** formal the process of coming or growing together to form one thing or system: **2** specialized the process in which speech sounds are joined together because someone is talking fast

coalface /ˈkəʊl.feɪs/ US /ˈkoʊl-/ **noun** [C] the surface from which coal is cut

IDIOM **at the coalface** UK doing the work involved in a job, in real working conditions, rather than planning or talking about it: *At the coalface with a deadline looming, you sometimes feel under a lot of pressure.*

coalfield /ˈkəʊl.fiːld/ US /ˈkoʊl-/ **noun** [C] an area where there is a lot of coal in the ground

ˈ**coal-fired** adj using coal as a fuel: *a coal-fired boiler*

coalition /kəʊ.əˈlɪʃ.ᵊn/ US /koʊ-/ **noun** [C or U] the joining together of different political parties or groups for a particular purpose, usually for a limited time: *By **forming** a coalition, the rebels and the opposition parties defeated the government.* ◦ *a coalition government*

ˈ**coal** ˌ**mine** noun [C] the deep hole or system of holes under the ground from which coal is removed • ˈ**coal** ˌ**mining** noun [U] the business, job, or process of removing coal from the ground

ˈcoal ˌminer noun [C] a person who works in a coal mine removing coal from the ground

ˈcoal ˌscuttle noun [C] a container with a handle in which coal is kept inside a house

ˈcoal ˌtar noun [U] a sticky, black substance, made from coal, that is used to make various chemical products

coarse /kɔːs/ (US) /kɔːrs/ adj ROUGH ▷ **1** rough and not smooth or soft, or not in very small pieces: *coarse sand/breadcrumbs* ◦ *Linen is a coarse-**grained** fabric.* RUDE ▷ **2** rude and offensive: *a coarse joke* ◦ *coarse language* • **coarsely** /-li/ adv • **coarseness** /-nəs/ noun [U] *The coarseness of the cloth irritated her skin.* ◦ *I can't stand his coarseness and stupidity.*

coarsen /ˈkɔː.sən/ (US) /ˈkɔːr-/ verb [I or T] to become rough or cause something to become rough

coarticulation /ˌkəʊ.ɑːtɪk.jəˈleɪ.ʃən/ (US) /ˌkoʊ.ɑːr-/ noun [U] specialized the fact that the pronunciation of a sound in a word is affected by the sounds before and after it

coast /kəʊst/ (US) /koʊst/ noun; verb

▸noun [C] **1** B1 the land next to or close to the sea: *Rimini is a thriving holiday resort **on** the east coast of Italy.* ◦ *The accident happened three miles **off** the coast (= in the sea three miles from land).* ◦ *We spent a week **by/on** the coast (= by the sea).* **2 coast to coast** from one side of the country to the other: *We travelled across America coast to coast.*

IDIOM **the coast is clear** it is safe to do something or go somewhere because no one is watching or listening who would prevent you or catch you: *You can come out now, the coast is clear.*

▸verb [I] **1** to move forward in a vehicle without using the engine, usually down a hill: *At the top of the hill I switched off the engine and we just coasted down the other side.* **2** to progress or succeed without any effort or difficulty: *While I struggled, my sister coasted through school with top grades.*

coastal /ˈkəʊ.stəl/ (US) /ˈkoʊ-/ adj B2 positioned on, or relating to the coast: *a coastal town*

coaster /ˈkəʊ.stər/ (US) /ˈkoʊ.stɚ/ noun [C] OBJECT ▷ **1** a small piece of wood, plastic, or other material that you put a glass or cup on to protect a surface from heat or liquid BOAT ▷ **2** a ship which sails between ports along a coast

coastguard /ˈkəʊst.gɑːd/ (US) /ˈkoʊst.gɑːrd/ noun **1** [C] an official who is employed to watch the sea near to a coast for ships that are in danger or involved with illegal activities **2 the coastguard** [S] the official organization which coastguards belong to

coastline /ˈkəʊst.laɪn/ (US) /ˈkoʊst-/ noun [C or U] C2 the particular shape of the coast, especially as seen from above, from the sea, or on a map

coat /kəʊt/ (US) /koʊt/ noun; verb

▸noun [C] CLOTHING ▷ **1** A1 an outer piece of clothing with sleeves that is worn over other clothes, usually for warmth: *Do your coat up, Joe, or you'll freeze.* ◦ *We need a coat **hook** on the back of this door.* **2** used as a combining form: *an overcoat* ◦ *a raincoat* ANIMAL ▷ **3** the hair, wool, or fur covering an animal: *a thick/glossy/matted coat* COVER ▷ **4** (also **coating** /kəʊ.tɪŋ/ (US) /koʊ.t̬ɪŋ/) a layer of a particular substance that covers something: *I'll **give** the walls **a** quick coat **of** paint.* ◦ *two coats of varnish* ◦ *a thick coating of chocolate*

▸verb [T] to cover something with a layer of a particular substance: *When the biscuits are cool, you coat them **in/with** melted chocolate.*

coated /ˈkəʊ.tɪd/ (US) /ˈkoʊ.t̬ɪd/ adj thickly covered: *Your trousers are coated **in** mud!*

-coated /-kəʊ.tɪd/ (US) /-koʊ.t̬ɪd/ suffix COVER ▷ **1** with a covering of the stated substance: ***sugar**-coated almonds* ANIMAL ▷ **2** (of an animal) with a coat (= hair, wool, or fur) of the stated type: *a smooth-coated dog*

ˈcoat ˌhanger noun [C] a **hanger**

ˌcoat of ˈarms noun [C] (plural **coats of arms**) a special SHIELD or shield-shaped pattern that is the sign of a family, university, or city

ˈcoat-tails noun [plural] the long divided pieces of cloth that hang down from the back of an old-fashioned, formal type of man's jacket → See also **tailcoat**

co-ˈauthor noun; verb

▸noun [C] (US **coauthor**) one of two or more people who write a book, article, report, etc. together

▸verb [T] (US **coauthor**) to write a book, article, report, etc. together with another person or other people: *Robert and his daughter have co-authored a diet book specifically written for young women.*

coax /kəʊks/ (US) /koʊks/ verb [T] to persuade someone gently to do something or go somewhere, by being kind and patient, or by appearing to be: *Perhaps you could coax your father **into** tak**ing** you to the station.* ◦ *He has some information I want, so I'm going to try to coax it **out of** him over a drink.* ◦ *A mother was coaxing her reluctant child into the water.* ◦ *a coaxing voice* • **coaxing** /ˈkəʊk.sɪŋ/ (US) /ˈkoʊk-/ noun [U] *A bit of gentle coaxing is all that's required and he'll come, I'm sure.* • **coaxingly** /ˈkəʊk.sɪŋ.li/ (US) /ˈkoʊk-/ adv

cob /kɒb/ (US) /kɑːb/ noun [C] HORSE ▷ **1** a strong horse with short legs BIRD ▷ **2** a male SWAN BREAD ▷ **3** UK a round LOAF of bread → See also **corn on the cob**

cobalt /ˈkəʊ.bɒlt/ (US) /ˈkoʊ.bɑːlt/ noun; adj

▸noun [U] (symbol **Co**) **1** a chemical element that is a hard silver-white metal, used in metal mixtures and for making materials blue **2** (also **cobalt blue**) a deep blue or greenish-blue colour

▸adj (also **cobalt blue**) having a deep blue or greenish-blue colour

cobber /ˈkɒb.ər/ (US) /ˈkɑː.bɚ/ noun [C] Australian English old-fashioned informal (used especially by a man speaking to or about another man) a friend

cobble /ˈkɒb.l̩/ (US) /ˈkɑː.bl̩/ noun; verb

▸noun [C usually plural] (also **cobblestone**) a rounded stone used on the surface of an old-fashioned road: *The cart rumbled over the cobbles.* • **cobbled** /ˈkɒb.l̩d/ (US) /ˈkɑː.bl̩d/ adj made of cobbles: *cobbled **streets***

▸verb

PHRASAL VERB **cobble sth together** to do or make something quickly and not very carefully: *I just had to cobble this meal together from what I had in the fridge.*

cobbler /ˈkɒb.lər/ (US) /ˈkɑː.blɚ/ noun JOB ▷ **1** [C] a person who repairs shoes NONSENSE ▷ **2 cobblers** [U] UK slang nonsense or lies: ***a load of old** cobblers*

cobnut /ˈkɒb.nʌt/ (US) /ˈkɑːb-/ noun [C] a **hazelnut**

cobra /ˈkəʊ.brə/ (US) /ˈkoʊ-/ noun [C] a poisonous snake from Africa or southern Asia which makes itself look bigger and more threatening by spreading the skin at the back of its head

ˈco-brother noun [C] Indian English the husband of your wife's sister

cobweb

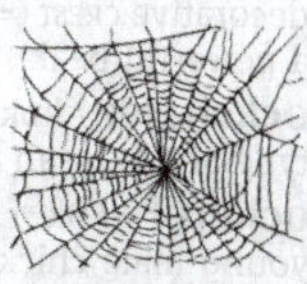

cobweb /ˈkɒb.web/ (US) /ˈkɑːb-/ noun [C] a structure like a net of sticky SILK threads made by a SPIDER for catching insects

C

Coca-Cola /ˌkəʊ.kəˈkəʊ.lə/ (US) /ˌkoʊ.kəˈkoʊ.lə/ **noun** [C or U] (informal **Coke**) trademark a sweet, dark-brown FIZZY drink (= one with bubbles)

cocaine /kəʊˈkeɪn/, /kə-/ (US) /koʊ-/ **noun** [U] a drug used in medicine to prevent pain and also used illegally, often in the form of a white powder that is breathed in through the nose

coccyx /ˈkɒk.sɪks/ (US) /ˈkɑːk-/ **noun** [C] (plural **coccyxes** or **coccyges** /-saɪ.dʒiːz/) specialized a small bone at the base of the SPINE of humans and some APES

cochineal /ˌkɒtʃ.ɪˈniːl/ (US) /ˈkɑː.tʃɪ-/ **noun** [U] a bright red substance used to make food red in colour, made from a type of small South American insect

cochlea /ˈkɒk.li.ə/ (US) /ˈkɑːk-/ **noun** [C] (plural **cochleae** /-iː/ or **cochleas**) specialized a twisted tube inside the INNER EAR that is the main organ of hearing

cock /kɒk/ (US) /kɑːk/ **noun; verb**

▸noun **BIRD** ▷ **1** [C] (US also **rooster**) an adult male chicken: *The cock started to **crow**.* **2** [C] used with the name of a bird to refer to the adult male of that type: *a cock robin* ◦ *a cock pheasant* **PENIS** ▷ **3** [C] offensive a PENIS **FORM OF ADDRESS** ▷ **4** (also **cocker**) UK old-fashioned informal a friendly form of address, used especially by a man talking to another man: *Wotcher, cock! How's things?*

▸verb **TURN** ▷ **1** [T] to move a part of your body upwards or in a particular direction: *He cocked his **head** on one side with a slight frown.* ◦ *The dog cocked its **leg** (= urinated) against a tree.* ◦ *to cock an ear/eyebrow* **PREPARE GUN** ▷ **2** [T] to push the necessary piece of a gun up into position so that it is ready to FIRE: *He cocked his rifle and took aim.* **3 cock a snook at sb/sth** UK to do something intentionally to show you have no respect for someone or something: *He could seldom resist an opportunity to cock a snook at traditional English life.* • **cocked** /kɒkt/ (US) /kɑːkt/ **adj** *Her hat was cocked **at a** jaunty **angle**.*

PHRASAL VERB **cock sth up** UK slang to do something wrong or badly: *David cocked up the arrangements and we ended up missing the reception.* ◦ *'How did the exam go?' 'Terrible – I panicked and really cocked it up.'*

cockade /kɒkˈeɪd/ (US) /kɑːˈkeɪd/ **noun** [C] a decorative knot of cloth worn in the hat, often for official ceremonies, to show rank

cock-a-doodle-doo /ˌkɒk.ə.duː.dlˈduː/ (US) /ˌkɑːk-/ noun [C] child's word the long call that a cock makes

ˌcock-aˈhoop **adj** [after verb] extremely happy and excited about something: *Graeme was cock-a-hoop when Scotland won the championship.*

cock-a-leekie /kɒk.əˈliː.ki/ (US) /kɑːk-/ **noun** [U] a soup, originally from Scotland, made from boiled chicken and vegetables

cockamamie /ˌkɒk.əˈmeɪ.mi/ (US) /ˌkɑːk-/ **adj** US slang stupid or silly: *He had some cockamamie **idea** about turning waste paper into animal food.*

ˌcock-and-bull ˈstory **noun** [C] informal disapproving a story that is obviously not true, especially one given as an excuse: *He **gave me** some cock-and-bull story about having to be at his cousin's engagement party.*

cockatoo /ˌkɒk.əˈtuː/ (US) /ˈkɑː.kə.tuː/ **noun** [C] (plural **cockatoos** or **cockatoo**) an Australian bird with a decorative CREST (= growth of feathers) on its head and a powerful beak

cockchafer /ˈkɒkˌtʃeɪ.fəʳ/ (US) /ˈkɑːkˌtʃeɪ.fɚ/ **noun** [C] a type of European BEETLE which causes damage to trees

cockerel /ˈkɒk.ər.əl/, /-rəl/ (US) /ˈkɑː.kɚ-/ **noun** [C] a young male chicken

ˌcocker ˈspaniel **noun** [C] a breed of dog with long ears, short legs, and fur that is white and brown or white and black

cockeyed /ˌkɒkˈaɪd/ (US) /ˌkɑːk-/ **adj** **SLOPING** ▷ **1** informal not straight, but sloping to one side: *Would you straighten that picture over there? – It's a bit cockeyed.* **STUPID** ▷ **2** describes a plan or idea that is stupid, not suitable, or not likely to be successful: *The government has dreamed up some cockeyed **scheme** for getting unemployed youngsters back into work.*

cockfight /ˈkɒk.faɪt/ (US) /kɑːk-/ **noun** [C] an activity, illegal in the UK, in which people watch as two COCKS attack each other and BET on which one will win

cockle /ˈkɒk.l/ (US) /ˈkɑː.kl/ **noun** [C] a small rounded sea creature with a shell, common in Europe, which can be eaten

cockney /ˈkɒk.ni/ (US) /ˈkɑːk-/ **noun** **1** [U] the type of speech used in East London, especially the poorer part **2** [C] a person from East London, who speaks cockney • **cockney adj** *a cockney accent*

ˌcockney ˈrhyming ˌslang **noun** [U] a type of slang in which certain words are used instead of other words that they RHYME with: *In cockney rhyming slang, 'apples and pears' means 'stairs'.*

cockpit /ˈkɒk.pɪt/ (US) /ˈkɑːk-/ **noun** [C] the small closed space where the pilot sits in an aircraft, or where the driver sits in a racing car

cockroach /ˈkɒk.rəʊtʃ/ (US) /ˈkɑːk.roʊtʃ/ **noun** [C] a flat brown or black insect sometimes found in the home

cockscomb /ˈkɒks.kəʊm/ (US) /ˈkɑːks.koʊm/ **noun** [C] (also **comb**) the soft red growth on the head of a male chicken

cocksure /ˌkɒkˈʃɔːʳ/ (US) /ˌkɑːkˈʃɝː/ **adj** informal disapproving too confident, in a way that is slightly unpleasant or rude: *a cocksure young man*

cocktail /ˈkɒk.teɪl/ (US) /ˈkɑːk-/ **noun** **DRINK** ▷ **1** [C] a drink, usually an alcoholic one, made by mixing two or more drinks together: *We were all in the bar **sipping** cocktails.* **MIXTURE** ▷ **2** [C usually singular] a mixture of different things, often an unexpected, dangerous, or exciting one: *The inquest heard that the guitarist died from a cocktail **of** drink and drugs.* ◦ *Cars produce a **lethal** cocktail **of** gasses.* **DISH** ▷ **3** [C or U] a cold dish, often eaten at the start of a meal, consisting of small pieces of food: *fruit cocktail* ◦ *a prawn/seafood cocktail*

ˈcocktail ˌdress **noun** [C] a dress worn for a special social occasion in the evening, such as a party or dance

ˈcocktail ˌlounge **noun** [C] a large comfortable room in a hotel where you can meet people and be served alcoholic drinks

ˈcocktail ˌparty **noun** [C] a formal party with alcoholic drinks, usually in the early evening

ˈcocktail ˌstick **noun** [C] a small pointed wooden or plastic stick on which small pieces of food, such as cheese or sausage, are served to guests at parties

ˈcock-up **noun** [C] UK slang something that is done wrong or badly: *Gerry's **made** a right cock-up **with/of** those figures!* ◦ *So it was delivered to the wrong place? **What a** cock-up!*

cocky /ˈkɒk.i/ (US) /ˈkɑː.ki/ **adj** informal disapproving describes a young person who is confident in a way that is unpleasant and sometimes rude: *He's a bit cocky for my liking.*

cocoa /ˈkəʊ.kəʊ/ (US) /ˈkoʊ.koʊ/ **noun** [U] **1** a dark brown powder made from cocoa beans, used to make chocolate and add a chocolate flavour to food and drink **2** a sweet chocolate drink that is made with cocoa powder: *a nice hot mug of cocoa*

C

ˈ**cocoa ˌbean** noun [C] the seed of the tropical CACAO tree

ˈ**cocoa ˌbutter** noun [U] a substance from the cocoa bean that contains a lot of fat and is used in some foods and also in products for the skin and hair

coconut /ˈkəʊ.kə.nʌt/ ⓊⓈ /ˈkoʊ-/ noun **1** B1 [C] a large fruit like a nut with a thick, hard, brown shell containing hard, white flesh that can be eaten and a clear liquid **2** B1 [U] the white flesh of the coconut, often used in cooking: ***grated/shredded*** *coconut*

ˈ**coconut ˌshy** noun [C] UK a game at a FAIR where you throw balls at a row of coconuts and try to knock them down to win them

cocoon /kəˈkuːn/ noun; verb

▸noun **COVER** ▷ **1** [C] the covering made of soft smooth threads that surrounds and protects particular insects during the PUPA stage as they develop into adult form **PROTECTED PLACE** ▷ **2** [C usually singular] a safe quiet place: *the warm, safe cocoon of childhood*

▸verb [T usually passive] to protect someone or something from pain or an unpleasant situation: *As a student you're cocooned* ***against/from*** *the real world.*

cod /kɒd/ ⓊⓈ /kɑːd/ noun [C or U] (plural **cod**) B1 a large sea fish that can be eaten: *Cod and chips, please.*

COD /ˌsiː.əʊˈdiː/ ⓊⓈ /-oʊˈ-/ adv abbreviation for cash on delivery: payment will be made when goods are DELIVERED

coda /ˈkəʊ.də/ ⓊⓈ /ˈkoʊ-/ noun [C] **1** specialized a piece of music at the end of a longer piece of music, usually separate from the basic structure **2** formal the final or extra part of a speech, event, or piece of writing: *In a coda* ***to*** *the main exhibition are various works that were once attributed to Rembrandt.* **3** specialized the end of a syllable

coddle /ˈkɒd.l̩/ ⓊⓈ /ˈkɑː.dl̩/ verb [T] **COOK** ▷ **1** to cook food, especially eggs, in water just below boiling temperature: *coddled eggs* **PROTECT** ▷ **2** to protect someone or something too much: *The steel industry is coddled by trade protection and massive subsidies.*

code /kəʊd/ ⓊⓈ /koʊd/ noun; verb

▸noun **LANGUAGE** ▷ **1** B2 [C or U] a system of words, letters, or signs used to represent a message in secret form, or a system of numbers, letters, or signals used to represent something in a shorter or more convenient form: *The message was written* ***in*** *code.* ◦ *She managed to* ***decipher/break/crack*** *(= succeed in understanding) the code.* ◦ *Each entry in this dictionary has a grammar code.* **RULES** ▷ **2** C1 [C] a set of rules that are accepted as general principles, or a set of written rules that say how people in a particular organization or country should behave: *Clinics will be subject to a new code* ***of conduct*** *and stronger controls by local authorities.* **3** [C] a set of principles that are accepted and used by society or a particular group of people: *a moral code* ◦ *a code of behaviour/ethics*

▸verb [T] to represent a message in code so that it can only be understood by the person who is meant to receive it

coded /kəʊd.ɪd/ ⓊⓈ /koʊd-/ adj written or sent in code: *a coded message/warning*

codeine /ˈkəʊ.diːn/ ⓊⓈ /ˈkoʊ-/ noun [U] a drug made from OPIUM that is used to reduce pain

ˈ**code ˌname** noun [C] a special word or name that is used instead of the real name of someone or something to keep the real name secret: *Her code name is 'Running Bear'.* • ˈ**code-name** verb [T] [+ noun] *We've code-named the new project 'Entropy'.*

ˌ**code of ˈpractice** noun [C] a set of standards agreed on by a group of people who do a particular job

codependency /ˌkəʊ.dɪˈpen.dənts.i/ noun [U] the situation when someone has too strong an emotional need to help someone else in their family who has an alcohol problem, mental illness, etc. • **codependent** /-dənt/ adj

ˈ**code switching** noun [U] specialized the act of changing between two or more languages when you are speaking

codex /ˈkəʊ.deks/ ⓊⓈ /ˈkoʊ-/ noun [C] (plural **codices** /-dɪ.siːz/) specialized an ancient book which was written by hand

codger /ˈkɒdʒ.əʳ/ ⓊⓈ /ˈkɑː.dʒɚ/ noun [C] informal an old man, especially one who is strange or humorous in some way: *A couple of* ***old*** *codgers were sitting on the park bench, grumbling about the children.*

codicil /ˈkəʊ.dɪ.sɪl/ ⓊⓈ /ˈkɑː-/ noun [C] legal an instruction that is added to a WILL (= a document stating what should be done with a person's possessions after his or her death)

codify /ˈkəʊ.dɪ.faɪ/ ⓊⓈ /ˈkɑː-/ verb [T] formal to arrange something, such as laws or rules, into a system

ˌ**cod liver ˈoil** noun [U] a thick, yellow oil that contains VITAMINS A and D, which some people take to keep healthy

codpiece /ˈkɒd.piːs/ ⓊⓈ /ˈkɑːd-/ noun [C] a small piece of clothing like a bag that was used in the past to cover the opening at the front of men's clothes for the lower body

codswallop /ˈkɒdzˌwɒl.əp/ ⓊⓈ /ˈkɑːdzˌwɑː.ləp/ noun [U] UK slang nonsense: *What* ***a load of*** *codswallop!*

coed /ˌkəʊˈed/ ⓊⓈ /ˌkoʊ-/ adj; noun

▸adj informal for **coeducational**

▸noun [C] US old-fashioned informal a female student in a college with male and female students

coeducation /ˌkəʊ.ed.jʊˈkeɪ.ʃən/ ⓊⓈ /ˌkoʊ-/ noun [U] the teaching of male and female students together

coeducational /ˌkəʊ.ed.jʊˈkeɪ.ʃən.əl/ ⓊⓈ /ˌkoʊ-/ adj (informal **coed**) having male and female students being taught together in the same school or college rather than separately: *Girls tend to do better academically in single-sex schools than in coeducational ones.*

coefficient /ˌkəʊ.ɪˈfɪʃ.ənt/ ⓊⓈ /ˌkoʊ-/ noun [C] specialized a value, in mathematics, that appears in front of and multiplies another value: *In 2x + 4y = 7, 2 is* ***the*** *coefficient* ***of*** *x.*

coelenterate /sɪˈlen.tə.reɪt/ noun [C] specialized a type of sea creature that has a simple body with TENTACLES and a single opening at the centre, such as a JELLYFISH or a SEA ANEMONE

coeliac disease UK (US **celiac disease**) /ˈsiː.liː.æk.dɪˌziːz/ noun [U] a medical condition in which the INTESTINE reacts badly to a type of PROTEIN contained in GLUTEN (= a substance found in some grains): *People with coeliac disease need to keep to a gluten-free diet.*

coequal /ˌkəʊˈiː.kwəl/ ⓊⓈ /ˌkoʊ-/ adj formal equal in rank, ability, or power to another person or thing • **coequal** noun [C]

coerce /kəʊˈɜːs/ ⓊⓈ /koʊˈɝːs/ verb [T] formal to persuade someone forcefully to do something which they are unwilling to do: *The court heard that the six defendants had been coerced* ***into*** *making a confession.*

coercion /kəʊˈɜː.ʃən/ ⓊⓈ /koʊˈɝː-/ noun [U] formal the use of force to persuade someone to do something which they are unwilling to do

coercive /kəʊˈɜː.sɪv/ ⓊⓈ /koʊˈɝː-/ adj formal using force to persuade people to do things which they are unwilling to do: *The president relied on the coercive **powers** of the military.* ◦ *coercive measures/tactics*

coeval /kəʊˈiː.vəl/ (US) /koʊ-/ **adj; noun**

▸**adj** formal of the same age or existing at the same time as another person or thing: *The abundant reef growth on Gotland was shown to be coeval **with** that in Estonia.*

▸**noun** [C] formal someone or something coeval

ˌco-eˈxist (also **coexist**) **verb** [I] to live or exist together at the same time or in the same place: *He does not believe that modern medicine can co-exist **with** faith-healing.* • **coexistence** /-ˈzɪs.tənts/ **noun** [U] *The two communities enjoyed a period of **peaceful** coexistence.*

ˌC of ˈE **adj, noun** [U] abbreviation for **the Church of England**: *a C of E service*

coffee /ˈkɒf.i/ (US) /ˈkɑː.fi/ **noun** [C or U] (A1) a dark brown powder with a strong flavour and smell that is made by crushing coffee beans, or a hot drink made from this powder: *decaffeinated coffee* ◦ *fresh/instant coffee* ◦ *a **cup of** coffee* ◦ *Would you get some coffee when you go shopping?* ◦ *If I drink too much coffee, I can't sleep.* ◦ *Can I get you a coffee (= cup of coffee)?* ◦ *I'd like a **black** coffee (= a cup of coffee without milk), please.* ◦ *Do you **take** (= drink) your coffee white (= with milk)?*

ˈcoffee ˌbar **noun** [C] UK (US **ˈcoffee ˌshop**) a small, informal restaurant where hot drinks, cakes, and often small meals are served

ˈcoffee ˌbean **noun** [C] a seed of a tropical bush that is heated until it is brown and then crushed to make coffee

ˈcoffee ˌbreak **noun** [C] a short rest from work in the morning or afternoon

ˈcoffee ˌcake **noun** [C or U] **1** UK a cake that has a coffee flavour **2** US a type of sweet bread made with nuts or fruit

ˈcoffee-coloured **adj** having a pale brown colour, like coffee with milk: *We've just bought a new coffee-coloured rug for the living room.*

ˈcoffee ˌgrinder **noun** [C] (also **ˈcoffee ˌmill**) a machine that crushes coffee beans to make coffee powder

ˈcoffee ˌhouse **noun** [C] a restaurant, especially in central and northern Europe, where people have coffee or other drinks, cakes, and small meals

coffee klatch /ˈkɒf.iˌklætʃ/ (US) /ˈkɑː.fi-/ **noun** [C] US an occasion when people meet socially to talk and drink coffee

ˈcoffee ˌmorning **noun** [C] UK a social event where people meet to talk, drink coffee, and eat cakes, often giving money to a CHARITY or other organization

ˈcoffee ˌpot **noun** [C] a container with a handle and shaped opening, for making and serving coffee in

ˈcoffee ˌshop **noun** [C] **1** (A1) (UK also **coffee bar**) a small informal restaurant where drinks and small meals are served, sometimes in a larger shop or building: *the hospital/theatre coffee shop* **2** (A1) a shop where different types of coffee are sold, either to drink or as beans or powder

ˈcoffee ˌtable **noun** [C] a small low table on which coffee is served or books and magazines are arranged

ˈcoffee-table ˌbook **noun** [C] a large expensive book with a lot of pictures, intended to be looked at rather than read

coffer /ˈkɒf.ər/ (US) /ˈkɑː.fə/ **noun** **1** [C] a large strong box in which money or valuable objects are kept **2** **coffers** [plural] the money that an organization has in its bank accounts and available to spend: *government/party coffers*

cofferdam /ˈkɒf.ə.dæm/ (US) /ˈkɑː.fə-/ **noun** [C] specialized a large box filled with air which allows people to work underwater, for example while building bridges

coffin /ˈkɒf.ɪn/ (US) /ˈkɑː.fɪn/ **noun** [C] (US also **casket**) a long box in which the body of a dead person is buried or burned

cog /kɒg/ (US) /kɑːg/ **noun** [C] **1** one of the tooth-like parts around the edge of a wheel in a machine which fits between those of a similar wheel, causing both wheels to move **2** (also **cogwheel**) a wheel with cogs around its edge, used to turn another wheel or part in a machine

cog

IDIOM **a cog in a/the machine** disapproving a member of a large organization whose job, although necessary, makes them feel as if they are not important: *I decided to set up my own business because I was tired of just being a cog in a machine.*

cogent /ˈkəʊ.dʒənt/ (US) /ˈkoʊ-/ **adj** formal describes an argument or reason, etc. that is clearly expressed and persuades people to believe it • **cogency** /-dʒən.si/ **noun** [U] • **cogently** /-li/ **adv** *She **argued** most cogently for a relaxation of the sanctions.*

cogitate /ˈkɒdʒ.ɪ.teɪt/ (US) /ˈkɑː.dʒɪ-/ **verb** [I] formal to spend time thinking very carefully about a subject • **cogitation** /kɒdʒ.ɪˈteɪ.ʃən/ (US) /kɑː.dʒɪ-/ **noun** [C or U]

cognac /ˈkɒn.jæk/ (US) /ˈkoʊ.njæk/ **noun** [C or U] high quality BRANDY (= strong alcoholic drink) made in western France, or a glass of this: *a bottle of cognac* ◦ *Would you like another cognac?*

cognate /ˈkɒg.neɪt/ (US) /ˈkɑːg-/ **adj; noun**

▸**adj** specialized describes languages and words that have the same origin, or that are related and in some way similar: *The Italian word 'mangiare' (= to eat) is cognate **with** the French 'manger'.*

▸**noun** [C] specialized a word that has the same origin, or that is related in some way, to a word in another language

cognition /kɒgˈnɪʃ.ən/ (US) /kɑːg-/ **noun** [U] formal or specialized the use of a conscious mental process: *a book on human learning, memory, and cognition*

cognitive /ˈkɒg.nɪ.tɪv/ (US) /ˈkɑːg.nɪ.t̬ɪv/ **adj** [before noun] specialized connected with thinking or conscious mental processes: *Some of her cognitive **functions** have been impaired.* ◦ *cognitive behaviour/development* ◦ *cognitive psychology*

ˌcognitive ˈtherapy **noun** [U] (also **ˌcognitive beˌhavioural ˈtherapy, CBT**) a treatment for people suffering from mental illnesses that tries to change the way they think

cognizance /ˈkɒg.nɪ.zənts/ (US) /ˈkɑːg-/ **noun** formal or legal **take cognizance of sth** to take notice of and consider something, especially when judging: *The lawyer asked the jury to take cognizance of the defendant's generosity in giving to charity.* • **cognizant** /-zənt/ **adj** formal *Unfortunately, we were not cognizant **of** (= did not know) the full facts.*

cognoscenti /ˌkɒn.jəˈʃen.tiː/ (US) /ˌkɑː.njə-/ **noun** [plural] formal a group of people who have a great knowledge and understanding of a particular subject, especially one of the arts: *Not being **one of the** cognoscenti, I failed to understand the ballet's subtler points.*

cogwheel /ˈkɒg.wiːl/ US /ˈkɑːg-/ noun [C] a **cog**

cohabit /kəʊˈhæb.ɪt/ US /koʊ-/ verb [I] formal If two people, especially a man and woman who are not married, cohabit, they live together and have a sexual relationship: *About 23 percent of men and women aged 25 to 34 told researchers they had previously cohabited **with** a partner without it leading to marriage.* ◦ *cohabiting couples* • **cohabitation** /kəʊ.hæb.ɪˈteɪ.ʃən/ US /koʊ-/ noun [U] *a cohabitation agreement*

cohabitant /kəʊˈhæb.ɪ.tənt/ US /koʊˈhæb.ɪ.t̬ənt/ noun [C] (also **cohabitee** /ˌkəʊ.hæb.ɪˈtiː/) the official word for someone who lives in the same house, apartment, etc. as someone else: *Is Mr Jones one of the cohabitants at this address?*

cohere /kəʊˈhɪər/ US /koʊˈhɪr/ verb [I] formal **1** If an argument or theory coheres, all the different stages fit together to form a reasonable whole. **2** to unite or to hold together as a unit: *His vision is of a world that coheres through human connection rather than rules.*

coherence /kəʊˈhɪə.rəns/ US /koʊˈhɪr.əns/ noun [U] C2 the situation when the parts of something fit together in a natural or reasonable way: *There was no coherence **between** the first and the second half of the movie.*

coherent /kəʊˈhɪə.rənt/ US /koʊˈhɪr.ənt/ adj **1** C2 If an argument, set of ideas, or a plan is coherent, it is clear and carefully considered, and each part of it connects or follows in a natural or reasonable way. **2** C2 If someone is coherent, you can understand what they say: *When she calmed down, she was more coherent (= able to speak clearly and be understood).* • **coherently** /-li/ adv

cohesion /kəʊˈhiː.ʒən/ US /koʊ-/ noun [U] (also **cohesiveness**) the situation when the members of a group or society are united: *social/national cohesion* ◦ *The **lack of** cohesion within the party lost them votes in the election.*

cohesive /kəʊˈhiː.sɪv/ US /koʊ-/ adj formal united and working together effectively: *a cohesive group* ◦ *cohesive forces*

cohort /ˈkəʊ.hɔːt/ US /ˈkoʊ.hɔːrt/ noun [C, + sing/pl verb] **1** specialized a group of people who share a characteristic, usually age: *This study followed up a cohort of 386 patients aged 65+ for six months after their discharge home.* **2** disapproving a group of people who support a particular person, usually a leader: *The Mayor and his cohorts have abused their positions of power.*

coiffed /kwɒft/ US /kwɑːft/ adj often humorous describes hair that is carefully arranged in an attractive style: *How do those TV mothers always manage to look so **immaculately** coiffed as they do the housework?*

coiffure /kwɒfˈjʊər/ US /kwɑːˈfjʊr/ noun [C] formal the style in which someone's hair is cut and arranged

coil /kɔɪl/ noun; verb

▸noun [C] **CIRCLE** ▷ **1** a length of rope, hair, or wire, arranged into a series of circles, one above the other: *A coil of rope lay on the beach.* ◦ figurative *A coil of thick blue smoke rose up from his pipe.* **2** specialized a twisted length of wire through which an electric current travels **MEDICAL** ▷ **3** UK informal an IUD (= a medical device to stop a woman becoming pregnant)

▸verb [I or T] to arrange something in a coil: *She coiled her hair **into** a neat bun on top of her head.* ◦ *The snake coiled it**self** tightly **around** the deer.* • **coiled** /kɔɪld/ adj *a coiled spring*

coin /kɔɪn/ noun; verb

▸noun **1** B1 [C] a small round piece of metal, usually silver or COPPER coloured, that is used as money: *a 10p/ten pence coin* ◦ *a pound coin* ◦ *a ten-cent coin* ◦ *gold coins* ◦ *I asked for £10 **in** 20p coins.* ◦ *That machine doesn't **take** 50p coins.* **2** [U] money in the form of metal coins

▸verb **INVENT** ▷ **1** C2 [T] to invent a new word or expression, or to use one in a particular way for the first time: *Allen Ginsberg coined the term 'flower power'.* **MONEY** ▷ **2** **coining it (in)** UK informal to be earning a lot of money quickly

IDIOM **to coin a phrase** humorous something you say before using an expression that has been very popular or used too much: *I was, to coin a phrase, gobsmacked!*

coinage /ˈkɔɪ.nɪdʒ/ noun **MONEY** ▷ **1** [U] a set of coins of different values used in a country's money system: *decimal coinage* **NEW WORD** ▷ **2** [C or U] (the inventing of) a new word or phrase in a language: *The expression 'boy band' is a 1990s coinage.*

coincide /ˌkəʊ.ɪnˈsaɪd/ US /ˌkoʊ-/ verb [I] **1** C2 to happen at or near the same time: *I timed my holiday to coincide **with** the children's school holiday.* ◦ *If the heavy rain had coincided **with** an extreme high tide, serious flooding would have resulted.* **2** C2 to be the same or similar: *Our views coincide on a range of subjects.* ◦ *If our schedules coincide, we'll go to Spain together.*

coincidence /kəʊˈɪn.sɪ.dəns/ US /koʊ-/ noun **1** B2 [C] an occasion when two or more similar things happen at the same time, especially in a way that is unlikely and surprising: *You chose exactly the same wallpaper as us – **what a** coincidence!* ◦ *Is it just a coincidence that the wife of the man who ran the competition won first prize?* ◦ *a series of strange/amazing coincidences* **2** B2 [U] chance or luck: *Just **by** coincidence, I met my old school-mate again 50 years later.* ◦ [+ that] ***It** was **pure/sheer** coincidence **that** I remembered his phone number.* ◦ *By some **strange** coincidence, he was passing the house just when it happened.*

coincident /kəʊˈɪn.sɪ.dənt/ US /koʊ-/ adj formal happening at the same time: *His birth was coincident **with** the end of the war.*

coincidental /kəʊˌɪn.sɪˈden.təl/ US /koʊˌɪn.sɪˈden.t̬əl/ adj happening by coincidence • **coincidentally** /-i/ adv *The highest scorers, coincidentally, were all women.*

coitus /ˈkɔɪ.təs/ US /-t̬əs/ noun [U] specialized the sexual act in which a man puts his PENIS into a woman's VAGINA • **coital** /ˈkɔɪ.təl/ US /-t̬əl/ adj

coitus interruptus /ˌkɔɪ.təs.ɪn.təˈrʌp.təs/ US /-t̬əs.ɪn.t̬ə-/ noun [U] a method of preventing pregnancy in which the man removes his PENIS from the woman's VAGINA before SPERM is released

coke /kəʊk/ US /koʊk/ noun [U] **FUEL** ▷ **1** a solid, grey substance that is burned as a fuel, left after coal is heated and the gas and TAR removed **DRUG** ▷ **2** slang for **cocaine**

Coke /kəʊk/ US /koʊk/ noun [C or U] trademark → **Coca-Cola**

col. noun [C] written abbreviation for **column**

col- /kɒl-/ US /kɑːl-/ prefix together; with: *colleagues*

Col. noun [C] written abbreviation for **colonel**: *Col. (Angus) Ferguson*

cola /ˈkəʊ.lə/ US /koʊ-/ noun [C or U] A2 a sweet, brown FIZZY drink (= one with bubbles) which does not contain alcohol: *Coke and Pepsi are types of cola.*

colander /ˈkɒl.ən.dər/ US /ˈkɑː.lən.dɚ/ noun [C] a bowl with small holes in it, used for washing food or for emptying food into when it has been cooked in water: *After four minutes, pour the pasta into a colander to drain.*

C

cold /kəʊld/ (US) /koʊld/ **adj; noun**

▸**adj** LOW TEMPERATURE ▷ **1** (A1) at a low temperature, especially when compared to the temperature of the human body, and not hot or warm: *a cold day/ house* ◦ *cold food/water* ◦ *cold hands* ◦ *cold weather* ◦ *My feet are so cold.* ◦ ***It's freezing** cold today.* ◦ *You'll feel cold if you don't wear a coat.* UNFRIENDLY ▷ **2** (B1) not showing kindness, love, or emotion and not friendly: *His handshake was cold, and his eyes lifeless.* ◦ *He stared into her cold blue eyes.* ◦ *The school was a cold, unwelcoming place.* • **coldness** /ˈkəʊld.nəs/ (US) /ˈkoʊld-/ **noun** [U] (C2) *It was the coldness of her manner that struck me.*

> **Other ways of saying cold**
>
> If the weather outside or the temperature inside is very cold, you can use the adjectives **bitter** or **freezing**:
>
> *Wrap up warmly – it's **bitter** outside!*
>
> *It's absolutely **freezing** in here!*
>
> If the weather, especially the wind, is so cold that it is unpleasant to be in, the adjectives **biting** and **icy** are sometimes used:
>
> *A **biting/icy** wind blew in her face as she opened the door.*
>
> The adjective **chilly** is often used to describe weather or temperatures that feel slightly cold and unpleasant:
>
> *It's a bit **chilly** in here – can you turn up the heating?*
>
> If the temperature feels cold but pleasant, you can say that it is **cool**:
>
> *That's a nice **cool** breeze.*
>
> Cold weather in autumn or winter that is dry and pleasant is sometimes described as **crisp**:
>
> *We walked through the forest on a **crisp** autumn day.*

IDIOMS **be (as) cold as ice** to be extremely cold: *Feel my toes – they're as cold as ice.* • **be cold comfort** When being told a particular thing about a bad situation is cold comfort, it does not make you feel better although it is intended to. • **get cold feet** to suddenly become too frightened to do something you had planned to do, especially something important such as getting married • **give sb the cold shoulder** to deliberately ignore someone in an unfriendly way: *I tried to be pleasant to her but she gave me the cold shoulder.* → See also **cold-shoulder** • **in cold blood** (C2) If someone kills in cold blood, they kill in a way that seems especially cruel because they show no emotion. • **in the cold light of day** If you think about something in the cold light of day, you think about it clearly and calmly, without the emotions you had at the time it happened, and you often feel sorry or ashamed about it: *The next morning, in the cold light of day, Sarah realized what a complete idiot she had been.* • **pour/throw cold water on sth** to criticize someone's opinions or ideas and stop people believing them or being excited about them • **you're getting colder** said by children playing a guessing or searching game to tell the person who is guessing or searching that they are getting further away from the answer or hidden object

▸**noun** ILLNESS ▷ **1** (A2) [C] a common infection especially in the nose and throat which often causes a cough, a slight fever, and sometimes some pain in the muscles: *I've **got a** cold.* ◦ *She **caught a** cold at school.* ◦ UK informal *Don't come near me – I've got a **stinking/streaming** cold (= extremely bad cold).* LOW TEMPERATURE ▷ **2** (B1) [S or U] cold weather or temperatures: *Don't stand out there in **the** cold, come in here and get warm.* ◦ *Old people tend to **feel the** cold (= feel uncomfortable in cold temperatures) more than the young.* ◦ *My feet were numb with cold.*

ˌcold-ˈblooded **adj** **1** describes animals that can only control their body heat by taking in heat from the outside or by being very active: *Snakes and lizards are cold-blooded animals.* → Compare **warm-blooded** **2** behaving in a very cruel way with no sympathy for other people: *a cold-blooded murder*

ˈcold-ˌcalling **noun** [U] the activity of phoning or visiting a possible customer to try to sell them something without being asked by the customer to do so • **ˈcold-ˌcall** **verb** [T] *We were cold-called by a company offering savings on our phone bill.*

ˈcold ˌcream **noun** [U] a thick white substance used to clean the skin and stop it from becoming too dry

ˈcold ˌcuts **noun** [plural] mainly US thin flat slices of cold cooked meat

ˌcold ˈfish **noun** [S] someone who seems unfriendly and who does not share their feelings

ˈcold ˌframe **noun** [C] a glass or plastic box, with a top which can be left open, into which young plants are put for a short time, especially in order to help them grow faster or to protect them from cold weather

ˌcold ˈfront **noun** [C] the weather condition in which a moving mass of cold air pushes into a mass of warm air resulting in a fall in temperature

ˌcold-ˈhearted **adj** disapproving showing no understanding for or not feeling sorry about another person's suffering: *a cold-hearted killer*

coldly /ˈkəʊld.li/ (US) /ˈkoʊld-/ **adv** in an unfriendly way and without emotion: *'That's your problem,' she said coldly.*

ˌcold-ˈshoulder **verb** [T] to deliberately ignore someone in an unfriendly way: *He found himself being cold-shouldered by his former colleagues.*

ˈcold ˌsnap **noun** [C] a short period of cold weather

ˈcold ˌsore **noun** [C] a painful, red swelling, especially on the lips or nose, that is caused by a virus

ˌcold ˈstorage **noun** [U] If something, usually food, is kept in cold storage, it is put in artificially cold conditions, usually to stop it from decaying.

ˌcold ˈsweat **noun** [C] a state of extreme worry and fear: *I **break out in** a cold sweat (= become extremely worried) just thinking about public speaking.*

ˌcold ˈturkey **noun** [U] slang the period of extreme suffering which comes immediately after a person has stopped taking a drug on which they depend: *Six years ago she **went** cold turkey on (= stopped completely) a three-pack-a-day smoking habit.*

ˌcold ˈwar **noun** [C] a state of extreme unfriendliness existing between countries, especially with opposing political systems, which expresses itself not through fighting but through political pressure and threats. The expression is usually used of the relationship between the US and the Soviet Union after the Second World War.

coleslaw /ˈkəʊl.slɔː/ (US) /ˈkoʊl.slɑː/ **noun** [U] cold, uncooked CABBAGE, CARROT, and onion, cut into long, thin strips and covered in a thick, cold sauce

coley /ˈkəʊ.li/ (US) /ˈkoʊ-/ **noun** [C or U] (plural **coley**) a fish that lives in the North Atlantic, or the flesh of this fish eaten as food

colic /ˈkɒl.ɪk/ (US) /ˈkɑː.lɪk/ **noun** [U] a severe but not continuous pain in the bottom part of the stomach or bowels, especially of babies • **colicky** /ˈkɒl.ɪ.ki/ (US) /ˈkɑː.lɪ-/ **adj** *a colicky baby*

colitis /kəˈlaɪ.təs/ (US) /koʊˈlaɪ.t̬əs/ **noun** [U] an illness of the COLON (= part of the bowels) in which the contents of the bowels are passed out of the body too often

collaborate /kəˈlæb.ə.reɪt/ **verb** [I] **WORK WITH** ▷ **1** (C1) to work with someone else for a special purpose: *Two writers collaborated **on** the script for the film.* ◦ *A German company collaborated **with** a Swiss firm **to** develop the product.* ◦ *The British and Italian police collaborated **in** catch**ing** the terrorists.* **SUPPORT AN ENEMY** ▷ **2** disapproving to work with an enemy who has taken control of your own country: *Anyone who was suspected of collaborating **with** the occupying forces was arrested.*

collaboration /kəˌlæb.əˈreɪ.ʃən/ **noun** **WORKING WITH** ▷ **1** (C1) [C or U] the situation of two or more people working together to create or achieve the same thing: *The two playwrights worked **in close** collaboration (**with** each other) on the script.* ◦ *The new airport is a collaboration **between** two of the best architects in the country.* **HELPING AN ENEMY** ▷ **2** [U] disapproving the situation of people working with an enemy who has taken control of their country: *She was accused of collaboration.*

collaborationist /kəˌlæb.əˈreɪ.ʃən.ɪst/ **adj** disapproving describes a person or group who works with an enemy who has taken control of their country: *a collaborationist government*

collaborative /kəˈlæb.ər.ə.tɪv/ (US) /-ɚ.ə.t̬ɪv/ **adj** [before noun] involving two or more people working together for a special purpose: *The presentation was a collaborative **effort** by all the children in the class.*

collaborator /kəˈlæb.ə.reɪ.təʳ/ (US) /-t̬ɚ/ **noun** [C] **ENEMY SUPPORTER** ▷ **1** disapproving a person who works with an enemy who has taken control of their country: *wartime collaborators* ◦ *a Nazi collaborator* **WORKING WITH** ▷ **2** a person who works together with others for a special purpose: *a new production by Andrew Davies and collaborators*

collage /ˈkɒl.ɑːʒ/ (US) /ˈkɑː.lɑːʒ/ **noun** [C or U] (the art of making) a picture in which various materials or objects, for example paper, cloth, or photographs, are stuck onto a larger surface: *The children made a collage of postcards.* → Compare **assemblage**

collagen /ˈkɒl.ə.dʒən/ (US) /ˈkɑː.lə-/ **noun** [U] **1** a PROTEIN found especially in the JOINTS (= places where two bones are connected) of humans and animals **2 collagen implant/injection** an INJECTION of collagen into the lips or skin to make the lips appear larger or the skin appear younger and smoother

collapse /kəˈlæps/ **verb; noun**

▸**verb** **FALL** ▷ **1** (B2) [I] to fall down suddenly because of pressure or having no strength or support: *Thousands of buildings collapsed in the earthquake.* ◦ *The chair collapsed **under** her **weight**.* ◦ figurative *He thought his whole world had collapsed when his wife died.* **2** (B2) [I] If someone collapses, they fall down because they are ill or weak: *He collapsed and died of a heart attack.* **3** [I or T] to fold something into a smaller shape, usually so it can be stored, or (especially of furniture) to fold in this way: *All chairs collapse for easy storage.* **FAIL** ▷ **4** (C2) [I] (of people and business) to suddenly be unable to continue or work correctly: *Lots of people lost their jobs when the property market collapsed.* ◦ *Talks between management and unions have collapsed.* ◦ *Share prices collapsed (= became lower suddenly) after news of poor trading.*

▸**noun** **FAILURE** ▷ **1** (B2) [C or U] the sudden failure of a system, organization, business, etc.: *I don't know what caused the collapse **of** her marriage.* ◦ *A poor economy has caused the collapse **of** thousands of small businesses.* ◦ *Negotiations between the two countries are **on the brink/verge of** collapse (= very soon going to fail).* ◦ *He **suffered a mental/nervous** collapse after ten years' teaching.* **FALL** ▷ **2** [S or U] the sudden falling movement of a person or structure that has become too weak to stand: *He was taken to hospital after his collapse on the pitch.* ◦ *the collapse of a tower block during the earthquake*

collapsed /kəˈlæpst/ **adj** describes a lung or BLOOD VESSEL (= tube that carries blood in the body) that is not able to work because disease or injury has caused it to become flat

collapsible /kəˈlæp.sɪ.bl/ **adj** describes furniture that can be folded, usually so it can be put or stored in a smaller space: *collapsible chairs*

collar /ˈkɒl.əʳ/ (US) /ˈkɑː.lɚ/ **noun; verb**

▸**noun** [C] **1** (B1) the part around the neck of a piece of clothing, usually sewn on and sometimes made of different material: *a shirt collar* ◦ *a fur collar* ◦ *a dress with a big collar* **2** (B2) a strap made of leather or other strong material that is put around the neck of an animal, especially a dog or cat: *I grabbed the dog by the collar and dragged it out of the room.* **3** a type of NECKLACE (= a piece of jewellery worn around the neck): *a diamond collar* **4** specialized an area around the neck of an animal that is coloured differently from the other parts of the body: *The bird has grey feathers with a lighter collar.* **5** specialized a strip of strong material that is put round a pipe or a piece of machinery to make it stronger or to join two parts together

▸**verb** [T] informal **1** to catch and hold someone so that they cannot escape: *She was collared by the police at the airport.* **2** to find someone and stop them going somewhere, often so that you can talk to them about something: *I was collared by Pete as I was coming out of the meeting this morning.*

collarbone /ˈkɒl.ə.bəʊn/ (US) /ˈkɑː.lɚ.boʊn/ **noun** [C] (specialized **clavicle**) a bone between your shoulder and neck on each side of your body

collate /kəˈleɪt/ **verb** [T] **1** formal to bring together different pieces of written information so that the similarities and differences can be seen: *to collate data/information* **2** to collect and arrange the sheets of a report, book, etc., in the correct order: *The photocopier will collate the documents for you.*

collateral /kəˈlæt.ər.əl/ (US) /-ˈlæt̬.ɚ-/ **noun; adj**

▸**noun** [U] specialized valuable property owned by someone who wants to borrow money which they agree will become the property of the company or person who lends the money if the debt is not paid back: *She **used/put up** her house as collateral for a loan.*

▸**adj** formal connected but less important, or of the same family although not directly related: *collateral senses of a word* ◦ *a collateral branch of the family*

colˌlateral ˈdamage **noun** [U] during a war, the unintentional deaths and injuries of people who are not soldiers, and damage that is caused to their homes, hospitals, schools, etc.

collation /kəˈleɪ.ʃən/ **noun** **1** [C] formal a meal, especially one left ready for people to serve themselves **2** [C or U] the act or an example of collating

> **! Common mistake: colleague**
>
> **Warning:** Check your spelling!
>
> **Colleague** is one of the 50 words most often spelled wrongly by learners.

colleague /ˈkɒl.iːɡ/ (US) /ˈkɑː.liːɡ/ **noun** [C] (A2) one of a group of people who work together: *We're entertaining some colleagues of Ben's tonight.*

collect /kəˈlekt/ **verb; noun; adj, adv**

▸**verb** AS A HOBBY ▷ **1** (A2) [T] to get and keep things of one type such as stamps or coins as a hobby: *She collects dolls.* ◦ *So when did you start collecting antique glass?* GET ▷ **2** (A2) [T] UK to go to a place and bring someone or something away from it: *Your shoes will be repaired and ready for you to collect on Thursday.* ◦ *I'll collect you* ***from*** *the station.* BRING TOGETHER ▷ **3** (B1) [T] to bring something together from different places or over a period of time: *After the party I collected (****up****) bottles from various parts of the house.* ◦ *These china ornaments just collect* ***dust****.* MONEY ▷ **4** (B2) [T or I] to ask people to give you money for something, for example a charity: *We're collecting (money) for the homeless.* **5** [T] to take money such as taxes, rents, etc.: *The state collected about $1.2 million in taxes in January.* COME TOGETHER ▷ **6** [I] to come together from different places or over a period of time: *A large crowd of reporters collected outside the prime minister's house.* ◦ *Rainwater collects in the barrel in the garden.* **7 collect yourself/your thoughts** (C2) formal to get control of your feelings and thoughts, especially after shock, surprise, or laughter: *I was so stunned by what he'd said I had to collect myself before I could reply.*

▸**noun** [C] a short prayer that is said during some Christian religious ceremonies

▸**adj, adv** US When you phone collect or make a collect phone call, the person you call pays for the call: *I'd like to make a collect* ***call****.* ◦ *She called me collect.*

collectable /kəˈlek.tə.bl̩/ (US) /-t̬ə-/ **noun; adj**

▸**noun** [C] (also **collectible**) any object which people want to collect as a hobby

▸**adj** (also **collectible**) describes something that is considered to be worth collecting as a hobby: *Comics from the 1960s are highly collectable.*

collected /kəˈlek.tɪd/ **adj** GATHERED ▷ **1** [before noun] brought together in one book or series of books: *His collected poems were published in 1928.* CONTROLLED ▷ **2** showing control over your feelings: *She appeared* ***calm and*** *collected.*

colˈlecting ˌflask noun [C] specialized a wide glass container with a flat base, used in scientific work for collecting liquids

collection /kəˈlek.ʃən/ **noun** THINGS TOGETHER ▷ **1** (B1) [C] a group of objects of one type that have been collected by one person or in one place: *a private art collection* ◦ *a valuable stamp collection* **2** [C] an amount of money collected from several people, or the act of collecting money: *We're* ***having*** *a collection for Tom's retirement present.* **3** (B1) [C] a lot of things or people: *There's quite a collection of toothbrushes in the bathroom.* **4** [C] a range of new clothes produced by one clothes DESIGNER: *Kenzo's summer/winter collection* GETTING ▷ **5** (B2) [C or U] the act of taking something away from a place: *The photos will be* ***ready for*** *collection on Tuesday afternoon.* ◦ *Which day is the rubbish collection?* ◦ UK *There are three collections a day from the post box on the corner.*

> **Word partners for collection**
>
> a collection *of* sth • an *extensive/fine/large/priceless* collection • a *museum/private* collection • *display/exhibit/house* a collection • *add* sth *to* a collection

collective /kəˈlek.tɪv/ **adj; noun**

▸**adj** [before noun] of or shared by every member of a group of people: *a collective decision/effort* ◦ *collective responsibility/leadership*

▸**noun** [C] an organization or business that is owned and controlled by the people who work in it

colˌlective ˈbargaining noun [U] the system in which employees talk as a group with their employers to try to agree on matters such as pay and working conditions

colˌlective ˈfarm noun [C] (originally in countries which had a COMMUNIST system of government) a large farm or group of farms owned by the state but controlled by the workers

collectively /kəˈlek.tɪv.li/ **adv** as a group: *She has a staff of four who collectively earn almost $200,000.*

colˌlective ˈnoun noun [C] specialized a noun which describes a group of things or people as a unit: *'Family' and 'flock' are examples of collective nouns.*

collectivism /kəˈlek.tɪ.vɪ.zəm/ (US) /-t̬ə-/ **noun** [U] specialized a theory or political system based on the principle that all of the farms, factories, and other places of work in a country should be owned by or for all the people in that country

collector /kəˈlek.tər/ (US) /-t̬ɚ/ **noun** [C] HOBBY ▷ **1** (B2) someone who collects objects because they are beautiful, valuable, or interesting: *a keen stamp/antiques collector* ◦ *a collector of modern art* JOB ▷ **2** someone whose job is to collect tickets or money from people: *a tax/ticket collector* **3** Indian English the person who is in charge of the local government in a particular town or area of the country

colˈlector's ˌitem noun [C] (also **colˈlector's ˌpiece**) an object that is very valuable to a person who collects such objects as a hobby

colleen /kɒlˈiːn/ (US) /kɑːˈliːn/ **noun** [C] **1** Irish a girl or young woman **2** US a girl from Ireland

college /ˈkɒl.ɪdʒ/ (US) /ˈkɑː.lɪdʒ/ **noun** EDUCATION ▷ **1** (A2) [C or U] any place for specialized education after the age of 16 where people study or train to get knowledge and/or skills: *a teacher training college* ◦ *a secretarial college* ◦ *a Naval college* ◦ UK *a sixth form college* ◦ *She's* ***at*** *art college.* **2** [C or U] US university: *You have to* ***go to*** *(= study at) college for many years if you want to be a doctor.* **3** [C] one of the separate and named parts into which some universities are divided: *I attended the College* ***of*** *Arts and Sciences at New York University.* ◦ *Cambridge has some very fine old colleges (= college buildings).* **4** [C] in Britain and Australia, used in the names of some schools for children, especially those where education is paid for: *Cheltenham Ladies' College* GROUP ▷ **5** [C] a group of people with a particular job, purpose, duty, or power who are organized into a group for sharing ideas, making decisions, etc.: *the Royal College of Medicine/Nursing*

collegial /kəˈliː.dʒi.əl/ **adj** formal **1** relating to a friendly relationship between COLLEAGUES (= people who work together): *The organization has a welcoming collegial atmosphere.* **2** used to describe a method of working in which responsibility is shared between several people: *The new chair quickly upset council members, who were used to a more collegial style.*

collegiate /kəˈliː.dʒi.ət/ (US) /-dʒɪt/ **adj** **1** of or belonging to a college or its students: *a collegiate theatre* ◦ *collegiate sports* **2** UK formed of colleges: *Oxford and Cambridge are both collegiate* ***universities****.*

collide /kəˈlaɪd/ **verb** [I] (especially of moving objects) to hit something violently: *The two vans collided at the* *crossroads.* ◦ *It was predicted that a comet would collide* ***with*** *one of the planets.*

collie /ˈkɒl.i/ US /ˈkɑː.li/ **noun** [C] any of several breeds of dog with long hair that are bred for controlling sheep

collier /ˈkɒl.i.əʳ/ US /ˈkɑː.ljɚ/ **noun** [C] **1** formal a **coal miner 2** a ship used for carrying coal

colliery /ˈkɒl.i.əʳ.i/ US /ˈkɑː.ljɚ-/ **noun** [C] a COAL MINE and all the buildings, machines, etc. connected with it

collision /kəˈlɪʒ.ən/ **noun** **ACCIDENT** ▷ **1** [C or U] an accident that happens when two vehicles hit each other with force: *There has been a collision on the southbound stretch of the motorway.* ◦ *Two drivers were killed in a* ***head-on*** *(= direct) collision* ***between*** *a car and a taxi last night.* ◦ *The cyclist was* ***in*** *collision* ***with*** *a bus.* **DIFFERENCE** ▷ **2** [C] a strong disagreement: *There was a collision of interests/opinions.*

IDIOM **be on a collision course** If two or more people or groups are on a collision course, they are doing or saying things that are certain to cause a serious disagreement or fight between them: *All attempts at diplomacy have broken down and the two states now appear to be on a collision course.*

collocate /ˈkɒl.ə.keɪt/ US /ˈkɑː.lə-/ **verb** [I] specialized (of words and phrases) to often be used together in a way that sounds correct to people who have spoken the language all their lives, but might not be expected from the meaning

collocation /ˌkɒl.əˈkeɪ.ʃən/ US /ˌkɑː.lə-/ **noun** specialized **1** B2 [C] (also **collocate**) a word or phrase that is often used with another word or phrase, in a way that sounds correct to people who have spoken the language all their lives, but might not be expected from the meaning: *In the phrase 'a hard frost', 'hard' is a collocation of 'frost' and 'strong' would not sound natural.* **2** B2 [C] the combination of words formed when two or more words are often used together in a way that sounds correct: *The phrase 'a hard frost' is a collocation.* **3** [U] the regular use of some words and phrases with others, especially in a way that is difficult to guess

colloquial /kəˈləʊ.kwi.əl/ US /-ˈloʊ-/ **adj** specialized (of words and expressions) informal and more suitable for use in speech than in writing: *colloquial speech* • **colloquially** /-i/ **adv**

colloquialism /kəˈləʊ.kwi.əl.ɪ.zəm/ US /-ˈloʊ-/ **noun** [C] an informal word or expression that is more suitable for use in speech than in writing

colloquy /ˈkɒl.ə.kwi/ US /ˈkɑː.lə-/ **noun** [C] formal a formal conversation

collude /kəˈluːd/ **verb** [I] formal to act together secretly or illegally in order to deceive or cheat someone: *It was suspected that the police had colluded* ***with*** *the witnesses.*

collusion /kəˈluː.ʒən/ **noun** [U] formal agreement between people to act together secretly or illegally in order to deceive or cheat someone: *It is thought that they worked* ***in*** *collusion* ***with*** *the terrorist network.* • **collusive** /-sɪv/ **adj**

cologne /kəˈləʊn/ US /-ˈloʊn/ **noun** [U or C] (also ˌ**eau de coˈlogne**) a type of PERFUME (= liquid with a pleasant smell, used on the skin)

colon /ˈkəʊ.lɒn/ US /ˈkoʊ.lən/ **noun** [C] **BODY PART** ▷ **1** the lower and bigger half of the bowels in which water is removed from solid waste **SIGN** ▷ **2** B2 the symbol : used in writing, especially to introduce a list of things or a sentence or phrase taken from somewhere else

colón /kɒlˈɒn/ US /kəˈloʊn/ **noun** [C] (plural **colones** /-es/) the standard unit of money used in Costa Rica and El Salvador

colonel /ˈkɜː.nəl/ US /ˈkɝː-/ **noun** [C] (also **Colonel**, written abbreviation **Col.**) an officer of high rank in the army or air force: *Colonel is the military rank between lieutenant-colonel and brigadier.* ◦ *Colonel Furlong* ◦ [as form of address] *Yes, Colonel.*

ˌ**Colonel ˈBlimp** **noun** [C] UK old-fashioned an old man who has old-fashioned ideas and believes he is very important

colonial /kəˈləʊ.ni.əl/ US /-ˈloʊ-/ **adj; noun**

▸**adj 1** [before noun] relating to a COLONY or colonialism: *Turkey was once an important colonial power.* ◦ *Various parts of Africa have suffered* ***under*** *colonial* ***rule.*** ◦ *a colonial mentality* **2** describes furniture or buildings in the style of a period when a country was a COLONY: *colonial architecture* ◦ *colonial-style houses*

▸**noun** [C] a person from another country who lives in a COLONY, especially as part of its system of government

colonialism /kəˈləʊ.ni.ə.lɪ.zəm/ US /-ˈloʊ-/ **noun** [U] the belief in and support for the system of one country controlling another

colonialist /kəˈləʊ.ni.əl.ɪst/ US /-ˈloʊ-/ **adj; noun**

▸**adj** relating to colonialism: *the colonialist powers* ◦ *colonialist ideology*

▸**noun** [C] a supporter of colonialism

colonist /ˈkɒl.ə.nɪst/ US /ˈkɑː.lə-/ **noun** [C] someone who lives in or goes to live in a country or area that is a COLONY

colonize (UK usually **colonise**) /ˈkɒl.ə.naɪz/ US /ˈkɑː.lə-/ **verb** [T often passive] to send people to live in and govern another country: *Peru was colonized by the Spanish in the 16th century.* • **colonization** (UK usually **colonisation**) /ˌkɒl.ə.naɪˈzeɪ.ʃən/ US /ˌkɑː.lə.nə-/ **noun** [U]

colonnade /ˌkɒl.əˈneɪd/ US /ˌkɑː.lə-/ **noun** [C] a row of columns separated from each other by an equal distance

colonoscopy /ˌkəʊ.ləˈnɒs.kə.pi/ US /ˌkoʊ.ləˈnɑː.skə-/ **noun** [C or U] specialized a medical examination of the COLON (= the lower part of the tube that takes solid waste out of your body)

colony /ˈkɒl.ə.ni/ US /ˈkɑː.lə-/ **noun** [C] **GROUP** ▷ **1** a country or area controlled politically by a more powerful country that is often far away: *Australia and New Zealand are* ***former*** *British colonies.* **2** a group of people who live in a colony **3** a group of people with a shared interest or job who live together in a way that is separate from other people: *an artists' colony* ◦ *a nudist colony* **4** specialized a group of animals, insects, or plants of the same type that live together: *a colony of ants/termites/bacteria* **HOUSES** ▷ **5** Indian English an area surrounded by fences or walls that contains a group of houses, for example houses that have been built by an employer for its workers

color /ˈkʌl.əʳ/ US /-ɚ/ **noun** US for colour

Colorado beetle /ˌkɒl.ə.rɑː.dəʊˈbiː.tl/ US /-doʊˈbiː.t̬l/ **noun** [C] (US usually ˌ**Colorado ˈpotato ˌbeetle**) a type of BEETLE with black and yellow lines on its body that attacks potato plants

coloration /ˌkʌl.əˈreɪ.ʃən/ **noun** [U] specialized the fact of colour being present on an animal or plant and the pattern that the colour makes

ˈ**color ˌline** **noun** [C usually singular] US for **colour bar**

colossal /kəˈlɒs.əl/ US /-ˈlɑː.səl/ **adj** extremely large: *In the centre of the hall stood a colossal wooden statue,* *decorated in ivory and gold.* ◦ *They were asking a colossal amount of money for the house.*

colossus /kəˈlɒs.əs/ (US) /-ˈlɑː.səs/ **noun** [C] (plural **colossi** /-aɪ/ or **colossuses**) **1** a person or thing of great size, influence, or ability: *She has been described as the creative colossus of the literary world.* **2** a very large STATUE (= large artistic object) or building

colour /ˈkʌl.əʳ/ (US) /-ɚ/ **noun; adj; verb**

▸**noun** UK (US **color**) **APPEARANCE** ▷ **1** (A1) [C or U] red, blue, green, yellow, etc.: *What's your favourite colour?* ◦ *She wears a lot of bright colours.* ◦ *What colour are your eyes?* ◦ *Does the shirt come* ***in*** *any other colour?* ◦ *I like rich jewel colours, such as purple, blue, and green.* ◦ *Are the photos* ***in*** *colour or black and white?* **2** [U] the pleasant effect of a bright colour or of a lot of colours together: *I think we need a bit of colour in this room.* ◦ *Red and yellow peppers give a little colour to the sauce.* ◦ literary *The whole garden was* ***ablaze with/a riot of*** *colour (= full of different bright colours).* **3** [C] a substance, such as a paint or DYE, that you add to something to give it a particular colour: *I put my new green shirt in a hot wash and the colour* ***ran*** *(= the colour came out of the material).* **4** [U] a pink colour in someone's face, often showing good health or showing feelings such as embarrassment or excitement: *That walk has* ***put some*** *colour* ***in your cheeks.*** ◦ *I watched the colour* ***drain from*** *her face as she heard the news.* ◦ *She has a high colour (= the natural colour of her face is red).* **INTEREST** ▷ **5** (C2) [U] interesting or exciting qualities or details: *We added your story for a bit of local colour.* ◦ *Michael was there so that added a bit of colour to the evening's proceedings.* **RACE** ▷ **6** (C2) [C or U] the natural colour of a person's skin which shows which race they belong to: *She felt she had not been given the job because of her colour.* ◦ *There should be no discrimination on the grounds of colour.* **SYMBOL** ▷ **7 colours** [plural] **a** (at school, college, or university) an honour given to people who have been chosen for a sports team, often represented by a special symbol on a shirt or tie: *She was awarded her colours* ***for*** *hockey/her hockey colours at the end of term.* **b** the official flag of a country, ship, or military group: *regimental colours*

IDIOMS **see sb's true colours** to see someone's real character for the first time, especially when it is unpleasant: *It was only when they started to work together that she began to see his true colours.* • **show sb in their true colours** to show what someone's real character is, especially when it is unpleasant

▸**adj** UK (US **color**) Colour television, photography, or printing shows things in all their colours, not just in black and white.

▸**verb** UK (US **color**) **BECOME A COLOUR** ▷ **1** (A1) [I or T] to become a particular colour, or to make something a particular colour: *Do you think he colours his hair?* ◦ *He drew a heart and coloured it red.* ◦ *Fry the onions till they start to colour.* **2** [I] to become red in the face because you are embarrassed **INFLUENCE** ▷ **3** (C2) [T often passive] If something colours your opinion of something, it influences your opinion in a negative way: *I'm sure my views on marriage are coloured by my parents' divorce.* ◦ *I'm trying not to let my judgment be coloured by that one incident.*

PHRASAL VERB **colour sth in** to fill an area with colour using paint, coloured pencils, etc.: *Rosie drew an elephant and coloured it in.*

ˈcolour ˌbar **noun** [C usually singular] UK (US **ˈcolor ˌbarrier**) a social and legal system in which people of different races are separated and not given the same rights and opportunities

ˈcolour-blind UK (US **colorblind**) **adj** unable to see the difference between particular colours, especially green and red

ˈcolour-ˌcoded **adj** If a set of objects such as books or wires are colour-coded, they are in different colours so that people can recognize them as being different or separate.

coloured /ˈkʌl.əd/ (US) /-ɚd/ **adj; noun**

▸**adj** UK (US **colored**) **APPEARANCE** ▷ **1** having or producing a colour or colours: *coloured lights/pencils* **RACE** ▷ **2** old-fashioned used to describe a person who has black or brown skin. This word is now considered offensive by most people: *Coloured* ***people*** *were not allowed to use the same facilities as whites.* **3** in South Africa, used to describe a person of mixed race

▸**noun** UK (US **colored**) **RACE** ▷ **1** [C] old-fashioned a person who has black or brown skin. This word is now considered offensive by most people. **2 Coloured** [C] in South Africa, a person of mixed race **APPEARANCE** ▷ **3 coloureds** [plural] clothes that are any colour except white

-coloured UK (US **-colored**) /-kʌl.əd/ (US) /-ɚd/ **suffix** of the colour or colours described: *a multicoloured scarf* ◦ *brightly-coloured flowers* ◦ *flesh-coloured tights*

ˈcolour-fast **adj** If a piece of clothing or material is colour-fast, its colour will not change or lose brightness when it is washed.

colourful UK (US **colorful**) /ˈkʌl.ə.fəl/ (US) /-ɚ-/ **adj** **APPEARANCE** ▷ **1** (B1) having bright colours or a lot of different colours: *a colourful painting* ◦ *colourful costumes* **INTERESTING** ▷ **2** (B2) interesting and exciting: *a colourful character* ◦ *The town, of course, has a very colourful history/past.* ◦ *The old city around the cathedral is the most colourful part of town.* • **colourfully** (US **colorfully**) /-i/ **adv**

colouring UK (US **coloring**) /ˈkʌl.əʳr.ɪŋ/ (US) /-ɚ-/ **noun** **APPEARANCE** ▷ **1** [S] the combined effect of a person's hair, skin, and eye colour: *Their colouring is so totally different that you would never think they were sisters.* **SUBSTANCE** ▷ **2** [C or U] a substance that is added to food or drink to change its colour artificially: *It says on the label that no preservatives or* ***artificial*** *colourings have been added.*

colourless UK (US **colorless**) /ˈkʌl.ə.ləs/ (US) /-ɚ-/ **adj** **NO COLOUR** ▷ **1** having no colour: *Water and glass are colourless.* ◦ *Carbon monoxide is a colourless, odourless, poisonous gas.* **BORING** ▷ **2** not exciting or not interesting: *It is a rather grey, colourless city, with few interesting sights.*

ˈcolour ˌprejudice **noun** [U] an unreasonable dislike of people who have a different skin colour which results in the unfair treatment of members of different races

ˈcolour ˌscheme **noun** [C] UK a combination of colours that has been chosen for a particular room

ˈcolour ˌsupplement **noun** [C] mainly UK a magazine with colour pictures that is given free with a newspaper, especially on Saturdays and Sundays

colourway /ˈkʌl.ə.weɪ/ (US) /-ɚ-/ **noun** [C] UK specialized a combination of colours in which cloth or paper is printed: *The sweaters are available* ***in*** *two colourways: grey/pink or blue/white.*

colt /kəʊlt/ (US) /koʊlt/ **noun** [C] a young male horse under the age of four → Compare **filly** • **coltish** /ˈkəʊl.tɪʃ/ (US) /ˈkoʊl-/ **adj** describes a person who is young and energetic but awkward: *coltish limbs*

columbine /ˈkɒl.əm.baɪn/ (US) /ˈkɑː.ləm-/ **noun** [C] a plant that has brightly coloured flowers with five pointed PETALS that hang down

Columbus Day /kəˈlʌm.bəsˌdeɪ/ **noun** a US holiday on the second Monday in October when people in some states remember Christopher Columbus, who discovered the Americas → See also **Indigenous People's Day**

column /ˈkɒl.əm/ (US) /ˈkɑː.ləm/ **noun** [C] **PRINTING** ▷ **1** B2 one of several vertical blocks of print into which a page of a newspaper or magazine is divided: *I didn't have time to read the whole article – just the first column.* **2** a piece of writing in a newspaper or magazine, usually on a particular subject, that is always written by the same person and appears regularly: *She writes a weekly **fashion/gossip** column for the Evening Standard.* **3** C1 any vertical block of words or numbers: *Add the column of figures and divide the sum by three.* **BUILDING** ▷ **4** B2 a tall, vertical stone post, used as a support for a roof or in CLASSICAL buildings (= in the style of ancient Greece or Rome) for decoration, or standing alone as a MONUMENT (= a symbol of respect for a special person or event): *The roof of the temple was held up by a row of thick stone columns.* ◦ *Nelson's Column in Trafalgar Square* → See also **spinal column** **5 column of sth** something with a tall narrow shape: *A column of smoke rose from the chimney.* **6** a line of moving people or vehicles: *a column of refugees*

columnist /ˈkɒl.əm.nɪst/ (US) /ˈkɑː.ləm.nɪst/ **noun** [C] someone who writes a regular article for a newspaper or magazine: *a gossip/sports columnist* ◦ *She's a columnist for USA Today.*

com- /kɒm-/ (US) /kɑːm-/ **prefix** together; with: *combination* ◦ *community* ◦ *companions*

coma /ˈkəʊ.mə/ (US) /ˈkoʊ-/ **noun** [C] a state in which a person is unconscious and cannot be woken, caused by damage to the brain after an accident or illness: *He's been **in** a coma for the past six weeks.* ◦ *She **went into** a deep coma after taking an overdose of sleeping pills.*

comatose /ˈkəʊ.mə.təʊs/ (US) /ˈkoʊ.mə.toʊs/ **adj** **1** specialized in a coma **2** informal very tired or in a deep sleep because of extreme tiredness, hard work, or too much alcohol: *By midnight I was virtually comatose.*

comb /kəʊm/ (US) /koʊm/ **noun; verb**

▸**noun** [C] **FOR HAIR** ▷ **1** A2 a flat piece of plastic, wood or metal with a thin row of long, narrow parts along one side, which you use to tidy and arrange your hair **2** a small comb-shaped object which women put in their hair to hold their hair away from their face or for decoration **CHICKEN** ▷ **3** a soft red growth on a chicken's head → Synonym **cockscomb**

▸**verb** [T] **TIDY HAIR** ▷ **1** B1 to tidy your hair using a comb: *She combed her hair and put on some lipstick.* ◦ *I've been trying to comb **out** (= remove using a comb) the knots in her hair.* **SEARCH** ▷ **2** to search a place or an area very carefully in order to find something: *The police combed the whole area **for** evidence.* ◦ *Investigators combed **through** the wreckage.*

combat **noun; verb**

▸**noun** /ˈkɒm.bæt/ (US) /ˈkɑːm-/ **1** C2 [C or U] a fight, especially during a war: *There was fierce combat **between** the two sides.* ◦ *No one knew how many troops had died **in** combat.* ◦ *The soldiers were engaged in **hand-to-hand** combat.* ◦ ***armed** combat (= fighting with weapons)* ◦ ***unarmed** combat (= fighting without weapons)* **2** [C] a fight between two people or things: *The film explores the combat **between** good and evil.*

▸**verb** [T] /kəmˈbæt/ (US) /ˈkɑːm.bæt/ (**-tt-** or **-t-**) C2 to try to stop something unpleasant or harmful from happening or increasing: *to combat crime/terrorism/inflation/disease* ◦ *The government is spending millions of dollars in its attempt to combat drug abuse.* ◦ *I have to combat this constant desire to eat chocolate.*

combatant /ˈkɒm.bə.tᵊnt/ (US) /ˈkɑːm.bə.tᵊnt/ **noun** [C] formal a person who fights in a war

combative /ˈkɒm.bə.tɪv/ (US) /ˈkɑːm.bə.t̬ɪv/ **adj** formal eager to fight or argue: *The prime minister was in a combative mood, twice accusing the opposition of gross incompetence.*

ˈcombat ˌtrousers **noun** [plural] (also **combats**) loose trousers made of strong material with large pockets on the outside of the legs

combi **noun** [C] South African English a **kombi**

combination /ˌkɒm.bɪˈneɪ.ʃᵊn/ (US) /ˌkɑːm-/ **noun** **1** B2 [C or U] the mixture you get when two or more things are combined: *Strawberries and cream – a perfect combination.* ◦ *A combination of tiredness and boredom caused me to fall asleep.* ◦ *This drug can be safely used **in** combination **with** other medicines.* ◦ *Her experience and energy are a **winning** combination (= a successful mixture) in business.* **2** [C] specialized an arrangement in a different order: *From the letters X Y Z, we can get three combinations of two letters: XY, XZ, and YZ.* **3** [C] a set of letters or numbers in a particular order that can be used to open some types of locks: *a combination **lock***

combine **verb; noun**

▸**verb** /kəmˈbaɪn/ **1** B2 [I or T] to (cause to) exist together, or join together to make a single thing or group: *None of us has much money so let's combine what we've got.* ◦ *Sickness, **combined with** (= together with) terrible weather, contrived to ruin the trip.* ◦ *The two countries combined **against** their common enemy.* ◦ [+ to infinitive] *These normally harmless substances combine **to** form a highly poisonous gas.* **2** [T] If someone combines two or more qualities, they have both of those qualities: *As a writer, he combined wit **and/with** passion.* **3** [T] to do two activities at the same time: *She manages to successfully combine family life **and/with** a career.*

▸**noun** /ˈkɒm.baɪn/ (US) /ˈkɑːm-/ **GROUP** ▷ **1** [C, + sing/pl verb] a group of people or organizations acting together in business: *a Japanese industrial combine* **MACHINE** ▷ **2** [C] (also **combine harvester**) a large farming machine which cuts the plant, separates the seed from the stem, and cleans the grain as it moves across a field

comˈbining ˌform **noun** [C] specialized a word or group of letters that is added to the beginning or end of words to change or add meaning: *The combining form 'Anglo' combines to make various words, including Anglo-American and Anglophile.*

combo /ˈkɒm.bəʊ/ (US) /ˈkɑːm.boʊ/ **noun** (plural **combos**) informal **MUSICIANS** ▷ **1** [C, + sing/pl verb] a small group of musicians who play dance and JAZZ music **MIXTURE** ▷ **2** [C] a combination of different things: *That's a funny combo – pink and orange.* ◦ *I'll have the burrito and taco combo, please.*

ˈcomb-ˌover **noun** [C] a hairstyle in which a man brushes hair from the side of his head across the top of his head because he has no hair there

combustible /kəmˈbʌs.tɪ.bl/ **adj** formal able to burn easily: *Wood and coal are both combustible substances.*

combustion /kəmˈbʌs.tʃᵊn/ **noun** [U] **1** the process of burning **2** specialized the chemical process in which substances mix with OXYGEN in the air to produce heat and light

comˈbustion ˌchamber **noun** [C] a closed space in which combustion happens

come /kʌm/ verb; noun

▸verb (**came**, **come**) **MOVE TO SPEAKER** ▷ **1** A1 [I] to move or travel towards the speaker or with the speaker: *Are you coming* ***with*** *me?* ◦ *There's a car coming!* ◦ *Can you come* ***to*** *my party?* ◦ ***Here*** *comes Adam.* ◦ *She's come 500 km (= has travelled 500 km) to be here with us tonight.* ◦ *If you're ever in Dublin, come* ***and*** *visit us.* ◦ *We came* ***by*** *car.* ◦ *Your father will come* ***for*** *(= to collect) you at four o'clock.* ◦ *Come forward a bit and stand on the line.* ◦ *I've come straight* ***from*** *the airport.* ◦ *The door opened and a nurse came* ***into*** *the room.* ◦ [+ to infinitive] *A man's coming* ***to*** *mend the boiler this afternoon.* ◦ *As he came towards me, I could see he'd been crying.* ◦ *He thought we'd been picking his apples and came* ***after*** *(= chased) us with a stick.* ◦ [+ -ing verb] *He came rush****ing*** *over when I fell.*

> **! Common mistake: come**
>
> **Remember: come** is used to talk about movement towards where the speaker is:
>
> *He came to my office today to ask me for help.*
>
> To talk about movement to another place, away from the speaker, don't say 'come', say **go**:
>
> ~~*If I came there again one day, I would probably be disappointed.*~~
>
> *If I went there again one day, I would probably be disappointed.*

> **! Common mistake: come**
>
> **Warning:** choose the correct preposition!
>
> To talk about moving towards a town, country, etc. where the speaker is or going there with the speaker, don't say 'come in/at', say **come to** a town, country, etc.:
>
> ~~*Next time you come in London please stay at my house.*~~
>
> *Next time you come to London please stay at my house.*

MOVE TO LISTENER ▷ **2** A1 [I] to move or travel in the direction of the person being spoken to: *'Sal, are you ready?' 'Coming.'* ◦ *I'll come* ***and*** *pick you up in the car if you like.* ◦ *I've come* ***for*** *(= come to collect) your census form.* ◦ [+ to infinitive] *I've come* ***to*** *read the gas meter.* **ARRIVE** ▷ **3** A1 [I] to get to a particular place: *Has she come yet?* ◦ *When does the post come?* ◦ *Hasn't his train come* ***in*** *yet?* **LEAVE** ▷ **4** [I + adv/prep] to leave a place: *I had to come* ***away from*** *the party early.* ◦ *The police watched him come* ***out of*** *the house.* **DIFFERENT STATE** ▷ **5** C2 [L] to change or develop so as to be in a different position or condition: *Those pictures will have to come* ***down*** *(= be removed from the wall).* ◦ *He pulled the knob and it just came* ***off*** *(in his hand).* ◦ *How many times have you come* ***off*** *that horse?* ◦ *Two of his teeth came* ***out*** *after he got hit in the face.* ◦ *Can you get this cork to come* ***out of*** *the bottle?* ◦ *When does the heating come* ***on*** *(= start working)?* ◦ [+ adj] *A wire has come* ***loose*** *at the back.* ◦ *The door came* ***open*** *for no apparent reason.* **HAPPEN** ▷ **6** B2 [I] to happen: *Spring has come early.* ◦ *The announcement came at a bad time.* ◦ *Her resignation came* ***as*** *quite a shock.* ◦ informal *Come Monday morning (= when it is Monday morning) you'll regret staying up all night.* ◦ *I'm afraid those days are gone and they'll never come* ***again.*** **7 come after, first, last, etc.** B1 to have or achieve a particular position in a race, competition, list, etc.: *She came second* (US *came* ***in*** *second*) *in the 100 metres.* ◦ *Z comes* ***after*** *Y in the alphabet.* ◦ *Which king came* ***after*** *Edward?* ◦ *April comes* ***before*** *May.* ◦ *I know the first verse of the song, but I don't know what comes* ***next.*** **EXIST** ▷ **8** A2 [I + adv/prep, not continuous] to exist or be available: *Do these trousers come* ***in*** *any other colour?* ◦ *Runners come* ***in*** *all shapes and sizes – fat and thin, short and tall.* ◦ *This cuddly baby doll comes* ***with*** *her own blanket and bottle.* ◦ *They're the best sunglasses you can buy, but they* ***don't*** *come* ***cheap*** *(= they are expensive).* **9 come to do sth** C2 to start to do something: *I've come to like her over the months.* ◦ *It used to hold paper bags, but gradually came to be used for magazines.* ◦ *How did that phrase come to mean (= develop so that it means) that?* **SEX** ▷ **10** [I] to have an ORGASM

> **! Common mistake: come**
>
> **Warning:** Check your verb endings!
>
> Many learners make mistakes when using **come** in the **-ing** form. Don't write 'comming' or 'comeing', write **coming**.

IDIOMS **as it comes** UK If someone asks how they should prepare your drink and you say as it comes, you mean that any way they prepare it will be acceptable: *'How do you like your coffee?' 'Oh, as it comes.'* • **be as crazy, rich, etc. as they come** to be very crazy, rich, etc.: *He's as mean as they come.* • **come again?** informal used to ask someone to repeat something that you have not heard or understood • **come and go** to exist or happen somewhere for a short time and then go away: *The feeling of nausea comes and goes.* • **come down on sb like a ton of bricks** to punish someone very quickly and severely: *Do that once more and I'll come down on you like a ton of bricks!* • **come from behind** to succeed in winning after being in a losing position in a game: *England came from behind to beat Scotland 2–1.* • **come off it!** informal used to tell someone that you do not believe what they are saying is true, or that you strongly disagree with them: *Ask Simon to cook the meal? Come off it, he can hardly boil an egg!* • **come the sth** disapproving to pretend to be or feel something: *Don't come the poor little innocent* ***with*** *me!* • **come to pass** old use to happen: *It came to pass that their love for each other grew and grew.* • **come to sb's attention/notice** If something comes to your attention, you notice it: *It has recently come to my attention that some of the younger boys are not using the toilets for the proper purpose.* • **come to that** informal in fact: *'I owe you a fiver, don't I?' 'Yes, and come to that, you never paid me back the other money I lent you.'* • **come what may** whatever happens: *I shall be there tonight come what may.* ◦ *It's always good to know that, come what may, your job is safe.* • **the days/week(s)/year(s) to come** the following or next days/week(s)/year(s): *What are your plans for the year to come (= next year)?* • **had it coming (to you)** informal If someone had it coming, something bad happened to them that they deserved: *He's been sacked but, with all that time he took off, he had it coming really.* • **have sth coming out of your ears** informal to have more of something than you want or need: *He's going to have money coming out of his ears if this deal comes off.* • **how come?** informal C1 used to ask how or why something has happened: *So how come you missed the train?* ◦ *'We had to stop in Birmingham.' 'How come?'* • **not know whether you are coming or going** to be in a very confused state: *I'm so busy, I don't know whether I'm coming or going.*

PHRASAL VERBS **come about** C2 to happen, or start to happen: *How did the problem come about in the first place?* • **come across sth** B2 to find something by chance: *He came across some of his old love letters in his wife's desk.* • **come across** **BEHAVE** ▷ **1** C1 to behave in a way that makes people believe that you have a particular characteristic: *She comes across really well (= creates a positive image) on television.* ◦ *He comes across* ***as*** *a bit of a bore in interview.* **EXPRESS** ▷ **2** Ⓒ2 If an idea or emotion comes across in writing, film, music, or when someone is speaking, it is expressed clearly and people notice it: *What comes across in his later poetry is a great sense of sadness.* • **come along ARRIVE** ▷ **1** Ⓑ2 to arrive or appear at a place: *Go now and I'll come along later.* ◦ *You wait half an hour for a bus, then three come along at once!* **GO WITH SOMEONE** ▷ **2** Ⓑ1 to go somewhere with someone: *We're going to the cinema. Do you want to come along?* **3** UK used to tell someone to hurry: *Come along – we don't want to be late!* **EXIST** ▷ **4** Ⓒ2 to start to exist: *I gave up climbing when my first child came along.* **DEVELOP** ▷ **5** Ⓒ2 If something is coming along, it is developing or improving: *Hassan's English is really coming along.* • **come apart** Ⓒ2 to separate into several pieces: *I picked up the book and it came apart in my hands.* ◦ *My boots are coming apart at the seams.* • **come around** US for **come round** • **come at sb** to move towards someone in order to attack them: *He came at me* ***with*** *a knife.* • **come away** If something comes away from something else, it becomes separated from it: *I just opened the drawer as usual and the handle came away* ***in my hand****.* ◦ *The paper has started to come away* ***from*** *the walls.* • **come back RETURN** ▷ **1** Ⓐ2 to return to a place: *I'll come back and pick you up in half an hour.* ◦ *We've just come back* ***from*** *Amsterdam.* **FASHION** ▷ **2** If a style or a fashion comes back, it becomes popular again after being unpopular for a period of time: *Padded shoulders are coming back, apparently.* ◦ *Long hair on men seems to be coming back* ***into fashion****.* • **come back to sb** If something comes back to you, you start to remember it: *I can't think of her name – it'll come back to me later.* ◦ *It's all coming back to me!* • **come before sth/sb IMPORTANCE** ▷ **1** to be more important than, or to be treated as more important than, another thing or person: *My children will always come before my career.* **COURT** ▷ **2** legal If a legal case comes before a law court or a judge, it is dealt with by them, and when someone comes before a court or judge, they are present while their case is dealt with. • **come between sb** Ⓒ2 If something comes between two people, it harms their relationship: *Don't let one little quarrel come between you.* • **come between sth** to stop someone from doing something that they like doing: *Nothing comes between Jim and his food.* • **come by sth** Ⓒ2 to get something, using effort, by chance or in a way that has not been explained: *Cheap organic food is still difficult to come by.* ◦ *I'd like to know how she came by that black eye.* • **come by (somewhere)** to visit a place for a short time, often when you are going somewhere else: *I'll come by (the office/your house) one day this week and we can have a chat.* • **come down LAND** ▷ **1** Ⓑ2 to fall and land on the ground: *A lot of trees came down in the storm.* ◦ *Our plane came down in a field.* ◦ *The snow came down during the night.* **LOWER LEVEL** ▷ **2** Ⓑ2 If a price or a level comes down, it becomes lower: *House prices have come down recently.* ◦ *Inflation is coming down.* **3** informal to feel less excited after a very enjoyable experience: *The whole weekend was so wonderful I haven't come down yet.* **SUPPORT** ▷ **4** [+ adv/prep] to decide that you support a particular person or side in an argument, etc.: *The government has come down* ***on the side of*** *military action.* **DRUGS** ▷ **5** informal If a person comes down from a drug, they stop feeling its effects. **UNIVERSITY** ▷ **6** UK old-fashioned If you come down (from a college or university, especially Oxford or Cambridge University), you leave your studies either permanently or for a short time. **TRAVEL SOUTH** ▷ **7** to go to a place that is south of where you live: *My boyfriend's coming down* ***from*** *Scotland this weekend.* ◦ *They don't come down* ***to*** *London much because it's too tiring with the kids.* • **come down on sb/sth** to punish or criticize a person or activity very strongly: *They're coming down* ***heavily*** *on people* ***for*** *not paying their licence fees.* ◦ *The authorities plan to come down* ***hard*** *on truancy in future.* • **come down to sth** Ⓒ2 If a situation or decision comes down to something, that is the thing that influences it most: *What* ***it all*** *comes down to is your incredible insecurity.* ◦ [+ question word] *Eventually our choice of hotel will come down to how much we can afford.* • **come down with sth** Ⓑ2 to start to suffer from an illness, especially one that is not serious: *I think I'm coming down with flu.* • **come forward** to offer to give help or information: *Nobody has yet come forward* ***with*** *any information relating to the girl's death.* • **come from somewhere/sth** Ⓐ1 to be born, got from, or made in a particular place: *She comes from Italy.* ◦ *Some of the best wines come from France.* ◦ *Does that quote come from Shakespeare?* ◦ *She could hear banging coming from the room upstairs.* ◦ *Where will the money for the project come from?* • **come from sth** to be caused by something: *'I feel awful.' 'That comes from eating too much.'* • **come in ENTER** ▷ **1** Ⓐ2 to enter a room or building: *Do you want to come in for a cup of tea?* ◦ *Hi, come in – lovely to see you!* **FASHION** ▷ **2** If a fashion or product comes in, it becomes available or popular: *Flared trousers first came in during the 1970s.* **3 come in handy, useful, etc.** to be useful for a particular purpose: *Keep it, it might come in useful.* ◦ *The money will come in handy when I want to travel.* **BE RECEIVED** ▷ **4** When news or information comes in, it is received: *Reports are just coming in of a major accident on the motorway.* **5** If you have money coming in, you receive it as income: *With Dave unemployed, we haven't got much money coming in at the moment.* **BE INVOLVED** ▷ **6** Ⓒ2 informal to become involved in a situation, story, or plan: *We need expert advice, and that's where you come in.* **7 come in first, second, etc.** to finish a race in first, second, etc. position **SEA** ▷ **8** When the sea or the TIDE comes in, the water moves forwards to cover more of the beach. → Compare **go out** • **come in for sth** Ⓒ2 to receive blame or criticism: *The director has come in for a lot of criticism over his handling of the affair.* • **come into sth MONEY** ▷ **1** Ⓒ2 If someone comes into money, property, or a title, they receive it as a result of the death of a relation: *She came into a bit of money when her grandfather died.* **INFLUENCE** ▷ **2** If a particular emotion or quality comes into a situation, it influences that situation: *She married for money – love didn't come into* ***it****.*

> **! Note:**
> This sense is usually used in negative sentences.

• **come of sth** to happen as a result of something: *Did anything come of all those job applications?* • **come off 1** Ⓒ1 informal to happen as planned or to succeed: *There was some sort of property deal that didn't come off.* ◦ *I tried telling a few jokes but they didn't come off* (*= no one laughed*). **2 come off better/worse/badly/well** to finish in a particular condition after a fight, argument, etc., especially compared to someone else: *The smaller dog actually came off better, with only a few scratches.* ◦ *I always come off worse when we argue.* • **come off sth STOP USING** ▷ **1** mainly UK If you come off medicine or drugs, you stop using them:

C

He's come off the tablets because they were making him dizzy. **COMPLETE** ▷ **2** US to have recently finished a period of time when something very successful or very difficult happened: *The company was coming off one of its best years ever.* • **come on START** ▷ **1** C1 to start to happen or work: *The heating comes on at six in the morning.* **2** If you have got an illness coming on, it is starting gradually: *I think I've got a cold coming on.* **3** UK informal If a woman comes on, her period (= the blood coming from the WOMB that happens every month) starts. **ENCOURAGE** ▷ **4** B1 said to encourage someone to do something, especially to hurry or try harder, or to tell you something: *Come on – we're going to be late if you don't hurry!* ◦ *Come on, Helen, you can tell me. I won't tell anyone.* **SEXUAL INTEREST** ▷ **5** informal to make your sexual interest known to someone: *Then his wife left the room and he started coming on **to** me.* ◦ *She was coming on **strong** and, naturally, I responded.* **APPEAR** ▷ **6** (of an actor) to walk onto the stage: *There was great applause when the Russian ballerina came on.* **NOT BELIEVE** ▷ **7** informal used to tell someone that you do not believe them or that you disagree with them, or to show that you are angry with them: *Oh come on, Ian, you made the same excuse last week!* • **come on/along** C2 to make progress: *Your piano playing has really come on since I last heard you play.* ◦ *How's your English coming on?* • **come out SOCIAL EVENT** ▷ **1** UK to go somewhere with someone for a social event: *Would you like to come out for a drink sometime?* **BE PUBLISHED** ▷ **2** B1 If a book, record, film, etc. comes out, it becomes available for people to buy or see: *When does their new album come out?* **APPEAR** ▷ **3** B1 When the sun, moon, or stars come out, they appear in the sky: *The clouds finally parted and the sun came out.* **BECOME KNOWN** ▷ **4** C2 If something comes out, it becomes known publicly after it has been kept secret: *After her death, **it** came out **that** she'd lied about her age.* ◦ *When the truth came out, there was public outrage.* **5** B2 If information or results come out, they are given to people: *The exam results come out in August.* **6** C2 to tell people that you are gay, often after having kept this secret for some time **RESULT** ▷ **7** [+ adv/prep or adjective] If you describe how something or someone comes out at the end of a process or activity, you say what condition they are in or what they have achieved: *She came out **of** the divorce settlement a rich woman.* ◦ *These figures have come out wrong! I don't understand it.* ◦ *Your painting has come out really well.* ◦ *He hasn't exactly come out **of** the scandal **with** his reputation enhanced.* **BE REMOVED** ▷ **8** C2 If dirt or a mark comes out, it disappears from something when it is cleaned: *Did the red wine stain come out?* **PHOTO** ▷ **9** If a photo or part of a photo comes out, the picture can be seen clearly: *The photos didn't come out because the room was so dark.* ◦ *He's in the picture, but his face hasn't come out very clearly.* **GIVE OPINION** ▷ **10** [+ adv/prep] to express an opinion: *In the survey politicians came out overwhelmingly **in favour of** capital punishment.* ◦ *Some of the members supported the changes, but the majority came out **against**.* **BE SAID** ▷ **11** C2 If something you say comes out in a particular way, that is how you say it: *I didn't mean to be rude – it just came out like that.* ◦ *When I tried to tell her that I loved her it came out **all wrong**.* **STOP WORK** ▷ **12** UK If workers come out, they stop working because of a disagreement: *The postal workers have come out in support of their pay claim.* **OPEN** ▷ **13** When flowers come out, they open: *Daffodils come out in spring.* • **come out in sth** If you come out in something, such as spots, they appear on your skin: *This heat has made me come out in an itchy red rash.* • **come out of sth** C2 If something comes out of a process or event, it is one of the results: *I hope something good can come out of this mess.* • **come out with sth** to say something suddenly and unexpectedly: *She comes out with some good ideas though.* • **come over SEEM** ▷ **1** C2 to seem to be a particular type of person: *I watched the interview and felt he came over **as** quite arrogant.* **MOVE** ▷ **2** C1 to come to a place, move from one place to another, or move towards someone: *Come over here!* ◦ *Are your family coming over from Greece for the wedding?* **FEEL** ▷ **3** [L only + adj] UK to be influenced suddenly and unexpectedly by a strange feeling: *I stood up too quickly and came over **all** dizzy/faint/peculiar.* • **come over sb** C1 to influence someone suddenly to behave in a particular way: *I'm sorry! That was a stupid thing to say – I don't know **what** came over me.* ◦ humorous *He gave you a present! **What's** come over him?* • **come round** UK (US **come around**) **VISIT** ▷ **1** A2 to visit someone in their home: *Come round tonight and we'll watch a video.* **CHANGE YOUR MIND** ▷ **2** C2 to change your opinion of something, often influenced by another person's opinion: *He'll come round **to** my point of view, given a bit of time.* ◦ *Do you still dislike your office, or have you come round **to** think**ing** it's all right?* **HAPPEN** ▷ **3** If an event that happens regularly comes round/around, it happens at its usual time: *Christmas comes round so quickly!* **BECOME CONSCIOUS** ▷ **4** C1 to become conscious again after an accident or operation: *She hasn't come round **from** the anaesthetic yet.* • **come through INFORMATION** ▷ **1** C2 If a piece of information or a document comes through, you receive it: *Have the test results come through yet?* ◦ *My visa still hasn't come through.* **EMOTION** ▷ **2** If an emotion comes through, other people can notice it: *His nervousness came through when he spoke.* • **come through (sth)** C2 to manage to get to the end of a difficult or dangerous situation: *We've had some hard times, but we've come through.* • **come to** to become conscious again after an accident or operation • **come to sb** If a thought or idea comes to you, you suddenly remember or start to think about it: *I can't remember his name – it'll come to me in a minute.* • **come to sth TOTAL** ▷ **1** B2 to be a particular total when numbers or amounts are added together: *That comes to £25.* **REACH** ▷ **2** B2 to reach a particular point or state: *His hair comes right **down** to his shoulders.* ◦ *He's tiny, he doesn't even come **up** to my chest!* ◦ *And now I come to (= I will mention) my main point.* ◦ *The war had just come to **an end** (= ended).* ◦ *The car spun off the road, turned over twice and came to **rest** (= stopped moving) in a field.* ◦ *We may have to sell the house, but I hope it won't come to **that**.* **3 come to nothing** If plans come to nothing, they fail: *So much effort and planning and it's all come to nothing.* **DECIDE** ▷ **4** If you come to a decision, arrangement, etc., you make a decision or decide what to think about something: *We haven't come to a decision on the matter yet.* ◦ *Have you come to any conclusions about the story yet?* • **come under sth EXPERIENCE** ▷ **1** C1 If you come under something, you suddenly experience or suffer it: *Our armies have come under heavy bombardment.* ◦ *The government are coming under pressure to change the law.* **IN A BOOK** ▷ **2** C1 If a piece of information comes under a particular part of a list, book, or collection of things, you can find it in that part: *Swimming pools usually come under 'leisure centres' in the phone directory.* **IN AN ORGANIZATION** ▷ **3** to be controlled or dealt with by an official organization or a particular part of it: *Playground*

C

guidelines come under the Department of Health and Safety. • **come up** MOVE TOWARDS ▷ **1** B2 to move towards someone: *A young girl came up **to** me and asked for money.* BE MENTIONED ▷ **2** B2 to be mentioned or talked about in conversation: *What points came up at the meeting?* APPEAR ▷ **3** B2 When the sun or moon comes up, it rises. **4** C1 If information comes up on a computer screen, it appears there. BECOME AVAILABLE ▷ **5** C1 If a job or opportunity comes up, it becomes available: *A position has come up in the accounts department.* HAPPEN ▷ **6** C1 to happen, usually unexpectedly: *I've got to go – something has just come up at home and I'm needed there.* **7 be coming up** B2 to be happening soon: *My exams are coming up soon.* • **come up against sth** C1 to have to deal with a problem: *If you come up against difficulties, let me know and I'll help out.* • **come up to sth** to reach the usual or necessary standard: *The essay didn't come up to his usual standards.* ◦ *The food didn't come up to my expectations.* • **come up with sth** B2 to suggest or think of an idea or plan: *She's come up with some amazing scheme to double her income.* • **come upon sb/sth** formal to find something or meet someone unexpectedly: *I came upon this book in the attic – would you like it?*

▸noun [U] slang **semen** (= the liquid containing sperm)

comeback /ˈkʌm.bæk/ **noun** [C] C1 an attempt to become famous, powerful, or important again after a period of being much less famous, etc.: *She's trying to **make a** comeback with her first album for 20 years.*

comedian /kəˈmiː.di.ən/ **noun** [C] (female also **comedienne** /kəˌmiː.diˈen/) B2 a person whose job is to make people laugh by telling jokes and funny stories or by copying the behaviour or speech of famous people: *a stand-up comedian*

comedic /kəˈmiː.dɪk/ **adj** relating to or involving comedy: *a comedic actor/actress* ◦ *His comedic **timing** is perfect.* • **comedically** /-dɪ.kəl.i/ **adv**

comedown /ˈkʌm.daʊn/ **noun** [S] informal a situation that is not as good as the one you were in before: *These days he plays to audiences of a hundred or fewer which is **a bit of a** comedown after Wembley Stadium.*

comedy /ˈkɒm.ə.di/ US /ˈkɑː.mə-/ **noun** **1** B1 [C] a (type of) film, play, or book that is intentionally funny either in its characters or its action: *His latest film is described as a 'romantic comedy'.* ◦ *I prefer Shakespeare's comedies to his tragedies.* **2** [U] the humorous part of a situation: *The vicar's forgetting his lines in the middle of the speech provided some good comedy.* **3 comedy of manners** a type of comedy in which the social behaviour of a particular group of people is made to appear silly

ˌcome-ˈhither **adj** [before noun] old-fashioned informal describes a way of looking at someone that shows you are sexually interested in them: *come-hither eyes*

comely /ˈkʌm.li/ **adj** old-fashioned or literary describes a woman who is attractive in appearance

ˈcome-on **noun** [C] informal **1** a remark that shows someone that you are sexually interested in them: *He was **giving me the** come-on.* **2** something which someone who is selling a product uses to interest a customer

ˈcome-on ˌline **noun** [C] US for **chat-up line**

comestibles /kəˈmes.tɪ.blz/ **noun** [plural] formal things that are for eating

comet /ˈkɒm.ɪt/ US /ˈkɑː.mɪt/ **noun** [C] an object that moves around the sun, usually at a great distance from it, that is seen on rare occasions from Earth as a bright line in the sky

comeuppance /kʌmˈʌp.əns/, /kəˈmʌp-/ **noun** [S] informal humorous a person's bad luck that is considered to be a fair and deserved punishment for something bad that they have done: *She'll **get** her comeuppance.*

comfort /ˈkʌm.fət/ US /-fɚt/ **noun; verb**

▸noun NO PAIN ▷ **1** B1 [U] a pleasant feeling of being relaxed and free from pain: *She evidently dresses **for** comfort.* ◦ *It's a little too hot for comfort.* ◦ *Now you can watch the latest films **in the** comfort **of** your own room.* FOR SADNESS ▷ **2** C2 [C or U] the state of feeling better after feeling sad or worried, or something that makes you feel better in this way: *The letters that people wrote after his death gave me a lot of comfort.* ◦ *It's some comfort to his wife (= it makes her feel less sad) to know that he died instantly and didn't suffer.* ◦ *I've got to take an exam too, **if it's** any comfort (= if it makes you feel better to know that we share the same problem or bad luck).* ◦ *I know she goes out a lot at night, but I **draw/take** comfort **from** the fact that she's always with friends.* ◦ *He's a great comfort **to** his mother.* ENOUGH MONEY ▷ **3** C2 [U] the state of having a pleasant life with enough money for everything that you need: *He could retire now and **live in** comfort for the rest of his life.* PLEASANT THING ▷ **4** C1 [C usually plural] something that makes your life easy and pleasant: *After the trip, it was nice getting back to a few **home** comforts.* ◦ *She's always liked her **creature** comforts (= the type of pleasure found in the house, for example warmth, food, etc.).*

▸verb [T] C2 to make someone feel better when they are sad or worried: *The girl's mother was at home today, being comforted by relatives.*

> **!** Common mistake: **comfortable**
> **Warning:** Check your spelling!
> **Comfortable** is one of the 50 words most often spelled wrongly by learners. Remember: the correct spelling has 'm', and not 'n'.

comfortable /ˈkʌm.fə.tə.bl/ US /-fɚ.t̬ə-/ **adj** CLOTHES/FURNITURE ▷ **1** A2 describes furniture and clothes that provide a pleasant feeling and that do not give you any physical problems: *a comfortable bed/sofa* ◦ *comfortable shoes/trousers* PHYSICALLY OKAY ▷ **2** B1 relaxed and free from pain: *Are you comfortable or shall I turn the heat down?* ◦ *I don't feel comfortable in high heels.* ◦ *Do sit down and **make yourself** comfortable.* **3** describes an ill or injured person in hospital who is not feeling too much pain NO PROBLEMS ▷ **4** B2 If you are comfortable with a situation, you are not worried about it: *I'm not comfortable **with** the idea of leaving her on her own.* ENOUGH MONEY ▷ **5** C2 having enough money for a good standard of living: *They're not fabulously rich or anything, but they're quite comfortable.* EASY WIN ▷ **6** If you win a game or competition by a comfortable amount, you win easily: *a comfortable lead/victory*

comfortably /ˈkʌmf.tə.bli/ **adv** **1** in a comfortable way: *Are you sitting comfortably? Then I'll begin.* **2** without financial or other problems: *We could live fairly comfortably on Edward's salary.* **3 comfortably off** having enough money to lead a good life

ˈcomfort ˌbreak **noun** [C] (also **ˈcomfort ˌstop**) UK a short pause in a meeting to allow people to go to a toilet: *Shall we have a comfort break?*

ˈcomfort ˌeating **noun** [U] eating because you are feeling worried or upset and not because you are hungry • **ˈcomfort-ˌeat verb** [I]

comforter /ˈkʌm.fə.tər/ US /-t̬ɚ/ **noun** [C] US (UK

duvet) a large soft flat bag filled with feathers or artificial material used on a bed

ˈcomfort ˌfood noun [C or U] the type of food which people eat when they are sad or worried, often sweet food or food that people ate as children

C

comforting /ˈkʌm.fə.tɪŋ/ US /-fɚ.t̬ɪŋ/ **adj** C2 making you feel less sad or worried: *I found her words very comforting.* ◦ *Hot soup is very comforting on a cold winter's day.*

comfortingly /ˈkʌm.fə.tɪŋ.li/ US /-fɚ.t̬ɪŋ-/ **adv** in a way that makes you feel less sad or worried: *'It'll be all right,' she said comfortingly.*

comfortless /ˈkʌm.fət.ləs/ US /-fɚt-/ **adj** formal without anything that gives physical comfort

ˈcomfort ˌstation noun [C] US old-fashioned a public toilet

ˈcomfort ˌstop noun [C] UK a short pause in a journey to allow passengers to go to a toilet

ˈcomfort ˌzone noun [C] a situation in which you feel comfortable and in which your ability and determination are not being tested: *Rock climbing pushes many people beyond their comfort zones.*

comfy /ˈkʌm.fi/ **adj** informal for comfortable: *a comfy chair*

comic /ˈkɒm.ɪk/ US /ˈkɑː.mɪk/ **adj; noun**

▸**adj** B1 funny and making you want to laugh: *a comic actor/performance*

▸**noun** [C] **MAGAZINE** ▷ **1** A2 (US also **comic book**) a magazine, especially for children, which contains a set of stories told in pictures with a small amount of writing **PERSON** ▷ **2** someone who entertains people by telling jokes

comical /ˈkɒm.ɪ.kəl/ US /ˈkɑː.mɪ-/ **adj** funny in a strange or silly way: *He looked so comical in that hat.* • **comically adv**

ˌcomic ˈopera noun [C or U] a play that is humorous and in which there is a lot of music and singing

ˈcomic ˌstrip noun [C] (also **carˈtoon ˌstrip**) a short series of funny drawings with a small amount of writing, often published in a newspaper

coming /ˈkʌm.ɪŋ/ **adj** [before noun] happening soon: *We look forward to greater success in the coming year.* ◦ *I'll be back* ***this*** *coming Friday.*

ˌcoming of ˈage noun [S] **1** Someone's coming of age is the time when they legally become an adult and are old enough to vote. **2** the time when something starts to become successful: *the coming of age of democracy in the country* • **ˌcoming-of-ˈage adj** [before noun] done to celebrate the fact that someone is legally an adult and old enough to vote: *a coming-of-age party*

comings /ˈkʌm.ɪŋz/ **noun** [plural] **the comings and goings** the movements of people arriving at places and leaving places: *I sometimes just look out the window and watch the comings and goings of everyone in the street.*

comma /ˈkɒm.ə/ US /ˈkɑː.mə/ **noun** [C] B1 the symbol , used in writing to separate parts of a sentence showing a slight pause, or to separate the single things in a list

command /kəˈmɑːnd/ US /-ˈmænd/ **noun; verb**

▸**noun ORDER** ▷ **1** B2 [C] an order, especially one given by a soldier: *You will run forward* ***at*** *(= when you hear) my command.* ◦ *When I* ***give*** *the command, fire!* ◦ *He hated being in the army because he had to* ***obey*** *commands.* **2** C2 [U] control over someone or something and responsibility for them: *Colonel Sailing* ***has*** *command* ***over/is in*** *command* ***of*** *the Guards Regiment.* ◦ *Lee* ***took*** *command* ***of*** *the Confederate Army in 1862.* ◦ *The soldiers were* ***under the*** *command* ***of*** *a tough sergeant major.* **COMPUTER** ▷ **3** C1 [C] an instruction to a computer to perform a particular action **KNOWLEDGE** ▷ **4** B2 [S or U] a great knowledge of a subject and an ability to use that knowledge: *She* ***has an*** *impressive command* ***of*** *the English language.* **VIEW** ▷ **5** [S] formal a view: *the castle's position with its command of the surrounding countryside*

IDIOMS **at your command 1** If you have particular qualities at your command, you are able to use them effectively: *As a writer, she has both style and humour at her command.* **2** humorous If someone says that they are at your command, they mean they are willing to do what you ask: *'I can't reach my zip – could you unfasten it, please?' 'I'm at your command!'* • **be in command (of yourself)** to be calm and completely in control of your behaviour and emotions: *Suntanned and relaxed, looking calmly about the room, he appeared completely in command.*

▸**verb ORDER** ▷ **1** [I or T] to give someone an order: [+ to infinitive] *The officer commanded his men* ***to*** *shoot.* ◦ [+ that] *He commanded* ***that*** *the troops (should) cross the water.* **2** [I or T] to control someone or something and tell them what to do: *Colonel Sailing commands the Guards Regiment.* **RECEIVE** ▷ **3** [T] to deserve and get something good, such as attention, respect, or a lot of money: *She was one of those teachers who just commanded* ***respect.*** ◦ *She commands one of the highest fees per film in Hollywood.* **VIEW** ▷ **4** [T] formal to give a view: *The master bedroom commands a* ***view*** *of rolling green hills.*

Command /kəˈmɑːnd/ US /-ˈmænd/ **noun** [C] a group of soldiers or an area controlled by a commander

commandant /ˈkɒm.ən.dænt/ US /ˈkɑː-/ **noun** [C] an officer who is in charge of a military organization or building, such as a prison for soldiers used during a war

commandeer /ˌkɒm.ənˈdɪəʳ/ US /ˌkɑː.mənˈdɪr/ **verb** [T] to take possession of or control private property by force or for military use

commander /kəˈmɑːn.dəʳ/ US /-ˈmæn.dɚ/ **noun** [C] C2 (also **Commander**) an officer who is in charge of a military operation, or an officer of a particular rank in the British Royal Navy: *Commander Phillips/James Phillips* ◦ [as form of address] *Yes, Commander.*

comˌmander-in-ˈchief noun [C] (plural **commanders-in-chief**) (abbreviation **ˌC.-in-ˈC.**) a commander in charge of all the armed forces of a country or of all the forces fighting in a particular area or operation

commanding /kəˈmɑːn.dɪŋ/ US /-ˈmæn-/ **adj WITH AUTHORITY** ▷ **1** [before noun] having the authority to give orders: *a commanding officer* **2** describes a voice or manner which seems to have authority and therefore demands your attention: *his commanding presence* **STRONG POSITION** ▷ **3** [before noun] in a very successful position and likely to win or succeed: *He has a commanding* ***lead*** *in the championships.* **4 a commanding position/view** formal a position or view from which a lot of land can be seen: *The house occupies a commanding position at the top of the valley.*

commandment /kəˈmɑːnd.mənt/ US /-ˈmænd-/ **noun** [C] often literary an order, especially one of the TEN COMMANDMENTS

commando /kəˈmɑːn.dəʊ/ US /-ˈmæn.doʊ/ **noun** [C] (plural **commandos** or **commandoes**) (a member of) a small group of soldiers that are specially trained to make attacks on enemy areas that are very dangerous or difficult to attack

IDIOM **go commando** informal to not wear any underwear

comˈmand perˌformance noun [C] a special performance of a play or film that is given because a royal or very important person has asked for it

comme il faut /ˌkɒm.ɪlˈfəʊ/ (US) /ˌkɑː.mɪlˈfoʊ/ adj [after verb] formal behaving or dressing in the right way in public according to formal rules of social behaviour: *Trust me – it's not comme il faut to wear a pink tie to a funeral.*

commemorate /kəˈmem.ə.reɪt/ verb [T] C2 to remember officially and give respect to a great person or event, especially by a public ceremony or by making a STATUE or special building: *Gathered all together in this church, we commemorate those who lost their lives in the war.* ◦ *A statue has been built to commemorate the 100th anniversary of the poet's birthday.*

commemoration /kəˌmem.əˈreɪ.ʃən/ noun [C or U] something that is done to remember officially and give respect to a great person or event: *A set of stamps has been commissioned **in** commemoration **of** Independence Day.* ◦ *Thousands of veterans will take part in a commemoration of the battle.* • **commemorative** /kəˈmem.ər.ə.tɪv/ (US) /-ə.ə.t̬ɪv/ adj *a commemorative statue/stamp/service/plaque*

commence /kəˈmens/ verb [I or T] formal C2 to begin something: *We will commence building work in August of next year.* ◦ *Shall we let the meeting commence?* ◦ [+ -ing verb] *Unfortunately, he commenced speak**ing** before all the guests had finished eating.*

commencement /kəˈmens.mənt/ noun **1** [C or U] formal the beginning of something: *Would passengers please turn off their mobile phones before the commencement of the flight.* **2** [C] US a ceremony at which students formally receive their degree

commend /kəˈmend/ verb [T] to formally praise someone or something: *The judge commended her **for/on** her bravery.* ◦ *For a low-budget film, it has much to commend it (= it deserves praise).* ◦ *It says on the back cover of the book '**highly** commended'.*

commendable /kəˈmen.də.bl/ adj formal deserving praise: *commendable efforts/behaviour/bravery* • **commendably** /-bli/ adv

commendation /ˌkɒm.enˈdeɪ.ʃən/ (US) /ˌkɑː.mən-/ noun [C or U] formal praise, or an official statement which praises someone

commensalism /kəˈmen.səl.ɪ.zəm/ noun [U] specialized a relationship between two SPECIES in which one gets an advantage from living closely with the other and the other is not affected by it

commensurate /kəˈmen.sjər.ət/ (US) /-sjə-/ adj formal in a correct and suitable amount compared to something else: *a salary that is commensurate **with** skills and experience*

comment /ˈkɒm.ent/ (US) /ˈkɑː.ment/ noun; verb
▸noun [C or U] **1** B1 something that you say or write that expresses your opinion: *I don't want any comments **on/about** my new haircut, thank you!* ◦ *He made negative comments to the press.* ◦ *I suppose his criticism was **fair** comment (= a reasonable opinion).* ◦ *She was asked about the pay increase but made **no** comment (= did not give an opinion).* **2 no comment** C2 used to say that you do not want to answer someone's question

> **Word partners for comment noun**
>
> *make* a comment • *pass* comment • *attract/draw/excite* comment • *adverse/caustic/critical/disparaging* comments • *favourable* comments • a *casual/general/passing* comment • *fair* comment • comments *about/on* sth • *without* comment

▸verb [I or T] B2 to make a comment: *My mum always comments **on** what I'm wearing.* ◦ [+ that] *He commented **that** the two essays were rather similar.* ◦ *The official **refused to/declined to** comment on the matter.*

commentary /ˈkɒm.ən.tər.i/ (US) /ˈkɑː.mən.ter-/ noun [C or U] **1** a spoken description of an event on the radio or television that is broadcast as the event happens: *The commentary **on** the Olympic Games was much better on the other channel.* **2** a set of written remarks on an event, book, or person which explains its subject or expresses an opinion on it: *There's good arts coverage in the newspaper, but not much political commentary.* **3 running commentary** (a) continuous description of events as they are happening

ˈcommentary ˌbox noun [C] a room or place for a radio or television REPORTER at a special event, especially a sports competition, from which they report what is happening

commentator /ˈkɒm.ən.teɪ.təʳ/ (US) /ˈkɑː.mən.teɪ.t̬ə/ noun [C] a REPORTER for radio or television who provides a spoken description of and remarks on an event, especially a sports competition, as it happens: *a radio commentator* ◦ *a sports/football commentator.* • **commentate** /-teɪt/ verb [I] *She commentates **on** the tennis each year at Wimbledon.*

commerce /ˈkɒm.ɜːs/ (US) /ˈkɑː.mɝːs/ noun [U] B2 the activities involved in buying and selling things: *the world of commerce and industry*

commercial /kəˈmɜː.ʃəl/ (US) /-ˈmɝː-/ adj; noun
▸adj **1** B2 related to buying and selling things: *a commercial organization/venture/success* ◦ *commercial law* ◦ *The commercial future of the company looks very promising.* **2** disapproving describes a record, film, book, etc. that has been produced with the aim of making money and as a result has little artistic value **3** [before noun] describes a product that can be bought by or is intended to be bought by the general public **4** C2 [before noun] refers to radio or television paid for by advertisements that are broadcast between and during programmes • **commercially** /-i/ adv *Does the market research show that the product will succeed commercially (= make a profit)?* ◦ *The drug won't be commercially **available** (= able to be bought) until it has been thoroughly tested.*
▸noun [C] B1 an advertisement that is broadcast on television or radio: *a commercial break*

commercialism /kəˈmɜː.ʃəl.ɪ.zəm/ (US) /-ˈmɝː-/ noun [U] the principles and activity of commerce, especially those connected with profit rather than quality or doing good

commercialize (UK usually **commercialise**) /kəˈmɜː.ʃəl.aɪz/ (US) /-ˈmɝː-/ verb [T usually passive] to organize something to make a profit • **commercialization** disapproving (UK usually **commercialisation**) /kəˌmɜː.ʃəl.aɪˈzeɪ.ʃən/ (US) /-ˌmɝː-/ noun [U] *The commercialization of football has turned it from a sport into a business.* • **commercialized** disapproving (UK usually **commercialised**) /-aɪzd/ adj *It's a pity Christmas has become so commercialized.*

commie /ˈkɒm.i/ (US) /ˈkɑː.mi/ noun [C], adj informal disapproving for **communist (communism)**

commiserate /kəˈmɪz.ə.reɪt/ verb [I] to express sympathy to someone about some bad luck: *I began by commiserating **with** her **over** the defeat.*

commiseration /kəˌmɪz.əˈreɪ.ʃən/ noun **1 commiserations** [plural] an expression of sympathy for someone, especially someone who has lost a competition: *Commiserations **on** losing the match!* ◦ *Our commiserations **to** the losing side!* **2** [U] a feeling or expression of sympathy for someone about some bad luck: *She gave me a look of commiseration as I entered the room.*

commissar /ˌkɒm.ɪˈsɑːʳ/ (US) /ˈkɑː.mɪ.sɑːr/ **noun** [C] (in the Soviet Union until 1946) the official title of the head of a government department, or an official responsible for political education, especially in a military group

commissariat /ˌkɒm.ɪˈseə.ri.ət/ (US) /ˌkɑː.məˈser-/ **noun** [C, + sing/pl verb] a military department which supplies food and equipment

commissary /ˈkɒm.ɪ.səʳr.i/ (US) /ˈkɑː.mə.ser-/ **noun** [C] US a shop which supplies food and goods, especially to people in the army or in prison

commission /kəˈmɪʃ.ən/ **verb**; **noun**

▸**verb** **WORK** ▷ **1** [T] to formally choose someone to do a special piece of work: *The newspaper commissioned a series of articles on the worst excesses of the fashion industry.* **MILITARY** ▷ **2** [T usually passive] to give someone the official authority to be an officer in the armed forces: *Grandfather was commissioned **as** Group Captain in the RAF just before the war.*

▸**noun** **GROUP** ▷ **1** [C, + sing/pl verb] a group of people who have been formally chosen to discover information about a problem or examine the reasons why the problem exists: *a commission **on** alcohol abuse/racial tension* ◦ *The government have **set up/established** a commission to investigate the problem of inner city violence.* **PAYMENT** ▷ **2** [C or U] a payment to someone who sells goods that is directly related to the amount of goods sold, or a system that uses such payments: *Is she paid a regular wage or is it **on/by** commission only?* ◦ *She **gets** a 15 percent commission **on** every machine she sells.* **WORK** ▷ **3** [C] a request to do a special piece of work: [+ to infinitive] *She's just got a commission **to** paint Sir Ellis Pike's wife.* ◦ *Do you **do/take** commissions?* **CRIME** ▷ **4** [U] formal or legal the act of committing a crime: *the commission of the crime/offence/murder* **MILITARY** ▷ **5** [C] the official authority to be an officer in the armed forces

IDIOMS **in commission** If something, such as a machine or a military ship, is in commission it is working and ready for use. • **out of commission** If something, such as a machine or a military ship, is out of commission it is broken or not available to be used.

commissionaire /kəˌmɪʃ.ənˈeəʳ/ (US) /-ˈer/ **noun** [C] mainly UK a person wearing a uniform who stands at the entrance of a hotel, theatre, etc. and whose job is to open the door for guests and generally be helpful to them when they arrive

comˌmissioned ˈofficer **noun** [C] a type of officer in the armed forces → Compare **NCO**

commissioner /kəˈmɪʃ.ən.əʳ/ (US) /-ɚ/ **noun** [C] an important official who has responsibility in a government department or another organization: *the commissioner in charge of the police force*

commit /kəˈmɪt/ **verb** (-tt-) **CRIME** ▷ **1** (B2) [T] to do something illegal or something that is considered wrong: *He was sent to prison for a crime that he didn't commit.* ◦ *to commit adultery/murder* ◦ *to commit an offence* **PROMISE** ▷ **2** (C2) [I or T] to promise or give your loyalty, time, or money to a particular principle, person, or plan of action: *Like so many men, he has problems committing him**self to** a relationship.* ◦ *The government must commit itself **to** improv**ing** healthcare.* ◦ *Once we have committed **to** this course of action there is no going back.* **3 commit yourself** to express an opinion or to make a decision that you tell people about: *I think I can come but I won't commit myself till I know for sure.* **4 commit sth to memory** to make certain that you remember something **5 commit sth to paper** to write something down: *Perhaps we should commit these ideas to paper before we forget them.* **SEND** ▷ **6** [T] formal to send someone officially to prison or hospital: *He's been committed **to** prison for fraud.*

> **!** Common mistake: **commit**
>
> **Warning:** Check your verb endings!
> Many learners make mistakes when using **commit** in the past tense. The past simple and past participle have 'tt'. Don't write 'comited', write **committed**. The **-ing** form is **committing**.

IDIOM **commit suicide** If a person commits suicide, they kill themselves.

commitment /kəˈmɪt.mənt/ **noun** **1** (B2) [C or U] a willingness to give your time and energy to something that you believe in, or a promise or firm decision to do something: *Players must **make** a commitment to play for a full season.* ◦ *her commitment **to** left-wing politics/the cause of feminism/the company* ◦ *She is known chiefly for her commitment **to** nuclear disarmament.* ◦ *I'd like to thank the staff for having shown such commitment.* ◦ *Try the product out in the comfort of your own home with absolutely no commitment **to** buy!* **2** (B2) [C] something that you must do or deal with that takes your time: *family/work commitments* ◦ *I've got too many commitments at the moment to do an evening class.* ◦ *Children are such a commitment.*

committal /kəˈmɪt.əl/ (US) /-ˈmɪţ-/ **noun** [U] specialized the process of sending someone to a prison or mental hospital: *The psychiatric team decided that committal would not be beneficial in her case.*

committed /kəˈmɪt.ɪd/ (US) /-ˈmɪţ-/ **adj** **1** (C2) loyal and willing to give your time and energy to something that you believe in: *a committed socialist/Christian/teacher* **2** [after verb] having promised to be involved in a plan of action: *We are committed **to** withdraw**ing** our troops by the end of the year.*

committee /kəˈmɪt.i/ (US) /-ˈmɪţ-/ **noun** [C, + sing/pl verb] (B2) a small group of people chosen to represent a larger organization and either make decisions or collect information for it: *She **sits on/is on** the school's development committee.* ◦ *The local council have just set up a committee to study recycling.* ◦ *a committee **meeting***

> **!** Common mistake: **committee**
>
> **Warning:** Check your spelling!
> **Committee** is one of the 50 words most often spelled wrongly by learners. Remember: the correct spelling has 'mm', 'tt', and 'ee'.

commode /kəˈməʊd/ (US) /-ˈmoʊd/ **noun** [C] a piece of furniture that looks like a chair but has a container in the seat which people who are ill or old can use as a toilet

commodious /kəˈməʊ.di.əs/ (US) /-ˈmoʊ-/ **adj** formal describes a room or house that has a lot of space

commodity /kəˈmɒd.ə.ti/ (US) /-ˈmɑː.də.ţi/ **noun** [C] **1** (C1) a substance or product that can be traded, bought, or sold: *The country's most valuable commodities include tin and diamonds.* ◦ *the international commodities market* **2** a valuable quality: *If you're going into teaching, energy is a necessary commodity.*

commodore /ˈkɒm.ə.dɔːʳ/ (US) /ˈkɑː.mə.dɔːr/ **noun** [C] (also **Commodore**) an officer of high rank in the navy, or the person in charge of a sailing organization: *Commodore Perry/Matthew Perry* ◦ [as form of address] *Yes, Commodore.*

common /ˈkɒm.ən/ (US) /ˈkɑː.mən/ **adj; noun**

▸adj **USUAL** ▷ **1** (B1) the same in a lot of places or for a lot of people: *It's quite common to see couples who dress alike.* ◦ *The surname 'Smith' is very common in Britain.* **2 common courtesy/decency** the basic level of politeness which you expect from someone **3 common knowledge** (B2) a fact that everyone knows: [+ that] *It's common knowledge that they live together.*

> **!** Common mistake: **common or ordinary?**
>
> **Warning: common** is used disapprovingly to talk about people and things that are from a low social class.
>
> To say that people or things are not different, special, or unexpected in any way, don't use 'common', use **ordinary**:
>
> ~~*The programme shows how common Romanians live today.*~~
>
> *The programme shows how ordinary Romanians live today.*

SHARED ▷ **4** (B1) belonging to or shared by two or more people or things: *a common goal/interest* ◦ *English has some features common* ***to*** *many languages.* → See also **common ground 5 for the common good** If something is done for the common good, it is done to help everyone. **6 make common cause with sb** formal to act together with someone in order to achieve something: *Environmental protesters have made common cause with local people to stop the motorway being built.* **LOW CLASS** ▷ **7** disapproving typical of a low social class: *My mum thinks dyed blonde hair is a bit common.*

IDIOMS **the common man** ordinary people: *How can anyone so privileged have any understanding of the common man?* • **the common touch** the ability of an important or rich person to communicate well with and understand ordinary people

▸noun **LAND** ▷ **1** [C] (US also **commons**) an area of grass which everyone is allowed to use, usually in or near a village **SHARED** ▷ **2 have sth in common** (B1) to share interests, experiences, or other characteristics with someone or something: *We don't really have much in common.* **3 in common with sb/sth** (C1) in the same way as someone or something: *In common with many mothers, she feels torn between her family and her work.*

commonality /ˌkɒm.ənˈæl.ə.ti/ (US) /ˌkɑː.mənˈæl.ə.t̬i/ **noun** [C or U] formal the fact of sharing interests, experiences, or other characteristics with someone or something: *They found a commonality in discussing their experiences.* ◦ *There are some commonalities between the different stories.*

the ˌcommon ˈcold noun [S] a slight illness that a lot of people catch, causing a cough, sore throat, and blocked nose

ˌcommon deˈnominator noun [C] **NUMBER** ▷ **1** specialized a number that can be divided exactly by all the DENOMINATORS (= numbers under the line) in a group of FRACTIONS: *12 is a common denominator* ***of*** *⅓ and ¼.* **SIMILARITY** ▷ **2** something that is the same for all the members of a group and might bring them together: *The common denominator was that we had all worked for the same company.*

commoner /ˈkɒm.ə.nər/ (US) /ˈkɑː.mə.nɚ/ **noun** [C] a person who is not born into a position of high social rank: *It is now accepted that a member of the royal family can marry a commoner.*

ˌCommon ˈEra noun [S] (also **ˌCurrent ˈEra**, **ˌChristian ˈEra**) the period from the birth of Jesus Christ, when the Christian CALENDAR starts counting years as AD: *Synagogues have been excavated here dating from the first century of the Common Era.* → See also **CE, BCE**

ˌcommon ˈfactor noun [C] specialized a number that a set of two or more different numbers can be divided by exactly: *Three is a common factor* ***of*** *18 and 24.*

ˌcommon ˈfraction noun [C] specialized a FRACTION in which there is a horizontal line with one number above it and one number below it → Synonym **vulgar fraction** → See also **denominator, numerator**

ˌcommon ˈground noun [U] shared interests, beliefs, or opinions between two people or groups of people who disagree about most other subjects: *It seems increasingly unlikely that the two sides will find any common ground.*

ˌcommon ˈlaw noun [U] the legal system in England and most of the US that has developed over a period of time from old customs and court decisions, rather than laws made in Parliament

ˈcommon-law adj common-law wife/husband someone who is not officially a wife or husband but is considered to be one because she or he has been living with their partner for a long time

commonly /ˈkɒm.ən.li/ (US) /ˈkɑː.mən-/ **adv USUALLY** ▷ **1** (C1) often or usually: *Elbow injuries are commonly found among tennis players.* **SHARED** ▷ **2** shared by two or more people: *a commonly held belief*

the ˌCommon ˈMarket noun the former name of **the European Union** or **the European Community**

ˌcommon ˈmultiple noun [C] specialized a number that can be divided exactly by two or more different numbers: *24 is a common multiple* ***of*** *3, 4, and 6.*

ˌcommon ˈnoun noun [C] specialized a noun that is the name of a group of similar things, such as 'table' or 'book', and not of a single person, place or thing → Compare **proper noun**

ˌcommon or ˈgarden adj [before noun] UK informal very ordinary: *It's a common or garden washing machine, but it works perfectly well.*

commonplace /ˈkɒm.ən.pleɪs/ (US) /ˈkɑː.mən-/ **adj; noun**

▸adj happening often or often seen or experienced and so not considered to be special: *Electric cars are increasingly commonplace.*

▸noun [C] formal a boring remark that is used very often and does not have much meaning: *We exchanged commonplaces about the weather over cups of tea.*

ˈcommon ˌroom noun [C] mainly UK a room in a school or college where students or teachers can sit together and talk when they are not working

the ˈCommons noun the House of Commons: *The bill was defeated in the Commons by 249 votes to 131.* ◦ *a Commons committee*

ˌcommon ˈsense noun [U] (B1) the basic level of practical knowledge and judgment that we all need to help us live in a reasonable and safe way: *Windsurfing is perfectly safe as long as you have/use some common sense.* ◦ *a matter of common sense* • **commonsensical** /ˌkɒm.ənˈsen.sɪ.kəl/ (US) /ˌkɑː.mən-/ **adj** *He described the report as 'rigorous and commonsensical'.*

commonwealth /ˈkɒm.ən.welθ/ (US) /ˈkɑː.mən-/ **noun** [C] **1** a country or part of a country that is governed by its people or REPRESENTATIVES elected by

C

its people **2** formal a group of countries with the same political or economic aims

the ˌCommonwealth of ˈNations noun (also **the ˈCommonwealth**) an organization of independent countries which in the past belonged to the British EMPIRE and now still have friendly and practical connections with each other

commotion /kəˈməʊ.ʃən/ (US) /-ˈmoʊ-/ noun [S or U] a sudden short period of noise, confusion, or excited movement: *His arrival* ***caused*** *quite a commotion.* ◦ *He looked up to see what all the commotion was about.*

communal /ˈkɒm.jʊ.nəl/, /kəˈmjuː-/ (US) /ˈkɑː.mjə-/ adj SHARED ▷ **1** belonging to or used by a group of people rather than one single person: *communal facilities/food/property* ◦ *We each have a separate bedroom but share a communal kitchen.* **2** describes a society in which everyone lives and works together and property and possessions are shared rather than being owned by a particular person IN A COMMUNITY ▷ **3** involving different social or religious groups within a COMMUNITY: *Communal riots/disturbances have once again broken out between the two ethnic groups.* ◦ *communal harmony/solidarity* • **communally** /-i/ adv

commune /ˈkɒm.juːn/ (US) /ˈkɑː.mjuːn/ noun; verb

▸noun GROUP ▷ **1** [C, + sing/pl verb] a group of families or single people who live and work together sharing possessions and responsibilities: *She left her husband to* ***join*** *a women's commune.* GOVERNMENT ▷ **2** [C] in some countries, a unit of local government

▸verb [I] formal to get very close to someone or something by exchanging feelings or thoughts: *Lying naked in the grass, among the trees and birds, he felt he was communing* ***with*** *nature.*

communicable /kəˈmjuː.nɪ.kə.bl̩/ adj formal able to be given from one person to another: *In this period, there were 974 outbreaks of communicable* ***disease*** *attributed to the consumption of raw milk.* ◦ *communicable ideas/emotions*

communicant /kəˈmjuː.nɪ.kənt/ noun [C] a person who is involved in HOLY COMMUNION (= a Christian religious ceremony) and is therefore considered to be an active member of a Church

communicate /kəˈmjuː.nɪ.keɪt/ verb SHARE INFORMATION ▷ **1** (B1) [I or T] to share information with others by speaking, writing, moving your body, or using other signals: *We can now communicate instantly* ***with*** *people on the other side of the world.* ◦ *Unable to speak a word of the language, he communicated* ***with*** *(= using) his hands.* ◦ *Has the news been communicated* ***to*** *the staff yet?* ◦ *As an actor he could communicate a whole range of emotions.* **2** (B2) [I] to talk about your thoughts and feelings, and help other people to understand them: *I find I just can't communicate* ***with*** *her.* DISEASE ▷ **3** [T] specialized to pass a disease from one person or animal to another ROOMS ▷ **4** [I] formal If one room communicates with another, it connects with it through a door: *The bedroom communicates* ***with*** *both bathroom and hall.* ◦ *communicating rooms*

communication /kəˌmjuː.nɪˈkeɪ.ʃən/ noun **1** (B1) [U] the act of communicating with people: *Television is an increasingly important* ***means of*** *communication.* ◦ *We are* ***in*** *direct communication* ***with*** *Moscow.* ◦ *With no decent phone signal, communication is difficult.* ◦ *There's very little communication* ***between*** *mother and daughter (= they do not have a good relationship).* ◦ *a course on communication skills* **2** [C] formal a message or a letter: *We received your communication of 11 March and are sorry to inform you that we won't be attending the conference.* **3 communications** [plural] **a** the various methods of sending information between people and places, especially phones, computers, radio, etc.: *the communications industry* **b** ways of moving between one place and another: *Its commercial success as a city is partly due to its excellent rail and road communications.*

> **Word partners for communication**
>
> *establish/improve* communication • communication *breaks down* • *direct/effective/good/poor* communication • a *lack of/breakdown in* communication • a *form/means/method/mode* of communication • *channels/lines* of communication • communication *between* sb/sth • communication *with* sb/sth

communiˈcation ˌcord noun [C] UK (US **eˈmergency ˌcord**) a chain in a train CARRIAGE which a passenger can pull in an emergency to stop the train

communiˈcations ˌsatellite noun [C] an artificial object in space used to send out television and radio signals around the Earth's surface

communicative /kəˈmjuː.nɪ.kə.tɪv/ (US) /-t̬ɪv/ adj **1** (B2) willing to talk to people and give them information: *He was in a bad mood at breakfast and wasn't very communicative.* **2** relating to communication: *The communicative ability of the whale is thought to be highly developed.*

communicator /kəˈmjuː.nɪ.keɪ.təʳ/ (US) /-t̬ɚ/ noun [C] someone who is able to talk about their ideas and emotions in a way that other people understand: *Obviously teachers have to be good communicators.*

communion /kəˈmjuː.ni.ən/ noun **1** [U] formal a close relationship with someone in which feelings and thoughts are exchanged: *He lived* ***in*** *close communion* ***with*** *nature/God.* **2** [C, + sing/pl verb] literary a group of people who are united by the same, especially religious, beliefs

Communion /kəˈmjuː.ni.ən/ noun [U] (formal **ˌHoly Comˈmunion**) a Christian ceremony based on Jesus' last meal with his DISCIPLES (= the twelve men who first believed in him)

communiqué /kəˈmjuː.nɪ.keɪ/ noun [C] an official piece of news or an announcement, especially to the public or newspapers: *The palace have* ***issued*** *a communiqué denying the rumour.*

communism (also **Communism**) /ˈkɒm.jʊ.nɪ.zəm/ (US) /ˈkɑː.mjə-/ noun [U] the belief in a society without different social classes in which the methods of production are owned and controlled by all its members and everyone works as much as they can and receives what they need → Compare **capitalism**, **socialism** • **communist** (also **Communist**) /-nɪst/ adj, noun *the Communist Party* ◦ *communist ideology* ◦ *Was she ever a Communist?*

community /kəˈmjuː.nə.ti/ (US) /-t̬i/ noun [C, + sing/pl verb] **1** (B2) the people living in one particular area or people who are considered as a unit because of their common interests, social group, or nationality: *He's well known in the* ***local*** *community.* ◦ *There's a large* ***black/white/Jewish*** *community living in this area.* ◦ *Her speech caused outrage among the* ***gay*** *community.* ◦ *Drug trafficking is a matter of considerable concern for the entire* ***international*** *community (= all the countries of the world).* ◦ *There's a real* ***sense of*** *community (= caring and friendly feeling) in this neighbourhood.* **2** specialized a group of animals or plants that live or grow together **3 the community** [S] the general public: *Unlike the present government, we believe in* ***serving*** *the community.*

comˈmunity ˌcentre noun [C] a place where people who live in an area can meet each other and play sports, take courses, etc.

comˈmunity ˌchest noun [C] US an amount of money that has been given and collected by the people of a particular area to help people who are old or ill and in need of help

comˈmunity ˌcollege noun [C] **1** UK a school for children between the ages of eleven and 18 that also provides different types of classes, sports, etc. for adults from the local area **2** US a two-year college where students can learn a skill or prepare to enter a university

comˌmunity ˈservice noun [U] work done without payment to help other people that criminals whose crime was not serious enough for them to be put in prison are sometimes ordered to do

comˈmunity ˌspirit noun [U] friendliness and understanding between local people: *The presence of so many outsiders has ruined the community spirit.*

commutation /ˌkɒm.jʊˈteɪ.ʃən/ US /ˌkɑː.mjə-/ noun [U] legal the act of changing a punishment to one that is less severe

commutator /ˈkɒm.jʊ.teɪ.tər/ US /ˈkɑː.mjə.teɪ.t̬ɚ/ noun [C] specialized a device used in some types of electric motors to change the direction in which an electric current is flowing

commute /kəˈmjuːt/ verb; noun

▸verb **TRAVEL** ▷ **1** C1 [I] to make the same journey regularly between work and home: *It's exhausting commuting **from** Brighton **to** London every day.* **CHANGE** ▷ **2** [T] formal to change one thing into another: *People used to believe that you could commute base metals **into** gold.* **3** [T] specialized to exchange one type of payment for a different type: *I think I'll commute my life insurance **into** an annuity.* **4** [T] legal to change a punishment to one that is less severe: *Her sentence was commuted **from** death **to** life imprisonment.*

▸noun [C] informal a regular journey between work and home: *It's at least an hour's commute to work.*

commuter /kəˈmjuː.tər/ US /-t̬ɚ/ noun [C] someone who regularly travels between work and home: *The train was packed with commuters.*

comˈmuter ˌtrain noun [C] a train service especially for people travelling between home and work

compact adj; noun; verb

▸adj /kəmˈpækt/ consisting of parts that are positioned together closely or in a tidy way, using very little space: *compact soil/sand* ◦ *a compact camera/bag* ◦ *What a compact office! How did you fit so much into so little space?* • **compactly** /-li/ adv • **compactness** /-nəs/ noun [U]

▸noun [C] /ˈkɒm.pækt/ US /ˈkɑːm-/ **CASE** ▷ **1** a small, flat case which contains women's face powder: *a powder compact* **CAR** ▷ **2** US a small car **AGREEMENT** ▷ **3** formal a formal agreement between two or more people, organizations, or countries: [+ to infinitive] *They made a compact not **to** reveal any details.*

▸verb [T] /kəmˈpækt/ formal to press something together in a tight and solid way: *Cars had compacted the snow until it was like ice.*

ˌcompact ˈdisc noun [C] a **CD**

companion /kəmˈpæn.jən/ noun [C] **PERSON** ▷ **1** B2 a person you spend a lot of time with often because you are friends or because you are travelling together: *The dog has been her **constant** companion these past ten years.* ◦ *a travelling companion* **2** in the past, a young woman who was paid to care for and provide friendship for an old or ill woman, especially while she was travelling **OBJECT** ▷ **3** old-fashioned either of two matching objects: *I've still got one of the candlesticks but I've lost its companion.* **BOOK** ▷ **4** used in the title of the type of book which gives you information on a particular subject or tells you how to do something: *the Music Lover's Companion*

companionable /kəmˈpæn.jən.ə.bl/ adj friendly and pleasant to be with

companionship /kəmˈpæn.jən.ʃɪp/ noun [U] the enjoyment of spending time with other people: *I lived on my own for a while but I missed the companionship of others.*

companionway /kəmˈpæn.jən.weɪ/ noun [C] specialized the steps which lead from one DECK (= level) of a ship to another

company /ˈkʌm.pə.ni/ noun **BUSINESS** ▷ **1** A2 [C] an organization which sells goods or services in order to make money: *He works for a software company/a company that makes software.* ◦ *I work for Duggan and Company.* ◦ *No smoking is company **policy**.*

> **! Common mistake: company**
>
> **Warning:** Irregular plural!
>
> If you want to form the plural of **company**, don't write 'companys', write **companies**.

OTHER PEOPLE ▷ **2** B2 [U] the fact of being with a person or people, or the person or people you are with: *I just enjoy his company.* ◦ *It was a long trip and I was grateful for his company.* ◦ *I enjoy my **own** company* (= I like being alone). ◦ *I travelled **in the** company **of*** (= with) *two teachers as far as Istanbul.* ◦ *I'd rather you didn't mention it when we're **in** company* (= with other people). ◦ *I didn't realize you **had** company* (= were with someone/people). ◦ *Margot came to stay for a week as company **for** my mother while I was away.* ◦ *With only her thoughts for company* (= being alone), *she walked slowly along the beach.* → See also **accompany** **3** **be good company** C1 to be pleasant and entertaining to be with: *You'll like Rosie – she's good company.* **4** **for company** If you do something for company, you do it to make you feel as if you are not alone: *I usually have the radio on for company.* **5** **keep sb company** B2 to stay with someone so that they are not alone: *I'll keep you company till the train comes.* **THEATRICAL GROUP** ▷ **6** [C] a group of actors, singers, or dancers who perform together: *She's in the National Theatre Company.* **GROUP** ▷ **7** [C, + sing/pl verb] a large group of soldiers, especially a division of a BATTALION

> **Word partners for company (BUSINESS)**
>
> *create/establish/set up* a company • *buy/buy out/take over* a company • *run* a company • *join/leave* a company • companies *merge* • company *executives/policy/profits*

> **Word partners for company (OTHER PEOPLE)**
>
> *want* company • the company *of* sb • *in* the company *of* sb

IDIOMS **be in good company** to have the same problem as many other people: *'I can't play tennis – I'm hopeless at it!' 'Oh well, you're in good company.'* • **the company sb keeps** the influence of the people that someone spends time with: *'Where does he pick up words like that?' 'It's the company he keeps.'* ◦ *He's been keeping bad company* (= spending time with unsuitable people).

ˌcompany ˈcar noun [C] a car owned by a company

or other organization that is used by an employee for his or her work

ˈcompany ˌtown noun [C] US a city or town in which most of the workers are employed by a single organization

C

comparable /ˈkɒm.pər.ə.bl̩/ (US) /ˈkɑːm.pɚ-/ adj (C1) similar in size, amount or quality to something else: *The girls are of comparable ages.* ◦ *Our prices are comparable* ***to/with*** *those in other shops.* ◦ *The two experiences aren't comparable.* • **comparably** /-bli/ adv *comparably priced tickets*

comparative /kəmˈpær.ə.tɪv/ (US) /-ˈper.ə.t̬ɪv/ noun; adj

▸noun [C] specialized (A2) the form of an adjective or adverb that expresses a difference in amount, number, degree, or quality: *'Fatter' is the comparative* ***of*** *'fat'.* ◦ *'More difficult' is the comparative* ***of*** *'difficult'.*

▸adj EXAMINING DIFFERENCES ▷ **1** (C1) comparing different things: *She's carrying out a comparative study of health in inner cities and rural areas.* **2 comparative comfort/freedom/silence, etc.** (C2) a situation that is comfortable, free, silent, etc. when compared to another situation or what is normal: *I enjoyed the comparative calm of his flat after the busy office.* WORD FORM ▷ **3** specialized relating to the form of an adjective or adverb that expresses a difference in amount, number, degree, or quality: *The comparative* ***form*** *of 'slow' is 'slower'.*

comparatively /kəmˈpær.ə.tɪv.li/ (US) /-ˈper.ə.t̬ɪv-/ adv (C1) as compared to something else: *We couldn't afford it and yet we're comparatively well off* (= we are richer than most people). ◦ *Comparatively* ***speaking****, this machine is easy to use.*

compare /kəmˈpeər/ (US) /-per/ verb; noun

▸verb [T] EXAMINE DIFFERENCES ▷ **1** (B1) to examine or look for the difference between two or more things: *If you compare house prices in the two areas, it's quite amazing how different they are.* ◦ *That seems expensive – have you compared prices in other shops?* ◦ *Compare some recent work* ***with*** *your older stuff and you'll see how much you've improved.* ◦ *This road is quite busy compared* ***to/with*** *ours.* ◦ *Children seem to learn more interesting things compared* ***to/with*** *when we were at school.* CONSIDER SIMILARITIES ▷ **2** to judge, suggest, or consider that something is similar or of equal quality to something else: *The poet compares his lover's tongue* ***to*** *a razor blade.* ◦ *Still only 25, she has been compared* ***to*** *the greatest dancer of all time.* ◦ *People compared her* ***to*** *Elizabeth Taylor.* ◦ *You can't compare the two cities – they're totally different.* **3 does not compare** If something or someone does not compare with something or someone else, the second thing is very much better than the first: *Instant coffee just doesn't compare* ***with*** *freshly ground coffee.* **4 compare favourably** If something compares favourably with something else, it is better than it: *The hotel certainly compared favourably* ***with*** *the one we stayed in last year.*

> **! Common mistake: compared with/to**
>
> **Remember:** to describe the differences or similarities between two or more things, use 'compare' in the past tense.
>
> Don't say 'compare with/to', or 'comparing with/to', say **compared with/to**:
>
> ~~*Her garden is big comparing to mine.*~~
>
> *Her garden is big compared to mine.*

IDIOM **compare notes** (C1) If two people compare notes, they tell each other what they think about something they have both done: *We'd both been out with the same man at different points in our lives so it was interesting to compare notes.*

▸noun literary **beyond compare** so good that everyone or everything else is of worse quality: *Her beauty is beyond compare.*

comparison /kəmˈpær.ɪ.sən/ (US) /-ˈper-/ noun [C or U] EXAMINING DIFFERENCES ▷ **1** (B2) the act of comparing two or more people or things: *They* ***made a*** *comparison of different countries' eating habits.* ◦ ***By/In*** *comparison* ***with*** *the French, the British eat far less fish.* CONSIDERING SIMILARITIES ▷ **2** (B2) the fact of considering something similar or of equal quality to something else: *She* ***drew a*** *comparison* ***between*** *life in the army and life in prison.* ◦ *To my mind* ***there's no*** *comparison between the two restaurants* (= one is much better than the other). ◦ *He's a good writer but he doesn't* ***bear/stand*** *comparison* ***with*** *Shakespeare* (= he is not nearly as good as Shakespeare).

> **Word partners for comparison**
>
> ***draw/make*** a comparison • ***bear/stand*** comparison ***with*** sb/sth • ***invite*** comparison • a ***detailed/direct/inevitable*** comparison • a ***fair/favourable/unfair/unfavourable*** comparison • [dull/easy, etc.] ***by/in*** comparison • ***in*** comparison ***to/with*** sb or sth • a comparison ***between/with*** sb or sth

compartment /kəmˈpɑːt.mənt/ (US) /-ˈpɑːrt-/ noun [C] **1** one of the separate areas inside a vehicle, especially a train: *a first-class compartment* **2** a separate part of a piece of furniture or equipment or a container with a particular purpose: *a fridge with a small freezer compartment* ◦ *the sleeping/inner compartment in a tent*

compartmentalize (UK usually **compartmentalise**) /ˌkɒm.pɑːtˈmen.təl.aɪz/ (US) /ˌkɑːm.pɑːrtˈmen.t̬əl-/ verb [T] to separate something into parts and not allow those parts to mix together: *His life was carefully compartmentalized, with his work in one city and his social life in another.*

compass /ˈkʌm.pəs/ noun DIRECTION DEVICE ▷ **1** [C] a device for finding direction with a needle that can move easily and that always points to MAGNETIC NORTH MEASURING DEVICE ▷ **2 compasses** [plural] a V-shaped device that is used for drawing circles or measuring distances on maps LIMIT ▷ **3** [U] formal a particular range (of ability, activity, interest, etc.): *The discussion went* ***beyond the*** *compass* ***of*** *my brain.*

compass

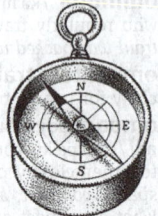

compassion /kəmˈpæʃ.ən/ noun [U] approving a strong feeling of sympathy and sadness for the suffering or bad luck of others and a wish to help them: *I was hoping she might* ***show*** *a little compassion.*

compassionate /kəmˈpæʃ.ən.ət/ adj approving showing compassion: *The public's response to the crisis appeal was generous and compassionate.* • **compassionately** /-li/ adv

comˌpassionate ˈleave noun [U] UK a period of time that a company allows you not to come to work because a member of your family has died or is ill

comˈpassion faˌtigue noun [U] the situation in which people stop thinking or worrying about a problem that is affecting a lot of people and stop giving money to them because the problem has continued for too long

ˈcompass ˌpoint noun [C] any of the 32 marks on the COMPASS that show direction

compatible /kəmˈpæt.ɪ.bl/ US /-ˈpæţ-/ adj C1 able to exist, live together, or work successfully with something or someone else: *It was when we started living together that we found we just weren't compatible.* ◦ *This software may not be compatible* ***with*** *older operating systems.* ◦ *Such policies are not compatible* ***with*** *democratic government.* ◦ *Are their two blood groups compatible (= can blood from one person be given to the other person)?* • **compatibility** /kəmˌpæt.əˈbɪl.ɪ.ti/ US /-ˌpæţ.əˈbɪl.ə.ţi/ noun [U] • **compatibly** /-bli/ adv

compatriot /kəmˈpæt.ri.ət/ US /-ˈpeɪ.tri-/ noun [C] **1** formal a person who comes from the same country **2** US a friend or someone you work with

compel /kəmˈpel/ verb [T] (-ll-) **1** to force someone to do something: [+ to infinitive] *As a school boy he was compelled* ***to*** *wear shorts even in winter.* ◦ formal *The new circumstances compelled a change in policy.* → See also **compulsion 2** formal to produce a strong feeling or reaction: *Over the years her work has compelled universal admiration and trust.*

compelled /kəmˈpeld/ adj [after verb] C1 having to do something, because you are forced to or feel it is necessary: [+ to infinitive] *He* ***felt*** *compelled* ***to*** *report the incident.*

compelling /kəmˈpel.ɪŋ/ adj STRONG ▷ **1** If a reason, argument, etc. is compelling, it makes you believe it or accept it because it is so strong: *compelling evidence* ◦ *It's a fairly compelling argument for going.* EXCITING ▷ **2** very exciting and interesting and making you want to watch or listen: *I found the whole film very compelling.* ◦ *a compelling story*

compendium /kəmˈpen.di.əm/ noun [C] (plural **compendiums** or **compendia** /-ə/) a short but complete account of a particular subject, especially in the form of a book: *the Gardener's Compendium*

compensate /ˈkɒm.pən.seɪt/ US /ˈkɑːm-/ verb PAY MONEY ▷ **1** C1 [T] to pay someone money in exchange for something that has been lost or damaged or for some problem: *Victims of the crash will be compensated* ***for*** *their injuries.* EXCHANGE ▷ **2** C2 [I] to provide something good or useful in place of something or to make someone feel better about something that has failed or been lost or missed: *Nothing will ever compensate* ***for*** *his lost childhood.* ◦ *His enthusiasm* ***more than*** *compensates for his lack of experience.* ◦ *We were late and I was driving fast to compensate.*

> **Common mistake: compensate**
>
> When **compensate** is followed by a direct object, remember to use the preposition **for**.
>
> Don't say 'compensate something', say **compensate for something**:
>
> ~~*The beautiful weather compensates the difficult journey.*~~
>
> *The beautiful weather compensates for the difficult journey.*

compensation /ˌkɒm.penˈseɪ.ʃən/ US /ˌkɑːm-/ noun MONEY ▷ **1** [U] money that is paid to someone in exchange for something that has been lost or damaged or for some problem: *She received £40,000* ***in*** *compensation* ***for*** *a lost eye.* ◦ *You should* ***claim/seek*** *compensation.* ◦ *a compensation* ***claim*** EXCHANGE ▷ **2** [C or U] something that makes you feel better when you have suffered something bad: *I have to spend three months of the year away from home – but there are compensations like the chance to meet new people.* ◦ *Free food was no compensation for a very boring evening.* JOB PAYMENT ▷ **3** [U] the combination of money and other BENEFITS (= rewards) that an employee receives for doing their job: ***Annual*** *compensation for our executives includes salary and bonus under our incentive plan.* • **compensatory** /ˌkɒm.pənˈseɪt.ər.i/ US /kəmˈpen.sə.tɔːr.i/ adj mainly US *He was awarded $3 million in compensatory* ***damages.***

compere /ˈkɒm.peəʳ/ US /ˈkɑː.m.per/ noun; verb
▸**noun** [C] UK (US **emcee**) a person whose job is to introduce performers in a television, radio, or stage show: *He started his career as a TV compere.*
▸**verb** [I or T] UK (US **emcee**) to act as a compere: *She comperes that awful game show on Saturday night.*

compete /kəmˈpiːt/ verb [I] **1** B2 to try to be more successful than someone or something else: *It's difficult for a small shop to compete* ***against/with*** *the big supermarkets.* ◦ *Both girls compete* ***for*** *their father's attention.* ◦ figurative *Turn the music down – I'm not competing* ***against/with*** *that noise (= I can't/won't try to speak louder than that music)!* **2** B1 to take part in a race or competition: *Are you competing* ***in*** *the 100 metres?* ◦ *The two athletes are competing* ***for*** *the gold medal.*

competence /ˈkɒm.pɪ.tᵊns/ US /ˈkɑːm-/ noun [C or U] (also **competency**) C1 the ability to do something well: *Her competence as a teacher is unquestionable.* ◦ *He reached a reasonable level of competence* ***in*** *his English.* → Opposite **incompetence**

competency /ˈkɒm.pɪ.tᵊn.si/ US /ˈkɑːm-/ noun [C] an important skill that is needed to do a job: *managerial competencies*

competent /ˈkɒm.pɪ.tᵊnt/ US /ˈkɑː.m.pə.ţᵊnt/ adj C1 able to do something well: *a competent secretary/horse-rider/cook* ◦ *I wouldn't say he was brilliant but he is competent* ***at*** *his job.* → Opposite **incompetent** • **competently** /-li/ adv *I thought she played the role very competently.*

> **Word partners for competition**
>
> *face* competition • *enter/take part in* a competition • *win* a competition • *withdraw from* a competition • a competition *takes place* • *fierce/intense/stiff/strong* competition • *growing/healthy/increasing* competition • *in* competition *with* sb • competition *among/between* sb or sth • *level* of competition

competition /ˌkɒm.pəˈtɪʃ.ᵊn/ US /ˌkɑːm-/ noun **1** B2 [U] a situation in which someone is trying to win something or be more successful than someone else: *Competition for jobs is intense.* ◦ *There's a lot of competition* ***between*** *computer companies.* ◦ *The two companies are* ***in*** *competition* ***with*** *each other.* ◦ [+ to infinitive] *There's fierce competition* ***to*** *get into that school.* ◦ *Foreign competition (= similar products from other countries) had reduced their sales.* ◦ *Why are you jealous of her? She's* ***no*** *competition!* **2** A2 [C] an organized event in which people try to win a prize by being the best, fastest, etc.: *a swimming/chess competition* ◦ *She's* ***entered*** *a crossword competition.* ◦ humorous *You don't need to eat so quickly! It's not a competition.* **3 the competition** [S] the person or people you are trying to be better than: *The competition on the track looked fierce and her heart sank.*

competitive /kəmˈpet.ɪ.tɪv/ US /-ˈpeţ.ə.ţɪv/ adj **1** B2 involving competition: *competitive sports* ◦ *a highly competitive industry* ◦ *Acting is very competitive – you've got to really push yourself if you want to succeed.* **2** B2 wanting very much to win or be more successful than other people: *You're very competitive –*

it's meant to be a friendly match! ◦ I could never play team sports – I lack the competitive **spirit** (= a strong wish to beat others). **3** B2 Competitive prices, services, etc. are as good as or better than other prices, services, etc. • **competitively** /-li/ **adv** *competitively **priced** goods* • **competitiveness** /-nəs/ **noun** [U]

C

competitor /kəmˈpet.ɪ.tər/ US /-ˈpet̬.ɪ.t̬ɚ/ **noun** [C] B1 a person, team, or company that is competing against others: *Their prices are better than any of their competitors.* ◦ *How many competitors took part in the race?*

compilation /ˌkɒm.pɪˈleɪ.ʃən/ US /ˌkɑːm-/ **noun** **1** [U] the act of compiling something: *A team of four were involved in the compilation of the book.* **2** [C] a book, CD, etc. that has been made from several separate parts: *a compilation of their greatest hits*

compile /kəmˈpaɪl/ **verb** [T] **GATHER TOGETHER** ▷ **1** C1 to collect information from different places and arrange it in a book, report, or list: *We're compiling some facts and figures for a documentary on the subject.* **CHANGE INSTRUCTIONS** ▷ **2** specialized to change a computer program into a machine language

compiler /kəmˈpaɪ.lər/ US /-lɚ/ **noun** [C] **PERSON** ▷ **1** a person who compiles something: *a dictionary compiler* **COMPUTER PROGRAM** ▷ **2** specialized a computer program that changes instructions into machine language: *She ran her code through the compiler.*

complacency /kəmˈpleɪ.sən.si/ **noun** [U] (also **complacence**) a feeling of calm satisfaction with your own abilities or situation that prevents you from trying harder: *What annoys me about these girls is their complacency – they seem to have no desire to expand their horizons.* ◦ *There's no **room for** complacency if we want to stay in this competition!*

complacent /kəmˈpleɪ.sənt/ **adj** disapproving feeling so satisfied with your own abilities or situation that you feel you do not need to try any harder: *a complacent smile/attitude* ◦ *We can't afford to become complacent about any of our products.* • **complacently** /-li/ **adv**

> **Other ways of saying complain**
>
> The verbs **grumble** and **whine** are sometimes used when someone is complaining about things which are not important:
>
> *She's always **grumbling** about something.*
>
> *I hope you don't think I'm just **whining**.*
>
> If someone, especially a child, complains in an annoying way, **whine** is often used:
>
> *Stop **whining**, Tom – it's not that bad!*
>
> The expression **make a fuss** is sometimes used in informal contexts, especially when someone is complaining that something has not happened in the way he or she wanted:
>
> *If the food doesn't come soon, I'm going to **make a fuss**.*
>
> If you complain formally to someone in authority, you can use the phrase **file a complaint**:
>
> *I've **filed a complaint** with the police about the noise.*

complain /kəmˈpleɪn/ **verb** [I] **1** B1 to say that something is wrong or not satisfactory: *Lots of people have complained **about** the noise.* ◦ *You're always complaining!* ◦ [+ that] *He complained **that** his boss was useless and he had too much work.* **2** B1 to tell someone formally that something is wrong: *If the service was so bad why didn't you complain **to** the manager?* • **complainingly** /kəmˈpleɪ.nɪŋ.li/ **adv**

> **Common mistake: complain**
>
> Remember to use the preposition **about**.
>
> Don't say 'complain something', say **complain about something**:
>
> ~~*I want to complain the quality of the food in the canteen.*~~
>
> *I want to complain about the quality of the food in the canteen.*

PHRASAL VERB **complain of sth** B1 to tell other people that something is making you feel ill: *She's been complaining of a bad back recently.*

complainant /kəmˈpleɪ.nənt/ **noun** [C] legal a person who makes a formal complaint in a law court

complaint /kəmˈpleɪnt/ **noun** **REPORT OF A PROBLEM** ▷ **1** B1 [C or U] a statement that something is wrong or not satisfactory: *We've received a complaint from one of our listeners **about** offensive language.* ◦ *I've **made a** complaint (= formally complained) **to** the police about the noise.* ◦ [+ that] *We've had complaints **that** you've been playing your radio too loud.* ◦ *Do you have any **grounds for** complaint (= reason to formally complain)?* **ILLNESS** ▷ **2** [C] an illness: *a heart/stomach complaint*

> **Common mistake: complaint or complain?**
>
> **Warning:** do not confuse the noun **complaint** with the verb **complain**:
>
> ~~*I want to complaint about the service in your restaurant.*~~
>
> *I want to complain about the service in your restaurant.*

> **Word partners for complaint**
>
> *make* a complaint • *file/lodge* a complaint • *get/receive* a complaint • *deal with/handle/investigate* a complaint • a *formal/official* complaint • a *common/frequent* complaint • a complaint *about/against* sb/sth • *cause/grounds* for complaint • a complaints *department/procedure*

complaisance /kəmˈpleɪ.zəns/ US /-səns/ **noun** [U] formal willingness to please others by being polite and fitting in with their plans • **complaisant** /-zənt/ US /-sənt/ **adj**

complement /ˈkɒm.plɪ.ment/ US /ˈkɑːm-/ **verb** [T] to make something else seem better or more attractive when combining with it: *Strawberries and cream complement **each other** perfectly.* ◦ *The music complements her voice perfectly.*

> **Note:**
>
> Do not confuse with **compliment**.

complementary /ˌkɒm.plɪˈmen.tər.i/ US /ˈkɑːm.plɪˈmen.t̬ɚ-/ **adj** useful or attractive together: *complementary colours/flavours/skills* ◦ *My family and my job both play an important part in my life, fulfilling separate but complementary needs.*

compleˌmentary ˈangle **noun** [C usually plural] one of two angles which together add up to 90°

compleˌmentary ˈmedicine **noun** [U] a wide range of treatments for medical conditions which people use instead of or in addition to ordinary medicine: *Acupuncture, reflexology, and homeopathy are all forms of complementary medicine.*

complete /kəmˈpliːt/ **verb; adj**

▸**verb** [T] **MAKE WHOLE** ▷ **1** A2 to make whole or

perfect: *Complete the sentence with one of the adjectives provided.* ◦ *He only needs two more cards to complete the set.* ◦ *All she needed to complete her happiness was a baby.* **2** A2 to write all the details asked for on a form or other document: *Have you completed your application form yet?* **FINISH** ▷ **3** A2 to finish doing something: *He's just completed filming his 17th feature film.* ◦ *The palace took over 20 years to complete.* ◦ *She will complete her studies in France.*

▸**adj VERY GREAT** ▷ **1** B1 [before noun] very great or to the largest degree possible: *The man's a complete fool!* ◦ *I need a break, a complete change of scene.* ◦ *I made a complete **and utter** mess of it!* **WHOLE** ▷ **2** B1 with all the parts: *the complete works of Oscar Wilde* ◦ *The report comes complete **with** (= including) diagrams and colour photographs.* ◦ *Sun, sand, and romance – her holiday was complete.*

completely /kəmˈpliːt.li/ **adv** B1 in every way or as much as possible: *I agree with you completely.* ◦ *She's completely mad.* ◦ *He'd completely changed – I didn't recognize him.*

> **!** Common mistake: **completely**
>
> **Warning:** do not confuse the adverb **completely** with the adjective **complete**:
>
> ~~*My tour of France was a completely disaster.*~~
>
> *My tour of France was a complete disaster.*

> **!** Common mistake: **completely**
>
> **Warning:** Common word-building error!
>
> If an adjective ends with 'te', just add 'ly' to make an adverb. Don't write 'completly', write **completely**.

completeness /kəmˈpliːt.nəs/ **noun** [U] the quality of being whole or perfect and having nothing missing: *For the sake of completeness, I should also mention two other minor developments.*

completion /kəmˈpliː.ʃən/ **noun** [U] C1 the act of finishing something that you are doing or making: *You'll be paid **on** completion **of** the project.* ◦ *The road repair work is **nearing** completion (= almost finished).*

complex adj; noun

▸**adj** /ˈkɒm.pleks/, /kəmˈpleks/ US /ˈkɑːm-/ **1** B2 involving a lot of different but related parts: *a complex molecule/carbohydrate* ◦ *a complex network of roads* ◦ *a complex procedure* ◦ *The company has a complex organizational structure.* **2** B2 difficult to understand or find an answer to because of having many different parts: *It's a very complex issue to which there is no straightforward answer.* ◦ *The film's plot was so complex that I couldn't follow it.*

▸**noun** [C] /ˈkɒm.pleks/ US /ˈkɑːm-/ **BUILDING** ▷ **1** C1 a large building with various connected rooms or a related group of buildings: *a shopping/sports and leisure complex* ◦ US *They live in a large apartment complex.* **BAD FEELING** ▷ **2** C2 a particular ANXIETY or unconscious fear that a person has, especially as a result of an unpleasant experience that they have had in the past or because they have a low opinion of their own worth: *an inferiority complex* ◦ *I think he's **got** a complex **about** being bald.* ◦ *Don't go on about her weight – you'll **give** her a complex!*

complexion /kəmˈplek.ʃən/ **noun** [C] **FACE** ▷ **1** C2 the natural appearance of the skin on a person's face, especially its colour or quality: *a dark/fair complexion* ◦ *a healthy/clear/spotty complexion* **CHARACTER** ▷ **2** the general character of something: *What Pablo has just said **puts an entirely/completely new** complexion **on** (= changes) things.*

complexity /kəmˈplek.sɪ.ti/ US /-sə.t̬i/ **noun** **1** C2 [U] the state of having many parts and being difficult to understand or find an answer to: *a problem of great complexity* **2** **complexities** [plural] the features of something which make it difficult to understand or find an answer to: *There are a lot of complexities surrounding this issue.*

complex ˈsentence **noun** [C] specialized in grammar, a sentence which contains a main part and one or more other parts

compliance /kəmˈplaɪ.əns/ **noun** [U] **1** formal the act of obeying an order, rule,or request: *It is the job of the inspectors to enforce compliance **with** the regulations.* ◦ *The company said that it had always acted **in** compliance **with** environmental laws.* **2** mainly disapproving the state of being too willing to do what other people want you to do: *It's his compliance that amazes me.*

compliant /kəmˈplaɪ.ənt/ **adj** **1** formal willing to do what other people want you to do: *a compliant child* **2** used to describe something that obeys a particular rule or law: *The company expects to be reclassified soon as its factories are fully compliant **with** the Federal Clean Air Act.*

complicate /ˈkɒm.plɪ.keɪt/ US /ˈkɑːm-/ **verb** [T] **1** C1 to make something more difficult to deal with, do, or understand: *It will only complicate the situation if we invite his old girlfriend as well.* ◦ *The rescue operation has been complicated by bad weather.* ◦ *These new rules have complicated the tax system even further.* **2** If one illness complicates another illness, it makes the other illness worse: *The breathing problem has now been complicated by a chest infection.*

complicated /ˈkɒm.plɪ.keɪ.tɪd/ US /ˈkɑːm.plɪ.keɪ.t̬ɪd/ **adj** B1 involving a lot of different parts, in a way that is difficult to understand: *complicated instructions* ◦ *I had to fill in this really complicated form.* ◦ *The rules are rather complicated to follow.* ◦ *The relationship is a bit complicated. He's my mother's cousin's daughter's child.*

complication /ˌkɒm.plɪˈkeɪ.ʃən/ US /ˌkɑːm-/ **noun** **1** C1 [C or U] something that makes a situation more difficult, or the act of doing this: *Dave couldn't find his passport at the airport and then there were **further** complications when Fiona lost her baggage.* ◦ *If any complications **arise**, let me know and I'll help.* **2** C2 [C] an extra medical problem which makes it more difficult to treat an existing illness: *If there are no complications, the doctor says that she'll be able to come home within two weeks.*

complicit /kəmˈplɪs.ɪt/ **adj** involved in or knowing about a crime or some activity that is wrong: *She was accused of being complicit **in** her husband's death.*

complicity /kəmˈplɪs.ɪ.ti/ US /-ə.t̬i/ **noun** [U] formal involvement in a crime or some activity that is wrong: *She is suspected of complicity **in** the fraud.*

compliment /ˈkɒm.plɪ.mənt/ US /ˈkɑːm-/ **noun; verb**

▸**noun** **1** C2 [C] a remark that expresses approval, admiration, or respect: *She complained that her husband never **paid** her any compliments any more.* ◦ *I **take it as** a compliment (= I am pleased) when people say I look like my mother.* ◦ *Are you **fishing for** (= trying to get) compliments?*

> **!** Note:
>
> Do not confuse with **complement**.

2 C2 [S] an action which expresses approval or respect: *You should **take it as** a compliment when I fall asleep in your company – it means I'm relaxed.* ◦ *Thank you so much for your help – I hope one day I'll be able to **return/repay the** compliment (= do some-*

thing good for you). **3 my compliments...** formal an expression of your admiration or respect: *That was an excellent meal! My compliments* ***to*** *the chef.* **4 with your compliments** (C2) formal If you give something to someone with your compliments, you give it to them free: *We enclose a copy of our latest brochure, with our compliments.*

▸verb [T] (C1) to praise or express admiration for someone: *I was just complimenting Robert* ***on*** *his wonderful food.* ◦ *I must compliment you* ***on*** *your handling of a very difficult situation.*

complimentary /ˌkɒm.plɪˈmen.tᵊr.i/ (US) /ˌkɑːm.plɪˈmen.t̬ɚ-/ adj **PRAISING** ▷ **1** praising or expressing admiration for someone: *The reviews of his latest film have been highly complimentary.* ◦ *She wasn't very complimentary* ***about*** *your performance, was she?* ◦ *Our guests said some very complimentary things about the meal I'd cooked.* → Opposite **uncomplimentary** **FREE** ▷ **2** (C2) If tickets, books, etc. are complimentary, they are given free, especially by a business.

ˈcompliment(s) ˌslip noun [C] a piece of paper printed with the name and address of a company, sent with a parcel in place of a letter

comply /kəmˈplaɪ/ verb [I] formal (C1) to act according to an order, set of rules, or request: *He's been ordered to have the dog destroyed because it's dangerous, but he refuses to comply.* ◦ *There are serious penalties for failure to comply* ***with*** *the regulations.*

component /kəmˈpəʊ.nənt/ (US) /-ˈpoʊ-/ noun [C] (C1) a part which combines with other parts to form something bigger: *television/aircraft/computer components* ◦ *The factory supplies electrical components for cars.* ◦ *The course has four main components: business law, finance, computing, and management skills.* ◦ *Fresh fruit and vegetables are an* ***essential*** *component* ***of*** *a healthy diet.* ◦ *The control of inflation is a* ***key*** *component* ***of*** *the government's economic policy.*

comport /kəmˈpɔːt/ (US) /-ˈpɔːrt/ verb **BEHAVE** ▷ **1 comport yourself** to behave in a particular way: *She comported herself with great dignity at her husband's funeral.* **BE SIMILAR** ▷ **2** [I] US formal If an idea or statement, etc. comports, it matches or is similar to something else: *The findings of this research do not comport* ***with*** *accepted theory.* • **comportment** /-mənt/ noun [U] formal *This scandal raises new questions about the president's private comportment.*

compose /kəmˈpəʊz/ (US) /-ˈpoʊz/ verb **PRODUCE ART** ▷ **1** (B2) [I or T] to produce music, poetry, or formal writing: *The music was specially composed* ***for*** *the film.* ◦ *a piece of music composed* ***for*** *the flute* ◦ *He composed this poem* ***for*** *his wife.* ◦ formal *My lawyer is going to compose a letter of complaint.* **FORM** ▷ **2 be composed of sth** (B2) to be formed from various things: *Air is composed mainly of nitrogen and oxygen.* ◦ *The committee is composed of MPs, doctors, academics and members of the public.* ◦ *The audience was composed largely of young people.* **3** [T] to be the parts that something is made of: *At that time, women composed only 1.6 percent of the US forces.* **BECOME CALM** ▷ **4 compose yourself** to make yourself calm again after being angry or upset: *She finally stopped crying and composed herself.* **5 compose your features/thoughts** to try to make yourself look or feel calm after being angry or upset: *I tried to compose my features into a smile.* ◦ *He took a minute or two to compose his thoughts before he replied.* **ARRANGE TEXT** ▷ **6** [T] specialized to arrange words, sentences, pages, etc. in preparation for printing

composed /kəmˈpəʊzd/ (US) /-ˈpoʊzd/ adj calm and in control of your emotions: *She looked remarkably composed throughout the funeral.* • **composedly** /-ˈpəʊ.zɪd.li/ (US) /-ˈpoʊ.zɪd.li/ adv

composer /kəmˈpəʊ.zəʳ/ (US) /-ˈpoʊ.zɚ/ noun [C] (B2) a person who writes music

composite /ˈkɒm.pə.zɪt/ (US) /kɑːm-/ noun [C] something that is made of various different parts: *The main character in her latest novel is a composite* ***of*** *several public figures of that era.* ◦ *Scientists have put together a composite picture of what the Earth's crust is like.*

composition /ˌkɒm.pəˈzɪʃ.ᵊn/ (US) /ˌkɑːm-/ noun **MUSIC/ART** ▷ **1** (B2) [C] a piece of music that someone has written: *This concerto is one of her earlier/later compositions.* **2** (C2) [U] the process or skill of writing music: *At music school I studied piano and composition.* **3** (C2) [C] the way that people or things are arranged in a painting or photograph: *a group composition* **PIECE OF WRITING** ▷ **4** (B1) [C or U] old-fashioned a short piece of writing about a particular subject, done by a student: *a 200-word composition* **FORMED FROM** ▷ **5** (C2) [U] the parts, substances, etc. that something is made of: *the composition of the atmosphere*

compositor /kəmˈpɒz.ɪ.təʳ/ (US) /-ˈpɑː.zɪ.t̬ɚ/ noun [C] a person whose job is to arrange the letters, words, sentences, etc. of a book or a magazine before it is printed

compos mentis /ˌkɒm.pɒsˈmen.tɪs/ (US) /ˌkɑːm.pəs ˈmen.t̬əs/ adj [after verb] humorous able to think clearly and be in control of and responsible for your actions: *She was very old but still compos mentis.*

compost /ˈkɒm.pɒst/ (US) /ˈkɑːm.poʊst/ noun [U] decaying plant material that is added to soil to improve its quality • **compost** verb [T]

compostable /kɒmˈpɒs.tə.bᵊl/ (US) /kɑːmˈpoʊst.ə-/ adj Something that is compostable can be used as compost when it decays: *compostable garden waste*

composure /kəmˈpəʊ.ʒəʳ/ (US) /-ˈpoʊ.ʒɚ/ noun [U] the feeling of being calm, confident, and in control: *I didn't want to* ***lose*** *my composure in front of her.*

compote /ˈkɒm.pɒt/ (US) /ˈkɑːm.poʊt/ noun [C or U] a sweet dish made of cooked fruit

compound noun; verb; adj

▸noun [C] /ˈkɒm.paʊnd/ (US) /ˈkɑːm-/ **COMBINATION** ▷ **1** a chemical that combines two or more elements: *Salt is a compound* ***of*** *sodium and chlorine.* **2** formal something consisting of two or more different parts: *Then there was his manner, a curious compound of humour and severity.* **3** in grammar, a word that combines two or more different words. Often, the meaning of the compound cannot be discovered by knowing the meaning of the different words that form it. Compounds may be written either as one word or as separate words: *'Bodyguard' and 'floppy disk' are two examples of compounds.* **AREA** ▷ **4** an area surrounded by fences or walls which contains a group of buildings: *The gates opened and the troops marched into their compound.* ◦ *The embassy compound has been closed to the public because of a bomb threat.*

▸verb /kəmˈpaʊnd/ **WORSEN** ▷ **1** [T often passive] to make a problem or difficult situation worse: *His financial problems were compounded when he unexpectedly lost his job.* ◦ *Severe drought has compounded food shortages in the region.* **COMBINE** ▷ **2** [T] to mix two things together: *Most tyres are made of rubber compounded* ***with*** *other chemicals and materials.*

▸adj /ˈkɒm.paʊnd/ (US) /ˈkɑːm-/ **1** consisting of two or more parts **2** used to refer to a system of paying interest in which interest is paid both on the original amount of money INVESTED (= given to companies hoping to get more back) or borrowed and on the interest that has collected over a period of time:

compound interest ◦ The investment fund has achieved annual compound returns of 18.2 percent.

ˌcompound ˈeye noun [C] specialized an eye made of a large number of parts, each with a separate LENS, as found in insects

ˌcompound ˈfracture noun [C] an injury caused by a bone breaking or CRACKING and cutting through the surrounding flesh → Compare **simple fracture**

ˌcompound ˈleaf noun [C] a type of leaf that is formed from a number of smaller leaves all joined to one stem

comprehend /ˌkɒm.prɪˈhend/ ⓤⓢ /ˌkɑːm-/ verb [I or T, not continuous] formal to understand something completely: *I fail to comprehend their attitude. ◦ He doesn't seem to comprehend the scale of the problem ◦* [+ question word] *I'll never comprehend **why** she did what she did. ◦* [+ that] *I don't think he **fully** comprehends **that** she won't be here to help him.*

comprehensible /ˌkɒm.prɪˈhen.sɪ.bl̩/ ⓤⓢ /ˌkɑːm-/ adj able to be understood: *It's written in clear, comprehensible English. ◦ Her writing is barely comprehensible **to** me.* → Opposite **incomprehensible** • **comprehensibility** /-hen.sɪˈbɪl.ɪ.ti/ ⓤⓢ /-hen.səˈbɪl.ə.t̬i/ noun [U] • **comprehensibly** /-bli/ adv

comprehension /ˌkɒm.prɪˈhen.ʃən/ ⓤⓢ /ˌkɑːm-/ noun **1** [U] the ability to understand completely and be familiar with a situation, facts, etc.: *He has no comprehension **of** the size of the problem. ◦ How she manages to fit so much into a working day is **beyond** my comprehension* (= I cannot understand it). **2** [C or U] UK a test to find out how well students understand written or spoken language: *a **listening/reading** comprehension*

comprehensive /ˌkɒm.prɪˈhen.sɪv/ ⓤⓢ /ˌkɑːm-/ adj C1 complete and including everything that is necessary: *We offer you a comprehensive training in all aspects of the business. ◦ Is this list comprehensive or are there some names missing? ◦ He has written a **fully** comprehensive guide to Rome.*

compreˈhensive (ˌschool) noun [C] UK a school in the UK for children above the age of eleven of all abilities: *the local comprehensive ◦ a comprehensive education*

compreˌhensive inˈsurance noun [U] INSURANCE which financially protects any other vehicles and people that are involved in a car accident with you, in addition to yourself

comprehensively /ˌkɒm.prɪˈhen.sɪv.li/ ⓤⓢ /ˌkɑːm-/ adv C1 completely: *a comprehensively illustrated book ◦ The plan was comprehensively rejected.*

compress verb; noun

▸verb [T] /kəmˈpres/ **1** to press something into a smaller space: *Firmly compress the soil in the pot so that the plant is secure. ◦ compressed air* **2** to make information, a piece of writing, etc. shorter: *The course compresses two year's training **into** six intensive months. ◦ I managed to compress ten pages of notes **into** four paragraphs.* **3** to make a computer file use less space when it is stored in the MEMORY of a computer or on a disk, by using a special program: *to compress data/files* • **compression** /-ˈpreʃ.ən/ noun [U] the action of compressing or being compressed • **compressible** /-ɪ.bl̩/ adj

▸noun [C] /ˈkɒm.pres/ ⓤⓢ /ˈkɑːm-/ a thick, soft piece of cloth that is pressed to a part of a person's body to stop BLEEDING or to reduce pain or swelling: *a cold/hot compress*

compressor /kəmˈpres.ər/ ⓤⓢ /-ɚ/ noun [C] a (part of a) machine which presses gas or air into less space

comprise /kəmˈpraɪz/ verb [T, L only + noun, not continuous] formal C1 to have as parts or members, or to be those parts or members: *The course comprises a class book, a practice book, and a CD. ◦ The class is comprised mainly **of** Italian and French students. ◦ Italian students comprise 60 percent **of** the class.*

compromise /ˈkɒm.prə.maɪz/ ⓤⓢ /ˈkɑːm-/ noun; verb

▸noun [C or U] B2 an agreement in an argument in which the people involved reduce their demands or change their opinion in order to agree: *It is hoped that a compromise will be **reached** in today's talks. ◦ In a compromise **between** management and unions, a four percent pay rise was agreed in return for an increase in productivity. ◦ The government has said that there will be no compromise **with** terrorists.*

▸verb **AGREEMENT** ▷ **1** B2 [I] to accept that you will reduce your demands or change your opinion in order to reach an agreement with someone: *Party unity is threatened when members will not compromise. ◦ Well, you want $400 and I say $300, so let's compromise **at/on** $350.* **LOWER STANDARDS** ▷ **2** [T] disapproving to allow your principles to be less strong or your standards or morals to be lower: *Don't compromise your **beliefs/principles** for the sake of being accepted. ◦ If we back down on this issue, our **reputation** will be compromised. ◦ His political career ended when he compromised him**self** by accepting bribes.* **HARM** ▷ **3** C2 [T] to risk having a harmful effect on something: *We would never compromise the safety of our passengers.*

compromising /ˈkɒm.prə.maɪ.zɪŋ/ ⓤⓢ /ˈkɑːm-/ adj causing damage to the reputation of someone, especially making known that they have had a sexual relationship with someone who is considered unsuitable: *Photographs were published of her in a compromising **position/situation** with her bodyguard.*

comptroller /kənˈtrəʊ.lər/ ⓤⓢ /-ˈtroʊ.lɚ/ noun [C] formal a CONTROLLER, especially in the job titles of people who have important financial jobs

compulsion /kəmˈpʌl.ʃən/ noun **WANT** ▷ **1** [C] a very strong feeling of wanting to do something repeatedly that is difficult to control: *For many people, dieting is a compulsion. ◦* [+ to infinitive] *I seem to **have** a **constant** compulsion **to** eat.* **FORCE** ▷ **2** [S or U] a force that makes you do something: *He seems to be driven by some kind of inner compulsion. ◦* [+ to infinitive] *We were **under no** compulsion **to** attend. ◦ Don't feel **under any** compulsion **to** take me with you.* → See also **compel**

compulsive /kəmˈpʌl.sɪv/ adj **1** C2 doing something a lot and unable to stop doing it: *a compulsive liar/thief/eater ◦ compulsive gambling ◦ a compulsive eating disorder* **2** C2 describes a film, play, sports event, book, etc. that is so interesting or exciting that you do not want to stop watching or reading it: *I always find programmes about hospitals compulsive **viewing**. ◦ Her latest book is compulsive **reading**/a compulsive **read**.* • **compulsively** /-li/ adv too much and in a way that shows you are unable to stop: *She exercises/cleans/works compulsively.* • **compulsiveness** /-nəs/ noun [U]

compulsory /kəmˈpʌl.sər.i/ ⓤⓢ /-sɚ-/ adj B2 If something is compulsory, you must do it because of a rule or law: *Swimming was compulsory at my school. ◦ The law made wearing seat belts in cars compulsory.* • **compulsorily** /-əl.i/ adv *Patients can now be compulsorily detained in hospital only under tightly drawn criteria.*

compunction /kəmˈpʌŋk.ʃən/ noun [U] formal a slight guilty feeling about something you have done or might do: *I wouldn't have any compunction **about** telling him to leave.*

C

computational /kɒm.pju'teɪ.ʃən.əl/ (US) /kɑːm.pjə-/ **adj** **1** formal involving the calculation of answers, amounts, results, etc.: *The children had limited linguistic and computational skills.* ◦ *computational techniques* **2** using computers to study something: *computational chemistry*

compu,tational lin'guistics noun [U] the study of language and speech using computers

compute /kəm'pjuːt/ verb [T] formal to calculate an answer or amount by using a machine • **computation** /ˌkɒm.pju'teɪ.ʃən/ (US) /ˌkɑːm.pjə-/ noun [C or U]

computer /kəm'pjuː.tər/ (US) /-t̬ɚ/ noun [C or U] A1 an electronic machine that is used for storing, organizing, and finding words, numbers, and pictures, for doing calculations, and for controlling other machines: *a personal/home computer* ◦ *All our customer orders are handled* ***by*** *computer.* ◦ *We've put all our records* ***on*** *computer.* ◦ *computer software/hardware* ◦ *computer graphics* ◦ *a computer program*

> Word partners for **computer**
>
> *restart/shut down/start up* a computer • be *connected to/hooked up to* a computer • a computer *crashes* • *use* a computer • *on* a computer • *by* computer • computer *equipment/hardware/programs/software* • computer *literacy*

com,puter-aided de'sign noun [U] (abbreviation **CAD**) the use of computers to design objects

com'puter-,animated adj Computer-animated films use computers to make the characters look as if they are moving: *'Toy Story' is a computer-animated film.*

computerate /kəm'pjuː.tər.ət/ (US) /-t̬ɚ-/ adj able to use computers well

com,puter 'dating noun [U] a way of helping people find suitable romantic partners by using a computer to match them with people of similar interests

com'puter ,game noun [C] a game that is played on a computer, in which the pictures that appear on the screen are controlled by pressing keys or moving a JOYSTICK

com,puter-generated 'imagery noun [U] (abbreviation **CGI**) the process of using computers to create pictures or characters in film and television

computerize (UK usually **computerise**) /kəm'pjuː.tər.aɪz/ (US) /-t̬ə.raɪz/ verb [T] to use a computer to do something that was done by people or other machines before: *They've just computerized the whole system.* • **computerization** (UK usually **computerisation**) /kəmˌpjuː.tər.aɪ'zeɪ.ʃən/ (US) /-t̬ɚ-/ noun [U]

com,puter-'literate adj able to use computers well • **com,puter-'literacy** noun [U]

com,puter 'science noun [U] the study of computers and how they can be used

computing /kəm'pjuː.tɪŋ/ (US) /-t̬ɪŋ/ noun [U] the study or use of computers: *a degree in computing*

comrade /'kɒm.reɪd/ (US) /'kɑːm.ræd/ noun [C] **FRIEND** ▷ **1** old-fashioned (UK ,**comrade-in-'arms**) a friend, especially one who you have been involved in difficult or dangerous, usually military, activities with: *Many of his comrades were killed in the battle.* **POLITICAL MEMBER** ▷ **2** a member of the same political group, especially a COMMUNIST or SOCIALIST group or a TRADE UNION: *I know my opinion is shared by many of my comrades in the Labour movement.* ◦ [as form of address] *Welcome to the conference, comrades.* • **comradely** /-li/ adj like a comrade

comradeship /'kɒm.reɪd.ʃɪp/ (US) /'kɑːm-/ noun [U] the feeling of friendship between people who live or work together, especially in a difficult situation

con /kɒn/ (US) /kɑːn/ verb; noun

▸**verb** [T] (**-nn-**) informal to make someone believe something false, usually so that they will give you their money or possessions: *She felt she had been conned* ***into*** *buy****ing*** *the car.* ◦ *Thieves conned him* ***out of*** *his life savings.* ◦ *He managed to con £20* ***out of*** *them (= get that amount from them by deceiving them).*

▸**noun** **TRICK** ▷ **1** [C] informal a trick to get someone's money, or make them do what you want: *It's a con – you get half the food for twice the price!* ◦ *a con trick* **DISADVANTAGE** ▷ **2** [C usually plural] informal a disadvantage or a reason for not doing something: *One of the cons of buying a bigger car is that it costs more to run.* ◦ *You have to weigh up all the* ***pros and*** *cons of the matter before you make a decision.* **PRISONER** ▷ **3** [C] slang a **convict**

con- /kən-/ prefix together; with: *conspiracy* ◦ *consortium*

Con. adj written abbreviation for **Conservative**

'con ,artist noun [C] (also **'con ,man**) a person who deceives other people by making them believe something false or making them give money away

concatenate /kən'kæt.ə.neɪt/ (US) /-'kæt̬-/ verb [T] formal or specialized to put things together as a connected series: *The filename is a series of concatenated words with no spaces.*

concatenation /kənˌkæt.ə.neɪ.ʃən/ (US) /-'kæt̬-/ noun [C] formal a series of events, ideas, or things that are connected: *a concatenation of circumstances/events*

concave /'kɒŋ.keɪv/ (US) /'kɑːn-/ adj curving in: *a concave lens* → Compare **convex** • **concavity** /ˌkɒn'kæv.ɪ.ti/ (US) /ˌkɑːn.kæv.ə.t̬i/ noun [C or U] specialized

conceal /kən'siːl/ verb [T] C2 to prevent something from being seen or known about: *The listening device was concealed in a pen.* ◦ *I tried to conceal my surprise when she told me her age.* ◦ *It was said that the police concealed vital evidence.* ◦ *Is there something you're concealing* ***from*** *me?* → Synonym **hide** • **concealed** /-'siːld/ adj *The robbery had been recorded on a concealed security camera.* ◦ *He was carrying a concealed weapon.* ◦ *The room had concealed lighting.*

concealment /kən'siːl.mənt/ noun [U] the act of hiding something: *the concealment* ***of*** *evidence/facts/weapons*

concede /kən'siːd/ verb **ADMIT** ▷ **1** C2 [T] to admit, often unwillingly, that something is true: [+ (that)] *The government has conceded* (***that***) *the new tax policy has been a disaster.* ◦ [+ speech] *'Well okay, perhaps I was a little hard on her,' he conceded.* → See also **concession** **2** [I or T] to admit that you have lost in a competition: *He kept on arguing and wouldn't concede* ***defeat****.* ◦ *She conceded even before all the votes had been counted.* **GIVE AWAY** ▷ **3** C2 [T] to allow someone to have something, even if you do not want to: *The president is not expected to concede these reforms.* ◦ *He is not willing to concede any of his power/authority.* ◦ *Britain conceded (= allowed) independence* ***to*** *India in 1947.* **4 concede a goal/point** to fail to stop an opposing team or person from winning a point or game: *The team conceded two goals* (***to*** *the other side*) *in the first five minutes of the game.*

conceit /kən'siːt/ noun **PRIDE** ▷ **1** [U] the state of being too proud of yourself and your actions: *The conceit of that man is incredible!* **COMPARISON** ▷ **2** [C] literary a clever or surprising comparison, especially in a poem

conceited /kən'siː.tɪd/ (US) /-t̬ɪd/ adj disapproving C2 too proud of yourself and your actions and abilities: *Without wishing to sound conceited, I am the best salesperson in the company.* • **conceitedly** /-li/ **adv**

conceivable /kən'siː.və.bl̩/ **adj** possible to imagine or to believe: *Books on every conceivable subject lined one wall.* ◦ *It's **just** conceivable (= possible although difficult to imagine) (**that**) the hospital made a mistake.* • **conceivably** /-bli/ **adv** *She could conceivably (= possibly) have already left.*

conceive /kən'siːv/ **verb IMAGINE** ▷ **1** C2 [I or T] to imagine something: *I think my uncle still conceives **of** me **as** a four-year-old.* ◦ *He couldn't conceive **of** a time when he would have no job.* ◦ [+ question word] *I can't conceive (= it is too shocking to imagine) **how** anyone could behave so cruelly.* ◦ [+ that] *I find it hard to conceive (= it is too shocking to imagine) **that** people are still treated so badly.* **INVENT** ▷ **2** C2 [T] to invent a plan or an idea: *He conceived the plot for this film while he was still a student.* ◦ *The exhibition was conceived by the museum's director.* → See also **concept** **BECOME PREGNANT** ▷ **3** C2 [I or T] to become pregnant, or to cause a baby to begin to form: *Do you know exactly when you conceived?* ◦ *The baby was conceived in March, so will be born in December.* → See also **conception**

concentrate /'kɒn.sᵊn.treɪt/ (US) /'kɑːn-/ **verb**; **noun**
▸**verb GIVE ATTENTION** ▷ **1** B1 [I or T] to direct your attention or your efforts towards a particular activity, subject, or problem: *Come on, concentrate! We haven't got all day to do this.* ◦ *I can't concentrate **on** my work with all that noise.* ◦ *I find running concentrates **the mind** (= helps me to think).* ◦ *I'm going to concentrate **on** my writing for a while.* ◦ *The company is concentrating (its resources) **on** developing new products.* **COME TOGETHER** ▷ **2** C1 [T usually passive or I, usually + adv/prep] to bring or come together in a large number or amount in one particular area: *Most of the country's population is concentrated in the north.* ◦ *In the dry season, the animals tend to concentrate in the areas where there is water.* **REMOVE WATER** ▷ **3** [T] specialized to make a liquid or substance stronger and reduce its size by removing water from it
▸**noun** [C or U] **1** a liquid from which some of the water has been removed: *fruit-juice concentrate* **2** an ORE from which rock has been removed: *a mineral concentrate*

concentrated /'kɒn.sᵊn.treɪ.tɪd/ (US) /'kɑːn.sᵊn.treɪ.t̬ɪd/ **adj GIVING ATTENTION** ▷ **1** [before noun] using a lot of effort to succeed at one particular thing: *The company is making a concentrated effort to broaden its market.* **WATER REMOVED** ▷ **2** having had some liquid removed: *concentrated orange juice*

concentration /ˌkɒn.sᵊn'treɪ.ʃᵊn/ (US) /ˌkɑːn-/ **noun ATTENTION** ▷ **1** B2 [U] the ability to think carefully about something you are doing and nothing else: *The noise outside made concentration difficult.* ◦ *There was a look of **intense** concentration on her face.* ◦ *I find that yoga improves my **powers of** concentration.* ◦ *I found it hard to follow what the teacher was saying, and eventually I **lost** concentration.* ◦ *The government's concentration **on** tax reduction has won them a lot of support.* **AMOUNT** ▷ **2** C2 [C or U] a large number or amount of something in the same place: *There is a heavy concentration **of** troops in the area.* **3** [C or U] specialized the exact amount of one particular substance that is found in another substance: *a concentration of one part per million* ◦ *High concentrations **of** toxic elements were found in the polluted areas.*

concen'tration ˌcamp **noun** [C] a prison where people are kept in extremely bad conditions, especially for political reasons: *Nazi concentration camps*

concentric /kən'sen.trɪk/ **adj** describes circles and rings that have the same centre: *a concentric pattern*

concept /'kɒn.sept/ (US) /'kɑːn-/ **noun** [C] **1** B2 a principle or idea: *The very concept **of** free speech is unknown to them.* ◦ *It is very difficult to define the concept **of** beauty.* ◦ *I failed to grasp the film's central concept.* ◦ *Kleenbrite is a whole **new** concept **in** toothpaste!* **2 not have any concept/have no concept of sth** to not understand about something: *I don't think you have any concept of the pain you have caused her.*

conception /kən'sep.ʃᵊn/ **noun IDEA** ▷ **1** C2 [C or U] an idea of what something or someone is like, or a basic understanding of a situation or a principle: *People from different cultures have different conceptions **of** the world.* ◦ *She has a conception **of** people as being basically good.* ◦ *I thought the book's writing was dreadful, and its conception (= the ideas on which it was based) even worse.* ◦ *He has absolutely **no** conception **of** how a successful business should run.* **BABY** ▷ **2** [U] the process of a male and a female sex cell joining and causing a baby to start to form: *at/from the moment of conception*

conceptual /kən'sep.tju.əl/ **adj** based on ideas or principles: *The main weakness of the proposal is conceptual.*

conceptualize formal (UK usually **conceptualise**) /kən'sep.tju.ə.laɪz/ **verb** [I or T] to form an idea or principle in your mind: *He argued that morality could be conceptualized (= thought about) **as** a series of principles based on human reason.*

concern /kən'sɜːn/ (US) /-'sɝːn/ **verb**; **noun**
▸**verb WORRY** ▷ **1** C1 [T] to cause worry to someone: *The state of my father's health concerns us **greatly**.* ◦ [+ that] ***It** concerns me **that** he hasn't been in contact.*

> **!** Common mistake: **concern or concerned?**
> **Warning:** do not confuse the verb **concern** with the adjective **concerned**:
> ~~*These days, people are concern about their health.*~~
> *These days, people are concerned about their health.*

INVOLVE ▷ **2** B2 [T] to be important to someone or to involve someone directly: *Matters of pollution and the environment concern us all.* ◦ *What I have to say to Amy doesn't concern you.* **3** B2 [T] formal If a story, film, or article concerns a particular subject, person, etc., it is about that person or subject: *The film concerns a woman who goes to China as a missionary.* **4 concern yourself** to become involved with something, or worried about something: *There's no need for you to concern **yourself with** what happened.* ◦ *Don't concern yourself. She'll be home soon.* **5 to whom it may concern** something you write at the start of a formal letter or notice when you do not know exactly who it should be sent to
▸**noun WORRY** ▷ **1** B2 [C or U] a worried or nervous feeling about something, or something that makes you feel worried: *Concern **for** the safety of the two missing teenagers is **growing**.* ◦ *There's a lot of public concern **about/over** dangerous toxins recently found in food.* ◦ [+ that] *My concern is **that** you're not getting enough work done.* **BUSINESS** ▷ **2** [C] a company: *a family concern* ◦ *It started slowly, but the company is now a **going** concern (= doing business effectively).* **IMPORTANT TO** ▷ **3** B2 [C or U] something that is important to you, or the fact of being important: [+ to infinitive] *His concern **to** appear sophisticated amused everyone.* ◦ *The company's **sole** concern is **to** ensure the safety of its employees.* ◦ *There's **a matter of** some*

concern that I have to discuss with you. **4** [C or U] something that involves or affects you or is important to you: *What were the major concerns **of** the writers from this period?* ◦ *I don't want to hear about it – it's no concern **of** mine!* ◦ *'What's happening?' 'That's **none of/ not any of** your concern.'* **5 be of concern** to be important: *The results of the election are of concern **to** us all.*

C

concerned /kənˈsɜːnd/ (US) /-ˈsɝːnd/ adj **WORRIED** ▷ **1** (B2) worried: *I'm a bit concerned **about/for** your health.* ◦ [+ (that)] *Aren't you concerned (**that**) she might tell someone?* ◦ [+ to infinitive] *He was concerned **to** hear that two of his trusted workers were leaving.* ◦ *Concerned parents have complained about the dangerous playground.* **INVOLVED** ▷ **2** (C2) [after verb] involved in something or affected by it: *I'd like to thank everyone concerned for making the occasion run so smoothly.* ◦ *It was quite a shock for **all/everyone** concerned.* ◦ *Her job is something concerned **with** computers.* ◦ *I'm not very good **where** money is concerned* (= when dealing with money). **3 as far as sb is concerned** (B2) in a particular person's opinion: *As far as I'm concerned, feng shui is a load of rubbish.* **4 as far as sth is concerned** (B2) if we are discussing or thinking about a particular thing: *As far as unemployment's concerned, a change of government would be a good idea.* **5 be concerned with sth/sb** (C1) to be about a particular thing or person: *Today's lesson is concerned with punctuation.*

concernedly /kənˈsɜː.nɪd.li/ (US) /-ˈsɝː-/ adv in a way that shows you are worried: *'Are you sure you're all right?' she asked concernedly.*

concerning /kənˈsɜː.nɪŋ/ (US) /-ˈsɝː-/ preposition; adj
▸**preposition** formal (B2) about: *I've had a letter from the tax authorities concerning my tax payments.*

> **! Common mistake: concerning**
>
> Remember that **concerning** is never followed by 'to' or 'about'.
>
> Don't say 'concerning to something' or 'concerning about something', say **concerning something**:
>
> ~~*I am writing concerning to the article in yesterday's newspaper.*~~
>
> *I am writing concerning the article in yesterday's newspaper.*

▸**adj** formal not standard making you feel slightly worried: *The increase in crime in the area is very concerning.*

concert /ˈkɒn.sət/ (US) /ˈkɑːn.sɚt/ noun [C] (A2) a performance of music by one or more musicians or singers: *a pop/classical concert* ◦ *a school concert*

IDIOM **in concert 1** playing or singing with other musicians in a public performance: *She was appearing in concert at Carnegie Hall.* **2** formal together: *If the member countries would **act** in concert, the problem might be solved more easily.*

concerted /kənˈsɜː.tɪd/ (US) /-ˈsɝː.t̬ɪd/ adj [usually before noun] **1** planned or done together for a shared purpose: *The richer countries of the world should take concerted **action** to help the poorer countries.* ◦ *The D-Day invasion was a concerted **exercise** by the armed forces of Britain, the US, and Canada.* **2** describes an effort or attempt that is determined and serious: *There has been a concerted campaign against the proposals.* ◦ *He's making a concerted **effort** to improve his appearance.*

concertgoer /ˈkɒn.sətˌɡəʊ.əʳ/ (US) /ˈkɑːn.sɚtˌɡoʊ.ɚ/ noun [C] a person who often goes to concerts

ˌconcert ˈgrand noun [C] the biggest type of GRAND PIANO, usually used for concerts

ˈconcert ˌhall noun [C] a large building in which concerts are performed

concertina /ˌkɒn.səˈtiː.nə/ (US) /ˌkɑːn.sɚ-/ noun; verb
▸**noun** [C] a musical instrument with a folding middle part, which you play by pushing both ends together with the hands and pressing buttons
▸**verb** [I or T] UK to fold, crush, or push together: *In the accident, several cars concertinaed **into** each other.* ◦ figurative *Could we concertina the three meetings **into** one morning?*

concerto /kənˈtʃɜː.təʊ/ (US) /-ˈtʃer.t̬oʊ/ noun [C] (plural **concertos** or **concerti** /-ti/) a long piece of music for one or more main SOLO instruments and an ORCHESTRA: *a violin/piano concerto* ◦ *Mozart's **concerto for** flute and harp*

concession /kənˈseʃ.ən/ noun **SOMETHING ALLOWED** ▷ **1** (C2) [C or U] something that is allowed or given up, often in order to end a disagreement, or the act of allowing or giving this: *He stated firmly that no concessions will be **made to** the strikers.* → See also **concede 2** [U] the act of admitting defeat: *The former president's concession came even before all the votes had been counted.* ◦ *a concession speech* **LOWER PRICE** ▷ **3** (C2) [C] UK a reduction in the usual price of something, made available to students, old people, etc. **RIGHT** ▷ **4** [C] a special right to property or land **5** [C] the right to sell a product in a particular area

concessionaire /kənˌseʃ.ənˈeəʳ/ (US) /-ˈer/ noun [C] someone who has been given a concession to sell or do something

concessionary /kənˈseʃ.ən.ər.i/ (US) /-er-/ adj offered at a lower price than usual for certain people, for example students or old people: *a concessionary fare/ticket*

concessive clause /kənˌses.ɪvˈklɔːz/ (US) /-ˈklɑːz/ noun [C] specialized a CLAUSE, often beginning with 'though' or 'although', that expresses an idea that suggests the opposite of the main part of the sentence: *The sentence 'Although he's quiet, he's not shy' begins with a concessive clause.*

conch /kɒntʃ/, /kɒŋk/ (US) /kɑːntʃ/ /kɑːŋk/ noun [C] a large SPIRAL shell, or the tropical SNAIL-like sea creature which lives in it

conchie /ˈkɒn.tʃi/ (US) /ˈkɑːn-/ noun [C] old-fashioned informal for **conscientious objector** (= someone who refuses to work in the armed forces for moral or religious reasons)

concierge /ˌkɒn.siˈeəʒ/ (US) /kɑːn.siˈerʒ/ noun [C] **1** a person who is employed to take care of an apartment building, especially in France **2** someone who is employed in a hotel to help guests arrange things, such as theatre tickets and visits to restaurants

conciliate /kənˈsɪl.i.eɪt/ verb [I or T] to end a disagreement or someone's anger by acting in a friendly way or slightly changing your opinions, or to satisfy someone who disagrees with you by acting in this way: *An independent adviser has been brought in to conciliate **between** the two sides involved in the conflict.* ◦ *These changes have been made in an attempt to conciliate critics of the plan.* • **conciliation** /kənˌsɪl.iˈeɪ.ʃən/ noun [U] formal *All attempts at conciliation failed and the dispute continued.* • **conciliatory** /kənˈsɪl.i.ə.tər.i/ (US) /-tɔːr.i/ adj *a conciliatory gesture/remark*

concise /kənˈsaɪs/ adj short and clear, expressing what needs to be said without unnecessary words: *Make your answers clear and concise.* • **concisely** /-li/

adv • **conciseness** /-nəs/ noun [U] (also **concision** /-ˈsɪʒ.ən/)

conclave /ˈkɒŋ.kleɪv/ US /ˈkɑːn-/ noun [C] formal a private meeting at which the discussions are kept secret

conclude /kənˈkluːd/ verb **FINISH** ▷ **1** C1 [I or T] to end a speech, meeting, or piece of writing: *She concluded the speech* ***by*** *remind****ing*** *us of our responsibility.* ◦ *Before I conclude, I'd like to thank you all for coming.* ◦ *The concert concluded* ***with*** *a rousing chorus.* **2** [T] to complete an official agreement or task, or arrange a business deal **JUDGE** ▷ **3** C1 [T] to judge or decide something after thinking carefully about it: [+ that] *The jury concluded* ***from*** *the evidence* ***that*** *the defendant was innocent.* ◦ *The discussions continued late into the night, but nothing was concluded.*

concluding /kənˈkluː.dɪŋ/ adj [before noun] last in a series of things: *Don't miss tonight's concluding episode.*

conclusion /kənˈkluː.ʒən/ noun **LAST PART** ▷ **1** C2 [C] the final part of something: *I found the conclusion of the film rather irritating.* **2** **in conclusion** formal B2 finally: *In conclusion, I would like to thank our guest speaker.* **AGREEMENT** ▷ **3** [U] the act of arranging or agreeing something formally: *the conclusion of the deal/treaty* **JUDGMENT** ▷ **4** B1 [C] the opinion you have after considering all the information about something: *Did you* ***come to/reach/draw*** *any conclusions at the meeting this morning?* ◦ [+ that] *At first I thought he was a bit shy, but I've* ***come to*** *the conclusion* ***that*** *he's simply unfriendly!*

> **Word partners for conclusion**
>
> *arrive at/come to/draw/reach* a conclusion • *jump to/leap to* conclusions • *lead* sb *to* the conclusion (that) • *base* your conclusions *on* sth • a *foregone/inevitable/logical/obvious/unavoidable* conclusion • a *depressing/sobering/startling* conclusion • a conclusion *about/on* sth

conclusive /kənˈkluː.sɪv/ adj C2 proving that something is true, or ending any doubt: *They had conclusive* ***evidence/proof*** *of her guilt.* ◦ *a conclusive argument* → Opposite **inconclusive**

conclusively /kənˈkluː.sɪv.li/ adv C2 without any doubt: *It is impossible to* ***demonstrate/prove*** *conclusively that the factory is responsible for the pollution.*

concoct /kənˈkɒkt/ US /-ˈkɑːkt/ verb [T] **1** to make something, usually food, by adding several different parts together, often in a way that is original or not planned: *He concocted the most amazing dish from all sorts of unlikely ingredients.* **2** to invent an excuse, explanation, or story in order to deceive someone: *He concocted a story about working late at the office.*

concoction /kənˈkɒk.ʃən/ US /-ˈkɑːk-/ noun [C or U] the result or process of concocting something

concomitant /kənˈkɒm.ɪ.tənt/ US /-ˈkɑː.mə.t̬ənt/ noun; adj

▸noun [C] formal something that happens with something else and is connected with it: *Loss of memory is a natural concomitant* ***of*** *old age.*

▸adj formal happening and connected with another thing: *Any increase in students meant a concomitant increase in funding.* • **concomitantly** /-li/ adv

concord /ˈkɒŋ.kɔːd/ US /ˈkɑːŋ.kɔːrd/ noun [U] **1** formal agreement and peace between countries and people: *nations living* ***in*** *concord* → Compare **discord** **2** specialized the situation in which the words in a sentence match each other according to the rules of grammar, for example when the verb is plural because the subject of the sentence is plural

concordance /kənˈkɔː.dəns/ US /-ˈkɔːr-/ noun; verb

▸noun **1** [C] specialized a book or document that is an ALPHABETICAL list of the words used in a book or a writer's work, with information about where the words can be found and in which sentences: *a Shakespeare concordance* **2** [U] formal the state of there being agreement or similarity between things: *Last Thursday's show produced moments of inspired concordance* ***between*** *the dance forms.*

▸verb [T] specialized to collect all the words used in a book or a writer's work into a book or list in alphabetical order, with information about where the words can be found and in which sentences: *We've got a computer program which will concordance newspaper texts.*

concordat /kənˈkɔː.dæt/ US /-ˈkɔr-/ noun [C] specialized a formal agreement, especially on religious matters, between the Roman Catholic Church and a particular country

concourse /ˈkɒŋ.kɔːs/ US /ˈkɑːn.kɔːrs/ noun [C] a large space or room in a public building such as a station or airport which people meet in or pass through: *There's a ticket machine in the main concourse.*

concrete /ˈkɒŋ.kriːt/ US /ˈkɑːn-/ noun; verb; adj

▸noun [U] B2 a very hard building material made by mixing together CEMENT, sand, small stones, and water: *reinforced concrete* ◦ *a concrete floor/path* ◦ *a grey concrete building*

▸verb [T] to cover something in concrete: *Why did you concrete* ***over*** *that nice garden?*

▸adj C1 clear and certain, or real and existing in a form that can be seen or felt: *They think she killed her husband, but they've no concrete* ***evidence****.* ◦ *We've got a general idea of what we want, but nothing concrete at the moment.*

concrete ˈjungle noun [C usually singular] an ugly grey area of a city where people live in closely crowded apartment buildings and there is little space and no trees or grass

concrete ˈmixer noun [C] a **cement mixer**

concrete ˈnoun noun [C] a noun which refers to a real, physical object → Compare **abstract noun**

concubine /ˈkɒŋ.kjʊ.baɪn/ US /ˈkɑːn-/ noun [C] a woman who, in some societies, lives and has sex with a man she is not married to, and has a lower social rank than his wife or wives

concur /kənˈkɜːʳ/ US /-ˈkɝː/ verb [I] (-rr-) formal **1** to agree or have the same opinion: *The new report concurs* ***with*** *previous findings.* ◦ [+ that] *The board concurred* ***that*** *the editor should have full control over editorial matters.* ◦ [+ speech] *'I think you're absolutely right,' concurred Chris.* **2** If two or more events concur, they happen at the same time.

concurrence /kənˈkʌr.əns/ US /-ˈkɝː-/ noun [U] formal the situation in which people, things, or events concur

concurrent /kənˈkʌr.ənt/ US /-ˈkɝː-/ adj happening or existing at the same time: *The judge imposed concurrent sentences totalling 14 years for the attacks on the girls.* • **concurrently** /-li/ adv *Her two dramas are being shown concurrently (= at the same time) by rival television stations.*

concuss /kənˈkʌs/ verb [T often passive] to give someone concussion

concussed /kənˈkʌst/ adj suffering from concussion: *I hit my head and was concussed for several days.*

concussion /kən'kʌʃ.ən/ **noun** [U] temporary damage to the brain caused by a fall or hit on the head or by violent shaking: *He's been a bit dizzy and confused since the accident. Do you think it's mild concussion?*

condemn /kən'dem/ **verb** [T] C2 to criticize something or someone strongly, usually for moral reasons: *The terrorist action has been condemned **as** an act of barbarism and cowardice.* ◦ *The film was condemned **for** its sexism.*

PHRASAL VERBS **condemn sb to (do) sth** to say what the punishment of someone who has committed a serious crime will be: *She was condemned to **death** and executed two weeks later.* ◦ [often passive] *They were condemned to spend the rest of their lives in prison.* • **condemn sb to sth** to make someone suffer in a particular way: *Poor education condemns many young people to low-paid jobs.*

condemnation /ˌkɒn.dəm'neɪ.ʃən/ (US) /ˌkɑːn-/ **noun** [C or U] the act of condemning something or someone: *The shooting of the policeman has received universal condemnation.* • **condemnatory** /kən'dem.nə.tri/ (US) /-tɔːr.i/ **adj** *a condemnatory speech/tone*

condemned /kən'demd/ **adj** PERSON ▷ **1** A condemned person is someone who is going to be killed, especially as a punishment for having committed a very serious crime, such as murder. BUILDING ▷ **2** describes a building that has been officially judged not safe for people to live in or to use, or food that has been officially judged not safe to eat

conˌdemned ˈcell **noun** [C] a room in a prison for someone who is going to be killed as a legal punishment

condensation /ˌkɒn.den'seɪ.ʃən/ (US) /ˌkɑːn-/ **noun** [U] **1** the drops of water that appear on cold windows or other surfaces, as a result of hot air or steam becoming cool: *We get a lot of condensation on the walls in the winter.* **2** specialized the act or process of changing from a gas to a liquid or solid state

condense /kən'dens/ **verb** REDUCE ▷ **1** [T] to reduce something, such as a speech or piece of writing, in length: *I condensed ten pages of comments **into/to** two.* **2** [T] to make a liquid thicker by removing some of the water BECOME LIQUID ▷ **3** [I or T] to change or make something change from a gas to a liquid or solid state: *Water vapour in the air condenses into fog.* • **condensed** /-'denst/ **adj** *condensed soup*

conˌdensed ˈmilk **noun** [U] a thick and very sweet milk from which water has been removed

condenser /kən'den.səʳ/ (US) /-sɚ/ **noun** [C] specialized a piece of equipment that reduces gases to their liquid or solid form

condescend /ˌkɒn.dɪ'send/ (US) /ˌkɑːn-/ **verb** usually humorous **condescend to do sth** If you condescend to do something, you agree to do something that you do not consider to be good enough for your social position: *I wonder if Michael will condescend to visit us?* • **condescension** /-'sen.ʃən/ **noun** [U]

PHRASAL VERB **condescend to sb** to treat someone as if you are more important or more intelligent than them: *He explains things without condescending to his audience.*

condescending /ˌkɒn.dɪ'sen.dɪŋ/ (US) /ˌkɑːn-/ **adj** disapproving treating someone as if you are more important or more intelligent than them: *I hate the way he's so condescending to his staff!* • **condescendingly** /-li/ **adv**

condiment /'kɒn.dɪ.mənt/ (US) /'kɑːn-/ **noun** [C] formal a substance, such as salt, that you add to food to improve its taste

condition /kən'dɪʃ.ən/ **noun; verb**

▸**noun** STATE ▷ **1** B1 [S or U] the particular state that something or someone is in: *Mum's still got our pram – it's very old, but it's **in** perfect condition.* ◦ *They left the flat in a terrible condition – there was mess everywhere.* ◦ *The hospital say her condition (= state of health) is improving slowly.* ◦ *He's **in no** condition (= he is too ill or too drunk) **to** drive home.* **2 conditions** [plural] B1 the physical situation that someone or something is in and affected by: ***weather** conditions* ◦ ***working** conditions* ◦ *The prisoners were kept **in** the most appalling conditions.* ◦ ***Under** what conditions do plants grow best?* **3** B2 [C] any of different types of diseases: *to suffer from a heart/skin condition* ◦ *a medical condition* **4 out of condition** not healthy enough for hard physical exercise, as a result of not taking part in sport or other physical activities AGREED LIMIT ▷ **5** C1 [C] an arrangement that must exist before something else can happen: *We're not in a position to **make/set** any conditions – we'll have to accept what they offer us.* ◦ ***Under** the conditions of the agreement, she must vacate the house on 12 July .* **6 on (the) condition that** B2 only if: *I'll come to the party on the condition that you don't wear those ridiculous trousers!*

Word partners for condition (STATE)

in excellent/immaculate/mint/perfect condition • in a *critical/serious/stable* condition • the condition *of* sth

Word partners for conditions (STATE)

conditions *deteriorate/improve/worsen* • *appalling/atrocious/dangerous/treacherous* conditions • *poor/primitive/unhygienic* conditions • *cold/icy/wet/windy* conditions • *under* (harsh/terrible) conditions • conditions *for* sb/sth

Word partners for condition (AGREED LIMIT)

agree to/comply with/fulfil/meet conditions • *attach/impose/set* conditions • *under* the conditions *of* sth • a *necessary* condition (for/of sth)

▸**verb** [T] **1** C2 to train or influence a person or animal mentally so that they do or expect a particular thing without thinking about it: *a conditioned reflex/response* ◦ [+ to infinitive] *Pavlov conditioned dogs **to** salivate at the sound of a bell.* ◦ *Women were conditioned **to** expect lower wages than men.* **2** to try to improve the quality or appearance of your hair, skin, etc. by putting a conditioner on it • **conditioning** /-ɪŋ/ **noun** [U] *Conditioning starts as soon as boys are given guns to play with and girls are given dolls.*

conditional /kən'dɪʃ.ən.əl/ **adj, noun; adj**

▸**adj, noun** specialized SENTENCE FORM ▷ **1** [C] (relating to) a sentence, often starting with 'if' or 'unless', in which one half expresses something which depends on the other half: *a conditional clause* ◦ *'If I won a lot of money, I'd go travelling' is an example of a conditional (sentence).* VERB FORM ▷ **2** [S] (a form of a verb) expressing the idea that one thing depends on another thing: *In English, **the** conditional is expressed by 'would'.*

▸**adj** describes an offer or agreement that depends on something else being done: *The offer of a place on the nursing course is conditional **on/upon** my passing all three exams.* → Opposite **unconditional** • **conditionally** /-i/ **adv**

conditioner /kən'dɪʃ.ən.əʳ/ (US) /-ɚ/ **noun** [C or U] **1** a thick liquid that you put on and wash off your hair after you have washed it, to improve the quality and appearance of your hair **2** a thick liquid which you wash clothes in to make them feel soft: ***fabric*** *conditioner*

condo /ˈkɒn.dəʊ/ ⓤⓢ /ˈkɑːn.doʊ/ **noun** [C] US informal a **condominium**

condolence /kənˈdəʊ.ləns/ ⓤⓢ /-ˈdoʊ-/ **noun** [C usually plural, U] sympathy and sadness for the family or close friends of a person who has recently died, or an expression of this, especially in written form: *a letter of condolence* ◦ *Dignitaries from all over the world came to **offer** their condolences.*

condom /ˈkɒn.dɒm/ ⓤⓢ /ˈkɑːn.dəm/ **noun** [C] (UK also **sheath**) a thin rubber covering that a man can wear on his PENIS during sex to stop a woman becoming pregnant or to protect him or his partner against infectious diseases

condominium /ˌkɒn.dəˈmɪn.i.əm/ ⓤⓢ /ˌkɑːn-/ **noun** [C] **BUILDING** ▷ **1** US an apartment building in which each apartment is owned separately by the people living in it, but also containing shared areas **2** (informal **condo**) an apartment in a condominium

condone /kənˈdəʊn/ ⓤⓢ /-ˈdoʊn/ **verb** [T] to accept or allow behaviour that is wrong: *If the government is seen to condone **violence**, the bloodshed will never stop.*

condor /ˈkɒn.dɔːʳ/ ⓤⓢ /ˈkɑːn.dɔːr/ **noun** [C] a type of VULTURE (= a large bird which feeds on dead animals) from South America

conducive /kənˈdjuː.sɪv/ ⓤⓢ /-ˈduː-/ **adj** providing the right conditions for something good to happen or exist: *Such a noisy environment was not conducive **to** a good night's sleep.* ◦ *This is a more conducive atmosphere **for** studying.*

conduct **verb**; **noun**

▸**verb** /kənˈdʌkt/ **ORGANIZE** ▷ **1** Ⓑ2 [T] to organize and perform a particular activity: *We are conducting a survey to find out what our customers think of their local bus service.* ◦ *The experiments were conducted by scientists in New York.* ◦ *How you choose to conduct your private life is your own business!* **BEHAVE** ▷ **2 conduct yourself** Ⓒ2 to behave in a particular way, especially in a public or formal situation, or to organize the way in which you live in a particular way: *How should I conduct **myself** at these dinners? I know nothing about etiquette.* **SHOW WAY** ▷ **3** [T usually + adv/prep] formal to lead someone to a particular place: *May I conduct you **to** your table, sir, or would you prefer to have a drink at the bar first?* ◦ *The protesters were conducted from the courtroom by two police officers.* **4** [T] If you conduct a TOUR of a place, you take people round the place and show it to them: *A guide conducts **tours** of the cathedral every afternoon at 2.00.* ◦ *a conducted **tour** of the palace* **MUSIC** ▷ **5** Ⓑ2 [I or T] to direct the performance of musicians or a piece of music: *The orchestra was conducted by Mira Shapur.* ◦ *Who's conducting at tonight's concert?* **ALLOW THROUGH** ▷ **6** [T] to allow electricity or heat to go through: *Copper conducts electricity, but plastic does not.*

▸**noun** [U] /ˈkɒn.dʌkt/ ⓤⓢ /ˈkɑːn-/ **BEHAVIOUR** ▷ **1** behaviour: *bad/excellent/disgraceful conduct* ◦ *The club has a strict **code** (= set of rules) of conduct.* **ORGANIZATION** ▷ **2** formal the way in which an activity is organized and performed: *He was criticized for his conduct of the inquiry.*

conduction /kənˈdʌk.ʃᵊn/ **noun** [U] the process by which heat or electricity goes through a substance: *the conduction of electricity*

conductive /kənˈdʌk.tɪv/ ⓤⓢ /-t̬ɪv/ **adj** describes a substance that allows heat or electricity to go through it: *Aluminium is a conductive metal.* • **conductivity** /ˌkɒn.dʌkˈtɪv.ɪ.ti/ ⓤⓢ /ˌkɑːn.dʌkˈtɪv.ə.t̬i/ **noun** [U] *a high level of conductivity*

conductor /kənˈdʌk.təʳ/ ⓤⓢ /-tɚ/ **noun** [C] **PUBLIC TRANSPORT** ▷ **1** someone whose job is to sell tickets on a bus, train, or other public vehicle **MUSIC** ▷ **2** Ⓑ2 someone who directs the performance of musicians or a piece of music: *The conductor raised his baton.* ◦ *a guest conductor* **SUBSTANCE** ▷ **3** a substance that allows heat or electricity to go through it: *Metal is a good conductor of heat.*

conduit /ˈkɒn.djuː.ɪt/ ⓤⓢ /ˈkɑːn.duː-/ **noun** [C] **1** a pipe or passage for water or electrical wires to go through **2** a way of connecting two places: *There is growth in sales to Hong Kong, the conduit for Taiwan's exports to China.*

cone /kəʊn/ ⓤⓢ /koʊn/ **noun**; **verb**

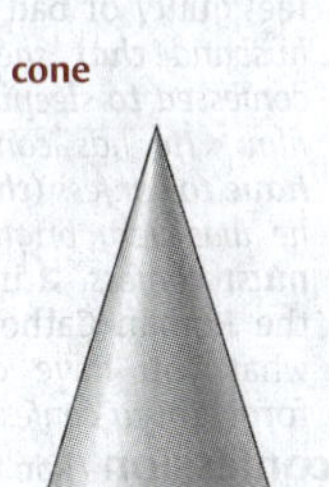
cone

▸**noun** [C] **SHAPE** ▷ **1** a shape with a flat, round, or oval base and a top which becomes narrower until it forms a point: *a **traffic** cone* **TREE** ▷ **2** the hard oval-shaped fruit of a CONIFER **FOOD** ▷ **3** a container made of very light thin biscuit, or one of these containing ICE CREAM: *an ice cream cone*

▸**verb**

PHRASAL VERB **cone sth off** to prevent traffic from using a road or area by putting special objects that are shaped like cones on it: *Part of the road had been coned off for repair work.*

coney /ˈkəʊ.ni/ ⓤⓢ /ˈkoʊ-/ **noun** [C or U] another spelling of **cony**

confab /ˈkɒn.fæb/ ⓤⓢ /ˈkɑːn-/ **noun** [C usually singular] old-fashioned humorous an informal discussion, usually about one particular subject: *They had a quick confab to decide on a possible design.*

confection /kənˈfek.ʃᵊn/ **noun** [C] formal a decorated cake or unusual sweet dish

confectioner /kənˈfek.ʃᵊn.əʳ/ ⓤⓢ /-ɚ/ **noun** [C] a company or person that makes or sells SWEETS or chocolates

conˌfectioner's ˈsugar **noun** [U] US for **icing sugar**

confectionery /kənˈfek.ʃᵊn.ri/ ⓤⓢ /-er.i/ **noun** [U] SWEETS (= small pieces of sweet food, made with sugar) or chocolates

confederacy /kənˈfed.ᵊr.ə.si/ ⓤⓢ /-ɚ-/ **noun** [C, + sing/pl verb] the situation in which states or people join together for a particular purpose, usually related to politics or trade

confederate /kənˈfed.ᵊr.ət/ ⓤⓢ /-ɚ-/ **noun**; **adj**

▸**noun** [C] formal someone you work together with in a secret, sometimes illegal, activity

▸**adj** united in or part of a confederacy: *confederate states*

confederation /kənˌfed.əˈreɪ.ʃᵊn/ **noun** [C, + sing/pl verb] an organization consisting of different groups of people working together for business or political reasons: *the Confederation of British Industry*

confer /kənˈfɜːʳ/ ⓤⓢ /-ˈfɝː/ **verb** (**-rr-**) **TALK** ▷ **1** [I] to exchange ideas on a particular subject, often in order to reach a decision on what action to take: *I should like some time to confer **with** my lawyer.* **GIVE** ▷ **2** [T] to give an official title, honour, or advantage to someone: *An honorary doctorate was conferred **on** him by Edinburgh University.*

C

conference /ˈkɒn.fər.əns/ (US) /ˈkɑːn.fɚ-/ **noun** [C] **1** (B1) an event, sometimes lasting a few days, at which there is a group of talks on a particular subject, or a meeting in which especially business matters are discussed formally: *a conference **on** women's rights* ◦ *They frequently **hold** conferences at that hotel.* ◦ *I'm speaking at/attending a conference next week.* ◦ *Should I book the conference **room** for the meeting?* **2 be in conference** formal to be in a meeting: *Ms O'Neill isn't available at present. She's in conference.*

ˈ**conference** ˌ**call** **noun** [C] a work phone call that involves three or more people

confess /kənˈfes/ **verb** [I or T] **1** (B2) to admit that you have done something wrong or something that you feel guilty or bad about: [+ that] *She confessed **to** her husband **that** she had sold her wedding ring.* ◦ *He confessed **to** sleep**ing**/hav**ing** slept through most of the film.* ◦ *He has confessed **to** the murder.* ◦ [+ (that)] *I **have to** confess (**that**) when I first met Ian I didn't think he was very bright.* ◦ *I found it all very confusing, I **must** confess.* **2** in the Christian religion, especially the Roman Catholic Church, to tell God or a priest what you have done wrong so that you can be forgiven: *to confess your sins*

confession /kənˈfeʃ.ən/ **noun** [C or U] **1** (B2) the act of admitting that you have done something wrong or illegal: *I've got a confession to **make** – I've lost that book you lent me.* ◦ *I can't ask for help. It feels like a confession **of** failure.* ◦ *Confession is the first stage of coming to terms with what you've done.* ◦ *He **made** a full confession to the police.* **2** an occasion when a Christian tells God or, especially in the Roman Catholic Church, tells a priest formally and privately, what they have done wrong so that they can be forgiven: *Have you been to confession recently?* ◦ *The priest **heard** his confession.*

confessional /kənˈfeʃ.ən.əl/ **noun** [C] a small structure like a box in a church, especially a Roman Catholic church, in which people can privately confess to a priest

confessor /kənˈfes.ər/ (US) /-ɚ/ **noun** [C] a priest who someone can confess to

confetti /kənˈfet.i/ (US) /-ˈfeţ-/ **noun** [U] small pieces of coloured paper that you throw at a celebration, especially over two people who have just been married

confetti

confidant /ˈkɒn.fɪ.dænt/ (US) /ˈkɑːn.fə-/ **noun** [C] (female also **confidante**) a person you trust and share your feelings and secrets with: *a **close** confidant*

confide /kənˈfaɪd/ **verb** [I or T] to tell something secret or personal to someone who you trust not to tell anyone else: [+ that] *He confided (**to** her) **that** his hair was not his own.* ◦ [+ speech] *'My husband doesn't know yet, but I'm going to leave him,' she confided.* • **confiding** /-ˈfaɪ.dɪŋ/ **adj** *a confiding tone/whisper* • **confidingly** /-ˈfaɪ.dɪŋ.li/ **adv** *She spoke in a low voice, leaning towards him confidingly.*

PHRASAL VERB **confide in sb** to share your feelings and secrets with someone because you trust them not to tell other people: *She's nice, but I don't feel I can confide in her.*

confidence /ˈkɒn.fɪ.dəns/ (US) /ˈkɑːn-/ **noun** CERTAINTY ▷ **1** (B2) [U] the quality of being certain of your abilities or of having trust in people, plans, or the future: [+ to infinitive] *He's got the confidence to walk into a room of strangers and immediately start a conversation.* ◦ *She's completely lacking in confidence.* ◦ *I **have every/complete** confidence **in** her. She'll be perfect for the job.* ◦ [+ that] *I don't share your confidence **that** the market will improve next year.* SECRET ▷ **2** [C] a secret that you tell someone: *They talked endlessly, **exchanging** confidences.* **3 in confidence** (C2) If you tell something to someone in confidence, you do not want them to tell anyone else. **4 take sb into your confidence** to share your secrets with someone, trusting them not to tell other people: *I should never have taken him into my confidence.*

> **Word partners for confidence**
>
> *boost/bolster/improve/increase* confidence • *dent/shake/shatter/undermine* confidence • *lack/lose* confidence • *have* confidence *in* sb/sth • *absolute/complete/full/total* confidence • a *degree/level/sense* of confidence • *with* confidence

ˈ**confidence** ˌ**trick** **noun** [C] a **con**

ˈ**confidence** ˌ**trickster** **noun** [C] a **con artist**

confident /ˈkɒn.fɪ.dənt/ (US) /ˈkɑːn-/ **adj** (B1) having confidence: *Be a bit more confident **in** yourself!* ◦ *They don't sound confident **about** the future of the industry.* ◦ *I'm confident **of** his skills as a manager.* ◦ [+ that] *Are you confident **that** enough people will attend the event?* ◦ *It was a confident performance.* • **confidently** /-li/ **adv** (B2) *Try to act confidently, even if you feel nervous.*

> **Other ways of saying confident**
>
> **Self-assured** and **self-confident** are words that mean the same as 'confident':
>
> *The interview showed her as a very **self-assured** woman.*
>
> **Assertive** can be used to describe people who are confident because they are not frightened to say what they want or believe:
>
> *You'll have to be more **assertive** if you want to be promoted.*
>
> **Bold** can be used when someone is very confident, especially in a way that shows a lack of respect:
>
> *He was a **bold** and defiant little boy.*
>
> The phrase **be sure of yourself** can be used when someone is very confident or too confident:
>
> *He seems very **sure of himself**.*
>
> If someone is confident in an unpleasant or rude way, you could use the adjective **cocky** in informal English or **brash**:
>
> *He's a **cocky** young man.*

confidential /ˌkɒn.fɪˈden.ʃəl/ (US) /ˌkɑːn-/ **adj** (C1) secret, often in a formal, business, or military situation: *All information will be treated as **strictly** confidential.* • **confidentially** /-i/ **adv** *Can I speak to you confidentially?* ◦ *All information supplied will be treated confidentially.*

confidentiality /ˌkɒn.fɪ.den.ʃiˈæl.ɪ.ti/ (US) /ˌkɑːn.fɪ.den.ʃiˈæl.ə.ţi/ **noun** [U] the state of being confidential: *patient/client confidentiality* ◦ *All replies will be treated with complete confidentiality.*

configuration /kənˌfɪg.əˈreɪ.ʃən/ **noun** **1** [C] formal or specialized the particular arrangement or pattern of a group of related things **2** [C or U] the way in which all the equipment that makes up a computer system is set to operate

configure /kənˈfɪg.ər/ (US) /kənˈfɪg.ɚ/ **verb** [T] to arrange something or change the controls on a computer or other device so that it can be used in a particular way: [+ to infinitive] *Some software can be configured* ***to*** *prevent children from giving out their phone numbers on the internet.*

confine /kən'faɪn/ **verb 1** C2 [T] to limit an activity, person, or problem in some way: *Let's confine our discussion* ***to*** *the matter in question, please!* ◦ *Please confine your use of the phone* ***to*** *business calls.* ◦ *By closing the infected farms we're hoping to confine the disease* ***to*** *the north of the region* (= stop it from spreading to other areas). **2** C2 [T usually passive] to keep someone closed in a place, often by force: *The hostages had been confined for so long that they couldn't cope with the outside world.* **3 be confined to somewhere/sth** to exist only in a particular area or group of people: *We know that the illness is not confined to any one group in society.* ◦ *This attitude seems to be confined to the upper classes.*

confinement /kən'faɪn.mənt/ **noun 1** [U] the situation in which a person or animal is kept somewhere, usually by force: *She spent most of those years under house arrest or* ***close*** *confinement.* **2** [C or U] old-fashioned or formal **labour** (= the process of giving birth to a baby)

confines /'kɒn.faɪnz/ US /'kɑːn-/ **noun** [plural] formal the outer limits of something: *the* ***narrow*** *confines* ***of*** *a religious life* ◦ ***within/beyond*** *the confines* ***of*** *the city*

confirm /kən'fɜːm/ US /-'fɜːm/ **verb** **MAKE CERTAIN** ▷ **1** B1 [I or T] to make an arrangement or meeting certain, often by phone or writing: [+ that] *Six people have confirmed* ***that*** *they will be attending and ten haven't replied yet.* ◦ *Flights should be confirmed 48 hours before departure.* ◦ *I've accepted the job over the phone, but I haven't confirmed in writing yet.* **PROVE TRUE** ▷ **2** B2 [T] to prove that a belief or an opinion that was previously not completely certain is true: [+ question word] *The smell of cigarette smoke confirmed* ***wh****at he had suspected: there had been a party in his absence.* ◦ [+ (that)] *Her announcement confirmed (****that****) she would be resigning as prime minister.* ◦ *The leader's speech was impressive and confirmed her faith in the party.* **RELIGION** ▷ **3** [T] to accept someone formally as a full member of the Christian Church at a special ceremony

confirmation /ˌkɒn.fə'meɪ.ʃən/ US /ˌkɑːn.fɚ-/ **noun** **CERTAIN** ▷ **1** B2 [C or U] a statement, often written, that an arrangement or meeting is certain: *a letter of confirmation* ◦ *We've only had five confirmations for the conference so far.* ◦ *We will send you* ***written*** *confirmation* ***of*** *our offer shortly.* **PROOF** ▷ **2** [U] a statement or proof that something is true: *We are still awaiting confirmation* ***of*** *the exact number of casualties.* ◦ *Her confession was no surprise to him, – just the confirmation* ***of*** *a long-held suspicion.* **RELIGION** ▷ **3** [C or U] a ceremony in which someone is confirmed into the Christian Church

confirmed /kən'fɜːmd/ US /-fɜːmd/ **adj** [before noun] describes someone who has had a particular habit or way of life for a long time and is unlikely to change: *a confirmed bachelor/atheist/tea drinker*

confiscate /'kɒn.fɪ.skeɪt/ US /'kɑːn-/ **verb** [T] to take a possession away from someone when you have the right to do so, usually as a punishment and often for a limited period, after which it is returned to the owner: *Miss Edwards has confiscated my phone!* ◦ *His passport was confiscated by the police to prevent him from leaving the country.* • **confiscation** /ˌkɒn.fɪ'skeɪ.ʃən/ US /ˌkɑːn-/ **noun** [C or U] *There was a record number of confiscations by customs officers last year.*

confit /kɒn'fiː/ US /koʊn'fiː/ **noun** [U] formal meat cooked slowly in its own fat: *confit of duck*

conflagration /ˌkɒn.flə'greɪ.ʃən/ US /ˌkɑːn-/ **noun** [C] formal **1** a large fire that causes a lot of damage **2** a large and violent event, such as a war, involving a lot of people

conflate /kən'fleɪt/ **verb** [T] to combine two or more separate things, especially pieces of text, to form a whole • **conflation** /-'fleɪ.ʃən/ **noun** [C or U]

conflict noun; verb

▸**noun** [C or U] /'kɒn.flɪkt/ US /'kɑːn-/ **1** B2 an active disagreement between people with opposing opinions or principles: *There was a lot of conflict* ***between*** *him and his father.* ◦ *It was an unpopular policy and caused a number of conflicts within the party.* ◦ *His outspoken views would frequently* ***bring*** *him* ***into*** *conflict* ***with*** *the president.* **2** B2 fighting between two or more groups of people or countries: *We wish to avoid conflict* ***between*** *our countries if at all possible.*

IDIOM **a conflict of interest** C2 a situation in which someone cannot make a fair decision because they will be affected by the result: *I need to* ***declare*** *a conflict of interest here – one of the candidates for the job is a friend of mine.*

▸**verb** [I] /kən'flɪkt/ **BE OPPOSITE** ▷ If beliefs, needs, or facts, etc. conflict, they are very different and cannot easily exist together or both be true: *The results of the new research would seem to conflict* ***with*** *existing theories.*

conflicted /kən'flɪk.tɪd/ **adj** [after verb] confused or worried because you cannot choose between very different ideas, feelings, or beliefs, and do not know what to do or believe: *It seems that politicians, like ordinary citizens, are conflicted* ***about*** *gambling.*

conflicting /kən'flɪk.tɪŋ/ **adj** describes beliefs, needs, facts, etc. that are different and opposing: *conflicting opinions/ideas/advice* ◦ *She was troubled by the conflicting* ***interests*** (= interests which are difficult to combine) *of a career and a family.* ◦ *The jury heard conflicting* ***evidence*** *from three different witnesses.*

confluence /'kɒn.fluː.əns/ US /'kɑːn-/ **noun** [C] specialized the place where two rivers flow together and become one larger river

conform /kən'fɔːm/ US /-'fɔːrm/ **verb** [I] to behave according to the usual standards of behaviour that are expected by a group or society: *At our school, you were required to conform, and there was no place for originality.*

PHRASAL VERB **conform to/with sth** to obey a rule or reach the necessary stated standard, or to do things in a traditional way: *Before buying a pram, make sure that it conforms to the official safety standards.* ◦ *Members must conform to a strict dress code.*

conformance /kən'fɔː.məns/ US /-'fɔːr-/ **noun** [U] **conformity**

conformist /kən'fɔː.mɪst/ US /-'fɔːr-/ **noun** [C] often disapproving someone who conforms • **conformist adj**

conformity /kən'fɔː.mɪ.ti/ US /-'fɔːr.mə.ţi/ **noun** [U] **1** behaviour that follows the usual standards that are expected by a group or society: *It's depressing how much conformity there is in such young children.* **2** (also **conformance**) the process of a product being made as it was designed, without mistakes or faults: *Our goal is to improve conformity* ***with*** *customer requirements.* ◦ *conformity* ***to specification***

confound /kən'faʊnd/ **verb** [T] to confuse and very much surprise someone, so that they are unable to explain or deal with a situation: *An elderly man from Hull has confounded doctors* ***by*** *recovering after he was officially declared dead.* ◦ *The singer confounded her critics* ***with*** *a remarkable follow-up album.*

C

confounded /kən'faʊn.dɪd/ **adj** [before noun] old-fashioned informal used to express anger: *What a confounded nuisance!*

confront /kən'frʌnt/ **verb** [T] C2 to face, meet, or deal with a difficult situation or person: *As she left the court, she was confronted* ***by*** *angry crowds who tried to block her way.* ◦ *It's an issue we'll have to confront at some point, no matter how unpleasant it is.* ◦ *I thought I would remain calm, but when I was confronted* ***with/by*** *the TV camera, I became very nervous.*

PHRASAL VERB **confront sb with sth** C2 to tell someone what they do not want to hear, often because it is about something bad that they have done or because it needs an explanation: *I know she's the one who made the error, but I don't want to confront her with it in case she breaks down.*

confrontation /ˌkɒn.frʌn'teɪ.ʃən/ US /ˌkɑːn.frən-/ **noun** [C or U] C2 a fight or argument: *She actually enjoys confrontation, whereas I prefer a quiet life.* ◦ *There were violent confrontations between police and demonstrators.* • **confrontational** /-əl/ **adj** *He's got a rather aggressive, confrontational manner.*

confuse /kən'fjuːz/ **verb** [T] **1** B2 to mix up someone's mind or ideas, or to make something difficult to understand: *You're confusing him! Tell him slowly and one thing at a time.* ◦ *Stop confusing the issue (= making the problem unnecessarily difficult)!* **2** B2 to mix up two separate things or people in your mind, imagining that they are one: *You're confusing me* ***with*** *my sister – she's the one studying drama.* ◦ *It's easy to confuse his films, because he tends to use the same actors.*

confused /kən'fjuːzd/ **adj** **1** B1 unable to think clearly or to understand something: *Grandfather gets quite confused sometimes, and doesn't even know what day it is.* ◦ *I'm a bit confused. Was that her husband or her son she was with?* **2** B2 not clear and therefore difficult to understand: *Your essay gets a bit confused halfway through when you introduce too many ideas at once.*

confusing /kən'fjuː.zɪŋ/ **adj** B1 describes something that makes you feel confused because it is difficult to understand: *We've got two people called Paul James working here, so it's a bit confusing!* ◦ *The instructions are terribly confusing. Could you help me with them, please?*

confusion /kən'fjuː.ʒən/ **noun** **1** B2 [C or U] a situation in which people do not understand what is happening, what they should do or who someone or something is: *There seems to be some confusion* ***over*** *who is actually giving the talk.* ◦ *To* ***avoid*** *confusion, the twins never wore the same clothes.* **2** B2 [U] a situation, often with a lot of activity and noise, in which people do not know what to do: *In the confusion after the bomb blast, I lost my bag and wasn't able to stop and look for it.*

> **Word partners for confusion**
>
> *general/total/utter/widespread* confusion • *cause/create/lead to/result in* confusion • *descend into/fall into/plunge* sth *into/throw* sth *into* confusion • *avoid/clear up/dispel/eliminate* confusion • confusion *surrounding* sth • confusion *among/amongst/within* • confusion *about/over* sth • a *sense/state* of confusion

confute /kən'fjuːt/ **verb** [T] formal to prove a person or an argument to be wrong

conga /'kɒŋ.gə/ US /'kɑːŋ-/ **noun** [C] **1** a Latin American dance in which a chain of people hold each other around the waist and follow the leader around using simple steps and kicks **2** a piece of music for the conga

congeal /kən'dʒiːl/ **verb** [I] to change from a liquid or soft state to a thick or solid state: *The blood had congealed in thick black clots.* • **congealed** /-'dʒiːld/ **adj** *congealed fat*

congenial /kən'dʒiː.ni.əl/ **adj** friendly and pleasant: *congenial company/surroundings*

congenital /kən'dʒen.ɪ.təl/ US /-t̬əl/ **adj** **1** specialized describes a disease or condition that exists at or from birth: *a congenital abnormality/disease* **2** describes someone who always shows a particular bad quality: *a congenital* ***liar***

conger eel /ˌkɒŋ.gə'riːl/ US /ˌkɑŋ.gɚ-/ **noun** [C] a long, powerful, snake-like sea fish

congested /kən'dʒes.tɪd/ **adj** **1** too blocked or crowded and causing difficulties **2** describes roads and towns where there is too much traffic and movement is made difficult **3** describes someone who cannot breathe through their nose because it is blocked, usually during an infection **4** describes lungs or other body parts that have become too full of blood or other liquid • **congestion** /-tʃən/ **noun** [U] C1 *The (****traffic****) congestion in the city gets worse during the summer.* ◦ *This spray helps to ease* ***nasal*** *congestion.*

con'gestion ˌcharge **noun** [C usually singular] UK an amount of money that you have to pay each day to drive into a city centre, charged in order to reduce traffic

conglomerate /kən'glɒm.ər.ət/ US /-'glɑː.mɚ-/ **noun** COMPANY ▷ **1** [C] a company that owns several smaller businesses whose products or services are usually very different: *a financial/industrial conglomerate* ROCK ▷ **2** [C or U] specialized a rock which consists of small rounded stones that are held together by clay and sand

conglomeration /kənˌglɒm.ə'reɪ.ʃən/ US /-ˌglɑː-/ **noun** [C usually singular, + sing/pl verb] a large group or mass of different things all collected together in an untidy or unusual way

congrats /kən'græts/ **exclamation, noun** [plural] informal **congratulation**

congratulate /kən'græt.jʊ.leɪt/ **verb** [T] B2 to praise someone and say that you approve of or are pleased about a special or unusual achievement: *I was just congratulating Ceri* ***on*** *winn****ing/on*** *hav****ing*** *won her race.* • **congratulatory** /kənˌgræt.jʊ'leɪ.tər.i/ US /-'grætʃ.əl.ə.tɔːr-/ **adj** *a congratulatory speech*

congratulation /kənˌgræt.jʊ'leɪ.ʃən/ **noun** **1 congratulations** [plural] A2 something that you say when you want to congratulate someone: *'I passed my driving test yesterday.' 'Did you? Congratulations!'* ◦ *Congratulations* ***on*** *your engagement!* **2** [U] the act of congratulating someone: *He sent her a note of congratulation on her election victory.*

congregate /'kɒŋ.grɪ.geɪt/ US /'kɑːŋ-/ **verb** [I] to come together in a large group of people or animals: *A crowd congregated* ***around*** *the entrance to the theatre, hoping to catch a glimpse of the stars of the show.*

congregation /ˌkɒŋ.grɪ'geɪ.ʃən/ US /ˌkɑːŋ-/ **noun** [C, + sing/pl verb] a group of people who have come together in a religious building for worship and prayer: *The vicar asked the congregation to kneel.* • **congregational** /-əl/ **adj** *congregational singing*

congress /'kɒŋ.gres/ US /'kɑːŋ-/ **noun** [C, + sing/pl verb] a large formal meeting of REPRESENTATIVES from countries or societies at which ideas are discussed and information is exchanged: *an international/*

medical congress ◦ *the congress* ***of*** *the Australian Council of Trade Unions*

Congress /ˈkɒŋ.ɡres/ Ⓤⓢ /ˈkɑːŋ-/ **noun** the elected group of politicians in the US who are responsible for making the law, consisting of the SENATE and the HOUSE OF REPRESENTATIVES: *Congress has rejected the recent presidential proposal on firearms.*

congressional /kəŋˈɡreʃ.ən.əl/ **adj** [before noun] belonging or related to the US Congress: *a congressional committee* ◦ *congressional elections*

congressman /ˈkɒŋ.ɡres.mən/ Ⓤⓢ /ˈkɑːŋ-/ **noun** [C] (plural **-men** /-mən/) a man who belongs to a CONGRESS, especially a member of the US HOUSE OF REPRESENTATIVES

congresswoman /ˈkɒŋ.ɡresˌwʊm.ən/ Ⓤⓢ /ˈkɑːŋ-/ **noun** [C] a woman who belongs to a CONGRESS, especially a member of the US HOUSE OF REPRESENTATIVES

congruent /ˈkɒŋ.ɡru.ənt/ Ⓤⓢ /ˈkɑːŋ-/ **adj** specialized describes a shape in mathematics that has the same shape and size as another: *congruent triangles* • **congruence** /-əns/ **noun** [U] • **congruently** /-li/ **adv**

conical /ˈkɒn.ɪ.kəl/ Ⓤⓢ /ˈkɑː.nɪ-/ **adj** shaped like a cone: *a conical hat*

ˌconical ˈflask noun [C] specialized a glass container with a flat base, a wide, rounded body, and a long neck, used in scientific work

conifer /ˈkɒn.ɪ.fər/ Ⓤⓢ /ˈkɑː.nɪ.fɚ/ **noun** [C] one of various types of EVERGREEN tree (= one that never loses its leaves) that produce fruit in the form of CONES • **coniferous** /kəˈnɪf.ər.əs/ Ⓤⓢ /-ɚ-/ **adj** *a coniferous forest*

conifer

conjecture /kənˈdʒek.tʃər/ Ⓤⓢ /-tʃɚ/ **noun; verb**

▸**noun** [C or U] a guess about something based on how it seems and not on proof: *There's been a lot of conjecture in the papers recently* ***about*** *the marriage.*

▸**verb** [I] formal to guess, based on the appearance of a situation and not on proof: *We'll never know exactly how she died; we can only conjecture.* ◦ [+ that] *He conjectured* ***that*** *the company would soon be in financial difficulties.* • **conjectural** /-əl/ **adj**

conjoined /kənˈdʒɔɪnd/ **adj** formal joined together

conˌjoined ˈtwins noun [plural] (old-fashioned **ˌSiamese ˈtwins**) a pair of TWINS who were born with some part of their bodies joined together

conjugal /ˈkɒn.dʒʊ.ɡəl/ Ⓤⓢ /ˈkɑːn-/ **adj** formal connected with marriage or the relationship between two married people, especially their sexual relationship: *conjugal happiness* ◦ *Some prisoners who want to start a family are to be permitted conjugal* ***visits***.

ˌconjugal ˈrights noun [plural] often humorous the right to have sex with the person you are married to: *He complained that he had been denied his conjugal rights.*

conjugate /ˈkɒn.dʒʊ.ɡeɪt/ Ⓤⓢ /ˈkɑːn-/ **verb** [I or T] specialized If a verb conjugates, it has different forms that show different TENSES, the number of people it refers to, etc., and if you conjugate a verb, you list its different forms: *The verb 'to be' conjugates irregularly.*

conjugation /ˌkɒn.dʒʊˈɡeɪ.ʃən/ Ⓤⓢ /ˌkɑːn-/ **noun** specialized **1** [C] a group of verbs that conjugate in the same way **2** [U] the way in which you conjugate a verb

conjunction /kənˈdʒʌŋk.ʃən/ **noun CONNECTING WORD** ▷ **1** Ⓑ2 [C] (written abbreviation **conj**) a word such as 'and', 'but', 'while', or 'although' that connects words, phrases, and CLAUSES in a sentence **COMBINATION** ▷ **2** Ⓒ2 [C or U] (formal **conjuncture** /kənˈdʒʌŋk.tʃər/) the situation in which events or conditions combine or happen together: *An unfortunate conjunction of circumstances led to his downfall.* ◦ *There is a team of writers working* ***in*** *conjunction* (***with*** *each other) on the book.* **3** [C or U] (formal **conjuncture**) in ASTROLOGY, the situation in which two planets appear to be in the same part of the sky as seen from Earth: *Mars and Venus will be* ***in*** *exact conjunction on 1 September.*

conjunctiva /ˌkɒn.dʒʌŋkˈtaɪ.və/ Ⓤⓢ /ˌkɑːn.dʒəŋk-/ **noun** [C usually singular] specialized the transparent layer of MUCOUS MEMBRANE that covers the inside of the EYELID and the front surface of the EYEBALL

conjunctivitis /kənˌdʒʌŋk.tɪˈvaɪ.tɪs/ Ⓤⓢ /-t̬ɪs/ **noun** [U] a painful infection of the eyes which makes them red and makes the EYELIDS swollen and sticky

conjure /ˈkʌn.dʒər/ Ⓤⓢ /-dʒɚ/ **verb** [I or T] to make something appear by magic, or as if by magic: *In an instant, the magician had conjured* (***up***) *a dove from his hat.*

PHRASAL VERBS **conjure sth up THINK OF** ▷ **1** to make a picture or idea appear in someone's mind: *The glittering ceremony conjured up images of Russia's imperial past.* ◦ *For some people, the word 'England' may still conjure up images of pretty gardens and tea parties.* **CREATE** ▷ **2** to make something in a quick and clever way, especially food: *How am I expected to conjure up a meal for six of his friends with almost nothing in the fridge?* • **conjure sb/sth up** to ask the spirit of a dead person or an imaginary being to appear, by using special words

conjurer (also **conjuror**) /ˈkʌn.dʒər.ər/ Ⓤⓢ /-dʒɚ.ɚ/ **noun** [C] a person who performs magic to entertain people

ˈconjuring ˌtrick noun [C] a trick in which something is made to appear as if by magic, often using a quick movement of the hand

conk /kɒŋk/ Ⓤⓢ /kɑːŋk/ **noun; verb**

▸**noun** [C] UK informal humorous a nose

▸**verb** [T] informal humorous to hit someone, usually on the head with a heavy object

PHRASAL VERB **conk out** informal **1** If vehicles and other machines conk out, they stop working or fail suddenly: *I was just two miles from home when my motorbike conked out!* **2** to go to sleep very quickly, or to suddenly become unconscious: *After a six-hour flight and a long day of meetings, it's not surprising you conked out.*

conker /ˈkɒŋ.kər/ Ⓤⓢ /ˈkɑːŋ.kɚ/ **noun** mainly UK **1** [C] the shiny brown poisonous nut of a HORSE CHESTNUT tree **2 conkers** [U] a children's game in which you have a conker with a string through it and try to break another child's conker by hitting it with yours

ˈcon ˌman (also **conman**) **noun** [C] a **con artist**

connect /kəˈnekt/ **verb JOIN** ▷ **1** Ⓑ1 [I or T] to join or be joined with something else: *Can I connect my printer* ***to*** *your computer?* ◦ *Where does the cooker connect* (***up***) ***to*** *the electricity?* ◦ *Has the phone/electricity/gas been connected (= switched on or joined to the main supply) in your new place yet?* **RELATE** ▷ **2** Ⓒ2 [T] to consider or show a person or thing to be related to someone or something else: *She's an actress I connect* ***with*** *the theatre rather than films.* ◦ *Police are connecting the break-in* ***with*** *other recent thefts in the area.* **PHONE** ▷ **3** [T] to make it possible for you to speak to someone else by phone: *Could you connect me* ***with/to*** *a number in Paris, please? I can't seem to get through.* **TRANSPORT** ▷ **4** [I] If two public transport vehicles connect, they arrive at suitable times to allow passengers to get off one and onto another: *Your flight arrives at 12.30, when it connects* ***with*** *a coach service to your hotel.* ◦ *There's a connecting train service between the airport and the city.*

connected /kəˈnek.tɪd/ **adj** **JOINED** ▷ **1** joined together: *The TV won't work if the aerial's not connected.* **RELATED** ▷ **2** related to someone or something: *They're not blood relations – they're only connected by marriage.* ◦ *He was connected in some way* ***with*** *that fraud scandal a couple of years back.* → See also **well connected**

connecting /kəˈnek.tɪŋ/ **adj** joining or being joined: *There's a connecting corridor between the buildings.* ◦ *connecting rooms*

conˈnecting ˌrod **noun** [C] (informal ˈ**con** ˌ**rod**) a rod that joins two particular moving parts in an engine, especially one joining the PISTON to the CRANKSHAFT in a motor vehicle

connection /kəˈnek.ʃən/ **noun** **RELATION** ▷ **1** B2 [C] the state of being related to someone or something else: *The connection* ***between*** *smoking* ***and*** *heart disease is well known.* ◦ *They're sisters, are they? I knew their surname was the same, but I never* ***made*** *(= thought of) the connection.* **2 in connection with sth** B2 on the subject of something: *They want to talk to you in connection with an unpaid tax bill.* **JOIN** ▷ **3** B1 [C or U] the act of joining or being joined to something else, or the part or process that makes this possible: *The electricity company guarantees connection within 24 hours.* ◦ *It's no wonder your shaver isn't working. There's a loose connection (= a connecting wire has become loose) in the plug.* **4** [C] the state of being joined or connected in some way **5 connections** [plural] the people you know and who can help you: *He only got the job because of his connections!* **PHONE** ▷ **6** [C] the way that two people can speak to each other by phone: *Sorry, could you repeat that? This is a very* ***bad*** *connection.* **TRANSPORT** ▷ **7** B2 [C] a bus, train, plane, etc. that arrives at a suitable time for passengers to get on after getting off another one so that they can continue their journey: *If the flight is late, we'll* ***miss*** *our connection.*

connective tissue /kəˌnek.tɪvˈtɪʃ.uː/, /-ˈtɪs.juː/ **noun** [U] specialized the strong material that supports and connects the organs in the body and is also found in the JOINTS (= places where two bones are connected)

connectivity /ˌkɒn.ekˈtɪv.ɪ.ti/ US /ˌkɑː.nekˈtɪv.ə.t̬i/ **noun** [U] specialized the ability of a computer, program, device, or system to connect with one or more others: *After installing, you should test for connectivity.*

connector /kəˈnek.təʳ/ US /-tɚ/ **noun** [C] specialized a device at the end of a wire in a piece of electrical equipment, which holds the wire in position: *electrical connectors*

connivance /kəˈnaɪ.vəns/ **noun** [U] the act of conniving, especially by knowing that something bad is happening and allowing it to continue: *Their appalling treatment of their child could only have happened* ***with*** *the connivance* ***of*** *their neighbours.*

connive /kəˈnaɪv/ **verb** [I] **1** to plan secretly and dishonestly for something to happen which will be to your advantage: *Civil servants and ministers were accused of conniving* ***with*** *the company* ***in*** *the supply of arms to Sierra Leone.* ◦ [+ to infinitive] *They connived* ***to*** *break the school rules at every opportunity.* **2** to allow something bad to happen although you know about it: *She had murdered or connived* ***at*** *the murder of one of her lovers.* ◦ *He called for checks to discover whether corrupt officials are being bribed to connive* ***in*** *shoddy construction.*

conniving /kəˈnaɪ.vɪŋ/ **adj** describes a person who deceives others for their own advantage: *He's a conniving bastard!*

connoisseur /ˌkɒn.əˈsɜːʳ/ US /ˌkɑː.nəˈsɝː/ **noun** [C] a person who knows a lot about and enjoys one of the arts, or food, drink, etc. and can judge quality and skill in that subject: *a wine/art connoisseur* ◦ *a connoisseur* ***of*** *ballet/cigars*

connotation /ˌkɒn.əˈteɪ.ʃən/ US /ˌkɑː.nə-/ **noun** [C] a feeling or idea that is suggested by a particular word although it need not be a part of the word's meaning, or something suggested by an object or situation: *The word 'lady' has connotations* ***of*** *refinement and excessive femininity that some women find offensive.* • **connote** /kəˈnəʊt/ US /-ˈnoʊt/ **verb** [T] formal *To me, chocolate connotes pleasure and indulgence.*

connubial /kəˈnjuː.bi.əl/ US /-ˈnuː-/ **adj** formal connected with marriage: *connubial bliss*

conquer /ˈkɒŋ.kəʳ/ US /ˈkɑːŋ.kɚ/ **verb** [T] **1** C1 to take control or possession of foreign land, or a group of people, by force: *The Spanish conquered the New World in the 16th century.* ◦ *The English were conquered by the Normans in 1066.* **2** to deal with or successfully fight against a problem or an unreasonable fear: *He has finally conquered his* ***fear*** *of spiders.* ◦ *It may be many years before this dreadful disease is conquered.*

conqueror /ˈkɒŋ.kər.əʳ/ US /ˈkɑːŋ.kɚ.ɚ/ **noun** [C] someone who has conquered a country or its people

conquest /ˈkɒŋ.kwest/ US /ˈkɑːŋ-/ **noun** **1** [C or U] the act of conquering a country, area, or situation **2** [C] humorous someone you have had sex with but probably not a relationship: *I was determined not to become just another of his conquests.*

conquistador /kɒnˈkwɪs.tə.dɔːʳ/ US /kɑːnˈkiː.stə.dɔːr/ **noun** [C] one of the Spanish people who travelled to America in the 16th century and took control of Mexico and Peru

conscience /ˈkɒn.ʃəns/ US /ˈkɑːn-/ **noun** [C or U] C2 the part of you that judges how moral your own actions are and makes you feel guilty about bad things that you have done or things you feel responsible for: *a* ***guilty*** *conscience* ◦ *a* ***question/matter of*** *conscience* ◦ *You didn't do anything wrong – you should have a* ***clear*** *conscience (= not feel guilty).* ◦ *My conscience would really trouble me if I wore a fur coat.* ◦ *He's got no conscience at all (= does not feel guilty)* ***about*** *leaving me to do the housework.*

> Word partners for **conscience**
>
> a *bad/guilty/troubled/uneasy* conscience • a *clean/clear/easy/good* conscience • *appease/ease/salve* sb's conscience • *prick/trouble/stir/weigh on* sb's conscience • *follow/listen to/wrestle with* your conscience • a *matter/question* of conscience • a *pang/prick/twinge* of conscience

IDIOMS **be/weigh on your conscience** to make you feel guilty: *Yesterday I ignored an old woman who asked me for money in the street, and it's been on my conscience ever since.* • **in all conscience** UK (US **in good conscience**) without feeling guilty: *You couldn't, in all conscience, ask her to pay the whole bill!*

ˈ**conscience-ˌstricken** **adj** feeling very sorry for something that you have done wrong

conscientious /ˌkɒn.ʃiˈen.ʃəs/ US /ˌkɑːn-/ **adj** C1

putting a lot of effort into your work: *a conscientious student* • **conscientiously** /-li/ **adv** • **conscientiousness** /-nəs/ **noun** [U]

consci͵entious obˈjector **noun** [C] a person who refuses to work in the armed forces for moral or religious reasons

conscious /ˈkɒn.ʃəs/ (US) /ˈkɑːn-/ **adj** NOTICING ▷ **1 be conscious of sth/sb** (B2) to notice that a particular thing or person exists or is present: *The tooth doesn't exactly hurt, but I'm conscious of it (= I can feel it) all the time.* ◦ [+ -ing verb] *I think she's very conscious of being the only person in the office who didn't have a university education.* ◦ [+ that] *He gradually became conscious (of the fact)* **that** *everyone else was wearing a suit.* → See also **subconscious** AWAKE ▷ **2** (C1) awake, thinking, and knowing what is happening around you: *He's still conscious but he's fairly badly injured.* ◦ *They've brought her out of the operating theatre, but she's not* **fully** *conscious yet.* ◦ figurative humorous *'Can I speak to Isobel, please?' 'She's still in bed. I'll just go and see if she's conscious (= awake) yet.'* → Opposite **unconscious** INTENTIONAL ▷ **3** (C2) determined and intentional: *He's obviously making a conscious* **effort** *to be nice to me at the moment.* ◦ *It wasn't a conscious* **decision** *to lose weight. It just happened.* • **consciously** /-li/ **adv** *I don't think she's consciously rude to people – it's just her manner.*

-conscious /-kɒn.ʃəs/ (US) /-kɑːn-/ **suffix** used after nouns and adverbs to mean 'knowing about and worried about a particular thing', or 'thinking that something is important': *fashion-conscious teenagers* ◦ *the health-conscious consumer* → See also **self-conscious**

consciousness /ˈkɒn.ʃəs.nəs/ (US) /ˈkɑːn-/ **noun** [U] UNDERSTANDING ▷ **1** (C1) the state of understanding and realizing something: [+ that] *Her consciousness* **that** *she's different makes her feel uneasy.* ◦ *Working in an unemployment office had helped to* **raise** *his political consciousness.* AWAKE ▷ **2** (B2) the state of being awake, thinking, and knowing what is happening around you: *He* **lost** *consciousness after his accident and never* **recovered/regained** *it.*

ˈconsciousness-͵raising **noun** [U] the attempt to increase people's knowledge of and interest in social and political matters

conscript /kənˈskrɪpt/ **verb** [T] (US usually **draft**) to force someone by law to serve in one of the armed forces: *He was conscripted* **into** *the army at the age of 18.* • **conscript** /ˈkɒn.skrɪpt/ (US) /ˈkɑːn-/ **noun** [C] (US usually **draftee**) *Over half the army was composed of conscripts.* → Compare **volunteer** • **conscript** /ˈkɒn.skrɪpt/ (US) /ˈkɑːn-/ **adj** [before noun] *a conscript army* • **conscription** /-ˈskrɪp.ʃən/ **noun** [U] *Ever since the war began he's been worried that the government will introduce conscription.*

consecrate /ˈkɒn.sɪ.kreɪt/ (US) /ˈkɑːn-/ **verb** [T] **1** to officially make something holy and able to be used for religious ceremonies: *The new cathedral was completed and consecrated in 2002.* **2** to officially give someone the title of BISHOP in the Christian Church in a religious ceremony • **consecrated** /-kreɪ.tɪd/ (US) /-kreɪ.t̬ɪd/ **adj** *consecrated bread/wine/ground* • **consecration** /͵kɒn.sɪˈkreɪ.ʃən/ (US) /͵kɑːn-/ **noun** [U] *the consecration of the new bishop*

consecutive /kənˈsek.jʊ.tɪv/ (US) /-t̬ɪv/ **adj** (C2) describes events, numbers, etc. that follow one after another without an interruption: *This is the fifth consecutive weekend that I've spent working, and I'm a bit fed up with it.* • **consecutively** /-li/ **adv** *Tickets are numbered consecutively.*

consensual /͵kɒnˈsen.sju.əl/ (US) /͵kɑːn-/ **adj** formal or legal with the willing agreement of all the people involved: *consensual sex*

consensus /kənˈsen.səs/ **noun** [S or U] (C2) a generally accepted opinion or decision among a group of people: *The* **general** *consensus in the office is that he's useless at his job.* ◦ *Could we* **reach** *a consensus* **on** *this matter? Let's take a vote.*

consent /kənˈsent/ **noun; verb**

▸**noun** [U] **1** (C1) permission or agreement: *They can't publish your name without your consent.* ◦ *You can only come on the trip if your parents* **give** *their consent.* **2 by common consent** most people agree: *Her latest film, by common consent, is her best yet.*

▸**verb** [I] formal (C2) to agree to do something, or to allow someone to do something: [+ to infinitive] *Very reluctantly, I've consented* **to** *lend her my car.* ◦ *My aunt never married because her father wouldn't consent* **to** *her marriage.*

con͵senting ˈadult **noun** [C] formal a person who is considered old enough, and therefore responsible enough, to decide if they want sex and who they want to have sex with

consequence /ˈkɒn.sɪ.kwəns/ (US) /ˈkɑːn-/ **noun** [C] **1** (B2) a result of a particular action or situation, often one that is bad or not convenient: *Not making a will can have* **serious** *consequences for the people you might wish to benefit.* ◦ *Scientists think it unlikely that any species will actually become extinct* **as a** *consequence* **of** *the oil spill.* ◦ *I told the hairdresser to do what she wanted to my hair, and* **look at the** *consequences!* ◦ *Well, if you insist on eating so much, you'll have to* **suffer/take** *(= accept and deal with) the consequences!* **2 of little/no consequence** (C1) (also **not of any/much consequence**) not important: *The money was of little consequence to Tony.*

> **Word partners for consequence**
>
> *adverse/grave/serious/unpleasant* consequences • *dire/disastrous/fatal/tragic* consequences • *enormous/far-reaching/long-term/major* consequences • a *possible/potential/unforeseen* consequence • a *direct* consequence of sth • *accept/deal with/face/suffer* the consequences • *as* a consequence (of sth) • consequences *for* sb/sth

consequent /ˈkɒn.sɪ.kwənt/ (US) /ˈkɑːn-/ **adj** (also **consequential** /͵kɒn.sɪˈkwen.tʃəl/) happening as a result of something: *Our use of harmful chemicals and the consequent damage to the environment is a very serious matter.*

consequently /ˈkɒn.sɪ.kwənt.li/ (US) /ˈkɑːn-/ **adv** (B2) as a result: *I spent most of my money in the first week and consequently had very little to eat by the end of the holiday.*

conservation /͵kɒn.səˈveɪ.ʃən/ (US) /͵kɑːn.sɚ-/ **noun** [U] **1** (B2) the protection of plants and animals, natural areas, and interesting and important structures and buildings, especially from the damaging effects of human activity: *wildlife conservation* ◦ *a conservation area* **2** (C1) carefully using valuable natural substances that exist in limited amounts in order to make certain that they will be available for as long a time as possible: *the conservation of coal/gas/oil reserves* ◦ **Energy** *conservation reduces your fuel bills and helps the environment.* • **conservationist** /-ɪst/ **noun** [C] *Conservationists are fighting to save the tiger.*

conservatism /kənˈsɜː.və.tɪ.zəm/ (US) /-ˈsɝː-/ **noun** [U] the quality of not usually liking or trusting change, especially sudden change

conservative /kənˈsɜː.və.tɪv/ (US) /-ˈsɝː.və.t̬ɪv/ **adj**

AGAINST CHANGE ▷ **1** Ⓒ not usually liking or trusting change, especially sudden change: *a conservative society/outlook* ◦ *Older people tend to be quite conservative and a bit suspicious of any supposed advances.* → Compare **liberal 2** If you are conservative in your appearance, you usually do not like fashionable or modern clothes or hairstyles: *He's a very conservative dresser – he always looks like he's wearing his father's clothes!* **LOW** ▷ **3** A conservative guess or calculation is likely to be less than the real amount: *If I said there were three million unemployed, that would be a conservative* ***estimate****.* • **conservatively** /-li/ **adv** *I dress more conservatively for the office.* ◦ *The costs of cleaning up the bay are estimated, conservatively, at $1 billion.*

C

Conservative /kən'sɜː.və.tɪv/ Ⓤⓢ /-'sɝː.və.t̬ɪv/ **adj** (also **Tory**) belonging to or supporting the British political party that traditionally supports business and opposes high taxes and government involvement in industry: *the Conservative Party* ◦ *Conservative policies* ◦ *a Conservative MP/government* ◦ *Did you* ***vote*** *Conservative at the last election?* • **Conservative noun** [C] (also **Tory**) *She's a* ***staunch*** *(= very loyal) Conservative.* • **Conservatism** /-tɪ.zᵊm/ **noun** [U] Conservative actions and beliefs

conservatory /kən'sɜː.və.tᵊr.i/ Ⓤⓢ /-'sɝː.və.tɔː.ri/ **noun** [C] **SCHOOL** ▷ **1** (UK also **conservatoire** /kən'sɜː.və.twɑːʳ/) a school for the teaching of music or sometimes acting or art **ROOM** ▷ **2** (US also **solarium**) a room with glass walls and a glass roof, usually connected to a house, used for growing plants or for relaxing in

conserve verb; noun

▸**verb** [T] /kən'sɜːv/ Ⓤⓢ /-'sɝːv/ to keep and protect something from damage, change, or waste: *To conserve electricity, we are cutting down on our central heating.* ◦ *The nationalists are very keen to conserve their customs and language.* ◦ *I'm not being lazy – I'm just conserving my* ***energy/strength*** *for later.*

▸**noun** [C or U] /'kɒn.sɜːv/ Ⓤⓢ /'kɑːn.sɝːv/ formal a type of jam in which the fruit is whole or in large pieces: *apricot/strawberry conserve*

> **! Common mistake: consider**
>
> Remember that **consider** is never followed by a preposition.
>
> Don't say 'consider about something', say **consider something**:
>
> ~~*I hope you will consider about my application.*~~
>
> *I hope you will consider my application.*

> **! Common mistake: consider**
>
> When **consider** is followed by a verb, that verb should be in the **-ing** form.
>
> Do not say 'consider to do something', say **consider doing something**:
>
> ~~*Please consider to pay my expenses.*~~
>
> *Please consider paying my expenses.*

consider /kən'sɪd.əʳ/ Ⓤⓢ /-ɚ/ **verb** **POSSIBILITY** ▷ **1** Ⓑ1 [I or T] to spend time thinking about a possibility or making a decision: *Don't make any decisions before you've considered the matter.* ◦ [+ question word] *Have you considered* ***what*** *you'll do if you don't get the job?* ◦ [+ -ing verb] *We're considering sell****ing*** *the house.* ◦ *She's being considered* ***for*** *the job.* ◦ *I'd like some time to consider before I make a decision.* **SUBJECT/FACT** ▷ **2** Ⓒ [T] to give attention to a particular subject or fact when judging something else: *You've got to consider the time element when planning the whole project.* ◦ [+ question word] *If you consider* ***how*** *long he's been learning the piano, he's not very good.* **CARE ABOUT** ▷ **3** Ⓒ2 [T] to care about or respect other people or their feelings and wishes: *Have you considered your mother and how she's going to feel about you leaving?* ◦ *She never considers anyone but herself – she's totally selfish!* **OPINION** ▷ **4** Ⓑ2 [T often + obj + (to be) + noun/adj] to believe someone or something to be, or think of them as something: *He is currently considered (to be) the best British athlete.* ◦ *We don't consider her suitable for the job.* ◦ [passive + obj + to infinitive] *It is considered bad manners in some cultures to speak with your mouth full of food.* ◦ *I consider my****self*** *lucky* ***that*** *I only hurt my arm in the accident.* ◦ *Do you consider him a friend of yours?* ◦ [+ (that)] *She considers (that) she has done enough to help already.* **5 be highly/well considered** to be very much admired: *I've never enjoyed her books, but I know she's very highly considered.*

considerable /kən'sɪd.ᵊr.ə.bl/ Ⓤⓢ /-ɚ-/ **adj** Ⓑ2 large or of noticeable importance: *The fire caused considerable damage to the church.* • **considerably** /-bli/ **adv** Ⓑ2 *He's considerably fatter than he was when I knew him.*

considerate /kən'sɪd.ᵊr.ət/ Ⓤⓢ /-ɚ-/ **adj** kind and helpful: *It wasn't very considerate of you to drink all the milk.* → Opposite **inconsiderate**

consideration /kən,sɪd.ə'reɪ.ʃᵊn/ **noun** **CAREFUL THINKING** ▷ **1** Ⓑ2 [U] the act of thinking about something carefully: *After some consideration, we've decided to sell the house.* ◦ *The whole matter needs (to be given)* ***careful*** *consideration.* **SUBJECT/FACT** ▷ **2** Ⓑ2 [C or U] attention to a particular subject or fact when judging something: *It may be fairly cheap to buy, but you've got to* ***take into*** *consideration the money you'll spend on repairs.* ◦ *Comfort/Safety is an important consideration.*

> **! Common mistake: take into consideration**
>
> **Remember:** use the correct preposition.
>
> Don't say 'take in/under/to consideration', say **take into consideration**:
>
> ~~*Please take all my suggestions in consideration.*~~
>
> *Please take all my suggestions into consideration.*

CARE ▷ **3** Ⓒ2 [U] behaviour that is kind and considers people's feelings: *You've got no consideration* ***for*** *others!* ◦ *Could you turn your music down and* ***show*** *a little consideration* ***for*** *the neighbours!* ◦ *We didn't publish the details,* ***out of*** *consideration* ***for*** *the victim's family.* **MONEY** ▷ **4** [C] old-fashioned or humorous a payment for a service: *For* ***a small*** *consideration, madam, I'll show you the way there myself.*

considered /kən'sɪd.əd/ Ⓤⓢ /-ɚd/ **adj** **considered opinion/view/decision** an opinion or decision that someone has reached after a lot of thought: [+ that] *It is* ***my*** *considered opinion* ***that*** *he should be promoted.*

considering /kən'sɪd.ᵊr.ɪŋ/ Ⓤⓢ /-ɚ-/ **preposition, conjunction, adv** Ⓑ2 used to mention a particular condition or fact about something, usually a disadvantage: *Considering the weather, we got here quite quickly.* ◦ *She did well to find the way, considering she'd only been there once before.*

consign /kən'saɪn/ **verb** [T] formal to send something to someone: *The goods have been consigned* ***to*** *you by air.* • **consignee** /,kɒn.saɪ'niː/ Ⓤⓢ /,kɑːn-/ **noun** [C] formal the person something is sent to: *Goods must be signed for by the consignee.*

PHRASAL VERB **consign sb/sth to sth** [often passive] to get rid of someone or something or to put them in an unpleasant place or situation: *to be consigned to prison*

consignment /kən'saɪn.mənt/ noun [C] **1** an amount of goods that is sent somewhere: *The most recent consignment **of** cloth was faulty.* **2 on consignment** If goods are on consignment, the person or company that receives them will only pay for them after they have been sold.

consist /kən'sɪst/ verb

PHRASAL VERBS **consist in sth** [L not continuous] formal to have something as a main and necessary part or quality: *The beauty of air travel consists in its speed and ease.* ◦ [+ -ing verb] *For her, happiness consists in watch**ing** television and reading magazines.* • **consist of sth** [L not continuous] B1 to be made of or formed from something: *The team consists of four Europeans and two Americans.* ◦ *It's a simple dish to prepare, consisting mainly of rice and vegetables.*

consistency /kən'sɪs.tᵊn.si/ noun **SUBSTANCE** ▷ **1** [C or U] the physical nature of a substance, especially a thick liquid, for example by being thick or thin, smooth or LUMPY: *She loved the creamy consistency of fresh paint.* ◦ *Melt the chocolate to a **pouring** (= easy to pour) consistency.* **BEING THE SAME** ▷ **2** [U] the quality of always behaving or performing in a similar way, or of always happening in a similar way: *They've won a few games this season but they lack consistency.* ◦ *It's important to show some consistency in your work.* → Opposite **inconsistency**

consistent /kən'sɪs.tᵊnt/ adj **NOT CHANGING** ▷ **1** C2 always behaving or happening in a similar, especially positive, way: *There has been a consistent improvement in her attitude.* → Opposite **inconsistent** **AGREEING** ▷ **2** C2 [after verb] in agreement with other facts or with typical or previous behaviour, or having the same principles as something else: *What the witness said in court was not consistent **with** the statement he made to the police.* ◦ *We do not consider his behaviour to be consistent **with** the holding of a high-ranking job.* • **consistently** /-li/ adv C2 *The president has consistently denied the rumours.*

consolation /ˌkɒn.sə'leɪ.ʃᵊn/ US /ˌkɑːn-/ noun [C or U] something that makes someone who is sad or disappointed feel better: ***If it's (of) any** consolation (**to** you), you're not the only one he was rude to.* ◦ *I didn't know what to say – I just offered a few **words of** consolation.* • **consolatory** /kən'sɒl.ə.tᵊr.i/ US /-'sɑː.lə.tɔːr.i/ adj formal *a consolatory remark*

conso'lation ˌprize noun [C] a small prize given to someone who has taken part in a competition, but who has not won

console verb; noun

▸verb [T] /kən'səʊl/ US /-'soʊl/ to make someone who is sad or disappointed feel better by giving them comfort or sympathy: *He tried to console her, but she kept saying it was all her own fault.* ◦ *I tried to console her **with** a box of chocolates.* ◦ *I was consoling Liz **on** hav**ing** broken up with her boyfriend.*

▸noun [C] /'kɒn.səʊl/ US /-soʊl/ a surface on which you find the controls for a piece of electrical equipment or a machine: *a computer console*

consolidate /kən'sɒl.ɪ.deɪt/ US /-'sɑː.lɪ-/ verb [I or T] **1** to become, or cause something to become, stronger, and more certain: *The success of their major product consolidated the firm's position in the market.* ◦ *She hoped that marriage would consolidate their relationship.* ◦ *The party consolidated its hold on power during its term of office.* ◦ *The company has been expanding rapidly and I feel it's now time to consolidate (= stop growing and make our present position stronger).* **2** to combine several things, especially businesses, so that they become more effective, or to be combined in this way: *The two firms consolidated to form a single company.* • **consolidated** /-deɪ.tɪd/ US /-deɪ.t̬ɪd/ adj *consolidated trading/accounts* • **consolidation** /kənˌsɒl.ɪ'deɪ.ʃᵊn/ US /-ˌsɑː.lɪ-/ noun [C or U] *The company is entering a period of consolidation (= becoming better and stronger at what it does).* ◦ *We have seen a similar consolidation (= joining together) of booksellers and distributors.*

consommé /kən'sɒm.eɪ/ US /ˌkɑːn.sə'meɪ/ noun [U or C] a thin, clear soup

consonant /'kɒn.sə.nənt/ US /'kɑːn-/ noun [C] B1 one of the speech sounds or letters of the alphabet that is not a vowel. Consonants are pronounced by stopping the air from flowing easily through the mouth, especially by closing the lips or touching the teeth with the tongue. → Compare **vowel**

consort verb; noun

▸verb [I + adv/prep] /kən'sɔːt/ US /-'sɔːrt/ to spend a lot of time in the company of a particular group of people, especially people whose character is not approved of: *They claimed he had been consorting **with** drug dealers.*

▸noun [C] /'kɒn.sɔːt/ US /'kɑːn.sɔːrt/ a wife or husband, especially of a ruler

consortium /kən'sɔː.ti.əm/ US /-'sɔːr.t̬i-/ noun [C] (plural **consortiums** or **consortia** /-ə/) an organization of several businesses or banks joining together as a group for a shared purpose: *a consortium **of** textile manufacturers*

conspicuous /kən'spɪk.ju.əs/ adj very noticeable or attracting attention, often in a way that is not wanted: *In China, her blonde hair was conspicuous.* ◦ *He tried not to **look** conspicuous and moved slowly along the back of the room.* → Opposite **inconspicuous** • **conspicuously** /-li/ adv in a way that is conspicuous: *The temple's grand white arches rose conspicuously over the dirty decaying city.* • **conspicuousness** /-nəs/ noun [U]

IDIOM **be conspicuous by your absence** mainly humorous to be absent when you should be present, in a way that other people notice: *Why wasn't Stephen at the meeting, then? He was conspicuous by his absence.*

conˌspicuous con'sumption noun [U] disapproving the situation in which people spend a lot of money intentionally so that other people notice and admire them for their WEALTH

conspiracy /kən'spɪr.ə.si/ noun [C or U] **1** the activity of secretly planning with other people to do something bad or illegal: *The three men are accused of conspiracy.* ◦ [+ to infinitive] *She has been charged with conspiracy **to** murder.* ◦ *I think there was a conspiracy **to** keep me out of the committee.* **2 conspiracy of silence** a general agreement to keep silent about a subject for the purpose of keeping it secret

con'spiracy ˌtheory noun [C] a belief that an unpleasant event or situation is the result of a secret plan made by powerful people • **con'spiracy ˌtheorist** noun [C] someone who believes in a conspiracy theory

conspirator /kən'spɪr.ə.tər/ US /-t̬ɚ/ noun [C] someone who conspires with other people to do something

conspiratorial /kənˌspɪr.ə'tɔː.ri.ᵊl/ US /-'tɔːr.i-/ adj **1** relating to a secret plan to do something bad, illegal, or against someone's wishes **2** showing that you share a secret: *They exchanged conspiratorial glances.* • **conspiratorially** /-i/ adv *She heard them whispering conspiratorially in the bedroom.*

conspire /kən'spaɪəʳ/ US /-'spaɪr/ **verb** [I] to plan secretly with other people to do something bad, illegal, or against someone's wishes: [+ to infinitive] *He felt that his colleagues were conspiring **together to** remove him from his job.* ◦ *As girls, the sisters used to conspire **with** each other **against** their brother.*

C

PHRASAL VERB **conspire against sth** (also **conspire to do sth**) If events or conditions conspire against something or conspire to do something, they combine in such a way that they spoil your plans: *The weather had conspired to ruin their day out.* ◦ *I'd planned a romantic evening together, but circumstances conspired against it – friends arrived unexpectedly and then Dave was called out to an emergency.*

constable /'kʌn.stə.bl/ US /'kɑːn-/ **noun** [C] a British police officer of the lowest rank

constabulary /kən'stæb.jʊ.lə.ri/ US /-je.ler.i/ **noun** [C, + sing/pl verb] the British police force for a particular area

constancy /'kɒn.stən.si/ US /'kɑːn-/ **noun** [U] formal **STAYING SAME** ▷ **1** the quality of staying the same, not getting less or more **LOYALTY** ▷ **2** loyalty: *Never doubt the constancy **of** my love for you.*

constant /'kɒn.stənt/ US /'kɑːn-/ **adj; noun**

▸**adj FREQUENT** ▷ **1** B2 happening a lot or all the time: *He's in constant trouble with the police.* ◦ *machines that are in constant use* **STAYING SAME** ▷ **2** C2 staying the same, or not getting less or more: *We've kept up a fairly constant **speed**.* ◦ *The fridge keeps food at a constant **temperature**.* **LOYAL** ▷ **3** describes a COMPANION or friend who is loyal to you

▸**noun** [C] specialized a particular number or amount that never changes

constantly /'kɒn.stənt.li/ US /'kɑːn-/ **adv** B2 all the time or often: *He's constantly changing his mind.* ◦ *She has the television on constantly.*

constellation /ˌkɒn.stə'leɪ.ʃən/ US /ˌkɑːn-/ **noun** [C] **1** any of the groups of stars in the sky which seem from Earth to form a pattern and have been given names **2** often humorous a group of famous or admired people all together in one place: *At our annual ceremony we had a whole constellation of film stars and directors.*

consternation /ˌkɒn.stə'neɪ.ʃən/ US /ˌkɑːn.stə-/ **noun** [U] a feeling of worry, shock, or confusion: *The prospect of so much work **filled** him **with** consternation.* ◦ ***To his** consternation, when he got to the airport he found he'd forgotten his passport.*

constipated /'kɒn.stɪ.peɪ.tɪd/ US /'kɑːn.stɪ.peɪ.t̬ɪd/ **adj** unable to empty your bowels as often as you should: *If you ate more fibre you wouldn't **get** constipated.* • **constipation** /ˌkɒn.stɪ'peɪ.ʃən/ US /ˌkɑːn-/ **noun** [U] *to get/have/suffer from constipation*

constituency /kən'stɪt.ju.ən.si/ **noun** [C] (the group of people who can vote belonging to) any of the official areas of a country that elect someone to represent them in parliament

constituent /kən'stɪt.ju.ənt/ **noun** [C] **PART** ▷ **1** one of the parts that a substance or combination is made of: *What are the basic constituents **of** the mixture?* **PERSON** ▷ **2** a VOTER (= person who can vote) in a particular area of the country: *The MP worked hard, always talking to his constituents and listening to their problems.* • **constituent** **adj** [before noun] *Let's look at the constituent **parts** of this sentence.*

constitute /'kɒn.stɪ.tjuːt/ US /'kɑːn.stɪ.tuːt/ **verb BE CONSIDERED AS** ▷ **1** C1 [L only + noun, not continuous] formal to be or be considered as something: *This latest defeat constitutes a major setback for the government.* **FORM PART OF** ▷ **2** C1 [L not continuous] to form or make something: *Women constitute about ten percent of Parliament.*

constitution /ˌkɒn.stɪ'tjuː.ʃən/ US /ˌkɑːn.stɪ'tuː-/ **noun** [C] **LAWS** ▷ **1** C1 the set of political principles by which a state or organization is governed, especially in relation to the rights of the people it governs: *Britain has no **written** constitution.* ◦ *the Constitution **of** the United States* ◦ ***Under** (= as part of) the union constitution, a new committee must be elected each year.* **HEALTH** ▷ **2** C2 the general state of someone's health: *He has a very **strong** constitution.* **PARTS** ▷ **3** how something is made up of different parts: *the constitution **of** a chemical compound*

constitutional /ˌkɒn.stɪ'tjuː.ʃən.əl/ US /ˌkɑːn.stɪ'tuː-/ **adj; noun**

▸**adj LAWS** ▷ **1** C2 allowed by or contained in a constitution: *Such a policy would not be constitutional.* ◦ *Freedom of speech should be a constitutional **right**.* → Opposite **unconstitutional** **HEALTH** ▷ **2** relating to someone's general state of health: *constitutional weakness*

▸**noun** [C] old-fashioned humorous a walk that you often do to keep yourself healthy: *She's nearly 86 and still **takes** a constitutional every morning.*

constitutionality /ˌkɒn.stɪ.tjuː.ʃən'æl.ɪ.ti/ US /ˌkɑːn.stɪ.tuː.ʃən'æl.ə.t̬i/ **noun** [U] US the quality of being allowed by or contained in a constitution: *The judge chose to ignore questions of the constitutionality of the Senator's actions.*

constitutionally /ˌkɒn.stɪ'tjuː.ʃən.əl.i/ US /ˌkɑːn.stɪ'tuː-/ **adv LAWS** ▷ **1** according to the rules in a constitution: *There was some doubt as to whether the government were behaving constitutionally.* **HEALTH** ▷ **2** in a way that relates to or is caused by your general health or your character: *constitutionally weak* ◦ humorous *She seems constitutionally unable to make decisions.*

ˌconstitutional ˈmonarchy **noun** [C] a system in which the king or queen's power is severely limited, because they act only on the advice of the politicians who form the government

constrain /kən'streɪn/ **verb** [T often passive] C2 to control and limit something: *The country's progress was constrained by a leader who refused to look forward.*

constrained /kən'streɪnd/ **adj** **1** **constrained to do sth** forced to do something against your will: *Don't feel constrained to do what he says – he's got no authority.* **2** describes behaviour that is forced and unnatural: *a constrained voice/manner*

constraint /kən'streɪnt/ **noun** **1** C2 [C] something that controls what you do by keeping you within particular limits: *The constraints **of** politeness wouldn't allow her to say what she really thought about his cooking.* ◦ ***Financial** constraints **on** the company are preventing them from employing new staff.* **2** [U] formal unnatural behaviour that is sometimes the result of forcing yourself to act in a particular way: *She tried to appear friendly, but her constraint was obvious.* **3** **under constraint** formal If you do something under constraint, you do it only because you have been forced to: *They confessed, but only under severe constraint.*

constrict /kən'strɪkt/ **verb BECOME TIGHTER** ▷ **1** [I or T] to become tighter and narrower, or to make something become tighter and narrower: *He hated wearing a tie – he felt it constricted his breathing.* ◦ *If you're going dancing, you don't want to wear anything that constricts your movements.* ◦ *The drug causes the*

C

blood vessels to constrict. **LIMIT** ▷ **2** [T] to limit an action or behaviour: *Too many rules had constricted her lifestyle.* • **constriction** /-ˈstrɪk.ʃən/ noun [C] *The constrictions (= limits) of prison life were inhuman.* ◦ *He felt a constriction (= a tight feeling) in his chest.*

constrictor /kənˈstrɪk.tər/ (US) /-tɚ/ **noun** [C] any snake that kills animals and birds by wrapping itself around them and crushing them → See also **boa**

construct verb; noun

▸**verb** [T] /kənˈstrʌkt/ B2 to build something or put together different parts to form something whole: *to construct a new bridge/building* ◦ *The walls are constructed* ***of*** *concrete.* ◦ *to construct a story/sentence/argument*

▸**noun** [C] /ˈkɒn.strʌkt/ (US) /ˈkɑːn-/ formal an idea or an imaginary situation: *His reputation as an eccentric is largely a media construct.*

construction /kənˈstrʌk.ʃən/ **noun BUILDING** ▷ **1** B2 [U] the work of building or making something, especially buildings, bridges, etc.: *She works* ***in*** *construction/in* ***the*** *construction* ***industry***. ◦ *The bridge is a marvellous work of engineering and construction.* ◦ *This website is currently* ***under*** *construction (= being created).* **2** [U] the particular type of structure, materials, etc. that something has: *The bridge is of lightweight construction.* **3** B2 [C] a building: *What's that concrete and metal construction over there?* **LANGUAGE** ▷ **4** B2 [C] specialized the way in which the words in a sentence or phrase are arranged: *The writer has used several complex grammatical constructions.* **5 put a construction on sth** formal **a** to understand something in a particular way: *How can they put such a damning construction on a perfectly innocent phrase?* **b** to understand something as having a particular meaning, especially other people's actions and statements: *I don't want them to* ***put*** *the wrong construction* ***on*** *my actions.* → See **construe**

constructive /kənˈstrʌk.tɪv/ **adj** C1 If advice, criticism, or actions are constructive, they are useful and intended to help or improve something: *She criticized my writing, but in a way that was very constructive.* ◦ *If you don't have anything constructive to say, I'd rather you kept quiet.* • **constructively** /-li/ **adv**

conˌstructive disˈmissal noun [C or U] mainly UK actions taken by an employer that intentionally make working conditions for an employee difficult or unfair so that the employee feels forced to leave their job

constructor /kənˈstrʌk.tər/ (US) /-tɚ/ **noun** [C] someone who builds something or puts it together from different parts: *The firm produces kits for amateur car constructors.*

construe /kənˈstruː/ verb formal **construe sth as sth** to understand the meaning, especially of other people's actions and statements, in a particular way: *Any change in plan would be construed as indecision.*

consul /ˈkɒn.səl/ (US) /ˈkɑːn-/ **noun** [C] an official chosen by a government to live in a foreign city, in order to take care of people from the official's own country who travel or live there, and to protect the trade interests of that government: *the British Consul*

consular /ˈkɒn.sjʊ.lər/ (US) /ˈkɑːn.sjə.lɚ/ **adj** [before noun] relating to a consul or a consulate: *the consular office*

consulate /ˈkɒn.sjʊ.lət/ (US) /ˈkɑːn.sjə-/ **noun** [C] the office where a consul works: *the Cuban consulate in Mexico City*

consult /kənˈsʌlt/ **verb 1** C1 [T] to get information or advice from a person, book, etc. with special knowledge on a particular subject: *If the symptoms get worse, consult your doctor.* ◦ *I'm not quite sure how to get there – I'd better consult a map.* **2** C1 [I or T] to discuss something with someone before you make a decision: *Why didn't you consult me about this?* ◦ *This afternoon the prime minister was consulting* ***with*** *his advisers.*

consultancy /kənˈsʌl.tənt.si/ **noun 1** [C] a company that gives advice on a particular subject: *a management/financial/recruitment consultancy* **2** [U] the activity of giving advice on a particular subject: *They pay me for IT consultancy.*

consultant /kənˈsʌl.tənt/ noun [C] **1** B2 someone who advises people on a particular subject: *a management/financial/computer consultant* ◦ *a firm of public relations consultants* **2** UK a **specialist** (= doctor with special training and knowledge in a particular area of medicine)

consultation /ˌkɒn.sʌlˈteɪ.ʃən/ (US) /ˌkɑːn-/ **noun 1** C2 [C] a meeting to discuss something or to get advice: *After consultations* ***with*** *our accountants, we've decided how to cut costs within the company.* **2** C2 [U] the process of discussing something with someone in order to get their advice or opinion about it: *He chose his study course* ***in*** *consultation* ***with*** *his parents and teachers.*

consultative /kənˈsʌl.tə.tɪv/ (US) /-t̬ə.t̬ɪv/ **adj** A consultative group or document gives advice about something: *She works for the firm in a consultative capacity.* ◦ *to set up a consultative committee*

consulting /kənˈsʌl.tɪŋ/ (US) /-t̬ɪŋ/ **adj** [before noun] giving advice on a particular subject: *a consulting lawyer/engineer*

conˈsulting ˌroom noun [C] an office where a doctor talks to and examines patients

consumables /kənˈsjuː.mə.bl̩z/ (US) /-suː-/ **noun** [plural] goods, especially food, or services which people buy regularly because they are quickly used and need to be replaced quite often: *At this hospital we use up bandages, disposable gloves, and other consumables at an alarming rate.*

consume /kənˈsjuːm/ (US) /-ˈsuːm/ **verb** [T] **USE RESOURCE** ▷ **1** C1 to use fuel, energy, or time, especially in large amounts: *Our high living standards cause our present population to consume 25 percent of the world's oil.* **2** B2 formal to eat or drink, especially a lot of something: *He consumes vast quantities of chips with every meal.* **DESTROY** ▷ **3** If a fire consumes something, it destroys it completely. **4 be consumed by/with sth** C2 to have so much of a feeling that it affects everything you do: *He was consumed with jealousy.*

consumer /kənˈsjuː.mər/ (US) /-ˈsuː.mɚ/ **noun** [C] B2 a person who buys goods or services for their own use: *The new rates will affect all consumers, including businesses.* ◦ *consumer rights/advice*

conˌsumer ˈdurables noun [plural] goods that last a long time and are not intended to be bought very often, such as televisions and cars

consumerism /kənˈsjuː.mə.rɪ.zəm/ (US) /-ˈsuː.mɚ.ɪ-/ **noun** [U] **1** the state of an advanced industrial society in which a lot of goods are bought and sold **2** disapproving the situation in which too much attention is given to buying and owning things: *He disliked Christmas and its* ***rampant*** *(= extreme) consumerism.*

conˌsumer ˈprice ˌindex noun [C usually singular] (abbreviation **CPI**) a measurement of the changes in the cost of basic goods and services

conˌsumer proˈtection noun [U] the protection of buyers of goods and services against low quality or dangerous products and advertisements that deceive people

conˈsumer soˌciety noun [C] a society in which people often buy new goods, especially goods that they do not need, and in which a high value is placed on owning many things

C

consuming /kənˈsjuː.mɪŋ/ (US) /-ˈsuː-/ **adj** describes an emotion that is very strong: *Running is a consuming passion with him.*

consummate adj; verb

▸**adj** [before noun] /ˈkɒn.sə.mət/ (US) /ˈkɑːn-/ formal perfect, or complete in every way: *a life of consummate happiness* ◦ *He's a consummate athlete/gentleman/liar.*

▸**verb** [T] /ˈkɒn.sjʊ.meɪt/ (US) /ˈkɑː.n.sə-/ **HAVE SEX** ▷ **1** legal to make a marriage or romantic relationship complete by having sex: *The marriage was never consummated.* **COMPLETE** ▷ **2** formal to make something complete or perfect

consummation /ˌkɒn.sjʊˈmeɪ.ʃən/ (US) /ˌkɑː.n.sə-/ noun [U] **SEX** ▷ **1** legal the act of making a marriage or romantic relationship complete by having sex **COMPLETION** ▷ **2** formal the act of making something complete or perfect

consumption /kənˈsʌmp.ʃən/ noun [U] **USE** ▷ **1** (C1) the amount used or eaten: *As a nation, our consumption of junk food is horrifying.* ◦ *We need to cut down on our fuel consumption by having fewer cars on the road.* **2** the act of using, eating, or drinking something: *The meat was clearly* ***unfit for human*** *consumption (= not suitable for people to eat).* ◦ *These products are not for national consumption, but for export.* **3** the situation in which information, entertainment, etc. is intended for a particular group of people: *This memo is for* ***internal*** *consumption only.* ◦ *The movie was not intended for* ***public*** *consumption.* **DISEASE** ▷ **4** old-fashioned for **tuberculosis** (= a serious disease of the lungs)

consumptive /kənˈsʌmp.tɪv/ adj, noun [C] old-fashioned (a person) suffering from consumption: *She didn't live very long – she was (a) consumptive.*

cont. adj (also **contd**) written abbreviation for continued

contact /ˈkɒn.tækt/ (US) /ˈkɑːn-/ **noun; verb**

▸**noun** **COMMUNICATION** ▷ **1** (B1) [U] communication with someone, especially by speaking or writing to them regularly: *'Have you been* ***in*** *contact* ***with*** *Andrew recently?' 'Only by phone.'* ◦ *I'm still* ***in*** *contact* ***with*** *her – we write a couple of times a year.* ◦ *There isn't enough contact* ***between*** *teachers and parents.* ◦ *I've been busy at home and have hardly* ***had*** *any contact* ***with*** *the outside world.* ◦ *I'd hate to* ***lose*** *contact* ***with*** *my old school friends.* ◦ *She finally* ***made*** *contact* ***with*** *him in Italy.* ◦ *Air traffic control* ***lost*** *radio contact* ***with*** *the pilot of the aircraft ten minutes before the accident.* ◦ *The school likes to have a contact* ***number*** *(= phone number, especially for emergencies) for parents during school hours.* **TOUCH** ▷ **2** (C1) [U] the fact of two people or things touching each other: *Don't let that glue* ***come into*** *contact* ***with*** *your skin.* ◦ *Have you been* ***in*** *contact* ***with*** *(= touched or been very near) anyone with the disease?* ◦ *He hates* ***physical*** *contact of any sort – he doesn't even like to shake your hand.* **PERSON** ▷ **3** (A2) [C] a person, especially someone in a high position, who can give you useful information or introductions which will help you at work or socially: *I don't really know how she got the job, but I suspect her mother's got contacts.* ◦ *If you need more stationery, I've got a good contact in a local printing firm.* ◦ *We're* ***building up*** *(= increasing the number of) our contacts in the business.* **ELECTRICITY** ▷ **4** [C] a part in a CIRCUIT which makes the CIRCUIT complete when it touches another part

> **Word partners for contact (COMMUNICATION)**
>
> *establish/get in/make* contact • *have/keep/maintain* contact • *be in/keep in/remain in/stay in* contact • *avoid/break off/lose* contact • *close/direct/frequent/regular* contact • contact *between* sb and sb • be *in* contact *with* sb

> **Word partners for contact (TOUCH)**
>
> *come in/into* contact with sb/sth • *bodily/physical/sexual* contact • *close/direct* contact • contact *with* sb/sth

> **Word partners for contact (PERSON)**
>
> *build up/make* contacts • *good/important/useful/valuable* contacts • a *network* of contacts

▸**verb** [T] (A2) to communicate with someone by phoning them or sending them a letter, email, etc.: *I tried to contact him at his office, but he wasn't in.* ◦ *You can contact me* ***on*** *(US* ***at****) (= speak to me by phoning) 388 9146.* ◦ *Unless the money is returned, we shall shortly be contacting our legal department.* • **contactable** /kənˈtæk.tə.bl̩/ **adj** *Is he contactable at his home number?*

> **Common mistake: contact**
>
> Remember that when **contact** is a verb it is never followed by a preposition.
>
> Don't say 'contact with someone' or 'contact to someone', say **contact someone**:
>
> ~~*You can contact with me by phone or email.*~~
>
> *You can contact me by phone or email.*

ˈcontact ˌlens noun [C] (C2) a small round curved piece of transparent plastic, worn on the surface of your eye to improve your sight: *I usually wear contact lenses, but I sometimes wear glasses when my eyes are tired.*

ˈcontact ˌsport noun [C] a sport such as RUGBY or American football in which players are allowed to touch each other when, for example, they are trying to get the ball

contagion /kənˈteɪ.dʒən/ noun [U] formal **1** the situation in which a disease is spread by touching someone or something: *The doctor says there's no chance/danger of contagion.* **2** the situation in which feelings, ideas, or problems spread from one place to another: *Brazil's stock markets were battered by contagion from the problems in other emerging markets.*

contagious /kənˈteɪ.dʒəs/ **adj** **1** describes a disease that can be caught by touching someone who has the disease or a piece of infected clothing: *The infection is* ***highly*** *contagious, so don't let anyone else use your towel.* **2** describes someone who has a contagious disease: *Keep him off school till he stops being contagious.* **3** A contagious feeling spreads quickly among people: *Fear is contagious.*

contain /kənˈteɪn/ **verb** **HOLD** ▷ **1** (B1) [T not continuous] to have something inside or include something as a part: *How much liquid do you think this bottle contains?* ◦ *I've lost a file containing a lot of important documents.* ◦ *Try to avoid foods which contain a lot of fat.* ◦ *The allegations contained* ***in*** *this report are very serious.* **CONTROL** ▷ **2** [T not continuous] to keep something harmful within limits and not allow it to spread: *Farms in the area have been closed off in an attempt to contain the disease.* ◦ *More police were sent to help contain the violence.* **3** (C2) [T often in negatives] to control or hide a strong emotion, such as excitement or anger: *She could no longer contain her anger and shouted at him uncontrollably.* ◦ humorous *Contain yourself! It's not that exciting.*

container /kən'teɪ.nəʳ/ (US) /-nɚ/ **noun** [C] **1** (B2) a hollow object, such as a box or a bottle, which can be used for holding something, especially to carry or store it: *an airtight container* ◦ *a plastic drinks container* **2** specialized a very large metal box used for transporting goods: *a container ship/lorry*

containerize (UK usually **containerise**) /kən'teɪ.nəʳ.aɪz/ (US) /-nə.raɪz/ **verb** [T] to put goods in a large metal box for transport, or to make a port, ship, etc. suitable for this method of transport: *containerized goods*

containment /kən'teɪn.mənt/ **noun** [U] **1** specialized the act of controlling or limiting something or someone harmful: *Containment of crowd violence was the police's main concern.* **2** an attempt to keep another country's political power within limits without having a war with them: *The government is pursuing a policy of containment.*

contaminant /kən'tæm.ɪ.nənt/ **noun** [C] specialized a substance that makes something less pure or makes it poisonous: *Make sure that all equipment is clean and free of contaminants.*

contaminate /kən'tæm.ɪ.neɪt/ **verb** [T] to make something less pure or make it poisonous: *Much of the coast has been contaminated by nuclear waste.* ◦ *The food which had been contaminated was destroyed.* • **contaminated** /-neɪ.tɪd/ (US) /-neɪ.t̬ɪd/ **adj** *The infection was probably caused by swimming in contaminated water/water contaminated* ***with*** *sewage.* • **contamination** /kənˌtæm.ɪ'neɪ.ʃᵊn/ **noun** [U] *The water supply is being tested for contamination (= the presence of unwanted or dangerous substances).*

contd **adj** (also **cont.**) written abbreviation for **continued**

contemplate /'kɒn.təm.pleɪt/ (US) /'kɑːn.t̬əm-/ **verb** [I or T] (C2) to spend time considering a possible future action, or to consider one particular thing for a long time in a serious and quiet way: [+ -ing verb] *I'm contemplating go****ing*** *abroad for a year.* ◦ *You're not contemplating a change of job, are you?* ◦ *It's* ***too*** *awful/horrific/dangerous* ***to*** *contemplate.*

contemplation /ˌkɒn.təm'pleɪ.ʃᵊn/ (US) /ˌkɑːn.t̬əm-/ **noun** [U] serious and quiet thought for a period of time: *She was staring out over the lake,* ***lost in*** *contemplation.* ◦ *The nuns have an hour for silent contemplation every morning.* • **contemplative** /kən'tem.plə.tɪv/ (US) /-t̬ɪv/ **adj** *Her mood was calm and contemplative.* • **contemplatively** /kən'tem.plə.tɪv.li/ (US) /-t̬ɪv-/ **adv**

contemporaneous /kənˌtem.pə'reɪ.ni.əs/ **adj** formal happening or existing at the same period of time: *The two events were more or less contemporaneous, with only months between them.* • **contemporaneously** /-li/ **adv**

contemporary /kən'tem.pᵊr.ᵊr.i/ (US) /-pə.rer-/ **adj; noun**

▸**adj** EXISTING NOW ▷ **1** (B2) existing or happening now: *contemporary music/literature/art/fashion* ◦ *Although the play was written hundreds of years ago, it still has a contemporary (= modern) feel to it.* OF SAME PERIOD ▷ **2** belonging to the same or a stated period in the past: *Almost all of the contemporary accounts of the event have been lost.* ◦ *Most of the writers he was contemporary* ***with*** *were interested in the same subjects.*

▸**noun** [C] **1** someone living during the same period as someone else: *Was he a contemporary of Shakespeare's?* **2** a person who is of the same age as you: *She didn't mix with her contemporaries, preferring the company of older people.*

contempt /kən'tempt/ **noun** [U] NO RESPECT ▷ **1** (C2) a strong feeling of disliking and having no respect for someone or something: *At school she had complete contempt* ***for*** *all her teachers.* ◦ *You should* ***treat*** *those remarks* ***with*** *the contempt that they deserve.* ◦ *She's* ***beneath*** *contempt (= I have no respect for her)!* **2 hold sb/sth in contempt** to feel contempt for someone or something NOT OBEYING ▷ **3** (also **contempt of court**) behaviour that is illegal because it does not obey or respect the rules of a law court: *The tobacco companies may be guilty of contempt of court for refusing to produce the documents.*

contemptible /kən'temp.tɪ.bl/ **adj** deserving contempt: *Her behaviour was contemptible.* • **contemptibly** /-bli/ **adv**

contemptuous /kən'temp.tju.əs/ **adj** expressing contempt: *a contemptuous manner/laugh* ◦ *He was very contemptuous* ***of*** *'popular' writers, whom he described as having no talent.* • **contemptuously** /-li/ **adv**

contend /kən'tend/ **verb** COMPETE ▷ **1** [I] to compete in order to win something: *There are three world-class tennis players contending* ***for*** *this title.* ◦ *He's contending* ***against*** *someone with twice his experience.* CLAIM ▷ **2** [T + (that)] formal to say that something is true or is a fact: *The lawyer contended (****that****) her client had never been near the scene of the crime.*

PHRASAL VERB **contend with sth** to have to deal with a difficult or unpleasant situation: *At the age of nine, he had the death of both parents to contend with.* ◦ *We don't need a computer failure to contend with as well as all our other problems.*

contender /kən'ten.dəʳ/ (US) /-dɚ/ **noun** [C] someone who competes with other people to try to win something: *Now aged 42, he is no longer considered a serious contender* ***for*** *the title.*

content **adj; noun; verb**

▸**adj** [after verb] /kən'tent/ (B2) pleased with your situation and not hoping for change or improvement: *He seems fairly content* ***with*** *(his) life.* ◦ [+ to infinitive] *They're content* ***to*** *socialize with a very small circle of people.* • **contentment** /-mənt/ **noun** [U] (also **content**) *His face wore a look of pure contentment.*

IDIOM **not content with sth/doing sth** in addition to something wrong or unpleasant you have done: *Not content with having upset my parents, he then insulted my sister!*

▸**noun** /'kɒn.tent/ (US) /'kɑːn-/ SUBJECT ▷ **1 contents** [plural] (B2) the list of articles or parts contained in a magazine or book, with the number of the page they begin on **2** (B2) [S or U] the ideas that are contained in a piece of writing, a speech, or a film: *It's a very stylish and beautiful film, but it lacks content.* ◦ *We've discussed the unusual form of the book – now, what about the content?* AMOUNT ▷ **3 contents** [plural] (B1) everything that is contained within something: *The contents* ***of*** *his bag spilled all over the floor.* ◦ *He hardly needed to open the letter because he already knew the contents.* **4** (C2) [S] the amount of a particular substance contained in something: *Chocolate has a* ***high*** *fat content.*

▸**verb** [T] /kən'tent/ to make someone feel happy and satisfied: *You're quite easily contented, aren't you?* ◦ *My explanation seemed to content him.*

PHRASAL VERB **content yourself with sth** to do something or have something although it is not exactly what you want: *I wanted to take two weeks' holiday, but had to content myself with one because the office was so busy.*

contented /kənˈten.tɪd/ (US) /-t̬ɪd/ **adj** happy and satisfied: *She smiled a contented* ***smile.*** ◦ *He won't be contented until he's upset everyone in the office.* • **contentedly** /-li/ **adv** *Finishing her meal, she sat back and sighed contentedly.*

contention /kənˈten.ʃᵊn/ **noun** DISAGREEMENT ▷ **1** [U] the disagreement that results from opposing arguments: *There's a lot of contention about that issue – for every person firmly in favour, there's someone fiercely against it.* ◦ *The matter has been settled – it's no longer* ***in*** *contention.* OPINION ▷ **2** [C] formal an opinion expressed in an argument: [+ that] *It is her contention* ***that*** *exercise is more important than diet if you want to lose weight.* IN A COMPETITION ▷ **3 be in/out of contention for sth** to be able/not able to achieve or win something, especially in sport: *This decisive defeat* ***puts*** *them* ***out of*** *contention for this year's championship finals.*

contentious /kənˈten.ʃəs/ **adj** causing or likely to cause disagreement: *a contentious decision/policy/issue/subject* ◦ *She has some rather contentious* ***views*** *on education.* • **contentiousness** /-nəs/ **noun** [U]

contest **noun**; **verb**

▸**noun** [C] /ˈkɒn.test/ (US) /ˈkɑːn-/ COMPETITION ▷ **1** (B1) a competition to do better than other people, usually in which prizes are given: *a dance/sports contest* ◦ *She's won a lot of* ***beauty*** *contests.* ATTEMPT ▷ **2** an attempt, usually against difficulties, to win an election or to get power or control: *The contest* ***for*** *deputy leadership of the party is gathering speed.*

▸**verb** [T] /kənˈtest/ ARGUE ▷ **1** If you contest a formal statement, a claim, a judge's decision, or a legal case, you say formally that it is wrong or unfair and try to have it changed: *We will certainly contest any claims made against the safety of our products.* COMPETE ▷ **2** to compete for something: *The medal is being keenly contested by eight gymnasts.* ATTEMPT ▷ **3** to attempt to win an election or to get power or control: *She stands a good chance, since only two people are contesting the seat and the other candidate is very unpopular.*

contestant /kənˈtes.tᵊnt/ (US) /-t̬ᵊnt/ **noun** [C] COMPETITION ▷ **1** (C1) someone who competes in a contest: *In tonight's quiz, our contestants have come from all over the country.* ATTEMPT ▷ **2** someone who attempts to win an election or get power or control: *Two main candidates are emerging as contestants* ***for*** *the presidency.*

context /ˈkɒn.tekst/ (US) /ˈkɑːn-/ **noun** [C] CAUSE OF EVENT ▷ **1** (B2) the situation within which something exists or happens, and that can help explain it: *It is important to see all the fighting and bloodshed in his plays* ***in*** *historical context.* ◦ *This small battle is very important* ***in the*** *context* ***of*** *Scottish history.* LANGUAGE ▷ **2** (C1) the text or speech that comes immediately before and after a particular phrase or piece of text and helps to explain its meaning: *In this exercise, a word is blanked out and you have to guess what it is by looking at the context.* **3 out of context** If words are used out of context, only a small separate part of what was originally said or written is reported, which causes their meaning to not be clear or understood: *The papers took my remarks completely out of context.*

contextual /kənˈtek.stju.əl/ **adj** formal or specialized related to the context of something: *It's impossible to understand the nuances of an isolated word without some contextual clues.* • **contextually** /-i/ **adv** formal or specialized

contextualize formal or specialized (UK usually **contextualise**) /kənˈtek.stju.ə.laɪz/ **verb** [T] to consider something in its context: *We must contextualize the problem before we can understand its origin.*

contiguous /kənˈtɪg.ju.əs/ **adj** formal next to or touching another, usually similar, thing: *The two states are contiguous* ***with/to*** *each other, but the laws are quite different.* • **contiguity** /ˌkɒn.tɪˈgjuː.ɪ.ti/ (US) /ˌkɑːn.t̬əˈgjuː.ə.t̬i/ **noun** [U]

continent /ˈkɒn.tɪ.nənt/ (US) /ˈkɑːn.t̬ᵊn.ənt/ **noun**; **adj**

▸**noun** [C] (B1) one of the seven large land masses on the Earth's surface, surrounded, or mainly surrounded, by sea and usually consisting of various countries: *the North American continent* ◦ *the continents of Asia and Africa* • **continental** /ˌkɒn.tɪˈnen.tᵊl/ (US) /ˌkɑːn.t̬ᵊnˈen.t̬ᵊl/ **adj** (C2) *continental waters*

▸**adj** **1** specialized able to control when you urinate and empty your bowels → Opposite **incontinent** **2** literary able to control your sexual DESIRES • **continence** /-nəns/ **noun** [U]

the ˈContinent **noun** [S] mainly UK Europe, especially western Europe, but not including the British Isles: *He found driving* ***on*** *the Continent very different to Britain.* • **Continental** (also **continental**) /ˌkɒn.tɪˈnen.tᵊl/ (US) /ˌkɑːn.t̬ᵊnˈen.t̬ᵊl/ **adj** *She preferred the continental way of life.* • **Continental** (also **continental**) /ˌkɒn.tɪˈnen.tᵊl/ (US) /ˌkɑːn.t̬ᵊnˈen.t̬ᵊl/ **noun** [C] mainly UK old-fashioned someone who comes from Europe but not the British Isles

ˌcontinental ˈbreakfast **noun** [C] a simple morning meal consisting of fruit juice, coffee, and bread with butter and jam

ˌcontinental ˈcrust **noun** [U] specialized the surface of the Earth that is about 35 kilometres thick and includes the land masses and the solid rock below them

ˌcontinental ˈdrift **noun** [U] specialized the very slow movement of continents over the Earth's surface

ˌcontinental ˈplate **noun** [C] specialized one of the large pieces of the surface of the Earth that move separately

ˌcontinental ˈquilt **noun** [C] UK old-fashioned a **duvet**

ˌcontinental ˈshelf **noun** [C usually singular] specialized the area of the bottom of the sea near the coast of a continent, where the sea is not very deep

contingency /kənˈtɪn.dʒᵊn.si/ **noun** [C] formal something that might possibly happen in the future, usually causing problems or making further arrangements necessary: *You must be able to deal with all possible contingencies.* ◦ *Have you made any contingency* ***plans?***

contingent /kənˈtɪn.dʒᵊnt/ **noun**; **adj**

▸**noun** [C, + sing/pl verb] a group of people representing an organization or country, or a part of a military force: *The French contingent certainly made their presence known at this year's conference.* ◦ *a large contingent of voluntary soldiers*

▸**adj** formal **contingent on/upon sth** depending on something else in the future in order to happen: *Outdoor arrangements are, as ever, contingent on the weather.* ◦ *Our success is contingent upon your support.*

continual /kənˈtɪn.ju.əl/ **adj** (C1) happening repeatedly, usually in an annoying or not convenient way: *I've had continual* ***problems*** *with this car ever since I bought it.* ◦ *I'm sorry – I can't work with these continual* *interruptions.* • **continually** /-i/ **adv** C1 *They argue continually.*

continuation /kən͵tɪn.ju'eɪ.ʃən/ **noun** [C or U] (formal **continuance** /kən'tɪn.ju.əns/) the fact of continuing or a thing that continues or follows from something else: *The continuation of the strike caused a lot of hardship.* ◦ *It's just a continuation of the bigger river, but with a different name.*

continue /kən'tɪn.juː/ **verb** **1** B1 [I or T] to keep happening, existing, or doing something, or to cause something or someone to do this: [+ to infinitive] *It's said that as the boat went down the band continued* ***to*** *play.* ◦ [+ -ing verb] *If she continues drink**ing** like that, I'll have to carry her home.* ◦ *Do you intend to continue (**with**) your studies?* ◦ *If the rain continues, we'll have to cancel tonight's plans.* ◦ *Sally Palmer will be continuing* ***as*** *chairperson this autumn.* ◦ *The article continues/is continued* ***on*** *page ten.* **2** B1 [I] to start to do something again after a pause: *After stopping for a quick drink, they continued* ***on*** *their way.* ◦ [+ -ing verb] *He paused for a moment to listen and then continued eat**ing**.* ◦ *The president continued* ***by*** *say**ing** that his country was a free country and would always remain so.* ◦ [+ speech] *'I don't like your weather!' she shouted, 'and I don't,' she continued, 'like your food!'*

continued /kən'tɪn.juːd/ **adj** [before noun] **1** (also **continuing**) still happening, existing, or done: *Continued fighting in the city is causing great concern.* **2** (written abbreviation **cont.**) often used at the bottom of a page to show that the story, article, etc. is not finished: *continued on page 7*

continuity /͵kɒn.tɪ'njuː.ɪ.ti/ US /͵kɑːn.tən'uː.ə.t̬i/ **noun** [U] **1** C2 the fact of something continuing for a long period of time without being changed or stopped: *There has been no continuity in that class – they've had a succession of different teachers.* **2** specialized the way in which film and television broadcasts are joined together so that the action happens without any pause or change

continuous /kən'tɪn.ju.əs/ **adj** B2 without a pause or interruption: *continuous pain* ◦ *My computer makes a continuous low buzzing noise.* ◦ *A continuous white line (= line without spaces) in the middle of the road means no overtaking.* • **continuously** /-li/ **adv** B2 *You can't work continuously for six hours without a break!*

con͵tinuous as'sessment **noun** [U] the system in which the quality of a student's work is judged by various pieces of work during a course and not by one final exam

continuum /kən'tɪn.ju.əm/ **noun** [C] (plural **continua** /-ə/ or **continuums**) specialized something that changes in character gradually or in very slight stages without any clear dividing points: *It's not 'left-wing or right-wing' – political opinion is a long continuum.*

contort /kən'tɔːt/ US /-'tɔːrt/ **verb** [I or T] to (cause something to) twist or bend violently and unnaturally into a different shape or form: *His face contorted* ***with*** *bitterness and rage.* • **contorted** /-'tɔː.tɪd/ US /-'tɔːr.t̬ɪd/ **adj** *contorted limbs/branches* • **contortion** /-'tɔː.ʃən/ US /-'tɔːr.ʃən/ **noun** [C or U] *facial/bodily contortions*

contortionist /kən'tɔː.ʃən.ɪst/ US /-'tɔːr-/ **noun** [C] someone who can twist their body into shapes and positions that ordinary people cannot

contour /'kɒn.tɔːr/ US /'kɑːn.tʊr/ **noun** [C] **1** the shape of a mass of land or other object, especially its surface or the shape formed by its outer edge: *the rugged contour of the coast* ◦ *He studied the contours of her face.* **2** (also **contour line**) a line on a map that joins points of equal height or depth, in a way that shows high and low areas of land: *a 400 ft contour line* ◦ *This map has contours marked at 250-metre intervals.*

contra- /'kɒn.trə/ US /'kɑːn-/ **prefix** against or opposite: *to contradict (= say the opposite)* ◦ *contraception (= something that is used to prevent pregnancy)*

contraband /'kɒn.trə.bænd/ US /'kɑːn-/ **noun** [U] goods that are brought into or taken out of the country secretly and illegally: *The lorry contained thousands of pounds worth of contraband.* • **contraband** **adj** *contraband cigarettes/goods*

contraception /͵kɒn.trə'sep.ʃən/ US /͵kɑːn-/ **noun** [U] C2 (the use of) any of various methods intended to prevent a woman becoming pregnant: *They offer impartial advice on contraception.* ◦ *What is the most reliable* ***form/method of*** *contraception?*

contraceptive /͵kɒn.trə'sep.tɪv/ US /͵kɑːn-/ **noun** [C] C2 any of various devices or drugs intended to prevent pregnancy: *The clinic provides a free supply of contraceptives on request.* • **contraceptive** **adj** *a contraceptive device/pill*

contract **noun**; **verb**

▸**noun** [C] /'kɒn.trækt/ US /'kɑːn-/ **1** B1 a legal document that states and explains a formal agreement between two different people or groups, or the agreement itself: *a contract of employment* ◦ *a temporary/building contract* ◦ *They could take legal action against you if you* ***break*** *(**the terms of**) the contract.* ◦ *My solicitor is* ***drawing up*** *(= writing) a contract.* ◦ *Don't* ***sign/enter into*** *any contract before examining its conditions carefully.* ◦ [+ to infinitive] *They're the firm of architects who* ***won*** *the contract* ***to*** *design the National Museum extension.* **2** **be under contract** to have formally agreed to work for a company or person on a stated job for a stated period of time

▸**verb** /kən'trækt/ **SHORTEN** ▷ **1** [I or T] to make or become shorter or narrower or generally smaller: *In spoken English, 'do not' often contracts* ***to*** *'don't'.* ◦ *As it cooled, the metal contracted.* **BECOME ILL** ▷ **2** C2 [T] formal to catch or become ill with a disease: *He contracted malaria while he was travelling.* **AGREEMENT** ▷ **3** C2 [I or T] to make a legal agreement with someone to do work or to have work done for you: [+ to infinitive] *They have just contracted our company* ***to*** *build shelters for the homeless.*

PHRASAL VERBS **contract in/out** UK to formally agree to take part/stop taking part in an official plan or system: *Have you contracted in* ***to*** *the pension scheme?* • **contract sth out** to formally arrange for other people to do a particular job: *The government contracted out hospital cleaning* ***to*** *private companies.*

contractile /kən'træk.taɪl/ US /-t̬əl/ **adj** specialized describes body tissue that is able to contract, or something that causes this to happen

contraction /kən'træk.ʃən/ **noun** [U] **REDUCTION** ▷ **1** the fact of something becoming smaller or shorter: *Cold causes contraction of the metal.* ◦ *The contraction of this muscle raises the lower arm.* **MUSCLE** ▷ **2** [C] one of the very strong and usually painful movements of the muscles in the WOMB that help to push the baby out of the mother's body during the process of birth: *She was* ***having*** *regular strong contractions every four minutes.* **WORD** ▷ **3** [C] a short form of a word or combination of words that is often used instead of the full form in spoken English: *'Won't' is a contraction of 'will not'.*

contractor /kən'træk.tər/ US /'kɑːn.træk.tɚ/ **noun** [C] a person or company that arranges to supply materials or workers for building or for moving goods

contractual /kənˈtræk.tju.əl/ **adj** relating to or contained within a CONTRACT (= legal agreement): *contractual conditions/terms* ◦ *Are you* ***under a*** *contractual* ***obligation*** *to any other company?* • **contractually** /-i/ **adv** *They are contractually* ***bound/obliged*** *to finish the work.*

contradict /ˌkɒn.trəˈdɪkt/ US /ˌkɑːn-/ **verb** [I or T] C1 (of people) to say the opposite of what someone else has said, or (of one fact or statement) to be so different from another fact or statement that one of them must be wrong: *If you're both going to lie, at least stick to the same story and don't contradict each other!* ◦ *He kept contradicting him****self*** *when we were arguing – I think he was a bit confused.* ◦ *How dare you contradict (me)!* ◦ *Recent evidence has tended to contradict established theories on this subject.*

contradiction /ˌkɒn.trəˈdɪk.ʃən/ US /ˌkɑːn-/ **noun** [C or U] **1** C2 the fact of something being the complete opposite of something else or very different from something else, so that one of them must be wrong: *You say that you're good friends and yet you don't trust him. Isn't that a bit of a contradiction?* **2 a contradiction in terms** a combination of words that is nonsense because some of the words suggest the opposite of some of the others: *Many people think that an honest politician is a contradiction in terms.*

contradictory /ˌkɒn.trəˈdɪk.tər.i/ US /ˌkɑːn.trəˈdɪk.tɚ-/ **adj** C2 If two or more facts, pieces of advice, etc. are contradictory, they are very different from each other: *I keep getting contradictory advice – some people tell me to keep it warm and some tell me to put ice on it.*

contraflow /ˈkɒn.trə.fləʊ/ US /ˈkɑːn.trə.floʊ/ **noun** [C] mainly UK a temporary traffic arrangement, usually on a main road, in which traffic travelling in both directions uses one side of the road while the other side is being repaired: *A contraflow is* ***in operation/in force*** *between junctions 13 and 14 on the motorway.*

contraindication /ˌkɒn.trəˌɪn.dɪˈkeɪ.ʃən/ US /ˌkɑːn-/ **noun** [C] specialized a sign that someone should not continue with a particular medicine or treatment because it is or might be harmful

contralto /kənˈtræl.təʊ/ US /-t̬oʊ/ **noun** [C] (plural **contraltos** or **contralti** /-ti/) a woman singer with the lowest female singing voice, or this type of voice

contraption /kənˈtræp.ʃən/ **noun** [C] a device or machine that looks awkward or old-fashioned, especially one that you do not know how to use: *Whatever's that* ***strange*** *contraption you've got in the garage?*

contrapuntal /ˌkɒn.trəˈpʌn.təl/ US /ˌkɑːn.trəˈpʌn.t̬əl/ **adj** specialized describes music in which two or more separate tunes happen at the same time

contrariness /kənˈtreə.ri.nəs/ US /-ˈtrer.i-/ **noun** [U] the quality of being someone who intentionally wants to disagree with and annoy other people

contrary noun; adj

▸**noun** [S] /ˈkɒn.trə.ri/ US /ˈkɑːn.tre-/ **1 the contrary** the opposite: *I was worried that it might be too difficult for me but I found the contrary.* **2 on the contrary** B2 used to show that you think or feel the opposite of what has just been stated: *'Didn't you find the film exciting?' 'On the contrary, I nearly fell asleep half way through it!'* **3 to the contrary** C1 saying or showing the opposite: *For a long time it was thought to be a harmless substance, but we now have* ***proof/evidence*** *to the contrary.*

> **! Common mistake: on the contrary or by/in contrast?**
>
> Use **on the contrary** to show that you think or feel the opposite of what has just been stated:
>
> *'You must be pleased with your exam results.' 'On the contrary, I thought they would be much better.'*
>
> If you are comparing two things and you want to say that the second thing is very different to the first, don't say 'on the contrary', say **by/in contrast**:
>
> ~~*Rory is always on time for work. On the contrary, Vicki is always late.*~~
>
> *Rory is always on time for work. By contrast, Vicki is always late.*

▸**adj** **OPPOSITE** ▷ **1** C1 /ˈkɒn.trə.ri/ US /ˈkɑːn.tre-/ opposite: *a contrary point of view* ◦ *Contrary* ***to*** *all our expectations, he's found a well-paid job and a nice girlfriend.* **2 contrary to popular opinion** /ˈkɒn.trə.ri/ US /ˈkɑːn.tre-/ in a different way from what most people believe: *Contrary to popular opinion, I don't dye my hair!* **NOT REASONABLE** ▷ **3** /kənˈtreə.ri/ US /-ˈtrer.i/ describes a person who wants to disagree with and annoy other people

contrast noun; verb

▸**noun** [C or U] /ˈkɒn.trɑːst/ US /ˈkɑːn.træst/ B2 an obvious difference between two or more things: *I like the contrast* ***of*** *the white trousers* ***with*** *the black jacket.* ◦ *The antique furnishing provides an unusual contrast* ***to*** *the modernity of the building.* ◦ *There's a* ***marked*** *contrast* ***between*** *his character* ***and*** *hers.* ◦ *Their economy has expanded enormously, while ours,* ***by/in*** *contrast, has declined.* ◦ *The amount spent on defence is* ***in stark/sharp*** *(= in very noticeable) contrast* ***to*** *that spent on housing and health.* ◦ *I love his use of contrast (= strong differences between light and darkness) in his later photographs.*

▸**verb** /kənˈtrɑːst/ US /-ˈtræst/ **1** C2 [T] to compare two people or things in order to show the differences between them: *If you contrast some of her early writing* ***with*** *her later work, you can see just how much she improved.* **2** C2 [I] If one thing contrasts with another, it is very different from it: *The styles of the two film makers contrast quite dramatically.* ◦ *The sharpness of the lemons contrasts* ***with*** *the sweetness of the honey.*

contrasting /kənˈtrɑː.stɪŋ/ US /-ˈtræs.tɪŋ/ **adj** very different: *contrasting colours/flavours* ◦ *the contrasting attitudes of different age-groups*

contrastive /kənˈtrɑː.stɪv/ US /-ˈtræs.tɪv/ **adj** showing the differences between things: *a contrastive analysis of English and Spanish*

contravene /ˌkɒn.trəˈviːn/ US /ˌkɑːn-/ **verb** [T] formal to do something that a law or rule does not allow, or to break a law or rule: *This contravenes the Race Relations Act.* • **contravention** /ˌkɒn.trəˈven.ʃən/ US /ˌkɑːn-/ **noun** [C or U] *By accepting the money, she was* ***in*** *contravention* ***of*** *company regulations.*

contretemps /ˈkɒn.trə.tɒ/ US /ˈkɑːn.trə.tɑː/ **noun** [C] (plural **contretemps**) a small argument or unlucky event, often happening in public and causing social embarrassment: *There was a slight contretemps* ***between*** *Richard and some bloke at the bar.* ◦ *Have you got over your little contretemps* ***with*** *the neighbour yet, or are you still not speaking?*

contribute /kənˈtrɪb.juːt/, /ˈkɒn.trɪ.bjuːt/ US /ˈkɑːn-/ **verb** [I or T] **1** B2 to give something, especially money, in order to provide or achieve something together with other people: *Aren't you going to contribute* ***towards*** *Jack's leaving present?* ◦ *Come to the meeting if you feel you have something to contribute.* ◦ *Her family have contributed £50,000* ***to*** *the fund.* **2** C1 to write articles for a newspaper, magazine, or book: *She contributes **to** several magazines.*

PHRASAL VERB **contribute to sth** to help to cause an event or situation: *Smoking contributed to his early death.*

> **! Common mistake: contribution**
>
> **Warning:** Choose the right verb!
>
> Don't say 'give/have/do a contribution', say **make a contribution**:
>
> ~~*She gave a useful contribution to the discussion.*~~
>
> *She made a useful contribution to the discussion.*

contribution /ˌkɒn.trɪˈbjuː.ʃən/ US /ˌkɑːn-/ noun [C or U] B2 something that you contribute or do to help produce or achieve something together with other people, or to help make something successful: *All contributions (= presents of money), no matter how small, will be much appreciated.* ◦ *All contributions (= articles to be printed) **for** the school magazine must be received by 1 August.* ◦ *This invention **made a** major contribution **to** road safety.* ◦ *She didn't **make** much of **a** contribution (= she did not say much) at today's meeting, did she?*

> **Word partners for contribution**
>
> *make* a contribution • a *big/enormous/great/massive* contribution • an *important/major/positive/valuable* contribution • a *genuine/individual/lasting/unique* contribution • a contribution *to/towards* sth • a contribution *from* sb

contributor /kənˈtrɪb.jʊ.təʳ/ US /-jə.t̬ɚ/ noun [C] **1** a person who contributes something, especially money, in order to provide or achieve something together with other people: *At the back of the programme, there is a list of contributors **to** the theatre appeal.* **2** someone who writes articles for a newspaper, magazine, or book

contributory /kənˈtrɪb.jʊ.təʳr.i/ US /-jə.tɔːr.i/ adj **1** describes something that you contribute to: *The company offers a contributory **pension plan** (= one to which both the employee and employer pay money).* → Opposite **non-contributory** **2** helping to cause something: *Too little exercise is a contributory **factor** in heart disease.*

conˌtributory ˈnegligence noun [U] UK legal a judgment in court that a person who has been hurt in an accident was partly responsible for their own injuries because they failed to act in a way that could have prevented the accident or the injuries

contrite /ˈkɒn.traɪt/ US /ˈkɑːn-/ adj formal feeling very sorry and guilty for something bad that you have done: *a contrite apology/expression* • **contritely** /-li/ adv • **contrition** /-ˈtrɪʃ.ən/ noun [U]

contrivance /kənˈtraɪ.vəns/ noun [C or U] formal the act of contriving something: disapproving *Because of the timing, I'm sure the salary freeze is a deliberate contrivance, not a coincidence.* ◦ *I think the meeting happened more by contrivance than chance.*

contrive /kənˈtraɪv/ verb [T] **1** to arrange a situation or event, or arrange for something to happen, using clever planning: *Couldn't you contrive a meeting between them? I think they'd be ideally suited.* ◦ [+ to infinitive] *Somehow she contrived **to** get tickets for the concert.* **2** to invent and/or make a device or other object in a clever and possibly unusual way: *Do you think you could contrive something for hanging my clothes on until I can get a wardrobe?*

contrived /kənˈtraɪvd/ adj disapproving **1** clever rather than honest: *His excuse sounded a bit contrived.* **2** artificial and difficult to believe: *I enjoyed the film, but felt the ending was a bit contrived.*

control /kənˈtrəʊl/ US /-ˈtroʊl/ verb; noun

▸verb [T] (-ll-) B1 to order, limit, or rule something, or someone's actions or behaviour: *If you can't control your dog, put it on a lead!* ◦ *You're going to have to learn to control your temper.* ◦ *The temperature is controlled by a thermostat.* ◦ *The laws controlling drugs are very strict in this country.* ◦ *The government is trying to control spending.*

▸noun **POWER** ▷ **1** B2 [C or U] the act of controlling something or someone, or the power to do this: *She's got no control **over** that child – it's terrible.* ◦ *He wants the government to **impose** strict controls **on** dog ownership.* ◦ *The dictator **took** control **of** the country in 1933.* ◦ *He felt he was **losing** control **of** events.* ◦ *You need to stay **in** control **of** your emotions.* ◦ *The car skidded and **went out of** control, crashing into an oncoming truck.* ◦ *There was nothing we could do about it – the situation was **out of/beyond/outside** our control.* ◦ *She criticized the police's methods of **crowd** control.* **2 under control** B2 being dealt with or limited successfully: *It seems that the disease is now under control.* ◦ *Everything is under control, sir.* ◦ *It took them two hours to **bring/get** the fire under control.* **SWITCH** ▷ **3** B2 [C] a switch or other device used to operate a machine such as a vehicle: *The main instruments are in the centre of the control **panel**.* ◦ *Captain Firth sat **at the** controls **of** the aircraft.* **4** [C usually singular] (also **control key**, written abbreviation **Ctrl**) a key on a computer keyboard that you press at the same time as other keys to make the keyboard operate in a particular way: *Press and hold down the control key while you press 9.* ◦ *I pressed Control Alt Delete but nothing happened.* **IN AN EXPERIMENT** ▷ **5** [C] specialized in an EXPERIMENT, an object or system that is not changed so that you can compare it with similar objects or systems that are intentionally changed

> **Word partners for control noun**
>
> *assume/have/take* control • *lose/relinquish* control • *gain/get/seize* control • *impose/strengthen/tighten* controls on sth • *complete/direct/full/total* control • *firm/strict/tight* control • control *of/on/over* sb/sth • *beyond/out of/under* sb's control

conˈtrol ˌfreak noun [C] informal disapproving someone who is determined to make things happen exactly in the way they want and who tries to make other people do what they want

conˈtrol ˌkey noun [C] the key on a computer keyboard that usually has 'Ctrl' printed on it and that is used together with other keys to do particular operations

controller /kənˈtrəʊ.ləʳ/ US /-ˈtroʊ.lɚ/ noun [C] a person who controls something, or someone who is responsible for what a particular organization does: *an air-traffic controller* ◦ *That was the year he became Controller of Radio 4.*

conˈtrol ˌtower noun [C] a building at an airport from which air traffic is watched and directed

controversial /ˌkɒn.trəˈvɜː.ʃəl/ US /ˌkɑːn.trəˈvɝː-/ adj B2 causing disagreement or discussion: *a controversial issue/decision/speech/figure* ◦ *The book was very controversial.* • **controversially** /-i/ adv

controversy /ˈkɒn.trə.vɜː.si/, /kənˈtrɒv.ə-/ US /ˈkɑːn.trə.vɝː-/ noun [C or U] C1 a lot of disagreement or argument about something, usually because it affects or is important to many people: *There was a big* *controversy **surrounding/over** the use of drugs in athletics.* ◦ *The policy has caused **fierce/heated** controversy ever since it was introduced.*

C

contusion /kənˈtjuː.ʒən/ ⓤⓢ /-ˈtuː-/ noun [C] specialized a **bruise** • **contuse** /kənˈtjuːz/ ⓤⓢ /-ˈtuːz/ verb [I or T] specialized to **bruise**

conundrum /kəˈnʌn.drəm/ noun [C] **1** a problem that is difficult to deal with: *Arranging childcare over the school holidays can be quite a conundrum for working parents.* **2** a question that is a trick, often involving a humorous use of words that have two meanings

conurbation /ˌkɒn.əˈbeɪ.ʃən/ ⓤⓢ /ˌkɑː.nɚ-/ noun [C] formal a city area containing a large number of people, formed by various towns growing and joining together

convalesce /ˌkɒn.vəˈles/ ⓤⓢ /ˌkɑːn-/ verb [I] to rest in order to get better after an illness: *After your operation, you'll need to convalesce for a week or two.*

convalescence /ˌkɒn.vəˈles.əns/ ⓤⓢ /ˌkɑːn-/ noun [S or U] a period in which you convalesce

convalescent /ˌkɒn.vəˈles.ənt/ ⓤⓢ /ˌkɑːn-/ **noun; adj**
▸**noun** [C] someone who is getting better after a serious illness or injury: *Most convalescents prefer to be cared for at home rather than in a hospital.*
▸**adj** (for or relating to) convalescing: *a convalescent **home/hospital***

convection /kənˈvek.ʃən/ noun [U] specialized the flow of heat through a gas or a liquid: *Warm air rises by the process of convection.*

convector /kənˈvek.təʳ/ ⓤⓢ /-tɚ/ noun [C] a device that warms a room by creating a current of hot air

convene /kənˈviːn/ verb [I or T] formal to bring together a group of people for a meeting, or to meet for a meeting: *The prime minister convened (a meeting of) his ministers to discuss the matter.* ◦ *The council will be convening on the morning of the 25th.*

convenience /kənˈviː.ni.əns/ noun **BEING EASY** ▷ **1** B2 [U] the state of being convenient: *I like the convenience of living so near work.* ◦ *Just for convenience, I'm going to live at my mother's place until my new house is ready.* **2 at your convenience** B2 when you want: *The goods will be delivered at your convenience.* **3 at your earliest convenience** as soon as you like or can: *Please return the completed form at your earliest convenience.* **MACHINE** ▷ **4** C1 [C] a device or machine, usually in the house, that operates quickly and needs little effort: *The house has every modern convenience.* **TOILET** ▷ **5** [C usually plural] (also **public convenience**) a public toilet

conˈvenience ˌfood noun [U or C] food that is almost ready to eat when it is bought and can be prepared quickly and easily

conˈvenience ˌstore noun [C] mainly US a shop that sells food, drinks, etc. and is usually open until late

convenient /kənˈviː.ni.ənt/ adj **1** B1 suitable for your purposes and needs and causing the least difficulty: *Our local shop has very convenient opening hours.* ◦ *A bike's a very convenient way of getting around.* ◦ [+ that] ***It's** very convenient **that** you live near the office.* ◦ [+ to infinitive] *I find **it** convenient **to** be able to do my banking online.* ◦ *What time would **it** be convenient **for** me **to** come round?* → Opposite **inconvenient** **2** B1 near or easy to get to or use: *a very convenient bus service* ◦ *Our new flat is very convenient **for** (*= near to*) the kids' school.* • **conveniently** /-li/ adv B2 *The house is conveniently situated near the station and the shops.* ◦ humorous *I asked her to tidy the kitchen but of course she conveniently forgot (= she forgot because she did not want to do it).*

> **!** Common mistake: **convenient**
> **Warning:** Check your spelling!
> **Convenient** is one of the 50 words most often spelled wrongly by learners.

convenor /kənˈviː.nəʳ/ ⓤⓢ /-nɚ/ noun [C] (also **convener**) an important TRADE UNION official who works in a particular factory or office

convent /ˈkɒn.vənt/ ⓤⓢ /ˈkɑːn-/ noun [C] a building in which NUNS (= members of a female religious order) live → Compare **monastery**

IDIOM **enter a convent** to become a NUN

convention /kənˈven.ʃən/ noun **MEETING** ▷ **1** C1 [C] a large formal meeting of people who do a particular job or have a similar interest, or a large meeting for a political party: *the national Democratic convention* ◦ *Where are they **holding** their party convention?* **CUSTOM** ▷ **2** C1 [C or U] a usual or accepted way of behaving, especially in social situations, often following an old way of thinking or a custom in one particular society: *They **defied/flouted/broke with** convention by giving up their jobs and becoming self-sufficient.* ◦ *Convention **dictates that** it is the man who asks the woman to marry him and not the reverse.* ◦ *In many countries it is the/a convention to wear black at funerals.* **3** [C] a common way of showing something in art or writing: *an artistic convention* **AGREEMENT** ▷ **4** [C] a formal agreement between country leaders, politicians, and states on a matter that involves them all: *the Geneva Convention* ◦ *a convention **on** human rights*

conventional /kənˈven.ʃən.əl/ adj **1** B2 traditional and ordinary: *conventional behaviour/attitudes/clothes* ◦ *conventional medicine/farming* ◦ *a conventional wedding* ◦ disapproving *I find his art rather dull and conventional.* → Opposite **unconventional** **2** describes weapons that are not nuclear, or methods of fighting a war that do not involve nuclear weapons: *conventional weapons/bombs* • **conventionality** /kənˌven.ʃənˈæl.ɪ.ti/ ⓤⓢ /-ə.t̬i/ noun [U] • **conventionally** /-i/ adv

ˈ**convent ˌschool** noun [C] a school in which the teachers are NUNS (= members of a female religious order)

converge /kənˈvɜːdʒ/ ⓤⓢ /-ˈvɝːdʒ/ verb [I] **1** If lines, roads, or paths converge, they move towards the same point where they join or meet: *The paths all converge **at** the main gate of the park.* ◦ *Due to roadworks, three lanes of traffic have to converge **into** two.* → Compare **diverge** **2** If ideas and opinions converge, they gradually become similar. **3** to come from other places to meet in a particular place: *Ambulances, police cars, and fire engines all converged **on** the scene.* ◦ *100,000 people are expected to converge **on** the town for the festival.* • **convergence** /kənˈvɜː.dʒəns/ ⓤⓢ /-ˈvɝː-/ noun [C or U] *a convergence **of** interests/opinions/ideas*

convergent /kənˈvɜː.dʒənt/ ⓤⓢ /kənˈvɝː-/ adj **1** coming closer together: *The rays become more convergent as they leave the lens.* **2** becoming more similar: *The two countries have convergent views on regional and international issues.*

conversant /kənˈvɜː.sənt/ ⓤⓢ /-ˈvɝː-/ adj formal **be conversant with sth** to be familiar with, and have knowledge or experience of the facts or rules of something: *I'm not conversant with the rules of chess.*

conversation /ˌkɒn.vəˈseɪ.ʃən/ ⓤⓢ /ˌkɑːn.vɚ-/ noun [C or U] A1 (a) talk between two or more people in which thoughts, feelings, and ideas are expressed, questions are asked and answered, or news and information is exchanged: *She **had** a strange conversation **with** the man who's moved in upstairs.* ◦ *It's impossible to **hold/carry on** a conversation with all this noise going on!* ◦ *I **struck up** (= started) an interesting conversation **with** your uncle.* ◦ *Whenever I'm in a social situation with my boss, we seem to **run out of** conversation (= things to say to each other) after two minutes!*

> Word partners for **conversation**
>
> *carry on/have/hold* a conversation (*with* sb) • *get into/strike up* a conversation (*with* sb) • *steer/turn* the conversation • a *brief/casual/long/private* conversation • a conversation *between* [two people] • a conversation *about* sth • *in* conversation • a *topic of* conversation

IDIOM **make conversation** to say things to someone who you do not know well, in order to be polite: *I was just trying to make conversation.*

conversational /ˌkɒn.vəˈseɪ.ʃən.əl/ (US) /ˌkɑːn.vɚ-/ **adj** relating to or like a conversation: *a conversational style of writing* ◦ *He seems to lack basic conversational skills.*

conversationalist /ˌkɒn.vəˈseɪ.ʃən.əl.ɪst/ (US) /ˌkɑːn.vɚ-/ **noun** [C] someone who enjoys or is good at talking with people

converˈsation ˌpiece **noun** [C] an unusual object that causes people to start talking

converse **noun; adj; verb**

▸**noun** /ˈkɒn.vɜːs/, /kənˈvɜːs/ (US) /ˈkɑːn.vɝːs/, /kənˈvɝːs/ **the converse** [S] the opposite: *In the US, you drive on the right-hand side of the road, but in Britain the converse applies.* ◦ *However, the converse of this theory may also be true.*

▸**adj** /ˈkɒn.vɜːs/, /kənˈvɜːs/ (US) /ˈkɑːn.vɝːs/, /kənˈvɝːs/ formal opposite: *a converse effect/opinion/argument* • **conversely** /kənˈvɜːs.li, ˈkɒn.vɜːs-/ (US) /kənˈvɝːs, ˈkɑːn.vɝːs-/ **adv** in an opposite way

▸**verb** [I] /kənˈvɜːs/ (US) /-ˈvɝːs/ formal to have a conversation with someone: *She's so shy that conversing **with** her can be quite difficult.*

conversion /kənˈvɜː.ʃən/, /-ʒən/ (US) /-ˈvɝː-/ **noun** CHANGE ▷ **1** (C2) [C or U] the process of converting something from one thing to another: *Solar power is the conversion **of** the sun's energy **into** heat and electricity.* **2** a process in which someone changes to a new religion or belief: *Her conversion **to** Buddhism/Islam was a very gradual process.* ◦ *He used to be very right-wing, but he's **undergone** something of a conversion recently.* **3** [C] a place for living in that has been changed from its previous use: *a barn/factory conversion* RUGBY ▷ **4** [C] in RUGBY, an attempt to score more points after a TRY by kicking the ball over the bar and between the two posts

convert **verb; noun**

▸**verb** /kənˈvɜːt/ (US) /-ˈvɝːt/ CHANGE ▷ **1** (B2) [I or T] to (cause something or someone to) change in form or character: *Could we convert the small bedroom **into** a second bathroom?* ◦ *What's the formula for converting pounds **into** kilos?* **2** (C2) [I or T] to change to a new religion, belief, opinion, etc., or to make someone do this: *He converted **to** (= started believing in) Catholicism when he got married.* ◦ *I used not to like exercise, but my sister has converted me (**to** it).* RUGBY ▷ **3** [T] in RUGBY, to score more points after a TRY by kicking the ball over the bar and between the posts

▸**noun** [C] /ˈkɒn.vɜːt/ (US) /ˈkɑːn.vɝːt/ someone who changes their beliefs, habits, or way of living: *a Christian/Buddhist convert* ◦ *a convert **to** vegetarianism/wholemeal bread*

converter /kənˈvɜː.təʳ/ (US) /-ˈvɝː.t̬ɚ/ **noun** [C] (also **convertor**) a machine or device that changes something into a different form

convertible /kənˈvɜː.tɪ.bl̩/ (US) /-ˈvɝː.t̬ə-/ **adj; noun**

▸**adj** **1** able to be arranged in a different way and used for a different purpose: *a convertible sofa bed* **2** specialized describes a type of money that can be easily exchanged into other types of money: *a convertible currency/bond*

▸**noun** [C] (also **ˈsoft top**) a car with a soft roof that can be folded back: *a Volkswagen convertible*

convex /ˈkɒn.veks/ (US) /ˈkɑːn-/ /kənˈveks/ **adj** curved or swelling out: *a convex lens/mirror* → Compare **concave**

convey /kənˈveɪ/ **verb** [T] COMMUNICATE ▷ **1** (C1) to express a thought, feeling, or idea so that it is understood by other people: *His poetry conveys a great sense of religious devotion.* ◦ *If you see James, do convey my apologies (**to** him).* ◦ [+ question word] *I tried to convey in my speech **how** grateful we all were for his help.* ◦ *You don't want to convey the impression **that** we're not interested.* TAKE ▷ **2** formal to take or carry someone or something to a particular place: *The goods are usually conveyed by sea.* ◦ *Could you convey a message **to** Mr Merrick for me, please?*

conveyance /kənˈveɪ.əns/ **noun** TRANSPORTATION ▷ **1** [U] formal the process of moving something or someone from one place to another: *the conveyance of water* **2** [C] Indian English or old-fashioned a vehicle or method of transport: *a horse-drawn/public conveyance* DOCUMENT ▷ **3** [C] legal a legal document that officially gives to someone the rights to land or property

conveyancing /kənˈveɪ.ən.sɪŋ/ **noun** [U] legal the process of moving the legal OWNERSHIP of property or land from one person to another: *When we bought our house, we did our own conveyancing instead of using a lawyer.*

conveyor belt

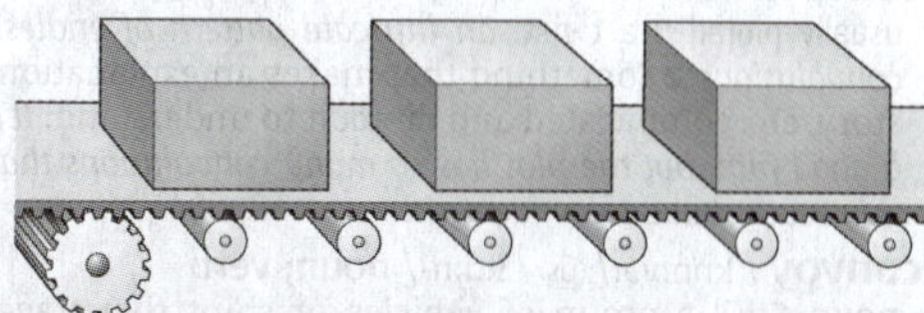

conveyor belt /kənˈveɪ.əˌbelt/ (US) /-ɚ-/ **noun** [C] (also **conveyor**) a continuous moving strip or surface that is used for transporting objects from one place to another

convict **verb; noun**

▸**verb** [T usually passive] /kənˈvɪkt/ (C2) to decide officially in a law court that someone is guilty of a crime: *He has twice been convicted **of** robbery/arson.* → Compare **acquit** • **convicted** /-ˈvɪk.tɪd/ **adj** *a convicted murderer*

▸**noun** [C] /ˈkɒn.vɪkt/ (US) /ˈkɑːn-/ someone who is in prison because they are guilty of a crime: *an escaped convict*

conviction /kənˈvɪk.ʃən/ **noun** CRIME ▷ **1** (C2) [C or U] the fact of officially being found to be guilty of a particular crime, or the act of officially finding someone guilty: *As it was her first conviction **for** stealing, she was given a less severe sentence.* ◦ *He has a long record of previous convictions **for** similar offences.* ◦ *The conviction **of** the three demonstrators has caused public outrage locally.* → Compare **acquittal** OPIN-

ION ▷ **2** C2 [C or U] a strong opinion or belief: *religious/moral convictions* ◦ *a* ***deep/strong/lifelong*** *conviction* ◦ [+ that] ***It's my*** *personal conviction* ***that*** *all rapists should be locked away for life.* **3** [U] a feeling of being certain about something: *He said he was enjoying his new job, but his voice* ***lacked*** *conviction.*

convince /kənˈvɪns/ **verb** [T] B1 to persuade someone or make them certain: *He managed to convince the jury* ***of*** *his innocence.* ◦ [+ (that)] *It's useless trying to convince her* ***(that)*** *she doesn't need to lose any weight.* ◦ [+ to infinitive] *I hope this will convince you* ***to*** *change your mind.*

convinced /kənˈvɪnst/ **adj** **1** B2 certain: *My boyfriend says I'd enjoy a walking holiday, but I'm not convinced.* ◦ [+ (that)] *I'm convinced* ***(that)*** *she is lying.* **2** certain of your beliefs: *a convinced Christian/atheist* ◦ *a convinced socialist*

convincing /kənˈvɪn.sɪŋ/ **adj** **1** C1 able to make you believe that something is true or right: *a convincing argument/explanation* ◦ *convincing evidence* ◦ *I didn't find the ending of the film very convincing.* **2** **a convincing win/victory** a VICTORY in which the person or team that wins is much better than the person or team they are competing against: *They won a convincing victory.* • **convincingly** /-li/ **adv**

convivial /kənˈvɪv.i.əl/ **adj** friendly and making you feel happy and welcome: *a convivial atmosphere/host* • **conviviality** /kənˌvɪv.iˈæl.ɪ.ti/ (US) /-ə.t̬i/ **noun** [U] • **convivially** /-i/ **adv**

convocation /ˌkɒn.vəˈkeɪ.ʃᵊn/ (US) /ˌkɑːn-/ **noun** formal **1** [C] a large formal meeting, especially of Church officials or of members of some universities in the UK: *a university convocation* **2** [U] the act of arranging a convocation

convoluted /ˈkɒn.və.luː.tɪd/ (US) /ˈkɑːn.və.luː.t̬ɪd/ **adj** **1** very twisted: *a very convoluted route/knot* **2** describes sentences, explanations, arguments, etc. that are unreasonably long and difficult to understand: *His grammar explanations are terribly convoluted.* ◦ *Her book is full of long, convoluted sentences.*

convolution /ˌkɒn.vəˈluː.ʃᵊn/ (US) /ˌkɑːn-/ **noun** [C usually plural] **1** a twist: *an intricate pattern of endless convolutions* **2** something that makes an explanation, story, etc. complicated and difficult to understand: *It's a good film, but the plot has so many convolutions that you really have to concentrate.*

convoy /ˈkɒn.vɔɪ/ (US) /ˈkɑːn-/ **noun; verb**

▸**noun** **1** [C] a group of vehicles or ships that travel together, especially for protection: *A convoy of trucks containing supplies was sent to the famine area.* **2** **in convoy** travelling one behind another in a row: *Shall we all drive to the party in convoy so we don't get lost?*

▸**verb** [T] to travel with a vehicle or group of people to make certain that they arrive safely: *Two tanks convoyed the trucks across the border.*

convulse /kənˈvʌls/ **verb** [I or T] to (cause to) shake violently with sudden uncontrolled movements: *to convulse* ***with*** *pain* ◦ *A racking cough convulsed her whole body.*

IDIOM **be convulsed with laughter, rage, etc.** to laugh or feel anger, etc. in a way that you cannot control

convulsion /kənˈvʌl.ʃᵊn/ **noun** [C usually plural] a sudden movement of the muscles in your body that you cannot control, caused by illness or drugs: *She* ***went into*** *convulsions and had to be rushed to hospital.*

IDIOM **be in convulsions** informal to be laughing in a way that you cannot control

convulsive /kənˈvʌl.sɪv/ **adj** describes sudden movements of the muscles in your body that you cannot control: *convulsive spasms*

cony /ˈkəʊ.ni/ (US) /ˈkoʊ-/ **noun** [C or U] (also **coney**) a RABBIT, or the fur of a rabbit

coo /kuː/ **verb** [I] (present tense **cooing**, past tense and past participle **cooed**) **1** When birds such as DOVES and PIGEONS coo, they make a low soft sound. **2** to speak in a soft, gentle, or loving way: *The baby lay in his cot, cooing and gurgling.* ◦ *It's sickening the way she coos* ***over*** *those cats of hers.* ◦ [+ speech] *'How wonderful to see you again, darling,' she cooed.*

cook /kʊk/ **verb; noun**

▸**verb** A1 [I or T] When you cook food, you prepare it to be eaten by heating it in a particular way, such as baking or boiling, and when food cooks, it is heated until it is ready to eat: *I don't cook meat very often.* ◦ [+ two objects] *He cooked us an enormous meal./He cooked an enormous meal* ***for*** *us.* ◦ *Let the fish cook for half an hour before you add the wine.*

IDIOMS **be cooking** US informal to be making good progress or doing something well: *'Look! I've found the missing puzzle pieces.' 'Now we're cooking!'* ◦ *Jean's new band was really cooking at the party last night.* • **cook sb's goose** to do something that spoils someone's plans and prevents them from succeeding: *Just tell her we can't – that'll cook her goose.* • **cook the books** informal to change numbers dishonestly in the ACCOUNTS (= financial records) of an organization, especially in order to steal money from it • **what's cooking?** old-fashioned slang used to ask about what is happening or what someone is planning: *I just saw the police arrive – what's cooking?*

PHRASAL VERB **cook sth up** informal to invent a story, plan, etc., usually dishonestly: *She'd cooked up some weird scheme that was going to earn her a fortune.* ◦ *I had to cook up an excuse about my car breaking down.*

▸**noun** [C] A2 someone who prepares and cooks food: *She's a wonderful cook.*

IDIOM **too many cooks spoil the broth** UK saying (US **too many cooks spoil the soup**) said when there are too many people doing the same piece of work at the same time, so that the final result will be spoiled

cookbook /ˈkʊk.bʊk/ **noun** [C] (UK also **ˈcookery ˌbook**) a book that explains how to prepare particular dishes

cooked /kʊkt/ **adj** describes food that has been prepared by heating: *cooked meat/vegetables* ◦ *Is that cake cooked properly in the middle?* → Opposite **raw**

ˌcooked ˈbreakfast **noun** [C] UK a dish eaten in the morning consisting of fried eggs, BACON, sausages, and TOAST

cooker /ˈkʊk.əʳ/ (US) /-ɚ/ **noun** [C] **1** A2 mainly UK (US **stove**) a large box-shaped device that is used to cook and heat food, either by putting the food inside or by putting it on the top: *a gas/electric cooker* **2** UK informal a **cooking apple**

cookery /ˈkʊk.ᵊr.i/ (US) /-ɚ-/ **noun** [U] UK the skill or activity of preparing and cooking food: *cookery classes* ◦ *cookery books*

cookie /ˈkʊk.i/ **noun** [C] **BISCUIT** ▷ **1** A2 mainly US a sweet biscuit: *chocolate-chip cookies* **TYPE OF PERSON** ▷ **2** US informal a person of the type mentioned: *She's a* ***smart/tough*** *cookie.* **COMPUTING** ▷ **3** C2 specialized a piece of information stored on your computer about internet documents that you have looked at

IDIOM **that's the way the cookie crumbles** saying said when something slightly unlucky has happened that could not have been prevented and so must be accepted

ˈcookie ˌcutter noun [C] mainly US a sharp metal or plastic device used to cut cookies into shapes before they are cooked

ˈcookie-ˌcutter adj US disapproving similar to other things of the same type, especially in a way that shows little imagination: *a row of cookie-cutter houses*

cooking /ˈkʊk.ɪŋ/ noun; adj
▸noun [U] A2 the activity of preparing or cooking food: *Who **does** the cooking in your house?* ◦ *I love my dad's cooking (= the food that he cooks).*
▸adj [before noun] suitable for cooking with: *cooking apples* ◦ *cooking oil*

ˈcooking ˌapple noun [C] (UK informal **cooker**) a sour and usually large apple that is used in cooking → Compare **eating apple**

cookout /ˈkʊk.aʊt/ noun [C] US informal a meal cooked and eaten outside, especially as part of a party

cool /kuːl/ adj; adj, exclamation; noun; verb
▸adj **COLD** ▷ **1** B1 slightly cold: *cool water* ◦ *cool weather* **2** B1 slightly cold in a pleasant way: *It was a lovely cool evening.* ◦ *How do you manage to look so cool in this hot weather?* **3** describes a temperature that is slightly too cold: ***It's a bit cool in here, isn't it?*** *I think I'll close the window.* **CALM** ▷ **4** C1 calm and not worried or frightened; not influenced by strong feeling of any kind: *He was very cool and calm about the mishap, and didn't shout or lose his temper.* ◦ ***Stay/Keep*** *cool (= do not become angry or excited).* **5 be cool with sth** informal to be happy to accept a situation or suggestion: *Yeah, we could leave later – I'm cool with that.* **COLOUR** ▷ **6** describes colours, such as blue or green, that make you feel calm and relaxed: *The bedroom was painted a lovely cool blue.* **UNFRIENDLY** ▷ **7** C2 unfriendly or not showing kindness or interest in something or someone: *She was decidedly cool **towards** me.* ◦ *I got a rather cool **reception/welcome** this evening. What do you think I've done wrong?* **FASHIONABLE** ▷ **8** A2 informal fashionable or attractive: *Angie's got some cool new sunglasses.*

IDIOMS **(as) cool as a cucumber** very calm or very calmly, especially when this is surprising: *She walked in as cool as a cucumber, as if nothing had happened.* • **cool customer** informal someone who stays calm and does not show their emotions, even in a difficult situation • **keep a cool head** C2 to stay calm in a difficult situation: *I don't know how you manage to keep **such** a cool head in such a hectic, stressful office!*

▸adj, exclamation informal A2 excellent; very good: *'So how was the concert?' 'It was cool!'* ◦ *'Do you want to come with us?' 'Yeah, cool!'*
▸noun **COLD** ▷ **1 the cool** [S] the pleasant, slightly cold temperature of a place: *He loved the cool **of** the early morning.* ◦ *She left the midday sun for the cool of the shade.* **CALM** ▷ **2** C1 [U] informal a person's ability to stay calm and not become angry or excited: ***keep*** *your cool* ◦ *He really **lost** his cool when he heard about what happened.*
▸verb **BECOME COLD** ▷ **1** B2 [I or T] to become or cause something to become slightly colder: *Leave the cake to cool for an hour before cutting it.* ◦ *He took off his shoes to cool his sweaty feet.* **BECOME LESS** ▷ **2** [I] (also **cool off**) If a feeling cools or cools off, it starts to become less strong: *Their interest in the project seems to be cooling.* **3** [I] (also **cool off**) If the economy, a business, etc. cools or cools off, it grows less fast than before: *The rise in share prices has cooled off.*

IDIOM **cool it** slang used to tell someone to become calm, rather than be angry or violent: *Just cool it everyone, fighting won't solve anything.*

PHRASAL VERBS **cool (sb/sth) down/off** B2 to become less hot, or to make someone or something become less hot: *She waited until her coffee had cooled down before taking a sip.* ◦ *We went for a swim to cool off.* • **cool (sb) down/off** B2 to stop feeling angry or to stop someone else feeling angry after an argument: *Leave her to cool off and then talk to her.*

coolant /ˈkuː.lənt/ noun [C or U] specialized a specially prepared liquid that is used to stop a machine from getting too hot while it is operating

ˈcool ˌbag noun [C] UK (US **ˈcooler ˌbag**) a bag made of a thick INSULATING material that keeps food and drink cold when you are travelling

ˈcool ˌbox noun [C] UK (US **cooler**) a container like a box with a lid, used for keeping food and drinks cool

cooler /ˈkuː.ləʳ/ (US) /-lɚ/ noun [C] **1** US for **cool box**: *We've brought a cooler full of beer with us.* **2** mainly US a cold drink, usually of wine, fruit juice, and FIZZY water (= with bubbles): *a wine/fruit cooler* **3** Indian English an **air-cooler**

ˈcooler ˌbag noun [C] US for **cool bag**

coolheaded /ˌkuːlˈhed.ɪd/ adj having the ability to stay calm and think clearly in difficult situations

coolhunter /ˈkuːl.hʌn.təʳ/ (US) /-t̬ɚ/ noun [C] informal a **trendspotter**

coolie /ˈkuː.li/ noun [C] old-fashioned offensive **1** an unskilled and cheaply employed worker in Asia **2** Indian English a person whose job is to carry things, especially travellers' bags at stations, airports, etc.

cooling /ˈkuː.lɪŋ/ adj causing you to feel less warm or hot: *a cooling breeze/drink/swim*

ˌcooling-ˈoff ˌperiod noun [C usually singular] an agreed length of time in which someone can decide not to buy something they have agreed to buy, or a period in which two groups who are arguing can try to improve the situation before taking further action: *There is a 20-day cooling-off period in which the investor can choose to back out of the contract.*

ˈcooling ˌtower noun [C] a tall, hollow structure that is used in industrial processes to reduce the temperature of something, especially water, so that it can be used to cool other parts of the system

coolly /ˈkuːl.li/ adv in an unfriendly way: *'How did he receive your suggestion?' 'Rather coolly – I don't think he was too keen.'*

coolness /ˈkuːl.nəs/ noun [U] **CALM** ▷ **1** C2 the ability to stay calm and act in a reasonable way even in difficult situations: *Her coolness in an emergency was admirable.* **UNFRIENDLINESS** ▷ **2** C2 behaviour that shows no warm feelings or friendliness: *I noticed a certain coolness between your parents.* **COLD** ▷ **3** C1 the quality of being slightly cold: *There's a slight coolness in the air – do you think it's going to rain?*

coon /kuːn/ noun [C] offensive a very offensive word for a black person

coop /kuːp/ noun; verb
▸noun [C] a CAGE (= a small space surrounded by bars, wire, etc.) where small animals are kept, especially chickens

▸verb

PHRASAL VERB **coop sb/sth up** to keep someone or something in a closed space

ˌcooped ˈup adj If you are cooped up somewhere, you are in a small closed space from which you cannot escape, or you feel as if you are: *Cooped up in a small, dark cell, the prisoner hadn't seen daylight for five years.* ◦ *It's such a tiny office – don't you ever feel cooped up here?*

cooperate (UK also **co-operate**) /kəʊˈɒp.ər.eɪt/ (US) /koʊˈɑː.pə.reɪt/ verb [I] (B2) to act or work together for a particular purpose, or to be helpful by doing what someone asks you to do: *I find it very hard to dress my two-year-old when she refuses to cooperate.* ◦ *The two companies have cooperated* ***in*** *joint ventures for the past several years.* ◦ *The Spanish authorities cooperated* ***with*** *the British police* ***in*** *finding the terrorists.*

cooperation (UK also **co-operation**) /kəʊˌɒp.ərˈeɪ.ʃən/ (US) /koʊˌɑː.pəˈreɪ-/ noun [U] (B2) the act of working together with someone or doing what they ask you: *This movie was made* ***with*** *the cooperation* ***of*** *the victims' families.* ◦ *There's very little cooperation* ***between*** *the two countries.* ◦ *The company produces computers* ***in*** *cooperation* ***with*** *a German firm.*

cooperative /kəʊˈɒp.ər.ə.tɪv/ (US) /koʊˈɑː.pə.ə.t̬ɪv/ adj; noun

▸adj (UK also **co-operative**) (B2) willing to help or do what people ask: *I've asked them not to play their music so loudly, but they're not being very cooperative.* → Opposite **uncooperative** • **cooperatively** (UK also **co-operatively**) /-li/ adv

▸noun [C] (UK also **co-operative**, abbreviation **co-op** /ˈkəʊɒp/ (US) /ˈkoʊɑː.p/) a company that is owned and managed by the people who work in it: *The magazine is run as a cooperative.*

co-ˈopt verb [T] **1** (of an elected group) to make someone a member through the choice of the present members: *She was co-opted* ***on to*** *the committee last June.* **2** to include someone in something, often against their will: *Whether they liked it or not, local people were co-opted* ***into*** *the victory parade.* **3** to use someone else's ideas

coordinate verb; noun

▸verb /kəʊˈɔː.dɪ.neɪt/ (US) /koʊˈɔːr-/ **COMBINE** ▷ **1** (UK also **co-ˈordinate**) [T] to make various different things work effectively as a whole: *We need someone to coordinate the whole campaign.* ◦ *A number of charities are coordinating their efforts to distribute food to the region.* **MATCH** ▷ **2** [I] to match or look attractive together: *The bed linen coordinates* ***with*** *the bedroom curtains.* ◦ *a coordinating jacket and skirt*

▸noun /kəʊˈɔː.dɪ.nət/ (US) /koʊˈɔːr-/ **POSITION** ▷ **1** [C usually plural] one of a pair of numbers and/or letters that show the exact position of a point on a map or GRAPH **CLOTHES** ▷ **2 coordinates** [plural] clothes, especially for women, that are made in matching colours or styles so that they can be worn together

coordinated /kəʊˈɔː.dɪ.neɪ.tɪd/ (US) /koʊˈɔːr.dɪ.neɪ.t̬ɪd/ adj **WELL ORGANIZED** ▷ **1** effectively organized so that all the parts work well together: *The rebel troops have launched a coordinated attack on government soldiers.* **2** If a person is coordinated, they move in a very easy and controlled way, especially when playing sports or dancing: *I wasn't a very coordinated child.* **WELL MATCHED** ▷ **3** arranged so that the colours, etc. match or look attractive together: *colour-coordinated decor* ◦ *The colour scheme of their living room is carefully coordinated.*

coordination /kəʊˌɔː.dɪˈneɪ.ʃən/ (US) /koʊˌɔːr-/ noun [U] **1** the act of making all the people involved in a plan or activity work together in an organized way: *There's absolutely no coordination* ***between*** *the different groups – nobody knows what anyone else is doing.* **2** the ability to make your arms, legs, and other body parts move in a controlled way: *Gymnastics is a sport that requires a lot of coordination.*

coordinator /kəʊˈɔː.dɪ.neɪ.təʳ/ (US) /koʊˈɔːr.dɪ.neɪ.t̬ɚ/ noun [C] someone whose job is to make different groups work together in an organized way to achieve something: *We've just appointed a coordinator who will oversee the whole project.*

coot /kuːt/ noun [C] **BIRD** ▷ **1** a small dark bird which lives near rivers and lakes **PERSON** ▷ **2** US informal a person, especially one who is not very clever: *He's a sweet* ***old*** *coot.*

cop /kɒp/ (US) /kɑːp/ noun; verb

▸noun **POLICE** ▷ **1** [C] (UK informal also **copper**) a **police officer**: *Quick, run – there's a cop coming!* **QUALITY** ▷ **2 not much cop** slang not very good: *His last book wasn't much cop.*

▸verb [T] (-pp-) **TAKE** ▷ slang to take or hold: *Cop (****hold of****) that, would you – I can't carry both myself.*

IDIOMS **cop a feel** US slang to touch someone in a sexual way without their permission • **cop a plea** slang US to admit to having committed a crime in order to avoid being punished for a more serious crime • **cop it** UK informal to be punished or spoken to severely because you have done something wrong: *You'll really cop it if your parents find out you've been stealing.*

PHRASAL VERB **cop out** slang to avoid doing something that you should do or that you have promised to do because you are frightened, shy, or you think it is too difficult: *She copped out* ***of*** *the parachute jump at the last minute with some feeble excuse.*

cope /kəʊp/ (US) /koʊp/ verb [I] (B2) to deal successfully with a difficult situation: *It must be difficult to cope* ***with*** *three small children and a job.* ◦ *The tyres on my car don't cope very well on wet roads.* ◦ *He had so much pressure on him in his job that eventually he just couldn't cope.*

copier /ˈkɒp.i.əʳ/ (US) /ˈkɑː.pi.ɚ/ noun [C] a **photocopier**

ˈco-ˌpilot noun [C] a pilot who helps the main pilot on an aircraft

copious /ˈkəʊ.pi.əs/ (US) /ˈkoʊ-/ adj in large amounts, or more than enough: *They drank copious* ***amounts*** *of wine.* ◦ *He took copious notes during the lecture.* • **copiously** /-li/ adv *We ate and drank copiously at the party.*

ˈcop-out noun [C usually singular] slang a way of avoiding doing something difficult or unpleasant that you should do, or the excuse that you use to do this: *She always thought that having a family instead of a career was a cop-out.*

copper /ˈkɒp.əʳ/ (US) /ˈkɑː.pɚ/ noun **METAL** ▷ **1** (B2) [U] (symbol **Cu**) a chemical element that is a reddish-brown metal, used especially for making wire and coins: *copper wire/pipes* ◦ *a copper alloy* **2** [U] the reddish-brown colour of the metal copper: *The copper of Rosie's hair shone in the sunlight.* **3** [C usually plural] UK informal a brown coin of low value: *I gave him a few coppers.* **POLICE** ▷ **4** [C] UK informal a **police officer** • **copper** adj of the reddish-brown colour of the metal copper

ˌcopper ˈbeech noun [C] a type of tree with reddish-brown leaves

ˌcopper-ˈbottomed adj **1** UK describes a plan, deal, or INVESTMENT that can be trusted completely because it is safe and certain to succeed **2** having a base made of copper: *a copper-bottomed saucepan*

copperplate /ˈkɒp.ə.pleɪt/ (US) /ˈkɑː.pɚ-/ **noun** [U] an old-fashioned decorative style of writing with long, flowing letters

coppery /ˈkɒp.ər.i/ (US) /ˈkɑː.pɚ.i/ **adj** reddish-brown: *The leaves on the trees have started to turn a rich coppery colour.*

coppice noun; verb
▸**noun** [C] /ˈkɒp.ɪs/ (US) /kɑː.pɪs/ an area of closely planted trees in which the trees are cut back regularly to provide wood: *a hazel/willow coppice*
▸**verb** [T] /ˈkɒp.ɪs/ (US) /ˈkɑː.pɪs/ specialized to cut trees or bushes back in order to form a small, closely planted area

ˌco-proˈduction noun [C] specialized a film, television programme, or theatre production organized by two or more people or organizations, rather than a single person or organization

copse /kɒps/ (US) /kɑːps/ **noun** [C] a small group of trees

ˈcop ˌshop noun [C] UK informal a **police station**

Coptic /ˈkɒp.tɪk/ (US) /ˈkɑːp-/ **adj** of or connected with the ancient Christian Church of Egypt, now based in Egypt and Ethiopia: *a Coptic monastery*

copula /ˈkɒp.jʊ.lə/ (US) /ˈkɑː.pjə-/ **noun** [C] specialized a type of verb, of which the most common is 'be', that joins the subject of the verb with a COMPLEMENT: *In the sentence 'You smell nice', 'smell' is a copula.*

copulate /ˈkɒp.jʊ.leɪt/ (US) /ˈkɑː.pjə-/ **verb** [I] specialized to have sex • **copulation** /ˌkɒp.jʊˈleɪ.ʃən/ (US) /ˌkɑː.pjə-/ **noun** [U] specialized

copy /ˈkɒp.i/ (US) /ˈkɑː.pi/ **verb; noun**
▸**verb** [I or T] **PRODUCE** ▷ **1** A2 to produce something so that it is the same as an original piece of work: *They've copied the basic design* ***from*** *the Japanese model and added a few of their own refinements.* ◦ *Patricia's going to copy her novel onto disk and send it to me.* ◦ disapproving *He was always copying* ***from/off*** *other children (= cheating by copying), but never got caught.* **BEHAVE** ▷ **2** B2 to behave, dress, speak, etc. in a way that is intended to be like someone else, for example, because you admire them: *He tends to copy his brother* ***in*** *the way he dresses.* **3 copy and paste** If you copy and paste something on a computer screen, you move it from one area to another.

PHRASAL VERBS **copy sth down** to write something that someone has said or written so that you can remember it • **copy sb in** to send someone a copy of an email that you are sending to someone else: *I'll copy you in* ***on*** *all emails relating to the project.* • **copy sth out** UK If you copy out a piece of writing, you write it out again on a piece of paper: *Copy out the poem on page six.*

▸**noun VERSION** ▷ **1** B1 [C] something that has been made to be exactly like something else: *This painting is only a copy – the original hangs in the Louvre.* ◦ *I always* ***keep*** *a copy* ***of*** *any official or important letters that I send off.* ◦ *Could you* ***make*** *a copy* ***of*** *(= use a special machine to copy) this for tomorrow's meeting, please?* **2** B2 [C] a single book, newspaper, record, or other printed or recorded text of which many have been produced: *Have you got a copy of last Saturday's 'Guardian', by any chance?* **TEXT** ▷ **3** [U] written text that is to be printed, or text that is intended to help with the sale of a product: *We need someone who can write good copy for our publicity department.*

> Word partners for **copy noun**
> *make* a copy • *have/keep* a copy • *download/get hold of/obtain* a copy • an *additional/extra/spare* copy • an *accurate/exact/identical* copy • a *cheap/poor* copy

C

copybook /ˈkɒp.i.bʊk/ (US) /ˈkɑː.pi-/ **adj** [before noun] UK approving exactly as is expected or following the rules connected with a situation: *a copybook musical performance* ◦ *a copybook military exercise*

copycat /ˈkɒp.i.kæt/ (US) /ˈkɑː.pi-/ **noun; adj**
▸**noun** [C] child's word someone who has few ideas of their own and does or says exactly the same as someone else: *You're just a copycat!*
▸**adj 1** done or made to be very similar to something else: *In the market you can buy affordable copycat (= very similar) versions of expensive perfumes.* **2** describes a crime that is believed to have been influenced by another, often famous, crime because it is so similar: *copycat murders*

copyright /ˈkɒp.i.raɪt/ (US) /ˈkɑː.pi-/ **noun** [C or U] the legal right to control the production and selling of a book, play, film, photograph, or piece of music: *Who* ***owns/holds*** *the copyright* ***on*** *this article?* ◦ *His work is no longer protected* ***by*** *copyright.* ◦ *The symbol © shows that something is protected by copyright.* • **copyright verb** [T]

copywriter /ˈkɒp.iˌraɪ.tər/ (US) /ˈkɑː.piˌraɪ.t̬ɚ/ **noun** [C] someone who writes the words for advertisements

coquette /kɒkˈet/ (US) /koʊˈket/ **noun** [C] literary a woman who likes to attract attention by behaving as if she is sexually interested in people, in a pleasant but not serious way • **coquetry** /ˈkɒk.ɪ.tri/ (US) /ˈkoʊ.kə-/ **noun** [U] • **coquettish** /kɒkˈet.ɪʃ/ (US) /koʊˈket̬-/ **adj** *She greeted him with a coquettish smile.* • **coquettishly** /kɒkˈet.ɪʃ.li/ (US) /koʊˈket̬-/ **adv**

cor /kɔːr/ (US) /kɔːr/ **exclamation** UK slang an expression of interest and admiration or surprise: *Cor! Did you see him in the blue swimming trunks?*

IDIOM **cor blimey!** UK old-fashioned slang a way of expressing surprise or anger: *Cor blimey, I didn't see you there!*

cor- /kər-/ (US) /kɚ-/ **prefix** together; with: *to correspond*

coracle /ˈkɒr.ə.kl̩/ (US) /ˈkɔːr-/ **noun** [C] a small, round boat that is made by stretching animal skin over a wooden frame

coral /ˈkɒr.əl/ (US) /ˈkɔːr-/ **noun; adj**
▸**noun** [U] **1** C2 a substance like rock, formed in the sea by groups of particular types of small animal, often used in jewellery: *a coral bracelet/necklace* **2** a colour between orange and pink
▸**adj** having a colour between orange and pink

ˌcoral ˈreef noun [C] an area of coral, the top of which can sometimes be seen just above the sea

cor anglais /ˌkɔː.rɒŋˈgleɪ/ (US) /ˌkɔːr.ɑːŋ-/ **noun** [C] (plural **cors anglais**) (US **ˈEnglish ˌhorn**) a musical instrument like an OBOE but with a lower sound

corbel /ˈkɔː.bəl/ (US) /ˈkɔːr-/ **noun** [C] specialized a support for an ARCH or similar heavy structure that sticks out of a wall and is usually made of stone or brick

cord /kɔːd/ (US) /kɔːrd/ **noun ROPE/WIRE** ▷ **1** [C or U] (a length of) rope or string made of twisted threads: *Where's the cord that ties back the curtains?* ◦ *Have you got some cord that I can tie this parcel up with?* **2** [C or U] (UK also **flex**) a piece of wire covered in plastic, used to connect electrical equipment to a power supply: *an* ***extension*** *cord* **CLOTH** ▷ **3** [U] UK **corduroy**: *a cord* *shirt/jacket* **4 cords** [plural] trousers made of CORDUROY material

cordial /ˈkɔː.di.əl/ (US) /ˈkɔːr.dʒəl/ **adj; noun**

▸**adj** formal **FRIENDLY** ▷ **1** friendly, but formal and polite: *a cordial smile/greeting/welcome/reception* ◦ *Relations between the two leaders are said to be cordial.* **STRONG** ▷ **2** (of a feeling, especially dislike) strong: *The two statesmen are known to have a cordial **dislike** for each other.* • **cordially** /-i/ **adv** formal *You are cordially **invited** to attend our annual wine-tasting evening.* ◦ *On a personal level, they came to be cordially **disliked**.*

▸**noun** [U] **1** UK a sweet drink made from fruit, to which water is usually added: *lime cordial* **2** US **liqueur**

cordiality /ˌkɔː.diˈæl.ɪ.ti/ (US) /ˌkɔːrˈdjæl.ə.t̬i/ **noun** [U] formal behaviour that is friendly, but formal and polite

cordite /ˈkɔː.daɪt/ (US) /ˈkɔːr-/ **noun** [U] specialized a type of explosive, especially used in bullets

cordless /ˈkɔːd.ləs/ (US) /ˈkɔːrd-/ **adj** describes an electrical tool or piece of equipment that operates without needing to be permanently connected by a wire to an electrical supply: *a cordless drill/iron*

cordon /ˈkɔː.dən/ (US) /ˈkɔːr-/ **noun; verb**

▸**noun** [C] a line of police, soldiers, vehicles, etc. positioned around a particular area in order to prevent people from entering it: *There was a **police** cordon around the building.*

▸**verb**

PHRASAL VERB **cordon sth off** If people in authority, such as the police, cordon off a building or area, they put something around it in order to stop people from entering it: *They've cordoned off the whole area because of a suspected bomb.*

cordon bleu /ˌkɔː.dɒ̃ˈblɜː/ (US) /ˌkɔːr.dɑ̃ːˈbluː/ **adj** **1** describes food prepared to the highest standard: *cordon bleu cuisine* **2** describes people who are able to cook food to the highest standard: *a cordon bleu chef*

cordon sanitaire /ˌkɔː.dɒ̃.sæn.ɪˈteəʳ/ (US) /kɔːr.dɑ̃ː.sɑː.niˈter/ **noun** [C] (plural **cordons sanitaires**) a guarded area around a place or country that prevents people from entering or leaving it: *NATO was accused of trying to throw a cordon sanitaire around Russia.*

corduroy /ˈkɔː.də.rɔɪ/ (US) /ˈkɔːr-/ **noun** [U] a thick cotton material with soft raised parallel lines, used especially for making clothes

core /kɔːʳ/ (US) /kɔːr/ **noun; adj; verb**

▸**noun** **IMPORTANT PART** ▷ **1** (C2) [S or U] the basic and most important part of something: *The lack of government funding is **at the** core of the problem.* **CENTRE** ▷ **2** (C2) [C] the hard central part of some fruits, such as apples, which contains the seeds: *Don't throw your apple core on the floor!* **3** [C] the centre of a planet: *The Earth's core is a hot, molten mix of iron and nickel.* **4** [C] specialized The core of a NUCLEAR REACTOR (= a device in which atoms are changed to produce energy) is the place where FISSION (= the dividing of atoms) happens. **5** [C] specialized a long, thin cylinder-shaped mass of material taken out of the Earth for study

IDIOM **to the core** **1** in every way: *He's a Conservative to the core.* **2** to an extreme degree: *I was shocked to the core.*

▸**adj** **IMPORTANT** ▷ **1** most important or most basic: *They are cutting back production of some of their core products.* **2 core value, belief, issue, etc.** a value, belief, etc. that is basic and more important than any other: *The final status negotiations would focus on the core issues of the peace process.* **3 core business/operations/activities** the most important or largest part of a company's business activities, which it depends on in order to continue trading: *The company's core operations include entertainment and aviation.* **4 core curriculum/subjects/courses** the most important parts of a course of study, that all students must do **5** the main part of the body, without the arms and legs: *Pilates is good for strengthening the core muscles.*

▸**verb** [T] to remove the core from a piece of fruit: *Peel and core the pears before cooking them.*

ˌco-reˈspondent **noun** [C] legal the person who a married person is said to have committed ADULTERY (= sex outside marriage) with: *He was **cited/named** as co-respondent in the divorce.* → Compare **respondent**

corgi /ˈkɔː.gi/ (US) /ˈkɔːr-/ **noun** [C] a breed of dog with a long, strong body, short legs, and a pointed nose

coriander /ˌkɒr.iˈæn.dəʳ/ (US) /ˈkɔːr.i.æn.dɚ/ **noun** [U] a plant whose leaves or seeds are added to food to give a special flavour

Corinthian /kəˈrɪn.θi.ən/ **adj** of or copying the most decorated of the three styles of ancient Greek building: *Corinthian columns* → Compare **Doric, Ionic**

cork /kɔːk/ (US) /kɔːrk/ **noun; verb**

▸**noun** **1** [U] the light, soft BARK (= outer covering) of a Mediterranean tree **2** [C] a short, cylinder-shaped piece of cork, plastic, or rubber that is put into the top of a bottle, especially a wine bottle, to close it: *I can't get the cork out of the bottle – can you try?*

▸**verb** [T] to close a bottle by putting a cork in it: *If you've drunk enough, I'll cork the bottle and we can have the rest later.*

PHRASAL VERB **cork sth up** informal to not allow yourself to express your anger, worry, or sadness

corkage /ˈkɔː.kɪdʒ/ (US) /ˈkɔːr-/ **noun** [U] the charge made by some restaurants for allowing customers to drink wine that has been bought from somewhere else

corked /kɔːkt/ (US) /kɔːrkt/ **adj** Wine is described as corked if its taste has been spoiled by the cork.

corker /ˈkɔː.kəʳ/ (US) /ˈkɔːr.kɚ/ **noun** [C] informal mainly humorous a person or thing that is especially good, attractive, or funny: *She told an absolute corker of a story about a priest she'd mistaken for an ex-lover.*

corkscrew /ˈkɔːk.skruː/ (US) /ˈkɔːrk-/ **noun; adj**

▸**noun** [C] a device for removing CORKS from bottles, that consists of a handle with a twisted metal rod to push into the CORK and pull it out

▸**adj** [before noun] tightly twisted or curled: *Her daughter's hair is a mass of wonderful red corkscrew curls.*

corm /kɔːm/ (US) /kɔːrm/ **noun** [C] specialized the short underground growth of particular plants from which the new stem grows each year

cormorant /ˈkɔː.mər.ənt/ (US) /ˈkɔːr.mɚ-/ **noun** [C] a large, black sea bird with a long neck and body

corn /kɔːn/ (US) /kɔːrn/ **noun** **FOOD** ▷ **1** (B1) [U] UK (the seeds of) plants, such as WHEAT, MAIZE, OATS, and BARLEY, that can be used to produce flour: *a sheaf of corn* ◦ *grains of corn* **2** [U] US the seeds of the MAIZE plant, or the plant itself **AREA OF SKIN** ▷ **3** [C] a small, painful area of hard skin that forms on the foot, especially on the toes **EMOTION** ▷ **4** [U] mainly US slang something that is old-fashioned, boring, or done to create emotion: *Everyone says it's a great movie, but I think it's **just** corn.*

cornball /ˈkɔːn.bɔːl/ (US) /ˈkɔːrn.bɑːl/ **adj** US describes a joke, film, story, etc. that has no new ideas and is not sincere, or is too often repeated and therefore not funny or interesting

ˈcorn ˌbread noun [U] a type of bread made from MAIZE

ˈcorn ˌchips noun [C usually plural] US thin, flat, CRISP pieces of food made from crushed MAIZE: *I love corn chips and beer.*

corncob /ˈkɔː.n.kɒb/ (US) /ˈkɔːrn.kɑːb/ **noun** [C] the part of the MAIZE plant on which the grain grows

corncrake /ˈkɔːn.kreɪk/ (US) /ˈkɔːrn-/ **noun** [C] a European bird with a loud cry

cornea /kɔːˈni.ə/ (US) /ˈkɔːr.ni-/ **noun** [C] the transparent outer covering of the eye

ˌcorned ˈbeef noun [U] cooked BEEF that has been preserved in salty water and spices, often sold in TINS (= metal containers)

corner /ˈkɔː.nəʳ/ (US) /ˈkɔːr.nɚ/ **noun; verb**

▸**noun** [C] **1** (A2) the point, area, or line that is formed by the meeting of two lines, surfaces, roads, etc.: *You drive round corners too fast – just slow down a bit!* ◦ *There's a postbox **on** the corner (= the place where the street crosses another).* ◦ *Click the icon **in** the bottom right-hand corner **of** the screen.* ◦ *I've got a bruise where I hit my leg against the corner of the table.* **2** (C2) a part of a larger area, often somewhere quiet or far away: *They live in a **remote** corner **of** Scotland, miles from the nearest store.* **3** a kick in football or a shot in HOCKEY that is taken from the corner of the playing area

IDIOMS **all/the four corners of the world/earth** many different parts of the world: *She had invited relatives from the four corners of the world to her 80th birthday party.* • **(just) around the corner** (C2) not far away, or going to happen soon: *There's a great restaurant just around the corner.* ◦ *Everything is a bit depressing at the moment, but good times are just around the corner.* • **be in a tight corner** to be in a difficult situation • **have a corner on a market** If a company has a corner on a particular market, it is more successful than any other company at selling a particular type of product. • **out of/from the corner of your eye** If you see something out of/from the corner of your eye, you see it but not clearly because it happens to the side of you: *I saw something move out of the corner of my eye.*

▸**verb TURN** ▷ **1** [I] If a vehicle corners well, badly, etc., it drives around corners in the stated way: *It's a powerful car, but it doesn't corner **well**.* **TRAP** ▷ **2** [T] to force a person or an animal into a place or situation from which they cannot easily escape: *Once the police had cornered her in the basement, she gave herself up.*

IDIOM **corner the market** If a company corners the market in a particular type of product, it is more successful than any other company at selling the product.

-cornered /-kɔː.nəd/ (US) /-kɔːr.nɚd/ **suffix** having the number of corners mentioned: *a three-cornered hat*

ˈcorner ˌshop noun [C] UK a small shop, especially on a corner of a road, that sells foods and other things that are often needed

cornerstone /ˈkɔː.nə.stəʊn/ (US) /ˈkɔːr.nɚ.stoʊn/ **noun** [C] **1** a stone in a corner of a building, especially one with the date when the building was made or other writing on it **2** something of great importance that everything else depends on: *In most countries, the family unit is still the cornerstone of society.*

cornet /ˈkɔː.nɪt/ (US) /ˈkɔːr-/ **noun** [C] **CONE** ▷ **1** UK a **cone INSTRUMENT** ▷ **2** a musical instrument made from metal, usually BRASS, that you play by blowing into it

cornfield /ˈkɔːn.fiəld/ (US) /ˈkɔːrn-/ **noun** [C] a field that is used for growing CORN

cornflakes /ˈkɔːn.fleɪks/ (US) /ˈkɔːrn-/ **noun** [plural] small, thin yellowish-orange pieces of dry food made from crushed MAIZE, often eaten with milk and sugar in the morning: *a bowl of cornflakes*

cornflour /ˈkɔːn.flaʊəʳ/ (US) /ˈkɔːrn.flaʊr/ **noun** [U] UK (US **cornstarch**) a white flour made from MAIZE, used in cooking for making liquids thicker

cornflower /ˈkɔːn.flaʊ.əʳ/ (US) /ˈkɔːrn.flaʊ.ɚ/ **noun** [C] a plant that grows in fields and gardens, usually with blue flowers

cornice /ˈkɔː.nɪs/ (US) /ˈkɔːr-/ **noun** [C] a decorative border found where the ceiling meets the walls in some rooms and also along the top of some walls and buildings

Cornish pasty /ˌkɔː.nɪʃˈpæs.ti/ (US) /ˈkɔːr-/ **noun** [C] UK a piece of pastry baked with a mixture of meat and vegetables inside it, usually for one person to eat

cornmeal /ˈkɔːn.mɪəl/ (US) /ˈkɔːrn-/ **noun** [U] rough, yellow flour made from MAIZE, used to make bread, TORTILLAS, etc.

ˈcorn oil noun [U] oil made from MAIZE, often used for cooking

ˌcorn on the ˈcob noun [U] the part of the MAIZE plant that is shaped like a cylinder, and is cooked with the sweet yellow or white grains on it

cornrow /ˈkɔːn.rəʊ/ (US) /ˈkɔːrn.roʊ/ **noun** [C] one of many strips of hair twisted together close to the head in thin rows: *Tyler likes her hair in cornrows, but braiding it takes a long time.* • **cornrow verb** [T] *Paul cornrowed her hair.*

cornstarch /ˈkɔːn.stɑːtʃ/ (US) /ˈkɔːrn.stɑːrtʃ/ **noun** [U] US for **cornflour**

ˌcorn ˈsyrup noun [U] a thick, sweet liquid made from MAIZE

cornucopia /ˌkɔː.njʊˈkəʊ.pi.ə/ (US) /ˌkɔːr.njəˈkoʊ-/ **noun** [S] formal a large amount or supply of something: *The table held a veritable cornucopia **of** every kind of food or drink you could want.*

corny /ˈkɔː.ni/ (US) /ˈkɔːr-/ **adj** informal (especially of jokes, films, stories, etc.) showing no new ideas or too often repeated, and therefore not funny or interesting: *corny **jokes*** ◦ *I couldn't watch the whole movie – it was just too corny.*

corolla /kəˈrɒl.ə/ (US) /-ˈroʊ.lə/ **noun** [C] specialized all of the PETALS of a flower as a group

corollary /kəˈrɒl.ᵊr.i/ (US) /ˈkɔːr.ə.ler.i/ **noun** [C] formal something that results from something else: *Unfortunately, violence is the inevitable corollary **of** such a revolutionary change in society.*

corona /kəˈrəʊ.nə/ (US) /-ˈroʊ-/ **noun** [C usually singular] (plural **coronae** /-niː/ (US) /-niː/) specialized a circle of light that can sometimes be seen around the moon at night, or around the sun during an ECLIPSE (= a time when the moon is positioned exactly between the sun and the Earth)

coronary /ˈkɒr.ᵊn.ᵊr.i/ (US) /ˈkɔːr.ə.ner-/ **noun; adj**

▸**noun** [C] (also specialized **ˌcoronary thromˈbosis**) an extremely dangerous medical condition in which the flow of blood to the heart is blocked by a blood CLOT (= a mass of blood): *He's in hospital after **having** a coronary last week.*

▸**adj** specialized relating to the ARTERIES (= thick tubes) that supply blood to the muscles of the heart: *Regular exercise reduces the risk of coronary **heart disease**.*

coronation /ˌkɒr.əˈneɪ.ʃᵊn/ (US) /ˌkɔːr-/ **noun** [C] a ceremony at which a person is made king or queen

coroner /ˈkɒr.ə.nər/ (US) /ˈkɔːr.ən.ɚ/ **noun** [C] an official who examines the reasons for a person's death, especially if it was violent or unexpected

coronet /ˈkɒr.ə.net/ (US) /ˌkɔːr.əˈnet/ **noun** [C] a small CROWN (= circular decoration for the head)

Corp. noun [C] **BUSINESS ▷ 1** written abbreviation for **corporation RANK ▷ 2** written abbreviation for **corporal**

corpora /ˈkɔː.pər.ə/ (US) /ˈkɔːr.pɚ-/ plural of **corpus**

corporal /ˈkɔː.pər.əl/ (US) /ˈkɔːr.pɚ-/ **adj; noun**
▸**adj** formal of or relating to the body
▸**noun** [C] (also **Corporal**, written abbreviation **Corp.**) a person of low rank in the army or the air force: *Corporal Green/Sam Green* ◦ [as form of address] *Thank you, Corporal.*

ˌcorporal ˈpunishment noun [U] the physical punishment of people, especially of children, by hitting them

corporate /ˈkɔː.pər.ət/ (US) /ˈkɔːr.pɚ-/ **adj 1** (C1) [before noun] relating to a large company: *corporate finance* ◦ *a corporate merger* ◦ *corporate executives* **2** formal of or shared by a whole group and not just of a single member: *All adults take corporate* ***responsibility*** *for the upbringing of the tribe's children.*

corporation /ˌkɔː.pərˈeɪ.ʃən/ (US) /ˌkɔːr.pəˈreɪ-/ **noun** [C, + sing/pl verb] **BUSINESS ▷ 1** (B2) (written abbreviation **Corp.**) a large company or group of companies that is controlled together as a single organization: *a multinational corporation* ◦ *the British Broadcasting Corporation* **LOCAL GOVERNMENT ▷ 2** mainly UK the organization in a particular town or city that is responsible for services such as cleaning roads: *a municipal corporation*

corpoˈration ˌtax noun [U] UK tax paid by businesses on their profits

corporeal /kɔːˈpɔː.ri.əl/ (US) /kɔːrˈpɔːr.i-/ **adj** formal **1** physical and not spiritual **2** relating to the body • **corporeally** /-i/ **adv**

corps /kɔːr/ (US) /kɔːr/ **noun** [C, + sing/pl verb] (plural **corps**) **MILITARY UNIT ▷ 1** a military unit trained to perform particular duties: *the Royal Army Medical Corps* ◦ *the intelligence corps* **GROUP ▷ 2** a group of people who are connected because they are involved in a particular activity: *the diplomatic corps* ◦ *the press corps* ◦ *A corps of technicians is accompanying the band on their tour.*

ˌcorps de ˈballet noun [S, + sing/pl verb] the members of a group of BALLET dancers who dance together, especially those who are not the main dancers

corpse /kɔːps/ (US) /kɔːrps/ **noun** [C] (C2) a dead body, usually of a person

corpulent /ˈkɔː.pjʊ.lənt/ (US) /ˈkɔːr-/ **adj** formal fat: *a corpulent gentleman* • **corpulence** /-ləns/ **noun** [U] formal

corpus /ˈkɔː.pəs/ (US) /ˈkɔːr-/ **noun** [C] (plural **corpora** /-pərə/ or **corpuses**) **1** a collection of written or spoken material stored on a computer and used to find out how language is used: *All the dictionary examples are taken from a corpus of billions of words.* **2** a collection of a single writer's work, or of writing about a particular subject

corpuscle /ˈkɔː.pʌs.l̩/ (US) /ˈkɔːr-/ **noun** [C] specialized any of the red or white cells in the blood

corral /kəˈrɑːl/ (US) /-ˈræl/ **noun; verb**
▸**noun** [C] an area surrounded by a fence for keeping horses or CATTLE in, especially in North America
▸**verb** [T] (-ll-) **1** to move horses or CATTLE into a corral **2** to bring a group of people together and keep them in one place, especially in order to control them: *Police corralled most of the demonstrators in a small area near the station.*

correct /kəˈrekt/ **adj; verb**
▸**adj 1** (A2) in agreement with the true facts or with what is generally accepted: *a correct answer* ◦ *'Is that the correct spelling?' 'I don't know – look it up in a dictionary.'* ◦ ***It's*** *not correct* ***to*** *describe them as 'students'.* ◦ formal *'Your name is Angela Black?' 'That is correct.'* → Synonym **right** → Opposite **incorrect 2** (B1) taking or showing great care to behave or speak in a way that is generally accepted and approved of: *He's very correct* ***in*** *his dress/speech/manner, isn't he?* • **correctly** /-li/ **adv** (B1) *Have I pronounced your name correctly?* • **correctness** /-nəs/ **noun** [U] *He speaks with such correctness (= care) that it sometimes sounds very formal.*

> **Other ways of saying correct**
>
> Instead of 'correct', the word **right** is often used:
>
> *All his answers were* ***right****.*
>
> If something is correct because there are no mistakes, you can use the adjective **accurate**:
>
> *Her novel is an* ***accurate*** *reflection of life in Spain.*
>
> The adjectives **exact** and **precise** can be used when something is exactly correct in every small detail:
>
> *'I still owe you $7.00, don't I?' 'Actually, it's $7.30 to be* ***exact****.'*
>
> *We still don't know the* ***precise*** *details of what happened.*

▸**verb** [T] **1** (B2) to show or tell someone that something is wrong and to make it right: *Students said it was helpful if the teacher corrected their pronunciation.* ◦ *I've got 30 exam papers to correct.* **2** If a medical treatment corrects a particular condition, it cures the condition or makes it easier to manage: *glasses to correct poor vision* ◦ *a chair that corrects bad posture* **3 correct me if I'm wrong but...** said as a polite and slightly formal way of disagreeing with someone: *Correct me if I'm wrong, but I think we arranged the meeting for the 12 December.*

correction /kəˈrek.ʃən/ **noun CHANGE ▷ 1** (B1) [C or U] a change made to something in order to correct or improve it, or the action of making such a change: *She was disappointed to see her essay returned with a mass of corrections in red ink.* **2** [C or U] (also **ˌmarket corrˈection**) a change in prices in a financial market, especially when they go down after a period of being too high in relation to the real situation in a company, the economy, etc.: *It looks like last week's correction is over and prices are going to go higher.* **PUNISHMENT ▷ 3** [U] old-fashioned punishment of a type that is intended to improve bad behaviour **4 corrections** [plural] US formal the set of methods available for punishing and treating people who have committed crimes: *a corrections officer*

> **Word partners for correction**
>
> *make* corrections • *need/require* correction • a *minor/small* correction • a correction *to* sth

correctional /kəˈrek.ʃən.əl/ **adj** mainly US formal relating to the punishment and treatment of people who have committed crimes: *a correctional program*

corˈrectional ˌcenter noun [C] (also **corˈrectional faˌcility**) US for **prison**

corrective /kəˈrek.tɪv/ **adj; noun**
▸**adj 1** intended to improve a situation: *corrective measures/action* **2** describes something that is intended to cure a medical condition: *corrective surgery*

▸**noun** [C] something that improves a situation: *This European report on the internet provides a corrective* ***to*** *the usual US-based views.*

correlate /ˈkɒr.ə.leɪt/ Ⓤⓢ /ˈkɔːr-/ **verb** [I or T] If two or more facts, numbers, etc. correlate or are correlated, there is a relationship between them: *Stress levels and heart disease are strongly correlated (= connected).*

correlation /ˌkɒr.əˈleɪ.ʃən/ Ⓤⓢ /ˌkɔːr-/ **noun** [C or U] a connection or relationship between two or more facts, numbers, etc.: *There's a correlation* ***between*** *smoking and cancer.*

correspond /ˌkɒr.ɪˈspɒnd/ Ⓤⓢ /ˌkɔːr.ɪˈspɑːnd/ **verb** [I] **MATCH** ▷ **1** Ⓑ② to match or be similar or equal: *The money I've saved corresponds roughly* ***to*** *the amount I need for my course.* ◦ *The American FBI corresponds* ***to*** *the British MI5.* ◦ *His story of what happened that night didn't correspond* ***with*** *the witness's version.* **WRITE** ▷ **2** Ⓑ② to communicate by writing a letter or sending an email: *I've been corresponding* ***with*** *several experts in the field.*

correspondence /ˌkɒr.ɪˈspɒn.dəns/ Ⓤⓢ /ˌkɔːr.ɪˈspɑːn-/ **noun** **WRITING** ▷ **1** [U] letters, especially official or business letters: *Any further correspondence should be sent to my new address.* **2** [U] the action of writing, receiving, and reading letters, especially between two people: *Her correspondence* ***with*** *Jim lasted many years.* **MATCH** ▷ **3** [C usually singular, U] a connection between two things: *The survey found no correspondence* ***between*** *crime and unemployment rates.*

correspondent /ˌkɒr.ɪˈspɒn.dənt/ Ⓤⓢ /ˌkɔːr.ɪˈspɑːn-/ **noun** [C] **REPORTER** ▷ **1** a person employed by a newspaper, a television station, etc. to report on a particular subject or send reports from a foreign country: *a war correspondent* ◦ *the education correspondent for the Guardian* **LETTER WRITER** ▷ **2** formal someone who writes letters: *I'm a terrible correspondent – I never seem to get the time to write.*

corresponding /ˌkɒr.ɪˈspɒn.dɪŋ/ Ⓤⓢ /ˌkɔːr.ɪˈspɑːn-/ **adj** Ⓒ② similar to, connected with, or caused by something else: *Company losses were 50 percent worse than in the corresponding period last year.* ◦ *As the course becomes more difficult, there's usually a corresponding drop in attendance.* • **correspondingly** /-li/ **adv** *Life in the city is more expensive, but salaries are correspondingly higher.*

corresˌponding ˈangle **noun** [C usually plural] specialized one of two equal angles on the same side of a line that crosses two parallel lines, and on the same side of each parallel line → Compare **alternate angle**

corridor /ˈkɒr.ɪ.dɔːr/ Ⓤⓢ /ˈkɔːr.ɪ.dɚ/ **noun** [C] **PASSAGE** ▷ **1** Ⓑ② a long passage in a building or train, especially with rooms on either side: *Her office is at the end of the corridor.* **LAND** ▷ **2** a long piece of one country's land that goes through another country: *the Polish corridor*

IDIOM **the corridors of power** the higher levels of government where the most important decisions are made

corrie /ˈkɒr.i/ Ⓤⓢ /ˈkɔr-/ **noun** [C] specialized a round hollow made in the side of a mountain by the action of a GLACIER

corroborate /kəˈrɒb.ə.reɪt/ Ⓤⓢ /-ˈrɑː.bə-/ **verb** [T] formal to add proof to an account, statement, idea, etc. with new information: *Recent research seems to corroborate his theory.* • **corroborating** /kəˈrɒb.ər.eɪ.tɪŋ/ Ⓤⓢ /-ˈrɑː.bə.reɪ.t̬ɪŋ/ **adj** (also **corroborative** /kəˈrɒb.ər.ə.tɪv/ Ⓤⓢ /kəˈrɑː.bɚ.ə.t̬ɪv/) *corroborating evidence/reports* • **corroboration** /kəˌrɒb.əˈreɪ.ʃən/ Ⓤⓢ /-ˌrɑː.bə-/ **noun** [U] *Without corroboration from forensic tests, it will be difficult to prove that the suspect is guilty.*

corrode /kəˈrəʊd/ Ⓤⓢ /-ˈroʊd/ **verb** [I or T] If metal corrodes, or if something corrodes it, it is slowly damaged by something such as rain or water: *Steel tends to corrode faster in a salty atmosphere, such as by the sea.*

corrosion /kəˈrəʊ.ʒən/ Ⓤⓢ /-ˈroʊ-/ **noun** [U] the process of corroding, or metal that has been corroded: *There was a lot of corrosion on the bottom of the car.* ◦ figurative *We are witnessing the corrosion of moral standards within our society.*

corrosive /kəˈrəʊ.sɪv/ Ⓤⓢ /-ˈroʊ-/ **adj** **1** A corrosive substance causes damage by chemical action: *a highly corrosive acid* **2** harmful and causing bad feelings: *the corrosive influence of racism* • **corrosively** /-li/ **adv**

corrugated /ˈkɒr.ə.geɪ.tɪd/ Ⓤⓢ /ˈkɔːr.ə.geɪ.t̬ɪd/ **adj** (especially of sheets of iron or cardboard) having parallel rows of folds that look like a series of waves when seen from the edge: *The roof is made from sheets of corrugated* ***iron****.*

corrupt /kəˈrʌpt/ **adj**; **verb**

▸**adj** **BAD** ▷ **1** Ⓒ① dishonestly using your position or power to get an advantage, especially for money: *Both companies are under investigation for corrupt practices.* ◦ *The whole system was corrupt – every official she approached wanted money before helping her.* **2** morally bad: *a corrupt society* **ON COMPUTER** ▷ **3** When information on a computer becomes corrupt, it cannot be used because it has changed and become wrong: *corrupt data* ◦ *a corrupt file*

▸**verb** [T] **MAKE BAD** ▷ **1** Ⓒ① to make someone or something become dishonest or IMMORAL: *The study claimed that violence on television corrupts the minds of children.* **ON COMPUTER** ▷ **2** to change information on a computer so that it is wrong and cannot be used: *Most of the data on the hard drive was corrupted by the power cut.* • **corruptible** /-ˈrʌp.tɪ.bl̩/ **adj**

corruption /kəˈrʌp.ʃən/ **noun** **BAD BEHAVIOUR** ▷ **1** Ⓒ① [U] illegal, bad, or dishonest behaviour, especially by people in positions of power: *The film is about a young police officer and his struggle to* ***expose*** *corruption in the force.* ◦ *Political corruption is widespread throughout the country.* **CHANGED WORD** ▷ **2** [C] in language, a word whose original form has been changed: *The swear word 'bloody' is wrongly thought by some to be a corruption of the words 'by our Lady'.* **ON COMPUTER** ▷ **3** [U] the fact of information on a computer being changed so that it is wrong and cannot be used: *data corruption*

corsage /kɔːˈsɑːʒ/ Ⓤⓢ /kɔːr-/ **noun** [C] a small, decorative group of flowers that a woman pins to her clothes or ties around her wrist, usually for a special occasion

corset /ˈkɔː.sɪt/ Ⓤⓢ /ˈkɔːr-/ **noun** [C] a tight piece of underwear worn on the middle part of a woman's body to make her waist appear smaller, especially in the past

cortege /kɔːˈteʒ/ Ⓤⓢ /kɔːr-/ **noun** [C] a slowly moving line of people or cars at a FUNERAL

cortex /ˈkɔː.teks/ Ⓤⓢ /ˈkɔːr-/ **noun** [C] (plural **cortices** /-ɪ.siːz/) specialized the outer layer, especially of the brain and other organs: *the cerebral cortex*

cortisone /ˈkɔː.tɪ.zəʊn/ Ⓤⓢ /ˈkɔːr.t̬ə.zoʊn/ **noun** [U] a HORMONE (= chemical made by living cells) that is used medically, especially for treating ARTHRITIS (= a painful condition of the JOINTS) and skin problems

coruscating /ˈkɒr.ə.skeɪ.tɪŋ/ Ⓤⓢ /ˈkɔːr.ə.skeɪ.t̬ɪŋ/ **adj**

1 literary flashing brightly **2** formal extremely clever and exciting or humorous: *He's known for his coruscating wit.* → Synonym **sparkling**

cos conjunction; noun
▸conjunction /kəz/ (also **'cos**) not standard for because: *You can cook dinner tonight cos I did it last night.*
▸noun specialized written abbreviation for **cosine**

cosh /kɒʃ/ (US) /kɑːʃ/ noun; verb
▸noun [C] UK (US **blackjack**) a short, heavy stick made of metal or rubber, used as a weapon
▸verb [T] UK to hit someone with a cosh: *He was coshed outside the pub.*

cosignatory /ˌkəʊˈsɪg.nə.tᵊr.i/ (US) /ˌkoʊˈsɪg.nə.tɔːr-/ noun [C] formal one of two or more people who sign an official agreement or document

cosily UK (US **cozily**) /ˈkəʊ.zɪ.li/ (US) /ˈkoʊ-/ adv in a comfortable, warm, and pleasant way: *The children are cosily tucked up in bed.*

cosine /ˈkəʊ.saɪn/ (US) /ˈkoʊ-/ noun [C] (written abbreviation **cos**) (in a triangle that has one angle of 90°) the RATIO of the length of the side next to an angle less than 90°, divided by the length of the HYPOTENUSE (= the side opposite the 90° angle) → Compare **sine, tangent**

ˈco-sister noun [C] Indian English the wife of your husband's brother

ˌcos ˈlettuce noun [C or U] (US **romaine**) UK a type of LETTUCE (= green salad vegetable) with long, narrow leaves

cosmetic /kɒzˈmet.ɪk/ (US) /kɑːzˈmet̬-/ noun; adj
▸noun **cosmetics** [plural] substances that you put on your face or body that are intended to improve your appearance: *We sell a wide range of cosmetics and toiletries at a very reasonable price.*
▸adj **1** disapproving describes changes, etc. that are intended to make you believe that something is better when, really, the problem has not been solved: *They were offered a few cosmetic improvements to their working conditions, but nothing of significance.* → Synonym **superficial** **2** [before noun] describes substances that you put on your face or body that are intended to improve your appearance: *a cosmetic cream* • **cosmetically** /-ɪ.kᵊl.i/ adv

cosˌmetic ˈsurgery noun [U] any medical operation that is intended to improve a person's appearance rather than their health

cosmic /ˈkɒz.mɪk/ (US) /ˈkɑːz-/ adj **1** relating to the universe and the natural processes that happen in it: *cosmic dust/radiation* **2** informal very great: *The earthquake was a disaster **of** cosmic **proportions/scale**.* • **cosmically** /-mɪ.kᵊl.i/ adv

cosmology /kɒzˈmɒl.ə.dʒi/ (US) /kɑːzˈmɑː.lə-/ noun [C] the study of the nature and origin of the universe • **cosmological** /ˌkɒz.məˈlɒdʒ.ɪ.kᵊl/ (US) /ˌkɑːz.məˈlɑː.dʒɪ-/ adj (also **cosmologic** /ˌkɒz.məˈlɒdʒ.ɪk/ (US) /ˌkɑːz.məˈlɑː.dʒɪk/) *Caltech in the 50s was an international centre of cosmological discovery.*

cosmonaut /ˈkɒz.mə.nɔːt/ (US) /ˈkɑːz.mə.nɑːt/ noun [C] an ASTRONAUT (= a person who travels into space) from Russia

cosmopolitan /ˌkɒz.məˈpɒl.ɪ.tᵊn/ (US) /ˌkɑːz.məˈpɑː.lɪ.t̬ᵊn/ adj; noun
▸adj usually approving (C1) containing or having experience of people and things from many different parts of the world: *New York is a highly cosmopolitan city.*
▸noun [C] usually approving someone who has experience of many different parts of the world: *Lisa is a real cosmopolitan.*

the cosmos /ˈkɒz.mɒs/ (US) /ˈkɑːz.moʊs/ noun [S] the universe considered as a system with an order and pattern

cosset /ˈkɒs.ɪt/ (US) /ˈkɑː.sɪt/ verb [T] (-**t**- or UK also -**tt**-) to give a lot of attention to making someone comfortable and to protecting them from anything unpleasant: *Children sometimes need to be cosseted.* ◦ disapproving *The country has been cosseted (= too protected) by the government for so long that people have forgotten how to take responsibility for themselves.*

cossie (also **cozzie**) /ˈkɒz.i/ (US) /kɑː.zi/ noun [C] UK informal for **swimming costume**

cost /kɒst/ (US) /kɑːst/ noun; verb
▸noun **MONEY SPENT** ▷ **1** (A2) [U] the amount of money needed to buy, do, or make something: *When you buy a new computer, you usually get software included **at** no extra cost (= for no additional money).* ◦ *For many parents, two salaries are essential to **cover** the cost of (= pay for) school fees.* ◦ *The supermarket chain announced that it was **cutting** the cost (= reducing the price) of all its fresh and frozen meat.* ◦ *It's difficult for most people to cope with the **rising** cost **of** (= increasing price of) healthcare.* ◦ *I was able to buy the damaged goods **at** cost (= for only the amount of money needed to produce or get the goods, without any extra money added for profit).* **2 costs** [plural] the amount of money needed for a business or to do a particular job: *We need to **cut** our advertising costs.* ◦ *The **estimated** costs of the building project are well over £1 million.* **SOMETHING LOST/GIVEN** ▷ **3** (B2) [S or U] something that is given, needed, or lost in order to get a particular thing: *We were going to paint the house ourselves, but when we considered the cost **in** time and effort, we decided to get a painter to do it for us.* ◦ *The driver managed not to hit the child who ran in front of his car, but only **at the** cost **of** injuring himself.* ◦ *She has finally got the job she wanted, but **at** great personal cost (= she has had to give up other things that were important to her).* ◦ *It's not worth getting into an argument with Tim, as I learned **to** my cost (= from my unpleasant experience of having done so).*

> **Word partners for cost (MONEY SPENT)**
>
> *cut/keep down/lower/reduce* the cost/costs • *push up/raise/increase* the cost/costs • *bear/cover/meet/pay* the cost • *escalating/high/rising/spiralling* cost/costs • the *actual/full/total* cost • *estimated/potential/projected* cost/costs • *additional/extra/hidden* cost • the cost *of* sth/doing sth • *at* a cost *of* [$5,000, £2,000, etc]

> **Word partners for cost (SOMETHING LOST/GIVEN)**
>
> *considerable/enormous/great/huge* cost • *at* (a) cost • *at* the cost *of* sth • *to* sb's cost • the cost *in* sth • cost *to* sb

IDIOM **at all cost(s)** (also **at any cost**) (B2) If something must be done or avoided at all costs, it must be done or avoided whatever happens: *Security during the president's visit must be maintained at all costs.* ◦ *He wanted her at any cost, even if it meant giving up everything he had.*

▸verb [T] **MONEY** ▷ **1** (A2) (**cost, cost**) If something costs an amount of money, you must pay that amount to buy or do it: *'How much does this book cost?' 'It costs £25.'* ◦ ***It** costs a lot **to** buy a house in this part of London.* ◦ [+ two objects] *The trip will cost you $1,000.* **2** (**costed, costed**) to calculate the future cost of something: *How carefully did you cost the materials for the new fence and gate?* ◦ *Has your scheme been* properly costed (*out*)? **DESTROY** ▷ **3** (B2) (**cost, cost**) to cause someone to lose or destroy something valuable: *Drinking and driving costs lives (= can cause accidents in which people die).* ◦ [+ two objects] *His affairs cost him his marriage (= his marriage ended because of them).*

IDIOMS **cost sb dear 1** to cause someone to spend a lot of money or lose money: *Buying that second-hand car without having it checked by a mechanic first cost us dear.* **2** to cause someone a lot of problems: *Later that year he attacked a photographer, an incident that cost him dear.* • **cost an arm and a leg/a small fortune** (UK also **cost a bomb/the earth/a packet**) to be extremely expensive: *I'd love to buy a Rolls-Royce, but they cost an arm and a leg.* • **it'll cost you** informal it will be very expensive: *It'll cost you to have your roof mended.*

ˈco-star noun; verb
▸noun [C] a famous actor appearing with another famous actor in a film or a play, when both have parts of equal importance: *The co-stars of 'Casablanca' are Ingrid Bergman and Humphrey Bogart.*
▸verb [I or T] (**-rr-**) to appear in a film or a play as a co-star: *Katharine Hepburn co-starred* ***with*** *Spencer Tracy in many films.*

ˈcost-ˌcutting noun [U] actions taken to reduce the amount that is spent on a service or within an organization: *The recovery was achieved in the old-fashioned way, with cost-cutting and price increases.* ◦ *a cost-cutting exercise* ◦ *cost-cutting measures*

ˌcost-eˈffective adj If an activity is cost-effective, it is good value for the amount of money paid: *It wouldn't be cost-effective to buy an expensive new computer when all you want to do is store your photos.*

costing /ˈkɒs.tɪŋ/ (US) /ˈkɑː.stɪŋ/ noun [C often plural, U] a calculation of the future cost of something such as a possible product: *We'll need accurate costings before we can agree to fund the scheme.*

costly /ˈkɒst.li/ (US) /ˈkɑːst-/ adj **EXPENSIVE** ▷ **1** expensive: *a costly item* ◦ *a costly purchase* ◦ disapproving *The project was subject to several costly* ***delays/setbacks.*** **DAMAGING** ▷ **2** involving a lot of loss or damage: *Building this bridge has already been too costly in terms of lives (= people have been killed while working on it).* • **costliness** /-nəs/ noun [U]

ˌcost of ˈliving noun [S] the amount of money that a person needs to live: *The increase in interest rates will* ***raise*** *the cost of living.*

ˌcost-of-ˈliving alˌlowance noun [C usually singular] an amount of money that an employee gets in addition to his or her normal pay, because the cost of living in a particular area is high: *Nurses working in London received an additional 7.5 percent cost-of-living allowance.*

ˌcost-of-ˈliving ˌindex noun [C usually singular] US for **retail price index**

ˈcost ˌprice noun [C] the price that it costs to make a product, without a profit being added: *We were able to buy the furniture from a friend* ***at*** *cost price.*

costume /ˈkɒs.tjuːm/ (US) /ˈkɑː.stuːm/ noun **1** (B2) [C or U] the set of clothes typical of a particular country or period of history, or suitable for a particular activity: *Singers performing Mozart's operas often* ***dress in/wear historical*** *costume.* ◦ *The dancers leading the procession were* ***in*** *colourful and elaborate costumes.* **2** (B2) [C] (UK also **fancy-dress costume**) a set of clothes worn in order to look like someone or something else, especially for a party or as part of an entertainment: *Our host was wearing a clown costume.* ◦ *The children were dressed in Halloween costumes.*

ˈcostume ˌdrama noun [C or U] a film, especially on television, about a period in the past, or films of this type

ˈcostume ˌjewellery noun [U] cheap jewellery made to look as if it is expensive

costumier /kɒsˈtjuː.mi.eɪ/ (US) /kɑːˈstuː.mi.ɚ/ noun [C] a person who makes and rents out costumes, especially for use in a theatre

cosy /ˈkəʊ.zi/ (US) /ˈkoʊ-/ adj; noun
▸adj UK (US **cozy**) **COMFORTABLE** ▷ **1** (B1) comfortable and pleasant, especially (of a building) because of being small and warm: *This room is* ***nice and*** *cosy in the winter.* ◦ *He showed me into a cosy* ***little*** *room.* **TOO CLOSE** ▷ **2** disapproving describes a situation that is convenient for those involved but may not be honest or legal: *He has some cosy arrangement/deal with his supplier, which means he's able to sell his goods more cheaply.*
▸noun [C] UK (US **cozy**) a cover that you put on a TEAPOT or a boiled egg to keep it warm: *a tea cosy* ◦ *an egg cosy*

cot /kɒt/ (US) /kɑːt/ noun [C] **1** UK (US **crib**) a small bed for a baby or young child with high bars around the sides so that the child cannot fall out **2** US for **camp bed** **3** Indian English a narrow bed

cot

ˈcot ˌdeath noun [C or U] (specialized **SIDS**) a medical condition in which a baby dies suddenly while it is sleeping for no obvious reason

coterie /ˈkəʊ.tᵊr.i/ (US) /ˈkoʊ.t̬ɚ-/ noun [C, + sing/pl verb] a small group of people with shared interests, often one that does not want other people to join them: *a coterie* ***of*** *writers*

coterminous /ˌkəʊˈtɜː.mɪ.nəs/ (US) /ˌkoʊˈtɝː-/ adj formal having or meeting at a shared border or limit: *France is coterminous* ***with*** *Italy.* • **coterminously** /-li/ adv

cottage /ˈkɒt.ɪdʒ/ (US) /ˈkɑː.t̬ɪdʒ/ noun [C] (B1) a small house, usually in the countryside: *They live in an idyllic* ***country/thatched*** *cottage, with roses around the door.*

ˌcottage ˈcheese noun [U] soft, white cheese made from milk CURDS (= the solid part of the milk) with some WHEY (= the liquid part) left in

ˌcottage ˈindustry noun [C] a small business run from home

ˌcottage ˈloaf noun [C] UK a LOAF of bread that has a smaller round part on top of a larger round part

ˌcottage ˈpie noun [C or U] a dish consisting of a layer of small pieces of meat covered with a thick layer of MASHED POTATO

cottaging /ˈkɒt.ɪ.dʒɪŋ/ (US) /ˈkɑː.t̬ɪ-/ noun [U] UK slang sexual activity between men in places such as public toilets

cotton /ˈkɒt.ᵊn/ (US) /ˈkɑː.tᵊn/ noun; verb
▸noun [U] **1** the threads that grow around the seeds of a tall plant grown especially in the US, China, and South Asia: *a bale of cotton* **2** (B1) thread or cloth made from the FIBRES of the cotton plant: *a shirt made of pure cotton* ◦ *She looked pretty in a simple cotton dress.* ◦ UK *a reel of cotton (= thread)* **3** US or Indian English for **cotton wool**

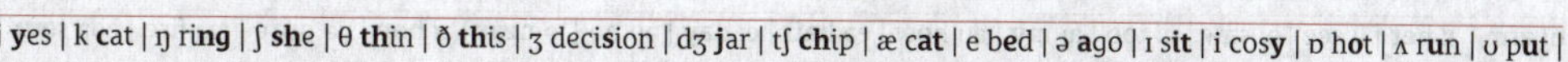

►verb

PHRASAL VERB **cotton on** informal to begin to understand a situation or fact: *I'd only just cottoned on* **to** *the fact that they were having a relationship.*

C

ˈ**cotton ˌbud** noun [C] UK (US trademark ˈ**Q-tip**) a short stick with a small amount of cotton on each end that is used for cleaning, especially the ears

ˌ**cotton ˈcandy** noun [U] US for **candyfloss**

ˈ**cotton ˌgin** noun [C] a machine used for separating the FIBRES of the cotton plant from the seeds

ˈ**cotton-ˌpicking** adj [before noun] US informal used to add emphasis when you are slightly annoyed: *Just wait one cotton-picking minute, will you?*

cottonwood /ˈkɒt.ən.wʊd/ (US) /ˈkɑː.t̬ən-/ noun [C] a North American tree whose seeds are covered with hairs that look like cotton

ˌ**cotton ˈwool** noun [U] UK (US **cotton**) cotton in the form of a soft mass, usually used for cleaning your skin: *cotton wool balls/pads*

cotyledon /ˌkɒt.ɪˈliː.dən/ (US) /ˌkɑː.t̬əˈliː-/ noun [C] specialized a type of leaf that is part of the developing plant inside a seed and either stores food or grows from the seed to produce food

couch /kaʊtʃ/ noun; verb

►noun [C] **SEAT** ▷ **1** (A2) a **sofa BED** ▷ **2** a type of high bed, especially one in a doctor's office

►verb formal **couch sth in/as sth** to express something in a particular way: [often passive] *I don't understand this form – it's all couched* **in** *legal terminology.*

couchette /kuːˈʃet/ noun [C] a bed in a train or on a boat that can either be folded away or used as an ordinary seat during the day

ˈ**couch poˌtato** noun [C] informal disapproving a person who watches a lot of television and does not have an active life

cougar /ˈkuː.gər/ (US) /-gɚ/ noun [C] **ANIMAL** ▷ **1** mainly US (UK usually **puma**) a large, brown wild cat that lives in North and South America **WOMAN** ▷ **2** informal an older woman who has sexual relationships with younger men

cough /kɒf/ (US) /kɑːf/ verb; noun

►verb [I] **1** (B1) to force air out of your lungs through your throat with a short, loud sound: *The smoke made me cough.* ◦ *I coughed all night long.* **2** to make a sound like a cough: *The car engine coughed a few times, but wouldn't start.*

PHRASAL VERBS **cough sth up** to make something come out of your throat or lungs when you cough: *Doctors were worried when she started to cough up blood.* • **cough (sth) up** informal to produce money or information unwillingly: *I've just had to cough up £40 for a parking fine.*

►noun [C] **1** (B1) the act of coughing, or the sound this makes: *a dry cough (= one that does not produce* MUCUS*)* ◦ *a hacking (= very bad and loud) cough* **2** an illness that makes you cough a lot: *a smoker's cough* ◦ *Emily has a very bad/nasty cough.*

ˈ**coughing ˌfit** noun [C] a sudden period of coughing

ˈ**cough ˌlolly** noun [C] Australian English a hard, sweet piece of medicine that you suck on to help a cough get better → Compare **cough sweet**

ˈ**cough ˌmedicine** noun [C or U] (also ˈ**cough ˌmixture**) medicine in the form of a liquid that helps a cough get better

ˈ**cough ˌsweet** noun [C] UK (US ˈ**cough ˌdrop**) a hard, sweet piece of medicine that you suck on to help a cough get better

could strong /kʊd/ weak /kəd/ verb; modal verb

►verb **CAN** ▷ (A2) past simple of can, used to talk about what someone or something was able or allowed to do: *When I was younger I could stay up all night and not get tired.* ◦ *It was so noisy that we couldn't hear ourselves speak.* ◦ *You said we could watch television when we've finished our homework.* ◦ *We asked if the computer could access the internet.*

> **!** Common mistake: **could**
>
> **Could** is followed by an infinitive verb without 'to'.
>
> Don't say 'could to do something', say **could do something**:
>
> ~~We're glad you could to come to our party.~~
>
> We're glad you could come to our party.

►modal verb **PERMISSION** ▷ **1** (B1) used as a more polite form of 'can' when asking for permission: *Could I speak to Mr Davis, please?* ◦ *Excuse me, could I just say something?* **REQUEST** ▷ **2** (A2) used as a more polite form of 'can' when asking someone to provide something or do something: *Could you lend me £5?* ◦ *Could you possibly turn that music down a little, please?* **POSSIBILITY** ▷ **3** (B1) used to express possibility, especially slight or uncertain possibility: *A lot of crime could be prevented.* ◦ *She could arrive anytime now.* ◦ *Be careful with that stick – it could* **have** *gone in my eye!* **SUGGESTION** ▷ **4** (B1) used for making a suggestion: *We could go for a drink after work tomorrow, if you like.* ◦ *You could* **always** *call Susie and see if she will babysit.* **SHOULD** ▷ **5** used for saying, especially angrily, what you think someone else should do: *Well, you could try to look a little more enthusiastic!* ◦ *I waited ages for you – you could have said that you weren't coming!*

IDIOM **could do with sth** informal If you could do with something, you want it very much: *I could do with a rest.*

couldn't /ˈkʊd.ənt/ short form of could not: *I couldn't find my keys this morning.*

coulis /ˈkuː.li/ noun [C or U] (plural **coulis** /ˈkuː.li/) a liquid made by cooking and crushing fruit: *raspberry coulis*

coulomb /ˈkuː.lɒm/ (US) /-lɑːm/ noun [C] specialized the standard unit of measurement for electric CHARGE, representing the CHARGE carried by one AMPERE (= unit of electric current) in one second

council /ˈkaʊn.səl/ noun [C, + sing/pl verb] **1** a group of people elected or chosen to make decisions or give advice on a particular subject, to represent a particular group of people, or to run a particular organization: *the United Nations Security Council* ◦ *This play is supported by a grant from the local arts council.* **2** (B2) the group of people elected to govern a particular area, town, or city, and organize services for it: *Edinburgh City Council* ◦ *The* **local** *council has/have decided not to allocate funds for the project.* ◦ *The* **town/city** *council is/are responsible for keeping the streets clean.*

ˈ**council eˌstate** noun [C] UK (US ˈ**housing ˌproject**) an area of a city in which there are council houses and apartments: *She was brought up on a council estate in Liverpool.*

ˈ**council ˌhouse/flat** noun [C] UK a house/flat owned by the local authority and rented to people at a low rent

ˈ**council ˌhousing** noun [U] UK (US ˌ**public** ˈ**housing**) houses or flats owned by the government for which the rent is lower than homes that are privately owned

councillor UK (US **councilor**) /ˈkaʊn.səl.ər/ (US) /-ɚ/

noun [C] (US also **councilman**, **councilwoman**) an elected member of a local government: *a town/city/county/local councillor* ◦ *Councillor Moore*

ˌcouncil of ˈwar noun [C] UK a meeting held to decide what action to take in a serious or difficult situation: *Parents are holding a council of war to decide what to do about the threatened closure of the school.*

counsel /ˈkaʊn.səl/ verb; noun

▸verb [T] (**-ll-** or US usually **-l-**) to give advice, especially on social or personal problems: *The police have provided experts to counsel local people affected by the tragedy.* ◦ *My job involves counselling unemployed people **on/about** how to find work.*

▸noun **1** [U] formal advice: *I should have listened to my father's wise counsel, and saved some money instead of spending it all.* **2** C2 [S] legal one or more of the lawyers taking part in a legal case: *The judge addressed counsel.* ◦ *Counsel **for the defence** (= the lawyer giving advice to the accused person) argued convincingly that his client was not guilty.*

IDIOM **keep your own counsel** to not say what your opinions are: *I'd love to know what Anna thinks, but she always keeps her own counsel.*

counselling (US usually **counseling**) /ˈkaʊn.səl.ɪŋ/ noun [U] C2 the job or process of listening to someone and giving them advice about their problems: *a counselling **service***

counsellor (US usually **counselor**) /ˈkaʊn.səl.əʳ/ US /-ɚ/ noun [C] **1** C2 someone who is trained to listen to people and give them advice about their problems: *a **marriage guidance** counsellor* **2** C2 US a lawyer: [as form of address] *I don't think that question is relevant, counselor.* **3** US someone who takes care of children at a summer CAMP

count /kaʊnt/ verb; noun

▸verb **NUMBER** ▷ **1** B1 [I or T] to say numbers one after the other in order, or to calculate the number of people or things in a group: *Let's count **out loud** (= speak the words) from one to ten.* ◦ *The teachers counted the students as they got on to the coach.* ◦ *Count your money carefully to make sure it's all there.* ◦ [+ question word] *We need to count **who**'s here, so we can make sure that no one's missing.* ◦ *There'll be eight for dinner, counting (= including) ourselves.* ◦ *We're still waiting for the votes to be counted (up).* **HAVE VALUE** ▷ **2** B2 [I] to have value or importance: *I've always believed that happiness counts more than money.* ◦ *My opinion doesn't count **for** anything around here (= no one values my opinion).* → Synonym **matter** **CONSIDER** ▷ **3** C2 [I or T] to consider or be considered as: *I count my**self** fortunate to have had such a good education.* ◦ *I've had three jobs in the last five years, but one of them was unpaid, so it doesn't count (= cannot be considered as a real job).* ◦ *I've always counted Lucy **among** my closest friends.* ◦ *I didn't think his grudging remarks really counted **as** an apology.*

IDIOMS **could count sth on (the fingers of) one hand** If you could count something on (the fingers of) one hand, it does not happen very often or exists in very small numbers: *I could count the number of times he's paid for a round of drinks on the fingers of one hand.* • **count your blessings** to be grateful for the good things in your life, often to stop yourself becoming too unhappy about the bad things • **count the cost** to start to understand how badly something has affected you: *I didn't read the contract fully before I signed it but I'm counting the cost now.* • **don't count your chickens before they're hatched** saying said to emphasize that you cannot depend on something happening before it has happened

PHRASAL VERBS **count against sb/sth** to make someone or something more likely to fail: *Gail's qualified for the job, but her lack of experience will count against her.* • **count sb in** informal C2 to include someone in an activity or arrangement: *'Do you want to come swimming tomorrow?' 'Yes, count me in.'* • **count on sb** B2 to be confident that you can depend on someone: *You can always count on Michael in a crisis.* ◦ [+ to infinitive] *I can count on my parents **to** help me.* • **count on sth** B2 to expect something to happen and make plans based on it: [+ -ing verb] *I'm counting on the meeting finish**ing** on time, or I'll miss my train.* ◦ *Sorry I'm late, I didn't count on be**ing** held up in the traffic.* • **count sth out** to count coins or notes one by one as you put them down: *She counted out five crisp new $100 bills.* • **count sb out** **NOT INCLUDE** ▷ **1** informal to keep someone out or not include them in an activity or arrangement: *Scuba diving? Oh no, count me out – I hate water!* **BOXING** ▷ **2** [often passive] In a BOXING competition, the REFEREE counts someone out by counting to ten when they fall to the floor and announcing that they have lost the fight if they fail to get up before the ten seconds is over. • **count towards sth** C2 to be part of what is needed to complete or achieve something: *The work that the students do during the year will count towards their final degrees.*

▸noun **NUMBER** ▷ **1** C2 [C] the act of counting, or the total number of things counted: *Early vote counts show Mr Adams in the lead.* ◦ *We had 450 members **at** the last count (= when they were last counted).* **2 keep count** UK to record how many of something there are, or how many times something has happened: *I'm trying to lose weight, so I'm keeping count of the number of calories I eat every day.* **3 lose count** C2 to not be able to remember how many times something has happened: *I've lost count of how many times she's been late for work this month.* **4** [C] a scientifically measured amount of something: *a high pollen count* ◦ *a low blood/sperm count* **5 on the count of three, four, five, etc.** when a particular number is reached: *On the count of three, I'd like you all to stand up.* **RANK** ▷ **6** [C] a European man of the same social rank as an English EARL → See also **countess** **CRIME** ▷ **7** [C] legal a particular crime that a person is accused of: *The prisoner was found guilty **on** two counts **of** murder.* **OPINION** ▷ **8** [C] an opinion in a discussion or argument: *I'm afraid I disagree with you **on** all/several counts (= I disagree with all/several of your opinions).*

IDIOM **be out for the count** to be sleeping, especially heavily: *It looks like Ben's out for the count.*

countable /ˈkaʊn.tə.bl̩/ US /-t̬ə-/ adj specialized a countable noun can be used with 'a' or 'an' and can be made plural: *An example of a countable noun is 'table', and an example of an uncountable noun is 'money'.* → Compare **uncountable**

ˌcountable ˈnoun noun [C] a **count noun**

countdown /ˈkaʊnt.daʊn/ noun **1** [C] the act of counting backwards to zero: *The countdown **to** the rocket launch will begin at 9.00 a.m.* **2** [S] a short period of time leading to an important event: *The countdown **to** the election has already begun.*

countenance /ˈkaʊn.tə.nəns/ US /-t̬ən.əns/ noun; verb

▸noun formal **FACE** ▷ **1** [C or U] the appearance or expression of someone's face: *He was of noble countenance.* **APPROVAL** ▷ **2** [U] approval: *We will not **give/lend** countenance **to** any kind of terrorism.*

▸verb [T] formal to approve of or give support to

something: *The school will not countenance bad behaviour.*

counter /ˈkaʊn.təʳ/ US /-t̬ɚ/ **noun; verb; adv**

▸**noun** [C] **SURFACE** ▷ **1** B2 a long, flat, narrow surface or table in a shop, bank, restaurant, etc. at which people are served: *There was nobody* ***behind/on*** *the counter when I went into the bank, and I had to wait to be served.* ◦ *You will find sausages* ***on*** *the meat counter/rolls* ***on*** *the bread counter.* **2** mainly US a flat surface in a kitchen, especially on top of low furniture, on which food can be prepared: *We stacked the dirty plates on the* ***kitchen*** *counter.* → See also **worktop** **OBJECT IN GAME** ▷ **3** C2 (US also **piece**) a small object used to mark someone's place in some games played on boards **DOING COUNTING** ▷ **4** a person or machine that counts → See also **Geiger counter**

IDIOMS **over the counter** Drugs that are bought over the counter are bought in a shop without first visiting a doctor: *You can buy most cold remedies over the counter.* ◦ [before noun] *over-the-counter medicines* • **under the counter** Things bought under the counter are bought secretly and illegally: *He'd managed to get cigarettes under the counter.*

▸**verb** [I or T] to react to something with an opposing opinion or action, or to defend yourself against something: *The prime minister countered the opposition's claims about health service cuts* ***by saying*** *that the government had increased spending in this area.* ◦ *When criticisms were made of the school's performance, the parents' group countered* ***with*** *details of its exam results.*

▸**adv** C2 in a way that opposes something: *Bob's decision not to take the job* ***ran*** *counter* ***to*** *his family's expectations.*

counter- /kaʊn.tə/ US /-t̬ɚ/ **prefix** opposing or as a reaction to something: *a counterattack* (= an attack on someone who has attacked you)

counteract /ˌkaʊn.tərˈækt/ US /-t̬ɚ.ækt/ **verb** [T] to reduce or remove the effect of something unwanted by producing an opposite effect: *Drinking a lot of water counteracts the dehydrating* ***effects*** *of hot weather.*

ˈcounter-argument **noun** [C] an argument against another argument, idea, or suggestion

counterattack /ˈkaʊn.tər.ə.tæk/ US /-t̬ɚ.ə-/ **noun** [C] an attack intended to stop or oppose an attack by an enemy or competitor: *The Republicans have* ***launched*** *a strong counterattack against the Democrats' manifesto.* • **counterattack** /ˌkaʊn.tər.əˈtæk/ US /-t̬ɚ.ə-/ **verb** [I or T] *The air force counterattacked and repelled the invasion.*

counterbalance /ˈkaʊn.təˌbæl.əns/ US /-t̬ɚ-/ **verb** [T] to have an equal but opposite effect on something so that it does not have too much of a particular characteristic: *The ugliness of the resort is counterbalanced by the excellence of the skiing.* • **counterbalance** **noun** [C usually singular] *Her calm nature served as a natural counterbalance* ***to*** *his excitable personality.*

counterclockwise /ˌkaʊn.təˈklɒk.waɪz/ US /-t̬ɚ-ˈklɑːk.waɪz/ **adj, adv** US for **anticlockwise**

ˈcounter-ˌculture **noun** [C or U] a way of life and a set of ideas that are completely different from those accepted by most of society, or the group of people who live this way

ˌcounter-ˈespionage **noun** [U] secret action taken by a country to prevent another country from discovering its military, industrial, or political secrets

counterfeit /ˈkaʊn.tə.fɪt/ US /-t̬ɚ-/ **adj** made to look like the original of something, usually for dishonest or illegal purposes: *counterfeit jewellery/passports/coins* • **counterfeit** **noun** [C] *This watch may be a counterfeit, but it looks just like the original.* • **counterfeit** **verb** [T] *Two women and a man have been convicted of counterfeiting $100 bills.* • **counterfeiter** /-ˌfɪt.əʳ/ US /-fɪt̬.ɚ/ **noun** [C]

counterfoil /ˈkaʊn.tə.fɔɪl/ US /-t̬ɚ-/ **noun** [C] UK (mainly US **stub**) the part of a ticket, CHEQUE, etc. that is kept as a record of payment

counterinsurgency /ˌkaʊn.tər.ɪnˈsɜː.dʒᵊn.si/ US /-t̬ɚ.ɪnˈsɝː-/ **noun** [U] military action taken by a government to prevent attacks by small groups of soldiers or fighters that are opposed to it → Compare **insurgency**

counterintelligence /ˌkaʊn.tər.ɪnˈtel.ɪ.dʒəns/ US /-t̬ɚ.ɪn-/ **noun** [U] secret action taken by a country to prevent another country from discovering its military, industrial, or political secrets

ˌcounter-inˈtuitive **adj** describes something that does not happen in the way you would expect it to: *Steering a yacht is counter-intuitive – you push the tiller the opposite way to the way you want to go.*

countermand /ˌkaʊn.təˈmɑːnd/ US /-t̬ɚˈmænd/ **verb** [T] formal to change an order that has already been given, especially by giving a new order

countermeasure /ˈkaʊn.təˌmeʒ.əʳ/ US /-t̬ɚˌmeʒ.ɚ/ **noun** [C] an action taken against an unwanted action or situation: *The Chancellor's countermeasures* ***against*** *inflation have been completely ineffective.*

counteroffensive /ˌkaʊn.tər.əˈfen.sɪv/ US /-t̬ɚ.ə-/ **noun** [C] a set of attacks that defend against enemy attacks

counterpane /ˈkaʊn.tə.peɪn/ US /-t̬ɚ-/ **noun** [C] UK old-fashioned a **bedspread**

counterpart /ˈkaʊn.tə.pɑːt/ US /-t̬ɚ.pɑːrt/ **noun** [C] C1 a person or thing that has the same purpose as another one in a different place or organization: *The prime minister is to meet his European counterparts to discuss the war against drugs.*

counterpoint /ˈkaʊn.tə.pɔɪnt/ US /-t̬ɚ-/ **noun** [U] specialized the combination of two or more different tunes played at the same time

counterproductive /ˌkaʊn.tə.prəˈdʌk.tɪv/ US /-t̬ɚ-/ **adj** having an effect that is opposite to the one intended or wanted: *Improved safety measures in cars can be counterproductive as they encourage people to drive faster.*

ˌcounter-revoˈlution **noun** [C] a political activity that happens as a reaction to an earlier political change • **ˌcounter-revoˈlutionary** **adj, noun** [C] *counter-revolutionary activities/literature* ◦ *She was tried and executed for being a counter-revolutionary.*

countersign /ˈkaʊn.tə.saɪn/ US /-t̬ɚ-/ **verb** [T] specialized to write your name on a document that already has the SIGNATURE (= name written) of another person, especially in order to show that you are certain that the first person is who they say they are

ˈcounter-suit **noun** [C] a legal claim that you make as a reaction to a claim made against you

countertenor /ˈkaʊn.təˌten.əʳ/ US /-t̬ɚˌten.ɚ/ **noun** [C] (also **alto**) a man with a singing voice that is higher than usual for a TENOR and similar to a low female voice

countertop /ˈkaʊn.tə.tɒp/ US /-t̬ɚ.tɑːp/ **noun** [C] mainly US a **counter** in a kitchen → See also **worktop**

countervailing /ˈkaʊn.təˌveɪ.lɪŋ/ US /-t̬ɚ-/ **adj** [before noun] formal having equal force but an opposite effect: *There was nobody strong enough to lead an effective* *countervailing **force** against the dictator.* ◦ *a countervailing argument*

counterweight /ˈkaʊn.tə.weɪt/ (US) /-t̬ɚ-/ noun [C] a weight that is as heavy as something else, so that the two objects can balance

countess /ˈkaʊn.tes/ (US) /-t̬əs/ noun [C] a woman of high social rank, or the wife of a COUNT or EARL: *the Countess of Abingdon*

countless /ˈkaʊnt.ləs/ adj C1 very many, or too many to be counted: *There are countless arguments against this ridiculous proposal.* ◦ *I've heard it played countless **times** on the radio.*

ˈcount ˌnoun noun [C] (also **ˈcountable ˌnoun**) B1 a noun that can be used in the singular and the plural: *Count nouns are shown in this dictionary with [C].*

countrified /ˈkʌn.trɪ.faɪd/ adj describes a person or thing that belongs to or is suited to the countryside: *I thought myself very sophisticated compared with my countrified relatives.*

country /ˈkʌn.tri/ noun **POLITICAL UNIT** ▷ **1** A1 [C] an area of land that has its own government, army, etc.: *Which is the largest country in Europe?* ◦ *Sri Lanka is my native country, but I've been living in Belgium for the past five years.* ◦ *The climate is cooler in the east of the country.* **2 the country** C2 all the people who live in a country: *The whole country celebrated the signing of the peace treaty.*

> **!** Common mistake: **country**
>
> **Warning:** Irregular plural!
>
> If you want to form the plural of **country**, don't write 'countrys', write **countries**.

> **!** Usage: **country, land, nation, or state?**
>
> **Country** is the most general of these words. It usually means an area of land with its own government and people:
>
> *China, Japan, and other countries in Asia*
>
> **Nation** is used to talk about a country, especially when you mean the people or the culture of that country:
>
> *The whole nation celebrated the 100th anniversary of independence.*
>
> **State** is used to talk about a country as a political or official area. Some countries are divided into political units that are also called **states**:
>
> *Belgium became an independent state in 1830.*
>
> *America is divided into 50 states.*
>
> *the State of Florida*
>
> **Land** means an area of ground, especially when used for farming or building. It can also be used to mean a country, but this is formal:
>
> *We bought some land to build a house on.*
>
> *He told stories of distant lands.*

NATURAL LAND ▷ **3** A2 [S or U] land that is not in towns, cities, or industrial areas and is either used for farming or left in its natural condition: *He lives out **in the** country somewhere.* ◦ *Would you prefer to live **in the** country instead of a town?* ◦ *Country life isn't always as peaceful as city-dwellers think.* ◦ *It's often quicker to travel **across** country and avoid the major roads altogether.* **PARTICULAR AREA** ▷ **4** [U] an area of land considered in relation to a particular feature: *Stratford-upon-Avon is the capital of Shakespeare country.* ◦ *The empty roads make this area good cycling country.* **MUSIC** ▷ **5** [U] (also **country and western**, also **country music**) popular music that is based on a type of traditional music from the western and southern US

> **!** Common mistake: **country**
>
> **Warning:** Check your spelling!
>
> **Country** is one of the 50 words most often spelled wrongly by learners.

IDIOMS **across country** travelling in a direction where roads or public transport do not go, or where main roads or railways do not go: *Getting a train across country from Cambridge to Chester can be difficult.* • **go to the country** UK to have an election: *The prime minister has decided to go to the country.*

ˈcountry ˌclub noun [C] a sports or social organization based in the countryside, often one that only allows people to become members if they are considered to have a suitable social position, job, or financial situation

ˌcountry ˈdance noun [C] a traditional dance for several pairs of male and female dancers who are arranged in circles, squares, or long rows

ˌcountry ˈhouse noun [C] a large traditional house in the countryside, especially one that has belonged to the same family for many years: *Through the trees we could see a beautiful Georgian country house.*

ˌcountry ˈliquor noun [U] Indian English alcoholic drink that is made in the local area and is often made illegally → Compare **foreign liquor**

countryman /ˈkʌn.trɪ.mən/ noun [C] (plural **-men** /-mən/) **FROM YOUR COUNTRY** ▷ **1** a person from your own country: *Didn't he feel guilty about betraying his **fellow** countrymen and women?* **FROM THE COUNTRYSIDE** ▷ **2** UK someone who lives in or who comes from the countryside and not a town

ˈcountry ˌmusic noun [U] **country**

ˌcountry ˈseat noun [C] UK a large house in the country with the land surrounding it, especially one that belongs to a member of the upper class

countryside /ˈkʌn.trɪ.saɪd/ noun [S or U] A2 land not in towns, cities, or industrial areas, that is either used for farming or left in its natural condition: *The countryside around there is lovely.* ◦ *The mansion is set in 90 acres of beautiful, unspoilt countryside.* ◦ *Every summer thousands of people flock to the countryside.*

> **!** Common mistake: **countryside**
>
> **Remember**: you usually use **the** before **countryside**:
>
> ~~*They live in a beautiful cottage in countryside.*~~
>
> *They live in a beautiful cottage in the countryside.*
>
> But before another noun, you do not have to use 'the':
>
> *The cottage is in a countryside location.*

countrywide /ˌkʌn.triˈwaɪd/ adj, adv existing in or involving all parts of a country: *a countrywide epidemic* ◦ *countrywide protests against the government* ◦ *The bank has three branches in Norwich, and over 300 countrywide.*

countrywoman /ˈkʌn.trɪˌwʊm.ən/ noun [C] (plural **-women** /-wɪmɪn/) a female COUNTRYMAN

county /ˈkaʊn.ti/ (US) /-t̬i/ noun [C] (written abbreviation **Co.**) B2 a political division of the UK or Ireland, forming the largest unit of local government, or the largest political division of a state in the US: *County Antrim* ◦ *Rutland is the smallest county in England.* ◦ *Texas is divided into 254 counties.*

ˌcounty ˈcouncil noun [C, + sing/pl verb] UK an elected group of people that forms the government of a county: *Northumberland County Council*

C

ˌcounty ˈcourt noun [C] a local law court in England and in some parts of the US that deals with cases that do not involve serious crime

ˌcounty ˈfair noun [C] a large public event that happens every summer in US counties, with RIDES, games, and competitions for the best animal, best cooked dish, etc.: *She won first prize for her raspberry jam at the Mitchell county fair.*

ˌcounty ˈtown noun [C] UK (US **ˌcounty ˈseat**) the most important town or city in a county, especially the one where the local government is based: *Cambridge is the county town of Cambridgeshire.*

countywide /ˌkaʊn.tiˈwaɪd/ (US) /-t̬i-/ adj, adv mainly US existing in or involving all parts of a county: *a countywide survey* ◦ *Countywide, exam results have improved by an average of eight percent.*

coup /kuː/ noun [C] **SUCCESS** ▷ **1** an unexpectedly successful achievement: *It was a tremendous coup for the local paper to get an exclusive interview with Prince Charles.* ◦ *I got him to come to a party, which was something of a coup.* **TAKE POWER** ▷ **2** (C2) (also **coup d'état** /ˌkuː.deɪˈtɑː/ (plural **coups d'état**)) a sudden illegal, often violent, taking of government power, especially by part of an army: *a **military** coup*

coup de grâce /ˌkuː.dəˈgrɑːs/ noun [S] formal an action that ends something that has been gradually getting worse, or that kills a person or animal in order to end their suffering: *Jane's affair was the coup de grâce **to** her disintegrating marriage.*

coupé /ˈkuː.peɪ/ (US) /kuˈpeɪ/ noun [C] a car with a fixed roof, two doors, two or four seats, and usually a sloping back

couple /ˈkʌp.l/ noun; verb

▸noun **SOME** ▷ **1** (B1) [S] two or a few things that are similar or the same, or two or a few people who are in some way connected: *The doctor said my leg should be better in **a** couple **of** days.* ◦ ***A** couple **of** people objected to the proposal, but the vast majority approved of it.* ◦ *We'll have to wait **another** couple **of** hours for the paint to dry.* ◦ *The weather's been terrible for **the last** couple **of** days.* ◦ *Many economists expect unemployment to fall over **the next** couple **of** months.* ◦ *I'm sorry I didn't phone you, but I've been very busy over **the past** couple **of** weeks.* **TWO PEOPLE** ▷ **2** (B1) [C, + sing/pl verb] two people who are married or in a romantic or sexual relationship, or two people who are together for a particular purpose: *a **married** couple* ◦ *An **elderly** couple live* (US *lives*) *next door.* ◦ *Should the government do more to help **young** couples buy their own homes?* ◦ *The couple skated spectacularly throughout the competition.*

▸verb **JOIN** ▷ **1** [T usually passive, usually + adv/prep] to join or combine: *The sleeping car and restaurant car were coupled **together**.* ◦ *High inflation coupled **with** low output spells disaster for the government in the election.* **HAVE SEX** ▷ **2** [I] formal When two people or two animals couple, they have sex.

couplet /ˈkʌp.lət/ noun [C] two lines of poetry next to each other, especially ones that RHYME (= have words with the same sounds) and have the same length and rhythm: *a **rhyming** couplet*

coupling /ˈkʌp.lɪŋ/ noun [C] a device that joins two things together: *The carriage at the end of the train was left stranded when the coupling broke.*

coupon /ˈkuː.pɒn/ (US) /-pɑːn/ noun [C] **1** a piece of paper that can be used to get something without paying for it, or at a reduced price: *If you **collect** ten coupons from the newspaper, you can get a free beach towel.* **2** a piece of paper, especially a part of an advertisement in a newspaper or magazine, that a reader can send to an organization in order to get information about its products or services

courage /ˈkʌr.ɪdʒ/ (US) /ˈkɝː-/ noun [U] **1** (B2) the ability to control your fear in a dangerous or difficult situation: *They showed great courage when they found out about their baby's disability.* ◦ [+ to infinitive] *People should have **the** courage **to** stand up for their beliefs.* ◦ *It took me ages to **summon/pluck up** the courage **to** ask for a promotion.* → Synonym **bravery** **2 have the courage of your convictions** to be brave and confident enough to do what you believe in: *Although many of his policies were unpopular, he had the courage of his convictions to see them through.*

courageous /kəˈreɪ.dʒəs/ adj (C1) having or showing courage: *It was a courageous decision to resign in protest at the company's pollution record.* ◦ *It was courageous **of** her to challenge the managing director's decision.* → Synonym **brave** • **courageously** /-li/ adv

courgette /kɔːˈʒet/ (US) /kʊr-/ noun [C] UK (US **zucchini**) (B2) a long, thin vegetable with a dark green skin. It is a type of small MARROW.

courier /ˈkʊr.i.əʳ/ (US) /-i.ɚ/ noun [C] **MESSENGER** ▷ **1** a person who carries important messages or documents for someone else: *I want to have this package delivered by motorcycle courier.* **ON HOLIDAY** ▷ **2** UK a person who takes care of a group of people on holiday, especially by giving them advice on what to do, what to see, etc.

course /kɔːs/ (US) /kɔːrs/ noun; verb

▸noun **CLASSES** ▷ **1** (A1) [C] a set of classes or a plan of study on a particular subject, usually leading to an exam or qualification: *Tim **did** a three-year course **in** linguistics at Newcastle.* ◦ *They're going away **on** a training course next week.* ◦ *I'd like to **do*** (US ***take***) *a writing course when I retire.*

> **!** Common mistake: **course**
>
> The correct preposition to use before **course** is **on**.
>
> Don't say 'to/at/in a course', say **on a course**:
>
> ~~*In this course you will learn how to manage your time.*~~
>
> *On this course you will learn how to manage your time.*

SPORTS AREA ▷ **2** (B1) [C] an area of land or water used for a sports event: *a golf course/cross-country course* → See also **racecourse** **DEVELOPMENT** ▷ **3** (C1) [S] the often gradual development of something, or the way something happens, or a way of doing something: *Did the scandal have any effect on the course of the election?* ◦ ***In the** course **of*** (= during) *the interview it became clear that he was not suitable for the job.* ◦ *What would be an appropriate course* (***of action***) *in such a situation?* ◦ *If our rivals are spending more on advertising, we'll have to follow the same course.* ◦ *The defendants are also accused of attempting to pervert the course **of justice**.* **4 in the course of time** UK after a period of time: *I expect they plan to have children in the course of time.* **5 in/with the course of time** gradually: *With the course of time, I've learned to live with my disability.* **DIRECTION** ▷ **6** (C1) [C usually singular, U] the direction in which a vehicle, especially an aircraft, spacecraft, or ship, moves, or the path along which a river flows: *The pilot avoided a collision by **changing** course.* ◦ *Changing the course of the river would cause serious environmental damage to the whole valley.* ◦ figurative *The debate completely changed course after Liz made her speech.* **7 on course** likely to happen, or likely to succeed as planned: *Because of the recession, we're on course **for/***

to have record unemployment levels. **MEAL** ▷ **8** (A2) [C] a part of a meal that is served separately from the other parts: *a four-course lunch* ◦ *A traditional British **main** course consists of a meat dish with potatoes and other vegetables.* **MEDICAL TREATMENT** ▷ **9** [C] a fixed number of regular medical treatments: *My doctor's **put** me **on** a course **of** antibiotics.* ◦ *She needed a six-month course of physiotherapy after she broke her leg.* **LAYER** ▷ **10** [C] specialized a continuous horizontal layer of bricks or other building material

> **Word partners for course (CLASSES)**
>
> *do/go on/take* a course • *offer/run* a course • *enrol on* a course • a *crash/intensive/short* course • *on* a course • a course *in* sth

> **Word partners for course (DEVELOPMENT)**
>
> *change* the course *of* sth • *follow/pursue/steer* a course • *set* the course *for* sth • *run/take* its course • *during/over* the course *of* sth • the *natural* course (of sth)

> **Word partners for course (DIRECTION)**
>
> *alter/change* course • *follow/pursue/steer* a course • *stray/veer* off course • *blow/knock* sb/sth off course

IDIOMS **of course 1** (A1) informal used to say 'yes' or to give someone permission to do something: *'Can you help me?' 'Of course.'* ◦ *'May I have a look at your newspaper?' 'Of course you can.'* ◦ *'Have you written your English essay yet?' 'Of course, I finished it last week.'* **2** (B1) used to show that what you are saying is obvious or already known: *The Second World War ended, of course, in 1945.* **3** used to show that a situation or a piece of information is not surprising: *We arrived at the restaurant 30 minutes late so, of course, our reservation had been cancelled.* • **of course not** (A2) used to emphasize that you disagree or that something is not true: *'Where did you get the money? Did you steal it?' 'Of course not. I borrowed it from Carol.'*

▸**verb** [I usually + adv/prep] formal to flow quickly or in large amounts: *Tears were coursing **down** his cheeks.* ◦ *You could almost hear the blood coursing **through** her veins as she passed the finishing line.* ◦ figurative *A new wave of idealism is coursing **through** our schools.*

> **Common mistake: course**
>
> **Warning:** Check your spelling!
> **Course** is one of the 50 words most often spelled wrongly by learners. Remember: the correct spelling has 'ou'.

coursebook /ˈkɔːs.bʊk/ (US) /ˈkɔːrs-/ **noun** [C] UK a book used by students when they do a particular course of study

coursework /ˈkɔːs.wɜːk/ (US) /ˈkɔːrs.wɜːk/ **noun** [U] work set at regular periods as part of an educational course

coursing /ˈkɔː.sɪŋ/ (US) /ˈkɔːr-/ **noun** [U] UK a sport in which RABBITS are chased by dogs

court /kɔːt/ (US) /kɔːrt/ **noun; verb**

▸**noun** **LAW** ▷ **1** (B2) [C usually singular, U] a place where trials and other legal cases happen, or the people present in such a place, especially the officials and those deciding if someone is guilty: *Protestors gathered outside the court to await the verdict.* ◦ *He's due to appear **in** court again on Monday.* ◦ *Please describe to the court exactly what you saw.* ◦ *the European Court of Human Rights* ◦ *The lack of evidence means that the case is unlikely to **go to** court.* **2 take sb to court** to take legal action against someone: *She's threatening to take me to court for not paying the bill on time.* **3 settle (a case) out of court** to solve a legal disagreement without taking legal action: *The newspaper has agreed to settle out of court.* **SPORT** ▷ **4** (B1) [C] an area drawn out on the ground that is used for playing sports such as tennis and BASKETBALL: *a tennis/volleyball/basketball/squash court* ◦ *They were penalized for having too many players **on** the court.* **OPEN AREA** ▷ **5** [C] an area or a short road that is not covered by a roof and is mostly or completely surrounded by buildings: *You really should go and see the lovely medieval court in the castle.* **6 Court** mainly UK used in the names of some roads, and buildings containing apartments **ROYALTY** ▷ **7** [C or U] the official home of a queen or king: *the courts of Renaissance Europe* ◦ *He quickly lost his popularity **at** court.* **8** [S, + sing/pl verb] the important people who live in the official home of a queen or king or who work for or advise them

▸**verb** **PLEASE** ▷ **1** [T] to try to please someone because you want them to join you: *Adams is being courted by a number of football clubs.* **TRY TO GET** ▷ **2** [T] to try to get something, especially attention or support from other people: *She courts publicity by inviting journalists to extravagant parties.* **RISK** ▷ **3** [T] to risk something unpleasant, especially by behaving stupidly or carelessly: *Drinking and driving is simply courting **disaster**.* **HAVE A RELATIONSHIP** ▷ **4** [I or T] old-fashioned to have a romantic relationship with someone that you hope to marry: *They courted for two years before getting married.*

courteous /ˈkɜː.ti.əs/ (US) /ˈkɝː.t̬i-/ **adj** (C2) polite and showing respect: *Although she often disagreed with me, she was always courteous.* → Synonym **well mannered** • **courteously** /-li/ **adv** *He's always behaved courteously toward my family.*

courtesan /ˌkɔː.tɪˈzæn/, /ˈkɔː.tɪ.zæn/ (US) /ˈkɔːr.t̬ɪ-/ **noun** [C] a woman, usually with a high social position, who in the past had sexual relationships with rich or important men in exchange for money

courtesy /ˈkɜː.tə.si/ (US) /ˈkɝː.t̬ə-/ **noun** [U or C] **1** (B2) polite behaviour, or a polite action or remark: *You might get on better with your parents if you showed them some courtesy.* ◦ [+ to infinitive] *He could at least have had the courtesy **to** say sorry.* ◦ *The president welcomed the Queen with the usual courtesies.* **2 (by) courtesy of a** by permission of: *Jessie J appears courtesy of Universal Records.* **b** because of: *Did the Conservatives win courtesy of the division of the opposition vote between Labour and the Liberal Democrats?*

courthouse /ˈkɔːt.haʊs/ (US) /ˈkɔːrt-/ **noun** [C] US a building that contains law courts: *a county/federal courthouse*

courtier /ˈkɔː.ti.əʳ/ (US) /ˈkɔːr.t̬i.ə/ **noun** [C] a COMPANION of a queen, king, or other ruler in their official home, especially in the past

courtly /ˈkɔːt.li/ (US) /ˈkɔːrt-/ **adj** polite and formal in behaviour • **courtliness** /-nəs/ **noun** [U]

court ˈmartial **noun** [C] (plural **court martials** or formal **courts martial**) (a trial in) a military court for members of the armed forces • **ˌcourt-ˈmartial verb** [T] *She is likely to be court-martialled for disobeying her commanding officer.*

ˌcourt of inˈquiry **noun** [C, + sing/pl verb] (plural **courts of inquiry**) UK a group of people, often with special knowledge or skill, who have been brought

C

together in order to examine the causes of an accident

ˌcourt ˈorder noun [C] an instruction given by a court telling someone what they can or cannot do

C

courtroom /ˈkɔːt.rʊm/, /-ruːm/ (US) /ˈkɔːrt-/ noun [C] a room where a law court meets: *The accused entered the courtroom handcuffed to two police officers.*

courtship /ˈkɔːt.ʃɪp/ (US) /ˈkɔːrt-/ noun [C or U] old-fashioned or formal the time when people have a romantic relationship with the intention of getting married: *They had a passionate courtship and a long, loving marriage.*

ˈcourt ˌshoe noun [C] UK (US **pump**) a type of plain shoe with a raised HEEL and no way of fastening it to the foot, worn by women

courtyard /ˈkɔːt.jɑːd/ (US) /ˈkɔːrt.jɑːrd/ noun [C] an area of flat ground outside that is partly or completely surrounded by the walls of a building

couscous /ˈkuːs.kuːs/ noun [U] a food, originally from North Africa, consisting of crushed WHEAT, that is often served with meat or vegetables

cousin /ˈkʌz.ᵊn/ noun [C] **1** A2 (also **first cousin**) a child of a person's aunt or uncle, or, more generally, a DISTANT (= not close) relation: *My brother's wife and I both had babies around the same time, so the cousins are very close in age.* ◦ *Many of our* ***distant*** *cousins, whom we hadn't seen for years, came to my sister's wedding.* **2** a member of a group of people with similar origins: *We Americans owe a great deal to our European cousins.*

ˈcousin-ˌbrother noun [C] Indian English a male cousin → Compare **cousin-sister**

ˈcousin-ˌsister noun [C] Indian English a female cousin → Compare **cousin-brother**

couture /kuːˈtjʊəʳ/ (US) /-ˈtʊr/ noun [U] (also **ˌhaute couˈture**) the designing, making, and selling of expensive fashionable clothing, or the clothes themselves: *a couture show/collection/house* • **couturier** /kuːˈtjʊə.ri.eɪ/ (US) /-ˈtʊr.i-/ noun [C] *In 1960 Pierre Cardin became the first couturier to design men's clothes.*

covalent bond /kəʊˌveɪ.ləntˈbɒnd/ (US) /koʊˌveɪ.ləntˈbɑːnd/ noun [C] specialized a chemical BOND in which two atoms share one or more pairs of ELECTRONS that hold them together

cove /kəʊv/ (US) /koʊv/ noun [C] **COAST** ▷ **1** a curved part of a coast that partly surrounds an area of water → Compare **bay** **MAN** ▷ **2** UK old-fashioned a man: *He's an odd-looking cove.*

coven /ˈkʌv.ᵊn/ noun [C, + sing/pl verb] a group or meeting of WITCHES

covenant /ˈkʌv.ᵊn.ᵊnt/ noun [C] **1** a formal agreement or promise between two or more people: *The contract contained a* ***restrictive*** *covenant against building on the land.* **2** UK specialized a formal agreement to pay a fixed amount of money regularly, especially to a CHARITY • **covenant** verb [T] *Five percent of our profits are covenanted* ***to*** *charity.*

cover /ˈkʌv.əʳ/ (US) /-ɚ/ verb; noun

▸verb **PLACE OVER** ▷ **1** A2 [T] to put or spread something over something, or to lie on the surface of something: *The light was so bright that I had to cover my eyes.* ◦ *Snow covered the hillsides.* ◦ *She covered him* (***up***) ***with*** *a blanket.* ◦ *Cover the meat* ***with*** *a layer of cheese.* ◦ *The bandages were covered* ***with/in*** *blood.* ◦ *How much of the Earth's surface is covered* ***by/with*** *water?* **DEAL WITH** ▷ **2** B1 [T] to deal with or direct attention to something: *This leaflet covers what we've just discussed in more detail.* ◦ *Do these parking restrictions cover residents as well as visitors?* ◦ *The new office will cover the whole of Scotland.* **REPORT** ▷ **3** C1 [T] to report the news about a particular important event: *She's covering the American election for BBC television.* **PROTECT** ▷ **4** C1 [T] to protect someone against loss, damage, accident, or having something stolen, by having INSURANCE: *Does your travel insurance cover you* ***against/for*** *the loss or theft of cash?* **5** to do something to protect yourself from blame or criticism in the future: *I kept copies of my expense receipts, just to cover myself.* **TRAVEL** ▷ **6** B2 [T] to travel a particular distance: *We covered 400 km in three hours.* **BE ENOUGH** ▷ **7** C1 [T] to be enough money to pay for something: *The selling price barely covered the cost of the raw materials.* ◦ *Would £50 cover your expenses?* **GIVE PROTECTION** ▷ **8** [T] to aim a gun or shoot at someone to try to stop them from shooting or escaping, or to protect someone else: *The police officer was covered by her colleagues while she ran towards the gunman's hideout.* **9** [T] When soldiers or police officers cover a place such as a road or building, they are in a position from which they can watch and defend it: *We've got all the exits covered, so they've no chance of escape.* **DO SOMEONE'S JOB** ▷ **10** [I or T] to do someone else's job or duty when they are absent: *I'm going to the doctor's tomorrow, so do you think you could cover my shift* ***for*** *me?* ◦ *Sorry, I'm already covering* ***for*** *someone else.* **RECORD** ▷ **11** [T] to make a recording of a song or tune that has already been recorded by someone else: *I think more singers have covered 'Yesterday' than any other song.*

IDIOMS **cover your ass, butt, backside, etc.** US offensive to do something to protect yourself from blame or criticism in the future: *He'd do anything to cover his ass, including lie, cheat, and murder.* • **cover your tracks** to hide or destroy the things that show where you have been or what you have been doing: *Roberts covered his tracks by throwing the knife in the river.*

PHRASAL VERB **cover sth up** C2 to stop people discovering the truth about something bad: *The company tried to cover up its employment of illegal immigrants.*

▸noun **SOMETHING PLACED OVER** ▷ **1** B1 [C] something that is put on or over something else, usually to protect it, to keep something in, etc.: *I keep my computer printer under a protective plastic cover.* ◦ *Remove the packaging and pierce the film cover before microwaving.* **2** B1 [C] the stiff outside part of a book or magazine, usually made of thick paper or cardboard: *Who should we put on the cover of the magazine this month?* ◦ *Paperback books have soft covers.* **3 read sth from cover to cover** to read a book, magazine, etc. all the way through from the beginning to the end **4** [C] Indian English an envelope **5 send sth under plain/separate cover** formal to send something in a plain/separate envelope **6 covers** [plural] the BLANKETS, SHEETS, etc. on a bed: *Martha threw back the covers and bounced out of bed.* **PROTECTION** ▷ **7** C1 [U] UK (US **coverage**) financial protection so that you get money if something bad happens: *I've got £20,000 worth of cover* ***for*** *the contents of my house.* ◦ *Have you got cover* ***for*** *accidental damage?* **8** [U] protection by someone who has a gun: *We needed more cover* ***from*** *the enemy aircraft.* **9** C1 [U] shelter or protection in an unpleasant or dangerous situation: *We* ***took*** *cover from the storm in a bus shelter.* ◦ *The burglar broke into the house* ***under*** *cover of darkness.* **10** [U] plants, especially bushes, that are used as shelter by animals **SONG** ▷ **11** [C] (also **ˈcover ˌversion**) a performance or recording of a song or tune that has already been recorded by someone else

coverage /ˈkʌv.ᵊr.ɪdʒ/ (US) /-ɚ-/ noun [U] **REPORT** ▷ **1** (C1) the reporting of a particular important event or subject: *What did you think of the BBC's election coverage?* **DEALING WITH** ▷ **2** the fact of dealing with or directing attention to something: *These books give very good grammar coverage (= they deal with grammar very well).*

coveralls /ˈkʌv.ə.rɔːlz/ (US) /-ɚ.ɑːlz/ noun [plural] US for **boiler suit**

ˈcover ˌcharge noun [C usually singular] a charge that is sometimes added to the amount that a customer pays for food, drinks, and service in a restaurant, or that is added in a NIGHTCLUB to pay for entertainment

-covered /-kʌv.əd/ (US) /-ɚd/ suffix covered in the way mentioned: ***snow**-covered hills*

ˈcover ˌgirl noun [C] an attractive, often famous, woman whose photograph appears on the front of a magazine

covering /ˈkʌv.ᵊr.ɪŋ/ (US) /-ɚ-/ noun [C] a layer of something that covers something else: *a light covering of snow*

ˈcovering ˌletter/ˌnote noun [C] (US **ˈcover ˌletter/ˌnote**) a letter or note that contains information about the thing it is sent with: *Please send a covering letter with your application form.*

coverlet /ˈkʌv.ə.lət/ (US) /-ɚ-/ noun [C] a **bedspread**

ˈcover ˌnote noun [C] UK specialized a document that is used temporarily as proof that someone is INSURED until the final official document is available

ˈcover ˌstory noun [C usually singular] a report or article connected with the picture on the front of a magazine

covert adj; noun

▸**adj** /ˈkəʊ.vɜːt/ (US) /ˈkoʊ.vɝːt/ hidden or secret: *covert actions* ◦ *The government was accused of covert military operations against the regime.* → Compare **overt**

▸**noun** [C] /ˈkʌv.ət/ (US) /-ɚt/ a group of bushes and small trees growing close together in which animals can hide, especially from people or other animals hunting them

covertly /ˈkəʊ.vɜːt.li/ (US) /koʊˈvɝːt.li/ adv secretly, or in a hidden way: *Terrorists have been operating covertly in England.*

ˈcover-up noun [C] an attempt to prevent the public from discovering information about a serious crime or mistake: *Allegations of a cover-up **of** the effects of pollution have been strongly denied.*

covet /ˈkʌv.ɪt/ verb [T] formal to want to have something very much, especially something that belongs to someone else: *She always coveted power but never quite achieved it.* ◦ *The Booker Prize is the most coveted British literary award.*

covetable /ˈkʌv.ɪ.tə.bl̩/ (US) /-t̬ə-/ adj UK formal describes something that people want to have

covetous /ˈkʌv.ɪ.təs/ (US) /-t̬əs/ adj formal disapproving wanting to have something too much, especially something that belongs to someone else: *People were casting covetous eyes over the large yacht moored in the harbour.* • **covetously** /-li/ adv *The boys looked covetously at the shiny new motorcycles.* • **covetousness** /-nəs/ noun [U]

cow /kaʊ/ noun; verb

▸**noun ANIMAL** ▷ **1** (A1) [C] a large female farm animal kept to produce meat and milk: *a **dairy** cow* **2** [C] a large female adult mammal such as an ELEPHANT, a WHALE, or a SEAL: *a cow elephant* **WOMAN** ▷ **3** [C] UK offensive an unkind or unpleasant woman: *You stupid cow!* **UNPLEASANT THING** ▷ **4** [S] Australian English informal something difficult or unpleasant: *It's been **a** cow **of a** day.*

IDIOM **till/until the cows come home** for a very long time: *I could sit here and argue with you till the cows come home, but it wouldn't solve anything.*

▸**verb** [T usually passive] to frighten someone into doing something, using threats or violence: *The protesters refused to be cowed **into** submission by the army.*

coward /ˈkaʊ.əd/ (US) /ˈkaʊ.ɚd/ noun [C] disapproving (B2) a person who is not brave and is too eager to avoid danger, difficulty, or pain: *They **branded** her a coward for informing on her colleagues during the interrogation.* • **cowardly** /-li/ adj (B2) *This was a particularly brutal and cowardly attack.* • **cowardice** /-ə.dɪs/ (US) /-ɚ.dɪs/ noun [U] *You can accuse me of cowardice, but I still wouldn't fight in a war.*

cowbell /ˈkaʊ.bel/ noun [C] a bell that is hung from a cow's neck so that the cow can be found, or a metal musical instrument in the shape of such a bell that is hit with a stick

cowboy /ˈkaʊ.bɔɪ/ noun [C] **FARM WORKER** ▷ **1** (also **cowhand** /-hænd/) a person, especially in the western US, whose job is to take care of CATTLE, and who usually rides a horse, or a similar character in a film: *The ranch employed ten or twelve cowboys.* **DISHONEST PERSON** ▷ **2** UK informal someone who is not honest, careful, or skilful in their trade or business, or someone who ignores rules that most people obey and is therefore not considered to be responsible: *Those builders are **a bunch of** cowboys – they made a terrible job of our extension.*

ˈcowboy ˌboots noun [plural] leather boots with a HEEL and pointed toes

ˈcowboy ˌfilm noun [C] UK (US **ˈcowboy ˌmovie**) a film based on stories about cowboys and life in the west of the US in the past

ˈcowboy ˌhat noun [C] a hat with a wide, curving lower edge, especially worn by cowboys

cowcatcher /ˈkaʊˌkætʃ.əʳ/ (US) /-ɚ/ noun [C] US a strong metal frame fixed to the front of a train that pushes objects off the track as the train moves forward

cower /ˈkaʊ.əʳ/ (US) /ˈkaʊ.ɚ/ verb [I] to lower your head or body in fear, often while moving backwards: *Stop cowering! I'm not going to hit you.*

cowgirl /ˈkaʊ.gɜːl/ (US) /-gɝːl/ noun [C] a female COWBOY

cowherd /ˈkaʊ.hɜːd/ (US) /-hɝːd/ noun [C] a person employed to take care of CATTLE

cowhide /ˈkaʊ.haɪd/ noun [C or U] (leather made from) the skin of a cow: *a cowhide briefcase*

cowl /kaʊl/ noun [C] **1** a large, loose covering for the head and sometimes shoulders, but not the face, worn especially by MONKS **2** a metal cover on the top of a CHIMNEY that helps smoke to go up it and prevents wind from blowing down it

cowlick /ˈkaʊ.lɪk/ noun [C] a piece of hair that always sticks out on someone's head

cowling /ˈkaʊ.lɪŋ/ noun [C] a metal cover for an engine, especially an aircraft engine

cowman /ˈkaʊ.mən/, /-mæn/ noun [C] (plural **-men** /-mən/, /-men/) **1** UK a male COWHERD **2** US a man who owns CATTLE

ˌco-ˈworker noun [C] a person who you work with, especially someone with a similar job or level of responsibility

ˈcow ˌparsley noun [U] UK (US **ˌQueen Anne's ˈlace**) a wild plant with delicate, white flowers

cowpat /ˈkaʊ.pæt/ noun [C] a round, flat mass of solid waste from a cow

cowpox /ˈkaʊ.pɒks/ (US) /-pɑːks/ noun [U] a disease in CATTLE

cowrie (also **cowry**) /ˈkaʊ.ri/ (US) /ˈkaʊr.i/ noun [C] a small sea creature with a soft body and a brightly coloured shell, or the shell itself used in the past as money in parts of Africa and southern Asia: *a cowrie shell*

ˈco-write verb [T] (**co-wrote**, **co-written**) to write something with someone else, especially a popular song, or something for television or the cinema: *Lennon and McCartney co-wrote most of the Beatles' songs.* • **ˈco-ˌwriter** noun [C] *Flanagan and McCulloch were co-writers **on** the television series 'Sleepers'.*

cowshed /ˈkaʊ.ʃed/ noun [C] a building where cows are kept while they are MILKED (= have milk taken from them) or where they are kept during winter or bad weather

cowslip /ˈkaʊ.slɪp/ noun [C] a small plant with yellow flowers that smell sweet

cox /kɒks/ (US) /kɑːks/ noun; verb

▸noun [C] (formal **coxswain** /ˈkɒk.sən/ (US) /ˈkɑːk-/) the person who sits at the back of a ROWING BOAT and controls which direction it moves in: *Coxes are often small, light people.*

▸verb [I or T] to act as a cox: *She coxed **for** her college for three seasons.* ◦ *He coxed the winning eight.*

coy /kɔɪ/ adj **SECRET** ▷ **1** intentionally keeping something secret: *She's very coy **about** her age.* **MODEST** ▷ **2** (especially of women) being or pretending to be shy, or like a child: *She gave me a coy look from under her schoolgirl's fringe.* • **coyly** /ˈkɔɪ.li/ adv *She smiled coyly.* • **coyness** /ˈkɔɪ.nəs/ noun [U]

coyote /kaɪˈəʊ.ti/ (US) /-ˈoʊ.t̬i/ noun [C] a small wild animal like a dog that lives in North America

coyote

coypu /ˈkɔɪ.puː/ noun [C] (plural **coypus** or **coypu**) a South American animal that lives near water and has valuable fur

cozily /ˈkəʊ.zɪ.li/ (US) /ˈkoʊ-/ adv US for **cosily**

cozy /ˈkəʊ.zi/ (US) /ˈkoʊ-/ adj, noun [C] US for **cosy**

cozzie /ˈkɒz.i/ (US) /ˈkɑː.zi/ noun [C] UK informal for **swimming costume**

CPR /ˌsiː.piːˈɑːr/ (US) /-ˈɑːr/ noun [U] abbreviation for cardiopulmonary resuscitation: a method used to keep someone alive in a medical emergency, in which you blow into their mouth then press on their chest and then repeat the process: *to administer/perform CPR*

CPU /ˌsiː.piːˈjuː/ noun [C] abbreviation for central processing unit: the part of a computer that controls all the other parts

crab /kræb/ noun [C or U] **SEA CREATURE** ▷ **1** (B2) a sea creature with five pairs of legs and a round, flat body covered by a shell, or its flesh eaten as food: *We walked along the beach collecting small crabs.* ◦ *This crab **meat/salad** is delicious!* **DISEASE** ▷ **2 crabs** [plural] (also **ˈcrab lice**) small insects that can live in the hair around the sex organs

the ˈCrab noun [S] the sign of the ZODIAC **Cancer**

ˈcrab ˌapple noun [C] (UK also **crab**) (the small, sour fruit of) a small tree that has attractive flowers: *a crab apple tree*

crabbed /kræbd/, /ˈkræb.ɪd/ adj old-fashioned describes writing that is written too closely together and therefore difficult to read

crabby /ˈkræb.i/ adj (old-fashioned **crabbed**) easily annoyed and complaining: *You're very crabby today. What's upset you?* • **crabbily** /-ɪ.li/ adv • **crabbiness** /-nəs/ noun [U]

crabgrass /ˈkræb.ɡrɑːs/ (US) /-ɡræs/ noun [U] US a type of WEED (= unwanted plant)

crabwise /ˈkræb.waɪz/ adv UK If you move crabwise, you move sideways or carefully and not directly.

crack /kræk/ verb; noun; adj

▸verb **BREAK** ▷ **1** (B2) [T or I] to break something so that it does not separate, but very thin lines appear on its surface, or to become broken in this way: *A stone hit the window and cracked the glass.* ◦ *I cracked my tooth as I fell.* ◦ *The walls cracked and the roof collapsed in the earthquake.* **2** [I] informal to become mentally and physically weak: *Stress and overwork are causing teachers to crack (**up**).* **3** [I] informal to fail as a result of problems: *Their relationship began to crack (**up**) after their child died.* **4** [I] If someone cracks, they begin to feel weak and agree that they have been defeated: *He cracked during questioning and told us where to find the stolen goods.* **GET INTO** ▷ **5** [T] to break something open, especially in order to reach or use what is inside: *Crack three **eggs** into a bowl and mix them together.* ◦ *He cracked (**open**) the **nuts** with his hands.* **6** [T] (also **crack into sth**) to get into someone else's computer system without permission and get information or do something illegal **7** [T] informal to copy computer programs or recorded material illegally **FIND ANSWER** ▷ **8** [T] to find a solution to a problem: *They cracked the **code** and read the secret message.* ◦ UK *I've been trying to solve this problem all week, but I still haven't cracked it.* **HIT** ▷ **9** [I or T, usually + adv/prep] to hit something or someone: *I cracked my head **on/against** the door.* ◦ *They cracked him **over** the head with a baseball bat.* **MAKE SOUND** ▷ **10** [I or T] to make a sudden, short noise, or to cause something to make this noise: *The whip cracked over the horses' heads.* **11** [I] If a voice cracks, its sound changes because the person is upset: *Her voice cracked **with** emotion as she told the story.* **MAKE JOKE** ▷ **12** (C1) [T] to make a joke or clever remark: *He's always cracking **jokes**.*

IDIOMS **crack the whip** to use your authority to make someone else behave better or work harder: *We were two months behind schedule, so I decided it was time to crack the whip.* • **get cracking** to start doing something quickly: *Get cracking (= hurry), or we'll miss the train.* ◦ *I'd better get cracking **with** these letters before I go home.*

PHRASAL VERBS **crack down** (C2) to start dealing with bad or illegal behaviour in a more severe way: *The library is cracking down **on** people who lose their books.* • **crack up** informal (C2) to become mentally ill: *I think she's cracking up.* • **crack (sb) up** informal (C2) to suddenly laugh a lot, or to make someone suddenly laugh a lot: *I took one look at her and cracked up.* ◦ *There's something about that guy's face that just cracks me up.*

▸noun **NARROW SPACE** ▷ **1** (C2) [C] a very narrow space between parts of something: *Cracks had appeared in the dry ground.* ◦ *We peered through the crack in the floorboards.* ◦ figurative *Cracks began to show in his façade of self-confidence.* **2 (just) a crack** so that there is a very small space: *She opened the door just a crack to listen to the conversation.* **SOUND** ▷ **3** [C] a sudden loud sound: *the crack of a rifle/whip/breaking branch* **ATTEMPT** ▷ **4** [C usually singular] informal an attempt: *It was her first crack **at** beating the record.* ◦ *It's not* something I've done before, but I'll *have/* (US *take*) *a crack* ***at*** *it.* **DRUG** ▷ **5** [U] (also ˌ**crack** ˈ**cocaine**) a powerful form of the drug COCAINE: *Several kilos of crack were found in her luggage.* ◦ *a crack addict* **ENJOYABLE TIME** ▷ **6** [U] **craic** **IN COMPUTER SYSTEM** ▷ **7** [C] informal a method of getting into someone else's computer system: *Find cracks for your shareware programs.* **JOKE** ▷ **8** [C] a **wisecrack**

IDIOM **at the crack of dawn** C2 very early in the morning, especially at the time when the sun first appears: *We'll have to leave at the crack of dawn.*

▸**adj** [before noun] excellent, or of the highest quality: *a crack regiment* ◦ *crack troops*

crackdown /ˈkræk.daʊn/ **noun** [C] C2 a situation in which someone starts to deal with bad or illegal behaviour in a more severe way: *There has been a series of government crackdowns* ***on*** *safety in factories.*

cracked /krækt/ **adj** **1** If something is cracked, it is damaged with one or more thin lines on its surface: *a cracked mirror/window* ◦ *cracked plates* **2** **crackers**

IDIOM **not be all it's cracked up to be** informal to be not as good as people say: *This new radio station's not all it's cracked up to be.*

cracker /ˈkræk.əʳ/ US /-ɚ/ **noun** **FOOD** ▷ **1** A1 [C] a thin, flat, hard biscuit, especially one eaten with cheese **DEVICE** ▷ **2** [C] UK a paper tube with small toys, small pieces of sweet food, etc. inside, that is covered with bright paper and makes a short, sharp sound when both ends are pulled: *Who wants to* ***pull*** *a cracker with me?* ◦ *a* ***Christmas*** *cracker* **3** [C] UK a FIREWORK that explodes with a loud noise **GOOD THING** ▷ **4** [S] UK informal a person or thing that is very good or has a special exciting quality: *She's written five books, and every one is a cracker.*

crackers /ˈkræk.əz/ US /-ɚz/ **adj** [after verb] (also **cracked**) silly, stupid, or slightly mentally ill

crackhead /ˈkræk.hed/ **noun** [C] slang a person who cannot stop using CRACK (= an illegal drug)

ˈ**crack** ˌ**house** **noun** [C] slang a house or flat where people use, sell, or buy CRACK (= an illegal drug)

cracking /ˈkræk.ɪŋ/ **adj** UK informal extremely good: *He scored with a cracking shot into the back of the goal.* ◦ *The marathon began at a cracking (= very fast) pace.*

crackle /ˈkræk.l/ **verb; noun**

▸**verb** [I] to make a lot of short, dry, sharp sounds: *The radio started to crackle.* ◦ *The logs crackled and popped in the fireplace.* • **crackly** /-li/ **adj** *a crackly voice*

▸**noun** [C or U] a short, dry, sharp sound: *the crackle of burning logs*

crackling /ˈkræk.lɪŋ/ **noun** [U] **FOOD** ▷ **1** (US also **cracklings** [plural]) the CRISP skin of cooked PORK (= meat from a pig) **SOUND** ▷ **2** short, dry, sharp sounds made by something: *We could hear the crackling of a fire.*

crackpot /ˈkræk.pɒt/ US /-pɑːt/ **noun** [C] informal a person who is silly or stupid • **crackpot adj** *crackpot ideas*

cradle /ˈkreɪ.dl/ **noun; verb**

▸**noun** [C] **BED** ▷ **1** a small bed for a baby, especially one that moves from side to side: *The nurse* ***rocked*** *the cradle.* **PHONE** ▷ **2** the object that you put a phone, camera, etc. into in order to RECHARGE (= put power into) its BATTERIES or connect it to a computer **EQUIPMENT** ▷ **3** UK (US **scaffold**) a frame that hangs on the side of a building, ship, etc. for people to work from

IDIOMS **the cradle of sth** literary the place where something started: *Fossil records indicate that Africa was the cradle of early human evolution.* ◦ *the cradle of civilization* • **from (the) cradle to (the) grave** for all of a person's life: *She lived in the same village from the cradle to the grave.*

▸**verb** [T] to hold something or someone gently, especially by supporting with the arms: *She cradled him tenderly* ***in her arms.***

ˈ**cradle-**ˌ**snatcher** **noun** [C] UK humorous or disapproving (US ˈ**cradle-**ˌ**robber**) a person whose sexual partner is much younger than they are

craft /krɑːft/ US /kræft/ **noun; verb**

▸**noun** **SKILL** ▷ **1** B2 [C or U] (plural **crafts**) (a job or activity needing) skill and experience, especially in relation to making objects: *the craft of furniture making/sewing/glassblowing* ◦ *political/literary craft* ◦ *rural/ancient/traditional crafts* ◦ *craft workers (= skilled workers)* **VEHICLE** ▷ **2** [C] (plural **craft**) a vehicle for travelling on water or through the air: *naval/civilian/patrol/rescue craft* ◦ *18 craft (= boats) set out in the race.* → See also **aircraft, hovercraft, spacecraft**

▸**verb** [T often passive] to make objects, especially in a skilled way: *These bracelets were crafted by Native Americans.* ◦ *a beautifully crafted silver brooch*

ˈ**craft** ˌ**fair** **noun** [C] an event where people sell decorative objects that they have made by hand

ˈ**craft** ˌ**shop** **noun** [C] a shop that sells decorative objects made by hand or the materials and tools used for making such objects

craftsman /ˈkrɑːfts.mən/ US /ˈkræfts-/ **noun** [C] (plural **-men** /-mən/) a person who is skilled in a particular craft

craftsmanship /ˈkrɑːfts.mən.ʃɪp/ US /ˈkræfts-/ **noun** [U] skill at making things: *The jewellery showed exquisite craftsmanship.*

craftswoman /ˈkrɑːftsˌwʊm.ən/ US /ˈkræfts-/ **noun** [C] (plural **-women** /-ˌwɪmɪn/) a female craftsman

crafty /ˈkrɑːf.ti/ US /ˈkræf-/ **adj** clever, especially in a dishonest or secret way: *I've had a crafty idea for getting round the regulations.* ◦ *She was a crafty old woman.* • **craftily** /-tɪ.li/ **adv** • **craftiness** /-nəs/ **noun** [U]

crag /kræg/ **noun** [C] a high, rough mass of rock that sticks out from the land around it

craggy /ˈkræg.i/ **adj** **1** having many crags: *a craggy coastline* **2** describes a man's face that is quite roughly formed and has loose skin but is also attractive: *a craggy face* ◦ *craggy features*

craic /kræk/ **noun** [U] (also **crack**) Irish enjoyable time spent with other people, especially when the conversation is entertaining and funny: *The boys went driving round the town just* ***for the*** *craic.*

cram /kræm/ **verb** (**-mm-**) **FIT A LOT IN** ▷ **1** [T usually + adv/prep] informal to force a lot of things into a small space: *Eight children were crammed* ***into*** *the back of the car.* ◦ *The room was packed and we were crammed* ***against*** *the door.* **2** [T usually + adv/prep] informal to do many things in a short period of time: *I managed to cram three countries* ***into*** *a week's business trip.* **LEARN** ▷ **3** [I] to try to learn a lot very quickly before an exam

PHRASAL VERB **cram sth down** informal to eat a lot of something quickly: *I just had time to cram down a few biscuits before we left.*

crammed /kræmd/ **adj** very full of people or things: *a crammed train/room* ◦ *The platform was crammed* ***with****/crammed* ***full of*** *people trying to board the train.*

crammer /ˈkræm.əʳ/ US /-ɚ/ **noun** [C] UK old-fashioned informal a school or a book that helps you to learn quickly for an exam

cramp /kræmp/ noun; verb

▸noun **1** [C or U] a sudden painful tightening in a muscle, often after a lot of exercise, that limits movement: *Several runners needed treatment for cramp (US cramps) and exhaustion.* ◦ *I've got cramp (US a cramp) in my foot.* ◦ ***stomach** cramps* **2 cramps** [plural] pains in the lower stomach caused by a woman's PERIOD

▸verb [T] to limit someone, especially to prevent them from enjoying a full life: *Worry and lack of money cramp the lives of the unemployed.*

IDIOM **cramp sb's style** informal humorous C2 to prevent someone from enjoying themselves as much as they would like, especially by going somewhere with them

cramped /kræmpt/ adj not having enough space or time: *a cramped room/house* ◦ *We have six desks in this room, so we're rather cramped (**for** space).* ◦ *I have a very cramped schedule.*

crampon /ˈkræm.pɒn/ US /-pɑːn/ noun [C] a metal frame with sharp points that is fixed to the bottom of a boot to make walking on ice or snow easier

cranberry /ˈkræn.bᵊr.i/ US /-ber-/ noun [C] a small, round, red fruit with a sour taste

crane /kreɪn/ noun; verb

▸noun [C] **MACHINE** ▷ **1** a tall metal structure with a long horizontal part, used for lifting and moving heavy objects: *The crane lifted the container off the ship.* **BIRD** ▷ **2** a tall bird with long, thin legs and a long neck

▸verb [I usually + adv/prep, T] to stretch in order to look at something: *He craned **forward** to see the procession.* ◦ *Mike was craning his **neck** to get the first glimpse of the car.*

ˈcrane ˌfly noun [C] a flying insect with a narrow body and very long legs

cranial /ˈkreɪ.ni.əl/ adj specialized of the SKULL

cranium /ˈkreɪ.ni.əm/ noun [C] (plural **craniums** or **crania**) specialized the hard bone case that gives an animal's or a human's head its shape and protects the brain

crank /kræŋk/ noun; verb

▸noun **PERSON** ▷ **1** [C] informal a person who has strange or unusual ideas and beliefs **2** [C] US, informal an unpleasant and easily annoyed person: *She's always a crank first thing in the morning.* **EQUIPMENT** ▷ **3** [C] a device that creates movement between parts of a machine or that changes backward and forward movement into circular movement: *a crank handle*

▸verb

PHRASAL VERBS **crank sth out** US informal to produce something with no special care or effort: *Like clockwork, he cranks out a new book every year.* • **crank sth up** informal to increase or improve something: *crank up the volume/pressure*

ˌcrank ˈcaller noun [C] someone who makes unpleasant phone calls to people they do not know

crankshaft /ˈkræŋk.ʃɑːft/ US /-ʃæft/ noun [C] a long metal rod, especially one in a car engine, that helps the engine turn the wheels: *a crankshaft bearing*

cranky /ˈkræŋ.ki/ adj **1** US informal easily annoyed or upset: *a cranky baby* ◦ *He's been cranky all day.* **2** informal strange and unusual: *She's a member of a group that promotes cranky ideas about food and exercise.*

cranny /ˈkræn.i/ noun [C] a small, narrow opening in something solid: *There were small plants growing in every **nook and** cranny of the wall.*

crap /kræp/ noun; adj; verb

▸noun **SOLID WASTE** ▷ **1** [S or U] offensive solid waste, or an occasion when an animal or person produces solid waste: *I stepped in a pile of crap.* ◦ *to **have** (US **take**) a crap* **BAD QUALITY** ▷ **2** [U] something that is not worth anything, not useful, nonsense, or of bad quality: *I can't believe she's trying to pass off this crap as art!* ◦ *I've only read one novel by him and it was **a load of** crap.* **GAME** ▷ **3 craps** [U] (also **crap**) US a game played with DICE for money

▸adj (**crapper**, **crappest**) offensive **1** of very bad quality: *A bad film? It was crap!* ◦ UK *He watches a lot of crap TV.* **2** not skilled or not organized: *He's totally crap **at** football.*

▸verb [I] (**-pp-**) offensive to produce solid waste: *The dog crapped right in the middle of the street.*

PHRASAL VERB **crap on** offensive to talk for a long time in a boring way

crape /kreɪp/ noun [U] UK for **crepe**

crapper /ˈkræp.əʳ/ US /-ɚ/ noun [C] offensive a toilet

crappy /ˈkræp.i/ adj offensive unpleasant or of very bad quality: *He's had a series of crappy jobs.*

crash /kræʃ/ verb; noun; adj

▸verb **HAVE AN ACCIDENT** ▷ **1** B1 [I or T] to have an accident, especially one that damages a vehicle: *We skidded on the ice and crashed.* ◦ *The plane crashed **into** a mountainside.* ◦ *Her brother borrowed her motorbike and crashed it.* **MAKE A NOISE** ▷ **2** [I or T, usually + adv/prep] to hit something, often making a loud noise or causing damage: *We could hear waves crashing **on/against** the shore.* ◦ *Suddenly, cymbals crashed and the orchestra began playing.* ◦ *Without warning, the tree crashed through the roof.* **FAIL** ▷ **3** C1 [I] If something such as a business crashes, it suddenly fails or becomes unsuccessful: *Investors were seriously worried when the stock market began to crash.* **4** B2 [I] If a computer or system crashes, it suddenly stops operating: *My laptop's crashed again.* **SLEEP** ▷ **5** [I] informal to sleep at someone else's house for the night, especially when you have not planned it: *They crashed on my floor after the party.* **ENTER WITHOUT PERMISSION** ▷ **6** [T] informal to go to a party or other event without an invitation: *We tried to crash the party, but the bouncers wouldn't let us in.* → See also **gatecrash**

IDIOM **crash and burn** informal to fail very suddenly, obviously, and completely: *In this business, new products often crash and burn.*

PHRASAL VERB **crash out** informal **SLEEP** ▷ **1** to go to sleep very quickly because you are very tired: *I just want to go home and crash out.* **LOSE** ▷ **2** UK to lose in a sports competition when you were expected to win: *He crashed out **of** the French Open in the second round.*

▸noun [C] **ACCIDENT** ▷ **1** B1 an accident, especially one that damages a vehicle: *a car crash* ◦ *She **had** a crash on the way to work.* ◦ *They were only slightly injured in the crash.* **NOISE** ▷ **2** B2 a sudden loud noise made when something breaks or falls: *I heard a loud crash in the kitchen.* ◦ *The vase landed on the floor with a crash.* **FAILURE** ▷ **3** C1 a sudden large fall in the value of a country's businesses: *They lost a lot of money in the Stock Market crash.* **4** a situation when a computer or system suddenly stops operating: *a computer crash*

▸adj [before noun] informal quick and involving a lot of effort: *The company undertook a crash programme of machine replacement.*

ˈcrash ˌbarrier noun [C] UK a strong fence that

separates the two sides of a large road or is built at a dangerous place at the edge of a road, to help prevent accidents

ˈcrash ˌcourse noun [C] a course that teaches you a lot of basic facts in a very short time: *I **did/took** a crash course **in** French before my trip to Paris.*

ˌcrash ˈdiet noun [C] a way of losing body weight quickly by eating very little

ˈcrash ˌhelmet noun [C] a hard hat that covers and protects the whole head, worn especially by MOTORCYCLISTS

crashing /ˈkræʃ.ɪŋ/ noun [U] loud noises made when things break or fall: *I could hear crashing in the next room.*

ˌcrashing ˈbore noun [C] informal someone or something that is extremely boring: *I love his books, but in person he's a crashing bore.*

ˈcrash-land verb [I or T] to land an aircraft suddenly because of an emergency, sometimes resulting in serious damage or injuries: *The jet crash-landed and burst into flames.* • **ˈcrash-landing** noun [C] *The pilot attempted a crash-landing on the beach.*

crass /kræs/ adj stupid and without considering how other people might feel: *a crass remark* ◦ *crass behaviour/ignorance* ◦ *a crass error of judgment* ◦ *He made crass comments about her worn-out clothes.* • **crassly** /-li/ adv • **crassness** /-nəs/ noun [U]

crate /kreɪt/ noun; verb
▸noun [C] a box made of wood, plastic, or metal, especially one divided into parts to hold bottles: *a milk crate* ◦ *a crate of empty bottles* ◦ *a packing crate*
▸verb [T] to put something into a crate, especially in order to move it

crater /ˈkreɪ.tər/ (US) /-t̬ɚ/ noun [C] the hole at the top of a VOLCANO, or a hole in the ground similar to this: *the huge crater of Vesuvius* ◦ *a bomb crater* ◦ *With a good telescope, you can see craters on the moon.* • **cratered** /-təd/ (US) /-t̬əd/ adj *a cratered surface*

ˈcrater ˌlake noun [C] specialized a round lake that has formed in the crater of a VOLCANO

cravat /krəˈvæt/ noun [C] a wide, straight piece of material worn loosely tied in the open neck of a shirt

crave /kreɪv/ verb [T] C2 to have a strong feeling of wanting something: *Many young children crave **attention**.*

craven /ˈkreɪ.vən/ adj formal extremely COWARDLY (= not brave): *a craven act of terrorism*

craving /ˈkreɪ.vɪŋ/ noun [C] C2 a strong feeling of wanting something: *I have a craving **for** chocolate.*

crawl /krɔːl/ (US) /krɑːl/ verb; noun
▸verb **MOVE** ▷ **1** B2 [I] to move slowly or with difficulty, especially with your body stretched out along the ground or on hands and knees: *The child crawled **across** the floor.* ◦ *The injured soldier crawled to safety.* ◦ *Megan has just learned to crawl.* ◦ *The lorry crawled noisily up the hill.* **TRY TO PLEASE** ▷ **2** [I] informal disapproving to try hard to please in order to get an advantage: *I don't like people who crawl.* ◦ UK *He crawled **to** the group leader because he wanted a promotion.* **FILL** ▷ **3** **be crawling with sth** C2 informal to be completely covered with or full of a particular type of thing: *The kitchen floor was crawling with ants.*

IDIOM **crawl back (to sb)** to admit that you were wrong and ask someone to forgive you or ask them for something that you refused in the past: *Don't **come** crawling back to me when she throws you out!*

▸noun **SWIMMING** ▷ **1** C1 [S or U] a style of swimming in which you move your arms over your head and

kick with straight legs **MOVEMENT** ▷ **2** C1 [S] a very slow speed: *Traffic moved forward **at a crawl**.*

crawler /ˈkrɔː.lər/ (US) /ˈkrɑː.lɚ/ noun [C] **MOVING** ▷ **1** UK a baby who has not yet learned to walk **2** something, such as a vehicle, that moves very slowly **TRYING TO PLEASE** ▷ **3** UK informal disapproving a person who tries hard to please others in order to get an advantage

C

crayfish /ˈkreɪ.fɪʃ/ noun [C or U] (plural **crayfish** or **crayfishes**) (US also **crawfish** /ˈkrɔː-/) a small animal that lives in rivers and is similar to a LOBSTER, or its flesh eaten as food

crayon /ˈkreɪ.ɒn/ (US) /-ɑːn/ noun; verb
▸noun [C] a small stick of coloured WAX used for drawing or writing: *wax crayons* ◦ *children's crayons*
▸verb [I or T] UK to draw something with a crayon: *When I left her she was busy crayoning.*

craze /kreɪz/ noun [C usually singular] an activity, object, or idea that is extremely popular, usually for a short time: *Cycling shorts were **the latest** craze/(**all**) the craze that year.* ◦ *The craze **for** health foods has become big business.*

crazed /kreɪzd/ adj behaving in a wild or strange way, especially because of strong emotions or extreme pain: *a crazed expression* ◦ *He became crazed **with** anger/jealousy/pain.* ◦ *The horses bolted, crazed **with** fear.*

crazy /ˈkreɪ.zi/ adj; noun
▸adj **NOT SENSIBLE** ▷ **1** A2 stupid or not reasonable: *It's a crazy idea.* ◦ *You're crazy **to** buy a house without seeing it.* **2** mentally ill: *I seriously think she'll **go** crazy if she doesn't have a holiday soon.* **ANGRY** ▷ **3** B2 annoyed or angry: *The constant noise **drove** me crazy (= made me become angry).* • **crazily** /-zɪ.li/ adv • **craziness** /-nəs/ noun [U]

IDIOMS **be crazy about sb/sth** A2 to be very interested in something or love someone very much: *Both my sons are crazy about old motorbikes.* ◦ *Lorna is completely crazy about her boyfriend.* • **like crazy** informal C1 If you do something like crazy, you do a lot of it or do it very quickly: *They were working like crazy to get the job done on time.*

▸noun [C] US slang a person who behaves in a way that is stupid or not reasonable, especially one who is mentally ill: *There's some old crazy over there shouting and spitting at people.*

ˌcrazy ˈpaving noun [U] UK a hard surface for paths made with broken pieces of stone or concrete

creak /kriːk/ verb; noun
▸verb [I] When a door, floorboard, etc. creaks, it makes a long low sound when it moves or is moved: *The door creaked on its hinges.*
▸noun [C] a noise made when something creaks: *I heard a creak on the stairs.*

creaky /ˈkriː.ki/ adj **1** describes something that creaks: *a creaky hinge/chair/bed* ◦ *creaky floorboards* **2** UK describes something that is old-fashioned and not now effective: *the creaky legal system* • **creakily** /-kɪ.li/ adv • **creakiness** /-nəs/ noun [U]

cream /kriːm/ noun; adj; verb
▸noun **1** A2 [U] the thick, yellowish-white liquid that forms on the top of milk: *strawberries and cream* ◦ *Do you like cream in your coffee?* ◦ UK *a cream cake (= cake with cream in it)* **2** A2 [U] the colour of cream **3** B1 [C or U] a soft substance that you rub into your skin: *face/hand cream* ◦ *moisturizing cream* ◦ *Put some **sun** cream on to protect your face.* **4** [C] a type of sweet that is soft inside: *chocolate/peppermint creams* **5** [U] a

thick liquid used for cleaning things: *cream cleaner* **6 cream of mushroom, tomato, etc. soup** soup that has been made into a smooth thick liquid and usually has cream in it

IDIOM **the cream of sth** C1 the best of a particular group of things or people: *The cream of this year's graduates have gone abroad for jobs.* ◦ *These artists are the best of our students – the **cream of the crop**.*

▸**adj** A2 having a yellowish-white colour: *a cream shirt*
▸**verb** [T] to make food into a smooth, thick liquid: *Cream the butter and sugar together.*

PHRASAL VERB **cream sth/sb off** to remove the best part of something or the best people in a group and use them for your own advantage: *They had a plan to cream off the brightest children and put them in separate schools.*

ˌcream ˈcheese noun [C or U] (a) soft, white cheese that you spread rather than cut

ˌcream ˈcracker noun [C] UK a hard biscuit that is not sweet and is often eaten with cheese

creamer /ˈkriː.məʳ/ US /-mɚ/ **noun 1** [U] a powder that is added to hot drinks instead of milk or cream: *I've run out of milk – would you like some creamer instead?* **2** [C] US a small container for serving cream in

ˌcream of ˈtartar noun [U] a white powder used in baking

ˌcream ˈsoda noun [C or U] US (a) FIZZY drink (= with bubbles) with a VANILLA flavour

ˌcream ˈtea noun [C] mainly UK a light meal of SCONES (= small cakes) with jam and thick cream

creamy /ˈkriː.mi/ adj like cream or containing cream: *The chocolate mousse was smooth and creamy.* ◦ *a creamy sauce* • **creaminess** /-nəs/ **noun** [U]

crease /kriːs/ noun; verb
▸**noun FOLD** ▷ **1** [C] a line on cloth or paper where it has been folded or crushed: *He ironed a crease down the front of each trouser leg.* **CRICKET** ▷ **2** [S] UK specialized a line drawn on the ground where the player stands to hit the ball in cricket
▸**verb** [I or T] If cloth, paper, etc. creases, or if you crease it, it gets a line in it where it has been folded or crushed: *The seat belt has creased my blouse.* ◦ *It's a nice dress, but it creases very easily.*

PHRASAL VERB **crease (sb) up** UK informal to laugh a lot, or make someone else laugh a lot: *The look on his face just creased me up.*

creased /kriːst/ adj with a crease or creases: *Can you iron my shirt? It's really creased.*

create /kriˈeɪt/ verb **MAKE** ▷ **1** B1 [T] to make something new, or invent something: *Charles Schulz created the characters 'Snoopy' and 'Charlie Brown'.* ◦ *The Bible says that God created the world.* ◦ *He created a wonderful meal **from** very few ingredients.* ◦ *It's important to create a good impression when you meet a new client.* **BE ANGRY** ▷ **2** [I] UK old-fashioned to show that you are angry: *If she sees you with an ice cream she'll only start creating.*

creation /kriˈeɪ.ʃən/ noun [C or U] B2 the act of creating something, or the thing that is created: *the creation **of** a new political party* ◦ *Their policies all emphasize the creation **of** wealth.* ◦ *This 25-foot-high sculpture is her latest creation.* ◦ *The fashion magazines were full of the latest Paris creations (= fashionable new clothes).*

the Creˈation noun [S] in the BIBLE, the making of the world by God

creationist /kriˈeɪ.ʃən.ɪst/ **noun** [C] a person who believes that the world was made by God exactly as described in the BIBLE

creative /kriˈeɪ.tɪv/ US /-t̬ɪv/ **adj; noun**
▸**adj** B1 producing or using original and unusual ideas: *a creative person/artist/designer/programmer* ◦ *creative talents/powers/abilities* ◦ *creative thinking* • **creatively** /-li/ **adv** • **creativity** /ˌkriː.eɪˈtɪv.ɪ.ti/ US /-ˈt̬ɪv.ə.t̬i/ **noun** [U] (also **creativeness** /-nəs/) B2 *Too many rules might deaden creativity.* ◦ *Creativity, ingenuity, and flair are the songwriter's real talents.*
▸**noun** [C] specialized an employee whose imagination and artistic skills are very important for a company: *Several leading creatives are involved in the advertising campaign.*

creˌative acˈcounting noun [U] disapproving ways of explaining how money has been spent, that hide what has really happened to it

creˌative ˈwriting noun [U] the activity of writing stories, poetry, etc., or the stories, poems, etc. that are written: *I'm taking a course in creative writing.*

creator /kriˈeɪ.təʳ/ US /-t̬ɚ/ **noun** [C] someone who has invented something: *He's the creator **of** a successful cartoon series.* ◦ *Who was the creator **of** the miniskirt?*

the Creˈator noun [S] God

creature /ˈkriː.tʃəʳ/ US /-tʃɚ/ **noun** [C] **1** B1 any large or small living thing that can move independently: *Rainforests are filled with amazing creatures.* ◦ *Don't all **living** creatures have certain rights?* ◦ *Blue whales are the largest creatures ever to have lived.* **2** used to refer to a life form that is unusual or imaginary: *The unicorn is a mythical creature.* ◦ *The film was about creatures from outer space.* ◦ *The duck-billed platypus is a truly bizarre creature.* **3** used to refer to a person when an opinion is being expressed about them: *John is a strange/weak/pathetic creature.* ◦ *A lovely blonde creature (= a beautiful blonde woman) walked into the room.*

IDIOMS **be the creature of sb/sth** formal disapproving to do everything that you are asked to do by a particular person or organization, without question: *He had become the creature of the secret police.* • **creature of habit** someone who always does the same thing in the same way: *My father's such a creature of habit – he always has to have a biscuit and a cup of tea at bedtime.*

ˌcreature ˈcomforts noun [plural] things that make life more pleasant, such as good food and a comfortable place to live

crèche /kreʃ/ **noun** [C] **CHILDCARE** ▷ **1** mainly UK a place where young children are cared for during the day while their parents do something else, especially work, study, or shop: *Does your employer provide a crèche?* **CHRISTMAS SCENE** ▷ **2** US (UK **crib**) a model of the people and animals present at the birth of Jesus, used as a decoration at Christmas

cred /kred/ **noun** [U] UK slang **street cred**

credence /ˈkriː.dəns/ **noun** [U] formal the belief that something is true: *I'm not prepared to **give** credence **to** anonymous complaints.* ◦ *His bruises **added/lent** credence **to** his statement that he had been beaten.*

credential /krɪˈden.ʃəl/ **noun 1 credentials** [plural] the abilities and experience that make someone suitable for a particular job or activity, or proof of someone's abilities and experience: *All the candidates had excellent academic credentials.* ◦ *She was asked to show her press credentials.* **2** [C] a piece of information that is sent from one computer to another to check that a user is who they say they are or to allow someone to see information

credibility /ˌkred.əˈbɪl.ɪ.ti/ (US) /-ə.t̬i/ **noun** [U] (C2) the fact that someone can be believed or trusted: *His arrest for lewd behaviour seriously damaged his credibility* ***as*** *a religious leader.* ◦ *He complained that we had tried to undermine his credibility within the company.*

crediˈbility ˌgap **noun** [S] a difference between what is promised and what really happens

credible /ˈkred.ɪ.bl̩/ **adj** able to be believed or trusted: *They haven't produced any credible* ***evidence*** *for convicting him.* ◦ *The story of what had happened to her was* ***barely*** *(= almost not) credible.* • **credibly** /-bli/ **adv** *The family in the television programme could not be credibly compared with a real one.*

credit /ˈkred.ɪt/ **noun; verb**

▸**noun** PRAISE ▷ **1** (B2) [U] praise, approval, or honour: *She* ***got*** *no credit for solving the problem.* ◦ *Her boss* ***took*** *credit* ***for*** *it/****took*** *(all)* ***the*** *credit instead.* ◦ ***To*** *her (great) credit, she admitted she was wrong.* ◦ *I* ***gave*** *him credit* ***for*** *(= thought that he would have) better judgment than he showed.* **2 be a credit to sb/sth** to do something that makes a person, group, or organization feel proud or receive praise: *She is a credit to her family.* **3 do your family, parents, teacher, etc. credit** to cause someone who has been or is responsible for you to receive praise by your good behaviour or successful actions: *She does her teachers credit.* **4 all credit to sb** used to show that you think a person deserves a lot of praise for something that they have done: *All credit to her, she did it all herself.* MONEY ▷ **5** (B1) [U] a method of paying for goods or services at a later time, usually paying interest as well as the original money: *They decided to buy the car* ***on*** *credit.* ◦ *The shop was offering six months' (****interest-free****) credit* ***on*** *electrical goods.* → Compare **debit 6** (B1) [C or U] money in your bank account: *I was relieved to see from my statement that my account was* ***in*** *credit.* COURSE UNIT ▷ **7** (B2) [C] a unit that represents a successfully finished part of an educational course: *He's already got a credit/three credits in earth science.* LIST OF NAMES ▷ **8 the credits** [plural] a list of people who helped to make a film or a television or radio programme, that is shown or announced at the beginning or the end of it

IDIOM **credit where credit's due** an expression which means that you should praise someone who deserves it, although you might dislike some things about them: *I don't especially like the woman but, credit where credit's due, she's very efficient.*

▸**verb** PAY ▷ **1** [T] to pay money into a bank account: *They credited my account* ***with*** *$20 after I pointed out the mistake.* BELIEVE ▷ **2** [T not continuous] to believe something that seems unlikely to be true: *He even tried to pretend he was my son – can you credit it?* ◦ ***It*** *was hard* ***to*** *credit some of the stories we heard about her.*

PHRASAL VERB **credit sb with sth 1** to consider that someone has a particular quality: *I had credited them with more integrity than they showed.* **2** to say that someone is responsible for something good: *She is credited with making the business a success.*

creditable /ˈkred.ɪ.tə.bl̩/ (US) /-t̬ə-/ **adj** deserving praise, trust, or respect: *Our team came in a creditable third in the competition.* ◦ *The other, less creditable, reason for their decision was personal gain.*

ˈcredit acˌcount **noun** [C] UK (US **ˈcharge acˌcount**) a formal agreement between a shop or other business and a customer, in which the customer can take goods and pay the shop or business for them at a later time

ˈcredit ˌcard **noun** [C] (A1) a small plastic card that can be used as a method of payment, the money being taken from you at a later time

ˈcredit ˌcrunch **noun** [C usually singular] (UK also **ˈcredit ˌsqueeze**) economic conditions that make financial organizations less willing to lend money, often causing serious economic problems

ˈcredit ˌlimit **noun** [C] the largest amount of money that a bank allows you to spend using a credit card

ˈcredit ˌnote **noun** [C] UK a piece of paper given by a shop when you return something you do not want, that allows you to buy other goods of the same value

creditor /ˈkred.ɪ.təʳ/ (US) /-t̬ɚ/ **noun** [C] someone who money is owed to: *The company couldn't pay its creditors.* → Compare **debtor**

ˈcredit ˌrating **noun** [C usually singular] a calculation of someone's ability to pay back money that they have borrowed

ˈcredit ˌrisk **noun** [C or U] **1** a calculation of how likely it is that a person or company will not be able to pay back money they have borrowed from a bank or organization: *The scheme assesses the credit risk of new borrowers.* **2** a possibility that someone may not be able to pay back money that they have borrowed from a bank or organization: *corporate bonds with little credit risk/efforts to reduce credit risk*

ˈcredit ˌsqueeze **noun** [C] (also **ˈcredit ˌcrunch**) UK **credit crunch**

ˈcredit ˌterms **noun** [plural] the arrangements made for giving CREDIT, especially the amount of money, the period of borrowing, etc.

creditworthy /ˈkred.ɪtˌwɜː.ði/ (US) /-ˌwɜː-/ **adj** describes someone who has enough money or property for banks and other organizations to be willing to lend them money • **creditworthiness** /-nəs/ **noun** [U]

credo /ˈkreɪ.dəʊ/ (US) /ˈkriː.doʊ/ **noun** [C] (plural **credos**) formal a set of beliefs that influences the way you live → Synonym **creed**

credulity /krəˈdjuː.lə.ti/ (US) /-ˈduː.lə.t̬i/ **noun** [U] (also **credulousness**) formal willingness to believe that something is real or true, especially when this is unlikely

credulous /ˈkred.jʊ.ləs/ **adj** formal too willing to believe what you are told and so easily deceived → Synonym **gullible** • **credulously** /-li/ **adv**

creed /kriːd/ **noun** [C] formal a set of beliefs that influences the way you live → Synonym **credo**

the Creed /kriːd/ **noun** [S] specialized a short, formal statement of Christian religious belief, said in church

creek /kriːk/ **noun** [C] **1** UK a narrow area of water that flows into the land from the sea, a lake, etc. **2** US a stream or narrow river

IDIOM **up the creek** informal in trouble: *If any more people resign, we'll be really up the creek.*

creep /kriːp/ **verb; noun**

▸**verb** [I usually + adv/prep] (**crept, crept**) (C2) to move slowly, quietly, and carefully, usually in order to avoid being noticed: *She turned off the light and crept* ***through*** *the door.* ◦ *Someone was creeping* ***around*** *outside my window.* ◦ *The spider crept up the wall.* ◦ *The traffic was creeping* ***along*** *at a snail's pace.*

PHRASAL VERBS **creep in/creep into sth 1** mainly UK If mistakes creep in or creep into a piece of text, they are included despite efforts not to include them: *A few mistakes always creep in during the editing process.* ◦ *One or two typing errors crept into the report.* **2** to gradually start to be noticeable: *Doubts began to creep into my **mind** about the likely success of the project.* • **creep over sb** If a bad feeling creeps over someone, they gradually start to feel it: *A dangerous tiredness crept over her as she drove.* • **creep up** If the value or amount of something creeps up, it slowly increases: *Over the last year, the rate of inflation has crept up to almost seven percent.* • **creep up on/behind sb** to surprise someone by moving closer to them without them seeing or hearing you: *Don't creep up on me like that!* ◦ *We crept up behind her and yelled 'Boo!'* • **creep up on sb** If a feeling or state creeps up on someone, they start to experience it so gradually that they do not realize it: *It was only after I turned 60 that old age began to creep up on me.*

▸**noun** informal **PERSON** ▷ **1** [C] UK someone who tries to make someone more important like them by being very polite and helpful in a way that is not sincere: *Making coffee for the boss again? You creep!* **2** Ⓒ [C] an unpleasant person, especially a man: *He was a real creep – he was always staring at me in the canteen.* ◦ [as form of address] *Leave me alone, creep!* **3 give sb the creeps** to cause someone to have uncomfortable feelings of nervousness or fear: *Living next to a graveyard would give me the creeps.*

creeper /ˈkriː.pəʳ/ ⓤⓢ /-pɚ/ **noun** [C] a plant that grows along the ground, or up walls or trees

creeping /kriː.pɪŋ/ **adj** [before noun] disapproving happening, developing, or moving slowly or gradually: *We are totally against any form of creeping Socialism.*

ˈcreeping ˌplant **noun** [C] a plant that grows along the ground

creepy /ˈkriː.pi/ **adj** informal strange or unnatural and making you feel frightened: *a creepy film* ◦ *a creepy smile*

creepy-crawly /ˌkriː.piˈkrɔː.li/ ⓤⓢ /-ˈkrɑː.li/ **noun** [C] informal a small insect that gives you a feeling of fear and dislike

cremate /krɪˈmeɪt/ ⓤⓢ /ˈkriː.meɪt/ **verb** [T] to burn a dead person's body, usually as part of a funeral ceremony • **cremation** /krɪˈmeɪ.ʃən/ **noun** [C or U]

crematorium /ˌkrem.əˈtɔː.ri.əm/ ⓤⓢ /-ˈtɔːr.i-/ **noun** [C] (plural **crematoriums** or **crematoria** /-ə/) (US also **crematory** /ˈkrem.ə.tər.i/ ⓤⓢ /ˈkriː.mə.tɔːr.i/) a building where dead people's bodies are burned, usually as part of a funeral ceremony

crème brûlée /ˌkrem.bruːˈleɪ/ **noun** [C or U] a sweet food made from CUSTARD (= a sweet, soft mixture of milk, eggs, and sugar) with hard, burnt sugar on top

crème caramel /ˌkrem.kær.əˈmel/ ⓤⓢ /-ker-/ **noun** [C or U] a sweet food made from CUSTARD (= a sweet, soft mixture of milk, eggs, and sugar) with soft, brown liquid sugar on top

the crème de la crème /ˌkrem.də.lɑːˈkrem/ **noun** [S] the best people in a group or the best type of a particular thing: *She was hoping to attract the crème de la crème **of** the art world to her exhibition.*

crème de menthe /ˌkrem.dəˈmɑːnθ/ **noun** [U] a sweet alcoholic drink with a MINT flavour

crème fraîche /ˌkremˈfreʃ/ **noun** [U] a type of thick cream with a slightly sour taste

crenellated specialized (US usually **crenelated**) /ˈkren.əl.eɪ.tɪd/ ⓤⓢ /-t̬ɪd/ **adj** having BATTLEMENTS (= castle walls with regular spaces along the top) • **crenellations** (US usually **crenelations**) /ˌkren.əlˈeɪ.ʃənz/ **noun** [plural]

creole /kriˈəʊl/ ⓤⓢ /-ˈoʊl/ **noun** [C or U] a language that has developed from a mixture of languages: *creole-speaking tribes*

Creole /kriˈəʊl/ ⓤⓢ /-ˈoʊl/ **noun** **LANGUAGE** ▷ **1** [C or U] an American or Caribbean language that is a combination of a European language and another language and is a main language in parts of the southern US and the Caribbean **PERSON** ▷ **2** [C] someone who is related to the first Europeans who came to the Caribbean or the southern US **3** [C] a person of mixed African and European origin who speaks Creole • **Creole adj** *I love Creole cooking, so hot and spicy.*

creosote /ˈkriː.ə.səʊt/ ⓤⓢ /-soʊt/ **noun**; **verb**

▸**noun** [U] a thick, brown liquid used especially for protecting wood

▸**verb** [T] to put creosote on something: *James and I creosoted the fence.*

crepe **noun** **FOOD** ▷ **1** (also **crêpe**) /krep/ [C] mainly US a thin, light PANCAKE **CLOTH** ▷ **2** (UK also **crêpe, crape**) /kreɪp/ [U] thin cloth with a surface that has WRINKLES (= small, thin folds): *a black crepe dress* ◦ *a crepe jacket* **RUBBER** ▷ **3** (also **crêpe**) /kreɪp/ [U] a strong type of rubber with a rough surface, used especially for making the bottom of shoes: *crepe-soled shoes*

ˌcrepe ˈpaper (UK also **ˌcrêpe ˈpaper**) **noun** [U] thin, usually brightly coloured paper, used especially for making party decorations

crept /krept/ **verb** past simple and past participle of **creep**

crepuscular /krɪˈpʌs.kjʊ.ləʳ/ ⓤⓢ /-lɚ/ **adj** literary relating to or like the time of day just before the sun goes down, when the light is not bright

crescendo /krɪˈʃen.dəʊ/ ⓤⓢ /-doʊ/ **noun** [C usually singular] (plural **crescendos**) **1** a gradual increase in loudness, or the moment when a noise or piece of music is at its loudest: *The music **reached** a crescendo.* **2** an increase in excitement, danger, or action: *There has been a **rising** crescendo **of** violence in the region.*

crescent /ˈkres.ənt/ **noun** [C] **1** (something with) a curved shape that has two narrow pointed ends, like the moon when it is less than half of a circle: *The moon was a brightly shining crescent.* **2** a row of houses or a road built in a curve: *They live at 15 Park Crescent.* • **crescent adj** *the crescent moon*

cress /kres/ **noun** [U] any of various plants with small, green leaves, used especially in salads: *egg and cress sandwiches* → See also **watercress**

crest /krest/ **noun** [C] **TOP** ▷ **1** the top or highest part of something such as a wave or a hill: *the crest of a hill/wave* **2** a growth of feathers, fur, or skin along the top of the heads of some animals **3** a decoration, usually made of feathers or animal hair, on the top of a soldier's hat, especially in the past **PICTURE** ▷ **4** a formal design that is used by a family, town, organization, etc. as the symbol that represents them: *a royal crest*

IDIOM **be riding/on the crest of a wave** to be very successful for a limited period of time: *Mrs Singh is still riding the crest of a wave **of** popularity.*

crested /ˈkres.tɪd/ **adj** **WITH TOP** ▷ **1** A crested bird has a growth of feathers on its head: *a crested grebe* **WITH PICTURE** ▷ **2** Crested paper has a crest (= design) at the top: *crested writing paper*

crestfallen /ˈkrestˌfɔː.lən/ ⓤⓢ /-ˌfɑː-/ **adj** disappointed and sad because of having failed unexpectedly: *He looked crestfallen at their decision.*

Cretaceous /krɪˈteɪ.ʃəs/ ⓤⓢ /kretˈeɪ-/ **adj** from or referring to the period of GEOLOGICAL time between around 144 and 65 million years ago, in which plants with flowers first appeared: *the Cretaceous age/*

period ◦ *Cretaceous rocks* • **the Cretaceous** noun the Cretaceous period

cretin /ˈkret.ɪn/ (US) /ˈkriː.t̬ən/ noun [C] offensive a very stupid person • **cretinous** /ˈkret.ɪ.nəs/ (US) /ˈkriː.t̬ən-/ adj

Creutzfeldt-Jakob disease /ˌkrɔɪts.feltˈjæk.ɒb.dɪˌziːz/ (US) /-ˈjɑː.kɑːb-/ noun [U] (abbreviation **CJD**) a disease that damages the brain and the main nerves connected to it and usually causes death

crevasse /krəˈvæs/ noun [C] a very deep CRACK in the thick ice of a GLACIER (= moving mass of ice)

crevice /ˈkrev.ɪs/ noun [C] a small, narrow CRACK or space, especially in the surface of rock

crew /kruː/ noun; verb

▸noun **1** B1 [C, + sing/pl verb] a group of people who work together, especially all those who work on and operate a ship, aircraft, etc.: *an ambulance/lifeboat crew* ◦ *a TV/film/camera crew* ◦ *The aircraft* ***has/carries*** *a crew of seven.* → See also **aircrew** **2** [C] the people who work on a ship, aircraft, etc. who are not officers: *Apart from the ten officers, a crew of 90 looks after the 300 passengers.*

▸verb [I or T] If you crew a boat, or crew for someone on their boat, you help to sail it.

ˈcrew ˌcut noun [C] (also **ˈbuzz ˌcut**) a hairstyle in which the hair is cut very short

ˈcrew ˌmember noun [C] (also **crewman** /kruː.mən/) a member of a group of people who work together, especially on a ship

ˈcrew ˌneck noun [C] a round neck hole on a shirt, or a shirt with a neck hole in this shape

crib /krɪb/ noun; verb

▸noun [C] **BED** ▷ **1** US for COT (= a small bed for a baby) **CHRISTMAS SCENE** ▷ **2** UK (US **crèche**) a model of the people and animals present at the birth of Jesus Christ, used as a decoration at Christmas **HOME** ▷ **3** US slang Someone's crib is their home or the place where they are living at present.

▸verb [I or T] (**-bb-**) informal disapproving to copy someone else's work, especially dishonestly: *I got chucked out of the exam for cribbing* ***from*** *the guy in front.*

ˈcrib ˌdeath noun [C or U] US for **cot death**

ˈcrib ˌsheet noun [C] (US **ˈcrib ˌnotes**) a piece of paper that contains notes or information, especially one used for cheating during an examination

crick /krɪk/ noun [C] a painful, usually sudden stiffness in a group of muscles in the neck or back: *I got a crick* ***in*** *my neck from painting the ceiling.* • **crick** verb [T] *I cricked my neck while I was painting the ceiling.*

cricket /ˈkrɪk.ɪt/ noun **GAME** ▷ **1** A2 [U] a sport in which two teams of eleven players try to score RUNS (= points) by hitting a small, hard ball with a BAT, and running between two sets of small wooden posts: *a cricket ball/bat* **INSECT** ▷ **2** C2 [C] a brown or black insect that makes short, loud noises by rubbing its wings together

IDIOM **not cricket** UK old-fashioned or humorous If behaviour is not cricket, it is not honest or moral: *It's simply not cricket to flirt with another man's wife.*

cricketer /ˈkrɪk.ɪ.təʳ/ (US) /-t̬ɚ/ noun [C] a cricket player

cricketing /ˈkrɪk.ɪ.tɪŋ/ (US) /-t̬ɪŋ/ adj [before noun] relating to the sport of cricket: *the cricketing* ***world***

cri de coeur /ˌkriː.dəˈkɜːʳ/ (US) /-ˈkɝː/ noun [C usually singular] (plural **cris de coeur**) an urgent and strongly felt request for help from someone in a very bad situation

cried /kraɪd/ verb past simple and past participle of **cry**

crikey /ˈkraɪ.ki/ exclamation UK old-fashioned informal an expression of surprise

crime /kraɪm/ noun **1** B1 [U] illegal activities: *a life of crime* ◦ *rising crime* ◦ *crime prevention* ◦ ***petty*** (= unimportant) *crime/****serious*** *crime* **2** B1 [C] an illegal act: *He has admitted* ***committing*** *several crimes, including fraud.* ◦ *The defendant is* ***accused of/charged with*** *a range of crimes, from theft to murder.* ◦ *A knife was found at* ***the scene of the*** *crime (= the place where the crime happened).* ◦ *Bombing civilians is a crime* ***against humanity*** *(= a cruel crime against many people).* **3** [S] an unacceptable or very silly act or situation: *To have hundreds of homeless people sleeping in the streets of a rich city like London is* ***a*** *crime.* ◦ ***It*** *would be* ***a*** *crime (= a waste)* ***to*** *spend such a beautiful day indoors.*

> **Word partners for crime**
>
> *commit* (a) crime • *combat/fight/reduce* crime • *accuse* sb of a crime • *investigate/solve* a crime • (a) *serious/violent* crime • *petty* crime • a crime *against* sth/sb

IDIOM **crime doesn't pay** saying said to emphasize that you believe criminals are always punished for their crimes

ˌcrime of ˈpassion noun [C] a crime committed because of very strong emotional feelings, especially in connection with a sexual relationship

ˈcrime-ridden adj used for describing an area where there is a lot of crime: *our crime-ridden streets*

ˈcrime ˌwave noun [C usually singular] a sudden increase in the number of crimes

criminal /ˈkrɪm.ɪ.nəl/ noun; adj

▸noun [C] B1 someone who commits a crime: *a dangerous/violent criminal*

▸adj [before noun] **1** B2 relating to crime: *criminal activity* ◦ *a criminal act/offence* ◦ *criminal behaviour* ◦ *a criminal investigation* **2** very bad or morally wrong: ***It's*** *criminal* ***to*** *charge so much for a book.* ◦ *The way we waste this planet's resources is criminal.* • **criminality** /ˌkrɪm.ɪˈnæl.ɪ.ti/ (US) /-ə.t̬i/ noun [U] • **criminally** /-i/ adv

ˌcriminal ˈcourt noun [C] a law court that deals with criminal cases

ˌcriminal ˈdamage noun [U] serious damage that is against the law

criminalize (UK usually **criminalise**) /ˈkrɪm.ɪ.nə.laɪz/ verb [T] to make something illegal: *The law has criminalized prostitution but not got rid of it.*

ˌcriminal ˈjustice ˌsystem noun [S] the system in a society by which people who are accused of crimes are judged in court

ˌcriminal ˈlaw noun [U] the part of the legal system that relates to punishing people who break the law

ˌcriminal ˈrecord noun [C] an official record of crimes that a person has committed: *They fired him when they found out he had a criminal record.*

criminology /ˌkrɪm.ɪˈnɒl.ə.dʒi/ (US) /-ˈnɑː.lə-/ noun [U] the scientific study of crime and criminals • **criminologist** /-dʒɪst/ noun [C] someone who studies crime and criminals

crimp /krɪmp/ verb [T] to press cloth, paper, etc. into small folds along its edges, or to press hair into a series of folds using a heated device

Crimplene /ˈkrɪm.pliːn/ noun [U] UK trademark an artificial cloth, used for clothes, that does not easily CREASE (= develop unwanted folds and lines)

crimson /ˈkrɪm.zən/ **adj; noun**

▸**adj 1** having a dark, deep red colour **2 go/turn crimson** If you go/turn crimson, your face becomes red because you are very embarrassed or angry: *She went crimson* ***with*** *embarrassment.*

▸**noun** [U] a dark, deep red colour

C

cringe /krɪndʒ/ **verb** [I] **1** to suddenly move away from someone or something because you are frightened **2** informal to feel very embarrassed: *I cringed* ***at*** *the sight of my dad dancing.*

ˈcringe-ˌmaking adj UK informal describes someone or something that is so bad that you feel embarrassed: *Then there were his cringe-making attempts at humour.*

crinkle /ˈkrɪŋ.kl̩/ **verb** [I or T] to become covered in many small lines and folds, or to cause something to do this: *She crinkled (****up****) her nose in distaste.* • **crinkle noun** [C] • **crinkled** /-kl̩d/ **adj** • **crinkly** /-kli/ **adj**

crinoline /ˈkrɪn.əl.ɪn/ **noun** [C] a stiff frame worn under a woman's skirt to give it a full appearance, especially in the 19th century

cripes /kraɪps/ **exclamation** UK old-fashioned informal an expression of surprise

cripple /ˈkrɪp.l̩/ **noun; verb**

▸**noun** [C] **1** offensive old-fashioned a person who cannot use their arms or legs in a normal way **2 emotional cripple** informal someone who finds it difficult to have or express feelings

▸**verb** [T] **1** to injure someone so that they are unable to walk or move in a normal way **2** to cause serious damage to someone or something, making them weak and not effective: *a country crippled by war* • **crippled** /-l̩d/ **adj** describes someone with serious injuries that affect their ability to walk or move: *Will she be crippled* ***for life****?* • **crippling** /-l̩.ɪŋ/, /-.lɪŋ/ **adj** describes something that causes someone serious injuries or harm: *A crippling attack of malaria kept him in bed for months.* ◦ *crippling debts*

crisis /ˈkraɪ.sɪs/ **noun** (plural **crises** /-siːz/) **1** B2 [C or U] a time of great disagreement, confusion, or suffering: *The country's leadership is* ***in crisis****.* ◦ *an economic/financial crisis* ◦ *I've got a family crisis on my hands – my 16-year-old sister is pregnant.* **2** [C] an extremely difficult or dangerous point in a situation: *crisis talks* ◦ *A mediator has been called in to* ***resolve*** *the crisis.* **3** [C] a moment during a serious illness when there is the possibility of suddenly getting either better or worse: *He's passed the crisis – the fever's started to go down.* **4 a crisis of confidence** a sudden loss of confidence: *With inflation at 500 percent, the country faces a crisis of confidence.*

crisp /krɪsp/ **adj; noun**

▸**adj** mainly approving **HARD** ▷ **1** hard enough to be broken easily **2** describes cooked foods, such as pastry and biscuits, that are well cooked so that they are just dry and hard enough **3** describes fruit or vegetables that are fresh and firm: *a crisp apple* **4** C2 describes paper or cloth that is stiff and smooth: *a crisp new £5 note/a crisp white tablecloth* **CLEAR** ▷ **5** describes sound or an image that is very clear: *Now that we have cable, we get a wonderfully crisp picture.* **6** describes a way of speaking, writing, or behaving that is quick, confident, and effective: *a crisp reply* ◦ *a crisp, efficient manner* **COLD** ▷ **7** C2 describes weather that is cold, dry, and bright: *a wonderful crisp spring morning* **8** describes air that is cold, dry, and fresh: *I breathed in deeply the crisp mountain air.* • **crisply** /-li/ **adv** • **crispness** /-nəs/ **noun** [U]

▸**noun POTATO** ▷ **1** A2 [C usually plural] UK (US **(potato) chip**) a very thin, often round piece of fried potato, sometimes with a flavour added, sold especially in plastic bags: ***a packet of*** *salt and vinegar crisps* **SWEET FOOD** ▷ **2** [C] US for **crumble**

crispbread /ˈkrɪsp.bred/ **noun** [C or U] UK a hard, dry, flat, salty biscuit, often eaten instead of bread by people trying to lose weight

crispy /ˈkrɪs.pi/ **adj** approving describes food that is hard enough to be broken easily: *crispy bacon*

criss-cross /ˈkrɪs.krɒs/ US /-krɑːs/ **verb** [I or T] to move or exist in a pattern of lines crossing something or each other: *This area of the city is criss-crossed by railway lines.* • **criss-cross adj** *a criss-cross pattern*

criterion /kraɪˈtɪə.ri.ən/ US /-ˈtɪr.i-/ **noun** [C] (plural **criteria** /-ri.ə/ US /-ˈtɪr.i.ə/) C1 a standard by which you judge, decide about, or deal with something: *The Health Service should not be judged by financial criteria alone.*

critic /ˈkrɪt.ɪk/ US /ˈkrɪţ-/ **noun** [C] **1** C1 someone who says that they do not approve of someone or something: *Her critics say she is leading the party to disaster.* **2** B2 someone whose job is to give their opinion about something, especially films, books, music, etc.: *She's a film/theatre critic for the 'Irish Times'.* ◦ *The play has been well received by the critics.*

critical /ˈkrɪt.ɪ.kəl/ US /ˈkrɪţ-/ **adj NOT PLEASED** ▷ **1** B2 saying that someone or something is bad or wrong: *a critical report* ◦ *The report is* ***highly*** *critical* ***of*** *safety standards at the factory.* **IMPORTANT** ▷ **2** B2 of the greatest importance to the way things might happen: *The president's support is critical (****to*** *this project).* ◦ *a critical decision* **GIVING OPINIONS** ▷ **3** C2 giving opinions or judgments on books, plays, films, etc.: *She has written a major critical appraisal/study of Saul Bellow's novels.* ◦ *His last film* ***won/received*** *critical* ***acclaim*** *(= was praised by film critics).* **SERIOUS** ▷ **4** B2 extremely serious or dangerous: *Both drivers are critical/in a critical* ***condition*** *(= so badly hurt that they might die) after the 120 mph crash.* • **critically** /-i/ **adv** B2 *a critically* ***acclaimed*** *TV series* ◦ *They were both critically* ***injured*** *in the crash.*

ˌcritical ˈmass noun [C usually singular or U] **1** specialized the smallest amount of matter that is needed to produce a nuclear CHAIN REACTION **2** the size that something needs to reach before a particular change, event, or development can happen

ˌcritical ˈthinking noun [U] the process of thinking carefully about a subject or idea, without allowing feelings or opinions to affect you

criticism /ˈkrɪt.ɪ.sɪ.zəm/ US /ˈkrɪţ-/ **noun** [C or U] **1** B2 the act of saying that something or someone is bad: *The designs for the new mosque have attracted* ***widespread*** *criticism.* ◦ *I have a few criticisms to make* ***of/about*** *your speech.* **2** the act of giving your opinion or judgment about the good or bad qualities of something or someone, especially books, films, etc.: ***literary*** *criticism* ◦ *If you've got any* ***constructive*** *(= helpful) criticism of the project, I'd be glad to hear it.*

criticize (UK usually **criticise**) /ˈkrɪt.ɪ.saɪz/ US /ˈkrɪţ-/ **verb 1** B2 [I, T often passive] to express disapproval of someone or something: *The government is being widely criticized in the press* ***for*** *fail****ing*** *to limit air pollution.* ◦ *We'll get nowhere if all you can do is criticize.* **2** [T] to give an opinion or judgment about a book, film, etc.: *We're a group of artists who meet to discuss ideas and criticize each other's work.*

critique /krɪˈtiːk/ **noun** [C] a report of something such as a political situation or system, or a person's work or ideas, that examines it and provides a

Other ways of saying criticize

Attack, **condemn**, and **denounce** can all be used when someone criticizes someone or something severely:

*She wrote an article **attacking** the judge and the way the trial had been conducted.*

*She was **condemned** for her comments about the candidate.*

*The government's economic policy has been **denounced** on all sides.*

If someone is criticized strongly and publicly, you could also use the phrase **come under fire**:

*The government programme has **come under fire** for mismanaging funds.*

A formal word that means the same as 'criticize' is **censure**:

*The trial judge was **censured** for incompetence.*

Blast and **pan** are both informal ways of saying 'criticize':

*The senator **blasted** the president's record on taxes, foreign policy, and the economy.*

*Her latest movie has been **panned** by critics.*

If a person criticizes someone in a very unpleasant way, you can also use the informal verb **bad-mouth**:

*The coach was suspended for **bad-mouthing** a referee.*

If you think someone is criticizing something unfairly, you could use the phrase **find fault with**:

*He's always **finding fault with** my work.*

If you think someone is criticizing a person or thing unfairly, you could use the verbs **knock** or **run down**:

*Don't **knock** him. He's trying his best.*

*Stop **running him down**.*

judgment, especially a negative one: *a Marxist critique of neo-liberal policy*

critter /ˈkrɪt.əʳ/ ⓤⓢ /ˈkrɪt̬.ɚ/ **noun** [C] (also **crittur**) US not standard a creature

croak /krəʊk/ ⓤⓢ /kroʊk/ **verb; noun**

▸**verb** MAKE SOUND ▷ **1** [I or T] When animals such as FROGS and CROWS croak, they make deep rough sounds. **2** If you croak, you speak with a rough voice because you have a sore or dry throat. DIE ▷ **3** [I] slang to die

▸**noun** [C] a deep, rough sound made by a person or animal

crochet /ˈkrəʊ.ʃeɪ/ ⓤⓢ /kroʊˈʃeɪ/ **verb** [I or T] to make clothes and other things using wool and a special needle with a HOOK (= curve) at one end • **crochet** noun [U] • **crocheted** /ˈkrəʊ.ʃeɪd/ ⓤⓢ /kroʊˈʃeɪd/ adj

ˈcrochet ˌhook **noun** [C] a needle with a HOOK at one end that is used to crochet with

crock /krɒk/ ⓤⓢ /krɑːk/ **noun** [C] CONTAINER ▷ **1** a container, usually one made of clay: *He keeps his coffee in an earthenware crock.* CAR/PERSON ▷ **2** UK slang an old person or car

IDIOM **a crock (of shit)** US offensive something that is not true or useful: *His presentation was a crock of shit.*

crockery /ˈkrɒk.ər.i/ ⓤⓢ /ˈkrɑː.kɚ-/ **noun** [U] UK old-fashioned cups, plates, bowls, etc., used to serve food and drink, especially made of CHINA → Compare **cutlery**

crocodile /ˈkrɒk.ə.daɪl/ ⓤⓢ /ˈkrɑː.kə-/ **noun** [C] (plural **crocodiles** or **crocodile**) ANIMAL ▷ **1** B2 (informal **croc** /krɒk/ ⓤⓢ /krɑːk/) a large reptile with a hard skin that lives in and near rivers and lakes in hot, wet parts of the world. It is like an ALLIGATOR, but it usually has a longer and narrower nose: *a crocodile-infested swamp* LINE ▷ **2** UK informal a line of people, especially children, who are walking in pairs

ˈcrocodile ˌtears **noun** [plural] tears that you cry when you are not really sad or sorry

crocus /ˈkrəʊ.kəs/ ⓤⓢ /ˈkroʊ-/ **noun** [C] a small yellow, white, or purple spring flower

croft /krɒft/ ⓤⓢ /krɑːft/ **noun** [C] UK (especially in Scotland) a very small farm around a house, or the house itself • **crofter** /ˈkrɒf.təʳ/ ⓤⓢ /ˈkrɑːf.tɚ/ **noun** [C] someone who lives and works on a croft

Crohn's disease /ˈkrəʊnz.dɪˌziːz/ ⓤⓢ /ˈkroʊnz-/ **noun** [S] a disease that makes the INTESTINES swollen and sore

croissant /ˈkwæs.ɒ̃ːŋ/ ⓤⓢ /kwɑːˈsɑ̃ː/ **noun** [C] a piece of light CRESCENT-shaped pastry, usually eaten in the morning

cromlech /ˈkrɒm.lek/ ⓤⓢ /ˈkrɑːm-/ **noun** [C] (plural **cromlechs**) a DOLMEN (= an ancient group of stones consisting of one large flat stone supported by several vertical ones)

crone /krəʊn/ ⓤⓢ /kroʊn/ **noun** [C] an unpleasant or ugly old woman

crony /ˈkrəʊ.ni/ ⓤⓢ /ˈkroʊ-/ **noun** [C] informal disapproving a friend, or a person who works for someone in authority, especially one who is willing to give and receive dishonest help: *The general and his cronies are now awaiting trial for drug smuggling.*

cronyism /ˈkrəʊ.ni.ɪzm/ ⓤⓢ /ˈkroʊ-/ **noun** [U] disapproving the situation in which someone important gives jobs to friends rather than to independent people who have the necessary skills and experience

crook /krʊk/ **noun; adj; verb**

▸**noun** CRIMINAL ▷ **1** [C] informal a very dishonest person, especially a criminal or a cheat: *These politicians are just a bunch of crooks.* BEND ▷ **2 the crook of your arm** the inside part of your arm where it bends STICK ▷ **3** [C] a long stick with a curved end, especially one carried by a SHEPHERD or a BISHOP

▸**adj** Australian English informal bad or ill

▸**verb** [T] old-fashioned to bend your arm or finger: *She delicately crooked her little finger as she picked up her cup.*

crooked /ˈkrʊk.ɪd/ **adj** BENT ▷ **1** not forming a straight line, or having many bends: *You have to drive slowly on these crooked country roads.* ◦ *His front teeth are crooked.* CRIMINAL ▷ **2** informal dishonest: *crooked police officers* • **crookedly** /-li/ adv *She smiled crookedly at me.*

croon /kruːn/ **verb** [I or T] to sing or talk in a sweet, low voice full of emotion

crooner /ˈkruː.nəʳ/ ⓤⓢ /-nɚ/ **noun** [C] old-fashioned a singer, especially a man, who sings love songs

crop /krɒp/ ⓤⓢ /krɑːp/ **noun; verb**

▸**noun** PLANT ▷ **1** B1 [C] (the total amount collected of) a plant such as a grain, fruit, or vegetable grown in large amounts: *The main crops grown for export are coffee and rice.* ◦ *a **bumper** (= very good) potato crop* GROUP ▷ **2** [C usually singular] informal a group of people or things with something in common, that exist at a particular time: *The judges will select the best from this year's crop **of** first novels.* HAIRSTYLE ▷ **3** [C] a short hairstyle: *She's had a very short crop.* THROAT ▷ **4** [C] a part of the throat in many birds where food is stored before going into the stomach STICK ▷ **5** [C] a short stick used to control a horse by hitting it

▸**verb** (-pp-) CUT ▷ **1** [T] to make something shorter or smaller, especially by cutting: *He had his hair cropped when he went into the army.* **2** [T] When animals such as sheep or horses crop grass or other plants, they eat the top parts. **3** [T] to remove some or all of the edges from a picture, leaving only the most important part: *He cropped the photo so that only the face remained.* **PLANT** ▷ **4** [I usually + adv/prep] If a plant crops, it produces fruit, flowers, etc.: *The carrots have cropped (= grown) well this year.* **5** [T usually passive] to grow crops on land: *The land is intensively cropped.*

PHRASAL VERB **crop up** informal to happen or appear unexpectedly: *Her name keeps cropping up **in** conversation.*

cropper /ˈkrɒp.əʳ/ ⓤⓢ /ˈkrɑː.pɚ/ **noun** informal **come a cropper** to fail badly, or to fall from a horse or have a bad accident in a vehicle: *Having reached the final, the British have come a cropper against the more experienced German team.* ◦ *She came an almighty cropper when her back wheels hit an icy patch.*

ˈcrop roˌtation noun [U] a method of farming where a number of different plants are grown one after the other on a field so that the soil stays healthy and FERTILE (= able to produce crops)

ˈcrop ˌspraying noun [U] (also **ˈcrop ˌdusting**) a way of covering crops with chemicals in order to kill harmful insects and diseases, sometimes from an aircraft

ˈcrop ˌtop noun [C] a piece of clothing for a woman's top half that does not cover her stomach

croquet /ˈkrəʊ.keɪ/ ⓤⓢ /kroʊˈkeɪ/ **noun** [U] a game in which two, three, or four players use MALLETS (= long wooden hammers) to hit wooden balls through small metal HOOPS (= curves) fixed into the grass

croquette /krəˈket/ ⓤⓢ /kroʊ-/ **noun** [C] a small, rounded mass of food, such as meat, fish, or potato, that has been cut into small pieces, pressed together, covered in BREADCRUMBS and fried

crore /krɔːʳ/ ⓤⓢ /krɔːr/ **number** Indian English ten million: *Private airlines owe a total of Rs 14,573 crore to state-run banks.*

crosier /ˈkrəʊ.zi.əʳ/ ⓤⓢ /ˈkroʊ.zi.ɚ/ **noun** [C] a **crozier**

cross /krɒs/ ⓤⓢ /krɑːs/ **verb; noun; adj**

▸**verb GO ACROSS** ▷ **1** Ⓐ2 [I or T] to go across from one side of something to the other: *It's not a good place to cross the road.* ◦ *Look both ways before you cross **over** (= cross the road).* ◦ *Cross the bridge and turn right.* ◦ *They crossed **from** Albania **into** Greece.* **2 cross sb's mind** Ⓑ2 If something crosses your mind, you think of it: *It crossed my mind yesterday that you must be a bit short of staff.* ◦ *It never once crossed my mind that she might be unhappy.* **3 cross your arms/fingers/legs** to put one of your arms, fingers, or legs over the top of the other: *She sat down and crossed her legs.* **ANNOY** ▷ **4** to annoy someone by not doing or saying what they want: *I wouldn't cross him if I were you, not if you value your life.* **MIX** ▷ **5** If you cross a plant or animal with another of a different type, you cause them to breed together in order to produce a new VARIETY (= type of plant or animal). **MAKE SIGN** ▷ **6** UK specialized to draw two lines across the middle of a CHEQUE to show that it must be paid into a bank account: *a crossed cheque* **7 cross yourself** UK specialized When Christians cross themselves, they move their hand down and then across their face or chest, making the shape of a cross.

IDIOMS **cross your fingers** to hope very much that something will happen: *I'm just going to cross my fingers and hope it works.* • **cross sb's hand/palm with silver** to give someone money so that they will tell you what will happen to you in the future • **cross my heart (and hope to die)** saying said to show that what you have just said or promised is completely true or sincere • **cross sb's path/cross paths with sb** Ⓒ2 to meet someone, especially by chance: *I hope I don't cross his path/cross paths with him again.* • **cross swords** to have an argument with someone • **I'll/we'll cross that bridge when I/we come/get to it** an expression that means you will not worry about a possible future problem but will deal with it if it happens

PHRASAL VERBS **cross sb/sth off (sth)** to remove someone or something, such as a name, from a list by drawing a line through it: *Did you cross her name off the guest list?* • **cross sth out** to draw a line through something you have written, usually because it is wrong: *If you think it's wrong, cross it out and write it again.*

▸**noun** [C] **MARK** ▷ **1** Ⓐ1 a written mark (x), usually used to show where something is, or that something has not been written correctly **2** Ⓑ1 an object in the shape of a cross (a long vertical line with a shorter horizontal line across it), used as a symbol of Christianity: *Christ died on the Cross.* ◦ *She wears a gold cross round her neck.* ◦ *The priest **made the sign of the** cross (= moved his or her hand down and then across the chest) over the dead bodies.* **3** a MEDAL in the shape of a cross: *In Britain, the Victoria Cross is awarded for acts of great bravery during wartime.* **MIXTURE** ▷ **4** a mixture of two different things that have been combined to produce something new: *Police dogs are often a cross **between** a retriever and an alsatian.* → See also **crossbreed**

IDIOM **a (heavy) cross to bear** an unpleasant or painful situation or person that you must accept and deal with, although you find it very difficult

▸**adj** annoyed or angry: *My Dad gets cross (**with** me) if I leave the kitchen in a mess.* • **crossly** /ˈkrɒs.li/ ⓤⓢ /ˈkrɑːs.li/ **adv** *'He's so unreliable!' she said crossly.*

cross- /krɒs/ ⓤⓢ /krɑːs/ **prefix** **1** across: *cross-border* **2** including different groups or subjects: *cross-cultural*

crossbar /ˈkrɒs.bɑːʳ/ ⓤⓢ /ˈkrɑːs.bɑːr/ **noun** [C] a horizontal bar, either the part that forms the top of a goal, or the part of a bicycle between the seat and the HANDLEBARS

ˌcross-ˈborder adj [before noun] between different countries, or involving people from different countries: *cross-border trade*

crossbow /ˈkrɒs.bəʊ/ ⓤⓢ /ˈkrɑːs.boʊ/ **noun** [C] a weapon, used especially in the past, that shoots a short arrow with great force

crossbow

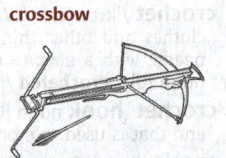

crossbreed /ˈkrɒs.briːd/ ⓤⓢ /ˈkrɑːs-/ **noun** [C] an animal or plant that is a mixture of breeds and is therefore a new VARIETY (= type of plant or animal) • **crossbred** /-bred/ **adj** • **crossbreed verb** [I or T] (**crossbred, crossbred**)

ˌcross-ˈChannel adj [before noun] connecting or happening between England and France, Belgium, or Holland: *a cross-Channel ferry/route*

crosscheck /ˈkrɒs.tʃek/ ⓤⓢ /ˈkrɑːs-/ /krɒsˈ-/ **verb** [I or T] to make certain that information, a calculation, etc. is correct, by asking a different person or using a different method of calculation

ˌcross-contamiˈnation noun [U] the process by which a substance that is harmful or dirty spreads from one area to another

ˌ**cross-ˈcountry** adj; adv
▸**adj** describes sports in which competitors race over long distances through the countryside: *cross-country skiing*
▸**adv** across the length of a country: *After high school we bought a camper van and travelled cross-country for two months.*

ˌ**cross-ˈdressing** noun [U] the act of wearing the clothes of the opposite sex • ˌ**cross-ˈdresser** noun [C]

ˌ**cross-eˈxamine** verb [T] (also ˌ**cross-ˈquestion**) to ask detailed questions of someone, especially a WITNESS in a trial, in order to discover if they have been telling the truth • ˌ**cross-examiˈnation** noun [C usually singular, U] ***Under*** *cross-examination, the witness admitted her evidence had been mostly lies.* • ˌ**cross-eˈxaminer** noun [C]

ˌ**cross-ˈeyed** adj having eyes that look in towards the nose

ˌ**cross-ˌfertiliˈzation** (UK usually ˌ**cross-ˌfertiliˈsation**) noun [U] the mixing of the ideas, customs, etc. of different places or groups of people, to produce a better result

crossfire /ˈkrɒs.faɪəʳ/ (US) /ˈkrɑːs.faɪr/ noun [U] bullets fired towards you from different directions: *One boat of refugees was* ***caught in (the)*** *naval crossfire and sunk.*

IDIOM **caught in the crossfire** to be involved in a situation where people around you are arguing: *The Health Minister, who resigned today, claims she is an innocent victim caught in the crossfire of the current battle over inflation.*

ˈ**cross-hatching** noun [U] two groups of parallel lines that are drawn close together across each other, especially at an angle of 90°, on parts of a picture to show differences of light and darkness • ˈ**cross-hatch** verb [I or T] (also **hatch**) • ˈ**cross-hatched** adj

crossing /ˈkrɒs.ɪŋ/ (US) /ˈkrɑː.sɪŋ/ noun [C] **1** (B1) a place where something such as a road, river, etc. can be crossed safely, or a place where a road and a railway meet and cross each other: *a border/river crossing* **2** (C1) a journey across something such as a sea, from one side to the other: *We had a really rough crossing – I was sick three times.*

cross-legged /ˌkrɒsˈlegd/, /-ɪd/ (US) /ˌkrɑːs-/ adv having your feet crossed over each other, but your knees wide apart, usually while sitting on the floor

crossover /ˈkrɒs.əʊ.vəʳ/ (US) /ˈkrɑːs.oʊ.vɚ/ noun [C] the process or result of changing from one activity or style to another: *a crossover artist/album*

ˌ**cross-ˈparty** adj [before noun] UK including different political parties: *He is calling for cross-party talks on social care.*

ˌ**cross-proˈmote** verb [T] to use one product to advertise another: *The company uses its TV shows to cross-promote its magazines.* • ˌ**cross-proˈmotion** noun [C or U]

ˌ**cross ˈpurposes** adv **at cross purposes** If two or more people are at cross purposes, they do not understand each other because they are talking about different subjects without realizing this: *I think we've been talking at cross purposes – I meant next year, not this year.*

ˌ**cross-ˈquestion** verb [T] to **cross-examine**

ˌ**cross-ˈreference** noun [C] a note in a book that tells you to look somewhere else in the book for more information about something • ˌ**cross-reˈfer** verb [T] *The main entry also cross-refers you* ***to*** *the appendix on page 259.*

crossroads /ˈkrɒs.rəʊdz/ (US) /ˈkrɑːs.roʊdz/ noun [C] (plural **crossroads**) (B2) a place where two roads meet and cross each other

IDIOM **be at a crossroads** to be at a stage in your life when you have to make a very important decision

ˈ**cross-section** noun [C] **1** something that has been cut in half so that you can see the inside, or a model or picture of this: *a cross-section of the human heart* **2** a small group that represents all of the different types within the total group: *The demonstrators seemed to be* ***from*** *a wide cross-section of society.*

ˌ**cross-ˈselling** noun [U] the activity of selling a different product to someone who is already buying a product from the same company

ˈ**cross-stitch** noun [U] a decorative style of sewing that uses STITCHES that cross each other to form an X

ˈ**cross-ˌtrainer** noun **1** [C] (also **elˈliptical ˌtrainer**) a piece of exercise equipment designed to exercise all of the body's main groups of muscles **2** [C usually plural] (also ˈ**cross-training ˌshoe**) a sports shoe that is suitable for wearing in the GYM (= a room or building where you can exercise) and also for running and other sports

ˈ**cross-ˌtraining** noun [U] exercise that makes your whole body stronger by combining several different activities: *a cross-training programme*

crosswalk /ˈkrɒs.wɔːk/ (US) /ˈkrɑːs.wɑːk/ noun [C] US for **pedestrian crossing**

crosswind /ˈkrɒs.wɪnd/ (US) /ˈkrɑːs-/ noun [C] a wind blowing at an angle to the direction a vehicle is travelling in

crosswise /ˈkrɒs.waɪz/ (US) /ˈkrɑːs-/ adv, adj crossing something, especially at an angle of 90°

crossword (puzzle) /ˈkrɒs.wɜːdˌpʌz.l̩/ (US) /ˈkrɑːs.wɝːd-/ noun [C] a game in which you write words that are the answers to questions in a pattern of black and white squares: *I* ***do*** *the Times crossword every morning.*

crostini /krɒsˈtiː.ni/ (US) /krɑːsˈ-/ noun [plural] thin pieces of cooked bread covered with food such as tomatoes or meat

crotch /krɒtʃ/ (US) /krɑːtʃ/ noun [C] (also **crutch**) the part of your body where your legs join at the top, or the part of trousers or underwear that covers this area

crotchet /ˈkrɒtʃ.ət/ (US) /ˈkrɑː.tʃət/ noun [C] (mainly US ˈ**quarter ˌnote**) a musical note with a time value equal to two QUAVERS or half a MINIM

crotchety /ˈkrɒtʃ.ɪ.ti/ (US) /ˈkrɑː.tʃə.t̬i/ adj informal often in a bad mood and easily annoyed: *By the time the meal began, the youngest children were getting tired and crotchety.*

crotchless /ˈkrɒtʃ.ləs/ (US) /ˈkrɑːtʃ-/ adj describes underwear that has no part covering the area where your legs join at the top

crouch /kraʊtʃ/ verb [I] to bend your knees and lower yourself so that you are close to the ground and leaning forward slightly: *She saw him coming and crouched (****down****) behind a bush.* • **crouch** noun [S]

croup /kruːp/ noun [U] a children's illness in which a child has noisy, difficult breathing and coughs a lot

croupier /ˈkruː.pi.eɪ/ noun [C] a person who works in a CASINO (= a place where people risk money in games) who is responsible for a particular table and whose job is to collect and pay out money and give out playing cards, etc.

crouton /ˈkruː.tɒ̃/ (US) /-t̬ɑːn/ noun [C usually plural] a small square piece of bread that is fried or TOASTED

(= heated until it is dry and brown), added to soup or a salad just before you eat it

crow /krəʊ/ (US) /kroʊ/ **noun; verb**

▸**noun** [C] a large, black bird with a loud, unpleasant cry

IDIOM **as the crow flies** describes a distance when measured in a straight line between two points or places

▸**verb** [I] (**crowed** or UK also **crew**) **CRY** ▷ **1** When a COCK (= an adult male chicken) crows, it makes a very long and loud sharp cry: *We were woken at dawn by a cock crowing repeatedly.* **2** When a baby crows, it makes sudden cries of happiness. **TALK PROUDLY** ▷ **3** disapproving to talk in a proud and annoying way about something you have done: *He's always crowing* ***about*** *his latest triumph.*

crowbar /ˈkrəʊ.bɑːʳ/ (US) /ˈkroʊ.bɑːr/ **noun** [C] a heavy iron bar with a bent end that is used to help lift heavy objects off the ground or to force things open

crowd /kraʊd/ **noun; verb**

▸**noun** [+ sing/pl verb] **1** (A2) [C] a large group of people who have come together: *A crowd of about 15,000 attended the concert.* **2** [S] informal a group of friends or a group of people with similar interests: *She goes around with a friendly crowd.* ◦ *'Who was there?' 'Oh, the usual crowd.'*

IDIOM **follow the crowd** disapproving to do what most other people do: *Think for yourself, don't just follow the crowd.*

▸**verb** [T] informal to make someone feel uncomfortable by standing too close to them or by watching them all the time: *I need some time to do this work properly, so don't crowd me.*

PHRASAL VERBS **crowd (sth) into sth** (C1) If people crowd or are crowded into a place, they fill it completely: *Hordes of commuters crowded into the train.* • **crowd sb/sth out** to not allow a person or thing any space or opportunity to grow or develop: *Small local businesses have been crowded out by large multinationals.* • **crowd round/around (sb/sth)** (C1) to come together closely in a crowd around someone or something: *As soon as he appeared, reporters crowded round.*

crowded /ˈkraʊ.dɪd/ **adj** (A2) If a place is crowded, it is full of people: *By ten o'clock the bar was crowded.*

crowd-puller /ˈkraʊdˌpʊl.əʳ/ (US) /-ɚ/ **noun** [C] a person or thing that attracts a lot of attention and that people will pay to see

crowdsource /ˈkraʊdˌsɔːs/ (US) /-sɔːrs/ **verb** [I or T] to give tasks to a large group of people or to the general public, for example, by asking for help on the internet, rather than having tasks done within a company by employees: *The company plans to crowdsource the translation of its new web app.* • **crowdsourcing** /-ˌsɔː.sɪŋ/ (US) /-ˌsɔːr.sɪŋ/ **noun** [U]

crown /kraʊn/ **noun; verb**

▸**noun** [C] **HEAD COVERING** ▷ **1** a circular decoration for the head, usually made of gold and JEWELS (= precious stones), and worn by a king or queen at official ceremonies **2** the act of winning a sports competition: *He plans to defend his Olympic crown.* **TOP PART** ▷ **3** the top part of a head, hat, or hill: *A pink ribbon had been tied around the crown of the hat.* **TOOTH** ▷ **4** an artificial piece used to cover a damaged tooth **COIN** ▷ **5** a British coin that is no longer used

▸**verb** [T] **HEAD COVERING** ▷ **1** to put a crown on someone's head in an official ceremony that makes them king or queen: *Queen Elizabeth II was crowned (**queen**) (= made queen in a special ceremony) in 1953.* → See also **coronation 2** If an event or achievement crowns something, it is the best or most successful part of it: *an acting career crowned by her final Oscar-winning performance* **TOP PART** ▷ **3** formal If something crowns something else, it is on or around the top of it: *The church was crowned with golden domes.* **4** slang to hit someone on the head **TOOTH** ▷ **5** to fit a crown (= tooth covering): *She's had her two front teeth crowned.*

IDIOM **to crown it all** UK informal used to say that something is the worst thing to happen in a series of unpleasant events: *I had lost my ticket, was soaked to the skin, and, to crown it all, discovered that my purse had been stolen.*

the ˈCrown **noun** [S] the royal governing power of a country that has a king or queen

ˌcrown ˈcolony **noun** [C] an area or country that is politically controlled by the UK and has a British GOVERNOR

ˌCrown ˈCourt **noun** [C] UK legal a law court in England or Wales where criminal cases are judged by a judge and JURY

ˌcrowned ˈhead **noun** [C usually plural] formal a king or queen: *Most of the crowned heads of Europe have been entertained in this palace.*

crowning /ˈkraʊ.nɪŋ/ **adj** A crowning event or achievement is the best or most important one: *the crowning* ***achievement*** *of her long career* ◦ *Walking on the moon was his crowning* ***glory*** *(= his most important achievement).*

ˌcrown ˈjewels **noun** [plural] the crown and other JEWELS (= precious stones) worn at important official ceremonies by the king or queen

ˌcrown ˈprince **noun** [C] the man who will be king of a country when the ruling king or queen dies

ˌcrown prinˈcess **noun** [C] the woman who will be queen of a country when the ruling king or queen dies, or is the wife of a crown prince

ˌCrown ˈprosecutor **noun** [C] UK legal an official who is responsible for trying to prove in a law court that people accused of crimes are guilty

ˈcrow's feet **noun** [plural] narrow lines around the outside corners of your eyes, that appear when you get older

ˈcrow's nest **noun** [C usually singular] a small closed space near the top of a ship's MAST, from which a person can see in all directions

crozier (also **crosier**) /ˈkrəʊ.zi.əʳ/ (US) /ˈkroʊ.zi.ɚ/ **noun** [C] a long stick with a decorative end that is curved or in the shape of a cross, carried by BISHOPS

CRT /ˌsiː.ɑːˈtiː/ (US) /-ɑːr-/ **noun** [C] abbreviation for **cathode ray tube**

crucial /ˈkruː.ʃəl/ **adj** (B2) extremely important or necessary: *a crucial decision/question* ◦ *Her work has been crucial* ***to*** *the project's success.* ◦ [+ that] *It is crucial* ***that*** *the problem is tackled immediately.* • **crucially** /-i/ **adv**

crucible /ˈkruː.sɪ.bl̩/ **noun** [C] **CONTAINER** ▷ **1** a container in which metals or other substances can be heated to very high temperatures **TEST** ▷ **2** formal a severe test **MIX** ▷ **3** formal a place or situation in which different cultures or styles can mix together to produce something new and exciting

crucifix /ˈkruː.sɪ.fɪks/ **noun** [C] a model or picture representing Jesus Christ on a cross: *She always wears a small gold crucifix round her neck.*

crucifixion /ˌkruː.sɪˈfɪk.ʃən/ **noun** [C or U] **1** the act of crucifying someone **2** a painting or other piece of art representing the crucifixion of Jesus Christ

the Cruci'fixion noun [S] the death of Jesus Christ on a cross

cruciform /ˈkruː.sɪ.fɔːm/ US /-fɔːrm/ adj formal in the shape of a cross

crucify /ˈkruː.sɪ.faɪ/ verb [T] **1** to kill someone by tying or fastening them with nails to a cross and leaving them there to die **2** informal to severely punish or damage someone or something: *He's going to crucify me when he finds out what I've done!*

crud /krʌd/ noun [U] informal something dirty and unpleasant • **cruddy** /ˈkrʌd.i/ adj

crude /kruːd/ adj; noun

▸adj **SIMPLE** ▷ **1** C2 simple and not skilfully done or made: *a crude device/weapon* **RUDE** ▷ **2** C2 rude and offensive: *a crude remark/comment* • **crudely** /ˈkruːd.li/ adv *a crudely made bomb* • **crudeness** /ˈkruːd.nəs/ noun [U] (also **crudity**)

▸noun [U] (also ˌ**crude 'oil**) oil from rocks underground in a natural state that has not yet been treated

crudités /ˈkruː.dɪ.teɪz/ US /ˌkruː.dɪˈteɪz/ noun [plural] small pieces of uncooked vegetables, often served with a DIP (= a cold, thick sauce) before a meal

cruel /ˈkruː.əl/, /krʊəl/ adj (**crueller**, **cruellest** or **crueler**, **cruelest**) **1** B1 extremely unkind and unpleasant and causing pain to people or animals intentionally: *Don't tease him about his weight – it's cruel.* ◦ *Children can be very cruel to each other.* **2** causing suffering: *His death was a cruel **blow**.* • **cruelly** /-i/ adv B2 in a cruel way

+ Other ways of saying cruel

If something is extremely cruel and unpleasant, you could describe it as **barbaric** or **inhumane**:

*The world must condemn their actions as **barbaric**.*

*We are trying to end the most **inhumane** forms of punishment.*

Callous, **cold-blooded**, or **ruthless** can be used when someone is very cruel and would hurt someone and not care if the person suffers:

*He had a **callous** disregard for the feelings of others.*

*The budget is based on a **cold-blooded** analysis of the markets.*

*He was a **ruthless** dictator.*

Heartless can be used about people who are cruel because they do not care about other people:

*He has been described as a **heartless** boss by several employees.*

If something is cruel because it is intended to upset or harm someone, the word **malicious** is often used:

*People were spreading **malicious** rumours about him.*

You could use **sadistic** if someone is cruel to other people and seems to enjoy it:

*He was described as cold, mean, vicious, and **sadistic**.*

If someone is slightly cruel to someone, you could use the words **nasty** or **mean** to describe them:

*Don't be so **nasty** to him!*

*Don't listen to him. He's just being **mean**.*

IDIOM **be cruel to be kind** to do or say something that causes someone pain because you believe that it will help them

cruelty /ˈkruː.əl.ti/, /ˈkrʊəl-/ US /-t̬i/ noun [U or C] B2 cruel behaviour or a cruel action: *The farmer was accused of cruelty **to** animals.*

cruet /ˈkruː.ɪt/ noun [C] **1** UK a container that holds smaller containers of salt and PEPPER, etc., used when having a meal **2** US a glass bottle that holds oil or VINEGAR for use during a meal

cruise /kruːz/ noun; verb

▸noun [C] B1 a journey on a large ship for pleasure, during which you visit several places

▸verb **1** B2 [I] to travel on ships for pleasure **2** [I] If a ship or aircraft cruises, it travels at a continuous speed. **3** [I or T] slang to go around public places looking for someone to have sex with: *He spends the weekends cruising the bars.* • **cruising** /ˈkruː.zɪŋ/ noun [U] *Mediterranean/luxury cruising* ◦ *a popular cruising area/ground*

ˌ**cruise 'missile** noun [C] a MISSILE (= flying weapon) that can be directed by a computer during its flight and that sometimes carries nuclear explosives

cruiser /ˈkruː.zəʳ/ US /-zɚ/ noun [C] **1** a large fast ship used in war **2** a boat with an engine and a CABIN in which people sail for pleasure

ˈ**cruise** ˌ**ship** noun [C] (also ˈ**cruise** ˌ**liner**) a large ship like a hotel, that people travel on for pleasure

crumb /krʌm/ noun [C] **1** a very small piece of bread, cake, or biscuit → See also **breadcrumbs** **2** a small amount of something: *a crumb of **hope/comfort***

crumble /ˈkrʌm.bl̩/ verb; noun

▸verb **1** C2 [I or T] to break, or cause something to break, into small pieces: *She nervously crumbled the bread between her fingers.* ◦ *The cliffs on which the houses are built are starting to crumble.* **2** [I] to become weaker in strength or influence: *Support for the government is crumbling.*

▸noun [C or U] UK (US **crisp**) a sweet dish made from fruit covered in a mixture of flour, butter, and sugar rubbed together into small pieces, baked, and eaten hot: *apple crumble*

crumbly /ˈkrʌm.bli/, /-bl̩.i/ adj breaking easily into small pieces: *bread with a crumbly texture*

crumbs /krʌmz/ exclamation UK old-fashioned informal an expression of surprise or worry

crummy /ˈkrʌm.i/ adj informal of very bad quality: *a crummy old carpet*

crumpet /ˈkrʌm.pɪt/ noun **BREAD** ▷ **1** [C] a small, round cake like bread with holes in one side that is eaten hot with butter **WOMAN** ▷ **2** [U] UK slang offensive one or more people, usually women, who are sexually attractive

crumple /ˈkrʌm.pl̩/ verb **1** [I or T] to become, or cause something to become, full of folds that are not equal in size: *This shirt crumples easily* **2** [I] If someone's face crumples, it becomes full of lines because of a strong emotion: *Her face crumpled **with** laughter.* **3** [I] If someone crumples, they fall to the ground suddenly: *The bullet hit him and he crumpled **into a heap** on the floor.*

PHRASAL VERB **crumple sth up** to crush a piece of paper until all of it is folded: *Sylvie crumpled up the letter and threw it in the bin.*

crumpled /ˈkrʌm.pl̩d/ adj full of folds: *crumpled clothes*

ˈ**crumple** ˌ**zone** noun [C] UK a part of a car that is designed to crumple easily in an accident and so protect the people inside from being hit too hard

crunch /krʌntʃ/ verb; noun

▸verb [I or T] to crush hard food loudly between the teeth, or to make a sound as if something is being crushed or broken: *She was crunching noisily **on** an* *apple.* ◦ *The gravel crunched underfoot as we walked up to the house.*

▸noun **SOUND** ▷ **1** [C usually singular] the sound of hard food being crushed between the teeth, or like something being crushed or broken: *The woods were silent apart from the crunch of our feet in the snow.* **DIFFICULTY** ▷ **2 the crunch** [S] informal a difficult situation that forces you to make a decision or do something: *The crunch **came** when she was forced to choose between her marriage and her career.* **EXERCISE** ▷ **3** [C usually plural] an exercise in which you lie on your back on the floor with your knees bent and your feet flat on the floor, and then raise your head and shoulders: *Doing crunches every day strengthens your abdominal muscles.*

IDIOM **if/when it comes to the crunch** UK if/when a situation becomes extremely serious and a decision must be made: *If it comes to the crunch and you and your husband do split up, you can always stay with us.*

crunchy /ˈkrʌn.tʃi/ **adj** describes food that is firm and makes a loud noise when it is eaten: *crunchy vegetables*

crunk /kruŋk/ **noun** [U] a type of pop music that people dance to, with a strong beat and repeated words that people shout

crusade /kruːˈseɪd/ **noun; verb**

▸noun **1** [C] a long and determined attempt to achieve something that you believe in strongly: *They have long been involved in a crusade **for** racial equality.* ◦ *a **moral** crusade against drugs* **2** [C often plural] (also **Crusade**) a war fought by Christians against Muslims, often in Palestine, in the 11th, 12th, 13th, and 17th centuries

▸verb [I] to make an effort to achieve something that you believe in strongly • **crusader** /-ˈseɪ.dəʳ/ (US) /-ˈseɪ.dɚ/ **noun** [C] *He caught the public imagination as a crusader **against** corruption.*

crush /krʌʃ/ **verb; noun**

▸verb **PRESS** ▷ **1** (C2) [T] to press something very hard so that it is broken or its shape is destroyed: *The package had been badly crushed in the post.* ◦ *Add three cloves of crushed garlic.* ◦ *His arm was badly crushed in the car accident.* **2** [T] to press paper or cloth so that it becomes full of folds and is no longer flat: *My dress got all crushed in my suitcase.* **3** [T] If people are crushed against other people or things, they are pressed against them: *Tragedy struck when several people were crushed **to death** in the crowd.* **SHOCK** ▷ **4** [T usually passive] to upset or shock someone badly: *He was crushed by the news of the accident.* **BEAT** ▷ **5** [T] to defeat someone completely: *The president called upon the army to help crush the rebellion.* ◦ *France crushed Wales by 36 to 3 in last Saturday's match in Paris.*

▸noun **LIKING** ▷ **1** (C2) [C] informal a strong but temporary feeling of liking someone: *She has a crush **on** one of her teachers at school.* **PRESS** ▷ **2** (C2) [S] a crowd of people forced to stand close together: *I had to struggle through the crush to get to the door.* ◦ *You can come in our car, but it'll be a bit of a crush (= there will be a lot of people in it).*

ˈcrush ˌbarrier **noun** [C] a strong fence that is used to divide a large crowd, for example at a football game, to stop them from being pressed too close together

crushing /ˈkrʌʃ.ɪŋ/ **adj** severe: *The news came as a crushing blow.* ◦ *Their army had suffered a crushing **defeat**.*

crust /krʌst/ **noun** **1** [C or U] a hard outer covering of something: *pie crust (= the cooked pastry on top)* ◦ *the Earth's crust* **2** [C] the outside layer of a LOAF of bread: *Could you cut the crusts off the sandwiches, please?* • **crusted** /ˈkrʌs.tɪd/ **adj** *crusted with mud*

crustacean /krʌsˈteɪ.ʃən/ **noun** [C] any of various types of animal that live in water and have a hard outer shell

crusty /ˈkrʌs.ti/ **adj; noun**

▸adj **HARD LAYER** ▷ **1** having a hard outer layer: *fresh, crusty bread* **EASILY ANNOYED** ▷ **2** (especially of older people) complaining and easily annoyed: *a crusty old man*

▸noun [C] UK informal a young person who does not live in a way that society considers normal, typically with untidy or dirty clothes and hair, and no regular job or permanent home: *Lots of crusties came into town for the festival.*

crutch /krʌtʃ/ **noun** **1** [C usually plural] a stick with a piece that fits under the arm, that you lean on for support if you have difficulty in walking because of a foot or leg injury: *Martin broke his leg and has been **on** crutches for the past six weeks.* **2** [S] often disapproving something that provides help and support and that you depend on, often too much: *As an atheist, he believes that religion is just an **emotional** crutch for the insecure.* **3** [C] **crotch**

the crux /ˈkrʌks/ **noun** [S] the most important or serious part of a matter, problem, or argument: *The crux **of** the country's economic problems is its foreign debt.* ◦ *The issue of an arms embargo will be at the crux of the negotiations in Geneva.*

cry /kraɪ/ **verb; noun**

▸verb [I or T] **PRODUCE TEARS** ▷ **1** (A2) to produce tears as the result of a strong emotion, such as unhappiness or pain: *I could hear someone crying in the next room.* ◦ *'There, there, don't cry,' she said.* ◦ *We all laughed until we cried.* ◦ *She cried bitter tears when she got the letter.* ◦ *He cried **for joy** when he heard that his son had been found alive and well.* **2 cry yourself to sleep** to cry for a long time until you start to sleep **SHOUT** ▷ **3** (B1) to call out loudly: [+ speech] *'Look out!' she cried.*

> **! Usage: cry, scream, or shout?**
>
> When **cry** is used to mean 'to call out loudly', it is usually only used in written English, when quoting direct speech:
>
> *'Get me out of here!' she cried.*
>
> The most common words used to mean 'to call out loudly' are **scream** or **shout**. **Scream** is usually something you do when you are frightened or being attacked and is often just sounds, not words:
>
> *As he grabbed her arm, she screamed and tried to get away.*
>
> ~~*As he grabbed her arm, she cried and tried to get away.*~~
>
> **Shout** is a more general word for 'to call out loudly':
>
> *Alex shouted something to me across the street.*
>
> ~~*Alex cried something to me across the street.*~~

IDIOMS **cry your eyes out** (C2) to cry a lot: *I was so upset that day, I cried my eyes out.* • **cry foul** to say that something that has happened is unfair or illegal: *The opposition parties have cried foul **at** the president's act, seeing it as a violation of democracy.* • **cry wolf** disapproving to ask for help when you do not need it: *If you cry wolf too often, people will stop believing you.* • **for crying out loud!** informal said when you are annoyed, and to emphasize what you are saying: *Oh,* *for crying out loud, why won't you listen to me!* • **it's no use crying over spilled milk** saying said to emphasize that it is not useful feeling sorry about something that has already happened

PHRASAL VERBS **cry off** informal to decide not to do something that you have arranged to do: *She usually says she'll be there and then cries off at the last minute.* • **cry out** C2 to shout or make a loud noise because you are frightened, hurt, etc.: *She cried out in pain as the bullet grazed her shoulder.* • **cry out against sth** to complain loudly about something that you do not approve of: *Women's rights groups have cried out against the proposed cut in benefit paid to single mothers.* • **cry out for sth** C2 to need a particular thing very much: *The country is crying out for a change in leadership.*

▸noun **SHOUT** ▷ **1** B1 [C] a loud, high sound that expresses an emotion: *a cry of despair* **2** B1 [C] a shout made to attract people's attention: *They were wakened by cries of 'Fire!' from the next room.* **3** C2 [C] the noise that a bird or animal makes: *an eagle's cry* **TEARS** ▷ **4** [S] a period of crying: *'Go on, have a **good** cry,' he said, stroking her hair.*

IDIOMS **a cry for help** a way of saying that you need help: *Most suicide attempts are really a cry for help.* • **in full cry** talking continuously about something in a noisy or eager way: *The opposition was in full cry in Parliament last night **over** the proposed changes to the education bill.*

ˈcry-ˌbaby noun [C] informal disapproving someone, usually a child, who cries a lot without good reason: *Don't be such a cry-baby – it's only a scratch.*

crying /ˈkraɪ.ɪŋ/ adj; noun

▸adj [before noun] very serious and needing urgent attention: *There's a crying **need** for a better education system.*

IDIOM **it's a crying shame** old-fashioned something that you say when you think a situation is wrong: *It's a crying shame **that** she's paid so little for what she does.*

▸noun [U] the act of crying, or the sound of someone crying: *She could hear crying coming from the next room.*

cryonics /ˌkraɪˈɒn.ɪks/ US /-ˈɑː.nɪks/ noun [U] the process of storing a dead body by freezing it until science has advanced to such a degree that it is able to bring that person back to life

crypt /krɪpt/ noun [C] a room under the floor of a church where bodies are buried

cryptic /ˈkrɪp.tɪk/ adj mysterious and difficult to understand: *I received a cryptic message through the post.* • **cryptically** /-tɪ.kəl.i/ adv

ˌcryptic ˈcrossword noun [C] a type of CROSSWORD (= word game) that has difficult CLUES (= pieces of information) that are not obvious in their meaning

crypto- /krɪp.təʊ-/ US /-toʊ-/ prefix hidden or secret: *The minister accused his opponent of being a crypto-communist.*

crystal /ˈkrɪs.təl/ noun **GLASS** ▷ **1** C2 [U] transparent glass of very high quality, usually with its surface cut into delicate patterns: *a crystal vase* **2** [C] US a transparent glass or plastic cover for a watch or clock **MINERAL** ▷ **3** [C] specialized a piece of a substance that has become solid, with a regular shape: *Cirrus clouds are composed of ice crystals.* **4** [C or U] clear, transparent rock that is used in jewellery, or a piece of this: *a pair of crystal earrings*

IDIOM **crystal clear 1** C1 extremely clear: *crystal clear water* **2** C2 very easy to understand: *The evidence is now crystal clear.* ◦ *She made it crystal clear **that** she was in charge.*

ˌcrystal ˈball noun [C usually singular] a transparent glass ball used by someone who says they can discover what will happen to you in the future by looking into it: *Looking into the crystal ball, it's safe to say that interest rates will rise next year.*

crystalline /ˈkrɪs.təl.aɪn/ US /-lən/ adj **CLEAR** ▷ **1** literary clear and bright like crystal: *Her singing voice has a pure, crystalline quality.* **SHAPE** ▷ **2** specialized describes a substance that has become solid, with regular shapes: *crystalline deposits*

crystallize specialized (UK usually **crystallise**) /ˈkrɪs.təl.aɪz/ verb **1** [I] If a liquid crystallizes, it turns into crystals. **2** [T] If something crystallizes your thoughts or opinions, it makes them clear and fixed: *The event helped to crystallize my thoughts.* • **crystallization** (UK usually **crystallisation**) /ˌkrɪs.təl.aɪˈzeɪ.ʃən/ noun [U]

crystallized (UK usually **crystallised**) /ˈkrɪs.təl.aɪzd/ adj SOAKED (= left to become completely wet) in melted sugar that has then become hard: *crystallized fruit*

ˌcrystal ˈmeth noun [U] informal **methamphetamine**

the CSA /ˌsiː.esˈeɪ/ noun abbreviation for the Child Support Agency: a British government organization that makes parents who do not live with their children continue to pay for their living costs

ˈC-ˌsection noun [C] a CAESAREAN (SECTION) (= an operation in which a woman's WOMB is cut open to allow a baby to be born)

CSF /ˌsiː.esˈef/ noun [C] specialized abbreviation for critical success factor: something that is necessary in order for a company or organization to achieve its aims

CS gas /ˌsiː.esˈgæs/ noun [U] a gas that causes painful breathing and tears, used by the army or police to control a person or crowd in a violent situation

Ctrl (key) written abbreviation for **control key**

CˈT scan noun [C] abbreviation for computerized tomography scan: another word for **CAT scan**

cu written abbreviation for see you: used when saying goodbye at the end of an email or text message to a friend

cub /kʌb/ noun [C] **YOUNG ANIMAL** ▷ **1** a young lion, BEAR, WOLF, etc. **BOY** ▷ **2** (also **Cub Scout**) a boy aged between eight and eleven years old who is a member of the international organization called the SCOUTS

cubbyhole /ˈkʌb.i.həʊl/ US /-hoʊl/ noun [C] a very small room or space for storing things

cube /kjuːb/ noun; verb

▸noun [C] **SHAPE** ▷ **1** a solid object with six square sides of equal size: *Cut the cheese into small cubes.* **NUMBER** ▷ **2** specialized the number made by multiplying a number twice by itself

▸verb [T] **SHAPE** ▷ **1** to cut food into cubes **NUMBER** ▷ **2** specialized If you cube a number, you multiply it twice by itself: *2 cubed (= 2 x 2 x 2) equals 8, and is written* 2^3.

ˌcube ˈroot noun [C] specialized The cube root of a number is another number that, when multiplied by itself twice, makes the first number: *The cube root of 125 is 5, because 5 x 5 x 5 = 125.*

cubic /ˈkjuː.bɪk/ adj specialized used in units of volume to show when the length of something has been multiplied by its width and height

cubicle /ˈkjuː.bɪ.kl̩/ noun [C] a small space with walls or curtains around it, that is separate from the rest of a room and where you can be private when taking clothes off, etc.: *a shower cubicle*

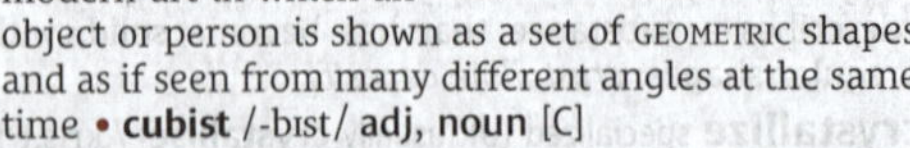

cubism /ˈkjuː.bɪ.zəm/ noun [U] a style of modern art in which an object or person is shown as a set of GEOMETRIC shapes and as if seen from many different angles at the same time • **cubist** /-bɪst/ adj, noun [C]

cuboid /ˈkjuː.bɔɪd/ noun; adj
▸noun [C] specialized a solid object with six rectangular sides
▸adj approximately in the shape of a CUBE (= a solid object with six square sides of equal size)

ˈcub reˌporter noun [C] a young person being trained to write articles for a newspaper

cuckold /ˈkʌk.əʊld/ (US) /-oʊld/ noun; verb
▸noun [C] old-fashioned disapproving a man whose wife deceives him by having a sexual relationship with another man
▸verb [T] old-fashioned disapproving If a man is cuckolded, his wife has a sexual relationship with another man.

cuckoo /ˈkʊk.uː/ noun; adj
▸noun [C] (plural **cuckoos**) a grey bird with a two-note call that sounds similar to its name. Cuckoos LAY their eggs in other birds' nests.
▸adj informal silly or crazy

ˈcuckoo ˌclock noun [C] a decorative clock with a little wooden bird inside it that comes out every hour and makes a quick two-note sound like a cuckoo

cucumber /ˈkjuː.kʌm.bər/ (US) /-bɚ/ noun [C or U] (B1) a long, thin, pale green vegetable with dark green skin, usually eaten uncooked in salads

cud /kʌd/ noun [U] food that has been eaten by an animal with more than one stomach, such as a cow, and that comes back into the animal's mouth to be CHEWED again before going into the second stomach: *a cow chewing the cud*

cuddle /ˈkʌd.l̩/ verb [I or T] to put your arms around someone and hold them in a loving way, or (of two people) to hold each other close to show love or for comfort: *She cuddled the baby and eventually it stopped crying.* ◦ *They sat in the back row of the cinema kissing and cuddling.* • **cuddle** noun [C] *Come here and give me a cuddle.*

PHRASAL VERB **cuddle up** informal to sit or lie very close to someone and put your arms around them: *We cuddled up together and tried to get warm.* ◦ *She cuddled up **to** her mother.*

cuddly /ˈkʌd.l̩i/ adj approving liking to cuddle, or making you want to cuddle: *a very cuddly child*

ˌcuddly ˈtoy noun [C] UK a toy animal that is soft and covered in fur

cudgel /ˈkʌdʒ.əl/ noun; verb
▸noun [C] a short, heavy stick used for hitting people

IDIOM **take up the cudgels for/against sb/sth** UK old-fashioned to argue strongly in support of, or against, someone or something: *Relatives have taken up the cudgels for two British women accused of murder.*

▸verb [T] (**-ll-** or US usually **-l-**) to hit someone with a cudgel

cue /kjuː/ noun; verb
▸noun [C] **SIGNAL** ▷ **1** a word or action in a play or film that is used as a signal by a performer to begin saying or doing something **2** a signal for someone to do something: [+ to infinitive] *They started washing up, so that was our cue **to** leave the party.* **3 on cue** If something happens on cue, it happens just after someone has said or thought it would happen: *I was just wondering where Sarah was, when, right on cue, she came in.* **4 take your cue from sb** to take notice of someone's words or behaviour so that you know what you should do: *She watched his lips carefully and took her cue from him.* **STICK** ▷ **5** a long, thin wooden pole with a small piece of leather at one end, used for hitting the ball in games such as BILLIARDS or SNOOKER

IDIOM **take your cue from sth/sb** to be strongly influenced by something or someone: *The architects took their cue for the design of the new pub from the nearby Aston Hall.*

▸verb [T] (present tense **cueing**, past tense and past participle **cued**) (also **cue in**) to give someone a signal to do something: *With a nod of his head, the drummer cued the lead singer **in**.*

cuff /kʌf/ noun; verb
▸noun [C] **MATERIAL ON CLOTHES** ▷ **1** the thicker material at the end of a sleeve nearest the hand **2** US (UK **ˈturn-up**) the part of a trouser leg that is turned up **HIT** ▷ **3** the act of hitting someone with your hand in a light, joking way: *She gave him a playful cuff on the shoulder.* **HANDCUFFS** ▷ **4 cuffs** [plural] informal for **handcuffs**

IDIOM **off the cuff** If you speak off the cuff, you say something without having prepared or thought about your words first: *I hadn't prepared a speech so I just said a few words off the cuff.* ◦ [before noun] *an off-the-cuff remark*

▸verb [T] **HIT** ▷ **1** to hit someone with your hand in a light, joking way: *His brother cuffed him playfully round the head.* **PUT IN HANDCUFFS** ▷ **2** informal to put someone's hands in HANDCUFFS: *He was led out of the dock with his hands cuffed behind his back.*

cufflink /ˈkʌf.lɪŋk/ noun [C] a small decorative object used to fasten shirt cuffs

cuisine /kwɪˈziːn/ noun [U] a style of cooking: *French cuisine* → See also **haute cuisine, nouvelle cuisine**

cul-de-sac /ˈkʌl.də.sæk/ noun [C] **1** a short road that is blocked off at one end **2** a situation that leads nowhere: *an intellectual cul-de-sac*

culinary /ˈkʌl.ɪ.nər.i/ (US) /ˈkʌl.ə.ner-/ adj formal connected with cooking or kitchens: *the culinary **delights** (= good food) of Beijing* ◦ *My culinary **skills** are rather limited, I'm afraid (= I am not very good at cooking)!*

cull /kʌl/ verb [T] When people cull animals, they kill them, especially the weaker members of a particular group of them, in order to reduce or limit their number. • **cull** noun [C] *the annual red deer cull*

PHRASAL VERB **cull sth from sth** [often passive] to collect ideas or information from various places: *Here are a few facts and figures I've culled from the week's papers.*

culminate /ˈkʌl.mɪ.neɪt/ verb **culminate in/with sth** If an event or series of events culminates in something, it ends with it, having developed until it reaches this point: *My arguments with the boss got worse and worse, and it all culminated in my deciding to change jobs.* ◦ *Their many years of research have finally culminated in a cure for the disease.* • **culmination** /ˌkʌl.mɪˈneɪ.ʃən/ noun [U] *Winning first prize was **the** culmination **of** years of practice and hard work.*

culottes /kuˈlɒts/ (US) /kjəˈlɑːts/ **noun** [plural] women's short trousers that look like a skirt: *a pair of culottes*

culpable /ˈkʌl.pə.bl̩/ **adj** formal deserving to be blamed or considered responsible for something bad: *He was **held** culpable (= blamed) **for** all that had happened.* • **culpability** /ˌkʌl.pəˈbɪl.ɪ.ti/ (US) /-ə.t̬i/ **noun** [U] *After the accident, the company refused to **accept** culpability.* • **culpably** /-bli/ **adv**

culprit /ˈkʌl.prɪt/ **noun** [C] **1** someone who has done something wrong: *Police hope the public will help them to find the culprits.* **2** a fact or situation that is the reason for something bad happening: *Children in this country are getting much too fat, and sugar and sweets are the main culprits.*

cult /kʌlt/ **noun**; **adj**

▸**noun** **RELIGION** ▷ **1** [C] a religious group, often living together, whose beliefs are considered extreme or strange by many people: *Their son ran away from home and joined a **religious** cult.* **2** [C] a particular system of religious belief: *the Hindu cult **of** Shiva* **POPULARITY** ▷ **3** [S] someone or something that has become very popular with a particular group of people: *the cult of celebrity* → See also **personality cult**

▸**adj** [before noun] liked very much by a particular group of people: *The singer had a cult **following** in the 1970s.* ◦ *a cult **figure/movie***

cultivable /ˈkʌl.tɪ.və.bl̩/ (US) /-t̬ə-/ **adj** describes land that can be used to grow crops: *Most of the island isn't cultivable – the soil is too rocky.*

cultivate /ˈkʌl.tɪ.veɪt/ (US) /-t̬ə-/ **verb** [T] **USE LAND** ▷ **1** (C1) to prepare land and grow crops on it, or to grow a particular crop: *Most of the land there is too poor to cultivate.* ◦ *The villagers cultivate mostly maize and beans.* **DEVELOP** ▷ **2** (C2) to try to develop and improve something: *She has cultivated **an image** as a tough negotiator.* **3** If you cultivate a relationship, you make a special effort to establish and develop it, because you think it might be useful to you: *The new prime minister is cultivating relationships with East Asian countries.* • **cultivation** /ˌkʌl.tɪˈveɪ.ʃən/ (US) /-t̬ə-/ **noun** [U]

cultivated /ˈkʌl.tɪ.veɪ.tɪd/ (US) /-t̬ə.veɪ.t̬ɪd/ **adj** **ART** ▷ **1** describes someone who has had a good education and knows a lot about and likes art, music, painting, etc. **LAND** ▷ **2** describes land that is used to grow crops: *cultivated fields/soil/land*

cultural /ˈkʌl.tʃər.əl/ (US) /-tʃɚ-/ **adj** **WAY OF LIFE** ▷ **1** (B1) relating to the habits, traditions, and beliefs of a society: *Australia has its own cultural **identity**, which is very different from that of Britain.* ◦ *cultural **diversity/differences*** ◦ *cultural **heritage** (= ways of living and thinking that have existed for a long time in a society)* **ART** ▷ **2** (B1) relating to music, art, theatre, literature, etc.: *cultural **activities*** ◦ *a cultural **centre** (= a place with a lot of museums, theatres, etc.)* ◦ *a cultural desert/wasteland (= a place without museums, theatres, etc.)* • **culturally** /-i/ **adv** (B2) *a culturally diverse society*

culture /ˈkʌl.tʃər/ (US) /-tʃɚ/ **noun**; **verb**

▸**noun** **WAY OF LIFE** ▷ **1** (B1) [C or U] the way of life, especially the general customs and beliefs, of a particular group of people at a particular time: *youth/working-class culture* ◦ *She's studying modern Japanese language and culture.* → See also **subculture** **ART** ▷ **2** (B1) [U] music, art, theatre, literature, etc.: *You won't find much culture in this sleepy little town, I'm afraid!* ◦ ***popular** culture (= the books, music, etc. liked by most people)* **GROWING** ▷ **3** [C or U] specialized cells, tissues, organs, or organisms grown for scientific purposes, or the activity of breeding and keeping particular living things in order to get the substances they produce

▸**verb** [T] specialized to breed and keep particular living things in order to get the substances they produce

cultured /ˈkʌl.tʃəd/ (US) /-tʃɚd/ **adj** describes someone who has had a good education and knows a lot about art, music, literature, etc.

ˌcultured ˈpearl **noun** [C] a PEARL (= a round, white precious stone) that has been formed artificially

ˈculture ˌmedium **noun** [C] (plural **culture media**) specialized a substance containing NUTRIENTS in which cells or MICROORGANISMS can be grown

ˈculture ˌshock **noun** [C or U] a feeling of confusion felt by someone visiting a country or place that they do not know: *It was a real culture shock to find herself in London after living on a small island.*

ˈculture ˌvulture **noun** [C] informal someone who is very interested in music, art, theatre, etc.: *He's a bit of a culture vulture – always out at galleries and theatres.*

culvert /ˈkʌl.vət/ (US) /-vɚt/ **noun** [C] a pipe for waste water that crosses under roads, railways, etc.

-cum- /-kʌm-/ **preposition** used to join two nouns, showing that a person or thing does two things or has two purposes; combined with: *This is my bedroom-cum-study.*

cumbersome /ˈkʌm.bə.səm/ (US) /-bɚ-/ **adj** awkward because of being large, heavy, or not effective: *cumbersome equipment* ◦ *cumbersome **bureaucracy***

cumin /ˈkjuː.mɪn/ **noun** [U] (a plant with) seeds that smell pleasant and are used as a spice, especially in South Asian and Middle Eastern cooking

cummerbund /ˈkʌm.ə.bʌnd/ (US) /-ɚ-/ **noun** [C] a wide piece of cloth worn round the waist, especially by men, as part of formal or Middle Eastern clothing

cumquat /ˈkʌm.kwɒt/ (US) /-kwɑːt/ **noun** [C] a **kumquat**

cumulative /ˈkjuː.mjʊ.lə.tɪv/ (US) /-t̬ɪv/ **adj** increasing by one addition after another: *The cumulative **effect** of using so many chemicals on the land could be disastrous.* • **cumulatively** /-li/ **adv**

cumulonimbus /ˌkjuː.mjə.ləʊˈnɪm.bəs/ (US) /-loʊ-/ **noun** [U] specialized a large, tall type of cumulus cloud that is often dark and brings heavy rain or a THUNDERSTORM

cumulus /ˈkjuː.mjʊ.ləs/ **noun** [U] specialized a type of tall, white cloud with a wide, flat base and rounded shape → Compare **cirrus, nimbus, stratus**

cuneiform /ˈkjuː.nɪ.fɔːm/ (US) /-fɔːrm/ **adj** of a form of writing used for over 3,000 years until the 1st century BC in the ancient countries of the Middle East • **cuneiform noun** [U]

cunnilingus /ˌkʌn.ɪˈlɪŋ.gəs/ **noun** [U] the sexual activity of moving the tongue across the female sex organs in order to give pleasure and excitement → Compare **fellatio**

cunning /ˈkʌn.ɪŋ/ **adj**; **noun**

▸**adj** **CLEVER** ▷ **1** (C2) describes people who are clever at planning something so that they get what they want, especially by tricking other people, or things that are cleverly made for a particular purpose: *a cunning **plan/ploy*** ◦ *He's a very cunning man.* **ATTRACTIVE** ▷ **2** US old-fashioned pretty and attractive: *a cunning little child/puppy/kitten* • **cunningly** /-li/ **adv**

▸**noun** [U] the quality or skill of being clever at planning something so you get what you want, especially by tricking other people: *We need to **show** a bit of cunning if we want to trick the enemy.*

cunt /kʌnt/ **noun** [C] offensive **1** an offensive word for a very unpleasant or stupid person: *You stupid cunt!* ◦ *He's a right cunt.* **2** offensive for the **vagina**

cup /kʌp/ noun; verb

▸noun DRINKING CONTAINER ▷ **1** A1 [C] a small, round container, often with a handle, used for drinking tea, coffee, etc.: *a cup and saucer* ◦ *a plastic/paper cup* ◦ *a coffee cup/teacup* **2** [C] US a container that holds nearly a quarter of a litre of liquid, used for measuring when cooking SPORT ▷ **3** B1 [C] a specially designed cup, usually with two handles and often made of silver, given as a prize in a sports competition or in a game or match in which the winner receives such a cup: *Sheila won this cup in the school squash championship.* ◦ *The Davis Cup is an important championship.* CONTAINER ▷ **4** [C] a bowl-shaped container: *an egg cup* **5** [C] one of the two parts that support the breasts in a woman's BRA (= piece of underwear): *'What size bra do you wear?' 'A 'C' cup.'* **6** [C] US (UK **box**) a curved piece of hard plastic that is worn by men while playing sports to protect their outer sex organs DRINK ▷ **7** [C or U] a mixture of several types of drink, often including one that is alcoholic, often drunk at parties and usually served from a bowl: *a strawberry/cider cup*

IDIOM **not be sb's cup of tea** If something or someone is not your cup of tea, they are not the type of thing or person that you like: *Thanks for inviting me, but ballet isn't really my cup of tea.*

▸verb [T] (**-pp-**) to hold your hands in the shape of a cup, often around something: *She gently cupped the small injured bird* ***in*** *her* ***hands****.*

cupboard /ˈkʌb.əd/ US /-ɚd/ noun [C] A2 a piece of furniture or a small part of a room with a door or doors behind which there is space for storing things, usually on shelves: *a kitchen cupboard* ◦ *Is there plenty of cupboard* ***space*** *(= are there many cupboards) in your new house?*

IDIOM **the cupboard is bare** used to say that there is no food in a house or that there is no money, etc. available: *I'd like to help you out, Paul, but I'm afraid the cupboard is bare.*

ˈcupboard ˌlove noun [U] love shown by someone, typically a child or an animal, in order to get something that they want such as food

cupcake /ˈkʌp.keɪk/ noun [C] **fairy cake**

ˌcup ˈfinal noun [C] UK the last game in a competition between teams, usually in football or RUGBY, for a CUP: *Manchester United has won the FA (= Football Association) Cup Final for the last two years in a row.*

cupful /ˈkʌp.fʊl/ noun [C] (plural **cupfuls** or US also **cupsful**) the amount held by a cup: *Add two cupfuls of milk to the mixture.*

ˈcup ˌholder noun [C] In team sports, the cup holders are the team that won the CUP (= prize) for the competition held during the previous year or season: *The cup holders began their defence of the trophy in fine style.*

cupid /ˈkjuː.pɪd/ noun [C] a model or painting of a little boy looking like Cupid

Cupid /ˈkjuː.pɪd/ noun the ancient Roman god of love, represented by a naked baby boy who has wings and shoots arrows at people to make them start to love each other

cupidity /kjuːˈpɪd.ɪ.ti/ US /-ə.t̬i/ noun [U] formal a strong feeling of wanting to have something, especially money or possessions

cupola /ˈkjuː.pəl.ə/ noun [C] a DOME (= round roof) on top of a building

cuppa /ˈkʌp.ə/ noun [C] mainly UK informal a cup of tea

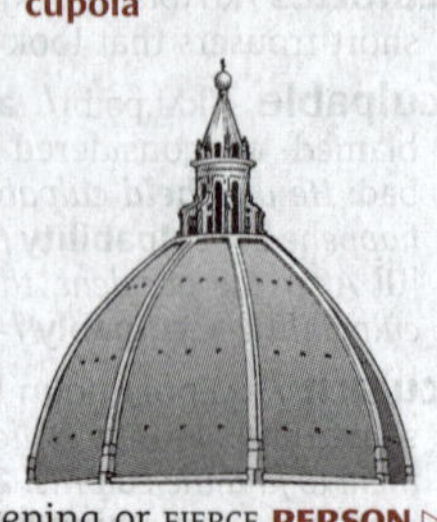
cupola

ˈcup ˌtie noun [C] UK a game between two teams trying to win a CUP (= prize), especially in football

cur /kɜːʳ/ US /kɜː/ noun [C] literary DOG ▷ **1** a MONGREL (= dog of mixed type), especially one that is frightening or FIERCE PERSON ▷ **2** a person who is thought to be worth nothing or COWARDLY (= not brave)

curable /ˈkjʊə.rə.bl̩/ US /ˈkjʊr-/ adj describes a disease that can be cured: *Many illnesses which once killed are today curable.* → Opposite **incurable** • **curability** /ˌkjʊə.rəˈbɪl.ɪ.ti/ US /ˌkjʊr.əˈbɪl.ə.t̬i/ noun [U]

curaçao /ˈkjʊə.rə.saʊ/ US /ˈkjʊr.ə.soʊ/ noun [U] a LIQUEUR (= type of strong alcoholic drink) with an orange flavour

curacy /ˈkjʊə.rə.si/ US /ˈkjʊr.ə-/ noun [C] a job or period of time as a curate: *He's got a curacy in the North of England.*

curate /ˈkjʊə.rət/ US /ˈkjʊr.ət/ noun [C] a priest of the lowest rank, especially in the Church of England, whose job is to help the VICAR (= priest of a particular area)

IDIOM **curate's egg** UK something that is partly good but mainly bad: *The film is a bit of a curate's egg.*

curative /ˈkjʊə.rə.tɪv/ US /ˈkjʊr.ə.t̬ɪv/ adj able to cure or cause to get better: *Do you believe in the curative* ***powers*** *of the local mineral water?*

curator /kjʊˈreɪ.təʳ/ US /kjɜːˈeɪ.t̬ɚ/ noun [C] a person in charge of a museum, library, etc.

curb /kɜːb/ US /kɜːb/ verb; noun

▸verb [T] C2 to control or limit something that is not wanted: *The government should act to curb tax evasion.*

▸noun [C] CONTROL ▷ **1** a limit on something that is not wanted: *You must try to put a curb* ***on*** *your bad temper/spending habits.* EDGE ▷ **2** US spelling of **kerb**

curbside /ˈkɜːb.saɪd/ US /ˈkɜːb-/ noun [U], adj [before noun] US spelling of **kerbside**

curd /kɜːd/ US /kɜːd/ noun [U] (also **curds** [plural]) the solid substance that forms when milk turns sour

ˌcurd ˈcheese noun [U] (also **curds**) mainly UK a soft, smooth, white cheese without a strong taste

curdle /ˈkɜː.dl̩/ US /ˈkɜː-/ verb [I or T] If a liquid curdles, or you curdle it, it gets thicker and develops LUMPS.

IDIOM **make sb's blood curdle** (also **curdle sb's blood**) to fill someone with fear: *The strange sound made his blood curdle.* → See also **bloodcurdling**

cure /kjʊəʳ/ US /kjʊr/ verb; noun

▸verb [T] MAKE WELL ▷ **1** B2 to make someone with an illness healthy again: *At one time doctors couldn't cure TB/cure people* ***of*** *TB.* **2** C1 to solve a problem: *Finance ministers meet this week to discuss how to cure inflation.* PRESERVE ▷ **3** to treat food, tobacco, etc. with smoke, salt, etc. in order to preserve it: *cured meats*

PHRASAL VERB **cure sb of sth** to stop someone doing or wanting something bad: *I ate so much of it one day I was sick and that cured me of my addiction.*

▸noun [C] **1** B2 something that makes someone who is sick healthy again: *There's still no cure* ***for*** *cancer.* ◦ *The disease has* ***no known*** *cure (= a cure has not yet been found).* **2** a solution to a problem: *The best cure* ***for*** *boredom is hard work!*

ˈcure-all noun [C] something that people think will solve any problem or cure any illness

curfew /ˈkɜː.fjuː/ US /ˈkɝː-/ noun [C or U] **1** a rule that everyone must stay at home between particular times, usually at night, especially during a war or a period of political trouble: *to* ***impose/lift*** *a curfew* ◦ *a midnight curfew* ◦ *He was shot for* ***breaking*** (= *not obeying*) *the curfew.* **2** mainly US a time by which a child must be home in the evening

the Curia /ˈkjʊə.ri.ə/ US /ˈkjʊr.i-/ noun [S] specialized the government and court of the Roman Catholic Church, with the Pope in the highest position

curio /ˈkjʊə.ri.əʊ/ US /ˈkjʊr.i.oʊ/ noun [C] (plural **curios**) an unusual object: *a shop full of antiques and curios*

curiosity /ˌkjʊə.riˈɒs.ɪ.ti/ US /ˌkjʊr.iˈɑː.sə.t̬i/ noun **INTEREST** ▷ **1** B2 [U] an eager wish to know or learn about something: *to* ***arouse/excite/satisfy*** *someone's curiosity* ◦ *I'm* ***burning with*** *curiosity – you must tell me who's won!* ◦ *She decided to call her ex-boyfriend* ***out of*** *curiosity.* ◦ *'Why do you ask?' 'Oh, just* ***idle*** *curiosity* (= *for no particular reason*).' **STRANGE OBJECT** ▷ **2** [C] something that is interesting because it is rare and unusual: *Cars like mine are curiosities nowadays.* ◦ *I kept this old pot for its curiosity* ***value*** (= *the interest it has because it is unusual*).

IDIOM **curiosity killed the cat** saying said to warn someone not to ask too many questions about something

curious /ˈkjʊə.ri.əs/ US /ˈkjʊr.i-/ adj **INTERESTED** ▷ **1** B1 interested in learning about people or things around you: *I was curious to know what would happen next.* ◦ *Babies are curious* ***about*** *everything around them.* ◦ *'Why did you ask?' 'I was just curious.'* **STRANGE** ▷ **2** strange and unusual: *There was a curious-****looking*** *man standing outside.* ◦ *A curious thing happened to me yesterday.* ◦ *It's curious (****that****) Billy hasn't phoned when he promised he would.* → Synonym **peculiar** • **curiously** /-li/ adv B2 *Curiously* (= *strangely*), *there didn't seem to be a bank in the town.*

curl /kɜːl/ US /kɝːl/ noun; verb

▸noun [C or U] a piece of hair that grows or has been formed into a curving shape, or something that is the same shape as this: *tight/loose curls* ◦ *Her hair fell* ***in*** *curls over her shoulders.* ◦ *Curls of smoke were rising from the chimney.* → Compare **wave**

▸verb [I or T] **1** to make something into the shape of a curl, or to grow or change into this shape: *Does your hair curl* ***naturally****, or is it permed?* ◦ *A new baby will automatically curl its fingers* ***round*** *any object it touches.* **2** **curl your lip** to show by an upward movement of one side of your mouth that you feel no respect for something or someone: *Her lip curled at what he said.*

IDIOM **curl up and die** informal to feel very ashamed and sorry: *I just wanted to curl up and die when I spilled coffee on their new carpet!*

PHRASAL VERB **curl up** **POSITION** ▷ **1** to sit or lie in a position with your arms and legs close to your body: *She curled up on the sofa to watch TV.* **EDGES** ▷ **2** If something flat, such as paper, curls up, the edges start to become rounded.

curler /ˈkɜː.ləʳ/ US /ˈkɝː.lɚ/ noun [C] (also **roller**) a small plastic tube that you twist hair around to make it curl

curlew /ˈkɜː.ljuː/ US /ˈkɝː-/ noun [C] a large, brownish-coloured bird with long legs and a very long, curved beak, usually found near water

curling /ˈkɜː.lɪŋ/ US /ˈkɝː-/ noun [U] a game played on ice in which special flat, round stones are slid towards a mark

curly /ˈkɜː.li/ US /ˈkɝː-/ adj B1 having curls or a curved shape: *He has blond, curly hair.* ◦ *These pigs all have curly tails.*

curmudgeon /kəˈmʌdʒ.ən/ US /kɚ-/ noun [C] old-fashioned an old person who is often in a bad mood • **curmudgeonly** /-li/ adj

currant /ˈkʌr.ənt/ US /ˈkɝː-/ noun [C] **DRY FRUIT** ▷ **1** a small, black dried GRAPE without seeds, used especially in cakes: *currant buns* **FRUIT** ▷ **2** a small, round fruit that grows on bushes and is eaten fresh or cooked: *blackcurrants/redcurrants* ◦ *currant bushes*

> **! Note:**
> This word is often used in compounds.

currency /ˈkʌr.ən.si/ US /ˈkɝː-/ noun **MONEY** ▷ **1** B1 [C or U] the money that is used in a particular country at a particular time: *foreign currency* **ACCEPTANCE** ▷ **2** [U] the state of being commonly known or accepted, or of being used in many places: *His ideas* ***enjoyed wide*** *currency during the last century.* ◦ *Many informal expressions are* ***gaining*** *currency in serious newspapers.*

current /ˈkʌr.ənt/ US /ˈkɝː-/ adj; noun

▸adj B2 of the present time: *Have you seen the current* ***issue*** *of* (= *the most recently published*) *Vogue magazine?* ◦ *The word is no longer* ***in*** *current* ***use****.* • **currently** /-li/ adv B2 *The Director is currently having talks in the US.*

▸noun [C] **FLOW** ▷ **1** a movement of water, air, or electricity in a particular direction: *to swim* ***against/with*** *the current* ◦ *He was swept out to sea by the* ***strong*** *current.* ◦ *Switch off the electric current before changing the bulb.* **FEELING** ▷ **2** a particular opinion or feeling that a group of people have: *There is a growing current of support for green issues among voters.*

ˌcurrent acˌcount noun [C] UK (US **ˈchecking acˌcount**) a bank account that you can take money from at any time and that usually earns little or no interest

ˌcurrent afˈfairs noun [plural] UK (US **ˌcurrent eˈvents**) political news about events happening now

curriculum /kəˈrɪk.jʊ.ləm/ noun [C] (plural **curricula** or **curriculums**) B1 the subjects studied in a school, college, etc. and what each subject includes: *the school curriculum* → See also **the national curriculum** • **curricular** /-ləʳ/ US /-lɚ/ adj specialized

curriculum vitae /kəˌrɪk.jʊ.ləmˈviː.taɪ/ noun [C] (plural **curricula vitae**) formal a **CV**

curry /ˈkʌr.i/ US /ˈkɝː-/ noun; verb

▸noun [C or U] A2 a dish, originally from South Asia, consisting of meat or vegetables cooked in a spicy sauce: *a hot* (= *very spicy*) *curry* ◦ *a mild* (= *slightly spicy*) *curry* ◦ *vegetable/chicken/lamb curry* ◦ *curry sauce* • **curried** /-id/ adj *curried eggs/fish*

▸verb **TRY TO PLEASE** ▷ **1** **curry favour** disapproving to praise someone, especially someone in authority, in a way that is not sincere, in order to get some advantage for yourself: *He's always trying to curry favour* ***with*** *the boss.* **FOOD** ▷ **2** [T] to make a curry with something: *Let's curry the leftover meat.*

ˌcurry ˈpaste noun [C or U] a soft mixture of spices and oil, used to flavour curries

ˈcurry ˌpowder noun [U] a dry mixture of spices used to flavour curries

curse /kɜːs/ US /kɝːs/ verb; noun

▸verb **SPEAK ANGRILY** ▷ **1** [I or T] to use a word or an expression that is not polite and shows that you are very angry: *We could hear him cursing and swearing as he tried to get the door open.* ◦ *I could curse her* ***for*** *losing my key!* **PERFORM MAGIC** ▷ **2** [T] to say magic words that are intended to bring bad luck to someone: *Things were going so badly – it was as if I'd been cursed.*

C

▸noun **MAGIC** ▷ **1** [C] magic words that are intended to bring bad luck to someone: *In the story, a wicked witch* ***puts a*** *curse* ***on*** *the princess for a hundred years.* **TROUBLE** ▷ **2** [C] a cause of trouble and unhappiness: *Noise is the curse of modern city life.* **BLOOD** ▷ **3 the curse** [S] old-fashioned or humorous a woman's PERIOD (= flow of blood each month) **ANGRY WORD** ▷ **4** [C] a rude word or phrase

cursed /kɜːst/, /ˈkɜː.sɪd/ (US) /ˈkɝːst/ **adj** **SHOWING ANGER** ▷ **1** [before noun] old-fashioned used to describe something that is annoying to you in an angry way: *It's a cursed nuisance, having to work late every evening!* → See also **accursed** **HAVING BAD LUCK** ▷ **2** experiencing problems and unhappiness: *In recent years I've been cursed* ***with*** *worsening eyesight.* **3** experiencing bad luck caused by a magic curse: humorous *I'm sure this car is cursed – it never starts when I need it.*

cursive /ˈkɜː.sɪv/ (US) /ˈkɝː-/ **adj** specialized describes writing that is written with rounded letters that are joined together

cursor /ˈkɜː.səʳ/ (US) /ˈkɝː.sɚ/ **noun** [C] (B2) a line on a computer screen that moves to show the point where work is being done: *You can* ***move*** *the cursor either by using the mouse or by using the arrow keys on the keyboard.*

cursory /ˈkɜː.sᵊr.i/ (US) /ˈkɝː.sɚ-/ **adj** quick and probably not detailed: *a cursory glance/look* ◦ *a cursory examination* • **cursorily** /-ᵊl.i/ (US) /ˈkɝː.sɚ-/ **adv**

curt /kɜːt/ (US) /kɝːt/ **adj** disapproving If someone's manner or speech is curt, it is rude as a result of being very quick: *to give a curt nod/reply* ◦ *The boss was rather curt* ***with*** *him.* • **curtly** /ˈkɜːt.li/ (US) /ˈkɝːt-/ **adv** *Steve answered curtly and turned his back on me.* • **curtness** /ˈkɜːt.nəs/ (US) /ˈkɝːt-/ **noun** [U] *Claire's curtness made him wonder what he'd done wrong.*

curtail /kəˈteɪl/ (US) /kɚ-/ **verb** [T] to stop something before it is finished, or to reduce or limit something: *to curtail your holiday/spending* ◦ *The last government* ***severely*** *curtailed trade union rights.* • **curtailment** /-mənt/ **noun** [C or U]

curtain /ˈkɜː.tᵊn/ (US) /ˈkɝː.t̬ᵊn/ **noun** [C] **1** (A2) a piece of material, especially cloth, that hangs across a window or opening to make a room or part of a room dark or private: *Heavy curtains blocked out the sunlight.* ◦ *to* ***draw*** *(= open or close) the curtains* **2** a thick layer of something that makes it difficult to see anything behind it: *They could see nothing through the curtain of rain/smoke.* **3** the large screen of heavy material in a theatre that separates the stage from the area where people are watching

IDIOM **be curtains for sb** informal used to say someone will die or have to stop doing something: *It'll be curtains for him if he doesn't do what I tell him!*

ˈcurtain ˌcall **noun** [C] the part at the end of a performance when actors come to the front of the stage and the people watching clap to show their enjoyment

ˈcurtain ˌrail **noun** [C] a fixed strip of plastic or metal from which a curtain hangs

ˈcurtain-ˌraiser **noun** [C] **1** a short play sometimes performed before the main play **2** a small event that happens before a bigger one and is a preparation for it

curtilage /ˈkɜː.tᵊl.ɪdʒ/ (US) /ˈkɝː.t̬ᵊl-/ **noun** [U] specialized the land surrounding a building that belongs to the owner of the building and for which he or she has responsibility

curtsy /ˈkɜːt.si/ (US) /ˈkɝːt-/ **verb**; **noun**

▸verb [I] (also **curtsey**) When a girl or woman curtsies, she bends quickly at the knees, with one foot in front of the other, often while holding her skirt, especially to show respect: *She curtsied* ***to*** *the Queen.* → Compare **bow**

▸noun [C] (also **curtsey**) a movement in which a girl or woman bends quickly at the knees, with one foot in front of the other, especially to show respect: *She* ***gave*** *a curtsy before presenting the flowers to the princess.*

curvaceous /kɜːˈveɪ.ʃəs/ (US) /kɝː-/ **adj** describes a woman who has a body with attractive curves

curvature /ˈkɜː.və.tʃəʳ/ (US) /ˈkɝː.və.tʃɚ/ **noun** [U or C] specialized the state of being curved or bent: *the curvature of the Earth's surface* ◦ *a pronounced curvature of the spine*

curve /kɜːv/ (US) /kɝːv/ **noun**; **verb**

▸noun [C] (B2) a line that bends continuously and has no straight parts: *a curve* ***in*** *the road*

▸verb [I] to form a curve, or move in the shape of a curve: *The road curves* ***round*** *to the left.* • **curved** /kɜːvd/ (US) /kɝːvd/ **adj** *a curved surface*

curveball /ˈkɜːv.bɔːl/ (US) /ˈkɝːv.bɑːl/ **noun** [C] mainly US **1** in the sport of baseball, a throw in which the ball curves as it moves towards the player with the BAT **2** something such as a question or event that is surprising or unexpected, and therefore difficult to deal with: *Every so often life will* ***throw*** *you a curveball.*

curvy /ˈkɜː.vi/ (US) /ˈkɝː-/ **adj** containing a lot of curves

cushion /ˈkʊʃ.ᵊn/ **noun**; **verb**

▸noun [C] **SOFT THING** ▷ **1** (B1) a bag made of cloth, plastic, or leather that is filled with soft material, often has an attractive cover, and is used especially on chairs for sitting or leaning on: *She sank back* ***against/into*** *the cushions.* → See also **pincushion** **2 cushion of air** specialized a layer of air often used to support a machine or vehicle: *A hovercraft travels on a cushion of air.* **PROTECTION** ▷ **3** (C2) something that makes the effects of a bad situation less severe: *You should aim to build up a cushion of money in case of emergencies.*

▸verb [T] to make the effect or force of something softer: *The soft grass cushioned his* ***fall.***

IDIOM **cushion the blow** to make a bad situation less serious: *He's lost his job, but the redundancy money will cushion the blow.*

cushy /ˈkʊʃ.i/ **adj** informal disapproving very easy: *a cushy job* ◦ UK *a cushy* ***number*** *(= an easy job or situation)*

cusp /kʌsp/ **noun** [S] the dividing line between two very different things: ***on the*** *cusp* ***of*** *adulthood*

cuspidor /ˈkʌs.pɪ.dɔːʳ/ (US) /-dɔːr/ **noun** [C] US for **spittoon**

cuss /kʌs/ **verb**; **noun**

▸verb [I] mainly US old-fashioned informal to say words that are not polite because you are angry → Compare **curse**

▸noun [C] US old-fashioned informal a person of the bad type mentioned: *Tom's an* ***awkward/stupid/irritable*** *(****old****) cuss!*

cussed /ˈkʌs.ɪd/ **adj** disapproving describes people who are unwilling to be helpful, or things that are annoying: *He's just* ***plain*** *cussed: he's only doing it because I asked him not to!* ◦ *It's a cussed nuisance.* • **cussedly** /ˈkʌs.ɪd.li/ **adv** • **cussedness** /ˈkʌs.ɪd.nəs/ **noun** [U] *He refused to help* ***out of sheer/pure*** *cussedness.*

custard /ˈkʌs.təd/ ⓤⓢ /-tɚd/ **noun** [U] a sweet sauce made from eggs, milk, and sugar and poured over sweet dishes: *apple pie and custard*

ˌcustard ˈpie **noun** [C] UK a flat, open pastry container filled with artificial custard, thrown at people's faces as part of a show to make people laugh

ˈcustard ˌpowder **noun** [U] UK a yellowish powder that you combine with milk to make custard

custodial /kʌsˈtəʊ.di.əl/ ⓤⓢ /-ˈtoʊ-/ **adj** PRISON ▷ **1** **custodial sentence** a period of time that someone must stay in prison CARE ▷ **2** relating to the legal right to care for someone or something, especially a child: *custodial care*

custodian /kʌsˈtəʊ.di.ən/ ⓤⓢ /-ˈtoʊ-/ **noun** [C] **1** formal a person with responsibility for protecting or taking care of something or keeping something in good condition: *the custodian* ***of*** *a museum/castle* **2** formal someone who tries to protect particular ideas or principles: *She sees herself as a custodian* ***of*** *the public's morals.* **3** US for **caretaker**

custody /ˈkʌs.tə.di/ **noun** [U] CARE ▷ **1** C2 the legal right or duty to care for someone or something, especially a child after its parents have separated or died: *The court* ***awarded/granted/gave*** *custody* ***of*** *the child to the father.* ◦ *The mother* ***got/received*** *custody* ***of*** *the child.* ◦ *The parents were given* ***joint*** *custody.* PRISON ▷ **2** C2 the state of being kept in prison, especially while waiting to go to court for trial: *You will be* ***remanded in*** *custody until your trial.*

custom /ˈkʌs.təm/ **noun** USUAL WAY ▷ **1** B1 [C or U] a way of behaving or a belief that has been established for a long time: *a local/ancient custom* ◦ [+ to infinitive] *In my country, it's* ***the*** *custom (****for*** *women)* ***to*** *get married in white.* **2** [S] something you usually do: *He left the house at nine exactly,* ***as is*** *his custom.* TRADE ▷ **3** [U] the support given to a business, especially a shop, by the people who buy things or services from it: *Most of our custom comes from tourists nowadays.* ◦ *If we don't give good service, people will* ***take*** *their custom* ***elsewhere***. OFFICIAL CHECK ▷ **4** **customs** [plural] B1 the place at a port, airport, or border where travellers' bags are looked at to find out if any goods are being carried illegally: *to* ***go through*** *customs*

custom- /kʌs.təm-/ **prefix** used before another word to mean 'specially designed for a particular person or purpose': *custom-designed* ◦ *custom-built software*

customary /ˈkʌs.tə.mᵊr.i/ ⓤⓢ /-mer-/ **adj** USUAL ▷ **1** C1 usual: *She's not her customary cheerful self today.* TRADITIONAL ▷ **2** C1 traditional: [+ to infinitive] *In my village,* ***it*** *is customary* ***for*** *a girl* ***to*** *take her mother's name.* • **customarily** /kʌs.təˈmer.ɪ.li/ **adv**

ˌcustom-ˈbuilt **adj** If a car, machine, etc. is custom-built, it is made according to the needs of a particular buyer.

customer /ˈkʌs.tə.məʳ/ ⓤⓢ /-mɚ/ **noun** [C] A2 a person who buys goods or a service: *a satisfied customer* ◦ *Mrs Wilson is one of our* ***regular*** *customers.*

> **! Common mistake: customer**
>
> **Warning:** Check your spelling!
>
> **Customer** is one of the 50 words most often spelled wrongly by learners. Remember: don't write 'costumer', write **customer**.

IDIOM **the customer is always right** saying said to emphasize that in business, it is very important not to disagree with a customer or make them angry

ˈcustomer ˌbase **noun** [C] the people who buy or use a particular product or service

ˈcustomer-ˌfacing **adj** customer-facing staff or jobs deal directly with people buying a product or using a service

ˌcustomer ˈservices **noun** [plural] the part of an organization that answers customers' questions, exchanges goods that are not satisfactory, etc.

customize (UK usually **customise**) /ˈkʌs.tə.maɪz/ **verb** [T] to make or change something according to the buyer's or user's needs • **customization** (UK usually **customisation**) /ˌkʌs.tə.maɪˈzeɪ.ʃᵊn/ **noun** [U] *The website allows users some customization.* • **customized** (UK usually **customised**) /-maɪzd/ **adj** *The company specializes in customized computer systems.*

ˌcustom-ˈmade **adj** If an article of clothing is custom-made, it is specially made for a particular buyer: *custom-made shoes*

ˌCustoms and ˈExcise **noun** [+ sing/pl verb] the former name for the UK government department that collects taxes, especially on goods leaving or entering the country

ˈcustoms ˌofficer **noun** [C] a person whose job is to make certain travellers are not taking goods into a country without paying taxes

cut /kʌt/ **verb; noun**

▸**verb** (present tense **cutting**, past tense and past participle **cut**) USE KNIFE ▷ **1** A2 [I or T] to break the surface of something, or to divide or make something smaller, using a sharp tool, especially a knife: *to cut a slice of bread* ◦ *I've cut myself/my hand* ***on*** *that glass/****with*** *that knife.* ◦ *Cut the meat* ***up*** *into small pieces.* ◦ *This knife doesn't cut very well.* ◦ *Where did you* ***have*** *your* ***hair cut?*** ◦ [+ obj + adj] *Firefighters had to cut the trapped driver* ***loose/free*** *(= cut the metal to allow the driver to get out of the car) using special equipment.* ◦ *He fell off the swing and cut his head* ***open*** *(= got a deep cut in his head).* ◦ *He cut the cake* ***in/into*** *six (pieces) and gave each child a slice.* REDUCE ▷ **2** B2 [T] to make something shorter, lower, smaller, etc.: *to cut prices/costs* ◦ *to cut overtime/wages* REMOVE ▷ **3** B2 [T] to remove something from something else: *The sex scenes had been cut* ***out of*** *the English version of the film.* **4** **cut and paste** to move words or pictures from one place to another in a computer document **5** **cut sb out of your will** to decide not to leave someone any of your money or possessions when you die MISS ▷ **6** [T] mainly US informal to not go, especially to a place where you should be: *Your son has been cutting* ***classes***. STOP ▷ **7** [I or T] to stop or interrupt something: *to cut an engine/a motor* ◦ *'Cut! (= stop filming!)' shouted the director.* **8** **cut sb short** to stop someone from talking before they have finished what they were saying: *He started to explain, but she cut him short.* **9** **cut it/that out!** informal used to tell someone to stop talking or stop behaving in an annoying way: ***Just*** *cut it out! I've had enough of your silly jokes.* GROW TEETH ▷ **10** **cut a tooth** (of a baby) to grow a new tooth: *The baby's cutting a tooth. That's why she's crying.* TAKE SHORT WAY ▷ **11** [I usually + adv/prep] to go through or across a place, especially in order to get somewhere quickly: *to cut* ***through*** *a passage* **12** **cut a corner** UK to fail to keep to your own side of the road when going round a corner CARDS ▷ **13** [I or T] to choose a playing card by dividing a pile of cards into two parts: *Who's going to cut the cards?* RECORD ▷

14 [T] to record music or speech on a record: *When did the Stones cut their first record?*

> **Other ways of saying cut**
>
> The verb **chop** means 'to cut something into pieces':
>
> *He was **chopping** vegetables to make a stew.*
>
> When you cut something into thin, flat pieces, you can use the word **slice**:
>
> ***Slice** the mushrooms and fry them in butter.*
>
> The verb **snip** means 'to cut something with scissors, usually with small quick cuts':
>
> *She **snipped** the corner off the soup packet.*
>
> If you make a long straight cut in something, the verb **slit** can be used:
>
> *He **slit** open the envelope with a knife.*
>
> If someone cuts stone or wood, the verb **carve** is often used:
>
> *He **carved** her name on a tree.*
>
> **Carve** can also be used when someone cuts slices off a large piece of meat:
>
> *Would you like me to **carve** the chicken?*
>
> If you cut a small amount of something in order to make it neater, you can use the verb **trim**:
>
> *I'm going to get my hair **trimmed**.*
>
> The verbs **slash** or **hack** can be used when someone cuts something in a rough or violent way:
>
> *The museum was broken into and several paintings were **slashed**.*
>
> *He **hacked** the wood with an axe.*

IDIOMS **be cut up** UK to be upset: *Philip was very cut up **about** his grandmother's death.* • **can't cut it** (also **can't cut the mustard**) mainly US to not be able to deal with problems or difficulties in a satisfactory way: *If he can't cut it, then we'll get someone else to do the job.* • **cut sb dead** to pretend you do not know someone in order to show you are angry: *I said 'Good morning' but he just cut me dead.* • **cut sb down to size** to show someone that they are not as clever or important as they think they are: *Someone should cut that man down to size!* • **cut your losses** to avoid losing any more money than you have already lost: *Let's cut our losses and sell the business before prices drop even further.* • **cut your political, professional, etc. teeth** to get your first experience of the type mentioned: *The minister cut her political teeth **on** student debates.* • **cut sb some slack** informal to not judge someone as severely as you usually would because they are having problems at the present time: *'Andrew's late again.' 'Cut him some slack – his wife's just had a baby.'* • **cut to the chase** informal to talk about or deal with the important parts of a subject and not waste time with things that are not important: *I didn't have long to talk so I cut to the chase and asked whether he was still married.* • **cut (sb) to the quick** to hurt someone's feelings a lot: *Her thoughtless remark cut him to the quick.* • **cut a fine figure** (also **cut quite a figure/dash**) to cause people to admire you because of your appearance: *The young soldier cut a fine figure in his smart new uniform.* • **cut a swathe through sth** to destroy a large part of something or kill many of a group of people: *The storm cut a swathe through the village.* • **cut both/two ways** If you say something cuts both/two ways, you think it has both a good and a bad side. • **cut corners** to do something in the easiest, cheapest, or fastest way • **cut it/things fine** to allow very little time for something: *She arrived ten minutes before her flight, so she was cutting it **a bit** fine.* • **cut loose** US to behave in an uncontrolled, wild way • **cut no ice with sb** to not cause someone to change their opinion or decision: *I've heard her excuses and they cut no ice with me.* • **cut off your nose to spite your face** to do something because you are angry, even if it will cause trouble for you • **cut the crap!** offensive a rude way of telling someone to stop saying things that are not true or not important • **cut the ground from under sb's feet** to make someone or their ideas seem less good, especially by doing something before them or better than them • **cut up rough** UK to become very angry, and often violent • **not be cut out for sth** C2 to not be the right type of person for something: *I'm not cut out for an office job.* • **you could cut the atmosphere with a knife** used to describe a situation in which everyone is feeling very angry or nervous and you feel that something unpleasant could soon happen • **cut your coat according to your cloth** UK said to emphasize that someone should do the best they can with the limited money they have

PHRASAL VERBS **cut across sth** CROSS ▷ **1** B2 to go straight from one side of an area to another instead of going around: *If we cut across the field, it'll save time.* AFFECT ▷ **2** C1 If a problem or subject cuts across different groups of people, all of those groups are affected by or interested in it: *Support for environmental issues cuts across traditional party lines.* • **cut back/down** B2 to do less of something or use something in smaller amounts: *The government has announced plans to cut back **on** defence spending by 10 percent next year.* ◦ *I'm trying to cut down **on** caffeine.* • **cut sth down** B2 to make a tree or other plant fall to the ground by cutting it near the bottom • **cut in** TALK ▷ **1** to interrupt what someone is saying by saying something yourself: *I was just talking to Jan, when Dave cut in (**on** us/our conversation).* DRIVE ▷ **2** to make a sudden sideways movement in order to position your car in front of another car, not leaving a safe distance between the two vehicles: *Did you see that white car cut in (**on** us/**in front of** us)?* → See also **cut sb up** DANCE ▷ **3** old-fashioned to interrupt two people who are dancing in order to dance with one of them • **cut sb in** to allow someone to take part in something, for example a game or business: *Shall we cut you in (**on** the deal/game)?* • **cut into sth** If an activity cuts into a period of time, it fills part of it, often a large part of it: *I don't like doing the shopping on a Saturday afternoon because it cuts into my weekend.* • **cut sth off** REMOVE ▷ **1** A2 to remove a part of something to make it smaller or shorter, using a sharp tool such as a knife: *Remember to cut off the fat before you fry the steak.* STOP ▷ **2** B2 to stop providing something such as electricity, supplies, etc.: *If this bill is not paid within five days, your gas supply will be cut off.* ◦ *The aim was to cut off the enemy's escape route/supplies.* • **cut sb off** PHONE ▷ **1** [usually passive] to stop people from continuing a phone conversation by breaking the phone connection: *We were cut off before she could give me directions.* DRINKS ▷ **2** US If someone serving drinks in a bar cuts you off, they stop serving you alcoholic drinks because they think you have drunk too many: *I'm glad the bartender cut Tommy off – he's already had too much to drink.* • **cut sb/sth off** B2 to cause a person or place to become separate, or cause someone to be or feel alone: *When his wife died, he cut himself off **from** other people.* ◦ *Many villages have been cut off **by** the heavy snow.* • **cut sth out** REMOVE ▷ **1** C1 to remove something or form a shape by cutting, usually from paper or cloth: *She cut* *out his picture from the magazine.* **STOP EATING** ▷ **2** C1 to stop eating or drinking something, usually to improve your health: *Since my heart attack, I've cut fatty foods out altogether.* • **cut sb out** to not allow someone to share something or be included in something: *They cut me out **of** the conversation.* • **cut out STOP WORKING** ▷ **1** If an engine, machine, or piece of equipment cuts out, it suddenly stops working: *One of the plane's engines cut out, so they had to land with only one.* **DRIVE** ▷ **2** US to make a sudden sideways movement out of a line of traffic: *Don't cut out when everyone is going fast.* • **cut through sth** If you cut through something difficult that usually causes problems, you quickly understand it or deal with it so that it does not cause problems for you: *She always manages to cut through the complex theory and get at the facts.* • **cut sth up** B1 to cut something into pieces • **cut sb up** UK (US **cut sb off**) to suddenly move your car sideways in front of another car which was in front of you, leaving too little space: *I **got/was** cut up several times on the motorway this morning – I've never seen such dangerous driving!* • **cut up** US to behave in a very active and silly way in order to make people laugh: *I hate it when Jane cuts up in class.*

▸**noun INJURY** ▷ **1** B1 [C] an injury made when the skin is cut with something sharp: *a deep cut* **MEAT** ▷ **2** [C] a piece of meat cut from a particular part of an animal: *Sirloin is the most expensive cut **of** beef.* **STYLE** ▷ **3** [S] the shape into which something is cut: *I don't like **the** cut **of** these jeans.* **REDUCTION** ▷ **4** C1 [C] a reduction in the number, amount, or rate of something: *a cut **in** expenditure/interest rates/hospital waiting lists* **5 cuts** [plural] reductions in public spending **PART REMOVED** ▷ **6** [C] the act of removing a part from a book, film, etc., or a part that is removed: *The movie contains some very violent scenes, so some cuts were **made** when it was shown on TV.* **SHARE** ▷ **7** [S] informal a share of something, usually money: *When am I going to get my cut?*

IDIOMS **a cut above** someone who is of a higher social class: *She thinks she's a cut above her neighbours.* • **cut and thrust** interesting and exciting arguments: *She enjoys the cut and thrust of party politics.*

ˌcut and ˈdried adj already decided and unlikely to be changed: *We need a cut-and-dried decision by the end of the week.*

cutback /ˈkʌt.bæk/ noun [C] C1 a reduction in something, made in order to save money: *The closure of the Manchester printing factory is the company's biggest single cutback so far.*

cute /kjuːt/ adj **ATTRACTIVE** ▷ **1** (especially of something or someone small or young) pleasant and attractive: *He's got a really cute baby brother.* **CLEVER** ▷ **2** US wishing to seem clever, sometimes in a rude or unpleasant way: *Don't be cute with me, Vicki.* • /ˈkjuːt.li/ adv • **cuteness** /ˈkjuːt.nəs/ noun [U]

cutesy /ˈkjuːt.si/ adj informal disapproving artificially attractive and pleasant, especially in a CHILDISH way

ˌcut ˈglass noun [U] glass with a decorative pattern cut into the surface: [before noun] *a cut-glass bowl*

ˌcut-ˈglass adj [before noun] UK used about a way of speaking in which words are pronounced very clearly and carefully, in a way that is typical of someone from a high social class: *a cut-glass accent*

cuticle /ˈkjuː.tɪ.kl/ US /-t̬ɪ-/ noun [C] the thin skin at the base of the nails on the fingers and toes

cutie (also **cutey**) /ˈkjuː.ti/ US /-t̬i/ noun [C] (also **ˈcutie ˌpie**) informal a woman or girl who you consider attractive or like a lot: *His daughter is a real cutie.* ◦ [as form of address] *Hi there, cutie, we were just talking about you.*

cutlass /ˈkʌt.ləs/ noun [C] a curved SWORD with a single sharp edge, especially as used in the past by PIRATES

cutlery /ˈkʌt.lə.ri/ US /-lɚ.i/ noun [U] UK (US usually **silverware**) C2 knives, forks, and spoons used for eating food → Compare **crockery**

cutlet /ˈkʌt.lət/ noun [C] **PIECE OF MEAT** ▷ **1** a small piece of meat still joined to the bone, especially from the animal's neck or RIBS: ***lamb** cutlets* **SAVOURY FOOD** ▷ **2** small pieces of vegetables, nuts, fish, or meat that have been pressed into a round flat shape: *a **nut** cutlet*

ˌcut ˈlunch noun [C] Australian English a light meal put in a container, usually to take with you somewhere to be eaten later → Compare **packed lunch**

cutoff /ˈkʌt.ɒf/ US /ˈkʌt̬.ɑːf/ noun [C] **STOP** ▷ **1** the act of stopping the supply of something: *The US has announced a cutoff **of** military aid to the country.* **2** a fixed point or level at which you stop including people or things: *31 March is the cutoff **date** for applications to be accepted.* **TROUSERS** ▷ **3 cutoffs** [plural] (also **cutoff jeans**) a pair of JEANS or trousers that has had the bottom parts of the legs removed

cutout /ˈkʌt.aʊt/ US /ˈkʌt̬-/ noun [C] **SHAPE** ▷ **1** a shape that has been cut out from something, especially a flat one that can stand vertically: *a life-size cutout **of** the actor* **SAFETY DEVICE** ▷ **2** a device that, for safety reasons, stops or interrupts a CIRCUIT, used, for example, in a motor or engine: *a cutout **fuse/switch***

cutpiece /ˈkʌt.piːs/ noun [C] Indian English a piece of cloth, usually the last piece left from a BALE (= a long, rolled piece of cloth); a **remnant**

ˌcut-ˈprice adj [before noun] **1** describes something that costs less than its usual price: *cut-price airline tickets* **2** A cut-price shop sells things at lower prices than other shops.

ˌcut-ˈrate adj [before noun] charged at a lower rate than usual: *We get cut-rate electricity for six hours each night.*

cutters /ˈkʌt.əz/ US /-ɚz/ noun [plural] a tool for cutting something: *wire cutters* ◦ *bolt cutters*

cutthroat /ˈkʌt.θrəʊt/ US /-θroʊt/ adj mainly UK not involving considering or worrying about any harm caused to others: *the cutthroat **world** of journalism* ◦ *The advertising world can be a very cutthroat **business**.*

ˌcutthroat ˈrazor noun [C] UK (US **ˌstraight ˈrazor**, **ˌstraight-edge ˈrazor**) a type of old-fashioned RAZOR with a long blade that folds out from the handle

cutting /ˈkʌt.ɪŋ/ US /ˈkʌt̬-/ noun; adj

▸**noun** [C] **ARTICLE** ▷ **1** UK (US also **clipping**) an article that has been cut from a newspaper or magazine **PLANT** ▷ **2** a piece cut off from a plant that can be used to grow another plant of the same type **PASSAGE** ▷ **3** (US **cut**) a deep, narrow passage made through a hill for a road, railway, or CANAL

▸**adj** unkind and intending to upset someone: *a cutting remark/comment* ◦ *He can be very cutting when he chooses to be!*

ˌcutting-ˈedge adj [before noun] C1 very modern and with all the newest features: *cutting-edge design/technology* → Compare **bleeding-edge**

the ˌcutting ˈedge noun [S] the most modern stage of development in a particular type of work or activity: *a company **at** the cutting edge **of** mobile communications technology*

cuttlefish /ˈkʌt.l̩.fɪʃ/ US /ˈkʌt̬-/ noun [C] (plural

cuttlefish or cuttlefishes) a sea creature with eight arms and two TENTACLES that has a wide, flat shell inside its body and lives in waters near the coast and near the bottom of the sea

cutup /ˈkʌt.ʌp/ (US) /ˈkʌṭ-/ **noun** [C] US someone who behaves in an active and silly way in order to make people laugh: *It's hard to believe Sally was a cutup in school – she's so quiet now.*

CV /ˌsiːˈviː/ **noun** [C] **1** B1 mainly UK (US usually **résumé**) abbreviation for **curriculum vitae**: a short written description of your education, qualifications, previous jobs, and sometimes also your personal interests, that you send to an employer when you are trying to get a job **2** US a written description of the previous work of someone who is looking for a job at a college or university: *Applicants interested in applying for the position should submit their CVs to the Anatomy Department no later than 15 February.*

cwt **noun** written abbreviation for **hundredweight**

cyan /ˈsaɪ.ən/ **noun** [U] a deep greenish-blue colour, one of the main colours that are used in colour printing and photography • **cyan** **adj** of a deep greenish-blue colour

cyanide /ˈsaɪə.naɪd/ **noun** [U] an extremely powerful poison that can kill people

cyber- /saɪ.bər-/ (US) /-bɚ-/ **prefix** involving, using, or relating to computers, especially the internet: *cybercrime* ◦ *cyberculture*

cyberattack /ˈsaɪ.bə.rəˌtæk/ (US) /-bɚ.əˌtæk/ **noun** [C] an illegal attempt to harm someone's computer system or the information on it, using the internet

cyberbully /ˈsaɪ.bəˌbʊl.i/ (US) /-bɚ-/ **noun** [C] someone who uses the internet to harm or frighten another person, especially by sending them unpleasant messages • **cyberbullying** /-ɪŋ/ **noun** [U]

cybercafé /ˈsaɪ.bəˌkæf.eɪ/ (US) /-bɚ-/ **noun** [C] a small, informal restaurant where you can pay to use the internet

cybercrime /ˈsaɪ.bə.kraɪm/ (US) /-bɚ-/ **noun** [U] crime or illegal activity that is done using the internet

cyberfraud /ˈsaɪ.bə.frɔːd/ (US) /-bɚ.frɑːd/ **noun** [U] the use of the internet to get money, goods, etc. from people illegally by deceiving them

cyberlaw /ˈsaɪ.bəˌlɔː/ (US) /-bɚˌlɑː/ **noun** [U or C] laws about how people should use computers, especially the internet, or one of these laws

cybernetics /ˌsaɪ.bəˈnet.ɪks/ (US) /-bɚˈneṭ-/ **noun** [U] the scientific study of how information is communicated in machines and electronic devices, comparing this with how information is communicated in the brain and nervous system

cyberpet /ˈsaɪ.bə.pet/ (US) /-bɚ-/ **noun** [C] an electronic toy that behaves like a pet

cyberpunk /ˈsaɪ.bə.pʌŋk/ (US) /-bɚ-/ **noun** [U] literature about an imaginary society controlled by computers: *cyberpunk science fiction*

cybersex /ˈsaɪ.bə.seks/ (US) /-bɚ-/ **noun** [U] any sexual entertainment or activity that involves using the internet

cyberspace /ˈsaɪ.bə.speɪs/ (US) /-bɚ-/ **noun** [U] the internet considered as an imaginary area without limits where you can meet people and discover information about any subject: *You can find the answer to almost any question in cyberspace.*

cybersquatting /ˈsaɪ.bəˌskwɒt.ɪŋ/ (US) /-bɚˌskwɑː.ṭɪŋ/ **noun** [U] the situation in which someone pays for a famous name as an internet address, so that they can later sell it for a high price to the person or organization with that name • **cybersquat** /-skwɒt/ (US) /-skwɑːt/ **verb** [I] (plural **-tt-**) • **cybersquatter** /-ˌskwɒt.əʳ/ (US) /-ˌskwɑː.ṭɚ/ **noun** [C]

cyberterrorism /ˈsaɪ.bəˌter.ə.rɪ.zəm/ (US) /-bɚˌter.ɚ.ɪ-/ **noun** [U] the use of the internet to damage or destroy computer systems for political or other reasons

cyberterrorist /ˈsaɪ.bəˌter.ə.rɪst/ (US) /-bɚˌter.ɚ.ɪst/ **noun** [C] someone who takes part in cyberterrorism: *Unidentified cyberterrorists gained access to emails and financial details of customers.*

cyberwarfare /ˌsaɪ.bəˈwɔː.feəʳ/ (US) /-bɚˈwɔːr.fer/ **noun** [U] the use of the internet to attack an enemy, by damaging things such as communication and transport systems or water and electricity supplies

cyclamen /ˈsɪk.lə.mən/ **noun** [C] a small plant with white, pink, purple, or red flowers whose PETALS turn backwards, and green and silver leaves

cycle /ˈsaɪ.kl̩/ **noun; verb**

▸**noun** **BICYCLE** ▷ **1** B2 [C] a bicycle **SERIES** ▷ **2** B2 [C] a group of events that happen in a particular order, one following the other, and are often repeated: *the life cycle of a moth* **3** [C] one in a series of movements that a machine performs: *the washing machine's spin cycle* **LITERATURE/MUSIC** ▷ **4** [C, + sing/pl verb] a group of plays, poems, songs, etc. written by one person and connected with each other by dealing with the same characters or ideas

▸**verb** [I] B1 to ride a bicycle • **cycling** /-klɪŋ/ **noun** [U] A2 *We did a lot of cycling in France last year.*

ˈcycle ˌclips **noun** [plural] thin straps that you wear around the bottom of your trousers when you are riding a bicycle to prevent the trousers from becoming caught in the bicycle's chain

ˈcycle ˌhelmet **noun** [C] (also **ˈcycling ˌhelmet**) a hard hat that you wear to protect your head if you have an accident while you are riding a bicycle

ˈcycle ˌlane/path **noun** [C] UK (US **ˈbike ˌlane**, **ˈbicycle ˌlane**) a part of the road or a special path for the use of people riding bicycles

ˈcycle ˌrack **noun** [C] UK (US **ˈbike ˌrack**) a row of frames where bicycles can be left

ˌcycle ˈrickshaw **noun** [C] a bicycle with three wheels, with a covered seat at the back for passengers, used as a form of taxi in some Asian countries

cyclical /ˈsaɪ.klɪ.kəl/, /ˈsɪk.lɪ-/ **adj** (also **cyclic**) describes a group of events that happen in a particular order, one following the other, and that are often repeated: *Changes in the economy have followed a cyclical pattern.*

ˈcycling ˌshorts **noun** [plural] (also **ˈcycle ˌshorts**) short, tight trousers worn by people involved in CYCLING sports

cyclist /ˈsaɪ.klɪst/ **noun** [C] B1 someone who rides a bicycle

cyclone /ˈsaɪ.kləʊn/ (US) /-kloʊn/ **noun** [C] a violent tropical storm or wind in which the air moves very fast in a circular direction

Cyclops /ˈsaɪ.klɒps/ (US) /-klɑːps/ **noun** in ancient Greek stories, a GIANT (= extremely tall creature) with one eye

cygnet /ˈsɪg.nət/ **noun** [C] a young SWAN (= a large, white bird with a long neck)

cylinder /ˈsɪl.ɪn.dəʳ/ (US) /-dɚ/ **noun** [C] **SHAPE** ▷ **1** a solid or hollow tube with long straight sides and two circular ends the same size, or an object shaped like this, often used as a container: *Deep-sea divers carry cylinders of oxygen on their backs.* **ENGINE PART** ▷ **2** the tube-shaped device, found especially in an engine, inside which the part of the engine that causes the fuel to produce power moves up and down: *a six-cylinder engine*

cylindrical /sɪˈlɪn.drɪ.kəl/ **adj** having the shape of a cylinder (= hollow tube)

cymbal /ˈsɪm.bəl/ **noun** [C usually plural] a flat round musical instrument made of BRASS, that makes a loud noise when hit with a stick or against another cymbal

cynic /ˈsɪn.ɪk/ **noun** [C] disapproving a person who believes that people are only interested in themselves and are not sincere: *I'm too much of a cynic to believe that he'll keep his promise.* ◦ *A cynic might say that the government has only taken this measure because it is concerned about its declining popularity.*

cynical /ˈsɪn.ɪ.kəl/ **adj** disapproving **1** C2 believing that people are only interested in themselves and are not sincere: *I think she takes a rather cynical* ***view*** *of men.* ◦ *I've always been* ***deeply*** *cynical* ***about*** *politicians.* **2** describes the use of someone's feelings or emotions to your own advantage: *He praises my cooking but it's just a cynical ploy to get me to make his meals.* • **cynically** /-kəl.i/ **adv** • **cynicism** /-sɪ.zəm/ **noun** [U]

cynosure /ˈsaɪ.nə.sjʊəʳ/ US /-ʃʊr/ **noun** [C] literary a person or thing that is so good or beautiful that it attracts a lot of attention

cypher /ˈsaɪ.fəʳ/ US /-fɚ/ **noun** [C or U] another spelling of **cipher**

cypress /ˈsaɪ.prəs/ **noun** [C] a type of CONIFER (= tree that never loses its leaves)

Cyrillic /sɪˈrɪl.ɪk/ **adj, noun** [U] (written in, or relating to) the alphabet used in some Slavonic languages, such as Russian

cyst /sɪst/ **noun** [C] a round mass growing just under the skin or deeper in the body, that contains liquid: *He had a cyst removed from near his eye.*

cystic fibrosis /ˌsɪs.tɪk.faɪˈbrəʊ.sɪs/ US /-ˈbroʊ-/ **noun** [U] a serious disease that causes GLANDS in the lungs and other organs, such as the LIVER and the PANCREAS, not to work correctly

cystitis /sɪˈstaɪ.tɪs/ US /-t̬ɪs/ **noun** [U] a disease, especially of women, in which the BLADDER becomes infected and there is pain when urinating

cytology /saɪˈtɒl.ə.dʒi/ US /-ˈtɑː.lə-/ **noun** [U] the scientific study of cells from living things

cytoplasm /ˈsaɪ.tə.plæz.əm/ US /-t̬ə-/ **noun** [U] specialized the substance inside a cell that surrounds the cell's NUCLEUS

czar /zɑːʳ/ US /zɑːr/ **noun** [C] mainly US for **tsar**

D

D

D, d /diː/ noun (plural **Ds, D's** or **d's**) LETTER ▷ **1** [C or U] the fourth letter of the English alphabet NUMBER ▷ **2** (also **d**) [C] the sign used in the Roman system for the number 500 MUSIC ▷ **3** [C or U] a note in Western music: *in (**the key of**) D*

d. written abbreviation for died: used when giving the dates of someone's birth and death: *John Winston Lennon (b. 9 October 1940, Liverpool, d. 8 December 1980, New York).*

'd /əd/ short form of **1** would: *I asked if she'd like to come tonight.* **2** had: *If you'd told me what was wrong I could have helped.*

DA /ˌdiːˈeɪ/ noun [C] US abbreviation for **district attorney**

dab /dæb/ verb; noun

▸verb [I or T] (-bb-) to touch something with quick light touches, or to put a substance on something with quick light touches: *She dabbed **at** her eyes with a tissue.* ◦ *She dabbed a little perfume behind her ears.*

▸noun [C] a small amount of a substance, or a light touch: *Can't you just put **a** dab **of** paint over the mark and cover it up?* ◦ *I'll give that stain a quick dab with a wet cloth.*

DAB /diː.eɪˈbiː/ noun [U] abbreviation for **digital audio broadcasting**

dabble /ˈdæb.l̩/ verb TRY ▷ **1** [I] to take a slight and not very serious interest in a subject, or try a particular activity for a short period: *He first dabbled **in** politics when he was at law school.* ◦ *She dabbled **with** drugs at university.* MOVE IN WATER ▷ **2** [T] to put part of your body, such as your hand or foot, into the water of a pool or stream, etc. and move it about • **dabbler** /-ləʳ/ (US) /-lɚ/ noun [C]

ˌdab ˈhand noun [C] UK informal someone who is very good at a particular activity: *Binns was a dab hand **at** cricket and played for his county in his youth.* ◦ *Carlo's a dab hand in the kitchen (= good at cooking), isn't he?*

dachshund /ˈdæk.sənd/ (US) /ˈdɑːks.hʊnd/ noun [C] (informal **ˈsausage ˌdog**, US informal **ˈwiener ˌdog**) a small dog with a long body and short legs

dacoit /dəˈkɔɪt/ noun [C] Indian English one of a group of thieves who carry weapons

Dacron /ˈdæk.rɒn/ (US) /-rɑːn/ noun [U] US trademark (cloth made from) an artificial thread

dad /dæd/ noun [C] informal (A1) a father: [as form of address] *Can you pick me up from the party tonight, Dad?* ◦ *It was lovely to see your **mum and** dad at the school concert last night.*

daddy /ˈdæd.i/ noun [C] child's word for father: [as form of address] *I'm tired, Daddy.* ◦ *Why don't you show your daddy your lovely picture?*

daddy longlegs /ˌdæd.iˈlɒŋ.legz/ (US) /-ˈlɑːŋ-/ noun [C] (plural **daddy longlegs**) informal for **crane fly**

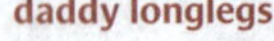

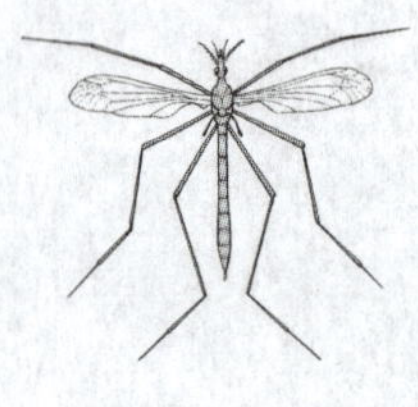

dado rail /ˈdeɪ.dəʊ.reɪl/ (US) /-doʊ-/ noun [C] a long thin piece of decorative wood fixed about one metre above the floor along all the walls of a room

daffodil /ˈdæf.ə.dɪl/ noun [C] a yellow, bell-shaped flower with a long stem that is commonly seen in the spring

daffy /ˈdæf.i/ adj informal strange or unusual, sometimes in a humorous way

daft /dɑːft/ (US) /dæft/ adj informal silly or stupid: *You daft idiot!* ◦ *It was a pretty daft idea anyway.* ◦ *Don't be daft – let me pay – you paid last time.*

IDIOM **be (as) daft as a brush** UK informal to be very silly: *He's a nice enough boy, but he's as daft as a brush.*

dag /dæg/ noun [C] Australian English informal a person who does not look attractive or who behaves in a way that is not attractive • **daggy** /ˈdæg.i/ adj Australian English and UK informal (of a person or their clothes) untidy or dirty

dagger /ˈdæg.əʳ/ (US) /-ɚ/ noun [C] a short, pointed knife that is sharp on both sides, used especially in the past as a weapon

dagger

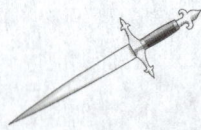

IDIOM **(at) daggers drawn** If two people, countries, etc. are at daggers drawn, they are in a state of extreme unfriendliness and do not trust each other.

dago /ˈdeɪ.gəʊ/ (US) /-goʊ/ noun [C] (plural **dagos** or **dagoes**) offensive a person from Spain, Portugal, Italy, or South America

daguerreotype /dəˈger.ə.taɪp/ noun [C] the first successfully produced type of photograph

dahlia /ˈdeɪ.li.ə/ (US) /ˈdeɪl.jə/ noun [C] a brightly coloured garden flower with long, thin PETALS in a shape like a ball

the Dáil /dɔɪl/ noun [S] one of the two law-making groups that together make up the parliament in Ireland

daily /ˈdeɪ.li/ adv, adj; noun

▸adv, adj (A2) happening on or relating to every day: *Take the tablets twice daily.* ◦ *Exercise has become part of my daily routine.* ◦ *We back up our computer files at work on a daily basis.* ◦ *She's looking forward to retiring and ending the daily **grind** (= hard, boring work or duty) of working in an office.*

▸noun [C] UK old-fashioned informal a person who is employed to clean someone else's home

ˌdaily ˈbread noun [U] informal the money you need to pay for necessary things, such as food

ˌdaily ˈpaper noun [C] (also **daily**) a newspaper that is published every day of the week except Sunday: UK *The story was covered in all the **national** dailies.*

ˌdaily ˈpassenger noun [C] Indian English someone who travels to work by train every day

daintily /ˈdeɪn.tɪ.li/ (US) /-t̬ɪ-/ adv in an attractive, careful way, especially with small movements or small pieces: *She skipped daintily down the street, holding her father's hand.* ◦ *He handed round a plate of tiny sandwiches, daintily arranged in rings.*

dainty /ˈdeɪn.ti/ (US) /-t̬i/ adj small, delicate, and often moving in a careful way: *She was a small, dainty child, unlike her sister who was large and had big feet.* ◦ *We were given tea, and some dainty little cakes.* • **daintiness** /-nəs/ noun [U]

daiquiri /ˈdæk.ɪ.ri/ (US) /-ɚ.i/ noun [C or U] an alcoholic drink made with RUM, LIME juice, sugar, and ice

dairy /ˈdeə.ri/ (US) /ˈder.i/ adj; noun

▸adj B2 used to refer to cows that are used for producing milk, rather than meat, or to foods that are made from milk, such as cream, butter, and cheese: *dairy cattle* ◦ *dairy farmers* ◦ *dairy products*

▸noun **1** [C] a place on a farm where milk and cream are kept and cheese and butter are made, or a company that supplies milk and products made from milk **2** [U] foods that are made from milk, such as cream, butter, and cheese: *a dairy-free diet* ◦ *I was advised not to eat too much dairy.*

ˈdairy ˌfarm noun [C] (US also **dairy**) a farm that only produces milk and products made from milk

dais /ˈdeɪ.ɪs/, /deɪs/ noun [C] a raised surface at one end of a meeting room which someone can stand on when speaking to a group

daisy /ˈdeɪ.zi/ noun [C] a small flower with white PETALS and a yellow centre that often grows in grass

dal (also **dhal**) /dɑːl/ noun [U] (in South Asia) LENTILS or a dish made from these

the Dalai Lama /ˌdæl.aɪˈlɑː.mə/ noun [S] the leader of the Tibetan Buddhist religion

dale /deɪl/ noun [C] **1** literary or Northern English a valley **2 the (Yorkshire) Dales** an area of northern England in which there are a lot of hills and valleys

Dalit /ˈdʌl.ɪt/ noun [C] (in the former CASTE system in South Asia) a member of the lowest caste

dalliance /ˈdæl.i.əns/ noun [C or U] **1** mainly humorous (involvement in) a sexual relationship that is not lasting or serious **2** an interest or involvement in an activity or belief that only lasts for a very short period: *The 1970s witnessed the first of the pop star's dalliances* ***with*** *communism.*

dally /ˈdæl.i/ verb [I] old-fashioned to waste time or do something slowly → See also **dilly-dally**

PHRASAL VERBS **dally with sb** (also **dally with sb's affections**) to be romantically or sexually involved with someone, usually for a short time, without really loving them: *It's cruel the way she just dallies with his affections.* • **dally with sth** to consider or imagine an idea, subject, or plan, but not in a serious way: *He had occasionally dallied with the idea of starting his own business, but he had never actually done anything about it.*

Dalmatian /dælˈmeɪ.ʃᵊn/ noun [C] a big dog with short, white fur and dark spots

dam /dæm/ noun; verb

▸noun [C] **1** a wall built across a river that stops the river's flow and collects the water, especially to make a RESERVOIR (= an artificial lake) that provides water for an area → Compare **dyke 2** a **dental dam**

▸verb [T] (**-mm-**) to build a dam across a river in order to store water

PHRASAL VERB **dam sth up** to build a dam across a river in order to store water

damage /ˈdæm.ɪdʒ/ verb; noun

▸verb [T] B1 to harm or spoil something: *Many buildings were* ***badly*** *damaged during the war.* ◦ *It was a scandal that damaged a lot of reputations.*

▸noun **1** B1 [U] harm or injury: *Strong winds had caused serious damage* ***to*** *the roof.* ◦ *Recent discoveries about corruption have* ***done*** *serious damage* ***to*** *the company's reputation.* ◦ *The doctors were worried that he might have suffered* ***brain*** *damage.* **2 damages** [plural] legal money that is paid to someone by a person or organization who has been responsible for causing them some injury or loss: *The politician was* ***awarded*** *£50,000 damages over false allegations made by the newspaper.* ◦ *The police have been ordered to* ***pay*** *substantial damages to the families of the two dead boys.*

! Common mistake: damage

In its first meaning, **damage** does not have a plural form and cannot be used with **a** or **an**.

To talk about an amount of **damage**, do not say 'damages', say **damage, some damage** or **a lot of damage**:

~~*Tourism causes damages to the environment.*~~

Tourism causes a lot of damage to the environment.

Word partners for damage noun

do/cause damage (to sb/sth) • *incur/suffer* damage • *considerable/extensive/serious/severe* damage • *minor/slight* damage • *irreparable/permanent* damage • damage *to* sth • [hundreds/thousands of pounds/dollars worth] *of* damage • the *extent* of the damage

Word partners for damages

award/pay damages • *claim/seek* damages • *receive/win* damages • an *action/claim for* damages • be *liable for* damages • [a thousand pounds, a million dollars, etc.] *in* damages • damages *of* [a thousand pounds, a million dollars, etc.]

IDIOMS **the damage is done** said to mean that it is too late to improve a bad situation: *I didn't even know I'd offended her till Colin told me and then it was too late – the damage was done.* • **what's the damage?** informal humorous used to ask how much something has cost you

damaged /ˈdæm.ɪdʒd/ adj B1 harmed or spoiled: *They're selling off damaged goods at reduced prices.* ◦ *Both the cars involved in the accident looked badly damaged.*

ˈdamage limiˌtation noun [U] the process of limiting the damaging effects of an action or mistake, or the attempt in war to use careful planning to avoid unnecessary death: *The government is involved in a damage-limitation* ***exercise*** *to minimize the effects of the scandal.*

damaging /ˈdæm.ɪ.dʒɪŋ/ adj causing harm: *Many chemicals have a damaging* ***effect*** *on the environment.* ◦ *These are very damaging allegations.*

damask /ˈdæm.əsk/ noun [U] a type of heavy cloth that has a pattern WOVEN into it that is the same colour as the cloth: *a white damask tablecloth*

dame /deɪm/ noun [C] **WOMAN** ▷ **1** US old-fashioned slang a woman **CHARACTER** ▷ **2** UK the funny character of an older woman in a PANTOMIME (= musical play for children) who is usually played by a man

Dame /deɪm/ noun [C] a title used in front of a woman's name that is given in Britain as a special honour, usually for valuable work done over a long period, or a woman having this honour: *Dame Judy Dench* → Compare **Sir, knight**

damn /dæm/ exclamation; adv; verb; adj;

▸noun exclamation informal (also **damn it**, also **dammit**) B1 an expression of anger: *Damn, I've spilled coffee down my blouse!* → See also **goddamn**

▸adv informal **1** used, especially when you are annoyed, to mean 'very': *He* ***knew*** *damn* ***well*** *how much trouble it would cause.* ◦ *Next time he can damn* ***well*** *do it* himself! ◦ *You were damn lucky not to have been killed!* **2 damn all** UK informal nothing: *I know damn all about computers.*

▸verb **BLAME** ▷ **1** [T] to blame or strongly criticize something or someone: *The inquiry into the disaster damns the company* ***for*** *its lack of safety precautions.* **PUNISH** ▷ **2** [T usually passive] (especially of God) to force someone to stay in hell and be punished for ever: *As a child she was taught that she would be damned for her sins.* **3 damn you, them, it, etc.** informal used to express anger with someone or something: *You got the last ticket – damn you, I wanted that!*

IDIOM **damn sb with faint praise** to praise someone so slightly that it suggests you do not really admire them

▸adj [before noun] informal (also **damned**) used to express anger with someone or something: *Damn* ***fool!***

▸noun informal

IDIOM **not give/care a damn** used as a way of saying you do not care about something, especially the annoying things that someone else is doing or saying: *He can think what he likes about me – I don't give a damn!*

damnable /ˈdæm.nə.bl̩/ adj old-fashioned informal very annoying • **damnably** /-bli/ adv

damnation /dæmˈneɪ.ʃən/ noun [U] the act of sending someone to hell or the state of being in hell: *He believed that he would be condemned to* ***eternal*** *damnation for what he had done.*

damned /dæmd/ adj; noun

▸adj [before noun] informal (also **damn**) used to express anger with someone or something: *This damned printer won't work.*

IDIOMS **be damned if you do and damned if you don't** used to say that you cannot escape being criticized, whatever you decide to do • **(well) I'll be damned!** an expression of complete surprise: *She's marrying a man who she met two months ago? – Well, I'll be damned!* • **I'm damned if** used to say that you will certainly not do something: *I'm polite to his ex-wife when I meet her, but I'm damned if I'm going to invite her round for dinner.*

▸noun **the damned** [plural] the people who have been sent to hell after their death

damnedest /ˈdæm.dɪst/ adj; noun

▸adj [before noun] mainly US informal very surprising or unusual: *Well that's the damnedest excuse I've ever heard!*

▸noun informal **do your damnedest** to try very hard: *I don't know if I'll succeed, but I'll do my damnedest.*

damning /ˈdæm.ɪŋ/ adj describes a report, judgment, remark, etc. which includes a lot of criticism or which shows clearly that someone is wrong, guilty or has behaved very badly: *He made some fairly damning remarks about the government's refusal to deal with the problem.* ◦ *The two men were convicted on some extremely damning* ***evidence.***

damp /dæmp/ adj; verb

▸adj **B2** slightly wet, especially in a way that is not pleasant or comfortable: *The grass is still damp.* ◦ *This shirt still feels a bit damp.* ◦ *It was a damp, misty morning.* • **dampness** noun [U] (UK also **damp**) *It's the dampness in the air that is bad for your lungs.*

▸verb

PHRASAL VERB **damp sth down** **FIRE** ▷ **1** to make a fire burn more slowly **FEELING** ▷ **2** to make a strong feeling be felt less strongly: *He had tried to damp down speculation about the state of his marriage.*

ˈdamp ˌcourse noun [C] (also **ˈdamp-proof ˌcourse**) UK a layer of material that is put in the bottom of a wall in order to stop water rising through the bricks

dampen /ˈdæm.pən/ verb [T] **MAKE WET** ▷ **1** (also **damp**) to make something slightly wet: *Rain had dampened the tent so we left it to dry in the afternoon sun.* **FEELINGS** ▷ **2** to make feelings, especially of excitement or enjoyment, less strong: *Nothing you can say will dampen her* ***enthusiasm.*** ◦ *I didn't want to dampen his* ***spirits.***

damper /ˈdæm.pər/ (US) /-pɚ/ noun informal **put a damper/dampener on sth** to stop an occasion from being enjoyable: *Both the kids were ill while we were in Boston, so that rather put a damper on things.*

ˌdamp ˈsquib noun [C] UK an event that is not as exciting or popular as people thought it would be: *After all that media attention, the whole event turned out to be a bit of a damp squib, with very few people attending.*

damsel /ˈdæm.zəl/ noun [C] old use a young woman who is not married

IDIOM **a damsel in distress** humorous a young woman who is in trouble and needs a man's help

damson /ˈdæm.zən/ noun [C] the sour dark-blue fruit of a type of PLUM tree: *damson jam*

dance /dɑːns/ (US) /dæns/ verb; noun

▸verb **1** **A1** [I or T] to move the body and feet to music: *We* ***went*** *dancing at a club.* ◦ *What sort of music do you like dancing* ***to****?* ◦ *Who was she dancing* ***with*** *at the party last night?* ◦ *Can you dance the tango?* ◦ *Colin would dance the night* ***away*** *at XXL.* **2** [I] literary to move quickly and lightly: *The daffodils were dancing in the breeze.* ◦ *She watched the sunlight dancing on the water.*

IDIOMS **be dancing in the streets** informal to be extremely happy about something that has happened: *Few people will be dancing in the streets* ***about*** *a two percent pay rise.* • **dance attendance on sb** UK to do everything that someone asks you to and treat them as if they are special: *I can't stand the way she has to have someone dancing attendance on her the whole time.* • **dance to sb's tune** to do what someone wants

▸noun **1** **A1** [C or U] the act of moving your feet and body to music: *We* ***had a*** *dance.* ◦ *a dance* ***class*** **2** **B1** [C] a particular series of movements that you perform to music or the type of music which is connected with it: *The band played a slow dance.* **3** **A2** [C] a social occasion where people dance, especially a formal occasion in a large room: *They're having an end-of-term dinner-dance.* **4** **A2** [U] the art of performing dances, especially as a form of entertainment: *The performers tell the story through song and dance.*

ˈdance ˌfloor noun [C] an area of a NIGHTCLUB, restaurant, etc. that is for dancing: *Have you seen him* ***on*** *the dance floor (= dancing)?*

ˈdance ˌhall noun [C] especially in the past, a special building or large room for dancing in

ˈdance ˌmusic noun [U] a type of music with a strong beat that people dance to in a NIGHTCLUB

dancer /ˈdɑːn.sər/ (US) /ˈdæn.sɚ/ noun [C] **A2** someone who dances either as a job or for pleasure: *He's a dancer in the Royal Ballet.* ◦ *I never knew you were such a good dancer.*

ˈdance ˌstudio noun [C] a place where people can go for dance classes

ˌ**D and ˈC** noun [C] specialized abbreviation for dilatation and curettage: an operation in which the inside surface of a woman's WOMB is removed for medical reasons

dandelion /ˈdæn.dɪ.laɪ.ən/ (US) /-də-/ **noun** [C] a common small, bright yellow wild flower that has a lot of long, thin PETALS arranged in a circular pattern around a round centre: *The children took turns blowing the dandelion* ***clock*** *(= the mass of white threads to which the seeds are attached).*

dander /ˈdæn.dəʳ/ (US) /-dɚ/ **noun** [U] **1** pieces of dry skin in an animal's fur or hair **2 have/get your dander up** mainly US informal to be or to become angry: *He had his dander up about the parking fine he'd just received.*

dandified /ˈdæn.dɪ.faɪd/ (US) /-də-/ **adj** looking or acting like a dandy: *An embroidered silk waistcoat contributed to his dandified appearance.*

dandle /ˈdæn.dl̩/ **verb** [T] old-fashioned to hold a baby or child on your knee and move it up and down in a PLAYFUL way

dandruff /ˈdæn.drʌf/ (US) /-drəf/ **noun** [U] small white pieces of dead skin from the head which collect in the hair or fall on the clothes

dandy /ˈdæn.di/ **noun; adj**

▸**noun** [C] a man, especially in the past, who dressed in expensive, fashionable clothes and was very interested in his own appearance: *an upper-class dandy*

▸**adj** (also ˌ**jim-ˈdandy**) US old-fashioned very good: *'Shall we meet at six?' 'Sure, that's just dandy.'*

dang /dæŋ/ **exclamation; adv**

▸**exclamation** US informal used to express anger: *Dang, I broke the glass!*

▸**adv** US informal used, especially when you are annoyed, to mean 'very': *He knows dang well I can't swim.*

danger /ˈdeɪn.dʒəʳ/ (US) /-dʒɚ/ **noun 1** (A2) [C or U] the possibility of harm or death to someone: *Danger! Keep out!* ◦ *He drove so fast that I really felt my life was* ***in*** *danger.* ◦ *The doctors say he is now* ***out of*** *danger (= is not expected to die although he has been extremely ill).* ◦ *the dangers of rock-climbing* **2** (B1) [C] something or someone that may harm you: *Icy roads are a danger* ***to*** *drivers.* ◦ *The judge described him as a danger* ***to*** *society.* **3 danger of sth** (A2) the possibility that something bad will happen: *If there's any danger of seeing Gary at the party, I'm not going.* ◦ *If he carries on like this he's* ***in*** *danger* ***of*** *losing his job.*

> Word partners for **danger**
>
> be *in* danger • *put* sb *in* danger • *pose* a danger • (a) *grave/great/serious* danger • a *hidden/obvious* danger • the danger *from/in/of* sth

IDIOM **there's no danger of that!** humorous said to mean that something certainly will not happen: *'Bye – don't work too hard!' 'There's no danger of that!'*

ˈ**danger** ˌ**list** noun **be on/off the danger list** to be expected/no longer expected to die from a serious injury or illness

ˈ**danger** ˌ**money** noun [U] UK (US ˌ**hazardous-ˈduty** ˌ**pay**) extra money that is paid to someone because their job is dangerous

dangerous /ˈdeɪn.dʒər.əs/ (US) /-dʒɚ-/ **adj** (A2) describes a person, animal, thing, or activity that could harm you: *dangerous chemicals* ◦ *The men are armed and dangerous.* ◦ *I've never played ice hockey – it's far too dangerous.* ◦ [+ to infinitive] ***It's*** *dangerous* ***to*** *take more than the recommended dose of tablets.*

> Other ways of saying **dangerous**
>
> If something is extremely dangerous, you can use the adjectives **hazardous**, **perilous**, or **treacherous**:
>
> *Ice had made the roads* ***treacherous****.*
>
> *Heavy rain is causing* ***hazardous*** *driving conditions.*
>
> *A* ***perilous*** *journey through the mountains was their only escape route.*
>
> Substances which are dangerous are often described as **harmful** or **hazardous**:
>
> *Please be aware that these chemicals are* ***harmful/hazardous*** *to human health.*
>
> If something is so dangerous that it is likely to kill someone, you can describe it as **lethal**:
>
> *These medications can be* ***lethal*** *if they get into the wrong hands.*
>
> If something is dangerous because something bad might happen, you can say that it is **risky**:
>
> *Surgery at his age would be too* ***risky****.*

dangerously /ˈdeɪn.dʒər.əs.li/ (US) /-dʒɚ-/ **adv** (B1) in a way that is dangerous: *She drives dangerously.* ◦ *He likes to* ***live*** *dangerously.*

dangle /ˈdæŋ.gl̩/ **verb 1** [I or T] to hang loosely, or to hold something so that it hangs loosely: *Loose electric wires were dangling* ***from*** *the wall.* ◦ *He dangled the puppet in front of the children.* **2** [T] to offer someone something that they want in order to persuade them to do something: *I've tried dangling all sorts of offers* ***before*** *him/****in front of*** *him to get him to work harder at school, but nothing works.*

dangly /ˈdæŋ.gli/ **adj** hanging loosely: *dangly* ***earrings***

Danish pastry /ˌdeɪ.nɪʃˈpeɪ.stri/ **noun** [C] (US usually **Danish**) a type of cake for one person, consisting of sweet pastry, often with fruit inside

dank /dæŋk/ **adj** (especially of buildings and air) wet, cold, and unpleasant: *a dank, dark cellar* • **dankness** /-nəs/ **noun** [U]

Daoism /ˈdaʊ.ɪ.zəm/ **noun** [U] **Taoism**

dapper /ˈdæp.əʳ/ (US) /-ɚ/ **adj** describes a man who is dressed in a fashionable and tidy way: *Hercule Poirot is the dapper detective of the Agatha Christie novels.*

dappled /ˈdæp.l̩d/ **adj** covered with spots of colour that are lighter or darker than the main colour, or covered with areas of light and darkness: *a dappled pony.* ◦ *The dappled sunlight fell across her face as she lay beneath the tree.*

dare /deəʳ/ (US) /der/ **verb; noun**

▸**verb BE BRAVE/RUDE** ▷ **1** (B2) [I not continuous] to be brave enough to do something difficult or dangerous, or to be rude or silly enough to do something that you have no right to do: *I was going to ask if his dog was any better, but I didn't dare in case it had died.* ◦ [+ (to) infinitive] *Everyone in the office complains that he smells awful, but nobody dares* ***(to)*** *mention it to him.* ◦ *Do you dare* ***(to)*** *tell him the news?* ◦ [+ infinitive without to] *I wouldn't dare have a party in my flat in case the neighbours complained.* ◦ *Dare you tell him the news?* ◦ *I daren't/don't dare think how much it's going to cost.* ◦ *I'd never dare* ***(to)*** *talk to my mother the way Ben talks to his.* ◦ [+ to infinitive] *He was under attack for daring* ***to*** *criticize the prime minister.* → See also **daresay ASK** ▷ **2** (C1) [T] to ask someone to do something which involves risk: *Wear the low-cut* blouse with your pink shorts – go on, I dare you! ◦ [+ to infinitive] I dare you **to** ask him to dance.

IDIOMS **don't you dare** informal C2 used to tell someone angrily not to do something: *'I think I'll just walk my dirty shoes over your nice clean floor.' 'Don't you dare!'* ◦ *Don't you dare go without me!* • **how dare she, you, etc.!** C1 used to express anger about something someone has done: *How dare you use my car without asking!* ◦ *How dare he tell me what to do!*

D

▸noun [C] something you do because someone dares you to: *He jumped in the river at twelve o'clock last night **as/for** (US **on**) a dare.*

daredevil /ˈdeəˌdev.əl/ US /ˈder-/ noun [C] informal a person who does dangerous things and takes risks • **daredevil adj** [before noun]

daren't /deənt/ US /dernt/ **short form of** dare(s) not: *I daren't tell him – he'll be so angry.*

daresay /ˌdeəˈseɪ/ US /ˌder-/ /ˈdeə.seɪ/ **verb I daresay** C2 (also **I dare say**) used to say that you agree or think that something is true: *'She's got a lot of admirers.' 'I daresay – she's very beautiful.'* ◦ *He gets paid a lot of money, but I daresay (**that**) he earns it.*

daring /ˈdeə.rɪŋ/ US /ˈder.ɪŋ/ **adj** brave and taking risks: *a daring escape* ◦ *This is a daring new film (= one willing to risk criticism) by one of our most original modern directors.* ◦ *She was wearing a rather daring (= short) skirt that only just covered her bottom.* • **daringly** /-li/ **adv** *a daringly short skirt*

dark /dɑːk/ US /dɑːrk/ **adj; noun**

▸adj **WITHOUT LIGHT** ▷ **1** A2 with little or no light: *It was too dark to see properly.* ◦ *What time does it **get** dark in the summer?* ◦ *Our bedroom was very dark until we put a larger window in.* **2** A1 nearer to black than white in colour: *dark blue/green* ◦ *dark clouds* ◦ *She has dark hair.* ◦ *He was tall, dark (= with black/brown hair) and handsome.* **SAD** ▷ **3** C1 [before noun] sad and without hope: *Her husband's sudden death was the start of a dark chapter in her life.* ◦ *This environmental report contains more dark predictions about the future of the Earth.* **EVIL** ▷ **4** C1 evil or threatening: *There's a darker side to his character.* • **darkness** /-nəs/ **noun** [U] B2 *The city centre was **plunged into** darkness by the power cut.*

IDIOM **the darkest hour is just before the dawn** saying said to emphasize that things often seem at their worst just before they get better

▸noun **1 the dark** B1 the fact of there being no light somewhere: *Cats can see in the dark.* ◦ *I've always been afraid of the dark.* **2 before/after dark** B1 before/after the sun has gone down: *It isn't safe to leave the house after dark.* ◦ *I want to be home before dark.*

IDIOM **be in the dark** C2 to not know about something that other people know about

the ˈdark ˌages noun [plural] **1 the Dark Ages** the period in European history from the end of the Roman EMPIRE in AD 476 to about AD 1000 **2** disapproving a time in the past considered to be not advanced and when people were unwilling to accept the beliefs or opinions of others: *This repressive law takes gay rights **back to** the dark ages.*

ˌdark ˈchocolate noun [C or U] (UK also **ˌplain ˈchocolate**) dark brown chocolate that has been made without milk

darken /ˈdɑː.kən/ US /ˈdɑːr-/ **verb** [I] to become dark: *The sky darkened as thick smoke billowed from the blazing oil well.* • **darkened** /-kənd/ **adj** *We crept slowly along the darkened (= without light) corridor.*

IDIOM **not darken sb's door** literary used to tell someone to never come back to a place: *Never darken my door again!*

ˌdark ˈglasses noun [plural] glasses with dark LENSES (= glass parts)

ˌdark ˈhorse noun [C usually singular] **SECRET** ▷ **1** UK a person who keeps their interests and ideas secret, especially someone who has a surprising ability or skill: *Anna's such a dark horse – I had no idea she'd published a novel.* **WINNER** ▷ **2** US a horse or a politician who wins a race or competition although no one expected them to

darkie offensive old-fashioned (US usually **darky**) /ˈdɑː.ki/ US /ˈdɑːr-/ **noun** [C] a person who has black or brown skin

ˌdark ˈl noun [C] specialized a way of saying an /l/ sound, in which the back of the tongue is raised slightly: *Dark l typically occurs before a consonant, as in 'help'.*

darkly /ˈdɑːk.li/ US /ˈdɑːrk-/ **adv THREATENING** ▷ **1** in a way that is threatening or frightening: *'Don't come any closer,' she said darkly.* **WITHOUT LIGHT** ▷ **2** in a way that has little or no light: *His figure could be seen darkly on the foggy moor.*

ˌdark ˈmeat noun [U] the dark-coloured meat that you find on the legs of birds that you eat, such as chicken

darkroom /ˈdɑːk.rʊm/, /-ruːm/ US /ˈdɑːrk-/ **noun** [C] a specially lit room where photographic film is PROCESSED

darling /ˈdɑː.lɪŋ/ US /ˈdɑːr-/ **noun; adj**

▸noun [C] B2 a person who is very much loved or liked: *Oh darling, I do love you.* ◦ *Here's your change, darling.* ◦ *In spite of his unpopularity in the USSR, Gorbachev remained **a/the** darling **of** (= very popular with) the West right to the end.*

> **Note:**
> This is used as a name between people who love each other and people who are being friendly. As a friendly way of talking to someone it is not usually used between men.

▸adj [before noun] **1** old-fashioned used when talking someone you love, for example in a letter, to say that you love them very much: *Darling Martha, It was lovely to see you at the weekend.* **2** very attractive: *They've just bought a darling little cottage.*

darn /dɑːn/ US /dɑːrn/ **verb; exclamation**

▸verb [T] to repair a hole or a piece of clothing with long STITCHES across the hole and other STITCHES across them: *She still darns the holes in her socks.* • **darn noun** [C]

▸exclamation informal used instead of DAMN to express anger: *Darn **it**! There goes my bus!* • **darn adj** [before noun], **adv** (also **darned**) informal *Getting off the bus while it was moving was a darn stupid thing to do.*

darning /ˈdɑː.nɪŋ/ US /ˈdɑːr-/ **noun** [U] things that need to be darned: *I don't think I'll ever finish that darning.*

darts

ˈdarning ˌneedle noun [C] a special large needle used for darning, or for sewing thick cloth

dart /dɑːt/ US /dɑːrt/ **noun; verb**

▸noun **POINTED OBJECT** ▷

D

1 [C] a small, thin object with a sharp point that is thrown by hand in a game, shot from a gun, or blown from a tube when used as a weapon → Compare **arrow** **2 darts** [U] a game in which darts are thrown at a circular board. The number of points won depends on where the darts land on the board: *a* ***game of*** *darts* ◦ *a darts tournament* **SEWN FOLD** ▷ **3** [C] a small fold, becoming narrower towards one end, that is sewn into a piece of clothing to make it fit better **QUICK MOVEMENT** ▷ **4** [C usually singular] a quick, sudden movement: *We* ***made*** *a dart* ***for*** *(= moved quickly towards) the exit.*

▸verb [I + adv/prep] **1** to move quickly or suddenly: *I darted behind the sofa and hid.* **2 dart a glance/look at sb** to look quickly at someone: *She darted an angry look at me.*

dartboard /ˈdɑːt.bɔːd/ (US) /ˈdɑːrt.bɔːrd/ noun [C] a circular board which darts are thrown at in a game

dash /dæʃ/ verb; noun; exclamation

▸verb **MOVE QUICKLY** ▷ **1** B2 [I] to go somewhere quickly: *I've been dashing* ***around*** *all day.* ◦ *I must dash – I've got to be home by seven.* **HIT** ▷ **2** [I or T, usually + prep] to hit something with great force, especially causing damage: *The tidal wave dashed the ship* ***against*** *the rocks.* ◦ *Waves dashed* ***against*** *the cliffs.*

IDIOM **dash sb's hopes** to destroy someone's hopes: *Saturday's 2–0 defeat dashed their hopes of reaching the final.*

PHRASAL VERB **dash sth off** to write something quickly, putting little effort into it: *She dashed the letter off in five minutes.*

▸noun **QUICK MOVEMENT** ▷ **1** B2 [S] the act of running somewhere very quickly: *I* ***made a*** *dash* ***for*** *the bathroom.* ◦ *There was a* ***mad*** *dash for the exit.* ◦ *As soon as the rain dies down I'm going to* ***make a*** *dash* ***for it*** *(= run somewhere very fast).* **2** [C usually singular] mainly US a race over a short distance: *Who won the 100-yard dash?* **PUNCTUATION** ▷ **3** B2 [C] the symbol – used to separate parts of a sentence → Compare **hyphen** **4** [C] a long sound or flash of light that is used with DOTS to send messages in MORSE (CODE) **SMALL AMOUNT** ▷ **5 a dash** C2 a small amount of something, especially liquid food, that is added to something else: *'Cream with your coffee, Madam?' 'Yes please – just a dash.'* ◦ figurative *a youthful ambience with a dash of (= small amount of) sophistication* **STYLE** ▷ **6** [U] old-fashioned style and confidence

▸exclamation UK old-fashioned informal used to express anger: *Oh dash (****it****)! I've left my umbrella in the office.*

dashboard /ˈdæʃ.bɔːd/ (US) /-bɔːrd/ noun [C] (mainly US **dash**, UK old-fashioned **fascia**) the part of a car which contains some of the controls used for driving and the devices for measuring speed and distance

dashed /dæʃt/ adj [before noun], adv mainly UK old-fashioned extremely: *Dashed decent of you, old boy!*

dashing /ˈdæʃ.ɪŋ/ adj old-fashioned attractive in a confident, exciting, and stylish way: *a dashing young soldier* • **dashingly** /-li/ adv

dastardly /ˈdæs.təd.li/ (US) /-tɚd-/ adj old-fashioned or humorous evil and cruel: *It's the story of a woman who plots a dastardly revenge on her unfaithful lover.*

DAT /dæt/ noun [C or U] abbreviation for **digital audio tape**

data /ˈdeɪ.tə/ (US) /-t̬ə/ noun [U, + sing/pl verb] B2 information, especially facts or numbers, collected to be examined and considered and used to help decision-making, or information in an electronic form that can be stored and used by a computer: *The data was/were collected by various researchers.* ◦ *Now the data is/are being transferred from magnetic tape to hard disk.*

ˈdata ˌbank noun [C] a large collection of information that can be searched through quickly, especially by a computer

database /ˈdeɪ.tə.beɪs/ (US) /-t̬ə-/ noun [C] B2 a large amount of information stored in a computer system in such a way that it can be easily looked at or changed: *We're linked to the on-line database at our head office.*

ˈdata ˌcapture noun [U] any method of collecting information and then changing it into a form that can be read and used by a computer

dataglove /ˈdeɪ.tə.glʌv/ (US) /-t̬ə-/ noun [C] an electronic GLOVE (= hand covering) which sends information about the hand movements of the person wearing it to a computer

ˈdata ˌprocessing noun [U] the use of a computer to perform calculations on DATA: *a data-processing bureau*

ˈdata proˌjector noun [C] a piece of electronic equipment that is used to show information from a computer screen on a large screen

date /deɪt/ noun; verb

▸noun [C] **DAY** ▷ **1** A1 a NUMBERED day in a month, often given with a combination of the name of the day, the month, and the year: *What's the date (today)?/What date is it?/What's today's date?* ◦ UK *Today's date is 11 June (the eleventh of June).* ◦ US *Today's date is June 11 (June the eleventh).* ◦ *What is your date* ***of birth****?* ◦ *The* ***closing*** *date for applications is the end of this month.* ◦ *We've agreed to meet again at a later date.* ◦ *I'd like to* ***fix*** *a date for our next meeting.* ◦ *I've* ***made a*** *date (= agreed a date and time) to see her about the house.* → See also **out of date, up to date** **2** a particular year: *The date on the coin is 1789.* ◦ *Albert Einstein's dates are 1879 to 1955 (= he was born in 1879 and died in 1955).* **3** a month and a year: *The* ***expiry*** *(US* ***expiration****) date of this certificate is August 2013.* **MEETING** ▷ **4** B1 a social meeting planned before it happens, especially one between two people who have or might have a romantic relationship: *He's asked her out* ***on a*** *date.* ◦ *She has a* ***hot*** *date (= an exciting meeting) tonight.* **5** mainly US a person you have a romantic meeting with: *Who's your date for the prom?* **PERFORMANCE** ▷ **6** a performance: *They've just finished an exhausting 75-date European tour.* **FRUIT** ▷ **7** C1 the sweet fruit of various types of PALM tree

IDIOMS **it's a date** informal used to say that a particular time is a suitable time to meet: *'I can't make it at seven o'clock. How about 9.30?' 'Sure, it's a date.'* • **to date** formal B2 up to the present time: *This novel is his best work to date.*

▸verb **TIME** ▷ **1** B1 [T] to write the day's date on something you have written or made: [+ obj + noun] *Thank you for your letter dated 30 August.* **2** [T] to say how long something has existed or when it was made: *Archaeologists have been unable to date these fossils.* ◦ *An antique dealer had dated the vase* ***at*** *(= said that it was made in) 1734.* **MEET** ▷ **3** [I or T] mainly US to regularly spend time with someone you have a romantic relationship with: *They dated for five years before they got married.* ◦ *How long have you been dating Nicky?* **BECOME OLD** ▷ **4** [I or T] to stop being fashionable or become old-fashioned, or to show the age of a person or thing: *Some James Bond films have dated more quickly than others.* ◦ *I can remember watching live TV coverage of the first lunar landing, so that dates me (= shows how old I am).*

PHRASAL VERBS **date back** B2 to have existed for a particular length of time or since a particular time: *This tradition dates back **to** medieval times.* • **date from sth** to have existed since a particular time: *This map dates from the 14th century.*

datebook /ˈdeɪt.bʊk/ noun [C] US (UK **diary**) a book showing the days of the year, used to keep a record of the meetings you have, used to keep a record of things you must do, people's addresses and phone numbers, etc.

D

dated /ˈdeɪ.tɪd/ US /-t̬ɪd/ adj C2 old-fashioned: *Spy thrillers with plots based on the Cold War look particularly dated nowadays.*

dateline /ˈdeɪt.laɪn/ noun [C] the line in a newspaper article which tells the place and date of writing → Compare **byline**

ˈdate ˌrape noun [C or U] (a case of) RAPE that happens when the ATTACKER is already known to the person who is attacked

ˈdating ˌagency noun [C] UK (US **ˈdating ˌservice**) an organization which introduces people with similar interests to each other, especially people who want to start a romantic or sexual relationship with someone: *She met her husband through a dating agency.*

dative /ˈdeɪ.tɪv/ US /-t̬ɪv/ noun [C or U] the form of a noun, PRONOUN, or adjective which in some languages marks the INDIRECT OBJECT of a verb that has two objects • **dative** adj *the dative case*

datum /ˈdeɪ.təm/ US /-t̬əm/ noun [C] (plural **data**) specialized a single piece of information

daub /dɔːb/ US /dɑːb/ verb; noun

▸verb [T] to spread a thick or sticky liquid on something or to cover something with a thick or sticky liquid, often quickly or carelessly: *The walls had been daubed **with** graffiti.* ◦ *The baby had daubed butter all **over** its hair and face.*

▸noun [C] **1** an area of thick or sticky liquid on something: *a daub of red paint* **2** a badly painted picture

daughter /ˈdɔː.təʳ/ US /ˈdɑː.t̬ɚ/ noun [C] A1 your female child: *Liz and Phil have a daughter and three sons.* → See also **stepdaughter**

ˈdaughter-in-law noun [C] (plural **daughters-in-law**) B2 the woman who is married to your son or daughter

daunt /dɔːnt/ US /dɑːnt/ verb [T often passive] to make someone feel slightly frightened or worried about their ability to achieve something: *She was not at all daunted by the size of the problem.* → Synonym **discourage**

IDIOM **nothing daunted** mainly UK still confident and enthusiastic despite a failure or problem: *She was rejected the first time she applied to the university, but, nothing daunted, reapplied the following year and was accepted.*

daunting /ˈdɔːn.tɪŋ/ US /ˈdɑːn.t̬ɪŋ/ adj making you feel slightly frightened or worried about your ability to achieve something: *The country was faced with the daunting prospect of overcoming four decades of division.*

dauntless /ˈdɔːnt.ləs/ US /ˈdɑːnt-/ adj literary showing determination and no fear: *In spite of the scale of the famine, the relief workers struggled on with dauntless optimism.*

dawdle /ˈdɔː.dl̩/ US /ˈdɑː-/ verb [I] to do something or go somewhere very slowly, taking more time than is necessary: *Stop dawdling! You'll be late for school!*

dawn /dɔːn/ US /dɑːn/ noun; verb

▸noun [C or U] **1** B2 the period in the day when light from the sun begins to appear in the sky: *We woke **at** dawn.* ◦ *We left as dawn was **breaking** (= starting).* ◦ *We left at the **break of** dawn.* ◦ *23 people were arrested and large quantities of heroin were seized in a dawn **raid** (= when police officers suddenly enter a building, in an attempt to catch people involved in illegal activities).* **2 the dawn of sth** C1 literary the start of a period of time or the beginning of something new: *The fall of the Berlin Wall marked the dawn **of a new era** in European history.* **3 from dawn to dusk** from early morning until night: *We worked from dawn to dusk, seven days a week.*

▸verb [I] **BEGIN** ▷ **1** If a day or period of time dawns, it begins: *He left the house just as the day was dawning.* ◦ *Few people could have predicted the dramatic changes that were to take place during that year.* **BECOME KNOWN** ▷ **2** to become known or obvious: *Gradually the truth about him dawned.* ◦ [+ that] ***It** eventually dawned **that** he wouldn't be coming back.*

PHRASAL VERB **dawn on sb** C2 If a fact dawns on you, you understand it after a period of not understanding it: [+ that] *I was about to pay for the shopping when **it** suddenly dawned on me **that** I'd left my cheque book at home.*

ˌdawn ˈchorus noun [S] mainly UK the singing of birds together, which happens just before dawn

> **! Common mistake: day**
>
> **Warning:** choose the correct preposition!
>
> To talk about when something happened or will happen, don't say 'in/at' this/that day, say **on this/that day**:
>
> ~~*I will always remember where I was in that day.*~~
>
> *I will always remember where I was on that day.*

day /deɪ/ noun [C] **1** A1 a period of 24 hours, especially from twelve o'clock one night to twelve o'clock the next night: *January has 31 days.* ◦ *the days of the week* ◦ *He runs five miles **every** day.* ◦ *It took us almost a day to get here.* ◦ *I saw him **the** day **before yesterday**.* ◦ *We leave **the** day **after tomorrow**.* ◦ *He was last seen alive five days **ago**.* ◦ *They haven't been seen **for** days (= for several days).* ◦ *I'll be seeing Pat **in a few** days/**in a few** days' **time**.* ◦ *How's your day been? (= Have you enjoyed today?)* ◦ *Have a nice day!* ◦ *I must get some sleep – I've got **a big** day (= an important day) tomorrow.* **2** A2 used to refer to the period in 24 hours when it is naturally light: *a bright sunny day* ◦ *It's rained **all** day today.* ◦ *These animals sleep during the day and hunt at night.* **3** A2 the time that you usually spend at work or at school: *a normal working day* ◦ *I work a seven-hour day.* ◦ *We're having to work a six-day week to cope with demand.* **4 day off** a day when you do not have to work, or do something that you normally do: *I won't be in on Thursday; I'm having a day off.* ◦ *She's taking three days off next week.* **5 the other day** B1 a few days ago: *Didn't I see you in the post office the other day?* **6 these days** A2 used to talk about the present time, in comparison with the past: *Vegetarianism is very popular these days.* **7 in those days** B2 in the past: *In those days people used to write a lot more letters.* **8 any day now** B2 very soon, especially within the next few days: *The baby's due any day now.* **9 by day** when it is naturally light: *I prefer travelling by day.* **10 day after day** B1 repeatedly, every day: *The same problems keep coming up day after day.* **11 day and night** all the time: *You can hear the traffic from your room day and night.* **12 day by day** B2 every day, or more and more as each day passes: *Day by day he became weaker.* **13 (from) day to day** If something changes (from) day to day, it changes often: *The symptoms of the disease change from day to day.* **14 the days** C1 a period in history: *How did people communicate in the days before email?* **15 to this day** until now: *To this day nobody knows what happened to him.*

IDIOMS **all in a day's work** If something difficult, unpleasant, or strange is all in a day's work for someone, it is a usual part of their job: *When you're a nurse, cleaning up vomit is all in a day's work.* • **the best/happiest days of your life** the most pleasant time you will ever have: *Adults are fond of telling children that their school years are the best days of their life.* • **day in day out** (especially of something boring) done or happening every day for a long period of time: *I have to do the same boring jobs day in day out.* • **sb's/sth's days are numbered** If someone or something's days are numbered, they will not exist for much longer: *The latest opinion polls suggest that his days **as** leader are numbered.* • **have had its/your day** to be much less popular than before: *She sold a lot of books in the 1990s, but she's had her day.* • **have your day in court** to get an opportunity to give your opinion on something or to explain your actions after they have been criticized: *She was determined to get her day in court and the TV interview would give it to her.* • **in all my (born) days** in all of my life: *I've never seen anything so strange in all my born days.* • **in my day** when I was young: *Children take so much for granted nowadays – in my day a new bike was really special.* • **in this day and age** at the present time: *You can't afford to run businesses inefficiently in this day and age.* • **make sb's day** C2 to make someone happy: *Seeing Adrian again after such a long time really made my day.* • **not be sb's day** If it is not your day, you are having a difficult or unpleasant day: *This really isn't my day – my wallet was stolen and now I've lost my car keys.* • **the old days** C1 times in the past: *In the old days we only had four or five TV channels.* • **one of these days** B1 some time in the near future: *You're going to get into serious trouble one of these days.* • **one of those days** a bad day, full of problems: *It's just been one of those days.* • **one/some day** B1 at some time in the future: *I'd love to go to China some/one day.* • **take each day as it comes/take it one day at a time** to deal with things as they happen, and not to make plans or to worry about the future: *I've lived through a lot of changes recently, but I've learned to take each day as it comes.* • **that'll be the day** something you say in order to show you think that something is unlikely to happen: *'Mike says he's going to give up smoking.' 'That'll be the day!'* • **those were the days** something you say that means life was better at the time in the past that you are talking about: *We were young and madly in love. Ah, those were the days!* • **to the day** exactly: *She died ten years ago to the day.*

ˈday ˌboy noun [C] a male DAY PUPIL

daybreak /ˈdeɪ.breɪk/ noun [U] **dawn**

ˈday ˌcare noun [U] C1 care or education provided during the day, especially for young children or old people: *a day care centre for the elderly*

daydream /ˈdeɪ.driːm/ noun [C usually singular] a series of pleasant thoughts about something you would prefer to be doing or something you would like to achieve in the future: *He never paid attention in class and seemed to be **in a** permanent daydream.* ◦ *I was just enjoying a daydream **about** winning the Nobel Prize for literature.* • **daydream** verb [I] C1 *Stop daydreaming and get on with your work!* • **daydreamer** /-driː.məʳ/ US /-driː.mɚ/ noun [C]

ˈday ˌgirl noun [C] a female DAY PUPIL

Day-Glo /ˈdeɪ.gləʊ/ US /-gloʊ/ adj trademark in or of a colour which seems to shine especially brightly in ordinary light: *Day-Glo swimsuits*

ˈday ˌjob noun [C] a job that you do to earn money so that you can do something else that you prefer but that does not pay you much money: *Many actors have day jobs too.*

IDIOM **don't give up the day job!** humorous used for telling someone that you do not think they are very good at something: *'What did you think of my singing, then?' 'Er, don't give up the day job!'*

daylight /ˈdeɪ.laɪt/ noun [U] B2 (the period when there is) natural light from the sun: *The colours look much better in daylight.*

IDIOMS **beat/knock the (living) daylights out of sb** informal to hit someone very hard, many times: *I'll knock the living daylights out of him if he says that again!* • **frighten, scare, etc. the (living) daylights out of sb** informal to frighten someone very much: *Don't jump out on me like that! You scared the living daylights out of me!*

ˌdaylight ˈrobbery noun [U] (US also **ˌhighway ˈrobbery**) a situation in which you are charged a lot too much for something: *£4 for an orange juice? That's just daylight robbery!*

ˌdaylight ˈsaving ˌtime noun [U] the time set usually one hour later in summer so that there is a longer period of daylight in the evening

ˈday ˌnursery noun [C] a place where young children are taken care of, especially while their parents are working

the ˌDay of Aˈtonement noun [U] **Yom Kippur**

the ˌDay of ˈJudgment noun [U] **Judgment Day**

ˌday of ˈreckoning noun [S] a time when the effect of a past mistake is experienced or when a crime is punished

ˈday ˌpupil noun [C] UK (US **ˈday ˌstudent**) a student who sleeps at home and studies at a school where some of the other students live → Compare **boarder**

ˈday reˌlease noun [U] UK a system in which people who work can study one day a week at a college

ˌday reˈturn noun [C] UK a ticket that can only be used for travelling to a place and back to where you started in a single day: *a day return to London*

ˈday ˌschool noun [C] a private school whose students return home in the evening

ˈday ˌstudent noun [C] US for **day pupil**

daytime /ˈdeɪ.taɪm/ noun [U] B2 the period between the time when the sun rises and the time it goes down, or the part of the day that is neither evening nor night: *I tend to sleep **in/during** the daytime and study at night.* ◦ *a regular daytime job* ◦ *a daytime phone number* ◦ *daytime television*

ˌday-to-ˈday adj [before noun] C1 happening every day as a regular part of your job or life: *day-to-day problems/responsibilities*

ˈday ˌtrip noun [C] a visit to a place in which you go there and come back on the same day: *Do you fancy coming **on** a day trip to Bath next Saturday?* • **ˈday-ˌtripper** noun [C] *The coast is full of day-trippers at this time of year.*

daze /deɪz/ noun **in a daze** unable to think clearly: *She was wandering around in a daze this morning.*

dazed /deɪzd/ adj C2 very confused and unable to think clearly: *You're looking rather dazed – is anything wrong?* ◦ *a dazed expression*

D

dazzle /ˈdæz.l/ verb **1** B2 [T] If light dazzles you, it makes you unable to see for a short time: *I was dazzled by the sunlight.* **2** C2 [T usually passive] If you are dazzled by someone or something, you think they are extremely good and exciting: *I was dazzled by his charm and good looks.*

dazzling /ˈdæz.lɪŋ/ adj **1** C2 A dazzling light is so bright that you cannot see for a short time after looking at it: *a dazzling white light* **2** C2 extremely attractive or exciting: *dazzling good looks* ◦ *a dazzling smile* ◦ *a dazzling performance/display* • **dazzlingly** /-li/ adv

D

DC /ˌdiːˈsiː/ noun [U] **ELECTRICITY** ▷ **1** abbreviation for direct current: electrical current which always flows in one direction → Compare **AC** **UNITED STATES** ▷ **2** abbreviation for the District of Columbia: an area of the eastern US that has the same borders as the US capital, Washington, and is not part of a US state

ˈD-Day noun [U] **1** the day during the Second World War when the ALLIES began their INVASION of Europe by attacking the coast of northern France: *The D-Day landings began on 6 June 1944, when Allied forces invaded Normandy.* **2** a day when something important will happen: *After four hectic weeks of electioneering, candidates are preparing themselves for D-Day (= election day) tomorrow.*

DDT /ˌdiː.diːˈtiː/ noun [U] a poisonous chemical for killing insects

de- /diː-/, /dɪ-/ prefix used to add the meaning 'opposite', 'remove', or 'reduce' to a noun or verb: *deforestation* ◦ *the denationalization of the coal industry* ◦ *Once you've written a computer program, you have to debug (= remove the errors from) it.*

deacon /ˈdiː.kən/ noun [C] in some Churches, an official, either male or female, who is below a priest in rank and who performs some of the duties of a priest

deaconess /ˌdiː.kəˈnes/ (US) /ˈdiː.kən.əs/ noun [C] in some Churches, a woman who performs particular duties but who is not a deacon

deactivate /ˌdiˈæk.tɪ.veɪt/ verb [T] to cause something to be no longer active or effective: *All chemical weapons facilities will be deactivated.* • **deactivation** /ˌdiː.æk.tɪˈveɪ.ʃən/ (US) /diˌæk-/ noun [U]

dead /ded/ adj; adj, adv; noun

▸adj **NOT LIVING** ▷ **1** A2 not now living: *She's been dead for 20 years now.* ◦ *The motorcyclist was dead **on arrival** at the hospital.* ◦ *He was **shot** dead (= killed by shooting) outside his home.* **2** C2 mainly UK If a part of your body is dead, you cannot feel it: *I've been sitting with my legs crossed for so long, my right leg has gone dead.* **NOT IN USE** ▷ **3** UK describes empty glasses and bottles that were previously full **4** In some sports, if a ball is dead, it is outside the area of play. **BORING** ▷ **5** C2 If a place is dead, it is too quiet and nothing interesting happens there: *The city centre's quite lively during the day, but it's totally dead at night.* **EQUIPMENT** ▷ **6** B2 If a piece of equipment is dead, it is not working: *a dead battery* ◦ *The phone suddenly **went** dead.*

IDIOMS **be (as) dead as a/the dodo** informal to not be important or popular any longer: *Letter-writing is as dead as the dodo.* • **be as dead as a doornail** informal to be clearly and obviously dead • **be dead in the water** If something is dead in the water, it has failed and it seems impossible that it will be successful in the future: *So how does a government revive an economy that is dead in the water?* • **be dead on your feet** to be very tired • **be dead to the world** to be sleeping: *'Is Georgie up yet?' 'I doubt it – she was dead to the world ten minutes ago.'* • **over my dead body** If you say something will happen over your dead body, you mean that you will do everything you can to prevent it: *'Joe says he's going to buy a motorbike.' 'Over my dead body!'*

▸adj [before noun], adv C1 complete(ly): *The conductor waited for dead **silence** before commencing the performance.* ◦ *You won't be able to change his mind – he's dead **against** the plan.* ◦ informal *I'm dead **certain** I left my purse on the desk.* ◦ informal *I'm dead (= very) hungry.* ◦ informal *The exam was dead (= very) **easy**.* ◦ UK informal *'How was the film?' 'It was dead good.'* ◦ *The post office is dead (= straight) **ahead**.* ◦ *Aim for the dead (= exact) centre of the target.* ◦ *I always try to arrive dead (= exactly) **on time**.* ◦ *Martha's dead **set on** having (= very much wants to have) a new bike.* ◦ *He's dead **set against** (= completely opposed to) living in the city.*

▸noun **the dead** [plural] dead people: *Three children were among the dead.* ◦ *A ceasefire has been called to allow the survivors to bury their dead.*

IDIOMS **come back from the dead** (also **rise from the dead**) to be successful or popular again after a period of not being successful or popular: *This was a company that had risen from the dead.* • **in the dead of night/winter** in the middle of night/winter: *The fire broke out in the dead of night.*

ˌdead ˈair noun [U] US a period of silence during a radio or television broadcast that is not intended

deadbeat /ˈded.biːt/ noun; adj

▸noun [C] mainly US informal **1** a person who is not willing to work does not behave in a responsible way and does not fit into ordinary society: *He's a **real** deadbeat who's never had a proper job.* ◦ [as form of address] *Come off it, deadbeat, you're never going to get anywhere.* **2** a person or company that is not willing to pay debts

▸adj [before noun] mainly US informal not willing to pay debts or accept responsibility: *The new law is aimed at deadbeat landlords who owe $22 million.*

deadbolt /ˈded.bəʊlt/ (US) /-boʊlt/ noun [C] US for **mortise lock**

ˌdead ˈcat ˌbounce noun [S] specialized a temporary increase in the value of SHARES after there has been a large reduction in their value: *Are we witnessing a genuine recovery in the share price, or is it just a dead cat bounce?*

ˌdead ˈduck noun [C usually singular] informal someone or something that is very unlikely to be successful, especially because of a mistake or bad judgment: *Thanks to the lack of market research, the project was a dead duck right from the start.*

deaden /ˈded.ən/ verb [T] to make something less painful or less strong: *Morphine is often used to deaden the pain of serious injuries.* ◦ *Double glazing has helped to deaden the noise from the motorway.*

ˌdead ˈend noun; verb

▸noun **1** [C] a road that is closed at one end, and does not lead anywhere: *a dead-end street* **2** [S] a situation that has no hope of making progress: *Negotiators have reached a dead end in their attempts to find a peaceful solution.*

▸verb [I] US (usually **dead-end**) If a road or path dead-ends, it is closed at one end, and does not lead anywhere: *The road dead-ended halfway up the mountain.*

ˌdead-end ˈjob noun [C] a job in which there is no chance of progressing to a better, more important job

deadhead noun; verb

▸noun [C] /ˈded.hed/ informal a person who is boring or stupid

►verb [T] /ˌdedˈhed/ to remove old flowers from a plant

ˌdead ˈheat noun [C] a competition in which two or more competitors finish at exactly the same time or with exactly the same result: *The race ended* ***in*** *a dead heat.* ◦ *The opinion polls show the three election candidates* ***in*** *a dead heat (****with*** *each other).*

ˌdead ˈlanguage noun [C] a language that is no longer spoken by anyone as their main language: *Latin is a dead language.*

ˌdead ˈletter noun **MAIL** ▷ **1** [C] a letter that cannot be DELIVERED to the address written on it and cannot be returned to the person who sent it: *the dead-letter office* **LAW/AGREEMENT** ▷ **2** [C usually singular] a law or agreement that is no longer effective

deadline /ˈded.laɪn/ noun [C] B2 a time or day by which something must be done: *There's no way I can* ***meet*** *that deadline.* ◦ *We're working to a* ***tight*** *deadline (= we do not have much time to finish the work).* ◦ *I'm afraid you've* ***missed*** *the deadline – the deadline* ***for*** *applications was 30 May.*

deadlock /ˈded.lɒk/ US /-lɑːk/ noun **1** [S or U] a situation in which agreement in an argument cannot be reached because neither side will change its demands or accept any of the demands of the other side: *Somebody will have to compromise if we are to* ***break*** *(= end) the deadlock* ***between*** *the two warring factions.* ◦ *Once again the talks have* ***ended in*** *deadlock.* ◦ *Deadlock* ***over*** *wage levels has prevented an agreement being reached.* → Synonym **stalemate** **2** [C] a lock that is inside the edge of a door, so that it cannot be seen or removed when the door is closed → See also **mortise lock**

deadlocked /ˈded.lɒkt/ US /-lɑːkt/ adj If a situation is deadlocked, agreement in an argument cannot be reached because neither side will change its demands or accept any of the demands of the other side: *The dispute has now been deadlocked for several months.*

ˌdead ˈloss noun [S] informal **1** an activity or process that is not at all effective or successful: *Yesterday's meeting was a dead loss – nothing was decided.* **2** a person who is not successful or useful: *I was a dead loss at languages at school.* ◦ *John was a dead loss – he just stood there and did nothing.*

deadly /ˈded.li/ adj; adv

►adj **VERY DANGEROUS** ▷ **1** B2 likely to cause death: *a deadly virus* ◦ *a deadly weapon* **COMPLETE** ▷ **2** complete or extreme: *They have been deadly* ***enemies*** *ever since Mark stole Greg's girlfriend.*

►adv C1 completely or extremely: *I thought she was joking but she was deadly* ***serious****.*

deadly nightshade /ˌded.liˈnaɪt.ʃeɪd/ noun [C or U] (also **belladonna**) a very poisonous plant with small black shiny fruits, which grows in Europe, North Africa, and West Asia

deadpan /ˈded.pæn/ adj looking or seeming serious when you are telling a joke: *a deadpan expression/voice*

ˌdead ˈreckoning noun [U] a way of calculating the position of a ship or aircraft using only information about the direction and distance it has travelled from a known point

ˌdead ˈringer noun [C usually singular] someone or something which looks very similar to someone or something else: *He's a dead ringer* ***for*** *Bono from U2.*

ˌdead ˈweight noun [C usually singular] the heaviness of a person or object that cannot or does not move by itself: *She may be small but, when I have to carry her upstairs after she's fallen asleep, she's a dead weight* (US also *she is dead weight*).

ˌdead ˈwood noun [U] people or things that are no longer useful: *She cleared out the dead wood as soon as she took over the company.*

ˈdead ˌzone noun [C] **1** a place where a mobile phone does not work because there is no signal **2** a place or time in which nothing happens: *The village is a dead zone for many young people.*

deaf /def/ adj; noun

►adj **1** B1 unable to hear, either completely or partly: *He's been totally/partially deaf since birth.* **2** disapproving unwilling to listen: *The local council has remained deaf* ***to*** *all the objections to its proposals.* • **deafness** /ˈdef.nəs/ noun [U]

IDIOM **(as) deaf as a post** informal completely deaf: *Grandad's as deaf as a post.*

►noun [plural] **the deaf** people who are unable to hear: *Many of the TV programmes are broadcast with subtitles for the deaf.*

ˈdeaf ˌaid noun [C] UK a **hearing aid**

deafen /ˈdef.ən/ verb [T] If a very loud noise deafens you, it makes you deaf, or makes you temporarily unable to hear the other sounds near you: *The explosion permanently deafened her in her right ear.*

deafening /ˈdef.ən.ɪŋ/ adj extremely loud: *The music was deafening.*

ˌdeaf-ˈmute noun [C] old-fashioned a person who can neither hear nor speak

deal /dɪəl/ noun; verb

►noun **AGREEMENT** ▷ **1** B2 [C] an agreement or an arrangement, especially in business: *a business deal* ◦ *The unions and management have* ***made*** *a two-year pay and productivity deal.* ◦ *I'll* ***make/do*** *a deal* ***with*** *you – you wash the car and I'll let you use it tonight.* ◦ *She got* ***a good*** *deal (= paid a low price)* ***on*** *her new house.* ◦ *Is industry* ***getting*** *a* ***raw/rough*** *deal from (= being unfairly/badly treated by) the EU?* **AMOUNT** ▷ **2 a good/great deal** B2 a large amount: *She spends a good deal of her time in Glasgow.* ◦ *A great deal of effort has gone into making the software reliable.* ◦ *They still need a great deal more money to finish the project.* **SHARING OUT** ▷ **3** [C] the act of dealing (= sharing out) something, especially playing cards: *It's your deal (= turn to deal).*

►verb [I or T] (**dealt, dealt**) **DO BUSINESS** ▷ **1** to do business: *We only deal* ***with*** *companies which have a good credit record.* ◦ slang *How long had she been dealing (= selling drugs) before she was arrested?* ◦ slang *He was suspected of dealing (= selling) cocaine.* **SHARE OUT** ▷ **2** to give or share out something, especially playing cards: *Whose turn is it to deal?* ◦ *Would you like to deal (****out****) the cards?* ◦ [+ two objects] *Deal them five cards each./Deal five cards* ***to*** *each of them.* ◦ *We have only a small amount of food and clothing to deal* ***out to*** *each refugee.* **3 deal a blow to sb/sth** (also **deal sb/sth a blow**) to cause someone or something, usually a plan or hope, to fail or to be affected very badly: *The latest trade figures have dealt a severe blow to hopes of an early economic recovery.*

PHRASAL VERBS **deal in sth** to buy and sell particular goods as a business: *They mainly deal in rare books.* • **deal with sb** B2 to talk to someone or meet someone, especially as part of your job: *She's used to dealing with difficult customers.* • **deal with sth TAKE ACTION** ▷ **1** B1 to take action in order to achieve something or in order to solve a problem: *How do you intend to deal with this problem?* ◦ *General enquiries are dealt with by our head office.* **BE ABOUT** ▷ **2** to be about or be on the subject of something: *Her new film deals with the relationship between a woman and her* *sick daughter.* ◦ *The author has tried to deal with (= write about) a very difficult subject.*

dealer /ˈdiː.ləʳ/ (US) /-lə/ **noun** [C] **1** (B2) a person who trades in something: *a second-hand car dealer* ◦ *an antiques dealer* ◦ *drug dealers* **2** the person who deals the cards in a game

dealership /ˈdiː.lə.ʃɪp/ (US) /-lə-/ **noun** [C] a company that has permission to sell a particular product: *Their company has just won the dealership **for** Rolls-Royce.*

dealings /ˈdiː.lɪŋz/ **noun** [plural] activities involving other people, especially in business: *Have you **had** any dealings **with** their Paris office?*

dealt /delt/ **verb** past simple and past participle of **deal**

dean /diːn/ **noun** [C] **LEADER** ▷ **1** an official of high rank in a college or university who is responsible for the organization of a department or departments: *She is the new dean of the Faculty of Social Sciences.* ◦ *the Dean of Medicine* **2** US someone among a group of people who has worked the longest in the particular job or activity they share, and who is their unofficial leader: *Parsons is the dean of the TV news correspondents at Channel Nine.* **CHURCH** ▷ **3** a priest of high rank in the Church of England or the Roman Catholic Church, who is in charge of managing a large church or CATHEDRAL

dear /dɪəʳ/ (US) /dɪr/ **adj; exclamation; noun**

▸**adj LOVED** ▷ **1** (B2) loved or liked very much: *She was a very dear friend.* ◦ *He was very dear **to** me.* ◦ *What a dear (= very attractive) little kitten!* ◦ ***My** dear Gina – how lovely to see you!* **2** (A1) used at the beginning of a letter to greet the person you are writing to: *Dear Kerry/Mum and Dad/Ms Smith/Sir* **EXPENSIVE** ▷ **3** costing too much: *The food was good but very dear.* → Synonym **expensive**

IDIOM **for dear life** If you do something for dear life, you do it with as much effort as possible, usually to avoid danger: *As the ship began to tilt, we clung on for dear life.*

▸**exclamation** (also old-fashioned **dearie**) (A2) used in expressions of anger, disappointment, sadness, or surprise: ***Oh** dear! I've lost my keys again.* ◦ *Dear **me**, it's already 4.30 and I said I'd be home by 5.00!* ◦ *Dearie **me**, what a mess!*

▸**noun 1** [C usually singular] informal a kind person: *Annie's such a dear – she's brought me breakfast in bed every morning this week.* **2** [as form of address] used to address someone you love or are being friendly to, not used between men: *Here's your receipt, dear.* ◦ *Would you like a drink, dear?* ◦ *Lovely to see you, **my** dear.*

dearie /ˈdɪə.ri/ (US) /ˈdɪr.i/ **noun** [as form of address] old-fashioned a friendly form of address, not used between men: *Here's your change, dearie.*

ˌ**Dear** ˈ**John (letter)** **noun** [C] a letter written to end a romantic relationship

dearly /ˈdɪə.li/ (US) /ˈdɪr-/ **adv 1** very much: *She will be dearly missed by her family and friends.* ◦ *We would dearly love to sell our flat and move to the country.* **2** in a way that is expensive: *dearly priced*

IDIOM **pay dearly** to suffer a lot as a result of a particular action or event: *If you refuse to cooperate with us, you will pay dearly **for** it.*

ˈ**dearness al**ˌ**lowance** **noun** [U] Indian English an amount of money that is added to a person's basic pay or PENSION because of rising prices and other costs

dearth /dɜːθ/ (US) /dɝːθ/ **noun** [S] formal an amount or supply that is not large enough: *a dearth **of** new homes in the region* → Synonym **lack of sth**

death /deθ/ **noun** [C or U] **1** (B1) the end of life: *The disease causes thousands of deaths a year.* ◦ *Do you believe in life after death?* ◦ *He never got over the death of his daughter.* ◦ *death threats* **2 bored, frightened, etc. to death** (B2) extremely bored, frightened, etc. **3 to death** (C2) until you die: *The animals burned to death in the barn.* ◦ *He choked to death on a fish bone.* ◦ *The traitor was **put** to death (= killed as a punishment).* **4 the death of sb/sth** the cause of the end of life, or the end or destruction of something: *The failure of the family business was the death of him.* ◦ *That child **will be** the death of me (= is always doing something which upsets me)!*

> **Word partners for death**
>
> *bleed/choke/freeze/starve* to death • be *beaten/crushed/stabbed/trampled* to death • *condemned to/put to/sentenced to* death • *escape* death • *mourn/get over* sb's death • *premature/sudden/tragic/untimely* death • a (leading/major) *cause* of death • death *from* sth

IDIOMS **be at death's door** informal to be very ill • **be in at the death** UK to be present at the important time when something comes to an end • **catch your death of cold** informal to catch a very bad cold because you are not wearing warm or dry clothes, etc. • **look/feel like death warmed up** UK (US **look/feel like death warmed over**) to look or feel very ill: *He shouldn't be working when he's so ill – he looks like death warmed up!*

deathbed /ˈdeθ.bed/ **noun** [C usually singular] the bed that someone dies in or is dying in: *She spoke to her family **from** her deathbed.*

IDIOM **be on your deathbed** to be dying

ˈ**death-de**ˌ**fying** **adj** [before noun] very dangerous: *a death-defying leap from an aircraft*

ˈ**death** ˌ**duty** **noun** [U] UK the unofficial name for tax on a person's money and possessions when they die

ˈ**death** ˌ**knell** **noun** [S] a warning of the end of something: *The opening of the superstore will **sound/toll the** death knell **for** (= cause the failure of) hundreds of small independent shops.*

deathless /ˈdeθ.ləs/ **adj** literary lasting for ever and never to be forgotten: *his deathless prose*

> **Note:**
>
> Often used humorously about writing of a low quality.

deathly /ˈdeθ.li/ **adj, adv** extreme in a way that is unpleasant: *After he had spoken, a deathly **silence/hush** fell on the room.* ◦ *She went deathly **pale**.*

ˈ**death** ˌ**mask** **noun** [C] a model of a dead person's face made by pressing WAX onto the face

the ˈ**death** ˌ**penalty** **noun** [S] the legal punishment of death for a crime

ˌ**death** ˈ**row** **noun** mainly US **on death row** in prison and waiting to be killed as a punishment for a crime

ˈ**death** ˌ**sentence** **noun** [C usually singular] a legal punishment of a crime by death: *In some countries, drug-smuggling still carries the death sentence.*

ˈ**death's head** **noun** [C] a picture of a human SKULL (= the hard structure of the head) used as a warning of danger or to frighten people

ˈ**death** ˌ**squad** **noun** [C, + sing/pl verb] an unofficial armed group who look for and illegally kill particular people, especially the enemies of a political party

ˈdeath ˌthroes noun [plural] literary the process of dying or ending in a very painful or unpleasant way: *The government was* ***in*** *its death throes.*

ˈdeath ˌtoll noun [C usually singular] the number of people who die because of an event such as a war or an accident: *The day after the explosion the death toll had risen to 90.*

ˈdeath ˌtrap noun [C usually singular] something that is very dangerous and could cause death: *The car he met me in was a death trap.*

ˈdeath ˌwarrant noun [C] an official document which says that someone must be killed as a punishment

deathwatch beetle /ˌdeθ.wɒtʃˈbiː.tl/ (US) /-wɑːtʃˈbiː.t̬l/ noun [C] an insect which eats wood, especially in old houses, causing serious damage

ˈdeath ˌwish noun [S] a DESIRE for death: *The chances he takes, you'd think he had a death wish.*

deb /deb/ noun [C] informal for **debutante**

debacle /deɪˈbɑː.kl/ noun [C] a complete failure, especially because of bad planning and organization: *The collapse of the company was described as the greatest financial debacle in US history.*

debar /dɪˈbɑːʳ/ (US) /diːˈbɑːr/ verb [T] (-rr-) formal to stop someone from doing something by law or by official agreement: *He was debarred* ***from*** *the club* ***for*** *unacceptable behaviour.*

debase /dɪˈbeɪs/ verb [T] **1** to reduce the quality or value of something: *Some argue that money has debased football.* ◦ *Our world view has become debased. We no longer have a sense of the sacred.* **2 debase the coinage/currency** • **debasement** /-mənt/ noun [U]

debatable /dɪˈbeɪ.tə.bl/ (US) /-t̬ə-/ adj not clear or certain because different people may have different opinions: [+ question word] ***It's*** *debatable* ***wh****ether a university degree helps at all.* ◦ *The value of some of the experiments is debatable.*

debate /dɪˈbeɪt/ noun; verb

▸noun [C or U] (B2) (a) serious discussion of a subject in which many people take part: *Education is the current focus of public debate.* ◦ *How we proceed from here is a matter* ***for*** *debate.* ◦ *Over the year we have had several debates* ***about*** *future policy.*

▸verb **1** (C2) [I or T] to discuss a subject in a formal way: *In Parliament today, MPs debated the Finance Bill.* ◦ *They had been debating for several hours without reaching a conclusion.* ◦ [+ question word] *The authorities debated* ***wh****ether to build a new car park.* **2** [T] to try to make a decision about something: [+ question word] *We debated* ***wh****ether to take the earlier train.* ◦ *I'm still debating* ***what*** *colour to paint the walls.* • **debater** /dɪˈbeɪ.təʳ/ (US) /-t̬ɚ/ noun [C] *She was a good speaker and an excellent debater.*

debauched /dɪˈbɔːtʃt/ (US) /-ˈbɑːtʃt/ adj made weaker or destroyed by bad sexual behaviour, drinking too much alcohol, taking drugs, etc.: *his debauched lifestyle* • **debauchee** /ˌdeb.ɔːˈtʃiː/ (US) /-ɑːˈʃiː/ noun [C] a debauched person: *He gave a convincing stage performance as the unpleasant young debauchee.*

debauchery /dɪˈbɔː.tʃəʳr.i/ (US) /-ˈbɑː.tʃɚ-/ noun [U] bad sexual behaviour, drinking too much alcohol, taking drugs, etc.: *a life of debauchery*

debenture /dɪˈben.tʃəʳ/, /-ˈbent.ʃɚ/ noun [C] specialized a type of LOAN, often used by companies to raise money, that is paid back over a long period of time and at a fixed rate of interest

debilitate /dɪˈbɪl.ɪ.teɪt/ verb [T] formal to make someone or something physically weak: *Chemotherapy exhausted and debilitated him.* • **debilitating** /-teɪ.tɪŋ/ (US) /-teɪ.t̬ɪŋ/ adj *a debilitating* ***condition/disease***

debility /dɪˈbɪl.ɪ.ti/ (US) /-ə.t̬i/ noun [U] formal physical weakness

debit /ˈdeb.ɪt/ noun; verb

▸noun [C or U] (B2) (a record of) money taken out of a bank account: *The account was* ***in*** *debit at the end of the month (= more money had been spent than was in the account at that time).* ◦ *Debits are shown in the left-hand column.* → Compare **credit**

▸verb [T] (B2) to take money out of an account or keep a record of this: *The bank debited my account.* ◦ *The bank debited the money* ***from*** *my account.* ◦ *The unauthorized borrowing fee will be debited* ***to*** *your account.*

ˈdebit ˌcard noun [C] (B2) a small plastic card that can be used as a method of payment, the money being taken from your bank account automatically: *I paid with my debit card.*

ˈdebit ˌcolumn noun [C] the list of numbers that shows amounts of money that have been spent from a bank account

debonair /ˌdeb.əˈneəʳ/ (US) /-ˈner/ adj old-fashioned (especially of men) attractive, confident, and carefully dressed: *a debonair appearance/manner* ◦ *a debonair young man*

debrief /ˌdiːˈbriːf/ verb [T] to question someone in detail about work they have done for you: *The pilots were thoroughly debriefed after every mission.* ◦ *a debriefing* ***session***

debris /ˈdeb.riː/, /ˈdeɪ.briː/ (US) /dəˈbriː/ noun [U] broken or torn pieces of something larger: *Debris from the aircraft was scattered over a large area.*

debt /det/ noun [C or U] (B2) something, especially money, that is owed to someone else, or the state of owing something: *He managed to* ***pay off*** *his debts in two years.* ◦ *The firm* ***ran up*** *huge debts.* ◦ *They are* ***in*** *debt* ***to*** *(= owe money to) the bank.* ◦ *He* ***ran/got into*** *debt (= borrowed money) after he lost his job.* ◦ *The company is* ***deep in*** *debt (= owes a lot of money).* → See also **indebted**

> **Word partners for debt**
>
> *be in/fall into/get into/run into* debt • *get out of* debt • *incur/run up* debts • *default on* a debt • *clear/pay off/repay/settle* a debt • *cancel/write off* a debt • be *deep/heavily* in debt • *crippling/heavy/mounting* debts • *outstanding/unpaid* debts

debtor /ˈdet.əʳ/ (US) /ˈdet̬.ɚ/ noun [C] someone who owes money

ˈdebt reˌlief noun [U] the situation in which a bank or a government tells a person, a company, or a government that they do not have to pay back the money they owe: *There are plans to provide full debt relief for some African countries.*

debug /ˌdiːˈbʌɡ/ verb [T] (-gg-) REMOVE MISTAKES ▷ **1** to remove BUGS (= mistakes) from a computer program: *to debug a program* REMOVE DEVICES ▷ **2** to look for and remove BUGS (= hidden listening or recording devices) from a place

debunk /ˌdiːˈbʌŋk/ verb [T] informal to show that something is less important, less good, or less true than it has been made to appear: *The writer's aim was to debunk the* ***myth*** *that had grown up around the actress.*

debut /ˈdeɪ.bju/ noun; verb

▸noun [C] (C1) the occasion when someone performs or presents something to the public for the first time: *She* ***made*** *her professional stage debut in Swan Lake.*

∘ *He started as an actor, **making** his debut **as** a director in 1990.* ∘ *her debut (= first) album*

▸**verb** [I usually + adv/prep] to perform or be introduced to the public for the first time: *The programme debuted last year to great acclaim.*

debutante /ˈdeb.juː.tɒnt/ US /-tɑːnt/ **noun** [C] (also **deb**) a rich young woman who, especially in the past in Britain, went to a number of social events as a way of being introduced to other young people of high social rank: *a debutantes' ball*

D

Dec. **noun** written abbreviation for **December**

deca- /ˈdek.ə-/ **prefix** ten: *decade*

decade /ˈdek.eɪd/, /dekˈeɪd/ **noun** [C] B2 a period of ten years, especially a period such as 2010 to 2019

decadence /ˈdek.ə.dᵊns/ **noun** [U] low moral standards and behaviour: *Western decadence*

decadent /ˈdek.ə.dᵊnt/ **adj** A decadent person or group has low moral standards: *a decadent society* ∘ *the decadent court surrounding the king* ∘ humorous *Champagne and chocolates for breakfast – how decadent!*

decaf /ˈdiː.kæf/ **noun** [C or U] informal for decaffeinated coffee: *a cup of decaf*

decaffeinated /diːˈkæf.ɪ.neɪ.tɪd/ US /dɪˈkæf.ɪ.neɪ.t̬ɪd/ **adj** C2 describes coffee or tea from which the CAFFEINE (= a chemical substance) has been removed

decal /ˈdiː.kæl/ **noun** [C] mainly US a picture or design printed on special paper, that can be put onto another surface, such as metal or glass

the Decalogue /ˈdek.ə.lɒg/ US /-lɑːg/ **noun** [S] specialized the rules of behaviour God gave to Israel through Moses on Mount Sinai → Synonym **the Ten Commandments**

decamp /diːˈkæmp/ **verb** [I] informal to leave suddenly and unexpectedly, usually without telling anyone: *He decamped from the hotel with someone else's luggage.*

decant /dɪˈkænt/ **verb** [T] to pour a liquid from one container into another

decanter /dɪˈkæn.təʳ/ US /-t̬ɚ/ **noun** [C] a decorative glass container for wine and other alcoholic drinks, with a part that fits into the top: *a cut-glass sherry decanter*

decapitate /dɪˈkæp.ɪ.teɪt/ **verb** [T] to cut off the head of a person • **decapitation** /dɪˌkæp.ɪˈteɪ.ʃᵊn/ **noun** [U]

decathlete /dɪˈkæθ.liːt/ **noun** [C] a man who competes in a decathlon

decathlon /dɪˈkæθ.lɒn/ US /-lɑːn/ **noun** [C] a competition in which an ATHLETE competes in ten sports events → Compare **biathlon, heptathlon, pentathlon**

decay /dɪˈkeɪ/ **verb; noun**

▸**verb** [I or T] B2 to (cause something to) become gradually damaged, worse, or less: *Sugar makes your teeth decay.* ∘ *The role of the extended family has been decaying for some time.* ∘ *Pollution has decayed the surface of the stonework on the front of the cathedral.* ∘ *the smell of decaying meat*

▸**noun** [U] C2 the process of decaying: *environmental/industrial/moral/urban decay* ∘ *dental/tooth decay* ∘ *The buildings had started to **fall into** decay.* ∘ *This industry has been **in** decay for some time.*

decease /dɪˈsiːs/ **noun** [U] formal a person's death: *The house will not be yours till after your mother's decease.*

deceased /dɪˈsiːst/ **adj; noun**

▸**adj** formal C2 dead: *the recently deceased Member of Parliament*

▸**noun** [C] (plural **the deceased**) formal **the deceased** C2 a person who has recently died: *The deceased shot her mother before killing herself.* ∘ *Five of the deceased were employed by the club.*

deceit /dɪˈsiːt/ **noun** [C or U] (an act of) keeping the truth hidden, especially to get an advantage: *The story is about theft, fraud, and deceit on an incredible scale.* • **deceitful** /-fᵊl/ **adj** *deceitful behaviour* • **deceitfully** /-fə.li/ **adv** • **deceitfulness** /-fᵊl.nəs/ **noun** [U]

deceive /dɪˈsiːv/ **verb** [T] **1** B2 to persuade someone that something false is the truth, or to keep the truth hidden from someone for your own advantage: *The company deceived customers by selling old computers as new ones.* ∘ *The sound of the door closing deceived me **into** thinking they had gone out.* → Synonym **trick** **2 deceive yourself** to refuse to accept the truth: *She thinks he'll come back, but she's deceiving herself.* • **deceiver** /-ˈsiː.vəʳ/ US /-ˈsiː.vɚ/ **noun** [C] someone who deceives people

IDIOM **are my eyes deceiving me?** something you say when you cannot believe what you see: *Is that snow in May, or are my eyes deceiving me?*

decelerate /ˌdiːˈsel.ᵊr.eɪt/ US /-ə.reɪt/ **verb** [I] **1** to reduce the speed that a vehicle is travelling at: *The car decelerated at the sight of the police car.* **2** to happen or make something happen more slowly → Compare **accelerate**

December /dɪˈsem.bəʳ/ US /-bɚ/ **noun** [C or U] (written abbreviation **Dec.**) A1 the twelfth and last month of the year, after November and before January: *My parents got married **in** December.* ∘ *We went to Mexico **on** 12 December.* ∘ *Their baby was born **last** December.*

decency /ˈdiː.sᵊn.si/ **noun** **1** [U] behaviour that is good, moral, and acceptable in society: *a sense of decency* ∘ [+ to infinitive] *She didn't even **have the** decency **to** apologize.* **2 the decencies** [plural] UK old-fashioned the acceptable or expected ways of doing something: *I hate going to funerals, but you must **observe** the decencies (= it is something you should do).*

decent /ˈdiː.sᵊnt/ **adj** **1** B2 socially acceptable or good: *Everyone should be entitled to a decent wage/standard of living.* ∘ *I thought he was a decent sort of person.* ∘ ***It** was very decent (= kind) **of** you **to** help.* ∘ *It made quite a decent-sized (= large) hole.* ∘ *After the recent scandal, the priest is expected to **do the** decent **thing** and resign from his position.* **2** informal dressed or wearing clothes: *Are you decent yet?* • **decently** /-li/ **adv**

decentralize (UK usually **decentralise**) /ˌdiːˈsen.trə.laɪz/ **verb** [I or T] to move the control of an organization or government from a single place to several smaller ones: *We decentralized our operations last year and opened several regional offices.* ∘ *Modern technology has made it easy for us to decentralize.* • **decentralization** (UK usually **decentralisation**) /ˌdiː.sen.trə.laɪˈzeɪ.ʃᵊn/ US /-ə-/ **noun** [U] *the decentralization of power*

deception /dɪˈsep.ʃᵊn/ **noun** [C or U] C2 the act of hiding the truth, especially to get an advantage: *He was found guilty of obtaining money by deception.*

deceptive /dɪˈsep.tɪv/ **adj** C2 making you believe something that is not true: *It's deceptive – from the outside the building looks small, but inside it's quite big.* • **deceptively** /-li/ **adv** *The plan seemed **deceptively simple** (= it seemed simple but was not in fact).* • **deceptiveness** /-nəs/ **noun** [U]

decibel /ˈdes.ɪ.bel/ **noun** [C] a unit for measuring the loudness of sound: *The typical lawn mower makes about 90 decibels of noise.*

decide /dɪˈsaɪd/ **verb** **1** A2 [I or T] to choose something, especially after thinking carefully about several possibilities: *They have to decide by next Friday.* ∘ *I don't mind which one we have – you decide.* ∘ [+ to infinitive] *In the end, we decided **to** go to the theatre.* ◦ [+ (that)] *She decided (**that**) she would retire to the country.* ◦ [+ question word] *I can't decide **what** to do.* ◦ *He can't decide **whether** to buy it.* ◦ *The committee decided **in favour of** (= made a formal judgment to choose) the cheapest option.* **2** C2 [T] to be the reason or situation that makes a particular result happen: *The weather decided the outcome of the cricket match.* ◦ *Tim's mistake decided the game (= caused him to lose).*

> **! Common mistake: decide**
>
> **Warning:** Check your spelling!
>
> **Decide** is one of the 50 words most often spelled wrongly by learners.

> **+ Other ways of saying decide**
>
> If someone is deciding a time or an amount, especially an exact date or price, the verbs **fix** and **set** are often used:
>
> *The price has been **set/fixed** at $10.*
>
> *Have you **set/fixed** a date for the wedding?*
>
> If someone makes a final and certain decision about a plan, date, etc., the verb **finalize** is sometimes used:
>
> *We've chosen a venue for the wedding, but we haven't **finalized** the details yet.*
>
> The verb **settle** and the phrasal verb **settle on/upon** are also often used when someone is making a final decision:
>
> *Have you **settled on** a place to live yet?*
>
> *OK then, we're going to Spain. That's **settled**.*
>
> To **resolve** to do something, is to decide definitely that you will do it:
>
> *Emma weighed herself and **resolved** to lose some weight.*
>
> The expression **make up your mind** is often used to mean 'to decide':
>
> *I like them both – I just can't **make up my mind** which one to pick.*
>
> *Have you **made up your mind** whether you're going?*
>
> If someone is unable to decide between two choices, in informal situations you can use the expression **be torn between** something **and** something else:
>
> *I'm **torn between** the fish **and** the beef.*

PHRASAL VERB **decide on sth/sb** to choose something or someone after careful thought: *I've decided on blue for the bathroom.*

decided /dɪˈsaɪ.dɪd/ **adj** [before noun] formal certain, obvious, or easy to notice: *She had a decided advantage over her opponent.*

decidedly /dɪˈsaɪ.dɪd.li/ **adv** certainly and obviously: *He was decidedly careful about what he told me.* ◦ *An agreement is looking decidedly difficult according to the newspapers.*

decider /dɪˈsaɪ.dəʳ/ US /-ɚ/ **noun** [C] informal a final game or competition which allows one person or team to win, or the winning point scored: *They lost what was regarded as the championship decider at Leeds.* ◦ *Jones scored the decider in the final minute.*

deciding /dɪˈsaɪ.dɪŋ/ **adj** [before noun] C2 A deciding event or action is more important than the rest because the final result, decision, or choice is changed by it: *The environmental argument was a deciding **factor**.* ◦ *The chairperson always has the deciding **vote**.* ◦ *Glennon scored the deciding goal in the final minute of the match.*

deciduous /dɪˈsɪd.ju.əs/ **adj** specialized A deciduous tree loses its leaves in autumn and grows new ones in the spring. → Compare **evergreen**

decimal /ˈdes.ɪ.məl/ **adj; noun**

▸**adj** relating to or expressed in a system of counting based on the number ten: *If you calculate the result **to** two decimal **places** (= give two numbers after the decimal point, as in 3.65), that should minimize any possible errors.*

▸**noun** [C] (specialized ˌ**decimal** ˈ**fraction**) a number expressed using a system of counting based on the number ten: *Three fifths expressed as a decimal is 0.6.*

ˌ**decimal** ˈ**currency** **noun** [C or U] a money system in which a smaller unit can be multiplied by ten or a 100 to make up a bigger unit

decimalization (UK usually **decimalisation**) /ˌdes.ɪ.mə.laɪˈzeɪ.ʃən/ US /-əˈ-/ **noun** [U] the changing of a system or number to a decimal form

ˌ**decimal** ˈ**place** **noun** [C] the position of a number after a decimal point: *The number is accurate to three decimal places.* ◦ *Pi expressed to five decimal places is 3.14159.*

ˌ**decimal** ˈ**point** **noun** [C] the DOT used between the whole numbers and the tenths of a decimal. In some countries a decimal COMMA is used instead: *To divide by ten, move the decimal point one place to the left.*

ˈ**decimal** ˌ**system** **noun** [S] a system of counting based on the number ten, with numbers from 0 to 9

decimate /ˈdes.ɪ.meɪt/ **verb** [T usually passive] to kill a large number of something, or to reduce something severely: *Populations of endangered animals have been decimated.*

decipher /dɪˈsaɪ.fəʳ/ US /-fɚ/ **verb** [T] to discover the meaning of something written badly or in a difficult or hidden way: *Can you decipher the writing on this envelope?*

decision /dɪˈsɪʒ.ən/ **noun** CHOICE ▷ **1** B1 [C] a choice that you make about something after thinking about several possibilities: *She has had to **make** some very difficult decisions.* ◦ *The company will **reach/come to/make** a decision shortly.* ◦ *Let me have a/your decision (= tell me what you have decided) by next week.* ◦ [+ to infinitive] *It was his decision **to** leave.* ◦ *The decision **about/on** whether he is innocent or guilty rests with the jury.* ◦ *We need to take a lot of factors into account in our decision-**making**.* ◦ [+ that] *I accepted his decision **that** he wished to die with dignity.* DECIDING QUICKLY ▷ **2** [U] approving the ability to decide quickly and without pausing because you are not certain: *She **acted with** decision, closing the bank account and phoning the police.* → Opposite **indecision**

> **Word partners for decision**
>
> ***make/take*** a decision • ***come to/reach*** a decision • ***overturn/reverse*** a decision • a ***difficult/hard/tough*** decision • a ***big/crucial/important*** decision • a ***conscious*** decision • a ***hasty/snap*** decision • a decision ***about/on*** sth

decisive /dɪˈsaɪ.sɪv/ **adj** **1** B2 able to make decisions quickly and confidently, or showing this quality: *You need to be more decisive.* ◦ *a decisive reply* → Opposite **indecisive** **2** C1 strongly affecting how a situation will progress or end: *These results could prove decisive in establishing the criminal's identity.* ◦ *a decisive role* ◦ *a decisive victory* • **decisively** /-li/ **adv** C2 *If we had acted earlier and more decisively (= more quickly and effectively) it might not have come to this.* • **decisiveness** /-nəs/ **noun** [U]

D

D

deck /dek/ noun; verb
▸noun [C] FLOOR ▷ **1** B2 a flat area for walking on, especially one built across the space between the sides of a boat or a bus: *We sat* ***on*** *deck until it was dark.* ◦ *The upper/top deck of the bus was always full of people smoking.* → See also **quarterdeck, sun deck** **2** a wooden floor built outside, where people can sit and relax **3** **below decks** on a level of a ship below the main deck: *Our cabin was below decks.* CARDS ▷ **4** A2 (also **pack**) mainly US a set of cards used for playing card games: *a new deck* ***of*** *cards*
▸verb [T] DECORATE ▷ **1** to decorate or add something to something to make an effect: *The room was decked* ***with*** *flowers.* ◦ *The wedding guests were decked* ***out in*** *their finery (= wearing their best clothes).* → See also **bedeck** HIT ▷ **2** slang to hit someone, especially to hit someone and knock them down: *Do that again and I'll deck you.*

deckchair /ˈdek.tʃeəʳ/ US /-tʃer/ noun [C] a folding chair for use outside, especially on the beach, on a ship, or in a park, with a long strip of material that forms a low seat when the chair is open

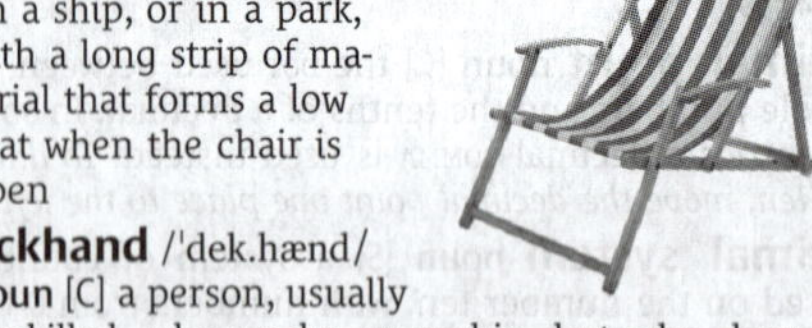
deckchair

deckhand /ˈdek.hænd/ noun [C] a person, usually unskilled, who works on a ship, but who does not serve the passengers or work in the engine room

decking /ˈdek.ɪŋ/ noun [U] a floor outside made of wood, or the long pieces of wood used to make this floor

declaim /dɪˈkleɪm/ verb [I or T] formal to express something with strong feeling, especially in a loud voice or with forceful language: [+ speech] *'The end of the world is at hand!' the poster declaimed.* ◦ *She declaimed* ***against*** *the evils of capitalism.*

declamation /ˌdek.ləˈmeɪ.ʃən/ noun [C or U] formal a strong statement or an occasion when you express something with a lot of feeling: *He subjected us to half an hour of impassioned declamation* ***against*** *the new motorway.* ◦ *Declamations* ***against*** *the press are common enough.*

declamatory /dɪˈklæm.ə.tər.i/ US /-tɔːr-/ adj formal expressing something with strong feeling, especially in a loud voice or with forceful language: *a declamatory style*

declaration /ˌdek.ləˈreɪ.ʃən/ noun [C] ANNOUNCEMENT ▷ **1** C1 an announcement, often one that is written and official: *Members of Parliament must* ***make*** *a declaration of their business interests.* ◦ *As witnesses to the accident, we were asked to* ***make*** *written declarations of what we had seen.* ◦ *The company made a declaration* ***of intent*** *to follow an equal opportunities policy.* CRICKET ▷ **2** in cricket, a situation in which a team stops BATTING (= hitting the ball) because they think they already have enough RUNS (= points) to win: *a cleverly timed declaration*

declare /dɪˈkleəʳ/ US /-ˈkler/ verb EXPRESS ▷ **1** B2 [T] to announce something clearly, firmly, publicly, or officially: *They declared their support for the proposal* ◦ [+ (that)] *She declared (that) it was the best chocolate cake she had ever tasted.* ◦ [+ obj + (to be) + noun/adj] *They declared themselves (to be) bankrupt.* ◦ [+ speech] *'I won't do it!' he declared.* ◦ *America declared* ***war on*** *Japan in 1941 (= announced officially that it was at war).* ◦ figurative *The government have declared* ***war on*** *(= publicly announced their opposition to) the drug dealers.* ◦ *The country declared* ***independence*** *in 1952 (= announced that it was no longer under the control of another country).* **2** B1 [T] to officially tell someone the value of goods you have bought, or the amount of money you have earned because you might have to pay tax: *Nothing to declare.* CRICKET ▷ **3** [I] If a cricket team declares, they stop BATTING (= hitting the ball) because they think they already have enough RUNS (= points) to win: *Pakistan declared* ***at*** *350 for 7.*

IDIOM **I declare** old-fashioned used to express surprise: *Well, I declare!*

PHRASAL VERB **declare for/against sth** to give/not give someone or something your public support: *She declared for the new airport plan.*

declared /dɪˈkleəd/ US /-ˈklerd/ adj A declared fact is one that someone has publicly said or admitted: *He is a declared supporter of the scheme.* ◦ *It has always been my declared intention to sail round the world.*

declassify /ˌdiːˈklæs.ɪ.faɪ/ verb [T] to say officially that political or military information is no longer secret: *Many government documents are declassified after 50 years.* • **declassification** /ˌdiː.klæs.ɪ.fɪˈkeɪ.ʃən/ noun [U]

declension /dɪˈklen.ʃən/ noun **1** [C] a group of nouns or adjectives that DECLINE in the same way: *How many declensions are there in German?* **2** [U] the act of DECLINING a word, or the way you DECLINE it → Compare **conjugation**

decline /dɪˈklaɪn/ verb; noun
▸verb GO DOWN ▷ **1** B2 [I] to gradually become less, worse, or lower: *His interest in the project declined after his wife died.* ◦ *The party's popularity has declined in the opinion polls.* ◦ formal *The land declines sharply away from the house.* REFUSE ▷ **2** B2 [I or T] formal to refuse: *I invited him to the meeting but he declined.* ◦ *He declined my offer.* ◦ [+ to infinitive] *They declined* ***to*** *tell me how they had got my address.* GRAMMAR ▷ **3** [I or T] specialized If a noun, PRONOUN, or adjective declines, it has different forms to show if it is the subject or object, etc. of a verb or if it is singular or plural, etc. If you decline such a word, you list its various forms: *In Latin we learned how to decline nouns.*

IDIOM **sb's declining years** the last years of someone's life: *He became very forgetful in his declining years.*

▸noun [S or U] B2 when something becomes less in amount, importance, quality, or strength: *industrial decline* ◦ *Home cooking seems to be* ***on the/in*** *decline (= not so many people are doing it).* ◦ *a decline* ***in*** *the number of unemployed* ◦ *She seemed to be recovering and then she went into a decline.*

decoction /dɪˈkɒk.ʃən/ US /-ˈkɑːk-/ noun [C] **1** a liquid made by boiling something such a plant in water **2** Indian English strong coffee or tea before milk or sugar are added

decode /diːˈkəʊd/ US /-ˈkoʊd/ verb **1** [T] to discover the meaning of information given in a secret or complicated way: *Decoding the paintings is not difficult once you know what the component parts symbolize.* → Compare **encode** **2** [I or T] specialized to understand the meaning of a word or phrase in a foreign language in the correct way: *Grammatical information helps learners to decode sentences.*

decoder /diːˈkəʊd.əʳ/ US /-ˈkoʊd.ə/ noun [C] specialized a piece of equipment that allows you to receive particular television signals

décolletage /ˌdeɪ.kɒl.ɪˈtɑːʒ/ US /-ˌkɑː.ləˈtɑːʒ/ noun [C or U] (the shoulders and chest of a woman's body shown by) the low top edge of a dress

decolonization (UK usually **decolonisation**) /diːˌkɒl.ə.naɪˈzeɪ.ʃən/ (US) /diːˌkɑː.lənə-/ **noun** [U] the process in which a country that was previously a COLONY (= controlled by another country) becomes politically independent

decommission /ˌdiː.kəˈmɪʃ.ən/ **verb** [T] to take equipment or weapons out of use: *The government has decided to decommission two battleships.* ◦ *It would cost $300 million to decommission the nuclear installation.*

decompose /ˌdiː.kəmˈpəʊz/ (US) /-ˈpoʊz/ **verb** [I or T] **1** to decay, or to cause something to decay: *The body must have been decomposing for several weeks.* **2** specialized to break, or to break something, into smaller parts: *Microbes decompose organic waste into a mixture of methane and carbon dioxide.* • **decomposition** /ˌdiː.kɒm.pəˈzɪʃ.ən/ (US) /-kɑːm-/ **noun** [U] *The corpse was in an advanced stage of decomposition.*

decomposer /ˌdiː.kəmˈpəʊz.əʳ/ (US) /ˈpoʊz.ɚ/ **noun** [C] specialized an organism such as a BACTERIUM or FUNGUS that makes dead plant and animal material decay

decompress /ˌdiː.kəmˈpres/ **verb** [I or T] to return to the original size or air pressure, or to cause something to do this: *If a plane window breaks, the cabin will rapidly decompress.* • **decompression** /-ˈpreʃ.ən/ **noun** [U]

decomˈpression ˌchamber noun [C] a small room in which a very high air pressure is reduced slowly to the normal level to prevent or treat decompression sickness

decomˈpression ˌsickness noun [U] specialized → **the bends** (= a serious medical condition caused by returning too quickly to the surface of the sea when DIVING with breathing equipment)

decongestant /ˌdiː.kənˈdʒes.tənt/ **noun** [C] a medicine which helps you to breathe more easily, especially when you have a cold

decontaminate /ˌdiː.kənˈtæm.ɪ.neɪt/ **verb** [T] to remove dangerous substances from something: *Estimates of the amount of money needed to decontaminate the heavily polluted chemical installations vary.* • **decontamination** /ˌdiː.kən.tæm.ɪˈneɪ.ʃən/ **noun** [U]

decontrol /ˌdiː.kənˈtrəʊl/ (US) /-ˈtroʊl/ **verb** [T] (**-ll-**) to remove official control on something, especially prices and businesses: *Prices have been decontrolled and markets are flourishing.*

decor /ˈdeɪ.kɔːʳ/, /ˈdek.ɔːʳ/ (US) /deɪˈkɔːr/ **noun** [S or U] the colour, style, and arrangement of the objects in a room: *elegant decor*

> **Other ways of saying decorate**
>
> The verbs **refurbish**, **renovate**, and **revamp** are common alternatives to 'decorate' when you are talking about improving the appearance of a room or building:
>
> *The University library is currently being **refurbished**.*
>
> *They were in the process of **renovating** an old barn.*
>
> *The restaurant has recently been **revamped**.*
>
> Another alternative used in more informal situations is the phrasal verb **do up**:
>
> *He's bought an old cottage and is gradually **doing it up**.*

decorate /ˈdek.ə.reɪt/ **verb** MAKE ATTRACTIVE ▷ **1** (B1) [T] to add something to an object or place, especially in order to make it more attractive: *They decorated the wedding car **with** ribbons and flowers.* **2** (B1) [I or T] to paint the inside or outside of a house or put paper on the inside walls: *We're going to decorate the kitchen next week.* ◦ *I hate the smell of paint when I'm decorating.* HONOUR ▷ **3** [T] to reward or honour a person by giving them something, especially a MEDAL: *They were decorated **for** their part in the rescue.*

decoration /ˌdek.əˈreɪ.ʃən/ **noun** MAKE ATTRACTIVE ▷ **1** (B2) [C or U] the activity of making something look more attractive by putting things on it or around it, or something that you use to do this: *Christmas/party/table/cake decorations* ◦ *He's good at cake decoration.* **2** (B2) [U] the activity of covering the walls or other surfaces of rooms or buildings with paint or paper: *This place is badly in need of decoration.* HONOUR ▷ **3** [C] a MEDAL given to someone and worn as an honour: *The Victoria Cross and George Cross are British decorations **for** bravery.*

decorative /ˈdek.ər.ə.tɪv/ (US) /-ɚ.ə.t̬ɪv/ **adj** (B2) made to look attractive: *a decorative display of plants and flowers* ◦ *a mirror in a decorative frame* • **decoratively** /-li/ **adv** *A shawl was arranged decoratively over the back of the chair.*

decorator /ˈdek.ər.eɪ.təʳ/ (US) /-ɚ.eɪ.t̬ɚ/ **noun** [C] a person whose job is to paint the inside or outside of buildings and to do other related work: *a firm of painters and decorators*

decorous /ˈdek.ə.rəs/ (US) /-ɚ.əs/ **adj** formal behaving politely and in a controlled way: *His manner, as ever, was decorous.* • **decorously** /-li/ **adv**

decorum /dɪˈkɔː.rəm/ (US) /-ˈkɔːr.əm/ **noun** [U] formal behaviour that is controlled, calm, and polite: *As young ladies we were expected to **act/behave with** proper decorum.*

decoy /ˈdiː.kɔɪ/ **noun** [C] something or someone used to trick or confuse other people or animals into doing something, especially something dangerous: *They used a girl hitch-hiker as the decoy to get him to stop.* • **decoy** /dɪˈkɔɪ/ **verb** [T]

> **Other ways of saying decrease**
>
> The verbs **lessen**, **lower**, and **reduce**, and the phrasal verb **bring down** are often used when someone decreases an amount or level:
>
> *They've just **lowered** the age at which you can join.*
>
> *Exercise **reduces** the chance of heart disease.*
>
> *They are **bringing down** their prices.*
>
> **Drop**, **fall**, **go down**, and **come down** are often used when a level or amount decreases:
>
> *Unemployment has **dropped/fallen** to six percent in the last year.*
>
> *Prices always **come/go down** in January.*
>
> If a level or amount decreases very quickly, the verbs **plummet** and **plunge** are sometimes used:
>
> *Temperatures last night **plummeted/plunged** below zero.*
>
> If a level or amount decreases gradually, the verbs **dwindle** and **decline** are sometimes used:
>
> *The number of students in the school has **dwindled** to around 200.*
>
> *The number of members has **declined** by 25 percent over the last 30 years.*
>
> If the size of something decreases, the verb **shrink** is sometimes used. The verb **contract** is used in technical contexts:
>
> *Forests have **shrunk** to almost half the size they were 20 years ago.*
>
> *As the metal cools, it **contracts**.*

decrease verb; noun
▸**verb** [I or T] /dɪˈkriːs/ (US) /ˈdiː.kriːs/ (B1) to become less,

or to make something become less: *Our share of the market has decreased sharply this year.* ◦ *We have decreased our involvement in children's books.* → Opposite **increase**

▸**noun** [C or U] /ˈdiː.kriːs/ B1 a reduction: *There has been a steady decrease **in** the number of visitors.* ◦ *I haven't noticed much decrease **in** interest.*

D

> **! Common mistake: decrease**
>
> When you are talking about the thing that has decreased, the most usual preposition to use after **decrease** is **in**.
>
> Don't say 'a decrease of something', say **a decrease in something**:
>
> *There has been a two percent decrease in the rate of unemployment.*
>
> When **decrease** is followed by an amount, the correct preposition is **of**:
>
> *There has been a decrease of two percent.*

decree /dɪˈkriː/ **noun; verb**

▸**noun** [C or U] formal an official statement that something must happen: *The decree stopped short of a full declaration of independence.* ◦ *More than 200 people were freed **by** military decree.*

▸**verb** [T] to officially decide or order that something must happen: *They decreed an end to discrimination on grounds of age.* ◦ [+ that] *The local council has decreed **that** the hospital should close.*

deˌcree ˈabsolute **noun** [S] legal the final stage of a DIVORCE (= a legal agreement to end a marriage), when people become free to marry again

decree nisi /dɪˌkriːˈnaɪ.saɪ/, /-si/ **noun** [S] legal the first stage of a DIVORCE (= a legal agreement to end a marriage)

decrepit /dɪˈkrep.ɪt/ **adj** in very bad condition because of being old, or not having been cared for, or having been used a lot: *Most of the buildings were old and decrepit.* ◦ *A decrepit old man sat on a park bench.* • **decrepitude** /-ɪ.tjuːd/ US /-ɪ.tuːd/ **noun** [U] formal *a state of decrepitude*

decriminalize (UK usually **decriminalise**) /ˌdiːˈkrɪm.ɪ.nə.laɪz/ **verb** [T] to stop something from being illegal: *the campaign to decriminalize cannabis* • **decriminalization** (UK usually **decriminalisation**) /ˌdiː.krɪm.ɪ.nə.laɪˈzeɪ.ʃən/ US /ˌdiː.krɪm.ɪ.nə.lə-/ **noun** [U]

decry /dɪˈkraɪ/ **verb** [T] formal to criticize something as bad, without value, or unnecessary: *She decried the appalling state of the British film industry.* → Synonym **condemn**

decrypt /dɪˈkrɪpt/ **verb** [T] to change electronic information or signals that were stored, written, or sent in the form of a secret CODE (= a system of letters, numbers, or symbols) back into a form that you can understand and use normally: *Messages encrypted using the public key can be decrypted only by someone with the private key.*

dedicate /ˈded.ɪ.keɪt/ **verb** [T] **GIVE TIME/ENERGY** ▷ **1** C1 to give your energy, time, etc. completely: *He has dedicated his life **to** scientific research.* ◦ *The new president said she would dedicate her**self to** protecting the rights of the sick and the homeless.* **BOOK, ETC.** ▷ **2** C2 If you dedicate a book, play, performance, etc. to someone or something, you publicly say that it is in their honour: *The book is dedicated to the author's husband.* **BUILDING** ▷ **3** formal When a building, especially a religious building, is dedicated, there is a ceremony at which it is formally opened for use and its particular purpose is stated: *The church was dedicated on 1 March 1805 **to** the local Saint Jude.*

dedicated /ˈded.ɪ.keɪ.tɪd/ US /-t̬ɪd/ **adj** **1** C1 believing that something is very important and giving a lot of time and energy to it: *a dedicated father/teacher* ◦ *She's completely dedicated **to** her work.* ◦ *The Green Party is dedicated to protect**ing** the environment.* **2** C2 specialized designed to be used for one particular purpose: *a dedicated computer* ◦ *a dedicated sports channel*

dedication /ˌded.ɪˈkeɪ.ʃən/ **noun** **TIME/ENERGY** ▷ **1** C1 [U] the willingness to give a lot of time and energy to something because it is important: *He has always shown great dedication **to** the cause.* ◦ *She thanked the staff for their dedication and enthusiasm.* **OF BOOK, ETC.** ▷ **2** [C] a statement which says in whose honour something has been written, made, performed, etc.: *The dedication at the front of the book read 'For my Father'.* **OF BUILDING** ▷ **3** [C] a ceremony in which a building, especially a religious building, is opened for use and its purpose is stated

deduce /dɪˈdjuːs/ US /-ˈduːs/ **verb** [T] C2 to reach an answer or a decision by thinking carefully about the known facts: *We cannot deduce much **from** these figures.* ◦ [+ that] *The police have deduced **that** he must have left his apartment yesterday evening.* • **deducible** /dɪˈdjuː.sɪ.bl/ US /-ˈduː-/ **adj** formal able to be deduced • **deductive** /dɪˈdʌk.tɪv/ **adj** *a deductive argument* ◦ *deductive logic/reasoning*

deduct /dɪˈdʌkt/ **verb** [T] to take away an amount or part from a total: *The player had **points** deducted (**from** his score) for arguing with the referee.*

deductable **adj** Australian English **deductible**

deductible /dɪˈdʌk.tɪ.bl/ US /-t̬ə-/ **adj; noun**

▸**adj** a deductible amount can be taken away from a total: *Expenses like office phone bills are **tax**-deductible (= you do not have to pay tax on them).*

▸**noun** [C usually plural] **1** an amount of money that is taken away from an employee's pay before they receive it: *Companies try to control the cost of healthcare by raising employees' deductibles.* **2** US (UK **excess**) a part of the cost of an accident, injury, etc. that you agree to pay yourself when you buy INSURANCE: *Customers can lower insurance premiums by taking higher deductibles.*

deduction /dɪˈdʌk.ʃən/ **noun** [C or U] **THINKING** ▷ **1** C2 the process of reaching a decision or answer by thinking about the known facts, or the decision that is reached: *Through a process of deduction, the detectives discovered the identity of the killer.* ◦ *All we can do is make deductions **from** the available facts.* **TAKING AWAY** ▷ **2** C1 the calculation of taking an amount or a part of something away from a total, or the amount that is taken away: *The interest I receive on my savings account is paid after the deduction **of** tax.* ◦ *After deductions (= expenses on which tax does not have to be paid), his taxable income is $30,000.* **3** US and Australian English an amount that is taken away from the money you are paid before you officially receive it → Compare **stoppage**

deed /diːd/ **noun** [C] **ACTION** ▷ **1** an intentional act, especially a very bad or very good one: *It seems to me that a lot of **evil** deeds are **done** in the name of religion.* ◦ *She's always helping people and **doing** other **good** deeds.* **DOCUMENT** ▷ **2** legal a legal document that is an official record of an agreement or official proof that someone owns land or a building

ˈdeed ˌbox **noun** [C usually singular] a metal box that can be locked, in which important documents are kept

ˈdeed ˌpoll **noun** [S or U] in Britain, a type of legal document, especially one that allows someone to officially change their name: *He changed his name* **by** *deed poll.*

deejay /ˈdiː.dʒeɪ/ **noun** [C] informal a **disc jockey**

deem /diːm/ **verb** [T not continuous] formal C2 to consider or judge something in a particular way: [+ obj + noun/adj] *The area has now been deemed safe.* ◦ [+ noun/adj] *We will provide help whenever you deem it appropriate.* ◦ [+ obj + to infinitive] *Anyone not paying the registration fee by 31 March will be deemed* **to** *have withdrawn from the scheme.*

deep /diːp/ **adj, adv; adj; noun**

▸**adj, adv** A2 going or being a long way down from the top or surface, or being of a particular distance from the top to the bottom: *a deep well/mine* ◦ *a deep river/sea* ◦ *a deep cut* ◦ *The hole is so deep you can't see the bottom.* ◦ *The water's not deep here – look, I can touch the bottom.* ◦ *Drill 20 holes, each 5 cm deep.* ◦ *The water's only* **ankle/knee/waist**-*deep, so we'll be able to get across the river easily.* ◦ *He thrust his hands deep* **in** *(***to***) his pockets.* ◦ *The submarine sailed deep* **under** *the ice cap.* ◦ *Take a few deep* **breaths** *(= breaths that fill the lungs with air) and calm down.*

IDIOMS **deep down** B2 felt strongly and often hidden from other people: *Deep down, I know you love me really.* • **deep pockets** If an organization or person has deep pockets, they have a lot of money: *Anyone who tries to help that company will need deep pockets – it is nearly bankrupt.*

▸**adj** **STRONGLY FELT** ▷ **1** B2 very strongly felt or experienced and usually lasting a long time: *Their son has been a deep disappointment to them.* ◦ *We're in deep trouble.* ◦ *She fell into a lovely deep sleep.* **LOW** ▷ **2** B2 (of a sound) low: *a wonderfully deep voice* **COMPLICATED** ▷ **3** C2 showing or needing serious thought, or not easy to understand: *His films are generally a bit deep for me.* **FRONT TO BACK** ▷ **4** B2 If something is deep, it has a large distance between its edges, especially between its front and back edges: *Is the alcove deep enough for bookshelves?* ◦ *The wardrobe is 2 m high, 1 m wide and 60 cm deep.* ◦ *By midnight, there were customers standing six deep (= in six rows) at the bar.* **5 deep in/inside/within sth** B1 near the middle of something, and a long distance from its edges: *Little Red Riding Hood's grandmother lived in a house deep in the forest.* **DARK** ▷ **6** B1 (of a colour) strong and dark: *The sky was deep blue.*

IDIOMS **be in deep water** (also **get into deep water**) to be in or get into serious trouble: *The government is in deep water* **over** *its plans for tax increases.* • **deep in thought** C2 thinking very hard: *She sat, not listening, but deep in thought.* • **go off the deep end** informal to get very angry about something or lose control of yourself • **jump in at the deep end** (also **throw sb in at the deep end**) C2 If you jump or are thrown in at the deep end, you start doing something new and difficult without help or preparation. • **run/go deep** C2 If a feeling or problem runs deep, it is strong or serious and has existed for a long time.

▸**noun** **the deep** literary the sea or the ocean

ˌdeep-ˈdown **adj** [before noun] B2 felt strongly and often hidden from other people: *a deep-down certainty*

deepen /ˈdiː.pᵊn/ **verb** **DOWN** ▷ **1** [I or T] to make something deeper, or to become deeper: *One way of preventing further flooding would be to deepen the river bed.* ◦ *The sea bed deepens here* **to** *5,000 metres.* **STRONGLY FELT** ▷ **2** C2 [I or T] to become more strongly felt or experienced, or to make something this way: *Over the years, her love for him deepened.* ◦ *The economic crisis is deepening.* ◦ *We must try not to deepen existing splits within the party.* **COMPLICATED** ▷ **3** C1 [I or T] to make something increase or become more serious: *It certainly helped to deepen my understanding of the situation.* **LOW** ▷ **4** [I] to become lower: *Boys' voices deepen in their early to mid-teens.* **DARK** ▷ **5** [I] to become darker: *The shadows deepened as the evening drew on.*

deepening /ˈdiː.pᵊn.ɪŋ/ **adj** increasing or becoming darker: *They felt a deepening sense of despair.*

ˌdeep ˈfreeze **noun** [C] a **freezer**

ˌdeep-ˈfry **verb** [T] to fry food in a deep pan in which the food is completely covered by oil • **ˈdeep-fried** **adj** *deep-fried chicken*

deeply /ˈdiː.pli/ **adv** B2 extremely or strongly: *I'm deeply grateful to you.* ◦ *He found her comments deeply irritating/offensive.* ◦ *We don't want to get too deeply involved with these people.* ◦ *After 20 years of marriage, they're still deeply in love.*

ˌdeep-ˈsea **adj** [before noun] happening in or relating to the deep parts of the sea : *deep-sea diving/fishing*

ˌdeep-ˈseated **adj** (also **ˌdeep-ˈrooted**, **ˌdeeply ˈrooted**) strongly felt or believed and very difficult to change or get rid of: *a deep-seated faith in God*

ˌdeep-ˈset **adj** describes eyes that are far back in the bones of the face

the ˌDeep ˈSouth **noun** the part of the US that is furthest to the south and east, including Alabama, Georgia, Louisiana, Mississippi, and South and North Carolina

ˌdeep ˌtissue ˈmassage **noun** [C or U] a type of MASSAGE in which the person giving the massage presses hard on areas of the body where the muscles are very stiff or painful

ˌdeep ˌvein thromˈbosis **noun** [U] (abbreviation **DVT**) a serious medical condition in which a blood CLOT (= a sticky mass of blood) forms in the VEINS of the legs or lungs

deer /dɪəʳ/ (US) /dɪr/ **noun** [C] (plural **deer**) B2 a quite large animal with four legs which eats grass and leaves. The male has ANTLERS (= wide horns like branches). The female is called a HIND or a DOE and the male a STAG or BUCK: *a* ***herd of*** *deer* → See also **reindeer**

deer

deerstalker /ˈdɪəˌstɔː.kəʳ/ (US) /ˈdɪrˌstɑː-/ **noun** [C] a soft hat with two PEAKS (= flat curved parts that stick out), one at the back and one at the front, and coverings for the ears that are usually worn turned up: *Sherlock Holmes's deerstalker*

ˌde-ˈescalate **verb** [I or T] to (cause to) become less dangerous or difficult: *The government has taken these measures in an attempt to de-escalate the conflict.* ◦ *There are signs that the confrontation is beginning to de-escalate.*

def /def/ **adj** slang very good: *They're one of the most def bands around.*

deface /dɪˈfeɪs/ **verb** [T] to damage and spoil the appearance of something by writing or drawing on it: *He was fined for defacing library books.*

de facto /ˌdeɪˈfæk.təʊ/ (US) /-toʊ/ **adj, adv; noun**

▸**adj** [before noun], **adv** formal existing in fact, although perhaps not intended, legal, or accepted: *The city is rapidly becoming the de facto centre of the financial world.* ◦ *He's her de facto husband though they're not* *actually married.* ◦ *If it is on British soil then it is de facto British.* → Compare **de jure**

▸**noun** [C] Australian English formal a person who someone lives with as a wife or a husband, although they are not married: *They've invited Joanne and her de facto for lunch on Sunday.*

defame /dɪˈfeɪm/ **verb** [T] formal to damage the reputation of a person or group by saying or writing bad things about them that are not true: *Mr Turnock claimed the editorial had defamed him.* → Compare **libel, slander** • **defamation** /ˌdef.əˈmeɪ.ʃᵊn/ **noun** [U] *He is suing for defamation **of character**.* • **defamatory** /dɪˈfæm.ə.tᵊr.i/ (US) /-tɔːr-/ **adj** *He claims the remarks were **highly** defamatory.*

default verb; noun

▸**verb** [I] /dɪˈfɒlt/ (US) /-ˈfɑːlt/ to fail to do something, such as pay a debt, that you legally have to do: *People who default **on** their mortgage repayments may have their home repossessed.*

PHRASAL VERB **default to sth** If a computer defaults to a way of operating, it automatically uses it if you do not intentionally change it.

▸**noun** /dɪˈfɒlt/, /ˈdiː.fɒlt/ (US) /-ˈfɑːlt/ **RESULT** ▷ **1** [U] what exists or happens if you do not change it intentionally by performing an action: *The computer will take 0 as the default **value**, unless you type in something different.* **FAIL** ▷ **2** [C or U] a failure to do something, such as pay a debt, that you legally have to do: *Defaults **on** loan repayments have reached 52,000 a month.* ◦ *Any default **on** your mortgage repayments may mean you will lose your house.* ◦ *Since they refuse to reply, I think we've won the argument **by** default (= because of their failure to act).* ◦ ***The** default **rate** (= the number of people failing to do something) is estimated at one in ten of taxpayers.*

defeat /dɪˈfiːt/ verb; noun

▸**verb** [T] **1** (B1) to win against someone in a fight, war, or competition: *Napoleon was defeated by the Duke of Wellington at the battle of Waterloo.* ◦ *If we can defeat the Italian team, we'll be through to the final.* → See also **self-defeating** **2** (B2) to cause someone or something to fail: *The proposal to change the rules was **narrowly** (= only just) defeated by 201 votes to 196.* ◦ *Our ambitions for this tournament have been defeated by the weather.* ◦ *I'm afraid anything that involves language learning has always defeated me (= I have been unable to do it).*

▸**noun** [C or U] **1** (B1) the fact of losing against someone in a fight or competition, or when someone or something is made to fail: *At the last General Election, they **suffered** a **crushing/humiliating** defeat.* ◦ *After their defeat in battle, the soldiers surrendered.* ◦ *She **admitted/conceded** defeat well before all the votes had been counted.* → Compare **victory** **2** **admit defeat** to accept that you cannot do something: *I thought I could mend the radio myself, but I've had to admit defeat.*

> Word partners for **defeat noun**
>
> *suffer* defeat • *face* defeat • *accept/admit/concede* defeat • a *crushing/heavy/humiliating/resounding* defeat • a *narrow* defeat • a defeat *against* sb/sth

defeatism /dɪˈfiː.tɪ.zᵊm/ (US) /-t̬ɪ-/ **noun** [U] disapproving a way of thinking or behaving that shows that you have no hope and expect to fail: *There is a spirit of defeatism among some members of the party.*

defeatist /dɪˈfiː.tɪst/ (US) /-t̬ɪst/ **adj** disapproving having no hope and expecting to fail: *Being defeatist will get us nowhere.* ◦ *He's got such a defeatist attitude.* • **defeatist noun** [C] *I can't believe it – you're such a defeatist!*

defecate /ˈdef.ə.keɪt/ **verb** [I] formal to pass the contents of the bowels out of the body • **defecation** /ˌdef.əˈkeɪ.ʃᵊn/ **noun** [U]

defect noun; verb

▸**noun** [C] /ˈdiː.fekt/ **1** (C1) a fault or problem in something or someone that spoils them or causes them not to work correctly: *All R45 aircraft have been grounded, after a defect **in** the engine cooling system was discovered.* ◦ *There are so many defects **in** our education system.* ◦ *It's a **character** defect **in** her that she can't ever accept that she's in the wrong.* **2** a physical condition in which something is wrong with a part of someone's body: *She suffers from a heart/sight/speech defect.* ◦ *The drug has been shown to cause **birth** defects.* ◦ *Cystic fibrosis is caused by a **genetic** defect.*

▸**verb** [I] /dɪˈfekt/ to leave a country, political party, etc., especially in order to join an opposing one: *When the national hockey team visited America, half the players defected.* ◦ *The British spy, Kim Philby, defected **to** the Soviet Union/defected **from** Britain in 1963.* • **defector** /dɪˈfek.təʳ/ (US) /-tɚ/ **noun** [C] *She was one of many Communist Party defectors.*

defection /dɪˈfek.ʃᵊn/ **noun** [C or U] the act of leaving a country, political party, etc. to go to another one: *Over the years there were hundreds of defections **to** the West/defections **from** the East.* ◦ *Recent changes in policy have resulted in large-scale defection **from** the party.*

defective /dɪˈfek.tɪv/ **adj** (C2) describes something that has a fault in it and does not work correctly: *defective brakes* ◦ *defective eyesight* ◦ *I think that theory is defective.*

defence UK (US **defense**) /dɪˈfens/ **noun** **PROTECTION** ▷ **1** (A2) [C or U] protection or support against attack, criticism, or infection: *The rebels' only form of defence **against** the soldiers' guns was sticks and stones.* ◦ *The war has ended but government spending on defence (= the country's armed forces) is still increasing.* ◦ *When Helen criticized me, Chris **came/rushed to** my defence (= quickly supported me).* ◦ *The book is a closely argued defence **of** (= something that supports) the economic theory of Keynes.* ◦ *The towers were once an important part of the city's defences.* ◦ *A good diet helps build the body's natural defences.* → See also **self-defence** **EXPLANATION** ▷ **2** [S or U] (an) argument or explanation which you use to prove that you are not guilty of something: *The judge remarked that ignorance was not a valid defence.* ◦ *All I can say, **in** defence **of** my actions, is that I had little choice.* **3** the things said in court to prove that a person did not commit a crime: *She said that she didn't want a lawyer and was going to **conduct** her own defence.* **4** **the defence** (C2) legal the person or people in a law case who have been accused of doing something illegal, and their lawyer(s): *a witness for the defence* ◦ *a defence lawyer* **SPORT** ▷ **5** (B1) [S or U] in some sports, the part of a team which tries to prevent the other team from scoring goals or points: *a strong defence* ◦ *I play **in** (US **on**) defence.*

> Word partners for **defence**
>
> *come to/jump to/leap to/spring to* sb's defence • *mount/put up* a defence • an *effective/spirited/strong/vigorous* defence • defence *against* sth • defence *of* sth • defence *budget/cuts/spending* • [first/last, etc.] *line of* defence

defenceless UK (US **defenseless**) /dɪˈfens.ləs/ **adj** describes people, animals, places, or things that are weak and unable to protect themselves from attack: *a small defenceless child* ◦ *a defenceless city* ◦ *They were quite defenceless* ***against*** *the enemy bombs.* • **defencelessness** (US **defenselessness**) /-nəs/ **noun** [U]

deˈfence ˌmechanism UK (US **deˈfense ˌmechanism**) **noun** [C] an automatic way of behaving or thinking by which you protect yourself from something, especially from feeling unpleasant emotions: *Arrogance is often a defence mechanism.*

defend /dɪˈfend/ **verb** PROTECT ▷ **1** B1 [T] to protect someone or something against attack or criticism: *How can we defend our homeland if we don't have an army?* ◦ *White blood cells help defend the body* ***against*** *infection.* ◦ *They are fighting to defend their* ***beliefs/interests/rights.*** ◦ *He vigorously defended his point of view.* ◦ *The Bank of England intervened this morning to defend the pound (= stop it from losing value).* ◦ *The prime minister was asked how he could defend (= explain his support for) a policy that increased unemployment.* ◦ *I'm going to karate lessons to learn how to defend my****self.*** ◦ *I can't afford a lawyer so I shall defend myself (= argue my own case in a law court).* → Compare **attack** SPORT ▷ **2** [T] to compete in a sports competition which you won before and try to win it again: *He will defend his 1500 metre title at the weekend.* ◦ *The defending champion will play her first match of the tournament tomorrow.* **3** [I] to try to prevent the opposing player or players from scoring points, goals, etc. in a sport: *In the last ten minutes of the match, we needed to defend.*

defendant /dɪˈfen.dənt/ **noun** [C] legal a person in a law case who is accused of having done something illegal → Compare **plaintiff**

defender /dɪˈfen.dəʳ/ US /-dɚ/ **noun** [C] **1** someone who protects a place against attack, or who believes in and supports a person, idea, plan, etc.: *The city's defenders were outnumbered by the besieging army.* ◦ *So far they have found few defenders* ***of*** *their point of view on campus.* **2** B2 someone in a sports team who tries to prevent the other team from scoring points, goals, etc.: *The Brazilian attack put France's defenders under pressure.*

defensible /dɪˈfen.sɪ.bl̩/ **adj** (US also **defendable**) able to be protected from attack, or able to be supported by argument: *A city built on an island is easily defensible.* ◦ *High petrol taxes are defensible on ecological grounds.*

defensive /dɪˈfen.sɪv/ **adj; noun**

▸**adj 1** used to protect someone or something against attack: *These are purely defensive weapons, not designed for attack.* → Opposite **offensive 2** C2 too quick to protect yourself from being criticized **3** in a sports event, trying to prevent the opposing player or players from scoring points, goals, etc.: *He's currently the best defensive player on the team.*

▸**noun on the defensive** ready to protect yourself because you are expecting to be criticized or attacked • **defensively** /-li/ **adv** • **defensiveness** /-nəs/ **noun** [U]

defer /dɪˈfɜːʳ/ US /-ˈfɝː/ **verb** [T] **(-rr-)** to delay something until a later time: *My bank has agreed to defer the* ***repayments*** *on my loan while I'm still a student.* ◦ [+ -ing verb] *Can we defer mak****ing*** *a decision until next week?* → Synonym **postpone** • **deferment** /-mənt/ **noun** [C or U] (also **deferral** /dɪˈfɜː.rəl/, /-ˈfɝː.əl/)

PHRASAL VERB **defer to sb/sth** formal to allow someone or something to make decisions for you or tell you what to do, even if you disagree with them, because of your respect for them or because of their higher rank, authority, knowledge, etc.: *I have to defer to my boss* ***on*** *important decisions.* ◦ *I defer to (= accept) your judgment.*

deference /ˈdef.ər.əns/ US /-ɚ-/ **noun** [U] formal respect and politeness: *He* ***treats*** *her* ***with*** *such deference.* ◦ *She covered her head* ***out of/in*** *deference* ***to*** *(= because of a polite respect for) Muslim custom.*

deferential /ˌdef.əˈren.ʃəl/ **adj** polite and showing respect: *She is always extremely deferential* ***to/towards*** *anyone in authority.* • **deferentially** /-i/ **adv** *They bowed deferentially as she came into the room.*

defiance /dɪˈfaɪ.əns/ **noun** [U] behaviour in which you refuse to obey someone or something: *The demonstration is a pointless* ***act/gesture*** *of defiance* ***against*** *the government.* ◦ ***In*** *defiance* ***of*** *the ceasefire, rebel troops are again firing on the capital.*

defiant /dɪˈfaɪ.ənt/ **adj 1** proudly refusing to obey authority: *a defiant attitude/gesture* ◦ *The protesters blocking the entrance to the offices remained defiant this morning.* **2** not willing to accept criticism or disapproval: *The prime minister was in defiant mood in the House of Commons.* • **defiantly** /-li/ **adv**

defibrillator /ˌdiːˈfɪb.rɪ.leɪ.təʳ/ US /-t̬ɚ/ **noun** [C] specialized a machine used especially in hospitals, which uses an electric current to stop any IRREGULAR and dangerous activity of the heart's muscles: *Defibrillators are used to restore normal rhythm to the heart.*

deficiency /dɪˈfɪʃ.ən.si/ **noun** [C or U] C1 a state of not having, or not having enough, of something that is needed: *Pregnant women often suffer from iron deficiency.* ◦ *Deficiencies* ***in*** *the education system have been much in the news.*

deficient /dɪˈfɪʃ.ənt/ **adj 1** not having enough of: *A diet deficient* ***in*** *vitamin D may cause the disease rickets.* **2** not good enough: *His theory is deficient in several respects.* • **deficiently** /-li/ **adv**

deficit /ˈdef.ɪ.sɪt/ **noun** [C] C1 the total amount by which money spent is more than money received: *The country is running a balance-of-payments/budget/trade deficit* ***of*** *$250 million.* ◦ *The UK's deficit* ***in*** *manufactured goods fell slightly in the last three months.*

defile /dɪˈfaɪl/ **verb; noun**

▸**verb** [T] formal to spoil something or someone so that they are less beautiful or pure: *It's a shame that such a beautiful area has been defiled by a rubbish dump.* ◦ *The soldiers deliberately defiled all the holy places.* • **defilement** /-mənt/ **noun** [U]

▸**noun** [C] literary a very narrow valley between two mountains

define /dɪˈfaɪn/ **verb** [T] EXPLAIN ▷ **1** B2 to say what the meaning of something, especially a word, is: *In this dictionary 'reality' is defined* ***as*** *'the state of things as they are, rather than as they are imagined to be'.* ◦ *Before I answer your question, could you define your* ***terms*** *a little more (= explain what you mean by the words you have used)?* → See also **well defined 2** B2 to explain and describe the meaning and exact limits of something: *Your rights and responsibilities are defined in the citizens' charter.* ◦ *Your role in the project will be strictly defined (= limited to particular areas).* ◦ *I'd hate to feel that I was defined* ***by*** *(= that my life got its meaning and importance only from) my job.* CLEARLY SHOW ▷ **3** to show clearly the edge of something: *The outline of the castle on the hill was clearly defined* ***against*** *the evening sky.* • **definable** /dɪˈfaɪ.nə.bl̩/ **adj** *definable rules of grammar/syntax*

deˌfining ˈmoment **noun** [C] the point at which a situation is clearly seen to start to change: *The end of* the Cold War was a defining moment for the world in more ways than one.

definite /ˈdef.ɪ.nət/ **adj; noun**

▸**adj** B2 fixed, certain, or clear: *The date for the meeting is now definite: 5 March .* ◦ *She has very definite opinions.* ◦ *We need a definite answer by tomorrow.* ◦ *'Are you sure I'm invited too?' 'Yes, Roger was quite definite* ***about*** *it on the phone.'* ◦ *There's been a definite improvement in your English since you arrived.*

▸**noun** [C] informal something that is certain to happen: *Let's make the 9th a definite – we'll have a curry and then go to the movies.* ◦ *She's a definite* ***for*** *the Olympic team.*

ˌdefinite ˈarticle noun [C] specialized B1 the grammatical name for the word 'the' in English, or the words in other languages that have a similar use → Compare **indefinite article**

definitely /ˈdef.ɪ.nət.li/ **adv** B1 without any doubt: *Have you definitely decided to go to America?* ◦ *He definitely said he'd be here.* ◦ *'Are you going to have children?' 'Oh, definitely (= without any doubt).'* ◦ *'Is she not coming, then?' 'No, definitely not.'*

> **!** Common mistake: **definitely**
>
> **Warning:** Check your spelling!
>
> **Definitely** is one of the 50 words most often spelled wrongly by learners.

definition /ˌdef.ɪˈnɪʃ.ᵊn/ **noun** EXPLANATION ▷ **1** B2 [C] a statement that explains the meaning of a word or phrase: *a dictionary definition* ◦ *What is the definition* ***of*** *'mood'?* **2** [C] a description of the features and limits of something: *The legal definition* ***of*** *what is and what is not pornography is very unsatisfactory.* **3 by definition** because of its own features: *Psychology is by definition an inexact science.* CLEARLY QUALITY ▷ **4** C1 [U] how clear an image or sound is: *The photograph rather lacks definition.*

definitive /dɪˈfɪn.ɪ.tɪv/ US /-ə.t̬ɪv/ **adj 1** C2 not able to be changed or improved: *a definitive judgment/ruling* ◦ *There are no definitive* ***answers/solutions*** *to this problem.* ◦ *The police have no definitive* ***proof*** *of her guilt.* **2** considered to be the best of its type: *He's written the definitive guide to Thailand.* • **definitively** /-li/ **adv**

deflate /dɪˈfleɪt/ **verb** MAKE SMALLER ▷ **1** [I or T] If something that has air or gas inside it deflates, or is deflated, it becomes smaller because it loses the air or gas: *to deflate a balloon/tyre* WEAKEN ▷ **2** [T often passive] to cause something to become weaker: *The party's ambitions have been rather deflated by the two recent by-election defeats.* **3** [T often passive] to make someone lose confidence or feel less important: *They were totally deflated by losing the match.* MONEY ▷ **4** [T] to reduce the supply of money in an economy

deflated /dɪˈfleɪ.tɪd/ US /-t̬ɪd/ **adj** feeling less confident and positive than before: *Her criticism left me feeling a bit deflated.*

deflation /dɪˈfleɪ.ʃᵊn/ **noun** [U] MAKING SMALLER ▷ **1** the situation in which something becomes smaller or weaker, or something or someone becomes less confident than before: *a feeling of deflation after the party* MONEY ▷ **2** a reduction of the supply of money in an economy, and therefore a reduction of economic activity, that is often part of an intentional government plan to reduce prices → Compare **inflation, reflation (reflate) 3** a reduction in value: *There has been a deflation* ***in/of*** *property values.* • **deflationary** /-ᵊr.i/ US /-er.i/ **adj**

deflect /dɪˈflekt/ **verb** [I or T] to (cause to) change direction: *The crowd cheered as the goalkeeper deflected the* ***shot****.* ◦ *He deflected the ball* ***away from*** *the goal.* ◦ *The prime minister deflected mounting* ***criticism*** *today by announcing tax cuts.* ◦ *The ball deflected* ***off*** *my hockey stick, straight into the goal.*

deflection /dɪˈflek.ʃᵊn/ **noun** [C or U] a change of direction: *The second goal was from a deflection* ***off*** *the Liverpool captain.* ◦ *The journalists were frustrated by her constant deflection* ***of*** *their questions.*

deflower /ˌdiːˈflaʊ.əʳ/ US /-ɚ/ **verb** [T] literary to have sex with a woman who has never had sex before

defog /ˌdiːˈfɒg/ US /-ˈfɑːg/ **verb** [T] **(-gg-)** US for **demist**

defogger /ˌdiːˈfɒg.əʳ/ US /-ˈfɑː.gɚ/ **noun** [C] US for **demister**

defoliant /ˌdiːˈfəʊ.li.ənt/ US /-ˈfoʊ-/ **noun** [C or U] a chemical that is used to make the leaves drop off plants

defoliate /ˌdiːˈfəʊ.li.eɪt/ US /-ˈfoʊ-/ **verb** [T] to make the leaves drop off a plant, especially by using strong chemicals • **defoliation** /ˌdiː.fəʊ.liˈeɪ.ʃᵊn/ US /-foʊ-/ **noun** [U]

deforestation /diːˌfɒr.ɪˈsteɪ.ʃᵊn/ US /-ˌfɔːr-/ **noun** [U] the cutting down of trees in a large area, or the destruction of forests by people: *Deforestation is destroying large areas of tropical rain forest.* • **deforest** /ˌdiːˈfɒr.ɪst/ US /-ˈfɔːr-/ **verb** [T]

deform /dɪˈfɔːm/ US /-ˈfɔːrm/ **verb 1** [T] to spoil the usual and true shape of something: *Age deforms the spine.* **2** [I] specialized If something deforms, its usual shape changes and becomes spoiled: *These plastics deform at temperatures of over 90°C.* • **deformation** /ˌdef.əˈmeɪ.ʃᵊn/ US /-ɚ-/ **noun** [U] *The deformation* ***of*** *the bones was caused by poor diet.*

deformed /dɪˈfɔːmd/ US /-ˈfɔːrmd/ **adj** with a shape that has not developed normally: *deformed hands*

deformity /dɪˈfɔː.mɪ.ti/ US /-ˈfɔːr.mə.t̬i/ **noun** [C or U] the situation in which a part of the body has not developed in the normal way or with the normal shape

defragment /ˌdiː.frægˈment/ US /ˌdiːˈfræg.ment/ **verb** [I or T] (informal **defrag** /ˌdiːˈfræg/ **(-gg-)**) to make a computer organize its files and free space so that it can operate more quickly: *Defragment your computer overnight.*

defraud /dɪˈfrɔːd/ US /-ˈfrɑːd/ **verb** [T] to take something illegally from a person, company, etc., or to prevent someone from having something that is legally theirs by deceiving them: *He was found guilty of defrauding the Internal Revenue Service.* ◦ *They are both charged with conspiracy to defraud an insurance company* ***of*** *$20,000.*

defray /dɪˈfreɪ/ **verb** [T] formal (especially of an organization) to pay the cost of something: *The company will defray all your expenses, including car hire.*

defriend /ˌdiːˈfrend/ **verb** [T] (also **unfriend**) to remove someone from your list of friends on a SOCIAL NETWORKING website: *How do I check who has defriended me on Facebook?*

defrock /ˌdiːˈfrɒk/ US /-ˈfrɑːk/ **verb** [T] formal or humorous to DISMISS a priest (= remove him from his job), usually because of bad behaviour

defrost /ˌdiːˈfrɒst/ US /-ˈfrɑːst/ **verb** [I or T] to (cause to) become free of ice, or to (cause to) become no longer frozen: *When you get a build-up of ice in your freezer, you know it's time to defrost it.* ◦ *Defrost the chicken thoroughly before cooking.* ◦ *Leave the chicken to defrost.*

defroster /dɪˈfrɒs.təʳ/ US /-ˈfrɑː.stɚ/ **noun** [C] US for a **demister**

deft /deft/ **adj** skilful, clever, or quick: *Her movements were deft and quick.* ◦ *She answered the journalist's questions with a deft touch.* ◦ *He's very deft **at** handling awkward situations.* • **deftly** /ˈdeft.li/ **adv** *He deftly (= skilfully) caught the ball.* • **deftness** /ˈdeft.nəs/ **noun** [U]

defunct /dɪˈfʌŋkt/ **adj** formal no longer existing, living, or working correctly: *members of a **now** defunct communist organization* ◦ humorous *I think this kettle is defunct!*

defuse /ˌdiːˈfjuːz/ **verb** [T] **BOMB** ▷ **1** to prevent a bomb from exploding: *Bomb disposal experts have defused a 110-pound bomb at Victoria Station.* **DIFFICULT SITUATION** ▷ **2** to make a difficult or dangerous situation calmer by reducing or removing its cause: *The two groups will meet next week to try to defuse the crisis/situation/tension.*

defy /dɪˈfaɪ/ **verb** [T] **1** (C2) to refuse to obey a person, decision, law, situation, etc.: *children openly defying their teachers* ◦ *A few workers have defied the majority decision and gone into work despite the strike.* ◦ *The fact that aircraft don't fall out of the sky always seems to me to defy (= act against) the **law** of gravity.* ◦ *A forest fire raging in the south of France is defying (= is not changed by) all attempts to control it.* **2 defy belief/description/explanation** (C2) to be extreme or very strange and therefore impossible to believe, describe, or explain: *The chaos at the airport defies description.* **3 defy sb to do sth** to tell someone to do something that you think will be impossible: *I defy you to prove your accusations.* ◦ *I defy you to tell where I've painted over the scratch on my car.*

degenerate verb; adj; noun

▸**verb** [I] /dɪˈdʒen.ə.reɪt/ to become worse in quality: *Educational standards are degenerating year by year because of a lack of funds.* ◦ *What was intended as a peaceful demonstration rapidly degenerated **into** violence.*

▸**adj** /dɪˈdʒen.ər.ət/ (US) /-ɚ-/ having low standards of behaviour: *a degenerate young man*

▸**noun** [C] /dɪˈdʒen.ər.ət/ (US) /-ɚ-/ formal disapproving someone with low standards of behaviour: *They're just **moral** degenerates with no sense of decency.*

degeneration /dɪˌdʒen.əˈreɪ.ʃən/ **noun** [S or U] the process by which something gets worse: *There has been a gradual degeneration **of** the judicial system in the last few years.* ◦ *High blood pressure can cause degeneration **of** the heart muscles.*

degenerative /dɪˈdʒen.ər.ə.tɪv/ (US) /-ɚ.ə.t̬ɪv/ **adj** describes an illness in which the body or a part of the body gradually stops working: *a degenerative disease/condition*

degradable /dɪˈɡreɪ.də.bl̩/ **adj** describes a substance that can change into a more simple chemical structure, especially over time: *These bags are made of degradable plastic.* → See also **biodegradable**

degradation /ˌdeɡ.rəˈdeɪ.ʃən/ **noun** [U] **1** the process in which the beauty or quality of something is destroyed or spoiled: *environmental degradation* **2** formal the situation in which people are made to feel they have no value: *the misery and degradation of prison life*

degrade /dɪˈɡreɪd/ **verb** **LOSE RESPECT** ▷ **1** [T] to cause people to feel that they or other people have no value and do not have the respect or good opinion of others: *Pornography degrades women.* **SPOIL** ▷ **2** [T] to spoil or destroy the beauty or quality of something: *Every day the environment is further degraded by toxic wastes.* **3** [I or T] specialized If the quality of something electrical or electronic degrades or is degraded, it becomes less good or less correct. **CHANGE STRUCTURE** ▷ **4** [I] specialized (of a substance) to change into a more simple chemical structure: *These chemicals quickly degrade **into** harmless compounds.* → See also **biodegrade (biodegradable)**

degrading /dɪˈɡreɪ.dɪŋ/ **adj** causing people to feel that they have no value: [+ to infinitive] *It is so degrading **to** have to ask for money.* ◦ *No one should have to suffer such degrading treatment.*

degree /dɪˈɡriː/ **noun** **AMOUNT** ▷ **1** (B2) [C usually singular, U] (an) amount or level of something: *This job demands a high degree **of** skill.* ◦ *There isn't the slightest degree **of** doubt that he's innocent.* ◦ *I have to warn you that there's **a** degree **of** (= some) danger involved in this.* ◦ *The number of terrorist attacks has increased **to** a terrifying degree.* ◦ *There was some degree **of** truth in what she said.* ◦ ***To what** degree do you think we will be providing a better service?* ◦ *'That's really bad.' 'Well, it's all a **matter/question of** degree (= there are other things better and other things worse).'* **UNIT** ▷ **2** (A2) [C] (written abbreviation **deg.**) any of various units of measurement, especially of temperature or angles, usually shown by the symbol ° written after a number: *a difference of three degrees* ◦ *Water boils at 212° **Fahrenheit** and 100° **Celsius/Centigrade**.* ◦ *A right angle is an angle of 90°.* ◦ *New York is on a **latitude of** 41°N and a **longitude of** 74°W.* **COURSE** ▷ **3** (B1) [C] a course of study at a college or university, or the qualification given to a student who has done this course: *'What degree did you **do** at York?' 'Geography.'* ◦ *She's **got** a physics degree/a degree **in** physics **from** Edinburgh.* ◦ mainly US *She's **got** a **bachelor's/master's** degree **in** history **from** Yale.*

IDIOMS **by degrees** gradually: *The economy seems to be improving by degrees.* • **to a/some degree** partly: *To some degree I think that's right, but there are other factors which affect the situation.*

-degree /-dɪ.ɡriː/ **suffix** used with an ORDINAL number to show how serious something is: *She suffered **first-/second-/third**-degree (= least serious/serious/very serious) burns on her legs.* ◦ US *He's being charged with **first**-degree (= the most serious type of) **murder**.*

dehumanize (UK usually **dehumanise**) /ˌdiːˈhjuː.mə.naɪz/ **verb** [T] to remove from a person the special human qualities of independent thought, feeling for other people, etc.: *It's a totalitarian regime that reduces and dehumanizes its population.*

dehydrate /ˌdiː.haɪˈdreɪt/ **verb** [I or T] to (cause to) lose water: *Air travel dehydrates the body.* ◦ *You'll dehydrate (= lose water from your body) very quickly in this heat, if you don't drink lots of water.* • **dehydration** /ˌdiː.haɪˈdreɪ.ʃən/ **noun** [U] *More than 11,000 children die every day around the world because of dehydration caused by diarrhoea.*

dehydrated /ˌdiː.haɪˈdreɪ.tɪd/ (US) /-ˈdreɪ.t̬ɪd/ **adj** not having the normal amount of water in your body so that you feel ill or weak

ˌde-ˈice **verb** [T] to remove ice from something: *to de-ice the car*

de-icer /ˌdiːˈaɪ.səʳ/ (US) /-sɚ/ **noun** [C] a substance for removing ice

deictic /ˈdaɪk.tɪk/, /ˈdeɪk-/ **adj** specialized relating to a word or phrase whose meaning depends on who is talking, who they are talking to, where they are, etc., for example 'me' and 'here'

deify /ˈdeɪ.ɪ.faɪ/ **verb** [T] **1** to make someone or something into a god: *The Romans used to deify their emperors.* **2** disapproving to consider someone or something to be more important than anything else: *Pelé was deified by his fans.* • **deification** /ˌdeɪ.ɪ.fɪˈkeɪ.ʃᵊn/ (US) /ˌdiː.ə-/ noun [U]

deign /deɪn/ verb disapproving **deign to do sth** to do something unwillingly and in a way that shows that you think you are too important to do it: *If she deigns to reply to my letter, I'll be extremely surprised.*

deindustrialization (UK usually **deindustrialisation**) /diː.ɪnˌdʌs.tri.ᵊl.aɪˈzeɪ.ʃᵊn/ noun [U] the process by which a country or area stops having industry as its main SOURCE (= cause) of work or income: *the deindustrialization of America/the Northeast of England*

deism /ˈdeɪ.ɪ.zᵊm/ noun [U] the belief in a single god who does not act to influence events, and whose existence has no connection with religions, religious buildings, or religious books, etc.

deity /ˈdeɪ.ɪ.ti/ (US) /ˈdiː.ə.t̬i/ noun [C] a god or GODDESS: *Ares and Aphrodite were the ancient Greek deities of war and love.*

the ˈDeity noun [S] formal God

déjà vu /ˌdeɪ.ʒɑːˈvuː/ noun [U] the strange feeling that in some way you have experienced already what is happening now: *When I met her, I had a strange **feeling of** déjà vu.* ◦ disapproving *The movie has a strong **sense of** déjà vu about it (= is similar to other films and does not contain new ideas).*

dejected /dɪˈdʒek.tɪd/ adj unhappy, disappointed, or without hope: *She looked a bit dejected when she was told that she hadn't got the job.* • **dejectedly** /-li/ adv • **dejection** /-ʃᵊn/ noun [U]

de jure /ˌdeɪˈdʒʊə.reɪ/, /ˌdiː-/ (US) /-ˈdʒʊr.i/ adj [before noun], adv formal having a right or existence as stated by law: *The country has de facto independence now, and it will soon be recognized de jure by the world's governments.* ◦ *The president aims to create a de jure one-party state.* → Compare **de facto**

delay /dɪˈleɪ/ verb; noun

▸verb **1** (A2) [I or T] to make something happen at a later time than originally planned or expected: *My plane was delayed by an hour.* ◦ *Could we delay the meeting a few days?* ◦ [+ -ing verb] *I think we should delay decid**ing** about this until next year.* **2** (B1) [T] to cause someone or something to be slow or late: *I was delayed by traffic.* **3** [I] to not act quickly or immediately: *If you delay now, the opportunity might be lost.*

▸noun [C or U] (A2) the situation in which you have to wait longer than expected for something to happen, or the time that you have to wait: *This situation needs to be tackled **without** delay.* ◦ *Long delays are predicted on the motorway because of the accident.* ◦ *There has been a delay **in** the book's publication.*

> Word partners for **delay noun**
>
> a *brief/short/slight* delay • a *considerable/lengthy/long/serious* delay • *cause* delays • *experience/face/suffer* delays • delays *due to* sth • a delay *in* sth/doing sth • a delay *of* [two hours, five days, etc.] • *without* delay

delayed /dɪˈleɪd/ adj [before noun] happening at a later time than expected or intended: *Officials said that the reason for the large number of delayed trains was the bad weather conditions.* ◦ *The protests are a delayed reaction to last week's announcement.* ◦ *He's suffering from delayed **shock**.*

delayering /diːˈleɪ.ər.ɪŋ/ (US) /-ɚ-/ noun [U] the process in which a company or organization reduces the number of its managers

deˈlaying tactics noun [plural] actions that are intended to make something happen more slowly, in order to win an advantage

delectable /dɪˈlek.tə.bl̩/ adj beautiful and giving great pleasure: *a delectable cheesecake* • **delectably** /-bli/ adv

delectation /ˌdiː.lekˈteɪ.ʃᵊn/ noun [U] formal great pleasure and enjoyment

delegate noun; verb

▸noun [C] /ˈdel.ɪ.gət/ (C1) a person chosen or elected by a group to speak, vote, etc. for them, especially at a meeting: *Delegates have voted in favour of the motion.* ◦ *Each union elects several delegates **to** the annual conference.*

▸verb /ˈdel.ɪ.geɪt/ GIVE ▷ **1** (C2) [I or T] to give a particular job, duty, right, etc. to someone else so that they do it for you: *As a boss you have to delegate (responsibilities **to** your staff).* ◦ *Authority to make financial decisions has been delegated **to** a special committee.* CHOOSE PERSON ▷ **2** [T + obj + to infinitive] to choose or elect someone to speak, vote, etc. for a group, especially at a meeting: *A group of four teachers were delegated **to** represent the school at the union conference.*

delegation /ˌdel.ɪˈgeɪ.ʃᵊn/ noun CHOSEN PEOPLE ▷ **1** (C2) [C, + sing/pl verb] a group of delegates: *A delegation from Spain has/have arrived for a month.* GIVING ▷ **2** [U] the act of delegating a particular job, duty, right, etc. to someone: *Delegation **of** responsibility is a key part of a manager's job.*

delete /dɪˈliːt/ verb [I or T] (B1) to remove or draw a line through something, especially a written word or words: *They insisted that all expletives be deleted **from** the article.* ◦ *Here is a list of possible answers. Please delete (= draw a line through them) as appropriate.*

deleterious /ˌdel.ɪˈtɪə.ri.əs/ (US) /-ˈtɪr.i-/ adj formal harmful: *These drugs have a proven deleterious **effect** on the nervous system.* • **deleteriously** /-li/ adv

deletion /dɪˈliː.ʃᵊn/ noun [C or U] the process of removing something, or what is removed: *In 2002, the management ordered the deletion of all computer files on this subject.* ◦ *There have been some deletions (= words have been removed) **from** this text.*

deli /ˈdel.i/ noun [C] informal for **delicatessen**

deliberate adj; verb

▸adj /dɪˈlɪb.ᵊr.ət/ (US) /-ɚ-/ **1** (B2) (often of something bad) intentional or planned: *a deliberate attack/insult/lie* ◦ *We made a deliberate decision to live apart for a while.* **2** describes a movement, action, or thought that is done carefully without hurrying: *From her slow, deliberate speech I guessed she must be drunk.*

▸verb [I or T] /dɪˈlɪb.ə.reɪt/ formal to think or talk seriously and carefully about something: *The jury took five days to deliberate **on** the case.* ◦ *The committee has deliberated the question at great length.* ◦ [+ question word] *He's deliberating **wh**ether or not to accept the new job that he's been offered.*

deliberately /dɪˈlɪb.ᵊr.ət.li/ (US) /-ɚ-/ adv **1** (B2) intentionally: *I'm sure he says these things deliberately to annoy me.* **2** slowly and carefully: *Calmly and deliberately, she poured petrol over the car and set it alight.*

deliberation /dɪˌlɪb.əˈreɪ.ʃᵊn/ noun DISCUSSION ▷ **1** [C or U] formal considering or discussing something: *After much deliberation, she decided to accept their offer.* ◦ *After five days of deliberations, the jury decided on a verdict.* CAREFUL ▷ **2** [U] a slow careful way of doing something: *Slowly and with deliberation she turned to me and told me to get out.*

delicacy /ˈdel.ɪ.kə.si/ noun FOOD ▷ **1** [C] something especially rare or expensive that is good to eat: *In some parts of the world, sheep's eyes are considered a*

***great** delicacy.* **POLITENESS** ▷ **2** [U] acting and speaking carefully so that no one is offended, or the possibility of causing offence: *He raised the matter with great delicacy.* ◦ *I don't think you quite appreciate the delicacy **of** the situation.* **BEING EASILY DAMAGED** ▷ **3** [U] the quality of being easy to damage or looking very easy to damage: *Because of their great delicacy, the books cannot be moved.* **CARE** ▷ **4** [U] the quality of being done carefully or gently: *We admired the delicacy of her brush strokes.*

delicate /ˈdel.ɪ.kət/ **adj** **EASILY DAMAGED** ▷ **1** (B2) needing careful treatment, especially because easily damaged: *Peaches have delicate skins which are easily bruised.* ◦ *Delicate plants need to be kept in a greenhouse during the winter.* ◦ *delicate china* ◦ *Molly's **health** has always been delicate (= she becomes ill easily).* **2** (C1) needing to be done carefully: *Repairing damaged nerves is a very delicate **operation/process**.* **DIFFICULT** ▷ **3 a delicate situation, matter, point, etc.** (C1) a situation. matter, etc. that needs to be dealt with carefully in order to avoid trouble or offence: *I need to speak to you about a rather delicate matter.* ◦ *The pay negotiations have reached a delicate point/ stage.* ◦ *Teachers need to strike a delicate (= carefully achieved) balance between instructing their pupils and letting them discover things for themselves.* **ACCURATE** ▷ **4** able to measure very small changes: *Weather-forecasters have extremely delicate **equipment** which helps them predict what the weather is going to be like.* **SOFT** ▷ **5** (B2) pleasantly soft or light: *a rose with a delicate scent* ◦ *a delicate shade of pink* ◦ *We chose a delicate floral pattern for our bedroom curtains.* **ATTRACTIVE** ▷ **6** (C2) having a thin, attractive shape: *She folded her delicate hands on the table.* • **delicately** /-li/ **adv** *I thought you handled the situation very delicately (= in a way that avoided causing offence).* ◦ *The pudding was delicately flavoured with vanilla.*

delicatessen /ˌdel.ɪ.kəˈtes.ᵊn/ **noun** [C] (informal **deli**) a small shop that sells high quality foods, such as types of cheese and cold cooked meat, which often come from other countries

delicious /dɪˈlɪʃ.əs/ **adj** **1** (B1) having a very pleasant taste or smell: *a delicious cake* ◦ *The delicious smell of freshly-made coffee came from the kitchen.* ◦ *This wine is delicious.* **2** describes a situation or activity that gives you great pleasure: *I've got some delicious gossip.* • **deliciousness** /-nəs/ **noun** [U]

deliciously /dɪˈlɪʃ.əs.li/ **adv** **1** with a very pleasant taste or smell: *a deliciously garlicky potato cake* **2** very pleasantly: *As she dived into the pool, the water felt deliciously cool on her skin.*

delight /dɪˈlaɪt/ **noun; verb**

▸**noun** [C or U] **1** (B2) (something or someone that gives) great pleasure, satisfaction, or happiness: *My sister's little boy is a real delight.* ◦ *I read your letter **with** great delight.* ◦ *The children squealed **in** delight when they saw all the presents under the Christmas tree.* ◦ *He seems to **take** great delight **in** (= enjoys) teasing his sister.* **2 the delights of sth** the pleasures of something: *We're just discovering the delights of being retired.*

▸**verb** [T] to give someone great pleasure or satisfaction: *Peter's success at college delighted his family.*

PHRASAL VERB **delight in sth** to get a lot of pleasure from something, especially something unpleasant: *Some people delight in the misfortunes of others.* ◦ *My brother always delights in tell**ing** me when I make a mistake.*

delighted /dɪˈlaɪ.tɪd/ (US) /-t̬ɪd/ **adj** (B1) very pleased: *a delighted audience* ◦ *Pat was delighted **with** her new flat.* ◦ *I was delighted **at/by** your news.* ◦ [+ that] *I'm **absolutely** delighted **that** you can come.* ◦ [+ to infinitive] *We'd be delighted **to** come to dinner on Friday.* • **delightedly** /-li/ **adv**

delightful /dɪˈlaɪt.fᵊl/ **adj** (B2) very pleasant, attractive, or enjoyable: *Our new neighbours are delightful.* ◦ *Thank you for a delightful evening.* • **delightfully** /-i/ **adv**

delimit /ˌdiːˈlɪm.ɪt/ **verb** [T] formal to mark or describe the limits of something: *Police powers are delimited by law.*

delineate /dɪˈlɪn.i.eɪt/ **verb** [T] formal to describe or mark the edge of something: *The main characters are clearly delineated in the first chapter.* ◦ *The boundary of the car park is delineated by a low brick wall.* • **delineation** /dɪˌlɪn.iˈeɪ.ʃᵊn/ **noun** [C or U]

delinquency /dɪˈlɪŋ.kwᵊn.si/ **noun** **BAD BEHAVIOUR** ▷ **1** [U] behaviour, especially of a young person, that is is illegal or not acceptable to most people: *There is a high rate of **juvenile** delinquency in this area.* **2** [C] formal an action that is illegal or not acceptable: *His past delinquencies have made it difficult for him to get a job.* **MONEY** ▷ **3** US a situation in which borrowed money is not paid back as agreed: *The consumer loan delinquency **rate** has increased 33 percent.*

delinquent /dɪˈlɪŋ.kwᵊnt/ **noun; adj**

▸**noun** [C] a person, usually young, who behaves in a way that is illegal or not acceptable to most people: ***juvenile** delinquents*

▸**adj** **1** being or behaving in ways that are illegal or not acceptable: *delinquent teenagers* ◦ *They are carrying out research on the causes of delinquent behaviour among young people.* **2** US formal late (in paying money owed): *She has been delinquent **in** paying her taxes.*

delirious /dɪˈlɪr.i.əs/ **adj** **1** unable to think or speak clearly because of fever or mental confusion: *She had a high temperature and was delirious.* **2** extremely happy or excited: *The Greek football team arrived home to a delirious reception in Athens.* • **deliriously** /-li/ **adv** *Kate and Peter are deliriously **happy** (= extremely happy) together.*

delirium /dɪˈlɪr.i.əm/ **noun** [U] **1** a state of being unable to think or speak clearly because of fever or mental confusion: *fever accompanied by delirium* **2** a state of extreme excitement or happiness: *I've never seen such delirium at a football match before.*

delirium tremens /dɪˌlɪr.i.əmˈtrem.ənz/, /-ˈtriː-/ **noun** [U] formal for **the DTs**

deliver /dɪˈlɪv.əʳ/ (US) /-ɚ/ **verb** **TAKE** ▷ **1** (B1) [T] to take goods, letters, parcels, etc. to people's houses or places of work: *Mail is delivered **to** our office twice a day.* ◦ *The shop is delivering our new bed on Thursday.* **GIVE** ▷ **2** (B2) [T] to give, direct, or aim something: *The priest delivered a passionate **sermon/speech** against war.* ◦ *The jury delivered a **verdict** of not guilty.* ◦ *The police said that it was the **blow** that had been delivered (= given) **to** her head that had killed her.* ◦ *The bowler tripped as he was delivering the ball (= throwing it towards the person with the bat).* **PRODUCE** ▷ **3** (C1) [I or T] to achieve or produce something that has been promised: *The government has failed to deliver (what it promised).* ◦ mainly US *The Republicans are relying on their agricultural policies to deliver the farmers' vote (= to persuade farmers to vote for them).* **GIVE BIRTH** ▷ **4** [T] to (help) give birth to a baby: *She delivered her third child at home.* ◦ *The baby was delivered by a midwife.* ◦ formal *The princess has been delivered **of** (= has given birth to) a healthy baby boy.* **SAVE** ▷ **5** [T] formal to save someone from a painful or bad experience: *Is there nothing that can be done to deliver these starving people **from** their suffering?* • **deliverance** /-ᵊns/ noun [U] formal *We pray for deliverance **from** our sins.* • **deliverer** /-əʳ/ (US) /-ɚ/ noun [C] formal *Moses was the deliverer **of** the Israelites from Egypt.*

D

deliverable /dɪˈlɪv.ᵊr.ə.bl̩/ (US) /-ɚ-/ noun; adj
▸noun [C] something that can be provided or achieved as a result of a process: *What are the project deliverables?*
▸adj able to be delivered: *The goods were not in a deliverable state.*

delivery /dɪˈlɪv.ᵊr.i/ (US) /-ɚ-/ noun LETTERS, ETC. ▷ **1** (B1) [C or U] the act of taking goods, letters, parcels, etc. to people's houses or places of work: *We get two deliveries **of** mail (= it is delivered twice) a day.* ◦ *You can pay for the carpet **on** delivery (= when it is delivered).* ◦ *We expect to **take** delivery **of** (= receive) our new car next week.* ◦ *a delivery **van*** GIVING ▷ **2** [S] the way in which someone speaks in public: *the actor's delivery* **3** [C or U] in some sports, such as cricket or baseball, the act of throwing the ball towards the person with the BAT, in order for that person to try to hit the ball: *That was a good delivery from Thompson.* BIRTH ▷ **4** [C] a birth

deliveryman /dɪˈlɪv.ᵊr.i.mæn/ (US) /-ɚ-/ noun [C] (plural **-men** /-mən/) a man who delivers goods to people's houses or places of work

deˈlivery ˌroom noun [C usually singular] a room in a hospital in which babies are born

delouse /ˌdiːˈlaʊs/ verb [T] to remove LICE (= a type of very small insect) from the body, hair, or clothing of a person or the fur of an animal

delphinium /delˈfɪn.i.əm/ noun [C] (also **larkspur**) a tall garden plant with blue flowers

delta /ˈdel.tə/ (US) /-t̬ə/ noun RIVER ▷ **1** [C] an area of low, flat land, sometimes shaped like a triangle, where a river divides into several smaller rivers before flowing into the sea: *the Mississippi delta* ◦ *the delta **of** the Nile* LETTER ▷ **2** [C or U] (symbol δ) the fourth letter of the Greek alphabet → Compare **alpha, beta, gamma**

deltoids /ˈdel.tɔɪdz/ noun [plural] (also ˌ**deltoid** ˈ**muscles**, also informal **delts**) the muscles on the tops of the shoulders

delude /dɪˈluːd/ verb [T] to make someone believe something that is not true: *He's deluding him**self** if he thinks he's going to be promoted this year.*

deluded /dɪˈluː.dɪd/ adj believing things that are not real or true: *Poor deluded girl, she thinks he's going to marry her.*

deluge /ˈdel.juːdʒ/ noun; verb
▸noun [C] **1** a very large amount of rain or water: *This little stream can become a deluge when it rains heavily.* **2 a deluge of sth** a lot of something: *The newspaper received a deluge of complaints/letters/phone calls about the article.*
▸verb [T usually passive] to cover something with a lot of water: *The city was deluged when the river burst its banks.* ◦ figurative *We've been deluged **with** (= have received a lot of) replies.*

delusion /dɪˈluː.ʒᵊn/ noun [C or U] belief in something that is not true: [+ that] *He's **under** the delusion **that** he will be promoted this year.*

IDIOM **delusions of grandeur** the belief that you are more important or powerful than you really are

delusional /dɪˈluː.ʒᵊn.ᵊl/ adj believing things that are not true: *Delusional thinking is common in schizophrenia.*

delusive /dɪˈluː.sɪv/ adj (also **delusory**) false: *I harboured the delusive hope that he would return my love.* • **delusively** /-li/ adv

deluxe /dɪˈlʌks/ adj [usually before noun] very comfortable and of very high quality: *a deluxe hotel in Paris*

delve /delv/ verb [I] to search, especially as if by digging, in order to find a thing or information: *She delved **into** her pocket to find some change.*

PHRASAL VERB **delve into sth** to examine something carefully in order to discover more information about someone or something: *It's not always a good idea to delve too deeply into someone's past.*

Dem. written abbreviation for **Democrat**

demagogue disapproving (US also **demagog**) /ˈdem.ə.ɡɒɡ/ (US) /-ɡɑːɡ/ noun [C] a person, especially a political leader, who wins support by exciting people's emotions rather than by having good ideas • **demagogic** /ˌdem.əˈɡɒdʒ.ɪk/ (US) /-ˈɡɑː.dʒɪ-/ adj • **demagogically** /ˌdem.əˈɡɒdʒ.ɪ.kᵊl.i/ (US) /-ˈɡɑː.dʒɪ-/ adv • **demagoguery** /ˌdem.əˈɡɒɡ.ə.ri/ (US) /-ˈɡɑː.ɡɚ.i/ noun [U]

demand /dɪˈmɑːnd/ (US) /-ˈmænd/ verb; noun
▸verb [T] REQUEST ▷ **1** (B1) to ask for something forcefully, in a way that shows that you do not expect to be refused: *I demanded an explanation.* ◦ *The car workers' union is demanding a seven percent pay rise this year.* ◦ *He has always demanded the highest standards of behaviour **from** his children.* ◦ [+ speech] *'And where do you think you're going?' demanded the police officer.* ◦ [+ to infinitive] *I demand **to** see the manager.* ◦ [+ that] *She demanded **that** he return the books he borrowed from her.* NEED ▷ **2** (B2) to need something such as time, effort, or a particular quality: *This is a very difficult piece of music to play – it demands a lot of concentration.* ◦ *He seems to lack many of the qualities demanded **of** (= needed by) a successful politician.*
▸noun REQUEST ▷ **1** (B1) [C] a strong request: *You can't give in to children's demands all the time.* ◦ *The government is unlikely to agree to the rebels' demands **for** independence.* ◦ UK *They received a **final** demand (= a last request) **for** payment.* NEED ▷ **2** (B2) [C or U] a need for something to be sold or supplied: *There was little demand **for** tickets.* ◦ *Good teachers are always **in** (**great**) demand (= are always needed).* **3 demands** [plural] the difficult things that you have to do: *The demands **of** nursing are too great for a lot of people.* ◦ *His new job **makes** a lot of demands **on** him (= he has to work very hard).*

> Word partners for **demand noun**
>
> *make* a demand • *comply with/give in to* a demand • *reject/resist* a demand • *fresh/new/renewed* demands • a *legitimate/reasonable* demand • a demand *for* sth

demanding /dɪˈmɑːn.dɪŋ/ (US) /-ˈmæn-/ adj (B2) needing a lot of time, attention, or energy: *She's a very demanding child.* ◦ *a demanding job/task*

demarcate /ˈdiː.mɑː.keɪt/ (US) /ˌdiːˈmɑːr-/ verb [T] (US also **demark**) to show the limits of something: *Parking spaces are demarcated by white lines.* ◦ *Responsibilities within the department are clearly demarcated.*

demarcation /ˌdiː.mɑːˈkeɪ.ʃᵊn/ (US) /-mɑːr-/ noun [C or U] (US also **demarkation**) a border or a rule that shows the limits of something or how things are divided: *The river serves as the **line of** demarcation (= the line showing the separation) **between** the two counties.* ◦ *In some schools there is little demarcation **between***

subjects (= subjects are not taught separately). ◦ *On this map, demarcations **between** regions are shown with dotted lines.*

demarˈcation ˌdispute noun [C] UK a disagreement between TRADE UNIONS (= organizations of workers) about what types of work should be done by the members of each of them

demean /dɪˈmiːn/ verb [T] to cause someone to become less respected: *The entire family was demeaned by his behaviour.* ◦ *I wouldn't demean my**self** by asking my parents for money.*

demeaning /dɪˈmiː.nɪŋ/ adj causing someone to become or feel less respected: *That advertisement is demeaning **to** women.* ◦ [+ to infinitive] ***It** was very demeaning **to** be criticized in front of all my colleagues.*

demeanour UK formal (US **demeanor**) /dɪˈmiː.nəʳ/ US /-nɚ/ noun [U] a way of looking and behaving: *There was nothing **in** his demeanour that suggested he was anxious.* ◦ *She **has** the demeanour **of** a woman who is contented with her life.*

demented /dɪˈmen.tɪd/ US /-t̬ɪd/ adj **1** unable to think or act clearly because you are extremely worried, angry, or excited by something: *She was nearly demented **with** worry when her son didn't come home.* **2** old-fashioned or informal crazy: *The man is demented – he's going to wreck the whole operation.* • **dementedly** /-li/ adv

dementia /dɪˈmen.ʃə/ noun [U] specialized a medical condition that affects especially old people, causing the memory and other mental abilities to gradually become worse, and leading to confused behaviour

demerara (sugar) /ˌdem.ə.reə.rəˈʃʊg.əʳ/ US /-ˌrɑːr.ə-ˈʃʊg.ɚ/ noun [U] rough pale brown sugar

demerit /ˌdiːˈmer.ɪt/ noun [C] **1** formal a fault or disadvantage: *We need to consider the merits and demerits **of** the plan.* **2** a mark given to someone, especially a student in a school, because they have done something wrong or broken a rule: *She got three demerits **for** lateness on this term's report.*

demigod /ˈdem.i.gɒd/ US /-gɑːd/ noun [C] (in ancient stories) a being who is partly human and partly a god: *Some football players become like demigods to their fans.*

demilitarize (UK usually **demilitarise**) /ˌdiːˈmɪl.ɪ.təʳ.aɪz/ US /-t̬ɚ-/ verb [T] to remove military forces from an area: *A demilitarized **zone** has been created on the border between the warring countries.* • **demilitarization** (UK usually **demilitarisation**) /diːˌmɪl.ɪ.təʳ.aɪˈzeɪ.ʃən/ US /diːˌmɪl.ɪ.t̬ɚ.əˈ-/ noun [C or U]

demise /dɪˈmaɪz/ noun [S] formal **1** death **2** the end of something that was previously considered to be powerful, such as a business, industry, or system: *The demise **of** the company was sudden and unexpected.*

demist /ˌdiːˈmɪst/ verb [T] UK (US **defrost**, also **defog**) to remove the MIST (= thin layer of liquid on a surface) from the window of a car, usually by blowing air over it

demister /ˌdiːˈmɪs.təʳ/ US /-tɚ/ noun [C] UK (US **defroster**, also **defogger**) a device for removing MIST (= thin layer of liquid on a surface) from a car window

demit /dɪˈmɪt/ verb [T] (-tt-) formal to give up a job or position by telling your employer that you are leaving: *Where an elected member of the Council fails to attend three meetings of the Council without apologies, they shall be deemed to have demitted office.* → Synonym **resign**

demo /ˈdem.əʊ/ US /-oʊ/ noun; verb
▸noun [C] (plural **demos**) **MARCH** ▷ **1** UK informal for **demonstration** (= a political march): *I went on lots of demos as a student.* **EXAMPLE** ▷ **2** an example of a product, especially a computer program or piece of recorded music, given or shown to someone to try to make them buy or support it: *a software demo* ◦ *A team of music industry figures will select bands and soloists from demo **tapes**.* **3** informal for **demonstration** (= when you show people how something works or how to do something): *a cookery demo*
▸verb [T] to show something and explain how it works, or to show or produce a demo: *to demo a new piece of software* ◦ *They've just completed a Christmas single and are also demoing lots of new songs.*

D

demob /ˌdiːˈmɒb/ US /-ˈmɑːb/ verb; noun
▸verb [T] (-bb-) informal for **demobilize**
▸noun [U] informal for **demobilization (demobilize)**

demobilize formal (UK usually **demobilise**) /ˌdiːˈməʊ.bɪ.laɪz/ US /-ˈmoʊ-/ verb [T] to release someone from one of the armed forces, especially at the end of a war: *He was demobilized in March 1946.* • **demobilization** (UK usually **demobilisation**) /diːˌməʊ.bɪ.laɪˈzeɪ.ʃən/ US /-ˌmoʊ.bɪ.ləˈ-/ noun [U]

democracy /dɪˈmɒk.rə.si/ US /-ˈmɑː.krə-/ noun **1** B2 [U] the belief in freedom and EQUALITY between people, or a system of government based on this belief, in which power is either held by elected REPRESENTATIVES or directly by the people themselves: *The government has promised to uphold the principles of democracy.* ◦ *The early 1990s saw the spread of democracy in Eastern Europe.* **2** B2 [C] a country in which power is held by elected REPRESENTATIVES: *Few of the Western democracies still have a royal family.*

democrat /ˈdem.ə.kræt/ noun [C] a person who believes in democracy

Democrat /ˈdem.ə.kræt/ noun [C] (written abbreviation **Dem.**) in the US, a member or supporter of the Democratic Party

democratic /ˌdem.əˈkræt.ɪk/ US /-ˈkræt̬-/ adj B2 based on the principles of democracy: *We must accept the results of a democratic election (= an election in which all people can vote).* ◦ *Do you think Australia is a more democratic country than Britain?* • **democratically** /-ɪ.kəl.i/ adv *We need to decide this democratically (= based on the wishes of most of the people).* ◦ *Yeltsin was Russia's first **democratically elected** president.*

the Demoˈcratic ˌParty noun one of the two main political parties in the US

democratize (UK usually **democratise**) /dɪˈmɒk.rə.taɪz/ US /-ˈmɑː.krə-/ verb [T] to make countries or organizations use democratic ways of making decisions: *It's about time we democratized the organization of this company.* • **democratization** (UK usually **democratisation**) /dɪˌmɒk.rə.taɪˈzeɪ.ʃən/ US /-ˌmɑː.krə.t̬ɪ-/ noun [U]

demographer /dɪˈmɒg.rə.fəʳ/ US /-ˈmɑː.grə.fɚ/ noun [C] a person who studies changes in numbers of births, marriages, deaths, etc. in an area over a period of time

demographic /ˌdem.əˈgræf.ɪk/ noun [C] a group of people, for example customers, who are similar in age, social class, etc.: *This demographic (young teenagers) is the fastest-growing age group using the site.*

demographics /ˌdem.əˈgræf.ɪks/ noun [plural] the quantity and characteristics of the people who live in a particular area, especially in relation to their age, how much money they have, and what they spend it on: ***The** demographics **of** the country have changed dramatically in recent years.*

demography /dɪˈmɒg.rə.fi/ US /-ˈmɑː.grə-/ noun [U] **1** the study of changes in the number of births, marriages, deaths, etc. in a particular area during a period of time: *historical demography* **2** The demography of an area is the number and characteristics of the people who live in an area, in relation to their age, sex, if they are married or not, etc.: *The increase in the number of young people leaving to work in the cities has had a dramatic impact on the demography of the villages.* • **demographic** /ˌdem.əˈgræf.ɪk/ **adj** *Current demographic **trends** suggest that there will be fewer school leavers coming into the workforce in ten years' time.*

D

demolish /dɪˈmɒl.ɪʃ/ (US) /-ˈmɑː.lɪʃ/ **verb** [T] **DESTROY** ▷ **1** B2 to completely destroy a building, especially in order to use the land for something else: *A number of houses were demolished so that the supermarket could be built.* **2** C2 to prove that an argument or theory is wrong: *He completely demolished all her arguments.* **DEFEAT** ▷ **3** to easily defeat someone: *In a surprise result, Aberdeen demolished Celtic 5–0.* **EAT** ▷ **4** humorous to quickly eat all the food you have been given: *Joe demolished an enormous plateful of sausages and chips.* • **demolition** /ˌdem.əˈlɪʃ.ᵊn/ **noun** [C or U] the act of destroying something such as a building: *the demolition of dangerous buildings*

demoˈlition ˌderby **noun** [C] a car race in which the drivers drive their cars into other cars intentionally, with the winner being the last car still able to move

demon /ˈdiː.mən/ **noun** **1** [C] an evil spirit **2** [C usually singular] approving a person who does a particular activity with great skill or energy: *She works like a demon.* ◦ *Stefan has a demon serve.* **3** [C] a negative feeling which causes you to worry or behave badly: *She had her demons and, later in life, they drove her to drink.*

IDIOM **the demon drink** (US **the demon alcohol**) alcohol and its unpleasant effects

demoniacal /ˌdiː.məˈnaɪ.ə.kᵊl/ **adj** (also **demoniac**) wild and evil: *A demoniacal light had entered his eyes.* • **demoniacally** /-i/ **adv**

demonic /dɪˈmɒn.ɪk/ (US) /-ˈmɑː.nɪk/ **adj** wild and evil: *He had a demonic (= cruel) gleam in his eye.* • **demonically** /-ˈmɒn.ɪ.kᵊl.i/ (US) /-ˈmɑː.nɪ-/ **adv**

demonize (UK usually **demonise**) /ˈdiː.mə.naɪz/ **verb** [T] to try to make someone or a group of people seem as if they are evil: *The Nazis used racist propaganda in an attempt to demonize the Jews.*

demonology /ˌdiː.məˈnɒl.ə.dʒi/ (US) /-ˈnɑː.lə-/ **noun** [U] the study of DEMONS and other evil creatures

demonstrable /dɪˈmɒn.strə.bl/ (US) /-ˈmɑːn-/ **adj** able to be proved: *The report contains numerous demonstrable errors.* • **demonstrability** /dɪˌmɒn.strəˈbɪl.ɪ.ti/ (US) /-ˌmɑːn.strəˈbɪl.ə.ţi/ **noun** [U] • **demonstrably** /-bli/ **adv** *That's demonstrably untrue!*

demonstrate /ˈdem.ən.streɪt/ **verb** **SHOW** ▷ **1** B2 [T] to show or make make something clear: *These figures **clearly** demonstrate the size of the economic problem facing the country.* ◦ [+ that] *Research has demonstrated **that** babies can recognize their mother's voice very soon after birth.* ◦ *These problems demonstrate the importance of strategic planning.* **2** C1 [T] to show something and explain how it works: *He's got a job demonstrating kitchen equipment in a department store.* ◦ [+ question word] *The teacher demonstrated **how** to use the equipment.* **EXPRESS** ▷ **3** C2 [T] to express or show that you have a particular feeling, quality, or ability: *He has demonstrated a genuine interest in the project.* ◦ *His answer demonstrated a complete lack of understanding of the question.* **PROTEST** ▷ **4** B2 [I] to make a public expression that you are not satisfied about something, especially by marching or having a meeting: *Thousands of people gathered to demonstrate **against** the new proposals.*

demonstration /ˌdem.ənˈstreɪ.ʃᵊn/ **noun** **SHOW** ▷ **1** C1 [C or U] the act of showing someone how to do something, or how something works: *This disaster is a clear demonstration **of** the need for tighter controls.* ◦ *Let me give you a demonstration **of** how the camera works.* ◦ *She told us how easy it was to use the computer, then by way of demonstration simply pressed a few keys on the keyboard.* ◦ *We're going to a cookery demonstration tonight.* **PROTEST** ▷ **2** B2 [C] (informal **demo**) an occasion when a group of people march or stand together to show that they disagree with or support something or someone: *The students are **holding** a demonstration to protest against the increase in their fees.* ◦ *Protesters **staged** an anti-war demonstration.* **EXPRESSION** ▷ **3** [C or U] a way of expressing a feeling or a quality: *Huge crowds followed the funeral procession in a public demonstration **of** grief.* ◦ *There has been little demonstration **of** support for the proposal so far.*

demonstrative /dɪˈmɒn.strə.tɪv/ (US) /-ˈmɑːn.strə.ţɪv/ **adj** **SHOWING FEELINGS** ▷ **1** If you are demonstrative, you show your feelings or behave in a way that shows your love: *We're a very demonstrative family.* **GRAMMAR** ▷ **2** describes words such as 'this', 'that', 'these', and 'those' that show which person or thing is being referred to: *In the sentence 'This is my brother', 'this' is a demonstrative pronoun.* **INDICATING** ▷ **3** **be demonstrative of sth** formal to show something or make something clear: *The findings of this survey are demonstrative of the need for further research.* • **demonstratively** /-li/ **adv** • **demonstrativeness** /dɪˈmɒn.strə.tɪv.nəs/ (US) /-ˈmɑːn.strə.ţɪv.nəs/ **noun** [U]

demonstrator /ˈdem.ən.streɪ.təʳ/ (US) /-ţɚ/ **noun** [C] **PERSON SHOWING** ▷ **1** a person who explains how something works or how to do something: *There was a special stand in the shop where a demonstrator was showing how the food processor worked.* **PROTESTER** ▷ **2** a person who marches or stands with a group of people to show that they disagree with or support something or someone: *Police arrested several of the demonstrators.*

demoralize (UK usually **demoralise**) /dɪˈmɒr.ə.laɪz/ (US) /-ˈmɔːr-/ **verb** [T] to make someone or something feel much less confident: *Losing several matches in succession had completely demoralized the team.*

demoralized (UK usually **demoralised**) /dɪˈmɒr.ə.laɪzd/ (US) /-ˈmɔːr-/ **adj** having lost your confidence, enthusiasm, and hope: *After the game, the players were tired and demoralized.* • **demoralization** (UK usually **demoralisation**) /dɪˌmɒr.ᵊl.aɪˈzeɪ.ʃᵊn/ (US) /-ˌmɔːr-/ **noun** [U] • **demoralizing** (UK usually **demoralising**) /-laɪ.zɪŋ/ **adj** *Being out of work for a long time is very demoralizing.*

demote /dɪˈməʊt/ (US) /-ˈmoʊt/ **verb** [T] to lower someone or something in rank or position: *The captain was demoted (**to** sergeant) for failing to fulfil his duties.* → Opposite **promote** • **demotion** /-ˈməʊ.ʃᵊn/ (US) /-ˈmoʊ.ʃᵊn/ **noun** [C or U]

demotic /dɪˈmɒt.ɪk/ (US) /-ˈmɑː.ţɪk/ **adj** formal (of or in a form of language) used by ordinary people

demotivate /ˌdiːˈməʊ.tɪ.veɪt/ (US) /-ˈmoʊ.ţɪ-/ **verb** [T] to make someone less enthusiastic about a job: *She was very demotivated by being told she had little chance of being promoted.* • **demotivating** /-veɪ.tɪŋ/ (US) /-veɪ.ţɪŋ/ **adj** *Constant criticism can be very demotivating.*

demur /dɪˈmɜːʳ/ (US) /-ˈmɜː/ **verb** [I] **(-rr-)** formal to express disagreement or refuse to do something: *The lawyer requested a break in the court case, but the judge* demurred. • **demur** noun [U] *She agreed to his request **without** demur.*

demure /dɪˈmjʊəʳ/ ⓤⓢ /-ˈmjʊr/ adj (especially of women) quiet and well behaved: *She gave him a demure smile.* • **demurely** /-li/ adv *She sat with her hands folded demurely in her lap.* • **demureness** /-nəs/ noun [U]

demurrage /dɪˈmʌr.ɪdʒ/ ⓤⓢ /dɪˈmɝː-/ noun [U] specialized money that must be paid when a CHARTERED (= rented) ship is used for longer than agreed, or when goods are collected later than the agreed time after being taken off a chartered ship

demystify /ˌdiːˈmɪs.tɪ.faɪ/ verb [T] to make something easier to understand: *What I need is a book that will demystify the workings of a car engine for me.*

demythologize (UK usually **demythologise**) /ˌdiː.mɪˈθɒl.ə.dʒaɪz/ ⓤⓢ /-ˈθɑː.lə-/ verb [T] to provide an explanation of something, or to present something, in a way which removes any mystery surrounding it

den /den/ noun [C] **FOR ANIMALS** ▷ **1** the home of particular types of wild animal **FOR CHILDREN** ▷ **2** a rough structure, usually built outside from pieces of wood, cardboard, etc., in which children play **ROOM** ▷ **3** mainly US a room in a house or apartment, used for activities not involving work: *The kids are watching television in the den.* **CRIME** ▷ **4** a place where people secretly plan or take part in dishonest or illegal activities: *a **drug/drinking/vice** den* ◦ often humorous *a den **of thieves/iniquity***

denationalize (UK usually **denationalise**) /ˌdiːˈnæʃ.ən.əl.aɪz/, /ˌdiːˈnæʃ.nə.laɪz/ verb [T] to change an industry from being publicly owned to being privately owned • **denationalization** (UK usually **denationalisation**) /diːˌnæʃ.ə n.əl.aɪˈzeɪ.ʃən/ ⓤⓢ /-əˈ-/ noun [C or U]

deniable /dɪˈnaɪ.ə.bl/ adj possible to DENY: *The facts are simply not deniable.*

denial /dɪˈnaɪ.əl/ noun **NOT TRUE** ▷ **1** Ⓒ2 [C] a statement that something is not true or does not exist: *The prime minister **issued** a denial **of** the report that she is about to resign.* ◦ [+ that] *Officials did not believe the runner's denial **that** he had taken drugs.* ◦ *His denial **of** responsibility for the accident was unconvincing.* **NOT ALLOW** ▷ **2** [U] the fact of not allowing someone to do or have something: ***a** gross denial **of** justice* → See also **self-denial** **NOT ACCEPT** ▷ **3** an unwillingness to accept that something unpleasant is true: *He's still **in denial** about the break-up of his relationship.* **AGAINST BELIEFS** ▷ **4** the situation in which someone behaves in a way that goes against their beliefs and what they think is right: *If I did what you ask, it would be a denial **of** everything I stand for (= believe in).*

denier /ˈden.i.əʳ/ ⓤⓢ /-jɚ/ noun [U] mainly UK a measure of the thickness of the WEAVE (= pattern of threads) of NYLON, SILK, etc. thread, especially thread used in making STOCKINGS or TIGHTS

denigrate /ˈden.ɪ.greɪt/ verb [T] to say that someone or something is not good or important: *You shouldn't denigrate people just because they have different beliefs from you.* • **denigration** /ˌden.ɪˈgreɪ.ʃən/ noun [U]

denim /ˈden.ɪm/ noun [U] **1** Ⓑ2 a thick, strong cotton cloth, often blue in colour, used especially for making JEANS: *a denim jacket and jeans* **2** **denims** UK informal clothes made of denim: *He's usually in denims.*

denitrify /diˈnaɪ.trɪ.faɪ/ verb [T] specialized to break up NITRATES (= chemicals containing NITROGEN and OXYGEN), for example in soil, and so release nitrogen into the air: *Denitrifying bacteria reduce the fertility of the soil.*

• **denitrification** /diˌnaɪ.trɪ.fɪˈkeɪ.ʃən/ noun [U] *biological/bacterial denitrification*

denizen /ˈden.ɪ.zən/ noun [C] literary an animal, plant, or person that lives in or is often in a particular place: *Deer and squirrels are among the denizens **of** the forest.*

denomination /dɪˌnɒm.ɪˈneɪ.ʃən/ ⓤⓢ /-ˌnɑː.mə-/ noun **RELIGIOUS GROUP** ▷ **1** [C, + sing/pl verb] a religious group that has slightly different beliefs from other groups that share the same religion: *Protestantism and Roman Catholicism are both denominations of the Christian faith.* **VALUE** ▷ **2** [C] a unit of value, especially of money: *It always takes time to get used to the different denominations **of** coins when you go to a foreign country.*

denominational /dɪˌnɒm.ɪˈneɪ.ʃən.əl/ ⓤⓢ /-ˌnɑː.mə-/ adj connected with a particular religious denomination → Opposite **non-denominational**

denominator /dɪˈnɒm.ɪ.neɪ.təʳ/ ⓤⓢ /-ˈnɑː.mə.neɪ.t̬ɚ/ noun [C] the number below the line in a FRACTION: *In the fraction ¾, 4 is the denominator.* → Compare **numerator**

denote /dɪˈnəʊt/ ⓤⓢ /-ˈnoʊt/ verb [T] to represent something: *The colour red is used to denote passion or danger.*

denouement /deɪˈnuː.mɒ̃/ ⓤⓢ /-mɑ̃ː/ noun [C] the end of a story, in which everything is explained, or the end result of a situation

denounce /dɪˈnaʊns/ verb [T] **CRITICIZE** ▷ **1** to criticize something or someone strongly and publicly: *The government's economic policy has been denounced on all sides.* **ACCUSE** ▷ **2** to accuse someone publicly of being something that is bad or wrong: *His former colleagues have denounced him **as** a spy.*

dense /dens/ adj **THICK** ▷ **1** Ⓑ2 having parts that are close together so that it is difficult to go or see through: *dense **fog*** ◦ *a dense forest* ◦ *The body was found hidden in dense **undergrowth**.* → Synonym **thick** **STUPID** ▷ **2** informal stupid: *We've got some really dense people in our class.* **MATTER** ▷ **3** specialized (of a substance) containing a lot of matter in a small space: *Plutonium is very dense.*

densely /ˈdens.li/ adv Ⓑ2 with a lot of things close together: *England was once a densely wooded country (= a lot of trees grew close together there).* ◦ *Mexico City is one of the most densely **populated** cities in the world (= a lot of people live close together there).* ◦ *His books tend to be rather densely written (= contain a lot of information and ideas and are difficult to understand).*

density /ˈden.sɪ.ti/ ⓤⓢ /-sə.t̬i/ noun [C or U] **THICKNESS** ▷ **1** Ⓒ1 (also **denseness**) the number of people or things in a place when compared with the size of the place: *The area has a **high/low** population density.* ◦ *We were unable to move because of the density **of** the crowd.* **OF MATTER** ▷ **2** specialized the relationship between the mass of a substance and its size: *Lead **has** a **high** density.* ◦ *Aluminium is **low in** density.*

dent /dent/ noun; verb

▸**noun** [C] a small hollow mark in the surface of something, caused by pressure or by being hit: *a dent in the door of a car*

IDIOM **make/put a dent in sth** to reduce an amount of money: *The holiday made a big dent in our savings.*

▸**verb** [T] **1** to make a small hollow mark in the surface of something: *I dropped a hammer on the floor, and it dented the floorboard.* **2** If you dent someone's confidence or PRIDE, you make them feel less confident or proud: *His confidence was **badly** dented when he didn't get into the football team.*

dental /ˈden.tᵊl/ (US) /-t̬ᵊl/ **adj; noun**
▸**adj** B2 relating to the teeth: *dental decay/treatment*
▸**noun** [C] specialized a speech sound in which your tongue touches your front teeth

ˈ**dental** ˌ**dam** noun [C] a piece of rubber that is used to keep the teeth dry during dental treatment, or that is used to prevent HIV infection during sexual activity in which someone touches someone else's sexual organs with their mouth or tongue

ˈ**dental** ˌ**floss** noun [U] a type of thread used for cleaning between the teeth

ˈ**dental hy**ˌ**gienist** noun [C] a person who works with a dentist and cleans people's teeth to keep them healthy

ˈ**dental prac**ˌ**titioner/**ˌ**surgeon** noun [C] formal a dentist

dentine /ˈden.tiːn/ noun [U] specialized a hard substance containing CALCIUM which forms the main part of a tooth and has ENAMEL (= a shiny white substance) covering it

dentist /ˈden.tɪst/ (US) /-t̬ɪst/ noun [C] **1** A2 a person whose job is treating people's teeth: *You should have your teeth checked by a dentist at least twice a year.* **2 dentist's** the place where a dentist carries out their job: *I've got to go to the dentist's on Friday.*

dentistry /ˈden.tɪ.stri/ (US) /-t̬ɪ-/ noun [U] the work of a dentist

dentition /denˈtɪʃ.ᵊn/ noun [U] specialized the number, type, and arrangement of teeth in a person or animal: *mixed/permanent/mammalian dentition*

dentures /ˈden.tʃəz/ (US) /-tʃɚz/ noun [plural] false teeth fixed to a small piece of plastic or similar material, which fits inside the mouth of someone who does not have their own teeth: *a set of dentures*

denude /dɪˈnjuːd/ (US) /-ˈnuːd/ verb [T] **1** to remove the covering of something, especially land: *The countryside has been denuded by war.* ◦ *Drought and years of heavy grazing by sheep have completely denuded the hills* ***of*** *grass.* **2** to remove a valuable possession or quality: *Any further cuts in the country's armed forces would leave its* ***defences*** *dangerously denuded.*

denunciation /dɪˌnʌn.siˈeɪ.ʃᵊn/ noun [C or U] **CRITICISM** ▷ **1** public criticism of something or someone **ACCUSATION** ▷ **2** the act of accusing someone in public of something bad: *his denunciation as a traitor*

ˌ**Denver** ˈ**boot** noun [C] (also **boot**) US a **wheel clamp**

deny /dɪˈnaɪ/ verb [T] **NOT TRUE** ▷ **1** B2 to say that something is not true: *He will not confirm or deny the* ***allegations.*** ◦ [+ that] *Neil denies* ***that*** *he broke the window, but I'm sure he did.* ◦ [+ -ing verb] *Neil denies break****ing*** *the window.* **2 there's no denying** it is true: *There's no denying* ***that*** *this has been a difficult year for the company.* **REFUSE** ▷ **3** B2 to not allow someone to have or do something: *Her request for time off work was denied.* ◦ *No one should be denied a good education./A good education should be denied* ***to*** *no one.* ◦ [+ two objects] *The goalkeeper denied him his third goal.* ◦ *I was denied the opportunity of learning French at school.* **4 deny yourself** to not allow yourself to have or do things: *Many parents deny themselves so that their children can have the best.* **NOT ADMIT** ▷ **5** to not admit that you have knowledge, responsibility, feelings, etc.: *He denied all responsibility for the rumours which have been circulating.* ◦ *Even under torture, he refused to deny his beliefs/faith.*

deodorant /diˈəʊ.dᵊr.ᵊnt/ (US) /-ˈoʊ.dɚ-/ noun [C or U] C1 a substance that you put on your body to prevent or hide unpleasant smells

dep. written abbreviation for **depart** or **departure** (used in TIMETABLES to show the time at which a bus, train or aircraft leaves a place): *Flight BA174, dep. Heathrow 07.45.*

depart /dɪˈpɑːt/ (US) /-ˈpɑːrt/ verb [I] formal B1 to go away or leave, especially on a journey: *The plane departs at 6 a.m.* ◦ *The train for London departs* ***from*** *platform 2.*

IDIOM **depart this life** to die: *In loving memory of my dear husband, who departed this life on 5 May, 2008.*

PHRASAL VERB **depart from sth** to be different from the usual or expected way of doing or thinking about something: *I see no reason for us to depart from our usual practice.*

departed /dɪˈpɑː.tɪd/ (US) /-ˈpɑːr.t̬ɪd/ **adj; noun**
▸**adj** literary dead: *We will always remember our* ***dear*** *departed friends.*
▸**noun the departed** formal a person who has died, or people who have died: *Let us remember the departed.*

department /dɪˈpɑːt.mənt/ (US) /-ˈpɑːrt-/ noun [C, + sing/pl verb] (written abbreviation **dept**) A2 a part of an organization such as a school, business, or government which deals with a particular area of study or work: *the geography department/the department* ***of*** *geography* ◦ *The accounts department is/are having a Christmas party this week.*

IDIOMS **be sb's department** informal to be a particular person's area of responsibility: *Wasn't buying the tickets your department, Kev?* • **in the brain/looks department** humorous in intelligence or beauty: *He's a bit lacking in the brain department.*

departmental /ˌdiː.pɑːtˈmen.tᵊl/ (US) /-pɑːrtˈmen.t̬ᵊl/ adj relating to a department: *Janet is now a departmental head/manager.* ◦ *a departmental meeting*

deˈ**partment** ˌ**store** noun [C] A2 a large shop divided into several different parts, each of which sells different things

departure /dɪˈpɑː.tʃəʳ/ (US) /-ˈpɑːr.tʃɚ/ noun [C] **LEAVING** ▷ **1** B1 the fact of a person, vehicle, etc. leaving somewhere: *There are several departures (= buses, trains, or aircraft leaving)* ***for*** *Paris every day.* ◦ *Our departure was delayed because of bad weather.* ◦ *departure time* **2** the act of leaving a job: *Everyone in the office was surprised by Graham's sudden departure.* **CHANGE** ▷ **3** a change from what is expected, or from what has happened before: *There can be no departure* ***from*** *the rules.* ◦ *Selling men's clothing is a* ***new*** *departure for the shop.*

deˈ**parture** ˌ**lounge** noun [C usually singular] the area in an airport where passengers wait before getting onto an aircraft

depend /dɪˈpend/ verb [I] **1** B1 to be decided by or to change according to the stated thing: *Whether or not we go to Spain for our holiday depends* ***on*** *the cost.* ◦ [+ question word] *I might go to the cinema tomorrow –* ***it*** *depends* ***wh****at time I get home from work.* **2 it (all) depends** B1 informal it is not decided yet: *'Are you going to Emma's party?' 'I don't know, it depends – we might be going away that weekend.'*

> **!** Common mistake: **depend**
>
> **Remember:** the most usual preposition to use after **depend** is **on**.
>
> Don't say 'depend from/of/at something', say **depend on something**:
>
> ~~*The journey takes half an hour, but it depends from the traffic.*~~

IDIOM **(you can) depend on/upon it** you can be certain: *You haven't heard the last of this, depend upon it.*

PHRASAL VERB **depend on/upon sb/sth** TRUST ▷ **1** B2 to trust someone or something and know that they will help you or do what you want or expect them to do: *You can always depend on Michael in a crisis.* ◦ [+ to infinitive] *I'm depending on you **to** keep your promise.* ◦ [+ -ing verb] *You can't always depend on the trains arriv**ing** on time.* ◦ humorous *You can depend on Jane **to** be late (= she is always late).* SUPPORT ▷ **2** B2 to need something, or need the help and support of someone or something, in order to live or continue as before: *The country depends **heavily** on foreign aid.* ◦ *Elaine depends upon Bob completely **for** her happiness.*

dependable /dɪˈpen.də.bl̩/ **adj** If someone or something is dependable, you can trust them or have confidence in them: *I need someone dependable to look after the children while I'm at work.* ◦ *a dependable car* • **dependability** /dɪˌpen.dəˈbɪl.ɪ.ti/ US /-ə.t̬i/ **noun** [U] *The car offers value for money, comfort, and dependability.* • **dependably** /-bli/ **adv**

dependant (mainly US **dependent**) /dɪˈpen.dᵊnt/ **noun** [C] someone who depends on you for financial support, such as a child or family member who does not work: *My pension will provide for my dependants.*

dependence (US also **dependance**) /dɪˈpen.dᵊns/ **noun** [S or U] (also **dependency**) C2 the situation in which you need something or someone all the time, especially in order to continue existing or operating: *The company needs to reduce its dependence **on** just one particular product.* ◦ *Drug dependence led to her early death.* ◦ *She has developed **a** deep dependence **on** him (= she needs him emotionally).*

dependency /dɪˈpen.dᵊn.si/ **noun** [C] a country that is supported and governed by another country

dependent /dɪˈpen.dᵊnt/ **adj** NEEDING HELP ▷ **1** B2 needing the support of something or someone in order to continue existing or operating: *He has three dependent children.* ◦ *It's very easy to become dependent **on** sleeping pills.* DECIDED BY ▷ **2** **dependent on/upon sth** C1 influenced or decided by something: *Whether I go to university or not is dependent on what exam grades I get.*

deˌpendent ˈclause **noun** [C] specialized in grammar, a CLAUSE that cannot form a separate sentence but can form a sentence when joined with a main clause → Synonym **subordinate clause**

deˌpendent ˈvariable **noun** [C] specialized a number or amount whose value depends on the value of another element in the same mathematical EXPRESSION (= group of symbols representing an amount or idea) → Compare **independent variable**

depersonalize (UK usually **depersonalise**) /ˌdiːˈpɜː.sᵊn.ᵊl.aɪz/ US /-ˈpɜː-/ **verb** [T] to remove from a person, organization, object, etc. the qualities or features which make them particular or special: *He thinks that wearing school uniform depersonalizes children.*

depict /dɪˈpɪkt/ **verb** [T] C2 to represent or show something in a picture or story: *Her paintings depict the lives of ordinary people in the last century.* ◦ *In the book, he depicts his father **as** a tyrant.* ◦ [+ -ing verb] *People were shocked by the advertisement which depicted a woman beat**ing** her husband.*

depiction /dɪˈpɪk.ʃᵊn/ **noun** [C or U] the way that something is represented or shown: *The painter's depictions **of** the horror of war won her a worldwide reputation.* ◦ *I disapprove of the depiction **of** violence on television.*

depilatory /dɪˈpɪl.ə.tᵊr.i/ US /-tɔːr-/ **noun** [C] a substance used for removing unwanted hair from the human body • **depilatory adj** *I use a depilatory **cream** under my arms.*

deplane /ˌdiːˈpleɪn/ **verb** [I] US to leave an aircraft: *Would all passengers please deplane by the rear doors.*

deplete /dɪˈpliːt/ **verb** [T] to reduce something in size or amount, especially supplies of energy, money, etc.: *If we continue to deplete the Earth's natural resources, we will cause serious damage to the environment.* ◦ *The illness depletes the body **of** important vitamins.* ◦ humorous *That last holiday has seriously depleted my bank account!*

depleted /dɪˈpliː.tɪd/ US /-t̬ɪd/ **adj** reduced: *Measures have been taken to protect the world's depleted elephant population.* ◦ *physically/emotionally depleted (= weakened)*

depletion /dɪˈpliː.ʃᵊn/ **noun** [S or U] (a) reduction: *the depletion **of** the ozone layer* ◦ *Increased expenditure has caused a depletion **in** our capital/funds.*

deplorable /dɪˈplɔː.rə.bl̩/ US /-ˈplɔːr.ə-/ **adj** formal very bad: *I thought his behaviour absolutely deplorable.* ◦ *They are forced to live in deplorable conditions.* • **deplorably** /-bli/ **adv** *He behaved deplorably.*

deplore /dɪˈplɔːʳ/ US /-ˈplɔːr/ **verb** [T not continuous] formal to say or think that something is very bad: *We deeply deplore the loss of life.* ◦ *He said that he deplored all violence.* ◦ UK *The attitude of the Minister is **to be** deplored (= is very bad).*

deploy /dɪˈplɔɪ/ **verb** [T] **1** to use something or someone, especially in an effective way: *The company is reconsidering the way in which it deploys its **resources/staff**.* ◦ *My job doesn't really allow me fully to deploy my skills/talents.* **2** to move soldiers or equipment to a place where they can be used when they are needed: *The decision has been made to deploy extra **troops**/more powerful **weapons**.*

deployment /dɪˈplɔɪ.mənt/ **noun** [U] **1** the use of something or someone in an effective way: *the deployment **of** technologies to address this challenge* **2** the movement of soldiers or equipment to a place where they can be used when they are needed: *The Chief of Police ordered the deployment **of** 2,000 troops to try to stop the rioting.*

depopulate /ˌdiːˈpɒp.jʊ.leɪt/ US /-ˈpɑː.pjə-/ **verb** [T] to cause a country or area to have fewer people living in it: *The region was depopulated by disease/famine/war.* • **depopulation** /diːˌpɒp.jʊˈleɪ.ʃᵊn/ US /-ˌpɑː.pjə-/ **noun** [U] *rural depopulation/depopulation **of** the rural areas*

deport /dɪˈpɔːt/ US /-ˈpɔːrt/ **verb** [T] to force someone to leave a country, especially someone who has no legal right to be there or who has broken the law: *Thousands of illegal immigrants are caught and deported every year.* ◦ *The refugees were deported back **to** their country of origin.* • **deportation** /ˌdiː.pɔːˈteɪ.ʃᵊn/ US /-pɔːr-/ **noun** [C or U] *There were **mass** deportations in the 1930s, when thousands of people were forced to leave the country.*

deporˈtation ˌorder **noun** [C] an official document stating that someone must be made to leave a country

deportee /ˌdiː.pɔːˈtiː/ US /-pɔːr-/ **noun** [C] a person who has been or is waiting to be deported

deportment /dɪˈpɔːt.mənt/ US /-ˈpɔːrt-/ **noun** [U] formal **1** the way a person walks and stands: *to have good/bad deportment* ◦ *speech and deportment lessons* **2** the way a person behaves: *Throughout the ordeal of her husband's funeral, Mrs Kennedy was a model of deportment (= behaved in a controlled and calm way).*

depose /dɪˈpəʊz/ (US) /-ˈpoʊz/ **verb** [T] to remove someone important from a powerful position: *Margaret Thatcher was deposed* ***as*** *leader of the British Conservative Party in 1991.* ◦ *King Charles I was deposed* ***from*** *the English throne in 1646.*

deposit /dɪˈpɒz.ɪt/ (US) /-ˈpɑː.zɪt/ **verb; noun**

▸**verb** LEAVE ▷ **1** [T usually + adv/prep] to leave something somewhere: *The flood waters fell, depositing mud over the whole area.* ◦ *The bus deposited me miles from anywhere.* ◦ *I deposited my luggage in a locker at the station.* MONEY ▷ **2** C1 [T] to put something valuable, especially money, in a bank or SAFE (= strong box or cupboard with locks): *There's a night safe outside the bank, so you can deposit money whenever you wish.* ◦ *I deposited £500* ***in*** *my account this morning.* **3** [T] to pay someone an amount of money when you make an agreement with them to pay for or buy something, that either will be returned to you later, if the agreed arrangement is kept, or which forms part of the total payment: *When we moved in, we had to deposit $1,000* ***with*** *the landlord in case we broke any of his things.* ◦ *You deposit 20 percent now and pay the rest when the car is delivered.*

▸**noun** LAYER ▷ **1** C2 [C or U] a substance or layer that is left, usually after a liquid is removed: *Decant the wine carefully, so that you leave the deposit in the bottom of the bottle.* ◦ *The flood left a thick deposit* ***of*** *mud over the entire ground floor of the house.* **2** C2 [C] specialized a layer that has formed under the ground, especially over a long period: *mineral/oil/coal deposits* MONEY ▷ **3** C1 [C] a payment, especially into a bank account: *To open an account, you need to* ***make*** *a minimum deposit* ***of*** *$500.* **4** B1 [C] an amount of money that you pay as the first part of the total payment for something: *The shop assistant says if I* ***leave*** *£10* ***as*** *a deposit, they'll keep the dress for me.* ◦ *We* ***paid/put*** *a deposit* ***of*** *£10,000* ***on*** *the house, and paid the balance four weeks later.* **5** C1 [C] an amount of money that you pay when you rent something, and is returned to you when you return the thing you have rented: *It costs £1,000 a week to hire the yacht, plus a £120* ***refundable/returnable*** *deposit.* ◦ *You pay a 10p deposit/deposit of 10p* ***on*** *the bottle, which you get back when you return the empty bottle.*

deˈposit acˌcount noun [C] UK (US ˈ**savings acˌcount**) a bank account that pays you interest, in which you usually leave money for a long time

deposition /ˌdep.əˈzɪʃ.ən/ **noun** STATEMENT ▷ **1** [C] legal a formal written statement made or used in a law court: *Before the court case, we had to* ***file/give*** *a deposition.* ◦ *Our lawyer* ***took*** *a deposition from us.* ◦ *a* ***sworn*** *deposition* REMOVAL ▷ **2** [U] formal the act of removing someone important from a powerful position

depositor /dɪˈpɒz.ɪ.tər/ (US) /-ˈpɑː.zə.t̬ɚ/ **noun** [C] someone who DEPOSITS money

depository /dɪˈpɒz.ɪ.tər.i/ (US) /-ˈpɑː.zə.tɔːr-/ **noun** [C] a place, especially a large building, for storing things: *The government is having difficulty finding a safe depository* ***for*** *nuclear waste.*

depot /ˈdep.əʊ/ (US) /ˈdiː.poʊ/ **noun** [C] **1** a building where supplies or vehicles, especially buses, are kept: *an arms/weapons depot* ◦ *a fuel/storage depot* ◦ *a bus depot* **2** US a bus station or train station

deprave /dɪˈpreɪv/ **verb** [T] formal to make someone depraved

depraved /dɪˈpreɪvd/ **adj** morally bad or evil: *a depraved character/mind* ◦ *Someone who can kill a child like that must be totally depraved.*

depravity /dɪˈpræv.ə.ti/ (US) /-t̬i/ **noun** [U or C] the state of being morally bad, or an action that is morally bad

deprecate /ˈdep.rə.keɪt/ **verb** formal NOT APPROVE ▷ **1** [T not continuous] to not approve of something or say that you do not approve of something: *We deprecate this use of company funds for political purposes.* NOT VALUE ▷ **2** [T] to say that you think something is of little value or importance: *He always deprecates my achievements.* • **deprecation** /ˌdep.rəˈkeɪ.ʃən/ **noun** [U]

deprecating /ˈdep.rə.keɪ.tɪŋ/ (US) /-t̬ɪŋ/ **adj** (also **deprecatory** /ˈdep.rə.kə.tər.i/ (US) /-tɔːr.i/) NOT VALUING ▷ **1** showing that you think something is of little value or importance: *Her deprecating smile clearly showed that she thought I'd said something stupid.* → See also **self-deprecating** **2** showing that you feel embarrassed, especially by praise: *She reacted to his compliments with a deprecating laugh.* NOT APPROVING ▷ **3** formal showing that you do not approve of something: *The teacher gave the boys a deprecating stare.* • **deprecatingly** /-li/ **adv**

depreciate /dɪˈpriː.ʃi.eɪt/ **verb** [I or T] to (cause something to) lose value, especially over time: *Our car depreciated* ***(by)*** *£1,500 in the first year we owned it.* ◦ *Since they set up a builder's yard next door, our house has depreciated* ***in value.*** → Compare **appreciate**

depreciation /dɪˌpriː.ʃiˈeɪ.ʃən/ **noun** [U] the process of losing value

depredation /ˌdep.rəˈdeɪ.ʃən/ **noun** [C usually plural, U] formal (an act causing) damage or destruction: *The entire area has suffered the depredations* ***of*** *war.* ◦ *Depredation* ***of*** *(= damage done to) the environment is destroying hundreds of species each year.*

depress /dɪˈpres/ **verb** [T] CAUSE SADNESS ▷ **1** to cause someone to feel unhappy and without hope: *This weather depresses me.* ◦ [+ -ing verb] *Doesn't* ***it*** *depress you listen****ing*** *to the news these days?* ◦ [+ to infinitive] ***It*** *depresses me* ***to*** *think that I'll probably still be doing exactly the same job in ten years' time.* REDUCE ▷ **2** to reduce the value of something, especially money: *A surplus of corn has helped depress the grain* ***market****/grain* ***prices.*** ◦ *The rise in the value of the dollar has depressed the company's* ***earnings/profits*** *this year.* **3** to reduce the amount of activity in something, especially a business operation: *High interest rates are continuing to depress the* ***economy.*** **4** to lower the level or amount of something: *This drug helps depress high hormone levels.* PRESS DOWN ▷ **5** formal to press down or lower: *Slowly depress the accelerator/brake pedal.*

depressant /dɪˈpres.ənt/ **noun** [C] a substance which causes you to feel unhappy and without hope: *Alcohol is a depressant.* • **depressant adj** *These drugs have a depressant effect.*

depressed /dɪˈprest/ **adj** SAD ▷ **1** B1 unhappy and without hope: *He seemed a bit depressed* ***about*** *his work situation.* ◦ *She became* ***deeply*** *depressed when her husband died.* REDUCED ▷ **2** C2 not having enough money, jobs, or business activity: *In a depressed market, it's difficult to sell goods unless you lower your prices.* ◦ *an economically depressed area*

depressing /dɪˈpres.ɪŋ/ **adj** B2 making you feel unhappy and without hope for the future: *I find this weather so depressing.* ◦ *Her letter made depressing reading.* ◦ [+ -ing verb] ***It*** *was very depressing watch****ing*** *the news on television tonight.* ◦ [+ to infinitive] ***It's*** *depressing* ***to*** *think that we've got five more years of this government!*

depressingly /dɪˈpres.ɪŋ.li/ **adv** in a way that makes you feel unhappy and without hope for the future:

My score was depressingly low. ◦ *The story was depressingly familiar.*

depression /dɪˈpreʃ.ən/ noun **UNHAPPINESS** ▷ **1** B2 [U] the state of feeling very unhappy and without hope for the future: *I was overwhelmed by feelings of depression.* **2** B2 [C or U] a mental illness in which a person is very unhappy and ANXIOUS (= worried and nervous) for long periods and cannot have a normal life during these periods: *Tiredness, loss of appetite, and sleeping problems are all classic symptoms of depression.* ◦ *If you **suffer from** depression, it's best to get professional help.* → See also **clinical depression** **NO ACTIVITY** ▷ **3** C2 [C] a period in which there is very little business activity and not many jobs: *The stock market crash marked the start of a severe depression.* **WEATHER** ▷ **4** [C] specialized an area where the air pressure is low: *The deep depression **over** the mid-Atlantic will gradually move eastwards during the day.* **HOLE** ▷ **5** [C] a part in a surface that is slightly lower than the rest: *There was a depression in the sand where he'd been lying.*

depressive /dɪˈpres.ɪv/ noun; adj
▸noun [C] a person who often suffers from depression
▸adj suffering from or relating to depression: *a depressive personality* ◦ *a depressive disorder/illness*

depressurize specialized (UK usually **depressurise**) /ˌdiːˈpreʃ.ə.raɪz/ verb [I or T] to (cause a closed space, especially the inside of an aircraft to) become lower in air pressure: *If the cabin depressurizes, oxygen masks will automatically drop down.*

deprivation /ˌdep.rɪˈveɪ.ʃən/ noun [C or U] C2 a situation in which you do not have things or conditions that are usually considered necessary for a pleasant life: *They used sleep deprivation as a form of torture.* ◦ *There is awful deprivation in the shanty towns.*

deprive /dɪˈpraɪv/ verb [T] B2 to take something, especially something necessary or pleasant, away from someone: *He claimed that he had been deprived **of** his freedom/rights.* ◦ *You can't function properly when you're deprived **of** sleep.*

deprived /dɪˈpraɪvd/ adj C1 not having the things that are necessary for a pleasant life, such as enough money, food or good living conditions: *She had a deprived childhood/comes from a deprived background.* ◦ *a deprived area*

dept noun written abbreviation for **department**

depth /depθ/ noun **DISTANCE DOWN** ▷ **1** B1 [C or U] the distance down either from the top of something to the bottom, or to a distance below the top surface of something: *the depth **of** a lake/pond* ◦ *There are very few fish **at** depths (= distances below the surface) below 3,000 metres.* ◦ *The river froze **to** a depth **of** over a metre.* **2 the depths** [plural] literary the lowest part of the sea: *The ship sank slowly to the depths **of** the ocean.* **SERIOUSNESS** ▷ **3** B2 [C or U] the state of having serious qualities or the ability to think seriously about something: *Terry **lacks** depth – he's a very superficial person.* ◦ *Her writing shows astonishing depth.* ◦ *Jo has **hidden** depths (= serious qualities that you do not see immediately).* **4 in depth** B2 in a serious and detailed way: *I'd like to look at this question in some depth.* **DISTANCE BACKWARDS** ▷ **5** [C or U] the distance from the front to the back of something: *Measure the depth **of** the cupboard/shelf.* **STRENGTH** ▷ **6** C2 [C or U] the fact of a feeling, state, or characteristic being strong, extreme, or detailed: *He spoke with great depth **of** feeling.* ◦ *I was amazed at the depth of her **knowledge**.* **7 in the depth(s) of sth a** experiencing an extreme and negative emotion: *He was in the depths of **despair/depression** about losing his job.* **b** during the worst period of a bad situation: *The company was started in the depth of the recession of the 1930s.* **LOW SOUND** ▷ **8** [U] the quality of having a low sound: *The depth **of** his voice makes him sound older than he is.* **DARKNESS** ▷ **9** [U] the fact of something, especially a colour, having the quality of being dark and strong: *I love the depth **of** colour in her early paintings.*

IDIOMS **in the depth(s) of somewhere** in the middle of somewhere, and a long distance from its edges: *a house in the depths of the forest* • **in the depth(s) of winter** in the middle of winter • **out of your depth** **1** C2 not having the knowledge, experience, or skills to deal with a particular subject or situation: *I was out of my depth in the advanced class, so I moved to the intermediate class.* **2** in water that is so deep that it goes over your head when you are standing: *I'm not a strong swimmer so I prefer not to go out of my depth.*

ˈdepth ˌcharge noun [C] a bomb that explodes underwater

deputation /ˌdep.jʊˈteɪ.ʃən/ noun [C, + sing/pl verb] a group of people sent to speak or act for others: *They sent a deputation **to** Parliament.* ◦ *The deputation **from** the EU arrives/arrive tomorrow.* ◦ *a deputation **of** local government officials* ◦ *She was sent **on** a deputation **to** see the Pope.*

depute /dɪˈpjuːt/ verb [T] formal to ask someone to act or speak for you: [+ to infinitive] *I've deputed Lara Brown **to** speak for me at the conference.*

deputize (UK usually **deputise**) /ˈdep.jʊ.taɪz/ verb [I] to act or speak for another person, especially at work: *I'm deputizing **for** (= doing the job of) the director during his absence.*

deputy /ˈdep.jʊ.ti/ US /-t̬i/ noun [C] C1 a person who is given the power to do something instead of another person, or the person whose rank is immediately below that of the leader of an organization: *I'd like you to meet Ann Gregory, my deputy.* ◦ *I'm **acting as** deputy while the boss is away.* ◦ *She's deputy (head) **of** a large North London school.* ◦ *the deputy chairperson/manager/sheriff*

derail /ˌdiːˈreɪl/ verb **TRAIN** ▷ **1** [I or T] If a train derails or is derailed, it comes off the railway tracks. **PLAN** ▷ **2** [T] to prevent a plan or process from succeeding: *Renewed fighting threatens to derail the peace talks.* • **derailment** /-mənt/ noun [C or U]

deranged /dɪˈreɪndʒd/ adj completely unable to think clearly or behave in a controlled way, especially because of mental illness: *a deranged criminal/mind/personality* ◦ *to be **mentally** deranged* • **derangement** /-mənt/ noun [U]

derby /ˈdɑː.bi/ US /ˈdɝː-/ noun [C] **SPORTING EVENT** ▷ **1** a sports event between teams in the same area: *a **local** derby between Manchester United and Manchester City* **2** mainly US a sports event in which any competitor can take part: *the annual New Hampshire fishing derby* **HAT** ▷ **3** US for **bowler hat**

Derby /ˈdɑː.bi/ US /ˈdɝː-/ noun [C usually singular] a type of horse race: *the Epsom/Kentucky Derby*

derecognize (UK usually **derecognise**) /ˌdiːˈrek.əg.naɪz/ verb [T] to no longer accept that something is true, legal, or important → Opposite **recognize**

deregulate /ˌdiːˈreg.jʊ.leɪt/ verb [T] to remove national or local government controls or rules from a business or other activity: *The government plans to deregulate the banking industry/the bus system.* • **deregulation** /ˌdiː.reg.jʊˈleɪ.ʃən/ noun [U] *Couldn't the deregulation **of** broadcasting lead to a lowering of standards?*

derelict /ˈder.ə.lɪkt/ adj; noun
▸adj describes buildings or places that are not cared for and are in bad condition: *a derelict site* ◦ *The theatre has been left to **stand/lie** derelict.*
▸noun [C] formal a person who has no home or money and often lives outside

dereliction /ˌder.əˈlɪk.ʃən/ noun **FAILURE** ▷ **1** [C or U] (a) failure to do what you should do: *What you did was a grave dereliction **of duty**.* **IN BAD CONDITION** ▷ **2** [U] (especially of a building) a state of not being cared for: *The old railway cottages were in a state of dereliction.*

deride /dɪˈraɪd/ verb [T] formal to laugh at someone or something in a way which shows you think they are stupid or of no value: *He derided my singing **as** pathetic.* ◦ *This building, once derided by critics, is now a major tourist attraction.*

de rigueur /də.rɪˈgɜːʳ/ ⓤⓢ /-ˈgɝː/ adj [after verb] formal demanded by fashion, custom, etc.: *Where I work, smart suits are de rigueur **for** the women.*

derision /dɪˈrɪʒ.ən/ noun [U] formal the situation in which someone or something is laughed at and considered stupid or of no value: *They treated his suggestion **with** derision.* ◦ *Her speech was met with **hoots/howls of** derision.*

derisive /dɪˈraɪ.sɪv/ adj (also **derisory**) showing derision: *derisive laughter* ◦ *a derisive comment/remark* • **derisively** /-li/ adv

derisory /dɪˈraɪ.sər.i/ ⓤⓢ /-ɚ.i/ adj formal disapproving describes an amount that is so small it is silly: *We were awarded a derisory sum.*

derivation /ˌder.ɪˈveɪ.ʃən/ noun [C or U] the origin of something, such as a word, from which another form has developed, or the new form itself

derivative adj; noun
▸adj /dɪˈrɪv.ə.tɪv/ ⓤⓢ /-t̬ɪv/ disapproving If something is derivative, it is not the result of new ideas, but has been developed from or copies something else: *His painting/style is very derivative.*
▸noun [C] /dɪˈrɪv.ɪ.tɪv/ ⓤⓢ /-ə.t̬ɪv/ specialized **FORM OF WORD, ETC.** ▷ **1** a form of something, such as a word, made or developed from another form: *'Detestable' is a derivative **of** 'detest'.* **FINANCIAL PRODUCT** ▷ **2** a financial product such as an OPTION (= the right to buy or sell something in the future) that has a value based on the value of another product, such as SHARES or BONDS

derive /dɪˈraɪv/ verb **derive sth from sth** Ⓒ1 to get something from something else: *The institute derives all its money from foreign investments.* ◦ *She derives great pleasure/satisfaction from playing the violin.*

PHRASAL VERB **derive from sth** [often passive] Ⓒ1 to come from something: *The English word 'olive' is derived from the Latin word 'oliva'.*

dermatitis /ˌdɜː.məˈtaɪ.təs/ ⓤⓢ /ˌdɝː.məˈtaɪ.t̬əs/ noun [U] specialized a disease in which the skin is red and painful

dermatologist /ˌdɜː.məˈtɒl.ə.dʒɪst/ ⓤⓢ /ˌdɝː.məˈtɑː.lə-/ noun [C] a doctor who studies and treats skin diseases

dermatology /ˌdɜː.məˈtɒl.ə.dʒi/ ⓤⓢ /ˌdɝː.məˈtɑː.lə-/ noun [U] the scientific study of the skin and its diseases

dermis /ˈdɜː.mɪs/ ⓤⓢ /ˈdɝː-/ noun [S] specialized the thick layer of skin under the EPIDERMIS (= thin outer layer) that contains BLOOD VESSELS, SWEAT GLANDS and NERVE ENDINGS

derogate /ˈder.ə.geɪt/ verb [T] formal **CRITICIZE** ▷ **1** to talk about or treat someone or something in a way that shows you do not respect them or it **LAW** ▷ **2** to officially state that a law or rule no longer needs to be obeyed because it no longer has any authority

PHRASAL VERB **derogate from sth MAKE LESS GOOD** ▷ **1** to make something seem less good or important **IGNORE RULES** ▷ **2** to not behave according to the rules of an agreement, acceptable behaviour, etc.

derogation /ˌder.əˈgeɪ.ʃən/ noun [U] formal **CRITICISM** ▷ **1** the act of talking about or treating someone in a way that shows you do not respect them or it **LAW** ▷ **2** the act of officially stating that a law or rule no longer needs to be obeyed

derogatory /dɪˈrɒg.ə.tər.i/, /-tri/ ⓤⓢ /-ˈrɑː.gə.tɔːr-/ adj showing strong disapproval and not showing respect: *He made some derogatory **comment/remark** about her appearance.*

derrick /ˈder.ɪk/ noun [C] specialized **1** a type of CRANE (= a machine with a part like an arm) used for moving things on and off ships **2** a tower above an OIL WELL which supports the DRILL (= machine for making a hole in the ground)

derricks

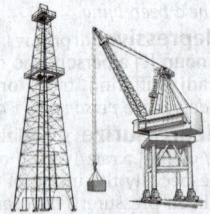

derrière /ˈder.i.eəʳ/ ⓤⓢ /-ˈer/ noun [C] humorous a person's bottom

derring-do /ˌder.ɪŋˈduː/ noun [U] old-fashioned or humorous brave action taken without considering the danger involved: ***deeds/feats of** derring-do*

derv /dɜːv/ ⓤⓢ /dɝːv/ noun [U] UK a type of liquid fuel used especially in trucks

dervish /ˈdɜː.vɪʃ/ ⓤⓢ /ˈdɝː-/ noun [C] a member of a Muslim religious group that has an energetic dance as part of its worship: *The children were spinning around like **whirling** dervishes.*

desalinate /ˌdiːˈsæl.ɪ.neɪt/ verb [T] to remove salt from sea water

desalination /ˌdiː.sæl.ɪˈneɪ.ʃən/ ⓤⓢ /diːˌsæl-/ noun [U] the process of removing salt from sea water: *a desalination **plant** (= factory)*

descale /ˌdiːˈskeɪl/ verb [T] to remove SCALE (= a layer of hard white material) from something: *This kettle needs descaling.*

descant /ˈdes.kænt/ noun [C] a part of a piece of music that is higher than the main tune: *Shall I sing the descant in the last verse?*

ˌdescant reˈcorder noun [C] a RECORDER (= a wind instrument) with a high sound

descend /dɪˈsend/ verb **POSITION** ▷ **1** Ⓑ2 [I or T] formal to go or come down: *The path descended steeply into the valley.* ◦ *Jane descended the stairs.* **2** [I] literary If darkness or night descends, it becomes dark and day changes to night. **NEGATIVE MOOD** ▷ **3** [I] literary If a negative or bad feeling descends, it is felt everywhere in a place or by everyone at the same time: *A feeling of despair descended (**on** us) as we realized that we were lost.* **4** [I] literary If a condition, usually a negative condition, descends, it quickly develops in every part of a place: *Silence descended **on** the room/**over** the countryside.*

PHRASAL VERBS **descend from sth 1** to have developed from something that existed in the past: *All living creatures are thought to descend from an organism that came into being three billion years ago.* **2 be descended from sb** Ⓒ2 to be related to a particular person or group of people who lived in the past: *Her* *father is descended from Greek royalty.* ◦ *Humans are descended from (= developed from) ape-like creatures.* • **descend into sth** formal If a situation descends into a particular state, it becomes worse: *The demonstrations in the capital rapidly descended into anarchy.* • **descend on/upon sb/sth** If a group of people descend on a place or person, they arrive, usually without warning or without being invited: *Sorry to descend on you like this, but we had no time to phone.* ◦ *The police descended on the house in the early hours of the morning.* • **descend to sth** to behave badly in a way that other people would not expect you to: *I never thought she would descend to stealing.*

descendant /dɪˈsen.dənt/ noun [C] C2 a person who is related to someone and who lives after them, such as their child or GRANDCHILD: *He has no descendants.* ◦ *They claim to be descendants **of** a French duke.* → Compare **ancestor**

descent /dɪˈsent/ noun **RELATION** ▷ **1** [U] the state or fact of being related to a particular person or group of people who lived in the past: *She's a woman **of** mixed/French descent.* ◦ *They trace their **line of** descent back to a French duke.* ◦ *He claims **direct** descent **from** Mohammed.* **ARRIVAL** ▷ **2** [U] an occasion when a group of people arrive somewhere, usually suddenly or unexpectedly: *We weren't prepared for the descent of thousands of journalists **on** the town.* **POSITION** ▷ **3** [C or U] a movement down: *The plane began (to **make**) its **final** descent into the airport.* ◦ *There is a steep descent (= way down, such as a path) to the village below.* **NEGATIVE CHANGE** ▷ **4** [S or U] a change in someone's behaviour, or in a situation, from good to bad: *His descent **into** crime was rapid.*

describe /dɪˈskraɪb/ verb [T] **1** A2 to say or write what someone or something is like: *Could you describe your attacker?* ◦ *He described the painting **in detail**.* ◦ [+ question word] *Let me describe (**to** you) **how** it happened.* ◦ *She described Gary **as** shy.* **2** formal If you describe a shape, you draw it or move in a direction that follows the line of it: *He used compasses to describe a circle.*

description /dɪˈskrɪp.ʃən/ noun [C or U] **1** B1 something that tells you what something or someone is like: *Write a description **of** your favourite seaside resort.* ◦ *She has **given** the police a very **detailed/full** description **of** the robber.* ◦ *A girl **answering** (= matching) the description **of** the missing teenager was spotted in Hull.* ◦ *Your essay contains too much description, and not enough discussion of the issues.* **2 of every description** of all types: *Boats of every description were entering the harbour.* **3 be beyond description** (also **defy description**) to be something that you cannot describe accurately because of its great size, quality, or level: *Her beauty is beyond description.* ◦ *The mess in Bart's room defies description (= is very bad)!*

> Word partners for **description**
>
> *give* a description • *fit/match* a description • an *accurate/complete/detailed/full* description • a *brief/short* description • a description *of* sth/sb

descriptive /dɪˈskrɪp.tɪv/ adj describing something, especially in a detailed, interesting way: *a descriptive essay/passage*

desecrate /ˈdes.ɪ.kreɪt/ verb [T] to damage or show no respect towards something holy or very much respected: *The mosque/shrine was desecrated by vandals.* • **desecration** /ˌdes.ɪˈkreɪ.ʃən/ noun [U] *People were horrified at the desecration **of** the cemetery.*

desegregate /ˌdiːˈseg.rɪ.geɪt/ verb [T] to end SEGREGATION (= separation) between races or sexes in an organization: *President Truman desegregated the American armed forces in 1948.* ◦ *Plans to desegregate the schools/universities met with opposition.* • **desegregation** /ˌdiː.seg.rɪˈgeɪ.ʃən/ noun [U]

deselect /ˌdiː.səˈlekt/ verb [T often passive] UK specialized to choose, as a local political party, not to have the person who now represents your party as your CANDIDATE at the next election • **deselection** noun [U]

desensitize (UK usually **desensitise**) /ˌdiːˈsen.sɪ.taɪz/ verb [T] to cause someone to experience something, usually an emotion or a pain, less strongly than before: *Seeing too much violence on television can desensitize people **to** it.* • **desensitization** (UK usually **desensitisation**) /diˌsen.sɪ.taɪˈzeɪ.ʃən/ noun [U]

desert noun; verb

▸noun [C or U] /ˈdez.ət/ US /-ət/ **1** A2 an area, often covered with sand or rocks, where there is very little rain and not many plants: *They were lost **in** the desert for nine days.* ◦ *We had to cross a large area of arid, featureless desert.* ◦ *the desert sun* **2 cultural, intellectual, etc. desert** disapproving a place that is considered to have no cultural, intellectual, etc. quality or interest: *This town is a cultural desert.*

▸verb /dɪˈzɜːt/ US /-ˈzɝːt/ **RUN AWAY** ▷ **1** [I or T] to leave the armed forces without permission and with no intention of returning: *Soldiers who deserted and were caught were shot.* ◦ *How many people desert **from** the army each year?* **LEAVE BEHIND** ▷ **2** [T] to leave someone without help or in a difficult situation and not come back: *He deserted his wife and family **for** another woman.* **3** [T] If a quality deserts you, you suddenly and temporarily lose it: *All my confidence/courage deserted me when I walked into the exam room.*

deserted /dɪˈzɜː.tɪd/ US /-ˈzɝː.t̬ɪd/ adj **EMPTY** ▷ **1** C1 If a place is deserted, there are no people in it: *a deserted building/street* ◦ *The coastal resorts are deserted (= do not have many visitors) in winter.* **LEFT BEHIND** ▷ **2** left alone in a difficult situation: *a deserted wife*

deserter /dɪˈzɜː.tər/ US /-ˈzɝː.t̬ɚ/ noun [C] a person who leaves the armed forces without permission

desertification /dɪˌzɜː.tɪ.fɪˈkeɪ.ʃən/ US /-ˌzɝː.t̬ə-/ noun [U] specialized the process by which land changes into desert, for example because there has been too much farming activity on it or because a lot of trees have been cut down

desertion /dɪˈzɜː.ʃən/ US /-ˈzɝː-/ noun **1** [C or U] the act of leaving the armed forces without permission: *During the war, desertion was punishable by death.* ◦ *There were thousands of desertions in the last weeks of the war.* ◦ figurative *There have been **mass** desertions **from** (= a lot of people have left) the party in recent months.* **2** [U] the act of leaving someone behind in a difficult situation: *Roger got his divorce on the grounds of desertion (= because his wife had left him).*

ˌdesert ˈisland noun [C] an island, especially in a warm region, where no people live

deserts /dɪˈzɜːts/ US /-ˈzɝːts/ noun [plural] **get your just deserts** to get what you deserve: *I'd say he got his just deserts **for** not sticking around to help with the children.*

deserve /dɪˈzɜːv/ US /-ˈzɝːv/ verb [T not continuous] B1 to have earned or to be given something because of the way you have behaved or the qualities you have: *After all that hard work, you deserve a holiday.* ◦ *Chris deserves our special **thanks** for all his efforts.* ◦ *I hope* they get the ***punishment*** they deserve. ◦ [+ to infinitive] *They certainly deserved **to** win that match.*

IDIOMS **sb deserves a medal** humorous said when you admire someone for dealing with a difficult person or situation for a long time: *She deserves a medal **for** putting up with that husband of hers.* • **he/she deserves whatever/everything he/she gets** said if you think someone should have to suffer because of their bad behaviour: *After all the harm she's done, she deserves whatever she gets.*

D

deserved /dɪˈzɜːvd/ Ⓤⓢ /-ˈzɝːvd/ **adj** describes something that you earn or are given because of your behaviour or qualities: *a **well**-deserved holiday/rest* ◦ *Their victory was **richly/thoroughly** deserved.*

deservedly /dɪˈzɜː.vɪd.li/ Ⓤⓢ /-ˈzɝː-/ **adv** If something happens to you deservedly, you deserve it to happen: *He won the award for best actor, **and** deservedly **so**.*

deserving /dɪˈzɜː.vɪŋ/ Ⓤⓢ /-ˈzɝː-/ **adj 1** If people or things are deserving, they should be helped because they have good qualities: *a deserving **cause/charity*** **2 be deserving of sth** formal to deserve to get something: *His efforts are certainly deserving of praise.*

desiccated /ˈdes.ɪ.keɪ.tɪd/ Ⓤⓢ /-t̬ɪd/ **adj** dried: *100 g of desiccated **coconut***

desiccation /ˌdes.ɪˈkeɪ.ʃən/ **noun** [U] specialized the process of becoming completely dried

design /dɪˈzaɪn/ **verb; noun**

▸**verb PLAN** ▷ **1** B1 [I or T] to make or draw plans for something, for example clothes or buildings: *Who designed this building/dress/furniture?* ◦ *This range of clothing is specially designed **for** shorter women.* **INTEND** ▷ **2** B2 [T usually passive] to intend: *This dictionary is designed **for** advanced learners of English.* ◦ [+ to infinitive] *These measures are designed **to** reduce pollution.*

▸**noun PLAN** ▷ **1** C1 [C] a drawing or set of drawings showing how a building or product is to be made and how it will work and look: *Have you seen the designs **for** the new shopping centre?* **2** B1 [U] (also **designing**) the art of making plans or drawings for something: *She's an expert on kitchen/software design.* ◦ *He's studying design at college.* **3** B1 [S or U] the way in which something is planned and made: *I don't like the design **of** this kettle.* ◦ *The building was originally Victorian **in** design.* ◦ *a serious design **fault*** ◦ *The car has some excellent design **features**.* **PATTERN** ▷ **4** B1 [C] a pattern used to decorate something: *a floral/abstract design* ◦ *I like the design **on** your sweatshirt.* **INTENTION** ▷ **5 by design** intentionally: *I'm sure he ignored you by accident and not by design.* **6 designs** [plural] plans, often ones that are not honest, to get something or someone for yourself: *to **have** territorial designs (**on** neighbouring countries)* ◦ humorous *I think Alan **has** designs **on** your job/wife!*

designate **verb; adj**

▸**verb** [T] /ˈdez.ɪg.neɪt/ **1** to choose someone officially to do a particular job: *Traditionally, the president designates his or her successor.* ◦ *Thompson has been designated (**as/to be**) team captain.* ◦ [+ to infinitive] *She has been designated **to** organize the meeting.* **2** to say officially that a place or thing has a particular character or purpose: *This area of the park has been **specially** designated **for** children.* ◦ *They officially designated the area (**as**) unsuitable for human habitation.*

▸**adj** [after noun] /ˈdez.ɪg.nət/, /-neɪt/ used after the title of a particular official job to refer to someone chosen to do that job, but who has not yet started doing it: *the Secretary General/Managing Director designate* → Compare **-elect**

ˌdesignated ˈdriver **noun** [C] one person in a group who agrees not to drink alcohol in order to drive the other people to and from a place where they will drink alcohol: *Tom said he'd be the designated driver when we go out tonight.*

designation /ˌdez.ɪgˈneɪ.ʃən/ **noun 1** [C] an official title or name: *What's her official designation now she's been promoted?* **2** [U] the act of designating a place or thing: *The area qualifies for designation **as** a site of special scientific interest.*

designer /dɪˈzaɪ.nəʳ/ Ⓤⓢ /-nɚ/ **noun; adj**

▸**noun** [C] B1 a person who imagines how something could be made and draws plans for it: *a fashion/software/theatrical designer*

▸**adj** [before noun] B2 made by a famous or fashionable designer: *designer jeans/sunglasses* ◦ *I can't afford designer **labels**/designer **label** clothes.*

deˈsigner ˌbaby **noun** [C] a baby whose GENES have been chosen by its parents and doctors so that it has particular characteristics

deˈsigner ˌdrug **noun** [C] any of various strong drugs that has been changed to give it a similar effect to an illegal drug such as COCAINE

deˌsigner ˈstubble **noun** [U] a BEARD (= hair on the chin) that has grown for one or two days and is then kept at this length in order to look fashionable

designing /dɪˈzaɪ.nɪŋ/ **adj** [before noun] formal describes someone who tries to get what they want for themselves, usually dishonestly

desirability /dɪˌzaɪə.rəˈbɪl.ɪ.ti/ Ⓤⓢ /dɪˌzaɪr.əˈbɪl.ə.t̬i/ **noun** [U] **1** the quality of being sexually attractive: *She need have no doubts about her desirability.* **2** the quality of being worth having: *Too much emphasis is placed on the desirability **of** being thin.*

desirable /dɪˈzaɪə.rə.bl̩/ Ⓤⓢ /-ˈzaɪr.ə-/ **adj WANTED** ▷ **1** B2 worth having and wanted by most people: *Reducing class sizes in schools is a desirable aim.* ◦ *It's regarded as a **highly** desirable job.* ◦ *The house is in a very desirable area of the city.* **ATTRACTIVE** ▷ **2** sexually attractive: *a **highly** desirable man* • **desirably** /-bli/ **adv**

desire /dɪˈzaɪəʳ/ Ⓤⓢ /-ˈzaɪr/ **verb; noun**

▸**verb** [T not continuous] formal **WANT** ▷ **1** C1 to want something, especially strongly: *I desire only to be left in peace.* ◦ *The hotel had everything you could possibly desire.* ◦ *What does her Ladyship desire me **to** do/desire **of** me?* ◦ [+ to infinitive] *The president desires **to** meet the new prime minister.* **SEXUAL** ▷ **2** to have a strong sexual attraction to someone

▸**noun WANT** ▷ **1** B2 [C or U] a strong feeling that you want something: *I certainly **have no** desire to have children.* ◦ *There is a strong desire **for** peace among the people.* ◦ *He needed to **satisfy** his desire **for** revenge.* ◦ [+ to infinitive] *She **had** a **burning/strong** desire **to** go back to her home country before she died.* **SEXUAL NEED** ▷ **2** [U] formal the strong feeling that you want to have sex with someone: *sexual desire* ◦ *Beatrice was the **object of** Dante's desire.*

IDIOM **sb's heart's desire** something that you want very much

desired /dɪˈzaɪəd/ Ⓤⓢ /-ˈzaɪrd/ **adj** C2 that is wanted: *His words had the desired **effect**.*

desirous /dɪˈzaɪə.rəs/ Ⓤⓢ /dəˈzaɪr.əs/ **adj** [after verb] old-fashioned formal wanting something: *The duke is desirous **of** meeting you.*

desist /dɪˈsɪst/ **verb** [I] formal to stop doing something, especially something that someone else does not want you to do: *The soldiers have been ordered to desist* *from firing their guns.* ◦ *The high winds are expected to desist tomorrow.*

desk /desk/ noun [C] **TABLE** ▷ **1** A1 a type of table that you can work at, often one with drawers: *an office/ school desk* ◦ *She sat* ***at*** *her desk writing letters.* ◦ *He had a pile of papers* ***on*** *his desk.* ◦ *The report arrived on/ landed on/reached my desk (= I received it) this morning.* **SERVICE AREA** ▷ **2** a place, often with a COUNTER (= a long flat narrow surface) especially in a hotel or airport, where you can get information or service: *a check-in/information/reception desk* **NEWSPAPER OFFICE** ▷ **3** an office which deals with a particular type of news for a newspaper or broadcasting company: *the foreign/sports desk*

deskbound /ˈdesk.baʊnd/ adj describes someone who has to work in an office, sitting at a desk

ˈdesk ˌclerk noun [C] US someone who is employed to welcome hotel guests when they arrive

deskill /ˌdiːˈskɪl/ verb [T] to reduce the amount of skill that someone needs to do a particular job: *New technology has been used to deskill many jobs.*

ˈdesk ˌjob noun [C] a job working in an office

ˈdesk ˌtidy noun [C] UK (US **ˈdesk ˌorganizer**) a container for holding pens, pencils, etc. that is kept on top of a desk

desktop /ˈdesk.tɒp/ US /-tɑːp/ noun **COMPUTING** ▷ **1** B2 [C] a view on a computer screen that contains ICONS (= small symbols or pictures) representing files, programs, and other features of the computer: *The menu bar with its windows is one of the features of the desktop.* **2** B2 [C] (also **desktop computer**) a type of computer that is small enough to fit on the top of a desk → Compare **laptop, notebook, palmtop** **FURNITURE** ▷ **3** [C usually singular] the top of a desk • **desktop** adj [before noun] *a desktop device/printer/system*

ˌdesktop ˈpublishing noun [U] (abbreviation **DTP**) the production of finished page designs for books or other printed material, using a small computer and printer

desolate /ˈdes.əl.ət/ adj **EMPTY** ▷ **1** describes a place that is empty and not attractive, with no people or nothing pleasant in it: *The house stood in a bleak and desolate landscape.* **SAD** ▷ **2** extremely sad and feeling alone: *She* ***felt*** *desolate when her closest friend moved away.* • **desolated** /ˈdes.əl.eɪ.tɪd/ US /-t̬ɪd/ adj [after verb] *She was desolated* ***at*** *the loss of her sister.* • **desolately** /-li/ adv

desolation /ˌdes.əlˈeɪ.ʃən/ noun [U] **EMPTINESS** ▷ **1** the state of a place that is empty or where everything has been destroyed: *a* ***scene of*** *desolation* **SADNESS** ▷ **2** the state of feeling sad and alone: *a feeling of utter desolation*

despair /dɪˈspeəʳ/ US /-ˈsper/ noun; verb

▸noun [U] **1** B2 the feeling that there is no hope and that you can do nothing to improve a difficult or worrying situation: *a* ***mood/sense of*** *despair* ◦ *They're* ***in*** *(****the depths of****) despair* ***over/about*** *the money they've lost.* ◦ ***To*** *her teacher's despair, Nicole never does the work that she's told to do.* ◦ *Their fourth year without rain* ***drove*** *many farmers* ***to*** *despair.* **2 be the despair of sb** to cause someone such difficulties that they do not know how to deal with you: *He's the despair of his parents because he shows no interest in getting a job.*

▸verb [I] to feel despair about something or someone: *Don't despair! We'll find a way out!* ◦ *I despair* ***at/over*** *the policies of this government.* ◦ *They began to despair* ***of*** *ever being rescued.* • **despairing** /-ˈspeə.rɪŋ/ US /-ˈsper.ɪŋ/ adj *a despairing glance/cry* • **despairingly** /-ˈspeə.rɪŋ.li/ US /-ˈsper.ɪŋ.li/ adv *He rubbed his hand despairingly over his face.*

despatch /dɪˈspætʃ/ noun, verb **dispatch**

desperado /ˌdes.pəˈrɑː.dəʊ/ US /-doʊ/ noun [C] (plural **desperados** or **desperadoes**) someone who is willing to do things that involve risk or danger, and often criminal things: *a gang of desperados*

desperate /ˈdes.pər.ət/ US /-pɚ-/ adj **SERIOUS** ▷ **1** C2 very serious or bad: *desperate poverty* ◦ *a desperate* ***shortage*** *of food/supplies* ◦ *The* ***situation*** *is desperate – we have no food, very little water and no medical supplies.* **2** very great or extreme: *The earthquake survivors are in desperate need of help.* ◦ *He has a desperate desire to succeed.* ◦ informal *I'm in a desperate hurry.* **WANTING** ▷ **3** B2 [usually after verb] needing or wanting something very much: *They are desperate* ***for*** *help.* ◦ humorous *I'm desperate* ***for*** *a drink!* ◦ [+ to infinitive] *He was desperate* ***to*** *tell someone his good news.* **RISKY** ▷ **4** B2 feeling that you have no hope and are ready to do anything to change the bad situation you are in: *The doctors made one last desperate* ***attempt/effort*** *to save the boy's life.* ◦ *Desperate* ***measures*** *are needed to deal with the growing drug problem.* ◦ *They made a desperate* ***plea*** *for help.* **5** willing to be violent, and therefore dangerous: *This man is desperate and should not be approached as he may have a gun.*

desperately /ˈdes.pər.ət.li/ US /-pɚ-/ adv **SERIOUSLY** ▷ **1** B2 extremely or very much: *He was desperately ill.* ◦ *She always seems to be desperately busy!* ◦ *I'm not desperately keen on football.* ◦ *They desperately wanted a child.* **TAKING RISKS** ▷ **2** B2 in a way that shows you are frightened and ready to try anything to change a situation: *They fought desperately for their lives.*

desperation /ˌdes.pəˈreɪ.ʃən/ noun [U] **1** C2 the feeling that you have when you are in such a bad situation that you are willing to take risks in order to change it: *There was a note of desperation in his voice.* ◦ ***In*** *desperation, they jumped out of the window to escape the fire.* ◦ ***an act of*** *desperation* **2** the feeling of needing or wanting something very much: *his desperation to survive*

despicable /dɪˈspɪk.ə.bl̩/ adj very unpleasant or bad, causing strong feelings of dislike: *despicable behaviour* ◦ *He's a despicable human being!* ◦ ***It*** *was despicable* ***of*** *her* ***to*** *lie about her friend.* • **despicably** /-bli/ adv *I think you behaved despicably.*

despise /dɪˈspaɪz/ verb [T not continuous] to feel a strong dislike for someone or something because you think they are bad or have no value: *The two groups despise each other.* ◦ *She despised him* ***for*** *the way he treated her sister.* ◦ *He despised him****self for*** *being such a coward.*

> **! Common mistake: despite**
>
> Remember that **despite** is never followed by 'of'.
> Don't say 'despite of something', say **despite something**:
>
> ~~*She is an excellent assistant, despite of her lack of computer skills.*~~
> *She is an excellent assistant, despite her lack of computer skills.*
>
> Note that **in spite** has a similar meaning but is always followed by 'of':
>
> *In spite of her lack of computer skills, she is an excellent assistant.*

despite /dɪˈspaɪt/ preposition **1** B1 without taking any notice of or being influenced by; not prevented by: *I still enjoyed the week despite the weather.* ◦ *Despite repeated assurances that the product is safe, many people have stopped buying it.* ◦ [+ -ing verb] *He* *managed to eat a big lunch despite having eaten an enormous breakfast.* **2 despite yourself** If you do something despite yourself, you do it although you do not want to or although you know you should not: *He laughed despite himself.* ◦ *She took the money from her mother's purse, despite herself.*

despoil /dɪˈspɔɪl/ (US) /ˌdiː-/ **verb** [T] formal to make a place less attractive especially by taking things away from it by force: *Many of the tombs had been despoiled.*

despondent /dɪˈspɒn.dənt/ (US) /-ˈspɑːn-/ **adj** unhappy and with no hope or enthusiasm: *He became/grew increasingly despondent when she failed to return his phone calls.* ◦ *She started to feel despondent* ***about*** *ever finding a job.* • **despondency** /-dən.si/ (US) /-ˈspɑːn-/ **noun** [U] • **despondently** /-li/ **adv** *'It's hopeless,' he said, shaking his head despondently.*

despot /ˈdes.pɒt/ (US) /-pɑːt/ **noun** [C] a person, especially a ruler, who has unlimited power over other people, and often uses it unfairly and cruelly: *an evil despot* ◦ *The king was regarded as having been an enlightened despot.* → See also **tyrant** • **despotic** /dɪˈspɒt.ɪk/ (US) /desˈpɑː.t̬ɪk/ **adj** *a despotic government/regime* • **despotically** /dɪˈspɒt.ɪ.kəl.i/ (US) /desˈpɑː.t̬ɪ-/ **adv** • **despotism** /ˈdes.pə.tɪ.zəm/ (US) /-t̬ɪ-/ **noun** [U] *After years of despotism, the country is now moving towards democracy.*

des res /ˌdezˈrez/ **noun** [C] UK informal humorous a very DESIRABLE RESIDENCE (= a nice house or apartment): *She's got a nice little des res in Chelsea.*

dessert /dɪˈzɜːt/ (US) /-ˈzɝːt/ **noun** [C or U] (A2) sweet food eaten at the end of a meal: *a dessert fork/spoon* ◦ ***For*** *dessert there's apple pie or fruit.* ◦ *If you make the main course, I'll make a dessert.*

dessertspoon /dɪˈzɜːt.spuːn/ (US) /-ˈzɝːt-/ **noun** [C] **1** a medium-sized spoon, used especially for eating sweet food at the end of a meal → Compare **teaspoon**, **tablespoon** **2** the amount that a dessertspoon holds, used for measuring food in cooking: *Add one dessertspoon* ***of*** *sugar.*

dessertspoonful /dɪˈzɜːtˌspuːn.fʊl/ (US) /-ˈzɝːt-/ **noun** [C] (plural **dessertspoonsful** or **dessertspoonfuls**) the amount that a dessertspoon holds

desˈsert ˌwine **noun** [C or U] a sweet wine, especially for drinking with sweet food

destabilize (UK usually **destabilise**) /ˌdiːˈsteɪ.bəl.aɪz/ **verb** [T] to make a government, area, or political group lose power or control, or to make a political or economic situation less strong or safe, by causing changes and problems: *They uncovered a plot to destabilize the government.* ◦ *Further increases in imports could destabilize the economy.* • **destabilization** (UK usually **destabilisation**) /diˌsteɪ.bəl.aɪˈzeɪ.ʃən/ **noun** [U] • **destabilizing** (UK usually **destabilising**) /-aɪ.zɪŋ/ **adj** [before noun] *The conflict had a seriously destabilizing* ***effect*** *on the region.*

destination /ˌdes.tɪˈneɪ.ʃən/ **noun** [C] (B1) the place where someone is going or where something is being sent or taken: *We* ***arrived at*** *our destination tired and hungry.* ◦ *His letter never* ***reached*** *its destination.* ◦ *The Caribbean is a popular* ***holiday*** *(US* ***vacation****) destination.*

destined /ˈdes.tɪnd/ **adj** PURPOSE ▷ **1** intended (for a particular purpose): *The money was destined* ***for*** *the relief of poverty, but was diverted by corrupt officials.* ◦ *These cars are destined* ***for*** *the European market.* PLACE ▷ **2** travelling or being sent to somewhere: *Customs officers have seized nearly a ton of heroin destined* ***for*** *New York.* FUTURE ▷ **3** controlled by FATE, and not by humans: *She is destined* ***for*** *an extremely successful career.* ◦ [+ to infinitive] *These plans are destined* ***to*** *fail.* ◦ [+ that] *Do you think* ***it*** *was destined* ***that*** *we should one day meet?*

destiny /ˈdes.tɪ.ni/ **noun** **1** (C1) [C] the things that will happen in the future: *The destiny* ***of*** *our nation depends on this vote!* ◦ *She felt that her destiny had been* ***shaped*** *by her gender.* ◦ *People want to* ***control/determine/take charge of*** *their own destinies.* **2** (C1) [U] the force that some people think controls what happens in the future, and is outside human control: *You can't fight destiny.* ◦ *He is a tragic victim of destiny.*

destitute /ˈdes.tɪ.tjuːt/ (US) /-t̬ɪ.tuːt/ **adj** without money, food, a home, or possessions: *The floods left thousands of people destitute.* • **destitution** /ˌdes.tɪˈtjuː.ʃən/ (US) /-ˈtuː-/ **noun** [U] *Destitution has become a major problem in the capital.*

destroy /dɪˈstrɔɪ/ **verb** [T] **1** (B1) to damage something so badly that it cannot be used: *Most of the old part of the city was destroyed by bombs during the war.* ◦ *The accident seemed to have* ***completely/totally*** *destroyed his confidence.* **2** to kill an animal because it is ill, in pain, or dangerous

destroyer /dɪˈstrɔɪ.ər/ (US) /-ɚ/ **noun** [C] **1** a small fast military ship **2** literary a person or thing that destroys something

destruction /dɪˈstrʌk.ʃən/ **noun** [U] (B2) the act of destroying something, or the fact of being destroyed: *Many people are very concerned about the destruction* ***of*** *the rainforests.* ◦ *Unusually high winds left a* ***trail of*** *destruction over the area.* ◦ *weapons of* ***mass*** *destruction (= those which kill or hurt large numbers of people)*

destructive /dɪˈstrʌk.tɪv/ **adj** causing, or wanting to cause, damage: *the destructive* ***power*** *of nuclear weapons* ◦ *I worry about the destructive effect that violent films may have on children.* ◦ *Lack of trust is very destructive in a relationship.* • **destructively** /-li/ **adv** • **destructiveness** /-nəs/ **noun** [U]

desultory /ˈdes.əl.tər.i/ (US) /-tɔːr-/ **adj** formal without a clear plan or purpose and showing little effort or interest: *She made a desultory attempt at conversation.* • **desultorily** /-əl.i/ **adv**

detach /dɪˈtætʃ/ **verb** [T] to separate or remove something from something else that it is connected to: *You can detach the hood if you prefer the coat without it.* ◦ *Detach the lower part of the form* ***from*** *this letter and return it to the above address.* → Compare **attach**

detachable /dɪˈtætʃ.ɪ.bl/ **adj** able to be detached: *a detachable collar/hood*

detached /dɪˈtætʃt/ **adj** SEPARATE ▷ **1** separated: *The label became detached* ***from*** *your parcel.* **2** (C1) describes a house that is not connected to any other building → Compare **semi-detached** WITHOUT EMOTION ▷ **3** (C2) describes someone who does not show any emotional involvement or interest in a situation: *She seemed a bit detached, as if her mind were on other things.* ◦ *Throughout the novel, the story is seen through the eyes of a detached observer.*

detachment /dɪˈtætʃ.mənt/ **noun** ARMY GROUP ▷ **1** [C, + sing/pl verb] a group of soldiers who are separated from the main group in order to perform a particular duty: *a* ***military*** *detachment* ◦ *A detachment* ***of*** *Italian soldiers was sent to the area.* NO EMOTION ▷ **2** [U] a feeling of not being emotionally involved: *to have an* ***air of*** *detachment*

detail **noun**; **verb**

▸**noun** /ˈdiː.teɪl/ (US) /dɪˈteɪl/ INFORMATION ▷ **1** (B1) [C] a single piece of information or fact about something: *She insisted on telling me every single detail* ***of*** *what* they did to her in hospital. ◦ We don't know the **full/precise** details of the story yet. ◦ She refused to **disclose/divulge** any details **about/of** the plan. **2 details** [plural] A2 information about someone or something: *Can I have your details (= name and address, etc.), please?* ◦ *I've sent off for the details **of** a job I saw advertised in the paper.* ◦ *A police officer **took down** the details **of** what happened.* **3** [U] the small features of something that you only notice when you look carefully: *I was just admiring the detail in the doll's house – even the tins of food have labels on them.* ◦ *It's his **eye for** (= ability to notice) detail that distinguishes him as a painter.* **4 in detail** B1 including or considering all the information about something or every part of something: *We haven't **discussed** the matter in detail yet.* ◦ *The book **described** her sufferings in graphic detail.* ◦ *He talked in **great** detail about the curtains he's chosen for his lounge.* **5 go into detail** B2 to tell or include all the facts about something: *I won't go into detail over the phone, but I've been having a few health problems recently.* **6** [C] a part of something which does not seem important: *As far as Tony's concerned, he's getting that car and finding the money to pay for it is just a detail.* **GROUP** ▷ **7** [C, + sing/pl verb] a group of people who have been given a particular task

> Word partners for **detail** noun (**INFORMATION**)
>
> *disclose/discuss/divulge/reveal* details • *spare* sb the details • *exact/full/precise/relevant* details • *final/further/the latest* details • *a minor* detail • *gory* details • *attention to* detail • details *about/of/on* sth

▸verb /ˈdiː.teɪl/ (US) /-ˈ-/ **GIVE INFORMATION** ▷ **1** [T] to describe something completely, giving all the facts: [+ question word] *Can you produce a report detailing **wh**at we've spent on the project so far?* **ORDER** ▷ **2** [T + to infinitive, often passive] to order someone, often a small group of soldiers or workers, to perform a particular task: *Four soldiers were detailed **to** check the road for troops.*

detailed /ˈdiː.teɪld/ (US) /dɪˈteɪld/ **adj** B2 giving a lot of information with many details: *A witness gave a detailed **description** of the man.*

detain /dɪˈteɪn/ **verb** [T often passive] **1** to force someone officially to stay in a place: *A suspect has been detained by the police for further questioning.* ◦ *Several of the injured were detained overnight in hospital.* **2** to delay someone for a short length of time: *I'm sorry I'm late – I was **unavoidably** detained.* **3 detain sb at His/Her Majesty's pleasure** UK legal to keep someone in prison for as long as the courts feel is necessary

detainee /ˌdiː.teɪˈniː/ **noun** [C] a person who has been officially ordered to stay in a prison or similar place, especially for political reasons: *a political detainee*

detect /dɪˈtekt/ **verb** [T] **1** C1 to notice something that is partly hidden or not clear, or to discover something, especially using a special method: *Some sounds cannot be detected by the human ear.* ◦ *Financial experts have detected signs that the economy is beginning to improve.* **2** C1 to discover something, usually using special equipment: *High levels of lead were detected in the atmosphere.* ◦ *Radar equipment is used to detect (= find the position of) enemy aircraft.* • **detectable** /dɪˈtek.tə.bl̩/ **adj** *There has been no detectable change in the patient's condition.*

detection /dɪˈtek.ʃᵊn/ **noun** [U] **1** the fact of noticing or discovering something: *Early detection **of** the cancer improves the chances of successful treatment.* ◦ *bomb detection* **2** the fact of the police discovering

information about crimes: *a low/high **crime** detection rate*

detective /dɪˈtek.tɪv/ **noun** [C] **1** B1 someone whose job is to discover information about crimes and find out who is responsible for them: *a private detective* ◦ *detective stories* **2** used as part of the title of particular ranks in the police force: *Detective Sergeant Lewis*

D

deˈtective ˌwork noun [U] the activity of searching for information about something, often over a long period: *After a lot of detective work, I managed to find out where he was living.*

detector /dɪˈtek.təʳ/ (US) /-tɚ/ **noun** [C] a device used to find particular substances or things, or measure their level: *a metal/smoke detector*

détente /deɪˈtɒnt/ (US) /-ˈtɑːnt/ **noun** [U] formal an improvement in the relationship between two countries that in the past were not friendly and did not trust each other: *The talks are aimed at furthering détente **between** the two countries.*

detention /dɪˈten.ʃᵊn/ **noun 1** [U] the act of officially DETAINING someone: *Concern has been expressed about the death **in** detention of a number of political prisoners.* **2** [C or U] a form of punishment in which children are made to stay at school for a short time after classes have ended: *She's had four detentions this term.*

deˈtention ˌcentre UK (US **deˈtention ˌcenter**) **noun** [C] **1** a type of prison where young people can be kept for short periods of time **2** a place where people who have entered a country without the necessary documents can be kept for short periods of time

detenu /dɪˈten.juː/ **noun** [C] Indian English for **detainee**

deter /dɪˈtɜːʳ/ (US) /-ˈtɜː/ **verb** [T] (**-rr-**) to prevent someone from doing something or to make someone less enthusiastic about doing something by making it difficult for them to do it or by threatening bad results if they do it: *These measures are designed to deter an enemy attack.* ◦ *High prices are deterring many young people **from** buy**ing** houses.*

detergent /dɪˈtɜː.dʒᵊnt/ (US) /-ˈtɜː-/ **noun** [C or U] a chemical substance in the form of a powder or a liquid for removing dirt from clothes, dishes, etc.

deteriorate /dɪˈtɪə.ri.ə.reɪt/ (US) /-ˈtɪr.i-/ **verb** [I] C1 to become worse: *She was taken into hospital last week when her **condition** suddenly deteriorated.* ◦ *The political **situation** in the region has deteriorated rapidly.* • **deterioration** /dɪˌtɪə.ri.əˈreɪ.ʃᵊn/ (US) /-ˌtɪr.i-/ **noun** [C or U] *We've seen a deterioration **in** relations between the countries.*

determinant /dɪˈtɜː.mɪ.nənt/ (US) /-ˈtɜː-/ **noun** [C] formal something that controls or affects what happens in a particular situation: *Soil and climate are the main determinants **of** how land is used.*

determinate /dɪˈtɜː.mɪ.nət/ (US) /-ˈtɜː-/ **adj** formal fixed or exact: *A determinate sentence of imprisonment was imposed.* → Compare **indeterminate**

determination /dɪˌtɜː.mɪˈneɪ.ʃᵊn/ (US) /-ˌtɜː-/ **noun TRYING HARD** ▷ **1** B2 [U] the ability to continue trying to do something, although it is very difficult: *a man of fierce/ruthless determination* ◦ [+ to infinitive] *You can't help but admire her determination **to** succeed.* → See also **self-determination DECISION** ▷ **2** [U] formal the process of controlling, influencing, or deciding something: *The determination of policy is not your business – your job is to implement it.*

determine /dɪˈtɜː.mɪn/ (US) /-ˈtɜː-/ **verb DECIDE** ▷ **1** C1 [T often passive] to control or influence something directly, or to decide what will happen: *The number of* *staff we can take on will be determined by how much money we're allowed to spend.* ◦ *Your health is determined in part by what you eat.* ◦ *Eye colour is genetically determined.* ◦ [+ question word] formal *A pitch inspection will determine **whether** or not the match will be played.* ◦ *People should be allowed to determine their own future.* **2** [T] formal to make a strong decision: [+ that] *She determined **that** one day she would be an actor.* ◦ [+ to infinitive] *On leaving jail, Joe determined **to** reform.* **DISCOVER** ▷ **3** C1 [T] formal to discover the facts or truth about something: *The police never actually determined the cause of death.* ◦ [+ question word] *It is the responsibility of the court to determine **whether** these men are innocent.* ◦ [+ that] *The jury determined **that** the men were guilty.*

determined /dɪˈtɜː.mɪnd/ US /-ˈtɝː-/ adj B2 wanting to do something very much and not allowing anyone or any difficulties to stop you: [+ to infinitive] *I'm determined **to** get this piece of work finished today.* ◦ *She's sure to get the job she wants – she's a very determined person.* • **determinedly** /-li/ adv *He continued determinedly despite his injury.*

determiner /dɪˈtɜː.mɪ.nəʳ/ US /-ˈtɝː.mɪ.nɚ/ noun [C] specialized B2 in grammar, a word that is used before a noun to show which particular example of the noun you are referring to: *In the phrases 'my first boyfriend' and 'that strange woman', the words 'my' and 'that' are determiners.*

determinism /dɪˈtɜː.mɪ.nɪ.zᵊm/ US /-ˈtɝː-/ noun [U] specialized the theory that everything which happens must happen as it does and could not have happened any other way

deterrence /dɪˈter.ᵊnts/ noun [U] the action or the fact of DETERRING people from doing something: *They believed in the principle of **nuclear** deterrence.*

deterrent /dɪˈter.ᵊnt/ noun [C] C2 something that DETERS people from doing something: *a **nuclear** deterrent* ◦ *Tougher prison sentences may **act/serve as** a deterrent **to** other would-be offenders.* • **deterrent** adj *a deterrent effect*

detest /dɪˈtest/ verb [T not continuous] to hate someone or something very much: *I detest any kind of cruelty.* ◦ [+ -ing verb] *I detest hav**ing** to get up when it's dark outside.* ◦ *her detested older brother* • **detestation** /ˌdiː.tesˈteɪ.ʃᵊn/ noun [U]

detestable /dɪˈtes.tə.bl̩/ adj formal describes people or things that you hate very much: *a detestable coward* • **detestably** /-bli/ adv

dethrone /diˈθrəʊn/ US /-ˈθroʊn/ verb [T] **1** to remove a king or queen from their position of power **2** to beat someone who is the best at something, especially a sport, and become the best yourself: *The world champion was dethroned by a young Swedish challenger.*

detonate /ˈdet.ᵊn.eɪt/ US /ˈdeţ-/ verb [I or T] to (cause something to) explode: *The device detonated unexpectedly.* ◦ *A remote control device was used to detonate the bomb.*

detonation /ˌdet.ᵊnˈeɪ.ʃᵊn/ US /ˌdeţ-/ noun [C or U] the fact of being detonated: *Underground nuclear detonations are believed to have been carried out.*

detonator /ˈdet.ᵊn.eɪ.təʳ/ US /ˈdeţ.ᵊn.eɪ.ţɚ/ noun [C] a small amount of explosive in a bomb that explodes first and causes a larger explosion, or an electrical device that is used from a distance to make a bomb explode

detour /ˈdiː.tɔːʳ/ US /-tʊr/ noun [C] a different or less direct route to a place that is used to avoid a problem or to visit somewhere or do something on the way: *You'd be wise to **make** (US also **take**) a detour to avoid the roadworks.* • **detour** verb [I or T] mainly US *We had to detour around the town, so it took us longer than usual.*

detox /ˈdiː.tɒks/ US /-tɑːks/ noun; verb

▸noun [S or U] **1** a period when you stop taking unhealthy or harmful foods, drinks or drugs into your body for a period of time, in order to improve your health: *a detox diet* **2** medical treatment in a special hospital to stop someone drinking too much alcohol or taking harmful drugs: *He'd spent 18 months **in** detox/at a detox centre fighting drug addiction.*

▸verb [I or T] **1** to stop taking unhealthy or harmful foods, drinks, and other substances into your body for a period of time, in order to improve your health: *If you have skin problems or feel sluggish and run-down, then it may be time to detox.* **2** to have medical treatment in a special hospital in order to stop drinking too much alcohol or taking harmful drugs

detoxification /diːˌtɒk.sɪ.fɪˈkeɪ.ʃᵊn/ US /-ˌtɑːk-/ noun [U] the process of removing harmful chemicals from something • **detoxify** /diːˈtɒk.sɪ.faɪ/ US /-ˈtɑːk-/ verb [I or T]

detract /dɪˈtrækt/ verb

PHRASAL VERB **detract from sth** [not continuous] to make something seem less valuable or less deserving of admiration than it really is or was thought to be: *All that make-up she wears actually detracts from her beauty, I think.*

detractor /dɪˈtræk.təʳ/ US /-tɚ/ noun [C] someone who criticizes something or someone, often unfairly: *His detractors claim that his fierce temper makes him unsuitable for party leadership.*

detriment /ˈdet.rɪ.mənt/ noun [U] formal harm or damage: *Are you sure that I can follow this diet **without** detriment **to** my health?* ◦ *She was very involved with sports at college, **to the** detriment **of** (= harming) her studies.*

detrimental /ˌdet.rɪˈmen.tᵊl/ US /-ţᵊl/ adj formal C2 causing harm or damage: *These chemicals have a detrimental **effect/impact** on the environment.* ◦ *Their decision could be detrimental **to** the future of the company.*

detritus /dɪˈtraɪ.təs/ US /-ţəs/ noun [U] **1** formal waste material or rubbish, especially left after a particular event: *The stadium was littered with the detritus **of** yesterday's rock concert.* **2** specialized a loose mass of decaying material

de trop /dəˈtrəʊ/ US /-ˈtroʊ/ adj [after verb] formal unnecessary, unwanted or more than is suitable: *I thought her remarks about Roger's recent problems were rather de trop.*

deuce /djuːs/ US /duːs/ noun [U] **1** the score in tennis when both players have 40 points **2** the word for 'two' in some card and DICE games **3 the deuce** old-fashioned informal used in questions to express anger or surprise: *What the deuce do you think you're doing?*

deus ex machina /ˌdeɪ.əs.eksˈmæk.ɪ.nə/ US /-ˈmɑː.kɪ-/ noun [S] formal an unnatural or very unlikely end to a story or event, that solves or removes any problems too easily

deuterium /djuːˈtɪə.ri.əm/ US /-tɪr-/ noun [U] specialized an ISOTOPE of HYDROGEN that is twice the mass of ordinary HYDROGEN: *The nucleus of a deuterium atom contains a proton and a neutron.*

Deutschmark /ˈdɔɪtʃ.mɑːk/ US /-mɑːrk/ noun [C] (also **mark**, abbreviation **DM**) the standard unit of money used in Germany before the introduction of the euro

devalue /ˌdiːˈvæl.juː/ verb **MONEY** ▷ **1** [I or T] to reduce the rate at which money can be exchanged for foreign money: *Last year Mexico was forced to devalue the peso.* **NOT VALUE** ▷ **2** [T] to cause someone or something to be considered less valuable or important: *I don't want to devalue your achievement, but you seem to have passed your exam without really doing any work.* • **devaluation** /ˌdiː.væl.juˈeɪ.ʃən/ **noun** [C or U] *The devaluation **of** the dollar had a strong effect on the financial markets.*

devastate /ˈdev.ə.steɪt/ **verb** [T] **DESTROY** ▷ **1** to destroy a place or thing completely or cause great damage **UPSET** ▷ **2** to make someone feel very shocked and upset

devastated /ˈdev.ə.steɪ.tɪd/ (US) /-t̬ɪd/ **adj** **DESTROYED** ▷ **1** completely destroyed: *Thousands of people have left their devastated villages and fled to the mountains.* **VERY UPSET** ▷ **2** (C1) very shocked and upset: *She was utterly devastated when her husband died.*

devastating /ˈdev.ə.steɪ.tɪŋ/ (US) /-t̬ɪŋ/ **adj** **VERY HARMFUL** ▷ **1** (C2) causing a lot of damage or destruction: *If the bomb had exploded in the main shopping area, it would have been devastating.* ◦ *The drought has had devastating **consequences/effects**.* **STRONG EFFECT** ▷ **2** (C1) making someone very shocked and upset: *devastating news* **3** describes a personal quality that has a powerful effect: *She had a devastating beauty/charm/smile that few men could resist.* • **devastatingly** /-li/ **adv** *devastatingly beautiful/powerful*

devastation /ˌdev.əˈsteɪ.ʃən/ **noun** [U] **DAMAGE** ▷ **1** damage and destruction: *If disease is allowed to spread, it will cause widespread devastation.* ◦ *The storm left behind it a **trail of** devastation.* **STRONG FEELING** ▷ **2** feeling very shocked or upset: *She had a look of utter devastation on her face.*

develop /dɪˈvel.əp/ **verb** **GROW** ▷ **1** (B1) [I or T] to (cause something to) grow or change into a more advanced, larger or stronger form: *It became clear that he wasn't developing like all the other little boys.* ◦ *The fear is that these minor clashes may develop **into** all-out confrontation.* ◦ *Over time, their acquaintance developed **into** a lasting friendship.* ◦ *This exercise is designed to develop the shoulder and back muscles.* ◦ *I'm looking for a job which will enable me to develop my skills/talents.* **START** ▷ **2** (B1) [T] to invent something or bring something into existence: *We must develop a new policy/strategy to deal with the problem.* ◦ *The company is spending $650 million on developing new products/technology.* **3** (C2) [I] to start to happen or exist: *Large cracks began to develop in the wall.* **4** (B2) [I or T] If you develop an illness or problem, or if it develops, you start to suffer from it: *The study showed that one in twelve women is likely to develop breast cancer.* ◦ *She's developed some very strange habits lately.* **5** [T] to build houses, factories, shops, etc. on a piece of land: *They're planning to develop the whole site **into** a shopping complex.* **PROCESS FILM** ▷ **6** [I or T] to make photographs or NEGATIVES from a film: *I haven't had my holiday photos developed yet.*

> **!** Common mistake: **develop**
>
> **Warning:** Check your verb endings!
> Many learners make mistakes when using **develop** in the past tense. The past simple and past participle have 'p'. Don't write 'developped', write **developed**. The **-ing** form is **developing**.

developed /dɪˈvel.əpt/ **adj** (B2) advanced or powerful: *Sharks have a **highly** developed sense of smell.* ◦ *less developed nations* → See also **well developed**

developer /dɪˈvel.ə.pər/ (US) /-pɚ/ **noun** **BUILDER** ▷ **1** (C2) [C] a person or company that makes money from buying land, building new houses, shops or offices, or by changing existing buildings to sell or rent: *a **property** developer* **OF PRODUCT** ▷ **2** (C1) [C] a person or company that creates new products, especially computer products such as SOFTWARE: *The company is a leading **software** developer.* **CHEMICAL** ▷ **3** [C or U] a chemical used for developing photographs or films **PERSON** ▷ **4** [C] someone, especially a child, whose physical or mental development can be described in a particular way: *Tom was a **late/slow** developer.*

D

developing /dɪˈvel.ə.pɪŋ/ **adj** **1** (B2) describes a country or area of the world that is poorer and has less advanced industries, especially in Africa, Latin America or Asia: *the developing world/countries/nations* **2** [before noun] growing or becoming stronger or more advanced

development /dɪˈvel.əp.mənt/ **noun** **GROWTH** ▷ **1** (B1) [U] the process in which someone or something grows or changes and becomes more advanced: *healthy growth and development* ◦ *The programme traced the development **of** popular music through the ages.* ◦ *The region suffers from under-/over-development (= having too little/much industry).* ◦ *a development project (= one to help improve industry) in Pakistan* **THING THAT HAPPENS** ▷ **2** (B2) [C] a recent event that is the latest in a series of related events: *an important development in the fuel crisis* ◦ *Phone me if there are any new developments.* **START** ▷ **3** (B1) [U] the process of developing something new: *Mr Berkowitz is in charge of **product** development.* **BUILDINGS** ▷ **4** [C] an area on which new buildings are built in order to make a profit: *a **housing** development* • **developmental** /dɪˌvel.əpˈmen.təl/ (US) /-t̬əl/ **adj** *a developmental process/problem*

> Word partners for **development**
>
> *aid/encourage/support* development • *hinder/restrict* development • *monitor/oversee* development • *gradual/rapid* development • *future* development • development *of* sth

deˈvelopment ˌarea **noun** [C] UK an area with many unemployed people where the government encourages new industries to start so that more jobs will be created

deviant /ˈdiː.vi.ənt/ **adj; noun**

▸**adj** (US also **deviate**) describes a person or behaviour that is not usual and is generally considered to be unacceptable

▸**noun** [C] disapproving someone whose behaviour, especially sexual behaviour, is deviant: *a sexual deviant* • **deviance** /-əns/ **noun** [U]

deviate /ˈdiː.vi.eɪt/ **verb** [I] **BEHAVIOUR** ▷ **1** to do something that is different from the usual or common way of behaving: *The recent pattern of weather deviates **from** the norm for this time of year.* **DIRECTION** ▷ **2** to go in a different direction: *The path follows the river closely, occasionally deviating round a clump of trees.* • **deviation** /ˌdiː.viˈeɪ.ʃən/ **noun** [C or U] *Any deviation **from** the party's faith is seen as betrayal.*

device /dɪˈvaɪs/ **noun** [C] **OBJECT** ▷ **1** (B2) an object or machine that has been invented for a particular purpose: *a contraceptive/electronic device* ◦ *Rescuers used a special device **for** finding people trapped in collapsed buildings.* **METHOD** ▷ **2** a method that is used to produce a particular effect: *a literary/rhetorical device* ◦ *A trademark can be a powerful marketing device.* ◦ [+ to infinitive] *Her cool manner is just a device **to** avoid having to talk to people.* **BOMB** ▷

3 a bomb or other explosive: *an explosive/incendiary/ nuclear device*

devil /ˈdev.əl/ noun **EVIL BEING** ▷ **1** B2 [C] an evil being, often represented in human form but with a tail and horns **2 the devil** [S] (often **the Devil**) a powerful evil force and the enemy of God in Christianity and Judaism **PERSON** ▷ **3** C2 [C] informal someone, especially a child, who behaves badly: *Those **little/young** devils broke my window.* **4** [C] informal humorous a person who enjoys doing things people might disapprove of: *'I'm going to wear a short black skirt and thigh-length boots.' 'Ooh, you devil!'* ◦ *Have another slice of cake – go on, **be** a devil!* **5** [C] informal used with an adjective to describe someone and express your opinion about something that has happened to them: *I hear you've got a new car, you **lucky** devil!* ◦ *He's been ill for weeks, **poor** devil.*

IDIOMS **be between the devil and the deep blue sea** to have two choices that are both equally unpleasant or not convenient • **(to) give the devil his due** said when you admit that someone you do not like or admire does have some good qualities: *I don't like the man but – give the devil his due – he works incredibly hard.* • **go to the devil** old-fashioned something you say to someone annoying or bad to tell them to go away for ever • **speak/talk of the devil** something you say when the person you were talking about appears unexpectedly: *Did you hear what happened to Anna yesterday – oh, speak of the devil, here she is.* • **the/a devil of a sth** old-fashioned an extremely difficult or serious type of something: *a devil of a mess/problem* ◦ *We had the devil of a **job/time** trying to find this place!* • **what/where/how/why the devil** old-fashioned informal used to give emphasis to a question: *What the devil are you doing?* ◦ *Where the devil have you been?*

devilish /ˈdev.əl.ɪʃ/ adj **BAD** ▷ **1** evil or morally bad: *a devilish plot* **2** morally bad but in an attractive way: *a devilish grin* **COMPLEX** ▷ **3** extremely difficult or clever: *devilish cunning*

devilishly /ˈdev.əl.ɪʃ.li/ adv extremely: *That's a devilishly **difficult** question.*

ˌdevil-may-ˈcare adj not considering or worrying about the results of your actions: *He has a rather devil-may-care **attitude** to his studies.*

devilment /ˈdev.əl.mənt/ noun [U] (also **devilry**) behaviour that causes trouble but is usually intended to be humorous: *He's up to some kind of devilment again, I'll be bound.*

ˌdevil's ˈadvocate noun [C usually singular] someone who pretends, in an argument or discussion, to be against an idea or plan which a lot of people support, in order to make people discuss and consider it in more detail: *I don't really believe all that – I was just **playing** devil's advocate.*

ˈdevil's food ˌcake noun [C or U] mainly US a strong-tasting dark chocolate cake

devious /ˈdiː.vi.əs/ adj **DISHONEST** ▷ **1** describes people or plans and methods that are dishonest, often in a complicated way, but often also clever and successful: *You have to be a bit devious if you're going to succeed in business.* ◦ *a devious scheme* **NOT DIRECT** ▷ **2** not direct: *He took a rather devious route which avoids the city centre.* • **deviously** /-li/ adv • **deviousness** /-nəs/ noun [U]

devise /dɪˈvaɪz/ verb [T] C2 to invent a plan, system, object, etc., usually cleverly or using imagination: *He's good at devising language games that you can play with students in class.* ◦ *The cartoon characters Snoopy and Charlie Brown were devised by Charles M. Schultz.*

devoice /ˌdiːˈvɔɪs/ verb [T] specialized to pronounce a sound that is usually VOICED, in a way that is not voiced

devoid /dɪˈvɔɪd/ adj formal **be devoid of sth** to lack or be without something that is necessary or usual: *Their apartment is devoid of **all** comforts.* ◦ *He seems to be devoid of compassion.*

devolution /ˌdiː.vəˈluː.ʃən/ noun [U] the moving of power or responsibility from a main organization to a lower level, or from a central government to a local government

devolve /dɪˈvɒlv/ US /-ˈvɑːlv/ verb [T] to (cause power or responsibility to) be given to other people: *To be a good manager, you must know how to devolve responsibility downwards.* ◦ formal *Those duties will necessarily devolve **on/upon** me.*

PHRASAL VERB **devolve sth to sb** formal to give power or responsibility to a person or organization at a lower or more local level: *The local education authorities have devolved financial control to individual schools.*

devote /dɪˈvəʊt/ US /-ˈvoʊt/ verb

PHRASAL VERB **devote sth to sth/sb 1** B2 to give all of something, especially your time, effort or love, or yourself, to something you believe in or to a person: *He left government to devote more **time** to his family.* ◦ *She has devoted all her **energies/life** to the care of homeless people.* ◦ *At the age of 25, he decided to devote him**self** to God.* **2** B2 [passive] to use a space, area, time, etc. for a particular purpose: *Over half his speech was devoted to the issue of unemployment.* ◦ *The report recommends that more **resources** be devoted to teaching four-year-olds.*

devoted /dɪˈvəʊ.tɪd/ US /-ˈvoʊ.t̬ɪd/ adj B2 extremely loving and loyal: *a devoted fan/husband* ◦ *Lucy is devoted **to** her cats.* • **devotedly** /-li/ adv

devotee /ˌdev.əˈtiː/ noun [C] a person who strongly admires a particular person or is extremely interested in a subject: *He is a great devotee **of** the prime minister.* ◦ *devotees of cricket*

devotion /dɪˈvəʊ.ʃən/ US /-ˈvoʊ-/ noun [U] **LOYALTY** ▷ **1** loyalty and love or care for someone or something: *He inspired respect and devotion from his pupils.* ◦ *She will be remembered for her selfless/unstinting devotion **to** the cause.* **RELIGION** ▷ **2** religious worship: *He knelt **in** humble devotion.* **3 devotions** [plural] acts of religious worship, especially prayers

devotional /dɪˈvəʊ.ʃən.əl/ US /-ˈvoʊ-/ adj connected with the act of religious worship: *devotional music/ poems/practices*

devour /dɪˈvaʊəʳ/ US /-ˈvaʊɚ/ verb [T] **1** to eat something eagerly and in large amounts so that nothing is left: *The young cubs hungrily devoured the deer.* **2** literary to destroy something completely: *The flames quickly devoured the building.* **3** to read books or literature quickly and eagerly: *She's a very keen reader – she devours one book after another.*

IDIOM **be devoured by sth** to feel an emotion, especially a bad emotion, very strongly so that it strongly influences your behaviour: *He was devoured by jealousy/hatred.*

devouring /dɪˈvaʊə.rɪŋ/ US /-ˈvaʊɚ.ɪŋ/ adj [before noun] literary a devouring emotion is extremely strong and usually causes damage: *She is driven by a devouring ambition/passion.*

devout /dɪˈvaʊt/ adj believing strongly in a religion and obeying all its rules or principles: *a devout*

Buddhist/Christian/churchgoer • **devoutness** /-nəs/ noun [U]

devoutly /dɪˈvaʊt.li/ adv **1** in a very religious way: *a devoutly Catholic family* **2** formal sincerely and strongly: *He devoutly **hoped** that they would reach a peaceful agreement.*

dew /djuː/ ⓤⓢ /duː/ noun [U] drops of water that form on the ground and other surfaces outside during the night • **dewy** /-i/ adj *a dewy morning*

dewdrop /ˈdjuː.drɒp/ ⓤⓢ /ˈduː.drɑːp/ noun [C] a drop of dew

ˌdewy-ˈeyed adj **1** having eyes that are wet with tears because you feel emotional: *dewy-eyed nostalgia* **2** not knowing about unpleasant things and having no experience of life: *a dewy-eyed bride* ◦ *dewy-eyed innocence*

dexterity /dekˈster.ə.ti/ ⓤⓢ /-t̬i/ noun [U] the ability to perform a difficult action quickly and skilfully with the hands, or the ability to think quickly and effectively: *He caught the ball **with** great dexterity.* ◦ *He answered the journalists' questions **with** all the dexterity **of** a politician.* • **dexterous** (also **dextrous**) /ˈdek.stər.əs/ ⓤⓢ /-stɚ-/ adj *a dexterous movement* • **dexterously** (also **dextrously**) /ˈdek.stər.əs.li/ ⓤⓢ /-stɚ-/ adv

dextrose /ˈdek.strəʊs/ ⓤⓢ /-stroʊs/ noun [U] specialized a type of sugar that is produced naturally and is found in fruits, HONEY, etc.

dhal noun [U] another spelling of **dal**

dhansak /ˈdʌn.sɑːk/, /ˈdæn.sæk/ noun [C or U] an Indian meat or vegetable dish cooked with LENTILS

dharna /ˈdɑː.nə/ ⓤⓢ /ˈdɑːr-/ noun [C or U] Indian English a way of showing your disagreement with something by refusing to leave a place: *The activists organized a dharna in front of the college.*

dhoti /ˈdəʊ.ti/ ⓤⓢ /ˈdoʊ.t̬i/ noun [C] a loose piece of clothing wrapped around the lower half of the body, worn by some men from South Asia

diabetes /ˌdaɪəˈbiː.tiːz/ ⓤⓢ /-t̬əs/ noun [U] a disease in which the body cannot control the level of sugar in the blood

diabetic /ˌdaɪəˈbet.ɪk/ ⓤⓢ /-ˈbet̬-/ noun; adj
▸noun [C] a person who has diabetes
▸adj **1** relating to diabetes: *a diabetic coma* **2** made for diabetic people to eat: *diabetic chocolate/jam*

diabolical /ˌdaɪəˈbɒl.ɪ.kəl/ ⓤⓢ /-ˈbɑː.lɪ.kəl/ adj (US also **diabolic**) **1** informal extremely bad or shocking: *Conditions in the prison were diabolical.* ◦ *His driving is diabolical!* **2** evil, or caused by the DEVIL • **diabolically** /-ˈbɒl.ɪ.kəl.i/ ⓤⓢ /-ˈbɑː.lɪ.kəl.i/ adv *diabolically (= extremely) clever/wicked*

diacritic /ˌdaɪəˈkrɪt.ɪk/ ⓤⓢ /-ˈkrɪt̬-/ noun [C] a mark written above or below a letter that changes its usual pronunciation

diadem /ˈdaɪ.ə.dem/ noun [C] a small CROWN (= circular decoration for the head) with JEWELS in it

diaeresis (plural **diaereses**) (mainly US **dieresis**) /daɪˈer.ə.sɪs/ noun [C] a mark written over a vowel that shows it is pronounced separately from the vowel immediately before it, for example in the word naïve

diagnose /ˈdaɪ.əg.nəʊz/ ⓤⓢ /ˌdaɪ.əgˈnoʊz/ verb [T] C2 to recognize and name the exact character of a disease or a problem, by examining it: *The specialist diagnosed cancer.* ◦ *His condition was diagnosed **as** some sort of blood disorder.* ◦ *She was diagnosed **with/as** having diabetes.* ◦ *The electrician has diagnosed a fault in the wiring.*

diagnosis /ˌdaɪ.əgˈnəʊ.sɪs/ ⓤⓢ /-ˈnoʊ-/ noun [C or U] (plural **diagnoses**) C2 a judgment about what a particular illness or problem is, made after examining it: *'What was the diagnosis?' 'Arthritis in both joints.'* ◦ *The doctor has **made** an initial diagnosis.* ◦ *Diagnosis **of** the disease is difficult in the early stages.* • **diagnostic** /ˌdaɪ.əgˈnɒs.tɪk/ ⓤⓢ /-ˈnɑː.stɪk/ adj *diagnostic **techniques/tests***

diagonal /daɪˈæg.ən.əl/ adj; noun
▸adj **1** A diagonal line is straight and sloping, not horizontal or vertical, for example joining two opposite corners of a square or other flat shape with four sides: *The book has a diagonal black stripe on the cover.* **2** moving in a diagonal line: *Peters received a diagonal pass and headed the ball into the net.* • **diagonally** /-i/ adv *It's quickest if you cut diagonally across the park.*
▸noun [C] specialized a straight line which joins two opposite corners of a four-sided flat shape, such as a square

diagram /ˈdaɪ.ə.græm/ noun [C] B1 a simple plan which represents a machine, system or idea, etc., often drawn to explain how it works: *The teacher drew a diagram showing how the blood flows through the heart.* • **diagrammatic** /ˌdaɪ.ə.grəˈmæt.ɪk/ ⓤⓢ /-ˈmæt̬-/ adj • **diagrammatically** /ˌdaɪ.ə.grəˈmæt.ɪ.kəl.i/ ⓤⓢ /-ˈmæt̬-/ adv using diagrams: *She explained the whole problem diagrammatically.*

dial /ˈdaɪ.əl/ verb; noun
▸verb [I or T] (-ll- or US usually -l-) B1 to operate a phone or make a phone call to someone by choosing a particular series of numbers on the phone: *Can I dial this number **direct**, or do I have to go through the operator?* ◦ *Dial 0 for the switchboard.*
▸noun [C] **MEASURING DEVICE** ▷ **1** the part of a machine or device which shows you a measurement of something such as speed or time: *Can you read what it says on the dial?* ◦ *The dial **of/on** his watch had a picture of Mickey Mouse on it.* **2** a device on an instrument which you move in order to control it or make changes to it: *You turn this dial to find a different radio station.* **PHONE** ▷ **3** the disc with numbers on old-fashioned phones that you turn when you make a call

dialect /ˈdaɪ.ə.lekt/ noun [C or U] C2 a form of a language that people speak in a particular part of a country, containing some different words and grammar, etc.: *a **regional** dialect* ◦ *The poem is written **in** northern dialect.*

dialectic /ˌdaɪ.əˈlek.tɪk/ noun [U] (also **dialectics**) a way of discovering what is true by considering opposite theories • **dialectical** /-tɪ.kəl/ adj

ˈdialling ˌcode noun [C] UK (US **ˈarea ˌcode**) a series of numbers used before the main phone number when you phone someone outside your own town or area

ˈdialling ˌtone noun [C usually singular] UK (US **ˈdial ˌtone**) a continuous sound which tells you that a phone is connected to the phone system and is ready to be used

ˈdialog ˌbox noun [C] a WINDOW (= a separate area on a computer screen) that appears and gives the person using the computer information about what they are doing

dialogue (US also **dialog**) /ˈdaɪ.ə.lɒg/ ⓤⓢ /-lɑːg/ noun [C or U] **1** B2 conversation that is written for a book, play or film: *The play contained some very snappy/witty dialogue.* ◦ *Act Two begins with a short dialogue **between** father and son.* **2** C2 formal talks between opposing countries, political groups, etc.: *The rebel leaders stated that they are willing to **enter into***

dialogue ***with*** *the government.* ◦ *The two sides have at last begun to* ***engage in*** *a constructive dialogue.*

ˈdial-up adj [before noun] Dial-up computer systems, devices, and internet services use a phone line to connect them: *a dial-up connection* ◦ *dial-up access/networking* ◦ *a dial-up account/modem*

dialysis /daɪˈæl.ə.sɪs/ **noun** [U] specialized a process of separating substances from liquid by putting them through a thin piece of skin-like material, especially to make pure the blood of people whose KIDNEYS are not working correctly: *a dialysis machine* ◦ ***kidney*** *dialysis* ◦ *She is* ***on*** *(= being treated by) dialysis.*

diamanté /diːəˈmɒn.teɪ/ US /-ˈmɑːn.t̬eɪ/ **noun** [U] artificial JEWELS which shine brightly: *a diamanté brooch/diamanté earrings*

diameter /daɪˈæm.ɪ.təʳ/ US /-ə.t̬ɚ/ **noun** [C or U] (the length of) a straight line that reaches from one point on the edge of a round shape or object, through its centre, to a point on the opposite edge: *The diameter measures twice the radius.* ◦ *The pond is six feet* ***in*** *diameter.*

diametrically /ˌdaɪ.əˈmet.rɪ.kəl.i/ **adv** completely: *The two politicians have diametrically* ***opposite*** *points of view/are diametrically* ***opposed.***

diamond /ˈdaɪə.mənd/ **noun** **STONE** ▷ **1** B2 [C or U] a transparent, extremely hard PRECIOUS STONE that is used in jewellery, and in industry for cutting hard things: *The tiara was set with diamonds and rubies.* ◦ *a diamond ring/necklace* ◦ *He had worked in the diamond mines of South Africa.* ◦ *diamond-tipped saw blades* **2 diamonds** [plural noun] jewellery made from diamonds: *Shall I wear the diamonds or the pearls with this dress?* **SHAPE** ▷ **3** B2 [C or U] a shape with four straight sides of equal length, forming two opposite angles that are wide and two that are narrow: *Joe's socks had diamond patterns on them.* **4** [C] the square part of a field on which baseball is played, surrounded by the four BASES, or the whole field on which the game is played **CARDS** ▷ **5 diamonds** [plural or U] one of the four SUITS in playing cards, shown by one or more red symbols in the shape of a diamond: *the six/jack* ***of*** *diamonds* **6** [C] a playing card from the SUIT of diamonds: *She played a diamond.*

ˌdiamond in the ˈrough noun [C usually singular] US for **rough diamond**

ˌdiamond ˈjubilee noun [C usually singular] mainly UK the day exactly 60 years after an important occasion, or a special event to celebrate this

ˌdiamond ˈwedding (anniˌversary) noun [C] the day exactly 60 years after a marriage, often celebrated with a party

diaper /ˈdaɪ.pəʳ/ US /-pɚ/ **noun** [C] US for **nappy**

diaphanous /daɪˈæf.ən.əs/ **adj** literary describes a substance, especially cloth, that is so delicate and thin that you can see through it: *a diaphanous silk veil*

diaphragm /ˈdaɪ.ə.fræm/ **noun** [C] **MUSCLE** ▷ **1** the muscle which separates the chest from the lower part of the body **BIRTH CONTROL** ▷ **2** a circular rubber device that a woman puts inside her VAGINA before having sex, to avoid becoming pregnant **COVER** ▷ **3** specialized any thin piece of material stretched across an opening

diarist /ˈdaɪə.rɪst/ **noun** [C] someone who is known for writing or having written a diary: *Anne Frank was a famous diarist of the Second World War.*

diarrhoea (mainly US **diarrhea**) /ˌdaɪ.əˈriː.ə/ **noun** [U] C2 an illness in which the body's solid waste is more liquid than usual and comes out of the body more often: *diarrhoea and sickness* ◦ ***an attack of*** *diarrhoea*

diary /ˈdaɪə.ri/ US /ˈdaɪr.i/ **noun** [C] **1** A2 a book with a separate space or page for each day, in which you write down your future arrangements, meetings, etc.: *Don't forget to write/enter the date of the meeting in your diary.* **2** a book in which you record your thoughts or feelings or what has happened each day: *While in hiding, Anne Frank* ***kept*** *a diary.*

diaspora /daɪˈæs.pər.ə/ US /-pɚ-/ **noun** [U] formal the spreading of people from one original country to other countries

the Diˈaspora noun [S, + sing/pl verb] the Jews living in different parts of the world outside Israel, or the various places outside Israel in which they live

diatomic /ˌdaɪ.əˈtɒm.ɪk/ **adj** specialized describes a MOLECULE that consists of two atoms of the same type: *The symbol for diatomic nitrogen is* N_2.

diatonic /daɪ.əˈtɒn.ɪk/ US /-ˈtɑː.nɪk/ **adj** specialized belonging or relating to a MAJOR or MINOR musical SCALE consisting of five full TONES and two SEMITONES

diatribe /ˈdaɪ.ə.traɪb/ **noun** [C] formal an angry speech or piece of writing which severely criticizes something or someone: *He* ***launched into*** *a long diatribe* ***against*** *the government's policies.*

dibs /dɪbz/ **noun** [plural] mainly US informal **dibs on sth** a right to have or get something from someone, or to use something: *Dibs on the front seat!* ◦ *The current owner might* ***have first*** *dibs on buying the rest of the property.*

dice /daɪs/ **noun; verb**

▸**noun** [C] (plural **dice**)
GAME ▷ **1** C2 (US also or old-fashioned **die**) a small CUBE (= object with six equal square sides) with a different number of spots on each side, used in games involving chance: *We need two dice to play the game.* ◦ *You* ***roll/throw*** *the dice and whoever gets the highest score goes first.* **2** [U] any game involving chance in which dice are thrown: *Let's play dice.* **PIECE** ▷ **3** a small square piece of something: *Cut the potatoes into small dice.*

dice

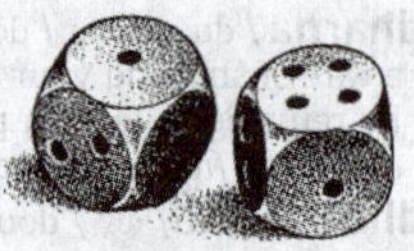

IDIOM **no dice** US informal something that people say when you may not or cannot do something: *I asked if we could go to the party, but Mom said no dice.*

▸**verb** **CUT** ▷ **1** C2 [T] to cut food into small squares: *Peel and dice the potatoes.* ◦ *diced carrots* **GAME** ▷ **2 dice with death** to do something extremely dangerous and silly: *You're dicing with death driving at that speed on icy roads.*

dicey /ˈdaɪ.si/ **adj** (**dicier**, **diciest**) mainly UK informal slightly dangerous or uncertain: *The company's finances look a bit dicey.*

dichotomy /daɪˈkɒt.ə.mi/ US /-ˈkɑː.t̬ə-/ **noun** [C usually singular] formal a difference between two completely opposite ideas or things: *There is often a dichotomy* ***between*** *what politicians say and what they do.*

dick /dɪk/ **noun** [C] **PENIS** ▷ **1** offensive a PENIS **PERSON** ▷ **2** offensive a stupid man: *That guy is such a dick.* **3** US old-fashioned informal a DETECTIVE (= someone whose job is to discover facts about a crime): *a private dick*

dickens /ˈdɪk.ɪnz/ **noun** [plural] old-fashioned informal **the dickens** used in questions to express anger or surprise: *What the dickens are you doing with that paint?*

Dickensian /dɪˈken.zi.ən/ **adj** **1** relating to or similar to something described in the books of the 19th-century English writer Charles Dickens, especially living or working conditions that are below an acceptable standard: *The bathrooms in this hotel are positively Dickensian – no hot water and grime everywhere.* **2** written by or in the style of Charles Dickens

dicker /ˈdɪk.əʳ/ US /-ɚ/ verb [I] US to argue with someone, especially about the price of goods: *She dickered **with** the driver **over** the fare.*

dickey /ˈdɪk.i/ noun [C] Indian English the covered space at the back of a car, where you can put luggage, etc. → See also **boot**

dickhead /ˈdɪk.hed/ noun [C] offensive a stupid person: *You dickhead – you've dented the back of my car!*

dicky /ˈdɪk.i/ adj UK informal weak, especially in health, and likely to fail or suffer from problems: *Grandad's got a dicky **heart**.*

ˈdicky bird noun [C] UK child's word a small bird

IDIOM **not a dicky bird** old-fashioned informal nothing at all: *We haven't **heard** a dicky bird from (= spoken to or received a letter from) Riza recently.*

dicky bow /ˈdɪk.iˌbəʊ/ US /-ˌboʊ/ noun [C] (also **dicky**) UK informal for **bow tie**

dicotyledon /ˌdaɪ.kɒt.ɪˈliː.dən/ US /-kɑː.t̬əlˈiː-/ noun [C] specialized a plant that produces flowers and has two COTYLEDONS (= leaf parts inside the seed) which develops wide leaves with VEINS • **dicotyledonous** /-əs/ adj

dicta /ˈdɪk.tə/ plural of **dictum**

Dictaphone /ˈdɪk.tə.fəʊn/ US /-foʊn/ noun [C] trademark a machine used in an office to record spoken words and later repeat them aloud so that they can be written down

dictate verb; noun

▸verb /dɪkˈteɪt/ US /ˈdɪk.teɪt/ **GIVE ORDERS** ▷ **1** C1 [I or T] to give orders, or tell someone exactly what they must do, with total authority: *The UN will dictate the terms of troop withdrawal from the region.* ◦ [+ question word] *He disagrees with the government dictating **wh**at children are taught in schools.* ◦ [+ that] *The tennis club rules dictate **that** suitable footwear must be worn on the courts.* **2** [T] to influence something or make it necessary: *The party's change of policy has been dictated by its need to win back the support of voters.* ◦ [+ that] *I wanted to take a year off, but my financial situation dictated **that** I got a job.* **SPEAK** ▷ **3** [I or T] to speak something aloud for a person or machine to record the words said, so that they can be written down: *I dictated my order over the phone.* ◦ *She spent the morning dictating letters **to** her secretary.*

PHRASAL VERB **dictate to sb** to tell someone what to do: *I will not be dictated to like that!*

▸noun [C usually plural] /ˈdɪk.teɪt/ formal an order which should be obeyed, often one which you give to yourself: *the dictates **of** conscience/common sense* → Compare **diktat**

dictation /dɪkˈteɪ.ʃən/ noun **1** [U] the activity of dictating something for someone else to write down: *I'll ask my assistant to **take** dictation (= write down what I say).* **2** [C] a test in which a piece of writing is dictated to students learning a foreign language, to test their ability to hear and write the language correctly: *Our French dictation lasted half an hour.*

dictator /dɪkˈteɪ.təʳ/ US /ˈdɪk.teɪ.t̬ɚ/ noun [C] disapproving **1** a leader who has complete power in a country and has not been elected by the people **2** a person who gives orders and behaves as if they have complete power: *My boss is a bit of a dictator.*

dictatorial /ˌdɪk.təˈtɔː.ri.əl/ US /-ˈtɔːr.i-/ adj disapproving liking to give orders: *a dictatorial ruler/government* ◦ *Her father is very dictatorial.*

dictatorship /dɪkˈteɪ.tə.ʃɪp/ US /-t̬ɚ-/ noun **1** [C] a country ruled by a dictator: *a **military** dictatorship* **2** [U] the state of being, or being ruled by, a dictator: *The dictatorship **of** Franco lasted for nearly 40 years.*

diction /ˈdɪk.ʃən/ noun [U] the manner in which words are pronounced: *It is very helpful for a language teacher to have good diction.*

dictionary /ˈdɪk.ʃən.ər.i/ US /-er.i/ noun [C] **1** A1 a book that contains a list of words in ALPHABETICAL order and that explains their meanings, or gives a word for them in another language; a similar product for use on a computer: *a French-English/English-French dictionary* ◦ *a bilingual/monolingual dictionary* ◦ *To check how a word is spelled, look it up in a dictionary.* **2** a book that gives information about a particular subject, in which the ENTRIES (= words or phrases) are given in alphabetical order: *a biographical/science dictionary* ◦ *a dictionary **of** quotations*

dictum /ˈdɪk.təm/ noun [C] (plural **dicta** or **dictums**) a short statement, especially one expressing advice or a general truth: *He followed the famous American dictum, 'Don't get mad, get even'.*

did /dɪd/ verb past simple of **do**

didactic /daɪˈdæk.tɪk/ adj **1** mainly disapproving intended to teach, especially in a way that is too determined or eager, and often fixed and unwilling to change: *a didactic approach to teaching* **2** intended to teach people a moral lesson: *didactic literature* • **didactically** /-tɪ.kəl.i/ adv

diddle /ˈdɪd.l̩/ verb **TRICK** ▷ [T] informal to get money from someone in a way that is not honest: *He diddled me! He said that there were six in a bag, but there were only five.* ◦ *I checked the bill and realized the restaurant had diddled me **out of** £5.*

diddly /ˈdɪd.l̩.i/ noun [U] (also **ˌdiddly-ˈsquat**) US informal anything: *He hasn't done diddly all day.* ◦ *There's no point in asking Ellen – she doesn't know diddly.*

diddums! /ˈdɪd.əmz/ exclamation UK humorous something you say to show that you feel no sympathy for someone who is behaving like a child: *He called you a bad name, did he? Ah, diddums!*

didgeridoo /ˌdɪdʒ.ə.riˈduː/ US /-ɚ.i-/ noun [C] (plural **didgeridoos**) a long wooden wind instrument played by Australian Aborigines to produce a long deep sound

didn't /ˈdɪd.ənt/ short form of did not: *We didn't arrive at our hotel until after midnight.*

> **! Common mistake: didn't**
>
> **Warning: didn't** is not followed by a verb in the past tense:
>
> Don't say 'didn't did something', say **didn't do something**:
>
> ~~*We didn't saw anything interesting on our visit.*~~
>
> *We didn't see anything interesting on our visit.*

die /daɪ/ verb; noun

▸verb [I] (present tense **dying**, past tense and past participle **died**) **1** A1 to stop living or existing, either suddenly or slowly: *Twelve people died in the accident.* ◦ *She died **of/from** hunger/cancer/a heart attack/her injuries.* ◦ *It is a brave person who will die **for** their beliefs.* ◦ *I should like to die **in my sleep** (= while I am sleeping).* ◦ *Many people have a fear of dying.* ◦ *Our love will never die.* ◦ *She will not tell anyone – the secret will die with her.* **2** **die a natural/violent death** to die naturally,

D

violently, etc.: *He died a violent death.* ◦ *My grandmother died a natural death (= did not die of illness or because she was killed), as she would have wanted.* **3** informal If a machine stops working, or if an object cannot be used or repaired any more, usually because it is very old, people sometimes say it has died: *The engine just died **on** us.* ◦ humorous *He wore his jeans until they died.*

D

Other ways of saying die

The phrasal verbs **pass away** or **pass on** are sometimes used to avoid saying 'die' in case it upsets someone:

*He **passed away** peacefully in hospital.*

If people die as the result of an accident or violence, you can say that they **were killed** or **lost their lives**:

*His sister **was killed** in a car accident.*

*Many people **lost their lives** in the war.*

Someone who dies very suddenly while doing something is sometimes said to have **dropped dead**:

*He **dropped dead** on the tennis court at the age of 42.*

You can use the verb **lose** to say that a person in someone's family has died:

*She **lost** her husband last year.*

In informal situations and if you are trying to be humorous, you can use the phrase **kick the bucket**:

*When I **kick the bucket**, you can do what you want.*

IDIOMS **almost/nearly die of sth** (also **could have died of sth**) to feel a particular feeling extremely strongly: *I almost/could have died of embarrassment.* • **be dying for/to do sth** B1 to be extremely eager to have or do something: *I'm dying to hear your news.* ◦ *I'm dying for a cup of tea.* • **die a/the death** UK (US **die a natural death**) to fail and end: *The play, like so many before it, died the death after a week.* • **die hard** If a belief or way of behaving dies hard, it takes a long time to disappear, and is not given up easily: *Old habits die hard.* → See also **diehard** • **do or die** said when you are in a situation in which you must take a big risk in order to avoid failure: *On Tuesday, **it's** do or die in the match against Brazil.* • **never say die** saying said to encourage people to keep trying • **or die in the attempt** said when someone would do anything to achieve what they want to achieve: *She'll finish the race or die in the attempt.* • **to die for** informal excellent or to be strongly wished for: *She has a figure to die for.* ◦ *That chocolate cake is to die for.* • **to/until my dying day** as long as I live: *I'll remember your kindness to my dying day.*

PHRASAL VERBS **die away** If something, especially a sound, dies away, it gradually becomes reduced until it stops existing or disappears: *The sound of his footsteps gradually died away.* • **die down** C2 If a sound or activity dies down, it becomes quieter or less obvious: *It was several minutes before the applause died down.* • **die off** If a group of plants, animals, or people dies off, all of that group dies over a period of time. • **die out** B2 to become less common and finally stop existing: *Dinosaurs died out millions of years ago.* ◦ *It's a custom which is beginning to die out.*

▸noun [C] **TOOL** ▷ **1** a shaped piece or MOULD (= hollow container) made of metal or other hard material, used to shape or put a pattern on metal or plastic **GAME** ▷ **2** old use or US for **dice**

IDIOM **the die is cast** said when a situation is certain to develop in a particular way because decisions have been taken which cannot be changed: *From the moment the negotiations failed, the die was cast and war was inevitable.*

ˈdie-cast verb [T] to make something by pouring liquid metal, plastic, etc., usually under pressure, into a MOULD (= hollow container) • **ˈdie-cast** adj *a die-cast toy*

diehard /ˈdaɪ.hɑːd/ US /-hɑːrd/ noun [C] disapproving someone who is unwilling to change or give up their ideas or ways of behaving, even when there are good reasons to do so: *a diehard conservative/fan*

diesel /ˈdiː.zəl/ noun **1** C1 [U] a type of heavy oil used as fuel: *a diesel engine* ◦ *My new car **runs on** (= uses) diesel.* **2** [C] any vehicle, especially a train, which has a diesel engine

diet /ˈdaɪ.ət/ noun; adj; verb

▸noun **1** B1 [C or U] the food and drink usually eaten or drunk by a person or group: *Diet varies between different countries in the world.* ◦ *a **healthy/balanced/varied** diet* ◦ *Rice is the **staple** diet (= most important food) of many people in China.* ◦ *The children seem to exist on a diet **of** burgers and chips.* **2** B1 [C] an eating plan in which someone eats less food, or only particular types of food, because they want to become thinner or for medical reasons: *I'm **going on** a diet next week and hope to lose ten pounds before Christmas.* ◦ *a **crash/strict/calorie-controlled** diet* ◦ *The doctor **put** me **on** a low-salt diet to reduce my blood pressure.* **3** [S] a particular type of thing that you experience or do regularly, or a limited range of activities: *He was brought up on a diet **of** political propaganda from birth.* ◦ *The TV only offers a diet **of** comedies and old movies every evening.*

Word partners for diet noun

eat/live on a diet *of* sth • *change/improve* your diet • *be put on/follow/go on/stick to* a diet • a *balanced/good/healthy/varied* diet • a *poor/unhealthy* diet • a *special/strict* diet • *staple* diet • a diet *high in/low in/rich in* sth • be *on* a diet • a diet *of* sth

▸adj [before noun] describes food or drink that contains less sugar or fat than the usual type, and often contains an artificial SWEETENER: *diet cola*

▸verb [I] to limit the food and/or drink that you have, especially in order to lose weight: *You should be able to reduce your weight by careful dieting.*

dietary /ˈdaɪ.ə.tər.i/ US /-ter-/ adj relating to your diet: *Dietary **habits** can be very difficult to change.* ◦ *Do you have any special dietary **requirements**?*

ˌdietary ˈfibre noun [U] **fibre**

dieter /ˈdaɪ.ə.tər/ US /-t̬ɚ/ noun [C] someone who is trying to lose weight by dieting

dietetics /ˌdaɪ.əˈtet.ɪks/ US /-ˈtet̬-/ noun [U] the scientific study of the food that people eat and its effects on health

dietitian (also **dietician**) /ˌdaɪ.əˈtɪʃ.ən/ noun [C] a person who scientifically studies and gives advice about food and eating

differ /ˈdɪf.ər/ US /-ɚ/ verb [I] **1** B2 to be not like something or someone else, either physically or in another way: *The twins look alike, but they differ **in** temperament.* ◦ *His views differ considerably **from** those of his parents.* ◦ *The findings of the various studies differ **significantly/markedly/radically**.* ◦ *The incidence of the illness differs greatly **between** men and women.* **2** formal to disagree: *Economists differ **on** the* *cause of inflation.* ◦ *I* ***beg to*** *differ* ***with*** *you on that point.*

difference /ˈdɪf.ər.əns/ ⓤⓢ /-ɚ-/ noun **NOT THE SAME** ▷ **1** A2 [C or U] the way in which two or more things which you are comparing are not the same: *What's the difference* ***between*** *an ape and a monkey?* ◦ *Is there any significant difference* ***in*** *quality* ***between*** *these two items?* **2 make a (big) difference** B2 (also **make all the difference**) to improve a situation (a lot): *Exercise can make a big difference* ***to*** *your state of health.* **3 not make any difference** B2 (also **not make the slightest difference**) to not change a situation in any way: *You can ask him again if you like, but it won't make any difference – he'll still say no.* ◦ *It makes no difference* ***wh****ere you put the aerial, the TV picture's still lousy.* **4 with a difference** describes something unusual, and more interesting or better than other things of the same type: *Try new Cremetti – the ice cream with a difference.*

> **! Common mistake: difference**
>
> **Warning:** choose the correct preposition!
>
> When you want to compare two or more things or people, the correct preposition to use is **between**.
>
> Don't say 'difference among/in/of', say **difference between**:
>
> *~~Children must learn the difference among right and wrong.~~*

NOT AGREEING ▷ **5** C2 [C usually plural] a disagreement: *They had an awful row several years ago, but now they've* ***settled/resolved*** *their differences.* **6 have a difference of opinion** to disagree: *They had a difference of opinion* ***about/over*** *their child's education.* **AMOUNT** ▷ **7** B1 [C or U] the amount by which one thing is different from another: *a(n)* ***age/price/temperature*** *difference* ◦ *There's a big difference* ***in*** *age* ***between*** *them.* ◦ *There's a difference* ***of*** *eight years* ***between*** *them.*

> **Word partners for difference**
>
> *know/tell* the difference • a *big/important/major/vast* difference • a *basic/fundamental* difference • a *marked/obvious* difference • a *slight/subtle* difference • a difference *in* sth • a difference *between* [two things]

different /ˈdɪf.ər.ənt/ ⓤⓢ /-ɚ-/ adj **1** A1 not the same: *She seems to wear something different every day.* ◦ *He's different now that he's been to college.* ◦ *We're reading a different book this week.* ◦ *Emily is* ***very/completely/entirely*** *different* ***from*** *her sister.* ◦ *Emily and her sister are quite (= completely) different.* ◦ *There are many different* ***types/kinds*** *of bacteria.* **2** informal describes something or someone you think is unusual or shows bad judgment: *What do I think of your purple shoes? Well, they're certainly different.* • **differently** /-li/ adv B1 *We want to do things differently.* ◦ *Are girls treated differently?*

> **! Common mistake: different**
>
> **Warning:** Check your spelling!
>
> **Different** is one of the 50 words most often spelled wrongly by learners.

> **! Common mistake: different or difference?**
>
> **Warning:** do not confuse the adjective **different** with the noun **difference**:
>
> *~~Children need to learn the different between right and wrong.~~*
>
> *Children need to learn the difference between right and wrong.*

> **Other ways of saying different**
>
> See also: **unusual**
>
> If something is different from what people normally expect, you can say that it is **unusual**:
>
> *Carina – that's quite an* ***unusual*** *name.*
>
> The adjective **alternative** is often used to describe something which is different from something else but can be used instead of it:
>
> *The hotel's being renovated, so we're looking for an* ***alternative*** *venue.*
>
> If something is very different and separate from other things, you can describe it as **distinct** or **distinctive**:
>
> *She's got really* ***distinctive*** *handwriting.*
>
> *The word has three* ***distinct*** *meanings.*
>
> The preposition **unlike** is often used to compare people or things that are very different from each other:
>
> *Dan's actually quite nice,* ***unlike*** *his father.*
>
> *The furniture was* ***unlike*** *anything she had ever seen.*

differential /ˌdɪf.əˈren.ʃəl/ **noun; adj**
▸noun [C] **GAP** ▷ **1** an amount of difference between things that are compared: *a* ***price*** *differential* ◦ *The* ***pay*** *differential* ***between*** *workers and management is too great.* **GEAR** ▷ **2** a **differential gear**
▸adj based on a difference: *We have a differential salary structure based on employees' experience.* • **differentially** /-i/ adv

ˌdifferential ˈcalculus noun [U] specialized the branch of CALCULUS in which rates of change and connected quantities are calculated

ˌdifferential ˈgear noun [C] specialized a device fitted to the AXLE of a vehicle that allows the wheels to turn at different rates when going round a corner

differentiate /ˌdɪf.əˈren.ʃi.eɪt/ verb **FIND DIFFERENCE** ▷ **1** C1 [I or T] to show or find the difference between things that are compared: *We do not differentiate* ***between*** *our workers on the basis of their background or ethnic origin.* **MAKE DIFFERENT** ▷ **2** C2 [T] to make someone or something different: *The slate roof differentiates this house* ***from*** *others in the area.*

differentiation /ˌdɪf.ər.en.ʃiˈeɪ.ʃən/ ⓤⓢ /-ə.ren-/ noun **1** [C] the act of differentiating: *a differentiation between mental illness and mental handicap* **2** [U] the process of becoming or making something different: *Product differentiation is essential to the future of the company.*

difficult /ˈdɪf.ɪ.kəlt/ adj **1** A1 needing skill or effort: *a difficult problem/choice/task/language* ◦ [+ to infinitive] ***It*** *will be very difficult* ***to*** *prove that they are guilty.* ◦ *Many things make* ***it*** *difficult* ***for*** *women* ***to*** *reach the top in US business.* ◦ [+ -ing verb] *He finds* ***it*** *extremely difficult be****ing*** *a single parent.* → Opposite **easy** **2** B1 not friendly, easy to deal with, or behaving well: [+ to infinitive] *The manager is difficult* ***to*** *deal with/a difficult person* ***to*** *deal with.* ◦ *His wife is a very difficult woman.* ◦ *Please children, don't be so difficult!*

difficulty /ˈdɪf.ɪ.kəl.ti/ ⓤⓢ /-t̬i/ **noun** **1** B1 [U] the fact of not being easy to do or understand: *We finished the job, but only* ***with*** *great difficulty.* ◦ *The difficulty* ***of*** *the task excited them.* ◦ *People with asthma have difficulty* ***in*** *breathing.* ◦ [+ -ing verb] *She* ***had*** *great difficulty finding a job.* **2** B2 [C] a problem: *to* ***have*** *financial/personal difficulties* ◦ *People learning a new language often* ***encounter*** *some difficulties at first.* ◦ *An unforeseen difficulty has* ***arisen****.* **3 be in difficulties** UK (US

D

Other ways of saying difficult

Hard is very often used instead of 'difficult' and means exactly the same:

*The exam was really **hard**.*

*It must be **hard** to study with all this noise.*

If something is difficult to understand or do because it has a lot of different parts or stages, you can say that it is **complicated** or **complex**:

*The instructions were so **complicated** I just couldn't follow them.*

*Designing a house is a **complex** process.*

Tricky describes something difficult that needs skill or needs you to be very careful:

*It's quite **tricky** getting the puzzle pieces to fit together.*

*It's a **tricky** situation – I don't want to upset anyone.*

Awkward describes something that is difficult to deal with and could cause problems:

*Luckily, she didn't ask any **awkward** questions.*

Demanding means 'needing a lot of your time, attention, or effort':

*She has a very **demanding** job.*

*Like most young children, he's very **demanding**.*

A situation or piece of work that is **challenging** is difficult and needs all your skills and determination:

*This has been a **challenging** time for us all.*

*I found the class very **challenging**.*

You say **easier said than done** about something that is impossible or very difficult to do:

*I know I should stop smoking but it's **easier said than done**.*

be in difficulty) to have problems or be in a difficult situation: *A ship is in difficulties off the coast of Ireland.*

Common mistake: difficulty

Warning: Choose the right verb!

Don't say 'find difficulty doing something', say **have difficulty doing something**:

~~*If you find difficulty understanding the instructions, call me.*~~

If you have difficulty understanding the instructions, call me.

Word partners for difficulty

have difficulty (*in*) doing sth • *encounter/experience/run into* difficulties • difficulties *arise* • *considerable/great/serious* difficulty • *fraught with* difficulty • (do sth) *with/without* difficulty • the difficulty *of* sth/doing sth

diffident /ˈdɪf.ɪ.dᵊnt/ **adj** shy and not confident of your abilities: *a diffident manner* ◦ *You shouldn't be so diffident **about** your achievements – you've done really well!* • **diffidence** /-dᵊns/ **noun** [U] • **diffidently** /-li/ **adv**

diffract /dɪˈfrækt/ **verb** [T] to break up light or sound waves by making them go through a narrow space or across an edge

diffraction /dɪˈfræk.ʃᵊn/ **noun** [U] specialized (a pattern caused by) a change in the direction of light, water or sound waves

diffuse verb; adj

▸verb [I or T] /dɪˈfjuːz/ **1** to (cause something to) spread in many directions: *Television is a powerful means of diffusing knowledge.* **2** to (cause a gas or liquid to) spread through or into a surrounding substance by mixing with it: *Oxygen diffuses from the lungs **into** the bloodstream.* • **diffusion** /dɪˈfjuː.ʒᵊn/ **noun** [U] *the process of diffusion in gases/liquids/solids*

▸adj /dɪˈfjuːs/ **SPREAD** ▷ **1** spread out and not directed in one place: *a diffuse light* ◦ *The company has become large and diffuse.* **NOT CLEAR** ▷ **2** disapproving not clear or easy to understand: *a diffuse literary style* • **diffusely** /-li/ adv

dig /dɪg/ verb; noun

▸verb (present tense **digging**, past tense and past participle **dug**) **MOVE SOIL** ▷ **1** B1 [I or T] to break up and move soil using a tool, a machine or your hands: *Digging (in) the garden is good exercise.* **2** B2 [T] to form a hole by moving soil: *The tunnel was dug with the aid of heavy machinery.* **SEARCH** ▷ **3** [I usually + adv/prep] to search for an object or information or to find it after looking: *He dug **into** his pocket and took out a few coins.* ◦ *As I dug **deeper into** his past (= found out more about it), I realized that there was a lot about this man that I didn't know.* **PRESS** ▷ **4 dig sb in the ribs** to push the side of someone's body quickly with your ELBOW (= the middle part of the arm where it bends) often as a way of sharing a private joke with them or to get their attention **APPROVE** ▷ **5** [T] old-fashioned slang to like or understand something: *Hey, I really dig those shoes!* ◦ *You dig my meaning, man?*

IDIOMS **dig your heels in** to refuse to change your plans or ideas, especially when someone is trying to persuade you to do so • **dig yourself into a hole** informal to get yourself into a difficult situation: *The government has really dug itself into a hole with its economic policies.* • **dig your own grave** to do something that causes you harm, sometimes serious harm: *She dug her own grave when she made fun of the boss.*

PHRASAL VERBS **dig (yourself) in** to make arrangements to protect yourself from an attack by the enemy in a war situation, for example by digging TRENCHES (= long, narrow holes) • **dig in** informal to start eating: *The food's going cold – dig in!* • **dig (sth) into sb/sth** to press or push, or to press or push an object, hard into someone or something: *A stone was digging into my heel.* ◦ *She dug her fingernails into my wrist.* • **dig sb/sth out** to get someone or something out of somewhere by digging: *Firefighters helped to dig out the people trapped in the snowdrift.* ◦ *The doctor used a sharp instrument to dig a piece of glass out of my finger.* • **dig sth out** informal to find something that you have not seen or used for a long time: *Mum dug out some old family photos to show me.* • **dig sth up MOVE SOIL** ▷ **1** to take something out of the ground by digging: *It's time we dug up those potatoes.* **2** to break the ground or to make a hole in it with a tool, machine, etc.: *They're digging up the road outside to repair the electricity cables.* **INFORMATION** ▷ **3** to discover secret or forgotten facts by searching very carefully: *I've been doing some research on our family history and I've dug up some interesting information.* ◦ *She's one of those journalists who's always trying to dig up **dirt on** (= unpleasant private details about) celebrities.*

▸noun [C] **REMARK** ▷ **1** a remark that is intended to criticize, embarrass, or make a joke about someone: *He's always **having/taking/making** digs **at** me.* **REMOVE SOIL** ▷ **2** the process of carefully removing soil and objects from an area of historical interest: *an **archaeological** dig* **ACCOMMODATION** ▷ **3 digs** [plural] mainly UK informal for **lodgings**: *Many students in London have to live **in** digs.*

the digerati /ˌdɪdʒ.əˈrɑː.tiː/ (US) /-əˈrɑː.t̬iː/ **noun** [plural] mainly humorous people who know a lot about computers and who use them a lot

digest verb; noun

▸**verb** /daɪˈdʒest/ **EAT** ▷ **1** (C1) [I or T] to change food in your stomach into substances that your body can use: *I find that I don't digest meat easily.* ◦ *Sit still and allow your meal to digest.* **UNDERSTAND** ▷ **2** (C1) [T] to read or hear new information and take the necessary time to understand it: *This chapter is so difficult to digest, I shall have to read it again later.*

▸**noun** [C] /ˈdaɪ.dʒest/ a short written report providing the most important parts of a larger piece of writing, or one containing recent news: *A digest **of** the research findings is now available.* ◦ *The company publishes a monthly digest of its activities.*

digestible /daɪˈdʒes.tə.bl̩/ **adj** **FOOD** ▷ **1** easy to digest **INFORMATION** ▷ **2** easy to understand

digestion /daɪˈdʒes.tʃən/ **noun** [C or U] (C1) the process in which your body digests food, or your ability to digest food: *a poor/good/strong digestion* ◦ *Discover how eating raw food helps balance your body and **aids** digestion.*

digestive /daɪˈdʒes.tɪv/ **adj; noun**

▸**adj** relating to the digestion of food: *the digestive process*

▸**noun** [C] (also **diˌgestive ˈbiscuit**) UK a slightly sweet biscuit made from WHOLEMEAL flour

diˈgestive ˌsystem **noun** [C usually singular] the organs in your body involved with the digestion of food

diˈgestive ˌtract **noun** [C usually singular] specialized the tube-like passage from the mouth, through the stomach and to the ANUS, through which food travels during digestion → Compare **alimentary canal**

digger /ˈdɪg.əʳ/ (US) /-ɚ/ **noun** [C] **1** a machine used for digging: *a mechanical digger* **2** Australian English a person who MINES for gold (= removes it from under the ground) → See also **gold digger**

digit /ˈdɪdʒ.ɪt/ **noun** [C] **NUMBER** ▷ **1** any one of the ten numbers 0 to 9: *The number 345 contains three digits.* **FINGER** ▷ **2** specialized a finger, thumb or toe

digital /ˈdɪdʒ.ɪ.təl/ (US) /-t̬əl/ **adj** **1** (A2) describes information, music, an image, etc. that is recorded or broadcast using computer TECHNOLOGY: *digital data* ◦ *a digital recording* ◦ *a digital camera* ◦ *digital TV* ◦ *digital compact/audio cassettes* **2** (B1) showing information in the form of an electronic image: *a digital clock/display* ◦ *a digital watch* • **digitally** /-i/ **adv** *Sound and pictures can be stored digitally, as on a CD.*

ˌdigital audio ˈbroadcasting **noun** [U] (abbreviation **DAB**) a system of broadcasting sound and written information using electronic signals which represent a series of the numbers 0 and 1

ˌdigital ˈaudio ˌtape **noun** [C or U] (abbreviation **DAT**) a MAGNETIC TAPE used to record high-quality sound by storing information as a series of the numbers 0 and 1 → See also **magnetic tape**

ˌdigital ˈcamera **noun** [C] (A2) a type of camera that records images that can be looked at on a computer

ˌdigital ˈradio **noun** **1** [U] the system of broadcasting using digital electronic signals that carry sound and information about what is being broadcast **2** [C] a piece of electronic equipment used to listen to digital radio broadcasts

digitize (UK usually **digitise**) /ˈdɪdʒ.ɪ.taɪz/ **verb** [T] to put information into the form of a series of the numbers 0 and 1, usually so that it can be understood and used by a computer

diglossia /ˌdaɪˈglɒs.i.ə/ (US) /-ˈglɑː.si-/ **noun** [U] specialized a situation in which there are two different forms of the same language used by a community, used in different social situations

dignified /ˈdɪg.nɪ.faɪd/ **adj** (C2) controlled, serious, and calm, and therefore deserving respect: *a tall, dignified woman* ◦ *He has maintained a dignified **silence** about the rumours.*

dignify /ˈdɪg.nɪ.faɪ/ **verb** [T] **1** to cause something to be respected and considered important **2** to cause something to be respected and considered important when that is not deserved: *I'm not even going to dignify that stupid question **with** an answer.*

dignitary /ˈdɪg.nɪ.tər.i/ (US) /-nə.ter-/ **noun** [C] a person who has an important position in a society: *Several foreign dignitaries attended the ceremony.*

dignity /ˈdɪg.nɪ.ti/ (US) /-ə.t̬i/ **noun** [U] **1** (C2) calm, serious, and controlled behaviour that makes people respect you: *He is a man of dignity and calm determination.* ◦ *She has **a** quiet dignity about her.* ◦ *I think everyone should be able to die with dignity.* **2** the importance and value that a person has, that makes other people respect them or makes them respect themselves: *How could you wear something so indecent? Have you no dignity?* ◦ *In hospital, she felt stripped of all her dignity.* ◦ *He longs for a society in which the dignity **of** all people is recognized.*

IDIOM **beneath your dignity** (C2) If something is beneath your dignity, you feel that you are too important to do it: *He felt cleaning of any description was beneath his dignity.*

digress /daɪˈgres/ **verb** [I] to move away from the main subject you are writing or talking about and to write or talk about something else: *But I digress. To get back to what I was saying, this poem reflects the poet's love of nature and his religious beliefs.* ◦ *The lecturer temporarily digressed **from** her subject to deal with a related theory.* • **digression** /-ˈgreʃ.ən/ **noun** [C or U] *Talking about money now would be a digression **from** the main purpose of this meeting.*

Dijon mustard /ˌdiː.ʒɒnˈmʌs.təd/ (US) /ˌdiː.ʒoʊnˈmʌs.tɚd/ **noun** [U] a type of smooth yellow MUSTARD, usually containing wine and originally made in Dijon, France

dike /daɪk/ **noun** [C] another spelling of **dyke**

diktat /ˈdɪk.tæt/ **noun** [C or U] disapproving an order that must be obeyed, or the act of giving such an order: *The coach issued a diktat that all team members must attend early-morning practice.* ◦ *The occupying force ruled by diktat.*

dilapidated /dɪˈlæp.ɪ.deɪ.tɪd/ (US) /-t̬ɪd/ **adj** describes something old and in poor condition: *The hotel we stayed in was really dilapidated.* ◦ *a dilapidated old car/shed* • **dilapidation** /dɪˌlæp.ɪˈdeɪ.ʃən/ **noun** [U] *The farmhouse fell into **a state of** dilapidation.*

dilate /daɪˈleɪt/ (US) /ˈdaɪ.leɪt/ **verb** [I or T] to (cause a part of the body to) become wider or further open: *The pupils of the eyes dilate as darkness increases.* ◦ *This drug will dilate the arteries.* • **dilation** /daɪˈleɪ.ʃən/ **noun** [U]

dilatory /ˈdɪl.ə.tər.i/ (US) /-tɔːr.i/ **adj** formal slow and likely to cause delay: *dilatory behaviour/tactics* ◦ *British institutions have been dilatory **in** cutting credit card charges.*

dildo /ˈdɪl.dəʊ/ (US) /-doʊ/ **noun** [C] (plural **dildos**) an object shaped like and used in place of a PENIS, for giving sexual pleasure

dilemma /daɪˈlem.ə/, /dɪ-/ **noun** [C] B2 a situation in which a difficult choice has to be made between two different things you could do: *The president is clearly* ***in*** *a dilemma* ***about/over*** *how to tackle the crisis.* ◦ *She* ***faces*** *the dilemma* ***of*** *disobeying her father or losing the man she loves.* ◦ *a* ***moral/ethical*** *dilemma*

dilettante /ˌdɪl.əˈtæn.ti/ **noun** [C] (plural **dilettanti** or **dilettantes**) usually disapproving a person who is or seems to be interested in a subject, but whose understanding of it is not very deep or serious: *He's a bit of a dilettante as far as wine is concerned.*

D

diligent /ˈdɪl.ɪ.dʒənt/ **adj 1** approving careful and using a lot of effort: *a diligent student* ◦ *Leo is very diligent* ***in/about*** *his work.* ◦ *Their lawyer was extremely diligent* ***in*** *preparing their case.* **2** done in a careful and detailed way: *The discovery was made after years of diligent research.* • **diligence** /-dʒəns/ **noun** [U] *She hoped that her diligence would be noticed at work.* • **diligently** /-li/ **adv**

dill /dɪl/ **noun** [U] a herb whose seeds and thin FEATHERY leaves are used in cooking: *1 tsp fresh dill, chopped*

dilly-dally /ˈdɪl.iˌdæl.i/ **verb** [I] old-fashioned informal to waste time, especially by being slow, or by not being able to make a decision: *Don't dilly-dally – just get your things and let's go!*

dilute /daɪˈluːt/ **verb; adj**

▸**verb** [T] **1** to make a liquid weaker by mixing in something else: *Dilute the juice (****with*** *water) before you drink it.* **2** to reduce the strength of a feeling, action, etc.: *These measures are designed to dilute public fears about the product's safety.* • **dilution** /-ˈluː.ʃən/ **noun** [C or U] *The drug's effectiveness is decreased by dilution.* ◦ *a dilution of standards*

▸**adj** (US usually **diluted**) made weaker by diluting: *dilute hydrochloric acid*

dim /dɪm/ **adj; verb**

▸**adj** (**dimmer**, **dimmest**) **NOT CLEAR** ▷ **1** C not giving or having much light: *The lamp gave out a dim light.* ◦ *He sat in a dim corner of the waiting room.* ◦ *We could see a dim (= not easily seen) shape in the fog.* **2** literary If your eyes are dim, you cannot see very well. **3 a dim memory, recollection, etc.** C something that you remember slightly, but not very well: *I had a dim recollection* ***of*** *having met her before.* **NOT CLEVER** ▷ **4** informal not very clever: *He's a nice guy, but a little dim.* ◦ *Don't be dim!* **NOT POSITIVE** ▷ **5** not likely to succeed: *The company's prospects for the future are rather dim.* • **dimly** /ˈdɪm.li/ **adv** *The room was dimly lit.* ◦ *I dimly remembered seeing the film before.* • **dimness** /ˈdɪm.nəs/ **noun** [U]

IDIOMS **dim and distant** mainly UK from the past and not clearly remembered: *The times of huge profits are now a dim and distant memory.* • **the dim and distant past** mainly UK a time in the past that is not clearly remembered: *I used to enjoy dancing, back in the dim and distant past.* • **take a dim view of sth** to disapprove of something: *I take a dim view of this kind of behaviour.*

▸**verb** [I or T] (**-mm-**) **1** C to (make something) become less bright: *Someone dimmed the lights.* ◦ *The lights dimmed and the curtains opened.* **2** literary to (make a positive feeling or quality) become less strong: *Our hopes/expectations dimmed as the hours passed.*

dime /daɪm/ **noun** [C] C1 an American or Canadian coin that has the value of ten CENTS

IDIOM **be a dime a dozen** US (UK also **be two/ten a penny**) to be common and/or of very little value: *Books like this are a dime a dozen.*

dimension /ˌdaɪˈmen.ʃən/, /ˌdɪ-/ **noun 1** B2 [C often plural] a measurement of something in a particular direction, especially its height, length or width: *Please specify the dimensions (= the height, length and width)* ***of*** *the room.* ◦ *a building of vast dimensions (= size)* **2** B2 [C] a part or feature or way of considering something: *His personality has several dimensions.* ◦ *These weapons add a* ***new*** *dimension to modern warfare.* ◦ *There is a spiritual dimension to her poetry.*

-dimensional /-daɪ.men.ʃən.əl/, /-dɪ-/ **suffix** having measurements in the stated directions: *a three-dimensional figure*

diminish /dɪˈmɪn.ɪʃ/ **verb** [I or T] C1 to reduce or be reduced in size or importance: *I don't want to diminish her achievements, but she did have a lot of help.* ◦ *These memories will not be diminished by time.* ◦ *What he did has seriously diminished him in many people's eyes.* ◦ *We've seen our house diminish* ***greatly/sharply/substantially*** *in value over the last six months.*

diˌminished responsiˈbility **noun** [U] UK (US **diˌminished caˈpacity**) the condition in which someone's mental state, etc. causes them not to be in full control of their actions: *The accused pleaded not guilty* ***on grounds of*** *diminished responsibility.*

diminution /ˌdɪm.ɪˈnjuː.ʃən/ US /-əˈnuː-/ **noun** [C or U] formal reduction in size or importance: *Regular exercise can result in a general diminution* ***in*** *stress levels.* ◦ *The company suffered a diminution in profits.*

diminutive /dɪˈmɪn.jʊ.tɪv/ US /-t̬ɪv/ **adj** very small: *He's a diminutive figure, less than five feet tall.*

dimmer /ˈdɪm.əʳ/ US /-ɚ/ **noun** [C] (also **ˈdimmer switch**) a device for changing the brightness of an electric light, often combined with a switch to turn the light on and off

dimple /ˈdɪm.pl̩/ **noun** [C] a small hollow place, especially one which appears on a person's face when they smile: *Freddie was an angelic-looking child with blond curly hair, blue eyes and dimples.* • **dimpled** /-pld/ **adj** *dimpled cheeks*

dimwit /ˈdɪm.wɪt/ **noun** [C] informal a stupid person: *I've forgotten what I came in here for – I'm such a dimwit!* ◦ *Look where you're going, dimwit!*

ˌdim-ˈwitted **adj** stupid: *Marilyn was portrayed as some sort of dim-witted blonde.*

din /dɪn/ **noun; verb**

▸**noun** [S] a loud unpleasant confused noise which lasts for a long time: *the din* ***of*** *the traffic* ◦ *I had to shout to make myself heard above the din.* ◦ *The children were* ***making*** *a terrible din.*

▸**verb** (**-nn-**)

PHRASAL VERB **din sth into sb** to say something forcefully and repeatedly to someone so that they remember it: *It was dinned into me that I mustn't be late.*

dinar /ˈdiː.nɑːʳ/ US /-nɑːr/ **noun** [C] the standard unit of money used in various countries in the Middle East and North Africa

dine /daɪn/ **verb** [I] formal to eat the main meal of the day, usually in the evening: *I hate dining alone.* ◦ *He once dined* ***with*** *the president of France.*

PHRASAL VERBS **dine on/upon sth** to eat something as a meal: *We dined on salmon and strawberries.* • **dine out** to go to a restaurant to eat your evening meal: *We rarely dine out these days.* • **dine out on sth** mainly UK to entertain people, especially at a meal, by telling them about an experience you have had: *For months*

I've been dining out on the story of what happened when my house got flooded.

diner /ˈdaɪ.nəʳ/ (US) /-nɚ/ noun [C] **1** someone who is eating a meal, especially in a restaurant **2** mainly US a small informal restaurant at the side of the road

ding /dɪŋ/ verb; noun

▸verb **MAKE SOUND** ▷ **1** [I] to make a short ringing sound like a bell **HIT** ▷ **2** [T] US to damage the surface of something slightly by hitting it: *She was worried she might ding the car beside her when she parked.*

▸noun [C] **SOUND** ▷ **1** a short ringing sound like that made by a bell **DAMAGE** ▷ **2** US a small damaged area on a surface where something has hit it: *She had the ding in the paintwork repaired.*

dingbat /ˈdɪŋ.bæt/ noun [C] slang a stupid or easily confused person: *Edith may seem like a dingbat, but she's quite clever really.*

ding-dong /ˈdɪŋ.dɒŋ/ (US) /-dɑːŋ/ noun **SOUND** ▷ **1** [U] used to represent the sound a bell makes **ARGUMENT** ▷ **2** [S] mainly UK informal a noisy argument or fight: *They **had** a real ding-dong in the middle of the restaurant.*

dinghy

dinghy /ˈdɪŋ.gi/ (US) /ˈdɪŋ.i/ noun [C] **1** a small open boat: *an inflatable/motorized dinghy* ◦ *He was transferred to the ship by dinghy.* **2** a small sailing boat: *a dinghy race*

dingo /ˈdɪŋ.gəʊ/ (US) /-goʊ/ noun [C] (plural **dingoes**) a type of wild dog found in Australia

dingy /ˈdɪn.dʒi/ adj dark and often also dirty: *a dingy room/corridor* ◦ *Her hair was a dingy brown colour.* • **dingily** /-dʒɪ.li/ adv

ˈ**dining** ˌ**car** noun [C usually singular] (UK also ˈ**restaurant** ˌ**car**) a part of a train in which passengers are served meals

ˈ**dining** ˌ**hall** noun [C usually singular] a large room in a school or other building, where many people can eat at the same time

ˈ**dining** ˌ**room** noun [C] (A1) a room in which meals are eaten

ˈ**dining** ˌ**table** noun [C] a table at which meals are eaten → Compare **the dinner table**

dinky /ˈdɪŋ.ki/ adj informal small: UK approving *She's got dinky little (= small and charming) feet.* ◦ US disapproving *They live in a dinky one-room apartment.*

dinner /ˈdɪn.əʳ/ (US) /-ɚ/ noun **1** (A1) [C or U] the main meal of the day, usually the meal you eat in the evening but sometimes, in Britain, the meal eaten in the middle of the day: *We were just **having** (our) dinner.* ◦ *We had some friends round for dinner on Saturday.* ◦ *a romantic **candlelit** dinner* → Compare **lunch 2** [C usually singular] a formal social occasion in the evening at which a meal is served: *They **held** a dinner to celebrate his retirement.* ◦ *a charity/society dinner*

ˈ**dinner** ˌ**dance** noun [C] a social occasion in the evening, at which there is a meal and dancing

ˈ**dinner** ˌ**jacket** noun [C] UK (abbreviation **DJ**, US **tuxedo**) a man's black or white jacket worn at formal social events, usually in the evening, with matching trousers and a BOW TIE

dinner jacket

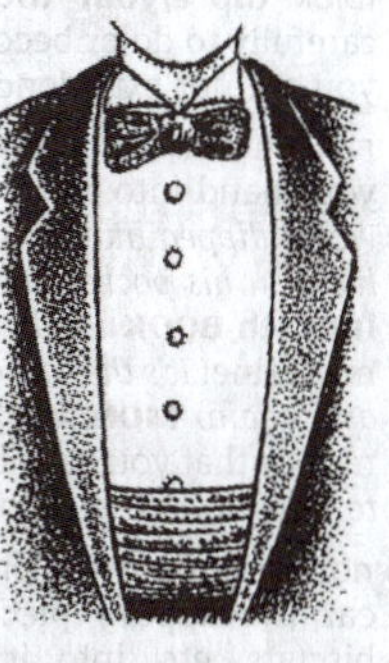

ˈ**dinner** ˌ**party** noun [C] a formal evening meal to which a small number of people are invited: *I'm **having/giving** a dinner party next week.*

ˈ**dinner** ˌ**service** noun [C] (also ˈ**dinner** ˌ**set**) a complete set of plates and dishes with the same design, used when serving a meal to several people

the ˈ**dinner** ˌ**table** noun [S] the table at which the main meal of the day is served, or the occasion when this meal is served: *They sat round the dinner table, arguing about politics.* ◦ *No reading **at** the dinner table!* ◦ *We usually talk about the day's events **over** the dinner table.* → Compare **dining table**

ˈ**dinner** ˌ**time** noun [U] the time at which the main meal of the day is eaten: *I didn't get home till after dinner time.*

dinosaur /ˈdaɪ.nə.sɔːʳ/ (US) /-sɔːr/ noun [C] **1** (A2) a type of reptile which stopped existing about 65,000,000 years ago. There were many different types of dinosaur, some of which were extremely large. **2** disapproving an old-fashioned person or thing that people no longer consider to be useful: *This typewriter's a bit of a dinosaur, isn't it?*

dint /dɪnt/ noun **BECAUSE OF** ▷ **1 by dint of sth** formal as a result of something: *She got what she wanted by dint of pleading and threatening.* **MARK** ▷ **2** [C] a small hollow mark in the surface of something, caused by pressure or by being hit

diocese /ˈdaɪ.ə.sɪs/ noun [C] (plural **dioceses**) an area controlled by a BISHOP • **diocesan** /daɪˈɒs.ɪ.zᵊn/ (US) /-ˈɑː.sə-/ adj

diode /ˈdaɪ.əʊd/ (US) /-oʊd/ noun [C] specialized a device which controls an electric current so that it can only flow in one direction

dioxide /daɪˈɒk.saɪd/ (US) /-ˈɑːk-/ noun [U] specialized a chemical substance consisting of two atoms of OXYGEN combined with one atom of another element: *carbon/sulphur dioxide*

dioxin /daɪˈɒk.sɪn/ (US) /-ˈɑːk-/ noun [C or U] a poisonous chemical of a type produced when substances used for killing plants are made: *Highly toxic dioxins were released into the air.*

dip /dɪp/ verb; noun

▸verb (**-pp-**) **PUT INTO LIQUID** ▷ **1** (B2) [T] to put something into a liquid for a short time: *Dip the fish **in** the batter, then drop it into the hot oil.* ◦ *She dipped her toe **into** the pool to see how cold it was.* **2** [T] to put sheep for a short time into a container of liquid containing chemicals that kill harmful insects on the sheep's bodies **DROP** ▷ **3** (B2) [I] to go down to a lower level: *As you turn the corner, the road dips suddenly.* ◦ *The sun dipped below the horizon.* ◦ *House prices dipped in the first three months of the year.* **4** [T] UK to make the beam from the lights at the front of a vehicle point down: *You'll dazzle oncoming drivers if you don't dip your headlights.*

D

IDIOM **dip a/your toe in (the water)** to start very carefully to do or become involved in something that you are not experienced at

PHRASAL VERBS **dip (sth) in/dip (sth) into sth** to put your hand into a container and take something out: *We all dipped into the box of chocolates.* ◦ *He dipped his hand in his pocket and brought out a few coins.* • **dip into sth** BOOK ▷ **1** UK to read small parts of a book or magazine: *It's the sort of book you can just dip into now and again.* MONEY ▷ **2** to spend part of a supply of money that you have been keeping or saving: *I've had to dip into my savings to pay for the repairs.*

▸noun LIQUID ▷ **1** [C or U] a cold, thick sauce that you eat by dipping pieces of uncooked vegetable or biscuits, etc. into it: *cheese/salsa dip* **2** [C usually singular] a quick swim: *a dip **in** the sea/pool* **3** [C or U] a special liquid used for cleaning, etc.: *a silver dip* ◦ *sheep dip* DROP ▷ **4** [C usually singular] a part of something that is at a lower level or a movement to a lower level: *a dip **in** the road* ◦ *a sudden dip **in** temperature* QUICK LOOK ▷ **5** [C usually singular] a short time spent considering a subject: *We begin our dip **into** local history by examining the town's origins.*

diphtheria /dɪfˈθɪə.ri.ə/, /dɪp-/ ⓤⓢ /-ˈθɪr.i-/ **noun** [U] a serious infectious disease that causes fever and difficulty in breathing and swallowing

diphthong /ˈdɪf.θɒŋ/, /ˈdɪp-/ ⓤⓢ /-θɑːŋ/ **noun** [C] specialized a vowel sound in which the tongue changes position to produce the sound of two vowels → Compare **monophthong, triphthong**

diploid /ˈdɪp.lɔɪd/ **adj** having two sets of CHROMOSOMES (= structures containing chemical patterns that control what a plant or animal is like), one from each parent: *a diploid cell* → Compare **haploid**

diploma /dɪˈpləʊ.mə/ ⓤⓢ /-ˈploʊ-/ **noun** [C] (A2) a document given by a college or university to show that you have passed a particular exam or finished a course: *a diploma **in** business studies* ◦ US *a high school diploma*

diplomacy /dɪˈpləʊ.mə.si/ ⓤⓢ /-ˈploʊ-/ **noun** [U] **1** (C2) the management of relationships between countries: *Diplomacy has so far failed to bring an end to the fighting.* **2** (C2) approving skill in dealing with people without offending or upsetting them: *It took all her tact and diplomacy to persuade him not to resign.*

diplomat /ˈdɪp.lə.mæt/ **noun** [C] **1** (B2) (old-fashioned **diplomatist**) an official whose job is to represent one country in another, and who usually works in an EMBASSY: *a Spanish/British diplomat* **2** approving a person who is skilled at dealing with difficult situations in a way which does not offend people

diplomatic /ˌdɪp.ləˈmæt.ɪk/ ⓤⓢ /-ˈmæţ-/ **adj 1** (C1) involving diplomats or the management of the relationships between countries: *diplomatic negotiations* **2** (C2) approving acting in a way that does not cause offence: *Ask him nicely – be diplomatic.* • **diplomatically** /-ɪ.kəl.i/ **adv**

diploˈmatic ˌbag **noun** [C usually singular] a container in which letters are sent between diplomats without being examined by CUSTOMS officials

diploˈmatic ˌcorps **noun** [C usually singular, + sing/pl verb] all the people from one country who work in another country as diplomats

ˌdiplomatic imˈmunity **noun** [U] the special rights that diplomats have while working in a country that is not their own, such as freedom from legal action: *He did not have to pay his speeding fine because he **pleaded** diplomatic immunity.*

ˌdiplomatic reˈlations **noun** [plural] the arrangement between two countries by which each has REPRESENTATIVES in the other country: *Britain threatened to **break off** diplomatic relations.*

the ˌdiplomatic ˈservice **noun** [S, + sing/pl verb] the government department that employs people to represent their country in other parts of the world

dippy /ˈdɪp.i/ **adj** informal silly: *You dippy thing!*

dipsomania /ˌdɪp.səˈmeɪ.ni.ə/ **noun** [U] a strong need to drink alcohol

dipsomaniac /ˌdɪp.səˈmeɪ.ni.æk/ **noun** [C] (informal **dipso**) someone suffering from dipsomania

dipstick /ˈdɪp.stɪk/ **noun** [C] MEASURE ▷ **1** a long thin stick for measuring the amount of liquid in a container, especially the oil in a car engine PERSON ▷ **2** slang a silly person

ˈdip switch **noun** [C] UK (US **ˈdimmer ˌswitch**) a switch for temporarily reducing the brightness of the lights of a vehicle

dire /daɪəʳ/ ⓤⓢ /daɪr/ **adj 1** very serious or extreme: *These people are in dire **need** of help.* ◦ *He gave a dire **warning** that an earthquake was imminent.* ◦ *This decision will have dire **consequences** for local people.* **2** informal very bad: *I thought that film was dire!*

direct **adj; verb; adv**

▸adj /daɪˈrekt/, /dɪ-/ STRAIGHT ▷ **1** (B1) going in a straight line towards somewhere or someone without stopping or changing direction: *a direct **route/line*** ◦ *Is there a direct train to Edinburgh?* **2** (B2) without anyone or anything else being involved or between: *She decided to take direct control of the project.* ◦ *He denied that he had any direct involvement in the deal.* ◦ *Have you any direct experience of this kind of work?* ◦ *He left as a direct **result/consequence** of what she said.* ◦ *There is a direct **link/connection** between smoking and lung cancer.* **3 direct light/heat** strong light or heat that has nothing protecting and separating you from it: *This plant should be kept out of direct sunlight.* **4 direct relation/relative/descendant** a relation who is related to you through one of your parents, not through an aunt or uncle, etc.: *Diana is a direct descendant of Robert Peel.* COMPLETE ▷ **5** complete: *a direct **contrast*** ◦ *She's very thoughtful – the direct **opposite** of her sister.* HONEST ▷ **6** (C1) describes someone who says what they think in a very honest way without worrying about other people's opinions: *I like her open and direct manner.* • **directness** /-nəs/ **noun** [U]

▸verb CONTROL ▷ **1** (C1) [T] to control or be in charge of an activity, organization, etc.: *There was a police officer directing the traffic.* ◦ *She directs a large charity.* **2** (B1) [I or T] to be in charge of a film or play and tell the actors how to play their parts: *He wanted to give up acting and start directing (his own films).* ◦ *'Jaws' was directed by Steven Spielberg.* → Compare **produce** AIM ▷ **3** (C1) [T usually + adv/prep] to aim something in a particular direction: *Was that remark directed **at/towards** me?* ◦ *Criticism was directed **against/at** the manufacturers of the product.* SAY WHERE ▷ **4** (B1) [T] to tell someone how to get somewhere: *Could you direct me **to** the airport?* ◦ *I couldn't find the station, so I asked someone if they could direct me.* ORDER ▷ **5** [T + obj + to infinitive] formal to order someone, especially officially: *The judge directed the defendant **to** remain silent.*

▸adv **1** without having to stop or change direction: *Does this train go direct to Edinburgh?* **2** without anything or anyone else being involved or in between: *Can I dial this number direct or do I have to go through the switchboard?*

ˌdirect ˈaction **noun** [U] the use of STRIKES, violence, or protests as a way of trying to get what you want, instead of talking

ˌdirect ˈcurrent noun [U] (abbreviation **DC**) electrical current which moves in one direction only → Compare **alternating current**

ˌdirect ˈdebit noun [C or U] UK an arrangement for making payments, usually to an organization, in which your bank moves money from your account into the organization's account at regular times: *I pay my electricity bill* ***by*** *direct debit.* → Compare **standing order**

ˌdirect deˈposit noun [U] US an arrangement in which money is moved electronically into a bank account

diˌrect ˈhit noun [C] an explosion or injury caused when a bomb or bullet hits an object accurately: *The house suffered a direct hit.*

direction /daɪˈrek.ʃən/, /dɪ-/ noun **POSITION** ▷ **1** B1 [C] the position towards which someone or something moves or faces: *'No, go that way,' I said, pointing* ***in*** *the opposite direction.* ◦ *He was going* ***in*** *the direction* ***of*** *the bedroom.* ◦ *They drove away in opposite directions.* **2 directions** A2 [plural] instructions that you give to someone about how to find a particular place: *Can you* ***give*** *me directions* ***to*** *your house?* ◦ *'Did you have any difficulty finding the theatre?' 'No, your directions were excellent.'* **3 sb's direction** B2 the area or position which someone is in: *She keeps looking* ***in*** *my direction.* **4 sense of direction** B2 the ability to find places or to know which direction to go: *a* ***good*** *sense of direction* ◦ *Which way is it? – I* ***have*** *no/a lousy sense of direction!* **CONTROL** ▷ **5** C1 [U] control or instruction: *The project was* ***under*** *the direction* ***of*** *a well-known academic.* **6 directions** C1 [plural] information or orders telling you what to do: *I couldn't understand* ***the*** *directions on the packet.* ◦ *He will be* ***giving/issuing*** *directions* ***to*** *judges* ***on*** *sentencing in the next few days.* **DEVELOPMENT** ▷ **7** C2 [C or U] the way that someone or something changes or develops: *There is disagreement over the direction the project* ***is taking.*** ◦ *Her latest album represents a* ***change of*** *direction for her.* ◦ *This plan isn't perfect, but it's* ***a step in the right*** *direction.*

IDIOM **lack direction** to not know what you really want to do: *She seems to lack direction in her life.*

directional /daɪˈrek.ʃən.əl/, /dɪ-/ adj **SIGNALS** ▷ **1** specialized Directional radio equipment receives or sends stronger signals in particular directions. **FASHION** ▷ **2** very fashionable: *She had a very directional look.*

directionless /daɪˈrek.ʃən.ləs/, /dɪ-/ adj not knowing what to do or what you want to do

directive /daɪˈrek.tɪv/, /dɪ-/ noun [C] formal an official instruction: *The boss* ***issued*** *a directive* ***about*** *not using the fax machine.*

directly /daɪˈrekt.li/, /dɪ-/ adv; conjunction

▸adv **STRAIGHT** ▷ **1** B1 without anything else being involved or in between: *Our hotel room was directly above a building site.* ◦ *The disease is directly linked to poor drainage systems.* ◦ *The sun shone directly in my eyes.* **HONEST** ▷ **2** B2 honestly, even when it might make people feel uncomfortable: *Let me answer that question directly.* ◦ *'Did you tell him to go?' 'Not directly, no.'* **SOON** ▷ **3** old-fashioned or formal very soon: *Dr Schwarz will be with you directly.* **4** old-fashioned immediately: *When you get home you're going directly to bed.*

▸conjunction **1** formal immediately after: *Directly he was paid, he went out shopping.* **2** formal as soon as: *I'll be with you directly I've finished this letter.*

ˌdirect ˈmail noun [U] the activity in which companies or organizations write to people to try to persuade them to buy their product or give money, etc.

ˌdirect ˈobject noun [C] specialized The direct object of a TRANSITIVE verb is the person or thing that is affected by the action of the verb. → Compare **indirect object**

director /daɪˈrek.təʳ/, /dɪ-/ noun [C] **MANAGER** ▷ **1** B1 a manager of an organization, company, college, etc.: *the* ***board of*** *directors* ◦ *She has become the director* ***of*** *the new information centre.* **FILM MAKER** ▷ **2** B1 a person who is in charge of a film or play and tells the actors how to play their parts: *a famous* ***film/movie*** *director* → Compare **producer** • **directorial** /ˌdɪr.ekˈtɔː.ri.əl/ US /-ˈtɔːr.i-/ adj *Is she ready for directorial responsibility?*

directorate /daɪˈrek.tər.ət/, /dɪ-/ noun [C] **1** a department or organization that is responsible for one particular thing: *the Norwegian fish and game directorate* **2** [+ sing/pl verb] a group of directors

diˌrector ˈgeneral noun [C usually singular] the person who is in charge of a big organization

Diˌrector of ˌPublic Proseˈcutions noun [S] the official title of the lawyer who works for the UK government and decides if someone formally accused of committing a crime should be made to appear in a law court

diˈrector's ˌcut noun [C] a later version of a film, that has been made in exactly the way the DIRECTOR originally wanted it to be

directorship /daɪˈrek.tə.ʃɪp/, /dɪ-/ noun [C] the position of being the DIRECTOR of a company: *He holds several company directorships.*

directory /dɪˈrek.tər.i/, /daɪ-/ US /-tɚ.i/ noun [C] C1 a book that gives a list of names, addresses or other facts: *a business directory* ◦ *a directory* ***of*** *hotels* ◦ *Look up their number in the telephone directory.*

Diˌrectory Enˈquiries noun [U, + sing/pl verb] UK (US **Diˌrectory Asˈsistance**) a service that you can phone in order to find out someone's phone number

ˌdirect ˈspeech noun [U] (US also **ˌdirect ˈdiscourse**) When you use direct speech, you repeat what someone has said using exactly the words they used: ***She said, 'If it rains, I won't go out.'*** *is an example of the use of direct speech.* → Compare **indirect speech**

ˌdirect ˈtax noun [C usually singular] the money that a person must pay to the government themselves, such as income tax, rather than through someone else → Compare **indirect tax** • **diˌrect taxˈation** noun [U]

dirge /dɜːdʒ/ US /dɝːdʒ/ noun [C] a slow sad song or piece of music, sometimes played because someone has died

dirham /ˈdɪ.ræm/ US /dɪrˈhæm/ noun [C] the standard unit of money used in the United Arab Emirates and Morocco

dirk /dɜːk/ US /dɝːk/ noun [C] a type of DAGGER (= small pointed knife) used as a weapon in Scotland in the past

dirndl (skirt) /ˌdɜːn.dlˈskɜːt/ US /ˌdɝːn.dlˈskɝːt/ noun [C] a wide skirt tightly GATHERED (= pulled into folds) at the waist

dirt /dɜːt/ US /dɝːt/ noun [U] **NOT CLEAN** ▷ **1** B1 dust, soil or any substance that makes a surface not clean: *His coat was covered with dirt.* **2** mainly US soil on the ground: *I've been digging in the dirt, planting seeds.* **3** informal solid waste: *I got some* ***dog*** *dirt on my shoes.* **GOSSIP** ▷ **4** informal unpleasant or bad details about someone's private life that are repeated or published to influence people's opinion of them in a negative way: *Journalists are always* ***digging for*** *(= trying to discover) dirt.*

ˌdirt ˈcheap adj, adv very cheap

dirtiness /ˈdɜː.ti.nəs/ US /ˈdɝː.t̬i-/ noun [U] the state of being dirty: *I don't mind untidiness – it's dirtiness I can't stand.*

ˌdirt ˈpoor adj US very poor

ˌdirt ˈroad noun [C] US (UK **ˌdirt track**) a road in the countryside made from soil

dirty /ˈdɜː.ti/ US /ˈdɝː.t̬i/ adj; adv; verb

▸adj **NOT CLEAN** ▷ **1** A2 not clean: *Her face was dirty and tear-stained.* **NOT HONEST** ▷ **2** informal unfair, dishonest, or unkind: *She played a dirty* ***trick*** *on me by telling me Diane was having a party when she wasn't.* ◦ *That's a dirty lie!* **NOT POLITE** ▷ **3** informal describes something that is connected with sex, in a way that many people think is offensive: *a dirty* ***magazine/film/joke*** ◦ *You've got a really dirty* ***mind!***

Other ways of saying dirty

If something is extremely dirty, you can say it is **filthy**:

Wash your hands before supper – they're ***filthy!***

If something or someone looks dirty and untidy, you can say that the person or thing is **scruffy** or **messy**:

He's the typical ***scruffy*** *student.*

Ben's bedroom is always really ***messy.***

If something is covered in dirt and needs washing, the adjectives **grimy** and **grubby** are often used:

Don't wipe your ***grimy*** *hands on that clean towel!*

He was wearing an old pair of jeans and a ***grubby*** *T-shirt.*

The adjective **soiled** is a rather formal way of describing something, especially something made of cloth, that is dirty:

Soiled *tablecloths should be soaked in detergent.*

If a place is extremely dirty and unpleasant, the adjective **squalid** is sometimes used:

He lived in a ***squalid*** *dormitory.*

IDIOMS **do sb's dirty work** to do something unpleasant or difficult for someone else because they do not want to do it themselves: *Tell her yourself – I'm not going to do your dirty work for you.* • **do the dirty on sb** UK informal to behave unfairly towards someone, usually without their knowledge: *He can't forgive her for doing the dirty on him and having an affair with his best friend.* • **give sb a dirty look** to look at someone in a disapproving way: *He gave me a really dirty look.*

▸adv **dirty great/big** very great/big: *The old power station's nothing but a dirty great blot on the landscape.*

IDIOM **play dirty** informal to behave dishonestly, especially by cheating in a game: *Dez likes football but he plays dirty.*

▸verb [T] to make something dirty: *Don't sit on the floor – you might dirty your dress.*

IDIOM **dirty your hands** to become involved in something unfair or dishonest: *He refused to dirty his hands by lying about what had happened.*

ˈdirty ˌbomb noun [C] a bomb that has RADIOACTIVE material added to it so that it causes serious damage to the environment

ˌdirty old ˈman noun [C] disapproving or humorous an older man who has an unpleasantly strong interest in sex

ˌdirty ˈtricks noun [plural] dishonest activities intended to harm someone you are competing against: *The airline was accused of a dirty tricks campaign against its main rival.*

ˌdirty weekˈend noun [C usually singular] mainly UK a weekend when two people go away together to have sex, especially secretly, because they are not married to each other

ˌdirty ˈword noun **1** [C] a word that is connected with sex and considered offensive by many people **2** [S] a word or an expression that refers to something that many people do not approve of: *For the environmentally aware, 'disposable' has become a dirty word.*

dis /dɪs/ verb [T] (-ss-) US slang **diss**

dis- /dɪs-/ prefix added to the front of some words to form their opposites: *to disagree* ◦ *a dishonest person* → Compare **in-, non-, un-**

disability /ˌdɪs.əˈbɪl.ɪ.ti/ US /-ə.t̬i/ noun [C or U] B2 an illness, injury, or condition that makes it difficult for someone to do the things that other people do: *a physical/learning disability* ◦ *She is deaf, but refuses to let her disability prevent her from doing what she wants to do.* ◦ *Trying to change attitudes to disability is an uphill struggle.* → Compare **inability**

disable /dɪˈseɪ.bl̩/ verb **PERSON** ▷ **1** [T often passive] to cause someone to have an illness, injury, or condition that makes it difficult for them to do the things that other people do: *She was disabled in the accident.* **MACHINE** ▷ **2** [T] to stop something such as (part of) a machine, system or weapon from working: *These guns will destroy or disable any incoming missile.* ◦ *Disable the alarm system and then enter the building.* • **disabling** /-blɪŋ/ adj *a disabling illness*

disabled /dɪˈseɪ.bl̩d/ adj; noun

▸adj **1** B1 not having one or more of the physical or mental abilities that most people have: *The accident left him severely disabled.* **2** B1 [before noun] specially relating to or intended for disabled people: *The library does not have disabled* ***access.***

▸noun [plural] **the disabled** people who are disabled: *It is often very difficult for the disabled to find jobs.*

disabuse /ˌdɪs.əˈbjuːz/ verb [T] formal to cause someone no longer to have a wrong idea: *He thought that all women liked children, but she soon disabused him* ***of*** *that (idea/notion).*

disaccharide /daɪˈsæk.ə.raɪd/ noun [C] specialized a sugar that is formed of two single sugar MOLECULES: *Sucrose is a disaccharide made of one fructose and one glucose molecule.*

disadvantage /ˌdɪs.ədˈvɑːn.tɪdʒ/ US /-ˈvæn.t̬ɪdʒ/ noun; verb

▸noun [C or U] **1** B1 a condition or situation which causes problems, especially one which causes something or someone to be less successful than other things or people: *One disadvantage of living in the town is the lack of safe places for the children to play.* ◦ *We need to consider whether the disadvantages of the plan outweigh the advantages.* **2 at a disadvantage** C2 in a situation in which you are less likely to succeed than others: *He's at a disadvantage being so shy.* ◦ *This new law* ***places/puts*** *poorer families at a distinct disadvantage.* • **disadvantageous** /ˌdɪs.æd.vənˈteɪ.dʒəs/ US /-væn-/ adj

▸verb [T] to cause someone or something to be less successful than most other people or things: *Teachers claim such measures could unfairly disadvantage ethnic minorities.*

disadvantaged /ˌdɪs.ədˈvɑːn.tɪdʒd/ (US) /-ˈvæn.t̬ɪdʒd/ adj; noun
▸adj (C1) not having the standard of living conditions, education, etc. that most people have: *A new educational programme has been set up for economically disadvantaged children.*
▸noun [plural] **the disadvantaged** people who do not have good living conditions, a good standard of education, etc., considered as a group: *These measures are intended to help the disadvantaged.*

disaffected /ˌdɪs.əˈfek.tɪd/ adj **1** no longer supporting or being satisfied with an organization or idea: *The party needs to take steps to attract disaffected voters.* **2** describes young people who are no longer satisfied with society's values: *The teacher said that he found it difficult to cope with a class of disaffected **teenagers**.* ◦ *disaffected youth* • **disaffection** /-ʃᵊn/ noun [U] *a growing disaffection with the country's political leaders*

disagree /ˌdɪs.əˈgriː/ verb [I] **1** (B1) to not have the same opinion, idea, etc.: *I'm afraid I have to disagree **with** you (**on** that issue).* ◦ [+ that] *Few people would disagree **that** something should be done to reduce crime in the area.* ◦ *I **profoundly/strongly** disagree **with** the decision that has been taken.* → Opposite **agree 2** If two or more statements, ideas, sets of numbers, etc. disagree, they are not the same.

PHRASAL VERB **disagree with sb** If a type of food disagrees with you, it makes you feel slightly ill or uncomfortable: *Spicy food disagrees with me.*

disagreeable /ˌdɪs.əˈgriː.ə.bl̩/ adj formal unpleasant: *a rather disagreeable young man* ◦ *She said some very disagreeable things.* • **disagreeably** /-bli/ adv

disagreement /ˌdɪs.əˈgriː.mənt/ noun [C or U] (B2) an argument or a situation in which people do not have the same opinion: *We had a disagreement **about/over** the fee for the work.* ◦ *Literary critics were **in** total disagreement (**about** the value of the book).*

disallow /ˌdɪs.əˈlaʊ/ verb [T] to say officially that something cannot be accepted because it has not been done in the correct way: *The England team had two goals disallowed.* → Opposite **allow**

disambiguate /ˌdɪs.æmˈbɪg.ju.eɪt/ verb [I or T] specialized to show the differences between two or more meanings clearly: *Good dictionary definitions disambiguate between similar meanings.* • **disambiguation** /ˌdɪs.æmˈbɪg.ju.eɪ.ʃᵊn/ noun [U]

> **Other ways of saying disappear**
>
> **Go away** is an alternative to 'disappear':
>
> *It was weeks before the bruises **went away**.*
>
> **Vanish** or the phrase **vanish into thin air** can be used when someone or something disappears, especially in a sudden and surprising way:
>
> *Dinosaurs **vanished** from the Earth 65 million years ago.*
>
> If people or things disappear and no one knows where they are, you can say that they **go missing**:
>
> *The computer files containing nuclear secrets **went missing** for a short time.*
>
> If something disappears slowly, you can say it **fades away**:
>
> *As the years passed, the memories **faded away**.*

disappear /ˌdɪs.əˈpɪəʳ/ (US) /-ˈpɪr/ verb [I] **1** (B1) If people or things disappear, they go somewhere where they cannot be seen or found: *The search was called off for the sailors who disappeared in the storm.* ◦ *I can't find my keys anywhere – they've completely disappeared.* ◦ *The sun disappeared **behind** a cloud.* ◦ *We looked for her but she had disappeared **into** the crowd.* ◦ *I don't know how it's possible for a person to **disappear without trace**.* **2** (B2) to no longer exist: *These flowers are disappearing **from** our countryside.* ◦ *This is a way of life that is fast disappearing.*

disappearance /ˌdɪs.əˈpɪə.rᵊns/ (US) /-ˈpɪr.ᵊns/ noun [C or U] (B2) the fact of someone or something disappearing: *A man was being questioned in connection with her disappearance.*

the disapˈpeared noun [plural] people who have been killed by a government or army, usually for political reasons, and whose bodies have not been found

disappoint /ˌdɪs.əˈpɔɪnt/ verb [I or T] (B1) to fail to satisfy someone or their hopes, wishes, etc., or to make someone feel unhappy: *I'm sorry to disappoint you, but I'm afraid I can't come after all.* ◦ *We don't want to disappoint the fans.*

disappointed /ˌdɪs.əˈpɔɪn.tɪd/ (US) /-t̬ɪd/ adj (B1) unhappy because someone or something was not as good as you hoped or expected, or because something did not happen: *We were **deeply** disappointed **at/about** the result.* ◦ *His parents were **bitterly** disappointed **in/with** him.* ◦ [+ (that)] *She was disappointed (**that**) they hadn't phoned.* ◦ [+ to infinitive] *He was disappointed **to** find they'd already gone.* ◦ *If you're expecting Dad to let you borrow his car, you're going to be **sorely** disappointed.* • **disappointedly** /-li/ adv

> **! Common mistake: disappointed**
>
> **Warning:** Check your spelling!
>
> **Disappointed** is one of the 50 words most often spelled wrongly by learners. Remember: the correct spelling has 's' and 'pp'.

> **Other ways of saying disappointed**
>
> If someone feels very disappointed about something that has happened, you can use the adjective **disheartened**:
>
> *He was very **disheartened** by the results of the test.*
>
> A person who does not do what he or she agreed to do can be said to have **let** *someone* **down**:
>
> *John had promised to go but he **let** me **down** at the last minute.*
>
> A situation that makes someone feel disappointed is often described as a **letdown**:
>
> *After finally winning the playoffs, the loss of the championship game was a real **letdown**.*
>
> An **anticlimactic** experience is a disappointing experience, often one that you thought would be exciting before it happened or one that comes after a more exciting experience:
>
> *After so much preparation, the party itself was a little **anticlimactic**.*

disappointing /ˌdɪs.əˈpɔɪn.tɪŋ/ (US) /-t̬ɪŋ/ adj (B1) making you feel disappointed: *What a disappointing result!* ◦ *The response to our advertisement has been somewhat disappointing.* • **disappointingly** /-li/ adv *The team played very disappointingly.*

disappointment /ˌdɪs.əˈpɔɪnt.mənt/ noun **1** (B1) [U] the feeling of being disappointed: *Book early to **avoid** disappointment.* ◦ ***To** my (**great**) disappointment (= sadness), he decided to leave.* **2** (B1) [C usually singular] something or someone that is not what you were hoping it would be: *The party turned out to be a huge* *disappointment.* ◦ *I'm afraid I've been rather a disappointment* ***to*** *my parents.*

disapprobation /ˌdɪsˌæp.rəˈbeɪ.ʃᵊn/ (US) /ˌdɪsˌæp-/ **noun** [U] formal strong feelings of not approving of something or someone: *She feared her father's disapprobation.*

disapproval /ˌdɪs.əˈpruː.vᵊl/ **noun** [U] **C1** the feeling of having a negative opinion of someone or something: *Although they said nothing, she could sense their disapproval* ***of*** *her suggestion.* ◦ *There was a note of disapproval in the teacher's voice.*

D

disapprove /ˌdɪs.əˈpruːv/ **verb** [I] **B2** to feel that something or someone is bad, wrong, etc.: *The survey showed that 32 percent of respondents approve, 54 percent disapprove, and the rest are undecided.* ◦ *I* ***strongly*** *disapprove,* ***of*** *underage drinking.* → Opposite **approve**

disapproving /ˌdɪs.əˈpruː.vɪŋ/ **adj** showing that you feel something or someone is bad or wrong: *a disapproving look* • **disapprovingly** /-li/ **adv** *They looked at her disapprovingly.*

disarm /dɪˈsɑːm/ (US) /-ˈsɑːrm/ **verb** **REMOVE WEAPONS** ▷ **1** [I or T] to take weapons away from someone, or to give up weapons or armies: *With one movement, she disarmed the man and pinned him against the wall.* ◦ *Many politicians argued that this was no time to disarm (= give up the country's weapons and army).* **PERSONALITY** ▷ **2** [T] to make someone like you, especially when they had not expected to: *His frankness completely disarmed her.* • **disarming** /-ˈsɑː.mɪŋ/ (US) /-ˈsɑːrmɪŋ/ **adj** approving *He displayed a disarming honesty by telling them about his father's bankruptcy.*

disarmament /dɪˈsɑː.mə.mənt/ (US) /-ˈsɑːr-/ **noun** [U] the act of taking away or giving up weapons: *She said she supported* ***nuclear*** *disarmament.* ◦ *the disarmament of the militia*

disarrange /ˌdɪs.əˈreɪndʒ/ **verb** [T] formal to make something untidy

disarray /ˌdɪs.əˈreɪ/ **noun** [U] formal the state of being confused and having no organization or of being untidy: *Ever since the oil crisis, the industry has been* ***in*** *(****a state of****) disarray.* ◦ *The news had* ***thrown*** *his plans* ***into*** *disarray.* ◦ *Her clothes were* ***in*** *disarray.*

disassemble /ˌdɪs.əˈsem.bl̩/ **verb** [T] to separate something into its different parts: *This video shows you how to disassemble a television set.*

disassociate /ˌdɪs.əˈsəʊ.si.eɪt/ (US) /-ˈsoʊ-/ **verb** [T] to DISSOCIATE

disaster /dɪˈzɑː.stəʳ/ (US) /-ˈzæs.tɚ/ **noun** [C or U] **1** **B2** (an event which results in) great harm, damage or death, or serious difficulty: *An inquiry was ordered into the recent rail disaster (= a serious train accident).* ◦ *It would be a disaster* ***for*** *me if I lost my job.* ◦ *This is one of the worst* ***natural*** *disasters ever to* ***befall*** *the area.* ◦ *Heavy and prolonged rain can* ***spell*** *disaster* ***for*** *many plants.* ◦ *Everything was going smoothly until suddenly disaster* ***struck****.* ◦ *Inviting James and Ivan to dinner on the same evening was a* ***recipe for*** *disaster (= caused a very difficult situation) – they always argue with each other.* **2 be a disaster** **B2** informal to be very unsuccessful or extremely bad: *The evening was a complete disaster.* ◦ *As an engineer, he was a disaster.*

> **Word partners for disaster**
>
> a *major/terrible* disaster • disaster *happens/strikes* • *end in/turn to* disaster • *spell* disaster • be *heading for* disaster • *avert/avoid/prevent* disaster • a disaster *for* sb/sth

diˈsaster ˌarea **noun** **1** [C usually singular] a place where a very serious accident, such as an EARTHQUAKE, has happened **2** [S] humorous an extremely untidy, dirty, or badly organized place: *After the party, the house was a complete disaster area.*

disastrous /dɪˈzɑː.strəs/ (US) /-ˈzæs.trəs/ **adj** **C1** extremely bad or unsuccessful: *Such a war would be disastrous* ***for*** *the country.* ◦ *This decision will have a disastrous impact on foreign policy.* ◦ *His first attempt was disastrous.* • **disastrously** /-li/ **adv** *Things began to go disastrously wrong.*

disavow /ˌdɪs.əˈvaʊ/ **verb** [T] formal to say that you know nothing about something, or that you have no responsibility for or connection with something: *She tried to disavow her past.* • **disavowal** /-ᵊl/ **noun** [C]

disband /dɪsˈbænd/ **verb** [I] to stop being a group: *She formed a political group which disbanded a year later.*

disbar /dɪsˈbɑːʳ/ (US) /-ˈbɑːr/ **verb** [T] (-rr-) legal to make someone unable to continue working as a lawyer, especially because they have done something wrong

disbelief /ˌdɪs.bɪˈliːf/ **noun** [U] the feeling of not being able to believe that something is true or real: *His response was one of complete disbelief.* ◦ *She shook her head* ***in*** *disbelief.*

disbelieve /ˌdɪs.bɪˈliːv/ **verb** [I or T] formal to not believe someone or something: *Do you disbelieve me?* ◦ *They said that they disbelieved the evidence.*

disburse /dɪsˈbɜːs/ (US) /-ˈbɝːs/ **verb** [T] formal to pay out money, usually from an amount that has been collected for a particular purpose: *The local authorities annually disburse between £50 million and £100 million on arts projects.*

disbursement /dɪsˈbɜːs.mənt/ (US) /-ˈbɝːs.mənt/ **noun** [C] an amount of money given for a particular purpose

disc (US also **disk**) /dɪsk/ **noun** [C] **1** **B2** a circular flat object: *The dog's name was engraved on a little metal disc attached to its collar.* **2** **C2** a small piece of CARTILAGE (= strong body tissue that stretches) between the bones in your back **3** **B1** a musical record or a COMPACT DISC → See also **CD**

discard /dɪˈskɑːd/ (US) /-ˈskɑːrd/ **verb; noun**

▸**verb** **1** [T] to throw something away or get rid of it because you no longer want or need it: *Discarded food containers and bottles littered the streets.* **2** [I or T] to get rid of a card you are holding during a card game

▸**noun** [C] in a card game, a card that you have got rid of

ˈdisc ˌbrake **noun** [C] a type of BRAKE where two pieces of material are pressed against a metal disc that is fixed to a wheel

discern /dɪˈsɜːn/ (US) /-ˈsɝːn/ **verb** [T] formal to see, recognize, or understand something that is not clear: *I could just discern a figure in the darkness.* ◦ *It is difficult to discern any pattern in these figures.*

discernible /dɪˈsɜː.nɪ.bl̩/ (US) /-ˈsɝː-/ **adj** formal able to be seen or understood: *The influence of Rodin is discernible in the younger artist.* ◦ *There is no discernible reason why this should be the case.* • **discernibly** /-bli/ **adv**

discerning /dɪˈsɜː.nɪŋ/ (US) /-ˈsɝː-/ **adj** formal approving showing good judgment, especially about style and quality: *a discerning customer*

discernment /dɪˈsɜːn.mənt/ (US) /-ˈsɝːn-/ **noun** [U] formal approving the ability to judge people and things well: *It's clear that you are a person of discernment.*

discharge verb; noun

▸**verb** /dɪsˈtʃɑːdʒ/ (US) /-ˈtʃɑːrdʒ/ **ALLOW TO LEAVE** ▷ **1** [T] to allow someone officially to leave somewhere, especially a hospital or a law court: *Patients were discharged* ***from*** *hospital because the beds were needed by other people.* ◦ *A peace protester was* ***conditionally*** *discharged for twelve months (= allowed to go free only if they do not commit a crime again for this period of time).* ◦ *More than half of all prisoners discharged are reconvicted within two years.* **SEND OUT** ▷ **2** [I or T] to send out a substance, especially waste liquid or gas: *Large amounts of dangerous waste are discharged daily by the factory.* ◦ *The oil which discharged* ***into*** *the sea seriously harmed a lot of birds and animals.* **PERFORM** ▷ **3** [T] formal to perform a task, especially an official one: *If the authority is to discharge its legal* ***duty*** *to house the homeless, it needs government support.* **4 discharge a debt** formal to pay back a debt completely **FIRE GUN** ▷ **5** [T] formal to fire a gun, or to fire a shot from a gun: *The police stated that some 50 rounds had been discharged.*

▸**noun** /ˈdɪs.tʃɑːdʒ/ (US) /-tʃɑːrdʒ/ **PERMISSION TO LEAVE** ▷ **1** [C or U] official permission to leave the armed forces, a prison, or a hospital: *The judge* ***gave*** *him a one-year* ***conditional*** *discharge.* ◦ *The soldier* ***received*** *a* ***dishonourable*** *discharge for a disciplinary offence.* **SUBSTANCE** ▷ **2** [C or U] the act of sending out waste liquid or gas: *Thousands of fish were killed as a result of a discharge* ***of*** *poisonous chemicals from a nearby factory.* **3** [C or U] liquid matter that comes from a part of the body and is often infected: *a vaginal discharge* **PERFORMANCE** ▷ **4** [U] formal the performance of duties or payment of money that is owed: *the discharge of his duties* **FIRING GUN** ▷ **5** [U] formal the action of firing a gun

disciple /dɪˈsaɪ.pl̩/ noun **1** [C] a person who believes in the ideas and principles of someone famous and tries to live the way they do or did: *an ardent disciple of the prime minister* **2 the disciples** [plural] (also **the Disciples**) the twelve men who followed Jesus during his life → See also **apostle**

disciplinarian /ˌdɪs.ə.plɪˈneə.ri.ən/ (US) /-ˈner.i-/ noun [C] someone who believes in keeping complete control of the people he or she is in charge of, especially by giving severe punishments: *a strict disciplinarian*

disciplinary /ˌdɪs.əˈplɪn.ər.i/ (US) /ˈdɪs.ə.plɪ.ner-/ adj relating to discipline: *disciplinary* ***measures/action*** *(= punishment)*

discipline /ˈdɪs.ə.plɪn/ noun; verb

▸**noun** **TRAINING** ▷ **1** (B2) [U] training that makes people more willing to obey or more able to control themselves, often in the form of rules, and punishments if these are broken, or the behaviour produced by this training: *parental/military/school discipline* ◦ *There should be better discipline in schools.* ◦ *I don't have enough (****self****) discipline to save money.* **2** [U] the ability to control yourself or other people, even in difficult situations: *Maintaining classroom discipline (= control of the students) is the first task of every teacher.* **SUBJECT** ▷ **3** (C2) [C] a particular area of study, especially a subject studied at a college or university

> Word partners for **discipline**
>
> *enforce/establish/restore* discipline • *firm/harsh/rigorous/tough* discipline • *lax/poor* discipline • a discipline *problem*

▸**verb** **PUNISH** ▷ **1** [T] to punish someone: *A senior civil servant has been disciplined* ***for*** *revealing secret government plans to the media.* **CONTROL** ▷ **2** [T] to teach someone to behave in a controlled way: [+ to infinitive] *I'm trying to discipline my****self to*** *eat less chocolate.*

disciplined /ˈdɪs.ə.plɪnd/ adj behaving in a very controlled way: *France play with more flair and inventiveness, whereas England are a more disciplined side.* ◦ *Those children are well disciplined.*

ˈdisc ˌjockey noun [C] (abbreviation **DJ**) (B1) someone who plays records and talks on the radio or at an event where people dance to recorded popular music, such as a NIGHTCLUB

D

disclaim /dɪˈskleɪm/ verb [T] formal to say that you have no responsibility for, or knowledge of, something that has happened or been done: *We disclaim all responsibility for this disaster.*

disclaimer /dɪˈskleɪ.mər/ (US) /-mɚ/ noun [C] **1** formal a formal statement saying that you are not legally responsible for something, such as the information given in a book or on the internet, or that you have no direct involvement in it **2** specialized a formal statement giving up your legal claim to something or ending your connection with it

disclose /dɪˈskləʊz/ (US) /-ˈskloʊz/ verb [I or T] formal (C2) to make something known publicly, or to show something that was hidden: *Several companies have disclosed profits of over £200 million.* ◦ [+ that] *The police have disclosed* ***that*** *two officers are under internal investigation.*

disclosure /dɪˈskləʊ.ʒər/ (US) /-ˈskloʊ.ʒɚ/ noun [C or U] formal the act of making something known or the fact that is made known: *Any public disclosure* ***of*** *this information would be very damaging to the company.* ◦ *The newspaper made damaging disclosures* ***of*** *management incompetence.*

disco /ˈdɪs.kəʊ/ (US) /-koʊ/ noun **DANCE** ▷ **1** (A2) [C] (plural **discos**) (old-fashioned **discotheque**) an event where people dance to modern recorded music for entertainment, or a place where this often happens: *disco lights* **MUSIC** ▷ **2** [U] (also **disco music**) a type of music that people dance to in a NIGHTCLUB, that was popular in the 1970s

ˈdisco ˌball noun [C] a round object covered with small mirrors that hangs from the ceiling and reflects light, for example in a disco

discolour UK (US **discolor**) /dɪˈskʌl.ər/ (US) /-ɚ/ verb [I or T] to (cause something to) change from the original colour and therefore to look unpleasant: *The coal fire had discoloured the paintwork.* • **discoloration** /dɪˌskʌl.əˈreɪ.ʃən/ noun [C or U]

discoloured UK (US **discolored**) /dɪˈskʌl.əd/ (US) /-ɚd/ adj describes something that has become a less attractive colour than it was originally: *discoloured teeth*

discombobulate /ˌdɪs.kəmˈbɒb.jə.leɪt/ (US) /-ˈbɑː.bjə-/ verb [T] informal mainly humorous to confuse someone or make someone feel uncomfortable • **discombobulation** /dɪs.kəmˌbɒb.jəˈleɪ.ʃən/ (US) /-ˌbɑː.bjə-/ noun [U]

discomfit /dɪˈskʌm.fɪt/ verb [T] formal to make someone feel uncomfortable, especially mentally • **discomfiture** /-tʃər/ (US) /-tʃɚ/ noun [U] *She turned away to hide her discomfiture.*

discomfort /dɪˈskʌm.fət/ (US) /-fɚt/ noun [C or U] (C1) a feeling of being uncomfortable physically or mentally, or something that causes this: *You may feel* ***a little*** *discomfort for a few days after the operation.*

ˈdisco ˌnap noun [C] informal a short sleep during the day, before you go out in the evening

D

disconcert /ˌdɪs.kənˈsɜːt/ (US) /-ˈsɝːt/ **verb** [I or T] to make someone feel suddenly uncertain and worried: *The whole experience had disconcerted him.* • **disconcerting** /-ˈsɜː.tɪŋ/ (US) /-ˈsɝː.t̬ɪŋ/ **adj** *There was a disconcerting silence.* • **disconcertingly** /-ˈsɜː.tɪŋ.li/ (US) /-ˈsɝː.t̬ɪŋ.li/ **adv**

disconcerted /ˌdɪs.kənˈsɜː.tɪd/ (US) /-ˈsɝː.t̬ɪd/ **adj** worried by something and uncertain: *I was a little disconcerted by his reply.*

disconnect verb; noun

▸**verb** [T] /ˌdɪs.kəˈnekt/ **1** to unfasten something, especially to break the connection between a supply of electricity, gas, water, etc. and a device or piece of equipment: *Never try to mend a broken machine without disconnecting it **from** the electricity supply.* **2** to stop supplying electricity/gas/water/phone services, especially because money has not been paid **3** If you are disconnected while speaking on the phone, the phone connection is suddenly broken and you can no longer continue your conversation. • **disconnection** /-ˈnek.ʃən/ **noun** [C or U]

▸**noun** [C] /ˈdɪs.kənekt/ a situation in which two or more things are not connected in the way that they should be: *The study found a disconnect **between** the state's social programs and some people who need government assistance.*

disconnected /ˌdɪs.kəˈnek.tɪd/ **adj** If ideas, remarks, etc. or the different parts of something are disconnected, they are not well joined together and it is difficult to see their purpose or pattern: *disconnected thoughts*

disconsolate /dɪˈskɒn.səl.ət/ (US) /-ˈskɑːn-/ **adj** formal extremely sad and disappointed: *The team were disconsolate after losing what should have been an easy game.* • **disconsolately** /-li/ **adv**

discontent /ˌdɪs.kənˈtent/ **noun** [U] (also **discontentment**) (C1) a feeling of wanting better treatment or an improved situation: *Discontent **among** junior ranks was rapidly spreading.* ◦ *There was **widespread** discontent **at/about/over/with** the plan.* • **discontented** /-ˈten.tɪd/ (US) /-ˈten.t̬ɪd/ **adj** • **discontentedly** /-ˈten.tɪd.li/ (US) /-ˈten.t̬ɪd.li/ **adv**

discontinue /ˌdɪs.kənˈtɪn.juː/ **verb** [T] formal to stop doing or providing something: *The bank is discontinuing its Saturday service.* • **discontinuation** /ˌdɪs.kənˌtɪn.juˈeɪ.ʃən/ **noun** [U] (also **discontinuance** /-əns/)

discontinued /ˌdɪs.kənˈtɪn.juːd/ **adj** describes a product or service that is no longer being produced or offered

discontinuous /ˌdɪs.kənˈtɪn.ju.əs/ **adj** formal with breaks, or stopping and starting again: *a discontinuous process* • **discontinuity** /ˌdɪs.kɒn.tɪˈnjuː.ɪ.ti/ (US) /-kɑːn.təˈnuː.ə.t̬i/ **noun** [C or U]

discord /ˈdɪs.kɔːd/ (US) /-kɔːrd/ **noun** DISAGREEMENT ▷ **1** [U] formal the state of not agreeing or sharing opinions: *marital discord* ◦ *A **note of** discord has crept into relations between the two countries.* → Compare **concord** SOUND ▷ **2** [C or U] specialized a group of musical notes which give an unpleasant sound when played together

discordant /dɪˈskɔː.dənt/ (US) /-ˈskɔːr-/ **adj** **1** producing an unpleasant sound **2 strike a discordant note** formal to look or sound different or wrong compared with everything else: *The contemporary dialogue for me struck a slightly discordant note.*

discotheque /ˈdɪs.kə.tek/ **noun** [C] old-fashioned a **disco**

discount noun; verb

▸**noun** [C] /ˈdɪs.kaʊnt/ (A2) a reduction in the usual price: *They usually **give** you a discount if you buy multiple copies.* ◦ *They offer a ten percent discount **on** rail travel for students.*

▸**verb** /dɪˈskaʊnt/ NOT CONSIDER ▷ **1** [T] to decide that something or someone is not worth considering or giving attention: *You shouldn't discount the possibility of him coming back.* REDUCE ▷ **2** [T often passive] to reduce the price of something: *discounted goods/rates*

ˈdiscount ˌstore **noun** [C] a shop which sells its goods at cheap prices

ˈdiscount ˌwarehouse **noun** [C] a large shop, usually not in the centre of a town, which sells goods at cheap prices, especially large goods or large quantities of goods

discourage /dɪˈskʌr.ɪdʒ/ (US) /-ˈskɝː-/ **verb** [T] MAKE LESS CONFIDENT ▷ **1** (B2) to make someone feel less confident, enthusiastic, and positive about something, or less willing to do something: *The thought of how much work she had to do discouraged her.* → Opposite **encourage** PREVENT ▷ **2** (B2) to prevent or try to prevent something happening or someone doing something, by making things difficult or unpleasant, or by showing disapproval: *a campaign to discourage people **from** smoking* ◦ *The authorities have put tanks on the streets to discourage any protest.* → Opposite **encourage** • **discouraging** /-ɪ.dʒɪŋ/ **adj** *discouraging results*

discouraged /dɪˈskʌr.ɪdʒd/ (US) /-ˈskɝː-/ **adj** having lost your confidence or enthusiasm for something: *I think he felt discouraged because of all the criticism he'd received.*

discouragement /dɪˈskʌr.ɪdʒ.mənt/ (US) /-ˈskɝː-/ **noun** MAKING LESS CONFIDENT ▷ **1** [C or U] the state of having lost your confidence or enthusiasm for something: *a feeling of discouragement* PREVENTING ▷ **2** [U] actions to prevent or try to prevent something from happening or someone from doing something: *the discouragement of any direct action*

discourse /ˈdɪs.kɔːs/ (US) /-kɔːrs/ **noun** formal **1** [U] communication in speech or writing **2** [C] a speech or piece of writing about a particular, usually serious, subject: *a discourse **on/upon** the nature of life after death*

discourteous /dɪˈskɜː.ti.əs/ (US) /-ˈskɝː.t̬i-/ **adj** formal rude and not considering other people's feelings: *The employees were found to be unhelpful and discourteous.* → Opposite **courteous** • **discourtesy** /dɪˈskɜː.tə.si/ (US) /-ˈskɝː.t̬ə-/ **noun** [C or U]

discover /dɪˈskʌv.ər/ (US) /-ɚ/ **verb** **1** (B1) [T] to find information, a place, or an object, especially for the first time: *Who discovered America?* ◦ *We searched all morning for the missing papers and finally discovered them in a drawer.* ◦ [+ question word] *Scientists have discovered **how** to predict an earthquake.* ◦ [+ (that)] *She discovered (**that**) her husband was having an affair.* ◦ [+ to infinitive] *Following a routine check-up, Mrs Mason was discovered **to** have heart disease.* ◦ [+ obj + -ing verb] *The boss discovered him (= unexpectedly found him) steal**ing** money from the till.* **2** [T often passive] to notice that a person has a special ability or quality and to help them to become successful: *Los Angeles is full of beautiful girls working as waitresses, hoping to be discovered by a movie agent.* • **discoverer** /-ər/ (US) /-ɚ/ **noun** [C] *Jim Watson and Francis Crick were the discoverers **of** the structure of DNA.*

discovery /dɪˈskʌv.ər.i/ (US) /-ɚ-/ **noun** [C or U] (B2) the process of finding information, a place, or an object, especially for the first time, or the thing that is found: *the discovery **of** electricity* ◦ *Leonardo **made** many scientific discoveries.* ◦ *a journey/voyage of discovery*

◦ *The discovery **of** a body in the undergrowth started a murder enquiry.*

> **Word partners for discovery**
>
> *make* a discovery • an *amazing/exciting/remarkable* discovery • a *chance/surprising/unexpected* discovery • a *new/recent* discovery • a *great/important/major/significant* discovery • a *grim/gruesome/shocking* discovery • the discovery *of* sth • a discovery *about* sth

discredit /dɪˈskred.ɪt/ verb; noun
▸verb [T] formal to cause people to stop respecting someone or believing in an idea or person: *Evidence of links with drug dealers has discredited the president.* ◦ *discredited theories* • **discreditable** /-ɪ.tə.bl̩/ US /-ə.t̬ə.bl̩/ adj • **discreditably** /dɪˈskred.ɪ.tə.bli/ US /-ə.t̬ə.bli/ adv
▸noun [U] formal loss of respect for or belief in someone or something: *The stupid behaviour of one pupil has **brought** discredit **on** the whole school.* ◦ ***To** her discredit, she never admitted her role in the scandal.*

discreet /dɪˈskriːt/ adj C2 careful not to cause embarrassment or attract too much attention, especially by keeping something secret: *The family made discreet enquiries about his background.* ◦ *They are very good assistants, very discreet – they wouldn't go shouting to the press.* • **discreetly** /-li/ adv

> **Note:**
>
> Do not confuse with **discrete**.

discrepancy /dɪˈskrep.ən.si/ noun [C or U] formal a difference between two things that should be the same: *There is some discrepancy **between** the two accounts.* ◦ *The committee is reportedly unhappy about the discrepancy **in** numbers.* • **discrepant** /-ənt/ adj *discrepant figures* ◦ *discrepant opinions/views*

discrete /dɪˈskriːt/ adj having a clear independent shape or form: *These small companies now have their own discrete identity.* → Synonym **separate**

> **Note:**
>
> Do not confuse with **discreet**.

discretion /dɪˈskreʃ.ən/ noun [U] **CAREFUL BEHAVIOUR** ▷ **1** C2 the ability to behave without causing embarrassment or attracting too much attention, especially by keeping information secret: *'Can you trust him with this?' 'Yes, he's **the soul of** discretion (= he will not tell other people).'* **RIGHT TO CHOOSE** ▷ **2** formal the right or ability to decide something: *Students can be expelled **at the** discretion of the headteacher (= if the headteacher decides it).* ◦ *I **leave** the decision **to** your discretion (= to your good judgment).*

IDIOM **discretion is the better part of valour** saying said when you believe it is wise to be careful and avoid unnecessary risks

discretionary /dɪˈskreʃ.ən.ər.i/ US /-er-/ adj formal decided by officials and not fixed by rules: *a discretionary grant* ◦ *Judges have great discretionary powers.*

discriminate /dɪˈskrɪm.ɪ.neɪt/ verb **TREAT DIFFERENTLY** ▷ **1** C1 [I] to treat a person or particular group of people differently, especially in a worse way from the way in which you treat other people, because of their skin colour, sex, SEXUALITY, etc.: *She felt she had been discriminated **against** because of her age.* ◦ *In order to increase the number of female representatives, the selection committee decided to discriminate **in favour of** women for three years.* **SEE A DIFFERENCE** ▷ **2** C2 [I + adv/prep] formal to be able to see the difference between two things or people: *Police dogs can discriminate **between** the different smells.* • **discriminatory** /-nə.tər.i/ US /-nə.tɔːri/ adj *discriminatory legislation/laws/practices*

discriminating /dɪˈskrɪm.ɪ.neɪ.tɪŋ/ US /-t̬ɪŋ/ adj formal approving able to know and act on the difference between good and bad: *They're discriminating shoppers.* ◦ *a discriminating palate*

discrimination /dɪˌskrɪm.ɪˈneɪ.ʃən/ noun [U] **DIFFERENT TREATMENT** ▷ **1** C1 treating a person or particular group of people differently, especially in a worse way from the way in which you treat other people, because of their skin colour, sex, SEXUALITY, etc.: ***racial/sex/age** discrimination* ◦ *Until 1986 most companies would not even allow women to take the exams, but such blatant discrimination is now disappearing.* **SEEING A DIFFERENCE** ▷ **2** formal the ability to see the difference between two things or people

discursive /dɪˈskɜː.sɪv/ US /-skɝː-/ adj **1** involving discussion: *a discursive essay* **2** formal mainly disapproving talking about or dealing with subjects that are only slightly connected with the main subject for longer than necessary: *a discursive writer/speech*

discus /ˈdɪs.kəs/ noun [C] **1** a heavy plate-shaped object that is thrown as part of a sports event **2 the discus** the event or sport in which a discus is thrown as far as possible

discuss /dɪˈskʌs/ verb [T] **1** A2 to talk about a subject with someone and tell each other your ideas or opinions: *The police want to discuss these recent racist attacks **with** local people.* **2** to talk or write about a subject in detail, especially considering different ideas and opinions related to it: *The later chapters discuss the effects on the environment.*

> **Common mistake: discuss**
>
> Remember that **discuss** is never followed by 'about'.
>
> Don't say 'discuss about something', say **discuss something**:
>
> ~~*We need to discuss about the new advertising campaign.*~~
>
> *We need to discuss the new advertising campaign.*

discussion /dɪˈskʌʃ.ən/ noun [C or U] B1 the activity in which people talk about something and tell each other their ideas or opinions: *I can say nothing – the matter is still **under** discussion (= being considered).* ◦ *a discussion group/document* ◦ *Management are **holding/having** discussions **with** employee representatives about possible redundancies.*

> **Word partners for discussion**
>
> *have/hold* a discussion • a *frank/heated* discussion • a *detailed/lengthy/long* discussion • a *subject/topic* of/for discussion • a discussion *about/on* sth • *under* discussion

disdain /dɪsˈdeɪn/ noun; verb
▸noun [U] formal the feeling of not liking someone or something and thinking that they do not deserve your interest or respect: *He regards the political process **with** disdain.* • **disdainful** /-fəl/ adj *a disdainful expression* • **disdainfully** /-fəl.i/ adv
▸verb [T] formal **1** to feel disdain for someone or something: *The older musicians disdain the new, rock-influenced music.* **2 disdain to do sth** to refuse to do something because you feel too important to do it

D

Word partners for disease

be affected by/have/suffer from a disease • *contract/develop* a disease • *cure/detect/diagnose/treat* a disease • *die from/of* a disease • *carry/cause/spread* disease • a *chronic/deadly/hereditary/infectious* disease • *signs/symptoms* of a disease • an *outbreak* of a disease

D

disease /dɪˈziːz/ **noun** **1** B1 [C or U] (an) illness of people, animals, plants, etc., caused by infection or a failure of health rather than by an accident: *a contagious/infectious disease* ◦ *a common/rare/incurable/fatal disease* ◦ *They reported a sudden* ***outbreak of*** *the disease in the south of the country.* ◦ *The first* ***symptom of*** *the disease is a very high temperature.* ◦ *She has* ***caught/contracted*** (= begun to have) *a lung disease/disease of the lungs.* ◦ *Starvation and disease have killed thousands of refugees.* **2** [C] something that is considered very bad in people or society: *The real disease affecting the country is inflation.*

diseased /dɪˈziːzd/ **adj** suffering from a disease: *a diseased lung/kidney* ◦ *Farmers were dumping or burying the diseased carcasses.* ◦ *a diseased mind/imagination* ◦ *a diseased society*

disembark /ˌdɪs.ɪmˈbɑːk/ US /-ˈbɑːrk/ **verb** [I] formal to leave a ship, aircraft, etc. after a journey • **disembarkation** /ˌdɪs.ɪm.bɑːˈkeɪ.ʃən/ US /-bɑːr-ˈ/ **noun** [U]

disembodied /ˌdɪs.ɪmˈbɒd.id/ US /-ˈbɑː.did/ **adj** seeming not to have a body or not to be connected to a body: *a disembodied* ***voice***

disembowel /ˌdɪs.ɪmˈbaʊ.əl/ **verb** [T] (**-ll-** or US usually **-l-**) to remove the stomach and bowels from a dead animal, or to kill a person in this way, especially in the past as a punishment

disenchanted /ˌdɪs.ɪnˈtʃɑːn.tɪd/ US /-ˈtʃæn.t̬ɪd/ **adj** no longer believing in the value of something, especially having learned of the problems with it: *Many voters have* ***become*** *disenchanted* ***with*** *the government.* • **disenchantment** /-ˈtʃɑːnt.mənt/ US /-ˈtʃænt.mənt/ **noun** [U] *There is (a) growing disenchantment* ***with*** *the way the country/school/club is being run.*

disenfranchise /ˌdɪs.ɪnˈfræn.tʃaɪz/ **verb** [T] (also MAINLY US **disfranchise**) to take away power or opportunities, especially the right to vote, from a person or group

disenfranchised /ˌdɪs.ɪnˈfræn.tʃaɪzd/ **adj** not having the right to vote, or a similar right, or having had that right taken away: *disenfranchised youth/communities/voters*

disengage /ˌdɪs.ɪŋˈgeɪdʒ/ **verb** **1** [I or T] to become separated from something, or to make two things become separate from each other: *They recognized that the country would revive only if it thoroughly disengaged* ***from*** *the chaos of the old regime.* ◦ *The number-one rule for being a good colleague is to disengage your emotions* ***from*** *the working relationship.* ◦ *Both children, disengaging them****selves from*** *their game, came to her side.* **2** [T] If you disengage the CLUTCH of a car, you stop the power produced by the engine being connected to the wheels. • **disengagement** /-mənt/ **noun** [U]

disentangle /ˌdɪs.ɪnˈtæŋ.gl/ **verb** [T] to separate things that have become joined or confused: *It's difficult to disentangle hard fact* ***from*** *myth, or truth* ***from*** *lies.* ◦ *I tried to disentangle the wires under my desk.*

disestablish /ˌdɪs.ɪˈstæb.lɪʃ/ **verb** [T] formal to take away official support and position from a Church or similar organized group • **disestablishment** /-mənt/ **noun** [U]

disfavour UK formal (US **disfavor**) /dɪsˈfeɪ.vəʳ/ US /-vɚ/ **noun** [U] a feeling of dislike or disapproval: *She sat down, regarding the plate in front of her* ***with*** *disfavour.*

disfigure /dɪsˈfɪg.əʳ/ US /-jɚ/ **verb** [T] to spoil the appearance of something or someone, especially their face, completely: *She was horribly disfigured by burns.* ◦ *This part of the old town has been disfigured by ugly new buildings.*

disfranchise /dɪsˈfræn.tʃaɪz/ **verb** [T] mainly US to **disenfranchise**

disgorge /dɪsˈgɔːdʒ/ US /-ˈgɔːrdʒ/ **verb** [T] **1** literary to release large amounts of liquid, gas or other contents: *The pipe was found to be disgorging dangerous chemicals into the sea.* **2** literary to send many people out of a place or vehicle at the same time: *The delayed commuter train disgorged hundreds of angry passengers.* **3** formal to force something up from the stomach and out through the mouth: *Flies disgorge digestive fluid onto their food to soften it up.* **4** literary to unwillingly release information or money: *The judge has forced EXIP to disgorge $400,000 in illegal profits.*

disgrace /dɪsˈgreɪs/ **noun; verb**

▸**noun** [U] **1** B2 embarrassment and the loss of other people's respect, or behaviour which causes this: *They were sent home* ***in*** *disgrace.* ◦ *He* ***brought*** *disgrace* ***on*** *the whole team by falsifying the results.* **2 be a disgrace** B2 to be a very bad situation: *Three families living in one room – it's a disgrace!* ◦ [+ that] ***It's*** *a disgrace* ***that*** *the government spends so much on guns and so little on education.* **3 be a disgrace to sb/sth** C2 to be so bad or unacceptable that you make people lose respect for the group or activity you are connected to: *You're a disgrace (to the family) – what a way to behave!*

▸**verb** [T] to make people stop respecting you or your family, team, etc. by doing something very bad: *You have disgraced us all with your behaviour.* • **disgraced** /-ˈgreɪst/ **adj** *a disgraced politician*

disgraceful /dɪsˈgreɪs.fəl/ **adj** very bad: *disgraceful behaviour/conduct* ◦ *a disgraceful situation* ◦ *She thought that their attitude was absolutely disgraceful.* ◦ [+ that] ***It*** *is disgraceful* ***that*** *children can get hold of drugs at school.* • **disgracefully** /-i/ **adv** *You've behaved disgracefully.*

disgruntled /dɪsˈgrʌn.tld/ US /-t̬ld/ **adj** unhappy, annoyed, and disappointed about something: *A disgruntled former employee is being blamed for the explosion.* ◦ *The players were disgruntled* ***with*** *the umpire.*

disguise /dɪsˈgaɪz/ **verb; noun**

▸**verb** [T] **1** B2 to give a new appearance to a person or thing, especially in order to hide its true form: *He disguised him****self*** *by wearing a false beard.* ◦ *Minor skin imperfections can usually be disguised with a spot of make-up.* ◦ *We tried to disguise the fact that it was just a school hall by putting up coloured lights and balloons.* **2** C2 to hide an opinion, a feeling, etc.: *I couldn't disguise my disappointment.*

▸**noun** [C or U] **1** B2 something that someone wears to hide their true appearance: *He put on a large hat and glasses as a disguise and hoped no one would recognize him.* **2 in disguise** B2 If people, objects, or activities are in disguise, they appear to be something which they are not, especially intentionally: *She usually goes out in disguise to avoid being bothered by the public.* ◦ *He claims that most Western aid to the Third World is just colonialism in disguise.*

disguised /dɪsˈgaɪzd/ **adj** having an appearance that

hides the true form: *In Shakespeare's play 'Twelfth Night', Duke Orsino falls in love with the disguised Viola.* ∘ *In the book, the author gives a* ***thinly*** *(= only slightly) disguised account of his own early teaching experiences.*

disgust /dɪsˈɡʌst/ **noun; verb**

▸**noun** [U] C2 a strong feeling of disapproval and dislike at a situation, person's behaviour, etc.: *She walked out* ***in*** *disgust.* ∘ *We are demonstrating to show our anger and disgust* ***at*** *the treatment of refugees.* ∘ *He resigned from the committee* ***in*** *disgust* ***at*** *the corruption.* ∘ *Beresford,* ***much to*** *his disgust, was fined for illegal parking.*

▸**verb** [T not continuous] to make you feel extreme dislike or disapproval: *Doesn't all this violence on TV disgust you?*

disgusted /dɪsˈɡʌs.tɪd/ **adj** C1 feeling extreme dislike or disapproval of something: *She was disgusted* ***at*** *the way they treated their children.* ∘ *I'm totally disgusted* ***with*** *your behaviour.* • **disgustedly** /-li/ **adv**

disgusting /dɪsˈɡʌs.tɪŋ/ **adj** B1 extremely unpleasant or unacceptable: *It's disgusting that there are no schools or hospitals for these people.* ∘ *Passengers were kept for three hours in a disgusting waiting room.* • **disgustingly** /-li/ **adv**

dish /dɪʃ/ **noun; verb**

▸**noun CONTAINER** ▷ **1** A2 [C] a container, flatter than a bowl and sometimes with a lid, from which food can be served or which can be used for cooking: *an oven-proof dish* → See also **satellite dish** **2 the dishes** A2 [plural] all the plates, glasses, knives, forks, etc. that have been used during a meal: *Have you* ***done/washed*** *the dishes?* **FOOD** ▷ **3** A2 [C] food prepared in a particular way as part of a meal: *a chicken/vegetarian dish* **ATTRACTIVE PERSON** ▷ **4** [S] old-fashioned a sexually attractive person: *He's gorgeous – what a dish!*

dish

▸**verb**

IDIOM **dish the dirt** to tell people unpleasant or shocking personal information about someone: *She agreed to dish the dirt* ***on*** *her ex-husband for a fee of £50,000.*

PHRASAL VERBS **dish sth out** informal **1** to give or say things to people without thinking about them carefully: *He's very keen to dish out criticism.* **2** to give or serve food to people: *Jon, could you dish the carrots out for me, please?* • **dish (sth) up** UK informal to make or serve a meal: *Come to the table everybody – I'm ready to dish (supper) up.* • **dish sth up** to produce something: *The offer is better than anything the other airlines can dish up.*

disharmony /dɪsˈhɑː.mə.ni/ US /-ˈhɑːr-/ **noun** [U] formal the situation in which there is disagreement and unpleasant feeling between people: *racial disharmony*

dishcloth /ˈdɪʃ.klɒθ/ US /-klɑːθ/ **noun** [C] a cloth for washing and cleaning dirty plates, cups, forks, etc.

dishearten /dɪsˈhɑː.tən/ US /-ˈhɑːr.t̬ən/ **verb** [T] to make a person lose confidence, hope, and energy → Synonym **discourage** • **disheartened** /-ˈhɑː.tənd/ US /-ˈhɑːr.t̬ənd/ **adj** *She was very disheartened by the results of the test.* • **disheartening** /ˈhɑː.tən.ɪŋ/ US /-ˈhɑːr.t̬ən.ɪŋ/ **adj** *disheartening news*

dishevelled (US usually **disheveled**) /dɪˈʃev.əld/ **adj** (of people or their appearance) very untidy: *dishevelled hair/clothes/appearance*

dishonest /dɪˈsɒn.ɪst/ US /-ˈsɑː.nɪst/ **adj** B2 not honest: *a dishonest lawyer* ∘ *a dishonest way of making money* ∘ *morally dishonest* ∘ *intellectually dishonest* ∘ *He's been dishonest* ***in*** *his dealings with us/****about*** *his past.* • **dishonestly** /-li/ **adv** C1 *The money was dishonestly obtained.* ∘ *She's been accused of acting dishonestly.* • **dishonesty** /-ˈsɒn.ɪ.sti/ US /-ˈsɑː.nə.sti/ **noun** [U] B2 *Her dishonesty landed her in prison.*

> **Other ways of saying dishonest**
>
> In informal situations, you can use the adjective **crooked** instead of 'dishonest':
>
> ***crooked*** *salesmen*
>
> **Unscrupulous** can be used when someone is dishonest or unfair in order to get what he or she wants:
>
> *This list will help you avoid* ***unscrupulous*** *financial advisers.*
>
> If you want to say that someone is dishonest in his or her job and tries to get money or use power wrongly, you can use the adjective **corrupt**:
>
> *There are always a few* ***corrupt*** *government officials who will accept bribes.*
>
> Someone who is hiding the truth can be described as **deceitful**:
>
> *He was being* ***deceitful*** *by not telling his parents that he was going to see a movie.*
>
> The adjective **devious** means that a person or plan is slightly dishonest, often in a way that is complicated but clever and successful:
>
> *You often have to be a bit* ***devious*** *if you're going to succeed in business.*
>
> **Fraudulent** is often used when someone is being deliberately dishonest to try and get money:
>
> ***fraudulent*** *insurance claims*

dishonour /dɪˈsɒn.əʳ/ US /-ˈsɑː.nɚ/ **noun; verb**

▸**noun** [U] UK formal (US **dishonor**) a feeling of embarrassment and loss of people's respect, or a situation in which you experience this: *Some of the leaders of the coup took their lives rather than face dishonour.*

▸**verb** [T] UK formal (US **dishonor**) **1** to cause someone or something to lose respect: *He felt that he had dishonoured his country.* **2** If you dishonour a promise or agreement, you do not do what you said you would do: *We suspect he means to dishonour the* ***agreement*** *made three years ago.* • **dishonourable** (US **dishonorable**) /-ə.bl̩/ **adj** *dishonourable actions*

ˈdish ˌsoap **noun** [U] US (also US **ˈdish ˌliquid**, UK **ˌwashing-ˈup ˌliquid**) a thick liquid soap used for washing plates, knives, forks, etc.

dishtowel /ˈdɪʃ.taʊəl/ **noun** [C] US for **tea towel**

dishwasher /ˈdɪʃˌwɒʃ.əʳ/ US /-ˌwɑː.ʃɚ/ **noun** [C] **1** B1 a machine that washes dirty plates, cups, forks, etc. **2** a person who washes dishes

dishwater /ˈdɪʃˌwɔː.təʳ/ US /-ˌwɑː.t̬ɚ/ **noun** [U] water in which dirty plates, cups, forks, etc. have been washed

IDIOM **like dishwater** informal disapproving describes a drink or liquid that is unpleasant because it contains too much water and has very little flavour: *This soup/tea* ***tastes*** *like dishwater.*

dishy /ˈdɪʃ.i/ **adj** UK old-fashioned informal sexually attractive: *What a dishy guy.*

disillusion /ˌdɪs.ɪˈluː.ʒən/ **verb** [T] to disappoint someone by telling them the unpleasant truth about something or someone that they had a good opinion of, or respected: ***I hate to/I'm sorry to***

disillusion you, but pregnancy is not always wonderful – I was sick every day for six months. • **disillusionment** /-mənt/ **noun** [U] (also **disillusion**) *There is increasing disillusionment* ***with*** *the government.*

disillusioned /ˌdɪs.ɪˈluː.ʒənd/ **adj** C2 disappointed and unhappy because of discovering the truth about something or someone that you liked or respected: *He's become a disillusioned man.* ◦ *All the other teachers are thoroughly disillusioned* ***with*** *their colleague.*

D

disincentive /ˌdɪs.ɪnˈsen.tɪv/ US /-t̬ɪv/ **noun** [C] something that makes people not want to do something or not work hard: *High taxes are a disincentive* ***to*** *business.*

disinclination /ˌdɪs.ɪŋ.klɪˈneɪ.ʃən/ **noun** [S or U] a feeling of not wanting to do something: [+ to infinitive] *I have a strong disinclination* ***to*** *do any work.*

disinclined /ˌdɪs.ɪŋˈklaɪnd/ **adj** **be/feel disinclined to do sth** to not want to do something: *I am/feel disinclined to offer him a job if he hasn't got a degree.*

disinfect /ˌdɪs.ɪnˈfekt/ **verb** [T] to clean something using chemicals that kill bacteria and other very small living things that cause disease: *disinfect the toilets/a wound*

disinfectant /ˌdɪs.ɪnˈfek.tənt/ US /-t̬ənt/ **noun** [C or U] a substance which contains chemicals that kill bacteria and is used especially for cleaning surfaces in toilets and kitchens

disinformation /ˌdɪs.ɪn.fəˈmeɪ.ʃən/ US /-fɚ-/ **noun** [U] false information spread in order to deceive people: *They claimed there was an official disinformation campaign by the government.*

disingenuous /ˌdɪs.ɪnˈdʒen.ju.əs/ **adj** formal (of a person or their behaviour) slightly dishonest; not speaking the complete truth: *It was disingenuous of her to claim she had no financial interest in the case.*

disinherit /ˌdɪs.ɪnˈher.ɪt/ **verb** [T] to prevent someone, especially a son or daughter who has made you angry, from receiving any of your property after your death: *Her father said he'd disinherit her if she married Stephen.*

disintegrate /dɪˈsɪn.tɪ.greɪt/ US /-t̬ə-/ **verb** [I] **1** to become weaker or be destroyed by breaking into small pieces: *The spacecraft disintegrated as it entered the Earth's atmosphere.* ◦ *The Ottoman Empire disintegrated* ***into*** *lots of small states.* **2** to become much worse: *The situation disintegrated* ***into*** *chaos.* • **disintegration** /dɪˌsɪn.tɪˈgreɪ.ʃən/ US /ˌdɪs.ɪn.t̬ə-/ **noun** [U] *social disintegration* ◦ *the gradual disintegration* ***of*** *family values*

disinter /ˌdɪs.ɪnˈtɜːr/ US /-ˈtɝː/ **verb** [T] (-rr-) **1** to dig up a dead body from the ground **2** to find and use something that has not been seen or used for a long time

disinterest /dɪsˈɪn.tər.est/ US /-t̬ɚ-/ **noun** [U] **NOT INTERESTED** ▷ **1** lack of interest: *Some kids become high-achievers to compensate for their parents' disinterest.* **NOT INVOLVED** ▷ **2** formal the fact of having no involvement in or receiving no special advantage or good from a situation or event: *Their close and financially rewarding relationship was sufficient to call into question the independence and disinterest of the directors.*

disinterested /dɪˈsɪn.trə.stɪd/ **adj** having no personal involvement or receiving no personal advantage, and therefore free to act fairly: *a disinterested observer/judgment* ◦ *a piece of disinterested advice*

> **! Note:**
> **Disinterested** is sometimes used to mean not interested, but many people consider this use to be incorrect. Compare **uninterested**.

disinvest /ˌdɪs.ɪnˈvest/ **verb** [I] (also **divest**) to sell your SHARES in a company or to stop taking part in a business activity • **disinvestment** /-mənt/ **noun** [U] (US also **divestiture**, **divestment**)

disjointed /dɪsˈdʒɔɪn.tɪd/ US /-t̬ɪd/ **adj** (especially of words or ideas) not well connected or well ordered: *The script was disjointed and hard to follow.*

disk (UK also **disc**) /dɪsk/ **noun** [C] B1 a flat circular device, usually inside a square container, which has a MAGNETIC covering and is used for storing computer information → See also **floppy, hard drive**

ˈ**disk** ˌ**drive** **noun** [C] a piece of computer equipment that allows information to be stored on and read from a disk

dislike /dɪˈslaɪk/ **verb; noun**

▸**verb** [T] B1 to not like someone or something: *Why do you dislike her so much?* ◦ [+ -ing verb] *I dislike walking and I hate the countryside.*

▸**noun 1** B2 [S or U] a feeling of not liking something or someone: *She has a dislike of cold weather.* ◦ *I'm afraid Dad* ***took*** *an instant dislike* ***to*** *this new boyfriend of yours.* **2** B1 [C usually plural] something that you do not like: *His main dislikes about work are the noise and dust in the factory.*

dislocate /ˈdɪs.lə.keɪt/ US /dɪˈsloʊ-/ **verb** [T] **1** to force a bone suddenly out of its correct position: *She dislocated her knee falling down some steps.* **2** to have a negative effect on the working of something • **dislocated** /-keɪ.tɪd/ US /-keɪ.t̬ɪd/ **adj** *a dislocated hip* • **dislocation** /ˌdɪs.ləˈkeɪ.ʃən/ US /-loʊ-/ **noun** [C or U] *Snow has caused serious dislocation* ***of/to*** *train services.*

dislodge /dɪˈslɒdʒ/ US /-ˈslɑːdʒ/ **verb** [T] to remove something or someone, especially by force, from a fixed position: *The earthquake dislodged stones* ***from*** *the walls and the roof.* ◦ *We need two wins to dislodge the French team* ***from*** *first place.*

disloyal /ˌdɪsˈlɔɪ.əl/ **adj** C2 not supporting someone that you should support: *His sisters thought that his autobiography was disloyal* ***to*** *the family.* → Opposite **loyal** • **disloyalty** /-ti/ **noun** [U] *They accused her of disloyalty.*

dismal /ˈdɪz.məl/ **adj** **1** sad and without hope: *a dismal expression* **2** informal very bad: *The acting was dismal, wasn't it?* ◦ *What dismal weather!* • **dismally** /-mə.li/ **adv**

dismantle /dɪˈsmæn.tl̩/ US /-t̬l̩/ **verb** **1** [I or T] to take a machine apart or to come apart into separate pieces: *She dismantled the washing machine to see what the problem was, but couldn't put it back together again.* ◦ *The good thing about the bike is that it dismantles if you want to put it in the back of the car.* **2** [T] to get rid of a system or organization, usually over a period of time: *Unions accuse the government of dismantling the National Health Service.*

dismay /dɪˈsmeɪ/ **noun** [U] C2 a feeling of unhappiness and disappointment: *Aid workers were said to have been* ***filled with*** *dismay by the appalling conditions that the refugees were living in.* ◦ *The supporters watched* ***in/with*** *dismay as their team lost 6–0.* ◦ *She discovered,* ***to*** *her dismay, that her exam was a whole month earlier than she'd expected.* • **dismay** **verb** [T] • **dismayed** /-ˈsmeɪd/ **adj** *I was dismayed to discover that he'd lied.*

dismember /dɪˈsmem.bər/ US /-bɚ/ **verb** [T] **1** to cut, tear, or pull the arms and legs off a human body: *The* police found the dismembered body of a young man in the murderer's freezer. **2** literary to divide a country or an EMPIRE into different parts: *The UN protested at the dismembering of Bosnia.* • **dismemberment** /-mənt/ noun [U] literary *the dismemberment of the empire*

dismiss /dɪˈsmɪs/ verb **NOT TAKE SERIOUSLY** ▷ **1** Ⓒ1 [T] to decide that something or someone is not important and not worth considering: *I think he'd dismissed me* ***as*** *an idiot within five minutes of meeting me.* ◦ *Let's not just dismiss the idea before we've even thought about it.* ◦ *Just dismiss those thoughts* ***from*** *your mind – they're crazy and not worth thinking about.* **END JOB** ▷ **2** Ⓒ1 [T often passive] to remove someone from their job, especially because they have done something wrong: *He has been dismissed* ***from*** *his job* ***for*** *incompetence.* **SEND AWAY** ▷ **3** [T] to formally ask or order someone to leave: *The teacher dismissed the class early because she had a meeting.* **4** [T] When a judge dismisses a court case, he or she formally stops the trial, often because there is not enough proof that someone is guilty: *The defending lawyer asked that the charge against his client be dismissed.*

dismissal /dɪˈsmɪs.əl/ noun **FROM JOB** ▷ **1** Ⓒ1 [C or U] the situation in which an employer officially makes someone leave their job: ***unfair/wrongful*** *dismissal* **OF IDEA, ETC** ▷ **2** Ⓒ1 [U] a decision that someone or something is not important

dismissive /dɪˈsmɪs.ɪv/ adj showing that you do not think something is worth considering: *He's so dismissive* ***of*** *anybody else's suggestions.* ◦ *a dismissive attitude* • **dismissively** /-li/ adv

dismount /dɪˈsmaʊnt/ verb [I] to get off a horse, bicycle, or motorcycle

disobedient /ˌdɪs.əˈbiː.di.ənt/ adj refusing to do what someone in authority tells you to do: *a disobedient* ***child*** • **disobedience** /-əns/ noun [U] • **disobediently** /-li/ adv

disobey /ˌdɪs.əˈbeɪ/ verb [I or T] to refuse to do something that you are told to do: *How dare you disobey me!* ◦ *to disobey orders* → Opposite **obey**

disobliging /ˌdɪs.əˈblaɪ.dʒɪŋ/ adj formal unwilling to help or do what you are asked to do

disorder /dɪˈsɔː.dər/ (US) /-ˈsɔːr.dɚ/ noun **CONFUSION** ▷ **1** Ⓒ2 [U] a state of untidiness or lack of organization: *The whole office was in a state of disorder.* ◦ *The opposition party have been in such disorder for so long that they pose no real threat to the present government.* **ILLNESS** ▷ **2** Ⓒ1 [C or U] an illness of the mind or body: *a* ***blood*** *disorder* ◦ *The family have a history of* ***mental*** *disorder.* **ANGRY SITUATION** ▷ **3** Ⓒ1 [U] an angry, possibly violent, expression of not being happy or satisfied about something, especially about a political matter, by crowds of people: *The trial was kept secret because of the risk of* ***public*** *disorder.*

disorderly /dɪˈsɔː.dəl.i/ (US) /-ˈsɔːr.dɚ.li/ adj **CONFUSED** ▷ **1** untidy and badly organized **ANGRY** ▷ **2** angry and violent: *The police feared that the crowd were becoming disorderly and so they moved in with horses.*

disorganized (UK usually **disorganised**) /dɪˈsɔː.gə.naɪzd/ (US) /-ˈsɔːr-/ adj **1** Ⓑ2 badly planned and without order: *The whole conference was totally disorganized – nobody knew what they were supposed to be doing.* **2** Ⓑ2 not good at planning or organizing things: *He's impossible to work for – he's so disorganized.* • **disorganization** (UK usually **disorganisation**) /dɪˌsɔː.gə.naɪˈzeɪ.ʃən/ (US) /-ˌsɔːr-/ noun [U]

disorientate /dɪˈsɔː.ri.ən.teɪt/ (US) /-ˈsɔːr.i-/ verb [T] (US usually **disorient**) to make someone confused about where they are and where they are going • **disorientating** /-teɪ.tɪŋ/ (US) /-teɪ.t̬ɪŋ/ adj (US usually **disorienting**)

disoriented /dɪˈsɔː.ri.ən.tɪd/ (US) /-ˈsɔːr.i.ən.t̬ɪd/ adj (UK also **disorientated**) confused and not knowing where to go or what to do: *Whales become disoriented in shallow water.*

disown /dɪˈsəʊn/ (US) /-ˈsoʊn/ verb [T not continuous] to make it known that you no longer have any connection with someone that you were closely connected with: *It's a story set in the last century about a girl whose parents disowned her when she married a foreigner.*

disparage /dɪˈspær.ɪdʒ/ (US) /-ˈsper-/ verb [T] to criticize someone or something in a way that shows you do not respect or value them: *The actor's work for charity has recently been disparaged in the press* ***as*** *an attempt to get publicity.* • **disparagement** /-mənt/ noun [U]

disparaging /dɪˈspær.ɪ.dʒɪŋ/ (US) /-ˈsper-/ adj criticizing someone, in a way that shows you do not respect or value them: *disparaging* ***remarks*** • **disparagingly** /-li/ adv

disparate /ˈdɪs.pər.ət/ (US) /-pɚ.ət/ adj formal different in every way: *The two cultures were so utterly disparate that she found it hard to adapt from one to the other.*

disparity /dɪˈspær.ə.ti/ (US) /-ˈper.ə.t̬i/ noun [C or U] formal lack of EQUALITY or similarity, especially in a way that is not fair: *the growing disparity* ***between*** *rich and poor*

dispassionate /dɪˈspæʃ.ən.ət/ adj able to think clearly or make good decisions because not influenced by emotions: *In all the media hysteria, there was one journalist whose comments were clear-sighted and dispassionate.* • **dispassionately** /-li/ adv

dispatch /dɪˈspætʃ/ verb; noun

▸verb [T] (UK also **despatch**) **SEND** ▷ **1** to send something, especially goods or a message, somewhere for a particular purpose: *Two loads of woollen cloth were dispatched to the factory on 12 December.* **KILL** ▷ **2** literary or old-fashioned to kill someone: *Our handsome hero manages to dispatch another five villains.*

▸noun (UK also **despatch**) **1** [U] the act of sending someone or something somewhere: *the dispatch* ***of*** *troops* **2** [C] a newspaper report sent by someone in a foreign country, often communicating war news, or an official report, often on a military matter: *In her latest dispatch, Clare Duggan, our war correspondent, reported an increase in fighting.* **3 be mentioned in dispatches** UK to be given a lot of praise for actions you have performed as a soldier: *Sergeant Havers was mentioned in dispatches for his courage.*

IDIOM **with dispatch** old-fashioned formal quickly and effectively

disˈpatch ˌbox noun [C] UK in Britain, the box on a table in the House of Commons which important politicians stand next to when they are formally speaking to the Members of Parliament

disˈpatch ˌrider noun [C] UK someone who travels between companies riding a motorcycle or bicycle, taking documents and parcels as quickly as possible

dispel /dɪˈspel/ verb [T] (-ll-) to remove fears, doubts, and false ideas, usually by proving them wrong or unnecessary: *I'd like to start the speech by dispelling a few rumours that have been spreading recently.*

dispensable /dɪˈspen.sə.bl̩/ adj more than you need and therefore not necessary; that can be got rid of: *It seemed the soldiers were regarded as dispensable – their deaths just didn't matter.* → Opposite **indispensable**

D

D

dispensary /dɪˈspen.sᵊr.i/ (US) /-sɚ.i/ noun [C] a place where medicines are prepared and given out, often in a hospital

dispensation /ˌdɪs.penˈseɪ.ʃᵊn/ noun formal **PERMISSION** ▷ **1** [C or U] special permission, especially from the Church, to do something that is not usually allowed: *The couple have requested (a)* ***special*** *dispensation* ***from*** *the Church to allow them to marry.* **SYSTEM** ▷ **2** [C] a political or religious system controlling a country at a particular time

dispense /dɪˈspens/ verb [T] **1** to give out things, especially products, services, or amounts of money: *There is a vending machine on the platform that dispenses snacks.* **2** to prepare and give out medicine: UK *a dispensing chemist*

PHRASAL VERB **dispense with sth/sb** to get rid of something or someone or stop using them because you do not need them: *They've had to dispense with a lot of luxuries since Mike lost his job.*

dispenser /dɪˈspen.sər/ (US) /-sɚ/ noun [C] a machine or container that you can get something from: *a cash/soap/drinks dispenser*

disˈpensing opˌtician noun [C] UK (US **optician**) a person whose job is fitting and selling glasses and CONTACT LENSES to correct sight problems, but who does not examine people's eyes → Compare **optician**

disperse /dɪˈspɜːs/ (US) /-ˈspɝːs/ verb [I or T] to spread across or move away over a large area, or to make something do this: *When the rain came down the crowds started to disperse.* ◦ *Police dispersed the crowd that had gathered.* • **dispersal** /-ˈspɜː.sᵊl/ (US) /-ˈspɝː.sᵊl/ noun [U]

dispersion /dɪˈspɜː.ʃᵊn/ (US) /-ˈspɝː-/ noun [U] **1** formal **dispersal** **2** specialized the separation of light into different colours

dispirited /dɪˈspɪr.ɪ.tɪd/ (US) /-t̬ɪd/ adj not feeling much hope about a particular situation or problem: *The troops were dispirited and disorganized.* • **dispiriting** /-tɪŋ/ (US) /-t̬ɪŋ/ adj *It was a bit dispiriting to see so few people arriving for the meeting.*

displace /dɪˈspleɪs/ verb [T] (C1) to force something or someone out of its usual or original position: *The building of a new dam will displace thousands of people who live in this area.* • **displaced** /-ˈspleɪst/ adj

disˌplaced ˈperson noun [C] (plural **displaced persons**) someone who has been forced to leave their home, especially because of war or a natural DISASTER (= something that causes a lot of damage) such as an EARTHQUAKE, flood, etc.

displacement /dɪˈspleɪs.mənt/ noun [U] **1** (C1) the situation in which people are forced to leave the place where they normally live: *The recent famine in these parts has caused the displacement of tens of thousands of people.* **2** specialized the weight of liquid that is forced out of position by an object that is floating on or in it

disˈplacement acˌtivity noun [C or U] specialized an unnecessary activity that you do because you are trying to delay doing a more difficult or unpleasant activity: *When I was studying for my exams I used to clean the house as a displacement activity.*

display /dɪˈspleɪ/ verb; noun

▸verb [T] **ARRANGE** ▷ **1** (B1) to arrange something or a collection of things so that they can be seen by the public: *Family photographs were displayed on the wall.* **SHOW** ▷ **2** (C2) to show a feeling: *The British traditionally tend not to display much emotion in public.* **3** to show words, pictures, etc. on a screen: *Retailers should display delivery times and costs on their websites.*

▸noun **ARRANGEMENT** ▷ **1** (B1) [C or U] a collection of objects or pictures arranged for people to look at, or a performance or show for people to watch: *There's an Egyptian art collection* ***on*** *display (= being shown) at the museum at the moment.* ◦ *a fireworks display* **SHOW** ▷ **2** (C2) [C or U] the fact of someone showing how they feel: *There's never much (of a) display* ***of*** *affection between them.* **3** (B1) [C] the fact of something being shown electronically, for example on a computer screen: *The display problems might be due to a shortage of disk space.*

displease /dɪˈspliːz/ verb [T] formal to cause someone to be annoyed or unhappy: *I wouldn't want to do anything to displease him.* • **displeased** /-ˈspliːzd/ adj • **displeasure** /-ˈpleʒ.ər/ (US) /-ˈpleʒ.ɚ/ noun [U] *Employees have publicly criticized the company's plans, much to the displeasure of the management.*

disport /dɪˈspɔːt/ (US) /-ˈspɔːrt/ verb old-fashioned or humorous **disport yourself** to enjoy yourself, especially by doing physical activity

disposable /dɪˈspəʊ.zə.bl̩/ (US) /-ˈspoʊ-/ adj; noun

▸adj (C2) describes a product that is intended to be thrown away after use: *disposable nappies* ◦ *a disposable camera* ◦ *daily disposable contact lenses*

▸noun [C usually plural] a disposable product, especially a disposable NAPPY: *paper/plastic/medical disposables* ◦ *Do you use disposables or washable nappies?*

disˌposable ˈincome noun [U] (C2) the money that you can spend as you want and not the money that you spend on taxes, food, and other basic needs

disposal /dɪˈspəʊ.zᵊl/ (US) /-ˈspoʊ-/ noun [U] **1** (B2) the act of getting rid of something, especially by throwing it away: *waste disposal* ◦ *the disposal of hazardous substances* **2 at sb's disposal** (B2) formal available to be used by someone: *I would take you if I could, but I don't have a car at my disposal this week.* ◦ *Having sold the house she had a large sum of money at her disposal (= to spend as she wanted).*

dispose /dɪˈspəʊz/ (US) /-ˈspoʊz/ verb formal **dispose sb to/towards sb/sth** to make someone feel a particular way towards someone or something: *His rudeness when we first met didn't dispose me very kindly* ***to/towards*** *him.*

PHRASAL VERB **dispose of sb/sth** (C1) to get rid of someone or something or deal with something so that the matter is finished: *How did they dispose of the body?* ◦ *It took a mere five minutes for the world champion to dispose of (= defeat) his opponent.*

disposed /dɪˈspəʊzd/ (US) /-ˈspoʊzd/ adj formal **1 be disposed to do sth** (C2) to be willing or likely to do something: *After all the trouble she put me to, I didn't feel disposed to help her.* **2 be well, favourably, etc. disposed to/towards sth/sb** to like or approve of something or someone: *She seems favourably disposed towards the idea.*

disposition /ˌdɪs.pəˈzɪʃ.ᵊn/ noun **1** (C2) [C usually singular] the particular type of character which a person naturally has: *She* ***is of*** *a nervous/cheerful/sunny disposition.* **2** [S + to infinitive] formal a natural TENDENCY to do something, or to have or develop something: *a disposition to deceive*

dispossess /ˌdɪs.pəˈzes/ verb [T] formal to take property, especially buildings or land, away from someone or a group of people: *A lot of people were dispossessed* ***of*** *their homes during the civil war.* → Compare **repossess** • **dispossession** /-ˈzeʃ.ᵊn/ noun [U]

dispossessed /ˌdɪs.pəˈzest/ **adj; noun**
▸**adj** dispossessed people have had their property taken away from them
▸**noun** [plural] **the dispossessed** formal dispossessed people: *the poor and the dispossessed*

disproportionate /ˌdɪs.prəˈpɔː.ʃᵊn.ət/ (US) /-ˈpɔːr-/ **adj** too large or too small in comparison to something else, or not deserving its importance or influence: *There are a disproportionate* ***number*** *of girls in the class.* ◦ *The country's great influence in the world is disproportionate* ***to*** *its relatively small size.* • **disproportion** /ˌdɪs.prəˈpɔː.ʃᵊn/ (US) /-ˈpɔːr-/ **noun** [U] formal • **disproportionately** /-li/ **adv**

disprove /dɪˈspruːv/ **verb** [T] to prove that something is not true: *The allegations have been disproved.*

disputable /dɪˈspjuː.tə.bl̩/ (US) /-t̬ə-/ **adj** not certain: *It's claimed that they produce the best athletes in the world but I think that's disputable.*

dispute noun; verb
▸**noun** [C or U] /dɪˈspjuːt/, /ˈdɪs.pjuːt/ **1** (C2) an argument or disagreement, especially an official one between, for example, workers and employers or two countries with a common border: *a bitter/long-running dispute* ◦ *a border dispute* ◦ *a pay/legal/trade dispute* ◦ *They have been unable to settle/resolve the dispute* ***over*** *working conditions.* ◦ *The unions are* ***in*** *dispute* ***with*** *management over pay.* **2 beyond (all) dispute** (C2) certainly: *He is beyond all dispute the finest actor in Hollywood today.* **3 in dispute** being doubted: *I don't think her ability is in dispute, what I question is her attitude.* **4 open to dispute** not certain: *He says it's the best musical equipment you can buy, but I think that's open to dispute.*
▸**verb** [I or T] /dɪˈspjuːt/ (C2) to disagree with something that someone says: *Few would dispute his status as the finest artist of the period.* ◦ *The circumstances of her death have been* ***hotly*** *disputed.* ◦ [+ (that)] *I don't dispute (****that****) Lucas' films are entertaining, but they haven't got much depth.* • **disputation** /ˌdɪs.pjʊˈteɪ.ʃᵊn/ (US) /-pjuː-/ **noun** [C or U] formal a disagreement • **disputatious** /ˌdɪs.pjʊˈteɪ.ʃəs/ (US) /-pjuː-/ **adj** old use *He's a disputatious young man (= he argues a lot).* • **disputed** /dɪˈspjuː.tɪd/ (US) /-t̬ɪd/ **adj** *a disputed border/goal* ◦ *disputed territory*

disqualify /dɪˈskwɒl.ɪ.faɪ/ (US) /-ˈskwɑː.lə-/ **verb** [T] (C2) to stop someone from being in a competition or doing something because they are unsuitable or they have done something wrong: *He's been disqualified* ***from*** *driving for a year.* ◦ *Two top athletes have been disqualified* ***from*** *the championship after positive drug tests.* • **disqualification** /dɪˌskwɒl.ɪ.fɪˈkeɪ.ʃᵊn/ (US) /-ˌskwɑː.lə-/ **noun** [C or U] *The fans' bad behaviour has resulted in the disqualification of their football team* ***from*** *the championship.*

disquiet /dɪˈskwaɪət/ **noun** [U] formal worry: *The leader's decline in popularity is causing disquiet among supporters.*

disquieting /dɪˈskwaɪə.tɪŋ/ (US) /-t̬ɪŋ/ **adj** formal causing worry: *The disquieting situation between these two neighbouring countries looks set to continue.*

disquisition /ˌdɪs.kwɪˈzɪʃ.ᵊn/ **noun** [C] formal a long and detailed explanation of a particular subject

disregard /ˌdɪs.rɪˈɡɑːd/ (US) /-ˈɡɑːrd/ **noun; verb**
▸**noun** [U] the fact of showing no care or respect for something: *What amazes me is her complete disregard* ***for*** *anyone else's opinion.*
▸**verb** [T] to ignore something: *He told us to disregard everything we'd learned so far and start again.*

disrepair /ˌdɪs.rɪˈpeəʳ/ (US) /-ˈper/ **noun** [U] the state of being broken or old and needing to be repaired: *The building has* ***fallen into*** *disrepair over the years.*

disreputable /dɪsˈrep.jʊ.tə.bl̩/ (US) /-jə.t̬ə-/ **adj** not trusted or respected; thought to have a bad character: *Some of the more disreputable newspapers made false claims about her private life.* ◦ *a disreputable young man* • **disreputably** /-bli/ **adv**

disrepute /ˌdɪs.rɪˈpjuːt/ **noun** [U] the state of not being trusted or respected: *Involvement with terrorist groups* ***brought*** *the political party* ***into*** *disrepute.*

disrespect /ˌdɪs.rɪˈspekt/ **noun; verb**
▸**noun** [U] **1** (C1) lack of respect: *a disrespect* ***for*** *authority* **2 no disrespect to sb** used before you criticize someone in order not to sound rude: *No disrespect to Julie, but this department worked perfectly well before she started here.* • **disrespectful** /-fᵊl/ **adj** (C2) *disrespectful behaviour* • **disrespectfully** /-fᵊl.i/ **adv**
▸**verb** [T] informal to show a lack of respect towards someone: *I don't want anyone disrespecting my son.*

disrobe /dɪsˈrəʊb/ (US) /-ˈroʊb/ **verb** [I] formal or humorous to remove your clothes, especially an outer or formal piece of clothing worn for ceremonies

disrupt /dɪsˈrʌpt/ **verb** [T] (B2) to prevent something, especially a system, process, or event, from continuing as usual or as expected: *A heavy fall of snow had disrupted the city's transport system.* ◦ *The meeting was disrupted by a group of protesters who shouted and threw fruit at the speaker.* • **disruption** /-ˈrʌp.ʃᵊn/ **noun** [C or U] (C1) *The accident on the main road through town is causing* ***widespread*** *disruption for motorists.*

disruptive /dɪsˈrʌp.tɪv/ **adj** (C2) causing trouble and therefore stopping something from continuing as usual: *His teacher described him as a noisy, disruptive* ***influence*** *in class.* • **disruptively** /-li/ **adv**

diss (-ss-) (also **dis**) /dɪs/ **verb** [T] US slang to speak or behave rudely to someone or to show them no respect: *Don't diss me, man!*

dissatisfied /ˌdɪsˈsæt.ɪs.faɪd/ (US) /-ˈsæt̬.əs-/ **adj** (B2) not pleased with something; feeling that something is not as good as it should be: *If you're dissatisfied* ***with*** *the service, why don't you complain to the hotel manager?* • **dissatisfaction** /dɪsˌsæt.ɪsˈfæk.ʃᵊn/ (US) /ˌdɪs.sæt̬.əs-/ **noun** [U] (B2) *At the moment she's experiencing a lot of dissatisfaction* ***with*** *her job.*

dissect /daɪˈsekt/, /dɪ-/ **verb** [T] **1** to cut open something, especially a dead body or a plant, and study its structure: *In biology classes at school we used to dissect rats.* **2** to examine or consider something in detail: *He's the sort of person who watches a film and then dissects it for hours.* • **dissection** /-ˈsek.ʃᵊn/ **noun** [C or U] *The novel is really a dissection of nationalism.*

dissemble /dɪˈsem.bl̩/ **verb** [I] formal to hide your real intentions and feelings or the facts: *He accused the government of dissembling.*

disseminate /dɪˈsem.ɪ.neɪt/ **verb** [T] formal to spread or give out something, especially news, information, ideas, etc., to a lot of people: *One of the organization's aims is to disseminate information about the disease.* • **dissemination** /dɪˌsem.ɪˈneɪ.ʃᵊn/ **noun** [U]

dissension /dɪˈsen.ʃᵊn/ **noun** [U] formal arguments and disagreement, especially in an organization, group, political party, etc.

dissent /dɪˈsent/ **noun; verb**
▸**noun** [U] formal strong difference of opinion on a particular subject, especially about an official suggestion or plan or a popular belief: *When the time came to approve the proposal, there were one or two* ***voices of*** *dissent.* → Synonym **disagreement** → Compare **assent**
▸**verb** [I] formal to disagree with other people about something: *Anyone wishing to dissent* ***from*** *the motion should now raise their hand.* • **dissenting** /-ˈsen.tɪŋ/ (US)

/-ˈsen.t̬ɪŋ/ **adj** formal *There was only one dissenting* ***voice*** *(= person who disagreed).*

dissenter /dɪˈsen.təʳ/ ⓤⓢ /-t̬ɚ/ **noun** [C] formal someone who dissents

dissertation /ˌdɪs.əˈteɪ.ʃən/ ⓤⓢ /-ɚ-/ **noun** [C] **C1** a long piece of writing on a particular subject, especially one that is done as a part of a course at college or university: *Ann did her dissertation* ***on*** *Baudelaire.*

D

disservice /ˌdɪsˈsɜː.vɪs/ ⓤⓢ /-ˈsɝː-/ **noun** [S] an action which harms something or someone: *She has* ***done*** *a great disservice* ***to*** *her cause by suggesting that violence is justifiable.*

dissident /ˈdɪs.ɪ.dənt/ **noun** [C] a person who publicly disagrees with and criticizes their government: *political dissidents* • **dissidence** /-dəns/ **noun** [U] • **dissident adj** *a dissident group/writer*

dissimilar /ˌdɪsˈsɪm.ɪ.ləʳ/ ⓤⓢ /-lɚ/ **adj** different: *The new house is* ***not*** *dissimilar (= is similar)* ***to*** *our old one except that it's a bit bigger.*

dissipate /ˈdɪs.ɪ.peɪt/ **verb** [I or T] formal to (cause to) gradually disappear or waste: *The heat gradually dissipates into the atmosphere.* ◦ *His anger dissipated as the situation became clear.* • **dissipation** /ˌdɪs.ɪˈpeɪ.ʃən/ **noun** [U] formal

dissipated /ˈdɪs.ɪ.peɪ.tɪd/ ⓤⓢ /-t̬ɪd/ **adj** formal disapproving spending too much time enjoying physical pleasures and harmful activities such as drinking too much alcohol: *He recalled his dissipated youth spent in nightclubs and bars.*

dissociate /dɪˈsəʊ.ʃi.eɪt/ ⓤⓢ /-ˈsoʊ-/ **verb** [T] (also **disassociate**) to consider as separate and not related: *I can't dissociate the man* ***from*** *his political opinions – they're one and the same thing.* • **dissociation** /dɪˌsəʊ.ʃiˈeɪ.ʃən/ ⓤⓢ /-ˌsoʊ-/ **noun** [U]

PHRASAL VERB **dissociate yourself from sth** to make it publicly known that you are not in any way connected to, or responsible for someone or something, often to avoid blame or embarrassment: *Most party members are keen to dissociate themselves from the extremists.*

dissolute /ˈdɪs.ə.luːt/ **adj** literary (of a person) living in a way that other people strongly disapprove of: *He led a dissolute life, drinking, and womanizing till his death.* → Synonym **immoral** • **dissolutely** /-li/ **adv** • **dissoluteness** /-nəs/ **noun** [U]

dissolution /ˌdɪs.əˈluː.ʃən/ **noun** [U] the act or process of ending an official organization or legal agreement: *the dissolution of parliament*

dissolve /dɪˈzɒlv/ ⓤⓢ /-ˈzɑːlv/ **verb** **BE ABSORBED** ▷ **1** **C2** [I or T] (of a solid) to be absorbed by a liquid, especially when mixed, or (of a liquid) to absorb a solid: *Dissolve two spoons of powder* ***in*** *warm water.* ◦ *Nitric acid will dissolve most animal tissue.* **END** ▷ **2** **C1** [T often passive] to end an official organization or a legal arrangement: *Parliament has been dissolved.* ◦ *Their marriage was dissolved in 1968.* **3** [I] to disappear: *The tension in the office just dissolves when she walks out.*

IDIOM **dissolve into tears/laughter** to suddenly start to cry or laugh: *When she saw his photograph, she dissolved into tears.*

dissonance /ˈdɪs.ən.əns/ ⓤⓢ /-ə.nəns/ **noun** [U] **1** specialized a combination of sounds or musical notes that are not pleasant when heard together: *the jarring dissonance of Klein's musical score* **2** formal disagreement • **dissonant** /-ən.ənt/ ⓤⓢ /-ə.nənt/ **adj** specialized or formal

dissuade /dɪˈsweɪd/ **verb** [T] to persuade someone not to do something: *I tried to dissuade her* ***from*** *leaving.*

distance /ˈdɪs.təns/ **noun; verb**

▸**noun** **SPACE** ▷ **1** **B1** [C or U] the amount of space between two places: *What's the distance* ***between*** *Madrid and Barcelona/****from*** *Madrid* ***to*** *Barcelona?* ◦ *He travels quite a distance (= a long way) to work every day.* ◦ *Does she live* ***within walking*** *distance of her parents?* **2 at/from a distance** **B2** from a place that is not near: *From a distance he looks a bit like James Bond.* **3 in the distance** **B2** at a point that is far away: *On a clear day you can see the temple in the distance.* **MANNER** ▷ **4** [S or U] behaviour that shows little interest or friendliness: *I noticed a certain distance* ***between*** *father and son.*

> **Word partners for distance**
>
> a *considerable/great/long/short* distance • a *safe* distance • in/within *striking/walking* distance • *travel* a [great/considerable, etc.] distance • the distance *from* sth *to* sth • the distance *between* [two things or places]

IDIOMS **go the distance** to manage to continue until the end of a competition • **keep your distance** to avoid going near someone or something, or to avoid getting too friendly with people: *I've tried being friendly but she keeps her distance.*

▸**verb**

PHRASAL VERB **distance yourself from sth** to become or seem less involved or connected with something: *The leader has recently distanced himself from the extremists in the party.*

ˈdistance ˌlearning **noun** [U] a way of studying, especially for a degree, where you study mostly at home, receiving and sending off work by post or over the internet

distance multiplier /ˈdɪs.tənsˌmʌl.tɪ.plaɪəʳ/ ⓤⓢ /-ɚ/ **noun** [C] specialized a system or machine, for example a bicycle, that uses effort over a short distance to move a LOAD through a longer distance → Compare **force multiplier**

distant /ˈdɪs.tənt/ **adj** **NOT CLOSE** ▷ **1** **B2** far away: *a distant country* ◦ *She could hear the distant sound of fireworks exploding.* **2** **C2** part of your family but not closely related: *a distant relative/cousin* **3 in the distant past/future** far away in the past or future: *At some point in the distant future I would like to have my own house.* **4 in the not-too-distant future** quite soon: *They plan to have children in the not-too-distant future.* **NOT FRIENDLY** ▷ **5** **C1** describes someone who does not show much emotion and is not friendly: *She seemed cold and distant.*

distantly /ˈdɪs.tənt.li/ **adv** **NOT CLOSE** ▷ **1** far away: *He heard, distantly, the sound of the sea.* ◦ *They're distantly related.* **NOT FRIENDLY** ▷ **2** in an unfriendly way, showing no emotion: *Sam smiled distantly.*

distaste /dɪˈsteɪst/ **noun** [U] a dislike of something which you find unpleasant or unacceptable: *His distaste* ***for*** *publicity of any sort is well known.* ◦ *She looked at the advertisement with distaste before walking quickly on.* • **distasteful** /-fəl/ **adj** *He found the subject of their conversation very distasteful.* • **distastefully** /-fəl.i/ **adv** • **distastefulness** /-fəl.nəs/ **noun** [U]

distemper /dɪˈstem.pəʳ/ ⓤⓢ /-pɚ/ **noun** [U] **PAINT** ▷ **1** a type of paint that is mixed with water and glue, used especially in the past for painting walls **DIS-**

EASE ▷ **2** a type of infectious disease that can be caught by animals, especially dogs

distend /dɪˈstend/ verb [I] (usually of the stomach or other part of the body) to swell and become large (as if) by pressure from inside: *In the refugee centres we saw many children whose stomachs were distended because of lack of food.* • **distension** /-ˈsten.ʃən/ noun [U] specialized

distil /dɪˈstɪl/ verb (-ll-) **LIQUID** ▷ **1** (US usually **distill**) [T] to make a liquid stronger or purer by heating it until it changes to a gas and then cooling it so that it changes back into a liquid: *Some strong alcoholic drinks such as whisky are made by distilling.* **INFORMATION** ▷ **2** [T usually passive] literary to get or show only the most important part of something: *Over 80 hours of footage have been distilled* ***into*** *these 40 minutes.* • **distillation** /ˌdɪs.tɪˈleɪ.ʃən/ noun [C or U]

disˌtilled ˈwater noun [U] specialized water that has been made purer by being heated until it becomes a gas and then cooled until it became a liquid again

distiller /dɪˈstɪl.ər/ (US) /-ɚ/ noun [C] a person or a company that makes strong alcoholic drinks by the process of distilling

distillery /dɪˈstɪl.ər.i/ (US) /-ɚ.i/ noun [C] a factory where strong alcoholic drinks are produced by the process of distilling: *a whisky distillery*

distinct /dɪˈstɪŋkt/ adj **NOTICEABLE** ▷ **1** (C1) [before noun] clearly noticeable; that certainly exists: *There's a distinct smell of cigarettes in here.* **DIFFERENT** ▷ **2** (C1) clearly separate and different (from something else): *The two concepts are quite distinct (****from*** *each other).* ◦ *There are two distinct factions within the one political party.* **3 as distinct from** rather than: *She's a personal assistant as distinct from a secretary.* • **distinctly** /-li/ adv *I distinctly remember asking him.*

distinction /dɪˈstɪŋk.ʃən/ noun **DIFFERENCE** ▷ **1** (B2) [C or U] a difference between two similar things: *There's a* ***clear*** *distinction* ***between*** *the dialects spoken in the two regions.* ◦ *This company* ***makes*** *no distinction* ***between*** *the sexes.* **HIGH QUALITY** ▷ **2** [U] the quality of being excellent: *a writer/scientist/wine* ***of*** *distinction* **3** [C] a mark given to students who produce work of an excellent standard **SPECIAL** ▷ **4** (C2) [S] the quality of being special or different: *She* ***has the*** *distinction* ***of*** *be****ing*** *one of the few people to have an honorary degree conferred on her by the university this year.*

distinctive /dɪˈstɪŋk.tɪv/ adj (C1) Something that is distinctive is easy to recognize because it is different from other things: *a distinctive smell/taste* ◦ *She's got a very distinctive voice.* • **distinctively** /-li/ adv • **distinctiveness** /-nəs/ noun [U]

distinguish /dɪˈstɪŋ.gwɪʃ/ verb **1** (B2) [I or T, not continuous] to notice or understand the difference between two things, or to make one person or thing seem different from another: *He's colour-blind and can't distinguish (the difference)* ***between*** *red and green easily.* ◦ *I sometimes have difficulty distinguishing Spanish* ***from*** *Portuguese.* ◦ *It's important to distinguish* ***between*** *business and pleasure.* ◦ *It's not the beauty so much as the range of his voice that distinguishes him* ***from*** *other tenors.* **2 distinguish yourself** to do something so well that you are admired and praised for it: *He distinguished himself in British theatre at a very early age.* • **distinguishable** /-gwɪ.ʃə.bl/ adj *There are at least 20 distinguishable dialects of the language just on the south island.*

distinguished /dɪˈstɪŋ.gwɪʃt/ adj **1** (B2) describes a respected and admired person, or their work: *a distinguished writer/director/politician* ◦ *a distinguished career* **2** describes a person, especially an older person, who looks formal, stylish, or wise: *I think grey hair on a man can look very distinguished.*

distinguishing /dɪˈstɪŋ.gwɪ.ʃɪŋ/ adj a distinguishing mark or feature is one that makes someone or something different from similar people or things: *The main distinguishing* ***feature*** *of the new car is its fast acceleration.*

distort /dɪˈstɔːt/ (US) /-ˈstɔːrt/ verb [T] (C1) to change something from its usual, original, natural, or intended meaning, condition, or shape: *My original statement has been completely distorted by the media.* • **distortion** /-ˈstɔː.ʃən/ (US) /-ˈstɔːr-/ noun [C or U] *a gross distortion* ***of*** *the facts*

distorted /dɪˈstɔː.tɪd/ (US) /-ˈstɔːr.t̬ɪd/ adj changed from the usual, original, natural, or intended form: *This report gives a somewhat distorted impression of what actually happened.* ◦ *The music just gets distorted when you play it so loud.* ◦ *His face was distorted in agony.*

distract /dɪˈstrækt/ verb [T] (B2) to make someone stop giving their attention to something: *Don't distract her (****from*** *her studies).* ◦ *He tried to distract* ***attention from*** *his own illegal activities.* • **distracting** /-ˈstræk.tɪŋ/ adj *Please turn your music down – it's very distracting.*

distracted /dɪˈstræk.tɪd/ adj nervous or confused because you are worried about something: *Gill seems rather distracted at the moment – I think she's worried about her exams.* • **distractedly** /-li/ adv

distraction /dɪˈstræk.ʃən/ noun **1** [U] the state of being very bored or annoyed: *His lessons bore me* ***to*** *distraction.* ◦ *That dreadful noise is* ***driving*** *me* ***to*** *distraction.* **2** (C1) [C or U] something that prevents someone from giving their attention to something else: *I can turn the television off if you find it a distraction.* **3** (C1) [C] an activity that you do for pleasure: *one of the distractions of city life*

distraught /dɪˈstrɔːt/ (US) /-ˈstrɑːt/ adj extremely worried, nervous, or upset: *The missing child's distraught parents made an emotional appeal for information on TV.*

distress /dɪˈstres/ noun; verb

▸**noun** [U] **1** (C1) a feeling of extreme worry, sadness, or pain: *She claimed that the way she had been treated at work had caused her extreme emotional and psychological distress.* ◦ *Many of the horses were showing signs of distress at the end of the race.* **2** (C2) a situation in which you are suffering or are in great danger and therefore in urgent need of help: *Six people were rescued by helicopter from a fishing boat* ***in*** *distress off the coast.* ◦ *a distress* ***signal***

▸**verb** [T] to make someone feel very upset or worried: *I hope I haven't distressed you with all these personal questions.*

distressed /dɪˈstrest/ adj **1** (C1) upset or worried: *She was* ***deeply*** *distressed by the news of his death.* **2** having problems because of having too little money: *The government is taking steps to stimulate business development in (****economically****) distressed areas.* **3** a distressed material has been treated to make it look as if it has been used for a long time: *distressed denim* ◦ *distressed leather chairs*

distressing /dɪˈstres.ɪŋ/ adj (US usually **distressful**) (B2) upsetting or worrying: *The television reports about the famine were particularly distressing.* ◦ ***It*** *was* ***deeply*** *distressing for him* ***to*** *see his wife in such pain.* • **distressingly** /-li/ adv

distribute /dɪˈstrɪb.juːt/, /ˈdɪs.trɪ.bjuːt/ (US) /-jʊt/ verb [T] (B2) to give something out to several people, or to spread or supply something: *The books will be* *distributed free* ***to*** *local schools.* ◦ *Several people were arrested for distributing racist leaflets/pamphlets* (***to*** *the spectators).* ◦ *The company aims eventually to distribute* (= *supply for sale*) *its products* ***throughout*** *the European Union.*

distribution /ˌdɪs.trɪˈbjuː.ʃᵊn/ **noun** [C or U] **1** C1 the process of giving things out to several people, or spreading or supplying something: *distribution costs* **2** C1 the way in which people or things are spread out in a place: *a map showing distribution* ***of*** *global population* ◦ *We must find a way of achieving* ***a*** *more* ***equitable*** *distribution (= sharing) of resources/wealth.*

D

distributor /dɪˈstrɪb.jʊ.təʳ/ US /-jə.t̬ɚ/ **noun** [C] GOODS ▷ **1** a person or organization that supplies goods to shops and companies: *a film distributor* ENGINE ▷ **2** a device in a petrol engine which sends electricity to each of the SPARK PLUGS (= devices which cause the engine to start) in the necessary order

district /ˈdɪs.trɪkt/ **noun** [C] B1 an area of a country or town that has fixed borders that are used for official purposes, or that has a particular feature that makes it different from surrounding areas: *South Cambridgeshire District Council* ◦ *the fashion district of New York*

ˌdistrict atˈtorney **noun** [C] (abbreviation **DA**) a lawyer whose job is to represent the government in a particular area of the US

ˌdistrict ˈnurse **noun** [C] UK a person who is employed in a particular area to care for people who are ill or injured, often visiting them in their homes

distrust /dɪˈstrʌst/ **noun; verb**

▸**noun** [U] the feeling of not trusting someone or something: *The two groups have existed in a state of* ***mutual*** *distrust for centuries.* ◦ *She has* ***a*** *(****deep****) distrust* ***of*** *journalists.* • **distrustful** /-fᵊl/ **adj**

▸**verb** [T] to not trust someone or something: *In spite of its election success, the government is still* ***deeply*** *distrusted on key issues.*

disturb /dɪˈstɜːb/ US /-ˈstɝːb/ **verb** [T] INTERRUPT ▷ **1** B2 to interrupt what someone is doing: *Please don't disturb Georgina – she's trying to do her homework.* ◦ *I'm sorry to disturb you so late, but my car's broken down and I was wondering if I could use your phone.* **2 disturb the peace** to break the law by behaving unpleasantly and noisily in public: *Several England supporters were arrested and charged with disturbing the peace after the match.* WORRY ▷ **3** C2 to cause someone to be worried or upset: *Some scenes are violent and may disturb younger viewers.* MOVE ▷ **4** to move or change something from its usual position, arrangement, condition, or shape: *The thief had disturbed the documents in her filing cabinet, but nothing had been taken.*

disturbance /dɪˈstɜː.bᵊns/ US /-ˈstɝː-/ **noun** [C or U] **1** C1 something that interrupts someone or makes them feel worried: *Residents are fed up with the disturbance caused by the nightclub.* ◦ *Phone calls are the biggest disturbance at work.* **2** C2 violence or trouble: *There was a minor disturbance during the demonstration, but nobody was injured.* **3 cause a disturbance** to break the law by fighting or behaving extremely noisily in public

disturbed /dɪˈstɜːbd/ US /-ˈstɝːbd/ **adj** C2 not thinking or behaving normally because of mental or emotional problems: *a centre for* ***emotionally/mentally*** *disturbed teenagers*

disturbing /dɪˈstɜː.bɪŋ/ US /-ˈstɝː-/ **adj** C2 making you feel worried or upset: *The Home Secretary described the latest crime figures as 'disturbing'.* ◦ *The following programme contains scenes that may be disturbing* ***to*** *some viewers.* • **disturbingly** /-li/ **adv** *Pollution has reached disturbingly high levels in some urban areas.*

disunite /ˌdɪs.juːˈnaɪt/ **verb** [T] to cause people to disagree so much that they can no longer work together effectively: *A publicly disunited party stands little chance of winning the election.* • **disunity** /dɪˈsjuː.nɪ.ti/ US /-nə.t̬i/ **noun** [U]

disuse /dɪˈsjuːs/ **noun** [U] the condition of not being used (any longer): *The church was recently restored after decades of disuse.* • **disused** /-ˈsjuːzd/ **adj** *Many disused railway lines have become public footpaths.*

disyllabic /ˌdaɪ.sɪˈlæb.ɪk/ **adj** specialized (of a word) having two syllables

ditch /dɪtʃ/ **noun; verb**

▸**noun** [C] a long, narrow open hole that is dug into the ground, usually at the side of a road or field, used especially for supplying or removing water or for dividing land

▸**verb** GET RID OF ▷ **1** [T] informal to get rid of something or someone that is no longer wanted: *The getaway car had been ditched a couple of kilometres away from the scene of the robbery.* ◦ *Did you know that Sarah has ditched (= ended her relationship with) her boyfriend?* AIRCRAFT ▷ **2** [I or T] to land an aircraft in water in an emergency

dither /ˈdɪð.əʳ/ US /-ɚ/ **verb; noun**

▸**verb** [I] disapproving to be unable to make a decision about doing something: *Stop dithering and choose which one you want!* ◦ *She's still dithering* ***over*** *whether to accept the job she's just been offered.* • **ditherer** /-əʳ/ US /-ɚ/ **noun** [C]

▸**noun** disapproving **be in a dither about sth** to be very nervous, excited or confused about something: *Gideon is in a bit of a dither about what to wear for the interview.*

ditransitive /ˌdaɪˈtræn.sə.tɪv/ US /-t̬ɪv/ **adj** specialized describes a verb that can be followed by two objects, one of which has the action of the verb done to it and the other of which has the action of the verb directed towards it. In this dictionary, ditransitive verbs are shown with the label [+ two objects]: *In the sentence 'I sent Victoria a letter', 'send' is ditransitive.*

ditto /ˈdɪt.əʊ/ US /ˈdɪt̬.oʊ/ **adv; noun**

▸**adv** used to agree with something that has just been said, or to avoid repeating something that has been said: *'I hate these reality TV shows' 'Ditto. What's on the other side?'* ◦ *Local residents are opposed to the proposal. Ditto many members of the council (= they are also opposed).*

▸**noun** [C usually singular] (also ˈ**ditto ˌmark**) a symbol " that means 'the same' and is used in a list to avoid writing again the word written immediately above it

ditty /ˈdɪt.i/ US /ˈdɪt̬-/ **noun** [C] a short simple song

diuretic /ˌdaɪ.jʊˈret.ɪk/ US /-jəˈret̬-/ **noun** [C] specialized a substance which causes an increase in the production of urine • **diuretic adj**

diurnal /ˌdaɪˈɜː.nəl/ US /-ˈɝː-/ **adj** specialized happening over a period of a day, or being active or happening during the day rather than at night → Compare **nocturnal** • **diurnally** /-nə.li/ **adv**

div /dɪv/ **noun** UK informal a **divvy**

diva /ˈdiː.və/ **noun** [C] **1** a very successful and famous female singer: *an Italian opera diva* ◦ *a pop diva* **2** usually disapproving a woman who behaves as if she is very special or important: *She has a reputation for being a diva.*

Divali /dɪˈvɑː.li/ **noun** [C or U] → **Diwali**: a Hindu holiday

D

divan /dɪˈvæn/ noun [C] **1** a long, comfortable seat for more than one person that has no back or arms **2** (also **divan bed**) UK a bed consisting of a MATTRESS and a base, with no boards at either end

dive /daɪv/ verb; noun

▸verb (**dived** or US also **dove**, **dived** or US also **dove**) **IN WATER** ▷ **1** **B1** to jump into water, especially with your head and arms going in first, or to move down under the water: *Look at those children diving* ***for*** *oysters over there!* ◦ *They ran to the pool, dived* ***in****, and swam to the other side.* ◦ *Mark dived* ***off*** *the bridge* ***into*** *the river.* ◦ *The submarine dived just in time to avoid the enemy attack.* → See also **nosedive** **2** **B1** [I] to swim underwater, usually with breathing equipment **BECOME LESS** ▷ **3** [I] to fall in value suddenly and by a large amount: *The company's shares dived* ***by*** *90p* ***to*** *65p on the stock market yesterday.* **MOVE QUICKLY** ▷ **4** [I] to go down very quickly: *The plane dived towards the ground and exploded in a ball of flame.* ◦ *The goalkeeper dived* ***for*** *the ball (= tried to catch the ball by jumping towards it and falling on the ground).* **5** [I usually + adv/prep] to move quickly, often in order to avoid something: *They dived* ***for*** *cover when they heard the shooting start.*

PHRASAL VERB **dive in/dive into sth** **C2** to start doing something suddenly and energetically, often without stopping to think: *If neighbouring countries are having a war, you can't just dive in.*

▸noun **INTO WATER** ▷ **1** **B2** [C] a jump into water with your head going in first: *the best dive of the competition* **LOSS** ▷ **2** [S] a sudden loss in value: *The firm's profits* ***took a*** *dive last month.* **QUICK MOVEMENT** ▷ **3** [C] a movement down onto the ground: *The goalkeeper made a valiant dive* ***for*** *the ball, but couldn't stop it going in the net.* ◦ *The plane went into a dive.* **4** [C] in sports like football, the action of falling deliberately to try to win an advantage **5** [C] a sudden quick movement: *He made a dive for the door.* **PLACE** ▷ **6** [C] informal a restaurant, hotel, bar, or place for entertainment or social activities that is unpleasant because of the condition of the building or the type of people that go there: *I know this place is a bit of a dive, but the drink's cheap and the food's great.*

ˈdive-bomb verb [I or T] to drop bombs on something or someone from a dive-bomber

ˈdive-ˌbomber noun [C] a military aircraft designed to dive quickly before dropping its bombs on a target

diver /ˈdaɪ.vəʳ/ (US) /-vɚ/ noun [C] **B1** a person who dives as a sport, or who works or searches for things underwater using special breathing equipment: *He was a diver on a North Sea oil rig.*

diverge /ˌdaɪˈvɜːdʒ/ (US) /dɪˈvɝːdʒ/ verb [I] to follow a different direction, or to be or become different: *They walked along the road together until they reached the village, but then their paths diverged.* ◦ *Although the two organizations have worked together for many years, their objectives have diverged recently.* → Opposite **converge** • **divergent** /-ˈvɜː.dʒᵊnt/ adj *They hold* ***widely*** *divergent opinions on controversial issues like abortion.*

divergence /ˌdaɪˈvɜː.dʒᵊns/ (US) /dɪˈvɝː-/ noun [C or U] the situation in which two things become different: *The divergence* ***between*** *the incomes of the rich and the poor countries seems to be increasing.* ◦ *Recently published figures show a divergence* ***from*** *previous trends.*

diverse /daɪˈvɜːs/ (US) /dɪˈvɝːs/ adj **B2** different or including many different types: *Students from countries as diverse as Colombia and Lithuania use Cambridge textbooks.* ◦ *New York is a very* ***culturally/ethnically*** *diverse city.*

diversify /daɪˈvɜː.sɪ.faɪ/ (US) /dɪˈvɝː-/ verb **1** [I] to start to include more different types or things: *Millions of years ago, changes in the Earth's climate caused animal and plant life to diversify.* **2** [I or T] If a business diversifies, it starts making new products or offering new services: *Many wheat farmers have begun to diversify* ***into*** *other forms of agriculture.* • **diversification** /daɪˌvɜː.sɪ.fɪˈkeɪ.ʃᵊn/ (US) /dɪˌvɝː-/ noun [U]

diversion /daɪˈvɜː.ʃᵊn/ (US) /dɪˈvɝː-/ noun **CHANGE OF DIRECTION** ▷ **1** [C] UK (US **detour**) a different route that is used because a road is closed: *Traffic diversions will be kept to a minimum throughout the festival.* **2** [C or U] the fact of something being sent somewhere different from where it was originally intended to go: *the diversion of money to other projects* **TAKING ATTENTION** ▷ **3** [C] something that takes your attention away from something else: *Shoplifters often work in pairs, with one* ***creating*** *a diversion to distract the shop assistants while the other steals the goods.* **4** [C] formal an activity you do for entertainment: *Reading is a pleasant diversion.* • **diversionary** /-ᵊr.i/ (US) /-er.i/ adj *The proposal was dismissed as a diversionary* ***tactic*** *intended to distract attention from the real problems.*

diversity /daɪˈvɜː.sɪ.ti/ (US) /dɪˈvɝː.sə.t̬i/ noun [S or U] **C1** the fact of many different types of things or people being included in something: *Does television adequately reflect the* ***ethnic*** *and* ***cultural*** *diversity of the country?* ◦ *There is* ***a*** *wide diversity* ***of*** *opinion on the question of unilateral disarmament.*

divert /daɪˈvɜːt/ (US) /dɪˈvɝːt/ verb [T] **CHANGE DIRECTION** ▷ **1** **C2** to cause something or someone to change direction: *Traffic will be diverted through the side streets while the main road is resurfaced.* ◦ *Our flight had to be diverted* ***to*** *Stansted because of the storm.* **2** to use something for a different purpose: *Should more* ***funds/money/resources*** *be diverted* ***from*** *roads* ***into*** *railways?* **TAKE ATTENTION AWAY** ▷ **3** **C1** to take someone's attention away from something: *The war has diverted* ***attention*** *(****away****)* ***from*** *the country's economic problems.* **4** formal to entertain someone: *It's a marvellous game for diverting restless children on long car journeys.*

divest /dɪˈvest/ verb [I or T] mainly US to sell something, especially a business or a part of a business: *The company is divesting its less profitable business operations.* ◦ *She has divested her****self of*** *(= sold) some of her share-holdings.*

PHRASAL VERB **divest sb of sth** formal to take something off or away from someone or yourself: *There is a growing movement to divest the monarchy of its remaining constitutional power.* ◦ *She divested her****self*** *of her cumbersome attire.*

divide /dɪˈvaɪd/ verb; noun

▸verb **SEPARATE** ▷ **1** **B1** [I or T] to (cause to) separate into parts or groups: *At the end of the lecture, I'd like all the students to divide* ***into*** *small discussion groups.* ◦ *After the Second World War Germany was divided* ***into*** *two separate countries.* **2** **C1** [T] to share: *I think we should divide (****up****) the costs equally* ***among/between*** *us.* **3** **B2** [T] If something divides two areas, it marks the edge or limit of them: *There's a narrow alley that divides our house* ***from*** *the one next door.* ◦ *This path marks the dividing* ***line*** *between my land and my neighbour's.* **4** [T] to use different amounts of something for different purposes or activities: *She divides her time* ***between*** *her apartment in New York and her cottage in Yorkshire.* **DISAGREE** ▷ **5** **B2** [T often passive] to cause a group of people to disagree about something: *The party is divided* ***on/over*** *the issue of*

D

capital punishment. **6 divide and rule** a way of keeping yourself in a position of power by causing disagreements among other people so that they are unable to oppose you **CALCULATE** ▷ **7 divide sth by sth** to calculate the number of times that one number fits (exactly) into another: *10 divided by 5 is/equals 2.* → Compare **multiply, subtract 8 divide (sth) into sth** C1 If a number divides into another number, it fits (exactly) into it when multiplied a particular number of times: *What do you get if you divide 6 into 18?* ◦ *2 divides into 10 five times.*

▸noun [C] C1 a difference or separation: *Because of debt repayments, the divide* ***between*** *rich and poor countries is continuing to grow.*

di,vided 'highway noun [C] US for **dual carriageway**

dividend /ˈdɪv.ɪ.dend/, /-dənd/ noun [C] (a part of) the profit of a company that is paid to the people who own SHARES in it: *Dividends will be sent to shareholders.*

dividers /dɪˈvaɪ.dəz/ US /-dɚz/ noun [plural] UK a piece of equipment used in mathematics consisting of two parts that are joined at one end and have sharp points at the other, used for measuring lines and angles and for making marks to show positions along lines

divination /ˌdɪv.ɪˈneɪ.ʃən/ noun [U] the skill or act of saying or discovering what will happen in the future

divine /dɪˈvaɪn/ adj; verb

▸adj **GOD-LIKE** ▷ **1** connected with a god, or like a god: *Some fans seem to regard footballers as divine beings.* ◦ *England have fallen so far behind in the championship that their only hope of victory is divine* ***intervention*** (= help from God). ◦ *Just because you've been promoted that doesn't give you a divine* ***right*** (= one like that of a god) *to tell us all what to do.* **SPLENDID** ▷ **2** old-fashioned extremely good, pleasant or enjoyable: *Their new house is quite divine!* • **divinely** /-li/ adv

▸verb **GUESS** ▷ **1** [T] to guess something: [+ that] *I divined* ***from*** *his grim expression* ***that*** *the news was not good.* **SEARCH** ▷ **2** [I or T] to search for water or minerals underground by holding horizontally in your hands a Y-shaped rod or stick, the end of which suddenly points down slightly when water or minerals are below it: *a divining* ***rod***

diviner /dɪˈvaɪ.nəʳ/ US /-nɚ/ noun [C] (also **dowser**) a person who divines for water or minerals

diving /ˈdaɪ.vɪŋ/ noun [U] B1 the sport of jumping into water, especially with your head and arms going in first, or of swimming underwater

'diving ,bell noun [C] a bell-shaped metal container without a base that is supplied with air so that a person can work in deep water

'diving ,board noun [C] a board that sticks out over a swimming pool, from which people can DIVE (= jump) into water below

divinity /dɪˈvɪn.ɪ.ti/ US /-ə.t̬i/ noun **1** [U] the state of being a god: *How can you be a Christian and dispute the divinity of Jesus?* **2** [C] a god or GODDESS

Divinity /dɪˈvɪn.ɪ.ti/ US /-ə.t̬i/ noun [U] old-fashioned the study of religion: *She has a Doctorate in Divinity from York University.*

divisible /dɪˈvɪz.ɪ.bl̩/ adj (US also **dividable**) that can be divided by another number: *A prime number is a whole number greater than 1 that is exactly divisible* ***by*** *itself and 1 but no other number.*

division /dɪˈvɪʒ.ən/ noun **PART** ▷ **1** B2 [U] the act of separating something into parts or groups, or the way that it is separated: *the equal division of labour between workers* **2** B2 [C] a separate part of an army or large organization: *the sales division* **3** B2 [C] a group of teams which play against each other in a particular sport: *Norwich are currently top of Division One.* **CALCULATION** ▷ **4** [U] the calculation of how many times one number goes into another **DISAGREEMENT** ▷ **5** [C or U] the situation in which people disagree about something: *Disagreements about defence cuts have opened up* ***deep*** *divisions* ***within*** *the military.* ◦ *Division* ***within*** *the party will limit its chances at the election.*

divisional /dɪˈvɪʒ.ən.əl/ adj relating to a division (= part) of an army or large organization: *the divisional commander/headquarters*

di'vision ,lobby noun [C] UK specialized one of two rooms to which a British Member of Parliament must go to show if they are voting for or against a suggested law

di,vision of 'labour noun [U] a way of organizing work, especially making things, so that it is done as a set of separate processes by different (groups of) people

divisive /dɪˈvaɪ.sɪv/ adj describes something that causes great and sometimes unfriendly disagreement within a group of people: *The Vietnam war was an extremely divisive issue in the US.* • **divisively** /-li/ adv • **divisiveness** /-nəs/ noun [U]

divisor /dɪˈvaɪ.zəʳ/ US /-zɚ/ noun [C] a number by which another number is divided in a calculation: *When you divide 21 by 7, 7 is the divisor.*

divorce /dɪˈvɔːs/ US /-ˈvɔːrs/ noun; verb

▸noun **PEOPLE** ▷ **1** B1 [C or U] an official or legal process to end a marriage: *The last I heard they were* ***getting a*** *divorce.* ◦ *Divorce is on the increase.* ◦ *Ellie wants a divorce.* ◦ *What are the chances of a marriage* ***ending in*** *divorce?* **SUBJECTS** ▷ **2** [C] formal a separation: *Why is there such a divorce* ***between*** *the arts and the sciences in this country's schools?*

▸verb **PEOPLE** ▷ **1** B2 [I or T] to end your marriage by an official or legal process: *She's divorcing her husband.* **SUBJECTS** ▷ **2** [T] to separate two subjects: *How can you divorce the issues of environmental protection and overpopulation?*

divorcé /dɪˌvɔːˈseɪ/ US /dəˌvɔːr-/ noun [C] US a man who is divorced and who has not married again → Compare **divorcee**

divorced /dɪˈvɔːst/ US /-ˈvɔːrst/ adj **PEOPLE** ▷ **1** B1 married in the past but not now married: *She's divorced.* ◦ *They* ***got*** *divorced after only six months of marriage.* **SUBJECTS** ▷ **2** not based on or affected by something: *Sometimes politicians seem to be divorced* ***from*** *reality.*

divorcee /dɪˌvɔːˈsiː/ US /dəˌvɔːrˈseɪ/ noun [C] **1** UK a man or a woman who is divorced and who has not married again **2** (also **divorcée**) US a woman who is divorced and who has not married again → Compare **divorcé**

divulge /daɪˈvʌldʒ/, /dɪ-/ verb [T] to make something secret known: *Journalists do not divulge their sources.* ◦ [+ question word] *The managing director refused to divulge* ***how*** *much she earned.*

divvy /ˈdɪv.i/ noun; verb

▸noun [C] (also **div**) UK informal a stupid person: *Don't be such a divvy!*

▸verb

PHRASAL VERB **divvy sth up** to share something between a number of people: *They haven't yet decided how to divvy up the proceeds from the sale.*

Diwali (also **Divali**) /dɪˈwɑː.li/ noun [C or U] a Hindu holiday in October/November that is a celebration of light and of hopes for the following year

dixieland /ˈdɪk.si.lænd/ **noun** [U] a style of traditional JAZZ music with a two-beat rhythm, which originally began in New Orleans in the US in the 1920s

DIY /ˌdiː.aɪˈwaɪ/ **noun** [U] UK abbreviation for do-it-yourself: the activity of decorating or repairing your home, or making things for your home yourself, rather than paying someone else to do it for you: *a DIY enthusiast* ◦ *a DIY superstore*

dizygotic /ˌdaɪ.zaɪˈɡɒt.ɪk/ (US) /-ˈɡɑː.t̬ɪk/ **adj** specialized If TWINS are dizygotic, they developed from two separate eggs. → Compare **monozygotic**

dizzy /ˈdɪz.i/ **adj** **FEELING** ▷ **1** B2 feeling as if everything is turning round and being unable to balance and about to fall down: *Going without sleep for a long time makes me feel dizzy and light-headed.* ◦ *I felt quite dizzy* ***with*** *excitement as I went up to collect the award.* **QUALITY** ▷ **2** [before noun] confusing and very fast: *Who could have predicted the dizzy* ***pace*** *of change in the country?* **3** informal describes a person who is silly, especially a woman: *In the film, she played the part of a dizzy* ***blonde.*** • **dizzily** /-ɪ.li/ **adv** in a dizzy way or a way that makes you feel dizzy: *The skyscrapers towered dizzily above us.* • **dizziness** /-nəs/ **noun** [U]

IDIOM **the dizzy heights of sth** humorous a very important position: *Do you think Tess will* ***reach*** *the dizzy heights of Senior Editor before she's 30?*

dizzying /ˈdɪz.i.ɪŋ/ **adj** **FEELING** ▷ **1** causing you to feel dizzy: *a dizzying display of acrobatics* **QUALITY** ▷ **2** very fast or confusing: *The dizzying* ***pace*** *of political change in the country caught many people by surprise.* • **dizzyingly** /-li/ **adv**

DJ /ˌdiːˈdʒeɪ/ **noun** [C] **PERSON** ▷ **1** B1 (also **deejay**) abbreviation for **disc jockey** **CLOTHING** ▷ **2** UK abbreviation for **dinner jacket**

DNA /ˌdiː.enˈeɪ/ **noun** [U] specialized C2 deoxyribonucleic acid: the chemical at the centre of the cells of living things, which controls the structure and purpose of each cell and carries GENETIC information during REPRODUCTION

do[1] **auxiliary verb; verb; noun**

▸**auxiliary verb** /də, du, duː/ (**did, done**) **FOR QUESTIONS/NEGATIVES** ▷ **1** A1 used with another verb to form questions and negative sentences, including negative orders, and sometimes in AFFIRMATIVE sentences for reasons of style: *Where do you work?* ◦ *Why did you do that?* ◦ *Why don't we have lunch together on Friday?* ◦ *Doesn't Matthew look old these days?* ◦ *'Didn't you realize she was deaf?' 'No I didn't.'/'Of course I did.'* ◦ *Not only did I speak to her, I even got her autograph!* ◦ formal *Never did I hear such a terrible noise.* ◦ *Don't (you) speak to me like that!* ◦ UK *Don't let's argue about it (= let's not argue about it).* ◦ formal *So quietly did she speak (= she spoke so quietly) that I could scarcely hear her.* ◦ ***Little*** *does he know (= he knows nothing about it), but we're flying to Geneva next weekend to celebrate his birthday.* ◦ *'I want two chocolate bars and an ice cream.' 'Do you* ***now/indeed****? (= that is surprising or unreasonable).'* **2** A2 used instead of the main verb in questions that are added to the end of a sentence to check information: *You met him at our dinner party, didn't you?* ◦ *You don't understand the question, do you?* **3** used instead of the main verb in questions that are added to the end of a sentence as a way of expressing surprise: *So Susannah and Guy finally got married, did they?* **TO AVOID REPEATING** ▷ **4** B1 used to avoid repeating a verb or verb phrase: *She runs much faster than he does.* ◦ *Maria looks much healthier than she did.* ◦ *'I don't like intense heat.'* ***'Nor/Neither*** *do I.'* ◦ *'I hate intense heat.'* ***'So*** *do I.'* ◦ *'You left your umbrella.'* ***'So*** *I did. I'm becoming so forgetful these days.'* ◦ *'Would you mind tidying up the kitchen?' 'I already have done.'* ◦ *'May I join you?' 'Please do!'* ◦ *'Who said that?' 'I did.'* ◦ *'Tilly speaks fluent Japanese.' 'Does she really?'* ◦ *'I thought I'd take a day off school today.' 'Oh no you don't (= I'm not going to let you do that)!'* **FOR EMPHASIS** ▷ **5** B2 [+ infinitive without to] used to give extra force to the main verb: *Do shut up, Georgia, and get on with your homework.* ◦ *'Can I buy stamps here?' 'Well, we do sell them, but we haven't got any at the moment.'*

▸**verb** /duː/ (**did, done**) **PERFORM** ▷ **1** A1 [T] to perform, take part in or achieve something: *That was a really stupid thing to do.* ◦ *Why were you sent home from school early? What have you done now?* ◦ *What are you doing over the weekend?* ◦ *The only thing we can do now is wait and see what happens.* ◦ *You should be able to do it by yourself/on your own.* ◦ *What have you done (= made happen)* ***to*** *her?* ◦ ***What*** *(****on earth****) were you doing in the library (= why were you there) at two o'clock in the morning?* ◦ *What are these toys doing here? (= Why are they here?)* ◦ ***What*** *do you do (****for a living****)? (= What is your job?)* ◦ ***What*** *can I do* ***for*** *you? (= How can I help you?)* ◦ *What have you done* ***with*** *(= where have you put) my coat?* ◦ *She just hasn't known what to do* ***with herself*** *(= how to keep herself busy) since she retired.* **2 do sth about sth** to take action to deal with something: *It's a global problem – what can individuals do about it?* **3 do well/badly by sb** formal to treat someone well or badly **ACT** ▷ **4** [I or T] to act or take action: *Stop arguing with me, Daryl, and do* ***as*** *you're told!* ◦ *She told me not to ask any questions, just to do* ***as*** *she did.* ◦ *'Was it wrong of me to go to the police?' 'Oh no, I'm sure you did right/did the right thing.'* ◦ *You'd do* ***well*** *to take some professional advice on this matter.* **CONNECTED** ▷ **5 to do with** B2 connected with: *'Why did you want to talk to me?' 'Well, it's to do with a complaint that's been made about your work.'* ◦ *'But I didn't have any money.' 'What* ***has*** *that got to do with it? You still shouldn't have taken my purse without asking me.'* ◦ *She's refused to* ***have anything*** *(****more****) to do with him since he was arrested for drinking and driving.* ◦ *'I thought I should tell you I saw your son smoking today.' 'Mind your own business, would you? It* ***has nothing*** *to do with you what my son does!'* **DEAL WITH** ▷ **6** A1 [T] to deal with or be responsible for something: *Lucia is going to do the publicity for the school play.* ◦ *If they ask any awkward questions, just let me do the talking.* **STUDY** ▷ **7** A1 [T] to study a subject: *Diane did anthropology at university.* **SOLVE** ▷ **8** [T] to solve, or find the answer to something: *to do a puzzle* ◦ *I've never been able to do crosswords.* **MAKE** ▷ **9** A2 [T] to make, produce, or create something: *I can't come out tonight – I've got to do my history essay.* ◦ [+ two objects] *Can you do me 20 photocopies of this report/do 20 photocopies of this report* ***for*** *me?* **FINISH** ▷ **10** [I] If you say that you have done with something or someone, or have done performing a particular action, you mean that you have finished what you were doing with something or someone, or what you were saying to someone, or that you have finished the action: *Have you done* ***with*** *those scissors yet?* ◦ *Where are you going? I haven't done* ***with*** *you yet.* ◦ [+ -ing verb] *I haven't done talk****ing*** *to you yet.* **CLEAN/MAKE TIDY** ▷ **11** B1 [I or T] to clean or tidy, or make something look attractive: *I want to do (= clean) the living room this afternoon.* ◦ *I cooked the dinner so you can do (= wash) the dishes.* ◦ *do your* ***hair/make-up/nails*** **ARRANGE** ▷ **12** [T] to arrange something: *You've done those flowers beautifully.*

D

D

◦ *Can anyone here do (= tie) bow-ties?* **TRAVEL** ▷ **13** [T] to travel a particular distance or to travel at a particular speed: *It's an old car and it's done over 80,000 miles.* ◦ *My new car does 50 miles to the gallon/30 km to the litre (= uses one* GALLON *of fuel to travel 50 miles, or one litre to travel 30 km).* ◦ *We were doing 150 (kilometres an hour) along the motorway.* **14** [T] to complete a journey: *We did the journey to Wales in five hours.* **BE ACCEPTABLE** ▷ **15** C1 [I or T] to be acceptable, suitable or enough: *Will this room do or would you prefer one with a shower?* ◦ *This kind of behaviour just won't do.* ◦ [+ to infinitive] ***It*** *doesn't do* ***to*** *criticize your parents.* ◦ *I haven't got any grapefruit juice, but I've got some orange juice. Will that do (you)?* ◦ *'Is that enough potato, or would you like some more?' 'That'll do (= be enough for) me, thanks.'* **CAUSE TO HAVE** ▷ **16** [T] to provide or sell something, or to cause someone to have something: *There's a special offer on and they're doing three for the price of two.* ◦ *Do you do travel insurance as well as flights?* ◦ *The pub only does food at lunchtimes, not in the evenings.* **COOK** ▷ **17** [T] to cook or prepare food: *Who's doing the food for your party?* ◦ [+ two objects] *I'll do you some scrambled eggs.* **MANAGE** ▷ **18** B1 [I usually + adverb] to develop or continue with the stated amount of success: ***How*** *is Mary doing in her new job/school?* ◦ *Both the new mother and her baby are doing very* ***well***. ◦ *Are your roses doing* ***all right*** *this year?* ◦ *Many shops are doing* ***badly*** *because of the economic situation.* ◦ *I did rather* ***well*** *when I traded in my car – they gave me a good price for it.* ◦ *Alexa has done* ***well for*** *her****self*** *(= has achieved great personal success), getting such a highly paid job.* → Synonym **manage** **PLAY** ▷ **19** [T] to perform a play or to play the part of a character: *The children are doing a play at the end of term.* ◦ *She's done all the important Shakespearean roles apart from Lady Macbeth.* ◦ *I hope she doesn't do* ***a*** *Helen (= do what Helen did) and get divorced six months after her wedding.* **VISIT** ▷ **20** [T] informal to visit the interesting places in a town or country, or to look around an interesting place: *We didn't manage to do Nice when we were in France.* **STEAL** ▷ **21** [T] informal to enter a building illegally and steal from it: *Our house was done while we were away.* **CHEAT** ▷ **22** [T] informal to cheat someone: *$50 for that old bike! You've been done!* ◦ *He did me* ***for*** *a thousand quid for that car.* **PRISON** ▷ **23** [T] informal to spend time in prison: *He did three years for his part in the robbery.* ◦ *If you're not careful you'll end up doing* ***time*** *again.* **PUNISH** ▷ **24** [T] mainly UK informal to punish someone: *I got done (= stopped by the police)* ***for*** *speeding on my way home last night.* **TAKE DRUG** ▷ **25** [T] informal to take an illegal drug: *I don't do drugs.* **HAPPEN** ▷ **26** **be doing** informal to be happening: *This town is so boring in the evening – there's never anything doing.*

IDIOMS **can't be doing with sth** UK informal to be unable to bear something, or to have no patience with it: *I can't be doing with all this shouting and screaming.* • **do as you would be done by** saying said to show that you believe in treating others as you would like them to treat you • **do it** informal to have sex • **do something, nothing, etc. for/to sb** informal to have a strong and positive effect on someone, or to be something or someone that they like or enjoy: *Watching that film really did something to me.* ◦ *Chopin has never really done* ***it/anything*** *for me.* • **that does it!** said when someone or something goes further than the limit of what is acceptable: *That does it! I will not tolerate that sort of behaviour in this class.* • **that will never do!** old-fashioned used to say that a situation is wrong and unacceptable: *'The dinner was excellent except that they served red wine with the chicken.' 'Dear me! That will never do!'* • **that'll do!** used to tell someone to stop behaving badly: *That'll do, Timothy! Please just sit down and keep quiet.* • **that's done it!** informal said when someone or something has caused damage or a difficulty: *'That's done it!' said Anna as she looked at the damage. 'Now I really will have to get a new car.'* • **what's done is done** saying said when you cannot change something that has already happened

PHRASAL VERBS **do away with sth** C1 to get rid of something or stop using something: *These ridiculous rules and regulations should have been done away with years ago.* ◦ *Computerization has enabled us to do away with a lot of paperwork.* ◦ *How on Earth could they do away with a lovely old building like that and put a car park there instead?* • **do away with sb** informal to murder someone • **do sb down** to criticize someone in order to make them feel ashamed or to make other people lose respect for them: *She felt that everyone in the meeting was trying to do her down.* ◦ *Stop doing your****self*** *down.* • **do for sb/sth** UK old-fashioned informal to seriously damage something, or to seriously hurt or kill someone: *Driving on those rough roads has really done for my car.* • **do sb in** **KILL** ▷ **1** slang to attack or kill someone: *They threatened to do me in if I didn't pay up by Friday.* **TIRE** ▷ **2** informal to make someone extremely tired: *That hockey match really did me in.* • **do yourself in** slang to kill yourself: *She threatened to do herself in when her husband ran off with her best friend.* • **do sth out** to decorate something: *They did the room out* ***with*** *balloons and streamers ready for the party.* ◦ *We've had the bathroom done out* ***in*** *pale yellow.* • **do sb out of sth** informal to stop someone from getting or keeping something, especially in a dishonest or unfair way: *Pensioners have been done out of millions of pounds as a result of the changes.* • **do sb over** mainly UK informal to attack someone violently: *They said they'd do me over if I refused to drive the getaway car.* • **do sth over** US to do something again because you did not do it well the first time: • **do (sth) up** to fasten something or become fastened: *Can you help me to do up my dress?* ◦ *Do your shoes/laces up before you trip over.* ◦ *These trousers must have shrunk – I can't do the zip up.* ◦ *Why won't this zip do up?* → Opposite **undo** • **do sth up** **REPAIR** ▷ **1** B2 to repair or decorate a building so that it looks attractive: *I'd like to buy a run-down cottage that I can do up.* **WRAP** ▷ **2** to wrap something in paper: *She always does her presents up beautifully* ***in*** *gold and silver paper.* • **do without (sth)** B2 to manage without having something: *There's no mayonnaise left, so I'm afraid you'll just have to do without.* ◦ *Thank you, Kate, we can do without language like that (= we don't want to hear your rude language).*

▸**noun** [C] /duː/ (plural **dos**) **TREATMENT** ▷ **1** UK informal a way of treating people: *There are no special privileges for the managers – we believe in* ***fair*** *dos all round (= equal treatment for everyone) in this company.* ◦ *It's a* ***poor*** *do (= a bad/unfair situation) when a so-called developed country can't even provide homes for all its citizens.* **RULE** ▷ **2** **dos and don'ts** → See at **dos and don'ts** **PARTY** ▷ **3** mainly UK informal a party or other social event: *Colin's having a* ***bit of a*** *do for his 50th birthday.* **HAIR** ▷ **4** US for **hairdo**

do² (also **doh**) /dəʊ/ US /doʊ/ **noun** [S] the first note of the SOL-FA musical SCALE: *Would you sing me a do, please?*

doable /ˈduː.ə.bl/ **adj** If something is doable, it can be achieved or performed: *This project may be difficult, but I still think it's doable.*

PHRASAL VERB **dob sb in** informal to secretly tell someone in authority that someone else has done something wrong: *Who was it who dobbed me* ***in*** *(****to*** *the teacher)?*

dobber /ˈdɒb.əʳ/ ⓤⓢ /ˈdɑː.bɚ/ noun [C] Australian English informal disapproving a person who secretly tells someone in authority that someone else has done something wrong → Compare **sneak, tell-tale**

doc /dɒk/ ⓤⓢ /dɑːk/ noun [C] informal a doctor: [as form of address] *You see, doc, I haven't been sleeping at all well recently.*

docile /ˈdəʊ.saɪl/ ⓤⓢ /ˈdɑː.səl/ adj quiet and easy to influence, persuade, or control: *The once docile population has finally risen up against the ruthless regime.* • **docility** /dəʊˈsɪl.ɪ.ti/ ⓤⓢ /dɑːˈsɪl.ə.t̬i/ noun [U]

dock /dɒk/ ⓤⓢ /dɑːk/ noun; verb

▸noun **FOR SHIPS** ▷ **1** C1 [C] an area of water in a port that can be closed off and that is used for putting goods onto and taking them off ships or repairing ships → Compare **harbour 2 docks** [plural] a group of these areas of water in a port and the buildings around them: *The strike has led to the cancellation of some ferry services and left hundreds of passengers stranded at the docks.* **3** [C] US a long structure built over water where passengers can get on or off a boat or where goods can be put on and taken off **LAW** ▷ **4 the dock** [S] mainly UK the place in a criminal law court where the accused person sits or stands during the trial: *The defendant seemed nervous as he left the dock and stepped up to the witness box.* ◦ *The company will find itself* ***in*** *the dock (= in court) if it continues to ignore the pollution regulations.* **PLANT** ▷ **5** [C or U] a common wild plant with large wide leaves that grows in some northern countries such as Britain: *Rubbing dock leaves on nettle stings helps to relieve the pain.* **EQUIPMENT** ▷ **6** [C] a **docking station**

▸verb **REMOVE** ▷ **1** [T] to remove part of something: *The university has docked lecturers' pay/wages* ***by*** *20 percent because of their refusal to mark exam papers.* ◦ *The lambs' tails are docked (= cut short) for hygiene reasons.* **SHIP** ▷ **2** [I or T] If a ship docks, it arrives at a dock and if someone docks a ship, they bring it into a dock: *Hundreds of people turned up to see the ship dock* ***at*** *Southampton.* ◦ *The Russians and Americans docked (= joined together in space) (their spacecraft) just after one o'clock this morning.*

docker /ˈdɒk.əʳ/ ⓤⓢ /ˈdɑː.kɚ/ noun [C] (also **dock-worker**) a person who works at a port, putting goods onto and taking them off ships

docket /ˈdɒk.ɪt/ ⓤⓢ /ˈdɑː.kɪt/ noun [C] **1** UK an official document describing something that is being DELIVERED or transported and giving details of where it is coming from and where it is going to **2** US a list of cases to be dealt with in a law court, or an AGENDA in business

ˈ**docking** ˌ**station** noun [C] (also **dock**) a piece of electrical equipment to which another piece of equipment can be connected: *Just plug the camera into the docking station to transfer pictures onto your computer.*

dockland /ˈdɒk.lænd/, /-lənd/ ⓤⓢ /ˈdɑːk-/ noun [C or U] UK the area that surrounds the DOCKS in a port

the dockside /ˈdɒk.saɪd/ ⓤⓢ /ˈdɑːk-/ noun [S] the area next to a dock where goods can be stored before being put onto or after being taken off ships

dockyard /ˈdɒk.jɑːd/ ⓤⓢ /ˈdɑːk.jɑːrd/ noun [C] (also **shipyard**) a place where ships are built, SERVICED (= kept in good condition), and repaired

doctor /ˈdɒk.təʳ/ ⓤⓢ /ˈdɑːk.tɚ/ noun; verb

dockyard

▸noun [C] **MEDICINE** ▷ **1** A1 (written abbreviation **Dr**) a person with a medical degree whose job is to treat people who are ill or hurt: *The doctor* ***prescribed*** *some pills.* ◦ *You should* ***see*** *a doctor about that cough.* ◦ [as form of address] *Good morning, Doctor Smith/Doctor.* **2 the doctor's** the place where a doctor, especially a GP, works: *He* ***went to*** *the doctor's this morning for a check-up.* **EDUCATION** ▷ **3** (written abbreviation **Dr**) a person who has the highest DEGREE (= qualification) from a college or university

IDIOM **just what the doctor ordered** exactly what is wanted or needed: *Ooh thank you, a nice cup of tea. Just what the doctor ordered.*

▸verb [T] **CHANGE** ▷ **1** to change a document in order to deceive people: *He was found to have provided the court with doctored evidence.* **2** to secretly put a harmful or poisonous substance into food or drink: *Bottles of lemonade doctored* ***with*** *rat poison were discovered in the kitchen.* **ANIMAL** ▷ **3** UK informal to remove the sexual organs of an animal in order to prevent it from producing young

doctorate /ˈdɒk.tər.ət/ ⓤⓢ /ˈdɑːk.tɚ-/ noun [C] the highest degree from a university: *She has a doctorate* ***in*** *physics from Norwich.* • **doctoral** /-əl/ adj [before noun] *a doctoral dissertation*

ˌ**doctor's** ˈ**orders** noun [plural] mainly humorous used to mean that you must do something because your doctor has told you to do it: *I have to have a week off work – it's doctor's orders!*

doctrinaire /ˌdɒk.trɪˈneəʳ/ ⓤⓢ /ˌdɑːk.trəˈner/ adj formal disapproving based on and following fixed beliefs rather than considering practical problems: *These principles are doctrinaire.*

doctrinal /dɒkˈtraɪ.nəl/ ⓤⓢ /ˈdɑːk.trɪ-/ adj formal relating to doctrine: *a doctrinal matter/approach*

doctrine /ˈdɒk.trɪn/ ⓤⓢ /ˈdɑːk-/ noun [C or U] a belief or set of beliefs, especially political or religious ones, that are taught and accepted by a particular group: *Christian doctrine* ◦ *The president said he would not go against sound military doctrine.*

docudrama /ˈdɒk.jʊˌdrɑː.mə/ ⓤⓢ /ˈdɑː.kjʊˌdrɑː.mə/ noun [C or U] a television programme whose story is based on an event or situation that really happened, although it is not intended to be accurate in every detail

> **Word partners for document**
>
> *draw up/produce* a document • *sign* a document • *examine/look over/read* a document • documents *describe/detail* sth • *official/confidential/forged* documents • *in* a document • a document *concerning/on* sth • a *copy* of a document

document noun; verb

▸noun [C] /ˈdɒk.jʊ.mənt/ ⓤⓢ /ˈdɑː.kjʊ-/ **1** A2 a paper or

set of papers with written or printed information, especially of an official type: ***official/confidential/ legal*** *documents* ◦ *They are charged with using* ***forged*** *documents.* **2** B1 a text that is written and stored on a computer: *I'll send you the document by email.*

▸**verb** [T] /ˈdɒk.jʊ.mənt/, /-ment/ US /ˈdɑː.kjʊ-/ to record the details of an event, a process, etc.: *His interest in cricket has been* ***well-****documented (= recorded and written about) by the media.*

D

documentary /ˌdɒk.jʊˈmen.tᵊr.i/ US /ˌdɑː.kjəˈmen. t̬ɚ-/ **noun; adj**

▸**noun** [C] B1 a film or television or radio programme that gives facts and information about a subject: *The documentary took a fresh look at the life of Darwin.* ◦ *They showed a documentary* ***on*** *animal communication.*

▸**adj** [before noun] **1** in the form of documents: *Human rights campaigners have discovered documentary* ***evidence*** *of torture.* **2** giving facts and information about a subject in the form of a film or television or radio programme: *Most of her films have a documentary style.*

documentation /ˌdɒk.jʊ.menˈteɪ.ʃᵊn/ US /ˌdɑː.kjʊ-/ **noun** [U] **1** pieces of paper containing official information: *Passengers without proper documentation (= official papers saying who they are) will not be allowed to travel.* **2** the instructions for using a computer device or program

docusoap /ˈdɒ.kjuː.səʊp/ US /ˈdɑː.kjuː.soʊp/ **noun** [C] an entertaining programme about the lives of real people, especially people who live in the same place or do the same job: *Have you seen the new docusoap about driving instructors?*

doddery /ˈdɒd.ᵊr.i/ US /ˈdɑː.dɚ-/ **adj** (also **doddering**) weak and unable to walk in a normal way, usually because you are old: *a doddery old man*

doddle /ˈdɒd.l̩/ US /ˈdɑː.dl̩/ **noun** [S] UK informal something that is very easy to do: *The exam was a doddle.*

dodecahedron /ˌdəʊ.dek.əˈhiː.drᵊn/ US /ˌdoʊ-/ **noun** [C] (plural **dodecahedrons** or **dodecahedra** /-drə/) specialized a solid shape that has twelve flat surfaces of equal size with five sides

dodge /dɒdʒ/ US /dɑːdʒ/ **verb; noun**

▸**verb 1** [I or T] to avoid being hit by something by moving quickly to one side: *He dodged to avoid the hurtling bicycle.* **2** [T] to avoid something unpleasant: *The minister dodged questions about his relationship with the actress.*

▸**noun** [C] informal a clever, dishonest way of avoiding something: *They bought another car as a* ***tax*** *dodge (= a way to avoid paying tax).*

dodgem (car) /ˈdɒdʒ.əm.kɑːʳ/ US /ˈdɑː.dʒəm.kɑːr/ **noun** [C usually plural] trademark a small electric car driven for entertainment in a special closed space where the aim is to try to hit other cars

dodger /ˈdɒdʒ.əʳ/ US /ˈdɑː.dʒɚ/ **noun** [C] a person who avoids doing what they should do: *a* ***tax*** *dodger*

dodgy /ˈdɒdʒ.i/ US /ˈdɑː.dʒi/ **adj** UK informal **NOT HONEST** ▷ **1** dishonest: *a dodgy deal* ◦ *They got involved with a dodgy businessman and lost all their savings.* **NOT RELIABLE** ▷ **2** likely to fail or cause problems: *The weather might be a bit dodgy at this time of year.* ◦ *I can't come in to work today – I've got a bit of a dodgy stomach.* ◦ *It was a dodgy situation.* **3** likely to break or cause pain: *Careful – that chair's a bit dodgy.* ◦ *Ever since the war I've had this dodgy leg.*

dodo /ˈdəʊ.dəʊ/ US /ˈdoʊ.doʊ/ **noun** [C] (plural **dodos**) a large bird, unable to fly, that no longer exists

doe /dəʊ/ US /doʊ/ **noun** [C] the female of animals such as the DEER or RABBIT → Compare **buck**

doer /ˈduː.əʳ/ US /-ɚ/ **noun** [C] someone who gets actively involved in something, rather than just thinking or talking about it: *There are too many thinkers and not enough doers in this office.*

does strong /dʌz/ weak /dəz/ **verb** he/she/it form of do

doesn't /ˈdʌz.ᵊnt/ **short form of** does not: *Doesn't she look lovely in that hat?*

doff /dɒf/ US /dɑːf/ **verb** [T] old-fashioned to remove your hat, usually to show respect → Compare **don**

IDIOM **doff your hat to sb/sth** literary to show respect to someone or something: *The song doffs its hat to the best soul traditions.*

dog /dɒg/ US /dɑːg/ **noun; verb**

▸**noun** [C] **ANIMAL** ▷ **1** A1 a common animal with four legs, especially kept by people as a pet or to hunt or guard things: *my pet dog* ◦ *wild dogs* ◦ *dog food* ◦ *We could hear dogs barking in the distance.* **PERSON** ▷ **2** slang a man who is unpleasant or not to be trusted: *He tried to steal my money, the* ***dirty*** *dog.* **3** offensive a woman who is not attractive

IDIOMS **a dog in the manger** someone who keeps something that they do not want in order to prevent someone else from getting it • **a dog's breakfast** UK informal something or someone that looks extremely untidy, or something that is very badly done • **the dog's bollocks** UK offensive something or someone that you think is extremely good • **a dog's life** a very unhappy and unpleasant life • **done up/dressed up like a dog's dinner** UK informal wearing very formal or decorative clothes in a way that attracts attention • **every dog has its day** saying said to emphasize that everyone is successful or happy at some time in their life • **give a dog a bad name** UK saying said when someone has been accused of behaving badly in the past, with the result that people expect them to behave like that in the future • **go to the dogs** If a country or organization is going to the dogs, it is becoming very much less successful than it was in the past. • **let sleeping dogs lie** said to warn someone that they should not talk about a bad situation that most people have forgotten about • **put on the dog** US informal to act as if you are more important than you are • **you can't teach an old dog new tricks** saying said to mean that it is very difficult to teach someone new skills or to change someone's habits or character

▸**verb** [T] (-gg-) **FOLLOW** ▷ **1** to follow someone closely and continuously: *Reporters dogged him for answers.* → See also **dogged** **CAUSE PROBLEMS** ▷ **2** to cause difficulties: *Technical problems dogged our trip from the outset.*

ˈdog ˌbiscuit **noun** [C] a hard baked biscuit for dogs

dogcatcher /ˈdɒgˌkætʃ.əʳ/ US /ˈdɑːgˌkætʃ.ɚ/ **noun** [C] a person whose job is to catch dogs and cats that have no home and take them to an official place where they are kept in CAGES (= boxes with bars or wire around them)

ˈdog ˌcollar **noun** [C] **DOG** ▷ **1** a strap worn around a dog's neck **PRIEST** ▷ **2** informal for **clerical collar**

ˈdog ˌdays **noun** [plural] the hottest days of the summer

ˈdog-eared **adj** A book or paper that is dog-eared has the pages turned down at the corners as a result of a lot of use.

ˌdog-eat-ˈdog **adj** disapproving used to describe a situation in which people will do anything to be successful, even if what they do harms other people: *It's a dog-eat-dog* ***world*** *out there.*

dogfight /ˈdɒg.faɪt/ (US) /ˈdɑːg-/ **noun** [C] **1** a fight between two military aircraft in which they fly very fast and very close to each other **2** a fight between dogs, usually organized as an illegal entertainment

dogfish /ˈdɒg.fɪʃ/ (US) /ˈdɑːg-/ **noun** [C] (plural **dogfish** or **dogfishes**) a type of small SHARK

dogged /ˈdɒg.ɪd/ (US) /ˈdɑː.gɪd/ **adj** very determined to do something, even if it is very difficult: *Her ambition and dogged determination ensured that she rose to the top of her profession.* • **doggedly** /-li/ **adv** • **doggedness** /-nəs/ **noun** [U]

doggerel /ˈdɒg.ər.əl/ (US) /ˈdɑː.gɚ-/ **noun** [U] poetry that is silly or badly written

dogging /ˈdɒg.ɪŋ/ (US) /ˈdɑːg-/ **noun** [U] slang sexual activity between people in a public place

doggone /ˈdɒg.ɒn/ (US) /ˈdɑː.gɑːn/ **exclamation, adj** [before noun] US informal used to express anger: *Doggone* (***it***)*, where's that letter?* ◦ *That doggone washing machine's broken again.*

doggy (also **doggie**) /ˈdɒg.i/ (US) /ˈdɑː.gi/ **noun** [C] child's word a dog

ˈdoggy ˌbag **noun** [C] a small bag that a restaurant provides so that you can take home any food you have not finished

ˈdoggy ˌpaddle **noun** [U] (US and Australian English also **ˈdog ˌpaddle**) a simple swimming action in which a person moves their arms and legs up and down in quick movements under the water

doghouse /ˈdɒg.haʊs/ (US) /ˈdɑːg-/ **noun** [C] US for **kennel** (= a small shelter for a dog to sleep in)

IDIOM **in the doghouse** UK and US informal If you are in the doghouse, someone is annoyed with you and shows their disapproval: *I'm in the doghouse – I broke Sara's favourite vase this morning.*

dogie /ˈdəʊ.gi/ (US) /ˈdoʊ-/ **noun** [C] US a CALF (= young cow) that has no mother

dogleg /ˈdɒg.leg/ (US) /ˈdɑːg-/ **noun** [C] a sharp bend, especially in a road or on a GOLF COURSE

dogma /ˈdɒg.mə/ (US) /ˈdɑːg-/ **noun** [C or U] disapproving a fixed, especially religious, belief or set of beliefs that people are expected to accept without any doubts

dogmatic /dɒgˈmæt.ɪk/ (US) /dɑːgˈmæţ-/ **adj** disapproving If someone is dogmatic, they are certain that they are right and that everyone else is wrong. • **dogmatically** /-ɪ.kəl.i/ **adv**

dogmatism /ˈdɒg.mə.tɪ.zəm/ (US) /ˈdɑːg.mə.ţɪ-/ **noun** [U] disapproving stating your opinions in a strong way and not accepting anyone else's opinions: *There is a note of dogmatism in the book.*

dogmatist /ˈdɒg.mə.tɪst/ (US) /ˈdɑːg.mə.ţɪst/ **noun** [C] disapproving a person who believes too strongly that their personal opinions or beliefs are correct

do-gooder /ˈduːˌgʊd.ər/ (US) /-ɚ/ **noun** [C] disapproving someone who does things that they think will help other people, although the other people might not find their actions helpful

ˈdog ˌpaddle **noun** [U] US and Australian English **doggy paddle**

dogsbody /ˈdɒgz.bɒd.i/ (US) /ˈdɑːgz.bɑː.di/ **noun** [C] UK informal a person who has to do all the boring or unpleasant jobs that other people do not want to do

dogsled /ˈdɒg.sled/ (US) /ˈdɑːg-/ **noun** [C] US a SLEDGE pulled by dogs

ˈdog ˌtag **noun** [C] US a small piece of metal worn round the neck by members of the US armed forces with their name and number on it

ˌdog-ˈtired **adj** informal extremely tired

dogwood /ˈdɒg.wʊd/ (US) /ˈdɑːg-/ **noun** [C or U] a bush that has flowers, growing either wild or in gardens

d'oh (also **duh**) /dəʊ/ (US) /doʊ/ **exclamation** informal said when you feel stupid, usually after doing something silly, or to show that you think what someone else has done or said is stupid: *I forgot to turn it on. D'oh!*

doh /dəʊ/ (US) /doʊ/ **noun** [S] the musical note **do**

doily /ˈdɔɪ.li/ **noun** [C] a small piece of paper or cloth with a pattern of little holes in it, used as a decoration on a plate or under a cake

doing /ˈduː.ɪŋ/ **noun** ACTION ▷ **1 be sb's doing** [U] to be done or caused by someone: *Is this your doing?* (= *Did you do this?*) ◦ *It was none of my doing.* → See also **deed 2 take some doing** [U] to be difficult to do and need a lot of effort: *Running a marathon takes some/a lot of doing.* **3 doings** [plural] UK someone's activities: *The doings* ***of*** *the British royal family have always been of interest to the media.* THING ▷ **4 doings** [C] (plural **doings**) UK informal anything, especially a small object, whose name you have forgotten or do not know: *I'm looking for a doings to hold up a curtain rail that's fallen down.*

ˌdo-it-yourˈself **noun** [U] **DIY**

the doldrums /ˈdɒl.drəmz/ (US) /ˈdoʊl-/ **noun** [plural] **in the doldrums a** informal unsuccessful or showing no activity or development: *Her career was in the doldrums during those years.* **b** UK informal sad and with no energy or enthusiasm

dole /dəʊl/ (US) /doʊl/ **verb; noun**

▸**verb**

PHRASAL VERB **dole sth out** informal (C2) to give something, usually money, to several people

▸**noun** [S] **the dole** UK informal the money that the government gives to people who are unemployed: *Young people* ***on*** *(= receiving) the dole are often bored and frustrated.* ◦ *If I can't find any work within a month, I'll have to* ***go on*** *the dole.*

doleful /ˈdəʊl.fəl/ (US) /ˈdoʊl-/ **adj** very sad: *a doleful expression* • **dolefully** /-i/ **adv**

doll /dɒl/ (US) /dɑːl/ **noun; verb**

▸**noun** [C] (A1) a child's toy in the shape of a small person or baby

▸**verb**

PHRASAL VERB **doll yourself up** often disapproving If a woman dolls herself up, she tries to make herself more attractive by putting on make-up and special clothes: *I'm not going to doll myself up just to go to the shops.*

dollar /ˈdɒl.ər/ (US) /ˈdɑː.lɚ/ **noun** [C] **1** (A1) (symbol $) the standard unit of money used in the US, Canada, Australia, New Zealand, and other countries: *Can I borrow $10?* ◦ *There are one hundred cents in a dollar.* ◦ *You can pay in euros or* ***in*** *US dollars.* ◦ *The suitcase was full of dollar* ***bills***. **2 the dollar** the value of the US dollar, used in comparing the values of different types of money from around the world: *In the financial markets today, the dollar* ***rose against/fell against*** *(= was worth more than/less than) the pound.*

ˈdollar ˌsign **noun** [C] the symbol $

ˌdolled ˈup **adj** [after verb] informal (of a woman) wearing make-up and special clothes in order to look attractive for a special occasion: *She spent two hours* ***getting*** *dolled up for the party.*

dollop /ˈdɒl.əp/ (US) /ˈdɑː.ləp/ **noun** [C] a small amount of something soft, especially food: *a dollop **of** ice cream/whipped cream*

ˈdoll's ˌhouse noun [C] UK (US **dollhouse**) a toy that is a very small house, often with furniture and small DOLLS in it

dolly /ˈdɒl.i/ (US) /ˈdɑː.li/ **noun** [C] child's word a **doll**

D

ˈdolly ˌbird noun [C] UK old-fashioned informal a young woman who is thought of as attractive but not very intelligent

dolmen /ˈdɒl.men/ (US) /ˈdoʊl-/ **noun** [C] specialized a group of stones consisting of one large flat stone supported by several vertical ones, built in ancient times

dolorous /ˈdɒl.ər.əs/ (US) /ˈdoʊ.lɚ-/ **adj** literary sad, or causing sadness or emotional suffering

dolphin /ˈdɒl.fɪn/ (US) /ˈdɑːl-/ **noun** [C] **B1** a sea mammal that is large, smooth, and grey, with a long, pointed mouth

dolt /dəʊlt/ (US) /doʊlt/ **noun** [C] disapproving a stupid person

domain /dəˈmeɪn/ (US) /doʊ-/ **noun** [C] **AREA** ▷ **1** **C1** an area of interest or an area over which a person has control: *She treated the business as her private domain.* ◦ *These documents are **in the public** domain (= available to everybody).* **INTERNET** ▷ **2** specialized a set of websites on the internet that end with the same letters, for example .com

doˈmain ˌname noun [C] specialized the part of an email or website address on the internet that shows the name of the organization that the address belongs to

dome /dəʊm/ (US) /doʊm/ **noun** [C] **1** a rounded roof on a building or a room, or a building with such a roof **2** a shape like one-half of a ball: *Gerald had a long grey beard and a shiny bald dome (= head).*

domed /dəʊmd/ (US) /doʊmd/ **adj** shaped like a dome or covered with a dome

domestic /dəˈmes.tɪk/ **adj; noun**

▸**adj** **COUNTRY** ▷ **1** **B2** relating to a person's own country: *domestic airlines/flights* ◦ *Domestic opinion had turned against the war.* **HOME** ▷ **2** **B2** belonging or relating to the home, house or family: *domestic chores/duties/arrangements* • **domestically** /-tɪ.kəl.i/ **adv** *Such a policy would be unacceptable both domestically and internationally.*

▸**noun** [C] (also **doˌmestic ˈhelp**) someone paid to do work, such as cleaning and cooking, in someone else's house

doˌmestic ˈanimal noun [C] an animal that is not wild and is kept as a pet or to produce food

doˌmestic apˈpliance noun [C] a large piece of electrical equipment used in the home, especially in the kitchen: *We stock a wide range of domestic appliances, including fridges, freezers and dishwashers.*

domesticate /dəˈmes.tɪ.keɪt/ **verb** [T often passive] to bring animals or plants under human control in order to provide food, power or company: *Dogs were probably the first animals to be domesticated.*

domesticated /dəˈmes.tɪ.keɪ.tɪd/ (US) /-t̬ɪd/ **adj** able or willing to do cleaning, cooking, and other jobs in the home, and to take care of children: *Since they had their baby they've both become quite domesticated.*

doˌmestic ˈgoddess noun [C] informal humorous a woman who is very good at cooking and keeping her house clean and organized

domesticity /ˌdəʊ.mesˈtɪs.ɪ.ti/ (US) /ˌdoʊ.mesˈtɪs.ə.t̬i/ **noun** [U] life at home taking care of your house and family: *She married young and settled happily into domesticity.*

doˌmestic ˈscience noun [U] UK old-fashioned for **home economics**

doˌmestic ˈviolence noun [U] the situation in which someone you live with attacks you and tries to hurt you: *victims of domestic violence* ◦ *domestic violence against women*

domicile /ˈdɒm.ɪ.saɪl/ (US) /ˈdɑː.mə-/ **noun** [C] formal or legal the place where a person lives

domiciled /ˈdɒm.ɪ.saɪld/ (US) /ˈdɑː.mə-/ **adj** [after verb] formal or legal being legally RESIDENT (= living) in a place: *He was domiciled **in** Saudi Arabia.*

domiciliary /ˌdɒm.ɪˈsɪl.i.ər.i/ (US) /ˌdɑː.məˈsɪl.i.er-/ **adj** formal relating to the home, especially to care that takes place in someone's home because they are ill or old: *domiciliary nursing*

dominant /ˈdɒm.ɪ.nənt/ (US) /ˈdɑː.mə-/ **adj** **1** **C1** more important, strong, or noticeable than anything else of the same type: *a dominant military power* ◦ *Unemployment will be a dominant **issue** at the next election.* **2 dominant gene** specialized a GENE which always produces a particular characteristic in a person, plant, or animal • **dominance** /-nəns/ **noun** [U] **C2** *Music companies have profited from the dominance of CDs over vinyl records.*

dominate /ˈdɒm.ɪ.neɪt/ (US) /ˈdɑː.mə-/ **verb** **HAVE CONTROL** ▷ **1** **B2** [I or T] to have control over a place or person: *He refuses to let others speak and dominates every meeting.* ◦ *They work as a group – no one person is allowed to dominate.* **BE IMPORTANT** ▷ **2** **C1** [T] to be the largest, most important, or most noticeable part of something: *The cathedral dominates the landscape for miles around.* ◦ *The dispute is likely to dominate the news.* • **dominating** /-neɪ.tɪŋ/ (US) /-neɪ.t̬ɪŋ/ **adj** *a dominating personality*

domination /ˌdɒm.ɪˈneɪ.ʃən/ (US) /ˌdɑː.mə-/ **noun** [U] **C1** power or control over other people or things: *The film was about a group of robots set on world domination (= control of all countries).*

dominatrix /ˌdɒm.ɪˈneɪ.trɪks/ (US) /ˌdɑː.mə-/ **noun** [C] (plural **dominatrices**) a woman who has power or control over her partner in a sexual relationship

domineering /ˌdɒm.ɪˈnɪə.rɪŋ/ (US) /ˌdɑː.məˈnɪr.ɪŋ/ **adj** disapproving trying to control other people without thinking about their feelings: *She found him arrogant and domineering.*

dominion /dəˈmɪn.jən/ **noun** formal **1** [U] control over a country or people: *God **has** dominion **over** (= controls) all his creatures.* **2** [C] the land that belongs to a ruler: *The chief's son would inherit all his dominions.*

domino /ˈdɒm.ɪ.nəʊ/ (US) /ˈdɑː.mə.noʊ/ **noun** (plural **dominoes**) **1** [C] a small, rectangular object with spots on it that is used in a game **2 dominoes** [U] a game using dominoes: *A group of old men sat **playing** dominoes.*

the ˈdomino efˌfect noun [S] the situation in which something, usually something bad, happens, causing other similar events to happen

don /dɒn/ (US) /dɑːn/ **noun; verb**

▸**noun** [C] UK a LECTURER (= college teacher), especially at Oxford or Cambridge University in England

▸**verb** [T] (-nn-) formal to put on a piece of clothing: *He donned his finest coat and hat.* → Compare **doff**

donate /dəʊˈneɪt/ (US) /ˈdoʊ.neɪt/ **verb** **1** **B2** [I or T] to give money or goods to help a person or organization: *An anonymous businesswoman donated one million dollars **to** the charity.* ◦ *Please donate generously.* **2** **C1** [T] to allow some of your blood or a part of your body to be used for medical purposes

donation /dəʊˈneɪ.ʃən/ (US) /doʊˈneɪ-/ noun [C or U] B2 money or goods that are given to help a person or organization, or the act of giving them: *donations of food and money* ◦ *I'd like to* ***make*** *a small donation in my mother's name.*

done /dʌn/ verb; adj
▸verb past participle of **do**
▸adj [after verb] **DEALT WITH** ▷ **1** finished: *The washing-up's done, but I've left the drying for you.* **2 a done deal** a plan that has been formally arranged or agreed and that is now certain to happen: *Although it has yet to happen, reform of the sector is regarded as a done deal.* **COOKED** ▷ **3** cooked: *Are the vegetables done (= have they finished cooking) yet?* ◦ *'How would you like your steak done?'* ***'Well*** *done (= cooked for a long time), please.'* → Compare **medium, rare**

IDIOMS **done!** said to show that you accept someone's offer or that you agree to something: *'I'll give you 20 quid for all five of them.' 'Done!'* • **done for 1** to be about to die or suffer very much because of a serious difficulty or danger: *We all thought we were done for when the boat started to sink.* **2** informal very tired: *I'm really done for – I'm going to bed.* • **done in** (US **all done in**) too tired to do any more: *I was/felt really done in after the match.*

döner kebab /ˌdɒn.ə.kɪˈbæb/ (US) /ˌdoʊ.nɚ.kɪˈbɑːb/ noun [C or U] (also **kebab**) UK flat pieces of cooked meat such as LAMB, served with salad in PITTA

donga /ˈdɒŋ.gə/ (US) /ˈdɑːŋ-/ noun [C] South African English a type of DITCH (= long, narrow, open hole in the ground)

dongle /ˈdɒŋ.gəl/ (US) /ˈdɑːŋ-/ noun [C] a piece of equipment that is connected to a computer so that the computer can run a particular piece of software or can use WIRELESS BROADBAND

Don Juan /ˌdɒnˈdʒuː.ən/, /-ˈhwɑːn/ (US) /ˌdɑːn-/ noun [C] a man who has had sex with a lot of women

donkey /ˈdɒŋ.ki/ (US) /ˈdɑːŋ-/ noun [C] B1 an animal like a small horse with long ears

IDIOMS **do (all) the donkey work** UK informal to do the hard, boring part of a job: *Why should I do all the donkey work while you sit around doing nothing?* • **donkey's years** UK informal a very long time: *She's been in the same job* ***for*** *donkey's years.*

ˈdonkey ˌjacket noun [C] UK a type of thick jacket, usually dark blue, often worn by men who work outside

donnish /ˈdɒn.ɪʃ/ (US) /ˈdɑː.nɪʃ/ adj UK intelligent, often in a way that is too serious: *He was a thin, donnish-looking man in a tweed jacket and sandals.*

donor /ˈdəʊ.nər/ (US) /ˈdoʊ.nɚ/ noun [C] **1** C2 a person who gives some of their blood or a part of their body to help someone who is ill: *a blood donor* ◦ *a kidney donor* **2** C2 a person who gives money or goods to an organization: *Thanks to a large gift from an anonymous donor, the charity was able to continue its work.*

ˈdonor ˌcard noun [C] a card you can carry that says you want doctors to use parts of your body to help ill people when you die

don't /dəʊnt/ (US) /doʊnt/ short form of do not: *Don't do that – it hurts!* • **don'ts** /dəʊnts/ (US) /doʊnts/ noun [plural] → See **dos and dont's**

donut /ˈdəʊ.nʌt/ (US) /ˈdoʊ-/ noun US for **doughnut**

dooce /duːs/ US verb **be/get dooced** slang to lose your job because you have written something bad about it on a BLOG

doodah /ˈduː.dɑː/ noun [C] UK (US **doodad**) anything whose name you cannot remember or do not know: *Have you got the doodah, you know, the thing you attach to the end of this?*

doodle /ˈduː.dl̩/ verb [I] to draw pictures or patterns while thinking about something else or when you are bored: *She'd doodled all over her textbooks.* • **doodle** noun [C]

doofus /ˈduːfəs/ noun [C] US informal a stupid person

doohickey /duːˈhɪk.i/ noun [C] US informal any small object whose name you cannot remember

doom /duːm/ noun; verb
▸noun [U] C2 death, destruction, or any very bad situation that cannot be avoided: *A sense of doom hung over the entire country.* ◦ *The newspapers are always full of doom* ***and gloom*** *(= bad news and unhappiness) these days.*
▸verb [T usually passive] to make someone or something certain to do or experience something unpleasant, or to make something bad certain to happen: [+ to infinitive] *Are we doomed* ***to*** *repeat the mistakes of the past?* ◦ *Mounting debts doomed the factory* ***to*** *closure.*

doomed /duːmd/ adj certain to fail, die, or be destroyed: *This is a doomed city.*

doomsday /ˈduːmz.deɪ/ noun [U] the end of the world, or a time when something very bad will happen: *Ecologists predict a doomsday* ***scenario*** *(= a time when death and destruction will happen) if global warming continues to increase at the present rate.* ◦ *You could talk* ***till/until*** *doomsday (= for a very long time), but they will never change their minds.*

doona /ˈduː.nə/ noun [C] Australian English trademark a large, soft, flat bag filled with feathers or artificial material, used on a bed

door /dɔːr/ (US) /dɔːr/ noun [C] **1** A1 a flat object that is used to close the entrance of something such as a room or building, or the entrance itself: *the front door* ◦ *the back door* ◦ *a car door* ◦ *a sliding door* ◦ *The door* ***to*** *his bedroom was locked.* ◦ *We could hear someone knocking* ***at/on*** *the door.* ◦ *Could you* ***open/close/shut*** *the door, please?* ◦ *She asked me to* ***answer*** *the door (= go and open it for someone).* **2 be on the door** to work at the entrance of a building, collecting tickets or preventing particular people from entering **3** used to refer to a house or other building: *Sam only lives a few doors* ***(away/up/down) from*** *us.* ◦ *The people* ***next*** *door* ***(to*** *us) (= living in the house next to us) aren't very friendly.* **4 out of doors** outside in the open air

IDIOMS **close/shut the door on sth** to make it impossible for something to happen, especially a plan or a solution to a problem: *There are fears that this latest move might have closed the door on a peaceful solution.* • **open the door to sth** to make something possible: *These discussions may well open the door to a peaceful solution.* • **shut/close the stable/barn door after the horse has bolted** to be so late in taking action to prevent something bad happening that the bad event has already happened

doorbell /ˈdɔː.bel/ (US) /ˈdɔːr-/ noun [C] a bell operated by a button on or next to the door of a house, which you press to tell the people inside that you are there

doorframe /ˈdɔː.freɪm/ (US) /ˈdɔːr-/ noun [C] the rectangular frame that surrounds an opening into which a door fits

doorjamb /ˈdɔː.dʒæm/ (US) /ˈdɔːr-/ noun [C] US for **doorpost**

doorknob /ˈdɔː.nɒb/ (US) /ˈdɔːr.nɑːb/ noun [C] a round handle that you turn to open a door

ˈdoor knocker noun [C] a **knocker**

doorman /ˈdɔː.mən/ (US) /ˈdɔːr-/ **noun** [C] (plural **-men** /-mən/) a person whose job is to stand by the door of a hotel or public building and allow people to go in or out, and to open their car doors, etc.

doormat /ˈdɔː.mæt/ (US) /ˈdɔːr-/ **noun** [C] **MAT** ▷ **1** a piece of thick material that is put on the floor by a door, used to clean your shoes on when you go into a building **PERSON** ▷ **2** informal disapproving a person who accepts being treated badly and does not complain: *He may be selfish and insensitive, but she is a bit of a doormat.*

D

doorpost /ˈdɔː.pəʊst/ (US) /ˈdɔːr.poʊst/ **noun** [C] (US also **doorjamb**) one of the two vertical posts on either side of an opening into which a door fits

doorstep /ˈdɔː.step/ (US) /ˈdɔːr-/ **noun; verb**

▸**noun** [C] **STEP** ▷ **1** a step in front of an outside door: *Don't keep her* ***on*** *the doorstep (= outside the door), Jamie, invite her in.* **BREAD** ▷ **2** UK a very thick piece of bread

IDIOM **on sb's doorstep** informal very close to where someone is or lives: *There's a lovely park right on our doorstep.*

▸**verb** (**-pp-**) [T often passive] UK disapproving If you are doorstepped by JOURNALISTS, they come to your house and ask you to speak or answer questions, even if you do not want them to: *He complained about being doorstepped by the press.*

doorstop /ˈdɔː.stɒp/ (US) /ˈdɔːr.stɑːp/ **noun** [C] a heavy object that is used to keep a door open

ˌdoor-to-ˈdoor **adj** [before noun] going from one house or building in an area to another: *He was a door-to-door* ***salesman*** *before he became an actor.*

doorway /ˈdɔː.weɪ/ (US) /ˈdɔːr-/ **noun** [C] (C2) the space in a wall where a door opens, or a covered area just outside a door

dope /dəʊp/ (US) /doʊp/ **noun; verb**

▸**noun** **DRUG** ▷ **1** [U] informal CANNABIS, or, more generally, any type of illegal drug: *They were arrested for* ***smoking/selling/buying*** *dope.* **PERSON** ▷ **2** [C] informal a silly person: *You shouldn't have told him, you dope!*

▸**verb** [T] **1** to give a person or an animal drugs in order to make them perform better or worse in a competition: *They were arrested for doping racehorses.* **2** to give a person or an animal a drug to make them want to sleep: *We always have to dope* ***up*** *our cat for long car journeys.*

ˌdoped ˈup **adj** (also **doped**) under the influence of drugs: *They were too doped up to notice what was happening.*

ˈdope ˌtest **noun** [C] an official test to discover if a person or an animal taking part in a competition has been given any drugs to make their performance better or worse

dopey /ˈdəʊ.pi/ (US) /ˈdoʊ-/ **adj** (**dopier**, **dopiest**) **DRUGGED** ▷ **1** wanting to sleep, because or as if you have taken a drug: *He'd taken a sleeping tablet the night before and still felt dopey.* **STUPID** ▷ **2** silly or stupid: *He's nice, but a bit dopey.*

dopiaza /ˈdəʊ.pi.ɑː.zə/ (US) /ˈdoʊ-/ **noun** [C or U] a South Asian meat dish cooked with onions

doping /ˈdəʊ.pɪŋ/ (US) /ˈdoʊ-/ **noun** [U] the act of giving a person or animal drugs in order to make them perform better or worse in a competition: *We are determined to stamp out doping in our sport.*

doppelgänger /ˈdɒp.əlˌɡæŋ.əʳ/ (US) /ˈdɑː.pəlˌɡæŋ.ɚ/ **noun** [C] a spirit that looks exactly like a living person, or a person who looks exactly like someone else but who is not related to them

Doppler effect /ˈdɒp.lə.rɪˌfekt/ (US) /ˈdɑː.plɚ.ɪ-/ **noun** [U] (also **ˈDoppler ˌshift**) a change that seems to happen in the rate of sound or light wave production of an object when its movement changes in relation to another object

Doric /ˈdɒr.ɪk/ (US) /ˈdɔːr-/ **adj** of or copying the simplest of the CLASSICAL styles of ancient Greek building: *a Doric column* → Compare **Corinthian**, **Ionic**

dork /dɔːk/ (US) /dɔːrk/ **noun** [C] slang a stupid awkward person

dormant /ˈdɔː.mənt/ (US) /ˈdɔːr-/ **adj** **1** describes something that is not active or growing but has the ability to be active at a later time: *The long-dormant volcano has recently shown signs of erupting.* ◦ *These investments have remained dormant for several years.* **2** **lie dormant** If something lies dormant, it is not active: *Her talent might have lain dormant had it not been for her aunt's encouragement.*

dormer (window) /ˌdɔː.məˈwɪn.dəʊ/ (US) /ˌdɔːr.mɚˈwɪn.doʊ/ **noun** [C] a window sticking out from a sloping roof

dormitory /ˈdɔː.mɪ.tər.i/ (US) /ˈdɔːr.mə.tɔːr-/ **noun** [C] (informal **dorm**) **ROOM** ▷ **1** UK a large room containing many beds, especially in a BOARDING school or university **BUILDING** ▷ **2** US a large building at a college or university where students live

ˈdormitory ˌsuburb **noun** [C] Australian English a place from which many people travel in order to work in a bigger town or city → Compare **dormitory town**

ˈdormitory ˌtown **noun** [C] UK (US **ˈbedroom comˌmunity**) a place from which many people travel in order to work in a bigger town or city

dormouse /ˈdɔː.maʊs/ (US) /ˈdɔːr-/ **noun** [C] (plural **dormice**) a small animal which looks like a mouse with a long tail covered in fur

dorsal /ˈdɔː.səl/ (US) /ˈdɔːr-/ **adj** [before noun] specialized of, on, or near the back of an animal: *a shark's dorsal fin* → Compare **ventral**

dory /ˈdɔː.ri/ (US) /ˈdɔːr.i/ **noun** [C] a **John Dory**

dos /duːz/ **noun** [plural] **dos and don'ts** rules about actions and activities which people should or should not perform or take part in: *At my school we had to put up with a lot of dos and don'ts.*

DOS /dɒs/ (US) /dɑːs/ **noun** [U] trademark abbreviation for disk operating system: a type of OPERATING SYSTEM for computers

dosage /ˈdəʊ.sɪdʒ/ (US) /ˈdoʊ-/ **noun** [C usually singular] formal the amount of medicine that you should take at one time: *You mustn't exceed the* ***recommended*** *dosage.*

dose /dəʊs/ (US) /doʊs/ **noun; verb**

▸**noun** [C] **1** (B2) a measured amount of something such as medicine: *a high/low dose* ◦ *a dose* ***of*** *penicillin* ◦ *The label says to take one dose three times a day.* ◦ *20 or 30 of these pills would be a* ***lethal*** *dose (= enough to kill you).* **2** (B2) an amount or experience of something bad or unpleasant: *The government received a hefty dose* ***of*** *bad news this week.* ◦ *She's got a nasty dose* ***of*** *flu.*

IDIOMS **in small doses** for short periods of time: *I can only stand opera in small doses.* • **like a dose of salts** UK informal very quickly: *The medicine went through me like a dose of salts.*

▸**verb** [T] to give someone a measured amount of medicine: informal *He dosed him****self*** ***(up) with*** *valium to calm his nerves.*

dosh /dɒʃ/ ⓤⓢ /dɑːʃ/ noun [U] UK slang money

doss /dɒs/ ⓤⓢ /dɑːs/ verb; noun

▸verb [I usually + adv/prep] UK slang **1** to sleep outside or in an empty building because you have no home and no money: *She was dossing in doorways until the police picked her up.* → See also **dosshouse 2** (also **doss down**) to sleep somewhere without a bed: *Can I doss down at your house tonight, after the party?*

PHRASAL VERB **doss about/around** to spend your time doing very little: *Come on, Peter, stop dossing around and get some work done.*

▸noun [S] UK slang **a doss** UK slang an activity that is easy or does not need hard work

dosser /ˈdɒs.əʳ/ ⓤⓢ /ˈdɑː.sɚ/ noun [C] UK slang **1** someone who has no home and no money **2** a very lazy person

dosshouse /ˈdɒs.haʊs/ ⓤⓢ /ˈdɑːs-/ noun [C] UK (US **flophouse**) an extremely cheap hotel for poor people who have no home in a city

dossier /ˈdɒs.i.eɪ/, /-əʳ/ ⓤⓢ /ˈdɑː.si.eɪ/ noun [C] a set of papers containing information about a person, often a criminal, or on any subject: *The secret service probably has a dossier **on** all of us.*

dot /dɒt/ ⓤⓢ /dɑːt/ noun; verb

▸noun **1** B2 [C] a very small round mark: *The full stop at the end of this sentence is a dot.* ◦ *Her skirt was blue with white dots.* **2** B1 [U] the spoken form of a FULL STOP in an internet or email address, or some computer files: *'What's the web address?' 'www dot cambridge dot org'.*

IDIOMS **on the dot** C2 exactly at the stated or expected time: *The plane landed at two o'clock on the dot.* ◦ UK *She came promptly on the dot **of eleven**.* • **the year dot** UK informal a very long time ago: *I've known Peter **since** the year dot.*

▸verb (-tt-) **1** [T] to put a dot or dots on something: *Your handwriting is difficult to read because you don't dot your i's.* **2** [T often passive] to be spread across an area, or to spread many similar things across an area: *We have offices dotted **about/all over** the region.* ◦ *The countryside is dotted **with** beautiful churches.*

IDIOM **dot the i's and cross the t's** to pay a great deal of attention to the details of something, especially when you are trying to complete a task: *The negotiations are nearly finished, but we still have to dot the i's and cross the t's.*

dotage /ˈdəʊ.tɪdʒ/ ⓤⓢ /ˈdoʊ.t̬ɪdʒ/ noun [U] old age, especially with some loss of mental ability

dotcom /ˌdɒtˈkɒm/ ⓤⓢ /ˌdɑːtˈkɑːm/ noun [C] a company that does most of its business on the internet • **dotcom** adj [before noun] *a dotcom firm/millionaire*

dote /dəʊt/ ⓤⓢ /doʊt/ verb

PHRASAL VERB **dote on sb** to love someone completely and believe they are perfect: *He dotes on the new baby.*

doting /ˈdəʊ.tɪŋ/ ⓤⓢ /ˈdoʊ.t̬ɪŋ/ adj [before noun] showing that you love someone very much: *We saw photographs of the doting father with the baby on his knee.*

ˌdotted ˈline noun [C] a line of DOTS: *Cut along the dotted line.*

dotty /ˈdɒt.i/ ⓤⓢ /ˈdɑː.t̬i/ adj **1** UK informal slightly strange or mentally ill: *a dotty old woman* **2 be dotty about sb/sth** UK old-fashioned to like or love someone or something very much or be very interested in them: *Jean's absolutely dotty about cats.* • **dottiness** /-nəs/ noun [U]

double /ˈdʌb.l̩/ adj; noun; verb; noun, predeterminer; adv

▸adj A2 twice the size, amount, price, etc., or consisting of two similar things together: *I ordered a double espresso (= two standard amounts in one cup).* ◦ *Go through the double **doors** and turn left.* ◦ *The word 'cool' has a double 'o' in the middle.* ◦ *Everything he says has a double **meaning** (= has two possible meanings).* ◦ *This painkiller is double **strength** (= has twice the normal amount of medicine).* ◦ UK *Sabiha's phone number is double three, one, five, double seven (= 331577).*

▸noun PERSON ▷ **1** [C usually singular] a person who looks exactly the same as someone else: *Hey, Tony, I met someone at a party last week who was your double.* TWO PLAYERS ▷ **2 doubles** [U] a game of tennis or a similar sport between two teams of two people: *men's/women's/mixed doubles* → Compare **singles** BASEBALL ▷ **3** [C] US in baseball, a hit that allows the BATTER (= person who hits the ball) to reach second BASE

IDIOM **at/on the double** old-fashioned informal very quickly and without any delay

▸verb [I or T] B2 to become twice as much or as many, or to make something twice as much or many: *The government aims to double the number of students in higher education within 25 years.* ◦ *Company profits have doubled since the introduction of new technology.*

PHRASAL VERBS **double (up) as sth** to be also used as something else: *The kitchen table doubles as my desk when I'm writing.* ◦ *Our spare bedroom doubles up as a study for Dan when he's working at home.* • **double back** to turn and go back in the direction you have come from: *We realized we had taken the wrong road and had to double back.* • **double (sb) up/over** If you double up/over, or if something doubles you up/over, you suddenly bend forwards and down, usually because of pain or laughter: *Most of the crowd doubled up with laughter **at** every joke.* ◦ *She was doubled up/over **with** the pain in her stomach.* • **double up** to share something, especially a room, with someone else: *Terry will have to double up with Bill in the front bedroom.*

▸noun, predeterminer B1 something that is twice the amount, size, strength, etc. of something else: *I paid double (= twice as much) for those trousers before the sale.* ◦ *Electrical goods are almost double **the** price they were a few years ago.* ◦ *'Would you like another whisky?' 'Yes. Make it a double (= two standard amounts in one glass).'*

IDIOM **double or quits** UK (US **double or nothing**) (in games where money is risked) an agreement that the player who owes money will owe twice as much if they lose, but will owe nothing if they win

▸adv **1** in two parts or layers: *Fold the blanket double (= so that it is in two layers) and then you won't be cold.* ◦ *They were bent double (= their heads and shoulders were bent forward and down) from decades of labour in the fields.* **2 see double** to have a problem with your eyes so that you see two of everything, usually because you are drunk or ill: *I started seeing double, then I fainted.*

ˌdouble ˈagent noun [C] a person employed by a government to discover secret information about enemy countries, but who is really working for one of these enemy countries

ˌdouble-ˈbarrelled adj (US usually **ˌdouble-ˈbarreled**) GUN ▷ **1** describes a gun that has two BARRELS (= parts shaped like tubes): *a double-barrelled shotgun* **TWO PURPOSES** ▷ **2** US having two purposes: *It was a double-barreled question.*

ˌdouble-barrelled ˈname noun [C] UK a family name with two joined parts, such as Harvey-Jones

ˌdouble ˈbass noun [C] (informal **bass**) the largest musical instrument of the VIOLIN family. It plays the lowest line of music in ORCHESTRAL music and in JAZZ.

D

ˌdouble ˈbed noun [C] a bed big enough for two people to sleep in

ˌdouble ˈbill noun [C] a cinema or theatre performance that consists of two main films or plays

ˌdouble ˈbind noun [C usually singular] a difficult situation in which, whatever action you decide to take, you cannot escape unpleasant results: *The headteacher is caught in a double bind because whether she expels the boy or lets him off, she still gets blamed.*

ˌdouble-ˈblind adj describes a study or TRIAL, especially in medicine, in which two groups of people are studied, for example with one group taking a new drug and one group taking something else, but neither the people in the study nor the doctor knows which person is in which group

ˌdouble ˈbluff noun [C] UK a clever attempt to deceive someone, especially by telling them the truth when they think you are telling lies

ˌdouble ˈbond noun [C] specialized a chemical BOND in which two atoms share two pairs of ELECTRONS, which BIND (= hold) them together

ˌdouble-ˈbook verb [I, T often passive] to promise the same room, seat, ticket, etc. to different people: *The room was double-booked so they had to give us a different one.*

ˌdouble-ˈbreasted adj A double-breasted jacket or coat has two sets of buttons and two wide parts at the front, one of which covers the other when the buttons are fastened.

ˌdouble-ˈcheck verb [T] If you double-check something, you make certain it is correct or safe, usually by examining it again.

ˌdouble ˈchin noun [C] a fold of skin between the face and neck, caused by a layer of fat developing under the skin

ˌdouble-ˈclick verb [I or T] to press a computer mouse twice in order to tell the computer to do something: *Double-click* (**on**) *the icon to start the program.*

ˌdouble ˈcream noun [U] UK (US **ˌheavy ˈcream**) very thick cream

ˌdouble-ˈcross verb [T] informal to deceive someone by working only for your own advantage in the (usually illegal) activities you have planned together: *The diamond thief double-crossed his partners and gave them only worthless fake jewels.* • **ˌdouble-ˈcross noun** [C]

ˌdouble-ˈdealing noun [U] dishonest behaviour and actions intended to deceive: *The local business community has been destroyed by corruption, cheating and double-dealing.*

double-decker /ˌdʌb.l̩ˈdek.əʳ/ (US) /-ɚ-/ noun [C] **BUS** ▷ **1** a bus with two levels **SANDWICH** ▷ **2** a sandwich made with three pieces of bread with food such as cold meat or cheese between them

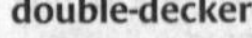
double-decker

ˌdouble-ˈdigit adj [before noun] relating to a number or series of numbers between 10 and 99: *Double-digit inflation continues to affect the country.*

ˌdouble-ˈdip verb; adj
▸verb [I] US to receive money from two places at the same time, sometimes in a way that is not legal
▸adj [before noun] used for describing a period of time during which economic activity gets weaker, increases a little, and then gets weaker again: *a double-dip* ***recession***

ˌdouble ˈDutch noun [U] **NONSENSE** ▷ **1** UK informal talk or writing that is nonsense or that you cannot understand **GAME** ▷ **2** US a game played by jumping over a rope

ˌdouble-ˈedged adj describes something that acts in two ways, often with one negative and one positive effect: *She paid me the double-edged compliment of saying my work was 'excellent for a beginner'.* ◦ *The government's programme to grow cash crops for export is a double-edged* ***sword*** *because it has created a local food shortage.* → See also **two-edged**

double entendre /ˌduː.bl̩.ɑːnˈtɑːn.drə/ noun [C] a word or phrase that might be understood in two ways, one of which is usually sexual

ˌdouble ˈfault noun [C] (in tennis and some other games) two mistakes made one after the other by a player who is beginning a game by hitting the ball

ˌdouble ˈfeature noun [C] the showing of two different films, one after the other, in a cinema

ˌdouble ˈglazing noun [U] windows that have two layers of glass to keep a building warm or to reduce noise from outside • **ˌdouble-ˈglaze verb** [T]

ˌdouble-ˈheader noun [C] two games of baseball or football played one after the other

ˌdouble ˈhelix noun [U] specialized the structure of a DNA MOLECULE

ˌdouble ˈjeopardy noun [U] the act of putting someone on trial twice for the same crime

ˌdouble-ˈjointed adj able to move your JOINTS in an unusual way so that, for example, you can bend your fingers or legs backwards as well as forwards

ˌdouble ˈmajor noun [C] US a university degree in which a person has gained enough CREDITS for two MAJORS instead of one

ˌdouble ˈnegative noun [C] in grammar, the use of two negatives (= words that mean 'no') in the same phrase or sentence: *The phrase 'a not unfamiliar situation' is an example of a double negative.*

ˌdouble-ˈpark verb [I or T] to park a car illegally next to a car that is already parked at the side of the road

ˌdouble ˈplay noun [C] the situation in baseball in which two players are put out after the ball is hit once

ˌdouble-ˈquick adv, adj UK informal **1** very quickly: *She left the room double-quick when I started singing.* **2 in double-quick time** very quickly, or as quickly as possible: *I shouted and he was gone in double-quick time.*

ˌdouble ˈroom noun [C] (informal **double**) a room in a hotel for two people

ˌdouble-ˈspace verb [T] If you double-space lines of text written on a computer, you put an empty line between each line of writing. • **ˌdouble-ˈspacing noun** [U]

doublespeak /ˈdʌb.l̩.spiːk/ noun [U] UK for **double-talk**

ˌdouble ˈstandard noun [C] a rule or standard of good behaviour which, unfairly, some people are expected to follow or achieve but other people are not: *The government is being accused of (**having**) double standards in being tough on law and order yet allowing its own MPs to escape prosecution for fraud.*

doublet /ˈdʌb.lɪt/ **noun** [C] a short, tight jacket worn by European men in the 15th, 16th, and 17th centuries

ˌdouble ˈtake **noun** informal **do a double take** to look at someone or something and then look again because you suddenly recognize them or notice that something unusual is happening: *I did a double take – I couldn't believe it was her.*

ˈdouble-talk **noun** [U] (UK also **doublespeak**) language that has no real meaning or has more than one meaning and is intended to hide the truth: *He accused the ambassador of diplomatic double-talk.*

ˈdouble-team **verb** [T] in BASKETBALL, to have two members of a team trying to prevent an opposing player from scoring: *They double-teamed Jordan in the second half.*

ˌdouble ˈtime **noun** [U] If you are paid double time, you are paid twice the usual amount for the time which you spend working, usually because you are working at the weekend or on an official holiday.

ˌdouble ˈtrouble **noun** [U] informal a situation in which there is twice the number of problems that usually exist: *Having twins usually means double trouble for the parents.*

ˌdouble ˈvision **noun** [U] a problem with your sight in which you see two of everything, usually with one image partly covering the other: *He suffered headaches and double vision after hitting his head in the accident.*

double whammy /ˌdʌb.lˈwæm.i/ **noun** [C usually singular] informal a situation when two unpleasant things happen at almost the same time: *Britain's farmers have faced the double whammy of a rising pound and falling agricultural prices.*

ˌdouble ˌyellow ˈline **noun** [C usually plural] in Britain, two lines of yellow paint that are put along the side of a road to show that vehicles may never be parked there: *It's an offence to park on double yellow lines.* → See also **yellow line**

doubly /ˈdʌb.li/ **adv** twice as much, or very much more: *Losing both the Cup and the League is doubly disappointing.*

doubt /daʊt/ **noun; verb**

▸**noun** [C or U] **1** B1 (a feeling of) not being certain about something, especially about how good or true it is: *I'm **having** doubts **about** his ability to do the job.* ◦ *If there's any doubt **about** the rocket's engines, we ought to cancel the launch.* ◦ *The prosecution has to establish his guilt **beyond reasonable** doubt* (US ***beyond a reasonable***) *doubt.* ◦ *This latest scandal has **raised** doubts **about** his suitability for the post.* ◦ [+ (that)] *I never had any doubt (**that**) you would win.* ◦ *He's the most attractive man in the room, **no doubt about that/it**.* **2 no doubt** C1 used to emphasize that what you are saying is true or likely to happen: *We will, no doubt, discuss these issues again at the next meeting.* ◦ *No doubt you'll want to unpack and have a rest before dinner.* **3 cast doubt on sth** C2 to make something seem uncertain: *Witnesses have cast doubt on the suspect's innocence.* **4 in doubt** B2 If the future or success of someone or something is in doubt, it is unlikely to continue or to be successful: *The future of the stadium is in doubt because of a lack of money.* **5 without (a) doubt** B2 used to emphasize your opinion: *She is without (a) doubt the best student I have ever taught.* → See also **undoubtedly**

▸**verb** [T] **1** B2 to not feel certain or confident about something or to think that something is not probable: *I doubt **whether/if** I can finish the work on time.* ◦ [+ that] *They had begun to doubt **that** it could be done.* ◦ *He may come back tomorrow with the money, but I very much doubt it.* ◦ *I don't doubt his abilities.* **2 doubt sb/doubt sb's word** C1 to not trust someone or believe what they say: *He's never lied to me before, so I have no reason to doubt his word.*

doubter /ˈdaʊ.tə^r/ US /-t̬ɚ/ **noun** [C] someone who doubts: *critics and doubters*

doubtful /ˈdaʊt.fəl/ **adj** **1** B2 If you are doubtful about something, you are uncertain about it: *The teacher is doubtful **about** having parents working as classroom assistants.* **2** B2 If a situation is doubtful, it is unlikely to happen or to be successful: ***It** is doubtful **whether/if** they ever reached the summit before they died.* ◦ ***It** was doubtful **that** the money would ever be found again.* • **doubtfully** /-i/ **adv** *'Are you telling me the truth?' he asked doubtfully.*

doubting Thomas /ˌdaʊ.tɪŋˈtɒm.əs/ US /-t̬ɪŋˈtɑː.məs/ **noun** [C usually singular] a person who refuses to believe anything until they are shown proof

doubtless /ˈdaʊt.ləs/ **adv** formal used to mean that you are certain that something will happen or is true: *They will doubtless protest, but there's nothing they can do.* ◦ *Doubtless you have heard the news already.*

douche /duːʃ/ **verb** [I or T] to put a liquid, usually water, into the VAGINA in order to wash it or treat it medically • **douche noun** [C]

dough /dəʊ/ US /doʊ/ **noun** **FLOUR** ▷ **1** [C or U] flour mixed with water and often YEAST, fat or sugar so that it is ready for baking: *bread dough* ◦ *pastry dough* ◦ *She **kneaded** the dough and left it to rise.* **MONEY** ▷ **2** [U] old-fashioned slang money: *I don't want to work but I need the dough.*

doughnut (US also **donut**) /ˈdəʊ.nʌt/ US /ˈdoʊ-/ **noun** [C] a small, circular cake, fried in hot fat, either with a hole in the middle or filled with jam: *a **jam** (US **jelly**) doughnut*

doughty /ˈdaʊ.ti/ US /-t̬i/ **adj** literary determined, brave, and unwilling ever to stop trying to achieve something: *She has been for many years a doughty campaigner for women's rights.*

doughy /ˈdəʊ.i/ US /ˈdoʊ-/ **adj** soft, thick, and sticky, like dough

dour /dʊə^r/ US /dʊr/ **adj** (usually of a person's appearance or manner) unfriendly, unhappy, and very serious: *The normally dour Mr James was photographed smiling and joking with friends.* • **dourly** /-li/ **adv**

douse (also **dowse**) /daʊs/ **verb** [T] **1** to make something or someone wet by throwing a lot of liquid over them: *We watched as demonstrators doused a car **in/with** petrol and set it alight.* **2** to stop a fire or light from burning or shining, especially by putting water on it or by covering it with something

dove **noun; verb**

▸**noun** [C] /dʌv/ **BIRD** ▷ **1** a white or grey bird, often used as a symbol of peace **PERSON** ▷ **2** a person in politics who prefers to solve problems using peaceful methods instead of force or violence → Compare **hawk**

▸**verb** /dəʊv/ US /doʊv/ mainly US past simple of **dive**

dovecote (also **dovecot**) /ˈdʌv.kət/ US /-koʊt/ **noun** [C] a small building for doves or similar birds to live in

ˌdove ˈgrey **noun** [U] UK a pale grey colour • **ˌdove-grey adj**

dovetail /ˈdʌv.teɪl/ **verb** [I or T] to cause something to fit exactly together: *Their results dovetail nicely* ***with*** *ours.*

ˈ**dovetail (ˌjoint)** **noun** [C] specialized a type of JOINT used to fix two pieces of wood firmly together

dowager /ˈdaʊə.dʒəʳ/ (US) /-dʒɚ/ **noun** [C] **1** specialized a woman of high social rank whose husband is dead but who has a title and property because of her marriage to him: *a dowager queen* **2** literary an old woman who is, or behaves as if she is, of high social rank

dowdy /ˈdaʊ.di/ **adj** disapproving (especially of clothes or the person wearing them) not attractive or fashionable: *a dowdy skirt* ◦ *She looked dowdy and plain.*

Dow Jones /ˌdaʊˈdʒəʊnz/ (US) /ˌdaʊˈdʒoʊnz/ **noun** [S] (also **the ˌDow Jones (Inˌdustrial) ˈAverage, the Dow**) an INDEX (= a system for comparing values) of the prices of SHARES in the 30 most important companies on the New York Stock Exchange → Compare **the FTSE 100, the Nikkei (index)**

down /daʊn/ **adv; preposition; verb; adj; noun**

▸**adv** **LOWER POSITION** ▷ **1** (A2) in or towards a low or lower position, from a higher one: *Is this lift going down?* ◦ *Don't look down! You'll get dizzy.* ◦ *The sun's going down and it'll be dark soon.* ◦ *The space capsule came down in the ocean.* ◦ *I bent down to look under the bed.* **2** (A1) moving from above and onto a surface: *Just as I was sitting down to watch TV, the phone rang.* ◦ *Why don't you lie down on the sofa for a while?* ◦ *This box is really heavy – can we put it down (on the floor) for a minute?* ◦ *Get down off that table immediately, you silly girl!* ◦ *The terrorists forced everybody to lie face down (= with the front part of the body below) on the floor.* **3** firmly in place or into position: *I put the loose floorboard back and nailed it down.* ◦ *He held my arms down by my sides.* **LOWER LEVEL** ▷ **4** in or towards a lower level, a smaller amount or a simpler state: *The rate of inflation is finally going down.* ◦ *Turn the TV down – it's way too loud!* ◦ *The nurse bandaged my sprained ankle to keep the swelling down (= to limit the swelling).* ◦ *If you wait a few months, the price will come down.* ◦ *Milan were three goals down (= losing by three goals) at half-time.* ◦ *The number of students at this school has* ***gone*** *down* ***from*** *500 last year* ***to*** *410.* **DESTROY** ▷ **5** If you burn, cut or knock something or someone down, you cause them to fall to the ground, usually damaged, destroyed or injured: *The house burned down many years ago.* ◦ *These trees will have to be cut down to make way for the new road.* ◦ UK *She was knocked down by a car and killed instantly.* **IN WRITING** ▷ **6** (B1) in writing or on paper: *I'll write it down now so I won't forget.* ◦ *Do you have it down* ***in writing/on paper****, or was it just a verbal agreement?* ◦ *I've* ***got/put*** *you down* ***for*** *(= have written that you want) three tickets each.* ◦ *The police officers were* ***taking*** *down the names of witnesses.* **FAR** ▷ **7** (B1) used, especially with prepositions, to emphasize that a place is far from you or from somewhere considered to be central: *I'll meet you down* ***at*** *the club after work.* ◦ *He has a house down* ***by*** *the harbour.* ◦ *I'm going down* ***to*** *the shop to buy some milk.* **8** in or towards the south: *Things are much more expensive down (in the) south.* ◦ *My parents live down in Florida, but they come up to Chicago every summer.* ◦ *We're moving down to London.* **OLDER TO YOUNGER** ▷ **9** from an older person to a younger one: *The necklace has been passed/handed down through seven generations.* ◦ *These myths have come down to us from prehistoric times.* **EATING** ▷ **10** inside your stomach: *You'll feel better once you've got some hot soup down you.* ◦ *He's getting weak because he can't keep anything down.* **MONEY** ▷ **11** at the time of buying: *I gave him £1,000 down, and paid the rest in instalments.*

IDIOMS **be down on sb** informal to criticize someone: *It's not fair of the boss to be so down on a new employee.* • **be down to sb** informal (C2) to be someone's responsibility or decision: *It's down to me to find a suitable person for the job.* • **come/go down in the world** mainly UK to lose the money and high social rank that you had in the past: *Fancy her taking a job like that – she's certainly come down in the world!* • **down sb's way** in the place where someone lives: *Down our way people don't take much interest in politics.* • **down under** UK and US informal (C2) (in or to) Australia or New Zealand: *She was born in Scotland, but she's been living down under for 22 years.* • **(right) down to** even including the following small or not important things or people: *Amalie was dressed completely in black, right down to black lipstick and a black earring.* ◦ *Everyone,* ***from*** *the Director down to the secretaries, was questioned by the police.* • **down with…!** something you say, write, or shout to show your opposition to someone or something, and to demand that they are removed from power or destroyed • **one, two, etc. down, one, two etc. to go.** an expression that is used to mean that you have done or dealt with the first, second, etc. of a series of things and have yet to do or deal with the rest: *'Have you done your exams?' 'Two down, three to go.'*

▸**preposition** **LOWER POSITION** ▷ **1** (A2) in or towards a low or lower position, from a higher one: *I slid down the hill.* ◦ *Aikiko fell down some stairs and broke her wrist.* **ALONG** ▷ **2** (A2) along: *We drove down the motorway as far as Bristol.* ◦ *Her office is down the corridor on the right.* ◦ *They sailed the boat down the river (= towards the sea).* **TO** ▷ **3** UK not standard to: *I went down the pub with my mates.* → Compare **up**

IDIOMS **down the drain** (Australian English also **down the gurgler**) (C2) If work or money is or goes down the drain, it is spoiled or wasted: *If the factory closes, that will be a million pounds' worth of investment down the drain.* • **down the toilet** (UK also **down the pan**) If something is or goes down the toilet, it is wasted or spoiled: *After the drugs scandal, his career went down the toilet.* • **down the road/line/track** in the future: *We have an idea to develop a talking book, but a marketable product is a long way down the road.*

▸**verb** [T] **LOWER POSITION** ▷ **1** to cause something or someone to fall to the ground: *We downed three enemy planes with our missiles.* ◦ *The ice storm has downed trees and power lines all over the region.* **EAT** ▷ **2** to eat or drink something quickly: *He'd downed four beers before I'd finished one.* **DEFEAT** ▷ **3** US to defeat someone, especially in sport: *The Yankees downed the Red Sox 7–0.*

IDIOM **down tools** UK to refuse to continue working, especially because you are not satisfied with your pay or working conditions: *The printers are threatening to down tools if the pay offer is not increased to eight percent.*

▸**adj** **UNHAPPY** ▷ **1** (B2) unhappy; unable to feel excited or energetic about anything: *She's been really down since her husband left.* ◦ *I've been (****feeling****)* ***a bit*** *down this week.* **NOT IN OPERATION** ▷ **2** (C1) [after verb] specialized (of a system or machine, especially a computer) not in operation or not working, usually only for a limited period of time: *The network will be down for an hour for routine maintenance.* ◦ *The whole system's* ***gone*** *down.* → See also **downtime**

IDIOM **kick/hit sb when they are down** to criticize or take unfair advantage of someone when they are in a weak position: *It's typical of the boss to kick someone when they're down.*

▸noun **FEATHERS** ▷ **1** [U] small soft feathers, especially those from a young bird: *goose/duck down* ◦ *a down jacket/pillow/sleeping bag* (= *a jacket/pillow/sleeping bag filled with down*) **2** [S or U] very soft thin hair **DISLIKE** ▷ **3 have a down on sb** UK informal to dislike someone, often unfairly: *Why do you have a down on him? I think he seems really nice.* → See also **downs**

down- /daʊn-/ prefix at or towards the end or the lower or worse part: *downhill* ◦ *downriver* ◦ *downmarket* ◦ *the downside*

ˌdown-and-ˈdirty adj US informal **1** down-and-dirty behaviour is not pleasant or honest: *a down-and-dirty political campaign* **2** something that is down-and-dirty is shocking, often because it is connected with sex: *He likes his films down-and-dirty.*

ˌdown-and-ˈout adj C2 having no luck, no money and no opportunities: *a down-and-out loser* ◦ *Nobody loves you when you're down and out.* • **ˈdown-and-out** noun [C] UK a person who has no money and no home

ˌdown-at-ˈheel adj UK (US **ˌdown-at-the-ˈheel**) wearing old clothes, or in a bad condition, because of not having much money: *She had a decidedly down-at-heel appearance.* ◦ *He worked in a down-at-the-heel café.*

downbeat /ˈdaʊn.biːt/ adj informal quiet and without much excitement: *The actual signing of the treaty was a downbeat affair without any ceremony.* ◦ *I thought he'd be really excited, but he seemed rather downbeat.* → Compare **upbeat**

downcast /ˈdaʊn.kɑːst/ US /-kæst/ adj **UNHAPPY** ▷ **1** formal sad and without hope: *I thought you were looking a little downcast this morning.* **EYES DOWN** ▷ **2** If someone's eyes are downcast, they are looking down.

downer /ˈdaʊ.nəʳ/ US /-nɚ/ noun informal **EXPERIENCE** ▷ **1** [C usually singular] an event or experience that makes you unhappy: *You lost your job? That's a real downer!* **DRUG** ▷ **2** [C] a drug that makes you feel calmer → Compare **upper**

downfall /ˈdaʊn.fɔːl/ US /-fɑːl/ noun [S] (something that causes) the usually sudden destruction of a person, organization or government and their loss of power, money or health: *Rampant corruption brought about the downfall of the government.* ◦ *In the end, it was the continual drinking that was his downfall.*

downgrade /ˌdaʊnˈɡreɪd/ verb; noun

▸verb [T] to reduce someone or something to a lower rank or position, or to cause something to be considered less important or valuable: *My job's been downgraded **to** that of ordinary editor.* ◦ *We mustn't let management downgrade the importance of safety at work.* → Compare **upgrade**

▸noun [C] the process of downgrading: *A **credit rating** downgrade would raise their cost of borrowing.*

downhearted /ˌdaʊnˈhɑː.tɪd/ US /-ˈhɑːr.t̬ɪd/ adj unhappy and having no hope, especially because of a disappointment or failure: *After hearing the news of the defeat, she told supporters not to be downhearted.*

downhill /ˌdaʊnˈhɪl/ adv, adj C2 (moving) towards the bottom of a hill: *It's so much easier running downhill!* ◦ *The route is all downhill from here to the finish.* → Compare **uphill**

IDIOMS **be (all) downhill** to be much easier: *Once we get the preparation done, it'll be downhill **all the way**.* ◦ *If I can just get through the training period, it'll be all downhill **from here**.* • **go downhill** C2 to gradually become worse: *After his wife died, his health started to go downhill.*

ˌdownhill ˈskiing noun [U] skiing down slopes, rather than along level ground

Downing Street /ˈdaʊ.nɪŋ.striːt/ noun **1** the road in central London where the official home of the UK prime minister is: *The prime minister lives at 10 Downing Street.* **2** [U, + sing/pl verb] the British government or the British prime minister: *The announcement took Washington and Paris by surprise, but Downing Street had been expecting it.*

ˌdown ˈjacket noun [C] US a warm jacket filled with the soft feathers of a DUCK or a GOOSE

downlighter /ˈdaʊn.laɪ.təʳ/ US /-t̬ɚ/ noun [C] (also **downlight**) a light that sends light down towards the floor

download verb; noun

▸verb [I or T] /ˌdaʊnˈləʊd/, /ˈdaʊn.ləʊd/ US /ˈdaʊn.loʊd/ A2 to copy or move programs or information into a computer's memory, especially from the internet or a larger computer

▸noun /ˈdaʊn.ləʊd/ US /-loʊd/ **1** B1 [C] a computer program or information that has been or can be copied into a computer's memory: *a free download* **2** [U] the act or process of copying programs or information into a computer's memory: *All of our products are available for download on our website.*

downloadable /ˌdaʊnˈləʊd.ə.bl̩/ US /-ˈloʊd-/ adj able to be downloaded: *downloadable documents/files/images* ◦ *downloadable software/music*

downmarket /ˌdaʊnˈmɑː.kɪt/ US /ˈdaʊnˌmɑːr-/ adj UK (US **downscale**) low in quality and cheap in price: *a downmarket tabloid newspaper* → Compare **upmarket** • **downmarket** adv *This catalogue has **gone** downmarket since the last time I bought something from it.*

ˌdown ˈpayment (also **downpayment**) noun [C] an amount of money that you pay at the time that you buy something but is only a part of the total cost of that thing. You usually pay the rest of the cost over a period of time: *I've **made/put** a down payment **on** a new TV and video.*

downpipe /ˈdaʊn.paɪp/ noun [C] UK (US **downspout**) a pipe that carries rain water from the roof of a building

downplay /ˌdaʊnˈpleɪ/ verb [T] to make something seem less important or less bad than it really is: *The government has been trying to downplay the crisis.*

downpour /ˈdaʊn.pɔːʳ/ US /-pɔːr/ noun [C usually singular] a lot of rain in a short time

downright /ˈdaʊn.raɪt/ adj [before noun], adv informal (especially of something bad) extremely or very great: *I think the way she's been treated is a downright disgrace.* ◦ *She's being downright difficult and obstructive.* ◦ *These working conditions are unhealthy, **if not** downright (= and probably extremely) dangerous.*

downriver /ˌdaʊnˈrɪv.əʳ/ US /-ɚ/ adv, adj → **downstream**

downs /daʊnz/ noun [plural] UK low hills covered in grass, especially used in the names of two such areas in southeast England: *the North Downs* ◦ *the South Downs*

downscale /ˈdaʊn.skeɪl/ adj US for **downmarket**

downshift /ˈdaʊn.ʃɪft/ verb [I] **WAY OF LIVING** ▷ **1** to leave a job that is well paid and difficult in order to do something that gives you more time and satisfaction but less money **VEHICLE** ▷ **2** US to change to a lower GEAR when driving, to reduce power and speed

• **downshifter** /-ʃɪf.tər/ (US) /-ʃɪf.tɚ/ **noun** [C] • **downshifting** /-ʃɪf.tɪŋ/ **noun** [U]

downside /ˈdaʊn.saɪd/ **noun** C1 a disadvantage of a situation: *The downside **of** living here, of course, is that it is expensive.* ◦ *Unemployment, inflation, and greater inequality are often the downside of a market economy.* → Compare **upside**

D

downsize /ˈdaʊn.saɪz/ **verb** [I or T] If you downsize a company or organization, you make it smaller by reducing the number of people working for it, and if it downsizes, it becomes smaller in this way: *to downsize your workforce/company* ◦ *The plight of the economy is forcing businesses to downsize.* • **downsizing** /-saɪ.zɪŋ/ **noun** [U] ***corporate** downsizing*

downspout /ˈdaʊn.spaʊt/ **noun** [C] US (UK **downpipe**) a pipe that carries rain water from the roof of a building

Down's syndrome /ˈdaʊnz ˌsɪn.drəʊm/ (US) /-droʊm/ **noun** [U] a GENETIC condition in which a person is born with learning difficulties and particular physical characteristics

downstage /ˌdaʊnˈsteɪdʒ/ (US) /ˈdaʊn.steɪdʒ/ **adv, adj** towards or at the front of the stage in a theatre → Compare **upstage**

downstairs /ˌdaʊnˈsteəz/ (US) /-ˈsterz/ **adv** A2 to or on a lower floor of a building, especially the ground floor: *I went downstairs to answer the phone.* → Compare **upstairs** • **downstairs adj** B1 *a downstairs bathroom* • **the downstairs noun** [S] *We've finished decorating upstairs but the downstairs still needs some work.*

downstream /ˌdaʊnˈstriːm/ **adv, adj 1** in the direction a river or stream is flowing: *The current carried her downstream.* **2** used to describe something that happens later in a process or series of events: *He has expanded the glass manufacturing firm by purchasing downstream **businesses** such as a glass distribution company.* → Opposite **upstream**

downswing /ˈdaʊn.swɪŋ/ **noun** [C usually singular] a **downturn**

downtime /ˈdaʊn.taɪm/ **noun** [U] **1** the time during which a machine, especially a computer, is not working or is not able to be used **2** informal time when you relax and do not do very much: *We've had a busy weekend so I'm planning to have some downtime tomorrow.*

ˌdown-to-ˈearth adj approving C1 practical, reasonable, and friendly: *She's a down-to-earth sort of woman with no pretensions.*

downtown /ˌdaʊnˈtaʊn/ **adj** [before noun], **adv** US A2 in or to the central part of a city: *downtown Los Angeles* ◦ *a downtown address* ◦ *I work downtown, but I live in the suburbs.* • **downtown noun** [U] *The hotel is situated two miles north of downtown.* → Compare **uptown**

downtrodden /ˈdaʊnˌtrɒd.ən/ (US) /-ˌtrɑː.dən/ **adj** treated badly and unfairly: *the downtrodden masses*

downturn /ˈdaʊn.tɜːn/ (US) /-tɝːn/ **noun** [C usually singular] a reduction in the amount or success of something, such as a country's economic activity: *the continuing economic downturn* ◦ *There is evidence of a downturn **in** the housing market.* → Compare **upturn**

ˌdown ˈvest noun [C] US a short, warm jacket without sleeves that is filled with the soft feathers of a DUCK or GOOSE

downward /ˈdaʊn.wəd/ (US) /-wɚd/ **adj** C1 moving towards a lower position: *a downward trend* ◦ *The country's economy is on a downward **spiral**.* → Compare **upward**

downwards /ˈdaʊn.wədz/ (US) /-wɚdz/ **adv** (US also **downward**) C1 towards a lower position: *The road slopes gently downwards for a mile or two.* ◦ *The water filters downwards through the rock for hundreds of feet.* ◦ *He was lying **face** downwards on the pavement.* ◦ *Casualty figures were **revised** downwards (= reduced) after the war had ended.* → Compare **upwards**

downwind /ˌdaʊnˈwɪnd/ **adv, adj** in the direction in which the wind blows; with the wind behind: *The smoke drifted downwind.* ◦ *They live downwind **of** a pig-farm and sometimes the smell is awful.* → Compare **upwind**

downy /ˈdaʊ.ni/ **adj 1** filled with feathers: *a downy nest* **2** covered with soft thin hair: *a tiny baby's downy head*

dowry /ˈdaʊ.ri/ **noun** [C] in some societies, an amount of money or property which a woman's parents give to the man she marries

dowse /daʊz/ **verb** SEARCH ▷ **1** [I] to DIVINE **MAKE WET** ▷ **2** [T] to DOUSE

doyen /ˈdɔɪ.en/, /dwaɪˈen/ **noun** [C usually singular] the oldest, most experienced, and often most respected person of all the people involved in a particular type of work

doyenne /dɔɪˈen/, /dwaɪˈen/ **noun** [C usually singular] the oldest, most experienced, and often most respected woman involved in a particular type of work: *The party was held in honour of Vivienne Westwood, that doyenne **of** British fashion.*

doze /dəʊz/ (US) /doʊz/ **verb** [I] to have a short sleep, especially during the day: *My cat likes dozing in front of the fire.* • **doze noun** [S] mainly UK *He's just **having a** little doze on the settee.*

PHRASAL VERB **doze off** informal If you doze off, you start to sleep, especially during the day: *The office was so hot I nearly dozed off at my desk.*

dozen /ˈdʌz.ən/ **noun** [C], **determiner** B1 twelve: *a dozen eggs* ◦ *This recipe makes three dozen cookies.* ◦ *Could you get me **half a** dozen (= six) eggs when you go to the shop?* ◦ informal *I've spoken to him dozens **of** (= many) times, but I still don't know his name!* ◦ *The refugees arrived **by the** dozen/**in their** dozens (= in large numbers).*

IDIOM **nineteen/ten to the dozen** UK informal If you are talking nineteen/ten to the dozen, you are talking very quickly and without stopping.

dozy /ˈdəʊ.zi/ (US) /ˈdoʊ-/ **adj 1** informal tired and wanting to sleep: *Drinking a beer at lunchtime makes me feel dozy all afternoon.* **2** UK informal thinking or reacting slowly: *He'd have driven straight into me if I hadn't seen him first – the dozy idiot!* • **dozily** /-zɪ.li/ **adv** • **doziness** /-nəs/ **noun** [U] informal

DPhil /ˌdiːˈfɪl/ **noun** [C] a **PhD**

Dr noun [before noun] A2 written abbreviation for Doctor: *An appointment has been made for you to see Dr Tracey Weaver on 19 July at 2.30 p.m.*

drab /dræb/ **adj** (**drabber**, **drabbest**) disapproving boring, especially in appearance; having little colour and excitement: *She walked through the city centre with its drab, grey buildings and felt depressed.* ◦ *I feel so drab in this grey uniform.* • **drabness** /ˈdræb.nəs/ **noun** [U] *It's the unrelieved drabness of big industrial cities that depresses me.*

drabs /dræbz/ **noun** [plural] **in dribs and drabs** in small amounts, a few at a time

drachma /ˈdræk.mə/ **noun** [C] the standard unit of

money used in Greece before the introduction of the euro

draconian /drəˈkəʊ.ni.ən/ (US) /-ˈkoʊ-/ **adj** formal describes laws, government actions, etc. that are extremely severe, or go further than what is right or necessary: *draconian laws/methods* ◦ *He criticized the draconian* ***measures*** *taken by the police in controlling the demonstrators.*

draft /drɑːft/ (US) /dræft/ **noun; verb; adj**
▸noun **PLAN** ▷ **1** (B2) [C] a piece of text, a formal suggestion, or a drawing in its original state, often containing the main ideas and intentions but not the developed form: *This is only a* ***rough*** *draft – the finished article will have pictures as well.* ◦ *She asked me to check the* ***(first)*** *draft of her proposal.* **MILITARY** ▷ **2 the draft** [S] mainly US (UK **conscription**) the system of ordering people by law to join the armed forces: *He avoided the draft because of a foot injury.* **MONEY** ▷ **3** [C] a written order for money to be paid by a bank, especially to another bank: *I arranged for some money to be sent from London to Madrid by* ***banker's*** *draft.* **COLD AIR** ▷ **4** [C] US for **draught**
▸verb UK **PLAN** ▷ **1** (C1) to write down a document for the first time, including the main points but not all the details: *Draft a proposal for the project and we can discuss it at the meeting.* **2** to draw the plans for a new building, structure, machine, etc.: *They hired an architect to draft the plans for their new home.* **MILITARY** ▷ **3** [T usually passive] mainly US (UK **conscript**) to order people by law to join the armed forces: *He was drafted* ***(into*** *the army) at 18.*

PHRASAL VERB **draft sb in** to bring someone somewhere to do a particular job: *Every Christmas thousands of people are drafted in to help with the mail.*

▸adj [before noun] describes a plan, document, etc. in its first form, including the main points but not all the details: *a draft plan/bill/proposal*

ˈdraft ˌdodger noun [C] mainly US a person who has not obeyed an official order to join the armed forces

draftee /ˌdrɑːfˈtiː/ (US) /ˌdræfˈt̬iː/ **noun** [C] US a person who has been ordered by law to join the armed forces

ˈdrafting ˌtable noun [C] a table with a top that can be moved so that it slopes at different angles, used for drawing or designing things on → See also **drawing board**

draftsman /ˈdrɑːfts.mən/ (US) /ˈdræfts-/ **noun** [C] (plural **-men** /-mən/) **1** US for **draughtsman 2** (US also **drafter**) someone who writes legal documents

draftsmanship /ˈdrɑːfts.mən.ʃɪp/ (US) /ˈdræfts-/ **noun** [U] US for **draughtsmanship**

draftswoman /ˈdrɑːftsˌwʊm.ən/ (US) /ˈdræfts-/ **noun** [C] (plural **-women** /-wɪmɪn/) **1** US for **draughtswoman 2** a woman who writes legal documents

drafty /ˈdrɑː.f.ti/ (US) /ˈdræf.t̬i/ **adj** US for **draughty**

drag /dræg/ **verb; noun**
▸verb (**-gg-**) **PULL** ▷ **1** (B2) [T] to move something by pulling it along a surface, usually the ground: *Pick the chair up instead of dragging it behind you!* ◦ *She dragged the canoe down to the water.* **2** (C2) [T + adv/prep] to make someone go somewhere they do not want to go: *She had to drag her child* ***away*** *from the toy shop.* ◦ *I really had to drag myself* ***out*** *of bed this morning.* **3** (B1) [T] to move something on a computer screen using a mouse **4** [T] If you drag a subject into a conversation, etc., you begin to talk about it even if it is not connected with what you are talking about: *She's always dragging sex* ***into*** *the conversation.* **5** [T] to pull nets or HOOKS (= curved wires) along the bottom of a river or lake in order to find something: *They found the man's body after dragging the canal.* **6 drag and drop** (B1) If you drag and drop something on a computer screen, you move it from one area to another using the MOUSE (DEVICE). **BORING** ▷ **7** (C2) [I] If something such as a film or performance drags, it seems to go slowly because it is boring: *The first half of the film was interesting but the second half dragged* ***(on)***.

IDIOMS **drag your heels/feet** to do something slowly because you do not want to do it: *I suspect the government is dragging its heels over this issue.* • **drag sb's name through the mire/mud** to damage someone's reputation by saying extremely insulting things about them

PHRASAL VERBS **drag sb away** informal to make someone leave a place or stop doing what they are doing so that they can go somewhere else or do something else: *I'm ready to go home now but I don't want to drag you away if you're enjoying yourself.* ◦ *I'll bring Tom, if I can drag him away from the football.* • **drag sb down** UK If an unpleasant situation drags someone down, it makes them feel unhappy or ill: *All that stress at work had begun to drag him down.* • **drag sb into sth** to force someone to become involved in an unpleasant or difficult situation: *Don't drag me into your argument! It's nothing to do with me.* • **drag sth out** to cause an event to continue for more time than is necessary or convenient: *I don't want to drag this meeting out too long, so could we run through the main points quickly?* • **drag sth out of sb** to force someone to say something, especially when they do not want to: *You never tell me how you feel – I always have to drag it out of you.*

▸noun **BORING THING** ▷ **1** [S] slang something that is not convenient and is boring or unpleasant: *Filling in forms is* ***such a*** *drag!* ◦ *I've got to go to the dentist's again – what* ***a*** *drag!* **PULL** ▷ **2** [S or U] specialized the force that acts against the forward movement of something that is passing through a gas or a liquid: *Engineers are always looking for ways to minimize drag when they design new aircraft.* **SUCK** ▷ **3** [C] slang the action of taking in air through a cigarette: *Taking a deep drag* ***of/on*** *his cigarette he closed his eyes and sighed.* **CLOTHES** ▷ **4** [U] informal the activity of dressing in clothes of the opposite sex, especially of a man dressing in women's clothes, often for humorous entertainment: *a man* ***in*** *drag*

IDIOM **be a drag on sb/sth** informal to slow down or limit the development of someone or something: *She didn't want a husband who would* ***be a drag on*** *her career.*

dragnet /ˈdræg.net/ **noun** [C] **1** a series of actions taken by the police that are intended to catch criminals: *The police have widened their dragnet in their search for the killer.* **2** a heavy net that is pulled along the bottom of a river or area of water when searching for something

dragon /ˈdræg.ən/ **noun** [C] **ANIMAL** ▷ **1** a large, frightening imaginary animal, often represented with wings, a long tail, and fire coming out of its mouth **2** any of various types of large LIZARD **WOMAN** ▷ **3** informal an unfriendly and frightening woman: *She's a real* ***old*** *dragon.*

dragon

dragonfly /ˈdræg.ən.flaɪ/ **noun** [C] a large insect with a long thin brightly coloured body and two pairs of transparent wings

dragoon /drəˈguːn/ noun; verb

▸noun [C] in the past, a soldier who rode on a horse and carried a gun

▸verb

PHRASAL VERB **dragoon sb into sth** [T often passive] to force or persuade someone to do something unpleasant: [+ -ing verb] *I've been dragooned into **giving** the after-dinner speech.*

D

ˈdrag ˌqueen noun [C] a man, often a gay man, who dresses as a woman for entertainment

ˈdrag ˌrace noun [C] US a car race over a very short distance • **ˈdrag ˌracing noun** [U]

dragster /ˈdræg.stəʳ/ (US) /-stɚ/ noun [C] a long, narrow, fast car that has been specially built to take part in drag races

drain /dreɪn/ verb; noun

▸verb **REMOVE LIQUID** ▷ **1** C2 [I or T] If you drain something, you remove the liquid from it, usually by pouring it away or allowing it to flow away, and if something drains, liquid flows away or out of it: *Drain the pasta thoroughly.* ◦ *We drained the pond and filled it with fresh water.* ◦ *Drain (**off**) any liquid that is left in the rice.* ◦ *Don't bother drying the pans – just leave them to drain.* **2** [T] If you drain a glass or cup, you drink all the liquid in it. **MAKE TIRED** ▷ **3** C2 [T] to make someone very tired: *The long journey completely drained me.* **REDUCE** ▷ **4** C2 [I or T] to reduce or cause something to reduce: *The long war had drained the resources of both countries.* ◦ *War drains a nation **of** its youth and its wealth (= uses them until they are gone).* **5** [I] If the blood/colour drains from someone's face, or if their face drains (of blood/colour), they turn very pale, often because they are shocked or ill: *The colour drained **from** his **face/cheeks** when they told him the results.*

PHRASAL VERB **drain (sth) away** If energy, colour, excitement, etc. drains away, it disappears completely, and if something drains it away, it completely removes it: *Stretching out her tired limbs, she felt the tensions of the day drain away.*

▸noun **PIPE** ▷ **1** C2 [C] a pipe or CHANNEL that is used to carry away waste matter and water from a building, or an opening in the road which rain water can flow down: *I think the kitchen drain is blocked.* ◦ *She accidentally dropped her ring down a drain in the road.* **2 drains** [plural] UK the system of pipes, openings in the ground or other devices that are used for carrying away waste matter and water: *There was an unpleasant smell coming from the drains.* **3** [C] US for **plughole** **MAKE TIRED** ▷ **4** [S] something that makes you feel very tired: *I think looking after her elderly mother is quite a drain **on** her energy.* **REDUCE** ▷ **5** C2 [S] something that uses more of your energy, money or time than you want to give: *Having a big mortgage is a real drain **on** your earnings.*

drainage /ˈdreɪ.nɪdʒ/ noun [U] **1** the system of water or waste liquids flowing away from somewhere into the ground or down pipes: *drainage channels/ditches/systems* **2** the ability of soil to allow water to flow away: *These plants need a sunny spot with good drainage.*

ˈdrainage ˌbasin noun [C] specialized an area of land from which the rain flows into a particular river or lake, etc.

drained /dreɪnd/ adj very tired: *You look completely drained – why don't you go to bed?*

drainer /ˈdreɪ.nəʳ/ (US) /-nɚ/ noun [C] a **draining board**

ˈdraining ˌboard noun [C usually singular] UK (US **drainboard**) the place next to a SINK where plates, knives, forks, etc. are left to dry after they have been washed

drainpipe /ˈdreɪn.paɪp/ noun [C] **1** a pipe that carries waste water or SEWAGE away from buildings **2 drainpipes** [plural] trousers that are very tight all the way down the legs

drake /dreɪk/ noun [C] a male DUCK (= water bird)

dram /dræm/ noun [C] mainly Scottish English a small amount of a strong alcoholic drink, especially WHISKY: *a dram **of** whisky*

drama /ˈdrɑː.mə/ (US) /ˈdræm.ə/ noun **THEATRE** ▷ **1** B1 [C or U] a play in a theatre or on television or radio, or plays and acting generally: *She's been in several **television** dramas.* ◦ *He's the drama critic for the Times.* ◦ *She studied English and drama at college.* **2** used in expressions which refer to the type of play or film: *a courtroom drama* ◦ *a historical drama* **EXCITEMENT** ▷ **3** B1 [C] an event or situation, especially an unexpected one, in which there is worry or excitement and usually a lot of action: *We had a little drama last night when the oil in the pan caught fire.* **4** [U] the excitement and energy that is created by a lot of action and arguments: *As a lawyer, he positively revelled in the drama of the courtroom.*

ˈdrama ˌqueen noun [C] informal disapproving someone who gets too upset or angry over small problems: *You're such a drama queen! I've never seen such a fuss.*

dramatic /drəˈmæt.ɪk/ (US) /-ˈmæt̬-/ adj **EXCITING** ▷ **1** B2 very sudden or noticeable, or full of action and excitement: *a dramatic change/improvement* ◦ *We watched scenes of the dramatic rescue on the news.* **THEATRE** ▷ **2** relating to plays and acting: *She bought me the complete dramatic works (= texts to be performed) of Brecht for my birthday.*

dramatically /drəˈmæt.ɪ.kəl.i/ (US) /-ˈmæt̬-/ adv **A LOT** ▷ **1** B2 suddenly or obviously: *Your life changes dramatically when you have a baby to take care of.* **THEATRE** ▷ **2** (as if) acting in a play: *She swept her hair back dramatically.*

dramatis personae /drəˌmɑː.tɪs.pɜːˈsəʊ.naɪ/ (US) /ˌdræm.ə.t̬ɪs.pɚˈsoʊ-/ noun [plural] formal all the characters in a play

dramatist /ˈdræm.ə.tɪst/ (US) /-t̬ɪst/ noun [C] a person who writes plays

dramatize (UK usually **dramatise**) /ˈdræm.ə.taɪz/ verb [T] **THEATRE** ▷ **1** When writers dramatize books, stories, poems, etc., they write them again in a form that can be performed. **MAKE EXCITING** ▷ **2** disapproving If someone dramatizes a report of what has happened to them, they make the story seem more exciting, important, or dangerous than it really is. • **dramatization** (UK usually **dramatisation**) /ˌdræm.ə.taɪˈzeɪ.ʃən/ (US) /ˌdræm.ə.t̬ə-/ noun [C] *a dramatization of a novel*

drank /dræŋk/ verb past simple of **drink**

drape /dreɪp/ verb; noun

▸verb **1 drape sth across, on, over, etc. sth** to put something such as cloth or a piece of clothing loosely over something: *He draped his jacket over the back of the chair and sat down to eat.* ◦ *She draped the scarf loosely around her shoulders.* **2 be draped in/with sth** to be loosely covered with a cloth: *The coffins were all draped with the national flag.*

IDIOM **draped all over sb** usually humorous very close to someone and with your arms around them: *I saw him* *last night in the pub with some woman draped all over him.*

►noun [C or U] **1** the way in which cloth folds or hangs as it covers something: *She liked the heavy drape of velvet.* **2 drapes** [plural] (also **draperies**) US heavy curtains made with thick cloth

draper /ˈdreɪ.pəʳ/ (US) /-pɚ/ noun [C] UK old-fashioned someone who, in the past, owned a shop selling cloth, curtains, etc.

drapery /ˈdreɪ.pəʳr.i/ (US) /-pɚ-/ noun [U] **1** cloth hanging or arranged in folds **2** UK (US **dry goods**) cloth, pins, thread, etc. used for sewing

drastic /ˈdræs.tɪk/ adj (C1) (especially of actions) severe and sudden or having very noticeable effects: *drastic **measures** ◦ Many employees have had to take drastic cuts in pay.* • **drastically** /-tɪ.kəl.i/ adv

drat (it) /ˈdræt.ɪt/ (US) /ˈdræt̬-/ exclamation old-fashioned informal used when you are slightly annoyed: *Oh drat! I've lost her phone number!*

draught /drɑːft/ (US) /dræft/ noun; adj

►noun UK (US **draft**) COLD AIR ▷ **1** (C1) [C] a current of unpleasantly cold air blowing through a room BOATS ▷ **2** [C] specialized the depth of water needed for a boat to be able to float: *A punt has a shallow draught.* BEER ▷ **3** [U] a system of storing and serving drinks from large containers, especially BARRELS: *Is the lager **on** draught or is it bottled?* GAME ▷ **4 draughts** [U] UK (US **checkers**) a game for two people, each with twelve circular pieces which they move on a board with black and white squares

►adj [before noun] UK (US **draft**) BEER ▷ **1** (of drinks such as beer) stored in and served from large containers, especially BARRELS: *draught beer/lager/cider* ANIMALS ▷ **2** (of animals) used for pulling heavy LOADS, vehicles, etc.: *a draught horse*

ˈdraught exˌcluder noun [C] UK **1** a long object that is put against the bottom of a door to stop cold air from entering a room **2** material, such as rubber or plastic, that is fixed in a long, thin strip around the edges of doors or windows to stop cold air from entering a room

draughtsman UK (US **draftsman**) /ˈdrɑːfts.mən/ (US) /ˈdræfts-/ noun [C] **1** someone whose job is to do detailed drawings of machines, new buildings, etc. **2** someone who draws well

draughtsmanship UK (US **draftsmanship**) /ˈdrɑːfts.mən.ʃɪp/ (US) /ˈdræfts-/ noun [U] the ability to draw well

draughtswoman /ˈdrɑːftsˌwʊm.ən/ (US) /ˈdræfts-/ noun [C] (plural **-women** /-wɪmɪn/) UK a female draughtsman

draughty (US **drafty**) /ˈdrɑːf.ti/ (US) /ˈdræf.t̬i/ adj describes a place, especially a room, that has currents of unpleasantly cold air blowing through it: *a draughty old house*

draw /drɔː/ (US) /drɑː/ verb; noun

►verb (**drew, drawn**) PICTURE ▷ **1** (A1) [I or T] to make a picture of something or someone with a pencil or pen: *Jonathan can draw brilliantly. ◦ The children drew pictures of their families. ◦ Draw a line at the bottom of the page.* ATTRACT ▷ **2** (B2) [T] to attract attention or interest: *He's an excellent speaker who always draws a crowd. ◦ Does he wear those ridiculous clothes to draw **attention**? ◦ Could I draw your **attention to** item number three on the agenda?* **3 draw sb's eye(s)** to attract someone's attention: *Her eyes were immediately drawn **to** the tall blond man standing at the bar.* MAKE ▷ **4** (C2) [T] formal to make or show a comparison between things: *You can't really draw a **comparison** between the two cases – they're entirely different. ◦ It's sometimes very difficult to draw a clear **distinction** between the meanings of different words.* **5 draw a conclusion** (B2) to consider the facts of a situation and make a decision about what is true, correct, likely to happen, etc.: *I'd seen them together so often I drew the logical conclusion that they were husband and wife.* MOVE ▷ **6** (B2) [I + adv/prep] to move in a particular direction, especially in a vehicle: *The train slowly drew **into** the station/drew **in**. ◦ As we drew **alongside** (= reached) the black car, I suddenly recognized my ex-boyfriend at the wheel. ◦ Montgomery drew **level with** Greene in the 100 metres final, but never passed him.* **7 draw near, close, etc.** (B2) to become nearer in space or time: *As Christmas draws nearer, the shops start to get unbearably crowded. ◦ As she drew closer I realized that I knew her.* **8 draw to a close/an end** (C2) to gradually finish: *As the evening drew to a close, people started reaching for their coats.* CAUSE ▷ **9** [T] If something draws a reaction, people react in the stated way: *Her speech last night in the Senate drew an angry **response**.* PULL ▷ **10** (C2) [T + adv/prep] to pull or direct something in a particular direction: *She drew her coat tightly around her shoulders. ◦ The crowd watched as the referee drew the player **aside/to one side** and spoke to him.* **11 draw the curtains** to pull curtains so that they are either together or apart CHOOSE ▷ **12** [I or T] to choose a number, card, etc. from several numbers, cards, etc. without first seeing it, in a competition or a game: *I was dealt two aces and I drew a third.* TAKE OUT ▷ **13** [T] to take something out of a container or your pocket, especially a weapon: *Suddenly he drew a **gun/knife** and held it to my throat.* **14** [T] to cause a substance, especially blood, to come out of a body: *He bit me so hard that it drew **blood**.* GET ▷ **15** [T] to get a feeling, idea, etc. from something or someone: *She drew comfort **from** the fact that he died peacefully.* BREATHE ▷ **16** [I or T] to take air or smoke into your lungs: *She drew a deep **breath** and plunged into the water.* EQUAL ▷ **17** (C1) [I] to finish a game with the same number of points as the other person or team: *Coventry drew 1–1 **with** United in the semifinal.* MONEY ▷ **18** [T + prep] to get money from a bank, account, etc. so that you can use it: *Alison drew some **money out** of her account to pay for our trip.* **19** [T] to receive money regularly, especially as an employee or from the government: *He's been drawing a pension for ten years.*

IDIOMS **draw a blank** informal to fail to get an answer or a result: *He asked me for my phone number and I drew a blank – I just couldn't remember it.* • **draw a veil over sth** UK If you draw a veil over a particular subject, you do not speak about it because it is unpleasant and you do not want to think about it: *Yes, well I think we'll just draw a veil over what went on last night.* • **draw breath** UK to pause for a moment to take a breath or breathe more slowly • **draw the line** (C2) to never do something because you think it is wrong: *I swear quite a lot but even I draw the line **at** saying certain words.*

PHRASAL VERBS **draw back** to move away from someone or something, usually because you are surprised or frightened: *She leaned forward to stroke the dog but quickly drew back when she saw its teeth.* • **draw sth down 1** to take an amount of money that has been made available: *We took out a bank loan which allowed us to draw down sums of money as we needed them.* **2** to use part of a supply of goods: *Consumers continue to draw down inventories of aluminum, copper and other metals at London Metal Exchange warehouses.* • **draw in** UK If days, evenings, or nights draw in, it becomes darker earlier because autumn or winter is coming. • **draw sb into sth** to make someone become involved in a difficult or unpleasant situation: *They tried to draw me into their argument but I refused.* • **draw sth off** to remove a small amount of liquid from a larger amount, especially by allowing it to flow through a pipe: *She drew off a little of her home-made wine just to taste.* • **draw on sth** C1 to use information or your knowledge of something to help you do something: *His novels draw heavily on his childhood.* ◦ *She had a wealth of experience to draw on.* • **draw sth out** to cause something to last longer than is usual or necessary: *The director drew the meeting out for another hour.* • **draw sb out** to help someone to express their thoughts and feelings more easily by making them feel less nervous: *Like all good interviewers he manages to draw people out of themselves.* • **draw sth up** PREPARE ▷ **1** C1 to prepare something, usually something official, in writing: *I've drawn up a list of candidates that I'd like to interview.* MOVE ▷ **2** to move a chair near to someone or something: *Draw up a chair and I'll tell you all about it.* • **draw yourself up** to make yourself look bigger by standing straight with your shoulders back, usually to try to seem more important: *Like a lot of short men, he tends to draw himself up to his full height in public.*

▸noun ATTRACTION ▷ **1** [C usually singular] someone or something that a lot of people are interested in: *We need someone at the event who'll be a **big** draw and attract the paying public.* EQUAL SCORE ▷ **2** [C] a situation in which each team in a game has equal points and neither side wins: *The result was a draw.* COMPETITION ▷ **3** [C] UK (US also **drawing**) a competition that is decided by choosing a particular ticket or number by chance

drawback /ˈdrɔː.bæk/ US /ˈdrɑː-/ noun [C] C1 a disadvantage or the negative part of a situation: *One of the drawbacks **of** living with someone is having to share a bathroom.*

drawbridge /ˈdrɔː.brɪdʒ/ US /ˈdrɑː-/ noun [C] a bridge that can be raised or brought down in order to protect a castle from attack or to allow big boats to go under it

drawdown /ˈdrɔː.daʊn/ US /ˈdrɑː-/ noun [C or U] a situation in which someone takes an amount of money that has been made available: *The income drawdown plan allows you to keep your fund invested in the stock market after retirement while you draw an annual income from it.*

drawer /drɔːʳ/ US /drɑː/ noun FURNITURE ▷ **1** A2 [C] a box-shaped container, without a top, that is part of a piece of furniture. It slides in and out to open and close and is used for keeping things in: *I keep my socks **in** the bottom drawer.* CLOTHES ▷ **2 drawers** [plural] old-fashioned **underpants**

drawing /ˈdrɔː.ɪŋ/ US /ˈdrɑː-/ noun [C or U] A2 the act of making a picture with a pencil or pen, or a picture made in this way: *Rosie loves drawing.* ◦ *She gave me a beautiful drawing **of** a horse.*

ˈdrawing ˌboard noun [C] a large, flat table, often with a top that can be moved into different positions, used as a desk for drawing or designing things

IDIOM **go back to the drawing board** to start planning something again because the first plan failed

ˈdrawing ˌpin noun [C] UK (US **thumbtack**) a short, sharp pin with a flat, round top, used especially for putting up notices

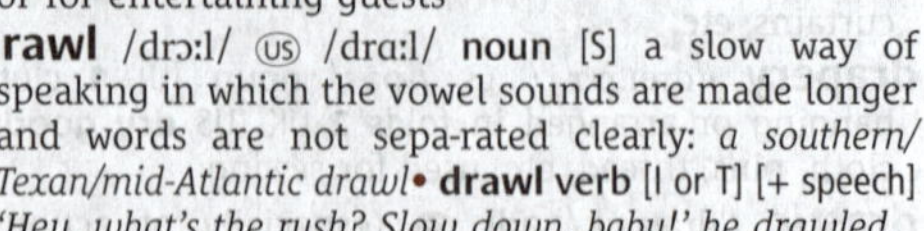

ˈdrawing ˌroom noun [C] formal a comfortable room in a large house used for relaxing or for entertaining guests

drawl /drɔːl/ US /drɑːl/ noun [S] a slow way of speaking in which the vowel sounds are made longer and words are not sepa-rated clearly: *a southern/ Texan/mid-Atlantic drawl* • **drawl** verb [I or T] [+ speech] *'Hey, what's the rush? Slow down, baby!' he drawled.*

drawn /drɔːn/ US /drɑːn/ verb; adj

▸verb past participle of **draw**

▸adj (usually of the face) very tired and showing suffering: *She looked pale and drawn after her ordeal.*

ˌdrawn-ˈout adj [before noun] lasting longer than is usual or necessary: *This dispute has been a **long** drawn-out affair.*

drawstring /ˈdrɔː.strɪŋ/ US /ˈdrɑː-/ noun [C] a thread or string which goes through an opening especially in the top of a bag or the waist of a piece of clothing and can be pulled to fasten it or make it tighter

dray /dreɪ/ noun [C] a large, low CARRIAGE with four wheels, pulled by horses

dread /dred/ verb; noun

▸verb [T] **1** C2 to feel extremely worried or frightened about something that is going to happen or that might happen: *He's dreading his driving test – he's sure he's going to fail.* ◦ [+ -ing verb] *I'm dreading hav**ing** to meet his parents.* **2 dread to think** C2 used to say that you do not want to think about something because it is too worrying: *I dread to think what would happen if he was left to cope on his own.*

▸noun [U] a strong feeling of fear or worry: *The prospect of working full-time **fills me with** dread.* ◦ *I **live in** dread **of** bumping into her in the street.* • **dread** adj [before noun] formal *The dread spectre of civil war looms over the country.* • **dreaded** /ˈdred.ɪd/ adj [before noun] humorous *My dreaded cousin is coming to stay!*

dreadful /ˈdred.fəl/ adj B2 very bad, of very low quality, or shocking and very sad: *The food was bad and the service was dreadful.* ◦ *I was beginning to think I'd made a dreadful **mistake**.* ◦ *The news report was so dreadful that I just had to switch it off.*

dreadfully /ˈdred.fəl.i/ adv BADLY ▷ **1** extremely badly: *She behaved dreadfully.* VERY ▷ **2** mainly UK extremely: *He was dreadfully upset.* ◦ *I'm dreadfully sorry – I really am.*

dreadlocks /ˈdred.lɒks/ US /-lɑːks/ noun [plural] (informal **dreads**) a hairstyle in which the hair hangs in long thick twisted pieces

dream /driːm/ noun; adj; verb

▸noun [C] SLEEP ▷ **1** A2 a series of events or images that happen in your mind when you are sleeping: *a good/bad dream* ◦ *a recurring dream* ◦ *I **had** a very odd dream **about** you last night.* ◦ [+ that] *Paul had a dream **that** he won the lottery.* HOPE ▷ **2** B1 something that you want to happen very much but that is not very likely: *It's always been my dream to have flying lessons.* ◦ *Winning all that money was a dream **come true**.* **3 of your dreams** the best that you can imagine: *Win the house of your dreams in our fantastic competition!*

IDIOMS **be (living) in a dream world** disapproving to have hopes and ideas that are not practical or possible: *If he thinks I'll forgive him, he's living in a dream world.* • **beyond your wildest dreams** C2 to a degree or in a way you had never thought possible: *Suddenly she was rich beyond her wildest dreams.* ◦ *The*

D

plan succeeded beyond my wildest dreams. • **in a dream** UK B2 not conscious of what is happening around you because other thoughts are filling your mind: *I didn't hear what you were saying – I was in a dream.* • **in your dreams!** humorous something you say to someone who has just told you about something they are hoping for, in order to show that you do not believe it will happen: *Dave, buy you a car? In your dreams!* • **not/never in your wildest dreams** C2 used to say that something is better than anything you could imagine or hope for: *Never in my wildest dreams did I imagine that one day I would run a marathon.* • **work/go like a dream** to work or go extremely well, without any problems: *The whole plan worked like a dream.* ◦ *He let me drive his new car last night – it goes like a dream.* • **wouldn't dream of sth/doing sth** C2 used to say that you would not do something because you think it is wrong or silly: *My father is very generous, but I wouldn't dream of actually asking him for money!*

▸adj **dream holiday, house, job, etc.** the perfect holiday, house, job, etc., that you want more than any other

▸verb (**dreamed** or **dreamt**, **dreamed** or **dreamt**) **SLEEP** ▷ **1** A2 [I or T] to experience events and images in your mind while you are sleeping: *What did you dream* ***about*** *last night?* ◦ *I often dream* ***about/of*** *flying.* ◦ [+ that] *I dreamed* ***that*** *I was having a baby.* **2** [I or T] mainly UK to imagine that you have heard, done or seen something when you have not: *Did you say that you were going tonight or did I dream it?* ◦ *I thought I'd bought some polish and it seems I haven't – I must have been dreaming.* **HOPE** ▷ **3** B1 [I] to imagine something that you would like to happen: *I dream* ***of*** *living on a tropical island.* ◦ [+ that] *He* ***never*** *dreamed* ***that*** *one day he would become president.* **4 dream on** informal used to tell someone that what they are hoping for is not likely to happen or to be true: *'Watch. All I have to do is wink at her, and she'll come over here.' 'Dream on, Dave!'*

> **! Common mistake: dream**
>
> Don't say 'dream to do something', say **dream about something/of doing something**:
>
> ~~*I have always dreamt to live by the sea.*~~
>
> *I have always dreamt of living by the sea.*

PHRASAL VERBS **dream about/of sth** to think about something that you want very much: *I dream of one day working for myself and not having a boss.* • **dream sth up** to invent something very unusual and usually silly: *This is the latest ploy dreamed up by advertising companies to sell their new products.*

dreamboat /ˈdriːm.bəʊt/ US /-boʊt/ **noun** [C] old-fashioned informal a very physically attractive person

dreamer /ˈdriː.məʳ/ US /-mɚ/ **noun** [C] a person who spends a lot of time thinking about or planning enjoyable events that are not likely to happen

dreamily /ˈdriː.mɪ.li/ **adv** If you say or do something dreamily, you do it as if you are not completely awake and are thinking of pleasant things: *'We had the most wonderful evening boating on the lake,' she said dreamily.*

dreamless /ˈdriːm.ləs/ **adj** describes sleep in which you do not dream: *I sank into a deep, dreamless sleep.*

dreamlike /ˈdriːm.laɪk/ **adj** as if in a dream and therefore not real: *There's a dreamlike quality to the final stages of the film.*

ˈdream ˌteam **noun** [C usually singular] a group of people who have been specially chosen to work together and are considered to be the best at what they do: *a dream team of lawyers/heart specialists/baseball players*

ˈdream ˌticket **noun** [C usually singular] a perfect combination, especially a combination of two politicians working for one party in an election

dreamy /ˈdriː.mi/ **adj 1** seeming to be in a dream and not paying attention to what is happening around you: *She gets this dreamy expression on her face when she talks about food.* **2** very pleasant or attractive: *The film opens with a dreamy shot of a sunset.* ◦ old-fashioned *He has these dreamy blue eyes.*

dreary /ˈdrɪə.ri/ US /ˈdrɪr.i/ **adj** boring and making you feel unhappy: *a dreary little town* ◦ *She had spent another dreary day in the office.* • **drearily** /ˈdrɪə.rə.li/ US /ˈdrɪr.əl-/ **adv** • **dreariness** /-nəs/ **noun** [U]

dreck /drek/ **noun** [U] informal something of poor quality: *Most of what's on TV is dreck.*

dredge /dredʒ/ **verb** [T] **REMOVE** ▷ **1** to remove unwanted things from the bottom of a river, lake, etc. using a boat or special device: *They have to dredge the canal regularly to keep it open.* **2** to search an area of water by dredging: *The police are dredging the lake* ***for*** *his body.* ◦ *They dredged* ***up*** *(= brought to the surface) all sorts of rubbish from the bottom of the river.* **FOOD** ▷ **3** to drop flour, sugar, etc. over food: *Lightly dredge the cake* ***with*** *icing sugar.*

PHRASAL VERB **dredge sth up** to talk about something bad or unpleasant that happened in the past: *The article dredged up details of her unhappy childhood.*

dredger /ˈdredʒ.əʳ/ US /-ɚ/ **noun** [C] (also **dredge**) a boat or a device that is used to dredge rivers, lakes, etc.

dregs /dregz/ **noun** [plural] the small solid pieces that sink to the bottom of some liquids, such as wine or coffee, that are not usually drunk: *In one swift go, she had drunk her coffee down* ***to the*** *dregs (= finished it).*

IDIOM **the dregs of society/humanity** a group of people in society who you consider to be IMMORAL and of no value: *People tend to regard drug addicts as the dregs of society.*

dreich /driːx/ **adj** Scottish English used for describing wet, dark, unpleasant weather

drench /drentʃ/ **verb** [T often passive] to make someone or something extremely wet: *A sudden thunderstorm had drenched us* ***to the skin.*** ◦ *The athletes were drenched* ***in/with*** *sweat.*

dress /dres/ **noun; verb; adj**

▸noun **1** A1 [C] a piece of clothing for women or girls which covers the top half of the body and hangs down over the legs: *a long/short dress* ◦ *a wedding dress* **2** B2 [U] used, especially in combination, to refer to clothes of a particular type, especially those worn in particular situations: *The queen, in full ceremonial dress, presided over the ceremony.*

▸verb **PUT ON CLOTHES** ▷ **1** A2 [I or T] to put clothes on yourself or someone else, especially a child: *My husband dresses the children while I make breakfast.* ◦ *He left very early and had to dress in the dark.* **2** B1 [I + adv/prep] to wear a particular type of clothes: *I have to dress quite smartly for work.* ◦ *Patricia always dresses* ***in*** *black (= wears black clothes).* **3 dress for dinner** to put on formal clothes for a meal: *It's the sort of hotel where you're expected to dress for dinner.* **PREPARE FOOD** ▷ **4** [T] to add a liquid, especially a mixture of oil and VINEGAR, to a salad for extra flavour: *a dressed salad* **5** [T] to prepare meat, chicken, fish, or CRAB so it can be eaten: *a whole dressed crab* **TREAT INJURY** ▷ **6** [T] to treat an injury by cleaning it and putting medicine or a covering on it to protect it: *Clean and dress the wound immediately.* **SHOP WINDOW** ▷ **7** [T] to decorate a shop window usually with an arrangement of the shop's goods: *They're dressing Harrods' windows for Christmas.*

PHRASAL VERBS **dress down** If you dress down for an occasion, you intentionally wear informal clothes of the type that will not attract attention: *She always made a point of dressing down on her first date with a man.* • **dress up 1** to put on formal clothes for a special occasion: *You don't need to dress up to go to the pub – jeans and a T-shirt will do.* **2** to put on special clothes in order to change your appearance: *Small children usually love dressing up* ***in*** *their mothers' clothes.* ◦ *He dressed up* ***as*** *a cowboy for the party.* • **dress sth up** If you dress something up, you add something to it in order to make it seem more interesting or pleasing than it really is: *I thought I'd dress up the frozen pizza* ***with*** *a few extra tomatoes and olives.* ◦ *Politicians tried to dress up the bill* ***as*** *a bold new strategy for combating poverty.*

▸adj [before noun] describes men's suits, shirts, or other clothes of the type that are worn at formal occasions: *a white dress shirt and bow tie*

dressage /ˈdres.ɑːʒ/ (US) /dresˈɑːʒ/ noun [U] the training of a horse to perform special, carefully controlled movements as directed by the rider, or the performance of these movements as a sport or in a competition: *a dressage competition*

ˈdress ˌcircle noun [C usually singular] UK the first level of seats above the main floor in a theatre

ˈdress ˌcode noun [C usually singular] **1** UK an accepted way of dressing for a particular occasion or in a particular social group: *Most evenings there's a party and the dress code is strict – black tie only.* **2** US a set of rules for what you can wear: *My school had a very strict dress code.*

dressed /drest/ adj [after verb] **1** (A2) wearing clothes and not naked: *I usually* ***get*** *dressed before I eat breakfast.* ◦ *He was dressed* ***in*** *a dark grey suit.* ◦ *They arrived early and I wasn't fully dressed (= didn't have all my clothes on).* **2** (B1) wearing clothing of a particular type: *a well-dressed/casually dressed man*

IDIOMS **dressed (up) to the nines** informal to be wearing fashionable or formal clothes for a special occasion: *Jackie went out dressed to the nines.* • **dressed to kill** intentionally wearing clothes that attract sexual attention and admiration

dresser /ˈdres.əʳ/ (US) /-ɚ/ noun [C] **FURNITURE** ▷ **1** UK a tall piece of furniture with cupboards below and shelves on the top half: *a kitchen dresser* **2** (A2) US a piece of bedroom furniture with drawers, usually with a mirror on top, used especially for keeping clothes in **CLOTHES** ▷ **3** used in phrases which describe the type of clothes that someone wears: *She was always a very stylish dresser.* **4** specialized a person who works in the theatre or in films, helping the actors to put on their clothes

dressing /ˈdres.ɪŋ/ noun **SALAD** ▷ **1** [C or U] a liquid mixture, often containing oil, VINEGAR, and herbs, added to food, especially salads **INJURY** ▷ **2** [C] a covering that is put on a cut or an area of damaged skin to protect it

ˌdressing-ˈdown noun [S] an act of speaking angrily to someone because they have done something wrong: *She* ***gave*** *me a dressing-down for being late.*

ˈdressing ˌgown noun [C] mainly UK (US usually **bathrobe**) a long loose piece of clothing, like a coat, which you wear informally inside the house

ˈdressing ˌroom noun [C] a room, especially in a theatre, in which actors put on clothes and make-up

ˈdressing ˌtable noun [C] mainly UK (US usually **vanity**) a piece of bedroom furniture like a table with a mirror and drawers

dressing table

dressmaker /ˈdresˌmeɪ.kəʳ/ (US) /-kɚ/ noun [C] someone who makes women's clothes, especially as a job • **dressmaking** /-kɪŋ/ noun [U]

ˈdress reˌhearsal noun [C] the last time a theatre work is practised before the real performance, when it is performed with the clothes, stage, and lighting exactly as they will be for the real performance

ˈdress ˌsense noun [U] the ability to dress well in attractive combinations of clothes that suit you

ˈdress-ˌup noun [U] US for **fancy dress**: *Everyone went to the party in dress-up.*

dressy /ˈdres.i/ adj **1** describes clothes that are suitable for formal occasions: *I need something a bit more dressy for the wedding.* **2** describes an occasion at which people wear very formal clothes: *a dressy affair/occasion*

drew /druː/ verb past simple of **draw**

dribble /ˈdrɪb.l̩/ verb; noun

▸verb [I or T] **FLOW SLOWLY** ▷ **1** to (cause a liquid to) flow very slowly in small amounts: *The water was barely dribbling* ***out of*** *the tap.* ◦ *Dribble the remaining olive oil over the tomatoes.* **FROM MOUTH** ▷ **2** to have liquid slowly coming out of your mouth: *Babies dribble constantly.* **MOVE BALL** ▷ **3** (in football or HOCKEY) to move a ball along the ground with repeated small kicks or hits, or (in BASKETBALL) to move a ball by repeatedly hitting it against the floor with your hand: *He dribbled the ball to the edge of the pitch.* ◦ *His speed allows him to easily dribble past defenders.* • **dribbler** /-əʳ/ (US) /-ɚ/ noun [C] *He's a good dribbler.* • **dribbling** /-ɪŋ/ noun [U]

▸noun **FROM MOUTH** ▷ **1** [C or U] liquid that comes out of your mouth: *There was dribble all over her chin.* ◦ *a dribble of saliva* **SLOW FLOW** ▷ **2** [C or U] a very slow flow of a liquid: *The flow of water was reduced to a dribble.* **MOVE BALL** ▷ **3** [C] in football, when a ball is moved along the ground with repeated kicks or, in BASKETBALL, when a ball is moved by repeatedly hitting it against the floor with your hand

dribs /drɪbz/ noun [plural] UK **in dribs and drabs** in small amounts, a few at a time: *The information has been released in dribs and drabs.*

dried /draɪd/ verb; adj

▸verb past simple and past participle of **dry**

▸adj Dried food or plants have had all their liquid removed, especially in order to stop them from decaying: *dried apricots/bananas/mushrooms* ◦ *dried flowers*

ˌdried ˈfruit noun [C or U] fruit that has been dried to stop it from decaying

ˌdried ˈmilk noun [U] milk in the form of a powder that you must add water to before you can drink it

drier /ˈdraɪ.əʳ/ (US) /-ɚ/ adj comparative of **dry** → See also **dryer**

driest /ˈdraɪ.əst/ adj superlative of **dry**

drift /drɪft/ verb; noun

▸verb [I usually + adv/prep] (C2) to move slowly, especially as a result of outside forces, with no control over direction: *No one noticed that the boat had begun to drift **out** to sea.* ◦ *A mist drifted **in** from the marshes.* ◦ *After the band stopped playing, people drifted **away** in twos and threes.* ◦ figurative *The talk drifted **aimlessly** from one subject to another.*

PHRASAL VERBS **drift apart** C2 If two people drift apart, they gradually become less friendly and their relationship ends. • **drift off** C2 to gradually start to sleep: *I couldn't help drifting off in the middle of that lecture – it was so boring!*

▸noun **MEANING** ▷ **1** [S] the general meaning without the details: *The **general** drift **of** the article was that society doesn't value older people.* **2 catch/get sb's drift** informal to understand the general meaning of what someone is saying **3 if you catch/get my drift** informal used to say that you have left out information or your opinion from what you have just said, but that you expect the person listening still to understand it: *She's married, but she doesn't act as if she is, if you get my drift.* **MOVEMENT** ▷ **4** [C] a pile of snow or something similar, formed by the wind: *The snow lay in deep drifts.* **5** [S or U] a general development or change in a situation: *The downward drift in copper prices looks set to continue.*

drifter /ˈdrɪf.təʳ/ (US) /-tɚ/ noun [C] disapproving someone who moves from one place to another or from one job to another without any purpose

ˈdrift net noun [C] a very large fishing net that hangs in the sea from devices floating on the surface

driftwood /ˈdrɪft.wʊd/ noun [U] wood that is floating on the sea or brought onto the beach by the sea

drill /drɪl/ noun; verb

▸noun [C] **TOOL** ▷ **1** a tool or machine which makes holes: *an electric/pneumatic drill* ◦ *a dentist's drill* ◦ *a drill **bit*** (= the sharp part of the drill which cuts the hole)

drill

REGULAR ACTIVITY ▷ **2** an activity which practises a particular skill and often involves repeating the same thing several times, especially a military exercise intended to train soldiers: *In some of these schools, army-style drills are used to instil a sense of discipline.* ◦ *a spelling/pronunciation drill*

IDIOM **what's the drill for sth?** informal used to ask what the usual, correct way of doing or getting something is: *What's the drill for getting money after four o'clock?*

▸verb **MAKE HOLE** ▷ **1** [I or T] to make a hole in something using a special tool: *Drill three holes in the wall for the screws.* ◦ *They are going to drill **for** oil nearby.* **PRACTISE** ▷ **2** [I or T] to practise something, especially military exercises, or to make someone do this: *We watched the soldiers drilling on the parade ground.* **3** [T usually + adv/prep] to tell someone something repeatedly to make them remember it: *It was drilled **into** us at an early age that we should always say 'please' and 'thank you'.* ◦ *He drilled the children **in** what they should say.*

PHRASAL VERB **drill down** to look for something on a computer or website by moving from general information to more detailed information: *Many websites have some form of hyperlink navigation as you drill down.*

drilldown /ˈdrɪl.daʊn/ noun [U] a system of moving from general information to more detailed information: *There are several ways to view the data, including drilldown.*

drily (also **dryly**) /ˈdraɪ.li/ adv being funny in a way that is not obvious: *'I know it sounds silly, but when I get to the beach I feel like a kid again.' 'We noticed,' she said drily.*

drink /drɪŋk/ noun; verb

▸noun [C or U] **LIQUID** ▷ **1** A1 (an amount of) liquid that is taken into the body through the mouth: *Would you like a drink **of** water/tea/juice?* ◦ *They'd had no food or drink for two days.* **ALCOHOL** ▷ **2** A2 alcoholic liquid: *Have we got time for a quick drink?* ◦ *Whose turn is it to buy the drinks?* ◦ UK *We ran out of drink at the party.* **3 drinks** [plural] a party at which you have drinks, especially alcoholic drinks: *Come for drinks on Saturday.* ◦ UK *We're having a small drinks **party** for one of our colleagues who's leaving next week.*

IDIOM **take to drink** old-fashioned to start drinking alcohol often, sometimes because of a personal problem: *He took to drink after his wife left him.*

▸verb (**drank, drunk**) **LIQUID** ▷ **1** A1 [I or T] to take liquid into the body through the mouth: *He drank three glasses of water.* ◦ *The animals came down to the waterhole to drink.* **ALCOHOL** ▷ **2** A2 [I] to drink alcohol: *'Would you like a glass of wine?' 'No thanks, I don't drink.'* ◦ *I didn't drink at all while I was pregnant.*

> **Other ways of saying drink**
>
> The verb **have** is often used instead of 'drink':
>
> *I'll just **have** a cup of coffee before we go out.*
>
> If someone drinks something taking only a small amount at a time, the verb **sip** is often used:
>
> *She **sipped** the tea carefully because it was hot.*
>
> The verb **swig** is often used when someone takes a large amount into their mouth:
>
> *He was **swigging** soda from the bottle.*
>
> When someone drinks something very quickly, you can use the verb **gulp down**:
>
> *She **gulped down** the rest of her coffee and then left.*
>
> The verb **slurp** can be used when someone drinks in a noisy way:
>
> *The children were eating pizza and **slurping** lemonade.*

IDIOMS **drink like a fish** informal to drink too much alcohol • **drink sb under the table** informal to drink a lot more alcohol than someone else

PHRASAL VERBS **drink sth in** to listen to, look at, or experience something with great interest and enjoyment: *They drank in the words of their leader.* • **drink to sth** If two or more people drink to something or someone, they hold their glasses up at the same time and then drink from them as a celebration, or to show respect or good wishes: *'Here's to a prosperous future then.' 'I'll drink to **that**!'* • **drink (sth) up** to finish your drink completely: *Drink up! It's time to go.*

drinkable /ˈdrɪŋ.kə.bl̩/ adj **1** clean and safe to drink: *Is the water drinkable?* **2** pleasant tasting: *'What's the wine like?' 'Oh, it's nice – very drinkable.'*

ˌdrink-ˈdriving noun [U] UK (US **ˌdrunk-ˈdriving**) driving a vehicle after drinking too much alcohol: *He was jailed for four months for drink-driving.*

drinker /ˈdrɪŋ.kəʳ/ (US) /-kɚ/ noun [C] **ALCOHOL** ▷ **1** someone who drinks alcohol: *He's a **heavy/light** drinker* (= drinks/does not drink a lot of alcohol). ◦ *I'm not much of a drinker* (= I don't drink much alcohol).

LIQUID ▷ **2** someone who drinks a particular drink: *I'm a tea drinker really – I don't like coffee.*

drinking /ˈdrɪŋ.kɪŋ/ noun [U] **ALCOHOL** ▷ **1** the activity of drinking alcohol: *I've **done** a lot of drinking since dad died.* ◦ *Drinking **and driving** is dangerous.* ◦ *The doctor told me to change my drinking **habits** (= not to drink so much alcohol).* **LIQUID** ▷ **2** the act of taking liquid in through your mouth: *This water is not for drinking.*

D

ˈdrinking ˌfountain noun [C] a device, usually in a public place, which supplies water for drinking

ˈdrinking ˌproblem noun [S] (UK also **ˈdrink ˌproblem**) a situation in which someone regularly drinks too much alcohol and finds it hard to stop: *I suspect he **has** a drinking problem.*

ˌdrinking-ˈup ˌtime noun [U] UK the short time allowed in a pub for people to finish their drinks before it closes

ˈdrinking ˌwater noun [U] water that is suitable for drinking

ˈdrink ˌproblem noun [S] UK for **drinking problem**

ˈdrinks maˌchine noun [C] UK (US **ˈvending ˌmachine**) a machine that sells drinks

drip /drɪp/ verb; noun

▸verb (**-pp-**) **1** [I or T] If a liquid drips, it falls in drops, or you make it fall in drops: *Water dripped **down** the wall.* ◦ *She dripped paint on the carpet.* **2** [I] to produce drops of liquid: *Watch out – the candle's dripping.*

▸noun **LIQUID** ▷ **1** [C] a drop of liquid: *drips of paint/sweat* **2** [S] the sound or action of liquid falling in drops: *All I could hear was **the** drip of the rain from the roof.* **3** [C] UK (US also **IV**) a method of slowly giving someone liquid medicine or food through a tube into one of their VEINS, or a piece of equipment for doing this: *He was **on** a drip for three days.* **PERSON** ▷ **4** [C] informal disapproving a boring person without a strong character: *Her husband is such a drip.*

IDIOM **drip, drip(, drip)** used to describe a process in which something bad happens very slowly: *the steady drip, drip, drip with which small independently owned shops are disappearing*

ˈdrip ˌcoffee noun [C or U] US for **filter coffee**

ˈdrip-dry adj; verb

▸adj Drip-dry clothing can be hung up to dry and does not need to be IRONED: *a drip-dry shirt*

▸verb [I or T] to dry a piece of clothing by hanging it up: *If I were you, I'd hang that sweater on the line and let it drip-dry.*

dripping /ˈdrɪp.ɪŋ/ noun; adj

▸noun [U] (US usually **drippings**) the fat that has come out of meat during cooking: *beef dripping*

▸adj [after verb] very wet: *It's raining really hard – I'm absolutely dripping (**wet**).* ◦ *Jim had just been on a run and was dripping **with** sweat.*

drippy /ˈdrɪp.i/ adj informal disapproving boring and without a strong character

drive /draɪv/ verb; noun

▸verb (**drove**, **driven**) **USE VEHICLE** ▷ **1** (A1) [I or T] to move or travel on land in a motor vehicle, especially as the person controlling the vehicle's movement: *I'm learning to drive.* ◦ *'Are you going by train?' 'No, I'm driving.'* ◦ *She drives a red sports car.* ◦ *They're driving to Scotland on Tuesday.* ◦ *We saw their car outside the house and drove **on/past/away**.* ◦ *I drove my daughter to school.* → Compare **ride 2** **driving while intoxicated** (abbreviation **DWI**) US legal the crime of operating a motor vehicle after having drunk more alcohol than you are legally allowed to: *Smith was arrested and charged with DWI.* **FORCE** ▷ **3** (C1) [T] to force someone or something to go somewhere or do something: *They used dogs to drive the sheep into a pen.* ◦ *A post had been driven (= hit hard) into the ground near the tree.* ◦ *By the end of the year, most of the occupying troops had been driven from the city.* ◦ [+ to infinitive] *In the end, it was his violent behaviour that drove her **to** leave home.* **4** (C1) [T] to force someone or something into a particular state, often an unpleasant one: *In the course of history, love has driven men and women **to** strange extremes.* ◦ *For the second time in ten years, the government has driven the economy into recession.* **5 drive sb mad, crazy, etc.** (B2) informal to make someone extremely annoyed: *My mother-in-law has been staying with us this past week and she's driving me crazy.* ◦ *He leaves dirty clothes all over the floor and it's driving me mad.* **6 drive sb wild** informal to make you very excited, especially sexually: *When he runs his fingers through my hair, it drives me wild!* **PROVIDE POWER** ▷ **7** (C2) [T] to provide the power to keep a machine working, or to make something happen: *The engine drives the wheels.* **8** [T] If you drive a ball, especially in GOLF, you hit it hard so that it travels a long way: *Slater drove the ball **down** the fairway.*

IDIOMS **be in the driving seat** UK (US **be in the driver's seat**) to be in charge or in control of a situation • **drive your message/point home** to state something in a very forceful and effective way: *The speaker really drove his message home, repeating his main point several times.* • **drive sb to drink** humorous to make someone extremely worried or unhappy: *These children will drive me to drink!* • **drive a coach and horses through sth** UK to completely destroy a rule, an argument or a plan • **drive a hard bargain** informal to expect a lot in exchange for what you pay or do • **drive a wedge between sb** to damage the good relationship that two people or groups of people have: *It would be silly to let things which have happened in the past drive a wedge between us now.*

PHRASAL VERBS **drive at sth** informal **be driving at sth** If you ask someone what they are driving at, you ask them what they really mean: *I don't see what you're driving at.* • **drive off** to leave in a car: *I got in the car and drove off.*

▸noun **ROAD** ▷ **1** [C] (also **driveway**) a short private road that leads from a public road to a house: *I parked **in** the drive.* **2** [C] used in the names of some roads, especially roads containing houses: *12 Cotswold Drive* **PLANNED EFFORT** ▷ **3** [C] a planned effort to achieve something: *The latest promotional material is all part of a **recruitment** drive.* ◦ *I'm meant to be **on** an **economy** drive at the moment, so I'm trying not to spend too much.* **COMPUTING** ▷ **4** (B1) [C] a device for storing computer information: *a hard drive* ◦ *a DVD drive* ◦ *a CD drive* **VEHICLE** ▷ **5** (B1) [C] a journey in a car: *It's a long drive from Glasgow to London.* ◦ *Shall we **go for a** drive this afternoon?* **6** [U] the system used to power a vehicle: *a car with **left-hand/right-hand** drive (= in which the driver sits in the seat on the left/right).* ◦ *a **four-wheel** drive vehicle* **POWER** ▷ **7** (C1) [U] energy and determination to achieve things: *We are looking for someone with drive and ambition.* ◦ [+ to infinitive] *He has the drive **to** succeed.* ◦ *Later on in life the **sex** drive tends to diminish.* **8** [C] (in sport, especially golf) a powerful hit which sends a ball a long way

ˈdrive-by adj [before noun] describes something that someone does as they drive past in a vehicle: *a drive-by shooting*

ˈdrive-in adj; noun

▸adj [before noun] mainly US A drive-in bank, cinema,

restaurant, etc. is one that you can use or visit without getting out of your car.
▸noun [C] a cinema or restaurant that you can visit without getting out of your car

drivel /ˈdrɪv.əl/ noun [U] disapproving nonsense or boring and unnecessary information: *You don't believe the drivel you read in the papers, do you?* ◦ *You're* ***talking*** *drivel as usual!* • **drivelling** /-ɪŋ/ adj *Who was that drivelling* ***idiot*** *on the radio this morning?*

driven /ˈdrɪv.ən/ adj describes someone who is so determined to achieve something or be successful that all their behaviour is directed towards this aim: *Like most of the lawyers that I know, Rachel is driven.*

-driven /-drɪv.ən/ suffix **POWER** ▷ **1** providing the power to keep a machine working, or to make something happen: *The new ships, propelled by gas turbines, require less maintenance than older, steam-driven ones.* ◦ *The fact remains that there are some public services that cannot be entirely* ***market****-driven (= controlled by economic forces).* **VEHICLE** ▷ **2** describing the person driving a vehicle: *He arrived every morning by* ***chauffeur****-driven car.*

driver /ˈdraɪ.vər/ (US) /-vɚ/ noun [C] **VEHICLE** ▷ **1** A1 someone who drives a vehicle: *a bus/lorry/truck/taxi driver* ◦ *The driver* ***of*** *the van was killed in the accident.* **COMPUTING** ▷ **2** specialized a computer program that makes it possible for a computer to use other pieces of equipment such as a printer **GOLF** ▷ **3** a type of CLUB (= long thin stick) with a wooden head, used in GOLF

ˈdrive ˌshaft noun [C] (in a vehicle) a rod that spins around and takes the power from the engine to the wheels

ˈdrive-through noun [C] a place where you can get some type of service by driving through it, without needing to get out of your car: *a drive-through restaurant*

ˈdrive ˌtime noun [U] used in connection with radio to refer to the times during the day when many people are listening in their cars travelling to or from work

driveway /ˈdraɪv.weɪ/ noun [C] a **drive**

driving /ˈdraɪ.vɪŋ/ noun; adj
▸noun [U] the ability to drive a car, the activity of driving, or the way someone drives: *a driving lesson/school* ◦ *Ashley passed her driving test first time!* ◦ *a driving lesson/school* ◦ *She has to* ***do*** *a lot of driving in her job.*
▸adj [before noun] **1** strong and powerful and therefore causing things to happen: *Driving* ***ambition*** *is what most great leaders have in common.* ◦ *She was always the driving* ***force*** *behind the plan.* **2 driving rain/snow** rain or snow that is falling fast and being blown by the wind: *Driving snow brought more problems on the roads last night.*

ˈdriving ˌlicence noun [C] UK (US **ˈdriver's ˌlicense**, Australian English **ˈdriver's ˌlicence**) A2 official permission for someone to drive a car, received after passing a driving test, or a document showing this

drizzle /ˈdrɪz.əl/ noun; verb
▸noun **RAIN** ▷ **1** [U] rain in very small light drops: *Tomorrow will be cloudy with outbreaks of rain and drizzle.* **LIQUID** ▷ **2** [S] a small amount of liquid that is lightly poured over something: *Serve the pasta with a drizzle of olive oil.*
▸verb **POUR** ▷ **1** [T] to pour liquid slowly over something, especially in a thin line or in small drops: *Drizzle the syrup* ***over*** *the warm cake.* **RAIN** ▷ **2** [I] to rain in small light drops: ***It's*** *been drizzling all day.*

drizzly /ˈdrɪz.li/ adj describes weather when it is raining in small light drops: *a drizzly afternoon*

droll /drəʊl/ (US) /droʊl/ adj humorous, especially in an unusual way: *a droll remark/expression/person* • **drolly** /ˈdrəʊ.li/ (US) /ˈdroʊ.li/ adv

dromedary /ˈdrɒm.ə.dər.i/ (US) /ˈdrɑː.mə.der-/ noun [C] a type of CAMEL (= a large animal that lives in the desert) with one HUMP (= raised area) on its back

drone /drəʊn/ (US) /droʊn/ noun; verb
▸noun **NOISE** ▷ **1** [S] a low continuous noise that does not change its note: *the drone* ***of*** *an engine* ◦ *Outside the tent I could hear* ***the*** *constant drone* ***of*** *insects.* ◦ ***The*** *drone* ***of*** *his voice made me feel sleepy.* **BEE** ▷ **2** [C] a male BEE **AIRCRAFT** ▷ **3** [C] a type of aircraft that does not have a pilot but is controlled by someone on the ground
▸verb [I] to make a low continuous noise that does not change its note: *An airplane droned in the background.*

PHRASAL VERB **drone on** disapproving to talk for a long time in a boring way: *He was droning on* ***(and on) about*** *his operation.*

drool /druːl/ verb; noun
▸verb [I] to allow SALIVA (= liquid in the mouth) to flow out of your mouth: *The dog lay drooling on the mat.*

PHRASAL VERB **drool over sb/sth** to show extreme and sometimes silly pleasure while looking at someone or something: *Roz and I sat by the swimming pool, drooling over all the gorgeous young men.* ◦ *I left Sara in the shop drooling over a green silk dress.*

▸noun [U] SALIVA that has come out of your mouth

droop /druːp/ verb [I] **1** to bend or hang down heavily: *The flowers were drooping in the heat.* ◦ *I can see you're tired because your eyelids have started to droop.* **2** If your SPIRITS (= feelings of happiness) droop, you start to feel less happy and energetic. • **drooping** adj *drooping branches* ◦ *Bloodhounds have drooping eyes and floppy ears.* • **droopy** /ˈdruː.pi/ adj informal *He had a long droopy* ***moustache****.*

drop /drɒp/ (US) /drɑːp/ verb; noun
▸verb (-pp-) **FALL** ▷ **1** B1 [I or T] to fall or to allow something to fall: *She dropped her keys.* ◦ *I'm always dropping things.* ◦ *Amanda dropped her sunglasses* ***in/into*** *the fountain.* ◦ *The book dropped* ***from/off*** *the shelf.* ◦ *Don't drop it!/Don't let it drop!* **2 drop dead** C2 to die suddenly and unexpectedly: *He dropped dead on the squash court at the age of 43.* **3 drop sb a line** informal to write someone a letter, especially a short informal one: *Just drop me a line when you've decided on a date.* **4 drop (sb) a hint** informal to tell someone something in a way that is not direct: *Margaret dropped a hint that she'd like to come to the party.* **5 drop your aitches/h's** UK to not pronounce the letter h at the beginning of words in which it should be pronounced **LOWER** ▷ **6** B2 [I or T] to move to a lower level, or cause something to move to a lower level: *The water level in the flooded region has finally begun to drop.* ◦ *The land drops* ***(away)*** *(= slopes down) sharply behind the barrier.* ◦ *We've had to drop our prices because of the recession.*

> **! Common mistake: drop**
>
> **Drop** meaning 'move to a lower level' is not usually followed by the adverb 'down', don't say 'drop down', say **drop**:
>
> ~~*The rate of unemployment dropped down significantly.*~~
>
> *The rate of unemployment dropped significantly.*

STOP ▷ **7** B2 [T] to stop doing or planning something, especially an activity: *I'm going to drop yoga and do aerobics instead.* ◦ *Can you drop what you're doing and help me with this report?* **8** [T] to stop including someone in a group or team: *He's been dropped* ***from*** *the team because of injury.* **TAKE** ▷ **9** Ⓒ1 [T + adv/prep] to take someone to a particular place, usually in a car, and leave them there: *They dropped me* ***off*** *at the main entrance.* ◦ *I dropped him* ***at*** *the library and went shopping.*

D

IDIOMS **be fit/ready to drop** informal to be extremely tired: *I'd just walked ten miles and was ready to drop.* • **drop sb/sth like a hot potato** informal to quickly stop being involved with someone or something because you stop liking them or you think they will cause problems for you: *He dropped the plan like a hot potato when he realized how much it would cost him.* • **drop a brick/clanger** UK to do or say something which makes you feel embarrassed • **drop dead!** slang a rude way of telling someone that you are angry with them and want them to go away or be quiet: *Oh, just drop dead!* • **drop everything** to stop whatever you are doing: *We just dropped everything and rushed to the hospital.* • **drop it/the subject** Ⓒ2 to stop talking about something, especially because it is upsetting or annoying: *I don't want to talk about it any more – let's drop the subject.* • **drop the ball** US informal to make a mistake, especially by doing something in a stupid or careless way: *For god's sake don't drop the ball on this – we're relying on you.*

PHRASAL VERBS **drop behind** to get further behind or away from something or someone: *As the pace quickened, Pepe began to drop behind.* ◦ *She stopped going to classes and dropped behind in her schoolwork.* • **drop by/in** informal to visit someone: *I dropped in* ***on*** *George on my way home from school.* ◦ *Drop by and pick up that book sometime.* • **drop off** **SLEEP** ▷ **1** to start to sleep **DECREASE** ▷ **2** If the amount, number, or quality of something drops off, it becomes less: *The demand for mobile phones shows no signs of dropping off.* • **drop sb/sth off** informal to take someone or something to a particular place, usually by car, as you travel to a different place: *We dropped our luggage off at the hotel and went sightseeing.* • **drop out 1** to not do something that you were going to do, or to stop doing something before you have completely finished: *He dropped out* ***of*** *the race after two laps.* **2** If a student drops out, they stop going to classes before they have finished their course.

▸noun **SMALL AMOUNT** ▷ **1** Ⓑ1 [C] a small round-shaped amount of liquid: *I thought I felt a drop* ***of*** *rain.* ◦ *There were little drops* ***of*** *paint on the kitchen floor.* **2** [S] a small amount of liquid you can drink: *I'll have a drop* ***more*** *juice, please.* ◦ *'Would you like some milk?' 'Just a drop, please.'* **3 drops** [plural] liquid medicine given in very small amounts: *eye/nose/ear drops* **4** [C] mainly UK a small piece of sweet food made of sugar: *fruit/pear drops* ◦ *chocolate drops* **LOWER** ▷ **5** Ⓒ1 [C usually singular] the distance from one thing to something lower: *There's a drop* ***of*** *two metres from the window to the ground.* **6** Ⓑ2 [C usually singular] a reduction in the amount or level of something: *The recent drop* ***in*** *magazine subscriptions is causing some concern.* **FALL** ▷ **7** [C] the act of DELIVERING things such as supplies, medicine, etc., often by dropping them from an aircraft: *The helicopter* ***made*** *a drop of much-needed supplies to the stranded hikers.*

IDIOMS **a drop in the ocean** UK (US **a drop in the bucket**) Ⓒ2 a very small amount compared to the amount needed: *My letter of protest was just a drop in the ocean.* • **a drop too much (to drink)** mainly UK too much alcohol to drink • **at the drop of a hat** If you do something at the drop of a hat, you do it immediately without stopping to think about it: *People will file lawsuits at the drop of a hat these days.*

ˈdrop-dead adv informal used to emphasize that someone or something is extremely attractive: *He's drop-dead* ***gorgeous!***

ˌdrop-down ˈmenu noun [C] a list of choices on a computer screen that is hidden until you choose to look at it

ˈdrop ˌkick noun [C] in RUGBY, a kick in which the ball is dropped to the ground before being kicked

ˌdrop-leaf ˈtable noun [C] a table whose sides can be folded down so that the table fits into a smaller space

droplet /ˈdrɒp.lət/ Ⓤⓢ /ˈdrɑːp-/ noun [C] a small drop of liquid

dropout /ˈdrɒp.aʊt/ Ⓤⓢ /ˈdrɑːp-/ noun [C] a person who leaves school, college or university before finishing a course, or a person who lives in an unusual way: *a high school/college dropout* ◦ *He was a loner and a dropout.*

dropper /ˈdrɒp.əʳ/ Ⓤⓢ /ˈdrɑː.pɚ/ noun [C] a small tube with a rubber container at one end that is filled with air and allows liquid to be given out in separate drops

droppings /ˈdrɒp.ɪŋz/ Ⓤⓢ /ˈdrɑː.pɪŋz/ noun [plural] solid waste produced by animals and birds

dross /drɒs/ Ⓤⓢ /drɑːs/ noun [U] mainly UK something that has no use or no value: *So much of what's on TV is pure dross.* ◦ *We read all the manuscripts but 95 percent are dross.*

drought /draʊt/ noun [C or U] Ⓒ2 a long period when there is little or no rain: *This year (a) severe drought has ruined the crops.*

drove /drəʊv/ Ⓤⓢ /droʊv/ verb; noun; verb
▸verb past simple of **drive**
▸noun [C] **1** mainly UK a large group of animals, especially CATTLE or sheep, moving from one place to another **2 droves** [plural] a large group, especially of people, moving towards a place: *Every summer droves of sightseers crowd the city.* ◦ *Fans came* ***in*** *droves to see her concerts.*
▸verb [T] (**drove**) UK specialized to move farm animals on foot from one place to another • **drover** /ˈdrəʊ.vəʳ/ Ⓤⓢ /ˈdroʊ.vɚ/ noun [C] *The drover walked alongside the oxen, gently tapping them with his stick.*

drown /draʊn/ verb **DIE** ▷ **1** Ⓑ2 [I or T] to (cause to) die by being unable to breathe underwater: *He drowned in a boating accident.* **COVER** ▷ **2** [T] to cover or be covered, especially with a liquid: *A whole valley was drowned when the river was dammed.* ◦ disapproving *He drowned his food* ***in/with*** *tomato sauce.*

IDIOMS **drown your sorrows** to drink alcohol in order to forget your problems • **look like a drowned rat** informal to be very wet, especially because you have been in heavy rain

PHRASAL VERBS **drown in sth** to have more of something than you are able to deal with: *I'm drowning in unpaid bills.* • **drown sth out** informal Ⓒ2 If a loud noise drowns out another noise, it prevents it from being heard.

drowning /ˈdraʊ.nɪŋ/ noun [C or U] (a) death caused by being underwater and not being able to breathe: *There were three drownings in the lake last year.*

drowsy /ˈdraʊ.zi/ adj being in a state between sleeping and being awake: *The room is so warm it's making me feel drowsy.* • **drowsily** /-zɪ.li/ adv • **drowsiness** /-nəs/ noun [U] *Seasickness tablets often cause drowsiness.*

drubbing /ˈdrʌb.ɪŋ/ noun [C usually singular] UK informal a beating or serious defeat, especially in a sports competition: *Norwich* ***got/received/took*** *a severe drubbing at the hands of Manchester United.*

drudgery /ˈdrʌdʒ.ər.i/ ⓤⓢ /-ɚ-/ noun [U] hard boring work: *the drudgery of housework* • **drudge** /drʌdʒ/ noun [C] *I feel like a real drudge – I've done nothing but clean all day!*

drug /drʌg/ noun; verb

▸noun [C] **MEDICINE** ▷ **1** B2 any natural or artificially made chemical that is used as a medicine: *anti-cancer/fertility/pain-killing drugs* ◦ *a* ***prescription*** *drug* ◦ *drug therapy* ◦ *He* ***takes*** *several drugs for his condition.* **ILLEGAL SUBSTANCE** ▷ **2** B2 any natural or artificially made chemical that is taken for pleasure, to improve someone's performance of an activity, or because a person cannot stop using it: *illegal drugs* ◦ *a drug* ***addict*** ◦ *drug* ***addiction/abuse*** ◦ *She began to suspect that her son was* ***on/taking/doing*** *drugs.* ◦ *She was suspected of being a drug* ***dealer.*** ◦ *His son died of a drug* ***overdose.*** **3** any activity that you cannot stop doing: *Work is a drug* ***for*** *him.*

▸verb [T] (**-gg-**) to give someone or something a chemical that causes them to lose feeling or to become unconscious: *The killer confessed that he often drugged his victims before he killed them.* ◦ *She was heavily drugged to ease the pain.* ◦ informal *We visited her in hospital but she was drugged* ***to the eyeballs*** *(= had been given a lot of drugs) and I don't think she even knew we were there.*

druggie /ˈdrʌg.i/ noun [C] informal a person who often uses illegal drugs

druggist /ˈdrʌg.ɪst/ noun [C] US for **chemist**

drugstore /ˈdrʌg.stɔːr/ ⓤⓢ /-stɔːr/ noun [C] B1 US for **chemist** (= a shop where you can buy medicines, make-up, sweets, cigarettes, etc.)

druid /ˈdruː.ɪd/ noun [C] a priest of a religion followed in Britain, Ireland, and France, especially in ancient times

drum /drʌm/ noun; verb

▸noun [C] **INSTRUMENT** ▷ **1** A2 a musical instrument, especially one made from a skin stretched over the end of a hollow tube or bowl, played by hitting with the hand or a stick: *a bass/snare/kettle drum* ◦ *They danced to the* ***beat*** *of the drums (= sound of the drums being hit).* **CONTAINER** ▷ **2** a large tube-like container: *an oil drum* ◦ *a drum* ***of*** *radioactive waste* **3** the hollow metal cylinder in a washing machine into which clothes and other things are put for washing

IDIOM **bang/beat the drum** UK to speak enthusiastically about a belief or idea in order to persuade other people to support it too: *Labour are banging the drum for a united Europe.*

▸verb [I or T] (**-mm-**) to hit a surface regularly and make a sound like a drum, or to make something do this: *She drummed her fingers impatiently* ***on*** *the table.* ◦ *The rain drummed loudly* ***on*** *the roof.*

PHRASAL VERBS **drum sth into sb** to teach something to someone by repeating it to them a lot: *The importance of good manners was drummed into us at an early age.* • **drum sb out of sth** to force someone to leave a job, group, etc., often because they have behaved in a way that is not considered acceptable: *The minister was drummed out of office when it was discovered that he had been taking bribes.* • **drum sth up** to increase interest in something or support for something: *He was trying to drum up some enthusiasm for the project.*

ˌdrum and ˈbass (also **ˌdrum 'n' ˈbass**) noun [U] a type of popular dance music with a fast, strong drum rhythm and a loud BASS

drumbeat /ˈdrʌm.biːt/ noun [C] (the sound of) a single hit on a drum

ˈdrum ˌkit noun [C] (US also **ˈdrum ˌset**) a set of drums and CYMBALS played by one person

drumlin /ˈdrʌm.lɪn/ noun [C] specialized a small hill formed by a GLACIER (= mass of moving ice), usually with a stretched, oval shape and found in groups

ˈdrum maˌchine noun [C] an electronic machine which produces the sound of drums

ˌdrum ˈmajor noun [C] the person who leads a marching musical group

ˌdrum majoˈrette noun [C] (also **majorette**) mainly US a girl or young woman who leads a marching musical group

drummer /ˈdrʌm.ər/ ⓤⓢ /-ɚ/ noun [C] someone who plays a drum or a set of drums, especially in a music group

drumstick /ˈdrʌm.stɪk/ noun [C] **MUSIC** ▷ **1** a stick for beating a drum **FOOD** ▷ **2** the lower part of the leg of a chicken or similar bird eaten as food: *chicken drumsticks*

drunk /drʌŋk/ verb; adj; noun

▸verb past participle of **drink**

▸adj [usually after verb] **1** B2 unable to speak or act in the usual way because of having had too much alcohol: *I* ***got*** *completely drunk at my sister's wedding.* ◦ *I'd had a couple of glasses of wine but I certainly wasn't drunk.* ◦ UK *He came home last night* ***blind*** *(= extremely) drunk.* **2 drunk and disorderly** legal the crime of behaving badly in public after drinking too much alcohol **3 drunk with power** having a strong and unreasonable feeling of being able to control other people

IDIOM **drunk as a lord** UK (US **drunk as a skunk**) extremely drunk: *Andy staggered in last night drunk as a lord.*

▸noun [C] (also **drunkard**) a person who drinks large amounts of alcohol very often and is unable to stop

ˌdrunk-ˈdial verb [T] informal to make a phone call when you are drunk: *She drunk-dialled her ex-boyfriend last night and told him that she still loved him.* • **ˌdrunk ˈdial** noun [C] informal a phone call that you make when you are drunk

ˌdrunk ˈdriving noun [U] US for **drink-driving**

drunken /ˈdrʌŋ.kən/ adj [before noun] disapproving **1** describes someone who is (often) under the influence of alcohol: *She was convicted of murdering her drunken and allegedly violent husband.* ◦ *Just before midnight, the square filled up with drunken revellers.* **2** describes a situation in which a lot of alcohol has been drunk: *a drunken* ***brawl*** ◦ *He came home and fell into a drunken* ***stupor*** *(= sleep).* • **drunkenly** /-li/ adv *He staggered drunkenly toward the door.* • **drunkenness** /-nəs/ noun [U]

dry /draɪ/ adj; noun; verb

▸adj (**drier, driest**) **NOT WET** ▷ **1** A2 describes something that has no water or other liquid in, on, or around it: *I hung his wet trousers on the radiator, but they're not dry yet.* ◦ *These plants grow well in dry soil/a dry climate.* ◦ *This cake's a bit dry – I think I overcooked it.* **2 run dry** If a river or other area of water runs dry, the water gradually disappears from it: *By this time all the wells had run dry.* **3** C1 describes hair or skin that does not have enough of the natural oils that make it soft and smooth: *a shampoo for dry hair* **4** describes bread when it is plain, without butter, jam, etc.: *All I was offered was a piece of dry bread and an apple!* **BORING** ▷ **5** C2 disapproving If a book, talk, subject, etc. is dry, it is not interesting. **NO ALCOHOL** ▷ **6** without alcoholic drinks: *a dry state (= a place that does not allow alcohol)* **NOT SWEET** ▷ **7** C1 If wine or another alcoholic drink is dry, it does not taste sweet: *dry cider/martini/sherry/wine* ◦ *On the whole, I prefer dry wines to sweet ones.* **HUMOUR** ▷ **8** approving Dry humour is very funny in a way that is clever and not obvious: *a dry* ***sense of humour*** ◦ *a dry wit* • **dryness** /ˈdraɪ.nəs/ **noun** [U] *The wine has just enough dryness to balance its fruitiness.*

IDIOMS **as dry as a bone** (also ˌ**bone** ˈ**dry**) extremely dry: *I don't think he's been watering these plants – the soil is as dry as a bone.* • **not a dry eye in the house** used to mean that all the people at a particular place felt very emotional about what they had seen or heard and many of them were crying

▸**noun** **the dry** UK a place where the conditions are not wet, especially when compared to somewhere where the conditions are wet: *You're soaked – come into the dry.*

▸**verb** [I or T] **1** A2 to become dry, or to make something become dry: *Will this paint dry by tomorrow?* ◦ *Hang the clothes up to dry.* ◦ *The fruit is dried in the sun.* **2 dry the dishes** (UK also **dry up (the dishes)**, UK **do the drying (up)**) to dry plates, knives, forks, etc. after they have been washed

IDIOM **dry your eyes** to stop crying: *Come on, Rosie, dry your eyes and we'll go and find Daddy.*

PHRASAL VERBS **dry (sb/sth) off** to make someone or something dry, or to become dry, especially on the surface: *I dried myself off and got dressed.* • **dry (sth) out** to make something dry, or to become dry: *If you don't keep food covered, it dries out.* • **dry out** informal Someone who dries out stops being DEPENDENT on (= unable to stop drinking) alcohol: *He went to a clinic in Arizona to dry out.* • **dry sth up** mainly UK to dry plates, cups, etc. with a cloth after they have been washed • **dry up** **WATER** ▷ **1** If a river, lake, etc. dries up, the water in it disappears. **END** ▷ **2** C2 If a supply of something dries up, it ends: *His main source of work had dried up, leaving him short of money.*

ˌ**dry-**ˈ**clean** **verb** [T] to clean clothes with chemicals, not water: *This dress has to be dry-cleaned.*

ˌ**dry-**ˈ**cleaner's** **noun** [C] a shop where clothes are cleaned with chemicals • ˌ**dry-**ˈ**cleaning** **noun** [U]

ˌ**dry** ˈ**dock** **noun** [C] an area of water that can be emptied and used for repairing ships

dryer (also **drier**) /ˈdraɪ.əʳ/ US /-ɚ/ **noun** [C] a machine that dries things: *a hair dryer* ◦ *a grain dryer* ◦ *Put those damp clothes in the (tumble) dryer.*

ˌ**dry-**ˈ**eyed** **adj** If someone is dry-eyed, they are not crying, especially in a situation in which you might expect them to be crying: *She accused me of being unfeeling because I left the cinema dry-eyed.*

ˈ**dry** ˌ**goods** **noun** [plural] **FOOD** ▷ **1** food, such as coffee and flour, that is solid and dry **CLOTH** ▷ **2** US for **drapery** (= cloth, pins, thread, etc. used for sewing)

ˌ**dry** ˈ**ice** **noun** [U] frozen CARBON DIOXIDE, used for keeping things very cold and for producing a gas that looks like smoke in musical and theatre performances

ˌ**dry** ˈ**land** **noun** [U] land and not sea or water: *We sailed for three days before we saw dry land.*

ˌ**dry** ˈ**rot** **noun** [U] a disease caused by a FUNGUS which destroys wood in houses and boats, etc.

ˌ**dry** ˈ**run** **noun** [C] informal a **dummy run**

ˈ**dry** ˌ**slope** **noun** [C] (also ˌ**dry** ˈ**ski** ˌ**slope**) a structure consisting of a slope covered with plastic or some other material on which people can ski in areas where there is no snow: *dry-slope skiing*

drystone wall /ˌdraɪ.stəʊnˈwɔːl/ US /-stoʊnˈwɑːl/ **noun** [C] a wall made with stones which fit together firmly without being stuck together with MORTAR

the DTs /ˌdiːˈtiːz/ **noun** [plural] informal abbreviation for delirium tremens: a physical condition, caused by drinking too much alcohol over a long period, in which you shake without being able to stop and see imaginary things: *He's got a bad case of the DTs.*

dual /ˈdjuː.əl/ US /ˈduː.əl/ **adj** [before noun] **1** C1 with two parts, or combining two things: *This room has a dual* ***purpose****, serving as both a study and a dining room.* ◦ *the dual* ***role*** *of chairman and chief executive* **2 dual controls** two sets of controls in a car, one for the person who is learning to drive and one for the teacher **3 dual nationality/citizenship** the nationality of two countries at the same time: *She has dual British and American nationality.*

ˌ**dual** ˈ**carriageway** **noun** [C] UK (US **di**ˌ**vided** ˈ**highway**) a road that has an area of land in the middle, dividing the rows of traffic that are moving in opposite directions

dualism /ˈdjuː.ə.lɪ.zəm/ US /ˈduː.əl.ɪ-/ **noun** [U] formal the belief that things are divided into two often very different or opposing parts: *Western dualism values mind over body.*

duality /djuːˈæl.ə.ti/ US /duːˈæl.ə.t̬i/ **noun** [U] formal the state of combining two different things: *His poems reveal the duality of his nature, the joy and hope, the fear and despair.*

ˌ**dual-**ˈ**purpose** **adj** able to be used to do two things: *a dual-purpose lawn-raking and leaf-collecting machine*

dub /dʌb/ **verb**; **noun**

▸**verb** (**-bb-**) **NAME** ▷ **1** [T + noun] to give something or someone a particular name, especially describing what you think of them: *She was dubbed by the newspapers 'The Angel of Death'.* **SOUNDS** ▷ **2** [T] to change the sounds and speech on a film or television programme, especially to a different language: *I'd rather watch a film with subtitles than one dubbed* ***into*** *English.* ◦ *To conceal his identity, the man's voice has been dubbed* ***over*** *(= an actor speaks his words).*

▸**noun** [U] a style of music or poetry connected with REGGAE in which the main part of the tune is removed and various special effects are added

dubious /ˈdjuː.bi.əs/ US /ˈduː-/ **adj** **1** C2 thought not to be completely true or not able to be trusted: *These claims are dubious and not scientifically proven.* ◦ *He has been associated with some dubious characters.* ◦ *Ruth Ellis has the dubious (= bad)* ***distinction*** *of being the last woman to be hanged in Britain.* **2** C2 feeling doubt or not feeling certain: *I'm dubious* ***about*** *his promises to change his ways.* • **dubiously** /-li/ **adv**

dubstep /ˈdʌb.step/ **noun** [U] mainly UK a type of electronic dance music

ducal /ˈdjuː.kəl/ US /ˈduː-/ **adj** of or connected with a DUKE

duchess /ˈdʌtʃ.es/ **noun** [C] (the title of) a woman who is married to a DUKE or who has the rank of DUKE: *the Duchess of Kent*

duchy /ˈdʌtʃ.i/ **noun** [C] the area of land owned or ruled by a DUKE or duchess

duck /dʌk/ **noun; verb**

▸**noun BIRD** ▷ **1** A2 [C] a bird that lives by water, has WEBBED feet (= feet with skin between the toes), a short neck and a large beak **2** [U] the meat of this bird **PERSON** ▷ **3** [C] (also **ducks**) UK old-fashioned informal a friendly way of talking to someone you like: [as form of address] *Come and sit beside me, duck.*

IDIOM **take to sth like a duck to water** informal to discover when you start to do something for the first time that you have a natural ability to do it: *He took to fatherhood like a duck to water.*

▸**verb 1** [I or T] to move your head or the top part of your body quickly down, especially to avoid being hit: *I saw the ball hurtling towards me and ducked (**down**).* ◦ *Duck your head or you'll bang it on the doorframe.* **2** [T] to push someone underwater for a short time: *The boys were splashing about and ducking each other in the pool.* **3** [I + adv/prep] to move quickly to a place, especially in order not to be seen: *When he saw them coming, he ducked **into** a doorway.*

PHRASAL VERB **duck out of sth** informal to avoid doing something: *You can't duck out of your responsibilities.*

ˌduck-billed ˈplatypus **noun** [C] a **platypus**

ducking /ˈdʌk.ɪŋ/ **noun** [C] an act or period of going below the surface of water: *The boat turned over and we all **got/had** a ducking.*

duckling /ˈdʌk.lɪŋ/ **noun** [C or U] a young DUCK, or its flesh when used as food

duckweed /ˈdʌk.wiːd/ **noun** [U] a plant that grows on the surface of some pools

duct /dʌkt/ **noun** [C] a tube or pipe that carries liquid or air, especially in and out of buildings or through the body: *Most office buildings have dozens of **air** ducts and vents.* ◦ *People with blocked **tear** ducts cannot cry.*

ductile /ˈdʌk.taɪl/ US /-tɪl/ **adj** specialized describes metals that can be bent easily

ˈduct ˌtape **noun** [U] a long, thin strip of very strong sticky material that is sold in a roll and is often used for covering holes or other repair jobs

dud /dʌd/ **noun; adj**

▸**noun** [C] informal something that has no value or that does not work: *Are there any more batteries? This one's a dud.* ◦ *He's made eleven films in the last 20 years and not one a dud.*

▸**adj** informal not working or not having any value: *A customer had tried to pay with a dud **cheque** (= one for which a bank will not give money).*

dude /duːd/ **noun** [C] mainly US slang a man: *Some dude just asked me if I knew you.* ◦ [as form of address] *Dude, where were you last night?* ◦ *Jason was one **cool** dude.*

ˈdude ˌranch **noun** [C] a holiday farm in the US that offers activities such as riding horses and CAMPING

dudgeon /ˈdʌdʒ.ən/ **noun** literary **in high dudgeon** If you do something in high dudgeon, you do it angrily, usually because of the way you have been treated: *After waiting an hour, he drove off in high dudgeon.*

due /djuː/ US /duː/ **adj; noun; adv**

▸**adj EXPECTED** ▷ **1** B1 expected to happen, arrive, etc. at a particular time: *What time is the next bus due?* ◦ *The next meeting is due **to** be held in three months' time.* ◦ *Their first baby is due in January.* **2 in due course** B2 formal at a suitable time in the future: *You will receive notification of the results in due course.* **RESULTING** ▷ **3 due to** B1 because of: *A lot of her unhappiness is due to boredom.* ◦ *Due to wet leaves on the line, this train will arrive an hour late.* **OWED** ▷ **4** C2 owed as a debt or as a right: *The rent is due (= should be paid) at the end of the month.* ◦ *£50 is due **to** me* (US *due me*) *from the people I worked for last month.* ◦ *Our thanks are due **to** everyone.* ◦ UK legal *He was found to have been driving without due (= the necessary) **care and attention**.* **5 be due for sth** C1 If you are due for something, you expect to receive it, because you deserve it: *I must be due for promotion soon.*

▸**noun 1 give sb their due** said when you are praising someone for something good they have done, although you dislike other things about them: *He failed again, but to give him his due, he did try hard.* **2 dues** [plural] the official payments that you make to an organization you belong to: *Members of the society pay $1,000 in annual dues.*

▸**adv** in a direction that is straight towards the north, south, east, or west: *From here, you go due east until you get to a forest.*

ˌdue ˈdiligence **noun** [U] **1** action that is considered reasonable for people to be expected to take in order to keep themselves or others and their property safe: *People have to exercise due diligence and watch what's being bought on their credit cards.* **2** specialized the detailed examination of a company and its financial records, done before becoming involved in a business arrangement with it

duel /ˈdjuː.əl/ US /ˈduː.əl/ **noun 1** [C] a formal fight in the past, using guns or SWORDS, arranged between two people as a way of deciding an argument: *The two men **fought** a duel **over** the lady.* ◦ *The composer Strauss was once **challenged to** a duel.* **2** [C usually singular] a difficult competition in which both sides show a lot of effort: *The two yachts are **locked in** a duel **for** the championship title.* • **duel verb** [I] (plural UK **-ll-** or US **-l-**) • **duelling** (US usually **dueling**) /-ə.lɪŋ/ **noun** [U] the activity of fighting duels

duet /djuˈet/ US /duː-/ **noun** [C] a song or other piece of music sung or played by two people

duff /dʌf/ **adj; noun; verb**

▸**adj** UK informal bad, not useful, or not working

▸**noun** [C] US informal a person's bottom: ***Get off** your duff and start working.*

▸**verb** [T]

PHRASAL VERB **duff sb up** UK informal to hit someone repeatedly: *Two of the robbers threatened to duff the witness up if he went to the police.*

duffel bag (also **duffle bag**) /ˈdʌf.lˌbæg/ **noun** [C] **1** UK a tube-shaped cloth bag with a circular bottom and a thick string at the top that is used to close it and carry it **2** US a long bag used for carrying clothes, etc. when you are travelling

duffel coat (also **duffle coat**) /ˈdʌf.lˌkəʊt/ US /-ˌkoʊt/ **noun** [C] a coat made of thick wool which has TOGGLE (= solid tube-shaped) buttons and usually has a HOOD (= head cover)

duffer /ˈdʌf.ər/ US /-ɚ/ **noun** [C] old-fashioned a person who has little skill or is slow to learn

dug /dʌg/ **verb** past simple and past participle of **dig**

dugout /ˈdʌg.aʊt/ **noun** [C] **SHELTER** ▷ **1** a shelter, usually for soldiers, made by digging a hole in the ground and covering it **2** a shelter for the members of a team at the side of a sports field **BOAT** ▷ **3** (also **dugout canoe**) a small light boat made by cutting out the middle of a tree TRUNK

duh /dɜː/ **exclamation** informal used to show that you think a person or statement is stupid, or that something is obvious

duke /djuːk/ US /duːk/ **noun** [C] a man of very high

rank in a country, or the ruler of a small independent country

dukedom /ˈdjuːk.dəm/ US /ˈduːk-/ noun [C] the rank of a duke, or the land owned by a duke

dulcet /ˈdʌl.sət/ adj **1** literary describes sounds that are soft and pleasant to listen to **2 sb's dulcet tones** humorous a person's voice

D

dulcimer /ˈdʌl.sɪ.məʳ/ US /-mɚ/ noun [C] a musical instrument, consisting of a wooden box with wire strings stretched over it, played by hitting the strings with a pair of light hammers

dull /dʌl/ adj; verb

▸adj **BORING** ▷ **1** B1 not interesting or exciting in any way: *She wrote dull, respectable articles for the local newspaper.* ◦ *He's pleasant enough, but **deadly** dull.* → Synonym **boring** **NOT BRIGHT** ▷ **2** C1 not clear, bright or shiny; dark: *We could just see a dull **glow** given off by the fire's last embers.* ◦ *The first day of our holiday was dull (= cloudy).* **NOT SHARP** ▷ **3** describes a sound or pain that is not sharp or clear: *I heard a dull **thud** from the kitchen and realized she must have fainted.* ◦ *The dull rumble of traffic woke her.* ◦ *She felt a dull **ache** at the back of her head.* **4** old-fashioned not intelligent • **dully** /ˈdʌl.li/ adv *The car lights glowed dully through the mist.* ◦ *My arm still ached dully.* • **dullness** /ˈdʌl.nəs/ noun [U]

IDIOM **be (as) dull as ditchwater** informal to be very boring

▸verb [T] to make something less severe: *Homeless children sniff glue to dull their hunger pains.*

dullard /ˈdʌl.əd/ US /-ɚd/ noun [C] old-fashioned a stupid person

duly /ˈdjuː.li/ US /ˈduː-/ adv in the correct way or at the correct time; as expected: *He knew he had been wrong, and duly apologized.* ◦ *She asked for his autograph and he duly **obliged** by signing her programme.*

dumb /dʌm/ adj; verb

▸adj **SILENT** ▷ **1** C1 permanently or temporarily unable to speak: *He's been deaf and dumb since birth.* ◦ *She was **struck** dumb by what she had seen.* **STUPID** ▷ **2** B2 mainly US informal stupid and annoying: *Are they brave or just dumb?* ◦ *What a dumb idea!* • **dumbness** /ˈdʌm.nəs/ noun [U]

▸verb

PHRASAL VERB **dumb sth down** informal disapproving to make something simpler and easier for people to understand, especially in order to make it more popular: *The General Synod accused broadcasters of dumbing down religious programmes.*

dumbbell /ˈdʌm.bel/ noun [C] **WEIGHT** ▷ **1** a short bar with a weight on each end that you lift up and down to make your arm and shoulder muscles stronger → Compare **barbell** **PERSON** ▷ **2** US for **dummy**

dumbfounded /ˌdʌmˈfaʊn.dɪd/ adj (also **dumbstruck**) so shocked that you cannot speak: *He was dumbfounded **by** the allegations.*

ˌdumbing-ˈdown noun [U] informal disapproving the act of making something simpler and easier for people to understand, especially in order to make it more popular: *the dumbing-down of television*

dumbly /ˈdʌm.li/ adv without speaking: *She stared dumbly into space.*

ˈdumb ˌshow noun [C or U] UK the use of hand movements and not speech in order to communicate what you mean, or an example of this

ˌdumb ˈwaiter noun [C] a small LIFT (= device used to move things from one level of a building to another) used especially in restaurants to bring food from the kitchen

dumdum (bullet) /ˈdʌm.dʌmˌbʊl.ɪt/ noun [C] a bullet with a soft front that increases in size when it hits someone, causing serious injuries

dummy /ˈdʌm.i/ noun; adj

▸noun [C] **MODEL** ▷ **1** a large model of a human, especially one used to show clothes in a shop: *a **shop** dummy* ◦ *a ventriloquist's dummy* **NOT REAL** ▷ **2** something that is not real and is used for practice or to deceive: *The device is not a real bomb but a dummy.* **3** (in some sports, especially football) when you pretend to hit the ball in a particular direction but do not, in order to deceive the other players **FOR BABY** ▷ **4** UK (US **pacifier**) a smooth rubber or plastic object that is given to a baby to suck in order to comfort it and make it stop crying **STUPID PERSON** ▷ **5** (US also **dumbbell**) a stupid or silly person: *Only a dummy would ignore the safety warnings.*

▸adj [before noun] not real: *an enormous dummy perfume bottle in the shop window*

ˌdummy ˈrun noun [C] (also **ˌdry ˈrun**) a practice of a particular activity or performance: *The local elections can be seen as a dummy run **for** the national election next year.*

dump /dʌmp/ verb; noun

▸verb [T] **PUT DOWN** ▷ **1** C2 to put down or drop something in a careless way: *He came in with four shopping bags and dumped them on the table.* **GET RID OF** ▷ **2** C1 to get rid of something unwanted, especially by leaving it in a place where it is not allowed to be: *The tax was so unpopular that the government decided to dump it.* ◦ *Toxic chemicals continue to be dumped in the North Sea.* **3** to sell unwanted goods very cheaply, usually in other countries: *They accused the West of dumping out-of-date medicines **on** Third World countries.* **4** specialized to move information from a computer's memory to another device **END RELATIONSHIP** ▷ **5** C2 informal to suddenly end a romantic relationship you have been having with someone: *If he's so awful, why don't you just dump him?*

▸noun [C] **1** C1 (UK also **rubbish dump**) a place where people are allowed to leave their rubbish: *I need to clear out the shed and take everything I don't want to the dump.* **2** C2 informal a very unpleasant and untidy place: *His room is an absolute dump!* **3** a place where things of a particular type are stored, especially by an army: *an ammunition/arms/weapons/food dump*

IDIOMS **(down) in the dumps** C2 unhappy: *She's a bit down in the dumps because she's got to take her exams again.* • **have/take a dump** offensive to pass the contents of the bowels out of the body

ˈdumper ˌtruck noun [C] UK (US **ˈdump ˌtruck**) a large truck for transporting heavy LOADS, with a back part that can be raised at one end so that its contents fall out

dumping /ˈdʌm.pɪŋ/ noun [U] the act of getting rid of something that is not wanted: *They have promised to limit the dumping **of** sewage sludge in the sea.*

ˈdumping ˌground noun [C usually singular] a place where something that is not wanted is left: *Most people do not want this country to become a dumping ground **for** toxic waste.*

dumpling /ˈdʌm.plɪŋ/ noun [C] **1** a small ball of DOUGH (= flour and water mixed together), cooked, and eaten with meat and vegetables **2** a small amount of fruit covered in a sweet DOUGH and baked: *apple dumplings*

Dumpster /ˈdʌmp.stəʳ/ (US) /-stɚ/ **noun** [C] US trademark **skip**

ˈ**dump** ˌ**truck** noun [C] US for **dumper truck**

dumpy /ˈdʌm.pi/ **adj** short and fat: *a dumpy little woman*

dun /dʌn/ **adj; verb**

▸**adj** of a greyish-brown colour

▸**verb** [T] (-nn-) US to demand money from someone: *He claimed he would rather go to prison than continue being dunned by the taxman.* ◦ *One of his jobs was dunning customers* ***for*** *money they owed.*

dunce /dʌns/ **noun** [C] disapproving a person who is slow to learn or stupid, especially at school

ˈ**dunce's** ˌ**cap** noun [C usually singular] (US usually ˈ**dunce** ˌ**cap**) a tall paper hat with a pointed end that in the past children had to wear in school if they had made many mistakes in their work

dunderhead /ˈdʌn.də.hed/ (US) /-dɚ-/ **noun** [C] old-fashioned informal a stupid person

dune /djuːn/ (US) /duːn/ **noun** [C] a hill of sand near a beach or in a desert

dung /dʌŋ/ **noun** [U] solid waste from animals, especially CATTLE and horses → Synonym **manure**

dungarees /ˌdʌŋ.gəˈriːz/ **noun** [plural] **1** UK (US **overalls**) a pair of trousers with an extra piece of cloth that covers the chest and is held in place by a strap over each shoulder **2** US old-fashioned trousers made of DENIM (= strong, blue cotton cloth)

dungeon /ˈdʌn.dʒən/ **noun** [C] an underground prison, especially in a castle

dunk /dʌŋk/ **verb** [T] **INTO LIQUID** ▷ **1** to put a biscuit, piece of bread, etc. into a liquid such as tea or soup for a short time before eating it: *She dunked a biscuit* ***in*** *her tea.* **BASKETBALL** ▷ **2** US to SLAM-DUNK

dunnit /ˈdʌn.ɪt/ **short form** not standard doesn't it: *That looks good, dunnit?*

dunno /dəˈnəʊ/ (US) /-ˈnoʊ/ **short form** not standard I don't know: *'Where are we exactly?' 'Dunno.'*

dunny /ˈdʌn.i/ **noun** [C] Australian English informal for **toilet**

duo /ˈdjuː.əʊ/ (US) /ˈduː.oʊ/ **noun** [C] (plural **duos**) two people, especially two singers, musicians, or other performers: *the comedy duo Laurel and Hardy*

duodecimal /ˌdjuː.əʊˈdes.ɪ.məl/ (US) /ˌduː.oʊˈ-/ **adj** specialized relating to or expressed in a system of counting based on the number twelve

duodenum /ˌdjuː.əˈdiː.nəm/ (US) /ˌduː.-/ **noun** [C] (plural **duodenums** or **duodena**) specialized the first part of the bowels just below the stomach • **duodenal** /-nəl/ **adj** specialized *duodenal* ***ulcers***

dupatta /duˈpʌt.ə/ (US) /-ˈpʌt̬.ə/ **noun** [C] a long piece of cloth worn around the head, neck, and shoulders by women from South Asia

dupe /djuːp/ (US) /duːp/ **verb; noun**

▸**verb** [T] to deceive someone, usually by making them do something that they did not intend to do: *The girls were duped by drug smugglers* ***into*** *carrying heroin for them.*

▸**noun** [C] someone who has been tricked: *an innocent dupe*

duplex /ˈdjuː.pleks/ (US) /ˈduː-/ **noun** [C] **ROOMS** ▷ **1** a set of rooms for living in that are on two floors of a building **TWO HOUSES** ▷ **2** Australian English a pair of small houses on a single floor that are joined together

duplicate verb; adj; noun

▸**verb** [T] /ˈdjuː.plɪ.keɪt/ (US) /ˈduː-/ to make an exact copy of something: *Can you duplicate (= use a special machine to copy) this document for me?* ◦ *Parenthood is an experience nothing else can duplicate.*

▸**adj** [before noun] /ˈdjuː.plɪ.kət/ (US) /ˈduː-/ being an exact copy of something: *The thieves were equipped with duplicate keys to the safe.*

▸**noun** [C] /ˈdjuː.plɪ.kət/ (US) /ˈduː-/ something that is an exact copy of something else: *I lost the original form so they sent me a duplicate.*

duplication /ˌdjuː.plɪˈkeɪ.ʃən/ (US) /ˌduː-/ **noun** [U] the act or process of making an exact copy of something

duplicitous /djʊˈplɪs.ɪ.təs/ (US) /duːˈplɪs.ə.t̬əs/ **adj** formal involving duplicity: *a duplicitous traitor/spy/politician*

duplicity /djʊˈplɪs.ɪ.ti/ (US) /duːˈplɪs.ə.t̬i/ **noun** [U] formal dishonest talk or behaviour, especially by saying different things to two people: *They were accused of duplicity* ***in*** *their dealings with both sides.*

durable /ˈdjʊə.rə.bl/ (US) /ˈdʊr.ə-/ **adj** able to last a long time without becoming damaged: *The machines have to be made of durable materials.* ◦ *The resolution calls for a durable peace settlement.* • **durability** /ˌdjʊə.rəˈbɪl.ɪ.ti/ (US) /ˌdʊr.əˈbɪl.ə.t̬i/ **noun** [U] *the durability of the materials used*

duration /djʊəˈreɪ.ʃən/ (US) /duː-/ **noun** [U] **1** (C1) the length of time that something lasts: *He planned a stay of two years' duration.* **2 for the duration** for as long as something lasts: *I suppose we're stuck with each other for the duration (of the journey).*

duress /djʊˈres/ (US) /duː-/ **noun** [U] formal threats used to force a person to do something: *He claimed that he signed the confession* ***under*** *duress.*

durian /ˈdjʊə.ri.ən/ (US) /ˈdʊr.i-/ **noun** [C] a large, oval, tropical fruit with a hard skin covered in sharp points, yellow, orange, or red flesh, and a very strong smell

during /ˈdjʊə.rɪŋ/ (US) /ˈdʊr.ɪŋ/ **preposition** **THROUGH** ▷ **1** (A2) from the beginning to the end of a particular period: *They work during the night and sleep by day.* ◦ *There were huge advances in aviation technology during the Second World War.* → Compare **while** **AT SOME TIME IN** ▷ **2** (A2) at some time between the beginning and the end of a period: *I woke up several times during the night.* ◦ *The programme will be shown on television during the weekend.*

durum wheat /ˈdjʊə.rəmˌwiːt/ (US) /ˈdʊr-/ **noun** [U] a type of WHEAT that is used to make PASTA

dusk /dʌsk/ **noun** [U] the time before night when it is not yet dark: *As dusk* ***fell****, bats began to fly between the trees.*

dusky /ˈdʌs.ki/ **adj** literary dark in colour: *In autumn, the leaves turn a dusky red.*

dust /dʌst/ **noun; verb**

▸**noun** [U] (B1) dry dirt in the form of powder that covers surfaces inside a building, or very small dry pieces of soil, sand or other substances: *The furniture was covered in dust and cobwebs.* ◦ *A cloud of dust rose in the air as the car roared past.* ◦ *coal dust*

IDIOMS **the dust settles** If the dust settles after an argument or big change, the situation becomes calmer: *We thought we'd* ***let*** *the dust settle before discussing the other matter.* • **turn to dust** literary to become worth nothing: *Every promise they have made has turned to dust.*

▸**verb** **CLEAN** ▷ **1** [I or T] to use a cloth to remove dust from the surface of something **COVER** ▷ **2** [T] to cover something with a light powder: *Dust the top of the cake* ***with*** *icing sugar.*

IDIOM **be done and dusted** UK informal to be complete and finished: *By now the deal was done and dusted.*

PHRASAL VERB **dust sth off** (UK also **dust down**) to prepare something for use, especially after it has not been used for a long time: *They brought out the old ambulances, dusted them down and put them back into service.*

dustbin /ˈdʌst.bɪn/ noun [C] UK (US ˈ**garbage** ˌ**can**, US also ˈ**trash** ˌ**can**) B1 a large container for rubbish from a house or other building, usually made of strong plastic or metal and kept outside

IDIOM **consign sth to the dustbin** to get rid of something: *Fox hunting, he claimed, should be consigned to the dustbin of history.*

ˈ**dust bowl** noun [C] an area of land where the ground is very dry and where the air is often full of dust

dustcart /ˈdʌst.kɑːt/ US /-kɑːrt/ noun [C] UK (US ˈ**garbage** ˌ**truck**) a large vehicle that is driven from one house to another to collect rubbish from the dustbins outside

dustcloth /ˈdʌst.klɒθ/ US /-klɑːθ/ noun [C] US a piece of cloth that is used for removing dust from furniture, books, surfaces, etc.

duster /ˈdʌs.təʳ/ US /-tɚ/ noun [C] **1** UK (US **dustcloth**) a piece of cloth that is used for removing dust from furniture, books, surfaces, etc. **2** US a **feather duster** (= a stick with feathers at one end, used for cleaning) or a similar object with cloth fixed to one end

dusting /ˈdʌs.tɪŋ/ noun [U] **THIN LAYER** ▷ a thin layer of powder, snow, etc.: *There was a dusting of snow on the lawn.*

ˈ**dust** ˌ**jacket** noun [C] a paper cover for a book, usually with the title of the book and the name of the AUTHOR (= writer) printed on it

dustman /ˈdʌst.mən/ noun [C] (plural **-men** /-mən/) UK (US **garbageman**, UK formal ˈ**refuse col**ˌ**lector**) a person whose job is to empty people's DUSTBINS and take the rubbish away

dustpan /ˈdʌst.pæn/ noun [C] a flat container with a handle into which you brush dust and dirt

brush and dustpan

dustsheet /ˈdʌst.ʃiːt/ noun [C] a large piece of cloth that is put over furniture to protect it from dust

ˈ**dust** ˌ**tea** noun [U] Indian English tea in the form of powder

ˈ**dust-up** noun [C usually singular] old-fashioned a fight or argument

dusty /ˈdʌs.ti/ adj **1** B1 covered in dust: *Heaps of dusty books lay on the floor.* ◦ *We drove along the dusty road.* **2** slightly grey in colour: *dusty pink*

Dutch /dʌtʃ/ adj; noun

▸adj from, belonging to, or relating to the Netherlands

IDIOM **go Dutch** informal to agree to share the cost of something, especially a meal

▸noun [U] the language of the Netherlands, also spoken in Belgium

ˌ**Dutch** ˈ**cap** noun [C] a **diaphragm**

ˌ**Dutch** ˈ**courage** noun [U] UK (US ˌ**liquid** ˈ**courage**) the confidence that some people get from drinking alcohol before they do something that needs courage

ˌ**Dutch** ˈ**elm di**ˌ**sease** noun [U] a disease that slowly kills ELM trees

Dutchman /ˈdʌtʃ.mən/ noun [C] (plural **-men** /-mən/) a man who comes from the Netherlands

IDIOM **I'm a Dutchman** UK humorous old-fashioned said after describing or hearing something that is very obviously not true: *If that's his real hair, then I'm a Dutchman.*

dutiable /ˈdjuː.ti.ə.bl/ US /ˈduː.t̬i-/ adj specialized describes goods on which duty must be paid

dutiful /ˈdjuː.tɪ.fəl/ US /ˈduː.t̬ɪ-/ adj doing everything that you should do: *a dutiful son/husband* • **dutifully** /-i/ adv

duty /ˈdjuː.ti/ US /ˈduː.t̬i/ noun [C or U] **RESPONSIBILITY** ▷ **1** B1 something that you have to do because it is part of your job, or something that you feel is the right thing to do: *The duty of the agency is to act in the best interests of the child.* ◦ [+ to infinitive] *I felt it was my duty* ***to*** *tell them the truth.* ◦ *You have a duty* ***to*** *yourself to take a holiday now and then.* ◦ *He only went to see her* ***out of*** *duty (= because he thought he should).* ◦ *You should* ***report for*** *duty (= arrive at work) at 8 a.m. on Monday.* ◦ *What time are you* ***off/on*** *duty (= when do you finish/start work) tomorrow?* **2 be duty bound to do sth** to have to do something because it is your duty: *We are duty bound to justify how we spend our funds.* **TAX** ▷ **3** a tax paid to the government, especially on things that you bring into a country: *There's a high duty* ***on*** *alcohol.*

> Word partners for **duty**
>
> *have* a duty (to do sth) • *carry out/do/fulfil/perform* a duty • *fail in/neglect* a duty • a *legal/moral* duty • a *sense* of duty • duty *to/towards* sb

ˌ**duty-**ˈ**free** adj; noun

▸adj B1 Duty-free goods are goods bought in special shops in airports, on ships, etc. on which you do not pay government tax: *He bought his wife some duty-free perfume.* ◦ *I almost missed my flight because there was a long queue in the duty-free* ***shop.***

▸noun **1** [U] goods that you can buy in special shops in airports, on ships, etc., without paying tax on them: *We can* ***buy*** *our duty-free while we're waiting at the airport.* **2** [C] (also ˌ**duty-free** ˈ**shop**) a shop at an airport, on a ship, etc. where you can buy duty-free goods: *There'll be a duty-free on the ferry.*

duvet /ˈduː.veɪ/ US /duːˈveɪ/ noun [C] UK (UK also **continental quilt**, US **comforter**) B1 a large, soft, flat bag filled with feathers or artificial material used as a covering on a bed

ˈ**duvet** ˌ**cover** noun [C] a cover for a duvet

DVD /ˌdiː.viːˈdiː/ noun [C] A1 abbreviation for digital versatile disc or digital video disc: a disc used for storing and playing music, films or information: *I got a DVD of 'Mary Poppins' for Christmas.* ◦ *Is the film available on DVD?* ◦ *a DVD drive/player*

'd've /dəv/ short form of would have: *I'd've invited you, but you weren't around.*

DVR /ˌdiː.viːˈɑːʳ/ US /-ˈɑːr/ noun [C] abbreviation for digital video recorder: a piece of electronic equipment that records television programmes onto a HARD DISK

DVT /ˌdiː.viːˈtiː/ noun [U] abbreviation for **deep vein thrombosis**

dwarf /dwɔːf/ US /dwɔːrf/ noun; adj; verb

▸noun [C] (plural **dwarfs** or **dwarves**) **1** in stories for children, a creature like a little man with magical powers: *Snow White and the Seven Dwarfs* **2** often offensive a person who is much smaller than the usual size

▸**adj** [before noun] very small: *You can grow dwarf conifers in pots on the patio.*

▸**verb** [T] If one thing dwarfs another, it makes it seem small by comparison: *The new skyscraper will dwarf all those near it.* ◦ *This new crisis may well dwarf most that have gone before.*

ˈdwarf ˌplanet noun [C] a round mass of metal and rock or gas, moving around the Sun or another star, that is not large enough to be considered a planet. Dwarf planets in the SOLAR SYSTEM include Ceres, Pluto, and Eris.

dweeb /dwiːb/ **noun** [C] US slang disapproving a person who is physically and socially awkward and has little confidence: *What a dweeb! Why doesn't she dump him?*

dwell /dwel/ **verb** [I usually + adv/prep] (**dwelt** or **dwelled**, **dwelt** or **dwelled**) formal to live in a place or in a particular way: *She dwelt **in** remote parts of Asia for many years.*

PHRASAL VERB **dwell on sth** C1 to keep thinking or talking about something, especially something bad or unpleasant: *In his speech, he dwelt on the plight of the sick and the hungry.*

dweller /ˈdwel.əʳ/ US /-ɚ/ **noun city, town, cave, etc. dweller** a person who lives in a city, town, cave, etc.

dwelling /ˈdwel.ɪŋ/ **noun** [C] formal a house or place to live in

DWI /ˌdiː.dʌb.l̩.juːˈaɪ/ US abbreviation for **driving while intoxicated (drive)**

dwindle /ˈdwɪn.dl̩/ **verb** [I] to become smaller in size or amount, or fewer in number: *The community has dwindled **to** a tenth of its former size in the last two years.* ◦ *Her hopes of success in the race dwindled last night as the weather became worse.* • **dwindling** /-ɪŋ/ **adj** *dwindling numbers/supplies*

d'ya /dʒə/ **short form** not standard do you: *Who d'ya think they'll believe, me or you?*

dye /daɪ/ **verb; noun**

▸**verb** [T] (present participle **dyeing**, past tense and past participle **dyed**) to change the colour of something using a special liquid: *For a change, why not dye your T-shirts?* ◦ [+ obj + adj] *He's dyed his hair black.*

▸**noun** [C or U] a substance used to change the colour of something: *She dipped the material into the dye.* ◦ *There are dozens of different dyes to choose from.*

ˌdyed-in-the-ˈwool If someone has dyed-in-the-wool opinions, they hold them strongly and will not change them: *He's a dyed-in-the-wool traditionalist where cooking is concerned – he won't have any modern gadgets in the kitchen.*

dying /ˈdaɪ.ɪŋ/ **adj; noun**

▸**adj 1** very ill and likely to die soon: *She nursed her dying husband for months.* **2** describes a tradition or industry that is becoming much less common or important **3** happening at the time someone dies, or connected with that time: *Beethoven's dying **words** are said to have been 'I shall hear in heaven.'*

▸**noun** [plural] **the dying** people who are about to die: *These nurses specialize in the care of the dying.*

dyke (also **dike**) /daɪk/ **noun** [C] **WALL** ▷ **1** a wall built to prevent the sea or a river from covering an area, or a CHANNEL dug to take water away from an area → Compare **dam** **WOMAN** ▷ **2** slang a **lesbian**. Many people consider this word offensive.

dynamic /daɪˈnæm.ɪk/ **adj 1** B2 having a lot of ideas and enthusiasm: *She's young and dynamic and will be a great addition to the team.* ◦ *We need a dynamic expansion of trade with other countries.* → Synonym **energetic 2** C2 continuously changing or developing: *Business innovation is a dynamic process.* ◦ *The situation is dynamic and may change at any time.* **3** relating to forces that produce movement: *a dynamic force* • **dynamically** /-ɪ.kəl.i/ **adv** *dynamically stable*

dynamics /daɪˈnæm.ɪks/ **noun 1** [plural] forces that produce movement: *This software is used for modelling atmospheric dynamics.* **2** [plural] forces or processes that produce change inside a group or system: *The fight for the leadership gave a fascinating insight into the group's dynamics.* **3** [plural] specialized changes in loudness in a piece of music **4** [U] specialized the scientific study of the forces that produce movement

dynamism /ˈdaɪ.nə.mɪ.zəm/ **noun** [U] the quality of being dynamic: *She has a freshness and dynamism about her.*

dynamite /ˈdaɪ.nə.maɪt/ **noun; verb**

▸**noun** [U] **1** a type of explosive: *a stick of dynamite* **2** informal something that causes or may cause great shock or excitement: *The issue of unemployment is **political** dynamite (= could cause big political problems) for the government.*

▸**verb** [T] to destroy something using dynamite: *The rebels had dynamited the railway line.*

dynamo /ˈdaɪ.nə.məʊ/ US /-moʊ/ **noun** (plural **dynamos**) **1** [C] a device which changes energy of movement into electrical energy: *A dynamo on a bicycle will power a pair of lights while the wheels are going round.* **2** [C usually singular] an energetic force: *Onstage she is a **human** dynamo, spending the hour in perpetual motion.*

dynasty /ˈdɪn.ə.sti/ US /ˈdaɪ.nə-/ **noun** [C] a series of rulers or leaders who are all from the same family, or a period when a country is ruled by them: *The Mogul dynasty ruled over India for centuries.* • **dynastic** /daɪˈnæs.tɪk/ **adj** formal

d'you strong /djuː/ weak /djə/ **short form** informal do you: *D'you come here often?*

dysentery /ˈdɪs.ən.tər.i/ US /-ter-/ **noun** [U] a disease of the bowels that causes the contents to be passed out of the body much more often and in a more liquid form than usual. It is caused by an infection that is spread by dirty water or food.

dysfunction /dɪsˈfʌŋk.ʃən/ **noun** [C] specialized a problem or fault in a part of the body or a machine: *There appears to be a dysfunction in the patient's respiratory system.*

dysfunctional /dɪsˈfʌŋk.ʃən.əl/ **adj** specialized not behaving or working normally: *a dysfunctional family*

dyslexia /dɪˈslek.si.ə/ **noun** [U] a difficulty with reading and writing caused by the brain's being unable to see the difference between some letter shapes

dyslexic /dɪˈslek.sɪk/ **adj, noun** [C] (someone) having dyslexia

dyspepsia /dɪˈspep.si.ə/ **noun** [U] specialized pain in the stomach → Synonym **indigestion**

dyspeptic /dɪˈspep.tɪk/ **adj 1** specialized having problems with digesting food **2** literary always angry or easily annoyed

dystopia /dɪsˈtəʊ.pi.ə/ US /-ˈtoʊ-/ **noun** [U] (the idea of) a society in which people do not work well with each other and are not happy • **dystopian** /-ən/ **adj** *dystopian movies*

D

E

E

E, e /iː/ noun; adj

▸noun (plural **Es**, **E's** or **es**) LETTER ▷ **1** [C or U] the fifth letter of the English alphabet MUSIC ▷ **2** [C or U] a note in Western music: *The piece is in (**the key of**) E.* ◦ *The bottom string on a guitar is an E.* MARK ▷ **3** [C or U] mainly UK a mark in an exam or for a piece of work that shows the work is considered to be very bad: *You might have to take the course again if you get many more Es.* **4** [C] US a mark in an examination or for a piece of work that shows the work is considered to be excellent EAST ▷ **5** [U] written abbreviation for **east** DRUG ▷ **6** [C or U] informal abbreviation for **ecstasy**

▸adj EAST ▷ written abbreviation for **east** or **eastern**

e- /iː/ prefix abbreviation for **electronic**: *e-ink* ◦ *e-commerce* ◦ *email*

each /iːtʃ/ pronoun, determiner **1** (A1) every thing, person, etc. in a group of two or more, considered separately: *When you run, each foot leaves the ground before the other comes down.* ◦ *There are five leaflets – please take one of each.* ◦ *Each **of** the companies supports a local charity.* ◦ *Each **and every one of** the flowers has its own colour and smell.* ◦ *We each (= every one of us) wanted the bedroom with the balcony, so we tossed a coin to decide.* ◦ *The bill comes to £79, so that's about £10 each.* **2 each to his/their own** (mainly US **to each their own**) used to say that everyone likes different things: *You actually like modern jazz, do you? Each to their own.* **3 each way** If you put an amount of money each way on a horse race, you will win money if the horse you have chosen comes first, second, or third.

ˌeach ˈother pronoun (also **ˌone aˈnother**) (A2) used to show that each person in a group of two or more people does something to the others: *They kept looking at each other and smiling.* ◦ *They're always wearing each other's clothes.* ◦ *Why are you always arguing **with** each other?* ◦ *They're so happy together – they were **made for** each other (= are perfectly matched).*

> **! Common mistake: each other**
>
> **Remember: each other** is not written as one word.
>
> Don't write 'eachother', write **each other**:
>
> ~~*It seemed as though they had known eachother for a long time.*~~

eager /ˈiː.gəʳ/ (US) /-gɚ/ adj (B2) wanting very much to do or have something, especially something interesting or enjoyable: *the children's eager faces* ◦ [+ to infinitive] *She sounded very eager **to** meet you.* ◦ *They crowded round the spokesperson, eager **for** any news.* • **eagerly** /-li/ adv (B2) *an eagerly **awaited** announcement* • **eagerness** /-nəs/ noun [U often + to infinitive] (B2) *In their eagerness **to** (= wanting so much to) find a solution, they have overlooked certain difficulties.*

ˌeager ˈbeaver noun [C] informal a person who is willing to work very hard

eagle /ˈiː.gl/ noun [C] (B2) a large strong bird with a curved beak which eats meat and can see very well

eagle

ˌeagle ˈeye noun [C usually singular] If someone has an eagle eye, they notice everything, even very small details: *We sat down and started the exam under the eagle eye of the teacher.* • **ˌeagle-ˈeyed** adj *My eagle-eyed mother noticed that some cakes had gone missing.*

> **+ Other ways of saying eager**
>
> **Avid** can be used about someone who is extremely eager or interested:
>
> *He took an **avid** interest in the project.*
>
> *an **avid** football fan*
>
> If someone is eager to be involved in something, you could describe that person as **enthusiastic**:
>
> *He was very **enthusiastic** about the idea of moving to Spain.*
>
> The phrases **be dying to** *do something* or **be dying for** *something* mean 'to be extremely eager to do or have something':
>
> *I'm **dying to** hear your news.*
>
> *I'm **dying for** a glass of water.*
>
> Someone who is **raring** to do something is very eager to start something:
>
> *I've bought all the paint and I'm **raring** to get started on the decorating.*
>
> Someone who accepts something in a very eager way can be said to **jump at** it:
>
> *She **jumped at** the chance of a trip to Paris.*

EAP /ˌiː.eɪˈpiː/ noun [U] abbreviation for English for Academic Purposes: the teaching of English to speakers of other languages who need English to study at a college or university

ˌear, nose, and ˈthroat noun [U] (abbreviation **ENT**) a department in a hospital that deals with diseases affecting the ear, nose, and throat

ear /ɪəʳ/ (US) /ɪr/ noun [C] BODY PART ▷ **1** (A1) either of the two organs, one on each side of the head, by which people or animals hear sounds, or the piece of skin and tissue outside the head connected to this organ: *The hearing in my left ear's not so good.* ◦ *She leaned over and whispered something in his ear.* → See also **aural** PLANT PART ▷ **2** the flower part of a plant like a grass, such as WHEAT, which later contains the grains that are used as food: *an ear of corn*

IDIOMS **be all ears** to be waiting eagerly to hear about something: *I'm all ears – tell us what they had to say.* • **be out on your ear** informal to be forced to leave a job or place, especially because you have done something wrong • **be up to your ears in sth** to be very busy, or to have more of something than you can manage: *I'm up to my ears in work.* ◦ *She's up to her ears in debt.* • **close your ears** to stop listening: *I tried to close my ears **to** the sounds coming from next door.* • **ears are flapping** informal If you say that someone's ears are flapping, you mean that they are trying to hear what you are saying, although they are not part of your conversation. • **your ears must be burning** informal something that you say to someone who is being talked about: *All this talk about Emma – her ears must be burning!* • **go in one ear and out the other** informal If you say that something you hear goes in one ear and out the other, you mean you quickly forget it: *If I have to listen to something I don't understand, it just goes in one ear and out the other.* • **grin/smile from ear to ear** to look extremely happy: *'We've had a fantastic response,' he said, grinning from ear to ear.* • **have an ear for sth** C1 If someone has an ear for music or languages, they are good at hearing, repeating or understanding these sounds: *She's never had much of an ear for languages.* • **have the ear of sb** If someone has the ear of an important person, their ideas are listened to and considered important by that person. • **have/keep your ear to the ground** to pay attention to everything that is happening around you and to what people are saying

earache /ˈɪə.reɪk/ US /ˈɪr.eɪk/ **noun** [C or U] B1 a pain in the inside part of your ear

earbashing /ˈɪəˌbæʃ.ɪn/ US /ˈɪr-/ **noun** [S] UK informal angry words spoken to someone who has done something wrong: *I got an earbashing from Sam for being late.*

earbuds /ˈɪə.bʌdz/ US /ˈɪr-/ **noun** [plural] very small HEADPHONES that you wear in your ears

ˈ**ear drops** **noun** [plural] liquid medicine put into the ears, usually to cure an ear infection

eardrum /ˈɪə.drʌm/ US /ˈɪr-/ **noun** [C] a thin piece of skin inside the ear that moves backwards and forwards very quickly when sound waves reach it, allowing you to hear sounds

-eared /-ɪəd/ US /-ɪrd/ **suffix** with ears of a particular type: *a long-eared rabbit*

ˈ**ear flap** **noun** [C] one of the two pieces of material or fur on some hats that can be pulled down to cover the ears

earful /ˈɪə.fʊl/ US /ˈɪr-/ **noun** informal **give sb an earful** to angrily complain to someone

earl /ɜːl/ US /ɝːl/ **noun** [C] (the title of) a British man of high social rank, between a MARQUIS and a VISCOUNT

earldom /ɜːl.dəm/ US /ɝːl-/ **noun** [C] the rank or lands of an earl or COUNTESS

ˌ**Earl** ˈ**Grey** **noun** [U] a type of tea flavoured with BERGAMOT

earlobe /ˈɪə.ləʊb/ US /ˈɪr.loʊb/ **noun** [C] (also **lobe**) the soft round part at the bottom of the ear

early /ˈɜː.li/ US /ˈɝː-/ **adj, adv** (**earlier, earliest**) **1** A1 near the beginning of a period of time, or before the usual, expected, or planned time: *If you finish early you can go home.* ◦ *If you arrived earlier, you'd have more time.* ◦ *I like being a little early for interviews.* ◦ *They scored two goals early* (**on**) **in** *the game.* ◦ *I hate having to get up early* (**in** *the morning*). ◦ *I'm going to have an early* **night** (= *go to sleep before my usual time*). ◦ *She was a poet living* **in** *the early 15th century.* ◦ *He learned to read at the early* **age** *of three.* ◦ **It's** *rather early* **to** *be sowing carrot seeds, isn't it?* ◦ *Mercedes were pioneers during the early* **days/years** *of car manufacture.* ◦ *My earliest (= first) memory is of being shown around our new house.* ◦ *These are some of my early (= first) attempts at sculpture.* ◦ *Here's a dish I prepared earlier (= I made a short time ago).* → Compare **late 2 at the earliest** C2 used after a date or time to show that something will not happen before then: *I'm very busy, so I won't be with you till four o'clock at the earliest.*

IDIOMS **drive/send sb to an early grave** to cause someone to die young: *Sometimes I think these children are going to drive me to an early grave!* • **the early bird catches the worm** saying said to advise someone that they will get an advantage if they do something immediately or before anyone else does it • **early to bed and early to rise (makes a man healthy, wealthy, and wise)** saying said to emphasize that someone who gets enough sleep and starts work early in the day will have a successful life • **it's early days** UK said when you think it is too soon to make a judgment about the likely result of something because a lot might still happen or change: *Our progress has been fairly slow so far, but it's early days.*

ˌ**early** ˈ**bird** **noun** [C] humorous a person who gets up or arrives early

ˌ**early** ˈ**childhood** ˌ**education** **noun** [U] (abbreviation **ECE**) US the study of the education of children from two to seven years of age

ˌ**early** ˈ**music** **noun** [U] Western music of the MIDDLE AGES or the RENAISSANCE, written before about 1650

early ˈ**warning** ˌ**system** **noun** [C] a military system of RADAR stations intended to give a warning as soon as enemy aircraft or bombs come near

earmark /ˈɪə.mɑːk/ US /ˈɪr.mɑːrk/ **verb** [T often passive] to keep or intend something for a particular purpose: *Five billion dollars of this year's budget is already earmarked* **for** *hospital improvements.*

earmuffs /ˈɪə.mʌfs/ US /ˈɪr-/ **noun** [plural] a pair of small pieces of material like fur worn over the ears with a strap that goes over the head to keep them on

earn /ɜːn/ US /ɝːn/ **verb** [I or T] **1** A2 to receive money as payment for work that you do: *I earn $80,000 a year.* ◦ *How much do you earn, if you don't mind me asking?* ◦ *You can't expect to earn* **a living** *(= be paid enough money to live on) from your painting.* ◦ [+ two objects] *Coffee exports earn (= give) Brazil many millions of pounds a year./Brazil earns many millions of pounds a year* **from** *coffee exports.* **2** C2 to get something that you deserve: *It's been a tough six months and I feel I've earned a few weeks off.* → See also **well earned**

earner /ˈɜː.nəʳ/ US /ˈɝː.nɚ/ **noun** [C] someone or something that earns money: *In most of these cases, the woman is the sole earner in the family.* ◦ informal *That hamburger stand is* **a nice little** *earner (= makes a lot of money).*

earnest /ˈɜː.nɪst/ US /ˈɝː-/ **adj** **1** serious or determined, especially too serious and unable to find your own actions funny: *He was a very earnest young man.* **2 in deadly earnest** completely serious: *These fanatics are in deadly earnest when they say they want to destroy all forms of government.* **3 in earnest** When something begins in earnest, it has already started but is now being done in a serious and complete way: *The election campaign has begun in earnest.* **4 be in earnest** to be speaking honestly: *I thought he was joking – I didn't realize he was in earnest.* • **earnestly** /-li/ **adv** • **earnestness** /ˈɜː.nɪst.nəs/ US /ˈɝː-/ **noun** [U]

earnings /ˈɜː.nɪŋz/ US /ˈɝː-/ **noun** [plural] **1** B2 the amount of money that someone is paid for the work they do: *Average earnings for skilled workers are rising.* **2** a company's profits in a particular period: *Sun Microsystems* **reported** *earnings that were slightly better than the market had been expecting.*

earphones /ˈiə.fəʊnz/ US /ˈɪr.foʊnz/ **noun** [plural] a piece of electronic equipment that you put over or in your ears so that you can listen privately to radio, recorded music, etc.: *a pair/set of earphones*

earpiece /ˈɪə.piːs/ US /ˈɪr-/ **noun** [C] the part of a phone in two parts that you hold near to your ear

ˈ**ear-piercing** **adj** **ear-splitting**

earplug /ˈɪə.plʌg/ US /ˈɪr-/ **noun** [C usually plural] a small piece of soft material, such as WAX, cotton, or plastic, that you put into your ear to keep out noise or water

earring /ˈɪə.rɪŋ/ US /ˈɪr.ɪŋ/ **noun** [C] A2 a piece of jewellery, usually one of a pair, worn in a hole in the ear or fixed to the ear by a CLIP: *gold earrings* ◦ *a pair* of **dangly** earrings ◦ He was **wearing** an earring in his left ear.

earshot /ˈɪə.ʃɒt/ (US) /ˈɪr.ʃɑːt/ **noun** [U] the range of distance within which it is possible to be heard or to hear what someone is saying: *I don't think you should say anything while the boss is still* ***in/within*** *earshot.* ◦ *Wait till she's* ***out of*** *earshot before you say anything.*

ˈear-ˌsplitting adj (also **ˈear-ˌpiercing**) describes a sound that is so loud or high that it hurts your ears: *an ear-splitting explosion*

E

earth /ɜːθ/ (US) /ɜːθ/ **noun; verb**

▸**noun PLANET** ▷ **1** B1 [S or U] (also **Earth**) the planet third in order of distance from the Sun, between VENUS and MARS; the world on which we live: *The Earth takes approximately 365¼ days to go round the Sun.* ◦ *The Circus has been described as the greatest show* ***on*** *earth (= in the world).* **SUBSTANCE** ▷ **2** B2 [U] the usually brown, heavy, loose substance of which a large part of the surface of the ground is made, and in which plants can grow; the land surface of the Earth rather than the sky or sea **WIRE** ▷ **3** [C usually singular] UK (US **ground**) a wire that makes a connection between a piece of electrical equipment and the ground, so the user is protected from feeling an electric shock if the equipment develops a fault **HOLE** ▷ **4** [C] a hole in the ground where an animal such as a FOX lives

IDIOMS **come back down to earth** (also **bring sb back down to earth**) to start dealing with life and problems again after you have had a very exciting time, or to make someone do this: *The realization of how little work I'd done for the exams brought me abruptly back down to Earth.* • **cost, charge, etc. the earth** to cost, charge, etc. a lot of money: *They charge the earth just for a cup of coffee.* • **the earth moved** informal If someone says the earth moved, they are joking about how good a sexual experience was. • **how, what, why, etc. on earth...** informal C1 used when you are extremely surprised, confused or angry about something: *How on earth did this happen?* ◦ *Why on earth didn't you tell me before?* • **like nothing (else) on earth** very strange, unusual or unpleasant: *With his make-up and strange clothes, he looked like nothing on earth.*

▸**verb** [T usually passive] UK (US **ground**) to put an earth (= wire) between a piece of electrical equipment and the ground: *You could get a nasty shock from that water heater if it isn't earthed properly.*

earthbound /ˈɜːθ.baʊnd/ (US) /ˈɜːθ-/ **adj 1** unable to leave the surface of the Earth: *The space shuttle remained earthbound because of a technical fault.* **2** not exciting or showing much imagination: *an uninspired and earthbound performance*

ˈearth ˌcolour noun [C] an **earth tone**

earthen /ˈɜː.θᵊn/ (US) /ˈɜː-/ **adj** made of earth or of baked clay: *an earthen casserole dish*

earthenware /ˈɜː.θᵊn.weəʳ/ (US) /ˈɜːr.θᵊn.wer/ **adj; noun**

▸**adj** made of quite rough clay, often shaped with the hands: *earthenware mugs/bowls*

▸**noun** [U] plates, bowls, cups, etc. that are made of rough clay

earthling /ˈɜːθ.lɪŋ/ (US) /ˈɜːθ-/ **noun** [C] in stories, a human being, especially when talked to or talked about by a creature from another planet

earthly /ˈɜːθ.li/ (US) /ˈɜːθ-/ **adj 1** literary happening in or related to this world and this physical life, not in heaven or relating to a spiritual life: *his earthly existence* ◦ *earthly powers* **2** used in questions or negatives to mean possible: *What earthly* ***reason*** *can she have for being so horrible to you?*

ˈearth ˌmother noun [C] informal a woman who seems full of emotional and spiritual understanding, and seems suited to having and loving children

earthquake /ˈɜːθ.kweɪk/ (US) /ˈɜːθ-/ **noun** [C] B2 a sudden violent movement of the earth's surface, sometimes causing great damage

ˈearth ˌscience noun [C or U] the scientific study of the structure, age, etc. of the Earth

ˈearth-ˌshattering adj (also **ˈearth-ˌshaking**) extremely important or very surprising: *an earth-shattering discovery*

ˈearth ˌtone noun [C usually plural] (also **ˈearth ˌcolour**) a rich dark colour which contains some brown

earthwards /ˈɜːθ.wədz/ (US) /ˈɜːθ.wədz/ **adv** (also **earthward** /-wəd/ (US) /-wəd/) towards the Earth, from the air or from space • **earthward adj**

earthwork /ˈɜːθ.wɜːk/ (US) /ˈɜːθ.wɜːrk/ **noun** [C usually plural] a bank of earth made, especially in the past, for defence against enemy attack

earthworm /ˈɜːθ.wɜːm/ (US) /ˈɜːθ.wɜːrm/ **noun** [C] a common type of WORM, which moves through the earth

earthy /ˈɜː.θi/ (US) /ˈɜː-/ **adj REFERRING TO SEX** ▷ **1** referring to sex and the human body in a direct way: *She has an earthy sense of humour.* **SUBSTANCE** ▷ **2** like or relating to earth: *an earthy smell* • **earthiness** /-nəs/ **noun** [U] *I like the earthiness of her writing.*

earwig /ˈɪə.wɪɡ/ (US) /ˈɪr-/ **noun** [C] a small insect with two PINCERS (= curved pointed parts) at the back end of its body

earworm /ˈɪə.wɜːm/ (US) /ˈɪr.wɜːm/ **noun** [C] (also **ˈsticky ˌtune**) a song that you keep hearing in your head

ease /iːz/ **verb; noun**

▸**verb MAKE LESS** ▷ **1** [I or T] to make or become less severe, difficult, unpleasant, painful, etc.: *To ease the* ***problem*** *of overcrowding, new prisons will be built.* ◦ *These pills should ease the* ***pain.*** ◦ *After the arrival of the United Nations soldiers, tension in the area began to ease.* **MOVE** ▷ **2** [T + adv/prep] to move or to make something move slowly and carefully in a particular direction or into a particular position: *She eased the key* ***into*** *the lock, anxious not to wake anyone.* ◦ *I eased myself out of the chair.*

IDIOM **ease sb's mind** to stop you from worrying: *If it will ease your mind, I'll have a word with Charlotte for you.*

PHRASAL VERBS **ease up/off STOP** ▷ **1** to gradually stop or become less: *At last the rain began to ease off.* **WORK LESS** ▷ **2** to start to work less or do things with less energy: *As he got older, he started to ease up a little.* **TREAT LESS SEVERELY** ▷ **3** to start to treat someone less severely: *I wish his supervisor would ease up* ***on*** *him a bit.* • **ease sb out** to make someone leave a job or powerful position: *The head teacher was eased out* ***of*** *his job after teachers and parents accused him of being autocratic.*

▸**noun** [U] **1** B2 the state of experiencing no difficulty, effort, pain, etc.: *She won the 400 metre race* ***with*** *ease.* ◦ *The doors are extra-wide* ***for*** *ease* ***of*** *access (= so that people can get in without difficulty).* **2 at (your) ease** B2 relaxed: *He felt completely at ease.* ◦ *She soon* ***put/set*** *me at ease (= made me relaxed).* **3 at ease** (also **standing at ease**) If someone, especially a soldier, is at ease, they are standing with their feet apart and their hands behind their back.

easel /ˈiː.zəl/ noun [C] a wooden frame, usually with legs, that holds a picture, especially one which an artist is painting or drawing

easel

easily /ˈiː.zɪ.li/ adv **NOT DIFFICULT** ▷ **1** A2 with no difficulty or effort: *I can easily be home early tonight, if you want.* ◦ *Ever since the illness I get tired very easily (= more quickly than usual).* **CERTAINLY** ▷ **2** C2 without doubt: *For me, Venice is easily the most beautiful city in Europe.* **LIKELY** ▷ **3** C1 very likely to happen or be true: *Prices could easily rise further.*

east /iːst/ noun; adj; adv

▸noun [U] (also **East**) (written abbrevia-tion **E**) **1** A2 the direction from which the sun rises in the morning, opposite to the west, or the part of an area or country that is in this direction: *The points of the compass are north, south, east, and west.* ◦ *Which way is east?* ◦ *Most of the country, except the east, is rural.* ◦ *Her home is **in** the east **of** France.* ◦ *According to the map, the village lies about ten kilometres **to** the east **of** here.* **2 the East a** B2 Asia, especially its eastern and southern parts: *She spent her childhood in the East – mostly in China.* **b** those countries in Europe that had COMMUNIST governments before the 1990s: *The collapse of Communism changed East-West relations for ever.*

IDIOM **back east** US to or in the east of the US: *Helen lived in Oregon for two years before moving back east.*

▸adj (also **East**) (written abbreviation **E**) **1** A2 in or forming the east part of something: *Cambridge is in East Anglia.* ◦ *The east wall of the mosque is covered with a beautiful mosaic.* **2 east wind** a wind coming from the east

▸adv (also **East**) (written abbreviation **E**) A2 towards the east: *We'll drive east for a few more miles, then turn south.* ◦ *They were the first people to travel east **of** the mountains (= into the area beyond and to the east of the mountains).* ◦ *We walked **due** (= directly) east for two kilometres.* ◦ *The garden **faces** east, so we'll get the morning sun.*

eastbound /ˈiːst.baʊnd/ adj, adv going or leading towards the east: *an eastbound train* ◦ *A flight eastbound causes more severe jetlag than flying west.*

the ˌEast ˈCoast noun in the US, the part of the country near the Atlantic Ocean, including cities such as New York, Boston, and Philadelphia

the ˌEast ˈEnd noun an area in the east of London

East Ender /iːstˈen.dəʳ/ US /-dɚ/ noun [C] someone who lives in the East End of London

Easter /ˈiː.stəʳ/ US /-stɚ/ noun [C or U] a Christian religious holiday to celebrate Jesus Christ's return to life after he was killed: *I get two weeks off school **at** Easter.*

ˌEaster ˈDay noun [C or U] **Easter Sunday**

ˈEaster ˌegg noun [C] chocolate in the shape of an egg, given as a present at Easter

easterly /ˈiː.stəl.i/ US /-stɚ.li/ adj; noun

▸adj **1** in or towards the east, or blowing from the east: *They were travelling in an easterly direction.* ◦ *The town is in the most easterly part of the country.* **2 easterly wind** a wind that blows from from the east

▸noun [C] a wind that blows from the east

eastern (also **Eastern**) /ˈiː.stən/ US /-stɚn/ adj (written abbreviation **E**) B1 in or from the east part of an area: *The eastern part of the country is very mountainous.* ◦ *Until about 1991, the Eastern **bloc** was the Soviet Union and the communist countries of Eastern Europe.* ◦ *Buddhism and other Eastern (= Asian) religions fascinate me.*

easterner (also **Easterner**) /ˈiː.stən.əʳ/ US /-ɚ/ noun [C] **1** a person who comes from a country in Asia: *He said that Americans need to understand the East, and Easterners need to understand the West.* **2** a person who comes from the east of a country, especially the US: *It's a popular ski resort with easterners.*

easternmost /ˈiː.stənˌməʊst/ US /-stɚnˌmoʊst/ adj furthest towards the east of an area: *Lowestoft is the easternmost town in Great Britain.*

ˌEastern ˈStandard ˌTime noun [U] the time on the eastern coast of the US and Canada

ˌEaster ˈSunday noun [C or U] (also **ˌEaster ˈDay**) the day on which Easter is celebrated

eastward /ˈiːst.wəd/ US /-wɚd/ adv; adj

▸adv (also **eastwards**) towards the east: *They marched eastward towards the capital.* ◦ *The storm is moving slowly eastwards.*

▸adj towards the east: *He was going in an eastward **direction**.*

easy /ˈiː.zi/ adj **NOT DIFFICULT** ▷ **1** A1 needing little effort: *an easy exam* ◦ *Would a ten o'clock appointment be easier **for** you?* ◦ [+ to infinitive] ***It's** easy **to** see why he's so popular.* ◦ *She's very easy **to** talk to.* ◦ *The easiest thing **to** do would be for us to take the train home.* ◦ ***It** isn't easy be**ing** a parent.* ◦ *Getting into the film business is **no** easy **matter**.* ◦ *I don't trust that easy (= relaxed) charm of his.* ◦ slang *My car can do 250 kph, easy.* → Opposite **difficult**

> **!** Common mistake: **easy or easily?**
>
> **Warning:** do not confuse the adjective **easy** with the adverb **easily**:
>
> ~~*You can easy find a job if you speak English.*~~
>
> *You can easily find a job if you speak English.*

COMFORTABLE ▷ **2** comfortable or calm; free from worry, pain, etc.: *They both retired and went off to lead an easy life in the Bahamas.* ◦ *I don't feel easy **about** leaving him alone in the house all day.* ◦ *With the harvest finished, I was able to relax **with an** easy **mind/conscience**.* • **easiness** /-nəs/ noun [U]

> **+** Other ways of saying **easy**
>
> If something is easy to do or understand, we often use the adjectives **simple** or **straightforward**:
>
> *The recipe is so **simple** – you just mix all the ingredients together.*
>
> *It seems like a fairly **straightforward** assignment.*
>
> If a machine or system is easy to use, we often describe it as **user-friendly**:
>
> *This latest version of the software is much more **user-friendly**.*
>
> In informal situations there are also some fixed expressions you can use to say that something is very easy to do, for example:
>
> *My last exam was **a piece of cake**.*
>
> *Once we reached the main road the trip was **plain sailing**.*
>
> In informal situations, you can use the word **cushy** if you think that someone's job or situation is too easy and you do not approve:
>
> *He has a very **cushy** job in an office.*

IDIOMS **an easy touch** informal someone who you can easily persuade or deceive into giving you something, usually money • **(as) easy as pie/ABC/anything/falling off a log** informal extremely easy • **easier said than done** informal C1 said when something seems like a good idea but it would be difficult to do: *'Why don't you just ask Simon to pay?' 'That's easier said than done.'* • **the easiest thing in the world** informal extremely easy: *Making bread is the easiest thing in the world.* • **easy come, easy go** informal said when something, especially money, is easily got and then soon spent or lost: *I lost £500 in a card game last night, but that's life – easy come, easy go.* • **easy does it!** informal used to tell someone to do something slowly and carefully • **be easy game/meat** UK (US **be an easy mark**) to be easily deceived: *Old ladies living alone are easy game **for** con-men.* • **easy on the eye/ear** pleasant to look at/listen to: *Her paintings are very easy on the eye.* • **go easy** informal **1** to not take or use too much of something: *Go easy **on/with** the cream – I haven't had any yet.* **2** to treat someone in a gentle way and not criticize them or punish them: *Go easy **on** the new students.* • **I'm easy** informal used to say that you do not mind which choice is made: *'Shall we go to the Indian restaurant, or would you prefer Chinese food?' 'I'm easy.'* • **on easy street** old-fashioned informal rich • **take it/things easy** B1 to relax and not use too much energy: *I wasn't feeling too good, so I thought I'd take it easy for a couple of days.*

ˌeasy ˈchair noun [C] a big soft comfortable chair with arms

ˌeasy-ˈgoing adj approving B1 relaxed and not easily upset or worried: *an easy-going attitude/manner* ◦ *a friendly, easy-going type of guy*

ˌeasy ˈlistening adj describes music that is not complicated, serious or difficult

easy ˈmoney noun [U] informal money that is easily and sometimes dishonestly earned

ˌeasy ˈoption noun [C] (UK also **ˈsoft ˌoption**) a decision or choice that is easy to make: *We'll have to make some tough decisions – there are no easy options.*

easy-peasy /ˌiː.ziˈpiː.zi/ adj UK informal or child's word very easy

eat /iːt/ verb [I or T] **(ate, eaten)** A1 to put or take food into the mouth, CHEW (= crush with the teeth) it, and swallow it: *Do you eat meat?* ◦ *When I've got a cold, I don't feel like eating.* ◦ *We usually eat (= have a meal) at about seven o'clock.*

IDIOMS **eaten up with/by sth** informal If someone is eaten up with/by a negative emotion, they are experiencing it very strongly: *He was so eaten up with guilt, he became ill.* • **eat sb alive** to criticize someone very angrily: *If we get our facts wrong we'll be eaten alive by the press.* • **eat sb for breakfast** informal to be able to very easily control or defeat someone: *He eats people like you for breakfast.* • **eat your heart out** humorous If someone says eat your heart out followed by the name of a famous person, they are joking that they are even better than that person: *I'm singing in the village production of Tosca next month – eat your heart out Pavarotti!* • **eat humble pie** (US also **eat crow**) to admit that you were wrong: *After boasting that his company could outperform the industry's best, he's been forced to eat humble pie.* • **eat like a horse** informal to always eat a lot of food: *She's so thin yet she eats like a horse.* • **eat sb out of house and home** humorous to eat a lot of the food someone has in their house • **eat your words** to admit that something you said before was wrong: *Sam said it would never sell, but when he sees these sales figures he'll have to eat his words.* • **have sb eating out of your hand** informal to easily make someone do or think what you want: *Within two minutes of walking into the classroom, she had the kids eating out of her hand.* • **I'll eat my hat** old-fashioned used to say that you are sure something will not happen: *If she actually marries him I'll eat my hat.* • **(I'm so hungry), I could eat a horse** humorous used to say that you are extremely hungry • **what's eating sb?** informal used to ask why someone seems angry or upset: *Jack's in a strange mood – I wonder what's eating him?*

Other ways of saying eat

Have is very often used instead of 'eat':

*I'll just **have** one more piece of chocolate cake.*

A more formal alternative is the verb **consume**:

*He **consumes** vast quantities of bread with every meal.*

If someone eats something quickly because that person is very hungry, the verb **devour** is sometimes used:

*The children **devoured** a whole box of cookies.*

Bolt down, **gobble up**, and **wolf down** are also used to describe the action of eating something very quickly:

*He **gobbled up** his food before anyone else had started.*

*I gave her a plate of pasta and she **wolfed** it **down**.*

The verb **scoff** (US **scarf**) can be used in informal situations when someone eats a lot of something very quickly:

*Who **scoffed** all the cake?*

The verb **snack** means 'to eat a little food between main meals':

*I've been **snacking** on potato chips all afternoon.*

To **eat out** is to eat in a restaurant:

*I thought we could **eat out** tonight.*

The phrasal verb **pick at** is sometimes used when someone eats only a little of something:

*He didn't feel hungry, and sat at the table **picking at** his food.*

The informal phrases **stuff yourself** and **stuff your face** mean 'to eat a lot':

*He'd been **stuffing himself** with snacks all afternoon and didn't want any dinner.*

*I've been **stuffing my face** all morning.*

PHRASAL VERBS **eat away at sth** to gradually damage or destroy something • **eat away at sb** If a bad memory or feeling eats away at someone, it makes them feel more and more unhappy. • **eat in** to have a meal at home rather than in a restaurant • **eat into sth** to use or take away a large part of something valuable, such as money or time: *The high cost of living in London is eating into my savings.* • **eat out** B1 to eat in a restaurant: *When I lived in Spain, I used to eat out all the time.* • **eat (sth) up** B2 to eat all the food that you have been given: *Be a good boy and eat up your vegetables.* • **eat up sth** to use or take away a large part of something valuable: *A big old car like that eats up petrol.*

eatable /ˈiː.tə.bl̩/ US /-t̬ə-/ adj describes food that is good enough to eat, but not excellent → Compare **edible**

eater /ˈiː.təʳ/ US /-t̬ɚ/ noun **a big/good/small eater** someone who always eats a lot/very little

eatery /ˈiː.tᵊr.i/ US /-t̬ɚ.ri/ noun [C] informal a

restaurant: *We met in a little eatery just off the main road.*

ˈeating ˌapple noun [C] an apple that can be eaten uncooked, rather than cooked → Compare **cooking apple**

ˈeating disˌorder noun [C] a mental illness in which people eat far too little or far too much food and are unhappy with their bodies

eats /iːts/ noun [plural] informal a small amount of food: *Would you like some eats?*

eau de cologne /ˌəʊ.də.kəˈləʊn/ noun [C or U] (plural **eaux de cologne**) a pleasant-smelling liquid that you put on your body to make yourself smell fresh

eaves /iːvz/ noun [plural] the edge of a roof that sticks out over the top of a wall

eavesdrop /ˈiːvz.drɒp/ (US) /-drɑːp/ verb [I] (-pp-) to listen to someone's private conversation without them knowing: *He was eavesdropping **on** our conversation.* • **eavesdropper** /-drɒp.əʳ/ (US) /-drɑː.pɚ/ noun [C]

ˈe-bank (also **ebank**) noun [C] a bank that operates over the internet

ˈe-ˌbanking (also **ebanking**) noun [U] the activity of managing a bank account or operating as a bank over the internet

ebb /eb/ verb; noun

▸verb [I] **WATER** ▷ **1** When the sea or TIDE ebbs, it moves away from the coast and falls to a lower level. **FEELING** ▷ **2** If a physical or emotional feeling ebbs, it becomes less strong or disappears: *He could feel his **strength** ebbing (**away**).*

▸noun **the ebb** the TIDE when it is moving away from the coast: *We'll sail **on** the ebb.*

IDIOMS **at a low ebb** in a bad or weak state: *Consumer confidence is currently at a low ebb.* • **ebb and flow** the way in which the level of something regularly becomes higher or lower in a situation: *You have to accept the ebb and flow **of** love in a relationship.*

ˈebb ˌtide noun [C usually singular] the regular movement of the sea away from the coast

Ebola /ɪˈbəʊ.lə/ (US) /-boʊ-/ noun [U] an infectious and very serious disease with fever and BLEEDING inside the body: *the Ebola virus*

Ebonics /ɪˈbɒn.ɪks/ (US) /ɪˈbɑː.nɪks/ noun [U] a type of English spoken by some African Americans

ebony /ˈeb.ən.i/ noun; adj

▸noun [U] **WOOD** ▷ a very hard dark wood of a tropical tree, used especially for making furniture

▸adj literary **BLACK** ▷ black: *her ebony hair*

ˈe-book noun [C] an **electronic book**

EBT /ˌiː.biːˈtiː/ noun [U] abbreviation for electronic benefit transfer: a system in the US in which the government gives money to poor people using a DEBIT CARD that they can use to buy food and other things

ebullient /ɪbˈʊl.i.ənt/ adj very energetic, positive, and happy: *He wasn't his usual ebullient self.* • **ebullience** /-əns/ noun [U] • **ebulliently** /-li/ adv

ˈe-ˌbusiness noun [C or U] the business of buying and selling goods and services on the internet, or a particular company which does this

the EC /ˌiːˈsiː/ noun abbreviation for **the European Community**

ˈe-cash noun [U] money from a special bank account that is used to buy goods and services over the internet by sending information from your computer

eccentric /ekˈsen.trɪk/ adj; noun

▸adj **STRANGE** ▷ **1** strange or unusual, sometimes in a humorous way: *eccentric behaviour* ◦ *eccentric clothes* **NOT CIRCULAR** ▷ **2** specialized not perfectly circular • **eccentrically** /-trɪ.kəl.i/ adv

▸noun [C] someone who behaves in an eccentric way: *My mother's a bit of an eccentric.*

eccentricity /ˌek.senˈtrɪs.ɪ.ti/ (US) /-t̬i/ noun **1** [U] the state of being eccentric: *His eccentricity now extends to never washing or changing his clothes.* **2** [C] an eccentric action: *Her eccentricities get stranger by the day.*

ecclesiastic /ɪˌkliː.ziˈæs.tɪk/ noun [C] formal or old-fashioned a Christian priest or official

ecclesiastical /ɪˌkliː.ziˈæs.tɪk.əl/ adj (also **ecclesiastic**) formal belonging to or connected with the Christian religion

ECE /ˌiː.siːˈiː/ noun [U] US abbreviation for **early childhood education**

ECG /ˌiː.siːˈdʒiː/ noun [C] abbreviation for **electrocardiogram** or **electrocardiograph**

echelon /ˈeʃ.ə.lɒn/ (US) /-lɑːn/ noun [C] **1** a particular level or group of people within an organization such as an army or company: *These salary increases will affect only the **highest** echelons of local government.* **2** specialized a special arrangement of soldiers, aircraft or ships

echidna /ɪˈkɪd.nə/ noun [C] a small Australian mammal that is covered with sharp SPINES, has a long nose, and eats ANTS and TERMITES

echinacea /ˌek.ɪˈneɪ.ʃə/ noun [U] a plant that is used as a medicine, especially to help your body fight illness

echinoderm /ɪˈkaɪ.nəʊ.dɜːm/ (US) /-dɝːm/ noun [C] specialized a type of sea creature with raised areas or sharp points on its skin and a body made of five equal parts arranged around the centre: *Echinoderms like the starfish live on the sea floor.*

echo /ˈek.əʊ/ (US) /-oʊ/ noun; verb

▸noun [C] (plural **echoes**) **SOUND** ▷ **1** (C2) a sound that is heard after it has been reflected off a surface such as a wall or a CLIFF: *The echoes of his scream sounded in the cave for several seconds.* ◦ *Thick carpet would reduce the echo in this hallway.* **SIMILAR DETAIL** ▷ **2** a detail that is similar to and makes you remember something else: *There are echoes **of** Mozart in her first piano compositions.*

▸verb **SOUND** ▷ **1** (C2) [I] If a sound echoes or a place echoes with a sound, you hear the sound again because you are in a large, empty space: *The sound of footsteps echoed **round** the hall.* ◦ *Suddenly, the building echoed **with** the sound of gunfire.* **SIMILAR DETAILS** ▷ **2** (C2) [T] to repeat details that are similar to, and make you think of, something else: *The design of the church echoes that of St. Paul's Cathedral.* ◦ *I've heard the prime minister's view echoed throughout the party.*

IDIOM **echo down/through the ages** to continue to have a particular effect for a long time: *The ideas of Plato have echoed through the ages.*

ˈecho ˌsounder noun [C] a piece of equipment, especially on a ship, which uses SOUND WAVES to discover water depth or the position of an object in the water

éclair /ɪˈkleəʳ/ (US) /-kler/ noun [C] a small thin cake made of pastry, with cream inside and usually chocolate on top

éclat /eɪˈklɑː/ noun [U] literary a strong and stylish effect: *She broke onto the music scene with great éclat.*

eclectic /ɪˈklek.tɪk/ adj formal Methods, beliefs, ideas, etc. that are eclectic combine whatever seem the best or most useful things from many different areas or systems, rather than following a single system: *an eclectic **style**/approach* ◦ *an eclectic **taste** in literature* • **eclectically** /-tɪ.kəl.i/ adv • **eclecticism** /-tɪ.sɪ.zəm/ noun [U]

eclipse /ɪˈklɪps/ noun; verb

▸noun **SUN** ▷ **1** [C] the situation when the sun disappears from view, either completely or partly, while the moon is moving between it and the Earth, or when the moon becomes darker while the SHADOW of the Earth moves over it: *a solar/lunar eclipse* ◦ *On Wednesday there will be a **total/partial** eclipse **of** the sun.* **IMPORTANCE** ▷ **2** [S or U] literary when something becomes less important: *The eclipse **of** the ruling political party was inevitable.* ◦ *His remarkable contribution to literature has been too long **in** eclipse.*

▸verb **SUN** ▷ **1** [T] to make an eclipse of the moon or sun: *The moon will be totally eclipsed at 12.10 p.m.* **IMPORTANCE** ▷ **2** [T often passive] to make another person or thing seem much less important, good or famous: *The economy has eclipsed all other issues during this election campaign.*

eco- /iː.kəʊ-/ Ⓤⓢ /-koʊ-/ prefix connected with the environment

ˈeco-ˌaudit noun [C] an examination of how the behaviour of a business or group of people affects the environment: *After our eco-audit, we switched to low-energy light bulbs.* • **ˈeco-ˌauditor** noun [C]

ˈeco-ˌfootprint noun [C] an **ecological footprint**

ˈeco-ˌfriendly adj UK describes a product that has been designed to do the least possible damage to the environment: *eco-friendly washing powder*

ˈeco-ˌlabel noun [C] an official symbol which shows that a product has been designed to do less harm to the environment than similar products • **ˈeco-ˌlabelling** UK (US **ˈeco-ˌlabeling**) noun [U]

E. coli /ˌiːˈkəʊ.laɪ/ Ⓤⓢ /ˌiːˈkoʊ.laɪ/ noun [U] abbreviation for Escherichia coli: a BACTERIUM (= small organism) that can exist in food that has not been cooked enough and can cause serious illness or death

ecological /ˌiː.kəˈlɒdʒ.ɪ.kəl/ Ⓤⓢ /-ˈlɑː.dʒɪ-/ adj **B2** relating to ecology or the environment: *The destruction of the rain forests is an ecological disaster.* • **ecologically** /-ɪ.kəl.i/ adv **B2** *It's an ecologically **friendly/sound** (= not harmful) means of transport.*

ecoˌlogical ˈfootprint noun [C] (also **ˈeco-ˌfootprint**) the amount of the Earth's energy that someone or something uses: *I'm trying to reduce my ecological footprint by cycling more and driving less.*

ecologist /ɪˈkɒl.ə.dʒɪst/ Ⓤⓢ /-ˈkɑː.lə-/ noun [C] a person who studies the natural relationships between the air, land, water, animals, plants, etc.

ecology /ɪˈkɒl.ə.dʒi/ Ⓤⓢ /-ˈkɑː.lə-/ noun [U] **C1** the relationships between the air, land, water, animals, plants, etc., usually of a particular area, or the scientific study of this: *The oil spill caused terrible damage to the fragile ecology **of** the coast.* ◦ *She hopes to study ecology at college.*

e-ˈcommerce noun [U] the business of buying and selling goods and services on the internet

econometrics /ɪˌkɒn.əˈmet.rɪks/ Ⓤⓢ /-ˌkɑː.nə-/ noun [U] specialized the testing of the performance of economies and economic theories using mathematical methods • **econometric** /-rɪk/ adj

economic /iː.kəˈnɒm.ɪk/, /ek.ə-/ Ⓤⓢ /-ˈnɑː.mɪk/ adj **COUNTRY'S ECONOMY** ▷ **1** **B2** [before noun] relating to trade, industry, and money: *The government's economic **policies** have led us into the worst recession for years.* **MAKING A PROFIT** ▷ **2** making a profit, or likely to make a profit: *We had to close our London office – with the rent so high it just wasn't economic.*

economical /ˌiː.kəˈnɒm.ɪ.kəl/, /ek.ə-/ Ⓤⓢ /-ˈnɑː.mɪ-/ adj **B2** not using a lot of fuel, money, etc.: *There's increasing demand for cars which are more economical **on** fuel.* ◦ *What's the most economical way of heating this building?*

> **!** Common mistake: **economical or economic?**
>
> **Warning:** choose the right adjective!
>
> To refer to the economy of a country or region, don't say 'economical', say **economic**:
>
> ~~*Unemployment causes a lot of economical problems.*~~
>
> *Unemployment causes a lot of economic problems.*

IDIOM **economical with the truth** humorous avoiding stating the true facts about a situation, or lying about it

economically /ˌiː.kəˈnɒm.ɪ.kəl.i/, /ek.ə-/ Ⓤⓢ /-ˈnɑː.mɪ-/ adv **SAVING MONEY** ▷ **1** using little money, time, etc.: *As a student she lived very economically, rarely going out and buying very few clothes.* **COUNTRY'S ECONOMY** ▷ **2** in a way that relates to a country's trade, industry, and money: *Economically the country has been improving steadily these past ten years.*

ecoˈnomic ˌmigrant noun [C] a person who leaves their home country to live in another country with better work or living conditions

economics /ˌiː.kəˈnɒm.ɪks/, /ek.ə-/ Ⓤⓢ /-ˈnɑː.mɪks/ noun [U] **B1** the way in which trade, industry or money is organized, or the study of this: *Their ideas sound fine in principle but they haven't worked out the economics behind the policies.* ◦ *She's in her third year of economics at York University.*

economist /ɪˈkɒn.ə.mɪst/ Ⓤⓢ /-ˈkɑː.nə-/ noun [C] **B2** a person who studies or has a special knowledge of economics

economize (UK usually **economise**) /ɪˈkɒn.ə.maɪz/ Ⓤⓢ /-ˈkɑː.nə-/ verb [I] to try to save money by reducing the amount that you are spending: *You could economize **on** food by not eating in restaurants all the time.* ◦ *A lot of companies are trying to economize by not taking on new staff.*

economy /ɪˈkɒn.ə.mi/ Ⓤⓢ /-ˈkɑː.nə-/ noun **SYSTEM** ▷ **1** **B2** [C] the system of trade and industry by which the WEALTH of a country is made and used: *the **global** economy* ◦ *the German/US economy* ◦ *the **state of** the economy* ◦ *a **weak/strong** economy* ◦ *Tourism contributes millions of pounds to the country's economy.* **SAVING MONEY** ▷ **2** [C or U] the intentional saving of money or, less commonly, the saving of time, energy, words, etc.: *They've had to **make** economies since Ian lost his job.* ◦ *This can be done by machines with more speed and economy.* ◦ *She writes with such economy – I've never known a writer say so much in so few words.*

> Word partners for **economy** (**SYSTEM**)
>
> a *booming/strong/stable/weak* economy • the *global/local/national* economy • *control/improve/revive/run/strengthen/wreck* the economy • the economy *grows/improves/slows/recovers* • the *state* of the economy

> Word partners for **economy** (**SAVING MONEY**)
>
> *achieve/make* economies • a *false* economy • an economy *drive*

eˈconomy ˌclass noun [U], adv (using) the cheapest

and least comfortable type of seats on an aircraft: *They always **fly** economy class.* ◦ *economy-class seats*

eˈconomy-class ˌsyndrome noun [U] informal **deep vein thrombosis** (= a sticky mass of blood in the lungs or in the tubes that carry blood to the heart) that someone develops after travelling on a plane

eˈconomy ˌdrive noun [C usually singular] an attempt to save money by spending as little as possible: *I don't think we'll be going anywhere expensive – Guy's **on** an economy drive.*

eˈconomy ˌpack noun [C] a larger amount of goods that you buy for a lower price

eˈconomy-ˌsized adj describes an amount of goods that is larger than normal and can be bought for a lower price

ecosystem /ˈiː.kəʊˌsɪs.təm/ (US) /-koʊ-/ noun [C] all the living things in an area and the way they affect each other and the environment: *Pollution can have disastrous effects on the delicately balanced ecosystem.*

ecotourism /ˈiː.kəʊˌtʊə.rɪ.zᵊm/ (US) /ˈiː.koʊ.tʊ.rɪ.zᵊm/ noun [U] the business of organizing holidays to places that people do not usually visit in a way which helps local people and does not damage the environment

ˈeco-ˌwarrior noun [C] UK a person who argues against and tries to stop activities which damage the environment

ecstasy /ˈek.stə.si/ noun **EMOTION** ▷ **1** [C or U] a state of extreme happiness, especially when feeling pleasure: *She threw her head back as if **in** ecstasy.* ◦ *sexual ecstasy* **DRUG** ▷ **2** [U] (abbreviation **E**) a powerful drug which makes you feel very active and can cause you to HALLUCINATE (= see or hear things that do not exist)

IDIOM **be/go into ecstasies about/over sth** informal to be or become very excited about something: *She went into ecstasies about the food there.*

ecstatic /ɪkˈstæt.ɪk/ (US) /-ˈstæţ-/ adj extremely happy: *The new president was greeted by an ecstatic crowd.* • **ecstatically** /-ɪ.kᵊl.i/ adv

ECT /ˌiː.siːˈtiː/ noun [U] abbreviation for **electroconvulsive therapy**

ectopic pregnancy /ekˌtɒp.ɪkˈpreg.nən.si/ (US) /-ˌtɑː.pɪk-/ noun [C] the development of the EMBRYO outside the usual position within the WOMB, usually inside one of the FALLOPIAN TUBES

ectoplasm /ˈek.tə.plæz.ᵊm/ (US) /-toʊ-/ noun [U] **1** specialized the outer layer of particular types of cell **2** a substance that is believed to surround GHOSTS and other creatures that are connected with spiritual activities

ecumenical /ˌiː.kjʊˈmen.ɪ.kᵊl/, /ˌek.jʊ-/ adj formal encouraging the different Christian Churches to unite: *an ecumenical service* • **ecumenicism** /-ɪ.sɪ.zᵊm/ noun [U]

eczema /ˈek.sɪ.mə/ noun [U] a skin condition in which areas of the skin become red, rough, and sore and make you want to rub them

-ed /-t/, /-d/, /-ɪd/, /-əd/ suffix (also **-d**) used to form the past simple and past participle of regular verbs: *called* ◦ *asked* ◦ *looked* ◦ *started* ◦ *played* ◦ *returned*

Edam /ˈiː.dæm/ noun [C or U] a hard, yellow cheese from the Netherlands that is covered with red WAX

edamame /ˌed.əˈmɑː.meɪ/ noun [U] a Japanese dish consisting of SOYBEANS in their PODS that have been boiled in water with salt

eddy /ˈed.i/ verb [I] If water, wind, smoke, etc. eddies, it moves fast in a circle: *The water eddied around in a whirlpool.* • **eddy** noun [C] *The bend in the river had caused an eddy of fast swirling water.*

edema /ɪˈdiː.mə/ noun [U] specialized US for **oedema**

Eden /ˈiː.dᵊn/ noun [S] (also **the ˌGarden of ˈEden**) in the Bible, the garden where the first humans, Adam and Eve, lived in perfect happiness before they did not obey God and were ordered by him to leave

edge /edʒ/ noun; verb

▸noun **OUTER POINT** ▷ **1** (B1) [C] the outer or furthest point of something: *He'd piped fresh cream around the edge **of** the cake.* ◦ *They built the church on the edge of the village.* ◦ *A man was standing at the water's edge with a small boy.* ◦ *I caught (= hit) my leg on the edge of the table as I walked past.* **BLADE** ▷ **2** (B2) [C] the side of a blade which cuts, or any sharp part of an object which could cut: *Careful with that open tin – it's got a very sharp edge.* **ALMOST** ▷ **3** [C usually singular] the point just before something very different and noticeable happens: *The company is **on** the edge **of** collapse.* ◦ *The government had **brought** the country **to** the edge of a catastrophe.* **4 push/drive sb over the edge** informal If an unpleasant event pushes someone over the edge, it makes them start to behave in a crazy way: *She had been driven over the edge by the separation from her husband.* **ADVANTAGE** ▷ **5** (C2) [S] an advantage over other people: *In terms of experience, she definitely **had** the edge **over** the other people that we interviewed.* **ANGER/NERVOUSNESS** ▷ **6** [U] a small but noticeable amount of anger in someone's voice: *There's a definite edge **to/in** her voice when she talks to her husband.* **7 on edge** (C2) nervous and not relaxed: *Is something wrong? You seem a bit on edge this morning.*

IDIOM **take the edge off sth** to make something unpleasant have less of an effect on someone: *Have an apple – it'll take the edge off your hunger.* ◦ *His apology took the edge off her anger.*

▸verb [I or T, + adv/prep] to move slowly with gradual movements or in gradual stages, or to make someone or something move in this way: *A long line of traffic edged **its way** forward.* ◦ *Inflation has edged **up** to five percent over the last two years.* ◦ *Those who disagreed with the director's viewpoint were gradually edged **out** of (= forced to leave) the company.*

edged /edʒd/ adj having something around the edge: *He bought a white tablecloth edged **with** a pretty pattern (= with a pattern around the outside).*

-edged /-edʒd/ suffix having a particular type of edge: *a double-edged blade* ◦ *a lace-edged collar*

edgeways /ˈedʒ.weɪz/ adv UK (US **edgewise** /ˈedʒ.waɪz/) with the narrowest part going first: *We should be able to get the sofa through edgeways.*

edging /ˈedʒ.ɪŋ/ noun [C or U] something that is put around the outside of something, usually to decorate it: *a tablecloth with (a) dark edging*

edgy /ˈedʒ.i/ adj informal nervous or worried • **edgily** /-ɪ.li/ adv

edible /ˈed.ɪ.bl̩/ adj (C1) suitable or safe for eating: *Only the leaves of the plant are edible.* → Compare **eatable** → Opposite **inedible**

edict /ˈiː.dɪkt/ noun [C] formal an official order, especially one that is given in a forceful and unfair way: *Most shops are ignoring the government's edict against Sunday trading.*

edification /ˌed.ɪ.fɪˈkeɪ.ʃᵊn/ noun [U] formal the improvement of the mind and understanding, especially by learning: *I tend to watch the television for pleasure rather than edification.*

edifice /ˈed.ɪ.fɪs/ noun [C] formal **1** a large building, especially an impressive one: *The town hall is the only edifice surviving from the 15th century.* **2** a system that has been established for a long time: *It looks as if the whole **political** edifice of the country is about to collapse.*

edify /ˈed.ɪ.faɪ/ **verb** [T] formal to improve someone's mind

edifying /ˈed.ɪ.faɪ.ɪŋ/ **adj** humorous or formal improving your mind: *Being left in a bar all afternoon with a load of football supporters is not the most edifying of experiences.*

E

edit /ˈed.ɪt/ **verb** [T] **1** B2 to make changes to a text or film, deciding what will be removed and what will be kept in, in order to prepare it for being printed or shown: *Janet edited books for a variety of publishers.* ◦ *The film's 129 minutes were edited **down** from 150 hours of footage.* **2** to be in charge of the reports in a newspaper or magazine, etc.: *He edits a national newspaper.* • **editing** /-.ɪ.tɪŋ/ US /-.ɪ.t̬ɪŋ/ **noun** [U] *Filming the documentary took two months, but editing took another four.*

PHRASAL VERB **edit sth out** to remove something before it is broadcast or printed: *Most of the violent scenes were edited out for television.*

edition /ɪˈdɪʃ.ən/ **noun** [C] **1** B2 a particular form in which a book, magazine or newspaper is published: *the **paperback/hardback** edition of the dictionary* ◦ *The regional editions of the paper contain specific information for that area.* **2** a single broadcast of a series of radio or television programmes: *This morning's edition of 'Women's Hour' is at the earlier time of a quarter to ten.* **3** the total number of copies of a particular book, newspaper, etc. that are published at the same time: *She collects **first** editions of 19th-century authors.* **4** US one of a series of repeated events: *The 77th edition of the Indianapolis 500 was held before an estimated 450,000 fans.*

editor /ˈed.ɪ.təʳ/ US /-t̬ɚ/ **noun** [C] B2 a person who corrects or changes pieces of text or films before they are printed or shown, or a person who is in charge of a newspaper or magazine: *She's a senior editor in the reference department of a publishing company.* ◦ *Who is the current editor of the Times?*

editorial /ˌed.ɪˈtɔː.ri.əl/ US /-əˈtɔːr.i-/ **noun; adj**
▸**noun** [C] (UK also **leader**, **ˌleading ˈarticle**) an article in a newspaper which expresses the editor's opinion on a subject of particular interest at the present time
▸**adj** relating to editors or editing, or to the editor of a newspaper or magazine: *editorial **staff*** ◦ *Editorial decisions are generally made by senior editors.* ◦ *It's plain reporting of the facts – there's not much editorial content (= opinion).*

editorialize disapproving (UK usually **editorialise**) /ˌed.ɪˈtɔː.ri.ə.laɪz/ US /-əˈtɔːr.i-/ **verb** [I] to express a personal opinion, especially when you should be giving a report of the facts only

educate /ˈed.jʊ.keɪt/ **verb** [T] B2 to teach someone, especially using the formal system of school, college, or university: *The form says he was educated in Africa.* ◦ *How much does it cost to educate a child privately?* ◦ *The government say they are trying to do more to educate the public **about** the consequences of drug abuse.*

educated /ˈed.jʊ.keɪ.tɪd/ US /-t̬ɪd/ **adj** B2 having learned a lot at school or university and having a good level of knowledge: *She was probably the most **highly** educated prime minister of this century.*

ˌeducated ˈguess **noun** [C usually singular] C2 a guess that is made using judgment and a particular level of knowledge and is therefore more likely to be correct

education /ˌed.jʊˈkeɪ.ʃən/ **noun** [S or U] B1 the process of teaching or learning in a school or college, or the knowledge that you get from this: *As a child he **received** most of his education at home.* ◦ *It's a country which places great importance on education.* ◦ *She lectures in education (= the study of education) at the teacher training college.* ◦ *It's important for children to get a good education.*

> **Word partners for education**
> *get/have/receive* an education • a *good* education • be *in* education • an education *authority/service/system*

educational /ˌed.jʊˈkeɪ.ʃən.əl/ **adj** B2 providing education or relating to education: *Reducing the size of classes may improve educational standards.* ◦ *She seems to have spent all her life studying in educational **establishments**.* ◦ humorous *My father has never been to a rock concert before – it'll be an educational **experience** for him (= a new experience from which he can learn).* • **educationally** /-i/ **adv**

educationalist /ˌed.jʊˈkeɪ.ʃən.əl.ɪst/ **noun** [C] (also **educationist**) a person who has a special knowledge of the principles and methods of teaching

educative /ˈed.jʊ.kə.tɪv/ US /-keɪ.t̬ɪv/ **adj** providing education: *Very few activities at this age have no educative value at all.*

educator /ˈed.jʊ.keɪ.təʳ/ US /-t̬ɚ/ **noun** [C] mainly US a person who teaches people

Edwardian /edˈwɔː.di.ən/ US /-ˈwɔːr-/ **adj; noun**
▸**adj** from the period when Edward VII was king of England (1901–10): *Edwardian architecture/clothes*
▸**noun** [C] a person from this period

-ee /-iː/, /-i/ **suffix** OBJECT ▷ **1** added to a verb to form a noun which refers to the person who the action of the verb is being done to: *an employee (= someone who is employed)* ◦ *the payee (= a person who money is paid to)* ◦ *an interviewee (= someone who is being interviewed for a job)* CONDITION ▷ **2** added to an adjective, noun, or verb to refer to a person who is in that condition or state: *a refugee (= someone who has taken refuge)* ◦ *an escapee (= someone who has escaped)*

EEG /ˌiː.iːˈdʒiː/ **noun** [C] abbreviation for **electroencephalogram** or **electroencephalograph**

eek /iːk/ **exclamation** informal mainly humorous an expression of worry or slight fear

eel /iːl/ **noun** [C] a long, thin, snake-like fish, some types of which are eaten: *jellied eels*

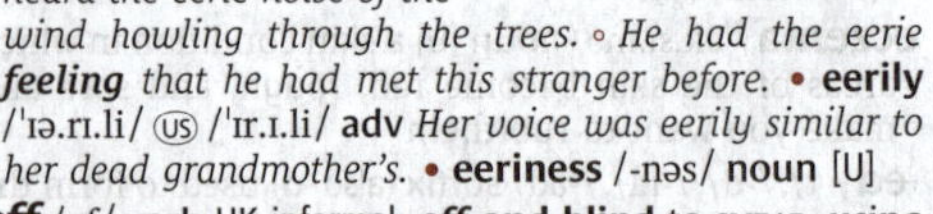

eerie /ˈɪə.ri/ US /ˈɪr.i/ **adj** strange in a frightening and mysterious way: *She heard the eerie noise of the wind howling through the trees.* ◦ *He had the eerie **feeling** that he had met this stranger before.* • **eerily** /ˈɪə.rɪ.li/ US /ˈɪr.ɪ.li/ **adv** *Her voice was eerily similar to her dead grandmother's.* • **eeriness** /-nəs/ **noun** [U]

eff /ef/ **verb** UK informal **eff and blind** to SWEAR, using words that are considered offensive

PHRASAL VERB **eff off!** offensive something that is said in order to tell someone rudely to go away

> **Note:**
> Although offensive, this is less offensive than **fuck off**.

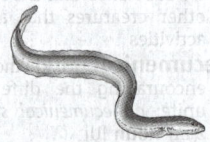

efface /ɪˈfeɪs/ **verb** REMOVE ▷ **1** [T] formal to remove something intentionally: *The whole country had tried* *to efface the memory of the old dictatorship.* **MODEST** ▷ **2 efface yourself** to behave in a MODEST way and treat the good things that you have achieved as if they were not important, often because you do not have much confidence → See also **self-effacing**

effect /ɪˈfekt/ noun; verb

▸noun **RESULT** ▷ **1** B1 [C or U] the result of a particular influence: *The radiation leak has had a disastrous effect* ***on/upon*** *the environment.* ◦ *I tried taking tablets for the headache but they didn't have any effect.* ◦ *I think I'm suffering from the effects of too little sleep.* ◦ *She has a lot of confidence which she uses* ***to good*** *effect (= to her advantage) in interviews.* → See also **aftereffects** **2 take effect** C1 to produce or achieve the results you want: *They had to wait ten minutes for the anaesthetic to take effect before they stitched up the cut.* **3 for effect** If you say or do something for effect, you intentionally do it to shock people or attract their attention: *I get the impression that she uses bad language in meetings for effect.* **4 in effect** C2 in fact, or in practice: *So in effect the government have lowered taxes for the rich and raised them for the poor.* **5 to that effect** (also **to the effect that**) used to express that what you are reporting is only a short and general form of what was really said: *She said she was unhappy, or* ***words*** *to that effect.* ◦ *He said something to the effect that he would have to change jobs if the situation continued.* **USE** ▷ **6** C2 [U] use: *The present system of payment will remain* ***in*** *effect (= be used) until the end of the rental agreement.* ◦ *When do the new driving laws* ***come into*** *effect?* ◦ *The new salary increases will* ***take*** *effect (= begin) from January onwards.* **THEATRE, ETC.** ▷ **7 effects** [plural] (also **special effects**) B1 lighting, sounds, and objects that are specially produced for the stage or a film and are intended to make something that does not exist seem real: *This is a movie worth seeing for its effects alone.* **POSSESSIONS** ▷ **8 effects** [plural] specialized a person's possessions, especially after their death: *It says on the form that the insurance covers all* ***personal*** *effects.*

> Word partners for **effect**
> *have/produce* an effect • *experience/feel/suffer* the effects • an *adverse/beneficial/profound/significant* effect • the *desired* effect • a *knock-on* effect • the effect *of* sth • an effect *on* sb/sth • *to/with* [devastating/no/little] effect

▸verb [T] formal to achieve something and cause it to happen: *As a political party they are trying to effect a change in the way that we think about our environment.*

effective /ɪˈfek.tɪv/ adj **SUCCESSFUL** ▷ **1** B2 successful or achieving the results that you want: *It's an extremely effective cure for a headache.* ◦ *The lighting for the production made a very effective use of shadow.* ◦ *She's a very effective teacher.* → Opposite **ineffective** **IN FACT** ▷ **2** [before noun] in fact, although not officially: *Although she's not officially our boss, she's in effective control of the office.* **IN USE** ▷ **3** If a law or rule becomes effective, it starts to be used: *The new laws will become effective next month.* • **effectiveness** /-nəs/ noun [U] C1 *There are doubts about the effectiveness of the new drug (= how successful it is) in treating the disease.*

effectively /ɪˈfek.tɪv.li/ adv **1** B2 in a way that is successful and achieves what you want: *The tablets work more effectively if you take a hot drink after them.* **2** C2 used when you describe what the real result of a situation is: *His wife left him when the children were small, so he effectively brought up the family himself.* ◦ *Effectively, we have to start again from scratch.*

effector /ɪˈfek.təʳ/ US /-tɚ/ noun [C] specialized a body part or cell that reacts to a STIMULUS in a particular way, or a cell or substance in the body that produces an effect: *effector cells* ◦ *In a reflex, the effector muscle acts before your brain is able to think.*

effectual /ɪˈfek.tju.əl/ adj formal effective and successful: *They wish to promote a real and effectual understanding between the two countries.* • **effectually** /-i/ adv

effeminate /ɪˈfem.ɪ.nət/ adj disapproving describes a man who behaves or looks similar to a woman: *He's got a very effeminate manner/voice.* • **effeminacy** /-nə.si/ noun [U] formal

effervesce /ˌef.əˈves/ US /-ɚ-/ verb [I] specialized If a liquid effervesces, it produces small bubbles.

effervescent /ˌef.əˈves.ənt/ US /-ɚ-/ adj **FIZZY** ▷ **1** describes a liquid that produces bubbles of gas: *effervescent vitamin C tablets* **ACTIVE** ▷ **2** full of energy, positive, and active: *She's one of those effervescent personalities that you often see presenting TV game shows.* • **effervescence** /-əns/ noun [U]

effete /ɪˈfiːt/ adj **1** literary disapproving weak and without much power: *With nothing to do all day the aristocracy had grown effete and lazy.* **2** disapproving more typical of a woman than of a man

efficacious /ˌef.ɪˈkeɪ.ʃəs/ adj formal able to produce the intended result → Synonym **effective**

efficacy /ˈef.ɪ.kə.si/ noun [U] formal an ability, especially of a medicine or a method of achieving something, to produce the intended result: *They recently ran a series of tests to measure the efficacy of the drug.* → Synonym **effectiveness**

efficiency /ɪˈfɪʃ.ən.si/ noun [U] **1** B2 the use of time and energy in a good way, without wasting any: *What is so impressive about their society is the efficiency of the public services.* ◦ *energy efficiency* **2** specialized the difference between the amount of energy that is put into a machine in the form of fuel, effort, etc. and the amount that comes out of it in the form of movement

efficient /ɪˈfɪʃ.ənt/ adj B1 working or operating quickly and effectively in an organized way: *The city's transport system is one of the most efficient in Europe.* ◦ *We need someone really efficient who can organize the office and make it run smoothly.* • **efficiently** /-li/ adv B2 *She runs the business very efficiently.*

effigy /ˈef.ɪ.dʒi/ noun [C] a model or other object that represents someone, especially one of a hated person that is hanged or burned in a public place

effing /ˈef.ɪŋ/ adj [before noun] UK slang used to add force to an expression. Some people might consider this offensive: *He's such an effing nuisance!*

efflorescence /ˌef.ləˈres.əns/ noun [U] **1** specialized the period when flowers start to appear on a plant **2** literary the production of a lot of art, especially of a high quality

effluent /ˈef.lu.ənt/ noun [C or U] specialized liquid waste that is sent out from factories or places where SEWAGE is dealt with, usually flowing into the sea or rivers: *Effluents from local factories are finding their way into the river.*

effort /ˈef.ət/ US /-ɚt/ noun **1** B1 [C or U] physical or mental activity needed to achieve something: [+ to infinitive] *If we could all* ***make*** *an effort* ***to*** *keep this office tidier it would help.* ◦ *You can't expect to have any friends if you don't* ***make*** *any effort with people.* ◦ ***In*** *their efforts* ***to*** *reduce crime the government expanded the police force.* ◦ *He's jogging round the park every* morning in an effort **to** get fit for the football season. ◦ It takes a long time to prepare the dish but the results are so good that it's **worth the** effort. **2** [C] the result of an attempt to produce something, especially when its quality is low or uncertain: *Do you want to have a look at his exam paper? It's a fairly poor effort.* **3 be an effort** C2 to be difficult, tiring or boring to do: *I'm exhausted all the time, and everything is a real effort.*

! Common mistake: effort

Warning: Choose the right verb!
Don't say 'do an effort', say **make an effort**:
~~*We must do an effort to improve our English.*~~
We must make an effort to improve our English.

Word partners for effort

make an effort • *demand/require/take* effort • a *considerable/great/tremendous* effort • a *concerted/determined/valiant* effort • a *conscious/deliberate* effort • a *joint/team* effort • *in* an effort to do sth • *with/without* effort

effortless /ˈef.ət.ləs/ US /-ət-/ **adj** approving seeming not to need any effort: *When you watch her dance it looks so effortless.* ◦ *He was an actor of effortless charm.* • **effortlessly** /-li/ **adv** *She runs so effortlessly as if it's the easiest thing in the world.* • **effortlessness** /ˈef.ət.ləs.nəs/ US /-ət-/ **noun** [U]

effrontery /ɪˈfrʌn.tᵊr.i/ US /-t̬ɚ-/ **noun** [U] formal extreme rudeness without any ability to understand that your behaviour is not acceptable to other people: *He was silent all through the meal and then had the effrontery to complain that I looked bored!*

effusion /ɪˈfjuː.ʒᵊn/ **noun** [C usually singular] literary a sudden and uncontrolled expression of strong emotion: *an effusion **of** anger and despair*

effusive /ɪˈfjuː.sɪv/ **adj** formal expressing welcome, approval or pleasure in a way that shows very strong feeling: *They gave us such an effusive welcome it was quite embarrassing.* • **effusively** /-li/ **adv**

E-FIT /ˈiː.fɪt/ **noun** [C] a picture of a person who is believed to have committed a crime or who is missing, created on a computer using the description of someone who saw them

EFL /ˌiː.efˈel/ **noun** [U] abbreviation for English as a Foreign Language: the teaching of English to students whose first language is not English: *Which bookshop has the largest selection of EFL materials?* → Compare **ESL**

e.g. (also **eg**) /iːˈdʒiː/ abbreviation for exempli gratia: a Latin phrase which means 'for example'. It can be pronounced as 'e.g.' or 'for example': *You should eat more food that contains a lot of fibre, e.g. fruit, vegetables, and bread.*

egalitarian /ɪˌgæl.ɪˈteə.ri.ən/ US /-ˈter.i-/ **adj; noun**
▸**adj** formal believing that all people are equally important and should have the same rights and opportunities in life: *an egalitarian society*
▸**noun** [C] formal a person who has egalitarian beliefs • **egalitarianism** /-ɪ.zᵊm/ **noun** [U] formal the belief in and actions taken according to egalitarian principles

egestion /ɪˈdʒes.tʃᵊn/ **noun** [C] specialized the process of removing undigested waste material from the body by EXCRETION

egg /eg/ **noun; verb**
▸**noun** FOOD ▷ **1** A1 [C or U] the oval object with a hard shell that is produced by female birds, especially chickens, eaten as food: *a hard-boiled/soft-boiled egg* ◦ *How do you like your eggs – fried or boiled?* **2** [C] an object that is made in the shape of a bird's egg: *a chocolate/marble egg* REPRODUCTION ▷ **3** B2 [C] an oval object, often with a hard shell, that is produced by female birds and particular reptiles and insects, and contains a baby animal that comes out when it is developed: *The cuckoo **lays** her egg in another bird's nest.* ◦ *After fourteen days the eggs **hatch**.* **4** [C] a cell produced by a woman or female animal from which a baby can develop if it combines with a male sex cell: *Identical twins develop from a single fertilized egg which then splits into two.*

IDIOMS **egg on sb's face** informal If someone has or gets egg on their face, they look stupid because of something that they have done: *This latest scandal has left the government with egg on its face.* • **put all your eggs in one basket** informal to depend for your success on a single person or plan of action: *I'm applying for several jobs because I don't really want to put all my eggs in one basket.*

▸**verb**

PHRASAL VERB **egg sb on** to strongly encourage someone to do something which might not be a very good idea: *Don't egg him on! He gets himself into enough trouble without your encouragement.*

ˌegg-and-ˈspoon ˌrace **noun** [C] a race in which people run with an egg balanced on a spoon

ˈegg ˌcup **noun** [C] a small container used to hold a boiled egg while you eat it

ˈegg ˌflip **noun** [U] UK **eggnog**

egghead /ˈeg.hed/ **noun** [C] humorous disapproving a person, especially a man, who is very clever and interested only in studying and other mental activities

eggnog /ˈeg.nɒg/ US /-nɑːg/ **noun** [U] (UK also **ˈegg ˌflip**) an alcoholic drink made from milk, sugar, and eggs mixed with brandy, rum, etc.

eggplant /ˈeg.plɑːnt/ US /-plænt/ **noun** [C] B2 US for **aubergine**

ˌegg ˈroll **noun** [C] US for **spring roll**

eggshell /ˈeg.ʃel/ **noun** [C or U] the hard outside covering of an egg

ˈegg ˌtimer **noun** [C] a device which helps you judge when a boiled egg has been cooked long enough to be eaten

ˈegg ˌwhite **noun** [C or U] the transparent part of an egg which turns white when it is cooked

eggy /ˈeg.i/ **adj** informal tasting or smelling of eggs

ˈegg ˌyolk **noun** [C or U] the yellow part of an egg

ego /ˈiː.gəʊ/ US /ˈiː.goʊ/ **noun** [C] (plural **egos**) **1** your idea or opinion of yourself, especially your feeling of your own importance and ability: *That man has such an enormous ego – I've never known anyone so full of themselves!* ◦ *I'm glad she got the job – she needed something to **boost/bolster** her ego* (= give her confidence). **2** specialized in PSYCHOANALYSIS, the part of a person's mind which tries to match the hidden DESIRES (= wishes) of the ID (= part of the unconscious mind) with the demands of the real world → See also **alter ego, superego**

egocentric /ˌiː.gəʊˈsen.trɪk/ US /-goʊ-/ **adj** thinking only about yourself and what will bring advantages for you: *Babies are entirely egocentric, concerned only with when they will next be fed.* • **egocentrically** /-trɪ.kᵊl.i/ **adv** • **egocentricity** /ˌiː.gəʊ.senˈtrɪs.ɪ.ti/ US /-goʊ.senˈtrɪs.ə.t̬i/ **noun** [U]

egoism /ˈiː.gəʊ.ɪ.zᵊm/ US /-goʊ-/ **noun** [U] **egotism**

egoist /ˈiː.gəʊ.ɪst/ US /-goʊ-/ **noun** [C] **egotist**

egoistic /ˌiː.ɡəʊˈɪs.tɪk/ ⓤⓢ /-ɡoʊ-/ **adj egotistic**

egomania /ˌiː.ɡəʊˈmeɪ.ni.ə/ ⓤⓢ /-ɡoʊ-/ **noun** [U] disapproving the state of considering yourself to be very important and able to do anything that you want to do • **egomaniac** /-æk/ **noun** [C] disapproving a person with egomania

egosurfing /ˈiː.ɡəʊˌsɜː.fɪŋ/ ⓤⓢ /-ɡoʊˌsɝː.f-/ **noun** [U] informal searching for your own name on the internet

egotism /ˈiː.ɡə.tɪ.zᵊm/ ⓤⓢ /-ɡoʊ-/ **noun** [U] (also **egoism**) thinking only about yourself and considering yourself better and more important than other people: *Finding herself world-famous by the time she was 18 only encouraged the actress's egotism.*

egotist /ˈiː.ɡə.tɪst/ ⓤⓢ /-ɡoʊ-/ **noun** [C] (also **egoist**) a person who considers himself or herself to be better or more important than other people: *Politicians are notorious egotists.*

egotistic (also **egotistical** /-tɪ.kᵊl/) /ˌiː.ɡəˈtɪs.tɪk/ ⓤⓢ /-ɡoʊ-/ **adj** considering yourself to be better or more important than other people • **egotistically** /-tɪ.kᵊli/ **adv**

ˈ**ego** ˌ**trip** **noun** [C] disapproving something that you do because it makes you feel important and also shows other people how important you are: *He was* ***on*** *another one of his ego trips, directing and taking the main part in a film.*

egregious /ɪˈɡriː.dʒəs/ **adj** formal disapproving often of mistakes, extremely bad: *It was an egregious* ***error*** *for a statesman to show such ignorance.*

egress /ˈiː.ɡres/ **noun** [C or U] formal the act or way of leaving a place: *The main egress from the restaurant had been blocked off.*

eh /eɪ/ **exclamation** (US usually **huh**) used to express surprise or confusion, to ask someone to repeat what they have said, or as a way of getting someone to give some type of reaction to a statement that you have made: *'Janet's leaving her husband.' 'Eh?'* ◦ *'Did you hear what I said?' 'Eh? Say it again – I wasn't listening.'* ◦ *Going overseas again, eh? It's a nice life for some!*

Eid /iːd/ **noun** [C or U] the name of two Muslim holidays. The more important of these is called Eid ul-Fitr and is celebrated to mark the end of RAMADAN.

eiderdown /ˈaɪ.də.daʊn/ ⓤⓢ /-dɚ-/ **noun** [C] a thick covering for the top of a bed, filled with soft feathers or warm material, used especially in the past

eight /eɪt/ **number** (A1) the number 8: *She was eight (years old) when her family moved here.* ◦ *We've got eight people coming to dinner.*

eighteen /ˌeɪˈtiːn/ **number** (A1) the number 18: *You are allowed to vote at eighteen (= when you are 18 years old)* ◦ *The table was set for eighteen people.*

eighteenth /ˌeɪˈtiːnθ/ **ordinal number** 18th written as a word: *Next Monday is* ***the*** *eighteenth (****of*** *February).*

eighth /eɪtθ/ **ordinal number; noun**

▸**ordinal number** (A2) 8th written as a word: *He* ***was/came*** *eighth in the race.* ◦ *Bob's birthday is on* ***the*** *eighth (****of*** *June).*

▸**noun** [C] one of eight equal parts of something: *An eighth of 32 is 4.*

ˈ**eighth** ˌ**note** **noun** [C] US for **quaver**

eighties /ˈeɪ.tiz/ ⓤⓢ /-t̬iz/ **noun** [plural] **1** (B2) A person's eighties are the period in which they are aged between 80 and 89: *My grandmother is* ***in*** *her eighties.* **2 the eighties a** the range of temperature between 80° and 89°: *The temperature is expected to be* ***in*** *the eighties tomorrow.* **b** (B2) the DECADE (= period of ten years) between 80 and 89 in any century, usually 1980–1989: *Margaret Thatcher was the UK prime minister* ***in/during*** *the eighties.*

eightieth /ˈeɪ.ti.əθ/ ⓤⓢ /-t̬i-/ **ordinal number** 80th written as a word

eighty /ˈeɪ.ti/ ⓤⓢ /-t̬i/ **number** (A2) the number 80: *seventy-nine, eighty, eight-one* ◦ *They've invited eighty (guests) to the wedding.*

ˈ**e-ink** **noun** [U] trademark a system used for showing words on an E-READER

either /ˈaɪ.ðəʳ/, /ˈiː-/ ⓤⓢ /-ðɚ/ **adv; determiner, pronoun, conjunction; determiner**

▸**adv** (B1) used in negative sentences instead of 'also' or 'too': *I don't eat meat and my husband doesn't either.* ◦ *'I've never been to the States.' 'I haven't either.'* ◦ *They do really good food at that restaurant and it's not very expensive either.*

▸**determiner, pronoun, conjunction** (B1) used when referring to a choice between two possibilities: *Either candidate would be ideal for the job.* ◦ *'Do you prefer pork or beef?' 'I don't like either.'* ◦ *'Would you like the metal or plastic one?' 'Either will do.'* ◦ *You can get there by train or bus – either* ***way/in*** *either* ***case*** *it'll take an hour.* ◦ *We can either eat now* ***or*** *after the show – it's up to you.* ◦ *Either you leave now* ***or*** *I call the police!*

▸**determiner** (B2) both: *Unfortunately I was sitting at the table with smokers on either side of me.*

ˌ**either-**ˈ**or** **adj** [before noun] describes a situation in which there is a choice between two different plans of action, but both together are not possible: *It's an either-or* ***situation*** *– we can buy a new car this year or we can go on holiday, but we can't do both.*

ejaculate /ɪˈdʒæk.jʊ.leɪt/ **verb** SPERM ▷ **1** [I or T] (of a man or male animal), to produce a sudden flow of SEMEN from the PENIS SAY ▷ **2** [T] old-fashioned or humorous to shout or say something suddenly: [+ speech] *'You've got my umbrella!' he ejaculated.*

ejaculation /ɪˌdʒæk.jʊˈleɪ.ʃᵊn/ **noun** SPERM ▷ **1** [C or U] the act of ejaculating SUDDEN REMARK ▷ **2** [C] old-fashioned or humorous something that someone says or shouts suddenly

eject /ɪˈdʒekt/ **verb 1** [T often passive] to force someone to leave a particular place: *A number of football fans had been ejected* ***from*** *the bar for causing trouble.* **2** [T] US (UK **send off**) to order a sports player to leave the playing area during a game because they have done something wrong **3** [I] to leave an aircraft in an emergency by being pushed while still in your seat **4** [I or T] to come out of a machine when a button is pressed, or to make something do this: *How do you eject the tape?*

ejection /ɪˈdʒek.ʃᵊn/ **noun** [C or U] the act of ejecting someone or something

eˈ**jection** ˌ**seat** **noun** [C] (UK also **ejector seat** /ɪˈdʒek.təˌsiːt/ ⓤⓢ /-tɚ-/) a seat that can throw out the person flying an aircraft if they suddenly have to leave it because they are in danger

eke /iːk/ **verb**

PHRASAL VERB **eke sth out** to use something slowly or carefully because you only have a small amount of it: *There wasn't much food left, but we just managed to eke it out.* ◦ *He managed to eke out* ***a living*** *(= earn just enough to live on) one summer by selling drinks on a beach.*

EKG /ˌiː.keɪˈdʒiː/ **noun** [C] US for **ECG**

elaborate **adj; verb**

▸**adj** /ɪˈlæb.ᵊr.ət/ ⓤⓢ /-ɚ-/ (C2) containing a lot of careful detail or many detailed parts: *You want a plain blouse to go with that skirt – nothing too elaborate.* ◦ *They're making the most elaborate preparations for the wedding.* ◦ *He came out with such an elaborate excuse*

E

that I didn't quite believe him. • **elaborately** /-li/ **adv** *It was the most elaborately decorated cake – all sugar flowers and bows.*

▸**verb** [I] /ɪˈlæb.ə.reɪt/ formal to add more information to or explain something that you have said: *The minister said he was resigning, but refused to elaborate **on** his reasons for doing so.* • **elaboration** /ɪˌlæb.əˈreɪ.ʃən/ **noun** [C or U] *This point needs greater elaboration.*

elan /eɪˈlæn/ **noun** [U] literary approving a combination of style and energetic confidence, especially in performances or manner: *She dances the role with such elan.*

elapse /ɪˈlæps/ **verb** [I] formal C2 If time elapses, it goes past: *Four years had elapsed since he left college and still he hadn't found a job.*

elastic /ɪˈlæs.tɪk/ **adj; noun**

▸**adj 1** describes material that is able to stretch and be returned to its original shape or size: *A lot of sportswear is made of very elastic material.* **2** able or likely to be changed: *The project has only just started so any plans are still very elastic.* ◦ *In this country, time is an elastic concept.*

▸**noun** [U] a type of rubber that is able to stretch and be returned to its original shape or size: *His trousers were held up with a piece of elastic.*

elasticated /ɪˈlæs.tɪ.keɪ.tɪd/ US /-t̬ɪd/ **adj** UK (US **elasticized**, Australian English **elasticised**) made with elastic material or thread: *a dress with an elasticated waist*

eˌlastic ˈband **noun** [C] UK for **rubber band**

elasticity /ˌɪl.æsˈtɪs.ɪ.ti/ US /-ə.t̬i/ **noun** [U] **1** the ability to stretch: *As the skin grows older it loses its elasticity.* **2** the ability to change: *There is some elasticity in our plans – nothing has been firmly decided yet.*

elasticized /ɪˈlæs.tɪ.saɪzd/ **adj** US for **elasticated**

elated /ɪˈleɪ.tɪd/ US /-t̬ɪd/ **adj** C2 extremely happy and excited, often because something has happened or been achieved: *The prince was reported to be elated **at/by** the birth of his daughter.*

elation /ɪˈleɪ.ʃən/ **noun** [U] a state of extreme happiness or excitement: *There's a sense of elation at having completed a race of such length.*

elbow /ˈel.bəʊ/ US /-boʊ/ **noun; verb**

▸**noun** [C] B1 the part in the middle of the arm where it bends, or the part of a piece of clothing which covers this area: *Her arm was bandaged from the elbow to the fingers.* ◦ *The sleeve of his shirt was torn **at the** elbow.*

IDIOMS **at sb's elbow** close to and a little behind someone: *During the visit, the interpreter was always at her elbow.* • **give sb the elbow** UK informal to end your romantic relationship with someone

▸**verb** [T usually + adv/prep] **1** disapproving to push someone rudely with your elbows so that you can move or have more space: *He elbowed **his way to** the front of the crowd.* ◦ *They elbowed the onlookers aside.* **2** to hit someone with your elbow, sometimes as a sign to make them notice or remember something: *She elbowed me **in the ribs** before I could say anything.*

PHRASAL VERB **elbow sb out** [M often passive] to force someone or something out of a position or job: *He resigned before he was elbowed out.*

ˈelbow ˌgrease **noun** [U] informal a lot of physical effort: *The polish needs a certain amount of elbow grease to apply.*

ˈelbow ˌroom **noun** [U] **1** space to move around in: *We were tightly squashed in at dinner, with very little elbow room.* **2** freedom to do what you want: *At first the management gave the new director plenty of elbow room.*

elder /ˈel.dər/ US /-dɚ/ **noun; adj**

▸**noun** [C] **1** C2 an older person, especially one with a respected position in society: *You should listen to the advice of your elders.* ◦ *They consulted the **village** elders.* ◦ formal *She is **my** elder **by** three years (= three years older than me).* **2** an official of a religious group: *a **church** elder* **3 elderberry**

▸**adj 1 elder sister/brother/son/daughter** B1 a sister/brother/son/daughter who is older than the other sister(s), brother(s), etc. **2 the elder a** B2 the older person of two people: *Of the two brothers Harvey is the elder.* **b** used after someone's name to show that they are the older of two people who have the same name, especially a father and son: *William Pitt the elder*

> **!** Common mistake: **elder or elderly?**
>
> **Warning:** choose the right adjective!
>
> To refer politely to a person who is old, don't say 'elder', say **elderly**:
>
> ~~*Loneliness is a big problem for elder people.*~~
>
> *Loneliness is a big problem for elderly people.*

elderberry /ˈel.dəˌber.i/ US /-dɚ-/ **noun** [C] (also **elder**) a small tree that grows wild or in gardens and has large flat groups of white flowers, or its nearly black fruit that can be used in cooking or making wine

elderly /ˈel.dəl.i/ US /-dɚ.li/ **adj; noun**

▸**adj** B1 polite word for old: *elderly **relatives/parents***

▸**noun** [plural] **the elderly** C1 old people considered as a group: *The city is building new housing for the elderly.*

ˌelder ˈstatesman **noun** [C] a respected leader, often one who no longer has an active job, who is thought of as having good advice to give: *He is one of the medical profession's elder statesmen.*

eldest /ˈel.dɪst/ **adj; noun**

▸**adj** [before noun] B1 being the oldest of three or more people, especially within a family: *Her eldest child is nearly 14.*

▸**noun** [S] **1 the eldest** B2 a person who is the oldest of three of more people: *He was the eldest of four kids.* **2** the oldest child in a family: *My eldest is at college.*

ˈe-ˌlearning **noun** [U] learning done by studying at home using computers and courses provided on the internet

elect /ɪˈlekt/ **verb; noun; adj**

▸**verb** [T] **1** B2 to decide on or choose, especially to choose a person for a particular job, by voting: *The government is elected for a five-year term of office.* ◦ [+ as + noun] *We elected him **as** our representative.* ◦ [+ noun] *She was elected Chair of the Board of Governors.* ◦ [+ to infinitive] *The group elected one of its members **to** be their spokesperson.* **2 elect to do sth** formal to choose to do a particular thing: *She elected to take early retirement instead of moving to the new location.*

▸**noun** [plural] **1 the elect** formal in the Bible, people who are chosen by God **2** humorous any group of people who have been specially chosen for their particular qualities

▸**adj** [after noun] **president elect, prime minister elect, etc.** the person who has been voted to be president, prime minister, etc. but has not yet started work: *The president elect has been preparing to take office in January.* → Compare **designate**

election /ɪˈlek.ʃən/ **noun** [C or U] B1 a time when people vote in order to choose someone for a political or official job: *The government is expected to* ***call*** *an election (= allow the country to vote) very soon.* ◦ *Local government elections will take place in May.* ◦ *The first election results have started to come in.* → See also **by-election, general election**

eˈlection camˌpaign noun [C] the period of weeks immediately before an election when politicians try to persuade people to vote for them

eˈlection ˌday noun [C usually singular] (UK also **ˈpolling ˌday**) the day when people vote in an election

electioneering /ɪˌlek.ʃəˈnɪə.rɪŋ/ ⓤⓢ /-ˈnɪr.ɪŋ/ noun [U] mainly disapproving the activity of trying to persuade people to vote for a particular political party: *The MP's speech was dismissed by her opponents as crude electioneering.*

elective /ɪˈlek.tɪv/ adj; noun

▸**adj** formal voted for or chosen: *an elective office* ◦ *elective surgery*

▸**noun** [C] a subject that someone can choose to study as part of a course: *During the MBA you will choose ten to twelve electives from a large and varied portfolio.*

elector /ɪˈlek.təʳ/ ⓤⓢ /-tɚ/ noun [C] a person who votes

electoral /ɪˈlek.tᵊr.ᵊl/ ⓤⓢ /-tɚ-/ adj [before noun] relating to an election: *the electoral* ***system*** ◦ *electoral law/reform/gains/defeat* • **electorally** /-ə.li/ adv

eˌlectoral ˈcollege noun [C] a group of people whose job is to choose a political or religious leader

eˌlectoral ˈregister noun [C] (also **eˌlectoral ˈroll**) UK the official list of people who are allowed to vote

electorate /ɪˈlek.tᵊr.ət/ ⓤⓢ /-tɚ-/ noun [C usually singular, + sing/pl verb] all the people who are allowed to vote: *The present voting system distorts the wishes of the electorate.*

electric /ɪˈlek.trɪk/ adj **POWER** ▷ **1** A2 using electricity for power: *an electric blanket/car/kettle/light* **EXCITING** ▷ **2** C1 very exciting and producing strong feelings: *an electric performance*

electrical /ɪˈlek.trɪ.kᵊl/ adj B1 related to electricity: *electrical equipment/goods/devices* ◦ *an electrical fuse/circuit/fault* • **electrically** /-i/ adv *an electrically powered car*

eˌlectrical enginˈeer noun [C] a trained expert in electrical systems, especially those which power and control machines or are involved in communication

eˌlectrical ˈstorm noun [C] (UK also **eˌlectric ˈstorm**) a storm with thunder and LIGHTNING

the eˌlectric ˈchair noun [S] in some parts of the US, a special chair that is used to kill a criminal with a current of electricity

eˌlectric ˈfence noun [C] a fence which produces a small electric current, usually to keep animals in a particular area

eˌlectric ˈheater noun [C] (UK also **ˌelectric ˈfire**) a device that uses electricity to produce heat, for example from metal bars that become red and hot when the current is switched on

electrician /ˌɪl.ekˈtrɪʃ.ᵊn/ noun [C] B2 a person who puts in and checks electrical wires

electricity /ɪˌlekˈtrɪs.ɪ.ti/ ⓤⓢ /-ə.t̬i/ noun [U] A2 a form of energy, produced in several ways, which provides power to devices that create light, heat, etc.: *The electricity has been turned off.* ◦ *an electricity generating company* ◦ *powered/heated by electricity* ◦ *an electricity bill*

eˌlectric ˈrazor noun [C] (also **shaver**) a device for removing hair that has different types of blades that turn or move backwards and forwards

electrics /ɪˈlek.trɪks/ noun [plural] UK the electrical system of something, especially a car: *I think the fault is in the electrics.*

eˌlectric ˈshock noun [C] (also **shock**) a sudden painful feeling that you get when electricity flows through your body: *He* ***got*** *an electric shock from one of the wires.*

electrification /ɪˌlek.trɪ.fɪˈkeɪ.ʃᵊn/ noun [U] the process of making a machine or system operate using electricity when it did not before: *the electrification of the railways* ◦ *electrification technology*

electrify /ɪˈlek.trɪ.faɪ/ verb [T] **POWER** ▷ **1** to make a machine or system operate using electricity when it did not before: *The east coast railway line has been electrified.* **MAKE EXCITED** ▷ **2** to make a person or group extremely excited by what you say or do: *She electrified her audience with her vivid stories.*

electrifying /ɪˈlek.trɪ.faɪ.ɪŋ/ adj very exciting: *an electrifying* ***performance***

electrocardiogram /ɪˌlek.trəˈkɑː.di.ə.græm/ ⓤⓢ /-ˈkɑːr-/ noun [C] (abbreviation **ECG**) a drawing or electronic image made by an electrocardiograph

electrocardiograph /ɪˌlek.trəˈkɑː.di.ə.græf, -grɑːf/ ⓤⓢ /-ˈkɑːrdi.ə.græf/ noun [C] (abbreviation **ECG**) a machine that records the electrical activity of the heart as it beats

electroconvulsive therapy /ɪˌlek.trəʊ.kᵊnˈvʌl.sɪv ˌθer.ə.pi/ ⓤⓢ /-troʊ-/ noun [U] (abbreviation **ECT**) the treatment of particular MENTAL ILLNESSES (= diseases which affect the mind) which involves sending an electric current through the brain

electrocute /ɪˈlek.trə.kjuːt/ verb [T often passive] to kill someone by causing electricity to flow through their body: *He was electrocuted when he touched the bare wires.* • **electrocution** /ɪˌlek.trəˈkjuː.ʃᵊn/ noun [C or U]

electrode /ɪˈlek.trəʊd/ ⓤⓢ /-troʊd/ noun [C] the point at which an electric current enters or leaves something, for example, a BATTERY

electroencephalogram /ɪˌlek.trəʊ.enˈsef.ə.lə.græm/ ⓤⓢ /-troʊ-/ noun [C] (abbreviation **EEG**) a drawing or image made by an electroencephalograph

electroencephalograph /ɪˌlek.trəʊ.enˈsef.ə.lə.græf, -grɑːf/ ⓤⓢ /-troʊ-/ noun [C] (abbreviation **EEG**) a machine that records the electrical activity of the brain

electrolysis /ɪˌlekˈtrɒl.ə.sɪs/ ⓤⓢ /-ˈtrɑː.lə-/ noun [U] **1** the use of an electric current to cause chemical change in a liquid **2** the process of using a very small electric current to remove hair and stop it from growing back

electrolyte /ɪˈlek.trə.laɪt/ noun [C] specialized a substance, usually a liquid, which electricity can go through or which breaks into its parts when electricity goes through it • **electrolytic** adj

electrolytic cell /ɪ.lek.trəˌlɪt.ɪkˈsel/ ⓤⓢ /-ˌlɪt̬-/ noun [C] specialized a device containing an electrolyte and two ELECTRODES, either used for producing electricity through a chemical reaction or for producing a chemical change in a liquid by ELECTROLYSIS

electromagnet /ɪˌlek.trəʊˈmæg.nət/ ⓤⓢ /-troʊ-/ noun [C] specialized a device made from a piece of iron that becomes MAGNETIC when a changing current is passed through the wire that goes round it

electromagnetic /ɪˌlek.trəʊ.mægˈnet.ɪk/ ⓤⓢ /-troʊ.mægˈnet̬-/ adj having MAGNETIC and electrical parts

electromagnetism /ɪˌlek.trəʊˈmæg.nə.tɪ.zᵊm/ ⓤⓢ

E

/-troʊˈmæg.nə.t̬ɪ-/ noun [U] specialized the science of MAGNETISM and electrical currents

electromotive /ɪˌlek.trəˈməʊ.tɪv/ (US) /-ˈmoʊ.t̬ɪv/ adj specialized **1** having an electric motor or relating to something that has an electric motor: *electromotive vehicles* **2** producing an electric current: *electromotive force*

electron /ɪˈlek.trɒn/ (US) /-trɑːn/ noun [C] an extremely small piece of matter with a negative electrical CHARGE → Compare **neutron, proton**

E

electronic /ɪˌlekˈtrɒn.ɪk/ (US) /-ˈtrɑː.nɪk/ adj **ELECTRICAL** ▷ **1** (B1) (especially of equipment), using, based on, or used in a system of operation which involves the control of electric current by various devices: *an electronic keyboard/game ◦ electronic components/devices* **COMPUTING** ▷ **2** (B1) relating to computers or something that is done by computers: *electronic communication/cash ◦ electronic publishing* • **electronically** /-ˈtrɒn.ɪ.kəl.i/ (US) /-ˈtrɑː.nɪ.kəl.i/ adv (B2) *electronically generated graphics ◦ electronically stored information*

elecˌtronic ˈbanking noun [U] (also **ˈe-ˌbanking**) the use of the internet to organize, examine, and make changes to your bank accounts and INVESTMENTS, etc. electronically, or the use of the internet by banks to operate accounts and services: *electronic banking services*

elecˌtronic ˈbook noun [C] (also **ˈe-book**) a book that is published in electronic form, for example on the internet or on a disk, and not printed on paper: *electronic book publishing ◦ an e-book publisher*

elecˌtronic ˈfootprint noun [C] something electronic, such as sending an email, using a CREDIT CARD, etc. which shows where you have been and what you have been doing: *Every website you visit leaves an electronic footprint of your surfing habits.*

elecˌtronic ˈmail noun [U] formal **email**

elecˌtronic ˈmailˌbox noun [C] a computer file where emails are stored

elecˌtronic ˈpublishing noun [U] the business of publishing information that is read using a computer: *an electronic publishing company/course*

electronics /ɪˌlekˈtrɒn.ɪks/ (US) /-ˈtrɑː.nɪks/ noun [U] (B2) the scientific study of electric current and the TECHNOLOGY that uses it: *a degree in electronics ◦ the electronics industry*

elecˌtronic ˈtagging noun [U] the use of an electronic device that is fastened to a person who has committed a crime, so that the police know where that person is

eˌlectron ˈmicroscope noun [C] a device that sends electrons through objects that are too small to be seen easily, to produce a picture that is more detailed than that produced by ordinary MICROSCOPES

electroplate /ɪˈlek.trəʊ.pleɪt/ (US) /-troʊ-/ verb [T] specialized to cover the surface of a metal object with a thin layer of a different metal, often silver, using ELECTROLYSIS (= method that uses electric current): *electroplated brass* • **electroplate** noun [U] objects that have been electroplated

electroshock therapy /ɪˌlek.trəʊˌʃɒkˈθer.ə.pi/ (US) /-troʊˌʃɑːk-/ noun [U] US **electroconvulsive therapy**

electrostatic /ɪˌlek.trəʊˈstæt.ɪk/ (US) /-troʊˈstæt̬-/ adj specialized connected with or caused by electricity which does not move in a current but is attracted to the surface of some objects: *an electrostatic charge*

elegant /ˈel.ɪ.gənt/ adj **1** (B2) GRACEFUL and attractive in appearance or behaviour: *an elegant woman ◦ a very elegant suit ◦ an elegant dining room* **2** describes an idea, plan, or solution that is clever but simple, and therefore attractive • **elegance** /-gəns/ noun [U] (C1) *It was her natural elegance that struck me. ◦ the elegance of her clothes* • **elegantly** /-li/ adv (B2) *elegantly dressed*

elegiac /ˌel.ɪˈdʒaɪ.ək/ (US) /ɪˈliː.dʒi.æk/ adj literary relating to an elegy

elegy /ˈel.ə.dʒi/ noun [C] a sad poem or song, especially remembering someone who has died or something in the past

element /ˈel.ɪ.mənt/ noun **PART** ▷ **1** (B2) [C] a part of something: *List the elements which make up a perfect dinner party. ◦ The film had all the elements of a good thriller. ◦ We weren't even taught the elements of (= basic information about) physics at school.* **AMOUNT** ▷ **2 an element of sth** (C2) a small amount of an emotion or quality: *There was certainly an element of truth in what she said. ◦ Don't you think there's an element of jealousy in all of this? ◦ We walked quietly up to the door to preserve the element of surprise.* **SIMPLE SUBSTANCE** ▷ **3** (B2) [C] a simple substance which cannot be reduced to smaller chemical parts: *Aluminium is an element.* **EARTH, AIR, ETC.** ▷ **4** [C] earth, air, fire, and water from which people in the past believed everything else was made **WEATHER** ▷ **5 the elements** [plural] the weather, usually bad weather: *We decided to **brave** the elements and go for a walk (= go for a walk despite the bad weather).* **HEAT** ▷ **6** [C] the part of an electrical device which produces heat: *a heating element ◦ The kettle needs a new element.*

IDIOMS **be in your element** to be happy because you are doing what you like or can do best: *Kate, of course, was in her element, making all the arrangements.* • **be out of your element** to be unhappy and feel uncomfortable in a particular situation

elemental /ˌel.ɪˈmen.təl/ adj **1** literary showing the strong power of nature: *elemental force/fury* **2** basic or most simple, but strong: *elemental needs/desires/feelings*

elementary /ˌel.ɪˈmen.tər.i/ (US) /-t̬ɚ-/ adj **1** basic: *I have an elementary **knowledge** of physics. ◦ They made some elementary **mistakes**. ◦ Millions of travellers fail to take even the most elementary of precautions.* **2** (B1) relating to the early stages of studying a subject: *This book contains a series of elementary exercises for learners.*

eleˌmentary ˈparticle noun [C] specialized one of the most simple parts of all matter, such as an ELECTRON, a PROTON or a NEUTRON

eleˈmentary ˌschool noun [C] UK old-fashioned or US (B1) a school which provides the first part of a child's education, usually for children between five and eleven years old

elephant /ˈel.ɪ.fənt/ noun [C] (A2) a very large grey mammal that has a TRUNK (= long nose) with which it can pick things up

IDIOM **an elephant in the room** informal If you say there is an elephant in the room, you mean that there is an obvious problem or difficult situation that people do not want to talk about.

elephantine /ˌel.ɪˈfæn.taɪn/ adj formal very large: *She's so tiny she makes me feel elephantine.*

elevate /ˈel.ɪ.veɪt/ verb [T] **1** formal to raise something or lift something up: *The platform was elevated by means of hydraulic legs.* **2** to make someone or something more important or to improve something: *They want to elevate the status of teachers. ◦ These factors helped to elevate the town into the list of the ten* *most attractive in the country.* **3 be elevated to sth** formal to be given a higher rank or social position: *He has been elevated to deputy manager.* ◦ *She was elevated to the peerage (= was given the title 'Lady').*

elevated /ˈel.ɪ.veɪ.tɪd/ (US) /-t̬ɪd/ **adj 1** raised: *The doctor said I was to keep my leg elevated.* ◦ *There is an elevated area at the back of the building.* **2** high or important: *She holds a more elevated position in the company.* **3** [before noun] greater than is normal or reasonable: *He has a rather elevated idea of his own importance.* **4** [before noun] formal formal or typical of language found in literature: *an elevated style/tone*

elevation /ˌel.ɪˈveɪ.ʃən/ **noun** **BUILDING** ▷ **1** [C] specialized the front or side of a building as shown on a drawing: *This plan shows the front, side and back elevations of the new supermarket.* **HEIGHT** ▷ **2** [C or U] formal the height of a place above the level of the sea: *Atmospheric pressure varies with elevation and temperature.* ◦ *The crop is not grown at high elevations/above an elevation of 1,000 metres.* **HILL** ▷ **3** [C] formal a hill: *The flagpole stands on a small elevation in front of the building.* **IMPORTANCE** ▷ **4** [U] formal the fact of being given a more important position: *His elevation to the presidency of the new republic was generally popular.*

elevator /ˈel.ɪ.veɪ.təʳ/ (US) /-t̬ɚ/ **noun** [C] **1** (A2) US (UK **lift**) a small room that carries people or goods up and down in tall buildings **2** a moving strip that can be used for removing goods from a ship, putting bags onto an aircraft, moving grain into a store, etc.

ˈelevator ˌmusic **noun** [U] US for **Muzak**

eleven /ɪˈlev.ən/ **number; noun**

▸**number** (A1) the number 11: *There are eleven girls in my class and ten boys.* ◦ *My younger brother is eleven.*

▸**noun** [C, + sing/pl verb] a team of eleven players

the eˌleven-ˈplus **noun** [S] UK in some parts of England, an exam taken by children aged eleven that affects what type of school they go to next

elevenses /ɪˈlev.ən.zɪz/ **noun** [plural] UK informal a drink and a small amount to eat between breakfast and LUNCH

eleventh /ɪˈlev.ənθ/ **ordinal number** 11th written as a word: *Her birthday is on* ***the*** *eleventh (****of*** *this month).*

IDIOM **the eleventh hour** the last moment or almost too late: *We only received the signatures* ***at*** *the eleventh hour.* ◦ *an eleventh-hour decision by the union to call off the strike*

elf /elf/ **noun** [C] (plural **elves**) a small person with pointed ears who has magic powers in children's stories

ELF /ˌiː.elˈef/ **noun** [U] **LANGUAGE** ▷ **1** abbreviation for English as a lingua franca: the type of English used by speakers of other languages as a way of communicating among themselves **COMPUTING** ▷ **2** abbreviation for executable and linkable format: a system for storing and moving computer files that contain programs

elfin /ˈel.fɪn/ **adj** describes a person who is small and delicate: *Her features were small, almost elfin.*

elicit /ɪˈlɪs.ɪt/ **verb** [T] formal to get or produce something, especially information or a reaction: *Have you managed to elicit a* ***response from*** *them yet?* ◦ *The questionnaire was intended to elicit* ***information*** *on eating habits.* ◦ *They were able to elicit the* ***support*** *of the public.* • **elicitation** /ɪˌlɪs.ɪˈteɪ.ʃən/ **noun** [U]

elide /ɪˈlaɪd/ **verb** [T] specialized to not pronounce a particular sound in a word: *The 't' of 'acts' is often elided if someone is speaking quickly.*

eligible /ˈel.ɪ.dʒə.bl̩/ **adj 1** (C1) having the necessary qualities or satisfying the necessary conditions: *Are you eligible* ***for*** *early retirement/maternity leave?* ◦ *You might be eligible for a grant.* ◦ *Only people over 18 are eligible* ***to*** *vote.* **2** describes someone who is not married and is thought to be a suitable future marriage partner, especially because they are rich and attractive: *I can think of several eligible* ***bachelors*** *of my acquaintance.* • **eligibility** /ˌel.ɪ.dʒəˈbɪl.ɪ.ti/ (US) /-ə.t̬i/ *I'll have to check her eligibility to take part.* ◦ *The eligibility rules prevent under-18s being in the team.*

eliminate /ɪˈlɪm.ɪ.neɪt/ **verb 1** (C1) [T] to remove or take away: *A move towards healthy eating could help eliminate heart disease.* ◦ *We eliminated the* ***possibility*** *that it could have been an accident.* ◦ *The police eliminated him* ***from*** *their enquiries.* **2** (C1) [T often passive] to defeat someone so that they cannot continue in a competition: *He was eliminated in the third round of the competition.* **3** [T] slang to murder: *A police officer was accused of helping a drug gang eliminate rivals.*

elimination /ɪˌlɪm.ɪˈneɪ.ʃən/ **noun** [U] **1** (C2) the process of removing something: *the elimination of disease/pain* ◦ *their elimination from the competition* **2 by a process of elimination** by removing from several possible answers the ones that are unlikely to be correct until only one is left: *We eventually found the answer by a process of elimination.*

elimiˈnation ˌtournament **noun** [C] US for **knockout**

eliminator /ɪˈlɪm.ɪ.neɪ.təʳ/ (US) /-t̬ɚ/ **noun** [C] UK a part of a competition in any game or sport where one person or team plays against another to decide which of them will continue to the next stage and which will be removed from the competition

elision /ɪˈlɪʒ.ən/ **noun** [C or U] specialized the fact of not pronouncing a particular sound in a word

elite /ɪˈliːt/ **noun; adj**

▸**noun** [C, + sing/pl verb] (C1) the richest, most powerful, best-educated, or best-trained group in a society: *the country's educated elite* ◦ *a member of the elite* ◦ disapproving *A powerful and corrupt elite has bled this country dry.*

▸**adj** [before noun] belonging to the richest, most powerful, best-educated, or best-trained group in a society: *Elite (= excellent) troops were airlifted to the trouble zone.*

elitist /ɪˈliː.tɪst/ **adj; noun**

▸**adj** mainly disapproving organized for the good of a few people who have special interests or abilities: *Many remember sport at school as elitist, focusing only on those who were good at it.* • **elitism** /-tɪ.zəm/ **noun** [U] mainly disapproving the quality of being elitist: *The accusation of elitism seems unfair as the festival presents a wide range of music, with something to please everyone.*

▸**noun** [C] mainly disapproving someone who believes that something should be controlled by the richest or best educated group in a society: *Hollywood elitists who give millions of dollars to the Democrat party*

elixir /ɪˈlɪk.sɪəʳ/ (US) /-sjɚ/ **noun** [C usually singular] literary a substance, usually a liquid, with a magical power to cure, improve, or preserve something: *It's yet another health product claiming to be the elixir* ***of life/youth*** *(= something to make you live longer/stay young).*

Elizabethan /ɪˌlɪz.əˈbiː.θən/ **adj; noun**

▸**adj** from the period when Queen Elizabeth I was the ruler of England (1558–1603)

▸**noun** [C] a person living during this period

elk /elk/ noun [C] (plural **elks** or **elk**) **1** US for **wapiti** **2** UK for **moose**

ellipse /ɪˈlɪps/ noun [C] a regular OVAL shape

ellipsis /ɪˈlɪp.sɪs/ noun (plural **ellipses**) specialized **LANGUAGE** ▷ **1** [C or U] the fact of words being left out of a sentence but the sentence can still be understood: *An example of ellipsis is 'What percentage was left?' '20' (= 20 percent).* **PRINTED MARK** ▷ **2** [C] three DOTS in a printed text, [...], which show where one or more words have been intentionally left out

E

elliptical /ɪˈlɪp.tɪ.kəl/ adj **SHAPE** ▷ **1** (also **elliptic**) having an oval shape **LANGUAGE** ▷ **2** formal Elliptical language has parts missing, so that it is sometimes difficult to understand: *His message was written in a deliberately elliptical style.* • **elliptically** /-i/ adv formal

elm /elm/ noun [C or U] a large tree which loses its leaves in winter, or the wood from this tree

El Niño /elˈniːn.jəʊ/ US /-joʊ/ noun [U] an unusual ocean current that happens along the coast of Peru every two to ten years, killing large numbers of sea creatures and causing noticeable and often severe changes in weather conditions in many areas of the world: *the El Niño weather pattern/system/phenomenon* ◦ *Rains came late to the region because of El Niño.*

elocution /ˌel.əˈkjuː.ʃən/ noun [U] the art of careful public speaking, using clear pronunciation and good breathing to control the voice: *classes in elocution*

elongate /ˈiː.lɒŋ.geɪt/ US /ɪˈlɑːŋ-/ verb [I or T] to become or make something become longer, and often thinner: *The cells elongate as they take in water.* • **elongation** /ˌiː.lɒŋˈgeɪ.ʃən/ US /ɪˌlɑːŋ-/ noun [U]

elongated /ˈiː.lɒŋ.geɪ.tɪd/ US /ɪˈlɑːŋ.geɪ.t̬ɪd/ adj (specialized **elongate**) longer and thinner than usual: *In the photo her face was slightly elongated.*

elope /ɪˈləʊp/ US /-ˈloʊp/ verb [I] to leave home secretly in order to get married without the permission of parents: *She eloped **with** an Army officer.* • **elopement** /-mənt/ noun [C]

eloquent /ˈel.ə.kwənt/ adj giving a clear, strong message: *She made an eloquent appeal for action.* • **eloquence** /-kwəns/ noun [U] • **eloquently** /-li/ adv *He spoke eloquently.*

else /els/ adv A2 used after words beginning with any-, every-, no-, and some-, or after how, what, where, who, why, but not which, to mean other, another, different, extra: *Everybody else has (= all the other people have) agreed except for you.* ◦ *If it doesn't work, try something else (= something different).* ◦ *Let's go before they ask us to visit anyone else (= another person).* ◦ *It's not my bag. It must be someone else's (= it must belong to another person).* ◦ *The book isn't here. Where else (= in what other place) should I look?* ◦ *He came to see you. Why else (= for what other reason) would he come?* ◦ *After I'd thanked them I didn't know what else (= what other things) to say.*

IDIOM **or else** **1** B2 used to say what will happen if another thing does not happen: *We must be there by six, or else we'll miss the beginning.* **2** B2 used to compare two different things or situations: *She's either really talkative and you can't shut her up or else she's silent.* **3** informal used as a threat, sometimes humorously: *He'd better find it quickly, or else (= or I will punish him in some way)!*

elsewhere /ˌelsˈweər/ US /ˈels.wer/ adv B2 at, in, from, or to another place or other places; anywhere or somewhere else: *The report looks at economic growth in Europe and elsewhere.* ◦ *They couldn't find what they wanted and decided to look elsewhere.*

ELT /ˌiː.elˈtiː/ noun [U] abbreviation for English Language Teaching: the teaching of English to speakers of other languages

elucidate /ɪˈluː.sɪ.deɪt/ verb [I or T] formal to explain or make clear: *I don't understand. You'll have to elucidate.* ◦ *The reasons for the change in weather conditions have been elucidated by several scientists.* • **elucidation** /ɪˌluː.sɪˈdeɪ.ʃən/ noun [U] *These figures need elucidation.*

elude /ɪˈluːd/ verb [T] **NOT ACHIEVE** ▷ **1** formal If something that you want eludes you, you do not succeed in achieving it: *The gold medal continues to elude her.* ◦ *They had minor breakthroughs but real success eluded them.* **NOT BE CAUGHT** ▷ **2** to not be caught by someone: *They eluded the police by fleeing.* **NOT REMEMBER** ▷ **3** formal If a piece of information eludes you, you cannot remember it: *I know who you mean but her name eludes me.*

elusive /ɪˈluː.sɪv/ adj C2 difficult to describe, find, achieve or remember: *The answers to these questions remain as elusive as ever.* ◦ *Success, however, remained elusive for her.* ◦ *elusive memories* • **elusively** /-li/ adv • **elusiveness** /-nəs/ noun [U]

elves /elvz/ plural of **elf**

'em /əm/ informal short form of them: *Tell 'em to go away.*

emaciated /ɪˈmeɪ.si.eɪ.tɪd/ US /-t̬ɪd/ adj formal very thin and weak, usually because of illness or extreme hunger: *There were pictures of emaciated children on the cover of the magazine.* • **emaciation** /ɪˌmeɪ.siˈeɪ.ʃən/ noun [U]

email /ˈiː.meɪl/ noun; verb

▸noun (also **ˈe-mail**) **1** A1 [U] the system for using computers to send messages over the internet: *You can contact us **by** email or fax.* ◦ *What's your **email address?*** **2** A1 [C] a message or document sent using this system: *I got an email from Danielle last week.*

▸verb [T] (also **ˈe-mail**) A2 to send an email to someone: *Email me when you've got time.* ◦ [+ two objects] *Has he emailed you that list of addresses yet?*

emanate /ˈem.ə.neɪt/ verb [T] formal to express a quality or feeling through the way that you look and behave: *Her face emanated sadness.* • **emanation** /ˌem.əˈneɪ.ʃən/ noun [C or U]

PHRASAL VERB **emanate from/through sth/sb** to come out of or be produced by something or someone: *Angry voices emanated from the room.*

emancipate /ɪˈmæn.sɪ.peɪt/ verb [T] to give people social or political freedom and rights

emancipated /ɪˈmæn.sɪ.peɪ.tɪd/ US /-t̬ɪd/ adj not limited socially or politically: *We live in more emancipated times.* ◦ *The 20s and 60s are often regarded as the most emancipated decades.*

emancipation /ɪˌmæn.sɪˈpeɪ.ʃən/ noun [U] the process of giving people social or political freedom and rights: ***women's/female** emancipation* ◦ ***black** emancipation*

emasculate /ɪˈmæs.kjʊ.leɪt/ verb [T] **1** formal to reduce the effectiveness of something: *They were accused of trying to emasculate the report's recommendations.* **2** formal to make a man feel less male by taking away his power and confidence: *A lot of men would feel emasculated if they stayed at home while their wives went out to work.* **3** specialized to remove the male parts of something • **emasculation** /ɪˌmæs.kjʊˈleɪ.ʃən/ noun [U] formal

embalm /ɪmˈbɑːm/ verb [T] to use chemicals to prevent a dead body from decaying • **embalmer** /-bɑː.məʳ/ US /-bɑː.mɚ/ noun [C]

embankment /ɪmˈbæŋk.mənt/ noun [C] an artificial slope made of earth and/or stones: *a river/road/railway embankment*

embargo /ɪmˈbɑː.gəʊ/ (US) /-goʊ/ noun; verb

▸noun [C] (plural **embargoes**) an order to temporarily stop something, especially trading or giving information: *They have **put** an embargo **on** imports of clothing.* ◦ *The police asked for a **news** embargo while they tried to find the kidnapper.*

▸verb [T] to officially stop trading with another country: *They are planning to embargo oil imports.*

embark /ɪmˈbɑːk/ (US) /-bɑːrk/ verb [I] formal to go onto a ship: *We embarked at Liverpool for New York.* → Opposite **disembark** • **embarkation** /ˌem.bɑːˈkeɪ.ʃən/ (US) /-bɑːr-/ noun [C or U] *You'll be asked for those documents **on** embarkation.*

PHRASAL VERB **embark on/upon sth** to start something new or important: *We're embarking upon a new project later this year.*

embarrass /ɪmˈbær.əs/ (US) /-ˈber-/ verb [T] C2 to cause someone to feel nervous, worried or uncomfortable: *You're embarrassing him with your compliments!* ◦ *I didn't want to embarrass her in front of her friends.*

embarrassed /ɪmˈbær.əst/ (US) /-ˈber-/ adj **1** B1 feeling ashamed or shy: *She felt embarrassed **about** undressing in front of the doctor.* ◦ [+ to infinitive] *I was too embarrassed to admit that I was scared.* **2 financially embarrassed** humorous having no money

embarrassing /ɪmˈbær.ə.sɪŋ/ (US) /-ˈber-/ adj B1 making you feel embarrassed: *an embarrassing situation* ◦ [+ to infinitive] ***It's** embarrassing **to** be caught telling a lie.* ◦ *My most embarrassing moment was trying to introduce a woman whose name I couldn't remember.* • **embarrassingly** /-li/ adv *an embarrassingly poor performance/loud voice*

> **!** Common mistake: **embarrassing**
>
> **Warning:** Check your spelling!
>
> **Embarrassing** is one of the 50 words most often spelled wrongly by learners. Remember: the correct spelling has 'rr' and 'ss'.

embarrassment /ɪmˈbær.əs.mənt/ (US) /-ˈber-/ noun [C or U] B2 the feeling of being embarrassed, or something that makes you feel embarrassed: *She blushed with embarrassment.* ◦ *My parents are **an** embarrassment **to** me!*

IDIOM **an embarrassment of riches** formal so many good things or people that it is impossible to decide which of them you want

embassy /ˈem.bə.si/ noun [C] **1** B1 the group of people who represent their country in a foreign country: *We used to be friendly with some people who worked **at** the Swedish Embassy.* **2** B1 the building that these people work in: *The Ambassador held a reception at the embassy.*

embattled /ɪmˈbæt.ld/ (US) /-ˈbæṭ-/ adj having a lot of problems or difficulties: *an embattled government*

embed (-dd-) (US also **imbed**) /ɪmˈbed/ verb [T] to fix something firmly into a substance

embedded (US also **imbedded**) /ɪmˈbed.ɪd/ adj FIXED ▷ **1** fixed into the surface of something: *The thorn was embedded **in** her thumb.* EMOTION ▷ **2** If an emotion, opinion, etc. is embedded in someone or something, it is a very strong or important part of them: *A sense of guilt was deeply embedded **in** my conscience.* PROTECTED BY SOLDIERS ▷ **3** An embedded JOURNALIST or REPORTER travels with and is protected by a unit of soldiers during a war.

embellish /ɪmˈbel.ɪʃ/ verb [T] to make something more beautiful or interesting by adding something to it: *The ceiling was embellished **with** flowers and leaves.* ◦ *He couldn't resist embellishing the story of his accident a little.* • **embellishment** /-mənt/ noun [C or U]

ember /ˈem.bər/ (US) /-bɚ/ noun [C usually plural] a piece of wood or coal, etc. which continues to burn after a fire has no more flames: *We sat by the **glowing/dying** embers of the fire.*

embezzle /ɪmˈbez.l/ verb [I or T] to secretly take money that is in your care or that belongs to an organization or business you work for: *She embezzled thousands of dollars **from** the charity.* • **embezzlement** /-mənt/ noun [U] *They were arrested for embezzlement **of** company funds.* • **embezzler** /-lər/ (US) /-lɚ/ noun [C]

embittered /ɪmˈbɪt.əd/ (US) /-ˈbɪṭ.ɚd/ adj very angry about unfair things that have happened to you: *He died a disillusioned and embittered old man.* • **embitter** /-ˈbɪt.ər/ (US) /-ˈbɪṭ.ɚ/ verb [T] to make someone feel embittered

emblazon /ɪmˈbleɪ.zən/ verb [T usually passive] (also **blazon**) to print or decorate something in a very noticeable way: *Her name was emblazoned **across** the front of the theatre.* ◦ *cars emblazoned **with** the company logo*

emblem /ˈem.bləm/ noun [C] a picture of an object that is used to represent a particular person, group, or idea: *A rose is the national emblem **of** England.*

emblematic /ˌem.bləˈmæt.ɪk/ (US) /-ˈmæṭ-/ adj formal representing a particular person, group or idea: *A sword is emblematic **of** power gained by violence.* • **emblematically** /-ɪ.kəl.i/ adv

embodiment /ɪmˈbɒd.ɪ.mənt/ (US) /-ˈbɑː.dɪ-/ noun **the embodiment of sth** someone or something that represents a quality or an idea exactly: *She was portrayed in the papers as the embodiment of evil.*

embody /ɪmˈbɒd.i/ (US) /-ˈbɑː.di/ verb [T] formal **1** C2 to represent a quality or an idea exactly: *She embodied good sportsmanship on the playing field.* **2** to include as part of something: *Kennett embodied in one man an unusual range of science, music and religion.*

embolden /ɪmˈbəʊl.dən/ (US) /-ˈboʊl-/ verb [T] formal to make someone brave: *Emboldened by drink, he walked over to speak to her.*

embolism /ˈem.bə.lɪ.zəm/ noun [C] specialized a bubble of air, a LUMP (= solid mass) of blood that has become hard or a small piece of fat which blocks a tube carrying blood around the body

emboss /ɪmˈbɒs/ (US) /-ˈbɑːs/ verb [T] to decorate an object, especially with letters, using special tools which make a raised mark on its surface: *She handed me a business card with her name neatly embossed on it.*

embrace /ɪmˈbreɪs/ verb; noun

▸verb ACCEPT ▷ **1** C1 [T] formal to accept something enthusiastically: *This was an opportunity that he would embrace.* HOLD ▷ **2** C2 [I or T] literary to hold someone tightly with both arms to express love, liking, or sympathy, or when greeting or leaving someone: *She saw them embrace on the station platform.* ◦ *He leaned over to embrace the child.* INCLUDE ▷ **3** C1 [T] formal to include something, often as one of a number of things: *Linguistics embraces a diverse range of subjects such as phonetics and stylistics.*

▸noun [C] C2 the act of holding someone tightly with both arms to express love, liking, or sympathy, or when greeting or leaving someone: *She greeted me with a warm embrace.*

embrocation /ˌem.brəˈkeɪ.ʃᵊn/ US /-broʊ-/ noun [C] mainly UK formal a liquid that is rubbed onto the body to reduce pain or stiffness in muscles

embroider /ɪmˈbrɔɪ.dəʳ/ US /-dɚ/ verb [I or T] **DECORATE CLOTH** ▷ **1** to decorate cloth or clothing with patterns or pictures consisting of STITCHES that are sewn directly onto the material: *I am embroidering this picture for my mother.* **ADD TO A STORY** ▷ **2** to make a story more entertaining by adding imaginary details to it: *Naturally, I embroidered the tale a little to make it more interesting.*

E

embroidery /ɪmˈbrɔɪ.dᵊr.i/ US /-dɚ-/ noun **SEWING** ▷ **1** [C or U] patterns or pictures that consist of STITCHES sewn directly onto cloth: *Let me show you Pat's embroideries.* ◦ *It was a beautiful piece of embroidery.* **2** [U] the activity of decorating a piece of cloth with STITCHES sewn onto it: *I'm not very good at embroidery.* **STORY** ▷ **3** [U] the way that someone makes a story more entertaining by adding imaginary details to it: *comic embroidery*

embroil /ɪmˈbrɔɪl/ verb [T] to cause someone to become involved in an argument or a difficult situation: *She had no desire to embroil her**self** **in** lengthy lawsuits with the tabloid newspapers.* ◦ *The United Nations was reluctant to get its forces embroiled **in** civil war.*

embryo /ˈem.bri.əʊ/ US /-oʊ/ noun [C] (plural **embryos**) **1** an animal that is developing either in its mother's WOMB or in an egg, or a plant that is developing in a seed: *Between the eighth week of development and birth a human embryo is called a foetus.* **2 in embryo** formal developing and not yet complete: *The department's plans for enlargement are still in embryo.*

embryology /ˌem.briˈɒl.ə.dʒi/ US /-ˈɑː.lə-/ noun [U] the study of animal development between the FERTILIZATION of the egg and the time when the animal is born • **embryologist** /-dʒɪst/ noun [C]

embryonic /ˌem.briˈɒn.ɪk/ US /-ˈɑː.nɪk/ adj **1** relating to an embryo **2** [before noun] formal starting to develop: *The project is still at an embryonic **stage**.*

emcee /ˌemˈsiː/ noun [C], verb US (to act as an) MC (= Master of Ceremonies)

emend /ɪˈmend/ verb [T] to correct or improve a text: *The text is currently being emended and will be published shortly.* • **emendation** /ˌiː.menˈdeɪ.ʃᵊn/ noun [C or U]

emerald /ˈem.ə.rəld/ noun **1** [C or U] a transparent bright green valuable stone that is often used in jewellery: *a ring with a large emerald* ◦ *an emerald necklace/ring* **2** [U] (also **ˌemerald ˈgreen**) a bright green colour • **emerald** /ˈem.ə.rəld/ adj (also **ˌemerald ˈgreen**) *emerald eyes*

the ˌEmerald ˈIsle noun literary Ireland

emerge /ɪˈmɜːdʒ/ US /-ˈmɝːdʒ/ verb [I] **APPEAR** ▷ **1** B2 to appear by coming out of something or out from behind something: *She emerged **from** the sea, blue with cold.* **2** to come to the end of a difficult period or experience: *The Prince emerged unscathed **from** the scandal.* **BECOME KNOWN** ▷ **3** C1 to become known, especially as a result of examining something or asking questions about it: *The facts behind the scandal are sure to emerge eventually.* ◦ [+ that] ***It** has emerged **that** secret talks had been going on between the two companies before the takeover was announced.* ◦ *She's the most exciting British singer to emerge on the pop scene for a decade.*

emergence /ɪˈmɜː.dʒᵊns/ US /-ˈmɝː-/ noun [U] **BECOMING KNOWN** ▷ **1** the fact of something becoming known or starting to exist: *China's emergence **as** an economic power* ◦ *the emergence **of** a new strain of the HIV virus* **APPEARING** ▷ **2** formal the fact of someone appearing by coming out from behind something: *Unfortunately, I misjudged the timing of my emergence.* **3** the fact of someone or something coming to the end of a difficult period or experience: *the country's emergence **from** bankruptcy*

emergency /ɪˈmɜː.dʒᵊn.si/ US /-ˈmɝː-/ noun [C or U] B1 something dangerous or serious, such as an accident, which happens suddenly or unexpectedly and needs fast action in order to avoid harmful results: *How would disabled people escape **in** an emergency?* ◦ *Is the emergency **exit** suitable for wheelchairs?* ◦ *The pilot of the aircraft was forced to make an emergency **landing** on Lake Geneva.*

> **Word partners for emergency**
>
> *cope with/deal with/respond to* an emergency • a *dire/real/sudden* emergency • *in* an emergency

eˈmergency ˌbrake noun US for **handbrake**

eˈmergency ˌroom noun (abbreviation **ER**) US for **casualty**

eˌmergency ˈservices noun [plural] mainly UK the organizations that deal with accidents and urgent problems such as fire, illness or crime

emerging /ɪˈmɜː.dʒɪŋ/ US /-ˈmɝː-/ adj [before noun] (formal **emergent**) starting to exist: *Western governments should be giving more aid to the emerging democracies of the Third World.* ◦ *emergent economies/markets*

emeritus /ɪˈmer.ɪ.təs/ US /-ţəs/ adj [before or after noun] no longer having a position, especially in a college or university, but keeping the title of the position: *She became Emeritus Professor of Linguistics when she retired.*

emery /ˈem.ᵊr.i/ US /-ɚ-/ noun [U] a very hard, dark grey substance, usually in the form of a powder, that is used to smooth or shape things

ˈemery ˌboard noun [C] a thin piece of cardboard with a rough surface used to shape FINGERNAILS

emetic /ɪˈmet.ɪk/ US /-ˈmeţ-/ noun [C] specialized a substance, especially a medicine, that causes vomiting • **emetic adj**

emigrant /ˈem.ɪ.grənt/ noun [C] a person who emigrates → Compare **immigrant**

emigrate /ˈem.ɪ.greɪt/ verb [I] to leave a country permanently and go to live in another one: *Millions of Germans emigrated **from** Europe **to** America in the 19th century.* ◦ *Thousands of Britons emigrate every year.* • **emigration** /ˌem.ɪˈgreɪ.ʃᵊn/ noun [C or U]

émigré (also **emigré**) /ˈem.ɪ.greɪ/ noun [C] someone who has had to leave their country permanently, usually for political reasons

eminence /ˈem.ɪ.nəns/ noun [U] the state of being famous, respected, or important: *his eminence as a film director*

Eminence /ˈem.ɪ.nəns/ noun [C] the title of a CARDINAL (= priest of very high rank in the Roman Catholic Church)

éminence grise /ˈem.ɪ.nõsˌgriːz/ noun [C] (also **ˌgrey ˈeminence**) someone without an official position who has power or influence over rulers or people who make decisions: *Civil servants are the ones who really have the power – they are the éminences grises behind the government ministers.*

eminent /ˈem.ɪ.nənt/ adj C2 famous, respected or important: *an eminent historian*

eminently /ˈem.ɪ.nənt.li/ **adv** formal very and obviously: *He is eminently qualified for the job.* ◦ *an eminently readable book*

emir /emˈɪəʳ/ (US) /-ˈɪr/ **noun** [C] a ruler of particular Muslim countries in the Middle East

emirate /ˈem.ɪ.rət/ **noun** [C] a country ruled by an emir

emissary /ˈem.ɪ.sᵊr.i/ (US) /-ser-/ **noun** [C] formal a person sent by one government or political leader to another to take messages or to take part in discussions: *The Foreign Secretary has flown to China as the personal emissary of the prime minister.*

emission /ɪˈmɪʃ.ᵊn/ **noun** **1** (C1) [U] the act of sending out gas, heat, light, etc.: *Environmental groups want a substantial reduction in the emission of greenhouse gases.* **2** (C1) [C] an amount of gas, heat, light, etc. that is sent out: *carbon dioxide emissions*

emit /ɪˈmɪt/ **verb** [T] **(-tt-)** (C2) to send out a beam, noise, smell, or gas: *The alarm emits infra-red rays which are used to detect any intruder.* ◦ *The machine emits a high-pitched sound when you press the button.*

Emmy /ˈem.i/ **noun** [C] (plural **Emmys**) one of a set of American prizes given each year to actors and other people involved in making television programmes

emo /ˈiː.məʊ/ (US) /-moʊ/ **noun** **1** [U] a type of popular PUNK music with words about people's feelings and emotions **2** [C] slang a young person who likes this music, wears mainly black clothes, and is often nervous, worried, and unhappy • **emo adj** relating to the music, clothes, opinions, and behaviour of emos

emollient /ɪˈmɒl.i.ənt/ (US) /-ˈmɑː.li-/ **noun; adj**
▸**noun** [C] a cream or liquid which makes dry or sore skin softer or less painful
▸**adj** **1** helping to treat dry, sore skin: *an emollient cream* **2** formal making people calm and avoiding argument: *an emollient mood/tone*

emolument /ɪˈmɒl.jʊ.mənt/ (US) /-ˈmɑːl-/ **noun** [C] UK formal a payment in money or some other form that is made for work that has been done

emoticon /ɪˈməʊ.tɪ.kɒn/ (US) /ɪˈmoʊ.t̬ɪ.kɑːn/ **noun** [C] (also **smiley**) an image made up of symbols such as PUNCTUATION MARKS, used in text messages, emails, etc. to express a particular emotion

emotion /ɪˈməʊ.ʃᵊn/ (US) /-ˈmoʊ-/ **noun** [C or U] (B2) a strong feeling such as love or anger, or strong feelings in general: *Like a lot of men, he finds it hard to express his emotions.* ◦ *My mother was overcome with emotion and burst into tears.*

> Word partners for **emotion**
>
> *display/express/show* emotion • *experience/feel* emotion • *be overcome by/with* emotion • *conflicting/mixed* emotions • a *deep/intense/powerful/strong* emotion • a *flicker/sign/trace* of emotion • a *display/expression* of emotion • *without* emotion

emotional /ɪˈməʊ.ʃᵊn.ᵊl/ (US) /-ˈmoʊ-/ **adj** **1** (B2) relating to the emotions: *a child's emotional development* ◦ *My doctor said the problem was more emotional than physical.* ◦ *Amnesia can be caused by emotional trauma.* **2** (B2) having and expressing strong feelings: *He's a very emotional man.* ◦ *I felt quite emotional during the wedding ceremony.* ◦ *He became very emotional when I told him I was pregnant.* ◦ *The president has made an emotional (= full of emotion) plea for the killing to stop.* • **emotionally** /-i/ **adv** (B2) *She spoke emotionally about her experiences as a war correspondent.* ◦ *Many children have become emotionally **disturbed** as a result of the abuse they have suffered.* ◦ *an emotionally **charged** (= causing strong feelings) issue*

eˌmotional ˈblackmail **noun** [U] a way of trying to make someone do something by making them feel guilty

eˌmotional inˈtelligence **noun** [U] the ability to understand the way people feel and react and to use this skill to make good judgments and to avoid or solve problems: *Individuals with even a small degree of emotional intelligence are a dream to work for.*

emotionalism /ɪˈməʊ.ʃᵊn.ᵊl.ɪ.zᵊm/ (US) /-ˈmoʊ-/ **noun** [U] disapproving showing too much emotion

emotionless /ɪˈməʊ.ʃᵊn.ləs/ (US) /-ˈmoʊ-/ **adj** not showing emotion

emotive /ɪˈməʊ.tɪv/ (US) /-ˈmoʊ.t̬ɪv/ **adj** causing strong feelings: *Animal experimentation is a highly emotive **issue**.* • **emotively** /-li/ **adv**

empanel (**-ll-** or US usually **-l-**) (also **impanel** (**-ll-** or US USUALLY **-l-**)) /ɪmˈpæn.ᵊl/ **verb** [T] specialized in a law court, to choose the people who will form the JURY for a trial

empathize (UK usually **empathise**) /ˈem.pə.θaɪz/ **verb** [I] to be able to understand how someone else feels: *It's very easy to empathize **with** the characters in her books.* → Compare **sympathize** • **empathetic** /ˌem.pəˈθet.ɪk/ (US) /-ˈθet̬-/ **adj** empathizing with someone

empathy /ˈem.pə.θi/ **noun** [U] (C2) the ability to share someone else's feelings or experiences by imagining what it would be like to be in their situation → Compare **sympathy**

emperor /ˈem.pᵊr.əʳ/ (US) /-pɚ.ɚ/ **noun** [C] (C1) a male ruler of an EMPIRE → See also **empress**

emphasis /ˈem.fə.sɪs/ **noun** [C or U] (plural **emphases**) **1** (B2) the particular importance or attention that you give to something: *I think we should put as much emphasis **on** preventing disease as we do on curing it.* ◦ *Schools here **put/place/lay** great emphasis **on** written work and grammar.* **2** the extra force that you give to a word or part of a word when you are saying it: *The emphasis is **on** the final syllable.* ◦ *Where do you **put** the emphasis in the word 'controversy'?*

emphasize (UK usually **emphasise**) /ˈem.fə.saɪz/ **verb** [T] **1** (B2) to show that something is very important or worth giving attention to: [+ question word] *I'd just like to emphasize **how** important it is for people to learn foreign languages.* ◦ [+ that] *He emphasized **that** all the people taking part in the research were volunteers.* ◦ *You can use italics or capitals to emphasize a word in a piece of writing.* **2** to make something more obvious: *Tight jeans will only emphasize any extra weight that you are carrying.*

emphatic /emˈfæt.ɪk/ (US) /-ˈfæt̬-/ **adj** done or said in a strong way and without any doubt: *Poland reached the final of the championship yesterday with an emphatic 5–0 **victory** over Italy.* ◦ *The minister has issued an emphatic rejection of the accusation.* • **emphatically** /-ɪ.kᵊl.i/ **adv** *Johnson has emphatically **denied** the allegations against him.*

emphysema /ˌem.fəˈsiː.mə/ **noun** [U] a condition in which the small bags in the lungs become filled with too much air, causing breathing difficulties and heart problems: *Heavy cigarette smoking often causes emphysema.*

empire /ˈem.paɪəʳ/ (US) /-paɪr/ **noun** [C] **COUNTRIES** ▷ **1** (C1) a group of countries ruled by a single person, government or country: *the Holy Roman Empire* → See also **imperial** **ORGANIZATION** ▷ **2** (C1) a very large and important business or organization: *In the space of* *just ten years, her company has grown from one small shop to a multi-million-pound empire.*

empirical /ɪm'pɪr.ɪ.kəl/ **adj** C2 based on what is experienced or seen rather than on theory: *This theory needs to be backed up with solid empirical **data/evidence**.* ◦ *Empirical **studies** show that some forms of alternative medicine are extremely effective.* • **empirically** /-i/ **adv**

empiricism /ɪm'pɪr.ɪ.sɪ.zəm/ **noun** [U] the belief in using empirical methods • **empiricist** /-sɪst/ **noun** [C]

emplacement /ɪm'pleɪs.mənt/ **noun** [C] specialized a position specially prepared for large pieces of military equipment

employ /ɪm'plɔɪ/ **verb; noun**

▸**verb** PROVIDE JOB ▷ **1** B1 [T] to have someone work or do a job for you and pay them for it: *How many people does your company employ?* ◦ *Can't we employ someone **as** an assistant to help with all this paperwork?* ◦ [+ to infinitive] *We've employed a market researcher **to** find out what people really want from a cable TV system.* ◦ *More people are now employed in service industries than in manufacturing.* USE ▷ **2** C1 [T] formal to use something: *Sophisticated statistical analysis was employed to obtain these results.* SPEND TIME ▷ **3 be employed in doing sth** formal to spend time doing something: *He was busily employed in lacing up his shoes.*

▸**noun** formal **be in sb's employ** to be working for someone

employable /ɪm'plɔɪ.ə.bl̩/ **adj** having enough skills and abilities for someone to employ you: *Computer skills make you far more employable.*

employee /ɪm'plɔɪ.iː/, /ˌem.plɔɪ'iː/ **noun** [C] B1 someone who is paid to work for someone else: *The number of employees in the company has trebled over the past decade.* ◦ *She's a former council employee/employee of the council.*

employer /ɪm'plɔɪ.əʳ/ US /-ɚ/ **noun** [C] B1 a person or organization that employs people: *We need a reference from your former employer.*

> **Common mistake: employer or employee?**
>
> **Warning:** Choose the right word!
>
> To talk about someone who is paid to work for someone else, don't say 'employer', say **employee**:
>
> ~~*We should send all our employers on a training course.*~~

employment /ɪm'plɔɪ.mənt/ **noun** [U] PROVIDE JOB ▷ **1** B1 the fact of someone being paid to work for a company or organization: *Employment levels are unlikely to rise significantly before the end of next year.* ◦ *How long have you been looking for employment?* **2 be in employment** formal to have a job: *Are you in employment at the moment?* USE ▷ **3** formal use: *How can you justify the employment **of** capital punishment?*

> **Word partners for employment**
>
> *look for/seek* employment • *create/offer/provide* employment • *full-time/part-time/permanent/temporary* employment • *full* employment • *gainful/paid* employment

em'ployment ˌagency **noun** [C] a business that finds suitable people to work for other businesses

emporium /ɪm'pɔː.ri.əm/ US /-pɔːr.i-/ **noun** [C] (plural **emporia** or **emporiums**) old-fashioned a large shop selling a large range of goods, or a shop selling a particular type of goods: *a video/ice cream/antiques emporium*

empower /ɪm'paʊəʳ/ US /-'paʊr/ **verb** [T] to give someone official authority or the freedom to do something: [+ to infinitive] *This amendment empowers the president **to** declare an emergency for a wide range of reasons.* ◦ *The first step in empowering the poorest sections of society is making sure they vote.* • **empowerment** /-mənt/ **noun** [U]

empowering /ɪm'paʊə.rɪŋ/ US /-'paʊr.ɪŋ/ **adj** Something that is empowering makes you more confident and makes you feel that you are in control of your life: *For me, learning to drive was an empowering experience.*

empress /'em.prəs/ **noun** [C] a female ruler of an EMPIRE, or the wife of a male ruler of an empire → See also **emperor**

emptiness /'emp.ti.nəs/ **noun** [U] EMPTY SPACE ▷ **1** empty space: *He gazed out over the emptiness of the moors.* NOT SINCERE ▷ **2** the fact of not being sincere or having no real meaning: *the emptiness of these political gestures* SAD FEELING ▷ **3** a sad feeling of having no emotion or purpose: *I was left with a horrible feeling of emptiness.*

empty /'emp.ti/ **adj; verb; noun**

▸**adj** NOTHING IN ▷ **1** A2 not containing any things or people: *an empty house/street* ◦ *Shall I take the empty bottles for recycling?* ◦ *The train was empty (= there were no passengers) by the time it reached London.* NOT SINCERE ▷ **2** C1 [usually before noun] not sincere or without any real meaning: *empty **threats/rhetoric*** ◦ *They're just empty **promises**.* WITHOUT PURPOSE ▷ **3** without purpose or interest: *He says his life has been completely empty since his wife died.* ◦ *I felt empty, like a part of me had died.* • **emptily** /-tɪ.li/ **adv**

> **Other ways of saying empty**
>
> If a place is empty because there are no people in it, you can describe it as **deserted**:
>
> *It was three o'clock in the morning and the streets were **deserted**.*
>
> **Desolate** can be used about places that are empty and unattractive:
>
> *The house stood in a bleak, **desolate** landscape.*
>
> If a place or building is empty because no people live there, you could use the word **uninhabited**:
>
> *The island is **uninhabited**.*
>
> If a room or building is empty because it has no furniture in it, you could describe it as **bare** or **unfurnished**:
>
> *The room was completely **bare**.*
>
> *The house was **unfurnished**.*
>
> **Vacant** is a word you can use to describe something that is empty and available to be used:
>
> *The hospital has no **vacant** beds.*
>
> **Blank** can be used about empty places on a piece of paper:
>
> *Sign your name in the **blank** space at the bottom of the form.*

IDIOM **on an empty stomach** without eating anything: *You should never go to work on an empty stomach.*

▸**verb** **1** [T] to remove everything from inside something: *I emptied the closet and put my belongings into the black overnight case.* ◦ *Would you mind emptying (**out**) your pockets?* ◦ *Empty the soup **into** a saucepan and simmer gently for ten minutes.* ◦ *She quickly emptied her glass (= drank its contents) and ordered another drink.* **2** [I] to become empty: *The place emptied pretty quickly when the fight started.*

PHRASAL VERB **empty into sth** If a river empties into a larger area of water, the water from it flows into that larger area: *The River Tees empties into the North Sea.*

▸**noun** [C usually plural] an empty drinks bottle: *Don't forget to take the empties to the bottle bank.*

ˌempty ˈcalories noun [plural] energy from food containing no NUTRIENTS (= substances which help you to be healthy)

ˌempty-ˈhanded adj [after verb] without bringing or taking anything: *We can't go to the party empty-handed.*

ˌempty-ˈheaded adj [after verb] silly, stupid, or not having good judgment

ˈempty ˌnester noun [C] informal someone whose children have grown up, and no longer live with them

empty ˈnest ˌsyndrome noun [U] the sad feelings which parents have when their children grow up and leave home: *The last of her children had recently moved out and she was suffering from empty nest syndrome.*

EMS /iː.emˈes/ noun **MONEY** ▷ **1 the EMS** [S] abbreviation for the European Monetary System: a system for limiting changes in the values of the different types of money used in countries in the European Union → Compare **ECU, EMU PHONE** ▷ **2** [U] abbreviation for enhanced messaging service: a system for sending text messages from one mobile phone to another

emu /ˈiː.mjuː/ noun [C] (plural **emu** or **emus**) a large Australian bird with a long neck and grey or brown feathers, which cannot fly but has long legs and can run quickly

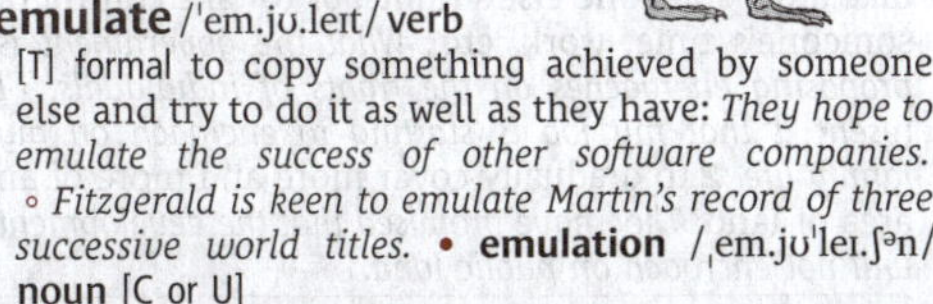
emu

EMU /ˌiː.emˈjuː/ noun [U] abbreviation for European Monetary Union: the process within the European Union of moving towards a single CURRENCY → Compare **ECU, EMS**

emulate /ˈem.jʊ.leɪt/ verb [T] formal to copy something achieved by someone else and try to do it as well as they have: *They hope to emulate the success of other software companies.* ◦ *Fitzgerald is keen to emulate Martin's record of three successive world titles.* • **emulation** /ˌem.jʊˈleɪ.ʃᵊn/ noun [C or U]

emulsifier /ɪˈmʌl.sɪ.faɪ.əʳ/ (US) /-ɚ/ noun [C] a substance which forms or keeps an emulsion and is often added to PROCESSED foods to prevent particular parts from separating

emulsify /ɪˈmʌl.sɪ.faɪ/ verb [I or T] If two liquids emulsify or are emulsified, they combine and become a smooth mixture.

emulsion /ɪˈmʌl.ʃᵊn/ noun [C or U] **1** a mixture that results when one liquid is added to another and is mixed with it but does not dissolve into it: *Mixing oil and vinegar together produces an emulsion.* **2** a water-based paint that is not shiny when dry: *emulsion paint*

en- /ɪn-/, /en-/ prefix (before b or p **em-**) **1** used to form verbs which mean to put into or onto something: *encase* ◦ *encircle* ◦ *endanger* **2** used to form verbs which mean to cause to be something: *enable* ◦ *endear* ◦ *enlarge* ◦ *enrich* **3** used to form verbs which mean to provide with something: *empower*

-en /-ᵊn/ suffix used to form verbs which mean to increase the stated quality: *Sweeten to taste with honey or brown sugar.* ◦ *I've had to loosen my belt.*

enable /ɪˈneɪ.bl̩/ verb [T] B2 to make someone able to do something, or to make something possible: [+ to infinitive] *Computerization should enable us* ***to*** *cut production costs by half.*

enabled /ɪˈneɪ.bl̩d/ adj, suffix **1** provided with a particular type of equipment or TECHNOLOGY, or having the necessary or correct system, device or arrangement to use it: *Their aim is to make sure that every home and business becomes* ***internet****-enabled in the next ten years.* **2** operated or made possible by the use of a particular thing: *voice-enabled software*

enabler /ɪˈneɪ.bləʳ/ (US) /-blɚ/ noun [C] a person or organization that allows other people to do things themselves instead of doing things for them

enact /ɪˈnækt/ verb **MAKE LAW** ▷ **1** [T often passive] specialized to put something into action, especially to change something into a law: *A package of economic sanctions is to be enacted against the country.* **PERFORM** ▷ **2** [T] formal to perform a story or play: *The stories are enacted using music, dance and mime.* • **enactment** /-mənt/ noun [C or U]

enamel /ɪˈnæm.ᵊl/ noun; verb

▸**noun 1** [C or U] a decorative substance like glass that is melted onto clay, metal, or glass objects and then left to cool and become hard, or an object covered with this substance **2** a type of paint which forms a shiny surface when dry **3** the hard white shiny substance which forms the covering of a tooth

▸**verb** [T] (**-ll-** or US usually **-l-**) to cover something with enamel

enamoured UK formal (US **enamored**) /ɪˈnæm.əd/ (US) /-ɚd/ adj [after verb] liking a lot: *I have to say I'm not exactly enamoured* ***with/of*** *this part of the country.*

en ˈbloc adv formal all together in a united group: *The ruling committee resigned en bloc to make way for a new election.*

enc. (also **encl.**) written abbreviation for **enclosed**

encamp /ɪnˈkæmp/ verb [I or T] mainly UK (US usually **camp**) to make an encampment or put someone in an encampment

encampment /ɪnˈkæmp.mənt/ noun [C] a group of tents or temporary shelters put in one place: *Many people are living in encampments around the city with no electricity or running water.*

encapsulate /ɪnˈkæp.sjʊ.leɪt/ verb [T] to express or show the most important facts about something: *It was very difficult to encapsulate the story of the revolution* ***in*** *a single one-hour documentary.* • **encapsulation** /ɪnˌkæp.sjʊˈleɪ.ʃᵊn/ noun [C or U]

encase /ɪnˈkeɪs/ verb [T] to cover or surround something or someone completely: *The nuclear waste is encased* ***in*** *concrete before being sent for storage in disused mines.*

-ence (also **-ance**) /-ᵊns/ suffix **ACTION** ▷ **1** used to form nouns which refer to an action or series of actions: *violence (= violent actions)* ◦ *a performance (= act of performing)* **STATE** ▷ **2** used to form nouns which describe a state or quality: *her long absence (= period during which she was absent)*

encephalitis /ˌen.kef.əˈlaɪ.tɪs/ (US) /enˌsef.əˈlaɪ.t̬ɪs/ noun [U] specialized a serious illness caused by an infection that makes the brain swell

enchant /ɪnˈtʃɑːnt/ (US) /-ˈtʃænt/ verb [T] **PLEASE** ▷ **1** to attract or please someone very much: *The audience was clearly enchanted by her performance.* **MAGIC** ▷ **2** to have a magical effect on someone or something

• **enchanter** /-ˈtʃɑːn.təʳ/ (US) /-ˈtʃæn.t̬ɚ/ **noun** [C] • **enchantment** /-mənt/ **noun** [C or U] *spells and enchantments*

enchanted /ɪnˈtʃɑːn.tɪd/ (US) /-ˈtʃæn.t̬ɪd/ **adj** affected by magic or seeming to be affected by magic: *They met in Paris one enchanted afternoon in early autumn.*

enchanting /ɪnˈtʃɑːn.tɪŋ/ (US) /-ˈtʃæn.t̬ɪŋ/ **adj** very pleasant: *It's described in the guide book as 'an enchanting medieval city'.*

E

enchantress /ɪnˈtʃɑːn.trəs/ (US) /-ˈtʃæn-/ **noun** [C] **1** a woman with magical powers **2** literary an extremely attractive and interesting woman

enchilada /ˌen.tʃɪˈlɑː.də/ **noun** [C] a type of food originally from Mexico consisting of a thin PANCAKE that is fried, filled with meat, and covered with a very spicy sauce

encircle /ɪnˈsɜː.kl/ (US) /-ˈsɝː-/ **verb** [T] to surround something, forming a circle around it: *The house is encircled by a high fence.* ◦ *Villaverde is one of the high-rise districts that encircle Madrid.*

enclave /ˈeŋ.kleɪv/ (US) /ˈɑːŋ-/ **noun** [C] a part of a country that is surrounded by another country, or a group of people who are different from the people living in the surrounding area: *Campione d'Italia is an Italian enclave in Switzerland.*

enclose /ɪnˈkləʊz/ (US) /-ˈkloʊz/ **verb** [T] **SURROUND** ▷ **1** (C1) to surround: *The park that encloses the monument has recently been enlarged.* **SEND** ▷ **2** (B2) to send something in the same envelope or parcel as something else: *Please enclose a curriculum vitae with your letter of application.*

enclosed /ɪnˈkləʊzd/ (US) /-ˈkloʊzd/ **adj** **SURROUNDED** ▷ **1** surrounded by walls, objects or structures: *He doesn't like enclosed* ***spaces****.* **SENT** ▷ **2** sent to someone in an envelope with a letter: *The enclosed card is for Julia.* ◦ formal *Please find enclosed a cheque in settlement of your invoice.*

enclosure /ɪnˈkləʊ.ʒəʳ/ (US) /-ˈkloʊ.ʒɚ/ **noun** **SURROUNDED** ▷ **1** [C] an area surrounded by fences or walls: *the members' enclosure* **2** [C or U] the act of putting fences around land: *An early example of privatization was the enclosure* ***of*** *public land for use by wealthy landlords.* **SENT** ▷ **3** [C] something that is put in the same envelope or parcel as something else

encode /ɪnˈkəʊd/ (US) /-ˈkoʊd/ **verb** **1** [T often passive] to change something into a system for sending messages secretly, or to represent complicated information in a simple or short way: *Many satellite broadcasts are encoded so that they can only be received by people who have paid to see them.* ◦ *Some music CDs are now encoded with information about the performers and their music.* **2** [I or T] specialized to use a word or phrase in a foreign language in the correct way: *Grammatical information helps learners to encode sentences.* → Compare **decode**

encompass /ɪnˈkʌm.pəs/ **verb** [T] formal to include, especially different types of things: *The festival is to encompass everything from music, theatre, and ballet to literature, cinema and the visual arts.*

encore! /ˈɒŋ.kɔːʳ/ (US) /ˈɑːŋ.kɔːr/ **exclamation** shouted at the end of a performance to get the performer to sing or play more

encore /ˈɒŋ.kɔːʳ/ (US) /ˈɑːŋ.kɔːr/ **noun** [C] an extra song or piece of music that is performed at the end of a show because the audience shout for it: *We were shouting for an encore.* ◦ *They did a few old hits* ***as/for*** *an encore.*

encounter /ɪnˈkaʊn.təʳ/ (US) /-t̬ɚ/ **noun; verb**

▸**noun** [C] **1** a meeting, especially one that happens by chance: *I had a rather alarming encounter* ***with*** *a wild pig.* ◦ *This meeting will be the first encounter* ***between*** *the party leaders since the election.* **2** an occasion when people have sex, usually with someone they have not met before **3** an occasion when two teams play against each other: *In their last encounter* ***with*** *Italy, England won 3–2.*

▸**verb** [T] **MEET** ▷ **1** formal to meet someone unexpectedly: *On their way home they encountered a woman selling flowers.* **EXPERIENCE** ▷ **2** (B2) to experience, especially something unpleasant: *When did you first encounter these difficulties?* ◦ *The army is reported to be encountering considerable resistance.*

encourage /ɪnˈkʌr.ɪdʒ/ (US) /-ˈkɝː-/ **verb** [T] **1** (B1) to make someone more likely to do something, or to make something more likely to happen: [T + to infinitive] *We were encouraged* ***to*** *learn foreign languages at school.* ◦ *The council is encouraging the development of the property for both employment and recreation.* **2** (B1) to talk or behave in a way that gives someone confidence to do something: *They've always encouraged me* ***in*** *everything I've wanted to do.*

encouraged /ɪnˈkʌr.ɪdʒd/ (US) /-ˈkɝː-/ **adj** [after verb] having more confidence or hope about something: *She felt encouraged by their promise of support.*

encouragement /ɪnˈkʌr.ɪdʒ.mənt/ (US) /-ˈkɝː-/ **noun** [C or U] **1** (B2) words or behaviour that give someone confidence to do something: *Children need lots of encouragement from their parents.* ◦ *I could never have achieved this without the encouragement* ***of*** *my husband and family.* **2** words or behaviour that make something more likely to happen: *The armed forces are now* ***giving*** *positive encouragement to applications from Asians and black people.*

encouraging /ɪnˈkʌr.ɪ.dʒɪŋ/ (US) /-ˈkɝː-/ **adj** (B2) making you feel more confidence or hope: *There was a lot of positive feedback which was very encouraging.* • **encouragingly** /-li/ **adv** *My mother smiled encouragingly at me as I went up on stage.*

encroach /ɪnˈkrəʊtʃ/ (US) /-ˈkroʊtʃ/ **verb**

PHRASAL VERB **encroach on/upon sth** **1** to gradually take away someone else's rights, or to take control of someone's time, work, etc.: *What the government is proposing encroaches on the rights of individuals.* ◦ *I resent it that my job is starting to encroach on my family life.* **2** to gradually cover more and more of an area of land: *They have promised that the development will not encroach on public land.*

encroachment /ɪnˈkrəʊtʃ.mənt/ (US) /-ˈkroʊtʃ-/ **noun** [C or U] the act of gradually taking away someone else's rights, or taking control of someone's time, work, etc.: *The new censorship laws are serious encroachments* ***on*** *freedom of expression.*

encrustation /ˌɪn.krʌsˈteɪ.ʃᵊn/ **noun** [C] US for **incrustation**

encrusted /ɪnˈkrʌs.tɪd/ **adj** covered with something hard or decorative: *She arrived home with her knees encrusted* ***with*** *mud.* ◦ *The manuscript is bound in gold and silver and encrusted* ***with*** *jewels.*

encrypt /ɪnˈkrɪpt/ **verb** [T usually passive] to change electronic information or signals into a secret CODE (= system of letters, numbers, or symbols) that people cannot understand or use on normal equipment: *Your financial information is fully encrypted and cannot be accessed.* • **encryption** /-ˈkrɪp.ʃᵊn/ **noun** [U]

encumber /ɪnˈkʌm.bəʳ/ (US) /-bɚ/ **verb** [T] formal to weigh someone or something down, or to make it difficult for someone to do something: *Today,* *thankfully, women tennis players are not encumbered* ***with/by*** *long, heavy skirts and high-necked blouses.* • **encumbrance** /-brᵊns/ **noun** [C] something that encumbers you: *When you're walking 30 miles a day, the fewer encumbrances the better.*

-ency (also **-ancy**) /-ᵊn.si/ **suffix** used to form nouns showing a state or quality: *her long presidency (= time during which she was president)* ◦ *a difficult pregnancy (= time during which a woman is pregnant)*

encyclopedia (also **encyclopaedia**) /ɪnˌsaɪ.kləˈpiː.di.ə/ **noun** [C] a book or set of books containing many articles arranged in ALPHABETICAL order that deal either with the whole of human knowledge or with a particular part of it, or a similar set of articles on the internet: *The Cambridge Encyclopedia of Language*

encyclopedic (also **encyclopaedic**) /ɪnˌsaɪ.kləˈpiː.dɪk/ **adj** **1** containing a lot of information **2** covering a large range of knowledge, often in great detail: *her encyclopedic knowledge of France*

end /end/ noun; verb

▸**noun** **LAST POINT** ▷ **1** A2 [C] the part of a place or thing that is furthest away from the centre: *This cable should have a plug* ***at*** *one end and a socket at the other.* ◦ *We damaged* ***the*** *end* ***of*** *the piano when we moved it.* ◦ *Get to* ***the*** *end* ***of*** *the queue and wait your turn like everyone else.* ◦ *Our house is the third from the end on the left.* ◦ *Is it safe to stand the computer on (its) end?* **2** A1 [C] the final part of something such as a period of time, activity, or story: *I always like to leave my desk clear* ***at the*** *end* ***of*** *the day.* ◦ *The end of the play was much more exciting than I'd expected.* ◦ *This latest injury must surely mean that her tennis career is now* ***at an*** *end (= finished).* ◦ *The statement said there would be* ***no*** *end* ***to*** *the violence until the terrorists' demands were met.* **3** [S] polite word for death: *We were all by her bedside when the end finally* ***came.*** ◦ *He* ***met his*** *end (= died) in a shoot-out with the police.* **4** [C] either of the two halves of a sports field: *The teams change ends at half-time so that neither side has an unfair advantage.* **5** [C] US one of the two players in American football who begin play furthest from the ball **6 bring sth to an end** C1 to make something finish: *Having agreed upon the matter of payment, he brought the interview to an end.* **7 in the end** B1 finally, after something has been thought about or discussed a lot: *We were thinking about going to Switzerland, but in the end we went to Austria.* **8 for hours, days, etc. on end** B2 for hours, days, etc. without stopping: *He used to lock himself in his bedroom for hours on end and refuse to talk to anyone.* **9 come to an end** B2 to finish: *Everyone wishes the war would come to an end soon.* **SMALL PART** ▷ **10** [C] a small unwanted part of something that is left after most of it has been used: *The floor was covered in cigarette ends.* **AIM** ▷ **11** [C] an aim, intention or purpose: *Do you have a particular end in mind?* **12 to this end** with this aim: *He wanted science students to take an interest in the arts, and to this end he ran literature classes at his home on Sunday afternoons.* **TYPE OF ACTIVITY** ▷ **13** [S] informal the parts of a task or process connected with one particular type of activity or person: *Rick's more involved with the financial end* ***of things.*** **14 sb's end of the bargain, deal, etc.** the area of activity for which someone is responsible: *We've kept our end of the deal – let's see if they keep theirs.*

IDIOMS **at the end of the day** UK something that you say before you give the most important fact of a situation: *Of course I'll listen to what she has to say but at the end of the day, it's my decision.* • **the end justifies the means** saying said about a situation in which the final aim is so important that any way of achieving it is acceptable • **end of** slang something you say to tell someone that you have made a final decision and you do not want to talk about it any more: *You're not going out tonight – end of!* • **end of story** informal something you say when you think that the opinion you have just expressed about something is correct and that there is no other way of thinking about it: *This woman is innocent – end of story.* • **the end of the line/road** the point where it is no longer possible to continue with a process or activity: *We've struggled on for as long as we could, but now we're* ***at*** *the end of the line.* ◦ *When the bank refused to lend us any more money we realized we'd* ***reached*** *the end of the road.* • **get/have your end away** UK informal If a man gets his end away, he has sex: *Did you get your end away last night, then?* • **keep/hold your end up** UK to continue to deal with difficulties bravely and successfully • **make ends meet** C1 to have just enough money to pay for the things that you need • **make both ends meet** Indian English **make ends meet** • **no end** very much: *It would please Granny no end if you wrote to her occasionally.* • **no end of sth** B2 a lot of: *If you don't want the job, there's no end of people willing to take your place.* • **not be the end of the world** informal C2 If something is not the end of the world, it will not cause very serious problems: *I'm really hoping to win, but it won't be the end of the world if I don't.* • **put an end to sth** B2 to make something stop happening or existing: *How can we put an end to the fighting?*

▸**verb** [I or T] A2 to finish or stop, or to make something finish or stop: *When is your meeting due to end?* ◦ *Her resignation ends months of speculation about her future.* ◦ *Their marriage ended in 1991.* ◦ *The match ended* ***in*** *a draw.* ◦ *I'd like to end* ***with*** *a song from my first album.* ◦ *She ended her speech on an optimistic note.*

IDIOMS **end it all** usually humorous to kill yourself: *And if this doesn't work, I'm just going to end it all.* • **it'll (all) end in tears.** something that you say which means something will end badly and the people involved will be upset: *She only met him in May and they were married by July. It'll end in tears, you'll see.*

PHRASAL VERB **end up** B1 to finally be in a particular place or situation: *They're travelling across Europe by train and are planning to end up* ***in*** *Moscow.* ◦ *Much of this meat will probably end up* ***as*** *dog food.* ◦ [L] *She'll end up penniless if she carries on spending like that.* ◦ [+ -ing verb] *After working her way around the world, she ended up teach****ing*** *English as a foreign language.*

endanger /ɪnˈdeɪn.dʒəʳ/ US /-dʒɚ/ **verb** [T] to put someone or something at risk or in danger of being harmed, damaged or destroyed: *He would never do anything to endanger the lives of his children.* ◦ *We must be careful not to do anything that might endanger the economic recovery.*

endangered /ɪnˈdeɪn.dʒəd/ US /-dʒɚd/ **adj** **endangered birds/plants/species** B2 animals or plants which may soon not exist because there are very few now alive

endear /ɪnˈdɪəʳ/ US /-dɪr/ verb

PHRASAL VERB **endear sb to sb** to cause someone to be liked by someone: *She is unlikely to endear her****self*** *to her colleagues with such an aggressive approach.*

endearing /ɪnˈdɪə.rɪŋ/ US /-ˈdɪr.ɪŋ/ **adj** making someone like you: *She laughs at herself a lot which is always endearing.* • **endearingly** /-li/ adv

endearment /ɪnˈdɪə.mənt/ US /-ˈdɪr-/ **noun** [C or U] a word or phrase that you use to show that you love someone: ***terms of*** endearment such as 'darling' or 'sweetheart' ◦ *Between kisses, he was murmuring endearments.*

endeavour /en'dev.əʳ/ (US) /-ɚ/ **verb; noun**
▸**verb** [I + to infinitive] UK (US **endeavor**) C1 to try to do something: *Engineers are endeavouring **to** locate the source of the problem.*
▸**noun** [C or U] UK (US **endeavor**) C1 an attempt to do something: *In spite of our best endeavours, it has proven impossible to contact her.* ◦ *Crossing the North Pole on foot was an amazing **feat of** human endeavour.* ◦ ***artistic*** *endeavour*

E

endemic /en'dem.ɪk/ **adj** especially of a disease or a condition, regularly found and very common among a particular group or in a particular area: *Malaria is endemic **in** many of the hotter regions of the world.* ◦ *The disease is endemic **among** British sheep/**to** many British flocks.* ◦ *There is endemic **racism/poverty/violence** in many of the country's cities.*

endgame /'end.geɪm/ **noun** [C usually singular] **1** specialized the last stage in a game of CHESS when only a few of the pieces are left on the board **2** the last stage of a process, especially one involving discussion: *A diplomatic endgame is under way to find a peaceful solution.*

ending /'en.dɪŋ/ **noun** [C] **STORY** ▷ **1** B1 the last part of a story: *People want love stories with **happy** endings.* **WORD** ▷ **2** B1 a part added to the end of a word: *To make the plural of 'dog', you add the plural ending '-s'.*

endive /'en.daɪv/ **noun** [C or U] **1** UK a plant with curly green leaves that are eaten uncooked in salads **2** US for **chicory**

endless /'end.ləs/ **adj** B2 never finishing, or seeming never to finish: *We used to have endless arguments about politics.* ◦ *He seems to think that I have an endless **supply** of money.* ◦ *The **possibilities** are endless.*
• **endlessly** /-li/ **adv**

endocrine gland /'en.də.krɪnˌglænd/ **noun** [C] specialized any of the organs of the body, such as the PITUITARY GLAND or the OVARIES, which produce and release HORMONES into the blood to be carried around the body

ˌend-of-'season **adj** [before noun] **1** describes a sports event which happens at the end of a SEASON (= the part of a year in which a sport is played): *the end-of-season **play-offs*** **2** relating to the end of a period of time when particular clothes, products, etc. are sold in shops: *Prices are reduced by up to 75 percent in our end-of-season **sale**.* ◦ *The store sells end-of-season stock at heavily discounted prices.*

ˌend-of-'terrace **adj** [before noun] UK describes a house at the end of a row of similar houses that are joined together

endogenous /en'dɒdʒ.ɪ.nəs/ (US) /-'dɑː.dʒə-/ **adj** specialized found or coming from within something, for example a system or a person's body or mind → Compare **exogenous**

endorphin /en'dɔː.fɪn/ (US) /-'dɔːr-/ **noun** [C] specialized a chemical naturally released in the brain to reduce pain, that in large amounts can make you feel relaxed or full of energy

endorse /ɪn'dɔːs/ (US) /-'dɔːrs/ **verb** [T] **SUPPORT** ▷ **1** C2 to make a public statement of your approval or support for something or someone: *The National Executive is expected to endorse these recommendations.* ◦ formal *I fully endorse* (= agree with) *everything the Chairperson has said.* **2** to appear in an advertisement, saying that you use and like a particular product: *They paid $2 million to the world champion to endorse their new aftershave.* **GIVE PERMISSION** ▷ **3** to write something in order to give permission for something, especially your name on the back of a CHEQUE, in order to make it able to be paid to someone else **PUNISH** ▷ **4** UK to officially record on a DRIVING LICENCE that the driver has been found guilty of driving in an illegal way

endorsement /ɪn'dɔːs.mənt/ (US) /-'dɔːrs-/ **noun** **APPROVAL** ▷ **1** [C or U] the act of saying that you approve of or support something or someone: *The campaign hasn't received any political endorsements.* ◦ *He hoped to secure quick endorsement **of** the plan from the president.* **2** [C or U] the fact of a famous person appearing in an advertisement saying that they use and like a product: *products which carry an endorsement **from** a famous person* **DRIVING LICENCE** ▷ **3** [C] UK a mark on a DRIVING LICENCE that shows the driver is guilty of driving in an illegal way: *He's got a couple of endorsements **on** his licence already.*

endoscope /'en.dəˌskəʊp/ (US) /-doʊˌskoʊp/ **noun** [C] specialized a long, thin medical device that is used to examine the hollow organs of the body such as the lungs

endoscopy /en'dɒs.kə.pi/ (US) /-'dɑː.skə-/ **noun** [C or U] specialized a medical examination of a hollow organ of the body

endoskeleton /ˌen.dəʊ'skel.ɪ.tən/ (US) /-doʊ'skel.ɪ.t̬ən/ **noun** [C] specialized a hard frame that supports the body of a VERTEBRATE animal on the inside, made of bone or CARTILAGE (= strong tissue) → Compare **exoskeleton**

endosperm /'en.dəʊ.spɜːm/ (US) /-doʊ.spɝːm/ **noun** [U] specialized the substance inside a plant seed that surrounds and provides food for the EMBRYO as it develops

endothermic reaction /en.dəʊˌθɜː.mɪk.ri'æk.ʃən/ (US) /-doʊˌθɝː-/ **noun** [C] specialized a chemical reaction in which heat is absorbed → Compare **exothermic reaction**

endow /ɪn'daʊ/ **verb** [T] to give a large amount of money to pay for creating a college or hospital, etc. or to provide an income for it: *The state of Michigan has endowed three institutes to do research for industry.* ◦ *This hospital was endowed by the citizens of Strasbourg in the 16th century.*

IDIOM **be endowed with sth** C2 to have a particular quality or feature: *Some lucky people are endowed with both brains and beauty.* ◦ *Sardinia is generously endowed with prehistoric sites.* → See also **well endowed**

endowment /ɪn'daʊ.mənt/ **noun** **1** [C or U] money that is given to a college or hospital, etc. in order to provide it with an income, or the giving of this money: *The school has received an endowment of £50,000 to buy new books for the library.* **2** [C] something that you have from birth, often a quality: *There are tests which can establish a baby's genetic endowment.*

enˌdowment 'mortgage **noun** [C] an arrangement in which you have an endowment policy which provides the money you need in order to buy a house

enˌdowment 'policy **noun** [C] an agreement where you pay money regularly so that you will receive a large agreed amount of money at an agreed later date or when you die

'end ˌproduct **noun** [C usually singular] something that is produced by an activity, especially by an industrial process

'end reˌsult **noun** [C usually singular] a result of a series of events or a long process: *The end result of these changes will be more bureaucracy and fewer resources.*

endurance /ɪnˈdjʊə.rᵊns/ US /-ˈdʊr.ᵊns/ **noun** [U] C2 the ability to keep doing something difficult, unpleasant, or painful for a long time: *Running a marathon is a test of human endurance.* ◦ *The pain was bad beyond endurance.*

endure /ɪnˈdjʊəʳ/ US /-ˈdʊr/ **verb** EXPERIENCE ▷ **1** B2 [T] to suffer something difficult, unpleasant or painful: *We had to endure a nine-hour delay at the airport.* ◦ *She's already had to endure three painful operations on her leg.* CONTINUE ▷ **2** [I] formal to continue to exist for a long time: *The political system established in 1400 endured until about 1650.* • **endurable** /-ˈdjʊə.rə.bl̩/ US /-ˈdʊr.ə.bl̩/ **adj**

enduring /ɪnˈdjʊə.rɪŋ/ US /-ˈdʊr.ɪŋ/ **adj** existing for a long time: *the enduring* ***appeal*** *of cartoons* ◦ *I shall be left with many enduring memories of the time I spent in India.* • **enduringly** /-li/ **adv** *enduringly popular*

ˈend ˌuser **noun** [C] the person or organization that uses something rather than an organization which trades in it: *The software can be modified to suit the particular needs of the end user.*

endways /ˈend.weɪz/ **adv** (US also **endwise**) with the end, rather than the side, facing or touching: *Looking at the sofa endways (****on****), I don't think it'll go through the door.*

enema /ˈen.ə.mə/ **noun** [C] cleaning or treatment of the bowels by filling them with a liquid through the ANUS

enemy /ˈen.ə.mi/ **noun** **1** B1 [C] a person who hates or opposes another person and tries to harm them or stop them from doing something: *He's* ***made*** *a few enemies in this company.* ◦ *Max stole Lee's girlfriend and they've been enemies ever since.* ◦ *political enemies* **2** B2 [C usually singular] a country, or the armed forces of a country, that is at war with another country: *The enemy had succeeded in stopping our supplies from getting through.* ◦ *an attack by enemy aircraft* ◦ *enemy forces/territory* **3 the enemy of sth** literary something that harms something else: *Familiarity is the enemy of desire.*

> Word partners for **enemy**
>
> *have/make* enemies • *attack/defeat* your enemy • *arch/bitter/deadly* enemies • enemy *aircraft/forces/troops/territory*

energetic /ˌen.əˈdʒet.ɪk/ US /-ɚˈdʒet̬-/ **adj** B2 having or involving a lot of energy: *an energetic young woman* ◦ *I tried aerobics but it was too energetic for me.* • **energetically** /-ɪ.kᵊl.i/ **adv**

energize (UK usually **energise**) /ˈen.ə.dʒaɪz/ US /-ɚ-/ **verb** [T] to make someone feel energetic or eager: *I felt very energized after my holiday.*

> Word partners for **energy** (STRENGTH)
>
> *have* the energy (to do sth) • *expend* energy • *devote/direct* energy *to/towards* sth • *need/require/take* energy • *save/waste* energy • *boundless/nervous/restless* energy • *full of/bursting with* energy

> Word partners for **energy** (POWER)
>
> *generate/produce* energy • *consume/use* energy • *conserve/save* energy • energy *consumption/demand/use* • energy *resources/source/supply*

energy /ˈen.ə.dʒi/ US /-ɚ-/ **noun** STRENGTH ▷ **1** B1 [U] the power and ability to be physically and mentally active: *Since I started eating more healthily I've got so much more energy.* ◦ *I was going to go out this evening, but I just haven't* ***got*** *the energy.* ◦ [+ to infinitive] *I didn't even have* ***the*** *energy* ***to*** *get out of bed.* ◦ approving *Her writing is full of passion and energy (= enthusiasm).* **2 energies** [plural] the total of all your power and ability to be mentally and physically active: *I'm going to channel all my energies into getting a better job.* POWER ▷ **3** B1 the power from something such as electricity or oil, which can do work, such as providing light and heat: *The energy generated by the windmill drives all the drainage pumps.* ◦ *energy* ***conservation/efficiency.*** ◦ ***nuclear*** *energy*

ˈenergy-eˌfficient **adj** using little electricity, gas, etc.: *energy-efficient homes/energy-efficient lighting*

enervate /ˈen.ə.veɪt/ US /-ɚ-/ **verb** [T] formal to make someone feel weak and without energy

enervating /ˈen.ə.veɪ.tɪŋ/ US /-ɚ.veɪ.t̬ɪŋ/ **adj** formal making you feel weak and without energy: *I find this heat very enervating.*

enfant terrible /ˌɑ̃ː.fɑ̃ː.terˈiː.blə/ **noun** [C] (plural **enfants terribles**) formal a famous or successful person who likes to shock people: *In the 70s he was the enfant terrible* ***of*** *the theatre.*

enfeeble /ɪnˈfiː.bl̩/ **verb** [T] formal to make someone or something very weak • **enfeebled** /-bl̩d/ **adj**

enfold /ɪnˈfəʊld/ US /-ˈfoʊld/ **verb** [T] literary to closely hold or completely cover someone or something: *He enfolded her* ***in*** *his* ***arms.***

enforce /ɪnˈfɔːs/ US /-ˈfɔːrs/ **verb** [T] C1 to make people obey a law, or to make a particular situation happen or be accepted: *It isn't always easy for the police to enforce speed limits.* ◦ *The new teacher had failed to enforce any sort of discipline.* • **enforceable** /-ˈfɔː.sə.bl̩/ US /-fɔːr.sə.bl̩/ **adj** • **enforcement** /-mənt/ **noun** [U] *law enforcement*

enfranchise /ɪnˈfræn.tʃaɪz/ **verb** [T] formal to give a person or group of people the right to vote in elections: *Women in Britain were first enfranchised in 1918.* • **enfranchisement** /-mənt/ **noun** [U]

engage /ɪnˈgeɪdʒ/ **verb** EMPLOY ▷ **1** [T] mainly UK formal to employ someone: [+ to infinitive] *I have engaged a secretary* ***to*** *deal with all my paperwork.* ◦ *We're engaging* ***the services of*** *a professional administrator.* INTEREST ▷ **2** C1 [T] formal to interest someone in something and keep them thinking about it: *The debate about food safety has engaged the whole nation.* ◦ *If a book doesn't engage my* ***interest*** *in the first few pages, I don't usually carry on reading it.* FIT TOGETHER ▷ **3** [I or T] to make one part of a machine fit into and move together with another part of a machine: *When the large cog wheel engages (****with*** *the smaller one), the mill stone will start to go round.* BEGIN FIGHTING ▷ **4** [I or T] specialized to attack or begin to fight someone: *Enemy planes engaged the troops as they advanced into the mountains.* TEACH ▷ **5** [T] Indian English to teach someone, especially a class of children, or to keep someone busy

PHRASAL VERB **engage in sth** formal **1** C2 to take part in something: *The two governments have agreed to engage in a comprehensive dialogue to resolve the problem.* **2 engage sb in conversation** formal to start a conversation with someone: *Once Mrs Kirkpatrick engages you in conversation, you're stuck with her for half an hour.*

engaged /ɪnˈgeɪdʒd/ **adj** MARRIAGE ▷ **1** B1 having formally agreed to marry: *Debbie and Christa have just* ***got*** *engaged.* ◦ *She was engaged* ***to*** *some guy in the army.* ◦ formal *They're engaged* ***to be married*** *in June.* INVOLVED/BUSY ▷ **2** [after verb] involved in something:

*They've been engaged **in** a legal battle with the council for several months.* ◦ *She's part of a team of scientists who are engaged **on/upon** cancer research.* **3** [after verb] formal busy doing something: *I'd come to the meeting on Tuesday but I'm afraid I'm **otherwise** engaged (= doing something else).* **IN USE** ▷ **4** B1 If a phone or public toilet is engaged, someone is already using it: *Every time I ring her, she/the phone/the number is engaged.* ◦ UK *I've been trying to call him all evening, but I keep **getting** the engaged **tone**.* ◦ *The sign on the toilet door said 'Engaged'.* → Compare **vacant**

E

engagement /ɪnˈgeɪdʒ.mənt/ **noun** **MARRIAGE** ▷ **1** [C] an agreement to marry someone: *They **announced** their engagement at the party on Saturday.* ◦ *an engagement **party*** **ARRANGEMENT** ▷ **2** [C] formal an arrangement to meet someone or do something at a particular time: *a dinner engagement* ◦ *I'm afraid I have a **previous/prior** engagement (= another arrangement already made).* **BEGIN FIGHTING** ▷ **3** [C or U] specialized the act of beginning to fight someone, or a period of time in a war

enˈgagement ˌring **noun** [C] a ring, usually with PRECIOUS STONES in it, that you give someone as a formal sign that you have decided to get married

engaging /ɪnˈgeɪ.dʒɪŋ/ **adj** approving pleasant, attractive, and CHARMING: *an engaging smile/manner/person*

engender /ɪnˈdʒen.dəʳ/ (US) /-dɚ/ **verb** [T] formal to make people have a particular feeling or make a situation start to exist: *Her latest book has engendered a lot of controversy.*

engine /ˈen.dʒɪn/ **noun** [C] **1** A2 a machine that uses the energy from liquid fuel or steam to produce movement: *a jet engine* ◦ *a car engine* ◦ *My car's been having engine trouble recently.* **2** (also **locomotive**) the part of a railway train that pulls it along **3** something that provides power, often economic power, for other things: *For much of the 19th century Britain was the workshop of the world and the engine **of economic growth**.*

-engined /-en.dʒɪnd/ **suffix** used for showing what type or number of engines something has: *twin-engined* ◦ *jet-engined*

ˈengine ˌdriver **noun** [C] UK (US usually **engineer**) a train driver

engineer /ˌen.dʒɪˈnɪəʳ/ (US) /-ˈnɪr/ **noun; verb**

▸**noun** [C] **1** A2 a person whose job is to design or build machines, engines, or electrical equipment, or things such as roads, railways, or bridges, using scientific principles: *a **civil** engineer* ◦ *a **mechanical/structural** engineer* ◦ *a **software** engineer* **2** a person whose job is to repair or control machines, engines, or electrical equipment: *a computer engineer* ◦ *The engineer is coming to repair our phone tomorrow morning.* **3** US an engine driver

▸**verb** [T] **ARRANGE** ▷ **1** to arrange cleverly and often secretly for something to happen, especially something that is to your advantage: *Left-wing groups engineered a coup against the military government.* ◦ *I'm trying to engineer a meeting between them.* **BUILD** ▷ **2** to design and build something using scientific principles

engineering /ˌen.dʒɪˈnɪə.rɪŋ/ (US) /-ˈnɪr.ɪŋ/ **noun** [U] B1 the work of an engineer, or the study of this work: *German/British engineering* ◦ *Richard studied engineering at Manchester University.*

English /ˈɪŋ.glɪʃ/ **noun; adj; noun**

▸**noun** [U] the language that is spoken in the UK, the US, and in many other countries: *American/British English* ◦ *Do you speak English?*

> **! Common mistake: English**
>
> **Remember:** English is always written with a capital 'E':
>
> ~~*I've been studying english since September.*~~
>
> *I've been studying English since September.*

▸**adj** **1** in or relating to the English language: *an English teacher* ◦ *an English translation* **2** relating to or from England: *English films/food/people* ◦ *English law* ◦ *Is she English?*

▸**noun** [plural] **the English** the people of England

ˌEnglish ˈbreakfast **noun** [C or U] UK a meal eaten in the morning consisting of cooked food such as fried eggs, tomatoes, and BACON

Englishman /ˈɪŋ.glɪʃ.mən/ **noun** [C] (plural **-men** /-mən/) a man who comes from England; → See table of **Geographical names**

IDIOM **an Englishman's home is his castle** UK old-fashioned saying used to show that English people believe that they should be able to control what happens in their own homes, and that no one else should tell them what to do there

ˌEnglish ˈmedicine **noun** [U] Indian English used to refer to the treatment of illness or injury in the way that is usual in Western countries

ˌEnglish ˈmuffin **noun** [C] US for **muffin**

Englishwoman /ˈɪŋ.glɪʃˌwʊm.ən/ **noun** [C] (plural **-women** /-wɪmɪn/) a woman who comes from England

engorged /ɪnˈgɔːdʒ/ (US) /-gɔːrdʒ/ **adj** specialized describes a part of the body that has become swollen or filled with a liquid, especially blood • **engorgement** /-ˈgɔːdʒ.mənt/ (US) /-ˈgɔːrdʒ.mənt/ **noun** [U]

engrave /ɪnˈgreɪv/ **verb** [T] to cut words, pictures, or patterns into the surface of metal, stone, etc.: *The jeweller skilfully engraved the initials **on** the ring.* ◦ *The bracelet was engraved **with** his name and date of birth.*

IDIOM **be engraved on sb's memory/mind** to be very difficult to forget: *That last conversation we had is engraved on my memory forever.*

engraver /ɪnˈgreɪ.vəʳ/ (US) /-vɚ/ **noun** [C] a person whose job is to engrave things

engraving /ɪnˈgreɪ.vɪŋ/ **noun** **1** [U] the activity of engraving **2** [C] a picture printed onto paper from a piece of wood or metal into which the design has been cut

engross /ɪnˈgrəʊs/ (US) /-ˈgroʊs/ **verb** [T] If something engrosses you, it is so interesting that you give it all your attention: *What is it about Harry Potter that so engrosses children?* → Synonym **absorb**

engrossed /ɪnˈgrəʊst/ (US) /-ˈgroʊst/ **adj** C2 giving all your attention to something: *She was so engrossed **by/in** the book that she forgot the cakes in the oven.* ◦ *They were so engrossed **in/with** what they were doing that they didn't hear me come in.* → Synonym **absorbed**

engrossing /ɪnˈgrəʊ.sɪŋ/ (US) /-ˈgroʊ-/ **adj** very interesting and needing all your attention: *an engrossing book/story* ◦ *I found the film completely engrossing from beginning to end.*

engulf /ɪnˈgʌlf/ **verb** [T] to surround and cover something or someone completely: *The flames rapidly engulfed the house.* ◦ *Northern areas of the country were engulfed **by/in** a snowstorm last night.* ◦ *The war is threatening to engulf the entire region.*

enhance /ɪnˈhɑːns/ (US) /-ˈhæns/ **verb** [T] C1 to improve the quality, amount or strength of something: *These scandals will not enhance the organization's reputation.* • **enhancement** /-mənt/ **noun** [C or U] • **-enhancing** /-ɪŋ/ **suffix** *Several athletes tested positive for illegal* ***performance****-enhancing drugs.*

enhancer /ɪnˈhɑːn.səʳ/ (US) /-ˈhæn.sɚ/ **noun** [C] something that is used to improve the quality of something. Enhancer is usually used as a combining form: *Music can be a* ***mood*** *enhancer.* ◦ *I don't like to use artificial* ***flavour*** *enhancers in my cooking.*

enigma /ɪˈnɪg.mə/ **noun** [C] something that is mysterious and seems impossible to understand completely: *She is a bit of an enigma.* ◦ *The newspapers were full of stories about the enigma of Lord Lucan's disappearance.*

enigmatic /ˌen.ɪgˈmæt.ɪk/ (US) /-ˈmæt̬-/ **adj** mysterious and impossible to understand completely: *The Mona Lisa has a famously enigmatic smile.* ◦ *He left an enigmatic message on my answering machine.* • **enigmatically** /-ɪ.kəl.i/ **adv** *'Who was that?' 'Just a man I know,' she said enigmatically.*

enjoin /ɪnˈdʒɔɪn/ **verb** [T] **1** formal to tell someone to do something or to behave in a particular way: [+ to infinitive] *We were all enjoined* ***to*** *be on our best behaviour.* ◦ *He enjoined (= suggested) caution.* **2** US legal to legally force someone to do something or stop doing something

> **+ Other ways of saying enjoy**
>
> A more formal way of saying 'enjoy' is **relish**:
>
> *Jonathan always* ***relishes*** *a challenge.*
>
> When someone enjoys a situation or activity very much, you can use the phrasal verbs **lap up** or **revel in**:
>
> *He* ***lapped up*** *all the attention they gave him.*
>
> *She* ***revelled in*** *her role as team manager.*
>
> If someone enjoys doing something that other people think is unpleasant, the phrasal verb **delight in** is sometimes used:
>
> *She seems to* ***delight in*** *making other people look stupid.*
>
> The verb **savour** is sometimes used when someone enjoys something slowly so that he or she can appreciate it as much as possible:
>
> *It was the first chocolate he'd had for over a year, so he* ***savoured*** *every mouthful.*
>
> When people enjoy themselves very much, in informal situations you can say that they are having a **ball** or a **whale of a** time:
>
> *We had a* ***ball*** *in Miami.*
>
> *I had* ***a whale of a*** *time on the class trip.*

> **! Common mistake: enjoy yourself**
>
> To talk about people getting pleasure from the situation they are in, remember to use a reflexive pronoun
>
> Don't say 'enjoy', say **enjoy yourself/himself/themselves**:
>
> ~~*I have made new friends and am enjoying in London.*~~
>
> *I have made new friends and am enjoying myself in London.*

enjoy /ɪnˈdʒɔɪ/ **verb** [T] **PLEASURE ▷ 1** (A1) to get pleasure from something: *I really enjoyed that film/book/concert/party/meal.* ◦ [+ -ing verb] *I want to travel because I enjoy meet****ing*** *people and see****ing*** *new places.* **2 enjoy yourself** (A2) to get pleasure from the situation which you are in: *I don't think Marie is enjoying herself very much at school.* ◦ *Come on, why aren't you dancing? Enjoy yourselves!* **3 enjoy!** informal something you say to someone when you have given them something and you want them to enjoy it: *Here are your drinks. Enjoy!*

ADVANTAGE ▷ 4 (C2) to have something good that is an advantage: *Even though he's 86, he enjoys excellent health.*

> **! Common mistake: enjoy**
>
> When **enjoy** is followed by a verb, that verb cannot be in the infinitive with 'to'.
>
> Do not say 'enjoy to do something', say **enjoy doing something**:
>
> ~~*My parents enjoy to walk in the mountains.*~~
>
> *My parents enjoy walking in the mountains.*

enjoyable /ɪnˈdʒɔɪ.ə.bl/ **adj** (B1) An enjoyable event or experience gives you pleasure: *a very enjoyable game/film* ◦ *Thank you for a most enjoyable evening.*

enjoyment /ɪnˈdʒɔɪ.mənt/ **noun** [U] (B2) the feeling of enjoying something: *Knowing the ending already didn't spoil my enjoyment* ***of*** *the movie.*

enlarge /ɪnˈlɑːdʒ/ (US) /-ˈlɑːrdʒ/ **verb 1** [I or T] to become bigger or to make something bigger: *They've enlarged the kitchen by building over part of the garden.* ◦ *an enlarged spleen* **2** [T] to print a bigger copy of a photograph or document

PHRASAL VERB **enlarge on/upon sth** formal to give more details about something you have said or written: *Would you care to enlarge on what you've just said?*

enlargement /ɪnˈlɑːdʒ.mənt/ (US) /-ˈlɑːrdʒ-/ **noun 1** [S or U] the fact of being enlarged: *I am pleased to announce the enlargement of the History Department by three new teachers.* **2** [C] something, especially a photograph, that has been enlarged: *I had an enlargement of my graduation photo done for my grandparents.*

enlarger /ɪnˈlɑː.dʒəʳ/ (US) /-ˈlɑːr.dʒɚ/ **noun** [C] a piece of equipment used especially by photographers to make pictures or photographs bigger

enlighten /ɪnˈlaɪ.tən/ (US) /-t̬ən/ **verb** [I or T] to provide someone with information and understanding; to explain the true facts about something to someone: *Should the function of children's television be to entertain or to enlighten?* ◦ *I don't understand this. Could you enlighten me?*

enlightened /ɪnˈlaɪ.tənd/ (US) /-t̬ənd/ **adj** approving **1** showing understanding, acting in a positive way, and not following old-fashioned or false beliefs: *The school has an enlightened policy of teaching boys to cook.* ◦ *These days she's much more enlightened in her views on education.* **2** knowing the truth about existence: *Buddha was an enlightened being.*

enlightening /ɪnˈlaɪ.tən.ɪŋ/ (US) /-t̬ən-/ **adj** giving you more information and understanding of something: *That was a very enlightening programme.* ◦ *The instruction manual that came with my new computer wasn't very enlightening* ***about*** *how to operate it.*

enlightenment /ɪnˈlaɪ.tən.mənt/ (US) /-t̬ən-/ **noun** [U] **1** the state of understanding something: *Can you give me any enlightenment* ***on*** *what happened?* **2** in Hinduism and Buddhism, the highest spiritual state that can be achieved

the Enˈlightenment noun [S] the period in the 18th century in Europe when many people began to emphasize the importance of science and reason, rather than religion and tradition

enlist /ɪnˈlɪst/ verb **JOIN** ▷ **1** [I] to join the armed forces: *They both enlisted (**in** the navy) a year before the war broke out.* **ASK FOR HELP** ▷ **2** [T] formal to ask for and get help or support from someone: *We've got to enlist some people to help prepare the food.* ◦ *The organization has enlisted the support of many famous people in raising money to help homeless children.* • **enlistment** /-mənt/ noun [C or U]

enlisted /ɪnˈlɪst.ɪd/ adj [before noun] US An enlisted man/woman is a member of the armed forces who is not an officer.

E

enliven /ɪnˈlaɪ.vᵊn/ verb [T] to make something more interesting: *The game was much enlivened when both teams scored within five minutes of each other.*

en masse /ˌɒ̃ˈmæs/ (US) /ˌɑ̃ː-/ adv If a group of people do something en masse, they do it together and at the same time: *The shop's 85 workers have resigned en masse.*

enmesh /enˈmeʃ/ verb [T] to catch or involve someone in something unpleasant or dangerous from which it is difficult to escape: *The whales are caught by being enmeshed **in** nets.* ◦ *She has become enmeshed **in** a tangle of drugs and petty crime.*

enmity /ˈen.mɪ.ti/ (US) /-t̬i/ noun [C or U] a feeling of hate: *She denied any personal enmity **towards** him.* ◦ *Bitter historical enmities underlie the present violence.*

ennoble /ɪˈnəʊ.bl/ (US) /-ˈnoʊ-/ verb [T] **1** to make someone a member of the NOBILITY (= highest social rank) **2** literary to make something or someone better so that people admire it or them more: *He has this theory that suffering can ennoble a person's character.*

ennui /ˌɒnˈwiː/ (US) /ˌɑːn-/ noun [U] literary a feeling of being bored and mentally tired caused by having nothing interesting or exciting to do: *The whole country seems to be affected by the ennui of winter.*

enormity /ɪˈnɔː.mɪ.ti/ (US) /-ˈnɔːr.mə.t̬i/ noun **SIZE** ▷ **1** [U] very great size or importance: *Nobody fully understands the enormity and complexity **of** the task of reviving the country's economy.* ◦ *I don't think you realize the enormity **of** the problem.* **EVIL ACT** ▷ **2** [C or U] formal an extremely evil act or the quality of being extremely evil

enormous /ɪˈnɔː.məs/ (US) /-ˈnɔːr-/ adj (B1) extremely large: *an enormous car/house* ◦ *He earns an enormous salary.* ◦ *I was absolutely enormous when I was pregnant.* ◦ *You've been an enormous help.* • **enormousness** /-nəs/ noun [U]

enormously /ɪˈnɔː.məs.li/ (US) /-ˈnɔːr-/ adv extremely or very much: *She worked enormously hard on the project.*

enough /ɪˈnʌf/ determiner, pronoun, adv; adv

▸**determiner, pronoun, adv 1** (A2) as much as is necessary; in the amount or to the degree needed: *Is there enough cake/Are there enough cakes **for** everyone?* ◦ *There are 25 textbooks per class. That should be enough.* ◦ *Have you had enough (**to** eat)?* ◦ *I know enough about art **to** recognize a masterpiece when I see one.* ◦ *He's tall enough to change the bulb without getting on a chair.* **2** (B2) as much as or more than is wanted: [+ to infinitive] *I've got enough work **to** do at the moment, without being given any more.* ◦ *Half an hour in his company is **quite** enough!* ◦ *Stop. You've made enough **of a** (= a lot of) mess already.* ◦ *You've drunk **more than** enough (= too much) already.* ◦ *I've **seen/heard** enough now (= I do not want to see/hear any more).* ◦ *I've **had** enough **of** your excuses (= I want them to stop).* ◦ *Enough **of this**! I don't want to discuss it any more.* ◦ *Enough **already**! (= No more!)* **3 enough is enough** something you say when you want something to stop: *Enough is enough – I don't want to argue with you any more.* **4 enough said** informal something you say to tell someone that you understand what they have said and that they do not need to say any more: *'Someone has to explain the situation to her.' 'Enough said.'* **5 have had enough** (C1) to want something to stop because it is annoying you: *I've had enough – I'm going home.* **6 that's enough** used to tell someone to stop behaving badly: *That's enough, Peter. Give those toys back, please.*

▸**adv 1** (A2) used after an adjective, adverb, or verb to mean to the necessary degree: *Is the water hot enough yet?* ◦ *I don't think he's really experienced enough for this sort of job.* ◦ *She told me it was brand new and I was stupid enough **to** believe her.* ◦ formal *Would you be **good** enough **to** take my bag upstairs for me?* **2** used after an adjective or adverb to mean quite: *He's bad enough, but his brother is far worse.* ◦ *She's gone away for six months, but strangely/oddly/funnily enough (= surprisingly), her boyfriend doesn't seem too unhappy about it.*

> **!** Common mistake: **enough**
>
> **Warning:** check your word order!
>
> When **enough** is used with an adjective, it always goes directly after the adjective.
>
> Don't say 'enough kind/healthy/brave', say **kind/healthy/brave enough**:
>
> *I hope my instructions are clear enough.*

en passant /ˌɒ̃ˈpæs.ɒ̃/ (US) /ˌɑ̃ː.pæˈsɑ̃ː/ adv formal If you say something en passant, you mention something quickly while talking about something else: *She mentioned, en passant, that she'd been in Brighton the previous week.*

enquire /ɪnˈkwaɪəʳ/ (US) /-ˈkwaɪr/ verb [I or T] UK (B2) to **inquire**

enquiry /ɪnˈkwaɪə.ri/ (US) /ˈɪn.kwə.ri/ noun [C or U] UK (B1) **inquiry**

enrage /ɪnˈreɪdʒ/ verb [T often passive] to cause someone to become very angry: *Plans to build a new nightclub in the neighbourhood have enraged local residents.* ◦ *He was enraged **at** the article about him.*

enraptured /ɪnˈræp.tʃəd/ (US) /-tʃɚd/ adj literary filled with great pleasure or extremely pleased by something: *The audience was enraptured by the young soloist's performance.*

enrich /ɪnˈrɪtʃ/ verb **IMPROVE** ▷ **1** (C1) [T] to improve the quality of something by adding something else: *Fertilizer helps to enrich the soil.* ◦ *My life was greatly enriched by knowing her.* **HAVE MORE MONEY** ▷ **2** [T] to make something or someone richer: *He claimed that the large stores were enriching them**selves** at the expense of their customers.* • **enrichment** /-mənt/ noun [U]

enrol (-ll-) UK (US usually **enroll**) /ɪnˈrəʊl/ (US) /-ˈroʊl/ verb [I or T] to put yourself or someone else onto the official list of members of a course, college or group: *Is it too late to enrol **at** the college?* ◦ *I enrolled **for/in/on** the modern art course.* ◦ *He is enrolled as a part-time student.* ◦ *They want to enrol their children in their local school.* • **enrolment** (US usually **enrollment**) /-mənt/ noun [C or U]

en ˈroute (US also **enroute**) adv on the way to or from somewhere: *I stopped en route (**to** the party) and got some wine.* ◦ *The bomb exploded while the plane was en route **from** Paris **to** Tokyo.*

ensconce /ɪnˈskɒns/ (US) /-ˈskɑːns/ verb literary **ensconce yourself** to make yourself very comfortable or safe in a place or position: *After dinner, I ensconced myself **in** an armchair with a book.*

ensconced /ɪnˈskɒnst/ ⓤⓢ /-ˈskɑːnst/ **adj** [after verb] literary positioned safely or comfortably somewhere: *The prime minister is now **firmly** ensconced **in** Downing Street with a large majority.*

ensemble /ˌɒnˈsɒm.bl̩/ ⓤⓢ /ˌɑːnˈsɑːm-/ **noun** [C, + sing/pl verb] a group of things or people acting or taken together as a whole, especially a group of musicians who regularly play together: *The Mozart Ensemble is/are playing at the Wigmore Hall tonight.* ◦ *She bought a dress and matching hat, gloves and shoes – in fact the **whole** ensemble.*

enshrine /ɪnˈʃraɪn/ **verb** [T usually + adv/prep] formal **1** to contain or keep as if in a holy place: *Almost two and a half million war dead are enshrined at Yasukuni.* ◦ *A lot of memories are enshrined **in** this photograph album.* **2 be enshrined in sth** If a political or social right is enshrined in something, it is protected by being included in it: *The right of freedom of speech is enshrined in **law**/in **the constitution**.*

enshroud /ɪnˈʃraʊd/ **verb** [T] **COVER ▷ 1** literary to cover something so that it cannot be seen clearly: *The planet Venus is enshrouded **in** thick clouds.* **KEEP SECRET ▷ 2** to make something difficult to know or understand: *The whole affair was enshrouded in secrecy.*

ensign /ˈen.sən/ **noun** [C] a flag on a ship that shows which country the ship belongs to

enslave /ɪnˈsleɪv/ **verb** [T often passive] **1** to control and keep someone forcefully in a bad situation, or to make a SLAVE of someone: *Women in this region were enslaved by poverty.* ◦ *The early settlers enslaved or killed much of the native population.* **2** literary to control someone's actions, thoughts, emotions, or life completely: *We are increasingly enslaved by technology.* ◦ *Guilt enslaved her.* • **enslavement** /-mənt/ **noun** [U]

ensnare /ɪnˈsneəʳ/ ⓤⓢ /-ˈsner/ **verb** [T] literary to catch or get control of something or someone: *Spiders ensnare flies and other insects in their webs.* ◦ *They wanted to make a formal complaint about their doctor, but ended up ensnared **in** the complexities of the legal system.*

ensue /ɪnˈsjuː/ ⓤⓢ /-ˈsuː/ **verb** [I] formal to happen after something else, especially as a result of it: *The police officer said that he had placed the man under arrest and that a scuffle had ensued.*

ensuing /ɪnˈsjuː.ɪŋ/ ⓤⓢ /-ˈsuː-/ **adj** [before noun] happening after something and because of it: *An argument broke out and in the ensuing fight, a gun went off.*

en suite /ˌɒnˈswiːt/ ⓤⓢ /ˌɑːn-/ **adv** describes a bathroom that is directly connected to a bedroom or a bedroom that is connected to a bathroom: *All four bedrooms in their new house are en suite.*

en-suite /ˌɒnˈswiːt/ ⓤⓢ /ˌɑːn-/ **adj** [before noun] describes a bathroom that is directly connected to a bedroom or a bedroom that is connected to a bathroom: *I want a hotel room with an en-suite **bathroom**.* • **en-suite noun** [C] *My room has an en-suite.*

ensure (US also **insure**) /ɪnˈʃɔːʳ/ ⓤⓢ /-ˈʃʊr/ **verb** [T] **B2** to make something certain to happen: *The airline is taking steps to ensure safety on its aircraft.* ◦ [+ (that)] *The role of the police is to ensure (**that**) the law is obeyed.* ◦ [+ two objects] *Their 2–0 victory today has ensured the Italian team a place in the Cup Final/ensured a place in the Cup Final **for** the Italian team.*

ENT /ˌiː.enˈtiː/ **noun** [U] abbreviation for **ear, nose, and throat**

entail /ɪnˈteɪl/ **verb** [T] formal to make something necessary, or to involve something: *Such a large investment inevitably entails some risk.* ◦ [+ -ing verb] *Repairing the roof will entail spend**ing** a lot of money.*

entangle /ɪnˈtæŋ.gl̩/ **verb** [T usually passive] **1** to cause something to become caught in something such as a net or ropes: *The dolphin had become entangled **in/with** the fishing nets.* **2 entangled in/with sth/sb** involved with something or someone in a way that makes it difficult to escape: *He went to the shop to buy bread, and got entangled **in/with** a carnival parade.* ◦ *The mayor and the city council are anxious to avoid getting entangled **in** the controversy.* ◦ *She seems to be romantically entangled **with** some artist in Rome.*

entanglement /ɪnˈtæŋ.gl̩.mənt/ **noun 1** [C] a situation or relationship that you are involved in and that is difficult to escape from: *The book describes the complex emotional and sexual entanglements between the members of the group.* **2** [C usually plural] UK specialized a fence made of wire with sharp points on it, intended to make it difficult for enemy soldiers to go across an area of land

entente (cordiale) /ˌɒn.tɒntˌkɔː.diˈɑːl/ ⓤⓢ /ˌɑːn.tɑːntˌkɔːr-/ **noun** [S or U] a friendly agreement or relationship between two countries

enter /ˈen.təʳ/ ⓤⓢ /-t̬ɚ/ **verb; noun**

▸**verb GO IN ▷ 1 A2** [I or T] to come or go into a particular place: *The police entered (the building) **through/by** the side door.* ◦ *You will begin to feel sleepy as the drug enters the **bloodstream**.*

> **!** Common mistake: **enter**
>
> **Warning:** when **enter** has a direct object, it is not followed by a preposition.
>
> Don't say 'enter in/into a place', say **enter a place**:
>
> *~~As you enter into the station, the shop is on the right.~~*
>
> *As you enter the station, the shop is on the right.*

COMPETITION ▷ 2 B1 [I or T] to be included in a competition, race, or exam, or to arrange for someone else to do this: *Both men have been entered **for/in** the 100 metres in Paris next month.* ◦ *All three companies have entered the **race** to develop a new system.* ◦ *Are you going to enter the photography **competition**?* **INFORMATION ▷ 3 B1** [T] to put information into a computer, book, or document: *You have to enter a **password** to access the database.* **4** [T] formal to make a particular type of statement officially: *The prisoner entered a **plea** of not guilty.* **ORGANIZATION ▷ 5** [T] to become a member of a particular organization, or to start working in a particular type of job: *Ms Doughty entered **politics/Parliament** after a career in banking.* **PERIOD ▷ 6 C1** [T] to begin a period of time: *The project is entering its final **stages**.* ◦ *The violence is now entering its third week.*

PHRASAL VERB **enter into sth** formal **1** to start to become involved in something, especially a discussion or agreement: *They refuse to enter into any **discussion** on this matter.* **2 not enter into sth** If you say that something does not enter into something else, it is not an important or necessary part of it: *The Council's opinion doesn't enter into it – it's up to us to make the decision.*

▸**noun** [S] the key on a computer keyboard that is used to say that the words or numbers on the screen are correct, or to say that an instruction should be performed, or to move down a line on the screen: *Move the cursor to where it says 'New File' and press enter.*

enterprise /ˈen.tə.praɪz/ ⓤⓢ /-t̬ɚ-/ **noun BUSINESS ▷**

E

1 C1 [C or U] an organization, especially a business, or a difficult and important plan, especially one that will earn money: *Don't forget this is a* ***commercial*** *enterprise – we're here to make money.* ◦ *Those were the years of* ***private*** *enterprise (= businesses being run privately, rather than by the government), when lots of small businesses were started.* ◦ *Her latest enterprise (= plan) is to climb Mount Everest.* **PERSONAL QUALITY** ▷ **2** C1 [U] eagerness to do something new and clever, despite any risks: *They've showed a lot of enterprise* ***in*** *sett****ing*** *up this project.* ◦ *We need someone with enterprise and imagination to design a marketing strategy.*

ˈenterprise ˌculture noun [S or U] a society in which personal achievement, the earning of money and the development of private business is encouraged

ˈenterprise ˌzone noun [C] an area with economic problems that has been given financial help by the government to encourage the growth of new businesses

enterprising /ˈen.tə.praɪ.zɪŋ/ US /-t̬ɚ-/ adj good at thinking of and doing new and difficult things, especially things that will make money: *The business was started by a couple of enterprising young women.* ◦ *That was very enterprising* ***of*** *you, Vijay!*

entertain /en.təˈteɪn/ US /-t̬ɚ-/ verb **AMUSE** ▷ **1** B1 [I or T] to keep a group of people interested or enjoying themselves: *We hired a magician to entertain the children.* **INVITE** ▷ **2** [I or T] to invite someone to your house and give food and drink to them: *We entertain a lot of people, mainly business associates of my wife's.* ◦ *Now that I live on my own, I don't entertain much.* **THINK ABOUT** ▷ **3** [T not continuous] formal to hold in your mind or to be willing to consider or accept: *The General refused to entertain the possibility of defeat.*

entertainer /en.təˈteɪ.nəʳ/ US /-t̬ɚˈteɪ.nɚ/ noun [C] B2 someone whose job is to entertain people by singing, telling jokes, etc.

entertaining /en.təˈteɪ.nɪŋ/ US /-t̬ɚ-/ adj; noun
▸**adj** B2 funny and enjoyable: *an entertaining story/film* ◦ *His books aren't particularly well-written, but they're always entertaining.* • **entertainingly** /-li/ adv
▸**noun** [U] the activity of inviting people to your house and giving them food and drink: *We do a lot of entertaining.*

entertainment /en.təˈteɪn.mənt/ US /-t̬ɚ-/ noun [C or U] B1 shows, films, television, or other performances or activities that entertain people, or a performance of this type: *There's not much in the way of entertainment in this town – just the cinema and a couple of pubs.* ◦ formal *This season's entertainments include five new plays and several concerts of Chinese and Indian music.*

enthral (-ll-) UK (US usually **enthrall**) /ɪnˈθrɔːl/ US /-ˈθrɑːl/ verb [I or T] to keep someone completely interested: *The baseball game completely enthralled the crowd.* ◦ *The audience was enthralled for two hours by a sparkling, dramatic performance.* ◦ *They listened enthralled to what he was saying.*

enthralling /ɪnˈθrɔː.lɪŋ/ US /-ˈθrɑː-/ adj keeping someone's interest and attention completely: *I found your book absolutely enthralling!*

enthrone /ɪnˈθrəʊn/ US /-ˈθroʊn/ verb **1** [T] formal to put a king, queen, etc. through the ceremony of sitting on a THRONE (= chair used in ceremonies) in order to mark the official beginning of their period in power **2** [T often passive] humorous to be positioned somewhere where you look or feel important: *She sat in the dining room, enthroned* ***on*** *an old high-backed chair.* • **enthronement** /-mənt/ noun [C or U]

enthuse /ɪnˈθjuːz/ US /-ˈθuːz/ verb **1** [I] to express excitement about something or great interest in it: *He was enthusing over a wonderful restaurant he'd been to.* ◦ [+ speech] *'She's the best leader that this country has ever known!' he enthused.* **2** [T] to give your feeling of excitement and interest in a particular subject to other people: *He was passionately interested in classical music but failed to enthuse his children (****with*** *it).*

enthusiasm /ɪnˈθjuː.zi.æz.əm/ US /-ˈθuː-/ noun **1** B2 [U] a feeling of energetic interest in a particular subject or activity and an eagerness to be involved in it: *One of the good things about teaching young children is their enthusiasm.* ◦ *After the accident he lost his enthusiasm* ***for*** *the sport.* ◦ *I just can't* ***work up*** *(= start to feel) any enthusiasm for the whole project.* **2** [C] a subject or activity that interests you very much: *One of his greatest enthusiasms was yoga.*

enthusiast /ɪnˈθjuː.zi.æst/ US /-ˈθuː-/ noun [C] a person who is very interested in and involved with a particular subject or activity: *a keep-fit enthusiast* ◦ *a model-aircraft enthusiast*

enthusiastic /ɪnˌθjuː.ziˈæs.tɪk/ US /-ˌθuː-/ adj B2 showing enthusiasm: *You don't seem very enthusiastic* ***about*** *the party – don't you want to go tonight?* • **enthusiastically** /-tɪ.kəl.i/ adv

entice /ɪnˈtaɪs/ verb [T] to persuade someone to do something by offering them something pleasant: *The adverts entice the customer* ***into*** *buy****ing*** *things they don't really want.* ◦ *People are being enticed* ***away from*** *the profession by higher salaries elsewhere.* ◦ [+ to infinitive] *A smell of coffee in the doorway enticed people* ***to*** *enter the shop.* • **enticement** /-mənt/ noun [C or U] *One of the enticements of the job is the company car.*

enticing /ɪnˈtaɪ.sɪŋ/ adj Something that is enticing attracts you to it by offering you advantages or pleasure: *an enticing smile* ◦ *an enticing job offer* • **enticingly** /-li/ adv

entire /ɪnˈtaɪəʳ/ US /-ˈtaɪr/ adj [before noun] B2 whole or complete, with nothing missing: *Between them they ate an entire cake.* ◦ *He'd spent the entire journey asleep.* ◦ *They got an entire set of silver cutlery as a wedding present.*

entirely /ɪnˈtaɪə.li/ US /-ˈtaɪr-/ adv B2 completely: *I admit it was entirely my fault.* ◦ *The company is run almost entirely by middle-aged men.*

entirety /ɪnˈtaɪə.rɪ.ti/ US /-ˈtaɪr.ə.t̬i/ noun formal **in its entirety** with all parts included: *I've never actually read the book in its entirety.*

entitle /ɪnˈtaɪ.tl̩/ US /-t̬l̩/ verb [T] **ALLOW** ▷ **1** B2 to give someone the right to do or have something: *Being unemployed entitles you* ***to*** *free medical treatment.* ◦ [+ to infinitive] *The employer is entitled* ***to*** *ask for references.* **GIVE TITLE** ▷ **2** C1 to give a title to a book, film, etc.: *Her latest novel, entitled 'The Forgotten Sex', is out this week.*

entitlement /ɪnˈtaɪ.tl̩.mənt/ US /-t̬l̩-/ noun [C or U] something that you have right to do or have, or when you have the right to do or have something: ***pension/holiday*** *entitlements* ◦ *Managers have generous leave entitlement.*

entity /ˈen.tɪ.ti/ US /-t̬ə.t̬i/ noun [C] formal C2 something which exists apart from other things, having its own independent existence: *The museums work closely together, but are separate legal entities.* ◦ *He regarded the north of the country as a separate cultural entity.*

entomb /ɪnˈtuːm/ verb [T often passive] formal to bury

someone or something: *The nuclear waste has been entombed* ***in*** *concrete many metres under the ground.*

entomology /ˌen.təˈmɒl.ə.dʒi/ (US) /-t̬əˈmɑː.lə-/ noun [U] specialized the scientific study of insects • **entomologist** /-dʒɪst/ noun [C]

entourage /ˈɒn.tʊ.rɑːʒ/ (US) /ˌɑːn.tʊˈrɑːʒ/ noun [C usually singular, + sing/pl verb] the group of people who travel with and work for an important or famous person: *The rock star arrived in London with her usual entourage of dancers and backing singers.*

entrails /ˈen.treɪlz/ noun [plural] the INTESTINES and other inside organs of an animal or person, when they are outside the body: *pig entrails* ◦ figurative *The sofa's entrails (= pieces of material from inside) were sticking out in places.*

entrance¹ /ˈen.trəns/ noun **1** (A2) [C] a door, gate, etc. by which you can enter a building or place: *There are two entrances – one at the front and one round the back.* → Compare **exit** **2** (C2) [C usually singular] the act of coming onto a stage, by an actor or dancer: *He* ***makes*** *a spectacular entrance in act two draped in a gold sheet.* **3** [C usually singular] the act of a person coming into a room in an ordinary situation, although often because there is something noticeable about it: *I noticed her entrance because she slipped and fell in the doorway.* **4** (B1) [U] the right to enter a place: *The management reserve the right to* ***refuse*** *entrance.*

entrance² /ɪnˈtrɑːns/ (US) /-ˈtræns/ verb [T] literary Someone or something that entrances you is so beautiful or interesting that you cannot stop listening to or watching them: *He has entranced millions of people with his beautifully illustrated books.* • **entrancing** /-ˈtrɑːn.sɪŋ/ (US) /-ˈtræn.sɪŋ/ adj *entrancing views*

entranced /ɪnˈtrɑːnst/ (US) /-ˈtrænst/ adj literary If you are entranced by someone or something, you cannot stop watching them because they are very interesting or very beautiful: *The children sat silent on the carpet, entranced* ***by*** *the puppet show.*

ˈentrance exˌam noun [C] an exam that you take to be accepted into a school, etc.

ˈentrance ˌfee noun [C] an amount of money that you pay in order to be allowed into a cinema, theatre, etc.

entrant /ˈen.trənt/ noun [C] **1** a person who becomes a member of a group or organization: *new entrants to the school/company* **2** a person who takes part in a competition or an exam: *All entrants complete two three-hour papers.* **3** a company that starts selling a particular product or service, or selling in a particular place, for the first time: *As a recent entrant* ***to*** *the Japanese market, the company is at a disadvantage compared to Japanese suppliers.*

entrap /ɪnˈtræp/ verb [T] (-pp-) formal to cause someone to do something that they would not usually do, by unfair methods: *I firmly believe my son has been entrapped by this cult.*

entrapment /ɪnˈtræp.mənt/ noun [U] formal the act of causing someone to do something they would not usually do by tricking them: *The police have been accused of using entrapment to bring charges against suspects.*

entreat /ɪnˈtriːt/ verb [T] to try very hard to persuade someone to do something: [+ to infinitive] *We would spend every meal time entreating the child* ***to*** *eat her vegetables.*

entreaty /ɪnˈtriː.ti/ (US) /-t̬i/ noun [C] an attempt to persuade someone to do something: *She refused to become involved with him despite his passionate entreaties.*

entrée /ˈɒn.treɪ/ (US) /ˈɑːn-/ noun FOOD ▷ **1** [C] US the main dish of a meal **2** [C] UK at very formal meals, a small dish served just before the main part ENTRY ▷ **3** [C or U] the right to join a group of people or enter a place

entrench /ɪnˈtrentʃ/ verb [T] mainly disapproving to firmly establish something, especially an idea or a problem, so that it cannot be changed: *The government's main task was to prevent inflation from entrenching it****self***.

entrenched /ɪnˈtrentʃt/ adj mainly disapproving Entrenched ideas are so fixed or have existed for so long that they cannot be changed: *It's very difficult to change attitudes that have become so* ***deeply*** *entrenched over the years.* ◦ *The organization was often criticized for being too entrenched* ***in*** *its views.*

entrenchment /ɪnˈtrentʃ.mənt/ noun [U] mainly disapproving the process by which ideas become fixed and cannot be changed: *There has been a shift in opinion on the issue after a decade of entrenchment.*

entre nous /ˌɒn.trəˈnuː/ (US) /ˌɑːn-/ adv [after verb], adj formal used when telling someone something that is secret and should not be told to anyone else: *He told me – and this is* ***strictly*** *entre nous – that he's going to ask Ruth to marry him.*

entrepreneur /ˌɒn.trə.prəˈnɜːʳ/ (US) /ˌɑːn.trə.prəˈnɝː/ noun [C] someone who starts their own business, especially when this involves seeing a new opportunity: *He was one of the entrepreneurs of the 80s who made their money in property.* • **entrepreneurial** /-ˈnɜː.ri.əl/ (US) /-ˈnɝː.i.əl/ adj *She'll make money – she's got that entrepreneurial* ***spirit***.

entrepreneurship /ˌɒn.trə.prəˈnɜː.ʃɪp/ (US) /ˌɑːn.trə.prəˈnɝː-/ noun [U] skill in starting new businesses, especially when this involves seeing new opportunities

entropy /ˈen.trə.pi/ noun [U] specialized the amount of order or lack of order in a system

entrust /ɪnˈtrʌst/ verb [T + adv/prep] to give someone a thing or a duty for which they are responsible: *He didn't look like the sort of man you should entrust your luggage* ***to***. ◦ *Two senior officials have been entrusted* ***with*** *organizing the auction.*

entry /ˈen.tri/ noun WAY IN ▷ **1** (B1) [C or U] the act of entering a place or joining a particular society or organization: *A flock of sheep blocked our entry* ***to*** *the farm.* ◦ *I can't go down that street – there's a 'No entry' sign.* ◦ *The actress's entry* ***into*** *the world of politics surprised most people.* ◦ *She* ***made*** *her entry to the ceremony surrounded by a group of photographers.* ◦ *The burglars* ***gained*** *entry by a top window.* **2** [C] a door, gate, etc. by which you enter a place INFORMATION ▷ **3** (B1) [C] a separate piece of information that is recorded in a book, computer, etc.: *They've updated a lot of the entries in the most recent edition of the encyclopedia.* ◦ *As his illness progressed, he* ***made*** *fewer entries in his diary.* COMPETITION ▷ **4** (B1) [C or U] a piece of work that you do in order to take part in a competition, or the act of taking part in a competition: *There have been a fantastic number of entries for this year's poetry competition.* ◦ *the* ***winning*** *entries* ◦ *Entry* ***to*** *the competition is restricted to those who have a ticket.* ◦ *Have you filled in your entry* ***form*** *yet?*

Word partners for entry

gain entry • *allow* (sb) entry • *deny/refuse* (sb) entry • entry *into/to* [a place] • *forced/illegal/unauthorized* entry • entry *qualifications/requirements*

ˈentry ˌlevel noun [U] **1** the lowest level of an organization, type of work, etc.: *E-commerce is presenting a lot of new jobs at entry level.* **2** the cheapest or simplest version of a particular product or service

ˈentry-ˌlevel adj [before noun] **1** at or relating to the lowest level of an organization, type of work, etc.: *entry-level **jobs/workers/salaries*** **2** used to describe a product that is cheaper or simpler than other similar products, and therefore suitable for someone who has not used or bought one before: *an entry-level **model/machine/PC***

entryphone /ˈen.tri.fəʊn/ (US) /-foʊn/ noun [C] UK trademark a phone at the entrance to a large building that people speak into when they want to speak to someone who is inside the building

entryphone

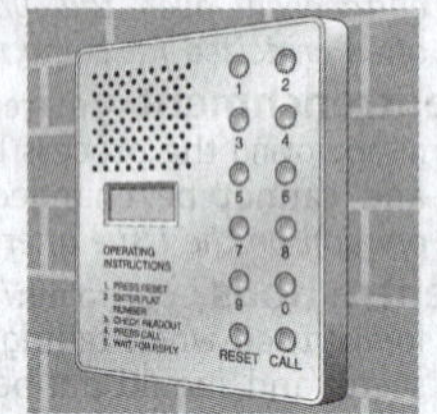

entryway /ˈen.tri.weɪ/ noun [C] US for **passage**

entwine /ɪnˈtwaɪn/ verb [T often passive] to twist something together or around something: *The picture captures the two lovers with their arms entwined.* • **entwined** /-ˈtwaɪnd/ adj closely connected or unable to be separated: *The fates of both countries seem somehow entwined.*

ˈE ˌnumber noun [C] any of a set of numbers with the letter E in front of them that are used on containers of food in the European Union to show which particular approved chemical has been added to the food

enumerate /ɪˈnjuː.mə.reɪt/ (US) /-ˈnuː.mə.eɪt/ verb [T] formal to name things separately, one by one: *He enumerated the benefits of the insurance scheme.* • **enumeration** /ɪˌnjuː.məˈreɪ.ʃən/ (US) /-ˌnuː-/ noun [U]

enunciate /ɪˈnʌn.si.eɪt/ verb formal **PRONOUNCE** ▷ **1** [I or T] to pronounce words or parts of words clearly: *He doesn't enunciate (his words) very clearly.* **EXPLAIN** ▷ **2** [T] to express and explain a plan or principle clearly or formally: *In the speech, the leader enunciated his party's proposals for tax reform.* • **enunciation** /ɪˌnʌn.siˈeɪ.ʃən/ noun [C or U]

envelop /ɪnˈvel.əp/ verb [T] literary to cover or surround something completely: *The graveyard looked ghostly, enveloped **in** mist.*

envelope /ˈen.və.ləʊp/ (US) /ˈɑːn.və.loʊp/ noun [C] (A2) a flat, usually square or rectangular, paper container for a letter

IDIOM **on the back of an envelope** in a hurried way, without much detail: *The prices were very roughly calculated – it looked as though he'd done them on the back of an envelope.*

enviable /ˈen.vi.ə.bl̩/ adj If someone is in an enviable situation, you wish you were also in that situation: *She's in the enviable **position** of being able to choose who she works for.* • **enviably** /-bli/ adv

envious /ˈen.vi.əs/ adj wishing you had what another person has: *I'm very envious **of** your new coat – it's lovely.* → Compare **jealous** → See also **envy** • **enviously** /-li/ adv *I was looking enviously at your plate, wishing I'd had the fish.* • **enviousness** /-nəs/ noun [U]

environment /ɪnˈvaɪ.rən.mənt/ (US) /-ˈvaɪr.ən-/ noun **NATURE** ▷ **1 the environment** [S] (B1) the air, water, and land in or on which people, animals, and plants live: *Certain chemicals have been banned because of their damaging effect on the environment.* ◦ *We're not doing enough to protect the environment from pollution.* **SURROUNDINGS** ▷ **2** (B2) [C] the conditions that you live or work in and the way that they influence how you feel or how effectively you can work: *The office is quite bright and airy – it's a pleasant **working** environment.* ◦ *As a parent you try to create a stable **home** environment.*

> **!** Common mistake: **environment**
>
> **Warning:** Check your spelling!
>
> **Environment** is one of the 50 words most often spelled wrongly by learners. Remember: the correct spelling has 'n' before the 'm'.

> Word partners for **the environment** (**NATURE**)
>
> *preserve/protect/safeguard* the environment • *damage/destroy/harm/pollute* the environment • *care about/be concerned about* the environment • be *harmful to* the environment • the *effect/impact* (of sth) *on* the environment

> Word partners for **environment** (**SURROUNDINGS**)
>
> a *familiar/pleasant/safe/stable* environment • a *dangerous/hostile/noisy* environment • the *right* environment for sth • *create/provide* an environment • *in* an environment

environmental /ɪnˌvaɪ.rənˈmen.təl/ (US) /-ˌvaɪr.ənˈmen.t̬əl/ adj (B1) relating to the environment: *People are becoming far more aware of environmental **issues**.* • **environmentally** /-i/ adv (B2) *environmentally damaging chemicals* ◦ *industries which work in an environmentally responsible way* ◦ *environmentally sensitive areas*

environˌmental ˈhealth noun [U] the activity of trying to prevent or protect against things that might harm people's health in the places where they work and live

environmentalism /ɪnˌvaɪ.rənˈmen.təl.ɪ.zəm/ (US) /-ˌvaɪr.ənˈmen.t̬əl-/ noun [U] an interest in or the study of the environment, in order to protect it from damage by human activities

environmentalist /ɪnˌvaɪ.rənˈmen.təl.ɪst/ (US) /-ˌvaɪr.ənˈmen.t̬əl-/ noun [C] (C1) a person who is interested in or studies the environment and who tries to protect it from being damaged by human activities

environˌmentally ˈfriendly adj (B2) not harmful to the environment: *environmentally-friendly washing powder*

environs /ɪnˈvaɪ.rənz/ (US) /-ˈvaɪr.ənz/ noun [plural] formal the area surrounding a place, especially a town

envisage /ɪnˈvɪz.ɪdʒ/ verb [T] formal (US also **envision**) **1** (C1) to imagine or expect something in the future, especially something good: *Train fare increases of 15 percent are envisaged for the next year.* ◦ [+ that] ***It's** envisaged **that** the building will start at the end of this year.* ◦ [+ -ing verb] *When do you envisage finish**ing** the project?* ◦ [+ question word] ***It's** hard to envisage **how** it might happen.* **2** to form a mental picture of something or someone you have never seen: *He wasn't what I'd expected – I'd envisaged someone much taller.*

envoy /ˈen.vɔɪ/ noun [C] someone who is sent as a REPRESENTATIVE from one government or organization to another: *a United Nations special envoy*

envy /ˈen.vi/ verb; noun

▸**verb** [T] (B2) to wish that you had something that another person has: *I envy her ability to talk to people*

she's never met before. ◦ [+ two objects] *I don't envy you the job of cooking for all those people.*
▸**noun** [U] **1** B2 the feeling that you wish you had something that someone else has: *I watched with envy as she set off for the airport.* → Compare **jealousy** **2 be the envy of sb** C2 to be liked and wanted by a lot of people: *Her hair is the envy of the office.*

enzyme /ˈen.zaɪm/ **noun** [C] any of a group of chemical substances that are produced by living cells and cause particular chemical reactions to happen while not being changed themselves: *An enzyme in the saliva of the mouth starts the process of breaking down the food.*

eolian /iˈəʊ.li.ən/ US /-ˈoʊ-/ **adj** specialized US for **aeolian**

eon (UK also **aeon**) /ˈiː.ɒn/ US /-ɑːn/ **noun** [C] a period of time that is so long that it cannot be measured: informal *I've been waiting eons for my new computer.*

epaulette UK (US **epaulet**) /ˌep.əˈlet/ **noun** [C] a decorative part on the shoulder of a piece of clothing, especially on a military coat, shirt, etc.

épée /ˈep.eɪ/ US /epˈeɪ/ **noun** [C] a thin SWORD used in the sport of FENCING that is heavier than a FOIL and has a larger, rounded part for protecting the hand of the user

EPG /ˌiː.piːˈdʒiː/ **noun** [C] abbreviation for electronic programme guide: a list on a television screen that says which programmes are going to be broadcast on which stations

ephemera /ɪˈfem.ər.ə/ US /-ɚ-/ **noun** [plural] the type of objects which, when they were produced, were not intended to last a long time or were specially produced for one occasion: *Amongst other pop ephemera, the auction will be selling off rock stars' stage clothes.*

ephemeral /ɪˈfem.ər.əl/ US /-ɚ-/ **adj** lasting for only a short time: *Fame in the world of rock and pop is largely ephemeral.*

epic /ˈep.ɪk/ **noun; adj**
▸**noun** [C] a film, poem, or book that is long and contains a lot of action, usually dealing with a historical subject
▸**adj** **1** in the style of an epic: *an epic **film** about the Roman Empire* **2** describes events that happen over a long period and involve a lot of action and difficulty: *an epic **journey/struggle*** **3** informal extremely large: *The problem of inflation has reached epic **proportions**.*

epicentre UK specialized (US **epicenter**) /ˈep.ɪ.sen.tər/ US /-t̬ɚ/ **noun** [C] the point on the Earth's surface directly above an EARTHQUAKE or atomic explosion

epicure /ˈep.ɪ.kjʊər/ US /-kjʊr/ **noun** [C] (also **epicurean**) a person who enjoys food and drink of a high quality → Synonym **gourmet**

epicurean /ˌep.ɪˈkjʊə.ri.ən/ US /-ˈkjʊr.i-/ **adj; noun**
▸**adj** formal getting pleasure from food and drink of a high quality
▸**noun** [C] formal an **epicure**

epidemic /ˌep.ɪˈdem.ɪk/ **noun; adj**
▸**noun DISEASE** ▷ **1** [C] the appearance of a particular disease in a large number of people at the same time: *a flu/AIDS epidemic* **PROBLEM** ▷ **2** [C usually singular] a particular problem that seriously affects many people at the same time: *a crime/unemployment epidemic*
▸**adj** happening a lot and affecting many people: *Poverty in this country has reached epidemic **proportions**.* ◦ *Crime and poverty are epidemic in the city.*

epidemiology /ˌep.ɪ.diː.miˈɒl.ə.dʒi/ US /-ə.diː.miˈɑː.lə-/ **noun** [U] the scientific study of diseases and how they are found, spread, and controlled in groups of people • **epidemiological** /ˌep.ɪ.diː.mi.əˈlɒdʒ.ɪ.kəl/ US /-ə.diː.mi.əˈlɑːdʒ-/ **adj** *epidemiological research*

epidermis /ˌep.ɪˈdɜː.mɪs/ US /-ˈdɝː-/ **noun** [S or U] specialized the thin outer layer of the skin

epidural /ˌep.ɪˈdjʊə.rəl/ US /-ˈdʊr.əl/ **noun** [C] an ANAESTHETIC (= substance which stops you feeling pain) that is put into the nerves in a person's lower back with a special needle: *They gave my wife an epidural when she was giving birth.*

epiglottis /ˌep.ɪˈglɒt.ɪs/ US /-ˈglɑː.t̬ɪs/ **noun** [C] specialized a small flat part at the back of the tongue which closes when you swallow to prevent food from entering the tube which goes to the lungs

epigram /ˈep.ɪ.græm/ **noun** [C] a short saying or poem which expresses an idea in a clever, funny way: *One of Oscar Wilde's most frequently quoted epigrams is 'I can resist everything except temptation'.* • **epigrammatic** /ˌep.ɪ.grəˈmæt.ɪk/ US /-ˈmæt̬-/ **adj**

epigraph /ˈep.ɪ.grɑːf/ US /-græf/ **noun** [C] specialized a saying or a part of a poem, play or book put at the beginning of a piece of writing to give the reader some idea of what the piece is about

epilator /ˈep.ɪ.leɪ.tər/ US /-t̬.ɚ/ **noun** [C] a electric device that removes hairs from someone's face or body by pulling them out

epilepsy /ˈep.ɪ.lep.si/ **noun** [U] a condition of the brain which causes a person to become unconscious for short periods or to move in a violent and uncontrolled way: *She can't drive because she **suffers from/has** epilepsy.*

epileptic /ˌep.ɪˈlep.tɪk/ **adj; noun**
▸**adj** suffering from, or caused by epilepsy: *an epileptic **fit*** ◦ *Her aunt is epileptic.*
▸**noun** [C] someone who has epilepsy

epilogue (US also **epilog**) /ˈep.ɪ.lɒg/ US /-lɑːg/ **noun** [C] a speech or piece of text that is added to the end of a play or book, often giving a short statement about what happens to the characters after the play or book finishes → Compare **prologue**

epiphany /ɪˈpɪf.ən.i/ **noun** [C or U] literary the moment when you suddenly feel that you understand, or suddenly become conscious of, something that is very important to you, or a powerful religious experience

Epiphany /ɪˈpɪf.ən.i/ **noun** [C or U] a Christian holy day in January that celebrates the REVELATION of the baby Jesus to the world

epiphyte /ˈep.ɪ.faɪt/ **noun** [C] specialized a plant that grows on another plant but does not feed from it, for example some MOSSES • **epiphytic** /ep.ɪˈfɪt.ɪk/ US /-ˈfɪt̬-/ **adj** *epiphytic orchids*

episcopal /ɪˈpɪs.kə.pəl/ **adj** formal of a BISHOP, or of a Church that is directed by BISHOPS

the Eˌpiscopal ˈChurch **noun** a part of the Anglican Church, especially in Scotland and the US

Episcopalian /ɪˌpɪs.kəˈpeɪ.li.ən/ **noun; adj**
▸**noun** [C] a member of the Episcopal Church
▸**adj** belonging or relating to the Episcopal Church

episode /ˈep.ɪ.səʊd/ US /-soʊd/ **noun** [C] **EVENT** ▷ **1** B2 a single event or group of related events: *This latest episode in the fraud scandal has shocked a lot of people.* ◦ *The drugs, the divorce and the depression – it's an episode in his life that he wants to forget.* **PART OF STORY** ▷ **2** B2 one of the single parts into which a story is divided, especially when it is broadcast on the television or radio

episodic /ˌep.ɪˈsɒd.ɪk/ US /-ˈsɑː.dɪk/ **adj** formal **NOT REGULAR** ▷ **1** happening only sometimes and not regularly: *The war between these two countries has been long-drawn-out and episodic.* **STORY** ▷ **2** describes stories that are divided into several parts, especially when they are broadcast on the television or radio: *an episodic drama series*

epistemic /ˌep.ɪˈstiː.mɪk/ **adj** formal relating to knowledge or the study of knowledge

epistemology /ɪˌpɪs.təˈmɒl.ə.dʒi/ US /-ˈmɑː.lə-/ **noun** [U] specialized the part of PHILOSOPHY that is about the study of how we know things • **epistemological** /ɪˌpɪs.tə.məˈlɒdʒ.ɪ.kəl/ US /-ˈlɑː.dʒɪ-/ **adj**

epistle /ɪˈpɪs.l̩/ **noun** [C] **1** formal a letter: humorous *Many thanks for your **lengthy** epistle which arrived in this morning's post.* **2** one of the letters written to the early Christians by the APOSTLES (= the first men who believed in Jesus Christ) • **epistolary** /-təl.ər.i/ US /–təl.er.i/ **adj** formal

epitaph /ˈep.ɪ.tɑːf/ US /-tæf/ **noun** [C] a short piece of writing or a poem about a dead person, especially one written on their GRAVESTONE

IDIOM **be your epitaph** to be something, especially something you say, that other people will remember you for

epithet /ˈep.ɪ.θet/ **noun** [C] formal an adjective added to a person's name or a phrase used instead of it, usually to criticize or praise them: *The singer's 104-kilo frame has earned him the epithet of 'Man Mountain' in the press.*

epitome /ɪˈpɪt.ə.mi/ US /-ˈpɪt̬-/ **noun** **the epitome of sth** the typical or highest example of a stated quality, as shown by a particular person or thing: *Even now in her sixties, she is the epitome of French elegance.*

epitomize (UK usually **epitomise**) /ɪˈpɪt.ə.maɪz/ US /-ˈpɪt̬-/ **verb** [T] to be a perfect example of a quality or type of thing: *With little equipment and unsuitable footwear, she epitomizes the inexperienced and unprepared mountain walker.*

epoch /ˈiː.pɒk/ US /-pɑːk/ **noun** [C] (plural **epochs**) a long period of time, especially one in which there are new developments and great change: *The president said that his country was moving into a new epoch which would be one of lasting peace.*

ˈepoch-ˌmaking **adj** [after verb] An event might be described as epoch-making if it has a great effect on the future.

eponym /ˈep.ə.nɪm/ **noun** [C] formal the name of an object or activity that is also the name of the person who first produced the object or did the activity

eponymous /ɪˈpɒn.ɪ.məs/ US /-ˈpɑː.nɪ-/ **adj** [before noun] literary An eponymous character in a play, book, etc. has the same name as the title.

epoxy /ɪˈpɒk.si/ US /-ˈpɑːk-/ **verb** [T] US informal to stick things together using epoxy resin: *I epoxied the broken chair.*

eˌpoxy ˈresin **noun** [C or U] a type of strong glue for sticking things together and covering surfaces

Epsom salts /ˌep.səmˈsɒlts/ US /-ˈsɑːlts/ **noun** [plural] a bitter white powder that is mixed with water to make a drink that helps people pass solid waste

equable /ˈek.wə.bl̩/ **adj** **1** always being pleasant: *Graham has a fairly equable **temperament** – I haven't often seen him really angry.* **2** not changing suddenly: *The south of the country enjoys an equable **climate**.* • **equably** /-bli/ **adv** *She deals with problems reasonably and equably, never losing her temper.*

equal /ˈiː.kwəl/ **adj; noun; verb**

▸**adj** **SAME** ▷ **1** B1 the same in amount, number or size: *One litre is equal **to** 1.76 imperial pints.* ◦ *One box may look bigger than the other, but in fact they are roughly (= almost) equal **in** volume.* **2** B1 the same in importance and deserving the same treatment: *All people are equal, deserving the same rights as each other.* ◦ *They've got a long way to go before they achieve equal **pay/status** for men and women.* ◦ *The government supports equal marriage (= the right of gay people to get married).* **ABLE** ▷ **3** [after verb] formal skilled or brave enough for a difficult duty or piece of work: *It's a challenging job but I'm sure you'll **prove** equal **to** it.* ◦ *Is he equal **to the task**?*

▸**noun** [C] B2 someone or something that has the same importance as someone or something else and deserves the same treatment: *The good thing about her as a boss is that she treats us all as equals.* ◦ *Throughout her marriage she never considered her husband as her intellectual equal.* ◦ *As an all-round athlete he **has no equal** (= no-one else is as good).*

▸**verb** [L only + noun, T] (**-ll-** or US usually **-l-**) **BE THE SAME** ▷ **1** to be the same in value or amount as something else: *16 ounces equals one pound.* **2** to achieve the same standard or level as someone else, or the same standard or level as you did before: *We raised over $500 for charity last year and we're hoping to equal that this year.* **RESULT IN** ▷ **3** to result in something: *He disputed the idea that more money equals better education.*

equality /ɪˈkwɒl.ɪ.ti/ US /-ˈkwɑː.lə.t̬i/ **noun** [U or C] B2 the right of different groups of people to have a similar social position and receive the same treatment: *equality **between** the sexes* ◦ ***racial** equality* ◦ *the government department responsible for equalities*

equalize (UK usually **equalise**) /ˈiː.kwə.laɪz/ **verb** **1** [T] to make things or people equal: *They are putting pressure on the government to equalize state pension ages between men and women.* **2** [I] UK to get the point in a game or competition that makes your score the same as that of the other team or player: *Spain managed to equalize in the last minute of the game.* • **equalization** (UK usually **equalisation**) /ˌiː.kwə.laɪˈzeɪ.ʃən/ **noun** [U]

equalizer (UK usually **equaliser**) /ˈiː.kwə.laɪ.zər/ US /-zə/ **noun** [C] the point in a game or competition which gives both teams or players the same score: *He **scored** an equalizer during the closing minutes of the match.*

equally /ˈiː.kwə.li/ **adv** **1** B2 fairly and in the same way: *In an ideal world, would everyone get treated equally?* **2** C1 in equal amounts: *The inheritance money was **shared** equally among the three sisters.* **3** C1 to the same degree: *You looked equally nice in both dresses.* **4** used for adding an idea that is as important as what you have just said: *Not all businesses are legitimate. Equally, not all customers are honest either.*

ˌequal opporˈtunity **noun** [C or U] (also **ˌequal opporˈtunities**) the principle of treating all people the same, and not being influenced by a person's sex, race, religion, etc.: *The advert said 'We are an equal opportunities employer'.*

ˈequal ˌsign **noun** [C] (also **ˈequals ˌsign**) the symbol =, used to show that two things are the same in value, size, meaning, etc.

equanimity /ˌek.wəˈnɪm.ɪ.ti/ US /-t̬i/ **noun** [U] formal a calm mental state, especially after a shock or disappointment or in a difficult situation: *He received the news of his mother's death **with** remarkable equanimity.*

equate /ɪˈkweɪt/ **verb** [T] C2 to consider one thing to be the same as or equal to another thing: *He* *complained that there was a tendency to equate right-wing politics* ***with*** *self-interest.*

PHRASAL VERB **equate to sth** to be the same in amount, number or size: *The price of such goods in those days equates to about $50 a kilo at current prices.*

equation /ɪˈkweɪ.ʒən/ noun **STATEMENT** ▷ **1** C1 [C] a mathematical statement in which you show that two amounts are equal using mathematical symbols: *In the equation 3x − 3 = 15, x = 6.* **2** [C] (also **chemical equation**) a statement containing chemical symbols, used to show the changes that happen during a particular chemical reaction **COMPLEX SITUATION** ▷ **3** [C usually singular] a difficult problem that can only be understood if all the different influences are considered: *Managing the economy is a complex equation* ***of*** *controlling inflation and reducing unemployment.* **THE SAME AS** ▷ **4** [U] the act of considering one thing to be the same as or equal to another: *There is a tendency in movies to* ***make*** *the equation* ***between*** *violence and excitement.*

equator /ɪˈkweɪ.təʳ/ US /-t̬ɚ/ noun [S] an imaginary line drawn around the middle of the Earth an equal distance from the North Pole and the South Pole: *Singapore* ***is/lies on*** *the Equator.*

equatorial /ˌek.wəˈtɔː.ri.əl/ US /-ˈt̬ɔːr.i-/ adj near the equator, or typical of places near the equator: *equatorial Africa*

equerry /ˈek.wə.ri/ US /-wɚ.i/ noun [C] an officer who works for a particular member of a royal family to help them in their official duties: *an equerry* ***to*** *the Queen*

equestrian /ɪˈkwes.tri.ən/ adj; noun

▸adj connected with the riding of horses: *They plan to hold the Olympics' equestrian* ***events*** *in another part of the city.*

▸noun [C] formal a person who rides horses, especially as a job or very skilfully

equi- /ek.wɪ-/ prefix equal or equally

equidistant /ˌek.wɪˈdɪs.tənt/, /ˌiː.kwɪ-/ adj equally far or close: *Australia is roughly equidistant* ***from*** *Africa and South America.*

equilateral /ˌiː.kwɪˈlæt.ər.əl/, /ˌek.wɪ-/ US /-læt̬-/ adj describes a shape whose sides are all the same length: *an equilateral* ***triangle***

equilibrium /ˌiː.kwɪˈlɪb.ri.əm/, /ˌek.wɪ-/ noun [S or U] formal **1** a state of balance: *The disease destroys much of the inner-ear, disturbing the animal's equilibrium.* ◦ *the country's economic equilibrium* **2** a calm mental state: *Yoga is said to restore one's inner equilibrium.*

equine /ˈek.waɪn/ adj formal connected with horses, or appearing similar to a horse: *equine flu*

equinox /ˈek.wɪ.nɒks/ US /-nɑːks/ noun [C] either of the two occasions in the year when day and night are of equal length: *the* ***vernal/autumn*** *equinox*

equip /ɪˈkwɪp/ verb [T] (-pp-) **PROVIDE** ▷ **1** B2 to provide a person or a place with objects that are necessary for a particular purpose: *It's going to cost $4 million to equip the hospital.* ◦ *All the police officers were equipped* ***with*** *shields to defend themselves against the rioters.* **PREPARE** ▷ **2** to give someone the skills they need to do a particular thing: *The course aims to equip people* ***with*** *the skills necessary for a job in this technological age.* ◦ *A degree in the history of art is very nice but it doesn't exactly equip you* ***for*** *many jobs.*

equipment /ɪˈkwɪp.mənt/ noun [U] **1** B1 the set of necessary tools, clothing, etc. for a particular purpose: *office/camping/kitchen equipment* ◦ *electrical equipment* **2** formal the act of equipping a person or place

! Common mistake: equipment

Equipment does not have a plural form and cannot be used with **a** or **an**.

To talk about an amount of **equipment**, do not say 'equipments', say **equipment**, **some equipment**, or **a lot of equipment**:

~~*We need to order more up-to-date office equipments.*~~

We need to order more up-to-date office equipment.

To talk about **equipment** in the singular, do not say 'an equipment', say **a piece of equipment**:

~~*A knife is a useful equipment to have when you are camping.*~~

A knife is a useful piece of equipment to have when you are camping.

Word partners for equipment

operate/use equipment • ***install/set up*** equipment • an ***item/piece*** of equipment • ***modern/new/the latest/sophisticated*** equipment • ***basic/vital*** equipment • ***specialist*** equipment • equipment ***for*** doing sth

equipped /ɪˈkwɪpt/ adj **PROVIDED** ▷ **1** C1 having the necessary tools, clothes, equipment, etc.: *Their schools are very poorly equipped.* ◦ *We were* ***well*** *equipped for the trip.* **PREPARED** ▷ **2** [+ to infinitive] having the skills needed to do something: *Many consider him the leader* ***best*** *equipped* ***to*** *be prime minister.* ◦ *Not being a specialist in the subject I don't feel very* ***well-****equipped* ***to*** *answer such questions.*

equitable /ˈek.wɪ.tə.bl/ US /-t̬ə-/ adj formal treating everyone in the same way: *an equitable tax system* → Synonym **fair** • **equitably** /-bli/ adv *If the law is to be effective it must be applied equitably.*

equity /ˈek.wɪ.ti/ US /-t̬i/ noun **VALUE** ▷ **1** [C or U] specialized the value of a company, divided into many equal parts owned by the SHAREHOLDERS, or one of the equal parts into which the value of a company is divided: *He sold his equity in the company last year.* ◦ *The rights give holders the opportunity to purchase additional equity interests in the company at a big discount.* **2** [U] the value of a property after you have paid any MORTGAGE or other charges relating to it **FAIRNESS** ▷ **3** [U] formal the situation in which everyone is treated fairly and equally: *a society based on equity and social justice*

! Note:

The opposite of equity is **inequity**.

4 [U] legal in English-speaking countries, a system of JUSTICE that allows a fair judgment of a case where the laws that already exist are not satisfactory

equivalent /ɪˈkwɪv.əl.ənt/ adj; noun

▸adj C1 having the same amount, value, purpose, qualities, etc.: *She's doing the equivalent job in the new company but for more money.* ◦ *Is $50 equivalent* ***to*** *about £30?*

▸noun [C usually singular] C1 something that has the same amount, value, purpose, qualities, etc. as something else: *There is no English equivalent* ***for*** *'bon appetit' so we have adopted the French expression.* ◦ *Ten thousand people a year die of the disease – that's the equivalent* ***of*** *the population of this town.* • **equivalence** /-əns/ noun [U] (also **equivalency** /-əns.i/) formal *There's a general equivalence between the two concepts.*

equivocal /ɪˈkwɪv.ə.kəl/ **adj** formal not clear and seeming to have two opposing meanings, or confusing and able to be understood in two different ways: *His words to the press were deliberately equivocal – he didn't deny the reports but neither did he confirm them.* → Opposite **unequivocal** • **equivocally** /-i/ **adv**

equivocate /ɪˈkwɪv.ə.keɪt/ **verb** [I] formal to speak in a way that is intentionally not clear and confusing to other people, especially to hide the truth: *She accused the minister of equivocating, claiming that he had deliberately avoided telling the public how bad the problem really was.* • **equivocation** /ɪˌkwɪv.əˈkeɪ.ʃən/ **noun** [U] *He answered openly and honestly without hesitation or equivocation.*

E

er /ɜːr/ (US) /ɜː/ **exclamation** the sound that people often make when they pause in the middle of what they are saying or pause before they speak, often because they are deciding what to say: *'What time shall we meet this evening?' 'Er, eight-ish?'*

-er /-ər/ (US) /-ɚ/ **suffix** **PERFORMER** ▷ **1** (also **-or**) added to some verbs to form nouns that refer to people or things that do that particular activity: *a singer (= a person who sings)* ◦ *a swimmer (= a person who swims)* ◦ *a dishwasher (= a machine or person that washes dishes)* ◦ *an actor (= a person who acts)* **SPECIALIST** ▷ **2** added to the names of particular subjects to form nouns that refer to people who have knowledge about or are studying that subject: *a philosopher (= a person who knows about/studies philosophy)* ◦ *an astronomer (= a person who knows about/studies astronomy)* **FROM A PLACE** ▷ **3** added to the names of particular places to form nouns referring to people who come from those places: *a Londoner (= a person who comes from London)* ◦ *a northerner (= a person who comes from the north)* **INVOLVED WITH** ▷ **4** added to nouns or adjectives to form nouns referring to people who are connected or involved with that particular thing: *a pensioner (= a person who receives a* PENSION*)* ◦ *first graders (= children who are in the first* GRADE *of an American school)* **CHARACTERISTICS** ▷ **5** added to nouns to form nouns or adjectives referring to people or things that have those particular characteristics: *a double-decker (= a bus with two* DECKS*)* ◦ *a big-spender (= someone who spends a lot of money)*

ER /ˌiːˈɑːr/ (US) /-ˈɑːr/ **noun** [C usually singular] **HOSPITAL** ▷ **1** US abbreviation for **emergency room** **THE QUEEN** ▷ **2** abbreviation for Elizabeth Regina: Queen Elizabeth II of England

era /ˈɪə.rə/ (US) /ˈɪr.ə/ **noun** [C] (B2) a period of time of which particular events or stages of development are typical: *the Clinton era* ◦ *a* ***bygone*** *(= past) era* ◦ *the post-war era* ◦ *They had worked for peace during the long era* ***of*** *conflict.* ◦ *The fall of the Berlin wall marked* ***the end of an*** *era.*

eradicate /ɪˈræd.ɪ.keɪt/ **verb** [T] formal (C2) to get rid of completely or destroy something bad: *The government claims to be doing all it can to eradicate corruption.* ◦ *The disease which once claimed millions of lives has now been eradicated.* • **eradication** /ɪˌræd.ɪˈkeɪ.ʃən/ **noun** [U]

erase /ɪˈreɪz/ (US) /-ˈreɪs/ **verb** [T] **MARK** ▷ **1** (B2) mainly US (UK usually **rub out**) to remove something, especially a pencil mark by rubbing it: *It's in pencil so you can just erase anything that's wrong.* **SOMETHING RECORDED** ▷ **2** to remove recordings or information from a MAGNETIC TAPE or disk: *A virus erased my hard disk.* **SOMETHING PAST** ▷ **3** to cause a feeling or memory, or a time to be completely forgotten: *Tiger Woods is determined to erase the* ***memory of*** *a disappointing Cup debut two years ago.* ◦ *Taylor wants a convincing victory to erase* ***doubts*** *about his team's ability to reach the World Cup finals.* ◦ *One election cannot erase 65 years of a corrupt one-party political process.* **4** literary to remove or destroy someone or something, or anything showing that they existed or happened: *The president said NATO expansion will finally erase the boundary line in Europe artificially created by the Cold War.* ◦ *Years of hard living had blurred but not erased her girlhood beauty.* ◦ *He was a man of mystery – erased from the history books.* • **erasure** /ɪˈreɪ.ʒər/ (US) /-ʒɚ/ **noun** [C or U] the act of erasing something: *the nuclear erasure of entire populations* ◦ *the erasure of police audiotapes*

eraser /ɪˈreɪ.zər/ (US) /-ˈreɪ.sɚ/ **noun** [C] mainly US (UK usually **rubber**) (A1) a small piece of rubber used to remove the marks made by a pencil: *If you draw or write in pencil you can always rub out your mistakes with an eraser.*

ere /eər/ (US) /er/ **preposition, conjunction** literary or old use before: *I shall be back ere nightfall.*

ˈ**e-reader** **noun** [C] a small electronic device with a screen that allows you to read books in an electronic form

erect /ɪˈrekt/ **verb; adj**

▸**verb** [T] formal **BUILD** ▷ **1** to build a building, wall, or other structure: *The war memorial was erected in 1950.* ◦ *The soldiers had erected barricades to protect themselves.* **MAKE VERTICAL** ▷ **2** to raise something to a vertical position: *They erected a marquee to accommodate 500 wedding guests.*

▸**adj** **1** standing with your back and neck very straight: *He's very tall and erect for his 78 years.* **2** When a part of the body, especially soft tissue, is erect, it is harder and bigger than usual, often pointing out or up: *an erect penis* ◦ *erect nipples*

erectile /ɪˈrek.taɪl/ (US) /-təl/ **adj** specialized (of body tissue) able to become larger and harder than usual by being filled with blood

erection /ɪˈrek.ʃən/ **noun** **BUILDING** ▷ **1** [U] formal the act of building or making a structure: *They approved the erection of an electrified fence around the prison.* **2** [C] mainly humorous a building: *This splendid if extraordinary erection from the last century is a local landmark.* **MAN'S PENIS** ▷ **3** [C] When a man has an erection, his PENIS is temporarily harder and bigger than usual and points up: *to* ***get/have*** *an erection*

erector (muscle) /ɪˈrek.təˌmʌs.l/ (US) /-tɚˌ-/ **noun** [C] specialized a muscle that can pull something, such as the human SPINE, into a vertical position

ergo /ˈɜː.gəʊ/ (US) /ˈer.goʊ/ **adv** formal therefore

ergonomics /ˌɜː.gəˈnɒm.ɪks/ (US) /ˌɝː.gəˈnɑː.mɪks/ **noun** [U] the scientific study of people and their working conditions, especially done in order to improve effectiveness • **ergonomic** /-ˈnɒm.ɪk/ (US) /-ˈnɑː.mɪk/ **adj** *ergonomic design/features* • **ergonomically** /-ˈnɒm.ɪ.kəl.i/ (US) /-ˈnɑː.mɪ.kəl.i/ **adv**

ermine /ˈɜː.mɪn/ (US) /ˈɝː-/ **noun** [U] expensive white fur with black spots that is the winter fur of the STOAT (= a small mammal) and is used to decorate formal clothes worn by kings, queens, judges, etc.

erode /ɪˈrəʊd/ (US) /-ˈroʊd/ **verb** [I or T] **DAMAGE PHYSICALLY** ▷ **1** (C2) to rub or be rubbed away gradually: *Wind and rain have eroded the statues into shapeless lumps of stone.* ◦ *The cliffs are eroding several feet a year.* **HAVE NEGATIVE EFFECT** ▷ **2** (C2) to slowly reduce or destroy: *His behaviour over the last few months has eroded my confidence in his judgment.*

erogenous /ɪˈrɒdʒ.ɪ.nəs/ Ⓤⓢ /ɪˈrɑː.dʒə-/ **adj** of areas of the body, able to feel sexual pleasure: *erogenous zones*

erosion /ɪˈrəʊ.ʒən/ Ⓤⓢ /-ˈroʊ.ʒən/ **noun** [U] **PHYSICAL DAMAGE** ▷ **1** C1 the fact of soil, stone, etc. being gradually damaged and removed by the sea, rain, or wind: ***soil/coastal** erosion* **NEGATIVE EFFECT** ▷ **2** C2 the fact of a good quality or situation being gradually lost or destroyed: *The survey reveals a gradual erosion of the president's popularity and support.*

erotic /ɪˈrɒt.ɪk/ Ⓤⓢ /-ˈrɑː.t̬ɪk/ **adj** related to sexual DESIRE and pleasure: *an erotic film* ◦ *erotic dreams/feelings* • **erotically** /ɪˈrɒt.ɪ.kəl.i/ Ⓤⓢ /ɪˈrɑː.t̬ɪ.kəl.i/ **adv**

erotica /ɪˈrɒt.ɪ.kə/ Ⓤⓢ /-ˈrɑː.t̬ɪ-/ **noun** [U] books, pictures, etc. which produce sexual DESIRE and pleasure

eroticism /ɪˈrɒt.ɪ.sɪ.zəm/ Ⓤⓢ /-ˈrɑː.t̬ə-/ **noun** [U] the quality of a picture, book, film, etc. being erotic: *The play's eroticism shocked audiences when it was first performed.*

err /ɜːr/, /eər/ Ⓤⓢ /ɜː/ /er/ **verb** [I] formal to make a mistake or to do something wrong: *He erred in agreeing to her appointment.*

IDIOM **err on the side of caution** to be especially careful rather than taking a risk or making a mistake: *25 people have replied to the invitation, but I've erred on the side of caution and put out 30 chairs.*

errand /ˈer.ənd/ **noun** [C] a short journey either to take a message or to take or collect something: *I'll meet you at six, I've got some errands to **do/run** first.*

IDIOM **ˌerrand of ˈmercy** literary an act of bringing help

ˈerrand ˌboy **noun** [C] old-fashioned a boy or young man employed by a shop or business to take messages, goods, etc.

errant /ˈer.ənt/ **adj** [before noun] formal behaving wrongly in some way, especially by leaving home: *an errant husband* ◦ *errant children*

errata /ɪˈrɑː.tə/ Ⓤⓢ /-t̬ə/ plural of **erratum**: *a list of errata*

erratic /ɪˈræt.ɪk/ Ⓤⓢ /-ˈræt̬-/ **adj** not regular, uncertain or without organization in movement or behaviour: *He drove in an erratic course down the road.* ◦ *She can be very erratic, one day she is friendly and the next she'll hardly speak to you.* • **erratically** /-ɪ.kəl.i/ **adv** *In her study, books were arranged erratically on chairs, tables and shelves.* ◦ *The machine is working erratically – there must be a loose connection.*

erratum /ɪˈrɑː.təm/ Ⓤⓢ /-t̬əm/ **noun** [C] (plural **errata**) formal a mistake in a printed or written document

erroneous /ɪˈrəʊ.ni.əs/ Ⓤⓢ /-ˈroʊ-/ **adj** formal wrong or false: *an erroneous **belief/impression*** • **erroneously** /-li/ **adv**

> **Word partners for error**
>
> *discover/correct/compound/make/spot* an error • a *fundamental/glaring/great/major* error • *human* error • a *margin* of/for error • do sth *in* error

error /ˈer.ər/ Ⓤⓢ /-ɚ/ **noun** [C or U] **1** B2 a mistake: *He admitted that he'd **made** an error.* ◦ *The letter contains a number of typing errors.* ◦ ***Human** error has been blamed for the air crash.* ◦ *With something as delicate as brain surgery, there is little **margin for** error* (= you must not make mistakes). **2 error of judgment** a wrong decision: *Not telling the staff before they read the news in the papers was an error of judgment.* **3 see the error of your ways** to understand that you were wrong to behave in a particular way and start to behave differently

ersatz /ˈeə.zæts/ Ⓤⓢ /ˈer.zɑːts/ **adj** disapproving used instead of something else, usually because the other thing is too expensive or rare: *I'm allowed to eat ersatz chocolate made from carob beans, but it's a poor substitute for the real thing.*

erstwhile /ˈɜːst.waɪl/ Ⓤⓢ /ˈɜːst-/ **adj** [before noun] formal previous → Synonym **former**

erudite /ˈer.ʊ.daɪt/ **adj** formal having or containing a lot of knowledge that is known by very few people: *He's the author of an erudite book on Scottish history.* • **erudition** /ˌer.ʊˈdɪʃ.ən/ **noun** [U] *a work of great erudition*

erupt /ɪˈrʌpt/ **verb** [I] **VOLCANO** ▷ **1** C2 When a VOLCANO erupts, it explodes and flames and rocks come out of it: *Since the volcano last erupted, many houses have been built in a dangerous position on its slopes.* **START SUDDENLY** ▷ **2** to start suddenly and violently: *At the end of a hot summer, **violence** erupted in the inner cities.* **3** to suddenly express your feelings in a noisy way: *The crowd erupted in applause and cheering.* **4** If spots erupt on your skin, they suddenly appear: *Two days after he'd been exposed to the substance, a painful rash erupted on his neck.* • **eruption** /ɪˈrʌp.ʃən/ **noun** [C or U] *a volcanic eruption* ◦ *There was a violent eruption of anti-government feeling.*

erythrocyte /ɪˈrɪθ.rəʊ.saɪt/ Ⓤⓢ /erˈɪθ.roʊ-/ **noun** [C] specialized any of the cells that carry OXYGEN around the body → Synonym **red blood cell**

escalate /ˈes.kə.leɪt/ **verb** [I or T] to make or become greater or more serious: *The decision to escalate UN involvement has been taken in the hopes of a swift end to the hostilities.* ◦ *His financial problems escalated after he became unemployed.* ◦ *The escalating rate of inflation will almost certainly bring escalating prices.* • **escalation** /ˌes.kəˈleɪ.ʃən/ **noun** [C or U] *It's difficult to explain the recent escalation **in/of** violent crime.*

escalator /ˈes.kə.leɪ.tər/ Ⓤⓢ /-t̬ɚ/ **noun** [C] B2 a set of stairs moved up or down by electric power on which people can stand and be taken from one level of a building to another, especially in shops, railway stations, and airports: *I'll meet you by the **up/down** escalator on the second floor.*

escalator

escalope /ˈes.kə.lɒp/ Ⓤⓢ /ɪˈskɑː.ləp/ **noun** [C] a thin piece of meat without bones: *veal/turkey escalopes*

escapade /ˈes.kə.peɪd/ **noun** [C] an act involving some danger, risk or excitement because it is different from usual or expected behaviour: *Her latest escapade was to camp outside a department store on the night before the sale.*

escape /ɪˈskeɪp/ **verb; noun**

▸**verb** **GET FREE** ▷ **1** B1 [I or T] to get free from something, or to avoid something: *Two prisoners have escaped.* ◦ *A lion has escaped **from** its cage.* ◦ *She was lucky to escape serious injury.* ◦ *He **narrowly*** (= only just) *escaped a fine.* ◦ *His **name** escapes me* (= I have forgotten his name). ◦ *Nothing important escapes her **notice/attention**.* **COMPUTER** ▷ **2** [I] specialized to press the key on a computer keyboard which allows you to leave a particular screen and return to the previous one or to interrupt a process: *Escape **from** this window and return to the main menu.*

IDIOM **there's no escaping the fact** used to mean that something is certain: *There's no escaping the fact (**that**) we won't be able to complete these orders without extra staff.*

▸noun GET FREE ▷ **1** C1 [C or U] the act of successfully getting out of a place or a dangerous or bad situation: *He **made** his escape on the back of a motorcycle.* ◦ *an escape **route*** ◦ *They **had a narrow** escape (= only just avoided injury or death) when their car crashed.* **2** [C] a loss that happens by accident: *an escape of radioactivity* FORGET ▷ **3** B2 [S] something that helps you to forget about your usual life or problems: *Romantic novels provide an escape **from** reality.* COMPUTER ▷ **4** [U] (also **escape key**, written abbreviation **Esc**) the key on a computer keyboard which allows you to leave a particular screen and return to the previous one or to interrupt a process: *Press Esc to return to the main menu.*

> Word partners for **escape noun**
>
> *have* a [*lucky/miraculous/narrow*] escape • *make* your escape • ***attempt/plan*** an escape • ***means*** of escape • an escape ***route***

escaped /ɪˈskeɪpt/ **adj** [before noun] having got free: *an escaped prisoner*

escapee /ˌɪskeɪˈpiː/ **noun** [C] a person who has escaped from a place: *The escapees were recaptured after three days on the run.*

eˈscape ˌhatch noun [C] the part of a SUBMARINE through which people can leave when it is underwater

escapism /ɪˈskeɪ.pɪ.zᵊm/ **noun** [U] a way of avoiding an unpleasant or boring life, especially by thinking, reading, etc. about more exciting but impossible activities: *These adventure movies are pure escapism.* ◦ *For many people going on holiday is a form of escapism.* • **escapist** /-pɪst/ **noun** [C], **adj** *escapist literature*

escapology /ˌes.kəˈpɒl.ə.dʒi/ US /-ˈpɑː.lə-/ **noun** [U] the activity of escaping from chains, boxes, etc. usually as part of an entertainment • **escapologist** /-dʒɪst/ **noun** [C] (US usually **escape artist**)

escarpment /ɪˈskɑːp.mənt/ US /-ˈskɑːrp-/ **noun** [C] a steep slope or CLIFF, such as one which marks the edge of a range of hills

eschew /ɪsˈtʃuː/ **verb** [T] formal to avoid something intentionally, or to give something up: *We won't have discussions with this group unless they eschew **violence**.*

escort verb; noun

▸verb [T] /ɪˈskɔːt/ US /-kɔːrt/ GO WITH ▷ **1** to go with someone or a vehicle especially to make certain that they arrive safely or that they leave a place: *Several little boats escorted the sailing ship into the harbour.* ◦ *The police escorted her **to** the airport, and made sure that she left the country.* **2** to go with someone and show them a place: *People on the tour will be escorted by an expert on archaeology.* SOCIAL COMPANION ▷ **3** formal to go to a social event with someone, especially a person of the opposite sex: *Who will be escorting her **to** the ball?*

▸noun /ˈes.kɔːt/ US /-kɔːrt/ SOCIAL COMPANION ▷ **1** [C] a person who goes with another person as a partner to a social event: *'But I can't go to the dance without an escort,' she protested.* **2** [C] someone who is paid to go out to social events with another person, and sometimes to have sex: *He hired an escort to go to the dinner with him.* GO WITH ▷ **3** [C] a person or vehicle that goes somewhere with someone to protect or guard them: *The members of the jury left the court with a **police** escort.* **4** [U] the state of having someone with you who gives you protection or guards you: *The prisoners were transported **under** military escort.*

ˈescort ˌagency noun [C] (also **ˈescort ˌservice**) a business that supplies people who work as escorts

escrow /ˈes.krəʊ/ US /-kroʊ/ **noun** [U] specialized an agreement between two people or organizations in which money or property is kept by a third person or organization until a particular condition is completed: *The money was placed **in** escrow.*

escudo /esˈkuː.dəʊ/ US /-doʊ/ **noun** [C] the standard unit of money used in Portugal before the introduction of the euro, and in Cape Verde

-ese /iːz/ **suffix** of a place, or the language spoken in a place: *Lebanese* ◦ *Chinese*

esker /ˈes.kəʳ/ US /-kɚ/ **noun** [C] specialized a long, narrow, raised line of earth, small stones and sand left on the earth's surface where melted ice once flowed under a GLACIER

Eskimo /ˈes.kɪ.məʊ/ US /-kə.moʊ/ **noun** [C] (plural **Eskimos** or **Eskimo**) a member of a race of people who live in the cold northern areas of North America, Greenland, and Siberia

> Note:
>
> Some of these people consider the term **Eskimo** offensive, and prefer the word **Inuit**.

ESL /ˌiː.esˈel/ **noun** [U] abbreviation for English as a Second Language: the teaching of English to speakers of other languages who live in a country where English is an official or important language → Compare **EFL**

ESOL /ˈiː.sɒl/ US /-sɑː.l/ **noun** [U] abbreviation for English for speakers of other languages: used, especially in the UK, to refer to to the teaching of English to students whose first language is not English, but who are living in an English-speaking country

esophagus /ɪˈsɒf.ə.gəs/ US /-ˈsɑː.fə-/ **noun** [C] (plural **esophagi** or **esophaguses**) US for **oesophagus**

esoteric /ˌiː.səˈter.ɪk/ US /ˌes.ə-/ **adj** very unusual and understood or liked by only a small number of people, especially those with special knowledge: *He has an esoteric collection of old toys and games.* ◦ disapproving or humorous *She has a rather esoteric **taste** in clothes.*

esp. adv written abbreviation for **especially**

ESP /ˌiː.esˈpiː/ **noun** [U] MIND ▷ **1** abbreviation for **extrasensory perception** LANGUAGE ▷ **2** abbreviation for English for specific/special purposes: the teaching of English for use in a particular area of activity, for example business or science

espadrille /ˈes.pə.drɪl/ **noun** [C] a shoe that is made from strong cloth, with a SOLE (= bottom part) made from rope

especial /ɪˈspeʃ.ᵊl/ **adj** [before noun] formal special

> Common mistake: **especially**
>
> **Warning:** Check your spelling!
>
> **Especially** is one of the 50 words most often spelled wrongly by learners.

especially /ɪˈspeʃ.ᵊl.i/ **adv** (also **specially**) **1** A2 very much; more than usual or more than other people or things: *She's not especially **interested** in sport.* ◦ *I love Australian wines, especially the white wines.* **2** for a particular reason: *I chose this especially **for** your new* house. ◦ They invited her to speak especially because of her experience in inner cities.

> **! Common mistake: especially or in particular?**
> **Warning:** do not use **especially** at the beginning of a sentence.
> When it refers to the subject of the sentence, **especially** usually comes directly after the subject:
> ~~Especially I enjoyed the boat trip on the Thames.~~
> *I especially enjoyed the boat trip on the Thames.*
> At the beginning of a sentence, don't say 'Especially', say **In particular**:
> *In particular, I enjoyed the boat trip on the Thames.*

Esperanto /ˌes.pᵊrˈæn.təʊ/ (US) /-pəˈræn.toʊ/ **noun** [U] an artificial language, made by combining features of several European languages, intended as a form of international communication

espionage /ˈes.pi.ə.nɑːʒ/ **noun** [U] the discovering of secrets, especially political or military information of another country or the industrial information of a business: ***military/industrial*** *espionage* → See also **spy**

esplanade /ˈes.plə.neɪd/ (US) /-nɑːd/ **noun** [C] old-fashioned a wide level path for walking along, often by the sea

espouse /esˈpaʊz/ **verb** [T] formal to become involved with or support an activity or opinion: *Vegetarianism is one cause she does not espouse.* • **espousal** /-ˈpaʊ.zᵊl/ **noun** [S or U] *Espousal **of** such liberal ideas won't make her very popular around here.*

espresso /esˈpres.əʊ/ (US) /-oʊ/ **noun** [C or U] (plural **espressos**) strong coffee, or a cup of this, made by forcing hot water through crushed coffee beans and served without milk: *Do you like espresso?* ◦ *Would you prefer an espresso or a cappuccino?*

esprit de corps /esˌpriː.dəˈkɔːʳ/ (US) /-ˈkɔːr/ **noun** [U] formal the feelings, such as being proud and loyal, shared by members of a group of people: *His leadership kept the team's esprit de corps intact during difficult periods.*

espy /esˈpaɪ/ **verb** [T] old-fashioned to suddenly or unexpectedly see something, especially something a long distance away: *She suddenly espied someone waving at her from the window.*

Esq. **noun** [after noun] **1** mainly UK formal written abbreviation for Esquire: a title added after a man's name on envelopes and official documents. If Esq. is used, Mr is not used before the name. **2** US written abbreviation usually used only after the full name of a man or woman who is a lawyer: *Address it to my lawyer, Steven A. Neil, Esq./Gloria Neil, Esq.*

-esque /-esk/ **suffix** like or in the style of someone or their work: *Dalí-esque* ◦ *Leonardo-esque* ◦ *Working there was like being trapped in a Kafkaesque nightmare.*

essay **noun; verb**
▸**noun** [C] /ˈes.eɪ/ UK (US **paper**) B1 a short piece of writing on a particular subject, especially one done by students as part of the work for a course: *For homework I want you to write an essay **on** endangered species.*
▸**verb** [T] /eˈseɪ/ old-fashioned to try to do something: *The procedure was first essayed in 1923.*

essayist /ˈes.eɪ.ɪst/ **noun** [C] a person who writes essays that are published: *a political essayist*

essence /ˈes.ᵊns/ **noun** IMPORTANCE ▷ **1** C2 [S or U] the basic or most important idea or quality of something: *The essence of his argument was that education should continue throughout life.* ◦ *Yet change is the very essence of life.* **2 in essence** C2 formal relating to the most important characteristics or ideas of something: *In essence, both sides agree on the issue.* **3 be of the essence** formal to be the most important thing: *In any of these discussions, of course, honesty is of the essence.* ◦ *Time is of the essence.* SMELL/TASTE ▷ **4** [C or U] a strong liquid, usually from a plant or flower, that is used to add a flavour or smell to something: ***vanilla*** *essence* ◦ *essence **of** violets*

essential /ɪˈsen.ʃᵊl/ **adj; noun**
▸**adj** B1 necessary or needed: *Government support will be essential if the project is to succeed.* ◦ *There is essential work to be done before the building can be re-occupied.* ◦ *Water is essential **for/to** living things.* ◦ ***It** is essential (**that**) our prices remain competitive.* ◦ [+ to infinitive] *For the experiment to be valid, it is essential **to** record the data accurately.*
▸**noun** [C usually plural] a basic thing that you cannot live without: *Because I live in a remote village, I regard my car as an essential.* ◦ *When we go on holiday, we only take **the bare** essentials.* ◦ *This leaflet will give you the essentials **of** how to use the word processor.*

essentially /ɪˈsen.ʃᵊl.i/ **adv** B2 relating to the most important characteristics or ideas of something: *What he's saying is essentially true.*

esˌsential ˈoil **noun** [C] an oil, usually with a strong smell, that is taken from a plant and is used to make PERFUME, or for rubbing into a person's body during MASSAGE: *Lavender, peppermint, and jasmine are essential oils which are widely available.*

esˌsential ˈservices **noun** [plural] basic public needs, such as water, gas, and electricity, that are often supplied to people's houses

est. **adj** **1** written abbreviation for **estimated**: *the town of Brownford (est. population 14,000)* **2** written abbreviation for established: used with a date to show when a company or organization was begun: *P. R. Jones & Co, Est. 1920*

-est /-ɪst/, /-əst/ **suffix** used to form the SUPERLATIVE of many adjectives and adverbs: *bravest* ◦ *latest*

establish /ɪˈstæb.lɪʃ/ **verb** START ▷ **1** B2 [T often passive] to start a company or organization that will continue for a long time: *The brewery was established in 1822.* ◦ *These methods of working were established in the last century.* **2** C1 [T often passive] to start having a relationship with, or communicating with another person, company, country, or organization: *There is a strong need to establish effective communication links between staff, parents, pupils, and external bodies.* ACCEPT ▷ **3** C1 [T] to cause to be accepted in or familiar with a place, position, etc.: *His reputation for carelessness was established long before the latest problems arose.* ◦ *He's established himself **as** a dependable source of information.* ◦ *After three months we were well established **in/at** our new house/new jobs.* **4 establish yourself** C1 formal to be in a successful position over a long period of time: *He has established himself as the leading candidate in the election.* DISCOVER ▷ **5** C2 [T] formal to discover or get proof of something: *Before we take any action we must establish the facts/truth.* ◦ [+ question word] *Can you establish **wh**at time she left home/**wh**ether she has left home.* ◦ [+ (that)] *We have established (**that**) she was born in 1900.*

established /ɪˈstæb.lɪʃt/ **adj** **1** accepted or respected because of having existed for a long period of time: *There are established procedures for dealing with emergencies.* ◦ *an established firm/brand* **2 get/become established a** to start to be successful or confident as a result of being in a particular place or doing a particular activity for a period of time: *The band doesn't make much money – it's just getting established.* **b** to start growing successfully somewhere: *As the plants get established, they will need frequent watering.* **3** used for describing someone who is known for doing a job well, because they have been doing it for a long time: *an established artist/star* **4** used for describing a Church or religion that is the official one of a country: *The Methodists broke away from the established Church.*

E

establishment /ɪˈstæb.lɪʃ.mənt/ noun **ORGANIZATION** ▷ **1** C1 [C] a business or other organization, or the place where an organization operates: *an educational/financial/religious establishment* **2 the establishment** [S, + sing/pl verb] the important and powerful people who control a country or an organization, especially those who support the existing situation: *Critics said judges were on the side of the establishment.* **START** ▷ **3** C1 [U] the process of starting or creating something, for example an organization: *Since its establishment two years ago, the advice centre has seen over 500 people a week.* ◦ *The establishment **of** new areas of employment is a priority.*

estate /ɪˈsteɪt/ noun **PROPERTY** ▷ **1** B2 [C] a large area of land in the country that is owned by a family or an organization and is often used for growing crops or raising animals: *It's a typical **country** estate with a large house for the owner, farm buildings and estate workers' houses.* **2** [C] legal everything that a person owns when they die: *She **left** her entire estate to her niece.* **BUILDINGS** ▷ **3** B2 [C] UK a group of houses or factories built in a planned way: *a **housing** estate* ◦ *an **industrial** estate (= a group of factories)* **CAR** ▷ **4** [C] UK (also **estate car**, US **station wagon**) a car with a lot of space behind the back seat and an extra door at the back for putting in large objects **STATE** ▷ **5** [U] old use a state of being: *the holy estate of marriage*

esˈtate ˌagency noun [C] UK (US **ˈreal esˌtate ˌoffice**, **realty office**) a business that arranges the selling, renting, or management of homes, land, and buildings for their owners

esˈtate ˌagent noun [C or] UK (US **ˈreal esˌtate ˌagent**, **realtor**) someone who works for an estate agency

esteem /ɪˈstiːm/ noun; verb

▸noun [U] formal respect for or a good opinion of someone: *There has been a drop in public esteem **for** teachers.* ◦ *Because of their achievements they were **held in** (= given) (**high**) esteem.*

▸verb [T not continuous] to respect someone or have a good opinion of them: *Her work is **highly** esteemed by all her colleagues.*

esthete /ˈes.θiːt/ noun [C] mainly US for **aesthete**

esthetic /esˈθet.ɪk/ US /-ˈθet̬-/ adj mainly US for **aesthetic**

estimable /ˈes.tɪ.mə.bl̩/ adj formal of a person or their behaviour, considered to be very good or deserving praise: *He writes estimable poetry under a pseudonym.*

estimate verb; noun

▸verb [T] /ˈes.tɪ.meɪt/ B2 to guess the cost, size, value, etc. of something: *Government sources estimate a long-term 50 percent increase in rail fares.* ◦ [+ (that)] *They estimate (**that**) the journey will take at least two weeks.* ◦ [+ question word] ***It** was difficult to estimate **how** many trees had been destroyed.* • **estimated** /-meɪ.tɪd/ US /-meɪ.t̬ɪd/ adj B2 *an estimated cost/value*

▸noun [C] /ˈes.tɪ.mət/ B2 a guess of what the size, value, amount, cost, etc. of something might be: *The number of people who applied for the course was 120 compared with an initial estimate **of** between 50 and 100.* ◦ *We'll accept the lowest of three estimates **for** the building work.* ◦ *a **conservative** (= low) estimate* ◦ *a **rough** (= not exact) estimate*

estimation /ˌes.tɪˈmeɪ.ʃən/ noun **OPINION** ▷ **1** [S] your opinion of someone or something: ***In** my estimation a lot of other banks are going to have the same problem.* ◦ *He **sank in** my estimation (= my opinion of him fell) when I saw how he treated his wife.* **GUESS** ▷ **2** [C or U] a guess about the cost, size, value, etc. of something: *computer-aided estimations* ◦ *estimation of the cost*

estoppel /ɪˈstɒp.əl/ US /-ˈstɑː.pəl/ noun [S or U] specialized a legal rule that prevents someone from changing their mind about something they have previously said is true in court

estranged /ɪˈstreɪndʒd/ adj **1** describes a husband or wife who is not now living with the person they are married to: *his estranged wife* **2** formal If you are estranged from your family or friends then you have seriously argued with them and are no longer friendly with them: *It's sad to see someone estranged **from** their parents.* • **estrangement** /ɪˈstreɪndʒ.mənt/ noun [C or U] formal (a period) when you are estranged from someone

estrogen /ˈes.trə.dʒən/ noun [U] mainly US for **oestrogen**

estuary /ˈes.tjʊə.ri/ US /-tu.er.i/ noun [C] the wide part of a river at the place where it joins the sea: *the Thames estuary* ◦ *the Rance estuary* • **estuarine** /-tjʊə.riːn/ US /-tjʊr.iːn/ adj specialized *estuarine species*

ˌEstuary ˈEnglish noun [U] a type of English spoken in southeast England that is a mixture of standard English and London English

ETA /ˌiː.tiːˈeɪ/ noun [S] abbreviation for estimated time of arrival: the time you expect to arrive: *What's your ETA?*

e-tailer /ˈiː.teɪ.lər/ US /-lɚ/ noun [C] UK a business that uses the internet to sell its products: *a music/wine/electrical e-tailer* • **e-tailing** /-lɪŋ/ noun [U]

et al. /etˈæl/ specialized abbreviation for et alia: and others. It is used in formal writing to avoid a long list of names of people who have written something together: *The method is described in an article by Feynman et al.*

etc. /ɪt.ˈset.ər.ə/ US /ˈset̬.ɚ-/ abbreviation for et cetera: and other similar things. It is used to avoid giving a complete list: *We saw lots of lions, tigers, elephants, etc.*

et cetera /ɪt.ˈset.ər.ə/ US /ˈset̬.ɚ-/ adv (abbreviation **etc.**) and other similar things

etch /etʃ/ verb [T] to cut a pattern, picture, etc. into a smooth surface, especially on metal or glass, using ACID or a sharp instrument: *He etched his name on a piece of glass.*

IDIOMS **be etched somewhere** (also **be etched with sth**) literary If a feeling, emotion, or shape is etched somewhere, it can be seen there very clearly: *His face was etched with pain.* ◦ *Confusion and sadness were etched **on** their faces.* ◦ *The foothills of the Himalayas were sharply etched against the pale blue sky.* • **be etched on/in sb's memory** to be something that you will continue to remember: *The scene will be etched on my memory forever.*

etcher /ˈetʃ.ər/ US /-ɚ/ noun [C] a person who makes etchings

etching /ˈetʃ.ɪŋ/ noun **1** [U] the act of etching **2** [C] a picture produced by printing from a metal plate that has been etched with ACID

eternal /ɪˈtɜː.nəl/ US /-ˈtɝː-/ adj lasting for ever or for a very long time: *The company is engaged in the* *eternal search for a product that will lead the market.* ◦ *Will you two never stop your eternal arguing!* • **eternally** /-i/ **adv** *the eternally changing seasons* ◦ formal *I'd be eternally (= very or always)* ***grateful*** *if you could arrange it.*

IDIOM **hope springs eternal** saying said when you continue to hope that something will happen, although it seems unlikely

eˌternal ˈstudent noun [C usually singular] humorous someone who tries to avoid getting a job for as long as possible by taking more educational courses

eternity /ɪˈtɜː.nɪ.ti/ ⓤⓢ /-ˈtɝː.nə.ţi/ **noun 1** [U] time that never ends or that has no limits: *They haven't been given these rights* ***for*** *(****all****) eternity – they should justify having them just like most other people have to.* ◦ *Religions gain some of their worldly power by claiming they have the key to eternity (= a state of existence outside normal life).* **2 an eternity** a very long time: *The film went on for what* ***seemed like*** *an eternity.* ◦ *Nine months is a long time for anyone, but it's an eternity for the very young.*

ethane /ˈiː.θeɪn/ **noun** [U] specialized a gas with no smell or colour that burns easily and is found in NATURAL GAS and PETROLEUM

ethanol /ˈeθ.ə.nɒl/ ⓤⓢ /-nɑːl/ **noun** [U] (also ˌ**ethyl** ˈ**alcohol**) a chemical COMPOUND that is a type of alcohol

ethene /ˈeθ.iːn/ **noun** [U] specialized **ethylene**

ether /ˈiː.θəʳ/ ⓤⓢ /-θɚ/ **noun MEDICAL** ▷ **1** [U] a clear liquid used, especially in the past, as an ANAESTHETIC to make people sleep before a medical operation **SKY** ▷ **2 the ether** [S] the sky or the air, especially considered as being full of radio waves

ethereal /ɪˈθɪə.ri.əl/ ⓤⓢ /-ˈθɪr.i-/ **adj** light and delicate, especially in an unnatural way: *an ethereal being* ◦ *ethereal beauty* • **ethereally** /-ə.li/ **adv**

Ethernet /ˈiː.θə.net/ ⓤⓢ /-θɚ-/ **noun** [S] a system for connecting computers into NETWORKS (= groups of computers that are used together)

ethic /ˈeθ.ɪk/ **noun 1** Ⓒ② [C usually plural] a system of accepted beliefs which control behaviour, especially such a system based on morals: *the (Protestant)* ***work*** *ethic* ◦ *The ethics of journalism are much debated.* ◦ *He said he was bound by a scientist's* ***code of*** *ethics.* ◦ *Publication of the article was a* ***breach of*** *ethics.* **2 ethics** Ⓒ② [U] the study of what is morally right and what is not

ethical /ˈeθ.ɪ.kəl/ **adj 1** Ⓒ② relating to beliefs about what is morally right and wrong: *ethical and legal issues* **2** Ⓒ② morally right: *ethical practice/trading* ◦ *a medical procedure which most people believe to be ethical* • **ethically** /-i/ **adv** *This action is ethically questionable.*

ethnic /ˈeθ.nɪk/ **adj; noun**

▸**adj 1** Ⓒ① relating to a particular race of people: *A question on ethnic* ***origin*** *was included in the census.* ◦ *The factory's workforce reflects the ethnic* ***mix*** *from which it draws its labour.* ◦ *Conflicts between the different ethnic* ***groups*** *in the country exploded into civil war.* **2** from a different race, or interesting because characteristic of an ethnic group that is very different from those that are common in western culture: *ethnic food* ◦ *ethnic costume* • **ethnically** /-nɪ.kəl.i/ **adv** *ethnically related communities* • **ethnicity** /eθˈnɪs.ɪ.ti/ ⓤⓢ /-ə.ţi/ **noun** [U] formal

▸**noun** [C] US a person belonging to an ethnic group

ˌethnic ˈcleansing noun [U] the organized attempt by a particular race or political group to completely remove from a country or area anyone who belongs to another particular race, using violence and often murder to achieve this

ˌethnic miˈnority noun [C] a group of people with a particular race or nationality living in a country or area where most people are from a different race or nationality

ethnocentric /ˌeθ.nəʊˈsen.trɪk/ ⓤⓢ /-noʊ-/ **adj** believing that the people, customs, and traditions of your own race or nationality are better than those of other races • **ethnocentrism** /-trɪ.zəm/ **noun** [U]

ethnographic /ˌeθ.nəˈɡræf.ɪk/ ⓤⓢ /-noʊ-/ **adj** related to ethnography: *ethnographic studies* • **ethnographically** /-ɪ.kəl.i/ **adv**

ethnography /eθˈnɒɡ.rə.fi/ ⓤⓢ /-ˈnɑː.ɡrə-/ **noun** [C or U] a scientific description of the culture of a society by someone who has lived in it, or a book containing this: *One of the aims of ethnography is to contribute to an understanding of the human race.* • **ethnographer** /-fəʳ/ ⓤⓢ /-fɚ/ **noun** [C]

ethnological /ˌeθ.nəˈlɒdʒ.ɪ.kəl/ ⓤⓢ /-noʊˈlɑː.dʒɪ.kəl/ **adj** (also **ethnologic** /-ˈlɒdʒ.ɪk/ ⓤⓢ /-ˈlɑː.dʒɪk/) relating to ethnology • **ethnologically** /-i/ **adv**

ethnology /eθˈnɒl.ə.dʒi/ ⓤⓢ /-ˈnɑː.lə-/ **noun** [U] the study of different societies and cultures • **ethnologist** /-dʒɪst/ **noun** [C]

ethos /ˈiː.θɒs/ ⓤⓢ /-θɑːs/ **noun** [S] the set of beliefs, ideas, etc. about social behaviour and relationships of a person or group: *national ethos* ◦ *working-class ethos* ◦ *The ethos* ***of*** *the traditional family firm is under threat.*

ˌethyl ˈalcohol noun [U] **ethanol**

ethylene /ˈeθ.ɪ.liːn/ ⓤⓢ /-ə-/ **noun** [U] specialized a gas with a slightly sweet smell that burns easily, used in industry and to make fruit RIPE (= ready to eat)

ˈe-ˌticket noun [C] a ticket, usually for someone to travel on an aircraft, that is held on a computer and is not printed on paper

etiolated /ˈiː.ti.ə.leɪ.tɪd/ ⓤⓢ /-ə.leɪ.ţɪd/ **adj** specialized especially of plants, pale and weak

etiology /ˌiː.tiˈɒl.ə.dʒi/ ⓤⓢ /-ˈɑː.lə-/ **noun** [U] the scientific study of the cause of diseases

etiquette /ˈet.ɪ.ket/ ⓤⓢ /ˈeţ.ɪ.kət/ **noun** [U] the set of rules or customs which control accepted behaviour in particular social groups or social situations: *(****Social****) etiquette dictates that men cannot sit while women are standing.* ◦ *Diplomatic etiquette forbids calling for the death of a national leader.*

etymology /ˌet.ɪˈmɒl.ə.dʒi/ ⓤⓢ /ˌeţ.ɪˈmɑː.lə-/ **noun** [C or U] the study of the origin and history of words, or a study of this type relating to one particular word: *At university she developed an interest in etymology.* ◦ *A list of selected words and their etymologies is printed at the back of the book.* • **etymological** /ˌet.ɪ.məˈlɒdʒ.ɪ.kəl/ ⓤⓢ /-ˈlɑː.dʒɪ-/ **adj** • **etymologically** /ˌet.ɪ.məˈlɒdʒ.ɪ.kəl.i/ ⓤⓢ /ˌeţ.ɪˈməˈlɑː.dʒɪ-/ **adv** • **etymologist** /-dʒɪst/ **noun** [C]

the EU /iːˈjuː/ **noun** abbreviation for **the European Union**

eucalyptus /juː.kəlˈɪp.təs/ **noun** [C or U] (also ˌ**eucalˈyptus ˌtree**, also ˈ**gum ˌtree**) any of several types of tree, found especially in Australia, that produce an oil with a strong smell used in medicine and industry: *eucalyptus* ***oil***

Eucharist /ˈjuː.kəʳ.ɪst/ **noun** [S or U] the Christian ceremony based on Jesus Christ's last meal with his DISCIPLES (= the first twelve men who believed in him) or the holy bread and wine used in this ceremony → See also **Communion** • **eucharistic** /juː.kəʳˈɪs.tɪk/ **adj**

eugenics /juːˈdʒen.ɪks/ **noun** [U] specialized the idea that it is possible to improve humans by allowing

E

only some people to produce children • **eugenic** /-ɪk/ **adj**

eulogize formal (UK usually **eulogise**) /ˈjuː.lə.dʒaɪz/ **verb** [T, I usually + adv/prep] to praise someone or something in a speech or piece of writing: *Critics everywhere have eulogized her new novel.* ◦ *They eulogized **over** the breathtaking views.*

eulogy /ˈjuː.lə.dʒi/ **noun** [C or U] formal a speech, piece of writing, poem, etc. containing great praise, especially for someone who recently died or stopped working: *He was the most self-effacing of men – the last thing he would have relished was a eulogy.* ◦ *The song was a eulogy **to** the joys of travelling.* • **eulogist** /-dʒɪst/ **noun** [C] • **eulogistic** /ˌjuː.ləˈdʒɪs.tɪk/ **adj**

eunuch /ˈjuː.nək/ **noun** [C] (plural **eunuchs**) a man who has had his TESTICLES removed

euphemism /ˈjuː.fə.mɪ.zəm/ **noun** [C or U] a word or phrase used to avoid saying an unpleasant or offensive word: *'Senior citizen' is a euphemism **for** 'old person'.* ◦ *The article made so much use of euphemism that often its meaning was unclear.* • **euphemistic** /ˌjuː.fəˈmɪs.tɪk/ **adj** • **euphemistically** /ˌjuː.fəˈmɪs.tɪ.kəl.i/ **adv**

euphonious /juːˈfəʊ.ni.əs/ (US) /-ˈfoʊ-/ **adj** formal having a pleasant sound

euphonium /juːˈfəʊ.ni.əm/ (US) /-ˈfoʊ-/ **noun** [C] a large musical instrument made from BRASS, that you play by blowing into it

euphoria /juːˈfɔː.ri.ə/ (US) /-ˈfɔːr.i-/ **noun** [U] extreme happiness, sometimes more than is reasonable in a particular situation: *They were in **a state of** euphoria for days after they won the prize.*

euphoric /juːˈfɒr.ɪk/ (US) /-ˈfɑːr-/ **adj** extremely happy and excited: *a euphoric mood* • **euphorically** /-ˈfɒr.ɪ.kəl.i/ (US) /-ˈfɑːr.ɪ.kəl.i/ **adv**

Eurasian /jʊˈreɪ.ʒən/ **adj** **1** describes a person with one European parent and one Asian parent **2** of or connected with Europe and Asia considered as a unit • **Eurasian noun** [C]

eureka /jʊˈriː.kə/ **exclamation** often humorous used to show that you have been successful in something you were trying to do: *'Eureka!' she shouted as the engine started.*

euro /ˈjʊə.rəʊ/ (US) /ˈjʊ.roʊ/ **noun** [C] **1** (A2) (symbol **€**) the unit of money used in most European Union countries: *You can usually find a hotel for €70 a night.* ◦ *I need to change my pounds into euros.* ◦ *a 20-euro note* **2 the euro** the value of the euro, used in comparing the values of different types of money from around the world: *The euro **fell/rose against** (= was worth less/more compared to) the pound today.*

Euro- /jʊə.rəʊ-/ (US) /jʊr.oʊ-/ **prefix** **1** relating to the European Union: *the Euro elections* ◦ *a Euro-MP (= a Member of the European Parliament)* **2** relating to Europe: *Europop (= modern, young people's music from Europe)*

Eurocrat /ˈjuː.rəʊ.kræt/ (US) /-roʊ-/ **noun** [C] an official, especially an important one, of the European Union

Europe /ˈjʊə.rəp/ (US) /ˈjʊ-/ **noun** **1** the continent that is to the east of the Atlantic Ocean, to the north of the Mediterranean and to the west of Asia **2** the European Union **3** UK the continent of Europe without including the UK

European /ˌjʊə.rəˈpiː.ən/ (US) /ˌjʊr.ə-/ **adj; noun**
▸**adj** of or from Europe: *a European city* ◦ *European history*
▸**noun** [C] someone who comes from Europe: *a party of Europeans*

the Euroˌpean Comˈmunity **noun** (abbreviation **the EC**) the organization through which particular European governments made decisions and agreed on shared action in social and economic matters until 1993, when it became the European Union

Euroˈpean ˌplan **noun** [U] US the situation when the price of a room in a hotel does not include meals

the Euroˌpean ˈUnion **noun** (abbreviation **the EU**) the organization, since 1993, through which European governments who choose to be members make decisions and agree on shared action in social and economic matters

Eurosceptic /ˈjʊə.rəʊˌskep.tɪk/ (US) /ˈjʊ.roʊ-/ **noun** [C] UK a person, especially a politician, who opposes closer connections between Britain and the European Union

the Eurozone /ˈjʊə.rə.zəʊn/ (US) /ˈjʊ.roʊ.zoʊn/ **noun** (also **Euroland** /-lænd/) the countries belonging to the European Union that use the euro as their unit of money

Eustachian tube /juːˈsteɪ.ʃənˈtjuːb/ (US) /-ˈtuːb/ **noun** [C] specialized either of the two passages between the MIDDLE EAR and the back of the nose which open to allow pressure to be kept equal on both sides of the EARDRUM

euthanasia /ˌjuː.θəˈneɪ.ʒə/ **noun** [U] the act of killing someone who is very ill or very old so that they do not suffer any more: *Although some people campaign for the right to euthanasia, it is still illegal in most countries.*

evacuate /ɪˈvæk.ju.eɪt/ **verb** [I or T] to move people from a dangerous place to somewhere safe: *The police evacuated the village shortly before the explosion.* ◦ *A thousand people were evacuated **from** their homes following the floods.* ◦ *When toxic fumes began to drift toward our homes, we were told to evacuate.* • **evacuation** /ɪˌvæk.juˈeɪ.ʃən/ **noun** [C or U] *The evacuation of civilians remains out of the question while the fighting continues.* ◦ *The first evacuations came ten days after the disaster.*

evacuee /ɪˌvæk.juˈiː/ **noun** [C] someone who is evacuated from a dangerous place, especially during a war: *Thousands of evacuees crossed the border to safety.*

evade /ɪˈveɪd/ **verb** [T] **1** formal to avoid or escape from someone or something: *The police have assured the public that the escaped prisoners will not evade recapture for long.* ◦ *She leaned forward to kiss him but he evaded her by pretending to sneeze.* ◦ *An Olympic gold medal is the only thing that has evaded her in her remarkable career.* ◦ [+ -ing verb] *He can't evade do**ing** military service forever.* **2 evade the issue, question, etc.** to intentionally not talk about something or not answer something: *Just give me an answer and stop evading the question!*

evaluate /ɪˈvæl.ju.eɪt/ **verb** [T] (C1) to judge or calculate the quality, importance, amount, or value of something: *It's impossible to evaluate these results without knowing more about the research methods employed.* ◦ [+ question word] *We shall need to evaluate **how** the new material stands up to wear and tear.* • **evaluation** /ɪˌvæl.juˈeɪ.ʃən/ **noun** [C or U] (C1) *Evaluation of this new treatment cannot take place until all the data has been collected.* • **evaluative** /ɪˈvæl.ju.ə.tɪv/ (US) /-eɪ.t̬ɪv/ **adj** formal *evaluative research*

evanescent /ˌiː.vəˈnes.ənt/ (US) /ˌev.ə-/ **adj** formal lasting for only a short time, then disappearing quickly and being forgotten • **evanescence** /-əns/ **noun** [U]

evangelical /ˌiː.vænˈdʒel.ɪ.kəl/ adj **RELIGION** ▷ **1** belonging to one of the Protestant Churches or Christian groups which believe the teaching of the BIBLE and persuading other people to join them to be extremely important: *the Evangelical movement* **OPINIONS** ▷ **2** having very strong beliefs and often trying to persuade other people to have the same beliefs: *Why is it that people who've given up smoking become so evangelical and intolerant of other smokers?* • **evangelical** noun [C] *The new Archbishop is an evangelical.* • **evangelicalism** /-ɪ.zəm/ noun [U]

evangelist /ɪˈvæn.dʒə.lɪst/ noun [C] a person who tries to persuade people to become Christians, often by travelling around and organizing religious meetings → See also **televangelist** • **evangelistic** /ɪˌvæn.dʒəˈlɪs.tɪk/ adj

Evangelist /ɪˈvæn.dʒə.lɪst/ noun [C] one of the writers of the four books in the Bible about Jesus Christ

evangelize (usually **evangelise**) /ɪˈvæn.dʒə.laɪz/ verb UK **OPINIONS** ▷ **1** [I] to talk about how good you think something is: *I wish she would stop evangelizing about the virtues of free market economics.* **RELIGION** ▷ **2** [T] to try to persuade people to become Christians • **evangelism** /-ɪ.zəm/ noun [U]

evaporate /ɪˈvæp.ər.eɪt/ (US) /-ɚ-/ verb **BECOME GAS** ▷ **1** [I or T] to cause a liquid to change to a gas, especially by heating: *The high concentration of sugars forms a syrup when the sap evaporates.* ◦ *Plants keep cool during the summer by evaporating water from their leaves.* **DISAPPEAR** ▷ **2** [I] to disappear: *Halfway through the film reality evaporates and we enter a world of pure fantasy.* • **evaporation** /ɪˌvæp.əˈreɪ.ʃən/ noun [U]

eˌvaporated ˈmilk noun [U] milk that has been made thicker by removing some of the water from it, used to make sweet dishes

eˈvaporating ˌdish noun [C] specialized a small, flat dish used in scientific work to heat and evaporate substances

evasion /ɪˈveɪ.ʒən/ noun [C or U] the act of avoiding something or someone: *Her speech was full of excuses and evasions and never properly addressed the issue.* ◦ ***tax** evasion (= illegally not paying tax)*

evasive /ɪˈveɪ.sɪv/ adj **1** answering questions in a way that is not direct or clear, especially because you do not want to give an honest answer: *The Minister was her usual evasive self, skilfully dodging reporters' questions about her possible resignation.* **2** done to avoid something bad happening: *By the time the pilot realized how close the plane was to the building, it was too late to take evasive **action**.* ◦ *Drivers had to make sudden evasive manoeuvres.* • **evasively** /-li/ adv • **evasiveness** /-nəs/ noun [U]

eve /iːv/ noun **1** [S] the period or day before an important event: *Mr Hurd was speaking to Arab journalists in London **on the** eve **of** his visit to Jordan and Saudi Arabia.* ◦ ***Christmas/New Year's** Eve* **2** [S or U] old use the evening

Eve /iːv/ noun [S] the first woman, according to the BIBLICAL story of how the world was made

even /ˈiː.vən/ adv; adj; verb

▸adv **SURPRISE** ▷ **1** (A2) used to show that something is surprising, unusual, unexpected, or extreme: *I don't even know where it is.* ◦ *Everyone I know likes the smell of bacon – even Mike does and he's a vegetarian.* ◦ *We were all on time – even Chris and he's usually late for everything.* ◦ *It's a very difficult job – it might even take a year to finish it.* ◦ *'I never cry.' 'Not even when you hurt yourself really badly?'* ◦ *Even with a load of electronic gadgetry, you still need some musical ability to write a successful song.* **2 even as** at the same time as: *I tried to reason with him, but even as I started to explain what had happened he stood up to leave.* **3 even if** (B2) used to say that if something is the case or not, the result is the same: *Even if you take a taxi, you'll still miss your train.* **4 even now/then** despite something: *I've thought about it so much, but even now I can't believe how lucky I was to survive the accident.* ◦ *I gave Jim very clear instructions, but even then he managed to make a mess of it.* **5 even so** (C1) despite what has just been said: *I had a terrible headache, but even so I went to the concert.* ◦ *An immediate interest cut might give a small boost to the economy. Even so, any recovery is likely to be very slow.* **6 even though** (B2) although: *Even though he left school at 16, he still managed to become prime minister.*

> **! Common mistake: even though**
>
> **Remember: even though** is never written as one word.
>
> Don't write 'eventhough', write **even though**:
>
> ~~*Eventhough I had a very nice time, I was glad to come home.*~~
>
> *Even though I had a very nice time, I was glad to come home.*

EMPHASIS ▷ **7** (B1) used to emphasize a comparison: *The next 36 hours will be even colder with snow showers becoming more widespread.* ◦ *Any devaluation of sterling would make it even more difficult to keep inflation low.* **MORE EXACTLY** ▷ **8** used when you want to be more exact or detailed about something you have just said: *I find some of his habits rather unpleasant, disgusting even.* ◦ *She has always been very kind to me, even generous on occasion.*

> **! Common mistake: even**
>
> **Warning:** check your word order!
>
> **Even** usually goes directly before the main verb in a sentence:
>
> ~~*I said 'Hello', but he even didn't look at me.*~~
>
> *I said 'Hello', but he didn't even look at me.*
>
> But if the main verb is **am/is/are/was/were**, **even** usually goes directly after it:
>
> ~~*He even is rude to his parents.*~~
>
> *He is even rude to his parents.*

▸adj **FLAT** ▷ **1** flat and smooth, or on the same level: *We resurfaced the floor because it wasn't even.* **CONTINUOUS** ▷ **2** continuous or regular: *You should try to work at an even rate instead of taking it easy one day and working flat out the next.* **EQUAL** ▷ **3** equal or equally balanced: *Both sides played well – it was a very even contest.* ◦ *The weather forecast said that there's an even chance of thunderstorms tonight (= that it is equally likely that there will or will not be storms).* **4** US (UK **evens**) equally likely to happen as to not happen: *The chances of her getting the job are about evens.* **5** describes a situation where you risk money on something where the risk is equally balanced, and will pay back twice the amount of money that is paid if it is successful: *an even bet* ◦ *If I were having a bet I'd take even **money** on United.* **NUMBER** ▷ **6** forming a whole number that can be divided exactly by two: *6 is an even number and 7 is an odd number.*

IDIOMS **get even with sb** informal to do something equally bad to someone who has done something bad to you • **on an even keel** regular and well-balanced and not likely to change suddenly: *The new manager succeeded in putting the business back on an even keel.*

►verb [T] to make two things equal: *Sheila was awarded a scholarship in Chemistry, and now her brother has evened **the score** with a scholarship in Economics.* ◦ *The whisky industry is campaigning for the taxes on different alcoholic drinks to be evened **up**.*

PHRASAL VERB **even (sth) out** to become equal, or to make something equal: *The university has a system designed to even out the differences between rich and poor colleges.*

ˌeven-ˈhanded adj treating everyone fairly and equally: *Several broadcasters have been criticized for failing to give even-handed treatment to all the parties during the election campaign.*

evening /ˈiːv.nɪŋ/ **noun; exclamation**
►noun [C or U] A1 the part of the day between the end of the afternoon and night: *a chilly evening* ◦ *I work in a restaurant and only get one evening **off** a week.* ◦ *Thank you for such a lovely evening.* ◦ *I always go to see a film **on** Friday evenings.* ◦ ***In the** evenings, I like to relax.* ◦ *I'm working late **this** evening.* ◦ *What are you doing **tomorrow** evening?* ◦ *It poured down **all** evening and most of the night as well.* ◦ *What time do you usually get home **in the** evening?*
►exclamation informal a friendly way of greeting someone when you meet them in the evening: *Evening, Tom! Where are you off to this evening?*
→ Compare **good evening**

ˈevening ˌclass noun [C] a class intended for adults rather than children which happens in the evening: *Pat teaches evening classes **in** yoga and relaxation.* ◦ *I've been going to evening classes to improve my German.*

ˈevening ˌdress noun **1** [U] special clothing worn for formal events, such as special evening meals: *The invitation says to wear evening dress.* **2** [C] a long dress worn by a woman to a formal party or social occasion

ˌevening ˈprimrose noun [C or U] a plant with pale yellow flowers. Its seeds are used to make an oil that is used to treat various medical conditions: *evening primrose oil*

evenings /ˈiːv.nɪŋz/ adv mainly US in the evening: *What time do you get home evenings?* ◦ *I work evenings.*

the ˌevening ˈstar noun [S] a planet, especially Venus, that can be seen shining brightly in the west just after the sun has gone down

evenly /ˈiː.vən.li/ adv **CALMLY** ▷ **1** If you say something evenly, you speak without showing emotion in your voice although you are angry or not satisfied in some way: *'We are not terrorists,' he said evenly. 'We are freedom fighters.'* **EQUALLY** ▷ **2** in or into equal amounts: *Divide the mixture evenly between the baking pans.* ◦ *Congress is still evenly divided on the issue.*

evensong /ˈiː.vən.sɒŋ/ US /-ˌsɑːŋ/ noun [U] the evening ceremony of the Church of England or the Roman Catholic Church

event /ɪˈvent/ noun [C] **1** B1 anything that happens, especially something important or unusual: *This year's Olympic Games will be the biggest ever **sporting** event.* ◦ *Susannah's party was the **social** event of the year.* ◦ *The police are trying to determine the **series of** events that led up to the murder.* **2** B1 one of a set of races or competitions: *The women's 200 metre event will be followed by the men's 100 metres.* **3 in the event** UK used to emphasize that what happened was not what you expected: *We had expected to arrive an hour late, but in the event we were early.* **4 in the event of sth** C1 if something happens: *In the event of a strike, the army will take over responsibility for firefighting.* **5 in any event** C1 (UK also **at all events**) whatever happens: *I might go home next month, but in any event, I'll be home for Christmas.* **6 in either event** in either of two situations: *I can't decide whether to accept the Cambridge or the London job, but in either event I'll have to move house.* **7 in that event** if that happens: *There's a possibility of my flight being delayed. In that event I'll phone to let you know.*

> Word partners for **event**
>
> an event *happens/occurs/takes place* • *witness* an event • an *important/major/significant* event • a *dramatic/horrific/tragic* event • a *rare* event • a *chain/sequence/series* of events • the *course* of events

ˌeven-ˈtempered adj approving always calm and never angry or too excited about anything

eventful /ɪˈvent.fəl/ adj C2 full of interesting or important events: *Her time at university was the most eventful period of her life.* ◦ *We had quite an eventful journey.*

eventide /ˈiː.vən.taɪd/ noun [C or U] literary evening

eventual /ɪˈven.tju.əl/ adj [before noun] C2 happening or existing at a later time or at the end, especially after a lot of effort, problems, etc.: *The Dukes were the eventual winners of the competition.* ◦ *Although the original budget for the project was $1 billion, the eventual cost is likely to be 50 percent higher.*

eventuality /ɪˌven.tjuˈæl.ɪ.ti/ US /-ə.t̬i/ noun [C] something unpleasant or unexpected that might happen or exist in the future: *We've tried to anticipate the most likely problems, but it's impossible to be prepared for **all** eventualities/**every** eventuality.* ◦ *I'm looking for a travel insurance policy that will cover me for **any** eventuality.*

eventually /ɪˈven.tju.əl.i/ adv B2 in the end, especially after a long time or a lot of effort, problems, etc.: *Although she had been ill for a long time, it still came as a shock when she eventually died.* ◦ *It might take him ages but he'll do it eventually.*

ever /ˈev.əʳ/ US /-ɚ/ adv **AT ANY TIME** ▷ **1** A2 at any time: *Nothing ever happens here in the evenings.* ◦ *Have you ever been to London?* ◦ *If you're ever/If ever you're in Cambridge, do give me a ring.* ◦ *He **hardly** ever (= almost never) washes the dishes and he **rarely, if** ever, (= probably never) does any cleaning.* ◦ *When there's a James Bond film on TV, I **never** ever miss it.* ◦ ***If** ever there was a cause for celebration, this peace treaty was it.* ◦ *The smell is worse **than** ever.* ◦ *I thought she was famous, but none of my friends have ever heard of her.* **2 better, bigger, more, etc. than ever** C1 better, bigger, etc. than at any time before: *We are spending more than ever on education.* **3 as big, fast, good, etc. as ever** as big, fast, etc. as at any time before: *The restaurants are as good as ever and no more expensive.* **ALWAYS** ▷ **4** C2 continuously: *United's record in cup competitions grows ever **more** impressive.* ◦ *The ever-**increasing** demand for private cars could be halted by more investment in public transport.* ◦ *nuclear devastation was an ever-**present** threat* ◦ *Susan and Guy moved to the country, where they lived **happily** ever **after**.* **5 ever since** B1 continuously since that time: *He's been depressed ever since he got divorced.* **6 as ever** in the same way as always: *As ever, I was the last to find out.* **7 yours ever** (also **ever yours**) UK formal used at the end of a letter as a way of saying goodbye to someone you know well: *Yours ever, Yvonne.* **EMPHASIS** ▷ **8** used for emphasizing an adjective: *The orchestra is to perform its last ever concert/last concert ever tomorrow night at* the Albert Hall. ◦ *Yesterday the company announced its* ***first*** *ever fall in profits.* ◦ *Was she ever a fast runner!* (= *She was a very fast runner!*) ◦ *'Are you looking forward to your vacation?' 'Am I ever!'* (= *Yes, very much!*) **9** in questions, used to emphasize the question word: *How ever did he manage that?* ◦ *What ever have you done to him?* ◦ *Why ever would anyone/Why would anyone ever want to hurt her?* **10 ever so/ever such a** B2 UK informal very/a very: *She's ever so pretty.* ◦ *She's ever such a pretty girl.*

IDIOM **if ever there was one** (also **if ever I saw one**) used to emphasize that what you are saying is true: *It was a brilliant performance if ever there was one.*

evergreen /ˈev.ə.griːn/ US /-ɚ-/ **adj; noun**
▸**adj 1** describes a plant, bush, or tree that has leaves for the whole year → Compare **deciduous 2** always seeming fresh or remaining popular: *that evergreen TV series 'The Good Life'*
▸**noun** [C] a plant, bush, or tree that has leaves for the whole year

everlasting /ˌev.əˈlɑː.stɪŋ/ US /-ɚˈlæs.tɪŋ/ **adj** lasting for ever or for a long time: *I wish someone would invent an everlasting light bulb.* ◦ *Their contributions to science have earned them an everlasting place in history.*

evermore /ˌev.əˈmɔːr/ US /-ɚˈmɔːr/ **adv** literary always in the future: *Their name will live on evermore.*

ˌever-ˈpresent adj used to describe something that is always there: *the ever-present danger of a terrorist attack*

every /ˈev.ri/ **determiner** ALL ▷ **1** A1 used when referring to all the members of a group of three or more: *The police want to interview every employee about the theft.* ◦ *The show will be broadcast every weekday morning between 9.00 and 10.00.* ◦ *We're open every day except Sunday.* ◦ *I've been out every night this week.* ◦ *Every time I go to London I get caught in a traffic jam.* ◦ *Ten pence is donated to charity for every bottle sold.* ◦ *These paintings may look like the real thing, but* ***(each and)*** *every* ***one*** *of them is a fake.* ◦ *That salmon was very expensive so make sure you eat up every* ***(single) bit.*** **2 every bit as** equally as: *Opponents of the war are considered every bit as patriotic as supporters.* **3 every last** every: *We catch the majority of people, but hunting down every last tax dodger is impossible.* **4 every which way** US in all directions: *The game was hindered by a fierce wind that swept the ball every which way.* **5 in every way** in all ways: *This movie is in every way a masterpiece of cinematography.* **6 (your) every need** all the things that you need or want: *There'll be an assistant there to see to your every need.*

> **! Common mistake: every time**
> **Remember:** when **every** is followed by **time**, it is written as two words.
> Don't write 'everytime', write **every time**:
> ~~*I see him everytime I take the dog for a walk.*~~
> *I see him every time I take the dog for a walk.*

REPEATED ▷ **7** A1 used to show that something is repeated regularly: *Computers can perform millions of calculations every second.* ◦ *Every four minutes a car is stolen in this city.* ◦ *Every day in the United States 25 people are murdered with handguns.* ◦ *Every* ***few*** *kilometres we passed a burned out jeep or truck at the side of the road.* ◦ *The conference takes place every* ***other/second*** *year.* **8 every now and again/then** C1 sometimes but not often: *Every now and again/then they'll have a beer together.* **9 every so often** C2 sometimes but not often: *Every so often I treat myself to a meal in an expensive restaurant.* GREATEST ▷ **10** B2 the greatest possible or that can be imagined: *I'd like to wish you every success in your new job/happiness in your new home.* ◦ *She has every reason to be unhappy after losing her job and her home.* ◦ *You had every opportunity to make a complaint.* ◦ *Every effort is being made to minimize civilian casualties.* ◦ *She has every right to be proud of her tremendous achievements.*

IDIOMS **every minute** describes the whole period that something lasted: *'Did you like the concert?' 'Yes, I enjoyed every minute* ***of*** *it.'* • **(your) every move** everything that you do: *I'd hate to be someone really famous with the press reporting my every move.* ◦ *After that, she was watching his every move.* • **(your) every word** all the things that you say: *She's such a fascinating lecturer – I was hanging on to her every word.* • **on/at every corner** in many places along the streets of a town or city: *After the match, police were stationed on every corner.*

everybody /ˈev.riˌbɒd.i/ US /-ˌbɑː.di/ **pronoun** A2 **everyone**

everyday /ˈev.ri.deɪ/ **adj** ordinary, typical or usual: *the everyday* ***lives*** *of ordinary Russian citizens* ◦ *Death was an everyday* ***occurrence*** *during the Civil War.*

> **! Common mistake: everyday**
> **Remember: everyday** is an adjective and is usually used before a noun.
> To describe how regularly something is repeated, don't write 'everyday', write **every day:**
> *I try to read English newspapers every day.*

everyone /ˈev.ri.wʌn/ **pronoun** (also **everybody**) A2 every person: *Would everyone who wishes to attend the dinner let me know by Friday afternoon?* ◦ *Everyone has their own ideas about the best way to bring up children.* ◦ *I've received replies from everybody but Jane.* ◦ *Do you agree with the principle that everyone should pay something towards the cost of health care?* ◦ *Everyone knows who stole it, but they're all afraid to tell anyone.* ◦ *Everyone involved in the accident has been questioned by the police.* ◦ *Goodbye, everybody – I'll see you next week.* ◦ *I'm sorry, but you'll just have to wait your turn like everybody* ***else.***

> **! Common mistake: everyone**
> **Remember: everyone** and **everybody** are usually written as one word.
> To refer to 'all the people' or 'all people', as a group, don't write 'every one' or 'every body', write **everyone/everybody**:
> ~~*He introduced me to every one at the party.*~~
> *He introduced me to everyone at the party.*
> **Every one** and **every body** are not common.
> Only write **every one** to refer to people as separate members of a group:
> *All his friends were there and he introduced me to every one.*
> *He introduced me to every one of his friends.*
> Only write **every body** to refer to separate physical bodies, especially dead bodies:
> *We will not know how many people died until the police have recovered every body.*

everyplace /ˈev.ri.pleɪs/ **adv** US informal everywhere

everything /ˈev.ri.θɪŋ/ **pronoun** A2 all things: *You can't blame him for everything.* ◦ *He's obsessed with Kylie Minogue and collects* ***anything and*** *everything connected with her.* ◦ *Jane's been unfaithful to Jim three* *times, but he still loves her* ***in spite of*** *everything.* ∘ *Money isn't everything (= the most important thing).* ∘ *His children are everything* ***to*** *him (= the most important part of his life).* ∘ *Have you been crying? Is everything all right?* ∘ *The thieves took everything.* ∘ *We did everything we could to save her but she died.* ∘ *We shall do everything* ***necessary*** *to bring the murderer to justice.* ∘ *They're very busy with their new house and everything (= all the things connected with it).*

> **! Common mistake: everything**
>
> **Remember:** when **every** is followed directly by **thing**, it is written as one word.
>
> Don't write 'every thing', write **everything**:
>
> ~~*I tell my best friend every thing.*~~
>
> *I tell my best friend everything.*
>
> **Every** and **thing** can appear with an adjective in between:
>
> *I tell her every little thing that happens to me.*

IDIOM **everything but/except the kitchen sink** humorous a much larger number of things than is necessary: *We're only going on vacation for a week, but John will insist on taking everything but the kitchen sink.*

everywhere /ˈev.ri.weəʳ/ ⓤⓢ /-wer/ **adv** (US informal **everyplace**) Ⓐ2 to, at or in all places or the whole of a place: *His children go everywhere with him.* ∘ *Everywhere looks so grey and depressing in winter.* ∘ *I looked everywhere for my keys.* ∘ *Reasonable people everywhere will be outraged by this atrocity.* ∘ *We had to stay in the sleaziest hotel in town as everywhere* ***else*** *(= all other places) was fully booked.*

ˈ**eve-teasing noun** [U] Indian English the act of annoying a woman or women in a public place, for example by making sexual comments

evict /ɪˈvɪkt/ **verb** [T] to force someone to leave somewhere: *Tenants who fall behind in their rent risk being evicted.* ∘ *He was evicted* ***from*** *the pub for drunken and violent behaviour.* • **eviction** /ɪˈvɪk.ʃᵊn/ **noun** [C or U] *After falling behind with his mortgage repayments he now faces eviction* ***from*** *his home.* ∘ *In this economically depressed area, evictions are common.*

evidence /ˈev.ɪ.dᵊns/ **noun** [U] Ⓑ2 one or more reasons for believing that something is or is not true: *The police have found no evidence* ***of*** *a terrorist link with the murder.* ∘ [+ to infinitive] *There is no* ***scientific*** *evidence* ***to*** *suggest that underwater births are dangerous.* ∘ [+ that] *Is there any scientific evidence* ***that*** *a person's character is reflected in their handwriting?* ∘ *Several experts are to* ***give*** *evidence on the subject.* ∘ *There is only* ***circumstantial*** *evidence against her, so she is unlikely to be convicted.* ∘ *Campaigners now have compelling* ***documentary*** *evidence of the human rights abuses that they had been alleging for several years.* ∘ ***Fresh*** *evidence suggests that the statement had been fabricated.* ∘ *The traces of petrol found on his clothing provided the* ***forensic*** *evidence proving that he had started the fire deliberately.* ∘ ***All the*** *evidence points to a substantial rise in traffic over the next few years.* ∘ *There is* ***growing/mounting/increasing*** *evidence* ***that*** *people whose diets are rich in vitamins are less likely to develop some types of cancer.* • **evidenced** /-dᵊnst/ **adj** mainly US shown to be true: *His desire to win an Olympic medal is evidenced* ***by*** *his performances throughout this season.*

evident /ˈev.ɪ.dᵊnt/ **adj** Ⓑ2 easily seen or understood: *The full extent of the damage only became evident the following morning.* ∘ ***From*** *the smell* ***it*** *was evident* ***that*** *the drains had been blocked for several days.* ∘ *Harry's courage during his illness was evident* ***to*** *everyone.* ∘ *Her love for him was evident* ***in*** *all that she did.* → Synonym **obvious** → See also **self-evident**

evidently /ˈev.ɪ.dᵊnt.li/ **adv 1** Ⓑ2 in a way that is easy to see: *He was evidently upset by the news of the accident.* ∘ *a thin although evidently pregnant woman* **2** used to say what people believe is true: *He had an accident, evidently because he was driving at excessive speed.*

evil /ˈiː.vᵊl/ **adj; noun**

▸**adj 1** Ⓑ2 morally bad, cruel, or very unpleasant: *an evil dictator* ∘ *These people are just evil.* **2** If the weather or a smell is evil, it is very unpleasant.

IDIOM **the evil eye** a magical power to injure or harm people by looking at them

▸**noun** [C or U] Ⓑ2 something that is very bad and harmful: *Each new leader would blame his predecessor for all the evils of the past.* ∘ *Drug addiction is one of today's great social evils.* ∘ *For the sake of long-term peace, the military option is the* ***lesser*** *evil/the* ***lesser of two*** *evils (= the less unpleasant of two bad choices).* ∘ *the battle between* ***good and*** *evil*

evildoer /ˈiː.vᵊlˌduː.əʳ/ ⓤⓢ /-ɚ/ **noun** [C] someone who does something evil: *The government has blamed the protests on a handful of evildoers.*

evince /ɪˈvɪns/ **verb** [T] formal to make obvious or show clearly: *In all the years I knew her, she never evinced any desire to do such a thing.*

eviscerate /ɪˈvɪs.ə.reɪt/ **verb** [T] specialized to remove one or all of the organs from the inside of a body • **evisceration** /ɪˌvɪs.əˈreɪ.ʃᵊn/ **noun** [U]

evocative /ɪˈvɒk.ə.tɪv/ ⓤⓢ /-ˈvɑː.kə.t̬ɪv/ **adj** making you remember or imagine something pleasant: *evocative* ***music*** ∘ *a sound evocative* ***of*** *the sea* • **evocatively** /-li/ **adv**

evoke /ɪˈvəʊk/ ⓤⓢ /-ˈvoʊk/ **verb** [T] to make someone remember something or feel an emotion: *That smell always evokes memories of my old school.* ∘ *a detergent designed to evoke the fresh smell of summer meadows* • **evocation** /ˌiː.vəˈkeɪ.ʃᵊn/ ⓤⓢ /ˌev.ə-/ **noun** [C or U]

evolution /ˌiː.vəˈluː.ʃᵊn/, /ˌev.ə-/ **noun** [U] **1** Ⓑ2 the way in which living things change and develop over millions of years: *Darwin's theory of evolution* **2** Ⓑ2 a gradual process of change and development: *the evolution of language*

evolutionary /ˌiː.vəˈluː.ʃᵊn.ᵊr.i/, /ˌev.əˈ-/ ⓤⓢ /-er-/ **adj 1** relating to the way in which living things develop over millions of years **2** involving a gradual process of change and development: *The change has been evolutionary rather than revolutionary.*

evolve /ɪˈvɒlv/ ⓤⓢ /-ˈvɑːlv/ **verb** [I or T] Ⓒ1 to develop gradually, or to cause something or someone to develop gradually: *Humans evolved* ***from*** *apes.* ∘ *The company has evolved over the years* ***into*** *a multi-million dollar organization.* ∘ *Bacteria are evolving resistance to antibiotics.*

evolved /ɪˈvɒlvd/ ⓤⓢ /-ˈvɑːlvd/ **adj** having developed through a gradual process: *Are humans just an evolved animal?*

ewe /juː/ **noun** [C] a female sheep, especially an adult one: *ewe's milk*

eww (also **ew**) /ˈiːuː/ **exclamation** an expression of DISGUST (= disapproval and dislike): *Eww – these socks smell!*

ex /eks/ **noun** [C] informal Someone's ex is a person who was their wife, husband, or partner in the past: *Is she still in touch with her ex?*

ex- /eks-/ **prefix** used to show that someone is no longer what they were: *ex-prisoners* ◦ *my ex-husband*

exacerbate /ɪɡˈzæs.ə.beɪt/ (US) /-ɚ-/ **verb** [T] to make something that is already bad even worse: *This attack will exacerbate the already tense relations between the two communities.* • **exacerbation** /ɪɡˌzæs.əˈbeɪ.ʃən/ (US) /-ɚ-/ **noun** [U]

exact /ɪɡˈzækt/ **adj**; **verb**

▸**adj** B1 in great detail, or complete, correct, or true in every way: *The exact distance is 1.838 metres.* ◦ *The exact time of the accident was 2.43 p.m.* ◦ *'I still owe you £7, don't I?' 'Actually, it's £7.30* ***to be*** *exact.'* ◦ *The exact location of the factory has yet to be decided.* ◦ *Unlike astronomy, astrology cannot be described as an exact science.* → Synonym **precise** • **exactness** /-nəs/ **noun** [U] (formal **exactitude** /-ˈzæk.tɪ.tʃuːd/ (US) /-ˈzæk.tə.tuːd/)

▸**verb** [T] formal to demand and get something, sometimes using force or threats, or to make something necessary: *to exact revenge on someone* ◦ *The blackmailers exacted a total of $100,000 from their victims.* ◦ *Heart surgery exacts tremendous skill and concentration.*

exacting /ɪɡˈzæk.tɪŋ/ **adj** demanding a lot of effort, care or attention: *an exacting training schedule* ◦ *exacting* ***standards***

exactly /ɪɡˈzækt.li/ **adv** **1** A2 used when you are giving or asking for information that is completely correct: *The journey took exactly three hours.* ◦ *That'll be £15 exactly, please.* ◦ *It tastes exactly the same as the real thing, but has half the fat.* ◦ *The building looks exactly as it did when it was built in 1877.* ◦ *'What you seem to be saying is that more should be invested in the road system and less in the railways.' 'Exactly' (= that is correct).* **2** B1 used to emphasize what you are saying: *Do exactly what I tell you and no one will get hurt!* ◦ *Exactly how do you propose to achieve this?* ◦ *What exactly do you mean?* **3 not exactly a** used for saying that someone or something is slightly different to a particular way of him, her, or it: *He's not exactly good-looking, but he has a certain attraction.* **b** B2 used for saying that something is not completely true: *'So you gave her your iPod?' 'Not exactly, I lent it to her.'* **c** used for saying that something is the opposite of a particular way of describing it: *Answer the question – it's not exactly difficult.*

exaggerate /ɪɡˈzædʒ.ə.reɪt/ (US) /-ɚ.eɪt/ **verb** [I or T] C1 to make something seem larger, more important, better or worse than it really is: *The threat of attack has been* ***greatly*** *exaggerated.* ◦ *Don't exaggerate – it wasn't that expensive.* ◦ *I'm not exaggerating – it was the worst meal I've ever eaten in my life.* • **exaggerated** /-ə.reɪ.tɪd/ (US) /-ɚ.eɪ.t̬ɪd/ **adj** *exaggerated reports of the problem* • **exaggeratedly** /-ə.reɪ.tɪd.li/ (US) /-ɚ.eɪ.t̬ɪd.li/ **adv**

exaggeration /ɪɡˌzædʒ.əˈreɪ.ʃən/ **noun** [C or U] C1 the fact of making something seem larger, more important, better or worse than it really is: *Sal reckons over 60 people were there but I think that's a slight exaggeration.* ◦ [+ to infinitive] ***It*** *would be* ***no*** *exaggeration* ***to*** *say that her work has saved lives.*

exalt /ɪɡˈzɒlt/ (US) /-ˈzɑːlt/ **verb** [T] **1** formal to raise someone to a higher rank or more powerful position **2** old use to praise someone a lot

exaltation /ˌeɡ.zɒlˈteɪ.ʃən/ (US) /-zɑːl-/ **noun** [U] **HAPPINESS** ▷ **1** formal a very strong feeling of happiness **MAKE IMPORTANT** ▷ **2** formal the act of raising someone to a higher rank or more powerful position **3** old use praise

exalted /ɪɡˈzɒl.tɪd/ (US) /-ˈzɑːl.t̬ɪd/ **adj** **IMPORTANT** ▷ **1** An exalted position in an organization is a very important one: *She rose to the exalted post of Foreign Secretary.* **HAPPY** ▷ **2** formal extremely happy

exam /ɪɡˈzæm/ **noun** [C] (formal **examination**) A2 a test of a student's knowledge or skill in a particular subject which results in a qualification if the student is successful: *How many pupils are* ***taking*** *the geography exam this term?* ◦ *I failed my physics exam, but I passed chemistry.* ◦ *an examination* ***paper*** ◦ *exam* ***results***

examination /ɪɡˌzæm.ɪˈneɪ.ʃən/ **noun** **1** B2 [C or U] the act of looking at or considering something carefully in order to discover something: *a post-mortem examination* ◦ *I had to* ***have/undergo*** *a medical examination when I started my pension scheme.* ◦ *The evidence is still* ***under*** *examination (= being examined).* ◦ *I thought it was paint at first, but* ***on closer*** *examination I realized it was dried blood.* **2** A2 [C] formal an exam

examine /ɪɡˈzæm.ɪn/ **verb** [T] **LOOK AT CAREFULLY** ▷ **1** B2 to look at or consider a person or thing carefully and in detail in order to discover something about them: *Forensic scientists are examining the wreckage* ***for*** *clues about the cause of the explosion.* ◦ *The council is to examine ways of reducing traffic in the city centre.* ◦ *The research examined the effects of alcohol on long-term memory.* ◦ [+ question word] *We need to examine* ***how*** *an accident like this can be avoided in the future.* ◦ *A psychiatrist was examined (= asked questions)* ***on*** *the mental state of the defendant.* **TEST** ▷ **2** C2 to test someone's knowledge or skill in a particular subject: *We were examined* ***on*** *European history.* ◦ UK *You'll be examined* ***in*** *three main areas; speaking, listening and reading comprehension.*

examiner /ɪɡˈzæm.ɪ.nər/ (US) /-nɚ/ **noun** [C] B1 someone whose job is to decide how well someone has done in an examination: *The candidates listed below have failed to satisfy the examiners.*

example /ɪɡˈzɑːm.pl̩/ (US) /-ˈzæm-/ **noun** [C] **TYPICAL CASE** ▷ **1** A1 something that is typical of the group of things that it is a member of: *Could you give me an example* ***of*** *the improvements you have mentioned?* ◦ *This painting is a marvellous example* ***of*** *her work.* → See also **exemplify** **2** A1 a way of helping someone to understand something by showing them how it is used: *Study the examples first of all, then attempt the exercises on the next page.* **3 for example** A1 used when giving an example of the type of thing you mean: *Offices can easily become more environmentally-friendly by, for example, using recycled paper.* **BEHAVIOUR** ▷ **4** B2 a person or a way of behaving that is considered suitable to be copied: *He's a very good example* ***to*** *the rest of the class.* ◦ *He's decided to* ***follow*** *the example of his father and study law.* **PUNISHMENT** ▷ **5** a punishment that is intended to warn others against doing the thing that is being punished, or a person who receives such a punishment: *The judge* ***made an*** *example* ***of*** *him and gave him the maximum possible sentence.*

IDIOM **set an example** B2 to behave in a way that other people should copy: *You should be setting a good example to your younger brother.*

exasperate /ɪɡˈzɑː.spə.reɪt/ (US) /-ˈzæs.pɚ.eɪt/ **verb** [T] to make someone very annoyed, usually when they can do nothing to solve a problem

exasperated /ɪɡˈzɑː.spə.reɪ.tɪd/ (US) /-ˈzæs.pɚ.eɪ.t̬ɪd/ **adj** annoyed: *He's becoming increasingly exasperated with the situation.* • **exasperatedly** /-li/ **adv**

exasperating /ɪɡˈzɑː.spə.reɪ.tɪŋ/ (US) /-ˈzæs.pɚ.eɪ.t̬ɪŋ/ **adj** extremely annoying: *It's so exasperating when he* *won't listen to a word that I say.* • **exasperatingly** /-li/ adv

exasperation /ɪɡˌzɑː.spəˈreɪ.ʃən/ (US) /-ˈzæs.pə-/ noun [U] anger: *There is growing exasperation within the government* ***at*** *the failure of these policies to reduce unemployment.* ◦ *After ten hours of fruitless negotiations, he stormed out of the meeting* ***in*** *exasperation.*

ex cathedra /ˌeks.kəˈθiː.drə/ adj [before noun], adv formal with complete authority, or said by the Pope to be true and so accepted by all members of the Roman Catholic Church

excavate /ˈek.skə.veɪt/ verb [I or T] **1** to remove earth that is covering very old objects buried in the ground in order to discover things about the past: *Tintagel Castle is being excavated.* **2** to dig a hole or CHANNEL in the ground, especially with a machine: *In tin mining today, workers excavate tunnels horizontally from a vertical shaft.* • **excavation** /ˌeks.kəˈveɪ.ʃən/ noun [C or U] *Excavation on the site is likely to continue for several years.*

excavator /ˈek.skə.veɪ.təʳ/ (US) /-t̬ɚ/ noun [C] UK (US ˈ**steam** ˌ**shovel**) a large, powerful machine with a container connected to a long arm, used for digging up the ground

exceed /ɪkˈsiːd/ verb [T] C1 to be greater than a number or amount, or to go past an allowed limit: *The final cost should not exceed $5,000.* ◦ *The success of our campaign has exceeded our wildest expectations.* ◦ *She was found guilty on three charges of exceeding the speed limit.*

exceedingly /ɪkˈsiː.dɪŋ.li/ adv formal to a very great degree: *He was clever, handsome, and exceedingly rich.* → Synonym **extremely**

excel /ɪkˈsel/ verb [I] (**-ll-**) **1** C2 to be extremely good at something: *Rebecca always excelled* ***in*** *languages at school.* **2 excel yourself** C2 to do something better than you usually do: *The British team have excelled themselves this year to reach the finals.*

excellence /ˈek.səl.əns/ noun [U] the quality of being excellent: *The school is noted for its academic excellence.*

Excellency /ˈek.səl.ən.si/ noun **Your Excellency/His Excellency** the title of someone in an important official position, especially someone, such as an AMBASSADOR, who represents their government in a foreign country: *His Excellency will be pleased to see you now.*

excellent /ˈek.səl.ənt/ adj A2 extremely good: *The food was excellent.* ◦ *Her car is in excellent condition.* ◦ *The fall in interest rates is excellent news for borrowers.* ◦ *'Our sales are up for the third year in a row.' 'Excellent.' (= I'm extremely pleased.)* • **excellently** /-li/ adv

> **!** Common mistake: **excellent**
>
> **Warning:** Check your spelling!
>
> **Excellent** is one of the 50 words most often spelled wrongly by learners.

except /ɪkˈsept/ preposition, conjunction A2 not including; but not: *The museum is open daily except Monday(s).* ◦ *The government has few options except to keep interest rates high.* ◦ *It's cool and quiet everywhere except in the kitchen.* ◦ *Everyone was there except* ***for*** *Sally.* ◦ *There is nothing to indicate the building's past, except (****for****) the fireplace.*

IDIOM **except that** B1 used to give a reason why something is not possible or true: *I want to go, except that I'm tired.* ◦ *The exam went pretty well, except that I misread the final question.*

excepted /ɪkˈsept.ɪd/ adj [after noun] formal not included: *I can't stand academics –* ***present company*** *excepted (= not including those who are being talked to).*

excepting /ɪkˈsep.tɪŋ/ preposition, conjunction formal not including: *All the people who were on the aircraft have now been identified, excepting one.*

exception /ɪkˈsep.ʃən/ noun [C or U] **1** B2 someone or something that is not included in a rule, group, or list or that does not behave in the expected way: *Men are usually quite good at map-reading but Tim is the exception.* ◦ *There are exceptions* ***to*** *every rule.* ◦ *I like all kinds of films* ***with the*** *exception* ***of*** *(= but not) horror films.* ◦ *Her books are always entertaining and this one is* ***no*** *exception.* ◦ *You must report here every Tuesday* ***without*** *exception.* **2 make an exception** C1 to not treat someone or something according to the usual rules: *We don't usually accept late applications, but in this case we will make an exception.* **3 take exception to sth/sb** C2 to be offended or made angry by something or someone: *Why did you take exception to what he said? He was only joking.*

IDIOM **the exception that proves the rule** something that emphasizes the general truth of a statement by disagreeing with it: *Most company directors are middle-aged men, but this 28-year-old woman is an exception that proves the rule.*

exceptionable /ɪkˈsep.ʃən.ə.bl/ adj formal offensive or upsetting: *exceptionable behaviour*

exceptional /ɪkˈsep.ʃən.əl/ adj approving B2 much greater than usual, especially in skill, intelligence, quality, etc.: *an exceptional student* ◦ *exceptional powers of concentration* ◦ *The company has shown exceptional growth over the past two years.* • **exceptionally** /-i/ adv *an exceptionally fine portrait*

excerpt /ˈek.sɜːpt/ (US) /-sɝːpt/ noun [C] a short part taken from a speech, book, film, etc.: *An excerpt* ***from*** *her new thriller will appear in this weekend's magazine.* • **excerpt** /ekˈsɜːpt/ (US) /-ˈsɝːpt/ verb [T] mainly US *This passage of text has been excerpted* ***from*** *her latest novel.*

excess noun; adj

►noun /ɪkˈses/, /ˈek.ses/ **TOO MUCH** ▷ **1** C1 [S or U] an amount that is more than acceptable, expected, or reasonable: *An excess* ***of*** *enthusiasm is not always a good thing.* ◦ *They both eat* ***to*** *excess (= too much).* ◦ *There will be an increase in tax for those earning* ***in*** *excess* ***of*** *(= more than) twice the national average wage.* **2 excesses** [plural] actions far past the limit of what is acceptable: *For many years people were trying to escape the excesses (= cruel actions) of the junta.* ◦ *As for shoes, her excesses (= the large number she owned) were well known.* **INSURANCE** ▷ **3** [U] UK (US **deductible**) a part of the cost of an accident, injury, etc. that you agree to pay yourself when you buy INSURANCE: *She has an excess of £200* ***on*** *her home insurance policy.*

►adj [before noun] /ˈek.ses/ C1 extra: *Cut off any excess pastry and put it to one side.*

exˌcess ˈbaggage noun [U] (UK also ˌ**excess** ˈ**luggage**) bags which weigh more than the allowed amount for a single passenger, or the money you are charged to take them onto an aircraft: *We had to pay excess baggage.* ◦ *He arrived with 88 pounds of excess baggage.*

excessive /ekˈses.ɪv/ adj C1 too much: *Excessive exercise can sometimes cause health problems.* ◦ *Any more pudding would simply be excessive.* • **excessively** /-li/ adv *She was polite but not excessively so.* ◦ *I don't drink excessively.*

exchange /ɪksˈtʃeɪndʒ/ noun; verb

►noun **GIVING AND GETTING** ▷ **1** B1 [C or U] the act of

giving something to someone and them giving you something else: *an exchange of ideas/information* ◦ *They were given food and shelter* ***in*** *exchange* ***for*** *work.* ◦ *She proposes an exchange of contracts at two o'clock.* ◦ *Several people were killed during the exchange of gunfire.* **2** [C] a short conversation or argument: *There was a* ***brief*** *exchange between the two leaders.* **STUDENTS** ▷ **3** B1 [C] an arrangement in which students from one country go to stay with students from another country: *Are you going on the French exchange this year?* ◦ *a German exchange student* **STOCK EXCHANGE** ▷ **4** [C usually singular] a STOCK EXCHANGE

▸**verb** [T] B1 to give something to someone and receive something from them: *It's traditional for the two teams to exchange shirts after the game.* ◦ *I exchanged those trousers* ***for*** *a larger size.* ◦ *Every month the group meets so its members can exchange their views/opinions (= have a discussion).* ◦ *We exchanged greetings before the meeting.* ◦ *We can exchange addresses when we see each other.* ◦ *Exchanging houses (= going to live in someone else's house while they live in yours) for a few weeks is a good way of having a holiday.* • **exchangeable** /-ˈtʃeɪn.dʒə.bl/ **adj** *Goods are exchangeable as long as they are returned in good condition.*

IDIOM **exchange words** to speak with someone: *We exchanged words after the meeting.*

exˈchange ˌrate noun [C] (also **ˌrate of exˈchange**) B1 the rate at which the money of one country can be changed for the money of another country

the Exchequer /ɪksˈtʃek.əʳ/ US /-ɚ/ **noun** the government department that receives and gives out public money, in the UK and some other countries

excise noun; verb

▸**noun** [U] /ˈek.saɪz/ a tax made by a government on some types of goods produced and used within their own country: *The excise* ***(duty) on*** *beer was increased under the last government.*

▸**verb** [T] /ekˈsaɪz/ formal to remove, especially by cutting: *During a three-hour operation six tumours were excised* ***from*** *the wall of the patient's stomach.* ◦ *The official censors have excised the controversial sections of the report.* • **excision** /-ˈsɪʒ.ən/ **noun** [C or U]

excitable /ɪkˈsaɪ.tə.bl/ US /-t̬ə-/ **adj** easily and often becoming excited: *an excitable child*

excite /ɪkˈsaɪt/ **verb** [T] **MAKE HAPPY** ▷ **1** to make someone have strong feelings of happiness and enthusiasm: *Nothing about my life excites me at present.* **CAUSE REACTION** ▷ **2** formal to cause a particular reaction in someone: *This product has excited a great deal of media* ***interest.*** ◦ *The statement excited new speculation that a senior minister may be about to resign.*

excited /ɪkˈsaɪ.tɪd/ US /-t̬ɪd/ **adj** A1 feeling very happy and enthusiastic: *Are you getting excited* ***about*** *your holiday?* ◦ *An excited crowd waited for the singer to arrive.* • **excitedly** /-li/ **adv** B1 *She ran excitedly down the hall to greet her cousins.*

IDIOM **be nothing to get excited about** to not be especially good: *It's a competent enough first novel but nothing to get excited about.*

excitement /ɪkˈsaɪt.mənt/ **noun** [C or U] B1 a feeling of being excited, or an exciting event: *Robin's heart was pounding with excitement.* ◦ *If you want excitement, you should try parachuting.* ◦ *the excitements of the previous day*

exciting /ɪkˈsaɪ.tɪŋ/ US /-t̬ɪŋ/ **adj** A1 making you feel excited: *an exciting film/soundtrack* ◦ *You're going to Africa? How exciting!* ◦ *It was a really exciting match.* • **excitingly** /-li/ **adv**

Word partners for excitement

feel excitement • *cause/create/generate* excitement • excitement *grows/mounts* • *great/growing/mounting/wild* excitement • *nervous* excitement • a *feeling/sense* of excitement • a *flurry/frisson/tingle* of excitement • excitement *about/at/over* sth

Other ways of saying exciting

If something is so exciting that it holds your attention completely, you can say that it is **gripping** or **riveting**:

The book was ***gripping*** *– I couldn't put it down.*

I found the movie absolutely ***riveting.***

Sports and outdoor activities which are exciting are often described as **exhilarating**:

I find skiing absolutely ***exhilarating.***

The adjective **action-packed** is often used to describe a story or period of time that is full of exciting events:

We had an ***action-packed*** *week of vacation.*

The movie is described as 'an ***action-packed*** *thriller'.*

If something is very exciting, especially because you are not sure what will happen, you can describe it as **thrilling**:

It was a ***thrilling*** *game in which both teams played well.*

An exciting atmosphere is sometimes described as **electric**:

The atmosphere backstage was ***electric.***

Vibrant is often used to describe places which are exciting:

This is one of the country's most ***vibrant*** *cities.*

excl. written abbreviation for **excluding** or **exclusive**, see at exclude

Note:

This abbreviation is used mainly in advertisements.

exclaim /ɪkˈskleɪm/ **verb** [I] C2 to say or shout something suddenly because of surprise, fear, pleasure, etc.: [+ speech] *'You can't leave now!' she exclaimed.* ◦ *She exclaimed* ***in*** *delight upon hearing the news.*

exclamation /ˌek.skləˈmeɪ.ʃən/ **noun** [C] something you say or shout suddenly because of surprise, fear, pleasure, etc.: *an exclamation of delight*

exclaˈmation ˌmark noun [C] (US **exclaˈmation ˌpoint**) B2 the symbol ! written immediately after an exclamation

exclude /ɪkˈskluːd/ **verb** [T] **1** C1 to prevent someone or something from entering a place or taking part in an activity: *Women are still excluded* ***from*** *the club.* ◦ *Microbes must, as far as possible, be excluded* ***from*** *the room during an operation.* ◦ *Tom has been excluded* ***from*** *school (= he is not allowed to go to school) for bad behaviour.* → Compare **include 2** C1 to intentionally not include something: *The price excludes local taxes.* → Compare **include 3** to decide that something is not true or possible: *We can't exclude the* ***possibility*** *that he is dead.*

excluding /ɪkˈskluː.dɪŋ/ **preposition** not including: *The aircraft carries 461 people excluding the crew and cabin staff.*

E

exclusion /ɪkˈskluː.ʒən/ noun [C or U] **1** the act of not allowing someone or something to take part in an activity or to enter a place: *her exclusion* ***from*** *the list of Oscar nominees* ◦ *the exclusion* ***of*** *disruptive students from school* **2 to the exclusion of** If you do something to the exclusion of something else, you do it so much that you do not have time for anything else.

exclusive /ɪkˈskluː.sɪv/ adj; noun
▸adj **1** C1 limited to only one person or group of people: *This room is for the exclusive* ***use*** *of guests.* ◦ *an exclusive* ***interview*** **2** B2 expensive and only for people who are rich or of a high social class: *an exclusive private club* ◦ *an exclusive part of town* **3 exclusive of sth** C2 not including something: *Is the total exclusive of service charges?* **4 mutually exclusive** not possible at the same time: *Some people think that uncontrolled economic growth and environmental stability are mutually exclusive.* • **exclusivity** /ˌek.skluːˈsɪv.ɪ.ti/ US /-ə.t̬i/ noun [U] (also **exclusiveness** /-nəs/) the quality of being exclusive
▸noun [C] a story that is published in one magazine, website, etc., and no others: *The newspaper published an exclusive about the escape.*

exclusively /ɪkˈskluː.sɪv.li/ adv C1 only: *This offer is available exclusively to our established customers.* ◦ *an exclusively female audience*

excommunicate /ˌek.skəˈmjuː.nɪ.keɪt/ verb [T] When the Christian Church, especially the Roman Catholic Church, excommunicates someone, it refuses to give them COMMUNION and does not allow them to be involved in the Church. • **excommunication** /ˌek.skəˌmjuː.nɪˈkeɪ.ʃən/ noun [C or U]

excoriate /ekˈskɔː.ri.eɪt/ US /-ˈskɔːr.i-/ verb [T] formal to write or say that a play, a book, a political action, etc. is very bad: *His latest novel received excoriating reviews.* ◦ *The president excoriated the Western press for their biased views.*

excrement /ˈek.skrɪ.mənt/ noun [U] formal the solid waste that is released from the bowels of a person or animal: *human excrement*

excrescence /ekˈskres.ənts/ noun [C] **1** formal an unusual growth on an animal or one of its organs or on a plant **2** literary something considered to be very ugly: *The new office development is an excrescence* ***on*** *the face of the city.*

excreta /ɪkˈskriː.tə/ US /-t̬ə/ noun [U] formal the waste material produced by a body, especially solid waste

excrete /ɪkˈskriːt/ verb [I or T] formal to get rid of material such as solid waste or urine from the body: *Most toxins are naturally excreted* ***from*** *the body.* • **excretion** /-ˈskriː.ʃən/ noun [C or U] *Excretion is one of several activities common to both plants and animals.*

excruciating /ɪkˈskruː.ʃi.eɪ.tɪŋ/ US /-t̬ɪŋ/ adj **1** extremely painful: *an excruciating* ***pain*** *in the lower back* **2** extremely boring or embarrassing: *excruciating boredom* ◦ *His confession, when it came, was excruciating.* • **excruciatingly** /-li/ adv *excruciatingly painful/uncomfortable* ◦ *excruciatingly embarrassing/boring/funny*

exculpate /ˈek.skəl.peɪt/ verb [T] formal to remove blame from someone: *The pilot of the aircraft will surely be exculpated when all the facts are known.* • **exculpatory** /ekˈskʌl.peɪ.tər.i/ US /-tɔː.ri/ adj

excursion /ɪkˈskɜː.ʃən/ US /-ˈskɝː-/ noun [C] **1** a short journey usually made for pleasure, often by a group of people: *This year's annual excursion will be* ***to*** *Lincoln.* ◦ *Next week we're* ***going on*** *an excursion.* **2 excursion into sth** a short involvement in a new activity: *A teacher by profession, this is her first excursion into writing.*

excusable /ɪkˈskjuː.zə.bl̩/ adj deserving to be forgiven: *Considering her difficult childhood her behaviour is excusable.* → Opposite **inexcusable**

excuse verb; noun
▸verb [T] /ɪkˈskjuːz/ **1** B1 to forgive someone: *Please excuse me* ***for*** *arriving late – the bus was delayed.* ◦ *Nothing can excuse that sort of behaviour.* ◦ *No amount of financial recompense can excuse the way in which the company carried out its policy.* ◦ *We cannot excuse him* ***for*** *these crimes.* ◦ *I asked the teacher if I could be excused* ***from*** (= allowed not to do) *football practice as my knee still hurt.* ◦ *Please excuse me* ***from*** (= allow me to miss) *the rest of the meeting – I've just received a phone call that requires my immediate attention.* **2 excuse me a** A1 a polite way of attracting the attention, especially of someone you do not know: *Excuse me, does this bus go to Oxford Street?* **b** used to politely ask someone to move so that you can walk past them: *Excuse me, can I just get past?* **c** used to tell someone politely that you are leaving: *Excuse me a moment, I'll be with you shortly.* **d** A2 used to say sorry for something you have done by accident: *Did I take your seat? Do excuse me.* **e** said before disagreeing with someone: *Excuse me but aren't you forgetting something?* **f** US (UK **pardon?**, **I beg your pardon?**) used to politely ask someone to repeat something they have said because you have not heard it
▸noun [C] /ɪkˈskjuːs/ **1** B1 a reason that you give to explain why you did something wrong: *He'd better have a* ***good*** *excuse* ***for*** *being late.* ◦ *I've never known him to miss a meeting – I'm sure he'll* ***have*** *an excuse.* ◦ *There's* ***no*** *excuse* ***for*** *that sort of behaviour.* **2** B1 a false reason that you give to explain why you do something: [+ to infinitive] *She was just looking for an excuse to call him.* ◦ *Any excuse* ***for*** *a holiday!* **3 make your excuses** to explain why you cannot be present somewhere: *Please make my excuses at the meeting on Friday.* **4 make excuses** to give false reasons why you cannot do something: *You're always making excuses* ***for*** *not helping me.*

> **Word partners for excuse noun**
> *have/make/offer/think up* an excuse • a *good/convenient/feeble/perfect/poor* excuse • *at* the *slightest* excuse • an excuse *for* sth

IDIOM **a miserable, poor, etc. excuse for sth** a very bad example of something: *It was a miserable excuse for a meal.*

ˌex-diˈrectory adj UK (US **unlisted**) refers to a phone number that is not made public by the phone company: *We've* ***gone*** *ex-directory because we were receiving so many unwanted calls.*

execrable /ˈek.sə.krə.bl̩/ adj formal very bad: *an execrable performance* ◦ *She's always had execrable taste in men.* • **execrably** /-bli/ adv *He was treated execrably.*

execute /ˈek.sɪ.kjuːt/ verb [T] KILL ▷ **1** C2 to kill someone as a legal punishment: *He was executed for murder.* DO ▷ **2** C2 formal to do or perform something, especially in a planned way: *to execute a deal/plan* ◦ *The whole play was executed with great precision.* **3 execute a will** legal If you execute someone's will, you deal with their money, property, etc., according to the instructions in it.

execution /ˌek.sɪˈkjuː.ʃən/ noun KILLING ▷ **1** [C or U] the legal punishment of killing someone: *Execution is still the penalty in some states for murder.* ◦ *The* *executions will be carried out by a firing squad.* **ACTION** ▷ **2** [U] the act of doing or performing something, especially in a planned way: *Sometimes* ***in the*** *execution* ***of*** *their duty the police have to use firearms.* ◦ *Although the original idea was good, its execution has been disappointing.*

executioner /ˌek.sɪˈkjuː.ʃən.ər/ (US) /-ɚ/ **noun** [C] someone whose job is to execute criminals

executive /ɪɡˈzek.jʊ.tɪv/ (US) /-jə.t̬ɪv/ **noun; adj**
▸noun [C] **1** (C1) (informal **exec**) someone in a high position, especially in business, who makes decisions and puts them into action: *She is now a* ***senior*** *executive, having worked her way up through the company.* **2 the executive** the part of a government that is responsible for making certain that laws and decisions are put into action **3** a group of people who run a business or an organization: *The executive of the health workers' union accepted the proposed pay increase on behalf of their members.*
▸adj [before noun] (C1) relating to making decisions and managing businesses, or suitable for people with important jobs in business: *His executive skills will be very useful to the company.* ◦ *executive cars* ◦ *an executive suite*

executor /ɪɡˈzek.jʊ.tər/ (US) /-jə.t̬ɚ/ **noun** [C] legal someone who makes sure that things are done according to the wishes in a dead person's will

exegesis /ˌek.sɪˈdʒiː.sɪs/ noun [C or U] (plural **exegeses**) specialized an explanation of a text, especially from the Bible, after its careful study

exemplar /ɪɡˈzem.plɑːr/ (US) /-plɑːr/ **noun** [C] formal a typical or good example of something

exemplary /ɪɡˈzem.plə.ri/ (US) /-plɚ.i/ **adj 1** very good and suitable to be copied by other people: *His tact was exemplary, especially considering the circumstances.* **2** [before noun] describes a punishment that is severe and intended as a warning to others: *The judge awarded exemplary* ***damages.***

exemplify /ɪɡˈzem.plɪ.faɪ/ **verb** [T] (C2) to be or give a typical example of something: *This painting perfectly exemplifies the naturalistic style which was so popular at the time.* • **exemplification** /ɪɡˌzem.plɪ.fɪˈkeɪ.ʃən/ **noun** [C or U]

exempt /ɪɡˈzempt/ **verb; adj**
▸verb [T] to excuse someone or something from a duty, payment, etc.: *Small businesses have been exempted* ***from*** *the tax increase.* • **exemption** /-ˈzemp.ʃən/ **noun** [C or U] *Candidates with a qualification in Chemistry have exemption* ***from*** *this course.*
▸adj with special permission not to do or pay something: *Goods exempt* ***from*** *this tax include books and children's clothes.* ◦ *Pregnant women are exempt* ***from*** *dental charges under the current health system.*

exercise /ˈek.sə.saɪz/ (US) /-sɚ-/ **noun; verb**
▸noun **HEALTHY ACTIVITY** ▷ **1** (A2) [C or U] physical activity that you do to make your body strong and healthy: *Swimming is my favourite* ***form of*** *exercise.* ◦ *You really should* ***take*** *more exercise.* ◦ *I* ***do*** *stomach exercises most days.* **PRACTICE** ▷ **2** (C2) [C] an action or actions intended to improve something or make something happen: *Ships from eight navies will be taking part in an exercise in the Pacific to improve their efficiency in combat.* ◦ *It would be a useful exercise for you to say the speech aloud several times.* ◦ *an exercise* ***in*** *public relations* **3** (A2) [C] a short piece of written work that you do to practise something you are learning: *The book has exercises at the end of every chapter.* **USE** ▷ **4** [U] formal the use of something: *The exercise* ***of*** *restraint may well be difficult.* **CEREMONY** ▷ **5 exercises** [plural] US formal a ceremony that includes speeches and usually traditional music or activities: *graduation exercises*

> **Word partners for exercise (HEALTHY ACTIVITY)**
> *do/get/take* exercise • be *good* exercise • *daily/regular* exercise • *strenuous/vigorous* exercise • *gentle/light/moderate* exercise • a *form of* exercise • an exercise *class/programme/routine*

> **Word partners for exercise (PRACTICE)**
> *perform/take part in* an exercise • the *aim/object/point/purpose* of the exercise • a *futile/pointless* exercise • a *useful/worthwhile* exercise • an exercise *in* sth

▸verb **DO HEALTHY ACTIVITY** ▷ **1** (B1) [I or T] to do physical activities to make your body strong and healthy: *She exercises most evenings usually by running.* ◦ *A work-out in the gym will exercise all the major muscle groups.* **2** [T] If you exercise an animal, you make it walk or run so that it stays strong and healthy: *Now he's retired he spends most afternoons exercising his dogs.* **USE** ▷ **3** (C2) [T] formal to use something: *I exercised my democratic* ***right*** *by not voting in the election.* ◦ *Always exercise* ***caution*** *when handling radioactive substances.* ◦ *We've decided to exercise the* ***option*** *(= use the part of a legal agreement) to buy the house we now lease.*

> **Common mistake: exercise**
> **Warning:** Check your spelling!
> **Exercise** is one of the 50 words most often spelled wrongly by learners.

IDIOM **exercise sb's mind** formal to worry you: *The whole situation is exercising our minds greatly.*

ˈexercise ˌbike noun [C] a machine for taking exercise which looks similar to and is used like a bicycle but does not move from one place

ˈexercise ˌbook noun [C] **1** UK a small book with BLANK (= empty) pages that students use to write their work in **2** US a book containing printed exercises

exert /ɪɡˈzɜːt/ (US) /-ˈzɜːt/ **verb USE** ▷ **1** [T] to use something such as authority, power, influence, etc. in order to make something happen: *If you were to exert your* ***influence*** *they might change their decision.* ◦ *Some managers exert considerable* ***pressure on*** *their staff to work extra hours without being paid.* **MAKE AN EFFORT** ▷ **2 exert yourself** to make a mental or physical effort: *I was too tired to exert myself.*

exertion /ɪɡˈzɜː.ʃən/ (US) /-ˈzɝː-/ **noun EFFORT** ▷ **1** [C or U] the use of a lot of mental or physical effort: *I get out of breath with any kind of* ***physical*** *exertion.* ◦ *We were exhausted after our exertions.* **USE** ▷ **2** [U] the use of something such as authority, power, influence, etc. in order to make something happen: *the exertion of influence over who was appointed to the job*

exfoliant /eksˈfəʊ.li.ənt/ (US) /-ˈfoʊ-/ **noun** [C or U] a substance with which you exfoliate

exfoliate /eksˈfəʊ.li.eɪt/ (US) /-ˈfoʊ-/ **verb** [I or T] to remove dead skin cells from the surface of the skin, in order to improve the appearance • **exfoliation** /eksˌfəʊ.liˈeɪ.ʃən/ (US) /-ˌfoʊ-/ **noun** [U]

ex gratia /eksˈɡreɪ.ʃə/ **adj, adv** formal An ex gratia payment is not necessary, especially legally, but is made to show good intentions: *Ex gratia* ***payments*** *were made to all those who had been affected by the spillage.*

exhale /eksˈheɪl/ **verb** [I or T] formal to send air out of your lungs: *Take a deep breath in then exhale into the mouthpiece.* → Compare **inhale** • **exhalation** /ˌeks.həˈleɪ.ʃən/ noun [C or U]

exhaust /ɪɡˈzɔːst/ (US) /-ˈzɑːst/ verb; noun

▸verb [T] TIRE ▷ **1** C1 to make someone extremely tired: *The long journey exhausted the children.* ◦ *I've exhausted myself with all that cleaning.* USE ▷ **2** to use something completely: *How long will it be before the world's fuel supplies are exhausted?* ◦ *I'm afraid he's exhausted my patience.* ◦ *We seem to have exhausted this topic of conversation (= we have nothing new to say about it).*

▸noun [U] C1 the waste gas from an engine, especially a car's, or the pipe the gas flows through: *Car exhaust is the main reason for the city's pollution.*

exhausted /ɪɡˈzɔː.stɪd/ (US) /-ˈzɑː-/ adj B1 extremely tired: *Exhausted, they fell asleep.* ◦ *By the time they reached the summit they were exhausted.*

exhaustible /ɪɡˈzɔː.stɪ.bl/ (US) /-ˈzɑː-/ adj describes supplies of something that can be used completely so there are none left: *It is clear that many of the Earth's resources are exhaustible.*

exhausting /ɪɡˈzɔː.stɪŋ/ (US) /-ˈzɑː-/ adj B2 making you feel extremely tired: *I've had an exhausting day.*

exhaustion /ɪɡˈzɔːs.tʃən/ (US) /-ˈzɑː-/ noun [U] B2 the state of being extremely tired: *She felt ill with/from exhaustion.*

exhaustive /ɪɡˈzɔː.stɪv/ (US) /-ˈzɑː-/ adj C1 complete and including everything: *an exhaustive study/report* • **exhaustively** /-li/ adv *The survey was exhaustively documented.*

exˈhaust ˌpipe noun [C] (US usually **tailpipe**) the pipe at the back of a vehicle through which waste gas escapes from the engine

exhibit /ɪɡˈzɪb.ɪt/ verb; noun

▸verb [I or T] C1 to show something publicly: *He frequently exhibits at the art gallery.* ◦ *In the summer the academy will exhibit several prints that are rarely seen.* ◦ *He exhibited great self-control considering her rudeness.*

▸noun [C] **1** C1 an object that is shown to the public in a museum, etc.: *The museum has a fascinating collection of exhibits ranging from Iron Age pottery to Inuit clothing.* **2** C1 US (UK **exhibition**) a collection of objects that is shown to the public in a museum, etc.: *Let's go see the new dinosaur exhibit.* **3** legal a thing used as EVIDENCE (= proof that something is true) in a trial: *Is exhibit C the weapon that you say was used?*

exhibition /ˌek.sɪˈbɪʃ.ən/ noun [C or U] B1 an event at which objects such as paintings are shown to the public, a situation in which someone shows a particular skill or quality to the public, or the act of showing these things: *The photographs will be **on** exhibition until the end of the month.* ◦ *There's a new exhibition **of** sculpture on at the city gallery.* ◦ *The athlete's third, and winning, jump was an exhibition of skill and strength.*

IDIOM **make an exhibition of yourself** disapproving to do something stupid in public: *I hope I didn't make an exhibition of myself last night.*

exhibitionism /ˌek.sɪˈbɪʃ.ən.ɪ.zəm/ noun [U] **1** disapproving behaviour which tries to attract attention: *It's exhibitionism to flaunt wealth so blatantly.* **2** formal someone's enjoyment of showing their sexual organs in public

exhibitionist /ˌek.sɪˈbɪʃ.ən.ɪst/ noun [C] **1** someone who tries to attract attention to themselves by their behaviour: *I have an exhibitionist streak that comes out on the dance floor.* **2** someone who shows their sexual organs in public

exhiˈbition ˌmatch noun [C] a single sports game that is not part of a larger competition, in which the players show their skills

exhibitor /ɪɡˈzɪb.ɪ.təʳ/ (US) /-t̬ɚ/ noun [C] someone who has made or owns something, especially a work of art, shown in an exhibition

exhilarate /ɪɡˈzɪl.ə.reɪt/ verb [T] to give someone strong feelings of happiness and excitement

exhilarated /ɪɡˈzɪl.ə.reɪ.tɪd/ (US) /-t̬ɪd/ adj very excited and happy: *At the end of the race I was exhilarated.*

exhilarating /ɪɡˈzɪl.ə.reɪ.tɪŋ/ (US) /-t̬ɪŋ/ adj making you feel very excited and happy: *an exhilarating walk in the mountains*

exhilaration /ɪɡˌzɪl.əˈreɪ.ʃən/ noun [U] excitement and happiness

exhort /ɪɡˈzɔːt/ (US) /-ˈzɔːrt/ verb [T + to infinitive] formal to strongly encourage or try to persuade someone to do something: *The governor exhorted the prisoners not **to** riot.* • **exhortation** /ˌeɡ.zɔːˈteɪ.ʃən/ (US) /-zɔːr-/ noun [C or U] *Despite the exhortations of the union leaders the workers voted to strike.* ◦ *The book is essentially an exhortation **to** religious tolerance.*

exhume /eksˈhjuːm/ (US) /eɡˈzuːm/ verb [T] formal to remove a dead body from the ground after it has been buried • **exhumation** /ˌeks.hjuːˈmeɪ.ʃən/ noun [C or U]

ex-ˈhusband noun [C] Someone's ex-husband is the man they were once married to.

exigency /ˈek.sɪ.dʒən.si/ noun [C or U] formal the difficulties of a situation, especially one which causes urgent demands: *the exigencies of war*

exigent /ˈek.sɪ.dʒənt/ adj formal needing urgent attention, or demanding too much from other people: *an exigent problem* ◦ *an exigent manager*

exile /ˈek.saɪl/, /ˈeɡ.zaɪl/ noun; verb

▸noun **1** C2 [U] the condition of someone being sent or kept away from their own country, village, etc., especially for political reasons: *The king **went into** exile because of the political situation in his country.* ◦ *The deposed leaders are currently **in** exile in the neighbouring country.* **2** [C] a person who is sent or kept away from their own country, etc. → See also **tax exile**

▸verb [T] to send someone away from their own country, village, etc., especially for political reasons: *The monarch was exiled because of the coup.* • **exiled** /-saɪld/, /-zaɪld/ adj *the exiled king*

exist /ɪɡˈzɪst/ verb [I] BE ▷ **1** B1 to be, or to be real: *I don't think ghosts exist.* ◦ *Poverty still exists in this country.* LIVE ▷ **2** C1 to live, or to live in difficult conditions: *Some species exist in this small area of forest and nowhere else on Earth.* ◦ *Few people can exist without water for more than a week.* ◦ *No one can be expected to exist **on** such a low salary.*

existence /ɪɡˈzɪs.təns/ noun **1** B2 [U] the fact of something or someone existing: *Many people question the existence **of** God.* ◦ *Modern cosmology believes the universe to have **come into** existence about 15 billion years ago.* ◦ *The theatre company that they started is still **in** existence today.* **2** C1 [C usually singular] a particular way of life: *She has a miserable existence living with him.*

existent /ɪɡˈzɪs.tənt/ adj formal existing now: *This carving is believed to be the only existent image of Saint Frideswide.*

existentialism /ˌeɡ.zɪˈsten.ʃəl.ɪ.zəm/ noun [U] specialized the modern system of belief made famous by Jean Paul Sartre in the 1940s in which the world has no meaning and each person is alone and completely responsible for their own actions, by which they make their own character • **existential** /-ʃᵊl/ **adj** (also **existentialist**) *an existential/existentialist argument/philosopher* • **existentialist** /-ɪst/ **noun** [C]

existing /ɪɡˈzɪs.tɪŋ/ **adj** [before noun] B2 describes something that exists now: *The existing laws covering libel in this country are thought by many to be inadequate.* ◦ *Under the existing conditions many children are going hungry.*

exit /ˈek.sɪt/, /ˈeɡ.zɪt/ **noun; verb**

▸**noun** [C] **DOOR** ▷ **1** A2 the door through which you might leave a building or large vehicle, or the act of leaving especially a theatre stage: *a **fire** exit* (= a door you can escape through if there is a fire) ◦ *an **emergency** exit* ◦ *He saw Emma arrive and **made** a quick exit.* ◦ *She **made** her exit from the stage to rapturous applause.* → Compare **entrance** **ROAD** ▷ **2** A2 a smaller road used to leave a main road: *Come off the motorway at the Duxford exit.*

▸**verb** [I or T] **LEAVE** ▷ **1** to leave a building or large vehicle: *I exited quickly before anyone could see me.* ◦ *Please exit the theatre by the side doors.* **COMPUTER** ▷ **2** B1 to end a computer program that you are using: *You have to exit the program before starting another.*

ˈexit ˌpoll **noun** [C] the activity of asking people about how they voted as they leave a POLLING STATION (= place at which people vote), to try to discover who will win the election

ˈexit ˌstrategy **noun** [C] a plan of how someone will end something such as a business deal or a military operation

Exocet /ˈek.sə.set/ US /-soʊ-/ **noun** [C] trademark a MISSILE (= flying weapon) that can be accurately directed over short distances, used especially against enemy ships

exodus /ˈek.sə.dəs/ **noun** [S] the movement of a lot of people from a place: *There has been a **mass** exodus of workers **from** the villages to the towns.*

Exodus /ˈek.sə.dəs/ **noun** [U] the second book of the Bible telling of Moses and the journey of the Israelites out of Egypt

ex officio /ˌeks.əˈfɪʃ.i.əʊ/ US /-oʊ/ **adj, adv** formal because of a person's position in a formal group: *The cabinet will also attend the meeting ex-officio.*

exogenous /ɪkˈsɒdʒ.ɪ.nəs/ US /-ˈsɑː.dʒə-/ **adj** specialized found or coming from outside something, for example a system or a person's body or mind → Compare **endogenous**

exonerate /ɪɡˈzɒn.ə.reɪt/ US /-ˈzɑː.nɚ.eɪt/ **verb** [T] formal to show or state that someone or something is not guilty of something: *The report exonerated the crew **from** all responsibility for the collision.* • **exoneration** /ɪɡˌzɒn.əˈreɪ.ʃᵊn/ US /-ˌzɑː.nə-/ **noun** [U]

exorbitant /ɪɡˈzɔː.bɪ.tᵊnt/ US /-ˈzɔːr.bə.t̬ᵊnt/ **adj** Exorbitant prices and demands, etc. are much too large: *The bill for dinner was exorbitant.*

exorcist /ˈek.sɔː.sɪst/ US /-sɔːr-/ **noun** [C] someone who forces an evil spirit to leave a person or place by using prayers or magic

exorcize (UK also **exorcise**) /ˈek.sɔː.saɪz/ US /-sɔːr-/ **verb** [T] **1** to force an evil spirit to leave a person or place by using prayers or magic: *After the priest exorcized the spirit/house/child, apparently, the strange noises stopped.* **2** to remove the bad effects of a frightening or upsetting event: *It will take a long time to exorcize the memory of the accident.* • **exorcism** /-sɪ.zᵊm/ **noun** [C or U]

exoskeleton /ˌek.səʊˈskel.ɪ.tᵊn/ US /ˌek.soʊˈskel.ə.t̬ən/ **noun** [C] specialized a hard outer layer that covers, supports, and protects the body of an INVERTEBRATE animal such as an insect or CRUSTACEAN → Compare **endoskeleton**

exothermic reaction /ek.səʊˌθɜː.mɪk.riˈæk.ʃᵊn/ US /-soʊˌθɝː-/ **noun** [C] specialized a chemical reaction in which heat is produced → Compare **endothermic reaction**

exotic /ɪɡˈzɒt.ɪk/ US /-ˈzɑː.t̬ɪk/ **adj** B2 unusual and often exciting because of coming (or seeming to come) from a far, especially tropical country: *exotic flowers/food/designs* • **exotically** /-ˈzɒt.ɪ.kᵊl.i/ US /-ˈzɑː.t̬ɪ.kᵊl.i/ **adv** *exotically dressed dancers* • **exoticism** /-ˈzɒt.ɪ.sɪ.zᵊm/ US /-ˈzɑː.t̬ɪ.sɪ.zᵊm/ **noun** [U]

exotica /ɪɡˈzɒt.ɪ.kə/ US /-ˈzɑː.t̬ɪ-/ **noun** [plural] unusual objects, often ones that have come from a far country

eˌxotic ˈdancer **noun** [C] a performer who removes her or his clothes in a sexually exciting way

expand /ɪkˈspænd/ **verb** [I or T] B2 to increase in size, number or importance, or to make something increase in this way: *The air in the balloon expands when heated.* ◦ *They expanded their retail operations during the 1980s.*

PHRASAL VERB **expand on sth** to give more details about something you have said or written: *She mentioned a few ideas, but she didn't expand on them.*

expandable /ɪkˈspæn.də.bl̩/ **adj** able to increase in size: *pregnancy trousers with expandable waists*

exˌpanded polyˈstyrene **noun** [U] a light plastic containing gas used for wrapping things in before putting them in boxes

expanse /ɪkˈspæns/ **noun** [C] a large, open area of land, sea, or sky: *She gazed at the immense expanse **of** the sea.* ◦ *vast expanses **of** sand and pine*

expansion /ɪkˈspæn.ʃᵊn/ **noun** [C or U] B2 the increase of something in size, number or importance: *the rapid expansion **of** the software industry* ◦ *Expansion **into** new areas of research is possible.* ◦ *an expansion of industry*

expansionism /ɪkˈspæn.ʃᵊn.ɪ.zᵊm/ **noun** [U] disapproving increasing the amount of land ruled by a country, or the business performed by a company: *As a consequence of expansionism by some European countries, many ancient cultures have suffered.* • **expansionist** /-ɪst/ **noun** [C], **adj**

expansive /ɪkˈspæn.sɪv/ **adj** **TALKING** ▷ **1** formal very happy to talk to people in a friendly way: *He was in an expansive **mood** on the night of the party.* **LARGE** ▷ **2** covering a large area: *There was an expansive view from the window.* ◦ *'All this is mine,' she said with an expansive (= using big movements) arm **gesture**.* • **expansively** /-li/ **adv** • **expansiveness** /-nəs/ **noun** [U]

expatiate /ekˈspeɪ.ʃi.eɪt/ **verb** [I] formal disapproving to speak or write about something in great detail or for a long time: *She expatiated **on/upon** her work for the duration of the meal.*

expatriate **noun; verb**

▸**noun** [C] /ekˈspæt.ri.ət/ US /-ˈspeɪ.tri-/ (informal **expat**) someone who does not live in their own country: *A large **community of** expatriates has settled there.* • **expatriate adj** *an expatriate Scot*

▸**verb** [T] /ekˈspæt.ri.eɪt/ US /-ˈspeɪ.tri-/ formal to use force or law to remove someone from their own country: *The new leaders expatriated the ruling family.*

expect /ɪkˈspekt/ **verb** **THINK** ▷ **1** B1 [T] to think or believe something will happen, or someone will arrive: *We are expecting a lot of applicants for the job.* ◦ [+ (that)] *I expect (**that**) you'll find it somewhere in* *your bedroom.* ◦ *I expect (**that**) he'd have left anyway.* ◦ [+ to infinitive] *He didn't expect **to** see me.* ◦ *The financial performance of the business is **fully** expected (= almost certain) **to** improve.* ◦ *We were **half** expecting you not **to** come back.* **2 (only) to be expected** normal and what usually happens: *All parents of small children get tired. It's to be expected.* **DEMAND** ▷ **3** B2 [T] to think that someone should behave in a particular way or do a particular thing: *I expect punctuality **from** my students.* ◦ [+ to infinitive] *Borrowers are expected **to** (= should) return books on time.* **BE PREGNANT** ▷ **4 be expecting (a baby)** B2 to be pregnant: *She shouldn't be lifting those boxes if she's expecting.* ◦ *Kate and Dom are expecting a baby.* • **expected** /-ˈspek.tɪd/ adj [before noun] B2 *The expected counter-attack never happened.*

E

expectancy /ɪkˈspek.tᵊn.si/ noun [U] the feeling that something exciting or pleasant is going to happen: *There was a general **air of** expectancy in the crowd.* → See also **life expectancy**

expectant /ɪkˈspek.tᵊnt/ adj **THINKING** ▷ **1** thinking that something pleasant or exciting is going to happen: *the children's expectant faces* **PREGNANT** ▷ **2** [before noun] describes a woman who is pregnant or a man whose partner is pregnant: *expectant mothers/fathers/couples* • **expectantly** /-li/ adv *The dog looked up at John expectantly.*

expectation /ˌek.spekˈteɪ.ʃᵊn/ noun **1** B2 [C usually plural] the feeling that good things are going to happen in the future: *The holiday **lived up to** all our expectations (= was as good as we were expecting).* ◦ *I **have high** expectations **for** this job (= I believe it will be good).* ◦ *We did so well – **beyond all** (= better than) our expectations.* ◦ *I think she had **unrealistic** expectations of motherhood.* **2** [C or U] the feeling of expecting something to happen: *Considering the injuries he's had there can be little expectation **of** him winning the race.* ◦ *Our expectations are **that** the UK will cut its interest rate.* **3 against/contrary to all expectations** different from what is expected: *Contrary to all expectations, she was accepted by the academy.*

expectorant /ɪkˈspek.tᵊr.ᵊnt/ noun [C] a type of cough medicine used to make PHLEGM (= thick liquid) less thick in the lungs

expectorate /ɪkˈspek.tᵊr.eɪt/ verb [I] specialized to bring up liquid from the throat or lungs and force it out of the mouth

expedience /ɪkˈspiː.di.ᵊns/ noun [U] (also **expediency**) the situation in which something is helpful or useful in a particular situation, but sometimes not morally acceptable: *As **a matter of** expedience, we will not be taking on any new staff this year.* ◦ *I think this government operates on the basis of expediency, not of principle.*

expedient /ɪkˈspiː.di.ᵊnt/ adj; noun
▸adj formal helpful or useful in a particular situation, but sometimes not morally acceptable: *It might be expedient not to pay him until the work is finished.* ◦ *The management has taken a series of expedient measures to improve the company's financial situation.* • **expediently** /-li/ adv
▸noun [C] formal an action that is expedient: *a **political** expedient*

expedite /ˈek.spə.daɪt/ verb [T] formal to make something happen more quickly: *Something needs to be done to expedite the process.*

expedition /ˌek.spəˈdɪʃ.ᵊn/ noun **JOURNEY** ▷ **1** B1 [C] an organized journey for a particular purpose: *We're **going on** a shopping expedition on Saturday.* ◦ *Scott died while he was **on** an expedition to the Antarctic in 1912.* **2** [C] the people, vehicles, animals, etc. taking part in an expedition: *The British expedition **to** Mount Everest is leaving next month.* **SPEED** ▷ **3** [U] formal speed in doing something: *We will deal with your order with the greatest possible expedition.*

expeditionary /ˌek.spəˈdɪʃ.ᵊn.ᵊr.i/ US /-er-/ adj **expeditionary force/unit** a group of soldiers sent to another country to fight in a war

expeditious /ˌek.spəˈdɪʃ.əs/ adj formal quick: *The bank was expeditious in replying to my letter.* • **expeditiously** /-li/ adv

expel /ɪkˈspel/ verb [T] (**-ll-**) **MAKE LEAVE** ▷ **1** to force someone to leave a school, organization, or country: *The new government has expelled all foreign diplomats.* ◦ *My brother was expelled **from** school for bad behaviour.* **AIR/LIQUID** ▷ **2** to force air or liquid out of something: *She took a deep breath, then expelled the air in short blasts.* ◦ *When you breathe out, you expel air **from** your lungs.*

expend /ɪkˈspend/ verb [T] formal to use or spend especially time, effort, or money: *You expend so much effort for so little return.* ◦ *Governments expend a lot of resources **on** war.*

expendable /ɪkˈspen.də.bl̩/ adj If someone or something is expendable, people can do something or deal with a situation without them: *No one likes to think that they're expendable.*

expenditure /ɪkˈspen.dɪ.tʃəʳ/ US /-tʃɚ/ noun **1** C2 [C or U] the total amount of money that a government or person spends: *The government's annual expenditure **on** arms has been reduced.* **2** [U] the act of using or spending energy, time, or money: *The expenditure of effort **on** this project has been enormous.*

expense /ɪkˈspens/ noun **1** B2 [U] the use of money, time or effort: *Buying a bigger car has proved to be well **worth the** expense.* ◦ *We've just had a new garage built **at great** expense.* ◦ *We went on holiday **at** my father's expense (= he paid for it).* ◦ *It's silly to **go to the** expense **of** (= spend money on) buying new clothes when you don't really need them.* **2** [C] something which causes you to spend money: *Our biggest expense this year was our summer holiday.* ◦ *We need to cut down on our expenses.* **3 expenses** C1 [plural] money that you spend when you are doing your job, that your employer will pay back to you: *I need to get my expenses approved.* ◦ UK *Don't worry about the cost of lunch – it's **on** expenses.*

IDIOMS **all expenses paid** If something is all expenses paid, it means that you do not have to pay for anything yourself: *She's going on a trip to New York, all expenses paid.* ◦ *an all expenses paid trip to New York* • **at the expense of sb** (also **at sb's expense**) C2 making another person look silly: *Would you stop making jokes at my expense?* • **at the expense of sth** C1 If you do one thing at the expense of another, doing the first thing harms the second thing: *He had no need to protect their reputation at the expense of his own.* • **blow/hang the expense** UK informal used for saying that you want something so much that you do not care how much it costs: *I'm going to book a holiday. Blow the expense!* • **no expense is spared** If no expense is spared in arranging something, a lot of money is spent to make it extremely good: *No expense was spared in making the guests feel comfortable.*

exˈpense acˌcount noun [C] an arrangement in which your employer will pay for the things you need to buy while doing your job: *I can **put** this lunch **on my** expense account.* ◦ *expense-account fraud*

expensive /ɪkˈspen.sɪv/ adj A1 costing a lot of money: *Rolls Royces are very expensive.* ◦ *Big houses* *are expensive* ***to*** *maintain.* ◦ *She has expensive* ***tastes*** *(= she likes things that cost a lot of money).* • **expensively** /-li/ **adv** *Sarah is always expensively dressed (= wearing expensive clothes).*

Other ways of saying expensive

The adjectives **costly** and **pricey** (*informal*) mean the same as 'expensive':

Consulting a lawyer can be a ***costly*** *business.*

I liked the shirt but I didn't buy it because it was a bit ***pricey.***

To talk about a place that is very expensive, you can use the adjectives **exclusive** or, in informal English, **fancy** or **posh**:

They have an apartment in an ***exclusive*** *part of town.*

We stayed in a ***fancy*** *hotel on the beach.*

He took me to a ***posh*** *restaurant.*

In informal situations, the expression **cost a fortune** or, more informally, the idiom **cost an arm and a leg** can be used to say that something is very expensive:

That coat must have ***cost a fortune.***

I'd love to buy a Rolls Royce but they ***cost an arm and a leg.***

If the price of something is more expensive than it should be, you can use the word **exorbitant** or in more informal situations, you could describe something as **steep** or a **rip-off**:

Customers are charged ***exorbitant*** *prices for drinks.*

Isn't £5 for a cup of coffee a little ***steep?***

You paid $300 for that shirt? That's a ***rip-off!***

experience /ɪkˈspɪə.ri.ənts/ (US) /-ˈspɪr.i-/ **noun; verb**

▸**noun 1** (B1) [U] (the process of getting) knowledge or skill from doing, seeing, or feeling things: *Do you have any experience* ***of*** *working with kids? (= Have you ever worked with them?)* ◦ *The best way to learn is* ***by*** *experience (= by doing things).* ◦ *I know* ***from*** *experience that Tony never keeps his promises.* ◦ *I don't think she has the experience* ***for*** *the job (= enough knowledge and skill for it).* ◦ ***In my*** *experience, people generally smile back if you smile at them.* ◦ *The experience* ***of*** *pain (= what pain feels like) varies from one person to another.* ◦ *There's nothing we can do about it now, we'll just have to* ***put it down to*** *experience (= consider it as a mistake we can learn from).* **2** (B1) [C] something that happens to you that affects how you feel: *I had a rather unpleasant experience at the dentist's.* ◦ *It was interesting hearing about his experiences as a policeman.* ◦ *I did meet him once and it was an experience I shall never forget.*

Common mistake: experience

The correct preposition to use after **experience** is **of**.

Don't say 'experience in/on doing something', say **experience of doing something**:

~~*I have two years' experience in working in a bank.*~~

I have two years' experience of working in a bank.

Common mistake: experience

Warning: Choose the right verb!

Don't say 'make an experience', say **have an experience:**

~~*I know several people who have made the same experience.*~~

I know several people who have had the same experience.

Word partners for experience noun

have (an) experience • *gain/lack* experience • experience *shows/suggests* that • *know/learn* from experience • a *bad/frightening/painful/traumatic* experience • an *amazing/great/pleasant/unforgettable* experience • *past/previous* experience • *good/useful/wide* experience • experience *in/of* sth • *in* my, your, etc experience • *by/from* experience

▸**verb** [T] (B1) If you experience something, it happens to you, or you feel it: *We experienced a lot of difficulty in selling our house.* ◦ *New companies often experience a loss in their first few years.* ◦ *It was the worst pain I'd ever experienced.*

Common mistake: experience

Warning: Check your spelling!

Experience is one of the 50 words most often spelled wrongly by learners.

experienced /ɪkˈspɪə.ri.ənst/ (US) /-ˈspɪr.i-/ **adj** approving (B1) having skill or knowledge because you have done something many times: *an experienced teacher* ◦ *She is very experienced* ***in*** *marketing.*

experiential /ɪkˌspɪə.riˈen.ʃəl/ (US) /-ˌspɪr.i-/ **adj** formal based on experience: *experiential learning*

experiment **noun; verb**

▸**noun** [C or U] /ɪkˈsper.ɪ.mənt/ (B1) a test done in order to learn something or to discover if something works or is true: *Some people believe that experiments* ***on*** *animals should be banned.* ◦ [+ to infinitive] *Scientists are* ***conducting/carrying out/doing*** *experiments* ***to*** *test the effectiveness of the new drug.* ◦ *I've bought a different kind of coffee this week* ***as*** *an experiment (= in order to see what it is like).* ◦ *We can only find the best solution* ***by*** *experiment.*

Word partners for experiment noun

carry out/conduct/do/perform an experiment • an experiment *involving* sth • an experiment *proves/shows* sth • a *bold/interesting/pioneering/simple* experiment • an experiment *on* sth

▸**verb** [I] /ɪkˈsper.ɪ.ment/ (B2) to try something in order to discover what it is like or find out more about it: *Things would never change if people weren't prepared to experiment.* ◦ *The school is experimenting* ***with*** *new teaching methods.* ◦ *Experimenting* ***on*** *mice can give us an idea of the effect of the disease in humans.* • **experimenter** /-men.təʳ/ (US) /-men.t̬ɚ/ **noun** [C]

experimental /ɪkˌsper.ɪˈmen.təl/ (US) /-t̬əl/ **adj** (C2) relating to tests, especially scientific ones: *The drug is still at the experimental stage (= is still being tested).* ◦ *The changes to the distribution system are purely experimental at the moment.* ◦ *experimental* ***psychology*** • **experimentally** /-i/ **adv**

experimentation /ɪkˌsper.ɪ.menˈteɪ.ʃən/ **noun** [U] the process of trying methods, activities, etc. to discover what effect they have: *Children need the opportunity for experimentation.* ◦ *Extensive experimentation is needed before new drugs can be sold.* ◦ *Experimentation* ***with*** *illegal drugs is dangerous.*

expert /ˈek.spɜːt/ (US) /-spɝːt/ **noun; adj**

▸**noun** [C] (B1) a person with a high level of knowledge or skill relating to a particular subject or activity: *a gardening/medical expert* ◦ *My mother is an expert* ***at*** *dress-making (= she does it very well).*

▸**adj** [before noun] (B2) having or showing a lot of knowledge or skill: *The centre provides expert* ***advice*** *for people with financial problems.* ◦ *What's your expert*

E

opinion? ◦ *an expert fisherman* • **expertly** /-li/ **adv** *He carved the meat expertly.*

expertise /ˌek.spɜːˈtiːz/ (US) /-spɝː-/ **noun** [U] a high level of knowledge or skill: *We admired the expertise with which he prepared the meal.* ◦ *I have no expertise **in** sewing/sewing expertise.*

ˈexpert ˌsystem **noun** [C] a computer system which asks questions and gives answers that have been thought of by a human expert

expiate /ˈek.spi.eɪt/ **verb** [T] formal to show that you are sorry for bad behaviour by doing something or accepting punishment: *to expiate a crime/sin* • **expiation** /ˌek.spiˈeɪ.ʃən/ **noun** [U] *the expiation of a sin*

E

expire /ɪkˈspaɪəʳ/ (US) /-ˈspaɪr/ **verb** [I] **END** ▷ **1** (C2) If something that lasts for a fixed length of time expires, it comes to an end or stops being in use: *Our television license expires next month.* ◦ *The contract between the two companies will expire at the end of the year.* **DIE** ▷ **2** literary to die

expiry /ɪkˈspaɪə.ri/ (US) /-ˈspaɪr.i/ **noun** [U] UK (US **expiration** /ˌek.spɪˈreɪ.ʃən/ /-spə-/) the situation in which something which lasts for a fixed length of time comes to an end or stops being in use: *the expiry of a lease/visa* ◦ *What is the expiry/expiration **date** of your credit card?* (= *What is the last date on which it can be used?*)

explain /ɪkˈspleɪn/ **verb** [I or T] **1** (A2) to make something clear or easy to understand by describing or giving information about it: *If there's anything you don't understand, I'll be happy to explain.* ◦ *The teacher explained the rules **to** the children.* ◦ [+ question word] *Our guide explained **wh**ere the cathedral was.* ◦ *He explained **how** the machine worked.* ◦ *Please could you explain **wh**y you're so late.* ◦ [+ that] *She explained **that** she was going to stay with her sister.* ◦ [+ speech] *'Someone must have hit the wrong button,' an official explained.* ◦ *Molly asked the teacher if she could explain her**self** a bit more clearly* (= *say more clearly what she meant*). ◦ *No one has been able to explain* (= *give the reason for*) *the accident.* **2 explain yourself** to give reasons for your behaviour: *He hadn't been home for three days so I asked him to explain himself.*

> **! Common mistake: explain**
>
> When **explain** is followed by an indirect object, remember to use the preposition **to**.
>
> Don't say 'explain someone', say **explain to someone**:
>
> *~~I had to explain him that I had lost his keys.~~*
>
> *I had to explain to him that I had lost his keys.*

> **+ Other ways of saying explain**
>
> If someone is explaining something in order to make it easier for someone else to understand, you can use the verb **clarify**:
>
> *Let me just **clarify** what I mean here.*
>
> The verb **define** is sometimes used when explaining exactly what something means:
>
> *Your responsibilities are clearly **defined** in the contract.*
>
> If something is being explained clearly in writing, the phrasal verb **set out** is sometimes used:
>
> *Your contract will **set out** the terms of your employment.*
>
> If something is being explained in great detail, the phrasal verb **spell out** is often used:
>
> *They sent me a letter **spelling out** the details of the agreement.*

PHRASAL VERB **explain sth away** to avoid blame for something that has happened by making it seem not important or not your fault: *I don't know how you're going to explain away that dent you made in dad's car.*

explaining /ɪkˈspleɪ.nɪŋ/ **noun** [U] the act of explaining or giving a good reason for your actions: *You'll **have** a lot of explaining **to do** when dad finds out what happened.*

explanation /ˌek.spləˈneɪ.ʃən/ **noun** [C or U] (B1) the details or reasons that someone gives to make something clear or easy to understand: *Could you **give** me a quick explanation **of** how it works?* ◦ *What was her explanation **for** why she was late?* ◦ [+ that] *The judge didn't believe his explanation **that** he had stolen the money in order to give it to charity.* ◦ *He said, **by way of** explanation, that he hadn't seen the traffic light change to red.*

> **Word partners for explanation**
>
> ***demand*** an explanation • ***give/offer/provide*** an explanation • ***owe*** sb an explanation • a ***clear/convincing/plausible/simple*** explanation • a ***detailed/full*** explanation • a ***likely/possible*** explanation • an explanation ***for*** sth • ***without*** explanation

explanatory /ɪkˈsplæn.ə.tər.i/ (US) /-tɔːr.i/ **adj** giving an explanation about something: *There are explanatory **notes** with the diagram.* → See also **self-explanatory**

expletive /ɪkˈspliː.tɪv/ (US) /ˈek.splə.t̬ɪv/ **noun** [C] formal a word that is considered offensive: *She dropped the book on her foot and **let out** a row/string of expletives.*

explicable /ekˈsplɪk.ə.bl̩/ **adj** able to be explained: *Under the circumstances, what happened was quite explicable.* • **explicably** /-bli/ **adv**

explicate /ˈek.splɪ.keɪt/ **verb** [T] formal to explain something, especially a piece of writing or an idea in detail: *This is a book which clearly explicates Marx's later writings.* • **explication** /ˌek.splɪˈkeɪ.ʃən/ **noun** [C or U]

explicit /ɪkˈsplɪs.ɪt/ **adj** **1** (C2) clear and exact: *I gave her very explicit directions how to get here.* ◦ *She was very explicit **about*** (= *said very clearly and exactly*) *what she thought was wrong with the plans.* ◦ *I wasn't aware that I would be paying – you certainly didn't **make** it explicit* (= *state it clearly*). → Compare **implicit** **2** (C2) showing or talking about sex or violence in a very detailed way: *a **sexually** explicit film* • **explicitly** /-li/ **adv** *I told you quite explicitly* (= *clearly*) *to be home by midnight.* • **explicitness** /-nəs/ **noun** [U]

explode /ɪkˈspləʊd/ (US) /-ˈsploʊd/ **verb** **BREAK APART** ▷ **1** (B1) [I or T] to (cause to) break up into pieces violently: *A **bomb** exploded at one of London's busiest railway stations this morning.* ◦ *He was driving so fast that his car tyre exploded.* → Compare **implode** **EMOTION** ▷ **2** [I] to react suddenly with a strong expression of emotion: [+ speech] *'What on Earth do you think you're doing?' she exploded* (= *said angrily*). ◦ *The children exploded **into** giggles* (= *suddenly started laughing uncontrollably*). **INCREASE** ▷ **3** [I] to increase very quickly: *The population has exploded in the last ten years.* **PROVE FALSE** ▷ **4** [T] to show something to be wrong: *This book finally explodes some of the **myths** about the origin of the universe.*

PHRASAL VERB **explode into sth** to suddenly change into something powerful or exciting: *London's parks have exploded into colour* (= *become very colourful because many flowers have opened*) *in the last week.*

exploit verb; noun

▸verb [T] /ɪkˈsplɔɪt/ **USE WELL** ▷ **1** (B2) to use something for advantage: *We need to make sure that we exploit our* ***resources*** *as fully as possible.* **USE UNFAIRLY** ▷ **2** B2 to use someone or something unfairly for your own advantage: *Laws exist to stop companies exploiting their employees.* • **exploitable** /-ˈsplɔɪ.tə.bl̩/ US /-ˈsplɔɪ.t̬ə.bl̩/ **adj** *The coal mine is no longer commercially exploitable (= can no longer be used for profit).* ◦ *The lack of jobs in this area means that the workforce is easily exploitable (= employers can use workers unfairly for their own advantage).*

▸**noun** [C usually plural] /ˈek.splɔɪt/ something unusual, brave or funny that someone has done: *She was telling me about her exploits while travelling around Africa.*

exploitation /ˌek.splɔɪˈteɪ.ʃən/ **noun** [U] **GOOD USE** ▷ **1** the use of something in order to get an advantage from it: *Britain's exploitation* ***of*** *its natural gas reserves began after the Second World War.* **UNFAIR USE** ▷ **2** the act of using someone unfairly for your own advantage: *Marx wrote about the exploitation* ***of*** *the workers.*

exploitative /ɪkˈsplɔɪ.tə.tɪv/ US /-t̬ə.t̬ɪv/ **adj** using someone else unfairly for your own advantage

exploiter /ɪkˈsplɔɪ.təʳ/ US /-t̬ɚ/ **noun** [C] someone who uses other people or things for his or her own profit or advantage

exploration /ˌek.spləˈreɪ.ʃən/ US /-splɚˈreɪ-/ **noun** [C or U] the activity of searching and finding out about something: *Livingstone was the first European to make an exploration* ***of*** *the Zambezi river (= to travel to it in order to discover more about it).* ◦ *We need to carry out a full exploration (= examination)* ***of*** *all the alternatives.* ◦ *The exploration (= search)* ***for*** *new sources of energy is vital for the future of our planet.*

exploratory /ekˈsplɒr.ə.tər.i/ US /-ˈsplɑː.rə.tɔːr.i/ **adj** done in order to discover more about something: *an exploratory expedition to Antarctica* ◦ *She's having some exploratory* ***tests*** *done to find out what's causing the illness.* ◦ *We're having an exploratory meeting next week to talk about merging the two companies.*

explore /ɪkˈsplɔːʳ/ US /-ˈsplɔːr/ **verb** [I or T] **1** B1 to search and discover (about something): *to explore space* ◦ *The best way to explore the countryside is on foot.* ◦ *The children have gone exploring in the woods.* **2** B2 to think or talk about something in order to find out more about it: *Let's explore this* ***issue/idea*** *more fully.*

explorer /ɪkˈsplɔː.rəʳ/ US /-rɚ/ **noun** [C] someone who travels to places where no one has ever been in order to find out what is there

explosion /ɪkˈspləʊ.ʒən/ US /-ˈsploʊ-/ **noun** **BURST** ▷ **1** B2 [C or U] the fact of something such as a bomb exploding: *The fire was thought to have been caused by a gas explosion.* ◦ *The explosion (= the intentional exploding)* ***of*** *nuclear devices in the Bikini Atoll was stopped in 1958.* **EMOTION** ▷ **2** [C] a sudden strong expression of emotion: *There was an explosion* ***of*** *applause from the audience at the end of the performance.* **INCREASE** ▷ **3** C1 [C] a large increase in the number of something that happens very quickly: *The government has had to take measures to halt the* ***population*** *explosion.* **FALSE IDEA** ▷ **4** [U] the act of proving that something is wrong: *the explosion of the conspiracy theories surrounding the death of the star*

explosive /ɪkˈspləʊ.sɪv/ US /-ˈsploʊ-/ **adj; noun**

▸**adj** **BURST** ▷ **1** C2 exploding or able to explode easily: *Certain gases are* ***highly*** *explosive.* ◦ *An explosive* ***device*** *(= a bomb) was found at one of London's busiest stations this morning.* **2** very loud and sudden, like an explosion: *There was an explosive clap of thunder overhead.* **EMOTION** ▷ **3** C2 describes a situation or emotion in which strong feelings are loudly or violently expressed: *The* ***situation*** *in some of America's cities has become explosive.* ◦ *Capital punishment is an explosive* ***issue.*** ◦ *She has an explosive* ***temper.*** **INCREASE** ▷ **4** describes an increase that is very large and quick: *The last few years have seen an explosive increase in the number of homeless people on our streets.* • **explosively** /-li/ **adv** • **explosiveness** /-nəs/ **noun** [U]

▸**noun** [C or U] C2 a substance or piece of equipment that can cause explosions

expo /ˈek.spəʊ/ US /-spoʊ/ **noun** [C] an **exposition**

exponent /ɪkˈspəʊ.nənt/ US /-ˈspoʊ-/ **noun** [C] **PERSON** ▷ **1** a person who supports an idea or belief or performs an activity: *Adam Smith was an exponent* ***of*** *free trade.* ◦ *Jacqueline du Pré was a leading exponent* ***of*** *the cello.* **NUMBER** ▷ **2** specialized a number or sign that shows how many times another number is to be multiplied by itself: *In* 6^4 *and* y^n, *4 and n are the exponents.*

exponential /ˌek.spəˈnen.ʃəl/ US /-spoʊ-/ **adj** **INCREASE** ▷ **1** formal describes a rate of increase which becomes quicker and quicker as the thing that increases becomes larger: *We are looking for exponential* ***growth*** *in our investment.* ◦ *There has been an exponential* ***increase*** *in the world population this century.* **NUMBER** ▷ **2** specialized containing an exponent (= a number or sign that shows how many times another number is to be multiplied by itself): 6^4 *is an exponential expression.* • **exponentially** /-i/ **adv** formal *Malthus wrote about the risks involved in the world's population* ***increasing*** *exponentially.*

export **verb; noun**

▸**verb** /ɪkˈspɔːt/ US /ˈek.spɔːrt/ **1** B2 [I or T] to send goods to another country for sale: *French cheeses are exported* ***to*** *many different countries.* ◦ *Our clothes sell so well in this country that we have no need to export.* → Compare **import** **2** [T] to put something from one country into use in other countries: *American culture has been exported all over the world.* **3** [T] If you export information from a computer, you copy a large amount of it to a different part of the computer's memory or to another device. • **exportable** /-ˈspɔː.tə.bl̩/ US /-ˈspɔːr.t̬ə.bl̩/ **adj** *The value of the new television technology to the company is that it is highly exportable (= can be sold in other countries).* • **exportation** /ˌek.spɔːˈteɪ.ʃən/ US /-spɔːr-/ **noun** [U] *These crates have been packed* ***for*** *exportation (= to be sent for sale in other countries).*

▸**noun** [C or U] /ˈek.spɔːt/ US /-spɔːrt/ B2 a product that you sell in another country, or the business of sending goods to another country in order to sell them there: *Coffee is one of Brazil's* ***main*** *exports.* ◦ *We plan to increase our exports over the next five years.* ◦ *The export* ***of*** *ivory is now strictly controlled.* ◦ *India grows tea* ***for*** *export.* ◦ *We are planning to develop our export* ***market/trade.***

exporter /ɪkˈspɔː.təʳ/ US /-ˈspɔːr.t̬ɚ/ **noun** [C] a person, country, or business that sells goods to another country: *Japan is a major exporter* ***of*** *cars.*

expose /ɪkˈspəʊz/ US /-ˈspoʊz/ **verb** [T] **UNCOVER** ▷ **1** to remove what is covering something so that it can be seen: *The plaster on the walls has been removed to expose the original bricks underneath.* ◦ *He damaged his leg so badly in the accident that the bone was exposed.* ◦ *This photograph was* ***under-/over-****exposed (= too little/too much light was allowed to reach the film).* **2** **expose yourself** If a man exposes himself, he shows his sexual organs in a public place to people he does not know. **MAKE PUBLIC** ▷ **3** B2 to make public something bad or dishonest: *The review exposed*

E

widespread ***corruption*** *in the police force.* ◦ *The newspaper story exposed him* ***as*** *(= showed that he was) a liar.*

PHRASAL VERB **expose sb to sth** [usually passive] B2 to make it likely that someone will experience something harmful or unpleasant: *About 800,000 children are exposed to poisons each year.* ◦ *It is feared that people living near the power station may have been exposed to radiation.*

exposé /ekˈspəʊ.zeɪ/ US /ˌek.spəˈzeɪ/ noun [C] a public report of the facts about a situation, especially one that is shocking or has been kept secret: *Today's newspaper contains a searing exposé* ***of*** *police corruption.*

exposed /ɪkˈspəʊzd/ US /-ˈspoʊzd/ adj having no protection from bad weather: *The house is in a very exposed* ***position****.*

exposition /ˌek.spəˈzɪʃ.ən/ noun EXPLANATION ▷ **1** [C or U] formal a clear and full explanation of an idea or theory: *It purports to be an exposition of Catholic social teaching.* SHOW ▷ **2** [C] (also **expo**) a show in which industrial goods, works of art, etc. are shown to the public: *the San Francisco exposition* ◦ *Expo 92 (= a show that happened in 1992)*

expository /ɪkˈspɒz.ɪ.tər.i/ US /-ˈspɑː.zə.tɔːr-/ adj formal explaining or describing something: *expository writing*

expostulate /ɪkˈspɒs.tjʊ.leɪt/ US /-ˈspɑː.stjʊ-/ verb [I] formal to express disagreement or complaint: *Walter expostulated* ***with*** *the waiter* ***about*** *the size of the bill.* • **expostulation** /ɪkˌspɒs.tjʊˈleɪ.ʃən/ US /-ˌspɑː.stjʊ-/ noun [C or U]

exposure /ɪkˈspəʊ.ʒər/ US /-ˈspoʊ.ʒɚ/ noun EXPERIENCE ▷ **1** C1 [C or U] the fact of experiencing something or being affected by it because of being in a particular situation or place: *You should always limit your exposure* ***to*** *the sun.* ◦ *Even a brief exposure* ***to*** *radiation is very dangerous.* MADE PUBLIC ▷ **2** [C or U] the fact of something bad that someone has done being made public]: *The exposure* ***of*** *the politician's love affair forced him to resign.* ATTENTION ▷ **3** [U] the fact of an event or information being often discussed in newspapers and on the television, etc.: *His last film* ***got*** *so much exposure in the press.* ILLNESS ▷ **4** [U] a serious medical condition that is caused by being outside in very cold weather: *All the members of the expedition to the South Pole died of exposure.* PHOTOGRAPH ▷ **5** [C] a single photograph on a piece of film, or the amount of time a piece of film is open to the light when making a photograph: *There are 24 exposures on this film.* DIRECTION ▷ **6** [S] the direction in which something faces: *Our dining room has a northern exposure (= faces north), so it's rather cold.*

expound /ɪkˈspaʊnd/ verb [I or T] formal to give a detailed explanation of something: *He's always expounding* ***on*** *what's wrong with the world.* ◦ *She uses her newspaper column to expound her* ***views*** *on environmental issues.*

express /ɪkˈspres/ verb; adj; adv; noun

▸verb [T] SHOW ▷ **1** B2 to show a feeling, opinion, or fact: *Her eyes expressed deep sadness.* ◦ *I would like to express my thanks for your kindness.* ◦ *Words can't express* ***how*** *happy I am.* ◦ *These figures are expressed* ***as*** *a percentage of the total.* **2 express yourself** B2 to communicate what you think or feel, by speaking or writing, or in some other way: *I'm afraid I'm not expressing myself very clearly.* ◦ *Children often express themselves in painting.* SEND FAST ▷ **3** mainly US to send something somewhere very quickly: *Your order will be expressed* ***to*** *you within 24 hours.*

▸adj [before noun] FAST ▷ **1** moving or being sent fast: *Please send this letter by express* ***delivery****.* ◦ *an express* ***train*** ◦ *The dry cleaners offer a normal or an express* ***service****.* CLEAR ▷ **2** clearly and intentionally stated: *It is my express* ***wish*** *that after my death, my books be given to my old college library.*

▸adv using a service which does something faster than usual: ***Send*** *this parcel express.*

▸noun **1** [C] a train or bus that takes less time to do a journey than other trains or buses: *The quickest way to get here is to take the uptown express.* ◦ *the Orient Express* **2** [U] a service which does something faster than usual: *This parcel needs to be sent* ***by*** *express.*

expression /ɪkˈspreʃ.ən/ noun SHOWING ▷ **1** B2 [C or U] the act of saying what you think or showing how you feel using words or actions: *He wrote her a poem as an expression* ***of*** *his love.* ◦ *We've received a lot of expressions* ***of*** *support for our campaign.* ◦ ***Freedom of*** *expression is a basic human right.* ◦ *It's better to* ***give*** *expression* ***to*** *(= show) your anger, rather than hiding it.* ◦ formal *His sadness at the death of his wife* ***found*** *expression (= was shown) in his music.* ◦ *She plays the violin with great expression (= feeling).* **2** B2 [C] the look on someone's face, showing what they feel or think: *I could tell from her expression that something serious had happened.* ◦ *Mark always has such a miserable expression on his face.* WORDS ▷ **3** B2 [C] a word or group of words used in a particular situation or by particular people: *He uses a lot of unusual expressions.* ◦ *'A can of worms' is an expression which means 'a difficult situation'.* NUMBERS ▷ **4** [C] in mathematics, a symbol or group of symbols which represent an amount: *$4xy^2$ is an expression.*

> Word partners for **expression** (SHOWING)
>
> *assume/wear* an expression • sb's expression *changes* • a *blank/dazed/pained/puzzled* expression • *without* expression • an expression *of* [anger/surprise/pain, etc]

expressionism /ɪkˈspreʃ.ən.ɪ.zəm/ noun [U] a style of art, music, or writing, found especially in the 1900s, that expresses extreme feelings • **expressionist** /-ɪst/ adj, noun [C]

expressionless /ɪkˈspreʃ.ən.ləs/ adj not showing what someone thinks or feels: *He has such an expressionless* ***face/voice****.*

expressive /ɪkˈspres.ɪv/ adj **1** C2 showing what someone thinks or feels: *an expressive* ***face*** ◦ *expressive* ***hands*** **2 be expressive of sth** formal showing a particular feeling: *The final movement of Beethoven's Ninth Symphony is expressive of joy.* • **expressively** /-li/ adv • **expressiveness** /-nəs/ noun [U]

expressly /ɪkˈspres.li/ adv **1** in a way that is clear: *I expressly* ***told*** *you to be home by midnight.* **2** for a particular purpose: *The farmer put up the fence expressly to stop people walking across his field.*

expressway /ɪkˈspres.weɪ/ noun [C] a wide road for fast-moving traffic, especially one in the US that goes through a city, with a limited number of places at which drivers can enter and leave it → Compare **freeway, motorway**

expropriate /ɪkˈsprəʊ.pri.eɪt/ US /-ˈsproʊ-/ verb [T] formal to take away money or property especially for public use without payment to the owner, or for personal use illegally: *He was discovered to have been expropriating company funds.* • **expropriation** /ɪkˌsprəʊ.priˈeɪ.ʃən/ US /-ˌsproʊ-/ noun [C or U] • **expropriator** /-eɪ.tər/ US /-eɪ.t̬ɚ/ noun [C]

expulsion /ɪkˈspʌl.ʃᵊn/ noun [C or U] **MAKE LEAVE ▷ 1** (the act of) forcing someone, or being forced, to leave a school, organization, or country: *They threatened him with expulsion* ***from*** *school.* ◦ *This is the second expulsion* ***of*** *a club member this year.* **AIR/LIQUID ▷ 2** (the act of) forcing air or liquid out of something

expunge /ɪkˈspʌndʒ/ verb [T] formal **1** to rub off or remove information from a piece of writing: *His name has been expunged* ***from*** *the list of members.* **2** to cause something to be forgotten: *She has been unable to expunge the details of the accident* ***from*** *her* ***memory.***

expurgate /ˈek.spə.ɡeɪt/ (US) /-spɚ-/ verb [T usually passive] formal to remove parts of a piece of writing that are considered likely to cause offence • **expurgated** /-ɡeɪ.tɪd/ (US) /-ɡeɪ.t̬ɪd/ adj *Only an expurgated* ***version*** *of the novel has been published so far.* • **expurgation** /ˌek.spəˈɡeɪ.ʃᵊn/ (US) /-spɚ-/ noun [C or U]

exquisite /ɪkˈskwɪz.ɪt/ adj **BEAUTIFUL ▷ 1** C2 very beautiful and delicate: *an exquisite piece of china* ◦ *Look at this exquisite painting* ◦ *She has exquisite taste.* **SHARP ▷ 2** literary describes feelings such as pleasure or pain that are extremely strong, or qualities that are extremely good; great: *exquisite joy* ◦ *The pain was quite exquisite.* ◦ *a vase of exquisite workmanship* ◦ *A good comedian needs to have an exquisite sense of timing.* • **exquisitely** /-li/ adv *Their house is exquisitely (= beautifully) furnished.* ◦ *an exquisitely painful disease* • **exquisiteness** /-nəs/ noun [U]

ˌex-ˈserviceman noun [C] (plural **-men**) a man who was a member of the armed services in the past

ˌex-ˈserviceˌwoman noun [C] (plural **-women**) a woman who was a member of the armed services in the past

extant /ekˈstænt/, /ˈek.stənt/ adj formal describes something very old that is still existing: *We have some extant parish records from the 16th century.*

extemporaneous /ekˌstem.pəˈreɪ.ni.əs/ adj formal done or said without any preparation or thought: *an extemporaneous* ***speech***

extempore /ekˈstem.pᵊr.i/ adj, adv formal done or said without any preparation or thought: *an extempore performance* ◦ *At the audition, the actors were asked to perform extempore.*

extemporize formal (UK usually **extemporise**) /ɪkˈstem.pᵊr.aɪz/ (US) /-pə.aɪz/ verb [I] to speak or perform without any preparation or thought: *I'd lost my notes and had to extemporize.*

extend /ɪkˈstend/ verb **INCREASE ▷ 1** B2 [T] to add to something in order to make it bigger or longer: *We have plans to extend our house (= to make it bigger).* ◦ *The government has produced a series of leaflets designed to extend (= increase) public awareness of the dangers of AIDS.* ◦ *We're planning to extend our publishing of children's books (= increase it).* **2** B2 [T] to make something last longer: *The pub has recently extended its opening hours (= made them longer).* ◦ *I need to extend my visa (= make it last longer).* **STRETCH ▷ 3** [T] to stretch something out: *We've extended a washing line (= made it reach) between two trees in the garden.* ◦ *He extended his hand as a greeting (= held out his hand for someone to shake it).* **REACH ▷ 4** B2 [I usually + adv/prep] to reach, stretch, or continue: *The Sahara Desert extends* ***for*** *miles.* ◦ *The path extends* ***beyond*** *the end of the road.* ◦ *Rain is expected to extend* ***to*** *(= arrive in) all parts of the country by this evening.* ◦ *The effects of this legislation will extend (= reach) further than the government intends.* **OFFER ▷ 5** [T] formal to offer or give: *I should like to extend my* ***thanks to*** *you for your kindness.* ◦ *The chairperson extended a warm* ***welcome to*** *the guest speaker.* ◦ *The government is extending (= giving) aid to people who have been affected by the earthquake.* ◦ [+ two objects] *The bank has agreed to extend us money/extend money* ***to*** *us (= lend us money) to buy our house.* **INCLUDE ▷ 6** [I + adv/prep] to include or affect someone or something: *Parking restrictions do not extend* ***to*** *disabled people.* ◦ *Her new-found tolerance does not extend to single mothers.* ◦ *The invitation did not extend to family members.* **USE ABILITY ▷ 7** [T] to cause someone to use all their ability: *She feels that her job doesn't extend her enough.*

E

extendable /ɪkˈsten.də.bl̩/ adj describes something that can be made longer: *an extendable ladder* ◦ *The lease on the office is extendable.*

extended /ɪkˈsten.dɪd/ adj [before noun] long or longer than usual: *They're going on an extended holiday to Australia.*

exˌtended ˈfamily noun [C usually singular, + sing/pl verb] a family unit that includes grandmothers, grandfathers, aunts, and uncles, etc. in addition to parents and children → Compare **nuclear family**

extension /ɪkˈsten.ʃᵊn/ noun **REACH ▷ 1** B2 [C or U] the fact of reaching, stretching, or continuing; the act of adding to something in order to make it bigger or longer: *Martin Luther King, Jr, campaigned for the extension* ***of*** *civil rights* ***to*** *(= for them to include) black people.* ◦ *The extension (= increasing)* ***of*** *police powers in the province has been heavily criticized.* ◦ *His report contained serious criticisms of the finance director, and,* ***by*** *extension (= therefore), of the entire board of management.* ◦ *The article is an extension* ***of*** *(= takes further) the ideas Professor Fox developed in an earlier book.* ◦ *I've applied for an extension* ***to*** *my visa (= asked for it to last longer).* ◦ *They are hoping to get an extension* ***of*** *their loan (= to be given a longer period of time in which to pay it back).* **BUILDING ▷ 2** [C] UK (US **addition**) a new part added to a house or other building: *We're building an extension* ***to/on*** *our house.* **PHONE ▷ 3** B2 [C] any of two or more phones in the same house which share the same number, or any of a number of phones connected to a SWITCHBOARD in a large building such as an office: *We have an extension in our bedroom.* ◦ *When you call, ask for extension 3276.* **COMPUTER ▷ 4** [C] the last part of the name of a computer file, which comes after a (.), and shows what type of file it is

exˈtension ˌcord noun [C] US (UK **exˈtension ˌlead**) an extra wire used to take electricity to a piece of electrical equipment when it is an extra distance from the nearest SOCKET

extensive /ɪkˈsten.sɪv/ adj B2 covering a large area; having a great range: *a school with extensive* ***grounds*** ◦ *extensive* ***repairs*** *to the motorway* ◦ *Her knowledge of music is extensive (= she knows a lot about music).* ◦ *The wedding received extensive coverage in the newspapers.* • **extensively** /-li/ adv *The house was extensively (= a large part of it was) rebuilt after the fire.* ◦ *The side effects of the new drug are being extensively researched (= are being studied in detail).*

extent /ɪkˈstent/ noun [S or U] **1** B2 area or length; amount: *From the top of the Empire State Building, you can see* ***the full*** *extent* ***of*** *Manhattan (= the area it covers).* ◦ *We don't yet know* ***the*** *extent* ***of*** *his injuries (= how bad his injuries are).* ◦ *Rosie's teacher was impressed by* ***the*** *extent* ***of*** *her knowledge (= how much she knew).* ◦ *The River Nile is over 6,500 kilometres* ***in*** *extent (= length).* **2 the extent to which** C2 the degree to which something happens or is likely to happen: *She had not realized the extent to which the children had been affected.* **3 to the extent of** so strongly that:

Some people hold their beliefs very strongly, even to the extent of being prepared to go to prison for them. **4 to the extent that** to a particular degree or stage, often causing particular results: *Sales have fallen badly this year, to the extent that we will have to close some of our shops.* **5 to the same extent** to the same degree as; as much as: *The rich will not benefit from the proposed changes to the tax system to the same extent as the lower paid.* **6 to some extent** B2 partly: *To some extent, she was responsible for the accident.* **7 to such an extent** so much: *The car was damaged to such an extent that it couldn't be repaired.* **8 to what extent?** how much: *To what extent will the budget have to be modified?* ◦ *To what extent do you think he's aware of the problem?* **9** :

extenuate /ɪkˈsten.ju.eɪt/ **verb** [T] formal to cause a wrong act to be judged less seriously by giving reasons for it: *He was unable to say anything that might have extenuated his behaviour.* • **extenuating** /-eɪ.tɪŋ/ US /-eɪ.t̬ɪŋ/ **adj** [before noun] formal *She was found guilty of theft, but because of extenuating* ***circumstances*** *(= a situation which made her crime seem less serious) was not sent to prison.* • **extenuation** /ɪkˌsten.juˈeɪ.ʃən/ **noun** [U] formal *Her plea of ignorance of the law* ***in*** *extenuation* ***of*** *(= as an excuse for) her crime was not accepted.*

exterior /ɪkˈstɪə.ri.əʳ/ US /-ˈstɪr.i.ɚ/ **adj; noun**
▸**adj** on or from the outside: *In some of the villages the exterior walls of the houses are painted pink.* ◦ *Exterior* ***to*** *the main house there is a small building that could be used as an office or studio.* → Synonym **external, outer**
▸**noun** [C] C1 the outside part of something or someone: *The Palace of Fontainebleau has a very grand exterior.* ◦ *The exterior* ***of*** *the house needs painting.* ◦ *Behind that cold exterior there's a passionate man.*

exterminate /ɪkˈstɜː.mɪ.neɪt/ US /-ˈstɝː-/ **verb** [T] to kill all the animals or people in a particular place or of a particular type: *Once cockroaches get into a building, it's very difficult to exterminate them.* ◦ *Millions of Jewish people were exterminated in concentration camps in the Second World War.* • **extermination** /ɪkˌstɜː.mɪˈneɪ.ʃən/ US /-ˌstɝː-/ **noun** [U] *International measures have been taken to prevent the extermination* ***of*** *the whale (= all of them being killed).* • **exterminator** /-neɪ.təʳ/ US /-neɪ.t̬ɚ/ **noun** [C]

external /ɪkˈstɜː.nəl/ US /-ˈstɝː-/ **adj** B2 of, on, for, or coming from the outside: *the external* ***walls*** *of the house* ◦ *Female kangaroos carry their young in pouches that are external* ***to*** *their bodies.* ◦ *This cream is* ***for*** *external* ***use*** *only (= it must not be put inside the body).* ◦ *In later years, his paintings began to show a number of external influences (= influences coming from other people).* ◦ *Most news magazines have a section devoted to external* ***affairs*** *(= foreign news).* ◦ *You shouldn't judge people by their external* ***appearances*** *(= what they appear to be like).* → See also **exterior** • **externally** /-i/ **adv** *Externally the house is in need of repair.* ◦ *Externally she appeared calm, but inside she was furious.*

exˌternal examinˈation **noun** [C] an exam arranged by people outside a student's own school, college, or university

exˌternal exˈaminer **noun** [C] someone from outside a student's own school, college, or university who judges an exam

externalize specialized (UK usually **externalise**) /ɪkˈstɜː.nə.laɪz/ US /-ˈstɝː-/ **verb** [T] to express feelings, especially bad feelings, such as anger: *You have to learn to externalize your anger.* • **externalization** (UK usually **externalisation**) /ɪkˌstɜː.nə.laɪˈzeɪ.ʃən/ US /-ˌstɝː.nə.lə-/ **noun** [C or U] *the externalization of negative feelings*

externals /ɪkˈstɜː.nəlz/ US /-ˈstɝː-/ **noun** [plural] the appearance of something or someone: *It's easy to be misled by externals.*

extinct /ɪkˈstɪŋkt/ **adj** **1** C1 not now existing: *There is concern that the giant panda will soon* ***become*** *extinct.* ◦ *Many tribes became extinct when they came into contact with Western illnesses.* ◦ *A lot of trades have become extinct because of the development of technology.* **2** An extinct volcano is one that is not now ACTIVE (= will not explode again).

extinction /ɪkˈstɪŋk.ʃən/ **noun** [U] C1 a situation in which something no longer exists: *The extinction* ***of*** *the dinosaurs occurred millions of years ago.* ◦ *Many species of plants and animals are* ***in danger of/ threatened with*** *extinction (= being destroyed so that they no longer exist).*

extinguish /ɪkˈstɪŋ.gwɪʃ/ **verb** [T] **FIRE/LIGHT** ▷ **1** to stop a fire or a light burning: *It took the firefighters several hours to extinguish the flames.* ◦ *to extinguish a cigarette* **FEELING/IDEA** ▷ **2** literary to stop or get rid of an idea or feeling: *Nothing could extinguish his love for her.*

extinguisher /ɪkˈstɪŋ.gwɪ.ʃəʳ/ US /-ɚ/ **noun** [C] a **fire extinguisher**

extirpate /ˈek.stɜː.peɪt/ US /-stɚ-/ **verb** [T] formal to remove or destroy something completely • **extirpation** /ˌek.stɜːˈpeɪ.ʃən/ US /-stɚ-/ **noun** [U]

extol /ɪkˈstəʊl/ US /-ˈstoʊl/ **verb** [T] (**-ll-**) formal to praise something or someone very much: *His book extolling the benefits of vegetarianism sold thousands of copies.* ◦ *She is forever extolling* ***the virtues of*** *her children.*

extort /ɪkˈstɔːt/ US /-ˈstɔːrt/ **verb** [T] to get something by force or threat, or with difficulty: *He had been extorting money* ***from*** *the old lady for years.* ◦ *Police have not so far been able to extort a confession* ***from*** *the people accused of the bombing.* • **extortion** /-ˈstɔː.ʃən/ US /-ˈstɔːr.ʃən/ **noun** [U] *He was found guilty of obtaining the money by extortion (= by forceful methods).*

extortionate /ɪkˈstɔː.ʃən.ət/ US /-ˈstɔːr-/ **adj** disapproving extremely expensive: *The price of books nowadays is extortionate.* • **extortionately** /-li/ **adv** *First-class travel is extortionately* ***expensive****.*

extortioner /ɪkˈstɔː.ʃən.əʳ/ US /-ˈstɔːr.ʃən.ɚ/ **noun** [C] (also **extortionist**) a person who obtains something by force or threat

extra /ˈek.strə/ **adj; adv; noun**
▸**adj** A2 added to what is normal: *If you need any extra help, just call me.* ◦ *Recently he's been working an extra two hours a day.* ◦ *The price includes travel and accommodation but meals are extra (= there is an additional charge for meals).*

IDIOM **go the extra mile** to make more effort than is expected of you: *He's a nice guy, always ready to go the extra mile* ***for*** *his friends.*

▸**adv** B1 more: *They pay her extra to work nights.* ◦ *We agreed on a price but afterwards they wanted £10 extra.* ◦ *I worked extra hard (= more than usual) on that essay.*
▸**noun** [C] **SOMETHING MORE** ▷ **1** B1 something that you can get with something else if you pay a little more money: *A sunroof is an* ***optional*** *extra on this model of the car.* **FILMS** ▷ **2** C1 a person in a film who does not have a speaking part and who is usually part of the SCENE, for example, in a crowd

extra- /ek.strə-/ **prefix** outside or in addition to: *extraterrestrial beings (= imaginary creatures which come from outside the planet Earth)* ◦ *an extramarital* affair (= *a sexual relationship of a married person with someone other than their husband or wife*) ◦ *extracurricular activities* (= *activities which are not part of the usual school or college course*)

extract verb; noun

▸verb [T] /ɪkˈstrækt/ **1** B2 to remove or take out something: *They used to extract iron ore* ***from*** *this site.* ◦ *The oil which is extracted* ***from*** *olives is used for cooking.* ◦ *The tooth was eventually extracted.* **2** to make someone give you something when they do not want to: *After much persuasion they managed to extract the information* ***from*** *him.*

▸noun /ˈek.strækt/ **PLANT** ▷ **1** [C or U] a substance taken from a plant, flower, etc. and used especially in food or medicine: *malt/yeast extract* ◦ *The cream contained extracts* ***of/from*** *several plants.* **WRITING** ▷ **2** B2 [C] a particular part of a book, poem, etc. that is chosen so that it can be used in a discussion, article, etc.: *They published an extract* ***from*** *his autobiography.*

extraction /ɪkˈstræk.ʃən/ noun **1** [U] the process of removing something, especially by force: *The extraction* ***of*** *minerals has damaged the countryside.* **2** [C] specialized the process of removing a tooth: *She had two extractions.* **3 be of French, German, Chinese, etc. extraction** to be from a family that originally came from another country

extractor /ɪkˈstræk.təʳ/ US /-tɚ/ noun [C] **1** a machine used to remove something: *a juice extractor* **2** (also **extractor fan**) a piece of equipment used to remove steam, smoke, or unpleasant smells from a room or building

extracurricular /ˌek.strə.kəˈrɪk.jʊ.ləʳ/ US /-jə.lɚ/ adj **1** describes an activity or subject that is not part of the usual school or college course **2** humorous used to refer to something a person does secretly or unofficially and not within their normal work or relationship, especially a sexual relationship: *He detailed the future president's extracurricular* ***activities*** *while governor.*

extraditable /ˈek.strə.daɪ.tə.bl̩/ US /-t̬ə-/ adj describes a crime for which a person can be extradited, or a person who can be extradited: *an extraditable crime/****offence***

extradite /ˈek.strə.daɪt/ verb [T] to make someone return for trial to another country where they have been accused of doing something illegal: *He will be extradited* ***to*** *Britain* ***from*** *France.* • **extradition** /ˌek.strəˈdɪʃ.ən/ noun [C or U] *They have applied for his extradition* ***to*** *Ireland.* ◦ *an extradition* ***treaty***

extramarital /ˌek.strəˈmær.ɪ.təl/ US /-ə.t̬əl/ adj describes a married person's sexual relationship with someone who is not their husband or wife: *an extramarital* ***affair***

extramural /ˌek.strəˈmjʊə.rəl/ US /-ˈmjʊr.əl/ adj mainly UK (US usually **extension**) organized especially by a college or university, etc. for people who are not students there: *extramural* ***classes/courses***

extraneous /ɪkˈstreɪ.ni.əs/ adj not directly connected with or related to something: *extraneous* ***information*** ◦ *These questions are extraneous* ***to*** *the issue being discussed.*

extranet /ˈeks.trə.net/ noun [C] a system of computers that makes it possible for particular organizations to communicate with each other and share information: *The extranet will link the company with its customers and suppliers.*

extraordinarily /ɪkˈstrɔː.dɪn.ər.əl.i/ US /-ˈstrɔr.dən.er-/ adv B2 very; more than usual: *She is, it must be said, extraordinarily beautiful.*

extraordinary /ɪkˈstrɔː.dɪn.ər.i/ US /-ˈstrɔːr.dən.er-/ adj **1** B1 very unusual, special, unexpected, or strange: *He told the extraordinary story of his escape.* ◦ *Her voice had an extraordinary hypnotic quality.* ◦ *an extraordinary coincidence* **2 extraordinary meeting** a special meeting which happens between regular meetings

extraˌordinary renˈdition noun [U] the act of taking prisoners to another country in order to do things to them that would not be allowed in your own country, for example TORTURING (= hurting) them in order to make them give you information

extrapolate /ɪkˈstræp.ə.leɪt/ verb [I or T] to guess or think about what might happen using information that is already known: *You can't really extrapolate a trend* ***from*** *such a small sample.* • **extrapolation** /ɪkˌstræp.əˈleɪ.ʃən/ noun [C or U]

ˌextra-ˈrare adj → **blue**

extrasensory /ˌek.strəˈsen.sər.i/ US /-sɚ-/ adj without the use of hearing, seeing, touch, taste, and smell

ˌextrasensory perˈception noun [U] (abbreviation **ESP**) the ability to know things without using hearing, seeing, touch, taste, or smell

extraterrestrial /ˌek.strə.təˈres.tri.əl/ adj (coming from) outside the planet Earth: *extraterrestrial beings*

extraterritorial /ˌek.strəˌter.ɪˈtɔː.ri.əl/ US /-ˈtɔːr.i-/ adj outside (the laws of) a country

ˌextra ˈtime noun [U] UK (US **overtime**) a period of time in a football game in which play continues if neither team has won in the usual time allowed for the game

extravagance /ɪkˈstræv.ə.gəns/ noun **1** [U] behaviour in which you spend more money than you need to: *I think she was shocked by my extravagance.* **2** [C] something expensive that you buy even though you do not need it: *Perfume is my greatest extravagance.*

extravagant /ɪkˈstræv.ə.gənt/ adj **1** C2 spending too much money, or using too much of something: *the extravagant lifestyle of a movie star* ◦ *That was very extravagant* ***of*** *you to buy strawberries out of season.* ◦ *He rarely used taxis, which he regarded as extravagant.* ◦ *the extravagant use of packaging on many products* **2** extreme and unreasonable: *The product does not live up to the extravagant claims of the advertisers.* • **extravagantly** /-li/ adv

extravaganza /ɪkˌstræv.əˈgæn.zə/ noun [C] a large, exciting, and expensive event or entertainment: *a* ***musical****/dance extravaganza*

extreme /ɪkˈstriːm/ adj; noun

▸adj **GREAT** ▷ **1** B2 very large in amount or degree: *extreme pain/stupidity/wealth* **BAD** ▷ **2** B2 very severe or bad: *extreme weather conditions* ◦ ***In*** *extreme* ***cases****, the disease can lead to blindness.* **BELIEFS** ▷ **3** C2 describes beliefs and political parties which most people consider unreasonable and unacceptable: *He has rather extreme* ***views****.* ◦ *He's on the extreme right wing of the party.* **FURTHEST POINT** ▷ **4** [before noun] at the furthest point, especially from the centre: *They live in the extreme south of the island.*

▸noun [C] **1** the largest possible amount or degree of something: *I've never witnessed such extremes of wealth and poverty.* ◦ *Most people I know work fairly hard but she* ***takes it to*** *extremes.* **2 in the extreme** used for emphasis; extremely: *Some of the scenes were unpleasant in the extreme.* **3** a situation, feeling, etc. that is the opposite or very different from another one: *My moods seem to* ***go from one*** *extreme* ***to another*** (= *my moods often change from very bad to very good*).

extremely /ɪkˈstriːm.li/ adv B1 very: *They played extremely well.* ◦ *She's extremely beautiful.*

exˌtreme ˈsport noun [C] B1 a sport that is very dangerous and exciting

extremism /ɪkˈstriː.mɪ.zəm/ noun [U] the fact of someone having beliefs that most people think are unreasonable and unacceptable: ***political*** *extremism*

extremist /ɪkˈstriː.mɪst/ noun [C] C2 someone who has beliefs which most people think are unreasonable and unacceptable: *a group of extremists* (= *people with extreme opinions*) • **extremist adj**

extremity /ɪkˈstrem.ɪ.ti/ US /-ə.t̬i/ noun **1** [C] the furthest point, especially from the centre: *The wood lies on the southern extremity of the estate.* **2 extremities** [plural] formal the parts of the human body furthest from the heart, for example, the fingers, toes, and nose

extricate /ˈek.strɪ.keɪt/ verb [T] formal to remove or set free something with difficulty: *It took hours to extricate the car* ***from*** *the sand.* ◦ *I tried to extricate my****self from*** *the situation.* • **extrication** /ˌek.strɪˈkeɪ.ʃən/ noun [U]

extrinsic /ekˈstrɪn.zɪk/ adj formal coming from outside, or not related to something: *Extrinsic forces were responsible for the breakdown of the peace talks.*

extrovert (also **extravert**) /ˈek.strə.vɜːt/ US /-vɝːt/ noun [C] C1 an energetic happy person who enjoys being with other people: *Most sales people are extroverts.* → Compare **introvert** • **extrovert** adj (also **extroverted**) *an extrovert personality*

extrude /ɪkˈstruːd/ verb [T] specialized to form something by forcing or pushing it out, especially through a small opening: *extruded aluminium rods* • **extrusion** /-ˈstruː.ʒən/ noun [U]

exuberant /ɪɡˈzjuː.bər.ənt/ US /-ˈzuː.bɚ-/ adj **PEOPLE** ▷ **1** (especially of people and their behaviour) very energetic: *Young and exuberant, he symbolizes Italy's new vitality.* **PLANTS** ▷ **2** (of plants) strong and growing quickly • **exuberance** /-əns/ noun [U]

exude /ɪɡˈzjuːd/ US /-ˈzuːd/ verb [T] **FEELING** ▷ **1** If you exude love, confidence, pain, etc., you show that you have a lot of that feeling: *She just exudes* ***confidence.*** **LIQUID/SMELL** ▷ **2** to produce a smell or liquid substance from inside: *Some trees exude* ***from*** *their bark a sap that repels insect parasites.*

exult /ɪɡˈzʌlt/ verb [I] formal to express great pleasure or happiness, especially at someone else's defeat or failure: *They exulted* ***at/over*** *their victory.* ◦ *She seems to exult* ***in*** *her power.* • **exultation** /ˌeɡ.zəlˈteɪ.ʃən/ noun [U]

exultant /ɪɡˈzʌl.tənt/ adj formal very happy, especially at someone else's defeat or failure: *an exultant cheer* ◦ *an exultant crowd* • **exultantly** /-li/ adv formal

ˌex-ˈwife noun [C] Someone's ex-wife is the woman they were once married to.

eye /aɪ/ noun; verb

▸noun [C] **BODY PART** ▷ **1** A1 one of the two organs in your face, which you use to see with: *He has no sight in his left eye.* ◦ *She's got beautiful green eyes.* ◦ *He closed his eyes and went to sleep.* **PLANT** ▷ **2** a dark spot on a potato or similar plant part, from which a new stem and leaves will grow **HOLE** ▷ **3** the hole in a needle through which you put the thread

IDIOMS **all eyes are on sb/sth** If all eyes are on someone or something, everyone is watching that person or thing and waiting to see what will happen: *All eyes are on the prime minister to see how he will respond to the challenge to his leadership.* • **an eye for an eye (and a tooth for a tooth)** saying said to show that you believe if someone does something wrong, they should be punished by having the same thing done to them • **as far as the eye can/could see** for a long distance until something is so far away and small it cannot be seen any more: *The road stretched into the distance as far as the eye could see.* • **be all eyes** to watch someone or something with a lot of interest: *We were all eyes as the celebrity guests emerged from the car.* • **be more to sth than meets the eye** If there is more to something than meets the eye, it is more difficult to understand or involves more things than you thought at the beginning. • **be one in the eye for sb** UK to be a disappointment or defeat for someone: *His promotion was one in the eye for his rivals.* • **be up to your eyes in sth** to be very busy doing something: *I'm up to my eyes in school reports this week.* • **before your very eyes** while you are watching: *Then, before my very eyes, she disappeared.* • **clap/lay/set eyes on sb/sth** to see someone or something for the first time: *Everyone keeps talking about Patrick, but I've never clapped eyes on the man.* • **sb's eyes are bigger than their belly/stomach** humorous something that you say when someone has taken more food than they can eat • **have an eye for sth** B2 to be good at noticing a particular type of thing: *She has an eye for* ***detail.*** • **have your eye on sth** to have seen something that you want and intend to get: *She's had her eye on a bike for some time.* • **have an eye to/for the main chance** UK Someone who has an eye to/for the main chance is always ready to use a situation to their own advantage. • **have eyes in the back of your head** to know everything that is happening around you: *Parents of young children need to have eyes in the back of their heads.* • **in sb's eyes** B2 in someone's opinion: *And although she was probably just an ordinary-looking kid, in my eyes she was the most beautiful child on the face of the planet.* • **keep your eye in** UK to continue to be good at a sport or other activity by practising it: *I try to play regularly to keep my eye in.* • **keep your/an eye on sth/sb** B2 to watch or take care of something or someone: *Will you keep your eye on my suitcase while I go to get the tickets?* • **keep your eye on the ball** to give your attention to what you are doing at the time: *You have to keep your eye on the ball in business.* • **keep your/an eye out for sb/sth** informal C1 to watch carefully for someone or something to appear: *Keep your eye out for signposts to Yosemite.* • **keep your eyes open for sb/sth** C2 to watch carefully for someone or something, often while you are doing something else: *While you are checking the animals, keep your eyes open for any signs of disease.* • **keep your eyes peeled/skinned** C2 to watch carefully for someone or something: *Keep your eyes peeled* ***for*** *Polly and Maisie.* • **make eyes at sb** old-fashioned to look at someone with sexual interest: *She was making eyes at him all evening.* • **not take your eyes off sb/sth** to not stop looking at someone or something: *He was so handsome – I couldn't take my eyes off him.* • **only have eyes for sb** to be interested in or attracted to only one person: *You've no need to be jealous. I only have eyes for you.* • **roll your eyes** to move your eyes upwards as a way of showing that you are annoyed or bored after someone has done or said something • **take your eye off the ball** to not give your attention to what you are doing at the time: *If you're a manager, you can't afford to take your eye off the ball for one minute.* • **to my eye** used when giving your opinion about the appearance of something or someone: *You see, to my eye, she looks better without make-up.* • **with your eyes open** knowing about all the problems there could be with something you want to do: *I went into this marriage with my eyes open.* • **with your eyes closed/shut 1** If someone could do something with their eyes closed or shut, they could do it very easily because they have done it many times: *I could do that journey with my eyes shut.* **2** noticing nothing: *Half the time you go around with your eyes shut.*

▸verb [T] (present tense **eyeing** or **eying**, past tense and past participle **eyed**) to look at someone or something with interest: *I could see her eyeing my lunch.* ◦ *She eyed me warily.*

PHRASAL VERBS **eye sb up** informal to look at someone with sexual interest: *That guy in the grey jacket has been eyeing you up all evening.* • **eye sth up** informal to look closely at something that you are interested in: *I saw you eyeing up that chocolate cake.*

eyeball /ˈaɪ.bɔːl/ (US) /-bɑːl/ **noun; verb**
▸noun [C] the whole eye, including the part that cannot usually be seen

IDIOMS **be up to your eyeballs in sth** to be very busy with something: *I'm up to my eyeballs in reports.* • **eyeball to eyeball** If you are eyeball to eyeball with an enemy or someone you are arguing with, you deal with them in a direct way.

▸verb [T] informal to look closely at someone: *He eyeballed me across the bar.*

eyebrow /ˈaɪ.braʊ/ **noun** [C] (B2) the line of short hairs above each eye in humans: *Do you* ***pluck*** *your eyebrows (= remove some of the hairs to change their shape)?* ◦ *He's got really* ***bushy*** *(= thick) eyebrows.*

IDIOM **raise your eyebrows** to show surprise by moving your eyebrows upwards

ˈeye ˌcandy noun [U] informal someone or something that is attractive but not very interesting or useful: *Most of the images on the website are not more than eye candy.*

ˈeye-ˌcatching adj very attractive or noticeable: *an eye-catching poster*

ˈeye ˌcontact noun [U] (C2) the situation when two people look at each other's eyes at the same time: *He's very shy and never* ***makes*** *eye contact.* ◦ *If you're telling the truth, why are you* ***avoiding*** *eye contact* ***with*** *me?*

-eyed /-aɪd/ **suffix** with the type of eyes described: *a brown-eyed baby girl* ◦ *She was wide-eyed in amazement.*

eyeful /ˈaɪ.fʊl/ **noun 1** [C] an amount of something, usually dust or dirt, that has entered the eye: *As the lorry went past, I got an eyeful* ***of*** *grit.* **2** [S] informal a very noticeable or attractive sight, often a sexually attractive person: *She's quite an eyeful.*

IDIOM **get an eyeful** informal to look at something or someone: *Hey, get an eyeful* ***of*** *this!*

eyeglasses /ˈaɪˌglɑː.sɪz/ (US) /-ˌglæs.ɪz/ **noun** [plural] US **glass**

eyehole /ˈaɪ.həʊl/ (US) /-hoʊl/ **noun** [C] UK for **peephole**

eyeing (US also **eying**) /ˈaɪ.ɪŋ/ present participle of **eye**

eyelash /ˈaɪ.læʃ/ **noun** [C] (B2) any of the short hairs which grow along the edges of the eye: ***long*** *eyelashes* ◦ ***false*** *eyelashes*

eyelet /ˈaɪ.lət/ **noun** [C] a small hole in material, the edge of which is protected by a ring of metal, through which a piece of string, a SHOELACE, etc. is put to fasten something

ˈeye ˌlevel noun [U] If something is at eye level, it is positioned at approximately the same height as your eyes.

eyelid /ˈaɪ.lɪd/ **noun** [C] (B2) either of the two pieces of skin that can close over each eye

eyeliner /ˈaɪˌlaɪ.nəʳ/ (US) /-nɚ/ **noun** [C or U] a coloured substance, usually contained in a pencil, that is put in a line just above or below the eyes in order to make them look more attractive

ˈeye-ˌopener noun [C usually singular] something that surprises you and teaches you new facts about life, people, etc.: *Living in another country can be a real eye-opener.*

eyepatch /ˈaɪ.pætʃ/ **noun** [C] a covering worn over the eye to protect it if it is damaged or sore

eyepiece /ˈaɪ.piːs/ **noun** [C] the part of a piece of equipment, for example a MICROSCOPE, through which you look

ˈeye ˌshadow noun [C or U] a coloured cream or powder that is put around the eyes to make them look larger or more attractive

eyesight /ˈaɪ.saɪt/ **noun** [U] (B2) the ability to see: *good/bad/poor eyesight* ◦ *You need to have your eyesight tested.*

ˈeye ˌsocket noun [C] one of the two round, low areas on each side of the nose which contain the eyes

eyesore /ˈaɪ.sɔːʳ/ (US) /-sɔːr/ **noun** [C] an unpleasant or ugly sight in a public place: *They think the new library building is an eyesore.*

eyestrain /ˈaɪ.streɪn/ **noun** [U] tired or painful eyes as a result of too much reading, looking at a computer screen, etc.

eyetooth /ˈaɪ.tuːθ/ **noun** [C] (plural **eyeteeth**) either of the two pointed teeth that are found one on each side of the top of the mouth → Synonym **canine**

IDIOM **give your eyeteeth for sth** If you would give your eyeteeth for something, you would like it very much: *Most women would give their eyeteeth for hair like yours.*

eyewash /ˈaɪ.wɒʃ/ (US) /-wɑːʃ/ **noun** **LIQUID** ▷ **1** [C or U] a liquid used to clean the eyes **NONSENSE** ▷ **2** [U] old-fashioned informal nonsense or something that is not true

eyewitness /ˈaɪˌwɪt.nəs/ **noun** [C] a person who saw something happen, for example a crime or an accident: *According to an eyewitness* ***account****, the thieves abandoned their vehicle near the scene of the robbery.*

eyrie /ˈɪə.ri/ (US) /ˈɪr.i/ **noun** [C] **BIRD'S NEST** ▷ **1** (mainly US **aerie**) the nest of an EAGLE or other large bird which eats meat, usually built in a high, far place **ROOM/APARTMENT** ▷ **2** a room or apartment that is high up in a building: *I interviewed the chairman of the company in his seventh-floor eyrie.*

ˈe-zine noun [C] a ZINE (= small magazine) that is available on the internet

F

F, f /ef/ noun (plural **Fs, F's** or **f's**) **LETTER** ▷ **1** [C or U] the sixth letter of the English alphabet **MUSIC** ▷ **2** [C or U] a note in Western music: *The song is in (**the key of**) F.* ◦ *Play an F followed by a G.* **TEMPERATURE** ▷ **3** [after noun] abbreviation for **Fahrenheit**: *Yesterday the temperature was 90°F.*

f2f written abbreviation for face to face: used in an email or internet CHAT ROOM to describe a situation where you meet and talk to someone, rather than communicate electronically

F

fa (also **fah**) /fɑː/ noun [S] the fourth note in the SOL-FA musical SCALE

the FA /ˌefˈeɪ/ noun abbreviation for the Football Association: the national organization for football in England

FAA /ˌef.eɪˈeɪ/ noun abbreviation for Federal Aviation Administration: a US government organization that makes the rules relating to planes and airports in the US and makes sure that these rules are obeyed

fab /fæb/ adj; noun

▸adj informal for **fabulous**: *I bought some fab jeans on Saturday.*

▸noun [C] (also ˈ**fab** ˌ**plant**) a factory for making advanced electronic products, for example SILICON CHIPS: *two major semiconductor fabs*

fable /ˈfeɪ.bl̩/ noun [C or U] a short story which tells a general truth or is only partly based on fact, or literature of this type: *the fable of the tortoise and the hare*

fabled /ˈfeɪ.bl̩d/ adj [before noun] literary describes something or someone who has been made very famous, especially by having many stories written about them: *the fabled film director Cecil B. De Mille*

fabric /ˈfæb.rɪk/ noun **CLOTH** ▷ **1** C1 [C or U] cloth or material for making clothes, covering furniture, etc.: *dress fabric* ◦ *cotton fabrics* **STRUCTURE** ▷ **2 the fabric of sth** C2 the structure or parts of something: *the fabric of society* ◦ *Unhappiness was woven into the natural fabric of people's lives.* ◦ *We must invest in the fabric of our hospitals and start rebuilding them.*

fabricate /ˈfæb.rɪ.keɪt/ verb [T] to invent or produce something false in order to deceive someone: *He was late, so he fabricated an excuse to avoid trouble.* ◦ *He claims that the police fabricated evidence against him.* • **fabrication** /ˌfæb.rɪˈkeɪ.ʃᵊn/ noun [C or U] *The evidence he gave in court was a **complete** fabrication.*

fabulous /ˈfæb.jʊ.ləs/ adj **GOOD** ▷ **1** very good; excellent: *She looked **absolutely** fabulous in her dress.* ◦ *They've got a fabulous apartment in the centre of Paris.* ◦ *We had a fabulous time at the party.* **NOT REAL** ▷ **2** imaginary, not existing in real life: *The unicorn is a fabulous **creature**.*

fabulously /ˈfæb.jʊ.ləs.li/ adv extremely: *fabulously rich/wealthy*

façade (also **facade**) /fəˈsɑːd/ noun **BUILDING** ▷ **1** [C] the front of a building, especially a large or attractive building: *the gallery's elegant 18th-century façade* **FALSE APPEARANCE** ▷ **2** [S] a false appearance that makes someone or something seem more pleasant or better than they really are: *Behind that amiable façade, he's a deeply unpleasant man.* ◦ *We are fed up with this façade of democracy.*

face /feɪs/ noun; verb

▸noun **HEAD** ▷ **1** A1 [C] the front of the head, where the eyes, nose, and mouth are: *She's got a long, thin face.* ◦ *She had a puzzled expression **on** her face.* **2** A1 [C] an expression on someone's face: *I was greeted by smiling faces.* ◦ *He had a face **like thunder*** (= he looked very angry). **3 make/pull a face** B1 to make a strange expression with your face, usually to show that you do not like someone or something: *'This tastes horrible,' said Tom, pulling a face at his glass.* ◦ *I was pulling silly faces to make the baby laugh.* **FRONT** ▷ **4** [C] the front or surface of an object: *the north face **of** a mountain* ◦ *the west face **of** the building* **5** [C] the front of a clock or watch that has the numbers or marks that show what time it is: *a watch face with Roman numerals* **RESPECT** ▷ **6** C2 [U] the respect and honour of others: *He thinks he would **lose** face if he admitted the mistake.* ◦ *She tried to **save** face by inventing a story about being overseas at the time.*

IDIOMS **be in sb's face** US informal If someone is in your face they criticize you all the time: *One of the managers is always in my face.* • **in your face** slang shocking and annoying in a way that is difficult to ignore: *dance music that is aggressive, sexy, and in your face* • **disappear off the face of the earth** (also **be wiped off the face of the earth**) to disappear completely: *The whole tribe seems to have disappeared off the face of the earth.* • **keep a straight face** C2 to manage to stop yourself from smiling or laughing: *She tried to keep a straight face but, unable to contain herself, burst into laughter.* • **sb's face doesn't fit** UK informal If someone's face doesn't fit, their appearance or personality are not suitable for a job or other activity. • **sb's face falls** If someone's face falls, they suddenly look very disappointed: *Her face fell when she heard he wasn't coming.* • **the face of sth** what you can see of something or what shows: *Poor quality is the **unacceptable** face of increased productivity.* • **get out of my face!** slang a rude way of telling someone that they are annoying you and should stop: *I said no! Now get out of my face!* • **have a face like the back end of a bus** UK informal to be very ugly • **in the face of sth** C2 despite having to deal with a difficult situation or problem: *She left home in the face of strong opposition from her parents.* • **on the face of it** C2 used when you are describing how a situation seems on the surface: *On the face of it, it seems like a bargain, but I bet there are hidden costs.* • **take sth at face value** C1 to accept something for what it appears to be rather than studying it more closely: *I took the offer at face value. I didn't think they might be trying to trick me.* • **to sb's face** C2 If you say something unpleasant to someone's face, you say it to them directly, when you are with them: *If you've got something to say, say it to my face.*

▸verb **DEAL WITH** ▷ **1** B2 [T] If you face a problem, or a problem faces you, you have to deal with it: *This is one of the many problems faced by working mothers.* ◦ *Passengers could face long delays.* ◦ *You're faced **with** a very difficult choice there.* **2** B2 [T] to accept that something unpleasant is true and start to deal with the situation: *I think Phil has to face **the fact that** she no longer loves him.* ◦ *We have to face **facts** here – we simply don't have enough money.* ◦ *He's dying but he refuses to face **the truth**.* **3 can't face sth/doing sth** B2 to not want to do or deal with something unpleasant: *I can't face walking up all those steps again.* ◦ *I know I've got to tell her but I can't face it.*

4 C2 [T] to deal with someone when the situation between you is difficult: *She half hoped he would not find her, though she knew she would have to face him sooner or later.* **TURN TOWARDS** ▷ **5** B1 [I usually + adv/prep, T] to turn or be turned towards something physically; to be opposite something: *The terrace faces towards the sea/faces south.* ◦ *Their houses face each other across the street.* **BUILDING** ▷ **6** [T] If you face a building, you put an extra layer in front of what is already there: *The house was built of wood but faced* ***in/with*** *brick.*

IDIOMS **face the music** C1 to accept criticism or punishment for something you have done • **let's face it** C2 something that you say before you say something that is unpleasant but true: *Let's face it, we both know why I stopped working there.*

PHRASAL VERB **face up to sth** B2 to accept that a difficult situation exists: *She's going to have to face up to the fact that he's not going to marry her.*

facebooking /ˈfeɪs.bʊk.ɪŋ/ **noun** [U] the activity of using the SOCIAL NETWORKING website Facebook™: *Facebooking takes up a lot of my time.*

facecloth /ˈfeɪs.klɒθ/ US /-klɑːθ/ **noun** [C] UK (US **washcloth**) a small cloth used to wash the body, especially the face and hands

ˈface ˌcream **noun** [C or U] cream which you put on your face to make the skin softer and less dry

-faced /-feɪst/ **suffix** with the type of face described: *round-faced* (= *having a round face*) ◦ *sad-faced* (= *having a sad face*) ◦ *red-faced* (= *embarrassed*)

faceless /ˈfeɪs.ləs/ **adj** disapproving having no clear characteristics and therefore not interesting: *faceless bureaucrats*

facelift /ˈfeɪs.lɪft/ **noun** **1** [C] a medical operation which tightens loose skin to make the face look younger **2** [S] treatment to make something look more attractive, for example a building: *The bank is planning to give its 1930s building a complete facelift.*

ˈface ˌpack **noun** [C] a substance like cream that is left on the face to dry and then removed, in order to improve the skin

ˈface ˌpowder **noun** [U] skin-coloured powder used on the face to make it look less shiny and more attractive

ˌface-recogˈnition ˌsoftware **noun** [U] (also **ˌfacial-recogˈnition ˌsoftware**) software that can recognize a person from a DIGITAL image of their face: *Face-recognition software allows you to log into your computer using your face as your password.*

ˈface-ˌsaving **adj** [before noun] done so that other people will continue to respect you: *a face-saving exercise/gesture*

facet /ˈfæs.ɪt/ **noun** [C] **1** one part of a subject, situation, etc. that has many parts: *She has so many facets to her personality.* **2** one of the small flat surfaces cut on a PRECIOUS STONE

facetious /fəˈsiː.ʃəs/ **adj** disapproving not serious about a serious subject, in an attempt to be funny or to appear clever: *facetious remarks* ◦ *He's just being facetious.* • **facetiously** /-li/ **adv** • **facetiousness** /-nəs/ **noun** [U]

ˌface-toˈface **adv** [before noun], **adj** B1 directly, meeting someone in the same place: *We've spoken on the phone but never face-to-face.* ◦ *She* ***came*** *face-to-face with the gunman as he strode into the playground.*

ˌface ˈvalue **noun** [C usually singular] the value or price that is shown on, for example, stamps, coins, or paper money

ˈface ˌwasher **noun** [C] Australian English a small cloth used to wash the body, especially the face and hands → Compare **facecloth**

facial /ˈfeɪ.ʃəl/ **adj**; **noun**

▸**adj** C2 of or on the face: *facial hair* ◦ *facial cleansers and moisturizers* ◦ *facial expressions*

▸**noun** [C] a beauty treatment which cleans and improves the skin of the face with creams and gentle rubbing: *Beauty treatments range from an eyelash tint at £8 to a deep cleansing facial costing £58.*

facile /ˈfæs.aɪl/ **adj** describes a remark or theory that is too simple and has not been thought about enough: *a facile explanation* ◦ *We must avoid facile recriminations about who was to blame.*

facilitate /fəˈsɪl.ɪ.teɪt/ **verb** [T] formal C1 to make something possible or easier: *The new ramp will facilitate the entry of wheelchairs.* ◦ *The current structure does not facilitate efficient work flow.*

facilitator /fəˈsɪl.ɪ.teɪ.təʳ/ US /-t̬ɚ/ **noun** [C] someone who helps a person or organization do something more easily or find the answer to a problem, by discussing things and suggesting ways of doing things: *I see my role as that of a facilitator, enabling other people to work in the way that suits them best.*

facility /fəˈsɪl.ɪ.ti/ US /-ə.t̬i/ **noun** **BUILDING** ▷ **1** B1 [C] a place, especially including buildings, where a particular activity happens: *a nuclear research facility* ◦ *a military facility* ◦ *a new sports facility* **2 facilities** B1 [plural] the buildings, equipment, and services provided for a particular purpose: *shopping facilities* ◦ *medical facilities* ◦ *sports facilities* **ABILITY** ▷ **3** B2 [C or U] an ability, feature, or quality: *His facility* ***for*** *languages is astonishing.* ◦ *a phone with a memory facility*

facing /ˈfeɪ.sɪŋ/ **noun** **1** [C] an outer layer covering a wall, etc.: *The wall was built of rubble with a facing of stone.* **2** [C or U] an extra layer of material sewn to the inside edge of a piece of clothing to make it stronger, or to the outside, especially of collars and the ends of sleeves, for decoration: *A blue jacket with white facing*

-facing /-feɪ.sɪŋ/ **suffix** turned towards the stated direction: *Most avalanche accidents occur on north- and east-facing slopes.*

facsimile /fækˈsɪm.ɪ.li/ **noun** [C] **1** an exact copy, especially of a document: *a facsimile* ***of*** *the original manuscript* **2** formal a **fax**

> **!** **Common mistake: in fact**
>
> **Remember: in fact** is not written as one word.
>
> Don't write 'infact', write **in fact**:
>
> ~~*It didn't rain at all. Infact, the weather was perfect.*~~

fact /fækt/ **noun** [C or U] **1** A2 something that is known to have happened or to exist, especially something for which proof exists, or about which there is information: *No decision will be made till we know all the facts.* ◦ *I don't know all the facts* ***about*** *the case.* ◦ *I'm not angry that you took my car – it's just the fact* ***that*** *you didn't ask me first.* ◦ *He knew* ***for a*** *fact that Natalie was lying.* ◦ *It's sometimes hard to separate fact from fiction.* **2 as a matter of fact** B1 (also **in (actual) fact**) used to add emphasis to what you are saying, or to show that it is the opposite of or different from what went before: *I don't work. In fact, I've never had a job.* ◦ *'Have you always lived here?' 'As a matter of fact (= the truth is) I've only lived here for the last three years.'* **3 a fact of life** something unpleasant that cannot be avoided: *Going bald is just a fact of life.* **4 facts and figures** exact detailed information: *We are getting some facts and figures together and we will then* *have a full board meeting.* **5 the facts of life** details about sexual activity and the way that babies are born

> Word partners for **fact**
>
> *accept/acknowledge/face up to* the fact (that) • *establish/find out* a fact • *account for/explain* the fact that • *hide/ignore* the fact that • *examine/look at* the facts • the fact *remains* that • the *mere/simple* fact that • the *basic* facts • the facts *about* sth • *apart from/despite/due to* the fact that

ˈfact-ˌfinding adj [before noun] done in order to discover information for your company, government, etc.: *a fact-finding mission/trip*

F

faction /ˈfæk.ʃᵊn/ noun [C] mainly disapproving a group within a larger group, especially one with slightly different ideas from the main group: *the left-wing faction of the party* • **factional** /-ᵊl/ adj *factional leaders* • **factionalism** /-ᵊl.ɪ.zᵊm/ noun [U] *Factionalism was tearing the party and the country apart.*

factitious /fækˈtɪʃ.əs/ adj formal false or artificial: *He has invented a wholly factitious story about his past.*

factoid /ˈfæk.tɔɪd/ noun [C] humorous an interesting piece of information

factor /ˈfæk.tᵊʳ/ (US) /-tɚ/ noun; verb

▸noun [C] **FACT** ▷ **1** B2 a fact or situation that influences the result of something: *People's voting habits are influenced by political, social and economic factors.* ◦ *Heavy snow was a* ***contributing*** *factor* ***in*** *the accident.* ◦ *Price will be a* ***major/crucial*** *factor* ***in*** *the success of this new product.* ◦ *The economy is regarded as the* ***decisive/key*** *factor in the outcome of the general election.* ◦ informal *The film's success is largely due to its* ***feel-good*** *factor (= its ability to make people feel happy).* **NUMBER** ▷ **2** specialized in mathematics, any whole number that is produced when you divide a larger number by another whole number: *Two, three, four and six are all factors of twelve.* **3** specialized a particular level on some systems of measurement: *a factor 20 suntan cream* ◦ *a wind chill factor of -20* **4 by a factor of** specialized If an amount becomes larger or smaller by a factor of a particular number, it becomes that number of times larger or smaller: *Cases of leukaemia in the area near the nuclear reactor have risen by a factor of four.*

▸verb

PHRASAL VERB **factor sth in** (also **factor sth into sth**) to include something when you are doing a calculation, or when you are trying to understand something: *People are earning more, but when inflation is factored in, they are no better off.* ◦ *The age of the patients and their overall health must be factored into the results.*

factorize (UK usually **factorise**) /ˈfæk.tᵊr.aɪz/ (US) /-tə.raɪz/ verb [T] (also **factor**) If you factorize a number, you divide it into factors.

factory /ˈfæk.tᵊr.i/ (US) /-tɚ.i/ noun [C] A1 a building or set of buildings where large amounts of goods are made using machines: *a car/shoe/textile factory* ◦ *a factory worker/manager*

ˌfactory ˈfarming noun [U] a system of farming in which a lot of animals are kept in a small closed area, in order to produce a large amount of meat, eggs, or milk as cheaply as possible: *a campaign against factory farming* • **ˌfactory-ˈfarmed** adj *factory-farmed chickens.*

ˌfactory ˈfloor noun [C] the area where the ordinary workers in a factory work: *The company has been criticized for the lack of safety on the factory floor.*

IDIOM **on the factory floor** involving ordinary workers rather than managers: *That sort of decision should be taken on the factory floor.*

ˈfactory ˌshop noun [C] (also **ˈfactory ˌstore, ˈfactory ˌoutlet**) a shop that sells things more cheaply because it sells them directly from the company which made them

factotum /fækˈtəʊ.təm/ (US) /-ˈtoʊ.t̬əm/ noun [C] formal a person employed to do all types of jobs for someone: *She was a* ***general*** *factotum at the restaurant – washing dishes, cleaning the floors and polishing the furniture.*

ˈfact ˌsheet noun [C] a written document containing information for the public: *A set of fact sheets accompanies the TV series.*

factual /ˈfæk.tjuəl/ adj using or consisting of facts: *She gave a clear, factual account of the attack to the police.* • **factually** /-tjuə.li/ adv *factually accurate*

faculty /ˈfæk.ᵊl.ti/ (US) /-t̬i/ noun **ABILITY** ▷ **1** C1 [C usually plural] a natural ability to hear, see, think, move, etc.: *Even at the age of 100, she still* ***had*** *all her faculties.* ◦ *Is he* ***in command/possession of*** *all his faculties (= can he still hear, speak, see, and think clearly)?* **2** [C] a special ability to do a particular thing: *She has a faculty* ***for*** *inspiring confidence in people.* ◦ *Studying has certainly* ***sharpened*** *my* ***critical*** *faculties (= taught me to think carefully about things using my judgment).* **IN A COLLEGE** ▷ **3** C1 [C] a group of departments in a college which specialize in a particular subject or group of subjects: *the Arts/Law Faculty* ◦ *the Faculty of Science* **4** B2 [C or S] US the people who teach in a department in a college

the ˌFA ˈCup noun [S] a competition for teams that belong to the Football Association, or the silver cup that is given as a prize in this competition: *Manchester United are hoping to win the FA Cup this year.* ◦ *It's the FA Cup* ***final*** *next week.*

fad /fæd/ noun [C] a style, activity, or interest that is very popular for a short period of time: *the latest health fad* ◦ *There was a fad* ***for*** *wearing ripped jeans a few years ago.*

faddy /ˈfæd.i/ adj (also **faddish** /ˈfæd.ɪʃ/) liking or disliking particular things, especially food, for no good reason: *I was a really faddy eater when I was young.* • **faddily** /-ɪ.li/ adv (also **faddishly** /ˈfæd.ɪʃ.li/) • **faddiness** /-nəs/ noun [U] (also **faddishness** /ˈfæd.ɪʃ.nəs/)

fade /feɪd/ verb [I or T] B2 to (cause to) lose colour, brightness or strength gradually: *If you hang your clothes out in the bright sun, they will fade.* ◦ *My suntan is already fading.* ◦ *They arrived home just as the light was fading (= as it was going dark).* ◦ *The sun had faded the blue walls.*

IDIOM **be fading away/fast** to be growing weaker and thinner and to be likely to die soon

PHRASAL VERBS **fade away** B2 to slowly disappear, lose importance, or become weaker: *The voices became louder and closer and then faded away again.* ◦ *As the years passed, the memories faded away.* • **fade (sth) in** If the picture or sound of a film or recording fades in, or someone fades it in, it becomes gradually stronger. • **fade (sth) out** If the picture or sound of a film or recording fades out or someone fades it out, it becomes gradually weaker.

faded /ˈfeɪ.dɪd/ adj less bright in colour than before: *faded* ***jeans*** ◦ *faded curtains/wallpaper* ◦ figurative *a faded beauty (= a woman who was beautiful in the past)*

faeces formal (mainly US **feces**) /ˈfiː.siːz/ noun [plural] the solid waste passed out of the body of a human or animal through the bowels: *The disease is spread by the contamination of food and water by faeces.* • **faecal** (mainly US **fecal**) /-kᵊl/ **adj** *faecal matter*

faff /fæf/ noun; verb
▸noun UK informal **be a faff** to need a lot of effort or cause slight problems: *Stripping the walls was a real faff.*
▸verb

PHRASAL VERB **faff about/around** UK informal to spend your time doing a lot of things that are not important instead of the thing that you should be doing: *I wish you'd stop faffing about and do something useful!*

fag /fæg/ noun; verb
▸noun **CIGARETTE** ▷ **1** [C] UK slang a cigarette: *a packet of fags* ◦ *She's gone outside for a quick fag.* ◦ *There were fag* ***ends*** *all over the floor.* **GAY MAN** ▷ **2** [C] US slang an offensive word for a gay man **TROUBLE** ▷ **3 be a fag** mainly UK informal to be boring and TIRING to do: *It's such a fag to have to make your bed every morning.* **YOUNG BOY** ▷ **4** [C] UK old-fashioned (at some large British private schools) a younger boy who has to do jobs for an older boy

IDIOM **the fag end of sth** UK informal the last, and often worst, part of something: *We always used to go on holiday at the fag end of the holiday season.*

▸verb [I] (-gg-) UK old-fashioned If a younger boy fags for an older boy at a British private school, he does jobs for him.

IDIOM **can't be fagged** UK informal If you can't be fagged to do something, you are unwilling to make the effort that is needed to do it: *I can't be fagged* ***to*** *walk all the way there.*

ˌfagged (ˈout) adj mainly UK informal tired and bored

faggot /ˈfæg.ət/ noun **GAY MAN** ▷ **1** [C] (informal **fag**) mainly US slang a gay man. This word is considered offensive when it is used by people who are not gay. **WOOD** ▷ **2** (US also **fagot**) [C usually plural] sticks of wood, tied together and used as fuel for a fire **FOOD** ▷ **3** [C usually plural] UK a ball of meat mixed with bread and herbs, fried or cooked in sauce

ˈfag ˌhag noun [C] slang a woman who likes to spend time with gay men

fah /fɑː/ noun [S] the musical note **fa**

Fahrenheit /ˈfær.ᵊn.haɪt/ adj, noun [U] (written abbreviation **F**) (of) a measurement of temperature on a standard in which 32° is the temperature at which water freezes and 212° that at which it boils: *Shall I give you the temperature in Celsius or* ***in*** *Fahrenheit?* ◦ *It was 80°F in the shade.* ◦ *Data are recorded in* ***degrees*** *Fahrenheit.* → Compare **Celsius**

fail verb; noun; exclamation
▸verb /feɪl/ **NOT SUCCEED** ▷ **1** (B2) [I] to not succeed in what you are trying to achieve or are expected to do: *She moved to London in the hope of finding work as a model, but failed.* ◦ *This method of growing tomatoes never fails.* ◦ *He failed* ***in*** *his attempt to break the record.* ◦ [+ to infinitive] *She failed* ***to*** *reach the Wimbledon Final this year.* ◦ *The reluctance of either side to compromise means that the talks are* ***doomed to*** *(= will certainly) fail.* **2 if all else fails** if none of our plans succeed: *If all else fails, we can always spend the holidays at home.* **EXAM** ▷ **3** (A2) [I or T] to be unsuccessful, or to judge that someone has been unsuccessful in a test or exam: *I passed in history but failed* ***in*** *chemistry.* ◦ *A lot of people fail their driving test the first time.* ◦ *The examiners failed him because he hadn't answered enough questions.* **NOT DO** ▷ **4** (B2) [I] to not do something that you should do: [+ to infinitive] *He failed* ***to*** *arrive on time.* ◦ *The club had been promised a grant from the council, but the money failed* ***to*** *(= did not) materialize.* ◦ *You couldn't fail* ***to*** *be (= it is impossible that you would not be) affected by the film.* ◦ *I'd be failing* ***in*** *my duty if I didn't tell you about the risks involved in the project.* **5 fail to see/understand** (C2) used when you do not accept something: *I fail to see* ***why*** *you can't work on a Saturday.* **STOP** ▷ **6** (B2) [I] to become weaker or stop working completely: *If my eyesight fails, I'll have to stop doing this job.* ◦ *The brakes failed and the car crashed into a tree.* ◦ *After talking non-stop for two hours, her voice started to fail.* ◦ *The old man was failing* ***fast*** *(= he was dying).* **7** [I] If a business fails, it is unable to continue because of money problems. **NOT HELP** ▷ **8** [T] to not help someone when you are expected to do so: *He failed her when she most needed him.* ◦ *When I looked down and saw how far I had to jump, my* ***courage*** *failed me (= I felt very frightened).*
▸noun [C] /feɪl/ **1** an unsuccessful result in a course, test, or exam: *John* ***got*** *three passes and four fails in his exams.* **2 without fail a** If you do something without fail, you always do it: *I go to the gym every Monday and Wednesday, without fail.* **b** used to tell someone that they must do something: *Be there at nine o'clock, without fail.*
▸exclamation US informal used for saying that you disapprove of what someone did: *You actually did his homework for him? Fail!*

failed /feɪld/ adj [before noun] having not succeeded: *a failed actress/writer* ◦ *She has two failed marriages behind her.*

ˌfailed ˈstate noun [C] a country whose government is considered to have failed at some of its basic responsibilities, for example keeping the legal system working correctly, and providing PUBLIC SERVICES (= electricity, water, education, hospitals, etc.): *Failed states are increasingly trapped in a cycle of poverty and violence.*

failing /ˈfeɪ.lɪŋ/ noun; preposition; adj
▸noun [C] a fault or weakness: *His one big failing is that he never says he's sorry.*
▸preposition if that is not possible: *Give her a book, or failing* ***that****, buy her something to wear.*
▸adj becoming weaker or less successful: *a failing business* ◦ *failing eyesight* ◦ *In the failing light, it was hard to read the signposts.*

ˈfail-safe adj **1** very unlikely to fail: *a fail-safe plan* **2** If something is fail-safe, it has been designed so that if one part of it does not work, the whole thing does not become dangerous: *a fail-safe device*

> **Word partners for failure**
>
> an *abject/complete/humiliating/total* failure • *be/feel* a failure • *end in/result in* failure • *admit* failure • be *doomed to* failure • a *fear/sense* of failure

failure /ˈfeɪ.ljəʳ/ (US) /-ljɚ/ noun **NO SUCCESS** ▷ **1** (B2) [C or U] the fact of someone or something not succeeding: *The meeting was a* ***complete/total*** *failure.* ◦ *I'm a bit of a failure* ***at*** *making (= I cannot make) cakes.* ◦ *I* ***feel such a*** *failure (= so unsuccessful).* ◦ *Their attempt to climb the Eiger* ***ended in*** *failure.* ◦ *The whole project was* ***doomed to*** *failure right from the start (= it could never have succeeded).* **NOT DO** ▷ **2** (B2) [U + to infinitive] the fact of not doing something that you must do or are expected to do: *His failure* ***to*** *return her phone call told her that something was wrong.* ◦ *Failure* ***to*** *keep the chemical at the right temperature could lead to an explosion.* **STOP** ▷ **3** (B2) [C or U] the fact of something not working, or stopping working as well as it should:

F

*He died of **heart/liver** failure.* ◦ *The accident was caused by the failure of the reactor's cooling system.* ◦ *The number of **business** failures rose steeply last year.* ◦ *After three **crop** failures in a row, the people face starvation.*

fain /feɪn/ **adv** old use willingly or happily: *I would fain forget what I had done.*

faint /feɪnt/ **adj**; **verb**; **noun**

▸**adj** **SLIGHT** ▷ **1** B2 not strong or clear; slight: *a faint sound/noise/smell* ◦ *The lamp gave out a faint glow.* ◦ *She gave me a faint smile of recognition.* ◦ *There's not the faintest hope of ever finding him.* ◦ *She bears a faint resemblance to my sister.* ◦ *I have a faint **suspicion** that you may be right!* **2 not have the faintest idea** C2 informal used to emphasize that you do not know something: *'Is she going to stay?' 'I haven't the faintest idea.'* ◦ *I haven't the faintest idea what you're talking about!* **UNWELL** ▷ **3 feel faint** C2 to feel weak, as if you are about to become unconscious: *She felt faint with hunger.*

▸**verb** [I] B2 to suddenly become unconscious for a short time, usually falling down: *He faints at the sight of blood.* ◦ *I nearly fainted in the heat.* ◦ *She took one look at the hypodermic needle and fainted (**dead**) **away** (= became unconscious immediately).*

▸**noun** [S] the act of suddenly becoming unconscious: *On receiving the news, she **fell into a dead** faint.*

fainthearted /ˌfeɪntˈhɑː.tɪd/ US /-ˈhɑːr.t̬ɪd/ **adj**; **noun**

▸**adj** [before noun] describes someone who is not confident or brave and dislikes taking unnecessary risks: *The terrorist threat in the region has kept fainthearted tourists away.*

▸**noun** [plural] **the fainthearted** people who are not brave: *The drive along the winding coast road is not for the fainthearted.*

faintly /ˈfeɪnt.li/ **adv** slightly or not strongly: *She seemed faintly embarrassed to see us there.* ◦ *A light flickered faintly in the distance.*

faintness /ˈfeɪnt.nəs/ **noun** [U] **NOT CLEAR** ▷ **1** the quality of not being strong or clear: *The faintness of the handwriting made the manuscript difficult to read.* **WEAK FEELING** ▷ **2** the feeling that you are about to become unconscious: *Faintness and morning sickness can be signs that you are pregnant.*

fair /feəʳ/ US /fer/ **adj**; **noun**; **verb**

▸**adj** **RIGHT** ▷ **1** B1 treating someone in a way that is right or reasonable, or treating a group of people equally and not allowing personal opinions to influence your judgment: *a fair trial* ◦ *Why should I have to do all the cleaning? **It's not** fair!* ◦ *It's not fair **on** Joe (= it is not right) to make him do all the work!* ◦ *It's not fair **that** she's allowed to go and I'm not!* ◦ *It's not fair **to** blame me for everything!* ◦ *She's **scrupulously** fair **with** all her employees (= she treats them all equally).* ◦ *She claims her article was a fair **comment** on (= a reasonable thing to say about) a matter of public interest.* ◦ *He offered to do all the cleaning if I did all the cooking, which seemed like a fair (= reasonable) **deal**.* **2** B1 If something, such as a price or share, is fair, it is reasonable and is what you expect or deserve: *I thought it was a fair **price** that she was offering.* ◦ *I'm willing to do my fair (= equal) **share** of the work.* ◦ *All the workers want is a fair **wage** for the work that they do.* **3** If a game or competition is fair, it is done according to the rules: *It was a fair fight.* **4 it's only fair** it is the right way to treat someone and what they deserve: *I think it's only fair to tell you that we have had over 300 applications for this job.* **5 it's fair to say** it is true to say: *I think it's fair to say (**that**) you've done less of the work than I have.* **6 to be fair** considering everything that has an effect on a situation, so that a fair judgment can be made: *He's done the job badly but, to be fair, I gave him very little time to do it.* **7 fair enough** B2 UK informal something you say to show that you understand why someone has done or said something: *'I'm just annoyed with him because he's behaved so badly.' 'Fair enough.'* **8 fair's fair** (also **fair dos**) something that you say when you want someone to behave reasonably or treat you the same as other people: *Come on, it's my turn. Fair's fair!* **9 a fair hearing** an opportunity to explain something or give your opinions, without other people trying to influence the situation: *He didn't feel he **got** a fair hearing in court.* **10 fair and square a** in an honest way and without any doubt: *We won the match fair and square.* **b** UK (US **squarely**) If you hit someone fair and square on a particular part of their body, you hit them hard, exactly on that part: *He hit me fair and square on the nose.* **PALE** ▷ **11** A2 (of skin) pale, or (of hair) pale yellow or gold: *She's got fair hair and blue eyes.* ◦ *a fair complexion* ◦ *My sister's dark and my brother's fair (= he has fair hair).* ◦ *He's fair-**haired**.* ◦ *All my family are fair-**skinned**.* **QUITE LARGE** ▷ **12** C2 [before noun] quite large: *We've had a fair **amount** of rain this week.* ◦ *We've had a fair **number** of applicants.* ◦ *It's a fair-**sized** garden.* ◦ *We've come a long way, but there's still a fair **way** (= quite a long distance) to go.* **AVERAGE** ▷ **13** C2 [after verb] neither very good nor very bad: *Films are rated on a scale of poor, fair, good and excellent.* ◦ *I was fair **at** science but it was never my thing.* **QUITE GOOD** ▷ **14** [before noun] (of an idea, guess or chance) good, but not excellent: *I think I've got a fair **idea** of (= I understand reasonably well) what you want.* ◦ *She's got a fair **chance** of winning (= there is a reasonable chance that she will win).* **WEATHER** ▷ **15** (of weather) pleasant and dry: *Fair weather was forecast for the following day.* **BEAUTIFUL** ▷ **16** old use or literary (of a woman) beautiful: *a fair maiden*

Other ways of saying fair

Right or **just** can be used when something is considered fair and morally acceptable by most people:

*I don't believe they should have put him in prison. It isn't **right**.*

*It wasn't a **just** punishment in my view.*

Even-handed or **balanced** can be used when something is fair because it does not favour one person more than another:

*The article contained very **even-handed** reporting.*

*The report gives a **balanced** view of what happened.*

If something is fair because everyone has the same opportunities and treatment, you could use the word **egalitarian** in formal English:

*We are working towards an **egalitarian** society.*

Equitable can also be used in formal English when a system is fair because everyone is treated in the same way:

*This is not an **equitable** tax system.*

When something is fair because a person is not influenced by their own opinions or trying to gain an advantage, you could use the words **unbiased** or **impartial**:

*The magazine provides **unbiased** information on the products available.*

*I want some **impartial** advice.*

If someone plays a game in a very fair way, you could describe them as **sportsmanlike**:

*That was very **sportsmanlike** of you.*

IDIOMS **all's fair in love and war** saying in love and war you do not have to obey the usual rules about reasonable behaviour • **by fair means or foul** If you try to achieve something by fair means or foul, you use any method you can to achieve it, even if it is not honest or fair. • **a fair crack of the whip** UK (US **a fair shake**) an equal chance to do something: *It's only right that all the candidates should be given a fair crack of the whip.* • **fair to middling** informal not very good but not bad: *'What's your French like?' 'Oh, fair to middling.'* • **it's a fair cop** UK informal something you say when someone has caught you doing something wrong and you agree that you were wrong • **with your own fair hand(s)** humorous used to say that you have made something yourself: *'Where did you get this cake?' 'I made it with my own fair hands.'*

▸**noun** [C] **1** a large public event where goods are bought and sold, usually from tables that have been specially arranged for the event, and where there is often entertainment: *I bought a wooden salad bowl at the local **craft** fair.* **2** B1 (UK also **funfair**, US also **carnival**) an outside event where you can ride on large machines for pleasure and play games to win prizes **3** C1 a large show at which people who work in a particular industry meet, and sell and advertise their products: *a book/antiques/toy fair* ◦ *a trade fair* **4** a public event in the countryside where farm animals and farm products are sold: *a cattle/agricultural fair* ◦ US *a county/state fair* **5** mainly US for **fete**
▸**verb** [T]

PHRASAL VERB **fair sth out** Indian English to make the final, corrected copy of a piece of written work

ˌfair ˈcopy noun [C usually singular] the final, corrected copy of a piece of written work

fair dinkum /ˌfeəˈdɪŋ.kəm/ US /ˌfer-/ **adj** [after verb], **adv, exclamation** Australian English informal honest(ly) or real(ly): *They beat us fair dinkum.*

ˌfair ˈgame noun [U] someone or something that should be allowed to be criticized: *Many journalists consider the royal family fair game.*

ˌfair ˈgo exclamation Australian English informal something you say when you want someone to act in a reasonable way: *Fair go mate, let the others have a turn!*

fairground /ˈfeə.graʊnd/ US /ˈfer-/ **noun** [C] a large outside area used for a fair: *There was a small fairground just by the river, with a carousel, a roller coaster and a Ferris wheel.*

ˌfair-haired ˈboy noun [C] US for **blue-eyed boy**

ˈFair ˌIsle noun [U] a style of KNITTED SWEATER with a repeated coloured pattern, originally made on the island of Fair Isle off the coast of Scotland: *a Fair Isle cardigan*

fairly /ˈfeə.li/ US /ˈfer-/ **adv QUITE** ▷ **1** B1 more than average, but less than very: *She's fairly tall.* ◦ *I'm fairly sure that this is the right address.* ◦ *We get on fairly well.* ◦ *I saw her fairly recently.* **2** literary used to emphasize FIGURATIVE expressions which describe what people or objects are doing: *The answer fairly jumps off the page at you!* ◦ *The dog fairly flew out of the door to greet him.* **IN THE RIGHT WAY** ▷ **3** B2 If you do something fairly, you do it in a way that is right and reasonable and treats people equally: *He claimed that he hadn't been **treated** fairly by his employers.* ◦ *Officials will ensure that the election is carried out fairly.* **4 fairly and squarely** UK (US **squarely**) completely: *She lays the blame for the recession fairly and squarely on the government.*

ˌfair-ˈminded adj treating everyone equally: *a fair-minded employer*

fairness /ˈfeə.nəs/ US /ˈfer-/ **noun** [U] **FAIR TREATMENT** ▷ **1** C1 the quality of treating people equally or in a way that is right or reasonable: *He had a real sense of fairness and hated injustice.* ◦ *The ban on media reporting has made some people question the fairness of the election (= ask whether it was fair).* **2 in (all) fairness** considering everything that has an effect on a situation, so that a fair judgment can be made: *In all fairness, he has been a hard worker.* ◦ *In fairness **to** Diana, she has at least been honest with you.* **BEAUTY** ▷ **3** old use beauty

ˌfair ˈplay noun [U] **1** in sport, the fact of playing according to the rules and not having an unfair advantage **2** C2 UK fair and honest treatment of people: *The committee's job is to ensure fair play between all the political parties during the election.*

the ˈfair ˌsex noun [S, + sing/pl verb] old-fashioned or humorous women in general

ˌfair ˈtrade (also **fairtrade**) noun [U] a way of buying and selling products that makes certain that the people who produce the goods receive a fair price: *Fair trade, say Oxfam, is about giving poor people power.* ◦ *fair trade coffee/chocolate* • **ˌfairly ˈtraded adv** *fairly traded bananas*

fairway /ˈfeə.weɪ/ US /ˈfer-/ **noun** [C] in GOLF, the area of short grass between the TEE (= place where you first hit the ball) and the GREEN (= place where the ball should enter a hole)

ˌfair-weather ˈfriend noun [C usually singular] disapproving someone who is a good friend when it is easy to be one and who stops being one when you are having problems

fairy /ˈfeə.ri/ US /ˈfer.i/ **noun** [C] **IMAGINARY CREATURE** ▷ **1** an imaginary creature with magic powers, usually represented as a very small person with wings: *Do you believe in fairies?* **2 be away with the fairies** humorous to behave in a way that is slightly strange: *It's no good asking her to look after the children – she's away with the fairies most of the time.* **GAY** ▷ **3** offensive a gay man

fairy

ˈfairy ˌcake noun [C] UK (US **cupcake**) a small light cake, often with ICING on top

ˈfairy floss noun [U] Australian English a large, soft ball of white or pink sugar in the form of thin threads, usually sold on a stick and eaten at FAIRS and AMUSEMENT PARKS → Compare **candyfloss**

ˌfairy ˈgodmother noun [C usually singular] **1** a magical character in some children's stories who helps someone who is in trouble: *Cinderella's fairy godmother helped her go to the ball.* **2** someone who unexpectedly arrives to solve your problems or make good things happen to you: *The company **played** fairy godmother by deciding to sponsor the club for a further five years.*

fairyland /ˈfeə.ri.lænd/ US /ˈfer.i-/ **noun** **1** [U] the place where FAIRIES (= imaginary creatures) are said to live **2** [S] approving a beautiful place with an attractive or special quality: *It had snowed heavily during the night and in the morning the garden was a white fairyland.*

ˈfairy ˌlights noun [plural] UK small electric lights on a

F

string used as decoration, especially on trees at Christmas

ˈfairy ˌtale noun [C] (also **ˈfairy ˌstory**) a traditional story written for children that usually involves imaginary creatures and magic

ˈfairy-tale adj [before noun] approving having a special and attractive or beautiful quality, like something in a fairy tale: *They had a fairy-tale* ***wedding***. ◦ *Sadly, there was no fairy-tale happy ending to the story.*

fait accompli /ˌfet.ə.kɒmˈpliː/ (US) /ˌfeɪt.ə.kɑːm-/ noun [C] (plural **faits accomplis**) something that has already happened or been done and cannot be changed: *The policy change was* ***presented to*** *us* ***as*** *a fait accompli, without consultation or discussion.*

F

faith /feɪθ/ noun **TRUST** ▷ **1** (B2) [U] great trust or confidence in something or someone: *She* ***has*** *no faith* ***in*** *modern medicine.* ◦ *You'll cope – I have* ***great*** *faith* ***in*** *you.* ◦ *After the trial, his family said they had* ***lost*** *all faith* ***in*** *the judicial system.* ◦ *Ministers must start keeping their promises if they want to* ***restore*** *faith* ***in*** *the government.* **RELIGION** ▷ **2** (B2) [C] a particular religion: *the Muslim/Christian/Jewish/Buddhist faith* ◦ *They were persecuted for their faith.* ◦ *He was forced to* ***practise*** *his faith in secret.* ◦ *a* ***multi-****faith society* ◦ *They were brought up in* ***the true*** *faith (= the religion which the speaker believes is the only true one).* **3** (B2) [U] strong belief in God or a particular religion: *Even in the bad times she never* ***lost*** *her faith.* ◦ *Her faith* ***in*** *God was shattered when her baby died.* ◦ *It's my faith that keeps me going.*

IDIOMS **accept/take sth on faith** to be willing to believe something without proof • **keep faith with sth/sb** to continue to support something or someone, or to do what you promised to do in a particular thing: *Despite the continuing recession, the government has asked people to keep faith with its reforms.* ◦ *The company has not kept faith with its promise to invest in training.* • **put/place your faith in sth/sb** to make a decision to trust something or someone: *Some people put their faith in strong leaders rather than sound policies.*

ˈfaith-ˌbased adj mainly US relating to organizations or government policies that are based on religious beliefs: *a faith-based community initiative*

faithful /ˈfeɪθ.fəl/ adj; noun; noun

▸adj **LOYAL** ▷ **1** (B2) firm and not changing in your friendship with or support for a person or an organization, or in your belief in your principles: *a faithful* ***friend*** ◦ *They are faithful supporters of the Labour Party.* ◦ *His faithful old dog accompanied him everywhere he went.* **2** (C2) If your husband, wife, or partner is faithful, he or she does not have a sexual relationship with anyone else: *Was your wife faithful during your marriage?* ◦ *He was faithful* ***to*** *his wife throughout their 30-year marriage.* **3 faithful to sth** continuing to support or follow something: *He remained faithful to the president's regime when so many others spoke out against it.* ◦ *Despite persecution, she remained faithful to her beliefs.* **ACCURATE** ▷ **4** true or not changing any of the details, facts, style, etc. of the original: *She gave a faithful* ***account*** *of what had happened on that night.* ◦ *I have tried to keep my translation as faithful as possible* ***to*** *the original book.* **RELIGIOUS** ▷ **5** following a particular religion: *faithful Christians* ◦ *faithful* ***followers*** *of Buddhism*

▸noun [C] **SUPPORTER** ▷ someone who continues to support someone or something: *He gave a rousing speech to a room full of* ***party*** *faithfuls.*

▸noun [plural] **the faithful a** people who are always loyal to a particular group or organization, especially a political party: *They asked for donations from the* ***party*** *faithful.* **b** the people who believe in a particular religion: *We heard bells calling the faithful to prayer.*

faithfully /ˈfeɪθ.fəl.i/ adv **LOYALLY** ▷ **1** in a loyal way or a way that can be trusted: *He served the family faithfully for 40 years.* ◦ *She* ***promised*** *faithfully (= made a firm promise) that she would never leave him.* **2 Yours faithfully** (B2) mainly UK used at the end of a formal letter beginning with 'Dear Sir' or 'Dear Madam'

> **!** Common mistake: **faithfully**
>
> **Remember:** a formal letter should end with **Yours faithfully** or **Yours sincerely.** If the letter is addressed to a particular person, don't write 'Yours faithfully', write **Yours sincerely**.

ACCURATELY ▷ **3** in a way that is true or accurate: *I always follow the instructions on medicine bottles faithfully (= exactly).*

faithfulness /ˈfeɪθ.fəl.nəs/ noun [U] the quality of being faithful to someone or something: *The bishop stressed the importance of faithfulness* ***in*** *marriage.*

ˈfaith ˌhealer noun [C] a person who cures ill people by using the power of prayer and belief • **ˈfaith ˌhealing** noun [U] *Despite all the advances in modern medicine, demand for alternative therapies and faith healing keeps growing.*

faithless /ˈfeɪθ.ləs/ adj **NOT LOYAL** ▷ **1** not loyal and not able to be trusted **2** not faithful sexually to your marriage partner or usual sexual partner: *a faithless husband* **NOT RELIGIOUS** ▷ **3** with no religious faith • **faithlessly** /-li/ adv • **faithlessness** /-nəs/ noun [U]

ˈfaith ˌschool noun [C] a school that is financially supported by a particular religious group, usually for children from that religion: *a Muslim faith school*

fajita /fəˈhiː.tə/ noun [C] a Mexican dish of meat and vegetables cut into strips, cooked, and wrapped inside a TORTILLA (= thin, round bread)

fake /feɪk/ noun; adj; verb

▸noun [C] **1** (C2) an object that is made to look real or valuable in order to deceive people: *Experts revealed that the painting was a fake.* ◦ *The gun in his hand was a fake.* **2** (C2) someone who is not what or who they say they are: *After working for ten years as a doctor, he was exposed as a fake.*

▸adj (C1) not real, but made to look or seem real: *He was charged with possessing a fake passport.* ◦ *fake fur/blood*

▸verb **FEELING/ILLNESS** ▷ **1** (C2) [I or T] to pretend that you have a feeling or illness: *to fake surprise* ◦ *to fake an orgasm* ◦ *She didn't want to go out, so she faked a headache.* ◦ *He faked a heart attack and persuaded prison staff to take him to hospital.* ◦ *He isn't really crying, he's just faking.* **OBJECT** ▷ **2** (C2) [T] to make an object look real or valuable in order to deceive people: *to fake a document/signature* • **faker** /ˈfeɪ.kər/ (US) /-kɚ/ noun [C]

ˌfake ˈtan noun [C or U] a substance that you put on your skin to make it look darker as if you have been in the sun: *Use a fake tan to make yourself look less pale.*

fakir (also **faqir**) /ˈfeɪ.kɪər/ (US) /fəˈkɪr/ noun [C] a member of an Islamic religious group, or a Hindu holy man

falafel (also **felafel**) /fəˈlæf.əl/ (US) /-ˈlɑː.fəl/ noun [C or U] fried balls of spicy food made from CHICKPEAS (= pale brown round seeds)

falcon /ˈfɒl.kᵊn/ Ⓤⓢ /ˈfɑːl-/ noun [C] a bird with pointed wings and a long tail which can be trained to hunt other birds and small animals

falcon

falconer /ˈfɒl.kᵊn.əʳ/ Ⓤⓢ /ˈfɑːl.kə.nɚ/ noun [C] a person who keeps and often trains falcons for hunting

falconry /ˈfɒl.kᵊn.ri/ Ⓤⓢ /ˈfɑːl-/ noun [U] the sport of hunting small animals and birds using falcons

fall /fɔːl/ Ⓤⓢ /fɑːl/ verb; noun

▸verb (**fell**, **fallen**) **HAVE AN ACCIDENT** ▷ **1** Ⓐ2 [I] to suddenly go down onto the ground or towards the ground without intending to or by accident: *The path's very steep, so be careful you don't fall.* ◦ *He fell badly and broke his leg.* ◦ *Athletes have to learn how to fall without hurting themselves.* ◦ *She fell under a bus and was killed instantly.* ◦ *The horse fell at the first fence.* ◦ *I fell* ***down*** *the stairs and injured my back.* ◦ *She had fallen, it appeared,* ***from*** *a great height.* ◦ *The water's deep here, so don't fall* ***in****!* ◦ *He fell* ***into*** *the river and drowned.* ◦ *If you fell* ***off*** *the roof, you'd kill yourself.* ◦ *He was leaning out of the window and fell* ***out****.* ◦ *She fell five metres* ***to*** *the bottom of the ravine.* ◦ *He fell* ***to*** *his* ***death*** *climbing the Matterhorn.* **2 fall flat on your face** informal to fall and land with your face down: *Poor Kathy fell flat on her face in the mud.* **BECOME LOWER** ▷ **3** Ⓑ1 [I] to become lower in size, amount, or strength: *Demand for new cars has fallen due to the recession.* ◦ *The standard of his work has fallen during the year.* ◦ *Salaries in the public sector are expected to fall by 15 percent this year.* ◦ *The temperature could fall* ***below*** *zero overnight.* ◦ *Average temperatures fell* ***by*** *ten degrees.* ◦ *The pound has fallen* ***to*** *its lowest-ever level against the dollar.* ◦ *When the teacher walked in, the children's voices fell* ***to a whisper*** *(= they became very quiet).* ◦ *Share prices fell* ***sharply*** *this week.*

> **!** Common mistake: **fall down or fall?**
>
> To talk about something becoming lower in size, amount or strength, don't say 'fall down', say **fall**:
>
> ~~*Last year the company's profits fell down dramatically.*~~
>
> *Last year the company's profits fell dramatically.*

COME DOWN ▷ **4** Ⓐ2 [I] to come down onto the ground or from a high position to a lower position: *The snow had been falling steadily all day.* ◦ *You can tell it's autumn because the leaves have started to fall.* ◦ *She fell* ***into*** *bed, completely exhausted.* ◦ *A bomb fell* ***on*** *the church and destroyed it.* ◦ *A huge meteor fell* ***to*** *Earth in the middle of the desert.* ◦ *He begged for mercy as the blows fell* ***on*** *him (= as he was being hit).* **5** [I] When the curtain falls in the theatre, it comes down because the play or performance has ended: *The audience was still laughing as the curtain fell.* **BELONG TO** ▷ **6** [I usually + adv/prep] to belong to a particular group, subject, or area: *The material falls* ***into*** *three categories.* ◦ *Matters of discipline fall* ***outside*** *my area of responsibility.* **BECOME** ▷ **7** Ⓑ1 [I + adv/prep, L] to change to a particular condition from a different one: *He always falls* ***asleep*** *after drinking red wine.* ◦ *Your rent falls* ***due*** *(= must be paid) on the first of the month.* ◦ *She suddenly fell* ***ill****.* ◦ *The book fell* ***open*** *(= opened by chance) at the page on Venice.* ◦ *The government has fallen strangely* ***silent*** *on the subject of tax cuts after all its promises at the last election.* ◦ ***Silence*** *fell* ***on*** *the group of men (= they became silent) as they received the news.* ◦ *She fell* ***under*** *the influence of (= began to be influenced by) an older student.* **BE DEFEATED** ▷ **8** Ⓒ2 [I] to be beaten or defeated: *The government finally fell after losing the support of the centre parties.* ◦ *The president fell* ***from power*** *during the military coup.* **9** Ⓒ2 [I] If a place falls in a war or an election, an enemy army or a different political party gets control of it: *Rome fell* ***to*** *the Vandals in 455 AD.* ◦ *The constituency fell* ***to*** *Labour at the last election, after ten years of Conservative rule.* **10** [I] literary If soldiers fall while fighting, they are killed: *Many brave men fell in the fight to save the city.* ◦ *During the war, he saw many of his comrades fall* ***in battle****.* **HAPPEN** ▷ **11** Ⓒ2 [I] to come at a particular time or happen in a particular place: *Easter falls late this year.* ◦ *My birthday will fall* ***on*** *a Friday this year.* ◦ ***Night/Darkness*** *had fallen by the time we got back to the camp.* ◦ *In the word 'table', the accent falls* ***on*** *the first syllable.* ◦ *The Treasury has still not decided where the cuts will fall.* **HANG DOWN** ▷ **12** Ⓒ2 [I usually + adv/prep] to hang down loosely: *The boy's hair fell* ***around*** *his shoulders in golden curls.* ◦ *The veil fell almost* ***to*** *her waist.* **UNHAPPY** ▷ **13 your face/spirits fall** If your face falls, you suddenly look unhappy or disappointed, and if your spirits fall, you suddenly feel unhappy or disappointed: *His spirits fell when he saw the distance he still had to go.* ◦ *As she read her exam results, her face fell.*

> **!** Common mistake: **fall**
>
> **Warning:** Check your verb endings!
>
> Many learners make mistakes when using **fall** in the past tense.
>
> The past simple of **fall** is **fell**:
>
> ~~*Paul felt off the roof and broke his leg.*~~
>
> *Paul fell off the roof and broke his leg.*
>
> **Felt** is the past simple and past participle of **feel**.

> **+** Other ways of saying **fall**
>
> **Drop** can sometimes be used instead of 'fall':
>
> *Several apples* ***dropped*** *from the tree.*
>
> **Collapse** can be used when someone or something falls down suddenly because of pressure or weakness:
>
> *Several buildings* ***collapsed*** *in the earthquake.*
>
> *He had a heart attack and* ***collapsed****.*
>
> If someone falls to the ground suddenly, you could use the verb **crumple**:
>
> *He fainted and* ***crumpled*** *into a heap on the floor.*
>
> **Tumble** means 'to fall quickly without control':
>
> *A huge rock* ***tumbled*** *down the mountain.*
>
> **Plunge** or **plummet** are verbs that are used when someone or something falls suddenly and a long way down or forward:
>
> *The car went out of control and* ***plunged/plummeted*** *over the cliff.*
>
> If you fall or almost fall because you step awkwardly while walking or running, the verb **stumble** could be used:
>
> *The waiter* ***stumbled*** *and dumped the food in my lap.*
>
> **Trip** could be used if you fall or almost fall after knocking your foot against something while you are walking or running:
>
> *She* ***tripped*** *over a crack in the pavement and broke her wrist.*

F

F

IDIOMS **fall between two stools** If something falls between two stools, it fails to achieve either of two aims: *The grammar guide falls between two stools – it's too difficult for a beginner but not detailed enough for an advanced student.* • **fall by the wayside** If someone falls by the wayside, they fail to finish an activity, and if something falls by the wayside, people stop doing it, making it, or using it: *So why does one company survive a recession while its competitors fall by the wayside?* • **fall flat** C1 If a joke, idea, or suggestion falls flat, it does not have the intended effect: *He made several jokes and each of them fell flat.* • **fall foul of sth** to break a rule or law, especially without intending to: *Manufacturers may fall foul of the new government guidelines.* • **fall foul of sb** to have a disagreement with someone: *Things were going well for her till she fell foul of the director..* • **fall in line** (also **fall into line**) If a person in an organization falls in/into line, they start to follow the rules and behave according to expected standards of behaviour: *Teachers who fail to fall in line **with** the new regulations may face dismissal.* • **fall in love** B1 to be very attracted to someone and begin to love them: *They met and fell **madly** in love.* ◦ *He fell in love **with** a young German student.* ◦ *I thought I was falling in love.* • **fall into sb's arms** literary When people fall into each other's arms, they hold each other tightly with both arms, to show their love for each other. • **fall into place 1** When things fall into place, they happen in a satisfactory way, without problems: *If you plan the project well, then everything should fall into place.* **2** C2 When events or details that you did not understand before fall into place, they become easy to understand: *Once I discovered that the woman whom he had been dancing with was his daughter, everything fell into place.* • **fall into the wrong hands** If something falls into the wrong hands, a dangerous person or an enemy starts to own or control it: *There are fears that the weapons might fall into the wrong hands.* • **fall into the/someone's trap** to make a mistake or get into a difficult situation by doing something or by trusting someone: *Don't fall into the trap **of** thinking you can learn a foreign language without doing any work.* ◦ *We fell right into the enemy's trap.* • **fall prey/victim to sth/sb** to suddenly begin to suffer as a result of something or someone bad: *Police fear that more pensioners could fall prey to the thieves.* • **fall short** C1 to fail to reach an amount or standard that was expected or hoped for, causing disappointment: *August car sales fell short **of** the industry's expectations.* • **nearly/almost fall off your chair** informal to be extremely surprised: *She nearly fell off her chair when she heard her exam result.* • **fall on deaf ears** C2 If a suggestion or warning falls on deaf ears, no one listens to it: *Their appeals to release the hostages fell on deaf ears.* • **fall on hard times** to lose your money and start to have a difficult life: *The scheme is designed to help children whose parents have fallen on hard times.*

PHRASAL VERBS **fall about** (also **fall about laughing**) UK informal to laugh without being able to stop: *We fell about when we heard her reply.* • **fall apart** **BREAK** ▷ **1** B2 to break into pieces: *My poor old boots are falling apart.* **STOP WORKING** ▷ **2** B2 If an organization, system, or agreement falls apart, it fails or stops working effectively: *The deal fell apart because of a lack of financing.* ◦ *Their marriage fell apart when she found out about her husband's affair.* **EMOTIONS** ▷ **3** informal to experience serious emotional problems that make you unable to think or act in the usual way: *After his wife died, he began to fall apart.* • **fall away** **BREAK** ▷ **1** If parts of something fall away, they break off and drop to the ground: *On the bathroom ceiling, some pieces of plaster had fallen away.* ◦ *The rear sections of the rocket fell away.* **TIME** ▷ **2** literary If a period of time falls away, it seems as if it has not happened: *As she looked at him, the years fell away, and she saw him again as a young boy.* **LAND** ▷ **3** If land falls away, it slopes down suddenly: *On the other side of the hill, the land falls away **sharply**.* • **fall away/off** to become smaller or lower in amount or rate: *Membership of the club has fallen away in recent months.* • **fall back 1** literary to move back suddenly from someone or something, often because you are frightened: *She fell back **in** horror/disgust.* **2** If an army falls back, it moves away from an enemy army in order to avoid fighting them: *The infantry fell back **in** disarray.* • **fall back on sth** C2 to use something for help because no other choice is available: *When the business failed, we had to fall back on our savings.* ◦ *If I lose my job, I'll have nothing to fall back on.* • **fall behind** to fail to do something fast enough or on time: *He was ill for six weeks and fell behind **with** his schoolwork.* ◦ *I've fallen behind **with** the mortgage payments.* • **fall down** **FALL** ▷ **1** B1 to fall to the ground: *Our apple tree fell down in the storm.* ◦ *He stumbled and fell down.* **2** If a building is falling down, it is in a very bad condition and there is a risk that it will break into pieces and drop to the ground: *Many buildings in the old part of the city are falling down.* **FAIL** ▷ **3** to fail: *Where do you think the plan falls down?* • **fall down on sth** to not be good at something in comparison with another thing: *I'm quite good at speaking Chinese, but I fall down on the written work.* • **fall for sb** informal B2 to suddenly have strong romantic feelings about someone: *She always falls for unsuitable men.* • **fall for sth** informal **1** to be tricked into believing something that is not true: *He told me he owned a mansion in Spain and I fell for it.* **2** **I'm not falling for that one!** informal said when you recognize a trick and refuse to be deceived by it: *'Lend me a fiver and I'll buy you a drink.' 'Oh no, I'm not falling for that one.'* • **fall in** **ROOF** ▷ **1** If a roof or ceiling falls in, it drops to the ground because it is damaged: *Ten miners were trapped underground when the roof of the tunnel fell in.* **SOLDIERS** ▷ **2** If soldiers fall in, they move into a line, one at the side of the other: *'Company, fall in!' shouted the sergeant-major.* ◦ *He started to march away, and the others fell in **behind** him.* → Compare **fall out**. • **fall in with sb** informal to become friendly with someone: *She fell in with a strange crowd of people at university.* • **fall in with sth** informal to accept and support a plan or suggestion: *It seemed like a good idea so we just fell in with it.* • **fall into sth** **START** ▷ **1** to start doing something, often without intending to: *We've fallen into the **habit** of getting up late on Saturday mornings.* ◦ *I fell into my job quite by accident.* ◦ *She fell into a conversation with a man at the bar.* **BECOME** ▷ **2** to gradually get into a particular condition, especially to get into a bad condition as a result of not being taken care of: *Over the years the house had fallen into disrepair.* ◦ *The old school fell into **disuse*** (= *people stopped using it*). • **fall off** If the amount, rate, or quality of something falls off, it becomes smaller or lower: *Sales have been falling off recently.* • **fall on/upon sb** literary to attack someone suddenly and unexpectedly: *The soldiers fell on the villagers and seized all their weapons.* • **fall on/upon sth** literary **NOTICE** ▷ **1** If your eyes fall on something, or your sight, eyes, etc. fall on something, you see and notice it: *Her gaze fell upon a small box at the back of the shop.* **EAT** ▷ **2** to start to eat food eagerly: *They fell on the* *bread as if they hadn't eaten for days.* • **fall on sb** When suspicion falls on a particular person, people think that they may be guilty of doing something bad: *He was the last person to see the woman alive, and suspicion immediately fell on him.* • **fall out** TOOTH/HAIR ▷ **1** If a tooth or your hair falls out, it becomes loose and separates from your mouth or head: *Her baby teeth are starting to fall out.* ◦ *A side effect of the treatment is that your hair starts to fall out.* ARGUE ▷ **2** B2 informal to argue with someone and stop being friendly with them: *He left home after falling out* ***with*** *his parents.* ◦ *She'd fallen out with her boyfriend* ***over*** *his ex-girlfriend.* SOLDIERS ▷ **3** If soldiers fall out, they move out of a line: *'Fall out, men!' shouted the sergeant-major.* → Compare **fall in** • **fall over 1** B1 If someone falls over, they fall to the ground: *She tripped and fell over.* **2** B1 If something falls over, it falls onto its side: *If you make the cake too high, it'll fall over.* • **fall over sth/sb** literary to cover something or someone: *A shadow fell over her work and she looked up to see who was there.* • **fall over yourself** UK (US **fall all over yourself**) to be very eager to do something: *Publishers are falling over themselves* ***to*** *produce non-fiction for seven-year-olds.* • **fall through** B2 to fail to happen: *We found a buyer for our house, but then the sale fell through.* • **fall to sb 1** to be or become the duty or job of someone: *The worst job fell to me.* **2 it falls to you** formal it is your duty: *It falls to me to thank you for all you have done for the association.* • **fall to** literary to begin doing something energetically: *There was a lot of work to do, so they fell to immediately.*

▸noun LOWER AMOUNT ▷ **1** B1 [C usually singular] the fact of the size, amount, or strength of something getting lower: *a fall* ***in*** *the price of petrol/the unemployment rate* ◦ *We could hear the* ***rise and fall*** *of voices in the other room.* ◦ *There was a fall* ***in*** *support for the Republican party at the last election.* SEASON ▷ **2** [C or U] US (UK **autumn**) the season after summer and before winter, when fruits and crops become ready to eat and the leaves fall off the trees: *I'm starting college* ***in the fall.*** ◦ ***Next*** *fall we'll be back in New York.* ◦ *a fall day/morning* ◦ *fall colours/foliage* ACCIDENT ▷ **3** B2 [C usually singular] the act of falling down to the ground, usually without intending to or by accident: *He* ***had/took*** *a nasty fall and hurt his back.* ◦ *the fall of the Berlin Wall (= when the Berlin Wall was destroyed)* MOVEMENT DOWNWARDS ▷ **4** [C usually singular] an amount of something that moves down onto the ground or from a higher position to a lower position: *a heavy fall of snow* → See also **rainfall** **5 falls** [plural] often used in place names to mean a very wide WATERFALL, often made of many separate WATERFALLS: *Niagara Falls* DEFEAT ▷ **6** C1 [C usually singular] the fact of being defeated or losing your power: *the fall of Rome* ◦ *The army took control of the city after the president's fall* ***from*** *power.*

IDIOMS **take a/the fall for sb** US informal to accept the blame for something another person did: *I wasn't going to take the fall for him.* • **fall from grace** a situation in which you do something that makes people in authority stop liking you or admiring you: *The finance minister's fall from grace gave his enemies great satisfaction.*

fallacious /fəˈleɪ.ʃəs/ adj formal not correct: *His argument is based on fallacious reasoning.* • **fallaciously** /-li/ adv • **fallaciousness** /-nəs/ noun [U]

fallacy /ˈfæl.ə.si/ noun [C] formal an idea that a lot of people think is true but is in fact false: [+ that] *It is a common fallacy* ***that*** *women are worse drivers than men.*

fallback /ˈfɔːl.bæk/ US /ˈfɑːl-/ adj [before noun] describes a plan or position that can be used if other plans do not succeed or other things are not available: *Do we have a fallback* ***position*** *for these negotiations?*

fallen /ˈfɔː.lən/ US /ˈfɑː-/ adj; noun
▸adj [before noun] LYING ON GROUND ▷ **1** lying on the ground, after falling down: *A fallen tree was blocking the road.* **2** having dropped down: *fallen leaves*
▸noun [plural] formal **the fallen** soldiers who have died in a war: *a statue in memory of the fallen*

ˌfallen ˈwoman noun [C] old-fashioned disapproving a woman who has lost her good reputation by having sex with someone before she is married

faller /ˈfɔː.ləʳ/ US /fɑː.lɚ/ noun [C] something such as a SHARE price or CURRENCY whose value has gone down during a particular period: *Among the fallers were the Canadian dollar and the yen.*

ˈfall ˌguy noun [C usually singular] informal a person who is falsely blamed for something that has gone wrong, or for a crime that they have not committed: *The governor was looking for a fall guy to take the blame for the corruption scandal.*

fallible /ˈfæl.ɪ.bl̩/ adj **1** able or likely to make mistakes: *We place our trust in doctors, but even they are fallible.* **2** A fallible object or system is likely not to work in a satisfactory way: *This method is more fallible than most because it depends on careful and accurate timing.* → Opposite **infallible** • **fallibility** /ˌfæl.ɪˈbɪl.ɪ.ti/ US /-ə.ţi/ noun [U] *The play deals with the fallibility of human nature.*

falling /ˈfɔː.lɪŋ/ US /fɑː-/ adj describes something that is becoming lower in size, amount or strength: *falling birth/interest rates* ◦ *falling standards*

ˌfalling-ˈoff noun [S] the fact of a rate, amount, or quantity becoming smaller or lower: *Travel agencies have recorded a falling-off in bookings this summer.*

ˌfalling-ˈout noun [S] informal an argument: *Rachel and Fi have* ***had*** *a falling-out and they're not speaking to each other.*

ˌfalling ˈstar noun [C] informal for **meteor**

fallopian tube /fəˌləʊ.pi.ənˈtjuːb/ US /-ˌloʊ.pi.ənˈtuːb/ noun [C usually plural] specialized either of the two tubes in a woman's body along which eggs travel from the OVARIES to the WOMB

fallout /ˈfɔːl.aʊt/ US /ˈfɑːl-/ noun [U] NUCLEAR ▷ **1** the RADIOACTIVE dust in the air after a nuclear explosion: *cancer deaths caused by fallout* ***from*** *weapons testing* UNPLEASANT RESULT ▷ **2** the unpleasant results or effects of an action or event: *The* ***political*** *fallout of the revelations has been immense.*

ˈfallout ˌshelter noun [C] a strong building, usually under the ground, intended to keep people safe from the dust in the air after a nuclear explosion

fallow /ˈfæl.əʊ/ US /-oʊ/ adj LAND ▷ **1** describes land that is not planted with crops, in order to improve the quality of the soil: *Farmers are eligible for government support if they let a certain amount of land* ***lie*** *fallow.* TIME ▷ **2** describes a period of time in which very little happens: *August is a fallow* ***period*** *in British politics.*

ˈfallow ˌdeer noun [C] (plural **fallow deer**) a small DEER of Europe and Asia that is grey in winter and pale brown with white spots in summer

false /fɒls/ US /fɑːls/ adj NOT REAL ▷ **1** B2 not real, but made to look or seem real: *false* ***eyelashes/teeth*** ◦ *Modern office buildings have false floors, under which computer and phone wires can be laid.* NOT TRUE ▷ **2** B1 disapproving not true, but made to seem true in order to deceive people: *She was charged with giving false **evidence** in court.* ◦ *When she was stopped by the police for speeding, she gave them a false **name** and address.* ◦ *He assumed a false **identity** (= pretended he was someone else) in order to escape from the police.* **3 under false pretences** disapproving If you do something under false pretences, you lie about who you are, what you are doing, or what you intend to do, in order to get something: *He was deported for entering the country under false pretences.* ◦ *If you're not going to offer me a job, then you've brought me here under false pretences (= you have deceived me in order to make me come here).* **NOT CORRECT** ▷ **4** B1 not correct: *'Three plus three is seven. True or false?' 'False.'* ◦ *The news report about the explosion turned out to be false.* ◦ *You'll get a false **impression/idea** of the town if you only visit the university.* **NOT SINCERE** ▷ **5** C1 disapproving not sincere or expressing real emotions: *a false smile/laugh* ◦ *I didn't like her – she seemed a bit false.* **NOT LOYAL** ▷ **6** literary disapproving A false friend is not loyal or cannot be trusted.

ˌfalse aˈlarm noun [C] an occasion when people wrongly believe that something dangerous or unpleasant is happening or will happen: *Three fire engines rushed to the school only to discover it was a false alarm.* ◦ *She thought she was pregnant, but it turned out to be a false alarm (= she was not).*

ˌfalse ˈdawn noun [C usually singular] something which seems to show that a successful period is beginning or that a situation is improving when it is not: *The increase in sales at the end of the year proved to be a false dawn.*

ˌfalse eˈconomy noun [C usually singular] an action that saves money at the beginning but, over a longer period of time, results in more money being wasted than being saved: *Buying cheap white goods is just a false economy – they're twice as likely to break down.*

ˌfalse ˈfriend noun [C] a word that is often confused with a word in another language with a different meaning because the two words look or sound similar: *The French word 'actuellement' and the English word 'actually' are false friends.*

falsehood /ˈfɒls.hʊd/ US /ˈfɑːls-/ noun formal **1** [U] lying: *She doesn't seem to understand the difference between truth and falsehood.* **2** [C] a lie or a statement that is not correct

ˌfalse ˈhopes noun [plural] confident feelings about something that might not be true: *I don't want to **raise** any false hopes, but I believe your son is still alive.*

ˌfalse imˈprisonment noun [C usually singular] legal the limiting of someone's freedom without the authority or right to do so: *He brought civil proceedings against the police for false imprisonment.*

falsely /ˈfɒls.li/ US /ˈfɑːls-/ adv **NOT TRUE** ▷ **1** in a way that is not true: *He claimed, falsely, that he was married.* **NOT CORRECTLY** ▷ **2** wrongly: *She was falsely accused of shoplifting.* **NOT SINCERELY** ▷ **3** disapproving in a way that is not sincere: *She tends to adopt a falsely cheerful tone when she's upset about something.*

ˌfalse ˈmodesty noun [U] behaviour in which a person pretends to have a low opinion of their own abilities or achievements

ˌfalse ˈmove noun [C usually singular] an unwise action that is likely to have an unpleasant or dangerous effect: *We can't afford to **make** any false moves once we're in enemy territory.* ◦ *'One false move and you're dead! (= I will kill you)' shouted the gunman.*

ˌfalse ˈstart noun [C usually singular] **RACE** ▷ **1** the start of a race in which one competitor starts too early, before the official signal to begin: *If an athlete **makes** a false start, the race must be restarted.* **PROBLEM** ▷ **2** an attempt to do something which fails because you are not ready or not able to do it: *We had a couple of false starts because of computer problems, but now the project is really under way.*

ˌfalse ˈteeth noun [plural] a set of artificial teeth fixed to a small piece of plastic or similar material, that fits inside the mouth of someone who does not have their own teeth: *a set of false teeth*

falsetto /fɔːlˈset.əʊ/ US /fɑːlˈset̬.oʊ/ noun; adj, adv
▸noun [C] (plural **falsettos**) a form of singing or speaking by men using an extremely high voice: *For his role as a young boy, he had to speak in a high falsetto.*
▸adj, adv describes an extremely high voice: *to sing falsetto*

falsies /ˈfɒl.siːz/ US /ˈfɑːl-/ noun [plural] informal thick soft pieces of material that can be worn inside a woman's clothing to make her breasts look bigger

falsify /ˈfɒl.sɪ.faɪ/ US /ˈfɑːl-/ verb [T] disapproving to change something, such as a document, in order to deceive people: *The certificate had clearly been falsified.* • **falsification** /ˌfɒl.sɪ.fɪˈkeɪ.ʃən/ US /ˌfɑːl-/ noun [U] *falsification of evidence*

falsity /ˈfɒl.sə.ti/ US /ˈfɑːl.sə.t̬i/ noun [U] (also **falseness**) **NOT CORRECT** ▷ **1** the state of not being correct **NOT SINCERE** ▷ **2** disapproving the state of not being sincere or of not expressing real emotions: *She left her career in television, saying she hated the falsity of it all.*

falter /ˈfɒl.təʳ/ US /ˈfɑːl.t̬ɚ/ verb [I] **1** to lose strength or purpose and stop, or almost stop: *The dinner party conversation faltered for a moment.* ◦ *Her friends never faltered in their belief in her.* ◦ *Nigel's voice faltered and he stopped speaking.* **2** to move awkwardly as if you might fall: *The nurse saw him falter and made him lean on her.* • **faltering** /-ɪŋ/ adj *She took a few faltering steps.* ◦ *This legislation is designed to stimulate the faltering economy.* • **falteringly** /-ɪŋ.li/ adv

fame /feɪm/ noun [U] B2 the state of being known or recognized by many people because of your achievements, skills, etc.: *She first **rose to** fame as a singer at the age of 16.* ◦ *She moved to London in search of fame **and fortune**.* ◦ *The town's fame rests on its beautiful cathedral.*

famed /feɪmd/ adj known or familiar to many people: *It's a city famed **for** its ski slopes and casinos.* ◦ *His famed calmness temporarily deserted him.*

familial /fəˈmɪl.i.əl/ adj [before noun] formal **1** similar to that in a family: *a familial relationship* **2** affecting several members of the same family: *a familial disease*

familiar /fəˈmɪl.i.əʳ/ US /-jɚ/ adj; noun
▸adj **EASY TO RECOGNIZE** ▷ **1** B1 easy to recognize because of being seen, met, heard, etc. before: *There were one or two familiar **faces** (= people I knew).* ◦ *The house looked **strangely** familiar, though she knew she'd never been there before.* ◦ *The street was familiar **to** me.* **2 be familiar with sth/sb** B2 to know something or someone well: *I'm sorry, I'm not familiar with your poetry.* **FRIENDLY** ▷ **3** informal and friendly, sometimes in a way that does not show respect to someone who is not a relation or close friend: *'That'll be five pounds, dear', he said in an irritatingly familiar way.* ◦ *He doesn't like to be too familiar **with** his staff.* • **familiarly** /-li/ adv *Henry Channon, known familiarly as 'Chips'*

IDIOM **be on familiar terms** to have a close and informal relationship: *We had met before, but we were hardly (= not) on familiar terms.*

▸noun [C] old use a close friend, or a spirit in the shape

of a cat, bird, or other animal that is the close COMPANION of a WITCH

familiarity /fəˌmɪl.iˈær.ə.ti/ (US) /-ˈer.ə.ţi/ noun [U] **KNOWLEDGE** ▷ **1** a good knowledge of something, or the fact that you know it so well: *Ellen's familiarity **with** pop music is astonishing.* ◦ *I love the familiarity of my old chair.* **FRIENDLINESS** ▷ **2** friendly and informal behaviour: *His excessive familiarity offended her.*

IDIOM **familiarity breeds contempt** saying said about someone you know very well and have stopped respecting because you have seen all their bad qualities

familiarize /fəˈmɪl.i.ər.aɪz/ verb

PHRASAL VERB **familiarize yourself with sth** (UK usually **familiarise yourself with sth**) C2 to learn about something: *We spent a few minutes familiarizing ourselves with the day's schedule.*

family /ˈfæm.əl.i/ noun **SOCIAL GROUP** ▷ **1** A1 [C or U, + sing/pl verb] a group of people who are related to each other, such as a mother, a father, and their children: *A new family has/have moved in next door.* ◦ *I come from a large family – I have three brothers and two sisters.* ◦ *He hasn't any family.* ◦ *He's American but his family (= relatives in the past) come/comes from Ireland.* ◦ *This film is good family entertainment (= something that can be enjoyed by parents and children together).* ◦ *How does family **life** (= being married, having children, etc.) suit you?* **2** B1 [C usually singular, U, + sing/pl verb] the children of a family: *Women shouldn't have to choose between career and family (= having children).* ◦ *Paul and Alison are hoping to **start** a family (= have children) soon.* ◦ *My dad died when we were small so my mum **raised** the family on her own.* **3** [C, + sing/pl verb] a pair of adult animals and their babies: *We've got a family **of** squirrels living in our garden.* **BIOLOGICAL GROUP** ▷ **4** [C] specialized a large group of related types of animal or plant: *The lion is a member of the cat family.*

> **Word partners for family**
>
> *come from* a [poor, large, etc] family • *bring up/raise/start* a family • *feed/support* a family • sth *runs in* the family • your *close/extended/immediate* family • a *big/close/single-parent* family • your mother's/father's *side of* the family • a *member of* sb's family • *in* sb's family

IDIOM **be in the family way** old-fashioned informal to be pregnant

ˌfamily ˈcredit noun [U] a payment made by the government in Britain to families with a low income

ˌfamily ˈdoctor noun [C] a **GP**

ˌfamily-ˈfriendly adj → **child-friendly**

ˈfamily ˌman noun [C] a man who has a wife and children, or who enjoys spending a lot of time with them

ˈfamily ˌname noun [C] a **surname**

ˌfamily ˈplanning noun [U] the use of CONTRACEPTION (= method of preventing a woman becoming pregnant) to control how many children you have and when you have them: *a family-planning clinic*

ˌfamily ˈtree noun [C] a drawing that shows the relationships between the different members of a family, especially over a long period of time

famine /ˈfæm.ɪn/ noun [C or U] C2 a situation in which there is not enough food for a great number of people, causing illness and death, or a particular period when this happens: *Another crop failure could*

*result in **widespread** famine.* ◦ *There were reports of refugees **dying of** famine.*

famished /ˈfæm.ɪʃt/ adj informal extremely hungry: *Have some dinner with us – you must be famished!*

famous /ˈfeɪ.məs/ adj A1 known and recognized by many people: *a famous actress/building* ◦ *Marie Curie is famous **for** her contribution to science.* ◦ *a city famous for its nightlife*

> **Other ways of saying famous**
>
> **Well known** or **renowned** are common alternatives to 'famous':
>
> *The area is **renowned** for its beauty.*
>
> *She's a **well-known** local artist.*
>
> If someone or something is famous everywhere, you can say **world-famous**:
>
> *a **world-famous** hotel*
>
> If someone or something is famous for some special quality or ability, you could use the word **celebrated**:
>
> *He's a **celebrated** writer of children's stories.*
>
> **Legendary** means 'very famous and admired or spoken about':
>
> *He once met the **legendary** singer, Eartha Kitt.*
>
> Someone who is famous in the entertainment business can be described as a **celebrity** or a **star**:
>
> *Many **celebrities** had been invited to the movie's premiere.*
>
> ***Stars** from the sports world attended the dinner.*
>
> **High-profile** and **prominent** can be used when someone is famous because of their importance:
>
> *He's a **prominent** member of the Saudi royal family.*
>
> ***high-profile** politicians*
>
> If someone is famous in a particular job or area of study, you could use **eminent** to describe them:
>
> *Darwin and other **eminent** scientists*
>
> **Infamous** and **notorious** are usually used when someone is famous for something bad:
>
> *He is one of history's most **notorious/infamous** criminals.*

IDIOM **famous last words** informal said when someone makes a statement that is shown very soon, and in an embarrassing way, to be wrong: *I told him categorically that we could never be anything more than friends. Famous last words! Within a few months we were engaged.*

famously /ˈfeɪ.məs.li/ adv **1** old-fashioned extremely well: *We **got along** famously.* **2** in a famous way: *He's designed dresses for many celebrities, most famously the Queen.*

fan /fæn/ noun; verb

▸noun [C] **PERSON** ▷ **1** A2 someone who admires and supports a person, sport, sports team, etc.: *More than 15,000 Liverpool fans attended Saturday's game.* ◦ *He's a big fan **of** country music.* ◦ *I'm pleased to meet you – I'm a great fan **of** your work.* **OBJECT/PIECE OF EQUIPMENT** ▷ **2** B1 a device that is used to move the air around, either an object made of folded paper or other material that you wave with your hand, or an electric device with wide blades that turn quickly: *There was no air conditioning, just a ceiling fan turning slowly.*

▸verb [T] (-nn-) **AIR** ▷ **1** to wave a fan, or something that acts as a fan, in front of your face: *It was so hot in the car that I tried to fan my**self with** the road map.* ◦ *She sat down and began fanning her face.* **2** to blow air at a

F

fans

fire to make it burn more strongly **MAKE WORSE** ▷ **3** literary to encourage bad emotions or behaviour to get worse: *to fan the violence/hatred* ◦ *The newspapers deliberately fanned the public's **fears** of losing their jobs.*

IDIOM **fan the flames** to make a dangerous or unpleasant mood or situation worse: *His speeches fanned the flames **of** racial tension.*

PHRASAL VERB **fan out** If a group of people fan out, they move in different directions from a single point.

fanatic /fəˈnæt.ɪk/ (US) /-ˈnæṭ-/ noun [C] (C2) a person whose strong admiration for something is considered to be extreme or unreasonable: *a fitness/film fanatic*

fanatical /fəˈnæt.ɪ.kəl/ (US) /-ˈnæṭ-/ adj describes someone whose admiration for something is considered to be extreme or unreasonable: *His enthusiasm for aerobics was almost fanatical.* ◦ *Gary's fanatical **about** football.* • **fanatically** /-i/ adv *The band has a fanatically loyal British following.* • **fanaticism** /-sɪ.zəm/ noun [U]

ˈfan ˌbelt noun [C] a strip of material that moves round continuously to make a fan turn and keep an engine cool

fanciable /ˈfæn.si.ə.bl̩/ adj UK informal sexually attractive: *This Ben bloke – is he fanciable?*

fancied /ˈfæn.sid/ adj mainly UK expected or thought likely to succeed: *She is the most fancied candidate for the next election.*

fancier /ˈfæn.si.əʳ/ (US) /-ɚ/ noun [C] someone who has an interest in and breeds a particular animal or plant: *a pigeon fancier*

fanciful /ˈfæn.sɪ.fəl/ adj not likely to succeed or happen in the real world: *He has some fanciful notion about converting one room of his apartment into a gallery.* • **fancifully** /-i/ adv

ˈfan ˌclub noun [C] an organization for people who admire the same music star, football team, etc.

fancy /ˈfæn.si/ verb; adj; noun

▸verb **LIKE** ▷ **1** (B1) [T] mainly UK to want to have or do something: *Do you fancy a drink this evening?* ◦ [+ -ing verb] *I didn't fancy swimm**ing** in that water.* **2** (B2) [T] mainly UK informal to be sexually attracted to someone: *He could tell she fancied him.* **3 fancy yourself** mainly UK disapproving to think you are very attractive or important: *That Dave really fancies himself, doesn't he?* **IMAGINE** ▷ **4** [I or T] to imagine or think that something is so: [+ (that)] UK *I fancied (**that**) I saw something moving in the corner.* ◦ *He fancies him**self as** a bit of a singer.* ◦ [+ to infinitive] *Who do you fancy **to** win the Cup this year?* ◦ UK old-fashioned *This isn't the first time this has happened, I fancy.* **5 fancy!** (C2) (also **fancy that!**) UK old-fashioned an expression of surprise: *'They have eight children.' 'Fancy that!'*

IDIOM **fancy sb's chances** mainly UK to think that someone is likely to succeed: *I don't fancy his chances **of** getting his novel published.*

▸adj **DECORATIVE** ▷ **1** decorative or complicated: *I wanted a simple black dress, nothing fancy.* ◦ *The decor was rather fancy for my tastes.* ◦ *fancy cakes* **EXPENSIVE** ▷ **2** informal expensive: *We stayed in a fancy hotel near the Champs-Élysées.* ◦ *a fancy restaurant*

▸noun **STH/SB YOU LIKE** ▷ **1 passing fancy** something that you like very much for a short period: *But for me, parachuting was no passing fancy.* **2 take a fancy to sth/sb** to start liking something or someone very much: *Laura's taken a fancy to Japanese food.* **3 take/tickle your fancy** informal If something takes/tickles your fancy, you like it and want to have or do it: *I looked in a lot of clothes shops but nothing really tickled my fancy.* **IMAGINATION** ▷ **4** [U] literary the imagination → See **flight of fancy**

ˌfancy ˈdress noun [U] UK (US **ˈdress-ˌup**) the special clothes that you wear for a party where everyone dresses as a particular type of character or thing: *a fancy-dress **party*** ◦ *I thought he was **in** fancy dress.*

ˌfancy-ˈfree adj [after verb] (also **ˈfootloose and ˌfancy-free**) free to do what you like and go where you like because you have no responsibilities such as a family or a relationship

ˈfancy ˌman/ˌwoman noun [C] old-fashioned the person you are having a sexual relationship with, but are not married to

fandango /fænˈdæŋ.gəʊ/ (US) /-goʊ/ noun [C] (plural **fandangos**) a fast Spanish dance performed by a man and a woman dancing close together

fanfare /ˈfæn.feəʳ/ (US) /-fer/ noun [C] a loud, short piece of music played on BRASS instruments, often to announce something important

fang /fæŋ/ noun [C] a long, sharp tooth: *The dog growled and bared its fangs.*

fangs

ˈfan ˌheater noun [C] a machine that runs on electricity, which blows heated air into a room

fanlight /ˈfæn.laɪt/ noun [C] (US usually **transom**) a small window over the top of a door

ˈfan ˌmail noun [U] letters that are sent to a famous person by people who admire that person

Fannie Mae /fæn.iˈmeɪ/ noun trademark Federal National Mortgage Association: a US government organization that buys and sells LOANS (= money that has been borrowed) on the financial markets in order to raise more money to lend to home buyers → Compare **Freddie Mac**

fanny /ˈfæn.i/ noun [C] **1** UK offensive a woman's sexual organs **2** US old-fashioned informal a person's bottom

ˈfanny ˌpack noun [C] US (UK **bumbag**) a small bag fixed to a long strap that you fasten around your waist, used for carrying money, keys, etc.

fansite /ˈfæn.saɪt/ noun [C] a website for people who like a particular actor, television programme, etc.

fantasia /fænˈteɪ.zi.ə/ noun [C] a piece of music with no fixed form, or one consisting of tunes that many people know or recognize

fantasist /ˈfæn.tə.sɪst/ noun [C] someone who often

has fantasies, or who confuses fantasy and what is real

fantasize (UK usually **fantasise**) /ˈfæn.tə.saɪz/ **verb** [I or T] to think about something very pleasant that is unlikely to happen: *He fantasized* ***about*** *winning the Nobel Prize.* ◦ [+ that] *As a child, Emma fantasized* ***that*** *she would do something heroic.*

fantastic /fænˈtæs.tɪk/ **adj** **GOOD** ▷ **1** A2 informal extremely good: *You look fantastic in that dress.* ◦ *We had a fantastic time.* ◦ *They've won a holiday? How fantastic!* **NOT REAL** ▷ **2** (also **fantastical** /-tɪ.kəl/) strange and imaginary, or not reasonable: *He drew fantastic animals with two heads and large wings.* ◦ *fantastical tales (= about imaginary things)* **3** very unusual, strange, or unexpected: *It* ***seemed*** *fantastic that they still remembered her 50 years later.* **LARGE** ▷ **4** A fantastic amount is very large: *She must be earning a fantastic amount of money.* • **fantastically** /-tɪ.kəl.i/ **adv** B2 *They're fantastically rich.* ◦ *They're doing fantastically well.*

fantasy /ˈfæn.tə.si/ **noun** [C or U] B2 a pleasant situation that you enjoy thinking about but is unlikely to happen, or the activity of thinking itself: *Steve's favourite fantasy was to own a big house and a flashy car.* ◦ ***sexual*** *fantasies* ◦ *She retreated into a fantasy* ***world****, where she could be anything she wanted.*

fanzine /ˈfæn.ziːn/ **noun** [C] a magazine written by people who admire a sports team, musicians, etc., for other people with the same special interest → See also **fan**

FAQ /ˌef.eɪˈkjuː/ **noun** [C] abbreviation for frequently asked question: a question in a list of questions and answers intended to help people understand a particular subject: *If you have any problems, consult the FAQs on our website.*

> **! Common mistake: far or away?**
>
> **Warning:** choose the correct adverb!
>
> **Far** is mainly used in questions and negative sentences to talk in general about distance in space or time:
>
> *How far is Cambridge from London?*
>
> *Cambridge isn't far from London.*
>
> To talk about a specific distance, don't say 'far', say **away**:
>
> ~~*My host family lived four miles far from the school.*~~
>
> *My host family lived four miles away from the school.*

far /fɑːr/ US /fɑːr/ **adv; adj**

▸**adv** (**farther**, **farthest** or **further**, **furthest**) **DISTANCE** ▷ **1** A2 at, to, or from a great distance in space or time: *How far is it* ***from*** *Australia to New Zealand?* ◦ *Is the station far* ***away****?* ◦ *She doesn't live far* ***from*** *here.* ◦ *He felt lonely and far* ***from*** *home.* ◦ *One day, perhaps far* ***in/into*** *the future, you'll regret what you've done.* **2 as/so far as I know** B2 used to say what you think is true, although you do not know all the facts: *He isn't coming today, as far as I know.* **3 as/so far as I'm concerned** B2 used to say what your personal opinion is about something: *She can come whenever she likes, as far as I'm concerned.* **4 as/so far as I can tell** used to say what you have noticed or understood: *There's been no change, as far as I can tell.* **5 far be it from me to** I certainly would not: *Far be it from me to tell you how to run your life.* **6 far from sth** C1 certainly not something: *The situation is far from clear.* **7 far from being/doing sth** C2 used to describe something that is almost the opposite of something else: *She insisted that, far from being easy, it would be a difficult period for all concerned.* **8 far from it** C1 certainly not: *He's not handsome – far from it.* **9 from far and wide** from a large number of places: *People came from far and wide to see the house.* **10 go so far as to do sth** C2 to be willing to do something that is extreme: *It's good, but I wouldn't go so far as to say that it's great.* **11 so far** B1 until now: *So far we've made £32,000.* **12 so far so good** C2 used to say that an activity has gone well until now: *I've found a tin of beans. So far so good, but where is the tin opener?* **AMOUNT** ▷ **13** B2 very much: *This car is far* ***better*** *than our old one.* ◦ *It cost far* ***more*** *(money) than I could afford.* ◦ *He loses his temper far* ***too*** *often.* ◦ *I'd far* ***rather/sooner*** *go to the theatre than watch a DVD.* **14 by far** B2 by a great amount: *They are by far* ***the best*** *students in the class.*

IDIOMS **as far as it goes** used to say that something has good qualities but could be better: *It's a good essay as far as it goes.* • **be a far cry from sth** C1 to be completely different from something: *This flat is a far cry from the house they had before.* • **go far** (also **go a long way**) informal to be very successful in the future: *She's a very talented writer – I'm sure she'll go far.* • **go too far** informal C2 to behave in a way that upsets or annoys people: *It's all very well having a joke but sometimes you go too far.*

▸**adj** **1** B2 describes something that is not near, or the part of something that is most DISTANT from the centre or from you: *The station isn't far – we could easily walk it.* ◦ [before noun] *The children ran to the far* ***side/corner*** *of the room.* **2 far left/right** C2 refers to political groups whose opinions are very extreme: *supporters of the far left*

faraway /ˌfɑː.rəˈweɪ/, /ˈfɑː.rə.weɪ/ US /ˌfɑːr.ə-/ **adj** [before noun] **1** C2 literary a long way away: *They travelled to faraway* ***lands/places****.* **2** C2 describes a person's expression which shows that they are not thinking about what is happening around them: *There was a faraway* ***look*** *in his eyes.*

farce /fɑːs/ US /fɑːrs/ **noun** **PLAY** ▷ **1** [C] a humorous play or film where the characters become involved in unlikely situations **2** [U] the style of writing or acting in this type of play: *The play suddenly changes from farce to tragedy.* **SITUATION** ▷ **3** [C] disapproving a silly or MEANINGLESS situation or action: *No one had prepared anything so the meeting was a bit of a farce.* • **farcical** /ˈfɑː.sɪ.kəl/ US /ˈfɑːr-/ **adj** disapproving *The whole situation has become farcical.* • **farcically** /ˈfɑː.sɪ.kəl.i/ US /ˈfɑːr-/ **adv** disapproving

fare /feər/ US /fer/ **noun; verb**

▸**noun** **PAYMENT** ▷ **1** B1 [C] the money that you pay for a journey on a vehicle such as a bus or train: *Train fares are going up again.* **2** [C] someone who pays to be driven somewhere in a taxi **FOOD** ▷ **3** [U] old-fashioned the type of food that is served in a restaurant: *a pub serving traditional British fare*

▸**verb** [I usually + adv/prep] old-fashioned to succeed or be treated in the stated way: *How did you fare in your exams?* ◦ *Low-paid workers will fare* ***badly/well*** *under this government.*

the ˌFar ˈEast **noun** the countries of East Asia, including China, Japan, North and South Korea, and Indonesia → Compare **the Middle East**

farewell /ˌfeəˈwel/ US /ˌfer-/ **exclamation; noun**

▸**exclamation** old-fashioned or formal goodbye

▸**noun** [C] formal an occasion when someone says goodbye: *We* ***said*** *our* ***sad*** *farewells and got on the bus.* ◦ *He* ***bid*** *us both a* ***fond*** *(= affectionate) farewell.* ◦ *a farewell party*

ˌfar-ˈfetched adj very unlikely to be true, and difficult to believe: *a far-fetched idea/story*

ˌfar-ˈflung adj literary describes places that are a great distance away, or something that is spread over a very large area: *The news spread to all corners of our far-flung empire.*

ˌfar ˈgone adj informal very drunk, ill, or in some other advanced and bad state: *He was so far gone that he could hardly walk.*

farm /fɑːm/ (US) /fɑːrm/ **noun; verb**
▸**noun** [C] **1** A1 an area of land, together with a house and buildings, used for growing crops and/or keeping animals as a business: *a dairy/arable farm* ◦ *farm animals* ◦ *fresh farm produce* ◦ *farm workers* ◦ *She spent the summer working* ***on a*** *farm.* **2** a place where a particular type of animal is raised in large numbers to be sold: *a sheep/fish farm*
▸**verb** [T] to use land for growing crops and/or raising animals as a business: *The Stamfords have farmed this land for over a hundred years.*

PHRASAL VERBS **farm sth out** to give work to other people to do: *Magazines often farm out articles* ***to*** *freelance journalists.* • **farm sb out** disapproving to arrange for another person to take care of someone, especially your child: *Almost since birth, their baby has been farmed out* ***to*** *nannies and nurseries.*

farmer /ˈfɑː.məʳ/ (US) /ˈfɑːr.mɚ/ **noun** [C] A2 someone who owns or takes care of a farm: *a dairy/sheep farmer*

ˈfarmers' ˌmarket noun [C] a regular event in a town or city when farmers come to sell their fruit, vegetables, eggs, meat, etc. directly to customers

farmhand /ˈfɑːm.hænd/ (US) /ˈfɑːrm-/ **noun** [C] a person who is paid to work on a farm

farmhouse /ˈfɑːm.haʊs/ (US) /ˈfɑːrm-/ **noun; adj**
▸**noun** [C] the main house on a farm where the farmer lives
▸**adj** [before noun] describes food that is made using traditional methods: *farmhouse cheddar*

farming /ˈfɑː.mɪŋ/ (US) /ˈfɑːr-/ **noun** [U] B1 the activity of working on a farm or organizing the work there

farmland /ˈfɑːm.lænd/ (US) /ˈfɑːrm-/ **noun** [U] land that is used for or is suitable for farming

farmstead /ˈfɑːm.sted/ (US) /ˈfɑːrm-/ **noun** [C] US the house belonging to a farm and the buildings around it

farmyard /ˈfɑːm.jɑːd/ (US) /ˈfɑːrm.jɑːrd/ **noun** [C] (US usually **barnyard**) an area surrounded by or near farm buildings: *farmyard animals/smells*

ˌfar-ˈoff adj **1** describes a time that is a long way from the present, or in the DISTANT past or future: *some point in the far-off future* **2** describes a place that is a great distance away

ˌfar ˈout adj; exclamation
▸**adj** slang strange and unusual: *I've seen the video – it's pretty far out.*
▸**exclamation** old-fashioned slang excellent: *You got the job? Far out!*

farrago /fəˈrɑː.gəʊ/ (US) /-goʊ/ **noun** [C] (plural **farragos** or US **farragoes**) US formal disapproving a confused mixture: *He told us a farrago* ***of*** *lies.*

ˌfar-ˈreaching adj Something far-reaching has a great influence on many people or things: *These new laws will have far-reaching benefits for all working mothers.*

farrier /ˈfær.i.əʳ/ (US) /-ɚ/ **noun** [C] specialized a person who makes and fits metal plates for horses' feet

ˌfar-ˈsighted adj **WISE** ▷ **1** UK having good judgment about what will be needed in the future and making wise decisions based on this: *Buying those shares was a very far-sighted move – they must be worth ten times their original value now.* **SEEING** ▷ **2** US (UK **ˌlong-ˈsighted**) describes someone who has difficulty seeing things that are close: *I'm so far-sighted, I can't read the newspaper without my glasses.*

fart /fɑːt/ (US) /fɑːrt/ **verb; noun**
▸**verb** [I] very informal to release gas from the bowels through the bottom

PHRASAL VERB **fart about/around** UK offensive to waste time doing silly or unnecessary things: *Stop farting about and help me tidy up.*

▸**noun** [C] **PERSON** ▷ **1** offensive a boring, annoying, or unpleasant person: *He's a pompous* ***old*** *fart.* **GAS** ▷ **2** very informal an escape of gas from the bowels: *to do a fart*

farther /ˈfɑː.ðəʳ/ (US) /ˈfɑːr.ðɚ/ **adv; adj**
▸**adv** comparative of **far**: to a greater distance: *How much farther is it to the airport?* ◦ *The fog's so thick, I can't see farther* ***than*** *about ten metres.*
▸**adj** a greater distance from something: *It was farther to the shops* ***than*** *I expected.* ◦ *He swam to the farther side of the lake.*

farthest /ˈfɑː.ðɪst/ (US) /ˈfɑːr-/ **adv; adj**
▸**adv** superlative of **far**: to the greatest distance: *What's the farthest you've ever run?*
▸**adj** at the greatest distance from sth: *The farthest landmark visible is about 30 km away.*

farthing /ˈfɑː.ðɪŋ/ (US) /ˈfɑːr-/ **noun** [C] a coin worth a quarter of a PENNY in old British money

fascia /ˈfeɪ.ʃə/ (US) /ˈfæ.ʃə/ **noun** [C] **VEHICLE** ▷ **1** UK formal the DASHBOARD in a motor vehicle **SHOP** ▷ **2** the sign above the window of a shop, where the shop's name is written **PHONE** ▷ **3** a cover for a mobile phone

fascinate /ˈfæs.ɪ.neɪt/ **verb** [T] C1 to interest someone a lot: *Science has always fascinated me.* ◦ *Anything to do with planes and flying fascinates him.*

fascinated /ˈfæs.ɪ.neɪ.tɪd/ (US) /-t̬ɪd/ **adj** B2 extremely interested: *We watched fascinated as he cleaned and repaired the watch.* ◦ *I was fascinated* ***to*** *hear about his travels in Japan.* ◦ *They were absolutely fascinated by the game.*

fascinating /ˈfæs.ɪ.neɪ.tɪŋ/ (US) /-t̬ɪŋ/ **adj** B2 extremely interesting: *The book offers a fascinating glimpse of the lives of the rich and famous.*

fascination /ˌfæs.ɪˈneɪ.ʃən/ **noun** [S or U] C1 the fact of finding someone or something fascinating: *Miller's fascination* ***with*** *medieval art dates from her childhood.* ◦ *Mass murders* ***hold*** *a gruesome fascination* ***for*** *the public.*

fascinator /ˈfæs.ɪ.neɪ.təʳ/ (US) /-t̬ɚ/ **noun** [C] a decoration for the head, like a small hat, that some women wear at formal events such as WEDDINGS

Fascism /ˈfæʃ.ɪ.zəm/ **noun** [U] a political system based on a very powerful leader, state control, and being extremely proud of country and race, and in which political opposition is not allowed

fascist /ˈfæʃ.ɪst/ **adj; noun**
▸**adj** (also **fascistic**) based on or supporting fascism: *fascist groups* ◦ *a fascist dictator/regime*
▸**noun** [C] **1** someone who supports fascism **2** a person of the far right in politics **3** disapproving someone who does not allow any OPPOSITION: *He reckons all policemen are fascists and bullies.*

fashion /ˈfæʃ.ən/ **noun; verb**
▸**noun POPULAR STYLE** ▷ **1** A2 [C or U] a style that is popular at a particular time, especially in clothes, hair, make-up, etc.: *Long hair is back* ***in*** *fashion for*

men. ◦ *Fur coats have gone* ***out of*** *fashion.* ◦ *a programme with features on sport and fashion* ◦ *She always wears* ***the latest*** *fashions.* ◦ *There was a fashion* ***for*** *keeping reptiles as pets.* **2 follow (a) fashion** to do what is popular at the time **3 like it's going out of fashion** informal If you use something like it's going out of fashion, you use large amounts of it very quickly: *Emma spends money like it's going out of fashion.* **MANNER** ▷ **4** [S] a way of doing things: *The rebel army behaved in a brutal fashion.* **5 after a fashion** If you can do something after a fashion, you can do it, but not well: *I can cook, after a fashion.*

> **Word partners for fashion**
>
> *follow* fashion • *come into/go out of* fashion • fashions *change* • the *latest* fashion • be *in* fashion • a fashion *for* sth

▸verb [T] formal to make something using your hands: *He fashioned a hat for himself* ***from/out of*** *newspaper.*

fashionable /ˈfæʃ.ən.ə.bl̩/ adj **1** B1 popular at a particular time: *a fashionable nightclub/restaurant* ◦ *fashionable ideas/clothes* ◦ ***It's*** *not fashionable* ***to*** *wear short skirts at the moment.* **2** wearing clothes, doing things, and going to places that are in fashion: *A fashionable couple posed elegantly at the next table.* • **fashionably** /-bli/ adv *fashionably dressed*

> **Other ways of saying fashionable**
>
> If something is fashionable, in informal English you can say that it is **in**:
>
> *Short jackets are* ***in*** *this season.*
>
> **Cool**, **hip**, and **trendy** are all informal words that mean 'fashionable':
>
> *He was wearing a pair of* ***cool*** *sunglasses.*
>
> ***trendy*** *clothes*
>
> A slang word for things which are fashionable in an unusual and noticeable way is **funky**:
>
> *You will look and feel great in these* ***funky*** *shoes.*
>
> **Chic** can be used about things that are very stylish and fashionable:
>
> *a* ***chic*** *restaurant*
>
> You can use the phrase **the latest thing** for something that is new and fashionable:
>
> *This doll is* ***the latest thing*** *for young girls.*
>
> If something is always fashionable because it has a simple style, you could describe it as **classic**:
>
> *She was wearing a* ***classic*** *black suit.*

ˈfashion-ˌconscious adj interested in the latest fashions and in wearing fashionable clothes: *your average fashion-conscious teenager*

ˌfashion-ˈforward adj informal **1** interested in fashion and wearing things that will soon become very fashionable: *clothes for fashion-forward teenagers* **2** more modern than things that are fashionable now: *fashion-forward jeans*

fashionista /fæʃ.ənˈiː.stə/ noun [C] someone who works in or writes about the fashion industry

ˈfashion ˌshow noun [C] a show for the public where MODELS wear new styles of clothes

ˈfashion ˌstatement noun [C] clothes that you wear or something else that you own in order to attract attention and show other people the type of person you are: *I thought I'd be bold and* ***make*** *a fashion statement.*

ˈfashion ˌvictim noun [C] someone who always wears very fashionable clothes even if the clothes sometimes make them look silly

fast /fɑːst/ (US) /fæst/ adj; adv; adv, adj; noun; verb

▸adj **QUICK** ▷ **1** A1 moving or happening quickly, or able to move or happen quickly: *fast cars* ◦ *a fast swimmer* ◦ *Computers are getting faster all the time.* ◦ *The fast train (= one that stops at fewer stations and travels quickly) to London takes less than an hour.* **2** If your watch or clock is fast, it shows a time that is later than the correct time. **3** specialized describes photographic film which allows you to take pictures when there is not much light or when things are moving quickly **4 fast and furious** describes something that is full of speed and excitement **IMMORAL** ▷ **5** old-fashioned disapproving without moral principles: *a fast crowd* ◦ *a fast woman* **FIXED** ▷ **6** If the colour of a piece of clothing is fast, the colour does not come out of the cloth when it is washed.

> **Other ways of saying fast**
>
> If you want to use 'fast' as an adjective, a very common alternative is **quick**:
>
> *I tried to catch him, but he was too* ***quick*** *for me.*
>
> If something is done fast, without waiting, you can use the adjectives **prompt**, **speedy**, or **swift**:
>
> *A* ***prompt*** *reply would be very much appreciated.*
>
> *He made a* ***speedy*** *recovery.*
>
> *His comments caused a* ***swift*** *response.*
>
> If something is done too fast, without thinking carefully, the adjectives **hasty** and **hurried** are often used:
>
> *I don't want to make a* ***hasty*** *decision.*
>
> *We left early after a* ***hurried*** *breakfast.*
>
> A fast walk is often described as **brisk**:
>
> *We took a* ***brisk*** *walk through the park.*
>
> The adjective **rapid** is often used to describe fast growth or change:
>
> *The 1990's were a period of* ***rapid*** *change/growth.*
>
> If you want to use 'fast' as an adverb, a very common alternative is **quickly**:
>
> *The problem needs to be solved as* ***quickly*** *as possible.*
>
> If someone does something very fast, in informal situations you can use the expression **in a flash**:
>
> *I'll be back* ***in a flash****.*

▸adv A2 quickly: *The accident was caused by people driving too fast in bad conditions.* ◦ *You'll have to act fast.* ◦ *Children's publishing is a fast-growing business.*

IDIOMS **as fast as your legs would carry you** as quickly as possible: *He scuttled back into the house as fast as his legs would carry him.* • **play fast and loose with sth/sb** to treat something or someone without enough care: *Like many film-makers, he plays fast and loose with the facts to tell his own version of the story.*

▸adv, adj C2 firmly fixed: *The glue had set and my hand was* ***stuck*** *fast.* ◦ *He tried to get away, but she held him fast.*

IDIOM **hold/stand fast** to firmly remain in the same position or keep the same opinion: *The rebels are standing fast and refuse to be defeated.* ◦ *He held fast* ***to*** *his principles.*

▸noun [C] a period of time when you eat no food: *Hundreds of prisoners began a fast in protest about prison conditions.*

▸verb [I] to eat no food for a period of time: *One day a week he fasts for health reasons.*

fastball /ˈfɑːst.bɔːl/ (US) /ˈfæst.bɑːl/ noun [C] US a type of high-speed throw in baseball: *The pitcher wound up and let loose a fastball.*

fasten /ˈfɑː.sən/ (US) /ˈfæs.ən/ verb **1** B1 [I or T] to (cause something to) become firmly fixed together, or in position, or closed: *Make sure your seat belt is securely fastened.* ◦ *This shirt fastens at the back.* **2 fasten sth on, together, etc.** B2 to fix one thing to another: *I fastened the sticker to the windscreen.*

PHRASAL VERB **fasten on/upon sth** to give attention to something, because it is of special interest or often because you think it is the cause of a problem: *The tabloid newspapers have fastened on popular psychology.* ◦ *My mind fastened on his admission that he was an agent.*

fastener /ˈfɑːs.ən.əʳ/ US /ˈfæs.ən.ɚ/ **noun** [C] a button, ZIP, or other device for temporarily joining together the parts of things such as clothes

fastening /ˈfɑː.sən.ɪŋ/ US /ˈfæs-/ **noun** [C] a device on a window, door, box, etc. for keeping it closed

ˌfast ˈfood **noun** [U] A2 hot food such as BURGERS that is quick to cook or is already cooked and is therefore served very quickly in a restaurant

ˌfast ˈfood ˌrestaurant **noun** [C] a restaurant that serves fast food such as BURGERS

ˌfast-ˈforward **verb** [I or T] If you fast-forward a recording, or if it fast-forwards, you make it play at very high speed so that you get to the end or a later part more quickly: *I hate this song – I'll fast-forward* ***to*** *the next one.* ◦ *The tape jammed while I was fast-forwarding it.*

fastidious /fæsˈtɪd.i.əs/ **adj 1** giving too much attention to small details and wanting everything to be correct and perfect: *He is very fastidious* ***about*** *how a suitcase should be packed.* **2** having a strong dislike of anything dirty or unpleasant: *They were too fastidious to eat in a fast-food restaurant.* • **fastidiously** /-li/ **adv** *fastidiously clean/dressed* • **fastidiousness** /-nəs/ **noun** [U]

ˈfast ˌlane **noun** [S] the part of a main road where vehicles travel at the fastest speed

IDIOM **life in the fast lane** C2 a way of living that is full of excitement, activity, and often danger: *Parties and women – his was a life in the fast lane.*

fastness /ˈfɑːst.nəs/ US /ˈfæst-/ **noun** FIXED ▷ **1** [U] how fast (= fixed) something is: *Test clothes for* ***colour*** *fastness before washing.* SAFE PLACE ▷ **2** [C] literary a safe place, such as a FORTRESS: *a mountain fastness*

ˈfast-talk **verb** [T] mainly US disapproving to persuade people with a lot of quick, clever, but usually dishonest talk: *He* ***fast-talked*** *his way* ***into*** *a powerful job.*

ˈfast-talker **noun** [C] informal disapproving someone who is good at persuading people to do what he or she wants

ˈfast ˌtrack **noun** [S] C2 the quickest route to a successful position: *A degree in computer science offers a fast track to the top.* • **ˈfast-track adj** [before noun] *fast-track opportunities* ◦ *They've introduced a fast-track* ***system*** *for brighter pupils which will allow thousands to take their GCSE exams two years early.*

fat /fæt/ **adj; noun**

▸**adj** (**fatter, fattest**) BIG ▷ **1** A1 having a lot of flesh on the body: *Like most women, she thinks she's fat.* ◦ *I have horrible fat thighs.* ◦ *He eats all the time but he never* ***gets*** *fat.* **2** thick or large: *He lifted a fat volume down from the shelf.* ◦ *Some producers of mineral water have made fat profits.* NO ▷ **3** [before noun] informal used in some phrases to mean very little or none: *A fat* ***lot*** *of use you are! (= You are not useful in any way.)*

IDIOM **fat chance** informal used to say that you certainly do not think that something is likely to happen: *'Perhaps they'll invite you.' 'Fat chance (of that)!'*

Other ways of saying fat

Overweight is another way of saying 'fat':

He used to be ***overweight****.*

If someone is extremely fat in a way that is bad for their health, you could use the word **obese**:

More and more children are becoming ***obese****.*

Plump is a polite way of saying that someone is fat:

He's got rather ***plump*** *since I last saw him.*

Chubby is often used about children who are fat in a pleasant and attractive way:

Look at the baby's ***chubby*** *little legs.*

Corpulent is a formal word that means 'fat':

He was ***corpulent*** *and red-faced.*

If an older man is fat, you could describe him as **portly**:

Dino was a ***portly*** *man with a bushy moustache.*

▸**noun 1** [U] the substance under the skin of humans and animals that stores energy and keeps them warm: *body fat* ◦ *Women have a layer of subcutaneous fat (= fat under the skin), which provides them with better insulation than men.* **2** B2 [C or U] a solid or liquid substance from animals or plants and used especially in cooking: *This product contains no animal fat.* ◦ *I only use vegetable fats in cooking.*

IDIOMS **the fat is in the fire** informal said when something has been said or done that will cause a lot of trouble • **live off the fat of the land** to be rich enough to enjoy the best of everything

fatal /ˈfeɪ.təl/ US /-t̬əl/ **adj 1** B2 A fatal illness, accident, etc. causes death: *This illness is fatal in almost all cases.* ◦ *the fatal shooting of an unarmed 15-year-old* **2** B2 very serious and having an important bad effect in the future: *He made the fatal* ***mistake/error*** *of believing what they told him.* ◦ *It just shows how you should never say how well things are going for you – it's fatal (= it causes bad things to happen).* • **fatally** /-i/ **adv** *Several people were injured, two fatally (= they died as a result).*

fatalism /ˈfeɪ.təl.ɪ.zəm/ US /-t̬əl-/ **noun** [U] the belief that people cannot change the way events will happen and that events, especially bad ones, cannot be avoided • **fatalist** /-ɪst/ **noun** [C] • **fatalistic** /ˌfeɪ.təlˈɪs.tɪk/ US /-t̬əl-/ **adj** • **fatalistically** /ˌfeɪ.təlˈɪs.tɪ.kəl.i/ US /-t̬əl-/ **adv**

fatality /fəˈtæl.ə.ti/ US /-t̬i/ **noun** [C] a death caused by an accident or by violence, or someone who has died in either of these ways: *Britain has thousands of road fatalities (= deaths on roads) every year.* ◦ *The first fatalities of the war were civilians.*

ˌfat ˈcat **noun** [C often plural] disapproving someone who has a lot of money, especially someone in charge of a company who has the power to increase their own pay: *fat cat bosses/directors*

fate /feɪt/ **noun 1** B2 [C usually singular] what happens to a particular person or thing, especially something final or negative, such as death or defeat: *We want to* ***decide*** *our own fate.* ◦ *His fate is now in the hands of the jury.* ◦ *The disciples were terrified that they would* ***suffer/meet*** *the same fate as Jesus.* **2** B2 [U] a power that some people believe causes and controls all events, so that you cannot change or control the way things will happen: *Fate has brought us together.*

IDIOMS **a fate worse than death** informal humorous something you do not want to experience because it is so unpleasant: *When you're 16, an evening at home with your parents seems like a fate worse than death.* • **the Fates** three GODDESSES who the ancient Greeks believed controlled people's lives and decided when people must die

fated /ˈfeɪ.tɪd/ (US) /-t̬ɪd/ **adj** [after verb] not able to be avoided because planned by a power that controls events: [+ that] *It seemed fated **that** we would get married.* ◦ [+ to infinitive] *She says she was fated **to** become a writer.*

fateful /ˈfeɪt.fəl/ **adj** [before noun] having an important and usually negative effect on the future: *the fateful **day** of President Kennedy's assassination* ◦ *He made the fateful decision to send in the troops.*

ˌfat ˈfinger noun [U] informal a situation in which you press the wrong button by accident when you are using a computer KEYBOARD • **ˌfat-ˈfinger verb** [T] informal to press the wrong button by accident when you are using a computer KEYBOARD: *I thought the computer wasn't working but I must have fat-fingered my password.* • **ˌfat-ˈfingered adj** informal *fat-fingered office workers*

ˌfat-ˈfree adj describes food that contains no fat

fathead /ˈfæt.hed/ noun [C] informal a stupid person • **fatheaded** /ˌfætˈhed.ɪd/ **adj**

father /ˈfɑː.ðər/ (US) /-ðɚ/ **noun; verb**

▸noun [C] **PARENT** ▷ **1** (A1) a male parent: *My father took me to watch the football every Saturday.* ◦ *The children's father came to collect them from school.* ◦ [as form of address] formal or old-fashioned *Please may I go, Father?* **IN RELIGION** ▷ **2** (also **Father**, written abbreviation **Fr**) (the title of) a Christian priest, especially a Roman Catholic or Orthodox priest: *Father O'Reilly* ◦ [as form of address] *Are you giving a sermon, Father?* **3** (also **Father**) a name for the Christian God: *God the Father* ◦ *Our Father, who art in heaven…*

IDIOM **the father of sth** the man who began something or first made something important: *Freud was the father of psychiatry.*

▸verb [T] to become the father of a child by making a woman pregnant: *He's fathered three children.*

ˌFather ˈChristmas noun mainly UK an imaginary old man with long white hair and a BEARD and a red coat who is believed by children to bring them presents at Christmas, or a person who dresses as this character for children

ˈfather ˌfigure noun [C] an older man who you treat like a father, especially by asking for his advice, help, or support

fatherhood /ˈfɑː.ðə.hʊd/ (US) /-ðɚ-/ noun [U] the state or time of being a father: *Fatherhood is a lifelong responsibility.*

ˈfather-in-law noun [C] (plural **fathers-in-law**) (B2) the father of your husband or wife

fatherland /ˈfɑː.ðə.lænd/ (US) /-ðɚ-/ noun [C usually singular] (also **motherland**) the country in which you were born, or the country with which you feel most connected

fatherless /ˈfɑː.ðə.ləs/ (US) /-ðɚ-/ **adj** without a father: *fatherless children*

fatherly /ˈfɑː.ðəl.i/ (US) /-ðɚ.li/ **adj** describes a man or male behaviour typical of a kind and loving father: *fatherly **advice***

fathom /ˈfæð.əm/ **noun; verb**

▸noun [C] a unit for measuring the depth of water, equal to 1.8 metres or 6 feet

▸verb [T] **1** to discover the meaning of something: *For years people have been trying to fathom **(out)** the mysteries of the whale's song.* **2** to understand someone or why someone acts as they do: *I can't fathom her at all.*

fathomless /ˈfæð.əm.ləs/ adj literary **DEEP** ▷ **1** too deep to be measured: *a fathomless ocean* ◦ figurative *She gazed into the fathomless **depths** of his brown eyes.* **MYSTERIOUS** ▷ **2** impossible to understand: *I'm afraid it's a fathomless mystery.*

fatigue /fəˈtiːɡ/ **noun; verb**

▸noun **TIREDNESS/WEAKNESS** ▷ **1** [U] formal extreme tiredness: *She was **suffering from** fatigue.* **2** [U] specialized weakness in something, such as a metal part or structure, often caused by repeated bending: *The crash was caused by **metal** fatigue in one of the propeller blades.* → See also **compassion fatigue** **ARMY** ▷ **3 fatigues** [plural] **a** specialized a loose, brownish-green uniform worn by soldiers: ***army** fatigues* **b** work such as cleaning or cooking, done by soldiers, often as punishment: *Get dressed right now or you'll find yourself **on** fatigues.*

▸verb [T] formal to make someone extremely tired: *The journey had fatigued him.*

fatigued /fəˈtiːɡd/ **adj** [after verb] formal tired

fatiguing /fəˈtiː.ɡɪŋ/ **adj** formal or old-fashioned making you feel tired: *Loading and unloading ships is fatiguing work.*

fatness /ˈfæt.nəs/ noun [U] the state of being fat: *Fatness often runs in families.*

fatso /ˈfæt.səʊ/ (US) /-soʊ/ noun [C] informal disapproving a fat person: *Hey, fatso!*

ˈfat ˌsuit noun [C] a set of clothes worn by an actor to make him or her look fatter: *He donned a dress and a fat suit to play the heroine's mother.*

ˈfat ˌtax noun [C] informal a tax on food that is bad for you because it makes you fat

fatten /ˈfæt.ən/ (US) /ˈfæt̬-/ **verb**

PHRASAL VERB **fatten sb/sth up** to give an animal or a thin person a lot of food so that they become fatter: *These cattle are being fattened up for slaughter.* ◦ humorous *You're just trying to fatten me up.*

fattening /ˈfæt.ən.ɪŋ/ (US) /ˈfæt̬-/ **adj** describes food that contains a lot of fat, sugar, etc. that would quickly make you fatter if you ate a lot of it: *fattening food, such as cheese and chocolate*

fattist /ˈfæt.ɪst/ (US) /ˈfæt̬-/ **adj** informal treating someone unfairly because they are fat

fatty /ˈfæt.i/ (US) /ˈfæt̬-/ **adj; noun**

▸adj (C1) containing a lot of fat: *Goose is a very fatty meat.*

▸noun [C] (also **fatso**) informal disapproving or humorous a fat person

ˌfatty ˈacid noun [C] any of a group of chemicals, most of which are involved in the way cells operate in the body

fatuous /ˈfæt.ju.əs/ **adj** formal stupid, not correct, or not carefully thought about: *a fatuous idea* • **fatuously** /-li/ **adv** • **fatuousness** /-nəs/ noun [U]

fatwa /ˈfæt.wɑː/ noun [C] an official statement or order from an Islamic religious leader

faucet /ˈfɔː.sɪt/ (US) /ˈfɑː-/ noun [C] (B1) US for **tap**

fault /fɒlt/ (US) /fɑːlt/ **noun; verb**

▸noun **MISTAKE** ▷ **1** (B1) [U] a mistake, especially something for which you are to blame: *It's not my fault she didn't come!* ◦ *She believes it was the doctor's fault that Peter died.* ◦ *The fault **was/lay with** the organizers, who failed to make the necessary arrangements for dealing with so many people.* ◦ ***Through no** fault **of his own**, he spent a week locked up in jail.* **2** (B2)

[C] a weakness in a person's character: *He has many faults, but dishonesty isn't one of them.* **3** B2 [C] a broken part or weakness in a machine or system: *The car has a serious design fault.* ◦ *I think it's got an **electrical** fault.* ◦ *For all its faults, our transport system is still better than that in many other countries.* **4** [C] a mistake made when hitting the ball over the net, in tennis or a similar game, to begin a game **5 be at fault** B2 to have done something wrong: *Her doctor was at fault **for/in** not sending her straight to a specialist.* **6 find fault with sb/sth** C2 to criticize someone or something, especially without good reasons: *He's always finding fault with my work.* **CRACK** ▷ **7** [C] specialized a CRACK in the Earth's surface where the rock has divided into two parts which move against each other: *Surveyors say the fault **line** is capable of generating a major earthquake once in a hundred years.*

> Word partners for **fault**
>
> *all/entirely* sb's fault • your *own* fault • the fault *lies with* sth/sb

IDIOM **be kind, generous, etc. to a fault** to be extremely kind, generous, etc.: *She's a really sweet person and she's generous to a fault.*

▸verb **CRITICIZE** ▷ **1** [T] to find a reason to criticize someone or something: *I can't fault the way they dealt with the complaint.* ◦ *I can't fault you **on** your logic.* **SPORTS** ▷ **2** [I] to hit a fault in tennis and other similar games: *That's the fourth serve he's faulted **on** today.*

faultless /ˈfɒlt.ləs/ (US) /ˈfɑːlt-/ **adj** approving C2 perfect and without any mistakes: *a faultless performance* ◦ *speaking faultless French* • **faultlessly** /-li/ **adv**

ˈfault ˌline **noun** [C] **CRACK** ▷ **1** a fault (= a break in the Earth's surface) **PROBLEM** ▷ **2** a problem that may not be obvious, which could cause something to fail: *The fault lines of imperfect peace deals are already showing.*

faulty /ˈfɒl.ti/ (US) /ˈfɑːl.t̬i/ **adj** B2 A faulty machine or device is not perfectly made or does not work correctly: *faulty wiring/brakes*

faun /fɔːn/ (US) /fɑːn/ **noun** [C] an imaginary creature that is like a small man with a GOAT's back legs, a tail, ears, and horns

fauna /ˈfɔː.nə/ (US) /ˈfɑː-/ **noun** [U, + sing/pl verb] specialized all the animals that live wild in a particular area: *an expedition to explore the **flora and** fauna of Hornchurch Wood*

faux /fəʊ/ (US) /foʊ/ **adj** [before noun] not real, but made to look or seem real: *faux fur* ◦ *a faux-brick wall*

faux pas /ˌfəʊˈpɑː/ (US) /ˌfoʊ-/ **noun** [C] (plural **faux pas**) words or behaviour that are a social mistake or not polite: *I made some remark about his wife's family then realized I'd **made** a serious faux pas.*

fave /feɪv/ **noun** [C], **adj** informal for **favourite**: *'Does anyone want a sweet?' 'Ooh thanks, they're my faves.'*

favour /ˈfeɪ.vəʳ/ (US) /-vɚ/ **noun; verb**

▸noun UK (US **favor**) **SUPPORT** ▷ **1** B2 [U] the support or approval of something or someone: *These plans are unlikely to **find** favour unless the cost is reduced.* ◦ *The Council voted **in** favour **of** a £200 million housing development.* ◦ *She is **out of** favour (= unpopular) **with** her colleagues.* ◦ *Her economic theories are **in** favour (= popular) **with** the current government.* ◦ *He sent her presents in an attempt to **win** her favour.* **2 in your favour** C1 When something is in your favour, it gives you an advantage: *This candidate has a lot in her favour, especially her experience of teaching.* **3 find in sb's favour** If a judge finds in someone's favour, they say that they are not guilty. **KIND ACT** ▷ **4** B1 [C] a kind action that you do for someone: *She rang up to **ask** me a favour.* ◦ *Could you **do** me a favour – would you feed my cat this weekend?* **5** [C usually plural] an advantage that you give to someone, such as money or a good job, especially when this is unfair: *Several politicians were accused of **dispensing** favours to people who voted for them.* **PRESENT** ▷ **6** [C usually plural] a small present that you give to every guest at a WEDDING, party, etc.: *wedding favours*

IDIOMS **be free with your favours** old-fashioned to be willing to have sex with a lot of people: *She's rather too free with her favours, from what I hear.* • **do me/us a favour!** informal something you say in answer to a stupid and impossible suggestion: *'Why don't you tell the police what happened?' 'Oh, do me a favour!'* • **not do sb any favours** to do something that is likely to have a bad effect on you or on another person: *You're not well, and you're not doing **yourself** any favours by taking on extra work.* ◦ [by + -ing verb] *The government isn't doing the families of the victims any favours **by hiding** the truth about what really happened.*

▸verb [T] UK (US **favor**) **1** to support or prefer one particular possibility: *These are the running shoes favoured by marathon runners.* ◦ *In the survey, a majority of people favoured higher taxes and better public services **over** (= rather than) tax cuts.* ◦ [+ -ing verb] *I generally favour travell**ing** by night, when the roads are quiet.* **2** to give an advantage to someone or something, in an unfair way: *A strong wind will favour the bigger boats.* ◦ *She always felt that her parents favoured her brother.* • **favoured** (US **favored**) /-vəd/ (US) /-vɚd/ **adj**

PHRASAL VERB **favour sb with sth** formal to be polite and kind enough to give something to someone: *I've no idea what is happening – David has not favoured me with an explanation.*

favourable UK (US **favorable**) /ˈfeɪ.vᵊr.ə.bl/ (US) /-vɚ-/ **adj** **1** B2 showing that you like or approve of someone or something: *We have had a favourable response to the plan so far.* **2** B2 making you support or approve of someone or something: *She made a very favourable impression on us.* **3** C2 giving you an advantage or more chance of success: *favourable weather conditions*

> **!** Note:
>
> opposite **unfavourable**

• **favourably** UK (US **favorably**) /-bli/ **adv** *Our products **compare** favourably **with** (= are as good as, or better than) all the leading brands.*

favourite /ˈfeɪ.vᵊr.ɪt/ **adj; noun**

▸adj [before noun] UK (US **favorite**) A1 best liked or most enjoyed: *'What's your favourite colour?' 'Green.'* ◦ *my favourite restaurant/book/song*

▸noun [C] UK (US **favorite**) **1** B1 a thing that someone likes best or enjoys most: *How clever of you to buy chocolate chip cookies – they're my favourites.* **2** a person who is treated with special kindness by someone in authority: *the teacher's favourite* **3** C2 the person or animal most people expect to win a race or competition: *Great Gold is **the** favourite in the 2.00 race at Epsom.* ◦ [+ to infinitive] *Brazil are favourites **to** win this year's World Cup.*

ˌfavourite ˈson UK (US **ˌfavorite ˈson**) **noun** [S] a famous person, especially a politician, who is supported and praised by people in the area they come from

favouritism UK disapproving (US **favoritism**) /ˈfeɪ.vᵊr.ɪ.tɪ.zᵊm/ **noun** [U] unfair support shown to one person or group, especially by someone in authority: *A parent must be careful not to **show** favouritism **towards** any one of their children.*

fawn /fɔːn/ (US) /fɑːn/ **noun; adj; verb**
▸**noun 1** [C] a young DEER **2** [U] a pale yellowish-brown colour
▸**adj** having a pale yellowish-brown colour
▸**verb**

PHRASAL VERBS **fawn on/upon sb** If an animal such as a dog fawns on/upon you, it is very friendly towards you and rubs itself against you. • **fawn over/on sb** disapproving to praise someone too much and give them a lot of attention that is not sincere, in order to get a positive reaction: *I hate waiters who fawn over you.*

fawning /ˈfɔː.nɪŋ/ (US) /ˈfɑː-/ **adj** disapproving praising someone too much and giving them a lot of attention that is not sincere in order to get a positive reaction: *a fawning young man*

fax /fæks/ **noun; verb**
▸**noun 1** [C] (a copy of) a document that travels in electronic form along a phone line and is then printed on paper: *I'll send you a fax with the details of the proposal.* **2** [C or U] (also **fax machine**) a device or system used to send and receive documents in electronic form along a phone line: *I'll send you the agenda **by** fax.* ◦ *Have you got a fax at home?*
▸**verb** [T] (B1) to send a document using a fax machine: *I'll fax it (through/over/across) **to** you.* ◦ [+ two objects] *Fax me your reply/Fax your reply **to** me.*

faze /feɪz/ **verb** [T; not continuous] informal to surprise and worry someone: *No one is fazed by the sight of guns here any more.*

the FBI /ˌef.biːˈaɪ/ **noun** [+ sing/pl verb] abbreviation for the Federal Bureau of Investigation: one of the national police forces in the US controlled by the central government

FCO /ˌef.siːˈəʊ/ (US) /-ˈoʊ/ **noun** abbreviation for **Foreign and Commonwealth Office**

fear /fɪəʳ/ (US) /fɪr/ **noun; verb**
▸**noun** [C or U] **1** (B1) an unpleasant emotion or thought that you have when you are frightened or worried by something dangerous, painful or bad that is happening or might happen: *Trembling with fear, she handed over the money to the gunman.* ◦ *Even when the waves grew big, the boy showed no (signs of) fear.* ◦ *I have **a** fear **of** heights.* ◦ *The low profit figures simply confirmed my **worst** fears.* ◦ [+ that] *There are fears **that** the disease will spread to other countries.* **2 be in fear of your life** to be frightened that you might be killed: *Lakisha sat inside, in fear of her life, until the police came.* **3 be no fear of sth** informal to be no possibility that a particular thing will happen: *Malcolm knows the city well, so there's no fear of us getting lost (= we will not get lost).* **4 for fear that/of sth** (C2) because you are worried that a particular thing might happen: *They wouldn't let their cat outside for fear (**that**) it would get run over.* ◦ *I didn't want to move for fear of wak**ing** her up.*

> **Word partners for fear noun**
> *cause/fuel/raise/spark* fears • *express/voice* your fears • *allay/calm/ease* (sb's) fears • *heighten* fears • *overcome* a fear • fears are *growing/mounting* • sth *holds* no fear for sb • sb's *biggest/greatest/worst* fear • fear *of* sth

IDIOMS **no fear!** UK informal certainly not: *'Are you coming to the concert?' 'No fear!'* • **put the fear of God into you** to frighten you a lot • **without fear or favour** in an equal and fair way: *The appointments are made without fear or favour.*

> **Other ways of saying fear**
> See also: **frightened**
> Extreme fear can be described as **terror**:
> *She fled from the attacker in **terror**.*
> Extreme fear about something which might happen can be described as **dread**:
> *The thought of giving a speech filled me with **dread**.*
> **Alarm** is often used when someone experiences sudden fear and worry that something dangerous might happen:
> *I don't want to cause you any **alarm**, but there's a rattlesnake in the path ahead of you.*
> **Fright** can be used when you have a sudden feeling of fear:
> *The family ran from their home in **fright** when the earthquake struck.*
> If fear is sudden and stops people from thinking and behaving normally, you could use the word **panic**:
> ***Panic** spread through the crowd when someone shouted 'Fire!'*
> A **phobia** is an extreme fear of a particular thing or situation:
> *I've got a **phobia** of worms.*

▸**verb 1** (B2) [T; not continuous] to be frightened of something or someone unpleasant: *Most older employees fear unemployment.* ◦ *What do you fear most?* **2** (B2) [T; not continuous] formal to be worried or frightened that something bad might happen or might have happened: [+ (that)] *Police fear (**that**) the couple may have drowned.* ◦ formal ***It is** feared (**that**) as many as two hundred passengers may have died in the crash.* ◦ *We huddled together, fearing we might be killed.* ◦ [+ to infinitive] *Fearing **to** go herself, she sent her son to find out the news.* **3 I fear** formal used to give someone news of something bad that has happened or might happen: [+ (that)] *I fear (**that**) she's already left.*

IDIOM **never fear** (also **fear not**) old use or humorous do not worry: *Never fear, I'll take good care of him.*

PHRASAL VERB **fear for sb/sth** formal to be worried about something, or to be worried that someone is in danger: *Her parents fear for her safety.*

fearful /ˈfɪə.fəl/ (US) /ˈfɪr-/ **adj** FRIGHTENED ▷ **1** (C2) formal frightened or worried about something: *He hesitated before ringing her, fearful **of** what she might say.* ◦ *She's fearful (**that**) she may lose custody of her children.* BAD ▷ **2** UK old-fashioned very bad: *a fearful argument* • **fearfulness** /-nəs/ **noun** [U]

fearfully /ˈfɪə.fəl.i/ (US) /ˈfɪr-/ **adv 1** with fear: *Fearfully, he walked closer to the edge.* **2** UK old-fashioned extremely: *These cakes are fearfully good.*

fearless /ˈfɪə.ləs/ (US) /ˈfɪr-/ **adj** (C2) having no fear: *a fearless fighter* • **fearlessly** /-li/ **adv** • **fearlessness** /-nəs/ **noun** [U]

fearsome /ˈfɪə.səm/ (US) /ˈfɪr-/ **adj** formal frightening: *a fearsome reputation* ◦ *a fearsome display of violence* • **fearsomely** /-li/ **adv**

feasibility /ˌfiː.zəˈbɪl.ɪ.ti/ (US) /-ə.t̬i/ **noun** [U] the possibility that can be made, done, or achieved, or is reasonable: *We're looking at the feasibility **of** building a shopping centre there.*

feasible /ˈfiː.zə.bl/ adj **1** C1 able to be made, done, or achieved: *With the extra resources, the scheme now seems feasible.* ◦ [+ to infinitive] *It may be feasible to clone human beings, but is it ethical?* **2** possible or reasonable: ***It's** quite feasible* (***that***) *we'll get the money.* • **feasibly** /-bli/ adv

feast /fiːst/ noun; verb
▸noun **FOOD** ▷ **1** C1 [C] a special meal with very good food or a large meal for many people: *'What a feast!' she said, surveying all the dishes on the table.* ◦ *a wedding feast* **ENJOYABLE THING** ▷ **2** [S] something that is very enjoyable to see, hear, experience, etc.: *a **visual** feast* ◦ *His food is a feast **for the eyes** as well as the palate.* **3** [S] a collection of something to be enjoyed: *The team contains a veritable feast **of** international talent.* **CELEBRATION** ▷ **4** [C] a day on which a religious event or person is remembered and celebrated: *the Feast of St James/the Passover* ◦ *a Muslim feast day*
▸verb

IDIOM **feast your eyes on sth/sb** literary to look at someone or something with great enjoyment: *As you cruise the waterways, feast your eyes on the gorgeous views of the illuminated city.*

PHRASAL VERB **feast on sth** literary C2 to eat a lot of good food and enjoy it very much: *We feasted on smoked salmon and champagne.*

feat /fiːt/ noun [C] C2 something difficult needing a lot of skill, strength, courage, etc. to achieve it: *The Eiffel Tower is a remarkable feat **of** engineering.* ◦ *She's performed remarkable feats of organization for the office.*

IDIOM **be no mean feat** informal C2 to be a great achievement: *Getting the job finished in under a week was no mean feat.*

feather /ˈfeð.əʳ/ US /-ɚ/ noun; verb
▸noun [C] B2 one of the many soft, light things which cover a bird's body, consisting of a long, thin central part with material like hairs along each side: *peacock/ostrich feathers* ◦ *feather **pillows*** (= *those containing feathers*) ◦ *The bird **ruffled** its feathers.*

IDIOMS **be (as) light as a feather** to be very light in weight • **a feather in your cap** an achievement to be proud of: *It's a real feather in our cap to be representing Britain in this contest.*

▸verb [T] specialized to turn OARS (= poles with flat ends used to move a boat) so that the flat parts are horizontal above the water while you prepare for the next pull

IDIOM **feather your own nest** to make yourself rich, especially in a way that is unfair or dishonest

featherbed /ˌfeð.əˈbed/ US /-ɚ-/ verb [T] (-dd-) disapproving to protect someone, especially a group of workers, too much and make things easy for them • **featherbedding** /-ɪŋ/ noun [U] *The taxpayer was forced to fund the featherbedding of a privatized rail company.*

ˌfeather ˈboa noun [C] a long, thin piece of clothing made of feathers, and worn around the neck, especially by women

featherbrained /ˈfeð.ə.breɪnd/ US /-ɚ-/ adj informal silly or often forgetting things

ˌfeather ˈduster noun [C] a stick with feathers fixed to one end, used for cleaning dust from delicate objects

feathered /ˈfeð.əd/ US /-ɚd/ adj having feathers: humorous *our feathered **friends*** (= *birds*)

featherweight /ˈfeð.ə.weɪt/ US /-ɚ-/ noun [C] a BOXER who weighs more than a BANTAMWEIGHT but less than a LIGHTWEIGHT

feathery /ˈfeð.ər.i/ US /-ɚ.i/ adj soft or delicate, or made of many very small and delicate pieces: *feathery clouds/foliage/leaves* ◦ *feathery blond hair*

feature /ˈfiː.tʃəʳ/ US /-tʃɚ/ noun; verb
▸noun **QUALITY** ▷ **1** B2 [C] a typical quality or an important part of something: *The town's main features are its beautiful mosque and ancient marketplace.* ◦ *Our latest model of phone has several new features.* ◦ *A unique feature of these rock shelters was that they were dry.* **2** [C] a part of a building or of an area of land: *a geographical feature* ◦ *This tour takes in the area's best-known natural features, including the Gullfoss waterfall.* ◦ *The most striking feature of the house was a huge two-storey room running the entire breadth and height of the building.* **3** B2 [C usually plural] one of the parts of someone's face that you notice when you look at them: *He has wonderful strong features.* ◦ ***regular*** (= *even and attractive*) *features* ◦ *Her eyes are her best feature.* **ARTICLE** ▷ **4** C2 [C] a special article in a newspaper or magazine, or a part of a television or radio broadcast, that deals with a particular subject: *a double-page feature **on** global warming* **FILM** ▷ **5** [C] (also **feature film**) a film that is usually 90 or more minutes long
▸verb [I + adv/prep, T] B2 to include someone or something as an important part: *The film features James Dean as a disaffected teenager.* ◦ *This week's broadcast features a report on victims of domestic violence.* ◦ *It's an Australian company whose logo features a red kangaroo.*

ˈfeature-length adj [before noun] describes a film or television play that is 90 or more minutes long

featureless /ˈfiː.tʃə.ləs/ US /-tʃɚ-/ adj looking the same in every part, usually in a way that most people consider to be boring: *a featureless desert* ◦ *a grey featureless landscape*

febrile /ˈfiː.braɪl/ US /ˈfeb.rɪl/ adj **ACTIVE** ▷ **1** literary extremely active, or too excited, IMAGINATIVE, or emotional: *She sang with febrile intensity.* ◦ *He has a febrile **imagination**.* **FEVER** ▷ **2** specialized caused by a fever: *febrile **convulsions***

February /ˈfeb.ru.ər.i/ US /-ruː.er-/ noun [C or U] (written abbreviation **Feb.**) A1 the second month of the year, after January and before March: *Building work is expected to start **in** February.* ◦ *I was born **on** 5 February.* ◦ *We moved house **last** February.*

feces /ˈfiː.siːz/ noun [plural] mainly US for **faeces**

feckless /ˈfek.ləs/ adj formal describes people or behaviour with no energy and enthusiasm: *He was portrayed as a feckless drunk.*

fecund /ˈfek.ənd/ adj formal **1** able to produce a lot of crops, fruit, babies, young animals, etc.: *fecund soil* **2** producing or creating a lot of new things, ideas, etc.: *a fecund imagination* • **fecundity** /fəˈkʌn.də.ti/ US /-t̬i/ noun [U]

fed /fed/ past simple and past participle of **feed**

Fed /fed/ noun [C] US informal a police officer or other officer who represents the central government: *The Feds completely screwed up the arrest.*

federal /ˈfed.ər.əl/ US /-ɚ.əl/ adj **1** C1 [before noun] relating to the central government, and not to the government of a region, of some countries such as the US: *the federal government* ◦ *a federal agency/employee* **2** A federal system of government consists of a group of regions that is controlled by a central government.

ˌfederal ˈholiday noun [C] US for **national holiday**

federalism /ˈfed.ᵊr.ᵊl.ɪ.zᵊm/ (US) /ˈ-ɚ-/ noun [U] the system of giving power to a central authority

federalist /ˈfed.ᵊr.ᵊl.ɪst/ (US) /ˈ-ɚ-/ noun [C] someone who supports a federal system of government

the ˌFederal Reˈserve noun (informal **the Fed**) the CENTRAL BANK of the US

federate /ˈfed.ᵊr.eɪt/ (US) /-ə.reɪt/ verb [I or T] to join to form a federation

federation /ˌfed.ᵊrˈeɪ.ʃᵊn/ (US) /-əˈreɪ-/ noun **1** C1 [C] a group of organizations, countries, regions, etc. that have joined together to form a larger organization or government: *The United States is a federation of 50 individual states.* **2** [U] the act of forming a federation: *The federation of the six original Australian states took place in 1901.* ◦ *He's against European federation.*

fedora /fəˈdɔː.rə/ (US) /-ˈdɔːr.ə/ noun [C] a man's hat, like a TRILBY but with a wider BRIM

ˌfed ˈup adj [after verb] informal B2 bored, annoyed, or disappointed, especially by something that you have experienced for too long: *I'm fed up **with** my job.* ◦ *He **got** fed up with all the travelling he had to do.*

IDIOM **fed up to the back teeth** mainly UK informal very fed up: *I'm fed up to the back teeth **with/of** being criticized all the time.*

fee /fiː/ noun [C] B1 an amount of money paid for a particular piece of work or for a particular right or service: *legal fees* ◦ *university fees* ◦ *an entrance/registration fee* ◦ *We couldn't pay the lawyer's fee.*

feeble /ˈfiː.bl/ adj **1** C2 weak and without energy, strength, or power: *He was a feeble, helpless old man.* ◦ *The little lamp gave only a feeble light.* ◦ *Opposition to the plan was rather feeble.* **2** C2 not effective or good: *a feeble **joke/excuse*** • **feebly** /-bli/ adv

ˌfeeble-ˈminded adj without an ordinary level of intelligence, or unable to act or think in an intelligent way

feed /fiːd/ verb; noun

▸verb (**fed, fed**) **GIVE FOOD** ▷ **1** B1 [T] to give food to a person, group, or animal: *I usually feed the neighbour's cat while she's away.* ◦ *Let's feed the kids first and have our dinner after.* ◦ [+ two objects] *Do you feed your chickens corn?* ◦ *If you feed your dog **on** cakes and biscuits, it's not surprising he's so fat.* ◦ *The kids love feeding bread **to** the ducks.* **2** C1 [I or T] If a baby or animal feeds, it eats or drinks milk: *The baby only feeds once a night at the moment, thank goodness.* ◦ *Most babies can feed them**selves** by the time they're a year old.* **3** [T] to be enough food for a group of people or animals: *This amount of pasta won't feed ten people.* **4** [T] to produce or supply enough food for someone or something: *If agriculture were given priority, the country would easily be able to feed **itself**.* ◦ *Feed the world/starving.* **5** [T] to give a plant substances that will help it grow: *Don't forget to feed the tomatoes.* **PUT** ▷ **6** C1 [I or T, usually + adv/prep] to supply something to a person or thing, or put something into a machine or system, especially in a regular or continuous way: *The vegetables are fed **into** the machine at this end.* ◦ *The images are fed **over** satellite networks to broadcasters throughout the world.* ◦ [+ two objects] *A member of staff had been feeding the newspaper information/feeding information **to** the newspaper.* ◦ *Several small streams feed **into** (= join) the river near here.* **7** [T] to put fuel on or inside something that burns, to keep it burning: *Remember to feed the fire while I'm out.*

IDIOMS **be like feeding time at the zoo** humorous to be very noisy and untidy and have no order: *Tea-time in our house is like feeding time at the zoo!* • **feed sb a line** disapproving to tell someone something that is not completely true, often as an excuse: *She fed me a line about not having budgeted for pay increases this year.*

PHRASAL VERBS **feed off/on sth** to increase because of something, or to use something to succeed or get advantages: *Fascism feeds off poverty.* • **feed sb/sth up** to make a person or animal healthier or fatter by giving them a lot of food: *You've lost a lot of weight – you need feeding up a bit.*

▸noun **FOOD** ▷ **1** [C] UK (US **feeding**) an occasion when a baby has something to eat or drink: *The baby had a feed an hour ago, so she can't be hungry.* **2** [U] food eaten by animals that are not kept as pets: *cattle/animal feed* → See also **chickenfeed** **3** [C] old-fashioned a large meal **MACHINE PART** ▷ **4** [C] the part of a machine through which it is supplied with fuel or with something else that it needs: *the car's oil feed* ◦ *the printer's paper feed*

feedback /ˈfiːd.bæk/ noun [U] **OPINION** ▷ **1** B2 information or statements of opinion about something, such as a new product, that can tell you if it is successful or liked: *Have you **had** any feedback **from** customers about the new soap?* ◦ *positive/negative feedback* **MACHINE** ▷ **2** the sudden, high, unpleasant noise sometimes produced by an AMPLIFIER when sound it produces is put back into it: *Jimi Hendrix loved to fling his guitar around to get weird and wonderful sounds from the feedback.*

feedbag /ˈfiːd.bæg/ noun [C] US for **nosebag**

feeder /ˈfiː.dəʳ/ (US) /ˈfiː.dɚ/ adj; noun

▸adj [before noun] describes something that leads to or supplies a larger thing of the same type: *a feeder **road*** ◦ *a feeder school*

▸noun [C] **1** a baby or animal that eats in a particular way: *a messy/slow feeder* **2** a container for giving food to animals: *a bird feeder* **3** old-fashioned a BIB for a young child

ˈfeeding ˌfrenzy noun [C] a situation in which people try to get as much as possible of something, for example information about an event, especially in an unpleasant way: *Her sudden death sparked a feeding frenzy in the media.*

feel /fiːl/ verb; noun

▸verb (**felt, felt**) **EXPERIENCE** ▷ **1** A1 [L or T] to experience something physical or emotional: *'How are you feeling?' 'Not too bad, but I've still got a slight headache.'* ◦ *How would you feel about moving to a different city?* ◦ *He's still feeling a bit weak after his operation.* ◦ *My eyes feel really sore.* ◦ *I never feel safe when I'm being driven by Richard.* ◦ *Never in her life had she felt so happy.* ◦ *My suitcase began to feel really heavy after a while.* ◦ *I felt (= thought that I was) a complete idiot/such a fool.* ◦ *She felt his hot breath on her neck.* ◦ [+ obj + -ing verb] *I could feel the sweat trickl**ing** down my back.* ◦ *By midday, we were really feeling (= suffering from) the heat.* **2 feel like sth a** B1 to have a wish for something, or to want to do something, at a particular moment: *I feel like (**going** for) a swim.* ◦ *I feel like (hav**ing**) a nice cool glass of lemonade.* ◦ *'Are you coming to aerobics?' 'No, I don't feel like **it** today.'* **b** [+ -ing verb] to want to do something that you do not do: *He was so rude I felt like slapp**ing** his face.* **3 feel the cold** to get cold quicker and more often than most people: *As you get* *older, you tend to feel the cold more.* **4 not feel a thing** informal to not feel any pain: *'Did it hurt?' 'Not at all – I didn't feel a thing.'* **OPINION** ▷ **5** B1 [I or T] to have a particular opinion about or attitude towards something: [+ (that)] *I feel* (***that***) *I should be doing more to help her.* ◦ [(+ to be) + adj] *He had always felt him**self*** (***to be***) *inferior to his brothers.* ◦ *Do you feel very strongly* (= *have strong opinions*) *about this?* ◦ *I feel certain I'm right.* **TOUCH** ▷ **6** B2 [I or T] to touch something in order to discover something about it: [+ question word] *Just feel **how** cold my hands are!* ◦ *He gently felt the softness of the baby's cheek.* ◦ *I was feeling* (***around***) (= *searching with my hand*) *in my bag **for** the keys.*

IDIOMS **feel your age** to realize that you are no longer young: *Everybody there looked under 20 and I really felt my age.* • **feel free** If someone tells you to feel free to do something, they mean that you can do it if you want to: *Feel free **to** help yourself to coffee.* • **feel it in your bones** to believe something strongly although you cannot explain why: *It's going to be a good summer – I can feel it in my bones.* • **feel the pinch** to have problems with money because you are earning less than before: *When my father lost his job and we had to live on my mother's earnings, we really started to feel the pinch.* • **feel your way 1** to judge where you are going by touching with your hands instead of looking: *The room was so dark, I had to feel my way along the wall to the door.* **2** to act slowly and carefully because you are not certain how to do something: *It's my first month in the job so I'm still feeling my way.*

PHRASAL VERBS **feel for sb** to experience sympathy and sadness for someone because they are suffering: *I know what it's like to be lonely, so I do feel for her.* • **feel sb up** slang to touch someone sexually, especially someone you do not know, for your own excitement: *That's the second time she's been felt up on the Metro.*

▸noun **TOUCH** ▷ **1** [S] the way that something feels: *She loved the feel of silk against her skin.* **2** [C] mainly UK informal the action of touching something: *Is that shirt silk? Ooh, let me **have a** feel!* **CHARACTER** ▷ **3** [S] (also **feeling**) the character of a place or situation: *I like the decoration – it's got quite a Spanish feel **to** it.* ◦ *There was **a** feel **of** mystery about the place.* ◦ *We were there for such a short time, we didn't really **get** the feel **of*** (= *get to know*) *the place.* **UNDERSTANDING** ▷ **4 a feel for sth** (also **feeling**) a natural understanding or ability, especially in a subject or activity: *She has a real feel for language.* ◦ *I tried learning the piano, but I never had much of a feel for it.* **5 get the feel of sth** (also **feeling**) to learn how to do something, usually a new activity: *Once you get the feel of it, using a mouse is easy.*

feeler /ˈfiː.ləʳ/ US /-lɚ/ noun [C usually plural] one of the two long parts on an insect's head with which it touches things in order to discover what is around it

IDIOM **put out feelers** to make informal suggestions as a way of testing other people's opinions on something before any decisions are made

ˈfeel-good adj [before noun] causing happy and positive feelings about life: *a feel-good movie* ◦ *With the housing market picking up and consumer spending buoyant, it appears that **the** feel-good **factor*** (= *a happy and positive feeling felt by people generally*) *has returned.*

feeling /ˈfiː.lɪŋ/ noun **SENSE** ▷ **1** B1 [C or U] the fact of feeling something physical: *I had a tingling feeling in my fingers.* ◦ *I've got this strange feeling **in** my stomach.* ◦ *My toes were so cold that I'd lost all feeling in them.* **EMOTION** ▷ **2** B1 [C or U] emotion: *The feeling **of** loneliness suddenly overwhelmed him.* ◦ *There's a feeling **of** dissatisfaction with the government.* ◦ [+ that] *I got the feeling **that** I was not welcome.* ◦ *Her performance seemed to me completely lacking in feeling.* **3 feelings** [plural] B1 emotions, especially those influenced by other people: *Some people say that dogs have feelings.* ◦ *I wanted to **spare** his feelings* (= *not to upset him*)*, so I didn't tell him what she'd said about him.* **OPINION** ▷ **4** B2 [C] opinion: *My feeling is that we had better act quickly or it will be too late.*

Word partners for feeling (SENSE, EMOTION)

give sb a feeling • ***know*** the feeling • a ***fantastic/good/great/wonderful*** feeling • a ***funny/horrible/sinking/unpleasant*** feeling • a ***dizzy/sick*** feeling • a ***general/growing*** feeling • a feeling ***of*** sth

Word partners for feelings (EMOTION)

express/hide/show your feelings • ***spare*** sb's feelings • ***hurt*** sb's feelings • have ***mixed*** feelings • feelings ***run high***

Word partners for feeling (OPINION)

a ***general/growing*** feeling • ***strong*** feelings • sb's ***gut/true*** feeling • sb's ***personal*** feeling • feelings ***about/on*** sth • a feeling ***among*** [a group of people]

Other ways of saying feeling

A very common alternative to the noun 'feeling' is **emotion**:

*He finds it hard to express his **emotions**.*

The nouns **pang** or **stab** are sometimes used to describe a sudden, strong, bad feeling:

*Amelia felt a sharp **pang** of jealousy when she saw her sister's new house.*

*He felt a **stab** of regret for having behaved so badly toward his friend.*

A small amount of a sad feeling is often described as a **tinge**:

*It was with a **tinge** of sadness that she finally said goodbye.*

IDIOMS **bad feeling** UK (US **bad feelings**) C1 a situation in which people are upset or angry with each other: *I'd like to complain to the neighbours about the noise, but I don't want to cause any bad feeling* (***between*** *us*). • **hurt sb's feelings** B1 to upset someone by criticizing them or by refusing something that they have offered you

feelingly /ˈfiː.lɪŋ.li/ adv with deep and sincere emotion: *'I've just had enough!' she said feelingly.*

ˈfee-ˌpaying adj UK describes a school where parents pay the school directly for their children's education

feet /fiːt/ plural of **foot**

feign /feɪn/ verb [T] to pretend to feel something, usually an emotion: *You know how everyone feigns surprise when you tell them how old you are.* ◦ *She responded to his remarks with feigned amusement.*

feint /feɪnt/ verb [I or T] (especially in football or BOXING) to pretend to move, or to make a move, in a particular direction in order to deceive an opponent: [+ to infinitive] *Callas feinted **to** pass the ball and then shot it into the net.* ◦ *He feinted a shot to the left.* • **feint** noun [C]

feisty /ˈfaɪ.sti/ adj active, forceful, and full of determination: *a feisty lady* ◦ *He launched a feisty attack on the government.*

felafel /fəˈlæf.əl/ US /-ˈlɑː.fəl/ noun [C or U] → **falafel**

feldspar /ˈfeld.spɑːr/ US /-spɑr/ noun [C or U] specialized a common type of mineral found especially in IGNEOUS rocks such as GRANITE

felicitous /fəˈlɪs.ɪ.təs/ US /-t̬əs/ adj literary suitable or right and expressing well the intended thought or feeling: *He summed up Jack's achievements in one or two felicitous* ***phrases.*** → Opposite **infelicitous** • **felicitously** /-li/ US /-t̬əs-/ adv *a felicitously phrased speech*

felicity /fəˈlɪs.ɪ.ti/ US /-ə.t̬i/ noun literary **HAPPINESS** ▷ **1** [U] happiness, luck, or a condition that produces positive results: *the dubious felicity of marriage* **SUITABLE WORDS** ▷ **2** [U] the fact that words or remarks are suitable and express what was intended: *As a songwriter, he combined great linguistic felicity with an ear for a tune.* **3** [C usually plural] a word or remark that is suitable or right and expresses well the intended thought or feeling: *Her article contained one or two verbal felicities that will stay in my mind for years.*

feline /ˈfiː.laɪn/ adj; noun
▸adj **1** belonging or relating to the cat family: *feline leukaemia* **2** appearing or behaving like a cat: *She had pretty, almost feline features.*
▸noun [C] specialized a member of the cat family: *a wildlife park with tigers and various other felines*

fell /fel/ verb; noun; adj
▸verb **FALL** ▷ **1** past simple of **fall** **CUT DOWN** ▷ **2** [T] to cut down a tree: *A great number of trees were felled to provide space for grazing.* **3** [T] to knock someone down, especially in sports: *The boxer was felled by a punch to the head.*
▸noun [C] a hill or other area of high land, especially in northwest England
▸adj **EVIL** ▷ **1** literary or old use evil or cruel **HILL** ▷ **2** [before noun] relating to fells (= hills): *We went fell* ***walking*** *last weekend.*

IDIOM **at/in one fell swoop** If you do something at/in one fell swoop, you do it all at the same time: *I got all my Christmas shopping done in one fell swoop.*

fella /ˈfel.ə/ noun [C] not standard **1** a man: *There were a couple of fellas leaning up by the bar.* **2** a male sexual partner or BOYFRIEND: *Was she with her fella?*

fellatio /fəˈleɪ.ʃi.əʊ/ US /-oʊ/ noun [U] the sexual activity of sucking or moving the tongue across the PENIS in order to give pleasure and excitement → Compare **cunnilingus** • **fellate** /felˈeɪt/ US /ˈfeleɪt/ verb [T] to perform fellatio on a man

feller /ˈfel.ər/ US /-ɚ/ noun [C] another spelling of fella

fellow /ˈfel.əʊ/ US /-oʊ/ adj; noun
▸adj [before noun] B2 describes someone who has the same job or interests as you, or is in the same situation as you: *She introduced me to some of her fellow students.* ◦ *Our fellow travellers were mostly Spanish-speaking tourists.*
▸noun [C] **MAN** ▷ **1** informal a man, used especially in the past by people in a higher social class: *He seemed like a decent sort of a fellow.* **MEMBER** ▷ **2** a member of a group of teachers of high rank at a particular college or university or of particular ACADEMIC societies: *Georgia's a fellow of Clare College, Cambridge.* **3** a member of an official organization for a particular subject or job: *He's a fellow of the Royal Institute of Chartered Surveyors.*

ˌfellow ˈfeeling noun [U] an understanding or sympathy that you feel for another person because you have a shared experience: *There was a fellow feeling between everyone who had lived through the war.*

ˌfellow ˈman/ˈmen noun **your fellow man/men** people generally or the people living around you: *He had very little love for his fellow men.*

fellowship /ˈfel.əʊ.ʃɪp/ US /-oʊ-/ noun **GROUP** ▷ **1** [C] formal a group of people or an organization with the same purpose: *the National Schizophrenia Fellowship* **2** [U] old-fashioned a friendly feeling that exists between people who have a shared interest or are doing something as a group: *He enjoyed the fellowship of other actors in the company.* ◦ *Christian fellowship* **EDUCATION** ▷ **3** [C] the position of a fellow (= a teacher of high rank at a college): *He's been* ***elected to*** *a fellowship at Merton College.* **4** [C] an amount of money that is given to POSTGRADUATES to allow them to study a subject at an advanced level: *She's applied for a* ***research*** *fellowship.*

felon /ˈfel.ən/ noun [C] legal a person who is guilty of a serious crime

felony /ˈfel.ə.ni/ noun [C or U] UK old-fashioned or US legal (an example of) serious crime that can be punished by one or more years in prison: *a felony charge* ◦ *He was convicted of felony.*

felt /felt/ verb; noun
▸verb past simple and past participle of **feel**
▸noun [U] a type of thick, soft cloth made from a pressed mass of wool and hair: *a felt hat*

ˌfelt-ˈtip noun [C] (also **ˌfelt-tip ˈpen**, UK also **ˌfibre-ˈtip**, **ˌfibre-tip ˈpen**) a pen that has a writing point made of felt

fem. adj written abbreviation for **feminine** or **female**

female /ˈfiː.meɪl/ adj; noun
▸adj **SEX** ▷ **1** B1 belonging or relating to women, or the sex that can give birth to young or produce eggs: *She was voted the best female vocalist.* ◦ *Female lions do not have manes.* → See also **feminine 2** describes plants which produce flowers that will later develop into fruit **CONNECTING PART** ▷ **3** specialized describes a piece of equipment that has a hole or space into which another part can be fitted: *a female plug/connector* → Compare **male** • **femaleness** /-nəs/ noun [U]
▸noun [C] **1** B2 a female animal or person: *The kitten was actually a female, not a male.* ◦ *Females (= women) represent 40 percent of the country's workforce.* **2** used to refer to a woman in a way that shows no respect: *I suspect the doctor thought I was just another hysterical female.*

feminine /ˈfem.ɪ.nɪn/ adj **FEMALE** ▷ **1** C1 acting, or having qualities that are traditionally considered to be suitable for a woman: *With his long dark eyelashes, he looked almost feminine.* ◦ *The current style in evening wear is soft, romantic, and feminine.* ◦ *Her clothes are always very feminine.* → Compare **masculine** **GRAMMAR** ▷ **2** (written abbreviation **fem.**, **f**) belonging to the group of nouns that, in some languages, are not MASCULINE or NEUTER: *In French, 'table' is feminine.* **3** describes a particular form of a noun in English, such as 'actress', that refers only to a female person. These feminine forms are now being used less often. • **femininity** /ˌfem.əˈnɪn.ɪ.ti/ US /-ə.t̬i/ noun [U] usually approving *Long hair was traditionally regarded as a sign of femininity.*

feminism /ˈfem.ɪ.nɪ.zəm/ noun [U] the belief that women should be allowed the same rights, power, and opportunities as men and be treated in the same way, or the set of activities intended to achieve this state: *She had a lifelong commitment to feminism.*

feminist /ˈfem.ɪ.nɪst/ noun; adj
▸noun [C] a person who believes in feminism, often

being involved in activities that are intended to achieve change: *All her life she was an ardent feminist.* ◦ *a radical feminist*
▸**adj** relating to feminism: *the feminist movement* ◦ *feminist issues/literature*

femme fatale /ˌfæm.fəˈtɑːl/ **noun** [C] (plural **femmes fatales**) a woman who is very attractive in a mysterious way, usually leading men into danger or causing their destruction

femur /ˈfiː.məʳ/ (US) /-mɚ/ **noun** [C] (plural **femurs** or **femora**) specialized the long bone in the upper part of the leg

fen /fen/ **noun** [C or U] (also **ˈfenland**) an area of low, flat, wet land: *areas of marsh and fen* ◦ *The road to Ely leads out across the fens.*

fence /fens/ **noun**; **verb**
fence
▸**noun** [C] **STRUCTURE** ▷ **1** B2 a structure which divides two areas of land, similar to a wall but made of wood or wire and supported with posts **CRIMINAL** ▷ **2** old-fashioned slang a person who buys and sells stolen goods
▸**verb** [I] to fight as a sport with a long thin SWORD
PHRASAL VERBS **fence sth in** to build a fence around an area: *She would need to fence in the field if she was to keep a horse there.* • **fence sb in** [often passive] informal to limit someone's activity in way that annoys them or makes them unhappy: *I feel a bit fenced in at work because my boss won't let me apply for promotion.* • **fence sth off** to separate an area with a fence in order to stop people or animals from entering it: *The hill had been fenced off to stop animals grazing on it.*

ˈfence-ˌmending **noun**; **adj**
▸**noun** [U] the act of trying to help opposing sides in a disagreement to agree: *Fence-mending is what she is best at; she's a wonderful listener.*
▸**adj** [before noun] trying to help opposing sides in a disagreement to agree: *The UN Secretary General is on a fence-mending mission.*

fencer /ˈfen.səʳ/ (US) /-sɚ/ **noun** [C] a person who fences as a sport

ˈfence-ˌsitter **noun** [C] disapproving someone who supports both sides in a disagreement because they cannot make a decision or do not want to annoy or offend either side • **ˈfence-ˌsitting noun** [U]

fencing /ˈfen.sɪŋ/ **noun** [U] **STRUCTURE** ▷ **1** fences, or the materials used to make fences: *wire/wooden fencing* **SPORT** ▷ **2** the sport of fighting with long thin SWORDS: *a fencing tournament/mask* ◦ *I did a bit of fencing while I was at college.*

fend /fend/ **verb**
PHRASAL VERBS **fend for yourself** C2 to take care of and provide for yourself without depending on anyone else: *Now that the children are old enough to fend for themselves, we can go away on holiday by ourselves.* • **fend sb off** to push or send away an ATTACKER or other unwanted person: *He managed to fend off his attackers with a stick.* ◦ *She spent the entire evening fending off unwanted admirers.* • **fend sth off** to avoid dealing with something that is unpleasant or difficult: *Somehow she managed to fend off the awkward questions.*

fender /ˈfen.dəʳ/ (US) /-dɚ/ **noun** [C] **FIRE** ▷ **1** a low metal frame around an open FIREPLACE which stops the coal or wood from falling out **CAR** ▷ **2** US for **wing** or **mudguard**

ˈfender ˌbender **noun** [C] US (UK **prang**) a road accident in which the vehicles involved are only slightly damaged

feng shui /ˌfʊŋˈʃweɪ/, /ˌfeŋˈʃuːi/ **noun** [U] an ancient Chinese belief that the way your house is built and the way that you arrange objects affects your success, health, and happiness: *It's **good** feng shui to have a loving animal in your home.* ◦ *a feng shui consultant*

fennel /ˈfen.əl/ **noun** [U] a plant with a large, rounded base that is eaten as a vegetable and small, pale leaves that are used as a herb

fenugreek /ˈfen.ʊ.griːk/ **noun** [U] a plant with hard, yellowish-brown seeds, used as a spice in South Asian cooking

feral /ˈfer.əl/ **adj** existing in a wild state, especially describing an animal that was previously kept by people: *feral dogs/cats*

ferment **verb**; **noun**
▸**verb** [I or T] /fəˈment/ (US) /fɚ-/ If food or drink ferments or if you ferment it, the sugar in it changes into alcohol because of a chemical process: *You make wine by leaving grape juice to ferment until all the sugar has turned to alcohol.* • **fermentation** /ˌfɜː.menˈteɪ.ʃən/ (US) /ˌfɜː-/ **noun** [U]
▸**noun** [U] /ˈfɜː.ment/ (US) /ˈfɜː-/ literary a state of confusion, change, and lack of order or fighting: *The resignation of the president has left the country **in** ferment.*

fern /fɜːn/ (US) /fɜːn/ **noun** [C] a green plant with long stems, leaves like feathers, and no flowers

fern

ferocious /fəˈrəʊ.ʃəs/ (US) /-ˈroʊ-/ **adj** frightening and violent: *a ferocious dog* ◦ *a ferocious battle* ◦ *She's got a ferocious (= very bad) temper.* ◦ *The president came in for some ferocious criticism.* • **ferociously** /-li/ **adv** *A female lion defends her young ferociously.* • **ferocity** /-ˈrɒs.ə.ti/ (US) /-ˈrɑː.sə.t̬i/ **noun** [U] (also **ferociousness**) *The ferocity of the attack shocked a lot of people.*

ferret /ˈfer.ɪt/ **noun**; **verb**
▸**noun** [C] a small, yellowish-white animal with a long body, bred for hunting RABBITS and other small animals
▸**verb** informal **1** [I + adv/prep] to search for something by moving things around with your hands, especially in a drawer, bag, or other closed space: *I was just ferreting **around** in my drawer for my passport.* **2** [I] to search for something or someone, by looking in many places or asking many questions: *After a bit of ferreting, I managed to find his address.*
PHRASAL VERB **ferret sth out** to find out a piece of information or find someone or something, after looking in many places or asking many questions: [+ question word] *I know his name but I haven't yet managed to ferret out **where** he lives.*

Ferris wheel /ˈfer.ɪsˌwiːl/ **noun** [C] mainly US for **big wheel**

ferrous /ˈfer.əs/ **adj** specialized containing or relating to iron: *ferrous metals/compounds*

ferry /ˈfer.i/ noun; verb
▸noun [C] (also ˈ**ferry** ˌ**boat**) B1 a boat or ship for taking passengers and often vehicles across an area of water, especially as a regular service: *a car ferry* ◦ *We're going across to France* ***by/on the*** *ferry.* ◦ *We* ***took*** *the ferry to Calais.*
▸verb [T usually + adv/prep] to transport people or goods in a vehicle, especially regularly and often: *I spend most of my time ferrying the children* ***about.***

fertile /ˈfɜː.taɪl/ US /ˈfɝː.t̬əl/ adj LAND ▷ **1** C2 describes land that can produce a large number of good quality crops → Compare **barren** PEOPLE/ANIMALS/PLANTS ▷ **2** describes animals or plants that are able to produce (a lot of) young or fruit: *People get less fertile as they get older.* → Opposite **infertile 3** describes a seed or egg that is able to develop into a new plant or animal IMAGINATION ▷ **4** A fertile mind or imagination is active and produces a lot of interesting and unusual ideas.

IDIOM **fertile ground for sth** a situation or place which produces good results or a lot of ideas: *British politics remains very fertile ground for comedy.*

fertility /fəˈtɪl.ɪ.ti/ US /fɚˈtɪl.ə.t̬i/ noun [U] PEOPLE/ANIMALS/PLANTS ▷ **1** (of animals and plants) the quality of being able to produce young or fruit: *a fertility symbol* ◦ *declining fertility* ***rates*** LAND ▷ **2** (of land) the quality of producing a large number of good quality crops: *the fertility of the soil* IMAGINATION ▷ **3** literary (of the mind or imagination) the quality of producing a lot of unusual and interesting ideas

fertilize (UK usually **fertilise**) /ˈfɜː.tɪ.laɪz/ US /ˈfɝː.t̬əl.aɪz/ verb [T] LAND ▷ **1** to spread a natural or chemical substance on land or plants, in order to make the plants grow well EGG/SEED ▷ **2** to cause an egg or seed to start to develop into a new young animal or plant by joining it with a male cell: *Bees fertilize the flowers by bringing pollen.* ◦ *Once an egg is fertilized by the sperm, it becomes an embryo.* • **fertilization** (UK usually **fertilisation**) /ˌfɜː.tɪ.laɪˈzeɪ.ʃən/ US /ˌfɝː.t̬əl.aɪ-/ noun [U] *In humans, fertilization is more likely to occur at certain times of the month.*

fertilizer (UK usually **fertiliser**) /ˈfɜː.tɪ.laɪ.zəʳ/ US /ˈfɝː.t̬əl.aɪ-/ noun [C or U] a natural or chemical substance that is spread on the land or given to plants, to make plants grow well: *organic fertilizer* ◦ *a liquid/chemical fertilizer*

fervent /ˈfɜː.vənt/ US /ˈfɝː-/ adj (also **fervid**) describes beliefs that are strongly and sincerely felt or people who have strong and sincere beliefs: *a fervent supporter of the communist party* ◦ *It is his fervent* ***hope*** *that a peaceful solution will soon be found.* • **fervently** /-li/ adv *The nationalists* ***believe*** *fervently in independence for their country.* • **fervour** UK (US **fervor**) /-vəʳ/ US /-vɚ/ noun [U] (also **fervency** /-vən.si/) *nationalist/religious fervour*

fess /fes/ verb

PHRASAL VERB **fess up** [I] informal to admit that you have done something that someone else will not like

fest /fest/ noun, suffix **a beer, film, jazz, etc. fest** a special event where people can enjoy a particular activity or thing: *a media-fest*

fester /ˈfes.təʳ/ US /-tɚ/ verb [I] INJURY ▷ **1** If a cut or other injury festers, it becomes infected and produces PUS: *a festering sore* FEELING ▷ **2** If an argument or bad feeling festers, it continues so that feelings of hate or lack of satisfaction increase: *It's better to express your anger than let it fester inside you.* ◦ *a festering argument/dispute*

festival /ˈfes.tɪ.vəl/ noun [C] **1** B1 a special day or period, usually in memory of a religious event, with its own social activities, food, or ceremonies: *a Jewish/Christian/Hindu festival* **2** B1 an organized set of special events, such as musical performances: *a folk/pop/rock festival* ◦ *The Brighton Festival is* ***held*** *every year around May time.* ◦ *the Cannes Film Festival*

festive /ˈfes.tɪv/ adj having or producing happy and enjoyable feelings suitable for a festival or other special occasion: *a festive mood/occasion* ◦ *The hall looked very festive with its Christmas tree.*

the ˈ**festive** ˌ**season** noun [S] UK the period around Christmas and New Year

festivity /fesˈtɪv.ɪ.ti/ US /-ə.t̬i/ noun **1 festivities** [plural] the parties, meals, and other social activities with which people celebrate a special occasion: *Come in and* ***join the*** *festivities!* **2** [U] a situation in which people are happy and celebrating

festoon /fesˈtuːn/ verb; noun
▸verb [T] to decorate a room or other place for a special occasion by hanging coloured paper, lights, or flowers around it, especially in curves: *The hall was festooned* ***with*** *Christmas lights and holly.*
▸noun [C] a decorative chain made of coloured paper, flowers, etc. hung in a curve between two points

feta /ˈfet.ə/ US /ˈfet̬-/ noun [U] a white Greek cheese, usually made from sheep's or GOAT's milk: *feta cheese*

fetal /ˈfiː.təl/ US /-t̬əl/ adj US for **foetal (foetus)**

fetch /fetʃ/ verb GET ▷ **1** B1 [T] to go to another place to get something or someone and bring them back: [+ two objects] *Could you fetch me my glasses/fetch my glasses* ***for*** *me from the other room, please?* ◦ *I have to fetch my mother from the station.* SELL ▷ **2** [T] to be sold for a particular amount of money: *The paintings fetched over a million dollars.* ◦ *The house didn't fetch as much as she was hoping it would.*

IDIOM **fetch and carry for sb** to do boring, unskilled jobs for someone, as if you were their servant

PHRASAL VERB **fetch up** mainly UK informal to arrive somewhere, especially without intending to: *After a whole hour of driving, we fetched up back where we started.*

fetching /ˈfetʃ.ɪŋ/ adj A fetching person or piece of clothing is attractive: *a rather fetching off-the-shoulder dress* ◦ *You* ***look*** *very fetching in your green shorts.* • **fetchingly** /-li/ adv

fete /feɪt/ noun; verb
▸noun [C] UK (also **fête**, US **fair**) a public event, often held outside, where you can take part in competitions and buy small things and food, often organized to collect money for a particular purpose: *a summer fete* ◦ *They're holding the* ***village*** *fete on the green.*
▸verb [T] to praise or to welcome someone publicly because of their achievements: *She was feted by audiences both in her own country and abroad.*

fetid formal (UK **foetid**) /ˈfet.ɪd/ US /ˈfet̬-/ adj smelling extremely bad and STALE: *fetid air/breath*

fetish /ˈfet.ɪʃ/ US /ˈfet̬-/ noun [C] INTEREST ▷ **1** a sexual interest in an object or a part of the body other than the sexual organs: *a rubber/foot fetish* ◦ *He has a fetish* ***about/for*** *high heels.* **2** an activity or object that you are so interested in that you spend an unreasonable amount of time thinking about it or doing it: *She* ***makes a*** *fetish* ***of*** *organization – it's quite obsessive.* ◦ *He* ***has*** *a fetish* ***for/about*** *cleanliness.* RELIGIOUS OBJECT ▷ **3** specialized an object that is worshipped in some societies because it is believed to have a spirit or special magical powers • **fetishism** /-ɪ.ʃɪ.zəm/ noun [U] • **fetishistic** /ˌfet.ɪˈʃɪs.tɪk/ US /ˌfet̬-/ adj

fetishist /ˈfet.ɪ.ʃɪst/ US /ˈfeţ-/ **noun** [C] a person who has a particular fetish: *a foot fetishist*

fetlock /ˈfet.lɒk/ US /-lɑːk/ **noun** [C] specialized the part of a horse's leg at the back, just above the foot, where longer hair grows

fetter /ˈfet.əʳ/ US /ˈfeţ.ɚ/ **verb** [T] **1** literary to keep someone within limits or stop them making progress: *He felt fettered* ***by*** *a nine-to-five office existence.* **2** to tie someone to a place by putting chains around their ANKLES

fetters /ˈfet.əz/ US /ˈfeţ.ɚz/ **noun** [plural] **1** old use a pair of chains which were tied round the legs of prisoners to prevent them from escaping **2** literary something which severely limits you: *the fetters* ***of*** *motherhood*

F

fettle /ˈfet.l̩/ US /ˈfeţ-/ old-fashioned informal **in fine/good fettle** healthy or strong, or in good condition: *'How was Jane?' 'Oh, she was in fine fettle.'*

fetus /ˈfiː.təs/ US /-ţəs/ **noun** [C] US for **foetus**

feud /fjuːd/ **noun; verb**

▸**noun** [C] an argument that has existed for a long time between two people or groups, causing a lot of anger or violence: *a* ***family*** *feud* ◦ *a ten-year-old feud* ***between*** *the two countries* ◦ *a bitter feud* ***over*** *land*

▸**verb** [I] to have a feud with someone: *They've been feuding* ***with*** *their neighbours for years* ***over*** *a boundary issue.*

feudal /ˈfjuː.dəl/ **adj** relating to the social system of Western Europe in the MIDDLE AGES or any society that is organized according to rank: *the feudal system* ◦ *a feudal lord/kingdom/society* • **feudalism** /-ɪ.zəm/ **noun** [U]

fever /ˈfiː.vəʳ/ US /-vɚ/ **noun** ILLNESS ▷ **1** B1 [C or U] a medical condition in which the body temperature is higher than usual and the heart beats very fast: *He's got a headache and a slight fever.* EXCITEMENT ▷ **2** C2 [U] a state of great excitement: *The whole country seems to be in the grip of football fever.*

fevered /ˈfiː.vəd/ US /-vɚd/ **adj** [usually before noun] EXCITED ▷ **1** disapproving unnaturally excited or active: *The film is clearly the product of a fevered* ***imagination****.* ILL ▷ **2** suffering from fever: *The nurse wiped my fevered brow.*

feverish /ˈfiː.vər.ɪʃ/ **adj** ILL ▷ **1** suffering from fever (= high body temperature): *I'm feeling a bit feverish – I hope it's not the start of flu.* EXCITED/ACTIVE ▷ **2** [before noun] unnaturally excited or active: *Have you seen the feverish* ***activity*** *in the kitchen?* • **feverishly** /-li/ **adv** *They* ***worked*** *feverishly to meet the deadline.*

ˈfever ˌpitch **noun** [U] a state of very strong emotion: *Excitement among the waiting crowd had* ***reached/was at*** *fever pitch.*

few /fjuː/ **determiner, pronoun; determiner, pronoun, noun, adj**

▸**determiner, pronoun** SOME ▷ **1 a few** A2 some, or a small number of something: *I need to get a few things in town.* ◦ *There are a few cakes left over from the party.* ◦ *We've been having a few problems with the new computer.* ◦ *If you can't fit all the cases in your car, I can take a few in mine.* ◦ *'How many potatoes do you want?' 'Oh, just a few, please.'* **2** A2 used in expressions such as 'quite a few' or 'a good few' to mean quite a large number: *I know quite a few people who've had the same problem.* ◦ *Lots of people at the club are under 20, but there are a good few who aren't.*

IDIOM **have a few (too many)** informal to drink quite a large number of, or too many, alcoholic drinks: *By the look of her, she'd had a few even before she arrived at the party.*

> **!** Note:
>
> **A few** is used with countable nouns. Compare **small**.

▸**determiner, pronoun, noun, adj** NOT MANY ▷ **1** B1 a small number, or not many: *It was embarrassing how few people attended the party.* ◦ *He is among the few people I can trust.* ◦ *Very few people can afford to pay those prices.* ◦ *We leave for France in a few days.* ◦ *Few of the children can read or write yet.* ◦ *Few things in this world give me more pleasure than a long bath.* ◦ *Fewer people smoke these days than used to.* ◦ *We get few complaints.* ◦ *According to the survey,* ***as*** *few* ***as*** *ten percent of us are happy with our jobs.* ◦ *The benefits of this scheme are few.* → Compare **little**

> **!** Note:
>
> **Few** is used with countable nouns.

2 few and far between C2 not happening or existing very often: *Flats which are both comfortable and reasonably priced are few and far between.*

> **!** Common mistake: **few or a few?**
>
> **Warning:** do not confuse 'few' and 'a few'.
>
> Use **few** to talk about a small number of things which is too small or not enough. This use is slightly formal:
>
> *Unfortunately, I have few opportunities to speak English.*
>
> To simply talk about a small number of things, don't say 'few', say **a few**:
>
> ~~*Luckily, I had few opportunities to speak English.*~~
>
> *Luckily, I had a few opportunities to speak English.*
>
> **Remember:** In spoken English it is more usual to use **not many** to talk about a small number that is not enough:
>
> *I don't get many opportunities to speak English.*

IDIOMS **a man/woman of few words** a man/woman who says very little: *My father was a man of few words, but when he spoke it was worth listening to.* • **no fewer than** formal used to show that you consider a number to be surprisingly large: *No fewer than five hundred delegates attended the conference.*

fey /feɪ/ **adj** literary often disapproving mysterious and strange, or trying to appear like this

fez /fez/ **noun** [C] (plural **fezzes**) a high, cone-shaped hat with a flat top and no BRIM, usually made of red material and with threads hanging from the top, especially as worn in the past by men in some Muslim countries

ff written abbreviation for and the following pages

fiancé /fiˈɒn.seɪ/ US /ˌfiː.ɑːnˈseɪ/ **noun** [C] the man who someone is ENGAGED to be married to: *Have you met Christina's fiancé?*

fiancée /fiˈɒn.seɪ/ US /ˌfiː.ɑːnˈseɪ/ **noun** [C] the woman who someone is ENGAGED to be married to

fiasco /fiˈæs.kəʊ/ US /-koʊ/ **noun** [C] (plural **fiascos** or mainly US **fiascoes**) something planned that goes wrong and is a complete failure, usually in an embarrassing way: *The show was a fiasco – one actor forgot his lines and another fell off the stage.*

fiat /ˈfiː.æt/ **noun** [C or U] formal an order given by a person in authority: *No company can set industry standards* ***by*** *fiat.*

fib /fɪb/ verb; noun
▸verb [I] (-bb-) informal to tell a small lie that does not cause any harm: *I can tell he's fibbing because he's smiling!*
▸noun [C] informal a small lie that does not cause any harm: *Don't believe him – he's **telling** fibs again.*

fibber /ˈfɪb.əʳ/ US /-ɚ/ noun [C] informal a person who tells fibs: *Fibber! You couldn't run ten kilometres, let alone a marathon!*

fibre UK (US **fiber**) /ˈfaɪ.bəʳ/ US /-bɚ/ noun THREAD ▷ **1** [C] any of the thread-like parts that form plant or artificial material and can be made into cloth: *The fibres are woven into fabric.* **2** [C or U] threads when they are in a mass that can be used for making products such as cloth and rope: *Natural fibres such as cotton tend to be cooler.* ◦ *artificial/man-made/natural fibre* **3** [C or U] one of various thread-like structures in the body, such as those found in muscle: *muscle fibre(s)* FOOD ▷ **4** C1 [U] a substance in certain foods, such as fruit, vegetables, and brown bread, that travels through the body as waste and helps the contents of the bowels to pass through the body easily: *You should eat more **dietary** fibre to reduce the risk of bowel cancer.* CHARACTER ▷ **5** [U] strength of character: *He lacked the **moral** fibre to be leader.*

IDIOM **with every fibre of your being** If you want or believe something with every fibre of your being, you want or believe it very much: *She wanted to win the race with every fibre of her being.*

fibreglass UK (US **fiberglass**) /ˈfaɪ.bəˌglɑːs/ US /-bɚˌglæs/ noun [U] a strong, light material made by twisting together small threads of glass and plastic, used especially for structures such as cars and boats: *a fibreglass hull/speedboat*

ˌfibre-optic ˈcable (US **ˌfiber-optic ˈcable**) noun [C or U] a very thin glass or plastic thread through which light can travel to carry information, especially in phone, television, and computer systems

ˌfibre ˈoptics noun [plural] specialized the use of very thin glass or plastic threads through which light can travel to carry information, especially in phone, television, and computer systems

fibrin /ˈfɪb.rɪn/ US /ˈfaɪ-/ noun [U] specialized a substance produced in the LIVER which makes the blood CLOT (= become solid)

fibrinogen /fɪˈbrɪn.ə.dʒən/ US /faɪˈbrɪn.ə-/ noun [U] specialized a substance produced in the LIVER that is changed into fibrin to CLOT the blood when body tissue is damaged

fibrous /ˈfaɪ.brəs/ adj THREAD ▷ **1** made of fibres, or like fibre FOOD ▷ **2** Food that is fibrous contains fibre.

fibula /ˈfɪb.jʊ.lə/ noun [C] (plural **fibulae** or **fibulas**) specialized the outer of the two bones in the lower part of the human leg

fickle /ˈfɪk.l̩/ adj disapproving **1** likely to change your opinion or your feelings suddenly and without a good reason: *She's so fickle – she's never been interested in the same man for more than a week!* ◦ *The world of popular music is notoriously fickle.* **2** describes conditions that are likely to change suddenly and without warning: *Fickle winds made sailing conditions difficult.* • **fickleness** /-nəs/ noun [U]

fiction /ˈfɪk.ʃən/ noun **1** B1 [U] the type of book or story that is written about imaginary characters and events and not based on real people and facts: *The book is a **work of** fiction and not intended as a historical account.* ◦ *a writer of children's fiction* **2** C1 [C or U] a false report or statement that you pretend is true: [+ that] *At work she kept up **the** fiction **that** she had a university degree.* ◦ *When he's telling you something, you never know what's fact and what's fiction.*

fictional /ˈfɪk.ʃən.əl/ adj C2 imaginary: *a fictional story* ◦ *fictional characters*

fictionalize (UK usually **fictionalise**) /ˈfɪk.ʃən.əl.aɪz/ verb [T] to write about a real event or character, but adding imaginary details and changing the real facts: *a fictionalized **account** of the life of St Francis* • **fictionalization** (UK usually **fictionalisation**) /ˌfɪk.ʃən.əl.aɪˈzeɪ.ʃən/ noun [C or U]

fictitious /fɪkˈtɪʃ.əs/ adj invented and not true or not existing: *He dismissed recent rumours about his private life as fictitious.* ◦ *Characters in this film are entirely fictitious.*

fiddle /ˈfɪd.l̩/ verb; noun
▸verb CHEAT ▷ **1** [T] informal to act dishonestly in order to get something for yourself, or to change something dishonestly, especially to your advantage: *She managed to fiddle a free trip to America.* ◦ *He had been fiddling **the accounts/books/finances** for years.* MOVE ABOUT ▷ **2** [I] to move things about or touch things with no particular purpose: *Put your papers down and stop fiddling!* INSTRUMENT ▷ **3** [I] informal to play the VIOLIN

PHRASAL VERBS **fiddle about/around** disapproving to spend time doing small things that are not important or necessary: *I was just fiddling around in the kitchen.* • **fiddle (about/around) with sth 1** to make small changes to something to try to make it work: *Stop fiddling about with your hair – it looks fine.* ◦ *Someone's been fiddling around with my computer!* **2** to touch or move things with your fingers because you are nervous or bored: *He was just fiddling around with the things on his desk.*

▸noun INSTRUMENT ▷ **1** [C] informal a VIOLIN: *to play the fiddle* DIFFICULTY ▷ **2** [S] UK informal something difficult to do, especially because the things involved are small or need careful use of the fingers: *I find threading a needle **a** terrible fiddle.* ◦ [+ to infinitive] ***It's a** real fiddle **to** assemble because of all the small parts.* DISHONEST BEHAVIOUR ▷ **3** [C or U] mainly UK informal something dishonest that someone does in order to get money or other advantages: *a tax fiddle* ◦ *Everyone suspected they were **on the** fiddle (= cheating).*

fiddler /ˈfɪd.ləʳ/ US /-lɚ/ noun [C] informal a VIOLIN player

fiddlesticks /ˈfɪd.l̩.stɪks/ exclamation (US also **fiddle-faddle** /ˈfɪd.l̩ˌfæd.l̩/) used to express disagreement or to say that something is nonsense

fiddling /ˈfɪd.lɪŋ/ adj [before noun] not important, or of no real interest: *fiddling little details* ◦ *fiddling restrictions*

fiddly /ˈfɪd.li/ adj informal difficult to do because the parts involved are small: *Repairing a watch is a very fiddly **job**.* ◦ *I hate painting the fiddly **bits** in the corner.*

fidelity /fɪˈdel.ə.ti/ US /-t̬i/ noun [U] LOYALTY ▷ **1** formal honest or lasting support, or loyalty, especially to a sexual partner: *Somerset Maugham's comedy of **marital** fidelity, 'The Constant Wife'* ◦ *How important do you think **sexual** fidelity is in a marriage?* EXACT COPY ▷ **2** approving the degree to which the detail and quality of an original, such as a picture, sound, or story, is copied exactly: *The best ink-jet printers can reproduce photographs with amazing fidelity.*

fidget /ˈfɪdʒ.ɪt/ verb; noun
▸verb [I] to make continuous small movements which

annoy other people: *Children can't sit still for long without fidgeting.* ◦ *Stop fidgeting* ***about!*** • **fidgety** /-ɪ.ti/ adj *a fidgety child/audience*

▸noun **1** [C] a person who often fidgets: *Tim's a terrible fidget.* **2 the fidgets** [plural] UK informal a state in which you keep fidgeting: *I got the fidgets halfway through the lecture.*

fiduciary /fɪˈdjuː.ʃi.ə.ri/ US /-ˈduː.ʃi.er-/ adj specialized relating to the responsibility to take care of someone else's money in a suitable way: *a breach of fiduciary duty*

fie /faɪ/ exclamation old use used to express anger, disapproval, or disappointment

F

field /fiːld/ noun; verb

▸noun **LAND** ▷ **1** A2 [C] an area of land, used for growing crops or keeping animals, usually surrounded by a fence: *We drove past fields of ripening wheat.* ◦ *The cows were all standing in one corner of the field.* **2 the field** an area of land in which you are working or studying: *I spoke to an aid worker who had recently returned from the field.* **SPORTS GROUND** ▷ **3** B1 [C] an area, usually covered with grass, used for playing sport: *the school* ***playing/sports*** *field* ◦ *a football/hockey/rugby field* **4 take the field** to go onto the field at the start of a game: *There were loud cheers as the Irish team took the field.* **AREA OF INTEREST** ▷ **5** B2 [C] an area of activity or interest: *the field* ***of*** *history/science/medicine* ◦ *Are you still in the same field (= are you doing the same type of work)?* **6 not be/be outside your field** to be something you do not know much about: *Programming really isn't my field – you'd better ask Phil.* **COMPETITORS** ▷ **7** C2 [S, + sing/pl verb] all the competitors taking part in a race or activity: *The race started with a field of eleven, but two horses fell.* ◦ *We have a* ***strong*** *field this afternoon.* ◦ *Jones finished ahead of* ***the*** *field.* **COMPUTER** ▷ **8** [C] specialized a division of a DATABASE (= collection of similar information on a computer) which contains a particular type of information, such as names or numbers

IDIOMS **sb's field of vision** the whole area that someone can see • **leave the field clear for sb** to stop competing with someone, making it possible for them to succeed: *John decided not to apply for the job, which left the field clear for Emma.*

▸verb **BALL** ▷ **1** [I or T] to catch or pick up the ball after it has been hit in a game such as cricket or baseball, and to try to prevent the other team from scoring: *He fielded the ball well.* ◦ *Our team is fielding first.* **ANSWER** ▷ **2** [T] to answer something cleverly or to avoid answering something directly: *He fielded some awkward questions very skilfully.* **TEAM** ▷ **3** [T] to have or produce a team of people to take part in an activity or event: *The company fielded a group of experts to take part in the conference.*

-field /-fiːld/ suffix an area of land containing a particular natural substance: *an oilfield* ◦ *a coalfield*

ˈfield ˌday noun [C] US a special day of organized sports or other outside activities for students

IDIOM **have a field day** to enjoy yourself very much or take advantage of an opportunity: *The newspapers had a field day when the wedding was announced (= they wrote a lot about it and printed many photographs of it).*

fielder /ˈfiːl.dəʳ/ US /-dɚ/ noun [C] any member of the team that is fielding in a game such as cricket or baseball and tries to prevent the other team from scoring

ˈfield eˌvent noun [C] a sports event in which competitors take part one after the other rather than racing or competing together: *High jump and javelin throwing are field events.*

ˈfield ˌglasses noun [plural] **binoculars**

ˈfield ˌhockey noun [C] US for **hockey**

ˈfield ˌmarshal noun [C] (also **Field Marshal**) a British army officer of the highest rank: *Field Marshal Davies/George Davies* ◦ [as form of address] *Yes, Field Marshal.*

ˈfield ˌtrip noun [C] a visit made by students to study something away from their school or college: *a geography field trip*

fieldwork /ˈfiːld.wɜːk/ US /-wɝːk/ noun [U] study which consists of practical activities that are done away from your school, college, or place of work: *They had to go to Africa to do their fieldwork.*

fiend /fiːnd/ noun [C] **1** an evil and cruel person: *He was portrayed in the media as a complete fiend.* **2** someone who likes something very much or is very interested in something: *a health/sex/chocolate fiend* ◦ *McCormack is a fiend* ***for*** *punctuality.*

fiendish /ˈfiːn.dɪʃ/ adj **1** evil and cruel: *a fiendish attack* **2** clever and difficult, sometimes in a bad way: *a fiendish crossword* ◦ *a fiendish plot/scheme* • **fiendishness** /-nəs/ noun [U]

fiendishly /ˈfiːn.dɪʃ.li/ adv informal extremely: *fiendishly* ***difficult***

fierce /fɪəs/ US /fɪrs/ adj **1** B2 physically violent and frightening: *a fierce attack/battle* ◦ *Two men were shot during fierce* ***fighting*** *last weekend.* **2** B2 strong and powerful: *Fierce winds/seas prevented the race from taking place.* ◦ *Fire fighters had to retreat from the fierce heat.* **3** B2 showing strong feeling or energetic activity: *The expansion plans will face fierce* ***opposition/resistance*** *from environmentalists.* ◦ *There is fierce* ***competition*** *to join the Special Branch.* **4** US informal difficult: *The chemistry exam was fierce!* • **fierceness**/-nəs/ noun [U]

IDIOM **something fierce** US informal very much: *I need a cold drink something fierce.*

fiercely /ˈfɪəs.li/ US /ˈfɪrs.li/ adv **1** in a frightening, violent, or powerful way: *to growl/fight fiercely* ◦ *to burn fiercely* **2** extremely: *She's fiercely competitive/independent.*

fiery /ˈfaɪə.ri/ adj **RED** ▷ **1** bright red, like fire: *a fiery sky/sunset* **FOOD** ▷ **2** describes food which causes a strong burning feeling in the mouth: *a fiery chilli sauce* **STRONG FEELINGS** ▷ **3** showing very strong feeling: *A fiery debate ensued.* ◦ *a fiery temperament/temper* ◦ *a fiery orator/speech*

fiesta /fiˈes.tə/ noun [C] a public celebration in Spain or Latin America, especially one on a religious holiday, with different types of entertainment and activities

fifteen /ˌfɪfˈtiːn/ number A1 the number 15: *They live about fifteen miles away.* ◦ *'How old is your sister?' 'Fifteen.'*

fifteenth /ˌfɪfˈtiːnθ/ ordinal number 15th written as a word: *Today is* ***the*** *fifteenth (****of*** *June).*

fifth /fɪfθ/ ordinal number A2 5th written as a word: *the fifth floor of the building* ◦ *Tomorrow is* ***the*** *fifth (****of*** *September).* ◦ *I* ***was/came*** *fifth in the race.*

IDIOM **I take/plead the Fifth (Amendment)** US humorous something that you say in order to tell someone you are not going to answer a question: *'So, who do you like best, Jenny or Kim?' 'Sorry, I take the Fifth on that.'*

▸**noun** [C] B1 one of five equal parts of something: *One fifth is the same as 20 percent.*

ˌfifth ˈcolumn **noun** [C] a group of people who support the enemies of the country they live in and secretly help them • **ˌfifth-ˈcolumnist** **noun** [C] a member of such a group

fifties /ˈfɪf.tiz/ **noun** [plural] **1** B2 A person's fifties are the period in which they are aged between 50 and 59: *My dad's* ***in*** *his fifties.* **2 the fifties a** the range of temperature between 50° and 59°: *It's been* ***in*** *the fifties all week.* **b** B2 the DECADE (= period of ten years) between 50 and 59 in any century, usually 1950–1959: *Rock and roll first became popular* ***in*** *the fifties.*

fiftieth /ˈfɪf.ti.əθ/ **ordinal number** 50th written as a word

fifty /ˈfɪf.ti/ **number** A2 the number 50: *forty-nine, fifty, fifty-one* ◦ *'How fast were they driving?' 'They were doing fifty (miles an hour).'*

ˌfifty-ˈfifty **adv, adj** (into) equal halves: *They divided the prize fifty-fifty.* ◦ *There's only* ***a*** *fifty-fifty* ***chance*** *that she'll survive the operation.*

fig. **noun; adj**
▸**noun** written abbreviation for **figure**
▸**adj** written abbreviation for **figurative**

fig /fɪg/ **noun** [C] a sweet, soft, purple or green fruit with many seeds, or a tree on which these grow

IDIOM **not care/give a fig** old-fashioned to not be at all worried by or interested in something: *They can say what they like. I don't give a fig.*

Other ways of saying fight

A noisy, rough fight between people in a public place can be described as a **brawl**:

He was injured in a ***brawl*** *outside the stadium.*

If a short fight starts suddenly, you can use the word **scuffle**:

There were a few ***scuffles*** *between fans after the match.*

A fight between large groups of people can be described as a **clash**:

Five people were injured in ***clashes*** *between strikers and owners.*

If someone fights against a person who is attacking them, you can describe it as a **struggle**:

He managed to escape after a ***struggle.***

The word **battle** is often used for a fight between armies:

Many soldiers were killed in the ***battle.***

fight /faɪt/ **verb; noun**
▸**verb** (**fought, fought**) **1** B1 [I or T] to use physical force to try to defeat another person or group of people: *There were children fighting in the playground.* ◦ *The soldiers fought from house to house.* ◦ *They fought* ***with*** *(= on the side of) the North* ***against*** *the South.* ◦ *The birds were fighting* ***over*** *(= competing for) a scrap of food.* ◦ *They fight* ***like cats and dogs*** *(= fight or argue very angrily and violently).* ◦ *They fought* ***to the bitter end/to the death*** *(= until everyone on one side was dead or completely defeated).* **2** B2 [I or T] to use a lot of effort to defeat or achieve something, or to stop something happening: *He fought the disease bravely for three years.* ◦ *We need the public's help in fighting* ***crime.*** ◦ *He fought* ***against*** *racism.* ◦ *Vitamin C is thought to help fight colds and flu.* ◦ *They had to fight hard* ***for*** *improvements to the road system.* ◦ *One of the passengers was* ***fighting for her life*** *(= so ill or injured that she might die) last night after receiving multiple injuries in the collision.* ◦ *With debts of over $2 million, the corporation is* ***fighting for its life*** *(= people are trying hard to stop it being destroyed)* ◦ *I had to fight (****back****) (= tried hard not to show or produce) the tears when he said he was leaving.* ◦ *The bank fought* ***off*** *(= successfully prevented) a takeover by another bank recently.* ◦ *I was getting a cold at the start of the week but I seem to have fought it* ***off*** *(= got rid of it).* **3** B2 [I] informal to argue: *I wish they wouldn't fight in front of the kids.* ◦ *I could hear them fighting* ***about*** *money again.*

IDIOMS **fight your corner** UK to defend something that you believe in by arguing: *You'll have to be prepared to fight your corner if you want them to extend the project.* • **fight a losing battle** to try hard to do something when there is no chance that you will succeed • **fight fire with fire** to use the same methods as someone else in order to defeat them • **fight it out** informal to argue about which of a group of people will get something good when there is only one or a few of that thing: *There's only one ticket so you'll have to fight it out between you.* • **fight shy of** UK to try to avoid something: *Before this course I'd always fought shy of technology.*

PHRASAL VERB **fight back** to defend yourself when someone attacks you or causes problems for you

▸**noun** **1** B1 [C] an argument or an occasion when someone uses physical force to try to defeat someone: *Jeff's always* ***getting into/starting*** *fights.* ◦ *The older boys* ***broke up*** *(= stopped) the fight.* ◦ UK *I had a* ***stand-up*** *fight* ***with*** *her (= we argued strongly)* ***about*** *the phone bill.* ◦ *Have you got tickets for* ***the*** *big fight (= boxing competition)?* ◦ *He* ***put up a*** *fight when the police tried to arrest him.* **2** B2 [C] a situation in which you use a lot of effort to defeat someone or achieve something, or to stop something happening: *We must continue* ***the*** *fight* ***against*** *homelessness.* ◦ *He died last week after a long fight* ***with*** *cancer.* ◦ *They* ***put up a good*** *fight (= played well)* ***against*** *a more experienced football team.* **3** [U] the wish or ability to fight or act energetically: *The team came out on the field full of fight.*

Word partners for fight noun

get into/have/pick/start a fight • *put up* a fight • *lose/win* a fight • *continue/join/keep up/give up* the fight • a *brave/desperate/long/tough* fight • *in* a fight • a fight *about/against/for/over* sth

IDIOM **a fight to the finish** a situation in which two groups or people intend to fight until one side has been defeated

fighter /ˈfaɪ.təʳ/ US /-t̬ɚ/ **noun** [C] **PERSON** ▷ **1** someone who fights: *She's a fighter (= she tries hard and will not easily give up).* **AIRCRAFT** ▷ **2** a small, fast military aircraft used for chasing and destroying enemy aircraft: *a fighter plane/aircraft* ◦ *a fighter pilot*

fighting /ˈfaɪ.tɪŋ/ US /-t̬ɪŋ/ **noun** [U] B2 the act of people fighting, especially in a war: *Fierce fighting has continued all day on the outskirts of the town.*

ˌfighting ˈchance **noun** [S] a small but real possibility that something can be done: *If we can raise enough money, there's a fighting chance (****that****) we can save the project.*

ˌfighting ˈfit **adj** [after verb] UK extremely healthy: *At 73, she's still fighting fit, walking five miles a day.*

ˌfighting ˈspirit **noun** [U] the willingness to compete or to do things that are difficult: *Don't take no for an answer – where's your fighting spirit?*

ˈ**fighting ˌwords** noun [U] (UK also ˈ**fighting ˌtalk**) speech that shows you are willing to fight

ˌ**fight-or-ˈflight** adj [before noun] used to describe the reaction that people have to a dangerous situation, that makes them either stay and deal with it, or run away: *a fight-or-flight response*

ˈ**fig ˌleaf** noun [C usually singular] **LEAF** ▷ **1** the type of leaf sometimes used in paintings to cover a naked person's sex organs **FALSE** ▷ **2** UK something that hides something else, especially something that is dishonest or embarrassing: *The spokesperson said the information campaign was a fig leaf to hide the most regressive tax in history.*

F

figment /ˈfɪg.mənt/ noun **a figment of sb's imagination** something which seems real but is not: *Was it just a figment of my imagination or did I hear John's voice in the other room?*

figurative /ˈfɪg.ər.ə.tɪv/ ⓤⓢ /-ɚ.ə.t̬ɪv/ adj **LANGUAGE** ▷ **1** (written abbreviation **fig.**) (of words and phrases) used not with their basic meaning but with a more IMAGINATIVE meaning: *Of course, she was using the term 'massacre' in the figurative sense.* → Compare **literal** **ART** ▷ **2** (of a painting, drawing, etc.) representing something as it really looks, rather than in an ABSTRACT way

figuratively /ˈfɪg.ər.ə.tɪv.li/ ⓤⓢ /-ɚ.ə.t̬ɪv-/ adv in a way which uses words and phrases with a more IMAGINATIVE meaning than usual: *Figuratively speaking, it was a blow right between the eyes (= it was a bad shock).*

figure /ˈfɪg.ər/ ⓤⓢ /-jʊr/ noun; verb

▸noun [C] **NUMBER** ▷ **1** **B1** the symbol for a number or an amount expressed in numbers: *Can you read this figure? Is it a three or an eight?* ◦ *Write the amount in both words and figures.* ◦ *I looked quickly down the **column of** figures.* ◦ *He earns a six-figure salary (= an amount of money with six figures).* **2 in single/double figures** **C2** between 1 and 9/between 10 and 99: *The job vacancies are now in double figures.* **SHAPE** ▷ **3** **B2** the shape of the human body, or a person: *I could see two tall figures in the distance.* ◦ *A strange bearded figure (= person) entered the room.* ◦ figurative *She was a **central/key/leading** figure in (= was an important person in) the movement for constitutional reform.* **4** a painting, drawing, or model of a person: *There are several reclining figures in the painting.* **5** **B1** a woman's body shape: *She's got a lovely figure.* ◦ *She **got** her figure **back** (= returned to her usual shape) after having the baby.* **PICTURE** ▷ **6** **B2** (written abbreviation **fig.**) a picture or drawing, often with a number, in a book or other document: *Please see figures 8 and 9.*

IDIOMS **a fine figure of a man/woman** often humorous a person who is tall, with a large, physically attractive body • **put a figure on it** to say exactly how much something is or costs: *I'm sure we'll make a good profit, but I couldn't put a figure on it.*

▸verb **EXPECT** ▷ **1** **B1** [I] mainly US to expect or think that something will happen: [+ (that)] *We figured (**that**) you'd want to rest after your journey.* **APPEAR** ▷ **2** [I usually + adv/prep] to be, appear, take part, or be included in something: *Their names did not figure **in** the list of finalists.* ◦ *They denied that violence and intimidation had figured prominently **in** achieving the decision.* **NUMBER** ▷ **3** [T] US to calculate an amount: *I'm still figuring my taxes.*

IDIOMS **go figure!** mainly US used when you tell someone a fact and you then want to say that the fact is surprising, strange or stupid: *It's a terrible movie and it made $200 million. Go figure!* • **it figures** (also **that figures**) used to say that you are not surprised by something unpleasant that has happened: *'Dad, Sadie spilled her milk all over the floor.' 'It figures.'*

PHRASAL VERB **figure sth/sb out** informal **B2** to finally understand something or someone, or find the solution to a problem after a lot of thought: [+ question word] *I can't figure out **why** he did it.* ◦ *I find him really odd – I can't figure him out at all.* ◦ *Can you figure out the answer to question 5?*

figurehead /ˈfɪg.ə.hed/ ⓤⓢ /-jə-/ noun [C] **PERSON** ▷ **1** someone who has the position of leader in an organization but who has no real power: *The president of this company is just a figurehead – the Chief Executive has day-to-day control.* **MODEL** ▷ **2** a painted model, usually of a person, which in the past was fixed to the front of a ship

ˈ**figure-ˌhugging** adj used to describe clothes that fit closely to your body: *a figure-hugging dress*

ˌ**figure of ˈeight** noun [C] UK (US ˌ**figure ˈeight**) the shape made when drawing an 8: *She skated a perfect figure of eight.*

ˌ**figure of ˈfun** noun [C usually singular] mainly UK someone who is laughed at unkindly

ˌ**figure of ˈspeech** noun [C] (plural **figures of speech**) an expression which uses words to mean something different from their ordinary meaning: *'Get up with the lark' is a figure of speech, meaning 'Get out of bed early'.*

ˈ**figure ˌskating** noun [U] a type of SKATING which involves circular patterns and often includes jumps

figurine /ˌfɪg.əˈriːn/ ⓤⓢ /-jə-/ noun [C] a small model of a human, usually made of clay or PORCELAIN

filament /ˈfɪl.ə.mənt/ noun [C] **1** a thin thread or FIBRE of natural or artificial material: *glass/silk filaments* **2** a thin wire, especially one which lights up inside an electric LIGHT BULB: *a tungsten filament*

filbert /ˈfɪl.bət/ ⓤⓢ /-bɚt/ noun [C] mainly US a **hazelnut**

filch /fɪltʃ/ verb [T] informal to steal something of little value: *Who's filched my pencils?*

file /faɪl/ noun; verb

▸noun **CONTAINER** ▷ **1** **A2** [C or U] any of several different types of container used to store papers, letters, and other documents in an ordered way, especially in an office: *a box/envelope file* ◦ *secret/confidential/personnel files* ◦ *You'll find it **in the** files under 'C'.* ◦ *We keep your records **on** file for five years.* **WRITTEN RECORD** ▷ **2** [C] written records that are kept about a particular person or subject: *The police have **opened a** file **on** local burglaries.* **COMPUTER** ▷ **3** **A2** [C] information stored on a computer as one unit with one name: *What's the file name?* ◦ *I'm going to copy/save this file.* **LINE** ▷ **4** [C or U] a long line of people or animals, one behind another: *They were horrified to see files **of** ants marching through the kitchen.* ◦ *They walked **in (single)** file (= one behind another).* **TOOL** ▷ **5** [C] a thin, flat or rounded metal tool, which has rough surfaces for rubbing wooden or metal objects to make them smooth or to change their shape

▸verb **STORE/RECORD INFORMATION** ▷ **1** [T] to store information in a careful and particular way: *We file these reports (= put them in a file) **under** country of origin.* **2** [T] legal to officially record something, especially in a law court: *The police filed charges against the two suspects.* **3** [T] News REPORTERS file a story by sending it to their office, usually by phone, email, or other electronic method **WALK IN A LINE** ▷ **4** [I usually + adv/prep] to walk in a line, one behind another: *The visitors filed **through** the entrance to the ticket offices.* **TOOL** ▷ **5** [I + adv/prep, T] to use a file in order to make an object smooth or to change its shape: *File* (***down***) *the sharp edges.* ◦ [+ obj + adj] *The surface had been filed smooth.* ◦ *She filed her* ***nails.***

PHRASAL VERB **file for sth** legal to make an official request for something such as DIVORCE or BANKRUPTCY

ˈfile ˌcabinet noun [C] US for **filing cabinet**

ˈfile exˌtension noun [C] a DOT followed by three letters, such as .doc or .jpg, that forms the end of the name of a computer document: *Be sure to type in the document name and file extension before you click 'save'.*

ˈfile ˌsharing noun [U] the activity of putting a file from your computer onto a special place on your computer so that other people can copy it, or look at it using the internet

filet /ˈfɪl.eɪ/ (US) /fɪˈleɪ/ noun [C], verb [T] US for **fillet**

filial /ˈfɪl.i.əl/ adj formal of a son or daughter: *filial duty/respect/affection*

filibuster /ˈfɪl.ɪ.bʌs.təʳ/ (US) /-tɚ/ verb [I or T] mainly US to make a long speech in order to delay or prevent a new law being made: *Conceivably, supporters of the law could filibuster to prevent it from being revised.* • **filibuster** noun [C]

filigree /ˈfɪl.ɪ.griː/ noun [U] delicate jewellery made from twisted, especially silver, wire: *a beautiful filigree brooch* ◦ *filigree ironwork*

filing /ˈfaɪ.lɪŋ/ noun **PUTTING IN A CONTAINER** ▷ **1** [U] the activity of putting documents, electronic information, etc. into files: *a filing cabinet* ◦ *Her job involves filing and other general office work.* **RECORD** ▷ **2** [C] legal an official record of something: *a bankruptcy filing* **METAL PIECES** ▷ **3 filings** [plural] small pieces of metal that are removed from a larger piece by filing: *iron filings*

ˈfiling ˌcabinet noun [C] UK (US **ˈfile ˌcabinet**) a large piece of furniture in an office, used for holding documents

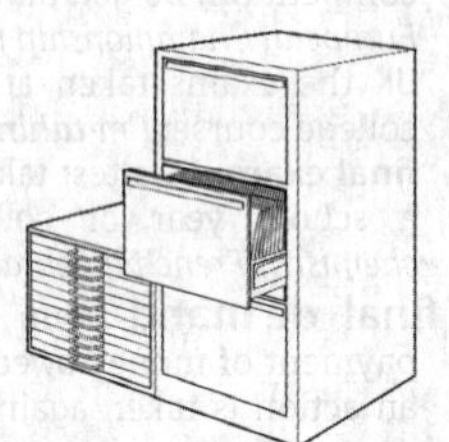
filing cabinet

fill /fɪl/ verb; noun

▸verb **SPACE** ▷ **1** (A2) [I or T] to make or become full; to use empty space: *I filled the bucket* ***with*** *water.* ◦ *I could hear the cistern filling.* ◦ *I went to the library to fill* (***in***) ***an hour*** (= *use that period of time*) *until the meeting.* ◦ figurative *Happy sounds filled the room* (= *could be heard everywhere in the room*). ◦ figurative *The thought of it fills me* ***with*** (= *makes me feel*) *dread.* **2** (C2) [I or T] to put a substance into an empty space: *Before painting, fill* (***in***) *all the cracks in the plaster.* ◦ *These cakes are filled* ***with*** *cream.* ◦ figurative *The product clearly filled a* ***need/gap in the market.*** **3** [T] to put a substance into a hole in a tooth to repair it: *You should get that cavity filled.* **JOB** ▷ **4** (C1) [T] to give a job or position to someone: *I'm sorry, the* ***job/post/vacancy*** *has already been filled.* ◦ *We would prefer to fill the post* ***with*** (= *give it to*) *a recent graduate.*

PHRASAL VERBS **fill sth in/out** (A2) to write the necessary information on an official document: *to fill in a form/questionnaire* • **fill sb in** to give someone extra or missing information: *I filled her in* ***on*** *the latest gossip.* • **fill in** to do someone else's work for them because they cannot or will not do it themselves: *Volunteers would fill in* ***for*** *teachers in the event of a strike.* ◦ *I'm not her regular secretary – I'm just filling in.* • **fill out** If someone who is thin fills out, they become heavier and more rounded, often because they have grown older. • **fill (sth) up** (B1) to become full, or to make

something become full: *The seats in the hall were filling up fast.* ◦ *As she read the poem, their eyes filled up* ***with*** *tears.* • **fill sb up** If food fills you up, it makes you feel as if you have eaten enough: *That sandwich really filled me up.*

▸noun [U] someone's fill is as much as they want or as much as they can deal with: *He took only a few minutes to* ***eat/drink*** *his fill.* ◦ *I'd had my fill* ***of*** *his rude remarks.*

-filled /-fɪld/ suffix full of the stated thing: *a smoke-filled room* ◦ *a fun-filled weekend*

filler /ˈfɪl.əʳ/ (US) /-ɚ/ noun **1** [C or U] a substance that is used to fill small holes and CRACKS, especially in wood and walls **2** [C] a short text or drawings used to fill extra space in a magazine or newspaper, or talk, music, etc. used to fill extra time in a radio or television broadcast

fillet /ˈfɪl.ɪt/ noun; verb

▸noun [C or U] UK (US **filet**) a piece of meat or fish without bones: *a piece of cod fillet* ◦ *fillet* ***of*** *plaice* ◦ *small trout fillets* ◦ *fillet steak* ◦ *fillet of beef*

▸verb [T] UK (US **filet**) to cut a piece of meat or fish from the bones

filling /ˈfɪl.ɪŋ/ noun; adj

▸noun **1** [U] any material used to fill something: *duvets with synthetic filling* **2** [C or U] the layer of food inside a sandwich, cake, etc.: *pies with sweet or savoury fillings* ◦ *sandwich fillings* **3** [C] the artificial substance put into holes in teeth to repair them

▸adj If food is filling, you feel full after you have eaten only a little of it.

ˈfilling ˌstation noun [C] UK and US for **petrol station**

fillip /ˈfɪl.ɪp/ noun [C usually singular] something which causes a sudden improvement: *The athletics win* ***provided*** *a much-needed fillip* ***to/for*** *national pride.* ◦ *The news* ***gave*** *the stock market a* ***big*** *fillip.*

filly /ˈfɪl.i/ noun [C] a young female horse → Compare **colt**

film /fɪlm/ noun; verb

▸noun **MOVING PICTURES** ▷ **1** (A1) [C or U] (US **movie**) a series of moving pictures, usually shown in a cinema or on television and often telling a story: *What's your favourite film?* ◦ *We took the children to* (***see***) *a film.* ◦ *She had a long career in films/film* (= *the business of making films*). ◦ *a film star/critic* ◦ *the film industry* ◦ *a film-maker* ◦ *Her last film was* ***shot*** (= *made*) *on location in South America.* ◦ *I hate people talking while I'm* ***watching*** *a film.* ◦ *Would you like to go and see a film tonight?* **MATERIAL** ▷ **2** [C or U] (a length of) dark plastic-like material that can record images as photographs or as a moving picture: *a* ***roll of*** *film* ◦ *a 24 exposure/16 mm/high-speed film* ◦ *A passer-by recorded the incident* ***on*** *film.* **LAYER** ▷ **3** (C2) [C] a thin layer of something on a surface: *a film* ***of*** *dust/oil/grease* ◦ *a film* ***of*** *smoke*

▸verb [I or T] (B1) to record moving pictures with a camera, usually to make a film for the cinema or television: *Most of the scenes were filmed in a studio.* ◦ *They filmed for a week in Spain.*

PHRASAL VERB **film over** If something films over, it becomes lightly covered with a thin layer of something: *Her eyes suddenly filmed over* (***with*** *tears*).

ˈfilm diˌrector noun [C] a person who is in charge of a film and tells the actors how to play their parts

filmgoer /ˈfɪlmˌgəʊ.əʳ/ (US) /-ˌgoʊ.ɚ/ noun [C] (mainly US **moviegoer**) a person who regularly goes to watch films at the cinema • **filmgoing** /-ɪŋ/ noun [U], adj

F

[before noun] UK (mainly US **moviegoing**) *the filmgoing public*

filming /ˈfɪl.mɪŋ/ **noun** [U] the activity of making a film: *Filming was halted after the lead actor became ill.*

filmmaker /ˈfɪlmˌmeɪ.kəʳ/ US /-kɚ/ **noun** [C] B1 someone who is in charge of making a film • **filmmaking** /-kɪŋ/ **noun** [U]

ˌfilm ˈnoir **noun** [U] a style of film that presents the world as being unpleasant, strange, or cruel

ˈfilm ˌstar **noun** [C] mainly UK (mainly US **ˈmovie ˌstar**) a famous cinema actor

filmy /ˈfɪl.mi/ **adj** very thin and often transparent: *filmy material* ◦ *a filmy dress* • **filminess** /-nəs/ **noun** [U]

F

filo pastry UK (US **phyllo pastry**) /ˌfiː.ləʊˈpeɪ.stri/ US /-loʊ/ **noun** [U] (also **filo**, **phyllo**) a type of pastry made in thin, almost transparent layers

filter /ˈfɪl.təʳ/ US /-t̬ɚ/ **noun**; **verb**

▸**noun** [C] **EQUIPMENT** ▷ **1** C2 any of several types of equipment or devices for removing solids from liquids or gases, or for removing particular types of light: *a water filter* ◦ *a dust filter* ◦ *I like to experiment with different light filters on my camera.* ◦ *Ozone is the Earth's primary filter for ultraviolet radiation.* **TRAFFIC** ▷ **2** UK a green, arrow-shaped light that is part of a set of TRAFFIC LIGHTS and tells drivers when they can turn left or right: *a traffic filter* ◦ *a left/right filter*

▸**verb** **APPEAR GRADUALLY** ▷ **1** C2 [I + adv/prep] to appear or happen gradually or to a limited degree: *News filtered **down** to us during the day.* ◦ *Reports about an accident began to filter **in**.* ◦ *Sunlight filtered **through** the branches.* **REMOVE** ▷ **2** C2 [T] to remove solids from liquids or gases, or to remove particular types of light, using special equipment: *The water is filtered to remove any impurities.* ◦ *Devices in the two chimneys would filter* (*out*) (= *remove*) *radioactive dust.*

PHRASAL VERB **filter in** UK to join a line of moving traffic without causing other vehicles to slow down

ˈfilter ˌbed **noun** [C] an area of stones and sand through which water flows to be cleaned

ˈfilter ˌcoffee **noun** [C or U] UK (also **ˈfiltered ˌcoffee**, US **ˈdrip ˌcoffee**) coffee made by slowly pouring hot water through crushed coffee beans in a coffee filter

ˈfilter ˌpaper **noun** **1** [U] thin paper that allows only liquid to flow through **2** [C] UK a paper cone that allows only water through and is used to make filter coffee

ˈfilter ˌtip **noun** [C] (also **ˌfilter-tipped cigaˈrette**) a cigarette with a filter on the end to remove TAR from the tobacco

filth /fɪlθ/ **noun** [U] **DIRT** ▷ **1** thick, unpleasant dirt: *The floor was covered in filth.* **OFFENSIVE WORDS/PICTURES** ▷ **2** sexually offensive words or pictures: *People complain about the filth on TV and in the press.*

filthiness /ˈfɪl.θi.nəs/ **noun** [U] the quality of being very dirty

filthy /ˈfɪl.θi/ **adj**; **adv**

▸**adj** **DIRTY** ▷ **1** C1 extremely or unpleasantly dirty: *Wash your hands – they're filthy!* ◦ *Look at this cloth – it's filthy!* ◦ *I've never smoked – it's a filthy **habit**.* ◦ figurative *That girl just gave me a filthy **look*** (= *looked at me in a very unpleasant, disapproving way*). ◦ UK *He was in a filthy* (= *a very bad*) ***temper/mood***. **OFFENSIVE** ▷ **2** C1 containing sexually offensive words or pictures: *filthy language* ◦ *a filthy joke* ◦ humorous *You've got a filthy mind!*

▸**adv** **1** **filthy dirty** extremely dirty **2** **filthy rich** informal extremely rich

filtrate /ˈfɪl.treɪt/ **noun** [C] specialized a liquid, gas, or other substance that has passed through a filter

filtration /fɪlˈtreɪ.ʃən/ **noun** [U] the act of passing a liquid or gas through a piece of equipment in order to remove solid pieces or other substances: *a filtration unit/plant* ◦ *The technology exists to remove all of these contaminants through filtration.*

fin /fɪn/ **noun** [C] a thin vertical part sticking out of the body of especially a fish or an aircraft which helps balance and movement: *We could see the fin of a shark as it slowly circled our boat.* ◦ *a fish's dorsal fin* ◦ *The aircraft has a long tail fin.*

finagle /fɪˈneɪ.gl̩/ **verb** [I or T] US to use tricks and dishonest methods to get what you want: *He somehow finagled his way into the army as a lieutenant.*

final /ˈfaɪ.nəl/ **adj**; **noun**

▸**adj** **1** A2 last: *a final warning/offer* ◦ *the final chapters of a book* ◦ *the final years* ◦ *The game is **in** its final **stages**.* **2** **in the final analysis** used when you are talking about what is most important or true in a situation: *In the final analysis, it is the drug companies that are going to profit from this policy.* **3** **that's final** used to show that you are certain you will not change your decision about something: *It's no use begging me – I'm not coming and that's final.*

▸**noun** **COMPETITION** ▷ **1** B1 [C] the last in a series of games, races, or competitions, usually the one in which the winner is chosen: *Last year we got **through to** the final.* ◦ *The men's basketball final will be on Sunday.* **2** **the finals** [plural] the last set of games in a competition: *Do you think Scotland will qualify for the European Championship finals?* **EXAM** ▷ **3** **finals** [plural] UK the exams taken at the end of a university or college course: *I'm **taking** my finals in June.* **4** [C] (also **final exam**) US a test taken on a subject at the end of a school year or college course: *When is your chemistry/French/algebra final?*

ˌfinal deˈmand **noun** [C] the last request for the payment of money owed for goods or services before an action is taken against the person who owes that money

finale /fɪˈnɑː.li/ **noun** [C usually singular] the last part of especially a musical or theatre performance, especially when this is very exciting or emotional: *All the dancers come on stage during the **grand** finale.* ◦ figurative *What better finale **to** her career than this extravagant gesture?*

finalist /ˈfaɪ.nə.lɪst/ **noun** [C] a person or group competing in a final

finality /faɪˈnæl.ə.ti/ US /-t̬i/ **noun** [U] formal the quality of being finished and therefore not able to be changed: *the finality of death*

finalize (UK usually **finalise**) /ˈfaɪ.nə.laɪz/ **verb** [T] to make a final and certain decision about a plan, date, etc.: *We'll finalize the details later.* • **finalization** (UK usually **finalisation**) /ˌfaɪ.nə.laɪˈzeɪ.ʃən/ **noun** [U] *the finalization of negotiations*

finally /ˈfaɪ.nə.li/ **adv** **AFTER TIME** ▷ **1** A2 after a long time or some difficulty: *We finally got home at midnight.* ◦ *After months of looking he finally found a job.* **LAST** ▷ **2** B1 used especially at the beginning of a sentence to introduce the last point or idea: *Finally, I'd like to thank everyone for coming this evening.* **CERTAINLY** ▷ **3** in a way that will not be changed: *The plan hasn't been finally approved.*

! Common mistake: finally

Warning: Common word-building error!

If an adjective ends with 'l', add '-ly' to make an adverb. Don't write 'finaly', write **finally**.

finance /ˈfaɪ.næns/ **noun; verb**

▸**noun 1** B2 [U] (the management of) a supply of money: *corporate/personal/public finance* ◦ *the minister of finance/the finance minister* ◦ *You need to speak to someone in the finance* ***department****.* ◦ *The finance* ***committee*** *controls the school's budget.* **2 finances** [plural] B2 the money which a person or company has: *We keep a tight control on the organization's finances.* ◦ UK informal *My finances won't* ***run to*** *(= I do not have enough money to buy) a new car this year.*

▸**verb** [T] B2 to provide the money needed for something to happen: *The local authority has refused to finance the scheme.*

financial /faɪˈnæn.ʃəl/, /fɪ-/ **adj** B1 relating to money or how money is managed: *financial difficulties/success* • **financially** /-i/ **adv** B2 *The project is not financially* ***viable*** *(= will not produce enough money).* ◦ *He's still financially* ***dependent on*** *(= regularly receives money to live from) his parents.*

fiˌnancial adˈviser noun [C] (also **fiˌnancial adˈvisor**) a person whose job is to give advice to other people about money and INVESTMENTS

fiˌnancial ˈservices noun [plural] business services relating to money and INVESTMENTS, for example those offered by banks: *the financial services industry*

fiˌnancial ˈyear noun [C] a period of twelve months (not always January to December) for which a business, government, etc. plans its management of money

financier /fɪˈnæn.si.əʳ/ US /-ɚ/ **noun** [C] a person who has control of a large amount of money and can give or lend it to people or organizations

finch /fɪntʃ/ **noun** [C] any of various types of small singing bird with a short, wide, pointed beak → See also **bullfinch, chaffinch**

find /faɪnd/ **verb; noun**

▸**verb (found, found) DISCOVER** ▷ **1** A1 [T] to discover, especially where a thing or person is, either unexpectedly or by searching, or to discover where to get or how to achieve something: *I've just found a ten-pound note in my pocket.* ◦ *I couldn't find Andrew's phone number.* ◦ *You'll find the knives and forks in the left-hand drawer.* ◦ *Researchers are hoping to find a cure for the disease.* ◦ [+ two objects] *Has he found himself a place to live yet?* ◦ [+ obj + adj] *She was found unconscious and bleeding.* ◦ [+ that] *The study found* ***that*** *men who were married lived longer than those who were not.* ◦ *Do you think they'll ever find a way of bringing peace to the region?* ◦ *We're really struggling to find (= get) enough money to pay the rent at the moment.* ◦ *After years of abuse from her husband, she eventually found the courage to leave him.* ◦ *I wish I could find (the) time to do more reading.* **2** B1 [T] to realize that something exists or has happened: [+ (that)] *We came home to find (****that****) the cat had had kittens.* ◦ *I found (****that****) I could easily swim a mile.* **3 be found** B2 to exist or be present somewhere: *Many plant and animal species are found only in the rainforests.* ◦ *Vitamin C is found in citrus fruit.* **4 find your way** to get somewhere you are trying to reach: *I had a map but I still couldn't find my way back to the hotel.* **5 find fault with** to criticize someone or something: *She's always finding fault with the way he works.* **6 find yourself a** B2 to realize that you are in a particular situation or place, or doing a particular thing, when you did not intend to: *He'll find himself with no friends at all if he carries on behaving this way.* ◦ *We fell asleep on the train and woke up to find ourselves* ***in*** *Calais.* **b** often humorous If you go somewhere or do something to find yourself, you go there or do it to discover your true character: *Simon spent a year in an ashram in India to find himself.*

! Common mistake: find out or find?

Warning: choose the correct verb!

To talk about discovering where a thing or person is or how to obtain or achieve something, don't say 'find out', say **find**:

We need to find a solution to this problem.

EXPERIENCE A FEELING ▷ **7** B1 [T] to think or feel a particular way about someone or something: [+ obj + noun/adj] *Do you find Clive difficult to talk to?* ◦ *I don't find him an easy person to get on with.* ◦ *She doesn't find it easy to talk about her problems.* ◦ [+ -ing verb] *I find living in the city quite stressful.*

! Common mistake: find

Remember: when **find** is followed by an adjective, it also needs an object noun or pronoun.

To talk about feeling a particular way about something, don't say 'find easy/difficult', say **find it easy/difficult**:

~~*I find difficult to understand his accent.*~~

I find it difficult to understand his accent.

JUDGE ▷ **8** B2 [I or T] legal to make a judgment in a law court: [+ obj + adj] *In a unanimous verdict, the jury found him* ***guilty/not guilty*** *of the murder.*

+ Other ways of saying find

A very common alternative to 'find' is the verb **discover**:

The missing wallet was ***discovered*** *under the chair.*

I finally ***discovered*** *the letters in a drawer.*

If someone finds the exact position of someone or something, in formal situations the verb **locate** is sometimes used:

Police are still trying to ***locate*** *the suspect.*

If someone finds something that has been secret or hidden, then the verbs **uncover** or **unearth** are sometimes used:

Reporters ***uncovered/unearthed*** *evidence of corruption.*

The phrasal verbs **come across** and **stumble across/on** are used when someone finds something by chance:

I ***stumbled upon*** *these photographs when I was cleaning out my desk.*

We ***came across*** *a lovely little restaurant in the village.*

If someone finds something or someone after looking carefully in different places, you can use the verb **trace** or the phrasal verb **track down**:

Police have so far failed to ***trace/track down*** *the missing woman.*

IDIOMS **find your feet** to become familiar with and confident in a new situation: *Did it take you long to find your feet when you started your new job?* • **find it in your heart to do sth** to be willing and able to do something unpleasant or difficult: *Could you find it in your heart to forgive her?* • **find your tongue** (US also **find your voice**) to become willing to talk: *Witnesses* *often find their tongues when they hear a reward has been offered.*

PHRASAL VERBS **find (sth) out** A2 to get information about something because you want to know more about it, or to learn a fact or piece of information for the first time: *How did you find out* ***about*** *the party?* ◦ *The holiday was a complete surprise – I only found out* ***about*** *it the day before we left.* ◦ [+ question word] *I'll just go and find out* ***what****'s going on outside.* ◦ [+ that] *Too late, she found out* ***that*** *the train had been cancelled.* • **find sb out** [M usually passive] to discover that someone has done something wrong: *He lived in dread of being found out.*

▸**noun** [C] a good or valuable thing or a special person that has been discovered but was not known about before: *This café's quite a find – I had no idea there was anywhere like it around here.* ◦ *A recent find* ***of*** *ancient artefacts is on display at the local museum.*

finder /ˈfaɪn.dəʳ/ US /-dɚ/ **noun** [C] someone who finds something

IDIOM **finders keepers (losers weepers)** saying said by a child who has found an object to the child who has lost it, to show that they intend to keep it

fin-de-siècle /ˌfæn.də.siːˈek.lə/ **adj** [before noun] relating to the end of the 19th century, especially the art, culture, and morals of the period: *The novel begins with an evocative description of fin-de-siècle Paris.*

finding /ˈfaɪn.dɪŋ/ **noun** DISCOVERY ▷ **1** [C] a piece of information that is discovered during an official examination of a problem, situation, or object: *The report's finding on the decrease in violent crime supports the police chief's claims.* JUDGMENT ▷ **2** [C usually singular] a judgment made at the end of an official legal INQUIRY (= a process to discover the answer to something)

fine /faɪn/ **adj; noun; verb; adv**

▸**adj** SATISFACTORY ▷ **1** A1 [after verb] good or good enough; healthy and well: *I felt terrible last night but I feel fine this morning.* ◦ *The apartments are very small, which is fine for one person.* ◦ *'Are you all right?' 'Everything's just fine, thanks.'* ◦ *'I'll come round to your place at eight.' 'Fine. See you then.'* EXCELLENT ▷ **2** B2 excellent or much better than average: *purveyors of fine wines and gourmet food* ◦ *The world's finest collection of Impressionist paintings is housed in the Musée d'Orsay in Paris.* ◦ *This building is the finest example of its type.* THIN ▷ **3** C2 very thin or in very small pieces or drops: *The baby's head was covered in fine blond hair.* ◦ *The eruption had covered the town with a fine layer of ash.* ◦ *Apply a fine line of highlighter along the middle of your top lip.* ◦ *She has inherited her mother's fine (= delicate and beautiful)* ***features****.* EXACT ▷ **4** C1 [usually before noun] very exact and delicate, or needing to be done, treated, or considered very carefully: *I understood in general what she was talking about, but some of the finer* ***details/points*** *were beyond me.* SUNNY ▷ **5** B1 mainly UK SUNNY and dry: *The forecast said it would be fine and dry today.* BAD ▷ **6** informal bad or not convenient: *That's a fine (= very unpleasant) thing to say about your father after all he's done for you!* ◦ *He picked a fine time to leave us.*

IDIOMS **a fine line** C1 If you say that there is a fine line between one thing and another, you mean that they are very similar. You often say this when one thing is acceptable and the other is not: *As a parent, I knew that there was a fine line between panic and caution.* • **have sth down to a fine art** (UK also **have sth off to a fine art**) to be able to do something very well or quickly, often because you have done it so many times • **not to put too fine a point on** to be completely direct and honest: *I think she's wrong – not to put too fine a point on it.*

▸**noun** [C] B1 an amount of money that has to be paid as a punishment for not obeying a rule or law: *The maximum penalty for the offence is a $1,000 fine.* ◦ *If found guilty, he faces six months in jail and a* ***heavy*** *(= severe) fine.*

▸**verb** [T] B2 to charge someone an amount of money as a punishment for not obeying a rule or law: *Drivers who exceed the speed limit can expect to be fined heavily.* ◦ [+ two objects] *They fined him $100* ***for*** *using threatening behaviour.*

▸**adv** B2 in a satisfactory way: *'Will a loan of $500 be sufficient?' 'That will* ***suit*** *me fine.'* ◦ *It was working fine yesterday.*

ˌfine ˈart noun 1 [U] drawings, paintings, and SCULPTURES that are admired for their beauty and have no practical use **2 fine arts** [plural] painting and SCULPTURE: *a fine arts degree* ◦ *The fine arts have suffered from a lack of government funding.*

ˌfine ˈdining noun [U] a style of eating that usually takes place in expensive restaurants, where especially good food is served to people, often in a formal way

finely /ˈfaɪn.li/ **adv** THINLY ▷ **1** B2 into very thin or small pieces: *Chop the herbs very finely.* EXACTLY ▷ **2** to an exact degree: *a finely-tuned engine* ◦ *a finely-executed manoeuvre* EXCELLENTLY ▷ **3** beautifully

fineness /ˈfaɪn.nəs/ **noun** [U] THIN QUALITY ▷ **1** the quality of being very thin: *It's the fineness of the thread that makes the cloth so soft.* EXACTNESS ▷ **2** the quality of being very exact and delicate: *When I look at her paintings I'm always struck by the fineness of the details.*

ˌfine ˈprint noun [U] US for **small print**

finery /ˈfaɪ.nəʳr.i/ US /-nɚ.i/ **noun** [U] beautiful clothing and jewellery worn on a special occasion: *There we all were* ***in our*** *finery, waiting for the bride and groom to arrive.*

fines herbes /fiːnˈeəb/ US /-ˈzerb/ **noun** [plural] a mixture of fresh or dried herbs that are used to flavour food

finesse /fɪˈnes/ **noun; verb**

▸**noun** [U] great skill or style: *It was a disappointing performance which lacked finesse.*

▸**verb** [T] to deal with a situation or a person in a skilful and often slightly dishonest way: *She finessed the interview by playing down her lack of experience and talking about her long-standing interest in the field.*

finest /ˈfaɪ.nɪst/ **noun** [U] **1** the best example of its type: *This 100-year-old restaurant is among London's finest.* **2** US informal A city's finest is its police force: *New York's finest*

ˌfine-tooth ˈcomb noun with a fine-tooth comb If you go through something with a fine-tooth comb, you examine it in great detail and with great care: *We have gone through the evidence with a fine-tooth comb.*

ˌfine-ˈtune verb [T] to make very small changes to something in order to make it work as well as possible: *She spent hours fine-tuning her speech.*

finger /ˈfɪŋ.gəʳ/ US /-gɚ/ **noun; verb**

▸**noun** [C] **1** A2 any of the long, thin, separate parts of the hand, especially those that are not thumbs: *He noticed her long delicate fingers.* ◦ *I cut my finger chopping onions last night.* → See also **forefinger, index finger, ring finger, little finger 2** a part of a GLOVE (= hand covering) that covers a finger

IDIOMS **be all fingers and thumbs** UK (US **be all thumbs**) to move your hands in an awkward way: *I'm all fingers and thumbs today. That's the second plate I've dropped this morning.* • **cross your fingers** (also **keep your fingers crossed**) C2 to hope that things will happen in the way that you want them to: *She has her exam this morning so cross your fingers.* ◦ *We're just hoping the weather stays nice and keeping our fingers crossed.* • **give sb the finger** US to show someone in an offensive way that you are angry with them by turning the back of your hand towards them and putting your middle finger up • **have a finger in every pie** to be involved in and have influence over many different activities, often in a way that people do not approve of • **have a finger in the pie** to be involved in something, often when your involvement is not wanted • **have your fingers in the till** UK to steal money from the place where you work • **have your finger on the trigger** used to say that someone is ready and prepared to do something, especially something violent: *They have their finger on the trigger to start a nuclear war.* • **not lift/raise a finger** to not make any effort to help: *He never lifts a finger to help with the housework.* • **point the finger at sb** to accuse someone of being responsible for something bad that has happened • **pull/get your finger out** UK informal to start working hard, especially after a period of low activity: *She's really going to have to pull her finger out if she wants to finish before Friday.* • **put your finger on sth** C2 to discover the exact reason why a situation is the way it is, especially when something is wrong: *There's something odd about him, but I can't quite put my finger on it.*

▸verb [T] **TOUCH** ▷ **1** to touch or feel something with your fingers: *She fingered her necklace absent-mindedly as she talked.* **TELL THE POLICE** ▷ **2** informal If you finger someone, you tell the police that they are guilty of a crime.

fingerboard /ˈfɪŋ.ɡə.bɔːd/ US /-ɡɚ.bɔːrd/ **noun** [C] the long strip of wood on a STRINGED musical instrument against which the strings are pressed by the fingers in order to change the note that is played: *Guitars and banjos have fingerboards.*

ˈfinger ˌbowl **noun** [C] a small bowl filled with water that a person can use to wash their fingers during a meal

ˈfinger ˌbuffet **noun** [C] a meal, often on a special occasion, in which the food is eaten with the fingers, often by guests who are standing

ˈfinger ˌchip **noun** [C] Indian English a CHIP (= a long, thin piece of potato that is fried and usually eaten hot)

-fingered /-fɪŋ.ɡəd/ US /-ɡɚd/ **suffix** with or using the stated number of fingers: *two-fingered typing*

ˈfinger ˌfood **noun** [U] food that you can eat without using knives, forks, or spoons

fingering /ˈfɪŋ.ɡər.ɪŋ/ US /-ɡɚ-/ **noun** [U] The fingering of a piece of music is the way that fingers are used to play particular notes, or the numbers on a sheet of music that show which fingers should play which notes.

fingerless glove /ˌfɪŋ.ɡə.ləsˈɡlʌv/ US /ˌfɪŋ.ɡɚ-/ **noun** [C] a type of GLOVE (= piece of clothing for the hand and wrist) that does not cover the fingers

fingermark /ˈfɪŋ.ɡə.mɑːk/ US /-ɡɚ.mɑːrk/ **noun** [C] UK (US usually **fingerprint**) a mark left by dirt or oil from someone's finger on a clean surface: *He'd left sticky fingermarks all over the glass.*

fingernail /ˈfɪŋ.ɡə.neɪl/ US /-ɡɚ-/ **noun** [C] (also **nail**) B2 the hard, slightly curved part that covers and protects the top of the end of a finger: *dirty fingernails* ◦ *She had long red fingernails.*

ˈfinger-ˌpointing **noun** [U] a situation in which someone is blamed for something that goes wrong: *There's the usual finger-pointing when mistakes are made.*

fingerprint /ˈfɪŋ.ɡə.prɪnt/ US /-ɡɚ-/ **noun; verb**

▸**noun** [C] **1** (informal **print**) the pattern of curved lines on the end of a finger or thumb that is different in every person, or a mark left by this pattern: *His fingerprints were all over the gun.* ◦ *The police have **taken** fingerprints from every man in the neighbourhood.* **2** a **fingermark**

▸**verb** [T] to record the pattern of someone's fingerprints: *We would like to fingerprint every one of your employees.*

fingertip /ˈfɪŋ.ɡə.tɪp/ US /-ɡɚ-/ **noun** [C] the end of a finger: *Use your fingertips to gently flatten the pastry.*

IDIOMS **at your fingertips** C2 If you have information at your fingertips, you can get it and use it very easily: *He has all the latest statistics at his fingertips.* • **be an artist, professional, etc. to your fingertips** UK to be a perfect or typical example of something: *Mark, a professional to his fingertips, insisted that we follow the correct procedures.*

finicky /ˈfɪn.ɪ.ki/ **adj** **1** disapproving difficult to please: *a finicky eater* ◦ *He's terribly finicky **about** his food.* **2** needing a lot of attention to detail: *Repairing watches must be a very finicky job.*

Other ways of saying finish

The verb **end** is a common alternative to 'finish' when it means 'stop':

*What time does the concert **end**?*

When someone finishes doing or making something, the verb **complete** is sometimes used:

*Have you **completed** all the questions?*

*The project took five years to **complete**.*

The verb **conclude** is used when someone finishes a speech, meeting, or piece of writing by doing something:

*She **concluded** her speech by thanking everyone who had helped her.*

If someone finishes something quickly and easily, especially food or a piece of work, in informal situations you can use the phrasal verb **polish off**:

*He's just **polished off** two huge bowls of pasta.*

The phrasal verb **wind up** is sometimes used when an activity is gradually finishing:

*It's time to **wind up** the game now.*

finish /ˈfɪn.ɪʃ/ **verb; noun**

▸**verb** **COMPLETE/END** ▷ **1** A1 [I or T] to complete something or come to the end of an activity: *I'll call you when I've finished my homework.* ◦ *Please place your questionnaire in the box when you've finished.* ◦ *She finished (the concert) **with** a song from her first album.* ◦ *She finished second (= in second place) in the finals.* ◦ [+ -ing verb] *Have you finished read**ing** that magazine?* ◦ *They've already run out of money and the building isn't even **half**-finished (= half of it has not been completed).* **2** A1 [I] to end: *The meeting should finish around four o'clock.* ◦ *The play finishes with a song.* **3** B1 [T] to eat, drink, or use something completely so that none remains: *Make sure she finishes her dinner.* ◦ *He finished his drink and left.* ◦ *We finished (= ate all of) the pie last night.* **WOOD** ▷ **4** [T] If you finish something made of wood, you give it a last covering of paint, POLISH, or VARNISH so that it is ready to be used.

IDIOM **put the finishing touches to** UK (US **put the finishing touches on**) to add the final improvements to something so that you are satisfied with it or certain that it is complete

PHRASAL VERBS **finish sth off** **COMPLETE** ▷ **1** B2 to complete the last part of something that you are doing: *I want to finish off this essay before I go to bed.* **USE** ▷ **2** to eat, drink, or use the last part of something: *We may as well finish off this pie – there's only a little bit left.* • **finish sb/sth off** **KILL** ▷ **1** informal to kill someone or something, especially if they have already been injured: *A third heart attack finally finished off the old man.* **DEFEAT** ▷ **2** to defeat a person or team that you are competing against in a sports event: *He could spar well enough but he couldn't seem to finish off his opponents.* • **finish sb off** informal to make someone extremely tired, weak, or unhappy: *That game of football has really finished me off.* • **finish up** [I or L] UK If you finish up in a particular place or situation, that is the place or situation that you are in finally: *You'll finish up dead if you carry on drinking like that.* ◦ *She married a Spaniard and finished up in Barcelona.* • **finish (sth) up** to eat or drink all of what you are eating or drinking: *Finish up your dinner and you can have dessert.* • **finish with sth** to stop using or needing something: *Have you finished with that magazine?* • **finish with sb** UK B2 to stop having a romantic relationship with someone: *She finished with him when she discovered he was having an affair.*

▸noun [C] **COMPLETE/END** ▷ **1** B1 the end of a race, or the last part of something: *a close finish* ◦ *They replayed the finish in slow motion.* **WOOD** ▷ **2** the condition of the surface of a material such as wood: *Look at the lovely shiny finish on that piano.* **3** the last covering of VARNISH, POLISH, or paint, that is put onto something: *Even a clear finish will alter the colour of wood slightly.*

finished /ˈfɪn.ɪʃt/ adj ended or final: *How much does the finished product cost?* ◦ *Are you finished **with** that drill?* ◦ *When do you expect to be finished?* ◦ UK *The rebels' ammunition is almost finished (= completely used) and it is only a matter of time before they surrender.* ◦ *This financial crisis means that the government's economic policy is finished (= destroyed).*

finisher /ˈfɪn.ɪ.ʃəʳ/ US /-ʃɚ/ noun [C usually plural] a person or animal that finishes an ATHLETIC competition

ˈ**finishing** ˌ**school** noun [C] a school or college where young women from rich families learn how to behave in high-class society

finite /ˈfaɪ.naɪt/ adj **LIMITED** ▷ **1** C2 having a limit or end: *The funds available for the health service are finite and we cannot afford to waste money.* ◦ *We only have a finite **amount** of time to complete this task – we can't continue indefinitely.* **GRAMMAR** ▷ **2** in a form that shows the TENSE and subject of a verb, rather than the INFINITIVE form or a participle: *In the following sentence 'go' is finite: 'I often go to the cinema.'*

finito /fɪˈniː.təʊ/ US /-toʊ/ adj [after verb] informal finished: *As far as I am concerned the relationship is over – finito.*

fink /fɪŋk/ noun; verb

▸noun [C] US informal someone who tells secret and damaging information about someone else, or an unpleasant person: *Kelly's such a fink – she told Mom I was smoking again.*

▸verb

PHRASAL VERB **fink on sb** US old-fashioned slang to tell other people secret and damaging information about someone

fiord /fjɔːd/ US /fjɔːrd/ noun [C] a **fjord**

fir /ˈfɜːʳ/ US /ˈfɝː/ noun [C] (also ˈ**fir** ˌ**tree**) a tall EVERGREEN tree (= one that never loses its leaves) that grows in cold countries and has leaves that are like needles

fire /faɪəʳ/ US /faɪr/ noun; verb

▸noun **FLAMES** ▷ **1** A2 [C or U] (material that is in) the state of burning that produces flames that send out heat and light, and might produce smoke: *Animals are usually afraid of fire.* ◦ *The fire was **started** by children playing with matches.* ◦ *40 people helped to **put out** (= stop) the fire.* ◦ *The library was badly damaged **in** the fire.* ◦ *How many historic buildings are damaged **by** fire each year?* ◦ *She had to be rescued when her house **caught** (US **caught on**) fire (= started to burn).* **2** B1 [C] a small controlled fire that is used for heating or cooking: *It's very cold in here – should I **light** a fire?* ◦ *We **built** a fire on the beach.* ◦ *We put up our tents and **made** a small fire.* **3 on fire** B1 If something is on fire, it is burning when it should not be: *If your home was on fire and you could save only one thing, what would it be?* **4** [C] UK a gas or ELECTRIC HEATER that is used to warm up a room: *a gas/electric fire* ◦ *If you're cold just put the fire on.* **SHOOT** ▷ **5** C2 [U] the shooting of guns or other weapons: *The police **opened** fire **on** (= started shooting at) the protesters.* ◦ *The command was given to **cease** fire (= stop shooting).* ◦ *The city **came under** fire **from** anti-government forces last night.* **EMOTION** ▷ **6** [U] strong emotion: *The fire in her speech inspired everyone.* → See also **fiery**

> **Word partners for fire noun**
>
> ***light/make/put out/start*** a fire • ***catch*** fire • a fire ***breaks out/burns/rages*** • a ***blazing/roaring*** fire • be ***on*** fire • a fire ***hazard***

IDIOMS **come under fire** C2 to be criticized: *The government has come under fire for its decision to close the mines.* • **fire and brimstone** used to mean the threat of Hell or DAMNATION (= punishment that lasts for ever) after death: *The preacher's sermon was full of fire and brimstone.* • **go through fire and water** UK old-fashioned to experience many difficulties or dangers in order to achieve something • **hang/hold fire** UK to delay making a decision • **play with fire** C2 to act in a way that is very dangerous and to take risks • **set sth/sb on fire** to cause something or someone to start burning: *A peace campaigner had set herself on fire in protest over the government's involvement in the war.* • **set fire to sth/sb** mainly UK C2 to cause something or someone to start burning: *Soldiers had chased the protesters into a warehouse and set fire to it.*

▸verb **SHOOT** ▷ **1** B2 [I or T] to cause a weapon to shoot bullets, arrows, or MISSILES: *He fired his gun into the air.* ◦ *Someone started firing **at** us.* ◦ *Without warning he started firing **into** the crowd.* ◦ *I just prayed that he would stop firing.* ◦ *The ambassador denied that any missiles had been fired across the border.* **2** [T or I] to direct a series of questions or criticisms at someone: *The journalists were firing questions at me for two whole hours.* ◦ *'I'd like to ask you some questions about your childhood, if I may.' 'Fire **away**!' (= You can start asking them now.)* **REMOVE FROM A JOB** ▷ **3** B2 [T] to remove someone from their job, either because they have done something wrong or badly, or as a way of saving the cost of employing them: *She was fired after she* *was caught stealing from her employer.* ◦ *He was fired* ***from*** *his $165,000 job* ***for*** *poor performance.* ◦ *She has just been fired as editor of the newspaper.* ◦ *The company is reducing its workforce by firing 500 employees.* **EXCITE** ▷ **4** C2 [T] to cause a strong emotion in someone: *I had a brilliant English teacher who fired me* ***with*** *enthusiasm for literature at an early age.* ◦ *Talk of treasure and lost cities had fired their* ***imaginations***. **HEAT** ▷ **5** [T] to heat objects made of clay in a KILN (= a special oven) so that they become hard

IDIOMS **be firing on all cylinders** to be operating as powerfully and effectively as possible: *Dawson will be firing on all cylinders after two months of fitness training.* • **in the firing line** (also **in the line of fire**, US also **on the firing line**) likely to be criticized, attacked, or got rid of: *He found himself in the firing line for his sexist remarks.*

PHRASAL VERBS **fire sth off SHOT** ▷ **1** to fire a shot from a gun: *They fired off several shots to frighten us.* **LETTER** ▷ **2** to write and send an angry letter to someone: *He fired off an angry letter to the editor.* • **fire sb up** to make someone become excited or angry: *We had an argument about it and she got all fired up.* • **fire sth up** to start a machine or computer program: *The old plane was firing up its engines.* ◦ *This system uses voice activation to fire up its web browser.*

ˈfire aˌlarm noun [C] a device such as a bell or SIREN that warns the people in a building that the building is on fire: *If the fire alarm* ***goes off*** *(= starts making a sound), leave the building calmly.*

firearm /ˈfaɪər.ɑːm/ US /ˈfaɪr.ɑːrm/ **noun** [C] formal a gun that can be carried easily: *He was found guilty of possessing an unlicensed firearm.*

fireball /ˈfaɪə.bɔːl/ US /ˈfaɪr.bɑːl/ **noun** [C] a large ball of fire, especially one caused by a very powerful explosion: *Witnesses reported seeing a huge orange fireball as the oil refinery exploded.*

ˈfire ˌblanket noun [C] a type of cover made of a material which does not burn very easily, which you throw over a fire to put it out or stop it from spreading

firebomb /ˈfaɪə.bɒm/ US /ˈfaɪr.bɑːm/ **noun** [C] a bomb that causes destruction by starting a fire rather than exploding • **firebomb verb** [T] to damage a place with a firebomb: *Animal rights extremists have threatened to firebomb any stores that stock fur coats.*

firebrand /ˈfaɪə.brænd/ US /ˈfaɪr-/ **noun** [C] a person who causes political or social trouble by opposing authority and encouraging others to do so

firebreak /ˈfaɪə.breɪk/ US /ˈfaɪr-/ **noun** [C] (Australian English also **firetrail**) a strip of land in a wood or forest from which the trees have been removed to prevent a fire from spreading

ˈfire briˌgade noun [C, + sing/pl verb] UK (US **ˈfire deˌpartment**) B2 an organization that is in charge of preventing and stopping unwanted fires

firecracker /ˈfaɪəˌkræk.əʳ/ US /ˈfaɪrˌkræk.ɚ/ **noun** [C] a FIREWORK that makes a loud noise when it explodes

-fired /-faɪəd/ US /-faɪrd/ **suffix** using the stated type of fuel: ***Gas****-fired power stations are expected to produce cheaper electricity than* ***coal****-fired ones.*

ˈfire ˌdoor noun [C] a door made of material that cannot burn, used to prevent a fire from spreading within a building

ˈfire ˌdrill noun [C] the set of actions that should be performed in order to leave a building such as an office, factory, or school safely when it is on fire, or an occasion when this is practised

ˈfire-ˌeater noun [C] a performer who entertains people by seeming to swallow flames

ˈfire ˌengine noun [C] (US also **ˈfire ˌtruck**) a large vehicle that carries FIREFIGHTERS and their equipment to a fire

ˈfire esˌcape noun [C] a set of metal stairs, especially on the outside of a building, which allows people to escape from a burning building

ˈfire exˌtinguisher noun [C] a device which contains water or a special gas, powder, or FOAM (= a mass of small bubbles) that is put onto a fire to stop it burning

fire extinguisher

firefight /ˈfaɪə.faɪt/ US /ˈfaɪr-/ **noun; verb**

▸**noun** [C] a fight, often unexpected, between opposing groups of soldiers in which they shoot at each other

▸**verb** [I] to spend time on problems that need to be dealt with quickly, instead of working in a calm, planned way: *Will the new manager be able to do anything other than firefight?*

firefighter /ˈfaɪəˌfaɪ.təʳ/ US /ˈfaɪrˌfaɪ.t̬ɚ/ **noun** [C] B1 a person whose job is to stop fires from burning

firefighting /ˈfaɪəˌfaɪ.tɪŋ/ US /ˈfaɪrˌfaɪ.t̬ɪŋ/ **noun** [U] **BURNING** ▷ **1** the activity of stopping fires burning **PROBLEMS** ▷ **2** spending time on problems that need to be dealt with quickly, instead of working in a calm, planned way: *I spend all my time firefighting rather than making any progress.*

firefly /ˈfaɪə.flaɪ/ US /ˈfaɪr-/ **noun** [C] an insect that is active during the night and whose tail produces light

fireguard /ˈfaɪə.gɑːd/ US /ˈfaɪr.gɑːrd/ **noun** [C] (US also **firescreen**) a metal frame that is put in front of a FIREPLACE to prevent burning wood or coal from falling onto the floor, or to prevent children or pets from burning themselves

ˈfire ˌhydrant noun [C] (US also **ˈfire ˌplug**) a large pipe in the street that FIREFIGHTERS can get water from to use to stop fires burning

firelight /ˈfaɪə.laɪt/ US /ˈfaɪr-/ **noun** [U] the light produced by a fire, especially one in a FIREPLACE

firelighter /ˈfaɪəˌlaɪ.təʳ/ US /ˈfaɪrˌlaɪ.t̬ɚ/ **noun** [C] (US usually **ˈfire ˌstarter**) a small block of material that burns very easily and is used for helping to start wood or coal fires

fireman /ˈfaɪə.mən/ US /ˈfaɪr-/ **noun** [C] a man whose job is to stop unwanted fires from burning

fireplace /ˈfaɪə.pleɪs/ US /ˈfaɪr-/ **noun** [C] C2 a space in the wall of a room for a fire to burn in, or the decorated part which surrounds this space: *She swept the ashes from the fireplace.*

ˈfire ˌplug noun [C] US informal for **fire hydrant**

firepower /ˈfaɪə.paʊəʳ/ US /ˈfaɪr.paʊɚ/ **noun** [U] the number and size of guns that a military group has available: *Although badly out-numbered by the enemy, we had vastly superior firepower.*

fireproof /ˈfaɪə.pruːf/ US /ˈfaɪr-/ **adj** unable to be damaged by fire: *She keeps all her important papers in a fireproof safe.*

ˈfire-ˌraising noun [U] UK for **arson** • **ˈfire-ˌraiser** noun [C] UK for **arsonist**

ˈfire ˌsale noun [C] **1** a sale of goods at reduced prices, especially because the shop has been damaged by fire

2 a sale of a business or part of a business at a low price because it needs money or is BANKRUPT

firescreen /ˈfaɪə.skriːn/ (US) /ˈfaɪr-/ **noun** [C] US for **fireguard**

fireside /ˈfaɪə.saɪd/ (US) /ˈfaɪr-/ **noun** [C usually singular] the part of a room which surrounds a FIREPLACE: *She sat reading* ***by*** *the fireside.*

ˈfire ˌstation **noun** [C] (US also **firehouse** /ˈfaɪə.haʊs/ (US) /ˈfaɪr-/) **B1** a building where FIRE ENGINES are kept and where FIREFIGHTERS work and stay in the hours they are working

firestorm /ˈfaɪə.stɔːm/ (US) /ˈfaɪr.stɔːrm/ **noun** [C] a very large fire that is impossible to control, sometimes caused by heavy bombing from aircraft

firetrail /ˈfaɪə.treil/ (US) /ˈfaɪr-/ **noun** [C] Australian English a strip of land in a wood or forest from which the trees have been removed to prevent a fire from spreading → Compare **firebreak**

firetrap /ˈfaɪə.træp/ (US) /ˈfaɪr-/ **noun** [C] (a part of) a building that would burn easily if a fire started by accident or would be difficult to escape from during a fire

ˈfire ˌtruck **noun** [C] US for **fire engine**

firewall /ˈfaɪə.wɔːl/ **noun** [C] specialized a device or program that stops people seeing or using information on a computer without permission while it is connected to the internet

firewater /ˈfaɪəˌwɔː.təʳ/ (US) /ˈfaɪrˌwɑː.t̬ɚ/ **noun** [U] informal humorous a very strong alcoholic drink, especially WHISKY

firewood /ˈfaɪə.wʊd/ (US) /ˈfaɪr-/ **noun** [U] wood used as fuel for a fire: *We can use those old shelves as firewood.*

firework /ˈfaɪə.wɜːk/ (US) /ˈfaɪr.wɝːk/ **noun** **EXPLOSIVE** ▷ **1** **B1** [C] a small container filled with explosive chemicals which produce bright coloured patterns or loud noises when they explode: *a firework display* ◦ *When it gets dark we'll* ***let off*** (US ***set off***) (= light) *the fireworks.* ◦ *What time do the fireworks start?* **SHOUTING** ▷ **2** **fireworks** [plural] informal humorous a lot of angry shouting: *I have to go home now – there'll be fireworks if I'm late!*

firing /ˈfaɪə.rɪŋ/ (US) /ˈfaɪ.rɪŋ/ **noun** [C] **DISMISSAL** ▷ **1** mainly US an act of removing someone from their job: ***hirings and*** *firings* **CRITICISM** ▷ **2** Indian English an act of speaking angrily to someone because you disapprove of what they have done: *The official couldn't escape the firing by his superintendent.*

ˈfiring ˌsquad **noun** [C] a group of soldiers who are ordered to shoot and kill a prisoner

firm /fɜːm/ (US) /fɝːm/ **adj; noun; verb**

▸**adj** **HARD** ▷ **1** **B2** not soft but not completely hard: *I'd rather sleep on a firm mattress than a soft one.* ◦ *These pears are still too firm to eat.* **FIXED** ▷ **2** well fixed in place or position: *The bridge provided a firm platform for the bungee jumpers.* **3** fixed at the same level or opinion and not changing: *The government remains firm in its opposition to tax reform.* **STRONG** ▷ **4** **C2** strong and tight: *a firm handshake* ◦ *Keep a firm hold of the handrail as you go down.* ◦ figurative *No one seems to have a firm* ***grip on*** *the company at the moment.* ◦ figurative *You need a firm* ***grasp of*** *mathematics to become an astronaut.* **CERTAIN** ▷ **5** **B2** certain and not likely to change: *He is a firm believer in traditional family values.* ◦ *Some people still claim that there is no firm evidence linking smoking with lung cancer.* **FORCEFUL** ▷ **6** **C2** forceful and making people do what you want: *I was always very firm with my children – they knew the rules and I made sure they kept to them.*

IDIOMS **a firm hand** strong control: *Reforming these young offenders will require a firm hand.* • **hold/stand firm** to remain in the same place or at the same level: *The protesters stood firm as the police tried to disperse them.* ◦ *The pound held firm* ***against*** *the Swiss franc today.*

▸**noun** [C] **B1** a company or business: *He's just started working for an accountancy firm/a firm* ***of*** *accountants in Cambridge.*

▸**verb** **MAKE HARD** ▷ **1** [T] to make soil harder by pressing on it: *Firm the soil around the cuttings and water them in.* **STOP CHANGING** ▷ **2** [I] specialized to stop changing or to remain at the same level, amount, etc.: *After a turbulent week on the markets, share prices firmed today.*

PHRASAL VERBS **firm sth up** to make something more certain or less likely to change: *Could we have a meeting so we can firm up the details of our agreement?* • **firm (sth) up** to make a part of your body have less fat and more muscle by doing exercise: *Cycling is one of the best ways to firm up your thighs.*

the firmament /ˈfɜː.mə.mənt/ (US) /ˈfɝː-/ **noun** [S] literary the sky: figurative *She is one of the rising stars in the political firmament.*

firmly /ˈfɜːm.li/ (US) /ˈfɝːm-/ **adv** **NOT LOOSELY** ▷ **1** **B2** in a way that will not become loose: *Make sure the rope is firmly attached before attempting to climb down it.* **STRONGLY** ▷ **2** **B2** strongly and tightly: *He shook my hand firmly and climbed into the taxi.* **FORCEFULLY** ▷ **3** forcefully: *'You're not going to the party and that's that!' she said firmly.* **CERTAINLY** ▷ **4** **B2** in a way that is certain or not likely to change: *We are firmly committed to reducing unemployment.*

firmness /ˈfɜːm.nəs/ (US) /ˈfɝːm-/ **noun** [U] **HARDNESS** ▷ **1** the quality of not being soft, but not completely hard: *The bed's firmness suited him.* **STRENGTH/TIGHTNESS** ▷ **2** the quality of being strong and tight: *The firmness of his handshake reassured me.* **FORCEFUL QUALITY** ▷ **3** the quality of being forceful and making people do what you want: *The new teacher has a reputation for firmness.* **CERTAINTY** ▷ **4** the quality of being certain and not likely to change

firmware /ˈfɜːm.weəʳ/ (US) /ˈfɝːm.wer/ **noun** [U] a set of instructions that form part of an electronic device and allow it to communicate with a computer or with other electronic devices

first /ˈfɜːst/ (US) /ˈfɝːst/ **ordinal number, determiner; adv; noun**

▸**ordinal number, determiner** **1** **A1** (a person or thing) coming before all others in order, time, amount, quality, or importance: *This is my first visit to New York.* ◦ *I fell in love with him* ***the first time*** *I saw him.* ◦ *I'm always nervous for the first* ***few*** *minutes of an exam.* ◦ *Today is* ***the*** *first (****of*** *August).* **2 in the first place** **B2** in or at the beginning (of a series of events): *The trousers shrank when I washed them, but they weren't really big enough in the first place.* ◦ *Thankfully, he wasn't hurt, but he never should have been there in the first place.* **3 in the first instance** UK as the first attempt or effort: *Enquiries about the post should be addressed in the first instance to the personnel manager.*

4 first thing at the earliest time in the day: *He said he'd phone back first thing tomorrow.*

IDIOMS **be in the first flush of** to be at the start of something: *He's no longer in the first flush of* ***youth.*** • **first things first** used to tell someone that more important things should be done before less important things: *First things first, let's have something to eat.*

▸**adv 1** A1 before all others in order, time, amount, quality, or importance: *Tom* ***came*** *first in the race.* ◦ *Who finished first?* ◦ *If you get home first, can you put the kettle on?* **2** B1 for the first time: *When did you first meet each other?* ◦ *The company was still very small when I first joined.* **3** A2 (also **firstly**) used at the beginning of a list of things you want to say or write: *First, I want to thank my parents.* ◦ *First* (***of all***) (= *before anything else*)*, I'd like to ask you a few questions.* ◦ UK *First* ***off*** (= *before anything else*)*, let me introduce myself.*

IDIOMS **at first** B1 in or at the beginning: *At first I thought he was joking but then I realized he meant it.* • **come first** C1 to be the most important person or thing to someone: *Her family will always come first with her.* • **first among equals** UK a member of a group who is officially on the same level as the other members but who in fact has slightly more responsibility or power: *The prime minister is first among equals in the cabinet.* • **first and foremost** C1 more than anything else: *In spite of being elected to office, she remains first and foremost a writer.* • **first and last** as the most important fact: *Don was, first and last, a good friend.* • **first come, first served** used to mean that people will receive something or be dealt with in the order in which they ask or arrive • **put sb/sth first** C2 to treat someone or something as being more important than anyone or anything else: *She all too often puts others first and never stops to think of herself.*

▸**noun THING/PERSON** ▷ **1** B1 [S] the first person or thing to do or be something, or the first person or thing mentioned: [+ to infinitive] *She was* ***one of the*** *first* ***to*** *arrive.* ◦ *He is* ***the*** *first* (= *very willing*) ***to*** *admit that much of his success is due to his good looks.* ◦ *Tonight sees the first of three documentaries about cancer.* **2 from the (very) first** from the beginning: *I've opposed the proposal from the very first.* **NEVER BEFORE** ▷ **3** C2 [S] something that has never happened or been done before: *This new surgical technique is* ***a*** *first* ***for*** (= *has never been done before in*) *Britain.* **QUALIFICATION** ▷ **4** [C] (also ˌ**first-class deˈgree**) UK the best possible degree you can get from a British university: *She has a first* ***in*** *English from Newcastle University.* **VEHICLE** ▷ **5** [U] (also **first gear**) (in a vehicle) the GEAR used when starting to drive forward or when driving up a steep hill

ˌfirst ˈaid noun [U] basic medical treatment that is given to someone as soon as possible after they have been hurt in an accident or suddenly become ill: *Did you learn any first aid at school?* ◦ *first-aid equipment*

first-aider /ˌfɜːstˈeɪ.dəʳ/ US /ˌfɝːstˈeɪ.dɚ/ noun [C] UK someone who is trained to give first aid: *How many first-aiders are there in your office?*

ˌfirst ˈbase noun [C usually singular] in baseball, the first of four places you must run to after hitting the ball and before scoring a point, or the position of a player defending this place: *Mattingly* ***played*** *first base for the Yankees.*

IDIOMS **get to first base** US informal humorous to kiss someone in a sexual way • **get to/reach first base** US informal to have the first achievement or agreement that is needed for later success: *The proposal is so poorly designed, they won't even get to first base with the directors.*

firstborn (child) /ˌfɜːst.bɔːnˈtʃaɪld/ US /ˌfɝːst.bɔːrn-/ noun [C usually singular] the first child of a set of parents: *Olaf is my firstborn.*

ˌfirst ˈclass adj; adv; noun

▸**adj** (also ˌ**first-ˈclass**) **EXCELLENT** ▷ **1** excellent: *She's made a first-class job of decorating the living room.* **QUALIFICATION** ▷ **2** best possible degree you can get from a British university **MOST EXPENSIVE** ▷ **3** relating to the most expensive and highest quality service on a plane or train, or in a hotel: *a first-class ticket* ◦ *first-class accommodation/travel* **4** UK relating to the most expensive and fastest service for sending post: *first-class mail/postage* ◦ *How much is a first-class stamp?*

▸**adv 1** If you travel first class in a train, aircraft, etc., you use the best and most expensive type of service: *She always travels first class.* **2** UK If you send something first class, you use the most expensive and fastest type of post: *How much more would it cost to send it first class?*

▸**noun** [U] **1** the best and most expensive seats on a plane or in a train: *Because of the delay, we were offered seats* ***in*** *first class.* **2** UK the most expensive and fastest post service: *First class costs more, but it will arrive tomorrow.*

ˌfirst ˈcousin noun [C] a child of your aunt or uncle

ˌfirst-deˈgree adj [before noun] US used to describe a crime that is the most serious of its type, especially because of being planned and intended: *first-degree* ***murder/felony/assault*** → Compare **second-degree**

ˌfirst-degree ˈburn noun [C] the least serious type of burn that needs medical treatment → Compare **second-degree burn, third-degree burn**

the ˌFirst ˈFleet noun [S, + sing/pl verb] Australian English the ships that brought the first Europeans to Australia

First Fleeter /ˌfɜːstˈfliː.təʳ/ US /ˌfɝːstˈfliː.t̬ɚ/ noun [C] Australian English someone who is related to a person who travelled in the First Fleet

the ˌfirst ˈfloor noun [S] B1 in British English, the floor of a building that is directly above ground level, or in American English, the floor at ground level: *She works* ***on the first floor.*** • ˌ**first-ˈfloor** adj [before noun] B1 *a first-floor flat/apartment/office*

ˌfirst ˌfruit noun [C usually plural] mainly UK the first result of someone's effort or work: *These improvements in quality are the first fruits of our investment.*

firsthand /ˌfɜːstˈhænd/ US /ˌfɝːst-/ adv If you experience something firsthand, you experience it yourself: *Most of the older reporters have experienced war firsthand.* • **firsthand** adj [before noun] *Most of us have firsthand experience of teaching.*

ˌfirst ˈlady noun [C] a woman who is married to the political leader of a country or a part of a country

ˌfirst ˈlanguage noun [C] B2 the language that someone learns to speak first

ˌfirst ˈlight noun [U] the time when the sun first appears in the morning: *We'll leave* ***at*** *first light.*

firstly /ˈfɜːst.li/ US /ˈfɝːst-/ adv (also **first**) B2 used to refer to the first thing in a list: *There are two very good reasons why we can't do it. Firstly, we don't have enough money, and secondly, we don't have enough time.*

ˌfirst ˈmate noun [C] the second most important officer on a ship that is not part of the navy

ˌfirst ˈminister noun [C] (in some areas or countries,

for example Scotland and Wales) the leader of the ruling political party: *the Scottish first minister*

ˌfirst ˌname noun [C] **1** A2 the name that was given to you when you were born and that comes before your family name: *It can be rude to **call** someone **by** their first name if they are much older or more important than you.* **2 on first-name terms** UK (US **on a first-name basis**) friendly or familiar enough with someone to call them by their first name

ˌfirst ˈnight noun [C] UK (US **ˈopening ˌnight**) the first public performance of a play

ˌfirst ofˈfender noun [C] someone who has been officially judged to be guilty of a crime for the first time

ˌfirst ˈofficer noun [C] **first mate**

ˌfirst-past-the-ˈpost adj UK using a voting system in which a person is elected because they get more votes than anyone else in the area that they want to represent → Compare **proportional representation**

the ˌfirst ˈperson noun [S] B2 the form of a verb or PRONOUN that is used when people are speaking or writing about themselves: *Autobiographies are written **in** the first person.* ◦ *'I' and 'we' are first-person pronouns.*

ˌfirst ˈprinciples noun [plural] UK the basic and most important reasons for doing or believing something: *We seem to have forgotten why we're fighting this campaign – we really need to return to first principles.*

ˌfirst-ˈrate adj extremely good: *a first-rate restaurant*

ˌfirst reˈfusal noun [U] the opportunity to buy something before it is offered to anyone else: *My sister's selling her car and she's offered me first refusal on it.*

ˌfirst ˈstrike noun [C] in a nuclear war, an attack intended to destroy the enemy's ability to fire before they have had an opportunity to do so

ˌfirst-time ˈbuyer noun [C] UK someone who is buying their own house or apartment for the first time, especially by borrowing money from a bank or similar organization

the ˌFirst ˌWorld ˈWar noun [S] the war from 1914 to 1918 in which many countries fought

firth /fɜːθ/ US /fɝːθ/ noun [C] Scottish English a long strip of sea reaching into the land: *the Firth of Forth*

fiscal /ˈfɪs.kəl/ adj specialized connected with (public) money: *fiscal policy* • **fiscally** /-i/ adv

ˈfiscal ˌyear noun [C] **financial year**

fish /fɪʃ/ noun; verb

▸noun (plural **fish** or **fishes**) **1** A1 [C or U] an animal which lives in water, is covered with SCALES, and breathes by taking water in through its mouth, or the flesh of these animals eaten as food: *Several large fish live in the pond.* ◦ *Sanjay **caught** the biggest fish I've ever seen.* ◦ *I don't like fish (= don't like to eat fish).* **2 an odd/queer fish** mainly UK old-fashioned a strange person

IDIOMS **be a big fish in a small pond** to have a lot of influence only over a small area • **be like a fish out of water** to feel awkward because you are in a situation which you have not experienced before or because you are very different from the people around you • **be neither fish nor fowl** like one thing in some ways and like another thing in other ways • **have bigger/other fish to fry** informal to have something more important to do • **there are plenty more fish in the sea** used to say that there are many other people or possibilities, especially when one person or thing has been unsuitable or unsuccessful: *Don't cry over Pierre – there are plenty more fish in the sea!*

▸verb **SEARCH** ▷ **1** [I usually + adv/prep] to search, especially in difficult conditions: *She fished **in** her tool box **for** the right spanner.* ◦ *The director was fishing **for** information about our strategy.* ◦ *He's always fishing **for compliments** (= trying to make people say good things about him).* **ANIMAL** ▷ **2** B1 [I or T] to catch fish from a river, sea, lake, etc., or to try to do this: *They're fishing **for** tuna.* ◦ *The sea here has been fished intensely over the last ten years.* **3 fished out** If an area of water has been fished out, all or most of the fish in it have been caught.

IDIOMS **a fishing expedition** mainly US an attempt to discover the facts about something by collecting a lot of information, often secretly: *The investigators' request for the company's accounts is simply a fishing expedition – they have no real evidence of wrongdoing.* • **fish in troubled waters** UK to try to win an advantage from a difficult situation or from someone else's problems • **fish or cut bait** US informal used to tell someone to take action or to stop saying that they will: *He's been promising voters that he'll support gun control, now it's time to fish or cut bait.*

PHRASAL VERB **fish sth out** informal to pull something out of water or take something out of a bag or pocket: *Police fished a body out **of** the river this morning.* ◦ *He fished out a coin **from** his pocket.*

ˌfish and ˈchips noun [U] fish covered with BATTER (= a mixture of flour, eggs, and milk) and then fried and served with pieces of fried potato

fishbowl /ˈfɪʃ.bəʊl/ US /-boʊl/ noun [C] US for **goldfish bowl**

fishcake /ˈfɪʃ.keɪk/ noun [C] a mixture of fish and potato that has been formed into small, flat round shapes, covered with BREADCRUMBS, and then cooked in oil

fisherman /ˈfɪʃ.ə.mən/ US /-ɚ-/ noun [C] (plural **-men** /-mən/) B2 someone who catches fish, especially as their job

fishery /ˈfɪʃ.ər.i/ US /-ɚ.i/ noun [C] an area of water where fish are caught so they can be sold: *an offshore fishery*

fisheye lens /ˌfɪʃ.aɪˈlenz/ noun [C] specialized a camera LENS that curves out from the camera and gives a view of an extremely wide area, with the central objects appearing closer than those at the edge

ˈfish ˌfarm noun [C] a special area of water used for breeding and growing fish

ˌfish ˈfinger noun [C] UK (US **ˈfish ˌstick**) a rectangular piece of fish covered in BREADCRUMBS and cooked

fishing /ˈfɪʃ.ɪŋ/ noun [U] A2 the sport or job of catching fish: *My dad loves to **go** fishing.* ◦ *salmon/trout fishing* ◦ *fishing tackle (= equipment used for catching fish)* ◦ *Fishing is still their main source of income.*

ˈfishing ˌpole noun [C] US for **fishing rod**

ˈfishing ˌrod noun [C] (US **ˈfishing ˌpole**) a long pole made of wood, plastic, etc. with a line attached to it and a HOOK at the end of the line, used for catching fish

ˈfish ˌkettle noun [C] a large metal pan for cooking fish

ˈfish ˌknife noun [C] a knife for eating fish, with a wide blade and a round edge

fishmonger /ˈfɪʃˌmʌŋ.gəʳ/ US /-gɚ/ noun [C] mainly UK **1** someone who sells fish, especially from a shop **2 fishmonger's** (plural **fishmongers**) a shop that sells fish: *I'll stop at the fishmonger's on my way home from work.*

fishnet /ˈfɪʃ.net/ noun [U] a type of material which looks like net: *She was wearing black fishnet* ***stockings***.

ˈfish ˌoil noun [C or U] oil from fish such as TUNA or SALMON, thought to be good for your health

ˈfish ˌslice noun [C] mainly UK (US usually **spatula**) a kitchen tool that has a wide, flat blade with long holes in it, used for lifting and turning food while cooking

ˈfish ˌtank noun [C] a glass container used for keeping fish in, especially pet tropical fish

fishwife /ˈfɪʃ.waɪf/ noun [C] (plural **fishwives**) UK old-fashioned a loud, unpleasant woman

fishy /ˈfɪʃ.i/ adj **DISHONEST** ▷ **1** informal seeming dishonest or false: *There's something fishy going on here.* **LIKE FISH** ▷ **2** tasting or smelling of fish

IDIOM **smell fishy** informal If a situation or an explanation smells fishy, it causes you to think that someone is being dishonest.

fissile /ˈfɪs.aɪl/ (US) /-əl/ adj specialized **1** (of rock) able to be divided easily into pieces: *Because of its layered structure, mica is fissile.* **2** (of atoms) able to produce nuclear fission: *An amount of fissile material went missing as a result of the accident.*

fission /ˈfɪʃ.ən/ noun [U] specialized the process of dividing the NUCLEUS of an atom, which results in the release of a large amount of energy, or the division of a living cell as part of REPRODUCTION: ***nuclear*** *fission* ◦ *The fission* ***of*** *the cell could be inhibited with certain chemicals.*

fissure /ˈfɪʃ.əʳ/ (US) /-ɚ/ noun [C] a deep, narrow CRACK in rock or the earth

fist /fɪst/ noun [C] (C2) a hand with the fingers and thumb held tightly in: *She* ***clenched*** *her fists.* ◦ *Protestors were* ***shaking*** *their fists at the soldiers.*

fistfight /ˈfɪst.faɪt/ noun [C] a fight between people using their hands but no weapons

fistful /ˈfɪst.fʊl/ noun [C] **1** an amount of something that you can hold in your fist: *He held out a fistful of crumpled notes.* **2** informal a large collection or number: *He has a fistful of acting awards.*

fisticuffs /ˈfɪs.tɪ.kʌfs/ noun [plural] old-fashioned or humorous fighting in which people hit each other with their fists

fit /fɪt/ verb; adj; noun

▸verb (-tt-) **CORRECT SIZE** ▷ **1** (B1) [I or T] to be the right size or shape for someone or something: *That jacket fits you perfectly.* ◦ *The dress fits* ***like a glove*** *(= very well).* ◦ *Our new sofa doesn't fit* ***through*** *the door.* ◦ *I don't think another desk will fit* ***into*** *this classroom.* ◦ *My car's too big to fit* ***in*** *this space.* **BE SUITABLE** ▷ **2** (C1) [T] to be suitable for something: *With her qualifications, she should fit the job perfectly.* ◦ *Let the punishment fit the crime.* ◦ *I'm sure we'll have something to fit your requirements, Madam.*

> **!** Common mistake: **fit or suit?**
>
> **Warning:** choose the correct verb!
>
> To talk about something being right for a particular person, situation, or occasion, don't say 'fit', say **suit**:
>
> ~~*Life in a small village didn't fit him.*~~
>
> *Life in a small village didn't suit him.*

PUT IN POSITION ▷ **3** (B2) [T] to provide something and put it in the correct position: *All the carpets we sell are fitted free.* ◦ *She's been fitted with an artificial leg.* **ILLNESS** ▷ **4** [I] UK specialized to have a fit (= sudden attack of uncontrolled movements)

IDIOMS **fit the bill** to be suitable for a particular purpose: *This new software certainly fits the bill.* • **fit to drop** mainly UK extremely tired: *After the run they were fit to drop.* • **if the cap fits, wear it** UK saying (US **if the shoe fits (wear it)**) used to tell someone that if they are guilty of bad behaviour, they should accept criticism

PHRASAL VERBS **fit in 1** (C1) to feel that you belong to a particular group and are accepted by them: *It's no surprise she's leaving – she never really fitted in.* **2** (B2) If one thing fits in with another thing, they look pleasant together or are suitable for each other: *It's a very nice sofa but it doesn't fit in* ***with*** *the rest of the room.* • **fit sb/sth in** to find time to do or deal with something or someone: *Dr Jones is very busy but I'm sure she'll be able to fit you in tomorrow.* • **fit in with sth** If one activity or event fits in with another, they exist or happen together in a way that is convenient. • **fit sth out** [M usually passive] to supply someone or something with all of the things which will be needed: *The ship will be in dock for eight months to be fitted out for its new duties.* • **fit sth up** UK to put furniture in a room or building: *We've fitted up the spare room* ***as*** *a nursery.* • **fit sb up** UK slang to make someone appear guilty: *Of course she didn't do it – someone fitted her up.*

▸adj (**fitter**, **fittest**) **HEALTHY** ▷ **1** (A2) healthy and strong, especially as a result of exercise: *I jog to* ***keep*** *fit.* ◦ *You need to be very fit to hike the Inca Trail.* → Opposite **unfit** **SUITABLE** ▷ **2** (C1) suitable for a particular purpose or activity: *She's not fit* ***for*** *the level of responsibility she's been given.* → Opposite **unfit 3 be in no fit state to do sth** to not be able to do something because you are upset, ill, drunk, etc.: *He's very upset and is in no fit state to drive.* **4 fit for human consumption** safe for people to eat **5 (not) fit for purpose** Something that is fit for purpose does what it is meant to do. **6 see/think fit** (C1) to consider an action or decision to be correct for the situation: *Just do whatever you think fit – I'm sure you'll make the right decision.* **ATTRACTIVE** ▷ **7** UK slang sexually attractive: *I met this really fit bloke in the pub last night.*

IDIOMS **be (as) fit as a fiddle** (UK also **be (as) fit as a flea**) to be very healthy and strong: *My grandmother's 89, but she's as fit as a fiddle.* • **fit to be tied** US informal extremely angry

▸noun **ILLNESS** ▷ **1** [C] a sudden attack of illness when someone cannot control their movements and becomes unconscious: *an epileptic fit* ◦ *He* ***had*** *a fit at work and collapsed.* **SHORT PERIOD** ▷ **2** [C] a sudden, uncontrolled period of doing something or feeling something: *a coughing/sneezing fit* ◦ *She hit him* ***in a*** *fit* ***of*** *anger.* **CORRECT SIZE** ▷ **3** [S] the way that something fits: *The trousers were a good fit but the jacket was too small.* ◦ *Check the fit* ***of*** *the pieces before gluing them in place.*

IDIOMS **have/throw a fit** informal to become very angry or worried, often shouting a lot: *She'll throw a fit when she sees the mess you've made.* • **in fits (of laughter)** UK informal laughing a lot: *His stories had them in fits of laughter.* • **in/by fits and starts** If something happens in fits and starts, it often stops and then starts again: *Replies to the advertisement are arriving in fits and starts.*

fitful /ˈfɪt.fəl/ **adj** often stopping and starting and not happening in a regular or continuous way: *fitful breathing* ◦ *a fitful sleep* • **fitfully** /-i/ **adv** *She **slept** fitfully (= only for short, irregular periods) throughout the night and arose before dawn.*

fitment /ˈfɪt.mənt/ **noun** [C usually plural] mainly UK a piece of furniture or equipment made especially for a particular room or space: *kitchen/bathroom fitments*

fitness /ˈfɪt.nəs/ **noun** [U] **HEALTH** ▷ **1** B1 the condition of being physically strong and healthy: *I'm trying to improve my fitness by cycling to work.* **SUITABLE QUALITY** ▷ **2** how suitable someone or something is: *His fitness **for** the new position is not in question.* ◦ [+ to infinitive] *Many people are concerned about her fitness **to** govern.*

F

ˈfitness ˌcentre **noun** [C] a place where you go to exercise, for example by lifting weights or using other equipment

fitted /ˈfɪt.ɪd/ US /ˈfɪţ-/ **adj** [before noun] **MADE TO FIT** ▷ **1** made to fit the shape of someone or something: *a fitted jacket/shirt* ◦ *fitted sheets* **FIXED** ▷ **2** mainly UK permanently fixed in position: *a fitted wardrobe/cupboard* ◦ *We're having a new fitted kitchen put in.*

ˌfitted ˈcarpet **noun** [C or U] UK (US **ˌwall-to-wall ˈcarpet**) a carpet that is cut to cover the whole floor in a room

fitter /ˈfɪt.əʳ/ US /ˈfɪţ.ɚ/ **noun** [C] **1** someone whose job is to repair or put together equipment or machines: *an engine fitter* ◦ *a gas fitter* **2** someone whose job is to cut and fit especially clothes or carpets: *a carpet fitter*

fitting /ˈfɪt.ɪŋ/ US /ˈfɪţ-/ **adj; noun**

▸**adj** formal suitable or right for a particular situation or occasion: *a fitting tribute* ◦ [+ that] ***It** is fitting **that** we should remember those who died.*

▸**noun** **CLOTHES** ▷ **1** [C] an occasion when someone who is having clothes made for them puts on the clothes before they are finished to make certain they will fit: *I'm having the final fitting of my wedding dress on Thursday.* **SMALL PART** ▷ **2** [C usually plural] a small part or thing: *plumbing fittings* ◦ *electric light fittings* → Compare **fixture** **IN A HOUSE** ▷ **3** [C usually plural] UK (US **furnishing**) an object in a house, such as a cooker or a shelf, that is not permanently fixed, and can be either taken away or left when the people who live there move to another house: *The house price, including **fixtures and** fittings, is £200,000.*

ˈfitting ˌroom **noun** [C] a room or area in a shop where you can put on clothes to check that they fit before you buy them

five /faɪv/ **number** A1 the number 5: *Five, four, three, two, one, blast-off!* ◦ *I work five days a week.* → See also **high five**

IDIOMS **give sb (a) five** informal to hit someone's open hand with your own to celebrate doing something well or achieving something, especially in sports • **take five** US informal used to tell someone to stop working and relax for a short period of time

ˌfive-a-side ˈfootball **noun** [U] UK football played by teams of five players, not the usual eleven players

ˌfive o'clock ˈshadow **noun** [S] the slight darkness on a man's face, especially his chin, caused by the growth of hair during the day

fiver /ˈfaɪ.vəʳ/ US /-vɚ/ **noun** [C] UK informal five pounds, or a note worth five pounds: *This CD only cost me a fiver.* → See also **tenner**

ˌfive-ˈstar **adj** [before noun] describes a hotel or service that is of the best possible quality: *a five-star hotel*

fix /fɪks/ **verb; noun**

▸**verb** **REPAIR** ▷ **1** B1 [T] to repair something: *They couldn't fix my old computer, so I bought a new one.* **ARRANGE** ▷ **2** B2 [I or T] mainly UK to arrange or agree a time, place, price, etc.: *Shall we fix a time for our next meeting?* ◦ *I understand the rent is fixed **at** £750 a month.* **FASTEN** ▷ **3** B2 [T + adv/prep] to fasten something in position so that it cannot move: *We fixed the bookcase **to** the wall.* **SIGHT** ▷ **4** C2 [T] to keep something or someone in sight: *His eyes were fixed **on** the distant yacht.* ◦ *She fixed the child **with** a stare of such disapproval he did not dare move.* **KEEP** ▷ **5** [T usually + adv/prep] to continue to think about or remember something: *It is somehow fixed **in** my **mind** that my fate and that woman's are intertwined.* ◦ *She was so frightened that she could not fix her thoughts **on** anything.* **CHEAT** ▷ **6** [T often passive] to do something dishonest to make certain that a competition, race, or election is won by a particular person: *Several jockeys were arrested on suspicion of fixing the race.* ◦ *It sounds like the election was fixed.* **HAIR/MAKE-UP/CLOTHES** ▷ **7** B1 [T] to make your hair, make-up, clothes, etc. look tidy: *Give me a couple of minutes while I fix my hair.* **PREPARE FOOD** ▷ **8** B2 [T] mainly US informal to cook or prepare food or drink: *Whose turn is it to fix dinner?* ◦ [+ two objects] *Can I fix you a drink?/Can I fix a drink **for** you?* **PUNISH** ▷ **9** [T] slang to punish especially someone who has been unfair: *I'm gonna fix her if she doesn't stop telling lies about me!* **PRESERVE COLOURS** ▷ **10** [T] specialized to treat something, especially photographic material, with chemicals to prevent its colours becoming pale **STOP REPRODUCTION** ▷ **11** [T] US informal to remove the REPRODUCTIVE organs of an animal so that it is unable to produce young animals **DRUG** ▷ **12** [I] slang to INJECT (= put into the body through a needle) an illegal drug

PHRASAL VERBS **fix sth up** **ARRANGE** ▷ **1** C1 to arrange a meeting, date, event, etc.: *I'd like to fix up a meeting with you next week sometime.* **REPAIR** ▷ **2** to repair or change something in order to improve it: *Nick loves fixing up old cars.* • **fix sb up** **PROVIDE** ▷ **1** to provide someone with something that they need: *Can he fix us up **with** somewhere to stay?* **FIND A PARTNER** ▷ **2** informal to find a romantic partner for someone: *Jacques tried to fix me up **with** his older sister.*

▸**noun** **CHEAT** ▷ **1** [C usually singular] a situation in which someone does something dishonest to make certain that a competition, race, or election is won by a particular person: *The result was a fix!* **AWKWARD SITUATION** ▷ **2** [C usually singular] informal an awkward or difficult situation: *I'm **in** a bit of a fix with the arrangements.* **DRUG** ▷ **3** [C] slang an amount of an illegal drug, or of another substance that has an effect on someone if they take it: *He was shaking badly and needed a fix.* ◦ humorous *Ginny needs her daily fix of chocolate.* **POSITION** ▷ **4** [C] (the calculation of) the position of a vehicle, usually in relation to the Earth: *Do we still have a fix **on** that jet?*

fixated /fɪkˈseɪ.tɪd/ US /ˈfɪk.seɪ.ţɪd/ **adj** [after verb] unable to stop thinking about something: *a nation fixated **on** the past* ◦ *Back in London, he became fixated **with** his best friend's daughter.*

fixation /fɪkˈseɪ.ʃən/ **noun** [C] the state of being unable to stop thinking about something or someone, or an unnaturally strong interest in them: *Liz has a fixation **with*** (US ***on***) *food.* ◦ *a mother fixation*

fixative /ˈfɪk.sə.tɪv/ US /-ţɪv/ **noun** [C or U] **1** a substance which holds something in position: *a fixative for dentures* **2** a chemical used to treat photographic material in order to preserve its colour

fixed /fɪkst/ **adj** **ARRANGED** ▷ **1** B2 arranged or decided already and not able to be changed: *a fixed price ◦ fixed interest rates ◦ Is the date of the wedding fixed yet?* **FASTENED** ▷ **2** fastened somewhere and not able to be moved

IDIOMS **be of/have no fixed abode/address** legal to not have a permanent home • **how are you fixed for sth?** informal used to ask how much of something someone has, or to ask about someone's arrangements: *How are you fixed for cash? ◦ How are you fixed for Saturday evening?*

ˌfixed ˈassets noun [plural] in business, buildings, equipment, and land owned by a company

fixedly /ˈfɪk.sɪd.li/ adv **gaze/look/stare fixedly** to look continuously at one thing: *Taylor was staring fixedly at her.*

ˌfixed ˈpenalty noun [C] a fixed amount of money you have to pay as a punishment for a driving offence, without having to go to court

fixer /ˈfɪk.səʳ/ US /-sɚ/ noun [C] informal someone who is skilled at arranging for things to happen, especially dishonestly

fixing /ˈfɪk.sɪŋ/ noun [U] dishonest activity to make certain that a competition, race, or election is won by a particular person: *Seven jockeys were arrested and charged with race fixing. ◦ After several days of questioning, he admitted to match fixing.*

fixity /ˈfɪk.sə.ti/ US /-t̬i/ noun [U] formal the quality of not changing

fixture /ˈfɪks.tʃəʳ/ US /-tʃɚ/ noun [C] **FIXED OBJECT** ▷ **1** mainly UK a permanently fixed piece of furniture in a house, such as a bath, which would not be taken by someone when they move to a new home: *All fixtures **and fittings** are included in the house price.* ◦ figurative *They've been together so long he's become a permanent fixture in her life.* → Compare **fitting** **SPORTS EVENT** ▷ **2** UK a day and usually a time agreed for a sports event: *Next season's fixtures will be published early next month.*

fizz /fɪz/ verb; noun

▸verb [I] **PRODUCE GAS** ▷ If a liquid fizzes, it produces a lot of bubbles and makes a continuous 's' sound: *I could hear the champagne fizz as he poured it into my glass.*

▸noun [U] **GAS BUBBLES** ▷ **1** bubbles of gas in a liquid **2** UK informal a fizzy drink, especially CHAMPAGNE: *Who'd like some fizz?*

fizzle /ˈfɪz.əl/ verb [I] **1** mainly US to gradually end: *Interest in the project fizzled after the funding was withdrawn.* **2** UK to make a weak continuous 's' sound: *The fire fizzled miserably in the rain.*

PHRASAL VERB **fizzle out** to gradually end, often in a disappointing or weak way: *They went off to different universities and their relationship just fizzled out.*

fizzy /ˈfɪz.i/ adj having a lot of bubbles: *fizzy orange/mineral water* • **fizziness** /-nəs/ noun [U]

fjord (also **fiord**) /fjɔːd/ US /fjɔːrd/ noun [C] a long strip of sea between steep hills, found especially in Norway

flab /flæb/ noun [U] informal disapproving soft, loose flesh on someone's body: *I've got to lose this flab on my belly!*

flabbergast /ˈflæb.ə.ɡɑːst/ US /-ɚ.ɡæst/ verb [T often passive] informal to shock someone, usually by telling them something they were not expecting: *He was flabbergasted when we told him how cheap it was.* • **flabbergasted** /-ɡɑː.stɪd/ US /-ɚ.ɡæs.tɪd/ adj *When they announced her name, the winner just sat there, flabbergasted.*

flabby /ˈflæb.i/ adj **FAT** ▷ **1** informal disapproving soft and fat: *flabby arms/thighs ◦ I was starting to get a bit flabby around my waist.* **WEAK** ▷ **2** weak and without force: *a flabby argument* • **flabbiness** /-nəs/ noun [U]

flaccid /ˈflæs.ɪd/ adj **1** formal soft or weak rather than firm: *The penis is usually in a flaccid state.* **2** disapproving weak and not effective

flack /flæk/ noun **1** [U] **flak 2** [C] US informal a person chosen by a group or organization that is in a difficult situation to speak officially for them to the public and answer questions and criticisms

flag /flæɡ/ noun; verb

▸noun [C] **SYMBOL** ▷ **1** B1 a piece of cloth, usually rectangular and fixed to a pole at one edge, that has a pattern which shows it represents a country or a group, or has a particular meaning: *Flags of all the participating countries are **flying** outside the stadium. ◦ Flags were flapping/fluttering in the breeze. ◦ The guard **waved** his flag and the train pulled away from the station.* **STONE** ▷ **2** a **flagstone**

IDIOMS **keep the flag flying** mainly UK to act or speak for the country or group which a flag represents • **put the flags out!** UK humorous something that you say when you are pleased and surprised that something has happened: *Josh has cleaned the bathroom – put the flags out!* • **wave/show/fly the flag** UK to show support for the country, group, or organization that you belong to

▸verb (-gg-) **MARK** ▷ **1** [T] to put a mark on something so it can be found easily among other similar things: *Flag any files which might be useful later.* **BECOME TIRED** ▷ **2** [I] to become tired or less interested: *I was starting to flag after the ninth mile. ◦ The conversation was flagging.*

PHRASAL VERB **flag sth/sb down** to cause a vehicle to stop by waving at its driver: *I managed to flag down a passing police car.*

ˈflag ˌday noun [C] UK a day when money is collected in public places for a CHARITY

ˈFlag ˌDay noun [U] 14 June, a holiday in the US to remember the day in 1777 when the US first officially used its flag

flagellant /ˈflædʒ.ɪ.lənt/ noun [C] formal someone who WHIPS himself or herself or someone else for religious reasons

flagellate /ˈflædʒ.ə.leɪt/ verb [T] formal to WHIP yourself or someone else, especially as a religious act • **flagellation** /ˌflædʒ.əˈleɪ.ʃən/ noun [U]

flagged /flæɡd/ adj mainly UK made of or covered in FLAGSTONES: *a flagged path*

flagging /flæɡ/ adj becoming weaker: *flagging energy/enthusiasm*

ˌflag of conˈvenience noun [C usually singular] UK If a ship sails under a flag of convenience, it means it is operated or taxed under the laws of a country different from its home country in order to save money: *They always register their ships **under** a flag of convenience.*

flagon /ˈflæɡ.ən/ noun [C] a large container for especially alcoholic drink, used in the past: *a flagon of wine*

flagpole /ˈflæɡ.pəʊl/ US /-poʊl/ noun [C] (also **flagstaff**) a long pole which a flag is fastened to

flagrant /ˈfleɪ.ɡrənt/ adj (of a bad action, situation, person, etc.) shocking because of being so obvious: *a flagrant misuse of funds/privilege ◦ a flagrant breach of trust ◦ a flagrant disregard for the law* • **flagrantly** /-li/

F

adv *The organization flagrantly promotes the use of violence.*

flagship /ˈflæɡ.ʃɪp/ noun [C] **BEST PRODUCT** ▷ **1** the best or most important product, idea, building, etc. that an organization owns or produces: *This machine is the flagship in our new range of computers.* ◦ *The company's flagship* ***store*** *is in New York.* **SHIP** ▷ **2** the ship within a group on which the most important officer sails

flagstaff /ˈflæɡ.stɑːf/ US /-stæf/ noun [C] a **flagpole**

flagstone /ˈflæɡ.stəʊn/ US /-stoʊn/ noun [C] (also **flag**) a large, flat piece of stone or concrete used for paths, floors, etc.

F

ˈflag-ˌwaving noun [U] disapproving the strong expression of support for a country or group, sometimes with military intention

flail /fleɪl/ verb; noun

▸verb [I or T] (also **flail about/around**) (especially of arms and legs) to move energetically in an uncontrolled way: *A wasp came towards us and Howard started flailing his arms around.* ◦ *She ran from the house in a terrible rage, her arms flailing in the air.*

▸noun [C] a tool consisting of a rod which hangs from a long handle, used especially in the past for THRESHING grain

flair /fleəʳ/ US /fler/ noun **1** C1 [S] natural ability to do something well: *He has a flair* ***for*** *languages.* **2** C2 [U] a situation in which something is done in an exciting and interesting way: *He played with great imagination and flair.* ◦ *It's a competent enough piece of writing but it lacks flair.*

flak (also **flack**) /flæk/ noun [U] **CRITICISM** ▷ **1** informal strong criticism or opposition: *She* ***took/caught*** *some flak from her parents about her new dress.* **FIRING OF GUNS** ▷ **2** the firing of guns from the ground at enemy aircraft, or the bullets, etc. that the guns fire: *They flew into heavy flak over the target area.*

flake /fleɪk/ noun; verb

▸noun [C] **SMALL PIECE** ▷ **1** a small, thin piece of something, especially if it has come from a surface covered with a layer of something: *flakes of snow* ◦ *soap flakes* ◦ *This room needs decorating – flakes of paint keep coming off the walls.* **PERSON** ▷ **2** US informal a person who you cannot trust to remember things or to do what they say they will do, or someone who behaves in a strange way

▸verb [I] to come off a surface in small, thin pieces: *Patches of skin are starting to flake* ***off.***

PHRASAL VERB **flake out** informal to suddenly go to sleep or feel weak because you are extremely tired: *I got home and flaked out on the sofa.*

ˈflak ˌjacket noun [C] a special piece of clothing worn by soldiers and police to protect them from bullets and weapons

flaky /ˈfleɪ.ki/ adj **SMALL PIECE** ▷ **1** coming off easily in small, flat, thin pieces: *dry, flaky skin* ◦ *a flaky scalp* **PERSON** ▷ **2** mainly US informal behaving in a way that is not responsible or expected: *The central character of the play is a flaky neurotic.*

flambé /ˈflɒm.beɪ/ US /flɑːmˈbeɪ/ verb [T] to pour alcohol over food and set fire to it during cooking: *flambéed pancakes* • **flambé** adj [after noun] *steak flambé*

flamboyant /flæmˈbɔɪ.ənt/ adj very confident in behaviour, or intended to be noticed, especially by being brightly coloured: *a flamboyant gesture* ◦ *The writer's flamboyant lifestyle was well known.* ◦ *His clothes were rather flamboyant for such a serious occasion.* • **flamboyance** /-əns/ noun [U] *Her flamboyance annoys some people but delights others.* • **flamboyantly** /-li/ adv

flame /fleɪm/ noun; verb

▸noun **FIRE** ▷ **1** B2 [C or U] burning gas (from something on fire) which produces usually yellow light: *The flames grew larger as the fire spread.* ◦ *The car flipped over and* ***burst into*** *flames (= started burning immediately).* ◦ *When the fire engine arrived the house was already* ***in*** *flames (= burning).* **EMOTION** ▷ **2** [C] literary a powerful feeling: *Flames* ***of*** *passion swept through both of them.* → See also **old flame** **COMPUTING** ▷ **3** [C] slang an angry or offensive email: *flame wars*

IDIOM **go up in flames** **1** to burn or be destroyed by fire: *The factory went up in flames.* **2** to be damaged or destroyed: *His career went up in flames when he was jailed for theft.*

▸verb **BURN** ▷ **1** [I] literary to burn (more) brightly: *The fire flamed cosily in the hearth.* ◦ *The fire suddenly flamed (****up****).* **EMOTION** ▷ **2** [I] literary If an emotion flames, you feel it suddenly and strongly: *Seeing the damage made hatred flame* ***within*** *her.* **3** [I] literary to suddenly become hot and red with emotion: *His face flamed (****red****) with anger.* **COMPUTING** ▷ **4** [T] slang to send an angry or insulting email: *Please don't flame me if you disagree with this message.*

flamenco /fləˈmeŋ.kəʊ/ US /-koʊ/ noun [C or U] (plural **flamencos**) a type of Spanish dance music, or the dance performed to this music: *flamenco music/dancers*

flameproof /ˈfleɪm.pruːf/ adj not likely to burn or be damaged by fire: *flameproof clothing*

flamer /ˈfleɪ.məʳ/ US /-mɚ/ noun [C] slang someone who sends an angry or insulting email

ˈflame-reˌtardant adj If a substance is flame-retardant, it will slow down the spread of fire.

flamethrower /ˈfleɪmˌθrəʊ.əʳ/ US /-ˌθroʊ.ɚ/ noun [C] a device that produces a stream of burning liquid and is used for military purposes or for removing plants from an area of wild land

flaming /ˈfleɪ.mɪŋ/ adj; noun

▸adj **1** [before noun] UK slang used to add force, especially anger, to something that is said: *Put that down you flaming idiot!* **2** **a flaming row** informal a very angry argument in which people shout at each other: *We had a flaming row over it last night.*

▸noun [U] the act of sending an angry or insulting email

flamingo /fləˈmɪŋ.ɡəʊ/ US /-ɡoʊ/ noun [C] (plural **flamingos** or **flamingoes**) a large bird with pink feathers, long thin legs, a long neck, and a beak that curves down

flammable /ˈflæm.ə.bl/ adj describes something that burns easily: *Caution! This solvent is highly flammable.*

flan /flæn/ noun [C] **1** UK a case of pastry or cake without a top, containing fruit or something SAVOURY (= not sweet) such as cheese: *a pear flan* ◦ *a flan dish* **2** US a sweet, soft food made from milk, eggs, and sugar

flange /flændʒ/ noun [C] a flat surface sticking out from an object, used to fix it to something or to make it stronger: *The flange around the wheels on railway trains helps to keep them on the rails.*

flank /flæŋk/ noun; verb

▸noun [C] **BODY** ▷ **1** the area of the body between the RIBS and the hips of an animal or a person **SIDE** ▷ **2** the side of something: *right/left flank* ◦ *A small group of houses clings to the eastern flank of the mountain.*

►verb [T usually passive] to be at the side of someone or something: *The president was flanked by senior ministers.*

ˈflank ˌsteak noun [C or U] US a cheap piece of meat cut from the side of a cow: *Marinated grilled flank steak is a good substitute for prime cuts of beef.*

flannel /ˈflæn.əl/ noun; verb

►noun **PIECE OF CLOTH** ▷ **1** [C] UK for FACECLOTH (= a small cloth used to wash the body, especially the face and hands) **TYPE OF CLOTH** ▷ **2** [U] a light cloth usually made from wool, used especially for making clothes: *flannel trousers* **3 flannels** [plural] UK trousers made of flannel: *Traditionally, white flannels are worn when playing cricket.* **UNNECESSARY WORDS** ▷ **4** [U] UK informal speech containing a lot of words that is used to avoid telling the truth or answering a question, and is often intended to deceive: *Leave out the flannel and answer the question!*

►verb [I or T] (-ll-) UK informal to use a lot of words to avoid telling the truth or answering a question, often in order to deceive

flannelette /ˌflæn.əlˈet/ noun [U] a soft cloth made of cotton: *flannelette sheets/pyjamas*

flap /flæp/ verb; noun

►verb (-pp-) **WAVE** ▷ **1** [I or T] to wave something, especially wings when or as if flying: *A small bird flapped its wings furiously and flew off.* ◦ *Flags flapped in the breeze above their tents.* **BEHAVE NERVOUSLY** ▷ **2** [I] UK informal to behave in a nervous and excited way: *Don't flap – there's plenty of time to cook before they arrive.* ◦ *Stop flapping* ***about/around****!*

►noun **ADDITIONAL PIECE** ▷ **1** [C] a piece of cloth or other material fixed along one edge, especially used for covering or closing something: *a pocket flap* ◦ *a tent flap (= a piece of cloth that acts like a door)* ◦ *A small flap of skin can be seen above the wound.* **EXCITEMENT** ▷ **2** [S] informal a state of nervous excitement: *She's* ***in a*** *flap because her parents are coming to visit.* **3** [S] US a lot of public anger, excitement, or discussion: *She claimed to have had an affair with the candidate, which produced a huge media flap.* **AIRCRAFT PART** ▷ **4** [C] specialized part of the back of an aircraft wing that can be moved up or down to help the aircraft go up or down **WAVE** ▷ **5** [C] the action of a bird waving its wings when flying, or of something else moving in this way: *A few flaps of its long wings and the bird was gone.* **SPEECH SOUND** ▷ **6** [C] specialized a consonant sound made when the tongue moves forward and down, and quickly touches the ALVEOLAR RIDGE

flapjack /ˈflæp.dʒæk/ noun [C] **1** UK a type of sweet, CHEWY cake made from OATS **2** US a PANCAKE (= a sweet, thick cake eaten hot, usually for breakfast)

flapper /ˈflæp.əʳ/ (US) /-ɚ/ noun [C] in the 1920s, a fashionable young woman, especially one showing independent behaviour

flare /fleəʳ/ (US) /fler/ verb; noun

►verb **BURN BRIGHTLY** ▷ **1** [I] to burn brightly either for a short time or not regularly: *The flame above the oil well flared (****up****) into the dark sky.* **GET WORSE** ▷ **2** [I] (also **flare up**) When something bad such as violence, pain, or anger flares (up), it suddenly starts or gets much worse: *Violence flared up again last night.* ◦ ***Tempers*** *flared after a three-hour delay at Gatwick Airport yesterday.* **MAKE WIDER** ▷ **3** [I or T] to (cause to) become wider: *The horse's nostrils flared.* ◦ *The skirt fits tightly over the hips and flares just below the knees.*

►noun **BRIGHTNESS** ▷ **1** [C] a sudden increase in the brightness of a fire: *There was a sudden flare when she threw the petrol onto the fire.* **2** [C] a very bright light or coloured smoke that can be used as a signal, or a device that produces this: *We set off a flare to help guide our rescuers.* **CLOTHES** ▷ **3 flares** [plural] UK trousers that get wider below the knee **4** [C usually singular] the fact of something, especially clothing, becoming wider at one end: *This skirt has a definite flare.*

flared /fleəd/ (US) /flerd/ adj becoming wider at one end: *flared trousers*

ˈflare-up noun [C usually singular] a situation in which something such as violence, pain, or anger suddenly starts or gets much worse: *There was another flare-up* ***of*** *rioting later that day.*

flash /flæʃ/ verb; noun; adj

►verb **SHINE SUDDENLY** ▷ **1** (B2) [I or T] to shine brightly and suddenly, or to make something shine in this way: *Stop flashing that light* ***in*** *my eyes!* ◦ *The lightning flashed and distant thunder rolled.* ◦ *You'd better slow down, that car was flashing (its lights)* ***at*** *you.* **2** [I] literary If someone's eyes flash, they look bright because of the anger or excitement the person is feeling. **MOVE FAST** ▷ **3** (C2) [I usually + adv/prep] to move very fast: *They flashed* ***past/by*** *on a motorcycle.* **SHOW QUICKLY** ▷ **4** (C2) [T] to show something for a short time: *He flashed a smile and offered to buy me a drink.* **5** [I or T] informal If someone flashes, they show their sexual organs in public: *He came out of the bushes and flashed at me.* **COMMUNICATE** ▷ **6** [T usually + adv/prep] to communicate something quickly, especially using radio or light waves: *Within moments of an event happening, the news can be flashed around the world.* **SUDDEN EXPERIENCE** ▷ **7** [I + adv/prep] If something flashes through/across your mind, you suddenly or quickly think of it: *The thought suddenly flashed through my mind that she didn't want to be here.*

PHRASAL VERBS **flash sth around/about** informal to intentionally make people understand that you have something valuable, especially in order to make them feel unhappy because they do not have it: *She was flashing her engagement ring around.* • **flash back** If your mind or thoughts flash back to something that happened in the past, you suddenly remember it: *Her mind flashed back* ***to*** *the day of their divorce.*

►noun **BRIGHT LIGHT** ▷ **1** (B2) [C] a sudden bright light that quickly disappears: *a flash of lightning* ◦ *The bomb exploded in a flash* ***of*** *yellow light.* **SUDDEN EXPERIENCE** ▷ **2** CB [C usually singular] a sudden, powerful emotional or mental experience: *The idea came to her in a flash* ***of*** *inspiration/genius.* **PHOTOGRAPHY** ▷ **3** (B2) [C or U] the device or system used to produce a bright light for a short time when taking a photograph: *Where's the flash for the camera?* ◦ *It's quite dark in here, I'll have to use flash.* **MILITARY SIGN** ▷ **4** [C] UK a small object or piece of material worn on a military uniform as a sign of rank, or (on clothing) a strip or mark of colour different from the main colour **QUICK LOOK** ▷ **5** [C] humorous a quick look at something: *She leaned over and I caught a flash of pink underwear.*

IDIOMS **a flash in the pan** something that happened only once or for a short time and was not repeated: *Sadly, their success was just a flash in the pan.* • **in a flash** (also **quick as a flash**) (C2) quickly or suddenly: *The ceremony was over in a flash.*

►adj UK looking expensive in a way that attracts attention: *That's a very flash suit he's wearing.*

flashback /ˈflæʃ.bæk/ noun **1** (C2) [C or U] a short part of a film, story, or play that goes back to events in the

F

past: *The novel began with a flashback* ***to*** *the hero's experiences in the war.* **2** Ⓒ2 [C usually plural] a sudden, clear memory of a past event or time, usually one that was bad: *I kept* ***having*** *flashbacks* ***of*** *her lying there bleeding.*

flashbulb /ˈflæʃ.bʌlb/ **noun** [C] specialized a small electric light that can be fixed to a camera and makes a bright flash so that photographs can be taken inside or when it is dark

ˈflash ˌcard **noun** [C] a card with a word or picture on it that is used to help students learn

ˈflash ˌdrive **noun** [C] (also **Memory Stick**, **pen drive**) a small piece of equipment that you connect to a computer or other piece of electronic equipment to copy and store information

flasher /ˈflæʃ.əʳ/ Ⓤ /-ɚ/ **noun** [C] informal someone who shows their sexual organs in public

ˌflash ˈflood **noun** [C] a sudden and severe flood

ˌflash-ˈfry **verb** [T] to fry something quickly on both sides in very hot oil

flashgun /ˈflæʃ.gʌn/ **noun** [C] specialized a device usually held away from a camera which automatically makes a flash when a camera is taking a picture

flashlight /ˈflæʃ.laɪt/ **noun** [C] Ⓑ2 US for TORCH (= a small light that you can carry with you)

flashmob /ˈflæʃ.mɒb/ Ⓤ /-mɑːb/ **noun** [C] a group of people who arrange, by email or mobile phone, to come together in a place and do something funny or silly and then leave

flashpoint /ˈflæʃ.pɔɪnt/ **noun** **VIOLENCE** ▷ **1** [C] a place or stage at which violence might be expected to begin: *Because of the army's presence, the city is seen to be the flashpoint of the area.* **TEMPERATURE** ▷ **2** [C usually singular] specialized The flashpoint of a liquid is the lowest temperature at which the VAPOUR it produces will burn in air.

flashy /ˈflæʃ.i/ **adj** disapproving looking too bright, big, and expensive in a way that is intended to get attention and admiration: *flashy clothes* ◦ *a flashy car* ◦ *flashy gold jewellery* • **flashily** /-ɪ.li/ **adv** *flashily dressed* • **flashiness** /-i.nəs/ **noun** [U]

flask /flɑːsk/ Ⓤ /flæsk/ **noun** [C] **HOT DRINKS** ▷ **1** UK (US trademark **Thermos**) a special container that keeps drinks hot or cold: *a flask of coffee/tea* **ALCOHOL** ▷ **2** a flat bottle that is used to carry alcohol in your pocket: *a* ***hip*** *flask* **SCIENCE** ▷ **3** a glass container for liquids with a wide base and a narrow neck, used in scientific work

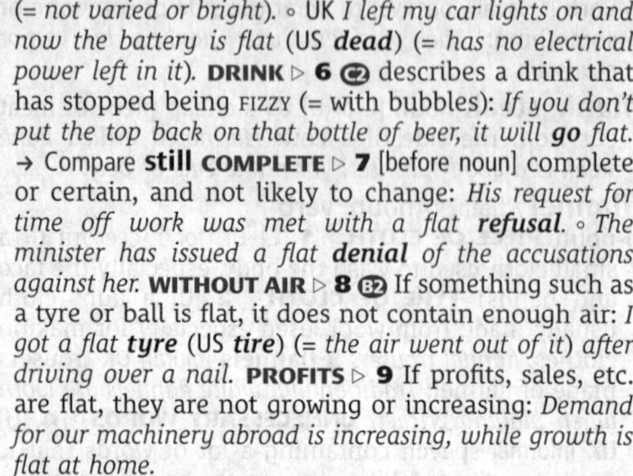
flask

flat /flæt/ **adj**; **noun**; **adj**, **adv**; **adv**

▸**adj** (**flatter**, **flattest**) **LEVEL** ▷ **1** Ⓑ1 level and smooth, with no curved, high, or hollow parts: *An ice rink needs to be completely flat.* ◦ *Roll out the pastry on a flat surface.* ◦ *Much of the countryside in East Anglia is very flat.* **NOT HIGH** ▷ **2** Ⓑ1 level but having little or no height: *flat shoes* (= *ones without a raised heel*) **3** describes bread that is made without YEAST, and therefore does not rise: *Pitta and nan are two types of flat bread.* **4 flat cap/hat** UK a hat that is not rounded on top and has little height **NOT ACTIVE** ▷ **5** not interesting, or without emotion or excitement: *After the excitement of the party, life seems rather flat now.* ◦ *I thought her performance a little flat.* ◦ *I think the colours in this painting are rather flat* (= *not varied or bright*). ◦ UK *I left my car lights on and now the battery is flat* (US ***dead***) (= *has no electrical power left in it*). **DRINK** ▷ **6** Ⓒ2 describes a drink that has stopped being FIZZY (= with bubbles): *If you don't put the top back on that bottle of beer, it will* ***go*** *flat.* → Compare **still** **COMPLETE** ▷ **7** [before noun] complete or certain, and not likely to change: *His request for time off work was met with a flat* ***refusal***. ◦ *The minister has issued a flat* ***denial*** *of the accusations against her.* **WITHOUT AIR** ▷ **8** Ⓑ2 If something such as a tyre or ball is flat, it does not contain enough air: *I got a flat* ***tyre*** (US ***tire***) (= *the air went out of it*) *after driving over a nail.* **PROFITS** ▷ **9** If profits, sales, etc. are flat, they are not growing or increasing: *Demand for our machinery abroad is increasing, while growth is flat at home.*

IDIOM **be (as) flat as a pancake** informal to be very flat: *The countryside around Cambridge is as flat as a pancake.*

▸**noun** **HOME** ▷ **1** Ⓐ1 [C] UK (US **apartment**) a set of rooms for living in that are part of a larger building and are usually all on one floor: *a furnished/unfurnished flat* ◦ *a* ***block*** *of flats* ◦ *They have a house in the country and a flat in London.* → See also **flatmate** **LEVEL GROUND** ▷ **2** [C often plural] an area of low, level ground, often near water: *The* ***salt*** *flats are used for motor racing.* ◦ *The* ***mud*** *flats attract large numbers of birds.* **3 the flat of your hand** the PALM and fingers when they are held straight and level: *He hit me with the flat of his hand.* **4 be on the flat** to be on a level surface, not on a slope or hill: *Most of the path is on the flat.* **TYRE WITHOUT AIR** ▷ **5** [C usually singular] mainly US informal a **flat tyre**: *We were late because we had to stop and fix a flat.* **SHOES** ▷ **6 flats** [plural] women's shoes without high HEELS: *I feel more comfortable in flats.* **MUSIC** ▷ **7** [C] (a symbol for) a note that is a SEMITONE lower than a stated note

▸**adj**, **adv** (**flatter**, **flattest**) **MUSIC** ▷ (in music) lower than a particular note or the correct note: *The top string on your violin is flat.* ◦ *She sang flat throughout the song* (= *all the notes she sang were too low*). → Compare **natural**, **sharp**

▸**adv** (**flatter**, **flattest**) **LEVEL** ▷ **1** Ⓑ2 in a level position, often against another surface: *Lay the cloth flat across the table.* **NOT HIGH** ▷ **2** into a flat shape without height: *These garden chairs will fold flat for storage.* **COMPLETELY** ▷ **3** informal completely or to the greatest degree possible: *She told him flat* (US also ***flat out***) *that she would not go to the show.* ◦ *Could you lend me some money, I'm flat* ***broke*** (= *I have no money*). → See also **stony broke** **4 three minutes, half an hour, etc. flat** informal exactly three minutes, half an hour, etc.: *We managed to get to the station in five minutes flat.* **5 flat out** informal as fast or as hard as possible: *My car only does about 60 mph, even when it's going flat out.* ◦ *We've been working flat out to get this done.*

flatbed /ˈflæt.bed/ **noun** [C] a truck with a flat area at the back with no roof or sides, for transporting large items

ˌflat-ˈchested **adj** A woman who is flat-chested has small breasts.

ˌflat ˈfeet **noun** [plural] feet that are level across the bottom instead of curved

flatfish /ˈflæt.fɪʃ/ **noun** [C] (plural **flatfish**) any thin, flat sea fish, such as a PLAICE or a SOLE

ˌflat-ˈfooted **adj** having feet whose bottom part is flat against the ground and not curved up in an ARCH

flathead /ˈflæt.hed/ **noun** [C] a thin, flat tropical sea fish that can be eaten

flatlet /ˈflæt.lət/ **noun** [C] UK a very small flat

flatline /ˈflæt.laɪn/ verb [I] informal **1** to be at a low level and not increase: *Have widescreen TV prices finally flatlined?* **2** to stop being popular or successful: *Her acting career has flatlined.* **3** to die • **flatlining** /-ɪŋ/ **noun** [U] *The effects of the music industry's flatlining have been felt by retailers.*

flatly /ˈflæt.li/ adv **WITHOUT EMOTION** ▷ **1** in a way that shows no emotion or interest: *The witness responded flatly to the judge's questions.* **COMPLETELY** ▷ **2** If you flatly DENY, refuse, or disagree with something or someone, you do it completely or in a very clear and firm way.

flatmate /ˈflæt.meɪt/ noun [C] UK a person who shares an apartment with another person

flatness /ˈflæt.nəs/ noun [U] **LEVEL QUALITY** ▷ **1** the quality of being level and without curved, high, or hollow parts: *The flatness* ***of*** *the desert was broken only by a few large piles of rocks.* **NO EMOTION** ▷ **2** the fact that someone or something shows no emotion or interest: *All the critics remarked on the flatness of the performance.*

ˌ**flat out** adv; adj
▸**adv** mainly US completely; used for emphasis: *When I asked him about it, he flat-out denied it.*
▸**adj** [before noun] mainly US complete; used for emphasis: *That was just a flat-out lie.*

flatpack /ˈflæt.pæk/ noun [C] UK a piece of furniture that is sold in pieces inside a flat box, ready for the buyer to put them together

ˈ**flat ˌracing** noun [U] a type of horse racing where the horses do not jump over fences

ˈ**flat ˌrate** noun [C] UK a charge that is the same for everyone: *Clients are charged a flat rate of £15 monthly.* ◦ *a flat-rate contribution*

ˌ**flat ˈscreen** noun [C] specialized a computer MONITOR or a television that is thin and flat: *a flat-screen TV*

flatten /ˈflæt.ən/ (US) /ˈflæţ-/ verb [I or T] **BECOME LEVEL** ▷ **1** (C2) to become level or cause something to become level: *Several trees were flattened (= knocked down) by the storm.* ◦ *The path flattens* (***out***) *(= does not go up so much) as it reaches the top of the hill.* **MAKE THINNER** ▷ **2** (C2) to become level and thinner or to cause something to become level and thinner: *Flatten the pastry into a thin disc with your hands.* ◦ *The biscuits will flatten out as they cook.*

flatter /ˈflæt.əʳ/ (US) /ˈflæţ.ɚ/ verb [T] **1** to praise someone in order to make them feel attractive or important, sometimes in a way that is not sincere: *I knew he was only flattering me because he wanted to borrow some money.* **2 flatter yourself** to believe something good about yourself although it might not be true: [+ that] *Clive flatters himself* ***that*** *he's an excellent speaker.* **3 flatter to deceive** to give the appearance of being better than the true situation: *I suspect these statistics flatter to deceive.* **4 be/feel flattered** to feel very pleased and proud because someone has said good things about you or has made you feel important: *She was flattered by his attention.* ◦ *They were flattered* ***to*** *be invited to dinner by the mayor.* ◦ *We felt flattered* ***that*** *so many people came to our party.* **5** to make someone look more attractive than usual: *That new hairstyle really flatters her.*

flatterer /ˈflæt.ər.əʳ/ (US) /ˈflæţ.ɚ.ɚ/ noun [C] someone who praises people without being sincere: *You can't believe a word Tony says, he's a real flatterer.*

flattering /ˈflæt.ər.ɪŋ/ (US) /ˈflæţ.ɚ-/ adj making someone look or seem better or more attractive than usual: *a flattering photograph* ◦ *That suit is very flattering.* ◦ *He's always making flattering* ***remarks.***

flattery /ˈflæt.ər.i/ (US) /ˈflæţ-/ noun [U] the act of praising someone, often in a way that is not sincere because you want something from them: *I was really pleased when he said how well I'd done, because he isn't known for flattery.*

IDIOM **flattery will get you nowhere** humorous saying used to tell someone that their praise will not persuade you to do anything you do not want to do

flatties /ˈflæt.iːz/ (US) /ˈflæţ-/ **noun** [plural] UK informal women's shoes without high HEELS

flattop /ˈflæt.tɒp/ (US) /-tɑːp/ **noun** [C] a short hairstyle, usually for a man, in which the hair is cut so that the top of the head seems flat

ˌ**flat ˈtyre** noun [C usually singular] (mainly US informal **flat**) a tyre that does not have any or enough air in it → See also **puncture**

flatulence /ˈflæt.jʊ.lənts/ noun [U] formal gas in the stomach and bowels: *Eating beans can cause flatulence.* • **flatulent** /-lənt/ **adj**

flatware /ˈflæt.weəʳ/ (US) /-wer/ **noun** [U] US **cutlery**

flatworm /ˈflæt.wɜːm/ (US) /-wɝːm/ **noun** [C] a creature with a flat body that can live inside the bodies of people and animals and often causes disease

flaunt /flɔːnt/ (US) /flɑːnt/ **verb** [T] disapproving **1** to show or make obvious something you are proud of in order to get admiration: *He's got a lot of money but he doesn't flaunt it.* ◦ *Flavio was flaunting his tan in a pair of white trunks.* **2 flaunt yourself** to show your body in a confident and sexual manner

flautist /ˈflɔː.tɪst/ (US) /ˈflɑː.ţɪst/ noun [C] (US also **flutist**) a person who plays the FLUTE

flavonoid /ˈflæv.ə.nɔɪd/ noun [C] (also **bioflavonoid**) a substance in fruit and vegetables that may help protect people against some types of CANCER or heart disease

flavour /ˈfleɪ.vəʳ/ (US) /-vɚ/ **noun; verb**
▸**noun** UK (US **flavor**) **1** (B1) [C or U] how food or drink tastes, or a particular taste itself: *Add a little salt to bring out the flavour* ***of*** *the herbs.* ◦ *My fish was delicious but Charles' beef had almost no flavour (= did not taste of anything).* ◦ *This wine has a light, fruity flavour (= the taste of fruit).* ◦ *We sell 32 different flavours (= particular types of taste) of ice cream.* **2** (C2) [S] a particular quality or character: *The resort has a nautical flavour.* **3** [S] an idea or quick experience of something: *To give you a flavour of what the book is like Jilly is going to read out a brief extract.*

IDIOM **flavour of the month** UK informal the most popular person at a particular time: *Andy is certainly flavour of the month with the boss.*

▸**verb** [T often passive] UK (US **flavor**) to give a particular taste to food or drink: *This sauce is flavoured with garlic and herbs.* ◦ *You can use fresh herbs to flavour the soup.*

-flavoured UK (US **-flavored**) /-fleɪ.vəd/ (US) /-vɚd/ **suffix** tasting of the thing stated: *orange-flavoured chocolate* ◦ *mint-flavoured sweets*

ˈ**flavour enˌhancer** noun [C] UK a substance used to improve the taste of a food or drink

flavourful UK (US **flavorful**) /ˈfleɪ.və.fʊl/ (US) /-vɚ-/ **adj** full of flavour: *a flavourful sauce*

flavouring UK (US **flavoring**) /ˈfleɪ.vər.ɪŋ/ (US) /-vɚ-/ noun [C or U] something that is added to food or drink to give it a particular taste: *artificial/natural flavouring(s)*

flavourless UK (US **flavorless**) /ˈfleɪ.və.ləs/ (US) /-vɚ-/

adj having little or no flavour: *These grapes are completely flavourless.*

flavoursome /ˈfleɪ.və.səm/ ⓤⓢ /-vɚ-/ **adj** UK having good flavour or a lot of flavour: *flavoursome wine*

flaw /flɔː/ ⓤⓢ /flɑː/ **noun; verb**

▸**noun** [C] C1 a fault, mistake, or weakness, especially one that happens while something is being planned or made, or which causes something not to be perfect: *I returned the material because it had a flaw **in** it.* ◦ *There's a **fatal** flaw in your reasoning.* ◦ *This report is full of flaws.* ◦ *a character flaw*

▸**verb** [T] to cause something to be not perfect: *A tiny mark flawed the otherwise perfect silk shirt.*

F

flawed /flɔːd/ ⓤⓢ /flɑːd/ **adj** C2 not perfect, or containing mistakes: *Diamonds are still valuable, even when they are flawed.* ◦ *His argument is deeply flawed.* ◦ *flawed beauty*

flawless /ˈflɔː.ləs/ ⓤⓢ /ˈflɑː-/ **adj** C2 perfect or without mistakes: *a flawless complexion* ◦ *a flawless performance* • **flawlessly** /-li/ **adv**

flax /flæks/ **noun** [U] a plant with blue flowers grown for its stems or seeds, or the thread made from this plant

flaxen /ˈflæk.sᵊn/ **adj** literary (of hair) pale yellow: *a flaxen-haired youth*

flaxseed oil /ˈflæks.siːdˌɔɪl/ **noun** [U] **linseed oil**

flay /fleɪ/ **verb** [T] **1** to remove the skin from a person's or animal's body **2** to WHIP a person or animal so hard that some of their skin comes off: figurative *The critics really flayed (= severely criticized) his new book.*

IDIOM **flay sb alive** informal to punish or tell someone off severely: *I'll be flayed alive when she finds out!*

flea /fliː/ **noun** [C] a very small jumping insect which feeds on the blood of animals and humans

IDIOM **send sb away with a flea in their ear** UK informal to angrily tell someone to go away: *A young kid came asking for money but I sent him away with a flea in his ear.*

fleabag /ˈfliː.bæg/ **noun** [C] PERSON/ANIMAL ▷ **1** UK informal a dirty and/or unpleasant person or animal HOTEL ▷ **2** US a cheap, dirty hotel

fleabite /ˈfliː.baɪt/ **noun** [C] the bite of a flea

fleabitten /ˈfliː.bɪt.ᵊn/ ⓤⓢ /-bɪṭ-/ **adj** informal dirty and in bad condition: *I'm not going to stay in that fleabitten old place.*

ˈ**flea** ˌ**collar** **noun** [C] a collar for dogs and cats that has been treated with chemicals which kill FLEAS

ˈ**flea** ˌ**market** **noun** [C] a market, which usually takes place outside, where old or used goods are sold cheaply

fleapit /ˈfliː.pɪt/ **noun** [C] UK old-fashioned informal an old, dirty cinema or theatre

fleck /flek/ **noun** [C usually plural] a small mark or spot: *Blackbirds' eggs are pale blue with brown flecks on them.* ◦ *I got a few flecks **of** paint on the window.*

flecked /flekt/ **adj** having small marks or spots: *It's a dark grey material but it's flecked **with** white.*

fled /fled/ past simple and past participle of **flee**

fledged /fledʒd/ **adj** (of young birds) able to fly → See **fully fledged**

fledgling /ˈfledʒ.lɪŋ/ **noun; adj**

▸**noun** [C] (also **fledgeling**) a young bird that has grown feathers and is learning to fly

▸**adj** [before noun] (also **fledgeling**) new and without experience: *The current economic climate is particularly difficult for fledgling businesses.*

flee /fliː/ **verb** [I or T, never passive] (present tense **fleeing**, past tense and past participle **fled**) **1** C1 to escape by running away, especially because of danger or fear: *She fled **(from)** the room in tears.* ◦ *In order to escape capture, he fled **to** the mountains.* **2 flee the country** to quickly go to another country in order to escape from something or someone: *It is likely that the suspects have fled the country by now.*

fleece /fliːs/ **noun; verb**

▸**noun** [C or U] **1** the thick covering of wool on a sheep, or this covering used to make a piece of clothing: *My jacket is lined with fleece/is fleece-**lined**.* **2** a type of warm soft material, or a jacket made from this

▸**verb** [T] informal to take someone's money dishonestly, by charging too much money or by cheating them: *That restaurant really fleeced us!*

fleecy /ˈfliː.si/ **adj** soft and like a sheep's wool, or looking like this: *fleecy clouds*

fleet /fliːt/ **noun; adj**

▸**noun** [C] SHIPS ▷ **1** C1 a group of ships, or all of the ships in a country's navy: *a fleet **of** 20 sailing ships* ◦ *a fishing fleet* ◦ *The British fleet sailed from Southampton early this morning.* VEHICLES ▷ **2** C1 a number of buses, aircraft, etc. under the control of one person or organization: *He owns a fleet of taxis.*

▸**adj** literary able to run quickly: *She was slight and fleet **of foot/fleet-footed**.* • **fleetness** /-nəs/ **noun** [U]

ˌ**fleet** ˈ**admiral** **noun** [C] (also **Fleet Admiral**) an officer of the highest rank in the US Navy: *Fleet Admiral Nimitz/Chester Nimitz* ◦ [as form of address] *Yes, Fleet Admiral.*

fleeting /ˈfliː.tɪŋ/ ⓤⓢ /-ṭɪŋ/ **adj** short or quick: *a fleeting **glimpse*** ◦ *This is just a fleeting visit.* • **fleetingly** /-li/ **adv** *I glimpsed her fleetingly through the window.*

ˈ**Fleet** ˌ**Street** **noun** the road in London where most of Britain's national newspapers were produced in the past, often used to refer to British national newspapers in general: *He's a Fleet Street journalist.*

flesh /fleʃ/ **noun; verb**

▸**noun** **1** C2 [U] the soft part of the body of a person or animal that is between the skin and the bones, or the soft inside part of a fruit or vegetable: *The thorn went deep into the flesh of my hand.* ◦ *The flesh of the fruit is white.* ◦ *Vegetarians don't eat animal flesh (= meat).* **2 the flesh** [S] literary the physical body and not the mind or the SOUL: *This left him plenty of time to indulge in **the pleasures of** the flesh (= physical pleasures, such as sex or eating).* → See also **fleshpot**

IDIOMS **be (only) flesh and blood** to have normal human limits, needs, etc.: *Of course I find pretty young women attractive – I'm only flesh and blood.* • **be sb's own flesh and blood** C2 to be someone's relation: *I couldn't send him away – he's my own flesh and blood.* • **in the flesh** in real life, and not on TV, in a film, in a picture, etc.: *I've seen her perform on television, but never in the flesh.* • **make your flesh crawl/creep** to make someone very worried or frightened: *I don't mind spiders but worms make my flesh crawl.* • **put flesh on (the bones of) sth** to add more details to a plan, idea, argument, etc. to make it better or more complete

▸**verb**

PHRASAL VERB **flesh sth out** to add more details or information to something: *These plans need to be fleshed out **with** some more figures.*

ˈ**flesh-**ˌ**coloured** UK (US ˈ**flesh-**ˌ**colored**) **adj** approximately the colour of white people's skin: *a pair of flesh-coloured tights*

fleshpot /ˈfleʃ.pɒt/ ⓤⓢ /-pɑːt/ **noun** [C usually plural] humorous a place which supplies sexual entertainment and food and drink

ˈflesh ˌwound noun [C] an injury that does not damage the bones or INNER organs

fleshy /ˈfleʃ.i/ adj having a lot of soft flesh • **fleshiness** /-nəs/ noun [U]

fleur-de-lis /ˌflɜː.dəˈliːs/ (US) /ˌflɜː-/ noun [C] (plural **fleurs-de-lis** /ˌflɜː.dəˈliːs/ (US) /ˌflɜː-/) (also **fleur-de-lys**) a pattern representing a flower with three separate parts joined at the bottom, used in COATS OF ARMS

flew /fluː/ past simple and past participle of **fly**

flex /fleks/ verb; noun

▸verb [T] to bend an arm, leg, etc. or tighten a muscle: *First, straighten your legs, then flex your feet.* ◦ *He tried to impress me by flexing his huge muscles.*

IDIOM **flex your muscles** to try to worry an opponent or enemy by publicly showing military, political, or financial power: *The parade is the first sign of the new regime flexing its military muscles.* → See also **muscle-flexing**

▸noun [C or U] UK (US **cord**) (a length of) wire with a plastic cover used for connecting a piece of electrical equipment to a supply of electricity: *The flex on this iron isn't long enough to reach the socket.*

flex

flexible /ˈflek.sɪ.bl/ adj ABLE TO CHANGE ▷ **1** (B2) able to change or be changed easily according to the situation: *My schedule is quite flexible – I could arrange to meet with you any day next week.* ABLE TO BEND ▷ **2** (C2) able to bend or to be bent easily without breaking: *Rubber is a flexible substance.* ◦ *Dancers and gymnasts need to be very flexible (= able to bend their bodies easily).* • **flexibility** /ˌflek.sɪˈbɪl.ɪ.ti/ (US) /-ə.t̬i/ noun [U] (B2) *The advantage of this system is its flexibility.* • **flexibly** /-bli/ adv *Today's schedule of events is organized flexibly so that people can decide for themselves what they want to do.*

ˌflexible ˈworking noun [U] a situation in which an employer allows people to choose the times that they work so that they can do other things, for example spend time with their children: *Employers can help women by offering childcare and flexible working.*

flexitime /ˈflek.si.taɪm/ noun [U] UK (US **flextime**) a system of working in which people work a set number of hours within a fixed period of time, but can change the time they start or finish work

flibbertigibbet /ˌflɪb.ə.tiˈdʒɪb.ɪt/ (US) /-ɚ.t̬i-/ noun [C] UK old-fashioned a silly person who talks too much

flick /flɪk/ verb; noun

▸verb [I + adv/prep, T] to move or hit something with a short, sudden movement: *He carefully flicked the loose hairs* ***from*** *the shoulders of his jacket.* ◦ *She quickly flicked the crumbs* ***off*** *the table.* ◦ *The lizard flicked* ***out*** *its tongue at a fly.*

PHRASAL VERBS **flick sth on/off** to move a switch in order to make electrical equipment start/stop working: *Could you flick the light switch on for me, please?* • **flick through sth** (C2) to look quickly at the pages of a magazine, book, etc.

▸noun [C] QUICK MOVEMENT ▷ **1** a sudden, quick movement: *With a flick* ***of*** *its tail, the cat was gone.* ◦ *A flick* ***of a switch*** *turns the machine on.* **2 have a flick through sth** to quickly look at the pages of a book, magazine, etc.: *I've had a flick through their brochure and it looks quite interesting.* FILM ▷ **3** UK old-fashioned informal a film → See **skin flick, chick flick 4 the flicks** [plural] UK old-fashioned informal the cinema: *What's on at the flicks this week?*

flicker /ˈflɪk.əʳ/ (US) /-ɚ/ verb; noun

▸verb **1** [I] to shine with a light that is sometimes bright and sometimes weak: *I felt a cold draft and the candle started to flicker.* **2** [I or T] to appear for a short time or to make a sudden movement: *A smile flickered across her face.* ◦ *He'd been in a coma for weeks, when all of a sudden he flickered an eyelid.* • **flickering** /-ɪŋ/ adj *a flickering candle/fire* ◦ *a flickering hope*

▸noun [C usually singular] LIGHT ▷ **1** a situation in which a light is sometimes bright and sometimes weak: *the soft flicker of candlelight* FEELING ▷ **2** a feeling or expression of an emotion or quality that does not last very long: *There was a flicker* ***of*** *hope in his eyes.*

ˈflick ˌknife noun [C] UK (US **switchblade**) a knife with a blade hidden inside its handle which springs out when a button is pressed

flier noun [C] US spelling of **flyer**

flies /flaɪz/ noun INSECT ▷ **1** plural of **fly** TROUSERS ▷ **2** [plural] UK for **fly**

flight /flaɪt/ noun JOURNEY ▷ **1** (A2) [C] a journey in an aircraft: *I'll never forget my first flight.* ◦ *How was your flight?* ◦ *All flights to New York today are delayed because of bad weather.* ◦ *My flight was cancelled.* AIRCRAFT ▷ **2** [C] an aircraft that is making a particular journey: *Flight 474 to Buenos Aires is now boarding at gate 9.* MOVEMENT ▷ **3** [U] an occasion when something flies or moves through the air: *an eagle* ***in*** *flight* ◦ *Suddenly the whole flock of geese* ***took*** *flight (= started flying).* **4** [C] a group of birds, aircraft, etc. flying together: *a flight of geese/swans* ESCAPE ▷ **5** [U] (an act or example of) escape, running away, or avoiding something: *They lost all their possessions during their flight* ***from*** *the invading army.* **6 put sb to flight** UK old-fashioned to defeat someone and force them to run away **7 take flight** to run away: *The burglars took flight when the alarm sounded.* STAIRS ▷ **8** (C2) [C] a set of steps or stairs, usually between two floors of a building: *We live up three flights of stairs.*

IDIOMS **flight of fancy** an idea that shows a lot of imagination but is not practical: *He was talking about cycling across the US or was that just another flight of fancy?* • **the top flight** UK the highest level in a job or sport: *The Sheffield Eagles move down to the second division after two seasons in the top flight.*

ˈflight atˌtendant noun [C] someone who serves passengers on an aircraft

ˈflight ˌdeck noun [C] AIRCRAFT ▷ **1** the part of an aircraft where the pilot sits and where the controls are SHIP ▷ **2** a flat, open surface on a ship from which aircraft take off

flightless /ˈflaɪt.ləs/ adj not able to fly: *The ostrich is a flightless bird.*

ˌflight lieuˈtenant noun [C] an officer in the British air force

ˈflight ˌpath noun [C] a route followed by an aircraft

ˈflight reˌcorder noun [C] a device which records information about an aircraft while it is flying → See also **black box**

ˈflight ˌsergeant noun [C] the next rank above SERGEANT in the British air force

ˈflight ˌsimulator noun [C] a piece of equipment that represents the conditions inside an aircraft, that can be used for learning to fly a plane

flighty /ˈflaɪ.ti/ (US) /-t̬i/ adj disapproving (especially of a woman) not responsible and likely to change activities, jobs, partners, etc. often: *a flighty young woman* • **flightiness** /-nəs/ noun [U]

flimflam /ˈflɪm.flæm/ noun [U] old-fashioned informal talk that is confusing and intended to deceive

flimsy /ˈflɪm.zi/ adj **THIN ▷ 1** very thin, or easily broken or destroyed: *You won't be warm enough in that flimsy dress.* ◦ *We spent the night in a flimsy wooden hut.* **DIFFICULT TO BELIEVE ▷ 2** A flimsy argument, excuse, etc. is weak and difficult to believe: *When I asked him why he was late, he gave me some flimsy **excuse** about having car trouble.* • **flimsily** /-zɪ.li/ adv • **flimsiness** /-nəs/ noun [U]

F

flinch /flɪntʃ/ verb [I] to make a sudden, small movement because of pain or fear: *He didn't even flinch when the nurse cleaned the wound.*

PHRASAL VERB **flinch from sth/doing sth** to avoid doing something that you consider unpleasant or painful: *We must not flinch from difficult decisions.*

fling /flɪŋ/ verb; noun

▸verb (**flung**, **flung**) **THROW ▷ 1** [T usually + adv/prep] to throw something or someone suddenly and with a lot of force: *He crumpled up the letter and flung it into the fire.* ◦ *'And you can take your ring back too!' she cried, flinging it down on the table.* ◦ informal *Could you fling the paper over here (= give me the paper)?* **MOVE/DO ▷ 2** [T usually + adv/prep] to move or do something quickly and energetically: *She flung her arms around his neck.* ◦ *The door was flung open by the wind.* ◦ *Sergei flung himself down on the sofa.* ◦ informal *Let me just fling (= quickly put) a few things into my bag, and I'll be right with you.* ◦ informal *They were flung (= quickly put) in prison.* **SAY ANGRILY ▷ 3** [I or T, usually + adv/prep] to say something angrily: *They were flinging bitter accusations **at** each other.* ◦ [+ speech] *'I don't care what you think', she flung (**back**) **at** him.*

IDIOM **fling up your hands** to show that you are very shocked or frightened: *They flung up their hands **in** horror at the cost of the trip.*

PHRASAL VERBS **fling yourself at sb** informal disapproving to make it very obvious to someone that you want to have a sexual relationship with them • **fling yourself into sth** to do something with a lot of enthusiasm: *Tom has really flung himself into his work this year.* • **fling sth on/off** to quickly put on/remove something, especially a piece of clothing: *We were so hot we flung off our clothes and dived into the swimming pool.* • **fling sth/sb out** mainly UK informal to get rid of something you do not want, or to make someone leave a place when they do not want to: *I think it's about time we flung out these old magazines.* ◦ *They were flung out of the pub for fighting.*

▸noun [C usually singular] informal a short period of enjoyment: *The students are **having a final/last** fling before they leave university and start work.*

IDIOM **have a fling** to have a short sexual relationship with someone: *She's been having a fling **with** her boss.*

flint /flɪnt/ noun [C or U] **1** (a piece of) shiny grey or black stone that is like glass **2** (a piece of) stone or metal used in a MUSKET to make it fire or in a cigarette LIGHTER to produce a flame

flinty /ˈflɪn.ti/ (US) /-t̬i/ adj **1** made of or like flint: *a flinty material* **2** severe and determined: *The head teacher has a rather flinty manner.*

flip /flɪp/ verb; noun; adj

▸verb (**-pp-**) **1** [I or T, usually + adv/prep] If you flip something, you turn it over quickly one or more times, and if something flips, it turns over quickly: *I flipped the book (**over**) to look at the back cover.* ◦ *I lost my place in my book when the pages flipped **over** in the wind.* ◦ *You turn the machine on by flipping (= operating) the **switch** on the side.* ◦ *The captains flipped a **coin** into the air (= made it turn over in the air to see which side it landed on) to decide which side would bat first.* **2** [T] to cook something by turning it over several times over heat: *I don't want to spend the rest of my life flipping burgers.* **3** [T] US to buy a house, improve it a little, then sell it quickly for more money: *I am going to take three weeks' vacation and flip this house.*

IDIOM **flip (your lid)** informal to become very angry: *She'll flip her lid if I'm late again.*

PHRASAL VERB **flip through sth** to look quickly at the pages of a magazine, book, etc.

▸noun [C] an occasion when something turns over quickly or repeatedly: *a flip of a coin* ◦ *The acrobats were doing somersaults and flips (= jumping and turning their bodies over in the air).*

▸adj (**flipper**, **flippest**) informal for **flippant**

flipback /ˈflɪp.bæk/ noun [C] a style of book that is smaller than usual and that you open with the longer side towards you and read from the top of the page to the bottom, rather than from right to left

ˈ**flip ˌchart** noun [C] a board standing on legs with large pieces of paper fixed to the top which can be turned over

ˈ**flip-flop** noun; verb

▸noun **SHOE ▷ 1** [C usually plural] (US and Australian English **thong**) a type of open shoe, often made of rubber, with a V-shaped strap which goes between the big toe and the toe next to it **CHANGE ▷ 2** US informal an occasion when someone completely changes a plan

▸verb [I] US informal to change a plan completely

flippant /ˈflɪp.ənt/ adj (UK informal **flip**) not serious about a serious subject, in an attempt to be funny or to appear clever: *a flippant remark/attitude* ◦ *It's easy to be flippant, but we have a serious problem to deal with here.* ◦ *I think she just thought I was being flippant.* • **flippancy** /-ən.si/ noun [U] • **flippantly** /-li/ adv

flipper /ˈflɪp.əʳ/ (US) /-ɚ/ noun [C] **PART OF CREATURE ▷ 1** one of two parts like arms on the bodies of some sea creatures, such as SEALS and PENGUINS, used for swimming **SHOE ▷ 2** (US also **fin**) a type of large, flat rubber shoe, used for swimming, especially underwater

flipping /ˈflɪp.ɪŋ/ adj, adv UK slang used to emphasize what is being said, or to express anger: *It's a flipping nuisance!* ◦ *You'll do as you're flipping well told!*

ˈ**flip ˌside** noun [S] **1** the opposite, less good, or less popular side of something: *We're now starting to see the flip side **of** the government's economic policy.* **2** old-fashioned the less popular side of a record

flirt /flɜːt/ (US) /flɝːt/ verb; noun

▸verb [I] to behave as if sexually attracted to someone, although not seriously: *Christina was flirting **with** just about every man in the room.*

PHRASAL VERB **flirt with sth CONSIDER ▷ 1** to consider doing something, but not seriously, or to be interested in something for a short time: *I'm flirting with **the idea of** taking a year off and travelling round the world.* **DANGER ▷ 2** to intentionally take risks and put yourself in a dangerous or difficult situation: *Like a lot of young men, he flirts with **danger**.*

▸noun [C] someone who behaves as if they are sexually attracted to a lot of people • **flirty** adj behaving as if you are sexually attracted to someone, although not seriously: *flirty comments* ◦ *a flirty woman*

flirtation /flɜːˈteɪ.ʃən/ (US) /flɝː-/ **noun** **SEXUAL ATTRACTION** ▷ **1** [C or U] a situation in which someone behaves as if they are sexually attracted to another person, without being seriously interested: *It was a harmless flirtation and nothing more.* **INTEREST** ▷ **2** [S] a short period of being interested in something or doing something: *a brief flirtation with Communism*

flirtatious /flɜːˈteɪ.ʃəs/ (US) /flɝː-/ **adj** behaving as if you are sexually attracted to someone, especially not in a serious way: *She's very flirtatious.* ◦ *a flirtatious relationship* • **flirtatiously** /-li/ **adv** • **flirtatiousness** /-nəs/ **noun** [U]

flit /flɪt/ **verb** [I usually + adv/prep] (**-tt-**) **1** to fly or move quickly and lightly: *In the fading light we saw bats flitting* ***around/about*** *in the garden.* ◦ figurative *Sara finds it very difficult to settle – she's always flitting* ***from*** *one thing* ***to*** *another (= changing her activities).* **2** to appear or exist suddenly and for a short time in someone's mind or on their face: *A ghost of a smile flitted across his face.* • **flit** **noun** [C] UK

float /fləʊt/ (US) /floʊt/ **verb; noun**

▸**verb** **NOT SINK** ▷ **1** (B1) [I] to stay on the surface of a liquid and not sink: *An empty bottle will float.* ◦ *You can float very easily* ***in/on*** *the Dead Sea because it's so salty.* **MOVE** ▷ **2** (B1) [I or T, usually + adv/prep] to (cause to) move easily through, or along the surface of a liquid, or to (cause to) move easily through air: *We spent a lazy afternoon floating* ***down/along*** *the river.* ◦ *He tossed the bottle into the waves and watched it float* ***out to*** *sea.* ◦ *The children enjoy floating their boats* ***on*** *the pond in the park.* ◦ *Fluffy white clouds were floating across the sky.* ◦ figurative *The sound of piano-playing floated out through the open window.* **3** [I usually + adv/prep] literary to move smoothly and attractively: *She sort of floats around, like a ballet dancer.* **4** [I usually + adv/prep] to move or act without purpose: *Since he lost his job, he's just floated* ***around/about*** *doing nothing.* **SUGGEST** ▷ **5** [T] to suggest a plan or an idea to be considered: *Ian has floated the* ***idea*** *that we should think about expanding into Europe next year.* **CHANGE VALUE** ▷ **6** [I or T] specialized to allow the value of a country's money to change according to the value of other countries' money: *The government has decided to float the pound.* **BUSINESS** ▷ **7** [T] to start selling SHARES in a business or company for the first time

IDIOMS **be floating on air** mainly UK to be very happy: *When he got his exam results he was floating on air.* • **float sb's boat** informal to be what someone likes or is interested in: *Motor racing doesn't really float my boat.*

PHRASAL VERB **float around/about** informal **OBJECT** ▷ **1** You say that an object is floating around when you think it is not far away but you cannot see exactly where: *I can't find my purse, but it must be floating around here somewhere.* **IDEA** ▷ **2** If an idea or story floats around, it is discussed or repeated by a lot of people: *rumours floating around*

▸**noun** **MONEY** ▷ **1** [S] UK a small amount of money kept by someone who works in a bar, etc., used for giving customers their change **VEHICLE** ▷ **2** [C] a large vehicle with a flat surface that is decorated and used in FESTIVALS: *carnival floats* **NOT SINK** ▷ **3** [C] a piece of wood or other light material that stays on the surface of water: *Fishing nets are often held in position by floats.* **DRINK** ▷ **4** [C] a drink with ice cream on the top: *I'll have a root beer float, please.*

floatation /fləʊˈteɪ.ʃən/ (US) /floʊ-/ **noun** [U] UK **flotation**

floating /ˈfləʊ.tɪŋ/ (US) /ˈfloʊ.t̬ɪŋ/ **adj** [before noun] **1** not fixed in one position, place, or level: *The city has a large floating* ***population*** *(= people who move around a lot).* ◦ *The bank has offered us a loan with a floating* ***interest rate.*** **2** specialized describes a part of the body that is out of its usual position, or not connected to another part of the body: *a floating rib*

ˌfloating ˈvoter **noun** [C] UK someone who does not always vote for the same political party

floaty /ˈfləʊ.ti/ (US) /ˈfloʊ.t̬i/ **adj** describes material that is very light and moves in the air: *floaty dresses*

flock /flɒk/ (US) /flɑːk/ **noun; verb**

▸**noun** **GROUP** ▷ **1** [C, + sing/pl verb] a group of sheep, goats or birds, or a group of people: *a flock* ***of*** *sheep/goats/geese* ◦ *The shepherd is bringing his flock down from the hills.* ◦ *A noisy flock* ***of*** *tourists came into the building.* ◦ *The vicar invited all the members of his flock (= all the people who go to his church) to attend the special service.* **MATERIAL** ▷ **2** [U] (US also **flocking**) soft material used for filling objects such as CUSHIONS, or soft material that forms a raised pattern on WALLPAPER or curtains

▸**verb** [I usually + adv/prep] to move or come together in large numbers: *Hundreds of people flocked* ***to*** *the football match.* ◦ [+ to infinitive] *Crowds of people flocked to see the Picasso exhibition.*

floe /fləʊ/ (US) /floʊ/ **noun** [C] (also **ˈice floe**) a large area of ice floating in the sea

flog /flɒg/ (US) /flɑːg/ **verb** [T] (**-gg-**) **PUNISH** ▷ **1** to beat someone very hard with a WHIP (= a long, thin piece of rope, leather, etc.) or a stick, as a punishment: *Soldiers used to be flogged for disobedience.* **SELL** ▷ **2** UK informal to sell something, especially quickly or cheaply: *He tried to flog his old car, but no one would buy it.*

IDIOMS **flog yourself to death** (also **flog yourself into the ground**) UK informal to work too hard • **flog sth to death** UK informal to use, do, or say something so often that it is no longer interesting: *It's a theme that's been flogged to death.* • **flog a dead horse** UK informal to waste effort on something when there is no chance of succeeding: *He keeps trying to get it published but I think he's flogging a dead horse.*

flogging /ˈflɒg.ɪŋ/ (US) /ˈflɑː.gɪŋ/ **noun** [C or U] a punishment in which someone is beaten severely with a WHIP or a stick

flood /flʌd/ **verb; noun**

▸**verb** **COVER WITH WATER** ▷ **1** (B1) [I or T] to cause to fill or become covered with water, especially in a way that causes problems: *Our washing machine broke down yesterday and flooded the kitchen.* ◦ *The whole town flooded when the river burst its banks.* ◦ *Several families living by the river were flooded* ***out*** *(= forced to leave their houses because they became covered with water).* **ARRIVE** ▷ **2** (B2) [I usually + adv/prep, T] to fill or enter a place in large numbers or amounts: *Donations are flooding* ***into*** *the appeal office.* ◦ *She drew back the curtains and the sunlight came flooding* ***in.*** ◦ *Japanese cars have flooded the* ***market*** *(= a lot of them are on sale).* ◦ *He was flooded* ***with*** *(= suddenly felt a lot of) joy when his first child was born.* ◦ *For Proust, the taste of a madeleine brought childhood memories flooding* ***back*** *(= made him suddenly remember a lot of things).*

PHRASAL VERB **flood sth with sth** (C2) If you are flooded with letters, phone calls, messages, etc., you receive so many that you cannot deal with them: *We were flooded with calls from worried parents.*

▸**noun** **WATER** ▷ **1** (B1) [C or U] a large amount of water covering an area that is usually dry: *After the flood it took weeks for the water level to go down.* ◦ *The river is* ***in*** *flood (= water has flowed over its banks) again.* **2 in floods of tears** UK crying a lot: *I found her in floods of*

F

tears in the toilets. **3 the Flood** (in the Bible) a flood sent by God that covered the whole Earth as a punishment **LARGE AMOUNT** ▷ **4** C2 [C] a large amount or number of something: *A flood **of** cheap imports has come into the country.*

IDIOM **before the Flood** UK humorous a very long time ago

flooded /ˈflʌd.ɪd/ adj **WATER** ▷ **1** covered with water: *flooded fields* **FULL OF** ▷ **2** containing a large amount or number of something: *The **market** is flooded **with** cheap imports.*

floodgate /ˈflʌd.geɪt/ noun [C usually plural] a gate that can be opened or closed to control a flow of water

IDIOM **open the floodgates** If an action or a decision opens the floodgates, it allows something to happen a lot or allows many people to do something that was not previously allowed: *Officials are worried that allowing these refugees into the country will open the floodgates **to** thousands more.*

flooding /ˈflʌd.ɪŋ/ noun [U] a situation in which an area is covered with water, especially from rain: *Some roads have been closed because of flooding.*

floodlight /ˈflʌd.laɪt/ noun [C usually plural] a large, powerful electric light used for lighting outside areas, such as sports fields or buildings, in the dark: *This evening's match will be played **under** floodlights.*

floodlight

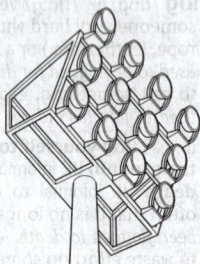

floodlit /ˈflʌd.lɪt/ adj lit by floodlights: *a floodlit stadium*

floodplain /ˈflʌdˌpleɪn/ noun [C] an area of flat land near a river that is often flooded when the river becomes too full

ˈ**flood** ˌ**tide** noun [C] the regular movement of the sea in towards the coast → Compare **ebb tide**

floor /flɔːʳ/ US /flɔːr/ noun; verb

▸noun **SURFACE** ▷ **1** A1 [C usually singular] the flat surface of a room on which you walk: *The floor was partly covered with a dirty old rug.* ◦ *The bathroom floor needs cleaning.* ◦ *The children sat playing **on** the floor.* ◦ *There's barely enough floor **space** to fit a bed in this room.* **LEVEL OF BUILDING** ▷ **2** A2 [C] a level of a building: *This building has five floors.* ◦ *Take the elevator to the 51st floor.* ◦ *We live **on** the third floor.* ◦ *a ground floor apartment*

> **!** Common mistake: **floor**
>
> **Remember:** to talk about the particular level of a building where something is, the correct preposition is **on.**
>
> Don't say 'in the ... floor' or 'at the ... floor', say **on the ... floor**:
>
> ~~*Their office is in the 12th floor.*~~
>
> *Their office is on the 12th floor.*

OPEN SPACE ▷ **3** B1 [C usually singular] a public space for activities such as dancing and having formal discussions: *a dance floor* ◦ *The new proposal will be discussed **on the** floor **of** the House of Commons (= in Parliament) tomorrow.* ◦ *He spent several years working on the **factory** floor (= in the factory) before becoming a manager.* ◦ *The chairman said that he would now take questions **from the** floor (= from the audience).* **4 have the floor** to have the right to speak: *Silence, please, the prime minister has the floor.* **5 take (to) the floor** to stand and begin to dance: *The newlyweds were the first to take the floor.* **6 take the floor** start speaking: *The Chancellor of the Exchequer will take the floor for his Budget speech at 3.00 p.m.* **BOTTOM** ▷ **7 the floor** the bottom surface of the sea, a forest, a cave, etc.: *the floor **of** the ocean/the ocean floor*

IDIOM **go through the floor** to fall to very low levels: *House prices have gone through the floor this year.*

▸verb **HIT** ▷ **1** [T] to hit someone and cause them to fall: *He was floored with a single punch to the head.* **SURPRISE/CONFUSE** ▷ **2** [T often passive] informal to surprise or confuse someone so much that they are unable to think what to say or do next: *I didn't know what to say – I was completely floored.*

floorboard /ˈflɔː.bɔːd/ US /ˈflɔːr.bɔːrd/ noun [C] one of the long, straight pieces of wood used to make a floor

flooring /ˈflɔː.rɪŋ/ US /ˈflɔː-/ noun [U] the material that a floor is made of: *wooden/marble/vinyl flooring*

ˈ**floor** ˌ**lamp** noun [C] US for **standard lamp**

ˈ**floor** ˌ**show** noun [C] a set of musical, dance, or COMEDY acts performed in a restaurant

floozy (also **floozie**) /ˈfluː.zi/ noun [C] old-fashioned informal a woman who has a lot of sexual relationships, or who wears clothes that attract sexual attention in a way that is too obvious

flop /flɒp/ US /flɑːp/ verb; noun

▸verb **(-pp-) FALL** ▷ **1** [I usually + adv/prep] to fall or drop heavily: *Hugh's hair keeps flopping **over/into** his eyes.* ◦ *When she gets home from school, she's so tired all she can do is flop **down** in front of the television.* **FAIL** ▷ **2** [I] If a book, play, film, etc. flops, it is not successful.

▸noun **FAILURE** ▷ **1** [C usually singular] informal a failure: *The play was a **complete/total** flop.* **FALL** ▷ **2** [S] an occasion when someone or something falls or drops heavily: *He fell with a flop on the bed.*

flophouse /ˈflɒp.haʊs/ US /ˈflɑːp-/ noun [C] US for **dosshouse**

floppy /ˈflɒp.i/ US /ˈflɑː.pi/ adj C2 soft and not able to keep a firm shape or position: *a floppy **hat*** ◦ *a dog with big floppy ears* ◦ *He's got floppy blond hair that's always falling in his eyes.* • **floppiness** /-nəs/ noun [U]

flora /ˈflɔː.rə/ US /ˈflɔːr.ə/ noun [U] specialized all the plants of a particular place or from a particular time in history: *the flora of the Balearic Islands*

ˌ**flora and** ˈ**fauna** noun [plural] specialized The flora and fauna of a place are its plants and animals.

floral /ˈflɔː.rəl/ US /ˈflɔːr.ᵊl/ adj made of flowers, or decorated with pictures of flowers: *floral curtains/print/wallpaper* ◦ *a floral display/tribute*

floret /ˈflɒr.ət/ US /ˈflɔːr-/ noun [C] a small part of a vegetable that is shaped like a flower: ***broccoli/cauliflower** florets*

florid /ˈflɒr.ɪd/ US /ˈflɔːr-/ adj **DECORATED** ▷ **1** with too much decoration or detail: *a florid architectural style* ◦ *florid prose/rhetoric* **RED** ▷ **2** formal (of a person's face) too red, especially in a way that is unhealthy: *a florid **complexion*** • **floridly** /-li/ adv

florist /ˈflɒr.ɪst/ US /ˈflɔːr-/ noun [C] **1** a person who works in a shop which sells cut flowers and plants for inside the house **2 florist's** a shop which sells cut flowers and plants for inside the house

floss /flɒs/ US /flɑːs/ noun; verb

▸noun [U] **TEETH** ▷ **1 dental floss THREAD** ▷ **2** a mass of soft, smooth threads especially produced by particular insects and plants → See also **candyfloss**

►verb [I or T] to clean between your teeth using DENTAL FLOSS: *It's important to floss every day.*

flotation (UK also **floatation**) /fləʊˈteɪ.ʃən/ (US) /floʊ-/ noun **BUSINESS** ▷ **1** [C or U] an occasion when a company's SHARES are sold to the public for the first time: *The Glasgow-based company is to launch a* ***stock market*** *flotation this summer.* **FLOAT** ▷ **2** [U] the action of floating **3 flotation chamber/compartment/tank** a container filled with water in which people float in order to relax

flotilla /fləˈtɪl.ə/ noun [C] a large group of boats or small ships → See also **fleet**

flotsam /ˈflɒt.səm/ (US) /ˈflɑːt-/ noun [U] (also ˌ**flotsam and** ˈ**jetsam**) **1** pieces of broken wood and other waste materials found on the beach or floating on the sea: *We wandered along the shore, stepping over the flotsam that had washed up in the night.* **2** anything or anyone that is not wanted or not considered to be important or useful: *The homeless sleep in doorways and stations – we step over their bodies like so much human flotsam.*

flounce /flaʊns/ verb; noun

►verb [I usually + adv/prep] to walk with large, noticeable movements, especially to attract attention or show that you are angry: *'Right, don't expect any help from me in future!' he said and flounced* ***out of*** *the room.*

►noun [C] a wide strip of cloth sewn along the edge of especially a dress or skirt for decoration

flouncy /ˈflaʊn.si/ adj (also **flounced**) Flouncy clothes are loose and have a lot of material: *She was wearing a dreadful pink flouncy skirt.*

flounder /ˈflaʊn.dər/ (US) /-dɚ/ verb; noun

►verb [I] to experience great difficulties or be completely unable to decide what to do or say next: *He lost the next page of his speech and floundered* (***about/around***) *for a few seconds.* ◦ *Although his business was a success, his marriage was floundering.* ◦ *In 1986 Richardson resigned as chairman, leaving the company floundering.*

►noun [C or U] (plural **flounder** or **flounders**) a flat fish that lives in the sea, or its flesh eaten as food

flour /flaʊər/ (US) /flaʊɚ/ noun; verb

►noun [U] (B1) powder made from grain, especially WHEAT, used for making bread, cakes, PASTA, pastry, etc. → See also **cornflour**

►verb [T] to put flour on a surface to prevent food from sticking: *Grease and flour the tins thoroughly.*

flourish /ˈflʌr.ɪʃ/ (US) /ˈflɝː-/ verb; noun

►verb **SUCCEED** ▷ **1** (C2) [I] to grow or develop successfully: *My tomatoes are flourishing this summer – it must be the warm weather.* ◦ *Watercolour painting began to flourish in Britain around 1750.* **WAVE** ▷ **2** [T] to move something in your hand in order to make people look at it: *She came in smiling, flourishing her exam results.*

►noun **with a flourish** If you do something with a flourish, you do it with one big, noticeable movement: *He took off his hat with a flourish.*

flourishing /ˈflʌr.ɪ.ʃɪŋ/ (US) /ˈflɝː-/ adj growing or developing successfully: *There's a flourishing* ***trade*** *in second-hand video machines.*

floury /ˈflaʊə.ri/ (US) /ˈflaʊɚ.i/ adj **1** covered in flour, or tasting or feeling like flour: *She wiped her floury hands on a cloth.* **2** UK describes potatoes that are dry and break into small pieces when they are cooked

flout /flaʊt/ verb [T] to intentionally not obey a rule, law, or custom: *Many motorcyclists flout the law by not wearing helmets.* ◦ *The orchestra decided to flout* ***convention/tradition****, and wear their everyday clothes for the concert.*

flow /fləʊ/ (US) /floʊ/ verb; noun

►verb [I] **MOVE** ▷ **1** (B1) (especially of liquids, gases, or electricity) to move in one direction, especially continuously and easily: *Lava from the volcano was flowing* ***down*** *the hillside.* ◦ *Many short rivers flow* ***into*** *the Pacific Ocean.* ◦ *The river flows* ***through*** *three counties before flowing* ***into*** *the sea just south of here.* ◦ *With fewer cars on the roads,* ***traffic*** *is flowing (= moving forward) more smoothly than usual.* **CONTINUE** ▷ **2** to continue to arrive or be produced: *Please keep the money flowing* ***in****!* ◦ *Offers of help are flowing* ***into*** *the disaster area from all over the country.* ◦ *My* ***thoughts*** *flow more easily if I work on a word processor.* ◦ *By eleven o'clock, the* ***wine*** *was starting to flow.* ◦ *After they'd all had a drink or two, the* ***conversation*** *began to flow.* **HANG DOWN** ▷ **3** to hang down loosely and often attractively: *Her long red hair flowed down over her shoulders.*

►noun **MOVEMENT** ▷ **1** (B2) [C usually singular] the movement of something in one direction: *the flow* ***of*** *a river* ◦ *the flow* ***of*** *traffic* ◦ *the flow* ***of*** *blood* **CONTINUOUS NUMBER** ▷ **2** [C usually singular] a regular and quite large number of something: *There's been a* ***steady*** *flow* ***of*** *visitors.* **3** [S] a situation in which something is produced or moved continuously: *the flow* ***of*** *ideas/information*

IDIOMS **go against the flow** to do or say the opposite of what most people are doing or saying: *With this new book, she is going against the flow.* • **go with the flow** informal (C2) to do what other people are doing or to agree with other people because it is the easiest thing to do: *Just relax and go with the flow!*

flowchart /ˈfləʊ.tʃɑːt/ (US) /ˈfloʊ.tʃɑːrt/ noun [C] (also ˈ**flow** ˌ**diagram**) a DIAGRAM (= simple plan) that shows the stages of a process

flower /ˈflaʊ.ər/ (US) /ˈflaʊ.ɚ/ noun; verb

►noun [C] (A1) the part of a plant that is often brightly coloured and has a pleasant smell, or the type of plant that produces these: *wild flowers* ◦ *to pick flowers* ◦ *a bunch/bouquet of flowers* ◦ *cut/dried flowers*

IDIOMS **the flower of sth** literary the best of a particular group or type: *The flower of the nation's youth were killed in the war.* • **in flower** describes a plant that has open flowers: *Our roses are usually in flower from April to November.* • **in the flower of sb's youth** literary the time when someone was young and in the best and most active period of life: *He died in the very flower of his youth.*

►verb [I] **DEVELOP** ▷ **1** literary to develop completely and become obvious: *Her talent flowered during her later years.* **PLANT** ▷ **2** to produce flowers: *When does this plant flower?*

ˈ**flower ar**ˌ**ranging** noun [U] the skill or activity of arranging flowers in an attractive or artistic way: *flower-arranging classes*

ˈ**flower** ˌ**bed** noun [C] a part of a garden where flowers are planted

ˈ**flower** ˌ**child** noun [C] a **hippie**

flowerpot /ˈflaʊ.ə.pɒt/ (US) /-ɚ.pɑːt/ noun [C] a container usually made of clay or plastic in which a plant is grown

ˈ**flower** ˌ**power** noun [U] the ideas and beliefs of some young people in the 1960s and 1970s who opposed war and encouraged people to love each other

flowery /ˈflaʊ.ə.ri/ (US) /ˈflaʊ.ɚ.i/ adj **FLOWERS** ▷ **1** (also **flowered**) decorated with pictures of flowers: *a flowery material/dress* ◦ *flowery curtains/wallpaper* **WORDS** ▷ **2** disapproving If a speech or writing style is flowery, it uses too many complicated words or phrases in an attempt to sound skilful: *a flowery description/speech*

flowing /ˈfləʊ.ɪŋ/ (US) /ˈfloʊ-/ adj **MOVING** ▷ **1** moving in one direction, especially continuously and easily: *a* ***fast****-flowing river* **SMOOTH AND CONTINUOUS** ▷ **2** produced in a smooth, continuous or relaxed style: *flowing movements/lines* **HANGING DOWN** ▷ **3** describes hair and clothes that are long and hang down loosely: *I remember her as a young girl with flowing black hair.* ◦ *Everyone on stage was dressed in flowing white* ***robes****.*

flown /fləʊn/ (US) /floʊn/ past participle of **fly**

fl oz written abbreviation for **fluid ounce**

F

flu /fluː/ noun [U] (formal **influenza**) (B1) an common infectious illness that causes fever and HEADACHE: *a flu virus* ◦ *to catch/get/have (the) flu*

fluctuate /ˈflʌk.tju.eɪt/ verb [I] (C2) to change, especially continuously and between one level or thing and another: *Vegetable prices fluctuate* ***according to*** *the season.* ◦ *Her wages fluctuate* ***between*** *£150 and £200 a week.* ◦ *Her weight fluctuates* ***wildly****.* ◦ *fluctuating prices* • **fluctuation** /ˌflʌk.tjuˈeɪ.ʃən/ noun [C or U] *fluctuations* ***in*** *share prices/the exchange rate/temperature*

flue /fluː/ noun [C] a pipe which leads from a fire or HEATER to the outside of a building, taking smoke, gases, or hot air away

fluent /ˈfluː.ənt/ adj **1** (B2) When a person is fluent, they can speak a language easily, well, and quickly: *She's fluent* ***in*** *French.* ◦ *He's a fluent Russian speaker.* **2** (B2) When a language is fluent, it is spoken easily and without many pauses: *He speaks fluent Chinese.* • **fluency** /-ən.si/ noun [U] (B2) *One of the requirements of the job is fluency* ***in*** *two or more African languages.* • **fluently** /-li/ adv (B2) *I'd like to speak English fluently.*

fluff /flʌf/ noun; verb

▸noun [U] **SOFT MASS** ▷ **1** small, loose pieces of wool or other soft material, or the DOWN (= soft new hairs) on a young animal: *He brushed the fluff off his coat.* **ENTERTAINMENT** ▷ **2** US entertainment that is not serious or valuable

▸verb [T] (US also **flub**) to fail something or do it badly: *I fluffed my driving test three times before I finally got it.* ◦ *All the time I was acting with him, I never once heard him fluff* ***his lines*** *(= say something wrong when acting).*

PHRASAL VERB **fluff sth up** to make something appear bigger or full of air by hitting or shaking it: *I'll just fluff up your pillows for you.*

fluffy /ˈflʌf.i/ adj **1** soft and like wool or like fur: *fluffy toys* **2** light and full of air: *Beat the eggs and sugar together until they are pale and fluffy.* • **fluffiness** /-nəs/ noun [U]

flugelhorn /ˈfluː.gəl.hɔːn/ (US) /-hɔːrn/ noun [C] a musical instrument that is similar to a TRUMPET but smaller and with a wider tube

fluid /ˈfluː.ɪd/ noun; adj

▸noun [C or U] (C2) a substance which flows and is not solid: *If you have a fever you should drink plenty of fluid(s).* ◦ *The virus is contracted through exchange of* ***bodily*** *fluids.*

▸adj **MOVEMENT** ▷ **1** (C2) smooth and continuous: *fluid movements* **LIKELY TO CHANGE** ▷ **2** If situations, ideas, or plans are fluid, they are not fixed and are likely to change, often repeatedly and unexpectedly: *The military situation is still very fluid.*

fluidity /fluˈɪd.ɪ.ti/ (US) /-ə.t̬i/ noun [U] **CHANGE** ▷ **1** the quality of being likely to change repeatedly and unexpectedly: *the fluidity of the political situation* **MOVEMENT** ▷ **2** formal the quality of being smooth and continuous: *Durante dances with fluidity and grace.* **LIQUID** ▷ **3** (of a substance) the quality of being not solid and able to flow

ˌfluid ˈounce noun [C] (written abbreviation **fl oz**) a measurement of liquid equal to UK 0.024 or US 0.030 of a litre

fluke /fluːk/ noun [C usually singular] informal something good that has happened that is the result of chance instead of skill or planning: *The first goal was just a fluke.* • **fluky** (**flukier**, **flukiest**) (also **flukey**) /ˈfluː.ki/ adj

flume /fluːm/ noun [C] **1** a narrow CHANNEL made for carrying water, for example to factories that produce electricity **2** a structure for people to slide down at a SWIMMING POOL or WATER PARK, shaped like a large tube with water flowing through it

flummox /ˈflʌm.əks/ verb [T] informal to confuse someone so much that they do not know what to do: *I have to say that last question flummoxed me.* • **flummoxed** /-əkst/ adj *He looked completely flummoxed.*

flung /flʌŋ/ past simple and past participle of **fling**

flunk /flʌŋk/ verb [T] mainly US informal to fail an exam or course of study: *I flunked my second-year exams and was lucky not to be thrown out of college.*

PHRASAL VERB **flunk out** US informal to have to leave school or college because your work is not good enough: *Dan won't be in college next year – he flunked out.*

flunky /ˈflʌŋ.ki/ noun [C] (also **flunkey**) a male servant wearing a uniform

fluorescent /flʊəˈres.ənt/ (US) /flʊ-/ adj **LIGHT** ▷ **1** Fluorescent lights are very bright, tube-shaped electric lights, often used in offices: *fluorescent lighting* **COLOUR** ▷ **2** Fluorescent colours are very bright and can be seen in the dark: *fluorescent green* • **fluorescence** /-əns/ noun [U]

fluoridate /ˈflʊə.rɪ.deɪt/ (US) /ˈflʊ-/ verb [T] to add fluoride to water • **fluoridation** /ˌflʊə.rɪˈdeɪ.ʃən/ (US) /ˌflʊ-/ noun [U]

fluoride /ˈflʊə.raɪd/ (US) /ˈflʊ-/ noun [U] a chemical substance sometimes added to water or TOOTHPASTE (= substance for cleaning teeth) in order to help keep teeth healthy

fluorine /ˈflʊə.riːn/ (US) /ˈflʊ-/ noun [U] (symbol **F**) a chemical element that is a poisonous, pale yellow gas

fluorocarbon /ˌflʊə.rəˈkɑː.bən/ (US) /ˌflʊ.roʊˈkɑːr-/ noun [C] specialized a chemical containing fluorine and carbon, with various industrial uses → See also **CFC**

flurry /ˈflʌr.i/ (US) /ˈflɜː-/ noun **SNOW** ▷ **1** [C] a sudden light fall of snow, blown in different directions by the wind: *There may be the odd flurry* ***of snow*** *over the hills.* **ACTIVITY** ▷ **2** [C usually singular] a sudden, short period of activity, excitement, or interest: *The prince's words on marriage have prompted a flurry* ***of*** *speculation in the press this week.* ◦ *a flurry of activity*

flush /flʌʃ/ verb; adj; noun

▸verb **BECOME RED** ▷ **1** [I] When you flush, you become red in the face, especially as a result of strong emotions, heat, or alcohol: *She flushed* ***with*** *pleasure as she accepted the prize.* ◦ *The champagne had caused his face to flush.* **TOILET** ▷ **2** [I or T] If you flush a toilet, or if a toilet flushes, its contents empty and it fills with water again: *My children never flush* ***the loo/toilet*** *after them.* ◦ *I can't get the toilet to flush.* **3 flush sth down the toilet** to get rid of something by putting it in the toilet and operating the toilet: *I tend to flush old medicines down the toilet.*

PHRASAL VERBS **flush sb/sth out** to force a person or animal to leave a place where they are hiding: *Planes bombed the guerrilla positions yesterday in an attempt to flush out snipers from underground tunnels.* ◦ *We used a dog to flush the rabbits out.* • **flush sb out** to do something in order to discover people who have been dishonest: *By cross-checking claims, we will flush out the fraudsters.* • **flush sth out** to remove something using a sudden flow of water: *Drink a lot of water to flush the toxins out of your system.*

▸adj **LEVEL** ▷ **1** at the same level as another surface: *I want the light fittings to be flush* ***with*** *the ceiling.* **RICH** ▷ **2** [after verb] informal having a lot of money: *I've just been paid so I'm feeling flush.*

▸noun **RED COLOUR** ▷ **1** [C] a red colour that appears on your face or body because you are embarrassed, hot, etc.: *A faint pink flush coloured her cheeks.* → See also **hot flush** **SUDDEN FEELING** ▷ **2 a flush of anger, excitement, pleasure, etc.** a sudden strong feeling of anger, excitement, pleasure, etc. **TOILET** ▷ **3** [C] an occasion when the contents of a toilet empty and it fills with water **4** the handle or button that you push to make a toilet empty and fill with water: *He pressed the flush with his hand.* **CARD GAMES** ▷ **5** [C] a number of playing cards held by one player that are all from the same suit

flushed /flʌʃt/ adj red in the face: *You look a bit flushed – are you hot?* ◦ *flushed* ***cheeks*** ◦ *flushed* ***with*** *anger/embarrassment*

IDIOM **flushed with success** feeling excited and confident after achieving something: *Flushed with success after their surprise win against Italy, Belgium are preparing for Saturday's game against Spain.*

fluster /ˈflʌs.təʳ/ (US) /-tɚ/ verb; noun

▸verb [T] to make someone upset and confused, especially when they are trying to do something

▸noun [S] an upset and confused state: *The important thing when you're cooking for a lot of people is not to get* ***in a*** *fluster.*

flustered /ˈflʌs.təd/ (US) /-tɚd/ adj upset and confused: *She seemed a bit flustered.* ◦ *If I look flustered it's because I'm trying to do so many things at once.*

flute /fluːt/ noun [C] **1** (B1) a tube-shaped musical instrument with a hole that you blow across at one end while holding the tube out horizontally to one side **2** a **champagne flute**

fluted /ˈfluː.tɪd/ (US) /ˈfluː.t̬ɪd/ adj If an object, especially a round object, is fluted, its edges have many curves that go in and out: *a flan dish with fluted edges* ◦ *fluted columns/pillars*

flutist /ˈfluː.tɪst/ (US) /-t̬ɪst/ noun [C] US for **flautist**

flutter /ˈflʌt.əʳ/ (US) /ˈflʌt̬.ɚ/ verb; noun

▸verb **MOVE** ▷ **1** [I or T] to make a series of quick delicate movements up and down or from side to side, or to cause something to do this: *Brightly coloured flags were fluttering in the breeze.* ◦ *Leaves fluttered* ***down*** *onto the path.* ◦ *Butterflies fluttered* ***about*** *in the sunshine.* ◦ *A white bird poised on a wire and fluttered its wings.* **HEART/STOMACH** ▷ **2** [I] If your heart or stomach flutters, you feel slightly uncomfortable because you are excited or nervous: *Every time I think about my exams my stomach flutters!*

IDIOMS **flutter your eyelashes** humorous If a woman flutters her eyelashes at a man, she uses the fact that she is attractive to persuade him to do something for her: *Go and flutter your eyelashes* ***at*** *the barman, Janet, and see if you can get him to serve us.* • **make sb's heart flutter** If someone makes your heart flutter, you find them very physically attractive and you feel excited when you see or talk to them: *James has been making hearts flutter ever since he joined the company.*

▸noun **EXCITEMENT** ▷ **1** [C usually singular] a short period of excited activity: *The publication of her first novel last autumn caused a flutter* ***of excitement***. **MONEY** ▷ **2** [C usually singular] UK informal a small BET (= money risked), especially on a horse race: *Auntie Paula likes to* ***have*** *a bit of a flutter* ***on*** *the horses.* **MOVEMENT** ▷ **3** [S] a quick up-and-down movement

IDIOMS **all of a flutter** in a state of nervous excitement: *Peter was coming round for dinner and I was all of a flutter.* • **in a flutter** in a confused and excited state: *When economic statistics are first published they grab headlines and put markets in a flutter.*

fluvial /ˈfluː.vi.əl/ adj specialized of a river: *a fluvial basin* ◦ *fluvial ice*

flux /flʌks/ noun [U] **CHANGE** ▷ **1** continuous change: *Our plans are* ***in a state of*** *flux at the moment.* **SUBSTANCE** ▷ **2** specialized a substance added to a metal to make it easier to SOLDER (= join by melting) to another metal

fly /flaɪ/ verb; noun

▸verb (**flew**, **flown**) **TRAVEL** ▷ **1** (A2) [I] When a bird, insect, or aircraft flies, it moves through the air: *The poor bird couldn't fly because it had a broken wing.* ◦ *As soon as it saw us, the bird flew* ***away/off***. **2** (A1) [I or T] to travel by aircraft, or to go somewhere or cross something in an aircraft: *We flew* ***to*** *Paris.* ◦ *We fly* ***from/out from/out of*** *Heathrow, but fly* ***back (in)to*** *Gatwick.* ◦ *We are flying* ***at*** *a height of 9,000 metres.* ◦ *She has to fly thousands of miles every year for her job.* ◦ *Who was the first person to fly* ***(across)*** *the Atlantic?* **3** [T] to use a particular company to travel by aircraft: *I usually fly Lufthansa/Japan Airlines/El Al.* **4** (C2) [T] to transport people or goods by aircraft: *The restaurant flies its fish* ***in*** *daily from Scotland.* ◦ *We will be flying 100 badly wounded civilians* ***out*** *of the battle zone tonight.* **5** (B2) [I or T] to control an aircraft: *I learned to fly when I was in Australia.* **MOVE QUICKLY** ▷ **6** [I] to move or go quickly: *With the explosion, glass flew* ***across*** *the room.* ◦ *Cathy flew* ***by/past*** *me in the corridor.* ◦ *My holiday seems to have flown* ***(by)*** *(= passed very quickly) this year.* ◦ *The door/window suddenly flew* ***open***. ◦ informal *Anyway, I* ***must*** *fly (= leave quickly) – I didn't realize how late it was!* **WAVE** ▷ **7** [I or T] to wave or move about in the air while being fixed at one end: *The ship was flying the Spanish flag.* ◦ *The flag was flying* ***at half-mast*** *(= brought down to a point half way down the pole) to mark the death of the president.* ◦ *There isn't really enough wind to fly a kite today.*

IDIOMS **be flying high 1** If a person or a company is flying high, they are very successful: *The company was flying high as a maker of personal computers.* **2** US informal to be very excited or happy, often because of the effect of drugs: *The guy was on drugs – flying high and scaring everyone around him.* ◦ *When the winter Olympics came to Canada, the whole country was flying high.* • **fly in the face of sth** (C2) to completely oppose what seems sensible or normal: *This is an argument that seems to fly in the face of* ***common sense***. • **fly into a rage** (UK also **fly into a temper/fury**) to suddenly become very angry: *I asked to speak to her boss and she just flew into a rage.* • **fly off the handle** to react in a very angry way to something that someone says or does: *He's extremely irritable – he flies off the handle at the slightest thing.* • **go fly a kite** mainly US informal used to tell someone who is being annoying to go away • **go/send sth/sb flying** informal to fall, or to cause something or someone to fall or move through the air, suddenly and by accident: *I tripped going up the stairs and I/my books went flying.* • **with flying colours** C1 If you do something such as pass an exam with flying colours, you do it very successfully.

PHRASAL VERBS **fly about/around** informal If ideas, remarks, or ACCUSATIONS are flying about/around, they are passed quickly from one person to another and cause excitement: *All kinds of rumours are flying around about the school closing.* • **fly at sb/sth** to attack another person or animal suddenly: *He flew at his brother like a mad thing.*

F

▸noun [C] **INSECT** ▷ **1** B1 a small insect with two wings **TROUSERS** ▷ **2** (UK also **flies**) the opening at the front of a pair of trousers: *Hey Chris, your fly's undone!* **FISHING** ▷ **3** a HOOK (= curved piece of wire) with coloured threads fastened to it, fixed to the end of a fishing line to attract fish **TENT** ▷ **4** mainly US for **flysheet**

IDIOMS **drop like flies** informal **1** If people are dropping like flies they are dying or falling down in large numbers: *The heat was overwhelming and people were dropping like flies.* **2** to stop doing an activity in large numbers: *There used to be over 20 of us in our aerobics class but they're dropping like flies.* • **fly in the ointment** informal a single thing or person that is spoiling a situation which could have been very positive or enjoyable: *I'm looking forward to Sunday, the only fly in the ointment being the fact that I shall have to sit next to my mother-in-law.* • **fly on the wall** If you say that you would like to be a fly on the wall on an occasion, you mean that you would like to hear what will be said or see what will happen while not being noticed: *I'd love to be a fly on the wall when those two get home!* → See also **fly-on-the-wall** • **no flies on sb** If you say there are no flies on someone, you mean that they cannot easily be deceived. • **wouldn't harm/hurt a fly** informal If you say that someone wouldn't harm/hurt a fly, you mean they are gentle and would not do anything to injure or offend anyone.

flyaway /ˈflaɪ.ə.weɪ/ **adj** describes hair that is soft, light, and difficult to keep in place

flyby /ˈflaɪ.baɪ/ **noun** [C] (plural **flybys**) **1** a flight, especially in a spacecraft, past a particular point in space **2** US for **flypast**

ˈfly-by-night adj [before noun] informal disapproving Fly-by-night companies or business people cannot be trusted because they are likely to get into debt and close down the business to avoid paying the debts or satisfying agreements: *a fly-by-night operator/organization*

flycatcher /ˈflaɪˌkætʃ.əʳ/ (US) /-ɚ/ **noun** [C] a small bird which catches insects in the air

ˌfly-drive ˈholiday noun [C] UK (US **ˌfly-drive vaˈcation**) an organized holiday which includes your air ticket and the use of a car

flyer (US usually **flier**) /ˈflaɪ.əʳ/ (US) /-ɚ/ **noun** [C] **INFORMATION** ▷ **1** a small piece of paper with information on it about a product or event **TRAVEL** ▷ **2** a person who travels by air: ***Frequent** flyers receive travel privileges.*

ˈfly ˌfishing noun [U] the activity of trying to catch fish using a fly to attract the fish

flying /ˈflaɪ.ɪŋ/ **noun** [U] travel by air: *Annette's scared of flying.*

ˌflying ˈbuttress noun [C] specialized an ARCH built against a wall, especially of a church, to support its weight

ˌflying ˈdoctor noun [C] a doctor, usually in Australia, who travels by air to see ill people who live a long way from a city

ˌflying ˈfish noun [C] a tropical fish that can jump above the surface of the water using its very large FINS

ˌflying ˈfox noun [C] a large BAT that eats fruit

ˌflying ˈpicket noun [C] mainly UK a worker who travels to support workers who are on STRIKE at another place of work

ˌflying ˈsaucer noun [C] old-fashioned for **UFO**

ˌflying ˌsquad noun [C] a small group of police officers that is trained to act quickly, especially when there is a serious crime

ˌflying ˈstart noun [C usually singular] an instance of one competitor in a race starting more quickly than the others: figurative *She's **got off to** a flying start (= has begun very well) in her new job.*

ˌflying ˈvisit noun [C usually singular] a very short visit

flyleaf /ˈflaɪ.liːf/ **noun** [C] (plural **flyleaves**) an empty page at the beginning or end of a book next to the cover

ˌfly-on-the-ˈwall adj [before noun] UK describes a television programme in which the people involved behave normally, as if they are not being filmed: *a fly-on-the-wall documentary*

flyover /ˈflaɪˌəʊ.vəʳ/ (US) /-ˌoʊ.vɚ/ **noun** **BRIDGE** ▷ **1** [C] UK (US **overpass**) a bridge that carries a road or railway over another road **AIRCRAFT** ▷ **2** [C usually singular] US for **flypast**

flypaper /ˈflaɪˌpeɪ.pəʳ/ (US) /-pɚ/ **noun** [C or U] a long strip of sticky paper which you hang in a room to catch flies

flypast /ˈflaɪ.pɑːst/ (US) /-pæst/ **noun** [C usually singular] UK (US **flyby**, **flyover**) an occasion when a group of aircraft flies in a special pattern as a part of a ceremony

ˈfly-ˌposting noun [U] UK illegally sticking a political or other POSTER (= notice) on a public wall, fence, etc. • **ˈfly-ˌposter** noun [C] a person who goes fly-posting or the POSTER (= notice) they put up: *Fly-posters will be prosecuted.*

flysheet /ˈflaɪ.ʃiːt/ **noun** [C] UK (mainly US **fly**) an extra sheet of CANVAS (= strong cloth) stretched over the outside of a tent to keep the rain out

ˈfly-ˌtipping noun [U] illegally leaving things that you do not want next to a road, in fields, in rivers, etc. • **ˈfly-tip** verb [T]

flyweight /ˈflaɪ.weɪt/ **noun** [C] specialized a BOXER who is in the lightest weight group, weighing 51 kilograms or less

flywheel /ˈflaɪ.wiːl/ **noun** [C] specialized a heavy wheel in a machine which helps the machine to work at a regular speed

FM /ˌefˈem/ **noun** [U] abbreviation for frequency modulation: a radio system for broadcasting which produces a very clear sound

foal /fəʊl/ (US) /foʊl/ **noun; verb**

▸noun [C] a young horse

IDIOM **in foal** (of a female horse) pregnant

▸verb [I] If a MARE (= a female horse) foals, she gives birth to a baby horse.

foam /fəʊm/ (US) /foʊm/ **noun; verb**

▸noun [U] **BUBBLES** ▷ **1** a mass of very small bubbles formed on the surface of a liquid **2** a substance like cream that is filled with bubbles of air: ***shaving** foam*

SOFT MATERIAL ▷ **3** a soft material used to fill furniture and other objects
▸verb [I] **1** to produce small bubbles **2 foam at the mouth** If a person or an animal foams at the mouth, they have bubbles coming out of their mouth as a result of a disease.

IDIOM **be foaming at the mouth** to be extremely angry: *The Almeida theatre's recent staging of the opera had critics foaming at the mouth.*

ˌfoam ˈpie noun [C] an amount of SHAVING FOAM on a paper plate, etc. that is thrown at someone's face to make people laugh or as a protest: *He was attacked by a protester with a foam pie.*

ˌfoam ˈrubber noun [U] soft rubber with air bubbles in it

foamy /ˈfəʊ.mi/ (US) /ˈfoʊ-/ adj made of or producing a mass of very small bubbles: *foamy beer* ◦ *foamy shampoo*

fob /fɒb/ (US) /fɑːb/ noun; verb
▸noun [C] a piece of leather or other material to which a group of keys is fastened, or a chain or piece of material used, especially in the past, to fasten a watch to a man's WAISTCOAT: *a fob watch*
▸verb (-bb-)

PHRASAL VERB **fob sb off** (also **fob sth off on sb**) UK to persuade someone to accept something that is of a low quality or different to what they really wanted: *Well, he wants the report ready by tomorrow but I can always fob him off* ***with*** *some excuse.*

focal /ˈfəʊ.kəl/ (US) /ˈfoʊ-/ adj central and important: *The focal* ***figure*** *of the film is Annette Corley, a dancer who has boyfriend troubles.*

ˌfocal ˈlength noun [C usually singular] specialized the distance between a point where waves of light meet and the centre of a LENS

ˌfocal ˈpoint noun **INTEREST** ▷ **1** [C usually singular] the thing that everyone looks at or is interested in: *The television is usually the focal point of the living room.* **SCIENCE** ▷ **2** [C] specialized (in physics) the point where waves of light or sound that are moving towards each other meet

focus /ˈfəʊ.kəs/ (US) /ˈfoʊ-/ noun; verb
▸noun [C] (plural **focuses** or formal **foci**) **CENTRE** ▷ **1** (C1) the main or central point of something, especially of attention or interest: *I think Dave likes to be the focus* ***of attention.*** ◦ *The main focus* ***of interest*** *at the fashion show was Christian Lacroix's outrageous evening wear.* ◦ *The media focus* ***on*** *politicians' private lives inevitably switches the attention away from the real issues.* **SCIENCE** ▷ **2** (in physics) the point where waves of light or sound that are moving towards each other meet: *the focus of a lens* **3 be in/out of focus** describes a photograph that is clear/not clear
▸verb (-s-) **1** [T] If you focus a device such as a camera or MICROSCOPE, you move a device on the LENS so that you can see a clear picture. **2** [I or T] If you focus your eyes, or if your eyes focus, you try to look directly at an object so that you can see it more clearly: *When they first took the bandages off, she/her eyes couldn't focus properly (= she couldn't see clearly).*

PHRASAL VERB **focus (sth) on/upon sb/sth** (B2) to give a lot of attention to one particular person, subject, or thing: *Tonight's programme focuses on the way that homelessness affects the young.* ◦ *When the kitchen is finished I'm going to focus* ***my attention*** *on the garden and get that sorted out.*

focused /ˈfəʊ.kəst/ (US) /ˈfoʊ-/ adj (also **focussed**) **GIVING ATTENTION** ▷ **1** giving a lot of attention to one particular thing: *the need for more focused research* **PHOTOGRAPH** ▷ **2** clear: *a focused image*

ˈfocus ˌgroup noun [C, + sing/pl verb] a group of people who have been brought together to discuss a particular subject in order to solve a problem or suggest ideas

fodder /ˈfɒd.əʳ/ (US) /ˈfɑː.dɚ/ noun [U] **ANIMAL FOOD** ▷ **1** food that is given to cows, horses, and other farm animals **USEFUL PEOPLE/THINGS** ▷ **2** people or things that are useful for the stated purpose: *Politicians are always good fodder* ***for*** *comedians (= they make jokes about them).* → See **cannon fodder**

foe /fəʊ/ (US) /foʊ/ noun [C] literary an enemy: *The two countries have united against their common foe.* ◦ *They were* ***bitter*** *foes for many years.* ◦ *Foes* ***of*** *the government will be delighting in its current difficulties.*

F

FoE /ˌef.əʊˈiː/ (US) /-oʊˈ-/ noun abbreviation for **Friends of the Earth**

foetid /ˈfet.ɪd/ (US) /ˈfet̬-/ adj UK **fetid**

foetus (US also **fetus**) /ˈfiː.təs/ (US) /-t̬əs/ noun [C] a young human being or animal before birth, after the organs have started to develop • **foetal** (US also **fetal**) /-təl/ (US) /-t̬əl/ adj *foetal abnormalities* ◦ *foetal position*

fog /fɒg/ (US) /fɑːg/ noun; verb
▸noun **WEATHER** ▷ **1** (A2) [C or U] a weather condition in which very small drops of water come together to form a thick cloud close to the land or sea, making it difficult to see: ***Thick/Heavy/Dense*** *fog has made driving conditions dangerous.* ◦ *Mists,* ***freezing*** *fogs and snow are common in this area.* ◦ *It took several hours for the fog to* ***lift.*** **CONFUSION** ▷ **2** [S] informal a confused or uncertain state, usually mentally or emotionally: *I went home* ***in a fog of*** *disbelief.*
▸verb [T] (-gg-) to make something or someone confused or uncertain: *Alcohol fogs the brain.* ◦ *The minister's speech had merely fogged the issue.*

PHRASAL VERB **fog up** If a glass surface fogs up, a thin layer of liquid develops on it so that it is difficult to see through: *I couldn't see a thing because my glasses had fogged up.*

fogbound /ˈfɒg.baʊnd/ (US) /ˈfɑːg-/ adj prevented from operating as usual or travelling because of fog: *Their flight was cancelled because the* ***airport*** *was fogbound.*

fogey (also **fogy**) /ˈfəʊ.gi/ (US) /ˈfoʊ-/ noun [C] informal disapproving a person who is old-fashioned and likes traditional ways of doing things: *The party is run by a bunch of* ***old*** *fogeys who resist progress.*

foggy /ˈfɒg.i/ (US) /ˈfɑː.gi/ adj (A2) with fog: *a cold, foggy day*

IDIOM **not have the foggiest (idea)** informal to not know or understand something at all: *I hadn't the foggiest idea what he was talking about.*

foghorn /ˈfɒg.hɔːn/ (US) /ˈfɑːg.hɔːrn/ noun [C] a horn that makes a very loud sound to warn ships that they are close to land or other ships: *He has a* ***voice like a*** *foghorn (= an unpleasantly loud voice).*

foible /ˈfɔɪ.bl̩/ noun [C usually plural] a strange habit or characteristic that is seen as not important and not harming anyone: *We all have our little foibles.*

foil /fɔɪl/ noun; verb
▸noun **METAL SHEET** ▷ **1** [U] a very thin sheet of metal, especially used to wrap food in to keep it fresh: *tin/silver foil* ◦ UK *aluminium* (US *aluminum*) *foil* **COMPARISON** ▷ **2** [C] something or someone that makes another's good or bad qualities more noticeable: *The older, cynical character in the play is the perfect foil*

for the innocent William. **SWORD** ▷ **3** [C] a thin, light SWORD used in the sport of FENCING
▸verb [T] to prevent someone or something from being successful: *The prisoners' attempt to escape was foiled at the last minute when police received a tip-off.*

foist /fɔɪst/ verb

PHRASAL VERB **foist sth on/upon sb** to force someone to have or experience something they do not want: *I try not to foist my values on the children but it's hard.*

fold /fəʊld/ ⓤⓢ /foʊld/ verb; noun
▸verb **BEND** ▷ **1** B1 [I or T] to bend something, especially paper or cloth, so that one part of it lies on the other part, or to be able to be bent in this way: *I folded the letter (**in half**) and put it in an envelope.* ◦ *He had a **neatly** folded handkerchief in his jacket pocket.* ◦ *Will you help me to fold (**up**) the sheets?* ◦ *The table folds up when not in use.* **2** [T] to wrap: *She folded her baby **in** a blanket.* ◦ *He folded his arms **around** her.* **3 fold your arms** to bring your arms close to your chest and hold them together **4** [T] to move a part of your body into a position where it is close to your body: *She sat with her legs folded **under** her.* **FAIL** ▷ **5** [I] (of a business) to close because of failure: *Many small businesses fold within the first year.*

PHRASAL VERB **fold sth in/fold sth into something** (in cooking) to mix a substance into another substance by turning it gently with a spoon: *Fold the egg whites into the cake mixture.* ◦ *Fold in the flour.*

▸noun [C] **BEND** ▷ **1** a line or mark where paper, cloth, etc. was or is folded: *Make a fold across the centre of the card.* **2** specialized a bend in a layer of rock under the Earth's surface caused by movement there **SHELTER** ▷ **3** a small area of a field surrounded by a fence where sheep can be put for shelter for the night **4 the fold** your home or an organization where you feel you belong: *Her children are all away at college now, but they always **return to** the fold in the holidays.*

-fold /-fəʊld/ ⓤⓢ /-foʊld/ **suffix** having the stated number of parts, or multiplied by the stated number: *threefold* ◦ *fourfold* ◦ *The problems are twofold – firstly, economic, and secondly, political.* ◦ *In the last 50 years, there has been a 33-fold increase in the amount of pesticide used in farming.*

foldaway /ˈfəʊld.ə.weɪ/ ⓤⓢ /ˈfoʊld-/ **adj** able to be folded away out of sight: *a foldaway bed*

folder /ˈfəʊl.dər/ ⓤⓢ /ˈfoʊl.dɚ/ noun [C] **FOR PAPERS** ▷ **1** A2 a piece of plastic or cardboard folded down the middle and used for keeping loose papers in **COMPUTER** ▷ **2** B1 a place on a computer where FILES or PROGRAMS can be stored

folding /ˈfəʊl.dɪŋ/ ⓤⓢ /ˈfoʊl-/ **adj** [before noun] **1** describes a chair, bed, bicycle, etc. that can be folded into a smaller size to make it easier to store or carry **2** describes a door made of several parts joined together that can be folded against each other when the door is opened

foliage /ˈfəʊ.li.ɪdʒ/ ⓤⓢ /ˈfoʊ-/ noun [U] the leaves of a plant or tree, or leaves on the stems or branches on which they are growing: *The **dense** foliage overhead almost blocked out the sun.*

folic acid /ˌfəʊ.lɪkˈæs.ɪd/ ⓤⓢ /ˌfoʊ-/ noun [U] a VITAMIN, found in the leaves of plants and in LIVER, that is needed by the body for the production of red blood cells

folio /ˈfəʊ.li.əʊ/ ⓤⓢ /ˈfoʊ.li.oʊ/ noun [C] (plural **folios**) **1** a book made of paper of a large size, especially one of the earliest books printed in Europe **2** a single sheet of paper from a book

folk /fəʊk/ ⓤⓢ /foʊk/ noun; adj
▸noun **PEOPLE** ▷ **1** B2 [plural] (mainly US **folks**) people, especially those of a particular group or type: ***old** folk* ◦ ***Ordinary** folk can't afford cars like that.* **2 folks** [plural] **a** [as form of address] informal used when speaking informally to a group of people: *All right, folks, dinner's ready!* **b** B2 mainly US someone's parents: *I'm going home to see my folks.* **MUSIC** ▷ **3** B1 [U] modern music and songs that are written in a style similar to that of traditional music: *I enjoy listening to folk (**music**).* ◦ *folk **singers*** ◦ *a folk **club/festival***
▸adj [before noun] **1** traditional to or typical of a particular group or country, especially one where people mainly live in the countryside, and usually passed on from parents to their children over a long period of time: *folk culture* **2** B1 describes art that expresses something about the lives and feelings of ordinary people in a particular group or country, especially those living in the countryside: *folk art* ◦ *folk dancing*

ˈfolk ˌhero noun [C] someone who is popular with and respected by ordinary people

folklore /ˈfəʊk.lɔːr/ ⓤⓢ /ˈfoʊk.lɔːr/ noun [U] the traditional stories and culture of a group of people: *In Irish folklore, the leprechaun had a large piece of gold.* ◦ *Arguments between directors and stars are part of the folklore of Hollywood.*

ˈfolk ˌmemory noun [C usually singular] the knowledge that people have about something that happened in the past because parents have spoken to their children about it over many years

ˈfolk ˌsong noun [C] a traditional song from a particular region, or a modern song, usually with a tune played on a guitar, that is written in a style similar to that of traditional music

folksy /ˈfəʊk.si/ ⓤⓢ /ˈfoʊk-/ **adj** having a traditional, simple artistic or musical style, or pretending to have such a style: *The book has a certain folksy charm.*

ˈfolk ˌtale noun [C] a story that parents have passed on to their children through speech over many years

follicle /ˈfɒl.ɪ.kl̩/ ⓤⓢ /ˈfɑː.lɪ-/ noun [C] any of the very small holes in the skin, especially one that a hair grows from

follow /ˈfɒl.əʊ/ ⓤⓢ /ˈfɑː.loʊ/ verb **GO** ▷ **1** A2 [I or T] to move behind someone or something and go where they go: *A dog followed us home.* ◦ *She followed me into the kitchen.* ◦ *The book was delivered yesterday with a note saying the bill for it would follow in a day or two.* ◦ *He had the feeling he was being followed (= someone was going after him to catch him or see where he was going).* ◦ *I could feel them following me with their eyes (= watching my movements closely).* ◦ *Follow (= go in the same direction as) the road for two miles, then turn left.* ◦ *Do your own thing, don't just follow **the crowd** (= do what everyone else does).* **2 follow suit** C2 to do the same thing as someone else: *When one airline reduces its prices, the rest soon follow suit.* **HAPPEN** ▷ **3** B1 [I or T] to happen or come after something: *We were not prepared for the events that followed (= happened next).* ◦ *The meal consisted of smoked salmon, followed by guinea fowl (= with this as the next part).* ◦ *She published a book of poems and followed it (**up**) **with** (= next produced) a novel.* **4 as follows** B2 said to introduce a list of things: *The winners are as follows – Woods, Smith, and Cassidy.* **OBEY** ▷ **5** B1 [T] to obey or to act as ordered by someone: *Follow the **instructions** on the back of the packet carefully.* ◦ *I decided to follow her **advice** and go to bed early.* ◦ *Muslims follow the **teachings** of the Koran.* **HAVE INTEREST IN** ▷ **6** C1 [T] to have a great interest in something or watch something closely: *He* *follows most sports avidly.* ◦ *They followed her academic progress closely.* **BE RESULT** ▷ **7** C2 [not continuous] to happen as a result, or to be a likely result: [+ that] *Just because I agreed last time,* ***it*** *doesn't* ***necessarily*** *follow* ***that*** *I will do so again.* **UNDERSTAND** ▷ **8** B1 [I or T] to understand something as it is being said or done: *I'm sorry, I don't quite follow (you).* ◦ *His lecture was complicated and difficult to follow.* **READ** ▷ **9** [T] To follow a piece of music or writing is to read the notes or words at the same time as they are being played or said. **SOCIAL MEDIA** ▷ **10** [T] If you follow a particular person on TWITTER™ (= a website where people can publish short remarks or pieces of information), you choose to see the messages that that person POSTS (= publishes) on the website.

> **Other ways of saying follow**
>
> The verbs **chase** or **pursue** can be used when someone follows and tries to catch someone else:
>
> *He was running and the dog was* ***chasing*** *him.*
>
> *The robber was* ***pursued*** *by several members of the public.*
>
> If someone is following someone else in order to watch that person and find out where her or she goes, the verbs **tail** or **shadow** can be used:
>
> *The car was* ***tailed*** *by police for several hours.*
>
> *The police think the robbers* ***shadowed*** *their victims for days before the crime.*
>
> If someone is following another person very closely to try to catch that person, you can use the idiom **in hot pursuit**:
>
> *She ran down the steps with a group of journalists* ***in hot pursuit****.*

IDIOMS **follow your nose** informal **1** to trust your own feelings rather than obeying rules or allowing yourself to be influenced by other people's opinions: *Take a chance and follow your nose – you may be right!* **2** go in a straight line: *Turn left, then just follow your nose and you'll see the shop on your left.* • **follow in sb's footsteps** C2 to do the same thing as someone else did previously: *She followed in her mother's footsteps, starting her own business.*

PHRASAL VERBS **follow on** mainly UK to happen or exist as the next part of something: *Following on* ***from*** *what I said earlier...* • **follow (sth) through** to do something as the next part of an activity or period of development: *The essay started interestingly, but failed to follow through (its argument).* • **follow through** to complete the movement of hitting, kicking, or throwing a ball by continuing to move your arm or leg in the same direction: *You need to follow through more on your backhand.* • **follow sth up** (US also **follow up on sth**) B2 to find out more about something, or take further action connected with it: *The idea sounded interesting and I decided to follow it up.* ◦ *He decided to follow up on his initial research and write a book.*

follower /ˈfɒl.əʊ.ər/ US /ˈfɑː.loʊ.ɚ/ noun [C] **SUPPORTER** ▷ **1** someone who has a great interest in something: *They are keen followers* ***of*** *their local football team.* **2** C2 someone who supports, admires, or believes in a particular person, group, or idea: *followers* ***of*** *the Dalai Lama/Buddhism* **PERSON WHO OBEYS** ▷ **3** a person who does what someone else does or suggests doing: *Be a leader, not a follower!* **SOCIAL MEDIA** ▷ **4** someone who chooses to see a particular person's POSTS (= messages) on TWITTER™ (= a website where people can publish short remarks or pieces of information): *She has over 100,000 followers on Twitter.*

following /ˈfɒl.əʊ.ɪŋ/ US /ˈfɑː.loʊ-/ **preposition; adj; noun**

▸**preposition** B2 after: *The weeks following the riots were extremely tense.* ◦ *Following the dinner, there will be a dance.*

▸**adj 1** B1 [before noun] The following day, morning, etc. is the next one. **2 following wind** a wind that is blowing in the same direction as the one in which you are going

▸**noun** [S] **NEXT** ▷ **1 the following** B2 (often used to introduce a list, report, etc.) of what comes next: *The following is an extract from her diary.* **PEOPLE** ▷ **2** a group of people who admire something or someone: *She has* ***attracted*** *a large following among the rich and famous.* ◦ *The shop has a small but* ***loyal/devoted*** *following.* **3** a group of people who support, admire or believe in a particular person, group, or idea

ˌfollow-my-ˈleader noun [U] UK (US **ˌfollow-the-ˈleader**) a children's game in which one child is followed by a line of other children, who have to copy everything the first child does

ˈfollow-up noun [C] a further action connected with something that happened before: *This meeting is a follow-up* ***to*** *the one we had last month.*

folly /ˈfɒl.i/ US /ˈfɑː.li/ noun **STUPIDITY** ▷ **1** [C or U] formal the fact of being stupid, or a stupid action, idea, etc.: *She said that the idea was folly.* ◦ [+ to infinitive] ***It*** *would be folly* ***for*** *the country* ***to*** *become involved in the war.* **BUILDING** ▷ **2** [C] (especially in Britain) a building in the form of a small castle, TEMPLE, etc., that has been built as a decoration in a large garden or park: *a Gothic garden folly*

foment /fəʊˈment/ US /foʊ-/ **verb** [T] formal to cause trouble to develop: *The song was banned on the grounds that it might foment racial tension.*

fond /fɒnd/ US /fɑːnd/ **adj LIKING** ▷ **1** B1 [before noun] having a great liking for someone or something: *She was very fond* ***of*** *horses.* ◦ *'I'm very fond* ***of*** *you, you know,' he said.* ◦ *My brother is fond* ***of*** *pointing out my mistakes.* ◦ *Many of us have fond* ***memories*** *of our childhoods.* ◦ *We said a fond* ***farewell*** *to each other (= we said goodbye in a loving way) and promised to write.* **FOOLISH** ▷ **2 a fond belief/hope** something that you would like to be true but that is probably not: *I waited in all evening in the fond hope that he might call.*

fondant /ˈfɒn.dənt/ US /ˈfɑːn-/ **noun** [C or U] a thick, soft, sweet food, made mainly of sugar and used to cover cakes, or a small soft sweet made mainly from sugar

fondle /ˈfɒn.dl/ US /ˈfɑːn-/ **verb** [T] to touch gently and in a loving way, or to touch in a sexual way: *She fondled the puppies.* ◦ *He gently fondled the baby's feet.* ◦ *She accused him of fondling her (= touching her in a sexual way) in the back of a taxi.*

fondly /ˈfɒnd.li/ US /ˈfɑːnd-/ **adv LIKING** ▷ **1** in a way that shows love or great liking: *He smiled fondly at the children.* **HOPING** ▷ **2** hoping that something will be true when it probably will not: *She fondly believed that he might come.*

fondness /ˈfɒnd.nəs/ US /ˈfɑːnd-/ **noun** [U] a liking: *George's fondness* ***for*** *pink gins was well known.*

fondue /fɒnˈduː/ US /fɑːn-/ **noun** [C] a hot dish prepared by keeping a container of either hot oil or melted cheese over a flame at the table and putting pieces of meat in the oil to be cooked or pieces of bread into the cheese: *a cheese fondue* ◦ *a meat fondue*

ˈfondue ˌset noun [C] the equipment needed to make a fondue

font /fɒnt/ (US) /fɑːnt/ noun [C] **IN A CHURCH** ▷ **1** a large, usually stone, container in a church, which holds the water used for BAPTISMS **LETTERS** ▷ **2** a set of letters and symbols in a particular design and size

food /fuːd/ noun [C or U] (A1) something that people and animals eat, or plants absorb, to keep them alive: *baby food* ◦ *cat food* ◦ *plant food* ◦ *There was lots of food **and drink** at the party.* ◦ *I'm allergic to certain foods.*

Word partners for food

buy/chew/cook/eat/prepare food • *delicious/good/nutritious/plain* food • *cold/hot/savoury/sweet* food

F

IDIOMS **be off your food** to not want to eat, usually because you are ill • **give sb food for thought** to make someone think seriously about something

ˈfood ˌadditive noun [C] an artificial substance added to food to give it taste or colour

the ˈfood ˌchain noun [S] a series of living things that are connected because each group of things eats the group below it in the series

ˈfood ˌcourt noun [C] a large covered area or room, for example inside a shopping centre, where there are small restaurants selling many different types of food that you can eat at tables in the middle of the area

ˈfood ˌgroup noun [C] one of the main groups that foods belong to: *There are five major food groups: carbohydrate, protein, fat, vitamin and mineral*

foodie /ˈfuː.di/ noun [C] informal a person who loves food and is very interested in different types of food

ˌfooding and ˈlodging noun [U] Indian English → **boarding and lodging**

ˈfood ˌmiles noun [plural] the distance between the place where food is grown or made and the place where it is eaten

ˈfood ˌpoisoning noun [U] an illness usually caused by eating food that contains harmful bacteria

ˈfood ˌprocessor noun [C] an electric machine that cuts, slices, and mixes food quickly

ˈfood ˌstamp noun [C] US a piece of paper that is given to poor people by the government and with which they can then buy food

foodstuff /ˈfuːd.stʌf/ noun [C] any substance that is used as food or to make food: *They lack basic foodstuffs, such as bread and milk.*

fool /fuːl/ noun; verb; adj

▸noun **PERSON** ▷ **1** (B1) [C] a person who behaves in a silly way without thinking: [as form of address] *You fool, you've missed your chance!* ◦ *He's a fool if he thinks she still loves him.* ◦ [+ to infinitive] *He's a fool **to** think she still loves him.* ◦ *He's fool **enough to** think she still loves him.* ◦ *My fool **of a** (= silly) husband has gone out and taken my keys!* **2** [C] in the past, a person who was employed in the court of a king or queen to make them laugh by telling jokes and doing funny things **3 act/play the fool** to behave in a silly way, often intentionally to make people laugh: *Stop acting the fool, I'm trying to talk to you.* **4 any fool** anyone: *Any fool could tell that she was joking.* **5 make a fool of sb** (B2) to trick someone or make them appear stupid in some way **6 make a fool of yourself** (B2) to do something that makes other people think you are silly or not to be respected: *I got a bit drunk and made a fool of myself.* **7 more fool sb** mainly UK said to mean that you think someone is being unwise: *'I lent Rhoda $100 and she hasn't paid me back.' 'More fool you – you know what she's like!'* **8 be no fool** (also **be nobody's fool**) to not be stupid or easily deceived: *I notice Ed didn't offer to pay for her – he's no fool.* **SWEET DISH** ▷ **9** [C or U] a sweet, soft food made of crushed fruit, cream, and sugar: ***gooseberry** fool*

▸verb **1** (B2) [I or T] to trick someone: *Don't be fooled by his appearance.* ◦ *She said she was doing it to help me but I wasn't fooled.* ◦ *Tim was fooled **into** believing that he'd won a lot of money.* **2 you could have fooled me!** informal used to tell someone that you do not believe what they have just said: *'Really, I'm very happy.' 'You could have fooled me.'*

PHRASAL VERB **fool around/about** **SILLY** ▷ **1** to behave in a silly way, especially in a way that might have dangerous results: *Don't fool around **with** matches.* **FUNNY** ▷ **2** to behave in a humorous way in order to make other people laugh: *He's always getting into trouble for fooling around in class.* **NOT USEFUL** ▷ **3** to spend your time doing nothing useful **HAVE A SEXUAL RELATIONSHIP** ▷ **4** mainly US If a married person fools around, they have a sexual relationship with someone who is not their husband or wife: *She'd been fooling around **with** someone at work.*

▸adj [before noun] mainly US informal silly: *You've done some fool things in your time, but this beats everything.*

foolery /ˈfuː.lᵊr.i/ (US) /-lɚ.i/ noun UK old-fashioned silly behaviour

foolhardy /ˈfuːlˌhɑː.di/ (US) /-ˌhɑːr-/ adj brave in a silly way, taking unnecessary risks: *a foolhardy decision* ◦ *Sailing the Atlantic in such a tiny boat wasn't so much brave as foolhardy.* ◦ ***It** would be foolhardy **to** try and predict the outcome of the talks at this stage.*

foolish /ˈfuː.lɪʃ/ adj (B2) unwise, stupid, or not showing good judgment: *That was a rather foolish thing to do.* ◦ *She was afraid that she would look foolish if she refused.* ◦ ***It was foolish of** them **to** pay so much.* • **foolishly** /-li/ adv (B2) *Foolishly, I didn't write the phone number down.* • **foolishness** /-nəs/ noun [U]

Other ways of saying foolish

Some common alternatives to 'foolish' are **stupid** and **silly**:

*She was really **stupid** to quit her job like that.*

*It was **silly** of you to go out in the sun without a hat.*

If something or someone is so foolish that that thing or person is funny or strange, you can use the words **absurd**, **ridiculous**, or **ludicrous**:

*What an **absurd** thing to say!*

*Do I look **ridiculous** in this hat?*

*I think giving young children such expensive jewellery is a **ludicrous** idea.*

You can describe a foolish person as a **fool** or an **idiot**:

*You were a **fool** not to take that job.*

*Some **idiot** put a lit match in the wastepaper basket.*

In informal situations, if you think people have been foolish, you can say that they are **out of their minds**:

*You must be **out of your mind** spending so much money on a car.*

foolproof /ˈfuːl.pruːf/ adj (of a plan or machine) so simple and easy to understand that it is unable to go wrong or be used wrongly: *I don't believe there's any such thing as a foolproof scheme for making money.* ◦ *This new DVD player is supposed to be foolproof.*

foolscap /ˈfuːl.skæp/ noun [U] paper of a standard size, measuring 17.2 cm x 21.6 cm

ˌfool's ˈgold noun [U] **1** a mineral that is found in

rocks and looks like gold but is not worth anything **2** something that you think will be very pleasant or successful but is not

ˌfool's ˈparadise noun **live in a fool's paradise** to be happy because you do not know or will not accept how bad a situation really is

foosball /ˈfuːz.bɑːl/ noun [U] US a game played on a table using a small ball and model players fixed to poles, based on football → Compare **table football**

foot /fʊt/ noun; verb

▸noun **BODY PART** ▷ **1** A1 [C] (plural **feet**) the part of the body at the bottom of the leg on which a person or animal stands: *I've got a blister on my left foot.* ◦ *I've been* ***on*** *my feet (= standing) all day and I'm exhausted.* ◦ informal *You look tired. Why don't you* ***put*** *your feet* ***up*** *(= sit or lie down with your feet resting on something)?* ◦ *Please wipe your feet (= clean the bottom of your shoes) before you come into the house.* **2 get/rise to your feet** C2 to stand up after you have been sitting: *He rose to his feet when she walked in.* **3 on foot** A2 walking: *Are you going by bicycle or on foot?* **MEASUREMENT** ▷ **4** B1 [C] (plural **feet** or **foot**) (written abbreviation **ft**) a unit of measurement, equal to twelve INCHES or 0.3048 metres, sometimes shown by the symbol ': *The man was standing only a few feet away.* ◦ *She is five feet/foot three inches tall.* ◦ *She is 5' 3" tall.* **BOTTOM** ▷ **5** C1 [S] the bottom or lower end of a space or object: *They built a house at the foot* ***of*** *a cliff.* ◦ *She dreamed she saw someone standing at the foot* ***of*** *her bed.* ◦ *There's a note to that effect at the foot* ***of*** *the page.* **POETRY** ▷ **6** [C] (plural **feet**) specialized a unit of division of a line of poetry containing one strong beat and one or two weaker ones

IDIOMS **be back on your feet** to be healthy again after a period of illness: *'We'll soon have you back on your feet again,' said the nurse.* • **fall/land on your feet** to be successful or lucky, especially after a period of not having success or luck: *She's really fallen on her feet with that new job.* • **get a/your foot in the door** to enter a business or organization at a low level, but with a chance of being more successful in the future: *Making contacts can help you get a foot in the door when it comes to getting a job.* • **get off on the right/wrong foot** C2 to make a successful/unsuccessful start in something • **have a foot in both camps** to be connected to two groups with opposing interests • **have feet of clay** to have a bad quality that you keep hidden: *Some of the greatest geniuses in history had feet of clay.* • **have one foot in the grave** humorous to be very old and near death • **have/keep your feet on the ground** (also **have both feet on the ground**) to be very practical and see things as they really are • **my foot** informal old-fashioned used to mean that you do not believe what another person has just told you: *'He says his car isn't working.' 'Not working my foot. He's just too lazy to come.'* • **not put a foot wrong** to not make any mistakes • **put your foot down 1** C2 to use your authority to stop something happening: *When she started borrowing my clothes without asking, I had to put my foot down.* **2** UK (US **floor it**) to increase your speed when you are driving: *The road ahead was clear, so I put my foot down.* • **put your foot in it** (mainly US **put your foot in your mouth**) C2 to say something by accident that embarrasses or upsets someone: *I really put my foot in it with Alison. I had no idea she was divorced.* • **hardly/barely put one foot in front of the other** If you can hardly/barely put one foot in front of the other, you are having difficulty walking: *I was so tired that I could hardly put one foot in front of the other.* • **rush/run sb off their feet** to cause someone to be very busy: *I've been rushed off my feet all morning.* • **set foot in somewhere** C1 to go to a place: *He refuses to set foot in an art gallery.* • **under your feet** If someone is under your feet, they are near you in a way that is difficult and prevents you from doing what you want to do: *The children were under my feet all day so I couldn't get anything done.*

▸verb [T] informal to pay an amount of money: *His parents footed* ***the bill*** *for his course fees.* ◦ *They refused to foot* ***the cost*** *of the wedding.* ◦ *The company will foot her* ***expenses.***

footage /ˈfʊt.ɪdʒ/ (US) /ˈfʊt̬-/ noun [U] (a piece of) film especially one showing an event: *Woody Allen's film 'Zelig' contains early* ***newsreel*** *footage.*

ˌfoot-and-ˈmouth noun [U] UK (UK also **ˌfoot-and-ˈmouth diˌsease**, US **hoof-and-mouth**) an infectious disease of CATTLE, sheep, pigs, and goats that causes painful areas in the mouth and on the feet

football /ˈfʊt.bɔːl/ (US) /-bɑːl/ noun **1** A1 [U] UK (UK and US **soccer**) a game played between two teams of eleven people, where each team tries to win by kicking a ball into the other team's goal: *a football player/team* ◦ *He's playing football.* ◦ *Are you coming to the football* ***match****?* ◦ *I'm not a big football fan.* **2** [U] US (UK **American football**) a game for two teams of eleven players in which an oval ball is moved along the field by running with it or throwing it: *a football game* **3** A1 [C] a large ball made of leather or plastic and filled with air, used in games of football

footballer /ˈfʊt.bɔː.ləʳ/ (US) /-bɑː.lɚ/ noun [C] UK A2 someone who plays football, especially as their job: *professional footballers*

footballing /ˈfʊt.bɔː.lɪŋ/ (US) /-bɑː.lɪŋ/ adj [before noun] relating to or playing football: *It was the high point of his footballing career.*

ˈfootball ˌpools noun [plural] UK **the pools**

footbridge /ˈfʊt.brɪdʒ/ noun [C] a narrow bridge that is only used by people who are walking

-footed /-fʊt.ɪd/ (US) /-fʊt̬-/ suffix with feet of the stated type or number: *our four-footed friends (= animals having four feet)* ◦ *bare-footed children (= children wearing no shoes)*

footer /ˈfʊt.əʳ/ (US) /ˈfʊt̬.ɚ/ noun [C] specialized a piece of text, such as a page number or a title, that appears at the bottom of every page of a document or book → Compare **header**

-footer /-fʊt.əʳ/ (US) /-fʊt̬.ɚ/ suffix the stated number of feet in length: *Our boat's a 40-footer.*

footfall /ˈfʊt.fɔːl/ (US) /-fɑːl/ noun **SOUND OF FEET** ▷ **1** [C] literary the sound of a person's foot hitting the ground as they walk: *I heard echoing footfalls in the corridor.* **BUSINESS** ▷ **2** [U] specialized the number of people who go into a shop or business in a particular period of time: *Footfall is an important indicator of how successful a company's advertising is at bringing people into its shops.*

ˈfoot ˌfault noun [C] in tennis, when a player steps over the back line of the COURT while SERVING

foothill /ˈfʊt.hɪl/ noun [C usually plural] a low mountain or low hill at the bottom of a larger mountain or range of mountains: *the foothills of the Pyrenees*

foothold /ˈfʊt.həʊld/ (US) /-hoʊld/ noun [C] **ROCK CLIMBING** ▷ **1** a place such as a hole in a rock where you can put your foot safely when climbing **STRONG POSITION** ▷ **2** a strong first position from which further progress can be made: *We are still trying to* ***get/gain*** *a foothold in the Japanese market.*

footing /ˈfʊt.ɪŋ/ (US) /ˈfʊt̬-/ noun [S] **FEET** ▷ **1** the fact of standing firmly on a slope or other dangerous surface: *I **lost/missed** my footing and fell.* ◦ *It was a struggle just to **keep** my footing.* **SITUATION** ▷ **2** the way in which something operates and the set of conditions that influences it: *The council wants to put the bus service on a commercial footing.* **3 be on an equal, firm, etc. footing** to be in an equal, safe, etc. situation: *Men and women ought to be able to compete for jobs on an equal footing.*

footlights /ˈfʊt.laɪts/ **noun** [plural] a row of lights along the front of a stage at a theatre

footling /ˈfuː.tḷ.ɪŋ/ ⓤⓢ /-t̬ḷ-/ **adj** old-fashioned silly or not important: *He could always do something useful instead of wasting my time with footling queries.*

F

footloose /ˈfʊt.luːs/ **adj** free to do what you like and go where you like because you have no responsibilities: *My sister's married but I'm still footloose **and fancy-free**.*

footman /ˈfʊt.mən/ **noun** [C] (plural **-men** /-mən/) a male servant whose job includes opening doors and serving food, and who often wears a uniform

footnote /ˈfʊt.nəʊt/ ⓤⓢ /-noʊt/ **noun 1** [C] a note printed at the bottom of a page that gives extra information about something that has been written on that page **2** [C usually singular] an event, subject, or detail that is not important: *His tumultuous triumph five years ago now seems a mere footnote **in history**.*

footpath /ˈfʊt.pɑːθ/ ⓤⓢ /-pæθ/ **noun** [C] a path, especially in the countryside, for walking on

footplate /ˈfʊt.pleɪt/ **noun** [C] the part of a steam railway engine on which the driver stands

footprint /ˈfʊt.prɪnt/ **noun** [C] **FOOT** ▷ **1** the mark made by a person's or animal's foot **SIZE** ▷ **2** specialized the amount of space on a surface that something needs: *The new computer has a smaller footprint.* ◦ *The footprint of the new Treasury building* **3** specialized a measurement of the size, effect, etc. of something: *We took the decision to invest in new countries and grow our **global** footprint.*

footsie /ˈfʊt.si/ **noun** [U] **play footsie**, see at **play**

Footsie /ˈfʊt.si/ **noun** informal for **the FTSE 100**

footslogging /ˈfʊtˌslɒg.ɪŋ/ ⓤⓢ /-ˌslɑː.gɪŋ/ **noun** [U] UK informal the action of walking over a long distance or from place to place so that you become tired

ˈfoot ˌsoldier noun [C] an **infantryman**

footsore /ˈfʊt.sɔːʳ/ ⓤⓢ /-sɔːr/ **adj** having painful, tired feet, especially after a lot of walking

footstep /ˈfʊt.step/ **noun** [C] **1** Ⓒ1 the sound made by a person walking as their foot touches the ground, or a STEP (= foot movement): *Walking along the darkened street, he heard footsteps close behind him.* **2 footsteps** [plural] the route a person has taken in order to reach a place or to achieve something: *When he realized he'd lost his wallet, he **retraced** his footsteps (= went back the way he had come).*

footstool /ˈfʊt.stuːl/ **noun** [C] a low support on which a person who is sitting can place their feet

footwear /ˈfʊt.weəʳ/ ⓤⓢ /-wer/ **noun** [U] shoes, boots, or any other outer covering for the human foot: *You'll need some fairly tough footwear to go walking up mountains.*

footwork /ˈfʊt.wɜːk/ ⓤⓢ /-wɝːk/ **noun** [U] the way in which the feet are used in sports or dancing, especially when it is skilful

footy (also **footie**) /ˈfʊt.i/ ⓤⓢ /ˈfʊt̬-/ **noun** [U] **1** UK informal football **2** Australian English informal **rugby**

fop /fɒp/ ⓤⓢ /fɑːp/ **noun** [C] (especially in the past) a man who is extremely interested in his appearance and who wears very decorative clothes • **foppish** /ˈfɒp.ɪʃ/ ⓤⓢ /ˈfɑː.pɪʃ/ **adj** old use disapproving

for strong /fɔːʳ/ ⓤⓢ /fɔːr/ weak /fəʳ/ ⓤⓢ /fɚ/ **preposition; conjunction**

▸**preposition INTENDED FOR** ▷ **1** Ⓐ1 intended to be given to: *There's a phone message for you.* ◦ *I'd better buy something for the new baby.* ◦ *There's a prize for the fastest three runners in each category.* **PURPOSE** ▷ **2** Ⓐ2 having the purpose of: *There's a sign there saying 'boats for hire'.* ◦ *This pool is for the use of hotel residents only.* ◦ *I'm sorry, the books are not for sale.* ◦ *They've invited us round for dinner on Saturday.* ◦ *Everyone in the office is contributing money for his leaving present.* ◦ *I need some money for tonight.* ◦ *Which vitamins should you take for (= in order to cure) skin problems?* ◦ *Put those clothes in a pile for wash**ing** (= so that they can be washed).* **BECAUSE OF** ▷ **3** Ⓐ2 because of or as a result of something: *I'm feeling all the better for my holiday.* ◦ *'How are you?' 'Fine, and all the better for see**ing** you!'* ◦ *She did 15 years in prison for murder.* ◦ *I don't eat meat for various reasons.* ◦ *I couldn't see for the tears in my eyes.* ◦ *The things you do for love!* ◦ *He's widely disliked in the company for his arrogance.* ◦ *She couldn't talk for cough**ing** (= she was coughing too much to talk).* ◦ *Scotland is famous for its spectacular countryside.* ◦ *He's best remembered for his novels.* ◦ *I didn't dare say anything for fear of (= because I was frightened of) offending him.* **4 if it wasn't/weren't for** (also **if it hadn't been for**) without: *If it wasn't for the life jacket, I would have drowned.* **TIME/DISTANCE** ▷ **5** Ⓐ1 used to show an amount of time or distance: *We walked for miles.* ◦ *She's out of the office for a few days next week.* ◦ *I'm just going to bed for an hour or so.* ◦ *I haven't played tennis for years.* **OCCASION** ▷ **6** Ⓐ2 on the occasion of or at the time of: *What did you buy him for Christmas?* ◦ *I'd like an appointment with the doctor for some time this week.* ◦ *We're having a party for Jim's 60th birthday.* ◦ *I've booked a table at the restaurant for nine o'clock.* **COMPARING** ▷ **7** Ⓒ1 used for comparing one thing with others of the same type: *She's very mature for her age.* ◦ *For every two people in favour of the law there are three against.* ◦ *The summer has been quite hot for England.* ◦ *It was a difficult decision, especially for a child.* ◦ *For a man of his wealth he's not exactly generous.* **RESPONSIBILITY** ▷ **8** Ⓒ1 used to say whose responsibility something is: *She knew the driver of the other car was not responsible for her son's death.* **SUPPORT** ▷ **9** Ⓑ2 in support of or in agreement with: *I voted for the Greens at the last election.* ◦ *Those voting for the motion, 96, and those voting against, 54.* ◦ *So let's hear some applause for these talented young performers.* ◦ *Who's for (= who wants to play) tennis?* **10 be all for sth** to approve of or support something very much: *I've got nothing against change – I'm all for it.* ◦ *I'm all for sexual equality, but I don't want my wife earning more than I do.* **HELP** ▷ **11** Ⓑ1 in order to help someone: *Let me carry those bags for you.* ◦ *Hello, what can I do for you?* ◦ *My sister will take care of the dog for us while we're away.* **IN RELATION TO** ▷ **12** in relation to someone or something: *Her feelings for him had changed.* ◦ *He felt nothing but contempt for her.* ◦ *I've got a lot of admiration for people who do that sort of work.* ◦ *The ice-cream was a little bit sweet for me.* ◦ *That jacket looks a bit big for you.* ◦ *Jackie's already left and, **as** for me, I'm going at the end of the month.* ◦ *Luckily for me (= I was lucky), I already had another job when the redundancies were announced.* ◦ *How are you doing for money/time (= have you got enough money/time)?* **13 for all** Ⓒ2 despite: *For all her qualifications, she's still useless at the job.* **PAYMENT** ▷ **14** Ⓐ2 (getting) in exchange: *How much did you pay* for your glasses? ◦ I've sponsored her £1 for every mile that she runs. ◦ She sold the house for quite a lot of money. ◦ They've said they'll repair my car for £300. **REPRESENTING ▷ 15** B1 being employed by or representing a company, country, etc.: *She works for a charity. ◦ He used to swim for his country when he was younger.* **TOWARDS ▷ 16** A2 towards; in the direction of: *They looked as if they were heading for the train station. ◦ Just follow signs for the town centre. ◦ This time tomorrow we'll be setting off for the States. ◦ It says this train is for (= going to stop at) Birmingham and Coventry only.* **MEANING ▷ 17** A2 showing meaning: *What's the Spanish word for 'vegetarian'? ◦ What does the 'M.J.' **stand** for? Maria Jose?* **TO GET ▷ 18** A2 in order to get or achieve: *I hate waiting for public transport. ◦ I had to run for the bus. ◦ Did you send off for details of the competition? ◦ I've applied for a job with another computer company.* **DUTY ▷ 19** the duty or responsibility of: *As to whether you should marry him – that's for you to decide. ◦ It's not for me to tell her what she should do with her life. ◦ As to how many she invites, it's not really for me to say.* **IN TROUBLE ▷ 20 for it** informal in trouble: *You'll be for it when she finds out!*

IDIOMS **for all sb cares/knows** informal said to show that something is not important to someone: *You could be the Queen of England, for all I care – you're not coming in here without a ticket.* • **that/there's ... for you** disapproving describes something that you think is a typical example of something bad: *You spend two hours cooking a meal and they say 'it's disgusting' – that's children for you!* • **what ... for?** why: *What did you do that for? ◦ What are you emptying that cupboard for?*

▸**conjunction** old-fashioned or literary **BECAUSE ▷** because; as: *She remained silent, for her heart was heavy and her spirits low.*

> **! Common mistake: for**
>
> **Remember: for** is only usually used to mean 'because' in old-fashioned or literary English.
>
> In ordinary language, don't say 'for', say **because**:
>
> ~~*Erik ate nothing for he was feeling sick.*~~
>
> *Erik ate nothing because he was feeling sick.*

forage /ˈfɒr.ɪdʒ/ US /ˈfɔːr-/ verb; noun

▸**verb** [I] to go from place to place searching, especially for food: *The children had been living on the streets, foraging **for** scraps and sleeping rough. ◦ The pigs foraged in the woods **for** acorns.*

▸**noun** [U] food grown for horses and farm animals: *winter forage ◦ forage crops.*

foray /ˈfɒr.eɪ/ US /ˈfɔːr-/ noun [C] **ATTEMPT ▷ 1** a short period of time being involved in an activity that is different from and outside the range of a usual set of activities: *She **made** a brief foray **into** acting before becoming a teacher.* **VISIT ▷ 2** a short visit, especially with a known purpose: *I **made** a quick foray **into** town before lunch to get my sister a present.* **ATTACK ▷ 3** the act of an army suddenly and quickly entering the area belonging to the enemy in order to attack them or steal their supplies

forbear verb; noun

▸**verb** [I] /fɔːˈbeəʳ/ US /fɔːrˈber/ (**forbore, forborne**) formal to prevent yourself from saying or doing something, especially in a way that shows control, good judgment, or kindness to others: *His plan was such a success that even his original critics could scarcely forbear **from** congratulat**ing** him. ◦ The doctor said she was optimistic about the outcome of the operation but forbore **to** make any promises at this early stage.*

▸**noun** [C usually plural] /ˈfɔː.beəʳ/ US /ˈfɔːr.ber/ a **forebear**

forbearance /fɔːˈbeə.rᵊns/ US /fɔːr-/ noun [U] formal the quality of being patient and being able to forgive someone or control yourself in a difficult situation: [+ (that)] *He thanked his employees for the forbearance (**that**) they had shown during the company's difficult times.*

forbearing /fɔːˈbeə.rɪŋ/ US /fɔːrˈber.ɪŋ/ adj formal patient and forgiving

forbid /fəˈbɪd/ US /fɚ-/ verb [T] (present participle **forbidding**, past tense **forbade** or old use **forbad**, past participle **forbidden**) B2 to refuse to allow something, especially officially, or to prevent a particular plan of action by making it impossible: *The law forbids the sale of cigarettes to people under the age of 16.* ◦ [+ to infinitive] *He's obviously quite embarrassed about it because he forbade me **to** tell anyone. ◦ He is forbidden **from** leav**ing** the country.*

> **+ Other ways of saying forbid**
>
> A common alternative to 'forbid' is the phrase **not allow** or **not let**:
>
> *My parents do**n't let** me stay out late.*
>
> The verbs **ban, prohibit,** or **outlaw** can be used to talk about officially forbidding something using a rule or law:
>
> *The government has **banned** the sale of lead-based paint.*
>
> *Vehicles are **prohibited** from parking on the grass.*
>
> *The new law **outlaws** smoking in public places.*
>
> If someone uses official authority to forbid something, the verb **veto** can be used:
>
> *The president **vetoed** the law after it was passed by a narrow margin in the Senate.*
>
> If you forbid someone from taking part in an activity, especially because that person has done something wrong, you can use the verbs **disqualify** or **bar**:
>
> *She was **disqualified** from the competition for cheating.*
>
> *The incident led to him being **barred** from playing for the rest of the season.*

IDIOM **heaven forbid** (also **God forbid**) a way of saying that you hope something does not happen: *Heaven forbid (**that**) his parents should ever find out.*

forbidden /fəˈbɪd.ᵊn/ US /fɚ-/ adj B1 not allowed, especially by law: *Smoking is forbidden in the cinema.*

IDIOM **forbidden fruit** literary something, especially something sexual, that is even more attractive because it is not allowed: *He was always drawn to other men's wives – the forbidden fruit.*

forbidding /fəˈbɪd.ɪŋ/ US /fɚ-/ adj unfriendly and likely to be unpleasant or harmful: *a forbidding row of security guards ◦ With storm clouds rushing over them, the mountains looked dark and forbidding.* • **forbiddingly** /-li/ adv

forbore /fɔːˈbɔːʳ/ US /fɔːrˈbɔːr/ past simple of **forbear**

forborne /fɔːˈbɔːn/ US /fɔːrˈbɔːrn/ past participle of **forbear**

force /fɔːs/ US /fɔːrs/ noun; verb

▸**noun PHYSICAL ▷ 1** B2 [U] physical, especially violent, strength or power: *The force of the wind had brought down a great many trees in the area. ◦ She slapped his face with unexpected force. ◦ Teachers aren't allowed to use force in controlling their pupils. ◦ The police were* able to control the crowd by sheer force **of numbers** (= because there were more police than there were people in the crowd). **2 in force** in large numbers: *Photographers were out in force at the palace today* **3** [C or U] specialized in scientific use, (a measure of) the influence which changes movement: *the force of gravity* **4 combine/join forces** C2 to work with someone else in order to achieve something which you both want **INFLUENCE** ▷ **5** C2 [C or U] (a person or thing with a lot of) influence and energy: *He was a powerful force in British politics during the war years.* ◦ *A united Europe, he said, would be a great force in world affairs.* ◦ literary *Fishermen are always at the mercy of* ***the forces of nature*** (= *bad weather conditions*). **6 a force to be reckoned with** C2 If an organization or a person is described as a force to be reckoned with, it means that they are powerful and have a lot of influence: *The United Nations is now a force to be reckoned with.* **7 force of habit** If you do something from force of habit, you do it without thinking because you have done it so often before. **GROUP** ▷ **8** B2 [C] a group of people organized and trained, especially for a particular purpose: *the security forces* ◦ *the work force* ◦ *He joined the* ***police*** *force straight after school.* **9 the forces** [plural] the military organizations for air, land, and sea **IN OPERATION** ▷ **10 in/into force** C2 (of laws, rules, or systems) existing and being used: *New driving regulations are going to* ***come*** *into force this year.*

> **Word partners for force (PHYSICAL)**
> *brute/sheer* force • *excessive/reasonable* force • *exert/use* force • the *use of* force • do sth *by* force • the force *of* sth

> **Word partners for force (INFLUENCE)**
> a *major/powerful* force • the (*driving*) force *behind* sth • a force *for* [change/good/peace, etc]

> **Word partners for force (GROUP)**
> *deploy/mobilize/withdraw* forces

IDIOM **the forces of evil** things that have a very bad influence or effect: *Poverty and ignorance, the bishop said, were the forces of evil in our society today.*

▸**verb** [T] **GIVE NO CHOICE** ▷ **1** B2 to make something happen or make someone do something difficult, unpleasant, or unusual, especially by threatening or not offering the possibility of choice: [+ to infinitive] *I really have to force my**self to** be pleasant to him.* ◦ [+ to infinitive] *You can't force her* ***to*** *make a decision.* ◦ *Hospitals are being forced* ***to*** *close departments because of lack of money.* ◦ *You could tell he was having to force* ***back*** *the tears (= stop himself from crying).* ◦ *I didn't actually want any more dessert, but Julia forced it* ***on*** *me (= made me accept it).* ◦ *I couldn't stay at their flat – I'd feel as if I was forcing my**self on** them (= making them allow me to stay).* ◦ *You never tell me how you're feeling – I have to force it* ***out of*** *you (= make you tell me)!* **2 force a laugh/smile** to manage, with difficulty, to laugh or smile: *I managed to force a smile as they were leaving.* **3 force an/the issue** to take action to make certain that an urgent problem or matter is dealt with now **USE PHYSICAL POWER** ▷ **4** C2 to use physical strength or effort to make something move or open: *Move your leg up gently when you're doing this exercise, but don't force it.* ◦ *If you force the zip, it'll break.* ◦ *She forced her way through the crowds.* **5** to break a lock, door, window, etc. in order to allow someone to get in: *I forgot my key, so I had to force a window.* ◦ [+ adj] *The police had forced* ***open*** *the door because nobody had answered.* ◦ *The burglar forced* ***an entry*** *(= broke a window, door, etc. to get into the house).*

IDIOM **force sb's hand** to make someone do something they do not want to do, or act sooner than they had intended

forced /fɔːst/ US /fɔːrst/ **adj** **1** done against your wishes: *forced repatriation* **2** describes an action that is done because it is suddenly made necessary by a new and usually unexpected situation: *The plane had to make a forced* ***landing*** *because one of the engines cut out.* **3** describes laughter, a smile, or an emotion that is produced with effort and is not sincerely felt: *She tried hard to smile but suspected that it looked forced.*

ˈ**force-feed** verb [T] to force a person or animal to eat and drink, often putting food into the stomach through a pipe in the mouth: *Eventually, the hunger strikers were force-fed.* ◦ figurative *The whole nation was force-fed government propaganda about how well the country was doing.*

forceful /ˈfɔːs.fəl/ US /ˈfɔːrs-/ **adj** C2 expressing opinions strongly and demanding attention or action: *The opposition leader led a very forceful attack on the government in parliament this morning.* ◦ *She has a very forceful personality which will serve her well in politics.* • **forcefully** /-i/ **adv** *He argued forcefully that stricter laws were necessary to deal with the problem.* • **forcefulness** /-nəs/ **noun** [U]

force multiplier /ˈfɔːsˌmʌl.tɪ.plaɪ.əʳ/ US /ˈfɔːrsˌmʌl.t̬ɪ.plaɪ.ɚ/ **noun** [C] specialized in physics, something that increases the effect of a force

forceps /ˈfɔː.seps/ US /ˈfɔːr-/ **noun** [plural] a metal instrument with two handles used in medical operations for picking up, pulling, and holding things

forceps

forcible /ˈfɔː.sɪ.bl/ US /ˈfɔːr-/ **adj** **USING PHYSICAL POWER** ▷ **1** describes actions that involve the use of physical power or of violence: *The police's forcible entry into the building has come under a lot of criticism.* **GIVING NO CHOICE** ▷ **2** happening or done against someone's wishes, especially with the use of physical force: *There's a law to protect refugees from forcible return to countries where they face persecution.* • **forcibly** /-bli/ **adv** *Several rioters were forcibly removed from the town square.*

ford /fɔːd/ US /fɔːrd/ **noun; verb**

▸**noun** [C] an area in a river or stream that is not deep and can be crossed on foot or in a vehicle

▸**verb** [T] to cross a river, where it is not deep, on foot or in a vehicle

fore /fɔːʳ/ US /fɔːr/ **noun; adv, adj**

▸**noun** **to the fore** to public attention or into a noticeable position: *Various ecological issues have* ***come to*** *the fore since the discovery of the hole in the Earth's ozone layer.* ◦ *The prime minister has deliberately* ***brought to*** *the fore those ministers with a more caring image.* → See also **the forefront**

▸**adv** [before noun], **adj** (especially on ships) towards or in the front

fore- /fɔːʳ-/ US /fɔːr-/ **prefix** at or towards the front: *the forelegs (= front legs) of a horse* ◦ *the foreground (= things that seem nearest to you) of a picture*

forearm /ˈfɔː.rɑːm/ US /ˈfɔːr.ɑːrm/ **noun** [C] the lower part of the arm, between the wrist and the ELBOW (= the middle of the arm where it bends)

forearmed /fɔːˈrɑːmd/ ⓤⓢ /fɔːrˈɑːrmd/ **adj fore-warned is forearmed** → See at **forewarn**

forebear (also **forbear**) /ˈfɔː.beəʳ/ ⓤⓢ /ˈfɔːr.ber/ **noun** [C usually plural] formal a relation who lived in the past → Synonym **ancestor**

foreboding /fɔːˈbəʊ.dɪŋ/ ⓤⓢ /fɔːrˈboʊ-/ **noun** [C or U] literary a feeling that something very bad is going to happen soon: *There's a **sense of** foreboding in the capital, as if fighting might at any minute break out.* ◦ *Her forebodings about the future were to prove justified.* ◦ [+ (that)] *He had a strange foreboding (**that**) something would go wrong.*

forecast /ˈfɔː.kɑːst/ ⓤⓢ /ˈfɔːr.kæst/ **noun; verb**

▸**noun** [C] **B1** a statement of what is judged likely to happen in the future, especially in connection with a particular situation, or the expected weather conditions: ***economic** forecasts* ◦ *The **weather** forecast said it was going to rain later today.*

▸**verb** [T] (**forecast** or **forecasted**, **forecast** or **forecasted**) to say what you expect to happen in the future: *They forecast a large drop in unemployment over the next two years.* ◦ *Snow has been forecast **for** tonight.* ◦ [+ to infinitive] *Oil prices are forecast **to** increase by less than two percent this year.*

forecaster /ˈfɔː.kɑː.stəʳ/ ⓤⓢ /ˈfɔːr.kæs.tɚ/ **noun** [C] a person who tells you what particular conditions are expected to be like: *an economic forecaster* ◦ *a weather forecaster*

foreclose /fɔːˈkləʊz/ ⓤⓢ /fɔːrˈkloʊz/ **verb** **TAKE POSSESSION** ▷ **1** [I or T] specialized (especially of banks) to take back property that was bought with borrowed money because the money was not being paid back as formally agreed **PREVENT** ▷ **2** [T] formal to prevent something from being considered as a possibility in the future: *The leader's aggressive stance seems to have foreclosed any chance of diplomatic compromise.* • **foreclosure** /-ˈkləʊ.ʒəʳ/ ⓤⓢ /-ˈkloʊ.ʒɚ/ **noun** [U] specialized

forecourt /ˈfɔː.kɔːt/ ⓤⓢ /ˈfɔːr.kɔːrt/ **noun** [C] **1** a flat area in front of a large building: *the garage forecourt* **2** specialized the area next to the net in sports such as tennis

foredoomed /fɔːˈduːmd/ ⓤⓢ /fɔːr-/ **adj** literary (especially of planned activities) going to fail, or extremely unlucky from the beginning: *The whole project seemed foredoomed **to** failure from the start.*

forefathers /ˈfɔːˌfɑː.ðəz/ ⓤⓢ /ˈfɔːrˌfɑː.ðɚz/ **noun** [plural] literary someone's relations who lived a long time ago

forefinger /ˈfɔːˌfɪŋ.gəʳ/ ⓤⓢ /ˈfɔːrˌfɪŋ.gɚ/ **noun** [C] (also **ˈindex ˌfinger**) the finger next to the thumb

forefoot /ˈfɔː.fʊt/ ⓤⓢ /ˈfɔːr-/ **noun** [C] (plural **forefeet**) one of the two front feet of an animal with four legs

the forefront /ˈfɔː.frʌnt/ ⓤⓢ /ˈfɔːr-/ **noun** [S] the most noticeable or important position: *She was one of the politicians **at/in** the forefront **of** the campaign to free the prisoners.* ◦ *His team are **at** the forefront **of** scientific research into vaccines.*

forego /fɔːˈgəʊ/ ⓤⓢ /fɔːrˈgoʊ/ **verb** [T] (present participle **foregoing**, past tense **forewent**, past participle **foregone**) to **forgo**

the ˈforegoing **noun** [S] formal what has just been mentioned or described: *I can testify to the foregoing since I was actually present when it happened.* • **foregoing adj** [before noun] *The foregoing account was written 50 years after the incident.*

ˌforegone conˈclusion **noun** [C usually singular] a result that is obvious to everyone even before it happens: *The result of the election seems to be a foregone conclusion.*

foreground /ˈfɔː.graʊnd/ ⓤⓢ /ˈfɔːr-/ **noun** [S] **the foreground a** the people, objects, countryside, etc. in a picture or photograph that seem nearest to you and form its main part: ***In** the foreground of the painting is a horse and cart.* → Compare **background b** the area that is of most importance and activity, or that people pay attention to: *Historically, issues of this kind have not occupied the foreground **of** political debate.*

forehand /ˈfɔː.hænd/ ⓤⓢ /ˈfɔːr-/ **noun** [C] (in sports such as tennis) a hit in which the PALM of the hand that is holding the RACKET faces the same direction as the hit itself, or the player's ability to perform this hit: *a forehand volley* ◦ *His forehand is his weakest shot.* ◦ *serve to her forehand* → Compare **backhand**

F

forehead /ˈfɒr.ɪd/, /ˈfɔː.hed/ ⓤⓢ /ˈfɑː.rɪd/ **noun** [C] **B1** the flat part of the face, above the eyes and below the hair: *She's got a **high** forehead.*

foreign /ˈfɒr.ən/ ⓤⓢ /ˈfɔːr-/ **adj 1** **A2** belonging or connected to a country that is not your own: *Spain was the first foreign country she had visited.* ◦ *foreign languages* ◦ *His work provided him with the opportunity for a lot of foreign travel.* **2 foreign to** formal **C2** Something can be described as foreign to a particular person if they do not know about it or it is not within their experience: *The whole concept of democracy, she claimed, was utterly foreign to the present government.* **3** describes an object or substance that has entered something else, possibly by accident, and does not belong there: *a foreign object/substance* ◦ *foreign matter*

ˌforeign afˈfairs **noun** [plural] matters that are connected with other countries

ˌforeign ˈaid **noun** [U] the help that is given by a richer country to a poorer one, usually in the form of money or food

ˌForeign and ˌCommonwealth ˌOffice **noun** (also **ˈForeign ˌOffice**, abbreviation **FCO**) the UK government department that deals with relationships with other countries and with British people travelling to other countries

foreigner /ˈfɒr.ə.nəʳ/ ⓤⓢ /ˈfɔːr.ə.nɚ/ **noun** [C] **B1** a person who comes from another country

ˌforeign exˈchange **noun** [C usually singular] the system by which the type of money used in one country is exchanged for another country's money, making international trade easier: *On the foreign-exchange markets the pound remained firm.*

ˌforeign ˈliquor **noun** [U] Indian English alcoholic drink that is made outside India → Compare **country liquor**

the ˈForeign ˌOffice **noun** in the UK, the department of the government that deals with relations with other countries

ˌforeign ˈpolicy **noun** [U] a government's policy on dealing with other countries, for example in matters relating to trade or defence: *He advises the president on foreign policy **issues**.*

ˌforeign-reˈturned **adj** Indian English used for describing someone who has returned to India after being educated in a different country: *foreign-returned doctors*

ˌForeign ˈSecretary **noun** [C] the British government politician who is responsible for dealing with other countries and who controls the FOREIGN AND COMMONWEALTH OFFICE

foreknowledge /fɔːˈnɒl.ɪdʒ/ Ⓤⓢ /fɔːrˈnɑː.lɪdʒ/ **noun** [U] formal knowledge of an event before it happens

foreleg /ˈfɔː.leg/ Ⓤⓢ /ˈfɔːr-/ **noun** [C] one of the two front legs of an animal with four legs

forelock /ˈfɔː.lɒk/ Ⓤⓢ /ˈfɔːr.lɑːk/ **noun** [C] a piece of hair which grows or falls over the FOREHEAD (= part of the face above the eyes) or the part of a horse's MANE that falls forward between its ears

IDIOM **tug at/touch your forelock** to show respect to someone in a higher position than you in a way that seems old-fashioned

F

foreman /ˈfɔː.mən/ Ⓤⓢ /ˈfɔːr-/ **noun** [C] (plural **-men** /-mən/) **PERSON AT WORK** ▷ **1** specialized a skilled person with experience who is in charge of and watches over a group of workers **IN COURT** ▷ **2** in a law court, one member of the JURY who is chosen to be in charge of their discussions and to speak officially for them

foremost /ˈfɔː.məʊst/ Ⓤⓢ /ˈfɔːr.moʊst/ **adj** C2 most important or best; leading: *This is one of the country's foremost arts centres.* ◦ *She's one of the foremost experts on child psychology.*

forename /ˈfɔː.neɪm/ Ⓤⓢ /ˈfɔːr-/ **noun** [C] formal the name that is chosen for you at birth and goes before your family name

forensic /fəˈren.zɪk/ **adj** [before noun] related to scientific methods of solving crimes, involving examining the objects or substances that are involved in the crime: *forensic evidence/medicine/science*

foreplay /ˈfɔː.pleɪ/ Ⓤⓢ /ˈfɔːr-/ **noun** [U] the sexual activity such as kissing and touching that people do before they have sex

forerunner /ˈfɔːˌrʌn.əʳ/ Ⓤⓢ /ˈfɔːrˌrʌn.ɚ/ **noun** [C] something or someone that acts as an early and less advanced model for what will appear in the future, or a warning or sign of what is to follow: *Germany's Green party was said to be the forerunner **of** environmental parties throughout Europe.* ◦ *The drop in share prices in March was a forerunner **of** the financial crash that followed in June.*

foresee /fəˈsiː/ Ⓤⓢ /fɚ-/ **verb** [T] (present participle **foreseeing**, past tense **foresaw**, past participle **foreseen**) C1 to know about something before it happens: *I don't foresee any difficulties so long as we keep within budget.*

foreseeable /fɔːˈsiː.ə.bl̩/ Ⓤⓢ /fɔːr-/ **adj 1** A foreseeable event or situation is one that can be known about or guessed before it happens. **2 in/for the foreseeable future** C2 as far into the future as you can imagine or plan for: *I'll certainly carry on living here for the foreseeable future.* ◦ *He asked me if there was any point in the foreseeable future when I'd like to have children.*

foreshadow /fɔːˈʃæd.əʊ/ Ⓤⓢ /fɔːrˈʃæd.oʊ/ **verb** [T] formal to act as a warning or sign of a future event: *The recent outbreak of violence was foreshadowed by isolated incidents in the city earlier this year.*

the foreshore /ˈfɔː.ʃɔːʳ/ Ⓤⓢ /ˈfɔːr.ʃɔːr/ **noun** [S] specialized the part of the land next to the sea that is between the limits reached by high and low TIDE, or any part of this land that does not have grass or buildings on it

foreshorten /fɔːˈʃɔː.tᵊn/ Ⓤⓢ /fɔːrˈʃɔːr.t̬ᵊn/ **verb** [T] **1** to reduce something or make it shorter: *Smoking was certainly one of the factors that foreshortened his life.* **2** specialized to draw, paint, or photograph people or objects to make them seem smaller or closer together than they really are • **foreshortened** /-tᵊnd/ Ⓤⓢ /-t̬ᵊnd/ **adj**

foresight /ˈfɔː.saɪt/ Ⓤⓢ /ˈfɔːr-/ **noun** [U] the ability to judge correctly what is going to happen in the future and plan your actions based on this knowledge: *She'd **had the** foresight to sell her apartment just before house prices came down.*

foreskin /ˈfɔː.skɪn/ Ⓤⓢ /ˈfɔːr-/ **noun** [C] the loose skin which covers the end of the PENIS

forest /ˈfɒr.ɪst/ Ⓤⓢ /ˈfɔːr-/ **noun** [C or U] A2 a large area of land covered with trees and plants, usually larger than a wood, or the trees and plants themselves: *the Black Forest* ◦ *The children got lost **in** the forest.*

forestall /fɔːˈstɔːl/ Ⓤⓢ /fɔːrˈstɑːl/ **verb** [T] to prevent something from happening by acting first: *The government forestalled criticism by holding a public enquiry into the matter.*

forester /ˈfɒr.ɪ.stəʳ/ Ⓤⓢ /ˈfɔːr.ɪ.stɚ/ **noun** [C] a person who is in charge of taking care of a forest

forestry /ˈfɒr.ɪ.stri/ Ⓤⓢ /ˈfɔːr-/ **noun** [U] the science of planting and taking care of large areas of trees

foretaste /ˈfɔː.teɪst/ Ⓤⓢ /ˈfɔːr-/ **noun** [S] something that gives you an idea of what something else is like by allowing you to experience a small example of it before it happens: *a foretaste of spring* ◦ *The recent factory closures and job losses are just a foretaste of the recession that is to come.*

foretell /fɔːˈtel/ Ⓤⓢ /fɔːr-/ **verb** [T] (**foretold**) literary to say what is going to happen in the future: [+ question word] *He was a 16th-century prophet who foretold **how** the world would end.*

forethought /ˈfɔː.θɔːt/ Ⓤⓢ /ˈfɔːr.θɑːt/ **noun** [U] the good judgment to consider the near future in your present actions: *I'm glad I had the forethought to make a copy of the letter, as proof of what had been promised.*

forever (UK also **ˌfor ˈever**) /fəˈre.vəʳ/ Ⓤⓢ /fɔːˈrev.ɚ/ **adv 1** B1 for all time: *I like the house but I don't imagine I'll live there forever.* **2** informal very often: *She's forever telling him she's going to leave him but she never actually does.* **3** B2 for an extremely long time or too much time: *We'd better walk a bit quicker – it's going to **take** forever if we go at this pace.*

forewarn /fɔːˈwɔːn/ Ⓤⓢ /fɔːrˈwɔːrn/ **verb** [T] to tell someone that something unpleasant is going to happen: [+ (that)] *The employees had been forewarned (**that**) the end-of-year financial results would be poor.*

IDIOM **forewarned is forearmed** saying said to mean that if you know about something before it happens, you can be prepared for it

forewoman /ˈfɔːˌwʊm.ən/ Ⓤⓢ /ˈfɔːr-/ **noun** [C] (plural **-women** /-wɪmɪn/) a female FOREMAN

foreword /ˈfɔː.wɜːd/ Ⓤⓢ /ˈfɔːr.wɝːd/ **noun** [C] a short piece of writing at the beginning of a book, sometimes praise by a famous person or someone who is not the writer

forfeit /ˈfɔː.fɪt/ Ⓤⓢ /ˈfɔːr-/ **verb; noun; adj**

▸**verb** [T] to lose the right to do or have something because you have broken a rule: *If you cancel now I'm afraid you forfeit your deposit.* ◦ *These people have forfeited the right to live in society.*

▸**noun** [C] **1** something that you have lost the right to do or have because you have broken a rule **2 pay a forfeit** to give up something, especially in a game

▸**adj** [after verb] formal taken away from someone as a punishment

forfeiture /ˈfɔː.fɪ.tʃəʳ/ Ⓤⓢ /ˈfɔːr.fɪ.tʃɚ/ **noun** [C or U] legal the loss of rights, property, or money, especially as a result of breaking a legal agreement

forgave /fəˈgeɪv/ Ⓤⓢ /fɚ-/ past simple of **forgive**

forge /fɔːdʒ/ Ⓤⓢ /fɔːrdʒ/ **verb; noun**

▸**verb COPY** ▷ **1** [T] to make an illegal copy of

something in order to deceive: *a forged passport* ◦ *a forged signature* ◦ *A number of forged works of art have been sold as genuine.* **CREATE** ▷ **2** [T] to make or produce something, especially with some difficulty: *The accident forged a* ***close bond*** *between the two families.* ◦ *She forged a new career for herself as a singer.* **MOVE** ▷ **3** [I + adv/prep] formal to suddenly and quickly move forward: *Just 100 metres from the finishing line Jackson forged* ***ahead***.

PHRASAL VERB **forge ahead** to suddenly make a lot of progress with something: *The organizers are forging ahead with a programme of public events.*

▸**noun** [C] a working area with a fire for heating metal until it is soft enough to be beaten into different shapes: *a blacksmith's forge*

forger /ˈfɔː.dʒəʳ/ US /ˈfɔːr.dʒɚ/ **noun** [C] someone who makes forged copies: *an art forger*

forgery /ˈfɔː.dʒəʳ.i/ US /ˈfɔːr.dʒɚ.i/ **noun** [C or U] C2 an illegal copy of a document, painting, etc. or the crime of making such illegal copies: *These banknotes are forgeries.* ◦ *He increased his income by forgery.*

> **Other ways of saying forget**
>
> The expression **slip someone's mind** is often used informally when someone forgets to do something:
>
> *I meant to tell you that he'd phoned, but it completely* ***slipped my mind***.
>
> If a word is **on the tip of your tongue**, you have forgotten it but think that you will very soon remember it:
>
> *Oh, what was that movie called? It's* ***on the tip of my tongue***.
>
> If something such as a name **escapes** you, you cannot remember it:
>
> *The name of her book* ***escapes*** *me at the moment.*
>
> If someone suddenly forgets something, you can say their **mind goes blank**:
>
> *I tried to remember her name but my* ***mind went blank***.

forget /fəˈget/ US /fɚ-/ **verb** (present participle **forgetting**, past tense **forgot**, past participle **forgotten**) **NOT REMEMBER** ▷ **1** B1 [I or T] to be unable to remember a fact, something that happened, or how to do something: *I'm sorry, I've forgotten your name.* ◦ *Let me write down that date before I forget it.* ◦ *I completely forgot* ***about*** *Gemma's party.* ◦ [+ (that)] *We had forgotten (****that****) she doesn't come on Thursdays.* ◦ *I'm sorry, I was forgetting (= I had forgotten) (****that****) you would be away in August.* ◦ [+ -ing verb] *She would never forget see****ing*** *the Himalayas for the first time.* ◦ [+ question word] *I've forgotten* ***wh****at you do next/****how*** *to do it.* ◦ *I never forget* ***a face*** *(= I'm good at remembering people).* **2 not forgetting** including: *This is where we keep all the books, not forgetting the magazines and newspapers.* **NOT DO** ▷ **3** A1 [I + to infinitive, T] to not remember to do something: *Don't forget to lock the door.* ◦ *Dad's always forgetting (to take) his pills.* **NOT BRING** ▷ **4** A2 [T] to not bring something with you because you did not remember it: *I've forgotten my keys.* **STOP THINKING** ▷ **5** B1 [I or T] to stop thinking about someone or something: *He tried to forget her.* ◦ *It seemed unlikely that the debt would ever be paid so we just forgot (****about****) it.* **BEHAVE BADLY** ▷ **6 forget yourself** to act in a socially unacceptable way because you have lost control of your emotions: *He was so angry he forgot himself and swore loudly.*

IDIOMS **and don't you forget it** used to tell someone that a particular fact is important and it should influence the way they behave: *I've been in the job*

longer than you and don't you forget it! • **forget it** informal **1** used to tell someone that what they want is impossible: *'I'd like to take a week's holiday.' 'Forget it, we're way too busy.'* **2** B2 used to tell someone that something is not important and not to worry about it: *'I'm so sorry about that cup.' 'Oh, forget it – I've got plenty.'*

forgetful /fəˈget.fəl/ US /fɚ-/ **adj** often forgetting things: *She's getting very forgetful in her old age.* • **forgetfully** /-i/ **adv** • **forgetfulness** /-nəs/ **noun** [U]

forˈget-me-not **noun** [C] a small garden plant with blue or pink flowers that grows from seed every year

forgettable /fəˈget.ə.bl̩/ US /fɚˈget̬-/ **adj** not important or good enough to be remembered: *a forgettable film/song* ◦ *Dennis White scored the only goal in an otherwise forgettable match.*

forgivable /fəˈgɪv.ə.bl̩/ US /fɚ-/ **adj** describes something that you are able to forgive because you understand it: *a forgivable mistake*

forgive /fəˈgɪv/ US /fɚ-/ **verb** [I or T, not continuous] (**forgave**, **forgiven**) **1** B1 to stop blaming or being angry with someone for something they have done, or not punish them for something: *I don't think she's ever quite forgiven me* ***for*** *getting her name wrong that time.* ◦ *I've never found it easy to forgive* ***and forget*** *(= to behave as if something wrong had never happened).* ◦ *I'd never forgive my****self*** *if anything happened to the kids.* **2 forgive me** B2 formal used before you ask or say something that might seem rude: *Forgive me for asking, but how much did you pay for your bag?*

forgiveness /fəˈgɪv.nəs/ US /fɚ-/ **noun** [U] C2 the act of forgiving or the willingness to forgive: *to ask for/beg forgiveness*

forgiving /fəˈgɪv.ɪŋ/ US /fɚ-/ **adj** **1** willing to forgive: *She's very forgiving.* **2** Something that is forgiving allows you to make mistakes or allows for your weaknesses: *They flew back to a cooler and more forgiving climate.*

forgo /fɔːˈgəʊ/ US /fɔːrˈgoʊ/ **verb** [T] (present participle **forgoing**, past tense **forwent**, past participle **forgone**) (also **forego**) to not have or do something enjoyable: *I shall have to forgo* ***the pleasure of*** *seeing you this week.*

fork /fɔːk/ US /fɔːrk/ **noun**; **verb**

▸**noun** [C] **FOOD** ▷ **1** A2 a small object with three or four points and a handle, that you use to pick up food and eat with: *a* ***knife and*** *fork.* **GARDEN** ▷ **2** a tool with a long handle and three or four points, used for digging and breaking soil into pieces: *a* ***garden*** *fork.* **DIVISION** ▷ **3** a place where a road, river, etc. divides into two parts, or either of those two parts: *When you reach a fork* ***in the road*** *take the right-hand path.* ◦ *Take the left-hand fork.*

▸**verb** **DIVIDE** ▷ **1** [I] If a road or river forks, it divides into two parts: *The pub is near where the road forks.* **2** [I + adv/prep] UK to turn in one of two different directions: *Fork* ***left/right*** *where the road divides.* **GARDEN** ▷ **3** [T] to move or dig something with a fork

PHRASAL VERBS **fork out (sth)** informal to pay, especially unwillingly: *I forked out ten quid* ***for/on*** *the ticket.* ◦ *I couldn't persuade him to fork out* ***for*** *a new one.* • **fork over/up sth** US informal to give something, especially money to someone, especially when you do not want to: *We had to fork over ten bucks to park near the stadium.* ◦ *Hey, that's mine. Fork it over!*

forked /fɔːkt/ US /fɔːrkt/ **adj** with one end divided into two parts: *a forked tail* ◦ *forked lightning*

F

ˌforked ˈtongue noun **speak with a forked tongue** to tell lies or say one thing and mean something else

forkful /ˈfɔːk.fʊl/ (US) /ˈfɔːrk-/ noun [C] the amount of food that can be held on a fork: *a forkful of baked beans*

forklift (truck) /ˌfɔːk.lɪftˈtrʌk/ (US) /ˌfɔːrk-/ noun [C] a small vehicle that has two strong bars of metal fixed to the front used for lifting piles of goods

forlorn /fəˈlɔːn/ (US) /fɚˈlɔːrn/ adj **SAD** ▷ **1** literary alone and unhappy; left alone and not cared for: *She looked a forlorn figure standing at the bus stop.* **UNLIKELY TO SUCCEED** ▷ **2** [before noun] very unlikely to be achieved or to succeed: *Their only hope now is that the outside world will intervene but it is an increasingly forlorn* ***hope***. ◦ *She appeared on daytime TV in a forlorn* ***attempt*** *to persuade the public of her innocence.* • **forlornly** /-li/ adv *She sat forlornly (= alone and unhappy) looking out to sea.*

form /fɔːm/ (US) /fɔːrm/ verb; noun

▸verb **1** B2 [I or T] to begin to exist or to make something begin to exist: *A crowd formed around the accident.* ◦ *A solution began to form in her mind.* ◦ *She formed the clay* ***into*** *a small bowl.* ◦ *I formed* ***the impression*** *(= the way she behaved suggested to me) that she didn't really want to come.* **2** B1 [L only + noun] to make or be something: *The lorries formed a barricade across the road.* ◦ *Together they would form the next government.* ◦ *This information formed the basis of the report.* **3** [I] (also **form up**) formal If separate things form, they come together to make a whole: *The children formed into lines.* ◦ *The procession formed up and moved off slowly.*

▸noun **DOCUMENT** ▷ **1** A2 [C] a paper or set of papers printed with spaces in which answers to questions can be written or information can be recorded in an organized way: *an* ***application*** *form (= document used for asking officially for something, for example a job)* ◦ *an* ***entry*** *form (= document used to enter a competition)* ◦ *Please* ***fill in/out*** *the form with black ink.* ◦ *When you have* ***completed*** *the form, hand it in at the desk.* **TYPE** ▷ **2** B2 [C] a type of something: *Swimming is the best form* ***of*** *exercise.* **SHAPE** ▷ **3** C1 [C] the shape or appearance of something: *I could just about make out his sleeping form on the bed.* ◦ *The moon highlighted the shadowy forms of the hills.* ◦ *The lawn was laid out* ***in the*** *form* ***of*** *the figure eight.* **4 take form** to gradually be seen or gradually develop: *Trees and hedges started to take form as the fog cleared.* ◦ *As they chatted, the idea of a holiday together gradually took form.* **ABILITY** ▷ **5** [U] A competitor's form is their ability to be successful over a period of time: *Both horses have shown good form over the last season.* ◦ *After a bad year, she has regained her form.* **6 be on good, great, etc. form** C2 UK (US **be in good, great, etc. form**) to be feeling or performing well: *Paul was on good form at the wedding and kept everyone entertained.* **GRAMMAR** ▷ **7** B1 [C] a part of a verb, or a different but related word: *The continuous form of 'stand' is 'standing'.* ◦ *'Stood' is an inflected form of 'stand'.* ◦ *'Hers' is the possessive form of 'her'.* ◦ *'Isn't' is the short form of 'is not'.* **SCHOOL GROUP** ▷ **8** B1 [C] in the UK, a class of school children or a group of classes of children of a similar age **BEHAVIOUR** ▷ **9 bad form** old-fashioned rude behaviour: *Was that bad form then, leaving so early?*

formal /ˈfɔː.məl/ (US) /ˈfɔːr-/ adj **OFFICIAL** ▷ **1** C1 public or official: *formal procedures* ◦ *a formal announcement* **2** in appearance or by name only: *I am the formal leader of the project but the everyday management is in the hands of my assistant.* **SERIOUS** ▷ **3** B2 describes language, clothes, and behaviour that are suitable for serious or official occasions: *a formal dinner party* **EDUCATION** ▷ **4** C1 describes education or training received in a school or college: *Tom had little in the way of a formal* ***education***. **GARDEN** ▷ **5** A formal garden is carefully designed and kept according to a plan, and it is not allowed to grow naturally.

formality /fɔːˈmæl.ə.ti/ (US) /-t̬i/ noun **ACTION** ▷ **1** [C] something that has to be done but has no real importance: *You'll have to sign the visitors' book, but* ***it's just a*** *formality.* **2 formalities** [plural] something that the law or an official process says must be done: *We'll have to* ***observe the*** *formalities (= do what is expected).* **SERIOUSNESS** ▷ **3** [U] the quality of being suitable for serious or official occasions: *She found the formality of the occasion rather daunting.* ◦ *A note of formality in his voice alerted her to the fact that others were listening.*

formalize (UK usually **formalise**) /ˈfɔː.mə.laɪz/ (US) /ˈfɔːr-/ verb [T] to make something official or decide to arrange it according to a fixed structure: *They started as informal gatherings but they have become increasingly formalized in the last few years.* ◦ *We need to formalize our initial thoughts about the way to proceed.*

formally /ˈfɔː.mə.li/ (US) /ˈfɔːr-/ adv **OFFICIALLY** ▷ **1** C1 officially: *The deal will be formally announced on Tuesday.* **SERIOUSLY/CORRECTLY** ▷ **2** C1 in a serious and correct way: *He was formally dressed in a grey suit.* ◦ *The headteacher greeted us very formally.* **GARDEN** ▷ **3** (of garden design) in a way that is carefully designed and kept according to a plan

format /ˈfɔː.mæt/ (US) /ˈfɔːr-/ noun; verb

▸noun [C or U] **1** C1 a pattern, plan or arrangement: *The meeting will have the usual format – introductory session, group work and then a time for reporting back.* **2** C1 specialized the way in which information is arranged and stored on a computer

▸verb [T] (-tt-) **1** to organize or arrange text, especially on a computer, according to a chosen pattern **2** to prepare a computer disk for use with a particular type of computer

formation /fɔːˈmeɪ.ʃən/ (US) /fɔːr-/ noun **1** C2 [C] the way something is naturally made or the way it has been arranged: *a rock formation* ◦ *cloud formations* **2** C2 [U] the development of something into a particular thing or shape: *the formation of a crystal* **3 in formation** Activities that are done in formation are done in a pattern by a number of people, vehicles, etc. moving together: *marching in close formation*

formative /ˈfɔː.mə.tɪv/ (US) /ˈfɔːr.mə.t̬ɪv/ adj formal relating to the time when someone or something is starting to develop in character: *She spent her formative* ***years*** *in Africa.* ◦ *a formative experience* ◦ *a formative period*

former /ˈfɔː.məʳ/ (US) /ˈfɔːr.mɚ/ adj; noun

▸adj [before noun] B1 of or in an earlier time; before the present time or in the past: *his former wife* ◦ *a former employer* ◦ *the former president of the United States* ◦ *The house, a former barn, has been attractively converted.* ◦ *The painting was then restored to its former* ***glory*** *(= returned to its original good condition).* ◦ *It was a long time after the accident before he seemed like his former* ***self*** *(= behaved in the way he had done before).*

▸noun [S] **the former** B2 the first of two people, things, or groups previously mentioned: *Of the two suggestions, I prefer the former.* → Compare **latter**

-former /-fɔː.məʳ/ (US) /-fɔːr.mɚ/ suffix a student of the stated class group: *sixth-formers (= students usually aged 16–18)*

formerly /ˈfɔː.mə.li/ (US) /ˈfɔːr.mɚ-/ adv formal B2 in the past: *The European Union was formerly called the European Community.*

Formica /fɔːˈmaɪ.kə/ (US) /fɔːr-/ noun [U] trademark a type of hard plastic made into a thin sheet that is used to cover table tops and other pieces of furniture, especially kitchen furniture

formidable /fɔːˈmɪ.də.bl̩/ (US) /fɔːr-/ adj C2 causing you to have fear or respect for something or someone because they are large, powerful, or difficult: *a formidable obstacle/task ◦ a formidable adversary/enemy/opponent ◦ a formidable intellect ◦* disapproving *the director and his formidable wife* • **formidably** /-bli/ adv

formless /ˈfɔːm.ləs/ (US) /ˈfɔːrm-/ adj without clear shape or structure

ˈform ˌroom noun [C] UK (US **homeroom**) a room in a school where members of a particular FORM (= group of students) go for their teacher to record that they are present, usually at the beginning of the day

formula /ˈfɔː.mjʊ.lə/ (US) /ˈfɔːr-/ noun (plural **formulas** or **formulae**) **METHOD/RULE** ▷ **1** C1 [C] a standard or accepted way of doing or making something, the things needed for it, or a mathematical rule expressed in a set of numbers and letters: *We have changed the formula **of** the washing powder. ◦ We had to learn chemical formulae at school, but I can only remember H_2O for water. ◦ There's no magic formula **for** success.* **BABY'S MILK** ▷ **2** [U] artificial milk that can be given to babies instead of milk from their mother

formulaic /ˌfɔː.mjəˈleɪ.ɪk/ (US) /ˌfɔːr-/ adj formal containing or consisting of fixed and repeated groups of words or ideas: *The text was dull and formulaic.*

formulate /ˈfɔː.mjʊ.leɪt/ (US) /ˈfɔːr-/ verb [T] C2 to develop all the details of a plan for doing something: *to formulate a new plan ◦ to formulate legislation* • **formulation** /ˌfɔː.mjʊˈleɪ.ʃən/ (US) /ˌfɔːr-/ noun [C or U]

fornicate /ˈfɔː.nɪ.keɪt/ (US) /ˈfɔːr-/ verb [I] formal disapproving to have sex with someone who you are not married to • **fornication** /ˌfɔː.nɪˈkeɪ.ʃən/ (US) /ˌfɔːr-/ noun [U] • **fornicator** /-keɪ.təʳ/ (US) /-keɪ.t̬ɚ/ noun [C]

forsake /fɔːˈseɪk/ (US) /fɔːr-/ verb [T] (**forsook, forsaken**) **LEAVE** ▷ **1** literary to leave someone for ever, especially when they need you: *Do not forsake me!* **STOP** ▷ **2** formal to stop doing or having something: *He decided to forsake politics for journalism.*

forswear /fɔːˈsweəʳ/ (US) /fɔːrˈswer/ verb [T] (**forswore, forsworn**) formal to make a serious decision to stop doing something: *to forswear alcohol*

forsythia /fɔːˈsaɪ.θi.ə/ (US) /fɔːr-/ noun [C] a medium-sized bush, grown in gardens, that has yellow flowers before the leaves appear

fort /fɔːt/ (US) /fɔːrt/ noun [C] a military building designed to be defended from attack, consisting of an area surrounded by a strong wall, in which soldiers are based: *The remains of the Roman fort are well preserved.*

forte /ˈfɔː.teɪ/ (US) /ˈfɔːr-/ noun [C usually singular] a strong ability, something that a person can do well: *I'm afraid sewing isn't one of my fortes.*

forth /fɔːθ/ (US) /fɔːrθ/ adv formal (from a place) out or away, or (from a point in time) forward: *They **set** forth on their travels in early June. ◦ **From that day forth** he never drank again.*

forthcoming /ˈfɔːθˌkʌm.ɪŋ/ (US) /ˈfɔːrθ-/ adj **SOON** ▷ **1** B2 [before noun] happening soon: *We have just received the information about the forthcoming conference.* **WILLING** ▷ **2** friendly and helpful, willing to give information or to talk: *I had difficulty getting any details. He wasn't very forthcoming.* **SUPPLIED** ▷ **3** C1 [after verb] produced, supplied, or given: *No explanation for his absence was forthcoming. ◦ Will financial support for the theatre project be forthcoming?*

forthright /ˈfɔːθ.raɪt/ (US) /ˈfɔːrθ-/ adj (too) honest or direct in behaviour: *His forthright manner can be mistaken for rudeness. ◦ I admire her forthright way of dealing with people.* • **forthrightness** /-nəs/ noun [U]

forthwith /ˌfɔːθˈwɪθ/ (US) /ˌfɔːrθ-/ adv formal immediately: *We expect these practices to cease forthwith.*

forties /ˈfɔː.tiz/ (US) /ˈfɔːr.t̬iz/ noun [plural] **1** B2 A person's forties are the period in which they are aged between 40 and 49: *She's probably **in** her early forties.* **2 the forties** the range of temperature between 40° and 49°: *The temperature is expected to be **in** the forties tomorrow.* **3** B2 the DECADE (= period of ten years) between 40 and 49 in any century, usually 1940–1949: *Our house was built some time **in** the forties.*

fortieth /ˈfɔː.ti.əθ/ (US) /ˈfɔːr.t̬i-/ ordinal number 40th written as a word

fortification /ˌfɔː.tɪ.fɪˈkeɪ.ʃən/ (US) /ˌfɔːr.t̬ə-/ noun **1** [C usually plural] strong walls, towers, etc. that are built to protect a place: *Some of the old fortifications still exist.* **2** [U] the act of fortifying something

ˌfortified ˈwine noun [C or U] a wine that contains more alcohol than wines usually do: *Sherry and Martini are fortified wines.*

fortify /ˈfɔː.tɪ.faɪ/ (US) /ˈfɔːr.t̬ə-/ verb [T] to make something stronger, especially in order to protect it: *a fortified town ◦ They hurriedly fortified the village **with** barricades of carts. ◦ The argument had fortified her resolve to prove she was right. ◦ He fortified himself **with** a drink and a sandwich before driving on. ◦ a fruit drink fortified **with** vitamin C (= with vitamin C added)*

fortis /ˈfɔː.tɪs/ (US) /ˈfɔːr.t̬ɪs/ adj specialized (of a speech sound) made with a greater than usual amount of force

fortitude /ˈfɔː.tɪ.tjuːd/ (US) /ˈfɔːr.t̬ə.tuːd/ noun [U] formal courage over a long period: *I thought she showed remarkable fortitude during that period.*

Fort Knox /ˌfɔːtˈnɒks/ (US) /ˌfɔːrtˈnɑːks/ noun humorous **be like Fort Knox** If a building or an area is like Fort Knox, it is impossible to enter or leave it because it is so well protected.

fortnight /ˈfɔːt.naɪt/ (US) /ˈfɔːrt-/ noun [C usually singular] UK B1 a period of two weeks: *a fortnight's holiday ◦ once a fortnight ◦ a fortnight ago* • **fortnightly** /-li/ adj, adv happening every two weeks: *We make a fortnightly check on supplies.*

fortress /ˈfɔː.trəs/ (US) /ˈfɔːr-/ noun [C] a large, strong building or group of buildings that can be defended from attack

fortuitous /fɔːˈtjuː.ɪ.təs/ (US) /fɔːrˈtuː.ə.t̬əs/ adj formal (of something that is to your advantage) not planned, happening by chance: *The timing of the meeting is certainly fortuitous.* • **fortuitously** /-li/ adv • **fortuitousness** /-nəs/ noun [U]

fortunate /ˈfɔː.tʃən.ət/ (US) /ˈfɔːr-/ adj approving B2 lucky: [+ to infinitive] *You're very fortunate **to** have found such a lovely house. ◦ He was fortunate **in** his choice of assistant. ◦* [+ that] ***It** was fortunate **that** they had left in plenty of time.* → Opposite **unfortunate**

fortunately /ˈfɔː.tʃən.ət.li/ (US) /ˈfɔːr-/ adv B1 happening because of good luck: *Fortunately, we got home before it started to rain.* → Opposite **unfortunately**

fortune /ˈfɔː.tʃuːn/ (US) /ˈfɔːr-/ noun **WEALTH** ▷ **1** B2 [C] a large amount of money, goods, property, etc.: *She* *inherited a fortune from her grandmother.* ◦ *He lost a fortune gambling.* ◦ *You can* ***make*** *a fortune out of junk if you call it 'antiques'.* ◦ *This dress* ***cost*** *a* ***(small)*** *fortune.* ◦ *Any painting by Van Gogh is* ***worth*** *a fortune.* **CHANCE** ▷ **2** B2 [C or U] chance and the way it affects your life: *He* ***had*** *the* ***(good)*** *fortune* ***to*** *train with some of the world's top athletes.* ◦ *The family's fortunes changed overnight.* **3 tell sb's fortune** to discover what will happen to someone in the future, for example by looking at the lines on their hands or using a special set of cards

IDIOM **fortune smiles on sb** If fortune smiles on you, you are lucky and good things happen to you.

F

ˈfortune ˌcookie noun [C] a biscuit containing a message, usually about your future, eaten especially after a Chinese meal

ˈfortune ˌhunter noun [C] disapproving someone who tries to marry a person who has a lot of money

ˈfortune ˌteller noun [C] a person who tells you what they think will happen to you in the future

forty /ˈfɔː.ti/ US /ˈfɔːr.t̬i/ **number** A2 the number 40: *thirty-nine, forty, forty-one* ◦ *He looks about forty.*

ˌforty ˈwinks noun [plural] informal a short sleep during the day: *He usually has forty winks going home on the train.*

forum /ˈfɔː.rəm/ US /ˈfɔːr.əm/ **noun** [C] **MEETING** ▷ **1** a situation or meeting in which people can talk about a problem or matter especially of public interest: *a forum for debate/discussion* **INTERNET** ▷ **2** a place on the internet where people can leave messages or discuss particular subjects with other people at the same time: ***Discussion*** *forums are a way of contacting people with similar interests from all over the world.* **ANCIENT ROME** ▷ **3** in ancient Rome, the area in the middle of the town used for public business

> **!** Common mistake: **forward**
>
> **Warning:** Check your spelling! **Forward** is one of the 50 words most often spelled wrongly by learners. **Remember**: the correct spelling has 'r' before the 'w'.

forward /ˈfɔː.wəd/ US /ˈfɔːr.wɚd/ **adv; adj; verb; noun**

▸**adv** (also **forwards**) **DIRECTION** ▷ **1** B1 towards the direction that is in front of you: *She leaned forward to whisper something in my ear.* **FUTURE** ▷ **2** B2 towards the future: *I always look forward, not back.* **3 from that day forward** formal after that point: *From that day forward they never spoke to each other.* **PROGRESS** ▷ **4** C1 used in expressions related to progress: *This is a big* ***step*** *forward for democracy.*

▸**adj DIRECTION** ▷ **1** towards the direction that is in front of you: *forward motion/movement* **FUTURE** ▷ **2** relating to the future: *forward planning/thinking* **CONFIDENT** ▷ **3** disapproving confident and honest in a way that ignores the usual social rules and might seem rude: *Do you think it was forward of me to invite her to dinner when we'd only just met?*

▸**verb** [T] to send a letter, etc., especially from someone's old address to their new address, or to send a letter, email, etc. that you have received to someone else: *I'll forward any mail* ***to*** *your new address.* ◦ *I'll forward his email to you if you're interested.*

▸**noun** [C] a player who is in an attacking position in a team

ˈforwarding adˌdress noun [C usually singular] where you want your post sent after you have left the address at which it will arrive

ˈforward-ˌlooking adj Someone who is forward-looking always plans for the future.

forwardness /ˈfɔː.wəd.nəs/ US /ˈfɔːr.wɚd-/ **noun** [U] disapproving the quality of being confident and honest in a way that ignores the usual social rules and might seem rude

forwards /ˈfɔː.wədz/ US /ˈfɔːr.wɚdz/ **adv forward** → Compare **backwards**

ˈforward ˌslash noun [C] specialized the symbol / used in computer instructions and internet addresses

forwent /fɔːˈwent/ US /fɔːr-/ past simple of **forgo**

fossil /ˈfɒs.əl/ US /ˈfɑː.səl/ **noun** [C] **IN ROCK** ▷ **1** the shape of a bone, a shell, or a plant or animal that has been preserved in rock for a very long period **PERSON** ▷ **2** informal humorous an old person, especially one who will not accept new ideas

ˈfossil ˌfuel noun [C or U] fuels, such as gas, coal, and oil, that were formed underground from plant and animal remains millions of years ago

fossilize (UK usually **fossilise**) /ˈfɒs.ɪ.laɪz/ US /ˈfɑː.səl.aɪz/ **verb** [I] to become a fossil: *The remains gradually fossilized.* • **fossilization** (UK usually **fossilisation**) /ˌfɒs.ɪ.laɪˈzeɪ.ʃən/ US /ˌfɑː.səl.aɪ-/ **noun** [U]

fossilized (UK usually **fossilised**) /ˈfɒs.ɪ.laɪzd/ US /ˈfɑː.səl.aɪzd/ **adj 1** having become a fossil: *fossilized bones* **2** old-fashioned and never changing

foster /ˈfɒs.təʳ/ US /ˈfɑː.stɚ/ **verb; adj**

▸**verb TAKE CARE OF** ▷ **1** [I or T] to take care of a child, usually for a limited time, without being the child's legal parent: *Would you consider fostering* ***(a child)****?* → Compare **adopt ENCOURAGE** ▷ **2** [T] to encourage the development or growth of ideas or feelings: *I'm trying to foster an interest in classical music* ***in*** *my children.* ◦ *They were discussing the best way to foster democracy and prosperity in the former communist countries.*

▸**adj** [before noun] describes someone or something connected with the care of children, usually for a limited time, by someone who is not the child's legal parent: *a foster care/home/child/mother* ◦ *She was taken into care by the local council and placed with a foster* ***family.*** ◦ *As a child, he had lived with a succession of foster* ***parents.***

fought /fɔːt/ US /fɑːt/ past simple and past participle of **fight**

foul /faʊl/ **adj; noun; verb**

▸**adj 1** C1 extremely unpleasant: *Those toilets smell foul!* ◦ *I've had a foul day at work.* ◦ *Why are you in such a foul mood this morning?* ◦ *What foul weather!* **2** C1 describes speech or other language that is offensive, rude, or shocking: *There's too much foul* ***language*** *on TV these days.*

▸**noun** [C] C2 an act that is against the rules of a sport, often causing injury to another player: *He was sent off for a foul* ***on*** *the French captain.*

▸**verb MAKE DIRTY** ▷ **1** [T] formal to spoil or damage something by making it dirty: *Penalty for dogs fouling the pavement – £50.* **SPORT** ▷ **2** [I or T] to do something against the rules of a sport, often causing injury to another player

PHRASAL VERB **foul (sth) up** informal to spoil something by making a mistake or doing something stupid: *I don't want David organizing this party after the way he fouled things up last year.*

ˌfoul-ˈmouthed adj If someone is foul-mouthed, they use a lot of offensive language.

ˌfoul ˈplay noun [U] **CRIME** ▷ **1** a criminal act that results in serious damage or injury, especially murder: *It is not clear what caused the explosion, but the police do not* ***suspect*** *foul play.* **SPORT** ▷ **2** in sport, the act of playing unfairly or doing something that is against the rules

ˈfoul-up noun [C] informal an occasion when something is spoiled by a stupid mistake: *This investigation has been mismanaged right from the start – I've never seen such a foul-up.*

found /faʊnd/ verb **FIND** ▷ **1** past simple and past participle of **find** **BEGIN** ▷ **2** B2 [T] to bring something into existence: *York was founded by the Romans in the year 71 AD.* ◦ *She left a large sum of money in her will to found a wildlife sanctuary.* ◦ *We are planning a dinner to celebrate the 50th anniversary of the founding of the company.* **BUILD** ▷ **3** [T usually + adv/prep] specialized to build a support in the ground for a large structure such as a building or road **BASE** ▷ **4** C2 [T + adv/prep] to base a belief, claim, idea, etc. on something: *Her lawyer accused the prosecution of founding its case* ***on*** *insufficient evidence.* ◦ *I'd like to see the research that these recommendations are founded* ***on***. ◦ *a society founded* ***on*** *egalitarian principles*

foundation /faʊnˈdeɪ.ʃən/ noun **BEGIN** ▷ **1** C1 [U] an occasion when an organization, state, etc. is established: *the foundation of a new state* **2** C1 [C] an organization that has been created in order to provide money for a particular group of people in need of help or for a particular type of study: *the British Heart Foundation* ◦ *the Environmental Research Foundation* **3** [U] UK the first year of INFANT school, previously known as RECEPTION: *a foundation class/teacher* ◦ *Her youngest child starts (in) foundation in September.* **BUILDING** ▷ **4 foundations** [plural] the structures below the surface of the ground that support a building: *The foundations will have to be reinforced to prevent the house from sinking further into the ground.* **UNTRUE** ▷ **5 be without foundation** [U] (also **have no foundation**) C2 to be untrue: *These allegations are completely without foundation.* **MAKE-UP** ▷ **6** [U] a type of make-up that is spread over the skin of the face, usually before other make-up is put on, giving it a better and more even colour and hiding unwanted marks

IDIOMS **lay the foundations of/for** C2 to produce the basic ideas or structures from which something much larger develops: *The two leaders have laid the foundations of a new era in cooperation between their countries.* • **shake/rock sth to its foundations** to seriously damage, upset, or change an organization or someone's beliefs: *The scandal has shaken the Democratic Party to its foundations.*

founˈdation ˌcourse noun [C] UK (US **introˈductory ˌcourse**) a college or university course that introduces students to a subject and prepares them for studying it at a higher level

founˈdation ˌstone noun [C] a large block of stone that is put in position at the start of work on a public building, often with a ceremony

founder /ˈfaʊn.dər/ (US) /-dɚ/ noun; verb
▸noun [C] C2 someone who establishes an organization: *She is the founder and managing director of the company.*
▸verb [I] **1** (especially of a boat) to fill with water and sink: *The ferry foundered in a heavy storm, taking many of the passengers and crew with it.* **2** to be unsuccessful: *Teaching computers to read and write has always foundered* ***on*** *the unpredictable human element in language.*

ˌfounder ˈmember noun [C] UK (US **ˈfounding ˌmember**) one of the original members of an organization or rock group

ˌfounding ˈfather noun [C] someone who establishes an important organization or idea

foundling /ˈfaʊnd.lɪŋ/ noun [C] old-fashioned a young child who is left by its parents and then found and cared for by someone else

foundry /ˈfaʊn.dri/ noun [C] a factory where metal is melted and poured into specially shaped containers to produce objects such as wheels and bars

fount /faʊnt/ noun literary or humorous **the fount of all knowledge, gossip, wisdom, etc.** the person or place from which all information on a particular subject comes: *He's renowned as the fount of all knowledge on the disease.*

fountain /ˈfaʊn.tɪn/ noun [C] B1 a stream of water that is forced up into the air through a small hole, especially for decorative effect, or the structure in a lake or pool from which this flows

fountain

ˈfountain ˌpen noun [C] a pen whose NIB (= point at the end which you write with) is supplied with ink from a container inside it

four /fɔːr/ (US) /fɔːr/ number; noun
▸number A1 the number 4: *Most animals have four legs.* ◦ *Their little girl is nearly four.*
▸noun [C, + sing/pl verb] **1** a team of four people in ROWING, or the boat that they use **2 hit a four**

IDIOM **on all fours** with your hands and knees on the ground: *You'll have to get down on all fours to clean behind the toilet.*

ˌfour-by-ˈfour noun [C] (written abbreviation **4x4**) a vehicle whose engine supplies power to all four wheels instead of the usual two, so that it can travel easily over difficult ground → See also **four-wheel drive**

ˈfour-eyes noun [S] informal an offensive way of talking to someone who wears glasses

ˌfour-leaf ˈclover noun [C] (also **ˌfour-leaved ˈclover**) a CLOVER (= small plant) with a leaf that is divided into four parts rather than the usual three, thought to bring good luck to anyone who finds it

ˌfour-letter ˈword noun [C] a short word that is considered to be extremely rude and offensive: *Four-letter words are often edited out of films before they are shown on television.*

ˌfour-oh-ˈfour (also **404**) adj [after verb] humorous disapproving describes someone stupid who does not know how to use email and computers: *Don't bother asking him. He's 404, man.*

ˌfour-poster ˈbed noun [C] (also **four-ˈposter**) a large, old-fashioned bed with tall posts at each corner supporting a frame from which curtains hang

four-poster bed

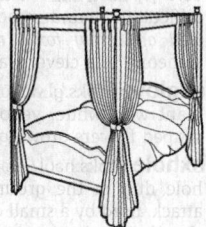

foursome /ˈfɔː.səm/ (US) /ˈfɔːr-/ noun [C] (also **four**) a group of four people meeting for a social activity, such as playing a game or having a meal: *Why don't we invite Caroline and Mark and* ***make up a foursome?***

ˈfour-square adj; adv
▸adj square or wide and built strongly and firmly: *The architecture tends to be four-square and unimaginative.*
▸adv with determination: *Clarke said he* ***stood*** *four-square* ***behind*** *(= believed strongly in) the prime minister's decision.*

ˌfour-ˈstar adj; noun
▸adj [before noun] describes a restaurant or hotel of a very high standard
▸noun [U] UK (also **ˌfour-star ˈpetrol**, US **premium**) the highest quality LEADED fuel that can be used in cars

fourteen /ˌfɔːˈtiːn/ (US) /ˌfɔːr-/ number (A1) the number 14: *Her baby is fourteen months old.* ◦ *Luisa is going to be fourteen next month.*

fourteenth /ˌfɔːˈtiːnθ/ (US) /ˌfɔːr-/ ordinal number 14th written as a word: *Valentine's Day is* ***the*** *fourteenth (****of*** *February).*

fourth /fɔːθ/ (US) /fɔːrθ/ ordinal number; noun
▸ordinal number (A2) 4th written as a word: *My birthday is on* ***the*** *fourth (****of*** *December).* ◦ *Daniel* ***was/came*** *fourth in the race.*
▸noun [C] mainly US a **quarter**: *Three fourths of his students, or 75 percent, come from the local area.*

the ˌfourth diˈmension noun [S] refers to time, especially in SCIENCE FICTION

the ˌFourth Esˈtate noun [S] newspapers, magazines, television, and radio stations and the people who work for them who are thought to have a lot of political influence

the ˌFourth of Juˈly noun [S] (formal **Indeˈpendence Day**) a national holiday in the US that celebrates the country's INDEPENDENCE from Great Britain in 1776

ˌfour-wheel ˈdrive noun **1** [C or U] (also **4x4**, written abbreviation **4WD**) If a vehicle has four-wheel drive, its engine supplies power to all four wheels instead of the usual two, so that the vehicle can travel easily over difficult ground. → Compare **all-wheel drive** **2** [C] a vehicle that uses this system • **ˈfour-wheel drive** adj *a four-wheel drive car*

ˌfour-ˈwheeler noun [C] Indian English a vehicle, especially a car

fowl /faʊl/ noun [C or U] (plural **fowl** or **fowls**) **1** a bird of a type that is used to produce meat or eggs **2** old use any bird → See also **waterfowl, wildfowl**

fox /fɒks/ (US) /fɑːks/ noun; verb
▸noun ANIMAL ▷ **1** (B2) [C] a wild mammal belonging to the dog family which has a pointed face and ears, a wide tail covered in fur, and often reddish-brown fur **2** [U] the skin of this animal used to make coats and hats CLEVER PERSON ▷ **3** [C usually singular] someone who is clever and good at deceiving people: *He's a cunning/sly/wily old fox.* WOMAN ▷ **4** [C] US informal a sexually attractive woman
▸verb [T] CONFUSE ▷ **1** to confuse someone or be too difficult to be understood by someone: *This puzzle has well and truly foxed me!* DECEIVE ▷ **2** to deceive someone in a clever way

foxglove /ˈfɒks.ɡlʌv/ (US) /ˈfɑːks-/ noun [C] a tall, thin plant with white, yellow, pink, red, or purple bell-shaped flowers growing all the way up its stem

foxhole /ˈfɒks.həʊl/ (US) /ˈfɑːks.hoʊl/ noun [C] a small hole dug in the ground during a war or military attack, used by a small group of soldiers as a base for shooting at the enemy and as a shelter from attack → Compare **trench**

foxhound /ˈfɒks.haʊnd/ (US) /ˈfɑːks-/ noun [C] a type of small dog with ears that hang down and short, smooth, usually black, white, and light brown fur

ˈfox ˌhunting noun [U] the activity of hunting foxes for entertainment in which people on horses follow dogs which chase a fox and kill it when they catch it • **ˈfox hunt** noun [C]

ˌfox ˈterrier noun [C] a small dog with smooth or rough fur that is white with black or pale brown marks

foxtrot /ˈfɒks.trɒt/ (US) /ˈfɑːks.trɑːt/ noun [C] (a piece of music for) a type of formal BALLROOM dance that combines short, quick steps with longer ones in various patterns

foxy /ˈfɒk.si/ (US) /ˈfɑːk-/ adj ANIMAL ▷ **1** like a fox in appearance GOOD AT DECEIVING ▷ **2** good at deceiving people WOMAN ▷ **3** informal sexually attractive: *a foxy chick*

foyer /ˈfɔɪ.eɪ/ noun [C] **1** a large open area just inside the entrance of a public building such as a theatre or a hotel, where people can wait and meet each other: *I'll see you downstairs* ***in*** *the foyer in half an hour.* **2** US (UK **hall**) the room in a house or apartment leading from the front door to other rooms, where things like coats and hats are kept

Fr. noun [before noun] written abbreviation for **Father** when used as a title of a Christian priest, especially a Roman Catholic or Orthodox priest: *Fr. McDonald conducted the mass.*

fracas /ˈfræk.ɑː/ (US) /ˈfreɪ.kəs/ noun [S] a noisy argument or fight: *He was injured in a Saturday-night fracas outside a disco.* ◦ *The prime minister has joined the fracas* ***over*** *the proposed changes to the health service.*

fracking /ˈfræk.ɪŋ/ noun [U] a method of getting oil or gas from the rock below the surface of the ground by making large CRACKS in it. Fracking is short for 'hydraulic fracturing'.

fractal /ˈfræk.təl/ noun [C] specialized a complicated pattern in mathematics built from simple repeated shapes that are reduced in size every time they are repeated: *The way that the trunk of a tree divides into smaller and smaller branches and twigs is an approximate fractal pattern.*

fraction /ˈfræk.ʃən/ noun [C] (C2) a number that results from dividing one whole number by another, or a small part of something: *¼ and 0.25 are different ways of representing the same fraction.* ◦ *Although sexual and violent crimes have increased by 13 percent, they remain* ***only a tiny/small*** *fraction* ***of*** *the total number of crimes committed each year.* ◦ *They can produce it* ***at a*** *fraction* ***of*** *the cost of (= much more cheaply than) traditional methods.*

fractional /ˈfræk.ʃən.əl/ adj **1** extremely small: *The fall in the value of the yen might result in a fractional increase in interest rates of perhaps a quarter of one percent.* **2** relating to only a part of something: *fractional* ***ownership*** • **fractionally** /-i/ adv *Despite substantial price cuts, sales have increased only fractionally (= by a very small amount).*

ˌfractional distilˈlation noun [U] specialized the chemical process of separating different substances that have different BOILING POINTS by heating a liquid mixture until it turns into gas and then cooling and collecting each substance separately

fractious /ˈfræk.ʃəs/ adj easily upset or annoyed, and often complaining: *a fractious child* • **fractiousness** /-nəs/ noun [U]

fracture /ˈfræk.tʃər/ (US) /-tʃɚ/ verb; noun
▸verb [I or T] **1** If something hard, such as a bone, fractures or is fractured, it breaks or CRACKS: *She*

fractured her ***skull*** *in the accident.* ◦ *Two of her ribs fractured when she was thrown from her horse.* ◦ *A fractured pipe at a steelworks has leaked 20 tons of oil into the Severn estuary.* **2** formal to divide an organization or society, or (of an organization or society) to be divided: *Intense disagreement over economic policy risks fracturing the coalition government.*

▸**noun** [C] a break or CRACK in something hard, especially a bone: *He suffered/sustained* ***multiple*** *fractures in a motorcycle accident.* ◦ *He has a* ***hairline*** *fracture (= a thin broken line in the bone) of the wrist.*

fragile /ˈfrædʒ.aɪl/ (US) /ˈfrædʒ.ᵊl/ **adj** (C2) easily damaged, broken, or harmed: *Be careful with that vase – it's very fragile.* ◦ *The assassination could do serious damage to the fragile peace agreement that was signed last month.* ◦ *I felt rather fragile (= weak) for a few days after the operation.* ◦ humorous *No breakfast for me, thanks – I'm feeling rather fragile (= ill, upset, or tired) after last night's party.* • **fragility** /frəˈdʒɪl.ɪ.ti/ (US) /-t̬i/ **noun** [U] *The collapse of the bank is an ominous reminder of the fragility of the world's banking system.*

fragment noun; verb

▸**noun** [C] /ˈfræg.mənt/ a small piece or a part, especially when broken from something whole: *The road was covered with fragments* ***of*** *glass from the shattered window.*

▸**verb** [I or T] /frægˈment/ to break something into small parts or to be broken up in this way: *The satellite will fragment and burn up as it falls through the Earth's atmosphere.* ◦ *The government is planning to fragment the industry before privatizing it.* • **fragmentation** /ˌfræg.menˈteɪ.ʃᵊn/ **noun** [U] *It was partly the fragmentation of the opposition which helped to get the Republicans re-elected.*

fragmentary /frægˈmen.tᵊr.i/ (US) /ˈfræg.mən.ter-/ **adj** formal existing only in small parts and not complete: *Reports are still fragmentary but it is already clear that the explosion has left many dead and injured.*

fragmented /frægˈmen.tɪd/ (US) /-t̬ɪd/ **adj** consisting of several separate parts: *In this increasingly fragmented society, a sense of community is a thing of the past.* ◦ *The president has only held onto power because the opposition is so fragmented.* • **fragmentation noun** [U] *the fragmentation of the country's banking system*

fragrance /ˈfreɪ.grᵊns/ **noun** [C or U] **1** (C2) a sweet or pleasant smell: *the delicate fragrance of roses* **2** a liquid which people put on their bodies to make themselves smell pleasant: *a brand new fragrance for men*

fragrant /ˈfreɪ.grᵊnt/ **adj** (C2) with a pleasant smell: *fragrant flowers* ◦ *The sauce itself was light, fragrant and slightly sweet.*

frail /freɪl/ **adj** (C2) weak or unhealthy, or easily damaged, broken, or harmed: *a frail old lady* ◦ *I last saw him just last week and thought how old and frail he looked.* ◦ *the country's frail economy*

frailty /ˈfreɪl.ti/ (US) /-t̬i/ **noun 1** [U] weakness and lack of health or strength: *Though ill for most of her life, physical frailty never stopped her from working.* **2** [C or U] moral weakness: *Most of the characters in the novel exhibit those common* ***human*** *frailties – ignorance and greed.* ◦ *Tolerant of* ***human*** *frailty in whatever form, she almost never judged people.*

frame /freɪm/ **noun; verb**

▸**noun** [C] **BORDER** ▷ **1** (B1) a border that surrounds and supports a picture, door, or window: *a picture frame* **2 frames** the plastic or metal structure that holds together a pair of glasses **STRUCTURE** ▷ **3** (B2) the basic structure of a building, vehicle, or piece of furniture that other parts are added onto: *a bicycle frame* **4** UK (US **rack**) a wooden or plastic triangle used to put the balls into position at the start of a game such as BILLIARDS or SNOOKER **5** the size and shape of someone's body **6 frame of mind** (C2) the way someone thinks or feels about something at a particular time: *The most important thing is to go into the exam* ***in*** *a positive frame of mind.* **7 frame of reference** a set of ideas or facts accepted by a person that explains their behaviour, opinions, or decisions: *How can Christians and atheists ever come to understand each other when their frames of reference are so different?* **GAME** ▷ **8** a period of play in some games, such as SNOOKER: *She lost the next two frames.* **PHOTOGRAPH** ▷ **9** specialized one of the pictures on a strip of photographic film, or one of the single pictures that together form a television or cinema film

▸**verb EXPRESS** ▷ **1** [T] to express something choosing your words carefully: *The interview would have been more productive if the questions had been framed more precisely.* **MAKE GUILTY** ▷ **2** [T often passive] informal to make a person seem to be guilty of a crime when they are not, by producing facts or information that are not true: *He claimed he'd been framed by the police.* **BORDER** ▷ **3** [T] to fix a border around a picture, etc. and often glass in front of it: *I keep meaning to get that photo framed.* **4** [T] to form an edge to something in an attractive way: *Her new hairstyle frames her face in a much more flattering way.*

framed /freɪmd/ **adj** surrounded by a border: *a framed photograph* ◦ *a pair of silver-framed spectacles*

ˈframe-up noun [C] informal a situation in which someone is made to seem guilty of a crime although they have not done it: *The organization protested that it was the victim of a politically motivated frame-up.*

framework /ˈfreɪm.wɜːk/ (US) /-wɝːk/ **noun 1** [C] a supporting structure around which something can be built **2** (C2) a system of rules, ideas, or beliefs that is used to plan or decide something: *a legal framework for resolving disputes*

franc /fræŋk/ **noun** [C] (written abbreviation **fr**) the standard unit of money used in France, Belgium, and Luxembourg before the introduction of the euro, and also used in Switzerland and in many African countries

franchise /ˈfræn.tʃaɪz/ **noun; verb**

▸**noun BUSINESS** ▷ **1** [C] a right to sell a company's products in a particular area using the company's name: *a fast-food franchise* ◦ *a franchise holder* **VOTE** ▷ **2 the franchise** [S] the right to vote in an election, especially in order to elect a parliament or similar law-making organization: *In 1918 the suffragists* ***won the*** *franchise for UK women over the age of 29.*

▸**verb** [T] to give or sell a franchise to someone • **franchising** /-tʃaɪ.zɪŋ/ **noun** [U]

franchisee /ˌfræn.tʃaɪˈziː/ **noun** [C] someone who is given or sold a franchise

franchiser (also **franchisor**) /ˈfræn.tʃaɪ.zəʳ/ (US) /-zɚ/ **noun** [C] someone who gives or sells a franchise

Franciscan /frænˈsɪs.kən/ **noun** [C] a person belonging to a Christian group originally established by St Francis of Assisi in 1209 • **Franciscan adj**

Franco- /fræŋ.kəʊ-/ (US) /-koʊ-/ **prefix** of or connected with France: *the Franco-German border (= the border between France and Germany)* ◦ *a francophile (= someone who loves France)*

francophone /ˈfræŋ.kə.fəʊn/ (US) /ˈfræŋ.koʊ.foʊn/ **adj** [before noun] speaking French as the main or official language: *francophone Africa* • **francophone noun** [C] *Most of the francophones live in these two provinces.*

frank /fræŋk/ adj; verb
▸adj honest, sincere, and telling the truth, even when this might be awkward or make other people uncomfortable: *a full and frank discussion* ◦ *There followed a frank exchange of views.* ◦ *The magazine, which gives frank advice about sex and romance, is aimed at the teenage market.* ◦ ***To be perfectly** frank with you, I don't think she's the woman for the job.*
▸verb [T] to print a mark on a stamp so that the stamp cannot be used again, or to print a mark on an envelope to show that the cost of sending it has been paid

Frankenstein /ˈfræŋ.kən.staɪn/ noun [C] (also ˌ**Frankenstein's** ˈ**monster**) something that destroys or harms the person or people who created it: *In arming the dictator, the US was creating a Frankenstein.*

frankfurter /ˈfræŋk.fɜː.təʳ/ (US) /-fɝː.t̬ɚ/ noun [C] a thin, red-brown sausage, preserved using smoke or chemicals and often eaten with bread

frankincense /ˈfræŋ.kɪn.sens/ noun [U] a thick sticky liquid that produces a sweet smell when burned and comes from a tree that grows in eastern Africa and Asia

frankly /ˈfræŋ.kli/ adv **1** in an honest and direct way: *She spoke very frankly about her experiences.* **2** (B2) used when giving an honest and direct opinion, often one that might upset someone: ***Quite** frankly, I think this whole situation is ridiculous.* ◦ *That's a frankly absurd suggestion.*

frankness /ˈfræŋk.nəs/ noun [U] honesty

frantic /ˈfræn.tɪk/ (US) /-t̬ɪk/ adj **VERY WORRIED/FRIGHTENED** ▷ **1** (C2) almost out of control because of extreme emotion, such as worry: *Where on earth have you been? We've been frantic **with** worry.* **HURRIED** ▷ **2** (C2) done or arranged in a hurry and a state of excitement or confusion: *Share prices have soared to a new all-time high in a day of frantic trading on the stock market.* ◦ *Rescuers were engaged in a frantic all-night effort to reach the survivors before their supply of air ran out.*

frantically /ˈfræn.tɪ.kəl.i/ (US) /-t̬ɪ-/ adv **HURRIEDLY** ▷ **1** done in a hurried way and in a state of excitement or confusion: *I've been working frantically all week to get it finished on time.* ◦ *I got home to find Lara frantically searching for her keys.* **SHOWING WORRY/FEAR** ▷ **2** in a way that is almost out of control because of extreme emotion, such as worry: *As the helicopter flew overhead, they waved frantically, trying to attract its attention.*

frappé /ˈfræp.eɪ/ (US) /fræpˈeɪ/ noun [C] a partly frozen drink made of milk or fruit juice, or a strongly alcoholic drink served with ice: *a chocolate/strawberry/crème de menthe frappé*

frat /fræt/ noun [C] US informal for fraternity (= a social organization for male university students in the US and Canada)

fraternal /frəˈtɜː.nəl/ (US) /-ˈtɝː-/ adj **1** relating to brothers: *fraternal rivalry* **2** friendly, like brothers: *The president's official visit marks the start of a more fraternal relationship between the two countries.* • **fraternally** /-nə.li/ (US) /-ˈtɝː-/ adv

fraternity /frəˈtɜː.nə.ti/ (US) /-ˈtɝː.nə.t̬i/ noun **GROUP** ▷ **1** [C, + sing/pl verb] a group of people who have the same job or interest: *the legal fraternity* (= lawyers) ◦ *the criminal fraternity* (= criminals) ◦ *The racing world is a pretty **close-knit** fraternity.* **2** [C, + sing/pl verb] (informal **frat**) US a social organization for male students at an American or Canadian college → Compare **sorority** **FRIENDSHIP** ▷ **3** [U] a feeling of friendship and support: *He described sport as a symbol of peace and a means of promoting fraternity between nations.*

fraternize (UK usually **fraternise**) /ˈfræt.ə.naɪz/ (US) /-ɚ-/ verb [I] to meet someone socially, especially someone who belongs to an opposing army or team, or has a different social position: *Do the doctors fraternize much **with** the nurses here?* ◦ *He accused the England team of fraternizing too much **with** the opposition.* • **fraternization** (UK usually **fraternisation**) /ˌfræt.ən.aɪˈzeɪ.ʃən/ (US) /-ɚ.nɪ-/ noun [U]

fratricide /ˈfræt.rɪ.saɪd/ noun [U] formal the crime of murdering your brother, or killing members of your own group or country • **fratricidal** /ˌfræt.rɪˈsaɪ.dəl/ adj

fraud /frɔːd/ (US) /frɑːd/ noun **CRIME** ▷ **1** (C2) [C or U] the crime of getting money by deceiving people: *credit card fraud* ◦ *He is fighting extradition to Hong Kong to face trial on fraud **charges**.* **FALSE** ▷ **2** (C2) [C] someone or something that deceives people by saying that they are someone or something that they are not: *She was a psychic who was later revealed to be a fraud.*

the ˈ**fraud** ˌ**squad** noun [S, + sing/pl verb] a department in the British police that discovers and takes action against business fraud

fraudster /ˈfrɔːd.stəʳ/ (US) /ˈfrɑːd.stɚ/ noun [C] someone who gets money by deceiving people

fraudulent /ˈfrɔː.djʊ.lənt/ (US) /ˈfrɑː-/ adj **CRIME** ▷ **1** (C2) dishonest and illegal: *A worrying trend for insurers has been a rise in fraudulent **claims**.* **FALSE** ▷ **2** intended to deceive: *They claim that the fall in unemployment is based on a fraudulent manipulation of statistics.* • **fraudulence** /-ləns/ noun [U] • **fraudulently** /-li/ adv

fraught /frɔːt/ (US) /frɑːt/ adj **FULL OF** ▷ **1** **fraught with** full of unpleasant things such as problems or dangers: *The negotiations have been fraught with **difficulties/problems** right from the start.* ◦ *From beginning to end, the airlift was fraught with **risks**.* **ANXIOUS** ▷ **2** causing or having extreme worry or ANXIETY: *This is one of the most fraught weekends of the year for the security forces.* ◦ *The atmosphere in the office is rather fraught.*

fray /freɪ/ verb; noun
▸verb **CLOTH** ▷ **1** [I or T] to become or to cause the threads in cloth or rope to become slightly separated, forming loose threads at the edge or end: *Denim frays so easily.* ◦ *I'd frayed the edges of my jeans as that was the fashion in those days.* **BECOME ANNOYED** ▷ **2** [I] If your temper frays or your nerves fray, you gradually become upset or annoyed: *Tempers frayed as thousands of motorists began the Christmas holiday with long waits in traffic jams.*

IDIOM **fray around/at the edges** to start to become less effective or successful: *Without the unifying forces of the army and the monarchy, it seems, the nation would begin to fray at the edges.*

▸noun [S] **the fray** an energetic and often not well organized effort, activity, fight, or disagreement: *With a third country about to **enter** (= take part in) the fray, the fighting looks set to continue.* ◦ *A good holiday should leave you feeling refreshed and **ready for** the fray (= ready to work) again.*

frayed /freɪd/ adj **CLOTH** ▷ **1** with the threads at the edge coming loose: *frayed cuffs* **ANNOYED** ▷ **2** describes someone's mood when they are feeling worried, upset, or annoyed: *The whole experience left me with frayed **nerves** (= feeling worried).*

frazzle /ˈfræz.l̩/ noun [S] **TIRED STATE** ▷ **1** informal a state of being very tired in a nervous or slightly ANXIOUS (= worried and nervous) way after a lot of mental or physical effort: *She's **worn** herself **to a***

frazzle (= made herself very tired and nervous) trying to meet the deadline. **BURNED** ▷ **2** UK informal a state of being completely burned or tired out: *I went to answer the phone and when I came back the eggs were* ***burned to a*** *frazzle.*

frazzled /ˈfræz.l̩d/ adj **TIRED** ▷ **1** informal extremely tired in a nervous or slightly worried way after a lot of mental or physical effort: *I've had a stressful day at work and it's left me feeling a bit frazzled.* **BURNED** ▷ **2** UK informal burned or dried out after being in the sun or cooking for too long: *I'd only been in the sun a couple of hours and my back was frazzled.*

freak /friːk/ noun; verb; adj

▸**noun STRANGE** ▷ **1** [C] a thing, person, animal, or event that is extremely unusual or unlikely, and not like any other of its type: *I was born with black hair all over my back, like some sort of freak.* ◦ *The pearl is so big that it has been described as a freak* ***of nature.*** ◦ humorous *At my school you were regarded as a freak if you weren't interested in sport.* **ENTHUSIASTIC PERSON** ▷ **2 a health, computer, surf, etc. freak** informal someone who is extremely interested in a particular subject or activity

▸**verb** [I or T] informal to become or cause someone to become extremely emotional: *My parents freaked when I told them I was pregnant.* ◦ *He freaked* ***out*** *when he heard he'd got the job.* ◦ *This song just freaks me* ***out*** *whenever I hear it.*

▸**adj** [before noun] very unusual or unexpected: *She was crushed in a freak (= very unlikely)* ***accident*** *in a cave in France.* ◦ *A freak whirlwind has destroyed over 20 caravans in west Wales.*

freakish /ˈfriː.kɪʃ/ adj (informal **freaky**) very unusual or unexpected, especially in an unpleasant or strange way: *Freakish weather conditions have caused massive traffic hold-ups in the area.* ◦ *When you're a child you always imagine that your own bodily imperfections are somehow freakish.* • **freakishly** /-li/ adv • **freakishness** /-nəs/ noun [U]

ˈfreak ˌshow noun [C] in the past, an event at which the public came to look at people and animals that had not developed normally: *She felt like something out of a freak show.*

freckle /ˈfrek.l̩/ noun [C] a small, pale brown spot on the skin, usually on the face, especially of a person with pale skin: *He has red hair and freckles.* → Compare **mole** • **freckled** /-l̩d/ adj (also **freckly** /-əl.i/) *a freckly complexion*

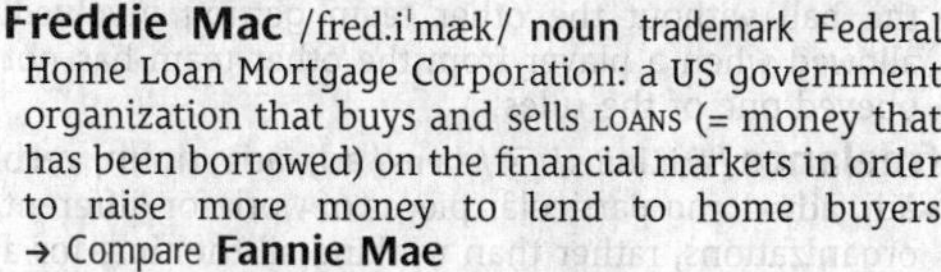
freckles

ˈfreckle-faced adj having a lot of freckles on the face

Freddie Mac /fred.iˈmæk/ **noun** trademark Federal Home Loan Mortgage Corporation: a US government organization that buys and sells LOANS (= money that has been borrowed) on the financial markets in order to raise more money to lend to home buyers → Compare **Fannie Mae**

free /friː/ adj, adv; adj; verb

▸**adj, adv NOT LIMITED** ▷ **1** B2 not limited or controlled: [+ to infinitive] *Am I free (= do I have permission)* ***to*** *leave now?* ◦ *I'll give you a key then you're free* ***to*** *come and go as you please.* ◦ *Please* ***feel*** *free* ***to*** *interrupt me if you don't understand anything.* ◦ *The agreement gives companies free* ***access*** *to the markets of member countries.* ◦ *A great deal has been achieved, most notably free* ***elections*** *(= elections in which people can vote as they wish).* **2 free and easy** relaxed and informal: *The atmosphere in the office is fairly free and easy.* **NO CHARGE** ▷ **3** A2 costing nothing; not needing to be paid for: *I got some free cinema tickets.* ◦ *Members all receive a free copy of the monthly newsletter.* ◦ *The elderly travel free on public transport.* ◦ *We will install your washing machine free* ***of charge/for*** *free (= without charge).* **NOT IN PRISON** ▷ **4** B2 not a prisoner any longer, or having unlimited movement: *She left the court a free woman after the case against her collapsed because of a legal technicality.* ◦ *The new government has decided to* ***set*** *all political prisoners free.* ◦ *She* ***went/walked*** *free after the charges against her were dropped.* ◦ *I let the dogs run free in the park.* **LOOSE** ▷ **5** not in a fixed position or not joined to anything: *Both bookcases stand free* ***of*** *the wall.* ◦ *The bolts have worked themselves free because of the vibrations.* ◦ *Rescuers took several hours to cut the survivors free* ***from*** *the wreckage.*

▸**adj NOT BUSY** ▷ **1** A2 not doing anything planned or important, or available to be used: *I do a lot of reading in my free* ***time.*** ◦ *She's in a meeting at the moment, but she should be free* ***to*** *see you in ten minutes.* ◦ *I'm working in the café all this week, but I've got a free evening next Monday.* ◦ *Excuse me, is this seat free (= is anyone intending to sit in this seat)?* ◦ *We queued for half an hour waiting for a free space in the car park.* ◦ *If you take these bags that will give me a free hand to open the door.* **WITHOUT** ▷ **2** C1 [after verb] not having something that is unwanted or unpleasant: *Because the organization is a charitable enterprise it is free* ***from*** *tax worldwide.* ◦ *She'll never be completely free* ***of*** *the disease.* ◦ *Ensure the wound is free* ***from/of*** *dirt before applying the bandage.* **GIVING/USING OFTEN** ▷ **3 free with** giving or using often or in large amounts: *He's rather free with his wife's money.* ◦ *He's very free with his criticism!* **4 make free with** disapproving to use something that belongs to someone else a lot: *Don't her parents mind her making free with their house while they're on holiday?* **CHEMICAL** ▷ **5** In chemistry, if an element is free, it is not combined with anything else or attached to anything else: *free oxygen/nitrogen*

IDIOMS **a free ride** an opportunity or advantage that someone gets without having done anything to deserve it: *Just because he was the boss's son didn't mean Tim got a free ride.* • **there's no such thing as a free lunch** saying said to emphasize that you cannot get something for nothing: *'I get to travel with my job but the downside is I have to give talks.' 'Well, there's no such thing as a free lunch.'*

▸**verb NOT IN PRISON** ▷ **1** B2 [T] to allow someone to leave a prison or place where they have been kept: *After a ten-hour siege the gunman agreed to free the hostages.* ◦ *Anti-vivisectionists last night freed a number of animals* ***from*** *a laboratory.* **MAKE LOOSE** ▷ **2** [T] to move or make loose someone or something that is caught or held somewhere: *Both men were freed from the wreckage after a four-hour operation.* ◦ *In vain he tried to free the rope around his hands.* **REMOVE LIMITS** ▷ **3** [T + obj + to infinitive] to remove the limits or controls on someone or something: *Her retirement from politics will free her (= provide her with enough time)* ***to*** *write her memoirs.* **MAKE AVAILABLE** ▷ **4** [T] to make something available for someone to use: *They planned to extend the car park, freeing existing parking spaces for visitors.* ◦ *Can you cancel my meetings – I need to free (****up****) the afternoon to write this report.*

PHRASAL VERB **free sb from/of sth** to help or make life better for someone by taking something unpleasant away from them: *He dedicated his life to freeing the world from famine and disease.* ◦ *I'd like to free my**self** of some of the responsibilities of this job.*

-free /-friː/ suffix **NO CHARGE** ▷ **1** used at the end of words to mean 'without having to pay': *They agreed to let us live there rent-free.* ◦ *Many banks are now offering interest-free overdrafts to students.* **WITHOUT** ▷ **2** used at the end of words to mean 'without': *lead-free fuel* ◦ *No working environment is entirely stress-free.*

ˌfree ˈagent noun [C] someone whose actions are not limited or controlled by anyone else

ˌfree assoc iˈation noun [U] a method of trying to see how the human mind works, in which a person says the first word that they think of after hearing a word that is spoken to them

freebasing /ˈfriː.beɪ.sɪŋ/ noun [U] slang the activity of smoking a specially prepared form of the drug COCAINE • **freebase** /-beɪs/ **verb** [I]

freebie /ˈfriː.bi/ noun [C] informal something that is given to you without you having to pay for it, especially as a way of attracting your support for or interest in something: *The company's marketing rep was giving out pens and mugs – the usual freebies.* ◦ *The journalists were all given a freebie lunch.*

ˌFree ˈChurch noun [C usually singular] a Protestant Church that is not part of a country's officially accepted Church

ˌfree collective ˈbargaining noun [U] UK specialized formal discussions between workers and employers that are not limited by the law or government, about pay, working hours, and conditions at work → See also **collective bargaining**

freedom /ˈfriː.dəm/ noun **1** B2 [C or U] the condition or right of being able or allowed to do, say, think, etc. whatever you want to, without being controlled or limited: *I felt such a sense of freedom, up in the hills alone.* ◦ *Children are allowed much more freedom these days.* ◦ [+ to infinitive] *At university, you **have** the freedom **to** do what you want.* ◦ *Everyone should be allowed freedom **of choice** (= the ability to make their own choices).* ◦ *Freedom **of speech** and freedom **of thought** (= the ability to say and think whatever you want) were both denied under the dictatorship.* ◦ *They are campaigning for freedom **of information** (= for any information to be allowed to be given to anyone who wants it).* ◦ *We demand freedom **from** injustice/persecution (= the condition of not having to suffer these things).* → Compare **liberty 2** [C] a right to act in the way you think you should: *Being able to vote as you want to is an important political/democratic freedom.* **3** [U] the state of not being in prison: *They regained their freedom after ten years of unjust imprisonment.* **4 give sb the freedom of** in Britain, to honour someone by giving them special rights in a particular city → See also **freeman**

ˈfreedom ˌfighter noun [C] a person who uses violent methods to try to remove a government from power: *It's often said that one person's freedom fighter is another person's terrorist.*

ˌfree ˈenterprise noun [U] an economic system in which private businesses compete with each other to sell goods and services in order to make a profit, and in which government control is limited to protecting the public and running the economy

ˌfree ˈfall noun [U] **1** an occasion when something or someone falls quickly under the influence of GRAVITY **2** informal the process of failing or losing value or strength quickly and continuously: *Only massive changes in government policies will prevent the peso **going into** free fall (= falling quickly in value by a large amount).*

ˌfree-ˈfloating adj **1** not supporting any particular political party **2** not fixed to anything: *free-floating aquatic plants* **3** not controlled by any particular system: *a free-floating exchange rate system* **4** a free-floating feeling is one that is general and does not have an obvious cause: *free-floating anxiety*

ˈfree-ˌflowing adj **1** Something that is free-flowing is able to move without anything stopping it: *free-flowing rivers* ◦ *free-flowing traffic* **2** happening or done in a continuous and natural way: *a free-flowing discussion* ◦ *a free-flowing style of rugby* **3** easily available in large amounts: *There was free-flowing champagne at the party.*

Freefone /ˈfriː.fəʊn/ US /-foʊn/ noun [U] UK trademark **Freephone**

ˌfree-for-ˈall noun [S] a situation without limits or controls in which people can have or do what they want: *The row between the prime minister and the opposition leader soon developed into a free-for-all between MPs from all parties.*

ˈfree-form adj not having or following a particular style or structure: *free-form skating*

freegan /ˈfriː.gən/ noun [C] a person who chooses to eat food that is not bought from a shop, especially food that other people, shops, or organizations throw away, so that food is not wasted

ˌfree ˈgift noun [C] a product that is given to a customer free when they buy something in order to encourage people to buy more of it: *You get a free gift if you spend more than £20.*

freehand /ˈfriː.hænd/ adj, adv (of a drawing) done without the help of any special equipment for accurately creating circles, straight lines, symbols, etc.: *a freehand sketch*

ˌfree ˈhand noun [S] C2 the right or authority to do anything you consider necessary: *The company's **given** me a free hand **to** negotiate a deal.*

freehold /ˈfriː.həʊld/ US /-hoʊld/ noun [C] the legal right to own and use a building or piece of land for an unlimited time: *Who owns the freehold **of/on** the property?* → Compare **leasehold** • **freehold adj** *Are those flats freehold or leasehold?*

freeholder /ˈfriː.həʊl.dər/ US /-hoʊl.dɚ/ noun [C] an owner of a particular building or piece of land

ˌfree ˈhouse noun [C] UK a type of bar in the UK that is not owned and controlled by a BREWERY (= a business that makes beer) so the range of beers and other drinks that it can sell is not limited → Compare **tied house**

ˌfree ˈjazz noun [U] a type of modern music in which the players do not follow any written structure

ˌfree ˈkick noun [C] in football, an opportunity to kick the ball without the other team getting involved, allowed when a player from the other team has not obeyed one of the rules

freelance /ˈfriː.lɑːns/ US /-læns/ adj, adv; noun; verb
▸adj, adv doing particular pieces of work for different organizations, rather than working all the time for a single organization: *Most of the journalists I know are/work freelance.* ◦ *a freelance artist*
▸noun [C] (also **freelancer**) someone who is freelance: *The firm employs several freelances.*
▸verb [I] to work freelance: *I prefer to freelance from home rather than to work in an office.*

freeloader /ˈfriːˌləʊ.dər/ US /-ˌloʊ.dɚ/ noun [C] disapproving a person who uses money, food, a room in a house, etc. given by other people, but who gives nothing to them in exchange • **freeloading** /-ˌləʊ.dɪŋ/ (US) /-ˌloʊ.dɪŋ/ noun [U]

ˌfree ˈlove noun [U] old-fashioned sexual activity with several partners which does not involve loyalty to any particular person

freely /ˈfriː.li/ adv **NOT LIMITED** ▷ **1** B2 without being controlled or limited: *For the first time in months she could move freely.* ◦ *Exotic foods are freely available in supermarkets.* ◦ *She freely (= willingly)* ***admits*** *that she's not as fast a runner as she used to be.* ◦ *We encourage the victims to talk freely (= talk a lot and honestly) about their experiences.* **ABLE TO MOVE EASILY** ▷ **2** in a way that is not fixed or joined to anything, so able to move easily: *Remember to apply plenty of oil so that the wheel can rotate freely.*

freeman /ˈfriː.mən/, /-mæn/ noun [C] (plural **-men** /-mən/) UK a person who has been given particular special rights in a city, as an honour: *Paul McCartney was made a freeman* ***of*** *the City of Liverpool.*

ˌfree ˈmarket noun [S] an economic system with only a small amount of government control, in which prices and earnings are decided by the level of demand for, and production of goods and services: *In a free market, if demand for a product increases then so does its price.* ◦ *the free-market* ***economy***

Freemason /ˈfriːˌmeɪ.sᵊn/ noun [C] (also **Mason**) a member of a large and old secret society for men in which all the members help each other and use secret signs to communicate with each other

Freemasonry /ˈfriːˌmeɪ.sᵊn.ri/ noun [U] (also **Masonry**) Freemasons considered as a group, or their beliefs and activities

ˌfree ˈpardon noun [C usually singular] UK (US **pardon**) an occasion when someone who has committed a crime is officially forgiven: *The new government is to grant a free pardon to all political prisoners.* → Compare **royal pardon**

Freephone (trademark **Freefone**) /ˈfriː.fəʊn/ (US) /-foʊn/ noun [U] a system in the UK which allows you to phone particular organizations without paying for the call, because the organizations will pay the cost: *a 24-hour freephone customer ordering service* ◦ *For further details, call Freephone 0800 123456/call our Freephone number 0800 123456.*

ˌfree ˈport noun [C] an area near a port or airport to which goods from foreign countries can be brought without tax being paid if they are sent to another country when they leave this area

Freepost /ˈfriː.pəʊst/ (US) /-poʊst/ noun [U] UK a system which allows you to send something by post to particular organizations without payment, because the organizations will pay the cost

ˌfree ˈradical noun [C often plural] specialized a MOLECULE that has an extra ELECTRON and therefore reacts very easily with other MOLECULES: *Free radicals have been implicated in cancer and many other serious diseases.*

ˌfree-ˈrange adj relating to or produced by farm animals that are allowed to move around outside and are not kept in CAGES: *free-range eggs/chickens*

ˌfree ˈrunning (also **freerunning**) noun [U] (also **parkour**) an activity in which people move quickly around buildings and objects in a city while performing jumps and other skilful movements

freesheet /ˈfriː.ʃiːt/ noun [C] UK a free newspaper that gives local news and information, and in which local businesses can advertise

freeship /ˈfriː.ʃɪp/ noun [C] Indian English an agreement that you do not have to pay for a place at a school, college, or university that you would usually have to pay for → Compare **scholarship**

freesia /ˈfriː.ʒə/ noun [C] a plant with pleasant-smelling yellow, white, pink, or purple flowers

ˌfree ˈspeech noun [U] the right to express your opinions publicly

ˌfree ˈspirit noun [C usually singular] a person who does what they want with enjoyment and pleasure and does not feel limited by the usual rules of social behaviour

freestanding /ˌfriːˈstæn.dɪŋ/ adj standing alone and not fixed to a wall, etc.: *a freestanding bookshelf* ◦ figurative *The electronics division was split off into a freestanding company.*

freestyle /ˈfriː.staɪl/ noun [S] a sports competition, especially a swimming race, in which each competitor can use any style or method they choose: *He won the 400 metres freestyle.*

freethinker /ˌfriːˈθɪŋ.kəʳ/ (US) /-kɚ/ noun [C] old-fashioned someone who forms their own opinions and beliefs, especially about religion or politics, rather than just accepting what is officially or commonly believed and taught • **freethinking** /-kɪŋ/ adj

ˌfree ˈthrow noun [C] in BASKETBALL, an opportunity to score extra points that is given to a member of one team if a player from the other team has broken a rule

ˌfree ˈtrade noun [U] international buying and selling of goods, without limits on the amount of goods that one country can sell to another, and without special taxes on the goods bought from a foreign country: *a free-trade agreement*

ˌfree ˈverse noun [U] poetry whose lines do not have a regular pattern

freeware /ˈfriː.weəʳ/ (US) /ˈfriː.wer/ noun [U] computer programs that you can often copy from the internet and do not have to pay for

freeway /ˈfriː.weɪ/ noun [C] a wide road for fast-moving traffic, especially in the US, with a limited number of places at which drivers can enter and leave it: *the Santa Monica freeway* → Compare **expressway, motorway**

freewheel /ˈfriː.wiːl/ verb [I] (also **coast**) UK to travel, especially down a hill, on a bicycle or in a vehicle without using the legs or engine to provide power

freewheeling /ˈfri.wiː.lɪŋ/ adj informal not limited by rules or accepted ways of doing things: *a freewheeling lifestyle/society*

ˌfree ˈwill noun [U] the ability to decide what to do independently of any outside influence: *No one told me to do it – I did it* ***of*** *my* ***own*** *free will.*

freeze /friːz/ verb; noun

▸verb (**froze, frozen**) **COLD** ▷ **1** B1 [I or T] If you freeze something, you lower its temperature below 0°C, causing it to become cold and often hard, and if something freezes, its temperature goes below 0°C: *Water freezes to ice at a temperature of 0°C.* ◦ *The ground had frozen* ***hard/solid****.* ◦ *When the lake freezes (****over****) (= turns into ice on the surface), we can go skating on it.* ◦ *Our pipes froze (****up****) (= the water in them turned to ice) several times last winter.* ◦ *The weather forecast says that* ***it*** *is going to freeze tonight (= that the temperature will be at or below 0°C).* ◦ *Without a sleeping bag, you would freeze* ***to death*** *(= become so cold that you die) out there on the mountainside.* **2** B1 [I or T] to make food last a long time by storing it at a very low temperature so that it becomes hard: *I'll*

F

freeze any food that's left over. ◦ *Most soups freeze (= can be preserved by being stored at a very low temperature) well.* **STOP WORKING** ▷ **3** [I] (also **freeze up**) US If an engine or lock freezes, it stops working because its parts have become stuck and can no longer move: *My old bicycle was so rusty that the gears had frozen.* ◦ *If the lock has frozen up, try lubricating it with oil.* **STOP MOVING** ▷ **4** B2 [I] If a person or animal that is moving freezes, it stops suddenly and becomes completely still, especially because of fear: *She saw someone outside the window and froze.* ◦ *'Freeze (= don't move) or I'll shoot', screamed the gunman.* **MONEY/PROPERTY** ▷ **5** [T] To freeze something such as pay or prices is to fix them at a particular level and not allow any increases: *The government has frozen pensions until the end of next year.* **6** [T] to officially and legally prevent money or property from being used or moved: *When it was obvious the company was going bankrupt, the government ordered all their assets to be frozen.*

IDIOM **be cold enough to freeze the balls off a brass monkey** humorous to be very cold

PHRASAL VERB **freeze sb out** to make someone feel that they are not part of a group by being unfriendly towards them, or to stop someone from being included in an arrangement or activity: *I felt I was being frozen out* ***of/from*** *the discussions.* ◦ *He believed that organizations like theirs were being frozen out.*

▸noun **COLD WEATHER** ▷ **1** [S] a period of extremely cold weather **STOP** ▷ **2** [C] a temporary stopping of something: *The government has imposed a wage freeze/ a freeze* ***on*** *wage increases.*

ˌfreeze-ˈdry verb [T] to preserve something, especially food, by freezing and then drying it: *freeze-dried coffee*

ˈfreeze-ˌframe noun [C] a single picture from a film, or the device that allows you to stop a film at a particular point and look at a single picture

freezer /ˈfriː.zəʳ/ US /-zɚ/ noun [C] (also **ˌdeep ˈfreeze**) B1 a container, operated by electricity, which stores food at a very cold temperature so that it becomes solid and can be kept safely for a long time: *a chest/ upright freezer*

ˈfreezer comˌpartment noun [C] a small, very cold part of a fridge used for keeping food at a very cold temperature for long periods so that it stays fresh

ˈfreezer ˌpack noun [C] a plastic container filled with water or other liquid which can be frozen and then put in a container holding food and drink, in order to keep the food and drink cold

freezing /ˈfriː.zɪŋ/ adj, adv; adj; noun

▸adj, adv B1 extremely cold: ***It's freezing*** *in here – can I close the window?* ◦ *They survived for four hours in the freezing water.* ◦ *After walking through the snow, my feet were freezing.* ◦ *I had to wait for hours on the freezing* ***cold*** *station platform.*

▸adj turning to ice: *Freezing fog and icy patches are expected to cause problems for motorists tonight.*

▸noun [U] (also **ˈfreezing ˌpoint**) the temperature (0°C) at which water becomes ice: *The temperature was below freezing for most of the day.*

freight /freɪt/ noun; verb; adv

▸noun [U] **1** goods, but not passengers, that are carried from one place to another, by ship, aircraft, train, or truck, or the system of transporting these goods: *The ship* ***carries*** *both freight and passengers.* ◦ *a freight company* ◦ *Will the goods be sent by* ***air*** *or* ***sea*** *freight?* ◦ *freight* ***trains*** ◦ US *The escaped prisoner made his getaway in a freight car/wagon on a train.* **2** the money paid for transporting goods

▸verb [T] to send goods by air, sea, or train: *Grapes from this region are freighted all over the world.*

▸adv transported as part of a large group of things, by ship, aircraft, train, or truck: *It would be much cheaper to send the goods freight.*

freighter /ˈfreɪ.təʳ/ US /-t̬ɚ/ noun [C] a large ship or aircraft for carrying goods

French /frentʃ/ noun; adj

▸noun [U] **1** the language that people speak in France, Belgium, parts of Canada and other countries **2 the French** [plural] the people of France

IDIOM **excuse/pardon my French!** old-fashioned humorous said when you are pretending to be sorry for using a word that may be considered offensive: *That sod Wilkins, excuse my French, has taken my bloody parking space.*

▸adj from, belonging to, or relating to France: *French food/culture/music*

ˌFrench ˈbean noun [C] UK for **green bean**

ˌFrench Caˈnadian noun [C], adj a person from Canada whose first language is French, or of or from that part of Canada where French is spoken

ˌFrench ˈdoors noun [plural] mainly US for **French windows**

ˌFrench ˈdressing noun [U] **1** UK a mixture of oil, VINEGAR, and spices, used to flavour salad: *She tossed the lettuce in French dressing.* **2** US a mixture of oil, MAYONNAISE (= a thick, cold, white sauce), and KETCHUP (= a thick, cold, red sauce) used to flavour salad

ˌFrench ˈfries noun [plural] (also **fries**) mainly US long, thin pieces of fried potato

ˌFrench ˈhorn noun [C] a musical instrument which consists of a long metal tube bent into circles, with a wide opening at one end, played by blowing down the tube and moving the fingers on VALVES

ˌFrench ˈkiss noun [C] a kiss with the lips apart and the tongues touching

ˌFrench ˈknickers noun [plural] loose KNICKERS (= women's underwear) with wide legs

ˌFrench ˈletter noun [C] UK old-fashioned informal for **condom**

Frenchman /ˈfrentʃ.mən/ noun [C] (plural **-men** /-mən/) a man who comes from France; → See table of **Geographical names**

ˌFrench ˈpolish noun [U] UK a very shiny VARNISH used on furniture • **ˌfrench-ˈpolish verb** [T]

ˌFrench ˈstick noun [C] UK for **baguette**

ˌFrench ˈtoast noun [U] bread that has been covered in egg and fried

ˌFrench ˈwindows noun [plural] a pair of glass doors, usually opening from the back of a house into its garden

Frenchwoman /ˈfrentʃˌwʊm.ən/ noun [C] (plural **-women** /-wɪmɪn/) a woman who comes from France; → See table of **Geographical names**

frenemy /ˈfren.ə.mi/ noun [C] informal a person who pretends to be your friend but is in fact an enemy: *Her only friends are a trio of catty frenemies she hasn't seen in months.*

frenetic /frəˈnet.ɪk/ US /-net̬-/ adj involving a lot of excited movement or activity: *After weeks of frenetic* ***activity****, the job was finally finished.* ◦ *There was frenetic trading on the Stock Exchange yesterday.* • **frenetically** /-ɪ.kəl.i/ adv

frenzied /ˈfren.ziːd/ adj uncontrolled and excited, sometimes violent: *The office was a scene of frenzied*

activity *this morning.* ◦ *As the evening wore on the* ***dancing*** *got more and more frenzied.*

frenzy /ˈfren.zi/ noun [C or U] C2 (an example of) uncontrolled and excited behaviour or emotion that is sometimes violent: *In a frenzy* ***of*** *rage she hit him.* ◦ *the media frenzy over the royal wedding* ◦ *The audience* ***worked/whipped themselves up into*** *a frenzy as they waited for her to come on stage.* ◦ *There was a frenzy* ***of*** *activity on the financial markets yesterday.* ◦ *In a moment of jealous frenzy, she cut the sleeves off all his shirts.*

frequency /ˈfriː.kwən.si/ noun **HAPPENING** ▷ **1** [C or U] the number of times something happens within a particular period, or the fact of something happening often or a large number or times: *Complaints about the frequency* ***of*** *trains rose by 201 percent in the last year.* ◦ *the increasing frequency* ***of*** *terrorist attacks* ◦ *It's not the duration of his absences from work so much as the frequency that worries me.* **LIGHT/SOUND/RADIO** ▷ **2** [U] specialized the number of times that a wave, especially a light, sound, or radio wave, is produced within a particular period, especially one second: *the frequency of light* ◦ *low frequency radiation* ◦ *The human ear cannot hear very high-frequency sounds.* **3** [C] specialized a particular number of radio waves produced in a second at which a radio signal is broadcast: *Do you know what frequency the BBC World Service is* ***on****?*

frequent adj; verb

▸adj /ˈfriː.kwᵊnt/ B1 happening often; common: *a frequent visitor to the US* ◦ *A frequent criticism of the proposal has been its high cost.* ◦ *The most frequent cause of death is heart attack.* ◦ *The attacks were increasingly frequent and serious.*

▸verb [T] /frɪˈkwent/ US /ˈfriː.kwᵊnt/ formal to be in or visit a particular place often: *a bar frequented by criminals*

frequently /ˈfriː.kwᵊnt.li/ adv B1 often: *frequently asked questions* ◦ *I see him quite frequently.* ◦ *The buses run less frequently on Sundays.*

fresco /ˈfres.kəʊ/ US /-koʊ/ noun [C or U] (plural **frescoes** or **frescos**) (a picture made by) painting on wet PLASTER on a wall or ceiling

fresh /freʃ/ adj **NEW** ▷ **1** B1 [before noun] new; different or another: *The original orders were cancelled and I was given fresh instructions.* ◦ *Fresh evidence has emerged that casts doubts on the men's conviction.* ◦ *We need to take a fresh look at the problem.* ◦ *Your coffee is cold – let me make you a fresh cup.* ◦ *There has been fresh fighting between police and demonstrators.* ◦ *They decided to move abroad and* ***make a*** *fresh* ***start.*** **2** [before noun] approving new and therefore interesting or exciting: *His book offers some fresh insights into the events leading up to the war.* ◦ *We have tried to come up with a fresh new approach.* **RECENT** ▷ **3** B2 recently made, done, arrived, etc., and especially not yet changed by time: *There was a fresh fall of snow during the night.* ◦ *There's nothing better than fresh bread, straight from the oven.* ◦ *The house, with its fresh coat of paint, looked lovely in the sunshine.* ◦ *She's fresh* ***out of/from*** *university and very bright.* ◦ *The events of last year are still fresh in people's minds (= people can remember them easily).* **4 be fresh out** mainly US If you are fresh out of something, you have just finished or sold all of it, so that there is no more left. **NATURAL** ▷ **5** A2 (of food or flowers) in a natural condition rather than artificially preserved by a process such as freezing: *fresh fruit and vegetables* ◦ *fresh fish/meat* ◦ *fresh coffee* **AIR** ▷ **6** B1 (of air) clean and cool; found outside rather than in a room: *I opened the window to let some fresh air in.* ◦ *fresh mountain air* ◦ *I'm just going out for a breath of fresh air.* **7** describes weather that is cool, sometimes with wind: *It was a lovely, fresh spring morning.* ◦ *There's quite a fresh breeze today.* **CLEAN** ▷ **8** B1 clean and pleasant: *I felt wonderfully clean and fresh after my shower.* ◦ *I use a mouthwash to keep my breath fresh.* ◦ *This wine has a light, fresh taste.* **NOT TIRED** ▷ **9** C1 [after verb] energetic, enthusiastic, and not tired: *I'll deal with this problem in the morning when I'm fresh.* ◦ *Try and get some sleep on the plane, then you'll arrive feeling fresh.* **SKIN** ▷ **10** C2 (of a face) natural, healthy, and young looking: *She has a lovely fresh (= clear and smooth)* ***complexion.*** **NOT SALTY** ▷ **11** C2 [before noun] (of water) not salty: *Trout are fresh water fish (= live in water that is not salty).* ◦ *These plants are found in fresh water lakes and rivers (= those containing water that is not salty).* **TOO CONFIDENT** ▷ **12** informal being too confident and showing no respect, or showing by your actions or words that you want to have sex with someone: *Don't you* ***get*** *fresh* ***with*** *me, young woman!* ◦ *He started* ***getting*** *fresh (= behaving in a sexual way) in the cinema, so she slapped his face.* • **freshness** /ˈfreʃ.nəs/ noun [U]

IDIOM **be as fresh as a daisy** to be full of energy and enthusiasm: *After a good night's sleep I'll be as fresh as a daisy.*

fresh- /freʃ-/ prefix recently done: *fresh-baked bread* ◦ *fresh-cut flowers*

freshen /ˈfreʃ.ᵊn/ verb **AIR** ▷ **1** [T] (also **freshen up**) to make something cleaner and/or cooler: *She opened a window to freshen up the room.* **2** [I] If a wind freshens, it becomes stronger and cooler: *The wind is expected to freshen as it moves in from the east.* **DRINK** ▷ **3** [T] (also **freshen up**) mainly US If you freshen someone's especially alcoholic drink, you add more to it: *Here, let me freshen your drink.* • **freshener** /-əʳ/ US /-ɚ/ noun [C]

PHRASAL VERBS **freshen (sb/sth) up** to make someone or something clean and pleasant: *Would you like to freshen up after your journey?* ◦ *I'm just going to have a shower to freshen my****self*** *up.* • **freshen sth up** to make something different and more interesting or attractive: *The prime minister has freshened up her Cabinet with a few new faces.*

fresher /ˈfreʃ.əʳ/ US /-ɚ/ noun [C] UK informal a student who has recently started studying at a college or university

ˈ**fresh-faced** adj looking young: *fresh-faced 18 and 19-year-old soldiers*

freshly /ˈfreʃ.li/ adv recently done: *freshly baked bread* ◦ *freshly made sandwiches* ◦ *freshly washed hair*

freshman /ˈfreʃ.mən/ noun [C] (plural **-men** /-mən/) US **1** (informal **frosh**) a student in the first year of HIGH SCHOOL, college, or university: *He's a freshman at Harvard.* ◦ *Greg and Jody met in their freshman year at college and married soon after they graduated.* **2** someone who has recently started any particular job or activity: *a freshman in Congress* ◦ *a freshman football player*

freshwater /ˈfreʃˌwɔː.təʳ/ US /-ˌwɑː.t̬ɚ/ adj [before noun] living in or containing water that is not salty: *freshwater fish* ◦ *a freshwater lake/river* → Compare **salt water**

fret /fret/ verb; noun

▸verb [I] (-tt-) to be nervous or worried: *Don't fret – I'm sure he's OK.* ◦ *She spent the day fretting* ***about/over*** *what she'd said to Nicky.*

▸noun [C] any of the small raised metal bars across the long thin part of a STRINGED musical instrument such as a guitar, that show you where to put your fingers on the strings in order to produce different notes • **fretted** /ˈfret.ɪd/ (US) /ˈfret̬-/ **adj** *Guitars and lutes are fretted musical instruments.*

fretboard /ˈfret.bɔːd/ (US) /-bɔːrd/ **noun** [C] a long strip of wood on a musical instrument, such as a guitar, that has frets and against which the strings are pressed by the fingers in order to change the note that is played

fretful /ˈfret.fəl/ **adj** behaving in a way that shows you are unhappy, worried, or uncomfortable: *By midnight the children were tired and fretful (= complaining a lot because they were unhappy).* • **fretfully** /-i/ **adv**

F

fretsaw /ˈfret.sɔː/ (US) /-sɑː/ **noun** [C] a saw for cutting curves and inside corners in wood

fretwork /ˈfret.wɜːk/ (US) /-wɝːk/ **noun** [U] decorative open patterns especially cut out of wood or metal or made in EMBROIDERY

Freudian /ˈfrɔɪ.di.ən/ **adj** relating to the ideas or methods of Sigmund Freud, especially his ideas about the way in which people's hidden thoughts and feelings influence their behaviour

ˌFreudian ˈslip **noun** [C] something that you say that seems to show your true thoughts in a way that you do not intend

FRG /ef.ɑːˈdʒiː/ (US) /-ɑːr-/ abbreviation for Federal Republic of Germany

Fri. **noun** written abbreviation for Friday

friable /ˈfraɪ.ə.bl/ **adj** specialized easily broken into small pieces

friar /fraɪəʳ/ (US) /fraɪr/ **noun** [C] a man belonging to one of several Roman Catholic religious groups, whose members often promise to stay poor

friary /ˈfraɪə.ri/ (US) /ˈfraɪɚ.i/ **noun** [C] a building in which friars live

fricassee /ˈfrɪk.ə.siː/ **noun** [C or U] a dish made of pieces of meat, especially chicken or VEAL (= meat from young cows) cooked and served in a white sauce

fricative /ˈfrɪk.ə.tɪv/ (US) /-t̬ɪv/ **noun** [C] specialized a consonant sound that is made by forcing air through a narrow space: *The /s/ in 'said' and the /z/ in 'zoo' are fricatives.*

friction /ˈfrɪk.ʃən/ **noun** [U] **FORCE** ▷ **1** the force which makes it difficult for one object to slide along the surface of another or to move through a liquid or gas: *When you rub your hands together the friction produces heat.* **DISAGREEMENT** ▷ **2** disagreement or unfriendliness caused by people having different opinions: *There's a lot of friction* ***between*** *my wife and my mother.* ◦ *Politics is a source of considerable friction in our family.* ◦ *Border clashes have led to increased friction* ***between*** *the two countries.* • **frictional** /-əl/ **adj**

Friday /ˈfraɪ.deɪ/ **noun** [C or U] (written abbreviation **Fri.**) (A1) the day of the week after Thursday and before Saturday: *Shall we go to the theatre* ***on*** *Friday?* ◦ *I leave work early* ***on*** *Fridays.* ◦ *We're going to Paris for the weekend* ***next*** *Friday.* ◦ *I haven't spoken to him since* ***last*** *Friday.* ◦ *Our next meeting is on the 5th, which is a Friday.* ◦ *Friday* ***morning/afternoon/evening/night***

fridge /frɪdʒ/ **noun** [C] (also **refrigerator**, US old-fashioned **icebox**) (A2) a piece of kitchen equipment which uses electricity to preserve food at a cold temperature: *Don't forget to put the milk back in the fridge.*

ˌfridge-ˈfreezer **noun** [C] (US usually **reˌfrigerator-ˈfreezer**) a piece of kitchen equipment that includes a fridge and a FREEZER, designed to keep food fresh

ˈfridge ˌmagnet **noun** [C] a small decorative MAGNET used for fastening messages and notes to a fridge

fried /fraɪd/ **adj** (A2) cooked in hot oil or fat: *a fried egg*

friend /frend/ **noun; verb**

▸**noun** [C] **PERSON YOU LIKE** ▷ **1** (A1) a person who you know well and who you like a lot, but who is usually not a member of your family: *She's my* ***best/oldest/closest*** *friend – we've known each other since we were five.* ◦ *He's a* ***family*** *friend/friend* ***of the family.*** ◦ *This restaurant was recommended to me by a friend* ***of*** *mine.* ◦ *We've been friends for years.* ◦ *José and Pilar are* (***good***) *friends* ***of*** *ours.* ◦ *We're* (***good***) *friends* ***with*** *José and Pilar.* ◦ *She said that she and Peter were* ***just*** (***good***) *friends (= they were not having a sexual relationship).* ◦ *I've* ***made*** *a lot of friends in this job.* ◦ *He finds it difficult to* ***make*** *friends.* → See also **befriend** **2** someone who is not an enemy and who you can trust: *You don't have to pretend any more – you're among friends now.*

> **! Common mistake: friend**
>
> **Warning:** Choose the correct verb!
>
> To talk about starting a friendly relationship with someone, don't say 'meet/find/get friends', say **make friends**:
>
> ~~*If you don't speak English, it's hard to meet friends.*~~
>
> *If you don't speak English, it's hard to make friends.*

PERSON GIVING MONEY ▷ **3** someone who gives money to an arts organization or CHARITY in order to support it: *The Friends of the Royal Academy raised £10,000 towards the cost of the exhibition.*

> **Word partners for friend**
>
> *have/find/make* friends • *be/become* friends *with* sb • sb's *best/closest/oldest* friend

> **Other ways of saying friend**
>
> The words **chum** and **pal** are informal words for 'friend':
>
> *Pete was there with a couple of his* ***chums.***
>
> An **old friend** is someone you have known and liked for many years:
>
> *Rachel is one of my* ***oldest friends.***
>
> An **acquaintance** is someone you know, but do not know well:
>
> *He had a few business* ***acquaintances.***
>
> A **confidant** is a friend whom you can talk to about your feelings and secrets:
>
> *Sarah was my* ***confidant*** *throughout this period and I told her everything.*
>
> A group of friends with similar interests are sometimes described informally as a **crowd**:
>
> *'Who was there?' 'Oh, you know, Dave, Fiona, and all that* ***crowd.'***
>
> The informal word **crony** is sometimes used disapprovingly to describe one of a group of friends who help each other in an unfair way:
>
> *He always gives his* ***cronies*** *all the best jobs.*

IDIOMS **a friend in need is a friend indeed** saying This means that a friend who helps you when you really need help is a true friend. • **have friends in high places** to know important people who can help you get what you want • **what are friends for?** (also **that's what friends are for**) said to a friend who has thanked you for doing something special for them • **with friends like you, who needs enemies?** humorous saying said to or about someone who says he or she is your friend but who is treating you very badly

▸verb [T] informal to invite someone to be your friend on a SOCIAL NETWORKING website: *I friended her and sent her a message.*

Friend /frend/ noun [C] a **Quaker**

friendless /ˈfrend.ləs/ adj without friends: *Friendless and jobless, he wondered how he would survive the year.*

friendly /ˈfrend.li/ adj; noun

▸adj **1** A2 behaving in a pleasant, kind way towards someone: *a friendly face/smile ◦ Our neighbours have always been very friendly **to/towards** us. ◦ I'm on quite friendly **terms** with my daughter's teacher. ◦ Are you friendly **with** (= a friend of) Graham?* → Opposite **unfriendly 2** describes a place that is pleasant and that makes you feel happy and comfortable: *It's a friendly little restaurant.* **3** A friendly game or argument is one that you play or have for pleasure and in order to practise your skills, rather than playing or arguing seriously with the aim of winning: *We were having a friendly argument about Green politics. ◦ The teams are playing a friendly match on Sunday.* **4** Friendly countries and friendly soldiers are ones who are not your enemies and who are working or fighting with you. • **friendliness** /-nəs/ noun [U]

▸noun [C] a game that is played for enjoyment and in order to practise, not with the aim of winning points as part of a serious competition: *The rugby club has a friendly next week against the Giants.*

-friendly /-frend.li/ suffix **1** used at the end of words to mean 'not harmful': *ozone-friendly aerosols ◦ dolphin-friendly tuna (= fish caught without harming* DOLPHINS*).* **2** used at the end of words to mean 'suitable for particular people to use': *a family-friendly restaurant*

ˌfriendly ˈfire noun [U] during a war, shooting that is hitting you from your own side, not from the enemy: *Three soldiers were killed by friendly fire when a mortar bomb hit their truck.*

ˈfriendly soˌciety noun [C] in Britain, an organization to which members pay small amounts of money over a long period so that when they are ill or old they will receive money back

friendship /ˈfrend.ʃɪp/ noun [C or U] B1 a situation in which two people are friends: *Their friendship goes back to when they were at school together. ◦ Did you **form** any close/lasting friendships in college? ◦ I value her friendship above anything else.*

frier /ˈfraɪ.əʳ/ US /-ɚ/ noun [C] a **fryer**

fries /fraɪz/ noun [plural] **French fries**

Friesian /ˈfriː.ʒən/ noun [C] mainly UK (mainly US **Holstein**) a black and white cow that produces a large amount of milk

frieze /friːz/ noun [C] a narrow piece of decoration along a wall, either inside a room or on the outside of a building just under the roof

frig /frɪg/ verb (-gg-)

PHRASAL VERB **frig about/around** slang to behave stupidly: *Stop frigging about, will you!*

frigate /ˈfrɪg.ət/ noun [C] a small, fast military ship

frigging /ˈfrɪg.ɪŋ/ adj [before noun], adv offensive used to give more force to an expression of anger: *You frigging idiot!*

fright /fraɪt/ noun [S or U] **1** C1 the feeling of fear, especially if felt suddenly, or an experience of fear which happens suddenly: *I lay in bed shaking with fright. ◦ You **gave** her such a fright turning the lights out like that. ◦ You gave me **the fright of my life** (= a very severe fright), jumping out of the shadows like that!* **2 take fright** to feel fear: *Our dog took fright **at** the noise of the fireworks and ran indoors.*

IDIOM **look a fright** old-fashioned informal to look ugly or untidy: *Didn't she look a fright in that dress?*

frighten /ˈfraɪ.tən/ verb [T] B2 to make someone feel fear: *He frightens me when he drives so fast. ◦ You'll frighten the baby wearing that mask. ◦ The noise frightened me **to death/out of** my **wits** (= gave me a severe fright).*

PHRASAL VERBS **frighten sb/sth away/off 1** to make a person or animal feel fear in order to make them go away: *Be quiet or you'll frighten the deer off.* **2** to make someone so nervous that they decide not to do something: *Many potential buyers were frightened off by the £1 million price tag.* • **frighten sb into sth** to make someone so frightened that they do something they did not want to do

frightened /ˈfraɪ.tənd/ adj B1 feeling fear or worry: *She **gets** frightened when he shouts at her. ◦ The policewoman found a frightened child in the hut. ◦ Are you frightened **of** spiders? ◦ I was frightened (**that**) you would fall. ◦ Don't be frightened **to** complain if the service is bad.*

Other ways of saying frightened

Other common ways of saying 'frightened' are **afraid** and **scared.**

If someone is extremely frightened, then you can use adjectives like **petrified**, **terrified**, **panic-stricken**, or the informal phrase **scared to death**:

*I'm **terrified** of flying.*

*She was **panic-stricken** when her little boy disappeared.*

*He's **scared to death** of having the operation.*

If someone is frightened because he or she is worrying about something, then you can use the adjectives **afraid** or **worried**:

*I'm **worried** that something will go wrong.*

If someone is frightened about something that might happen in the future, you can use the adjectives **apprehensive** or **uneasy**:

*He's a bit **apprehensive** about living away from home.*

To talk about things that make you feel uncomfortable and scared, you could use the phrase **give** *me* **the creeps**:

*Being alone in that big house **gives me the creeps**.*

To talk about something that is frightening in a shocking way, you could use the adjective **hair-raising**:

*The pilots are trained to do **hair-raising** stunts at low altitude.*

frighteners /ˈfraɪ.tən.əz/ US /-ɚz/ noun [plural] UK old-fashioned **put the frighteners on sb** to threaten someone: *He said he wouldn't pay up so I sent my brother round to put the frighteners on him.*

frightening /ˈfraɪ.tən.ɪŋ/ adj B1 making you feel fear: *a frightening thought ◦ a frightening film ◦ **It** is frightening **to** think what might happen if she left him.* • **frighteningly** /-li/ adv *She looked frighteningly thin.*

frightful /ˈfraɪt.fəl/ adj old-fashioned informal used to emphasize what you are saying, especially how bad something is: *He made a frightful mess in the kitchen. ◦ Of course the cleaning is a frightful bore.*

frightfully /ˈfraɪt.fəl.i/ adv old-fashioned informal very: *I'm frightfully sorry about the noise last night.*

frigid /ˈfrɪdʒ.ɪd/ adj **DISLIKING SEX** ▷ **1** (of a woman) having difficulty in becoming sexually excited **UNFRIENDLY** ▷ **2** unfriendly or very formal: *There's a rather frigid atmosphere in the school.* **COLD** ▷ **3** (of weather conditions or the conditions in a room) extremely cold: *Few plants can grow in such a frigid environment.* • **frigidity** /frɪˈdʒɪd.ɪ.ti/ (US) /-t̬i/ noun [U] • **frigidly** /-li/ adv *Sarah shook his hand frigidly.*

ˈfrigid ˌzone noun specialized one of the two cold areas inside the ARCTIC and ANTARCTIC Circles, which receive very little light from the sun

F

frill /frɪl/ noun **1** [C] a long, narrow strip of cloth with folds along one side that is sewn along the edge of a piece of clothing or material for decoration: *You could always sew a frill or two around the bottom of the skirt if you think it's too plain.* **2 frills** [plural] informal extra things that are added to something to make it more pleasant or more attractive, but that are not necessary: *a cheap, no frills airline*

frilly /ˈfrɪl.i/ adj (also **frilled**) with a lot of frills: *a baby in a white frilly dress*

fringe /frɪndʒ/ noun; verb

▸noun [C] **EDGE** ▷ **1** (C2) the outer or less important part of an area, group, or activity: *the southern fringe of the city* ◦ *the radical fringes of the party* ◦ *He attended several of the fringe* ***meetings*** *at the conference.* **DECORATION** ▷ **2** a decorative edge of hanging narrow strips of material or threads on a piece of clothing or material: *a fringe around the edge of a tablecloth* **HAIR** ▷ **3** (C2) UK (US **bangs**) an area of hair hanging over the FOREHEAD (= part of the face above the eyes) that is cut shorter than the rest of the hair: *a short fringe*

▸verb **be fringed with sth** If a place is fringed with something, that thing forms a border along the edge: *The river is fringed with wild flowers.*

ˈfringe ˌbenefit noun [C usually plural] something that you get for working, in addition to your pay, that is not in the form of money: *Fringe benefits include a company car and free health insurance.*

fringed /frɪndʒd/ adj with a fringe: *a fringed denim skirt* ◦ *a robe fringed with fur*

frippery /ˈfrɪp.ər.i/ (US) /ˈ-ɚ-/ noun [C or U] disapproving a silly decoration or other unnecessary object: *fashion fripperies*

Frisbee /ˈfrɪz.bi/ noun [C] trademark a circular piece of plastic with a curved edge that is thrown between people as a game

frisée /ˈfriː.zeɪ/ noun [U] a plant that has green leaves with curly edges, eaten uncooked in salads

frisk /frɪsk/ verb **1** [T] to use your hands to search someone's body when they are wearing clothes to see if they are hiding illegal objects or weapons: *We were all frisked at the airport.* **2** [I] to move around in a happy, energetic way: *a postcard with a picture of lambs frisking in the fields*

frisky /ˈfrɪs.ki/ adj informal (of a person or an animal) liking to play or full of activity: *It's a beautiful horse but a bit too frisky for an inexperienced rider.* • **friskily** /-kɪ.li/ adv • **friskiness** /-nəs/ noun [U]

frisson /ˈfriː.sɒ/ (US) /-ˈsoʊn/ noun [C usually singular] a sudden feeling of excitement or fear, especially when you think that something is about to happen: *As the music stopped, a frisson* ***of*** *excitement ran through the crowd.*

frittata /frɪˈtɑː.tə/ (US) /-ˈtæ.t̬ə/ noun [C or U] an Italian dish made by mixing eggs and frying them with small pieces of other food such as cheese, potatoes, or vegetables

fritter /ˈfrɪt.əʳ/ (US) /ˈfrɪt̬.ɚ/ noun; verb

▸noun [C] a slice of fruit, vegetable, or meat covered with BATTER (= a mixture of flour, egg, and milk) and then fried: *banana/apple fritters*

▸verb

PHRASAL VERB **fritter sth away** disapproving to waste money, time, or an opportunity: *She fritters so much money away* ***on*** *expensive make-up.*

fritz /frɪts/ noun [S] **on the fritz** US informal broken or not working: *The fridge is on the fritz.*

frivolity /frɪˈvɒl.ə.ti/ (US) /-ˈvɑː.lə.t̬i/ noun [C or U] behaviour that is silly and not serious, or things that are silly and not important: *You shouldn't treat such a serious subject with frivolity.* ◦ *I'm far too busy to waste time on frivolities like going to the cinema.*

frivolous /ˈfrɪv.əl.əs/ adj **1** behaving in a silly way and not taking anything seriously: *I think he sees her as a frivolous young woman.* **2** describes an activity or object that is silly or not important rather than useful or serious: *I feel like doing something completely frivolous today.* • **frivolously** /-li/ adv • **frivolousness** /-nəs/ noun [U]

frizz /frɪz/ noun; verb

▸noun [U] the quality of hair being frizzy: *This mousse says it's designed to eliminate frizz and make hair glossy and easier to manage.*

▸verb [T] informal to make hair frizzy: *She's just had her hair frizzed, and I didn't recognize her at first.*

frizzled /ˈfrɪz.əld/ adj (of food) fried for too long, making it burnt and unpleasant to eat: *frizzled bacon*

frizzy /ˈfrɪz.i/ adj disapproving (of hair) very curly and not smooth or shiny: *My hair goes all frizzy if it gets rained on.*

fro /frəʊ/ (US) /froʊ/ adv → See **to and fro**

frock /frɒk/ (US) /frɑːk/ noun [C] old-fashioned a dress: *a little girl in a pretty frock*

ˈfrock ˌcoat noun [C] a coat that reaches the knees, worn by men, especially in the past

frog /frɒg/ (US) /frɑːg/ noun [C] (B1) a small animal that has smooth skin, lives in water and on land, has long powerful back legs with which it jumps from place to place, has no tail, and is usually greenish-brown in colour: *Frogs make a low noise called a croak.* → See also **bullfrog**

IDIOM **have a frog in your throat** to have difficulty in speaking because your throat feels dry and you want to cough

Frog /frɒg/ (US) /frɑːg/ noun [C] UK offensive a French person

frogman /ˈfrɒg.mən/ (US) /ˈfrɑːg-/ noun [C] (plural **-men** /-mən/) someone who swims or works underwater for a long time wearing breathing equipment, FLIPPERS (= rubber or plastic shoes that are longer than the feet), and usually a rubber suit: *police frogmen*

frogmarch /ˈfrɒg.mɑːtʃ/ (US) /ˈfrɑːg.mɑːrtʃ/ verb [T usually + adv/prep] to force someone who is unwilling to move forward by holding the person's arms behind their back and then pushing them forward: *He was frogmarched* ***off*** *by two police officers.*

frogspawn /ˈfrɒg.spɔːn/ (US) /ˈfrɑːg.spɑːn/ noun [U] a close group of frog's eggs, each egg being a small almost transparent ball with a black grain near its centre

frolic /ˈfrɒl.ɪk/ (US) /ˈfrɑː.lɪk/ verb; noun

▸verb [I] (present tense **frolicking**, past tense and past participle **frolicked**) to play and behave in a happy way: *A group of suntanned children were frolicking on the beach.*

▸**noun** [C or U] old-fashioned happy behaviour, like that of children playing: *a harmless frolic* ◦ *It was all* ***fun and*** *frolics until it began to pour down with rain.*

frolicsome /ˈfrɒl.ɪk.səm/ (US) /ˈfrɑː.lɪk-/ **adj** literary enthusiastic and liking to play

from strong /frɒm/ (US) /frɑːm/ weak /frəm/ **preposition** **PLACE** ▷ **1** (A1) used to show the place where someone or something starts: *What time does the flight from Amsterdam arrive?* ◦ *The wind is coming from the north.* ◦ *She sent me a postcard from Majorca.* ◦ *He took a handkerchief from his pocket.* ◦ *She took her hairbrush from her handbag and began to brush her hair.* ◦ *So did you really walk all the way from Bond Street?* **TIME** ▷ **2** (A1) used to show the time when something starts or the time when it was made or first existed: *Drinks will be served from seven o'clock.* ◦ *The price of petrol will rise by 5p a gallon from tomorrow.* ◦ *Most of the tapestries in this room date from the 17th century.* ◦ *The museum is open from 9.30* ***to*** *6.00 Tuesday to Sunday.* **3 from that day/time on(wards)** (C1) literary starting at that time and then continuing: *From that day on, she vowed never to trust him again.* **DISTANCE** ▷ **4** (A1) used to show the distance between two places: *It's about two kilometres from the airport* ***to*** *your hotel.* ◦ *We're about a mile from home.* **ORIGIN** ▷ **5** (A1) used to show the origin of something or someone: *'Where are you from?' 'I'm from Italy.'* ◦ *I wonder who this card is from.* ◦ *Could I speak to someone from the sales department?* ◦ *The sales executive from Unilever is here to see you.* ◦ *What sort of reaction did you get from him?* **MATERIAL** ▷ **6** (A2) used to show the material of which something is made: *The desk is made from pine.* ◦ *Meringues are made from sugar and egg whites.* **LEVEL** ▷ **7** used to show the level at which a range of things begins, such as numbers or prices: *Prices start from £2.99.* ◦ *Tickets will cost from $10* ***to*** *$45.* ◦ *The number of people employed by the company has risen from 25* ***to*** *200 in three years.* **CHANGE** ▷ **8** (B2) used to show a change in the state of someone or something: *Things went from bad* ***to*** *worse.* ◦ *She has been promoted from deputy manager* ***to*** *senior manager.* ◦ *Since the success of her first play, she has gone from strength* ***to*** *strength (= her success has continued to increase).* **CAUSE** ▷ **9** (B2) used to show the cause of something or the reason why something happens: *He was rushed to hospital but died from his injuries.* ◦ *She made her money from investing in property.* ◦ *You could tell she wasn't lying from the fear in her voice.* ◦ *Wearing the correct type of clothing will reduce the risk from radiation.* **CONSIDERING** ▷ **10** used to show the facts or opinions you consider before making a judgment or decision: *Just from looking at the clouds, I would say it's going to rain.* ◦ *It's difficult to guess what they will conclude from the evidence.* **REMOVE** ▷ **11** used to show that someone has left a place, or that something has been removed or taken away: *They were exiled from their homes during the war.* ◦ *Her handbag was snatched from her in the street.* ◦ *A refining process is used to extract usable fuel from crude oil.* **12** If you take a smaller amount from a larger amount, you reduce the larger amount by the smaller one: *3 from 16 is 13.* **DIFFERENCE** ▷ **13** (B1) used to show a difference between two people or things: *His opinion could hardly be more different from mine.* ◦ *The two sisters are so similar that it's almost impossible to tell one from the other.* **POSITION** ▷ **14** (B2) used to show the position of something in comparison with other things, or the point of view of someone when considering a matter or problem: *From the restaurant there is a beautiful view of Siena.* ◦ *She was talking from her own experience of the problem.* ◦ *From our point of view, we do not see how these changes will be beneficial to the company.* **PROTECTION** ▷ **15** used to show what someone is being protected against: *They found shelter from the storm under a large oak tree.* **PREVENTING** ▷ **16** (B2) used to show what someone is not allowed to do or know, or what has been stopped happening: *He's been banned from driving for six months.* ◦ *For many years, the truth was kept from the public.* ◦ *The bank loan saved her company from bankruptcy.*

fromage frais /ˌfrɒm.ɑːʒˈfreɪ/ (US) /frəˌmɑːʒ-/ **noun** [C or U] a type of soft cheese that is often produced with fruit flavours and sugar added

frond /frɒnd/ (US) /frɑːnd/ **noun** [C] specialized a long thin leaf of a plant: *Ferns and palms have fronds.*

front /frʌnt/ **noun; adj; verb**

▸**noun** [C usually singular] **PLACE** ▷ **1** (A2) the part of a building, object, or person's body that faces forward or is most often seen or used: *The front of the museum is very impressive.* ◦ *He spilled soup all down his front.* ◦ *He was lying on his front.* ◦ *The* ***shop*** *front occupies a very prominent position on the main street.* **2** (A2) the part of a vehicle that is nearest to its direction of movement: *Do you want to sit* ***in the*** *front (= next to the driver)?* ◦ *If we sit near the front of the bus, we'll have a better view.* **3** the outside part or cover of a book, newspaper, or magazine: *There was a picture of the Trevi fountain* ***on*** *the front of the book.* **4** one of the first pages in a book: *There's an inscription* ***in*** *the front of the book.* **5 in front a** (B1) further forward than someone or something else: *The car in front suddenly stopped and I went into the back of it.* ◦ *She started talking to the man in front* ***of*** *her.* **b** winning a game or competition: *By half time the Italians were well in front.* **6 in front of a** (A2) close to the front part of something: *There's parking space in front of the hotel.* **b** (A2) where someone can see or hear you: *Please don't swear in front of the children.* **7 up front** If you give someone an amount of money up front, you pay them before they do something for you: *He wants all the money up front or he won't do the job.* **AREA OF ACTIVITY** ▷ **8** a particular area of activity: *How are things on the work front? (= Is the situation at work satisfactory?)* ◦ *She's very creative on the design front (= she is very good at design).* **APPEARANCE** ▷ **9** [C usually singular] the character or qualities that a person or organization appears to have in public that are different from their real character or qualities, and whose purpose is often to deceive people or hide an illegal activity: *Don't be fooled by his kindness and sensitivity – it's just a front.* ◦ *She presents such a cheerful front that you'd never guess she's ill.* ◦ *The machinery company was a front operation for arms smuggling.* ◦ *Several trading companies were set up in the early 1960s to act as fronts* ***for*** *money-laundering operations.* **LAND** ▷ **10** [C usually singular] land near the sea or a lake, or the part of a town near the beach that often has a wide road or path along it: *Let's go for a stroll along the front.* **WEATHER** ▷ **11** [C] specialized the place where two masses of air that have different temperatures meet: *A* ***cold/warm*** *front is approaching from the west.*

▸**adj** [before noun] (B1) in or at the front of something: *One of his front teeth is missing.* ◦ *I'd like seats on the front row of the stalls.* ◦ *a dog's front paws*

▸**verb 1** [I or T] (also **front onto**) If a building or area fronts (onto) a particular place, it is near it and faces it: *All the apartments front onto the sea.* **2** [T] to lead an

F

organization or group of musicians: *She fronts a large IT company.* **3 be fronted with** If a building is fronted with something, its surface is covered with it: *a brick house fronted on three sides with timber*

PHRASAL VERB **front for sth** If a person fronts for an illegal organization, they help that organization by using their good reputation to hide its secret activities: *The police suspect him of fronting for a crime syndicate.*

Front /frʌnt/ **noun** [C usually singular] a group of people sharing a political belief who perform actions in public to achieve their aims: *The National Front is an extremely right-wing political party in Britain.* ◦ *The Animal Liberation Front has claimed responsibility for releasing the monkeys from the laboratory.*

frontage /ˈfrʌn.tɪdʒ/ US /-t̬ɪdʒ/ **noun** [C] formal the front part of a building which faces a road or river, or land near a road or river: *These apartments all have a delightful dockside frontage.*

frontal /ˈfrʌn.təl/ US /-t̬əl/ **adj** [before noun] formal or specialized **1** relating to the front of something: *the frontal lobes/regions of the brain* → See also **full-frontal** **2 frontal assault/attack** very strong criticism of someone or something: *a frontal attack **on** the politician*

ˈ**frontal ˌsystem** **noun** [C] specialized a combination of weather conditions in which one or more weather fronts can be recognized: *With so many frontal systems so close together, we can expect the weather to be highly changeable over the next few days.*

ˌ**front ˈbench** **noun** [C] one of the two rows of seats in the UK parliament used by leading members of the government and leading members of the main OPPOSITION party (= the party not in government), or the people who sit in these seats: *The prime minister's reply was met with howls of laughter from the opposition front bench.* ◦ *a former front-bench Treasury spokeswoman* → Compare **backbench**

frontbencher /ˌfrʌntˈben.tʃər/ US /-tʃɚ/ **noun** [C] a politician who sits on the front benches of the UK parliament: *He is the government's longest serving frontbencher.* → Compare **backbencher**

ˌ**front ˈdoor** **noun** [C] the main entrance to a building, especially a house, which usually faces the road

frontier /ˈfrʌn.tɪər/, /frʌnˈtɪər/ US /-ˈtɪr/ **noun** [C] C2 a border between two countries, or (especially in the past in the US) a border between land used to grow crops where people live and wild land: *Some of the frontier **between** Germany and Poland follows the course of the river Oder* ◦ *Nepal has frontiers **with** both India and China.* ◦ *They lived in a town close to **the** frontier.*

IDIOM **the frontiers of sth** C2 the limits of what is known or what has been done before in an area of knowledge or an activity: *the frontiers of science and technology*

frontiersman /frʌnˈtɪəz.mən/ US /-ˈtɪrz-/ **noun** [C] (plural **-men** /-mən/) a person who lives on the border between CULTIVATED land (= land used to grow crops) and wild land, especially in the past in the US: *The book portrays him as a heroic frontiersman of the Wild West.*

frontispiece /ˈfrʌn.tɪ.spiːs/ US /-t̬ɪ-/ **noun** [C] the picture which faces the page of a book with the title on: *A photograph of the author forms the frontispiece to the book.*

the ˌfront ˈline **noun** [S] a place where opposing armies face each other in war and where fighting happens: *Tens of thousands of soldiers died **at the** front line.*

IDIOM **be in the front line** to be in an important position where you have influence, but where you are likely to be criticized or attacked: *Many social workers are in the front line of racial tension.*

frontman /ˈfrʌnt.mæn/ **noun** [C] (plural **-men** /men/) **1** the lead singer or leader of a musical group: *Franz Ferdinand frontman Alex Kapranos* **2** someone who appears to be in charge of or representing an organization or group, but who may not have real authority **3** UK someone who presents a television programme

ˌ**front-of-ˈhouse** **noun** [U] specialized the area in a theatre that is used by the public

ˌ**front-ˈpage** **adj** [before noun] describes information that is so important that it deserves to be printed on the front page of a newspaper: *The story made front-page news.*

ˌ**front ˈroom** **noun** [C] mainly UK old-fashioned a LIVING ROOM (= room in a house used for relaxing, but not for eating in) that faces the road

ˌ**front-ˈrunner** **noun** [C] the person, animal, or organization that is most likely to win something: *She is one of the front-runners in the contest.*

ˌ**front-wheel ˈdrive** **noun** [C] a vehicle in which the power from the engine is put directly to the front wheels rather than the back wheels

frosh /frɒʃ/ US /frɑːʃ/ **noun** [C] US informal for **freshman** (= a first-year student in high school, college, or university)

frost /frɒst/ US /frɑːst/ **noun; verb**

▸**noun** [C or U] B2 (a period of time in which there is) an air temperature below the freezing point of water, or the thin, white layer of ice which forms in these conditions, especially outside at night: *There was a frost last night.* ◦ *When I woke up this morning the ground was covered with frost.* ◦ *There were a lot of **hard/heavy** (= severe) frosts that winter.*

▸**verb** **COLD** ▷ **1** [I or T] to become covered in frost: *Our bedroom window frosted **up**.* ◦ *Our lawn is frosted **over**.* **CAKE** ▷ **2** [T] US (UK **ice**) to cover a cake with FROSTING: *Leave the cake to cool before frosting it.* **HAIR** ▷ **3** [T] US to make narrow strips of a person's hair a more pale colour than the surrounding hair **GLASS** ▷ **4** [T] to intentionally make glass less smooth to stop it being transparent

frostbite /ˈfrɒst.baɪt/ US /ˈfrɑːst-/ **noun** [U] injury to someone caused by severe cold, usually to their toes, fingers, ears, or nose • **frostbitten** /-ˌbɪt.ən/ US /-ˌbɪt̬.ən/ **adj** *frostbitten fingers/toes*

frosted /ˈfrɒs.tɪd/ US /ˈfrɑː.stɪd/ **adj** Frosted glass is less smooth to stop it being transparent: *We had frosted glass put in the bathroom window.*

frostily /ˈfrɒs.tɪ.li/ US /ˈfrɑː.stə-/ **adv** in an unfriendly way: *'I didn't ask you to come,' she said frostily.*

frosting /ˈfrɒs.tɪŋ/ US /ˈfrɑː.stɪŋ/ **noun** [U] US (UK **icing**) a sweet food used to cover or fill cakes, made from sugar and water or sugar and butter

frosty /ˈfrɒs.ti/ US /ˈfrɑː.sti/ **adj** **1** very cold, with a thin layer of white ice covering everything: *Be careful – the pavements are very frosty.* ◦ *It was a cold and frosty morning.* **2** If someone or their behaviour is frosty, they are unfriendly and not welcoming: *He gave me a frosty look.* ◦ *The chairperson's plan received a frosty **reception** from the committee.* • **frostiness** /-nəs/ **noun** [U]

froth /frɒθ/ (US) /frɑːθ/ noun; verb
▸noun [U] **BUBBLES** ▷ **1** small, white bubbles on the surface of a liquid: *I like the froth on the top of the coffee.* **NOT SERIOUS** ▷ **2** something that is not serious and has no real value, but is entertaining or attractive: *His books are just froth, but they're enjoyable enough.*
▸verb [I or T] **1** to (cause a liquid to) have or produce a lot of small bubbles which often rise to the surface: *The waves frothed as they crashed onto the beach.* ◦ *Shake the drink before serving it to froth it* ***up.*** **2 froth at the mouth a** If a person or animal froths at the mouth, a mass of small bubbles appears from their mouth as the result of a disease. **b** informal to be extremely angry

frothy /ˈfrɒθ.i/ (US) /ˈfrɑː.θi/ adj (of a liquid) with small white bubbles on the surface: *Beat the mixture until it becomes frothy.* ◦ *frothy coffee*

frou-frou /ˈfruː.fruː/ noun [U] decorative pieces added to women's clothing: *a frou-frou gown/skirt*

frown /fraʊn/ verb [I] (C2) to bring your EYEBROWS together so that there are lines on your face above your eyes to show that you are annoyed or worried: *She frowned* ***at*** *me, clearly annoyed.* ◦ *He frowned as he read the instructions, as if puzzled.* • **frown** noun [C] (C2) *'Leave me alone!' she said with a frown.*

PHRASAL VERB **frown on/upon sth** [often passive] (C2) to disapprove of something: *Smoking is frowned upon in many societies.*

frowsty /ˈfraʊ.sti/ adj mainly UK informal disapproving (of a room) having an unpleasant smell because of having no fresh air

froze /frəʊz/ (US) /froʊz/ past simple of **freeze**

frozen /ˈfrəʊ.zᵊn/ (US) /ˈfroʊ-/ verb; adj
▸verb past participle of **freeze**
▸adj **1** (B1) (of water) turned into ice, or (of food) preserved by freezing: *They skated over the frozen lake.* ◦ *We don't have any fresh vegetables, only frozen peas.* **2** (B1) If a person, or a part of their body is frozen, they are very cold: *I'm frozen – could you close the window?* ◦ *After walking through the snow, my feet were frozen* ***stiff.***

fructose /ˈfrʊk.təʊs/ (US) /-toʊs/ noun [U] a type of sugar found in HONEY and many fruits

frugal /ˈfruː.gᵊl/ adj careful when using money or food, or (of a meal) cheap or small in amount: *a frugal lifestyle* ◦ *a frugal meal of bread and soup* • **frugality** /fruːˈgæl.ə.ti/ (US) /-t̬i/ noun [U] • **frugally** /-i/ adv *We had very little money, so we ate frugally in cheap cafés.*

fruit /fruːt/ noun; verb
▸noun **PLANT PART** ▷ **1** (A1) [C or U] the soft part containing seeds that is produced by a plant. Many types of fruit are sweet and can be eaten: *Apricots are the one fruit I don't like.* ◦ *Oranges, apples, pears, and bananas are all types of fruit.* ◦ *Would you like some fruit for dessert?* ◦ *The cherry tree in our garden is* ***in*** *fruit (= it has fruit growing on it).* ◦ *I like* ***exotic*** *fruit, like mangoes and papayas.* ◦ *How many pieces of* ***fresh*** *fruit do you eat in a day?* ◦ *fruit trees* ◦ *He runs a fruit* ***and vegetable*** *stall in the market.* → Compare **vegetable 2** [C] specialized the part of any plant that holds the seeds **RESULT** ▷ **3 the fruit/fruits of sth** (C2) the pleasant or successful result of work or actions: *This book is the fruit of 15 years' research.* ◦ *It's been hard work, but now the business is running smoothly you can sit back and enjoy the fruits* ***of your labours.*** **PERSON** ▷ **4** [C] slang a gay man. Many people consider this word offensive.

IDIOM **fruits of the earth** literary types of food that have come from plants, such as vegetables or grain
▸verb [I] specialized When a plant fruits, it produces fruit: *Over the last few years, our apple trees have been fruiting much earlier than usual.*

ˈfruit ˌbat noun [C] (also **flying ˈfox**) a large flying mammal that eats fruit and lives in warm or hot countries

fruitcake /ˈfruːt.keɪk/ noun **CAKE** ▷ **1** [C or U] a cake containing a lot of dried fruit, such as RAISINS **PERSON** ▷ **2** [C] UK slang a crazy person: *My teacher's a bit of a fruitcake.*

fruiterer /ˈfruː.tᵊr.əʳ/ (US) /-t̬ɚ.ɚ/ noun [C] mainly UK old-fashioned a person who sells fruit in a shop or market

ˈfruit ˌfly noun [C] a small flying insect which feeds on plants and leaves its eggs on the leaves of plants

fruitful /ˈfruːt.fᵊl/ adj **1** (C1) formal producing good results: *It was a most fruitful discussion, with both sides agreeing to adopt a common policy.* → Opposite **fruitless 2** old use If a person is fruitful, they produce a lot of children. • **fruitfully** /-i/ adv

fruitfulness /ˈfruːt.fᵊl.nəs/ noun [U] **GOOD RESULT** ▷ **1** the fact that something produces good results **PLANT** ▷ **2** literary the fact that plants produce a lot of fruit: *She loved the beauty and fruitfulness of the autumn, when the whole countryside was ablaze with rich golden colours.*

fruition /fruːˈɪʃ.ᵊn/ noun [U] formal an occasion when a plan or an idea begins to happen, exist, or be successful: *None of his grand plans for a TV series ever* ***came to*** *fruition.*

fruitless /ˈfruːt.ləs/ adj If an action or attempt to do something is fruitless, it is unsuccessful or produces nothing of value: *All diplomatic attempts at a peaceful solution to the crisis have been fruitless.* → Opposite **fruitful** • **fruitlessly** /-li/ adv • **fruitlessness** /-nəs/ noun [U]

ˈfruit maˌchine noun [C] UK a **slot machine**

ˌfruit ˈsalad noun [C or U] a mixture of pieces of different types of fruit that is usually served at the end of a meal

fruity /ˈfruː.ti/ (US) /-t̬i/ adj **SMELL/TASTE** ▷ **1** smelling or tasting of fruit: *This wine has a delicious fruity flavour.* **REMARK** ▷ **2** (of a remark) humorous in a slightly shocking way: *He was well known for his fruity jokes.* **VOICE** ▷ **3** informal approving (of a voice) deep and pleasant • **fruitiness** /-nəs/ noun [U] *a lively wine with a refreshing, lemon fruitiness*

frump /frʌmp/ noun [C] disapproving a woman who wears old-fashioned clothes which do not look attractive: *She looked a frump in her shapeless skirt and flat shoes.*

frumpy /ˈfrʌm.pi/ adj (also **frumpish**) (of a person or their clothes) old-fashioned and not attractive: *I felt fat and frumpy.* ◦ *a frumpy cardigan*

frustrate /frʌsˈtreɪt/ verb [T] **DISCOURAGE** ▷ **1** to make someone feel annoyed or less confident because they cannot achieve what they want: *It frustrates me that I'm not able to put any of my ideas into practice.* **PREVENT** ▷ **2** to prevent the plans or efforts of someone or something from being achieved: *The continuing civil war is frustrating the efforts of relief agencies.*

frustrated /frʌsˈtreɪ.tɪd/ (US) /-t̬ɪd/ adj **1** (C1) feeling annoyed or less confident because you cannot achieve what you want: *Are you feeling frustrated in your present job?* **2** [before noun] describes a person who has not succeeded in a particular type of job:

Frustrated writers often end up in publishing. **3** [before noun] A frustrated emotion is one that you are not able to express: *her frustrated love for him* **4** [before noun] unhappy because you are not having as much sex as you want

frustrating /frʌsˈtreɪ.tɪŋ/ (US) /-t̬ɪŋ/ adj **C1** making you feel annoyed or less confident because you cannot achieve what you want: *He doesn't listen to what I say and it's so frustrating.*

frustration /frʌsˈtreɪ.ʃən/ noun **FEELING** ▷ **1** **B2** [C or U] the feeling of being annoyed or less confident because you cannot achieve what you want; something that makes you feel like this: *I could sense his frustration* ***at*** *not being able to help.* ◦ *This job has more than its fair share of frustrations.* **PREVENTING** ▷ **2** [U] the fact that something prevents plans or efforts from being successful

F

fry /fraɪ/ verb; noun
▸verb [I or T] **B1** to cook food in hot oil or fat: *Fry the mushrooms in a little butter.* ◦ informal figurative *You'll fry (= burn) if you lie in the sun all day.*
▸noun [plural] young, small fish

fryer (also **frier**) /ˈfraɪ.əʳ/ (US) /-ɚ/ noun [C] **1** a large deep pan in which food is fried: *I've just bought a* ***deep-fat*** *fryer for cooking chips.* **2** US a chicken suitable for frying

ˈfrying ˌpan noun [C] (US also **skillet**) **B1** a flat metal pan with a long handle, used for frying food

frying pan

IDIOM **out of the frying pan into the fire** saying said when you move from a bad or difficult situation to one that is worse

ˈfry-up noun [C] UK informal a meal consisting of fried meat, eggs, and vegetables

ft noun [C] (plural **ft**) written abbreviation for **foot**: *The main bedroom measures 24 ft by 18 ft (24' x 18').*

the FTSE 100 /ˌfʊt.si.wʌnˌhʌn.drəd/ noun [S] (informal **the Footsie**) trademark a number that expresses the value of the SHARE prices of the 100 most important British companies, published by the Financial Times: *The FTSE 100 closed 31.6 points down at 2459.3 in today's trading.* → Compare **Dow Jones, the Nikkei (index)**

fuchsia /ˈfjuː.ʃə/ noun; adj
▸noun **1** [C] a small plant, often grown in gardens, which has red, purple, or white flowers that hang down **2** [U] a colour between pink and purple
▸adj having a colour between pink and purple

fuck /fʌk/ verb; exclamation; noun
▸verb [I or T] offensive to have sex with someone

PHRASAL VERBS **fuck about/around** to behave stupidly, or to waste time doing things that are not important: *Stop fucking around!* • **fuck sb about** to treat someone badly by wasting their time or causing them problems: *I'm warning you, don't fuck me about!* • **fuck off** to leave or go away, used especially as a rude way of telling someone to go away: *Just fuck off and leave me alone!* ◦ *He's fucked off somewhere and left me to do all the work.* • **fuck sb off** to annoy or upset someone very much: *You speak to me as if I'm stupid and it really fucks me off.* • **fuck (sth) up** to damage, harm, or upset someone or something, or to do something very badly: *Her parents' divorce really fucked her up.* ◦ *I fucked up the interview.* ◦ *The exam was a disaster – I really fucked up.*

▸exclamation offensive used when expressing extreme anger, or to add force to what is being said: *Fuck – the bloody car won't start!* ◦ *Shut* ***the*** *fuck up!* ◦ *Who the fuck does she think she is, telling me what to do?*
▸noun [C] offensive **1** an act of having sex **2** a sexual partner

fuck ˈall noun; determiner
▸noun [U] offensive nothing: *Don't blame me, mate – I had fuck all to do with it!* ◦ *I've had fuck all to eat all day.*
▸determiner offensive no; not any: *Now that the wheel's broken, it's fuck all use to anyone.*

fucker /ˈfʌk.əʳ/ (US) /-ɚ/ noun [C] offensive a stupid person: *You stupid fucker!*

fucking /ˈfʌk.ɪŋ/ adj, adv offensive used to emphasize a statement, especially an angry one: *What a fucking waste of time!* ◦ *He's a fucking idiot.* ◦ *He'd fucking well better do it.*

ˈfuck-up noun [C] offensive a serious problem: *It's been one fuck-up after another since she took charge.*

fuckwit /ˈfʌk.wɪt/ noun [C] offensive a stupid person: *Some fuckwit walked off with my bag.*

fuddle /ˈfʌd.l̩/ verb; noun
▸verb [T] informal to confuse someone and make them unable to think clearly: *The heat had fuddled my brain.*
▸noun [C usually singular] informal a confused state: *Sometimes he gets in a fuddle and then he can't find things.*

fuddy-duddy /ˈfʌd.iˌdʌd.i/ noun [C] disapproving a person who has old-fashioned ideas and opinions: *They think I'm an old fuddy-duddy because I don't approve of tattoos.*

fudge /fʌdʒ/ noun; verb
▸noun **SWEET** ▷ **1** [U] a soft sweet made from sugar, butter, and milk **AVOID** ▷ **2** [C usually singular] a plan or action which avoids making a clear decision or giving a clear answer: *It's a bit of a fudge but we could put the cost through on next year's budget.*
▸verb [T] to avoid making a decision or giving a clear answer about something: *The government continues to fudge* ***the issue*** *by refusing to give exact figures.*

fuel /fjʊəl/ noun; verb
▸noun **1** **B1** [C or U] a substance that is used to provide heat or power, usually by being burned: *Wood, coal, oil, petrol and gas are all different kinds of fuel.* ◦ *Plutonium is a fuel used to produce nuclear energy.* ◦ ***nuclear*** *fuel* ◦ ***unleaded*** *fuel* ◦ *The new exhaust system, it is claimed, will lower fuel* ***consumption***. **2** [U] anything that keeps people's ideas or feelings active, or makes them stronger: *Reports in today's newspapers have* ***added*** *fuel* ***to*** *the controversy (= made it worse).*

IDIOM **add fuel to the fire/flames** to make an argument or bad situation worse: *The discovery that the government was aware of the cover-up has really added fuel to the fire.*

▸verb [T] (**-ll-** or US usually **-l-**) **1** to supply a system with a substance that can be burned to provide heat or power: *Our heating system is fuelled* ***by*** *gas.* ◦ *We have a gas-fuelled heating system.* ◦ *petrol/hydrogen-fuelled cars* **2** Something that fuels a feeling or a type of behaviour increases it or makes it stronger: *The rapid promotion of the director's son has itself fuelled resentment within the company.* ◦ *The prime minister's speech fuelled* ***speculation*** *that she is about to resign.*

ˈfuel ˌcell noun [C] a device that changes the chemical energy from a fuel into electricity: *Car manufacturers are looking at alternative sources of energy such as hydrogen fuel cells.*

ˌfuel-efˈficient adj working in a way that does not

waste fuel: *They are replacing their old aircraft with more fuel-efficient models.*

ˈfuel inˌjection noun [U] a system in a vehicle that directs an exact amount of fuel into the engine when it is needed • **ˈfuel-inˌjected** adj *a fuel-injected engine/car*

ˌfuel ˈpoverty noun [U] mainly UK the condition of having too little money to be able to keep your home warm: *Rising gas costs have pushed more families into fuel poverty.*

ˈfuel ˌrod noun [C] a part of a device that produces nuclear power

fug /fʌg/ noun [S] a condition that can exist in a small, crowded place when the air is not pure, especially because of smoke or heat: *We smiled at each other through a grey fug of cigarette smoke.* • **fuggy** /ˈfʌg.i/ adj

fugitive /ˈfjuː.dʒɪ.tɪv/ (US) /-t̬ɪv/ noun; adj
▸noun [C] a person who is running away or hiding from the police or a dangerous situation: *Thousands of fugitives are fleeing from the war-torn area.* ◦ *Butch Cassidy and the Sundance Kid were fugitives* ***from justice*** *(= they ran away to avoid being tried in court).*
▸adj **TEMPORARY** ▷ **1** formal (especially of thoughts or feelings) lasting for only a short time: *a fugitive impression* → Synonym **fleeting** **PERSON** ▷ **2** [before noun] relating to a fugitive: *Fugitive families who have fled the fighting in the cities are now trying to survive in the mountains.*

fugly /ˈfʌg.li/ adj very informal very ugly: *Oh, that girl is fugly!*

fugue /fjuːg/ noun [C] a piece of music consisting of three or more tunes played together: *a Bach organ fugue*

-ful /-fəl/, /-fʊl/ suffix **HAVING** ▷ **1** having the stated quality to a high degree, or causing it: *colourful* ◦ *powerful* ◦ *painful* ◦ *truthful* ◦ *beautiful* **AMOUNT** ▷ **2** the amount of something needed to fill the stated container or place: *a spoonful* ***of*** *sugar* ◦ *a mouthful* ***of*** *tea* ◦ *a houseful* ***of*** *people*

fulcrum /ˈfʊl.krəm/ noun (plural **fulcrums** or specialized **fulcra**) **1** [C] specialized the point at which a bar, or something that is balancing, is supported or balances: *A seesaw balances at its fulcrum.* **2** [S] formal the main thing or person needed to support something or to make it work or happen: *The fulcrum* ***of*** *the* ***debate/argument*** *is the individual's right to choose.*

fulfil (-ll-) (US usually **fulfill**) /fʊlˈfɪl/ verb [T] **MAKE HAPPEN** ▷ **1** (C1) to do something that is expected, hoped for, or promised or to cause it to happen: *A school fails if it does not fulfil the* ***needs/requirements*** *of its pupils.* ◦ *At the age of 45, she finally fulfilled her* ***ambition*** *to run a marathon.* ◦ *Zoos fulfil an important* ***function*** *in the protection of rare species.* ◦ *He has failed to fulfil his* ***duties*** *as a father.* ◦ *We're looking for a very specific sort of person and this woman seems to fulfil all of our* ***criteria***. ◦ *So did the course fulfil all your* ***expectations***? ◦ *We're suing our suppliers for failing to fulfil their contract.* **SATISFY** ▷ **2** (C2) to satisfy someone or make them feel happy: *I don't feel that my present way of life really fulfils me.* ◦ *I've finally found a job in which I can fulfil my****self*** *(= completely develop my abilities and interests).*

fulfilled /fʊlˈfɪld/ adj feeling happy because you are getting everything that you want from life: *For the first time in my life, I feel really fulfilled.*

fulfilling /fʊlˈfɪl.ɪŋ/ adj (C2) making you feel happy and satisfied: *Nursing is hard work, but it can be very fulfilling.*

fulfilment (US usually **fulfillment**) /fʊlˈfɪl.mənt/ noun [U] **STH YOU DO** ▷ **1** (C2) the fact of doing something that is necessary or something that someone has wanted or promised to do: *For many women, the fulfilment of family* ***obligations*** *prevents the furtherance of their career.* **FEELING** ▷ **2** (C2) a feeling of pleasure because you are getting what you want from life: *She finally* ***found*** *fulfilment in motherhood.* ◦ *sexual fulfilment*

full /fʊl/ adj; adv; noun
▸adj **CONTAINING A LOT** ▷ **1** (A2) (of a container or a space) holding or containing as much as possible or a lot: *This cup is very full so be careful with it.* ◦ *My plate was already full.* ◦ *I tried to get in the cinema last night but it was full.* ◦ *Don't talk with your* ***mouth*** *full!* ◦ *The shelves were full* ***of*** *books.* ◦ *When she looked at him her eyes were full* ***of*** *tears.* ◦ *I tried to get on the 8.45 train but it was full* ***(up)***. ◦ *Don't* ***fill*** *your glass too full or you'll spill it.* ◦ *The theatre was only* ***half*** *full.* **2** (A2) containing a lot of things or people or a lot of something: *This sweater is full* ***of*** *holes.* ◦ *His essay was full* ***of*** *spelling errors.* ◦ *I'm full* ***of*** *admiration for you.* ◦ *You're always so full* ***of*** *energy.* **3** involving a lot of activities: *I've got rather a full week next week – could we postpone our meeting?* ◦ *She has a very full life.* **4 be full of sth** to be talking or thinking a lot about something that you have enjoyed or found exciting: *'Did the kids enjoy their trip to the zoo?' 'Oh, yes, they were full of it when they got back this afternoon.'* **5 be full of your own importance** disapproving to think and act as if you are very important: *Since he got his new job, he's been very full of his own importance.* **6 be full of yourself** (C2) disapproving to think that you are very important in a way that annoys other people: *I can't stand her – she's so full of herself.* **COMPLETE** ▷ **7** (A2) [before noun] complete, whole, or containing a lot of detail: *Please give your full name and address.* ◦ *We do not yet have full details of the story.* ◦ *Few journalists have managed to convey the full horror of the situation.* ◦ *The full impact of the tax changes is yet to be felt.* ◦ *Today's my last full day in Paris.* ◦ *He unwound the rope to its full extent.* ◦ *Are you a full* ***member*** *(= do you have all the membership rights) of the club?* ◦ *Some plants need to be in full sun (= to have the sun shining on them) all the time.* **8 in full** (B1) completely: *The bill must be paid in full by the end of the month.* **9 in full flow** If an activity is in full flow, it is happening fast and with energy: *Preparations for the event are now in full flow.* **10 be in full swing** If an event is in full swing, it has already been happening for a period of time and there is a lot of activity: *The party was in full swing by the time we arrived.* **11 in full view** able to be seen by other people: *Andy and Vicki had a furious row outside their house, in full view* ***of*** *the neighbours.* **GREATEST POSSIBLE** ▷ **12** (B1) [before noun] the greatest possible: *James is very bright, but he doesn't make full use of his abilities.* ◦ *Nobody got full* ***marks*** *(= all the answers right) in the spelling test.* ◦ *It doesn't seem likely that we will see a return to full employment (= that all the people in the country will have a job) in the near future.* **FOOD** ▷ **13** (B2) (also **full up**) having eaten so much food that you cannot eat any more: *No more cake for me, thanks, I'm full.* **14 on a full stomach** (also **full up**) having recently eaten: *Never go swimming on a full stomach.* **LARGE** ▷ **15** (of clothing) loose or containing a lot of material, or (of parts of the body) quite large and rounded: *a full skirt* ◦ *Women often have full* ***faces****/become full* ***in the face*** *when they're pregnant.* ◦ *She has wonderful full lips.* **16** used to avoid saying 'fat': *They advertise clothes 'for the fuller* ***figure***'. **STRONG** ▷ **17** (of a flavour, sound, smell, etc.) strong or deep: *This wine*

F

has a full fruity flavour. ◦ *A cello has a fuller sound than a violin.*

IDIOMS **(at) full blast** as loud as possible: *He had the television on at full blast.* • **(at) full speed/tilt/pelt** as fast as possible: *He was driving at full speed down the motorway when it happened.* • **(at) full stretch** UK working as hard as possible, so that you could not manage to do any more: *The emergency services are **working** at full stretch today to cope with the accident.* • **be full of beans** informal to have a lot of energy and enthusiasm: *I've never known anyone be so full of beans before breakfast.* • **be full of the joys of spring** humorous to be very happy: *He bounced into the office, full of the joys of spring.* • **be in full cry** to criticize someone or something in a noisy and eager way: *The opposition was in full cry over the changes to the education bill.* • **come/go/turn full circle** If something or someone has come full circle after changing a lot, they are now the same as they were in the beginning: *Things have come full circle now that long skirts are back in fashion.* • **full marks to sb** something you say to praise someone for something clever or good that they have said or done: *Full marks to Jo for spotting the error in time.* • **full steam ahead** with all your energy and enthusiasm: *Now that problem is out of the way, it's full steam ahead to get the job finished.*

▸adv **COMPLETE** ▷ **1 know full well** to understand a situation completely: *You know full well that you're not supposed to go there without asking me!* **STRAIGHT** ▷ **2** straight; directly: *He was kicked full **in** the stomach.* ◦ *The intruders turned and ran as the police shone their torches full **on** them.*

▸noun **to the full** as much or as well as possible: *She certainly lives life to the full.*

fullback /ˈfʊl.bæk/ noun [C] a defending player in games such as football and HOCKEY who plays near the end of the field, or a player in American football whose team has control of the ball

ˌfull-ˈblooded adj [before noun] **RACE** ▷ **1** having parents, grandparents, and earlier relations all belonging to the same race: *a full-blooded Maori* **ENTHUSIASTIC** ▷ **2** enthusiastic and loyal: *a full-blooded Liverpool supporter*

ˌfull-ˈblown adj [before noun] (also **ˌfully ˈblown**) completely developed: *full-blown AIDS*

ˌfull ˈboard noun [U] UK (US **Aˈmerican ˌplan**) an arrangement in which all your meals are provided at the hotel or rooms that you are paying to stay in: *The price of the holiday includes flights, full board, and all extras.* → Compare **half board**

ˌfull-ˈbodied adj describes wine with a strong, satisfying quality and taste

ˌfull-ˈfat adj containing all of the FAT that something naturally has, with none removed: *full-fat milk/cheese*

ˌfull-ˈfrontal adj; noun

▸adj [before noun] **NO CLOTHES** ▷ **1** showing someone's body naked and from the front: *full-frontal nudity* ◦ *full-frontal pictures* **STRONG** ▷ **2** informal very strongly and clearly expressed: *Cash Junior made a full-frontal **assault/attack** on Hollywood's 'moral delinquency'.*

▸noun [C] a photograph or picture showing someone's body naked and from the front

ˌfull-ˈgrown adj (mainly UK **ˌfully ˈgrown**) describes people and other living things that have finished their physical growth and will not grow taller: *A full-grown giraffe is 5.5 m tall.*

ˌfull ˈhouse noun **AUDIENCE** ▷ **1** [C usually singular] a situation in which every seat in a cinema, theatre, CONCERT, etc. is filled: *We're expecting a full house tonight.* **CARD GAME** ▷ **2** [C] an occasion when a card player has three cards of one type and two cards of another: *Steve won the poker game with a full house.*

ˌfull-ˈlength adj; adv

▸adj **REACHING FLOOR** ▷ **1** describes a mirror, curtain, or piece of clothing that reaches the floor: *Victoria wore a full-length evening gown to the ball.* **USUAL LENGTH** ▷ **2** of the usual length and not made shorter: *a full-length feature film*

▸adv describes the way a person moves or lies so that their whole body is flat on the floor: *He was lying full-length on the grass.*

the full monty /ˌfʊlˈmɒn.ti/ (US) /-mɑːn.t̬i/ noun UK informal the most or best that you can have, do, get, or achieve, or all that you want or need: *When we bought the television, we decided to go for the full monty.*

IDIOM **do the full monty** to take off all your clothes in front of other people

ˌfull ˈmoon noun [S] the moon when it is shaped like a complete disc, or a time when it is: *There's a full moon tonight.*

fullness (also **fulness**) /ˈfʊl.nəs/ noun [U] **CONTAINING A LOT** ▷ **1** the fact that something is full **COMPLETE** ▷ **2** the quality of being complete or containing a lot of detail: *The fullness **of** the research report (= how much detail it contains) has been widely praised.* ◦ *I envy him the fullness **of** his life (= how busy and interesting his life is).* **FOOD** ▷ **3** having eaten a lot: *I've always disliked that feeling of fullness after a large meal.* **STRONG QUALITY** ▷ **4** the quality of having a strong flavour, sound, smell, etc.: *I like this cheese for the fullness **of** its flavour.* **LARGE** ▷ **5** the quality of being large or loose

IDIOM **in the fullness of time** If you say something will happen in the fullness of time, you mean that it will happen if you wait long enough: *Everything will become clear in the fullness of time.*

ˌfull-ˈon adj **VERY GREAT** ▷ **1** very great or to the greatest degree: *The hotel specializes in full-on luxury.* **ENTHUSIASTIC** ▷ **2** [after verb] very serious and enthusiastic, often in a way that is annoying to other people

ˌfull-ˈpage adj [before noun] filling a complete page of a newspaper or book: *a full-page advertisement*

ˌfull-ˈscale adj **FULL SIZE** ▷ **1** describes a model of the same size as the original thing: *full-scale models of dinosaurs* **COMPLETE** ▷ **2** [before noun] complete or using all available methods, equipment, money, etc.: *a full-scale investigation* ◦ *a full-scale attack*

ˌfull-ˈservice adj [before noun] US **1** used to describe a business that provides customers with a complete range of services: *I need to find a good full-service bank.* **2** used to describe a restaurant or petrol station where you are served by an employee rather than collecting food or filling your car yourself: *Some motorists with a disability depend on full-service stations.* → Compare **self-service**

ˌfull ˈstop noun; adv

▸noun [C] UK (US **period**) (B1) the symbol . used in writing at the end of a sentence or at the end of the short form of a word

IDIOM **come to a full stop** to end, especially because of problems: *It looks like negotiations between the two sides have come to a full stop.*

▸adv UK (US **period**) used at the end of a sentence, usually when you are angry, to say you will not continue to discuss a subject: *Look, I'm not lending you my car, full stop!*

ˌ**full ˈtime** noun [U] UK the end of a sports match: *The score was 2–2 at full time.* → Compare **half-time**

ˌ**full-ˈtime** adj, adv **1** B1 (of work or education) done for the whole of a working week: *a full-time* ***job*** ◦ *Most children in the UK remain in full-time education until they are at least 16 years old.* ◦ *She went back to work full-time when her youngest child went to school.* **2 full-time job/activity** an activity which uses a lot of your time: *Keeping a garden tidy is a full-time job.*

> **!** Common mistake: **full-time**
>
> Remember that **full-time** has a hyphen between 'full' and 'time':
>
> ~~*I am looking for a full time job for the summer.*~~
>
> *I am looking for a full-time job for the summer.*

fully /ˈfʊl.i/ adv **COMPLETELY** ▷ **1** B1 completely: *Have you fully recovered from your illness?* ◦ *I'd fully intended to call you last night.* ◦ *I'm sorry, madam, the restaurant is fully booked.* ◦ *a fully qualified teacher* **GREATEST POSSIBLE** ▷ **2** as much as possible: *Kate has always participated fully in the life of the school.* ◦ *Students are advised to answer all questions as fully as possible.*

-fully /-fəl.i/, /-fʊ.li/ suffix in a way that shows the stated quality: *powerfully* ◦ *tearfully* ◦ *truthfully*

ˌ**fully ˈfledged** adj UK (US ˌ**full-ˈfledged**) completely developed or trained: *What started as a small business is now a fully fledged company.* ◦ *After years of study, Tim is now a fully fledged architect.*

fulminate /ˈfʊl.mɪ.neɪt/ verb [I usually + adv/prep] formal to criticize strongly: *I had to listen to Michael fulminating* ***against*** *the government.* • **fulmination** /ˌfʊl.mɪˈneɪ.ʃən/ noun [C or U]

fulsome /ˈfʊl.səm/ adj formal expressing a lot of admiration or praise for someone, often too much, in a way that does not sound sincere: *Her new book has received fulsome* ***praise*** *from the critics.* ◦ *Our guests were fulsome* ***in*** *their compliments about the food.* • **fulsomely** /-li/ adv *He thanked her fulsomely for her help.* • **fulsomeness** /-nəs/ noun [U]

fumble /ˈfʌm.bl̩/ verb **DO STH AWKWARDLY** ▷ **1** [I usually + adv/prep] to do something awkwardly, especially when using your hands: *I fumbled* ***with*** *the lock.* ◦ *He fumbled* ***in*** *his pockets* ***for*** *some change.* ◦ *She fumbled* ***around/about*** *in her handbag, looking for her key.* ◦ *They fumbled* ***around/about*** *(= moved awkwardly) in the dark, trying to find their way out of the cinema.* **SPORT** ▷ **2** [T] in sport, to fail to catch a ball: *If Wilson hadn't fumbled that* ***catch****, we might have won the match.* **THINK OF A WORD** ▷ **3** [I usually + adv/prep] to have difficulty saying or thinking of suitable words: *I was fumbling* ***for*** *the right word.*

fume /fjuːm/ verb [I] to be very angry, sometimes without expressing it: *I saw her a week after they'd had the argument and she was still fuming.* ◦ *The whole episode left me fuming* ***at*** *the injustice of it all.*

fumes /fjuːmz/ noun [plural] C1 strong, unpleasant, and sometimes dangerous gas or smoke: ***exhaust*** *fumes* ◦ ***Petrol*** *fumes always make me feel ill.* ◦ *cigar fumes*

fumigate /ˈfjuː.mɪ.geɪt/ verb [T] to use poisonous gas to remove harmful insects, bacteria, disease, etc. from somewhere or something: *We had to fumigate the cellar to get rid of cockroaches.* • **fumigation** /ˌfjuː.mɪˈgeɪ.ʃən/ noun [U]

fun /fʌn/ noun; adj

▸noun [U] **PLEASURE** ▷ **1** A1 pleasure, enjoyment, or entertainment: ***Have*** *fun (= enjoy yourself)!* ◦ *Having fun (= are you enjoying yourself)?* ◦ *I really enjoyed your party – it was such* ***good*** *fun.* ◦ *She's great fun to be with.* ◦ *Mark was ill for most of the holiday so that* ***took*** *all the fun* ***out of*** *it.* ◦ *It's* ***no*** *fun/****not much*** *fun (= not enjoyable) having to work on Saturdays.* ◦ *a fun-****loving*** *girl* ◦ *'We're going on a picnic at the weekend.' '****What*** *fun (= how enjoyable)!'* ◦ *The relationship was never going to work, but it was fun while it lasted.* → See Note **funny 2 for fun** (also **for the fun of it**) B1 for pleasure: *I ran but just for fun.* **3 make fun of sb/sth** B2 to make a joke about someone or something in a way that is not kind: *The other children were always making fun of him because he was fat and wore glasses.* **GAME/JOKE** ▷ **4** behaviour or activities that are not serious; games or jokes: *The children are always* ***full of*** *fun.* ◦ *I didn't mean to upset her – it was just* ***a bit of*** *fun.* ◦ *I didn't mean what I said, it was only* ***in*** *fun (= a joke).*

IDIOMS **have fun and games** humorous to have difficulty doing something: *We had real fun and games trying to bath the dog.* • **not be all fun and games** If an activity is not all fun and games, parts of it are difficult or unpleasant: *It's not all fun and games being a tour representative.*

▸adj [before noun] A2 enjoyable: *There are lots of fun things to do here.*

function /ˈfʌŋk.ʃən/ noun; verb

▸noun **PURPOSE** ▷ **1** B2 [C] the natural purpose (of something) or the duty (of a person): *The function* ***of*** *the veins is to carry blood to the heart.* ◦ *I'm not quite sure what my function is within the company.* ◦ *A thermostat* ***performs*** *the function* ***of*** *controlling temperature.* **CEREMONY** ▷ **2** C1 [C] an official ceremony or a formal social event, such as a party or a special meal, at which a lot of people are usually present: *As a mayor, he has a lot of* ***official*** *functions to* ***attend****.* ◦ *I see her two or three times a year, usually at* ***social*** *functions.* **WORK** ▷ **3** [U] the way in which something works or operates: *It's a disease that affects the function* ***of*** *the nervous system.* ◦ *Studies suggest that regular intake of the vitamin significantly improves brain function.* **COMPUTER** ▷ **4** [C] specialized a process that a computer or a computer program uses to complete a task: *a search/save/sort function* **RESULT** ▷ **5 a function of sth** formal something that results from something else, or is the way it is because of something else: *His success is a function of his having worked so hard.* ◦ *The low temperatures here are a function of the terrain as much as* ***of*** *the climate.* **VALUE** ▷ **6** [C] specialized (in mathematics) a quantity whose value depends on another value and changes with that value: *x is a function* ***of*** *y.*

> Word partners for **function** noun
>
> *carry out/fulfil/perform/serve* a function • the *basic/main/primary* function • an *important/useful/vital* function • the function *of* sth

▸verb [I] to work or operate: *You'll soon learn how the office functions.* ◦ *The television was functioning normally until yesterday.* ◦ *I'm so tired today, I can barely function.*

PHRASAL VERB **function as sth/sb** to perform the purpose of a particular thing or the duties of a particular person: *We have a spare bedroom that also functions as a study.*

functional /ˈfʌŋk.ʃən.əl/ adj **USEFUL** ▷ **1** B2 designed to be practical and useful rather than attractive: *functional clothing* **WORKING NORMALLY** ▷ **2** (of a machine, system, etc.) working in the usual way: *Is the central heating functional yet?* **3** performing a particular operation: *a functional disorder (= when an organ does not work as it should)*

ˌfunctional ˈfood noun [C] **nutraceutical**

ˌfunctional ilˈliterate noun [C] mainly US specialized someone who is able to live and possibly work in society, but who cannot read and write • **functional illiteracy** noun [U] *There's a high **rate of** functional illiteracy here.*

functionalism /ˈfʌŋk.ʃən.əl.ɪ.zəm/ noun [U] the principle that the most important thing about an object such as a building is its use rather than what it looks like • **functionalist** /-ɪst/ adj

F

functionality /ˌfʌŋk.ʃənˈæl.ə.ti/ (US) /-ə.t̬i/ noun [C or U] any or all of the operations performed by a piece of equipment or a software program

functionally /ˈfʌŋk.ʃən.əl.i/ adv **IN A PRACTICAL WAY** ▷ **1** in a way that is practical and useful rather than attractive: *The office is functionally designed.* **WORK** ▷ **2** in a way that works normally

functionary /ˈfʌŋk.ʃən.ər.i/ (US) /-er-/ noun [C] formal a person who has official duties, especially in a government or political party: *The visitors were met by a functionary who escorted them to the director's office.* ◦ *a government functionary*

ˈfunction ˌkey noun [C] one of the keys at the top of the keyboard which make the computer perform particular operations

ˈfunction ˌword noun [C] specialized in grammar, a word such as a CONJUNCTION, preposition, or PRONOUN that is used to show the relationship between other words in a sentence or phrase

fund /fʌnd/ noun; verb

▸noun **1** (C1) [C] an amount of money saved, collected, or provided for a particular purpose: *a **pension/trust** fund* ◦ *The hospital has **set up** a special fund to buy new equipment.* ◦ *Contributions are being sought for the disaster fund.* **2 funds** (C1) [plural] money needed or available to spend on something: *Following the repairs to the roof, church funds are now seriously depleted.* ◦ *The president has agreed to allocate further funds to develop the new submarine.* ◦ informal *I'd love to come on holiday with you, but I'm a bit **short of/low on** funds (= I have little money) at the moment.* **3 a fund of sth** a lot of something: *She has a fund of **knowledge** on the subject.*

▸verb [T] (C1) to provide the money to pay for an event, activity, or organization: *The company has agreed to fund my trip to Australia.* ◦ *The new college is being privately funded (= money for it is not being provided from taxes).*

fundamental /ˌfʌn.dəˈmen.təl/ (US) /-t̬əl/ adj **1** (C2) forming the base, from which everything else develops: *We need to make fundamental **changes** to the way in which we treat our environment.* ◦ *It's one of the fundamental **differences** between men and women.* ◦ *The school is based on the fundamental **principle** that each child should develop its full potential.* ◦ *Diversity is **of** fundamental **importance** to all ecosystems and all economies.* **2** (C2) more important than anything else: *Some understanding of grammar is fundamental **to** learning a language.*

fundamentalism /ˌfʌn.dəˈmen.təl.ɪ.zəm/ (US) /-t̬əl-/ noun [U] the belief in old and traditional forms of religion, or the belief that what is written in a holy book, such as the Christian Bible, is completely true: *Recent years have witnessed a growth in religious fundamentalism.* • **fundamentalist** /-ɪst/ noun [C] • **fundamentalist** /-ɪst/ adj

fundamentally /ˌfʌn.dəˈmen.təl.i/ (US) /-t̬əl-/ adv (C2) in a basic and important way: *Our new managing director has reorganized the company a bit, but nothing has fundamentally **changed/altered** (= its basic character has not changed).* ◦ *I still believe that people are fundamentally good.* ◦ *I disagree fundamentally with what you're saying.*

fundamentals /ˌfʌn.dəˈmen.təlz/ (US) /-t̬əlz/ noun [plural] the main or most important rules or parts: *It's important for children to be taught the fundamentals **of** science.*

funding /ˈfʌn.dɪŋ/ noun [U] (C1) money given by a government or organization for an event or activity: *Ian is trying to get funding for his research.* ◦ *They received state funding for the project.*

fundraiser /ˈfʌndˌreɪ.zər/ (US) /-zɚ/ noun [C] a person or event involved in collecting money for a particular purpose, especially a CHARITY

fundraising /ˈfʌndˌreɪ.zɪŋ/ noun [U] the act of collecting or producing money for a particular purpose, especially for a CHARITY: *The dinner is a fundraising **event** for the museum.*

funeral /ˈfjuː.nər.əl/ (US) /-nɚ.əl/ noun [C] (B2) a (usually religious) ceremony for burying or burning the body of a dead person: *The funeral will be **held** next Friday.* ◦ *Over 300 mourners attended the funeral.* ◦ *a funeral **procession***

IDIOM **that's/it's your funeral!** informal something that you say which means that if someone suffers bad results from their actions, it will be their fault

ˈfuneral diˌrector noun [C] a person whose job it is to arrange for the bodies of dead people to be buried or burned

ˈfuneral ˌhome noun [C] US for **funeral parlour**

ˈfuneral ˌparlour UK (US **ˈfuneral parlor**) noun [C] a place where the bodies of dead people are prepared to be buried or burned

funereal /fjuːˈnɪə.ri.əl/ (US) /-ˈnɪr.i-/ adj formal suitable for a funeral: *funereal music* ◦ *dressed in funereal black*

funfair /ˈfʌn.feər/ (US) /-fer/ noun [C] UK (US **aˈmusement ˌpark**) a place of outside entertainment where there are machines for riding on and games that can be played for prizes

ˈfun ˌfur noun [C or U] artificial fur that is used in clothing, often brightly coloured in a way that is obviously not natural

fungal /ˈfʌŋ.gəl/ adj caused by a fungus: *a fungal infection*

fungible /ˈfʌn.dʒɪ.bl/ adj specialized easy to exchange or trade for something else of the same type and value: *fungible goods/commodities* ◦ *fungible assets/bonds*

fungicide /ˈfʌn.dʒɪ.saɪd/, /ˈfʌŋ.gɪ-/ noun [C or U] a chemical substance used to kill fungus or prevent it from growing

fungoid /ˈfʌŋ.gɔɪd/ adj specialized like a fungus

fungus /ˈfʌŋ.gəs/ noun [C or U] (plural **fungi** /-gaɪ/ or **funguses**) any of various types of organism that get their food from decaying material or other living things: *Mushrooms and mould are fungi.*

funhouse /ˈfʌn.haʊs/ noun [C] US a building at a fair containing frightening or humorous objects and devices

funicular (railway) /fjʊˌnɪk.jʊ.ləˈreɪl.weɪ/ (US) /-juː.lɚ-/ noun [C] a special type of railway which travels up and down steep slopes, with the CARRIAGES being pulled by a strong metal rope

funk /fʌŋk/ noun [U] a style of music, usually for

dancing to, with a strong rhythm based on JAZZ and a tune that repeats: *James Brown is the master of funk.*

IDIOM **be in a funk** US informal to be very unhappy and without hope: *He's been in a real funk since she left him.*

funky /ˈfʌŋ.ki/ adj **MUSIC** ▷ **1** describes a style of music, usually for dancing to, with a strong rhythm based on JAZZ and a tune that repeats **FASHIONABLE** ▷ **2** slang fashionable in an unusual and noticeable way: *She has some really funky clothes.*

funnel /ˈfʌn.əl/ noun; verb

▸noun [C] **TUBE** ▷ **1** an object that has a wide round opening at the top, sloping sides, and a narrow tube at the bottom, used for pouring liquids or powders into containers with narrow necks: *When you've ground the coffee, use a funnel to pour it into the jar.* **ON A SHIP/TRAIN** ▷ **2** (US also **smokestack**) a vertical metal pipe on the top of a ship or steam train through which smoke comes out

▸verb (**-ll-** or US usually **-l-**) [I or T, usually + adv/prep] to put something, or to travel, through a funnel or something that acts like a funnel: *The wind funnels* ***down*** *these narrow streets.* ◦ *The children funnelled* ***along*** *the corridor into the school hall.* ◦ *If you funnel the oil* ***into*** *the engine, you're less likely to spill it.*

ˈfunnel-web noun [C] (also **ˌfunnel-web ˈspider**) any of various poisonous SPIDERS that make a WEB (= sticky net) with a funnel-shaped entrance

funnily /ˈfʌn.ɪ.li/ adv strangely: *If I'm talking a bit funnily it's because I've just had an injection in my mouth.*

IDIOM **funnily enough** strangely, in a way that is surprising: *Funnily enough, I was just thinking about you when you called.*

funny /ˈfʌn.i/ adj; noun

▸adj **HUMOROUS** ▷ **1** A1 humorous; causing laughter: *Do you know any funny jokes?* ◦ *I've never found Charlie Chaplin very funny.* ◦ *It's a really funny film.* ◦ *It's not funny – don't laugh!* ◦ *Breaking your leg isn't funny (= is serious), I can assure you.* ◦ *No matter how disastrous the situation there always seems to be a funny* ***side to it***. ◦ *Don't you try to be funny* ***with*** *me (= be serious and show respect), young man!*

> **Common mistake: funny or fun?**
>
> **Warning:** choose the right word!
>
> To say that something is enjoyable, don't say 'funny', say it is **fun**:
>
> ~~*It was a funny game and the score was 2–2.*~~
>
> *The game was fun and the score was 2–2.*
>
> **Remember:** to describe something you enjoy very much, don't say it is 'very funny', say it is **good** or **great fun**:
>
> ~~*The music festival is always very funny.*~~
>
> *The music festival is always great fun.*

STRANGE ▷ **2** B1 strange, surprising, unexpected, or difficult to explain or understand: *The washing machine is making a funny noise again.* ◦ *He's got some funny ideas about how to bring up children.* ◦ ***That's*** *funny – I'm sure I left my keys here.* ◦ *A funny* ***thing*** *happened to me on the way to the crematorium.* ◦ *Do you think this jacket looks* ***a bit*** *funny with these trousers?* ◦ *It's funny* ***how*** *Alec always disappears whenever there's work to be done.* ◦ *She's a funny girl (= she is strange and difficult to understand).* ◦ UK informal *The television's* ***gone*** *funny (= isn't working correctly).* **DISHONEST** ▷ **3** informal dishonest; involving cheating: *I think there's something funny* ***going on*** *next door.* **UNFRIENDLY** ▷ **4** [after verb] UK informal unfriendly or seeming to be offended: *I'm not being funny or anything but I think I'd rather go on my own.* ◦ *She sounded a bit funny with me on the phone last night and I wondered if I'd offended her.* **ILL** ▷ **5** [after verb] informal slightly ill: *I don't know if it was something I ate but I'm feeling a bit funny.* **CRAZY** ▷ **6** UK informal slightly crazy: *All the stress made him* ***go*** *a bit funny.*

> **Other ways of saying funny**
>
> The adjective **amusing** is a more formal alternative to 'funny':
>
> *I gave her an article that I thought she would find* ***amusing****.*
>
> If a remark, story, piece of writing, etc., is funny, you can describe it as **humorous**:
>
> *She wrote a* ***humorous*** *account of her teenage years.*
>
> If something is extremely funny, you can use the adjectives **hilarious** or (*informal*) **hysterical**:
>
> *I've just read his autobiography – it's absolutely* ***hysterical****.*
>
> If someone talks in a way that is clever and funny, you can use the adjective **witty**:
>
> *He was a very* ***witty*** *man.*
>
> The adjective **comical** is sometimes used if someone or something looks funny:
>
> *She looked so* ***comical*** *in that hat!*
>
> You can describe a person or situation that is very funny informally as a **laugh** or a **scream**:
>
> *You'd like Amanda – she's a real* ***scream****.*

IDIOM **it's a funny old world** UK saying said when someone has told you something that is strange or surprising

▸noun **the funnies** [plural] mainly US the series of drawings in a newspaper that tell a humorous story → See also **comic strip**

ˈfunny ˌbone noun [C] informal the outer part of the ELBOW (= the middle part of the arm where it bends) which hurts a lot if it is knocked

ˈfunny ˌbusiness noun [U] dishonest actions or behaviour intended to trick someone: *If you try any funny business you'll be sorry.*

the ˈfunny ˌfarm noun [S] UK informal sometimes used in a humorous or offensive way to refer to a hospital for mentally ill people: *If things get much worse, I'll soon be carted off to the funny farm.*

ˈfun ˌrun noun [C] an event in which people run a certain distance for pleasure, usually to make money for CHARITY

fur /fɜːr/ (US) /fɝː/ noun; verb

▸noun **HAIR** ▷ **1** B1 [C or U] the thick hair that covers the bodies of some animals, or the hair-covered skin (s) of animals, removed from their bodies: *She stroked the rabbit's soft fur.* ◦ *'Is that real fur on your collar?' 'Certainly not – I only wear* ***fake*** *fur.'* ◦ *a fur* ***coat*** ◦ *Native Americans traded furs with early European settlers.* **GREY SUBSTANCE** ▷ **2** [U] a hard pale grey substance that can form on the inside of water pipes, KETTLES, etc. **TONGUE** ▷ **3** [U] a greyish covering on the tongue, caused by illness or by smoking cigarettes

IDIOM **the fur flies** If the fur flies, people have a bad argument: *The fur was really flying during that meeting.*

▸verb [I] (**-rr-**) **1** If water pipes, KETTLES, etc. fur, a hard grey substance forms on the inside: *Over the years, the pipes in our house have slowly furred (up).* **2** (also **fur up**) If someone's ARTERIES (= tubes that carry blood

F

from your heart) fur, or something furs them, they become slightly blocked: *Eating too much fat furs up your arteries which slows down the flow of blood.*

furious /ˈfjʊə.ri.əs/ (US) /ˈfjɝː.i-/ adj ANGRY ▷ **1** B2 extremely angry: *I was late and he was furious* ***with*** *me.* ◦ *He's furious* ***about/at*** *the way he's been treated.* ◦ *We had a furious row last night.* STRONG ▷ **2** using a lot of effort or strength: *There is a furious struggle going on between the two presidential candidates.* ◦ *He set off running at a furious pace.* • **furiousness** /-nəs/ noun [U]

furiously /ˈfjʊə.ri.əs.li/ (US) /ˈfjɝː.i-/ adv ANGRY WAY ▷ **1** B2 in a very angry way: *'Get out of here!' she shouted furiously.* WITH STRENGTH ▷ **2** with as much effort or strength as possible: *I was pedalling furiously to try to keep up with the other children.*

F

furl /fɜːl/ (US) /fɝːl/ verb [T] to fold and roll something such as a flag, sail, or UMBRELLA into a tight tube shape

furlong /ˈfɜː.lɒŋ/ (US) /ˈfɝː.lɑːŋ/ noun [C] a unit of length equal to 201 metres or 1/8 mile, used especially in horse racing: *a five-furlong race*

furlough /ˈfɜː.ləʊ/ (US) /ˈfɝː.loʊ/ noun; verb
▸noun [C] US a period of time that a worker or a soldier is allowed to be absent, especially to return temporarily to their own town or country
▸verb [T] US to allow or force someone to be absent temporarily from work: *After safety concerns, the company furloughed all 4,000 of its employees.*

furnace /ˈfɜː.nɪs/ (US) /ˈfɝː-/ noun [C] **1** a container that is heated to a very high temperature, so that substances that are put inside it, such as metal, will melt or burn: *People who work with furnaces in a steel factory need to wear protective clothing.* ◦ *This room's* ***like*** *a furnace (= is very hot)!* **2** US a piece of equipment for heating a building: *It's cold in here – should I turn on the furnace?*

furnish /ˈfɜː.nɪʃ/ (US) /ˈfɝː-/ verb [T] to put furniture in something: *They've furnished the room very simply.*

PHRASAL VERB **furnish sb with sth** formal to provide someone with something: *Furnished with a compass and sandwiches, they set off for a day's hiking.*

furnished /ˈfɜː.nɪʃt/ (US) /ˈfɝː-/ adj C1 containing furniture or containing furniture of a particular type: *She's looking for a furnished* ***flat/apartment****.* ◦ *Their house is expensively furnished.*

furnishings /ˈfɜː.nɪ.ʃɪŋz/ (US) /ˈfɝː-/ noun [plural] the furniture, curtains, and other decorations in a room or building: *Bathroom furnishings are in the basement of the store, Sir.*

furniture /ˈfɜː.nɪ.tʃəʳ/ (US) /ˈfɝː.nɪ.tʃɚ/ noun [U] A2 things such as chairs, tables, beds, cupboards, etc. that are put into a house or other building to make it suitable and comfortable for living or working in: *They have a lot of antique furniture.* ◦ *The only* ***piece/item of*** *furniture he has in his bedroom is a bed.* ◦ *We've just bought some new garden furniture (= tables, chairs, etc. for use in the garden).*

> **!** Common mistake: **furniture**
> **Furniture** does not have a plural form.
> Do not say 'furnitures'. Only say **furniture**:
> ~~*The furnitures are not very comfortable.*~~
> *The furniture is not very comfortable.*

furore UK (US **furor**) /ˈfjʊ.rɔːʳ/ (US) /-rɔːr/ noun [S] a sudden excited or angry reaction to something by a lot of people: *The government's decision to raise taxes has caused a great furore.* ◦ *the furore* ***over*** *his latest film*

furphy /ˈfɜː.fi/ (US) /ˈfɝː-/ noun [C] Australian English slang a RUMOUR (= unofficial interesting story or piece of news that might be either true or invented)

furred /fɜːd/ (US) /fɝːd/ adj **1** describes a tongue that is covered in a substance because of illness, smoking, etc.: *He had the furred tongue of a sick man.* **2** describes ARTERIES (= tubes that carry blood from your heart) that are slightly blocked: *furred arteries from eating too many fatty foods*

furrier /ˈfʌr.i.əʳ/ (US) /ˈfɝː.i.ɚ/ noun [C] a person who makes or sells clothes made from fur

furrow /ˈfʌr.əʊ/ (US) /ˈfɝː.oʊ/ noun; verb
▸noun [C] a long line or hollow that is formed or cut into the surface of something: *A deep furrow has formed in the rock, where water has run over it for centuries.* ◦ *Years of anxiety have lined her brow with deep furrows.*
▸verb [T] to form or cut a long line or hollow in the surface of something: *The wheels of the heavy tractor furrowed the soft ground.* ◦ *The pain of the headache made him furrow his* ***brow*** *(= make lines in the skin above his eyes).*

furrowed /ˈfʌr.əʊd/ (US) /ˈfɝː.oʊd/ adj **a furrowed brow** a FOREHEAD (= part of the face above the eyes) that has lines in the skin, usually caused by worry

furry /ˈfɜː.ri/ (US) /ˈfɝː.i/ adj **1** covered with fur: *small furry animals* **2** describes things that are made from a soft material that looks like fur: *furry* ***slippers***

further /ˈfɜː.ðəʳ/ (US) /ˈfɝː.ðɚ/ adv; adj; adj, adv; verb
▸adv **1** B1 comparative of **far**: to a greater distance or degree, or at a more advanced level: *I'm afraid I never got further than the first five pages of 'Ulysses'.* ◦ *We discussed the problem but we didn't* ***get*** *much further in actually solving it.* ◦ *The whole matter is further complicated by the fact that Amanda and Jo refuse to speak to each other.* ◦ *Every day she sinks further and further into depression.* **2 go further/take sth further** If you go or take something further, you take it to a more advanced stage: *Before we go any further with the project I think we should check that there's enough money to fund it.* ◦ *If you wish to take* ***the matter*** *further, you can file charges against him.*

IDIOM **nothing could have been further from my mind/thoughts** used to say that you certainly did not intend something: *I certainly wasn't trying to get money off him – nothing could have been further from my mind!*

▸adj at a greater distance: *It was much further to the town centre than I remembered.* ◦ *Fourteen miles is further than you'd think once you start to run it.* ◦ *Is that her at the further (= other) end of the room?*
▸adj, adv **1** A2 more or extra: *Have you anything further to add?* ◦ *If you have any further problems do let me know.* ◦ *It cost me £50 a day and a further £60 for insurance.* ◦ *This shop will be closed until further notice.* ◦ *We need to talk further about this.* **2 further to** mainly UK formal used in business letters to refer to an earlier letter, conversation, meeting, etc.: *Further to your letter of 11 March, I should like to inform you of a number of recent developments regarding the Saffron Hill site.*
▸verb [T] C2 to develop or make progress in something: *He has probably done more to further* ***the cause*** *of interracial harmony than any other person.* ◦ *Additional training is probably the best way to further your career these days.* • **furtherance** /-ᵊns/ noun [U] formal *The charter states that the press shall be devoted to printing and publishing* ***in*** *the furtherance and dissemination* ***of*** *knowledge.*

ˌ**further eduˈcation** noun [U] UK (US ˌ**adult eduˈcation**) education below the level of a university degree for people who are older than school age: *She teaches at a college of further education.*

furthermore /ˌfɜː.ðəˈmɔːr/ (US) /ˈfɝː.ðɚ.mɔːr/ adv formal (B2) in addition; more importantly: *I suggest we use Barkers as our main suppliers – they're good and furthermore they're cheap.*

> **! Common mistake: furthermore**
> Remember that **furthermore** is written as one word. Don't write 'further more', write **furthermore**.

furthermost /ˈfɜː.ðə.məʊst/ (US) /ˈfɝː.ðɚ.moʊst/ adj formal The furthermost place or places are those at the greatest distance away: *the furthermost ports of northern Europe*

furthest /ˈfɜː.ðɪst/ (US) /ˈfɝː-/ adv (B1) superlative of **far**: *That's the furthest I can see without glasses.* ◦ *I wanted to be an actress but the furthest I ever got was selling ice-creams in a theatre.* • **furthest** adj *The novel explores the furthest extremes of human experience.*

furtive /ˈfɜː.tɪv/ (US) /ˈfɝː.t̬ɪv/ adj (of people) behaving secretly and often dishonestly, or (of actions) done secretly and often dishonestly: *I saw him cast a furtive **glance** at the woman at the table to his right.* ◦ *He made one or two furtive phone calls.* ◦ *There was something furtive **about** his behaviour and I immediately felt suspicious.* • **furtively** /-li/ adv *As she turned away I saw him sniff furtively under his arm.* • **furtiveness** /-nəs/ noun [U]

fury /ˈfjʊə.ri/ (US) /ˈfjɝː.i/ noun [S or U] (C2) extreme anger: *He could hardly contain his fury.* ◦ *She flew into a fury at the suggestion.*

IDIOM **like fury** old-fashioned with great energy and determination: *I've been working like fury these past few days to catch up.*

fuse /fjuːz/ noun; verb

▸noun [C] **SAFETY PART** ▷ **1** a small safety part in an electrical device or piece of machinery which causes it to stop working if the electric current is too high, and so prevents fires or other dangers: *My hairdryer's stopped working – I think the fuse has **blown** (= broken).* ◦ *Have you tried **changing** the fuse?* **DEVICE ON EXPLOSIVE** ▷ **2** a string or piece of paper connected to a FIREWORK or other explosive product by which it is lit, or a device inside a bomb which causes it to explode after a fixed length of time or when it hits or is near something: *He **lit** the fuse and ran.*

IDIOM **have a short fuse** to get angry very easily

▸verb [I or T] **JOIN** ▷ **1** to join or become combined: *Genes determine how we develop from the moment the sperm fuses with the egg.* ◦ *The bones of the skull are not properly fused at birth.* ◦ *In Istanbul, East and West fuse together in a way that is fascinating to observe.* **MELT** ▷ **2** to (cause to) melt (together) especially at a high temperature: *The heat of the fire fused many of the machine's parts together.* **STOP WORKING** ▷ **3** UK When an electrical device or piece of machinery fuses, or when someone or something fuses it, it stops working because the electric current is too high: *Either my headlights have fused or the bulbs have gone.* ◦ *The kids were messing around with the switches and they fused the lights.*

ˈ**fuse** ˌ**box** noun [C] a container holding several fuses, such as all the fuses for the electrical system of a single house

fused /fjuːzd/ adj describes an electrical device or a piece of machinery that has a fuse in it

fuselage /ˈfjuː.zəl.ɑːʒ/ noun [C] the main body of an aircraft: *A close inspection revealed minute cracks in the aircraft's fuselage and wings.*

fusilier /ˌfjuː.zɪˈlɪər/ (US) /-ˈlɪr/ noun [C] UK a British soldier of low rank who is in the INFANTRY

fusillade /ˌfjuː.zɪˈleɪd/ noun [C] a large number of bullets FIRED at the same time or one after another very quickly: *a fusillade **of** automatic fire* ◦ formal figurative *A fusillade (= sudden large amount) **of** questions greeted the president at this afternoon's press conference.*

fusion /ˈfjuː.ʒən/ noun [U] an occasion when two or more things join or are combined: ***nuclear** fusion* ◦ *Their music is described as 'an explosive fusion of Latin American and modern jazz rhythms'.*

fuss /fʌs/ noun; verb

▸noun **TOO MUCH OF A FEELING** ▷ **1** (C1) [S or U] a show of anger, worry, or excitement that is unnecessary or greater than the situation deserves: *She **made such a** fuss when Richard spilled a drop of wine on her blouse!* ◦ *It's all a fuss **about nothing.*** ◦ *I don't see **what the** fuss **is about** – he seems like a fairly ordinary looking guy to me.* ◦ *We tried to arrange a ceremony with as little fuss as possible.* **2 make a fuss of/over sb** to give someone a lot of attention and treat them well: *She doesn't see her grandchildren very often so she makes a real fuss of them when she does.* **ATTENTION** ▷ **3** [U] attention given to small matters that are not important

▸verb **GIVE ATTENTION TO** ▷ **1** [I] to give too much attention to small matters that are not important, usually in a way which shows that you are worried and not relaxed: *Please, stop fussing – the food's cooking and there's nothing more to do until the guests arrive.* ◦ *It irritates me the way she's always fussing **with** her hair!* **MAKE NERVOUS/ANGRY** ▷ **2** [T] US to make someone nervous and angry by trying to get their attention when they are very busy: *Don't fuss me, honey, I've got a whole pile of work to do.*

PHRASAL VERB **fuss over sb/sth** to give someone or something too much attention because you want to show that you like them: *She's always fussing over that son of hers as if he were a little boy.*

fusspot /ˈfʌs.pɒt/ (US) /-pɑːt/ noun [C] (US also **fussbudget**) a person who is often not satisfied and complains about things that are not important: *'I can't eat this meat – it's too tough.' 'You old fusspot – give it here and I'll eat it!'*

fussy /ˈfʌs.i/ adj disapproving **NOT EASILY SATISFIED** ▷ **1** (C2) not easily satisfied, or having very high standards about particular things: *All my children were fussy eaters.* ◦ *He's so fussy **about** the house – everything has to be absolutely perfect.* ◦ *'I haven't met a man I've fancied for ages!' 'You're too fussy – that's your problem!'* **DECORATED TOO MUCH** ▷ **2** having too much decoration and too many small details, in a way that is not stylish: *They've got those curtains that tie up with big bows – they're a bit fussy for my taste.* • **fussily** /-ɪ.li/ adv *fussily decorated* • **fussiness** /-i.nəs/ noun [U]

IDIOM **I'm not fussy/fussed** UK informal something that you say when you would be satisfied with either choice that is offered you: *'Red wine or white?' 'I'm not fussy – either would be lovely.'*

fustian /ˈfʌs.ti.ən/ (US) /-tʃən/ noun [U] a thick, rough cotton cloth that lasts for a long time • **fustian** adj

fusty /ˈfʌs.ti/ adj disapproving **SMELL** ▷ **1** not fresh and smelling unpleasant especially because of being left slightly wet: *This room smells a bit fusty – I think I'll* *just open a window.* **OLD-FASHIONED** ▷ **2** old-fashioned in ideas and beliefs: *Rupert's father belongs to some fusty old gentleman's club in London where they don't allow women in.*

futile /ˈfjuː.taɪl/ (US) /-t̬əl/ **adj** (of actions) having no effect or achieving nothing: *Attempts to get supplies to the region are futile because troops will not allow the aid convoy to enter the city.* ◦ *It's quite futile **trying** to reason with him – he just won't listen.* ◦ *All my attempts to cheer her up **proved** futile.* • **futility** /fjuːˈtɪl.ɪ.ti/ (US) /-t̬i/ **noun** [U] *'What's his latest book about?' 'Oh, the usual – the transience of love and the futility of life.'*

futon /ˈfuː.tɒn/ (US) /-tɑːn/ **noun** [C] a MATTRESS that is used on the floor or on a wooden frame

F

future /ˈfjuː.tʃəʳ/ (US) /-tʃɚ/ **noun; adj**

▸**noun TIME TO COME** ▷ **1 the future** [S] **a** (B1) a period of time that is to come: *Sometimes I worry about the future.* ◦ *I wonder what the future **holds** for (= what will happen to) you and me.* ◦ *I'm sure at some point **in** the future I'll want a baby.* ◦ *We need to plan for the future.* ◦ *Do you plan to leave London in the **distant** future or the **near** future?* ◦ *I can see those two getting married in the **not too distant** future (= quite soon).* **b** (A2) in grammar, the form of a verb which you use when talking about something that will happen or exist: *In the sentence 'Who will look after the dog?' the verb phrase 'will look' is **in** the future.* **2** (C2) [C] what will happen to someone or something in the time that is to come: *Torn apart by war, its economy virtually destroyed, this country now faces a very **uncertain** future.* ◦ *She's a very talented young singer, Mike, and I personally think she's got a **great** future ahead of her!* ◦ *The future isn't looking too rosy for these companies.* **3** (B1) [S or U] the chance of continuing success or existence for something: *With falling audiences, the future of this theatre is in doubt.* **4 in future** mainly UK (US usually **in the future**) (B1) used at the beginning or end of a sentence in which there is a decision about a plan of action or a warning: *Could you be more careful in future?* ◦ *In future I won't bother asking him out anywhere if he's just going to complain that he's bored!* ◦ *In future I'm going to check every single piece of work that you do!*

> **!** Common mistake: **in future or in the future?**
>
> **Remember:** in UK English, 'in future' is used to talk about what will happen starting from now.
>
> To talk about what will happen in a period of time that is to come, don't say 'in future', say **in the future**:
>
> ~~*I believe that in future all our clothes will be made of plastic.*~~
>
> *I believe that in the future all our clothes will be made of plastic.*

MONEY ▷ **5 futures** [plural] agreements for the buying and selling of goods, in which the price is agreed before a particular future time at which the goods will be provided: *the futures market* ◦ *She works in futures.*

> Word partners for **the future**
>
> the *distant/foreseeable/near* future • what the future *holds* • *plan for/predict* the future • *in* the future

▸**adj** [before noun] **1** (B1) happening or existing in the future: *Of course we'll keep you up to date with any future developments.* ◦ *There's an old superstition that young girls going to bed on this night dream of their future husbands.* **2** In grammar, the future form of a verb is used when talking about something that will happen or exist: *How do you say that in the future **tense**?* **3 for future reference** used when you tell someone something so that it will be known about and can be used in the future: *For future reference, could you use the headed paper for any correspondence that leaves this office?*

the ˌfuture ˈperfect noun [S] the form of the verb that is used to show that an action will have been performed by a particular time. In English it is formed by 'will have' or 'shall have' and a past participle: *In the sentence 'By that time I will have finished' the verb phrase 'will have finished' is **in** the future perfect.*

ˈfuture-proof verb; adj

▸**verb** [T] to design software, a computer, etc. so that it can still be used in the future, even when TECHNOLOGY changes: *Here are some tips for future-proofing your computer network.*

▸**adj** Future-proof software, computer equipment, etc. is designed so that it can still be used even when TECHNOLOGY changes: *Is it possible to build a future-proof PC?*

futurism /ˈfjuː.tʃəʳr.ɪ.zəm/ (US) /-tʃɚ-/ **noun** [U] a new way of thinking in the arts that started in the 1920s and 1930s, which tried to express through a range of art forms the characteristics and images of the modern age, such as machines, speed, movement, and power • **futurist** /-ɪst/ **adj, noun** [C] *a futurist painter*

futuristic /ˌfjuː.tʃəˈrɪs.tɪk/ **adj** strange and very modern, or intended or seeming to come from some imagined time in the future: *At the unspoiled North Bay, three white pyramids rise like futuristic sails from the sea.* ◦ *Her latest novel is a futuristic thriller, set some time in the late 21st century.*

fuzz /fʌz/ **noun** [U] **HAIR** ▷ **1** informal a covering of short thin soft hairs, or a mass of tightly curled and often untidy hair: *He's got that bit of adolescent fuzz on his upper lip.* **POLICE** ▷ **2** UK and US old-fashioned slang or Australian English informal the police: *Watch out! It's the fuzz.*

fuzzy /ˈfʌz.i/ **adj NOT CLEAR** ▷ **1** (of an image) having shapes that do not have clear edges, or (of a sound, especially from a television, radio, etc.) not clear, usually because of other unwanted noises making it difficult to hear: *Is the picture always fuzzy on your TV?* ◦ *You can pick up a lot of stations on the car radio but the sound is usually a bit fuzzy.* **2** informal not clear: *The basic facts of the story are starting to emerge though the details are still fuzzy.* ◦ *My head's a bit fuzzy (= I cannot think clearly) this morning after all that wine last night.* **HAIR/FUR** ▷ **3** (of hair) in an untidy mass of tight curls: *Oh no, it's raining – my hair will go all fuzzy.* **4** describes a surface that feels like short fur: *the fuzzy skin of a peach* • **fuzzily** /-ɪ.li/ **adv** • **fuzziness** /-nəs/ **noun** [U]

ˌfuzzy ˈlogic noun [U] a system of theories used in mathematics, COMPUTING, and PHILOSOPHY to deal with statements that are neither true nor false

fwiw written abbreviation for for what it's worth: used, for example in emails, when you are giving someone information and you do not know if it is useful or not

the ˈF-ˌword noun [S] polite word for **fuck**

fya written abbreviation for for your amusement: used when you send someone a joke by email

fyi written abbreviation for for your information: used, for example in emails, when you send someone an announcement or tell them something that you think they should know

G, g /dʒiː/ noun (plural **Gs**, **G's** or **g'd**) **LETTER** ▷ **1** [C or U] the seventh letter of the English alphabet **MUSIC** ▷ **2** [C or U] a note in Western music **FILM** ▷ **3** [C] in the US, a symbol that marks a film that is considered suitable for children of any age **MONEY** ▷ **4** [C] US informal 1,000 dollars: *You've got six Gs' worth of machinery here – you should get it insured.*

g /dʒiː/ noun **FORCE** ▷ **1** [C] (plural **g**) specialized a unit of measurement of the ACCELERATION (= rate of change of speed) of an object caused by GRAVITY **MASS** ▷ **2** (also **gm**) written abbreviation for **gram**

gab /gæb/ verb [I] (**-bb-**) informal disapproving to talk continuously and eagerly, especially about things that are not important: *I got so bored listening to him gabbing* ***on*** *about nothing.*

gabardine (also **gaberdine**) /ˈgæb.ə.diːn/ (US) /-ɚ-/ noun [C or U] a thick cloth that is especially used for making coats, or a long coat made from this cloth

gabble /ˈgæb.l̩/ verb; noun
▸verb [I or T] to speak quickly and not clearly so that it is difficult to understand: *She started gabbling* ***away*** *at me in Spanish and I didn't understand a word.* ◦ *Gina, as usual, was gabbling* ***away*** *on the phone!*
▸noun [U] fast conversation or speech that is difficult to understand, often because many people are talking at the same time

gable /ˈgeɪ.bl̩/ noun [C] the top end of the wall of a building, in the shape of a triangle, where it meets the sloping parts of a roof

gabled /ˈgeɪ.bl̩d/ adj with gables: *a house with a gabled end*

gad /gæd/ verb (**-dd-**)

PHRASAL VERB **gad about/around (somewhere)** old-fashioned to visit or travel to a lot of different places, enjoying yourself and not worrying about other things you should be doing: *We spent the weekend gadding about London and generally enjoying ourselves.*

gadabout /ˈgæd.ə.baʊt/ noun [C] old-fashioned humorous a person who goes out a lot and does not worry about other things they should be doing: *Where have you been, you young gadabout!*

gadget /ˈgædʒ.ɪt/ noun [C] (C1) a small device or machine with a particular purpose: *kitchen gadgets* ◦ *Have you seen this handy little gadget – it's for separating egg yolks from whites.* • **gadgetry** /-ə.tri/ noun [U] *We've got a juicer, a blender, a coffee grinder – all manner of kitchen gadgetry.*

Gaelic /ˈgeɪ.lɪk/, /ˈgæl.ɪk/ noun [U] a group of languages spoken in parts of Ireland, Scotland, and, in the past, the Isle of Man • **Gaelic** adj

gaff /gæf/ noun [C] UK informal someone's house or home: *Have you ever been round his gaff?*

gaffe /gæf/ noun [C] a remark or action that is a social mistake and not considered polite: *I* ***made*** *a real gaffe – I called his new wife 'Judy', which is the name of his ex-wife.* → Synonym **faux pas**

gaffer /ˈgæf.əʳ/ (US) /-ɚ/ noun [C] **MAN IN CHARGE** ▷ **1** UK informal a man who is in charge of other workers **FILM** ▷ **2** specialized the person responsible for the lights and other electrical equipment used when making a film or television programme **OLD MAN** ▷ **3** informal an old man

ˈgaffer ˌtape noun [U] strong TAPE (= a long strip of material) that is sticky on one side, used for holding things in place: *The cables should be fixed to the floor with gaffer tape so that nobody trips over them.*

gag /gæg/ noun; verb
▸noun [C] **PIECE OF CLOTH** ▷ **1** a piece of cloth that is tied around a person's mouth or put inside it in order to stop them from speaking, shouting, or calling for help: *Her hands and feet were tied and a gag placed over her mouth.* **JOKE** ▷ **2** informal a joke or funny story, especially one told by a COMEDIAN (= person whose job is to make people laugh): *I did a few opening gags about the band that had been on before me.* **3** US a trick played on someone or an action performed to entertain other people
▸verb (**-gg-**) **ALMOST VOMIT** ▷ **1** [I] to experience the sudden uncomfortable feeling of tightness in the throat and stomach that makes you feel you are going to vomit: *Just the smell of liver cooking makes me gag.* ◦ *I tried my best to eat it but the meat was so fatty I gagged* ***on*** *it.* **PREVENT FROM TALKING** ▷ **2** [T] to put a gag on someone's mouth: *He was* ***bound and gagged*** *and left in a cell for three days.* **3** [T often passive] to prevent a person or organization from talking or writing about a particular subject: *The media have obviously been gagged because nothing has been reported.* **BE EAGER** ▷ **4 be gagging for/to do sth** UK slang to be very eager to do something: *I was gagging for a pint of cold lager.* **5 be gagging for it** slang to be very eager to have sex

gaga /ˈgɑː.gɑː/ adj informal **MENTALLY UNCLEAR** ▷ **1** unable to think clearly and make decisions because of old age: *My granny's 94 and she's a bit gaga.* ◦ *I know I'm 73 but I haven't* ***gone*** *gaga yet!* → Compare **senile IN LOVE** ▷ **2** [after verb] having a strong but usually temporary love for someone: *She's totally gaga* ***about/over*** *him!* ◦ *Just standing near her makes him* ***go*** *gaga!*

ˈgagging ˌorder noun [C] UK (US **ˈgag ˌorder**) an official order not to discuss something, especially a legal case: *The judge* ***issued*** *a gagging order to prevent the witnesses from speaking to the press.*

gaggle /ˈgæg.l̩/ noun [C, + sing/pl verb] **1** a group of GEESE **2** disapproving a group of noisy or silly people: *There was the usual gaggle* ***of*** *journalists waiting for the star.*

gaiety /ˈgeɪ.ə.ti/ (US) /-t̬i/ noun [U] old-fashioned happiness and excitement: *I felt there was an air of forced gaiety about her manner.*

gaily /ˈgeɪ.li/ adv old-fashioned happily or brightly: *I could hear her gaily singing in her bedroom.* ◦ *The tree lights twinkled gaily across the lake.*

gain /geɪn/ verb; noun
▸verb [I or T] **GET** ▷ **1** (B1) to get something that is useful, that gives you an advantage, or that is in some way positive, especially over a period of time: *The Nationalist Party have gained a lot of support in the south of the country.* ◦ *What do you hope to gain* ***from*** *the course?* ◦ *Alternative medicine has only just started to gain respectability in our society.* ◦ [+ two objects] *It was her performances in Aida which gained her an international reputation as a soprano.* ◦ *After you've gained some experience teaching abroad you can come home and get a job.* ◦ *From the late 19th century, European powers began to gain control of parts of the*

G

Ottoman Empire. ◦ *She's certainly gained* (**in**) *confidence over the last couple of years.* ◦ *The data exists all right – the difficulty is in gaining access to it.* ◦ *The thieves gained entrance through an upstairs window that was left open.* **2 gain ground** C1 If a political party or an idea or belief gains ground, it becomes more popular or accepted: *The Republicans are gaining ground in the southern states.* **INCREASE** ▷ **3** B1 to increase in weight, speed, height or amount: *I gained a lot of weight while I was on holiday.* ◦ *The car gained speed going down the hill.* ◦ *Good economic indicators caused the share index to gain* (**by**) *ten points.* ◦ *The campaign has been gaining momentum ever since the television appeal.* **CLOCK/WATCH** ▷ **4** If a clock or watch gains, it works too quickly and shows a time that is later than the real time: *My watch has gained* (**by**) *ten minutes over the last 24 hours.*

G

PHRASAL VERB **gain on sb/sth** to get nearer to someone or something that you are chasing: *Garcia was gaining on her opponent throughout the race, but only overtook her at the very end.*

▸**noun** [C or U] **SOMETHING OBTAINED** ▷ **1** C1 an occasion when you get something useful or positive: *Whatever the objections to this sort of treatment, the gains in terms of the number of lives saved are substantial.* ◦ *The minister was sacked for abusing power for his* ***personal*** *gain.* **INCREASE** ▷ **2** C1 an increase in something such as size, weight or amount: *Side effects of the drugs may include tiredness, headaches, or weight gain.* ◦ *Having deducted costs we still made a net gain of £5,000.* ◦ *Oil prices rose again today after yesterday's gains.*

gainer /ˈgeɪ.nəʳ/ US /-nɚ/ **noun** [C] something or someone that is in a better position or has more value at the end of a process: *There were both gainers and losers as a result of the tax changes.*

gainful /ˈgeɪn.fəl/ **adj** formal providing money or something else that is useful: *Many graduates tell of months spent in search of gainful* ***employment***. • **gainfully** /-i/ **adv** *His estate continues to keep lawyers gainfully* ***employed*** *even seven years after his death.*

gainsay /ˌgeɪnˈseɪ/ **verb** [T often in negatives] (**gainsaid, gainsaid**) formal to refuse to accept something as the truth: *Certainly there's no gainsaying* (= *it is not possible to doubt*) *the technical brilliance of his performance.*

gait /geɪt/ **noun** [C] formal a particular way of walking: *He walked* ***with*** *a slow stiff gait.*

gaiters /ˈgeɪ.təz/ US /-t̬ɚz/ **noun** [plural] a pair of coverings for the lower half of the legs, often worn in the past but worn now mainly by people who go walking or climbing in order to stop earth and water from entering their boots

gal /gæl/ **noun** **GIRL** ▷ **1** [C] (plural **gals**) informal or humorous a woman or girl: *You're just an old-fashioned gal, aren't you, honey!* **UNIT OF MEASUREMENT** ▷ **2** (UK also **gall**) written abbreviation for **gallon**

gala /ˈgɑː.lə/ US /ˈgeɪ-/ **noun** [C] **CELEBRATION** ▷ **1** a special public occasion at which there is a lot of entertainment, usually in the form of different types of performances: *There will be many stars performing in the Royal Ballet's Gala Night, held in aid of children's charities.* **SPORTS EVENT** ▷ **2** UK a sports competition, especially in swimming: *a* ***swimming*** *gala*

galactic /gəˈlæk.tɪk/ **adj** relating to the Galaxy or other galaxies: *inter-galactic travel*

galah /gəˈlɑː/ **noun** [C] **BIRD** ▷ **1** a medium-sized COCKATOO (= type of bird) common in most parts of Australia, that has a grey upper part of its body and a pink lower part **PERSON** ▷ **2** Australian English informal a stupid person

galaxy /ˈgæl.ək.si/ **noun** **1** [C] one of the independent groups of stars in the universe **2** [C] a meeting of rich and famous people: *Present tonight at the long-awaited opening of this film are a whole galaxy* ***of*** *stars from the acting and musical professions.* **3 the Galaxy** (also **the Milky Way**) the very large group of stars that contains the SOLAR SYSTEM (= the sun and all the planets, including the Earth, that go round it)

gale /geɪl/ **noun** [C] a very strong wind: *Hundreds of old trees were blown down in the gales.*

IDIOM **gales of laughter** a lot of loud laughter: *I could hear gales of laughter coming from downstairs.*

galette /gæˈlet/ **noun** [C] a type of PANCAKE that is not sweet

gall /gɔːl/ US /gɑːl/ **noun; verb**

▸**noun** [U] rudeness and the quality of being unable to understand that your behaviour or what you say is not acceptable to other people: [+ to infinitive] *Considering that he never even bothers to visit my parents I'm amazed that Tim* ***has the*** *gall* ***to*** *ask them for money!*

▸**verb** [T] to make someone feel annoyed: *I think it galls him to take orders from a younger and less experienced colleague.*

gallant /ˈgæl.ənt/ US /gəˈlænt/ **adj** **BRAVE** ▷ **1** formal approving showing no fear of dangerous or difficult things: *Despite fierce competition she made a gallant effort to win the first medal of the championships.* **POLITE** ▷ **2** formal (of a man) polite and kind towards women, especially when in public: *That wasn't very gallant of you, Paul, pushing a young lady out of the way like that!* • **gallantly** /-li/ **adv** • **gallantry** /-ən.tri/ **noun** [U] *The speech praised those who had displayed gallantry in the liberation of their country.*

ˈ**gall bladder** **noun** [C] a small organ in the body like a bag connected to the LIVER which stores BILE (= a bitter liquid that helps to digest food): *She had an operation to remove a stone from her gall bladder.*

galleon /ˈgæl.i.ən/ **noun** [C] a large sailing ship with three or four MASTS, used both in trade and war from the 15th to the 18th centuries

gallery /ˈgæl.ər.i/ US /-ɚ-/ **noun** [C] **BUILDING** ▷ **1** B1 a room or building that is used for showing works of art, sometimes so that they can be sold: *the National Portrait Gallery* ◦ *a contemporary* ***art*** *gallery* **RAISED AREA** ▷ **2** a raised area around the sides or at the back of a large room that provides extra space for people to sit or stand, or the highest floor in a theatre that contains the cheapest seats → Compare **circle, stalls**

galley /ˈgæl.i/ **noun** [C] **KITCHEN** ▷ **1** a kitchen in a ship or aircraft **BOAT** ▷ **2** (in the past) a long low ship which had sails and was usually ROWED by prisoners and SLAVES: *a galley slave*

Gallic /ˈgæl.ɪk/ **adj** French or typically French: *Catherine Deneuve seemed to typify cool Gallic elegance.*

galling /ˈgɔː.lɪŋ/ US /ˈgɑː-/ **adj** annoying: [+ to infinitive] *It was very galling* ***to*** *have a younger brother who did everything better than me.*

gallivant /ˈgæl.ɪ.vænt/ **verb** [I usually + adv/prep] humorous to visit or go to a lot of different places, enjoying yourself and not worrying about other things you should be doing: *Well you won't be able to go off gallivanting* ***around*** *like this when there's a baby to be taken care of.*

gallon /ˈgæl.ən/ **noun** **1** [C] a unit for measuring volume: *An imperial gallon, used in Britain, is equal to 4,546 cubic centimetres.* ◦ *A US gallon is equal to 3,785 cubic centimetres.* **2** [C usually plural] informal a large amount of liquid: *I love milk – I drink gallons of the stuff.*

gallop /ˈgæl.əp/ **verb; noun**

▸**verb 1** [I or T] (of a horse) to run fast so that all four feet come off the ground together in each act of forward movement, or (of a person) to ride a horse that is running in this way: *We galloped through the woods.* → Compare **canter, trot 2** [I usually + adv/prep] informal to move or act quickly: *It is the height of folly and a tragic waste to gallop into war.*

PHRASAL VERB **gallop through sth** informal to perform, read, or do something very quickly and without enough care: *They often gallop through ten news items in 20 minutes.*

▸**noun** [S] **RUN** ▷ **1** the fast run or speed of a horse when it is galloping, or an act of galloping: *At the sound of gunfire the horse suddenly* ***broke into*** *a gallop.* **SPEED** ▷ **2** a fast speed: *We had to complete the work* ***at a*** *gallop (= very quickly).*

galloping /ˈgæl.ə.pɪŋ/ **adj** [before noun] increasing or developing at a very fast rate that cannot be controlled: *galloping* ***inflation***

gallows /ˈgæl.əʊz/ (US) /-oʊz/ **noun** [C] (plural **gallows**) a wooden structure used, especially in the past, to hang criminals from as a form of EXECUTION (= killing as a punishment): *New witnesses have cast doubt on some of the evidence that* ***sent*** *the 19-year-old* ***to the*** *gallows.*

ˌ**gallows** ˈ**humour noun** [U] jokes or humorous remarks that are made about unpleasant or worrying subjects such as death and illness

gallstone /ˈgɔːl.stəʊn/ (US) /ˈgɑːl.stoʊn/ **noun** [C] a small piece of hard material which sometimes forms in the GALL BLADDER (= an organ in the body) and can cause great pain

Gallup poll /ˈgæl.əpˌpəʊl/ (US) /-ˌpoʊl/ **noun** [C] trademark a series of questions asked of a group of people in order to find out what they think about a particular subject or how they will vote in an election

galore /gəˈlɔːr/ (US) /-ˈlɔːr/ **adj** [after noun] old-fashioned informal in great amounts or numbers: *And for the sweet-toothed, this café has desserts galore.*

galoshes /gəˈlɒʃ.ɪz/ (US) /-ˈlɑː.ʃɪz/ **noun** [plural] US for **overshoes**

galumphing /gəˈlʌm.fɪŋ/ **adj** UK informal moving about or behaving in an awkward manner: *In his galumphing way he managed to wake the whole house on his return.*

galvanize (UK usually **galvanise**) /ˈgæl.və.naɪz/ **verb** [T] to cause someone to suddenly take action, especially by shocking or exciting them in some way: *Western charities were galvanized by TV pictures of starving people.* ◦ *The prospect of his mother coming to stay galvanized him* ***into action*** *and he set about cleaning the house.*

galvanized (UK usually **galvanised**) /ˈgæl.və.naɪzd/ **adj** describes metal, or something made of metal, that is covered with a thin layer of ZINC to protect it: *galvanized iron/steel* ◦ *galvanized nails/rivets*

gambit /ˈgæm.bɪt/ **noun** [C] **CLEVER ACTION** ▷ **1** a clever action in a game or other situation that is intended to achieve an advantage and usually involves taking a risk: *Her clever* ***opening*** *gambit gave her an early advantage.* ◦ *Their promise to lower taxes is clearly an election-year gambit.* **2** specialized a way of beginning a game of CHESS, in which you intentionally lose a PAWN (= game piece) in order to win some other form of advantage later **REMARK** ▷ **3** a remark that you make to someone in order to start a conversation: *'I hear you're a friend of Jamie's' was her* ***opening*** *gambit.*

gamble /ˈgæm.bl̩/ **verb; noun**

▸**verb 1** [I] to do something that involves risks that might result in loss of money or failure, hoping to get money or achieve success: *Anyone who gambles* ***on*** *the stock exchange has to be prepared to lose money.* **2** (C2) [I or T] to risk money, for example in a game or on a horse race: *I like to gamble when I play cards – it makes it more interesting.* ◦ *He gambles* ***on*** *the horses (= horse races).* ◦ *He gambled* ***away*** *all of our savings.*

PHRASAL VERB **gamble on sth** to take a risk that something will happen: *You're rather gambling on it being a nice day by holding the party in the garden, aren't you?*

▸**noun** [C usually singular] (C2) a risk that might result in loss of money or failure: *Her publishers knew they were* ***taking*** *a gamble when they agreed to publish such an unusual novel.* ◦ *It was a gamble using such an inexperienced director, but it* ***paid off*** *(= was successful).*

gambler /ˈgæm.bləʳ/ (US) /-blɚ/ **noun** [C] someone who often gambles, for example in a game or on a horse race: *a self-help group for* ***compulsive*** *gamblers*

gambling /ˈgæm.blɪŋ/ **noun** [U] (B2) the activity of BETTING money, for example in a game or on a horse race: *Gambling can be an addictive habit.* ◦ *He had to borrow money to pay off his gambling debts.*

gambol /ˈgæm.bᵊl/ **verb** [I] (**-ll-** or US usually **-l-**) literary to run and jump in a happy way: *Lambs were gambolling* ***(about/around)*** *in the spring sunshine.*

game /geɪm/ **noun; adj**

▸**noun FUN ACTIVITY/SPORT** ▷ **1** (A1) [C] an entertaining activity or sport, especially one played by children, or the equipment needed for such an activity: *a board game* ◦ *indoor/computer games* ◦ *The children played a game* ***of*** *cops and robbers.* ◦ *I told the children to put their toys and games away.* **2** (A2) [C] a particular competition, match, or occasion when people play a game: *a game* ***of*** *chess/tennis/baseball* **3** [C] one part of a competition in activities such as tennis: *I won the first game, and then lost the next two.* **4 games** [plural] **a** UK organized sports activities that children do at school: *the games teacher* ◦ *It's games this afternoon.* **b** an organized competition consisting of several different sports events: *the Olympic/Commonwealth Games* **5** [U] the way in which a person plays a particular sport: *Susan is playing golf every day to try to improve her game.* **6** [S] something that is not treated seriously: *Love is just a game to him.* **ACTIVITY** ▷ **7** [S] informal an illegal or secret activity **8** [S] old-fashioned informal a type of business activity: *I'm in the stocks and shares game.* **9 on the game** UK informal working as a PROSTITUTE: *She* ***went*** *on the game to pay for her drug habit.* **ANIMALS** ▷ **10** [U] wild animals and birds that are hunted for food or sport: *game* ***birds***

> **Word partners for game**
>
> *lose/play/win* a game • a *ball/board/computer/ indoor/outdoor* game • a game *of* sth

IDIOMS **be ahead of the game** to know more about the most recent developments in a particular subject or activity than the people or companies you are competing against: *A very extensive research and development programme ensures that we're ahead of the game.* • **be new to this game** to be involved in an activity or situation that you have not experienced before • **the game is up** used to tell someone that you know what their secret activities or plans are and they cannot continue • **give the game away** informal to spoil a surprise or a joke by telling someone something that should have been kept secret: *It's a secret, so don't give the game away, will you?* • **what's your game?** UK informal something you ask when you want to know what someone is doing or secretly planning to do: *The porter saw me climbing over the wall and shouted 'Hey you, what's your game?'*

▸adj willing to do things that are new, difficult, or that involve risks: *It was a difficult challenge, but Roberta was game.* ◦ *She's game **for** anything.* • **gamely** /-li/ adv *'I'll look after the baby,' he said gamely (= bravely).*

G

ˈgame ˌchanger noun [C] **1** something or someone that affects the result of a game very much: *As a player he can be a game changer.* **2** something such as a product or event that affects a situation or area of business very much: *The hit show has been a game changer for the network.*

ˈgame-ˌchanging adj **1** affecting the result of a game very much: *Every day, referees make game-changing decisions.* **2** having a big effect on the conditions in an area such as business: *New technology can create a game-changing shift in a market.*

gamekeeper /ˈgeɪmˌkiː.pəʳ/ (US) /-pɚ/ noun [C] a person whose job is to take care of wild animals and birds that are kept especially for hunting

gamelan /ˈgæm.ə.læn/ noun [C] an Indonesian ORCHESTRA consisting of PERCUSSION instruments, such as GONGS or CHIMES, and often FLUTES and STRINGED INSTRUMENTS: *gamelan music*

gamepad /ˈgeɪm.pæd/ noun [C] a piece of equipment with buttons for controlling an electronic game, that you hold in two hands

ˈgame ˌplan noun [C] a plan for achieving success: *You need to come up with a game plan, and stick to it.*

gamer /ˈgeɪm.əʳ/ (US) /-ɚ/ noun [C] **1** someone who likes playing computer games **2** a sports player who enjoys their sport very much and works very hard

ˈgame ˌshow noun [C] a television programme where people score points by answering questions or doing things: *a game show **host** (= a person who introduces the programme and asks the questions)*

gamesmanship /ˈgeɪmz.mən.ʃɪp/ noun [U] informal the activity of trying to win a game by doing things that are not really breaking the rules but are intended to destroy the confidence of the other player

gamete /ˈgæm.iːt/ noun [C] specialized a cell connected with sexual REPRODUCTION, either a male SPERM or a female egg

gamine /ˈgæm.iːn/ adj approving describes a girl or young woman who is thin, has short hair and is attractively like a young boy in appearance • **gamine** noun [C]

gaming /ˈgeɪ.mɪŋ/ noun [U] **BETTING** ▷ **1** the risking of money in games of chance, especially at a CASINO: *gaming machines/tables* **COMPUTER GAMES** ▷ **2** the activity of playing VIDEO GAMES

gamma /ˈgæm.ə/ noun [C or U] (symbol γ) the third letter of the Greek alphabet → Compare **alpha, beta, delta**

gamma globulin /ˌgæm.əˈglɒb.jʊ.lɪn/ (US) /-ˈglɑː.bjə-/ noun [U] a natural substance in the blood that gives protection against disease

ˌgamma radiˈation noun [U] a type of RADIATION with a very short WAVELENGTH, which passes through most solid objects

ˈgamma ˌray noun [C usually plural] a beam of gamma radiation

gammon /ˈgæm.ən/ noun [U] mainly UK (US usually **ham**) meat taken from the back leg or side of a pig and preserved with smoke or salt

gammy /ˈgæm.i/ adj UK informal A gammy leg or other body part is damaged or does not work correctly: *I've got a gammy knee.*

the gamut /ˈgæm.ət/ noun [S] **1** the whole range of things that can be included in something: *In her stories she expresses the **whole** gamut **of** emotions, from happiness to sorrow.* **2 run the gamut of sth** to experience or show the whole range of something: *Jonson has run the gamut of hotel work, from porter to owner of a large chain of hotels.*

gamy /ˈgeɪ.mi/ adj (**gamier**, **gamiest**) having the strong smell or taste of **game** (= wild animals or birds that are killed to eat)

gander /ˈgæn.dəʳ/ (US) /-dɚ/ noun **BIRD** ▷ **1** [C] a male GOOSE **LOOK** ▷ **2 have/take a gander** informal to have a quick look: *Let's take a gander **at** your new car, then.*

gang /gæŋ/ noun; verb

▸noun [C, + sing/pl verb] **1** (B2) a group of young people, especially young men, who spend time together, often fighting with other groups and behaving badly: *Fights among rival gangs account for most murders in the city.* **2** (B2) a group of criminals who work together: *a gang of armed robbers* **3** (C2) informal a group of friends: *She was in our gang at school.* ◦ *I went out with the usual gang from college on Friday night.* **4** a group of workers or prisoners who work together: *a gang of labourers*

▸verb

PHRASAL VERB **gang up** disapproving to unite as a group against someone: *They all ganged up to try and get him to change his decision.* ◦ *The whole class ganged up **against/on** her because she was the teacher's pet.*

ˈgang bang noun [C] slang → **gang rape** • **ˈgang-bang** verb [T] slang

gangbanger /ˈgæŋˌbæŋ.əʳ/ (US) /-ɚ/ noun [C] US slang a member of a violent group of young men, especially ones who use guns and commit crimes

gangland /ˈgæŋ.lænd/ noun [U] the people and places involved in violent crime: *a gangland feud/murder*

ganglion /ˈgæŋ.gli.ən/ noun [C] (plural **ganglia** or **ganglions**) specialized **1** a swelling, often on the back of the hand **2** a mass of nerve cells, especially appearing outside the brain or SPINE

gangly /ˈgæŋ.gli/ adj (also **gangling** /ˈgæŋ.glɪŋ/) describes someone, usually a boy or young man, who is very tall and thin and moves awkwardly: *a gangly youth*

gangmaster /ˈgæŋˌmɑː.stəʳ/ (US) /-ˌmæs.tɚ/ noun [C] UK someone who employs a large number of workers, often illegally and for very little money: *The Home Secretary has promised that the gangmasters responsible for immigration crime would be ruthlessly targeted.*

gangplank /ˈgæŋ.plæŋk/ noun [C] a board or similar object put between a boat or ship and the land, so that people can get on and off

ˈgang ˌrape noun [C] an occasion when a group of people use violence or threatening behaviour to force someone to have sex with all of them • **ˈgang-rape** verb [T]

gangrene /ˈgæŋ.griːn/ (US) /gæŋˈgriːn/ noun [U] the decay of a part of a person's body because the blood has stopped flowing there: *They had to amputate his leg because gangrene had **set in**.* • **gangrenous** /-grɪ.nəs/ adj

gangsta rap /ˈgæŋ.stə,ræp/ US /-stɚ-/ noun [U] a type of RAP music that is about life in the poor parts of cities, especially violence and drugs

gangster /ˈgæŋ.stəʳ/ US /-stɚ/ noun [C] a member of an organized group of violent criminals

gangway! /ˈgæŋ.weɪ/ exclamation something you shout when you want people to move so that you can get someone or something through a crowd quickly

gangway /ˈgæŋ.weɪ/ noun [C] **1** a passage between two rows of seats, for example in a cinema or bus: *His suitcase was blocking the gangway.* **2** a wide or big GANGPLANK

ganja /ˈgæn.dʒə/ noun [U] slang **marijuana**

gannet /ˈgæn.ɪt/ noun [C] a large bird with mainly white feathers and a yellow beak that lives by the sea

gantry /ˈgæn.tri/ noun [C] a tall metal frame that supports heavy machines such as CRANES, railway signals, or other equipment

Gantt chart /ˈgænt.tʃɑːt/ US /-tʃɑːrt/ noun [C] specialized a DIAGRAM (= picture) of the stages of a piece of work, showing stages that can be done at the same time, and stages that must be completed before others can start: *The activities and their durations are entered on the Gantt chart and the end date is displayed.*

gaol /dʒeɪl/ noun, verb UK old-fashioned for **jail**

gaoler /ˈdʒeɪ.ləʳ/ US /-lɚ/ noun [C] UK old-fashioned for **jailer**

gap /gæp/ noun **HOLE** ▷ **1** B1 [C] an empty space or opening in the middle of something or between two things: *The children squeezed through a gap* ***in*** *the wall.* ◦ *She has a small gap* ***between*** *her front teeth.* **2 gap in the market** C2 [C] an opportunity for a product or service that does not already exist: *There is a gap in the magazine market that needs to be filled.* **DIFFERENCE** ▷ **3** B2 [S] a difference between two things: *The gap* ***between*** *rich and poor is still widening (= becoming greater).* **4** B2 [C usually singular] a period of time spent doing something different: *After a gap* ***of*** *five years, Jennifer decided to go back to work full-time.*

IDIOM **bridge a/the gap** to connect two things or to make the difference between them smaller: *The president singled out education as a vital tool in bridging the gap* ***between*** *rich and poor.* ◦ *This collection of stories bridges the gap between history and fiction.*

gape /geɪp/ verb [I] **LOOK** ▷ **1** to look in great surprise at someone or something, especially with an open mouth: *They stood gaping* ***at*** *the pig in the kitchen.* **OPEN** ▷ **2** to be or become wide open: *Peter's jacket gaped at the seams.*

gaping /ˈgeɪ.pɪŋ/ adj describes a hole or other opening that is very large: *The bomb had left gaping holes in the wall.*

ˌgap-ˈtoothed adj having spaces between the front teeth

ˈgap ˌyear noun [C] UK a year between leaving school and starting university that is usually spent travelling or working: *I didn't* ***take*** *a gap year. Did you?*

garage /ˈgær.ɑːʒ/, /-ɪdʒ/ US /gəˈrɑːʒ/ noun; verb

▸**noun CARS** ▷ **1** A2 [C] a building where a car is kept, built next to or as part of a house: *Did you put the car in the garage?* **2** B1 [C] a place where cars are repaired: *The car's still* ***at*** *the garage getting fixed.* **3** [C] UK (US **gas station**) a place where fuel is sold for cars and other vehicles **MUSIC** ▷ **4** [U] fast, electronic dance music with a strong beat, keyboards, and singing

▸**verb** [T] to put or keep a vehicle in a garage: *If your car is garaged, you get much cheaper insurance.*

ˈgarage ˌsale noun [C] an occasion when people sell things, often in their garage or outside their house, that they no longer want

garam masala /ˌgɑː.rəm.məˈsɑː.lə/ noun [U] a mixture of ground spices, such as CUMIN, CORIANDER, and CARDAMOM, used in Indian cooking

garb /gɑːb/ US /gɑːrb/ noun [U] literary clothes of a particular type: *prison/clerical/military garb*

garbage /ˈgɑː.bɪdʒ/ US /ˈgɑːr-/ noun [U] **1** B1 US (UK **rubbish**) waste material or unwanted things that you throw away **2** nonsense or stupid ideas: *He talks a lot of garbage about education.*

IDIOM **garbage in, garbage out** mainly US saying something you say that means that something produced from materials of low quality will also be of low quality: *The meals are pretty poor but then they never use fresh ingredients – garbage in, garbage out.*

ˈgarbage ˌbag noun [C] US for **dustbin bag**

ˈgarbage ˌcan noun [C] US for **dustbin**

ˈgarbage colˌlector noun [C] US for **dustman**

ˈgarbage disˌposal noun [C] US for **waste disposal**

garbageman /ˈgɑː.bɪdʒˌmæn/ US /ˈgɑːr-/ noun [C] (plural **-men** /-men/) US for **dustman**

ˈgarbage ˌtruck noun [C] US for **dustcart**

garˈbanzo ˌbean noun [C] US for **chickpea**

garbled /ˈgɑː.bld/ US /ˈgɑːr-/ adj If words or messages are garbled, they are not clear and are very difficult to understand, often giving a false idea of the facts: *He left a rather garbled* ***message*** *on my answerphone.*

garçon /ˈgɑː.sɒn/ US /gɑːrˈsoʊn/ noun [C] old-fashioned a WAITER in a French restaurant

garden /ˈgɑː.dən/ US /ˈgɑːr-/ noun **1** A1 [C] (US usually **yard**) a piece of land next to and belonging to a house, where flowers and other plants are grown, and often containing an area of grass: *garden tools/furniture* ◦ *a garden shed* ◦ mainly UK *The house has a large* ***back*** *garden, and a small* ***front*** *garden.* **2** C1 [C usually plural] a public park with flowers, plants, and places to sit: *the Botanical Gardens*

ˈgarden ˌcentre noun [C] a place where you can buy things such as plants and equipment for your garden

ˌgarden ˈcity noun [C] UK a town that has been planned to include a lot of trees, plants, and open spaces

gardener /ˈgɑː.dən.əʳ/ US /ˈgɑːr.dən.ɚ/ noun [C] B2 someone who works in a garden, growing and taking care of plants: *I'm not much of a gardener (= not very good at taking care of my garden).*

ˈgarden ˌflat noun [C] UK an apartment that is on the ground level of a building and has its own garden

gardenia /gɑːˈdiː.ni.ə/ US /gɑːr-/ noun [C] a large white or yellow flower with a pleasant smell, or the bush that produces this

gardening /ˈgɑː.dən.ɪŋ/ US /ˈgɑːr-/ noun [U] B2 the job or activity of working in a garden, growing and taking care of the plants, and keeping it attractive: *Many people in Britain are fond of gardening.* ◦ *gardening gloves*

ˈgardening ˌleave noun [U] UK a period of time after an employee leaves a job when they continue to be paid but are not allowed to go to work or to begin a new job: *He is currently* ***on*** *gardening leave and may not take up his new post until May.*

the ˌgarden of ˈEden noun [S] literary the beautiful garden, described in the Bible, made by God for Adam and Eve

ˌgarden ˈparty noun [C] (US also **ˈlawn ˌparty**) a formal party that happens outside in the afternoon, often in a large private garden

gargantuan /ɡɑːˈɡæn.tju.ən/ (US) /ɡɑːr-/ **adj** very large: *a problem **of** gargantuan **proportions*** ◦ *a gargantuan appetite*

gargle /ˈɡɑː.ɡl/ (US) /ˈɡɑːr-/ **verb** [I] to move a liquid around in your throat without swallowing, especially to clean it or stop it feeling painful • **gargle noun** [S] *Have **a** gargle with this mouthwash.*

gargoyle /ˈɡɑː.ɡɔɪl/ (US) /ˈɡɑːr-/ **noun** [C] an ugly creature or head cut from stone and fixed to the roof of an old church, etc., often with an open mouth through which rain water flows away

garish /ˈɡeə.rɪʃ/ (US) /ˈɡer.ɪʃ/ **adj** disapproving unpleasantly bright: *a pair of garish Bermuda shorts*

G

garland /ˈɡɑː.lənd/ (US) /ˈɡɑːr-/ **noun; verb**

▸**noun** [C] a circle made of flowers and leaves worn around the neck or head as a decoration: *a garland of white roses*

▸**verb** [T] to put garlands on someone or something: *They garlanded the visitors **with** scented flowers.*

garlic /ˈɡɑː.lɪk/ (US) /ˈɡɑːr-/ **noun** [U] (A2) a plant of the onion family that has a strong taste and smell and is used in cooking to add flavour: *For this recipe you need four **cloves** (= single pieces) of garlic, crushed.* ◦ *a garlic bulb*

ˌgarlic ˈbread noun [U] bread that has been spread with a mixture of butter, garlic, and herbs before being baked

garlicky /ˈɡɑː.lɪ.ki/ (US) /ˈɡɑːr-/ **adj** containing, tasting, or smelling of garlic: *garlicky food/breath*

garment /ˈɡɑː.mənt/ (US) /ˈɡɑːr-/ **noun** [C] formal (C1) a piece of clothing

garner /ˈɡɑː.nəʳ/ (US) /ˈɡɑːr.nɚ/ **verb** [T] literary to collect something, usually after much work or with difficulty: *Coppola garnered several Oscar awards for 'The Godfather'.*

garnet /ˈɡɑː.nɪt/ (US) /ˈɡɑːr-/ **noun** [C] a hard, dark red stone used in jewellery

garnish /ˈɡɑː.nɪʃ/ (US) /ˈɡɑːr-/ **verb; noun**

▸**verb** [T] to decorate food with a small amount of different food: *Garnish the dish **with** parsley before serving.*

▸**noun** [C or U] a small amount of different food used to decorate a dish or serving of food: *a lemon and herb garnish*

garret /ˈɡær.ɪt/ **noun** [C] literary a very small uncomfortable room at the top of a house

garrison /ˈɡær.ɪ.sᵊn/ (US) /ˈɡer-/ **noun; verb**

▸**noun** [C, + sing/pl verb] a group of soldiers living in or defending a town or building, or the buildings that the soldiers live in: *The 100-strong garrison has/have received no supplies for a week.* ◦ *a garrison **town***

▸**verb** [T usually passive + adv/prep] to put a group of soldiers in a place in order to live there and defend it: *British troops are garrisoned in the area.*

garrotte /ɡəˈrɒt/ (US) /-ˈrɑːt/ **verb; noun**

▸**verb** [T] (also **garotte**, US also **garrote**) to kill someone by putting a metal wire or collar around their neck to break their neck or stop them breathing

▸**noun** [C] (also **garotte**, US also **garrote**) a metal wire or collar used to kill someone

garrulous /ˈɡær.ᵊl.əs/ (US) /ˈɡer-/ **adj** having the habit of talking a lot, especially about things that are not important • **garrulously** /-li/ **adv** • **garrulousness** /-nəs/ **noun** [U]

garter /ˈɡɑː.təʳ/ (US) /ˈɡɑːr.t̬ɚ/ **noun 1** [C] a piece of ELASTIC (= material that stretches) used, especially in the past, for holding up a STOCKING or sock **2 garters** [plural] US for **suspenders**

gas /ɡæs/ **noun; verb**

▸**noun AIR SUBSTANCE** ▷ **1** (B2) [C or U] a substance in a form like air that is neither solid nor liquid: *Oxygen, hydrogen and nitrogen are all gases.* ◦ *poisonous/inflammable/toxic gas* **2** (A2) [C or U] a substance in a form like air that is used as a fuel for heating and cooking: *Do you prefer cooking with electricity or gas?* ◦ UK *A leak in the gas **mains** (= pipes) caused a major explosion.* ◦ *a gas-**fired** power station* **3** [U] informal a substance in a form like air used for medical purposes to prevent people feeling pain or being conscious during an operation: *I had/was given gas when I got my wisdom teeth out.* **4** [U] mainly US for **wind**: *Beer gives me gas.* **LIQUID FUEL** ▷ **5** (A2) [U] US for **petrol**: *I'll stop and get some gas – we're running low.* ◦ *a gas tank/pump* **6 the gas** [S] US the part of a car that you push with your foot to make it go faster: *Step on the gas (= drive faster)!* **ENJOYABLE SITUATION** ▷ **7** [S] mainly US informal a funny or enjoyable situation: *Some kids put on a show for the moms and dads, – it was **a** gas.*

▸**verb** (-ss-) **POISON** ▷ **1** [T] to kill or injure a person by making them breathe poisonous gas **TALK** ▷ **2** [I] old-fashioned informal to talk for a long time about things that are not important: *Susan came round and we sat gassing for hours.*

PHRASAL VERB **gas (sth) up** US to fill a vehicle's fuel container with fuel: *I want to gas up when we get to the next town.*

gasbag /ˈɡæs.bæɡ/ **noun** [C] informal a person who always talks too much

ˈgas ˌchamber noun [C] a room that can be filled with poisonous gas in order to kill the people or animals inside it

gaseous /ˈɡeɪ.si.əs/ (US) /ˈɡæ.si.əs/ **adj** specialized consisting of gas or gases, or like gas: *a gaseous mixture* ◦ *Steam is water in its gaseous form.*

ˌgas ˈfire noun [C] UK (US **ˈgas ˌheater**) a fire that uses gas as a fuel to heat a room

ˌgas-ˈfired adj UK using gas as a fuel: *gas-fired central heating*

gas guzzler /ˈɡæsˌɡʌz.ləʳ/ (US) /-lɚ/ **noun** [C] mainly US informal a car that uses a lot of fuel • **ˈgas-ˌguzzling** adj [before noun]

gash /ɡæʃ/ **noun; verb**

▸**noun** [C] a long, deep cut, especially in the skin

▸**verb** [T] to make a long, deep cut in something, especially the skin on a part of the body: *She slipped on a rock and gashed her knee.*

gasket /ˈɡæs.kɪt/ **noun** [C] a flat piece of soft material or rubber that is put between two joined metal surfaces to prevent gas, oil, or steam from escaping: *The gasket has **blown** (= allowed gas, oil, or steam to escape).* → See also **blow a fuse/gasket**

gaslight /ˈɡæs.laɪt/ **noun** [C or U] a light that uses gas as fuel, or the light that is produced by this

gasman /ˈɡæs.mæn/ **noun** [C] (plural **-men** /-men/) UK informal a man whose job is reading gas METERS and repairing gas systems

ˈgas ˌmark noun [U] UK one of a set of numbers on a gas cooker that is used instead of the temperature to show how hot it is: *Preheat the oven to gas mark 4.*

ˈgas ˌmask noun [C] a device worn over the face to prevent you from breathing in poisonous gases

gasoline /ˈɡæs.ᵊl.iːn/ **noun** [U] US (B2) formal for **gas**

gasometer /ɡæsˈɒm.ɪ.təʳ/ (US) /-ˈɑː.mə.t̬ɚ/ **noun** [C] (also **gasholder**) a large metal container where gas is stored before it is supplied to customers

gasp /gɑːsp/ (US) /gæsp/ **verb; noun**

▸**verb** [I] **1** (C2) to take a short, quick breath through the mouth, especially because of surprise, pain, or shock: *When she saw the money hidden in the box she gasped **in** surprise.* ◦ [+ speech] *'Help me!' he gasped.* **2** (C2) to breathe loudly and with difficulty, trying to get more air: *He pulled her aboard the boat and she sprawled on the deck, coughing and gasping **for** breath.*

IDIOMS **be gasping** UK informal to be very thirsty • **be gasping for sth** UK informal to want or need something very much: *I'm absolutely gasping for a cigarette.*

▸**noun** [C] (C2) an act of gasping: *He gave a gasp **of** amazement.*

ˈgas ˌpedal noun [C usually singular] US **accelerator**

ˌgas-ˈpermeable adj used to describe CONTACT LENSES that allow gases to pass through them

gasses /ˈgæs.ɪz/ plural of **gas**

ˈgas ˌstation noun [C] (A2) US for **petrol station**

gassy /ˈgæs.i/ adj containing a lot of gas → Synonym **fizzy**

gastric /ˈgæs.trɪk/ adj specialized relating to the stomach: *gastric juices* ◦ *a gastric ulcer*

ˌgastric ˈband noun [C] a strip of material that can be put around part of someone's stomach in a medical operation so that the person feels less hungry, eats less food, and loses weight

gastritis /gæsˈtraɪ.tɪs/ (US) /-t̬əs/ noun [U] specialized an illness in which the stomach walls become swollen and painful

gastroenteritis /ˌgæs.trəʊˌen.təˈraɪ.tɪs/ (US) /-troʊˌen.t̬əˈraɪ.t̬əs/ noun [U] specialized an illness which causes the stomach and bowels to become swollen and painful

gastrointestinal /ˌgæs.trəʊˌɪn.tesˈtaɪ.nəl/ (US) /-troʊ.ɪnˈtes.tən.əl/ adj in or relating to both the stomach and the INTESTINE (= long tube food passes through after the stomach): *the gastrointestinal **tract*** ◦ *gastrointestinal bleeding*

gastronome /ˈgæs.trə.nəʊm/ (US) /-noʊm/ noun [C] someone who enjoys and knows about high-quality food and drink

gastronomic /ˌgæs.trəˈnɒm.ɪk/ (US) /-ˈnɑː.mɪk/ adj (also **gastronomical**) relating to the preparation and CONSUMPTION (= eating) of good food: *This dish is a gastronomic delight.*

gastronomy /gæsˈtrɒn.ə.mi/ (US) /-ˈtrɑː.nə-/ noun [U] formal the art and knowledge involved in preparing and eating good food

gastropod /ˈgæs.trəʊ.pɒd/ (US) /-trə.pɑːd/ noun [C] specialized a type of animal with no SPINE, a soft body with a flat base used for moving, and often a shell, for example a SNAIL or a SLUG

gastropub /ˈgæs.trəʊ.pʌb/ (US) /-troʊ-/ noun [C] a bar where high quality food is served: *an organic gastropub*

gasworks /ˈgæs.wɜːks/ (US) /-wɝːks/ noun [C, + sing/pl verb] (plural **gasworks**) a factory where coal is made into gas for use as fuel for heating and cooking

gate /geɪt/ noun [C] **STRUCTURE** ▷ **1** (A2) a part of a fence or outside wall that is fixed at one side and opens and closes like a door, usually made of metal or wooden strips **2** a similar device that slides across an opening, often folding into a smaller space as it is opened: *The lift won't move if the safety gate isn't shut properly.* **3** (B1) a part of an airport where travellers are allowed to get on or off a particular aircraft: *All passengers for flight LH103 please proceed to gate 16.* **PEOPLE** ▷ **4** UK informal the number of people that go to see a sports event or other large event, or the amount of money people pay to see it: *Gates at football matches were lower than average last season.*

gateau /ˈgæt.əʊ/ (US) /gæt̬ˈoʊ/ noun [C or U] (plural **gateaus** or **gateaux**) a large, sweet cake, usually with cream or fruit in it: *a chocolate/raspberry gateau*

gatecrash /ˈgeɪt.kræʃ/ verb [I or T] informal to go to a party or other event when you have not been invited: *He decided to gatecrash the wedding.* • **gatecrasher** /-əʳ/ (US) /-ɚ/ noun [C]

ˌgated comˈmunity noun [U] mainly US a group of houses surrounded by fences or walls, that can only be entered by the people who live there: *The neighborhood is a gated community with a security guard to protect residents from intruders.*

gatefold /ˈgeɪt.fəʊld/ (US) /-foʊld/ noun [C] a cover for a book, magazine, or set of CDs or DVDs that is folded in the middle and opens out so that it is twice as big

gatehouse /ˈgeɪt.haʊs/ noun [C] a small house at the gate into a castle, park, or other large building or area of land, often lived in by someone employed to take care of it

gatekeeper /ˈgeɪtˌkiː.pəʳ/ (US) /-pɚ/ noun [C] **1** a person whose job is to open and close a gate and to prevent people entering without permission **2** a person or organization that has control over allowing people to have or use a particular service: *British Telecom lost its gatekeeper status when it was forced to open up the local network to other companies.*

gatepost /ˈgeɪt.pəʊst/ (US) /-poʊst/ noun [C] a post to which a gate is fixed, or to which it fastens when closed

IDIOM **between you, me, and the gatepost** (also **between you and me**) an expression used to tell someone that what you are about to say should be kept secret

gateway /ˈgeɪt.weɪ/ noun [C] **1** an entrance through a wall, fence, etc. where there is a gate **2** **gateway to somewhere** a place through which you have to go to get to a particular area: *Manchester is known as the gateway to the north.* **3** something in a system that allows you to use its other parts: *The bank is your gateway to a whole range of financial services.*

gather /ˈgæð.əʳ/ (US) /-ɚ/ **verb; noun**

▸**verb** **COLLECT** ▷ **1** (B2) [T] to collect several things, often from different places or people: *I went to several libraries to gather information about the scheme.* ◦ *We gathered blackberries from the hedgerow.* ◦ *She gathered **up** the newspapers that were scattered around the floor.* ◦ *We gathered our things **together** and left quickly.* **2** [T + adv/prep] to put your arms around someone and hold or carry them in a careful or loving way: *He gathered her **in** his arms and kissed her.* ◦ *She gathered the children up and hurried into the house.* **3** **gather speed, strength, momentum, etc.** (C1) to become faster, stronger, etc.: *The bicycle gathered speed as it went down the hill.* ◦ *Economic recovery is gathering pace.* **4** **gather (up) strength/courage** to prepare to make a great effort to be strong or brave: *I spent a week gathering the courage to say no.* **COME TOGETHER** ▷ **5** (B2) [I] When people or animals gather, they come together in a group: *A crowd had gathered to hear her speak.* ◦ *Gather **round**, children, and I'll tell you a story.* **6** [I] literary to get thicker and closer: *Storm **clouds** were gathering.* **UNDERSTAND** ▷ **7** (C1) [T] to understand or believe something as a result of something that has been said or done: *Harry loves his new job, I gather.* ◦ [+ (that)]

From the look on their faces, she gathered (**that**) *they were annoyed with her.* ◦ [+ question word] *I never really gathered* ***why*** *he left his job.* ◦ *I didn't gather much from his lecture.* **CLOTH** ▷ **8** [T] to pull cloth into small folds by sewing a thread through it and then pulling the thread tight: *a gathered skirt* **9** [T] If you gather a piece of clothing or loose cloth about/around yourself, you pull it close to your body: *She shivered, and gathered the blanket* ***around*** *her.*

IDIOM **gather dust** to not be used for a long time: *My guitar has just been gathering dust since I injured my hand.*

▸noun [C usually plural] a small fold that has been sewn into cloth: *a skirt with gathers at the back*

gathering /ˈgæð.ər.ɪŋ/ ⓤⓢ /-ɚ-/ noun [C] C1 a party or a meeting when many people come together as a group: *There will be a gathering* ***of*** *world leaders in Vienna next month.* ◦ *a* ***social*** *gathering (= when people meet for pleasure not work)*

gator /ˈgeɪ.təʳ/ ⓤⓢ /-t̬ɚ/ noun [C] US informal for **alligator**

gauche /gəʊʃ/ ⓤⓢ /goʊʃ/ adj awkward and uncomfortable with other people, especially because young and without experience: *She had grown from a gauche teenager to a self-assured young woman.*

gaucho /ˈgaʊ.tʃəʊ/ ⓤⓢ /-tʃoʊ/ noun [C] (plural **gauchos**) a South American COWBOY (= person who takes care of male and female cows)

gaudy /ˈgɔː.di/ ⓤⓢ /ˈgɑː-/ adj unpleasantly bright in colour or decoration: *gaudy plastic flowers* • **gaudily** /-dɪ.li/ adv • **gaudiness** /-nəs/ noun [U]

gauge /geɪdʒ/ verb; noun

▸verb [T] (US also **gage**) **MEASURE** ▷ **1** to calculate an amount, especially by using a measuring device: *Use a thermometer to gauge the temperature.* ◦ *I tried to gauge (= guess) the weight of the box.* **JUDGE** ▷ **2** to make a judgment about something, usually people's feelings: *A poll was conducted to gauge consumers' attitudes.* ◦ [+ question word] *It's difficult to gauge* ***how*** *they'll react.*

▸noun (US also **gage**) **MEASURE** ▷ **1** [C] a device for measuring the amount or size of something: *a fuel/rain/temperature gauge* **2** [C] specialized the distance between the RAILS (= the two long metal bars fixed to the ground) on a railway line: *a* ***narrow/standard*** *gauge railway* **3** [C] specialized the thickness of something, especially metal or wire **JUDGING** ▷ **4** [S] a way of judging or showing something, especially how successful or popular something is: *The fact that the play has transferred to New York is a gauge* ***of*** *its success.*

gaunt /gɔːnt/ ⓤⓢ /gɑːnt/ adj **1** very thin, especially because of sickness or hunger: *Her face was gaunt and grey.* **2** literary empty and not attractive • **gauntness** /-nəs/ noun [U]

gauntlet /ˈgɔːnt.lət/ ⓤⓢ /ˈgɑːnt-/ noun [C] a long, thick GLOVE (= hand covering), worn for protection

IDIOMS **run the gauntlet** to have to deal with a lot of people who are criticizing or attacking you: *Every day they had to run the gauntlet* ***of*** *hostile journalists on their way to school.* • **take/pick up the gauntlet** to agree to fight or compete with someone • **throw down the gauntlet** to invite someone to fight or compete with you: *A price war looks likely now that a leading supermarket has thrown down the gauntlet to its competitors.*

gauze /gɔːz/ ⓤⓢ /gɑːz/ noun **1** [U] a very thin, light cloth, used to make clothing, to cover cuts, and to separate solids from liquids, etc.: *a gauze skirt* ◦ *a piece of sterile gauze* **2** [C or U] a material like a net formed by wires crossing over each other: ***wire*** *gauze* • **gauzy** /ˈgɔː.zi/ ⓤⓢ /ˈgɑː-/ adj

gave /geɪv/ past simple of **give**

gavel /ˈgæv.əl/ noun [C] a small hammer which an official in charge of a meeting hits against a wooden block or table to get people to be quiet and listen

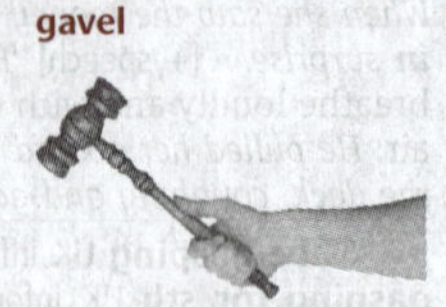
gavel

ˌgavel-to-ˈgavel adj US lasting from the beginning to the end of an event: *Broadcasters provided gavel-to-gavel coverage of the trial.*

gavotte /gəˈvɒt/ ⓤⓢ /-ˈvɑːt/ noun [C] a fast dance from France, popular in the past, or a piece of music for this

Gawd (also **gawd**) /gɔːd/ ⓤⓢ /gɑːd/ mainly humorous an informal way of writing the word god, when used in expressions of fear, surprise, etc.: *'Gawd help us,' she cried out.* ◦ *Oh gawd! You don't believe that do you?*

gawk /gɔːk/ ⓤⓢ /gɑːk/ verb [I] (UK also **gawp**) to look at something or someone in a stupid or rude way: *Don't sit there gawking like that – give me a hand!* ◦ UK *They just stood there gawping* ***at*** *me.*

gawky /ˈgɔː.ki/ ⓤⓢ /ˈgɑː-/ adj informal tall and awkward: *a gawky teenager*

gawp /gɔːp/ ⓤⓢ /gɑːp/ verb [I] UK for **gawk**

gay /geɪ/ adj; noun

▸adj **SEXUALITY** ▷ **1** B1 sexually attracted to people of the same sex and not to people of the opposite sex: *gay rights* ◦ *Mark knew he was gay by the time he was fourteen.* ◦ *the lesbian and gay community* **HAPPY** ▷ **2** old-fashioned happy: *We had a gay old time down at the dance hall.* **3** old-fashioned If a place is gay, it is bright and attractive: *The streets were gay and full of people.* **BAD QUALITY** ▷ **4** slang offensive not good, reasonable, or suitable • **gayness** /ˈgeɪ.nəs/ noun [U]

▸noun [C] a gay person, especially a man

ˈgay-ˌbasher noun [C] (also **ˈqueer-ˌbasher**) slang disapproving someone who hates gay people and attacks them violently • **ˈgay-ˌbashing** noun [U] (also **ˈqueer-ˌbashing**) violence directed at gay people

gaydar /ˈgeɪ.dɑːʳ/ ⓤⓢ /-dɑːr/ noun [U] humorous an ability to notice that someone is gay

ˌgay liberˈation noun [U] the principle that gay people should be treated equally in society: *the gay liberation movement*

ˌgay ˈpride noun [U] the idea that gay people should not keep the fact of their SEXUALITY secret and that they should be proud of it instead, or the social and political movement that is based on this idea: *a gay pride rally*

ˌgay ˈrights noun [plural] the principle that gay people should have the same legal and political rights as everyone else

gaze /geɪz/ verb; noun

▸verb [I usually + adv/prep] B2 to look at something or someone for a long time, especially in surprise or admiration or because you are thinking about something else: *Annette gazed admiringly* ***at*** *Warren as he spoke.* ◦ *He spends hours gazing* ***out of*** *the window when he should be working.*

▸noun [S] C2 a long look, usually of a particular kind: *a* ***steady*** *gaze* ◦ *an* ***innocent/admiring*** *gaze* ◦ literary *As I looked out, my gaze fell on a small child by the road.*

gazebo /gəˈziː.bəʊ/ ⓤⓢ /-boʊ/ noun [C] (plural **gazebos**) a small decorated building, usually in a garden, giving a good view of the surrounding countryside

gazelle /gəˈzel/ **noun** [C] an African or Asian mammal with HOOFS and large eyes that moves quickly and lightly

gazette /gəˈzet/ **noun** [C] **1** old-fashioned a newspaper **2** used in the titles of some newspapers and magazines: *the Montreal Gazette*

gazetteer /ˌgæz.əˈtɪəʳ/ (US) /-ˈtɪr/ **noun** [C] a book or part of a book that contains a list of names of places, usually with some extra information: *the Cambridge Gazetteer of the United States and Canada*

gazpacho /gæsˈpætʃ.əʊ/ (US) /-pɑː.tʃoʊ/ **noun** [U or C] a soup made from tomatoes and uncooked vegetables, and eaten cold

gazump /gəˈzʌmp/ **verb** [T often passive] UK informal to refuse to sell a house that you own to someone you have agreed to sell it to, and to sell it instead to someone who offers to pay more for it: *Sally's offer for the house has been accepted, but she's worried she might be gazumped.* • **gazumping** /-ˈzʌm.pɪŋ/ **noun** [U] *During the 1980s, practices like gazumping gave the property business in England a bad name.*

gazunder /gəˈzʌn.dəʳ/ (US) /-dɚ/ **verb** [T often passive] UK informal to unfairly demand a reduction in the price you have agreed to pay for a house just before you buy it • **gazundering** /-ɪŋ/ **noun** [U]

GB /ˌdʒiːˈbiː/ **noun** abbreviation for Great Britain

GBH /ˌdʒiː.biːˈeɪtʃ/ **noun** [U] abbreviation for **grievous bodily harm**

GCE /ˌdʒiː.siːˈiː/ **noun** [C] abbreviation for General Certificate of Education: before 1988, an English and Welsh public exam taken in various subjects, especially one taken at the age of about 16

GCSE /ˌdʒiː.siː.esˈiː/ **noun** [C or U] General Certificate of Secondary Education: a system of public exams taken in various subjects from the age of about 16, or one of these exams, or a qualification from this system: *I'm taking six subjects for GCSE.* ◦ *Owen is retaking two of his GCSEs.* ◦ *She's got nine GCSEs, all at grade A.*

GDA /ˌdʒiː.diːˈeɪ/ **noun** [U] abbreviation for Guideline Daily Amount: used on food packaging to tell you how much of something you should eat each day in order to stay healthy

g'day /gəˈdeɪ/ **exclamation** Australian English informal used when meeting or greeting someone

GDP /ˌdʒiː.diːˈpiː/ **noun** [U] specialized abbreviation for Gross Domestic Product: the total value of goods and services produced by a country in a year: *If the GDP continues to shrink, the country will be in a recession.* → Compare **GNP**

gear /gɪəʳ/ (US) /gɪr/ **noun; verb**

▸**noun ENGINE PART** ▷ **1** (B2) [C or U] a device, often consisting of connecting sets of wheels with teeth (= points) around the edge, that controls how much power from an engine goes to the moving parts of a machine: *Does your car have four or five gears?* ◦ *I couldn't find reverse gear.* ◦ *The car should be **in** gear (= with its gears in position, allowing the vehicle to move).* ◦ *When you start a car you need to be **in** first* (US also ***low***) *gear.* ◦ figurative *After a slow start, the leadership campaign suddenly shifted into **top** gear (= started to advance very quickly).* **2 change gear** UK (US also **shift gear**) to change the position of the gears to make a vehicle go faster or more slowly **CLOTHES/EQUIPMENT** ▷ **3** (B2) [U] the equipment, clothes, etc. that you use to do a particular activity: *fishing/camping gear* ◦ *Police in **riot** gear (= protective clothing) arrived to control the protesters.* → See also **headgear 4** (B2) informal clothes: *She wears all the latest gear.* **DRUGS** ▷ **5** [U] UK slang drugs: *The traffickers knew that there would always be someone willing to move the gear.*

IDIOM **step/move up a gear** informal to start to do something better, especially in sports, in a way that is easy to see: *After a disappointing first half, United moved up a gear and took control of the game.*

▸**verb**

PHRASAL VERBS **gear sth to/towards sb/sth** to design or organize something so that it is suitable for a particular purpose, situation, or group of people: *Most public places are simply not geared to the needs of people with disabilities.* ◦ *The workshops are geared towards helping people to become more employable.* ◦ *These advertisements are geared towards a younger audience.* • **gear (sb/sth) up** to prepare for something that you have to do, or to prepare someone else for something: *Politicians are already gearing up **for** the election.* ◦ [+ to infinitive] *I'm gearing my**self** up **to** ask him to give me my money back.* ◦ *I'm trying to gear my**self** up **for** tomorrow's exam.*

gearbox /ˈgɪə.bɒks/ (US) /ˈgɪr.bɑːks/ **noun** [C] specialized a metal box containing the gears in a vehicle

gearing /ˈgɪə.rɪŋ/ (US) /ˈgɪr.ɪŋ/ **noun** [U] (also **leverage**) UK SPECIALIZED the amount a company has borrowed compared to its SHARE CAPITAL: *You must look at the company's gearing **level** and its ability to service its debt.*

ˈgear ˌlever **noun** [C] (also **gearstick** /ˈgɪə.stɪk/ (US) /ˈgɪr-/) UK a metal rod that you use to change gear in a car or other vehicle

gearshift /ˈgɪə.ʃɪft/ (US) /ˈgɪr-/ **noun** [C] US for **gear lever**

gecko /ˈgek.əʊ/ (US) /-oʊ/ **noun** [C] (plural **geckos** or **geckoes**) a small LIZARD with wide feet, found especially in warm countries

GED /ˌdʒiː.iːˈdiː/ **noun** [C] abbreviation for General Equivalency Diploma: an official document in the US that is given to someone who did not complete HIGH SCHOOL (= school for students aged 15–18) but who has passed a government exam instead

geddit? /ˈged.ɪt/ **exclamation** UK informal used at the end of saying something to attract attention to a joke that has been made with two meanings of a word: *'The new series of plays on Channel Four is called 4-Play. Geddit?'*

gee /dʒiː/ **exclamation; verb**

▸**exclamation** mainly US informal an expression of surprise or enthusiasm: *Gee, honey, is that all your own hair?*

▸**verb**

PHRASAL VERBS **gee sb up** UK informal to encourage someone to show more effort or enthusiasm • **gee up!** UK informal something that you say to a horse to make it move faster: *Gee up, Neddy!*

ˈgee-gee **noun 1** [C] UK child's word a horse **2 the gee-gees** informal horse races where you try to win money by correctly guessing which horse will win: *He won some money on the gee-gees.*

geek /giːk/ **noun** [C] informal a person, especially a man, who is boring and not fashionable: *He's such a geek.*

geeky /ˈgiː.ki/ **adj** informal boring and not fashionable: *a geeky-looking guy in glasses*

geese /giːs/ plural of **goose**

ˌgee ˈwhiz exclamation old-fashioned an expression of surprise or enthusiasm

geezer /ˈgiː.zəʳ/ (US) /-zɚ/ noun [C] UK informal a man, often old or unusual in some way: *a funny old geezer* ◦ *She got talking to some geezer in the pub.*

Geiger counter /ˈgaɪ.gəˌkaʊn.təʳ/ (US) /-gɚˌkaʊn.t̬ɚ/ noun [C] an electronic device for measuring the level of RADIOACTIVITY

geisha /ˈgeɪ.ʃə/ noun [C] a Japanese woman trained in music and dancing whose job is entertaining men

gel /dʒel/ noun; verb

▸noun [U] a thick, clear, liquid substance, especially one used on the hair or body: *shower gel* ◦ *hair gel*

▸verb (-ll-) **BECOME FIRM** ▷ **1** (US also **jell**) [I] to change from a liquid into a thick, soft solid **2** (US also **jell**) [I] If an idea or situation gels, it starts to become more clear and fixed: *The race issue gelled in the 1960s.* **3** (US also **jell**) [I] If two or more people gel, they form a good relationship or become friends: *The team really gelled during the first few games of the season.* **ON HAIR** ▷ **4** [T] to put gel on your hair

G

gelatine (US usually **gelatin**) /ˈdʒel.ə.tiːn/ noun [U] a clear substance, often sold in the form of a powder, made from animal bones and used especially to make JELLY

gelatinous /dʒəˈlæt.ɪ.nəs/ (US) /-læt̬-/ adj thick and like JELLY: *The liquid solidifies into a gelatinous mass.*

geld /geld/ verb [T] to remove the TESTICLES of a male horse or similar animal

gelding /ˈgel.dɪŋ/ noun [C] a male horse that has been gelded

gelignite /ˈdʒel.ɪg.naɪt/ noun [U] a very powerful explosive substance, similar to DYNAMITE

gem /dʒem/ noun [C] **JEWEL** ▷ **1** (also **gemstone**) a JEWEL (= precious stone), especially when cut into a particular regular shape **VERY GOOD** ▷ **2** someone or something that is very good, pleasing, or useful: *You've been an* ***absolute*** *gem – I couldn't have managed without your help.* ◦ *He came out with a gem (= clever or pleasing remark) about the absurdity of the situation.*

Gemini /ˈdʒem.ɪ.naɪ/ noun [C or U] the third sign of the ZODIAC, relating to the period 23 May to 21 June, represented by TWINS (= two people born together), or a person born during this period

gen /dʒen/ noun; verb

▸noun [U] UK old-fashioned informal information about a particular subject: *So who's going to* ***give*** *me* ***the*** *gen* ***on*** *what's been happening while I've been away?*

▸verb (-nn-)

PHRASAL VERB **gen up** UK old-fashioned informal to find out as much information as possible: *Derek genned up* ***on*** *the country's history before going there.*

gender /ˈdʒen.dəʳ/ (US) /-dɚ/ noun **SEX** ▷ **1** (B2) [U] the physical and/or social condition of being male or female: *Does this test show the gender of the baby?* ◦ *Discrimination on the basis of race, gender, age or disability is not allowed.* → Compare **sex 2** [C, + sing/pl verb] all males, or all females, considered as one group: *I think both genders are capable of looking after children.* → Compare **sex** **GRAMMAR** ▷ **3** (B2) [C] specialized the grammatical arrangement of nouns, PRONOUNS and adjectives into MASCULINE, FEMININE, and NEUTER types in some languages

ˌgender discriminˈation noun [U] (also **ˌgender ˈbias**) a situation in which someone is treated less well because of their sex, usually when a woman is treated less well than a man: *The report will examine unequal pay as well as other types of gender discrimination in the workplace.*

ˌgender-ˈneutral adj relating to people and not especially to men or to women: *gender-neutral words such as 'person'*

ˌgender reasˈsignment noun [C or U] a process, including medical operations, by which someone's sex is changed from male to female or female to male

gene /dʒiːn/ noun [C] (C1) a part of the DNA in a cell that controls the physical development, behaviour, etc. of an individual plant or animal and is passed on from its parents: *The illness is believed to be caused by a defective gene.*

genealogy /ˌdʒiː.niˈæl.ə.dʒi/ noun **1** [U] (the study of) the history of the past and present members of a family: *I became interested in the genealogy* ***of*** *my family.* **2** [C] a drawing showing the history of a family with all past and present members joined together by lines • **genealogical** /ˌdʒiː.ni.əˈlɒdʒ.ɪ.kəl/ (US) /ˈlɑː.dʒɪ-/ adj • **genealogically** /ˌdʒiː.ni.əˈlɒdʒ.ɪ.kəl.i/ (US) /ˈlɑː.dʒɪ-/ adv • **genealogist** /-dʒɪst/ noun [C] someone who studies genealogy

ˈgene ˌpool noun [C] all the genes of a particular group of people or animals

genera /ˈdʒen.ər.ə/ (US) /-ɚ-/ plural of **genus**

general /ˈdʒen.ər.əl/ (US) /-ɚ-/ adj; noun

▸adj **COMMON** ▷ **1** (B2) involving or relating to most or all people, things, or places, especially when these are considered as a unit: *The general feeling at the meeting was that a vote should be taken.* ◦ *There is general concern about rising crime rates.* ◦ *My general impression of the place was good.* ◦ *The talk is intended to be of general* ***interest*** *(= of interest to most people).* ◦ UK formal *Rain will become more general in the southeast during the afternoon.* **2 in general a** (B1) (also **as a general rule**) usually, or in most situations: *In general, men are taller than women.* ◦ *As a general rule, we don't allow children in the bar.* **b** (B2) considering the whole of someone or something, and not just a particular part of them: *So, apart from the bad ankle, how are you in general?* **3 be in the general interest** formal to be a good thing for the public: *The government will only say it is not in the general interest to reveal any more information.* **NOT DETAILED** ▷ **4** (B1) not detailed, but including the most basic or necessary information: *What he said was very general.* ◦ *The school aims to give children a general background in a variety of subjects.* ◦ *I'm not an expert, so I can only speak* ***in*** *general* ***terms*** *on this matter.* **5 the general** things considered as a unit and without giving attention to details: *His book moves from the general to the particular.* **NOT LIMITED** ▷ **6** (B2) including a lot of things or subjects and not limited to only one or a few: *general knowledge* **7** used as part of the title of a job of someone who is in charge of a whole organization or company: *the general* ***manager*** ◦ *the General Secretary of the UN*

▸noun [C] (also **General**) an officer of very high rank, especially in the army: *He was promoted to the rank of general.* ◦ *General Brown/Roger Brown* ◦ [as form of address] *Thank you, General.*

ˌgeneral anaesˈthetic noun [C or U] a drug that is used to make you unconscious when you have an operation, so that you do not feel any pain

ˌgeneral deˈlivery noun [U] US for **poste restante**

ˌgeneral eˈlection noun [C] an election in which the people living in a country vote to choose the government

generalist /ˈdʒen.ər.əl.ɪst/ (US) /-ɚ-/ adj, noun [C] formal (someone who is) not specialized: *Children of this age need specialist rather than generalist teachers.*

generality /ˌdʒen.əˈræl.ɪ.ti/ (US) /-ə.t̬i/ **noun** [C usually plural, U] **NO DETAILS** ▷ **1** an occasion when what someone says contains no details, and often very little meaning, or a statement of this type: *We need to get away from generalities and focus on the issues.* **MOST** ▷ **2 the generality** [S] formal most: *For the generality* ***of*** *young people, university is not an option.*

generalization (UK usually **generalisation**) /ˌdʒen.ᵊr.ᵊl.aɪˈzeɪ.ʃᵊn/ (US) /-ə·-/ **noun** [C or U] C1 a written or spoken statement in which you say or write something very basic, based on limited facts, that is partly or sometimes true, but not always, or when someone generalizes by using such statements: *The report is full of errors and* ***sweeping*** *(= extreme) generalizations.* ◦ *Generalization can be dangerous.*

generalize (UK usually **generalise**) /ˈdʒen.ᵊ r.ə.laɪz/ (US) /-ɚ-/ **verb** [I] C1 to say or write something very basic, based on limited facts, that is partly or sometimes true, but not always: *You can't generalize* ***about*** *a continent as varied as Europe.*

generalized (UK usually **generalised**) /ˈdʒen.ᵊr.ə.laɪzd/ (US) /-ɚ-/ **adj** involving a lot of people, places or things: *He spoke of generalized corruption in the government.* ◦ *Isolated showers will give way to more generalized rain later in the day.* → Opposite **localized**

ˌgeneral ˈknowledge **noun** [U] information on many different subjects that you collect gradually, from reading, television, etc., rather than detailed information on subjects that you have studied formally

generally /ˈdʒen.ᵊ r.ᵊl.i/ (US) /-ɚ-/ **adv** **1** B2 considering the whole of someone or something, and not just a particular part of them: *Your health is generally good, but you do have a few minor problems.* ◦ *He wants more money to be given to the arts generally.* ◦ *I shall now develop my previous point more generally (= to say more about what it includes).* **2** B1 usually, or in most situations: *The baby generally wakes up three times during the night.* ◦ *Well, generally* ***speaking*** *(= in most situations), it's quicker on public transport.* **3** B2 by most people, or to most people: *It was generally believed at the time that both men were guilty.* ◦ *The proposal has received a generally favourable reaction.*

ˌgeneral ˈpractice **noun** [C or U] UK the work of a GP (= a doctor) who treats the people who live in the local area and treats conditions that do not need a hospital visit • **ˌgeneral pracˈtitioner** **noun** [C]

the ˌgeneral ˈpublic **noun** [S, + sing/pl verb] ordinary people, especially all the people who are not members of a particular organization or who do not have any special type of knowledge: *This is a matter of great concern to the general public.*

general-ˈpurpose **adj** a general-purpose product is used for many different things, rather than one particular thing: *a general-purpose PC*

ˌgeneral ˈstaff **noun** [C, + sing/pl verb] the group of army officers who work for and give advice to a COMMANDING officer

ˌgeneral ˈstore **noun** [C] (UK also **ˌgeneral ˈstores**) a shop that sells food and a wide range of products, often the only shop in a village

ˌgeneral ˈstrike **noun** [C] a STRIKE in which most people in a country refuse to work until they are given higher pay or something else that they want

generate /ˈdʒen.ᵊr.eɪt/ (US) /-ɚ-/ **verb** [T] **CREATE** ▷ **1** B2 to cause something to exist: *Her latest film has generated a lot of* ***interest/excitement****.* ◦ *The new development will generate 1,500 new jobs.* ◦ *These measures will increase the club's ability to generate* ***revenue/income****.* **MAKE ENERGY** ▷ **2** B2 to produce energy in a particular form: *The wind farm may be able to generate enough* ***electricity/power*** *for 2,000 homes.*

generation /ˌdʒen.əˈreɪ.ʃᵊn/ **noun** **AGE GROUP** ▷ **1** B1 [C, + sing/pl verb] all the people of about the same age within a society or within a particular family: *The* ***younger*** *generation smoke/smokes less than their parents did.* ◦ *There were at least three generations – grandparents, parents and children – at the wedding.* ◦ *It's our duty to preserve the planet for* ***future*** *generations.* ◦ *This painting has been in the family* ***for*** *generations.* **2** B2 [C, + sing/pl verb] a period of about 23 to 30 years, in which most human babies become adults and have their own children: *A generation ago, home computers were virtually unknown.* **3 first, second, third, etc. generation** describes the nationality of someone belonging to the first, second, third, etc. group of people of the same age in the family to have been born in that country: *She's a second-generation American (= her parents were American, although their parents were not).* **ENERGY** ▷ **4** B2 [U] the production of energy in a particular form: ***electricity*** *generation from wind and wave power* **PRODUCT** ▷ **5** B2 [C, + sing/pl verb] a group of products or machines that are all at the same stage of development: *a* ***new*** *generation of low-fat margarines* ◦ *Scientists are working on developing the* ***next*** *generation of supercomputers.*

the geneˈration ˌgap **noun** [S] a situation in which older and younger people do not understand each other because of their different experiences, opinions, habits, and behaviour: *She's a young politician who manages to* ***bridge/cross*** *(= understand both groups in) the generation gap.*

ˌGeneration ˈX **noun** [U] a way of referring to the group of people who were born in the 1960s and 1970s: *Members of Generation X are often portrayed as having no clear direction to their lives.* → Compare **baby-boomer, Generation Y**

ˌGeneration ˈY **noun** [U] a way of referring to the group of people who were born in the 1980s and early 1990s: *Generation Y, the baby-boomers' children, will be the most adept ever with emerging technology.* → Compare **baby-boomer, Generation X**

generative /ˈdʒen.ᵊr.ə.tɪv/ (US) /-ɚ.ə.t̬ɪv/ **adj** specialized able to produce or create something: *the generative power of the mind*

generator /ˈdʒen.ə.reɪ.təʳ/ (US) /-ə.eɪ.t̬ɚ/ **noun** [C] a machine which produces something, especially electricity

generic /dʒəˈner.ɪk/ **adj** **1** formal shared by, typical of, or relating to a whole group of similar things, rather than to any particular thing: *The new range of engines all had a generic problem with their fan blades.* **2** generic drugs or other products do not have a TRADEMARK and are sold without the name of the company that produced them

generically /dʒəˈner.ɪ.kᵊl.i/ **adv** relating to generic products, especially medical drugs: *The drug is generically known under another name.*

geˌneric ˈbrand **noun** [C] a product that is advertised with the name of the shop where you buy it, rather than the name of the company that made it → Compare **own brand**

generosity /ˌdʒen.əˈrɒs.ɪ.ti/ (US) /-ˈrɑː.sə.t̬i/ **noun** [U] B2 the quality or condition of being generous: *Her friends take advantage of (= benefit unfairly from) her generosity.*

generous /ˈdʒen.ər.əs/ (US) /-ɚ-/ **adj** CHARACTER ▷ **1** B1 willing to give money, help, kindness, etc., especially more than is usual or expected: *a very generous man* ◦ [+ to infinitive] ***It*** *was most generous* ***of*** *you* ***to*** *lend me the money.* ◦ *She's been very generous* ***with*** *her time.* ◦ *There's a generous (= kinder than deserved) review of the book in today's newspaper.* SIZE ▷ **2** C1 larger than usual or expected: *a generous slice of cake* ◦ *a generous pay increase* • **generously** /-li/ **adv** B2 *Please* ***give*** *generously to Children in Need.*

genesis /ˈdʒen.ə.sɪs/ **noun** [S] formal the origin of something, when it is begun or starts to exist: *In her autobiography, she describes the song's genesis in a Dublin bar.* ◦ *research into* ***the*** *genesis* ***of*** *cancer*

Genesis /ˈdʒen.ə.sɪs/ **noun** [S] the first book of the Bible, which describes how God made the world

G

ˈgene ˌtherapy noun [U] the science of changing GENES in order to stop or prevent a disease

genetic /dʒəˈnet.ɪk/ (US) /-ˈnet̬-/ **adj** C1 belonging or relating to GENES (= parts of the DNA in cells) received by each animal or plant from its parents: *a genetic* ***defect/disease*** • **genetically** /-ɪ.kəl.i/ **adv**

geˌnetically enginˈeered adj genetically modified

geˌnetically ˈmodified adj (also **geˌnetically engiˈneered**) C1 describes a plant or animal that has had some of its GENES changed scientifically: *genetically modified* ***food/crops***

geˌnetic ˈcode noun [C] the arrangement of GENES which controls the development of characteristics and qualities in a living thing

geˌnetic enginˈeering noun [U] (the science of) changing the structure of the GENES of a living thing in order to make it healthier or stronger or more useful to humans

geˌnetic ˈfingerprinting noun [U] the process of recording and/or examining a person's pattern of GENES, often to prove that they did or did not commit a crime

geneticist /dʒəˈnet.ɪ.sɪst/ (US) /-ˈnet̬-/ **noun** [C] a person who studies genetics

geˌnetic modifiˈcation noun [U] specialized the process of changing the structure of the GENES of a living thing in order to make it healthier, stronger, or more useful to humans → Compare **genetic engineering**

genetics /dʒəˈnet.ɪks/ (US) /-ˈnet̬-/ **noun** [U] B2 the study of how, in all living things, the characteristics and qualities of parents are given to their children by their GENES

genial /ˈdʒiː.ni.əl/ **adj** friendly and pleasant: *The headteacher is very genial/has a genial manner.* • **geniality** /ˌdʒiː.niˈæl.ɪ.ti/ (US) /-ə.t̬i/ **noun** [U] *His geniality, reliability and ability made him a popular figure.* • **genially** /-i/ **adv**

genie /ˈdʒiː.ni/ **noun** [C] (plural **genies** or **genii**) a magical spirit, originally in Arab traditional stories, who does or provides whatever the person who controls it asks

genitals /ˈdʒen.ɪ.təlz/ (US) /-t̬əlz/ **noun** [plural] (also **genitalia**) the outer sexual organs, especially the PENIS or VULVA • **genital adj** *the genital area/organs*

genitive /ˈdʒen.ɪ.tɪv/ (US) /-t̬ɪv/ **noun** [C] specialized the form of a noun, PRONOUN, etc. in the grammar of some languages, which shows that the noun, pronoun, etc. has or owns something • **genitive adj** *the genitive form of a noun*

genius /ˈdʒiː.ni.əs/ **noun** [C or U] (plural **geniuses**) **1** C1 very great and rare natural ability or skill, especially in a particular area such as science or art, or a person who has this: *(an) artistic/creative/musical genius* ◦ *Einstein was a (mathematical) genius.* ◦ *From the age of three, she showed signs of genius.* ◦ *It was such a brilliant idea – a real* ***stroke of*** *genius.* **2 evil genius** literary **3 have a genius for sth** to be especially skilled at a particular activity: *She has a genius for raising money.*

ˌgenned ˈup adj [after verb] UK old-fashioned informal having found out as much information as possible about something: *I got myself genned up* ***on*** *the company before my interview.*

genocide /ˈdʒen.ə.saɪd/ **noun** [U] the murder of a whole group of people, especially a whole nation, race, or religious group: *victims of genocide* • **genocidal** /ˌdʒen.əˈsaɪ.dəl/ **adj** *a genocidal war/regime*

genome /ˈdʒiː.nəʊm/ (US) /-noʊm/ **noun** [C] specialized the complete set of GENETIC material of a human, animal, plant or other living thing

genomics /dʒəˈnəʊm.ɪks/ (US) /-ˈnoʊm.ɪks/ **noun** [U] the study of the genomes of living things: *She is a specialist in animal genomics.*

genotype /ˈdʒen.ə.taɪp/ (US) /-oʊ-/ **noun** [C] specialized the particular type and arrangement of GENES that each organism has → Compare **phenotype**

genre /ˈʒɑ̃ː.rə/, /ˈʒɒn-/ **noun; adj**

▸**noun** [C] formal a style, especially in the arts, that involves a particular set of characteristics: *What genre does the book fall into – comedy or tragedy?* ◦ *a literary/musical/film genre*

▸**adj** produced according to a particular model or style: *a genre movie* ◦ *genre fiction*

gent /dʒent/ **noun 1** [C] old-fashioned a GENTLEMAN (= polite man who behaves well towards other people, especially women) **2 the gents** [S, + sing/pl verb] UK a public toilet for men

genteel /dʒenˈtiːl/ **adj 1** typical of a high social class: *a genteel old lady* ◦ *The mansion had an atmosphere of genteel elegance and decay.* **2** being very polite, or trying too hard to seem of a higher social class than you really are: *He took elocution lessons to try to make his accent sound more genteel.* **3** calm and gentle: *The game seemed to be a more genteel version of American football.* • **genteelly** /-li/ **adv**

Gentile /ˈdʒen.taɪl/ **noun** [C] a person who is not Jewish: *The war memorial was dedicated to both* ***Jews and*** *Gentiles.* • **Gentile adj**

gentility /dʒenˈtɪl.ɪ.ti/ (US) /-ə.t̬i/ **noun** [U] the quality of being GENTEEL: *an air (= manner) of gentility*

gentle /ˈdʒen.tl̩/ (US) /-t̬l̩/ **adj 1** B1 calm, kind, or soft: *a gentle smile* ◦ *He's very gentle with his kids.* **2** B1 not violent, severe, or strong: *gentle* ***exercise*** ◦ *a gentle* ***breeze*** ◦ *You can actually accomplish a lot more by gentle* ***persuasion.*** **3** C1 not steep or sudden: *The path has a gentle* ***slope/gradient.*** • **gentleness** /-nəs/ **noun** [U] the quality of being gentle

gentleman /ˈdʒen.tl̩.mən/ (US) /-t̬l̩-/ **noun** [C] (plural **-men** /-mən/) **1** B2 a polite way of talking to or referring to a man: ***Ladies and*** *gentlemen, the show is about to begin.* ◦ *Excuse me, this gentleman has a question for you.* **2** approving a man who is polite and behaves well towards other people, especially women: *He was a perfect gentleman.* ◦ *Not holding a door for a lady? You're no gentleman, are you?* **3** a man of a high social class: *a gentlemen's club*

gentlemanly /ˈdʒen.tl̩.mən.li/ (US) /-t̬l̩-/ **adj** typical of a polite gentleman: *a gentlemanly manner*

ˌgentleman's aˈgreement noun [C] an agreement that is based on trust and is not written down

gentlewoman /ˈdʒen.tlˌwʊm.ən/ (US) /-t̬l-/ **noun** [C] (plural **-women** /-wɪmɪn/) old-fashioned a woman who belongs to a high social class, or who is kind, polite, and honest

gently /ˈdʒent.li/ **adv** **1** (B2) calmly, kindly, or softly: *He lifted the baby gently out of its cot.* ◦ *to smile/laugh/blow gently* **2** without force or strength: *The door closed gently.* **3** slightly or gradually: *gently rolling hills*

IDIOM **gently does it!** UK (US **easy does it!**) used when telling someone to be slow and careful

gentrify /ˈdʒen.trɪ.faɪ/ **verb** [T often passive] disapproving to change a place from being a poor area to a richer one, by people of a higher social class moving to live there: *The area where I grew up has been all modernized and gentrified, and has lost all its old character.* • **gentrification** /ˌdʒen.trɪ.fɪˈkeɪ.ʃən/ **noun** [U] the process by which an area is gentrified

the gentry /ˈdʒen.tri/ **noun** [plural] people of high social class, especially in the past: *a member of the **landed** gentry (= those who own a lot of land)*

genuflect /ˈdʒen.jʊ.flekt/ **verb** [I] to bend one or both knees as a sign of respect to God, especially when entering or leaving a Catholic church: *People were genuflecting in front of the altar.*

genuflection /ˌdʒen.jʊˈflek.ʃən/ **noun** [C or U] the act of genuflecting

genuine /ˈdʒen.ju.ɪn/ **adj** **1** (B2) If something is genuine, it is real and exactly what it appears to be: *genuine leather* ◦ *If it is a genuine Michelangelo drawing, it will sell for millions.* **2** (C1) If people or emotions are genuine, they are honest and sincere: *He's a very genuine person.* ◦ *Machiko looked at me in genuine surprise – 'Are you really going?' she said.* • **genuinely** /-li/ **adv** (B2) really: *I'm genuinely sorry for what I said, I really am.* • **genuineness** /-nəs/ **noun** [U]

IDIOM **the genuine article** informal a good and real example of a particular thing: *Those cowboy boots sure look like the genuine article.*

genus /ˈdʒiː.nəs/ **noun** [C] (plural **genera**) specialized a group of animals or plants, more closely related than a family, but less similar than a SPECIES

geo- /dʒiː.əʊ-/ (US) /-oʊ-/ **prefix** of or relating to the Earth: *geophysics* ◦ *geology*

geocentric /ˌdʒiː.əʊˈsen.trɪk/ (US) /-oʊ-/ **adj** specialized having the Earth as its centre

geodesic dome /dʒiː.əˌdesɪk ˈdəʊm/ (US) /-ˈdoʊm/ **noun** [C] a structure or building shaped like half a ball, made up of many parts that form triangles and other shapes with several sides

geoengineering /ˌdʒiː.əʊ.en.dʒɪˈnɪə.rɪŋ/ (US) /ˌdʒiː.oʊ.en.dʒɪˈnɪr.ɪŋ/ **noun** [U] the study and activity of finding ways to change the earth's ATMOSPHERE in order to reduce GLOBAL WARMING (= the gradual increase in world temperatures): *One geoengineering project is tree planting.*

geographer /dʒiˈɒg.rə.fər/ (US) /dʒiˈɑː.grə.fɚ/ **noun** [C] a person who studies geography

geographical /ˌdʒi.əˈgræf.ɪ.kəl/ **adj** (mainly US **geographic** /-ɪk/) relating to geography, or to the geography of a particular area or place: *a geographical region* ◦ *geographical features* • **geographically** /-i/ **adv**

geography /dʒiˈɒg.rə.fi/ (US) /dʒiˈɑː.grə-/ **noun** [U] **1** (A2) the study of the systems and processes involved in the world's weather, mountains, seas, lakes, etc. and of the ways in which countries and people organize life within an area → See also **physical geography** **2 the geography of somewhere** the way all the parts of an area are arranged within it: *the geography of Australia* ◦ *It's impossible to work out the geography of this hospital.*

geolocation /ˌdʒiː.əʊ.ləʊˈkeɪ.ʃən/ (US) /-oʊ.loʊ-/ **noun** [U] TECHNOLOGY that shows the place where someone is when they are using the internet or a mobile phone

geological /ˌdʒi.əˈlɒdʒ.ɪ.kəl/ (US) /-ˈlɑː.dʒɪ-/ **adj** relating to geology, or to the geology of a particular area or place: *a geological survey/map* ◦ *the complex geological structure of the region* • **geologically** /-i/ **adv**

geologist /dʒiˈɒl.ə.dʒɪst/ (US) /-ˈɑː.lə-/ **noun** [C] a person who studies geology

geology /dʒiˈɒl.ə.dʒi/ (US) /-ˈɑː.lə-/ **noun** [U] **1** (C1) the study of the rocks and similar substances that make up the Earth's surface: *a geology course/teacher* **2 the geology of somewhere** the particular rocks and similar substances that form an area of the earth, and their arrangement

geometric /ˌdʒiː.əˈmet.rɪk/ **adj** (also **geometrical** /-rɪ.kəl/) describes a pattern or arrangement that is made up of shapes such as squares, triangles, or rectangles: *a geometric design of overlapping circles* • **geometrically** /-rɪ.kəl.i/ **adv** *geometrically patterned*

geoˌmetric(al) proˈgression **noun** [C] an ordered set of numbers, where each number in turn is multiplied by a fixed amount to produce the next

geometry /dʒiˈɒm.ə.tri/ (US) /dʒiˈɑː.mə-/ **noun** [U] **1** the area of mathematics relating to the study of space and the relationships between points, lines, curves, and surfaces: *the laws of geometry* ◦ *a geometry lesson* **2 the geometry of sth** the way the parts of a particular object fit together: *the geometry of a DNA molecule*

geophysicist /ˌdʒi.əˈfɪz.ɪ.sɪst/ **noun** [C] specialized a person who studies geophysics

geophysics /ˌdʒiː.əˈfɪz.ɪks/ **noun** [U] specialized the study of the rocks and other substances that make up the Earth and the physical processes happening on, in, and above the Earth • **geophysical** /-ɪ.kəl/ **adj** *geophysical and geological phenomena*

geopolitics /ˌdʒiː.əʊˈpɒl.ə.tɪks/ (US) /-oʊˈpɑː.lə.t̬ɪks/ **noun** [U] the study of the way a country's size, position, etc. influence its power and its relationships with other countries • **geopolitical** /-pəˈlɪt.ɪ.kəl/ (US) /-pəˈlɪt̬.ɪ.kəl/ **adj**

Geordie /ˈdʒɔː.di/ (US) /ˈdʒɔːr-/ **noun** **1** [C] someone who comes from Tyneside in Northeast England **2** [U] the type of English spoken by someone from Tyneside: *a Geordie accent*

georgette /dʒɔːˈdʒet/ (US) /ˈdʒɔːr-/ **noun** [U] a very thin SILK OR POLYESTER cloth, used for making clothes

Georgian /ˈdʒɔː.dʒən/ (US) /ˈdʒɔːr-/ **adj** **1** relating to the period when Kings George I, II, III, and IV were kings of Britain, from 1714 to 1830: *Georgian furniture/architecture* **2** relating to the period when Kings George V and VI were kings of Britain, from 1910 to 1952

geostationary orbit /dʒiː.əʊˌsteɪ.ʃən.ər.iˈɔː.bɪt/ (US) /-oʊˈsteɪ.ʃən.er.iˈɔːr-/ **noun** [C] specialized an ORBIT (= path travelled around an object in space) in which a SATELLITE always remains over the same place on the Earth's surface because it moves at the same speed as the Earth turns

geothermal /ˌdʒiː.əʊˈθɜː.məl/ (US) /-oʊˈθɝː-/ **adj** specialized of or connected with the heat inside the Earth: *a geothermal power station*

geranium /dʒəˈreɪ.ni.əm/ **noun** [C] a plant with red,

pink, or white flowers, often grown in containers and gardens

gerbil /ˈdʒɜː.bᵊl/ US /ˈdʒɝː-/ noun [C] a small animal similar to a mouse with long back legs that is often kept as a pet

geriatric /ˌdʒer.iˈæt.rɪk/ adj; noun
▸adj **1** for or relating to old people, especially those who are ill: *a geriatric hospital/ward/nurse* **2** informal disapproving old and weak: *Who's going to elect a geriatric President?*
▸noun [C] **1** an old person who needs medical care: *a clinic for the care of geria-trics* **2** informal disapproving someone who is old and weak: *They were a bunch of hopeless geriatrics.*

geriatrician /ˌdʒer.i.əˈtrɪʃ.ᵊn/ noun [C] specialized a doctor who specializes in the care and treatment of old people who are ill

geriatrics /ˌdʒer.iˈæt.rɪks/ noun [U] specialized the care and treatment of old people who are ill

germ /dʒɜːm/ US /dʒɝːm/ noun ORGANISM ▷ **1** C1 [C usually plural] a very small organism that causes disease: *Wash your hands so you don't get germs on the food.* ◦ *Rats and flies* ***spread*** *germs.* AMOUNT ▷ **2 germ of sth** C2 [S] a small amount, usually one which develops into something large or important: *He found the germ of* ***an idea*** *in an old newspaper.*

germane /dʒɜːˈmeɪn/ US /dʒɝː-/ adj formal describes ideas or information connected with and important to a particular subject or situation: *Her remarks could not have been more germane* ***to*** *the discussion.*

Germanic /dʒəˈmæn.ɪk/ US /dʒɚ-/ adj **1** typical of German people or things: *Germanic efficiency* **2** specialized belonging or relating to the group of languages that includes German, English, and Swedish: *a Germanic language*

germanium /dʒəˈmeɪ.ni.əm/ US /dʒɚ-/ noun [U] specialized a chemical element with unusual electrical characteristics that allow it to be used in SEMICONDUCTORS

ˌGerman ˈmeasles noun [U] (specialized **rubella**) an infectious disease which causes red spots on your skin, a cough, and a sore throat

ˌGerman ˈshepherd noun [C] mainly US for **Alsatian**

germicide /ˈdʒɜː.mɪ.saɪd/ US /ˈdʒɝː-/ noun [C or U] a substance that kills GERMS • **germicidal** /ˌdʒɜː.mɪˈsaɪ.dᵊl/ US /ˌdʒɝː-/ adj

germinate /ˈdʒɜː.mɪ.neɪt/ US /ˈdʒɝː-/ verb SEED ▷ **1** [I or T] specialized to (cause a seed to) start growing: *The beans will only germinate if the temperature is warm enough.* IDEA ▷ **2** [I] to start developing: *I felt an idea germinating in my head/mind.* • **germination** /ˌdʒɜː.mɪˈneɪ.ʃᵊn/ US /ˌdʒɝː-/ noun [U]

ˌgerm ˈwarfare noun [U] (also **bioˌlogical ˈwarfare**) the use of GERMS (= extremely small organisms) during periods of war to cause disease among enemy soldiers or among crops in enemy countries

gerontologist /ˌdʒer.ənˈtɒl.ə.dʒɪst/ US /-ˈtɑː.lə-/ noun [C] specialized a person who studies old age

gerontology /ˌdʒer.ənˈtɒl.ə.dʒi/ US /-ˈtɑː.lə-/ noun [U] specialized the study of old age and of the problems and diseases of old people • **gerontological** /-təˈlɒdʒ.ɪ.kᵊl/ US /-təˈlɑː.dʒɪ.kᵊl/ adj

gerrymandering /ˈdʒer.iˌmæn.dᵊr.ɪŋ/ US /-dɚ-/ noun [U] an occasion when someone in authority changes the borders of an area in order to increase the number of people within that area who will vote for a particular party or person: *The boundary changes were denounced as blatant gerrymandering.* • **gerrymander** /-dəʳ/ US /-dɚ/ verb [I or T]

gerund /ˈdʒer.ᵊnd/ noun [C] specialized C1 a word that ends in '-ing' that is made from a verb and used like a noun: *In the sentence 'Everyone enjoyed Tyler's singing', the word 'singing' is a gerund.*

gestation /dʒesˈteɪ.ʃᵊn/ noun [U] BABY ▷ **1** specialized (the period of) the development of a child or young animal while it is still inside its mother's body: *The baby was born prematurely at 28 weeks gestation.* ◦ *The* ***period of*** *gestation* ***of*** *rats is 21 days.* IDEA ▷ **2** (the period of) the development of ideas, thoughts, or plans: *The scheme had a very long gestation* ***period.*** • **gestate** /-ˈteɪt/ verb [I]

gesticulate /dʒesˈtɪk.jʊ.leɪt/ verb [I] formal to make movements with your hands or arms, to express something or to emphasize what you are saying: *There was a man outside the window gesticulating* ***wildly.*** • **gesticulation** /dʒesˌtɪk.jʊˈleɪ.ʃᵊn/ noun [C or U]

gesture /ˈdʒes.tʃəʳ/ US /-tʃɚ/ noun; verb
▸noun [C] MOVEMENT ▷ **1** C1 a movement of the hands, arms, or head, etc. to express an idea or feeling: *The prisoner raised his fist in a gesture* ***of*** *defiance as he was led out of the courtroom.* ◦ *She* ***made*** *a rude gesture at the other driver.* SYMBOLIC ACT ▷ **2** C1 an action that you take which expresses your feelings or intentions, although it might have little practical effect: *The government donated £500,000 as a gesture* ***of*** *goodwill.* ◦ *Not having butter on his potatoes was his only gesture towards healthy eating.*
▸verb [I] C2 to use a gesture to express or emphasize something: *When he asked where the children were, she gestured vaguely in the direction of the beach.* ◦ *He made no answer but walked on, gesturing* ***for*** *me* ***to*** *follow.*

gesundheit /gəˈzʊnt.haɪt/ exclamation mainly US said to someone after they have SNEEZED → See also **bless you!**

get /get/ verb (present participle **getting**, past tense **got**, past participle **got** or US **gotten**) OBTAIN ▷ **1** A1 [T] to obtain, buy, or earn something: *He's gone down to the corner shop to get some milk.* ◦ *I think she gets about £40,000 a year.* ◦ *We stopped off on the way to get some breakfast.* ◦ *I managed to get all three suitcases* ***for*** *under $200.* ◦ *How much did he get* ***for*** *his car? (= How much money did he sell it for?)* ◦ *Where did you get your radio* ***from?*** **2** A1 [T] to receive or be given something: *I got quite a surprise when I saw her with short hair.* ◦ *When did you get the news about Sam?* ◦ *I got a phone call* ***from*** *Phil last night.* ◦ *What grade did he get for the exam?* ◦ *I got the impression that they'd rather be alone.* ◦ *What did you get* ***for*** *your birthday?* ◦ *We don't get much snow (= it does not often snow) here.* ◦ *I managed to get a glimpse of him (= see him for a moment) through the crowds.* ◦ *If you get a moment (= have time available), could you help me fill in that form?* ◦ *She gets such pleasure* ***from*** *her garden.* ◦ *If you can get some time* ***off*** *work, we could finish the decorating.* ◦ *I can never get her* ***to myself*** *(= be alone with her) because she's always surrounded by people.* **3** A2 [T] to go somewhere and bring back someone or something: *I must just get the washing* ***in.*** ◦ [+ two objects] *Can I get you a drink?* **4** [T] to take someone or something into your possession by force: *Have the police got the man who did it yet?* ◦ *Your cat got a bird this morning!* REACH ▷ **5** A1 [I usually + adv/prep, T] to reach or arrive at a particular place: *We hadn't even got as far as London when the car broke down.* ◦ *What time does he normally get home (from work)?* ◦ *If you get **to** the restaurant before us, just wait at the bar.* **6** [I usually + adv/prep] to reach a particular stage, condition, or time: *You earn loads if you get **to** the top in that profession.* ◦ *It got **to** Thursday and she still hadn't heard any news.* ◦ informal *I'm getting **to** the stage now where I just want to give up.* **7 get far/somewhere/anywhere** to make progress or to improve: *She's taking flute lessons, but she really doesn't seem to be getting anywhere with it.* ◦ *It's been hard settling in, but I feel I'm getting somewhere at last.* **BECOME ILL WITH** ▷ **8** B1 [T] to become ill with a disease, virus, etc.: *I got food poisoning at that cheap little seafood restaurant.* ◦ *Kids get all kinds of bugs at school.* **START TO BE** ▷ **9** B1 [L] to become or start to be: *He gets really upset if you mention his baldness.* ◦ *Is your cold getting any better?* ◦ *Your coffee's getting cold.* ◦ *After a while you get used to all the noise.* ◦ *You're getting quite a big boy now, aren't you!* ◦ [+ to infinitive] *How did you get **to** be a belly dancer?* **10 get going/moving** C2 informal to start to go or move: *We'd better get moving or we'll be late.* **CAUSE** ▷ **11** B1 [T] to cause something to happen, or cause someone or something to do something: [+ adj] *She had to get the kids **ready** for school.* ◦ [+ past participle] *I'm trying to get this article finish**ed** for Thursday.* ◦ *We get our milk deliver**ed**.* ◦ [+ -ing verb] *Haven't you got the photocopier work**ing** yet?* ◦ [+ to infinitive] *I can't get my computer **to** work!* **12** B2 [T + obj + to infinitive] to persuade someone to do something: *Why don't you get Nicole **to** come to the party?* **13** [T + past participle] to do something to something or someone without intending to or by accident: *He got his bag caught in the train doors as they were closing.* ◦ *I always get the two youngest sisters' names confus**ed**.* **BE** ▷ **14** B1 [L + past participle] sometimes used instead of 'be' to form the PASSIVE: *I got shout**ed** at by some idiot for walking past his house.* ◦ *They're getting marri**ed** later this year.* ◦ *This window seems to have got broken.* **MOVE** ▷ **15** B1 [I usually + adv/prep] to move to a different place or into a different position: *I hit my head as I was getting **into** the car.* ◦ *Get **out of** here now or I'll call the police.* ◦ *The bed is too wide – we'll never get it through the door.* ◦ *Getting **up** the ladder was easy enough – it was coming down that was the problem.* ◦ *He got **down** on his knees and asked me to marry him!* **TRAVEL** ▷ **16** A1 [T] to travel somewhere in a train, bus, or other vehicle: *Shall we get a taxi to the station?* **DEAL WITH** ▷ **17** B1 [T] to deal with or answer a ringing phone, knock on the door, etc.: *Hey, Ty, someone's at the door – would you get it, please?* **HAVE CHANCE** ▷ **18** B2 [I + to infinitive] to have the chance to do something: *I never get **to** see her now that she's left the company.* **UNDERSTAND/HEAR** ▷ **19** B2 [T] to understand or hear something: *I didn't get what he said because the music was so loud.* ◦ *I told that joke to Sophia, but she didn't get it.* **PREPARE** ▷ **20** [T] to prepare a meal: *I'll put the kids to bed while you're getting the dinner.* **PAY** ▷ **21** [I or T] to pay for something: *Put your money away – I'll get these drinks.* **CONFUSE** ▷ **22** [T] informal to confuse someone and make them completely unable to understand or explain: *Give him a technical question – that'll really get him!* **23 you've got me there!** informal something that you say when you do not know the answer to a question: *'How many ounces in a kilo?' 'You've got me there.'* **ANNOY** ▷ **24** [T] informal to annoy someone: *It really gets me the way we're expected to actually laugh at his pathetic jokes!* **EMOTION** ▷ **25** [T] informal to make someone feel strongly emotional and often cry: *That bit in the film when he finds out that his daughter is alive – that always gets me!* **HIT** ▷ **26** [T] to hit someone, especially with a bullet or something thrown: *The bullet got her in the leg.*

IDIOMS **get away with murder** informal to be allowed to do things that other people would be punished or criticized for: *He's so charming that he really does get away with murder.* • **get him, her, you, etc.!** informal UK said to make the person you are with look at or notice someone, and usually laugh at them: *Get him in his new clothes!* • **get it on** slang to have sex: *Did you get it on **with** him?* • **get it together** informal to make a decision or take positive action in your life: *Brian has really got it together since I last saw him – he has started a new job and lost a lot of weight.*

PHRASAL VERBS **get about** UK (US **get around**) **TRAVEL** ▷ **1** to travel to a lot of places: *Spain last week and Germany this week – he gets about, doesn't he!* **MOVE** ▷ **2** to be able to go to different places without difficulty, especially if you are old or ill: *My gran is finding it harder to get about these days.* • **get sth across** B2 to manage to make someone understand or believe something: *This is the **message** that we want to get across to the public.* • **get ahead** to be successful in the work that you do: *It's tough for a woman to get ahead **in** politics.* • **get along** mainly US (mainly UK **get on**) **BE FRIENDLY** ▷ **1** If two or more people get along, they like each other and are friendly to each other: *I don't really get along with my sister's husband.* **DEAL WITH** ▷ **2** to deal with a situation, usually successfully: *I wonder how Michael is getting along in his new job?* • **get around** mainly US for **get round (somewhere)**: *News of Helen's pregnancy soon got around the office.* • **get at sb** informal **CRITICIZE** ▷ **1** UK (US usually **get on sb**) to criticize a person repeatedly: *He keeps getting at me and I really don't know what I've done wrong.* **INFLUENCE** ▷ **2** to influence a person illegally, usually by offering them money or threatening them: *The accused claimed that the witness had been got at.* • **get at sth** **REACH** ▷ **1** B2 to reach or obtain something, especially something that is difficult to get: *I've put the cake on a high shelf where he can't get at it.* **SUGGEST** ▷ **2** C1 informal When someone is getting at something, they mean it or are trying to express it: *I'm not sure **what** you're getting at – don't you think I should come tonight?* ◦ ***What** do you think the poet is getting at in these lines?* • **get away 1** B2 to leave or escape from a person or place, often when it is difficult to do this: *We walked to the next beach to get away from the crowds.* ◦ *I'll get away from work as soon as I can.* **2** B2 to go somewhere to have a holiday, often because you need to rest: *I just need to get away for a few days.* ◦ *We've decided to go to Scotland to get away **from it all**.* • **get away (with you)!** UK old-fashioned informal said when you do not believe or agree with what someone is saying: *'Ralph painted that, you know.' 'Get away!'* • **get away with sth** **AVOID PUNISHMENT** ▷ **1** B2 to succeed in avoiding punishment for something: *If I thought I could get away with it, I wouldn't pay any tax at all.* **SUCCEED** ▷ **2** to do something successfully although it is not the best way of doing it: *Do you think we could get away with just one coat of paint on that wall?* • **get back** A2 to return to a place after you have been somewhere else: *When we got back to the hotel, Ann had already left.* • **get sb back** (also **get back at sb**) to do something unpleasant to someone because they have done something unpleasant to you: *I'll get you back for this, just you wait!* ◦ *I think he's trying to get back at*

G

her *for* those remarks she made in the meeting. • **get sth back** B1 to be given something again that you had before: *He went next door to get his ball back.* ◦ *Don't lend him money, you'll never get it back.* • **get back to sb** C1 to talk to someone again, usually on the phone, in order to give them some information or because you were not able to speak to them before: *I'll get back to you later with those figures.* • **get back to sth** to start doing or talking about something again: *Anyway, I'd better get back to work.* • **get behind** to fail to do as much work or pay as much money as you should by a particular time: *She got behind* ***with*** *her mortgage and the house was repossessed.* • **get by** to be able to live or deal with a situation with difficulty, usually by having just enough of something you need, such as money: *How can he get by* ***on*** *so little money?* ◦ *We can get by* ***with*** *four computers at the moment, but we'll need a couple more when the new staff arrive.* • **get sb down** B2 If something gets you down, it makes you feel unhappy or DEPRESSED.: *The chaos in his house was starting to get him down.* ◦ *I know it's frustrating, but don't let it get you down.* • **get sth down** to write something, especially something that someone has said: *I didn't manage to get down that last bit she said, about the meeting.* • **get sth down (sb)** to succeed in swallowing something although it is difficult: *Her throat was so swollen that she couldn't get the tablets down.* ◦ informal humorous *Your dinner is on the table and you've got ten minutes to get it down (you).* • **get down to sth** B2 to start to direct your efforts and attention towards something: *I've got a lot of work to do, but I can't seem to get down to* ***it***. ◦ [+ -ing verb] *I must get down to book****ing*** *the hotels.* • **get in** ENTER ▷ **1** B1 to succeed in entering a place, especially by using force or a trick: *They must have got in through the bathroom window.* ARRIVE ▷ **2** B1 to arrive at your home or the place where you work: *What time did you get in last night?* **3** B1 If a train or other vehicle gets in at a particular time, that is when it arrives: *What time is the plane expected to get in?* **4 get in there!** UK informal something you say when something good happens to someone • **get in/get into sth** B2 to succeed in being chosen or elected: *He wanted to go to Cambridge, but he didn't get in.* ◦ *The Republicans are bound to get in at the next elections.* • **get sth in** SEND ▷ **1** to send something so that it arrives by a particular time: *I have to get my application in by Thursday.* SAY ▷ **2** to succeed in saying something, although it is difficult to do this because other people are talking too: *He couldn't get a word in because she was talking so much.* FIND TIME ▷ **3** informal to manage to find time to do something or deal with someone: *I get in a bit of gardening most evenings.* BUY ▷ **4** UK informal to buy a supply of something, usually food or drink, so that you will have enough of what you need: *We'll have to get some food in for the weekend if we're having visitors.* • **get sb in** to ask a trained person to come to your home to do some paid work: *We'll have to get a plumber in to look at that water tank.* • **get in on sth** to start to take part in an activity that is already happening because you will win an advantage from it: *A Japanese company tried to get in on the deal.* • **get into sb** If you do not know what has got into someone, you do not understand why they are behaving strangely: *I can't think what's got into him. He doesn't usually make such a fuss.* • **get into sth** C1 to become interested in an activity or subject, or start being involved in an activity: *She's been getting into yoga recently – she does three classes a week.* • **get (sb) into sth** to (cause someone to) become involved in a difficult situation, often without intending to: *After he lost his job, he got into debt.* ◦ *Are you trying to get me into trouble?* • **get off 1** to leave a place, usually in order to start a journey: *If we can get off by seven o'clock, the roads will be clearer.* **2** informal to leave work with permission, usually at the end of the day: *How early can you get off this afternoon?* • **get off (sth)** A2 to leave a train, bus, or aircraft: *Get off at Camden Town.* ◦ *I tripped as I got off the bus.* • **get sth off** to send a letter or parcel to someone: *I got that letter off this morning.* • **get (sb) off** SLEEP ▷ **1** to start sleeping, or to help a baby to start sleeping: *It was so hot that I didn't get off (****to sleep****) till three o'clock.* ◦ *I've been trying to get the baby off (****to sleep****) for an hour!* PLEASURE ▷ **2** mainly US slang to have or give someone an ORGASM: *They got off at the same time.* • **get (sb) off (sth) 1** to avoid punishment, or to help another person to avoid punishment for something: *She was charged with fraud, but her lawyer managed to get her off.* ◦ *'Was he found guilty?' 'No, he got off.'* ◦ *She got off* ***with*** (= her only punishment was) *a small fine.* **2 get off lightly** to experience less serious punishment, injury, or harm than you might have expected: *I think I got off quite lightly with one or two cuts, bearing in mind how damaged the car was.* • **get sth off (sth)** informal to remove a part of your body from a particular place: *Get your dirty feet off the settee!* ◦ *Get your hands off me!* • **get off on sth** informal to find something exciting, especially in a sexual way: *Dave likes power – he gets off on it.* • **get off with sb** UK slang to begin a sexual relationship with someone: *She'd got off with some bloke at the party.* • **get on** RELATIONSHIP ▷ **1** B1 mainly UK (mainly US **get along**) to have a good relationship: *We're getting on much better now that we don't live together.* ◦ *He doesn't get on* ***with*** *his daughter.* MANAGE ▷ **2** B1 mainly UK (mainly US **get along**) to manage or deal with a situation, especially successfully: *How are you getting on in your new home?* ◦ *We're getting on quite well* ***with*** *the decorating.* CONTINUE ▷ **3** B2 to continue doing something, especially work: *I'll leave you to get on then, shall I?* OLD ▷ **4 be getting on** informal to be getting old: *He's getting on (****a bit****) – he'll be 76 next birthday.* LATE ▷ **5 be getting on** informal If you say it's getting on, or time is getting on, you mean it is becoming late: *It's getting on – we'd better be going.* **6 getting on for** UK (US **going on**) almost: *He must be getting on for 80 now.* ◦ *It was getting on for midnight.* • **get on (sth)** A2 to go onto a bus, train, aircraft, or boat: *I think we got on the wrong bus.* • **get on to/onto sth** SUBJECT ▷ **1** to start talking about a different subject: *How did we get on to (the subject of) your grandmother's cat?* PERSON ▷ **2** UK to speak or write to a person or organization because you want them or it to help you in some way: *Did you remember to get on to the plumber about the shower?* • **get on with sth** to start or continue doing something, especially work: *Stop talking and get on with it.* ◦ *I like to be left to get on with the job.* ◦ *I suppose I could get on with the ironing while I'm waiting.* • **get out** LEAVE ▷ **1** B1 to leave a closed vehicle, building, etc.: *I'll get out when you stop at the traffic lights.* VISIT PLACES ▷ **2** C1 to go out to different places, spend time with people, and enjoy yourself: *We don't get out much since we had the children.* **3 you should get out more** humorous used to tell someone that they are spending too much time doing things that are boring or not important: *'I've ordered all my CDs alphabetically.' 'Mmm, I think you should get out more, Mike.'* BECOME KNOWN ▷ **4** If news or information gets out, people hear about it although someone is trying to keep it secret: *I don't want it to get out that I'm leaving before I've had a* *chance to tell Anthony.* • **get (sb/sth) out** C1 to (help someone or something to) escape from or leave a place: *I left the door open and the cat got out.* ◦ *A team of commandos got the hostages out* ***from*** *the rebel base.* • **get out of sth** AVOID ▷ **1** B2 to avoid doing something that you do not want to do, especially by giving an excuse: *I reckon her backache was just a way of getting out of the housework.* ◦ [+ -ing verb] *If I can get out of go****ing*** *to the meeting tonight I will.* STOP ▷ **2** to give up or stop a habit or a regular activity: *I must get out of* ***the habit of*** *finishing off people's sentences for them.* ◦ *If you get out of a routine, it's very hard to get back into it.* • **get sth out of sth** to enjoy something or think something is useful: *It was a really boring course and I don't think I got much out of it.* • **get sth out of sb** to persuade or force someone to tell or give you something: *He was determined to get the truth out of her.* • **get over sth/sb 1** B2 to get better after an illness, or feel better after something or someone has made you unhappy: *She was only just getting over the flu when she got a stomach bug.* ◦ *It took him years to get over the shock of his wife dying.* ◦ *It took her months to get over Rupert when he finished the relationship.* **2 get over yourself!** informal something you say to tell someone to stop thinking that they are more important than other people, especially when they are complaining about something **3 not get over sth** B2 When you say that you can't get over something, you mean that you are very surprised by it: *I can't get over the way he behaved at your party – it was appalling!* • **get sth over with** C2 to do or finish an unpleasant but necessary piece of work or duty so that you do not have to worry about it in the future: *I'll be glad to get these exams over with.* • **get round (somewhere)** UK (US **get around (somewhere)**) If news or information gets round, a lot of people hear about it: *News of her pregnancy soon got round (the office).* • **get round sb** UK to persuade someone to allow you something by using your CHARM: [+ to infinitive] *See if you can get round your father* ***to*** *take you to the game.* • **get round sth** UK (US **get around sth**) to succeed in avoiding or solving a problem: *We can get round the problem of space by building an extension.* • **get round to sth** UK B2 to do something that you have intended to do for a long time: *I still haven't got round to fixing that tap.* • **get through** to succeed in talking to someone on the phone: *I tried to phone her but couldn't get through.* ◦ *I got through* ***to*** *the wrong department.* • **get through sth** EXAM ▷ **1** B2 to succeed in an exam or competition: *She got through her exams without too much trouble.* FINISH ▷ **2** C2 to finish something: *I can get through a lot more work when I'm on my own.* ◦ *We've got a lot to get through today.* USE UP ▷ **3** UK (US **go through**) to use up something: *We're getting through a lot of coffee/toilet paper.* ◦ *She gets through ten bars of chocolate each week.* • **get (sb) through sth** C1 to deal with a difficult or unpleasant experience, or to help someone do this: *I don't know how I got through the first couple of months after Andy's death.* ◦ *We need to conserve our supplies so we can get through the winter.* • **get (sth) through (to sb)** C1 to succeed in making someone understand or believe something: [+ question word] *We can't get through to the government just* ***how*** *serious the problem is!* ◦ *I don't seem to be able to get through to (= communicate with) him these days.* • **get to** B2 You ask where people or things have got to when they do not arrive or are not where you expect them to be and you want to know where they are: *I wonder where my glasses have got to.* ◦ *Where's Annabel got to? She should be here by now.* • **get to sb** informal SUFFER ▷ **1** If something gets to you, it makes you suffer: *The heat was beginning to get to me, so I went indoors.* UPSET ▷ **2** C2 If someone gets to you, they make you feel upset or angry: *I know he's annoying, but you shouldn't let him get to you.* • **get together** MEET ▷ **1** B1 If two or more people get together, they meet each other, having arranged it before: *Shall we get together on Friday and go for a drink or something?* → See also **get-together** START ▷ **2** informal to start a romantic relationship: *She got together with Paul two years ago.* ◦ *They finally get* ***it*** *together right at the end of the film.* • **get up** STAND ▷ **1** B2 to stand up: *The whole audience got up and started clapping.* GROW STRONG ▷ **2** UK If the wind gets up, it starts to grow stronger: *The wind is getting up.* • **get (sb) up** A1 to wake up and get out of bed, or to tell or help someone to do this: *I got up at five o'clock this morning!* ◦ *It's dreadful trying to get the kids up on school days.* • **get sth up** UK to organize a group of people to do something: *He's getting up a small group to go carol-singing for charity.* • **get yourself/sb up** UK informal to dress yourself or someone else in particular clothing, especially clothing that is strange and unusual and intended to achieve a particular effect: *He'd got him****self*** *up* ***as*** *a Roman emperor for the party.* • **get up to sth** UK C2 to do something, often something that other people would disapprove of: *She's been getting up to all sorts of* ***mischief*** *lately.*

getaway /ˈget.ə.weɪ/ /ˈget̬-/ noun [C] informal an occasion when someone leaves a place quickly, usually after committing a crime: *The two masked men* ***made*** *their getaway in a stolen van.* ◦ *a getaway* ***car*** → See also **get away**

ˈget-out ˌclause noun [C] UK a part of an agreement that allows someone to avoid doing something that they normally would have to do

ˌget-rich-ˈquick adj [before noun] disapproving used to describe a plan or wish to make a lot of money in a short time: *He refused to get involved in a friend's unrealistic get-rich-quick* ***scheme***. ◦ *People love the get-rich-quick promise of gambling.*

ˈget-toˌgether noun [C] an informal meeting or social occasion, often arranged for a particular purpose: *a family get-together* → See also **get together**

ˈget-up noun [C] informal a set of clothes, especially strange and unusual ones: *He was in a sort of Mafia get-up, with a pinstriped suit and wide tie.*

ˌget-up-and-ˈgo noun [U] informal the quality of being positive and having a lot of new ideas, determination, and energy: *This job needs someone with a bit of get-up-and-go.*

get-ˈwell ˌcard noun [C] a card that you give or send to someone who is ill, to say that you hope they are well again soon: *Everyone at work signed a get-well card for me.*

geyser /ˈgiː.zəʳ/ US /ˈgaɪ.zɚ/ noun [C] a hole in the ground from which hot water and steam are sent out

ghastly /ˈgɑːst.li/ US /ˈgæst-/ adj **1** informal unpleasant and shocking: *Today's newspaper gives all the ghastly details of the murder.* **2** informal extremely bad: *What ghastly* ***weather***! ◦ *It was all a ghastly* ***mistake***. ◦ *I thought her outfit was ghastly.* **3** literary describes someone who looks very ill or very shocked, especially with a very pale face: *You look ghastly – are you okay?* • **ghastliness** /-nəs/ noun [U]

ghat /gɑːt/ noun [C] Indian English AREA NEAR RIVER ▷ **1** a set of steps leading down to a river or lake **2** (also **burning ghat**) a place at the edge of a river where

Hindus CREMATE (= burn) dead people **ROAD** ▷ **3** a road or path through mountains

ghee /giː/ noun [U] a type of clear butter used in South Asian cooking

gherao /gəˈraʊ/ noun [C] Indian English an occasion when people show that they disagree with something by standing around a person in authority and not letting them leave until they agree to do what the people want • **gherao** verb [T]

gherkin /ˈgɜː.kɪn/ (US) /ˈgɝː-/ noun [C] a small type of CUCUMBER (= long, thin, green vegetable) that is often PICKLED (= preserved in VINEGAR): *a pickled gherkin*

ghetto /ˈget.əʊ/ (US) /ˈgeţ.oʊ/ noun [C] (plural **ghettos** or **ghettoes**) **1** an area of a city, especially a very poor area, where people of a particular race or religion live closely together and apart from other people: *As a child she lived in one of New York's poorest ghettos.* ◦ *to live in ghetto conditions* **2** in the past, an area of a city where Jews were made to live

G

ghost /gəʊst/ (US) /goʊst/ noun **SPIRIT** ▷ **1** B1 [C] the spirit of a dead person, sometimes represented as a pale, almost transparent image of that person, which some people believe appears to people who are alive: *Do you **believe in** ghosts?* ◦ *The gardens are said to be **haunted** by the ghost **of** a child who drowned in the river.* **MEMORY** ▷ **2** [S] literary a memory, usually of something or someone bad: *The ghost **of** the old dictator still lingers on.*

IDIOMS **give up the ghost 1** to die **2** humorous If a machine gives up the ghost, it stops working: *We've had the same TV for over ten years and it's just given up the ghost.* • **look like/as though you've seen a ghost** to look very shocked: *Whatever's the matter? You look as though you've just seen a ghost!* • **not have a/the ghost of a chance** informal to have no chance at all: *They haven't got a ghost of a chance **of** winning.*

ghostly /ˈgəʊst.li/ (US) /ˈgoʊst-/ adj **1** pale and transparent: *a ghostly figure/apparition* **2** not loud or clear: *a ghostly voice/echo* • **ghostliness** /-nəs/ noun [U]

ˈghost ˌstory noun [C] a frightening story about ghosts and their activities

ˈghost ˌtown noun [C] a town where few or no people now live

ˈghost ˌtrain noun [C] an entertainment for adults and children, in which you travel in a vehicle through a set of exciting and frightening experiences

ghostwrite /ˈgəʊst.raɪt/ (US) /ˈgoʊst-/ verb [T] (also **ghost**) to write a book or article, etc. for another person, so that they can pretend it is their own or use it themselves: *His autobiography was ghostwritten.* • **ghostwriter** /-ˌraɪ.təʳ/ (US) /-ˌraɪ.ţɚ/ noun [C]

ghoul /guːl/ noun [C] **1** an evil spirit that eats dead bodies **2** informal someone who is very interested in death and unpleasant things

ghoulish /ˈguː.lɪʃ/ adj **1** ugly and unpleasant, or frightening: *ghoulish faces* **2** disapproving connected with death and unpleasant things: *He takes a ghoulish delight in reading about horrific murders.* • **ghoulishly** /-li/ adv

GHQ /ˌdʒiː.eɪtʃˈkjuː/ noun [U] abbreviation for General Headquarters: the main centre from which a military operation is controlled

GI /ˌdʒiːˈaɪ/ noun **SOLDIER** ▷ **1** [C] informal a soldier in the US army, especially in the Second World War **FOOD** ▷ **2** [S] abbreviation for glycaemic index: a system for listing foods according to how quickly they increase the level of sugar in your blood: ***low** GI foods such as peanuts, milk, and lentils* ◦ ***high** GI foods such as sweets and white bread*

giant /ˈdʒaɪ.ənt/ noun; adj

▸noun [C] **VERY TALL PERSON** ▷ **1** B1 an imaginary creature like a man but extremely tall, strong, and usually very cruel, appearing especially in children's stories → See also **gigantic 2** someone who is taller or larger than usual **LARGE BUSINESS** ▷ **3** C2 a very successful and powerful person or organization: *He was one of the intellectual/political giants of this century.* ◦ *The takeover battle is between two of America's industrial/retail giants (= large companies).*

▸adj extremely large: *a giant earth-moving machine* ◦ *to take giant steps*

ˌgiant ˈpanda noun [C] a **panda**

gibber /ˈdʒɪb.əʳ/ (US) /-ɚ/ verb [I] mainly disapproving to speak quickly in a way that cannot be understood, usually when you are very frightened or confused: *Stop gibbering, man, and tell us what you saw.* • **gibbering** /-ɪŋ/ adj *I stood there like a gibbering **idiot**.*

gibberish /ˈdʒɪb.ər.ɪʃ/ (US) /-ɚ-/ noun [U] disapproving spoken or written words that have no meaning: *I was so nervous, I just started **talking** gibberish.*

gibbet /ˈdʒɪb.ɪt/ noun [C] a wooden structure from which criminals were hanged, in the past, as a form of EXECUTION (= killing as a punishment) → Compare **gallows**

gibbon /ˈgɪb.ən/ noun [C] a small APE with long arms which lives in trees in the forests of South Asia

gibe /dʒaɪb/ noun [C], verb [I] **jibe**

giblets /ˈdʒɪb.ləts/ noun [plural] the inside parts and neck of a bird, usually removed before it is cooked, that are often used to flavour sauces, etc.

giddy /ˈgɪd.i/ adj **dizzy**

gift /gɪft/ noun; verb

▸noun **PRESENT** ▷ **1** A2 [C] a present or something that is given: *a birthday/wedding gift* ◦ *The guests all arrived **bearing** (= bringing) gifts.* **2** [C usually singular] informal something that is surprisingly easy or cheap: *That goal was a gift!* ◦ *£100 for a good leather coat? It's a gift!* **ABILITY** ▷ **3** C1 [C usually singular] a special ability to do something: *He has a gift **for** languages.*

IDIOMS **a gift from the gods** an especially good or lucky thing or person that comes to you • **the gift of the gab** UK (US **the gift of gab**) the ability to speak easily and confidently in a way that makes people want to listen to you and believe you: *She's got the gift of the gab – she should work in sales and marketing.*

▸verb [T] to give something in an official or formal way: *I gifted to my husband my 50 percent share of the property.*

gifted /ˈgɪf.tɪd/ adj **1** C1 having special ability in a particular subject or activity: *a gifted dancer/musician* **2** clever, or having a special ability: *Schools often fail to cater for the needs of gifted **children**.*

ˈgift ˌshop noun [C] a shop that sells goods that are suitable for giving as presents

ˈgift ˌtoken noun [C] UK (UK also **ˈgift ˌvoucher**, US **ˈgift cerˌtificate**) a card or piece of paper that can be exchanged in a shop for goods of the value that is printed on it

ˈgift-wrapped adj A present that is gift-wrapped has been put in decorative paper ready for giving.

gig /gɪg/ noun; verb

▸noun [C] **PERFORMANCE** ▷ **1** informal a single performance by a musician or group of musicians, especially playing modern or pop music: *This week the band **did** the last gig of their world tour.* **CAR-**

RIAGE ▷ **2** a light two-wheeled CARRIAGE pulled by one horse, used especially in the past **UNIT** ▷ **3** a **gigabyte**
▸verb [I] (-gg-) (of a musician or group of musicians) to perform gigs: *Gigging around the London clubs helped the band develop their own sound.*

giga- /ˈgɪg.ə-/ **prefix** used to form words with the meaning 1,000,000,000: *gigavolt* ◦ *gigahertz* ◦ *gigawatt*

gigabit /ˈgɪg.ə.bɪt/ **noun** [C] (abbreviation **Gb**) a unit of computer information, consisting of 1,000,000,000 BITS, or 125 MEGABYTES: *The new cable will carry up to 120 gigabits of data traffic.*

gigabyte /ˈgɪg.ə.baɪt/ **noun** [C] (written abbreviation **GB**) (also **gig**) specialized a unit of computer information, consisting of 1,024 MEGABYTES

gigantic /dʒaɪˈgæn.tɪk/ (US) /-t̬ɪk/ **adj** extremely large: *a gigantic statue* ◦ *The cost has been gigantic.* • **gigantically** /-tɪ.kəl.i/ (US) /-t̬ɪ.kəl.i/ **adv**

giggle /ˈgɪg.l̩/ **verb; noun**
▸verb [I] ⓒ to laugh repeatedly in a quiet but uncontrolled way, often at something silly or rude or when you are nervous: *Stop that giggling at the back!*
▸noun **LAUGHTER** ▷ **1** [C] a nervous or silly laugh: *There were a few* ***nervous*** *giggles from people in the audience.* ◦ *I caught Roz* ***having*** *a giggle over some of Janet's awful poetry.* **2 the giggles** [plural] informal an occasion when you can't stop giggling: *I often used to* ***get/have*** *the giggles in lectures when I was at college.* **FUNNY SITUATION** ▷ **3** [S] UK informal something that is funny, often when it involves laughing at someone else: *Just* ***for a*** *giggle, we hid his trousers while he was in the water.*

giggler /ˈgɪg.ləʳ/ (US) /-lɚ/ **noun** [C] a person who often giggles

giggly /ˈgɪg.l̩.i/, /-li/ **adj** mainly disapproving giggling a lot: *a load of giggly school kids*

gigolo /ˈdʒɪg.ə.ləʊ/ (US) /-loʊ/ **noun** [C] (plural **gigolos**) old-fashioned a man who is paid by a woman to have sex with her or spend time with her

gild /gɪld/ **verb** [T] **1** to cover a surface with a thin layer of gold or a substance that looks like gold **2** literary to cover the surface of something with bright gold light: *Sunlight gilded the children's faces.*

IDIOM **gild the lily** disapproving to improve or decorate something that is already perfect and therefore spoil it: *Should I add a scarf to this jacket or would it be gilding the lily?*

gilded /ˈgɪl.dɪd/ **adj 1** [before noun] covered with a thin layer of gold or a substance that looks like gold: *The gilded dome of the cathedral rises above the city.* → Synonym **gilt 2** literary rich or of a higher social class: *The story revolves around the gilded* ***youth*** *of the 1920s and their glittering lifestyles.*

gilet /ˈʒɪ.leɪ/ **noun** [C] mainly UK a piece of clothing that is worn over other clothes and that is like a jacket without sleeves

gill **noun** **FISH** ▷ **1** /gɪl/ [C usually plural] the organ through which fish and other water creatures breathe **MEASUREMENT** ▷ **2** /dʒɪl/ [C] a measure of liquid that is equal to 0.142 litres or a quarter of a PINT

IDIOMS **be green about the gills** humorous to look ill and pale: *Matt was out drinking last night and he's a bit green about the gills this morning!* • **to the gills** informal used in expressions to mean completely full: *By the time the fourth course was served, I was* ***stuffed*** *to the gills.* ◦ *The restaurant was* ***packed*** *to the gills.*

gilt /gɪlt/ **adj; noun**
▸adj covered with a thin layer of gold or a substance that is intended to look like it: *a gilt picture frame* ◦ *It's not solid gold – it's just gilt.*
▸noun **SURFACE** ▷ **1** [U] a very thin layer of gold, silver, or a similar substance, used to cover the surface of something: *a silver gilt crucifix* **MONEY** ▷ **2 gilts** [plural] (also ˌ**gilt-edged seˈcurities**) UK specialized a type of INVESTMENT offered by the government that pays a fixed rate of interest and is considered low-risk

gimcrack /ˈdʒɪm.kræk/ **adj** disapproving attractive on the surface but badly made and of no real or permanent value

gimlet /ˈgɪm.lət/ **noun** [C] **TOOL** ▷ **1** a small tool used for making holes in wood **DRINK** ▷ **2** US a drink made with GIN or VODKA and LIME juice

IDIOM **have gimlet eyes** (also **be ˈgimlet-eyed**) to look at things very carefully and not miss anything

gimme /ˈgɪm.i/ **short form; noun**
▸short form not standard give me: *Gimme that pen back!*
▸noun [C usually singular] US slang something that is extremely easy to do: *That first test question was a gimme, for sure.*

gimmick /ˈgɪm.ɪk/ **noun** [C] mainly disapproving something that is not serious or of real value that is used to attract people's attention or interest temporarily, especially to make them buy something: *a* ***publicity*** *gimmick* ◦ *They give away free gifts with children's meals as a* ***sales/marketing*** *gimmick.* • **gimmicky** /-ɪ.ki/ **adj** disapproving *gimmicky foods/fashions*

gimmickry /ˈgɪm.ɪ.kri/ **noun** [U] disapproving the act of using gimmicks, especially in order to make a product or activity more successful

gin /dʒɪn/ **noun** [C or U] a clear, strong alcoholic drink flavoured with JUNIPER BERRIES (= small fruits): *a bottle of gin* ◦ *a gin and tonic*

ginger /ˈdʒɪn.dʒəʳ/ (US) /-dʒɚ/ **noun; adj; verb**
▸noun **SPICE** ▷ **1** [U] the spicy root of a tropical plant that is used in cooking or preserved in sugar: ***ground*** *(= powdered) ginger* ◦ ***crystallized*** *ginger* ◦ *ginger* ***biscuits/cake*** **COLOUR** ▷ **2** [U] a red or orange-brown colour **PERSON** ▷ **3** [S] UK offensive a person who has red or orange-brown hair: [as form of address] *Hey, ginger, what are you doing?* **DRINK** ▷ **4** [C or U] UK **ginger ale**: *rum and ginger* • **gingery** /-i/ **adj** *a gingery taste/colour*
▸adj **COLOUR** ▷ having a red or orange-brown colour: *His nickname was Ginger because of his ginger* ***hair***. ◦ *a ginger cat*
▸verb

PHRASAL VERB **ginger sth up** to make something more exciting, interesting or active: *They've gingered up the book cover with a new design, but the contents are the same.*

ˌ**ginger ˈale** **noun** [C or U] (UK also **ginger**, ˌ**dry ˈginger**) a FIZZY drink (= one with bubbles) containing ginger, sometimes mixed with an alcoholic drink

ˌ**ginger ˈbeer** **noun** [C or U] a British FIZZY drink (= one with bubbles) containing ginger and a small amount of alcohol

gingerbread /ˈdʒɪn.dʒə.bred/ (US) /-dʒɚ-/ **noun** [U] a type of cake, usually very dark brown and soft, which contains ginger

ˈ**gingerbread** ˌ**man** **noun** [C] a hard ginger biscuit shaped like a person

gingerly /ˈdʒɪn.dʒə.li/ (US) /-dʒɚ-/ **adv** in a way that is careful or CAUTIOUS: *Holding her painful back, she sat down gingerly on the bench.*

ˈginger ˌsnap noun [C] (UK also **ˈginger ˌnut**) a type of hard biscuit with a ginger flavour

gingham /ˈgɪŋ.əm/ noun [U] a cotton cloth that has a pattern of coloured squares on a white surface: *a gingham dress/tablecloth*

gingivitis /ˌdʒɪn.dʒɪˈvaɪ.tɪs/ (US) /-t̬əs/ **noun** [U] specialized an infection of the GUMS (= the part of the mouth from which the teeth grow) which causes swelling, pain, and sometimes BLEEDING

ginormous /ˌdʒaɪˈnɔː.məs/ (US) /-ˈnɔːr-/ **adj** UK informal extremely large: *Even little Billie ate his way through a ginormous ice cream sundae.*

ˌgin ˈrummy noun [U] a card game that is a type of RUMMY

ginseng /ˈdʒɪn.seŋ/ **noun** [U] the root of a tropical plant, especially from China, used as a medicine and to improve health

G

gipsy /ˈdʒɪp.si/ noun [C] mainly UK a **gypsy**

giraffe /dʒɪˈrɑːf/ (US) /-ˈræf/ noun [C] (plural **giraffes** or **giraffe**) B1 a large African animal with a very long neck and long legs

giraffe

gird /gɜːd/ (US) /gɝːd/ **verb** [T] (**girded**, **girded** or **girt**, **girt**) old use to tie something around your body or part of your body: *The knights girded them**selves for** battle (= put on their swords and fighting clothes).*

IDIOM **gird yourself** (also **gird (up) your loins**) literary or humorous to get ready to do something or deal with something: *We girded ourselves for **the fray** (= prepared for action or trouble).* ◦ *Europe's finest golfers are girding their loins for the challenge of the Ryder Cup.*

girder /ˈgɜː.dəʳ/ (US) /ˈgɝː.dɚ/ **noun** [C] a long, thick piece of metal or concrete, etc. which supports a roof, floor, bridge or other large structure: *steel roof girders*

girdle /ˈgɜː.dl̩/ (US) /ˈgɝː-/ **noun** **1** [C] old-fashioned a piece of underwear for women worn around the waist and bottom that stretches to shape the body **2** [C] a long strip of cloth worn tied around the waist, especially in the past

girl /gɜːl/ (US) /gɝːl/ **noun** **1** A1 [C] a female child or young woman, especially one still at school: *Two girls showed us round the classrooms.* **2** A1 [C] a daughter: *We have two girls.* ◦ *My little girl is five.* **3** [C usually plural] a woman worker, especially when seen as one of a group: *shop/office girls* **4** **the girls** B1 [plural] a group of female friends: *I'm going out with the girls tonight.* ◦ *The girls at work gave it to me.*

ˌgirl ˈFriday noun [C] old-fashioned a female office worker who does different types of work

girlfriend /ˈgɜːl.frend/ (US) /ˈgɝːl-/ noun [C] **1** A2 a woman or girl who a person is having a romantic or sexual relationship with: *I've never met his girlfriend.* → Compare **boyfriend** **2** A2 the female friend of a woman: *Susan was going out to lunch with her girlfriends.* **3** slang often humorous used, usually by a woman, when talking to a woman: *You'd better listen to me, girlfriend.*

ˌGirl ˈGuide noun [C] UK old-fashioned a member of the GUIDES organization

girlhood /ˈgɜːl.hʊd/ (US) /ˈgɝːl-/ noun [C or U] old-fashioned the period when a person is a girl, and not yet a woman, or the state of being a girl: *She lived in India during her girlhood.* → See also **boyhood, childhood**

girlie (also **girly**) /ˈgɜː.li/ (US) /ˈgɝː-/ **adj** **1** **girlie magazine, picture, etc.** a magazine, picture, etc. that shows women wearing few or no clothes **2** informal typical of females, or suitable for females rather than males: *We had a real girlie chat.* ◦ disapproving *Sometimes she speaks in this silly, girlie voice.*

girlish /ˈgɜː.lɪʃ/ (US) /ˈgɝː-/ **adj** usually approving describes behaviour or characteristics that are typical of a girl: *a girlish laugh* ◦ *His eyelashes were long and girlish.* • **girlishly** /-li/ **adv**

ˈgirl ˌpower noun [U] the idea that women and girls should be confident, make decisions and achieve things independently of men, or the social and political movement that is based on this idea

ˌGirl ˈScout noun [C] US a girl or young woman who belongs to an organization similar to the GUIDES and SCOUTS

giro /ˈdʒaɪ.rəʊ/ (US) /-roʊ/ **noun** **1** [U] a system used between European banks and similar organizations, in which money can be moved from one account to another by a central computer: *The money was **transferred by** giro.* **2** [C] UK a CHEQUE which provides money from the government, through the giro, to someone unemployed, ill, or with very little income: *a giro cheque* ◦ *She didn't know how she would manage until her next giro.*

girth /gɜːθ/ (US) /gɝːθ/ **noun** MEASUREMENT ▷ **1** [C or U] the distance around the outside of a thick or fat object, like a tree or a body: *The oak was two metres **in** girth.* ◦ humorous *His **ample** girth was evidence of his love of good food.* HORSE EQUIPMENT ▷ **2** [C] the strap which goes around the middle of a horse to keep the SADDLE (= rider's seat) or the LOAD in the right position: *Loosen the girth a little.*

gismo /ˈgɪz.məʊ/ (US) /-moʊ/ **noun** [C] (plural **gismos**) another spelling of **gizmo**

the gist /dʒɪst/ **noun** [S] the most important pieces of information about something, or general information without details: *That was the gist **of** what he said.* ◦ *I think I **got** (= understood) the gist **of** what she was saying.*

git /gɪt/ **noun** [C] UK informal a person, especially a man, who is stupid or unpleasant: *You stupid/lying git!*

gîte /ʒiːt/ **noun** [C] UK a holiday house for renting in France

give /gɪv/ verb; noun

▸verb (**gave**, **given**) PROVIDE ▷ **1** A1 [I or T] to offer something to someone, or to provide them with it: [+ two objects] *She gave us a set of saucepans as a wedding present.* ◦ *Can you give me a date for another appointment?* ◦ *They never gave me a chance/choice.* ◦ *Has the director given you permission to do that?* ◦ [+ adv/prep] *We always try to give **to** charity.* ◦ *We're collecting for the children's home – please give generously.* ◦ *The police gave (**out**) road-safety booklets **to** the children (= gave them to all the children).* ◦ *Please give (**up**) your **seat** to an elderly or disabled person if they require it.* **2** B1 [T] to pay someone a particular amount: *I gave £40 **for** this pump and it's broken already!* **3** **give of your money, time, etc.** formal to give your money, time, or best efforts, especially in a way that seems generous: *We're very grateful to all the people who have given of their time.* ◦ UK *She wasn't feeling well, so I don't think she gave of her **best** tonight.* **4** **give (sth) your all** (US also **give (sth) your best**) to put a lot of effort into doing something: *We must be finished by tonight, so I want you to give it your all.* **5** (A2) [T] to tell someone something: *The winner's name was given (**out**)/They gave the winner's name (**out**) on the news.* ◦ [+ two objects] *Can you give Jo a message for me?* **6** [T] to punish someone by making them go to prison for a particular period: [+ two objects] *If you're found guilty, they'll give you three years.* **7** (B1) [T] to allow a person or activity a particular amount of time: [+ two objects] *I'm nearly ready – just give me a couple of minutes.* **8** [T] informal to calculate that something will last a particular amount of time: [+ two objects] *Look at that old car she's bought – I give it two weeks before it breaks down.*

! Common mistake: give

Warning: when talking about giving a physical object, the indirect object can go before or after the direct object:

He gave the flowers to his mother.

He gave his mother the flowers.

When the indirect object comes before the direct object, don't say 'give to someone something', just say **give someone something**:

~~*He gave to his mother the flowers.*~~

Remember: when the object of **give** is something that you cannot touch, such as advice or an opinion or feeling, the indirect object must come before the direct object.

Don't say 'give advice/your opinion/a shock to someone', say **give someone advice/your opinion/a shock**:

~~*What he said gave an idea to me.*~~

What he said gave me an idea.

CAUSE ▷ **9** (B1) [T] to produce or cause something: [+ two objects] *The fresh air gave us an appetite* (= made us hungry). ◦ *What you said has given me an idea.* ◦ *The alarm gave (**out**) a high-pitched sound.* **10 give sb to understand sth** formal to tell someone something or cause them to think that something is true: *I was given to understand she was staying at this hotel.* DO ▷ **11** (A2) [T] to perform an action: [+ two objects] *She gave me a smile/strange look.* ◦ *They had to give the car a **push** to start it.* ◦ *Give me a **call/ring** (= phone me) when you get back from holiday.* ◦ *Who is giving the speech/lecture/concert?* **12** (A2) [T] to organize a party, meal, etc.: *They're always giving parties.* ◦ *The ambassador is giving a banquet for the visiting president.* **13 give sth a go** to attempt something: *Only a few people are successful as sports professionals, but it's worth giving **it** a go.* **14** [T + two objects] formal to say publicly that everyone present at a formal occasion, especially a meal, should drink a TOAST to someone (= have a drink in honour of someone): *Gentlemen, I give you the Queen!* STRETCH ▷ **15** [I] If something gives, it stretches, bends, or breaks, or becomes less firm or tight, under pressure: *The rope gave **under/with** the weight of the load.* ◦ *The shoes will give a little after you've worn them once or twice.* ◦ figurative *You can't work so hard all the time – something will have to give* (= change). ◦ figurative *Suddenly her patience gave (**out**) and she shouted crossly at the children.* DECIDE ▷ **16** [T + obj + adj] UK in some sports, to decide and state officially that a player or the ball is in a particular condition or place: *The umpire gave the batsman out.* ◦ *The ball was clearly out, but the line judge gave it in.*

IDIOMS **don't give me that!** informal don't expect me to believe that, because I know it is untrue: *'But I was going to let you have it tomorrow.' 'Don't give me that!'* • **give as good as you get** to be strong and confident

+ Other ways of saying give

Very common alternatives to 'give' are verbs such as **offer**, **provide**, and **supply**:

*This booklet **provides** useful information about local services.*

*Your doctor should be able to **offer** advice.*

*The lake **supplies** the whole town with water.*

The verb **donate** is often used when someone gives money or goods to an organization that needs help:

*Four hundred dollars has been **donated** to the school book fund.*

If one of many people gives something, especially money, in order to provide or achieve something, the verb **contribute** is used:

*I **contributed** £20 towards Jamie's present.*

If you put something from your hand into someone else's hand, you can use verbs such as **pass** and **hand**:

*Could you **hand** me that book, please?*

*He **passed** a note to her during the meeting.*

The phrasal verb **hand in** is sometimes used when you give something to someone in a position of authority:

*Have you **handed in** your history essay yet?*

The phrasal verb **pass on** is often used when you ask someone to give something to someone else:

*Could you **pass** this **on** to Laura when you've finished reading it?*

If something like a prize or an amount of money is given in an official way, you can use verbs like **award** or **present**:

*She was **presented** with a bouquet of flowers and a cheque for £100.*

*He was **awarded** the Nobel Prize for Physics.*

enough to treat people in the same way that they treat you, especially in an argument or a fight: *There's a lot of teasing and fighting among the crew, and you have to be able to give as good as you get.* • **give or take** possibly a little more or less than the amount or time mentioned: *It'll be ready at six, give or take a few minutes.* ◦ *It cost £200, give or take.* • **give me ... any day/every time!** informal used to say that you always like or prefer a particular thing: *This new stuff is all very well, but give me the old-style weather forecast any day!* • **give way 1** (C1) UK to allow other vehicles to go past before you move onto a road: *You have to give way **to** traffic coming from the right.* **2** (C2) to break, especially when under pressure from strong forces: *Because of an unusually strong current, the bridge's central support gave way, tipping a coach into the river.* **3** to stop arguing or fighting against someone or something: *Neither of them will give way, so they could be arguing for a very long time.* ◦ *Don't give way **to** your fears.* • **give sb what for** old-fashioned informal to speak angrily to someone whose behaviour you strongly disapprove of • **given the chance/choice** (also **given half a chance**) if I were allowed to, or if I could choose: *Given the chance, I'd spend all day reading.* • **what I wouldn't give for sth** (also **what wouldn't I give for sth**) used to say that you want something very much: *What I wouldn't give for a cold drink!* • **I would give anything/a lot** (also **I would give my eye teeth/right arm**) used to say that you would like to have or to do something very much: *I'd give anything to see the Taj Mahal.* ◦ *Janice would give her eye teeth **for** a house like that.*

PHRASAL VERBS **give sth away** **FREE** ▷ **1** B1 to give something to someone without asking for payment: *The shop is giving away a sample pack to every customer.* ◦ *Nobody wants this type of heater any more – I can't even give it away!* → See also **giveaway** **SECRET** ▷ **2** B2 to tell people something secret, often without intending to: *The party was meant to be a surprise, but Sharon gave it away.* ◦ *I won't give **the game** (= the information or plan) away.* • **give sb away** **SHOW** ▷ **1** to show someone's secret feelings: *She thinks no one knows how much she likes him, but her face when I said he'd be there really gave her away!* **MARRIAGE** ▷ **2** formal in a marriage ceremony, to formally bring a woman who is getting married to the front of the church so that she is standing at the side of her future partner, and then to give permission for her to marry: *The bride was given away by her father.* • **give sth back** A2 to return something to the person who gave it to you: *Has she given you those books back yet?* • **give in** **AGREE** ▷ **1** B1 to finally agree to what someone wants, after refusing for a period of time: *He nagged me so much for a new bike that eventually I gave in.* ◦ *The government cannot be seen to give in to terrorists' demands.* **ADMIT DEFEAT** ▷ **2** B2 to accept that you have been defeated and agree to stop competing or fighting: *You'll never guess the answer – do you give in?* • **give sth in** UK B1 to give a piece of written work or a document to someone for them to read, judge, or deal with: *Have you given that essay in yet?* • **give sth off** to produce heat, light, a smell, or a gas: *That tiny radiator doesn't give off much heat.* • **give onto sth** to open in the direction of something: *The patio doors give onto a small courtyard.* • **give out** If a machine or part of your body gives out, it stops working: *At the end of the race his legs gave out and he collapsed on the ground.* • **give over** UK old-fashioned informal to stop doing something, usually something annoying: *Oh (do) give over (= stop complaining), it's not my fault!* ◦ [+ -ing verb] *It's time you gave over pretend**ing** you're still a teenager.* • **give sth over to sth/sb** to give another person the use of something, or the responsibility for something or someone: *We've given the attic over to the children.* • **give yourself over/up to sth** to spend all your time and energy doing or feeling something: *After her death he gave himself over to grief.* • **give up** to stop trying to guess: *You'll never guess the answer – do you give up?* ◦ *I give up – how many were there?* • **give up sth** **1** to stop owning and using something: *They were forced to give up their home because they couldn't pay the mortgage.* **2** **give up hope** to stop hoping that a particular thing will happen: *We still haven't given up hope **of** finding her alive.* • **give up (sth)** B2 to stop doing something before you have finished it, usually because it is too difficult: [+ -ing verb] *I've given up try**ing** to help her.* • **give (sth) up** B1 If you give up a habit, such as smoking, or something such as alcohol, you stop doing it or using it: [+ -ing verb] *I gave up smok**ing** two years ago.* ◦ *Don't offer him a cigarette, he's trying to give up.* • **give sth up** B1 to stop doing a regular activity or job: [+ -ing verb] *He's given up driv**ing** since his illness.* ◦ *We're going to give up our sports club membership after this year.* • **give it up for sb** used to ask people to clap their hands to show their enjoyment or approval of a performance: *Ladies and gentlemen, will you give it up for Danny Jones.* • **give sb up** **END FRIENDSHIP** ▷ **1** to stop having a friendship with someone: *She seems to have given up all her old friends.* **NOT EXPECT** ▷ **2** (also **give up on sb**) to stop expecting that someone will arrive: *I've been waiting half an hour – I'd almost given you up.* **3** **give sb up for dead** (also **give up on sb**) to think that someone is certain to die or to be dead: *The hospital had virtually given her up for dead, but she eventually recovered.* ◦ *After a three-day search on the mountain, they gave him up for dead.* • **give yourself up** to allow the police or an enemy to take you as a prisoner: *The gunman gave himself up to the police.* → See also **give yourself over/up to sth**

▸**noun** [U] the quality of stretching, bending, or breaking, or becoming less firm or tight, under pressure: *A sweater knitted in pure cotton hasn't much give (= will not stretch much).*

ˌgive and ˈtake noun **1** C2 [U] willingness to accept suggestions from another person and give up some of your own: *In every friendship there has to be some give and take.* **2** [S] US an exchange of ideas or statements: *The candidates engaged in a **lively** give and take, witnessed by a huge television audience.*

giveaway /ˈɡɪv.əˌweɪ/ **noun; adj**

▸**noun** [C] **GIFT** ▷ **1** something that is given free to a customer **TRUTH** ▷ **2** informal something that tells or shows something secret, often without intending to: *He said he'd given up smoking, but the empty packets in the bin were **a dead** giveaway (= clearly showed the secret truth).*

▸**adj** [before noun] describes a price that is very low: *The furniture shop's offering three-piece suites at giveaway **prices**.*

given /ˈɡɪv.ən/ **verb; preposition; adj; noun**

▸**verb** past participle of **give**

▸**preposition** knowing about or considering a particular thing: *Given his age, he's a remarkably fast runner.* ◦ *Given **(the fact) that** he's had six months to do this, he hasn't made much progress.*

▸**adj** **ARRANGED** ▷ **1** already decided, arranged or agreed: *At the given signal, the group rushed forward to the barrier.* ◦ *The bomb could go off at **any** given (= any) time and in **any** given (= any) place.* **HAVE HABIT** ▷ **2** **be given to sth** to do something regularly or as a habit: *She was given to staying in bed till lunchtime.*

▸**noun** [C] something that is certain to happen: *You can **take** it **as** a given that there will be champagne at the wedding.*

ˈgiven ˌname noun [C] US (UK **ˈfirst ˌname**) the name that is chosen for you at birth and is not your family name: *Her family name is Smith and her given names are Mary Elizabeth.*

gizmo (plural **gizmos**) (also **gismo** (plural **gismos**)) /ˈɡɪz.məʊ/ US /-moʊ/ **noun** [C] informal any small device with a particular purpose: *electronic gizmos*

glacé /ˈɡlæs.eɪ/ US /ɡlæsˈeɪ/ **adj** [before noun] (US also **glacéed**) preserved in liquid sugar and then dried: *glacé fruit*

glacial /ˈɡleɪ.ʃəl/ **adj** **ICE/COLD** ▷ **1** made or left by a glacier: *glacial deposits* **2** extremely cold: *glacial temperatures* **NOT FRIENDLY** ▷ **3** extremely unfriendly: *She gave me a glacial smile/stare.*

ˈglacial ˌperiod noun [C] (also **ˈice ˌage**) a time in the past when the temperature was very cold and glaciers covered large parts of the earth

glaciation /ˌɡleɪ.siˈeɪ.ʃən/ **noun** [U] the forming, existence, or movement of glaciers over the surface of the Earth: *This landscape shows many clear features of glaciation.*

glacier /ˈɡlæs.i.ər/ US /ˈɡleɪ.si.ər/ **noun** [C] a large mass of ice which moves slowly

>**glad** /glæd/ adj (**gladder**, **gladdest**) A2 pleased and happy: *We were glad **about** her success.* ◦ *I'm glad (**that**) you came.* ◦ *I'm glad **to** know the parcel arrived safely.* ◦ *I'd be (**only too**) glad **to** help you.* ◦ *We'd be glad **of** the chance to meet her.* • **gladness** /-nəs/ noun [U]

gladden /ˈglæd.ən/ verb [T] literary to make someone or something glad: *The news gladdened his **heart**.*

glade /gleɪd/ noun [C] literary a small area of grass without trees in a wood

ˈglad-ˌhanding noun [U] informal being very friendly to people you have not met before, as a way of trying to get an advantage: *political glad-handing* • **ˈglad-hand** verb [I or T]

gladiator /ˈglæd.i.eɪ.təʳ/ US /-t̬ɚ/ noun [C] in ancient Rome, a man who fought another man or an animal, usually until one of them died, for public entertainment

gladiatorial /ˌglæd.i.əˈtɔː.ri.əl/ US /-ˈtɔːr.i-/ adj literary relating to violent fighting in which only one person or group can win: *gladiatorial combat*

gladiolus /ˌglæd.iˈəʊ.ləs/ US /-ˈoʊ-/ noun [C] (plural **gladioli** /-laɪ/) a garden plant that has a long stem and many brightly coloured flowers

gladly /ˈglæd.li/ adv willingly or happily: *I'd gladly meet her, but I'm on holiday that week.*

ˈglad ˌrags noun [plural] humorous Someone's glad rags are their best clothes: *Let's put on our glad rags and go out tonight!*

glam /glæm/ adj; verb

▸adj informal short form of glamorous: *You look dead glam in that dress!*

▸verb (**-mm-**)

PHRASAL VERB **glam (yourself) up** UK informal to dress yourself attractively and put on make-up, etc.: *Have I got time to glam (myself) up?*

ˌglammed ˈup adj UK informal dressed attractively and wearing make-up: *She **got/was** all glammed up for the party.*

glamorize (UK usually **glamorise**) /ˈglæm.ə.raɪz/ US /-ɚ.aɪz/ verb [T] to make something seem better than it is and therefore more attractive: *The ad glamorized life in the army, emphasizing travel and adventure.*

glamorous /ˈglæm.ər.əs/ US /-ɚ-/ adj (mainly UK informal **glam**) attractive in an exciting and special way: *a glamorous woman/outfit* ◦ *a glamorous job.* • **glamorously** /-li/ adv

glamour UK (US **glamor**) /ˈglæm.əʳ/ US /-ɚ/ noun [U] C1 the special exciting and attractive quality of a person, place, or activity: *Who can resist the glamour **of** Hollywood?*

glance /glɑːns/ US /glæns/ verb; noun

▸verb **LOOK** ▷ **1** B1 [I usually + adv/prep] to give a quick short look: *She glanced **around/round** the room to see who was there.* ◦ *He glanced **up** from his book as I passed.* ◦ *Could you glance **over/through** this letter and see if it's alright?* **SHINE** ▷ **2** [I + adv/prep] to shine, reflect light, or SPARKLE: *The sunlight glanced **on** the lake.*

PHRASAL VERB **glance off (sth)** to hit or touch something quickly and lightly at an angle and move away in another direction: *The bullets glanced off the car.*

▸noun [C] **1** B2 a quick short look: *She **took/cast** a glance **at** her watch.* **2 at a glance** C1 immediately: *He could **tell** at a glance that something was wrong.* **3 at first glance** when first looking: *At first glance I thought it was a dog (but I was mistaken).*

glancing /ˈglɑːn.sɪŋ/ US /ˈglæn-/ adj [before noun] hitting quickly and lightly at an angle: *a glancing **blow** to the head*

gland /glænd/ noun [C] an organ of the body or of a plant which SECRETES (= produces) liquid chemicals that have various purposes: *The glands in my neck are a bit swollen.*

glandular /ˈglæn.djʊ.ləʳ/ US /-dʒə.lɚ/ adj belonging or relating to, or produced or caused by, a gland or glands: *a glandular problem* ◦ *glandular secretions*

ˌglandular ˈfever noun [U] UK (US **mononucleosis**) an infectious disease that has an effect on particular glands and makes you feel weak and sick for a long time

glare /gleəʳ/ US /gler/ noun; verb

▸noun **LOOK** ▷ **1** C2 [C] a long angry look: *She gave me a fierce glare.* **LIGHT** ▷ **2** C2 [U] unpleasantly bright or strong light: *Tinted windows will cut down **the** glare/the sun's glare.* ◦ *This screen **gives off** a lot of glare.*

IDIOM **the/a glare of sth** an occasion when something receives a very large amount of public attention: *The actor's wedding took place **in** the **full** glare of **publicity/the media**.*

▸verb [I] **SHINE** ▷ **1** to shine too brightly: *The sun was glaring right in my eyes.* **LOOK** ▷ **2** C2 to look directly and continuously at someone or something in an angry way: *She glared angrily **at** everyone and stormed out of the room.*

glaring /ˈgleə.rɪŋ/ US /ˈgler.ɪŋ/ adj **OBVIOUS** ▷ **1** describes something bad that is very obvious: *glaring errors* ◦ *a glaring injustice* **SHINING** ▷ **2** shining too brightly: *glaring light* ◦ *glaring colours* • **glaringly** /-li/ adv *glaringly obvious*

glass /glɑːs/ US /glæs/ noun; verb

▸noun **SUBSTANCE** ▷ **1** A1 [U] a hard, transparent material, used to make windows, bottles, and other objects: *coloured/broken glass* ◦ *a glass jar/dish/ornament* ◦ *It's a huge window made from a single **pane of** glass.* **2** [U] objects made from glass when thought of as a group: *The museum has a fine collection of valuable glass.* **3 under glass** in a GLASSHOUSE: *In cool climates you have to grow tropical plants under glass.* **CONTAINER** ▷ **4** A1 [C] a small container for drinks made of glass or similar material, with a flat base and usually with no handle: *a **beer/wine** glass* ◦ *She poured some milk into a glass.* **5 a glass of sth** A1 a type or amount of drink contained in a glass: *Would you like a glass of water?* ◦ *Two glasses of lemonade, please.* **FOR IMPROVING SIGHT** ▷ **6 glasses** [plural] A1 two small pieces of special glass or plastic in a frame worn in front of the eyes to improve sight: *a **pair of** glasses* ◦ ***reading** glasses* **DEVICE** ▷ **7 the glass** [S] old-fashioned a **barometer**: *The glass has been **falling/rising** (= showing a change to bad/good weather) all day.*

▸verb

PHRASAL VERB **glass sth in/over** to use glass to fill the open spaces in something or to cover something: *We glassed in the porch to make a small conservatory.* ◦ *The manuscripts are now glassed over, to stop them being damaged.*

glassblower /ˈglɑːsˌbləʊ.əʳ/ US /ˈglæsˌbloʊ.ɚ/ noun [C] someone who blows air down a tube to form heated glass into objects • **glassblowing** /-ɪŋ/ noun [U]

ˌglass ˈceiling noun [C usually singular] a point after which you cannot go, usually in improving your position at work: *Various reasons are given for the apparent glass ceiling women hit in many professions.*

G

ˌglass ˈfibre noun [U] UK **fibreglass**

glassful /ˈglɑːs.fʊl/ (US) /ˈglæs-/ noun [C] an amount contained in a glass: *She drank two whole glassfuls **of** orange juice.*

glasshouse /ˈglɑːs.haʊs/ (US) /ˈglæs-/ noun [C] (US usually **greenhouse**) a large building with glass sides and roof for growing plants in

glassware /ˈglɑːs.weəʳ/ (US) /ˈglæs.wer/ noun [U] drinking glasses or other objects made of glass: *a display/collection of ornamental glassware*

glassy /ˈglɑː.si/ (US) /ˈglæs.i/ adj **SURFACE** ▷ **1** literary describes a surface that is smooth and shiny, like glass: *a glassy sea/lake* **EYES** ▷ **2** describes a person's eyes when they have a fixed expression and seem unable to see anything: *Her eyes were glassy and her skin pale.*

Glaswegian /glæzˈwiː.dʒən/ noun [C] a person from Glasgow, the largest city in Scotland • **Glaswegian** adj *Steven has a Glaswegian accent.*

glaucoma /glaʊˈkəʊ.mə/ (US) /-ˈkoʊ-/ noun [U] a disease of the eye that can cause a person to gradually lose their sight

glaze /gleɪz/ verb; noun

▸verb **GLASS** ▷ **1** [T] to put a piece of glass into a window or the windows of a building: *The house is nearly finished but it hasn't been glazed yet.* **SHINY** ▷ **2** [T] to make a surface shiny by putting a liquid substance onto it and leaving it or heating it until it dries: *Glaze the pastry with beaten egg.* ◦ *The pot had been badly glazed.* **BORED** ▷ **3** [I] (also **glaze over**) If your eyes glaze or glaze over, they stay still and stop showing any emotion because you are bored or tired or have stopped listening: *Among the audience, eyes glazed over and a few heads started to nod.* • **glazed** /gleɪzd/ adj *All the rooms have glazed doors.* ◦ *a glazed **expression/look***

▸noun [C] a substance used to glaze something: *a cake with a redcurrant glaze* ◦ *pottery with a fine translucent glaze*

glazier /ˈgleɪ.zi.əʳ/ (US) /-ɚ/ noun [C] a person who sells glass or fits it into windows

glazing /ˈgleɪ.zɪŋ/ noun [U] the glass used for windows

gleam /gliːm/ verb; noun

▸verb [I] **1** to produce or reflect a small, bright light: *He polished the table until it gleamed.* **2** When eyes gleam, they shine in a way that expresses a particular emotion: *His eyes gleamed **with/in** triumph.*

▸noun [C usually singular] an occasion when something gleams

gleaming /ˈgliː.mɪŋ/ adj bright and shiny from being cleaned: *a gleaming kitchen* ◦ *gleaming windows*

glean /gliːn/ verb [T] to collect information in small amounts and often with difficulty: *From what I was able to glean, the news isn't good.* ◦ *They're leaving on Tuesday – I managed to glean that much (**from** them).*

glee /gliː/ noun [U] happiness, excitement or pleasure: *She opened her presents with glee.* • **gleeful** /-fəl/ adj *a gleeful smile/shout* • **gleefully** /-fəl.i/ adv

ˈglee ˌclub noun [C] US an organization for people who like to sing together: *He sang with the school's glee club.*

glen /glen/ noun [C] a deep narrow valley, especially among mountains: *the glens of Scotland* ◦ *Glen Maye*

glib /glɪb/ adj (**glibber, glibbest**) speaking or spoken in a confident way, but without careful thought or honesty: *He's a glib, self-centred man.* ◦ *No one was convinced by his glib **answers/explanations**.* • **glibly** /ˈglɪb.li/ adv • **glibness** /ˈglɪb.nəs/ noun [U]

glide /glaɪd/ verb **MOVE** ▷ **1** [I usually + adv/prep] to move easily without stopping and without effort or noise: *She came gliding gracefully into the ballroom in a long, flowing gown.* ◦ *I love my new pen – it just glides across/over the paper.* **2** [I usually + adv/prep] to move or progress without difficulty or effort: *Some people glide effortlessly through life with no real worries.* **FLY** ▷ **3** [I] to fly by floating on air currents instead of using power from wings or an engine: *We saw a condor gliding high above the mountains.* ◦ *Unlike other spacecraft, the shuttle can glide back **through** the atmosphere, land safely, and be reused.* • **glide** noun [C]

glider /ˈglaɪ.dəʳ/ (US) /-dɚ/ noun [C] an aircraft without an engine and with long fixed wings, which flies by gliding

gliding /glaɪ.dɪŋ/ noun [U] the sport or activity of flying in a glider

glimmer /ˈglɪm.əʳ/ (US) /-ɚ/ verb; noun

▸verb [I] to shine with a weak light or a light that is not continuous: *The lights of the village were glimmering in the distance.* ◦ *The sky glimmered **with** stars.* ◦ *a glimmering candle* ◦ figurative *The first faint signs of an agreement began to glimmer through (= appear).*

▸noun [C] (also **glimmering**) **LIGHT** ▷ **1** a light that glimmers weakly: *We saw a glimmer **of light** in the distance.* **SIGN** ▷ **2** a slight sign of something good or positive: *This month's sales figures offer a glimmer **of hope** for the depressed economy.* ◦ *She's never shown a glimmer **of interest** in classical music.* ◦ *The first glimmer **of light** (= sign of development or understanding) has appeared in the peace talks.*

glimpse /glɪmps/ verb; noun

▸verb [T] to see something or someone for a very short time or only partly: *We glimpsed the ruined abbey from the windows of the train.*

▸noun [C] **1** (C1) an occasion when you see something or someone for a very short time: *I only **caught** (= had) a **fleeting** glimpse **of** the driver of the getaway car, but I know I would recognize her if I saw her again.* **2** a quick idea or understanding of what something is like: *This biography offers a few glimpses **of** his life before he became famous.*

glint /glɪnt/ verb; noun

▸verb [I] **1** to produce small bright flashes of light reflected from a surface: *The stream glinted in the moonlight.* ◦ *A large diamond glinted on her finger.* **2** When someone's eyes glint, they look bright, expressing a strong emotion: *She smiled at him, her eyes glinting **with** mischief.*

▸noun [C usually singular] an occasion when something glints: *the glint **of** a knife* ◦ *a mischievous glint in his eye*

glisten /ˈglɪs.ən/ verb [I] to shine by reflecting light from a wet or smooth surface: *The grass glistened in the early-morning dew.* ◦ *His eyes glistened **with** tears.*

glitch /glɪtʃ/ noun [C] a small problem or fault that prevents something from being successful or working as well as it should: *We'd expected a few glitches, but everything's gone remarkably smoothly.* ◦ *The system has been plagued with glitches ever since its launch.*

glitter /ˈglɪt.əʳ/ (US) /ˈglɪt̬.ɚ/ verb; noun

▸verb [I] **1** to produce a lot of small bright flashes of reflected light: *Her diamond necklace glittered brilliantly under the spotlights.* **2** literary If someone's eyes glitter, they look bright and express strong feeling: *His dark eyes glittered **with** anger behind his spectacles.*

IDIOM **all that glitters is not gold** saying said about something that seems to be good on the surface, but might not be when you look at it more closely

▸noun [U] EXCITEMENT ▷ **1** the excitement and attractive quality connected with rich and famous people: *He was attracted by the glitter **of** Hollywood.* BRIGHT LIGHT ▷ **2** an occasion when something glitters: *the glitter **of** the fireworks* DECORATION ▷ **3** very small pieces of shiny material used to decorate the skin or used by children to make pictures

glitterati /ˌglɪt.əˈrɑː.ti/ (US) /ˌglɪt̬.əˈrɑː.t̬i/ **noun** [plural] rich, famous, and fashionable people whose activities are of interest to the public and are written about in some newspapers and magazines: *The restaurant is popular with the glitterati **of** the music world.* → Compare **literati**

glittering /ˈglɪt.ər.ɪŋ/ (US) /ˈglɪt̬.ɚ-/ **adj** EXCITING ▷ **1** exciting or admired by many people, usually relating to rich and famous people: *a glittering career* ◦ *The Cannes Film Festival is one of the most glittering occasions in the movie world.* BRIGHT LIGHT ▷ **2** shining with a lot of small bright flashes of light: *the glittering skyline of Manhattan*

glittery /ˈglɪt.ər.i/ (US) /ˈglɪt̬.ɚ-/ **adj** producing a lot of small flashes of reflected light: *glittery eye shadow* ◦ *a glittery dress*

glitzy /ˈglɪt.si/ **adj** having a fashionable appearance intended to attract attention: *He celebrated his birthday at a glitzy party in Beverly Hills.* • **glitz** /glɪts/ **noun** [U] *The party's electoral message may be obscured by the glitz **and glamour** of its presentation.*

gloat /gləʊt/ (US) /gloʊt/ **verb; noun**

▸verb [I] to feel or express great pleasure or satisfaction because of your own success or good luck, or someone else's failure or bad luck: *She's continually gloating **over/about** her new job.* ◦ *I know I shouldn't gloat, but it really serves him right.* ◦ *His enemies were quick to gloat **at** his humiliation.* ◦ [+ speech] *'This is our fourth victory in a row,' he gloated.* • **gloatingly** /ˈgləʊ.tɪŋ.li/ (US) /ˈgloʊ.t̬ɪŋ-/ **adv**

▸noun [C usually singular] an occasion when you gloat about something: *to have a gloat at/over/about something*

glob /glɒb/ (US) /glɑːb/ **noun** [C] informal a round mass of a thick liquid or a sticky substance: *a glob **of** ketchup/yogurt*

global /ˈgləʊ.bəl/ (US) /ˈgloʊ-/ **adj** WORLD ▷ **1** (B2) relating to the whole world: *a global catastrophe/problem* ALL PARTS ▷ **2** considering or relating to all parts of a situation or subject: *This report gives a global picture of the company's finances.* • **globally** /-i/ **adv** (B2) *The company has to be able to compete globally (= across the whole world).* ◦ *We need to look at this issue globally (= to look at all parts of it).*

globalism /ˈgləʊ.bəl.ɪ.zəm/ (US) /ˈgloʊ-/ **noun** [U] the idea that events in one country cannot be separated from those in another and that a government should therefore consider the effects of its actions in other countries as well as its own → Compare **isolationism**

globalization (UK usually **globalisation**) /ˌgləʊ.bəl.aɪˈzeɪ.ʃən/ (US) /ˌgloʊ-/ **noun** [U] **1** (C1) the increase of trade around the world, especially by large companies producing and trading goods in many different countries: *We must take advantage of the increased globalization of the commodity trading business.* **2** a situation in which available goods and services, or social and cultural influences, gradually become similar in all parts of the world: *the globalization of fashion/American youth culture*

globalize (UK usually **globalise**) /ˈgləʊ.bəl.aɪz/ (US) /ˈgloʊ-/ **verb** [I or T] to (make a company or system) spread or operate internationally: *Satellite broadcasting is helping to globalize television.* ◦ *As the economy develops, it will continue to globalize.*

ˌglobal ˈwarming **noun** [U] (B2) a gradual increase in world temperatures caused by gases such as CARBON DIOXIDE that are collecting in the air around the Earth and stopping heat escaping into space

globe /gləʊb/ (US) /gloʊb/ **noun** WORLD ▷ **1 the globe** (C2) [S] the world: *His greatest ambition is to sail **round** the globe.* ◦ *She is a superstar all **around** the globe.* **2** [C] a map of the world made in the shape of a ball and fixed to a support, that can be turned around at the same angle as the Earth turns in space: *She **spun** the globe, and pointed to the Solomon Islands.* ROUND OBJECT ▷ **3** [C] any ball-shaped object **4** [C] Australian English a **light globe**

ˌglobe ˈartichoke **noun** [C] a plant with a round mass of pointed parts like leaves surrounding its flower that are eaten as a vegetable

globetrotter /ˈgləʊbˌtrɒt.ər/ (US) /ˈgloʊbˌtrɑː.t̬ɚ/ **noun** [C] someone who often travels to a lot of different countries: *Japan last month, New York next month – you've become a regular globetrotter, haven't you?* • **globetrotting** /-ˌtrɒt.ɪŋ/ (US) /-ˌtrɑː.t̬ɪŋ/ **adj, noun** [U]

globular /ˈglɒb.jʊ.lər/ (US) /ˈglɑː.b.jə.lɚ/ **adj** shaped like a ball

globule /ˈglɒb.juːl/ (US) /ˈglɑːb-/ **noun** [C] a small ball of something, especially a drop of liquid: *The disease is caused by globules of fat blocking the blood vessels.*

glockenspiel /ˈglɒk.ən.ʃpiːl/ (US) /ˈglɑː.kən.spiːl/ **noun** [C] a musical instrument made of flat metal bars of different lengths which you hit with a pair of small hammers

glom /glɒm/ (US) /glɑːm/ **verb**

PHRASAL VERB **glom onto sth/sb** US informal **1** to become very interested in something such as a new idea or fashion or in someone: *Retailers are glomming onto a new fashion among teens for outsize clothes.* ◦ *This guy glommed onto me at Tasha's party and wouldn't take no for an answer.* **2** to get or take something that you want: *He's glommed onto a couple of my comics and I can't get them back off him.*

gloom /gluːm/ **noun** [U] WITHOUT HOPE ▷ **1** feelings of great unhappiness and loss of hope: *Bergman's films are often full of gloom and despair.* ◦ *There is widespread gloom **and doom** about the company's future.* DARKNESS ▷ **2** a situation in which it is nearly dark and difficult to see well: *She peered into the gloom, but she couldn't see where the noise was coming from.* ◦ *A figure emerged from the gloom of the corridor.*

gloomy /ˈgluː.mi/ **adj** WITHOUT HOPE ▷ **1** unhappy and without hope: *a gloomy person/expression* ◦ *The cemetery is a gloomy place.* **2** not expecting or believing anything good in a situation: *The vet is rather gloomy about my cat's chances of recovery.* ◦ *a gloomy economic forecast* DARK ▷ **3** dark in a way that is unpleasant and makes it difficult to see: *What gloomy weather we're having!* ◦ *We waited in a gloomy waiting room.* • **gloomily** /-mɪ.li/ **adv** • **gloominess** /-nəs/ **noun** [U]

gloop /gluːp/ **noun** [U] UK informal any thick liquid or sticky substance • **gloopy** /ˈgluː.p.iː/ **adj** UK

glop /glɒp/ (US) /glɑːp/ **noun** [U] informal any thick, unpleasant liquid, especially food: *The soup was a greyish glop, with bits in it.*

G

glorify /ˈglɔː.rɪ.faɪ/ (US) /ˈglɔːr.ɪ-/ **verb** [T] **1** to praise and honour God or a person: *There are 99 prayer beads – one for each way Allah can be glorified in the Koran.* ◦ *A statue was erected to glorify the country's national heroes.* **2** to describe or represent something in a way that makes it seem better or more important than it really is: *I didn't like the way the film glorified war/violence.* ◦ informal *The limousine was really just a glorified taxi.* • **glorification** /ˌglɔː.rɪ.fɪˈkeɪ.ʃən/ (US) /ˌglɔːr.ɪ-/ **noun** [U] *He criticized the entertainment industry for the glorification of violence.* ◦ *Cathedrals are built for the glorification of God.*

glorious /ˈglɔː.ri.əs/ (US) /ˈglɔːr.i-/ **adj** DESERVING ADMIRATION ▷ **1** deserving great admiration, praise, and honour: *a glorious victory* BEAUTIFUL/NICE ▷ **2** very beautiful: *The beetroot had turned the soup a glorious pink.* ◦ *Your roses are glorious!* **3** describes weather that is very pleasant, especially weather that is hot and SUNNY: *They had glorious weather for their wedding.* ◦ *It was a glorious winter day – crisp and clear.* **4** very enjoyable or giving great pleasure: *This wine is absolutely glorious.* ◦ *We had a glorious time in the south of France last summer.* • **gloriously** /-li/ **adv** *We've had gloriously sunny weather.* ◦ *They looked gloriously happy.*

the ˌGlorious ˈTwelfth noun [S] UK 12 August, the start of the GROUSE shooting season in Britain

glory /ˈglɔː.ri/ (US) /ˈglɔːr.i/ **noun; verb**

▸**noun** ADMIRATION/PRAISE ▷ **1** [U] praise and thanks, especially as given to God: *Glory be to God!* ◦ *He dedicated his poetry to the glory of God.* **2** (C1) [U] great admiration, honour, and praise which you earn by doing something successfully: *He revelled in the glory **of** scoring three goals in the final eight minutes.* ◦ *This was her final professional match, and she wanted to end her career in **a blaze of** glory.* **3** [C] an important achievement which earns someone great admiration, honour, and praise: *The reunion is an opportunity for the soldiers to remember their past glories.* BEAUTY ▷ **4** (C1) [C or U] great beauty, or something special or extremely beautiful, which gives great pleasure: *They want to restore the castle to its former glory.* ◦ *The garden **in all** its glory is now open to the public.*

IDIOMS **bask/bathe in reflected glory** to feel successful and admired for something, despite the fact that you did not achieve it yourself but were only connected to it in some way: *The government is bathing in the reflected glory of its victorious military forces.* • **cover yourself in/with glory** to be very successful and earn admiration: *He didn't exactly cover himself with glory in his last job.* • **crowning glory** the greatest or most beautiful thing: *The ballroom is the crowning glory **of** the palace.* ◦ *Her hair is her crowning glory.*

▸**verb**

PHRASAL VERB **glory in sth** to feel or show that you are very proud and happy about something: *He is still glorying in the success of his first Hollywood film.* ◦ *She glories in the fact that she's much better qualified than her sister.*

ˈglory ˌdays noun [plural] Someone's glory days are a period of time when they were very successful: *Her popularity as a singer has waned since the glory days of the 1980s.*

gloss /glɒs/ (US) /glɑːs/ **noun; verb**

▸**noun** APPEARANCE ▷ **1** [S or U] a smooth, shiny appearance on the surface of something, or paint or a similar substance that produces this appearance: *Marble can be polished to **a** high gloss.* ◦ *This varnish provides a long-lasting and hard-wearing gloss **finish**.* ◦ ***lip** gloss* ◦ *We'll need a litre of gloss (**paint**) to cover the woodwork.* EXPLANATION ▷ **2** [C] an explanation for a word or phrase: *Difficult expressions are explained in the glosses at the bottom of the page.*

IDIOMS **put a gloss on sth** to emphasize the good parts of something that has been done, especially those that are to your advantage, and to avoid the bad parts: *Politics is all about putting a **good** gloss on unpleasant or difficult situations.* • **take the gloss off sth** to make an event or occasion less special and enjoyable: *The bad weather really took the gloss off our trip to the zoo.*

▸**verb** [T] to provide an explanation for a word or phrase: *In the school edition of the book, the older and more rare words have been glossed.*

PHRASAL VERB **gloss over sth** to avoid considering something, such as an embarrassing mistake, to make it seem not important, and to quickly continue talking about something else: *She glossed over the company's fall in profits.* ◦ *The film was well researched, but it glossed over the important issues.*

glossary /ˈglɒs.ər.i/ (US) /ˈglɑː.sɚ-/ **noun** [C] an ALPHABETICAL list, with meanings, of the words or phrases in a text that are difficult to understand: *a glossary **of** technical terms*

glossy /ˈglɒs.i/ (US) /ˈglɑː.si/ **adj; noun**

▸**adj 1** smooth and shiny: *She has wonderfully glossy hair.* ◦ *a dog with a glossy coat* **2** describes a book or magazine that has been produced on shiny and expensive paper and contains many colour pictures: *a glossy coffee-table book* ◦ *a pile of glossy magazines/car brochures* • **glossiness** /-nəs/ **noun** [U]

▸**noun** [C] **1** a glossy magazine **2** US a photograph printed on smooth shiny paper

ˌglossy magaˈzine noun [C] (also **glossy**) a magazine printed on shiny, high-quality paper, containing a lot of colour photographs and advertisements, and usually about famous people, fashion, and beauty

ˌglottal ˈstop noun [C] specialized a speech sound produced by closing the VOCAL CORDS and then opening them quickly so that the air from the lungs is released with force

glottis /ˈglɒt.ɪs/ (US) /ˈglɑː.t̬ɪs/ **noun** [C usually singular] (plural **glottises** or **glottides**) specialized the thin opening between the VOCAL CORDS at the top of the LARYNX (= the organ in the throat), that is closed by the EPIGLOTTIS when you swallow • **glottal** /ˈglɒt.əl/ (US) /ˈglɑː.t̬əl/ **adj**

glove /glʌv/ **noun; verb**

▸**noun** [C] (A2) a piece of clothing that is worn on the hand and wrist for warmth or protection, with separate parts for each finger: *leather/woollen/rubber gloves* ◦ *a **pair of** gloves*

▸**verb** [T] US **1** to put gloves on your hands: *She gloved her hands to protect them from the chemicals.* **2** to catch a ball when playing baseball: *He gloved the ball, turned and threw in one motion.*

ˈglove ˌbox noun [C] IN A LABORATORY ▷ specialized a closed transparent container in which poisonous or RADIOACTIVE substances can be touched safely using gloves fixed to holes in one side of the container

ˈglove comˌpartment noun [C] (also **ˈglove ˌbox**) a small cupboard or shelf in the front of a car, used for storing small things

gloved /glʌvd/ **adj** having a glove or gloves on: *She held out a gloved hand.*

ˈglove ˌpuppet noun [C] UK (US **ˈhand ˌpuppet**) a toy person or animal that has a soft, hollow body so that you can put your hand inside and move its head and arms with your fingers

glow /gləʊ/ (US) /gloʊ/ **verb; noun**

▶**verb** [I] **1** to produce a continuous light and sometimes heat: *A nightlight glowed dimly in the corner of the children's bedroom.* ◦ *This substance is so radioactive that it glows in the dark.* **2** to look attractive because you are happy or healthy, especially with eyes that are shining: *The children's faces were glowing **with** excitement.* ◦ *They came back from their week by the sea, glowing **with** health.* **3 be glowing**

▶**noun** [S] **LIGHT** ▷ **1** continuous light and/or heat that is produced by something: *the glow **of** the fire* ◦ *Neon emits a characteristic red glow.* **SKIN** ▷ **2** the fact of your face feeling or appearing warm and healthy: *Like all the staff at the health club she had the healthy glow of the young and fit.* **FEELING** ▷ **3** a positive feeling: *They felt a glow **of** pride as they watched their daughter collect the award.* ◦ *She felt a **warm** glow **of** satisfaction.*

glower /ˈglaʊ.əʳ/ (US) /-ɚ/ **verb** [I] to look very angry, annoyed or threatening: *There's no point glowering **at** me like that – you know the rules.* ◦ figurative *Large black rain clouds glowered (= looked likely to produce rain) in the sky.* • **glower noun** [C usually singular] *an angry glower*

glowing /ˈgləʊ.ɪŋ/ (US) /ˈgloʊ-/ **adj** praising with enthusiasm: *In her speech, she paid a glowing **tribute** to her predecessor.* ◦ *His latest book has received glowing **reviews**.* • **glowingly** /-li/ **adv**

ˈglow-worm **noun** [C] a BEETLE, the females and young of which produce a green light from the tail

glucose /ˈgluː.kəʊs/ (US) /-koʊs/ **noun** [U] a type of sugar that is found in plants, especially fruit, and supplies an important part of the energy that animals need

glue /gluː/ **noun; verb**

▶**noun** [U] a sticky substance that is used for joining things together permanently, produced from animal bones and skins or by a chemical process

▶**verb** [T usually + adv/prep] (present tense **glueing** or **gluing**, past tense and past participle **glued**) to join things together using glue: *Is it worth trying to glue this plate back together?* ◦ *I've nearly finished making my plane – I just have to glue the wings **on**.*

IDIOMS **be glued to sth** informal to be unable to stop watching something: *We were glued to the television watching the election results come in.* • **glued to the spot** informal unable to move because you are very frightened, nervous, or interested: *I just stood there, glued to the spot.*

ˈglue-ˌsniffer **noun** [C] someone who breathes in the dangerous gases produced by some types of glue in order to feel excited • **ˈglue-sniffing noun** [U] *Glue-sniffing is prevalent amongst the older teenagers.*

gluey /ˈgluː.i/ **adj** (**gluier**, **gluiest**) covered with glue

glum /glʌm/ **adj** (**glummer**, **glummest**) informal disappointed or unhappy, and quiet: *You look glum. What's up?* ◦ *He's very glum **about** the company's prospects.* • **glumly** /ˈglʌm.li/ **adv** *'I'll never find another job at my age,' she said glumly.* • **glumness** /ˈglʌm.nəs/ **noun** [U]

glut /glʌt/ **noun** [C] a supply of something that is much greater than can be sold or is needed or wanted: *The fall in demand for coffee could cause a glut **on/in the market**.* ◦ *The current glut **of** graduates means that many of them will not be able to find jobs.* • **glut verb** [T often passive] (plural **-tt-**) *Higher mortgage rates and over-building left some markets glutted with unsold houses.*

glute /gluːt/ **noun** [C usually plural] informal **gluteus**: *Squats are ideal for developing and toning the glutes.* ◦ *Step up, squeezing the right glute as you lift.*

gluten /ˈgluː.tᵊn/ (US) /-tᵊn/ **noun** [U] a PROTEIN that is contained in WHEAT and some other grains: *a gluten-free diet*

gluteus /ˈgluː.ti.əs/ **noun** [C] (plural **glutei**) (informal **glute**) any of the large muscles in each BUTTOCK

glutinous /ˈgluː.tɪ.nəs/ (US) /-t̬ɪ-/ **adj** sticky: *Short-grain rice turns into a soft, glutinous mass when cooked.*

glutton /ˈglʌt.ᵊn/ (US) /ˈglʌt̬-/ **noun** [C] disapproving a person who regularly eats and drinks more than is needed

IDIOMS **be a glutton for sth** to like something very much: *Sophie is a glutton for books.* • **be a glutton for punishment** to be someone who seems to enjoy doing something that you consider unpleasant: *He's a real glutton for punishment, taking on all that extra work without getting paid for it.*

gluttonous /ˈglʌt.ᵊn.əs/ (US) /ˈglʌt̬-/ **adj** disapproving eating and drinking more than you need • **gluttonously** /-li/ **adv**

gluttony /ˈglʌt.ᵊn.i/ (US) /ˈglʌt̬-/ **noun** [U] disapproving a situation in which people eat and drink more than they need to: *They treat Christmas as just another excuse for gluttony.*

glyˌcaemic ˈindex (mainly US **glyˌcemic ˈindex**) **noun** [S] (abbreviation **GI**) a system for listing foods according to how quickly they increase the level of sugar in your blood

glycerine (US also **glycerin**) /ˈglɪs.ᵊr.iːn/, /-ɪn/ (US) /-ɚ.rɪn/ **noun** [U] a sweet, thick, clear liquid used in making explosives and medicines and for making food sweet → Compare **nitroglycerine**

glycerol /ˈglɪs.ᵊ.rɒl/ (US) /-rɑːl/ **noun** [U] specialized **glycerine**

glycogen /ˈglaɪ.kəʊ.dʒən/ (US) /-koʊ-/ **noun** [U] specialized a substance found in the LIVER and muscles which stores CARBOHYDRATE and is important in controlling sugar levels in the blood

gm **noun** written abbreviation for **gram**

GM /ˌdʒiːˈem/ **adj** [before noun] abbreviation for **genetically modified**

GˌM ˈfood **noun** [C or U] genetically modified food: food from crops whose GENES have been scientifically changed: *Agricultural companies have failed to convince consumers that GM foods are safe.*

GMO /ˌdʒiː.emˈəʊ/ (US) /-ˈoʊ/ **noun** [C] abbreviation for genetically modified organism: a plant or animal whose GENES have been scientifically changed

GMT /ˌdʒiː.emˈtiː/ **noun** [U] abbreviation for **Greenwich Mean Time**

gnarled /nɑːld/ (US) /nɑːrld/ **adj** rough and twisted, especially because of old age or no protection from bad weather: *a gnarled tree trunk* ◦ *The old man drew a long gnarled finger across his throat.*

gnarly /ˈnɑː.li/ (US) /ˈnɑːr.li/ **adj** **EXCITING** ▷ **1** mainly US slang used to describe something extreme, especially something that is very dangerous and exciting: *The waves were what surfers would call 'pretty gnarly'.* **SHAPE** ▷ **2 gnarled**: *There were low trees with thick, gnarly branches.*

gnash /næʃ/ **verb**

IDIOMS **gnash your teeth** to bring your teeth forcefully together when you are angry: *The monster* roared and gnashed its teeth. • **gnashing of teeth** (also ˈ**teeth-ˌgnashing**) angry noise and upset: *There has been much gnashing of teeth about the proposal to close the hospital.*

gnat /næt/ **noun** [C] a very small flying insect that bites animals and people

gnaw /nɔː/ (US) /nɑː/ **verb** [I + prep, T] **BITE** ▷ **1** to bite or CHEW something repeatedly, usually making a hole in it or gradually destroying it: *Babies like to gnaw hard objects when they're teething.* ◦ *A dog lay under the table, gnawing* ***on*** *a bone.* **FEEL WORRIED** ▷ **2** to make you feel worried or uncomfortable: *The feeling that I've forgotten something has been gnawing* ***at*** *me all day.*

PHRASAL VERB **gnaw away at sth** to gradually reduce or spoil something: *Bad debts are continuing to gnaw away at the bank's profits.*

G

gnawing /ˈnɔː.ɪŋ/ (US) /ˈnɑː-/ **adj** continuously uncomfortable, worrying or painful: *I've had gnawing doubts about this project for some time.* ◦ *After three days, we felt an agonizing, gnawing* ***hunger****.*

gneiss /naɪs/ **noun** [U] specialized a type of METAMORPHIC rock that contains light and dark layers formed of minerals such as QUARTZ and MICA

gnocchi /ˈnjɒk.i/ (US) /ˈnjɑː.ki/ **noun** [plural] small round balls made from potato or WHEAT flour mixed with water, that you eat in soup or with sauce

gnome /nəʊm/ (US) /noʊm/ **noun** [C] **1** an imaginary, very small, old man with a BEARD and a pointed hat, in traditional children's stories **2** a model of a gnome used as a garden decoration: *I don't think* ***garden*** *gnomes are in very good taste.* **3 the gnomes of Zurich** disapproving the powerful BANKERS (= people who own or control banks) from Switzerland who control a lot of money, much of it belonging to foreign governments

gnomic /ˈnəʊ.mɪk/ (US) /ˈnoʊ-/ **adj** formal describes something spoken or written that is short, mysterious, and not easily understood, but often seems wise: *Peter is always coming out with gnomic utterances/pronouncements.*

GNP /ˌdʒiː.enˈpiː/ **noun** [U] specialized abbreviation for Gross National Product: the total value of goods and services produced by a country in one year, including profits made in foreign countries → Compare **GDP**

gnu /nuː/ **noun** [C] (plural **gnu** or **gnus**) a large African animal with a long tail and horns that curve to the sides, which lives in areas covered with grass

go /gəʊ/ (US) /goʊ/ **verb; noun**

▸**verb** (present participle **going**, past tense **went**, past participle **gone**) **MOVE/TRAVEL** ▷ **1** (A1) [I usually + adv/prep] to travel or move to another place: *We went into the house.* ◦ *I went* ***to*** *Paris last summer. Have you ever been there?* ◦ *We don't go* ***to*** *the cinema very often these days.* ◦ *Wouldn't it be quicker to go* ***by*** *train?* ◦ *Does this train go* ***to*** *Newcastle?* ◦ *Where do you think you're going? Shouldn't you be at school?* **2** (A1) [I usually + adv/prep] to be in the process of moving: *Can't we go any faster?* ◦ *We were going* ***along*** *at about 50 miles an hour.* ◦ *to go* ***down*** *the road* ◦ *to go* ***up/down*** *stairs* ◦ *to go* ***over*** *the bridge* ◦ *to go* ***through*** *a tunnel* ◦ figurative *I've got a tune going* ***around/round*** *in my head (= I am continually hearing it) and I just can't remember the name of it.* **3** (A1) [I] to move or travel somewhere in order to do something: [+ -ing verb] *We go shopp****ing*** *every Friday night.* ◦ *I've never gone ski****ing****.* ◦ *They've gone* ***for*** *a walk, but they should be back soon.* ◦ [+ to infinitive] *She's gone* ***to*** *meet Brian at the station.* ◦ *There's a good film on at the Odeon. Shall we go?* **4 where has/have sth gone?** said when you cannot find something: *Where have my keys gone?*

> **! Common mistake: go**
>
> When talking about travelling or moving to another place, the most usual preposition to use with 'go' is **to**.
>
> Don't say 'go in/at/on a place', say **go to a place**:
>
> ~~*I want to go in/at/on England/the cinema/university.*~~
>
> *I want to go to England/the cinema/university.*

> **! Common mistake: go or come?**
>
> **Remember: go** is used to talk about movement to another place, away from where the speaker is:
>
> *I am going to London next week.*
>
> To talk about movement towards where the speaker is, don't say 'go', say **come**:
>
> ~~*You can go to visit me here whenever you want.*~~
>
> *You can come to visit me here whenever you want.*

> **! Common mistake: go or get?**
>
> **Warning:** choose the correct verb!
>
> To talk about reaching or arriving at a particular place, don't say 'go to', say **get to**:
>
> ~~*It takes two hours to go to London from here.*~~
>
> *It takes two hours to get to London from here.*

> **! Usage: gone or been?**
>
> The past participle of 'go' is **gone**:
>
> *I'm sorry but she's gone abroad on business – she'll be back next week.*
>
> Sometimes, however, **been** is used to say that someone has gone somewhere and come back, or to say that someone has visited somewhere:
>
> *He's been abroad many times.*

LEAVE ▷ **5** (B1) [I] to leave a place, especially in order to travel to somewhere else: *Is it midnight already? I really must go/must be going.* ◦ *She wasn't feeling well, so she went* ***home*** *early.* ◦ mainly UK *What time does the last train to Bath go?* ◦ *I'm afraid he'll have to go (= be dismissed from his job) – he's far too inefficient to continue working for us.* ◦ *This carpet's terribly old and worn – it really will have to go (= be got rid of).* **6 to go** mainly US If you ask for some food to go at a restaurant, you want it wrapped up so that you can take it away with you instead of eating it in the restaurant: *I'd like a cheeseburger and strawberry milkshake to go, please.* → See also **takeaway** **7** [I] polite word for to die: *She went peacefully in her sleep.* **LEAD** ▷ **8** (B1) [I + adv/prep] If a road, path, etc. goes in a particular direction, it leads there: *This road goes* ***to*** *Birmingham.* ◦ *A huge crack went* ***from*** *the top* ***to*** *the bottom of the wall.* **9** [I usually + adv/prep] to continue for a particular length: *The tree's roots go* ***down*** *three metres.* **FUTURE TIME** ▷ **10 be going to do/be sth a** (A2) to intend to do or be something in the future: *Are you going to go to Claire's party?* ◦ *He wants me to mend his shirt for him, but I'm not going to!* ◦ *I'm going to be a famous pop star when I'm older.* **b** (A2) to be certain or expected to happen in the future: *They're going to have a baby in the spring.* ◦ *There's going to be trouble when Paul finds out about this.* ◦ *The forecast said it was going to be hot and sunny tomorrow.* **BECOME** ▷ **11** (B1) [L only + adj] to become: *The idea of going grey doesn't bother me, but I'd hate to go bald.* ◦ *Her father's going senile/blind/deaf.* ◦ *If anything goes* ***wrong****, you can call our emergency hotline free of charge.* ◦ *After twelve* *years of Republican presidents, the US went Democratic in 1992.* **MOVE BODY** ▷ **12** [I usually + adv/prep] to move a part of the body in a particular way or the way that is shown: *Go* ***like this with*** *your hand to show that you're turning left.* **OPERATE** ▷ **13** [I] to operate (in the right way): *Have you any idea why this watch won't go?* ◦ *Can you help me get my car going?* ◦ *Our company has been going (= has been in business) for 20 years.* **TIME** ▷ **14** B2 [I] If a period of time goes, it passes: *I had a wonderful weekend but it went awfully quickly.* ◦ *Time seems to go faster as you get older.* ◦ *There's only a week* ***to*** *go before (= until) my exam results come out.* **BE** ▷ **15** [L only + adj] to be or stay in a particular, especially unpleasant, condition: *In spite of the relief effort, thousands of people continue to go hungry.* ◦ *Why do so many rapes go unreported?* **16 as...go** in comparison with most other things of a particular type, especially when you do not think that type of thing is very good: *It was quite a good film, as horror films go.* ◦ *I suppose the concert was OK, as* ***these things*** *go.* **17 go to prove/show** to prove that something is true: *Your daughter's attitude* ***only*** *goes to prove how much society has changed over the last 30 years.* **START** ▷ **18** [I] to start doing or using something: *I'll just connect up the printer to the computer and then we'll be ready to go.* **PLAY GAME** ▷ **19** [I] to use your opportunity to play in a game: *It's your turn to go now.* **DIVIDE** ▷ **20** [I not continuous] (of a number) to fit into another number especially resulting in a whole number: *5* ***into*** *11 won't go.* ◦ *5 goes* ***into*** *11 twice with 1 left over.* **SAY** ▷ **21** [+ speech] informal to say, especially when a story is being told: *'I never want to see you ever again,' he goes, and storms out the house.* **WEAKEN** ▷ **22** [I] to become weak or damaged, especially from being used (too much), or to stop working: *After a gruelling six months singing on a world tour, it is hardly surprising that her voice is starting to go.* ◦ *I really must get a new jacket – this one's starting to go at the elbows.* ◦ *Her hearing is going, but otherwise she's remarkably fit for a 95-year-old.* **NOISE** ▷ **23** C2 [I or T] to produce a noise: *I think I heard the doorbell go (= ring) just now.* ◦ *I wish my computer would stop going 'beep' whenever I do something wrong.* **BE EXPRESSED** ▷ **24** B2 [I not continuous] to be expressed, sung or played: *I can never remember* ***how*** *that song goes.* ◦ *'Doesn't it go something* ***like*** *this?' said Joan, and played the first couple of bars on her guitar.* ◦ [+ (that)] *The story goes (= people say)* (***that***) *he was sacked after he was caught stealing company property.* ◦ *A headless ghost walks the castle at night – or* ***so*** *the story goes (= so people say).* **HAPPEN** ▷ **25** [I usually + adv/prep] to happen or be found regularly or typically with each other or another: *Wisdom and maturity don't necessarily go* ***together.*** ◦ *She knows all about the health problems that go* ***with*** *smok****ing****.* ◦ *Great wealth often goes* ***hand in hand with*** *meanness.* **BE SITUATED** ▷ **26** [I usually + adv/prep, not continuous] to be put in a particular place, especially as the usual place: *The sofa went* ***against*** *that wall before we had the radiator put in.* ◦ *I'll put it all away if you tell me* ***where*** *everything goes.* **BE SOLD** ▷ **27** [I] to be sold or be available: *The shop is having a closing-down sale – everything must go.* ◦ *The painting will go* ***to*** *the highest bidder.* ◦ *I bought some flowers that were going* ***cheap.*** ◦ *'Going... going... gone! (= Sold!)' said the auctioneer, banging down the hammer.* **BE ACCEPTABLE** ▷ **28** B1 [I not continuous] to look or be acceptable or suitable: *That picture would go* ***well*** *on the wall in the living room.* ◦ *The TV would go nicely* ***in*** *that corner, wouldn't it?* ◦ *If I wear the orange hat with the blue dress, do you think it will go?* ◦ *Just remember that I'm the boss and what I say goes (= you have to accept what I say).* ◦ *My parents don't worry too much about what I get up to, and most of the time* ***anything*** *goes (= I can do what I want).* **BE KNOWN** ▷ **29** [I usually + adv/prep] to be known (by a particular name): *He had a scruffy old teddy bear which went* ***by the name of*** *Augustus.* ◦ *In Britain, this flour usually goes* ***under the name of*** *maize meal.* **DEVELOP** ▷ **30** B1 [I usually + adv/prep] to develop or happen: *'****How*** *did the interview go?' 'It went very well, thanks.'* ◦ *Things have gone badly* ***for*** *him since his business collapsed.*

IDIOMS **be gone on sb** informal to like someone a lot: *Nicky's really gone on Marty.* • **go about your business** to continue doing what you usually do: *In spite of last night's terrorist attack, most people seem to be going about their business as if nothing had happened.* • **go and...** informal used to express disapproval of something that is done: *He's gone and lost (= he has lost) that wallet I gave him for his birthday.* ◦ *Mike's really gone and* ***done it*** *now – he'll be in terrible trouble for breaking that window.* • **go for it** informal to do anything you have to in order to get something: *'I'm thinking of applying for that job.' 'Go for it!'* • **go it alone** to do something without other people: *He's decided to leave the band and go it alone as a singer.* • **sth gone mad** a particular type of thing that has gone out of control: *He described the new regulations as bureaucracy gone mad.* • **have sth going for you** If someone or something has something going for them, that thing causes them to have a lot of advantages and to be successful: *They've got a happy marriage, brilliant careers, wonderful kids – in fact they've got* ***everything*** *going for them.* • **not go there** to not start to think about or discuss a subject: *'Then there's the guilt I feel about leaving her for seven hours every day.' 'Don't* ***even*** *go there!'* • **the same/that goes for sb/sth** what I have said about one person or thing is also true for or relates to another person or thing: *You really need to smarten up your appearance, Chris – and the same goes for the rest of you.* • **what are you going to do?** US informal used to say that there is nothing you can do to make a situation better

PHRASAL VERBS **go about sth** to begin to do something or deal with something: *What's the best way of going about this?* ◦ [+ -ing verb] *How can we go about solv****ing*** *this problem?* • **go after sb** to chase or follow someone in order to catch them: *The police went after him but he got away.* • **go after sth** informal to try to get something: *Are you planning to go after Paul's job when he leaves?* • **go against sb** If a decision or vote goes against someone, they do not get the result that they needed: *The judge's decision went against us.* ◦ *The vote went against her (= she lost the vote).* • **go against sth/sb** to oppose or disagree with something or someone: *Public opinion is going against the government on this issue.* ◦ *What you're asking me to do goes against everything I believe in.* • **go ahead 1** B2 to start to do something: *We've received permission to go ahead* ***with*** *the music festival in spite of opposition from local residents.* ◦ *I got so fed up with waiting for him to do it that I just went ahead and did it myself.* **2** B2 informal said to someone in order to give them permission to start to do something: *'Could I ask you a rather personal question?' 'Sure, go ahead.'* **3** If an event goes ahead, it happens: *The festival is now going ahead as planned.* • **go along PLACE** ▷ **1** UK to go to a place or event, usually without much planning: *I might go along* ***to*** *the party later.* **ACTIVITY** ▷ **2 as you go along** as you are doing a job or activity: *We have a flexible approach to what we're doing that allows us to*

G

make any necessary changes as we go along. ◦ *I'll explain the rules as we go along.* • **go along with sth/sb** to support an idea, or to agree with someone's opinion: *Kate's already agreed, but it's going to be harder persuading Mike to go along with it.* • **go around** US for **go round** • **go at sb** to attack someone: *Suddenly, he went at me with a knife.* • **go at sth** informal to start doing something with a lot of energy and enthusiasm: *He went at (= ate eagerly) his dinner as if he hadn't had anything to eat for weeks.* • **go away** LEAVE ▷ **1** B1 to leave a place: *Go away and leave me alone!* **2** B1 to leave your home in order to spend time somewhere else, usually for a holiday: *We usually go away for the summer.* ◦ *He goes away on business a lot.* DISAPPEAR ▷ **3** to disappear: *It was weeks before the bruises went away.* • **go back** RETURN ▷ **1** B1 to return: *That restaurant was terrible – I'm never going back there again.* ◦ *I'll have to go back* ***for*** *my umbrella.* ◦ *Do you think you'll ever go back* ***to*** *London?* ◦ *When do you go back* ***to*** *school?* ◦ *Let's go back* ***to*** *the beginning and start again.* ◦ *We can always go back* ***to*** *the original plan if necessary.* **2** to be returned: *When are these library books due to go back?* ◦ *That TV will have to go back* ***to*** *the shop – it hasn't worked properly ever since I bought it.* ORIGIN ▷ **3** to have existed since a time in the past: *Their relationship goes back* ***to*** *when they were at university together.* ◦ *Our house goes back* ***to*** *(= has existed since) the 18th century.* • **go back on sth** to fail to keep a promise, or to change a decision or agreement: *The government looks likely to go back on its decision to close the mines.* ◦ *She's gone back on* ***her word*** *and decided not to give me the job after all.* • **go back to sb** to start a relationship again with a person you had a romantic relationship with in the past: *I hear he's ended the affair and gone back to his wife.* • **go back to sth** to start doing something again that you were doing before: *It's time to go back to work.* • **go by 1** B2 to move past, in space or time: *You can watch the trains going by from this window.* ◦ *You can't let an opportunity like that go by – it's too good to miss.* ◦ *Hardly a day goes by when I don't think about her.* **2 in days gone by** in the past: *The house was a railway station in days gone by.* • **go by sth** FOLLOW ▷ **1** to follow something or be shown the way by something: *I'm sorry, madam, but we have to go by the rules.* BASE ▷ **2** to base an opinion, decision or judgment on something: *What do you go by when you're deciding whether or not to employ someone?* ◦ *Going by what she said yesterday, I would say she's about to resign.* ◦ ***If*** *past experience* ***is anything to*** *go by, he'll completely ignore our suggestions and then change his mind at the last minute.* • **go down (sth)** MOVE DOWN ▷ **1** to move down to a lower level or place: *He went down on his knees and begged for forgiveness.* ◦ *He first went down the mines when he was 17.* ◦ *The plane went down (= fell to the ground because of an accident, bomb, etc.) ten minutes after take-off.* ◦ *Everyone took to the lifeboats when the ship started to go down (= sink).* ◦ *Could I have a glass of water to help these pills go down (= to help me swallow them)?* REACH ▷ **2** to reach or go as far as: *Its roots can go down three metres.* ◦ *This path goes down* ***to*** *the river.* ◦ *Go down to (= read as far as) the bottom of the page.* • **go down** SUN ▷ **1** B1 When the sun goes down, it moves down in the sky until it cannot be seen any more: *On summer evenings we would sit on the veranda and watch the sun go down.* BE REDUCED ▷ **2** B1 to be reduced in price, value, amount, quality, level or size: *The temperature went down* ***to*** *minus ten last night.* ◦ *The company's shares went down 7p* ***to*** *53p.* ◦ *The swelling's gone down but there's still a lot of bruising.* ◦ *He went down in my* ***estimation*** *when he started trying to be a singer as well as an actor.* BE REMEMBERED ▷ **3** C2 to be remembered or recorded in a particular way: *Hurricane Katrina will go down* ***in*** *the record books* ***as*** *the costliest storm ever faced by insurers.* BE RECEIVED ▷ **4** to be received in a particular way: *I think my speech went down rather* ***well****, don't you?* LOSE ▷ **5** to lose or be defeated: *England's unbeaten run of ten games ended last night when they went down 4–2 to France.* ◦ *Dictators rarely go down without a fight.* PRISON ▷ **6** UK slang to be put in prison: *She went down* ***for*** *three years for her part in the robbery.* COMPUTER ▷ **7** If a computer system goes down, it stops working: *The battery should prevent the computer system from going down in the event of a power cut.* HAPPEN ▷ **8** US slang If an event such as a crime or a DEAL goes down, it happens: *I tried to tell Tyrell what was going down, but he wouldn't listen.* LEAVE ▷ **9** UK old-fashioned If you go down from a college or university, especially Oxford University or Cambridge University, you leave either permanently or for a holiday. • **go down on sb** slang to use the tongue and lips to touch someone's sexual organs in order to give pleasure • **go down with sth** (also **come down with sth**) UK B2 to start to suffer from an infectious disease: *Half of Martha's class has gone down with flu.* • **go for sb** to attack someone: *Their dog had to be put to sleep after it went for the postwoman.* • **go for sth** CHOOSE ▷ **1** B1 to choose something: *Instead of butter, I always go for margarine or a low-fat spread.* LIKE ▷ **2** to like or admire: *I don't go for war films in a big way (= very much).* ◦ *What sort of men do you go for (= are you attracted to)?* TRY ▷ **3** B2 to try to have or achieve something: *She tripped me as I went for the ball.* ◦ *Are you planning to go for that scholarship to Harvard University?* ◦ *The Russian relay team will again be going for the gold medal at the Olympic Games.* MONEY ▷ **4** If something goes for a certain amount of money, it is sold for that amount: *The painting is expected to go for at least a million dollars.* • **go in** ENTER ▷ **1** A2 to enter a place: *I looked through the window, but I didn't actually go in.* BECOME HIDDEN ▷ **2** If the sun goes in, it becomes hidden from view by clouds. BE UNDERSTOOD ▷ **3** mainly UK informal If a fact or piece of information goes in, you understand it or remember it: *No matter how many times you tell him something, it never seems to go in.* • **go in for sth** ENJOY ▷ **1** to do something regularly, or to enjoy something: *I've never really gone in for classical music, but I love jazz.* COMPETE ▷ **2** to take part in a competition: *Are you planning to go in for the 100 metres race?* • **go into sth** START ▷ **1** C1 to start doing a particular type of work: *My son's planning to go into journalism.* ◦ *She's decided to go into business* ***as*** *a freelance computer programmer.* **2** to start an activity, or start to be in a particular state or condition: *The drug is still being tested and will not go into commercial* ***production*** *for at least two years.* ◦ *How many companies have gone into* ***liquidation/receivership*** *during the current recession?* ◦ *Repeated death threats have forced them to go into* ***hiding****.* ◦ *Her baby was born three hours after she went into* ***labour****.* ◦ *Some of the fans seemed to go into* ***a trance*** *when she appeared on stage.* DISCUSS ▷ **3** C2 to discuss, examine, describe or explain something in a detailed or careful way: *This is the first book to go into her personal life as well as her work.* ◦ *I'd rather not go into that now. Can we discuss it later?* ◦ *I'm unable to go into* ***detail(s)*** *at this stage because I still have very little information about how the accident happened.* BE USED ▷ **4** C1 mainly UK If time, money, or effort goes into a product or activity, it is used when producing or doing it: *A considerable amount of time and effort has gone into this exhibition.* **HIT** ▷ **5** If a vehicle goes into something such as a tree or a wall, it hits it: *Their car was travelling at 50 miles an hour when it went into the tree.* → Compare **collide** • **go off STOP WORKING** ▷ **1** B1 If a light or a machine goes off, it stops working: *The lights went off in several villages because of the storm.* **EXPLODE** ▷ **2** C1 If a bomb goes off, it explodes: *The* ***bomb*** *went off at midday.* **3** C1 If a gun goes off, it fires: *His gun went off accidentally.* **FOOD** ▷ **4** B2 UK If food or drink goes off, it is not good to eat or drink any more because it is too old: *This bacon smells a bit funny – do you think it's gone off?* → See also **off NOISE** ▷ **5** B2 If a warning device goes off, it starts to ring loudly or make a loud noise: *The* ***alarm*** *should go off automatically as soon as smoke is detected.* ◦ *Didn't you hear your* ***alarm clock*** *going off this morning?* **LEAVE** ▷ **6** B1 to leave a place and go somewhere else: *She's gone off to the pub with Tony* **HAPPEN** ▷ **7** to happen in a particular way: *The protest march went off peacefully.* **BECOME WORSE** ▷ **8** UK to become worse in quality: *That paper's really gone off since they got that new editor.* • **go off sb/sth** B2 to stop liking or being interested in someone or something: *I went off beefburgers after I got food poisoning from a takeaway.* ◦ *I went off Peter when he said those dreadful things about Clare.* • **go off with sb** to leave a wife, husband or partner in order to have a sexual or romantic relationship with someone else: *Did you know that Hugh had gone off with his sister-in-law?* • **go off with sth** to take something without getting permission from the owner first: *I do wish you'd stop going off with my car without asking me beforehand.* • **go on HAPPEN** ▷ **1** B1 to happen: *I'm sure we never hear about a lot of what goes on in government.* ◦ *This war has been going on for years.* **CONTINUE** ▷ **2** B1 to continue or move to the next thing: *Please go on* ***with*** *what you're doing and don't let us interrupt you.* ◦ [+ -ing verb] *We really can't go on liv****ing*** *like this – we'll have to find a bigger house.* ◦ [+ to infinitive] *She admitted her company's responsibility for the disaster and went on* ***to*** *explain how compensation would be paid to the victims.* ◦ *What proportion of people who are HIV-positive go on* ***to*** *develop (= later develop) AIDS?* ◦ *If you go on (= continue behaving) like this you won't have any friends left at all.* **OPERATE** ▷ **3** to start operating: *The spotlights go on automatically when an intruder is detected in the garden.* ◦ *When does the heating go on?* **TALK AGAIN** ▷ **4** B2 to start talking again after a pause: *She paused to light another cigarette and then went on* ***with*** *her account of the accident.* ◦ [+ speech] *'What I want more than anything else,' he went on, 'is a house in the country with a large garden for the children to play in.'* **5** informal something that you say to encourage someone to say or do something: *Go on, what happened next?* **TALK A LOT** ▷ **6** C2 UK to talk in an annoying way about something for a long time: *I just wish he'd stop going on* ***about*** *how brilliant his daughter is.' 'Yes, he does go on (****a bit****), doesn't he?'* ◦ *I wish you'd stop going on* ***at*** *(= criticizing repeatedly) me about my haircut.* **PLEASE DO** ▷ **7** used when encouraging or asking someone to do something: *Go on, have another drink.* ◦ *'I don't really feel like seeing a film tonight.' 'Oh go on. We haven't been to the cinema for ages.'* **AGREE** ▷ **8** informal something that you say in order to agree to do or allow something that you did not want to do or to allow before: *'Are you sure you don't want another slice of cake?' 'Oh go on* ***then****, but just a small one.'* **TIME** ▷ **9** to continue or pass: *Tomorrow will start cold but it should get warmer as the day goes on.* ◦ *As the evening went on it became clear that we should never have agreed to see each other again.* **NOT BELIEVE** ▷ **10 go on!** mainly UK old-fashioned used when you do not believe someone • **go on sth** to use a piece of information in order to help you discover or understand something: *I'm only going on what I overheard him saying to Chris, but I think he's planning to leave next month.* ◦ *The investigation has only just started so the police* ***haven't got much*** *to go on at the moment.* • **go out LEAVE** ▷ **1** A1 to leave a room or building, especially in order to do something for entertainment: *Please close the door as you go out.* ◦ *Do you fancy going out* ***for*** *a meal after work?* ◦ *It's terribly smoky in here – I'm just going out* ***for*** *a breath of fresh air.* ◦ [+ -ing verb] *I wish you'd spend more time at home instead of going out drink****ing*** *with your friends every night.* **RELATIONSHIP** ▷ **2** B1 to have a romantic and usually sexual relationship with someone: *How long have you been going out* ***with*** *him?* ◦ *They'd been going out (****together/ with each other****) for almost five years before he moved in with her.* **SEA** ▷ **3** If the TIDE goes out, it moves back and covers less of the beach. → Compare **come in LIGHT/FIRE** ▷ **4** B1 If a light or something that is burning goes out, it stops producing light or heat: *When I woke up the fire had gone out.* **SPORT** ▷ **5** UK to lose when you are playing in a sports competition, so that you must stop playing in the competition: *England went out* ***to*** *France in the second round of the championship.* • **go out to sb** If your thoughts or sympathies go out to someone in a difficult or sad situation, you think of them and feel sorry for them: *Our deepest sympathies go out to her husband and children.* • **go over** US for **go down** • **go over sth EXAMINE** ▷ **1** B2 to examine or look at something in a careful or detailed way: *Forensic scientists are going over the victim's flat in a search for clues about the murderer.* ◦ *Remember to go over your essay checking for grammar and spelling mistakes before you hand it in to me.* ◦ *I've gone over the problem several times, but I can't think of a solution.* **STUDY** ▷ **2** to study or explain something: *I always go over my revision notes just before I go into an exam.* ◦ *Could you go over the main points of your argument again, Professor?* • **go over to sth 1** to change to something new or to a new way of doing things: *Many firms are going over to new technologies.* ◦ *She went over (= changed her support) to the Democrats at the last election.* **2** to change to a different person speaking or a different place during a television or radio programme: *We're now going over to Kate Adie speaking live from Baghdad.* ◦ *Later in this bulletin we will be going over to our Westminster studio for an update on the situation.* • **go round** UK (US **go around**) **SPIN** ▷ **1** to SPIN like a wheel → Compare **revolve, rotate BE ENOUGH** ▷ **2** If there is enough of something to go round, there is enough for everyone in a group of people: *Are there enough pencils to go round?* **BEHAVE BADLY** ▷ **3** to spend your time behaving in the stated way: [+ -ing verb] *You can't go round be****ing*** *rude to people.* **VISIT** ▷ **4** to visit someone in their home: *I'm just going round* ***to*** *Martha's for half an hour.* ◦ *Why didn't you tell me Perry had been round?* • **go round sth** UK (US **go around**) to travel to all, or the main, parts of a place that you are visiting in order to find out what it is like or to learn about it: *For a few weeks in the summer, visitors are able to go round Buckingham Palace.* • **go round (somewhere)** UK (US **go around (somewhere)**) to go or be given from one person to another, or to move from one place to another: *A nasty flu bug's going round (the school) at the moment.* ◦ *There's a rumour going round (the village) that they're having an affair.* • **go through** If a law, plan, or DEAL goes through, it is officially accepted or approved: *A council spokeswoman said that the proposals for the new shopping centre were unlikely to go through.* • **go through sth** EXPERIENCE ▷ **1** B2 to experience a difficult or unpleasant situation: *I've been going through a bad patch recently.* ◦ *You'd think his children would be more sympathetic towards him **after all** he's gone through (= the many bad things he has experienced).* EXAMINE ▷ **2** B2 to examine something which contains a collection of things carefully in order to organize them or find something: *I'm going through my wardrobe and throwing out all the clothes I don't wear any more.* ◦ *Remember to go through the pockets before you put those trousers in the washing machine.* PRACTISE ▷ **3** to do something in order to practise or as a test: *I'd like you to go through that manoeuvre again and then bring the car to a halt.* USE ▷ **4** to use a lot of something: *Before I gave up smoking I was going through 40 cigarettes a day.* ◦ *I went through a hundred quid on my last trip to London.* • **go through with sth** C2 to do something unpleasant or difficult that has already been agreed or promised: *He'd threatened to divorce her but I never thought he'd go through with it.* • **go to sb** to be given or sold to someone: *Who did the award for Best Actress go to?* ◦ *All the money raised will go to charity.* ◦ *The painting went to the highest bidder.* • **go together** LOOK GOOD ▷ **1** B1 to look good together: *Do you think the cream dress and the blue jacket go together?* → Compare **match, suit** BE FOUND ▷ **2** to happen or be found together: *Wisdom and maturity don't necessarily go together.* RELATIONSHIP ▷ **3** informal If two people are going together, they have a romantic or sexual relationship with each other. • **go under** SINK ▷ **1** to sink: *The ship went under just minutes after the last passenger had been rescued.* FAIL ▷ **2** If a company goes under, it fails financially: *The charity will go under unless a generous donor can be found within the next few months.* • **go up** RISE ▷ **1** B1 to move higher, rise, or increase: *The average cost of a new house has gone up **by** five percent **to** £276,500.* EXPLODE ▷ **2** C2 to suddenly explode: *There's a gas leak and the whole building could go up at any moment.* BE FIXED ▷ **3** If a sign goes up, it is fixed into position: *The new 'No Parking' signs went up yesterday.* BUILD ▷ **4** If a building goes up, it is built: *A new factory is going up on the old airport.* UNIVERSITY ▷ **5** UK old-fashioned If you go up to a college or university, especially Oxford University or Cambridge University, you begin studying there, or continue studying after a holiday. • **go up to sth** to reach as far as something: *The path going up to the back door is very muddy.* ◦ *This edition's rather out-of-date and only goes up to 1989.* • **go with sth** SUIT ▷ **1** B1 If one thing goes with another, they suit each other or they look or taste good together: *This wine goes particularly well with seafood.* ◦ *I'm not sure that this hat really goes **with** this dress.* → Compare **match, suit** RESULT ▷ **2** If a problem, activity, or quality goes with another one, they often happen or exist together and the first thing is often caused by the second: [+ -ing verb] *What are the main health problems that go with smok**ing**?* • **go with sb** informal to have a romantic or sexual relationship with someone: *Did he ever go with anyone else while they were living together?* • **go with sb/sth** informal to accept an idea or agree with a person: *I think we can go with the advertising agency's suggestions, don't you?* • **go without (sth)** C2 to not have something or to manage to live despite not having something: *If you don't want fish for dinner, then you'll just have to go without!* ◦ *I'd rather go without food than work for him.*

▸**noun** (plural **goes**) ATTEMPT ▷ **1** B2 [C] (US usually **try**) an attempt to do something: *Georgina passed her driving test (**on** her) first go.* ◦ *'This jar is impossible to open.' 'Here, let me **have a** go.'* ◦ *I want to **have a** go **at** finish**ing** my essay tonight.* ◦ *We can't do the work **all in one** go (= all at the same time).* **2 make a go of sth** (US usually **try**) C2 to try to make something succeed, usually by working hard: *She's really making a go of her new antique shop.* ◦ *I can't see him ever making a go of accountancy.* OPPORTUNITY ▷ **3** B1 [C] (US usually **turn**) an opportunity to play in a game, or to do or use something: *Hey, it's Ken's go now! You've just had your go.* ◦ *Please can I **have a** go (= can I ride) on your bike?* ◦ *I'll **have a** go **at** driv**ing** for a while if you're tired.* CRITICIZE ▷ **4 have a go at sb** UK to criticize someone: *My Dad's always having a go at me about getting a proper job.* ENERGY ▷ **5** [U] the condition of being energetic and active: *You're full of go this morning.* ◦ *He doesn't have much go about him, does he?* → See also **get-up-and-go**

IDIOM **be no go** informal to be impossible or not effective, or to not happen: *They tried for hours to get her to come down from the roof, but it was no go.* ◦ *The launch was no go due to the weather.*

goad /gəʊd/ US /goʊd/ **verb** [T] to make a person or an animal react or do something by continuously annoying or upsetting them: *Will the pressure applied by environmentalists be enough to goad the industrialized nations **into** us**ing** less fossil fuels?* ◦ *He refused to be goaded by their insults.* ◦ *The team were goaded **on** by their desire to be first to complete the course.* ◦ *A group of children were goading (= laughing at or pushing) another child in the school playground.* • **goad noun** [S] *The thought of exams next week is a great goad to the students to work hard.*

go-ahead noun; adj

▸**noun** [S] an occasion when permission is given for someone to start doing something or for an event or activity to happen: *The government has **given the** go-ahead for a multi-billion pound road-building project.* ◦ *We're ready to start but we're still waiting to **get the** go-ahead from our head office.* → See also **go ahead**

▸**adj** enthusiastic about using new products and modern methods of doing things

goal /gəʊl/ US /goʊl/ **noun** [C] SPORT ▷ **1** A2 an area on a playing field, that usually has two posts with a net fixed behind them, where players try to send the ball in order to score in sports such as football and HOCKEY: *Black kicked/headed the ball **into/towards** the goal.* **2** A2 a point scored in some sports, such as football or HOCKEY, when a player gets the ball into this area: *Brazil won by three goals to one.* ◦ *Only one goal was **scored** in the entire match.* **3 be/play in goal** UK to be the player who tries to prevent the other team from scoring goals: *Who is playing in goal for Milan this evening?* AIM ▷ **4** B1 an aim or purpose: *Our goal is for the country to be fully independent within two years.* ◦ *They have set themselves a series of goals to achieve by the end of the month.* ◦ *Do you think I'll be able to **achieve** my goal **of** los**ing** five kilos before the summer?*

goalkeeper /ˈɡəʊlˌkiː.pər/ (US) /ˈɡoʊlˌkiː.pɚ/ **noun** [C] UK (informal **goalie**, US **goaltender**) (B1) the player who stands in the team's goal to try to stop the other team from scoring

goalless /ˈɡəʊl.ləs/ (US) /ˈɡoʊl-/ **adj** without any goals being scored: *The match ended in a goalless* ***draw***.

ˈgoal ˌline noun [C] the line between the two posts that mark the goal, over which the ball must pass if a point is to be scored

goalmouth /ˈɡəʊl.maʊθ/ (US) /ˈɡoʊl-/ **noun** [C] the area exactly in front of the goal

goalpost /ˈɡəʊl.pəʊst/ (US) /ˈɡoʊl.poʊst/ **noun** [C] (also **post**, UK also **upright**) in some sports, one of the two vertical posts, often painted white, that are connected with a CROSSBAR to form a goal

IDIOM **move the goalposts** UK informal disapproving to change the rules while someone is trying to do something in order to make it more difficult for them: *We'd almost signed the contract when the other guys moved the goalposts and said they wanted more money.*

goalscorer /ˈɡəʊlˌskɔː.rər/ (US) /ˈɡoʊlˌskɔːr.ɚ/ **noun** [C] mainly UK a person who scores goals for their team in games such as football: *Le Tissier was Southampton's* ***leading/top*** *goalscorer that season.* • **goalscoring** /-ˌskɔː.rɪŋ/ (US) /-ˌskɔːr.ɪŋ/ **noun** [U]

goaltender /ˈɡəʊlˌten.dər/ (US) /ˈɡoʊlˌten.dɚ/ **noun** [C] **1** the person who stands in goal in ICE HOCKEY (= a game played by two teams on ice) and tries to stop the opposing team from scoring **2** US a **goalkeeper**

goanna /ɡəʊˈæn.ə/ (US) /ɡoʊ-/ **noun** [C] a type of large LIZARD that is common in Australia

goat /ɡəʊt/ (US) /ɡoʊt/ **noun** [C] **ANIMAL** ▷ **1** (B1) an animal related to sheep that usually has horns and a BEARD. Goats live wild on mountains or are kept on farms to provide milk, meat, wool, etc.: *goat's milk/cheese* **MAN** ▷ **2** informal disapproving a man who is very active sexually, or would like to be and makes it obvious: *an* ***old*** *goat*

IDIOMS **act/play the goat** UK informal to behave in a silly way: *Stop acting the goat!* • **get sb's goat** (Australian English also **get on sb's goat**) to annoy someone very much: *That sort of attitude really gets my goat.*

goatee

goatee /ɡəʊˈtiː/ (US) /ɡoʊ-/ **noun** [C] a small usually pointed BEARD grown only on the chin, not the cheeks

goatherd /ˈɡəʊt.hɜːd/ (US) /ˈɡoʊt.hɝːd/ **noun** [C] a person who takes care of a FLOCK (= group) of goats

goatskin /ˈɡəʊt.skɪn/ (US) /ˈɡoʊt-/ **noun** [C or U] the skin of a single goat, or leather made from the skin

gob /ɡɒb/ (US) /ɡɑːb/ **noun; verb**
▸**noun** [C] UK slang **1** a mouth **2 keep your gob shut** UK to not say anything: *You'd better keep your gob shut about what happened.*
▸**verb** [I] (**-bb-**) UK slang to SPIT

gobbet /ˈɡɒb.ɪt/ (US) /ˈɡɑː.bɪt/ **noun** [C] informal a small piece or LUMP of something, especially food

gobble /ˈɡɒb.l̩/ (US) /ˈɡɑː.bl̩/ **verb** **EAT** ▷ **1** [I or T] informal to eat food too fast: *She gobbled her dinner* ***(down/up)***. **MAKE NOISE** ▷ **2** [I] to make the sound of a male TURKEY

PHRASAL VERB **gobble sth up** informal **1** to gobble **2** to use a lot of your supply of something, usually money: *The mounting legal costs quickly gobbled up their savings.*

gobbledegook (also **gobbledygook**) /ˈɡɒb.l̩.di.ɡuːk/ (US) /ˈɡɑː.bl̩-/ **noun** [U] informal disapproving language, especially used in official letters, forms, and statements, that seems difficult or to mean nothing because you do not understand it: *This computer manual is complete gobbledegook.*

ˈgo-beˌtween noun [C] someone who takes messages between people who are unable or unwilling to meet: *The ambassador has offered to* ***act as*** *a go-between for the two countries involved in the conflict.*

goblet /ˈɡɒb.lət/ (US) /ˈɡɑː.blət/ **noun** [C] a container from which drink, especially wine, is drunk, usually made of glass or metal, and with a stem and a base but no handles

goblin /ˈɡɒb.lɪn/ (US) /ˈɡɑː.blɪn/ **noun** [C] (in stories) a small, ugly creature that is harmful to humans → See also **hobgoblin**

gobsmacked /ˈɡɒb.smækt/ (US) /ˈɡɑːb-/ **adj** UK informal so shocked that you cannot speak: *He was gobsmacked when he heard of the redundancies.*

gobstopper /ˈɡɒbˌstɒp.ər/ (US) /ˈɡɑːbˌstɑː.pɚ/ **noun** [C] UK (US **jawbreaker**) a large round hard sweet which often has different coloured layers

god /ɡɒd/ (US) /ɡɑːd/ **noun** [C] **SPIRIT** ▷ **1** (B2) a spirit or being believed to control some part of the universe or life and often worshipped for doing so, or something that represents this spirit or being: *the ancient Greek gods and goddesses* **ADMIRED PERSON** ▷ **2** someone who is very important to you, who you admire very much, and who strongly influences you **THEATRE** ▷ **3 the gods** [plural] UK informal the seats in a theatre that are at the highest level and the furthest distance from the stage

God /ɡɒd/ (US) /ɡɑːd/ **noun** [S not after the] (A2) (in some religions) the being who made the universe and is believed to have an effect on all things: *Do you believe in God?*

IDIOMS **(oh my) God!** informal (B1) used to emphasize how surprised, angry, shocked, etc. you are: *My God, what a mess!* ◦ *Oh my God, I've never seen anything like it!* • **God knows** informal used to emphasize that you do not understand something at all or have no knowledge of something at all: *God knows* ***where*** *he's put the keys!* ◦ *'What did he mean by that?' 'God knows!'* • **God willing** used to say you hope everything happens in the way you want: *We'll be there tomorrow, God willing!* • **hope/wish/swear to God** informal used for emphasis: *I hope to God* ***(that)*** *he turns up.* ◦ *I swear to God* ***(that)*** *I didn't know about it.* • **thank God** informal (B1) something you say when you are happy because something bad did not happen: *Thank God nobody was hurt in the accident.* ◦ *Oh, there's my wallet. Thank God.* • **there is a God!** humorous said in a bad situation when something good happens unexpectedly

ˈgod-ˌawful adj informal very bad, difficult or unpleasant: *That was a god-awful meal.*

godchild /ˈɡɒd.tʃaɪld/ (US) /ˈɡɑːd-/ **noun** [C] (plural **godchildren**) in the Christian religion, a child whose moral and religious development is partly the responsibility of two or more GODPARENTS (= adults who promise to take this responsibility at a ceremony)

goddamn very informal (US also **God damn, goddamned, goddam**) /ˈgɒd.dæm/ (US) /ˌgɑːdˈdæm/ exclamation, adj, adv used to add emphasis to what is being said: *Goddamn (**it**), how much longer will it take?* ◦ *Don't drive so goddamn fast!* → See also **damn**

goddaughter /ˈgɒdˌdɔː.təʳ/ (US) /ˈgɑːdˌdɑː.t̬ɚ/ noun [C] a female godchild

goddess /ˈgɒd.es/ (US) /ˈgɑː.des/ noun [C] a female god: *Aphrodite was the ancient Greek goddess **of** love.*

godfather /ˈgɒdˌfɑː.ðəʳ/ (US) /ˈgɑːdˌfɑː.ðɚ/ noun [C] **1** a male GODPARENT **2** the leader of a criminal group, especially a MAFIA family

ˈGod-ˌfearing adj old-fashioned Someone who is god-fearing is religious and tries to live in the way they believe God would wish them to.

G

godforsaken /ˈgɒd.fə.seɪ.kᵊn/ (US) /ˈgɑːd.fɚ-/ adj [before noun] disapproving describes a place that is not attractive and contains nothing interesting or pleasant: *The town is a godforsaken place at night.*

ˈGod-ˌgiven adj **1** If you say something is God-given, you mean that it has not been made by people: *She has a God-given talent as a painter.* **2** having to be obeyed: *She seems to think she has a God-given **right** to tell us all what to do.*

godless /ˈgɒd.ləs/ (US) /ˈgɑːd-/ adj **1** not having or believing in God or gods: *a godless society* **2** bad or evil • **godlessly** /-li/ adv • **godlessness** /-nəs/ noun [U]

godlike /ˈgɒd.laɪk/ (US) /ˈgɑːd-/ adj like God or a god in some way: *godlike powers*

godly /ˈgɒd.li/ (US) /ˈgɑːd-/ adj obeying and respecting God: *a godly woman* • **godliness** /-nəs/ noun [U]

godmother /ˈgɒdˌmʌð.əʳ/ (US) /ˈgɑːdˌmʌð.ɚ/ noun [C] a female godparent → See also **fairy godmother**

godown /ˈgəʊ.daʊn/ (US) /ˈgoʊ-/ noun [C] Indian English for **warehouse**

godparent /ˈgɒdˌpeə.rənt/ (US) /ˈgɑːdˌper.ᵊnt/ noun [C] (in the Christian religion) a person who, at a BAPTISM ceremony, promises to help a new member of the religion, usually a child, in religious and moral matters

godsend /ˈgɒd.send/ (US) /ˈgɑːd-/ noun [S] informal something good which happens unexpectedly, especially at a time when it is needed: *The grant was a **real** godsend, especially considering the theatre was due to close next month.*

ˌGod's ˈgift noun [U] disapproving If you say that someone thinks or behaves as if they are God's gift (to someone or something), you mean that they believe that they are better than anyone else: *He **thinks** he's God's gift **to women** (= he thinks he is extremely attractive to women).*

godson /ˈgɒd.sʌn/ (US) /ˈgɑːd-/ noun [C] a male GODCHILD

the ˈGod squad noun [C, + sing/pl verb] informal mainly disapproving EVANGELICAL Christians , whose members are generally thought to be too forceful in trying to persuade other people to believe as they do

ˌGod's ˈtruth exclamation said to emphasize that something is the complete truth: *I didn't know she would be there – God's **honest** truth.*

goer /ˈgəʊ.əʳ/ (US) /ˈgoʊ.ɚ/ noun [C] informal a woman who is sexually active with a lot of people: *Apparently, she was a bit of a goer before she got married.*

-goer /-gəʊ.əʳ/ (US) /-goʊ.ɚ/ suffix a person who goes to the stated type of place: *regular filmgoers*

goes /gəʊz/ (US) /goʊz/ he/she/it form of **go**

gofer /ˈgəʊ.fəʳ/ (US) /ˈgoʊ.fɚ/ noun [C] US informal someone whose job is to be sent to get and carry things such as messages, drinks, etc. for other people in a company

go-getter /ˈgəʊˌget.əʳ/ (US) /ˈgoʊˌget̬.ɚ/ noun [C] someone who is very energetic, determined to be successful, and able to deal with new or difficult situations easily • **ˈgo-getting** adj *He's a go-getting, high-powered business manager.*

gogga /ˈxɒ.xə/ (US) /ˈxɑː-/ noun [C] South African English an insect of any type

goggle /ˈgɒg.l/ (US) /ˈgɑː.gl/ verb [I] informal to look with the eyes wide open because you are surprised: *The cathedral was full of goggling tourists.*

ˈgoggle-box noun [C usually singular] UK old-fashioned informal for television

ˌgoggle-ˈeyed adj informal If someone is goggle-eyed, their eyes are very wide open, usually because of surprise.

goggles /ˈgɒg.lz/ (US) /ˈgɑː.glz/ noun [plural] special glasses which fit close to the face to protect the eyes from chemicals, wind, water, etc.: *ski goggles* ◦ *(**a pair of**) safety goggles*

goggles

ˈgo-go ˌdancer noun [C] a dancer who performs in places such as bars, dancing energetically in a sexually exciting manner while wearing very little clothing

going /ˈgəʊ.ɪŋ/ (US) /ˈgoʊ-/ noun; adj

▸noun **SPEED** ▷ **1** [U] how quickly you do something: *Cambridge to Newcastle in four hours is **good** going – you must have been driving flat out.* **DIFFICULTY** ▷ **2** [U] how easy or difficult something is: *She's obviously very intelligent, but her lectures are **heavy** going (= they are difficult to understand).* ◦ *He found three 400 metre races in two days **hard** going (= difficult).* **GROUND** ▷ **3** [U] the condition of the ground for walking or riding, etc.: *After an inch of rain at the racecourse overnight, the going is described as good to soft.* **LEAVING** ▷ **4** [S] an occasion when someone leaves somewhere: *His going came as as shock.*

IDIOMS **when the going gets rough/tough** when a situation becomes difficult or unpleasant: *I run the farm on my own but a local boy helps me out when the going gets tough.* • **while the going is good** while an opportunity lasts: *Many people fear that the newly elected government will be ousted in a military coup and are leaving their country while the going is good.*

▸adj [after noun] available or existing: *I wouldn't trust him if I were you – he's the biggest crook going (= he's the most dishonest person that exists).* ◦ *I don't suppose there's any left-over pie going, is there?*

-going /-gəʊ.ɪŋ/ (US) /-goʊ-/ suffix refers to the activity of going to the stated place: *He grew up in a strict church-going family.*

ˈgoing ˌon adv, preposition **1** (UK also **going on for**) nearly or almost (a particular number, age, time, or amount): *It was going on midnight when we left the party.* ◦ *There were going on 200 people at their wedding.* **2** humorous used for saying that someone behaves like a much older person: *'How old is Brian?' '30 going on 50.'*

ˌgoing-ˈover noun [S] **1** an activity such as cleaning that is done carefully and completely: *This carpet's filthy! It needs a really good going-over.* ◦ *Detectives have **given** the flat a thorough going-over (= examined it carefully).* **2** informal an occasion when someone is hit repeatedly: *They said I'd get a real going-over if I didn't pay them by tomorrow.*

ˌgoings-ˈon noun [plural] strange, unusual, humorous, or unsuitable events or activities: *There've been a lot of **strange/odd** goings-on in that house recently.*

goitre /ˈɡɔɪ.təʳ/ ⓤⓢ /-t̬ɚ/ noun [U] UK (US **goiter**) a swelling at the front of the neck caused by an increase in size of the THYROID GLAND

go-kart (also **go-cart**) /ˈɡəʊ.kɑːt/ ⓤⓢ /ˈɡoʊ.kɑːrt/ noun [C] a small, low car used for racing, or a toy car which you operate with your feet

go-karting (also **go-carting**) /ˈɡəʊˌkɑː.tɪŋ/ ⓤⓢ /ˈɡoʊˌkɑːr.t̬ɪŋ/ noun [U] racing in go-karts

gold /ɡəʊld/ ⓤⓢ /ɡoʊld/ noun; adj

▸noun **1** A2 [U] (symbol **Au**) a chemical element that is a valuable, shiny, yellow metal used to make coins and jewellery: *gold jewellery/bullion ◦ a gold watch/necklace* **2** [C] (also **gold medal**) a small disc of gold that is given to the person who wins a competition, especially in a sport: *He's running so well, surely he'll take the gold.*

▸adj A2 made of gold, or the colour of gold: *a gold dome ◦ gold paint*

IDIOM **go gold** If a recording of a popular song, or of a collection of popular songs, goes gold, it sells a large number of copies.

ˌgold ˈcard noun [C] a CREDIT CARD which you can get if you earn a lot of money

ˈgold ˌdigger noun [C] disapproving someone, usually a woman, who tries to attract a rich person, usually a man, in order to get presents or money

ˌgold ˈdisc noun [C] a prize given to the performer(s) of a popular song, or a collection of popular songs, when a large number of copies of the recording of it have been sold

ˈgold ˌdust noun [U] gold in powder form

IDIOM **like gold dust** mainly UK said about something that is very difficult to get because a lot of people want it: *Tickets for the concert are like gold dust.*

golden /ˈɡəʊl.dᵊn/ ⓤⓢ /ˈɡoʊl-/ adj GOLD ▷ **1** A2 made of gold: *a golden necklace* **2** A2 the colour of gold: *golden hair/skin ◦ miles of golden beaches* SPECIAL ▷ **3** B2 [before noun] special, successful, or giving someone an advantage: *the golden days of our youth ◦ He's got a place at university which gives him a golden **opportunity** to do research in the subject which interests him. ◦ I like listening to those radio stations that play all the golden **oldies** (= old popular songs which people still like or which have become liked again).*

ˌgolden ˈage noun [C usually singular] a period of time, sometimes imaginary, when everyone was happy, or when a particular art, business, etc. was very successful: *Adults often look back on their childhood as a golden age. ◦ She was an actress from the golden age **of** the cinema.*

ˈgolden ˌboy/girl noun [C] a person who is very successful and is much admired, although often only temporarily: *She's the current golden girl **of** American ice-skating.*

ˌgolden ˈeagle noun [C] a large flesh-eating bird with brown feathers on its back, which lives in northern parts of the world

ˌgolden ˌgoal noun [C] the first goal scored during a period of extra time in a football game, which ends the game and means that the team who scored it wins

ˌgolden ˈgoose noun [C usually singular] something which gives you an advantage, especially a financial advantage

ˌgolden ˈhandcuffs noun [plural] slang payments made to employees, especially those in a high position, as a way of persuading them not to leave their jobs and go and work somewhere else

ˌgolden ˈhandshake noun [C usually singular] informal a usually large payment made to someone when they leave their job, either when their employer has asked them to leave or when they are leaving at the end of their working life, as a reward for very long or good service in their job

ˌgolden helˈlo noun [C] UK an extra payment that is given to someone for accepting a new job

ˌgolden ˈjubilee noun [C usually singular] mainly UK the day exactly 50 years after an important occasion, or a special event to celebrate this: *The local hospital will be **celebrating** its golden jubilee on Thursday.*

ˌgolden ˈparachute noun [C] informal a large payment made to someone who has an important job with a company when they are forced to leave their job

ˌgolden reˈtriever noun [C] a large dog that has gold or cream-coloured fur

ˌgolden ˈrule noun [C usually singular] an important rule or principle, especially in a particular situation: *The golden rule for working in any factory is to observe its safety regulations.*

ˌgolden ˈsyrup noun [U] UK a thick, sweet, gold-coloured liquid used in cooking to make food sweet

ˌgolden ˈwedding (anniˌversary) noun [C] the day exactly 50 years after a marriage, often celebrated with a party

goldfield /ˈɡəʊld.fiːld/ ⓤⓢ /ˈɡoʊld-/ noun [C] an area where gold is found in the ground

goldfish /ˈɡəʊld.fɪʃ/ ⓤⓢ /ˈɡoʊld-/ noun [C] (plural **goldfish** or **goldfishes**) a small, shiny, gold or orange fish that is often kept as a pet in a bowl or garden pool

ˈgoldfish ˌbowl noun [C] (US also **fishbowl**) a bowl that is usually round and made of glass and is used for keeping pet fish in, especially goldfish: figurative *There are so many windows in the office, it's **like** being in **a** goldfish bowl (= people can easily see what you are doing)!*

goldish /ˈɡəʊld.ɪʃ/ ⓤⓢ /ˈɡoʊld-/ adj slightly gold in colour

ˌgold ˈleaf noun [U] gold in the form of very thin sheets, often used to cover objects, such as decorative details in a building

ˈgold ˌmine noun **1** [C] a place where gold is taken from the ground **2** [S] something which produces WEALTH or information: *The archive is a gold mine for historians.*

ˌgold-ˈplated adj covered with a very thin layer of gold: *gold-plated earrings*

ˈgold reˌserve noun [C] the amount of gold held by a national bank, used for dealing with the national banks of other countries

ˈgold ˌrush noun [C usually singular] a situation in which a lot of people move to a place to try to find gold because they have heard that gold has been found there

goldsmith /ˈɡəʊld.smɪθ/ ⓤⓢ /ˈɡoʊld-/ noun [C] someone who makes objects from gold

ˈgold ˌstandard noun [S] FINANCIAL SYSTEM ▷ **1** a system of providing and controlling the exchange of money in a country, in which the value of money (compared to foreign money) is fixed against that of gold GOOD THING ▷ **2** something that is very good and is used for measuring how good other similar things are: *I think 'Sesame Street' is still the gold standard for preschool television.*

golf /gɒlf/ US /gɑːlf/ **noun** [U] A2 a game played outside on grass in which each player tries to hit a small ball into a series of nine or 18 small holes, using a long thin stick: *We often play a* ***round*** *(= game) of golf at the weekend.* • **golfer** /ˈgɒl.fəʳ/ US /ˈgɑːl.fɚ/ **noun** [C] *He's one of the highest-earning professional golfers in the world.* • **golfing** /ˈgɒl.fɪŋ/ US /ˈgɑːl-/ **noun** [U] *a golfing* ***holiday***

ˈgolf ˌball noun [C] **SPORT** ▷ a small, hard, white ball used for playing golf

ˈgolf ˌclub noun [C] **STICK** ▷ **1** one of a set of specially shaped wooden or metal sticks used for hitting a golf ball **CLUB** ▷ **2** an organized group of golf players, or the building in which they meet and the area on which they play

ˈgolf ˌcourse noun [C] an area of land used for playing golf

Goliath /gəˈlaɪ.əθ/ **noun** **1** [C usually singular] (also **goliath**) a very large and powerful person or organization **2** [S not after the] in the Bible, a GIANT (= extremely tall man) who was killed by the boy David throwing a stone at him

golliwog /ˈgɒl.ɪ.wɒg/ US /ˈgɑː.lɪ.wɑːg/ **noun** [C] (also **golly**) UK old-fashioned a child's toy made of soft material, in the form of a small man with a black face and stiff black hair, now often considered offensive to black people

golly /ˈgɒl.i/ US /ˈgɑː.li/ **exclamation; noun**
▸**exclamation** old-fashioned informal used to show surprise: *Grandad might be 70 but he said he'd finish the marathon and,* ***by*** *golly, he did.*
▸**noun** [C] old-fashioned informal a golliwog

gonad /ˈgəʊ.næd/ US /ˈgoʊ-/ **noun** [C] specialized one of the organs in a male or female animal that produces sex cells

gondola /ˈgɒn.dəl.ə/ US /ˈgɑːn-/ **noun** [C] **1** a narrow boat with a raised point at both ends, used on CANALS in Venice **2** in a CABLE CAR, SKI LIFT, AMUSEMENT PARK ride, etc., a hanging part that people sit or travel in

gondola

gondolier /ˌgɒn.dəˈlɪəʳ/ US /ˌgɑːn.dəˈlɪr/ **noun** [C] a man who takes people from one place to another in a gondola

gone /gɒn/ US /gɑːn/ **verb; preposition; adj**
▸**verb** past participle of **go**
▸**preposition** UK later or older than: *I said I'd be home by six and it's already gone seven.*
▸**adj** **LEFT** ▷ **1** [after verb] If something is gone, there is none of it left: *All my money is gone and I have nothing to buy food with.* **2** [after verb] dead: *Fortunately I'll be* ***dead and*** *gone long before the money runs out.* ◦ *They did everything they could to save him, but he was already* ***too far*** *gone (= too close to death) when the ambulance arrived.* **PREGNANT** ▷ **3** [after noun] informal pregnant: *How far gone is she? (= How long has she been pregnant?)*

goner /ˈgɒn.əʳ/ US /ˈgɑː.nɚ/ **noun** [C usually singular] informal a person or thing that has no chance of continuing to live: *I thought I was a goner when I saw that car heading towards me.*

gong /gɒŋ/ US /gɑːŋ/ **noun** [C] **1** a round piece of metal that is hung in a frame and hit with a stick to produce a sound as a signal, also used as a musical instrument **2** UK informal an honour that is given to someone for the public service they have done, or to a performer for a particular acting or singing performance

gonna /ˈgə.nə/ US /ˈgɑː.nə/ mainly US informal for going to: *What are you gonna do?*

> **! Common mistake: gonna**
> **Remember: gonna** is only used in informal English. In ordinary or more formal language, don't say 'gonna', say **going to.**

gonorrhoea (mainly US **gonorrhea**) /ˌgɒn.əˈriː.ə/ US /ˌgɑː.nəˈ-/ **noun** [U] (slang **clap**) a disease of the sexual organs that can be given from one person to another during sex

gonzo /ˈgɒn.zəʊ/ US /gɑːn.zoʊ/ **adj** US slang (especially used of pieces of writing in newspapers) intended to be shocking and exciting rather than give information: *gonzo* ***journalism***

goo /guː/ **noun** [U] informal an unpleasantly sticky substance

good /gʊd/ **adj; noun**
▸**adj** (**better, best**) **PLEASANT/SATISFACTORY** ▷ **1** A1 very satisfactory, enjoyable, pleasant, or interesting: *a good book* ◦ *Did you have a good time at the party?* ◦ *The weather has been really good for the time of year.* ◦ *I've just had some very good news.* ◦ ***It's*** *so good* ***to*** *see you after all this time!* **2** used in greetings: *good morning/afternoon/evening*

> **! Common mistake: good or well?**
> **Remember: good** is not used as an adverb.
> To talk about something being done in a good way or to a high standard, don't say 'good', say **well:**
> ~~*She did her work very good, but she was often late.*~~
> *She did her work very well, but she was often late.*
> **Warning:** Some US English speakers use 'good' as an adverb, but many people consider this incorrect and it should not be used in exams.

HEALTHY ▷ **3** A1 healthy or well: *I didn't go into work because I wasn't feeling too good.* ◦ *'How's your mother?' 'She's good, thanks.'* **4 I'm good** used as a general reply when someone greets you: *'How are you doing?' 'I'm good, thanks.'* **HIGH QUALITY** ▷ **5** A1 of a high quality or level: *She speaks very good French.* ◦ *I've heard it's a very good school.* ◦ *The apple pie was* ***as*** *good* ***as*** *the one my grandmother used to make.* ◦ *This restaurant has a good* ***reputation.*** **6** used to express praise: *Good man! Splendid catch.* **SUCCESSFUL** ▷ **7** A1 successful, or able to do something well: *Kate's a good cook.* ◦ *She's very good* ***at*** *geography.* ◦ *They have a good relationship.* ◦ *She's very good* ***with*** *children.* **8 be no good** (also **be not any/much good**) B2 to be of low quality or not useful: *Shoes are no good if they let in water.* ◦ *Food aid isn't much good until the fighting stops.* **9 get off to a good start** to begin an activity successfully: *I didn't get off to a very good start this morning – I'd been at work five minutes and my computer stopped working!* **KIND** ▷ **10** A1 kind or helpful: *a good friend* ◦ ***It's*** *good* ***of*** *you to offer to help.* ◦ *He's very good* ***to*** *his mother.* **11 be so good as to** (also **be good enough to**) used to make a polite request: *Be so good as to close the door when you leave.* **12 do (sb) a good turn** old-fashioned to do something kind that helps someone else **MORALLY RIGHT** ▷ **13** B1 morally right or based on religious principles: *She led a good life.* ◦ *Try to set a good example to the children.* **POSITIVE** ▷ **14** A1 having a positive or useful effect, especially on the health: *Too much sugar in your diet isn't good* ***for*** *you.* **BEHAVIOUR** ▷ **15** A2 A good child or animal behaves well: *If you're a good boy at the doctor's, I'll take you swimming afterwards.* **16** able to be trusted: *Her credit is good (= she can be trusted to pay her debts).* **SUITABLE** ▷ **17** A2 suitable, convenient, or satisfactory: *When would be a good time to phone?* **LARGE** ▷ **18** C1 [before noun] used to emphasize the large number, amount, or level of something: *We've walked a good distance today.* ◦ *There was a good-sized crowd at the airport waiting for the plane to land.* ◦ *Not all of his films have been successful – there were* ***a*** *good* ***few*** *(= several) failures in the early years.* ◦ *Have a good think about it and let me know tomorrow.* ◦ *You have a good cry and you'll feel better after.* ◦ *There's a good chance the operation will be successful.* → See also **good money** **19 a good deal of** B2 much: *The new law met with a good deal of opposition at the local level.* **20 a good …** C2 (also **a good …'s**) more than: *It's a good half hour's walk to the station from here.* ◦ *The police said a good 20 kilos of explosive were found during the raid.* ◦ *Driving through the deserted town we saw a good* ***many*** *(= a lot of) burned-out houses.* **SATISFACTION** ▷ **21** A1 said when you are satisfied or pleased about something, or to show agreement with a decision: *Oh good, he's arrived at last.* ◦ *Good, I'll tell her it's all arranged, then.* **22 I'm good** used to tell someone that you have everything that you need: *'More coffee?' 'No, I'm good, thanks.'*

IDIOMS **be a good job/thing** B2 used to mean 'it is lucky': *It's a good job they didn't go camping last weekend – the weather was awful.* • **all in good time** used to tell someone to be patient because the thing they are eager for will happen when the time is right: *Be patient, you'll hear the result all in good time.* • **as good as** almost: *The decorating is as good as finished – I just need to finish off the painting.* • **be (as) good as gold** (of a child) to behave very well • **be (as) good as new** to be in very good condition: *A coat of paint and it will be as good as new.* • **be as good as your word** to do everything that you promise someone you will: *He said he'd call every day and he was as good as his word.* • **be good for sth** informal to be able and willing to provide something: *Bette is* ***always*** *good for a laugh.* ◦ *Dad will probably be good for a few pounds, if we ask him.* • **be good to go** US informal to be prepared and ready to do something: *Let me grab a jacket and then I'm good to go.* • **for good measure** in addition: *The concert was excellent – there were lots of well-known songs with some new ones* ***thrown in*** *for good measure.* • **good and …** informal very: *Drink your coffee while it's good and hot.* • **good and proper** informal completely: *The table is broken good and proper.* • **good for you!** (Australian English also **good on you!**) B2 used to show approval for someone's success or good luck: *You passed your exam – good for you!* • **good heavens/grief/gracious!** (also **Good God/Lord!**) used to emphasize how surprised, angry, shocked, etc. you are • **the good old days** If you talk about the good old days, you mean a time in the past when you believe life was better: *I wish my grandma would stop going on about the good old days.* • **good show** UK old-fashioned used as an expression of approval: *Good show chaps, you completed the course in the time allowed.* • **have a good innings** UK informal If you say that someone has had a good innings, you mean that they have had a long and successful life: *He was 86 when he died so I suppose he'd had a good innings.* • **in good faith** If something is done in good faith, it is done sincerely and honestly: *She was* ***acting*** *in good faith for her client.* • **in good time** mainly UK early: *We'll be at the airport in good time.* • **make good 1** to succeed and become rich: *a working-class boy made good* **2** When someone makes good something, they either pay for it, or make it happen: *The shortfall in the budget will be made good by selling further shares.* • **make good time** to complete a journey quickly

▸noun **THINGS** ▷ **1 goods** [plural] **a** B1 things for sale, or the things that you own: *There is a 25 percent discount on all electrical goods until the end of the week.* ◦ *The house insurance will not cover your personal goods.* **b** UK things, but not people, that are transported by railway or road: *a goods train* **HELP** ▷ **2** B2 [U] something that is an advantage or help to a person or situation: *Even a small donation can do* ***a lot of*** *good.* ◦ *I'm telling you* ***for*** *your* ***own*** *good.* **HEALTH** ▷ **3** [U] the state of being healthy or in a satisfactory condition: *You should stop smoking* ***for*** *your* ***own*** *good (= for your health).* ◦ *He goes running every day* ***for the*** *good* ***of*** *his* ***health.*** ◦ *Modernizing historic buildings can often* ***do more harm than*** *good.* ◦ *The decision has been postponed* ***for the*** *good* ***of*** *all concerned.* → Synonym **benefit** **4 do sb good** B2 to improve someone's health or life: *You can't work all the time – it does you good* ***to*** *go out and enjoy yourself sometimes.* ◦ *Take the medicine – it will do you (****a power/world of****) good (= improve your health a lot).* **MORALLY RIGHT** ▷ **5** C2 [U] that which is morally right: *There is an eternal struggle between good (= the force that produces morally right action) and evil.* ◦ *Ambition can sometimes be a force* ***for*** *good.* **6 the good** [plural] all the people who are morally good: *You can't buy your way into the ranks of the good.* **TIME** ▷ **7 for good** C1 for ever: *She's gone and this time it's for good.*

IDIOMS **be up to no good** informal to be behaving in a dishonest or bad way: *He certainly looked as if he was up to no good.* • **come up with the goods** (also **deliver the goods**) to produce what is wanted: *What they promise sounds impressive enough – let's see if they come up with the goods.* • **no good** informal old-fashioned morally bad: *I'd keep away from him if I were you – he's no good.* • **to the good** generally helpful: *Greater international stability can surely only be to the good.* • **what good is …** (also **what's the good of …**) a way of asking what the purpose of (doing) something is: *What good is sitting alone in your room?*

ˌgood ˌafterˈnoon exclamation A1 something you say to greet someone politely when you meet them in the afternoon → Compare **afternoon**

the ˌGood ˈBook noun [S] old-fashioned the Bible

goodbye /gʊdˈbaɪ/ exclamation; noun

▸exclamation (informal **bye**) A1 used when someone leaves or is left: *Goodbye Bill! See you next week.*

▸noun [C] the words or actions that are used when someone leaves or is left: *Don't go without* ***saying*** *goodbye* ***to*** *me, will you?* ◦ *She* ***kissed*** *her children goodbye before leaving for work.* ◦ *We* ***said*** *our goodbyes, and left.* ◦ *I hate long drawn-out goodbyes (= acts of leaving).*

IDIOM **goodbye to sth** used when accepting that there is no possibility of getting, keeping, or achieving a particular thing: *She only finished sixth – that surely* ***means*** *goodbye to a place in the final.*

ˌgood ˈday exclamation old-fashioned used as a greeting or when saying goodbye during the day → See also **g'day**

ˌgood ˈevening exclamation A1 something you say to greet someone politely when you meet them in the evening → Compare **evening**

ˈgood-faith adj [before noun] mainly US **1** done in an honest and sincere way: *A good-faith effort has been made by both parties to settle.* → Compare **bad-faith** **2** used to describe money that is paid to show that you are serious about doing something or entering an agreement: *What we're asking is that they make a good-faith payment on what they owe.*

ˌgood-for-ˈnothing noun; adj
▸noun [C] informal a person who is lazy and not helpful or useful: *She told him he was a lazy good-for-nothing and should get a job.*
▸adj [before noun] not helpful or useful: *They're all good-for-nothing* ***layabouts.***

ˌGood ˈFriday noun [C or U] the Friday before Easter Sunday, the day in the Christian religion on which the death of Jesus is especially remembered

G

ˌgood-ˈhearted adj kind and generous

ˌgood-ˈhumoured adj friendly or in a good mood: *a good-humoured remark* ◦ *The walkers were good-humoured despite the bad weather.*

goodish /ˈgʊd.ɪʃ/ adj [before noun] UK informal **1** good but not very good **2** quite large: *a goodish distance/number*

ˌgood-ˈlooking adj (A2) describes a physically attractive man or woman: *He's very good-looking but not terribly bright.*

ˌgood ˈlooks noun [plural] an especially attractive appearance: *his boyish good looks*

goodly /ˈgʊd.li/ adj [before noun] old-fashioned great or large

ˌgood ˈmoney noun [U] an amount of money that you think is large: *I paid good money for it.*

ˌgood ˈmorning exclamation (A1) something you say to greet someone politely when you meet them in the morning → Compare **morning**

ˌgood-ˈnatured adj pleasant or friendly: *a good-natured face/crowd*

goodness /ˈgʊd.nəs/ noun; exclamation
▸noun [U] **HEALTH** ▷ **1** the part of something, especially of food, that is good for health: *Don't cook vegetables for too long – they'll lose all their goodness.* **CHARACTER** ▷ **2** (C2) the personal quality of being morally good: *Mother Teresa's goodness is an example to us all.*
▸exclamation (also **ˌgoodness ˈgracious**) used to express any strong emotion, especially surprise: *Goodness gracious (**me**), what a terrible thought!*

ˌgood ˈnight exclamation (A1) said when people leave each other in the evening or before going to bed or to sleep: *Well, good night – sleep well.* ◦ *Give the children a good-night kiss.* → Compare **night**

goodo /ˌgʊdˈəʊ/ (US) /-ˈoʊ/ exclamation [after verb], adj, adv Australian English informal for good

ˈgood old ˌboy noun [C] informal a man from the southern US who enjoys spending time with his friends, and disapproves of ideas or ways of behaving that are different from his own

ˌgoods and ˈchattels noun [plural] legal the things that you own other than land and buildings

ˈgood-time ˌgirl noun [C] old-fashioned a young woman who is only interested in pleasure, not in serious activities, work, etc.

goodwill /gʊdˈwɪl/ noun [U] **1** friendly and helpful feelings: *The school has to rely on the goodwill of the parents to help it raise money.* ◦ *Releasing the hostages has been seen as a* ***gesture of*** *goodwill/a goodwill* ***gesture.*** **2** part of a company's value that includes things that cannot be directly measured, for example, its good reputation or its customers' loyalty: *The company's assets are worth £200 million, plus goodwill.*

goody /ˈgʊd.i/ noun; exclamation
▸noun informal **PLEASANT THING** ▷ **1** [C usually plural] an object which people want or enjoy, often something nice to eat: *All the children were given a bag of goodies – mostly sweets and toys.* **PERSON** ▷ **2** [C] someone, especially in a film or story, who is good: *It's one of those films where you don't know until the last moment who are the goodies and who are the baddies.*
▸exclamation informal or child's word used to show pleasure: *Oh goody! Chocolate cake.*

ˈgoody-ˌgoody noun [C] informal disapproving someone who behaves in a way intended to please people in authority

gooey /ˈguː.i/ adj (**gooier**, **gooiest**) soft and sticky: *a gooey cake*

goof /guːf/ verb; noun
▸verb [I or T] mainly US informal to make a silly mistake: *If Tom hadn't goofed and missed that shot, we'd have won the game.* ◦ *She goofed her lines (= said the words in the play wrong).*

PHRASAL VERBS **goof around** US informal to spend time doing nothing important or behaving in a silly way • **goof off** US informal to avoid doing any work: *They've goofed off and gone to the ball game.*

▸noun [C] **MISTAKE** ▷ **1** mainly US informal a silly mistake: *I* ***made*** *a real goof by forgetting his name.* **PERSON** ▷ **2** US informal a silly or stupid person

goofy /ˈguː.fi/ adj mainly US informal silly: *That was a real goofy thing to do.* ◦ *I like Jim, but he's a little goofy.*

Google /ˈguː.gl/ verb [I or T] trademark (B2) to search for something on the internet using the Google SEARCH ENGINE (= computer program that finds information)

googol /ˈguː.gəl/ noun [C] the number 10 to the 100th power (10 followed by 100 zeros)

googolplex /ˈguː.gəl.pleks/ number the number ten to the power of a GOOGOL

goon /guːn/ noun [C] **SILLY PERSON** ▷ **1** old-fashioned informal a silly or stupid person **CRIMINAL** ▷ **2** US informal a violent criminal who is paid to hurt or threaten people

goonda /ˈguːn.də/ noun [C] Indian English a person who is paid to hurt people or cause damage

goop /guːp/ noun [U] informal any thick liquid or sticky substance

goose /guːs/ noun; verb
▸noun (plural **geese**) **BIRD** ▷ **1** [C or U] a large water bird similar to a DUCK but larger, or the meat from this bird

> **! Note:**
> The female bird is called a goose and the male bird is called a **gander**.

PERSON ▷ **2** [C] old-fashioned informal a silly person
▸verb [T] **TOUCH** ▷ **1** informal to press or take hold of someone's bottom **MAKE ACTIVE** ▷ **2** US informal to encourage or cause something or someone to be more active

gooseberry /ˈgʊz.bər.i/ noun [C] a small green fruit covered with short hairs, which grows on a bush and has a sour taste: *Gooseberries are used for making pies and jam.*

IDIOM **play gooseberry** (also **feel like a gooseberry**) UK informal to be an unwanted third person who is present when two other people, especially two people having a romantic relationship, want to be alone

goosebumps /ˈguːs.bʌmps/ noun [plural] (UK also **ˈgoose ˌpimples**) small raised areas that appear on the skin because of cold, fear, or excitement: *You're cold – look, you've got goosebumps!*

gooseflesh /ˈguːs.fleʃ/ noun [U] UK **goosebumps**

ˈ**goose step** noun [S] a special way of marching with the legs lifted high and straight: *Hitler's soldiers used to **do** (**the**) goose step.* • ˈ**goose-step** verb [I] (plural **-pp-**)

the GOP /ˌdʒiː.əʊˈpiː/ noun abbreviation for the Grand Old Party: the Republican political party in the US

gopher /ˈɡəʊ.fəʳ/ (US) /ˈɡoʊ.fɚ/ noun [C] a North American animal which lives in holes that it makes in the ground

Gordian knot /ˌɡɔː.di.ənˈnɒt/ (US) /ˌɡɔːr.di.ənˈnɑːt/ noun [S] a difficult problem or situation: *to **cut** the Gordian knot (= to deal with problems by taking forceful action)*

Gordon Bennett /ˌɡɔː.dənˈben.ɪt/ (US) /ˌɡɔːr-/ exclamation UK old-fashioned slang used to express great surprise or anger

gore /ɡɔːʳ/ (US) /ɡɔːr/ noun; verb
▸noun [U] blood that has come from an injury and become thick: *It's a good film, but there's a lot of **blood and** gore in it (= pictures of people being badly injured).*
▸verb [T] (of an animal) to cause an injury to someone, or damage something, with the horns or TUSKS: *gored by a bull*

gorge /ɡɔːdʒ/ (US) /ɡɔːrdʒ/ noun; verb
▸noun **VALLEY** ▷ **1** [C] a deep narrow valley with steep sides, usually formed by a river or stream cutting through hard rock **ANGER** ▷ **2 make someone's gorge rise** to make someone feel shocked and angry
▸verb [I or T] to eat until you are unable to eat any more: *If you gorge your**self on** crisps like that, you won't eat your dinner.*

gorgeous /ˈɡɔː.dʒəs/ (US) /ˈɡɔːr-/ adj (B1) very beautiful or pleasant: *What a gorgeous room/dress/colour!* ◦ *The bride looked gorgeous.* ◦ *The weather was so gorgeous.* • **gorgeously** /-li/ adv • **gorgeousness** /-nəs/ noun [U]

gorgon /ˈɡɔː.ɡən/ (US) /ˈɡɔːr-/ noun [C] informal a woman whose appearance and behaviour causes fear: *Our teacher is a real gorgon!*

Gorgon /ˈɡɔː.ɡən/ (US) /ˈɡɔːr-/ noun [C] one of three sisters in ancient Greek stories who had snakes on their heads instead of hair, and who turned anyone who looked at them into stone

gorilla /ɡəˈrɪl.ə/ noun [C] a large APE that comes from western Africa

gorilla

gormless /ˈɡɔːm.ləs/ (US) /ˈɡɔːrm-/ adj UK informal stupid and slow to understand: *He looks really gormless.*

gorse /ɡɔːs/ (US) /ɡɔːrs/ noun [U] (also **furze**) a bush with sharp THORNS and small, yellow flowers, which grows in the countryside

gory /ˈɡɔː.ri/ (US) /ˈɡɔːr.i/ adj involving violence and blood: *a very gory film* ◦ *a gory description of the operation*

IDIOM **the gory details** the interesting and usually personal pieces of information about a person or event: *Come on, I want to know all the gory details about your date with Jon.*

gosh /ɡɒʃ/ (US) /ɡɑːʃ/ exclamation informal old-fashioned used to express surprise or strength of feeling: *Gosh, I didn't expect to see you here!*

gosling /ˈɡɒz.lɪŋ/ (US) /ˈɡɑːz-/ noun [C] a young GOOSE

ˈ**go-slow** noun [C usually singular] UK (US **slowdown**) an occasion when employees work more slowly and with less effort than usual to try to persuade an employer to agree to higher pay or better working conditions

gospel /ˈɡɒs.pəl/ (US) /ˈɡɑː.spəl/ noun **CHRISTIANITY** ▷ **1** [C] any of the four books of the Bible which contain details of the life of Jesus Christ: *St Mark's Gospel/the Gospel **according to** St Mark* **2 the gospel** [S] the teachings of Jesus Christ: *to **preach/spread** the gospel* **TRUTH** ▷ **3** [U] (also **gospel truth**) informal the complete truth: *If Mary tells you something, you can **take** it **as** gospel.* **MUSIC** ▷ **4** [U] (also **gospel music**) a style of religious music originally performed by black Americans **BELIEFS** ▷ **5** [S] literary a set of principles or ideas which someone believes in: *the gospel **of** hard work*

gossamer /ˈɡɒs.ə.məʳ/ (US) /ˈɡɑː.sə.mɚ/ noun; adj
▸noun [U] the very thin thread that SPIDERS produce to make WEBS
▸adj [before noun] literary very delicate and light: *gossamer wings* ◦ *a gossamer veil*

gossip /ˈɡɒs.ɪp/ (US) /ˈɡɑː.səp/ noun; verb
▸noun **1** (B2) [S or U] conversation or reports about other people's private lives which might be unkind, disapproving, or not true: *Her letter was full of gossip.* ◦ *Jane and Lyn sat in the kitchen **having** a good gossip **about** their friends.* ◦ *I don't like all this **idle** gossip.* ◦ *I've got some **juicy** gossip for you.* ◦ *Have you heard **the** (**latest**) gossip?* **2** [C] disapproving (mainly UK **gossipmonger**) someone who enjoys talking about other people and their private lives: *She's a terrible gossip.* • **gossipy** /ˈɡɒs.ɪ.pi/ (US) /ˈɡɑː.sɪ.pi/ adj *a gossipy letter* ◦ *gossipy people*
▸verb [I] (B2) to talk about other people's private lives: *Stop gossiping and get on with some work.* ◦ *People have started to gossip **about** us.*

ˈ**gossip** ˌ**column** noun [C] the part of a newspaper in which you find stories about the social and private lives of famous people

got /ɡɒt/ (US) /ɡɑːt/ past simple and past participle of **get**

gotcha /ˈɡɒtʃ.ə/ (US) /ˈɡɑːtʃ-/ exclamation slang said to mean 'I have got you' in order to surprise or frighten someone you have caught, or to show that you have an advantage over them

goth /ɡɒθ/ (US) /ˈɡɑː.θ/ noun **1** [U] a type of ROCK MUSIC which often has words expressing ideas about death or the end of the world **2** [C] someone who likes goth music, and wears black clothes and white make-up

Gothic /ˈɡɒθ.ɪk/ (US) /ˈɡɑː.θɪk/ adj **BUILDING** ▷ **1** of or like a style of building that was common in Europe between the 12th and 16th centuries and whose characteristics are pointed ARCHES and windows, high ceilings, and tall, thin columns: *a Gothic cathedral* ◦ *Gothic arches* **STORIES** ▷ **2** describes writing or films in which strange things happen in frightening places

ˌ**go-**ˈ**to** adj [before noun] mainly US used to describe the best person to deal with a particular problem or do a particular thing, or the best place to get a particular thing or service: *He was the company's go-to **guy** for new ideas.* ◦ *He is the go-to politician for all federal matters in the state.* ◦ *For 20 years, Wild Mountain was the go-to store for outdoor enthusiasts.*

gotta /ˈɡɒt.ə/ (US) /ˈɡɑː.t̬ə/ short form not standard 'have got to': *I gotta go now.*

gotten /ˈɡɒt.ən/ (US) /ˈɡɑː.t̬ən/ US past participle of **get**: *They were so pleased that they'd finally gotten to visit (= succeeded in visiting) England.*

gouge /ɡaʊdʒ/ verb; noun
▸verb [T] to make a hole in something in a rough or

violent way: *He drove into some railings and gouged a **hole** in the back of his car.*

PHRASAL VERB **gouge sth out** to remove something by digging or cutting it out of a surface: *In Shakespeare's play, 'King Lear', the Earl of Gloucester's eyes are gouged out.*

▸**noun** [C] a hole that has been made roughly or violently

goulash /ˈguː.læʃ/ **noun** [U] a dish, originally from Hungary, consisting of meat cooked in a sauce with PAPRIKA (= a spice that tastes hot)

gourd /gʊəd/, /gɔːd/ (US) /gɔːrd/ **noun** [C] a large fruit that has a hard shell and cannot be eaten, or the shell of this fruit used as a container

G

gourmand /gɔːˈmɑ̃ː/ (US) /ˈgʊr.mɑːnd/ **noun** [C] a person who enjoys eating large amounts of food

gourmet /ˈgɔː.meɪ/ (US) /ˈgʊr.meɪ/ **adj; noun**

▸**adj** [before noun] **1** (of food) very high quality: *gourmet coffee* ◦ *a gourmet meal* **2** producing or serving food that is very high quality: *a gourmet restaurant* ◦ *a gourmet chef*

▸**noun** [C] a person who knows a lot about food and cooking, and who enjoys eating high-quality food

gout /gaʊt/ **noun** [U] a painful disease that makes the JOINTS (= places where two bones are connected), especially the feet, knees, and hands, swell • **gouty** /ˈgaʊ.ti/ (US) /-t̬i/ **adj**

govern /ˈgʌv.ən/ (US) /-ən/ **verb** **RULE** ▷ **1** (B2) [I or T] to control and direct the public business of a country, city, group of people, etc.: *The country is now being governed by the Labour Party.* ◦ *They accused the government of being unfit to govern.* **INFLUENCE** ▷ **2** [T] to have a controlling influence on something: *Prices of goods are governed by the cost of the raw materials, as well as by the cost of production and distribution.*

governance /ˈgʌv.ən.ənts/ (US) /ˈgʌv.ɚ.nənts/ **noun** [U] the way that organizations or countries are managed at the highest level, and the systems for doing this: *We aim to promote and maintain the highest standards of directorship and **corporate** governance.*

governess /ˈgʌv.ən.əs/ (US) /-ɚ.nəs/ **noun** [C] (especially in the past) a woman who lives with a family and teaches their children at home

governing /ˈgʌv.ən.ɪŋ/ (US) /-ɚ.nɪŋ/ **adj** [before noun] **RULING** ▷ **1** having the power to govern a country or an organization: *the governing **body** of the school* **INFLUENCING** ▷ **2** having a controlling influence on something: *a governing **principle/factor***

> **! Common mistake: government**
>
> **Remember:** to talk about the group of people who officially control a particular country, use the definite article, **the**.
>
> Don't say 'government', say **the government**:
>
> ~~*Government should do more to help the unemployed.*~~
>
> *The government should do more to help the unemployed.*

government /ˈgʌv.ən.mənt/, /-əm-/ (US) /-ən-/ **noun** **GROUP** ▷ **1** (B1) [C, + sing/pl verb] (written abbreviation **govt**) the group of people who officially control a country: *the government of Israel* ◦ *The government is/are expected to announce its/their tax proposals today.* ◦ *The minister has announced that there will be no change in government policy.* ◦ *Senior government officials will be attending a meeting tomorrow.* ◦ *Theatre companies are very concerned about cuts in government grants to the arts.* ◦ *A government enquiry has been launched.* **SYSTEM** ▷ **2** (B2) [U] the system used for controlling a country, city, or group of people: *The 1990s saw a shift to democratic government in Eastern Europe.* ◦ *What this state needs is really strong government.* **3** (B2) [U] the activities involved in controlling a country, city, group of people, etc.: *The party that was elected to power has no experience of government.* ◦ UK *The party was **in** government (= controlled the country) for four years in the 1960s.* **4 Her/His Majesty's Government** the government of the UK

> **Word partners for government**
>
> *elect* a government • *establish/form* a government • *bring down/overthrow/topple* a government • a *democratic/elected* government • government *plans/policy/spending* • a government *department/leader/minister/official* • a *change* of government • be *in* government

governmental /ˌgʌv.ənˈmen.təl/, /-əˈmen-/ (US) /-ən-ˈmen.t̬əl/ **adj** belonging or relating to government or the government: *We await a governmental decision about the future of the programme.*

governor /ˈgʌv.ən.əʳ/ (US) /-ɚ.nɚ/ **noun** [C] (written abbreviation **Gov.**) **1** a person in charge of a particular political unit: *the governor of Texas* → See also **gubernatorial, guvnor** **2** mainly UK a person in charge of a particular organization: *a prison/school governor*

ˌgovernor ˈgeneral **noun** [C] (plural **governors general**) the main REPRESENTATIVE of a country in another country that is controlled by the first country, especially the representative of the British king or queen in a country that is a member of the COMMONWEALTH

governorship /ˈgʌv.ən.ə.ʃɪp/ (US) /-ɚ.nɚ-/ **noun** [U] the period of time that someone is a governor: *His governorship was marked by fairness and prosperity.*

gown /gaʊn/ **noun** [C] a woman's dress, especially a long one worn on formal occasions, or a long loose piece of clothing worn over other clothes for a particular purpose: *a **ball** gown* ◦ *a **hospital** gown*

GP /ˌdʒiːˈpiː/ **noun** [C] mainly UK abbreviation for general practitioner: a doctor who provides general medical treatment for people who live in a particular area: *I went along to the **local** GP.*

GPRS /ˌdʒiː.piː.ɑːˈres/ **noun** [U] abbreviation for general packet radio service: a system for sending and receiving images and other information using mobile phones

GPS /ˌdʒiː.piːˈes/ **noun** [U] abbreviation for global positioning system: a system that can show the exact position of a person or thing by using signals from SATELLITES (= objects in space that send signals to Earth)

grab /græb/ **verb; noun**

▸**verb** (**-bb-**) **TAKE WITH HAND** ▷ **1** (B1) [I or T] to take hold of something or someone suddenly and roughly: *A mugger grabbed her handbag as she was walking across the park.* ◦ *He grabbed (**hold of**) his child's arm to stop her from running into the road.* **TAKE OPPORTUNITY** ▷ **2** (B2) [T] informal to take the opportunity to get, use, or enjoy something quickly: *If you don't grab this opportunity, you might not get another one.* ◦ *We'd better get there early, or someone else will grab the best seats.* ◦ *Let's just grab a quick bite.* **3 grab sb's attention** (C1) to attract someone's attention: *With your first sentence you must grab the reader's attention.*

IDIOM **how does... grab you?** informal used to ask if someone would like to do something or is interested in something: *We could have a picnic in the park. How does that grab you?*

PHRASAL VERB **grab at sth/sb** to try to get hold of someone or something quickly, with your hand

▸noun [C] a sudden attempt to hold, get, or take something: *The two children both* ***made*** *a grab* ***for*** *the same cake.* • **grabby** /ˈɡræb.i/ informal *Don't be so grabby (= trying to take things for yourself), Shirley. Let the others have their share.*

IDIOM **up for grabs** available and ready to be won or taken: *There are hundreds of prizes up for grabs.*

ˈgrab ˌbag noun [C] **1** US for **lucky dip 2** US any mixed collection of things

-grabbing /-ɡræb.ɪŋ/ suffix getting or taking a lot of the stated thing: *a* ***money****-grabbing scheme* ◦ *a* ***headline****-grabbing court case (= one which is being written about a lot in newspapers)*

grace /ɡreɪs/ noun; verb

▸noun MOVEMENT ▷ **1** C1 [U] a quality of moving in a smooth, relaxed, and attractive way: *Joanna has natural grace and elegance.* POLITENESS ▷ **2** C2 [U] the quality of being pleasantly polite, or a willingness to be fair and honest: *They accepted their defeat* ***with good*** *grace.* **3 graces** /ɡreɪsɪz/ [plural] ways of behaving that are considered polite and pleasant: *Ken is sadly lacking in* ***social*** *graces.* APPROVAL ▷ **4** [U] formal approval or kindness, especially (in the Christian religion) that is freely given by God to all humans: *Betty believed that it was through* ***divine*** *grace that her husband had recovered from his illness.* **5 by the grace of God** formal through the kindness or help of God: *By the grace of God, the pilot managed to land the damaged plane safely.* PRAYER ▷ **6** [C or U] a prayer said by Christians before a meal to thank God for the food: *The children always* ***say*** *grace at school.* TIME ▷ **7** [U] a period of time left or allowed before something happens or before something must be done: *The exams have been postponed, so the students have a few days' grace before they start.*

IDIOM **there but for the grace of God (go I)** saying said when something bad that has happened to someone else could have happened to you

▸verb [T] **1** C2 When a person or thing graces a place or thing, they make it more attractive: *Her face has graced the covers of magazines across the world.* **2 grace sb with your presence** to honour people by taking part in something: *We are delighted that the mayor will be gracing us with his presence at our annual dinner.* ◦ humorous *So you've finally decided to grace us with your presence, have you? (= You are late.)*

Grace /ɡreɪs/ noun **Your/His/Her Grace** used to address or refer to a DUKE, DUCHESS or ARCHBISHOP

graceful /ˈɡreɪs.fəl/ adj MOVEMENT ▷ **1** C1 moving in a smooth, relaxed, attractive way, or having a smooth, attractive shape: *graceful movements* ◦ *a graceful neck* BEHAVIOUR ▷ **2** C2 behaving in a polite and pleasant way: *She finally apologized, but she wasn't very graceful about it.* • **gracefully** /-i/ adv

graceless /ˈɡreɪs.ləs/ adj NO BEAUTY ▷ **1** without beauty: *graceless movements* NOT POLITE ▷ **2** without politeness: *a graceless manner* • **gracelessly** /-li/ adv

gracious /ˈɡreɪ.ʃəs/ adj; exclamation

▸adj PLEASANT ▷ **1** behaving in a pleasant, polite, calm way: *a gracious smile* ◦ *He was gracious* ***enough*** *to thank me.* ◦ *The losing team were gracious* ***in*** *defeat.* COMFORTABLE ▷ **2** having the qualities of great comfort, beauty, and freedom made possible by being rich: *We can't afford gracious* ***living****.* • **graciously** /-li/ adv *She graciously accepted the flowers that were presented to her.* • **graciousness** /-nəs/ noun [U]

▸exclamation old-fashioned used to express surprise or to emphasize what is being said: *Gracious* ***(me)/Good gracious (me)****, I never thought he'd do that!*

grad /ɡræd/ noun [C] mainly US informal for **graduate**

gradable /ˈɡreɪ.də.bl/ adj A gradable adjective or adverb is one that can be used in the COMPARATIVE or SUPERLATIVE, or that can be QUALIFIED by words such as 'very' or 'quite'. • **gradability** /ɡreɪ.dəˈbɪl.ɪ.ti/ US /-ə.t̬i/ noun [U]

gradation /ɡrəˈdeɪ.ʃən/ US /ɡreɪ-/ noun [C or U] CHANGE ▷ **1** a gradual change, or a stage in the process of change: *The gradation* ***in/of*** *tempo in this piece of music is very subtle.* MARK ▷ **2** (one of) a set of marks showing units of measurement on a JUG, tube or instrument: *the gradations on a ruler*

G

grade /ɡreɪd/ noun; verb

▸noun [C] LEVEL ▷ **1** B2 a level of quality, size, importance, etc.: *He's suffering from some kind of* ***low****-grade (= slight) infection, which he can't seem to get rid of.* ◦ *There's some really* ***high****-grade (= high quality) musicianship on this recording.* ◦ *Bill has been* ***on*** *(US* ***at****) the same grade (= his job has been of the same level of importance, or he has had the same level of pay) for several years now.* **2** B1 a number or letter that shows how good someone's work or performance is: *Steve never studies, but he always gets good grades.* ◦ UK *Carla got a grade A in German.* SCHOOL ▷ **3** A2 US a school class or group of classes in which all the children are of a similar age or ability: *Jackie is in the sixth grade.* SLOPE ▷ **4** US for **gradient**

IDIOM **make the grade** to perform well enough to succeed in something: *Ian wanted to be an actor, but he didn't make the grade.*

▸verb [T] **1** C1 to separate people or things into different levels of quality, size, importance, etc.: *The fruit is washed and then graded* ***by*** *size.* ◦ *The books are graded according to the difficulty of the language.* **2** C1 US (UK **mark**) to give a score to a student's piece of work: *to grade work/papers*

ˈgrade ˌcrossing noun [C] US for **level crossing**

ˌgraded ˈreader noun [C] one of a series of books of increasing levels of difficulty, used for teaching people to read, or to help them learn a foreign language by reading

ˈgrade-point ˌaverage noun [C] (abbreviation **GPA**) US a number that is the average mark received for all the courses a student takes and shows how well the student is doing

-grader /-ɡreɪ.dəʳ/ US /-ɡreɪ.dɚ/ suffix US a student in the stated class level at school: *an eighth-grader*

ˈgrade ˌschool noun [C] US a school for children from the age of five to the age of ten or 14

gradient /ˈɡreɪ.di.ənt/ noun [C] (US also **grade**) how steep a slope is: *a* ***steep/gentle*** *gradient*

gradual /ˈɡræd.ju.əl/, /ˈɡrædʒ.u.əl/ adj B2 happening or changing slowly over a long period of time or distance: *There has been a gradual* ***improvement*** *in our sales figures over the last two years.* ◦ *As you go further south, you will notice a gradual* ***change*** *of climate.*

gradually /ˈɡræd.ju.li/, /ˈɡrædʒ.u.li/ adv B2 slowly over a period of time or a distance: *Gradually, she realized that he wasn't telling her the truth.* ◦ *The bank slopes gradually down to the river.*

graduate noun; verb

▸noun [C] /ˈɡrædʒ.u.ət/ **1** B2 UK a person who has a first degree from a university or college: *a Cambridge graduate ◦ Chris is a physics graduate.* → See also **postgraduate, undergraduate 2** A2 (informal **grad**) US a person who has finished their school, college, or university education: *high-school graduates ◦ a graduate **of** Yale*

▸verb /ˈɡrædʒ.u.eɪt/ **QUALIFY** ▷ **1** B2 [I] UK to complete a first university degree successfully: *Lorna graduated **from** the University of London. ◦ Tom has just graduated **with** first-class **honours in** psychology.* **2** B2 [I or T] US to complete school, college, or university correctly: *After he graduated high school, he joined the Army.* **PROGRESS** ▷ **3** [I] to move forward or improve: *She graduated **from** being a secretary **to** running her own department.*

graduated /ˈɡræd.ju.eɪ.tɪd/ US /-t̬ɪd/ **adj** divided into levels or stages: *The books that the children are using to learn to read are on a graduated **scale** of difficulty.*

ˈgraduate ˌschool noun [C] US a college or a college department where students who already have a first degree are taught

graduation /ˌɡrædʒ.uˈeɪ.ʃən/ **noun** [C or U] B1 the fact of finishing a degree or other course of study at a university or school, or the ceremony at which you are officially said to have finished: *a graduation ceremony*

Graeco- /ɡriː.kəʊ-/, /ɡrek.əʊ-/ US /ɡrek.oʊ-/ **prefix** UK spelling of **Greco-**

graffiti /ɡrəˈfiː.ti/ US /-t̬i/ **noun** [plural], **noun** [U] words or drawings, especially humorous, rude, or political, on walls, doors, etc. in public places: *The subway walls are covered in graffiti.*

graft /ɡrɑːft/ US /ɡræft/ **noun; verb**

▸noun **PIECE** ▷ **1** [C] a piece of healthy skin or bone cut from one part of a person's body and used to repair another damaged part, or a piece cut from one living plant and fixed to another plant so that it grows there: *He has had a **skin** graft on his badly burned arm.* **WORK** ▷ **2** [U] UK informal work: *I've never been afraid of **hard** graft.* **INFLUENCE** ▷ **3** [U] mainly US the act of getting money or advantage through the dishonest use of political power and influence: *The whole government was riddled with graft, bribery, and corruption.*

▸verb **ADD PIECE** ▷ **1** [T] to take and put in place a graft: *Skin was removed from her leg and grafted **on/onto** her face.* **2** [T] to join or add something new: *The management tried unsuccessfully to graft new working methods **onto** the existing ways of doing things.* **WORK** ▷ **3** [I] UK informal to work hard: *It was very sad that after spending all those years grafting (**away**), he died so soon after he retired.* • **grafter** /ˈɡrɑː.f.təʳ/ US /ˈɡræf.tɚ/ **noun** [C] UK informal a hard worker

the Grail /ˈɡreɪl/ **noun** [S] → **the holy grail**

grain /ɡreɪn/ **noun** **SEED** ▷ **1** C2 [C or U] a seed or seeds from a plant, especially a plant like a grass such as rice or WHEAT: *grains of wheat/rice ◦ Grain (= the crop from food plants like grasses) is one of the main exports of the American Midwest.* → See also **wholegrain** **SMALL PIECE** ▷ **2** C2 [C] a very small piece of a hard substance: *grains **of sand*** **3** C2 [S] a very small amount of a particular quality: *There wasn't a grain **of truth** in anything she said. ◦ Anyone with a grain of common sense would have known what to do.* **WOOD/CLOTH** ▷ **4 the grain** [S] the natural patterns of lines in the surface of wood or cloth: *to cut something **along/against** the grain* **WEIGHT** ▷ **5** [C] old-fashioned a unit of mass, equal to 0.0648 grams

IDIOM **go against the grain** C2 If something goes against the grain, you would not usually do it because it would be unusual or morally wrong: *These days it goes against the grain to show respect for authority.*

grainy /ˈɡreɪ.ni/ **adj** If photographs are grainy, they are not clear because the many black and white or coloured DOTS that make up the image can be seen.

gram (UK also **gramme**) /ɡræm/ **noun** [C] (written abbreviation **g, gm**) A2 a unit of mass equal to 0.001 kilograms

grammar /ˈɡræm.əʳ/ US /-ɚ/ **noun** **1** A2 [U] (the study or use of) the rules about how words change their form and combine with other words to make sentences **2** [C] mainly UK a book of grammar rules: *a German grammar*

grammarian /ɡrəˈmeə.ri.ən/ US /-ˈmer.i-/ **noun** [C] a person who studies grammar and usually writes books about it

ˈgrammar ˌschool noun [C] **1** in the UK, a school for children aged between eleven and 18 who are good at studying **2** in the US, a school for children aged between five and 12 or 14

grammatical /ɡrəˈmæt.ɪ.kəl/ US /-ˈmæt̬-/ **adj** C2 relating to grammar or obeying the rules of grammar: *a grammatical (= grammatically correct) sentence* • **grammatically** /-i/ **adv**

gramme /ɡræm/ **noun** [C] UK spelling of **gram**

Grammy /ˈɡræm.i/ **noun** [C] (plural **Grammys**) trademark in the US, one of a set of prizes given each year to people involved in different areas of the music industry: *She's won five Grammys.*

gramophone /ˈɡræm.ə.fəʊn/ US /-foʊn/ **noun** [C] old-fashioned for **record player**

gran /ɡræn/ **noun** [C] informal a grandmother: [as form of address] *I love you, Gran.*

granary /ˈɡræn.ər.i/ US /-ɚ-/ **noun** **1** [C] a large building for storing grain **2** [S] an area where a lot of grain is grown: *Punjab, the granary of India*

Granary /ˈɡræn.ər.i/ US /-ɚ-/ **noun** [U] UK trademark (US **ˌwholewheat ˈbread**) Granary bread contains whole seeds of WHEAT.

grand /ɡrænd/ **adj; noun**

▸adj **IMPORTANT** ▷ **1** important and large in degree: *She has all kinds of grand ideas. ◦ His job has a grand title, but he's little more than a clerk.* **SPLENDID** ▷ **2** C1 impressive and large or important: *The Palace of Versailles is very grand. ◦ They always entertain their guests **in** grand **style**.* **3** used in the name of a place or building to show that it is large or beautiful and deserves to be admired: *the Grand Hotel ◦ the Grand Canyon ◦ the Grand Canal* **EXCELLENT** ▷ **4** old-fashioned informal or Irish English excellent or enjoyable: *We had grand weather on our holiday. ◦ My grandson is a grand little chap. ◦ You've done a grand job.* • **grandness** /ˈɡrænd.nəs/ **noun** [U]

IDIOMS **grand old age** If a person or animal lives to a grand old age, they live until they are very old: *He lived to the grand old age **of** 97.* • **the grand old man of sth** humorous a man who has been involved in a particular activity for a long time and is known and respected by a lot of people: *He's been called the grand old man of cricket.*

▸noun [C] (plural **grand**) **MONEY** ▷ **1** (US **G**) £1,000 or $1,000: *John's new car cost him 20 grand!* **INSTRUMENT** ▷ **2** informal for **grand piano**

grandad (also **granddad**) /ˈɡræn.dæd/ **noun** [C] informal **1** A2 a grandfather: *My grandad was a coal* miner. ◦ [as form of address] *Do you want a cup of tea, Grandad?* **2** used rudely or humorously to address an old man: *Come on, grandad!*

grandaddy (also **granddaddy**) /ˈɡræn.dæd.i/ **noun** [C] US informal a grandfather: *I never knew my grandaddy.*

IDIOM **the grandaddy of sth** mainly US informal the biggest, most important or most powerful event or person of their type: *'Modern Times' is a classic comedy starring Charlie Chaplin, the grandaddy of comic film actors.*

grandchild /ˈɡræn.tʃaɪld/ **noun** [C] (plural **grandchildren**) A2 the child of a person's son or daughter

granddaughter /ˈɡræn.dɔː.təʳ/ US /-dɑː.t̬ɚ/ **noun** [C] A2 the daughter of a person's son or daughter

grande dame /ˌɡrɑːndˈdɑːm/ **noun** [C usually singular] a woman who is respected because of her experience and knowledge of a particular subject: *Vivienne Westwood is the grande dame **of** British fashion.*

grandee /ɡrænˈdiː/ **noun** [C] an important person, especially in a particular job or area of public life

grandeur /ˈɡræn.djəʳ/ US /-dʒɚ/ **noun** [U] the quality of being very large and special or beautiful: *the silent grandeur **of** the desert* ◦ *the grandeur **of** Wagner's music*

grandfather /ˈɡræn.fɑː.ðəʳ/ US /-ðɚ/ **noun** [C] (informal **grandpa**, **grandad**) A2 the father of a person's mother or father: *Her grandfather on her mother's side was Italian.* ◦ [as form of address] formal or old-fashioned *Let me help you, Grandfather.*

ˈgrandfather ˌclock **noun** [C] a tall clock in a wooden case which stands on the floor

grandiloquent /ɡrænˈdɪl.ə.kwənt/ **adj** formal mainly disapproving describes a style or a way of using language that is complicated in order to attract admiration and attention, especially in order to make someone or something seem important: *Her speech was full of grandiloquent language, but it contained no new ideas.* • **grandiloquence** /-kwəns/ **noun** [U] • **grandiloquently** /-li/ **adv**

grandiose /ˈɡræn.di.əʊs/ US /-oʊs/ **adj** disapproving larger and containing more detail than necessary, or intended to seem important or great: *grandiose **plans/schemes/ideas** for making money*

ˌgrand ˈjury **noun** [C] in the US, a group of people who decide if a person who has been charged with a crime should be given a trial in a law court

grandly /ˈɡrænd.li/ **adv** IMPORTANTLY ▷ **1** in a way suggesting that something or someone has great importance ATTRACTING ADMIRATION ▷ **2** in a way that attracts admiration and attention: *Their house is very grandly furnished.*

grandma /ˈɡræn.mɑː/, /ˈɡræm-/ **noun** [C] informal A2 a grandmother: *I'm going to visit my grandma on Sunday.* ◦ [as form of address] *I love you, Grandma.*

grandmaster /ˈɡrændˌmɑː.stəʳ/ US /-ˌmæs.tɚ/ **noun** [C] (written abbreviation **GM**) (the rank of) a person who plays the game of CHESS with the highest level of skill

grandmother /ˈɡræn.mʌð.əʳ/, /ˈɡræm-/ US /-ɚ/ **noun** [C] (informal **grandma**, **granny**, **gran**) A2 the mother of a person's father or mother: *Both my grandmothers were from Scotland.* ◦ [as form of address] formal or old-fashioned *Sit down here, Grandmother, and rest.*

IDIOM **teach your grandmother to suck eggs** UK disapproving to give advice to someone about a subject that they already know more about than you

ˌgrand ˈopera **noun** [U] a type of serious OPERA

grandpa /ˈɡræn.pɑː/, /ˈɡræm-/ **noun** [C] informal A2 a grandfather: [as form of address] *I love you, Grandpa.*

grandparent /ˈɡræn.peə.rənt/ US /-per.ənt/ **noun** [C] A2 the father or mother of a person's father or mother

ˌgrand piˈano **noun** [C] (informal **grand**) a large piano that has horizontal strings in a case supported on three legs

grand prix /ˌɡrɑ̃ːˈpriː/ US /ˌɡrɑːn-/ **noun** [C] (plural **grands prix**) one of a series of important international races for very fast and powerful cars: *the Italian Grand Prix*

ˌgrand ˈslam **noun** WINNING EVERYTHING ▷ **1** [C usually singular] an occasion when someone wins all of a set of important sports competitions CARDS ▷ **2** [C usually singular] an occasion when someone wins all the cards in a card game, especially BRIDGE BASEBALL ▷ **3** [C] in baseball, the hitting of a HOME RUN with runners at all three BASES, so that four points are scored

grandson /ˈɡræn.sʌn/ **noun** [C] A2 the son of a person's son or daughter

grandstand /ˈɡræn.stænd/ **noun** [C] a set of seats arranged in rising rows, sometimes covered by a roof, from which people can easily watch sports or other events

IDIOM **have a grandstand view** informal to be in a position where you can see something very well: *From our hotel room window, we had a grandstand view **of** the parade.*

grandstanding /ˈɡrænˌstæn.dɪŋ/ **noun** [U] US informal acting or speaking in a way intended to attract the good opinion of other people who are watching

ˌgrand ˈtotal **noun** [C] the complete number after everything has been added up: *The school bazaar raised a/the grand total of £550.*

ˌgrand ˈtour **noun** [C] **1** (also **Grand Tour**) a visit to the most important countries and cities of Europe which rich young people made in the past as part of their education **2** often humorous an occasion when someone shows you round a house or other building: *Let me give you a grand tour **of** the house.*

grange /ɡreɪndʒ/ **noun** [C] **1** a large house in the countryside with farm buildings connected to it: *Chiltern Grange* **2** US for **farm**

granita /ɡrəˈniː.tə/ US /-t̬ə/ **noun** [C or U] an Italian sweet dish made from crushed ice and sugar mixed with fruit, coffee, or nuts

granite /ˈɡræn.ɪt/ **noun** [U] a very hard, grey, pink, or black rock, used for building

granny /ˈɡræn.i/ **noun; adj**

▸**noun** [C] (also **grannie**) informal **1** A2 a grandmother: *Your granny is going to look after you today.* ◦ [as form of address] *Granny, can I have a drink?* **2** an old woman: *There were a few grannies sitting on the bench chatting.*

▸**adj** (also **grannie**) UK informal used of something that you wear, to mean having a style like those worn by old women: *granny glasses/shoes*

ˈgranny ˌflat **noun** [C] UK a set of rooms, often connected to or part of a relation's house, in which an old person lives

ˈgranny ˌknot **noun** [C] a type of simple knot that can be easily unfastened

granola /ɡrəˈnəʊ.lə/ US /-ˈnoʊ-/ **noun** [U] US a food made of baked grains, nuts, and dried fruit, usually eaten in the morning: *Granola is a lot like muesli, only crunchier.*

grant /ɡrɑːnt/ US /ɡrænt/ **noun; verb**

▸**noun** [C] B1 an amount of money given especially by the government to a person or organization for a special purpose: *a student/research grant* ◦ *a local* *authority/government grant* ◦ [+ to infinitive] *They **gave/awarded** her a grant **to** study abroad for one year.*

▸verb **GIVE** ▷ **1** (B2) [T] to give or allow someone something, usually in an official way: [+ two objects] *They granted her an entry visa.* ◦ *He was granted asylum.* ◦ formal *She granted their request/wish.* **ACCEPT** ▷ **2** [T + (that)] to accept that something is true, often before expressing an opposite opinion: *I grant **that** it must have been upsetting but even so I think she made a bit of a fuss.* ◦ ***I grant you*** *(= it is true that), it's a difficult situation but I feel sure he could have handled it more sensitively.* **3 take sth for granted** (B2) to believe something to be the truth without even thinking about it: *I didn't realize that Melanie hadn't been to college – I suppose I just took it for granted.* **4 take sth or sb for granted** (B2) If you take situations or people for granted, you do not realize or show that you are grateful for how much you get from them. • **granted** /ˈɡrɑːn.tɪd/ (US) /ˈɡræn.t̬ɪd/ **conjunction** used to mean 'if you accept' something: *Granted **(that)** the story's true, what are you going to do about it?*

granular /ˈɡræn.jʊ.ləʳ/ (US) /-jə.lɚ/ **adj** **TEXTURE** ▷ **1** made of, or seeming like, granules: *a granular texture* **DETAILS** ▷ **2** including small details: *The analysis needs to be more granular.*

granularity /ˌɡræn.jəˈlær.ə.ti/ (US) /-jəˈler.ə.t̬i/ **noun** [U] the quality of including a lot of small details: *The marketing analysis offers a high level of granularity.*

granulated /ˈɡræn.jʊ.leɪ.tɪd/ (US) /-t̬ɪd/ **adj** in small grains: *granulated **sugar***

granule /ˈɡræn.juːl/ **noun** [C] a small piece like a grain of something: *coffee granules*

grape /ɡreɪp/ **noun** **1** (A2) [C] a small round purple or pale green fruit that you can eat or make into wine: *black/white/red/green grapes* ◦ *a bunch of grapes* ◦ *seedless grapes* ◦ *grape juice* **2 the grape** [S] humorous wine

grapefruit /ˈɡreɪp.fruːt/ **noun** [C] (plural **grapefruit** or **grapefruits**) a fruit that is like a large orange, but has a yellow skin and tastes less sweet

grapevine /ˈɡreɪp.vaɪn/ **noun** [C] (also **vine**) a type of climbing plant on which grapes grow

IDIOM **hear (sth) on/through the grapevine** to hear news from someone who heard the news from someone else: *I heard on the grapevine **that** he was leaving – is it true?*

graph /ɡrɑːf/, /ɡræf/ **noun** [C] (B2) a picture which shows how two sets of information or VARIABLES (= amounts that can change) are related, usually by lines or curves: *This graph shows how crime has varied in relationship to unemployment over the last 20 years.*

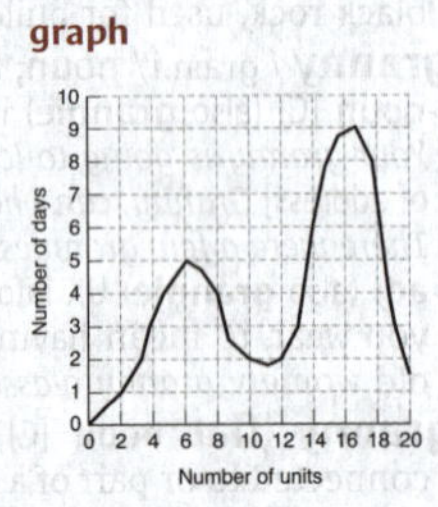

graphic /ˈɡræf.ɪk/ **adj** **CLEAR** ▷ **1** very clear and powerful: *a graphic description/account* ◦ *He insisted on describing his operation **in** graphic **detail** while we were eating lunch.* **DRAWING** ▷ **2** [before noun] related to drawing or printing: *a graphic artist* **GRAPH** ▷ **3** (mainly UK **graphical**) relating to, using, or consisting of a graph or graphs

graphically /ˈɡræf.ɪ.kəl.i/ **adv** **CLEARLY** ▷ **1** in a very clear and powerful way: *The incident graphically illustrates just how dangerous the situation in the war zone has become.* **IN PICTURES** ▷ **2** in a way that uses, consists of, or relates to graphs, or to drawing or printing: *Include a diagram that represents this data graphically.*

ˌgraphical ˌuser ˈinterface **noun** [C] (abbreviation **GUI**) a way of arranging information on a computer screen that is easy to understand and use because it uses ICONS (= pictures), MENUS, and a mouse rather than only text

ˌgraphic deˈsign **noun** [U] the art of designing pictures and text for books, magazines, advertising, etc. • **ˌgraphic deˈsigner** **noun** [C] someone who works in graphic design

ˌgraphic ˈnovel **noun** [C] a book containing a long story told mostly in pictures but with some writing: *Art Spiegelman's 'Maus' is a very well-known graphic novel.*

graphics /ˈɡræf.ɪks/ **noun** [plural] (B1) images and designs used in books, magazines, etc.: ***computer** graphics*

ˈgraphics ˌcard **noun** [C] (also **ˈvideo ˌcard**) a CIRCUIT BOARD (= small piece of electronic equipment) inside a computer that allows it to receive and show pictures and video

graphite /ˈɡræf.aɪt/ **noun** [U] a soft, dark grey form of carbon, used in the middle of pencils, as a LUBRICANT in machines, and in some NUCLEAR REACTORS

graphology /ɡrəˈfɒl.ə.dʒi/ (US) /-ˈfɑː.lə-/ **noun** [U] the study of the way people write letters and words, especially in order to discover things about their characters • **graphologist** /-dʒɪst/ **noun** [C]

ˈgraph ˌpaper **noun** [U] specialized a type of paper covered with small squares, for drawing graphs on

grapnel /ˈɡræp.nəl/ **noun** [C] (also **ˈgrappling ˌiron**, **ˈgrappling ˌhook**) a device that consists of several HOOKS (= curved devices) on the end of a rope, used especially in the past on ships

grappa /ˈɡræp.ə/ (US) /ˈɡrɑː.pə/ **noun** [U] a type of BRANDY (= strong alcoholic drink) made from GRAPES

grapple /ˈɡræp.l̩/ **verb** [I] to fight, especially in order to win something: *The children grappled **for** the ball.*

PHRASAL VERBS **grapple with sb** to hold onto someone and fight with them: *Two officers grappled with the gunman.* • **grapple with sth** to try to deal with or understand a difficult problem or subject: *Today, many Americans are still grappling with the issue of race.*

ˈgrappling ˌiron/ˌhook **noun** [C] a **grapnel**

grasp /ɡrɑːsp/ (US) /ɡræsp/ **verb; noun**

▸verb [T] **TAKE** ▷ **1** (C1) to quickly take something in your hand(s) and hold it firmly: *Rosie suddenly grasped my hand.* **2** If you grasp an opportunity, you take it eagerly. **UNDERSTAND** ▷ **3** (C1) to understand something, especially something difficult: *I think I managed to grasp the main points of the lecture.* ◦ *The government has acknowledged that homelessness is a problem but it has failed to grasp the scale of the problem.*

IDIOM **grasp the nettle** UK (C2) to force yourself to be brave and do something that is difficult or unpleasant: *You've been putting off making that phone call for days – I think it's about time you grasped the nettle!*

PHRASAL VERB **grasp at sth** **OPPORTUNITY** ▷ **1** to try to take an opportunity: *Certainly if the job were offered me I'd grasp at the chance.* **OBJECT** ▷ **2** (C2) to try to hold or touch something: *She grasped at his shirt as he ran past.*

▸noun **HOLD** ▷ **1** (C2) [S] the act of holding onto someone or something: *He shook my hand with a* *very firm grasp.* **2** [C2] [U] the ability to get, achieve, or keep something: *The presidency at last looked* ***within*** *her grasp (= it looked possible that she might become president).* ◦ *Why is success always* ***beyond*** *my grasp (= impossible to get)?* ◦ *The gold medal* ***slipped from*** *his grasp (= he was unable to get it) in the last moments of the race.* ◦ *I sometimes think that he's* ***losing*** *his grasp* ***on*** *reality (= his ability to judge what is real and what is not).* **UNDERSTANDING** ▷ **3** [C2] [S or U] understanding: *I'm afraid my grasp of economics is rather limited.*

grasping /ˈɡrɑː.spɪŋ/ (US) /ˈɡræs.pɪŋ/ **adj** disapproving (of people) always trying to get and keep more of something, especially money: *a grasping, greedy man*

grass /ɡrɑːs/ (US) /ɡræs/ **noun; verb**

▸**noun** **PLANT** ▷ **1** [A1] [U or C] a low, green plant that grows naturally over a lot of the Earth's surface, having groups of very thin leaves that grow close together in large numbers: *a blade of grass* ◦ ***cut*** *the grass* ◦ *a vase of dried flowers and grasses (= different types of grass)* **2** [U] slang **cannabis** **PERSON** ▷ **3** [C] UK slang a person, usually a criminal, who tells the police about other criminals' activities → See also **supergrass**

IDIOMS **the grass is always greener on the other side (of the fence)** saying something that you say which means that other people always seem to be in a better situation than you, although they may not be • **put sb out to grass** informal to make someone stop work permanently because they are too old

▸**verb**

PHRASAL VERBS **grass on sb** UK slang If a person grasses on someone else, they tell the police or someone in authority about something bad that that person has done: *Dan grassed on them* ***to*** *the local police.* • **grass sth over** to grow grass on an area of land

grasshopper /ˈɡrɑːsˌhɒp.əʳ/ (US) /ˈɡræsˌhɑː.pɚ/ noun [C] a plant-eating insect with long back legs that can jump very high and makes a sharp high noise using its back legs or wings

grasshopper

grassland /ˈɡrɑːs.lænd/, /-lənd/ (US) /ˈɡræs-/ **noun** [C or U] a large area of land covered with grass: *the grasslands of North America*

grassroots /ˈɡrɑːs.ruːts/ (US) /ˈɡræs-/ **noun; adj**

▸**noun** [plural] **the grassroots** the ordinary people in a society or an organization, especially a political party: *The feeling among the grassroots of the Party is that the leaders are not radical enough.*

▸**adj** [before noun] involving the ordinary people in a society or an organization: *grassroots support* ◦ *a grassroots movement/campaign*

ˌgrass ˈskirt noun [C] a skirt made of long pieces of real or artificial grass, traditionally worn by dancers in the Pacific islands

ˌgrass ˈwidow noun [C] humorous a woman who spends a lot of time apart from her partner, often because he or she is working in a different place

grassy /ˈɡrɑː.si/ (US) /ˈɡræs.i/ **adj** covered with grass: *a grassy slope/hillside*

grate /ɡreɪt/ **verb; noun**

▸**verb** **COOKING** ▷ **1** [T] to rub food against a grater in order to cut it into a lot of small pieces: *grated cheese* **RUB TOGETHER** ▷ **2** [I] When two hard objects grate, they rub together, sometimes making a sharp unpleasant sound. **ANNOY** ▷ **3** [I] When a noise or behaviour grates, it annoys you: *After a while her voice really started to grate* ***on*** *me.* ◦ *It's the way she's always talking about herself – it just grates* ***on*** *me.*

▸**noun** [C] a metal structure which holds coal or wood in a FIREPLACE

grateful /ˈɡreɪt.fəl/ **adj** [B1] showing or expressing thanks, especially to another person: *I'm so grateful* ***(to*** *you)* ***for*** *all that you've done.* ◦ *If you could get that report finished by Thursday I'd be very grateful.* ◦ *After the earthquake we felt grateful* ***to*** *be alive.* ◦ *I'm just grateful* ***that*** *I'm not still working for him.* ◦ formal *I would be* ***most*** *grateful if you would send me the book immediately.* → Opposite **ungrateful** • **gratefully** /-i/ **adv** *She smiled at me gratefully.*

> **!** Common mistake: **grateful**
>
> **Warning:** Check your spelling!
> **Grateful** is one of the 50 words most often spelled wrongly by learners. **Remember**: the correct spelling has 'ate', and not 'eat'.

> **+** Other ways of saying **grateful**
>
> The adjective **appreciative** is sometimes used to show that someone is grateful, or you can use the verb **appreciate** to express the same idea:
> *I'm really* ***appreciative*** *of all the help you've given me.*
> *I really* ***appreciate*** *all the help you've given me.*
> The expression **be glad of** is another alternative:
> *We* ***were*** *very* ***glad of*** *some extra help.*
> The expression **be indebted to** is a more formal way of saying that someone is very grateful for something:
> ***I'm indebted to*** *my parents for all their love and support.*
> The adjectives **thankful** or **relieved** are often used when a person is grateful that something unpleasant did not happen:
> *I'm just* ***thankful*** *that she's safe and well.*
> If a person is grateful that someone has done something kind, the adjective **touched** is sometimes used:
> *She was really* ***touched*** *that he remembered her birthday.*

grater /ˈɡreɪ.təʳ/ (US) /-t̬ɚ/ **noun** [C] a metal device with holes surrounded by sharp edges used to cut food into small pieces

gratify /ˈɡræt.ɪ.faɪ/ (US) /ˈɡræt̬.ə-/ **verb** [T] to please someone, or to satisfy a wish or need: *We were gratified* ***by*** *the response to our appeal.* ◦ [+ to infinitive] *He was gratified* ***to*** *see how well his students had done.* • **gratification** /ˌɡræt.ɪ.fɪˈkeɪ.ʃən/ (US) /ˌɡræt̬.ə-/ **noun** [U] *sexual gratification* ◦ *Some people expect* ***instant*** *gratification (= to get what they want immediately).*

gratifying /ˈɡræt.ɪ.faɪ.ɪŋ/ (US) /ˈɡræt̬-/ **adj** pleasing and satisfying: [+ to infinitive] *It must be very gratifying* ***to*** *see all your children grown up and happy.* • **gratifyingly** /-li/ **adv** *The success rate in the exam was gratifyingly high.*

gratin /ˈɡræt.æ̃/ (US) /ˈɡrɑː.t̬ən/ **noun** [C or U], **adj** [after noun] in cooking, a dish that has a thin layer of cheese and often BREADCRUMBS on top: *aubergine and tomato gratin*

grating /ˈɡreɪ.tɪŋ/ (US) /-t̬ɪŋ/ **adj; noun**

▸**adj** describes a sound that is unpleasant and annoying

▸**noun** [C] a structure made of metal bars that covers a hole, especially in the ground over a DRAIN

G

gratis /ˈgræ.tɪs/ **adv** [after verb], **adj** free: *I'll give it to you, gratis!*

gratitude /ˈgræt.ɪ.tjuːd/ (US) /ˈgræt̬.ə.tuːd/ **noun** [U] (also **gratefulness**) the feeling or quality of being grateful: *deep/eternal gratitude* ◦ *She sent them a present to* ***show/express*** *her gratitude.* ◦ *Take this* ***as a token of*** *my gratitude for all your help.*

gratuitous /grəˈtjuː.ɪ.təs/ (US) /-ˈtuː.ə.t̬əs/ **adj** disapproving (of something such as bad behaviour) not necessary, or with no cause: *A lot of viewers complained that there was too much gratuitous* ***sex*** *and* ***violence*** *in the film.* • **gratuitously** /-li/ **adv** *gratuitously violent* • **gratuitousness** /-nəs/ **noun** [U]

gratuity /grəˈtjuː.ə.ti/ (US) /-ˈtuː.ə.t̬i/ **noun** [C] an amount of money given as a reward for a service: formal *The guides sometimes receive gratuities from the tourists which supplement their salaries.* ◦ UK *After he was disabled in the accident, he left the army with a one-off gratuity of £5,000.*

G

gravadlax /ˈgræv.əd.læks/ (US) /ˈgrɑː.vəd.lɑːks/ **noun** [U] thin pieces of SALMON (= a type of fish) that have been dried with salt and herbs

grave /greɪv/ **noun**; **adj**

▸**noun** [C] (B1) a place in the ground where a dead person is buried: *a mass grave* ◦ *an unmarked grave* ◦ *a grave digger* ◦ *He visits his mother's grave every Sunday.*

IDIOMS **beyond the grave** after death: *Do you think there's life beyond the grave?* • **turn in your grave** UK (US **turn over/spin in your grave**) If you say that a dead person would turn in their grave, you mean that they would be very angry or upset about something if they knew about it: *She'd turn in her grave if she knew what he was spending his inheritance on.*

▸**adj** seriously bad: *a grave situation* • **gravely** /ˈgreɪv.li/ **adv** *gravely ill*

grave (accent) /ˌgrɑːv ˈæks^ə^nt/ **noun** [C] a symbol used over a letter in some languages, for example the letter 'è' in French, to show that it is pronounced in a particular way

gravel /ˈgræv.^ə^l/ **noun** [U] small rounded stones, often mixed with sand: *a gravel path*

gravelled (US usually **graveled**) /ˈgræv.^ə^ld/ **adj** covered with gravel: *a gravelled driveway*

gravelly /ˈgræv.^ə^l.i/ **adj** VOICE ▷ **1** If a voice, especially a man's voice, is gravelly, it is low and rough. SUBSTANCE ▷ **2** like or containing gravel: *gravelly soil*

ˈgravel ˌpit **noun** [C] a place where gravel is dug out of the ground

graven image /ˌgreɪ.v^ə^nˈɪm.ɪdʒ/ **noun** [C] disapproving an object made especially from wood, stone, etc. and used for religious worship

graveside /ˈgreɪv.saɪd/ **noun** [C usually singular] the area next to a GRAVE: *He made a short speech* ***at the*** *graveside, then the body was finally buried.*

gravestone /ˈgreɪv.stəʊn/ (US) /-stoʊn/ **noun** [C] a stone that shows where a dead person is buried, usually with the name and the years of birth and death of that person written on it → Compare **headstone**

graveyard /ˈgreɪv.jɑːd/ (US) /-jɑːrd/ **noun** [C] a place, often next to a church where dead people are buried

ˈgraveyard ˌshift **noun** [C] informal a period of work, for example in a factory, which begins late at night and ends early in the morning: *to work* ***the*** *graveyard shift*

gravitas /ˈgræv.ɪ.tæs/ **noun** [U] formal seriousness and importance of manner, causing feelings of respect and trust in others: *He's an effective enough politician but somehow he lacks the statesmanlike gravitas of a world leader.*

gravitate /ˈgræv.ɪ.teɪt/ **verb**

PHRASAL VERB **gravitate towards/to sth/sb** UK (US **gravitate toward sth/sb**) to be attracted by or to move in the direction of something or someone: *Susie always gravitates towards the older children in her playgroup.*

gravitation /ˌgræv.ɪˈteɪ.ʃ^ə^n/ **noun** FORCE ▷ **1** [U] in science, the force that attracts all objects towards one another: *Particles are attracted to each other by gravitation.* MOVEMENT TOWARDS ▷ **2** [S or U] an occasion when someone or something moves or is attracted in the direction of a particular thing or person: *The gravitation of country people* ***to/towards*** *the capital began in the 1920s.* • **gravitational** /-^ə^l/ **adj** relating to gravity or gravitation: *gravitational forces*

gravity /ˈgræv.ɪ.ti/ (US) /-ə.t̬i/ **noun** [U] FORCE ▷ **1** the force which attracts objects towards one another, especially the force that makes things fall to the ground: *the laws of gravity* SERIOUS ▷ **2** seriousness: *I don't think you understand the gravity of the situation.*

gravy /ˈgreɪ.vi/ **noun** [U] a sauce made with meat juices and flour, served with meat and vegetables

ˈgravy ˌboat **noun** [C] a long low container with a handle, used for serving gravy at the table

ˈgravy ˌtrain **noun** [C usually singular] informal a way of making money quickly, easily, and often dishonestly

gray /greɪ/ **adj** US spelling of grey

graze /greɪz/ **verb**; **noun**

▸**verb** SURFACE ▷ **1** [T] to break the surface of the skin by rubbing against something rough: *He fell down and grazed his* ***knee.*** ◦ *He was lucky, the bullet just grazed his leg.* **2** [T] If an object grazes something, it touches its surface lightly when it passes it: *The aircraft's landing gear grazed the treetops as it landed.* FOOD ▷ **3** [I or T] to (cause animals to) eat grass: *The cows were grazing.* ◦ *The farmer grazes cattle on this land in the summer months.* **4** [I] informal to eat small amounts of food many times during the day instead of sitting down to eat meals at particular times: *No dinner for me, thanks – I've been grazing all day.*

▸**noun** [C] an injury on the surface of your skin caused by rubbing it against something rough: *Her legs were covered with cuts and grazes.*

ˈgrazing (ˌland) **noun** [U] land where farm animals feed on grass

grease /griːs/ **noun**; **verb**

▸**noun** [U] animal or vegetable fat that is soft after melting, or more generally, any thick oil-like substance: *The dinner plates were thick with grease.* ◦ *You'll have to put some grease on those ball bearings.*

▸**verb** [T] to put fat or oil on something: *Grease the tins well before adding the cake mixture.*

IDIOMS **grease sb's palm** disapproving to secretly give someone money in order to persuade them to do something for you • **like greased lightning** very fast: *As soon as I mentioned work, he was out of the door like greased lightning!*

ˈgrease ˌmonkey **noun** [C] old-fashioned informal someone whose job is repairing car or aircraft engines

greasepaint /ˈgriːs.peɪnt/ **noun** [U] make-up as used by actors in the theatre

greaseproof paper /ˌgriːs.pruːfˈpeɪ.pə^r^/ (US) /-pɚ/ **noun** [U] UK paper which does not allow oil through, used especially in cooking: *Line the tins with greaseproof paper.*

greasy /ˈgriː.si/ **adj** covered with or full of fat or oil: *greasy food/dishes/skin/hair* • **greasiness** /-nəs/ **noun** [U]

ˌgreasy ˈspoon **noun** [C usually singular] slang a small, cheap restaurant, especially one which sells a lot of fried food

great /greɪt/ **adj; adv, adj; noun**
▸**adj** BIG ▷ **1** A2 large in amount, size or degree: *an enormous great hole* ◦ *A great crowd had gathered outside the president's palace.* ◦ *The improvement in water standards over the last 50 years has been very great.* ◦ *A great many people would agree.* ◦ ***The** great **majority of** (= almost all) people would agree.* ◦ formal *It gives us great **pleasure** to announce the engagement of our daughter Maria.* ◦ formal *It is with great **sorrow** that I inform you of the death of our director.* ◦ *I have great **sympathy** for you.* ◦ *I spent a great **deal of** time there.* **2** [before noun] used in names, especially to mean large or important: *a Great Dane (= large type of dog)* ◦ *Catherine the Great* ◦ *the Great Wall of China* ◦ *the Great Bear (= group of stars)* FAMOUS ▷ **3** B2 approving famous, powerful, or important as one of a particular type: *a great politician/leader/artist/man/woman* ◦ *This is one of Rembrandt's greatest paintings.* EXTREME ▷ **4** B1 extreme: *great success/difficulty* GOOD ▷ **5** A1 informal very good: *a great idea* ◦ *We had a great time last night at the party.* ◦ ***It's** great **to** see you after all this time!* ◦ *'I'll lend you the car if you like.' 'Great! Thanks a lot!'* ◦ *'What's your new teacher like?' 'Oh, he's great.'* ◦ *'How are you feeling now?' 'Great.'* **6** informal used to mean that something is very bad: *Oh great! That's all I need – more bills!* • **greatness** /ˈgreɪt.nəs/ **noun** [U] B2 skill and importance: *Her greatness as a writer is unquestioned.*

IDIOMS **be a great one for sth** to enjoy or do something a lot: *He's a great one for getting other people to do his work for him, old Peter!* • **go great guns** old-fashioned informal to go fast or successfully: *For the first 400 metres he was going great guns, but then he fell and that lost him the race.* • **great minds think alike** humorous said to someone just after you have discovered that they have had the same idea as you • **no great shakes** informal not very good: *I'm afraid I am no great shakes **as** a cook/**at** cooking!*

▸**adv** [before noun], **adj** informal B2 used to emphasize the meaning of another word: *a great big spider* ◦ *a great long queue* ◦ *You great idiot!*
▸**noun** [C] a famous person in a particular area of activity: *former tennis great Arthur Ashe* ◦ *Woody Allen, one of the **all-time** greats of the cinema*

IDIOM **the great and the good** UK important people: *The great and the good are calling on the government to support the arts.*

great- /greɪt-/ **prefix** used with a word for a family member to mean one GENERATION away from that member: *your great-grandmother (= the grandmother of one of your parents)* ◦ *your great-grandson (= the grandson of your child)*

ˌGreat ˈBritain **noun** England, Scotland, and Wales

greatcoat /ˈgreɪt.kəʊt/ US /-koʊt/ **noun** [C] a long, heavy, warm coat, worn especially by soldiers over their uniform

Greater /ˈgreɪ.təʳ/ US /-t̬ɚ/ **adj** [before noun] used before names of some cities to refer to both the city itself and the area around it: *Greater Manchester*

greatly /ˈgreɪt.li/ **adv** B2 very much, used especially to show how much you feel or experience something: *I greatly regret not having told the truth.* ◦ *Her piano playing has greatly improved/has improved greatly.*

the ˌGreat ˈWar **noun** [S] UK **the First World War**

grebe /griːb/ **noun** [C] any of a family of grey or brown water birds which swim on or under the water

Grecian /ˈgriː.ʃən/ **adj** (especially of building styles or a person's appearance) beautiful and simple, in the style of Ancient Greece: *a Grecian column*

Greco- (also **Graeco-**) /griː.kəʊ-/, /grek.əʊ-/ US /grek.oʊ-/ **prefix** of or connected with ancient Greece: *splendid Greco-Roman ruins*

greed /griːd/ **noun** [U] C1 a very strong wish to continuously get more of something, especially food or money: *I don't know why I'm eating more – it's not hunger, it's just greed!* ◦ *He was unsympathetic with many house sellers, complaining that they were motivated by greed.*

greedy /ˈgriː.di/ **adj** B2 wanting a lot more food, money, etc. than you need: *greedy, selfish people* ◦ *He's greedy **for** power/success.* • **greedily** /-dɪ.li/ **adv** *He ate the bread greedily.* • **greediness** /-nəs/ **noun** [U]

ˈgreedy guts **noun** [S] UK informal or child's word someone who eats too much

Greek /griːk/ **adj; noun**
▸**adj** from, belonging to, or relating to Greece: *Greek history/culture* ◦ *Greek food* → See table of **Geographical names**

IDIOM **it's all Greek to me.** a way of saying that you do not understand something that is said or written

▸**noun 1** [U] the language of Greece: *modern/ancient Greek* **2** [C] a person from Greece → See also **Grecian**

ˌGreek ˈcross **noun** [C] a cross with four arms that are all the same length

green /griːn/ **adj; noun**
▸**adj** COLOUR ▷ **1** A1 of a colour between blue and yellow; of the colour of grass: *green vegetables* POLITICAL ▷ **2** B2 relating to the protection of the environment: *green politics/issues* ◦ *a green campaigner/activist* ◦ *the Green **Party*** **3 go green** to do more to protect nature and the environment: *The Chancellor proposed a crackdown on car and plane emissions, and the introduction of tax incentives to go green.* PLANTS ▷ **4** B1 covered with grass, trees, and other plants: *the green hills of Ireland* NOT READY ▷ **5** (especially of fruit) not ready to eat, or (of wood) not dry enough to use: *green bananas/tomatoes* NOT EXPERIENCED ▷ **6** not experienced or trained: *I was very green when I started working there.* • **greenness** /ˈgriːn.nəs/ **noun** [U] the quality of being green: *What first struck her when she arrived in England was the greenness of the countryside.*

IDIOMS **be green with envy** C2 to be very unhappy because someone has something that you want: *Ben's heading off to Spain for the week, and I'm green with envy.* • **give the green light to sth** to give permission for someone to do something or for something to happen: *The council has given the green light to the new shopping development.* • **go/turn green** to look pale and ill as if you are going to vomit

▸**noun** COLOUR ▷ **1** A2 [C or U] the colour of grass; a colour between blue and yellow: *light/pale green* ◦ *dark/bottle green* GRASS ▷ **2** [C] an area planted with grass, especially for use by the public: *Children were playing on the **village** green.* **3** [C] used as a part of a name: *Sheep's Green* **4** [C] a flat area of grass surrounding the hole on a GOLF COURSE FOOD ▷ **5 greens** [plural] the leaves of green vegetables such

G

as SPINACH or CABBAGE when eaten as food

Green /griːn/ noun [C] a member of the Green Party: *He used to be a Liberal, but now he's a Green.*

ˈgreen ˌaudit noun [C] an official examination of the effects a company or other organization has on the environment, especially the damage that it causes: *Management refused to **carry out/conduct** a green audit.*

greenback /ˈgriːn.bæk/ noun [C] US old-fashioned slang a US dollar

ˌgreen ˈbean noun [C] (UK also **ˌFrench ˈbean**) a type of long, green bean that you can eat

ˈgreen ˌbelt noun [C usually singular] a strip of countryside round a city or town where building is not allowed

ˌgreen ˈcard noun [C] **WORK** ▷ **1** a document giving someone who is not a US CITIZEN permission to live and work in the US **CAR** ▷ **2** UK a document which INSURES your car against accidents (= protects you financially if you have a car accident) when travelling in other countries

greenery /ˈgriː.nᵊr.i/ noun [U] green plants or branches, especially when cut and used as decoration

greenfield /ˈgriːn.fiːld/ adj [before noun] UK describes land that has not yet been built on, or buildings built on land that had never been used before for building: *a greenfield site*

greenfinch /ˈgriːn.fɪntʃ/ noun [C] a medium-sized greenish bird, common in Europe

ˌgreen ˈfingers noun [plural] UK (US **ˌgreen ˈthumb**) the ability to make plants grow • **ˌgreen-ˈfingered** adj (US **ˌgreen-ˈthumbed**)

greenfly /ˈgriːn.flaɪ/ noun [C] (plural **greenfly** or **greenflies**) a very small pale green insect that often harms plants

greengage /ˈgriːŋ.geɪdʒ/ noun [C] a small, greenish-yellow PLUM (= a soft fruit)

greengrocer /ˈgriːŋ.grəʊ.səʳ/ ⓤⓢ /-groʊ.sɚ/ noun [C] mainly UK **1** a person who owns or works in a shop that sells fresh vegetables and fruit **2** (also **greengrocer's**) a shop in which fresh vegetables and fruit are sold

greenhorn /ˈgriːn.hɔːn/ ⓤⓢ /-hɔːrn/ noun [C] a person who is not experienced

greenhouse /ˈgriːn.haʊs/ noun [C] a building with a roof and sides made of glass, used for growing plants that need warmth and protection

greenhouse

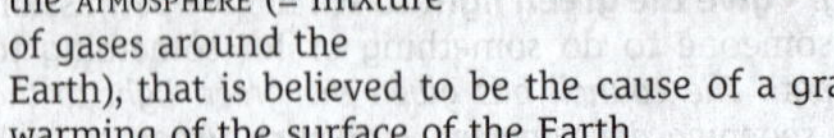

the ˈgreenhouse efˌfect noun [S] an increase in the amount of CARBON DIOXIDE and other gases in the ATMOSPHERE (= mixture of gases around the Earth), that is believed to be the cause of a gradual warming of the surface of the Earth

ˌgreenhouse ˈgas noun [C] a gas which causes the greenhouse effect, especially CARBON DIOXIDE

greening /ˈgriː.nɪŋ/ noun [S] **POLITICS** ▷ **1** the process of becoming more active about protecting the environment: *The next ten years, he predicted, would see **the** greening **of** America (= Americans starting to take more care of the environment).* **PLANTS** ▷ **2** the process of making somewhere greener by planting grass, trees, and plants there: *Concern about the ugly effects of industrialization has led to **the** greening **of** many of our cities.*

greenish /ˈgriː.nɪʃ/ adj slightly green in colour: *a slightly greenish complexion* ◦ *greenish-blue eyes*

ˌgreen ˈonion noun [C] US for **spring onion**

ˌGreen ˈPaper noun [C] in various countries, a government document that anyone who is interested can study and make suggestions about, especially before a law is changed or a new law is made → Compare **White Paper**

ˌgreen ˈpepper noun [C] a shiny green vegetable with a hollow centre which can be eaten uncooked or cooked

ˈgreen ˌroom noun [C] a room, for example in a theatre, where performers can relax

ˌgreen ˈsalad noun [C or U] UK a salad which consists of LETTUCE and other uncooked green vegetables

ˌgreen ˈshoots noun [plural] (used especially in newspapers) the first signs of an improvement in an economy that is performing badly: *the green shoots of recovery*

ˌgreen ˈtea noun [U] the light-coloured tea drunk especially in China and Japan

greenwash /ˈgriːn.wɒʃ/ ⓤⓢ /-wɑːʃ/ verb [I or T] to make people believe that your company is doing more to protect the environment than it really is

Greenwich Mean Time /ˌgren.ɪtʃˈmiːn.taɪm/ noun [U] (abbreviation **GMT**) the time at Greenwich, Greater London, that world TIME ZONES are based on → See also **British Summer Time**

greet /griːt/ verb **1** (B1) [T] to welcome someone with particular words or a particular action, or to react to something in the stated way: *He greeted me at the door.* ◦ *The teacher greeted each child **with** a friendly 'Hello!'* ◦ *The unions have greeted the decision **with** delight/anger.* **2** [T often passive] If you are greeted by a sight, sound, or smell, you notice it immediately when you arrive somewhere: *As we walked into the house, we were greeted by a wonderful smell of baking.*

greeting /ˈgriː.tɪŋ/ ⓤⓢ /-t̬ɪŋ/ noun **1** (B1) [C or U] something friendly or polite that you say or do when you meet or welcome someone: *They briskly **exchanged** greetings before starting the session.* ◦ *He nodded his head **in** greeting.* **2** **greetings** [plural] a message that says you hope someone is well, happy, etc.: *birthday/Christmas greetings* ◦ formal *My father **sends** his greetings.* ◦ formal *Greetings to you, my friends and colleagues.*

ˈgreetings ˌcard noun [C] UK (US **ˈgreeting ˌcard**) a piece of thick paper folded in half with a picture on the outside and a message inside, that you write in and send or give to someone, for example at Christmas or on their birthday

gregarious /grɪˈgeə.ri.əs/ ⓤⓢ /-ˈger.i-/ adj (of people) liking to be with other people, or (especially of animals) living in groups: *Emma's a gregarious, outgoing sort of person.* → See also **sociable** • **gregariously** /-li/ adv • **gregariousness** /grɪˈgeə.ri.əs.nəs/ ⓤⓢ /-ˈger.i-/ noun [U]

the Gregorian calendar /grɪˌgɔː.ri.ənˈkæl.ɪn.dəʳ/ ⓤⓢ /-ˌgɔːr.i.ənˈkæl.ɪn.dɚ/ noun [S] the system used in many parts of the world to divide the 365 days of the year into weeks and months, and to number the years

Gregorian chant /grɪˌgɔː.ri.ənˈtʃɑːnt/ ⓤⓢ /-ˌgɔːr.i.ənˈtʃænt/ noun [C or U] a type of Christian church music for voices alone, used since the Middle Ages → Compare **plainsong**

gremlin /ˈgrem.lɪn/ noun [C] an imaginary little creature which gets inside things, especially machines, and makes them stop working: *We must have a gremlin in the engine – it isn't working properly.*

grenade /grəˈneɪd/ **noun** [C] a small bomb thrown by hand or shot from a gun: *a hand grenade*

grenadier /ˌgren.əˈdɪəʳ/ (US) /-ˈdɪr/ **noun** [C] a member of the Grenadier Guards (= a special part of the British, Canadian, or other army)

grenadine /ˈgren.ə.diːn/ **noun** [U] a sweet liquid made from the juice of the POMEGRANATE and used to colour drinks and make them sweeter

grew /gruː/ past simple of **grow**

grey /greɪ/ **adj; noun; verb**

▸**adj** (US usually **gray**) **COLOUR** ▷ **1** (A1) of the colour that is a mixture of black and white, the colour of rain clouds: *a grey sky* **2** (C2) having hair that has become grey or white, usually because of age: *He started to **go/turn** grey in his mid-forties.* **3** (B2) describes the weather when there are a lot of clouds and little light: *Night turned into morning, grey and cold.* **BORING** ▷ **4** (C1) boring and sad: *He saw a grey future stretch ahead of him.* • **greyness** (US usually **grayness**) /ˈgreɪ.nəs/ **noun** [U]

▸**noun** [C or U] (US usually **gray**) (A2) the colour that is a mixture of black and white, the colour of rain clouds: *She was dressed in grey.*

▸**verb** [I] (US usually **gray**) **HAIR** ▷ **1** If a person or their hair greys, their hair becomes grey or white, usually because of age: *I'm greying at the sides.* **GET OLDER** ▷ **2** If a group of people is greying, it contains an increasing number of older people: *Italy is greying faster than any other European country.*

ˌgrey ˈarea **noun** [C usually singular] (US usually **ˌgray ˈarea**) a situation that is not clear or where the rules are not known: *The difference between gross negligence and recklessness is a legal grey area.*

greyhound /ˈgreɪ.haʊnd/ **noun** [C] a type of dog that has a thin body and long thin legs and can run fast, especially in races

greying (US usually **graying**) /ˈgreɪ.ɪŋ/ **adj** **HAIR** ▷ **1** becoming grey or white: *He is short, with a greying beard.* **OLDER** ▷ **2** containing an increasing number of older people: *Japan's graying population will drive up medical and pension payments.*

greyish (US usually **grayish**) /ˈgreɪ.ɪʃ/ **adj** slightly grey in colour

the ˈgrey ˌmarket **noun** [S] (US usually **the ˈgray ˌmarket**) **1** an unofficial but not completely illegal system in which products are bought and sold: *The store sells designer clothes and shoes sourced from the grey market.* → Compare **black market** **2** buying and selling of a company's shares before they are available officially: *First dealings in the company's shares will start on the grey market on 27 March and formal trading begins on 2 April.* **3** people over about 50, considered as a group to which products can be sold: *Motorbike manufacturers are selling to the grey market as much as to younger people.*

ˈgrey ˌmatter **noun** [U] informal (US usually **ˈgray ˌmatter**) a person's intelligence: *It's not the sort of movie that stimulates the old grey matter much.*

the ˌgrey ˈpound **noun** [S] UK (US **the ˌgray ˈdollar**) the money that all old people as a group have available to spend

ˈgrey ˌwater **noun** [U] (US usually **ˈgray ˌwater**) water that has been used before, for example for washing, that can be stored and used again, for example in toilets: *Water companies are testing recycling units which take grey water and clean it up sufficiently for flushing toilets.*

grid /grɪd/ **noun** [C] **PATTERN/STRUCTURE** ▷ **1** a pattern or structure made from horizontal and vertical lines crossing each other to form squares: *A metal grid had been placed across the hole to stop people falling in.* ◦ *In Barcelona the streets are laid out in/on a grid **system**.* → See also **gridiron** **ELECTRICITY** ▷ **2** a system of wires through which electricity is connected to different power stations across a region: *the national grid* **MAP** ▷ **3** a pattern of squares with numbers or letters used to find places on a map

griddle /ˈgrɪd.l̩/ **noun** [C] a round, flat piece of metal used for cooking over a fire or cooker

gridiron /ˈgrɪd.aɪən/ (US) /-aɪrn/ **noun** [C] US a field painted with lines for American football

gridlock /ˈgrɪd.lɒk/ (US) /-lɑːk/ **noun** [U] **1** a situation where roads in a town become so blocked by cars that it is impossible for any traffic to move: *A car breaking down at rush hour could cause gridlock across half the city.* **2** a situation in which no progress can be made

ˈgrid ˌreference **noun** [C] a position on a map that has been divided into squares by NUMBERED lines going from one side to the other and from top to bottom so that you can find places easily on it: *What's the grid reference of the village on this map?*

grief /griːf/ **noun** [C or U] **1** (B2) very great sadness, especially at the death of someone: *Her grief at her son's death was terrible.* ◦ *newspaper pictures of grief-**stricken** relatives* **2 come to grief** to suddenly fail in what you are doing, often because you have an accident: *The Italian champion was in second position when he came to grief on the third lap.* **3 give sb grief** informal to criticize someone angrily **4 get grief** informal to be criticized angrily: *I got a load of grief off Esther because I was ten minutes late.*

ˈgrief ˌtourist **noun** [C] informal someone who visits a place because something bad happened there: *Grief tourists continue to visit the house where the girls were murdered.*

grievance /ˈgriː.vᵊns/ **noun** [C or U] a complaint or a strong feeling that you have been treated unfairly: *A special committee has been appointed to handle prisoners' grievances.* ◦ *Bill still **harbours/nurses** a grievance **against** his employers for not promoting him.*

grieve /griːv/ **verb** **1** [I] to feel or express great sadness, especially when someone dies: *He is still grieving **for/over** his wife.* **2** [T] formal to make you feel sad and angry: [+ obj + to infinitive] *It grieves me **to** see all this food going to waste.*

grieving /ˈgriː.vɪŋ/ **adj** feeling very sad because someone has died: *grieving relatives*

grievous /ˈgriː.vəs/ **adj** formal having very serious effects or causing great pain: *Her death is a grievous loss to the whole of the community.* ◦ *grievous wounds* • **grievously** /-li/ **adv**

ˌgrievous bodily ˈharm **noun** [U] (abbreviation **GBH**) UK legal a crime in which one person does serious physical injury to another

griffin /ˈgrɪf.ɪn/ **noun** [C] (also **gryphon**) an imaginary creature with the head and wings of an EAGLE and the body of a lion

grill /grɪl/ **noun; verb**

▸**noun** [C] **1** (B1) UK (US **broiler**) the surface in a cooker that can be heated to very high temperatures and under which you put food to be cooked **2** (B1) a frame of metal bars over a fire on which food can be put to be cooked **3** mainly US an informal restaurant

▸**verb** [T] **COOK** ▷ **1** (B1) to cook food over fire or hot coals, usually on a metal frame: *Dad was grilling chicken in the back yard.* **2** (B1) UK (US **broil**) to cook something under a very hot surface in a cooker: *I'll*

G

grill the bacon rather than fry it. **QUESTION** ▷ **3** to ask someone a lot of questions for a long time: *After being grilled by the police for two days, Johnson signed a confession.* ◦ *Her parents would grill her* ***about*** *where she'd been.*

grille /grɪl/ **noun** [C] a frame of metal bars used to cover something such as a window or a machine: *a security grille* ◦ *A grille separated the prisoners from their visitors.*

grilled /grɪld/ **adj 1** (of food) cooked over fire or hot coals, usually on a metal frame: *grilled shrimp* **2** UK (US **broiled**) (of food) cooked under a very hot surface in a cooker: *Do you want your fish pan-fried or grilled?*

grilling /ˈgrɪl.ɪŋ/ **noun** [C usually singular] informal an occasion when someone is asked a lot of questions for a long time: *She faced a grilling when she got home.*

G

ˈgrill ˌpan noun [C] UK (US **ˈbroiler ˌpan**, Australian English **ˈgrill ˌtray**) an open, rectangular metal container, often with a frame of metal bars inside, on which food is cooked under a grill

grim /grɪm/ **adj** (**grimmer**, **grimmest**) **WITHOUT HOPE** ▷ **1** Ⓒ worrying, without hope: *The future* ***looks*** *grim.* **SERIOUS** ▷ **2** Ⓒ worried and serious or sad: *Her face was grim as she told them the bad news.* ◦ *The expression on his face was one of grim* ***determination****.* ◦ *Later Mr Ashby left the court, grim-faced and silent.* **UNPLEASANT** ▷ **3** Ⓒ informal very unpleasant or ugly: *a grim-looking block of flats* • **grimly** /ˈgrɪm.li/ **adv** • **grimness** /ˈgrɪm.nəs/ **noun** [U]

IDIOM **hang/hold on like grim death** UK to hold on very tightly to something, despite great difficulty: *Darren always drives and I sit behind him, hanging on like grim death.*

grimace /ˈgrɪ.məs/ **verb** [I] to make an expression of pain, strong dislike, etc. in which the face twists in an ugly way: *He tried to stand and grimaced* ***with*** *pain.* • **grimace noun** [C] *Helen made a grimace* ***of*** *disgust when she saw the raw meat.*

grime /graɪm/ **noun** [U] a layer of dirt on skin or on a building: *The walls were covered in grime.*

the Grim Reaper /ˌgrɪmˈriː.pəʳ/ Ⓤⓢ /-pɚ/ **noun** [S] literary death, imagined as a SKELETON with a large curved tool used for cutting crops

grimy /ˈgraɪ.mi/ **adj** dirty: *The child's face was grimy and streaked with tears.*

grin /grɪn/ **noun; verb**

▸**noun** [C] Ⓒ a wide smile: *I assumed things had gone well for him as he had a big grin on his face.* ◦ *a broad/sheepish grin*

▸**verb** [I] (**-nn-**) Ⓒ to smile a wide smile: *He grinned* ***at*** *me from the doorway.* ◦ *What are you grinning about?*

IDIOM **grin and bear it** Ⓒ to accept something bad without complaining: *I really don't want to go but I guess I'll just have to grin and bear it.*

grind /graɪnd/ **verb; noun**

▸**verb** [T] (**ground**, **ground**) **MAKE SMALLER** ▷ **1** to make something into small pieces or a powder by pressing between hard surfaces: *to grind coffee* ◦ *Shall I grind a little black pepper over your pizza?* ◦ *They grind the grain* ***into*** *flour (= make flour by crushing grain) between two large stones.* **RUB** ▷ **2** to rub something against a hard surface, in order to make it sharper or smoother: *She has a set of chef's knives which she grinds every week.* ◦ *He ground* ***down*** *the sharp metal edges to make them smooth.* ◦ *The car engine was making a strange grinding noise.* → See also **grindstone 3 grind your teeth** to make a noise by rubbing your teeth together: *She grinds her teeth in her sleep.*

IDIOM **grind to a halt/standstill** to stop slowly: *The car ground to a halt right in the middle of the road.* ◦ figurative *If we don't do something soon, the industry could grind to a halt (= stop operating).*

PHRASAL VERBS **grind sb down** to treat someone so badly for such a long time that they are no longer able to fight back: *Ground down by years of abuse, she did not have the confidence to leave him.* • **grind sth into sth** to press something hard into something else using a twisting movement: *Sara angrily ground her cigarette into the ashtray.* • **grind sth out** to produce the same thing, especially a boring thing, again and again: *The band ground out the same tunes it had been playing for 20 years.*

▸**noun** [S] informal a difficult or boring activity which needs a lot of effort: *Having to type up my handwritten work was a real grind.* ◦ *The* ***daily*** *grind of looking after three children was wearing her down.*

grinder /ˈgraɪn.dəʳ/ Ⓤⓢ /-dɚ/ **noun** [C] **1** a machine used to rub or press something until it becomes a powder: *a coffee/pepper grinder* **2** US (also **meat grinder**, UK **mincer**) a machine used for cutting meat into small pieces **3 knife grinder** a device for making knives sharper, or a person whose job is to do this

grinding /ˈgraɪn.dɪŋ/ **adj** literary **grinding poverty** a situation in which people are extremely poor over a long period

grindstone /ˈgraɪnd.stəʊn/ Ⓤⓢ /-stoʊn/ **noun** [C] a large round stone that is turned by a machine and is used to make tools sharper or sharp edges smooth

gringo /ˈgrɪŋ.gəʊ/ Ⓤⓢ /-goʊ/ **noun** [C] (plural **gringos**) informal disapproving used in Latin American countries to refer to people from the US or other English-speaking countries

grip /grɪp/ **verb; noun**

▸**verb** (**-pp-**) **HOLD** ▷ **1** Ⓑ② [I or T] to hold very tightly: *The baby gripped my finger with her tiny hand.* ◦ *Old tyres won't grip (= stay on the surface of the road) in the rain very well.* **INTEREST** ▷ **2** Ⓒ [T] to keep someone's attention completely: *This trial has gripped the whole nation.* ◦ *I was gripped throughout the entire two hours of the film.* **EMOTION** ▷ **3** Ⓒ [T usually passive] When an emotion such as fear grips you, you feel it strongly: *Then he turned towards me and I was suddenly gripped* ***by*** *fear.*

▸**noun CONTROL** ▷ **1** [S] control over something or someone: *Rebels have tightened their grip* ***on*** *the city.* **HOLD** ▷ **2** Ⓑ② [C usually singular] a tight hold on something or someone: *She tightened her grip* ***on*** *my arm.* ◦ *She would not loosen her grip* ***on*** *my arm.* **BAG** ▷ **3** [C] old-fashioned a bag for travelling that is smaller than a SUITCASE

IDIOMS **get/keep a grip on yourself** Ⓒ① to make an effort to control your emotions and behave more calmly: *I just think he ought to get a grip on himself – he's behaving like a child.* • **be in the grip of sth** to be experiencing something unpleasant that you have no control over: *The country is currently in the grip of the worst recession for 20 years.* • **come/get to grips with sth** Ⓒ to make an effort to understand and deal with a problem or situation: *The government have failed to come to grips with the two most important social issues of our time.* ◦ *I can't seem to get to grips with this problem.*

gripe /graɪp/ **noun** [C] informal a strong complaint: *Her main gripe is that she's not being trained properly.*

• **gripe** verb [I] *There's no point griping* ***about*** *the price of things.*

ˈGripe ˌWater noun [U] UK trademark a medicine given to babies to cure stomach pain

gripping /ˈgrɪp.ɪŋ/ adj C1 describes something that is so interesting or exciting that it holds your attention completely: *I found the book so gripping that I couldn't put it down.*

grisly /ˈgrɪz.li/ adj extremely unpleasant, especially because death or blood is involved: *a grisly murder*

grist /grɪst/ noun **grist to the mill** UK (US **grist for sb's mill**) anything that can be used to your advantage: *I might as well learn another language,* ***it's all*** *grist to the mill when it comes to getting a job.*

gristle /ˈgrɪs.l/ noun [U] a solid white substance in meat that comes from near the bone and is hard to CHEW (= crush with the teeth) • **gristly** /-li/ adj

grit /grɪt/ noun; verb

▸noun [U] **STONES** ▷ **1** very small pieces of stone or sand: *The road had been covered with grit.* **COURAGE** ▷ **2** courage and determination despite difficulty: *It takes* ***true*** *(= real) grit to stand up to a bully.* **FOOD** ▷ **3 grits** [plural] US a dish of HOMINY grain eaten especially as a morning meal

▸verb [T] (-tt-) to put small stones on a road or path that is covered in ice, in order to make it safer: *Council lorries had been out gritting the icy roads the night before.*

IDIOM **grit your teeth 1** to press your top and bottom teeth together, often in anger: *He gritted his teeth in silent fury.* **2** C2 to accept a difficult situation and deal with it in a determined way: *We had to grit our teeth and agree with their conditions because we wanted the contract.*

gritter /ˈgrɪt.əʳ/ US /ˈgrɪt̬.ɚ/ noun [C] UK (US **sander**) a special vehicle that spreads grit on the roads when they are covered with ice

gritty /ˈgrɪt.i/ US /ˈgrɪt̬.i/ adj **SANDY** ▷ **1** containing grit or like grit **BRAVE** ▷ **2** brave and determined: *He showed the gritty determination that we've come to expect from him.* **UNPLEASANT AND TRUE** ▷ **3** showing all the unpleasant but true details of a situation: *a gritty portrayal of inner-city poverty* ◦ *a gritty documentary*

grizzle /ˈgrɪz.əl/ verb [I] disapproving (especially of a young child) to cry continuously but not very loudly, or to complain all the time: *The baby was cutting a tooth and grizzled all day long.* ◦ *They're always grizzling (= complaining)* ***about*** *how nobody invites them anywhere.*

grizzled /ˈgrɪz.əld/ adj literary having hair that is grey or becoming grey: *Grizzled veterans in uniform gathered at the war monument.*

grizzly bear /ˌgrɪz.liˈbeəʳ/ US /-ˈber/ noun [C] (also **grizzly**) a very large, greyish-brown BEAR from North America

groan /grəʊn/ US /groʊn/ noun; verb

▸noun [C] **1** C2 a deep, long sound showing great pain or unhappiness: *We could hear the groans of the wounded soldiers.* **2** a complaining noise or phrase: *He looked at the piles of dirty dishes and gave a groan* ***of*** *dismay.*

▸verb [I] **1** C2 to make a deep long sound showing great pain or unhappiness: *He collapsed, groaning with pain.* ◦ [+ speech] *'Not again,' he groaned (= said in a low unhappy voice).* **2** to complain or speak unhappily: *She's always* ***moaning and*** *groaning (= complaining a lot) about the weather.*

IDIOM **groan with/under (the weight of) sth** humorous to carry a very large quantity of something: *The tables were positively groaning with food.*

grocer /ˈgrəʊ.səʳ/ US /ˈgroʊ.sɚ/ noun [C] old-fashioned a person who owns or works in a shop selling food and small things for the home → See also **greengrocer**

grocer's /ˈgrəʊ.səz/ US /ˈgroʊ.sɚz/ noun [C] (plural **grocers**) old-fashioned the shop where a grocer works: *I popped into the grocer's on the way home from work to get some cheese.*

grocery /ˈgrəʊ.sər.i/ US /ˈgroʊ.sɚ-/ noun **FOOD** ▷ **groceries** B1 [plural] the food that you buy in a grocer's shop or SUPERMARKET

grog /grɒg/ US /grɑːg/ noun [U] **1** old-fashioned strong alcohol, such as RUM, that has been mixed with water **2** mainly Australian English any alcoholic drink

groggy /ˈgrɒg.i/ US /ˈgrɑː.gi/ adj informal weak and unable to think clearly or walk correctly, usually because of tiredness or illness: *I felt a bit groggy for a couple of days after the operation.*

groin /grɔɪn/ noun [C] **BODY** ▷ **1** the place where your legs meet the front of your body: *He pulled a muscle in his groin.* ◦ *a groin strain* **2** the male sex organs: *He was kicked in the stomach and the groin.* **SEA** ▷ **3** a **groyne**

groom /gruːm/ verb; noun

▸verb [T] **CLEAN** ▷ **1** to clean an animal, often by brushing its fur: *Polly spends hours in the stables grooming her pony.* **PREPARE** ▷ **2** to prepare someone for a special job or activity: *She was being groomed* ***for*** *leadership.* ◦ [+ to infinitive] *My boss is grooming me* ***to*** *take over his job next year.* **SEX** ▷ **3** to become friends with a child, especially over the internet, with the intention of committing a sexual offence

▸noun [C] **MAN** ▷ **1** B1 a **bridegroom**: *The* ***bride and*** *groom walked down the aisle together.* **HORSES** ▷ **2** a person whose job is to take care of and clean horses

groomed /gruːmd/ adj having a tidy and pleasant appearance that is produced with care: *His mother was always impeccably groomed.* → See also **well groomed**

grooming /ˈgruː.mɪŋ/ noun [U] **TIDYING** ▷ **1** the things that you do to make your appearance tidy and pleasant, for example brushing your hair, or the things that you do to keep an animal's hair or fur clean and tidy **SEX** ▷ **2** the criminal activity of becoming friends with a child, especially over the internet, in order to try to persuade the child to have a sexual relationship with you

groove /gruːv/ noun [C] a long, narrow, hollow space cut into a surface: *The window slides along a deep metal groove to open and close.*

IDIOMS **be in the groove** informal to be operating or performing successfully: *Alex Popov proved he was back in the groove by winning the 100 metres freestyle.*

• **be stuck in a groove** to be bored because you are doing the same things that you have done for a long time: *We never do anything exciting any more – we seem to be stuck in a groove.*

grooved /gruːvd/ adj having a groove or grooves

groovy /ˈgruː.vi/ adj old-fashioned slang very fashionable and interesting: *That's a groovy hat you're wearing, did you knit it yourself?*

grope /grəʊp/ US /groʊp/ verb; noun

G

▸**verb 1** [I or T] to feel with your hands, especially in order to find or move towards something when you cannot see easily: *She groped **for** her glasses on the bedside table.* ◦ *I had to grope my **way** up the dark stairs.* **2** [T] informal to touch someone's body in order to get sexual pleasure, usually when the person does not want you to do this: *He groped me as I was going to the bar.*

PHRASAL VERB **grope for sth** to try to think of something, especially the right words, the correct answer, etc.: *I'm groping for the right words here.*

▸**noun** [C] informal a sexual touch, usually an unwanted and unpleasant one

groper /ˈgrəʊ.pəʳ/ US /ˈgroʊ.pɚ/ **noun** [C] PERSON ▷ **1** informal someone who touches another person's body in order to get sexual pleasure, when the person does not want them to: *gropers on crowded trains* FISH ▷ **2** Australian English a **grouper**

G

gross /grəʊs/ US /groʊs/ **adj, adv; adj; verb; noun**

▸**adj, adv** C1 (in) total: *A person's gross **income** is the money they earn before tax is deducted from it.* ◦ *Once wrapped, the gross **weight** of the package is 2.1 kg.* ◦ *She earns £30,000 a year gross.* → Compare **net**

▸**adj** UNACCEPTABLE ▷ **1** C1 [before noun] formal (especially in law) unacceptable because clearly wrong: *gross misconduct/indecency* ◦ *a gross violation of justice* FAT ▷ **2** extremely fat or large and ugly: *I'd put on ten kilos and felt gross in my bikini.* UNPLEASANT ▷ **3** informal extremely unpleasant: *'Oh, gross!' she said, looking at the flies buzzing above the piles of dirty plates.*

▸**verb** [T] to earn a particular amount of money before tax is paid or costs are taken away: *The film has grossed over $200 million this year.*

PHRASAL VERB **gross sb out** mainly US informal If something grosses you out, you think it is very unpleasant or DISGUSTING: *He smells and he's dirty – he really grosses me out.*

▸**noun** [C] (plural **gross**) old-fashioned (a group of) 144

grossly /ˈgrəʊs.li/ US /ˈgroʊs-/ **adv** extremely: *It was grossly unfair to demand such a high interest rate on the loan.* ◦ *He's grossly overweight.*

ˈ**gross-out adj** [before noun] informal deliberately showing things or making jokes about things that the audience may find unpleasant or DISGUSTING, in a humorous way: *a gross-out movie/comedy*

grotesque /grəʊˈtesk/ US /groʊ-/ **adj; noun**

▸**adj** strange and unpleasant, especially in a silly or slightly frightening way: *By now she'd had so much cosmetic surgery that she looked quite grotesque.* ◦ *Gothic churches are full of devils and grotesque figures.* • **grotesquely** /-li/ **adv** *a grotesquely fat man* ◦ *My views were grotesquely (= extremely) misrepresented.*

▸**noun** [C] a painting or other artistic work with an image of a person that is ugly or unpleasant as its subject: *Spencer's grotesques are his best works.*

grotto /ˈgrɒt.əʊ/ US /ˈgrɑː.t̬oʊ/ **noun** [C] (plural **grottoes** or **grottos**) a small cave, especially an artificial one that is made to look attractive

grotty /ˈgrɒt.i/ US /ˈgrɑː.t̬i/ **adj** informal unpleasant or of bad quality: *a grotty little room*

grouch /graʊtʃ/ **verb; noun**

▸**verb** [I] informal to complain in an angry way: *Oh, stop grouching!*

▸**noun** [C] informal a person who often complains

grouchy /ˈgraʊ.tʃi/ **adj** informal easily annoyed and complaining: *Don't be so grouchy!* • **grouchiness** /-nəs/ **noun** [U]

ground /graʊnd/ **noun; verb**

▸**noun** LAND ▷ **1 the ground** [S] B1 the surface of the Earth: *I sat down on the ground.* **2** B2 [U] soil: *soft/stony ground* ◦ *The ground was frozen hard and was impossible to dig.* **3** B1 [C] an area of land used for a particular purpose or activity: *a football ground* **4 grounds** [plural] C2 the gardens and land that surround a building and often have a wall or fence around them: *We went for a walk around the hospital grounds.* CAUSE ▷ **5** C2 [C usually plural] a reason, cause, or argument: *She is suing the company **on** grounds **of** unfair dismissal.* ◦ *Do you have any ground **for** suspecting them?* ◦ [+ to infinitive] *We have grounds **to** believe that you have been lying to us.* ◦ [+ that] *He refused to answer **on the** grounds **that** she was unfairly dismissed.* AREA OF KNOWLEDGE ▷ **6** C2 [U] an area of knowledge or experience: *When the conversation turns to politics he's **on familiar** ground (= he knows a lot about this subject).* ◦ *Once we'd found some **common** ground (= things we both knew about) we got on very well together.* ◦ *The lectures **covered a lot of** ground (= included information on many different subjects).* ◦ *I enjoyed her first novel, but I felt in the second she was **going over the same** ground (= dealing with the same area of experience).* WIRE ▷ **7** [C usually singular] US for **earth** COFFEE ▷ **8 grounds** [plural] the small grains of coffee left at the bottom of a cup or other container that has had coffee in it → See also **grind**

IDIOMS **drive/work yourself into the ground** to make yourself tired or ill by working too hard • **get (sth) off the ground** If a plan or activity gets off the ground or you get it off the ground, it starts or succeeds: *A lot more money will be required to get this project off the ground.* • **go/be run to ground** to hide in order to escape someone or something following you: *He found the media attention intolerable and went to ground for several months.* • **on the ground** among the general public: *Their political ideas have a lot of support on the ground.*

▸**verb** GRIND ▷ **1** past simple and past participle of **grind** KEEP ON LAND ▷ **2 be grounded** If a ship is grounded, it cannot move because it has hit solid ground: *The oil tanker was grounded **on** a sandbank.* **3** [T often passive] If aircraft are grounded, they are prevented from flying or ordered not to fly: *The snowstorm meant that all planes were grounded.* PUNISH ▷ **4** [T] to FORBID (= refuse to allow) a child or young person from going out as a punishment: *My parents have grounded me for a week.* CAUSE ▷ **5 be grounded in sth** formal to be based firmly on something: *Fiction should be grounded in reality.* ◦ *Most phobias are grounded in childhood experiences.* → See also **well grounded**

ˈ**ground ˌball noun** [C] US a **grounder**

ˌ**ground ˈbeef noun** [U] US for **mince**

groundbreaking (also ˈ**ground-ˌbreaking**) /ˈgraʊndˌbreɪ.kɪŋ/ **adj** If something is groundbreaking, it is very new and a big change from other things of its type: *His latest movie is interesting, but not groundbreaking.*

groundcloth /ˈgraʊnd.klɒθ/ US /-klɑːθ/ **noun** [C] US for **groundsheet**

ˈ**ground ˌcover noun** [U] plants which grow thickly and close to the ground, sometimes used in gardens to prevent WEEDS from growing: *This plant grows quickly and provides excellent ground cover.*

ˈ**ground ˌcrew noun** [C, + sing/pl verb] the people at

an airport who take care of the aircraft while it is on the ground

grounded /ˈɡraʊn.dɪd/ adj **SENSIBLE** ▷ **1** Someone who is grounded makes good decisions and does not say or do stupid things: *He's very grounded even though he has so much money.* **UNABLE TO MOVE** ▷ **2** describes an aircraft that is prevented from flying for some reason, or a ship that cannot move because it has hit solid ground **PUNISHED** ▷ **3** A child or young person who is grounded is not allowed to go out as a punishment: *I smashed some stuff and now I'm grounded for a week.*

grounder /ˈɡraʊn.dəʳ/ (US) /-dɚ/ noun [C] (also **ˈground ˌball**) US a ball that moves along the ground rather than through the air when it has been hit in a game of baseball

ˌground ˈfloor noun [C] the level of a building that is at the same level as the street: *Her flat is on the ground floor.* ◦ *a ground-floor room/window/flat* → See also **first floor**

IDIOM **be/get in on the ground floor** to be or become involved in something from the beginning: *He was sure that he was getting in on the ground floor with the next big thing.*

the ˌground ˈfloor noun [S] UK (US usually **ˌfirst ˈfloor**) (B1) the floor of a building that is at the same level as the ground outside: *My flat is on the ground floor.* • **ˌground-ˈfloor** adj [before noun] *a ground-floor office*

ˈground ˌfrost noun [C usually singular] a temperature at or below FREEZING POINT on and near the ground during the night which can damage plants

groundhog /ˈɡraʊnd.hɒɡ/ (US) /-hɑːɡ/ noun [C] US a **woodchuck**

grounding /ˈɡraʊn.dɪŋ/ noun [U] a knowledge of the basic facts about a particular subject: *This course is designed to give drivers a grounding **in** car maintenance.*

groundless /ˈɡraʊnd.ləs/ adj without cause: *My fears turned out to be groundless.*

ˈground ˌlevel noun [S] the same level as the surface of the ground

groundnut /ˈɡraʊnd.nʌt/ noun [C] a **peanut**, especially as a crop or when used in particular products: *groundnut oil*

groundout /ˈɡraʊnd.aʊt/ noun [C] US in baseball, the act of hitting a ball along the ground so that it is caught by someone on the other team who then causes the BATTER (= person who hits the ball) to be out

ˈground ˌplan noun [C usually singular] **BUILDING** ▷ **1** the plan that has been drawn of a building **ACTION** ▷ **2** mainly US the basic plan of action for something: *He doesn't have a ground plan, he just makes decisions as the need arises.*

ˈground ˌrent noun [C usually singular] money paid by the owner of a building or apartment to the person who owns the land on which it has been built

ˈground ˌrules noun [plural] the principles on which future behaviour is based: *In all relationships a few ground rules have to be established.*

groundsheet /ˈɡraʊnd.ʃiːt/ noun [C] (US also **groundcloth**) a piece of WATERPROOF material that you put on the ground to sleep on in a tent

groundsman /ˈɡraʊndz.mən/ noun [C] (plural **-men** /-mən/) UK (US **groundskeeper**) a man whose job is to take care of a sports ground or park

ˈground ˌspeed noun [C usually singular] specialized An aircraft's ground speed is its speed when measured against the ground rather than the air through which it moves.

ˈground ˌstaff noun [plural] the people whose job is to take care of a sports ground and its equipment

groundstroke /ˈɡraʊnd.strəʊk/ (US) /-stroʊk/ noun [C] in tennis and similar games, the action of hitting the ball after it has hit the ground

groundswell /ˈɡraʊnd.swel/ noun [S] a growth of strong feeling among a large group of people: *There is a groundswell **of** opinion against the new rules.*

ˈground ˌwater noun [U] underground water that is held in the soil and rocks

groundwork /ˈɡraʊnd.wɜːk/ (US) /-wɝːk/ noun [U] work that is done as a preparation for work that will be done later: *The committee will meet today to **lay** the groundwork **for** inter-party talks next month.*

ˌground ˈzero noun **1** [C usually singular] the exact place where a nuclear bomb explodes: *The blast was felt as far as 30 miles from ground zero.* **2 Ground Zero** the place where the World Trade Center stood in New York City before it was destroyed in an attack on 11 September, 2001

group /ɡruːp/ noun; verb

▸noun **SET** ▷ **1** (A1) [C] a number of people or things that are put together or considered as a unit: *I'm meeting a group **of** friends for dinner tonight.* ◦ *The car was parked near a small group **of** trees.* ◦ *She showed me another group **of** pictures, this time of children playing.* **MUSIC** ▷ **2** (A1) [C, + sing/pl verb] a number of people who play music together, especially pop music: *What's your favourite group?* ◦ *a pop/rock group* **BUSINESS** ▷ **3** [C] a business that contains several different companies: *United News Media, the national newspaper and television group*

> **Word partners for group noun**
>
> a *large/small* group • a *member of* a group • *belong to/form/join/start* a group • *divide/split* (sth) *into* groups • a group *of* [things/people]

▸verb [I or T, + adv/prep] (C1) to form a group or put people or things into a group: *We all grouped together round the bride for a family photograph.* ◦ *I grouped the children according to age.* ◦ *The books were grouped by size.*

ˈgroup ˌcaptain noun [C] an officer in the British air force

grouper /ˈɡruː.pəʳ/ (US) /-pɚ/ noun [C] a large fish with a big head and a wide mouth that lives in warm seas and can be eaten

groupie /ˈɡruː.pi/ noun [C] a person who likes a particular singer or other famous person and follows them to try to meet them, especially in order to have sex with them

grouping /ˈɡruː.pɪŋ/ noun [C] several people or things when they have been arranged into a group or are being considered as a group: *political groupings*

ˌgroup ˈpractice noun [C] a group of several doctors who work together in the same place

ˌgroup ˈtherapy noun [U] treatment in which people meet in a group to talk about their emotional problems, with a trained leader or doctor present

grouse /ɡraʊs/ noun; verb

▸noun [C] **BIRD** ▷ **1** (plural **grouse**) a small fat bird, shot for sport and food **COMPLAINT** ▷ **2** (plural **grouses**) informal an angry complaint

▸verb [I] informal to complain angrily: *She's always grousing **about** how she's been treated by the management.*

grout /graʊt/ verb; noun
▸verb [T] to put a thin line of MORTAR in the spaces between TILES: *We spent the weekend grouting the bathroom.*
▸noun [U] (also **grouting**) MORTAR used for grouting

grove /grəʊv/ (US) /groʊv/ noun [C] **1** a group of trees planted close together **2 Grove** used in some road and place names: *Camberwell Grove*

IDIOM **the groves of academe** universities considered as a whole: *It's yet another novel set in the groves of academe.*

grovel /ˈgrɒv.əl/ (US) /ˈgrɑː.vəl/ verb [I] (-ll- or US usually -l-) **TRY TO PLEASE** ▷ **1** to behave with too much respect towards someone to show them that you are very eager to please them: *He sent a grovelling note of apology.* **MOVE** ▷ **2** to move close to or on the ground: *I was grovelling under the sofa, trying to find my contact lens.*

G

grow /grəʊ/ (US) /groʊ/ verb (**grew**, **grown**) **INCREASE** ▷ **1** (A2) [I or L or T] to increase in size or amount, or to become more advanced or developed: *Children grow so quickly.* ◦ *This plant grows best in the shade.* ◦ *She's grown three centimetres this year.* ◦ *Football's popularity continues to grow.* ◦ *The labour force is expected to grow by two percent next year.* ◦ *The male deer grows large branching horns called antlers.* **2** (B1) [I or T] If your hair or nails grow, or if you grow them, they become longer: *Lottie wants to grow her hair long.* ◦ *Are you growing a beard?* ◦ *Wow, your hair's grown!* **3** (A2) [I] If a plant grows in a particular place, it exists and develops there: *There were roses growing up against the wall of the cottage.* **4** (A2) [T] If you grow a plant, you put it in the ground and take care of it, usually in order to sell it: *The villagers grow coffee and maize to sell in the market.* **5** [T] to make a business bigger by increasing sales, employing more people, etc.: *We aim to grow the company by giving the customer a better deal.* **BECOME** ▷ **6 grow tired, old, calm, etc.** (B2) to gradually become tired, old, calm, etc.: *He grew bored of the countryside.* ◦ *Growing old is so awful.* **7 grow to do sth** to gradually start to do something: *I've grown to like her over the months.*

PHRASAL VERBS **grow apart** (also **grow away from sb**) If two people in a close relationship grow apart or if they grow away from each other, they gradually begin to have a less close relationship, usually because they no longer have the same interests and want the same things: *There was nobody else involved, we just grew apart.* • **grow into sb/sth** to develop into a particular type of person or thing: *He's grown into a fine, responsible young man.* • **grow into sth** If children grow into clothes, they gradually become big enough to wear them. • **grow on sb** If someone or something grows on you, you like them more and more although you did not like them at first: *I wasn't sure about this album when I bought it but it's really grown on me.* • **grow out of sth CLOTHES** ▷ **1** If children grow out of clothes, they become too big to fit into them. **INTEREST** ▷ **2** If you grow out of an interest or way of behaving, you stop having or doing it as you become older: *He wants to join the army when he leaves school, but I hope he'll grow out of the idea.* **IDEA** ▷ **3** If an idea grows out of another one, it develops from it: *The idea for the story grew out of a strange experience I had last year.* • **grow up PERSON** ▷ **1** (A2) to gradually become an adult: *I grew up in Scotland* (= *I lived there when I was young*). ◦ *Taking responsibility for yourself is part of the process of growing up.* **CITY** ▷ **2** If a town or city grows up in a particular place or way, it develops there or in that way: *The city grew up originally as a crossing point on the river.*

grower /ˈgrəʊ.əʳ/ (US) /ˈgroʊ.ɚ/ noun [C] **1** a person who grows large amounts of a particular plant or crop in order to sell them **2** a plant that grows in a particular way: *The new varieties of wheat are good growers even in poor soil.*

growing /ˈgrəʊ.ɪŋ/ (US) /ˈgroʊ-/ adj (B2) increasing in size or quantity: *There is a growing awareness of the seriousness of this disease.* ◦ *A growing boy needs his food.*

ˈgrowing ˌpains noun [plural] **PHYSICAL PAIN** ▷ **1** pains felt by young people in the bones or JOINTS (= places where two bones are connected) of their legs **DIFFICULTIES** ▷ **2** the problems of a new organization or activity

growl /graʊl/ verb [I] to make a low, rough sound, usually in anger: *The dog growled **at** her and snapped at her ankles.* ◦ [+ speech] *'Not now, I'm busy,' he growled.* • **growl** noun [C] *The dog eyed me suspiciously and gave a low growl.*

grown /grəʊn/ (US) /groʊn/ adj **a grown man/woman** an adult: *I don't like to see a grown man in tears.*

ˌgrown ˈup adj (B2) If you say that someone is grown up, you mean that they are an adult or that they behave in a responsible way: *He seems very grown up for a ten-year-old.* ◦ *This book is a bit too grown up for you* (= *you are too young to understand this book*). ◦ [before noun] *She has two grown-up children who work in the family business.*

ˈgrown-up noun [C] (B2) an adult, used especially when talking to children: *Ask a grown-up to cut the shape out for you.*

growth /grəʊθ/ (US) /groʊθ/ noun **1** (B2) [U] The growth of a person, animal, or plant is its process of increasing in size: *A balanced diet is essential for healthy growth.* ◦ *Plant growth is most noticeable in spring and early summer.* **2** (B2) [U] an increase in the size or the importance of something: *The government is trying to limit population growth.* ◦ *The rapid growth of opposition to the plan has surprised the council.* ◦ *Electronic publishing is a growth **area*** (= *an area of activity that is increasing in size and developing quickly*). **3** [C] a LUMP (= solid mass) growing on the outside or inside of a person, animal, or plant that is caused by a disease: *a cancerous growth on the liver* **4** [C or U] something that has grown: *Graham came back from holiday with a week's growth of beard on his chin.*

groyne /grɔɪn/ noun [C] (also **groin**) a low wall built out from the coast into the sea, to prevent the repeated movement of the waves from removing parts of the land

grub /grʌb/ noun; verb
▸noun **INSECT** ▷ **1** [C] an insect in the stage when it has just come out of its egg: *A grub looks like a short, fat worm.* **FOOD** ▷ **2** [U] informal food: *They do really good grub in our local pub.*
▸verb (-bb-) **SEARCH** ▷ **1** [I usually + adv/prep] to search for something by digging or turning over earth: *The dog was grubbing **around/about** in the mud for a bone.* **TAKE** ▷ **2** [T usually + adv/prep] US slang to ask someone for something without intending to pay for it: *Could I grub a cigarette **off** you?*

PHRASAL VERB **grub sth up/out** to dig something out of the ground to get rid of it: *She spent the morning in the garden, grubbing up weeds.*

grubby /ˈgrʌb.i/ adj **1** informal dirty: *He was wearing some old shorts and a grubby T-shirt.* ◦ *Don't wipe your* *grubby hands on my clean towel!* **2** disapproving If you describe an activity or someone's behaviour as grubby, you do not think that it is honest, fair, or acceptable: *She sees the business of making money as just grubby opportunism.* ◦ *He doesn't want this story to get into the grubby hands of the tabloid press (= to be obtained by newspapers who are not honest and fair).*

grudge /grʌdʒ/ **noun; verb**
▸**noun** [C] a strong feeling of anger and dislike for a person who you feel has treated you badly, which often lasts for a long time: *I don't* ***bear*** *any grudge* ***against*** *you.* ◦ *Philippa still* ***has/holds*** *a grudge against me for refusing to lend her that money.*
▸**verb** [T] **1** to not want to spend time or money on someone or something, or to not want to give something to someone: *She grudged every hour she spent helping him.* **2** to think that someone does not deserve something good that they have: [+ two objects] *I don't grudge you your holiday, it's just that you've chosen a bad time to go.*

grudging /ˈgrʌdʒ.ɪŋ/ **adj** A grudging action or feeling is one which you do or have unwillingly: *She won the grudging respect of her boss.* • **grudgingly** /-li/ **adv** *She grudgingly (= unwillingly) admitted that she had been wrong to criticize him.*

gruel /ˈgruː.əl/ **noun** [U] a cheap simple food made especially in the past by boiling OATS with water or milk

gruelling (US usually **grueling**) /ˈgruː.ə.lɪŋ/ **adj** extremely TIRING and difficult, and demanding great effort and determination: *Junior doctors often have to work a gruelling 100-hour week.* • **gruellingly** (US **gruelingly**) /-li/ **adv**

gruesome /ˈgruː.səm/ **adj** extremely unpleasant and shocking, and usually dealing with death or injury: *The newspaper article included a gruesome description of the murder.* • **gruesomely** /-li/ **adv**

gruff /grʌf/ **adj** (of a person's voice) low and unfriendly, or (of a person's behaviour) unfriendly or showing no patience: *'If you must,' came the gruff reply.* ◦ *He's quite a sweet man beneath the gruff exterior.* • **gruffly** /-li/ **adv** • **gruffness** /-nəs/ **noun** [U]

grumble /ˈgrʌm.bl̩/ **verb; noun**
▸**verb** [I] **1** to complain about someone or something in an annoyed way: *She spent the evening grumbling to me* ***about*** *her job.* ◦ [+ speech] *'You never hang your coat up,' she grumbled.* **2** If your stomach grumbles, it makes a low, continuous noise, usually because you are hungry. • **grumbler** /-bləʳ/ (US) /-blɚ/ **noun** [C] a person who complains a lot

IDIOM **mustn't grumble** UK humorous something you say to mean that your life is not bad and that you should not complain about it: *'How's it going then, Mike?' 'Oh, all right. Mustn't grumble.'*

▸**noun** [C usually plural] a complaint: *If I hear any more grumbles about the food, you can do the cooking yourself!*

ˌgrumbling apˈpendix noun [C usually singular] UK a medical condition in which the APPENDIX (= the tube-shaped part that is joined to the INTESTINES) causes you slight pain over a period of time

grump /grʌmp/ **noun** [C] informal someone who is easily annoyed and complains a lot

grumpy /ˈgrʌm.pi/ **adj** informal C1 easily annoyed and complaining: *I hadn't had enough sleep and was feeling a bit grumpy.* ◦ *a grumpy old man* • **grumpily** /-pɪ.li/ **adv** • **grumpiness** /-nəs/ **noun** [U]

grunge /grʌndʒ/ **noun** [U] a type of ROCK MUSIC and a fashion for untidy clothes, which were popular in the early 1990s: *Nirvana was one of the most famous grunge bands.*

grungy /ˈgrʌn.dʒi/ **adj** informal (of a person) feeling tired and dirty, or (of a thing) dirty: *He showed up for the interview wearing some grungy old sweatshirt and jeans.*

grunt /grʌnt/ **verb** [I] **1** (of a pig) to make a low, rough noise: *The pigs were grunting contentedly as they ate their food.* **2** (of a person) to make a short, low sound instead of speaking, usually because of anger or pain: *He hauled himself over the wall, grunting with the effort.* ◦ [+ speech] *'Too tired,' he grunted and sat down.* • **grunt** **noun** [C] *Loud grunts were coming from the pig sty.*

Gruyère /ˈgruː.jeəʳ/ (US) /gruˈjer/ **noun** [U] a hard, pale yellow, strong-tasting cheese which was originally made in Switzerland

GSM /ˌdʒiː.esˈem/ **noun** [S] trademark abbreviation for global system for mobile telecommunications: a technical system for mobile phones used in many countries: *The phone company has placed a large order for GSM* ***network*** *equipment.*

GSOH **noun** [U] written abbreviation for good sense of humour: used in newspapers and magazine advertisements by people looking for a new friend or sexual partner: *Male non-smoker, 36, GSOH, would like to meet interesting female.*

ˈG-spot **noun** [C usually singular] a small area inside the VAGINA that is believed to increase sexual pleasure when rubbed

ˈG-string **noun** [C] a narrow piece of cloth worn between a person's legs to cover their sexual organs, held in place by a piece of string around their waist

gtg written abbreviation for got to go, used in emails, etc.

GTi /ˌdʒiː.tiːˈaɪ/ **noun** [C] abbreviation for Gran Turismo injection: a version of a car that is comfortable, expensive, and very powerful

guacamole /ˌgwæk.əˈməʊ.li/ (US) /-ˈmoʊ-/ **noun** [U] a thick mixture of AVOCADO (= a green tropical fruit), tomato, onion, and spices, usually eaten cold

guano /ˈgwɑː.nəʊ/ (US) /-noʊ/ **noun** [U] the EXCREMENT (= solid waste) of sea birds: *Guano is often used as a fertilizer.*

guarantee /ˌgær.ənˈtiː/ **noun; verb**
▸**noun** **1** B2 [C or U] a promise that something will be done or will happen, especially a written promise by a company to repair or change a product that develops a fault within a particular period of time: *The system costs £99.95 including postage, packing and a twelve-month guarantee.* ◦ *The TV* ***comes with/has*** *a two-year guarantee.* ◦ *a money-back guarantee* ◦ [+ that] *The United Nations has demanded a guarantee from the army* ***that*** *food convoys will not be attacked.* ◦ [+ (that)] *There is no guarantee* ***(that)*** *the discussions will lead to a deal.* ◦ *A product as good as that is a guarantee* ***of*** *commercial success (= it is certain to be successful).* ◦ *The shop said they would replace the television as it was still* ***under*** *guarantee.* **2** [C] a formal agreement to take responsibility for something, such as the payment of someone else's debt **3** [C] specialized something valuable that you give to someone temporarily while you do what you promised to do for them, that they will keep if you fail to do it
▸**verb** [T] PROMISE ▷ **1** If a product is guaranteed, the company that made it promises to repair or change it if a fault develops within a particular period of time: *The fridge is guaranteed* ***for*** *three years.* **2** B2 to promise that something will happen or exist: [+ two objects] *European Airlines guarantees its customers top-*

quality service. ◦ *The label on this bread says it is guaranteed* ***free of/from*** *preservatives (= it contains no preservatives).* **3** If you guarantee someone's debt, you formally promise to accept the responsibility for that debt if the person fails to pay it. **MAKE CERTAIN** ▷ **4** If something guarantees something else, it makes certain that it will happen: [+ (that)] *The £50 deposit guarantees (****that****) people return the boats after their hour has finished.* **5** If something is guaranteed to happen or have a particular result, it is certain that it will happen or have that result: [+ to infinitive] *Just looking at a picture of the sea is guaranteed* ***to*** *make me feel sick.*

guarantor /ˌgær.ənˈtɔːr/ (US) /-ˈtɔːr/ **noun** [C] **1** formal a person who makes certain that something happens or that something is protected: *The armed forces see themselves as the guarantors of free elections in the country.* **2** legal someone who formally accepts responsibility for you or for something that belongs to you: *You must have a guarantor in order to get a visa to enter the country.* **3** specialized a person or organization that promises to pay back a LOAN (= borrowed money) if the person or organization that borrowed it cannot pay it back: *The private investor acted as guarantor to £160 million of the company's bank borrowings.*

G

guard /gɑːd/ (US) /gɑːrd/ **noun; verb**

▸**noun** [C] **PERSON WHO PROTECTS** ▷ **1** (B1) a person or group of people whose job is to protect a person, place, or thing from danger or attack, or to prevent a person such as a criminal from escaping: *prison guards* ◦ *security guards* ◦ *There are guards* ***posted*** *(= standing and watching) at every entrance.* ◦ ***Armed*** *guards are posted around the site.* ◦ *The frontier is patrolled by* ***border*** *guards.* **2 be under guard** to be kept in a place by a group of people who have weapons: *The ex-president was under* ***armed*** *guard in the palace.* **3 stand/keep guard** (also **be on guard**) to be responsible for protecting someone or something, or for preventing someone from escaping: *Two of the soldiers kept guard* ***over*** *the captured guns.* ◦ *Armed police stand guard outside the house.* **4 the changing of the guard** a ceremony held outside Buckingham Palace in London when one set of soldiers replaces the soldiers who have finished their time on duty standing outside the palace **ON A TRAIN** ▷ **5** UK (US **conductor**) a railway official who travels on and is responsible for a train **DEVICE** ▷ **6** a device that protects a dangerous part of something or that protects something from getting damaged: *a fire guard* ◦ *a trigger guard* ◦ *The helmet has a face guard attached.*

IDIOMS **be on your guard** (C2) to be careful to avoid being tricked or getting into a dangerous situation: *You always have to be on your guard* ***against*** *pickpockets.* • **catch sb off guard** (C2) to surprise someone by doing something which they are not expecting and are not ready for • **drop/lower your guard** (C2) to stop being careful to avoid danger or difficulty: *Once he knew I wasn't a journalist, he dropped his guard and even let me take a photograph of him.*

▸**verb** [T] **WATCH** ▷ **1** (B2) to protect someone or something from being attacked or stolen: *Soldiers guard the main doors of the embassy.* **2** (B2) to watch someone and make certain they do not escape from a place: *Five prison officers guarded the prisoners.* **NOT TELL** ▷ **3** to keep information secret: *Journalists* ***jealously*** *(= carefully) guard their sources of information.*

PHRASAL VERB **guard against sth** to take careful action in order to try to prevent something from happening: *Regular exercise helps guard against heart disease.*

ˈ**guard** ˌ**cell** **noun** [C] specialized on a leaf, one of a pair of cells positioned around each STOMA (= small hole in the surface) which open it to release gases or close it to prevent water from being lost

ˈ**guard** ˌ**dog** **noun** [C] a dog trained to protect a place

guarded /ˈgɑː.dɪd/ (US) /ˈgɑːr-/ **adj** careful not to give too much information or show how you really feel: *a guarded response* • **guardedly** /-li/ **adv**

guardhouse /ˈgɑːd.haʊs/ (US) /ˈgɑːrd-/ **noun** [C] a building for the soldiers who are protecting a place

guardian /ˈgɑː.di.ən/ (US) /ˈgɑːr-/ **noun** [C] **1** a person who has the legal right and responsibility of taking care of someone who cannot take care of themselves, such as a child whose parents have died: *The child's parents or guardians must give their consent before she has the operation.* **2** formal someone who protects something: *These three official bodies are the guardians* ***of*** *the nation's countryside.* ◦ *a self-appointed guardian* ***of*** *public morals*

ˌ**guardian** ˈ**angel** **noun** [C] a spirit who is believed to protect and help a particular person

guardianship /ˈgɑː.di.ən.ʃɪp/ (US) /ˈgɑːr-/ **noun** [U] the state or duty of being a guardian

ˌ**guard of** ˈ**honour** **noun** [C usually singular] a group of people, usually soldiers, who are arranged in a row at a special occasion such as a marriage ceremony or an official visit, to honour someone very important

ˈ**guard** ˌ**post** **noun** [C] a small building for the soldiers who are protecting a place

ˈ**guard** ˌ**rail** **noun** [C] a bar along the edge of something steep, such as stairs or a CLIFF, to prevent people from falling off

guardroom /ˈgɑːd.rʊm/, /-ruːm/ (US) /ˈgɑːrd-/ **noun** [C] a room for soldiers who are protecting a place

Guards /gɑːdz/ (US) /gɑːrdz/ **noun** [plural] used in the name of several important REGIMENTS (= units) in an army: *the Grenadier Guards*

guardsman /ˈgɑːdz.mən/ (US) /ˈgɑːrdz-/ **noun** [C] a soldier who is a member of the Guards (= a particular army unit)

ˈ**guard's van** **noun** [C] UK (US **caboose**) a small train CARRIAGE, usually at the back of a train, in which the guard travels

guava /ˈgwɑː.və/ **noun** [C] a round yellow tropical fruit with pink or white flesh and hard seeds, or the small tropical tree on which it grows

gubbins /ˈgʌb.ɪnz/ **noun** [U] UK informal a collection of objects that are not important: *I've just got to clear all this gubbins off my desk before I start working.*

gubernatorial /ˌguː.bən.əˈtɔː.ri.əl/ (US) /-bɚ.nəˈtɔːr.i-/ **adj** US specialized relating to a GOVERNOR (= the official leader of a state in the US)

guerrilla /gəˈrɪl.ə/ **noun; adj**

▸**noun** [C] (also **guerilla**) a member of an unofficial military group that is trying to change the government by making sudden, unexpected attacks on the official army forces: *A small band of guerrillas has blown up a train in the mountains.* ◦ *guerrilla* ***warfare***

▸**adj** using unusual methods to get attention for your ideas, products, etc.: *guerrilla marketing*

guess /ges/ **verb; noun**

▸**verb** [I or T] **1** (A2) to give an answer to a particular question when you do not have all the facts and so cannot be certain if you are correct: *I didn't know the answer, so I had to guess.* ◦ *On the last question, she guessed* ***right/wrong.*** ◦ [+ question word] *Guess* ***when*** this was built. ◦ [+ (that)] *I guessed (**that**) she was your sister.* ◦ *She asked me to guess her age.* ◦ *I guessed the total amount **to be** about £50,000.* **2** A2 to give the correct answer or make the correct judgment: [+ question word] *I bet you can't guess **how** old he is.* ◦ *She guessed the answer first time.* ◦ *'You've got a new job, haven't you?' 'Yes, how did you guess?'* **3 guess what?** A2 informal used before telling someone something interesting or surprising: *Guess what? We won the match 4–0.* **4 I guess** B1 informal used when you believe something is true or likely but are not certain: [+ (that)] *I guess (**that**) things are pretty hard for you now.*

Other ways of saying guess

Estimate can be used when someone guesses the cost, size, value, etc. of something, based on his or her knowledge:

*They **estimate** that the work will take at least ten weeks.*

Divine is a formal word that means 'guess':

*Mum had **divined** my state of mind rather shrewdly.*

Surmise or **conjecture** are formal words that mean 'to guess, based on the appearance of a situation and not on facts':

*From the expression on his face, she **surmised** that something bad had happened.*

*It would be reasonable to **conjecture** that lack of exercise contributed to his obesity.*

If someone guesses possible answers to a question without having enough information to be certain, you could use the verb **speculate**:

*A spokesperson declined to **speculate** on the cause of the plane crash.*

IDIOM **keep sb guessing** to not tell someone what you are going to do next

PHRASAL VERB **guess at sth** [T] to try to imagine something when you have little knowledge or experience of it: *There are no photographs of him so we can only guess at what he looked like.*

▸**noun** [C] **1** B1 an attempt to give the right answer when you are not certain if you are correct: *Go on – **have/make** (US **take**) a guess.* ◦ *Both teams made some **wild** guesses (= made without much thought), none of which were right.* ◦ *'What's the time?' 'It's about five o'clock, **at a** guess (= without knowing exactly).'* **2** someone's opinion about something that is formed without any knowledge of the situation: *'I wonder why she's not here.' 'My guess is that her car has broken down.'* **3 be anyone's guess** If a piece of information is anyone's guess, no one knows it: *'So what's going to happen now?' 'That's anyone's guess.'*

IDIOM **your guess is as good as mine** informal something you say when you do not know the answer to a question: *'What's he doing?' 'Your guess is as good as mine.'*

guesstimate (also **guestimate**) /ˈges.tə.mət/ noun [C] informal an approximate calculation of the size or amount of something when you do not know all the facts: *Current guesstimates are that the company's turnover will increase by six percent this year.*

guesswork /ˈges.wɜːk/ US /-wɝːk/ noun [U] the process of making a guess when you do not know all the facts: *The projected sales figures are **pure** guesswork on our part.*

guest /gest/ noun; verb

▸**noun** [C] **1** A2 a person who is staying with you, or a person you have invited to a social occasion, such as a party or a meal: *150 guests were invited to the wedding.* ◦ *We have guests (US **houseguests**) staying this weekend.* ◦ *Is he on the guest **list**?* ◦ *He is a **paying** guest (= he pays for the use of a room in someone's home).* **2** A2 a person who is staying in a hotel: *We would like to remind all our guests to leave their keys at reception before they depart.* **3** B2 a person, such as an ENTERTAINER, who has been invited to appear on a television or radio programme or in a performance: *Our special guest on the programme tonight is Robert de Niro.* ◦ *Madonna made a guest appearance at the concert.* ◦ *Simon Rattle will be the guest conductor with the London Symphony Orchestra.*

Word partners for guest

a *frequent/occasional/regular* guest • *entertain/invite/welcome* guests • the guest *list* • a guest *of* sb • *as* sb's guest

IDIOM **be my guest!** something you say when you give someone permission to do or use something: *'Can I try out your new bicycle?' 'Be my guest.'*

▸**verb** [I] If a person, especially an ENTERTAINER, guests on a programme or show, they are invited to appear or perform on it.

ˈguest ˌbook noun [C] a book in which people write their names and addresses when they have been staying at a hotel

guesthouse /ˈgest.haʊs/ noun [C] a small cheap hotel

ˌguest of ˈhonour UK (US **ˌguest of ˈhonor**) noun [C] the most important person at a social occasion: *The prime minister was guest of honour at the dinner.*

ˈguest room noun [C] a bedroom in a house for visitors to sleep in

ˈguest ˌworker noun [C] a person who lives and works in a foreign country for a limited period of time, doing low-paid and usually unskilled work

guff /gʌf/ noun [U] informal speech or writing that is nonsense

guffaw /gʌfˈɔː/ US /-ˈɑː/ verb [I] to laugh loudly, especially at something stupid that someone has said or done: *He guffawed with delight when he heard the news.* • **guffaw** noun [C] *She let out a loud guffaw.*

GUI /ˈguː.i/ noun abbreviation for **graphical user interface**

guidance /ˈgaɪ.dᵊns/ noun [U] **1** B2 help and advice about how to do something or about how to deal with problems connected with your work, education, or personal relationships: *I've always looked to my father for guidance in these matters.* ◦ *careers guidance* **2** the process of directing the flight of a MISSILE or ROCKET: *a missile guidance system*

ˈguidance ˌcounselor noun [C] US someone whose job is to help people choose a job or CAREER

guide /gaɪd/ noun; verb

▸**noun** [C] **BOOK** ▷ **1** B1 a book which gives you the most important information about a particular subject: *a hotel/wine guide* ◦ *a guide **to** the birds of North America* **2** a guidebook: *a guide **to** the British Isles* ◦ ***tourist** guides* **HELP** ▷ **3** something that helps you form an opinion or make a decision about something else: *I never follow recipes exactly when I cook – I just use them as **rough** guides.* **PERSON** ▷ **4** A2 a person whose job is showing a place or a particular route to visitors: *We hired a guide to take us up into the mountains.* ◦ *a **tour** guide* **INFLUENCE** ▷ **5** a person or thing that influences what you do or think: *Let your conscience be your guide.*

G

▸verb **HELP** ▷ **1** [T] to show someone how to do something difficult: *Our lawyer guided us* ***through*** *the more complicated questions on the form.* **SHOW WAY** ▷ **2** B1 [T] to show people round a place: *The curator guided us* ***round*** *the gallery, pointing out the most famous paintings in the collection.* ◦ *a guided* ***tour*** *of the city* **3** B1 [T] to take someone somewhere or show them how to get there: *The shop assistant guided me* ***to*** *the shelf where the gardening books were displayed.* ◦ *The runway lights guide the plane in to land.* **4** [T usually + adv/prep] to take hold of part of someone's body, especially their arm, and take them somewhere: *He took my arm and guided me to the bar.* **MAKE MOVE** ▷ **5** [T usually + adv/prep] to make something move in the direction in which you want it to go: *The pilot guided the plane onto the runway.* ◦ *She guided the child's head and arms into the T-shirt.* **INFLUENCE** ▷ **6** [T] to influence someone's behaviour: *Trust your own judgment and don't be guided by what anyone else thinks.*

G

Guide /gaɪd/ noun **1** [C] (also **Girl Guide**) a girl between ten and 14 years old who is a member of the Guides organization **2 the Guides** [plural] an international organization for young women which encourages them to take part in different activities and to become responsible and independent → Compare **the Scouts**

guidebook /ˈgaɪd.bʊk/ noun [C] (also **guide**) A2 a book which gives information for visitors about a place, such as a city or country: *a guidebook* ***to*** *Montreal*

ˌguided ˈmissile noun [C] an explosive weapon whose direction is controlled electronically during its flight

ˈguide ˌdog noun [C] a dog that has been specially trained to help a blind person travel around safely: *guide dogs for the blind*

guideline /ˈgaɪd.laɪn/ noun [C usually plural] C1 information intended to advise people on how something should be done or what something should be: *The EU has* ***issued*** *guidelines on appropriate levels of pay for part-time manual workers.*

ˈguide ˌprice noun [C] the price that something is expected to be sold for, especially in an AUCTION: *The guide price for the farmhouse is £475,000.*

ˈguide ˌword noun [C] In this dictionary, guide words help you find the explanation you are looking for when a word has more than one main meaning. They are printed in small, coloured capital letters.

ˌguiding ˈprinciple noun [C] an idea which influences you very much when making a decision or considering a matter: *Equality of opportunity has been the government's guiding principle in its education reforms.*

ˌguiding ˈspirit noun [C usually singular] (also **ˌguiding ˈlight**) a person who influences a person or group and shows them how to do something successfully: *She was the founder of the company and its guiding spirit.*

guild /gɪld/ noun [C] an organization of people who do the same job or have the same interests: *the Writers' Guild* ◦ *the Fashion Designers' Guild*

guilder /ˈgɪl.dəʳ/ US /-dɚ/ noun [C] the standard unit of money used in the Netherlands before the introduction of the euro

guildhall /ˈgɪld.hɔːl/ US /-hɑːl/ noun [C usually singular] (in the UK) a building in the centre of a town in which members of a guild met in the past, now often used as a place for meetings or performances or as local government offices

guile /gaɪl/ noun [U] formal clever but sometimes dishonest behaviour that you use to deceive someone: *The president will need to use all her political guile to stay in power.* ◦ *He is a simple man, totally lacking in guile.*

guileless /ˈgaɪl.ləs/ adj formal honest, not able to deceive: *She regarded him with wide, guileless blue eyes.*

guillemet /ˈgiːmeɪ/ noun [C] each of the pair of punctuation marks << and >> used around a word or phrase in French and some other languages to show that someone else has written or said it

guillemot /ˈgɪl.ɪ.mɒt/ US /-ə.mɑːt/ noun [C] a black and white sea bird with a long narrow beak that lives in northern parts of the world

guillotine /ˈgɪl.ə.tiːn/ noun; verb

▸noun **DEVICE** ▷ **1** [C or S] a device, invented in France, consisting of a sharp blade in a tall frame, used in the past for killing criminals by cutting off their heads: *King Louis XVI and Marie Antoinette* ***went to*** *the guillotine (= were killed by the guillotine) during the French Revolution.* **2** [C] UK a device with a long sharp blade that is used for cutting large quantities of paper **LIMIT** ▷ **3** [C] UK specialized a limit on the amount of discussion allowed about a particular law in Parliament, made by setting a fixed time before a final vote must be taken

▸verb [T] **KILL** ▷ **1** to cut someone's head off using a guillotine: *During the French Revolution, thousands of people were guillotined.* **LIMIT** ▷ **2** UK specialized to set a fixed time before a final vote must be taken on a particular law in Parliament: *The bill was guillotined at the committee stage.*

guilt /gɪlt/ noun [U] **FEELING** ▷ **1** B2 a feeling of worry or unhappiness that you have because you have done something wrong, such as causing harm to another person: *He suffered such feelings of guilt over leaving his children.* ◦ *She remembered with* ***a pang of*** *guilt that she hadn't called her mother.* **RESPONSIBILITY** ▷ **2** B2 the fact of having done something wrong or committed a crime: *Both suspects* ***admitted*** *their guilt to the police.* ◦ *The prosecution's task in a case is to* ***establish*** *a person's guilt beyond any reasonable doubt.* → Compare **innocence**

ˈguilt ˌcomplex noun [C] a very strong feeling of guilt which you cannot get rid of: *She has a guilt complex about inheriting so much money.*

ˈguilt-free adj allowing you to enjoy something without feeling unhappy that you are doing something bad: *a guilt-free chocolate cake made without fat* ◦ *The travel company offers guilt-free trips that won't damage the environment.*

guiltless /ˈgɪlt.ləs/ adj not responsible for doing something wrong or committing a crime

ˈguilt-ˌridden adj feeling very guilty

ˈguilt ˌtrip noun [C] informal a strong feeling of guilt because of something you have done wrong or forgotten to do

ˈguilt-trip verb [T] (-pp-) informal to make someone feel guilty, usually in order to make them do something

guilty /ˈgɪl.ti/ US /-t̬i/ adj **FEELING** ▷ **1** B1 feeling guilt: *I feel so guilty* ***about*** *forgetting her birthday.* ◦ *She must have done something wrong, because she's looking so guilty.* ◦ *You've got a guilty* ***conscience*** *– that's why you can't sleep.* **RESPONSIBLE** ▷ **2** B2 responsible for breaking a law: *The jury has to decide whether a person is guilty or innocent* ***of*** *a crime.* ◦ *A person accused of a* *crime is presumed innocent until* ***proven*** *guilty.* ◦ *The company* ***pleaded*** *guilty (= they formally admitted their guilt in court)* ***to*** *the charge of manslaughter.* → Compare **innocent 3 the guilty party** the person who has done something wrong or who has committed a crime • **guiltily** /-tɪ.li/ (US) /-t̬ɪ.li/ adv • **guiltiness** /-nəs/ noun [U]

guinea /ˈgɪn.i/ noun [C] an old British gold coin worth £1.05

ˈguinea ˌfowl noun [C] (plural **guinea fowl**) a large grey and white African bird, kept for its eggs and meat

ˈguinea ˌpig noun [C] **ANIMAL** ▷ **1** a small animal covered in fur with rounded ears, short legs and no tail, often kept as a pet by children **TEST** ▷ **2** a person used in a scientific test, usually to discover the effect of a drug on humans: *They're asking for students to be guinea pigs in their research into the common cold.*

guise /gaɪz/ noun [U] the appearance of someone or something, especially when intended to deceive: *The men who arrived* ***in the*** *guise* ***of*** *drug dealers were actually undercover police officers.* ◦ *The company has been accused of trying to sell their products* ***under the*** *guise* ***of*** *market research.*

guitar /gɪˈtɑːʳ/ (US) /-ˈtɑːr/ noun [C] (A1) a musical instrument, usually made of wood, with six strings and a long neck, played with the fingers or a PLECTRUM: *He sat on the grass, strumming his guitar.* ◦ *an acoustic guitar* ◦ *an electric guitar*

guitarist /gɪˈtɑː.rɪst/ (US) /-ˈtɑːr.ɪst/ noun [C] (B1) a person who plays the guitar: *a classical/folk/rock guitarist*

the gulag /ˈguː.læg/ noun [S] severe work prisons for people found guilty of crimes against their country

gulch /gʌltʃ/ noun [C] US for **gully**

gulf /gʌlf/ noun **AREA** ▷ **1** (B2) [C] a very large area of sea surrounded on three sides by a coast: *the Gulf of Mexico* **2 the Gulf** [S] the Persian Gulf and the countries around it: *The Gulf states include Saudi Arabia, Kuwait, Bahrain, Oman, Qatar, and the United Arab Emirates.* **3** [C] formal a very large deep hole in the ground **DIFFERENCE** ▷ **4** (C2) [C usually singular] an important difference between the ideas, opinions, or situations of two groups of people: *There is a widening gulf* ***between*** *the middle classes and the poorest sections of society.* ◦ *It is hoped that the peace plan will* ***bridge*** *the gulf (= reduce the very large difference)* ***between*** *the government and the rebels.*

the ˈGulf ˌStream noun [S] the current of warm water that flows across the Atlantic Ocean from the Gulf of Mexico towards Europe

gull /gʌl/ noun [C] (also **seagull**) a bird that lives near the coast with black and white or grey and white feathers

gullet /ˈgʌl.ət/ noun [C] old-fashioned the tube which food travels down from the mouth to the stomach

gullible /ˈgʌl.ə.bl/ adj easily deceived or tricked, and too willing to believe everything that other people say: *There are any number of miracle cures on the market for people gullible enough to buy them.*

gully (US also **gulley**) /ˈgʌl.i/ noun [C] (also **gulch**) a narrow valley or CHANNEL with steep sides, made by a fast-flowing stream

gulp /gʌlp/ verb; noun

▸verb **1** [I or T] to eat or drink food or liquid quickly by swallowing it in large amounts, or to make a swallowing movement because of fear, surprise, or excitement: *She gulped* ***down*** *her drink and made a hasty exit.* ◦ *When it was his turn to dive, he gulped and stepped up onto the diving board.* **2** [T] to breathe in a large amount of air very quickly

PHRASAL VERB **gulp sth back** to try not to show that you are upset, usually by swallowing hard: *She gulped back* ***the tears****.*

▸noun [C] an act of gulping: *He swallowed his drink in one gulp.* ◦ *She rose to the surface of the water once every minute to get/take a gulp of air.*

gum /gʌm/ noun; verb

▸noun **MOUTH** ▷ **1** (B2) [C] either of the two areas of firm pink flesh inside the mouth that cover the bones into which the teeth are fixed: *sore gums* **STICKY SUBSTANCE** ▷ **2** [U] a sticky substance that comes from the stems of some trees and plants **3** [U] a type of glue used for sticking together pieces of paper **4** [U] **chewing gum** or **bubble gum** (= a soft sweet that you crush with your teeth but do not swallow) **5** [C] UK used in the names of some CHEWY sweets with fruit flavours: *fruit/wine gums*

IDIOM **by gum!** UK old-fashioned informal used to express surprise: *By gum, he's a big lad!*

▸verb [T] (-mm-) old-fashioned If you gum one piece of paper to another, you stick them together using glue: *The labels were already gummed to the envelopes.*

PHRASAL VERB **gum sth up** [M often passive] to prevent something from working or opening in the usual way by covering it with a sticky substance: *When I woke up this morning my eyes were all gummed up.*

gumbo /ˈgʌm.bəʊ/ (US) /-boʊ/ noun (plural **gumbos**) **1** [C or U] a thick soup made with OKRA (= a small green vegetable) and meat or fish, which comes from America **2** [U] US for **okra**

gumboot /ˈgʌm.buːt/ noun [C] UK old-fashioned for **wellington**

gumdrop /ˈgʌm.drɒp/ (US) /-drɑːp/ noun [C] (also **gum**) a CHEWY sweet that usually has a fruit flavour

gummed /gʌmd/ adj (also **gummy**) sticky or with glue on the surface: *gummed labels/envelopes*

gummy /ˈgʌm.i/ adj **MOUTH** ▷ **1** showing the gums **STICKY** ▷ **2** gummed: *a gummy label*

gumption /ˈgʌmp.ʃᵊn/ noun [U] informal the ability to decide what is the best thing to do in a particular situation, and to do it with energy and determination: *She* ***had the*** *gumption* ***to*** *write directly to the company manager and persuade him to give her a job.*

gumshield /ˈgʌm.ʃiːld/ noun [C] UK a device that BOXERS put inside their mouths in order to protect their teeth and gums during fights

gumshoe /ˈgʌm.ʃuː/ noun [C] US old-fashioned informal for **detective** (= someone whose job is to discover facts about a crime)

ˈgum ˌtree noun [C] a **eucalyptus**

gun /gʌn/ noun; verb

▸noun [C] **1** (B1) a weapon from which bullets or SHELLS (= explosive containers) are fired: *The British police do not* ***carry*** *guns.* ◦ *You could hear the noise of guns* ***firing*** *in the distance.* **2** in sport, a device which makes a very loud sudden noise as a signal to start a race: ***At the*** *gun, the runners sprinted away down the track.* **3** a device which you hold in your hand and use for sending out a liquid or object: *a spray gun* → See also **staple gun 4 hired gun** mainly US informal a person who is paid to shoot and kill someone

IDIOMS **be under the gun** mainly US to feel worried because you have to do something by a particular time or in a particular way: *Al's under the gun to decide by the end of the month whether to move with his* *company.* • **with guns blazing** (also **all guns blazing**) If you do something, especially argue, with guns blazing, you do it with a lot of force and energy: *I went into the meeting with guns blazing, determined not to let him win.*

▸**verb** [T] (**-nn-**) mainly US old-fashioned informal to make an engine operate at a higher speed: *You must have been really gunning the engine to get here on time.*

IDIOM **be gunning for sb** informal to often criticize someone or be trying to cause trouble for them: *She's been gunning for me ever since I got the promotion she wanted.*

PHRASAL VERB **gun sb down** to shoot someone and kill or seriously injure them, often when they cannot defend themselves: *The police officer was gunned down as he took his children to school.*

G

gunboat /ˈgʌn.bəʊt/ US /-boʊt/ noun [C] a small military ship with large guns, used especially in areas near the coast

ˌgunboat diˈplomacy noun [U] disapproving the use of military threats by a strong country against a weaker country in order to make that country obey it

ˈgun ˌcarriage noun [C] a frame on wheels for a CANNON (= a large powerful gun)

ˈgun conˌtrol noun [U] laws that control the sale and use of guns and who is allowed to own them: *He is a social conservative and an opponent of gun control.*

ˈgun ˌdog noun [C] (US also **ˈbird ˌdog**) a dog used by people who hunt to find and collect birds they have shot

gunfight /ˈgʌn.faɪt/ noun [C] a fight using guns between two or more people, especially COWBOYS • **gunfighter** /-faɪ.təʳ/ US /-faɪ.t̬ɚ/ noun [C]

gunfire /ˈgʌn.faɪəʳ/ US /-faɪr/ noun [U] the usually repeated shooting of one or more guns: *The sound of gunfire echoed into the night.*

gunge /gʌndʒ/ noun [U] (also **gunk**) any unpleasant soft dirty substance, often one which you cannot recognize: *It was amazing how much gunge had accumulated in the pipe.*

gung-ho /ˌgʌŋˈhəʊ/ US /-ˈhoʊ/ adj informal extremely enthusiastic about doing something, especially going to war

gunman /ˈgʌn.mən/ noun [C] (plural **-men** /-mən/) a man, usually a criminal, who is armed with a gun: *The three men were held hostage for two days by masked gunmen.*

gunmetal grey /ˌgʌnˌmet.əlˈgreɪ/ US /-ˌmet̬-/ noun [U] a dark grey colour • **ˌgunmetal-ˈgrey adj**

gunnel /ˈgʌn.əl/ noun [C] a **gunwale**

gunner /ˈgʌn.əʳ/ US /-ɚ/ noun [C] a member of the armed forces who is trained to use ARTILLERY (= very large guns)

gunnery /ˈgʌn.əʳr.i/ US /-ɚ-/ noun [U] the skill or activity of shooting with ARTILLERY (= very large guns)

gunpoint /ˈgʌn.pɔɪnt/ noun **at gunpoint** experiencing or using a threat of killing with a gun: *The family were held at gunpoint for an hour while the men raided their house.*

gunpowder /ˈgʌnˌpaʊ.dəʳ/ US /-dɚ/ noun [U] an explosive mixture of substances in the form of a powder, used for making explosive devices and FIREWORKS

ˈgun-ˌrunner noun [C] a person who illegally brings guns into a country

ˈgun-ˌrunning noun [U] the activity of bringing guns and other weapons into a country illegally, especially for use against the government

gunshot /ˈgʌn.ʃɒt/ US /-ʃɑːt/ noun [C] (the sound of) the shooting of a gun: *I then heard what sounded like a gunshot in the hall.* ◦ *gunshot* ***wounds***

gunslinger /ˈgʌnˌslɪŋ.əʳ/ US /-ɚ/ noun [C] especially in the past in North America, someone who is good at shooting guns and is employed for protection or to kill people

gunsmith /ˈgʌn.smɪθ/ noun [C] a person who makes and repairs guns, especially small guns

gunwale /ˈgʌn.əl/ noun [C] (also **gunnel**) the upper edge of the side of a boat or ship

IDIOM **to the gunwales** old-fashioned If something is filled to the gunwales, it is extremely full: *A crowd of 50,000 packed the stadium almost to the gunwales.*

gurdwara /gɜːˈdwɑː.rə/ US /gɝː-/ noun [C] a Sikh TEMPLE (= religious building where people worship)

gurgle /ˈgɜː.gl/ US /ˈgɝː-/ verb [I] (of babies) to make a happy sound with the back of the throat, or (of water, especially small streams) to flow quickly while making a low, pleasant sound: *The baby lay gurgling in her cot.* ◦ *Outside of her window the stream gurgled over the rocks.* • **gurgle** noun [C] *The water went down the plughole with a loud gurgle.*

gurgler /ˈgɜː.gləʳ/ US /ˈgɝː.glɚ/ noun [C] Australian English informal a **plughole**

IDIOM **go down the gurgler** Australian English If work or money goes down the gurgler, it is wasted: *So say he gives up his training, that's four thousand dollars down the gurgler.*

gurney /ˈgɜː.ni/ US /ˈgɝː-/ noun [C] US a light bed on wheels, used to move patients in a hospital

guru /ˈgʊr.uː/ noun [C] **1** a religious leader or teacher in the Hindu or Sikh religion **2** informal a person skilled in something who gives advice: *a management guru* ◦ *a lifestyle guru*

gush /gʌʃ/ verb; noun

▸**verb** FLOW ▷ **1** [I usually + adv/prep, T] to flow or send out quickly and in large amounts: *Oil gushed* (***out***) ***from*** *the hole in the tanker.* ◦ *Blood was gushing* ***from*** *his nose.* ◦ *Her arm gushed blood where the knife had gone in.* EXPRESS ▷ **2** [I or T] to express a positive feeling, especially praise, in such a strong way that it does not sound sincere: [+ speech] *'You're just so talented!' she gushed.*

▸**noun** [S] FLOW ▷ **1** a large amount of liquid or gas that flows quickly: *Showers with pumps are more expensive, but they deliver* ***a*** *really powerful gush* ***of*** *water.* EXPRESSION ▷ **2** a sudden strong and positive feeling, or an expression of positive feeling, usually so strong it does not sound sincere

gusher /ˈgʌʃ.əʳ/ US /-ɚ/ noun [C] an OIL WELL from which oil flows without the use of a PUMP

gushing /ˈgʌʃ.ɪŋ/ adj (also **gushy**) expressing a positive feeling, especially praise, in such a strong way that it does not sound sincere: *One of the more gushing newspapers described the occasion as 'a fairy-tale wedding'.* • **gushingly** /-li/ adv (also **gushily** /ˈgʌʃ.ɪ.li/)

gusset /ˈgʌs.ɪt/ noun [C] a second layer of cloth that is sewn into a piece of clothing to make it larger, stronger, or more comfortable: *silk panties with a cotton gusset*

gust /gʌst/ noun; verb

▸**noun** [C] a sudden strong wind: *A sudden gust* ***of*** *wind blew his umbrella inside out.* ◦ figurative *She could hear gusts* ***of*** *laughter (= sudden, loud laughter) from within the room.*

►verb [I] to blow strongly: *Winds gusting **to** 50 mph brought down power cables.*

gustatory /ˈɡʌs.tə.tᵊr.i/ (US) /-tɔː.ri/ **adj** specialized connected with taste: *gustatory pleasures*

gusto /ˈɡʌs.təʊ/ (US) /-toʊ/ **noun** [U] great energy, enthusiasm, and enjoyment that is experienced by someone taking part in an activity, especially a performance: *Everyone joined in the singing **with** great gusto.*

gusty /ˈɡʌs.ti/ **adj** with sudden, strong winds: *The forecast was for gusty winds and rain.*

gut /ɡʌt/ **noun; verb**

►noun **BOWELS** ▷ **1** [U] the long tube in the body of a person or animal, through which food moves during the process of digesting food: *Meat stays in the gut longer than vegetable matter.* **2** [C] informal a person's stomach when it is extremely large: *He's got a huge **beer** gut (= large stomach caused by drinking beer).* **3 guts** (C2) [plural] bowels: *My guts hurt.* ◦ *He got a knife in the guts.* **4 gut feeling/reaction** informal a strong belief about someone or something which cannot completely be explained and does not have to be decided by reasoning: *I have a gut feeling that the relationship won't last.* **5** [U] a strong thread made from an animal's bowels used, especially in the past, for making musical instruments and sports RACKETS **BRAVERY** ▷ **6 guts** (B2) [plural] informal courage in dealing with danger or uncertainty: [+ to infinitive] ***It takes** a lot of guts **to** admit to so many people that you've made a mistake.*

IDIOMS **have sb's guts for garters** UK informal If you say you will have someone's guts for garters, you mean that you will punish them severely: *If that boy has taken my bike again, I'll have his guts for garters!* • **slog/sweat/work your guts out** informal to work extremely hard: *I've been slogging my guts out these past few weeks and all he can do is criticize.*

►verb [T] (-tt-) **EMPTY A BUILDING** ▷ **1** to destroy the inside of a building completely, usually by fire: *A fire gutted the bookshop last week.* **2** to remove the inside parts and contents of a building, usually so that it can be decorated in a completely new way **REMOVE ORGANS** ▷ **3** to remove the INNER organs of an animal, especially in preparation for eating it: *She gutted the fish and cut off their heads.*

gutless /ˈɡʌt.ləs/ **adj** informal showing no courage: *This government is too gutless to take on the big long-term problems such as pollution.*

gutsy /ˈɡʌt.si/ **adj** informal brave and determined: *a gutsy performance*

gutted /ˈɡʌt.ɪd/ (US) /ˈɡʌt̬-/ **adj** UK slang extremely disappointed and unhappy: *He was gutted when she finished the relationship.*

gutter /ˈɡʌt.əʳ/ (US) /ˈɡʌt̬.ɚ/ **noun; verb**

►noun **CHANNEL** ▷ **1** [C] the edge of a road where rain flows away **2** [C] an open pipe at the lower edge of a roof which collects and carries away rain **SOCIAL LEVEL** ▷ **3 the gutter** [S] the lowest level, especially of society: *Born to a poverty-stricken family, she dragged herself out of the gutter to become one of the wealthiest people in Britain today.*

►verb [I] literary (of a flame or candle) to burn UNEVENLY and weakly, especially before completely stopping burning: *a guttering candle*

guttering /ˈɡʌt.ᵊr.ɪŋ/ (US) /ˈɡʌt̬.ɚ-/ **noun** [U] UK the system of open pipes on a building which collects and carries away rain

the ˌgutter ˈpress **noun** [S] UK disapproving the type of newspapers that pay more attention to shocking stories about crime and sex than to serious matters

guttersnipe /ˈɡʌt.ə.snaɪp/ (US) /ˈɡʌt̬.ɚ-/ **noun** [C] old-fashioned a child from a poor area of a town who is dirty and dressed badly: *a Victorian guttersnipe*

guttural /ˈɡʌt.ᵊr.ᵊl/ (US) /ˈɡʌt̬.ɚ-/ **adj** (of speech sounds) produced at the back of the throat and therefore deep: *Two Egyptians were arguing outside the room, their voices loud and guttural.*

ˈgut-ˌwrenching **adj** informal making you want to vomit: *gut-wrenching scenes of bloodshed*

guv /ɡʌv/ **noun** [S] UK old-fashioned slang **1** used to address a man: *Excuse me, guv, could you spare an old man the price of a cup of tea?* **2** guvnor: *Check with the guv first.*

guvnor /ˈɡʌv.nəʳ/ (US) /-nɚ/ **noun** [C] (also **guv**) UK old-fashioned slang a man who is in a position of authority over you: *If you want any time off work, you'll have to ask the guvnor.*

guy /ɡaɪ/ **noun MAN** ▷ **1** (A2) [C] informal a man: *He's a really nice guy.* ◦ *Do you mean the guy with the blonde hair and glasses?* **2 guys** (B1) [plural] mainly US used to address a group of people of either sex: *Come on, you guys, let's go.* **3** [C] in the UK, a model of a man that is burned on a large fire on Guy Fawkes Night **ROPE** ▷ **4** [C] (also **guy rope**, US also **guyline**) a rope which at one end is connected to a tent or pole and at the other end is fastened to the ground by a PEG, keeping the tent or pole in position

Guy Fawkes Night /ˈɡaɪ.fɔːksˌnaɪt/ (US) /-fɔːrks-/ **noun** [C or U] (also **ˈBonfire ˌNight**) UK in the UK, the evening of 5 November when models of men, called GUYS, are burned on large fires outside and there are FIREWORK DISPLAYS. This is in memory of the failed attempt by Guy Fawkes to destroy the Houses of Parliament in London in 1605 with explosives.

guzzle /ˈɡʌz.ᵊl/ **verb** [I or T] informal to eat or drink quickly, eagerly, and usually in large amounts: *I'm not surprised you feel sick after guzzling three ice creams!* ◦ *You're bound to get indigestion if you guzzle like that!* • **guzzler** /-əʳ/ (US) /-ɚ/ **noun** [C] *She's a real guzzler!*

gym /dʒɪm/ **noun** **1** (A2) [U] gymnastics, especially when done as a subject at school: *a gym skirt* ◦ *gym shoes* ◦ *Class 3 do gym on a Wednesday afternoon.* **2** (A2) [C] a large room with weights for lifting and other equipment for exercising the body and increasing strength: *I go to the gym twice a week.* **3** [U] US for **physical education**

gymkhana /dʒɪmˈkɑː.nə/ **noun** [C] mainly UK an event at which people ride horses, taking part in various competitions involving horse racing and jumping over special fences

gymnasium /dʒɪmˈneɪ.zi.əm/ **noun** [C] (also **gym**) a large room with weights for lifting and other equipment for exercising the body and increasing strength

gymnast /ˈdʒɪm.næst/ **noun** [C] a person who is skilled in gymnastics, often someone who competes in gymnastic competitions: *a great Russian gymnast*

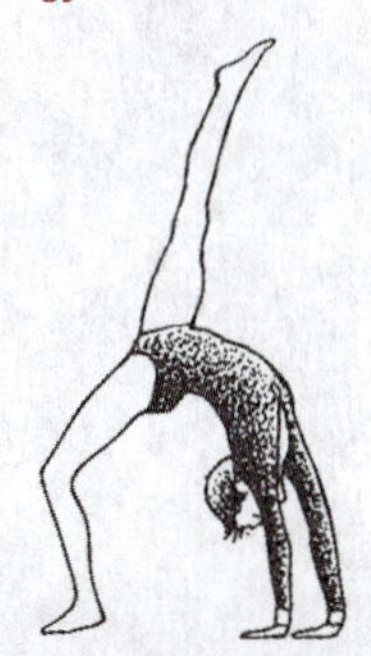
gymnast

gymnastics /dʒɪmˈnæs.tɪks/ **noun** [U] (B1) physical exercises and activities performed inside, often using equipment such as bars and ropes, intended to increase the body's strength and the ability to move and bend easily: *the US women's gymnastics team* ◦ figurative *Legal arguments require incredible* ***mental/verbal*** *gymnastics (= the ability to think/speak cleverly and quickly).* • **gymnastic** /-tɪk/ **adj** [before noun] B2 *a gymnastic display*

gymslip /ˈdʒɪm.slɪp/ **noun** [C] UK a plain dress without sleeves usually worn over a shirt, especially in the past, by girls as a part of their school uniform

gynaecologist UK (US **gynecologist**) /ˌgaɪ.nəˈkɒl.ə.dʒɪst/ US /-ˈkɑː.lə-/ **noun** [C] a doctor skilled in the treatment of women's diseases, especially those of the REPRODUCTIVE organs

gynaecology UK (US **gynecology**) /ˌgaɪ.nəˈkɒl.ə.dʒi/ US /-ˈkɑː.lə-/ **noun** [U] the area of medicine which involves the treatment of women's diseases, especially those of the REPRODUCTIVE organs • **gynaecological** (US **gynecological**) /-kəˈlɒdʒ.ɪ.kəl/ US /-kəˈlɑː.dʒɪ.kəl/ **adj** *gynaecological problems*

gyp /dʒɪp/ **noun** [U] UK informal pain or trouble: *My knee has been* ***giving*** *me gyp since I started running.*

gypsum /ˈdʒɪp.səm/ **noun** [U] a hard white substance that is used in making PLASTER OF PARIS

gypsy (UK also **gipsy**) /ˈdʒɪp.si/ **noun** [C] (also **Romany**) a member of a race of people originally from northern India who typically used to travel from place to place, and now live especially in Europe and North America: *a gypsy caravan/encampment*

gyrate /dʒaɪˈreɪt/ US /ˈdʒaɪ.reɪt/ **verb** [I] **1** to turn around and around on a fixed point, usually quickly **2** to dance, especially in a sexual way • **gyration** /ˌdʒaɪˈreɪ.ʃən/ **noun** [C or U]

gyro **noun** [C] (plural **gyros**) **DEVICE** ▷ **1** /ˈdʒaɪ.rəʊ/ US /-roʊ/ a gyroscope **FOOD** ▷ **2** /ˈjɪə.rəʊ/, /ˈdʒɪə-/ US /ˈjɪr.oʊ/ US a food consisting of PITTA bread filled with LAMB and vegetables

gyroscope /ˈdʒaɪ.rə.skəʊp/ US /-skoʊp/ **noun** [C] (also **gyro**) a device containing a wheel which SPINS freely within a frame, used on aircraft and ships to help keep them horizontal, and as a children's toy

H, h /eɪtʃ/ **noun** [C or U] (plural **Hs**, **H's** or **h's**) the eighth letter of the English alphabet

ha (also **hah**) /hɑː/, /hæ/ **exclamation** used to express satisfaction that something bad has happened to someone who deserved it, or to show that you have succeeded in something: *He's left her has he? Ha! That'll teach her to go chasing other women's husbands!* ◦ *Ha! So I am right after all!*

habeas corpus /ˌheɪ.bi.əsˈkɔː.pəs/ ⓤⓢ /-ˈkɔːr-/ **noun** [U] legal a legal order which states that a person in prison must appear before and be judged by a law court before he or she can be forced by law to stay in prison

haberdashery /ˌhæb.əˈdæʃ.ər.i/ ⓤⓢ /-ɚˈdæʃ.ɚ-/ **noun** [C or U] **CLOTH** ▷ **1** UK (US **notions**) cloth, pins, thread, etc. used for sewing, or a shop or a department of a large shop which sells these **MEN'S CLOTHES** ▷ **2** US old-fashioned clothing for men, or a shop or department in a large shop which sells this

habit /ˈhæb.ɪt/ **noun** **REPEATED ACTION** ▷ **1** B1 [C or U] something which you do often and regularly, sometimes without knowing that you are doing it: *I always buy the same brand of toothpaste just **out of** (= because of) habit.* ◦ *I'm trying not to **get into** (= start) the habit of always having biscuits with my coffee.* ◦ *I used to swim twice a week, but I seem to have **got out of** (= ended) the habit recently.* ◦ *I was taught to drive by my boyfriend and I'm afraid I've **picked up** (= caught) some of his bad habits.* ◦ *His eating habits are extraordinary.* ◦ *I'm trying to get him to **break** (= end intentionally) the habit of switching on the TV when he comes home at night.* ◦ *I don't mind being woken up once or twice in the middle of the night by my flatmate so long as she doesn't **make a habit of it** (= do it frequently).* ◦ *I'm not really **in the** habit **of** looking at (= I don't usually look at) other people's clothes, but even I noticed that awful suit!* **2** B2 [C] something annoying that someone often does: *She **has a** habit **of** finishing off other people's sentences.* **3** B2 [C] a strong physical need to keep having a particular drug: *a cocaine habit* ◦ figurative humorous *I'm afraid I've got a chocolate habit.* **CLOTHING** ▷ **4** [C] a special piece of long clothing worn by MONKS and NUNS

Word partners for habit

have a habit • *get into/get out of* the habit of doing sth • *have/make* a habit *of* doing sth • sth *becomes* a habit • *acquire/develop/pick up* a habit • *break/kick* a habit • an *annoying/bad/good/nasty* habit • be *in* the habit of doing sth • do sth *from/out of/through* habit

habitable /ˈhæb.ɪ.tə.bl̩/ ⓤⓢ /-t̬ə-/ **adj** (also **inhabitable**) providing conditions that are good enough to live in or on: *A lot of improvements would have to be made before the building was habitable.* ◦ *Some areas of the country are just too cold to be habitable.* → Opposite **uninhabitable**

habitat /ˈhæb.ɪ.tæt/ **noun** [C or U] C1 the natural environment in which an animal or plant usually lives: *With so many areas of woodland being cut down, a lot of wildlife is losing its natural habitat.*

habitation /ˌhæb.ɪˈteɪ.ʃən/ **noun** [U] formal **1** the act of living in a building **2 unfit for human habitation** describes a house that is too dirty or dangerous for people to be allowed to live in it

ˈhabit-ˌforming adj A habit-forming activity or drug makes you want to do or have it repeatedly.

habitual /həˈbɪtʃ.u.əl/ **adj** formal usual or repeated: *a habitual thief* ◦ *habitual drug use* ◦ *dressed in his habitual black* ◦ *her habitual meanness* • **habitually** /-ə.li/ **adv** *There is something wrong with anyone who is so habitually rude.*

habituated /həˈbɪtʃ.u.eɪ.tɪd/ ⓤⓢ /-t̬ɪd/ **adj** formal used to something, especially something unpleasant: *We find children's emotional needs difficult to respond to because we are habituated **to** disregarding our own.*

habitué /hæˈbɪt.juː.eɪ/ **noun** [C] literary a person who regularly visits a particular place

hack /hæk/ **verb; noun**

▸**verb** **CUT** ▷ **1** [I or T, + adv/prep] to cut into pieces in a rough and violent way, often without aiming exactly: *Three villagers were hacked **to death** in a savage attack.* ◦ *The butcher hacked **off** a large chunk of meat.* ◦ UK figurative *The article had been hacked **about** (= carelessly changed) so much it was scarcely recognizable.* **2** [T usually + adv/prep] UK in football and RUGBY, to kick the ball away or to FOUL (= act against the rules) by kicking another player in the leg: *He was twice hacked **down** in the second half by the other team's sweeper.* **INFORMATION** ▷ **3** [I or T] to get into someone else's computer system without permission in order to find out information or do something illegal: ***Computer** hacking has become very widespread over the last decade.* ◦ *A programmer had managed to hack **into** some top-secret government data.* ◦ *He claimed they had spied on him and tried to hack his computer.* **4** [I or T] to use someone else's phone system without permission, especially to listen to their spoken messages: *Police told the actor that his phone had been hacked.* **MANAGE** ▷ **5** [T usually in negatives] informal to manage to deal successfully with something: *I tried working on the night shift for a while, but I just **couldn't** hack it.* **HORSE** ▷ **6** [I usually + adv/prep] (also **go hacking**) to ride a horse in the countryside

PHRASAL VERB **hack sb off** mainly UK informal to make someone feel annoyed: *He leaves all the difficult stuff for me to do and it really hacks me off.*

▸**noun** [C] **WRITER** ▷ **1** disapproving a JOURNALIST (= writer for newspapers or magazines) whose work is low in quality or does not have much imagination: *Fleet Street hacks* **POLITICIAN** ▷ **2** disapproving a politician, especially one who is not important: *tired old **party** hacks* **HORSE** ▷ **3** a ride on a horse in the countryside **DRIVER/CAR** ▷ **4** US informal (the driver of) a car that is available for rent, especially a taxi

ˌhacked ˈoff adj [after verb] informal unhappy, tired, or annoyed, especially because of the situation you are in: *She's getting a bit hacked off **with** all the travelling she has to do.*

hacker /ˈhæk.ər/ ⓤⓢ /-ɚ/ **noun** [C] **1** (also **computer hacker**) someone who hacks into other people's computer systems **2** (also **phone hacker**) someone who hacks into another person's phone and listens to their messages

ˌhacking ˈcough noun [C usually singular] a loud cough that sounds painful

hackles /ˈhæk.l̩z/ **noun** [plural] the hairs on the back of some animals or the feathers on the back of the neck of some birds which rise when the animal or bird is frightened or about to fight

IDIOM **make (sb's) hackles rise** (also **raise (sb's) hackles**) to annoy someone: *The prime minister's speech has raised hackles among the opposition.*

hackney carriage /ˌhæk.ni'kær.ɪdʒ/ (US) /-'ker-/ **noun** [C] **1** (also **hackney cab**) UK formal a taxi **2** UK a CARRIAGE pulled by a horse that can be rented with a driver for making short journeys, used especially in the past

hackneyed /'hæk.nid/ **adj** disapproving describes a phrase or an idea that has been said or used so often that it has become boring and has no meaning: *The plot of the film is just a hackneyed boy-meets-girl scenario.*

hacksaw /'hæk.sɔː/ (US) /-sɑː/ **noun** [C] a small saw used especially for cutting metal

hacksaw

had **verb; adj**
▸**verb** strong /hæd/ weak /həd/ /əd/ **HAVE** ▷ **1** (also **'d**) past simple and past participle of **have**, also used with the past participle of other verbs to form the past perfect: *When I was a child I had a dog.* ◦ *No more food please – I've had enough.* ◦ *I had heard/I'd heard they were planning to move to Boston.* ◦ formal *Had I known (= if I had known), I would have come home sooner.* **FINISHED** ▷ **2 have had it** informal (of a machine, etc.) to be in such a bad condition that it is not useful or (of a person, team, etc.) to be doing so badly that they are certain to fail: *I think this kettle's had it.* ◦ *Liverpool have had it for this season.*

IDIOMS **had better/best do sth** If you had better/best do something, you should do it or it would be good to do it: *I'd better leave a note so they'll know I'll be late.* • **have had it (up to here) with** to have suffered because of someone or something and to be no longer able to bear them: *I've had it up to here with you – get out!* ◦ *I've had it with foreign holidays.*

▸**adj** /hæd/ **be had** informal to be tricked and given less than you agreed or paid for: *'I paid £2,000 for this car.' 'You've been had, mate. It's not worth more than £1,000.'*

haddock /'hæd.ək/ **noun** [C or U] (plural **haddock**) a fish that can be eaten, found in the North Atlantic

Hades /'heɪ.diːz/ **noun** (in stories about Ancient Greece) a place under the earth where the spirits of the dead go → Compare **underworld**

hadj /hædʒ/ **noun** [C] (plural **hadjes**) a **hajj**

hadn't /'hæd.ənt/ **short form of** had not: *If you hadn't told him he would never have known.*

haematite UK specialized (US **hematite**) /'hiː.mə.taɪt/ **noun** [U] a common dark red or grey rock from which iron is obtained

haematology UK specialized (US **hematology**) /ˌhiː.mə'tɒl.ə.dʒi/ (US) /-'tɑː.lə-/ **noun** [U] the scientific study of blood and the body tissues which make it • **haematological** (US **hematological**) /-tə'lɒdʒ.ɪ.kəl/ (US) /-tə'lɑː.dʒɪkəl/ **adj** • **haematologist** (US **hematologist**) /-dʒɪst/ **noun** [C]

haemoglobin UK (US **hemoglobin**) /ˌhiː.mə'gləʊ.bɪn/ (US) /-gloʊ-/ **noun** [U] a substance in red blood cells that combines with and carries OXYGEN around the body, and gives blood its red colour

haemophilia UK (US **hemophilia**) /ˌhiː.mə'fɪl.i.ə/ **noun** [U] a rare blood disease in which blood continues to flow after a cut or other injury because one of the substances which causes it to CLOT does not work correctly

haemophiliac UK (US **hemophiliac**) /ˌhiː.mə'fɪl.i.æk/ **noun** [C] a person who suffers from haemophilia

haemorrhage /'hem.ər.ɪdʒ/ (US) /-ɚ-/ **noun; verb**
▸**noun** [C] UK (US **hemorrhage**) **1** a large flow of blood from a damaged BLOOD VESSEL (= tube carrying blood around the body): *a brain haemorrhage* **2** a sudden or serious loss: *The higher salaries paid overseas have caused a haemorrhage of talent from this country.*
▸**verb** UK (US **hemorrhage**) **1** [I] to lose a large amount of blood in a short time: *She started haemorrhaging while giving birth to the baby.* **2** [I or T] to lose large amounts of something such as money over a period of time and be unable to stop this happening: *The business has been haemorrhaging **money** for several months.*

haemorrhoids UK specialized (US **hemorrhoids**) /'hem.ər.ɔɪdz/ (US) /-ɚ-/ **noun** [plural] a medical condition in which the VEINS at the ANUS become swollen and painful and sometimes BLEED → Synonym **piles**

hag /hæg/ **noun** [C] disapproving an ugly old woman

haggard /'hæg.əd/ (US) /-ɚd/ **adj** looking ill or tired, often with dark skin under the eyes: *He'd been drinking the night before and was looking a bit haggard.*

haggis /'hæg.ɪs/ **noun** [U] a dish which comes from Scotland consisting of different sheep's organs cut up with onions and spices and cooked inside a sheep's stomach

haggle /'hæg.l/ **verb** [I or T] to attempt to decide on a price or conditions that are acceptable to the person selling the goods and the person buying them, usually by arguing: *It's traditional that you haggle **over/about** the price of things in the market.*

hagiography /ˌhæg.i'ɒg.rə.fi/ (US) /-'ɑː.grə-/ **noun 1** [C or U] a very admiring book about someone or a description of someone that represents the person as perfect or much better than they really are, or the activity of writing about someone in this way **2** [U] specialized writings about the lives of holy people such as SAINTS

hah /hɑː/, /hæ/ **exclamation ha**

ha ha /hə'hɑː/, /'hɑː.hɑː/ **exclamation** used in writing to represent a shout of laughter, or said by children or by adults behaving like children as a way of making someone look silly

haiku /'haɪ.kuː/ **noun** [C] (plural **haiku**) a short Japanese poem in 17 syllables

hail /heɪl/ **noun; verb**
▸**noun 1** (C2) [U] small hard balls of ice which fall from the sky like rain **2 a hail of sth** a lot of similar things or remarks, thrown or shouted at someone at the same time: *a hail of bullets* ◦ *The prime minister was greeted with a hail of insults as she arrived at the students' union.*
▸**verb** **CALL** ▷ **1** (C2) [T] formal to call someone in order to attract their attention: *Shall we hail a taxi?* ◦ *I tried to hail her from across the room.* **ICE** ▷ **2** (C2) [I] If it hails, small hard balls of ice fall from the sky like rain.

IDIOM **be within hailing distance of somewhere** old-fashioned to be near somewhere

PHRASAL VERBS **hail sb/sth as sth** [often passive] (C2) to praise a person or an achievement by saying that they are similar to someone or something very good: *She's being hailed as one of the best up-and-coming young dancers today.* ◦ *The film was hailed as a masterpiece in its day.* • **hail from somewhere** formal to come from or to have been born in a particular place: *Joe originally hails from Toronto.*

ˌhail-fellow-well-ˈmet adj old-fashioned If a man or his actions are described as hail-fellow-well-met, they are very friendly and enthusiastic, sometimes in a way that is not sincere: *He was greeted with the usual hail-fellow-well-met slap on the back and handshake.*

Hail Mary /ˌheɪlˈmeə.ri/ (US) /-ˈmer.i/ **noun** [C] a Catholic prayer to Mary, the mother of Jesus Christ

hailstone /ˈheɪl.stəʊn/ (US) /-stoʊn/ **noun** [C] a small hard ball of ice that falls from the sky like rain

hailstorm /ˈheɪl.stɔːm/ (US) /-stɔːrm/ **noun** [C] a sudden heavy fall of HAIL

hair /heəʳ/ (US) /her/ **noun** [C or U] **A1** the mass of thin thread-like structures on the head of a person, or any of these structures that grow out of the skin of a person or animal: *He's got short dark hair.* ◦ *I'm going to **have/get** my hair **cut**.* ◦ *She brushed her long red hair.* ◦ *He had lost his hair by the time he was 25.* ◦ *He's starting to get a few grey hairs now.* ◦ *I found a hair in my soup.*

IDIOMS **a hair's breadth** a very small distance or amount: *His finger was **within** a hair's breadth **of** touch**ing** the alarm.* ◦ *She came within a hair's breadth of losing her life (= she nearly died).* • **get in sb's hair** informal to annoy someone, usually by being present all the time: *My flatmate has been getting in my hair a bit recently.* • **the hair of the dog (that bit you)** humorous an alcoholic drink taken as a cure the morning after an occasion when you have drunk too much alcohol • **keep your hair on** UK informal said to tell someone to stop being so angry or upset: *Keep your hair on! You car isn't badly damaged.* • **make sb's hair stand on end** informal to make someone very frightened: *The thought of jumping out of a plane makes my hair stand on end.* • **not a hair out of place** If someone does not have a hair out of place, their appearance is very tidy: *She was immaculate as ever, not a hair out of place.* • **that'll put hairs on your chest!** humorous something that is said to someone who is going to drink something that is very strongly alcoholic or eat something satisfying that will make their stomach feel full

hairband /ˈheə.bænd/ (US) /ˈher-/ **noun** [C] (UK also **ˈAlice ˌband**) a strip of cloth or curved plastic strip worn in the hair, that fits closely over the top of the head and behind the ears

hairbrush /ˈheə.brʌʃ/ (US) /ˈher-/ **noun** [C] a brush used for making the hair on your head tidy and smooth

haircut /ˈheə.kʌt/ (US) /ˈher-/ **noun** [C] **HAIR** ▷ **1** **B1** the style in which someone's hair is cut, or an occasion of cutting the hair: *She has a really awful haircut.* ◦ *I wish he'd **get/have** a haircut.* **MONEY** ▷ **2** specialized a reduction in an amount of money, such as the price of a SHARE or BOND: *The crisis means that lenders will have to take a haircut.*

hairdo /ˈheə.duː/ (US) /ˈher-/ **noun** [C] (plural **hairdos**) old-fashioned the style in which a person, especially a woman, has had their hair cut and arranged, especially if it is unusual or done for a particular occasion

hairdresser /ˈheəˌdres.əʳ/ (US) /ˈherˌdres.ɚ/ **noun** [C] **B1** a person who cuts people's hair and puts it into a style, usually working in a special shop, called a hairdresser's: *I'm going to change my hairdresser.* ◦ *I've got a four o'clock appointment at the hairdresser's.* • **hairdressing** /-ɪŋ/ **noun** [U] *a hairdressing salon*

hairdryer /ˈheəˌdraɪ.əʳ/ (US) /ˈherˌdraɪ.ɚ/ **noun** [C] (also **hairdrier**) **B1** an electrical device, usually held in the hand, which blows out hot air and is used for drying a person's hair

-haired /-heəd/ (US) /-herd/ **suffix** with the hair described: *dark-haired* ◦ *short-haired*

ˈhair exˌtension **noun** [C usually plural] a long piece of hair that is added to a person's own hair in order to make the hair longer

ˈhair ˌgel **noun** [C or U] a thick liquid substance that is put in the hair to help the hair keep a particular shape or style

hairgrip /ˈheə.grɪp/ (US) /ˈher-/ **noun** [C] UK (US **ˈbobby ˌpin**) a U-shaped metal pin that is tightly bent and slides into the hair in order to keep it back off the face or to keep part of the hair in position

ˈhair ˌlacquer **noun** [U] UK **hair spray**

hairless /ˈheə.ləs/ (US) /ˈher-/ **adj** without hair

hairline /ˈheə.laɪn/ (US) /ˈher-/ **noun; adj**

▸**noun** [C] the edge of a person's hair, especially along the top of the FOREHEAD (= part of the face above the eyes): *He's got a **receding** hairline (= he's losing his hair at the front of the head).*

▸**adj** [before noun] (of CRACKS or lines) very narrow: *a hairline **fracture***

ˈhair ˌmousse **noun** [C or U] a light substance that is put in the hair to help the hair keep a particular shape or style

hairnet /ˈheə.net/ (US) /ˈher-/ **noun** [C] a light net that some women wear over their hair to keep it in place

hairpiece /ˈheə.piːs/ (US) /ˈher-/ **noun** [C] an artificial covering of hair used to hide an area of the head where there is no hair: *Do you think he **wears** a hairpiece?*

hairpin /ˈheə.pɪn/ (US) /ˈher-/ **noun** [C] a thin, U-shaped metal pin that is used to hold part of the hair in a suitable position

ˌhairpin ˈbend **noun** [C] UK (US **ˌhairpin ˈturn**) a bend in the road that is so sharp that it almost turns back in the opposite direction

ˈhair-ˌraising **adj** very frightening: *She gave a hair-raising account of her escape through the desert.*

ˈhair ˌsalon **noun** [C] a shop where people go to have their hair cut and put into a particular style

ˈhair ˌslide **noun** [C] UK (US **barrette**) a small, decorative piece of plastic, metal, or wood that a woman or girl wears in her hair, often to stop it falling in front of her face

ˈhair ˌspray **noun** [C or U] (UK also **ˈhair ˌlacquer**) a sticky liquid that is SPRAYED (= forced out in small drops) onto someone's hair to keep it in a particular shape

hairstyle /ˈheə.staɪl/ (US) /ˈher-/ **noun** [C] the style in which someone's hair is cut and arranged

ˌhair-ˈtrigger **adj** informal **a hair-trigger temper** the characteristic of becoming very angry very easily

hairy /ˈheə.ri/ (US) /ˈher.i/ **adj** **WITH HAIR** ▷ **1** having a lot of hair, especially on parts of the body other than the head: *hairy armpits/legs* ◦ *a hairy chest* **FRIGHTENING** ▷ **2** informal frightening or dangerous, especially in a way that is exciting: *I like going on the back of Laurent's motorbike, though it can get a bit hairy.* • **hairiness** /-nəs/ **noun** [U]

hajj (plural **hajjes**) (also **haj** (plural **hajes**), **hadj** (plural **hadjes**)) /hædʒ/ **noun** [C] the religious journey to Mecca which all Muslims try to make at least once in their life

haka /ˈhæ.kə/ **noun** [C] a traditional war dance of the Maori people of New Zealand, or a similar performance before a sports event that is intended to give support to one team while making the opposing team less confident

hake /heɪk/ noun [C or U] (plural **hake** or **hakes**) a big sea fish that can be eaten

halal /hæˈlæl/ adj [before noun] describes meat from an animal that has been killed in the way that is demanded by Islamic law, or someone who sells this meat: *halal meat* ◦ *a halal butcher*

halcyon days /ˌhæl.si.ənˈdeɪz/ noun [plural] literary a very happy or successful period in the past: *She recalled the halcyon days of her youth.*

hale and hearty /ˌheɪl.ənd ˈhɑː.ti/ Ⓤⓢ /-ˈhɑːr.t̬i/ adj old-fashioned (especially of old people) healthy and strong

half /hɑːf/ Ⓤⓢ /hæf/ noun, pronoun, predeterminer, adj, adv; noun

▸**noun, pronoun, predeterminer, adj, adv 1** A2 either of the two equal or nearly equal parts that together make up a whole: *'What's half of 96?' '48.'* ◦ *Roughly half* (**of**) *the class are Spanish and the others are a mixture of nationalities.* ◦ *Cut the apple* **in** *half/***into** *halves* (= *into two equal parts*). ◦ *My little brother is half* **as** *tall as me/half my height.* ◦ *half* **a dozen** (= *six*) *eggs* ◦ *Half* **of** *me would just like to give it all up and travel around the world* (= *partly I would like to, but partly I would not*). ◦ *She was born in the latter half of the 18th century.* ◦ *The recipe tells you to use a pound and a half of butter.* **2** B2 informal a lot: *She invited a lot of people to the party but half of them didn't turn up.* ◦ *I don't even know where she is half* (**of**) **the time**. **3 half past** A1 Half past a particular hour is 30 minutes later than that hour: *I'll meet you at half past nine* (= *09.30 or 21.30*). ◦ UK informal *I'll meet you at half seven* (= *half past seven*). **4** B1 only partly: *He answered the door half naked.* ◦ *I was half expecting to see her at the party.* ◦ *I'm half inclined to take the job just because it's in London.* ◦ *He was being funny but I think he was half serious.* ◦ *The bottle's half empty.* **5 go halves** informal to divide the cost of something with someone: *Shall we go halves* **on** *a bottle of champagne?* ◦ *I'll go halves* **with** *you on a bottle of champagne.* **6 half and half** equal amounts of two different things: *'Do you use milk or cream in the recipe?' 'Half and half.'* **7 half as much again** (US also **half again as much**) 50 percent more of the existing number or amount

IDIOMS **be half the battle** to be the most difficult part of a process so that once you have finished this part, you have almost succeeded: *For a lot of jobs, getting an interview is half the battle.* • **be half the dancer, writer, etc. you used to be** to be much less good at doing something than you used to be: *She's half the tennis player she used to be.* • **given half a/the chance** informal If someone would do something given half a chance, they would certainly do it if they had the opportunity: *I'd give up work given half a chance.* • **how the other half lives** humorous something people say when they see or hear about the lives of people who are richer than them • **not do things by halves** humorous If someone does not do things by halves, they put a lot of effort and enthusiasm into doing things, often more than is necessary: *'I didn't realize you were decorating the whole house.' 'Oh, we don't do things by halves round here.'* • **not half** UK informal used in spoken English to express a positive statement more strongly: *It wasn't half crowded in the club last night* (= *it was very crowded*). ◦ *She didn't half shout at him* (= *she shouted a lot at him*). ◦ *'You enjoyed yourself last night, didn't you?' 'Not half!'* (= *Very much!*) • **not half as** (also **not half such a**) B2 not nearly as: *It wasn't half as good as that other restaurant we went to.* • **not know the half of it** (also **have not heard the half of it**) If someone does not know the half of it, they know that a situation is bad but they do not know how serious it is: *'I hear things aren't going too well at work.' 'You don't know the half of it!'* • **that was a game, meal, walk, etc. and a half!** informal something that you say about something that was very surprising, very good, or took a lot of time

▸**noun** [C] (plural **halves**) DRINK ▷ **1** UK informal half a PINT of a drink, especially beer: *A pint of lager and two halves, please.* TICKET ▷ **2** UK a ticket that is cheaper because it is for a child: *Two adults and three halves to Manchester, please.* SPORT ▷ **3 first/second half** either of two periods of time into which a game is divided

ˈhalf-assed slang disapproving (UK also **ˈhalf-arsed**) adj A half-assed idea or plan is stupid or has not been considered carefully enough: *It's another one of her half-assed ideas for getting rich.*

halfback /ˈhɑːf.bæk/ Ⓤⓢ /ˈhæf-/ noun [C] (also **half**) (in football and other sports) a player who plays in the middle of the field, in front of the FULLBACKS and behind the FORWARDS

ˌhalf-ˈbaked adj informal disapproving A half-baked idea or plan has not been considered carefully enough.

ˌhalf ˈboard noun [U] UK (US **ˈmodified AˌmericanˌIplan**) a hotel room combined with breakfast and another meal either in the evening or in the middle of the day: *Expect to pay about £350 for a week's half board in a three-star hotel.* ◦ *half-board* **accommodation** → Compare **full board**

ˈhalf-ˌbrother noun [C] a brother who is the son of only one of your parents

ˈhalf-caste noun [C] a person whose parents are from different races. This word is considered offensive. • **ˈhalf-caste** adj

ˌhalf-ˈcock adj old-fashioned **go off at half-cock** UK (US **go off ˌhalf-ˈcocked**) to start before arrangements are complete, and failing as a result

ˌhalf-ˈcut adj [after verb] UK informal drunk: *He looked half-cut to me.*

ˌhalf ˈdead adj [after verb] informal extremely tired

ˌhalf ˈdecent adj informal quite good or skilled: [before noun] *Any half-decent sprinter can run 100 metres in eleven seconds.*

ˌhalf-ˈhearted adj showing no enthusiasm and interest: *He made a rather half-hearted* **attempt** *to clear up the rubbish.* • **ˌhalf-ˈheartedly** adv *The audience applauded half-heartedly.*

ˌhalf ˈhour noun [C] (also **ˌhalf an ˈhour**) a period of 30 minutes: *The dollar surged against the yen in the final half hour of trading.* ◦ *Half an hour later, she was smiling and chatting as if nothing had happened.* ◦ *She is to host a new half-hour show which will be broadcast every weekday evening.* ◦ *Trains for Washington depart* **on the/every** *half hour* (= *at 10.30, 11.30, etc.*).

ˌhalf-ˈhourly adj [before noun], adv happening twice every hour: *There's a half-hourly train service to London from here.*

ˈhalf-life noun [C] specialized the length of time needed for the RADIOACTIVITY of a RADIOACTIVE substance to be reduced by half

ˈhalf-light noun [U] a low light in which you cannot see things well: *In the dim half-light of evening, I was unable to tell whether it was Mary or her sister.*

ˌhalf-ˈmarathon noun [C] a running race over a distance of about 21 kilometres

ˌhalf-ˈmast noun (US also **ˌhalf-ˈstaff**) **at half-mast** describes a flag that has been brought down to a point half the way down the pole as an expression of sadness at someone's death: *The palace flags were all **flying at** half-mast.*

ˌhalf ˈmeasures noun [plural] disapproving actions which only achieve part of what they are intended to achieve: *I'm not interested in half measures.*

ˌhalf-ˈmoon noun [C usually singular] (something shaped like) the moon when only half of the surface facing the Earth is lit by light from the sun

ˈhalf ˌnote noun [C] mainly US for **minim**

ˈhalf-pant noun [C] Indian English trousers that end above the knee or reach the knee; **shorts**

ˈhalf ˌpipe noun [C] a U-shaped structure on which people SKATEBOARD, SNOWBOARD, etc.

ˌhalf-ˈprice adj, adv A2 costing half the usual price: *I got some half-price pizzas at the supermarket.* ◦ *The railcard allows students and young people to travel half-price on most trains.*

ˈhalf-ˌsister noun [C] a sister who is the daughter of only one of your parents

ˈhalf-size noun [C] a size of clothing that is between two full sizes

ˈhalf-sleeve adj Indian English (of a shirt) with short sleeves

ˈhalf ˌstep noun [C] US for **semitone**

ˌhalf-ˈterm noun [C usually singular] in the UK, a short holiday in the middle of each of the three periods into which the school year is divided

ˌhalf-ˈtimbered adj A half-timbered building has a wooden frame whose spaces are filled with brick or stone to form the walls, so that the wood still shows on the surface.

ˌhalf-ˈtime noun [U] a short rest period between the two parts of a sports game: *Italy had a comfortable three-goal lead over France by half-time.* ◦ *What was the half-time score?* → Compare **full time**

halftone /ˌhɑːfˈtəʊn/ US /ˈhæf.toʊn/ noun PRINTING ▷ [C or U] (a method of printing) a picture built up from a pattern of very small black spots

ˈhalf-truth noun [C] a statement that is intended to deceive by being only partly true

ˌhalf-ˈvolley noun [C] a shot in a game such as tennis in which the ball is hit just after it has BOUNCED

halfway /ˌhɑːfˈweɪ/ US /ˌhæf-/ adj, adv; adv

▸adj, adv in the middle of something, or at a place that is equally far from two other places: *York is halfway **between** Edinburgh and London.* ◦ *I'd like you to look at the diagram that is halfway **down** page 27.* ◦ *She started feeling sick halfway **through** dinner.* ◦ *The management's proposals don't even **go** halfway **towards** meeting our demands.*

▸adv not very, but enough to be satisfactory: *Any halfway **decent** teacher should be able to explain the difference between transitive and intransitive verbs.*

ˌhalfway ˈhouse noun **1** [C usually singular] something which combines particular features of two other things, especially in order to try to please people who do not like the two things on their own: *The new proposals are a halfway house **between** the original treaty and the British government's revised version.* **2** [C] a place where prisoners or people with mental health problems stay after they leave prison or hospital and before they start to live on their own

ˈhalf-wit noun [C] disapproving a stupid person

ˌhalf-ˈwitted adj disapproving stupid: *a half-witted remark*

halibut /ˈhæl.ɪ.bət/ noun [C] (plural **halibut**) a big, flat sea fish that can be eaten

halitosis /ˌhæl.ɪˈtəʊ.sɪs/ US /-ˈtoʊ-/ noun [U] (also ˌ**bad ˈbreath**) breath that smells unpleasant when it comes out of the mouth

hall /hɔːl/ US /hɑːl/ noun [C] BUILDING ▷ **1** A2 a building or large room used for events involving a lot of people: *the Royal Albert Hall* ◦ *a **concert** hall* ◦ *the school **sports** hall* ◦ *I'm playing in a concert at the **village/church** hall.* ENTRANCE ▷ **2** A2 (also **hallway**) the room just inside the main entrance of a house, apartment or other building which leads to other rooms and usually to the stairs: *I've left my bags **in** the hall.*

hallah /ˈhɒ.lə/ noun [U] **challah**

hallelujah (also **alleluia**) /ˌhæl.ɪˈluː.jə/ exclamation, noun [C] **1** (an emotional expression of) praise and thanks to God **2** informal humorous said to express surprise and pleasure that something positive that you were certain would not happen has happened: *At last, Richard's found himself a girlfriend – hallelujah!*

hallmark /ˈhɔːl.mɑːk/ US /ˈhɑːl.mɑːrk/ noun; verb

▸noun [C] MARK ▷ **1** in the UK, an official mark put on objects made of gold or silver which shows their place and year of origin and how pure the metal is that is used to make them CHARACTERISTIC ▷ **2** a typical characteristic or feature of a person or thing: *Simplicity is a hallmark **of** this design.* ◦ *This explosion **bears/has all the** hallmarks **of** (= is extremely likely to have been) a terrorist attack.*

▸verb [T] to put an official mark on an object made of gold or silver

hallo /hælˈəʊ/ US /-ˈoʊ/ noun [C] (plural **hallos**) mainly UK for **hello**

ˌHall of ˈFame noun [C usually singular] mainly US a building which contains images of famous people and interesting things that are connected with them

ˌhall of ˈresidence noun [C] UK (US **dormitory**) a college building where students live

halloumi /hæˈluː.mi/ noun [U] a white cheese from Cyprus, usually made from sheep's and GOAT's milk

hallowed /ˈhæl.əʊd/ US /-oʊd/ adj **1** very respected and praised because of great importance or great age: *hallowed icons such as Marilyn Monroe and James Dean* **2** holy: *Can atheists be buried in hallowed ground?*

Halloween (also **Hallowe'en**) /ˌhæl.əʊˈiːn/ US /-oʊ-/ noun [C or U] the night of 31 October when children dress in special clothes and people try to frighten each other

hallucinate /həˈluː.sɪ.neɪt/ verb [I] to seem to see, hear, feel, or smell something which does not exist, usually because you are ill or have taken a drug: *Mental disorders, drug use and hypnosis can all cause people to hallucinate.*

hallucination /həˌluː.sɪˈneɪ.ʃᵊn/ noun [C or U] an experience in which you see, hear, feel, or smell something which does not exist, usually because you are ill or have taken a drug: *A high temperature can cause hallucinations.* ◦ *auditory/olfactory hallucinations*

hallucinatory /həˈluː.sɪ.nə.tᵊr.i/ US /-tɔːr.i/ adj relating to or causing hallucinations: *In some patients the drug has been found to have hallucinatory side effects.*

hallucinogen /ˌhæl.uːˈsɪn.ə.dʒᵊn/ US /həˈluː.sɪ.nə.dʒen/ noun [C] a drug which makes people hallucinate: *hallucinogens such as acid and ecstasy*

hallucinogenic /həˌluː.sɪ.nəˈdʒen.ɪk/ adj causing hallucinations: *LSD is a hallucinogenic **drug**.*

hallway /ˈhɔːl.weɪ/ US /ˈhɑːl-/ noun [C] a **hall**

halo /ˈheɪ.ləʊ/ US /-loʊ/ noun (plural **haloes** or **halos**) **1** [C] a ring of light around the head of a holy person in a religious drawing or painting **2** [C usually singular] a bright circle of light around something, or something that looks like this: *the halo around the moon* ◦ *a halo of blonde curls*

halogen /ˈhæl.ə.dʒen/ **noun** [C] a member of a group of five particular chemical elements: *Chlorine and iodine are halogens.*

halt /hɒlt/ Ⓤⓢ /hɑːlt/ **verb; noun**

▸**verb** [I or T] to (cause to) stop moving or doing something or happening: *'Halt!' called the guard.* *'You can't go any further without a permit.'* ◦ *Production has halted at all of the company's factories because of the pay dispute.* ◦ *Security forces halted the demonstrators by blocking the road.*

▸**noun** [S] **1** an occasion when something stops moving or happening: *the recent halt* ***in*** *production* ◦ *Severe flooding has* ***brought*** *trains* ***to a*** *halt (= prevented them from moving) on several lines in Scotland.* ◦ *The bus* ***came to a*** *halt (= stopped) just in time to avoid hitting the wall.* ◦ *If traffic increases beyond a certain level, the city* ***grinds to a*** *halt (= stops completely).* ◦ *The car* ***screeched to a*** *halt (= suddenly and noisily stopped) just as the lights turned red.* **2 call a halt to sth** to prevent something from continuing: *How many more people will have to die before they call a halt to the fighting?*

halter /ˈhɒl.təʳ/ Ⓤⓢ /ˈhɑːl.t̬ɚ/ **noun** ROPE ▷ **1** [C] a piece of rope or a leather strap that is tied around an animal's head so that it can be led by someone or tied to something CLOTHING ▷ **2** US for **halterneck**

halterneck /ˈhɒl.tə.nek/ Ⓤⓢ /ˈhɑːl.t̬ɚ-/ **noun** [C] UK (US **halter**, ˈ**halter** ˌ**top**) a piece of women's clothing that is held in position by a strap which goes behind the neck so that the upper back and shoulders are not covered: *a halterneck dress/swimsuit*

halting /ˈhɒl.tɪŋ/ Ⓤⓢ /ˈhɑːl.t̬ɪŋ/ **adj** stopping often while you are saying or doing something, especially because you are nervous: *He spoke quietly, in halting English.* • **haltingly** /-li/ **adv** *He spoke haltingly (= often stopping) about his experiences as a hostage.*

halva (also **halvah**) /ˈhæl.və/ **noun** [U] a sweet food made of crushed SESAME seeds and HONEY

halve /hɑːv/ Ⓤⓢ /hæv/ **verb 1** [T] to reduce something by half or divide something into two equal pieces: *In the past eight years, the elephant population in Africa has been halved.* ◦ *The potatoes will cook more quickly if you halve them before you put them in the oven.* **2** [I] If something halves, it is reduced by half: *Their profits have halved in the last six months.*

halves /hɑːvz/ Ⓤⓢ /hævz/ plural of **half**

ham /hæm/ **noun; verb**

▸**noun** MEAT ▷ **1** Ⓐ② [C or U] pig's meat from the leg or shoulder, preserved with salt or smoke ACTOR ▷ **2** [C] informal an actor whose style of acting is artificial and old-fashioned, often using movements and emotions that are too obvious: *They had some dreadful* ***old*** *ham in the main part.* ◦ *a ham* ***actor*** RADIO ▷ **3** [C] a person who operates a radio station as a hobby rather than as a job: *He's a* ***radio*** *ham.*

▸**verb** (-mm-)

PHRASAL VERB **ham it up** informal to perform or behave in a false way, especially in a way that is too obvious or that makes people laugh

hamburger /ˈhæmˌbɜː.gəʳ/ Ⓤⓢ /-ˌbɜː.gɚ/ **noun 1** [C] (informal **burger**, UK also **beefburger**) a round, flat piece of MINCED BEEF, fried and eaten between two halves of a bread ROLL **2** [U] US (UK **mince**) BEEF that is cut into very small pieces, used to make hamburgers

ˌ**ham-ˈfisted** **adj** mainly UK (US ˌ**ham-ˈhanded**) doing things in an awkward or unskilled way when using the hands or dealing with people: *The report criticizes the ham-fisted way in which complaints were dealt with.*

hamlet /ˈhæm.lət/ **noun** [C] a small village, usually without a church

hammer /ˈhæm.əʳ/ Ⓤⓢ /-ɚ/ **noun; verb**

hammer

▸**noun** [C] TOOL ▷ **1** Ⓑ② a tool con-sisting of a piece of metal with a flat end that is fixed onto the end of a long, thin, usually wooden handle, used for hitting things SPORT ▷ **2** a heavy metal ball attached to a chain that is thrown as part of a sports event **3 the hammer** the event or sport in which a hammer is thrown as far as possible: *She qualified for the women's hammer final.* PART OF GUN ▷ **4** the part of a gun that hits another part when you pull the TRIGGER to send out the bullet PART OF PIANO ▷ **5** one of the parts of a piano that hits the strings to make a sound

IDIOMS **be/go at it hammer and tongs** informal to do something, especially to argue, with a lot of energy or violence • **come/go under the hammer** to be sold at an AUCTION (= public sale where objects are bought by the people who offer the most money): *A private collection of her early paintings is expected to go under the hammer next year.*

▸**verb** USE TOOL ▷ **1** [I or T, usually + adv/prep] to hit something with a hammer: *Can you hold this nail in position while I hammer it* ***into*** *the door?* ◦ *I could hear you hammering upstairs.* ◦ *My car's got a dent, and I was hoping they'd be able to hammer it* ***out*** *(= remove it by hammering).* HIT WITH FORCE ▷ **2** [I or T, usually + adv/prep] to hit or kick something with a lot of force: *I was woken up suddenly by the sound of someone hammering* ***on/at*** *the front door.* ◦ *He hammered the ball* ***into*** *the net, giving France a 3–2 win over Italy.* DEFEAT ▷ **3** [T] informal to defeat someone completely in a game or a fight: *We were hammered in both games.* CRITICIZE ▷ **4** [T] informal to criticize someone or something strongly: *Her latest film has been hammered by the critics.*

IDIOM **hammer sth home** to make certain that something is understood by expressing it clearly and forcefully: *The advertising campaign will try to hammer home the message that excessive drinking is a health risk.*

PHRASAL VERBS **hammer away at sth** informal to work without stopping and with a lot of effort • **hammer sth into sb** (also **hammer sth in**) to force someone to understand something by repeating it a lot: *I always had it hammered into me that I mustn't lie.* • **hammer sth out** to reach an agreement or solution after a lot of argument or discussion: *Three years after the accident the lawyers finally managed to hammer out a settlement with the insurance company.*

ˌ**hammer and ˈsickle** **noun** [S] a symbol of COMMUNISM, which was based on tools used by workers in factories and on farms

hammered /ˈhæm.əd/ Ⓤⓢ /-ɚd/ **adj** [after verb] informal very drunk

hammering /ˈhæm.ᵊr.ɪŋ/ Ⓤⓢ /-ɚ-/ **noun** [S] DEFEAT ▷ **1** an occasion when someone is defeated completely: *You should have seen the hammering I* ***gave*** *her in the second game.* ◦ *Both countries* ***took*** *a tremendous hammering in the war.* CRITICIZE ▷ **2** strong criticism:

*Store cards have **taken** a hammering in recent years because of their high interest rates.*

ˈhammer ˌthrowing noun [U] a sport in which a heavy metal ball joined by a wire to a handle is thrown as far as possible

hammock /ˈhæm.ək/ noun [C] a type of bed used especially outside, consisting of a net or long piece of strong cloth which you tie between two trees or poles so that it SWINGS (= moves sideways through the air)

hammy /ˈhæm.i/ adj informal describes an actor or acting that is unnatural and uses too much emotion: *a hammy performance*

hamper /ˈhæm.pəʳ/ US /-pɚ/ verb; noun

hamper

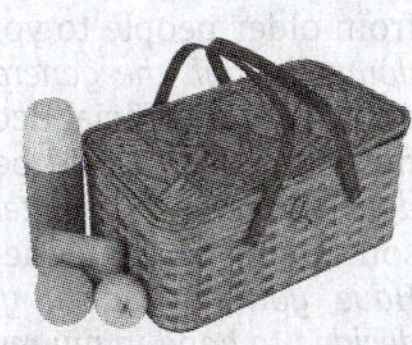

▸**verb** [T] to prevent someone doing something easily: *Fierce storms have been hampering rescue efforts and there is now little chance of finding more survivors.*

▸**noun** [C] **1** a large, rectangular container with a lid: *a **picnic** hamper* **2** UK a box containing food and drink, usually given as a present, for example at Christmas **3** US old-fashioned a container used for carrying dirty clothes and bed sheets and for storing them while they are waiting to be washed

hamster /ˈhæm.stəʳ/ US /-stɚ/ noun [C] a small animal covered in fur with a short tail and large spaces in each side of its mouth for storing food. It is often kept as a pet.

hamstring /ˈhæm.strɪŋ/ verb; noun

▸**verb** [T often passive] (**hamstrung**) to limit the amount of something that can be done or the ability or power of someone to do something: *The company was hamstrung by traditional but inefficient ways of conducting business.*

▸**noun** [C] any of five TENDONS (= pieces of tissue connecting muscles to bones) at the back of the knee: *He **pulled** (= injured) a hamstring while playing rugby.*

> **!** Common mistake: **on the one hand ... on the other hand**
>
> **Warning:** the correct preposition to use in this expression is **on**.
>
> Don't say 'in/at the one hand', say **on the one hand**:
>
> ~~*In the one hand mobile phones are convenient, but in the other hand they are expensive.*~~
>
> *On the one hand mobile phones are convenient, but on the other hand they are expensive.*

hand /hænd/ noun; verb

▸**noun** **BODY PART** ▷ **1** A1 [C] the part of the body at the end of the arm that is used for holding, moving, touching, and feeling things: *All their toys are made **by** hand.* ◦ *I delivered her invitation **by** hand (= not using the postal service).* ◦ informal ***Get** your hands **off** (= stop touching) my bike!* ◦ *He can mend anything – he's so **good with** his hands.* ◦ *You have to **hold** my hand when we cross the road.* ◦ *They walked by, **holding** hands.* ◦ *Hold your fork **in** your left hand and your knife **in** your right hand.* ◦ *She sat, pen **in** hand (= with a pen in her hand), searching for the right words.* ◦ *They can't **keep** their hands **off** each other – they never stop kissing and cuddling.* ◦ *'Congratulations!' she said and **shook** me **by the** hand/**shook** my hand/**shook** hands **with** me.* ◦ *She **took** me **by the** hand and led me into the cave.* ◦ *a hand **towel*** **CLOCK/WATCH** ▷ **2** [C] one of the long, thin pieces that point to the numbers on a clock or watch: *Does anyone have a watch with a **second** hand?* **CARDS** ▷ **3** [C] a (single part of a) game of cards, or the set of cards that a player has in a game: *Who's for a hand **of** poker?* ◦ *You **dealt** me an appalling hand in that game.* **HELP** ▷ **4** B1 [S] help with doing something that needs a lot of effort: [+ -ing verb] *Would you like **a** hand carry**ing** those bags?* ◦ *Could you **give/lend** me **a** hand **with** (= help me to move) the table, please?* ◦ *I think Matthew might **need a** hand **with** his maths homework.* ◦ *I could really **use a** hand **with** these accounts if you could spare a moment.* **PERSON** ▷ **5** [C] a person who does physical work or is skilled or experienced in something: *How many extra hands will we need to help with the harvest?* ◦ *I joined the firm as a **factory** hand and gradually worked my way up to the top.* → See also **farmhand** **6** [C] a sailor: *All hands on deck!* **CONTROL** ▷ **7** C2 [U] control or responsibility: *Things **got** a little **out of** hand (= the situation stopped being controlled) at the party and three windows were broken.* ◦ *In my first year at college my drinking got completely out of hand.* ◦ *The police have the situation **in** hand (= under control).* ◦ *How come there's a problem? I thought you had everything **in** hand (= arranged and organized).* ◦ *Their youngest child needs **taking in** hand (= they should start to control her) if you ask me.* **8 hands** C2 [plural] control or responsibility: *I'm worried about confidential information **falling into the wrong** hands (= being received by people who could use it against us).* ◦ *Are you sure your money's **in safe** hands?* ◦ *You're **in** excellent hands with her – she's a very good doctor.* ◦ *Unless I receive a satisfactory response from you within a month I shall put this matter **in(to) the** hands of (= make it the responsibility of) my solicitor.* ◦ *They're trying to **get** old stock **off** their hands by cutting prices.* ◦ *We **get** Daryl **off** our hands one evening a week when my mother looks after him.* ◦ *The court will decide how much money you get – the decision is **out of our hands** (= is not our responsibility).* ◦ *He's got a real problem **on his** hands (= he has something difficult to deal with).* ◦ *I don't **have** enough **time on my** hands (= I do not have enough time) to work and look after the children.* **INVOLVEMENT** ▷ **9** [S] involvement in or influence over an event: *It is not thought that terrorists **had a** hand **in** the explosion.* **CLAP** ▷ **10** [S] clapping for a performer: *So please **give a big** hand **to** (= welcome with clapping) your host for the evening, Bill Cronshaw!* **WRITING** ▷ **11** [S] old use a person's writing: *an untidy hand* **MEASUREMENT** ▷ **12** [C] a unit for measuring the height of a horse up to its shoulder: *One hand equals four inches (= 10.16 centimetres).*

IDIOMS **at hand** C1 near in time or position: *We want to ensure that **help** is at hand (= easily available) for all children suffering abuse.* • **at the hands of sb** C2 If you suffer at the hands of someone, they hurt you or treat you badly: *How many people have died at the hands of terrorist organizations?* • **get/lay/put your hands on sb** informal to catch someone: *I'll kill him if I ever get my hands on him.* • **get/lay/put your hands on sth** informal C2 to find something: *I can never lay my hands on a stapler in this office.* • **go hand in hand with sth** C1 If something goes hand in hand with something else, it is closely related to it and happens at the same time as it or as a result of it: *Prosperity goes hand in hand with investment.* • **hand in glove** (US also **hand and glove**) working together, often to do something dishonest: *It was rumoured at the time that some of the gangs were working hand in glove with the police.* • **hand in hand** B2 holding each other's hand: *I saw them walking hand in hand through town the other day.* • **hand to hand** involving people who are close enough to touch: *Conflicts used to be settled by men fighting hand to hand.* • **hand over fist** If you make or lose money hand over fist, you make or lose a lot of money very quickly: *Business was good and we were making money hand over fist.* • **sb's hands are tied** If someone's hands are tied, they are not free to behave in the way that they would like: *I'd like to raise people's salaries but my hands are tied.* • **have your hands full** C2 to be so busy that you do not have time to do anything else: *I'd love to help but I've got my hands full organizing the school play.* • **have sth in hand** mainly UK If you have something in hand, you have not yet used it and it is still available: *I've got enough money in hand to buy a new car.* ◦ *Italy are three points behind France in the championship, but they have one game in hand (= one game more than France still to play).* • **have sth on your hands** If you have a difficult situation on your hands, you have to deal with it: *If the police carry on like this they'll have a riot on their hands.* • **hold/put your hands up** to admit that something bad is true or that you have made a mistake: *I know I'm bossy and I hold my hands up* ***to*** *that.* • **in hand** C2 being worked on or dealt with now: *They've had plenty of time to prepare, so the arrangements should be* ***well*** *in hand (= almost ready).* • **the job/matter in hand** UK (US **the job/matter at hand**) the job or matter that is important at the present moment: *Could you just concentrate on the job in hand?* ◦ *If we could return to the matter in hand, we can discuss other issues later.* • **keep your hand in** to practise a skill often enough so that you do not lose the skill: *I do a bit of teaching now and then just to keep my hand in.* • **keep a firm hand on sth** to control something or someone carefully: *Susan keeps a firm hand on everything that goes on in the office.* • **live (from) hand to mouth** to have just enough money to live on and nothing extra: *My father earned very little and there were four kids, so we lived from hand to mouth.* • **on hand** (UK also **to hand**) C2 near to someone or something, and ready to help or be used if necessary: *A 1,200-strong military force will be on hand to monitor the ceasefire.* ◦ *For those of you who don't have an atlas to hand, Newcastle is a city in the northeast of England.* • **on the one hand ... on the other hand** B2 used when you are comparing two different facts or two opposite ways of thinking about a situation: *On the one hand I'd like a job that pays more, but on the other hand I enjoy the work I'm doing at the moment.* • **out of hand** If you refuse something out of hand, you refuse it completely without thinking about or discussing it: *Moving to London is certainly a possibility – I wouldn't dismiss it out of hand.* • **put your hand in your pocket** to give money to someone or to CHARITY (= organizations that collect money to give to poor people, ill people, etc.): *People are more inclined to put their hands in their pockets to help children.* • **a safe pair of hands** someone who you can trust to do an important job well, without making mistakes • **win (sth) hands down** (also **beat sb hands down**) to win something/beat someone very easily: *She won the debate hands down.* ◦ *The last time we played squash he beat me hands down.*

►**verb** [T] B1 to put something into someone's hand from your own hand: [+ two objects] *The waiter smiled politely as he handed me my bill/handed my bill* ***to*** *me.* ◦ *Please read this memo carefully and hand it* ***on*** *(****to*** *your colleagues).*

IDIOM **have (got) to hand it to sb** C2 If you say you have (got) to hand it to someone you mean that they have been very successful or skilful: *I mean you've got to hand it to her, she's brought up those three children all on her own.*

PHRASAL VERBS **hand sth around** (UK also **hand round**) to pass or offer something to all the people in a group: *Ben, could you hand round the biscuits?* • **hand sth back** to return something to the person who gave it to you: [+ two objects] *'No, I've never seen him before,' I said, handing her back the photograph.* • **hand sth down** OBJECT ▷ **1** C2 to give something to someone younger than you in the family because you want them to have it or because you no longer need it: *This necklace was handed down to my mother by my grandmother.* TRADITION ▷**2** C2 to pass traditions from older people to younger ones: *a custom handed down through the generations* DECISION ▷**3** formal to announce an official decision, often a decision about how someone should be punished: *The court handed down an eight-year sentence.* • **hand sth in** B1 to give something to someone in a position of authority: *Have you handed in your history essay yet?* ◦ *I've decided to hand in my resignation (= tell my employer I am leaving my job).* • **hand sth out** B1 to give something to each person in a group or place: *The teacher asked her to hand out the worksheets.* ◦ *They stood on the street corner handing out leaflets.* • **hand sth over** B2 to give something to someone else: *We were ordered to hand over our passports.* → See also **handover** • **hand sth/sb over** B2 to give another person control of someone or something, or responsibility for dealing with them: *The hijacker was handed over* ***to*** *the French police.* ◦ *If you'll hold the line a moment I'll hand you over to someone who might be able to help.* → See also **handover**

handbag /ˈhænd.bæg/ **noun** [C] (US also **purse**) A2 a small bag for money, keys, make-up, etc. carried especially by women

handball /ˈhænd.bɔːl/ (US) /-bɑːl/ **noun 1** A2 [U] in the US, a game in which players hit a small hard rubber ball against a wall with their hands **2** [C or U] in football, the act of intentionally touching the ball with your hand or arm **3** [U] a game similar to football, played by hitting a ball with your hands instead of your feet

handbill /ˈhænd.bɪl/ **noun** [C] a small printed advertisement or notice that is given to people by hand

handbook /ˈhænd.bʊk/ **noun** [C] a book which contains instructions or advice about how to do something or the most important and useful information about a subject: *The student handbook gives details of all courses.*

handbrake /ˈhænd.breɪk/ **noun** [C] UK (US **eˈmergency ˌbrake**, US also **ˈparking ˌbrake**) a device operated by hand which locks into position and prevents a vehicle from moving: *You're supposed to* ***put*** *the handbrake* ***on*** *whenever you stop on a hill.*

handcart /ˈhænd.kɑːt/ (US) /-kɑːrt/ **noun** [C] a small vehicle with two wheels and two long handles that is pushed or pulled with your hands, used for carrying goods

handcraft /ˈhænd.krɑːft/ (US) /-kræft/ **noun** [C usually plural] Australian English a skilled activity in which something is made in a traditional way with the hands rather than being produced by machines in a factory, or an object made by such an activity → Compare **handicraft**

handcrafts /ˈhænd.krɑːfts/ (US) /-kræfts/ **noun** [C or U] Australian English **handicraft**

handcuff /ˈhænd.kʌf/ verb [T often passive] (informal **cuff**) to put handcuffs on someone: *He arrived in court handcuffed* ***to*** *two police officers.*

handcuffs

handcuffs /ˈhænd.kʌfs/ noun [plural] (informal **cuffs**) two metal or plastic rings joined by a short chain that lock around a prisoner's wrists: *a pair of handcuffs* ◦ *She was taken to the police station* ***in*** *handcuffs.*

handful /ˈhænd.fʊl/ noun **AMOUNT** ▷ **1** [C] an amount of something that can be held in one hand: *He pulled out a handful of coins from his pocket.* **A FEW** ▷ **2** B2 [S] a small number of people or things: *She invited loads of friends to her party, but only a handful of them turned up.* **DIFFICULT PERSON** ▷ **3** [S] a person, often a child, who is difficult to control: *Her older son is fine but the little one is a bit of a handful.*

ˈhand greˌnade noun [C] a small bomb consisting of explosive material in a metal or plastic container that can be thrown easily

handgun /ˈhænd.gʌn/ noun [C] a gun that can be held in one hand and does not need to be supported against the shoulder when you shoot with it

handheld adj; noun

▸adj [before noun] /ˌhændˈheld/ B1 describes something that has been designed so that it can be held and used easily with one or two hands: *a handheld computer/device*

▸noun [C] /ˈhændˌheld/ a **PDA**

handhold /ˈhænd.həʊld/ US /-hoʊld/ noun [C] a thing you can hold on to with your hand as a support

handicap /ˈhæn.dɪ.kæp/ noun; verb

▸noun **CONDITION** ▷ **1** [C or U] old-fashioned something that is wrong with your mind or body permanently. This word is now considered offensive by many people, who prefer the word disability: *a* ***physical*** *handicap* ◦ *In cases of severe* ***mental*** *handicap, constant supervision is recommended.* **DIFFICULTY** ▷ **2** [C] something which makes it difficult for you to do something: *I found not having a car quite a handicap in the country.* **COMPETITION** ▷ **3** [C] a disadvantage given to a person taking part in a game or competition in order to reduce their chances of winning, or a sports event in which such disadvantages are given: *Handicaps give people with different abilities an equal chance of winning.* ◦ *My current golf handicap is nine.*

▸verb [T] (-pp-) to make something more difficult to do: *Rescue efforts have been handicapped by rough seas and hurricane-force winds.*

handicapped /ˈhæn.dɪ.kæpt/ adj; noun

▸adj old-fashioned not able to use part of your body or your mind because it has been damaged in some way. This word is now considered offensive by many people, who prefer the word disabled: *What's the best way of improving theatre access for people who are physically handicapped?*

▸noun [plural] **the handicapped** people who cannot use part of their body or mind because it has been damaged in some way

handicraft /ˈhæn.dɪ.krɑːft/ US /-kræft/ noun [C usually plural] a skilled activity in which something is made in a traditional way with the hands rather than being produced by machines in a factory, or an object made by such an activity

handily /ˈhæn.dɪ.li/ adv **IN A USEFUL WAY** ▷ **1** in a useful or convenient way: *An additional power switch for the radio is handily located next to the steering wheel.* **EASILY** ▷ **2** US easily: *The Yankees handily* ***defeated*** *the Boston Red Sox.*

handiwork /ˈhæn.dɪ.wɜːk/ US /-wɝːk/ noun [U] **1** work done skilfully with the hands: *Susannah put down the paintbrush and stood back to admire her handiwork.* **2** something that you have done or caused, usually something bad: *'Is this your handiwork?' he asked, pointing at the graffiti on the wall.*

handkerchief /ˈhæŋ.kə.tʃiːf/ US /-kɚ-/ noun [C] (plural **handkerchiefs** or UK also **handkerchieves**) (informal **hanky**) B1 a square piece of cloth or paper used for cleaning the nose or drying the eyes when they are wet with tears: *She took out her handkerchief and blew her nose loudly.* → Compare **tissue**

handknitted /ˌhændˈnɪt.ɪd/ US /-ˈnɪţ-/ adj UK **handknit**

handle /ˈhæn.dəl/ noun; verb

▸noun [C] **PART** ▷ **1** B2 a part of an object designed for holding, moving, or carrying the object easily: *a door handle* ◦ *the handle on a suitcase* ◦ *I can't pick the kettle up – the handle's too hot.* ◦ *She* ***turned*** *the handle and slowly opened the door.* **NAME** ▷ **2** informal a name of a person or place, especially a strange one: *That's some handle to go through life with!*

▸verb **DEAL WITH** ▷ **1** B1 [T] to deal with, have responsibility for, or be in charge of: *I thought he handled the situation very well.* ◦ *Some people are brilliant with computers, but have no idea how to handle (= behave with) other people.* ◦ *Who handles the marketing in your company?* **TOUCH** ▷ **2** C2 [T] to pick something up and touch, hold, or move it with your hands: *Always wash your hands before handling food.* ◦ *Please don't handle the vases – they're very fragile.* **OPERATE** ▷ **3** [T] to operate or control something which could be difficult or dangerous: *Have you ever handled a gun before?* **4** [I usually + adv/prep] If a car handles well, it is easy and pleasant to drive. **SELL** ▷ **5** [T] to buy and sell goods: *We only handle cosmetics which have not been tested on animals.* ◦ mainly UK *He's been arrested for handling stolen goods.*

ˌhandlebar mouˈstache noun [C] a thick, wide MOUSTACHE with curled ends in the shape of handlebars

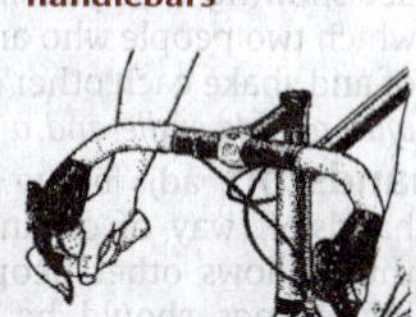

handlebars /ˈhæn.dl.bɑːz/ US /-bɑːrz/ noun [plural] a bar with curved ends forming handles which turns the front wheel of a bicycle or motorcycle so that it points in a different direction

handler /ˈhænd.ləʳ/ US /-lɚ/ noun [C] **TRAINER** ▷ **1** a person who trains and is in charge of animals, especially dogs: *police dog handlers* **ADVISER** ▷ **2** US someone who advises someone important: *The president's handlers are telling him to pull out of the talks.* **CARRY** ▷ **3** someone who carries or moves things as part of their job: *airport baggage handlers*

handling /ˈhænd.lɪŋ/ noun [U] **DEALING WITH** ▷ **1** the way that someone deals with a situation or person: *President Kennedy made his reputation with his handling* ***of*** *the Cuban missile crisis.* **OPERATING** ▷ **2** how easy a vehicle is to control: *Power steering can dramatically improve a car's handling.*

ˈhand ˌluggage noun [U] (US **ˈcarry-on ˌbaggage**) the small cases or bags that a passenger can carry onto an aircraft or bus: *How many items of hand luggage am I allowed to take onto the plane?*

handmade /ˌhændˈmeɪd/ adj made using the hands rather than a machine: *handmade chocolates/paper/shoes*

handmaiden /ˈhændˌmeɪ.dən/ noun [C] **1** (also **handmaid**) a female servant **2** formal something, such as an idea, which helps and supports something else: *Technique is the handmaiden of art.*

ˈhand-me-ˌdown noun [C] a piece of clothing which someone has given to a younger person because they no longer want it: *I got fed up with having to wear my sister's hand-me-downs.*

handout /ˈhænd.aʊt/ noun [C] **INFORMATION** ▷ **1** B2 a document given to students or REPORTERS which contains information about a particular subject: *On page two of your handout you will find a list of the books that I have referred to during the lecture.* **PRESENT** ▷ **2** often disapproving something such as food, clothing, or money that is given free to someone who has a great need for it: *I'm not interested in **government** handouts – all I want is a job.*

handover /ˈhæn.dəʊ.vəʳ/ US /-doʊ.vɚ/ noun [U] the giving of control of or responsibility for something to someone else: *The United Nations is to supervise the handover of the prisoners of war.* → See also **hand sth over**

handpicked /ˌhændˈpɪkt/ adj Someone who is handpicked has been carefully chosen for a special job or purpose: *a handpicked audience*

handrail /ˈhænd.reɪl/ noun [C] a long narrow bar of wood or metal which people can hold on to for support, especially when going up or down stairs

handset /ˈhænd.set/ noun [C] **1** the outer part of a mobile phone which does not include the BATTERY or the SIM CARD **2** the part of a phone in two parts that you hold in front of your mouth and against your ear

ˌhands-ˈfree adj; noun
▸adj describes a piece of equipment, especially a phone, that you can use without needing to hold it in your hand: *a hands-free car phone*
▸noun [C] a piece of equipment, especially a phone, that you can use without needing to hold it in your hand

handshake /ˈhænd.ʃeɪk/ noun [C] a greeting, or an act showing that you have made an agreement, in which two people who are facing each other take hold of and shake each other's right hand: *He welcomed me with a wide smile and a warm handshake.*

ˌhands-ˈoff adj [before noun] Someone who has a hands-off way of organizing or dealing with something allows other people to make decisions about how things should be done and avoids becoming directly involved: *Paul has a hands-off style of management.*

handsome /ˈhæn.səm/ adj **ATTRACTIVE** ▷ **1** B1 describes a man who is physically attractive in a traditional, male way: *She's dreaming she'll be whisked off her feet by a **tall, dark** handsome stranger.* **2** describes a woman who is attractive but in a strong way: *a handsome woman in her fifties* **LARGE AMOUNT** ▷ **3** C2 [before noun] large in amount: *They made a handsome profit on their house.* • **handsomely** /-li/ adv *He said if his results were good, he would **reward** him handsomely.*

ˌhands-ˈon adj [before noun] **INVOLVED** ▷ **1** Someone with a hands-on way of doing things becomes closely involved in managing and organizing things and in making decisions: *She's very much a hands-on manager.* **PRACTICAL EXPERIENCE** ▷ **2** Someone who has hands-on experience of something has done or used it rather than just read or learned about it: *Many employers consider hands-on experience to be as useful as academic qualifications.*

handstand /ˈhænd.stænd/ noun [C] an action in which you balance vertically on your hands with your legs pointing straight up in the air

ˌhand-to-ˈhand adj [before noun] Hand-to-hand fighting involves people who are very near or touching each other, rather than shooting at each other from a long way away: *hand-to-hand **combat***

ˌhand-to-ˈmouth adj having only just enough money to live: *Low wages mean a hand-to-mouth **existence** for many people.*

handwriting /ˈhændˌraɪ.tɪŋ/ US /-t̬ɪŋ/ noun [U] **1** B1 writing with a pen or pencil: *We need to ensure that handwriting is properly taught in our primary schools.* **2** B1 the particular way in which someone forms letters with a pen or pencil: *His handwriting is illegible.*

handwritten /ˌhændˈrɪt.ən/ US /-ˈrɪt̬-/ adj written using your hand rather than printed by a machine

handy /ˈhæn.di/ adj **USEFUL** ▷ **1** C2 useful or convenient: *a handy container/tool* ◦ *First-time visitors to France will find this guide particularly handy.* ◦ *It's a nice house and it's handy **for** (= near) the station.* ◦ informal *Don't throw those bottles away – they'll **come in** handy (= be useful) **for** the picnic next Sunday.* **SKILFUL** ▷ **2** [after verb] able to use something skilfully: *Jonathan's good at wallpapering but he's not so handy **with** a paintbrush.* ◦ *Susannah's very handy (= good at doing things which need skilled use of the hands) **about** the house.*

handyman /ˈhæn.di.mæn/ noun [C] (plural **-men** /-men/) a man who is skilled at repairing and making things inside or outside the house and who does this in his own home or as a job

hang /hæŋ/ verb; noun
▸verb **FIX AT TOP** ▷ **1** B1 [I or T, + adv/prep] (**hung, hung**) to fasten or support something at the top leaving the other parts free to move, or to be held in this way: *A heavy gold necklace hung **around** her neck.* ◦ *Long creepers hung (**down**) **from** the trees.* ◦ *The curtains hung **in** thick folds.* ◦ *Hang your coat and hat (**up**) on the rack over there.* ◦ *Many of his finest pictures hang/are hung (= are fixed to the wall so that they can be seen) in the National Gallery.* ◦ *Hang the pheasant/Let the pheasant hang for a few days for the flavour to improve before you cook it.* **2** [T] (**hung, hung**) If you hang WALLPAPER, you fix it to the wall. **KILL** ▷ **3** B2 [I or T] (**hanged** or **hung, hanged** or **hung**) to kill someone, especially as punishment for a serious crime, by dropping them with a rope tied around their neck, or to die in this way: *He was found guilty and hanged later that year.* ◦ *With so little evidence to prove her guilt, few people thought she should hang.* ◦ *The woman tried to hang her**self** with a sheet.* → See also **hangman** **STAY** ▷ **4** C2 [I] (**hung, hung**) to stay in the air: *The falcon seemed to hang **in the air** for a moment before diving onto its prey.* ◦ *Smoke from the houses hung **above** the village.* ◦ literary *The sound of the bells hung in the midnight air.* **BEND DOWN** ▷ **5** [I or T] (**hung, hung**) to curve down: *The branches hung heavy with snow.* ◦ *He knew he'd done something wrong and hung his head in shame.*

IDIOMS **go hang (yourself)** informal You say that someone can go hang (themselves) if you do not care what they say or do about something: *If she's expecting the report by tomorrow she can go hang herself.* • **hang by a thread** If a serious situation hangs by a thread, it means that even a slight change can decide what will happen and that a bad result such as death, failure, etc. is likely: *The mayor's political future has been hanging by a thread since the fraud scandal.* • **hang on in there** (also **hang in there**) said as a way of telling someone to not give up, despite difficulties: *Work can get tough in the middle of a term but hang on in there and it'll be OK.* • **hang the cost/expense** the cost is not important: *Just buy it and hang the expense!* • **hang tough** US informal to not change your actions or opinions although other people try to make you do this: *The president is hanging tough on the hostage crisis.* • **have sb/sth hanging round your neck** informal disapproving to be limited in what you can do by someone or something: *The last thing I want is a couple of kids hanging round my neck!* • **hung, drawn, and quartered** In the past, if someone was hung, drawn, and quartered, they were hanged by the neck and their body was cut into pieces. • **I'll be hanged if...** UK old-fashioned used to express your determination not to do something or not to allow someone else to do something: *I'll be hanged if I'm going to clean up after him!* • **I'll be hanged if I know** (also **I'm hanged if I know**) UK old-fashioned informal used to say that you certainly do not know

PHRASAL VERBS **hang around** (UK also **hang about**) to move or do things slowly: *Go and pack but don't hang around – we have to go in an hour.* • **hang around (somewhere)** (UK also **hang about**) B1 to wait or spend time somewhere, usually for no particular reason: *I spent most of my youth hanging around the bars of Dublin.* ◦ *I thought I'd hang around for a while and see if she comes.* • **hang around with sb** (UK also **hang about with sb**) to spend time with someone: *I got into drugs because I was hanging around with the wrong people.* • **hang back** to be slow to do something, often because of fear or having no confidence: *There's no need to hang back – you can sing as well as anyone.* • **hang on** WAIT ▷ **1** B1 informal to wait for a short time: *Sally's on the other phone – would you like to hang on?* ◦ *Do you need the toilet right now or can you hang on for a while?* ◦ *Hang on a minute – I'll be with you in a moment!* HOLD ▷ **2** to hold or continue holding onto something: *Hang on tight – it's going to be a very bumpy ride.* → See also **hanger-on** • **hang sth on sb** informal to blame someone for something, especially something they did not do: *I wasn't anywhere near the house when the window was broken, so you can't hang that on me!* • **hang on/upon sth** GIVE ATTENTION ▷ **1** to give careful attention to something, especially something that someone says: *He hangs on her **every word** as if she were some sort of goddess.* DEPEND ON ▷ **2** to depend on something: *The safety of air travel hangs partly on the thoroughness of baggage checking.* • **hang onto sth** to keep something: *You should hang onto that painting – it might be valuable.* • **hang out** informal B1 to spend a lot of time in a place or with someone: *You still hang out **at** the pool hall?* ◦ *I've been hanging out backstage **with** the band.* • **hang over sth** If a threat or doubt hangs over a place or a situation, it exists: *Uncertainty again hangs over the project.* • **hang together** STAY TOGETHER ▷ **1** If people hang together, they help each other and work together to achieve something: *If the opposition party can hang together over the next six months, they might just stand a chance of being elected.* SEEM TRUE ▷ **2** If the parts of something hang together, they are well organized or they seem to be true or correct: *Somehow her story doesn't quite hang together.* • **hang up** B1 to end a phone conversation: *He started shouting so I hung up (**on** him).* ◦ *Let me speak to Melanie before you hang up.* • **hang sth up** to stop using and needing something because you have given up the sport or activity it is used for: *So when did you hang up your boxing gloves/golf clubs/ballet shoes?*

▸noun **1 get the hang of sth** C2 informal to learn how to do something, especially if it is not obvious or simple: *'I've never used this program before.' 'Don't worry – you'll soon get the hang of **it**.'* **2 the hang** the way something made of cloth looks when it is hanging: *That coat fits you so well – the hang is perfect.*

hangar /ˈhæŋ.əʳ/ US /-ɚ/ noun [C] a large building in which aircraft are kept

hangdog /ˈhæŋ.dɒɡ/ US /-dɑːɡ/ adj [before noun] (of an expression on a face) unhappy or ashamed, especially because of feeling guilty: *a hangdog look/expression*

hanger /ˈhæŋ.əʳ/ US /-ɚ/ noun [C] (also **ˈclothes ˌhanger**, **ˈcoat ˌhanger**) a curved piece of wire, wood, or plastic on which clothes are hung while they are being stored

ˌhanger-ˈon noun [C] (plural **hangers-on**) disapproving a person who tries to be friendly and spend time with rich and important people, especially to get an advantage: *Wherever there is royalty, there are always hangers-on.*

ˈhang-ˌglider noun [C] a very small aircraft without an engine. It consists of a frame covered in cloth, which forms a wing, and the pilot hangs from this frame. • **ˈhang-ˌgliding noun** [U] the activity of using a hang-glider: *She's taken up hang-gliding.*

hanging /ˈhæŋ.ɪŋ/ noun KILL ▷ **1** [C or U] the act of killing someone, especially as a punishment for a serious crime, by dropping them with a rope tied around their neck PICTURE ▷ **2** [C usually plural] a large piece of cloth, often with a picture on it, that is hung on a wall for decoration: *The castle's great hall was decorated with sumptuous **wall** hangings.*

ˌhanging ˈbasket noun [C] an open container with plants and flowers in it, which hangs outside a building

ˌhanging ˈvalley noun [C] specialized a valley that ends suddenly with a steep CLIFF or WATERFALL where it meets the side of a larger, deeper valley

hangman /ˈhæŋ.mən/, /-mæn/ noun [C] (plural **-men** /-mən/) a person whose job is to operate the device which kills criminals by hanging them from a rope by their necks

hangout /ˈhæŋ.aʊt/ noun [C] informal a place where someone spends a lot of time or where they live: *The café is a favourite hangout of artists.*

hangover /ˈhæŋ,əʊ.vəʳ/ US /-ˌoʊ.vɚ/ noun [C] ILLNESS ▷ **1** a feeling of illness after drinking too much alcohol: *I **had** a terrible hangover the next morning.* ◦ *a hangover cure* → See also **hungover** CONTINUING ▷ **2** something that continues from an earlier time: *The present political system is a hangover **from** the colonial era.*

ˈhang-up noun [C] informal a permanent and unreasonable feeling of ANXIETY about a particular feature of yourself: ***sexual** hang-ups* ◦ *He's one of these men who went bald very young and has a terrible hang-up **about** it.*

hanker /ˈhæŋ.kəʳ/ US /-kɚ/ verb

PHRASAL VERB **hanker after/for sth** to have a strong wish for something, especially if you cannot or should not have it: *What did you hanker after most when you were in prison?* ◦ *Even after all these years, I still hanker for a motorbike.*

hankering /ˈhæŋ.kᵊr.ɪŋ/ US /-kɚ-/ noun [C] a strong wish: *Don't you ever* ***have*** *a hankering* ***for*** *a different lifestyle?*

hanky /ˈhæŋ.ki/ noun [C] (also **hankie**) a HANDKERCHIEF (= square piece of cloth or paper used for cleaning the nose and drying the eyes)

hanky-panky /ˌhæŋ.kɪˈpæŋ.ki/ noun [U] old-fashioned informal unacceptable or dishonest behaviour, especially involving sexual activity or money: *There was a bit of hanky-panky going on at the Christmas party.*

Hansard /ˈhæn.sɑːd/ US /-sɚd/ noun [S] the official record of what is said and done in the British, Australian, New Zealand, Canadian, and South African parliaments

hansom (cab) /ˈhæn.səmˌkæb/ noun [C] a two-wheeled CARRIAGE pulled by a horse, used like a taxi in the past

H

Hanukkah /ˈhɑː.nə.kə/ noun [C or U] (also **Chanukah**) a Jewish religious holiday lasting for eight days in December

haphazard /ˌhæpˈhæz.əd/ US /-ɚd/ adj disapproving not having an obvious order or plan: *He tackled the problem in a typically haphazard manner.* • **haphazardly** /-li/ adv disapproving

hapless /ˈhæp.ləs/ adj [before noun] formal unlucky and usually unhappy: *Many children are hapless* ***victims*** *of this war.* • **haplessly** /-li/ adv formal

haploid /ˈhæp.lɔɪd/ adj having a single set of CHROMOSOMES (= structures containing chemical patterns that control what a plant or animal is like) that comes from one parent only: *a haploid cell* ◦ *Sex cells such as eggs and sperm are haploid.* → Compare **diploid**

ha'porth /ˈheɪ.pəθ/ US /-pɚθ/ noun UK old-fashioned informal **(not) a ha'porth of difference** (not) any difference: *You can shout as much as you like but it won't make a ha'porth of difference – you're not going.*

happen /ˈhæp.ᵊn/ verb; adv

▸verb [I] HAVE EXISTENCE ▷ **1** A2 (of a situation or an event) to have existence or come into existence: *No one knows exactly what happened but several people have been hurt.* ◦ *Anything could happen in the next half hour.* ◦ *A funny thing happened in the office today.* ◦ *I don't like to think what might have happened if he'd been driving any faster.* **2 happen to sb** A2 If something happens to someone or something, it has an effect on them and changes them in some way: *I don't know what I'd do if anything happened to him (= if he was hurt, became ill, or died).* ◦ *What happened to your jacket? There's a big rip in the sleeve.* ◦ *What's happened to my pen? (= Where is it?) I put it down there a few moments ago.* CHANCE ▷ **3** C1 to do or be by chance: [+ to infinitive] *They happened* ***to*** *look (= looked by chance) in the right place almost immediately.* ◦ [+ (that)] *Fortunately* ***it*** *happened (****that****) there was no one in the house at the time of the explosion.* ◦ [+ that] ***It just so*** *happens* ***that*** *I have her phone number right here.* ◦ *She happens* ***to*** *like cleaning (= she likes cleaning, although that is surprising).* ◦ *I happen* ***to*** *think he's right (= I do think so, although you do not).* ◦ ***As it*** *happened (= although it was not planned), I had a few minutes to spare.*

> **! Common mistake: happen**
>
> **Warning:** Check your verb endings!
>
> Many learners make mistakes when using **happen** in the past tense. In the past simple and past participle, don't write 'happenned' or 'happended', write **happened**. The **-ing** form is **happening**.

PHRASAL VERBS **happen along/by (somewhere)** mainly US to go to a place by chance or without planning to: *I'd have drowned if he hadn't happened along and pulled me out of the river.* • **happen on/upon sth/sb** literary to find or meet something or someone by chance: *Eventually they happened on a road leading across the desert.*

▸adv Northern English perhaps: *Happen it'll rain later on.*

happening /ˈhæp.ᵊn.ɪŋ/ noun; adj

▸noun [C usually plural] **1** something that has happened: *Recent happenings on the money markets can be interpreted in various ways.* **2** a performance or similar event that happens without preparation

▸adj informal describes a place that is extremely fashionable and exciting

happenstance /ˈhæp.ᵊn.stɑːns/ US /-stæns/ noun [C or U] mainly US chance or a chance situation, especially one producing a good result: *By (a strange) happenstance they were both in Paris at the same time.*

happily /ˈhæp.ɪ.li/ adv PLEASED ▷ **1** B1 in a happy way: *He was happily* ***married*** *with two young children.* ◦ *She munched happily on her chocolate bar.* **2** B2 willingly: *I'd happily offer to help him if I thought it would make any difference.* LUCKY ▷ **3** C1 having a good or lucky result: *Happily, the weather remained fine throughout the afternoon.*

happiness /ˈhæp.i.nəs/ noun [U] B1 the feeling of being happy: *It was only later in life that she found happiness and peace of mind.* ◦ formal *Will you join me in wishing the bride and groom* ***every*** *happiness?*

> **+ Other ways of saying happy**
>
> A person who seems happy may be described as **cheerful**:
>
> *She's always very* ***cheerful****.*
>
> If someone is happy at a particular time, you can describe them as being **in a good mood**:
>
> *You're* ***in a good mood*** *this morning!*
>
> Someone who is happy because of something may be described as **pleased** or **glad**, and somone who is extremely happy because of something may be described as **delighted**:
>
> *He was* ***pleased*** *that she had come back.*
>
> *I was so* ***glad*** *to see her.*
>
> *They are* ***delighted*** *with their new car.*
>
> Someone who is extremely happy and excited may be described as **ecstatic** or **elated**:
>
> *The new president was greeted by an* ***ecstatic*** *crowd.*
>
> *We were* ***elated*** *at the news.*
>
> The expression **on cloud nine** can be used informally to say that someone is extremely happy because something good has happened:
>
> *I was* ***on cloud nine*** *after being offered the job.*
>
> Someone who seems to be happy most of the time can be described as **contented**:
>
> *She's a very* ***contented*** *little baby.*

happy /ˈhæp.i/ adj PLEASED ▷ **1** A1 feeling, showing, or causing pleasure or satisfaction: *a happy marriage/childhood* ◦ *She looks so happy.* ◦ *School days are said to be the happiest days of your life.* ◦ *Nicky seems a lot happier since she met Steve.* ◦ *You'll be happy* ***to*** *know that Jean is coming with us.* ◦ *I'm perfectly happy* ***to*** *(= I will willingly) help out.* ◦ *I'm so happy (****that****) everything is working out for you.* ◦ *Barry seems happy enough working for himself.* ◦ *Are you happy* ***about/with*** *(= satisfied with) your new working arrangements?* ◦ *Your mother's not going to be very happy when she sees the mess you've made!* ◦ formal

The manager will be happy (= is willing) ***to*** *see you this afternoon.* **GREETING ▷ 2** A1 [before noun] (used in greetings for special occasions) full of enjoyment and pleasure: *Happy Birthday! ◦ Happy Anniversary! ◦ Happy New Year!* **LUCKY ▷ 3** [before noun] (of a condition or situation) lucky: *We hadn't planned to be in France at the same time as Ann and Charles – it was just a happy* ***coincidence***. **SUITABLE ▷ 4** literary (of words or behaviour) suitable: *It wasn't a happy choice of phrase given the circumstances.*

IDIOMS **the happy day** humorous a marriage: *So when's the happy day then?* • **the happy event** (US also **the blessed event**) the birth of a child • **not be a happy bunny** UK humorous to be annoyed about a situation: *Her computer crashed an hour ago and she's lost a morning's work – she's not a happy bunny at the moment.*

ˌhappy ˈcamper noun [C] humorous someone who is happy with the situation they are in: *She's just found out about the pay cut and she's not a happy camper.*

happy-clappy /ˌhæp.iˈklæp.i/ adj UK informal often disapproving describes Christians who sing, talk, and shout enthusiastically during their religious ceremonies and who try to persuade other people to join them

ˌhappy-go-ˈlucky adj describes someone who does not plan much and accepts what happens without becoming worried

ˈhappy ˌhour noun [C usually singular] a period of time, usually in the early evening, when drinks are sold cheaply in a bar or a pub

ˌhappy ˈmedium noun [S] approving a state or way of doing something which avoids being extreme, often combining the best of two opposite states or ways of doing something: *I try to* ***strike a*** *(= achieve a) happy medium when I'm on holiday, and spend half my time doing things and the other half just relaxing.*

hara-kiri /ˌhær.əˈkiː.ri/ noun [U] (in Japan, especially in the past) a formal way of killing yourself by cutting open your stomach with a SWORD

harangue /həˈræŋ/ verb [T] disapproving to speak to someone or a group of people, often for a long time, in a forceful and sometimes angry way, especially to persuade them: *A drunk in the station was haranguing passers-by.* • **harangue** noun [C] *The team were given the usual half-time harangue by their manager.*

harass /ˈhær.əs/ verb [T] to continue to annoy or upset someone over a period of time: *Stop harassing me!*

harassed /ˈhær.əst/ adj worried, annoyed, and tired, especially because you have too many things to deal with: *harassed-looking mothers with young children*

harassment /ˈhær.əs.mənt/ noun [U] C1 behaviour that annoys or upsets someone: ***sexual*** *harassment*

harbinger /ˈhɑː.bɪn.dʒəʳ/ US /ˈhɑːr.bɪn.dʒɚ/ noun [C] literary a person or thing that shows that something is going to happen soon, especially something bad: *a harbinger* ***of doom***

harbour /ˈhɑː.bəʳ/ US /ˈhɑːr.bɚ/ noun; verb

harbour

▸noun [C or U] UK (US **harbor**) B1 an area of water next to the coast, often protected from the sea by a thick wall, where ships and boats can shelter: *Our hotel room overlooked a pretty little fishing harbour.* → Compare **dock**

▸verb [T] UK (US **harbor**) **HAVE IN MIND ▷ 1** to think about or feel something, usually over a long period: *He's been harbouring a* ***grudge*** *against her ever since his promotion was refused. ◦ There are those who harbour suspicions about his motives. ◦ Powell remains non-committal about any political ambitions he may harbour.* **HIDE ▷ 2** to protect someone or something bad, especially by hiding them when the police are looking for them: *to harbour a criminal* **CONTAIN ▷ 3** to contain the bacteria, etc. that can cause a disease to spread: *Bathroom door handles can harbour germs.*

ˈharbour ˌmaster noun [C] the official who is in charge of a harbour

hard /hɑːd/ US /hɑːrd/ adj; adv

▸adj **SOLID ▷ 1** A2 not easy to bend, cut, or break: *a hard surface ◦ There was a heavy frost last night and the ground is still hard. ◦ Heating the clay makes it hard.* → Opposite **soft** **DIFFICULT ▷ 2** A1 difficult to understand, do, experience, or deal with: *There were some really hard questions in the exam. ◦* ***It's*** *hard* ***to say*** *which of them is lying. ◦* ***It's*** *hard be****ing*** *a single mother. ◦ Her handwriting is very hard* ***to*** *read. ◦ He's a hard man* ***to please****. ◦ The topics* ***get*** *harder later in the course. ◦ I feel sorry for the kids, too – they've had a hard* ***time****.* → Opposite **easy** **USING EFFORT ▷ 3** B1 needing or using a lot of physical or mental effort: *Go on – give it a good hard push! ◦ It was hard* ***work*** *on the farm but satisfying.* **SEVERE ▷ 4** B2 not pleasant or gentle; severe: *You have to be quite hard to succeed in the property business. ◦ Ooh, you're a hard woman, Elaine! ◦ Our boss has been giving us all a hard* ***time*** *at work (= making our time at work difficult).* **5 be hard on sb** B2 to criticize someone severely, or to treat them unfairly: *Don't be too hard on him – he's new to the job.* **ALCOHOL ▷ 6** [before noun] describes a drink that contains a high level of alcohol: *hard* ***liquor*** **WATER ▷ 7** describes water which contains a lot of LIME which prevents soap from cleaning **CLEAR ▷ 8** [before noun] able to be proved: *hard facts/evidence* **WEATHER ▷ 9** describes a time when there is bad weather: *We had a very hard* ***winter*** *last year.* • **hardness** /-nəs/ noun [U]

> **Other ways of saying hard**
>
> You can use **stiff** when something is hard so that it does not bend very easily:
>
> ***stiff*** *cardboard*
>
> If something is so hard that it cannot be bent at all, you could use the adjective **rigid**:
>
> *a* ***rigid*** *steel and concrete structure*
>
> **Solid** can be used when something is hard and keeps its shape:
>
> *a* ***solid*** *object*
>
> If something is not soft, you could describe it as **firm**:
>
> *a* ***firm*** *mattress*
>
> Food that is hard in a pleasant way can be described as **crisp**:
>
> ***crisp*** *crackers*
>
> *a* ***crisp*** *apple*

IDIOMS **be no hard and fast rules** If there are no hard and fast rules, there are no clear rules for you to follow. • **hard feelings** anger towards someone that you have argued with: *So we're friends again, are we? No hard feelings?* • **hard luck!** mainly UK used to express sympathy to someone because something slightly bad has happened: *'We lost again.' 'Oh, hard luck!'* • **(that's) your hard luck** UK informal said if you think that it is someone's own fault that something bad has happened to them: *Well, if you missed the presentation because you couldn't be bothered to turn up on time, that's your hard luck!* • **hard to swallow** difficult to believe: *I found her story rather hard to swallow.* • **the hard way 1** a way of doing something which makes it more difficult than it needs to be: *She always does things the hard way.* **2** C2 If you learn something the hard way, you learn from unpleasant experiences rather than by being taught: *If she won't listen, she'll have to* ***learn/find out*** *the hard way.* • **take a hard line on sb/sth** to be very severe in the way that you deal with someone or something

▸adv USING EFFORT ▷ **1** A1 with a lot of physical or mental effort: *Work hard and play hard, that's my motto.* ◦ *I'm not surprised he failed his exam – he didn't exactly try very hard!* WEATHER ▷ **2** B1 If it rains or snows hard, it rains or snows a lot: *It had been raining hard most of the afternoon.*

IDIOMS **feel hard done-by** (also **feel ˌhard ˈdone-to**) UK to feel that you have been treated unfairly: *I'm feeling hard done-by because I've been looking after the kids all week and Steve's been out every night.* • **hard at it** UK informal putting a lot of effort into what you are doing: *That's what I like to see – everybody hard at it!*

hardback /ˈhɑːd.bæk/ US /ˈhɑːrd-/ **noun** [C or U] (US also **hardcover**) a book that has a stiff cover: *His latest novel will be published* ***in*** *hardback later this month.* → Compare **paperback, softback**

hardball /ˈhɑːd.bɔːl/ US /ˈhɑːrd.bɑːl/ **noun** [U] US for **baseball** → Compare **softball**

ˌhard-ˈbitten adj If someone is hard-bitten, their character has been made stronger as a result of difficult experiences in the past, and they control and do not show their emotions: *This particular murder case was so horrific that it shocked even the most hard-bitten of New York police officers.*

hardboard /ˈhɑːd.bɔːd/ US /ˈhɑːrd.bɔːrd/ **noun** [U] a substance made of very small pieces of wood, mixed with glue and pressed into large, thin, flat pieces

ˌhard-ˈboiled adj EGG ▷ **1** describes an egg that has been heated in its shell in boiling water until both the white and yellow parts are solid STRONG ▷ **2** informal describes a strong and determined person who shows little emotion: *The film stars Kathleen Turner as the hard-boiled detective of Sarah Paretsky's novel.*

ˌhard ˈby adv, **preposition** literary or old-fashioned very near: *The house where he lived as a child is hard by the main plaza.*

ˌhard ˈcase noun [C usually singular] (also **ˌhard ˈnut**) mainly UK informal someone who is difficult to deal with and possibly angry and violent

ˌhard ˈcash noun [U] money in the form of coins or notes but not CHEQUES or a CREDIT CARD

ˌhard ˈcider noun [U] US for **cider**

ˌhard ˈcopy noun [C or U] information from a computer that has been printed on paper

ˈhard ˌcore noun STONE/BRICK ▷ **1** [U] mainly UK the pieces of broken stone, brick, etc. used to make the base under a floor, path, or road BELIEF ▷ **2** (also **ˈhard-ˌcore**) [S, + sing/pl verb] a small group of people within a larger group, who strongly believe in the group's principles and usually have a lot of power in it: *The hard core of the party has not lost sight of the original ideals.*

ˌhard-ˈcore adj SEX ▷ **1** showing sexual acts clearly and in detail: *hard-core pornography* BELIEF ▷ **2** describes people who strongly believe in something: *hard-core party members*

hardcover /ˈhɑːdˌkʌv.əʳ/ US /ˈhɑːrdˌkʌv.ɚ/ **noun** [C or U] US for **hardback**: *The novel was published* ***in*** *hardcover.*

ˌhard ˈcurrency noun [U] money that is valuable and can be exchanged easily because it comes from a powerful country

ˈhard ˌdisk noun [C] B2 a device that is fixed inside a computer and is used to store programs and information

ˌhard ˈdrinker noun [C] someone who often drinks a lot of alcohol

ˈhard ˌdrive noun [C] B2 a part of a computer that reads information on a hard disk, or a separate device that can be connected to a computer in order to do this

ˌhard ˈdrug noun [C usually plural] a very strong, illegal drug

ˌhard-ˈearned adj If something such as a holiday is hard-earned, you deserve it because you have been working very hard.

harden /ˈhɑː.dᵊn/ US /ˈhɑːr-/ **verb** [I or T] SOLID ▷ **1** to become or make hard: *The mixture hardens as it cools.* ◦ *It is thought that high cholesterol levels in the blood can harden the arteries (= make them thicker and stiffer, causing disease).* SEVERE ▷ **2** to become more severe, determined or unpleasant: *Living rough in the desert hardened the recruits a lot (= made them stronger).* ◦ *As the war progressed, attitudes on both sides hardened (= became more severe and determined).* • **hardening** /-ɪŋ/ **noun** [U or S] *There has been a hardening of government policy since the invasion.*

IDIOM **harden your heart** to make yourself stop feeling kind or friendly towards someone: *You've just got to harden your heart and tell him to leave.*

hardened /ˈhɑː.dᵊnd/ US /ˈhɑːr-/ **adj 1** [before noun] used to describe someone who has had a lot of bad experiences and as a result no longer gets upset or shocked: *hardened detectives/reporters* **2** [before noun] no longer likely to change a bad way of life or feel sorry about it: *a hardened* ***criminal*** **3 be/become hardened to sth** to develop a way of dealing with a sad situation so that it no longer upsets you: *You see all sorts of terrible things when you're a nurse so you become hardened to it.*

ˌhard-ˈfought adj achieved after a lot of difficulty or fighting: *a hard-fought victory*

ˌhard ˈgoing adj [after verb] informal difficult and TIRING to do, deal with, or make progress with: *I find her books a bit hard going.*

ˈhard ˌhat noun [C] a hat made of a strong substance that is worn by workers to protect their heads

ˌhard-ˈheaded adj not influenced by emotions: *a hard-headed approach to problems*

ˌhard-ˈhearted adj disapproving If someone is hard-hearted, they are not kind or not able to feel sympathy. → Compare **kind-hearted, soft-hearted**

ˌhard-ˈhitting adj A speech or piece of writing that is hard-hitting includes strong criticism of something: *The committee published a hard-hitting report on the bank's management.*

ˌhard ˈlabour UK (US **ˌhard ˈlabor**) **noun** [U] a punishment for criminals, especially used in the past, which involves a lot of TIRING, physical work

ˌhard ˈline noun [S] the fact of being very severe, for example in refusing to allow something or to give people what they want: *The government wants to* ***take*** *a hard line against the strikers.*

ˌhard-ˈline adj extreme and severe and not likely to change: *a hard-line manifesto* ◦ *a hard-line politician*

• ˌhard-ˈliner noun [C] *He needs to persuade the hard-liners in the cabinet.*

ˌhard-ˈluck ˌstory noun [C] informal disapproving a story or piece of information that someone tells you or writes about themselves, intended to make you feel feel sympathy for them: *She came out with some hard-luck story about never having been loved by her mother.*

hardly /ˈhɑːd.li/ ⓤⓢ /ˈhɑːrd-/ adv **ONLY JUST** ▷ **1** B1 only just; almost not: *I* ***could*** *hardly hear her at the back.* ◦ *The party had hardly started when she left.* ◦ *He hardly ate anything/He ate hardly anything.* ◦ *We hardly* ***ever*** *(= almost never) go to concerts.* ◦ *Hardly had a moment passed before the door creaked open.* **CERTAINLY NOT** ▷ **2** B2 certainly not: *You* ***can*** *hardly expect a pay rise when you've only been working for the company for two weeks!* ◦ *Well don't be angry with me – it's hardly my fault that it's raining!*

> **!** Common mistake: **hardly**
>
> **Warning:** check your word order!
>
> **Hardly** usually goes directly before the main verb in a sentence.
>
> Don't say 'hardly could/can do something', say **could/can hardly do something**:
>
> ~~*I hardly could recognize him after so many years.*~~
>
> *I could hardly recognize him after so many years.*
>
> But if the main verb is **am/is/are/was/were**, **hardly** usually goes directly after it:
>
> ~~*There hardly were any shops in the town.*~~
>
> *There were hardly any shops in the town.*

ˌhard-ˈnosed adj practical and determined: *His hard-nosed business approach is combined with a very real concern for the less fortunate in society.*

ˌhard of ˈhearing adj [after verb] not able to hear well: *My father is quite old now and he's increasingly hard of hearing.*

ˈhard-on noun [C] offensive an ERECTION (= the condition of the PENIS when it is stiff): *to have a hard-on*

ˌhard ˈpalate noun [C] specialized the hard part that forms the top of the mouth, behind the front teeth → Compare **soft palate**

ˌhard ˈporn noun [U] PORNOGRAPHY (= books, films, etc. showing sexual acts) which shows sex in a very detailed way → Compare **soft porn**

ˌhard-ˈpressed adj having a lot of difficulties doing something, especially because there is not enough time or money: *The latest education reforms have put extra pressure on teachers who are already hard-pressed.* ◦ *Because of shortages, the emergency services were hard-pressed* ***to*** *deal with the accident.* ◦ *Most people would be hard-pressed (= would find it difficult)* ***to*** *name more than half a dozen members of the government.*

ˌhard ˈrock noun [U] a type of ROCK MUSIC with a strong beat in which drums and electric guitars are played very loudly

ˌhard ˈscience noun [C or U] science, or a branch of science in which facts and theories can be firmly and exactly measured, tested, or proved

ˌhard ˈsell noun [S] a method of selling in which the person selling tries very hard to persuade the customer to buy something

hardship /ˈhɑːd.ʃɪp/ ⓤⓢ /ˈhɑːrd-/ noun [C or U] C1 (something which causes) difficult or unpleasant conditions of life, or an example of this: *economic hardship*

ˌhard ˈshoulder noun [C usually singular] UK (US **shoulder**, Irish English **ˌhard ˈmargin**) a hard area at the side of a main road where a driver can stop if there is a serious problem

the ˈhard ˌstuff noun [S] informal humorous strong alcohol: *Would you like* ***a drop of*** *the hard stuff?*

hardtop /ˈhɑːd.tɒp/ ⓤⓢ /ˈhɑːrd.tɑːp/ noun [C] a car with a metal roof

ˌhard ˈup adj informal having very little money: *We're a bit hard up at the moment so we're not thinking in terms of holidays.* ◦ [before noun] *hard-up pensioners*

hardware /ˈhɑːd.weəʳ/ ⓤⓢ /ˈhɑːrd.wer/ noun [U] **COMPUTER** ▷ **1** B1 the physical and electronic parts of a computer, rather than the instructions it follows → Compare **software** **TOOLS** ▷ **2** metal tools, materials, and equipment used in a house or a garden, such as hammers, nails, and SCREWS **MILITARY** ▷ **3** informal equipment, especially if it is for military use or if it is heavy

ˌhard-ˈwearing adj If something, especially clothing or material, is hard-wearing it lasts for a long time and looks good even if it is used a lot.

hardwired /hɑːdˈwaɪəd/ ⓤⓢ /haəedˈwaɪəd/ adj **1** specialized A computer or electronic device that is hardwired is built to work in a particular way and you cannot change the way it performs with new software, etc. **2** informal If someone or something is hardwired to do a particular thing, they automatically do it and cannot change that behaviour: *Humans are hardwired to love fattening foods.*

ˌhard-ˈwon adj If something is hard-won, it was only achieved after a lot of effort: *a hard-won battle*

hardwood /ˈhɑːd.wʊd/ ⓤⓢ /ˈhɑːrd-/ noun [C or U] strong, heavy wood or the tree it comes from → Compare **softwood**

ˌhard-ˈworking adj B2 always doing a lot of work: *She was always very hard-working at school.*

hardy /ˈhɑː.di/ ⓤⓢ /ˈhɑːr-/ adj **1** strong enough to bear extreme conditions or difficult situations: *A few hardy souls continue to swim in the sea even in the middle of winter.* **2** describes a plant that can live through the winter without protection from the weather: *a hardy perennial* • **hardiness** /-nəs/ noun [U]

hare /heəʳ/ ⓤⓢ /her/ noun; verb

▸noun [C] (plural **hares** or **hare**) an animal like a large RABBIT that can run very fast and has long ears

▸verb [I + adv/prep] mainly UK to run or go very quickly, usually in an uncontrolled way: *I saw her haring* ***off*** *down the road after Molly.*

harebell /ˈheə.bel/ ⓤⓢ /ˈher-/ noun [C] a wild plant found in northern parts of the world which has blue, cup-shaped flowers

harebrained /ˈheə.breɪnd/ ⓤⓢ /ˈher-/ adj informal (of plans or people) not practical or silly: *That sounds like another of his harebrained* ***schemes!***

ˈhare ˌcoursing noun [U] mainly UK the activity of chasing a hare using dogs

Hare Krishna /ˌhær.iˈkrɪʃ.nə/ ⓤⓢ /ˌhɑː.riˈ-/ noun **1** [U] a modern type of Hinduism in which the god KRISHNA is especially worshipped **2** [C] informal a member of this religion

harelip /ˌheəˈlɪp/ ⓤⓢ /ˌher-/ noun [C] old-fashioned a **cleft lip**

harem /ˈhɑː.riːm/, /hɑːˈriːm/ ⓤⓢ /ˈher.əm/ noun [C] especially in the past in some Muslim societies, the wives or other female sexual partners of a man, or the part of a house in which they live

haricot (bean) /ˌhær.ɪ.kəʊˈbiːn/ ⓤⓢ /-koʊ-/ noun [C] a small, usually white bean

hark /hɑːk/ ⓤⓢ /hɑːrk/ verb [I] (also **hearken**) old use used to tell someone to listen: *Hark, I hear a distant trumpet!*

IDIOM **hark at sb!** humorous said to someone who has just accused you of something that you think they are guilty of themselves: *Hark at him calling me lazy when he never walks anywhere if he can drive!*

PHRASAL VERB **hark back to sth** REPEAT ▷ **1** If someone harks back to something in the past, they talk about it again and again, often in a way which annoys other people: *He's always harking back to his childhood and saying how things were better then.* BE SIMILAR ▷ **2** If something harks back to something in the past, it is similar to it: *The director's latest film harks back to the early years of cinema.*

Harley Street /ˈhɑː.li.striːt/, /ˈhɑːr-/ noun (the area around) a road in central London where many respected and well-known doctors treat their patients

H

harlot /ˈhɑː.lət/ (US) /ˈhɑːr-/ noun [C] old use disapproving a female PROSTITUTE

harm /hɑːm/ (US) /hɑːrm/ noun; verb

▸noun [U] B2 physical or other injury or damage: *Both deny conspiring to cause actual bodily harm.* ◦ *A mistake like that will* **do** *his credibility a lot of harm.* ◦ *Missing a meal once in a while never* **did** *anyone any harm.* ◦ *You could always ask Jim if they need any more staff in his office –* **(there's) no** *harm* **in** *asking (= no one will be annoyed and you might benefit).* ◦ *She* **meant no** *harm (= did not intend to offend), she was joking.* ◦ *She was frightened by the experience but she* **came to** *no harm (= was not hurt).*

> Word partners for **harm noun**
>
> *cause/do* (sb/sth) harm • not *mean* (sb) any harm • not *come to* any harm • *great/real/serious/irreparable* harm • *there's no harm in* (doing) sth • harm *to* sb/sth

IDIOMS **do more harm than good** to be damaging and not helpful: *Getting involved at this stage would do more harm than good.* • **out of harm's way** in a position that is safe from harm or from which harm cannot be done: *The children will be here soon – you'd better put that plate out of harm's way.*

▸verb [T] B2 to hurt someone or damage something: *Thankfully no one was harmed in the accident.* ◦ *The government's reputation has already been harmed by a series of scandals.*

IDIOM **harm a hair on sb's head** to hurt someone: *If he so much as harms a hair on her head I won't be responsible for my actions.*

harmful /ˈhɑːm.fəl/ (US) /ˈhɑːrm-/ adj B2 causing harm: *This group of chemicals is known to be harmful* **to** *people with asthma.* • **harmfully** /-i/ adv • **harmfulness** /-nəs/ noun [U]

harmless /ˈhɑːm.ləs/ (US) /ˈhɑːrm-/ adj B2 not able or not likely to cause harm: *Peter might look a bit fierce, but actually he's fairly harmless.* ◦ *There were those who found the joke offensive, but Johnson insisted it was just a bit of harmless* **fun**. • **harmlessly** /-li/ adv • **harmlessness** /-nəs/ noun [U]

harmonic /hɑːˈmɒn.ɪk/ (US) /hɑːrˈmɑː.nɪk/ adj; noun

▸adj relating to harmony

▸noun [C] specialized a special note that sounds when a musical note is played that is different from the main note

harmonica /hɑːˈmɒn.ɪ.kə/ (US) /hɑːrˈmɑː.nɪ-/ noun [C] (also ˈ**mouth** ˌ**organ**) a small, rectangular musical instrument, played by blowing and sucking air through it

harmonious /hɑːˈməʊ.ni.əs/ (US) /hɑːrˈmoʊ-/ adj MUSIC ▷ **1** having a pleasant tune or harmony PLEASANT ▷ **2** friendly and peaceful: *harmonious relations between the country's ethnic groups* • **harmoniously** /-li/ adv

harmonize (UK usually **harmonise**) /ˈhɑː.mə.naɪz/ (US) /ˈhɑːr-/ verb [I or T] MUSIC ▷ **1** to add harmonies to a tune MATCH ▷ **2** to be suitable together, or to make different people, plans, situations, etc. suitable for each other: *The garden has been designed to harmonize* **with** *the natural landscape.* ◦ *The plan is to harmonize (= make similar) safety standards across all the countries involved.* • **harmonization** (UK usually **harmonisation**) /ˌhɑː.mə.naɪˈzeɪ.ʃən/ (US) /ˌhɑːr-/ noun [U]

harmony /ˈhɑː.mə.ni/ (US) /ˈhɑːr-/ noun MUSIC ▷ **1** C2 [C or U] a pleasant musical sound made by different notes being played or sung at the same time: *singing* **in** *harmony* ◦ *It is a simple melody with complex harmonies.* MATCH ▷ **2** B2 [U] a situation in which people are peaceful and agree with each other, or when things seem right or suitable together: *racial harmony (= good feelings between different races)* ◦ *domestic harmony (= good feelings in the family or home)* ◦ *Imagine a society in which everyone lived together* **in (perfect)** *harmony.* ◦ *We must ensure that tourism develops* **in** *harmony* **with** *the environment.*

harness /ˈhɑː.nəs/ (US) /ˈhɑːr-/ noun; verb

▸noun [C] a piece of equipment with straps and belts, used to control or hold in place a person, animal or object: *a safety harness* ◦ *a baby harness* ◦ *a parachute harness*

IDIOMS **be back in harness** to have returned to work after being away for a period of time • **in harness with** working together to achieve something

▸verb [T] **1** to put a harness on a horse, or to connect a horse to a vehicle using a harness **2** to control something, usually in order to use its power: *There is a great deal of interest in harnessing wind and waves as new sources of power.*

harp /hɑːp/ (US) /hɑːrp/ noun; verb

▸noun [C] a large, wooden musical instrument with many strings that you play with the fingers

▸verb

PHRASAL VERB **harp on** informal disapproving to talk or complain about something many times: *He's always harping on* **about** *lack of discipline.* ◦ *I know you want to go to Paris. Don't keep harping on (***about** *it)!*

harpist /ˈhɑː.pɪst/ (US) /ˈhɑːr-/ noun [C] a person who plays the harp

harpoon /hɑːˈpuːn/ (US) /hɑːr-/ noun; verb

▸noun [C] a long, heavy SPEAR (= a long sharp weapon) fixed to a rope, used for killing large fish or WHALES

▸verb [T] to hit or kill a fish or WHALE with a harpoon

harpsichord /ˈhɑːp.sɪ.kɔːd/ (US) /ˈhɑːrp.sɪ.kɔːrd/ noun [C] a musical instrument similar to a piano. It was played especially in the 17th and 18th centuries.

harpy /ˈhɑː.pi/ (US) /ˈhɑːr-/ noun [C] **1** in Greek MYTHOLOGY, a creature with the head of a woman and the body of a bird **2** literary a cruel, unpleasant woman who shouts a lot

harridan /ˈhær.ɪ.dən/ (US) /ˈher-/ noun [C] old-fashioned disapproving an unpleasant woman, especially an older one, who is often angry and often tells other people what to do

harrow /ˈhær.əʊ/ (US) /ˈher.oʊ/ noun [C] a large piece of equipment that is pulled behind a TRACTOR (= a farm vehicle) to break the earth into small pieces ready for planting • **harrow** verb [I or T]

harrowed /ˈhær.əʊd/ (US) /ˈher.oʊd/ **adj** looking as if you have suffered: *His face was harrowed.*

harrowing /ˈhær.əʊ.ɪŋ/ (US) /ˈher.oʊ-/ **adj** extremely upsetting because connected with suffering: *a harrowing story* ◦ *For many women, the harrowing prospect of giving evidence in a rape case can be too much to bear.*

harry /ˈhær.i/ **verb** [T] formal to repeatedly demand something from someone, often causing them to feel worried or angry: *She harried the authorities, writing letters and getting up petitions.* • **harried** /-id/ **adj** *I saw a harried-looking mother at the checkout trying to manage two small children and a mountain of shopping.*

harsh /hɑːʃ/ (US) /hɑːrʃ/ **adj** **UNKIND** ▷ **1** C1 unpleasant, unkind, cruel, or more severe than is necessary: *harsh criticism* ◦ *The children had had a harsh upbringing.* ◦ *We thought the punishment was rather harsh for such a minor offence.* ◦ *'There is no alternative,' she said in a harsh voice.* ◦ *He said some harsh* ***words*** (= spoke unkindly) *about his brother.* **TOO STRONG** ▷ **2** C1 too strong, bright, loud, etc.: *harsh chemicals/lighting* • **harshly** /-li/ **adv** C2 *I thought she'd been treated rather harshly.* • **harshness** /-nəs/ **noun** [U]

hart /hɑːt/ (US) /hɑːrt/ **noun** [C] (plural **hart** or **harts**) a male DEER, especially a RED DEER → Compare **hind**

hartal /ˈhɑː.tɑːl/ (US) /ˈhɑːr-/ **noun** [C] Indian English a period of time, usually one day, when workers do not work because of an argument with an employer, or as a mark of respect for someone who has died

harum-scarum /ˌheə.rəmˈskeə.rəm/ (US) /ˌher.əmˈsker.əm/ **adv, adj** old-fashioned (behaving) in an uncontrolled way

harvest /ˈhɑː.vɪst/ (US) /ˈhɑːr-/ **noun; verb**

▸**noun** [C or U] B2 the time of year when crops are cut and collected from the fields, or the activity of cutting and collecting them, or the crops that are cut and collected: *the grain/potato/grape harvest* ◦ *We had a good harvest this year.* ◦ *Farmers are reporting a* ***bumper*** *(= very big) harvest this year.* ◦ *It won't be long now till harvest (time).*

▸**verb** [I or T] **CROPS** ▷ **1** to pick and collect crops, or to collect plants, animals, or fish to eat: *In the US, winter wheat is harvested in the early summer.* **BODY PARTS** ▷ **2** to take cells or other body parts from someone for medical use: *The donor organ is harvested at the accident scene and rushed to a hospital.* ◦ *There is a lot of controversy surrounding the harvesting of stem cells.*

harvester /ˈhɑː.vɪ.stəʳ/ (US) /ˈhɑːr.vɪ.stɚ/ **noun** [C] **1** a machine for harvesting crops **2** old use a person who harvests crops

ˌharvest ˈfestival **noun** [C usually singular] a celebration that is held in churches and schools in the autumn to give thanks for crops and food

has strong /hæz/ weak /həz/ /əz/ he/she/it form of **have**

ˈhas-been **noun** [C] informal disapproving a person who in the past was famous, important, admired, or good at something, but is no longer any of these

hash /hæʃ/ **noun; verb**

▸**noun** **FAILURE** ▷ **1** **make a hash of sth** [S] UK informal to do something very badly: *He made a complete hash of the last question.* **FOOD** ▷ **2** [U] a mixture of meat, potatoes, and vegetables cut into small pieces and baked or fried: *corned beef hash* ◦ US *eggs and hash* **DRUGS** ▷ **3** [U] informal for **hashish** **SYMBOL** ▷ **4** [C, usually singular] a symbol (#) on a phone or computer keyboard: *Please press the hash* ***key*** *to continue.*

▸**verb**

PHRASAL VERB **hash sth up** UK informal to spoil something by doing it badly: *The first interview was all right but I rather think I hashed up the second one.*

ˌhash ˈbrowns **noun** [plural] small pieces of potato pressed into flat shapes and fried

hashish /hæʃˈiːʃ/ **noun** [U] a drug, illegal in many countries, made from the CANNABIS plant and usually smoked

hashtag /ˈhæʃ.tæg/ **noun** [C] the symbol # on a phone or computer keyboard, used on TWITTER for describing the general subject of a TWEET (= message)

hasn't /ˈhæz.ənt/ short form of has not: *He hasn't done his homework.* ◦ *Hasn't he grown!*

hasp /hɑːsp/ (US) /hæsp/ **noun** [C] a piece of metal that fastens a box or door, used with a PADLOCK (= lock that can be removed)

hassle /ˈhæs.l/ **noun; verb**

▸**noun** [C or U] informal (a situation causing) difficulty or trouble: *I can't face the hassle of moving house again.* ◦ *My boss has been* ***giving*** *me a lot of hassle this week.* ◦ *It's one of the few bars that women can go to and not* ***get*** *any hassle from men.* ◦ *It was such a hassle trying to get my bank account changed that I nearly gave up.* ◦ *I should have taken it back to the shop but I just didn't think it was worth* (***all***) *the hassle.*

▸**verb** [T] to annoy someone, especially by repeatedly asking them something: *I'll do it in my own time – just stop hassling me!* ◦ [+ to infinitive] *The children keep hassling me* ***to*** *take them to Disneyland.*

haste /heɪst/ **noun** [U] disapproving (too much) speed: *Unfortunately the report was prepared* ***in*** *haste and contained several inaccuracies.* ◦ [+ to infinitive] ***In*** *her haste* ***to*** *get up from the table, she knocked over a cup.*

IDIOMS **make haste** old-fashioned hurry up: *Make haste!* • **more haste, less speed** UK saying said to mean that if you try to do things too quickly, it will take you longer in the end

hasten /ˈheɪ.sən/ **verb** formal **1** [T] to make something happen sooner or more quickly: *There is little doubt that poor medical treatment hastened her death.* ◦ *These recent poor results have hastened the manager's departure.* **2** [+ to infinitive] If you hasten to do something, you quickly do it: *The president hastened to reassure his people that he was in perfect health.* **3** [+ to infinitive] If you hasten to say something, you want to make it clear: *It was an unfortunate decision and I hasten* ***to*** *say it had nothing to do with me.* ◦ *'People round here dress so badly – except you, Justin,' she hastened* ***to*** *add.*

hasty /ˈheɪ.sti/ **adj** describes something that is done in a hurry, sometimes without the necessary care or thought: *He warned against making hasty decisions.* ◦ *Now let's not leap to any hasty conclusions.* ◦ *We saw the rain and made a hasty retreat into the bar.* ◦ *I think perhaps we were a little hasty* ***in*** *judging him.* • **hastily** /-stɪ.li/ **adv** *'He looks good for his age. Not that 55 is old,' she hastily added.* • **hastiness** /-nəs/ **noun** [U]

hat /hæt/ **noun** [C] **1** A1 a covering for the head that is not part of a piece of clothing: *a straw hat* ◦ *a woolly hat* ◦ *a wide-brimmed hat* **2** used to refer to one of the various jobs or responsibilities that someone has: *For this movie, she is* ***wearing*** *the hats of director and actress.* ◦ *This is me* ***with my*** *manager's hat* ***on*** *talking.*

IDIOMS **take your hat off to sb** If you say that you take your hat off to someone, you mean that you admire them for an achievement: *So Emma actually manages*

H

to juggle two small children and a full-time job, does she? Well, I take my hat off to her. • **throw your hat into the ring** to announce your intention of entering a competition or election

hatband /ˈhæt.bænd/ **noun** [C] a strip of material fixed around the outside of a hat

hatbox /ˈhæt.bɒks/ ⓤⓢ /-bɑːks/ **noun** [C] a round container for storing or carrying hats

hatch /hætʃ/ **verb; noun**

▸**verb** EGG ▷ **1** [I or T] to (cause an egg to) break in order to allow a young animal to come out PLAN ▷ **2** [T] to make a plan, especially a secret plan: *It was in August of 1978 that the Bolton brothers hatched their plot to kill their parents.*

▸**noun** [C] (also **hatchway**) an opening through a wall, floor, etc., or the cover for it: *an escape hatch* ◦ *a serving hatch*

IDIOM **down the hatch!** informal said before swallowing a drink, especially an alcoholic one

hatchback /ˈhætʃ.bæk/ **noun** [C] a car that has an extra door at the back that can be lifted up to allow things to be put in

hatchery /ˈhætʃ.ər.i/ ⓤⓢ /-ɚ-/ **noun** [C] a place for hatching large numbers of eggs, especially fish or chicken eggs

hatchet /ˈhætʃ.ɪt/ **noun** [C] a small AXE (= tool with a blade which cuts when you hit things with it)

hatchet

ˈ**hatchet-**ˌ**faced** adj Someone who is hatchet-faced has a thin, hard, and unpleasant face.

ˈ**hatchet** ˌ**job** **noun** [C usually singular] informal a cruel written or spoken attack on someone or something: *Fleck was certainly not the only critic to* ***do*** *a hatchet job* ***on*** *his latest novel.*

ˈ**hatchet** ˌ**man** **noun** [C usually singular] informal someone who is used for unpleasant and difficult or violent jobs

hate /heɪt/ **verb; noun**

▸**verb** [I or T] Ⓐ② to dislike someone or something very much: *Kelly hates her teacher.* ◦ *She hated the cold dark days of winter.* ◦ *I hate it when you do that.* ◦ [+ -ing verb] *I have always hated speak****ing*** *in public.* ◦ *I hate him tell****ing*** *me what do to all the time.* ◦ [+ to infinitive] *I hate (= do not want)* ***to*** *interrupt, but it's time we left.* ◦ *I'd hate (= would not like) you* ***to*** *think I didn't appreciate what you'd done.* • **hated** /ˈheɪ.tɪd/ ⓤⓢ /-t̬ɪd/ **adj** *He was the most hated teacher in the school.*

IDIOM **hate sb's guts** informal to dislike someone very much

▸**noun** [C or U] Ⓒ① an extremely strong dislike: *She gave him a look of pure hate.* ◦ *The feelings of hate grew stronger every day.* ◦ UK *One of my* ***pet*** *hates (= one of the main things I dislike) is people who use your name all the while when they're speaking to you.* → See also **hatred**

hateful /ˈheɪt.fəl/ **adj** old-fashioned very unpleasant: *I never wear grey because it reminds me of my hateful school uniform.*

ˈ**hate** ˌ**mail** **noun** [U] unpleasant or cruel letters from someone who dislikes you

hater /ˈheɪ.təʳ/ ⓤⓢ /-t̬ɚ/ **noun** [C] informal a person who says or writes unpleasant things about someone or

+ Other ways of saying hate

Detest and **loathe** are strong words that can be used instead of 'hate':

I ***detest*** *any kind of cruelty.*

'Do you like cabbage?' 'No, I ***loathe*** *it.'*

Despise is used when you hate someone and have no respect for them:

She ***despised*** *him for the way he treated her.*

A phrase which means the same as 'hate' is **can't stand**:

I ***can't stand*** *the sight of blood.*

Abhor or **deplore** are formal words that mean the same as 'hate' when someone hates a way of thinking or behaving:

I ***abhor*** *all forms of racism.*

He said that he ***deplored*** *all violence.*

If you want to say humorously that someone hates something, you can say that the person is **allergic to** it:

I'm ***allergic to*** *housework.*

In informal English if someone hates another person very much, you can use the phrase **hate** *someone's* **guts**:

I ***hate his guts*** *and wouldn't care if I never saw him again.*

criticizes their achievements, especially on the internet: *Forget the haters – they're just jealous.*

-hater /-heɪ.təʳ/ ⓤⓢ /-t̬ɚ/ **suffix** someone who dislikes the stated thing: *He thinks I'm a real* ***man****-hater.*

hatpin /ˈhæt.pɪn/ **noun** [C] a long metal pin, often with a decorated end, that is pushed through a woman's hat and hair to keep the hat on the head

hatred /ˈheɪ.trɪd/ **noun** [U] Ⓒ① an extremely strong feeling of dislike: *What is very clear in these letters is Clark's passionate hatred* ***of*** *his father.* ◦ *The motive for this shocking attack seems to be racial hatred.*

hatstand /ˈhæt.stænd/ **noun** [C] a vertical pole with HOOKS (= curved parts) at the top for hanging hats and coats on

hatter /ˈhæt.əʳ/ ⓤⓢ /ˈhæt̬.ɚ/ **noun** [C] old-fashioned someone who makes hats → See also **(as) mad as a hatter/Marchhare**

ˈ**hat** ˌ**trick** **noun** [C] an occasion when a player scores three times in the same game, especially in football, or when someone is successful at achieving something three times: *Goal! Fowler makes it a hat trick!* ◦ *After two election victories the government clearly has hopes of a hat trick.*

haughty /ˈhɔː.ti/ ⓤⓢ /ˈhɑː.t̬i/ **adj** disapproving unfriendly and seeming to consider yourself better than other people: *She has a rather haughty manner.* • **haughtily** /-tɪ.li/ ⓤⓢ /-t̬ɪ.li/ **adv** • **haughtiness** /-nəs/ **noun** [U]

haul /hɔːl/ ⓤⓢ /hɑːl/ **verb; noun**

▸**verb** [T] Ⓒ② to pull something heavy slowly and with difficulty: *They hauled the boat out of the water.* ◦ *She hauled herself* ***up*** *into the tree.*

IDIOM **haul ass** US offensive to move very quickly to a different place: *When the shooting started we hauled ass out of there.*

PHRASAL VERB **haul sb up** [M often passive] informal to force someone to go somewhere or see someone in order to be punished or to answer questions about their behaviour: *He was hauled up in court/in front of a magistrate.*

▸**noun** [C] AMOUNT ▷ **1** Ⓒ② a usually large amount of something that has been stolen or is illegal: *a haul of* *arms/drugs* **FISH** ▷ **2** the amount of fish caught: *Fishermen have been complaining of poor hauls all year.* **PERIOD OF TIME** ▷ **3** a journey, often a difficult one, or a period of effort: *From there it was a **long** haul/only a **short** haul (= long and difficult/short and easy journey) back to our camp.* ◦ *It was a long haul (= it took a long time and was difficult), but the alterations to the house are finished at last.* **4 long-haul flight/short-haul flight** a long/short journey by air

haulage /ˈhɔː.lɪdʒ/ (US) /ˈhɑː-/ noun [U] UK the business of moving things by road or railway: *a road haulage firm*

haulier /ˈhɔː.li.əʳ/ (US) /ˈhɑː.li.ɚ/ noun [C] UK (US **hauler**) a business or a person involved in a business which transports goods by road

haunch /hɔːntʃ/ (US) /hɑːntʃ/ noun **1** [C] one of the back legs of an animal with four legs that is used for meat: *a haunch of venison* **2 haunches** [plural] the top of a person's legs and their bottom: *She was sitting/squatting on her haunches.*

haunt /hɔːnt/ (US) /hɑːnt/ verb; noun

▸verb [T] **REPEATEDLY TROUBLE** ▷ **1** B2 to cause repeated suffering or ANXIETY: *Fighting in Vietnam was an experience that would haunt him for the rest of his life.* ◦ *30 years after the fire he is still haunted by images of death and destruction.* **SPIRIT** ▷ **2** B2 (of a GHOST) to appear in a place repeatedly: *A ghostly lady is said to haunt the stairway looking for her children.*

▸noun [C] a place often visited: *This pub used to be one of your **old** haunts, didn't it Jim?*

haunted /ˈhɔːn.tɪd/ (US) /ˈhɑːn.t̬ɪd/ adj **ANXIOUS** ▷ **1** showing signs of suffering or severe ANXIETY: *He had a haunted **look** about him.* **SPIRIT** ▷ **2** describes a place where GHOSTS often appear: *a haunted **house***

haunting /ˈhɔːn.tɪŋ/ (US) /ˈhɑːn.t̬ɪŋ/ adj beautiful, but in a sad way and often in a way which cannot be forgotten: *a haunting melody* ◦ *the haunting beauty of Africa*

haute couture /ˌəʊt.kuːˈtjʊəʳ/ (US) /ˌoʊt.kuːˈtʊr/ noun [U] (the business of making) expensive clothes of original design and high quality

haute cuisine /ˌəʊt.kwɪˈziːn/ (US) /oʊt-/ noun [U] cooking of a high standard, typically French cooking

hauteur /əʊˈtɜːʳ/ (US) /hoʊˈtɝː/ noun [U] literary a formal and unfriendly way of behaving which suggests that the person thinks they are better than other people

have strong /hæv/ weak /həv, əv/ **auxiliary verb; verb; modal verb**

▸auxiliary verb [+ past participle] **(had, had)** (also **'ve/'s**) A2 used with the past participle of other verbs to form the PRESENT PERFECT and PAST PERFECT: *I've heard that story before.* ◦ *Diane's already gone.* ◦ *John hasn't phoned.* ◦ *I haven't visited London before.* ◦ *Have you seen Roz?* ◦ *Has she been invited?* ◦ *They still hadn't had any news when I spoke to them yesterday.* ◦ formal *Had I known (= if I had known) you were coming, I'd have booked a larger room.*

▸verb **(had) POSSESS** ▷ **1** A1 [T not continuous] (also **'ve/'s**, mainly UK **have got**) to own: *They have a beautiful home.* ◦ *He has plenty of money but no style.* ◦ *I've got two brothers.* ◦ *Have you got time to finish the report today?* ◦ *I've got a suggestion/an idea.* **2 have the decency, good sense, etc. to do sth** to do one good thing, although you do other bad or silly things: ***At least** he had the good sense to turn the gas off.* ◦ ***At least** she had the decency to apologize.* **BE ILL** ▷ **3** A1 [T] (mainly UK **have got**) If you have a particular illness, you suffer from it: *Have you ever had measles?* ◦ *I've got a cold.* **DO** ▷ **4** A2 [T] to perform the action mentioned: *have a wash/bath/shower* ◦ *I had a swim.* ◦ *We had a short walk after lunch.* ◦ *I've never done it before but I'd like to have a try (= to try).* ◦ *Why don't you have a rest?* **EAT/DRINK** ▷ **5** A1 [T] to eat or drink something: *I had prawns and rice for lunch.* ◦ *Can I have a drink of water?* ◦ *When are we having dinner?* **RECEIVE/ALLOW** ▷ **6** [T] to receive, accept or allow something to happen: *Here, have some more coffee.* ◦ [+ to infinitive] *My mother's having visitors (**to** stay) next week.* ◦ *Let me have the book **back** next week.* ◦ *In the end they solved their problems and she had him **back** (= allowed him to come and live with her again).* ◦ *I looked in all the shops for string but there was **none to be** had (= none that anyone could obtain).* ◦ *I kept telling him that you were French but he **wouldn't** have **it** (= would not accept that it was true).* ◦ [+ -ing verb] *I **won't** have those kids runn**ing** all over my flowerbeds (= I refuse to allow them to do this).* **MAKE HAPPEN** ▷ **7** B1 [T] to cause something to happen or someone to do something: [+ past participle] *We're having the house painted next month.* ◦ [+ infinitive without to] *If you wait, I'll have someone collect it for you.* ◦ [+ obj + -ing verb] *The film soon had us cry**ing**.* ◦ *Guy'll have it work**ing** in no time.* ◦ *She had her parents **down** (= invited them to stay) for a week in the summer.* ◦ *We had the boat **out** (= went out in the boat) for the first time this week.* ◦ *We often have friends **over/round** (= invite them to come) on a Saturday night.* **SUFFER** ▷ **8** B1 [T + past participle] to suffer something that someone does to you: *She had her car stolen (= it was stolen) last week.* **EXPERIENCE** ▷ **9** A2 [T] to experience something: *We're having a wonderful time here in Venice.* ◦ *We didn't have any difficulty/problem finding the house.* ◦ *He hasn't been having much luck recently.* **BABY** ▷ **10** A2 [T] to give birth to a baby: *Elaine had a baby girl yesterday.* **11 be having a baby, twins, etc.** to be pregnant: *I hear his wife's having a baby.* **SEX** ▷ **12** [T not continuous] slang to have sex with someone: *He asked me how many men I'd had.*

IDIOMS **and have done with it** (also **and be done with it**) to deal with and finish the whole matter: *I think I'll just sell all the furniture and have done with it.* • **a good time was had by all** said to mean that everyone enjoyed themselves • **have it in you** to have a particular quality or ability: *His speech was really funny – we didn't know he had it in him.* • **have it in for sb** informal C2 to be determined to harm or criticize someone: *She's always had it in for me.* • **have it off** (also **have it away**) UK slang to have sex: *He was having it off **with** his friend's wife.* • **have it out with sb** to talk to someone about something they have done which makes you angry, in order to try to solve the problem: *She'd been late for work every morning and I thought I'd better have it out with her.* • **have nothing on sb or sth** informal to not be as good as someone or something: *He's a good player, but he's got nothing on his brother.* • **not have any of it** informal to be completely unwilling or to refuse: *I asked him to help out, but he wasn't having any of it.*

PHRASAL VERBS **have sb on** UK (US **put sb on**) to persuade someone that something is true when it is not, usually as a joke: *That's your new car? You're having me on!* • **have (got) sth on 1** B1 If you have clothes or shoes on, you are wearing them: *I loved that dress you had on last night.* **2** If you have something on, you have planned to do it: *Have you got anything on this week?* • **have sth out** to have something removed from your body: *You'll have to have that tooth out.* ◦ *He had his appendix out last week.* • **have sb up** [usually passive] UK informal to take someone to court for a trial: *He was had up **for** burglary.*

▸modal verb **have (got) to do sth a** A2 to need to or be forced: *I have to go to Manchester tomorrow on business.* ◦ *What time have you got to be there?* ◦ *Do we have to finish this today?* ◦ *We'll have to start keeping detailed records.* ◦ *Jackie's ill so they've had to change their plans.* **b** C2 used to say that something must be true: *That total has to be right – I've checked it twice.*

ˌhave-a-go ˈhero noun [C] UK informal an ordinary person who does something brave in order to try and stop a crime

haven /ˈheɪ.vᵊn/ noun [C] a safe or peaceful place: *The garden was a haven* ***from*** *the noise and bustle of the city.* ◦ *They wanted to provide* ***safe*** *havens for the refugees.*

haven't /ˈhæv.ᵊnt/ short form of have not: *I haven't been to Australia.*

haversack /ˈhæv.ə.sæk/ US /-ɚ-/ noun [C] old-fashioned a bag, often made from strong rough cloth, with one or two shoulder straps

haves /hævz/ noun [plural] **the haves and have-nots** the people who are not poor and the people who are poor: *The government's change of policy is intended to reduce the gap between the haves and have-nots in our society.*

havoc /ˈhæv.ək/ noun [U] confusion and lack of order, especially causing damage or trouble: *The storm* ***wreaked*** *(= caused) havoc in the garden, uprooting trees and blowing a fence down.* ◦ *The delay* ***played*** *(= caused) havoc* ***with*** *their travel arrangements.*

haw /hɔː/ US /hɑː/ verb → See **hum and haw**

hawk /hɔːk/ US /hɑːk/ noun; verb

▸noun [C] BIRD ▷ **1** a type of large bird which catches small birds and animals for food PERSON ▷ **2** a person who strongly supports the use of force in political relationships rather than discussion or other more peaceful solutions → Compare **dove**

▸verb [T] to sell goods informally in public places: *On every street corner there were traders hawking their wares.*

hawker /ˈhɔː.kəʳ/ US /ˈhɑː.kɚ/ noun [C] someone who sells goods informally in public places

ˈhawk-eyed adj Someone who is hawk-eyed watches and notices everything that happens: *Hawk-eyed store detectives stood by the doors.*

hawkish /ˈhɔː.kɪʃ/ US /ˈhɑː-/ adj supporting the use of force in political relationships rather than discussion or other more peaceful solutions: *The president is hawkish on foreign policy.*

hawser /ˈhɔː.zəʳ/ US /ˈhɑː.zɚ/ noun [C] a strong thick rope, often made of STEEL

hawthorn /ˈhɔː.θɔːn/ US /ˈhɑː.θɔːrn/ noun [C or U] a type of small wild tree with THORNS (= sharp points), white or pink flowers in spring and small, red fruits in the autumn

hay /heɪ/ noun [U] grass that is cut and dried and used as animal food

IDIOM **make hay while the sun shines** to make good use of an opportunity while it lasts

ˈhay ˌfever noun [U] an illness like a cold, caused by POLLEN: *She gets really bad hay fever.* ◦ *hay fever sufferers*

haystack /ˈheɪ.stæk/ noun [C] a large tall pile of hay in a field

haywire /ˈheɪ.waɪəʳ/ US /-waɪr/ adj informal **go haywire** to stop working, often in a way that is very sudden and noticeable: *The television's gone haywire.*

hazard /ˈhæz.əd/ US /-ɚd/ noun; verb

▸noun [C] C1 something that is dangerous and likely to cause damage: *a health/fire hazard* ◦ *The busy traffic entrance was a hazard* ***to*** *pedestrians.*

▸verb [T] to risk doing something, especially making a guess, suggestion, etc.: *I wouldn't like to hazard a* ***guess***.

ˌhazard (ˈwarning) ˌlight noun [C] one of the orange lights at the front and back of a car which turn on and off repeatedly to warn other drivers of danger

hazardous /ˈhæz.ə.dəs/ US /-ɚ-/ adj C2 dangerous: *a hazardous journey/occupation*

haze /heɪz/ noun; verb

▸noun [C or U] something such as heat or smoke in the air which makes it less clear, so that it is difficult to see well: *The road through the desert shimmered in the haze.* ◦ *I saw her through a haze of cigarette smoke.*

▸verb

PHRASAL VERB **haze over** If the sky hazes over, the air becomes less clear because of something such as heat or smoke: *The sky began to haze over during the afternoon.*

hazel /ˈheɪ.zᵊl/ noun; adj

▸noun **1** [C] a small tree that produces nuts that can be eaten **2** [U] a greenish-brown or yellowish-brown colour

▸adj (especially of eyes) greenish-brown or yellowish-brown in colour

hazelnut /ˈheɪ.zᵊl.nʌt/ noun [C] the nut of the hazel tree which has a hard brown shell

hazmat /ˈhæz.mæt/ noun [U] abbreviation for hazardous material: a dangerous substance: *Each volunteer was given a disposable white hazmat* ***suit*** *(= a suit that protects against dangerous substances)* ◦ *Over the past two weeks, hazmat crews have been flooded with anthrax false alarms.*

hazy /ˈheɪ.zi/ adj WEATHER ▷ **1** describes air or weather that is not clear, especially because of heat: *hazy sunshine* ◦ *the hazy days of summer* MEMORY ▷ **2** not remembering things clearly: *hazy memories of childhood* • **hazily** /-zɪ.li/ adv *She only hazily (= unclearly) remembered her previous visit.*

ˈH-bomb noun [C] a **hydrogen bomb**

HCF /ˌeɪtʃ.siːˈef/ specialized abbreviation for highest common factor: the highest number that a set of two or more different numbers can be divided by exactly

HD /ˌeɪtʃˈdiː/ adj abbreviation for high-definition: used to describe a system for showing very clear pictures on a television or computer screen or for producing very clear sound: *The series was shot entirely in HD.* ◦ *HDTV sets*

> **! Usage: he (avoiding sexist language)**
>
> Many people do not like the use of **he** to refer to a person whose sex is not known, as it seems unfair to women. Instead, they prefer to use **they**:
>
> *'Someone's on the phone.' 'What do they want?'*
>
> **He or she** can be used, but this can be repetitive in normal conversation. **He/she** and **s/he** are sometimes used in writing, but **they** is also accepted now, even in formal writing. The same is true of **his/their** and **him/them**:
>
> *Somebody called and left their number.*
>
> *If anybody needs to speak to me, tell them I'll be in the office this afternoon.*

he pronoun; noun

▸pronoun strong /hiː/ weak /hi, i/ **1** A1 used as the subject of a verb to refer to a man, boy, or male animal that has already been mentioned: *Don't ask*

Andrew, he won't know. ◦ *There's no need to be frightened – he's a very friendly dog.* **2** old-fashioned used to refer to a person whose sex is not known: *The modern traveller can go where he likes.* ◦ *As soon as the baby is born he'll start to take an interest in the world around him.*
▸**noun** [C] /hiː/ a male: *How can you tell whether the fish is a he or a she?*

head /hed/ noun; verb
▸**noun** BODY PART ▷ **1** A1 [C] the part of the body above the neck where the eyes, nose, mouth, ears, and brain are: *Put this hat on to keep your head warm.* ◦ *He banged his head on the car as he was getting in.* ◦ *She **nodded/shook** her head (= showed her agreement/disagreement).* **2** [S] a person or animal when considered as a unit: *Dinner will cost £20 a/per head (= for each person).* ◦ *I did a quick head **count** (= calculated how many people there were).* ◦ *They own a hundred head of (= 100) cattle.* **3** [S] a measure of length or height equal to the size of a head: *Her horse won **by a** head.* ◦ *Paul is **a** head taller than Andrew.* MIND ▷ **4** B1 [C] the mind and mental abilities: *You need a **clear** head to be able to drive safely.* ◦ *What put that (**idea**) **into** your head? (= What made you think that?)* ◦ *I can't get that tune/that man **out of** my head (= I cannot stop hearing the tune in my mind/thinking about that man).* ◦ ***Use** your head (= think more carefully)!* ◦ *Harriet has **a** (**good**) head **for** figures (= she is very clever at calculating numbers).* ◦ UK *Do you have **a** head **for heights** (= are you able to be in high places without fear)?* LEADER ▷ **5** B1 [C] someone in charge of or leading an organization, group, etc.: *the head of the History department* ◦ *the head chef* **6** A2 [C] mainly UK a **headteacher** **7** **head boy/girl** mainly UK a boy or girl who is the leader of the other PREFECTS and often represents his or her school on formal occasions TOP PART ▷ **8** C2 [S] the top part or beginning of something: *the head of the queue* ◦ *the head of the page* ◦ *Diana, the guest of honour, sat at the head of the table (= the most important end of it).* **9** [C] the larger end of a nail, hammer, etc. **10** [C] the top part of a plant where a flower or leaves grow: *a head of lettuce* **11** [C] the layer of white bubbles on top of beer after it has been poured **12** [C] the upper part of a river, where it begins **13** [C] the top part of a spot when it contains PUS (= yellow liquid) COIN SIDE ▷ **14** **heads** [U] the side of a coin that has a picture of someone's head on it → Compare **tail** DEVICE ▷ **15** [C] the part of a TAPE or video RECORDER (= machine for recording sound or pictures) which touches the tape to record and play music, speech, etc.

IDIOMS **a head of steam** **1** the force produced by a large amount of steam in a closed space **2** a situation in which a person or an activity starts to become very active or successful: *They're really beginning to **build up** a head of steam for their campaign.* • **an old/a wise head on young shoulders** a child or young person who thinks and talks like an older person who has more experience of life • **be banging, etc. your head against a brick wall** informal to try to do something that is very difficult or impossible to achieve and therefore causes you to feel annoyed: *I keep asking her not to park there but it's like banging your head against a brick wall.* • **be in over your head** informal to be involved in a difficult situation that you cannot get out of: *Sean tried to pay his gambling debts, but he was in over his head.* • **be off your head** informal **1** to be crazy: *You must be off your head going out in this weather!* **2** to not be in control of your behaviour because you have drunk too much alcohol or taken drugs: *Hannah was off her head as usual.* • **bite/snap sb's head off** informal to speak to someone angrily: *I asked what was wrong, but he just bit my head off.* • **bury/have your head in the sand** to refuse to think about unpleasant facts, although they will have an influence on your situation: *You've got to face facts here – you can't just bury your head in the sand.* • **can't get your head around sth** informal If you say that you can't get your head around something, you mean that you cannot understand it: *I just can't get my head around these tax forms.* • **can't make head nor tail of sth** to not be able to understand something • **come to a head** (also **bring sth to a head**) If something comes to a head or someone brings something to a head, a situation reaches a point where something must be done about it: *Things hadn't been good between us for a while and this incident just brought it to a head.* • **do sb's head in** UK informal to make someone feel confused and unhappy: *Getting up at four o'clock every morning was doing my head in.* ◦ *I've been trying to make sense of all these figures and it's doing my head in.* • **from head to foot/toe** completely covering your body: *The dog was covered in mud from head to foot.* • **a full, good, thick, etc. head of hair** a lot of hair: *Even as a tiny baby, she had a thick head of hair.* • **get your head down** UK informal to direct all your efforts into the particular task you are involved in: *I'm going to get my head down and try and finish this report before I go home today.* • **get sth into your head** to start to believe something: *When will you get it into your head that he's not coming back?* ◦ *One day, she got it into her head (= decided for no reason) that we all hated her.* • **get/put your head down** informal to sleep: *I'm just going to put my head down for a couple of hours.* • **give head** offensive to perform FELLATIO or CUNNILINGUS • **give sb their head** old-fashioned to allow someone to do what they want to do without trying to help them or give them advice • **go over sb's head** to speak to or ask permission from someone who has more authority than the person who you would normally go to in that situation: *Amanda was refusing to give me the week off so I went over her head and spoke to the boss.* • **go to sb's head** **1** If something goes to someone's head, it makes them think that they are very important and makes them a less pleasant person: *Don't let fame/success go to your head.* **2** If alcohol goes to your head, it makes you feel slightly drunk: *Champagne always goes straight to my head.* • **have your business, sensible, etc. head on** informal used for saying that you are considering something from a particular way of thinking: *I had my sensible head on that morning and knew we couldn't afford to buy the car.* • **have your head (buried/stuck) in a book** to be reading: *Rose always has her head buried in a book.* • **have your head in the clouds** to not know the facts of a situation • **have your head screwed on (the right way)** informal to be practical and wise: *Ask Lois to help – she's got her head screwed on the right way.* • **head and shoulders above** If someone or something is head and shoulders above other people or things, they are a lot better than them: *There's no competition – they're head and shoulders above the rest.* • **head first** with the head going first: *She **dived** head first **into** the pool.* • **head over heels (in love)** completely in love • **heads I win, tails you lose** humorous said about a situation in which you will win whatever happens • **heads or tails?** asked before you throw a coin into the air and want someone else to guess which side it will land on • **heads will roll!** something that is said to mean that people will be punished for something bad that has happened • **keep your head** (also **keep a cool head**) C2 to stay calm despite great difficulties: *She kept her*

H

head under pressure and went on to win the race. • **keep your head above water** C2 to just be able to manage, especially when you have financial difficulties: *The business is in trouble, but we are just about keeping our heads above water.* • **keep your head down** to avoid trouble: *He's in a bad mood today – I'm just keeping my head down.* • **laugh, shout, scream, etc. your head off** informal C2 to laugh, shout, scream, etc. very noisily and for a long time: *There I was lying face down on the pavement and you two were laughing your heads off!* • **over your head** too difficult or strange for you to understand: *I tried to take in what he was saying about nuclear fusion, but most of it* ***went*** *over my head.* • **put their heads together** If two or more people put their heads together, they plan something together: *If we put our heads together, we can think of a solution.* • **take it into your head to do sth** to suddenly decide to do something, often something silly or surprising: *Anyway, they took it into their heads to get married.*

H

▸verb **GO** ▷ **1** B2 [I + adv/prep] to go in a particular direction: *I was heading* ***out of*** *the room when she called me back.* ◦ *We were heading* ***towards*** *Kumasi when our truck broke down.* ◦ *He headed straight* ***for*** (= *went towards*) *the fridge.* ◦ *I think we ought to head* ***back/home*** (= *return to where we started*) *now, before it gets too dark.* **LEADER** ▷ **2** B2 [T] to be in charge of a group or organization: *She heads one of Britain's leading travel firms.* ◦ *Judge Hawthorne was chosen to head the team investigating the allegations of abuse.* **TOP PART** ▷ **3** C1 [T] to be at the front or top of something: *The Queen's carriage headed the procession.* ◦ *Jo's name headed the list of candidates.* **SPORT** ▷ **4** [T] to hit a ball with your head: *Owen headed the ball into the back of the net.*

PHRASAL VERBS **head for sth** B2 If you are heading for a bad situation, you are likely to experience it soon, because of your own actions or behaviour: *They're heading for disaster if they're not careful.* ◦ *The country is heading for recession.* • **head off** C1 to start a journey or leave a place: *What time are you heading off?* • **head sb/sth off** to force someone or something to change direction: *I tried to head the dog off by running towards it.* • **head sth off** to prevent a difficult or unpleasant situation from happening: *The company is putting up wages to head off a strike.*

-head /-hed/ **suffix** a person with a particular strong interest or ADDICTION: *a crack-head* (= *someone who depends on the drug* CRACK)

headache /ˈhed.eɪk/ **noun** [C] **PAIN** ▷ **1** A2 a pain you feel inside your head: *I've* ***got*** *a* ***splitting*** (= *severe*) *headache.* **DIFFICULTY** ▷ **2** something that causes you great difficulty and worry: *Finding a babysitter for Saturday evening will be a major headache.*

headachy /ˈhedˌeɪ.ki/ **adj** having a headache: *I knew I was getting a cold when I started feeling tired and headachy.*

headband /ˈhed.bænd/ **noun** [C] a narrow strip of material worn around the head, usually to keep your hair or SWEAT out of your eyes

headbanger /ˈhedˌbæŋ.əʳ/ (US) /-ɚ/ **noun** [C] **1** someone, especially a boy or young man, who enjoys listening to loud, energetic ROCK MUSIC **2** UK a stupid or silly person

headbanging /ˈhedˌbæŋ.ɪŋ/ **noun** [U] the activity of shaking your head up and down with great force to the beat of ROCK MUSIC

headboard /ˈhed.bɔːd/ (US) /-bɔːrd/ **noun** [C] a vertical board at the end of a bed behind where your head rests

ˈ**head-butt verb** [T] to hit someone violently on the head or in the face using the front of your head • ˈ**head-butt noun** [C]

headcase /ˈhed.keɪs/ **noun** [C] UK informal a person who behaves strangely or who is very silly or violent

headcheese /ˈhed.tʃiːz/ **noun** [U] US for **brawn**

ˈ**head** ˌ**cold noun** [C] a cold when your nose feels very blocked

headcount /ˈhed.kaʊnt/ **noun** [C] **1** the act of counting how many people are present in a place: *The teacher* ***did*** *a quick headcount before we all got back on the bus.* **2** the number of people who are in a place, at an event, or employed by a company: *Times were hard, and the company was unwilling to increase the headcount* (= *employ more people*).

headdress /ˈhed.dres/ **noun** [C] a decorative covering for the head

headed /ˈhed.ɪd/ **adj** [after verb] going in a particular direction: *Which way are you headed?*

-headed /-hed.ɪd/ **suffix** having the number or type of heads mentioned: *a many-headed monster*

ˌ**headed** ˈ**notepaper noun** [U] writing paper with a person's or organization's name and address printed at the top of it

header /ˈhed.əʳ/ (US) /-ɚ/ **noun** [C] **FOOTBALL** ▷ **1** the act of hitting the ball with your head in football: *A fine header!* **TEXT** ▷ **2** specialized a piece of text, such as a page number or a title, that appears at the top of every page in a document or book → Compare **footer**

ˌ**head-**ˈ**first adj** [before noun] (US also **headlong**) with the head going first

headgear /ˈhed.gɪəʳ/ (US) /-gɪr/ **noun** [U] a hat or other covering that is worn on the head: *When riding a bicycle, you should wear the proper headgear.*

headhunt /ˈhed.hʌnt/ **verb** [T] to persuade someone to leave their job by offering them another job with more pay and a higher position: *She was headhunted by a rival firm.*

headhunter /ˈhedˌhʌn.təʳ/ (US) /-t̬ɚ/ **noun** [C] **JOB** ▷ **1** a person who tries to persuade someone to leave their job by offering them another job with more pay and a higher position **FIGHTER** ▷ **2** a member of a group of people that keeps the heads of the enemies that it has killed

heading /ˈhed.ɪŋ/ **noun** [C] C1 words written or printed at the top of a text as a title

headland /ˈhed.lənd/, /-lænd/ **noun** [C] a piece of land that sticks out from the coast into the sea

headless /ˈhed.ləs/ **adj** without a head: *a headless corpse*

IDIOM **run round like a headless chicken** to be very busy doing a lot of things, but in a way that is not very effective

headlight /ˈhed.laɪt/ **noun** [C usually plural] (UK also **headlamp**) a large, powerful light at the front of a vehicle, usually one of two: *I could see a car's headlights coming towards me.* ◦ *It was foggy, and all the cars had their headlights* ***on.*** ◦ *to* ***dip*** *your headlights* (= *make them shine downwards*) → Compare **sidelight**

IDIOM **be like a deer/rabbit caught in the headlights** to be so frightened or surprised that you cannot move or think: *Each time they asked him a question he was like a deer caught in the headlights.*

headline /ˈhed.laɪn/ **noun; verb; adj**

▸noun [C] B1 a line of words printed in large letters as

the title of a story in a newspaper, or the main points of the news that are broadcast on television or radio: *The news of his death was splashed in headlines across all the newspapers.* ◦ *the eight o'clock headlines* → Compare **byline**
▸verb [T + obj + noun] **1** to have something as a headline or as the main story: *The story was headlined 'Killer dogs on the loose'.* **2** to be the main performer at an entertainment event: *The band's headlining appearance at the Reading Festival could be their last.*
▸adj [before noun] a headline amount, number, or rate is the most important one or the one that people notice most: *The credit card company will cut its headline* ***rate of interest*** *to 19.9 percent.* ◦ *The headline* ***figure*** *of 3.6 percent isn't as bad as it looks if you exclude the effects of oil prices.*

headlong /ˈhed.lɒŋ/ (US) /-lɑːŋ/ **adv, adj 1** [before noun] with great speed or without thinking: *The car skidded and* ***plunged*** *headlong over the cliff.* ◦ *In the headlong* ***rush*** *to buy houses, many people got into debt.* **2** US for **head-first**

headman /ˈhed.mæn/ **noun** [C] (plural **-men** /-mən/, /-men/) the CHIEF (= leader) of a village or group of people

headmaster /ˌhedˈmɑː.stər/ (US) /ˈhedˌmæs.tɚ/ **noun** [C] mainly UK a male HEADTEACHER

headmistress /ˌhedˈmɪs.trəs/ (US) /ˈhedˌmɪs-/ **noun** [C] mainly UK a female HEADTEACHER

ˌhead ˈoffice noun [C usually singular, + sing/pl verb] the most important office of an organization or company, or the people working there: *Paul was transferred to our head office in London.* ◦ *Head office have asked for a report.*

ˌhead of ˈstate noun [C] the official leader of a country, often someone who has few or no real political powers

ˌhead-ˈon adj [before noun], **adv** describes an accident in which the fronts of two vehicles hit each other: *The car crossed the road and hit a truck head-on.* ◦ *a head-on collision*

headphones /ˈhed.fəʊnz/ (US) /-foʊnz/ **noun** [plural] a device with a part to cover each ear through which you can listen to music, radio broadcasts, etc. without other people hearing

headquarters /ˌhedˈkwɔː.təz/ (US) /-ˌkwɔːr.tɚz/ **noun** [C, + sing/pl verb] (plural **headquarters**) (abbreviation **HQ**) B2 the main offices of an organization such as the army, the police, or a business company: *The company's headquarters is/are in Amsterdam.*

headrest /ˈhed.rest/ **noun** [C] the part of a chair that supports the head, especially a support fixed to the back of the seat of a car

headroom /ˈhed.ruːm/, /-rʊm/ **noun** [U] the amount of space below a roof or bridge: *It's a small car but there's lots of headroom.*

headscarf /ˈhed.skɑːf/ (US) /-skɑːrf/ **noun** [C] (plural **headscarves**) a square piece of material worn on the head by women, often folded into a triangle and tied under the chin: *a silk headscarf*

headset /ˈhed.set/ **noun** [C] a set of HEADPHONES, especially one with a MICROPHONE fixed to it

headship /ˈhed.ʃɪp/ **noun** mainly UK **1** [C] the position of being in charge of an organization or school: *Dozens of well-qualified teachers applied for the headship.* **2** [C usually singular] the period during which a particular person is in charge of a school or other organization: *A lot of changes have taken place during her headship.*

headstand /ˈhed.stænd/ **noun** [C] the act of balancing upside down on your head, using your hands to support you

ˌhead ˈstart noun [C usually singular] an advantage that someone has over other people in something such as a competition or race: *You've got a head start* ***over/on*** *others trying to get the job because you've got relevant work experience.*

headstone /ˈhed.stəʊn/ (US) /-stoʊn/ **noun** [C] a large stone that is put at one end of a GRAVE with the name of the person who has died and other details such as the year they died

headstrong /ˈhed.strɒŋ/ (US) /-strɑːŋ/ **adj** very determined to do what you want without listening to others: *She was a headstrong child, always getting into trouble.*

ˈheads-up noun [C usually singular] informal **1** a warning that something is going to happen, usually so that you can prepare for it: *This note is just to* ***give*** *you a heads-up that Vicky will be arriving next week.* **2** UK a short talk or statement about how a situation or plan is developing: *The boss called a meeting to* ***give*** *us a heads-up on the way the project was going.*

headteacher /ˌhedˈtiː.tʃər/ (US) /ˈhedˌtiː.tʃɚ/ **noun** [C] mainly UK (US usually **principal**, UK also **head**) A2 someone who is in charge of a school

ˌhead-to-ˈhead adj [before noun], **adv** involving a direct competition between two people or teams: *a head-to-head contest*

headway /ˈhed.weɪ/ **noun make headway** to make progress or get closer to achieving something: *I'm trying to learn to drive, but I'm not making much headway* (***with*** *it*).

headwind /ˈhed.wɪnd/ **noun** [C] a wind blowing in the opposite direction to the one you are moving in: *The runners had to battle against a* ***stiff/strong*** *headwind.*

heady /ˈhed.i/ **adj** having a powerful effect, making you feel slightly drunk or excited: *a heady wine/perfume* ◦ *In the heady* ***days*** *of their youth, they thought anything was possible.*

heal /hiːl/ **verb** [I or T] **1** B2 to make or become well again, especially after a cut or other injury: *The wounds were gradually healing* (***up***). ◦ *The plaster cast helps to heal the broken bone.* **2** If a bad situation or painful emotion heals, it ends or improves, and if something heals it, it makes it end or improve: *Peace talks were held to try to heal the growing rift between the two sides.* • **healing** /ˈhiː.lɪŋ/ **noun** [U] *This herb has been used in healing for centuries.*

healer /ˈhɪə.lər/ (US) /-lɚ/ **noun** [C] a person who has the power to cure ill people without using ordinary medicines: *a spiritual healer*

health /helθ/ **noun** [U] **1** A2 the condition of the body and the degree to which it is free from illness, or the state of being well: *to be in good/poor health* ◦ *Regular exercise is good for your health.* ◦ *I had to give up drinking for health reasons.* ◦ *He gave up work because of* ***ill*** *health.* **2** the condition of something that changes or develops, such as an organization or system: *the financial health of the business*

> Word partners for **health**
>
> sb's *state of* health • (in) ***excellent/good/ill/poor*** health • sb's health ***deteriorates/improves/worsens*** • ***damage/improve*** sb's health • health ***benefits/effects/problems***

ˌhealth and ˈsafety noun [U] the laws, rules, and principles that are intended to keep people safe from

H

injury or disease at work and in public places: *Tonight's performance has had to be cancelled for health and safety reasons.*

ˈhealth auˌthority noun [C usually singular] in the UK, an organization that is responsible for hospitals and medical services in a particular area

healthcare /ˈhelθ.keəʳ/ (US) /-ker/ **noun** [U] C1 the set of services provided by a country or an organization for the treatment of the physically and the mentally ill: *Healthcare workers are some of the lowest paid people in the country.*

ˈhealth ˌcentre UK (US **ˈhealth ˌcenter**) **noun** [C] a building in which several doctors have offices and where people go to visit them

ˈhealth ˌfood noun [C or U] food that is believed to be good for you because it does not contain artificial chemicals or much sugar or fat → Compare **junk food**

healthful /ˈhelθ.fəl/ adj US helping to produce good health: *A healthful diet includes lots of green vegetables.*

ˈhealth inˌsurance noun [U] an arrangement in which you make regular payments to an INSURANCE company in exchange for that company paying most or all of the costs of your medical care

ˈhealth ˌservice noun [C] a public service which provides medical treatment

ˈhealth ˌspa noun [C] (UK also **ˈhealth ˌfarm**) a place where you go for a holiday and eat healthy food, take exercise, etc.

ˈhealth ˌvisitor noun [C] UK a person employed to give advice to people, especially older people and the parents of very young children, about health matters, sometimes by visiting them in their own homes

healthy /ˈhel.θi/ adj **HEALTH** ▷ **1** A2 strong and well: *She's a normal healthy child.* ◦ *He looks healthy enough.* **2** showing that you are strong and well: *The walk had given her a healthy glow.* ◦ *a healthy appetite* **3** A2 good for your health: *a healthy diet* ◦ *a good healthy walk*

> **!** Common mistake: **healthy or health?**
>
> **Warning:** do not confuse the adjective **healthy** with the noun **health:**
>
> ~~*I enjoy cycling and it is good for my healthy.*~~
>
> *I enjoy cycling and it is good for my health.*

SUCCESSFUL ▷ **4** C2 successful and strong: *a healthy economy* **NORMAL** ▷ **5** normal and showing good judgment: *a healthy disrespect for authority* • **healthily** /-θɪ.li/ **adv** *Eat healthily (= eat foods that are good for you) and take plenty of exercise.*

heap /hiːp/ **noun; verb**

▸**noun** [C] C2 an untidy pile or mass of things: *a heap of clothes/rubbish*

IDIOMS **the bottom of the heap** People who are at the bottom of the heap are poor and unsuccessful and have the lowest position in society. • **collapse/fall in a heap** to fall down heavily and lie on the ground without moving: *The woman staggered and collapsed in a heap.* • **a (whole) heap of sth** informal a lot of something: *I've got a whole heap of work to do.*

▸**verb** [T + adv/prep] to put things into a large untidy pile: *He heaped more food* ***onto*** *his plate.*

PHRASAL VERB **heap sth on sb** to give someone a lot of praise, criticism, etc.: *He deals well with all the criticism heaped on him.*

heaped /hiːpt/ **adj** UK (US **heaping** (of a spoon or plate) containing as much as possible: *Add a heaped teaspoonful of sugar.*

heaping /ˈhiː.pɪŋ/ **adj** [before noun] US **1** large: *For less than $5, you get a sandwich, a heaping* ***helping*** *of fries, and a soft drink.* **2** (UK **heaped**) (of a spoon or plate) containing as much as possible: *Add a heaping teaspoonful of sugar.*

heaps /hiːps/ **noun** [plural], **adv** informal C2 a lot: *Let Sarah pay for dinner, she's got heaps* ***of*** *money.* ◦ *Our new house is heaps bigger than our last one.*

hear /hɪəʳ/ (US) /hɪr/ **verb** (**heard, heard**) **RECEIVE SOUND** ▷ **1** A1 [I or T] to receive or become conscious of a sound using your ears: *She heard a noise outside.* ◦ *My grandfather is getting old and can't hear very well.* ◦ *You'll have to speak up, I can't hear you.* ◦ [+ obj + -ing verb] *I heard/I could hear someone call****ing*** *my name.* ◦ [+ obj + infinitive without to] *At eight o'clock Jane heard him go out.* **BE TOLD** ▷ **2** B1 [I or T] to be told information about something: *Have you heard the news?* ◦ *If you haven't heard by Friday, assume I'm not coming.* ◦ [+ question word] *Have you heard* ***what's*** *happened?* ◦ [+ (that)] *I hear* ***(that)*** *you're leaving.*

> **!** Common mistake: **hear from *sb***
>
> To talk about getting a letter, email, or telephone call from someone, remember to use the preposition **from.**
>
> Don't say 'hear someone', say **hear from someone:**
>
> ~~*I look forward to hearing you.*~~

LISTEN ▷ **3** A2 [T] to listen to someone or something with great attention or officially in court: *I heard a really interesting programme on the radio this morning.* ◦ [+ infinitive without to] *I heard the orchestra play at Carnegie Hall last summer.* ◦ *An audience gathered to hear him speak.* ◦ formal *Lord, hear our prayers.* ◦ *The case will be heard (= officially listened to) by the High Court.*

IDIOMS **can't hear yourself think** If you cannot hear yourself think, you cannot give your attention to anything because there is so much noise: *There was so much noise in the classroom that I could hardly hear myself think.* • **do you hear?** a way of emphasizing that you want people to give their attention to what you are saying: *I won't stand for this rudeness, do you hear?* • **hear tell (of)** old-fashioned If you hear tell (of) something, someone tells you about it. • **hear wedding bells** informal to think that someone is going to get married: *She knew that if she brought her boyfriend home her mother would start hearing wedding bells.* • **hear, hear!** said to strongly agree with what someone else has just said • **I must be hearing things** humorous said when you cannot believe something because it is so unlikely: *He's offered to wash the dishes – I must be hearing things.* • **not hear the end/last of sth** to be told repeatedly about something: *We'll never hear the last of it if they win that competition.* • **will never hear the end of it** informal If you say you will never hear the end of it, you mean that someone is repeatedly going to speak proudly, disapprovingly, etc. about something: *If Linda gets that promotion, we'll never hear the end of it.* • **won't hear a word (said) against sb/sth** If you won't hear a word said against someone or something, you refuse to believe anything bad about them: *He's completely infatuated with the woman and won't hear a word said against her.* • **you could have heard a pin drop** something that you say in order to describe a situation where there was complete silence, especially because people were very interested or very surprised by what was happening:

Margaret's ex-husband turned up at the wedding. Honestly, you could have heard a pin drop.

PHRASAL VERBS **hear from sb** B1 If you hear from someone, you get a letter, email, or phone call from them, or they tell you something: *We haven't heard from her for ages.* ◦ *You'll be hearing from my solicitors (= they will write to you about my complaint).* • **hear of sb/sth** B2 If you have heard of someone or something, you know that that person or thing exists: *I'd never heard of him before he won the prize.* ◦ *It's a tiny country that most people have never heard of.* • **not hear of sth** If someone says they will not hear of something, they mean they will not allow it, usually when you want to do something good for them: *I wanted to pay but she wouldn't hear of it.* • **hear sth of sb** to receive news about someone: *We haven't heard anything of Jan for months.* • **hear sb out** to listen to someone until they have said everything they want to say: *At least hear me out before making up your mind.*

hearer /ˈhɪə.rəʳ/ US /ˈhɪr.ɚ/ noun [C] a person who hears or listens to something: *Jokes establish an intimacy between the teller and the hearer.*

hearing /ˈhɪə.rɪŋ/ US /ˈhɪr.ɪŋ/ noun **MEETING** ▷ **1** [C] an official meeting that is held to collect the facts about an event or problem: *A disciplinary hearing will examine charges of serious professional misconduct against three surgeons.* ◦ *I think we should give him a (**fair**) hearing (= we should listen to what he wants to say).* **ABILITY** ▷ **2** [U] the ability to hear: *He's getting old and his hearing isn't very good.*

ˈhearing ˌaid noun [C] a device worn inside or next to the ear by people who cannot hear well in order to help them to hear better

ˈhearing-imˌpaired adj A person who is hearing-impaired cannot hear or cannot hear well.

hearken /ˈhɑː.kən/ US /ˈhɑːr-/ verb [I] literary to listen

hearsay /ˈhɪə.seɪ/ US /ˈhɪr-/ noun [U] information that you have heard but do not know to be true: *The evidence against them is all hearsay.*

hearse /hɜːs/ US /hɝːs/ noun [C] a vehicle used to carry a body in a COFFIN to a funeral

heart /hɑːt/ US /hɑːrt/ noun; verb

▸noun **ORGAN** ▷ **1** A2 [C] the organ in your chest that sends the blood around your body: *He's got a weak/bad heart (= his heart is not healthy).* ◦ *Isabel's heart was beating fast with fright.* **EMOTIONS** ▷ **2** B1 [C or U] used to refer to a person's character, or the place within a person where feelings or emotions are considered to come from: *She has a good heart (= she is a kind person).* ◦ *I love you, and I mean it **from the bottom of** my heart (= very sincerely).* ◦ *I love you **with all** my heart (= very much).* ◦ *He said he'd never marry but he had a **change of** heart (= his feelings changed) when he met her.* ◦ *Homelessness is a subject very **close/dear to** her heart (= is very important to her and she has strong feelings about it).* ◦ *He **broke** her heart (= made her very sad) when he left her for another woman.* ◦ *It **breaks** my heart (= makes me feel very sad) to see him so unhappy.* ◦ *They say he died of a **broken** heart (= because he was so sad).* ◦ old-fashioned *It **does** my heart **good** (= makes me very happy) to see those children so happy.* ◦ *His heart **leaped** (= he suddenly felt very excited and happy) when the phone rang.* **CENTRAL PART** ▷ **3** B1 [S] the central or most important part: *The demonstrators will march through **the** heart **of** the capital.* ◦ *A disagreement about boundaries is **at the** heart **of** the dispute.* ◦ *Let's get to the heart **of the matter**.* **4** [C] the firm central part of a vegetable, especially one with a lot of leaves: *artichoke hearts* ◦ *the heart of a lettuce* **COURAGE** ▷ **5** C2 [U] courage or determination or hope: *You're doing really well – don't **lose** heart now.* ◦ ***Take** heart – things can only get better.* **SHAPE** ▷ **6** B2 [C] a shape, consisting of two half circles next to each other at the top and a V shape at the bottom, often coloured pink or red and used to represent love **CARDS** ▷ **7 hearts** [plural or U] one of the four SUITS in playing cards, which has one or more red heart shapes: *the seven/ace **of** hearts* **8** [C] a playing card from the SUIT of hearts: *In this game, a heart beats a club.*

IDIOMS **after your own heart** having the same opinions or interests as you: *She's a woman after my own heart.* • **at heart** C2 used to say what someone is really like: *He had dozens of friends, but he was a private person at heart.* • **be all heart** to be very kind and generous. This phrase is often used humorously, especially in the UK, to mean the opposite: *She's all heart.* ◦ humorous *'He deserves all he gets.' 'Oh, you're all heart (= you are not kind)!'* • **(off) by heart** B2 learned in such a way that you can say it from memory: *My father can still recite the poems he learned off by heart at school.* • **have a heart!** used to ask someone to be kinder to you: *Don't make me write it again! Have a heart!* • **have a heart of gold** to be very kind and generous • **have a heart of stone** to be unkind or cruel • **your heart aches** If your heart aches, you feel sad or feel sympathy and sadness for the suffering of other people: *His heart ached with pity for her.* • **heart and soul** literary completely: *She loves those children heart and soul.* • **your heart goes out to sb** If your heart goes out to someone who is in trouble, you feel sympathy for them: *Our hearts go out to the families of the victims of this terrible tragedy.* • **sb's heart is in their boots** UK informal If someone's heart is in their boots, they feel very sad, disappointed, worried, etc.: *Their hearts were in their boots when they realized that they would have to do the work all over again.* • **sb's heart is in their mouth** If someone's heart is in their mouth, they are feeling extremely nervous: *My heart was in my mouth when I opened the letter.* • **her/his heart is in the right place** used to say that someone has good intentions: *He's an odd man but his heart is in the right place.* • **your heart isn't in it** If your heart isn't in it, you do not feel interested or enthusiastic about something. • **your heart skips/misses a beat** When your heart skips/misses a beat, you feel very excited or nervous: *Every time he looks at me my heart skips a beat.* • **your heart's desire** literary the thing or person you most want • **in your heart of hearts** C1 in your most secret and true thoughts: *I didn't want to believe it, but in my heart of hearts I knew that it was true.* • **my heart bleeds for sb** used to say that you feel great sadness for someone. This phrase is often used humorously to mean the opposite: humorous *John complains he only has two cars – my heart bleeds for him (= I certainly do not feel sadness about that)!* • **not have the heart to do sth** to feel unable to do something because you feel it would be unkind: *She asked me to go with her and I didn't have the heart to refuse.* • **put your heart and soul into sth** to make a lot of effort to do something: *She puts her heart and soul into her work.* • **sb's heart sinks** to feel disappointed or to lose hope: *My heart sank when I realized we couldn't afford the new house.* • **set your heart on sth/doing sth** to want to get or achieve something very much: *She's set her heart on having a pony.* • **take sth to heart** C2 If you take criticism or advice to heart, you think about it seriously, often because it upsets you: *Don't take it to heart – he was only joking about your hair.* • **to your heart's content**

H

If you do something to your heart's content, you do something enjoyable for as long as you want to do it: *You've got a whole week to yourself and you can read to your heart's content.*

▸verb [T] informal mainly humorous used to say that you like someone or something very much: *I heart New York.*

heartache /ˈhɑː.teɪk/ US /ˈhɑːrt-/ **noun** [C or U] literary feelings of great sadness: *You've caused me nothing but heartache.*

ˈheart atˌtack noun [C] B1 a serious medical condition in which the heart does not get enough blood, causing great pain and often leading to death: *John* ***had*** *a heart attack three years ago.*

IDIOM **nearly/almost have a heart attack** informal to be extremely surprised or shocked: *I almost had a heart attack when I found out how much the meal cost.*

H

heartbeat /ˈhɑː.biːt/ US /ˈhɑːrt-/ **noun 1** [C or U] the regular movement or sound that the heart makes as it sends blood around your body: *a steady heartbeat* **2 the heartbeat of sth** [S] the person or thing that is most important in forming the character of a place, organization, etc. and giving it energy: *Keane was the heartbeat of the team.*

IDIOM **in a heartbeat** very quickly, without needing to think about it: *I'd do it again in a heartbeat.*

heartbreak /ˈhɑː.breɪk/ US /ˈhɑːrt-/ **noun** [U] feelings of great sadness or disappointment: *The kidnap has caused the family months of heartbreak and suffering.*

heartbreaking /ˈhɑːtˌbreɪ.kɪŋ/ US /ˈhɑːrt-/ **adj** causing extreme sadness: *a heartbreaking story* ◦ ***It*** *is heartbreaking* (***for*** *him*) ***that*** *he cannot see his children.* → See also **heartrending**

heartbroken /ˈhɑːtˌbrəʊ.kᵊn/ US /ˈhɑːrtˌbroʊ-/ **adj** extremely sad: *If she ever left him he would be heartbroken.*

heartburn /ˈhɑːt.bɜːn/ US /ˈhɑːrt.bɝːn/ **noun** [U] a painful burning feeling in the lower chest caused by the stomach not digesting food correctly

ˈheart disˌease noun [U] a medical condition affecting the heart: *Heart disease is the leading cause of death in many Western countries.*

-hearted /-hɑː.tɪd/ US /-hɑːr.t̬ɪd/ **suffix** having a character or feelings of the stated type: *a light-hearted play* • **-heartedly** /-li/ suffix • **-heartedness** /-nəs/ suffix

hearten /ˈhɑː.tᵊn/ US /ˈhɑːr.t̬ᵊn/ **verb** [T] to make someone feel happier and more positive about a situation: *Anti-government protesters have been heartened by recent government promises of free and fair elections.* → Opposite **dishearten**

heartened /ˈhɑː.tᵊnd/ US /ˈhɑːr.t̬ᵊnd/ **adj** [after verb] feeling happier and more positive about something: *I was heartened* ***to*** *hear reports that the tickets for the show were selling well.* ◦ *We all felt heartened by the news.*

heartening /ˈhɑː.tᵊn.ɪŋ/ US /ˈhɑːr.t̬ᵊn-/ **adj** making you feel happier and more positive: ***It*** *was heartening* ***to*** *see so many people at the rally.*

ˈheart ˌfailure noun [U] an occasion when the heart stops working correctly or stops completely

heartfelt /ˈhɑːt.felt/ US /ˈhɑːrt-/ **adj** strongly felt and sincere: *heartfelt relief* ◦ formal *Please accept my heartfelt* ***apologies/thanks.***

hearth /hɑːθ/ US /hɑːrθ/ **noun** [C] **1** the area around a FIREPLACE or the area of floor in front of it: *A bright fire was burning in the hearth.* **2** literary a home, especially when seen as a place of comfort and love: *They were reluctant to leave hearth* ***and home.***

heartily /ˈhɑː.tɪ.li/ US /ˈhɑːr.t̬ɪ-/ **adv** ENTHUSIASTIC ▷ **1** enthusiastically, energetically, and often loudly: *She laughed heartily at the joke.* LARGE ▷ **2** completely or very much: *I am heartily sick of the whole situation.*

heartland /ˈhɑːt.lænd/ US /ˈhɑːrt-/ **noun** [C] the central or most important area: *the Labour/Tory heartlands*

heartless /ˈhɑːt.ləs/ US /ˈhɑːrt-/ **adj** cruel and not worrying about other people: *Don't be so heartless!*

ˈheart ˌmurmur noun [C usually singular] a condition in which unusual sounds can be heard in the heart, sometimes as a result of a fault in its structure

heartrending /ˈhɑːtˌren.dɪŋ/ US /ˈhɑːrt-/ **adj** causing great sympathy or sadness: *a heartrending story* → See also **heartbreaking**

ˈheart-ˌsearching noun [U] the act of thinking very seriously about your feelings, usually before making an important decision: *After a lot of heart-searching, we decided to split up.*

heartsick /ˈhɑːt.sɪk/ US /ˈhɑːrt-/ **adj** literary very sad or disappointed

heartstrings /ˈhɑːt.strɪŋz/ US /ˈhɑːrt-/ **noun** [plural] **pull, tug, etc. at the heartstrings** to cause strong feelings of love or sympathy: *It's the story of a lost child – guaranteed to tug at the heartstrings.*

heartthrob /ˈhɑːt.θrɒb/ US /ˈhɑːrt.θrɑːb/ **noun** [C] informal a famous man, often a singer or an actor, who is attractive to many women

ˌheart-to-ˈheart noun [C usually singular] a serious conversation between two people, usually close friends, in which they talk honestly about their feelings: *We* ***had*** *a heart-to-heart over a bottle of wine.* ◦ *a heart-to-heart talk/chat*

heartwarming /ˈhɑːtˌwɔː.mɪŋ/ US /ˈhɑːrtˌwɔːr-/ **adj** (especially of an event, action, or story) seeming to be something positive and good and therefore causing feelings of pleasure and happiness: *a heart-warming tale of triumph over adversity*

hearty /ˈhɑː.ti/ US /ˈhɑːr.t̬i/ **adj** ENTHUSIASTIC ▷ **1** enthusiastic, energetic, and often loudly expressed: *a hearty welcome* ◦ *a hearty laugh* LARGE ▷ **2** large or (especially of food) in large amounts: *We ate a hearty breakfast before we set off.* ◦ *She's got a hearty* ***appetite*** *(= she eats a lot).* **3** old-fashioned very great: *She has a hearty dislike of any sort of office work.*

heat /hiːt/ **noun; verb**

▸noun TEMPERATURE ▷ **1** B1 [S or U] the quality of being hot or warm, or the temperature of something: *the heat of the sun/fire* ◦ *How do you manage to work in this heat without air conditioning?* ◦ *She always wore a coat, even in the heat of summer.* ◦ *Cook the meat* ***on*** *a* ***high/low*** *heat (= at a high/low temperature).* RACE ▷ **2** [C] a less important race or competition in which it is decided who will compete in the final event ANIMAL ▷ **3 on heat** UK (US **in heat**) describes an animal that is in a state of sexual excitement and ready to breed

> **Word partners for heat noun**
>
> *feel/generate/give out/withstand* heat • *great/intense/searing* heat • a *high/low* heat

IDIOMS **in the heat of the moment** If you say or do something in the heat of the moment, you say or do it without thinking because you are very angry or excited: *He didn't mean it – he said it in the heat of the moment.* • **if you can't stand the heat, get out of the**

kitchen saying used as a way to tell someone that they should either stop complaining about a difficult or unpleasant activity, or stop doing it • **put the heat on sb** informal to try to persuade or force someone to do something • **take the heat off sb** informal If someone or something takes the heat off you, they reduce the amount of criticism you have to deal with: *The deputy's resignation over the scandal has taken some of the heat off his superior.* • **the heat is on** slang If you say the heat is on, you mean that a time of great activity and/or pressure has begun: *With only months to go before the deadline, the heat is on.*

▸verb [I or T] B2 to make something hot or warm, or to become hot or warm: *A large house like this must be expensive to heat.* ◦ *Shall I heat* ***up*** *some soup for lunch?*

heated /ˈhiː.tɪd/ US /-t̬ɪd/ adj TEMPERATURE ▷ **1** describes something that has been made hot or warm: *a heated towel rail* ◦ *a heated swimming pool* EMOTION ▷ **2** excited or angry: *a heated debate*

heatedly /ˈhiː.tɪd.li/ US /-t̬ɪd-/ adv in an excited or angry way

heater /ˈhiː.təʳ/ US /-t̬ɚ/ noun [C] B1 a device which produces heat: *a gas/electric heater*

ˈheat exˌhaustion noun [U] (US also **ˈheat prosˌtration**) a condition in which you feel very weak and sick after being in a very hot place for too long

heath /hiːθ/ noun [C] an area of land that is not used for growing crops, where grass and other small plants grow, but where there are few trees or bushes

ˈheat ˌhaze noun [U] UK (US **haze**) an effect of very hot sun, making it difficult to see objects clearly: *When the heat haze lifted, the island could be seen clearly.*

heathen /ˈhiː.ðən/ adj; noun

▸adj old-fashioned disapproving offensive (of people or their way of life, activities, and ideas) having no religion, or belonging to a religion that is not Christianity, Judaism, or Islam

▸noun [C] **1** old use disapproving offensive a person who has no religion, or who belongs to a religion that is not Christianity, Judaism, or Islam **2 the heathen** [plural] old-fashioned heathen people: *Those who attempted to* ***convert*** *the heathen were put to death.* **3** humorous someone who behaves as if they are not educated: *He's such a heathen – he's never even heard of Puccini.*

heather /ˈheð.əʳ/ US /-ɚ/ noun [C or U] a low, spreading bush with small pink, purple or white flowers, which grows wild, especially on hills

heathland /ˈhiːθ.lənd/ noun [C or U] an area of heath

Heath Robinson /ˌhiːθˈrɒb.ɪn.sən/ US /-ˈrɑː.bɪn-/ adj UK humorous old-fashioned describes a machine that is very cleverly made and is complicated in a silly or humorous way, but has no practical use: *a Heath Robinson contraption*

heating /ˈhiː.tɪŋ/ US /-t̬ɪŋ/ noun [U] (US **heat**) A2 the system that keeps a building warm: *Is the heating* ***on****?* → See also **central heating**

ˈheat ˌrash noun [C or U] (also **ˌprickly ˈheat**) a condition in which the skin feels uncomfortable and is covered with red spots

ˈheat-ˌseeking adj [before noun] describes a weapon that can direct itself towards something hot, especially the hot engine of an aircraft: *heat-seeking* ***missiles***

ˈheat ˌshield noun [C] the part of a spacecraft's structure which prevents it from getting too hot as it returns to Earth

heatstroke /ˈhiːt.strəʊk/ US /-stroʊk/ noun [U] a condition that can lead to death, caused by being too long in a very hot place

ˈheat ˌtreatment noun [C usually singular] medical treatment in which a part of the body is heated with an electrical device, usually in order to relax it

heatwave /ˈhiːt.weɪv/ noun [C usually singular] a period of time such as a few weeks when the weather is much hotter than usual

heave /hiːv/ verb; noun

▸verb MOVE ▷ **1** [I or T, usually + adv/prep] to move something heavy using a lot of effort: *He heaved the bag onto his shoulder* ◦ *He cleared a space, heaving boxes out of the way.* **2** [T usually + adv/prep] informal to throw something forcefully, especially something large and heavy: *She picked up a great book and heaved it at him.* **3** [I] If something heaves, it makes one or more large movements up and down: *As the wind increased, the deck of the ship began to heave beneath his feet.* VOMIT ▷ **4** [I] to feel as if you are going to vomit: *The smell of the fish made me/my stomach heave.*

IDIOM **heave a sigh of relief** to suddenly feel very happy because something unpleasant has not happened or has ended: *We both heaved a sigh of relief when she left.*

▸noun [C] the act of throwing, pushing, or pulling something with a lot of effort: *They* ***gave*** *a great heave and rolled the boulder out of the way.*

heave-ˈho exclamation; noun

▸exclamation old-fashioned a phrase that you say or shout when you are making a big effort to pull or lift something

▸noun

IDIOM **give sb the heave-ho** informal humorous **1** to take someone's job away from them, usually because they have done something wrong **2** to end a romantic relationship with someone

heaven /ˈhev.ən/ noun **1** B2 [U] in some religions, the place, sometimes imagined to be in the sky, where God or the gods live and where good people are believed to go after they die, so that they can enjoy perfect happiness **2** B2 [U] informal a situation that gives you great pleasure: *I just lay in the sun for a week and did nothing – it was heaven.* **3 the heavens** [plural] the sky: *We stared up at the heavens trying to see the comet.*

IDIOMS **heavens (above)!** (also **good heavens!**) used to express surprise or anger • **the heavens open** If the heavens open, it suddenly starts to rain a lot: *Just as we got to the park, the heavens opened.*

heavenly /ˈhev.ən.li/ adj **1** of heaven: *heavenly music* ◦ *heavenly light* **2** C1 giving great pleasure: *It was a good party and the food was heavenly.*

ˌheavenly ˈbody noun [C] any object existing in space, especially a planet, star, or the moon

ˌheavenly ˈhost noun [C] literary a group of ANGELS

ˌheaven-ˈsent adj If someone or something is heaven-sent, they arrive or happen, usually unexpectedly, at the time when they are most useful.

heavenward /ˈhev.ən.wəd/ US /-wɚd/ adv (also **heavenwards**) upwards: *She raised her eyes heavenward.*

heavily /ˈhev.ɪ.li/ adv TO A GREAT DEGREE ▷ **1** B1 to a great degree: *The terrorists are heavily armed.* ◦ *The compound is heavily guarded.* ◦ *She's heavily involved in the project.* WEIGHING A LOT ▷ **2** in a way which needs a lot of effort to move or lift: *The news she had*

H

received **weighed** heavily **on** her (= worried her). **SOLID** ▷ **3** in a strong, thick, or solid way: *He's a heavily **built** (= large and strong) man.*

IDIOM **be heavily into sth** informal to be very interested in and involved with something: *When I was younger I was heavily into politics.*

heaviness /ˈhev.i.nəs/ noun [U] **WEIGHING A LOT** ▷ **1** the quality of weighing a lot **TO A GREAT DEGREE** ▷ **2** the quality of being done or happening to a great degree: *We were delayed by the heaviness of the traffic.*

heaving /ˈhiː.vɪŋ/ adj **BUSY** ▷ **1** informal full of people: *The bar was absolutely heaving.* **MOVING** ▷ **2** moving in large movements up and down: *He stood on the heaving deck.*

heavy /ˈhev.i/ adj; noun

▸adj **WEIGHING A LOT** ▷ **1** A2 weighing a lot, and needing effort to move or lift: *heavy equipment* ◦ *heavy work/lifting* ◦ ***How** heavy is that box?* (= How much does it weigh?) **TO A GREAT DEGREE** ▷ **2** B1 (especially of something unpleasant) of very or especially great force, amount, or degree: *a heavy blow to the head* ◦ *heavy fighting* ◦ *heavy traffic* ◦ *heavy rain/snow* ◦ *a heavy smoker/drinker* ◦ *a heavy sleeper* **3 heavy seas** sea that is rough with large waves **SOLID** ▷ **4** thick, strong, solid, or strongly made: *a heavy winter coat* ◦ *a heavy meal (= a large amount of solid food)* ◦ *a big man with heavy features* **5** describes soil that is thick and difficult to dig or walk through **6** thick, solid-looking, and not delicate: *The sun disappeared behind heavy clouds.* **MACHINES** ▷ **7** C2 describes machines or vehicles that are very large and powerful: *heavy artillery/machinery* **UNPLEASANT** ▷ **8** old-fashioned slang describes something such as a situation that is dangerous or unpleasant: *Then the police arrived and things got really heavy.*

IDIOMS **a heavy date** US and Australian English informal a planned meeting between two people who are very interested in having a romantic or sexual relationship: *I think Carol has a heavy date – she's been in the bathroom for over an hour.* • **have a heavy foot** US informal to drive a car too fast: *She has a heavy foot – does the trip in half the time it takes me!* • **a heavy heart** a feeling of unhappiness: ***With** a heavy heart, she turned to wave goodbye.* • **a heavy hitter** mainly US someone who is powerful and has achieved a lot: *Have you seen his résumé? He's a real heavy hitter.* • **be heavy on sb** to treat or punish someone severely: *I think his parents are being a bit heavy on him.* • **be/go heavy on sth** to use a lot of something: *The engine is heavy on fuel.* • **heavy with** If something is heavy with something else, it has a lot of it or is full of it: *The trees were heavy with fruit.* ◦ *The atmosphere was heavy with menace.* • **make heavy weather of sth** UK disapproving to find something hard to do and spend a lot of time on it, although it is not difficult: *She's making such heavy weather of that report she's writing.*

▸noun [C] slang a large strong man employed to protect someone else or to frighten other people: *Frank always took a couple of heavies along with him when he went collecting his debts.*

ˌheavy ˈbreather noun [C] a man who gets sexual pleasure from making phone calls, saying nothing, and breathing noisily

ˌheavy-ˈduty adj [before noun] describes clothing, machinery or equipment that is stronger than usual so that it can be used a lot, especially in difficult conditions: *heavy-duty tools/shoes*

ˌheavy ˈgoing adj difficult to read or understand: *I liked the film but the book was rather heavy going.* ◦ *I'm **finding** the advanced physics a bit heavy going.*

ˌheavy ˈgoods vehicle noun [C] (abbreviation **HGV**) UK a large truck used for transporting goods

ˌheavy-ˈhanded adj disapproving using too much force in dealing with someone: *The protestors accused the police of using heavy-handed **tactics**.*

ˌheavy ˈindustry noun [C usually singular] industry that uses large machines to produce either materials such as STEEL or large goods such as ships and trains

ˌheavy ˈmetal noun **METAL** ▷ **1** [C] specialized a DENSE (= heavy in relation to its size) and usually poisonous metal, such as lead **MUSIC** ▷ **2** [U] a style of ROCK MUSIC with a strong beat, played very loudly using electric guitars

ˌheavy ˈpetting noun [U] an occasion when two people kiss, hold, and touch each other in a sexual way, but do not have sex

heavyset /ˌhev.iˈset/ adj Someone who is heavyset has a large, wide, strong body.

heavyweight /ˈhev.ɪ.weɪt/ noun [C] **1** a BOXER who weighs more than 175 pounds (79.5 kilograms) and is therefore in the heaviest group: *Mike Tyson was heavyweight champion of the world.* → Compare **lightweight** **2** a person or thing that is important or serious and that other people notice: *Her extraordinary intelligence and speaking ability made her a political heavyweight.*

Hebrew /ˈhiː.bruː/ noun **1** [U] the ancient language of the Jewish people and the official language of modern Israel **2** [C] a Jewish person, used especially about the Jews of ancient Israel • **Hebraic** /hɪˈbreɪ.ɪk/ adj *Hebraic studies* • **Hebrew adj**

heck /hek/ exclamation, noun informal an expression of usually slight anger or surprise, or a way of adding force to a statement, question, etc.: *Oh heck! It's later than I thought.* ◦ *Where the heck have you been?*

IDIOMS **a heck of a** used for emphasis to mean 'very': *It's a heck of a long way to the nearest shop from here.* • **what the heck** used to say that you will do something although you know you should not do it: *The doctor said I shouldn't drink, but what the heck.*

heckle /ˈhek.l̩/ verb [I or T] to interrupt a public speech or performance with loud unfriendly statements or questions: *A few angry locals started heckling (the speaker).* • **heckler** /-ləʳ/ US /-lɚ/ noun [C] *The heckler was ejected from the hall by a couple of police officers.*

hectare /ˈhek.teəʳ/ US /-ter/ noun [C] a unit of measurement of an area of land (10,000 m²)

hectic /ˈhek.tɪk/ adj C1 full of activity, or very busy and fast: *a hectic schedule* ◦ *The area has become a haven for people tired of the hectic **pace** of city life.*

hector /ˈhek.təʳ/ US /-tɚ/ verb [T] disapproving to talk and behave towards someone in a loud and unpleasantly forceful way, especially in order to get them to act or think as you want them to • **hectoring** /-ɪŋ/ adj *He had a loud, hectoring manner.*

he'd /hiːd/ short form of **1** he had: *He'd already spent all his money by the second day of the trip.* **2** he would: *He'd be able to do it, if anyone could.*

hedge /hedʒ/ noun; verb

▸noun [C] **BUSHES** ▷ **1** B2 a line of bushes or small trees planted very close together, especially along the edge of a garden, field, or road: *a privet hedge* **PROTECTION** ▷ **2** a way of protecting, controlling, or limiting something: *She'd made some overseas invest-*

ments as a hedge **against** rising inflation in this country.

▸verb **1** [T + adv/prep, usually passive] to limit something severely: *We've got permission, but it's hedged **about/around with** strict conditions.* **2** [I] to try to avoid giving an answer or taking any action: *Stop hedging and tell me what you really think.*

IDIOM **hedge your bets** to protect yourself against loss by supporting more than one possible result or both sides in a competition

ˈhedge ˌfund noun [C] a type of INVESTMENT that can make a lot of profit but involves a large risk: *a hedge fund **manager***

hedgehog /ˈhedʒ.hɒg/ (US) /-hɑːg/ noun [C] a small brown mammal with a covering of sharp SPINES on its back

hedgehog

hedgerow /ˈhedʒ.rəʊ/ (US) /-roʊ/ noun [C] a line of different types of bushes and small trees growing very close together, especially between fields or along the sides of roads in the countryside

ˈhedge ˌtrimmers noun [plural] a tool with which you cut a garden hedge to keep it tidy

hedonism /ˈhed.ən.ɪ.zəm/ noun [U] living and behaving in ways that mean you get as much pleasure out of life as possible, according to the belief that the most important thing in life is to enjoy yourself • **hedonist** /-ɪst/ noun [C] • **hedonistic** /ˌhed.ənˈɪs.tɪk/ adj

the heebie-jeebies /ˌhiː.biˈdʒiː.biz/ noun [plural] informal strong feelings of fear or worry: *Don't start talking about ghosts – they **give** me the heebie-jeebies.*

heed /hiːd/ verb; noun

▸verb [T] formal to pay attention to something, especially advice or a warning: *The airline has been criticized for failing to heed **advice/warnings** about lack of safety routines.*

▸noun [U] formal attention: *The company **took** no heed **of*** (= did not consider) *public opposition to the plans.*

heedless /ˈhiːd.ləs/ adj formal not giving attention to a risk or possible difficulty: *Heedless destruction of the rainforests is contributing to global warming.* ◦ *Journalists had insisted on getting to the front line of the battle, heedless **of** the risks.* • **heedlessly** /-li/ adv

hee-haw /ˈhiː.hɔː/ (US) /-hɑː/ noun [C] the sound that a DONKEY makes

heel /hiːl/ noun; verb; exclamation

▸noun [C] **BODY PART** ▷ **1** (B2) the rounded back part of the foot → See also **well heeled** **2** the part of a sock or shoe which covers the heel of the foot **3** (B1) the raised part at the back of a shoe, under your heel **PERSON** ▷ **4** old-fashioned informal a person who treats other people badly and unfairly: *I felt like a real heel when I saw how I'd upset her.* **HAND** ▷ **5** the raised part of the PALM of your hand nearest the wrist **END PART** ▷ **6** the end part of something, especially of a LOAF of bread, that is usually left after the rest has been eaten or used

IDIOMS **bring/call sth/sb to heel** **1** to order a dog to come close to you **2** to force someone to obey you • **come to heel** If a person or organization comes to heel, they agree to obey, usually because they have been forcefully persuaded to do so. • **come/follow hard/hot on the heels of sth** to happen very soon after something: *For Walter, disaster followed hard on the heels of his initial success.* • **hard/hot on sb's heels** following someone very closely: *She ran down the steps with a group of journalists hard on her heels.* • **take to your heels** to quickly run away: *When they saw the soldiers coming, they took to their heels.* • **under the heel of sth/sb** disapproving completely controlled by something or someone: *This country would never submit to living under the heel of a foreign power.*

▸verb [T] **1** to repair the heel of a shoe **2** specialized In RUGBY, to heel the ball is to kick it backwards with the heel.

▸exclamation said to a dog to order it to come and stand close to you or to walk close to your side as you walk

ˈheel bar noun [C] UK a small shop that repairs shoes, especially while a customer waits

heft /heft/ verb [T usually + adv/prep] to lift, hold or carry something heavy using your hands: *I watched him heft the heavy sack onto his shoulder.*

hefty /ˈhef.ti/ adj large in amount, size, force, etc.: *a hefty bill/fine* ◦ *Her salary will go up by a hefty 13 percent.* ◦ *a hefty woman with dyed blond hair*

hegemony /hɪˈgem.ə.ni/, /-ˈdʒem-/ (US) /-ˈdʒem-/ /ˈhedʒ.ə.moʊ-/ noun [U] formal (especially of countries) the position of being the strongest and most powerful and therefore able to control others: *The three nations competed for regional hegemony.* • **hegemonic** /ˌheg.ɪˈmɒn.ɪk/, /ˌhedʒ-/ (US) /ˌhedʒ.ɪˈmɑː.nɪk/ adj

heifer /ˈhef.əʳ/ (US) /-ɚ/ noun [C] a young cow, especially one that has not yet given birth to a CALF (= baby cow)

heigh-ho /ˈheɪ.həʊ/ (US) /-hoʊ/ exclamation used to express the fact that you cannot change a situation so you must accept it

height /haɪt/ noun [C or U] **1** (B1) the distance from the top to the bottom of something, or the quality of being tall: *The sheer height of New York's skyscrapers is so impressive.* ◦ *She's about average height* (= neither short nor tall). **2** (B1) the particular distance that something is above a surface: *The bullet entered the body at chest height.* **3 heights a** high places, or the top of hills: *Don't go up the tower if you're **afraid of** heights.* ◦ *Machine guns were mounted along the heights behind the town.* **b** a high level of success: *He **reached** the heights **of** his profession at the age of 35.* ◦ *Share prices **scaled** new heights yesterday.* ◦ *Her husband **rose to** the **dizzy/lofty** heights of transport minister.* **4 the height of sth a** (C2) the time when a situation or event is strongest or most full of activity: *August is the height of the tourist season.* ◦ *At the height of the violence/crisis we were left without any help.* **b** an extreme example of something: *the height of fashion* **c** the time when you are most successful in what you do: *She was **at** the height of her career when he first met her.*

> **Word partners for height**
>
> *grow to/reach* a height of sth • *average/full/great/maximum* height • be [3 metres, etc.] *in* height

heighten /ˈhaɪ.tən/ (US) /-t̬ən/ verb [I or T] to increase or make something increase, especially an emotion or effect: *The strong police presence only heightened the tension among the crowd.*

heinous /ˈheɪː.nəs/ adj formal very bad and shocking: *a heinous **crime***

heir /eəʳ/ (US) /er/ noun **1** (C2) [C] a person who will legally receive money, property, or a title from another person, especially an older member of the same family, when that other person dies: *The guest of honour was the Romanov heir **to** the throne of all*

Russia. ◦ *Despite having a large family, they still had no **son and** heir.* → See also **heiress 2** [C usually singular] someone who now has responsibility for dealing with a problem or situation that existed or was created earlier: *The French finance minister is heir **to** a tradition of central control that goes back to Louis XIV's minister, Colbert.* **3** [C usually singular] someone who continues to do the work of someone important who has died or who has the same position as they had

ˌheir apˈparent noun [C usually singular] **1** the person with the automatic right to legally receive all or most of the money, property, titles, etc. from another person when they die: *The Prince of Wales is the heir apparent **to** the throne.* **2** a person who seems certain to take the place of someone in power when they stop working

heiress /ˈeə.res/ (US) /ˈer.es/ noun [C] a woman or girl who will receive or already has received a lot of money, property, or a title from another person, especially an older member of the same family, when that person dies: *the heiress **to** the throne* ◦ *a Texan oil heiress* → See also **heir**

heirloom /ˈeə.luːm/ (US) /ˈer-/ noun [C] a valuable object that has been given by older members of a family to younger members of the same family over many years: *This ring is a family heirloom.*

heist /haɪst/ noun [C] informal a crime in which valuable things are taken illegally and often violently from a place or person: *a $2 million jewellery heist*

held /held/ verb; adj

▸verb past simple and past participle of **hold**

▸adj kept or MAINTAINED: *firmly held beliefs* ◦ *widely held opinions*

helicopter /ˈhel.ɪˌkɒp.təʳ/ (US) /-ˌkɑːp.tɚ/ noun [C] (A2) a type of aircraft without wings, that has one or two sets of large blades which go round very fast on top. It can land and take off vertically and can stay in one place in the air: *The injured were ferried to hospital **by** helicopter.* ◦ *a helicopter pilot*

ˌhelicopter ˈparent noun [C] informal disapproving a parent who is closely involved with their child's life and tries to control it, especially their child's education

heliˌcopter ˈview noun [C] a general description or opinion of a situation, rather than a detailed one

helipad /ˈhel.ɪ.pæd/ noun [C] a place where a single helicopter can take off and land

heliport /ˈhel.ɪ.pɔːt/ (US) /-pɔːrt/ noun [C] an airport for helicopters

helium /ˈhiː.li.əm/ noun [U] (symbol **He**) a chemical element that is a gas lighter than air, that will not burn and is used in BALLOONS, AIRSHIPS, and some types of lights

helix /ˈhiː.lɪks/ noun [C] (plural **helices**) specialized a curve that goes around a central tube or cone shape in the form of a SPIRAL • **helical** /-lɪ.kᵊl/ adj specialized in the shape of a helix: *helical molecules* ◦ *a helical structure*

he'll /hiːl/ short form he will: *He'll be there, don't worry.*

hell /hel/ noun; exclamation, noun

▸noun **1** (B2) [S or U] an extremely unpleasant or difficult place, situation, or experience: *Work is **sheer** hell at the moment.* ◦ *The last few months have been absolute hell.* → See also **hellhole, infernal 2** (B2) [S] (also **Hell**) in some religions, the place where some people are believed to go after death to be punished for ever for the bad things they have done during their lives: *I'll go to Hell for this.* **3 make sb's life hell** (also **make life hell for sb**) to cause a lot of problems for someone and make them very unhappy: *I worked for her for two years and she made my life hell.*

IDIOMS **all hell breaks loose** informal If all hell breaks loose, a situation suddenly becomes violent and noisy, especially with people arguing or fighting: *One policeman drew his gun and then suddenly all hell broke loose.* • **come hell or high water** informal If you say that you will do something come hell or high water, you mean that you are determined to do it, despite any difficulties that there might be: *I'll get you to the airport by noon, come hell or high water!* • **for the hell of it** informal If you do something for the hell of it, you do it without having any particular purpose or wish, but usually for enjoyment • **from hell** informal used to say that someone or something is extremely bad: *Now Miranda – she was the housemate from hell.* ◦ *Poor Ann has the mother-in-law from hell.* • **give sb hell** informal **1** If someone gives you hell, they criticize you severely: *She gave me hell for being 20 minutes late.* **2** If something gives you hell, it causes you a lot of pain: *These new shoes are giving me hell.* • **go to hell** informal used to angrily tell someone to stop talking and go away: *'Anyway, it's your own fault.' 'Oh, go to hell!'* • **go to hell and back** informal to live through an extremely unpleasant, difficult or painful experience: *I've been to hell and back over this court case.* • **hell for leather** old-fashioned informal If you go, run, ride, etc. hell for leather, you go as fast as you can. • **hell on earth** informal an extremely unpleasant place or situation: *Soldiers who survived the war described it as hell on earth.* • **be hell on wheels** US informal to behave in an angry or difficult way: *When he was drinking, Ken was hell on wheels.* • **there'll be hell to pay** informal something you say which means someone will be very angry if something happens: *There'll be hell to pay if she doesn't get the money in time.* • **when hell freezes over** old-fashioned informal If you say that something will happen when hell freezes over, you mean that it will never happen.

▸exclamation, noun [U] (B2) used to express anger or to add emphasis: *Oh hell, I've forgotten my key!* ◦ ***What the** hell was that noise?* ◦ *We haven't got a **hope in** hell (= we have no hope) of meeting such a tight deadline.*

IDIOMS **annoy, frighten, scare, etc. the hell out of sb** informal to make someone extremely annoyed, frightened, etc.: *He jumped out from behind a wall and scared the hell out of her.* • **(as) ... as hell** informal used to emphasize a description of an unpleasant characteristic: *She's really quite unpleasant about other people and she's as mean as hell.* • **be hell-bent on sth** informal to be extremely determined to do something, without considering the risks or possible dangerous results: *He was hell-bent on revenge.* • **beat the hell out of sb** informal to hit someone repeatedly with great force • **get the hell out of somewhere** informal to leave a place quickly: *Let's get the hell out of here, before any shooting starts.* • **the hell you do** US informal used to tell someone that you do not believe what they have said or that you will not allow them to do what they want: *'I don't need your advice, Gene, I know what's good for me.' 'The hell you do!'* • **hell of a** (also **helluva**) informal (C2) extremely, or extremely big: *It's a/one hell of a big decision to take.* ◦ *The house was in a/one hell of a mess.* • **like hell** informal **1** (C2) very much: *We ran like hell.* ◦ *We worked like hell to finish the job.* ◦ *It hurt like hell.* **2** certainly not: *'Try to be polite to him.' 'Like hell I will!'* • **to hell** informal If you wish or hope to hell that something is true or that it will happen, you are saying how strongly you want it to be true or to happen: *I hope to hell she hasn't missed that plane.* • **what the hell** informal said when you suddenly realize that your plan is not important to you and that you will do something else: *I was supposed to be working this evening but what the hell – I'll see you in the pub in half an hour.*

Hellenic /hə'len.ɪk/ **adj** of or relating to the ancient or modern Greeks, and their history, art, etc.

hellfire /'hel.faɪəʳ/ (US) /-faɪr/ **noun** [U] the punishment that some religious people believe bad people will suffer after they die: *He certainly believed in preaching hellfire **and damnation**.*

hellhole /'hel.həʊl/ (US) /-hoʊl/ **noun** [C] informal an extremely unpleasant place

hellish /'hel.ɪʃ/ **adj** very bad or unpleasant: *a hellish experience* • **hellishly** /-li/ **adv** *a hellishly (= very unpleasantly) busy week*

hello /hel'əʊ/ (US) /-'oʊ/ **exclamation, noun** (UK also **hallo, hullo**) **1** (A1) used when meeting or greeting someone: *Hello, Paul. I haven't seen you for ages.* ◦ *I know her vaguely – we've exchanged hellos a few times.* ◦ *I just thought I'd call by and **say** hello.* ◦ *And **a big** hello (= welcome) to all the parents who've come to see the show.* **2** (A1) something that is said at the beginning of a phone conversation: *'Hello, I'd like some information about your flights to the US, please.'* **3** something that is said to attract someone's attention: *The front door was open so she walked inside and called out, 'Hello! Is there anybody in?'* **4** informal said to someone who has just said or done something stupid, especially something that shows they are not noticing what is happening around them: *She asked me if I'd just arrived and I was like 'hello, I've been here for an hour.'* **5** old-fashioned an expression of surprise: *Hello, this is very strange – I know that man.*

hell's 'bells **exclamation** old-fashioned informal (UK also **hell's 'teeth**) used to express anger or surprise: *Hell's bells, can't you do anything right?*

helluva /'hel.ə.və/ **adj, adv** (also **hell of a**) informal **1** extremely, or extremely big: *It's a helluva nice place.* **2 a helluva guy, woman, teacher, etc.** a man, woman, teacher, etc. that you admire very much

helm /helm/ **noun** [C] **1** the handle or wheel which controls the direction in which a ship or boat travels: *Who was **at** the helm when the collision occurred?* **2 at the helm** officially controlling an organization or company: *With Steve Lewis at the helm, we are certain of success.* **3 take the helm** to start to officially control an organization or company

helmet /'hel.mət/ **noun** [C] (B2) a strong hard hat that covers and protects the head: *a crash helmet* ◦ *a cycle helmet*

helmeted /'hel.mə.tɪd/ (US) /-t̬ɪd/ **adj** wearing a helmet: *Helmeted, baton-wielding police forced back the crowd.*

helmsman /'helmz.mən/ **noun** [C] (plural **-men** /-mən/) a person who directs a ship or boat, using a handle or wheel

help /help/ **verb; noun; exclamation**

▸**verb** MAKE EASIER ▷ **1** (A1) [I or T] to make it possible or easier for someone to do something, by doing part of the work yourself or by providing advice, money, support, etc.: *How can I help you?* ◦ *I wonder if you could help me – I'd like some information about flights to New Zealand.* ◦ *My dad said he would help **with** the costs of (= give part of the cost of) buying a house.* ◦ [+ obj + (to) infinitive] *The £10,000 loan from the bank helped her (**to**) start her own business.* ◦ *I feel that learning English will help (= improve) my chances of promotion at work.* ◦ *Nothing can help her now (= her situation is too bad for anyone to be able to improve it).* → See also **helpline** **2** (B2) [I or T] If something helps a difficult or painful situation, it improves it or makes it easier or less painful: *The morphine didn't seem to help (the pain).* **3** [+ (to) infinitive] If something or someone helps to do something, they are one of several reasons for it happening: *The drought has helped (**to**) make this a disastrous year for Somalia.*

> **! Common mistake: help**
>
> When **help** meaning 'make easier' is followed by another verb, that verb cannot be in the **-ing** form. Do not say 'help doing something', or 'help someone doing something'. **Help** is followed by an infinitive verb, either with or without 'to':
>
> **help someone (to) do something**:
>
> *I helped Mary to do her homework.*
>
> You can also say **help someone with something**:
>
> *I helped Mary with her homework.*

> **+ Other ways of saying help**
>
> The verbs **aid** and **assist** are more formal alternatives to 'help':
>
> *The army arrived to **assist** in the search.*
>
> *The project is designed to **aid** poorer countries.*
>
> If two or more people help each other in order to achieve the same thing, verbs such as **collaborate** or **cooperate** are sometimes used:
>
> *Several countries are **collaborating/cooperating** in the relief effort.*
>
> The verb **benefit** is sometimes used when someone is helped by something:
>
> *The children have **benefited** greatly from the new facilities.*
>
> If someone is asking for help, in informal situations the expressions **give** someone **a hand** or **do** someone **a favour** are sometimes used:
>
> *Do you think you could **give me a hand** with these heavy boxes?*
>
> *Could you **do me a favour** and buy me some milk while you're out?*

STOP YOURSELF ▷ **4 can't/couldn't help** (B1) If you can't/couldn't help something, such as acting in a particular way or making a particular remark, you are/were not able to control or stop it: *It was awful, but I couldn't help laugh**ing**.* ◦ *'Stop giggling!' 'I can't help it!'* ◦ *I can't help think**ing** (= my true feeling is that) she'd be better off without him.* GIVE/TAKE ▷ **5** (B1) [T] to give something to someone: *Shall I help you **to** some more soup?* **6 help yourself** (B1) to take something for yourself: *'Might I have some more bread?' 'Please, help **yourself**!'*

IDIOMS **give/lend sb a helping hand** to help someone • **God help sb** (also **heaven help sb**) used to give force to a statement of the danger or seriousness of a situation or action: *God help us if they attack now while we're still unprepared.* • **it can't be helped** used to say that an unpleasant or painful situation, or an unwanted duty cannot be avoided and must be accepted: *I really didn't want to go away this weekend but, oh well, it can't be helped.* • **so help me (God)** formal used to make a promise in a very formal and serious way: *Everything I have said is true, so help me God.*

PHRASAL VERB **help (sb) out** (B2) If you help out, you do a part of someone's work or give someone money: *Her parents helped (her) out with a £500 loan.*

▸**noun 1** A2 [U] the act of helping another person: *Do you need any help with those boxes? ◦ Her parents gave her some help **with** her bank loan (= paid some of it).* **2** B2 [S] something or someone that helps: *Having a satnav would be a help. ◦ He was a great help (**to** me) while my husband was away.* **3** [C] someone, usually a woman, who is employed to clean your house and do other small jobs: *a home help*

> **Word partners for help noun**
>
> *ask for/need/seek/want* help • *give/offer/provide* help • *enlist* the help of sb • *refuse* help • *extra/financial/professional* help • a *big/enormous/great/real* help • help *from* sb/sth • help *with* sth • *with/without* help

IDIOM **there's no help for it** mainly UK there is no other choice in this situation: *If you catch them stealing again, there'll be no help for it **but** (= except) **to** call the police.*

▸**exclamation help!** A2 shouted by a person who is asking for someone to come and save them from a dangerous situation

ˈhelp ˌdesk noun [C] a service which provides information and help to people using a computer NETWORK

helper /ˈhel.pəʳ/ (US) /-pɚ/ noun [C] B2 someone who helps with an activity: *The teachers make great use of volunteer helpers.*

helpful /ˈhelp.fᵊl/ adj B1 willing to help, or useful: *She's such a pleasant, helpful child! ◦ I'm sorry, I was only trying to be helpful. ◦ He made several helpful suggestions.* • **helpfully** /-i/ adv *The manufacturers helpfully provide an instruction manual.* • **helpfulness** /-nəs/ noun [U]

> **Common mistake: helpful**
>
> **Warning:** Common word-building error!
> Adjectives which end in the suffix **-ful** have only one 'l'. Don't write 'helpfull', write **helpful**.

helping /ˈhel.pɪŋ/ noun [C] an amount of food given to one person at one time: *a small/large helping **of** pasta*

helpless /ˈhelp.ləs/ adj C1 unable to do anything to help yourself or anyone else: *a helpless two-day-old baby ◦ You feel so helpless because there's nothing you can do to make the child better. ◦ The government is helpless (**to** act) **against** these crooks.* • **helplessly** /-li/ adv *Unable to swim, he watched helplessly as the child struggled desperately in the water.* • **helplessness** /-nəs/ noun [U] *I was overwhelmed by a feeling of helplessness as I was wheeled into the operating theatre.*

helpline /ˈhelp.laɪn/ noun [C] a service providing advice and comfort to worried or unhappy people on the phone: *A new helpline is now available for people trying to stop smoking.*

ˈhelp ˌscreen noun [C] information or instructions which you can ask the computer to show you if you are having difficulty using the computer

helter-skelter /ˌhel.təˈskel.təʳ/ (US) /-t̬ɚˈskel.t̬ɚ/ adv; noun

▸**adv** quickly and in all directions: *People were screaming and running helter-skelter down the steps to escape the flames.*

▸**noun** [C] UK a tall structure at a fair which you slide down and around for enjoyment

hem /hem/ noun; verb

▸**noun** [C] the edge of a piece of cloth, such as the bottom edge of a skirt or dress, that is folded over and sewn so that it does not develop loose threads: *I **took** the hem **up/let** the hem **down**.*

▸**verb** [T] (**-mm-**) to sew a hem on a piece of clothing or cloth: *I need to hem those curtains.*

PHRASAL VERB **hem sb in** to surround someone and prevent them from moving or doing what they want to do: *When they reached Trafalgar Square, the demonstrators were hemmed in by the police.*

ˈhe-man noun [C usually singular] (plural **-men**) informal a man who is very strong and who likes to show everyone how strong he is

hematite /ˈhiː.mə.taɪt/ noun [C] US for **haematite**

hematology /ˌhiː.məˈtɒl.ə.dʒi/ (US) /-ˈtɑː.lə-/ noun [U] mainly US for **haematology**

hemisphere /ˈhem.ɪ.sfɪəʳ/ (US) /-sfɪr/ noun [C] half of a SPHERE, especially the Earth: *the northern hemisphere*

hemline /ˈhem.laɪn/ noun [C] the length of a skirt or dress, or the lower edge of a skirt or dress

hemlock /ˈhem.lɒk/ (US) /-lɑːk/ noun [U] a type of poison made from a plant that has small white flowers and divided leaves

hemoglobin /ˌhiː.məˈgləʊ.bɪn/ (US) /-gloʊ-/ noun [U] mainly US for **haemoglobin**

hemophilia /ˌhiː.məˈfɪl.i.ə/ noun [U] mainly US for **haemophilia**

hemorrhage /ˈhem.ᵊr.ɪdʒ/ (US) /-ɚ-/ noun [C], verb [I] US for **haemorrhage**

hemorrhoids /ˈhem.ᵊr.ɔɪdz/ (US) /-ɚ-/ noun [plural] mainly US for **haemorrhoids**

hemp /hemp/ noun [U] a family of plants, some of which are used to make rope and strong rough cloth and others of which are used to produce the drug CANNABIS

hen /hen/ noun [C] **1** an adult female chicken, often kept for its eggs **2** the female of any bird **3** Scottish English informal used as a way of talking to a woman or girl, especially someone that you like: *'Are you not feeling too good, hen?'*

hence /hens/ adv formal THEREFORE ▷ **1** C1 that is the reason or explanation for: *His mother was Italian, hence his name – Luca.* → Synonym **therefore** FROM NOW ▷ **2** from this time: *The project will be completed at the end of the decade, two years hence.*

henceforth /ˌhensˈfɔːθ/ (US) /-ˈfɔːrθ/ adv (also **henceforward**) formal or legal starting from this time: *Henceforth, the said building shall be the property of Brendan Duggan.*

henchman /ˈhentʃ.mən/ noun [C] (plural **-men** /-mən/) disapproving someone who does unpleasant or illegal things for a powerful person: *Like other dictators, he tried to distance himself from the dirty deeds carried out by his henchmen.*

henna /ˈhen.ə/ noun; verb

▸**noun** [U] a reddish-brown DYE, used mainly for changing the colour of the hair and skin

▸**verb** [T] (present tense **hennaing**, past tense and past participle **hennaed**) to put henna on the hair or skin in order to change its colour: *Is her hair hennaed or is that a natural red?*

ˈhen ˌnight noun [C] (also **ˈhen ˌparty**) UK a party for women only, usually one held for a woman before she is married → Compare **stag night/party**

henpecked /ˈhen.pekt/ adj disapproving A henpecked man is controlled by and a little frightened of a woman, especially his wife.

hepatic /hepˈæt.ɪk/ (US) /-ˈæt̬-/ adj specialized relating to the LIVER

hepatitis /ˌhep.əˈtaɪ.tɪs/ (US) /-t̬ɪs/ noun [U] a serious disease of the LIVER. There are three main types of hepatitis: hepatitis A, B, and C.

heptagon /ˈhep.tə.gᵊn/ (US) /-gɑːn/ noun [C] a shape with seven straight sides • **heptagonal** /hepˈtæg.ᵊn.ᵊl/ adj

heptathlon /hepˈtæθ.lɒn/ (US) /-lɑːn/ noun [C] a competition in which ATHLETES compete in seven sports events → Compare **biathlon, decathlon, pentathlon** • **heptathlete** /-liːt/ noun [C]

her /hɜːʳ/ (US) /hɝː, ɚ/ weak /həʳ, əʳ/ (US) /hɚ, ɚ/ **pronoun; determiner**

▸**pronoun** strong **1** A1 used, usually as the object of a verb or preposition, to refer to a woman, girl, or female animal that has just been mentioned or is just about to be mentioned: *If your sister's around, bring her too.* ◦ *I gave her the letter.* ◦ *She's a beautiful horse – how long have you had her?* → See also **hers 2** old-fashioned used to refer to a country, a boat or a car: *God bless this ship and all who sail in her.*

▸**determiner 1** belonging to or connected with a woman, girl, or female animal that has just been mentioned or is known about: *I'll see if Louisa will bring her guitar to the party.* ◦ *I don't know why she quit her job.* ◦ *We saw a mother duck with her ducklings.* **2** old-fashioned belonging to a country, a boat or a car: *The boat sank with all her crew.*

herald /ˈher.ᵊld/ **verb; noun**

▸**verb** [T] formal to be a sign that something important, and often good, is starting to happen, or to make something publicly known, especially by celebrating or praising it: *The president's speech heralds a new era in foreign policy.* ◦ *This drug has been heralded **as** a major breakthrough in the fight against breast cancer.*

▸**noun** [C] **1** formal a sign that something will happen, change, etc.: *If this first opera of the season is a herald (= sign) **of** what is to come, we can expect great things.* **2** in the past, a person who carried important messages and made announcements

heraldry /ˈher.ᵊl.dri/ noun [U] the study of COATS OF ARMS and the history of the families which they belong to • **heraldic** /herˈæl.dɪk/ adj *a heraldic banner*

herb /hɜːb/ (US) /ɜːb/ noun [C] B1 a type of plant whose leaves are used in cooking to give flavour to particular dishes or in making medicine: *dried/fresh herbs* ◦ *Basil, oregano, thyme, and rosemary are all herbs.* ◦ *A large range of herbs **and spices** are used in South Asian cookery.*

herbaceous /hɜːˈbeɪ.ʃəs/ (US) /hɚ-/ adj specialized (of plants) soft and not WOODY

herˌbaceous ˈborder noun [C] a narrow strip of land in a garden, planted with different types of plants that produce flowers that mainly live for more than two years

herbal /ˈhɜː.bᵊl/ (US) /ˈɜː-/ adj relating to or made from herbs: *herbal tea* ◦ *herbal cigarettes/remedies*

herbalist /ˈhɜː.bᵊl.ɪst/ (US) /ˈɜː-/ noun [C] a person who grows or sells herbs for use as medicine

herbicide /ˈhɜː.bɪ.saɪd/ (US) /ˈhɝː-/ noun [C or U] a chemical that is used to destroy plants, especially WEEDS → Compare **insecticide, pesticide**

herbivore /ˈhɜː.bɪ.vɔːʳ/ (US) /ˈhɝː.bə.vɔːr/ noun [C] an animal that eats only plants: *Cows and sheep are herbivores.* → Compare **carnivore** • **herbivorous** /hɜːˈbɪv.ᵊr.əs/ (US) /hɝːˈbɪv.ɚ-/ adj

herby /ˈhɜː.bi/ (US) /ˈɜː-/ adj informal tasting or smelling of herbs: *This salad dressing is nice and herby.*

Herculean /ˌhɜː.kjʊˈliː.ən/ (US) /ˌhɝː-/ adj needing great strength and determination: *a Herculean **effort*** ◦ *She faces the Herculean **task** of bringing up four children single-handedly.*

herd /hɜːd/ (US) /hɝːd/ **noun; verb**

▸**noun** [C, + sing/pl verb] **1** a large group of animals of the same type that live and feed together: *a herd **of** cattle/elephants/goats* **2** mainly disapproving a large group of people that is considered together as a group and not separately: *Poor Janine – she just follows the herd (= does what all the other people are doing).*

▸**verb 1** [I or T, + adv/prep] to make animals move together as a group: *An old woman was herding the goats.* **2** [T + adv/prep] mainly disapproving to make people move somewhere as a group, often with force or against their wishes: *The football fans complained that they had been herded into a small alley.*

ˈherd ˌinstinct noun [S] disapproving a situation in which people act like everyone else without considering the reason why

herdsman /ˈhɜːdz.mən/ (US) /ˈhɝːdz-/ noun [C] (plural **-men** /-mən/) a man who takes care of a large group of animals of the same type

H

here /hɪəʳ/ (US) /hɪr/ adv **1** A1 in, at, or to this place: *I've lived here for about two years.* ◦ *I like it here.* ◦ *London is only 50 miles **from** here.* ◦ ***Come** here – I've got something to show you.* ◦ *How long are you **over** here (= in this country)?* **2** A2 used at the beginning of a statement to introduce someone or something: *Here's Fiona – let me introduce you to her.* ◦ *Here's the book I said I'd lend you.* **3** A2 used to show that someone has arrived or that something has started: *Here they are! We thought you'd never come!* ◦ *Here we are (= we have arrived) – I said it wouldn't take more than half an hour by car.* ◦ *Now that Christmas is here (= has begun), I might as well give up my diet.* **4** A1 describes someone or something that is near you: *I don't know anything about this, but I'm sure my colleague here can help you.* ◦ *It says here (= in this piece of writing) that she was born in 1943.* **5** B2 now: *Shall we break here and have a coffee?* ◦ *Where do we go/Where do we take it **from** here? (= What should we do next?)* **6 here (you are)** A2 used when giving something to someone: *'Could you pass the sugar, please?' 'Here you are.'* ◦ *Here, try some of this – it's delicious!*

IDIOMS **the here and now** the present time: *Most people can't be bothered thinking about their retirement – they're too busy concentrating on the here and now.* • **here and there** B2 in different places: *There were a few books here and there, but apart from that the room was quite bare.* • **here goes!** (also **here goes nothing!**) said just before you do something brave or something that you have never done before: *Well, I've never ridden a motorbike before, so here goes!* • **here today, gone tomorrow** saying said about something which lasts only a short time: *A lot of new internet companies are here today and gone tomorrow.* • **here we go** informal a phrase often sung repeatedly by British football crowds when their team is successful • **here we go (again)** informal said when something bad starts happening again: *Oh, here we go again! Claude's just asked to borrow some more money from me.* • **here's to …** said when asking a group of people to hold up their glasses and then drink as an expression of good wishes to someone or hope for the success of something: *Here's to the happy couple!*

hereabouts /ˌhɪə.rəˈbaʊts/ (US) /ˌhɪr.ə-/ adv UK (US **hereabout**) in this area, or near this place: *Any trouble hereabouts is swiftly dealt with by the police.*

hereafter /ˌhɪəˈrɑːf.təʳ/ (US) /ˌhɪrˈæf.tɚ/ **adv; noun**

▸**adv** (also **hereinafter**) formal or legal starting from this

time; in the future: *Elizabeth Gaskell's novel 'Ruth' will hereafter be cited within the text as EG.*
▸**noun** [S] formal **the hereafter** life after death: *She had a firm conviction that they would meet again **in** the hereafter.*

hereby /ˌhɪəˈbaɪ/ ⓤⓢ /ˌhɪr-/ **adv** formal or legal with these words or with this action: *I hereby pronounce you man and wife.*

hereditary /həˈred.ɪ.tᵊr.i/ **adj** (of characteristics or diseases) passed from the GENES of a parent to a child, or (of titles and positions in society) passed from parent to a child as a right: *a hereditary disease* ◦ *Depression is often hereditary.* ◦ *It is a hereditary **title**, so Mark Howard will become Sir Mark Howard on his father's death.*

heˌreditary ˈpeer **noun** [C] someone whose parent passed on a PEERAGE (= high social rank) to them when they died, and who can pass it on to their oldest child

H

heredity /həˈred.ə.ti/ **noun** [U] the process by which characteristics are given from a parent to their child through the GENES: *Diet and exercise can influence a person's weight, but heredity is also a factor.*

herein /ˌhɪəˈrɪn/ ⓤⓢ /ˌhɪr-/ **adv** formal or legal in this: *The people have no faith in their government, and herein **lies** the root of the problem.*

hereinafter /ˌhɪə.rɪnˈɑːf.təʳ/ ⓤⓢ /ˌhɪr.ɪnˈæf.tɚ/ **adv** formal or legal **hereafter**

heresy /ˈher.ə.si/ **noun** **1** [C or U] (the act of having) an opinion or belief that is the opposite of or against what is the official or popular opinion, or an action that shows that you have no respect for the official opinion: *Radical remarks like this amount to heresy for most members of the Republican party.* ◦ *She committed the heresy of playing a Madonna song on a classical music station.* **2** [U] a belief that is against the principles of a particular religion: *He was burned at the stake for heresy in the 15th century.*

heretic /ˈher.ə.tɪk/ **noun** [C] a person who is guilty of heresy • **heretical** /həˈret.ɪ.kᵊl/ ⓤⓢ /-ˈret̬-/ **adj** *Her belief that a split would be good for the party was regarded as heretical.*

hereto /ˌhɪəˈtuː/ ⓤⓢ /ˌhɪr-/ **adv** formal or legal to this matter or document: *You will find attached hereto the text of the Treaty on European Union.*

heretofore /ˌhɪə.tʊˈfɔːʳ/ ⓤⓢ /ˌhɪr.tʊˈfɔːr/ **adv** formal or legal before this point in time → Synonym **previously**

hereupon /ˌhɪə.rəˈpɒn/ ⓤⓢ /ˌhɪr.əˈpɑːn/ **adv** formal at this point in time

herewith /ˌhɪəˈwɪð/, /-ˈwɪθ/ ⓤⓢ /ˌhɪr-/ **adv** formal or legal together with this letter or other official written material: *I enclose three documents herewith.*

heritage /ˈher.ɪ.tɪdʒ/ ⓤⓢ /-t̬ɪdʒ/ **noun** [U] Ⓒ2 features belonging to the culture of a particular society, such as traditions, languages, or buildings, that were created in the past and still have historical importance: *These monuments are a vital part of the **cultural** heritage of South America.*

ˌheritage-listed ˈbuilding **noun** [C] Australian English a building of great historical or artistic value that has official protection to prevent it from being changed or destroyed → Compare **listed building**

hermaphrodite /hɜːˈmæf.rə.daɪt/ ⓤⓢ /hɝː-/ **noun** [C] a plant, animal, or person with both male and female sex organs

hermetic /hɜːˈmet.ɪk/ ⓤⓢ /hɚˈmet̬-/ **adj** **1** specialized (of a container) so tightly closed that no air can leave or enter: *a hermetic **seal*** **2** formal If a particular group is hermetic, the people who live within it don't often communicate with those who live outside it.

hermetically sealed /hɜːˌmet.ɪ.kliˈsiːld/ ⓤⓢ /hɚˌmet̬-/ **adj** **1** specialized describes a container or space that is so tightly closed that no air can leave or enter it **2** disapproving separated and protected from very different conditions outside, in an unnatural way: *We drove past a row of squalid shacks on the way to our hotel, where we slept in air-conditioned, hermetically sealed rooms.*

hermit /ˈhɜː.mɪt/ ⓤⓢ /ˈhɝː-/ **noun** [C] a person who lives alone and apart from the rest of society, especially for religious reasons

hermitage /ˈhɜː.mɪ.tɪdʒ/ ⓤⓢ /ˈhɝː.mɪ.t̬ɪdʒ/ **noun** [C] a place where a religious person lives on their own, apart from the rest of society

hernia /ˈhɜː.ni.ə/ ⓤⓢ /ˈhɝː-/ **noun** [C] a medical condition in which an organ pushes through the muscle which surrounds it

hero /ˈhɪə.rəʊ/ ⓤⓢ /ˈhɪr.oʊ/ **noun** [C] (plural **heroes**) **PERSON** ▷ **1** Ⓑ1 (female **heroine**) a person who is admired for having done something very brave or having achieved something great: *a war hero* ◦ *He became a national hero for his part in the revolution.* ◦ humorous *Graham says he'll take my parents to the airport at four o'clock in the morning – what a hero!* → See also **antihero** **2** Ⓑ1 (female **heroine**) the main male character in a book or film who is usually good: *the hero of her latest novel* **3** someone who you admire very much: *Humphrey Bogart's my hero – I've seen every one of his films.* **FOOD** ▷ **4** US a long sandwich filled with cold meat, cheese, salad, etc.

heroic /hɪˈrəʊ.ɪk/ ⓤⓢ /-ˈroʊ-/ **adj** **1** Ⓒ1 very brave or great: *a heroic act/deed* **2** Ⓒ1 informal If you make a heroic attempt or effort to do something, you try very hard to do it: *Despite Roz's heroic efforts to liven it up, the party was a disaster.* • **heroically** /-ɪ.kᵊl.i/ **adv** *She fought heroically against the disease.*

heroics /hɪˈrəʊ.ɪks/ ⓤⓢ /-ˈroʊ-/ **noun** [plural] mainly disapproving dangerous or silly actions that are only done to make other people admire you

heroin /ˈher.əʊ.ɪn/ ⓤⓢ /-oʊ-/ **noun** [U] a powerful illegal drug: *Heroin is obtained from morphine and is extremely addictive.* ◦ *a heroin addict* ◦ *She died from a heroin overdose.*

heroine → See **hero**

heroism /ˈher.əʊ.ɪ.zᵊm/ ⓤⓢ /-oʊ-/ **noun** [U] great courage: *an act of heroism*

heron /ˈher.ᵊn/ **noun** [C] (plural **herons** or **heron**) a large bird with long legs, a long neck and grey or white feathers that lives near water

ˈhero ˌworship **noun** [U] a feeling of extreme admiration for someone, imagining that they have qualities or abilities that are better than anyone else's • **ˈhero-ˌworship** **verb** [T] (plural **-pp-** or US also **-p-**) *She hero-worshipped her elder brother, and she was devastated when he died.*

herpes /ˈhɜː.piːz/ ⓤⓢ /ˈhɝː-/ **noun** [U] an infectious disease which causes painful red spots to appear on the skin, especially on the lips or sexual organs

herringbone

herring /ˈher.ɪŋ/ **noun** [C or U] (plural **herrings** or **herring**) a long silver-coloured fish which swims in large groups in the sea, or its flesh eaten as food

herringbone /ˈher.ɪŋ.bəʊn/ ⓤⓢ /-boʊn/ **noun** [U]

a pattern, used especially in cloth, which consists of rows of V shapes: *herringbone tweed*

hers /hɜːz/ (US) /hɝːz/ **pronoun** A2 the one(s) belonging to or con-nected with a woman, girl, or female animal that has been mentioned or is known about: *Nicky and I both have red hair but hers is lighter than mine.* ◦ *'Do you know Tina?' 'Yes, I'm a friend* ***of*** *hers.'* ◦ *Hers is the big house on the corner.*

herself /hɜːˈself/ (US) /hɝː-/ **pronoun 1** A2 used to refer to a female object of a verb, that is the same person or animal as the subject of the verb: *She kept telling herself that nothing was wrong.* ◦ *My mother would worry herself to death if she knew what I was doing.* **2** B2 used to emphasize a particular woman, girl, or female animal: *She decorated the cake herself.* ◦ *She herself admitted that it was wrong.* **3 (all) by herself** A2 If a woman or girl does something by herself, she does it alone or without help from anyone else: *She lives by herself in an enormous house.* ◦ *Holly's only three but she wrote her name all by herself.* **4 (all) to herself** for her use only: *Mum's got the house to herself this weekend.* **5 not be/seem/feel herself** not to be, seem, or feel as happy or healthy as usual: *Is Michelle all right? She doesn't seem quite herself at the moment.* **6 in herself** UK informal used when describing or asking about a woman's state of mind when she is physically ill: *I know she's got back trouble but how is she in herself?*

IDIOM **keep (herself) to herself** to spend a lot of time alone, not talking to other people very much: *My neighbour was an elderly lady who kept to herself.*

hertz /hɜːts/ (US) /hɝːts/ **noun** [C] (plural **hertz**) (written abbreviation **Hz**) a unit for measuring the number of CYCLES (= events that are repeated) which happen every second, used especially in ELECTRONICS → See also **kilohertz, megahertz**

he's /hiːz/ **short form 1** he is: *He's a great guy.* **2** he has: *He's just bought a new digital camera.*

hesitant /ˈhez.ɪ.tᵊnt/ **adj** If you are hesitant, you do not do something immediately or quickly because you are nervous or not certain: *You seemed a bit hesitant* ***about*** *recommend****ing*** *that restaurant – is something wrong with it?* ◦ *She gave me a hesitant smile.* • **hesitancy** /-tᵊn.si/ **noun** [U] *The president is not known for his hesitancy in such matters.* • **hesitantly** /-li/ **adv** *She approached the teacher hesitantly.*

hesitate /ˈhez.ɪ.teɪt/ **verb** [I] B2 to pause before you do or say something, often because you are uncertain or nervous about it: *She hesitated slightly before answering the inspector's question.* ◦ *'Do you love me?' she asked. He hesitated and then said, 'I'm not sure'.* ◦ [+ to infinitive] *If you need anything, don't hesitate* ***to*** *call me.*

hesitation /ˌhez.ɪˈteɪ.ʃᵊn/ **noun** [C or U] C1 the act of pausing before doing something, especially because you are nervous or not certain: *After a slight hesitation, she began to speak.* ◦ *Any hesitation on the part of the government will be seen as weakness.* ◦ formal *I have no hesitation* ***in*** *recommend****ing*** *Ms Shapur for the job.*

hessian /ˈhes.i.ən/ **noun** [U] UK (US **burlap**) a type of thick, rough cloth used for things and coverings which must be strong

hetero /ˈhet.ᵊr.əʊ/ (US) /ˈhet̬.ɚ.oʊ/ **noun** [C] (plural **heteros**) informal for **heterosexual**

heterodox /ˈhet.ᵊr.ə.dɒks/ (US) /ˈhet̬.ɚ.ə.dɑːks/ **adj** formal (of beliefs, ideas, or activities) different to and opposing generally accepted beliefs or standards: *His opinions have always been distinctly heterodox.* → Compare **orthodox** • **heterodoxy** /-dɒk.si/ (US) /-dɑːk.si/ **noun** [U]

heterogeneous /ˌhet.ᵊr.əˈdʒiː.ni.əs/ (US) /ˌhet̬.ə.roʊ-/ **adj** formal consisting of parts or things that are very different from each other: *Switzerland is a heterogeneous confederation of 26 self-governing cantons.* → Compare **homogeneous** • **heterogeneity** /ˌhet.ᵊr.ə.dʒəˈneɪ.ɪ.ti/ (US) /ˌhet̬.ə.roʊ.dʒəˈneɪ.ə.t̬i/ **noun** [U] *Archaeological studies of the tombs have shown the heterogeneity of religious practices in the region.*

heterosexual /ˌhet.ᵊr.əˈsek.sju.ᵊl/ (US) /ˌhet̬.ə.roʊ-/ **noun** [C] (informal **hetero**) a person who is sexually attracted to people of the opposite sex → Compare **bisexual, homosexual** • **heterosexual adj** *heterosexual sex/relationships* • **heterosexuality** /ˌhet.ᵊr.əˌsek.sjuˈæl.ə.ti/ (US) /ˌhet̬.ə.roʊˌsek.ʃuˈæl.ə.t̬i/ **noun** [U] • **heterosexually** /-i/ **adv** *I don't think he's heterosexually inclined.*

heterozygous /ˌhet.ᵊr.əʊˈzaɪ.fəs/ (US) /ˌhet̬.ə.roʊˈ-/ **adj** specialized having two different forms of a GENE (= part of a cell containing DNA information) that controls a particular characteristic, one INHERITED from each parent, and therefore able to pass on either form: *a heterozygous cell* → Compare **homozygous** • **heterozygote** /-ɡəʊt/ (US) /-ɡoʊt/ **noun** [C] specialized a heterozygous person, animal, or organism

het up /ˌhetˈʌp/ (US) /ˌhet̬-/ **adj** [after verb] UK informal worried or angry and not calm: *There's no need to* ***get*** *so het up* ***about*** *a few dirty dishes in the sink!*

heuristic /hjʊˈrɪs.tɪk/ **adj** specialized (of a method of teaching) allowing students to learn by discovering things themselves and learning from their own experiences rather than by telling them things

hew /hjuː/ **verb** [T] (**hewed, hewed** or **hewn**) to cut a large piece out of rock, stone, or another hard material in a rough way: *The monument was hewn* ***out of*** *the side of a mountain.*

hex /heks/ **noun** [C] US informal an evil spell, bringing bad luck and trouble: *Someone's* ***put*** *a hex* ***on*** *my computer this morning – it keeps on crashing.*

hexagon /ˈhek.sə.ɡən/ (US) /-ɡɑːn/ **noun** [C] a shape that has six straight sides • **hexagonal** /hekˈsæɡ.ᵊn.ᵊl/ **adj** *a hexagonal building/object*

hey /heɪ/ **exclamation** informal A2 used as a way of attracting someone's attention, sometimes in a way that is not very polite: *Hey! What are you doing with my car?* ◦ *Hey, are you guys coming to Angela's party?*

heyday /ˈheɪ.deɪ/ **noun** [C usually singular] the most successful or popular period of someone or something: *In their heyday, they sold as many records as all the other groups in the country put together.*

hey presto /ˌheɪˈpres.təʊ/ (US) /-toʊ/ **exclamation** UK (US **presto**) said when something appears or happens so quickly or easily that it seems to be magic: *You put your money in the machine and, hey presto, the coffee comes out!*

HGV /ˌeɪtʃ.dʒiːˈviː/ **noun** [C] UK abbreviation for **heavy goods vehicle**

hhok written abbreviation for ha ha only kidding: used in an email or in a discussion in an internet CHAT ROOM to show that you have written something that is not true and is a joke

hi /haɪ/ **exclamation** informal A1 used as an informal greeting, usually to people who you know: *Hi, there!* ◦ *Hi, how are you doing?*

hiatus /haɪˈeɪ.təs/ (US) /-t̬əs/ **noun** [C usually singular] formal a short pause in which nothing happens or is said, or a space where something is missing: *The*

H

company expects to resume production of the vehicle again after a two-month hiatus.

hibernate /ˈhaɪ.bə.neɪt/ US /-bɚ-/ **verb** [I] (of some animals) to spend the winter sleeping: *The turtle hibernates in a shallow burrow for six months of the year.* • **hibernation** /ˌhaɪ.bəˈneɪ.ʃən/ US /-bɚ-/ **noun** [U] *Bears* ***go into*** *hibernation in the autumn.*

hibiscus /hɪˈbɪs.kəs/ **noun** [C] a tropical plant or bush with large brightly coloured flowers

hiccup /ˈhɪk.ʌp/ **noun; verb**

▸**noun** (also **hiccough**) **NOISE** ▷ **1** [C usually plural] a loud noise that you make in the throat without wanting to, caused by a sudden tightening of a muscle just below the chest and usually happening repeatedly **2 the hiccups** [plural] a series of hiccups: *I've* ***got*** *the hiccups.* ◦ *an attack of the hiccups* **PROBLEM** ▷ **3** [C] a problem that delays or interrupts something for a while, but does not usually cause serious difficulties: *We've had one or two* ***slight*** *hiccups, but progress has generally been quite steady.*

▸**verb** [I] (**-p-**) (also **hiccough**) to make a hiccup: *I can't stop hiccuping – does anyone know a good cure?*

hick /hɪk/ **noun** [C] US informal disapproving a person from the countryside who is considered to be stupid and without experience: *a hick* ***town*** *(= a small town which is a long way from a city)*

hickey /ˈhɪk.i/ **noun** [C] US (UK ˈ**love** ˌ**bite**) a temporary red mark on someone's skin, often their neck, where someone has sucked or bitten it as a sexual act

hickory /ˈhɪk.ər.i/ US /-ɚ-/ **noun** [C or U] a small tree from North America or East Asia which has nuts that can be eaten, or the hard wood from this tree

ˈ**hickory** ˌ**chips** **noun** [plural] small pieces of hickory wood used as a fuel for a BARBECUE (= a method of cooking outside) which give food a special taste

hicksville /ˈhɪks.vɪl/ **noun** [U] US informal disapproving a small town or village that is not interesting and not modern

hidden /ˈhɪd.ən/ **adj** [usually before noun] **NOT EASY TO FIND** ▷ **1** B1 not easy to find: *a hidden valley* ◦ *There were hidden microphones in the room to record their conversation.* **NOT KNOWN ABOUT** ▷ **2** B2 that most people do not know about: *hidden* ***costs/taxes*** ◦ *Hidden problems may lead to an increase in costs.*

ˌ**hidden aˈgenda** **noun** [C] a secret reason for doing something: [+ to infinitive] *The prime minister denied that the new visa requirements were part of a hidden agenda* ***to*** *reduce immigration.*

hide /haɪd/ **verb; noun**

▸**verb** (**hid, hidden**) **1** B1 [I or T] to put something or someone in a place where they cannot be seen or found, or to put yourself somewhere where you cannot be seen or found: *She used to hide her diary under her pillow.* ◦ *A kilo of heroin was found hidden inside the lining of the suitcase.* ◦ *I like wearing sunglasses – I feel I can hide* ***behind*** *them.* **2** [T] to prevent something from being seen: *He tries to hide his bald patch by sweeping his hair over to one side.* **3** B1 [T] to not show an emotion: *She tried to hide her disappointment at not getting the promotion.* **4** B1 [T] If you hide information from someone, you do not allow that person to know it: *I feel sure there's something about her past that she's trying to hide* ***from*** *me.*

IDIOM **hide your light under a bushel** to keep your good qualities and abilities secret from other people

▸**noun** **SKIN** ▷ **1** [C or U] the strong, thick skin of an animal, used for making leather **FOR WATCHING BIRDS/ANIMALS** ▷ **2** [C] UK (US **blind**) a place where people can watch wild animals or birds without being noticed by them

ˌ**hide-and-ˈseek** **noun** [U] a children's game in which a group of children hide in secret places and then one child has to go to look for them

hideaway /ˈhaɪd.əˌweɪ/ **noun** [C] informal a place where someone goes when they want to relax away from other people

hidebound /ˈhaɪd.baʊnd/ **adj** disapproving having fixed opinions and ways of doing things and not willing to change or be influenced, especially by new or modern ideas

hideous /ˈhɪd.i.əs/ **adj** extremely ugly or bad: *They've just built some hideous new apartment blocks on the seafront.* • **hideousness** /-nəs/ **noun** [U]

hideously /ˈhɪd.i.əs.li/ **adv** **1** in an extremely ugly way: *hideously fat/ugly* ◦ *a hideously misshapen body* **2** informal used to emphasize the great degree of something: *a hideously expensive restaurant*

hideout /ˈhaɪd.aʊt/ **noun** [C] a secret place where someone can go when they do not want to be found by other people

hidey-hole /ˈhaɪd.i.həʊl/ US /-hoʊl/ **noun** [C] (also **hidy-hole**) UK informal a small place for hiding things in

hiding /ˈhaɪ.dɪŋ/ **noun** **1** [C usually singular] old-fashioned a punishment by being beaten repeatedly **2** [C usually singular] UK informal a total defeat: *'How did the French team get on in their match against Italy?' 'They got a real hiding!'* **3 be in hiding/go into hiding** to be/go somewhere where you cannot be found

IDIOM **be on a hiding to nothing** UK informal to be trying to do something when there is no chance that you will succeed

ˈ**hiding** ˌ**place** **noun** [C] a place where something can be hidden

hie /haɪ/ **verb** [I or T] (present tense **hies**, present participle **hieing**, past tense and past participle **hied**) old use or humorous to go quickly or to hurry yourself: *I must hie* ***me to*** *the sales before all the bargains are gone.*

hierarchy /ˈhaɪə.rɑː.ki/ US /ˈhaɪr.ɑːr-/ **noun** [C] **1** C2 a system in which people or things are arranged according to their importance: *Some monkeys have a very complex* ***social*** *hierarchy.* ◦ *He rose quickly through the* ***political*** *hierarchy to become party leader.* **2** the people in the upper levels of an organization who control it • **hierarchical** /ˌhaɪəˈrɑː.kɪ.kəl/ US /ˌhaɪr-ˈɑːr-/ **adj** C2 *It's a very hierarchical organization in which everyone's status is clearly defined.* • **hierarchically** /ˌhaɪəˈrɑː.kɪ.kəl.i/ US /ˌhaɪrˈɑːr-/ **adv** *The company is hierarchically structured.*

hieroglyph /ˈhaɪə.rəˌglɪf/ US /-roʊ-/ **noun** [C] a picture or symbol that represents a word, used in some writing systems, such as the one used in ancient Egypt

hieroglyphics /ˌhaɪə.rəˈglɪf.ɪks/ US /-roʊ-/ **noun** [plural] a system of writing which uses pictures instead of words, especially as used in ancient Egypt

hi-fi /ˈhaɪ.faɪ/ **noun** **1** [C or U] electronic equipment used to play recorded sound, especially music: *I've just bought a new hi-fi.* ◦ *hi-fi equipment* **2** [U] abbreviation for **high fidelity**

higgledy-piggledy /ˌhɪg.l̩.diˈpɪg.l̩.di/ **adj, adv** informal mixed up and in no particular order: *My clothes are all higgledy-piggledy in my drawers.*

high /haɪ/ **adj; noun; adv**

▸**adj** **DISTANCE** ▷ **1** A2 (especially of things that are not living) being a large distance from top to bottom or a long way above the ground, or having the stated distance from top to bottom: *a high building/ mountain* ◦ *high ceilings* ◦ *It's two and a half metres high and one metre wide.* ◦ *The corn grew waist-high (= as high as a person's waist) in the fields.* **ABOVE AVERAGE** ▷ **2** B1 greater than the usual level or amount: *The job demands **a** high **level of** concentration.* ◦ *He suffers from high blood pressure.* ◦ *Antique furniture fetches very high prices these days.* ◦ *She got very high marks in her geography exam.* ◦ *It's very dangerous to drive at high speed when the roads are wet.* ◦ *He's in a high-security prison.* **3 high in sth** C1 containing a large quantity of something: *I avoid foods that are high in fat.* **4 high standards/principles** B1 very good or very moral standards: *She was a woman of high principles.* ◦ *She demands very high standards from the people who work for her.* **5 high winds** fast, strong wind: *High winds caused delays on the ferries.* **IMPORTANT** ▷ **6** B2 having power, an important position, or great influence: *an officer of high rank* **SOUND** ▷ **7** near or at the top of the range of sounds: *I can't reach the high notes.* **BAD** ▷ **8** UK (of food) smelling bad and no longer good to eat: *This meat is rather high – shall I throw it out?* **MENTAL STATE** ▷ **9** C2 not thinking or behaving normally because of taking drugs: *He was high **on** heroin at the time.*

IDIOMS **be as high as a kite 1** informal to behave in a silly or excited way because you have taken drugs or drunk a lot of alcohol: *I tried to talk to her after the party, but she was as high as a kite.* **2** to feel very happy and excited: *I was a high as a kite when I heard I'd got the job.* • **come/get (down) off your high horse** to stop talking as if you were better or more clever than other people: *It's time you came down off your high horse and admitted you were wrong.* • **get on your high horse** to start talking angrily about something bad that someone else has done as if you feel you are better or more clever than they are • **high and mighty** disapproving Someone who is high and mighty behaves as if they are more important than other people. • **hunt/search high and low** to search everywhere for something: *I've been hunting high and low for that certificate and I still can't find it!* • **leave sb high and dry** informal to do something that is not at all convenient for someone and put them in a very difficult situation: *They pulled out of the deal at the last minute leaving us high and dry.* • **live high on/ off the hog** US informal often disapproving to live in great comfort with a lot of money • **on high 1** literary in heaven: *God looked down from on high.* **2** mainly humorous If an order comes from on high, it comes from someone in a position of authority: *Instructions came from on high to reduce our travel expenses.*

▸noun **ABOVE AVERAGE** ▷ **1** [C] a higher level than has ever been reached previously: *Interest rates have reached an **all-time/record** high.* **MENTAL STATE** ▷ **2** [C usually singular] a period of extreme excitement or happiness when you feel full of energy, often caused by a feeling of success, or by drugs or alcohol or a religious experience: *Exercise gives you a high.* ◦ *She's been **on** a high ever since she got her article published in the Times.* ◦ *There are lots of highs **and lows** in this job.* **EDUCATION** ▷ **3** [S] US informal for **high school** (when used in the name of a school): *I go to Santa Ana High.*

▸adv B1 at or to a large distance from the ground: *Concorde flew much higher than most planes.*

highball /ˈhaɪ.bɔːl/ US /-bɑːl/ noun [C] mainly US an alcoholic drink made with WHISKY a MIXER, and ice, served in a tall glass

ˈ**high** ˌ**beams** noun [plural] US car HEADLIGHTS that are on as brightly as possible

highbrow /ˈhaɪ.braʊ/ adj mainly disapproving (of books, plays, etc.) involving serious and complicated or artistic ideas, or (of people) interested in serious and complicated subjects → Compare **lowbrow, middlebrow** • **highbrow** noun [C]

ˈ**high** ˌ**chair** noun [C] a chair with long legs, for a baby or a small child, usually with a small table connected to it for the child to eat from

High ˈ**Church** adj related to the part of the Church of England that is closest to the Roman Catholic Church and contains a lot of ceremonies → Compare **Low Church**

high-ˈ**class** adj of very good quality, or of high social rank

ˌ**High Com**ˈ**mission** noun [C usually singular] **1** the **embassy** of one COMMONWEALTH country in another Commonwealth country **2** an international organization that has been created for a particular purpose: *the United Nations High Commission for Refugees*

ˌ**High Com**ˈ**missioner** noun [C] the main REPRESENTATIVE of one COMMONWEALTH country in another Commonwealth country, or a person in charge of a High Commission

ˌ**High** ˈ**Court** noun [C usually singular] **1** UK a law court in England and Wales for trials of CIVIL rather than criminal cases and where decisions made in local courts can be considered again **2 high court** US **the Supreme Court**

ˌ**high** ˈ**def** noun [U] abbreviation for high definition: a system for showing very clear pictures on a television or computer screen or for producing very clear sound: *With high def, you can recognize faces in the crowd.*

ˌ**high-def** adj abbreviation for high-definition: used to describe a system for showing very clear pictures on a television or computer screen or for producing very clear sound: *a high-def channel/video/television*

ˌ**high defi**ˈ**nition** noun [U] (abbreviation ˌ**high** ˈ**def**) a system for showing very clear pictures on a television or computer screen or for producing very clear sound: *The 'Planet Earth' series, which is shot **in** high definition, captures the beauty of nature.*

ˌ**high-defi**ˈ**nition** adj [before noun] (abbreviation **HD**, ˈ**high-def**) used to describe a system for showing very clear pictures on a television or computer screen or for producing very clear sound: *high-definition television*

ˌ**high-**ˈ**end** adj **1** intended for people who want very good quality products and who do not mind how much they cost: *high-end video equipment/a high-end department store* **2** wanting very good quality products, and willing to pay a lot of money for them: *high-end consumers*

higher /ˈhaɪ.əʳ/ US /-ɚ/ adj **HIGH** ▷ **1** comparative of **high** **EDUCATION** ▷ **2** [before noun] describes an advanced level of education: *A greater proportion of people with first degrees are now going on to study for higher degrees.*

Higher /ˈhaɪ.əʳ/ US /-ɚ/ noun [C] in Scotland, an

H

official exam that is taken in schools, usually by students aged 16 – 18 who want to study at college or university → Compare **AS level, A level**

ˌhigher eduˈcation noun [U] education at a college or university where subjects are studied at an advanced level

ˌhigher-ˈup noun [C] informal someone with a more important position than you in an organization: *They're still waiting for a decision about the extra money from the higher-ups.*

ˌhighest common ˈfactor noun [C] specialized the highest number that a set of two or more different numbers can be divided by exactly: *4 is the highest common factor **of** 8 and 12.*

ˌhigh exˈplosive noun [C or U] a very powerful explosive that can damage a large area

highfalutin /ˌhaɪ.fəˈluː.tɪn/ (US) /-t̬ɪn/ adj informal trying to seem very important or serious, but without having a good reason for doing so and looking silly as a result

H

ˌhigh fiˈdelity noun [U] (abbreviation **hi-fi**) the production by electrical equipment of very good quality sound that is as similar as possible to the original sound: *a major manufacturer of high-fidelity audio equipment*

ˌhigh ˈfive noun [C] a greeting or an expression of admiration in which two people each raise a hand above their shoulder and bring the fronts of their hands together with force • **ˌhigh-ˈfive** verb [I or T] to give someone a high five: *As the show ended, Chris high-fived his friends.*

ˌhigh-ˈflown adj disapproving describes language, ideas, or behaviour that is meant to make you admire someone

ˌhigh-ˈflyer noun **1** (US usually **highflier**) [C] someone who has a lot of ability and a strong wish to be successful and is therefore expected to achieve a lot **2** [C, + sing/pl verb] mainly UK an extremely successful organization, business, or team

ˌhigh-ˈflying adj [before noun] extremely successful: *a high-flying investment banker*

ˌhigh-ˈgrade adj [before noun] of very good quality or of better quality than usual: *high-grade petrol*

ˌhigh-ˈhanded adj disapproving Someone who is high-handed uses their power or authority more forcefully than is needed without thinking about the feelings or wishes of other people. • **high-handedness** /-nəs/ noun [U]

ˌhigh ˈheels noun [plural] women's shoes in which the heels are raised high off the ground • **ˌhigh-ˈheeled** adj [before noun] *high-heeled shoes*

high jinks informal (US also **hijinks**) /ˈhaɪˈdʒɪŋks/ noun [plural] energetic and excited behaviour in which people do funny things or play tricks on someone

the ˈhigh jump noun [S] a sport in which competitors try to jump over a bar supported on two poles. The height of the bar is gradually raised and the winner is the person who jumps highest without knocking the bar off the poles.

IDIOM **be for the high jump** UK to be going to be punished for something you have done wrong

ˈhigh ˌjumper noun [C] someone who competes in the high jump

ˌHighland ˈcow noun [C] (plural **Highland cows** or **Highland cattle**) a cow of a breed with thick long hair and large horns

Highlander /ˈhaɪ.lən.dəʳ/ (US) /-dɚ/ noun [C] a person who comes from the Scottish Highlands

ˌHighland ˈfling noun [C usually singular] an energetic Scottish dance

ˌHighland ˈGames noun [plural] an event that involves traditional Scottish dancing, music, and sports competitions

highlands /ˈhaɪ.ləndz/ noun [plural] a MOUNTAINOUS area of a country: *Most villages in the highlands are now connected by roads.* • **highland** /-lənd/ adj [before noun] in or relating to an area with mountains or hills: *highland springs*

the ˈHighlands noun [plural] a MOUNTAINOUS area in northern Scotland: *the Scottish Highlands* • **Highland** adj [before noun] related to or connected with the Scottish Highlands: *a Highland reel*

ˌhigh-ˈlevel adj If discussions are high-level, very important people are involved in them: *high-level meetings/talks between the two sides*

ˌhigh-level ˈlanguage noun [C] specialized a language for writing computer programs which looks more like human language than computer language and is therefore easier to understand

the ˈhigh ˌlife noun [S] an exciting way of living in which rich and successful people enjoy themselves by spending a lot of time and money in fashionable places

highlight /ˈhaɪ.laɪt/ verb; noun

▸verb [T] (B2) to attract attention to or emphasize something important: *The report highlights the need for improved safety.* ◦ *The spelling mistakes in the text had been highlighted **in** green.*

▸noun BEST PART ▷ **1** (B2) [C] the best or most exciting, entertaining, or interesting part of something: *Highlights **of** the match will be shown after the news.* HAIR ▷ **2** [C usually plural] a narrow strip of hair on a person's head which has been made a lighter colour than the surrounding hair

highlighter /ˈhaɪˌlaɪ.təʳ/ (US) /-t̬ɚ/ noun [C] a special pen containing bright ink, used to mark words in a book, magazine, etc.

highly /ˈhaɪ.li/ adv ABOVE AVERAGE ▷ **1** (B2) very, to a large degree, or at a high level: *a highly **paid** job* ◦ *a highly profitable line of products* ◦ *For our country to remain competitive, we need a highly skilled, highly educated workforce.* **2 think/speak highly of sb** (C2) to admire/say admiring things about someone: *He's very highly thought of within the company.* IMPORTANT ▷ **3** in an important or INFLUENTIAL (= having a lot of influence) position: *According to one highly **placed** source, the prime minister had threatened to resign over this issue.*

ˌhighly ˈstrung adj (US **ˌhigh-ˈstrung**) very nervous and easily upset: *a highly strung racehorse*

ˌhigh-ˈminded adj having very high moral standards of behaviour

Highness /ˈhaɪ.nəs/ noun formal **Her/His/Your Highness** used when you are speaking to or about a royal person: [as form of address] *Will that be all, Your Highness?*

ˌhigh ˈnoon noun [U] exactly twelve o'clock, when the sun should be at its highest point in the sky

ˌhigh-ˈoctane adj [before noun] **1** describes fuel that is of very good quality: *high-octane fuel* ◦ *high-octane petrol* (US *gas*) **2** full of energy or very powerful: *a high-octane performance*

ˌhigh-ˈpitched adj VOICE ▷ **1** A voice that is high-pitched is higher than usual. NOISE ▷ **2** describes a noise that is high and sometimes also loud or unpleasant: *the high-pitched scream of the fire alarm*

ˈ**high ˌpoint** noun [S] the best part of an experience: *The high point of the trip for me was visiting the Pyramids.*

ˌ**high-ˈpowered** adj **POWERFUL** ▷ **1** (of machines) very powerful: *a high-powered motorbike* **IMPORTANT JOB** ▷ **2** (of people) very successful or having a very important job: *a high-powered attorney*

ˌ**high-ˈpressure** adj [before noun] **PRESSURE** ▷ **1** involving pressure that is greater than usual: *They used special high-pressure hoses to help them put out the fires.* **SELLING** ▷ **2** describes methods of selling that involve persuading people in a forceful way to buy something that often they do not want: *I refuse to be intimidated by high-pressure sales techniques.* **WORRY** ▷ **3** involving a lot of responsibility or worry: *a high-pressure job in advertising*

ˌ**high ˈpriest** noun [C] (female ˌ**high prieˈstess**) **1** a very important priest or PRIESTESS in a religious or spiritual organization **2** the most important or famous person in a particular area of interest: *She is widely regarded as the high priestess **of** contemporary dance.*

ˌ**high-ˈprofile** adj [before noun] C2 attracting a lot of attention and interest from the public and newspapers, television, etc.: *high-profile politicians* ◦ *He resigned from a high-profile job as economic adviser to the prime minister.*

ˌ**high-ˈranking** adj having an important position in an organization

ˌ**high-resoˈlution** adj (also informal **hi-res**) used to describe something such as a screen or photograph that shows an image extremely clearly: *high-resolution graphics*

ˈ**high-rise** noun; adj

▸noun [C] a tall modern building with many floors: *She lives in a high-rise overlooking the river.*

▸adj *a high-rise office building*

ˌ**high-ˈrisk** adj [before noun] involving a greater than usual amount of risk: *Only people who can afford to lose their money should make high-risk investments.*

ˌ**high ˈroller** noun [C] someone who spends a lot of money or who GAMBLES with large amounts of money

ˈ**high ˌschool** noun [C] **1** A2 (informal **high**) a school in the US for children aged from 14 to 18, or from 16 to 18 if there is also a JUNIOR HIGH SCHOOL: *Diane goes to Santa Ana High.* **2** in the UK and Australia, sometimes used in the names of schools for children aged from eleven to 18

the ˌhigh ˈseas noun [plural] the seas that are not controlled by any country

ˌ**high ˈseason** noun [U] the time of year when the greatest number of people visit a place and when the prices are at their highest level: *People on limited budgets should avoid travelling **in/during** high season.* → Compare **low season**

ˌ**high-ˈspeed** adj [before noun] describes something that moves or operates very quickly: *a high-speed train/ferry* ◦ *a high-speed computer* ◦ *high-speed data transmission*

ˌ**high-ˈspirited** adj **PERSON** ▷ **1** Someone who is high-spirited is energetic and happy and likes doing exciting and enjoyable things. **ANIMAL** ▷ **2** describes a very active horse that is difficult to control

ˌ**high ˈspirits** noun [plural] If someone is in high spirits, they are extremely happy and enjoying themselves: *They'd had a couple of drinks and were **in** high spirits.*

ˈ**high ˌstreet** noun UK **1** [C] a street where the most important shops and businesses in a town are: *There's a new Italian restaurant opening **on** the high street.* **2 the high street** business done in shops: *There are signs of economic recovery in the high street.*

ˈ**high-street** adj **1** relating to business done in shops: *There was a modest rise in high-street spending last month.* **2** describes products, especially clothes, that are intended for the ordinary public and not for rich people: *high-street fashions*

ˌ**high ˈtable** noun [C or U] UK a table at a formal meal where the most important guests sit

hightail /ˈhaɪ.teɪl/ verb mainly US informal **hightail it** to leave or go somewhere in a great hurry: *As soon as I heard he was coming I hightailed it **out** of there.*

ˌ**high ˈtea** noun [C or U] UK a light meal eaten in the late afternoon or early evening which usually includes cooked food, cakes, and tea to drink

ˌ**high-ˈtech** adj **1** B2 (also **hi-tech**) using the most advanced and developed machines and methods: *This weapons system is an affordable, hi-tech solution.* → Compare **low-tech** **2** very modern looking or made with modern materials: *high-tech architecture*

ˌ**high techˈnology** noun [U] the most advanced and developed machines and methods: *a thriving economy built on high technology*

ˌ**high-ˈtension** adj [before noun] old-fashioned **high-voltage**: *a high-tension cable*

ˌ**high ˈtide** noun **SEA/RIVER** ▷ **1** [C or U] the time when the sea or a river reaches its highest level and comes furthest up the beach or the bank **SUCCESSFUL POINT** ▷ **2** [S] UK Something's high tide is its most successful point: *The signing of the peace treaty was the high tide **of** her presidency.*

ˈ**high-top** (also ˈ**hi-ˌtop**) noun [C] a type of shoe that covers the foot and the ANKLE: *high-top trainers*

ˌ**high ˈtreason** noun [U] the committing of a crime which seriously threatens the safety of your country

ˌ**high ˈup** adj [after verb] Someone who is high up in an organization has an important position in it.

ˌ**high-visiˈbility** adj **1** (also informal **high-vis** /ˌhaɪˈvɪz/) easy to see in all conditions because of being a very bright colour: *a security guard in a high-vis **jacket*** **2** noticed by many people: *There is a lot of stress in such a high-visibility job.* ◦ *High-visibility policing acts as a deterrent to crime.*

ˌ**high-ˈvoltage** adj **ELECTRICITY** ▷ **1** relating to or containing large amounts of electricity **EXCITING** ▷ **2** informal very exciting and full of energy: *Sara Hughes gives a high-voltage performance in one of the most exciting plays to hit London this year.*

ˌ**high ˈwater** noun [U] UK for **high tide**

ˌ**high ˈwater ˌmark** noun [C usually singular] **SEA/RIVER** ▷ **1** a mark which shows the highest level that the sea or river reaches at a particular place **SUCCESSFUL POINT** ▷ **2** the most successful point of something: *His 1991 election victory was probably the high water mark **of** his popularity.*

highway /ˈhaɪ.weɪ/ noun [C] US or UK formal A2 a public road, especially an important road that joins cities or towns together: *a coastal/interstate highway* → See also **superhighway**

the ˌHighway ˈCode noun [S] UK the set of official rules, published in a small book, that have to be obeyed by drivers in the UK

highwayman /ˈhaɪ.weɪ.mən/ noun [C] (plural **-men** /-mən/) in the past, a man on a horse and carrying a gun who stopped people travelling on public roads and stole from them

hijab /ˈhɪ.dʒæb/ noun **1** [C] the head covering that some Muslim women wear when they are outside

2 [U] the religious law that controls the clothes that Muslim women can wear

hijack /ˈhaɪ.dʒæk/ **verb; noun**

▸**verb** [T] **1** to take control of an aircraft or other vehicle during a journey, especially using violence: *Two men hijacked a jet travelling to Paris and demanded $125,000.* **2** disapproving to take control of or use something that does not belong to you for your own advantage: *He resents the way his ideas have been hijacked by others in the department.* • **hijacker** /-əʳ/ (US) /-ɚ/ **noun** [C]

▸**noun** [C or U] (also **hijacking**) an occasion when someone uses force to take control of an aircraft or other vehicle: *The hijack ended with the release of all the plane's passengers unharmed.*

hike /haɪk/ **noun; verb**

▸**noun** [C] **WALK** ▷ **1** a long walk, especially in the countryside **INCREASE** ▷ **2** an increase in the cost of something, especially a large or unwanted increase: *The recent hike* ***in*** *train fares came as a shock to commuters.*

IDIOM **take a hike!** US informal a rude way of telling someone to leave

▸**verb** **WALK** ▷ **1** [I] to go for a long walk in the countryside **INCREASE** ▷ **2** [T] to increase the cost of something: *The Chancellor has hiked* (***up***) *interest rates again.*

PHRASAL VERB **hike sth up** informal to lift or raise something with a quick movement: *She hiked up her skirt and climbed onto the bicycle.*

hiker /ˈhaɪ.kəʳ/ (US) /-kɚ/ **noun** [C] a person who goes for a long walk in the countryside: *On sunny days the trails are full of hikers.*

hiking /ˈhaɪ.kɪŋ/ **noun** [U] (A2) the activity of going for long walks in the countryside: *We're* ***going*** *hiking in the Lake District next weekend.*

hilarious /hɪˈleə.ri.əs/ (US) /-ˈler.i-/ **adj** (C1) extremely funny and causing a lot of laughter: *He didn't like the film at all – I thought it was hilarious.* • **hilariously** /-li/ **adv** *Her new book's hilariously funny.*

hilarity /hɪˈlær.ə.ti/ (US) /-ˈler.ə.t̬i/ **noun** [U] a situation in which people laugh very loudly and think something is very funny: *What was all the hilarity about?*

hill /hɪl/ **noun** [C] **1** (A2) an area of land that is higher than the surrounding land: *Hills are not as high as mountains.* ◦ *Their house is on the top of a hill.* ◦ *In the summer, the shepherds move their sheep up into* ***the*** *hills* (= an area where there are hills). **2** a slope in a road: *That hill's far too steep to cycle up.*

IDIOM **over the hill** often humorous used for describing someone who is old and no longer useful or attractive

hillbilly /ˈhɪlˌbɪl.i/ **noun** [C] US old-fashioned disapproving a person from a MOUNTAINOUS area of the US who has a simple way of life and is considered to be slightly stupid by people living in towns and cities

hillock /ˈhɪl.ək/ **noun** [C] a small hill

hillside /ˈhɪl.saɪd/ **noun** [C] the sloping surface of a hill, rather than the level surface at the top of it

ˈhill ˌstation **noun** [C] UK a village or town high up in the hills, especially in South Asia, where people go in the summer to escape from the heat

hilltop /ˈhɪl.tɒp/ (US) /-tɑːp/ **noun** [C] the top part of a hill, rather than its sloping sides

hilly /ˈhɪl.i/ **adj** having a lot of hills: *hilly countryside*

hilt /hɪlt/ **noun** [C] the handle of a sharp pointed weapon such as a SWORD

IDIOM **(up) to the hilt** Something that is done (up) to the hilt is done completely and without any limits: *The government is already borrowing up to the hilt.*

him strong /hɪm/ weak /ɪm/ **pronoun** **MALE** ▷ **1** (A1) used, usually as the object of a verb or preposition, to refer to a man, boy, or male animal that has just been mentioned or is just about to be mentioned: *If you see Kevin give him my love.* ◦ *What's Terry up to – I haven't seen him for ages.* ◦ *Why don't you give him his present?* ◦ *We've just got a new cat, but we haven't named him yet.* **FEMALE/MALE** ▷ **2** used, especially in formal situations, usually after a verb or preposition, to refer to a person or animal that has just been mentioned or is just about to be mentioned and whose sex is not known or not considered to be important: *Man's ability to talk makes him unlike any other animal.*

> **! Note:**
>
> Many people prefer to use **them**, and this can sometimes mean changing other words in the sentence:
>
> *Human beings' ability to talk makes them unlike any other animal.*
>
> **It** can be used for animals. See note at **he**.

himself /hɪmˈself/ **pronoun** **MALE** ▷ **1** (A2) used to refer to a male object of a verb that is the same person or animal as the subject of the verb: *He'd cut himself shaving.* ◦ *Most nights he would cry himself to sleep.* **2** (B2) used to emphasize a particular man, boy, or male animal: *Did you want to talk to the chairman himself, or could his personal assistant help you?* ◦ *Guy was going to buy a bookcase, but in the end he made one himself.* **3 (all) by himself** (A2) If a man or boy does something by himself, he does it alone or without help from anyone else: *Little Timmy made that snowman all by himself.* ◦ *Why did you leave your little brother by himself?* **4 (all) to himself** for his use only: *Johnny's got the apartment to himself next week.* **5 not be/seem/feel himself** not to be, seem, or feel as happy or as healthy as usual: *Is Tom all right? He doesn't seem quite himself this morning.* **6 in himself** UK informal used when describing or asking about a man's state of mind when he is physically ill: *He's well enough in himself – he just can't shake this cold off.* **FEMALE/MALE** ▷ **7** used to refer to an object of a verb that is the same person or animal as the subject of the verb, when referring to a person or animal whose sex is not known or not considered to be important: *Any fool can teach himself to type.*

IDIOM **keep (himself) to himself** to spend a lot of time alone, not talking to other people very much: *He was a quiet man who kept himself to himself.*

hind /haɪnd/ **adj; noun**

▸**adj** [before noun] at the back of an animal's body: *a hind leg*

▸**noun** [C] (plural **hinds** or **hind**) mainly UK a female DEER, especially a RED DEER → Compare **hart**

hinder /ˈhɪn.dəʳ/ (US) /-dɚ/ **verb** [T] (C2) to limit the ability of someone to do something, or to limit the development of something: *High winds have hindered firefighters* ***in*** *their efforts to put out the blaze.*

Hindi /ˈhɪn.di/ **noun** [U] one of the official languages of India, spoken especially in northern India

hindquarters /ˌhaɪndˈkwɔː.təz/ (US) /-ˈkwɔːr.t̬ɚz/ **noun** [plural] the back part of an animal with four legs

hindrance /ˈhɪn.drəns/ **noun** [C usually singular, U]

something which makes it more difficult for you to do something or for something to develop: *I've never considered my disability a hindrance, but other people have.*

hindsight /ˈhaɪnd.saɪt/ noun [U] the ability to understand an event or situation only after it has happened: ***With (the benefit/wisdom of)** hindsight, I should have taken the job.* ◦ ***In** hindsight, it would have been better to wait.*

Hindu /ˈhɪn.duː/ noun [C] someone who believes in Hinduism

Hinduism /ˈhɪn.duː.ɪ.zᵊm/ noun [U] an ancient religion with Indian origins whose characteristics include the worship of many gods and GODDESSES and the belief that when a person or creature dies, their spirit returns to life in another body

hinge /hɪndʒ/ noun; verb

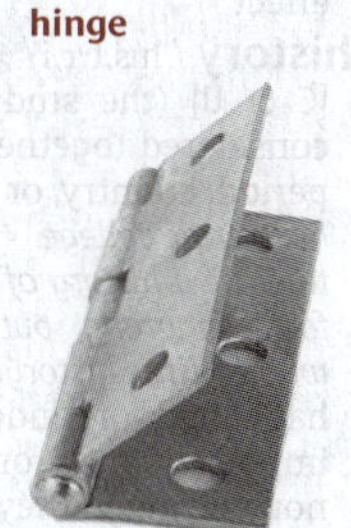

hinge

▸noun [C] a piece of metal that fastens the edge of a door, window, lid, etc. to something else and allows it to open or close: *We had to take the front door off its hinges to get our new sofa into the house.* • **hinged** /hɪndʒd/ adj *a hinged lid*

▸verb

PHRASAL VERB **hinge on/upon sth 1** If one thing hinges on another, the first thing depends on the second thing or is very influenced by it: *The prosecution's case hinged on the evidence of a witness who died before the trial.* **2** If a story or situation hinges on an idea or subject, it develops from that idea or that is the most important subject in it: *The film's plot hinges on a case of mistaken identity.*

Hinglish /ˈhɪŋ.glɪʃ/ noun [U] a mixture of the languages Hindi and English, especially the type of English used by speakers of Hindi

hint /hɪnt/ noun; verb

▸noun INDIRECT STATEMENT ▷ **1** B2 [C] something that you say or do that shows, but not directly, what you think or want: [+ that] *He's **dropped** (= given) several hints to the boss **that** he'll quit if he doesn't get a promotion.* ◦ *Did she **give** you any hints about where she was going?* ◦ *You can't **take** (= understand) a hint, can you? Just go away and leave me alone!* ADVICE ▷ **2** B2 [C] a piece of advice which helps you to do something: *Could you **give** us a hint **about** how to do this exercise, please?* ◦ *This recipe book is full of **handy** (= useful) hints.* SMALL AMOUNT ▷ **3** C2 [C usually singular] a very small amount of something: *There's just a hint **of** brandy in the sauce.* ◦ *I detected a hint **of** doubt in his voice.*

▸verb [I] to say or do something that shows, but not directly, what you think or want: [+ (that)] *Mum's hinted (**that**) she might pay for my trip to Mexico.* ◦ *He's hinted **at** the possibility of moving to America.*

hinterland /ˈhɪn.tə.lænd/ US /-t̬ɚ-/ noun **1** [C usually singular] the land behind the coast or the banks of a river, or an area of a country that is far away from cities **2 hinterlands** [plural] US a part of the country that is far away from the big city areas

hip /hɪp/ noun; adj; exclamation

▸noun [C] BODY PART ▷ **1** B2 the area below the waist and above the legs at either side of the body, or the JOINT which connects the leg to the upper part of the body: *This exercise is designed to trim your hips and stomach.* ◦ *The skirt was a bit tight across the hips.* FRUIT ▷ **2** mainly UK for **rose hip**

▸adj (**hipper, hippest**) informal fashionable

▸exclamation **hip, hip, hooray/hurray!** an expression that is called out, often by a group of people at the same time, to express approval of someone: *Three cheers for the bride and groom! Hip, hip, hooray!*

ˈhip bath noun [C] UK a small bath with a seat built into it, designed for sitting rather than lying in

ˈhip ˌflask noun [C] a small flat bottle that is used to carry alcohol in your pocket

hip flask

hip-hop noun [U] A2 a type of popular music in which the subject of the songs is often politics or society and the words are spoken rather than sung

hippie (also **hippy**) /ˈhɪp.i/ noun [C] a person, typically young, especially in the late 1960s and early 1970s, who believed in peace, was opposed to many of the accepted ideas about how to live, had long hair, and often lived in groups and took drugs

the Hippocratic oath /ˌhɪp.ə.kræt.ɪkˈəʊθ/ US /-kræt̬.ɪkˈoʊθ/ noun [S] a promise made by people when they become doctors to do everything possible to help their patients and to have high moral standards in their work

hippopotamus /ˌhɪp.əˈpɒt.ə.məs/ US /-ˈpɑː.t̬ə-/ noun [C] (plural **hippopotamuses** or **hippopotami**) (informal **hippo**) a very large animal with short legs and thick, dark grey skin which lives near water in Africa

hipster /ˈhɪp.stəʳ/ US /-stɚ/ noun PERSON ▷ **1** [C] informal someone who is very influenced by the most recent ideas and fashions TROUSERS ▷ **2 hipsters** [plural] UK (US **hiphuggers**) trousers which do not reach as high as the waist

hire /haɪəʳ/ US /haɪr/ verb; noun

▸verb [T] UK **1** B1 (US **rent**) to pay to use something for a short period: *How much would it cost to hire a car for a fortnight?* ◦ *You could always hire a dress for the ball if you can't afford to buy one.* **2** B2 to employ someone or pay them to do a particular job: *I was hired by the first company I applied to.* ◦ [+ to infinitive] *We ought to hire a public relations consultant **to** help improve our image.* • **hired** /haɪəd/ US /haɪrd/ adj UK *a hired car* ◦ *The police believe he was killed by a hired assassin.*

PHRASAL VERB **hire sth/sb out** to allow someone to use something or someone temporarily in exchange for money: *How much do you charge for hiring out a bicycle for a week?* ◦ *He's decided to go freelance and hire him**self** out as a technical writer.*

▸noun [U] UK an arrangement to use something by paying for it: *The price includes flights and **car** hire.* ◦ *There's a camping shop in town that has tents **for** hire (= available to be hired) at £10 a week.*

hireling /ˈhaɪə.lɪŋ/ US /ˈhaɪr-/ noun [C] UK disapproving someone who has been persuaded by an offer of money to do an unpleasant or unpopular job: *He's not the boss, he's just a hireling employed to do the dirty work.*

ˌhire ˈpurchase noun [U] UK (abbreviation **HP**, US **inˈstallment ˌplan**) a method of paying for some-

H

thing in which the buyer pays part of the cost immediately and then makes small regular payments until the debt is completely paid

hi-res (also **high-res**) /haɪˈrez/ **adj** abbreviation for **high-resolution**

hiring /ˈhaɪə.rɪŋ/ US /ˈhaɪr.ɪŋ/ **noun** [C usually plural] the act of starting to employ someone: *The office has completely changed in the past few weeks because there have been so many hirings* ***and firings*** *(= a lot of new people have been employed and a lot of others have lost their jobs).*

hirsute /ˈhɜː.sjuːt/ US /ˈhɝː.suːt/ **adj** literary or humorous having a lot of hair, especially on the face or body

his /hɪz/ **determiner; pronoun**

▸**determiner** **MALE** ▷ **1** A1 belonging to or connected with a man, boy, or male animal that has just been mentioned or is known about: *'Jo's got a new boyfriend.' 'Oh really? What's his name?'* ◦ *The bull tossed his horns.* ◦ formal *Did Chris tell you about his winning some money in the lottery?* **FEMALE/MALE** ▷ **2** belonging to or connected with a person or animal that has just been mentioned and whose sex is not known or not considered to be important: *Anyone who drives his car at 100 miles an hour is asking for trouble.* ◦ *What a lovely dog! What's his name?*

> **Note:**
> Many people prefer to use **their**, and this can sometimes mean changing other words in the sentence. **Its** can be used for animals. See note at **he**.

▸**pronoun** A1 the one(s) belonging to or connected with a man, boy, or male animal that has just been mentioned or is known about: *Mark just phoned to say he'd left his coat behind. Do you know if this is his?* ◦ *He introduced us to some colleagues* ***of*** *his.* ◦ *His is the office directly ahead of you, at the far end of the corridor.*

ˌhis and ˈhers **adj** [before noun] describes a pair of similar things designed for a man and woman in a romantic relationship to use: *My mum gave us his and hers matching dressing gowns for Christmas.*

Hispanic /hɪˈspæn.ɪk/ **adj** connected with Spain or Spanish-speaking countries, especially those countries in Latin America • **Hispanic noun** [C] *Hispanics make up a large proportion of the population of Miami.*

hiss /hɪs/ **verb; noun**

▸**verb** **1** [I] to make a noise like a long 's': *Why do snakes hiss?* ◦ *The iron was hissing and spluttering.* ◦ *People in the audience were hissing their disapproval.* **2** [T] to say something in a quiet angry way: *'Shut up, Tom!' she hissed.*

▸**noun** [C or U] a sound like the letter 's': *I heard a hiss and a pop as the cork came out of the bottle.*

hissy (fit) /ˈhɪs.iˌfɪt/ **noun** [C] informal a sudden period of uncontrolled and silly anger like a child's: *Sue* ***threw*** *a hissy when she found out.*

histamine /ˈhɪs.tə.miːn/ **noun** [U] specialized a chemical in the body that is released after an injury or during an ALLERGIC reaction

histogram /ˈhɪs.tə.græm/ **noun** [C] specialized a **bar chart/graph**

histology /hɪˈstɒl.ə.dʒi/ US /-ˈstɑː.lə-/ **noun** [U] specialized the scientific study of the structure of tissue from plants, animals, and other living things

historian /hɪˈstɔː.ri.ən/ US /-ˈstɔːr.i-/ **noun** [C] C1 someone who writes about or studies history

historic /hɪˈstɒr.ɪk/ US /-ˈstɔːr-/ **adj** B1 important or likely to be important in history: *historic buildings* ◦ *a historic day/moment* ◦ *In a historic vote, the Church of England decided to allow women to become priests.*

historical /hɪˈstɒr.ɪ.kəl/ US /-ˈstɔːr-/ **adj** **1** B1 connected with studying or representing things from the past: *Many important historical documents were destroyed when the library was bombed.* ◦ *She specializes in historical novels set in 18th-century England.* **2** used to describe prices, values, etc. in the past: *The table compares historical exchange rates for five different currencies.* • **historically** /-i/ **adv** C1 *The film makes no attempt to be historically accurate.* ◦ *Historically (= over a long period in the past), there have always been close links between France and Scotland.*

hisˌtoric ˈpresent **noun** [C usually singular] specialized the use of a verb in the present to describe past events, either informally, or to produce a special effect

history /ˈhɪs.tər.i/ US /-t̬ɚ-/ **noun** **PAST EVENTS** ▷ **1** A2 [C or U] (the study of or a record of) past events considered together, especially events of a particular period, country, or subject: *I studied modern European history at college.* ◦ *American history* ◦ *Annie's decided to write a history* ***of*** *electronic music.* ◦ *I only asked him for a cigarette, but two hours later he'd told me his whole* ***life*** *history.* **2** [U] informal something that happened or ended a long time ago and is not important now, or a person who is not important now, although they were in the past: *Last year's report is* ***ancient*** *history and totally irrelevant to the current situation.* ◦ *'What about Dan – are you still seeing him?' 'Oh, he's history.'* **PARTICULAR RECORD** ▷ **3** C1 [C usually singular] something that has been done or experienced by a particular person or thing repeatedly over a long period: *Her family* ***has a*** *history* ***of*** *heart problems.* ◦ *There's a long history* ***of*** *industrial disputes at the factory.* ◦ *He has a good* ***credit*** *history (= a good record of paying money that he owes).*

IDIOM **make history** to do something important that has not been done before and will be recorded publicly and remembered for a long time: *Margaret Thatcher made history when she became the first British woman prime minister.*

histrionic /ˌhɪs.triˈɒn.ɪk/ US /-ˈɑː.nɪk/ **adj** disapproving very emotional and energetic, but not sincere or without real meaning: *a histrionic outburst* ◦ *She put on a histrionic display of grief at the funeral.* • **histrionically** /-ˈɒn.ɪ.kəl.i/ US /-ˈɑː.nɪ.kəl.i/ **adv**

histrionics /ˌhɪs.triˈɒn.ɪks/ US /-ˈɑː.nɪks/ **noun** [plural] disapproving very emotional and energetic behaviour that is not sincere and has no real meaning: *I'd had enough of Lydia's histrionics.*

hit /hɪt/ **verb; noun**

▸**verb** (present tense **hitting**, past tense and past participle **hit**) **TOUCH** ▷ **1** A2 [T] to move your hand or an object onto the surface of something so that it touches it, usually with force: *Teachers are not allowed to hit their pupils.* ◦ *This type of glass won't shatter no matter how hard you hit it.* ◦ *She hit her thumb* ***with*** *the hammer.* **2** B1 [T] to touch something with sudden force: *They were going at about 60 kilometres an hour when their car hit the tree.* ◦ *One journalist was hit* ***in*** *the leg by a stray bullet.* ◦ *That new shelf in the bathroom is too low – I just hit my head* ***on*** *it.* **EFFECT** ▷ **3** B2 [T] to have an unpleasant or negative effect on a person or thing: *Production has been badly hit by the strike.* **4** C2 [T] If an idea or thought hits you, you suddenly think of it: *That's when it hit me that my life would never be the same again.* **SHOOT** ▷ **5** [T often passive] to shoot at or bomb a place or person, causing damage or injury: *Two schools were hit during the air raid.* ◦ *He was hit in* *the neck by a bullet from a sniper.* ◦ *Try to hit the middle of the target.* **REACH** ▷ **6** C1 [T] to arrive at a place or position: *If we turn left at the next junction, we should hit the main road after five miles or so.* **7** C1 [T] to succeed in reaching or achieving something: *Our profits hit an all-time high of £20 million last year.* ◦ *I just can't hit (= sing) those high notes like I used to.* **SUCCESS** ▷ **8 hit it off** informal B2 to like someone and become friendly immediately: *I didn't really hit it off **with** his friends.* ◦ *Jake and Sue hit it off immediately.* **ATTACK** ▷ **9** [T] mainly US slang to kill someone: *Three drug dealers were hit in the city over the weekend.*

Other ways of saying hit

Whack means the same as 'hit' but is slightly more informal:

*She **whacked** the water with her paddle.*

Bash is an informal word that means to hit someone or something hard:

*The swinging door **bashed** him in the face.*

Strike can be used when someone hits a person or thing hard:

*She had been **struck** on the head with a golf ball.*

If someone hits someone or something repeatedly, you could use the word **beat**:

*He was cruel to his dog and **beat** it with a stick.*

Punch or **thump** is used when someone hits a person with a fist:

*He **punched/thumped** me in the stomach.*

If someone hits a person with the flat part of the hand, the words **slap** or **smack** are often used:

*She **slapped** him across the face.*

*You shouldn't **smack** a child for lying.*

Deck is a slang word that you could use when someone hits a person so hard that the person falls over:

*If you do that again, I'll **deck** you.*

IDIOMS **hit sb between the eyes** to shock someone or have a sudden strong effect on them • **hit sb where it hurts** to do or say something to someone that will upset them as much as possible: *He's always worrying about his weight, so if you want to hit him where it hurts, tell him he's looking a bit fat.* • **hit home** to cause you to realize exactly how unpleasant or difficult something is: *The full horror of the war only hit home when we started seeing the television pictures of it in our living rooms.* • **hit the books** mainly US and Australian English informal to study: *I can't go out tonight. I've got to hit the books.* • **hit the bottle** to start to drink too much alcohol • **hit the ceiling/roof** to become extremely angry: *Dad'll hit the ceiling when he finds out I've left school.* • **hit the deck** to lie down quickly and suddenly so that you are hidden from view or protected from something dangerous • **hit the ground running** to immediately work hard and successfully at a new activity • **hit the hay/sack** informal to go to bed in order to sleep: *I've got a busy day tomorrow, so I think I'll hit the sack.* • **hit the headlines** to appear in the news suddenly or receive a lot of attention in news reports: *He hit the headlines two years ago when he was arrested for selling drugs to the prime minister's nephew.* • **hit the jackpot** to suddenly get or win a lot of money • **hit the nail on the head** to describe exactly what is causing a situation or problem: *I think Mick hit the nail on the head when he said that what's lacking in this company is a feeling of confidence.* • **hit the road** to leave a place or begin a journey: *I'd love to stay longer but I must be hitting the road.* • **hit the spot** to be exactly what is needed: *That bacon sandwich really hit the spot!* • **not know what hit you** to feel shocked or confused because something bad has happened to you suddenly when you were not expecting it

PHRASAL VERBS **hit back** to attack or criticize someone who has attacked or criticized you: *In tonight's speech, the minister is expected to hit back **at** critics who have attacked her handling of the crisis.* • **hit on sb** US slang to show someone that you are sexually attracted to them: *Some guy hit on me while I was standing at the bar.* • **hit on/upon sth** to think of an idea when you didn't expect or intend to, especially one that solves a problem • **hit out** to criticize something or someone strongly: *The Medical Association yesterday hit out **at** government cuts in healthcare services.* • **hit sb up** US informal to ask someone for something: *She hit me up **for** $20.*

▸noun [C] **SUCCESS** ▷ **1** B1 a thing or person that is very popular or successful: *The Beatles had a string of number-one hits in the 1960s.* ◦ *Your cake was a real hit at the party – everyone commented.* ◦ *They've just released an album of their **greatest** hits (= their most successful songs).* **INTERNET** ▷ **2** B2 a request to use a WEB PAGE on the internet that is then counted to calculate the number of people looking at the page: *Our page had 243 hits this week.* **TOUCH** ▷ **3** the act of hitting something or someone, or an occasion when something or someone hits you: *She gave him a hit **on** the head which knocked him flying.* **4** in baseball, when the BATTER (= person trying to hit the ball) safely reaches FIRST BASE after hitting the ball **SHOOT** ▷ **5** an occasion when something that has been thrown, dropped, shot, etc. at a place or object reaches that place or object: *The rebel headquarters took a **direct** hit from a bomb during the attack.* ◦ *I scored a hit on my second shot.* **ATTACK** ▷ **6** mainly US slang an act of murder: *He was the victim of a mafia hit.*

IDIOM **are/make a hit with** informal If you are/make a hit with someone, they like you a lot from the time that they first meet you: *You've made a big hit with my dad – he hasn't stopped talking about you.*

ˌhit-and-ˈmiss adj (also **ˌhit-or-ˈmiss**) If something is hit-and-miss you cannot depend on it to be of good quality, on time, accurate, etc.: *The trains are often late, so getting to work on time is a fairly hit-and-miss affair.*

ˌhit-and-ˈrun adj [before noun] **ACCIDENT** ▷ **1** describes a road accident in which the driver who caused the accident drives away without helping the other people involved and without telling the police: *a hit-and-run driver/accident* **MILITARY** ▷ **2** describes a military attack that needs to happen unexpectedly and quickly in order to be successful: *hit-and-run warfare*

hitch /hɪtʃ/ noun; verb

▸noun [C] a temporary difficulty which causes a short delay: *Due to a slight **technical** hitch the concert will be starting half an hour late.*

IDIOM **go (off) without a hitch** to happen successfully without any problems: *To the bride's relief, the wedding ceremony went off without a hitch.*

▸verb **RIDE** ▷ **1 hitch a lift/ride** informal to get a free ride in someone else's vehicle as a way of travelling: *They hitched a lift to Edinburgh from a passing car.* **FASTEN** ▷ **2** [T usually + adv/prep] to fasten something to another thing by tying it with a rope or using a metal HOOK: *The horses were hitched **to** a shiny black carriage.* ◦ *We just need to hitch the trailer (**on**)**to** the car and then we can go.*

PHRASAL VERB **hitch sth up** PULL STH UP ▷ **1** to pull something, especially trousers or a skirt, upwards to a slightly higher position: *She hitched her skirt up before wading across the stream.* CONNECT ▷ **2** If you hitch up a vehicle, you connect it so that it can be pulled, and if you hitch up an animal to a vehicle, you connect it so that it can pull the vehicle: *We watched as the farmer hitched up a team of oxen.*

hitched /hɪtʃt/ adj informal **get hitched** to get married: *Is Tracy really getting hitched then?*

hitchhike /ˈhɪtʃ.haɪk/ verb [I] B1 to travel by getting free rides in someone else's vehicle: *Women should never hitchhike on their own.* → See also **hitch** • **hitchhiker** /-haɪ.kəʳ/ US /–haɪ.kɚ/ noun [C] *Jack often* ***picks up*** *hitchhikers.*

hither /ˈhɪð.əʳ/ US /-ɚ/ adv old use or formal to or towards this place: *Come hither, young sir!*

H

IDIOM **hither and thither** (literary **hither and yon**) in many directions: *In clearer water, one encounters shoals of tiny fish, which dart hither and thither like flights of arrows.*

hitherto /ˌhɪð.əˈtuː/ US /-ɚ-/ adv formal until now or until a particular time: *Mira revealed hitherto* ***unsuspected*** *talents on the cricket pitch.*

ˈhit ˌlist noun [C usually singular] a list of people who someone intends to murder or take unpleasant action against: *The newspapers were sent a hit list of 100 military and political targets.*

hitman /ˈhɪt.mæn/ noun [C usually singular] (plural **-men** /-men/) a man who is paid to murder someone

ˈhit paˌrade noun [C] old-fashioned a list which shows which pop songs have sold the most copies in a particular week

HIV /ˌeɪtʃ.aɪˈviː/ noun [U] abbreviation for human immunodeficiency virus: the virus that causes AIDS (= a serious disease that destroys the body's ability to fight infection)

hive /haɪv/ noun; verb

▸noun BEES ▷ **1** [C, + sing/pl verb] a structure where BEES live, especially a BEEHIVE (= container like a box) or the group of bees living there SKIN CONDITION ▷ **2 hives** [U] a condition in which a person's skin develops red raised areas: *She* ***broke out in*** *hives after eating strawberries.*

IDIOM **a hive of activity/industry** a place where a lot of people are working very hard: *The whole house was a hive of activity on the day before the wedding.*

▸verb

PHRASAL VERB **hive sth off** UK to separate one part of a company, usually by selling it: *The plan is to hive off individual companies as soon as they are profitable.*

ˌHIV-ˈpositive adj If a person is HIV-positive, they are infected with HIV although they might not have AIDS (= a serious disease that destroys the body's ability to fight infection) or develop it for a long time.

hiya /ˈhaɪ.jə/ exclamation informal an expression said when people who know each other well meet: *Hiya, Pete, how're you doing?*

hmm /həm/ exclamation something you say when you pause while talking or when you are uncertain: *'Which one do you like best?' 'Hmm. I'm not sure.'*

HMP /ˌeɪtʃ.emˈpiː/ noun abbreviation for Her Majesty's Prison: used in the names of prisons in the UK: *He began his prison term at HMP Pentonville.*

HMS /ˌeɪtʃ.emˈes/ abbreviation for Her or His Majesty's Ship: used before the names of ships in the British navy: *HMS Illustrious*

HNC /ˌeɪtʃ.enˈsiː/ noun [C] abbreviation for Higher National Certificate: a qualification, especially in a scientific or technical subject, that is studied for at a British college

HND /ˌeɪtʃ.enˈdiː/ noun [C] abbreviation for Higher National Diploma: a qualification, especially in a scientific or technical subject, that is studied for at a British college

hoagie /ˈhəʊ.gi/ US /ˈhoʊ-/ noun [C] US a long thin LOAF of bread filled with salad and cold meat or cheese

hoard /hɔːd/ US /hɔːrd/ verb; noun

▸verb [T] to collect large amounts of something and keep it in a safe, often secret, place: *During the siege people began hoarding food and supplies.* • **hoarder** /ˈhɔː.dəʳ/ US /ˈhɔːr.dɚ/ noun [C]

▸noun [C] a large amount of something that someone has saved and hidden: *We found a huge hoard* ***of*** *tinned food in the basement.*

hoarding /ˈhɔː.dɪŋ/ US /ˈhɔːr-/ noun [C] UK ADVERTISEMENT ▷ **1** (US **billboard**) a very large board on which advertisements are shown, especially at the side of a road: *an advertising hoarding* FENCE ▷ **2** a temporary fence, usually made of boards, put around an area, especially one where people are building

hoarfrost /ˈhɔː.frɒst/ US /ˈhɔːr.frɑːst/ noun [U or C] a white layer of pieces of ice like needles that forms on objects outside when it is very cold

hoarse /hɔːs/ US /hɔːrs/ adj (of a voice or a person) having a rough voice, often because of a sore throat or a cold: *a hoarse* ***voice*** ◦ *She* ***sounded*** *a bit hoarse.* ◦ *You'll* ***make yourself*** *hoarse if you keep shouting like that!* → See also **husky** • **hoarsely** /hɔːs.li/ US /hɔːrs.li/ adv • **hoarseness** /hɔːs.nəs/ US /hɔːrs.nəs/ noun [U]

hoary /ˈhɔː.ri/ US /ˈhɔːr.i/ adj **1** old-fashioned very old and familiar and therefore not interesting or funny: *He told a few hoary* ***old*** *jokes and nobody laughed.* **2** literary (of a person) very old and with white or grey hair

hoax /həʊks/ US /hoʊks/ noun; verb

▸noun [C] a plan to deceive someone, such as telling the police there is a bomb somewhere when there is not one, or a trick: *The bomb threat turned out to be a hoax.* ◦ *He'd made a hoax* ***call*** *claiming to be the president.*

▸verb [T] to deceive, especially by playing a trick on someone • **hoaxer** /ˈhəʊk.səʳ/ US /ˈhoʊk.sɚ/ noun [C]

hob /hɒb/ US /hɑːb/ noun [C or] **1** UK (US **stove**, **stovetop**) the top part or surface of a cooker on which pans can be heated: *Most domestic hobs have four gas or electric rings.* **2** UK old-fashioned in the past, a metal shelf next to a FIREPLACE where pans were heated

hobble /ˈhɒb.l̩/ US /ˈhɑː.bl̩/ verb WALK ▷ **1** [I usually + adv/prep] to walk in an awkward way, usually because the feet or legs are injured: *The last time I saw Rachel she was hobbling around with a stick.* ◦ *Some of the runners could only manage to hobble over the finishing line.* LIMIT ▷ **2** [T] to limit something or control the freedom of someone: *A long list of amendments have hobbled the new legislation.* **3** [T] literary If you hobble an animal, especially a horse, you tie two of its legs together so that it cannot run away.

hobby /ˈhɒb.i/ US /ˈhɑː.bi/ noun [C] A2 an activity which someone does for pleasure when they are not working: *Ben's hobby is restoring vintage motorcycles.*

hobbyhorse /ˈhɒb.i.hɔːs/ US /ˈhɑː.bi.hɔːrs/ noun [C] SUBJECT ▷ **1** a subject that someone often talks about, usually for a long time: *Don't mention tax or Bernard'll* ***get on*** *his hobbyhorse again.* **TOY** ▷ **2** a toy made from a long stick with a shape like a horse's head at one end, which a child can pretend to ride

hobbyist /ˈhɒb.i.ɪst/ (US) /ˈhɑː.bi-/ **noun** [C] mainly US someone who does something as a hobby: *a computer hobbyist*

hobgoblin /ˌhɒbˈɡɒb.lɪn/ (US) /ˈhɑː.bˌɡɑː.blɪn/ **noun** [C] (in stories) a small ugly creature which causes trouble

hobnail boot /ˌhɒb.neɪlˈbuːt/ (US) /ˌhɑː.b-/ **noun** [C] (also ˌ**hobnailed** ˈ**boot**) a heavy boot or shoe that has NAILS fixed into the bottom to make it last longer

hobnob /ˈhɒb.nɒb/ (US) /ˈhɑː.b.nɑː.b/ **verb** [I] **(-bb-)** informal disapproving to spend time being friendly with someone who is important or famous: *She often has her picture in the papers, hobnobbing* ***with*** *the rich and famous.*

hobo /ˈhəʊ.bəʊ/ (US) /ˈhoʊ.boʊ/ **noun** [C] (plural **hoboes** or **hobos**) US someone who does not have a job or a house and who moves from one place to another

Hobson's choice /ˌhɒb.sənzˈtʃɔɪs/ (US) /ˌhɑː.b-/ **noun** [U] a situation in which it seems that you can choose between different things or actions, but there is really only one thing that you can take or do: *It's* ***a case of*** *Hobson's choice, because if I don't agree to their terms, I'll lose my job.*

hock /hɒk/ (US) /hɑːk/ **noun; verb**

▸**noun WINE** ▷ **1** [U] mainly UK a type of white wine from Germany **MONEY** ▷ **2 in hock a** in debt: *The company's entire assets are now in hock* ***to*** *the banks.* **b** Possessions that are in hock are PAWNED (= left temporarily with a person in exchange for an amount of money which must be paid back after a limited time to prevent the thing from being sold): *Most of her jewellery is in hock.* **ANIMAL** ▷ **3** [C] the middle JOINT in the back leg of an animal such as a horse **4** [C] mainly US the meat on the lower leg of an animal: *ham hocks*

▸**verb** [T] informal to sell something which you hope to buy back later because you need money now: *She had to hock her wedding ring.*

hockey /ˈhɒk.i/ (US) /ˈhɑː.ki/ **noun** [U] **1** A2 UK (US **field hockey**) a game played on a sports field between two teams of eleven players who each have a curved stick with which they try to put a small hard ball into the other team's goal **2** US for **ice hockey**

hocus-pocus /ˌhəʊ.kəsˈpəʊ.kəs/ (US) /ˌhoʊ.kəsˈpoʊ-/ **noun** [U] tricks used to deceive, or words used to hide what is happening or make it not clear

hod /hɒd/ (US) /hɑːd/ **noun** [C] a container for carrying bricks made of an open box on a pole that is held against the shoulder

hodgepodge /ˈhɒdʒ.pɒdʒ/ (US) /ˈhɑː.dʒ.pɑː.dʒ/ **noun** [C] a **hotchpotch**

hoe /həʊ/ (US) /hoʊ/ **noun** [C] a garden tool with a long handle and a short blade used to remove WEEDS and break up the surface of the ground

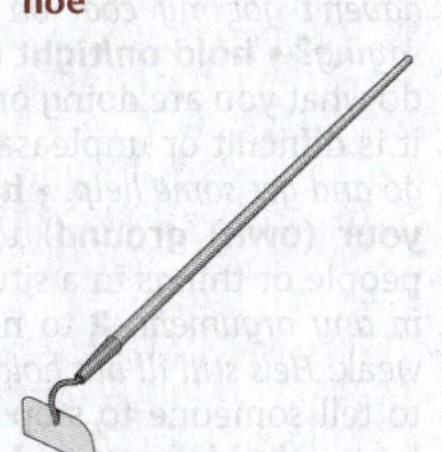

hoe

• **hoe verb** [I or T] **(hoeing, hoed, hoed)** *They spent the afternoon hoeing (the vegetable patch).*

hoedown /ˈhəʊ.daʊn/ (US) /ˈhoʊ-/ **noun** [C] in the US, a party, usually in the countryside, where there is traditional music and dancing

hog /hɒɡ/ (US) /hɑːɡ/ **noun; verb**

▸**noun** [C] **ANIMAL** ▷ **1** US a pig, especially one that is allowed to grow large so that it can be eaten **2** UK a male pig with its sexual organs removed, kept for its meat → Compare **boar, sow PERSON** ▷ **3** informal disapproving someone who takes much more than a fair share of something, especially by eating too much: *You've eaten it all? You hog!*

IDIOM **go hog wild** US informal to become too excited and eager about something, often so that you do too much: *There's no need to go hog wild just because it's Sarah's birthday – she won't want such a fuss.*

▸**verb** [T] **(-gg-)** informal to take or use more than your share of something: *He's always hogging the bathroom (= spending too much time in the bathroom, so that no one else can use it).*

IDIOM **hog the road** disapproving to drive so that other vehicles cannot go past

Hogmanay /ˈhɒɡ.mə.neɪ/ (US) /ˈhɑːɡ.mə.neɪ/ **noun** [C or U] UK in Scotland, the last day of the year and the parties to celebrate it which start in the evening and continue until the next day → See also **New Year's Eve**

hogwash /ˈhɒɡ.wɒʃ/ (US) /ˈhɑːɡ.wɑːʃ/ **noun** [U] informal nonsense, or words that are intended to deceive: *His answer was pure hogwash.*

ho-ho(-ho) /ˌhəʊˈhəʊ/ (US) /ˌhoʊˈhoʊ/ **exclamation** used in writing or sometimes spoken to represent the sound of laughter

ho-hum /ˌhəʊˈhʌm/ (US) /ˌhoʊ-/ **exclamation; adj**

▸**exclamation** an expression used when someone is bored, or when they accept that something unpleasant cannot be stopped from happening: *So I've got to do it all again. Ho-hum.*

▸**adj** boring or ordinary

hoick /hɔɪk/ **verb** [T + adv/prep] UK informal to raise or pull something, usually with a quick movement and with effort: *They hoicked the box onto the table.* ◦ *He hoicked* ***up*** *his trousers.*

the hoi polloi /ˌhɔɪ.pəˈlɔɪ/ **noun** [plural] disapproving or humorous ordinary people: *Anthony will be in the VIP lounge where he doesn't have to mix with the hoi polloi.*

hoist /hɔɪst/ **verb; noun**

▸**verb** [T] **1** to lift something heavy, sometimes using ropes or a machine: *A helicopter hoisted the final section of the bridge into place.* ◦ *With some difficulty he hoisted her onto his shoulders.* ◦ *I scrabbled for a handhold and hoisted my****self*** *up.* **2 hoist a flag** to raise a flag to the top of a pole using a rope

IDIOM **be hoist(ed) with/by your own petard** formal to suffer harm from a plan by which you had intended to harm someone else

▸**noun** [C] a device used for lifting heavy things

hoity-toity /ˌhɔɪ.tiˈtɔɪ.ti/ (US) /-t̬iˈtɔɪ.t̬i/ **adj** informal disapproving behaving as if you are better or more important than other people

hokey /ˈhəʊ.ki/ (US) /ˈhoʊ-/ **adj** US informal too emotional or artificial and therefore difficult to believe: *The ending of the movie was awful hokey.*

hoki /ˈhəʊ.ki/ (US) /ˈhoʊ-/ **noun** [C or U] a large sea fish from New Zealand which you can eat

hokum /ˈhəʊ.kəm/ (US) /ˈhoʊ-/ **noun** [U] mainly US informal a film, play, or television programme which does not show life as it really is: *As a whole the series was never less than watchable – hokum, perhaps, but entertaining.*

H

hold /həʊld/ (US) /hoʊld/ verb; noun

▸verb (**held, held**) **SUPPORT** ▷ **1** (A2) [T] to take and keep something in your hand or arms: *Can you hold the bag while I open the door?* ◦ *He was holding a gun.* ◦ *The little girl held her mother's* ***hand***. ◦ *He held her* ***in*** *his arms.* ◦ [+ obj + adj] *Could you hold the door* ***open****, please?* ◦ *Rosie held* ***out*** *an apple for the horse.* ◦ *All those who agree please hold* ***up*** *their hand (= raise their arm).* **2** [T] to support something: *Will the rope be strong enough to hold my weight?* ◦ *Each wheel is held* ***on*** *with four bolts.* ◦ *The parts are held* ***together*** *with glue.* **3 hold your nose** to press your nose tightly between thumb and finger in order to close it: *I have to hold my nose when I jump into water.* **4 hold hands** (A2) When two people hold hands, one person holds the other person's hand in their hand, especially to show that they love each other: *They walked along holding hands.* → See also **hand in hand** **CONTAIN** ▷ **5** (B1) [T not continuous] to contain or be able to contain something: *This jug holds exactly one pint.* ◦ *One bag won't hold all of the shopping – we'd better take two.* ◦ *Computers can hold huge amounts of information.* **6** [T not continuous] to have or contain something that a person will experience: *Who can tell what the future holds?* ◦ *She's very religious, so death holds no fear for her.* **CONTROL** ▷ **7** (C1) [T] to have something, especially a position or money, or to control something: *He currently holds the position of technical manager.* ◦ *The bank holds large reserves of gold.* ◦ *Despite incurring heavy losses, the rebels now hold the town and the surrounding hills.* **IN A COMPETITION** ▷ **8** (B2) [T] to have a particular position in a competition: *She holds the world* ***record***. ◦ *They held the* ***lead*** *until the 89th minute.* **KEEP** ▷ **9** (C1) [T] to keep something, especially when it might have been lost: *I asked the shop to hold the dress for me until this afternoon.* ◦ *You have to be a fairly good speaker to hold an audience's* ***attention/interest***. **10** (B2) [T] to keep someone in a place so that they cannot leave: *The police are holding several people* ***in custody*** *(= at the police station) for questioning.* ◦ [+ obj + noun] *The terrorists held him* ***hostage*** *for 18 months.* ◦ *I was held* ***prisoner*** *in a tiny attic room.* **MAKE HAPPEN** ▷ **11** (B1) [T] to have something such as a meeting or an election: *Could we hold a meeting to discuss this tomorrow afternoon?* ◦ *The election will be held on 8 August.* ◦ *I find it's almost impossible to hold a sensible conversation with her.* **CONTINUE** ▷ **12** [I or T] to cause to stay or continue in the same way as before: *Let's hope our good luck holds.* ◦ *I hope the repair holds until we get the car to a garage.* ◦ *The old adage that 'money talks' still holds* ***true*** *(= is still true).* ◦ *The government is committed to holding exports at their present level.* ◦ *The ship/aircraft held its course.* **BELIEVE** ▷ **13** [T not continuous] to believe an idea or opinion: [+ to infinitive] *Small amounts of alcohol are held* ***to*** *be good for the heart.* ◦ *You sold it to me, so if it breaks I'll hold you* ***responsible*** *(= make you take responsibility).* **DELAY** ▷ **14** [I or T] to wait, or to stop something temporarily: *They've decided to hold all future deliveries until the invoice has been paid.* ◦ *How long can you hold your* ***breath*** *(= stop breathing)?* ◦ *Will you hold my calls for the next half hour please?* ◦ *She's on the phone at the moment – will you hold (****the line****) (= wait on the phone until she can speak to you)?* **NOT INCLUDE** ▷ **15** [T] US If you ask someone to hold something, you do not want them to include it: *I'd like a ham sandwich on rye, hold the lettuce.*

IDIOMS **can't hold a candle to** to not be as good as the person or thing mentioned: *Her latest book is readable enough, but it can't hold a candle to her earlier work.* • **can't hold your drink** (US usually **can't hold your liquor**) If you can't hold your drink, you feel ill quickly when you drink alcohol. • **don't hold your breath** informal used to tell someone not to expect something to happen for a very long time: *She said she'd get back to us, but don't hold your breath!* • **hold all the cards** to be in a strong position when you are competing with someone else, because you have all the advantages: *Management holds all the cards when it comes to the negotiations over job cuts.* • **hold court** humorous to receive a lot of attention from other people who stand or sit round you to listen, especially on a social occasion • **hold down a job** (C2) to manage to keep a job for a period of time • **hold everything!** informal used to tell someone to stop what they are doing: *Hold everything! He's changed his mind again.* • **hold good** to continue to be true: *Their arguments were valid a hundred years ago and they still hold good today.* • **hold your head (up) high** to be very confident and proud: *If you know that you did your best, you can hold your head high.* • **hold your horses** old-fashioned informal used to tell someone to stop and consider carefully their decision or opinion about something: *Just hold your horses, Bill! Let's think about this for a moment.* • **hold it!** informal used to tell someone to wait or stop doing something: *Hold it! I haven't got my coat on yet.* ◦ *Hold it! What are you saying?* • **hold on/tight** to make yourself continue to do what you are doing or stay where you are although it is difficult or unpleasant: *If you can just hold on I'll go and get some help.* • **hold your own 1** (C2) (also **hold your (own) ground**) to be as successful as other people or things in a situation: *Josie can hold her own in any argument.* **2** to not become more ill or more weak: *He's still ill but holding his own.* • **hold still** used to tell someone to stop moving: *Hold still, this won't hurt.* • **hold sway** to have power or a very strong influence: *Fundamentalist beliefs hold sway* ***over*** *whole districts, ensuring the popularity of religious leaders.* • **hold that thought** used for telling someone

Other ways of saying **hold**

Clasp or **grip** can be used when you hold something very tightly:

The baby ***gripped*** *my finger with her tiny hand.*

He reached out to ***clasp*** *Lindsay's hand.*

Clutch is often used when someone holds something tightly, especially because of fear, anxiety, or pain:

Silent and pale, she ***clutched*** *her mother's hand.*

If someone holds something and does not want to let go, you could use the verb **cling**:

One little girl was ***clinging*** *onto a cuddly toy.*

Hang on is used when someone continues holding something:

The child was ***hanging on*** *to her mother's skirt.*

If you hold someone or something gently, especially by supporting that person or thing in your arms, you could use the verb **cradle**:

She ***cradled*** *him tenderly in her arms.*

Grasp or **grab** can be used when someone suddenly reaches out and holds something:

She ***grasped*** *his hand in a gesture of sympathy.*

He ***grabbed*** *the rope and pulled it hard.*

You could use the verb **wield** if someone is holding a weapon or tool and looks as if he or she is going to use it:

We found him ***wielding*** *a power drill on the deck of his beach house.*

to remember an idea or thought that has just been mentioned, especially because it will be useful later • **hold the floor** to speak to a group of people, often for a long time, without allowing anyone else to speak • **hold (down) the fort** humorous to have responsibility for something while someone is absent: *I'll be out of the office for a few hours – will you hold the fort until I get back?* • **hold the key** to have control of something: *Because the two main parties have won almost the same number of votes, the minority group holds the key **to** the result.* • **hold the reins** be in control • **hold the road** If a vehicle holds the road, its wheels stay firmly on the road and do not slide while moving. → See also **roadholding** • **hold your tongue** to not speak: *Hold your tongue, young man!* ◦ *I'm going to have to learn to hold my tongue (= to not say things that upset people).* • **hold water** C2 If a reason, argument, or explanation holds water, it is true: *Her alibi just didn't hold water.* • **there is no holding sb (back)** If there is no holding someone (back), they do something eagerly and cannot be stopped.

PHRASAL VERBS **hold it/that against sb** C2 to like someone less because they have done something wrong or behaved badly in the past: *He made a mistake but I don't hold it against him – we all make mistakes.* • **hold back** to not do something, often because of fear or because you do not want to make a bad situation worse: *He held back, terrified of going into the dark room.* • **hold sb/sth back** STOP DEVELOPMENT ▷ **1** C2 to stop someone or something developing or doing as well as they should: *She felt that having children would hold her back.* STOP MOVEMENT ▷ **2** C1 If you hold someone or something back, you stop them from coming or moving forward: *Sandbags will hold the flood waters back for a while.* • **hold sth back 1** C1 to keep information secret from someone deliberately **2** C2 to stop yourself showing an emotion: *He spoke slowly, to hold back his growing anger.* • **hold sb/sth down** to keep someone or something in a particular place or position and to stop them from moving: *He was struggling so much it took three officers to hold him down.* • **hold sth down** to keep something, especially costs, at a low level: *to hold down prices/wages* • **hold forth** usually disapproving to talk about a particular subject for a long time, often in a way that other people find boring: *She held forth all afternoon **about/on** government incompetence.* • **hold off** NOT DO ▷ **1** C2 to not do something immediately: [+ -ing verb] *Let's hold off mak**ing** a decision until next week.* ◦ US *They've decided to hold off **on** buy**ing** a car until they're both working.* RAIN/STORM ▷ **2** If rain or a storm holds off, it does not start immediately. • **hold sb off** to stop someone from attacking or defeating you: *How much longer will the resistance fighters be able to hold off the enemy?* • **hold on** WAIT ▷ **1** B1 informal used to tell someone to wait for a short time: *Hold on, I'll check in my diary.* **2** C1 informal used to say that you are confused or surprised by something that you have just heard or read and want to understand it: *Now hold on, Ed, that wasn't what we agreed at all!* **3** C1 to manage to stay alive or to deal with a difficult situation: *We just had to hold on until help arrived.* HOLD ▷ **4** to hold something or someone firmly with your hands or arms: *She held on tightly to his waist.* • **hold onto sb/sth** C2 to hold something or someone firmly with your hands or your arms: *Hold onto the rope and don't let go.* • **hold onto/on to sth** to keep something you have: *Hold on to your ticket – you'll need it later.* ◦ *Lewis held onto the lead until the final lap.* • **hold out** DEFEND ▷ **1** to continue to defend yourself against an enemy or attack without being defeated: *They won't be able to hold out much longer under this sort of bombardment.* SUPPLY OF STH ▷ **2** If a supply of something such as food or money holds out, there is enough of it to last for a particular period of time. • **hold sth out** C2 to offer a possibility, solution, hope, etc.: *Few people hold out any **hope** of finding more survivors.* • **hold out for sth** to wait until you get what you want: *The workers are holding out for a ten percent pay rise.* ◦ *The other side are holding out for a higher price.* • **hold out on sb 1** informal to refuse to give help or information to someone: *Don't hold out on me – I need to know who did it.* **2** mainly US informal to refuse to give money to someone • **hold sth over** US If a film, play, etc. is held over, it is shown or performed more times than was originally planned, usually because it is very popular with the public. • **hold sb to sth** to make someone do what they promised or agreed to do: *We'll hold him to the exact terms of the contract.* • **hold up** to remain strong or successful: *Will his alibi hold up (= continue to seem true) in court?* ◦ *I hope the repairs hold up until we can get to a garage.* • **hold sb/sth up** DELAY ▷ **1** B1 to delay someone or something: *Traffic was held up for several hours by the accident.* STEAL ▷ **2** to steal from someone using violence or the threat of violence: *They held the same bank up twice in one week.* ◦ *He was held up at gunpoint by a gang of masked youths.* • **hold sth up as sth** (also **hold up sth as sth**) to use someone or something as an example of something, especially something very good: *Sweden is often held up as an example of a successful social democracy.* • **not hold with sth** formal to not approve of an idea or activity

▸noun SUPPORT ▷ **1** B2 [S or U] the act of holding something or someone, or the way you do this: *Keep a tight hold **on** your tickets.* ◦ *Don't worry if you **lose** hold **of** the reins – the horse won't wander off.* → See also **foothold, handhold, toehold 2 catch/get/grab/take hold of sth/sb** B2 to start holding something or someone: *He took hold of one end of the carpet and tugged.* ◦ *I just managed to grab hold of Lucy before she fell in the pool.* **3** [C] in fighting sports, a position in which one person holds another person so that they cannot move part of their body **4** [C] a place to put the hands and feet, especially when climbing CONTROL ▷ **5** C2 [S] power or control over something or someone: *Their company has a **strong** hold **on/over** the computer market.* DELAY ▷ **6 on hold a** C1 If you are on hold when using the phone, you are waiting to speak to someone: *Mr Briggs is on hold.* ◦ *His phone is engaged – can I **put** you on hold?* **b** C1 If an activity is on hold, it has been intentionally delayed: *Everything's on hold again because of the bad weather.* ◦ *The film's been **put** on hold until the financial situation improves.* SPACE ▷ **7** [C] the space in a ship or aircraft in which goods are carried

IDIOMS **get hold of** UK (US **get ahold of**) **1** B2 informal to find someone or obtain something: *Where can I get hold of some stamps?* ◦ *How can I get ahold of Chris?* **2** mainly UK to understand something: *This is a very difficult concept to get hold of.* • **no holds barred** without limits or controls: *This is comedy with no holds barred.*

holdall /ˈhəʊld.ɔːl/ US /ˈhoʊld.ɑːl/ **noun** [C] mainly UK (US usually **carryall**) a small case used for carrying clothes and personal things when travelling

holder /ˈhəʊl.dəʳ/ US /ˈhoʊl.dɚ/ **noun** [C] CONTAINER ▷ **1** a device for putting objects in or for keeping them in place: *a toothbrush holder* ◦ *a cigarette holder* OWNER ▷ **2** someone who officially owns something:

an account/licence/passport holder ◦ Holders of shares in the company receive various benefits. → See also **shareholder**

holding /ˈhəʊl.dɪŋ/ (US) /ˈhoʊl-/ **noun** [C] something that you own such as SHARES in a company or buildings, or land which you rent and farm: *To ensure security the investment fund has holdings in many companies.*

ˈholding ˌcompany noun [C] a company whose main purpose is to control another company or companies through owning SHARES in it or them

ˈholding opeˌration noun [C usually singular] UK a temporary way of dealing with a situation until a new and better way can be introduced: *This is just a holding operation until we get the new management structure sorted out.*

holdout /ˈhəʊld.aʊt/ (US) /ˈhoʊld-/ **noun** [C] a person, organization, or country that continues to do something, despite other people trying to force them not to: *It's time to shame holdouts into signing the treaty.*

H

ˈhold-up noun **DELAY** ▷ **1** [C] informal a delay: *Come on, let's go. What's the hold-up?* **CRIME** ▷ **2** [C] an occasion when someone steals from someone else using violence or the threat of violence **CLOTHING** ▷ **3 hold-ups** [plural] STOCKINGS (= light coverings for the legs and feet) that hold themselves up by a piece of sticky material or ELASTIC at the top

hole /həʊl/ (US) /hoʊl/ **noun; verb**

▸**noun** [C] **SPACE** ▷ **1** (B1) an empty space in an object, usually with an opening to the object's surface, or an opening which goes completely through an object: *We **dug** a hole and planted the tree.* ◦ *My jumper's got a hole **in** it.* ◦ *Drill a hole through the back of the cupboard and pass the wires through.* **2** in GOLF, one of the small circular spaces in the ground into which the ball is hit **3** in golf, one of the usually 18 areas of play: *an 18-hole course* **PLACE** ▷ **4** a place in the ground where a small animal lives: *a mouse/rabbit/fox hole* **5** informal a small unpleasant place where someone lives: *What a hole that house was – I'm so pleased we moved.* → See also **hole in the wall** **FAULT** ▷ **6** a mistake or problem in an argument, discussion, plan, etc.: *The new proposal has several holes **in** it.*

> **!** Common mistake: **hole or whole?**
>
> **Warning:** Choose the right word!
> These two words sound the same, but they are spelled differently and have completely different meanings.

IDIOMS **be in a hole** UK informal to be in a difficult or an embarrassing situation: *We've lost the order and we're in a bit of a hole.* • **be in the hole** US informal to be in debt: *After selling all its assets, the bank was still half a million dollars in the hole.* • **a hole in one** in golf, an occasion when someone's ball goes into the hole the first time they hit it • **make a hole in sth** UK to reduce an amount of money by a lot: *The holiday made a big hole in our savings but I'm glad we went.* • **need sth like you need a hole in the head** humorous to not need or want something at all: *Extra work? I need that like I need a hole in the head.*

▸**verb** [T] specialized to make a hole in something, especially a ship or boat: *A torpedo holed the ship below the water and it quickly sank.*

IDIOM **be holed up** to be hiding in a safe place: *The robbers were holed up in a deserted warehouse.*

PHRASAL VERB **hole up (somewhere)** informal to stay in a safe place, often as a way of avoiding something or hiding from someone: *We'd better find some shelter and hole up until the storm passes.*

ˌhole in the ˈheart noun [C] a medical condition in which there is an extra opening between the main parts of the heart

ˌhole in the ˈwall noun [C usually singular] **MONEY** ▷ **1** UK informal for **cash machine** **BUILDING** ▷ **2** US a small, often unpleasant, shop, house, or restaurant: *It's just a hole in the wall but the food is good.*

ˈhole ˌpunch noun [C] (also **hole puncher** /ˈhəʊlˌpʌn.tʃəʳ/ (US) /ˈhoʊlˌpʌn.tʃɚ/) a device used for making holes in pieces of paper so that they can be fastened together

holiday /ˈhɒl.ɪ.deɪ/ (US) /ˈhɑː.lɪ-/ **noun; verb**

▸**noun 1** (A1) [C or U] UK (UK informal **holidays**, UK informal **hols**, US **vacation**) a time, often one or two weeks, when someone does not go to work or school but is free to do what they want, such as travel or relax: *a camping/skiing holiday* ◦ *Have you decided where you're going **for** your holiday(s) this year?* ◦ *Patricia is **on** holiday next week.* ◦ *How many days' holiday do you get with your new job?* ◦ *We thought we'd go to France for our **summer** holiday.* ◦ *Surely the **school** holidays start soon.* **2** (B1) [C] an official day when you do not have to go to work or school: *a public holiday* ◦ *St Patrick's Day is a holiday in Ireland.*

> Word partners for **holiday**
>
> *book/go on/have/take* a holiday • a *summer* holiday • a *lovely/wonderful* holiday • be *on* holiday

▸**verb** [I usually + adv/prep] UK (US **vacation**) to take a holiday: *My parents are holidaying **in** Spain this year.*

ˈholiday ˌcamp noun [C] UK a place where people on holiday can stay and different types of entertainment are provided for them

holidaymaker /ˈhɒl.ə.diˌmeɪ.kəʳ/ (US) /ˈhɑː.lə.deɪˌmeɪ.kɚ/ **noun** [C] UK (US **vacationer**) a person who is on holiday away from where they usually live

ˈholiday ˌpackage noun [C] Australian English a holiday at a fixed price in which the travel company arranges your travel, hotels, and sometimes meals for you → Compare **package tour**

the ˈholiday ˌseason noun [S] mainly US the period around Christmas and New Year

ˌholier-than-ˈthou adj disapproving If a person is holier-than-thou, they think that they are morally better than anyone else.

holiness /ˈhəʊ.li.nəs/ (US) /ˈhoʊ-/ **noun** [U] the quality of being holy

Holiness /ˈhəʊ.li.nəs/ (US) /ˈhoʊ-/ **noun His/Your Holiness** a title used when talking to or about the Pope: *Yes, Your Holiness.*

holism /ˈhəʊ.lɪ.zᵊm/ (US) /ˈhoʊl.ɪ-/ **noun** [U] the belief that each thing is a whole that is more important than the parts that make it up

holistic /həˈlɪs.tɪk/ (US) /hoʊlˈɪs-/ **adj** dealing with or treating the whole of something or someone and not just a part: *My doctor takes a holistic **approach** to disease.* ◦ *Ecological problems usually require holistic solutions.* • **holistically** /-tɪ.kᵊl.i/ **adv**

hoˌlistic ˈmedicine noun [U] treatment which deals with the whole person, not just the injury or disease

hollandaise /ˌhɒl.ənˈdeɪz/ (US) /ˌhɑː.lənˈ-/ **noun** [U] (also **ˌhollandaise ˈsauce**) a sauce made from egg YOLKS (= the yellow parts) and butter, usually with lemon juice added

holler /ˈhɒl.əʳ/ (US) /ˈhɑː.lɚ/ **verb** [I or T] mainly US informal to shout loudly: *He was hollering something* *about seeing a snake.* • **holler** noun [C] *He* ***let out*** *a holler as he fell.*

hollow /ˈhɒl.əʊ/ (US) /ˈhɑː.loʊ/ **adj; verb; noun**

▸adj **EMPTY** ▷ **1** (B2) having a hole or empty space inside: *a hollow tube* ◦ *Hollow blocks are used because they are lighter.* **2 hollow cheeks/eyes** If someone has hollow cheeks or eyes, their cheeks curve in or their eyes look deep in their head because they are old, tired, or ill. **NOT SINCERE** ▷ **3** (C2) (of situations, feelings, or words) without value, or not true or sincere: *It was something of* ***a*** *hollow* ***victory*** *– she won the case but lost all her savings in legal fees.* ◦ *Will their good intentions become realities or are they just hollow promises?* **SOUND** ▷ **4** (of sound) as if made by hitting an empty container: *a hollow sound* ◦ *This tree trunk* ***sounds*** *hollow.* • **hollowness** /-nəs/ **noun** [U] *the hollowness of fame/success*

IDIOM **ring/sound hollow** (C2) If something someone says rings hollow, it does not sound true or sincere.

▸verb

PHRASAL VERB **hollow sth out** to make an empty space inside something: *Sand carried by the wind has hollowed out the base of the cliff.*

▸noun [C] **1** a hole or empty space in something, or a low area in a surface: *The dog found a hollow in the ground to hide in from the wind.* **2** US a valley: *We used to go for long walks in the hollow.* ◦ *Sleepy Hollow*

ˌhollow-ˈcheeked adj describes a person whose face is too thin

ˌhollow-ˈeyed adj describes a person whose eyes seem to have sunk into their face because of illness or tiredness

hollowly /ˈhɒl.əʊ.li/ (US) /ˈhɑː.loʊ.li/ **adv** **NOT SINCERE** ▷ **1** in a way that does not sound true or sincere **SOUND** ▷ **2** making a sound as if hitting an empty container

holly /ˈhɒl.i/ (US) /ˈhɑː.li/ **noun** [C or U] a small EVERGREEN tree (= one that never loses its leaves) with shiny, sharp leaves and small, round, red fruit

hollyhock /ˈhɒl.i.hɒk/ (US) /ˈhɑː.li.hɑːk/ **noun** [C] a garden plant that has very tall stems covered with brightly coloured flowers

Hollywood /ˈhɒl.i.wʊd/ (US) /ˈhɑː.li-/ **noun** the centre of the US film industry

holocaust /ˈhɒl.ə.kɔːst/ (US) /ˈhɑː.lə.kɑːst/ **noun** [C] a very large amount of destruction, especially by fire or heat, or the killing of very large numbers of people: *A* ***nuclear*** *holocaust (= destruction caused by nuclear weapons) would leave few survivors.*

the Holocaust /ˈhɒl.ə.kɔːst/ (US) /ˈhɑː.lə.kɑːst/ **noun** [S] the killing of millions of Jews and others by the NAZIS before and during the Second World War

hologram /ˈhɒl.ə.græm/ (US) /ˈhɑː.lə-/ **noun** [C] a special type of photograph or image made with a LASER in which the objects shown look solid, as if they are real, rather than flat

holography /hɒlˈɒg.rə.fi/ (US) /hoʊˈlɑː.grə-/ **noun** [U] the activity of making holograms • **holographic** /ˌhɒl.əˈgræf.ɪk/ (US) /ˌhɑː.lə-/ **adj** *a holographic picture/image/projection*

hols /hɒlz/ (US) /hɑːlz/ **noun** [plural] UK informal for **holiday**

Holstein /ˈhɒl.staɪn/, /ˈhəʊl-/ (US) /ˈhoʊl.stiːn/ **noun** [C] US for **Friesian**

holster /ˈhəʊl.stəʳ/ (US) /ˈhoʊl.stɚ/ **noun** [C] a small case usually made of leather and fixed on a belt or a strap, used for carrying a gun

holy /ˈhəʊ.li/ (US) /ˈhoʊ-/ **adj** **RELIGIOUS** ▷ **1** (C1) related to a religion or a god: *holy scriptures/rites* **2** very religious or pure: *a holy person* **FOR EMPHASIS** ▷ **3 holy cow, mackerel, shit, etc.!** mainly US informal used to show surprise, fear, etc.: *Holy cow! How did you get that black eye?*

ˌHoly Comˈmunion noun [U] formal **Communion**

the ˌholy ˈgrail noun [S] **1** (also **the Holy Grail**) a cup believed to have been used by Jesus Christ at the meal before his death **2** something that is extremely difficult to find or get: *Sustained nuclear fusion is the holy grail of the power industry.*

the ˌholy of ˈholies noun [S] **1** the holiest part of a religious building, especially the Jewish TEMPLE **2** UK humorous any place that is very special: *This football stadium is the holy of holies to many fans.*

ˌholy ˈorders noun [plural] the ceremony by which someone becomes a priest in some parts of the Christian Church: *Will you be* ***taking*** *holy orders?*

the ˌHoly ˈSee noun the government of the Roman Catholic Church, under the POPE

ˌHoly ˈSpirit noun [S] (also **ˌHoly ˈGhost**) in the Christian Church, God in the form of a spirit

the ˌHoly ˈTrinity noun [S] **the Trinity**

ˌholy ˈwar noun [C] a war fought to defend religious beliefs or to force others to follow a different religion → See also **crusade, jihad**

ˈHoly ˌWeek noun [S] the week before Easter Sunday

homage /ˈhɒm.ɪdʒ/ (US) /ˈhɑː.mɪdʒ/ **noun** [U] deep respect and often praise shown for a person or god: *On this occasion we* ***pay*** *homage* ***to*** *him for his achievements.*

homburg /ˈhɒm.bɜːg/ (US) /ˈhɑːm.bɝːg/ **noun** [C] a man's hat with a wide curled BRIM and a fold in the middle of the top

> **! Common mistake: home**
>
> **Warning:** to talk about movement towards or away from someone's own home, you do not need a preposition.
>
> Don't say 'go/come/arrive/leave to/at home', say **go/come/arrive/leave home**:
>
> ~~*When I arrived to home, I realized my bag was missing.*~~
>
> *When I arrived home, I realized my bag was missing.*
>
> To talk about someone moving towards or away from a home that is not their own, it is usual to use a preposition:
>
> *You are welcome to come to my home.*

home /həʊm/ (US) /hoʊm/ **noun; adj; verb**

▸noun **HOUSE/APARTMENT** ▷ **1** (A1) [C or U] the house, apartment, etc. where you live, especially with your family: *The senator has two homes – an apartment in Washington and a house in Colorado.* ◦ *He was living on the streets for three months, and his home was a cardboard box.* ◦ *Phone me* ***at*** *home after four o'clock.* ◦ *I* ***took*** *home a couple of books to read.* ◦ *He* ***left*** *home (= stopped living with his parents) when he was 23.* ◦ *More and more couples are* ***setting up*** *home together without getting married.* **2** [C] a house, apartment, etc. when it is considered as property that you can buy or sell: *luxury/starter homes* **3** [C] the type of family you come from: *We had a happy home.* ◦ *children from a* ***broken*** *home (= from a family in which the parents had separated)* **4** (C1) [C] a place where people or animals live and are cared for by people who are not their relations or owners: *a children's home/an old people's home/a dogs' home* ◦ *He spent his early years* ***in a*** *home.*

H

ORIGIN ▷ **5** (A1) [C or U] someone's or something's place of origin, or the place where a person feels they belong: *I live in London, but my home (= where I was born) is in Yorkshire.* ◦ *I was actually born in New Zealand, but I've lived in England for so long that it **feels like** home now.* **COUNTRY** ▷ **6** [C or U] your own country or your own area: *I wonder what they're doing **back** home.* **7 be/play at home** If a sports team are/play at home, they play on their own sports field.

IDIOMS **be home and dry** (Australian English **be home and hosed**) to have successfully finished something: *We just have to finish this section, then we're home and dry.* • **be home free** US informal to be certain to succeed at something because you have done the most difficult part of it: *Once you leave the main road and cross the bridge, you're home free – we live just three houses further on.* • **be/feel at home** (B1) to feel comfortable and relaxed: *By the end of the week she was beginning to feel at home **in** her new job.* • **bring sth home (to sb)** to make someone understand something much more clearly than they did before, especially something unpleasant: *When I saw for myself the damage that had been caused, that really brought home to me the scale of the disaster.* • **come home to sb** If something comes home to someone, they understand it clearly: *The danger really came home to me when I saw the pictures on TV.* • **drive/hammer sth home** to say something clearly and with a lot of force so that you are certain people understand it: *She really drove home the message that we need to economize.* • **home from home** UK (US **home away from home**) a place where you feel as comfortable as you do in your own home: *The hotel was a real home from home.* • **make yourself at home** (C1) to relax and make yourself comfortable in someone else's home

▸**adj** [before noun] **DONE/USED AT HOME** ▷ **1** done at home, or intended to be used at home: *home cooking* ◦ *home-brewed beer* ◦ *a home computer* **COUNTRY** ▷ **2** connected with or done in your own country: *His books were a success in his home **market**, but failed to find an audience abroad.* **SPORTS** ▷ **3** relating to the place where a team is based and plays a lot of its games: *the home team/side* ◦ *a home match*

▸**verb**

PHRASAL VERB **home in on sth/sb** informal **1** to aim for: *The missile homed in on the ship.* **2** to find and give a lot of attention to something or someone: *The report homed in on the weaknesses in the management structure.*

ˌhome adˈdress noun [C usually singular] the address of the house or apartment you live in

ˌhome ˈbase noun **BASEBALL** ▷ **1** [U] **home plate** **PLACE** ▷ **2** [C usually singular] a place where someone or something usually lives, works, or operates from

homeboy /ˈhəʊm.bɔɪ/ (US) /hoʊm-/ noun [C] (also **homey**) US slang a boy or man from your own town, or someone who is a close friend or a member of your GANG

ˌhome ˈbrew noun [C or U] beer that someone makes at home

homecoming /ˈhəʊmˌkʌm.ɪŋ/ (US) /ˈhoʊm-/ noun **ARRIVAL** ▷ **1** [C] the fact of a person arriving home after being away for a long time: *They planned a special celebration for her homecoming.* **CELEBRATION** ▷ **2** [C or U] US a celebration at a school or a college to honour people who were students there earlier

the ˌHome ˈCounties noun [plural] the COUNTIES (= areas) around London in southeast England, considered to be a place where rich people live

ˌhome ecoˈnomics noun [U] at school, the study of cooking, sewing, and subjects relating to the management of a home

the ˌhome ˈfront noun [S] the people who stay in their own country during a foreign war

homegrown /ˌhəʊmˈgrəʊn/ (US) /ˌhoʊmˈgroʊn/ adj **1** from your own garden: *homegrown vegetables* **2** If someone or something is homegrown, they belong to or were developed in your own country: *She's a homegrown talent.*

ˌhome ˈhelp noun [C] UK someone who is paid to help someone else with the cleaning of their home

homeland /ˈhəʊm.lænd/ (US) /ˈhoʊm-/ noun [C] **1** the country you were born in **2** (in the past) one of the areas in South Africa in which black people were separated from whites under the political system of APARTHEID

ˌhomeland seˈcurity noun **1** [U] activities and organizations whose purpose is to protect the US from attacks within the country by TERRORISTS **2 Homeland Security** the department of the US government that deals with homeland security

homeless /ˈhəʊm.ləs/ (US) /ˈhoʊm-/ adj; noun

▸**adj** (C1) without a home

> **! Common mistake: homeless**
>
> **Remember: homeless** is an adjective.
>
> To talk about people who do not have a home, don't say 'homeless', say **the homeless** or **homeless people**:
>
> *The charity provides shelter for the homeless.*
>
> *The charity provides shelter for homeless people.*

▸**noun** [plural] **the homeless** (C1) people who do not have a home, usually because they are poor • **homelessness** /-nəs/ noun [U] (C2) *One common cause of homelessness is separation or divorce.*

ˈhome ˌloan noun [C] money borrowed from a bank or similar organization in order to buy a house or apartment

homely /ˈhəʊm.li/ (US) /ˈhoʊm-/ adj **PLAIN** ▷ **1** UK (US **homey**) plain or ordinary, but pleasant: *The hotel was homely and comfortable.* **UGLY** ▷ **2** US disapproving describes a person who is ugly • **homeliness** /-nəs/ noun [U]

homemade /ˌhəʊmˈmeɪd/ (US) /ˌhoʊm-/ adj made at home and not bought from a shop: *homemade bread/cakes* ◦ *homemade wine*

homemaker /ˈhəʊmˌmeɪ.kəʳ/ (US) /ˈhoʊmˌmeɪ.kɚ/ noun [C] mainly US a woman who manages a home and often raises children instead of earning money from a job → Compare **house husband**

ˌhome ˈmovie noun [C] a film that you make yourself using a VIDEO CAMERA, especially one of family or holiday activities

ˌhome (ˈphone) ˌnumber noun [C usually singular] the phone number at the house or apartment where you live

ˈHome ˌOffice noun the British government department that deals with matters inside Britain that are not the responsibility of other departments, for example JUSTICE and the rules for people from other countries entering Britain

homeopath (UK also **homoeopath**) /ˈhəʊ.mi.ə.pæθ/ (US) /ˈhoʊ.mi.oʊ-/ noun [C] a person who treats ill people by homeopathy

homeopathy (UK also **homoeopathy**) /ˌhəʊ.miˈɒp.ə.

θi/ (US) /ˌhoʊ.miˈɑː.pə-/ **noun** [U] a system of treating diseases in which ill people are given very small amounts of natural substances which, in healthy people, would produce the same effects as the diseases produce • **homeopathic** (UK also **homoeopathic**) /-əˈpæθ.ɪk/ (US) /-oʊˈpæθ.ɪk/ **adj** *homeopathic medicine/remedies*

homeostasis /ˌhəʊ.mi.əʊˈsteɪ.sɪs/ (US) /ˌhəʊ.mi.oʊˈ-/ **noun** [U] specialized the ability or TENDENCY of a living organism, cell, or group to keep the conditions inside it the same despite any changes in the conditions around it, or this state of INTERNAL balance: *Warm-blooded animals are able to achieve temperature homeostasis.*

homeothermic /ˌhəʊ.mi.əʊˈθɜː.mɪk/ (US) /ˌhəʊ.mi.oʊˈθɜː-/ **adj** specialized If a living organism is homeothermic, it is able to keep its body temperature at the same level despite any change in the temperature around it: *Homeothermic animals are often described as warm-blooded.* • **homeotherm** /ˈhəʊ.mi.əʊˌθɜː.m/ (US) /ˈhəʊ.mi.oʊˌθɜːm/ **noun** [C] specialized a homeothermic animal

homeowner /ˈhəʊmˌəʊ.nəʳ/ (US) /ˈhoʊmˌoʊ.nɚ/ **noun** [C] a person who owns their house or apartment

ˈhome ˌpage **noun** [C usually sing] **1** the first page of a website, which gives an introduction to the business or organization it belongs to and LINKS (= connections) to more detailed information on other pages **2** a WEB PAGE that you choose to appear on your computer screen when you first connect to the internet: *To make this your home page, click here.*

ˈhome ˌplate **noun** [S] (US informal **the plate**) in baseball, the place that the player has to stand next to in order to hit the ball, and the last place they have to touch to score a point

homer /ˈhəʊ.məʳ/ (US) /ˈhoʊ.mɚ/ **noun** [C] US informal a **home run**

homeroom /ˈhəʊm.ruːm/ (US) /ˈhoʊm-/ **noun** US **1** [C] (UK **form room**) a room in a school where members of a particular group of students go for their teacher to record that they are present, usually at the beginning of the day **2** [U] (UK **registration**) the period of time, usually at the beginning of the day, when students meet for their teacher to record that they are present, give out information, etc.

ˌhome ˈrule **noun** [U] a political arrangement in which a part of a country governs itself independently of the central government of the country

ˌhome ˈrun **noun** [C] (informal **homer**) US a point scored in baseball by hitting the ball so far that you have time to run all the way round the four corners of the playing field before it is returned

homeschool /ˌhəʊmˈskuːl/ (US) /ˌhoʊm-/ **verb** [I or T] to teach a child at home rather than sending him or her to school: *All her kids were homeschooled.*

homeschooling /ˌhəʊmˈskuː.lɪŋ/ (US) /ˌhoʊm-/ **noun** [U] the teaching of children at home, usually by parents

ˌHome ˈSecretary **noun** [C] the British government politician who controls the HOME OFFICE

ˌhome ˈshopping **noun** [U] shopping from home by ordering goods from a magazine, a television programme, or from the internet

homesick /ˈhəʊm.sɪk/ (US) /ˈhoʊm-/ **adj** unhappy because of being away from home for a long period: *As I read my mother's letter, I began to* ***feel*** *more and more homesick.* • **homesickness** /-nəs/ **noun** [U]

homespun /ˈhəʊm.spʌn/ (US) /ˈhoʊm-/ **adj** (of beliefs, theories, etc.) simple and ordinary: *homespun philosophy/wisdom*

homestead /ˈhəʊm.sted/ (US) /ˈhoʊm-/ **noun; verb**

▸**noun** [C] **1** mainly US a house and the surrounding area of land usually used as a farm **2** US in the past, land given by the government for farming

▸**verb** [I or T] US in the past, to build a house and grow crops on land given by the government

homesteader /ˈhəʊmˌsted.əʳ/ (US) /ˈhoʊmˌsted.ɚ/ **noun** [C] US someone who goes to live and grow crops on land given by the government, especially in the past: *In the 1800s, thousands of homesteaders settled on the prairies of the western US.*

ˌhome ˈstraight **noun** [S] UK (US **ˌhome ˈstretch**) **1** the last part of something that is being done: *It's taken three months, but we're* ***on*** *the home straight now.* **2** the last part of a race

hometown /ˈhəʊm.taʊn/ (US) /ˈhoʊm-/ **noun** [C] the town or city that a person is from, especially the one in which they were born and lived while they were young: *He was born in Bristol, but he considers London his hometown since he's lived there most of his life.*

ˌhome ˈtruth **noun** [C] mainly UK a true but unpleasant fact about yourself that another person tells you: *He decided it was time to tell her a few home truths.*

homewards /ˈhəʊm.wədz/ (US) /ˈhoʊm.wɚdz/ **adv** (also **homeward** /ˈhəʊm.wəd/ (US) /ˈhoʊm.wɚd/) towards home: *After three hours cycling we decided to turn homewards.* • **homeward adj**

homework /ˈhəʊm.wɜːk/ (US) /ˈhoʊm.wɜːk/ **noun** [U] (A1) work which teachers give their students to do at home: *You can't watch TV until you've* ***done*** *your homework.* ◦ *history/geography homework*

IDIOM **do your homework** to study a subject or situation carefully so that you know a lot about it and can deal with it successfully: *It was obvious that she had done her homework and thoroughly prepared for her interview.*

homeworker /ˈhəʊmˌwɜː.kəʳ/ (US) /ˈhoʊmˌwɜː.kɚ/ **noun** [C] someone who does their job at home rather than in an office, factory, etc.

homey /ˈhəʊ.mi/ (US) /ˈhoʊ-/ **noun; adj**

▸**noun** [C] (also **homie**) US slang **homeboy**

▸**adj** US for **homely**

homicidal /ˌhɒm.ɪˈsaɪ.dəl/ (US) /ˌhɑː.mə-/ **adj** likely to murder: *a homicidal* ***maniac***

homicide /ˈhɒm.ɪ.saɪd/ (US) /ˈhɑː.mə-/ **noun** [C or U] US formal or legal (an act of) murder: *He was convicted of homicide.* ◦ *The number of homicides in the city has risen sharply.*

homily /ˈhɒm.ɪ.li/ (US) /ˈhɑː.mə-/ **noun** [C] disapproving a piece of spoken or written advice about how someone should behave: *He launched into a homily* ***on*** *family relationships.*

homing /ˈhəʊ.mɪŋ/ (US) /ˈhoʊ-/ **adj** [before noun] **1** relating to the ability of some animals to find their way home: *Migrating birds and fish have a strong homing* ***instinct.*** **2** (of an electronic device) producing a special signal so that it can be found using electronic equipment: *The president's car is equipped with a homing* ***device.***

ˈhoming ˌpigeon **noun** [C] a PIGEON (= a type of bird) that is trained to return to its home from any place that it starts its journey → See also **carrier pigeon, racing pigeon**

hominy /ˈhɒm.ə.ni/ (US) /ˈhɑː.mə-/ **noun** [U] US dried MAIZE that is boiled and eaten

H

homoerotic /ˌhəʊ.məʊ.ɪˈrɒt.ɪk/ (US) /ˌhoʊ.moʊ.ɪˈrɑː.t̬ɪk/ **adj** (of art, literature, etc.) connected to or causing sexual DESIRE for a person of the same sex: *homoerotic photographs/literature*

homogeneous /ˌhɒm.əˈdʒiː.ni.əs/, /ˌhəʊ.mə-/ (US) /ˌhoʊ.moʊˈdʒiː-/ **adj** consisting of parts or people that are similar to each other or are of the same type: *a homogeneous group/society* ◦ *The population of the village has remained remarkably homogeneous.* → Compare **heterogeneous** • **homogeneity** /ˌhɒm.ə.dʒəˈneɪ.ɪ.ti/ (US) /ˌhɑː.mə.dʒəˈneɪ.ə.t̬i/ **noun** [U] *cultural/racial homogeneity*

homogenized specialized (UK usually **homogenised**) /həˈmɒdʒ.ɪ.naɪzd/ (US) /həˈmɑː.dʒə-/ **adj** describes milk that has been treated so that the cream is mixed into the other parts of the liquid

homogenous /ˌhɒm.əˈdʒiː.ni.əs/, /ˌhəʊ.mə-/ (US) /ˌhoʊ.moʊˈdʒiː-/ **adj** **homogeneous**

H

homograph /ˈhɒm.ə.grɑːf/ (US) /ˈhɑː.mə.græf/ **noun** [C] specialized a word that is spelled the same as another word but has a different meaning: *'Bow' meaning the front of a ship, 'bow' meaning a loop made in a string or ribbon and 'bow' meaning a device used to shoot arrows are all homographs.*

homologous /həˈmɒl.ə.gəs/ (US) /hoʊˈmɑː.lə-/ **adj** **1** formal having a similar position, structure, value, or purpose **2** specialized in biology, having the same origin although now having a different purpose or shape as a result of EVOLUTION (= gradual change over millions of years): *The wing of a bat and the arm of a man are homologous structures.*

homonym /ˈhɒm.ə.nɪm/ (US) /ˈhɑː.mə-/ **noun** [C] a word that sounds the same or is spelled the same as another word but has a different meaning: *'No' and 'know' are homonyms.* ◦ *'Bow' (= bend at the waist) and 'bow' (= weapon) are also homonyms.*

homophobia /ˌhəʊ.məˈfəʊ.bi.ə/ (US) /ˌhoʊ.məˈfoʊ-/ **noun** [U] a fear or dislike of gay people • **homophobic** /-bɪk/ **adj** *a homophobic attitude*

homophone /ˈhɒm.ə.fəʊn/ (US) /ˈhɑː.mə.foʊn/ **noun** [C] specialized a word that is pronounced the same as another word but has a different meaning or spelling, or both: *The words 'sow' and 'sew' are homophones.*

Homo sapiens /ˌhəʊ.məʊˈsæp.i.enz/ (US) /ˌhoʊ.moʊ-/ **noun** [U] specialized humans considered together as a type of animal

homosexual /ˌhəʊ.məˈsek.sju.əl/ (US) /ˌhoʊ.moʊˈsek.ʃu.əl/ **noun** [C] a person, especially a man, who is sexually attracted to people of the same sex and not to people of the opposite sex • **homosexual** **adj** *homosexual sex/relationships* • **homosexuality** /-ˌsek.sjuˈæl.ə.ti/ (US) /-sek.ʃuˈæl.ə.t̬i/ **noun** [U] *I've never been ashamed of my homosexuality.*

homozygous /ˌhɒm.əˈzaɪ.gəs/ (US) /ˌhoʊ.mə-/ **adj** specialized having two of the same form of GENE (= part of a cell containing DNA information) that controls a particular characteristic and is therefore able to pass on that form only: *a homozygous cell* → Compare **heterozygous** • **homozygote** /-gəʊt/ (US) /-goʊt/ **noun** [C] specialized a homozygous person, animal, or organism

Hon. /ɒn/ (US) /ɑːn/ **adj** [before noun] **1** abbreviation for **Honourable**, when used as a title: *The report was written by a recently appointed judge, the Hon. Mr Justice Carlton.* **2** UK abbreviation for **honorary**, when used as part of a title: *the Hon. Treasurer*

honcho /ˈhɒn.tʃəʊ/ (US) /ˈhɑːn.tʃoʊ/ **noun** [C] mainly US informal the person in charge: *Who's the **head** honcho round here?*

hone /həʊn/ (US) /hoʊn/ **verb** [T] **MAKE SHARP** ▷ **1** to make an object sharp: *The bone had been honed **to** a point.* **MAKE PERFECT** ▷ **2** to make something perfect or completely suitable for its purpose: *His physique was honed **to perfection**.* ◦ *Her debating skills were honed in the students' union.*

honest /ˈɒn.ɪst/ (US) /ˈɑː.nɪst/ **adj** (B1) telling the truth or able to be trusted and not likely to steal, cheat, or lie: *She's completely honest.* ◦ *I'd like you to give me an honest answer/your honest opinion.* ◦ *He had an honest face (= he looked like he could be trusted).* ◦ *To be honest (**with** you), I don't think it will be possible.* → Opposite **dishonest**

> **Other ways of saying honest**
>
> See also: **sincere**
>
> The adjective **straight** is often used instead of honest:
>
> *Just be **straight** with her and tell her how you feel.*
> *I don't think he is being entirely **straight** with me.*
>
> If someone is honest and does not tell lies, you can describe that person as **truthful**:
>
> *Are you being **truthful** with me?*
>
> If someone is honest and not likely to steal or cheat, you can describe that person as **trustworthy**:
>
> *In a small town, if someone isn't **trustworthy**, everyone knows it.*
>
> The adjective **reputable** is often used for a business that is honest and will not try to cheat people:
>
> *Make sure you insure your home with a **reputable** company.*
>
> A business arrangement that is honest can be described as **above board**:
>
> *The deal was completely open and **above board**.*
>
> The adjectives **candid**, **frank**, or **open** are used when someone is honest about personal feelings even if they are embarrassing:
>
> *We had a very **candid** discussion.*
> *He's quite **open** about his weaknesses.*
> *To be **frank**, I didn't know what I was doing.*

IDIOMS **honest (to God/goodness)** informal used to emphasize that what you are saying is true: *I tried to be nice to him, honest to God I did!* • **make an honest living** humorous to earn money by working hard at a job • **make an honest woman (out) of sb** informal humorous to marry a woman you are having a sexual relationship with

ˌhonest ˈbroker **noun** [C] someone who speaks to both sides involved in an argument or disagreement and tries to help them to agree

honestly /ˈɒn.ɪst.li/ (US) /ˈɑː.nɪst-/ **adv**; **adv, exclamation**

▸**adv** (B2) in a way that is honest: *They have always dealt honestly and fairly with their customers.* ◦ *I can't honestly say what time I'll be home.* ◦ *I'll do it tomorrow, honestly (= I promise that I will do it).*

▸**adv, exclamation** (B1) used to emphasize disapproval: *Honestly, you'd think she'd have asked you first!*

ˌhonest-to-ˈgoodness **adj** [before noun] real or true: *The book is an honest-to-goodness account of her early life.*

honesty /ˈɒn.ə.sti/ (US) /ˈɑː.nə-/ **noun** [U] (B2) the quality of being honest: *I appreciate your honesty.* ◦ *I must tell you **in all** honesty (= truthfully and hiding nothing) that there is little chance of the scheme being approved.*

IDIOM **honesty is the best policy** saying said to advise someone that it is better to tell the truth than to lie

honey /ˈhʌn.i/ **noun** **SWEET SUBSTANCE** ▷ **1** (A2) [U] a sweet, sticky, yellow substance made by BEES and used as food: UK *set honey/runny honey* ◦ *clover honey* **PERSON** ▷ **2** [as form of address] mainly US a name that you call someone you love or like very much: *Hi, honey, I'm home!*

honeybee /ˈhʌn.i.biː/ noun [C] a type of BEE that lives with others in a HIVE and makes honey

honeycomb /ˈhʌn.i.kəʊm/ (US) /-koʊm/ noun **1** [C or U] a WAX structure containing many small holes, made by BEES to store their honey **2** [C] something with a similar structure: *The hotel complex was a honeycomb **of** rooms and courtyards* (= there were many small rooms and passages). • **honeycombed** /-kəʊmd/ (US) /-koʊmd/ adj [after verb] *The tomb was honeycombed **with** passages and chambers.*

honeycomb

honeydew /ˈhʌn.i.djuː/ (US) /-duː/ noun **STICKY SUBSTANCE** ▷ **1** [U] a sticky substance similar to honey, left on leaves by some types of insect **FRUIT** ▷ **2** [C or U] (also **honeydew melon**) a type of MELON (= large fruit with a thick skin) that has white, green, or yellow skin and sweet flesh with a lot of juice

honeyed /ˈhʌn.id/ adj **honeyed tones/words/voice** describes speech or a person's voice when it is gentle and pleasant to listen to, sometimes in a way that is not sincere

honeymoon /ˈhʌn.i.muːn/ noun; verb

▸noun **1** (B1) [C or U] a holiday taken by a couple immediately after their marriage: *Where are you going **on** your honeymoon?* **2** [C usually singular] (also **honeymoon period**) a short period at the beginning of a new job, government, etc. when there is no criticism from anyone

▸verb [I usually + adv/prep] to go on a honeymoon: *They are honeymooning **in** the Bahamas.* • **honeymooners** /-muːnəz/ (US) /-muːnɚz/ noun [plural] people who are on their honeymoon: *The hotel is a favourite with honeymooners.*

honeysuckle /ˈhʌn.iˌsʌk.l̩/ noun [C or U] a climbing plant with flowers that smell sweet

ˈhoney ˌtrap noun [C usually singular] UK **1** something that is very attractive: *The Tower of London is a honey trap **for** tourists.* **2** the use of an attractive person to try to get information from someone: *Police set up a honey trap to get him to confess to the crime.*

honk /hɒŋk/ (US) /hɑːŋk/ verb; noun

▸verb [I or T] **SOUND** ▷ **1** If a GOOSE or a car horn honks, it makes a short, loud sound. **VOMIT** ▷ **2** UK slang to vomit: *He honked **(up)** all over the floor.*

▸noun [C] a short, loud sound made by a car horn or a GOOSE: *He gave us a honk on his horn as he drove off.*

honky /ˈhɒŋ.ki/ (US) /ˈhɑːŋ-/ noun [C] US slang offensive a word used by some black people to refer to a white person

honky-tonk /ˈhɒŋ.ki.tɒŋk/ (US) /ˈhɑːŋ.ki.tɑːŋk/ adj; noun

▸adj [before noun] connected with an informal type of JAZZ piano playing: *a honky-tonk piano* ◦ *honky-tonk music*

▸noun [C] US a noisy, cheap bar with loud jazz or COUNTRY (= traditional) music

honor /ˈɒn.əʳ/ (US) /ˈɑː.nɚ/ noun US for **honour**

honorable /ˈɒn.ər.ə.bl̩/ (US) /ˈɑː.nɚ-/ adj US for **honourable**

honorably /ˈɒn.ər.ə.bli/ (US) /ˈɑː.nɚ-/ adv US for **honourably**

honorarium /ˌɒn.əˈreə.ri.əm/ (US) /ˌɑː.nəˈrer.i-/ noun [C] (plural **honorariums** or **honoraria**) formal a usually small amount of money paid to someone for a service for which no official charge is made: *We usually offer our visiting lecturers an honorarium of £50.*

honorary /ˈɒn.ər.ə.ri/ (US) /ˈɑː.nə.rer.i/ adj **1** (especially of a degree) given as an honour to someone who has not done a course of study: *She received an honorary doctorate from Exeter University in recognition of her work for the homeless.* **2** An honorary position in an organization is one for which no payment is made: *Charities often have a well-known person as their honorary treasurer.*

honorific /ˌɒn.əˈrɪf.ɪk/ (US) /ˌɑː.nəˈrɪf-/ adj [before noun] formal showing or giving honour or respect: *an honorific title*

ˈhonors deˌgree noun [C] (formal **degree with honors**) in the US, a degree from a school, college, or university that shows that a student has done work of a very high standard → Compare **honours degree**

honour /ˈɒn.əʳ/ (US) /ˈɑː.nɚ/ noun; verb

▸noun UK (US **honor**) **RESPECT** ▷ **1** (B2) [U] a quality that combines respect, being proud, and honesty: *a man of honour* ◦ *We fought for the honour of our country.* **2 in honour of sb/sth** (B2) in order to celebrate or show great respect for someone or something: *a banquet in honour of the president* **3 be/feel honour bound to do sth** to feel you must do something because it is morally right, even if you do not want to do it: *I felt honour bound to tell him the truth.* **4 do sb the honour of doing sth** formal to make someone proud and happy by doing or being something: *Would you do me the honour of accompanying me to the New Year Ball?* **5 Your Honour** formal the way to address a judge **REWARD** ▷ **6** [C] a reward, prize, or title that publicly expresses admiration or respect: *She received an honour for her services to the community.* ◦ *He was buried with **full military honours*** (= with a special celebration to show respect). **7 with honours** If you complete a school or university qualification with honours, you achieve a high standard.

IDIOMS **be on your honour** old-fashioned If you are on your honour to do something, you are being trusted to do something that you have promised. • **do the honours** humorous to pour drinks or serve food: *John, will you do the honours?*

▸verb [T] UK (US **honor**) **RESPECT** ▷ **1** (C1) to show great respect for someone or something, especially in public: *He was honoured **for** his bravery.* ◦ formal *We are honoured* (= proud and happy) *to have you here tonight.* ◦ *I would be honoured to meet him.* **2** To honour a promise or agreement is to do what you said you would: *They decided not to honour an existing order for aircraft.* **REWARD** ▷ **3** to give someone public praise or a reward: *He was honoured **with** a knighthood.*

honourable UK (US **honorable**) /ˈɒn.ər.ə.bl̩/ (US) /ˈɑː.nɚ-/ adj honest and fair, or deserving praise and respect: *an honourable person* • **honourably** (US **honorably**) /-ə.bli/ adv

Honourable UK (US **Honorable**) /ˈɒn.ər.ə.bl̩/ (US) /ˈɑː.nɚ-/ adj (abbreviation **Hon.**) **the Honourable** a title used before the name of some government officials, and in the UK before the names of some people of high social rank: *the Honourable Andrew Robinson*

ˌhonourable ˈmention noun [C] a prize given in a competition for work of high quality which did not receive first, second, or third prize

H

ˈ**honours deˌgree** noun [C] (formal **degree with honours**) in the UK, a first university degree, based especially on one subject → Compare **honors degree**

ˈ**honours ˌlist** noun [S] in the UK, the list of people who receive a title and public praise as a reward for things they have done

hooch (also **hootch**) /huːtʃ/ noun [U] US slang strong alcohol, especially WHISKY

hood /hʊd/ noun [C] **CLOTHING** ▷ **1** B2 part of a piece of clothing that can be pulled up to cover the top and back of the head: *The coat has a detachable hood.* **2** a bag that is put over someone's head so that they cannot see or be recognized: *The prisoners had been tortured and made to wear hoods.* **COVER** ▷ **3** a part which covers or shelters a piece of equipment: *The hood over the air vent is loose.* **CAR** ▷ **4** US for **bonnet** **PLACE** ▷ **5** (also **'hood**) US slang a poor NEIGHBOURHOOD: *When he started he was just a poor boy from the hood – now he's a multimillionaire.*

-hood /-hʊd/ suffix used to form nouns describing the state of being a particular thing: *priesthood* ◦ *childhood/manhood* ◦ *nationhood*

hooded /ˈhʊd.ɪd/ adj **CLOTHES** ▷ **1** having a hood: *a hooded jacket* ◦ *armed and hooded intruders* **EYES** ▷ **2** describes EYELIDS that are large and cover the eyes more than usual: *He watched her from under hooded eyelids.*

hoodie (also **hoody**) /ˈhʊd.i/ noun [C] informal **1** a SWEATSHIRT (= cotton clothing for the upper body) that has a hood to cover the head **2** a person who wears a hoodie

hoodie

hoodlum /ˈhuːd.ləm/ noun [C] (also **hood**) a violent person, especially one who is member of a group of criminals

hoodwink /ˈhʊd.wɪŋk/ verb [T] to deceive or trick someone: *He hoodwinked us **into** agreeing.*

hoof /huːf/ noun; verb

▸noun [C] (plural **hoofs** or **hooves**) the hard part on the bottom of the feet of animals such as horses, sheep, and DEER → Compare **paw**

IDIOM **on the hoof** UK informal If you do something on the hoof, you do it while you are moving about or doing something else, often without giving it the attention it deserves: *I've got a meeting downtown in 20 minutes so I'll have lunch on the hoof.*

▸verb [T] informal to kick a ball: *The defender hoofed the ball up the field.*

IDIOM **hoof it** informal to walk somewhere, or to walk somewhere quickly: *We missed the bus and had to hoof it.*

ˌ**hoof-and-ˈmouth (diˌsease)** noun [U] US for **foot-and-mouth**

hoo-ha /ˈhuː.hɑː/ noun [S or U] informal an occasion when there is too much interest in or discussion about something that is not important: *One of the tabloids published the pictures and they caused a great hoo-ha.*

hook /hʊk/ noun; verb

▸noun [C] **DEVICE** ▷ **1** B2 a curved device used for catching or holding things, especially one fixed to a surface for hanging things on: *a coat/picture hook* ◦ *a fish hook* **HIT** ▷ **2** a way of hitting in BOXING, cricket, or GOLF: *a right/left hook* ◦ *a hook shot*

IDIOMS **by hook or by crook** by any method possible: *I decided I was going to get that job by hook or by crook.* • **fall for sth hook, line, and sinker** to completely believe something that someone tells you that is not true: *She told him she needed the money for her baby and he fell for it hook, line, and sinker.* • **get your hooks into sb/sth** to get control or influence over someone or something: *This product has really got its hooks into the American market.* • **off the hook 1** If you leave the phone off the hook, you do not put it back correctly and it will not ring. **2** If you are off the hook, you have escaped from a difficult situation: *John's agreed to go to the meeting in my place so that **gets/lets** me off the hook.*

▸verb **DEVICE** ▷ **1** [T] to fasten something with a hook, hang something on a hook, or catch something with a hook: *He hooked the trailer (= joined it with a hook) to his car.* ◦ *How many salmon did you hook (= catch) this afternoon?* ◦ *She hooked the shoe (= lifted it with a hook) out of the water.* **HAVE SEX** ▷ **2** [I] US informal to have sex for money

PHRASAL VERBS **hook up 1** informal to meet or begin to work with another person or other people: *He hooked up **with** the other members of the band in Amsterdam.* **2** informal to begin a romantic or sexual relationship with someone: *When did you two first hook up?* • **hook (sb/sth) up to sth** to connect a machine to a power supply or to another machine, or to connect a person to a piece of medical equipment: *Can we hook up to the electricity supply at the campsite?* ◦ *Helen was unconscious and hooked up to a life support machine.*

hookah /ˈhʊk.ə/ noun [C] a type of pipe which brings smoke through a container of water before it is breathed in

ˌ**hook and ˈeye** noun [C usually singular] a device for fastening clothes, consisting of a small bent piece of metal into which a hook fits

hooked /hʊkt/ adj **CANNOT STOP** ▷ **1** B2 [after verb] informal enjoying something so much that you are unable to stop having it, watching it, doing it, etc.: *I was hooked after two episodes.* **2** [after verb] informal unable to stop taking a drug: *to be hooked **on** cocaine* **NOSE** ▷ **3** describes a nose that is large and curved

hooker /ˈhʊk.əʳ/ US /-ɚ/ noun [C] **SEX** ▷ **1** informal a PROSTITUTE (= woman who has sex for money) **SPORT** ▷ **2** a RUGBY player who pulls the ball out of the SCRUM with his foot

ˌ**hook-ˈnosed** adj Someone who is hook-nosed has a large nose that curves out from the face.

hookup /ˈhʊk.ʌp/ noun [C] a connection between two or more things, places, or people using electronic equipment: *We hope to bring you a live report from Ouagadougou via our **satellite** hookup.*

hooky /ˈhʊk.i/ noun mainly US informal **play hooky** to stay away from school without permission

hooligan /ˈhuː.lɪ.gən/ noun [C] a violent person who fights or causes damage in public places: *Hooligans had sprayed paint all over the car.* • **hooliganism** /-ɪ.zəm/ noun [U] *football/soccer hooliganism*

hoop /huːp/ noun [C] **1** a ring of wood, metal, or plastic: *The dogs had been trained to jump through hoops.* **2** (also **hoop earring**) a ring-shaped EARRING (= a piece of jewellery which hangs from the ear): *She was wearing large gold hoops in her ears.*

IDIOM **go/jump through hoops** to do a lot of difficult things before you are allowed to have or do something you want

hoopla /ˈhuː.plɑː/ noun **GAME** ▷ **1** [U] UK (US **ringtoss**) a game in which a ring is thrown so that it falls over an object: *a game of hoopla* **EXCITEMENT** ▷ **2** [S or U] mainly US exciting noise and activity in celebration of an event

hooray /hʊˈreɪ/, /hə-/ exclamation, noun **hurray**

hooroo /hʊˈruː/ exclamation Australian English informal for **goodbye**

hoot /huːt/ noun; verb

▸noun [C] **1** a short loud high sound: *She gave three short hoots on the car horn.* ◦ *He gave a hoot **of** laughter/derision.* **2** the sound an OWL makes

IDIOMS **be a hoot** informal to be very funny: *He's an absolute hoot.* • **not care/give two hoots** (also **not care/give a hoot**) to not care about something or someone: *I don't give two hoots what she thinks.*

▸verb **1** [I or T] to make a short loud high sound: *She hooted her horn **at** the dog in the road.* ◦ *He hooted **with** laughter.* **2** [I] to make the sound that an OWL makes

hooter /ˈhuː.təʳ/ (US) /-t̬ɚ/ noun **NOSE** ▷ **1** [C] UK old-fashioned informal a nose **DEVICE** ▷ **2** [C] old-fashioned an electrical device which makes a loud noise, often to mark the start or end of work at a factory **BREASTS** ▷ **3 hooters** [plural] US slang a woman's breasts. This use of the word is considered offensive.

Hoover /ˈhuː.vəʳ/ (US) /-vɚ/ noun [C] UK trademark a **vacuum** • **hoover** verb [I or T] UK *He was busy hoovering the bedroom carpet when I got home.* • **hoovering** /-vəʳ.ɪŋ/ (US) /-vɚ.ɪŋ/ noun [U] *Could you **do** the hoovering?*

hooves /huːvz/ plural of **hoof**

hop /hɒp/ (US) /hɑːp/ verb; noun; adj

▸verb (**-pp-**) **1** C2 [I] to jump on one foot or to move about in this way: *I tried to hop on my good foot while holding onto Jim.* **2** C1 [I + adv/prep] informal to go somewhere quickly or to get into or out of a vehicle quickly: *We hopped over to Bruges for the weekend.* ◦ *I hopped on the bus at the traffic lights.* **3** C2 [I] If a small animal, bird, or insect hops, it moves by jumping on all or two of its feet at the same time: *The rabbit/bird hopped across the grass.*

IDIOMS **hop it** UK old-fashioned informal used to tell someone to go away • **hopping mad** old-fashioned very angry

▸noun **JUMP** ▷ **1** [C] a short jump by a person on one foot, or by a small animal, bird, or insect on all or two of its feet at the same time: *With his feet tied together he could only move in little hops.* **2 be a short hop** informal to be a short journey or distance, especially in an aircraft: *London to Edinburgh is just a short hop by plane.* **PLANT** ▷ **3 hops** [plural] the dried fruits of a climbing plant, used to give a bitter flavour to beer

IDIOM **catch sb on the hop** UK informal to do something when someone is not ready for it and is not able to deal with it: *I'm afraid you've caught me on the hop – I wasn't expecting you till next week.*

▸adj [before noun] relating to hops: *a hop plant*

hope /həʊp/ (US) /hoʊp/ verb; noun

▸verb [I or T] A2 to want something to happen or to be true, and usually have a good reason to think that it might: *I'm hoping **for** an interview next week.* ◦ [+ (that)] *She's hoping (**that**) she won't be away too long.* ◦ *I hope (**that**) she'll win.* ◦ *We have to hope **and pray** (**that**) the operation will go well.* ◦ [+ to infinitive] *They hope **to** visit us next year.* ◦ *It's good news, I hope.* ◦ *'Will you be at the meeting tomorrow?' 'I hope **not/so**'.* → Compare **wish**

> **!** Common mistake: **hope**
>
> **Remember:** when **hope** is followed by another verb, the verb must be in the infinitive with 'to'.
>
> Don't say 'hope to doing something', say **hope to do something**:
>
> ~~*I hope to hearing from you soon.*~~
>
> *I hope to hear from you soon.*

IDIOMS **hope against hope** to hope very strongly that something will happen, although you know it is not likely: *They're just hoping against hope that she's still alive.* • **hope for the best** to hope that something will be successful or happen in the way you want, even if it seems unlikely: *I've repaired it as well as I can – we'll just have to hope for the best.*

▸noun [C or U] B1 something good that you want to happen in the future, or a confident feeling about what will happen in the future: *What are your hopes and dreams **for** the future?* ◦ *Is there any hope **of** getting financial support for the project?* ◦ [+ that] *Is there any hope **that** they will be home in time?* ◦ *Young people are growing up in our cities without any hope **of** finding a job.* ◦ *His reply **dashed** (= destroyed) our hopes.* ◦ *They have **pinned** (**all**) their hopes **on** (= they are depending for success on) their new player.* ◦ *She's very ill, but there's still hope/we **live in** hope (= we think she might be cured).* ◦ *The situation is now **beyond/past** hope (= unlikely to produce the desired result).* ◦ *We never **gave up** hope (= stopped hoping) that she would be found alive.* ◦ *The letter offered us **a glimmer/ray of** (= a little) hope.* ◦ *I didn't phone till four o'clock **in the** hope **that** you'd be finished.* ◦ *I **don't hold out much** hope of getting (= I don't expect to be able to get) a ticket.*

> Word partners for **hope noun**
>
> *bring/give/offer* hope • *raise* (sb's) hopes • *abandon/give up/lose* hope • not *hold out any/much* hope • *pin* your hopes *on* sb/sth • *faint/fresh/great/vain* hope • a *glimmer/ray* of hope • hope *of* sth/doing sth

IDIOM **not have a hope in hell** informal to have no possibility of doing or achieving something: *We were so outclassed – we didn't have a hope in hell of winning.*

ˈhope ˌchest noun [C usually singular] US for **bottom drawer**

hopeful /ˈhəʊp.fəl/ (US) /ˈhoʊp-/ adj; noun

▸adj **1** B1 having hope: *He was hopeful **about** the outcome of the meeting.* ◦ *They were hopeful **of** a successful agreement.* ◦ *I'm hopeful (**that**) we can reach a compromise.* **2** C2 giving hope: *The green shoots were hopeful signs of spring.* • **hopefulness** /-nəs/ noun [U]

▸noun [C usually plural] a person who is trying to get a part in a film, play for a famous football team, etc.

hopefully /ˈhəʊp.fəl.i/ (US) /ˈhoʊp-/ adv **1** B1 used, often at the start of a sentence, to express what you would like to happen: *Hopefully it won't rain.* ◦ *Hopefully we'll be in Norwich by early evening.* **2** B2 in a hopeful way: *'Do you have a cigarette?' he asked hopefully.*

hopeless /ˈhəʊp.ləs/ (US) /ˈhoʊp-/ adj **1** B1 without hope: *a hopeless situation* ◦ *They searched for survivors but it was hopeless.* ◦ *She was depressed and felt totally hopeless about the future.* **2** B2 completely without skill

H

at a particular activity: *I'm hopeless **at** sports.* ◦ *He's a hopeless cook.* • **hopelessness** /-nəs/ noun [U] *I find the hopelessness of the situation very depressing.*

hopelessly /ˈhəʊp.ləs.li/ (US) /ˈhoʊp-/ adv (C2) extremely, or in a way that makes you lose hope: *They met at university and fell hopelessly in love.* ◦ *We were hopelessly lost.*

hopper /ˈhɒp.əʳ/ (US) /ˈhɑː.pɚ/ noun [C] specialized a large tube, wide at one end, through which large amounts of small separate things, for example seeds, can be moved from one container to another

hopscotch /ˈhɒp.skɒtʃ/ (US) /ˈhɑːp.skɑːtʃ/ noun [U] a game played by children, who throw a stone onto a set of joined squares drawn on the ground and jump on one leg and then on two legs into each square to get the stone

horde /hɔːd/ (US) /hɔːrd/ noun often disapproving **1** [C] a large group of people: *Hordes **of** students on bikes made crossing the road difficult.* **2 in their hordes** informal in very great numbers: *When they heard the concert was free, they came in their hordes.*

horizon /həˈraɪ.zən/ noun [S] (C2) the line at the farthest point that you can see, where the sky seems to touch the land or sea: *The moon rose slowly above the horizon.* ◦ *We could see a row of camels silhouetted **on** the horizon.*

IDIOMS **broaden/expand/widen sb's horizons** (C1) to increase the range of things that someone knows about or has experienced: *Travelling certainly broadens your horizons.* • **on the horizon** (C1) likely to happen or exist soon: *There is no new drug on the horizon that will make this disease easier to treat.*

horizontal /ˌhɒr.ɪˈzɒn.təl/ (US) /ˌhɔːr.ɪˈzɑːn.t̬əl/ adj; noun

▸**adj** (C1) parallel to the ground or to the bottom or top edge of something: *Draw a horizontal line across the bottom of the page.* ◦ *Keep the patient horizontal with the feet slightly raised.* → Compare **vertical** • **horizontally** /-i/ adv

▸**noun** [C usually singular] a horizontal line, surface, or position: *Rotate it slowly from **the** horizontal into a vertical position.*

horiˈzontal ˌaxis noun [S] specialized the **x-axis**

hormone /ˈhɔː.məʊn/ (US) /ˈhɔːr.moʊn/ noun [C] any of various chemicals made by living cells which influence the development, growth, sex, etc. of an animal and are carried around the body in the blood: *male and female hormones* ◦ *growth hormones* • **hormonal** /hɔːˈməʊ.nəl/ (US) /hɔːrˈmoʊ-/ adj *a hormonal imbalance*

ˌhormone reˈplacement ˌtherapy noun [U] (abbreviation **HRT**) a treatment for women whose levels of female hormones are low because they have reached the MENOPAUSE

horn /hɔːn/ (US) /hɔːrn/ noun; verb

▸**noun** **ANIMAL** ▷ **1** (C1) [C or U] a hard, pointed, often curved part that grows from the top of the head of some animals, or the hard substance of which a horn is made **VEHICLE** ▷ **2** (B2) [C] a device on a vehicle that is used to make a loud noise as a warning or signal to other people: *The driver **blew/sounded** (informal **honked**) her horn.* → See also **foghorn** **MUSIC** ▷ **3** (C2) [C] a curved metal musical instrument that is narrow at the end you blow into and much wider at the other end

IDIOMS **be on the horns of a dilemma** to be unable to decide which of two things to do because either could have bad results • **draw/pull in your horns** to behave in a more careful way than you did before, especially by spending less money: *He'll have to draw in his horns now he's lost his job.*

▸**verb**

PHRASAL VERB **horn in** US informal to try to become involved in a discussion or activity when you are not wanted: *She's always horning in **on** our conversations.*

horned /hɔːnd/ (US) /hɔːrnd/ adj describes an animal with horns: *horned cattle*

hornet /ˈhɔː.nɪt/ (US) /ˈhɔːr-/ noun [C] a large WASP (= type of flying insect) that can give you a bad STING

ˈhornet's ˌnest noun [C usually singular] a very difficult or unpleasant situation, especially in which a lot of people get very angry and complain: *His remarks about the lack of good women tennis players **stirred up a** (**real**) hornet's nest.*

horniness /ˈhɔː.ni.nəs/ (US) /ˈhɔːr-/ noun [U] informal sexual excitement or sexual ATTRACTION

ˌhorn-ˈrimmed adj [before noun] describes glasses with FRAMES that are coloured with a mixture of dark and light brown

horny /ˈhɔː.ni/ (US) /ˈhɔːr-/ adj **SEXUAL** ▷ **1** informal sexually excited: *She'd had a couple of drinks and was **feeling** horny.* **2** UK informal sexually attractive: *You look horny in that skirt.* **HARD** ▷ **3** made of a hard substance, like horn: *Birds have horny beaks.* **4** (especially of skin) hard and rough

horoscope /ˈhɒr.ə.skəʊp/ (US) /ˈhɔːr.ə.skoʊp/ noun [C] a description of what is going to happen to you, based on the position of the stars and planets at the time of your birth: *I **read** my horoscope most days.* ◦ *My horoscope said I was going to be lucky in love this month.*

horrendous /həˈren.dəs/ adj extremely unpleasant or bad: *a horrendous accident/tragedy/crime* ◦ *horrendous suffering/damage* ◦ *Conditions in the refugee camps were horrendous.* ◦ *The firm made horrendous (= very big) **losses** last year.* • **horrendously** /-li/ adv *horrendously **expensive** clothes* • **horrendousness** /-nəs/ noun [U]

horrible /ˈhɒr.ɪ.bl/ (US) /ˈhɔːr-/ adj **1** (A2) very unpleasant or bad: *He's got a horrible cold.* ◦ *What's that horrible smell?* ◦ *That was a horrible thing to say!* **2** very shocking and frightening: *a horrible crime*

horribly /ˈhɒr.ɪ.bli/ (US) /ˈhɔːr-/ adv extremely, especially in a very bad or unpleasant way: *His face was horribly scarred.* ◦ *Their plans went horribly wrong.*

horrid /ˈhɒr.ɪd/ (US) /ˈhɔːr-/ adj old-fashioned informal unpleasant or unkind: *Don't be so horrid!* ◦ *The medicine tasted horrid.* → Synonym **nasty** • **horridly** /-li/ adv informal • **horridness** /-nəs/ noun [U] informal

horrific /həˈrɪf.ɪk/ adj very bad and shocking: *a horrific accident/crime* ◦ *horrific injuries* • **horrifically** /həˈrɪf.ɪ.kəl.i/ adv

horrified /ˈhɒr.ɪ.faɪd/ (US) /ˈhɔːr-/ adj (C2) very shocked: *He looked horrified when I told him.* ◦ *We were horrified **at/by** the size of the bill.* ◦ *I was horrified **to** hear of his death.* ◦ *I was horrified **that** they hadn't included you.*

horrify /ˈhɒr.ɪ.faɪ/ (US) /ˈhɔːr-/ verb [T] to shock someone very much: *This news will horrify my parents.*

horrifying /ˈhɒr.ɪ.faɪ.ɪŋ/ (US) /ˈhɔːr-/ adj (C2) very shocking: *horrifying injuries/conditions/news* • **horrifyingly** /-li/ adv *The prediction of four million unemployed now looks horrifyingly realistic.*

horror /ˈhɒr.əʳ/ (US) /ˈhɔːr.ɚ/ noun **1** (B2) [U] an extremely strong feeling of fear and shock, or the frightening and shocking character of something: *The crowd cried out **in** horror as the car burst into flames.*

◦ *The thought of speaking in front of so many people* ***fills*** *me* ***with*** *horror.* ◦ *I then realized* ***to my*** *absolute horror, that I had forgotten the present.* ◦ *What the book does convey very successfully is the horror* ***of*** *war.* **2 horrors** [plural] things that are very shocking or frightening: *The population now faces the horrors of starvation.* **3** [C] UK informal a child who behaves very badly: *Her youngest boy is a* ***little*** *horror.*

IDIOMS **have a horror of sth** to hate something very much or be very frightened of something: *It may be childish but I have a horror of worms.* • **horror of horrors** UK humorous said when you are telling someone about a very bad or embarrassing situation: *Then I went to the toilets and, horror of horrors, discovered that my zip had been undone.*

ˈhorror ˌfilm noun [C] mainly UK (mainly US **ˈhorror ˌmovie**) B1 a film in which very frightening or unnatural things happen, for example dead people coming to life and people being murdered

ˈhorror ˌstory noun [C] **1** a story in which very frightening and unnatural things happen **2** a report of real events in which things have gone very wrong: *the usual travel horror stories about delays at the airport and flight cancellations*

ˈhorror-ˌstruck adj [after verb] (also **ˈhorror-ˌstricken**) extremely shocked and frightened: *They watched, horror-struck, as the car came off the road.*

hors d'oeuvre /ˌɔːˈdɜːv/ US /ˌɔːrˈdɜːv/ noun [C] (plural **hors d'oeuvre** or **hors d'oeuvres**) **1** UK a small SAVOURY (= not sweet) dish eaten at the start of a meal **2** US small pieces of food eaten at a party

horse /hɔːs/ US /hɔːrs/ noun; verb

▸noun **ANIMAL** ▷ **1** A1 [C] a large animal with four legs that people ride on or use for carrying things or pulling vehicles: *to ride a horse* ◦ *a horse and cart* **2 the horses** [plural] informal horse races where you try to win money by correctly guessing which horse will win: *He spends all his money on the horses.* **SPORTS EQUIPMENT** ▷ **3** [C] (also **vaulting horse**) a tall piece of equipment that people jump over in GYMNASTICS **DRUG** ▷ **4** [U] slang **heroin**

IDIOMS **(straight) from the horse's mouth** If you hear something (straight) from the horse's mouth, you hear it from the person who has direct personal knowledge of it. • **horses for courses** UK used for saying that it is important to choose suitable people for particular activities because everyone has different skills

▸verb

PHRASAL VERB **horse around/about** informal to behave in a silly and noisy way

horseback /ˈhɔːs.bæk/ US /ˈhɔːrs-/ adj; noun

▸adj [before noun] on a horse: *horseback riding* ◦ *a horseback rider*

▸noun **on horseback** riding a horse: *police on horseback*

horsebox

horsebox /ˈhɔːs.bɒks/ US /ˈhɔːrs.bɑːks/ noun [C] UK a vehicle for transporting horses, sometimes pulled by another vehicle

ˌhorse ˈchestnut noun [C] (the poisonous shiny brown nut from) a large tree with pink or white flowers → See also **conker**

ˈhorse-drawn adj [before noun] describes a vehicle pulled by a horse

ˈhorse ˌfloat noun [C] Australian English a vehicle for transporting horses, sometimes pulled by another vehicle → Compare **horsebox**

horsefly /ˈhɔːs.flaɪ/ US /ˈhɔːrs-/ noun [C] any of various large flying insects that bite horses, CATTLE, and sometimes people

horsehair /ˈhɔːs.heəʳ/ US /ˈhɔːrs.her/ noun [U] hairs from a horse's tail and MANE, used especially in the past as a soft filling for furniture

horseman /ˈhɔːs.mən/ US /ˈhɔːrs-/ noun [C] (plural **-men** /-mən/) a person who rides a horse, especially someone who rides well

horsemanship /ˈhɔːs.mən.ʃɪp/ US /ˈhɔːrs-/ noun [U] skill at riding horses

horseplay /ˈhɔːs.pleɪ/ US /ˈhɔːrs-/ noun [U] old-fashioned rough, noisy behaviour, especially when people push each other as a joke

horsepower /ˈhɔːs.paʊəʳ/ US /ˈhɔːrs.paʊr/ noun [C or U] (plural **horsepower**) (abbreviation **hp**) a unit for measuring the power of an engine: *a 100-horsepower engine*

ˈhorse ˌracing noun [U] a sport in which people race on horses, usually to win money for the horses' owners

horseradish /ˈhɔːsˌræd.ɪʃ/ US /ˈhɔːrs-/ noun [U] a plant with large, green leaves and a long, white root that has a strong sharp taste: *roast beef and horse-radish sauce*

ˈhorse ˌriding noun [U] UK (US **ˈhorseback ˌriding**) the sport or activity of riding a horse

ˌhorse's ˈass noun [C usually singular] US offensive a stupid and annoying person

ˈhorse ˌsense noun [U] old-fashioned practical knowledge and good judgment about ordinary life → Synonym **common sense**

horseshit /ˈhɔːs.ʃɪt/ US /ˈhɔːrs-/ noun [U] US offensive nonsense: *He described the film as 'middle-class, bourgeois horseshit'.*

horseshoe /ˈhɔːs.ʃuː/ US /ˈhɔːrs-/ noun **FOR A HORSE** ▷ **1** [C] a U-shaped piece of metal that is fixed to the bottom of a horse's HOOF to protect it: *For many people the horseshoe is a symbol of good luck.* **GAME** ▷ **2 horseshoes** [U] US a game in which horseshoes are thrown at a wooden or metal rod in the ground

ˈhorse-ˌtrading noun [U] often disapproving unofficial discussion in which people make agreements that provide both sides with advantages: *There's been a lot of* ***political*** *horse-trading while the parties try to form a government.* • **ˈhorse-ˌtrade** verb [I] disapproving

ˈhorse ˌtrailer noun [C] US (UK **horsebox**) a vehicle for transporting horses that is pulled behind another vehicle

horsewhip /ˈhɔːs.wɪp/ US /ˈhɔːrs-/ verb [T] (**-pp-**) to hit someone with a WHIP (= long thin piece of leather, rope, etc.)

horsewoman /ˈhɔːsˌwʊm.ən/ US /ˈhɔːrs-/ noun [C] (plural **-women** /-wɪmɪn/) a female HORSEMAN: *She's a keen horsewoman.*

horsey (**horsier**, **horsiest**) (also **horsy**) /ˈhɔː.si/ US

/ˈhɔːr-/ adj **1** informal liking horses and being involved with them **2** disapproving looking like a horse, usually in a way that is not attractive

horticulture /ˈhɔː.tɪ.kʌl.tʃəʳ/ (US) /ˈhɔːr.t̬ə.kʌl.tʃɚ/ noun [U] the study or activity of growing garden plants • **horticultural** /ˌhɔː.tɪˈkʌl.tʃər.əl/ (US) /ˌhɔːr.t̬əˈkʌl.tʃɚ.əl/ adj *a horticultural show* • **horticulturalist** /ˌhɔː.tɪˈkʌl.tʃər.əl.ɪst/ (US) /ˌhɔːr.t̬əˈkʌl.tʃɚ-/ noun [C] (also **horticulturist**)

hosanna /həʊˈzæn.ə/ (US) /hoʊ-/ exclamation a shout of praise to God

hose /həʊz/ (US) /hoʊz/ noun; verb

▸noun **PIPE** ▷ **1** [C] (UK also **hosepipe**) a long plastic or rubber pipe, used to direct water onto fires, gardens, etc.: *The severe drought has led to a hosepipe **ban** in eastern England.* **CLOTHES** ▷ **2** [U] specialized **hosiery** → See also **pantyhose**

▸verb [T] to direct water onto something using a hose: *He was covered in mud so we hosed him **down**.*

H

hoser /ˈhəʊ.zəʳ/ (US) /ˈhoʊ.zɚ/ noun [C] US slang a stupid or rude person

hosiery /ˈhəʊz.jə.ri/ (US) /ˈhoʊʒ.ɚ.i/ noun [U] (also **hose**) a word used especially in shops for things such as socks, TIGHTS, and STOCKINGS

hospice /ˈhɒs.pɪs/ (US) /ˈhɑː.spɪs/ noun [C] a hospital for people who are dying, especially from CANCER

hospitable /hɒsˈpɪt.ə.bl̩/ (US) /hɑːˈspɪt̬-/ adj **1** (C1) friendly and welcoming to guests and visitors: *The villagers were very hospitable **to/towards** anyone who passed through.* → Opposite **inhospitable** **2** providing good conditions for living or growing: *It's difficult to think of a less hospitable environment than the surface of the Moon.* • **hospitably** /-bli/ adv

hospital /ˈhɒs.pɪ.təl/ (US) /ˈhɑː.spɪ.t̬əl/ noun [C or U] (A1) a place where people who are ill or injured are treated and taken care of by doctors and nurses: *a general/children's/maternity hospital* ◦ *hospital patients/staff* ◦ UK *I've got to go **(in)to** hospital* (US **to** *the hospital*) *to have an operation.* ◦ UK *She spent a week **in** hospital* (US ***in the** hospital*) *last year.*

hospitality /ˌhɒs.pɪˈtæl.ə.ti/ (US) /ˌhɑː.spɪˈtæl.ə.t̬i/ noun [U] **1** (C1) the act of being friendly and welcoming to guests and visitors: *The local people showed me great hospitality.* **2** the food, drink, etc. that an organization provides in order to keep its guests or business partners happy: *The company's guests at Ascot are entertained in the **corporate** hospitality area.*

hospitalize (UK usually **hospitalise**) /ˈhɒs.pɪ.təl.aɪz/ (US) /ˈhɑː.spɪ.t̬əl-/ verb [T usually passive] to take someone to hospital and keep them there for treatment: *His wife's been hospitalized for depression.* • **hospitalization** (UK usually **hospitalisation**) /ˌhɒs.pɪ.təl.aɪˈzeɪ.ʃən/ (US) /ˌhɑː.spɪ.t̬əl.əˈ-/ noun [U]

host /həʊst/ (US) /hoʊst/ noun; verb

▸noun **PERSON WITH GUESTS** ▷ **1** (B2) [C] (female also **hostess**) someone who has guests: *We thanked our hosts for the lovely evening.* ◦ *The local language school is advertising for host **families** (= families people stay with when they are visiting another country).* **ON TELEVISION** ▷ **2** (C2) [C] (female also **hostess**) a person who introduces guests and performers, especially on television or radio: *Our host for tonight's show is Graham Norton.* **FOR AN EVENT** ▷ **3** [C] a place or organization that provides the space and other necessary things for a special event: *Japan is **playing** host **to** the next international conference.* ◦ *the host **nation** for the next World Cup* **ANIMAL/PLANT** ▷ **4** [C] specialized a plant or animal that another plant or animal lives on as a PARASITE **A LOT** ▷ **5 a host of** (C1) a large number of something: *There's a **whole** host of reasons why he didn't get the job.* **CHURCH** ▷ **6 the host** [S] specialized the holy bread that is eaten at COMMUNION (= a Christian religious ceremony) **INTERNET** ▷ **7** [C] a company which hosts a website on the internet

▸verb [T] **EVENT** ▷ **1** (C1) to provide the space and other things necessary for a special event: *Which country is hosting the next Olympic Games?* **TELEVISION SHOW** ▷ **2** to be the host of a television or radio programme: *to host a show/programme* **INTERNET** ▷ **3** to provide the computer HARDWARE and SOFTWARE which allows a website to exist on the internet: *I've written my website, now I just need to find a company to host it.*

hostage /ˈhɒs.tɪdʒ/ (US) /ˈhɑː.stɪdʒ/ noun [C] (C2) someone who is taken as a prisoner by an enemy in order to force the other people involved to do what the enemy wants: *She was **taken/held** hostage by the gunmen.* ◦ *The terrorists have **seized** 20 hostages and are threatening to kill one a day unless their demands are met.*

IDIOM **hostage to fortune** an action or statement that could create problems for you later: *The prime minister was extremely cautious, saying nothing inflammatory and **giving** no hostages to fortune.*

hostel /ˈhɒs.təl/ (US) /ˈhɑː.stəl/ noun [C] **1** (B1) a large house where people can stay free or cheaply: *a student hostel* → Compare **hotel** **2** (B1) UK (US **shelter**) a building where people with no home can live for a short time: *a hostel **for** the homeless* ◦ *a Salvation Army hostel*

hostelry /ˈhɒs.təl.ri/ (US) /ˈhɑː.stəl-/ noun [C] old use or humorous a bar or pub

hostess /ˈhəʊ.stes/ (US) /ˈhoʊ.stɪs/ noun [C] **1** a woman who has guests **2** a woman who entertains customers, especially men, at a NIGHTCLUB

hostile /ˈhɒs.taɪl/ (US) /ˈhɑː.stəl/ adj **UNFRIENDLY** ▷ **1** (C1) unfriendly and not liking or agreeing with something: *a hostile crowd* ◦ *The president had a hostile **reception** in Ohio this morning.* ◦ *I'm not hostile **to** (= against) the idea of change as such.* **DIFFICULT** ▷ **2** (C1) difficult or not suitable for living or growing: *hostile weather conditions* ◦ *a hostile climate/environment* **ENEMY** ▷ **3** [before noun] connected with the enemy in a war: *hostile aircraft/forces* **COMPANIES** ▷ **4** relating to situations in which one company wants to buy another company whose owners do not want to sell it: *The company convinced investors to reject a hostile **bid** from Enterprise Oil Plc worth £1.5 billion.* ◦ *a hostile **merger***

hostility /hɒsˈtɪl.ɪ.ti/ (US) /hɑːˈstɪl.ə.t̬i/ noun **UNFRIENDLINESS** ▷ **1** (C2) [U] an occasion when someone is unfriendly or shows that they do not agree with or like something: *They showed **open** (= obvious) hostility **to/towards** their new neighbours.* **FIGHTING** ▷ **2 hostilities** [plural] formal fighting in a war: *Hostilities **began/broke out** just after midnight.* ◦ *Hostilities were **suspended** (= fighting stopped temporarily) during the talks.*

hot /hɒt/ (US) /hɑːt/ adj; verb

▸adj (**hotter**, **hottest**) **VERY WARM** ▷ **1** (A1) having a high temperature: *a hot sunny day* ◦ *hot weather* ◦ *a hot drink/meal* ◦ *It's too hot in here, can we turn down the heating?* ◦ *Bake the cake in a hot oven, about 220°C, for 30 minutes.* ◦ *The food was **piping** hot (= very hot).* **SPICY** ▷ **2** (B1) describes food which causes a burning feeling in the mouth: *a hot curry* ◦ *hot spicy food* → Opposite **mild** **CAUSING DISAGREEMENT** ▷ **3** (C1) describes a subject which causes a lot of disagreement or discussion: *Global warming has become a very hot issue.* **NEW/EXCITING** ▷ **4** (C1) new and exciting:

Hollywood's hottest new actress ◦ *hot gossip* ◦ *This 21-year-old actor has become Hollywood's hottest* ***property***. **SKILFUL** ▷ **5** [after verb] informal knowing a lot or skilful: *I'm* ***not too*** *hot* ***on*** *Russian history.* **MOST LIKELY** ▷ **6 hot tip** informal an accurate piece of advice about who will win a race: *Have you got any hot tips for this afternoon's race?* **7 hot favourite** the person or animal that is most likely to win a race, competition, election, etc.: *He's the hot favourite* ***to*** *win the election.* **DEMANDING** ▷ **8 be hot on sth** informal to think that a particular thing is very important and to demand that it is done well or correctly: *They're very hot on dress at work so she always looks very smart for the office.* **STOLEN** ▷ **9** slang describes goods that have been recently stolen and are therefore difficult to sell or dangerous to deal with because the police are still looking for them **SEXY** ▷ **10** informal sexually attractive, or feeling sexually excited: *She's hot alright.* ◦ *I'm hot for you, baby.* ◦ *I've got a hot* ***date*** *tonight.* **ANGRY** ▷ **11 hot temper** If someone has a hot temper, they are easily made angry.

Other ways of saying hot

If the weather outside or the temperature inside is very hot, you can use the adjectives **scorching**, **boiling** (**hot**), or **sweltering**:

She won the race despite the ***sweltering*** *heat.*

a ***scorching*** *summer day*

If the temperature feels hot and unpleasant, you can say that it is **oppressive**:

The ***oppressive*** *afternoon heat was making him feel tired.*

Liquid that is extremely hot can be described as **scalding** (**hot**):

She burned herself on ***scalding*** *water from the kettle.*

If food is pleasantly very hot, you could describe it as **piping hot**:

She gave us a bowl of ***piping hot*** *soup.*

If something is not as hot as it should be, it could be described as **lukewarm**:

Yuck! This coffee's ***lukewarm***!

IDIOMS **be hot on sb's track/trail** to be very close to catching or finding someone • **be hot stuff** informal **1** to be very skilful: *She's really hot stuff* ***at*** *baseball.* **2** to be very sexually attractive: *Man, she's hot stuff!* • **be in hot water** (also **get into hot water**) to be in or get into a difficult situation in which you are in danger of being criticized or punished: *He found himself in hot water over his comments about immigration.* • **be too hot to handle** informal to be too difficult to deal with or talk about: *For many politicians, abortion is an issue that's too hot to handle.* • **go/sell like hot cakes** informal C2 to be bought quickly and in large numbers: *The new game is apparently selling like hot cakes.* • **hot air** informal If something that someone says is hot air, it is not sincere and will have no practical results: *His promises turned out to be so much hot air.* • **(all) hot and bothered** informal worried or angry, and sometimes physically hot • **hot and heavy** US informal If something or someone is hot and heavy, they are full of strong emotions or sexual feelings: *Guess who I saw getting hot and heavy on the dance floor?* • **hot dog!** US informal something that you say when you are very pleased about something: *You won your race? Hot dog!* • **hot off the press** News that is hot off the press has just been printed and often contains the most recent information about something. • **hot to trot** US informal sexually excited and wanting to find someone to have sex with • **hot under the collar** informal embarrassed or angry about something: *When I suggested he was mistaken he got rather hot under the collar.* • **in hot pursuit** following someone closely, trying hard to catch them: *The gang drove off, with the police in hot pursuit.* • **in the hot seat** in a position where you are responsible for important or difficult things

▸**verb** (**-tt-**)

PHRASAL VERB **hot up** UK informal If an event or situation hots up, it becomes more exciting and more things start to happen: *A few days before the elections, the pace began to hot up.* ◦ *The competition is really hotting up now.*

hot-ˈair balˌloon noun [C] an aircraft consisting of a very large bag filled with heated air or other gas, with a BASKET (= container) hanging under it in which people can ride

hot-ˈair ˌgun noun [C] an electrical tool which blows out hot air and is used to make paint on surfaces softer so that it can be removed more easily

hotbed /ˈhɒt.bed/ (US) /ˈhɑːt-/ noun **a hotbed of sth** a place or situation where a lot of a particular activity, especially an unwanted or unpleasant activity, is happening or might happen: *The police department was a hotbed of corruption.*

ˌhot-ˈblooded adj **SHOWING FEELINGS** ▷ **1** showing strong feelings very easily and quickly, especially anger or love **SEXUAL** ▷ **2** describes a person with strong sexual feelings and energy: *He's just your average 25-year-old hot-blooded* ***male***.

ˈhot ˌbutton noun [C] US informal a subject that is important to people and about which they have strong opinions: *Gender issues have become something of a hot button.* ◦ *Immigration has become a hot button* ***issue***.

ˌhot ˈchocolate noun [C or U] A2 a hot drink made from milk and/or water, powdered chocolate, and sugar

hotchpotch /ˈhɒtʃ.pɒtʃ/ (US) /ˈhɑːtʃ.pɑːtʃ/ noun [C] (US usually **hodgepodge**) a confused mixture of different things: *New Age thinking seems to be a hotchpotch* ***of*** *old and new ideas.*

ˌhot cross ˈbun noun [C] a round, sweet cake like bread with a cross painted on the top, eaten in some Christian countries at EASTER

ˌhot ˈdesk noun [C] a desk and computer in an office that are available to be used by any worker who needs it

ˌhot-ˈdesk verb [I] to work at whatever desk and computer is available in an office

ˌhot-ˈdesking noun [U] (US also **hoteling**) a way of saving office space in which workers do not have their own desk and are only given a desk when they need it: *Hot-desking allows a company to have significantly smaller premises.*

hotdog /ˈhɒt.dɒɡ/ (US) /ˈhɑːt.dɑːɡ/ verb [I] (**-gg-**) mainly US informal to make fast, skilful movements in particular sports, especially skiing, in order to make people notice you

ˈhot ˌdog noun [C] **FOOD** ▷ **1** B1 a cooked sausage eaten in a long soft piece of bread, often with fried onions **SPORT** ▷ **2** mainly US informal a person who makes fast, skilful movements in skiing, SNOWBOARDING, or SURFING in order to make people notice them

hotel /həʊˈtel/ (US) /hoʊ-/ noun [C] **PLACE TO STAY** ▷ **1** A1 a building where you pay to have a room to sleep in, and where you can sometimes eat meals: *a four-star hotel* ◦ *the Clarendon Hotel* ◦ *We stayed* ***in/at*** *a* *hotel on the seafront.* ◦ *hotel guests* → Compare **hostel** **PLACE TO DRINK** ▷ **2** Australian English a building where alcoholic drinks can be bought and drunk and where food is often available **PLACE TO EAT** ▷ **3** Indian English a restaurant

hotelier /həʊˈtel.i.əʳ/ (US) /ˌhoʊ.təlˈjeɪ/ noun [C] a person who manages or owns a hotel

hotelling (US usually **hoteling**) /həʊˈtel.ɪŋ/ (US) /ˌhoʊ-/ noun [U] US for **hot-desking**

ˌhot ˈflush noun [C] (US usually **ˌhot ˈflash**) a sudden hot, uncomfortable feeling experienced by some women during the MENOPAUSE

hotfoot adv; verb

▸adv /ˌhɒtˈfʊt/ (US) /ˈhɑːt.fʊt/ informal very quickly and without delay: *She'd come hotfoot from the palace with the latest news.*

▸verb /ˈhɒt.fʊt/ (US) /ˈhɑːt.fʊt/ **hotfoot it** informal to run or walk somewhere as quickly as possible: *He walked in and I hotfooted it out the back door.*

hothead /ˈhɒt.hed/ (US) /ˈhɑːt-/ noun [C] someone who does things or reacts to things quickly and without thinking carefully first • **hotheaded** /ˌhɒtˈhed.ɪd/ (US) /ˈhɑːtˌhed.ɪd/ adj *She's a bit hotheaded and rash.*

hothouse /ˈhɒt.haʊs/ (US) /ˈhɑːt-/ noun **FOR PLANTS** ▷ **1** [C] a heated glass building in which plants are grown: *hothouse tomatoes* **EDUCATION** ▷ **2** [C usually singular] often disapproving a place or environment in which people, especially children, are taught to develop skills and knowledge more quickly than usual: *He was attracted by the hothouse **atmosphere** of Britain's top schools.* **BUSY PLACE** ▷ **3** [C] a place where there is a lot of a particular activity: *a literary/political hothouse*

hothousing /ˈhɒt.haʊz.ɪŋ/ (US) /ˈhɑːt-/ noun [U] often disapproving the act of giving a child a lot of extra teaching or training in an activity or subject, because you want them to be very good at it • **hothouse** /-haʊs/ verb [T]

ˈhot ˌkey noun [C] specialized a key that starts a particular computer program or causes a series of actions to be performed automatically, sometimes when used in combination with another key → Synonym **shortcut**

hotline /ˈhɒt.laɪn/ (US) /ˈhɑːt-/ noun [C] a special direct phone connection for emergencies: *A national hotline has been set up for students suffering from stress.*

hotly /ˈhɒt.li/ (US) /ˈhɑːt.li/ adv **1** in an angry or excited way: *She hotly **denied** having taken the money.* **2** closely and with determination: *He ran down the street, hotly **pursued** by two police officers.* ◦ *a hotly contested election*

ˈhot pants noun [plural] very small, tight SHORTS (= short trousers) worn by women

hotplate /ˈhɒt.pleɪt/ (US) /ˈhɑːt-/ noun [C] **1** a small cooker that can be moved, on which pans of food are heated **2** UK a round flat metal surface on an electric cooker, on which pans of food are heated

hotpot /ˈhɒt.pɒt/ (US) /ˈhɑːt.pɑːt/ noun [C or U] a mixture of meat and vegetables, usually including sliced potatoes, cooked slowly in a covered dish inside a cooker

ˌhot poˈtato noun [C] a problem, situation, etc. that is difficult to deal with and causes a lot of disagreement: *The abortion issue is a **political** hot potato in the United States.*

hotrod /ˈhɒt.rɒd/ (US) /ˈhɑːt.rɑːd/ noun [C] old-fashioned slang a car that is specially built or changed so that it will go very fast

hots /hɒts/ (US) /hɑːts/ noun [plural]

IDIOM **have (got) the hots for sb** informal to be very sexually attracted to someone

hot ˈshit noun [U] US offensive someone or something that is very good

hotshot /ˈhɒt.ʃɒt/ (US) /ˈhɑːt.ʃɑːt/ noun [C] mainly US informal someone who is skilful and successful at something: *Now he's a lecturer, he thinks he's a **real** hotshot!* ◦ *She's quite a hotshot **at** chess.*

hotspot /ˈhɒt.spɒt/ (US) /ˈhɑːt.spɑːt/ noun [C] **FIGHTING** ▷ **1** a place where war or other fighting is likely to happen: *The border has become a major hotspot.* **POPULAR PLACE** ▷ **2** informal a popular and exciting place: *The Manhattan is one of the best hotspots in town.* **INTERNET ACCESS** ▷ **3** a public place where you can use a computer, mobile phone, etc. with WI-FI (= a system for connecting electronic equipment to the internet without using wires): *There are wi-fi hotspots in all our cafés.*

hottie /ˈhɒt.i/ (US) /ˈhɑː.t̬i/ noun [C] **PERSON** ▷ **1** informal someone who is very sexually attractive **THING** ▷ **2** UK informal a **hot-water bottle**

ˌhot ˈtub noun [C] a large, usually wooden, container full of hot water in which more than one person can sit

ˌhot-ˈwater ˌbottle noun [C] a rubber container which you fill with very hot water and use to warm a bed or a part of your body

hot-ˈwater ˌcylinder noun [C] UK (US and UK also **hot-ˈwater ˌtank**) a metal container, usually found in or near the bathroom, that holds and heats the water for a house

hot-wire /ˈhɒt.waɪəʳ/ (US) /ˈhɑːt.waɪr/ verb [T] informal to start a car engine without using the key, especially in order to steal the car

houmous (also **hummus**) /ˈhʊm.əs/ noun [U] a soft, smooth food made from crushed CHICKPEAS, oil, and lemon juice

hound /haʊnd/ noun; verb

▸noun [C] a type of dog used for hunting

▸verb [T] to chase someone or refuse to leave them alone, especially because you want to get something from them: *The reporters wouldn't stop hounding her.* → Synonym **harass**

PHRASAL VERB **hound sb out** to force someone to leave a job or a place: *He claims he was hounded out **of** his job by a group of students who disapproved of his views.*

hour /aʊəʳ/ (US) /aʊr/ noun **1** (A1) [C] a period of 60 minutes: *The exam lasted an hour and a half.* ◦ *There are 24 hours in a day.* ◦ *How many hours' sleep do you need?* ◦ *I'll be back in an hour's/two hours' **time** (= after one/two hours).* ◦ *The village is an hour from Doncaster/an hour away (= it takes an hour to travel there).* ◦ *He gets paid **by the** hour (= gets a particular amount of money for each hour he works).* ◦ *Trains leave **every** hour **on the** hour (= at exactly one o'clock, two o'clock, etc.).* ◦ *Buses leave at ten minutes **past/to the** hour (= at ten past/to one o'clock, two o'clock, etc.).* ◦ *War was declared at eighteen hundred/18.00 hours (= at six o'clock in the evening).* **2** [C usually plural] the period of time when a particular activity happens or when a shop or public building is open: *I did it in my lunch hour.* ◦ *office/working hours* ◦ *Our opening hours are from 8.00 to 6.00.* **3** (C2) [C] a particular time during the day or night: *Who could be phoning us at this **unearthly/ungodly** hour (= so late at night)?* ◦ *He returned in **the early/small** hours (= at night, after midnight).* **4 work long, regular, unsocial, etc. hours**

used to describe how many hours in the day you work or what part of the day you work: *She's a nurse so she often works unsocial hours.* ◦ *He's paid well but he works long hours.* **5 for hours (and hours)** B1 informal for a very long time: *I waited for him for hours.* **6 at all hours (of the day and night)** C1 disapproving repeatedly during the day and the night: *They keep ringing me up at all hours (of the day and night).*

IDIOMS **after hours** after the usual hours of work • **hour after hour** for many hours without stopping: *I sat by her bedside for hour after hour.* • **your hour has come** literary If you think your hour has come, you think you are going to die: *I thought my hour had come when he pointed his gun at me.* • **(from) hour to hour** If something changes from hour to hour, it is different every hour. • **in sb's hour of need** literary at a time when someone really needs help: *She helped me in my hour of need.* • **out of hours** mainly UK (US **after hours**) If you drink in a bar out of hours, you drink alcohol at a time when it is not allowed by law. • **till all hours** disapproving very late: *He stays up drinking till all hours.*

hourglass /ˈaʊə.ɡlɑːs/ US /ˈaʊr.ɡlæs/ noun [C] a glass container filled with sand that takes one hour to move from an upper to a lower part through a narrow opening in the middle, used especially in the past to measure time

hourglass

ˈhourglass ˌfigure noun [C usually singular] If a woman has an hourglass figure, she has a very small waist.

ˈhour ˌhand noun [C usually singular] the part on a clock or watch which points to the hours. It is shorter than the MINUTE HAND.

hourly /ˈaʊə.li/ US /ˈaʊr-/ adj; adv

▸adj **1** B2 done or happening every hour: *There's an hourly bus service into town.* ◦ *Take two tablets at hourly intervals.* **2 hourly fee, rate, etc.** B2 the amount that is charged or earned every hour

▸adv C1 once every hour: *Trains call here hourly.*

house noun; verb

▸noun /haʊs/ (plural **houses** /ˈhaʊzɪz/) **HOME** ▷ **1** A1 [C] a building that people, usually one family, live in: *a detached/semi-detached house* ◦ *to buy/rent a house* ◦ *house prices* ◦ *She lives in a little house* ***in*** *(US* ***on****) Cross Street.* → See also **farmhouse, roadhouse** **2** [C usually singular] all the people living in a house: *Try not to wake* ***the whole*** *house when you come in!* **3** [C] a building where animals are kept: *the monkey/lion house at the zoo* ◦ *a hen house* **PUBLIC BUILDING** ▷ **4** [C] a building or part of a building that is used for a special purpose: *the Sydney Opera House* ◦ *Broadcasting House* **BUSINESS** ▷ **5** a company that is involved in a particular area of business: *a publishing house* ◦ *a fashion house* ◦ UK *a curry house (= a South Asian restaurant)* **MUSIC** ▷ **6** [U] (also **ˈhouse ˌmusic**) popular dance music with a fast regular beat, usually produced on electronic equipment: *House music first appeared in the late 1980s.* **SCHOOL GROUP** ▷ **7** [C] UK any of a small number of groups that the children in a school are put in for sports and other competitions: *an inter-house football match* **FAMILY** ▷ **8** [C] an important family, especially a royal one: *The British Royal Family belong to the House of Windsor.* **POLITICS** ▷ **9** [C] an organization that makes laws, or its meeting place **10 the House** the members of the organization that makes laws: *The House began sitting at 3 p.m./rose at 2 a.m.* **11** [S] the group of people who suggest a subject for a DEBATE: *The motion for tonight's debate is, 'This house believes that capital punishment should be abolished.'* **PEOPLE AT THEATRE** ▷ **12** C2 [C] the people watching a performance, especially in a theatre: *The opera played to a* ***full/packed*** *house.*

> **Word partners for house**
>
> *build/buy/rent/sell* a house • a *beautiful/fine/derelict/rambling* house • a *terraced/semi-detached/detached* house

IDIOMS **get on like a house on fire** informal If two people get on like a house on fire, they like each other very much and become friends very quickly: *I was worried that they wouldn't like each other but in fact they're getting on like a house on fire.* • **get/put your own house in order** to solve your own problems: *You should put your own house in order before you start telling me what to do!* • **go (all) round the houses** UK to waste time doing or asking something in a very complicated way • **house of cards** a complicated organization or plan that is very weak and can easily be destroyed or easily go wrong • **on the house** If you have something on the house, it is given to you free by a business: *All the drinks were on the house.*

▸verb [T] /haʊz/ C2 to give a person or animal a place to live, or to provide space for something: *It will be difficult to house all the refugees.* ◦ *The museum houses the biggest collection of antique toys in Europe.*

ˈhouse arˌrest noun **under house arrest** legally forced to stay in your house as if it were a prison: *The opposition leader has just been* ***put/placed*** *under house arrest.*

houseboat /ˈhaʊs.bəʊt/ US /-boʊt/ noun [C] a boat which people use as their home, often kept in one place on a river or CANAL

housebound /ˈhaʊs.baʊnd/ adj unable to leave your home, especially because you are ill: *She's been housebound since the accident.*

housebreaker /ˈhaʊsˌbreɪ.kəʳ/ US /-kɚ/ noun [C] a person who illegally enters a house in order to steal something • **housebreaking** /-kɪŋ/ noun [U]

housebroken /ˈhaʊsˌbrəʊ.kən/ US /-ˌbroʊ-/ adj US for **house-trained**

housebuyer /ˈhaʊsˌbaɪ.əʳ/ US /-ɚ/ noun [C usually plural] a person who wants to buy, or is buying a house or other form of place to live in

ˈhouse ˌcall noun [C] an occasion when a doctor or other health worker comes to your home, usually to give treatment

ˈHouse Comˌmittee noun [C] in the US, a group of people chosen by the House of Representatives to consider a particular subject: *He appeared before the House Committee on Space, Science and Technology.*

housefly /ˈhaʊs.flaɪ/ noun [C] a small common fly often found in houses

houseful /ˈhaʊs.fʊl/ noun a lot of people or things in your house: *We've got a houseful* ***of*** *visitors at the moment.*

houseguest /ˈhaʊs.ɡest/ noun [C] mainly US a person who stays at someone else's house for one or more nights

household /ˈhaʊs.həʊld/ US /-hoʊld/ noun [C, + sing/pl verb] B2 a group of people, often a family, who live together: *By the 1960s, most households had a TV.* ◦ *household chores* ◦ *household expenses*

H

householder /ˈhaʊsˌhəʊl.dəʳ/ (US) /-ˌhoʊl.dɚ/ **noun** [C] the person who owns or is in charge of a house

ˌhousehold ˈname **noun** [C] a famous person that most people know of: *He was a household name in the 1950s.*

ˌhousehold ˈword **noun** [C usually singular] a word or name that everyone knows: *McDonalds quickly became a household word.*

ˈhouse-ˌhunting **noun** [U] the activity of looking for a house to live in: *We've been house-hunting for months.* ◦ *I'm* ***going*** *house-hunting later today.*

ˈhouse ˌhusband **noun** [C] a man who stays at home and cleans the house, takes care of the children, etc. while his partner goes out to work

ˈhouse ˌjournal **noun** [C] UK (US **ˈhouse ˌorgan**) a newspaper produced by a company to tell employees what is happening in the company

housekeeper /ˈhaʊsˌkiː.pəʳ/ (US) /-pɚ/ **noun** [C] a person, especially a woman, whose job is to organize another person's house and deal with cooking, cleaning, etc.

housekeeping (money) /ˈhaʊs.kiː.pɪŋˌmʌn.i/ **noun** [U] the money used for buying food and other things necessary for living in a house

ˈhouse ˌlights **noun** [plural] the lights in the place where the public sit in a theatre, cinema, etc.

housemaid /ˈhaʊs.meɪd/ **noun** [C] old-fashioned a woman servant whose job is to clean a large house, and who often lives there

houseman /ˈhaʊs.mən/, /-mæn/ **noun** [C] (plural **-men** /-mən/) UK (US **intern**) a male or female doctor who is still training, and who works in a hospital

ˈhouse ˌmartin **noun** [C] a small bird that makes its nest under the edge of the roof of a house

housemaster /ˈhaʊsˌmɑː.stəʳ/ (US) /-ˌmæs.tɚ/ **noun** [C] a male teacher who is in charge of the children who live in one of several separate buildings in a school

housemate /ˈhaʊs.meɪt/ **noun** [C] someone you live with in a house but are not related to and do not have a romantic or sexual relationship with

housemistress /ˈhaʊsˌmɪs.trəs/ **noun** [C] a female housemaster

the ˌHouse of ˈCommons **noun** (also **the Commons**) one of the two parts of parliament in the UK and Canada, whose members are each elected to represent a particular official area of the country, or its members, or the place where it meets: *The mood was sombre as the Commons sat down on Wednesday to debate the crisis.*

ˌhouse of corˈrection **noun** [C] US a building where people who have committed crimes that are not serious are sent to improve their behaviour

ˌhouse of ˈGod **noun** [S] literary a church

the ˌHouse of ˈLords **noun** (also **the Lords**) one of the two parts of the UK parliament, whose members are not elected but have a high social position, or its members, or the place where it meets

the ˌHouse of Repreˈsentatives **noun** the lower house of the parliaments of some countries, including the US, Australia, and New Zealand

houseplant /ˈhaʊs.plɑːnt/ (US) /-plænt/ **noun** [C] (UK also **ˈpot ˌplant**) a plant that is grown in a container inside a house

houseproud /ˈhaʊs.praʊd/ **adj** mainly UK very worried about your house being completely clean and tidy, and spending a lot of time making it so

ˈhouse-room **noun** **wouldn't give sth house-room** something that you say about something that you would not like to have in your house

ˈhouse-sit **verb** [I] to stay in someone's house while they are away in order to keep it safe • **ˈhouse-ˌsitter** **noun** [C] • **ˈhouse-ˌsitting** **noun** [U]

the ˌHouses of ˈParliament **noun** [plural] the UK parliament, consisting of the House of Commons and the House of Lords

ˈhouse ˌsparrow **noun** [C] a common small grey and brown bird

ˌhouse-to-ˈhouse **adj** [before noun], **adv** going to every house, or from one house to the next, in a particular area or road: *Police are making house-to-house enquiries.*

ˈhouse-trained **adj** mainly UK (US usually **house-broken**) describes a pet that has learned not to urinate or empty its bowels in your home

housewares /ˈhaʊs.weəz/ (US) /-werz/ **noun** [plural] US (UK **ˌhousehold ˈgoods**) equipment, tools, and machines used in a house, especially in the kitchen

housewarming (party) /ˈhaʊs.wɔː.mɪŋˌpɑː.ti/ (US) /-wɔːr.mɪŋˌpɑːr.t̬i/ **noun** [C] a party which you give when you move into a new house: *We're* ***having*** *a housewarming on Friday if you'd like to come.*

housewife /ˈhaʊs.waɪf/ **noun** [C] (plural **housewives**) (A2) a woman whose work is inside the home, doing the cleaning, cooking, etc., and who usually does not have any other job • **housewifely** /-li/ **adj**

housework /ˈhaʊs.wɜːk/ (US) /-wɜːk/ **noun** [U] (B1) the work of keeping a house clean and tidy: *I hate* ***doing*** *housework.*

housing /ˈhaʊ.zɪŋ/ **noun** [U] (C1) buildings for people to live in: *There's a shortage of cheap housing in the region.*

ˈhousing asˌsociation **noun** [C, + sing/pl verb] UK a group of people who join together so that they can build or buy houses or apartments at low cost

ˈhousing ˌbenefit **noun** [U] in the UK, money paid by the government to help people who are poor pay for a place to live in

ˈhousing esˌtate **noun** [C] UK (US **ˈhousing deˌvelopment**, US also **subdivision**) an area containing a large number of houses or apartments built close together at the same time: *They live* ***on/in*** *a housing estate.*

ˈhousing ˌproject **noun** [C] US (also **project**, UK **ˈcouncil eˌstate**) a group of houses or apartments, usually provided by the government for families who have low incomes

HOV /ˌeɪtʃ.əʊˈviː/ (US) /-oʊ-/ **noun** [C] US abbreviation for high-occupancy vehicle: a road vehicle that carries a lot of people such as a bus, or a car with more than one passenger: *Solo drivers can pay to ride on the HOV* ***lanes***. ◦ *In the morning and afternoon rush hours HOV restrictions are enforced.*

hove /həʊv/ (US) /hoʊv/ **verb** literary **hove in(to) sight/view** appeared: *After 30 minutes, a large ship hove into sight on the horizon.*

hovel /ˈhɒv.əl/ (US) /ˈhɑː.vəl/ **noun** [C] a small home that is dirty and in bad condition

hover /ˈhɒv.əʳ/ (US) /ˈhɑː.vɚ/ **verb** **1** [I usually + adv/prep] to stay in one place in the air, usually by moving the wings quickly: *A hawk hovered in the sky, waiting to swoop down on its prey.* ◦ *I heard the noise of a helicopter hovering overhead.* **2** [I usually + adv/prep] to stand somewhere, especially near another person, eagerly or nervously waiting for their attention: *A waiter hovered at the table, ready to take our order.* ◦ *I could sense him behind me, hovering and building up* *the courage to ask me a question.* **3** [I + prep] to stay at or near a particular level: *Inflation is hovering* ***at*** *three percent.* **4** [I + adv/prep, T] to put the CURSOR on a computer screen in a particular place without CLICKING on it: *The link changes to green when the mouse hovers* ***over*** *it.* ◦ *If you hover the mouse pointer over the entry, the full web address will be displayed.*

hovercraft /ˈhɒv.ə.krɑːft/ (US) /ˈhɑː.vɚ.kræft/ **noun** [C] (plural **hovercrafts** or **hovercraft**) a vehicle that travels quickly just above the surface of water or land by producing a current of air under it to support it

ˈ**hover** ˌ**mower** **noun** [C] UK a LAWNMOWER that cuts grass with blades that SPIN round, and that is held slightly above the ground by a current of air below it

how /haʊ/ **adv** **1** A2 in what way, or by what methods: *How do we get to the town from here?* ◦ *How did you hear about the concert?* ◦ *How does this machine work?* ◦ *How do you plan to spend your holiday?* ◦ *Roz doesn't know how* ***to*** *ride a bicycle.* ◦ *It all depends on how you look at it.* ◦ *I don't care about fashion, I dress how I please.* ◦ *I was horrified to hear about how (= the way) she had been treated.* ◦ *How* ***can/could*** *he be so stupid?* ◦ *I don't know how anyone* ***could*** *think that way.* **2** A2 used to mean in what condition, especially of physical or emotional health: *How is your mother?* ◦ *How are you feeling this morning?* **3** A1 used in questions which ask what an experience or event was like: *How was your flight?* ◦ *How did you* ***find*** *the lecture? (= did you think it was good)?* ◦ *How* ***did*** *you* ***like*** *the concert (= did you enjoy it)?* ◦ *She didn't say how* ***far*** *it is (= what the distance is) to her house.* ◦ *How* ***long*** *are you going to be (= what amount of time are you going to spend) in the bathroom?* ◦ *Do you know how* ***many*** *(= what number of) people are coming?* ◦ *How* ***much*** *does this cost (= what is its price)?* ◦ *How* ***old*** *is his daughter (= what age is she)?* ◦ *'Can you lift this case?' 'It depends on how heavy it is.'* ◦ *Do you remember how (= the fact that) we used to see every new film as soon as it came out?* **4** B1 used for emphasis: *I can't tell you how pleased I am (= I am very pleased) that you came.* ◦ *How (= it is very) nice to see you!* ◦ *'She paid for everything.' 'How (= that was very) generous.'* **5 how strange, stupid, weird, etc. is that?** C2 informal used to emphasize that something is strange, stupid, etc. **6 how are you?** A1 used to ask someone if they are well and happy: *'Hi, Lucy, how are you?' 'Fine, thanks, how are you?'* **7 how are things?** (also **how's everything?**, also **how's it going?**) used as greetings **8 how do you mean?** used when you want someone to explain what they have just said: *'I think we need to reconsider our position.' 'How do you mean?'* **9 how's that?** used when asking if something you have done for someone is satisfactory: *Let me put a cushion behind your back. How's that?* **10 and how!** informal used to show that you feel the same way as someone: *'I'll be so glad when this project is finished.' 'And how!'*

IDIOMS **how about...?** **1** A2 informal used to make a suggestion: *How about the cinema tonight?* ◦ *How about going to the cinema?* **2** used when asking someone about a different thing: *You don't eat meat, do you? How about fish?* • **how about that?** informal used to emphasize that something is surprising: *Sales are up by 36 percent. How about that?* • **how come?** informal C1 used to ask about the reason for something: *So how come you got an invitation and not me?* ◦ *'I don't think I'll be able to go swimming tomorrow.' 'How come?'* • **how do you do?** formal A2 a formal greeting for someone that you have not met before: *'I'm Jack Stewart.' 'How do you do? I'm Angela Black.'*

> **! Common mistake: how**
>
> **Warning:** check your word order!
>
> When **how** is used in a main clause to ask a question, the verb comes before the subject:
>
> *How can we solve this problem?*
>
> When **how** is used in a subordinate clause to talk about the way something can be done, do not put the verb before the subject:
>
> ~~*I have been wondering how can we solve this problem.*~~
>
> *I have been wondering how we can solve this problem.*

howdy /ˈhaʊ.di/ **exclamation** US informal hello

however /ˌhaʊˈev.əʳ/ (US) /-ɚ/ **adv** **1** B2 despite whatever amount or degree: *However hungry I am, I never seem to be able to finish off a whole pizza.* ◦ *If Emma likes something she'll buy it however much it costs.* ◦ *I'll see you after the show and give you £20 for the tickets, or however much (= whatever) they cost.* **2** used to express surprise: *However did you manage to get him to agree to that?* **3** C2 in whatever way: *However you look at it, it's still a mess.* ◦ *You can do it however you like, it really doesn't matter.* **4** A2 despite this: *This is one possible solution to the problem. However, there are others.* ◦ *There may, however, be other reasons that we don't know about.*

howitzer /ˈhaʊ.ɪt.səʳ/ (US) /-sɚ/ **noun** [C] a large gun which fires SHELLS (= very large bullets) high into the air so that they drop onto the place at which they are aimed

howl /haʊl/ **verb; noun**

▸**verb** PERSON/ANIMAL ▷ **1** [I] If a dog or WOLF howls, it makes a long, sad sound: *In the silence of the night, a lone* ***wolf*** *howled.* **2** [I or T] to make a loud sound, usually to express pain, sadness, or another strong emotion: *An injured dog lay in the middle of the road, howling* ***with/in*** *pain.* ◦ *We were howling* ***with laughter.*** ◦ figurative *The opposition howled* ***down*** *the government's proposal (= shouted loudly to express disapproval).* WIND ▷ **3** [I] If the wind howls, it blows hard and makes a lot of noise: *Is there someone outside, or is it just the* ***wind*** *howling in the trees?*

▸**noun** **1** [C] a long, loud, sad sound: *the howl of the wind in the trees* ◦ *He leaves his dog shut up in the house all day, and we can hear its howls.* ◦ *She let out a howl* ***of*** *pain.* **2** [C usually plural] a strong expression of emotion, such as anger or disagreement: *Plans to build a new supermarket have been greeted with howls* ***of*** *protest from local residents.*

howler /ˈhaʊ.ləʳ/ (US) /-lɚ/ **noun** [C] a stupid and obvious mistake, especially in something that someone says or writes: *I called her by the name of his first wife, which was a bit of a howler.*

howling /ˈhaʊ.lɪŋ/ **adj** **be a howling success** to be very successful: *Neither film was a howling success.*

howsoever /ˌhaʊ.səʊˈev.əʳ/ (US) /-soʊˈev.ɚ/ **adv** formal for **however**

ˌ**how-ˈto** **adj** [before noun] describes a book, video, or other product that provides advice on a particular activity: *How-to books on dieting are often at the top of the bestseller lists.*

howzit /ˈhaʊz.ɪt/ **exclamation** South African English informal hello

hp written abbreviation for **horsepower**

HP /ˌeɪtʃˈpiː/ **noun** [U] UK abbreviation for **hire purchase**: *We bought our television* ***on*** *HP.*

HQ /ˌeɪtʃˈkjuː/ **noun** [C, + sing/pl verb] abbreviation for **headquarters**: *We've just received instructions from HQ.*

hr **noun** [C] (plural **hrs**) written abbreviation for **hour**: *He ran the marathon in 2 hrs 48 mins.* ◦ *The plane departs at 15.00 hrs.*

HRH /ˌeɪtʃ.ɑːˈreɪtʃ/ (US) /-ɑːrˈeɪtʃ/ abbreviation for His or Her Royal Highness: a title of some members of a royal family: *HRH the Prince of Wales*

HRT /ˌeɪtʃ.ɑːˈtiː/ (US) /-ɑːr-/ **noun** [U] abbreviation for **hormone replacement therapy**

HSC /ˌeɪtʃ.esˈsiː/ **noun** [C] abbreviation for Higher School Certificate: an Australian exam taken in the last two years of school education

ht **noun** [U] written abbreviation for **height**: *Ht of bridge 1.8 m.*

hth written abbreviation for hope this helps: used, in an email for example, when you send someone information that you think is useful, often when answering a question

H

HTML /ˌeɪtʃ.tiː.emˈel/ **noun** [U] trademark abbreviation for hypertext markup language: a way of marking text so that it can be seen on the internet

http /ˌeɪtʃ.tiː.tiːˈpiː/ **noun** [U] trademark abbreviation for hypertext transfer protocol: a set of instructions made by a computer program that allows your computer to connect to an internet document: *http://www.cambridge.org*

hub /hʌb/ **noun** [C] **CENTRAL PART** ▷ **1** the central or main part of something where there is most activity: *The City of London is the hub* ***of*** *Britain's financial world.* ◦ *The computer department is* ***at the*** *hub* ***of*** *the company's operations.* **WHEEL** ▷ **2** the central part of a wheel into which the SPOKES (= bars connecting the central part to the outer edge of the wheel) are fixed

hubbub /ˈhʌb.ʌb/ **noun** [U] **1** a loud noise, especially caused by a lot of people all talking at the same time: *I could hardly hear myself speak above all the hubbub in the theatre bar.* **2** general excitement and activity: *Once the hubbub* ***of*** *the election had died down, it was back to normal for the president.*

hubby /ˈhʌb.i/ **noun** [C] informal for husband

hubcap /ˈhʌb.kæp/ **noun** [C] the circular metal covering over the hub

hubris /ˈhjuː.brɪs/ **noun** [U] literary a way of talking or behaving that is too proud: *He was punished for his hubris.*

huckleberry /ˈhʌk.lˌber.i/ **noun** [C] a small round dark blue fruit, or the low North American bush on which it grows

huckster /ˈhʌk.stəʳ/ (US) /-stɚ/ **noun** [C] US often disapproving a person who writes advertisements, especially for radio and television, or who sells things or brings ideas or people to the public's attention in a noisy annoying way

huddle /ˈhʌd.l/ **verb; noun**

▸**verb** [I usually + adv/prep] to come close together in a group, or to hold your arms and legs close to your body, especially because of cold or fear: *Everyone huddled* ***round*** *the fire to keep warm.* ◦ *It was so cold that we huddled* ***together*** *for warmth.* ◦ *Sophie was so frightened by the noise of the fireworks that she huddled (****up****) in a corner of the room.*

▸**noun** [C] **SMALL GROUP** ▷ **1** a small group of people or things that are close together: *A small group of people stood* ***in a*** *huddle at the bus stop.* **2 go into a huddle** to get into a group in order to talk secretly: *The judges went into a huddle to decide the winner.* **AMERICAN FOOTBALL** ▷ **3** US a group formed by the members of a team in American football before they separate and continue to play

huddled /ˈhʌd.ld/ **adj** standing or sitting close together: *We stood huddled* ***together*** *for warmth.*

hue /hjuː/ **noun** [C] **COLOUR** ▷ **1** (a degree of lightness, darkness, strength, etc. of) a colour: *In the Caribbean waters there are fish of every hue.* **TYPE** ▷ **2** literary a different type or group: *Politicians* ***of all*** *hues wish to get sleaze off the agenda so that they can discuss the real issues.*

IDIOM **hue and cry** a noisy expression of public anger or disapproval: *There has been a* ***great*** *hue and cry about the council's plans to close the school.*

huff /hʌf/ **noun; verb**

▸**noun** [C] informal **1** an angry and offended mood: *Ted's* ***gone into*** *one of his huffs again.* **2 in a huff** angry and offended: *She's in a real huff because I forgot her birthday.* ◦ *Julia criticized some aspect of his work and he* ***left/went off*** *in a huff.*

▸**verb** [I] to say something in an annoyed or offended way: *'Well if that's how you feel, I'll go,' she huffed.*

IDIOM **huff and puff 1** to breathe loudly, usually after physical exercise: *We were huffing and puffing by the time we'd climbed to the top of the hill.* **2** informal disapproving to complain loudly and express disapproval: *They huffed and puffed about the price but eventually they paid up.*

huffy /ˈhʌf.i/ **adj** angry and offended: *I told her she'd made a mistake and she* ***got*** *huffy* ***with*** *me.* • **huffily** /-ɪ.li/ **adv**

hug /hʌg/ **verb; noun**

▸**verb** [T] (**-gg-**) **1** (B1) to hold someone or something close to your body with your arms, usually to show that you like, love, or value them: *Have you hugged your child today?* ◦ *They hugged each other when they met at the station.* ◦ *Emily hugged her teddy bear* ***tightly*** *to her chest.* ◦ *She sat on the floor hugging her* ***knees*** *(= with her knees bent up against her chest and her arms around them).* ◦ *Whenever I travel in the city I make sure I hug my handbag tightly* ***to*** *me.* **2** to stay very close to something or someone: *The road hugs the coast for several miles, then turns inland.* ◦ *This type of car will hug (= not slide on) the road, even in the wettest conditions.* ◦ *a figure-hugging dress* **3** literary to keep something that makes you feel better or pleases you private or secret: *I hugged the idea* ***to myself*** *all through dinner.*

▸**noun** [C] (B1) the act of holding someone or something close to your body with your arms: *Come here and* ***give*** *me a* ***big*** *hug.* ◦ *We always exchange hugs* ***and kisses*** *when we meet.*

huge /hjuːdʒ/ **adj** (B1) extremely large in size or amount: *They live in a huge house.* ◦ *The costs involved in building a spacecraft are huge.* ◦ *A huge number of people attended.* ◦ *His last three films have all been huge successes.*

hugely /ˈhjuːdʒ.li/ **adv** to a great degree: *He gave her a hugely expensive diamond ring.* → Synonym **extremely**

huh /hə/ **exclamation 1** informal used to show that you have not heard or understood something: *'So what do you want to do tonight?' 'Huh? What did you say?'* ◦ *Huh? These instructions don't make sense!* **2** humorous used to express disapproval: *Huh, I don't think much of that idea!* **3** mainly US used at the end of a question or statement, especially when you want someone to agree with what you have said: *I'll bet you wish you hadn't done that, huh?* ◦ *Pretty cool, huh?*

ˈ**Hula-ˌHoop** US trademark (UK ˈ**hula ˌhoop**) **noun** [C] a large ring, usually made of plastic, that children play with by putting it around their waist and moving their body so that it SPINS

hulk /hʌlk/ noun [C] **SHIP** ▷ **1** the body of an old ship, car, or very large piece of equipment that is broken and no longer used: *Here and there the rusted hulk of an abandoned car dots the landscape.* **AWKWARD** ▷ **2** a large, heavy, awkward person or thing: *Henry's a real hulk of a man.*

hulking /ˈhʌl.kɪŋ/ adj large and heavy: *We were stopped by two hulking security guards.* ◦ *How do you expect me to lift that hulking **great** box?*

hull /hʌl/ noun; verb

▸noun [C] the body or frame of a ship, most of which goes under the water

▸verb [T] (US also **shuck**) to remove the covering or the stem and leaves from some fruits, vegetables, and seeds: *We sat in the garden hulling strawberries.*

hullabaloo /ˌhʌl.ə.bəˈluː/ noun [S] old-fashioned a loud noise made by people who are angry or annoyed: *There's a crowd of angry demonstrators **making** a real hullabaloo outside the Houses of Parliament.* ◦ *The minister resigned after all the hullabaloo (= public disapproval) over his affair with an actress.*

hullo /həˈləʊ/ US /-ˈloʊ/ exclamation, noun [C] (plural **hullos**) UK **hello**

hum /hʌm/ verb; noun

▸verb (**-mm-**) **1** [I] to make a continuous low sound: *The computers were humming in the background.* ◦ *What's that strange humming sound?* **2** [I or T] to sing without opening your mouth: *She hummed to herself as she walked to school.* **3** [I] informal to be busy and full of activity, excitement, sounds, or voices: *The pub was really humming last night.*

IDIOM **hum and haw** UK (US **hem and haw**) to be uncertain and take a long time deciding something: *We hummed and hawed for months before actually deciding to buy the house.*

▸noun [C usually singular] a continuous low noise: *Our house is on a main road, so we can hear the constant hum **of** traffic.* ◦ *There's an annoying hum on this computer.*

human /ˈhjuː.mən/ adj; noun

▸adj B1 of or typical of people: *The human **body** is composed of about 60 percent water.* ◦ *Early human **remains** were found in the Dordogne region of France.* ◦ *Victory in the war was achieved at the cost of great human **suffering**.* ◦ *The inspector declared the meat **fit for** human **consumption** (= in good enough condition for people to eat).* ◦ *Of course I make mistakes, I'm **only** human (= I am not perfect).* ◦ *The fault was due to human **error** (= a person making a mistake).*

▸noun [C] (also **ˌhuman ˈbeing**) B1 a man, woman, or child: *The greatest damage being done to our planet today is that being done by humans.*

humane /hjuːˈmeɪn/ adj showing kindness, care, and sympathy towards others, especially those who are suffering: *The humane way of dealing with a suffering animal (= the way that causes the least pain) is to kill it quickly.* → Opposite **inhumane** • **humanely** /-li/ adv *I don't support the death penalty, but if people are to be executed, it should be done humanely.*

ˌhuman immunodeˈficiency ˌvirus noun [S] (abbreviation **HIV**) the virus that causes AIDS (= a serious disease that destroys the body's ability to fight infection)

ˌhuman ˈinterest noun [U] details about people's experiences and feelings: *I like newspapers with lots of human interest **stories** in them.*

humanism /ˈhjuː.mə.nɪ.zəm/ noun [U] a belief system based on the principle that people's spiritual and emotional needs can be satisfied without following a god or religion • **humanist** /-nɪst/ noun [C] a person who believes in humanism • **humanist** adj *humanist beliefs/writers/ideas* • **humanistic** /ˌhjuː.məˈnɪs.tɪk/ adj *humanistic principles*

humanitarian /hjuːˌmæn.ɪˈteə.ri.ən/ US /-ˈter.i-/ adj, noun [C] C2 (a person who is) involved in or connected with improving people's lives and reducing suffering: *The prisoner has been released for humanitarian reasons.* ◦ *The United Nations is sending humanitarian **aid** (= food and supplies to help people) to the areas worst affected by the conflict.* ◦ *The well-known humanitarian, Joseph Rowntree, was concerned with the welfare of his employees.* • **humanitarianism** /-ə.nɪ.zəm/ noun [U]

humanity /hjuːˈmæn.ə.ti/ US /-t̬i/ noun **PEOPLE** ▷ **1** C1 [U] people in general: *The massacre was a crime against humanity.* **KINDNESS** ▷ **2** C2 [U] understanding and kindness towards other people: *If only he would **show/display** a little humanity for once.* **BEING HUMAN** ▷ **3** C2 [U] the condition of being human: *There is a sense of common humanity that unites people of all nations.* **SUBJECTS** ▷ **4** **(the) humanities** [plural] the study of subjects such as literature, language, history, and PHILOSOPHY: *I've always been more interested in the humanities than the sciences.*

humanize (UK usually **humanise**) /ˈhjuː.mə.naɪz/ verb [T] to make something less unpleasant and more suitable for people: *Steps are being taken to humanize the prison.* • **humanization** (UK usually **humanisation**) /ˌhjuː.mə.naɪˈzeɪ.ʃən/ US /-nəˈ-/ noun [U]

humankind /ˌhjuː.mənˈkaɪnd/ noun [U] all people, considered as a group

humanly /ˈhjuː.mən.li/ adv **humanly possible** able to be done by people: *Rescuers are doing everything that is humanly possible to free the trapped people.*

ˌhuman ˈnature noun [U] the natural ways of behaving that most people share: *You can't change human nature.* ◦ *It's **only** human nature (= it is natural) to want the best for your children.*

humanoid /ˈhjuː.mə.nɔɪd/ noun [C] a machine or creature with the appearance and qualities of a human • **humanoid** adj

the ˌhuman ˈrace noun [S] all the people in the world, considered as a group

ˌhuman reˈlations noun [plural] relationships between groups of people, especially between workers in a place of work, or the study of these relationships

ˌhuman reˈsources noun [plural] the department of an organization that deals with finding new employees, keeping records about all the organization's employees, and helping them with any problems

ˌhuman ˈrights noun [plural] B2 the basic rights which it is generally considered all people should have, such as JUSTICE and the freedom to say what you think: *She's claiming that her detention by the police was a violation of her human rights.*

ˌhuman ˈshield noun [C] a person or group of people kept in a particular place in order to stop an enemy from attacking that place: *Military bases were protected by captured enemy soldiers who were housed there as a human shield.*

the ˌhuman ˈtouch noun [S] a friendly and pleasant way of treating other people that makes them feel relaxed: *He is certainly an effective lawyer but colleagues say that he lacks the human touch.*

humble /ˈhʌm.bl̩/ adj; verb
▸adj **1** C2 not proud or not believing that you are important: *He's very humble about his success.* ◦ formal *Please accept our humble* ***apologies*** *for the error.* ◦ *In my humble* ***opinion*** (= *I want to emphasize that I think that*) *we should never have bought the car in the first place.* **2** C2 poor or of a low social rank: *Even when she became rich and famous, she never forgot her humble background.* **3** ordinary; not special or very important: *At that time she was just a humble mechanic.* ◦ humorous *Welcome to our humble* ***abode*** (= *our home*).
▸verb [T] to make someone understand that they are not as important or special as they thought they were: *He was humbled by the child's generosity.* ◦ *The world champion was humbled* (= *unexpectedly defeated*) *by an unknown outsider in last night's race.* • **humbling** /-blɪŋ/ adj *It's a humbling* ***experience*** *to see people being so positive about life when they have so little.*

H

humbly /ˈhʌm.bli/ adv in a way that shows that you do not think you are important: *He very humbly ascribes his success to his wife.*

humbug /ˈhʌm.bʌɡ/ noun **DISHONESTY** ▷ **1** [U] dishonest talk, writing, or behaviour that is intended to deceive people: *the usual political humbug* **SWEET** ▷ **2** [C] UK a hard sweet, usually with a MINT taste and strips of two different colours on the outside: *mint humbugs*

humdinger /ˌhʌmˈdɪŋ.əʳ/ US /-ɚ/ noun [S] humorous something or someone that is noticeable because it is a very good example of its type: *Annabel's party was a real humdinger.* ◦ *My brother and sister had a humdinger* ***of*** *a row last night.*

humdrum /ˈhʌm.drʌm/ adj having no excitement, interest, or new and different events: *We lead such a humdrum* ***life/existence***. ◦ *Most of the work is fairly humdrum.* → Synonym **ordinary**

humerus /ˈhjuː.mə.rəs/ noun [C] (plural **humeri**) specialized the long bone in the upper half of your arm, between your shoulder and your ELBOW (= the middle part of the arm where it bends)

humid /ˈhjuː.mɪd/ adj B1 (of air and weather conditions) containing extremely small drops of water in the air: *New York is very hot and humid in the summer.*

humidifier /hjuːˈmɪd.ɪ.faɪ.əʳ/ US /-ɚ/ noun [C] a machine which makes dry air in a room wetter

humidify /hjuːˈmɪd.ɪ.faɪ/ verb [T] to make dry air wetter: *If the air in a room is too dry, you can put a bowl of water near the radiator to humidify it.*

humidity /hjuːˈmɪd.ɪ.ti/ US /-ə.t̬i/ noun [U] **1** the quality of being humid: *I don't like the humidity of this climate.* **2** a measurement of how much water there is in the air: *The temperature is almost 80 degrees, and the humidity in the low thirties.*

humiliate /hjuːˈmɪl.i.eɪt/ verb [T] to make someone feel ashamed or lose their respect for themselves: *How could you humiliate me by questioning my judgment in front of everyone like that?* ◦ *England were humiliated* (= *completely defeated*) *in last night's match.* • **humiliation** /hjuːˌmɪl.iˈeɪ.ʃᵊn/ noun [C or U] *After the humiliation* ***of*** *last week's defeat, the Mets were back on form.* ◦ *Imagine the humiliation of having to apologize.*

humiliated /hjuːˈmɪl.i.eɪ.tɪd/ US /-t̬ɪd/ adj C2 describes someone who has been made to feel ashamed or stupid: *I've never felt so humiliated in my life.*

humiliating /hjuːˈmɪl.i.eɪ.tɪŋ/ US /-t̬ɪŋ/ adj C2 making you feel ashamed or stupid: *Losing my job was the most humiliating thing that ever happened to me.* ◦ *The government suffered a humiliating* ***defeat*** *in yesterday's debate.* ◦ *He found it humiliating* ***to*** *have to ask for money.*

humility /hjuːˈmɪl.ɪ.ti/ US /-ə.t̬i/ noun [U] C2 the quality of not being proud because you are aware of your bad qualities: *He doesn't have the humility to admit when he's wrong.* ◦ *They might be very rich, but it wouldn't hurt them to show a little humility.*

Hummer /ˈhʌm.əʳ/ US /-ɚ/ noun [C] trademark a type of FOUR-WHEEL DRIVE vehicle that is very wide and strong

hummingbird /ˈhʌm.ɪŋ.bɜːd/ US /-bɝːd/ noun [C] a very small brightly coloured bird with a long thin beak whose wings move very fast and make a HUMMING noise

hummingbird

hummock /ˈhʌm.ək/ noun [C] literary a very small hill or raised part of the ground: *a grassy hummock*

hummus /ˈhʊm.əs/ noun [U] **houmous**

humorist /ˈhjuː.mə.rɪst/ noun [C] a person who writes or tells funny stories

humorous /ˈhjuː.mə.rəs/ adj C1 funny, or making you laugh: *Her latest book is a humorous look at teenage life.* • **humorously** /-li/ adv

humour /ˈhjuː.məʳ/ US /-mɚ/ noun; verb
▸noun UK (US **humor**) **AMUSEMENT** ▷ **1** B1 [U] the ability to find things funny, the way in which people see that some things are funny, or the quality of being funny: *He's got a great* ***sense of*** *humour* (= *he is very able to see things as funny*). ◦ *I must say I find his* ***schoolboy*** (= *childish*) *humour rather tiresome.* **MOOD** ▷ **2** C2 [C or U] formal the state of your feelings: *You seem* ***in*** *a very good humour today.* → Synonym **mood**
▸verb [T] UK (US **humor**) to do what someone wants so that they do not become annoyed or upset: *I applied for the job just to humour my parents.*

-humoured /-hjuː.məd/ US /-mɝːd/ suffix (US **-humored**) used for describing the state of people's feelings: *The election campaign has been remarkably peaceful, even* ***good****-humoured.*

humourless /ˈhjuː.mə.ləs/ US /-mɚ-/ adj UK (US **humorless**) having no humour

hump /hʌmp/ noun; verb
▸noun **LUMP** ▷ **1** [C] a large, round raised area or part: *The car hit a hump in the road and swerved.* ◦ UK *Local residents are asking for* ***speed*** *humps* (= *raised areas across the road which make people drive slowly*) *to be installed in their street.* **2** [C] a round raised part on a person's or animal's back: *Some types of camel have two humps and others have one.* → See also **humpbacked**

IDIOMS **get the hump** UK informal to get upset and annoyed with someone because you think they have done something bad to you • **be over the hump** informal to be past the most difficult or dangerous part of an activity or period of time: *It's been hard work but I think we're over the hump now.*

▸verb **CARRY** ▷ **1** [T usually + adv/prep] informal to carry or lift something heavy with difficulty **HAVE SEX** ▷ **2** [I or T] offensive to have sex (with someone)

humpback bridge /ˌhʌmp.bæk ˈbrɪdʒ/ noun [C] (also ˌ**humpbacked** ˈ**bridge**) UK a small, steep road bridge

humpbacked /ˈhʌmp.bækt/ adj (of an animal)

having a round raised part on its back: *a humpbacked whale*

humph /hʌmf/ **exclamation** often humorous a short deep sound made with the lips closed, expressing anger or doubt, or pretended anger: *Humph, I see you've got yourself some lunch and you haven't made any for the rest of us!*

humungous UK informal (US **humongous**) /hjuː-ˈmʌŋ.gəs/ **adj** extremely large: *Zesto's restaurant serves humungous burgers.* ◦ *This minor glitch has turned into a humungous problem for the airline.*

humus /ˈhjuː.məs/ **noun** [U] dark earth made of ORGANIC material such as decayed leaves and plants

Humvee /ˈhʌm.viː/ **noun** [C] trademark a large, strong military vehicle used for travelling over rough ground

Hun /hʌn/ **noun** [C] a member of a group of people from Asia who attacked Europe in the 4th and 5th centuries

hunch /hʌntʃ/ **noun; verb**

▸**noun** [C] an idea that is based on feeling and for which there is no proof: [+ that] *I **had** a hunch **that** you'd be here.* ◦ *Sometimes you have to be prepared to **act on/follow** a hunch.*

▸**verb** [I or T] to lean forward with your shoulders raised or to bend your back and shoulders into a rounded shape: *We hunched round the fire to keep warm.* ◦ *Stand up straight and don't hunch your back.* • **hunched** /hʌntʃt/ **adj** *Sitting hunched **over** a computer all day can cause problems.*

hunchback /ˈhʌntʃ.bæk/ **noun** [C] old-fashioned (a person who has) a back with a large round LUMP (= raised area) on it, either because of illness or old age • **hunchbacked** /-bækt/ **adj**

hundred /ˈhʌn.drəd/ **number** (plural **hundred** or **hundreds**) **1** A2 the number 100: *We've driven a/one hundred miles in the last two hours.* ◦ *'How many children are there in the school?' 'About three hundred.'* ◦ *That dress costs hundreds **of** pounds.* **2 a hundred/hundreds of sth** B2 informal a large number: *There were hundreds of people at the pool today.* ◦ *There are a hundred shirts waiting to be ironed.* **3 the hundreds** numbers between 100 and 1,000: *He expects the total amount to be in the low hundreds.* **4 the eighteen hundreds, nineteen hundreds, etc.** the years of a particular century: *The house was built in the sixteen hundreds.* **5 one hundred, two hundred, etc. hours** used to say the time using the 24-hour system, especially used in the military: *Breakfast is at seven hundred hours.*

> **!** Common mistake: **hundreds or hundred?**
>
> When **hundred** is used after a particular number, it is used in the singular form and without 'of'.
>
> Don't say 'five/ten/fifteen hundred of sth', say five/ten/fifteen **hundred** sth:
>
> ~~*There were six hundreds of people at the conference.*~~
>
> *There were six hundred people at the conference.*
>
> When **hundred** is used without a particular number, it is used in the plural form and is sometimes followed by 'of':
>
> *There were hundreds (of people) at the conference.*

IDIOM **a/one hundred percent** completely: *I agree with you one hundred percent.* ◦ *I'm better than I was last week but I'm still not (feeling) a hundred percent (= I'm not completely well).*

hundredth /ˈhʌn.drətθ/ **ordinal number; noun**

▸**ordinal number** 100th written as a word: *He is now ranked one hundredth in world tennis.* ◦ *1991 was the two hundredth anniversary of Mozart's death.*

▸**noun** [C] one of a hundred equal parts of something: *She has knocked one/a hundredth **of** a second off the world record.*

hundredweight /ˈhʌn.drəd.weɪt/ **noun** [C] (plural **hundredweight**) (written abbreviation **cwt**) a measure of weight equal to 50.80 kilograms in Britain or 45.36 kilograms in the US: *We ordered a hundredweight **of** coal.*

hung /hʌŋ/ **verb; adj**

▸**verb** past simple and past participle of **hang**

▸**adj** having an equal or nearly equal number of members with opposing opinions, so that no decisions can be made: *The general election in Britain was expected to result in a hung **parliament**.* ◦ *a hung **jury***

hunger /ˈhʌŋ.gəʳ/ US /-gɚ/ **noun; verb**

▸**noun NEED FOR FOOD** ▷ **1** B1 [U] the feeling you have when you need to eat: *I can't believe that that enormous meal wasn't enough to **satisfy** your hunger.* ◦ *By about nine o'clock she started to feel **faint from/with** hunger.* ◦ *I often suffer from hunger **pangs** (= strong feelings of needing something to eat) in the middle of the afternoon.* **2** B2 [U] a situation in which the body does not have enough food: *All over the world, people **die of** hunger every day.* **DESIRE** ▷ **3** C1 [S or U] a strong wish or DESIRE: *a hunger **for** adventure/knowledge/success*

▸**verb**

PHRASAL VERB **hunger after/for sth** literary to want something very much: *I hunger **for** your touch.* ◦ *I've never hungered **after** power.*

ˈ**hunger** ˌ**strike** **noun** [C or U] the act of refusing to eat in order to make a protest: *The prisoners have **gone on** (a) hunger strike to protest about prison conditions.* • ˈ**hunger** ˌ**striker** **noun** [C]

hungover /ˌhʌŋˈəʊ.vəʳ/ US /-ˈoʊ.vɚ/ **adj** [after verb] feeling ill with a bad pain in the head and often wanting to vomit after having drunk too much alcohol: *That was a great party last night, but I'm (feeling) really hungover this morning.* → See also **hangover**

> **+** Other ways of saying **hungry**
>
> The adjective **ravenous** can be used to describe someone who is very hungry:
>
> *I'm **ravenous**; when's dinner ready?*
>
> Informal words which mean 'very hungry' are **famished** or **starving**:
>
> *I'm **famished**! I haven't eaten anything since this morning.*
>
> *Is there anything to eat? I'm **starving**!*
>
> The phrase **have a good appetite** can be used for someone who is often hungry and eats a lot of food:
>
> *Both my children **have** very **good appetites**.*

hungry /ˈhʌŋ.gri/ **adj NEEDING FOOD** ▷ **1** A1 wanting or needing food: *By four o'clock I **felt/was** really hungry.* ◦ *The children are always hungry when they get home from school.* ◦ *There are too many hungry people (= people without enough to eat) in the world.* ◦ *She often **goes** hungry herself (= does not eat) so that her children can have enough to eat.* ◦ *Digging the garden is hungry **work** (= makes you feel hunger).* **WANTING** ▷ **2** C2 having a strong wish or DESIRE for something: *She was so hungry **for** success that she'd do anything to achieve it.* ◦ *Journalists were hungry **for** details.* • **hungrily** /-grɪ.li/ **adv** *They sat down and ate*

H

hungrily. ◦ *He looked at her hungrily (= showing desire for her).*

-hungry /-hʌŋ.gri/ suffix having a strong wish or DESIRE for the stated thing: *power-hungry politicians*

ˌhung ˈup adj [after verb] informal having a HANG-UP (= feeling of worry about yourself): *Why are so many women so hung up **about** food?*

IDIOM **be hung up on sth** to be extremely interested in or worried by a particular subject and spend an unreasonably large amount of time thinking about it: *Why are you so hung up on getting everything right?*

hunk /hʌŋk/ noun [C] **PIECE** ▷ **1** a large thick piece, especially of food: *a hunk **of** bread/cheese/meat* **MAN** ▷ **2** informal approving a tall strong attractive man

hunker /ˈhʌŋ.kəʳ/ ⓤⓢ /-kɚ/ verb

PHRASAL VERB **hunker down** US **1** to sit down on your HEELS: *We hunkered down round the campfire, toasting marshmallows.* **2** to make yourself comfortable in a place or situation, or to prepare to stay in a place or position for a long time, usually in order to achieve something or for protection: *The press have hunkered down for the night outside the palace, waiting for news of the royal birth.*

H

hunky /ˈhʌŋ.ki/ adj informal approving describes a man who is sexually attractive and usually big and strong

hunky-dory /ˌhʌŋ.kiˈdɔː.ri/ ⓤⓢ /-ˈdɔːr.i/ adj [after verb] old-fashioned informal describes events or situations that are very satisfactory and pleasant: *You can't lose your temper one minute and then expect **everything** to be hunky-dory again the next.*

hunt /hʌnt/ verb; noun

▸verb [I or T] **CHASE** ▷ **1** (B1) to chase and try to catch and kill an animal or bird for food, sport, or profit: *Some animals hunt at night.* ◦ *When lion cubs are young, the mother stays with them while the father hunts **for** food.* ◦ *Jack and Charlie like to hunt/go hunting (= chase and kill animals for sport) at weekends.* ◦ *Cats like to hunt mice and birds.* ◦ *Elephants used to be hunted **for** the ivory from their tusks.* **2** in Britain, to chase and kill animals, especially FOXES, using dogs and riding on horses **SEARCH** ▷ **3** (B2) to try to find something or someone: *I've hunted all over the place, but I can't find that book.* ◦ *They are still hunting **for** the missing child.* ◦ *I've hunted **high and low** (= looked everywhere) **for** my gloves.* ◦ *Police are hunting the terrorists who planted the bomb.* ◦ *I'll try and hunt **out** (= find) those old photographs for you.* ◦ *They have spent months **house-/job-**hunting (= looking for a house/a job).*

PHRASAL VERB **hunt sb/sth down** to search everywhere for someone or something until you find them: *The terrorists must be hunted down and brought to justice.*

▸noun **SEARCH** ▷ **1** (C1) [C usually singular] a search for something or someone: *After a long hunt we finally found a house we liked.* ◦ *The hunt **for** the injured climber continued throughout the night.* ◦ *Police are **on the** hunt (= searching) **for** the kidnappers.* ◦ ***The** hunt **is on** (= the search has started) **for** a successor to Sir James Gordon.* **CHASE** ▷ **2** [C] the activity of people chasing wild animals in order to kill them: *to **go on** a fox/deer hunt* **3** [C] in the UK, a group of people who meet regularly in order to chase and kill animals, especially FOXES: *They are members of the local hunt.*

hunted /hʌn.tɪd/ ⓤⓢ /-t̬ɪd/ adj **1** looking frightened and worried: *Carla always has such a hunted **look**.* **2** [before noun] A hunted animal or person is being chased by someone.

hunter /ˈhʌn.təʳ/ ⓤⓢ /-t̬ɚ/ noun [C] **1** a person or an animal that hunts animals for food or for sport: *Animals in the cat family are hunters.* **2** a type of horse, especially one used in hunting animals

-hunter /-hʌn.təʳ/ ⓤⓢ /-t̬ɚ/ suffix **CHASE** ▷ **1** someone who hunts the stated animal: *a fox-hunter* **SEARCH** ▷ **2** someone who is trying to find or get the stated thing: *a job-hunter* ◦ *a house-hunter* ◦ *bargain-hunters*

ˌhunter-ˈgatherer noun [C] a member of a society that lives by hunting and collecting wild food, rather than by farming

hunting /ˈhʌn.tɪŋ/ ⓤⓢ /-t̬ɪŋ/ noun [U] **1** (B2) chasing and killing an animal or bird for food, sport, or profit: *deer hunting* ◦ *a hunting dog/rifle* **2** (B2) in Britain, the chasing and killing of animals, especially FOXES, for sport, using dogs and riding horses

ˈhunting ˌground noun [C] a place where you can find a lot of what you are looking for: *Flea markets are **happy** hunting grounds for people looking for antiques.*

ˈhunt saboˌteur noun [C] a person who tries to stop a hunt, especially a FOX hunt, because they think it is cruel to animals

huntsman /ˈhʌnts.mən/ noun [C] (plural **-men** /-mən/) **1** someone who hunts animals with a gun or other weapons **2** in Britain, someone who uses dogs and rides a horse to hunt animals, especially FOXES, for sport

hurdle /ˈhɜː.dl̩/ ⓤⓢ /ˈhɝː-/ noun; verb

▸noun **FENCE** ▷ **1** [C] a frame or fence for jumping over in a race: *He fell at the last hurdle.* ◦ *She **cleared** (= jumped over) all the hurdles easily and raced to the finishing line.* **2 hurdles** [plural] a race in which people or horses jump over hurdles: *the 400-metres hurdles* **PROBLEM** ▷ **3** a problem that you have to deal with before you can make progress: *Getting a work permit was the first hurdle to **overcome**.* ◦ *The cost of this exercise is proving a major hurdle.*

▸verb [I or T] to run in a race in which there are hurdles to be jumped over, or to jump over something while running: *He hurdled the gate and scrambled up the hill.*

hurdler /ˈhɜː.dləʳ/ ⓤⓢ /ˈhɝː.dlɚ/ noun [C] a person or horse that runs in races where there are hurdles

hurdy-gurdy /ˈhɜː.diˌgɜː.di/ ⓤⓢ /ˈhɝː.diˌgɝːr.di/ noun [C] a musical instrument that is played by turning a handle, causing a small wheel to be rubbed against a set of strings

hurl /hɜːl/ ⓤⓢ /hɝːl/ verb [T] **1** to throw something with a lot of force, usually in an angry or violent way: *In a fit of temper he hurled the book **across** the room.* ◦ *Youths hurled stones **at** the soldiers.* **2 hurl abuse, insults, etc. at sb** to shout insults or rude language at someone angrily

hurly-burly /ˈhɜː.liˌbɜː.li/ ⓤⓢ /ˈhɝː.liˌbɝːr-/ noun [U] noisy activity: *We got tired of the hurly-burly **of** city life, so we moved to the country.*

hurray /həˈreɪ/, /hʊ-/ exclamation (also **hooray**, also **hurrah**) used to express excitement, pleasure, or approval: *You won? Hurray!* ◦ *Hurray! It's time to go home.* → See also **hip**

hurricane /ˈhʌr.ɪ.kən/, /-keɪn/ ⓤⓢ /ˈhɝː-/ noun [C] a violent wind that has a circular movement, especially in the West Atlantic Ocean: *The state of Florida was **hit** by a hurricane that did serious damage.* ◦ *Hurricane force (= very strong) winds are expected tonight.*

ˈhurricane ˌlamp noun [C] a light produced by burning PARAFFIN, that has a strong glass cover to protect the flame from wind

hurried /ˈhʌr.id/ ⓤⓢ /ˈhɝː-/ adj done very or too quickly: *We left early, after a hurried breakfast.* ◦ *I'm sorry this is such a hurried note.* • **hurriedly** /-li/ adv

The party was a rather hurriedly (= quickly) arranged affair.

hurry /ˈhʌr.i/ (US) /ˈhɜː-/ **verb; noun**

▸**verb** [I or T] A2 to move or do things more quickly than normal or to make someone do this: *Hurry or you'll be late.* ◦ [+ to infinitive] *She hurried* ***to*** *answer the phone.* ◦ *I hate to hurry you, but I have to leave in a few minutes.* ◦ *Don't hurry your food (= don't eat it too quickly).* ◦ *I refuse to be hurried* ***into*** *a decision (= to be forced to make a decision too quickly).* ◦ *After spending her lunch hour shopping, she hurried* ***back*** *(= returned quickly) to work.*

PHRASAL VERB **hurry (sb/sth) up** B1 to move or do things more quickly than normal or to make someone do this: *Hurry up or we'll miss the train.* ◦ *Could you hurry the children up, or their dinner will get cold.*

▸**noun** [S] B1 the need to move or do things more quickly than normal: *We left* ***in*** *such* ***a*** *hurry that we forgot our tickets.* ◦ *'Can you wait a few minutes?' 'Yes, I'm not* ***in any*** *hurry/I'm* ***in no*** *hurry (= I can wait).'* ◦ *Are you* ***in a*** *hurry (= wanting)* ***to*** *leave?* ◦ *What's (all) the hurry (for)/Why (all) the hurry? (= Why are you acting or moving so quickly?)* ◦ *'I'll let you have this back next week.' 'That's all right, there's no (****great****) hurry/there isn't any (****great****) hurry (= no need to do it quickly).'*

hurt /hɜːt/ (US) /hɝːt/ **verb; adj; noun**

▸**verb** [I or T] (**hurt, hurt**) **1** A2 to feel pain in a part of your body, or to injure someone or cause them pain: *Tell me where it hurts.* ◦ *My head hurts.* ◦ *She says that her ear hurts her.* ◦ *Emma hurt her back when she fell off her horse.* ◦ *Several people were* ***seriously/badly*** *hurt in the explosion.* **2** B1 to cause emotional pain to someone: *She criticized my writing quite severely and that hurt.* ◦ *He was badly hurt by the end of his marriage.* **3** to cause harm or difficulty: *A lot of businesses are being hurt by the current high interest rates.* ◦ *These allegations have* ***seriously*** *hurt her reputation.* ◦ *Hard work* ***never*** *hurt anyone (= does no one any harm).* ◦ informal *One more drink won't hurt (= won't cause any harm).*

IDIOMS **it never hurts to do sth** it is wise: *It never hurts to check the flight departure time before you leave for the airport.* • **it wouldn't hurt you to do sth** informal something that you say when you think someone should do something because they do not often do it: *It wouldn't hurt you to do the ironing for once.*

▸**adj** [after verb] **1** B1 injured or in pain: *Let me help you up. Are you hurt?* ◦ *Put that knife away before someone* ***gets*** *hurt.* **2** B1 upset or unhappy: *I feel very hurt by what you said.* ◦ *'That was very unkind,' he said in a hurt voice.*

▸**noun** [S or U] emotional pain: *The hurt after a relationship breaks up can be awful.* ◦ *Her brave smile concealed a* ***deep*** *hurt.*

hurtful /ˈhɜːt.fᵊl/ (US) /ˈhɝːt-/ **adj** causing emotional pain: *That was a very hurtful remark!* ◦ *How can you be so hurtful?* • **hurtfully** /-i/ **adv** • **hurtfulness** /-nəs/ **noun** [U]

hurtle /ˈhɜː.tl/ (US) /ˈhɝː.t̬l/ **verb** [I usually + adv/prep] to move very fast, especially in a way that seems dangerous: *The truck came hurtling towards us.*

husband /ˈhʌz.bənd/ **noun; verb**

▸**noun** [C] A1 the man that you are married to: *I've never met Fiona's husband.*

IDIOM **as husband and wife** in the same way as two people who are married: *Although never married, they lived together as husband and wife for 50 years.*

▸**verb** [T] formal to use something carefully so that you do not use all of it

husbandry /ˈhʌz.bən.dri/ **noun** [U] **FARMING** ▷ **1** specialized farming: *He gave a lecture on crop and animal husbandry.* **CAREFUL USE** ▷ **2** old-fashioned the careful use of money, food, supplies, etc.

hush /hʌʃ/ **noun; verb; exclamation**

▸**noun** [S or U] a sudden calm silence: *There was a* ***deathly*** *hush after she made the announcement.* ◦ *A hush* ***fell*** *over the room.* ◦ informal *Let's have some hush, please! (= Be quiet, please!)*

▸**verb**

PHRASAL VERB **hush sth up** [M usually passive] disapproving to try to prevent people from discovering particular facts: *There was some financial scandal involving one of the ministers but it was all hushed up.*

▸**exclamation** used to tell someone to be quiet: *Hush! You'll wake the baby!*

hushed /hʌʃt/ **adj** quiet: *She stood up to address a hushed courtroom.* ◦ *People still speak in hushed* ***tones*** *(= very quietly) of the murders.*

ˌhush-ˈhush adj informal kept secret from people: *In the end he was forced to resign but it was all very hush-hush.*

ˈhush ˌmoney noun [U] informal money that is given to someone to make them keep something they know secret: *She claimed that the minister had offered her hush money to keep their child a secret.*

husk /hʌsk/ **noun** [C] the dry outer covering of some seeds

husky /ˈhʌs.ki/ **adj; noun**

▸**adj** **VOICE** ▷ **1** (of a person's voice) low and rough, often in an attractive way, or because of illness: *She's got a nice husky voice – very sexy.* ◦ *You sound husky – do you have a cold?* **STRONG** ▷ **2** US A husky man or boy is big and strong.

▸**noun** [C] a large dog with long thick fur, used for pulling SLEDGES over the snow

hussy /ˈhʌs.i/ **noun** [C] humorous a woman or girl who is sexually IMMORAL: *'You asked him out? Oh, you* ***brazen/shameless*** *hussy, you!'*

the hustings /ˈhʌs.tɪŋz/ **noun** [plural] UK the political activities and speeches that happen before an election and are intended to win votes: *Three weeks before the election the candidates are all out* ***on/at*** *the hustings.*

hustle /ˈhʌs.l/ **verb; noun**

▸**verb** **PUSH** ▷ **1** [T usually + adv/prep] to make someone move quickly by pushing or pulling them along: *After giving his speech, Johnson was hustled out of the hall by bodyguards.* **PERSUADE** ▷ **2** [I or T] mainly US informal to try to persuade someone, especially to buy something, often illegally: *to hustle for business/customers* ◦ *They made a living hustling stolen goods on the streets.*

▸**noun** [U] **hustle and bustle** noise and activity: *I love the hustle and bustle of the marketplace.*

hustler /ˈhʌs.ləʳ/ (US) /-lɚ/ **noun** [C] mainly US informal **1** someone who tries to deceive people into giving them money **2** a PROSTITUTE (= person who has sex for money): *The street was full of hustlers, drug addicts and pimps.*

hut /hʌt/ **noun** [C] B1 a small, simple building, usually consisting of one room: *a mountain hut* ◦ *a row of beach huts*

hutch /hʌtʃ/ **noun** [C] a box made of wood with a wire front where small animals such as RABBITS are kept

hyacinth /ˈhaɪ.ə.sɪnθ/ **noun** [C] a pleasant-smelling

H

plant with a lot of small flowers that grow close together around one thick stem

hybrid /ˈhaɪ.brɪd/ **noun** [C] **1** a plant or animal that has been produced from two different types of plant or animal, especially to get better characteristics, or anything that is a mixture of two very different things: *The garden strawberry is a large-fruited hybrid.* **2** (also **hybrid car**) a vehicle with an engine that uses both PETROL and another type of energy, usually electricity • **hybrid adj** figurative *His choreography is described as 'a hybrid **mix** of mime and circus tricks'.*

hydel /ˈhaɪ.del/ **adj** Indian English for **hydroelectric**: *hydel power*

hydra /ˈhaɪ.drə/ **noun** [C] **1** in ancient Greek stories, a creature with many heads that grew again when cut off **2** a difficult problem that keeps returning

hydrangea /haɪˈdreɪn.dʒə/ **noun** [C] a bush on which there are round groups of pink, white, or blue flowers

H

hydrant /ˈhaɪ.drənt/ **noun** [C] a vertical pipe, usually at the side of the road, that is connected to the main water system of a town and can supply water, especially for dealing with fires: *a fire hydrant*

hydrate /ˈhaɪ.dreɪt/ **noun** [C] specialized a chemical that contains water

hydraulic /haɪˈdrɒl.ɪk/ (US) /-ˈdrɑː.lɪk/ **adj** operated by or involving the pressure of water or some other liquid: *a hydraulic lift/platform/pump*

hyˌdraulic ˈfracturing

hydraulics /haɪˈdrɒl.ɪks/ (US) /-ˈdrɑː.lɪks/ **noun** [plural] a system of using water to produce power: *The hydraulics failed and the digger stopped.*

hydro- /haɪ.drəʊ-/, /-drə-/ (US) /-droʊ-/ **prefix** **WATER** ▷ **1** connected with or using the power of water: *hydroponic (= a method of growing plants in water)* **GAS** ▷ **2** showing that HYDROGEN is present

hydrocarbon /ˌhaɪ.drəʊˈkɑː.bᵊn/ (US) /-droʊˈkɑːr-/ **noun** [C] a chemical combination of HYDROGEN and carbon, such as in oil or petrol: *hydrocarbon emissions*

hydrochloric acid /ˌhaɪd.rə.klɒr.ɪk ˈæs.ɪd/ (US) /-klɔːr-/ **noun** [U] an ACID containing HYDROGEN and CHLORINE

hydroelectric /ˌhaɪ.drəʊ.ɪˈlek.trɪk/ (US) /-droʊ-/ **adj** producing electricity by the force of fast moving water such as rivers or WATERFALLS: *a hydroelectric power station* • **hydroelectricity** /-lekˈtrɪs.ɪ.ti/ (US) /-lekˈtrɪs.ə.t̬i/ **noun** [U]

hydrofoil /ˈhaɪ.drə.fɔɪl/ (US) /-droʊ-/ **noun** [C] a large boat that is able to travel quickly above the surface of the water on wing-like structures

hydrogen /ˈhaɪ.drɪ.dʒən/ **noun** [U] (symbol **H**) a chemical element that is the lightest gas, has no colour, taste, or smell, and combines with OXYGEN to form water

hydrogenated /haɪˈdrɒd.ɪ.neɪ.tɪd/ (US) /-ˈdrɑː.dʒə.neɪ.t̬ɪd/ **adj** describes fat in foods that has had hydrogen added to it. Hydrogenated fats are bad for your health.

hydrogenation /ˌhaɪ.drə.dʒəˈneɪ.ʃᵊn/ (US) /haɪˌdrɑː-/ **noun** [U] the process of producing hydrogenated fats

ˈhydrogen ˌbomb **noun** [C usually singular] (abbreviation **ˈH-bomb**) a nuclear bomb which explodes when the central parts of its hydrogen atoms join together

ˌhydrogen peˈroxide **noun** [U] (used on hair **peroxide**) a clear liquid chemical used to kill bacteria, to remove colour from cloth, and to BLEACH hair

hydrolysis /haɪˈdrɒl.ə.sɪs/ (US) /-ˈdrɑː.lə-/ **noun** [U] specialized a chemical reaction in which one substance reacts with water to produce another

hydrometer /haɪˈdrɒ.ɪ.təʳ/ (US) /-drɑː.mə.t̬ɚ/ **noun** [C] specialized a piece of equipment used to measure the DENSITY (= amount of matter in a particular quantity) of liquids, especially a long glass tube, closed and with a weight at one end so that it floats vertically

hydrophobia /ˌhaɪ.drəˈfəʊ.bi.ə/ (US) /-droʊˈfoʊ-/ **noun** [U] **1** specialized a great fear of drinking and water, often a sign of RABIES **2** old-fashioned the disease of RABIES

hydroplane /ˈhaɪ.drə.pleɪn/ (US) /-droʊ-/ **verb** [I] US for **aquaplane**

hydroplaning /ˈhaɪ.drə.pleɪn.ɪŋ/ (US) /-droʊ-/ **noun** [U] US for **aquaplaning**

hydroponics /ˌhaɪ.drəˈpɒn.ɪks/ (US) /-droʊˈpɑː.nɪks/ **noun** [U] specialized the method of growing plants in water to which special chemicals are added, rather than growing them in earth

hydropower /ˈhaɪd.rəʊ.paʊəʳ/ (US) /-roʊ.paʊr/ **noun** [U] HYDROELECTRIC power (= the production of electricity by the force of fast moving water)

hydrosphere /ˈhaɪ.drəʊ.sfɪəʳ/ (US) /-droʊ.sfɪɚ/ **noun** [C] specialized all of the water, ice, and WATER VAPOUR at or near the surface of the Earth, such as the seas and ice, clouds, and the water in and under the ground

hydrotherapy /ˌhaɪ.drəʊˈθer.ə.pi/ (US) /-droʊ-/ **noun** [U] a method of treating people with particular diseases or injuries by making them exercise in water

hydroxide /haɪˈdrɒk.saɪd/ (US) /-ˈdrɑːk-/ **noun** [C] specialized a chemical COMPOUND that contains the hydroxyl ion, or a COMPOUND of an OXIDE with water: *calcium hydroxide*

hydroxyl ion /haɪˌdrɒk.sɪlˈaɪən/ (US) /-ˈdrɑːk-/ **noun** [C] specialized an ION with a negative CHARGE, consisting of an OXYGEN atom and a HYDROGEN atom

hyena /haɪˈiː.nə/ **noun** [C] a wild animal from Africa and Asia that looks like a dog, hunts in groups, and makes a sound similar to a human laugh

hygiene /ˈhaɪ.dʒiːn/ **noun** [U] **C1** the degree to which people keep themselves or their environment clean, especially to prevent disease: *Poor standards of hygiene mean that the disease spreads fast.* ◦ *health and hygiene regulations* ◦ *dental/personal hygiene*

hygienic /haɪˈdʒiː.nɪk/ (US) /-ˈdʒen-/ **adj** **C2** clean, especially in order to prevent disease: *It isn't hygienic to let animals sit on the dining table.*

hygienist /haɪˈdʒiː.nɪst/ (US) /-ˈdʒen.ɪst/ **noun** [C] (also **ˌdental hyˈgienist**) a person who works with a dentist and cleans people's teeth to keep them healthy

hygrometer /haɪˈgrɒm.ɪ.təʳ/ (US) /ˈgrɑːm.ə.t̬ɚ/ **noun** [C] specialized a piece of equipment used to measure HUMIDITY (= how much water there is in the air)

hying /ˈhaɪ.ɪŋ/ present participle of **hie**

hymen /ˈhaɪ.mən/ **noun** [C] a thin piece of skin that partly covers the opening to a girl's or woman's VAGINA and breaks when she has sex for the first time

hymn /hɪm/ **noun** [C] a song of praise that Christians sing to God: *a hymn book*

hymnal /ˈhɪm.nᵊl/ **noun** [C] formal or old-fashioned a book containing hymns

hype /haɪp/ **noun; verb**

▸**noun** [U] informal a situation in which something is advertised and discussed in newspapers, on television, etc. a lot in order to attract everyone's interest: *media hype* ◦ *There's been a lot of hype **around/surrounding** his latest film.* ◦ *I've been put off reading the book by all the hype.*

▸**verb** [T often passive] (also **hype up**) to repeatedly advertise and discuss something in newspapers, on television, etc. in order to attract everyone's interest: *It's being hyped **as** the musical event of the year.*

ˌhyped ˈup adj [after verb] informal too excited or nervous and unable to rest or be calm: *I was hyped up because it was such a big race.*

hyper /ˈhaɪ.pəʳ/ Ⓤⓢ /-pɚ/ **adj** informal too excited and energetic → See also **hyperactive**

hyper- /haɪ.pəʳ-/ Ⓤⓢ /-pɚ-/ **prefix** having too much of a quality: *hyperactive ◦ hypercritical ◦ hypersensitive*

hyperactive /ˌhaɪ.pəʳˈæk.tɪv/ Ⓤⓢ /-pɚ-/ **adj** Someone who is hyperactive has more energy than is normal, gets excited easily, and cannot stay still or think about their work: *Hyperactive children often have poor concentration and require very little sleep.* → See also **hyper** • **hyperactivity** /-ækˈtɪv.ɪ.ti/ Ⓤⓢ /-ækˈtɪv.ə.t̬i/ **noun** [U]

hyperbola /haɪˈpɜː.bᵊl.ə/ Ⓤⓢ /-ˈpɝː-/ **noun** [C] specialized a curve whose ends continue to move apart from each other

hyperbole /haɪˈpɜː.bᵊl.i/ Ⓤⓢ /-ˈpɝː-/ **noun** [U] formal a way of speaking or writing that makes someone or something sound bigger, better, more, etc. than they are: *The blurb on the back of the book was full of the usual hyperbole – 'enthralling', 'fascinating', and so on.* • **hyperbolic** /ˌhaɪ.pəˈbɒl.ɪk/ Ⓤⓢ /-pɚˈbɑː.lɪk/ **adj** *hyperbolic rhetoric*

hypercritical /ˌhaɪ.pəˈkrɪt.ɪ.kᵊl/ Ⓤⓢ /-pɚˈkrɪt̬-/ **adj** extremely CRITICAL (= too eager to find mistakes in everything)

hyperinflation /ˌhaɪ.pə.rɪnˈfleɪ.ʃən/ Ⓤⓢ /-pɚ.ɪn-/ **noun** [U] a condition where the price of everything in a national economy goes out of control and increases very quickly

hyperlink /ˈhaɪ.pə.lɪŋk/ Ⓤⓢ /ˈhaɪ.pɚ.lɪŋk/ **noun** [C] a connection that allows you to move easily between two computer documents or two pages on the internet

hypermarket /ˈhaɪ.pəˌmɑː.kɪt/ Ⓤⓢ /-pɚˌmɑːr-/ **noun** [C] a very large shop, usually outside the centre of town

hypersensitive /ˌhaɪ.pəˈsen.sɪ.tɪv/ Ⓤⓢ /-pɚˈsen.sə.t̬ɪv/ **adj** **1** too easily upset by criticism: *He's hypersensitive **about** his height.* **2** very easily influenced, changed, or damaged, especially by a physical activity or effect: *hypersensitive skin*

hypertension /ˌhaɪ.pəˈten.ʃᵊn/ Ⓤⓢ /-pɚ-/ **noun** [U] specialized a medical condition in which your blood pressure is extremely high

hypertext /ˈhaɪ.pə.tekst/ Ⓤⓢ /-pɚ-/ **noun** [U] specialized a way of joining a word or image to another page, document, etc. on the internet or in another computer program so that you can move from one to the other easily: *The Web is based on hypertext **links** that allow people to easily move from document to document.*

hyperventilation /ˌhaɪ.pəˌven.tɪˈleɪ.ʃᵊn/ Ⓤⓢ /-pɚˌven.t̬ᵊlˈeɪ-/ **noun** [U] specialized breathing too quickly and so causing too much OXYGEN to enter the blood: *Hyperventilation can be caused by fear or panic.* • **hyperventilate** /-ˈven.tɪ.leɪt/ Ⓤⓢ /-ˈven.t̬ᵊl.eɪt/ **verb** [I]

hyphen /ˈhaɪ.fᵊn/ **noun** [C] Ⓑ② the symbol -, used to join two words together, or to show that a word has been divided into two parts at the end of one line and the beginning of the next: *There are hyphens in 'well-to-do'.* → Compare **dash**

hyphenate /ˈhaɪ.fᵊn.eɪt/ **verb** [T] to use a hyphen to join two words or two parts of a word • **hyphenation** /ˌhaɪ.fᵊnˈeɪ.ʃən/ **noun** [U] *the rules of hyphenation*

hyphenated /ˈhaɪ.fᵊn.eɪ.tɪd/ Ⓤⓢ /-t̬ɪd/ **adj** written with a hyphen: *hyphenated compounds*

hypnosis /hɪpˈnəʊ.sɪs/ Ⓤⓢ /-ˈnoʊ-/ **noun** [U] a mental state like sleep, in which a person's thoughts can be easily influenced by someone else: ***Under** deep hypnosis she remembered the traumatic events of that night.*

hypnotherapy /ˌhɪp.nəˈθer.ə.pi/ Ⓤⓢ /-noʊ-/ **noun** [U] the use of hypnosis to treat emotional problems

hypnotic /hɪpˈnɒt.ɪk/ Ⓤⓢ /-ˈnɑː.t̬ɪk/ **adj** **1** caused by hypnosis: *She went into a hypnotic **trance**.* **2** describes sounds or movements that are very regular and make you feel as if you want to sleep: *The beat of the music was strangely hypnotic.*

hypnotist /ˈhɪp.nə.tɪst/ Ⓤⓢ /-t̬ɪst/ **noun** [C] a person who uses hypnosis as a form of treatment, or sometimes entertainment

hypnotize (UK usually **hypnotise**) /ˈhɪp.nə.taɪz/ **verb** **1** to put someone in a state of hypnosis: *She agreed to be hypnotized to try to remember what had happened.* **2** [T usually passive] to keep your attention so strongly that you feel unable to move or look away: *I was hypnotized by his steely grey eyes.* • **hypnotism** /-tɪ.zᵊm/ **noun** [U] *Some people try hypnotism to cure themselves of addictions.*

hypoallergenic /ˌhaɪ.pəʊˌæl.əˈdʒen.ɪk/ Ⓤⓢ /-poʊˌæl.ɚ-/ **adj** designed to be less likely to cause ALLERGIC reactions (= physical problems caused by particular substances) in people who use a product: *hypoallergenic cosmetics/earrings*

hypochondria /ˌhaɪ.pəˈkɒn.dri.ə/ Ⓤⓢ /-poʊˈkɑːn-/ **noun** [U] a state in which a person continuously worries about their health without having any reason to do so: *I thought the doctor was going to accuse me of hypochondria.* • **hypochondriac** /-æk/ **noun** [C] *She's a terrible hypochondriac – she's always at the doctor's.* • **hypochondriac adj**

hypocrisy /hɪˈpɒk.rɪ.si/ Ⓤⓢ /-ˈpɑː.krə-/ **noun** [U] disapproving Ⓒ② a situation in which someone pretends to believe something that they do not really believe, or that is the opposite of what they do or say at another time: *There's one rule for her and another rule for everyone else and it's sheer hypocrisy.*

hypocrite /ˈhɪp.ə.krɪt/ **noun** [C] disapproving someone who says they have particular moral beliefs but behaves in way which shows these are not sincere: *He's a hypocrite – he's always lecturing other people on the environment but he drives around in a huge great car.*

hypocritical /ˌhɪp.əˈkrɪt.ɪ.kᵊl/ Ⓤⓢ /-əˈkrɪt̬-/ **adj** disapproving Ⓒ② saying that you have particular moral beliefs but behaving in a way that shows these are not sincere: *Their accusations of corruption are hypocritical – they have been just as corrupt themselves.* • **hypocritically** /-kᵊl.i/ **adv**

hypodermic /ˌhaɪ.pəˈdɜː.mɪk/ Ⓤⓢ /-poʊˈdɝː-/ **adj** specialized (of medical tools) used to INJECT drugs (= put them into the body) under a person's skin: *a hypodermic needle*

hypoglycaemia specialized (mainly US **hypoglycemia**) /ˌhaɪ.pəʊ.glaɪˈsiː.mi.ə/ Ⓤⓢ /-poʊ-/ **noun** [U] a medical condition resulting from dangerously low levels of sugar in the blood • **hypoglycaemic** (mainly US **hypoglycemic**) /-mɪk/ **adj** *As a diabetic she was accustomed to the occasional hypoglycaemic **attack**.*

hypotenuse /haɪˈpɒt.ᵊn.juːz/ Ⓤⓢ /-ˈpɑː.t̬ə.nuːz/ **noun** [C] specialized the longest side of any triangle that has one angle of 90°

H

hypothalamus /ˌhaɪ.pəʊˈθæl.ə.məs/ (US) /-poʊˈ-/ noun [S] specialized a small part in the brain that controls things such as body temperature and the release of HORMONES, that is below the THALAMUS

hypothermia /ˌhaɪ.pəˈθɜː.mi.ə/ (US) /-poʊˈθɝː-/ noun [U] a serious medical condition in which a person's body temperature falls below the usual level as a result of being in severe cold for a long time

hypothesis /haɪˈpɒθ.ə.sɪs/ (US) /-ˈpɑː.θə-/ noun [C] (plural **hypotheses**) C2 an idea or explanation for something that is based on known facts but has not yet been proved: *Several hypotheses for global warming have been suggested.*

hypothesize /haɪˈpɒθ.ə.saɪz/ (US) /-ˈpɑː.θə-/ verb [I or T] formal to give a possible but not yet proved explanation for something: *There's no point hypothesizing **about** how the accident happened, since we'll never really know.*

hypothetical /ˌhaɪ.pəˈθet.ɪ.kəl/ (US) /-ˈθeţ-/ adj imagined or suggested but not NECESSARILY real or true: *a hypothetical example/situation* ◦ *This is all very hypothetical but supposing Jackie got the job, how would that affect you?*

hysterectomy /ˌhɪs.tərˈek.tə.mi/ (US) /-təˈrek-/ noun [C] a medical operation to remove part or all of a woman's WOMB

hysteria /hɪˈstɪə.ri.ə/ (US) /-ˈstɪr.i-/ noun [U] extreme fear, excitement, anger, etc. which cannot be controlled: *One woman, close to hysteria, grabbed my arm.* ◦ *Tabloid hysteria about the murders has increased public fears.* ◦ *mass hysteria*

hysterical /hɪˈster.ɪ.kəl/ adj **1** C1 unable to control your feelings or behaviour because you are extremely frightened, angry, excited, etc.: *Calm down, you're getting hysterical.* ◦ *The police were accused of hysterical over-reaction.* ◦ *hysterical laughter* (= uncontrolled laughter) **2** informal extremely funny: *His last film was hysterical.* • **hysterically** /-i/ adv *She started laughing/crying hysterically (= without control).*

hysterics /hɪˈster.ɪks/ noun [plural] **1** uncontrolled behaviour or crying, usually caused by extreme fear or sadness: *Convinced the plane was about to crash, many people were sobbing and **in** hysterics.* **2** informal uncontrolled laughter: *He was hilarious – he had us all **in** hysterics.*

IDIOM **have hysterics** informal to get extremely angry or upset: *She'll have hysterics when she finds out how much money is missing.*

Hz written abbreviation for **hertz**

I

I, i /aɪ/ noun [C or U] (plural **Is, I's** or **i's**) **LETTER** ▷ **1** the ninth letter of the English alphabet **NUMBER** ▷ **2** (also **i**) the sign used in the Roman system for the number 1 and as part of the numbers 2 (ii), 3 (iii), 4 (iv), 6 (vi), 7 (vii), 8 (viii), and 9 (ix)

I /aɪ/ **pronoun** A1 used as the subject of a verb to refer to the person speaking or writing: *I love you.* ◦ *Am I invited?* ◦ *I'm not mistaken, am I?* ◦ *I'd like a coffee, please.*

> **!** Common mistake: **I**
>
> **Remember:** I is always written with a capital 'I'.
> Don't write 'i', write I:
> ~~*The next day i caught the first plane to Peru.*~~

iambic /aɪˈæm.bɪk/ **adj** specialized describes a RHYTHM (= pattern of words) used in poetry, in which each short SYLLABLE that is not STRESSED is followed by a long or STRESSED syllable: *Most of Shakespeare's verse is written in iambic* ***pentameter*** *(= rhythm with each line made of five iambic pairs).*

IB /ˌaɪˈbiː/ **noun** [S] abbreviation for **the International Baccalaureate**

Iberian /aɪˈbɪə.ri.ən/ US /-ˈbɪr.i-/ **adj** of Spain and Portugal: *the Iberian Peninsula*

ibid. /ˈɪb.ɪd/ **adv** specialized used in formal writing to refer to a book or article that has already been mentioned

-ibility /-ɪ.bɪl.ɪ.ti/ US /-ə.t̬i/ **suffix** used to form nouns from adjectives ending '-ible' or 'able': *accessibility*

-ible /-ɪ.bl̩/, /-ə.bl̩/ **suffix** (also **-able**) used to form adjectives meaning 'able to be': *convertible* ◦ *accessible* ◦ *permissible*

IBS /ˌaɪ.biːˈes/ **noun** [U] abbreviation for **irritable bowel syndrome**

ibuprofen /ˌaɪ.bjuːˈprəʊ.fen/ US /-ˈproʊ-/ **noun** [U] a drug used to reduce pain and swelling

-ic /-ɪk/ **suffix** (also **-ical**) used to form adjectives: *scenic* ◦ *economic*

-ical /-ɪ.kəl/ **suffix** added to nouns to form adjectives meaning 'relating to': *historical* ◦ *political*

ICBM /ˌaɪ.siː.biːˈem/ **noun** [C] abbreviation for intercontinental ballistic missile: a flying bomb that can travel a long distance

ice /aɪs/ **noun; verb**

▸**noun FROZEN WATER** ▷ **1** A2 [U] water that has frozen and become solid, or pieces of this: *The pond was covered in ice all winter.* ◦ *Would you like ice in your juice?* ◦ *I've put a couple of bottles of champagne* ***on*** *ice (= in a container of ice to get cold).* ◦ *He skidded on a patch of ice.* **ICE CREAM** ▷ **2** [C] UK old-fashioned an ice cream, especially one bought in a shop **JEWELLERY** ▷ **3** [U] informal jewellery, especially DIAMONDS

IDIOM **be on ice** If a plan is on ice, a decision has been made to delay it for a period of time: *Both projects are on ice until the question of funding is resolved.*

▸**verb** [T] **COVER CAKES** ▷ **1** UK (US **frost**) to cover a cake with ICING (= a food made mainly with sugar): *I've made her a chocolate cake – now I just need to ice it.* **KILL** ▷ **2** US slang to murder someone

PHRASAL VERBS **ice over** If an area of water ices over, it becomes covered with a layer of ice: *The lake has iced over.* • **ice up** to become covered in ice and often stop working: *The plane was delayed because the engine had iced up.*

ICE (number) /aɪ.siːˈiːˌnʌm.bər/ US /-ɚ/ **noun** [C] abbreviation for in case of emergency: the phone number of a friend or family member that should be told if you suddenly become ill or are involved in an accident

ˈice ˌage noun [C] (specialized **ˈglacial ˌperiod**) a time in the past when the temperature was very cold and GLACIERS (= large masses of ice) covered large parts of the earth

iceberg /ˈaɪs.bɜːɡ/ US /-bɝːɡ/ **noun** [C] a very large mass of ice that floats in the sea

iceblock /ˈaɪs.blɒk/ US /-blɑːk/ **noun** [C] Australian English a sweet piece of ice with a fruit flavour on a small stick → Compare **ice lolly**

icebox /ˈaɪs.bɒks/ US /-bɑːks/ **noun** [C] US old-fashioned a **fridge**

icebreaker /ˈaɪsˌbreɪ.kər/ US /-kɚ/ **noun** [C] **ACTIVITY** ▷ **1** a game or joke that makes people who do not know each other feel more relaxed together **SHIP** ▷ **2** a strong ship that can break a passage through ice

ˈice ˌbucket noun [C] a container in which pieces of ice for cooling drinks or bottles of wine are kept

ˈice ˌcap noun [C] (also **ˈice ˌsheet**) a thick layer of ice that permanently covers an area of land: *polar ice caps*

ˌice-ˈcold adj extremely cold: *I felt her hand and it was ice-cold.* ◦ *I'd love an ice-cold beer.*

ˌice ˈcream noun [C or U] A1 a very cold sweet food made from frozen milk or cream, sugar, and a flavour: *a tub of ice cream* ◦ *chocolate chip/vanilla ice cream*

ˌice cream ˈsoda noun [C] a sweet dish made from ice cream, thick fruit juice, and SODA (= water with bubbles), usually served in a tall glass

ˈice ˌcube noun [C] a small block of ice that you put into drinks to make them cold

iced /aɪst/ **adj** An iced drink has been made very cold, usually by having ice added to it: *iced tea* ◦ *iced water*

ˈice ˌfloe noun [C] a large area of ice floating in the sea

ˈice ˌhockey noun [U] (US also **hockey**) A2 a game played on ice between two teams of players who each have a curved stick with which they try to put a PUCK (= a small, hard disc) into the other team's goal

ˌice ˈlolly noun [C] UK (US trademark **Popsicle**) a sweet piece of ice with a fruit flavour on a small stick

icemaker /ˈaɪsˌmeɪ.kər/ US /-kɚ/ **noun** [C] a device that makes small pieces of ice to put in drinks, etc.

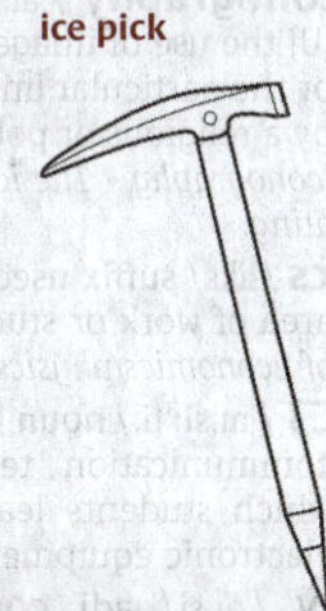

ˈice ˌpack noun [C] a bag containing ice that is put on a part of a person's body to make it cool and reduce swelling

ˈice ˌpick noun [C] a sharp tool for breaking large blocks of ice

ˈice ˌrink noun [C] a level area of ice, often inside a building, that is kept frozen for people to SKATE on

ˈice ˌskate noun [C] a special shoe with a thin metal bar fixed

I

to the bottom that you wear to move quickly on ice • ˈ**ice ˌskater noun** [C] • ˈ**ice ˌskating noun** [U] B1 *Would you like to go ice skating?*

ˈ**ice-skate verb** [I] to move across ice using ice skates

ˈ**ice ˌwater noun** [U] mainly US water that has been made extremely cold

icicle /ˈaɪ.sɪ.kl/ **noun** [C] a long pointed stick of ice that is formed when drops of water freeze: *Icicles hung from the roof.*

icing /ˈaɪ.sɪŋ/ **noun** [U] (US also **frosting**) a sweet food used to cover or fill cakes, made from sugar and water or sugar and butter: *chocolate butter icing*

IDIOM **the icing on the cake** UK (US **the frosting on the cake**) something which makes a good situation even better: *I was just content to see my daughter in such a stable relationship but a grandchild, that really was the icing on the cake.*

ˈ**icing ˌsugar noun** [U] UK (US ˌ**powdered** ˈ**sugar**, **con**ˌ**fectioner's** ˈ**sugar**) a soft powder made from sugar that is used to make icing for cakes

ick /ɪk/ **exclamation** US informal used to express a feeling of shock or dislike that makes you feel sick: *Then he kissed her! Ick!*

icky /ˈɪk.i/ **adj** informal unpleasant, especially to look at: *an icky shade of green*

icon /ˈaɪ.kɒn/ (US) /-kɑːn/ **noun** [C] **COMPUTER SYMBOL** ▷ **1** B2 a small picture or symbol on a computer screen that you point to and CLICK on (= press) with a mouse to give the computer an instruction **FAMOUS PERSON/THING** ▷ **2** B2 a very famous person or thing considered as representing a set of beliefs or a way of life: *Beckham has been one of the country's best-loved sporting icons.* **HOLY PAINTING** ▷ **3** (also **ikon**) a painting, usually on wood, of Jesus Christ, or of a person considered holy by some Christians, especially in Russia and Greece

iconic /aɪˈkɒn.ɪk/ (US) /-ˈkɑː.nɪk/ **adj** formal very famous or popular, especially being considered to represent particular opinions or a particular time

iconoclast /aɪˈkɒn.ə.klæst/ (US) /-ˈkɑː.nə-/ **noun** [C] formal a person who strongly opposes generally accepted beliefs and traditions: *Rogers, an iconoclast in architecture, is sometimes described as putting the insides of buildings on the outside.*

iconoclastic /aɪˌkɒn.əˈklæs.tɪk/ (US) /-kɑː.nə-/ **adj** strongly opposing generally accepted beliefs and traditions: *His plays were fairly iconoclastic in their day.* ◦ *iconoclastic views* • **iconoclasm** /aɪˈkɒn.əˌklæz.əm/ (US) /-ˈkɑː.nə-/ **noun** [U]

iconography /ˌaɪ.kəˈnɒg.rə.fi/ (US) /-ˈnɑː.grə-/ **noun** [U] the use of images and symbols to represent ideas, or the particular images and symbols used in this way by a religious or political group, etc.: *religious/political iconography* ◦ *The iconography* ***of*** *this picture is fascinating.*

-ics /-ɪks/ **suffix** used to form nouns which refer to an area of work or study: *the world of politics* ◦ *the study of economics/physics/ethics*

ICT /ˌaɪ.siːˈtiː/ **noun** [U] abbreviation for information and communication technology: a school subject in which students learn to use computers and other electronic equipment to store and send information

icy /ˈaɪ.si/ **adj COLD** ▷ **1** B1 covered in ice: *icy roads* ◦ *an icy pavement* **2** B1 extremely cold: *She opened the window and I was hit by an icy* ***blast*** *of air.* ◦ *He fell into the icy* ***waters*** *of the Moscow river.* ◦ *Her skin was icy to the touch.* **UNFRIENDLY** ▷ **3** B2 unfriendly and showing no emotion: *an icy stare* • **icily** /-sɪ.li/ **adv** C2 *She stared icily at us.*

id /ɪd/ **noun** [C] specialized in PSYCHOANALYSIS, the deepest part of the unconscious mind that represents the most basic natural human needs and emotions such as hunger, anger, and the wish for pleasure

I'd /aɪd/ **short form 1** I had: *I'd just got in the bath when the phone rang.* **2** I would: *Of course I'd love to see you.*

ID /ˌaɪˈdiː/ **noun; verb**

▸**noun** [U] informal A2 any official card or document with your name and photograph or other information on it that you use to prove who you are: *Have you got any ID? A driving licence or cheque card will do.*

▸**verb** [T] US informal to look at a person or a body and say who they are to someone in authority: *He had to go to the morgue to ID the body.*

ˌ**I'D ˌcard noun** [C] A2 an **identity card**

idea /aɪˈdɪə/ **noun SUGGESTION** ▷ **1** A2 [C] a suggestion or plan for doing something: *I've* ***had an*** *idea – why don't we go to the coast?* ◦ *'Let's go swimming.' 'That's a* ***good*** *idea!'* ◦ *If you have any ideas* ***for*** *what I could buy Jack, let me know.* ◦ *That's when I first had* ***the*** *idea* ***of starting*** *(= planned to start) my own business.* ◦ *I like the idea* ***of living*** *in the countryside but I'm not sure I'd like the reality.* ◦ *She's full of* ***bright*** *(= good) ideas.* ◦ [+ to infinitive] *It was Kate's idea* ***to*** *hire bikes.* ◦ ***It's*** *not a good idea* ***to*** *drive for hours without a rest.* **KNOWLEDGE** ▷ **2** B2 [S or U] an understanding, thought, or picture in your mind: *Do you* ***have any*** *idea* ***of*** *what he looks like?* ◦ *Can you* ***give*** *me an idea* ***of*** *the cost (= can you tell me approximately how much the cost is)?* ◦ *I don't like the idea* ***of living*** *so far away from my family.* ◦ [+ question word] *I haven't* ***the slightest/faintest*** *idea* ***wh****ere they've gone.* ◦ *I've got a* ***pretty good*** *idea* ***wh****y they left early.* **3 have no idea** B1 informal to not know something: *'Where's Serge?' 'I've no idea'.* **BELIEF** ▷ **4** B1 [C] a belief or opinion: *We have very different ideas* ***about*** *disciplining children.* ◦ [+ that] *Leach puts forward the idea* ***that*** *it is impossible to spoil a child.* ◦ *I'm not married – where did you get that idea (= what made you believe that)?* **PURPOSE** ▷ **5** C1 [S] a purpose or reason for doing something: *The idea* ***of*** *the game is to get rid of all your cards as soon as you can.* ◦ *The* ***whole*** *idea (= only purpose)* ***of*** *advertising is to make people buy things.* ◦ *The idea* ***behind*** *the national lottery is to raise money for good causes.*

> **Word partners for idea (SUGGESTION)**
>
> *come up with/have* an idea • *get* an idea • *toy with* the idea (**of** doing sth) • *hate/like/love* the idea **of** (doing) sth • *dismiss/reject* an idea • *exchange* ideas • a *bad/bright/good/stupid* idea

> **Word partners for idea (KNOWLEDGE)**
>
> *have no* idea/*not have* any idea • *have* an idea (that) • *give* sb an idea of sth • have a *general/rough/shrewd* idea • not have the *faintest/foggiest/slightest* idea

IDIOMS **your idea of sth** what you consider to be something: *Playing card games is not my idea of fun.* ◦ *Is this your idea of* ***a joke****? (= Do you think that this is amusing?)* • **put ideas into sb's head** to make someone want to do something they had not thought about before, especially something stupid: *Don't go putting ideas into his head. We can't afford a new car.* • **what an idea!** (also **the idea of it!**)

Other ways of saying idea

An idea about how to do something is often described as a **plan**, **thought**, or **suggestion**:

*The **plan** is to hire a car when we get there.*

*Have you got any **suggestions** for improvements?*

*Have you had any **thoughts** on presents for your mother?*

A sudden, clever idea is sometimes described as a **brainwave** in the UK and a **brainstorm** in the US:

*I wasn't sure what to do and then I had a **brainwave** – I could ask Anna for help.*

The noun **theory** is sometimes used to describe a set of ideas intended to explain something:

*He was giving a lecture on Einstein's **theory** of relativity.*

something you say to show that you think a suggestion is stupid: *I can't turn up at a funeral in a pink jacket. What an idea!* • **you have no idea** said for emphasis when you are describing how good or bad an experience is: *Flying a plane is wonderful, you have no idea.* ◦ *You have no idea **how** embarrassed I was.*

ideal /aɪˈdɪəl/ **adj; noun**

▸**adj** B2 perfect, or the best possible: *the ideal employer* ◦ *She's the ideal person (= exactly the right type of person) **for** the job.* ◦ *The television also comes in a compact 36 cm screen size, ideal **for** bedroom or kitchen use.* ◦ *It's the ideal **opportunity** to meet people.* ◦ ***In an** ideal **world** no one would go hungry.*

▸**noun** PRINCIPLE ▷ **1** [C] a principle or a way of behaving that is of a very high standard: *democratic ideals* ◦ *We are committed to the ideal of equality.* ◦ *They share the same high ideals.* PERFECT ▷ **2** [S] a perfect thing or situation: *The ideal would be to have a house in the town and one in the country.*

idealism /aɪˈdɪə.lɪ.zəm/ **noun** [U] **1** the belief that your ideals can be achieved, often when this does not seem likely to others: *She never lost her youthful idealism and campaigned for just causes all her life.* → Compare **realism 2** specialized the belief in PHILOSOPHY that objects in the world are ideas which only exist in the mind of God or people who see them

idealist /aɪˈdɪə.lɪst/ **noun** [C] someone who believes that very good things can be achieved, often when this does not seem likely to others • **idealistic** /ˌaɪ.dɪəˈlɪs.tɪk/ **adj** C1 *When I was young and idealistic I believed it was possible to change the world.* • **idealistically** /ˌaɪ.dɪəˈlɪs.tɪ.kəl.i/ **adv**

idealize (UK usually **idealise**) /aɪˈdɪə.laɪz/ **verb** [T] to think of or represent someone or something as better than they are: *Why do people idealize their school days?* • **idealized** (UK usually **idealised**) /aɪˈdɪə.laɪzd/ **adj** *The film presents a very idealized view of 19th-century Ireland (= making it seem more pleasant than it was).* • **idealization** (UK usually **idealisation**) /aɪˌdɪə.laɪˈzeɪ.ʃən/ US /aɪˌdɪə.ləˈ-/ **noun** [U]

ideally /aɪˈdɪə.li/ **adv** B2 used when describing the perfect situation: *Ideally, I'd like to work at home but it's just not practical.* ◦ *She's ideally (= perfectly) **suited** to the job.*

identical /aɪˈden.tɪ.kəl/ US /-t̬ə-/ **adj** B2 exactly the same, or very similar: *I've got three identical blue suits.* ◦ *The two rooms were virtually identical.* ◦ *The interests of both parties may not be identical, but they do overlap considerably.* ◦ *The tests are identical **to** those carried out last year.* • **identically** /-kəl.i/ **adv** *The two sisters were always dressed identically (= in the same clothes).*

iˌdentical ˈtwin **noun** [C usually plural] one of two babies of the same sex who were born at the same time, developed from the same egg, and look the same

identifiable /aɪˈden.tɪ.faɪ.ə.bl̩/ US /aɪˌden.t̬ə-/ **adj** able to be recognized: *In her bright yellow coat, she was easily identifiable in the crowd.*

identification /aɪˌden.tɪ.fɪˈkeɪ.ʃən/ US /-t̬ə-/ **noun** [U] **1** B2 the act of recognizing and naming someone or something: *Most of the bodies were badly burned, making identification almost impossible.* **2** A2 (also **ID**) an official document that shows or proves who you are: *We were asked to show some identification before the security guards would let us in.*

identify /aɪˈden.tɪ.faɪ/ US /-t̬ə-/ **verb** [T] **1** B2 to recognize someone or something and say or prove who or what they are: *Even the smallest baby can identify its mother by her voice.* ◦ *The gunman in Wednesday's attack has been identified as Lee Giggs, an unemployed truck driver.* ◦ *The police officer identified him**self** (= gave his name or proved who he was) and asked for our help.* **2** B2 to recognize a problem, need, fact, etc. and to show that it exists: *The research will be used to identify training needs.* ◦ *You need to identify your priorities.*

PHRASAL VERBS **identify with sb** B2 to feel that you are similar to someone in some way and that you can understand them or their situation because of this: *Many women of normal weight feel unable to identify with the super-thin models in glossy magazines.* • **identify sb/sth with sth** [usually passive] to believe that someone or something is closely connected or involved with something: *Many football fans are unfairly identified with violent behaviour.*

identikit /aɪˈden.tɪ.kɪt/ US /-t̬ə-/ **adj** [before noun] very similar in appearance, in a way that is boring and has no character

Identikit /aɪˈden.tɪ.kɪt/ US /-t̬ə-/ **noun** [C] UK trademark a picture of the face of someone who the police want to question, usually because that person is thought to have been involved in a crime. The picture is made from a collection of drawings of noses, eyes, ears, etc. and is based on the descriptions of WITNESSES to the crime: *an Identikit picture* ◦ *Police have issued an Identikit of the man they want to question.* → See also **photofit (picture)**

identity /aɪˈden.tɪ.ti/ US /-t̬ə.t̬i/ **noun** [C or U] B2 who a person is, or the qualities of a person or group which make them different from others: *The man's identity was being kept secret while he was helping police with enquiries.* ◦ *I cannot reveal the identity of my source.* ◦ *The informant was given a new identity (= a different name and new official documents) for protection.* ◦ *The newspaper photo apparently showed him in Rome but it was a case of **mistaken** identity (= it was the wrong person).* ◦ *In prison people often suffer from **a loss of** identity.* ◦ *I think my job gives me **a sense of** identity.*

iˈdentity ˌcard **noun** [C] (also **IˈD ˌcard**) B1 an official document or card with your name, date of birth, photograph, or other information on it that proves who you are

iˈdentity ˌcrisis **noun** [C usually singular] a feeling of being uncertain about who or what you are: *For some people, becoming a parent can bring on an identity crisis.*

iˈdentity paˌrade **noun** [C] UK (US **lineup**) a row of people, including a person who is believed to have committed a crime, who are shown to a WITNESS (= person who saw the crime) to find out if the WITNESS recognizes that person

ideogram /ˈɪd.i.ə.græm/ **noun** [C] (also **ideograph**) a written sign or symbol that represents an idea or object, used in some writing systems such as Chinese

ideological /ˌaɪ.di.əˈlɒdʒ.ɪ.kəl/ (US) /-ˈlɑː.dʒɪ-/ **adj** based on or relating to a particular set of ideas or beliefs: *ideological differences* ◦ *There are some fairly profound ideological disagreements within the movement.* • **ideologically** /-kəl.i/ **adv** *Little separates the two women ideologically (= they believe in similar things).*

ideologue /ˈaɪ.di.ə.lɒg/ (US) /-lɑːg/ **noun** [C] formal a person who believes very strongly in particular principles and tries to follow them carefully

ideology /ˌaɪ.diˈɒl.ə.dʒi/ (US) /-ˈɑː.lə-/ **noun** [C or U] a set of beliefs or principles, especially one on which a political system, party, or organization is based: *socialist/capitalist ideology* ◦ *The people are caught between two opposing ideologies.*

idiocy /ˈɪd.i.ə.si/ **noun** [C or U] a stupid action, or stupid behaviour: *the idiocies of war* ◦ *the idiocy of the whole scheme*

idiolect /ˈɪd.i.əʊ.lekt/ (US) /-oʊ-/ **noun** [C or U] the form of a language that a particular person speaks

idiom /ˈɪd.i.əm/ **noun** **1** (B2) [C] a group of words in a fixed order that have a particular meaning that is different from the meanings of each word on its own: *To 'have bitten off more than you can chew' is an idiom that means you have tried to do something which is too difficult for you.* **2** [C or U] formal the style of expression in writing, speech, or music that is typical of a particular period, person, or group: *Both operas are very much **in the modern** idiom.*

idiomatic /ˌɪd.i.əˈmæt.ɪk/ (US) /-ˈmæţ-/ **adj** **1** containing or consisting of an idiom: *'Bite the bullet' is an idiomatic expression that means to accept something unpleasant without complaining.* **2** containing expressions that are natural and correct: *She was born in Italy but her English is fluent and idiomatic.* • **idiomatically** /-kəl.i/ **adv**

idiosyncrasy /ˌɪd.i.əˈsɪŋ.krə.si/ **noun** [C usually plural] a strange or unusual habit, way of behaving, or feature that someone or something has: *She often cracks her knuckles when she's speaking – it's one of her **little** idiosyncrasies.* ◦ *One of the idiosyncrasies of this printer is that you can't stop it once it has started.* • **idiosyncratic** /-sɪŋˈkræt.ɪk/ (US) /-sɪŋˈkræţ.ɪk/ **adj** *The film, three hours long, is directed in his usual idiosyncratic style.*

idiot /ˈɪd.i.ət/ **noun** [C] (B2) a stupid person or someone who is behaving in a stupid way: *Some idiot left the tap running in the bathroom and there's water everywhere.* ◦ [as form of address] *You stupid idiot – that's a month's work you've lost!*

idiotic /ˌɪd.iˈɒt.ɪk/ (US) /-ˈɑː.ţɪk/ **adj** stupid • **idiotically** /-ˈɒt.ɪ.kəl.i/ (US) /-ˈɑː.ţɪ.kəl.i/ **adv**

ˈidiot-ˌproof **adj** extremely easy to use: *The DVD player comes with idiot-proof instructions.*

idle /ˈaɪ.dl/ **adj; verb**

▸**adj** **NOT WORKING** ▷ **1** (C1) not working or being used: *Half these factories now **stand** idle.* ◦ *It's crazy to have £7,000 **sitting** idle in the bank.* **2** An idle moment or period of time is one in which there is no work or activity: *If you have an idle moment, call me.* **3** without work: *Almost half of the workforce are now idle.* → Synonym **unemployed** **NO PURPOSE** ▷ **4** (C2) [before noun] without any particular purpose: *idle chatter/gossip/speculation* ◦ *an idle glance* ◦ *This is no idle threat.* **LAZY** ▷ **5** (C2) lazy and not willing to work: *He's a very able student, he's just **bone** idle (= very lazy).* • **idleness** /-nəs/ **noun** [U]

▸**verb** [I] (UK also **tick over**) If an engine or machine idles, it runs slowly but does not move or do any work: *He left the engine idling and ran into the shop.*

PHRASAL VERB **idle sth away** to spend a period of time relaxing and doing very little: *We idled away the hours drinking and playing cards.*

idly /ˈaɪd.li/ **adv** **1** without any particular purpose: *I was just glancing idly through a magazine.* **2** doing nothing: *She lay idly on the grass.* ◦ *We cannot **stand** idly **by** while these people suffer.*

idol /ˈaɪ.dəl/ **noun** [C] **1** (C1) someone who is admired and respected very much: *a pop/sporting idol* ◦ *The Hollywood film idols of the 1940s were glamorous figures, adored by millions.* **2** (C2) a picture or object that people pray to as part of their religion: *The ancient people of this area worshipped a huge bronze idol in the shape of an elephant.*

idolatry /aɪˈdɒl.ə.tri/ (US) /-ˈdɑː.lə-/ **noun** [U] often disapproving **1** very great admiration or respect for someone, often too great: *The youngster makes no attempt to conceal his idolatry **of** his team-mate.* ◦ *Newton was revered to the point of idolatry.* **2** the act of praying to a picture or object as part of a religion: *Father Brown considers the notes and flowers left near the statue to be close to idolatry.*

idolize (UK usually **idolise**) /ˈaɪ.dəl.aɪz/ **verb** [T] to admire and respect someone very much, often too much: *She idolized her father.*

idyll /ˈɪd.əl/ **noun** [C] a very happy, peaceful, and simple situation or period of time, especially in the countryside, or a piece of music, literature, etc. that describes this: *Every year thousands of people flee the big cities in search of the **pastoral/rural** idyll.*

idyllic /ɪˈdɪl.ɪk/ **adj** An idyllic place or experience is extremely pleasant, beautiful, or peaceful: *an idyllic childhood/summer* ◦ *an idyllic village in the Yorkshire Dales* • **idyllically** /-ɪ.kəl.i/ **adv** *They seem idyllically happy in their cottage.*

i.e. /ˌaɪˈiː/ used especially in writing before a piece of information that makes the meaning of something clearer or shows its true meaning: *The hotel is closed during low season, i.e. from October to March.* ◦ *The price must be more realistic, i.e. lower.*

IED /ˌaɪ.iːˈdiː/ **noun** [C] abbreviation for improvised explosive device: a type of bomb made and used by people who are not members of an official army, etc.: *Their truck was blown up by an IED.*

IELTS /ˈaɪ.elts/ **noun** [U] abbreviation for International English Language Testing System: a test in the ability to use the English language for people from other countries who need a qualification to study at a university or to work in Australia, Canada, Ireland, South Africa, New Zealand, or the UK

if /ɪf/ **conjunction; noun**

▸**conjunction** **IN THAT SITUATION** ▷ **1** (A2) used to say that a particular thing can or will happen only after something else happens or becomes true: *I'll pay you double if you get the work finished by Friday.* ◦ *We'll have the party in the garden if the weather's good. If **not** (= if the weather is not good), it'll have to be inside.* ◦ *If anyone rings for me, please tell them I'll be back in the office at four o'clock.* ◦ *If she hadn't called, I wouldn't have known.* ◦ *I wouldn't work for them (**even**) if they paid me twice my current salary.* ◦ *We'll deal with that problem if **and when** it arises.* ◦ *If disturbed, the bird may abandon the nest, leaving the chicks to die.* **2** although: *She's a lovely woman, **even** if she can be a bit tiring at times.* ◦ literary *It was a hot, if* windy day. **3** B1 every time: *If water is heated to 100°C it turns to steam.* ◦ *If I don't get enough sleep I get a headache.* **4** used to mean 'if it is true that': *I'm very sorry if I've offended you.*

> **! Common mistake: if**
>
> **Remember:** when you are using **if** to talk about something happening in the future, use the present simple tense.
>
> Don't say 'if something will happen', say **if something happens**:
>
> ~~*I will try to visit you if I will have time.*~~
>
> *I will try to visit you if I have time.*
>
> However, if a clause beginning with **if** is the object of the sentence, it is possible to use 'will':
>
> *I don't know if I will have time to visit you.*

WHETHER ▷ **5** B1 used to introduce a CLAUSE, often in INDIRECT SPEECH, that shows two or more possibilities: *Mrs Kramer rang half an hour ago to ask if her cake was ready.* ◦ *I don't care if he likes it or not – I'm coming!* ◦ *I was wondering if you'd like to come to the cinema with me this evening?* → Compare **whether** **REQUEST** ▷ **6** used when you want to make a polite request or remark: *If you'd like to take a seat, Mr Chang will be with you in a moment.* ◦ *Would you mind if I open/opened (= can I open) the window?* ◦ *There are, if you don't mind me saying so, one or two problems with this plan.*

IDIOM **if I were you** B1 used when you give someone advice: *If I were you, I'd probably go.* ◦ *I think I'd take the money if I were you.*

▸**noun** [C usually singular] informal something that is not certain or not yet decided: *There's a* ***big*** *if hanging over the project still (= it is uncertain whether the project will happen).*

IDIOM **no ifs and buts** UK (US **no ifs, ands or buts**) something that you say to a child to stop them arguing with you when you want them to do something: *I want no ifs and buts – just get on and tidy your room now.*

iffy /ˈɪf.i/ **adj** informal **1** not certain or decided: *Simon's still kind of iffy about going to Columbia.* **2** not completely good, honest, or suitable: *The milk smells a bit iffy.* ◦ *I was hoping to go to the park but the weather's looking a bit iffy.*

-ify (also **-fy**) /-ɪ.faɪ/ **suffix** used to form verbs meaning to cause an increase in the stated quality; to become: *simplify* ◦ *beautify*

igloo /ˈɪg.luː/ **noun** [C] (plural **igloos**) a circular house made of blocks of hard snow, especially as built by the Inuit people of northern North America

igloo

igneous /ˈɪg.ni.əs/ **adj** specialized (of rocks) formed from MAGMA (= very hot liquid rock that has cooled)

ignite /ɪgˈnaɪt/ **verb** **1** [I or T] formal to (cause to) start burning or explode: *The fuel spontaneously ignites because of the high temperature and pressure.* **2** [T] to cause a dangerous, excited, or angry situation to begin: *The proposed restrictions have ignited a storm of protest.*

ignition /ɪgˈnɪʃ.ən/ **noun** **1** [C usually singular] the electrical system in an engine that causes the fuel to burn or explode in order to start the engine: *Switch/Turn* ***the*** *ignition on.* ◦ *an ignition key* **2** [U] formal the act or process of something starting to burn

ignoble /ɪgˈnəʊ.bl/ US /-ˈnoʊ-/ **adj** formal morally bad and making you feel ashamed: *an ignoble action/idea* • **ignobly** /-bli/ **adv** literary

ignominious /ˌɪg.nəˈmɪn.i.əs/ **adj** literary (especially of events or behaviour) embarrassing because of being a complete failure: *an ignominious defeat/failure/retreat* • **ignominiously** /-li/ **adv**

ignominy /ˈɪg.nə.mɪ.ni/ **noun** [U] literary public embarrassment: *The Workers' Coalition experienced the ignominy of total defeat in the last election.*

ignoramus /ˌɪg.nəˈreɪ.məs/ **noun** [C] a person who knows nothing: *I'm a complete ignoramus where computers are concerned.*

ignorance /ˈɪg.nər.əns/ US /-nɚ-/ **noun** [U] C2 lack of knowledge, understanding, or information about something: *Public ignorance* ***about*** *the disease is still a cause for concern.* ◦ *Patients, it is claimed, were kept/left* ***in*** *ignorance* ***of*** *what was wrong with them.*

IDIOM **ignorance is bliss** saying said to emphasize that sometimes it is better for you if you do not know all the facts about a situation

ignorant /ˈɪg.nər.ənt/ US /-nɚ-/ **adj** **1** C2 not having enough knowledge, understanding, or information about something: *Many teenagers are surprisingly ignorant* ***about*** *current politics.* ◦ *We remained* ***blissfully*** *ignorant* ***of*** *the troubles that lay ahead.* **2** UK informal not polite or showing respect: *Ignorant lout!*

ignore /ɪgˈnɔːr/ US /-ˈnɔːr/ **verb** [T] B2 to intentionally not listen or give attention to: *She can be really irritating but I try to ignore her.* ◦ *Safety regulations are being ignored by company managers in the drive to increase profits.* ◦ *How can the government ignore the wishes of the majority?* ◦ *I smiled at her but she just ignored me.*

> **+ Other ways of saying ignore**
>
> **Disregard** can sometimes be used instead of 'ignore' when someone ignores suggestions, advice, rules, etc.:
>
> *He* ***disregarded*** *the advice of his doctor and went back to work.*
>
> The phrase **turn a blind eye** to something can be used when someone ignores something bad and pretends it is not happening:
>
> *Until now, the mayor has* ***turned a blind eye*** *to the city's homelessness problem.*
>
> If you ignore or avoid something regularly, you could use the verb **shun**:
>
> *As assistant to the president, he* ***shunned*** *the spotlight, but worked very hard behind the scenes.*
>
> The phrase **give someone the cold shoulder** can also be used when someone ignores a person in an unfriendly way:
>
> *I said hello to him and he just* ***gave me the cold shoulder.***

iguana /ɪˈgwɑː.nə/ **noun** [C] a large greyish-green LIZARD of tropical America

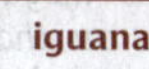

iguana

iirc written abbreviation for if I remember correctly, used in emails, etc.

ileum /ˈɪl.i.əm/ **noun** [C usually singular] (plural **ilea** /ˈɪl.i.ə/) specialized the last and narrowest part of the

SMALL INTESTINE (= part of bowels after the stomach), where substances from food are absorbed

ilk /ɪlk/ **noun** [S] mainly disapproving a particular type: *The worst of her criticism was reserved for journalists, photographers, and others* ***of*** *their ilk.*

ill /ɪl/ **adj; adv; noun**

▸**adj** **NOT WELL** ▷ **1** A2 not feeling well, or suffering from a disease: *I* ***felt*** *ill so I went home.* ◦ *He's been ill* ***with*** *meningitis.* ◦ *Sophia* ***fell*** *ill/****was taken*** *ill (= became ill) while on holiday.* ◦ *He is* ***critically*** *(= very badly) ill in hospital.* **BAD** ▷ **2** C1 [before noun] formal or old-fashioned bad: *ill health* ◦ *Did you experience any ill effects from the treatment?*

Other ways of saying ill

A common alternative is the adjective **sick**:

He was off work ***sick*** *last week.*

A more formal adjective meaning 'ill' is **unwell**:

I've felt a little ***unwell*** *all week.*

If you want to say that someone feels slightly ill, in informal situations you can also use the expressions **be/feel under the weather** and **be/feel below par**:

I don't think I'll be coming to the party – I'm ***feeling a bit under the weather.***

IDIOM **be ill at ease** C2 to be worried and not relaxed: *He seemed ill at ease and not his usual self.*

▸**adv** **1** literary badly: *He treated her very ill.* **2 speak ill of sb** formal or old-fashioned to say unkind things about someone: *I realize one shouldn't speak ill of the dead.* **3 augur/bode ill** formal or old-fashioned to be a sign of bad things in the future: *This weather bodes ill for the garden party tonight.* **4 can ill afford (to do sth)** formal or old-fashioned If you can ill afford to do something, it will cause problems for you if you do it: *We can ill afford to lose another member of staff.*

▸**noun** **1** [U] formal or old-fashioned harm: *I wish her no ill.* **2** [C usually plural] a problem: *There seems to be no cure for Britain's economic/social ills.*

ill- /ɪl/ **prefix** in a way that is bad or not suitable: *ill-prepared* ◦ *an ill-judged remark*

I'll /aɪl/ **short form** I shall or I will: *I'll be there at 6.00.*

ˌill-adˈvised **adj** not wise, and likely to cause problems in the future: *an ill-advised career move*

ˌill-aˈssorted **adj** mainly UK looking strange together and not seeming to be a good match: *ill-assorted furniture* ◦ *an ill-assorted couple*

ˌill-ˈbred **adj** old-fashioned rude and behaving badly: *an ill-bred young man*

ˌill-conˈceived **adj** badly planned and unwise: *The whole project was ill-conceived.*

ˌill-diˈsposed **adj** formal **be ill-disposed towards sb** to not be friendly to someone or not support them: *Most of the audience seemed ill-disposed towards the speaker.*

illegal /ɪˈliː.ɡəl/ **adj** B2 not allowed by law: *a campaign to stop the illegal sale of cigarettes to children under 16* ◦ *Prostitution is illegal in some countries.* ◦ ***It*** *is illegal* ***to*** *drive a car that is not taxed and insured.* ◦ *Cocaine, LSD, and heroin are all illegal* ***drugs/substances.*** • **illegally** /-i/ **adv** B2 *They entered the country illegally.* ◦ *an illegally parked car*

ilˌlegal ˈimmigrant **noun** [C] (US also **ilˌlegal ˈalien**) someone who goes to live or work in another country when they do not have the legal right to do this

illegality /ˌɪl.iːˈɡæl.ɪ.ti/ US /-ə.t̬i/ **noun** [C or U] the state of being illegal, or an illegal action

illegible /ɪˈledʒ.ə.bl/ **adj** (of writing or print) impossible or almost impossible to read because of being very untidy or not clear: *His writing is almost illegible.* • **illegibly** /-bli/ **adv**

illegitimate /ˌɪl.ɪˈdʒɪt.ə.mət/ US /-ˈdʒɪt̬-/ **adj** **1** born of parents not married to each other **2** formal not legal or fair: *The rebels regard the official parliament as illegitimate.* • **illegitimacy** /-mə.si/ **noun** [U]

ˌill-eˈquipped **adj** without the ability, qualities, or equipment to do something: [+ to infinitive] *He seems to me ill-equipped* ***to*** *cope with the responsibility.* ◦ *school leavers ill-equipped* ***for*** *adult life*

ˌill-ˈfated **adj** [before noun] unlucky and unsuccessful, often resulting in death: *The ill-fated aircraft later crashed into the hillside.*

ˌill-ˈfitting **adj** Ill-fitting clothes do not fit well.

ˌill-ˈgotten **adj** [before noun] mainly humorous dishonestly obtained: *He deposited his ill-gotten* ***gains*** *in foreign bank accounts.*

illiberal /ɪˈlɪb.ər.əl/ US /-ɚ-/ **adj** formal limiting freedom of expression, thought, behaviour, etc.: *illiberal policies*

illicit /ɪˈlɪs.ɪt/ **adj** illegal or disapproved of by society: *illicit drugs such as cocaine and cannabis* ◦ *an illicit love affair* • **illicitly** /-li/ **adv**

ˌill-inˈformed **adj** knowing less than you should about a particular subject

illiterate /ɪˈlɪt.ər.ət/ US /-ˈlɪt̬.ɚ-/ **adj; noun**

▸**adj** **1** C2 unable to read and write: *A surprising percentage of the population are illiterate.* → Compare **innumerate** **2** knowing little or nothing about a particular subject: *computer illiterate* ◦ *financially/technologically illiterate* • **illiteracy** /-ə.si/ **noun** [U] *In the rural areas, illiteracy is widespread.*

▸**noun** [C] someone who is illiterate

ˌill-ˈmannered **adj** rude and unpleasant

illness /ˈɪl.nəs/ **noun** **1** B1 [C] a disease of the body or mind: *He died at home after a long illness.* **2** B2 [U] the state of being ill: *She had five days off work due to illness.*

Word partners for illness

develop/have/suffer from an illness • *cause* an illness • *diagnose/prevent/treat* an illness • *recover from* an illness • a *chronic/rare/serious* illness • a *critical/fatal/terminal* illness • a *minor* illness • *because of/due to/through* illness

illogical /ɪˈlɒdʒ.ɪ.kəl/ US /-ˈlɑː.dʒɪ-/ **adj** not reasonable, wise, or practical, usually because directed by the emotions rather than by careful thought: *It is an illogical statement, because if one part is true, then the other must be false.* • **illogically** /-i/ **adv** • **illogicality** /ɪˌlɒdʒ.ɪˈkæl.ɪ.ti/ US /ɪˌlɑː.dʒɪˈkæl.ə.t̬i/ **noun** [U]

ˌill-ˈstarred **adj** [before noun] (also **ˌill-ˈomened**) **ill-fated**

ˌill-ˈtempered **adj** **1** formal easily annoyed **2** If an occasion, such as a game, is ill-tempered, people get angry during it: *An increasingly ill-tempered match saw three players sent off before half-time.*

ˌill-ˈtimed **adj** done or made at a wrong or unsuitable time: *an ill-timed comment*

ˌill-ˈtreat **verb** [T] to treat someone badly, especially by being violent or by not taking care of them: *The child had been severely ill-treated by his parents.*

illuminate /ɪˈluː.mɪ.neɪt/ **verb** [T] formal **1** to light something and make it brighter: *The streets were illuminated with strings of coloured lights.* **2** to explain and show more clearly something that is difficult to understand: *an article which illuminates the issues at stake*

illuminated /ɪˈluː.mɪ.neɪ.tɪd/ (US) /-t̬ɪd/ **adj** An illuminated book or other piece of writing is one decorated with added colour, gold paint, and small pictures: *an illuminated **manuscript***

illuminating /ɪˈluː.mɪ.neɪ.tɪŋ/ (US) /-t̬ɪŋ/ **adj** formal giving you new information about a subject or making it easier to understand: *The book is full of illuminating detail on the causes of the war.* ◦ *a most illuminating discussion*

illumination /ɪˌluː.mɪˈneɪ.ʃən/ **noun** formal **1** [C or U] light: *The only illumination was from a skylight.* **2 illuminations** [plural] mainly UK coloured decorative lights outside which make a town look bright and exciting at night: *the Blackpool illuminations*

illusion /ɪˈluː.ʒən/ **noun 1** C2 [C or U] an idea or belief that is not true: *He **had no** illusions **about** his talents as a singer.* ◦ *I'm **under no** illusions (= I understand the truth) about the man I married.* ◦ *My boss is **labouring under the** illusion **that** (= wrongly believes that) the project will be completed on time.* **2** C2 [C] something that is not really what it seems to be: *A large mirror in a room can **create the** illusion **of** space.* ◦ *The impression of calm in the office is just an illusion.*

illusionist /ɪˈluː.ʒən.ɪst/ **noun** [C] an ENTERTAINER who performs tricks where objects seem to appear and then disappear

illusory /ɪˈluː.sər.i/ (US) /-sɚ-/ **adj** (also **illusive**) not real and based on illusion: *Their hopes of a peaceful solution turned out to be illusory.*

illustrate /ˈɪl.ə.streɪt/ **verb** [T] **EXPLAIN** ▷ **1** C1 to show the meaning or truth of something more clearly, especially by giving examples: *The lecturer illustrated his point **with** a diagram on the blackboard.* ◦ *This latest conflict further illustrates the weakness of the UN.* ◦ [+ question word] *The exhibition will illustrate **how** life evolved from water.* **DRAW PICTURES** ▷ **2** B2 to draw pictures for a book, magazine, etc.: *a beautifully illustrated book/old manuscript*

illustration /ˌɪl.əˈstreɪ.ʃən/ **noun** [C or U] **EXAMPLE** ▷ **1** C2 an example that explains or proves something: *This delay is a perfect illustration **of** why we need a new computer system.* ◦ *A couple of examples are included, **by way of** illustration (= to show the meaning more clearly).* **PICTURE** ▷ **2** C1 a picture in a book, magazine, etc. or the process of illustrating something: *a full-page illustration* ◦ *colour/black and white illustrations*

illustrative /ˈɪl.ə.strə.tɪv/ (US) /ɪˈlʌs.trə.t̬ɪv/ **adj** formal helping to explain or prove something: *Falling house prices are illustrative **of** the crisis facing the construction industry.*

illustrator /ˈɪl.ə.streɪ.tər/ (US) /-t̬ɚ/ **noun** [C] a person who draws pictures, especially for books

illustrious /ɪˈlʌs.tri.əs/ **adj** formal famous, well respected and admired: *She comes from an illustrious political family which includes two former Cabinet ministers.*

ˌill ˈwill **noun** [U] **1** bad feelings between people because of things that happened in the past **2 bear sb ill will** formal to feel angry with someone because of something they have done: *I bear him no ill will.*

I'm /aɪm/ **short form** I am: *I'm so happy for you!*

image /ˈɪm.ɪdʒ/ **noun** **MENTAL PICTURE** ▷ **1** C2 [C] a picture in your mind or an idea of how someone or something is: *I have an image in my mind of how I want the garden to be.* ◦ *He doesn't **fit** (= he is different to) my image of how an actor should look.* **2** B2 [C or U] the way that something or someone is thought of by other people: *The aim is to improve the **public** image of the police.* ◦ *The company has made strenuous attempts to improve its image in recent years.* ◦ *He's terribly image-**conscious** (= tries to dress and behave in a way that other people will admire).* **3** [C] specialized a mental picture or idea which forms in a reader's or listener's mind from the words that they read or hear: *The poem is full of images of birth and new life.* **PICTURE** ▷ **4** B2 [C] any picture, especially one formed by a mirror or a LENS: *television images of starving children* ◦ *The image you see in the mirror.*

IDIOM **be the (living/spitting) image of sb** to look very similar to someone: *She's the spitting image of her mother.*

imagery /ˈɪm.ɪ.dʒər.i/ (US) /-dʒɚ-/ **noun** [U] the use of words or pictures in books, films, paintings, etc. to describe ideas or situations: *The imagery in the poem is mostly to do with death.*

imaginable /ɪˈmædʒ.ɪ.nə.bl/ **adj** possible to think of: *The school offers courses in every subject imaginable.* ◦ *ice cream of every imaginable flavour*

imaginary /ɪˈmædʒ.ɪ.nər.i/ (US) /-ə.ner-/ **adj** C1 describes something that is created by and exists only in the mind: *As a child I had an imaginary friend.* ◦ *The story is set in an imaginary world.* ◦ *imaginary fears*

imagination /ɪˌmædʒ.ɪˈneɪ.ʃən/ **noun 1** B1 [C or U] the ability to form pictures in the mind: *My younger son has a very **vivid** (= active) imagination.* ◦ *I can never make up stories – I have absolutely no imagination.* ◦ *For some reason the story **captured/caught the** imagination **of** the public (= made them very interested).* ◦ *It couldn't **by any stretch of the** imagination be described as a (= it is certainly not a) beautiful city.* ◦ *There's a sex scene in the film which apparently **leaves nothing to the** imagination (= shows sexual parts of the body very clearly).* **2** [U] something that you think exists or is true, although in fact it is not real or true: *Was she paying him a lot of attention or was it just my imagination?* ◦ *Is it my imagination or is David behaving strangely at the moment?* **3** B1 [U] the ability to think of new ideas: *It's a job that needs someone with a bit of imagination.*

> **Word partners for imagination**
>
> *have/lack/show* imagination • *use* your imagination • *take* imagination • *catch/capture* sb's imagination • *excite/fire/spark* sb's imagination • a *fertile/fevered/overactive/vivid* imagination • a *lack* of imagination • a *figment* of sb's imagination • *with* (a little) imagination

imaginative /ɪˈmædʒ.ɪ.nə.tɪv/ (US) /-t̬ɪv/ **adj** approving **1** C1 new, original, and clever: *an imaginative new approach/policy* ◦ *The architects have made imaginative use of glass and transparent plastic.* **2** C1 good at thinking of new, original, and clever ideas: *an imaginative designer* • **imaginatively** /-li/ **adv**

imagine /ɪˈmædʒ.ɪn/ **verb** [T] **1** B1 to form or have a mental picture or idea of something: *Imagine Robert Redford when he was young – that's what John looks like.* ◦ [+ (that)] *Imagine **(that)** you're eating an ice cream – try to feel how cold it is.* ◦ [+ question word] *Can you imagine **how** it feels to be blind?* ◦ [+ -ing verb] *She imagined herself sitt**ing** in her favourite armchair back home.* ◦ *They hadn't imagined (= expected) **(that)** it would be so difficult.* ◦ *I can't imagine (= I really don't know) what he wants from us.* **2** B2 to believe that something is probably true: [+ (that)] *I imagine **(that)** he's under a lot of pressure at the moment.* ◦ *I don't imagine **(that)** they have much money.* ◦ *'Will they change it?' 'I imagine **so**.'* **3** B1 to think that something exists or is true, although in fact it is not real or true: *'Did you hear a noise?' 'No, you're imagining **things**/No, you must have imagined it.'* ◦ *I've never heard her criticize you – I think you imagine it.* **4** used to express shock or surprise, often at someone else's behaviour: *She got married at 16! Imagine that!* ◦ [+ -ing verb] *Imagine spend**ing** all that money on a coat!* **5 you can't imagine** UK used to emphasize a statement: *You can't imagine what a mess the house was in after the party.*

imaging /ˈɪmɪdʒ.ɪŋ/ **noun** [U] specialized the process of producing an exact picture of something, especially on a computer screen: *computer/digital imaging*

imam /ɪˈmɑːm/ **noun** [C] a leader in the Islamic religion

IMAX /ˈaɪ.mæks/ **noun** [U] trademark a system for making and showing specially photographed films on an extremely large screen: *an IMAX cinema/theatre*

imbalance /ˌɪmˈbæl.ənts/ **noun** [C] a situation in which two things that should be equal or that are normally equal are not: *There is huge economic imbalance **between** the two countries.*

imbecile /ˈɪm.bə.siːl/ (US) /-sɪl/ **noun** [C] a person who behaves in a stupid way • **imbecilic** /ˌɪm.bəˈsɪl.ɪk/ **adj** (also **imbecile**)

imbed /ɪmˈbed/ **verb** (**-dd-**) US **embed**

imbibe /ɪmˈbaɪb/ **verb** [I or T] formal or humorous to drink, especially alcohol: *Have you been imbibing again?*

imbroglio /ɪmˈbrəʊ.li.əʊ/ (US) /-ˈbroʊ.li.oʊ/ **noun** [C] (plural **imbroglios**) formal an unwanted, difficult, and confusing situation, full of trouble and problems: *The Soviet Union became anxious to withdraw its soldiers from the Afghan imbroglio.*

imbue /ɪmˈbjuː/ **verb**

PHRASAL VERB **imbue sth/sb with sth** formal to fill something or someone with a particular feeling, quality, or idea: *His poetry is imbued with deep, religious feeling.*

the IMF /ˌaɪ.emˈef/ **noun** abbreviation for the International Monetary Fund: a part of the United Nations that encourages international trade and gives financial help to poor countries

imho written abbreviation for in my humble opinion: used when you tell someone your opinion, for example in an email

imitate /ˈɪm.ɪ.teɪt/ **verb** [T] (C1) to behave in a similar way to someone or something else, or to copy the speech or behaviour, etc. of someone or something: *Some of the younger pop bands try to imitate their musical heroes from the past.* ◦ *They produce artificial chemicals which exactly imitate particular natural ones.*

imitation /ˌɪm.ɪˈteɪ.ʃən/ **adj; noun**

▸**adj** made to look like something else: *an imitation leather watch-strap* ◦ *It's not real silk – it's just imitation.*

▸**noun 1** [C or U] an occasion when someone or something imitates another person or thing: *Ten-year-olds have started wearing lipstick and make-up **in** imitation **of** the older girls.* ◦ *She can **do** a wonderful imitation **of** a blackbird's song.* **2** (C2) [C] a copy: *His songs are just **cheap** (= low quality) imitations of Beatles tunes.*

> **Word partners for imitation**
>
> a *bad/cheap/pale/poor* imitation (of sth) • a *convincing/good* imitation (of sth)

imitative /ˈɪm.ɪ.tə.tɪv/ (US) /-teɪ.t̬ɪv/ **adj** mainly disapproving copying someone or something: *All these magazines are imitative **of** each other.* ◦ *He's an imitative artist, with very little originality in his work.*

imitator /ˈɪm.ɪ.teɪ.təʳ/ (US) /-t̬ɚ/ **noun** [C usually plural] a person who copies someone or something that they think is good: *The difference between Ms McArthur and her countless imitators is the elegance of her writing.*

immaculate /ɪˈmæk.jʊ.lət/ **adj** approving **1** perfectly clean or tidy: *dressed in an immaculate white suit* ◦ *an immaculate garden* **2** perfect and without any mistakes: *He gave an immaculate **performance** as the ageing hero.* • **immaculately** /-li/ **adv** *immaculately dressed*

the Imˌmaculate Conˈception **noun** [S] the Christian belief that Jesus Christ's mother Mary, or, more generally, Jesus Christ himself, was born free from SIN (= offence against religious law)

immaterial /ˌɪm.əˈtɪə.ri.əl/ (US) /-ˈtɪr.i-/ **adj** not important, or not relating to the subject you are thinking about: *Whether the book is well or badly written is immaterial (**to** me) – it has an important message.*

immature /ˌɪm.əˈtʃʊəʳ/ (US) /-ˈtʊr/ **adj 1** (C2) disapproving not behaving in a way that is as calm and wise as people expect from someone of your age: *Stop being so silly and immature, Ben!* ◦ *She's rather immature for her age, don't you think?* **2** disapproving not having much experience of something: *politically immature* **3** specialized not yet completely grown or developed: *While the animals are still immature, they do not breed.* • **immaturity** /-ˈtʃʊə.rɪ.ti/ (US) /-ˈtʊr.ə.t̬i/ **noun** [U]

immeasurable /ɪˈmeʒ.ər.ə.bl̩/ (US) /-ɚ-/ **adj** so large or great that it cannot be measured or known exactly: *Her films had an immeasurable effect on a generation of Americans.* • **immeasurably** /-bli/ **adv** *The damage from the 1956 hurricane was immeasurably greater.*

immediacy /ɪˈmiː.di.ə.si/ **noun** [U] the fact that something seems real and important, so that you feel involved with it: *Pre-recorded TV programmes have so much less immediacy and warmth than live theatre.*

immediate /ɪˈmiː.di.ət/ **adj 1** (B2) happening or done without delay or very soon after something else: *We must make an immediate response.* ◦ *Dioxin is a poison that takes immediate effect.* **2** (C1) describes something or someone that is close to, or is a cause of or an effect of, something or someone else: *There are few facilities in the immediate area.* ◦ *An immediate **result/effect** of the war was a breakdown of law and order.* **3** (B2) in the present or as soon as possible: *We have no immediate plans.* ◦ *MPs have demanded his immediate resignation.* **4 the immediate future** the period of time that is coming next **5 your immediate family** your closest relations, such as your parents, children, husband, or wife

immediately /ɪˈmiː.di.ət.li/ **adv; conjunction**

▸**adv 1** (A2) now or without waiting or thinking: *We really ought to leave immediately.* ◦ *The purpose of the meeting wasn't immediately obvious.* **2** (C1) close to something or someone in distance or time: *Milton Street is on the left, immediately **after** the bank.* ◦ *They moved in immediately before Christmas.* ◦ *We heard a loud crash from the room immediately above us.* **3** closely or directly: *The people most immediately affected by the drought are the farmers themselves.*

> **! Common mistake: immediately**
>
> **Warning:** Common word-building error!
> If an adjective ends with 'te', just add 'ly' to make an adverb. Don't write 'immediatly' or 'immediatelly', write **immediately**.

▸**conjunction** UK as soon as: *Immediately she'd gone,*

the boys started to mess about ◦ *I'll call you immediately I hear anything.*

immemorial /ˌɪm.əˈmɔː.ri.əl/ (US) /-ˈmɔːr.i-/ **adj from/since time immemorial** literary for a very long time: *Her family had farmed that land since time immemorial.*

immense /ɪˈmens/ **adj 1** C1 extremely large in size or degree: *immense wealth/value* ◦ *They spent an immense* ***amount*** *of time getting the engine into perfect condition.* **2** slang extremely good: *He's an immense goalkeeper.*

immensely /ɪˈmens.li/ **adv** C1 extremely: *He was immensely popular in his day.* ◦ *She's an immensely talented young athlete.*

immensity /ɪˈmen.sə.ti/ (US) /-t̬i/ **noun** [U] formal the extremely large size of something: *The immensity of the task is daunting.*

immerse /ɪˈmɜːs/ (US) /-ˈmɝːs/ **verb immerse yourself in sth a** to become completely involved in something: *She got some books out of the library and immersed herself in Jewish history and culture.* **b** [T] formal to put something or someone completely under the surface of a liquid: *The shells should be immersed* ***in*** *boiling water for two minutes.* • **immersion** /ɪˈmɜː.ʃən/ (US) /-ˈmɝː-/ **noun** [C or U]

imˈmersion (ˌheater) **noun** [C] an electric device used for heating water

immigrant /ˈɪm.ɪ.grənt/ **noun** [C] B2 a person who has come to a different country in order to live there permanently: *a large immigrant* ***population*** ◦ ***Illegal*** *immigrants are sent back across the border if they are caught.*

immigrate /ˈɪm.ɪ.greɪt/ **verb** [I] to come to live in a different country: *He immigrated with his parents in 1895, and grew up in Long Island.*

immigration /ˌɪm.ɪˈgreɪ.ʃən/ **noun** [U] **1** B2 the act of someone coming to live in a different country: *There are strict limits on immigration (****into*** *the country).* **2** B1 the process of examining your PASSPORT and other documents to make certain that you can be allowed to enter the country, or the place where this is done: *After you've been through immigration (****control****), you can go and get your luggage.* ◦ *immigration policy* ◦ *immigration officers*

imminent /ˈɪm.ɪ.nənt/ **adj** C2 coming or likely to happen very soon: *imminent disaster/danger* ◦ *A strike is imminent.* • **imminently** /-li/ **adv** • **imminence** /-nəns/ **noun** [U]

immiscible /ɪˈmɪs.ə.bəl/ **adj** specialized An immiscible liquid cannot be mixed with another liquid without separating from it: *Oil is immiscible* ***with/in*** *water.* → Compare **miscible**

immobile /ɪˈməʊ.baɪl/ (US) /-ˈmoʊ.bəl/ **adj** not moving or not able to move: *She sat immobile, wondering what to do next.* • **immobility** /ˌɪm.əˈbɪl.ə.ti/ (US) /-oʊˈbɪl.ə.t̬i/ **noun** [U]

immobilize (UK usually **immobilise**) /ɪˈməʊ.bəl.aɪz/ (US) /-ˈmoʊ-/ **verb** [T] to stop something or someone from moving: *You can immobilize the car by removing the spark plugs.* ◦ *The broken limb must be immobilized as soon as possible.* • **immobilization** (UK usually **immobilisation**) /ɪˌməʊ.bəl.aɪˈzeɪ.ʃən/ (US) /-ˌmoʊ.bə.lɪ-/ **noun** [U]

immobilizer (UK usually **immobiliser**) /ɪˈməʊ.bəl.aɪ.zər/ (US) /-zɚ/ **noun** [C] a device fitted to a car which stops it from moving so that it cannot be stolen

immoderate /ɪˈmɒd.ər.ət/ (US) /-ˈmɑː.dɚ-/ **adj** formal too much or many, or more than is usual or reasonable: *immoderate drinking* ◦ *immoderate demands* • **immoderately** /-li/ **adv**

immodest /ɪˈmɒd.ɪst/ (US) /-ˈmɑː.dɪst/ **adj** formal disapproving **1** having too high an opinion of yourself **2** showing too much of the body: *showing an immodest amount of leg* • **immodesty** /ɪˈmɒd.ə.sti/ (US) /-ˈmɑː.də-/ **noun** [U] formal

immolate /ˈɪm.ə.leɪt/ **verb** [T] formal to kill yourself or someone else, or to destroy something, usually by burning, in a formal ceremony • **immolation** /ˌɪm.əˈleɪ.ʃən/ **noun** [U]

immoral /ɪˈmɒr.əl/ (US) /-ˈmɑːr-/ **adj 1** B2 morally wrong, or outside society's standards of acceptable, honest, and moral behaviour: *an immoral act* ◦ *immoral behaviour* ◦ *It's an immoral tax, because the poor will pay relatively more.* → Compare **amoral, moral 2 immoral earnings** money earned from PROSTITUTION (= having sex in exchange for money): *If convicted, she could be jailed for five years for* ***living off*** *immoral earnings.* • **immorally** /-i/ **adv** • **immorality** /ˌɪm.əˈræl.ə.ti/ (US) /-ɑːˈræl.ə.t̬i/ **noun** [U]

immortal /ɪˈmɔː.təl/ (US) /-ˈmɔːr.t̬əl/ **adj; noun**

▸**adj 1** C2 living or lasting for ever: *immortal God* ◦ *The priest said he was endangering his immortal soul.* **2** C2 very special and famous and therefore likely to be remembered for a long time: *In the immortal* ***words*** *of Samuel Goldwyn, 'Include me out'.* • **immortality** /ˌɪm.ɔːˈtæl.ə.ti/ (US) /-ɔːrˈtæl.ə.t̬i/ **noun** [U] figurative *The Wright brothers achieved immortality with the first powered flight in 1903.*

▸**noun** literary **1** [C] someone who is so famous that they are remembered for a long time after they are dead: *She is one of the immortals of classical opera.* **2 the immortals** [plural] the Greek or Roman gods

immortalize (UK usually **immortalise**) /ɪˈmɔː.təl.aɪz/ (US) /-ˈmɔːr.t̬əl-/ **verb** [T often passive] to make someone or something so famous that they are remembered for a very long time: *Marlene Dietrich was immortalized through her roles* ***in*** *films like 'The Blue Angel'.*

immovable /ɪˈmuː.və.bl̩/ **adj 1** fixed and impossible to move: *The rock weighed over a ton and was completely immovable.* **2** describes a firm opinion that is impossible to change, or someone with such an opinion

immune /ɪˈmjuːn/ **adj 1** protected against a particular disease by particular substances in the blood: *Most people who've had chickenpox once are immune* ***to*** *it for the rest of their lives.* ◦ *He seems to be immune* ***to*** *colds – he just never gets them.* **2** C2 [after verb] not affected or upset by a particular type of behaviour or emotion: *The press had criticized her so often that in the end she had become immune (****to*** *it).* **3** [after verb] not able to be punished or damaged by something: *Journalists, he insisted, must be immune (= protected)* ***from*** *prosecution.*

imˈmune ˌsystem **noun** [C usually singular] C2 the cells and tissues in the body which make it able to protect itself against infection

immunity /ɪˈmjuː.nɪ.ti/ (US) /-ə.t̬i/ **noun** [U] a situation in which you are protected against disease or from legal action: *The vaccination gives you immunity* ***against*** *the disease for up to six months.* ◦ *He was granted immunity* ***from*** *prosecution because he confessed the names of the other spies.*

immunize (UK usually **immunise**) /ˈɪm.jʊ.naɪz/ **verb** [T] to protect a person or animal against a disease by putting a substance into their body, usually using a needle: *Children are routinely immunized* ***against*** *polio.* • **immunization** (UK usually **immunisation**) /ˌɪm.jʊ.naɪˈzeɪ.ʃən/ (US) /-nəˈ-/ **noun** [C or U]

immunodeficiency /ˌɪm.jʊ.nəʊ.dɪˈfɪʃ.ən.si/ (US) /-noʊ-/ **noun** [U] specialized a condition in which a body is unable to produce enough ANTIBODIES to fight bacteria and viruses, often resulting in infection and disease

immunology /ˌɪm.jəˈnɒl.ə.dʒi/ US /-ˈnɑː.lə-/ **noun** [U] specialized the study of how the body fights disease and infection

immured /ɪˈmjʊəd/ US /-ˈmjʊrd/ **adj** literary kept as a prisoner or closed away and out of sight: *Immured **in** a dark airless cell, the hostages waited six months for their release.*

immutable /ɪˈmjuː.tə.bl̩/ US /-t̬ə-/ **adj** formal not changing, or unable to be changed: *an immutable law* ◦ *Some people regard grammar as an immutable set of rules.* • **immutability** /ɪˌmjuː.təˈbɪl.ɪ.ti/ US /-t̬əˈbɪl.ə.t̬i/ **noun** [U]

imo written abbreviation for in my opinion: used when you tell someone your opinion, for example in an email

imp /ɪmp/ **noun** [C] **1** a small evil spirit **2** often humorous a child that behaves badly, but in a way that is funny rather than serious: *Come here, you little imp!*

impact **noun**; **verb**

▸**noun** [C usually singular, U] /ˈɪm.pækt/ **1** C2 the force or action of one object hitting another: *The impact of the crash reduced the car to a third of its original length.* ◦ *The bullet explodes **on** impact* (= when it hits another object). **2** B2 a powerful effect that something, especially something new, has on a situation or person: *The anti-smoking campaign had **had/made** quite an impact **on** young people.* ◦ *The new proposals were intended to **soften** the impact of the reformed tax system.*

▸**verb** [I or T] /ɪmˈpækt/ mainly US C1 to have an influence on something: *Falling export rates have impacted (**on**) the country's economy quite considerably.*

impacted /ɪmˈpæk.tɪd/ **adj** describes a tooth that cannot grow in the right way, usually because it is growing against another tooth below the GUM

impair /ɪmˈpeəʳ/ US /-ˈper/ **verb** [T] to spoil something or make it weaker so that it is less effective: *A recurring knee injury may have impaired his chances of winning the tournament.* • **impaired** /-ˈpeəd/ US /-ˈperd/ **adj** *She suffers from impaired vision/hearing.* • **impairment** /-mənt/ **noun** [U] *physical/mental impairment*

impale /ɪmˈpeɪl/ **verb** [T often passive] to push a sharp object through something, especially the body of an animal or person: *The dead deer was impaled **on** a spear.*

impalpable /ɪmˈpæl.pə.bl̩/ **adj** literary difficult to feel or understand: *an impalpable beauty/quality*

impanel /ɪmˈpæn.əl/ **verb** [T] to **empanel**

impart /ɪmˈpɑːt/ US /-ˈpɑːrt/ **verb** [T] formal **1** to communicate information to someone: *to impart the bad news* ◦ *I was rather quiet as I didn't feel I had much wisdom to impart on the subject.* **2** to give something a particular feeling, quality, or taste: *Preservatives can impart colour and flavour **to** a product.*

impartial /ɪmˈpɑː.ʃəl/ US /-pɑːr-/ **adj** not supporting any of the sides involved in an argument: *impartial advice* ◦ *A trial must be fair and impartial.* • **impartially** /-i/ **adv** • **impartiality** /ɪmˌpɑː.ʃiˈæl.ɪ.ti/ US /-ˌpɑːr.ʃiˈæl.ə.t̬i/ **noun** [U] *The state must ensure the independence and impartiality of the justice system.*

impassable /ɪmˈpɑː.sə.bl̩/ US /-ˈpæs.ə-/ **adj** describes a road or path that cannot be travelled on because of bad weather conditions or because it is blocked: *Many roads were flooded and impassable following the storm.*

impasse /æmˈpæs/ US /ˈɪm.pæs/ **noun** [U] a situation in which progress is impossible, especially because the people involved cannot agree: *The dispute had **reached** an impasse, as neither side would compromise.*

impassioned /ɪmˈpæʃ.ənd/ **adj** describes speech or writing that is full of strongly felt and strongly expressed emotion: *Relatives of the dead made an impassioned **plea** for the bodies to be flown back to this country.*

impassive /ɪmˈpæs.ɪv/ **adj** describes a person's face when it expresses no emotion, because they seem not to be affected by the situation they are experiencing • **impassively** /-li/ **adv** *The defendant sat impassively in the dock while evidence was given against him.* • **impassivity** /ˌɪm.pæsˈɪv.ɪ.ti/ US /-ə.t̬i/ **noun** [U]

impatience /ɪmˈpeɪ.ʃəns/ **noun** [U] **1** C2 the feeling of being annoyed by someone's mistakes or because you have to wait: *'I've shown you how to do this before,' she said, unable to disguise her impatience.* ◦ *There's a growing impatience among the electorate **with** the old two-party system.* **2** C2 the feeling of wanting something to happen as soon as possible: [+ to infinitive] *He was already half an hour late, which explains his impatience **to** leave.*

impatient /ɪmˈpeɪ.ʃənt/ **adj** **1** B2 easily annoyed by someone's mistakes or because you have to wait: *He's a good teacher, but inclined to be a bit impatient **with** slow learners.* ◦ *You'd be hopeless looking after children – you're far too impatient!* **2** B2 wanting something to happen as soon as possible: *He's got a lot of exciting ideas and he's impatient **to** get started.* ◦ *People are increasingly impatient **for** change in this country.* • **impatiently** /-li/ **adv** B2 *'Yes, you said that before,' she said impatiently.* ◦ *We were waiting impatiently for the show to begin (= wanting it to start).*

impeach /ɪmˈpiːtʃ/ **verb** [T] to make a formal statement saying that a public official is guilty of a serious offence in connection with their job, especially in the US: *The governor was impeached for wrongful use of state money.* • **impeachable** /-ˈpiː.tʃə.bl̩/ **adj** *an impeachable offence* • **impeachment** /-mənt/ **noun** [C or U]

impeccable /ɪmˈpek.ə.bl̩/ **adj** perfect, with no problems or bad parts: *impeccable taste/manners/credentials* ◦ *His English is impeccable.* • **impeccably** /-bli/ **adv** *She was impeccably dressed.*

impecunious /ˌɪm.pəˈkjuː.ni.əs/ **adj** formal having very little money: *I first knew him as an impecunious **student** living in a tiny bedsit.* → Synonym **poor**

impede /ɪmˈpiːd/ **verb** [T] formal to make it more difficult for something to happen or more difficult for someone to do something: *Although he's shy, it certainly hasn't impeded his career in any way.*

impediment /ɪmˈped.ɪ.mənt/ **noun** [C] formal something that makes progress, movement, or achieving something difficult or impossible: *In a number of developing countries, war has been an additional impediment **to** progress.* → See also **speech impediment**

impedimenta /ɪmˌped.ɪˈmen.tə/ **noun** [plural] mainly humorous the objects which you need for a particular activity that are heavy or difficult to carry: *We were weighed down with sleeping bags, gas cookers and pans – all the impedimenta of camping.*

impel /ɪmˈpel/ **verb** [T] (-ll-) to make someone feel that they must do something: [+ to infinitive] *She was in such a mess I **felt** impelled **to** (= felt I had to) offer your services.*

impending /ɪmˈpen.dɪŋ/ **adj** [before noun] describes an event, usually something unpleasant or unwanted, that is going to happen soon: *impending disaster/doom* ◦ *The player announced his impending retirement from international football.*

impenetrable /ɪmˈpen.ɪ.trə.bl̩/ adj **1** impossible to see through or go through: *Outside, the fog was thick and impenetrable.* ◦ *an impenetrable barrier* **2** impossible to understand: *Some of the lyrics on their latest album are completely impenetrable.* • **impenetrably** /-bli/ adv

imperative /ɪmˈper.ə.tɪv/ US /-t̬ɪv/ adj; noun

▸adj **URGENT** ▷ **1** C2 extremely important or urgent: [+ that] *The president said it was imperative* ***that*** *the release of all hostages be secured.* ◦ [+ to infinitive] *It's imperative* ***to*** *act now before the problem gets really serious.* **GRAMMAR** ▷ **2** specialized used to describe the form of a verb that is usually used for giving orders: *In the phrase 'Leave him alone!', the verb 'leave' is in the imperative form.*

▸noun **GRAMMAR** ▷ **1** B2 [S] specialized the form of a verb that is usually used for giving orders: *In the phrase 'Leave him alone!', the verb 'leave' is an imperative/is* ***in the*** *imperative.* **URGENT** ▷ **2** [C] something that is extremely important or urgent: *Getting the unemployed back to work, said the minister, is a* ***moral*** *imperative.*

imperceptible /ˌɪm.pəˈsep.tɪ.bl̩/ US /-pɚˈsep.tə-/ adj unable to be noticed or felt because of being very slight: *She heard a faint, almost imperceptible cry.* • **imperceptibly** /-bli/ US /-pɚˈsep.tə-/ adv *Gradually, almost imperceptibly, her condition had worsened.*

imperfect /ɪmˈpɜː.fekt/ US /-ˈpɝː-/ adj; noun

▸adj **NOT PERFECT** ▷ **1** C1 damaged, containing problems or not having something: *We're living in an imperfect world.* ◦ *I explained as well as I was able, given my own imperfect understanding of the situation.* **GRAMMAR** ▷ **2** specialized the imperfect form of a verb describes an action in the past which was continuous or was not completed: *In the sentence 'He was hit by a car as he was crossing the road', the verb 'cross' is* ***in*** *the imperfect form.* • **imperfectly** /-li/ adv

▸noun [S] **the imperfect** specialized in some languages, the form of a verb that is used for an action that has not been completed in the past, used, for example, to refer to an action that was happening when it was suddenly interrupted, or to describe an existing situation at the beginning of a story

imperfection /ˌɪm.pəˈfek.ʃən/ US /-pɚ-/ noun [C or U] a fault or weakness: *Gradually she began to notice one or two little imperfections in his character.* ◦ *She won't tolerate imperfection in her own or anyone else's work.*

imperial /ɪmˈpɪə.ri.əl/ US /-ˈpɪr.i-/ adj **EMPIRE** ▷ **1** belonging or relating to an EMPIRE or the person or country that rules it: *Imperial China* ◦ *Britain's imperial past* ◦ *the Imperial palace* ◦ *imperial grandeur* **MEASUREMENT** ▷ **2** describes a system of measurement that uses units such as INCHES, miles, and PINTS: *Imperial units have in many cases been replaced by metric ones in Britain.* → Compare **metric**

imperialism /ɪmˈpɪə.ri.ə.lɪ.zəm/ US /-ˈpɪr.i-/ noun [U] often disapproving **1** a system in which a country rules other countries, sometimes having used force to get power over them: *the age of imperialism* **2** a situation in which one country has a lot of power or influence over others, especially in political and economic matters: *She accused the United States of* ***economic*** *imperialism.*

imperialist /ɪmˈpɪə.ri.ə.lɪst/ US /-ˈpɪr.i-/ noun; adj

▸noun [C] often disapproving someone who supports imperialism

▸adj (also **imperialistic**) often disapproving supporting or relating to imperialism: *an imperialist power*

imperil /ɪmˈper.əl/ verb [T] (-**ll**- or US usually -**l**-) formal to put something or someone at risk or in danger of being harmed or destroyed: *A police raid would imperil the lives of the hostages.*

imperious /ɪmˈpɪə.ri.əs/ US /-ˈpɪr.i-/ adj unpleasantly proud and expecting to be obeyed: *an imperious manner/voice* ◦ *She sent them away with an imperious wave of the hand.* • **imperiously** /-li/ adv • **imperiousness** /-nəs/ noun [U]

imperishable /ɪmˈper.ɪ.ʃə.bl̩/ adj literary lasting for ever, or never becoming weaker with age

impermanent /ɪmˈpɜː.mə.nənt/ US /-ˈpɝː-/ adj not lasting for ever or not lasting for a long time: *Acrylic paint is quick-drying but impermanent.* • **impermanence** /-nəns/ noun [U] *the impermanence and fragility of life*

impermeable /ɪmˈpɜː.mi.ə.bl̩/ US /-ˈpɝː-/ adj not allowing liquid or gas to go through: *an impermeable membrane*

impermissible /ˌɪm.pəˈmɪs.ə.bl̩/ US /-pɚ-/ adj formal not allowed: *There are certain topics of conversation that are impermissible in polite society.*

impersonal /ɪmˈpɜː.sən.əl/ US /-ˈpɝː-/ adj disapproving C1 without human warmth and interest: *Hospitals always seem such impersonal places – rows of identical beds in dull grey rooms.* ◦ *She has a very cold and impersonal manner.*

impersonate /ɪmˈpɜː.sən.eɪt/ US /-ˈpɝː-/ verb [T] **1** to intentionally copy another person's characteristics, such as their behaviour, speech, appearance, or expressions, especially to make people laugh: *She's the woman who impersonates the Queen on TV.* **2** to attempt to deceive someone by pretending that you are another person: *He was fined for impersonating a police officer.* • **impersonation** /ɪmˌpɜː.sənˈeɪ.ʃən/ US /-ˌpɝː-/ noun [C or U] *He* ***does*** *a brilliant impersonation of Charles.*

impersonator /ɪmˈpɜː.sən.eɪ.təʳ/ US /-ˈpɝː.sən.eɪ.t̬ɚ/ noun [C] someone who impersonates another person: *an Elvis impersonator*

impertinent /ɪmˈpɜː.tɪ.nənt/ US /-ˈpɝː.t̬ən.ənt/ adj rude and not showing respect, especially towards someone older or in a higher position than you: *I hope he didn't think me impertinent when I asked him about his private life.* ◦ *an impertinent remark/question* • **impertinently** /-li/ adv • **impertinence** /-nəns/ noun [C or U] *She even* ***had*** *the impertinence* ***to*** *lecture Loretta on the importance of hygiene.*

imperturbable /ˌɪm.pəˈtɜː.bə.bl̩/ US /-pɚˈtɝː-/ adj formal always staying calm and controlled, even in difficult situations that would cause other people to worry • **imperturbably** /-bli/ adv formal

impervious /ɪmˈpɜː.vi.əs/ US /-ˈpɝː-/ adj **SUBSTANCE** ▷ **1** specialized not allowing liquid to go through: *How does glue bond with impervious substances like glass and metal?* **PERSON** ▷ **2** describes a person who is not influenced or affected by something: *He is impervious* ***to*** *criticism and rational argument.*

impetigo /ˌɪm.pəˈtaɪ.gəʊ/ US /-goʊ/ noun [U] an infectious skin disease in which yellowish areas appear on the body

impetuous /ɪmˈpet.ju.əs/ adj **1** likely to do something suddenly, without considering the results of your actions: *He's so impetuous – why can't he think things over before he rushes into them?* **2** An impetuous word or action is said or done suddenly, without considering the likely results: *The prime minister may now be regretting her impetuous promise to reduce* *unemployment by half.* • **impetuously** /-li/ adv • **impetuousness** /-nəs/ noun [U] (formal also **impetuosity**)

impetus /ˈɪm.pɪ.təs/ (US) /-pə.t̬əs/ noun [S or U] something which encourages a particular activity or makes that activity more energetic or effective: *The recent publicity surrounding homelessness has given **(a) fresh** impetus to the cause.*

impinge /ɪmˈpɪndʒ/ verb

PHRASAL VERB **impinge on/upon sb/sth** to have an effect on something, often causing problems by limiting it in some way: *The government's spending limits will seriously impinge on the education budget.*

impious /ˈɪm.pi.əs/ adj formal showing no respect, especially for God or religion • **impiousness** /-nəs/ noun [U] formal

impish /ˈɪm.pɪʃ/ adj showing a child's pleasure in enjoying yourself and making trouble: *At 70, he still retains his impish grin.* • **impishly** /-li/ adv • **impishness** /-nəs/ noun [U]

implacable /ɪmˈplæk.ə.bl/ adj formal describes (someone who has) strong opinions or feelings that are impossible to change: *an implacable enemy* ◦ *implacable hostility* • **implacably** /-bli/ adv

implant verb; noun

▸verb [T] /ɪmˈplɑːnt/ (US) /-ˈplænt/ **OBJECT** ▷ **1** to put an organ, group of cells, or device into the body in a medical operation: *The owner's name and address is stored on a microchip and implanted in the dog's body.* → Compare **transplant** **IDEA** ▷ **2** to fix ideas, feelings, or opinions in someone else's mind: *He implanted some very strange attitudes **in** his children.* ◦ *There is much debate on the issue of 'therapists' implanting false memories of sexual abuse **in** adults.*

▸noun [C] /ˈɪm.plɑːnt/ (US) /-plænt/ an organ, group of cells, or device that has been put into the body in a medical operation: *breast/heart valve implants*

implausible /ɪmˈplɔː.zɪ.bl/ (US) /-ˈplɑː.zə-/ adj difficult to believe, or unlikely: *The whole plot of the film is ridiculously implausible.* • **implausibly** /-bli/ adv • **implausibility** /ɪmˌplɔː.zɪˈbɪl.ɪ.ti/ (US) /-ˌplɑː.zəˈbɪl.ə.t̬i/ noun [U]

implement verb; noun

▸verb [T] /ˈɪm.plɪ.ment/ B2 to start using a plan or system: *The changes to the national health system will be implemented next year.* • **implementation** /ˌɪm.plɪ.menˈteɪ.ʃən/ noun [U] C2 *implementation of the law/agreement* ◦ *Various projects for constructing new schools are **under** implementation in the region.*

▸noun [C] /ˈɪm.plɪ.mənt/ a tool which works by being moved by hand or by being pulled across a surface: *garden/household/agricultural implements*

implicate /ˈɪm.plɪ.keɪt/ verb [T] to show that someone is involved in a crime or partly responsible for something bad that has happened: *Have they any evidence to implicate him **in** the robbery?*

implication /ˌɪm.plɪˈkeɪ.ʃən/ noun **1** C2 [C or U] an occasion when you seem to suggest something without saying it directly: [+ that] *From what she said, the implication was **that** they were splitting up.* ◦ *She accused the party and, **by** implication, its leader too.* **2** C1 [C usually plural] the effect that an action or decision will have on something else in the future: *The company is cutting back its spending and I wonder what the implications will be **for** our department.* ◦ *What are the implications **of** the new law?* **3** C2 [U] an occasion when you suggest or show that someone is involved in a crime: *The case depended upon his implication of his co-workers in the fraud.*

implicit /ɪmˈplɪs.ɪt/ adj **SUGGESTED** ▷ **1** C2 suggested but not communicated directly: *He interpreted her comments as an implicit **criticism** of the government.* ◦ *Implicit **in** the poem's closing lines are the poet's own religious doubts.* → Compare **explicit** **COMPLETE** ▷ **2** complete and without any doubts: *implicit **trust*** ◦ *All her life she had implicit **faith** in socialism.* • **implicitly** /-li/ adv *He trusts her implicitly.*

implode /ɪmˈpləʊd/ (US) /-ˈploʊd/ verb [I] **1** specialized to fall towards the inside with force: *The vacuum inside the tube caused it to implode when the external air pressure was increased.* → Compare **explode** **2** to fail suddenly and completely and be unable to operate: *Their economy is in danger of imploding.* • **implosion** /-ˈpləʊ.ʒən/ (US) /-ˈploʊ.ʒən/ noun [C or U] specialized

implore /ɪmˈplɔːr/ (US) /-ˈplɔːr/ verb **1** [T + to infinitive] to ask someone to do or not do something in a very sincere, emotional, and determined way: *She implored her parents not **to** send her away to school.* **2** [T] literary to ask for something in a sincere and emotional way: *She clasped her hands, and glancing upward, seemed to implore divine assistance.* • **imploring** /-ɪŋ/ adj *He had an imploring look in his eyes.* • **imploringly** /-ɪŋ.li/ adv

imply /ɪmˈplaɪ/ verb [T] **1** C2 to communicate an idea or feeling without saying it directly: [+ (that)] *Are you implying (**that**) I'm fat?* ◦ *I'm not implying anything about your cooking, but could we eat out tonight?* ◦ *I detected an implied **criticism** of the way he was treated.* **2 as sth implies** C2 used to show that the name, etc. of something tells you something about it: *Variable rate loans, as the name implies, have a variable interest rate.* **3** C2 formal to involve something or make it necessary: *Socialism implies equality.*

impolite /ˌɪm.pəlˈaɪt/ adj formal B2 rude: *impolite language/behaviour* ◦ *It is impolite **to** point at people.* • **impolitely** /-li/ adv

impolitic /ɪmˈpɒl.ɪ.tɪk/ (US) /-ˈpɑː.lə.t̬ɪk/ adj formal describes unwise words or actions that are likely to cause offence or problems, especially in social situations: *I thought it impolitic to ask any questions about her ex-husband.*

imponderable /ɪmˈpɒn.dər.ə.bl/ (US) /-ˈpɑːn-/ noun [C] formal something that cannot be guessed or calculated because it is completely unknown: *There are too many imponderables to make an accurate forecast.* • **imponderable** adj

import verb; noun

▸verb [T] /ɪmˈpɔːt/ (US) /ˈɪm.pɔːrt/ **1** B2 to buy or bring in products from another country: *We import a large number of cars **from** Japan.* → Compare **export** **2** to introduce new goods, customs, or ideas to one country from another: *The fashion for wearing baseball hats was imported directly **from** the States.* **3** specialized to copy information from one computer or computer program to another: *I need to import data from the database into my word processor.* ◦ *imported files*

▸noun /ˈɪm.pɔːt/ (US) /-pɔːrt/ **BRINGING IN** ▷ **1** C1 [C] goods bought by one country from another: *restrictions on foreign imports* **2** C2 [U] (also **importation**) the action of bringing goods or fashions into a country: *the illegal importation of drugs* ◦ *an import licence* ◦ *import duties* **IMPORTANCE** ▷ **3** [U] formal importance or meaning: *Whether it is to be a 'working' visit or an 'official' visit is of **little/no** import.*

importance /ɪmˈpɔː.təns/ (US) /-ˈpɔːr.t̬əns/ noun [U] B1 the quality of being important: *The health report stresses the importance **of** fresh food in a diet.* ◦ *She **attaches** a lot of importance **to** personal possessions.*

Word partners for importance

considerable/great/major/particular importance • ***crucial/paramount/the utmost/vital*** importance • ***growing/increasing*** importance • ***emphasize/highlight/stress/underline*** the importance of sth • ***attach/give*** (great/no/special) importance to sth • ***grasp/realize/recognize*** the importance of sth • the importance *of* sth

important /ɪmˈpɔː.tᵊnt/ (US) /-ˈpɔːr.t̬ᵊnt/ **adj 1** (A1) necessary or of great value: *I think his career is more important* ***to*** *him than I am.* ◦ ***It's*** *important* ***for*** *children* ***to*** *learn to get on with each other.* ◦ ***The*** *important* ***thing*** *is to keep the heat low or the sugar will burn.* ◦ *He's not amazingly handsome, but he's nice and that's more important.* → Opposite **unimportant 2** (B1) having great effect or influence: *He was one of the most important writers of that period.* ◦ *an important person/decision* • **importantly** /-li/ **adv** (B2) *If we served more soft drinks, there would be fewer hangovers and,* ***more*** *importantly, fewer drink-driving incidents.*

Common mistake: important

Remember: important must have a noun or pronoun that it refers to.

Don't say 'the important is', say **the important thing is**:

~~*The important is that nobody was injured.*~~

The important thing is that nobody was injured.

Other ways of saying important

Adjectives such as **big**, **major**, and **significant** are often used to mean 'important':

This is a ***big*** *game tonight – if we lose, we won't be in the playoffs.*

This is a ***major*** *decision so we'd better get it right.*

Did he make any ***significant*** *changes to my suggestions?*

Someone or something **of note** is important or famous:

Did she say anything ***of note*** *at the meeting?*

A person who is important and famous is sometimes described as **eminent**, **prominent**, or **great**:

Her father was an ***eminent*** *historian.*

importer /ɪmˈpɔː.təʳ/ (US) /-ˈpɔːr.t̬ɚ/ **noun** [C] a person, country, or company that buys products from another country in order to sell them: *After the USA, Japan is the second biggest importer of oil.*

importunate /ɪmˈpɔː.tjʊ.nət/ (US) /-ˈpɔːr.tʃə.nɪt/ **adj** *formal* **1** repeatedly asking for something, in a forceful and annoying way: *an importunate beggar/crowd* **2** An importunate request or question is repeated and forceful in an annoying way: *importunate demands*

importune /ˌɪm.pɔːˈtjuːn/ (US) /ˌɪm.pɔːrˈtuːn/ **verb** [T] *formal* to make repeated forceful requests for something, usually in a way that is annoying or causing slight problems: *As a tourist, you are importuned* ***for*** *money the moment you step outside your hotel.*

impose /ɪmˈpəʊz/ (US) /-ˈpoʊz/ **verb** FORCE ▷ **1** (C1) [T] to officially force a rule, tax, punishment, etc. to be obeyed or received: *Very high taxes have recently been imposed* ***on*** *cigarettes.* ◦ *Judges are imposing increasingly heavy fines for minor driving offences.* ◦ *The council has imposed a ban* ***on*** *alcohol in the city parks.* **2** (C1) [T] to force someone to accept something, especially a belief or way of living: *I don't want them to impose their religious beliefs* ***on*** *my children.* ◦ *We must impose some kind of order* ***on*** *the way this office is run.* EXPECT ▷ **3** [I] to expect someone to do something for you or spend time with you when they do not want to or when it is not convenient for them: *Are you sure it's all right for me to come tonight? I don't want to impose.* ◦ *She's always imposing* ***on*** *people – asking favours and getting everyone to do things for her.*

imposing /ɪmˈpəʊ.zɪŋ/ (US) /-ˈpoʊ-/ **adj** having an appearance which looks important or causes admiration: *an imposing mansion* ◦ *He was an imposing figure on stage.*

imposition /ˌɪm.pəˈzɪʃ.ᵊn/ **noun** EXPECTING ▷ **1** [S] a situation in which someone expects another person to do something that they do not want to do or that is not convenient: *Would it be too much of an imposition to ask you to pick my parents up from the airport?* NEW LAW ▷ **2** [U] the introduction of a new law or system: *the imposition* ***of*** *the death penalty/martial law/sanctions*

impossible /ɪmˈpɒs.ɪ.bl̩/ (US) /-ˈpɑː.sə-/ **adj**; **noun**

▸**adj 1** (B1) If an action or event is impossible, it cannot happen or be achieved: *It was impossible* ***to*** *sleep because of the noise.* ◦ *It seems impossible* ***that*** *I could have walked by without noticing her.* ◦ *He made it impossible for me to say no.* ◦ *She ate three plates of spaghetti and a dessert? That's impossible. I don't believe it!* **2** (C2) describes a situation that is extremely difficult to deal with or solve: *It's an impossible situation – she's got to leave him but she can't bear losing her children.* **3** (C2) describes a person who behaves very badly or is extremely difficult to deal with: *I had to leave the job because my boss was impossible.* ◦ *My niece is impossible when she's tired – you can't do anything to please her.* • **impossibility** /ɪmˌpɒs.ɪˈbɪl.ɪ.ti/ (US) /-ˌpɑː.səˈbɪl.ə.t̬i/ **noun** [C or U] (C2) *What you're asking just can't be done – it's an impossibility.*

▸**noun** [S] **the impossible** something that cannot be expected to happen or exist: *She wants a man who is attractive and funny as well, which is* ***asking*** *the impossible in my opinion.*

impossibly /ɪmˈpɒs.ɪ.bli/ (US) /-ˈpɑː.sə-/ **adv** extremely or more than is usual: *Doctors are being forced to work impossibly long hours.* ◦ *She has an impossibly thin waist.*

impostor (also **imposter**) /ɪmˈpɒs.təʳ/ (US) /-ˈpɑː.stɚ/ **noun** [C] a person who pretends to be someone else in order to deceive others: *He felt like an impostor among all those intelligent people, as if he had no right to be there.*

imposture /ɪmˈpɒs.tjəʳ/ (US) /-ˈpɑː.stjɚ/ **noun** [C or U] *formal* the act of pretending to be someone else in order to deceive others

impotence /ˈɪm.pə.tᵊns/ (US) /-t̬ᵊns/ **noun** [U] LACK OF POWER ▷ **1** lack of power to change or improve a situation: *political impotence* ◦ *a sense of impotence* SEXUAL PROBLEM ▷ **2** a medical condition in which a man cannot have sex because his PENIS cannot become hard or stay hard: *Men sometimes suffer from impotence after a serious illness.*

impotent /ˈɪm.pə.tᵊnt/ (US) /-t̬ᵊnt/ **adj** LACKING POWER ▷ **1** not having the power or ability to change or improve a situation: *You feel so impotent when your child is ill and you cannot help them.* SEXUAL PROBLEM ▷ **2** If a man is impotent, he cannot have sex because his PENIS cannot become hard or stay hard.

impound /ɪmˈpaʊnd/ **verb** [T] If the police or someone in authority impounds something that belongs to you, they take it away because you have broken the law: *The police impounded cars and other personal property belonging to the drug dealers.*

impoverished /ɪmˈpɒv.ər.ɪʃt/ US /-ˈpɑː.vɚ-/ **adj** formal **1** very poor: *an impoverished young actor* **2** made weaker or worse in quality: *He warned that the breakdown of the family unit would lead to an impoverished society.* • **impoverish** /-ɪʃ/ **verb** [T] formal *Excessive farming had impoverished the soil.* ◦ *The new law is likely to further impoverish single parents.* • **impoverishment** /-mənt/ **noun** [U] formal *cultural/economic/spiritual impoverishment*

impracticable /ɪmˈpræk.tɪ.kə.bl̩/ **adj** If a course of action, plan, etc. is impracticable, it is impossible to do in an effective way: *The changes to the tax system proved impracticable as they were impossible to enforce.*

impractical /ɪmˈpræk.tɪ.kəl/ **adj** **1** Impractical people are not naturally good at doing useful jobs such as making or repairing things. **2** Impractical arrangements, ideas, or methods cannot be done or used easily or effectively: *It's impractical to have so many people all trying to use this equipment at the same time.* **3** Impractical clothes, devices, etc. cause problems when used in normal situations: *I love high heels but they're rather impractical.*

imprecation /ˌɪm.prəˈkeɪ.ʃən/ **noun** [C] formal an offensive word: *The old woman walked along the street muttering imprecations.*

imprecise /ˌɪm.prɪˈsaɪs/ **adj** not accurate or exact: *The figures are imprecise because they're based on a prediction of next year's sales.* • **imprecision** /-ˈsɪʒ.ən/ **noun** [U]

impregnable /ɪmˈpreg.nə.bl̩/ **adj** **1** A building or other place that is impregnable is so strongly built and/or defended that it cannot be entered by force: *Despite burglar alarms and window locks, homes are never impregnable against determined thieves.* **2** mainly UK powerful and impossible to beat, especially in sport: *Surrey have been building up an impregnable **lead** in this season's County Championship.*

impregnate /ˈɪm.preg.neɪt/ US /ɪmˈpreg-/ **verb** [T] **ABSORB** ▷ **1** formal to cause something, usually a solid substance, to absorb something, usually a liquid: *This cloth has been impregnated **with** special chemicals for cleaning computer screens.* **MAKE PREGNANT** ▷ **2** specialized to make a woman or female animal pregnant

impresario /ˌɪm.prəˈsɑː.ri.əʊ/ US /-ˈsɑːr.i.oʊ/ **noun** [C] (plural **impresarios**) a person who arranges different types of public entertainment, such as theatre, musical, and dance events: *London's leading **theatrical** impresario*

impress /ɪmˈpres/ **verb** [I or T, not continuous] B2 to cause someone to admire or respect you: *I remember when I was a child being very impressed **with** how many toys she had.* ◦ *Your mother was clearly not impressed **by** our behaviour in the restaurant.* ◦ *He tried to impress me **with** his extensive knowledge of wine.* ◦ formal *I'm afraid the new theatre **fails to** impress.*

PHRASAL VERB **impress sth on/upon sb** to make someone understand or be familiar with the importance or value of something: *Mr Simmons tried to impress on me how much easier my life would be if I were better organized.*

impression /ɪmˈpreʃ.ən/ **noun** **OPINION** ▷ **1** B2 [C] an idea or opinion of what something or someone is like: *I didn't get much of an impression **of** the place because it was dark when we drove through it.* ◦ *What was your impression of Charlotte's husband?* ◦ *I don't tend to trust **first** impressions (= the opinion you form when you meet someone or see something for the first time).* ◦ [+ that] *When I first met him I **got/had** the impression **that** he was a shy sort of a bloke.* **2** **be under the impression** B2 to think that something is true, especially when it is not: *I was under the impression (**that**) you didn't get on too well.* ◦ *He was under the mistaken (= false) impression (**that**) you were married.* **EFFECT** ▷ **3** B2 [S] the way that something seems, looks, or feels to a particular person: *It **makes/gives/creates** a very bad impression if you're late for an interview.* ◦ [+ (that)] *He likes to **give** the impression (**that**) he's terribly popular and has loads of friends.* **COPY** ▷ **4** [C] an attempt at copying another person's manner and speech, etc. or an animal's behaviour, especially in order to make people laugh: *She **does** a really good impression **of** the president.* **MARK** ▷ **5** [C] a mark made on the surface of something by pressing an object onto it: *There were impressions round her ankles made by the tops of her socks.* **BOOKS** ▷ **6** [C usually singular] (US also **printing**) all the copies of a book that have been printed at the same time without any changes being made: *This is the second impression of the encyclopedia.*

> Word partners for **impression** (OPINION)
>
> *form/get/have* an impression • sb's *early/first/immediate/initial* impression • get/have the *distinct/vague* impression (that) • sb's *general/overall* impression • sb's impression *of* sb/sth

> Word partners for **impression** (EFFECT)
>
> *convey/create/give/make* an impression • a *favourable/good* impression • a *bad/false/misleading* impression • a *deep/indelible/lasting/strong* impression

IDIOM **make an impression on sb** to cause someone to notice and admire you: *He made quite an impression on the girls at the tennis club.*

impressionable /ɪmˈpreʃ.ən.ə.bl̩/ **adj** often disapproving describes someone, usually a young person, who is very easily influenced by the people around them and by what they are told, and who sometimes copies other people's behaviour: *He's **at that** impressionable **age** when he's very easily led by other children.*

Impressionism /ɪmˈpreʃ.ən.ɪ.zəm/ **noun** [U] a style of painting, which began in France in the 1860s, in which the artist tries to represent the effects of light on an object, person, area of countryside, etc.

impressionist /ɪmˈpreʃ.ən.ɪst/ **noun** [C] a person who copies other people's manner and speech in order to entertain other people and make them laugh

Impressionist /ɪmˈpreʃ.ən.ɪst/ **noun; adj**
▸**noun** [C] an artist who paints in the style of Impressionism: *Monet is one of the great Impressionists.*
▸**adj** relating to Impressionism: *Impressionist paintings*

impressionistic /ɪmˌpreʃ.ənˈɪs.tɪk/ **adj** giving a general view or idea of something instead of particular details or facts: *The new play at the Youth Theatre is an impressionistic view of life in the 50s.*

impressive /ɪmˈpres.ɪv/ **adj** **1** B2 If an object or achievement is impressive, you admire or respect it, usually because it is special, important, or very large: *That was an impressive performance from such a young tennis player.* ◦ *an impressive collection of modern paintings* ◦ *There are some very impressive buildings in the town.* → Opposite **unimpressive (unimpressed)** **2** B2 If someone is impressive, you admire or respect them for their special skills or abilities: *She's a very impressive public speaker.* • **impressively** /-li/ **adv**

imprimatur /ˌɪm.prɪˈmeɪ.tər/ US /-t̬ɚ/ **noun** [S] formal official permission to do something that is given by a person or group in a position of power: *When he* *suspended the constitution and dissolved Congress, he had the imprimatur **of** the armed forces.*

imprint verb; noun

▸verb [T] /ɪmˈprɪnt/ **1** to mark a surface by pressing something hard into it **2** to fix an event or experience so firmly in the memory that it cannot be forgotten although you do not try to remember it: *That look of grief would be imprinted **on** her mind forever.*

▸noun /ˈɪm.prɪnt/ **BOOK** ▷ **1** [C] the name of a publisher as it appears on a particular set of books **MARK** ▷ **2** [C usually singular] an occasion when an object presses on something and leaves a mark: *The button had left an imprint on my arm.* **3** [S] an occasion when an event or experience becomes fixed in someone's memory or leaves its mark in some way on their appearance: *War has left its imprint on the strained faces of these people.*

imprison /ɪmˈprɪz.ən/ verb [T usually passive] C1 to put someone in prison: *He was imprisoned in 1965 **for** attempted murder.* ◦ figurative *Unable to go out because of the deep snow, she felt imprisoned in her own house.* • **imprisonable** /-ə.bl/ adj *Driving whilst disqualified is an imprisonable **offence**.* • **imprisonment** /-mənt/ noun [C or U] C2 *She was sentenced to five years' imprisonment.*

improbable /ɪmˈprɒb.ə.bl/ US /-ˈprɑː.bə-/ adj not likely to happen or be true: ***It's highly** improbable **that** Norris will agree.* ◦ *an improbable-sounding excuse* • **improbably** /-bli/ adv *improbably cheap prices* ◦ *improbably large/long* • **improbability** /ɪmˌprɒb.əˈbɪl.ɪ.ti/ US /ˌɪm.prɑː.bəˈbɪl.ə.t̬i/ noun [C or U]

impromptu /ɪmˈprɒmp.tʃuː/ US /-tuː/ adj done or said without earlier planning or preparation: *an impromptu party/performance*

improper /ɪmˈprɒp.ər/ US /-ˈprɑː.pɚ/ adj **DISHONEST** ▷ **1** formal dishonest and against a law or a rule: *The governor has denied making improper **use** of state money.* **WRONG** ▷ **2** formal unsuitable or not correct for a particular use or occasion: *improper prescription of medicines* ◦ *Is it considered improper to wear such a short skirt to a formal occasion?* **RUDE** ▷ **3** related to sex in a way that is rude or socially unacceptable: *I trust you're not making improper **suggestions** to my husband!* • **improperly** /-li/ adv formal

imˌproper ˈfraction noun [C] specialized a FRACTION in which the number below the line is smaller than the number above it: *$^{9}/_{2}$ is an improper fraction.*

impropriety /ˌɪm.prəˈpraɪ.ə.ti/ US /-t̬i/ noun [C or U] formal behaviour that is dishonest, socially unacceptable, or unsuitable for a particular situation: *financial/legal impropriety* ◦ *allegations of **sexual** impropriety*

improve /ɪmˈpruːv/ verb [I or T] A2 to (cause something to) get better: *He did a lot to improve conditions for factory workers.* ◦ *I thought the best way to improve my French was to live in France.* ◦ *Her health has improved dramatically since she started on this new diet.*

> **Common mistake: improve or increase?**
>
> **Warning:** choose the correct verb!
>
> To talk about causing something to get better, don't say 'increase', say **improve**:
>
> ~~*We need to increase our relationship with our customers.*~~
>
> *We need to improve our relationship with our customers.*

PHRASAL VERB **improve on/upon sth** to do something in a better way or with better results than before: *Last time she ran the race in 20 minutes, so she's hoping to improve on that.*

> **Other ways of saying improve**
>
> A common alternative to 'improve' is **get better**:
>
> *The first part of the book isn't very good but it **gets better**.*
>
> If something improves after a period of doing badly, you can use the verbs **rally** and **recover**:
>
> *The team played badly in the first half but **rallied** in the second.*
>
> *We are still waiting for the economy to **recover**.*
>
> The phrasal verbs **look up** and **pick up** can be used informally to say that a situation is improving:
>
> *Our financial situation is **looking up**.*
>
> *Business is really beginning to **pick up**.*
>
> The phrasal verb **work on** means 'to try to improve something':
>
> *You need to **work on** your technique.*
>
> The verb **refine** can be used when someone improves something by making small changes:
>
> *A team of experts spent several months **refining** the software.*
>
> If someone or something improves very quickly, you can say that it is happening by/in **leaps and bounds**:
>
> *The sport's popularity has grown by **leaps and bounds** in the past decade.*

improvement /ɪmˈpruːv.mənt/ noun [C or U] B1 an occasion when something gets better or when you make it better: *a slight improvement **in** the economy* ◦ *home improvements* ◦ *These white walls are a big improvement **on** that disgusting old wallpaper.* ◦ *He's been having treatment for two months now without any improvement.*

> **Common mistake: improvement**
>
> **Warning:** Choose the right verb!
>
> Don't say 'do improvements', say **make improvements**:
>
> ~~*We need to do some improvements to the college canteen.*~~
>
> *We need to make some improvements to the college canteen.*

> **Word partners for improvement**
>
> a ***considerable/dramatic/great/substantial*** improvement • a ***marked/real/significant*** improvement • a ***slight/steady*** improvement • ***bring about/make/produce*** an improvement • ***show*** an improvement • ***notice/see*** an improvement • an improvement ***in*** sth • ***room/scope*** for improvement

improver /ɪmˈpruː.vər/ US /-ɚ/ noun [C] someone who is becoming better at a skill: *We run swimming classes for improvers.*

improvident /ɪmˈprɒv.ɪ.dənt/ US /-ˈprɑː.və-/ adj formal not planning carefully for the future, especially by spending money in a way that is unwise • **improvidence** /-dəns/ noun [U]

improvisation /ˌɪm.prə.vaɪˈzeɪ.ʃən/ US /ɪmˌprɑː.vɪ-/ noun [C or U] **1** a performance which an actor, musician, etc. has not practised or planned: *a blues/jazz improvisation* ◦ *There are classes in movement, dance, and improvisation.* **2** the act of making or doing something with whatever is available at the time: *I'm afraid we don't have all the necessary equipment, so a little improvisation might be required.*

improvise /ˈɪm.prə.vaɪz/ verb [I or T] **1** to invent or make something, such as a speech or a device, at the time when it is needed without already having planned it: *I hadn't prepared a speech so I suddenly had to improvise.* ◦ *To sleep on, we improvised a mattress **from** a pile of blankets.* **2** When actors or musicians improvise, they perform without prepared speech or music, making up the play, music, etc. as they perform it: *During certain scenes of the play there isn't any script and the actors just improvise (the dialogue).*

imprudent /ɪmˈpruː.dᵊnt/ **adj** formal unwise, by failing to consider the likely results of your actions: *The report criticizes the banks for being imprudent in their lending.* • **imprudence** /-dᵊns/ **noun** [U] formal

impudent /ˈɪm.pjʊ.dᵊnt/ **adj** rude and not showing respect, especially towards someone who is older or in a more important position: *an impudent remark/child* • **impudence** /-dᵊns/ **noun** [U]

impugn /ɪmˈpjuːn/ **verb** [T] formal to cause people to doubt someone's character, qualities, or reputation by criticizing them: *Are you impugning my competence as a professional designer?*

impulse /ˈɪm.pʌls/ **noun** **WISH** ▷ **1** C2 [C + to infinitive] a sudden strong wish to do something: *I had this sudden impulse **to** shout out 'Rubbish!' in the middle of her speech.* **2 on (an) impulse** C2 because you suddenly want to, although you haven't planned to: *'I didn't know you were looking for some new shoes.' 'Oh, I wasn't – I just bought them on impulse.'* **SIGNAL** ▷ **3** [C] a short electrical, radio or light signal which carries information or instructions between the parts of a system: *an electrical/nerve impulse* **REASON** ▷ **4** [C usually singular] formal something that is the force behind or reason for something else: *a creative/commercial impulse*

ˈimpulse ˌbuy **noun** [C] something that you buy suddenly and without thinking carefully: *I hadn't intended to get one – it was an impulse buy.* • **ˈimpulse ˌbuying noun** [U] the act of buying something that you had not planned to buy, because you suddenly want it when you see it: *They display chocolates next to supermarket checkouts to encourage impulse buying.*

impulsive /ɪmˈpʌl.sɪv/ **adj** C2 showing behaviour in which you do things suddenly without any planning and without considering the effects they may have: *Don't be so impulsive – think before you act.* ◦ *an impulsive man/decision/gesture* • **impulsively** /-li/ **adv**

impunity /ɪmˈpjuː.nɪ.ti/ (US) /-ə.t̬i/ **noun** [U] freedom from punishment or from the unpleasant results of something that has been done: *Criminal gangs are terrorizing the city **with** apparent impunity.*

impure /ɪmˈpjʊəʳ/ (US) /-ˈpjʊr/ **adj** **MIXED** ▷ **1** mixed with other substances and therefore lower in quality: *impure heroin/gold* **BAD** ▷ **2** literary or humorous involving sexual thoughts or behaviour that are wrong or not moral: *She was accused of having impure **thoughts** about her male students.*

impurity /ɪmˈpjʊə.rɪ.ti/ (US) /-ˈpjʊr.ə.t̬i/ **noun** **MIXED** ▷ **1** [C or U] the fact that a substance is dirty or lower in quality because it is mixed with another substance, or something that causes this: *Impurities are removed from the blood by the kidneys.* ◦ *The impurity of the water is a health risk.* **BAD** ▷ **2** [U] literary or humorous sexual thoughts or behaviour that are wrong or not moral

imputation /ˌɪm.pjʊˈteɪ.ʃᵊn/ **noun** [C or U] formal a suggestion that someone is guilty of something or has a particular bad quality: *imputations of dishonesty*

impute /ɪmˈpjuːt/ **verb**

PHRASAL VERB **impute sth to sb** formal **ACCUSE** ▷ **1** to say that someone is responsible for something that has happened, or that something is the cause of something else: *They imputed the error to the lawyer who was handling her case.* **BELIEVE** ▷ **2** to believe that someone or something has a particular characteristic, quality, or meaning: *He arrogantly imputed stupidity to anyone who disagreed with him.*

in /ɪn/ **preposition; adv; adj**

▸**preposition** **INSIDE** ▷ **1** A1 inside or towards the inside of a container, place or area, or surrounded or closed off by something: *Put the milk back in the fridge when you've finished with it.* ◦ *Is Mark still in bed?* ◦ *I got stuck in a traffic jam for half an hour.* ◦ *They live in a charming old cottage.* ◦ *How much is that coat on display in the window (= in the space behind the window of the shop)?* ◦ *I've got a pain in my back.* ◦ *What's that in your hand?* ◦ *I've got something in (= on the surface of) my eye.* ◦ *They used to live in Paris, but now they're somewhere in Austria.* ◦ *He's always looking at himself in the mirror (= at the image of his face produced by the mirror).* ◦ *I never know what's going on in her head (= what she's thinking about).* ◦ *My daughter's in hospital* (US *in the hospital*) *having her tonsils out.* ◦ US *Is Erika still in school (= does she still go to school)?* **INTO** ▷ **2** into something: *Come on, we're late – get in the car.* ◦ *Put it in the cupboard.* ◦ *They threw him in the swimming pool.* **PART** ▷ **3** A2 forming a part of something: *He used to be the lead singer in a rock 'n' roll band.* ◦ *There are too many spelling mistakes in this essay.* ◦ *I've been waiting in this queue for ages.* ◦ *What do you look for in a relationship?* ◦ *I can see a future champion in Joely (= I think that Joely might become a champion).* ◦ *Talent like hers is rare in someone so young.* **DURING** ▷ **4** A1 during part or all of a period of time: *We're going to Italy in April.* ◦ *Some trees lose their leaves in (the) autumn.* ◦ *I started working here in 2009.* ◦ *Life in the 19th century was very different from what it is now.* ◦ *Bye, see you in the morning (= tomorrow morning).* ◦ *She was a brilliant gymnast in her youth (= when she was young).* ◦ *How many civilians died in the Vietnam War?* ◦ *This is the first cigarette I've had in three years.* ◦ *I haven't had a decent night's sleep in years/ages (= for a long time).* **5 in between** between the two times mentioned: *I have breakfast at 7.30, lunch at 1.00, and sometimes a snack in between.* **NO MORE THAN** ▷ **6** A2 needing or using no more time than a particular amount of time: *Can you finish the job in two weeks?* ◦ *She could get that essay done in a couple of hours if she really tried.* ◦ *They completed the journey in record time (= faster than ever done before).* **BEFORE THE END** ▷ **7** A2 before or at the end of a particular period: *Dinner will be ready in ten minutes.* ◦ *We'll all be dead in a hundred years so there's no point worrying about it.* ◦ *I'm just setting off, so I should be with you in half an hour.* **EXPERIENCING** ▷ **8** B1 experiencing a situation or condition, or feeling an emotion: *We watched in horror as they pulled the bodies from the wreckage.* ◦ *He's living in luxury in the south of France.* ◦ *She left in a bit of a hurry.* ◦ *You're in great danger.* ◦ *Could I have a word with you in private?* ◦ *Have you ever been in love?* ◦ *Your car's in very good condition, considering how old it is.* **EXPRESSED** ▷ **9** B1 expressed or written in a particular way: *Cheques should be written in ink.* ◦ *She usually paints in watercolour.* ◦ *They spoke in Russian the whole time.* ◦ *He always talks in a whisper.* **RESULT** ▷ **10** B2 used when referring to something that is done as a result of something else: *I'd like to do something for you in **return/exchange** for everything you've done for me.* ◦ *The* changes are in **response** to demand from our customers. ◦ He refused to say anything in **reply** to the journalists' questions. **ARRANGEMENT** ▷ **11** B1 used to show how things or people are arranged or divided: *We all sat down in a circle. ◦ The desks were arranged in rows of ten. ◦ Discounts are available to people travelling in large groups. ◦ Sometimes customers buy books in twos and threes, but rarely in larger quantities than that. ◦ Cut the potatoes in two. ◦ People are dying in their thousands from cold and starvation.* **AGE/TEMPERATURE** ▷ **12** used when referring approximately to someone's age or the weather temperature: *Nowadays many women are in **their** late thirties when they have their first child. ◦ Temperatures will be in **the** mid-twenties (= about 25 degrees).* **INVOLVED** ▷ **13** B1 involved or connected with a particular subject or activity: *I never knew you were in publishing. ◦ a degree in philosophy ◦ advances in medical science* **WEARING** ▷ **14** B1 wearing: *Do you recognize that man in the grey suit? ◦ Pat can't resist men in uniform. ◦ You look nice in green (= green clothes).* **COMPARING AMOUNTS** ▷ **15** used to compare one part of an amount of something with the total amount of it: *Apparently one in ten people/one person in ten has problems with reading.* ◦ UK *The basic rate of income tax is 25 pence in* (US ***on***) *the pound.* **CHARACTERISTIC** ▷ **16** used to show which characteristic or part of a person or thing is being described: *The new version is worse in every respect – I much preferred the original. ◦ Are the two bags equal in weight? ◦ She's deaf in her left ear.* **CAUSE** ▷ **17** [+ -ing verb] used to show when doing one thing is the cause of another thing happening: *In refus**ing** (= because she refused) to work abroad, she missed an excellent job opportunity. ◦ The government banned tobacco advertising and, in **doing so** (= because of this), contributed greatly to the nation's health.* **18 in that** formal because: *This research is important in that it confirms the link between aggression and alcohol.*

IDIOMS **be nothing/not much/very little in it** informal said when two things that are being compared are the same or very similar: *One house has a slightly bigger garden, but there's really not much in it.* • **in all** B2 with everything added together to make a total: *The bill came to £25 in all.* • **in all honesty/seriousness/truthfulness** said when expressing your opinion honestly, seriously or TRUTHFULLY: *In all honesty, I do have some criticisms to make.*

▸**adv FROM OUTSIDE** ▷ **1** A2 from outside, or towards the centre: *Could you bring the clothes in for me? ◦ The roof of their house caved in during a hurricane. ◦ Cut the pastry into a square and turn in the corners.* **2 be in and out of somewhere** informal to often be staying in and receiving treatment in a particular place: *She's been in and out of hospitals ever since the accident.* **AT PLACE** ▷ **3** B1 at home or at work: *When did you get home? I never heard you come in. ◦ Mr Ellis isn't in this week.* **INSIDE** ▷ **4** within an object, area, or substance: *We've been shut in all day. ◦ Has the soup got any salt in?* **TRANSPORT** ▷ **5** B2 having arrived at the place where people can get on or off: *What time is Roz's flight due in?* **GIVEN** ▷ **6** B2 given or sent to someone official in order to be read: *When does your essay have to be in? ◦ Remember to get your application in by the end of the week.* **COAST** ▷ **7** towards the coast, beach, or HARBOUR: *The tide comes in very quickly here and you can soon find yourself stranded. ◦ We stood watching the ship come in.* **COMPLETION** ▷ **8** used to refer to an activity which makes something complete: *Just **pencil** in the answer unless you're sure it's correct. ◦ The text is finished, but the pictures will have to be pasted in later.* ◦ UK *Would you mind **filling** in a questionnaire about what you watch on television?* **SPORT** ▷ **9** If the ball is in during a game of tennis or a similar sport, it has not gone outside the edges of the area on which the game is played: *I won that point, I'm telling you! The ball was definitely in!* **10** taking your turn to play, especially taking your turn to hit the ball: *Who's in next for our team? ◦ It started to rain just as our team was going in to bat.*

IDIOMS **be/get in with sb** to be or become popular or friendly with someone: *He's trying to get in with the teachers.* • **in on sth** involved with or knowing about a particular activity or plan: *He seems to be in on everything that happens at work. ◦ She's trying to **get** in on a research project organized by the university.* • **be well in there** UK informal to be likely to experience something good because of a situation you are in: *She's well in there now that she's married her boss's son.*

▸**adj** informal fashionable or popular: *High heels are in this season. ◦ The new jazz club seems to be the in place to go at the moment.*

-in /ɪn/ **suffix** used to form a noun which describes an activity in which many people take part: *a sit-in/phone-in*

in- (before l **il-**, before b, m or p **im-**, before r **ir-**) /ɪn-/ **prefix** used to add the meaning 'not', 'lacking', or 'the opposite of' to adjectives and to words formed from adjectives: *incomplete/incompletely ◦ illegal/illegally ◦ impossible/impossibly ◦ irregular/irregularly* → Compare **dis-, non-, un-**

inability /ˌɪn.əˈbɪl.ɪ.ti/ US /-t̬i/ **noun** [S or U] C1 lack of ability to do something: [+ to infinitive] *Inability **to** use a computer is a serious disadvantage when you are applying for jobs.* → Compare **disability**

in absentia /ˌɪn.æbˈsen.ti.ə/, /-ʃi.ə/ **adv** formal while the person involved is not present: *An Italian court convicted him in absentia for his terrorist activities.*

inaccessible /ˌɪn.əkˈses.ɪ.bl̩/ **adj** **PLACE** ▷ **1** very difficult or impossible to travel to: *one of the most inaccessible places in the world ◦ Some of the houses on the hillside are inaccessible **to** cars.* **MEANING** ▷ **2** difficult to understand or admire: *Why is opera so inaccessible **to** so many people? ◦ I found his lecture completely inaccessible.* • **inaccessibility** /ˌɪn.əkˌses.ɪˈbɪl.ɪ.ti/ US /-ə.t̬i/ **noun** [U]

inaccuracy /ɪnˈæk.jʊ.rə.si/ US /-jɚ.ə-/ **noun** [C or U] C1 a situation in which a fact or measurement is not completely correct or exact: *The film is full of historical inaccuracies. ◦ The inaccuracy of the missiles greatly diminishes their effectiveness.*

inaccurate /ɪˈnæk.jʊ.rət/ US /-jɚ.ət/ **adj** B2 not completely correct or exact, or not able to do something correctly or exactly: *Their estimate of the cost of the project was **wildly** (= extremely) inaccurate. ◦ an inaccurate device/weapon* • **inaccurately** /-li/ **adv**

inaction /ɪnˈæk.ʃən/ **noun** [U] formal failure to do anything which might provide a solution to a problem: *The West's inaction has put millions of people at risk of starvation.*

inactive /ɪnˈæk.tɪv/ **adj** doing nothing: *It's bad for your health to be physically inactive. ◦ The property market remains largely inactive.* • **inactivity** /ˌɪn.ækˈtɪv.ɪ.ti/ US /-ə.t̬i/ **noun** [U] *a period of inactivity ◦ economic/physical inactivity*

inadequacy /ɪˈnæd.ɪ.kwə.si/ **noun** **1** [C or U] the fact that something is not good enough or is too small in amount: *Economic growth is hindered by the inadequacies of the public transport system. ◦ The inadequacy of the budget is likely to cause problems.* **2** [U] a lack of confidence which makes you feel unable to deal with a situation: *I always suffer from feelings of inadequacy when I'm with him.*

inadequate /ɪˈnæd.ɪ.kwət/ **adj 1** C1 not good enough or too low in quality: *This work is **woefully** (= extremely) inadequate – you'll have to do it again.* **2** C1 too small in amount: *She rejected the $2 million offer as totally inadequate.* **3** not confident enough to deal with a situation: *Maddie's a real expert on art, so I feel completely inadequate whenever I talk to her about it.* • **inadequately** /-li/ **adv** *Our scientific research is inadequately funded.*

inadmissible /ˌɪn.ədˈmɪs.ə.bl̩/ **adj** formal unable to be accepted in a law court: *Her confession was ruled inadmissible as evidence because it was given under pressure from the police.*

inadvertent /ˌɪn.ədˈvɜː.tənt/ US /-ˈvɝː.t̬ənt/ **adj** *All authors need to be wary of inadvertent copying of other people's ideas.* • **inadvertently** /-li/ **adv** not intentionally: *He inadvertently deleted the file.* • **inadvertence** /-təns/ **noun** [U]

inadvisable /ˌɪn.ədˈvaɪ.zə.bl̩/ **adj** unwise and likely to have unwanted results and therefore worth avoiding: *Skiing is inadvisable if you have a weak heart.* ◦ *It is inadvisable **to** generalize from the results of a single experiment.*

inalienable /ɪˈneɪ.li.ə.nə.bl̩/ **adj** formal unable to be removed: *an inalienable **right***

inane /ɪˈneɪn/ **adj** extremely silly or with no real meaning or importance: *He's always making inane remarks.* ◦ *There are too many inane quiz shows on television these days.* • **inanely** /-li/ **adv** *He grinned inanely.* • **inanity** /ɪˈnæn.ə.ti/ US /-t̬i/ **noun** [C or U] *His speech was full of inanities that were meant to be funny.* ◦ *I was amazed at the inanity of her comments.*

inanimate /ɪˈnæn.ɪ.mət/ **adj** having none of the characteristics of life that an animal or plant has: *He looks at me as if I'm an inanimate **object**.*

ˌin-ˈapp **adj** used for referring to services and features that are available from within a phone or computer APPLICATION or APP: *in-app advertising/billing*

inapplicable /ˌɪn.əˈplɪk.ə.bl̩/ **adj** not directed at, intended for, or suitable for someone or something: *These regulations are inapplicable **to** visitors from outside the European Community.*

inappropriate /ˌɪn.əˈprəʊ.pri.ət/ US /-ˈproʊ-/ **adj** C1 unsuitable: *His casual behaviour was wholly inappropriate **for** such a formal occasion.* ◦ *I think it would be inappropriate (**for** you) **to** invite her to a party so soon after her husband's death.* • **inappropriately** /-li/ **adv** • **inappropriateness** /-nəs/ **noun** [U]

inapt /ɪˈnæpt/ **adj** not suitable for the situation: *His comments were perhaps inapt.*

inarticulate /ˌɪn.ɑːˈtɪk.jʊ.lət/ US /-ɑːr-/ **adj** unable to express feelings or ideas clearly, or expressed in a way that is difficult to understand: *When it comes to expressing their emotions, some people are hopelessly inarticulate.* ◦ *His speech was inarticulate and it was obvious he had been drinking.* • **inarticulately** /-li/ **adv** • **inarticulacy** /-lə.si/ **noun** [U] (also **inarticulateness** /-nəs/)

inasmuch as /ɪ.nəˈsmʌtʃ.əz/ **conjunction** formal used to introduce a phrase which explains why or how much something described in another part of the sentence is true: *Inasmuch as you are their commanding officer, you are responsible for the behaviour of these men.*

inattention /ˌɪn.əˈten.ʃən/ **noun** [U] failure to give attention: *Her disappointing exam results are entirely due to her inattention in class.*

inattentive /ˌɪn.əˈten.tɪv/ US /-t̬ɪv/ **adj** disapproving not giving attention to someone or something: *He was wholly inattentive **to** the needs of his children.* • **inattentively** /-li/ **adv**

inaudible /ɪˈnɔː.dɪ.bl̩/ US /-ˈnɑː-/ **adj** unable to be heard: *The noise of the machinery made her voice inaudible.* • **inaudibly** /-bli/ **adv** • **inaudibility** /ɪˌnɔː.dəˈbɪl.ɪ.ti/ US /-ˌnɑː.dəˈbɪl.ə.t̬i/ **noun** [U]

inaugural /ɪˈnɔː.gjʊ.rəl/ US /-ˈnɑː.gjɚ-/ **adj** [before noun] **1** an inaugural speech is the first speech someone gives when starting an important new job: *the president's inaugural address to the nation* **2** an inaugural event is the first in a series of planned events: *the inaugural meeting of the archaeological society*

inaugurate /ɪˈnɔː.gjʊ.reɪt/ US /-ˈnɑː-/ **verb** [T] **1** to put someone into an official position with a ceremony: *American presidents are always inaugurated on 20 January.* **2** to put something into use or action officially: *The European Community inaugurated the Single European Market in 1993.* **3** to mark the beginning of a new period, style, or activity: *The change of government inaugurated a new era of economic prosperity.* • **inauguration** /ɪˌnɔː.gjʊˈreɪ.ʃən/ US /-ˌnɑː-/ **noun** [C or U] *an inauguration ceremony*

inauspicious /ˌɪn.ɔːˈspɪʃ.əs/ US /-ɑː-/ **adj** formal showing signs that something will not be successful or positive: *After an inauspicious **start**, Scotland went on to win the match.* • **inauspiciously** /-li/ **adv**

ˌin-beˈtween **adj** [before noun] between two clear or accepted stages or states, and therefore difficult to describe or know exactly: *He knows quite a lot of French, but he's at an in-between **stage** and not fluent yet.*

inborn /ˌɪnˈbɔːn/ US /ˈɪn.bɔːrn/ **adj** describes a mental or physical characteristic that someone has from birth: *Apparently some people have an inborn tendency to develop certain kinds of tumour.*

inbound /ˈɪn.baʊnd/ **adj** travelling towards a particular point: *We expect delays to both inbound and outbound trains.*

inbox /ˈɪn.bɒks/ US /-bɑːks/ **noun** [C] **1** a place on a computer where emails that are sent to you are kept **2** US for **in tray**

inbred /ˌɪnˈbred/ US /ˈɪn.bred/ **adj** ESTABLISHED ▷ **1** an inbred quality or characteristic is firmly established in a person: *an inbred sense of right and wrong* ◦ *inbred racism* RELATED ▷ **2** produced by breeding between closely related plants, animals, or people: *an inbred population/family/strain*

inbreeding /ˌɪnˈbriː.dɪŋ/ US /ˈɪn.briː-/ **noun** [U] a situation in which plants, animals, or people are produced by breeding between closely related plants, animals, or people: *the dangers/effects of inbreeding*

inbuilt /ˈɪn.bɪlt/ **adj** mainly UK (US usually **ˌbuilt-ˈin**) describes something that is an original part of something or someone and cannot be separated from them: *an inbuilt advantage/problem*

Inc. /ɪŋk/ **adj** [after noun] abbreviation for incorporated: used in the names of US companies that are legally established: *Bishop Computer Services, Inc.*

incalculable /ɪnˈkæl.kjʊ.lə.bl̩/ **adj** extremely large and therefore unable to be measured: *The ecological consequences of a nuclear war are incalculable.* • **incalculably** /-bli/ **adv**

incandescent /ˌɪn.kænˈdes.ənt/ **adj** LIGHT ▷ **1** producing a bright light from a heated FILAMENT or other part: *an incandescent lamp* **2** literary extremely bright:

The mountain's snow-white peak was incandescent against the blue sky. **QUALITY** ▷ **3** showing extreme anger or happiness: *He was incandescent **with rage**.* ◦ *Her beauty had an incandescent quality to it.* **4** extremely good, special, or skilled: *an incandescent performance/career* • **incandescence** /-ᵊns/ noun [U]

incantation /ˌɪn.kænˈteɪ.ʃᵊn/ noun [C or U] (the performance of) words that are believed to have a magical effect when spoken or sung: *Around the fire, tribal elders **chanted** incantations.*

incapable /ɪnˈkeɪ.pə.bl/ adj **C1** unable to do something: *He seems incapable **of** walk**ing** past a music shop without going in and buying another CD.* ◦ *I think she's incapable **of** love.*

incapacitate /ˌɪn.kəˈpæs.ɪ.teɪt/ verb [T often passive] to make someone unable to work or do things normally, or unable to do what they intended to do: *The accident left me incapacitated for seven months.* ◦ *Rubber bullets are designed to incapacitate people rather than kill them.* • **incapacitating** /-teɪ.tɪŋ/ US /-teɪ.t̬ɪŋ/ adj *Extreme shyness can be very incapacitating.*

incapacity /ˌɪn.kəˈpæs.ə.ti/ US /-t̬i/ noun [U] the fact that you are unable to do something because you do not have the ability or you are too weak: [+ to infinitive] *the incapacity of the police **to** limit the rise in crime*

incapping /ˈɪnˌkæp.ɪŋ/ noun [U] the use of a capital letter in the middle of a COMPOUND name or phrase → See also **camel case**

ˈin-car adj [before noun] used to describe a piece of equipment that is provided inside a car: *in-car entertainment/computer systems/stereo*

incarcerate /ɪnˈkɑː.sᵊr.eɪt/ US /-ˈkɑːr.sə.reɪt/ verb [T] **1** formal to put or keep someone in prison or in a place used as a prison: *Thousands of dissidents have been interrogated or incarcerated.* **2** to keep someone in a closed place and prevent them from leaving it: *We were incarcerated **in** that broken elevator for four hours.* • **incarceration** /ɪnˌkɑː.sᵊrˈeɪ.ʃᵊn/ US /-ˌkɑːr.səˈreɪ-/ noun [U]

incarnate /ɪnˈkɑː.nət/ US /-ˈkɑːr-/ adj [after noun] in human form: *One survivor described his torturers as **devils** incarnate.*

incarnation /ˌɪn.kɑːˈneɪ.ʃᵊn/ US /-kɑːr-/ noun **1** [C] a particular life, in religions that believe that we have many lives: *He believes that he was a Roman warrior in a **previous** incarnation.* → Compare **reincarnation** **2** [C] a particular physical form or condition of something or someone that is changing or developing: *This film is the latest incarnation of a fairy tale that dates back to the Middle Ages.* **3 the incarnation of sth** an extreme example, in human form, of a particular characteristic or type of behaviour: *He was **the** incarnation **of** evil* (= was extremely evil). ◦ *She's **the** incarnation **of** everything I hate about politics.* **4** [U] the appearance of a god as a human

incautious /ɪnˈkɔː.ʃəs/ US /-ˈkɑː-/ adj formal not showing or giving careful thought to the possible results: *Bill and Sandra haven't spoken to each other since he made an incautious **remark** about her husband's drinking problem.* • **incautiously** /-li/ adv

incendiary /ɪnˈsen.di.ᵊr.i/ US /-er.i/ adj **FIRE** ▷ **1** [before noun] designed to cause fires: *an incendiary bomb/device* **CAUSING ANGER** ▷ **2** likely to cause violence or strong feelings of anger: *incendiary remarks*

incense noun; verb

▸**noun** [U] /ˈɪn.sens/ a substance that is burnt to produce a sweet smell, especially as part of a religious ceremony: *an incense burner/stick*

▸**verb** [T usually passive] /ɪnˈsens/ to cause someone to be

extremely angry: *The editor said a lot of readers would be incensed by my article on class.* ◦ *I was so incensed by what he was saying I had to walk out.* • **incensed** /-ˈsenst/ adj extremely angry: *The villagers are incensed **at** the decision to close the railway station.*

incentive /ɪnˈsen.tɪv/ US /-t̬ɪv/ noun [C or U] **C2** something which encourages a person to do something: ***Tax** incentives have been very effective in encouraging people to save and invest more of their income.* ◦ [+ to infinitive] *There is little incentive **for** people **to** leave their cars at home when public transport remains so expensive.* ◦ *Bonus payments provide an incentive **to** work harder.*

incentivize (UK usually **incentivise**) /ɪnˈsen.tɪ.vaɪz/ US /-t̬ə-/ verb [T] to make someone want to do something: *We need to incentivize our sales managers to achieve these targets.*

inception /ɪnˈsep.ʃᵊn/ noun [S] the beginning of an organization or official activity: ***Since its** inception in 1968, the company has been at the forefront of computer development.*

incessant /ɪnˈses.ᵊnt/ adj never stopping, especially in an annoying or unpleasant way: *incessant rain/noise/complaints* • **incessantly** /-li/ adv *She talked incessantly about the most trivial things.*

incest /ˈɪn.sest/ noun [U] sexual activity involving people who are closely related and not legally allowed to marry: *a victim of incest*

incestuous /ɪnˈses.tju.əs/ adj **1** involving incest: *The film is about Auteil's incestuous love for his sister.* **2** disapproving involving only a close or limited group of people, who do not communicate or do business with people outside the group: *Journalists and politicians often have a rather incestuous **relationship**.* • **incestuously** /-li/ adv • **incestuousness** /-nəs/ noun [U]

inch /ɪntʃ/ noun; verb

▸**noun** [C] **B1** a unit used for measuring length, approximately equal to 2.54 centimetres, sometimes shown by the symbol ": *Twelve inches are equal to one foot.* ◦ *He had a cut an inch long above his left eye.* ◦ *The snow was six inches deep in some places.* ◦ *a piece of wood 2" by 2"*

IDIOMS **by inches** very closely or only just: *The car skidded and I avoided the dog by inches* (= *I very nearly hit the dog*). • **come within an inch of sth** to very nearly do something, especially something dangerous or exciting: *I came within an inch of losing my life on the rocks below.* • **every inch** exactly like: *She looked every inch a vampire in her costume.* • **every inch of sth/somewhere** all of a thing or place: *Every inch of her bedroom wall is covered with photos of pop stars.* • **inch by inch** in great detail and in many very small stages: *Detectives searched the area around the murder scene inch by inch.* • **not give/budge/move an inch** to not change your opinion: *She's definite that she wants to do it, and she'll not give an inch, however hard you try to persuade her.* • **give someone an inch and they'll take a mile** saying said about someone who has been given a small amount of power or freedom to do something, and then has tried to get a lot more

▸**verb** [I or T, + adv/prep] to move very slowly or in a lot of short stages: *We are inching **towards** an agreement.* ◦ *Share prices inched **up/higher** during the day.* ◦ *Residents watched the flames inch **closer** and closer.*

incharge /ˈɪn.tʃɑːdʒ/ US /-tʃɑːrdʒ/ adj [only before noun], noun Indian English (a person) having control or being responsible for someone or something: *the incharge officer*

inchoate /ɪnˈkəʊ.eɪt/ US /-ˈkoʊ-/ **adj** literary only recently or partly formed, or not completely developed or clear: *She had a child's inchoate awareness of language.*

incidence /ˈɪn.sɪ.dᵊns/ **noun** [C usually singular] formal an event, or the rate at which something happens: *There have been quite a few incidences of bullying in the school this year.* ◦ *an increased incidence* ***of*** *cancer near nuclear power stations*

incident /ˈɪn.sɪ.dᵊnt/ **noun** **1** B2 [C] an event that is either unpleasant or unusual: *an isolated/serious/unfortunate incident* ◦ *A youth was seriously injured in a shooting incident on Saturday night.* **2 without incident** with nothing unpleasant or unusual happening: *Despite fears of violence, the demonstration passed off without incident.*

incidental /ˌɪn.sɪˈden.tᵊl/ US /-t̬ᵊl/ **adj** less important than the thing something is connected with or part of: *Try not to be distracted by incidental details.*

incidentally /ˌɪn.sɪˈden.tᵊl.i/ US /-t̬ᵊl-/ **adv** **1** C1 used before saying something that is not as important as the main subject of conversation, but is connected to it in some way: *We had a marvellous meal at that restaurant you recommended – incidentally, I must give you the number of a similar one I know.* **2** used when mentioning a subject that has not been discussed before, often making it seem less important than it really is: *Incidentally, I wanted to have a word with you about your expenses claim.*

ˌincidental ˈmusic **noun** [U] music that is played during a film, broadcast, or play to create a particular mood

incidentals /ɪn.sɪˈden.tᵊlz/ US /-t̬ᵊlz/ **noun** [plural] details or costs that relate to something but are less important or smaller than the main ones: *Take some foreign currency to cover incidentals like the taxi fare to your hotel.*

ˈincident ˌray **noun** [C] specialized in physics, a RAY of light which hits a surface → Compare **reflected ray**

incinerate /ɪnˈsɪn.ᵊr.eɪt/ US /-ə.reɪt/ **verb** [T] to burn something completely: *to incinerate waste* ◦ *The spacecraft and its crew were incinerated by the billion-degree temperatures generated by the fireball.* • **incineration** /ɪnˌsɪn.ᵊrˈeɪ.ʃᵊn/ US /-əˈreɪ-/ **noun** [U]

incinerator /ɪnˈsɪn.ᵊr.eɪ.təʳ/ US /-ə.reɪ.t̬ɚ/ **noun** [C] a device for burning things that are no longer wanted: *a garbage/hazardous-waste incinerator* ◦ *a hospital incinerator*

incipient /ɪnˈsɪp.i.ᵊnt/ **adj** formal just beginning: *signs of incipient public frustration*

incise /ɪnˈsaɪz/ **verb** [T usually passive] formal to cut the surface of something carefully with a sharp tool: *The design is incised* ***into*** *a metal plate.* ◦ *a shield incised* ***with*** *Celtic symbols*

incision /ɪnˈsɪʒ.ᵊn/ **noun** [C or U] an opening that is made in something with a sharp tool, especially in someone's body during an operation: *The surgeon* ***makes*** *a small incision into which a tube is inserted.*

incisive /ɪnˈsaɪ.sɪv/ **adj** expressing an idea or opinion in a clear and direct way which shows good understanding of what is important: *incisive questions/comments* • **incisively** /-li/ **adv** • **incisiveness** /-nəs/ **noun** [U]

incisor /ɪnˈsaɪ.zəʳ/ US /-zɚ/ **noun** [C] one of the sharp teeth at the front of the mouth which cut food when you bite into it → Compare **canine, molar**

incite /ɪnˈsaɪt/ **verb** [T] to encourage someone to do or feel something unpleasant or violent: *She incited racial hatred by distributing anti-Semitic leaflets.* ◦ [+ to infinitive] *She was expelled for inciting her classmates* ***to*** *rebel against their teachers.* ◦ *They denied inciting the crowd* ***to*** *violence.* • **incitement** /-mənt/ **noun** [U] [+ to infinitive] *They were imprisoned for incitement* ***to*** *commit grievous bodily harm.*

incivility /ˌɪn.sɪˈvɪl.ɪ.ti/ US /-ə.t̬i/ **noun** [U] formal rudeness → See also **uncivil**

incl. written abbreviation for **including** or **inclusive**: *$449 incl. delivery* ◦ *car hire £35 per day incl.*

inclement /ɪnˈklem.ᵊnt/ **adj** formal describes weather that is unpleasant, especially cold wind and rain

inclination /ˌɪn.klɪˈneɪ.ʃᵊn/ **noun** **FEELING** ▷ **1** C2 [C or U] a feeling that you want to do a particular thing, or the fact that you prefer or are more likely to do a particular thing: [+ to infinitive] *My own inclination would be* ***to*** *look for another job.* ◦ *We should be basing our decisions on solid facts, not inclinations and hunches.* **MOVEMENT** ▷ **2** [C] formal a small downward movement: *a solemn inclination of the head* **ANGLE** ▷ **3** [C usually singular, U] specialized the angle at which something slopes

incline **verb; noun**

▸**verb** /ɪnˈklaɪn/ formal **FEEL** ▷ **1** [I or T, usually + adv/prep] to (make someone) feel something or want to do something: *The prime minister is believed to be inclining* ***towards*** *an April election.* **MOVE** ▷ **2** [T] to (cause to) slope at a particular angle: *The ground inclined steeply towards the ridge in the distance.* **3 incline your head** to bend your head slightly forward and down: *He inclined his head and said nothing.*

PHRASAL VERB **incline to/towards sth** to think that a belief or opinion is probably correct: *I incline to the view that peace can be achieved.*

▸**noun** [C] /ˈɪn.klaɪn/ formal a slope: *a steep/gentle incline*

inclined /ɪnˈklaɪnd/ **adj** [after verb, +, to, infinitive] **1** C2 likely or wanting to do something: *Tom is inclined* ***to*** *be lazy.* ◦ *No one seemed inclined* ***to*** *help.* **2 artistically, technically, etc. inclined** C2 having natural artistic, technical, etc. ability: *She's very bright, but she's not academically inclined.* **3 be inclined to agree, believe, think, etc.** C1 to have an opinion about something, but not a strong opinion: *He was inclined to agree with them.*

include /ɪnˈkluːd/ **verb** [T] A2 to contain something as a part of something else, or to make something part of something else: *The bill includes tax and service.* ◦ *Tax and service are included* ***in*** *the bill.* ◦ [+ -ing verb] *Your responsibilities will include mak****ing*** *appointments on my behalf.* → Compare **exclude** • **included** /-ˈkluː.dɪd/ **adj** [after noun] *The trip cost a total of £250, insurance included.* • **inclusion** /-ˈkluː.ʒᵊn/ **noun** [C or U] C1 *She is being considered for inclusion in the England team.* ◦ *Two last-minute inclusions in the team are Jim and Ahmed.*

including /ɪnˈkluː.dɪŋ/ **preposition** A2 used for saying that a person or thing is part of a particular group or amount: *Eight people, including two children, were injured in the explosion.* ◦ *Including Christmas Day and Boxing Day, I've got a week off work.*

inclusive /ɪnˈkluː.sɪv/ **adj** **1** C1 An inclusive price or amount includes everything: *My rent is $700 a month inclusive (****of*** *bills).* **2** [after noun] including the first and last date or number stated: *I'll be away from 20 to 31 May inclusive.* **3** describes a group or organization that tries to include many different types of people and treat them all fairly and equally: *Our aim is to create a fairer, more inclusive society.*

incognito /ˌɪn.kɒɡˈniː.təʊ/ (US) /-kɑːɡˈniː.t̬oʊ/ **adv** avoiding being recognized, by changing your name or appearance: *The prince often travelled abroad incognito.*

incoherent /ˌɪn.kəʊˈhɪə.rənt/ (US) /-koʊˈhɪr.ənt/ **adj** **1** expressing yourself in a way that is not clear: *He was confused and incoherent and I didn't get much sense out of him.* **2** expressed in a way that is not clear, especially with words or ideas that are joined together badly: *The talk she gave was incoherent and badly prepared.* • **incoherently** /-li/ **adv** *She was muttering incoherently.* • **incoherence** /-ˈhɪə.rəns/ (US) /-ˈhɪr.əns/ **noun** [U]

income /ˈɪn.kʌm/ **noun** [C or U] **1** (B2) money that is earned from doing work or received from INVESTMENTS: *Average incomes have risen by 4.5 percent over the past year.* ◦ *More help is needed for people on* ***low*** *incomes.* ◦ *I haven't had much income from my stocks and shares this year.* **2** a company's profit in a particular period of time: *The company's income has greatly improved: profit rose more than 50 percent last year.*

> Word partners for **income**
>
> *earn/get/have* an income • *generate/provide* an income • *increase/supplement* your income • a *low/average/good/high* income • an *annual/monthly/regular/steady* income • a *level* of income • a *source* of income • be *on* a (high/low) income

ˌincome supˈport **noun** [U] in the UK, money that is paid by the government to people who have no income or a very low income: *Many single mothers are* ***on*** *income support.*

ˈincome ˌtax **noun** [C or U] a tax that you have to pay on your income, usually higher for people with larger incomes

incoming /ˈɪnˌkʌm.ɪŋ/ **adj** [before noun] **1** arriving at or coming towards a place: *incoming mail/phone calls* ◦ *an incoming flight* **2** soon to start something such as a job because recently chosen or elected: *the incoming government* ◦ *What are the biggest problems faced by the incoming president?* ◦ US *Incoming freshmen (= students in the first year at college) start a week before everyone else.*

incommunicado /ˌɪn.kəˌmjuː.nɪˈkɑː.dəʊ/ (US) /-doʊ/ **adj** [after verb], **adv** formal not communicating with anyone else because you do not want to or are not allowed to: *His secretary says he will be incommunicado for the rest of the day.* ◦ *He was* ***held*** *incommunicado for the first 48 hours after he was arrested.*

incomparable /ɪnˈkɒm.pər.ə.bl̩/ (US) /-ˈkɑːm.pɚ-/ **adj** so good or great that nothing or no one else could achieve the same standard: *incomparable beauty/skill* ◦ *the incomparable Mohammed Ali* • **incomparably** /-bli/ **adv** *His second novel was incomparably better than his first.*

incompatible /ˌɪn.kəmˈpæt.ɪ.bl̩/ (US) /-ˈpæt̬.ə-/ **adj** not able to exist or work with another person or thing because of basic differences: *When we started living together we realized how incompatible we were – our interests were so different.* ◦ *Maintaining quality is incompatible* ***with*** *increasing output.* ◦ *Any new video system that is incompatible* ***with*** *existing ones has little chance of success.* • **incompatibility** /ˌɪn.kəmˌpæt.ɪˈbɪl.ɪ.ti/ (US) /-ˌpæt̬.əˈbɪl.ə.t̬i/ **noun** [U]

incompetence /ɪnˈkɒm.pɪ.təns/ (US) /-ˈkɑːm.pə.t̬əns/ **noun** [U] lack of ability to do something successfully or as it should be done: *Management have demonstrated almost unbelievable incompetence in their handling of the dispute.* ◦ *allegations/accusations of incompetence*

incompetent /ɪnˈkɒm.pɪ.tənt/ (US) /-ˈkɑːm.pə.t̬ənt/ **adj; noun**

▸**adj** not having the ability to do something as it should be done: *an incompetent teacher/doctor* ◦ *He has described the government as corrupt and incompetent.* • **incompetently** /-li/ **adv**

▸**noun** [C] someone who does not have the ability or skill to do something as it should be done: *The country's being governed by a* ***bunch of*** *incompetents.*

incomplete /ˌɪn.kəmˈpliːt/ **adj** not having some parts, or not finished: *The decision was based on incomplete or inaccurate information.* ◦ *The building is still incomplete.* • **incompletely** /-li/ **adv** *The chemical properties of coal are still incompletely understood.* • **incompleteness** /-nəs/ **noun** [U]

incomprehensible /ɪnˌkɒm.prɪˈhen.sɪ.bl̩/ (US) /-kɑːm-/ **adj** impossible or extremely difficult to understand: *These accounts are utterly incomprehensible. Can you explain them to me?* ◦ *It's incomprehensible* ***to*** *me why he would want to kill himself.* • **incomprehensibly** /-bli/ **adv** • **incomprehensibility** /ɪnˌkɒm.prɪˌhen.sɪˈbɪl.ɪ.ti/ (US) /ˌɪn.kɑːm.prɪ.hen.səˈbɪl.ə.t̬i/ **noun** [U]

incomprehension /ɪnˌkɒm.prɪˈhen.ʃən/ (US) /ˌɪn.kɑːm-/ **noun** [U] formal a person's failure or INABILITY to understand something: *She stared at him in total incomprehension.* ◦ *a look of blank incomprehension*

inconceivable /ˌɪn.kənˈsiː.və.bl̩/ **adj** **1** (C2) impossible to imagine or think of: *The idea that they might not win was inconceivable* ***to*** *them.* ◦ ***It*** *would be inconceivable* ***for*** *her* ***to*** *change her mind.* **2** extremely unlikely: *Another nuclear accident in the same place is* ***virtually/almost*** *inconceivable.* ◦ ***It*** *is not inconceivable (= it is possible)* ***that*** *she could be lying.* • **inconceivably** /-bli/ **adv**

inconclusive /ˌɪn.kəŋˈkluː.sɪv/ **adj** not giving or having a result or decision: *The evidence is inconclusive.* ◦ *The medical tests were inconclusive, and will need to be repeated.* • **inconclusively** /-li/ **adv**

incongruent /ɪnˈkɒŋ.gru.ənt/ (US) /-ˈkɑːŋ-/ **adj** **1** formal not suitable or not fitting well with something else: *Violence is incongruent* ***with*** *our values and legal system.* **2** specialized used to describe a shape in mathematics that does not have the same shape and size as another: *incongruent triangles* • **incongruence** /-əns/ **noun** [U]

incongruity /ˌɪn.kəŋˈgruː.ə.ti/ (US) /-kənˈgruː.ə.t̬i/ **noun** [C or U] formal the fact that something is incongruous

incongruous /ɪnˈkɒŋ.gru.əs/ (US) /-ˈkɑːŋ-/ **adj** unusual or different from what is around or from what is generally happening: *The new computer looked incongruous in the dark book-filled library.* ◦ *It* ***seems*** *incongruous to have a woman as the editor of a men's magazine.*

inconsequential /ɪnˌkɒn.sɪˈkwen.ʃəl/ (US) /-ˌkɑːn-/ **adj** not important: *an inconsequential matter/remark* ◦ *Most of what she said was pretty inconsequential.* • **inconsequentially** /-i/ **adv**

inconsiderable /ˌɪn.kənˈsɪd.ər.ə.bl̩/ (US) /-ɚ-/ **adj** [usually in negatives] very small and therefore not important or not worth considering: *He inherited a* ***not*** *inconsiderable (= a large)* ***sum/amount****.*

inconsiderate /ˌɪn.kənˈsɪd.ər.ət/ (US) /-ɚ-/ **adj** disapproving (C1) not thinking or worrying about other people or their feelings: *Our neighbours are very inconsiderate – they're always playing loud music late at night.* → Synonym **selfish** • **inconsiderately** /-li/ **adv**

inconsistent /ˌɪn.kənˈsɪs.tᵊnt/ **adj** NOT AGREEING ▷ **1** If a reason, idea, opinion, etc. is inconsistent, different parts of it do not agree, or it does not agree with something else: *These findings are inconsistent* ***with*** *those of previous studies.* CHANGING ▷ **2** not staying the same in behaviour or quality: *The teacher said that Alex's schoolwork was very inconsistent.* ◦ *Problems arise if the parents' approach to discipline is inconsistent.* • **inconsistently** /-li/ **adv** • **inconsistency** /-tᵊn.si/ **noun** [C or U] *There are a few inconsistencies in what you've written.* ◦ *Logan showed his inconsistency in missing half his kicks.*

inconsolable /ˌɪn.kənˈsəʊ.lə.bl̩/ (US) /-ˈsoʊ-/ **adj** so sad or disappointed that it is impossible for anyone to make you feel better: *They were inconsolable after the death of their young son.* • **inconsolably** /-bli/ (US) /-ˈsoʊ-/ **adv** *The child was crying inconsolably.*

inconspicuous /ˌɪn.kənˈspɪk.ju.əs/ **adj** not easily or quickly noticed or seen, or not attracting attention: *This type of bird is very inconspicuous because of its dull feathers.* ◦ *At parties, he always stands in a corner and tries to look inconspicuous.* • **inconspicuously** /-li/ **adv**

inconstant /ɪnˈkɒn.stᵊnt/ (US) /-ˈkɑːn-/ **adj** literary not staying the same, especially in emotion, behaviour, or choice of sexual partner: *an inconstant lover* • **inconstancy** /-stᵊn.si/ **noun** [U]

incontestable /ˌɪn.kənˈtes.tə.bl̩/ **adj** formal impossible to question because of being obviously true: *There is now incontestable* ***evidence*** *that the killings did take place.* • **incontestably** /-bli/ **adv**

incontinent /ɪnˈkɒn.tɪ.nənt/ (US) /-ˈkɑːn.tə-/ **adj** unable to control the EXCRETION of urine or the contents of the bowels: *Many of our elderly patients are incontinent.* ◦ *As the illness progressed, she became* ***doubly*** *incontinent (= unable to control the excretion both of urine and the contents of the bowels).* • **incontinence** /-nəns/ **noun** [U]

incontrovertible /ɪnˌkɒn.trəˈvɜː.tɪ.bl̩/ (US) /-ˌkɑːn.trəˈvɝː.t̬ə-/ **adj** formal impossible to doubt because of being obviously true: *incontrovertible* ***proof/evidence*** • **incontrovertibly** /ɪnˌkɒn.trəˈvɜː.tɪ.bli/ (US) /-ˌkɑːn.trəˈvɝː.t̬ə-/ **adv** *Your assertion is incontrovertibly true.*

inconvenience /ˌɪn.kənˈviː.ni.ᵊns/ **noun; verb**
▸**noun** [C or U] (C1) a state or an example of problems or trouble, which often causes a delay or loss of comfort: *We apologize for any inconvenience caused by the late arrival of the train.* ◦ *We had the inconvenience of being unable to use the kitchen for several weeks.* ◦ *Having to wait for ten minutes was a minor inconvenience.*
▸**verb** [T] to cause problems or difficulties for someone: *The strike inconvenienced many people.*

inconvenient /ˌɪn.kənˈviː.ni.ᵊnt/ **adj** (B2) causing problems or difficulties: *an inconvenient time/place* ◦ ***It*** *will be very inconvenient* ***for*** *me* ***to*** *have no car.* • **inconveniently** /-li/ **adv**

> **!** Common mistake: **inconvenient or inconvenience?**
>
> **Warning:** do not confuse the adjective **inconvenient** with the noun **inconvenience**:
>
> ~~*We apologize for any inconvenient.*~~
>
> *We apologize for any inconvenience.*

incorporate /ɪnˈkɔː.pᵊr.eɪt/ (US) /-ˈkɔːr.pə-/ **verb** [T] (C2) to include something as part of something larger: *Suggestions from the survey have been incorporated* ***into/in*** *the final design.* ◦ *This aircraft incorporates several new safety features.* • **incorporation** /ɪnˌkɔː.pᵊrˈeɪ.ʃᵊn/ (US) /-ˌkɔːr.pəˈreɪ-/ **noun** [U] *the regular incorporation* ***of*** *organic material into garden soil*

Incorporated /ɪnˈkɔː.pᵊr.eɪ.tɪd/ (US) /-ˈkɔːr.pə.reɪ.t̬ɪd/ **adj** [after noun] (abbreviation **Inc.**) used after the name of a company that is a CORPORATION (= a company or goup of companies controlled as one organization): *Bishop Computer Services Incorporated*

incorporeal /ˌɪn.kɔːˈpɔː.ri.əl/ (US) /ˌɪn.kɔːrˈpɔːr.i-/ **adj** formal not having a physical body but a spiritual form

incorrect /ˌɪn.kᵊrˈekt/ (US) /-kəˈrekt/ **adj** **1** (B1) not correct or not true: *an incorrect answer/diagnosis* ◦ *The assumptions made about the economy's rate of growth* ***proved*** *to be incorrect.* **2** not acceptable or not as it should be: *It's incorrect* ***to*** *address people by their first names at these formal events.* ◦ *incorrect grammar* • **incorrectly** /-li/ **adv** *For many years the sculpture was incorrectly thought to be by Donatello.*

incorrigible /ɪnˈkɒr.ɪ.dʒə.bl̩/ (US) /-ˈkɔːr-/ **adj** mainly humorous An incorrigible person or incorrigible behaviour is bad and impossible to change or improve: *an incorrigible* ***liar/rogue*** • **incorrigibly** /-bli/ **adv**

incorruptible /ˌɪn.kəˈrʌp.tɪ.bl̩/ **adj** **1** morally strong enough not to be persuaded to do something wrong: *Most politicians genuinely believe they are incorruptible.* **2** formal If something is incorruptible, it will not decay or be destroyed: *Some people think the soul, unlike the body, is incorruptible.* • **incorruptibly** /-bli/ **adv** • **incorruptibility** /ˌɪn.kə.rʌp.tɪˈbɪl.ɪ.ti/ (US) /-ə.t̬i/ **noun** [U]

increase **verb; noun**
▸**verb** [I or T] /ɪnˈkriːs/ (B1) to (make something) become larger in amount or size: *Incidents of armed robbery have increased over the last few years.* ◦ *The cost of the project has increased* ***dramatically/significantly*** *since it began.* ◦ *Gradually increase the temperature* ***to*** *boiling point.* ◦ *Increased/Increasing efforts are being made to end the dispute.* → Compare **decrease**

> **!** Common mistake: **increase**
>
> **Increase** is not usually followed by the adverb 'up'. Don't say 'increase up', say **increase**:
>
> ~~*The number of homeless people has increased up by five percent.*~~
>
> *The number of homeless people has increased by five percent.*

> **+** Other ways of saying **increase**
>
> The verbs **grow** and **rise** are common alternatives to 'increase':
>
> *The number of people living alone* ***grows*** *each year.*
>
> *Prices* ***rose*** *by 10 percent.*
>
> The phrasal verb **go up** is often used when prices increase:
>
> *House prices keep* ***going up****.*
>
> *The price of fuel has* ***gone up*** *by 5p a litre.*
>
> If something suddenly increases by a large amount, you can use verbs such as **escalate**, **rocket**, or **soar**:
>
> *Crime in the city has* ***escalated*** *in recent weeks.*
>
> *House prices have* ***soared*** *this year.*
>
> *Building costs have* ***rocketed*** *by 70 percent.*
>
> If someone makes something increase in size or amount, you can use verbs like **expand** or **extend**:
>
> *We're hoping to* ***expand/extend*** *our range of products.*
>
> The verb **maximize** is sometimes used when someone tries to increase something as much as possible:
>
> *We need to* ***maximize*** *profits.*

▸**noun** [C or U] /ˈɪn.kriːs/ **1** B2 a rise in the amount or size of something: ***price/tax** increases* ◦ *There were 39,000 new cases last year – an increase **of** six percent.* ◦ *Any increase **in** production would be helpful.* **2 on the increase** C1 increasing: *Homelessness is on the increase in many cities.*

> **Word partners for increase noun**
>
> a *dramatic/large/massive/substantial* increase • a *marked/significant* increase • a *rapid/sharp* increase • a *modest/slight/small* increase • a *gradual/steady* increase • an increase *in* sth • an increase *of* [ten percent/5,000/£300]

increasingly /ɪnˈkriː.sɪŋ.li/ adv B2 more and more: *to be increasingly important/common* ◦ *Increasingly, there is pressure on the council to reverse its decision.*

incredible /ɪnˈkred.ɪ.bl̩/ adj **DIFFICULT TO BELIEVE** ▷ **1** B2 impossible, or very difficult, to believe: *an incredible story* ◦ *The latest missiles can be fired with incredible accuracy.* ◦ ***It** seems incredible **that** no one foresaw the crisis.* **EXTREME** ▷ **2** B1 informal extremely good: *Yeah, it was an incredible performance.* ◦ *What an incredible motorbike!*

incredibly /ɪnˈkred.ɪ.bli/ adv **DIFFICULT TO BELIEVE** ▷ **1** C1 used for saying that something is very difficult to believe: *Incredibly, no one was hurt in the accident.* **EXTREMELY** ▷ **2** B2 extremely: *He was incredibly rich/angry/quick.* ◦ *An incredibly loud bang followed the flash.*

incredulous /ɪnˈkred.jʊ.ləs/ adj not wanting or not able to believe something, and usually showing this: *A few incredulous spectators watched on as Paterson, ranked 23rd in the world, beat the champion.* • **incredulously** /-li/ adv *'Did you see that?' she asked incredulously.* • **incredulity** /ˌɪn.krəˈdjuː.lɪ.ti/ US /-ˈduː.lə.t̬i/ noun [U] *He felt a sense of incredulity, anger, and pain at the accusation made against him.*

increment /ˈɪŋ.krə.mənt/ noun [C] one of a series of increases: *You will receive annual **salary/pay** increments every September.*

incremental /ˌɪŋ.krəˈmen.təl/ US /-t̬əl/ adj in a series of amounts: *Most research proceeds by small incremental advances.* • **incrementally** /-i/ adv

incriminate /ɪnˈkrɪm.ɪ.neɪt/ verb [T] to make someone seem guilty, especially of a crime: *A secret report incriminating the company was leaked last week.* ◦ *He refused to say anything on the grounds that he might incriminate him**self**.* • **incriminating** /-neɪ.tɪŋ/ US /-neɪ.t̬ɪŋ/ adj *incriminating remarks/statements* • **incrimination** /ɪnˌkrɪm.ɪˈneɪ.ʃən/ noun [U]

incrustation /ˌɪn.krʌsˈteɪ.ʃən/ noun [C] (US also **encrustation**) a layer of material, such as dirt or a chemical, which forms on something, especially slowly

incubate /ˈɪŋ.kjʊ.beɪt/ verb [I or T] **EGG** ▷ **1** When a bird, etc. incubates its eggs, it keeps them warm until the young come out, and when eggs incubate, they develop to the stage at which the young come out: *The female bird incubates the eggs for about 16 days.* **DISEASE** ▷ **2** When harmful bacteria or viruses incubate, or when a person or animal incubates them, they increase in size or number in the person's or animal's body but do not yet produce the effects of disease. • **incubation** /ˌɪŋ.kjʊˈbeɪ.ʃən/ noun [U] *The incubation **period** varies depending on the time of year when the eggs were laid.* ◦ *In smallpox, there is an incubation **period** of 8–18 days between initial infection and first symptoms.*

incubator /ˈɪŋ.kjʊ.beɪ.təʳ/ US /-t̬ɚ/ noun [C] **1** a container that has controlled air and temperature

conditions in which a weak or PREMATURE baby (= one which was born too early) can be kept alive **2** a device for keeping birds' eggs at the correct temperature to allow young birds to develop until they break out of the shell

inculcate /ˈɪŋ.kʌl.keɪt/ verb [T] formal to fix beliefs or ideas in someone's mind, especially by repeating them often: *Our football coach has worked hard to inculcate a team spirit **in/into** the players.* • **inculcation** /ˌɪŋ.kʌlˈkeɪ.ʃən/ noun [U]

incumbency /ɪnˈkʌm.bən.si/ noun [C] the period during which someone has a particular official position: *During her incumbency (**as** commissioner), several changes were introduced.*

incumbent /ɪnˈkʌm.bənt/ adj; noun

▸**adj** **1** [before noun] officially having the named position: *The incumbent president faces problems which began many years before he took office.* **2 be incumbent on/upon sb** formal to be necessary for someone: *She felt it incumbent upon/on her **to** raise the subject at their meeting.*

▸**noun** [C] the person who has or had a particular official position: *the first/last/previous incumbent* ◦ *The **present** incumbent (**of** the post) is due to retire next month.*

incur /ɪnˈkɜːʳ/ US /-ˈkɝː/ verb [T] (-rr-) formal C2 to experience something, usually something unpleasant, as a result of actions you have taken: *to incur debts/fines/bills* ◦ *The play has incurred **the wrath/anger** of both audiences and critics.* ◦ *Please detail any **costs/expenses** incurred by you in attending the interview.*

incurable /ɪnˈkjʊə.rə.bl̩/ US /-ˈkjʊr.ə-/ adj **DISEASE** ▷ **1** C2 not able to be cured: *Parkinson's disease is a debilitating and incurable **disease** of the nervous system.* **PERSONALITY** ▷ **2** [usually before noun] describes someone whose personality type does not change or cannot be changed: *an incurable romantic/optimist/pessimist* • **incurably** /-bli/ adv *She was told that she was incurably **ill**.* ◦ *He's incurably cheerful.*

incurious /ɪnˈkjʊə.ri.əs/ US /-ˈkjʊr.i-/ adj formal not interested in knowing what is happening, or not wanting to discover anything new: *He's strangely incurious **about** what goes on around him.*

incursion /ɪnˈkɜː.ʒən/ US /-ˈkɝː-/ noun [C] **1** a sudden attack on or act of going into a place, especially across a border: *incursions **into** enemy territory* **2** formal an occasion when people suddenly involve themselves in another person's private situation

incus /ˈɪŋ.kəs/ noun [C usually singular] (plural **incudes**) specialized one of three very small bones that carry sound from the EARDRUM to the INNER ear → Compare **malleus, stapes**

indaba /ɪnˈdɑː.bə/ noun [C] South African English a discussion or meeting

indebted /ɪnˈdet.ɪd/ US /-ˈdet̬-/ adj **GRATEFUL** ▷ **1** [after verb] grateful because of help given: *We're **deeply** indebted **to** you **for** your help.* **OWING** ▷ **2** owing money: *indebted countries* ◦ *The company is **heavily** indebted.* • **indebtedness** /-nəs/ noun [U]

indecency /ɪnˈdiː.sən.si/ noun [U] morally offensive behaviour: *acts of gross indecency*

indecent /ɪnˈdiː.sənt/ adj **IMMORAL** ▷ **1** morally offensive, especially in a sexual way: *an indecent act/photograph* **NOT SUITABLE** ▷ **2** not suitable or correct for a situation: *The premier left his residence with almost indecent **haste** following his resignation.* • **indecently** /-li/ adv

inˌdecent asˈsault noun [C or U] UK legal an attack

on someone that involves sexual actions but not RAPE (= forced sex)

in͵decent exˈposure noun [U] legal the act of showing the sexual organs in public in a way that is intended to upset people

indecipherable /ˌɪn.dɪˈsaɪ.fᵊr.ə.bl̩/ US /-fɚ-/ adj unable to be read or understood: *Her handwriting is virtually indecipherable.*

indecision /ˌɪn.dɪˈsɪʒ.ᵊn/ noun [U] (also **indecisiveness**) the state of being unable to make a choice: *A moment's indecision when you've got the ball and you could lose the game.* ◦ *There is a great deal of indecision **about/over** how to tackle the problem.*

indecisive /ˌɪn.dɪˈsaɪ.sɪv/ adj **1** not good at making decisions: *He is widely thought to be an indecisive leader.* **2** not having a clear meaning or producing a decision • **indecisively** /-li/ adv

indecorous /ɪnˈdek.ᵊr.əs/ US /-ɚ-/ adj formal behaving badly or rudely • **indecorously** /-li/ adv

indeed /ɪnˈdiːd/ adv; exclamation

▸**adv 1** B1 really or certainly, often used to emphasize something: *Indeed, it could be the worst environmental disaster in Western Europe this century.* ◦ *Evidence suggests that errors may indeed be occurring.* ◦ *We live in strange times indeed.* ◦ mainly UK *Many people are **very** poor indeed.* **2** used to express that something is correct: *'Is this your dog?' 'It is indeed.'/'Indeed it is.'* ◦ *Yes, I did indeed say that.* **3** C2 used to add some extra information which develops or supports something you have just said: *For such creatures, speed is not important – indeed it is counterproductive.* ◦ *I am happy, indeed proud, to be associated with this project.*

▸**exclamation** used to express surprise, anger, or lack of belief or interest: *'She said she won't come back until Monday.' 'Won't she, indeed?'* ◦ *'When will we get a pay rise?' 'When indeed?'*

indefatigable /ˌɪn.dɪˈfæt.ɪ.gə.bl̩/ US /-ˈfæţ-/ adj formal always determined and energetic in trying to achieve something and never willing to admit defeat: *Annie was an indefatigable campaigner for better community services.* • **indefatigably** /-bli/ adv

indefensible /ˌɪn.dɪˈfen.sɪ.bl̩/ adj **1** too bad to be protected from criticism: *The war is **morally** indefensible.* ◦ *His opinions/attitudes are completely indefensible.* **2** not able to be protected against attack: *indefensible borders* • **indefensibly** /-bli/ adv

indefinable /ˌɪn.dɪˈfaɪ.nə.bl̩/ adj (US also **undefinable**) impossible to clearly describe or explain: *She had that indefinable something that went beyond mere sex appeal.* • **indefinably** (US also **undefinably**) /-bli/ adv *The two versions are indefinably different.*

indefinite /ɪnˈdef.ɪ.nət/ adj not exact, not clear, or without clear limits: *The project has been postponed for an indefinite **period**.* ◦ *an indefinite **number** of people*

in͵definite ˈarticle noun [C] specialized B1 the grammatical name for the words 'a' and 'an' in English or words in other languages that have a similar use → Compare **definite article**

indefinitely /ɪnˈdef.ɪ.nət.li/ adv C2 for a period of time with no fixed end: *The negotiations have been **put off/postponed** indefinitely.*

indelible /ɪnˈdel.ɪ.bl̩/ adj **1** describes a mark or substance that is impossible to remove by washing or in any other way: *indelible ink* ◦ *The blood had left an indelible **mark** on her shirt.* **2** [before noun] Indelible memories or actions are impossible to forget, or have a permanent influence or effect: *I have an indelible **memory** of that meeting with Anastasia.* ◦ *In his 20 years working for the company, Joe Pearson made an indelible **impression** on it.* • **indelibly** /-bli/ adv

indelicate /ɪnˈdel.ɪ.kət/ adj describes words or actions that are not suitable for a situation and are likely to be offensive: *an indelicate comment* ◦ *Would **it** be indelicate **to** mention the fee at this point?* • **indelicacy** /-kə.si/ noun [U]

indemnify /ɪnˈdem.nɪ.faɪ/ verb [T] to protect someone or something against possible damage or loss by paying an indemnity to cover the costs: *The insurance also indemnifies the house **against** flooding.*

indemnity /ɪnˈdem.nə.ti/ US /-ţi/ noun [C or U] formal or specialized protection against possible damage or loss, especially a promise of payment, or the money paid if there is such damage or loss

indent verb; noun

▸**verb** [T] /ɪnˈdent/ **SPACE** ▷ **1** [T] to make a space in the edge or on the surface of something: *Each new paragraph should be indented about two centimetres **from** the margin.* **REQUEST** ▷ **2** [I] UK specialized to make an official request for goods: *We indented **for** the engine spares last month.*

▸**noun** [C] /ˈɪn.dent/ **SPACE** ▷ **1** a space at the edge or on the surface of something **REQUEST** ▷ **2** an official request for goods: *We **made** an indent **for** the engine spares last week.*

indentation /ˌɪn.denˈteɪ.ʃᵊn/ noun **HOLE** ▷ **1** [C] a hole or mark on the surface of something: *The heels of her shoes had left indentations in the mud.* **SPACE** ▷ **2** [C or U] a space left at the edge of a line of writing, or the process of leaving such a space

indenture /ɪnˈden.tʃəʳ/ US /-tʃɚ/ verb [T] (in the past) to officially agree that someone, often a young person, will work for someone else, especially in order to learn a job: *The land was worked on by indentured labourers.*

independence /ˌɪn.dɪˈpen.dᵊns/ noun [U] **1** B2 freedom from being governed or ruled by another country: *Mexico **gained** its independence **from** Spain in 1821.* **2** B1 the ability to live your life without being helped or influenced by other people: *It's important that parents should allow their children some independence.*

Indeˈpendence ͵Day noun [C] **US** ▷ **1** in the US, the official name for the FOURTH OF JULY holiday **OTHER COUNTRIES** ▷ **2** a day on which a country celebrates being independent from foreign rule

independent /ˌɪn.dɪˈpen.dᵊnt/ adj **NOT INFLUENCED** ▷ **1** B2 not influenced or controlled in any way by other people, events, or things: *an independent **enquiry/organization*** ◦ *They all made the same comment, quite independent **of** each other (= without deciding together to do so).* **2** describes a politician who does not agree or vote with any particular political party **3** specialized describes a grammatical CLAUSE which forms part of a sentence but can also form a separate sentence **NOT RULED** ▷ **4** B2 An independent country is not governed or ruled by another country: *Belize became fully independent **from** Britain in 1981.* ◦ *Tibet, once an independent country, is now ruled by China.* **NOT HELPED** ▷ **5** B1 not taking help or money from other people: *Grandma's very independent and does all her own shopping and cooking.* ◦ *I've always been **financially** independent.* • **independently** /-li/ adv B2 *The two scientists both made the same discovery independently, at roughly the same time.* ◦ *Each part of the organization operates independently **of** the others.*

͵independent ˈmeans noun [plural] income which you have from INVESTMENTS, etc. rather than from a job: *As a woman **of** independent means, she spent most* *of her life in voluntary work.* ◦ *He* ***has*** *independent means.*

ˌindependent ˈschool noun [C] in the UK, a school which does not receive money from the government → Compare **public school**

ˌindependent ˈvariable noun [C] specialized a number or amount whose value does not depend on the value of another element in the same mathematical EXPRESSION (= group of symbols representing an amount or idea) → Compare **dependent variable**

ˌin-ˈdepth adj [before noun] done carefully and in great detail: *an in-depth report/interview/analysis*

indescribable /ˌɪn.dɪˈskraɪ.bə.bl̩/ adj impossible to describe, especially because of being extremely good or bad: *a scene of indescribable beauty* ◦ *The pain was indescribable.* • **indescribably** /-bli/ adv *indescribably awful*

indestructible /ˌɪn.dɪˈstrʌk.tɪ.bl̩/ adj impossible to destroy or break: *These plastic cups are* ***virtually*** *indestructible.* ◦ *Whatever the degradation, the human spirit can be indestructible.* • **indestructibility** /ˌɪn.dɪ.strʌk.tɪˈbɪl.ɪ.ti/ (US) /-ə.t̬i/ noun [U]

indeterminate /ˌɪn.dɪˈtɜː.mɪ.nət/ (US) /-ˈtɝː-/ adj not measured, counted, or clearly known: *An indeterminate* ***number*** *of workers have already been exposed to the danger.* ◦ *a man of indeterminate* ***age*** • **indeterminacy** /-nə.si/ noun [U]

index /ˈɪn.deks/ noun; verb

▸noun (plural **indices** or **indexes**) **LIST** ▷ **1** (C1) [C] an ALPHABETICAL list, such as one printed at the back of a book showing which page a subject, name, etc. is on: *Try looking up 'heart disease'* ***in*** *the index.* **2** [C] a collection of information stored on a computer or on a set of cards, in ALPHABETICAL order: *He still has all his friends' names and addresses* ***on*** *a* ***card*** *index.* **COMPARISON** ▷ **3** [C] a system of numbers used for comparing values of things which change according to each other or a fixed standard: *the FTSE 100 Index* ◦ *the Dow Jones Index* ◦ *a wage/price index* **4** [C usually singular] something which shows how strong or common a condition or feeling is: *Consumer spending is often a good index* ***of*** *public confidence in the economy.*

▸verb [T] **MAKE LIST** ▷ **1** to prepare an index for a book or collection, or arrange it in an index: *Our computer indexes several thousand new records every second.* ◦ *The book contains a lot of information, but it's not very well indexed.* **COMPARE** ▷ **2** to change a system of numbers according to each other or a fixed standard: *Living expenses will be indexed* ***to/in line with*** *inflation (= to take inflation into consideration).*

indexation /ˌɪn.dekˈseɪ.ʃən/ noun [U] a system in which the value of something changes in relation to another value or fixed standard: *Indexation of pay rises* ***to*** *productivity will give people an incentive to work harder.*

ˈindex ˌfinger noun [C] the finger next to the thumb

ˌindex-ˈlinked adj UK (US **indexed**) describes an INVESTMENT or government payment that changes by the same amount as the general level of prices: *an index-linked pension/benefit*

Indian /ˈɪn.di.ən/ noun; adj

▸noun [C] **INDIA** ▷ **1** a person from India **AMERICA** ▷ **2** offensive old-fashioned a **Native American**: *playing cowboys and Indians*

▸adj **INDIA** ▷ **1** from, belonging to, or relating to India: *an Indian family* ◦ *the Indian ambassador* **AMERICA** ▷ **2** offensive old-fashioned belonging or relating to NATIVE AMERICANS: *an Indian chief*

Indian ˈclub noun [C] an object shaped like a bottle, used especially by JUGGLERS (= performers who throw objects into the air and catch them)

ˌIndian ˈink noun [U] UK (US **ˌIndia ˈink**) a thick, black ink used especially for drawing

Indian ˈmynah noun [C] Australian English a **mynah**

Indian ˈsummer noun [C] **WEATHER** ▷ **1** a period of calm warm weather which sometimes happens in the early autumn **SUCCESSFUL TIME** ▷ **2** a pleasant or successful time nearly at the end of someone's life, job, or other period: *A star of the 1960s, she's enjoying an Indian summer with her second highly acclaimed film this year.*

indicate /ˈɪn.dɪ.keɪt/ verb **SHOW** ▷ **1** (B2) [T] to show, point, or make clear in another way: *Exploratory investigations have indicated large amounts of oil below the sea bed.* ◦ [+ question word] *Please indicate* ***which*** *free gift you would like to receive.* ◦ [+ (that)] *She indicated* ***to*** *me* ***(that)*** *she didn't want me to say anything.* **SIGNAL** ▷ **2** [I or T] UK to show other road users that you intend to turn left or right when you are driving a vehicle **3** [T] When a device indicates a value or change, it signals it: *The gauge indicates a temperature below freezing point.* **SUGGEST** ▷ **4** [T] to suggest something as being suitable: specialized *Antihistamine is indicated for this patient as a treatment for her allergies.* ◦ humorous *I'm so hot and tired – I think a long cool drink is indicated!*

indication /ˌɪn.dɪˈkeɪ.ʃən/ noun **SIGN** ▷ **1** (C1) [C or U] a sign that something exists, is true, or is likely to happen: *There are few indications* ***(that)*** *the economy is on an upswing.* ◦ *Helen's face gave no indication* ***of*** *what she was thinking.* **SUGGESTION** ▷ **2** [C] a suitable action that is suggested by something: *The indication from the trade figures is to reduce stock by at least 30 percent.*

indicative /ɪnˈdɪk.ə.tɪv/ (US) /-t̬ɪv/ adj being or relating to a sign that something exists, is true, or is likely to happen: *Resumption of the talks is indicative* ***of*** *an improving relationship between the countries.*

indicator /ˈɪn.dɪ.keɪ.təʳ/ (US) /ˈɪn.dɪ.keɪ.t̬ɚ/ noun [C] **SHOWING** ▷ **1** (C2) something that shows what a situation is like: *Commodity prices can be a useful indicator* ***of*** *inflation, he claimed.* ◦ *an economic indicator* **SIGNAL** ▷ **2** UK (US **turn signal**) one of the lights at the front and back of a road vehicle which flash to show which way the vehicle is turning **3** a device which shows a value or a change in level, speed, etc.

indices /ˈɪn.dɪ.siːz/ plural of **index**

indict /ɪnˈdaɪt/ verb [T] legal If a law court or a GRAND JURY indicts someone, it accuses them officially of a crime: UK *He was indicted* ***on*** *drug* ***charges*** *at Snaresbrook Crown Court.* ◦ US *Five people were indicted* ***for*** *mak****ing*** *and sell****ing*** *counterfeit currency.* • **indictable** /ɪnˈdaɪ.tə.bl̩/ (US) /-t̬ə-/ adj *Robbery is an indictable* ***offence****.*

indictment /ɪnˈdaɪt.mənt/ noun **1** [C usually singular] a reason for giving blame: *This seems to me to be a* ***damning*** *indictment* ***of*** *education policy.* **2** [C] legal a formal statement of accusing someone: *The charges on the indictment include murder and attempted murder.*

indie /ˈɪn.di/ adj; noun

▸adj describes music or films made by small companies that are not owned by larger companies: *an indie movie/film/record label* ◦ *The popularity of indie bands has soared in recent years.*

▸noun [C] **1** a small music, film, or television company that is not owned by a larger company **2** a film or recording made by a small company that is not owned by a larger company

indifference /ɪnˈdɪf.ər.əns/, /-rəns/ US /-ɚ-/ **noun** [U] C2 lack of interest in someone or something: *Many native speakers of a language show indifference* ***to/towards*** *grammatical points.* ◦ *His attitude was one of bored indifference.*

indifferent /ɪnˈdɪf.ər.ənt/, /-rənt/ US /-ɚ-/ **adj** NOT INTERESTED ▷ **1** C2 not thinking about or interested in someone or something: *Why don't you vote – how can you be so indifferent (****to*** *what is going on)!* ◦ *He found it very hard teaching a class full of indifferent teenagers.* NOT GOOD ▷ **2** not good, but not very bad: *We didn't like the restaurant much – the food was indifferent and the service rather slow.* • **indifferently** /-li/ **adv** *She shrugged indifferently.*

indigenous /ɪnˈdɪdʒ.ɪ.nəs/ **adj** naturally existing in a place or country rather than arriving from another place: *Are there any species of frog indigenous* ***to*** *the area?* ◦ *So who are the indigenous people of this land?*

Inˌdigenous ˈPeople's ˌDay **noun** a US holiday on the second Monday of October when people in some states celebrate the Native Americans → See also **Columbus Day**

indigent /ˈɪn.dɪ.dʒənt/ **adj** formal very poor • **indigence** /-dʒəns/ **noun** [U]

indigestible /ˌɪn.dɪˈdʒes.tɪ.bl̩/ **adj** FOOD ▷ **1** describes food that is difficult or impossible for the stomach to break down: *a tough and indigestible piece of steak* INFORMATION ▷ **2** disapproving describes information that is difficult or impossible to understand: *The statistics are virtually indigestible presented in this form.* • **indigestibility** /ˌɪn.dɪ.dʒes.tɪˈbɪl.ɪ.ti/ US /-ə.t̬i/ **noun** [U]

indigestion /ˌɪn.dɪ.dʒes.tʃən/ **noun** [U] pain that you get in your stomach when you have eaten food that is difficult to digest: *Do you* ***suffer from*** *indigestion after you have eaten?* ◦ *You'll give yourself indigestion if you swallow your dinner so quickly.*

indignant /ɪnˈdɪg.nənt/ **adj** angry because of something that is wrong or not fair: *She wrote an indignant letter to the paper complaining about the council's action.* ◦ *He became very indignant when it was suggested he had made a mistake.* • **indignantly** /-li/ **adv** *'I said no such thing!' she cried indignantly.*

indignation /ˌɪn.dɪgˈneɪ.ʃən/ **noun** [U] anger about a situation that you think is wrong or not fair

indignity /ɪnˈdɪg.nɪ.ti/ US /-nə.t̬i/ **noun** [C or U] something that causes a loss of respect for someone or for yourself: *They were subjected to various indignities and discomforts, including having to get dressed and undressed in public.* ◦ *Clint* ***suffered*** *the indignity of being called 'Puppy' in front of his girlfriend.*

indigo /ˈɪn.dɪ.gəʊ/ US /-goʊ/ **noun** [U] a bluish-purple colour • **indigo adj** having a bluish-purple colour

indirect /ˌɪn.daɪˈrekt/, /-dɪ-/ **adj** NOT OBVIOUS ▷ **1** C2 happening in addition to an intended result, often in a way that is complicated or not obvious: *The benefits from pure research are often indirect.* ◦ *Indirect effects of the fighting include disease and food shortages.* **2** avoiding clearly mentioning or saying something: *indirect criticism* NOT STRAIGHT ▷ **3** C1 not following a straight line, or not directly or simply connected: *to take an indirect route/flight* • **indirectly** /-li/ **adv** C1 *She still controls the company indirectly through her son, who is the managing director.*

ˌindirect ˈcost **noun** [C] an amount of money spent by a business on things other than the products they make

ˌindirect ˈobject **noun** [C] specialized the person or thing that receives the effect of the action of a verb with two objects: *In the sentence 'Give Val some money', 'Val' is the indirect object.* → See also **object**

ˌindirect ˈquestion **noun** [C] specialized a question that is reported to other people in speech or writing, rather than the exact words of the original question, for example 'He asked me what was wrong.'

ˌindirect ˈspeech **noun** [U] (UK also **reˌported ˈspeech**, US also **ˌindirect ˈdiscourse**) the act of reporting something that was said, but not using exactly the same words → Compare **direct speech**

ˌindirect ˈtax **noun** [C] **1** UK a tax charged on goods and services rather than on the money that people earn → Compare **direct tax** **2** US a tax charged on goods before they reach their final buyer • **ˌindirect taxˈation** **noun** [U]

indiscernible /ˌɪn.dɪˈsɜː.nɪ.bl̩/ US /-ˈsɝː-/ **adj** impossible to see, see clearly, or understand: *an indiscernible change/shape/reason*

indiscipline /ɪnˈdɪs.ə.plɪn/ **noun** [U] formal a situation in which people do not control their behaviour or obey rules: *The school was given three months to sort out the problem of indiscipline.*

indiscreet /ˌɪn.dɪˈskriːt/ **adj** saying or doing things which tell people things that should be secret or which embarrass people: *In an indiscreet moment, the president let his genuine opinions be known.* ◦ *They have been rather indiscreet* ***about*** *their affair.* • **indiscreetly** /-li/ **adv**

indiscretion /ˌɪn.dɪˈskreʃ.ən/ **noun** **1** [U] the quality of being indiscreet: *Jones was censured for indiscretion in leaking a secret report to the press.* **2** [C] something, especially a sexual relationship, that is considered embarrassing or morally wrong: *We should forgive him a few* ***youthful*** *indiscretions.*

indiscriminate /ˌɪn.dɪˈskrɪm.ɪ.nət/ **adj** not showing careful thought or planning, especially so that harm results: *an indiscriminate terrorist attack on civilians* ◦ *The indiscriminate use of fertilizers can cause long-term problems.* • **indiscriminately** /-li/ **adv** *They fired indiscriminately into the crowd.*

indispensable /ˌɪn.dɪˈspen.sə.bl̩/ **adj** C2 Something or someone that is indispensable is so good or important that you could not manage without them: *This book is an indispensable resource for researchers.* ◦ *His long experience at the United Nations makes him indispensable* ***to*** *the talks.* • **indispensability** /ˌɪn.dɪ.spen.sɪˈbɪl.ɪ.ti/ US /-ə.t̬i/ **noun** [U]

indisposed /ˌɪn.dɪˈspəʊzd/ US /-ˈspoʊzd/ **adj** formal ILL ▷ **1** ill, especially in a way that makes you unable to do something: *Sheila Jones is indisposed, so the part of the Countess will be sung tonight by Della Drake.* NOT WILLING ▷ **2** [after verb + to, infinitive] not willing: *After their rude attitude in the past, we feel distinctly indisposed* ***to*** *help them now.*

indisposition /ˌɪn.dɪs.pəˈzɪʃ.ən/ **noun** [C or U] formal the fact that someone is unable to do something because they are ill or not willing: *an indisposition* ***to*** *cooperate*

indisputable /ˌɪn.dɪˈspjuː.tə.bl̩/ US /-t̬ə-/ **adj** C2 true, and impossible to doubt: *an artist of indisputable skill* ◦ *One fact is indisputable – this must never be allowed to happen again.* • **indisputably** /-bli/ **adv** *Segovia, she said, was indisputably the finest guitar player of the 20th century.*

indissoluble /ˌɪn.dɪˈsɒl.jʊ.bl̩/ US /-ˈsɑːl.jə-/ **adj** impossible to take apart or bring to an end, or existing for a very long time: *an indissoluble bond of friendship* • **indissolubly** /-bli/ adv • **indissolubility** /ˌɪn.dɪ.sɒl.jʊˈbɪl.ɪ.ti/ Ⓤⓢ /-ˌsɑːl.jəˈbɪl.ə.t̬i/ noun [U]

indistinct /ˌɪn.dɪˈstɪŋkt/ adj not clear: *an indistinct shape/sound/recollection* → Compare **distinct** • **indistinctly** /-li/ adv

indistinguishable /ˌɪn.dɪˈstɪŋ.gwɪ.ʃə.bl̩/ adj impossible to judge as being different when compared to another similar thing: *These forgeries are so good that they are more or less indistinguishable* ***from*** *the originals.*

individual /ˌɪn.dɪˈvɪd.ju.əl/ noun; adj

▸noun [C] **SINGLE** ▷ **1** B2 a single person or thing, especially when compared to the group or set to which they belong: *Every individual has rights which must never be taken away.* ◦ *Like many creative individuals, she can be very bad-tempered.* ◦ *We try to treat our students as individuals.* **DIFFERENT** ▷ **2** C2 a person who thinks or behaves in their own original way: *If nothing else, the school will turn her into an individual.*

▸adj **SINGLE** ▷ **1** B1 [before noun] existing and considered separately from the other things or people in a group: *Each individual table is finished by hand.* **2** B1 [before noun] given to or relating to a single, separate person or thing: *We deal with each case on an individual basis.* **DIFFERENT** ▷ **3** belonging or relating to, or suitable for, people or things that are different or particular in some way: *children with individual needs* ◦ *Marion has a very individual writing style.*

individualism /ˌɪn.dɪˈvɪd.ju.ə.lɪ.zᵊm/ noun [U] **DIFFERENT** ▷ the quality of being different or original • **individualistic** /ˌɪn.dɪˌvɪd.ju.əˈlɪs.tɪk/ Ⓤⓢ /-t̬ɪk/ adj *Her approach is highly individualistic and may not be suitable for everyone.* • **individualistically** /ˌɪn.dɪ.vɪd.ju.əˈlɪs.tɪ.kᵊl.i/ Ⓤⓢ /-t̬ɪ-/ adv

individualist /ˌɪn.dɪˈvɪd.ju.ə.lɪst/ noun [C] someone who is different or original • **individualist** adj

individuality /ˌɪn.dɪ.vɪd.juˈæl.ə.ti/ Ⓤⓢ /-t̬i/ noun [U] C2 the qualities that make a person or thing different from others: *It's a competent essay but it* ***lacks*** *individuality.*

individualized mainly US (UK usually **individualised**) /ˌɪn.dɪˈvɪd.ju.ə.laɪzd/ adj prepared or suitable for individual people: *The hospital gives individualized care/attention/treatment to all its patients.*

individually /ˌɪn.dɪˈvɪd.ju.ə.li/ adv **SINGLE** ▷ **1** C2 separately: *The children will first sing individually and then as a group.* **DIFFERENT** ▷ **2** in a different and usually original way

indivisible /ˌɪn.dɪˈvɪz.ɪ.bl̩/ adj not able to be separated from something else or into different parts: *He regards e-commerce as an indivisible* ***part*** *of modern retail.* ◦ *A country's language is indivisible* ***from*** *its culture.* • **indivisibly** /-bli/ adv • **indivisibility** /ˌɪn.dɪ.vɪz.ɪˈbɪl.ɪ.ti/ Ⓤⓢ /-ə.t̬i/ noun [U]

Indo- /ɪn.dəʊ-/ prefix of or connected with India: *Indo-European languages* ◦ *the Indo-Chinese border*

indoctrinate /ɪnˈdɒk.trɪ.neɪt/ Ⓤⓢ /-ˈdɑːk-/ verb [T] disapproving to often repeat an idea or belief to someone in order to persuade them to accept it: *Some parents were critical of attempts to indoctrinate children* ***in*** *green ideology.* ◦ *They have been indoctrinated by television to believe that violence is normal.* • **indoctrination** /ɪnˌdɒk.trɪˈneɪ.ʃᵊn/ Ⓤⓢ /-ˌdɑːk-/ noun [U] *religious/political/ideological indoctrination*

indolent /ˈɪn.dᵊl.ᵊn/ adj literary showing no real interest or effort: *an indolent wave of the hand* ◦ *an indolent reply* → Synonym **lazy** • **indolently** /-li/ adv

• **indolence** /ˈɪn.dᵊl.ᵊns/ noun [U] *After a sudden burst of activity, the team lapsed back into indolence.*

indomitable /ɪnˈdɒm.ɪ.tə.bl̩/ Ⓤⓢ /-ˈdɑː.mə.t̬ə-/ adj describes someone strong, brave, determined, and difficult to defeat or frighten: *The indomitable Mrs Furlong said she would continue to fight for justice.* • **indomitably** /-bli/ adv *indomitably cheerful* ◦ *to fight indomitably*

indoor /ˌɪnˈdɔːʳ/ Ⓤⓢ /-ˈdɔːr/ adj [before noun] A2 happening, used, or existing inside a building: *indoor sports/activities* ◦ *an indoor racetrack/swimming pool* → Opposite **outdoor**

indoors /ˌɪnˈdɔːz/ Ⓤⓢ /-ˈdɔːrz/ adv B1 into or inside a building: *Come indoors, it's cold outside.* ◦ *Spring bulbs can be grown indoors.*

indubitable /ɪnˈdjuː.bɪ.tə.bl̩/ Ⓤⓢ /-ˈduː.bɪ.t̬ə-/ adj formal that cannot be doubted: *an indubitable fact* • **indubitably** /-bli/ adv *He looked different, but it was indubitably John.*

induce /ɪnˈdjuːs/ Ⓤⓢ /-ˈduːs/ verb formal **PERSUADE** ▷ **1** [T + obj + to infinitive] to persuade someone to do something: *They induced her* ***to*** *take the job by promising editorial freedom.* ◦ ***Nothing could*** *induce me (= I definitely cannot be persuaded) to climb a mountain/ride a bike.* **CAUSE** ▷ **2** [T] to cause something to happen: *Pills for seasickness often induce drowsiness.* **3** [T] to use a drug to make a pregnant woman start giving birth: *In this hospital, twins are often induced.*

-induced /-in.djuːst/ Ⓤⓢ /-duːst/ suffix caused by the stated person or activity: *a self-induced illness* ◦ *work-induced stress*

inducement /ɪnˈdjuːs.mᵊnt/ Ⓤⓢ /-ˈduːs-/ noun [C or U] an act or thing that is intended to persuade someone or something: ***financial/cash*** *inducements* ◦ *Those tenants are not going to swap life-time security for shorter-term leases without some inducement.* ◦ [+ to infinitive] *They offered voters a massive inducement* ***to*** *oust the president by announcing that sanctions would be lifted if there was 'democratic change'.*

induct /ɪnˈdʌkt/ verb [T] formal to introduce someone formally or with a special ceremony to an organization or group, or to beliefs or ideas: *Li Xiannian was inducted* ***into*** *the Politburo in 1956.*

induction /ɪnˈdʌk.ʃᵊn/ noun **INTRODUCTION** ▷ **1** [C or U] an occasion when someone is formally introduced into a new job or organization, especially through a special ceremony: *Their induction* ***into*** *the church took place in June.* ◦ *Her induction* ***as*** *councillor took place in the town hall.* ◦ *an induction course/program/ceremony* **CAUSING** ▷ **2** [U] formal the act of causing an event or process to happen: *the induction* ***of labour*** **THINKING** ▷ **3** [U] specialized the process of discovering a general principle from a set of facts **ELECTRICITY** ▷ **4** [U] specialized an occasion when electrical power goes from one object to another without the objects touching: *an induction coil/motor*

inductive /ɪnˈdʌk.tɪv/ adj specialized using a particular set of facts or ideas to form a general principle: *inductive reasoning* • **inductively** /-li/ adv specialized

indulge /ɪnˈdʌldʒ/ verb **1** C2 [I or T] to allow yourself or another person to have something enjoyable, especially more than is good for you: *The soccer fans indulged their patriotism, waving flags and singing songs.* ◦ *I love champagne but I don't often indulge* ***myself.*** ◦ *We took a deliberate decision to indulge* ***in*** *a little nostalgia.* **2** [T] to give someone anything they want and not to mind if they behave badly: *My aunt indulges the children dreadfully.*

indulgence /ɪnˈdʌl.dʒəns/ noun **1** [C or U] an occasion when you allow someone or yourself to have something enjoyable, especially more than is good for you: *Chocolate is my only indulgence.* ◦ *All the pleasures and indulgences of the weekend are over, and I must get down to some serious hard work.* ◦ *His health suffered from **over**-indulgence **in** (= too much) rich food and drink.* → See also **self-indulgence (self-indulgent) 2** [U] an occasion when you allow or do not mind someone's failure or bad behaviour: *My inability to do needlework was treated with surprising indulgence by my teacher.*

indulgent /ɪnˈdʌl.dʒənt/ adj allowing someone to have or do what they want, especially when this is not good for them: *indulgent relatives* ◦ *an indulgent smile* ◦ *He had been a strict father but was indulgent **to/towards** his grandchildren.* • **indulgently** /-li/ adv

industrial /ɪnˈdʌs.tri.əl/ adj; noun
▸adj B2 in or related to industry, or having a lot of industry and factories, etc.: *industrial output* ◦ *industrial expansion* ◦ *an industrial landscape/nation* ◦ *He has an industrial background (= he has worked in industry).* • **industrially** /-ə.li/ adv
▸noun specialized **1** [C] a company whose main business is producing goods: *He owns a series of industrials across the US and beyond.* **2 industrials** [plural noun] shares in industrial companies: *On Thursday the industrials moved up more than 50 points.* ◦ *Industrials were up 1.2 percent at the close of trading.*

inˌdustrial ˈaction noun [U] an occasion when workers do something that is intended to force an employer to agree to something, especially by stopping work: *Workers at the plant are **threatening** industrial action.*

inˌdustrial ˈespionage noun [U] an occasion when one company steals secrets from another company with which it is competing

inˌdustrial esˈtate noun [C] UK (US **inˈdustrial ˌpark**) a special area on the edge of a town where there are a lot of factories and businesses

industrialism /ɪnˈdʌs.tri.ə.lɪ.zᵊm/ noun [U] the idea or state of having a country's economy, society, or political system based on industry

industrialist /ɪnˈdʌs.tri.ə.lɪst/ noun [C] an owner or an employee in a high position in industry

industrialization (UK usually **industrialisation**) /ɪnˌdʌs.tri.ə.laɪˈzeɪ.ʃᵊn/ US /-ləˈ-/ noun [U] C1 the process of developing industries in a country

industrialize (UK usually **industrialise**) /ɪnˈdʌs.tri.ə.laɪz/ verb [I or T] to develop industry: *It was the first country to industrialize.*

industrialized (UK usually **industrialised**) /ɪnˈdʌs.tri.ə.laɪzd/ adj C1 having developed a lot of industry: *industrialized nations/countries*

inˌdustrial reˈlations noun [plural] the relationships between companies and their workers

the Inˌdustrial Revoˈlution noun [S] the period of time during which work began to be done more by machines in factories than by hand at home

industrial-strength /ɪnˈdʌs.tri.əlˌstreŋθ/ adj **1** If a product is industrial strength, it is much stronger or more powerful than the product normally available to use: *an industrial-strength cleaner* **2** humorous extremely strong, or greater than necessary: *She arrived in a cloud of industrial-strength perfume.*

inˌdustrial triˈbunal noun [C] a type of law court that makes judgements on disagreements between companies and their workers

industrious /ɪnˈdʌs.tri.əs/ adj C2 describes a person who works hard: *an industrious worker* ◦ *She's extremely competent and industrious.* • **industriously** /-li/ adv *Marco was working industriously at his desk.* • **industriousness** /-nəs/ noun [U]

> Word partners for **industry**
>
> a *booming/important/major/thriving* industry • an industry *booms/grows* • an *area/sector* of industry • *in* an industry

industry /ˈɪn.də.stri/ noun **PRODUCTION** ▷ **1** B2 [U] the companies and activities involved in the process of producing goods for sale, especially in a factory or special area: *trade and industry* ◦ *industry and commerce* ◦ *The city needs to attract more industry.* ◦ *The strike seriously reduced coal deliveries to industry.* **TYPE OF WORK** ▷ **2** B1 [C] the people and activities involved in one type of business: *the gas/electricity industry* ◦ *the tourist industry* ◦ *manufacturing industries* ◦ *The computer industry has been booming.* **3** [C] disapproving something that is produced or is available in large quantities and makes a lot of money: *the heritage industry* **QUALITY** ▷ **4** [U] formal the quality of regularly working hard: *I must say that I'm very impressed by her industry.*

ˌindustryˈ-wide adj, adv happening or existing in all or most parts of a particular type of business: *an industry-wide practice* ◦ *Similar changes are happening industry-wide.*

inebriated /ɪˈniː.bri.eɪ.tɪd/ US /-t̬ɪd/ adj formal having drunk too much alcohol: *In her inebriated state, she was ready to agree to anything.* • **inebriation** /ɪˌniː.briˈeɪ.ʃᵊn/ noun [U] formal *He was in an advanced state of inebriation.*

inedible /ɪˈned.ɪ.bl̩/ adj C1 not suitable as food: *The meat was inedible.*

ineffable /ɪˈnef.ə.bl̩/ adj formal causing so much emotion, especially pleasure, that it cannot be described: *ineffable joy/beauty*

ineffective /ˌɪn.ɪˈfek.tɪv/ adj not producing the effects or results that are wanted: *They made an ineffective attempt to get the rules changed.* ◦ *The army has **proved** ineffective in protecting the civilian population.* • **ineffectively** /-li/ adv

ineffectual /ˌɪn.ɪˈfek.tju.ᵊl/ adj formal not skilled at achieving, or not able to produce, good results: *an ineffectual leader* ◦ *The teachers were ineffectual **at** maintaining discipline.* • **ineffectually** /-i/ adv

inefficient /ˌɪn.ɪˈfɪʃ.ᵊnt/ adj C1 not organized, skilled, or able to work in a satisfactory way: *Existing methods of production are expensive and inefficient.* ◦ *I'm hopelessly inefficient **at** mending things.* • **inefficiently** /-li/ adv *The hotel is inefficiently run.* • **inefficiency** /-ᵊn.si/ noun [C or U] *They were accused of **gross** inefficiency in their handling of the case.*

inelegant /ɪˈnel.ɪ.gᵊnt/ adj not attractive: *an inelegant posture* ◦ *inelegant surroundings*

ineligible /ɪˈnel.ɪ.dʒə.bl̩/ adj not allowed to do or have something, according to particular rules: *He was **declared** ineligible **for** the competition because he worked for the company that ran it.* ◦ *Many people became ineligible **to** receive state aid because their earnings were above the new limit.* • **ineligibility** /ɪˌnel.ɪ.dʒəˈbɪl.ɪ.ti/ US /-t̬i/ noun [U]

inept /ɪˈnept/ adj not skilled or effective: *an inept **comment/remark*** ◦ *He was always rather inept **at** sport.* ◦ *He was criticized for his inept **handling** of the situation.* ◦ *Dick was **socially** inept and uncomfortable in the presence of women.* • **ineptitude** /ɪˈnep.tɪ.tjuːd/

US /-t̬ɪ.tuːd/ **noun** [U] *political/social/economic ineptitude*

inequality /ˌɪn.ɪˈkwɒl.ə.ti/ US /-ˈkwɑː.lə.t̬i/ **noun** [C or U] C2 the unfair situation in society when some people have more opportunities, money, etc. than other people: *The law has done little to prevent racial discrimination and inequality.* ◦ ***sexual** inequality* ◦ *There remain major inequalities of opportunity in the workplace.*

inequitable /ɪˈnek.wɪ.tə.bl̩/ US /-wə.t̬ə-/ **adj** formal not fair: *The current healthcare system is inequitable and unjust, with huge disparities between rich and poor.* • **inequity** /ɪˈnek.wɪ.ti/ US /-t̬i/ **noun** [C or U] the fact that a situation is not fair: *inequities in the health care system*

ineradicable /ˌɪn.ɪˈræd.ɪ.kə.bl̩/ **adj** formal not able to be removed: *Some experiences in early life have ineradicable effects.*

inert /ɪˈnɜːt/ US /-ˈnɝːt/ **adj** **NOT MOVING** ▷ **1** not moving or not able to move: *The inert figure of a man could be seen lying in the front of the car.* **CHEMICAL** ▷ **2** specialized Inert substances do not produce a chemical reaction when another substance is added: *inert **gases*** • **inertly** /-li/ **adv**

inertia /ɪˈnɜː.ʃə/ US /-ˈnɝː-/ **noun** [U] **LACK OF ACTIVITY** ▷ **1** lack of activity or interest, or unwillingness to make an effort to do anything: *The organization is stifled by bureaucratic inertia.* **FORCE** ▷ **2** specialized the physical force that keeps something in the same position or moving in the same direction

inˈertia ˌselling **noun** [U] UK the act of sending products to people who have not asked for them, and then demanding payment

inescapable /ˌɪn.ɪˈskeɪ.pə.bl̩/ **adj** If a fact or a situation is inescapable, it cannot be ignored or avoided. • **inescapably** /-bli/ **adv** *We are inescapably conditioned by our upbringing.*

inessential /ˌɪn.ɪˈsen.ʃəl/ **adj** not necessary: *make-up and other inessential items* • **inessential** **noun** [C usually plural] something that is not necessary: *There's very little space for inessentials.*

inestimable /ɪˈnes.tɪ.mə.bl̩/ **adj** formal extremely great, or too great to be described or expressed exactly: *The medical importance of this discovery is **of** inestimable value.* • **inestimably** /-bli/ **adv**

inevitable /ɪˈnev.ɪ.tə.bl̩/ US /-t̬ə-/ **adj** **1** C1 certain to happen and unable to be avoided or prevented: *The accident was the inevitable consequence/result/outcome of carelessness.* **2 the inevitable** something that is certain to happen and cannot be prevented: *Eventually the inevitable happened and he had a heart attack.* • **inevitability** /ɪˌnev.ɪ.təˈbɪl.ɪ.ti/ US /-t̬əˈbɪl.ə.t̬i/ **noun** [U] *the inevitability of change*

inevitably /ɪˈnev.ɪ.tə.bli/ US /-t̬ə-/ **adv** C1 in a way that cannot be avoided: *Their arguments inevitably end in tears.*

inexact /ˌɪn.ɪɡˈzækt/ **adj** not exact or not known in detail: *Estimates of the numbers involved remain inexact.*

inexcusable /ˌɪn.ɪkˈskjuː.zə.bl̩/ **adj** (of behaviour) too bad to be accepted: *His drunken outbursts during the mayor's speech were inexcusable.* ◦ ***It's** inexcusable **that** such young children were left in the house alone.* • **inexcusably** /-bli/ **adv**

inexhaustible /ˌɪn.ɪɡˈzɔː.stɪ.bl̩/ US /-ˈzɑː-/ **adj** existing in very great amounts that will never be finished: *There seemed to be an inexhaustible **supply** of champagne at the wedding.*

inexorable /ɪˈnek.sər.ə.bl̩/ US /-sɚ-/ **adj** formal continuing without any possibility of being stopped: *the inexorable progress of science* • **inexorably** /-bli/ **adv** *These events led inexorably to war.* • **inexorability** /ɪˌnek.sər.əˈbɪl.ɪ.ti/ US /-sɚ.əˈbɪl.ə.t̬i/ **noun** [U]

inexpedient /ˌɪn.ɪkˈspiː.di.ənt/ **adj** [+ to infinitive] formal not suitable or convenient: ***It** was inexpedient **for** him **to** be seen to approve of the decision.*

inexpensive /ˌɪn.ɪkˈspen.sɪv/ **adj** B1 not costing a lot of money: *It's an inexpensive perfume.*

inexperience /ˌɪn.ɪkˈspɪə.ri.əns/ US /-ˈspɪr.i-/ **noun** [U] lack of knowledge or experience: *As a leader, he's been criticized for his inexperience **in** foreign affairs.*

inexperienced /ˌɪn.ɪkˈspɪə.ri.ənst/ US /-ˈspɪr.i-/ **adj** B2 having little knowledge or experience: *They are young inexperienced parents and need support.*

inexpert /ɪˈnek.spɜːt/ US /-spɝːt/ **adj** having little skill: *She had made an inexpert attempt to repair the car.* • **inexpertly** /-li/ **adv**

inexplicable /ˌɪn.ɪkˈsplɪk.ə.bl̩/ **adj** C2 unable to be explained or understood: *For some inexplicable reason, he's decided to cancel the project.* • **inexplicably** /-bli/ **adv** *Inexplicably, the men were never questioned about where the explosives came from.*

inexpressible /ˌɪn.ɪkˈspres.ɪ.bl̩/ **adj** describes a feeling that is too strong to be described: *The news filled him with inexpressible delight/joy/horror/pain.* • **inexpressibly** /-bli/ **adv** *The jokes were inexpressibly awful.*

inexpressive /ˌɪn.ɪkˈspres.ɪv/ **adj** showing no feelings: *Although the shock must have been great, her face remained inexpressive.*

inextinguishable /ˌɪn.ɪkˈstɪŋ.ɡwɪ.ʃə.bl̩/ **adj** unable to be stopped from burning or existing

in extremis /ˌɪn.ɪkˈstriː.mɪs/, /-ekˈstreɪ-/ **adv** **1** formal in an extremely difficult situation: *I'll only ask the bank for a loan in extremis.* **2** specialized at the moment of death

inextricable /ˌɪn.ɪkˈstrɪk.ə.bl̩/ **adj** unable to be separated, released, or escaped from: *In the case of King Arthur, legend and truth are often inextricable.* • **inextricably** /-bli/ **adv** *His name was inextricably **linked** with the environmental movement.*

infallible /ɪnˈfæl.ɪ.bl̩/ **adj** never wrong, failing, or making a mistake: *Even the experts are not infallible.* • **infallibility** /ɪnˌfæl.əˈbɪl.ɪ.ti/ US /-ə.t̬i/ **noun** [U]

infallibly /ɪnˈfæl.ɪ.bli/ **adv** always: *He's infallibly cheerful, despite his difficulties.*

infamous /ˈɪn.fə.məs/ **adj** famous for something considered bad: *The list included the infamous George Drake, a double murderer.* ◦ *He's infamous **for** his bigoted sense of humour.*

infamy /ˈɪn.fə.mi/ **noun** formal **1** [U] the quality of being famous for something considered bad: *The president described the attack as 'a day that will live in infamy'.* **2** [C] a bad and shocking act or event

infancy /ˈɪn.fən.si/ **noun** [U] **1** C2 the time when someone is a baby or a very young child: *Her youngest child died **in** infancy.* **2 be in its infancy** C2 to be very new and still developing: *The system is still in its infancy.*

infant /ˈɪn.fənt/ **noun; adj**

▸**noun** **YOUNG CHILD** ▷ **1** C2 [C] a baby or a very young child: *a **newborn** infant* **SCHOOL** ▷ **2** [C] UK a student at an INFANT SCHOOL: *Jenny is a top-year infant now.* **3 the infants** [plural] UK **infant school**: *Andrew's still **in** the infants.*

▸**adj** UK related to or connected with the first stage of school in the UK, for children aged four to seven years: *an infant teacher/class* → See also **junior school**

ˈinfant ˌformula noun [U] US for **baby milk**

infanticide /ɪnˈfæn.tɪ.saɪd/ US /-t̬ə-/ noun [U] formal the crime of killing a child

infantile /ˈɪn.fən.taɪl/ US /-tᵊl/ adj disapproving typical of a child and therefore unsuitable for an adult: *infantile behaviour*

infantilize (also **infantilise**) /ɪnˈfæn.tɪ.laɪz/ verb [T] UK usually disapproving to treat someone as if they are a child so that they start behaving like one: *He argues that giving money to the poor infantilizes them and stops them from helping themselves.*

infantry /ˈɪn.fən.tri/ noun [U, + sing/pl verb] the part of an army that fights on foot: *The infantry was/were sent into battle.* ◦ *It's a* ***light/heavy*** *infantry unit.* → Compare **cavalry**

infantryman /ˈɪn.fən.tri.mən/, /-mæn/ noun [C] (plural **-men** /-mən/, /-men/) a soldier who fights on foot

ˈinfant ˌschool noun [C] (also **the infants**) in the UK, a school or part of a school for children who are four to seven years old: *Erik starts infant school in September.*

infatuated /ɪnˈfæt.ju.eɪ.tɪd/ US /-t̬ɪd/ adj having a very strong but not usually lasting feeling of love or ATTRACTION for someone or something: *She was infatuated* ***with*** *her boss.*

infatuation /ɪnˌfæt.juˈeɪ.ʃᵊn/ noun [C or U] strong but not usually lasting feelings of love or ATTRACTION: *It's just an infatuation. She'll get over it.* ◦ *No one expected their infatuation* ***with*** *each other to last.*

infeasible /ɪnˈfiː.zɪ.bl̩/ adj US for **unfeasible**

infect /ɪnˈfekt/ verb [T] **DISEASE** ▷ **1** C1 to pass a disease to a person, animal, or plant: *The ward was full of children infected* ***with*** *TB.* ◦ *All the tomato plants are infected with a virus.* **2** C2 If a place, wound, or substance is infected, it contains bacteria or other things that can cause disease: *The meat had been infected by E. coli bacteria.* **FEELING** ▷ **3** to make someone have the same feeling or emotion as you: *Her optimism seemed to infect all those around her.* **COMPUTERS** ▷ **4** C1 to pass harmful programs from one computer to another, or within files in the same computer: *A computer virus may lurk unseen in a computer's memory, calling up and infecting each of the machine's data files in turn.*

infected /ɪnˈfek.tɪd/ adj **DISEASE** ▷ **1** containing bacteria or other things that can cause disease: *an infected wound/cut* ◦ *After the operation the wound became infected.* **COMPUTER** ▷ **2** An infected computer file contains a computer VIRUS (= a program that can harm computers and their files).

infection /ɪnˈfek.ʃᵊn/ noun [C or U] **DISEASE** ▷ **1** B2 a disease in a part of your body that is caused by bacteria or a virus: *a serious infection* ◦ *a throat infection* ◦ *Bandage the wound to reduce the* ***risk of*** *infection.* **COMPUTERS** ▷ **2** an act of passing harmful programs into a computer or file, or the harmful programs themselves: *You only have to open an attachment to pass the infection from computer to computer.*

infectious /ɪnˈfek.ʃəs/ adj **1** C2 able to pass a disease from one person, animal, or plant to another: *an infectious disease/patient* **2** C2 describes something that has an effect on everyone who is present and makes them want to join in: *an infectious laugh* ◦ *infectious enthusiasm*

infelicitous /ˌɪn.fəˈlɪs.ɪ.təs/ US /-t̬əs/ adj formal not suitable for the occasion: *an infelicitous remark* → Synonym **unfortunate** • **infelicity** /-ɪ.ti/ US /-ə.t̬i/ noun [C usually plural] formal *His article was full of mistakes and verbal infelicities (= unsuitable expressions).*

infer /ɪnˈfɜːʳ/ US /-ˈfɝː/ verb [T] (**-rr-**) formal C2 to form an opinion or guess that something is true because of the information that you have: *What do you infer* ***from*** *her refusal?* ◦ [+ that] *I inferred* ***from*** *her expression* ***that*** *she wanted to leave.*

inference /ˈɪn.fᵊr.ᵊns/ US /-fɚ-/ noun [C or U] formal a guess that you make or an opinion that you form based on the information that you have: *They were warned to expect a heavy air attack and* ***by*** *inference many casualties.* ◦ *His change of mind was recent and sudden, the inference being that someone had persuaded him.*

inferior /ɪnˈfɪə.ri.əʳ/ US /-ˈfɪr.i.ɚ/ adj; noun

▸adj **1** C1 not good, or not as good as someone or something else: *These products are inferior* ***to*** *those we bought last year.* ◦ *She cited cases in which women had received inferior healthcare.* ◦ *It was clear the group were regarded as* ***intellectually/morally/socially*** *inferior.* → Compare **superior 2** specialized lower, or of lower rank: *an inferior officer* → Compare **superior** • **inferiority** /ɪnˌfɪə.riˈɒr.ə.ti/ US /-ˌfɪr.iˈɔːr.ə.t̬i/ noun [U] C2 *His ill treatment as a child had given him a strong* ***sense of*** *inferiority.* → Compare **superiority**

▸noun [C] C2 someone who is considered to be less important than other people: *He regarded most men as his social, moral, and intellectual inferiors.*

inferiˈority ˌcomplex noun [C] a feeling that you are not as good, as intelligent, as attractive, etc. as other people: *He's always had an inferiority complex* ***about*** *his height.*

infernal /ɪnˈfɜː.nəl/ US /-ˈfɝː-/ adj **1** [before noun] old-fashioned very bad or unpleasant: *What an infernal* ***noise!*** **2** having the qualities of HELL (= place to which someone people believe bad people go after death): *He described a journey through the infernal world.*

inferno /ɪnˈfɜː.nəʊ/ US /-ˈfɝː.noʊ/ noun [C] (plural **infernos**) a very large uncontrolled fire: *a raging inferno* ◦ *The building was an inferno by the time the fire service arrived.*

infertile /ɪnˈfɜː.taɪl/ US /-ˈfɝː.tᵊl/ adj **1** An infertile person, animal, or plant cannot have babies, produce young, or produce new plants: *It has been estimated that one in eight couples is infertile.* **2** Infertile land or soil is not good enough for plants or crops to grow well there: *Poor farmers have little option but to try to grow food on these infertile* ***soils.*** • **infertility** /ˌɪn.fəˈtɪl.ɪ.ti/ US /-fɚˈtɪl.ə.t̬i/ noun [U] ***male/female*** *infertility*

inferˈtility ˌclinic noun [C] a special building or part of a hospital where people go to get medical treatment or advice when they are unable to produce children

infest /ɪnˈfest/ verb [T] (of animals and insects which carry disease) to cause a problem by being present in large numbers: *The barn was infested* ***with*** *rats.* • **infestation** /ˌɪn.fesˈteɪ.ʃᵊn/ noun [C or U] *a flea infestation* ◦ *an infestation* ***of*** *cockroaches/head lice*

infidel /ˈɪn.fɪ.dᵊl/ US /-fə.del/ noun [C or U] old use disapproving (used especially between Christians and Muslims) someone who does not have the same religious beliefs as the person speaking: *He lived among infidels/****the*** *infidel.* ◦ *infidel armies*

infidelity /ˌɪn.fɪˈdel.ə.ti/ US /-fəˈdel.ə.t̬i/ noun [C or U] (an act of) having sex with someone who is not your husband, wife, or regular sexual partner, or (an example of) not being loyal or FAITHFUL: ***marital/sexual*** *infidelity* ◦ *She could not forgive his many infidelities.*

the infield /ˈɪn.fiːld/ noun [S] the part of a cricket or baseball field that is closest to the player who hits the ball, or the group of players there → Compare **the outfield**

infielder /ˈɪnˌfiːl.dəʳ/ (US) /-dɚ/ noun [C] (In baseball) an infielder is any of the four players who regularly play between the positions of FIRST BASE and third BASE.

infighting /ˈɪnˌfaɪ.tɪŋ/ (US) /-t̬ɪŋ/ noun [U] competition between people within a group, especially to improve their own position or to get agreement for their ideas: *political infighting* ◦ *Years of infighting* ***among*** *the leaders have destroyed the party.*

infiltrate /ˈɪn.fɪl.treɪt/ verb [I + adv/prep, T] **1** to secretly become part of a group in order to get information or to influence the way that group thinks or behaves: *A journalist managed to infiltrate the powerful drug cartel.* **2** to move slowly into a substance, place, system, or organization: *At about this time the new ideas about 'corporate management' had begun to infiltrate* ***(into)*** *local government.* • **infiltration** /ˌɪn.fɪlˈtreɪ.ʃən/ noun [U]

infiltrator /ˈɪn.fɪl.treɪ.təʳ/ (US) /-t̬ɚ/ noun [C] a person who secretly becomes part of a group in order to get information or to influence the way the group thinks or behaves: *The infiltrator was identified and killed.*

infinite /ˈɪn.fɪ.nət/ adj; noun

►adj (C2) without limits; extremely large or great: *an infinite number/variety* ◦ *The universe is theoretically infinite.* ◦ *With infinite* ***patience****, she explained the complex procedure to us.*

IDIOM **in sb's infinite wisdom** disapproving used to show that you do not understand why someone has done something and that you think it was a stupid action: *The authorities, in their infinite wisdom, decided to close the advice centre.*

►noun **the Infinite** God

infinitely /ˈɪn.fɪ.nət.li/ adv (C2) very or very much: *Travel is infinitely more comfortable now than it used to be.*

infinitesimal /ˌɪn.fɪ.nɪˈtes.ɪ.məl/ adj formal extremely small: *The amounts of radioactivity present were infinitesimal.* • **infinitesimally** /-mə.li/ adv *infinitesimally small*

infinitive /ɪnˈfɪn.ɪ.tɪv/ (US) /-ə.t̬ɪv/ noun [C] specialized (B1) the basic form of a verb that usually follows 'to': *In the sentences 'I had to go' and 'I must go', 'go' is an infinitive.* ◦ *'Go' is the infinitive* ***form****.*

infinity /ɪnˈfɪn.ɪ.ti/ (US) /-ə.t̬i/ noun **1** [U] time or space that has no end: *the infinity of the universe* ◦ *the concept of infinity* **2** [U] a place that is so far away that it cannot be reached: figurative *The mountain range stretched away* ***into*** *infinity.* **3** [U] a number that is larger than all other numbers **4** [S] an extremely large number of something: *an infinity of stars in the galaxy*

infirm /ɪnˈfɜːm/ (US) /-ˈfɝːm/ adj; noun

►adj formal ill or needing care, especially for long periods and often because of old age: *She was too elderly and infirm to remain at home.*

►noun [plural] formal **the infirm** people who are ill for long periods: *The old and the infirm are the most susceptible to this disease.*

infirmary /ɪnˈfɜː.mə.ri/ (US) /-ˈfɝː.mɚ-/ noun [C] **1** UK old use a hospital. It is now used mainly in the names of hospitals: *Leeds General Infirmary* ◦ *the Royal Infirmary* **2** US In the US, an infirmary is a room in a school, college, or university where students who are injured or feeling ill can go to a nurse for treatment.

infirmity /ɪnˈfɜː.mə.ti/ (US) /-ˈfɝː.mə.t̬i/ noun [C or U] formal illness, especially for long periods or because of old age: *an advanced state of infirmity* ◦ *She suffered from a long list of infirmities.*

inflame /ɪnˈfleɪm/ verb [T] to cause or increase very strong feelings such as anger or excitement: *Reducing the number of staff is certain to inflame the already angry medical profession.* ◦ *Pictures of the bombed and burning city inflamed* ***feelings/passions*** *further.*

inflamed /ɪnˈfleɪmd/ adj (of a part of the body) red, painful, and swollen, especially because of infection: *an inflamed eye/toe* ◦ *You should call the doctor if the area around the wound becomes inflamed.*

inflammable /ɪnˈflæm.ə.bl̩/ adj **FIRE** ▷ **1** describes something that burns very easily: *a highly inflammable liquid such as petrol* **VIOLENCE** ▷ **2** likely to become violent or angry very quickly and in an uncontrolled way: *an inflammable situation/region* ◦ *a highly inflammable* ***mix*** *of outrage and bitterness*

inflammation /ˌɪn.fləˈmeɪ.ʃən/ noun [C or U] a red, painful, and often swollen area in or on a part of your body: *Aspirin reduces pain and inflammation.* ◦ *an inflammation of the eye/toe/ear*

inflammatory /ɪnˈflæm.ə.tᵊr.i/ (US) /-tɔːr-/ adj **ANGER** ▷ **1** intended or likely to cause anger or hate: *The men were using inflammatory* ***language****/ making inflammatory* ***remarks*** *about the other team's supporters.* **SWELLING** ▷ **2** specialized causing or related to swelling and pain in the body

inflatable /ɪnˈfleɪ.tə.bl̩/ (US) /-t̬ə-/ noun; adj

►noun [C] a boat or something similar which must be filled with air in order to float on the water

►adj able to be inflated: *inflatable pillows/mattresses*

inflate /ɪnˈfleɪt/ verb **FILL WITH AIR** ▷ **1** [I or T] to cause to increase in size by filling with air: *He inflated the balloons with helium.* ◦ *We watch the hot-air balloon slowly inflate.* **MAKE LARGER** ▷ **2** [T] to make something larger or more important: *They inflated their part in the rescue every time they told the story.*

inflate

inflated /ɪnˈfleɪ.tɪd/ (US) /-t̬ɪd/ adj Inflated prices, costs, numbers, etc. are higher than they should be, or higher than people think is reasonable.

inflation /ɪnˈfleɪ.ʃən/ noun [U] (B2) a general, continuous increase in prices: *high/low inflation* ◦ *the rate of inflation* ◦ *13 percent inflation* → Compare **deflation**

inflationary /ɪnˈfleɪ.ʃən.ər.i/ (US) /-er.i/ adj causing price increases and inflation: *inflationary policies/ pressures/trends*

inflected /ɪnˈflek.tɪd/ adj An inflected form of a word has a changed spelling or ending which shows the way it is used in sentences: *'Finds' and 'found' are inflected forms of 'find'.*

inˌflected ˈlanguage noun [C] a language that changes the form or ending of some words when the way in which they are used in sentences changes: *Latin, Polish, and Finnish are all highly inflected languages.*

inflection (UK also **inflexion**) /ɪnˈflek.ʃən/ noun **GRAMMAR** ▷ **1** [C] a change in or addition to the form of a word which shows a change in the way it is used in sentences: *If you add the plural inflection '-s' to 'dog' you get 'dogs'.* **SPEECH** ▷ **2** [C or U] the way in which the sound of your voice changes during speech, for example when you emphasize particular words: *His voice was low and flat, with almost no inflection.*

inflexible /ɪnˈflek.sɪ.bl̩/ **adj** usually disapproving (especially of opinions and rules) fixed and unable or unwilling to change: *The prime minister has adopted an inflexible position on immigration.* ◦ *This type of computer is too slow and inflexible to meet many business needs.* • **inflexibility** /ɪnˌflek.sɪˈbɪl.ɪ.ti/ (US) /-ə.t̬i/ **noun** [U]

inflict /ɪnˈflɪkt/ **verb** [T] to force someone to experience something very unpleasant: *These new bullets are capable of inflicting massive injuries.* ◦ *The suffering inflicted **on** these children was unimaginable.* • **infliction** /-ˈflɪk.ʃən/ **noun** [U]

ˈ**in-flight adj** [before noun] happening or available during a flight: *in-flight **entertainment*** ◦ *I always read the in-flight **magazine**.*

inflorescence /ˌɪn.flɔːˈres.ənts/ **noun** specialized **1** [C] in a plant, a flower or group of flowers on the stem, or the way they are arranged **2** [U] the forming of BUDS and flowers on a plant

inflow /ˈɪn.fləʊ/ (US) /-floʊ/ **noun** [C or U] the action of people or things arriving somewhere: *The government wanted an inflow **of** foreign investment.*

influence /ˈɪn.flu.əns/ **noun; verb**

▸**noun** [C or U] B2 the power to have an effect on people or things, or a person or thing that is able to do this: *Helen's a **bad/good** influence **on** him.* ◦ *He **has** a huge amount of influence **over** the city council.* ◦ *Christopher hoped to **exert** his influence to make them change their minds.* ◦ *At the time she was **under the** influence **of** her father.*

> **Word partners for influence**
>
> *have* an influence • *exert/wield* influence • *considerable/great/important/major* influence • a *bad/disruptive/good/powerful* influence • the influence *of* sb/sth • be *under* sb's influence • influence *on/over* sb/sth

IDIOM **under the influence** drunk: *Driving under the influence is a very serious offence.*

▸**verb** [T] B2 to affect or change how someone or something develops, behaves, or thinks: *She's very good at making friends and influencing people.* ◦ [+ obj + to infinitive] *What influenced you **to** choose a career in nursing?*

influential /ˌɪn.fluˈen.ʃəl/ **adj** C1 having a lot of influence on someone or something: *She wanted to work for a bigger and more influential (= powerful) newspaper.* ◦ *Johnson was influential (= important) **in** persuading the producers to put money into the film.*

influenza /ˌɪn.fluˈen.zə/ **noun** [U] formal for **flu**

influx /ˈɪn.flʌks/ **noun** [C usually singular] C2 the fact of a large number of people or things arriving at the same time: *Turkey is expecting an influx **of** several thousand refugees over the next few days.*

info /ˈɪn.fəʊ/ (US) /-foʊ/ **noun** [U] informal for **information**

infomercial /ˌɪn.fəʊˈmɜː.ʃəl/ (US) /ˈɪn.foʊ.mɝː-/ **noun** [C] mainly US a long television advertisement, that contains a lot of information and seems like a normal programme

inform /ɪnˈfɔːm/ (US) /-ˈfɔːrm/ **verb** [T] B1 to tell someone about particular facts: *The name of the dead man will not be released until his relatives have been informed.* ◦ *Why wasn't I informed **about** this earlier?* ◦ *Walters was not properly informed **of** the reasons for her arrest.* ◦ [+ that] *I informed my boss **that** I was going to be away next week.*

> **Common mistake: inform**
>
> **Remember: inform** must have a direct object.
>
> Don't say 'inform about/of something', say **inform someone about/of something**:
>
> ~~*I am writing to inform that I am leaving.*~~
>
> *I am writing to inform you that I am leaving.*

PHRASAL VERB **inform against/on sb** If you inform on/against someone, you give the police information, usually secretly, about that person, showing that he or she has done something wrong: *The terrorists said that anyone caught informing on them would be killed.*

informal /ɪnˈfɔː.məl/ (US) /-ˈfɔːr-/ **adj** B2 (of situations) not formal or official, or (of clothing, behaviour, speech) suitable when you are with friends and family but not for official occasions: *The two groups agreed to hold an informal meeting.* ◦ *'Hi' is an informal way of greeting people.* • **informally** /-i/ **adv** C1 *It's an outdoor party, so dress informally.* ◦ *They've agreed informally to separate.* • **informality** /ˌɪn.fɔːˈmæl.ə.ti/ (US) /-fɔːrˈmæl.ə.t̬i/ **noun** [U]

informant /ɪnˈfɔː.mənt/ (US) /-ˈfɔːr-/ **noun** [C] someone who gives information to another person or organization: *a police/secret informant* ◦ *Our survey is based on information from over 200 informants.*

> **Other ways of saying information**
>
> The plural noun **details** is often used to describe facts or pieces of information grouped together:
>
> *Please send me **details** of your training courses.*
>
> The plural nouns **directions** and **instructions** are often used to talk about information which describes how to do something:
>
> *Just follow the **directions** on the label.*
>
> The plural noun **directions** is also used to mean 'information about how to get to a place':
>
> *We had to stop and ask for **directions**.*
>
> The plural noun **guidelines** is used for information about the best way to do something:
>
> *The government has issued new **guidelines** on health and safety at work.*
>
> The noun **data** is sometimes used to describe information in the form of facts and numbers:
>
> *Our consultants have been collecting financial **data**.*
>
> The phrase **facts and figures** can be used for information which contains a lot of details which include facts and numbers:
>
> *Check the website for **facts and figures** on skin cancer.*
>
> Written information about a subject is sometimes described as **literature**:
>
> *Some **literature** on our current policy is enclosed.*

information /ˌɪn.fəˈmeɪ.ʃən/ (US) /-fɚ-/ **noun** [U] (informal **info**) A2 facts about a situation, person, event, etc.: *Do you have any information **about/on** train times?* ◦ *I read an interesting **bit/piece** of information in the newspaper.* ◦ ***For further** information (= if you want to know more), please contact your local library.* ◦ [+ that] *We have reliable information **that** a strike is planned next month.*

IDIOM **too much information** informal used when you want to tell someone that what they have said should be kept private or is embarrassing

informational /ɪn.fəˈmeɪ.ʃən.əl/ (US) /-fɚ/ **adj** containing information

Word partners for information

find/gather/get/obtain information • *divulge/give/provide* information • *additional/background/further* information • *accurate/detailed/factual* information • *relevant/useful/vital* information • a *bit/piece* of information • a *source* of information • information *about/on/regarding/relating to* sth

Common mistake: information

Information does not have a plural form and cannot be used with **a** or **an**.

To talk about an amount of **information**, do not say 'informations', say **information**, **some information**, or **a lot of information**:

~~*I found a lot of useful informations on their website.*~~

I found a lot of useful information on their website.

To talk about **information** in the singular, do not say 'an information', say **a piece/bit of information**:

~~*Sue has just told me a useful information.*~~

Sue has just told me a useful bit of information.

infor,mation 'overload noun [U] a situation in which you receive too much information at one time and cannot think about it in a clear way: *Spread your visit to the museum over two days if you want to avoid information overload.*

infor,mation re'trieval noun [U] the process of finding stored information on a computer

infor,mation super'highway noun [C usually singular] the internet and other systems that allow people to share information electronically: *Some saw the information superhighway as a research tool.*

infor,mation tech'nology noun [U] (abbreviation **IT**) the science and activity of using computers and other electronic equipment to store and send information

informative /ɪnˈfɔː.mə.tɪv/ (US) /-ˈfɔːr.mə.t̬ɪv/ **adj** C1 providing a lot of useful information

informed /ɪnˈfɔːmd/ (US) /-ˈfɔːrmd/ **adj** having a lot of knowledge or information about something: *an informed choice/opinion* ◦ *The school promised to* ***keep*** *parents informed* ***about*** *the situation.* ◦ *Elizabeth is remarkably* ***well****-informed.*

informer /ɪnˈfɔː.məʳ/ (US) /-ˈfɔːr.mɚ/ **noun** [C] a person who gives information in secret, especially to the police: *Most police informers receive a reward for their information.*

infotainment /ˌɪn.fəʊˈteɪn.mənt/ (US) /-foʊ-/ **noun** [U] (in television) the reporting of news and facts in an entertaining and humorous way rather than providing real information: *It wasn't a real documentary – it was more what you'd call infotainment.*

infraction /ɪnˈfræk.ʃən/ **noun** [C or U] formal an occasion when someone breaks a rule or law: *Any attempt to influence the judges will be seen as an infraction* ***of*** *the rules.*

infra dig /ˌɪn.frəˈdɪɡ/ **adj** [after verb] UK old-fashioned below what you consider to be socially acceptable: [+ to infinitive] *Diane thinks it's a bit infra dig* ***to*** *do her own housework.*

infrared /ˌɪn.frəˈred/ **adj** describes a type of light that feels warm but cannot be seen: *Their pilots are guided by an infrared optical system that shows images clearly even at night.*

infrastructure /ˈɪn.frəˌstrʌk.tʃəʳ/ (US) /-tʃɚ/ **noun** [C usually singular] C1 the basic systems and services, such as transport and power supplies, that a country or organization uses in order to work effectively

infrequent /ɪnˈfriː.kwənt/ **adj** not happening very often: *His letters became infrequent, then stopped completely.* • **infrequently** /-li/ **adv**

infringe /ɪnˈfrɪndʒ/ **verb** [T] formal to break a rule, law, etc.: *They infringed building regulations.*

PHRASAL VERB **infringe on/upon sth** If something infringes on/upon someone's rights or freedom, it takes away some of their rights or limits their freedom: *These restrictions infringe upon basic human rights.*

infringement /ɪnˈfrɪndʒ.mənt/ **noun** [C or U] an action that breaks a rule, law, etc.: *copyright infringement* ◦ *Even minor infringements* ***of*** *the law will be severely punished.*

infuriate /ɪnˈfjʊə.ri.eɪt/ (US) /-ˈfjʊr.i-/ **verb** [T] to make someone extremely angry: *His sexist attitude infuriates me.*

infuriating /ɪnˈfjʊə.ri.eɪ.tɪŋ/ (US) /-ˈfjʊr.i.eɪ.t̬ɪŋ/ **adj** extremely annoying: *It's infuriating when people keep spelling your name wrong, isn't it?*

infuse /ɪnˈfjuːz/ **verb** **EMOTION** ▷ **1** [T + obj + prep] to fill someone or something with an emotion or quality: *The pulling down of the Berlin Wall infused the world* ***with*** *optimism.* ◦ *The arrival of a group of friends on Saturday infused new life* ***into*** *the weekend.* **DRINK** ▷ **2** [I or T] If you infuse a drink or it infuses, you leave substances such as TEA LEAVES or herbs in hot water so that their flavour goes into the liquid: *Allow the tea to infuse for five minutes.*

infusion /ɪnˈfjuː.ʒən/ **noun** [C or U] the act of adding one thing to another to make it stronger or better: *An infusion of $100,000* ***into*** *the company is required.* ◦ *She drinks an infusion of herbs (= a drink made by leaving herbs in hot water).*

-ing /-ɪŋ/ **suffix** used to form the present participle of regular verbs: *calling* ◦ *asking*

ingenious /ɪnˈdʒiː.ni.əs/ **adj** (of a person) very clever and skilful, or (of a thing) cleverly made or planned and involving new ideas and methods: *an ingenious idea/method/solution* ◦ *Johnny is so ingenious – he can make the most remarkable sculptures from the most ordinary materials.* • **ingeniously** /-li/ **adv**

ingénue /ˈæ̃n.ʒeɪ.nuː/ (US) /ˈæn.ʒə-/ **noun** [C] formal a young woman who has little experience and is very trusting, especially as played in films and plays

ingenuity /ˌɪn.dʒəˈnjuː.ɪ.ti/ (US) /-ə.t̬i/ **noun** [U] someone's ability to think of clever new ways of doing something: *Drug smugglers constantly use their ingenuity to find new ways of getting drugs into a country.*

ingenuous /ɪnˈdʒen.ju.əs/ **adj** formal honest, sincere, and trusting, sometimes in a way that seems silly: *It has to be said it was rather ingenuous of him to ask a complete stranger to look after his luggage.* • **ingenuously** /-li/ **adv**

ingest /ɪnˈdʒest/ **verb** [T] specialized to eat or drink something: *The chemicals can be poisonous if ingested.* • **ingestion** /-ˈdʒes.tʃən/ **noun** [U]

inglenook

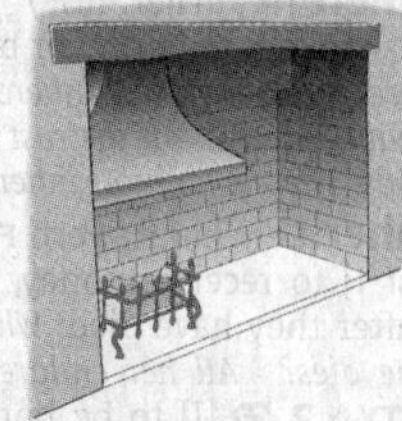

inglenook /ˈɪŋ.ɡl.nʊk/ **noun** [C] a partly closed space by a large open FIREPLACE built so that you can sit close to the fire

inglorious /ɪnˈglɔː.ri.əs/ (US) /-ˈglɔːr.i-/ **adj** literary not HONOURABLE (= fair and honest) or not to be proud of: *That country has a long, inglorious record of dealing harshly with political prisoners.*

ingot /ˈɪŋ.gət/ **noun** [C] a piece of metal, usually in the shape of a narrow brick: *a gold/silver ingot*

ingrained /ɪnˈgreɪnd/ **adj** **BELIEFS** ▷ **1** (of beliefs) so firmly held that they are not likely to change: *Such ingrained prejudices cannot be corrected easily.* ◦ *The belief that you should own your house is* ***deeply*** *ingrained* ***in*** *British society.* **DIRT** ▷ **2** Ingrained dirt has got under the surface of something and is difficult to remove: *The oil had become ingrained* ***in*** *his skin.*

ingrate /ˈɪŋ.greɪt/ **noun** [C] literary a person who is not grateful

ingratiate /ɪŋˈgreɪ.ʃiː.eɪt/ **verb** disapproving **ingratiate yourself** to make someone like you by praising or trying to please them: *He's always trying to ingratiate himself* ***with*** *his boss.*

ingratiating /ɪnˈgreɪ.ʃiː.eɪ.tɪŋ/ (US) /-t̬ɪŋ/ **adj** disapproving describes behaviour that is intended to make people like you: *an ingratiating smile/manner*

ingratitude /ɪnˈgræt.ɪ.tjuːd/ (US) /-ˈgræt̬.ə.tuːd/ **noun** [U] the fact that someone is not grateful for something

ingredient /ɪnˈgriː.di.ənt/ **noun** [C] **1** (B1) a food that is used with other foods in the preparation of a particular dish: *The* ***list of*** *ingredients included 250 g of almonds.* **2** (B2) one of the parts of something successful: *Trust is a vital ingredient in a successful marriage.*

ingress /ˈɪn.gres/ **noun** [C or U] formal the act of entering something: *There had been an ingress of water into the site.*

ˈin-group **noun** [C] mainly disapproving a social group whose members are very loyal to each other and share a lot of interests, and who usually try to keep other people out of the group

ingrowing /ˈɪŋˌgrəʊ.ɪŋ/ (US) /-groʊ-/ **adj** (US usually **ingrown**) growing into the flesh: *She's having an operation on an ingrowing* ***toenail.*** ◦ *an ingrowing hair*

inhabit /ɪnˈhæb.ɪt/ **verb** [T often passive] (C2) to live in a place: *These remote islands are inhabited only by birds.*

inhabitable /ɪnˈhæb.ɪ.tə.bl/ (US) /-t̬ə-/ **adj** able to be lived in or on → Opposite **uninhabitable**

inhabitant /ɪnˈhæb.ɪ.tənt/ **noun** [C] (B2) a person or animal that lives in a particular place: *a city of five million inhabitants*

inhale /ɪnˈheɪl/ **verb** **BREATHE** ▷ **1** [I or T] to breathe air, smoke, or gas into your lungs: *She flung open the window and inhaled deeply.* ◦ *She became ill shortly after inhaling the fumes.* → Compare **exhale** **EAT** ▷ **2** [T] US informal to eat something extremely fast: *Tony inhaled his burger.* • **inhalation** /ˌɪn.həˈleɪ.ʃən/ **noun** [U] *Two firefighters were treated for* ***smoke*** *inhalation.*

inhaler /ɪnˈheɪ.lər/ (US) /-lɚ/ **noun** [C] a small device you use to breathe in particular medicines

inherent /ɪnˈher.ənt/, /-ˈhɪə.rənt/ (US) /-ˈhɪr.ənt/ **adj** (C2) existing as a natural or basic part of something: *There are* ***dangers/risks*** *inherent* ***in*** *almost every sport.* ◦ *I have an inherent distrust of lawyers.* • **inherently** /-li/ **adv** *There's nothing inherently wrong with his ideas.*

inherit /ɪnˈher.ɪt/ **verb** **FROM DEAD PERSON** ▷ **1** (C2) [I or T] to receive money, a house, etc. from someone after they have died: *Who will inherit the house when he dies?* ◦ *All her children will inherit equally.* **QUALITY** ▷ **2** (C2) [T] to be born with the same physical or mental characteristics as one of your parents or grandparents: *Rosie inherited her red hair* ***from*** *her mother.* **PROBLEM** ▷ **3** [T] to begin to have responsibility for a problem or situation that previously existed or belonged to another person: *When I took on the job of manager, I inherited certain financial problems.*

inheritance /ɪnˈher.ɪ.təns/ **noun** [C usually singular, U] **FROM DEAD PERSON** ▷ **1** (C2) money or objects that someone gives you when they die: *The large inheritance* ***from*** *his aunt meant that he could buy his own boat.* ◦ *At 21 she* ***came into*** *her inheritance (= it was given to her).* **QUALITY** ▷ **2** a physical or mental characteristic inherited from your parents, or the process by which this happens: *genetic inheritance* ◦ *A particular gene is responsible for the inheritance of eye colour.*

inˈheritance ˌtax **noun** [C or U] a tax paid on money or property you have received from someone who has died

inheritor /ɪnˈher.ɪ.tər/ (US) /-t̬ɚ/ **noun** [C] a person who has been given something by someone who is dead: figurative *We are the inheritors* ***of*** *Greek and Roman culture.*

inhibit /ɪnˈhɪb.ɪt/ **verb** [T] to prevent someone from doing something, or to slow down a process or the growth of something: *Some workers were inhibited (****from*** *speaking) by the presence of their managers.* ◦ *This drug inhibits the growth of tumours.*

inhibited /ɪnˈhɪb.ɪ.tɪd/ (US) /-t̬ɪd/ **adj** not confident enough to say or do what you want: *The presence of strangers made her feel inhibited.*

inhibition /ˌɪn.hɪˈbɪʃ.ən/, /ˌɪn.ɪ-/ **noun** [C or U] (C2) a feeling of embarrassment or worry that prevents you from saying or doing what you want: *After a couple of drinks he* ***lost*** *his inhibition and started talking and laughing loudly.* ◦ *She was determined to shed her inhibitions and have a good time.*

ˌin-ˈhome **adj** [before noun] US provided at someone's home: *in-home care for the disabled*

inhospitable /ˌɪn.hɒsˈpɪt.ə.bl/, /ˌɪn.hɑːˈspɪt̬-/ **adj** **PERSON** ▷ **1** not welcoming or generous to people who visit you: *I'll have to cook them a meal or they'll think I'm inhospitable.* **PLACE** ▷ **2** describes an area that is not suitable for humans to live in: *They had to trek for miles through inhospitable countryside.*

ˌin-ˈhouse **adj, adv** Something that is done in-house is done within an organization or business by its employees rather than by other people: *an in-house training scheme* ◦ *All our advertising material is designed in-house.*

inhuman /ɪnˈhjuː.mən/ **adj** (C2) extremely cruel, or not human in an unusual or frightening way: *Prisoners of war were subjected to inhuman and degrading treatment.* ◦ *Most people feel that there is something almost inhuman about perfection.*

inhumane /ˌɪn.hjʊˈmeɪn/ **adj** cruel and causing suffering to people or animals: *Conditions for prisoners were described as inhumane.* • **inhumanely** /-li/ **adv**

inhumanity /ˌɪn.hjʊˈmæn.ə.ti/ (US) /-ə.t̬i/ **noun** [U] extremely cruel behaviour: *They were accused of inhumanity in their treatment of the hostages.*

inimical /ɪˈnɪm.ɪ.kəl/ **adj** formal harmful or limiting: *Excessive managerial control is inimical* ***to*** *creative expression.*

inimitable /ɪˈnɪm.ɪ.tə.bl̩/ (US) /-t̬ə-/ **adj** very unusual or of very high quality and therefore impossible to copy: *He was describing, in his* ***own*** *inimitable* ***style/way,*** *how to write a best-selling novel.* ◦ *She appeared* at the Oscar's wearing one of Versace's inimitable creations.

iniquitous /ɪˈnɪk.wɪ.təs/ (US) /-t̬əs/ **adj** formal very wrong and unfair: *It is an iniquitous **system** that allows a person to die because they have no money to pay for medicine.*

iniquity /ɪˈnɪk.wə.ti/ (US) /-t̬i/ **noun** [C or U] formal a very wrong and unfair action or situation: *They fought long and hard against the iniquities of apartheid.*

initial /ɪˈnɪʃ.əl/ **adj; noun; verb**

▸adj [before noun] B2 of or at the beginning: *My initial surprise was soon replaced by delight. ◦ Initial reports say that seven people have died, though this has not yet been confirmed.*

▸noun [C usually plural] B1 the first letter of a name, especially when used to represent a name: *He wrote his initials, P.M.R., at the bottom of the page. ◦ Paul M. Reynolds refused to say what the initial 'M' **stood for**. ◦ They carved their initials into a tree.*

▸verb [T] (-ll- or US usually -l-) to write your initials on something: *I initialled the documents and returned them to personnel.*

initialize /ɪˈnɪʃ.əl.aɪz/ **verb** [T] specialized to set the numbers, amounts, etc. in a computer program so that it is ready to start working

initially /ɪˈnɪʃ.əl.i/ **adv** B2 at the beginning: *Initially, most people approved of the new scheme. ◦ The damage was far more serious than initially believed.*

initiate **verb; noun**

▸verb [T] /ɪˈnɪʃ.i.eɪt/ **START** ▷ **1** C2 formal to cause something to begin: *Who initiated the violence?* **TEACH** ▷ **2** to teach someone about an area of knowledge, or to allow someone into a group by a special ceremony: *At the age of eleven, Harry was initiated **into** the art of golf by his father. ◦ Each culture had a special ritual to initiate boys **into** manhood.*

▸noun [C] /ɪˈnɪʃ.i.ət/ formal a person who has recently joined a group and has been taught its secrets

initiation /ɪˌnɪʃ.iˈeɪ.ʃən/ **noun** **START** ▷ **1** [U] formal an occasion when something starts: *Lawyers for the couple have announced the initiation of divorce proceedings.* **INTRODUCTION** ▷ **2** [C or U] an occasion when someone is first introduced to an activity or skill: *My initiation **into** the mysteries of home brewing was not a success.*

initiˈation ˌceremony **noun** [C] a process or event that a person takes part in to become an official member of a group

initiative /ɪˈnɪʃ.ə.tɪv/ (US) /-t̬ɪv/ **noun** **NEW PLAN** ▷ **1** C1 [C] a new plan or process to achieve something or solve a problem: *The **peace** initiative was welcomed by both sides.* **JUDGMENT** ▷ **2** C1 [U] the ability to use your judgment to make decisions and do things without needing to be told what to do: *Although she was quite young, she **showed** a lot of initiative and was promoted to manager after a year. ◦ I shouldn't always have to tell you what to do, **use** your initiative (= use your own judgment to decide what to do)!* **3 on your own initiative** If you do something on your own initiative, you plan it and decide to do it yourself without anyone telling you what to do. **ADVANTAGE** ▷ **4 the initiative** C1 [S] the power or opportunity to win an advantage: *to **seize/take/lose** the initiative*

inject /ɪnˈdʒekt/ **verb** [T] **DRUG** ▷ **1** to use a needle and SYRINGE (= small tube) to put a liquid such as a drug into a person's body: *Phil's a diabetic and has to inject himself **with** insulin every day.* **SOMETHING NEW** ▷ **2** to introduce something new that is necessary or helpful to a situation or process: *A large amount of money will have to be injected **into** the company if it is to survive. ◦ I tried to inject a little humour **into** the meeting.*

injection /ɪnˈdʒek.ʃən/ **noun** [C or U] **DRUG** ▷ **1** C2 the act of putting a liquid, especially a drug, into a person's body using a needle and a SYRINGE (= small tube): *Daily insulin injections are necessary for some diabetics. ◦ This steroid is sometimes given **by** injection.* **SOMETHING NEW** ▷ **2** C2 the introduction of something new that is necessary or helpful to a situation or process: *A cash injection of £20 million will be used to improve the health service. ◦ an injection of humour/excitement*

ˈin-joke **noun** [C] a private joke that can only be understood by a limited group of people who have a special knowledge of something that is referred to in the joke

injudicious /ˌɪn.dʒuːˈdɪʃ.əs/ **adj** formal showing bad judgment: *an injudicious remark* → Synonym **unwise**

injunction /ɪnˈdʒʌŋk.ʃən/ **noun** [C] an official order given by a law court, usually to stop someone from doing something: [+ to infinitive] *The court has **issued** an injunction **to** prevent the airline from increasing its prices. ◦* [+ -ing verb] *She is **seeking** an injunction bann**ing** the newspaper from publishing the photographs.*

injure /ˈɪn.dʒər/ (US) /-dʒɚ/ **verb** [T] B1 to hurt or cause physical harm to a person or animal: *A bomb exploded at the embassy, injuring several people. ◦ She fell and injured her shoulder. ◦ He was badly injured in the crash. ◦ He claimed that working too hard was injuring his health.*

injured /ˈɪn.dʒəd/ (US) /-dʒɚd/ **adj; noun**

▸adj **1** B2 hurt or physically harmed: *She was told to stay in bed to rest her injured back.* **2** If your feelings are injured, someone has offended or upset you: *It's nothing more than injured pride.*

▸noun [plural] **the injured** people who are injured, considered as a group: *The injured were taken to several nearby hospitals.*

injurious /ɪnˈdʒʊə.ri.əs/ (US) /-ˈdʒʊr.i-/ **adj** formal harmful: *Too much alcohol is injurious **to** your health.*

injury /ˈɪn.dʒər.i/ (US) /-dʒɚ-/ **noun** [C or U] B2 physical harm or damage to someone's body caused by an accident or an attack: *a head/back/knee injury ◦ Several train passengers **received/sustained** serious injuries in the crash. ◦ Injuries **to** the spine are common amongst these workers. ◦ They were lucky to **escape** (without) injury.*

> **Word partners for injury**
>
> *receive/suffer/sustain* an injury • *cause/inflict* an injury • *recover from* an injury • *escape/prevent* injury • a *fatal/horrific/serious/severe* injury • a *minor* injury • *multiple* injuries • an injury *to* sth

IDIOM **do yourself an injury** UK informal to hurt yourself: *Don't even think about lifting me up, Ted, you might do yourself an injury.*

ˈinjury ˌtime **noun** [U] UK a period of time added to the end of a sports game because play was stopped during the game to take care of players who were hurt

injustice /ɪnˈdʒʌs.tɪs/ **noun** [C or U] C1 (an example of) a situation in which there is no fairness and JUSTICE: *The sight of people suffering arouses a deep **sense of** injustice in her. ◦ They were aware of the injustices of the system.* → See also **unjust**

ink /ɪŋk/ **noun; verb**

▸noun [C or U] B1 coloured liquid used for writing,

printing, and drawing: *a bottle of ink ◦ blue/black/red ink ◦ Please write **in** ink, not in pencil. ◦ The book is printed in three different coloured inks.*

▸**verb** [T] specialized to put ink on something: *The printing plates have to be inked before they will print on the paper.*

inkblot test /ˈɪŋk.blɒtˌtest/ (US) /-blɑːt-/ **noun** [C] (also ˈ**Rorschach** ˌ**test**) a PSYCHOLOGICAL test in which a person is shown spots of ink and asked what they look like, as a way of learning about the person's personality or feelings

inkjet printer /ˈɪŋk.dʒetˌprɪn.təʳ/ (US) /-ˌprɪn.t̬ɚ/ **noun** [C] specialized an electronic printer which blows ink onto paper using very small JETS (= small openings which push out liquid)

inkling /ˈɪŋ.klɪŋ/ **noun** [C usually singular, U] a feeling that something is true or likely to happen, although you are not certain: [+ that] *I didn't **have** the slightest inkling **that** she was unhappy. ◦ He must have had some inkling **of** what was happening.*

inkstand /ˈɪŋk.stænd/ **noun** [C] a container for bottles of ink, pens and pencils, etc.

inkwell /ˈɪŋk.wel/ **noun** [C] a container for ink, used in the past, which fitted into a hole in a table

inky /ˈɪŋ.ki/ **adj** **1** covered with ink: *inky stains/fingers* **2** literary very dark: *It was night and the water looked cold and inky **black**.*

inland **adj**; **adv**

▸**adj** [before noun] /ˈɪn.lənd/, /-lænd/ in the middle of a country, away from the sea: *The Black Sea is a large inland sea.*

▸**adv** /ˈɪn.lænd/, /ɪnˈlænd/ towards the middle of a country, away from the sea: *Seabirds often come inland to find food.*

the ˌ**Inland** ˈ**Revenue** **noun** [+ sing/pl verb] the former name for the government office in the UK that collects the main taxes

ˈ**in-laws** **noun** [plural] informal the parents of your husband or wife and other members of their family

inlay /ˈɪn.leɪ/ **noun** [C or U] a decorative pattern put into the surface of an object: *The walls of the palace are marble with silver inlay.* • **inlaid** /-ˈleɪd/ **adj** *The top of the wooden chest was inlaid **with** ivory.*

inlet /ˈɪn.let/ **noun** [C] **CHANNEL** ▷ **1** a narrow strip of water that goes from a sea or lake into the land or between islands **MACHINE PART** ▷ **2** UK specialized the part of a machine through which liquid or gas enters: *an inlet pipe/manifold/valve*

ˌ**in-line** ˈ**skate** **noun** [C] US a SKATE with a single row of wheels on the bottom

ˌ**in-line** ˈ**skating** **noun** [U] the activity of SKATING while wearing special SKATES with a single row of wheels on the bottom of each one

in loco parentis /ɪnˌləʊ.kəʊ.pəˈren.tɪs/ (US) /-ˌloʊ.koʊ.pəˈren.t̬ɪs/ **adj** [after verb], **adv** formal being responsible for a child while the child's parents are absent: *While children are in school, teachers are legally in loco parentis.*

inmate /ˈɪn.meɪt/ **noun** [C] a person who is kept in a prison or a hospital for people who are mentally ill

inn /ɪn/ **noun** [C] **1** UK a pub where you can stay for the night, usually in the countryside **2** US a small hotel, usually in the countryside **3 Inn** used in the names of some hotels and restaurants: *the Holiday Inn*

innards /ˈɪn.ədz/ (US) /-ɚdz/ **noun** [plural] informal the organs inside a person or animal, or the inside parts of a machine

innate /ɪˈneɪt/ **adj** (C2) An innate quality or ability is one that you were born with, not one you have learned: *Cyril's most impressive quality was his innate goodness.* • **innately** /-li/ **adv** *I don't believe that human beings are innately evil.*

inner /ˈɪn.əʳ/ (US) /-ɚ/ **adj** [before noun] **1** (B2) inside or contained within something else: *Leading off the main hall is a series of small inner rooms. ◦* humorous *Few people ever managed to penetrate the director's **inner sanctum** (= very private room).* **2** (B2) Inner feelings or thoughts are ones that you do not show or tell other people: *Sarah seemed to have a profound sense of inner peace.*

ˌ**inner** ˈ**child** **noun** [C usually singular] Your inner child is the part of your personality that still reacts and feels like a child: *Many therapists think it's important for adults to get in touch with their inner child.*

ˌ**inner** ˈ**circle** **noun** [C] the small group of people who control an organization, political party, etc.: *Dr Simpson was a member of the inner circle **of** government officials.*

ˌ**inner** ˈ**city** **noun** [C] the central part of a city where people live and where there are often problems because people are poor and there are few jobs and bad houses: *a child from the inner city ◦ an inner-city area*

ˌ**inner** ˈ**ear** **noun** [C] the part inside the ear that controls balance and the ability to hear, and contains the COCHLEA

innermost /ˈɪn.ə.məʊst/ (US) /-ɚ.moʊst/ **adj** [before noun] (literary **inmost**) most secret and hidden, or nearest to the centre: *This was the diary in which Gina recorded her innermost thoughts and secrets. ◦ The spacecraft will fly through the innermost rings of Saturn.*

ˌ**inner** ˈ**ring** **noun** [C] US an area around the centre of a town or city where people live: *Population has ballooned in the inner ring.* • **inner-ˈring** **adj** [before noun] *inner-ring **suburbs*** → Compare **outer ring**

ˌ**inner** ˌ**tube** **noun** [C] a tube filled with air that fits inside a car or bicycle tyre

inning /ˈɪn.ɪŋ/ **noun** [C] one of the nine playing periods in a game of baseball

innings /ˈɪn.ɪŋz/ **noun** [C] (plural **innings**) the period in a game of cricket in which a team or a player BATS (= tries to hit the ball)

innit /ˈɪn.ɪt/ **short form** UK slang not standard isn't it. Used at the end of a statement for emphasis: *'It's wrong, innit?' ◦ 'They're such a wicked band, innit.'*

innkeeper /ˈɪnˌkiː.pəʳ/ (US) /-pɚ/ **noun** [C] old use a person who owns or manages an INN, especially in the past

innocence /ˈɪn.ə.sᵊns/ **noun** [U] **1** (C1) the fact that someone is not guilty of a crime: *She **pleaded** her innocence, but no one believed her. ◦ He was led away, **protesting** his innocence (= saying he was not guilty).* **2** (C2) the quality of not having much experience of life and not knowing about the bad things that happen in life: *She has a child-like innocence which I find very appealing.*

innocent /ˈɪn.ə.sᵊnt/ **adj**; **noun**

▸**adj** **NOT GUILTY** ▷ **1** (B2) (of a person) not guilty of a particular crime: *He firmly believes that she is innocent **of** the crime.* → Compare **guilty** **NO EXPERIENCE** ▷ **2** (B2) having no knowledge of the unpleasant and evil things in life: *She has such an innocent face that I find it hard to believe anything bad of her.* **NOT INVOLVED** ▷ **3** (B2) An innocent person is someone who is not involved with any military group or war: *Several innocent **bystanders** were injured in the explosion.* **NOT INTENDED TO HARM** ▷ **4** (C2) (of a thing) not intended to harm anyone: *It was an innocent remark, I didn't* *mean to hurt his feelings.* • **innocently** /-li/ **adv** B2 *'Have I done something wrong?', she asked innocently (= seeming not to have done anything wrong).* ◦ *He said he had obtained the television innocently, not knowing it had been stolen.*

▸**noun** [C] a person who has very little experience and does not know about the bad things that happen in life

innocuous /ɪˈnɒk.ju.əs/ US /-ˈnɑː.kju-/ **adj** completely HARMLESS (= causing no harm): *Some mushrooms look innocuous but are in fact poisonous.* • **innocuously** /-li/ **adv** • **innocuousness** /-nəs/ **noun** [U]

innovate /ˈɪn.ə.veɪt/ **verb** [I] to introduce changes and new ideas: *The fashion industry is always desperate to innovate.* • **innovator** /-veɪ.təʳ/ US /-veɪ.t̬ɚ/ **noun** [C] someone who introduces changes and new ideas

innovation /ˌɪn.əˈveɪ.ʃən/ **noun** [C or U] C1 (the use of) a new idea or method: *the latest innovations in computer technology*

innovative /ˈɪn.ə.və.tɪv/ US /-veɪ.t̬ɪv/ **adj** (UK also **innovatory** /ˈɪn.ə.veɪ.təʳ.i/) C1 using new methods or ideas: *innovative ideas/methods*

innuendo /ˌɪn.juˈen.dəʊ/ US /-doʊ/ **noun** [C or U] (plural **innuendos** or **innuendoes**) (the making of) a remark or remarks that suggest something sexual or something unpleasant but do not refer to it directly: *There's always an element of* ***sexual*** *innuendo in our conversations.*

innumerable /ɪˈnjuː.mər.ə.bl/ US /ɪˈnuː.mɚ-/ **adj** C2 too many to be counted: *The project has been delayed by innumerable problems.*

innumerate /ɪˈnjuː.mər.ət/ US /ɪˈnuː.mɚ.ət/ **adj** unable to understand and use numbers in calculations → Compare **illiterate** • **innumeracy** /-ə.si/ **noun** [U]

inoculate /ɪˈnɒk.jʊ.leɪt/ US /-ˈnɑː.kjə-/ **verb** [T] to give a weak form of a disease to a person or animal, usually by INJECTION, as a protection against that disease: *My children have been inoculated* ***against*** *polio.* • **inoculation** /ɪˌnɒk.jʊˈleɪ.ʃən/ US /-ˌnɑː.kjə-/ **noun** [C or U]

inoffensive /ˌɪn.əˈfen.sɪv/ **adj** (especially of a person or their behaviour) not causing any harm or offence: *an inoffensive article* ◦ *He seemed like a quiet, inoffensive sort of a guy.*

inoperable /ɪˈnɒp.ər.ə.bl/ US /ˌɪnˈɑː.pɚ-/ **adj** DISEASE ▷ **1** If a TUMOUR (= a growth) or other medical condition is inoperable, doctors are unable to remove or treat it with an operation. **NOT WORKING** ▷ **2** If a system, plan, machine, etc. is inoperable, it cannot be done or made to work.

inoperative /ɪˈnɒp.ər.ə.tɪv/ US /-ˈnɑː.pɚ.ə.t̬ɪv/ **adj** formal (of a law, rule, etc.) not having effect or power, or (of a machine, system, etc.) not working or not able to work as usual: *The old regulations became inoperative when the new ones were issued.*

inopportune /ɪˈnɒp.ə.tjuːn/ US /ɪˈnɑː.pɚ.tuːn/ **adj** formal happening or done at a time that is not suitable or convenient: *I'm sorry, you've called at an inopportune* ***moment.*** • **inopportunely** /-li/ **adv**

inordinate /ɪˈnɔː.dɪ.nət/ US /ˌɪnˈɔːr-/ **adj** formal much more than usual or expected: *Margot has always spent an inordinate* ***amount*** *of time on her appearance.* • **inordinately** /-li/ **adv** *She was inordinately fond of her pets.*

inorganic /ˌɪn.ɔːˈgæn.ɪk/ US /-ɔːr-/ **adj** specialized not being or consisting of living material, or (of chemical substances) containing no carbon or only small amounts of carbon: *Salt is an inorganic chemical.* ◦ *The meteorites contained only inorganic material.* → Compare **organic**

inorganic ˈchemistry **noun** [U] the scientific study of chemical substances which do not contain carbon

inpatient /ˈɪn.peɪ.ʃənt/ **noun** [C] a person who goes into hospital to receive medical care, and stays there one or more nights while they are being treated → Compare **outpatient**

input /ˈɪn.pʊt/ **noun; verb**

▸**noun 1** B2 [C or U] something such as energy, money, or information that is put into a system, organization, or machine so that it can operate: *I didn't have much input* ***into*** *the project (= the help I gave was small).* ◦ *The power input will come largely from hydroelectricity.* **2** [C] specialized the part that carries information to a machine, or the place where this is connected: *The inputs for the CD-ROM are at the back of the computer.* ◦ *an input device*

▸**verb** [T] (present tense **inputting**, past tense and past participle **inputted** or **input**) to put information into a computer or other piece of electronic equipment: *I've spent the morning inputting data* ***into*** *the computer.*

inquest /ˈɪŋ.kwest/ **noun** [C] **1** an official process to discover the cause of someone's death: *An inquest is always* ***held*** *if murder is suspected.* **2** an examination of or discussion about the reasons for someone's or something's failure: *an inquest* ***into*** *the department's poor performance*

inquire (UK also **enquire**) /ɪnˈkwaɪəʳ/ US /-ˈkwaɪr/ **verb** [I or T] B2 to ask for information: *Shall I inquire* ***about*** *the price of tickets?* ◦ [+ question word] *She rang up to inquire* ***when*** *her car would be ready.* ◦ [+ speech] *'Where are we going?' he inquired politely.*

IDIOM **inquire within** mainly UK written on a notice on a building, meaning that information can be found inside: *Saturday staff needed – Inquire within.*

PHRASAL VERBS **inquire after sb** mainly UK (UK also **enquire after sb**) to ask for information about someone, especially about their health, in order to be polite: *She inquired after his grandfather's health.* • **inquire into sth** formal (UK also **enquire into sth**) to try to discover the facts about something: *When the authorities inquired into his background, they found he had a criminal record.*

inquirer formal (UK also **enquirer**) /ɪnˈkwaɪə.rəʳ/ US /-ˈkwaɪr.ɚ/ **noun** [C] someone who asks about something

inquiring (UK also **enquiring**) /ɪnˈkwaɪə.rɪŋ/ US /-ˈkwaɪr.ɪŋ/ **adj** (of someone's behaviour) always wanting to learn new things, or (of someone's expression) wanting to know something: *You have a very inquiring* ***mind****, don't you?* ◦ *He gave her an inquiring look.* • **inquiringly** (UK also **enquiringly**) /-li/ **adv** *She* ***looked*** *at her mother inquiringly.*

inquiry (UK also **enquiry**) /ɪnˈkwaɪə.ri/ US /ˈɪŋ.kwɚ.i/ **noun** **QUESTION** ▷ **1** B1 [C or U] (the process of asking) a question: *I've been* ***making*** *inquiries* ***about/into*** *the cost of a round-the-world ticket.* ◦ formal *Inquiry* ***into*** *the matter is pointless – no one will tell you anything.* **PROCESS** ▷ **2** C2 [C] an official process to discover the facts about something bad that has happened: *a judicial inquiry* ◦ *Citizens have demanded a full inquiry* ***into*** *the government's handling of the epidemic.*

inquisition /ˌɪn.kwɪˈzɪʃ.ən/ **noun** [C] formal disapproving a period of asking questions in a detailed and unfriendly way: *The police* ***subjected*** *him* ***to*** *an inquisition that lasted twelve hours.*

the ˌInquiˈsition **noun** [S] in the past, an official

organization in the Roman Catholic Church whose purpose was to find and punish people who opposed its beliefs

inquisitive /ɪnˈkwɪz.ɪ.tɪv/ (US) /-t̬ɪv/ **adj** wanting to discover as much as you can about things, sometimes in a way that annoys people: *an inquisitive child* ◦ *an inquisitive mind* ◦ *She could see inquisitive faces looking out from the windows next door.* • **inquisitively** /-li/ **adv** *The mouse looked around the room inquisitively.* • **inquisitiveness** /-nəs/ **noun** [U]

inquisitor /ɪnˈkwɪz.ɪ.təʳ/ (US) /-t̬ɚ/ **noun** [C] formal disapproving someone who asks a lot of questions

inquisitorial /ɪnˌkwɪz.ɪˈtɔː.ri.əl/ (US) /-ˈtɔːr.i-/ **adj** formal disapproving asking a lot of questions, especially in a way that makes you feel annoyed: *an inquisitorial manner*

inquorate /ˌɪnˈkwɔː.reɪt/ (US) /-kwɔːr.eɪt/ **adj** mainly UK formal (of a meeting) not having enough people present and so unable to make any official decisions

in-ˈresidence **adj** [after noun] A painter, poet, etc. in-residence works with an organization, usually for a limited period.

inroads /ˈɪn.rəʊdz/ (US) /-roʊdz/ **noun** [plural] **make inroads** to start to have a direct and noticeable effect (on something): *The government is definitely making inroads* ***into*** *the problem of unemployment.*

insalubrious /ˌɪn.səˈluː.bri.əs/ **adj** formal unpleasant, dirty, or likely to cause disease

the ˌins and ˈouts **noun** [plural] (C2) the detailed or complicated facts of something: *I know how to use computers, but I don't really understand the ins and outs* ***of*** *how they work.*

insane /ɪnˈseɪn/ **adj; noun**

▸**adj 1** (C2) mentally ill: *For the last ten years of his life he was* ***clinically*** *insane.* ◦ informal *I sometimes think I'm* ***going*** *insane (= I feel very confused).* **2** (C1) extremely unreasonable or stupid: *It would be insane not to take advantage of this opportunity.*

▸**noun** [plural] **the insane** mentally ill people: *a hospital for the* ***criminally*** *insane*

insanely /ɪnˈseɪn.li/ **adv** extremely and unreasonably: *She gets insanely* ***jealous*** *if he so much as looks at another woman.*

insanitary /ɪnˈsæn.ə.tᵊr.i/ (US) /-ter.i/ **adj** UK for **unsanitary**

insanity /ɪnˈsæn.ə.ti/ (US) /-t̬i/ **noun** [U] **1** the condition of being seriously mentally ill: *He was found not guilty of murder by reason of insanity.* ◦ *He suffered from periodic* ***bouts of*** *insanity.* **2** an action that is stupid and likely to have extremely bad results: *It would be insanity to expand the business now.*

insatiable /ɪnˈseɪ.ʃə.bl̩/ **adj** (especially of a DESIRE or need) too great to be satisfied: *Like so many politicians, he had an insatiable* ***appetite/desire/hunger*** *for power.* ◦ *Nothing, it seemed, would satisfy his insatiable* ***curiosity***. • **insatiably** /-bli/ **adv**

inscribe /ɪnˈskraɪb/ **verb** [T] formal to write words in a book or CARVE (= cut) them on an object: *The prize winners each receive a book with their names inscribed* ***on*** *the first page.* ◦ *The wall of the church was inscribed* ***with*** *the names of the dead from the Great War.*

inscription /ɪnˈskrɪp.ʃᵊn/ **noun** [C] words that are written or cut in something: *The inscription read 'To darling Molly. Christmas 1904.'* ◦ *The inscriptions on the gravestones were worn away.*

inscrutable /ɪnˈskruː.tɪ.bl̩/ (US) /-t̬ə-/ **adj** (especially of a person or their expression) not showing emotions or thoughts and therefore very difficult to understand or get to know: *an inscrutable face/expression/smile* • **inscrutably** /-bli/ (US) /-t̬ə-/ **adv** *She smiled inscrutably.* • **inscrutability** /ɪnˌskruː.tɪˈbɪl.ɪ.ti/ (US) /-t̬əˈbɪl.ə.t̬i/ **noun** [U]

inseam /ˈɪn.siːm/ **noun** [C] US for **inside leg**

insect /ˈɪn.sekt/ **noun** [C] (A2) a type of very small animal with six legs, a body divided into three parts and usually two pairs of wings, or, more generally, any similar very small animal: *Ants, beetles, butterflies, and flies are all insects.* ◦ *I've got some sort of insect bite on my leg.*

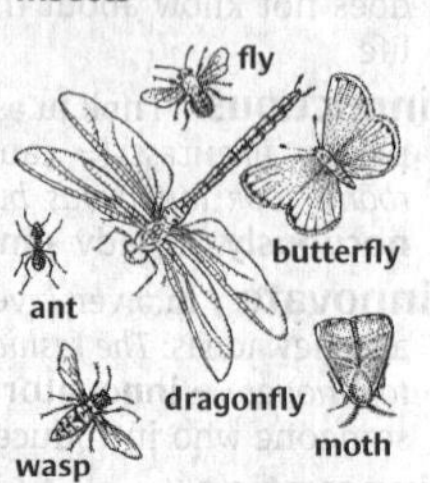

insecticide /ɪnˈsek.tɪ.saɪd/ **noun** [C or U] a chemical substance made and used for killing insects, especially those which eat plants → Compare **herbicide, pesticide**

insectivore /ɪnˈsek.tɪ.vɔːʳ/ (US) /-vɔːr/ **noun** [C] specialized an animal which eats only insects • **insectivorous** /ˌɪn.sekˈtɪv.ᵊr.əs/ (US) /-ɚ-/ **adj**

insecure /ˌɪn.sɪˈkjʊəʳ/ (US) /-ˈkjʊr/ **adj** NOT CONFIDENT ▷ **1** (C1) Insecure people have little confidence and are uncertain about their own abilities or if other people really like them: *I wonder what it was about her upbringing that made her so insecure.* ◦ *He still* ***feels*** *insecure* ***about*** *his ability to do the job.* NOT SAFE ▷ **2** (C2) (of objects or situations) not safe or not protected: *The situation is still insecure, with many of the rebels roaming the streets.* ◦ *Nations which are not self-sufficient in energy will face an insecure future.* ◦ *We've gone through a few financially insecure years.* • **insecurely** /-li/ **adv** *The shelves were insecurely fastened and fell to the floor.* • **insecurity** /-ˈkjʊə.rɪ.ti/ (US) /-ˈkjʊr.ə.t̬i/ **noun** [C or U] (C2) *a* ***sense/feeling of*** *insecurity* ◦ *She had developed an outgoing personality to mask her* ***deep*** *insecurities.* ◦ *financial insecurity*

inseminate /ɪnˈsem.ɪ.neɪt/ **verb** [T] to put a male animal's SPERM into a female animal, either by the sexual act or by an artificial method • **insemination** /ɪnˌsem.ɪˈneɪ.ʃᵊn/ **noun** [U] *artificial insemination*

insensible /ɪnˈsen.sɪ.bl̩/ **adj** formal **1** unconscious: *We found her lying on the floor, drunk and insensible.* **2 be insensible of/to sth** to not care about something or be unwilling to react to it • **insensibility** /ɪnˌsen.sɪˈbɪl.ɪ.ti/ (US) /-ə.t̬i/ **noun** [C or U]

insensitive /ɪnˈsen.sɪ.tɪv/ (US) /-sə.t̬ɪv/ **adj 1** (C1) disapproving (of a person or their behaviour) not feeling or showing sympathy for other people's feelings, or refusing to give importance to something: *It was a bit insensitive of Fiona to go on so much about fat people when she knows Mandy is desperate to lose weight.* ◦ *The police have been criticized for being insensitive* ***to*** *complaints from the public.* **2** specialized not showing the effect of something as a reaction to it, or unable to feel something: *The protective covering must be insensitive* ***to*** *light and heat.* ◦ *His feet seem to be insensitive* ***to*** *pain.* • **insensitively** /-li/ **adv** • **insensitivity** /ɪnˌsen.sɪˈtɪv.ɪ.ti/ (US) /-ə.t̬i/ **noun** [U] *His insensitivity* ***towards*** *the feelings of others is remarkable.* ◦ *an insensitivity* ***to*** *pain/light/noise*

inseparable /ɪnˈsep.rə.bl̩/ **adj** (C2) describes two or more people who are such good friends that they spend most of their time together, or two or more things that are so closely connected that they cannot be considered separately: *When we were kids Zoe and I were inseparable.* ◦ *Unemployment and inner city decay are inseparable issues which must be tackled* *together.* • **inseparably** /-bli/ **adv** *These two causes are inseparably linked.*

insert verb; noun

▸**verb** [T] /ɪnˈsɜːt/ (US) /-ˈsɝːt/ C1 to put something inside something else, or to add something, especially words, to something else: *Insert the key **in/into** the lock.* ◦ *I've filled in the form, but you still need to insert (= add) your bank details and date of birth.*

▸**noun** [C] /ˈɪn.sɜːt/ (US) /-sɝːt/ something that is made to go inside or into something else: *These magazines have too many annoying inserts (= extra loose pages) advertising various products.*

insertion /ɪnˈsɜː.ʃən/ (US) /-ˈsɝː-/ **noun** **1** [U] the act of putting something inside something else, or adding something, especially words to something else: *Scientists hope that the insertion of normal genes into the diseased cells will provide a cure.* **2** [C] something you put inside something else or something, especially words that you add to something else: *Any editorial insertions you make should be enclosed in square brackets.*

ˌin-ˈservice **adj** [before noun] happening during your time at work: *Instead of sending employees away on courses, the company relies on in-service **training**.*

inset /ˈɪn.set/ **noun** [C] specialized something positioned within a larger object: *The map has an inset (= small extra map) in the top corner, that shows the city centre in more detail.* • **inset** /ɪnˈset/ **adj** [after verb] *He bought her a gold necklace inset **with** rubies.*

inshore /ˈɪn.ʃɔːr/ (US) /-ʃɔːr/ **adj, adv** near or towards the coast: *an inshore fishing zone* ◦ *an inshore lifeboat* ◦ *The ships moved slowly inshore.*

inside noun; adv, preposition, adj; preposition; adj; adv

▸**noun** /ɪnˈsaɪd/ **1** B2 [C usually singular] the part, space, or side of something that is inside: *Did you clean the inside **of** the car?* ◦ *The hotel looked shabby from the street, but it was fine **on** the inside.* ◦ *the insides of people's houses* → Compare **outside** **2** [C usually singular] The inside of a part of the body such as the arm or leg is the part facing in towards the rest of the body: *She dabbed perfume on the inside of her wrist.* **3 insides** [plural] informal a person's or animal's INTERNAL organs, especially their stomach or bowels: *The dead seal's insides were spread all over the snow.*

IDIOM **on the inside** informal If someone is on the inside, they have a job or position in which they have special or secret information: *Who do we know on the inside who can help us?*

▸**adv, preposition, adj** /ɪnˈsaɪd/ **1** A1 in or into a room, building, container, or something similar: *'Is Anna in the garden?' 'No, she's inside (= in the house).'* ◦ *What's inside the box?* ◦ *Luckily, no one was inside the building when it collapsed.* ◦ figurative *She couldn't cope with the grief she felt inside.* ◦ figurative *Who can tell what goes on inside his head?* ◦ *He put the documents carefully in his inside **pocket** (= pocket on the inside of a jacket or coat).* **2 inside out** B2 If something is inside out, it has the usual inside part on the outside and the usual outside part on the inside: *She had her jumper on inside out.*

IDIOMS **know sth inside out** informal C1 to know everything about a subject: *He knows the system inside out.* • **turn a place inside out** UK informal to search every part of a place very carefully: *I've turned the house inside out but I still can't find my keys.*

▸**preposition** /ˌɪnˈsaɪd/ (also **inside of**) C2 If you do something or if something happens inside (of) a particular time or limit, you do it or it happens in less than that amount of time or under the limit: *The new faster trains can do the journey inside two hours.*

▸**adj** [before noun] /ˈɪn.saɪd/ C2 (of information) obtained by someone in a group, organization, or company and therefore involving special or secret knowledge: *inside information/knowledge* ◦ *I'll call up Clare and get **the** inside **story** (= a true report of the facts).*

IDIOM **have the inside track** to have a special position within an organization, or a special relationship with a person that gives you advantages that other people do not have

▸**adv** /ɪnˈsaɪd/ informal in prison: *Her husband's inside **for** armed robbery.*

ˈinside ˌjob **noun** [C] a crime, especially stealing, committed by someone in the place where they work

ˌinside ˈlane **noun** [C] ROAD ▷ **1** UK the part of the road nearest the edge, used especially by slower vehicles **2** US the part of the road nearest the vehicles going in the opposite direction RACE ▷ **3** the part of a RACETRACK nearest the middle

ˌinside ˈleg **noun** [C usually singular] UK (US **inseam**) the measurement from the top of your INNER leg to your ANKLE

insider /ɪnˈsaɪ.dər/ (US) /-dɚ/ **noun** [C] someone who is an accepted member of a group and who therefore has special or secret knowledge or influence: *According to insiders, the committee is having difficulty making up its mind.*

ˌinsider ˈdealing **noun** [U] (also **insider ˈtrading**) the illegal buying and selling of SHARES in a company by people who have special information because they are involved with the company

insidious /ɪnˈsɪd.i.əs/ **adj** (of something unpleasant or dangerous) gradually and secretly causing harm: *High-blood pressure is an insidious condition which has few symptoms.* • **insidiously** /-li/ **adv** • **insidiousness** /-nəs/ **noun** [U]

insight /ˈɪn.saɪt/ **noun** [C or U] C1 (the ability to have) a clear, deep, and sometimes sudden understanding of a complicated problem or situation: *It was an interesting book, full of fascinating insights **into** human relationships.* • **insightful** /-fəl/ **adj** approving

insignia /ɪnˈsɪg.ni.ə/ **noun** [C] (plural **insignia**) an object or mark which shows that a person belongs to a particular organization or group, or has a particular rank

insignificant /ˌɪn.sɪgˈnɪf.ɪ.kənt/ **adj** C1 not important or thought to be valuable, especially because of being small: *Why bother arguing about such an insignificant amount of money?* ◦ *The difference between the two results was insignificant.* • **insignificantly** /-li/ **adv** • **insignificance** /-kəns/ **noun** [U] *The traumas of my own upbringing **pale/fade into** insignificance (= seem very unimportant) when I hear stories about the way Peter's parents treated him.*

insincere /ˌɪn.sɪnˈsɪər/ (US) /-ˈsɪr/ **adj** disapproving pretending to feel something that you do not really feel, or not meaning what you say: *an insincere apology* ◦ *And all this praise just because the poor man has died – doesn't it strike you as a bit insincere?* • **insincerely** /-li/ (US) /-ˈsɪr-/ **adv** • **insincerity** /ˌɪn.sɪnˈser.ə.ti/ (US) /-t̬i/ **noun** [U]

insinuate /ɪnˈsɪn.ju.eɪt/ **verb** [T] to suggest, without being direct, that something unpleasant is true: [+ (that)] *Are you insinuating (**that**) I'm losing my nerve?* ◦ *What are you insinuating, Daniel?* • **insinuation** /ɪnˌsɪn.juˈeɪ.ʃən/ **noun** [C or U] [+ that] *We resent* *these insinuations* ***that*** *we are not capable of leading the company forward.*

PHRASAL VERB **insinuate yourself into sth** formal disapproving to use clever, secret, and often unpleasant methods to gradually become part of something: *Over the years she insinuated herself into the great man's life.*

insinuating /ɪnˈsɪn.ju.eɪ.tɪŋ/ US /-t̬ɪŋ/ **adj** suggesting ideas without saying them directly: *She didn't reply – she merely smiled that insinuating smile.* ◦ *Both songs are in danger of being banned for their sexy, insinuating lyrics.*

insipid /ɪnˈsɪp.ɪd/ **adj** disapproving not having a strong taste or character, or having no interest or energy: *a pale insipid wine* ◦ *He's an insipid old bore.* ◦ *Why anyone buys music with such insipid lyrics is a mystery.* • **insipidly** /-li/ **adv** • **insipidness** /-nəs/ **noun** [U] (also **insipidity**)

insist /ɪnˈsɪst/ **verb** [I] B1 to say firmly or demand forcefully, especially when others disagree with or oppose what you say: [+ (that)] *Greg still insists* ***(that)*** *he did nothing wrong.* ◦ *Please go first – I insist!* ◦ *She insisted* ***on*** *see****ing*** *her lawyer.*

PHRASAL VERB **insist on doing sth** C1 to keep doing something, even if it annoys other people, or people think it is not good for you: *I don't know why you insist on talking about it.*

insistence /ɪnˈsɪs.tᵊns/ **noun** [U] an occasion when you demand something and refuse to accept opposition, or when you say firmly that something is true: *Insistence* ***on*** *better working conditions by the union has resulted in fewer employee absences.* ◦ ***At*** *her father****'s*** *insistence, Amelia's been moved into a new class.* ◦ [+ that] *Her insistence* ***that*** *she should have the best room annoyed everyone.*

insistent /ɪnˈsɪs.tᵊnt/ **adj** firmly saying that something must be true or done: *insistent demands/appeals/signals* ◦ *The teacher is insistent* ***that*** *the school is not to blame for the situation.* • **insistently** /-li/ **adv**

in situ /ˌɪnˈsɪt.juː/ **adj, adv** formal in the original place instead of being moved to another place

insofar as /ˌɪn.səˈfɑːr.əz/ US /-ˈfɑːr-/ **conjunction** formal C2 to the degree that

insole /ˈɪn.səʊl/ US /-soʊl/ **noun** [C] (also ˌ**inner** ˈ**sole**) a piece of material inside a shoe on which your foot rests, or a piece of material that you put in a shoe to make it warmer or more comfortable

insolent /ˈɪn.sᵊl.ənt/ **adj** rude and not showing respect: *an insolent child/young man* ◦ *an insolent gesture/remark* • **insolently** /-li/ **adv** • **insolence** /-əns/ **noun** [U]

insoluble /ɪnˈsɒl.jʊ.bl/ US /-ˈsɑːl.jə-/ **adj** PROBLEM ▷ **1** (US also **insolvable**) (of a problem) so difficult that it is impossible to solve: *Traffic congestion in large cities seems to be an insoluble problem.* SUBSTANCE ▷ **2** (of a substance) impossible to dissolve: *These minerals are all insoluble in water.* • **insolubility** /ɪnˌsɒl.jʊˈbɪl.ɪ.ti/ US /-ˌsɑːl.jəˈbɪl.ə.t̬i/ **noun** [U]

insolvent /ɪnˈsɒl.vᵊnt/ US /-ˈsɑːl-/ **adj** specialized (especially of a company) not having enough money to pay debts, buy goods, etc. • **insolvency** /-vᵊn.si/ **noun** [U]

insomnia /ɪnˈsɒm.ni.ə/ US /-ˈsɑːm-/ **noun** [U] C2 the condition of being unable to sleep, over a period of time: *Holly* ***suffered from*** *insomnia caused by stress at work.*

insomniac /ɪnˈsɒm.ni.æk/ US /-ˈsɑːm-/ **noun** [C] someone who often finds it difficult to sleep

insouciance /ɪnˈsuː.si.əns/ **noun** [U] literary a relaxed and happy way of behaving without feeling worried or guilty: *I admired his youthful insouciance.* • **insouciant** /-ənt/ **adj**

inspect /ɪnˈspekt/ **verb** [T] **1** C1 to look at something or someone carefully in order to discover information, especially about their quality or condition: *After the crash both drivers got out and inspected their cars for damage.* ◦ *She held the bank note up to the light and inspected it* ***carefully.*** **2** to officially visit a place or a group of people in order to check that everything is correct and legal: *An official from the Department of Health will be inspecting the restaurant this afternoon.* ◦ *The King inspected the troops.*

inspection /ɪnˈspek.ʃᵊn/ **noun** [C or U] **1** C1 the act of looking at something carefully, or an official visit to a building or organization to check that everything is correct and legal: *Her passport seemed legitimate, but* ***on closer*** *inspection, it was found to have been altered.* ◦ *She arrived to* ***carry out/make*** *a health and safety inspection of the building.* **2** US and Australian English an examination of the structure of a building by a specially trained person → Compare **survey**

inspector /ɪnˈspek.təʳ/ **noun** [C] **1** B2 someone whose job is to officially inspect something: *a tax inspector* ◦ *a school inspector/an inspector of schools* **2** B2 UK a police officer of middle rank, above a SERGEANT and below a SUPERINTENDENT

inspectorate /ɪnˈspek.tᵊr.ət/ **noun** [C] mainly UK an official organization which sends inspectors to visit places and organizations in order to make certain they are in good condition and that the rules are being obeyed: *the education/pollution/schools inspectorate*

inspiration /ˌɪn.spɪˈreɪ.ʃᵊn/ **noun** **1** B2 [C or U] someone or something that gives you ideas for doing something: *The golden autumn light provided the inspiration* ***for*** *the painting.* ◦ *He went to church, perhaps seeking* ***divine*** *inspiration.* **2** C2 [C] a sudden good idea: *He* ***had*** *an inspiration – why not apply for some government money?* **3** C2 [S] someone that people admire and want to be like: *She has been* ***an*** *inspiration* ***to*** *us all.*

inspirational /ˌɪn.spɪˈreɪ.ʃᵊn.ᵊl/ **adj** making you feel full of hope or encouraged: *He gave an inspirational reading of his own poems.*

inspire /ɪnˈspaɪəʳ/ US /-ˈspaɪr/ **verb** [T] **1** B2 to make someone feel that they want to do something and can do it: *His confident leadership inspired his followers.* ◦ [+ to infinitive] *After her trip to Venezuela, she felt inspired* ***to*** *learn Spanish.* **2** B2 to make someone have a particular strong feeling or reaction: *She inspires great loyalty among her followers.* ◦ *The captain's heroic effort inspired them* ***with*** *determination.* **3** B2 to give someone an idea for a book, film, product, etc.: *a piece of music inspired by dolphin sounds* ◦ *The design of the car has inspired many imitations.*

inspired /ɪnˈspaɪəd/ US /-ˈspaɪrd/ **adj** excellent, or resulting from inspiration: *an inspired performance/choice* ◦ *an inspired suggestion/guess*

inspiring /ɪnˈspaɪə.rɪŋ/ US /-ˈspaɪr.ɪŋ/ **adj** encouraging, or making you feel you want to do something: *She was an inspiring example to her followers.*

instability /ˌɪn.stəˈbɪl.ɪ.ti/ US /-ə.t̬i/ **noun** [U] UNCERTAINTY caused by the possibility of a sudden change in the present situation: *political/economic instability* ◦ *The instability of the euro continues.* ◦ *The building's instability makes it extremely dangerous.*

install /ɪnˈstɔːl/ US /-ˈstɑːl/ **verb** [T] **READY TO USE** ▷ **1** B1 to put furniture, a machine, or a piece of equipment into position and make it ready to use: *The plumber is coming tomorrow to install the new washing machine.* **2** B1 specialized to put a computer program onto a computer so that the computer can use it: *Andrew, can you help me install this software?* **GIVE JOB** ▷ **3** to put someone in an important job or position: *She has installed a couple of young academics* ***as*** *her advisers.* **PLACE** ▷ **4 install sb/yourself in/at somewhere** UK to put someone/yourself in a comfortable position where you want to stay: *He seems to have installed himself* ***in*** *your spare room for good!*

installation /ˌɪn.stəˈleɪ.ʃən/ **noun** **EQUIPMENT/FURNITURE** ▷ **1** C1 [U] an occasion when equipment or furniture is put into position or made ready to use: *Do you have to pay extra for installation?* **PLACE** ▷ **2** [C] a nearly permanent place with people, buildings, and equipment that have a particular, especially military, purpose: *a nuclear installation* ◦ *The Americans still have several military bases and installations on the island.* **JOB** ▷ **3** [U] an occasion when someone is put in an important job or position: *The installation of the new archbishop will take place in January.* **ART** ▷ **4** [C] a form of modern SCULPTURE where the artist uses sound, movement, or space as well as objects in order to make an often temporary work of art

installer /ɪnˈstɔː.ləʳ/ US /.lɚ/ **noun** [C] **SOFTWARE** ▷ **1** software that tells your computer how to copy a program from a disk onto the computer: *Just pop the CD into your computer and start the installer.* **PERSON** ▷ **2** someone whose job is to put furniture, equipment, a machine, etc. into the correct position and make it ready to use: *a carpet installer* ◦ *a cable television installer*

inˈstallment ˌplan noun [C] US for **hire purchase**

instalment UK (US **installment**) /ɪnˈstɔːl.mənt/ US /-ˈstɑːl-/ **noun** [C] one of several parts into which a story, plan, or amount of money owed has been divided, so that each part happens or is paid at different times until the end or total is reached: *The novel has been serialized for radio* ***in*** *five instalments.* ◦ *We agreed to* ***pay for*** *the car* ***by/in*** *instalments.*

instance /ˈɪn.stəns/ **noun; verb**

▸**noun** [C] C1 a particular situation, event or fact, especially an example of something that happens generally: *There have been several instances* ***of*** *violence at the school.* ◦ *I don't usually side with the management, but* ***in this*** *instance I agree with what they're saying.*

IDIOM **for instance** B1 for example: *In the electronics industry, for instance, 5,000 jobs are being lost.*

▸**verb** [T] UK formal to give something as an example: *She argued the need for legal reform and instanced several recent cases with grossly unfair verdicts.*

instant /ˈɪn.stənt/ **adj; noun**

▸**adj 1** B2 happening immediately, without any delay: *This type of account offers you instant* ***access*** *to your money.* ◦ *Contrary to expectations, the film was an instant* ***success.*** **2** Instant food or drink is dried, usually in the form of a powder, and can be prepared very quickly by adding hot water: *instant coffee/soup*

▸**noun** [S] an extremely short period of time: ***In*** *an instant her mood had changed.* ◦ *The startled boy froze* ***for*** *an instant, then fled.* ◦ *'Stop that noise* ***this*** *instant (= now)!'* ◦ *I'll call you* ***the*** *instant (= as soon as) I get home.* → Synonym **moment**

instantaneous /ˌɪn.stənˈteɪ.ni.əs/ **adj** happening immediately, without any delay: *an instantaneous response/reply/reaction* • **instantaneously** /-li/ **adv**

instantly /ˈɪn.stənt.li/ **adv** B2 immediately: *Both drivers were killed instantly.*

ˌinstant ˈmessaging noun [U] a type of service available on the internet that allows you to exchange written messages with someone else who is using the service at the same time

ˌinstant ˈreplay noun [C] US for **action replay**

instead /ɪnˈsted/ **adv** A2 in place of someone or something else: *There's no coffee – would you like a cup of tea instead?* ◦ *You can go instead* ***of*** *me, if you want.*

instep /ˈɪn.step/ **noun** [C] the curved upper part of the foot between the toes and the HEEL, or the part of a shoe or sock which fits around this

instigate /ˈɪn.stɪ.geɪt/ **verb** [T] formal to cause an event or situation to happen by making a set of actions or a formal process begin: *The government will instigate new measures to combat terrorism.* ◦ *The revolt in the north is believed to have been instigated by a high-ranking general.* • **instigation** /ˌɪn.stɪˈgeɪ.ʃən/ **noun** [U] *The inquiry was begun* ***at the*** *instigation* ***of*** *a local MP.*

instigator /ˈɪn.stɪ.geɪ.təʳ/ US /-t̬ɚ/ **noun** [C] a person who causes something to happen, especially something bad: *The instigators of the disturbance have not yet been identified.*

instil (-ll-) UK (US **instill**) /ɪnˈstɪl/ **verb** [T] to put a feeling, idea, or principle gradually into someone's mind, so that it has a strong influence on the way they think or behave: *It is part of a teacher's job to instil* ***confidence in/into*** *his or her students.*

instinct /ˈɪn.stɪŋkt/ **noun** [C or U] C2 the way people or animals naturally react or behave, without having to think or learn about it: *All his instincts told him to stay near the car and wait for help.* ◦ [+ to infinitive] *Her* ***first*** *instinct was* ***to*** *run.* ◦ *It is instinct that tells the birds when to begin their migration.* ◦ figurative *Bob seems to* ***have*** *an instinct* ***for*** *(= is naturally good at) knowing which products will sell.*

instinctive /ɪnˈstɪŋk.tɪv/ **adj** Instinctive behaviour or reactions are not thought about, planned, or developed by training: *an instinctive reaction* • **instinctively** /-li/ **adv** *She knew instinctively that he was dangerous.*

institute /ˈɪn.stɪ.tjuːt/ US /-tuːt/ **noun; verb**

▸**noun** [C] B2 an organization where people do a particular type of scientific, educational, or social work, or the buildings which it uses: *the Massachusetts Institute of Technology*

▸**verb** [T] formal to start or cause a system, rule, legal action, etc. to exist: *She is threatening to institute legal proceedings against the hospital.*

institution /ˌɪn.stɪˈtjuː.ʃən/ US /-ˈtuː-/ **noun** **ORGANIZATION** ▷ **1** B2 [C] a large and important organization, such as a university or bank: *a medical/educational/financial institution* **PLACE** ▷ **2** B2 [C] mainly disapproving a building where people are sent to be cared for, especially a hospital or prison **CUSTOM** ▷ **3** C2 [C] a custom or tradition that has existed for a long time and is accepted as an important part of a particular society: *the venerable institution of marriage* ◦ figurative *Mrs Daly is an institution – she's been with the company 40 years and knows absolutely everyone.* **START** ▷ **4** [U] an occasion when a law, system, etc. begins or is introduced: *The institution of a Freedom of Information Act has had a significant effect.*

institutional /ˌɪn.stɪˈtjuː.ʃən.əl/ US /-ˈtuː-/ **adj** relating to an institution: *The hospital provides typically awful institutional food.*

institutionalize (UK usually **institutionalise**) /ˌɪn.stɪ-

ˈtjuː.ʃən.ə.laɪz/ (US) /-ˈtuː-/ **verb** [T] **PLACE** ▷ **1** to send someone, especially someone who is not able to live independently, to live in an institution **CUSTOM** ▷ **2** to make something become part of a particular society, system, or organization: *What was once an informal event has now become institutionalized.*

institutionalized mainly disapproving (UK usually **institutionalised**) /ˌɪn.stɪˈtjuː.ʃən.ə.laɪzd/ (US) /-ˈtuː-/ **adj** If someone becomes institutionalized, they gradually become less able to think and act independently, because they have lived for a long time under the rules of an institution: *We need to avoid long-stay patients in the hospital becoming institutionalized.*

instiˌtutionalized ˈracism **noun** [U] mainly UK RACISM (= when someone is treated unfairly because of their race) that has become part of the normal behaviour of people within an organization

ˌin-ˈstore **adj** [before noun] happening or existing inside a large shop, or available for customers to use or buy inside a large shop: *an in-store bakery/café* ◦ *in-store banking*

instruct /ɪnˈstrʌkt/ **verb** **ORDER** ▷ **1** C1 [T + to infinitive] to order or tell someone to do something, especially in a formal way: *The police have been instructed **to** patrol the building and surrounding area.* **2** [T] UK to employ a lawyer to represent you in court **3** [T] When a judge instructs a JURY, he or she tells it what the law means and how to use it. **TEACH** ▷ **4** C2 [T] to teach someone how to do something: *He works in a sports centre instructing people **in** the use of the gym equipment.*

instruction /ɪnˈstrʌk.ʃən/ **noun** **ORDER** ▷ **1** C2 [C usually plural] something that someone tells you to do: *The police who broke into the house were only acting **on/under** instructions.* ◦ [+ to infinitive] *He **gave** me strict instructions **to** get there by eight o'clock.* **TEACHING** ▷ **2 instructions** [plural] A2 advice and information about how to do or use something, often written in a small book or on the side of a container: *The cooking instructions say bake it for half an hour.* ◦ *You obviously didn't read the instructions properly.* ◦ *They need clear instructions **on** what to do next.* **3** C2 [U] the teaching of a particular skill or subject: *The video provides instruction **on** how to operate the computer.* ◦ *The course gives you **basic** instruction **in** car maintenance.* ◦ *Have you seen the instruction **manual** for the washing machine?*

instructive /ɪnˈstrʌk.tɪv/ **adj** approving giving useful or interesting information • **instructively** /-li/ **adv**

instructor /ɪnˈstrʌk.təʳ/ (US) /-tɚ/ **noun** [C] **1** B1 a person whose job is to teach people a practical skill: *an aerobics instructor* ◦ *a driving/ski/swimming instructor* **2** US a teacher of a college or university subject, who usually teaches a limited number of classes: *a history/science/sociology instructor.*

instrument /ˈɪn.strə.mənt/ **noun** [C] **MUSIC** ▷ **1** A2 (also **musical instrument**) an object, such as a piano, guitar, or drum, that is played to produce musical sounds: *Which instrument do you **play**?* **TOOL** ▷ **2** C1 a tool or other device, especially one without electrical power, used for performing a particular piece of work: *surgical instruments* ◦ *instruments of torture* ◦ *The man's injuries had obviously been caused by a blunt instrument.* **3** a device used for measuring speed, height, etc. in vehicles, especially aircraft: *the instrument panel* ◦ *The lightning had damaged the plane's instruments, and they weren't giving any readings.* **4** C2 formal a way of achieving or causing something: *He saw the theatre as an instrument **of** change – a way of forcing people to consider social and political issues.* **FINANCE** ▷ **5** a type of INVESTMENT in a company or in government debt that can be traded on the financial markets: *They trade in the **debt** instruments of developing countries.* ◦ *increasingly complex **financial** instruments*

instrumental /ˌɪn.strəˈmen.təl/ (US) /-t̬əl/ **adj; noun**
▸**adj** **INFLUENCE** ▷ **1** [after verb] formal If someone or something is instrumental in a process, plan, or system, they are one of the most important influences in causing it to happen: *She was instrumental **in** bring**ing** about the prison reform act.* **MUSIC** ▷ **2** involving only musical instruments, and no singing: *instrumental music* ◦ *an instrumental piece/arrangement*
▸**noun** [C] a piece of music without singing

instrumentalist /ˌɪn.strəˈmen.təl.ɪst/ (US) /-t̬əl-/ **noun** [C] a person who plays a musical instrument, especially as a job: *He was one of the finest instrumentalists of his day.*

instrumentation /ˌɪn.strə.menˈteɪ.ʃən/ **noun** [U] specialized **MUSIC** ▷ **1** the particular combination of musical instruments that are used to play a piece of music **TOOL** ▷ **2** the set of instruments that are used to operate a machine

insubordinate /ˌɪn.səˈbɔː.dɪ.nət/ (US) /-ˈbɔːr-/ **adj** disapproving (of a person) not willing to obey orders from people in authority, or (of actions and speech, etc.) showing that you are not willing to obey orders: *an insubordinate child*

insubordination /ˌɪn.səˌbɔː.dɪˈneɪ.ʃən/ (US) /-ˌbɔːr-/ **noun** [U] disapproving refusing to obey orders from people in authority: *an act of insubordination* ◦ *Several officers were arrested for insubordination.*

insubstantial /ˌɪn.səbˈstæn.ʃəl/, /-ˈstɑːn-/ **adj** **NOT ENOUGH** ▷ **1** not enough or not strong enough: *an insubstantial meal* ◦ *insubstantial evidence* **IMAGINARY** ▷ **2** literary not existing as a physical person or thing: *She seemed somehow insubstantial – a shadow of a woman.*

insufferable /ɪnˈsʌf.ər.ə.bl/ (US) /-ɚ-/ **adj** very annoying, unpleasant, or uncomfortable, and therefore extremely difficult to bear: *She disliked the president, whom she once described as an 'insufferable bore'.* ◦ *The metro is insufferable in this heat.* • **insufferably** /-bli/ **adv**

insufficient /ˌɪn.səˈfɪʃ.ənt/ **adj** C1 not enough: *insufficient information/time* ◦ [+ to infinitive] *There was insufficient money **to** fund the project.* • **insufficiently** /-li/ **adv** *I felt that the whole project was insufficiently researched.* • **insufficiency** /-ən.si/ **noun** [C or U]

insular /ˈɪn.sjʊ.ləʳ/ (US) /-lɚ/ **adj** disapproving interested only in your own country or group and not willing to accept different or foreign ideas • **insularity** /ˌɪn.sjʊˈlær.ə.ti/ (US) /-t̬i/ **noun** [U]

insulate /ˈɪn.sjʊ.leɪt/ **verb** [T] **COVER** ▷ **1** to cover and surround something with a material or substance in order to stop heat, sound, or electricity from escaping or entering: *You can insulate a house **against** heat loss by having the windows double-glazed.* **PROTECT** ▷ **2** to protect someone or something from harmful experiences or influences: *Children should be insulated **from** the horrors of war.* ◦ *Until recently the country's economy has been insulated **from** recession by its reserves of raw materials.*

ˈinsulating ˌtape **noun** [U] a strip of sticky material that is put around a piece of electrical wire in order to stop someone or something from being harmed by the electricity

insulation /ˌɪn.sjʊˈleɪ.ʃən/ **noun** [U] **1** the act of covering something to stop heat, sound, or electricity from escaping or entering, or the fact that something is covered in this way: *The animal's thick fur provides very good insulation **against** the arctic cold.* **2** material that is used to stop heat, sound, or electricity from escaping or entering: *Glass fibre is often used as **roof** insulation.*

insulator /ˈɪn.sjʊ.leɪ.təʳ/ (US) /-t̬ɚ/ **noun** [C] a material or covering which electricity, heat, or sound cannot go through: *Generally, plastics tend to be good insulators.*

insulin /ˈɪn.sjʊ.lɪn/ (US) /-sə-/ **noun** [U] a HORMONE in the body which controls the amount of sugar in the blood: *She has to have insulin injections for her diabetes.*

insult noun; verb

▸**noun** [C] /ˈɪn.sʌlt/ (B2) an offensive remark or action: *She **made** several insults about my appearance.* ◦ *The steelworkers' leader rejected the two percent pay-rise saying it was an insult **to** the profession.* ◦ *The instructions are so easy they are an insult **to your intelligence** (= they seem to suggest you are not clever if you need to use them).*

▸**verb** [T] /ɪnˈsʌlt/ (B2) to say or do something to someone that is rude or offensive: *First he drank all my wine and then he insulted all my friends.*

insulting /ɪnˈsʌl.tɪŋ/ (US) /-t̬ɪŋ/ **adj** rude or offensive • **insultingly** /-li/ **adv** *The questions were insultingly easy.*

insuperable /ɪnˈsjuː.pᵊr.ə.bl̩/ (US) /-ˈsuː.pɚ-/ **adj** formal (especially of a problem) so great or severe that it cannot be defeated or dealt with successfully • **insuperably** /-bli/ **adv**

insupportable /ˌɪn.səˈpɔː.tə.bl̩/ (US) /-ˈpɔːr.t̬ə-/ **adj** formal difficult or impossible to bear: *The war had put an insupportable financial burden on the country.*

insurance /ɪnˈʃɔː.rəns/ (US) /-ˈʃɔːr.ᵊns/ **noun** [U] (B2) an agreement in which you pay a company money and they pay your costs if you have an accident, injury, etc.: *life/health/car/travel insurance* ◦ *I'll need to **take out** extra car insurance for another driver.* ◦ *The insurance doesn't **cover** you for (= include) household items.* → Compare **assurance**

in'surance ˌpolicy **noun** [C] a written agreement for insurance between an insurance company and a person who wants insurance: *I **took out** a travel insurance policy before I boarded the plane.* ◦ figurative *There's one particular job I'm after but I'm applying for several others as an insurance policy (= because I might not get the job I want).*

insure /ɪnˈʃɔːʳ/ (US) /-ˈʃʊr/ **verb** **1** [I or T, usually + adv/prep] to protect yourself against risk by regularly paying a special company that will provide a fixed amount of money if you are killed or injured or if your home or possessions are damaged, destroyed, or stolen: *The house is insured **for** two million pounds.* ◦ *All our household goods are insured **against** accidental damage.* ◦ [+ obj + to infinitive] *I'm not insured **to** drive his car.* **2** [T] to provide insurance for someone or something: *They refused to insure us because they said we're too old.* ◦ *Many companies won't insure new or young drivers.*

PHRASAL VERB **insure against sth** to do something in order to prevent something unpleasant from happening or from affecting you: *We thought we'd insure against rain by putting a tent up where people could take shelter.*

insured /ɪnˈʃɔːd/ (US) /-ˈʃʊrd/ **noun** specialized **the insured** the person, group of people, or organization who is insured in a particular agreement

insurer /ɪnˈʃɔː.rəʳ/ (US) /-ˈʃʊr.ɚ/ **noun** [C] a person or company that insures someone or something: *Please contact your insurer if you have any inquiries.*

insurgency /ɪnˈsɜː.dʒᵊn.si/ (US) /-ˈsɝː-/ **noun** [U] an occasion when a group of people attempt to take control of their country by force: *The government is reported to be concerned about the growing insurgency in the South.* → Compare **counterinsurgency**

insurgent /ɪnˈsɜː.dʒᵊnt/ (US) /-ˈsɝː-/ **noun** **1** [C usually plural] formal someone who is fighting against the government in their own country: *All approaches to the capital are now under the control of the insurgents.* **2** [C] US someone who opposes political authority

insurmountable /ˌɪn.səˈmaʊn.tə.bl̩/ (US) /-sɚˈmaʊn.t̬ə-/ **adj** formal (especially of a problem or a difficulty) so great that it cannot be dealt with successfully: *insurmountable difficulties* ◦ *This small country is faced with an insurmountable debt.*

insurrection /ˌɪn.sᵊrˈek.ʃᵊn/ (US) /-sɚ-/ **noun** [C or U] an organized attempt by a group of people to defeat their government and take control of their country, usually by violence: *armed insurrection*

intact /ɪnˈtækt/ **adj** **1** (C2) complete and in the original state: *The church was destroyed in the bombing but the altar survived intact.* **2** (C2) not damaged: *It's difficult to emerge from such a scandal with your reputation still intact.*

intake /ˈɪn.teɪk/ **noun** **BREATH** ▷ **1** [C] an act of taking in something, especially breath: *I heard a **sharp** intake **of breath** behind me.* **AMOUNT** ▷ **2** [U] the amount of a particular substance that is eaten or drunk during a particular time: *It says on the packet that four slices of this bread contains one half of your recommended **daily** intake of fibre.* **3** [U] the number of people that are accepted at a particular time by an organization, especially a college or university **OPENING** ▷ **4** [C] an opening through which air, liquid, or gas is taken in: *The Tornado jet fighter-bomber has two **air** intakes, one at the base of each wing.*

intangible /ɪnˈtæn.dʒɪ.bl̩/ **adj** An intangible feeling or quality exists but you cannot describe it exactly or prove it: *She has that intangible quality which you might call charisma.* • **intangible** **noun** [C usually plural] *Common sense and creativity are some of the intangibles we're looking for in an employee.* • **intangibly** /-bli/ **adv**

inˌtangible ˈasset **noun** [C] something valuable that a company has which is not material, such as a good reputation

integer /ˈɪn.tɪ.dʒəʳ/ (US) /-dʒɚ/ **noun** [C] specialized a whole number and not a FRACTION: *The numbers -5, 0 and 3 are integers.*

integral /ˈɪn.tɪ.grəl/ (US) /-t̬ə-/ **adj** (C1) necessary and important as a part of, or contained within, a whole: *He's an integral **part** of the team and we can't do without him.* ◦ *Bars and terrace cafés are integral **to** the social life of the city.*

integrate /ˈɪn.tɪ.greɪt/ (US) /-t̬ə-/ **verb** **1** (C1) [I or T] to mix with and join society or a group of people, often changing to suit their way of life, habits, and customs: *He seems to find it difficult to integrate socially.* ◦ *It's very difficult to integrate your**self into** a society whose culture is so different from your own.* ◦ *Children are often very good at integrating **into** a new culture.* **2** [T] to combine two or more things in order to become more effective: *To get fitter you need to integrate exercise **into** your normal life.* ◦ *The idea with young children is to integrate learning **with** play.* • **integrated** /-greɪ.tɪd/ (US) /-greɪ.t̬ɪd/ **adj** *The town's* *modern architecture is very well integrated* ***with*** *the old.* • **integration** /ˌɪn.tɪˈɡreɪ.ʃən/ (US) /-t̬ə-/ noun [U] C1 *racial/cultural integration*

ˌintegrated ˈcircuit noun [C] (abbreviation **IC**) a very small electronic CIRCUIT which consists of a lot of small parts made on a piece of SEMICONDUCTING material

integrity /ɪnˈteɡ.rə.ti/ (US) /-t̬i/ noun [U] **HONESTY** ▷ **1** C2 approving the quality of being honest and having strong moral principles that you refuse to change: *No one doubted that the president was a man of the highest integrity.* **2 sb's artistic, professional, etc. integrity** approving someone's high artistic standards or standards of doing their job and their determination not to lower those standards: *Keen to preserve his artistic integrity, he refused several lucrative Hollywood offers.* **WHOLE** ▷ **3** formal the quality of being whole and complete: *A modern extension on the old building would ruin its architectural integrity.*

intellect /ˈɪn.təl.ekt/ (US) /-t̬ə-/ noun **1** C2 [U] the ability to understand and to think in an intelligent way: *Her energy and intellect are respected all over the world.* ◦ *He is a man more noted for his intellect than his charm.* **2** [C] formal a very educated person whose interests are studying and other activities that involve careful thinking

intellectual /ˌɪn.təlˈek.tju.əl/ (US) /-t̬əlˈek.tʃu-/ adj; noun

▸**adj** B2 relating to your ability to think and understand things, especially complicated ideas: *Looking after a baby at home all day is nice but it doesn't provide much intellectual* ***stimulation****.* ◦ *I like detective stories and romances – nothing too intellectual.* • **intellectually** /-ə.li/ adv C2 *She's hoping to find a job which is more demanding intellectually.*

▸**noun** [C] C2 a very educated person whose interests are studying and other activities that involve careful thinking and mental effort: *She was too much of an intellectual to find popular films interesting.*

intellectualize (UK usually **intellectualise**) /ˌɪn.təlˈek.tju.ə.laɪz/ (US) /-t̬əlˈek.tʃu-/ verb [I or T] to think about or discuss a subject in a detailed and intellectual way, without involving your emotions or feelings: *She couldn't stand all that pointless intellectualizing about subjects that just didn't matter.* • **intellectualism** /-lɪ.zəm/ noun [U] usually disapproving

intelˌlectual ˈproperty noun [U] legal (abbreviation **IP**) someone's idea, INVENTION, CREATION, etc., that can be protected by law from being copied by someone else

intelligence /ɪnˈtel.ɪ.dʒəns/ noun **ABILITY** ▷ **1** B2 [U] the ability to learn, understand, and make judgments or have opinions that are based on reason: *an intelligence test* ◦ *a child of high/average/low intelligence* ◦ *It's the intelligence of her writing that impresses me.* **SECRET INFORMATION** ▷ **2** [U, + sing/pl verb] secret information about the governments of other countries, especially enemy governments, or a group of people who collect and deal with this information: *the Central Intelligence Agency* ◦ *military intelligence* ◦ *They received intelligence (reports)* ***that*** *the factory was a target for the bombing.*

> **Word partners for intelligence (ABILITY)**
>
> of *average/great/high/low* intelligence • *have/show/use* intelligence • *have* the intelligence to do sth • *insult* sb's intelligence • a *lack/level/sign* of intelligence

> **Word partners for intelligence (SECRET INFORMATION)**
>
> a *piece* of intelligence • *secret/sensitive* intelligence • *gather/obtain* intelligence • intelligence *on* sb/sth

intelligent /ɪnˈtel.ɪ.dʒənt/ adj B1 showing intelligence, or able to learn and understand things easily: *a highly intelligent young man* ◦ *an intelligent remark* ◦ *Helen had a few intelligent things to say on the subject.* • **intelligently** /-li/ adv

> **Other ways of saying intelligent**
>
> The adjectives **smart** and **clever** (UK) are common alternatives to 'intelligent':
>
> *She's a very* ***smart*** *woman.*
>
> *She's the cleverest kid in the class.*
>
> Young people who are intelligent are sometimes described as **bright**:
>
> *Jacob was a very* ***bright*** *boy.*
>
> Someone who is extremely intelligent is sometimes described as **brilliant**:
>
> *William was a* ***brilliant*** *scholar.*
>
> An intelligent person who has a natural ability to do a particular thing very well can be described as **gifted**:
>
> *a* ***gifted*** *mathematician*
>
> The adjective **intellectual** can be used about someone who studies and understands complicated subjects and ideas:
>
> *This course examines the most influential* ***intellectual*** *thinkers of modern times.*
>
> **Wise** can be used to describe someone who is intelligent as the result of experience:
>
> *a* ***wise*** *old teacher*

inˌtelligent deˈsign noun [U] (abbreviation **ID**) the idea that the world is so complicated that it cannot have developed by chance, and must have been made by God or some other intelligent being

the intelligentsia /ɪnˌtel.ɪˈdʒent.si.ə/ noun [S, + sing/pl verb] very educated people in a society, especially those interested in the arts and in politics

intelligible /ɪnˈtel.ɪ.dʒɪ.bl/ adj (of speech and writing) clear enough to be understood: *She was so upset when she spoke that she was hardly intelligible.* → Opposite **unintelligible** • **intelligibly** /-bli/ adv • **intelligibility** /ɪnˌtel.ɪ.dʒəˈbɪl.ɪ.ti/ (US) /-ə.t̬i/ noun [U]

intemperate /ɪnˈtem.pər.ət/ (US) /-pɚ-/ adj formal (of a person or their behaviour or speech) not controlled and too extreme or violent: *an intemperate outburst* ◦ *intemperate language* ◦ *The governor said he would not be provoked into intemperate action.* • **intemperately** /-li/ adv • **intemperance** /-əns/ noun [U]

intend /ɪnˈtend/ verb [T] B1 to have as a plan or purpose: [+ to infinitive] *We intend* ***to*** *go to Australia next year.* ◦ *Somehow I offended him, which wasn't what I'd intended.* ◦ [+ obj + to infinitive] *I don't think she intended me* ***to*** *hear the remark.* ◦ *The course is intended* ***for*** *intermediate-level students.* ◦ *It was intended* ***as*** *a compliment, honestly!*

intended /ɪnˈten.dɪd/ noun [C usually singular] old-fashioned or humorous the person that you are going to marry: *I shall be there with my intended.*

intense /ɪnˈtens/ adj **1** C1 extreme and forceful or (of a feeling) very strong: *intense cold/heat/hatred* ◦ *an intense flavour/colour* ◦ *He suddenly felt an intense pain in his back.* **2** C2 Intense people are very serious, and usually have strong emotions or opinions: *an intense* *young man* • **intensely** /-li/ **adv** C2 *His strongest criticism is reserved for his father, whom he disliked intensely.*

intensifier /ɪnˈten.sɪ.faɪ.əʳ/ US /-ɚ/ **noun** [C] (also **intensive**) In English grammar, an intensifier is a word, especially an adverb or adjective, that has little meaning itself but is used to add force to another adjective, verb, or adverb: *In the phrases 'an extremely large man' and 'I strongly object', 'extremely' and 'strongly' are both intensifiers.*

intensify /ɪnˈten.sɪ.faɪ/ **verb** [I or T] C2 to become greater, more serious, or more extreme, or to make something do this: *Fighting around the capital has intensified in the last few hours.* • **intensification** /ɪnˌten.sɪ.fɪˈkeɪ.ʃᵊn/ **noun** [U]

intensity /ɪnˈten.sɪ.ti/ US /-sə.t̬i/ **noun** **1** C2 [U] the quality of being felt strongly or having a very strong effect: *The explosion was of such intensity that it was heard five miles away.* **2** [C or U] the strength of something that can be measured such as light, sound, etc.: *measures of light intensity* **3** [U] the quality of being very serious and having strong emotions or opinions: *The intensity of their relationship was causing problems.*

intensive /ɪnˈten.sɪv/ **adj** B2 involving a lot of effort or activity in a short period of time: *two weeks of intensive training* ◦ *an intensive course in English* ◦ *Intensive bombing had reduced the city to rubble.* • **intensively** /-li/ **adv**

inˌtensive ˈcare **noun** [U] **1** (in a hospital) continuous treatment for patients who are seriously ill, very badly injured, or who have just had an operation: *She needed intensive care for three weeks.* **2** (also **the intensive care unit**) the part of a hospital which provides intensive care: *He nearly died in the accident and was* ***in*** *intensive care for over a month.*

inˌtensive ˈfarming **noun** [U] a way of producing large amounts of crops, by using chemicals and machines: *The use of intensive farming can damage the environment.*

intent /ɪnˈtent/ **adj; noun**

▸**adj** **1** giving all your attention to something: *an intent stare* ◦ *She had an intent look on her face.* **2** **be intent on sth/doing sth** C2 to be determined to do or achieve something: *I've tried persuading her not to go but she's intent on it.* ◦ *He seems intent on upsetting everyone in the room!* • **intently** /-li/ **adv** *The child stared intently at her.*

▸**noun** [U] formal C2 the fact that you want and plan to do something: *I spent half the morning on the phone, which wasn't really my intent.* ◦ [+ to infinitive] *It was not his intent* ***to*** *hurt anyone.* ◦ legal *She was charged with possessing weapons* ***with*** *intent* ***to*** *endanger life.*

IDIOM **to/for all intents and purposes** C2 in all the most important ways: *For all intents and purposes, the project is completed.*

intention /ɪnˈten.ʃᵊn/ **noun** [C or U] B2 something that you want and plan to do: [+ to infinitive] *It wasn't my intention* ***to*** *exclude her from the list – I just forgot her.* ◦ *I've no intention* ***of*** *changing my plans just to fit in with his.* ◦ *He's full of* ***good*** *intentions, but he never does anything about them!* • **-intentioned** /-ʃᵊnd/ **suffix** *I'm sure he's* ***well****-intentioned – he wouldn't mean any harm.*

intentional /ɪnˈten.ʃᵊn.əl/ **adj** planned or intended: *Did you leave his name out by accident or was it intentional?* • **intentionally** /-i/ **adv** *I didn't ignore her intentionally – I just didn't recognize her.*

inter /ɪnˈtɜːʳ/ US /-ˈtɝː/ **verb** [T] **(-rr-)** formal to bury a dead body: *Many of the soldiers were interred* ***in*** *unmarked graves.*

inter- /ɪn.təʳ-/ US /-t̬ɚ-/ **prefix** used to form adjectives meaning 'between or among the people, things, or places mentioned': *international* ◦ *an interdepartmental meeting* ◦ *intercontinental missiles* → Compare **intra-**

interact /ˌɪn.təˈrækt/ US /-t̬ɚˈækt/ **verb** [I] B2 to communicate with or react to: *Dominique's teacher says that she interacts well* ***with*** *the other children.* ◦ *It's interesting at parties to see how people interact socially.* ◦ *We are studying how these two chemicals interact.*

interaction /ˌɪn.təˈræk.ʃᵊn/ US /-t̬ɚ-/ **noun** [C or U] C1 an occasion when two or more people or things communicate with or react to each other: *There's not enough interaction* ***between*** *the management and the workers.* ◦ *Language games are usually intended to encourage student interaction.* ◦ *The play follows the interactions of three very different characters.*

interactive /ˌɪn.təˈræk.tɪv/ US /-t̬ɚ-/ **adj** **1** B2 describes a system or computer program that is designed to involve the user in the exchange of information: *an interactive game/video* ◦ *This is an interactive museum where children can actively manipulate the exhibits.* **2** C1 involving communication between people: *interactive teaching methods* • **interactively** /-li/ **adv** *The program lets you work through a text interactively.*

inter alia /ˌɪn.təˈreɪ.li.ə/ US /-t̬ɚˈeɪ-/ **adv** formal among other things

interbreed /ˌɪn.təˈbriːd/ US /-t̬ɚ-/ **verb** [I or T] (**interbred, interbred**) to breed or cause to breed with members of another breed or group: *Some of the wolves had interbred* ***with*** *domestic dogs.* • **interbreeding** /-ˈbriː.dɪŋ/ **noun** [U]

intercede /ˌɪn.təˈsiːd/ US /-t̬ɚ-/ **verb** [I] formal to use your influence to persuade someone in authority to forgive another person, or save this person from punishment: *Several religious leaders have interceded* ***with*** *the authorities on behalf of the condemned prisoner.*

intercept /ˌɪn.təˈsept/ US /-tɚ-/ **verb** [T] to stop and catch something or someone before they are able to reach a particular place: *Law enforcement agents intercepted a shipment of drugs from Latin America.* ◦ *Barry intercepted Naylor's pass and scored the third goal.* • **interception** /-ˈsep.ʃᵊn/ **noun** [C or U] *the interception of enemy messages* ◦ *a pass interception*

interceptor /ˌɪn.təˈsep.təʳ/ US /-t̬ɚˈsep.t̬ɚ/ **noun** [C] a fast aircraft which attacks enemy aircraft

intercession /ˌɪn.təˈseʃ.ᵊn/ US /-t̬ɚ-/ **noun** **1** [U] the act of using your influence to make someone in authority forgive someone else or save them from punishment: *Several political prisoners have been released through the intercession of Amnesty International.* **2** [C or U] a prayer which asks God or a god to help or cure other people

interchange /ˌɪn.təˈtʃeɪndʒ/ US /-t̬ɚ-/ **noun; verb**

▸**noun** EXCHANGE ▷ **1** [C or U] formal an exchange, especially of ideas or information, between different people or groups ROAD ▷ **2** [C] UK a JUNCTION at which smaller roads meet a main road

▸**verb** [I or T] to exchange ideas or information

interchangeable /ˌɪn.təˈtʃeɪn.dʒə.bl̩/ US /-t̬ɚ-/ **adj** able to be exchanged with each other without making any difference or without being noticed: *interchangeable parts* ◦ *The terms 'drinking problem' and 'alcohol abuse' are often interchangeable.* • **interchangeably** /-bli/ **adv**

intercity /ˌɪn.təˈsɪt.i/ (US) /-t̬ɚˈsɪt̬-/ **adj** [before noun] travelling from one city to another, or happening between cities: *intercity bus/train/rail service*

intercollegiate /ˌɪn.tə.kəˈliː.dʒi.ət/ (US) /-t̬ɚ.kəˈliː.dʒɪt/ **adj** mainly US involving competition between different colleges: *intercollegiate sports/athletics/basketball*

intercom /ˈɪn.tə.kɒm/ (US) /-t̬ɚ.kɑːm/ **noun** [C] a device that people speak into when they want to communicate with someone who is inside a building, in a different room, in part of a plane, etc.

interconnect /ˌɪn.tə.kəˈnekt/ (US) /-t̬ɚ-/ **verb** [I or T] (of two or more things) to connect with or be related to each other: *The problems of poverty and unemployment are all interconnected.* • **interconnection** /-nek.ʃᵊn/ **noun** [C or U]

intercontinental /ˌɪn.təˌkɒn.tɪˈnen.tᵊl/ (US) /-t̬ɚˌkɑːn.t̬əˈnen.t̬ᵊl/ **adj** between continents: *intercontinental flights*

intercostal /ˌɪn.təˈkɒs.tᵊl/ (US) /-t̬ɚˈkɑː.stᵊl/ **adj** specialized between the RIBS (= bones around the chest): *intercostal* ***muscles*** ◦ *intercostal pain*

intercourse /ˈɪn.tə.kɔːs/ (US) /-t̬ɚ.kɔːrs/ **noun** [U] **SEX** ▷ **1** (also **sexual intercourse**) the act of having sex: *vaginal/anal intercourse* ◦ *Our survey reveals that most couples* ***have*** *intercourse once a week.* **CONVERSATION** ▷ **2** old-fashioned formal conversation and social activity between people

interdenominational /ˌɪn.tə.dɪˌnɒm.ɪˈneɪ.ʃᵊn.ᵊl/ (US) /-t̬ɚ.dɪˌnɑː.mə-/ **adj** shared by different groups of the Christian Church: *an interdenominational church service*

interdepartmental /ˌɪn.təˌdiː.pɑːtˈmen.tᵊl/ (US) /-t̬ɚˌdiː.pɑːrtˈmen.t̬ᵊl/ **adj** between or involving different departments of a school, university, business, etc.: *an interdepartmental committee/project*

interdependent /ˌɪn.tə.dɪˈpen.dᵊnt/ (US) /-t̬ɚ-/ **adj** depending on each other: *All living things are interdependent.* • **interdependence** /-dəns/ **noun** [U]

interdict /ˈɪn.tə.dɪkt/ (US) /-t̬ɚ-/ **noun** [C] specialized **1** an official instruction from a law court telling someone that they are not allowed to do something **2** an instruction from the Roman Catholic Church telling someone they are not allowed to take part in official Church activities

interdisciplinary /ˌɪn.təˈdɪs.ɪ.plɪ.nᵊr.i/ (US) /-t̬ɚˈdɪs.ə.plɪ.ner-/ **adj** involving two or more different subjects or areas of knowledge: *interdisciplinary courses*

> **! Common mistake: interest**
>
> The most usual preposition to use after the noun **interest** is **in**.
>
> Don't say 'interest for/on/about' something, say **interest in** something:
>
> ~~*He has never shown an interest for learning English.*~~
>
> *He has never shown an interest in learning English.*

interest /ˈɪn.trəst/ (US) /-trɪst/ **noun; verb**

▸**noun INVOLVEMENT** ▷ **1** (B1) [S or U] the feeling of wanting to give your attention to something or of wanting to be involved with and to discover more about something: *I've always* ***had*** *an interest* ***in*** *astronomy.* ◦ *He never seems to* ***show*** *any interest* ***in*** *his children.* ◦ *Unfortunately, I* ***lost*** *interest half way through the film.* ◦ *She* ***takes*** *more of* ***an*** *interest in politics these days.* ◦ informal *Just* ***out of*** *interest, how old is your wife?* **2** (B1) [C] Your interests are the activities that you enjoy doing and the subjects that you like to spend time learning about: *On his form he lists his interests as cycling and cooking.* **3** (B1) [U] the quality that makes you think that something is interesting: *Would this book* ***be of*** *any interest* ***to*** *you?* **ADVANTAGE** ▷ **4** (C1) [C usually plural, U] something that brings advantages to or affects someone or something: *A union looks after the interests of its members.* ◦ *It's* ***in his*** *interests to keep careful records.* ◦ ***In the*** *interests* ***of*** *safety, please do not smoke.* ◦ *Despite what you think, I'm only acting in your* ***best*** *interests* (= doing what is best for you). → See also **vested interest** **MONEY** ▷ **5** (C1) [U] money that is charged by a bank or other financial organization for borrowing money: *Interest* ***charges*** *on an overdraft are usually quite high.* **6** (C1) [U] money that you earn from keeping your money in an account in a bank or other financial organization: *You should put the money in a savings account where it will* ***earn*** *interest.* **LEGAL RIGHT** ▷ **7** [C] an involvement or a legal right, usually relating to a business or possessions: *He is a multi-millionaire with business interests around the world.* ◦ specialized *When they divorced she retained a legal interest in the property.*

> **Word partners for interest (INVOLVEMENT)**
>
> *develop/have/pursue/take* an interest • *express/indicate/show* an interest • *arouse/attract/generate/spark* interest • *lose* interest • a *genuine/great/keen/special* interest • an interest *in* sth • *with* interest • be *of* interest (to sb)

> **Word partners for interest (ADVANTAGE)**
>
> *protect/safeguard* sb's interests • *advance/promote* sb's interests • be *in* sb's interests to do sth • *in* the interest **of** sb/sth

▸**verb** [T] (B1) If someone or something interests you, you want to give them your attention and discover more about them: *Sport has never really interested me.*

PHRASAL VERB **interest sb in sth** Someone might ask if they can interest you in something when they are trying to persuade you to buy something or when they are offering you something: *Can I interest you in our new range of kitchen fittings, madam?* ◦ *I don't suppose I can interest you in a quick drink after work, can I?*

ˈinterest-ˌbearing **adj** [before noun] used to describe a financial product that pays money in the form of interest: *an interest-bearing account*

interested /ˈɪn.trəs.tɪd/ (US) /-trɪs-/ **adj** **INVOLVED** ▷ **1** (A2) wanting to give your attention to something and discover more about it: *He didn't seem very interested* ***in*** *what I was saying.* ◦ *She's at that age where she's starting to get interested* ***in*** *boys.* ◦ *I'd be interested* ***to*** *hear more about your work.* ◦ *'Really?' he said, with an interested look on his face.* ◦ *Yes, I'd be very interested* ***in*** *know****ing*** *more about the services your firm offers.* → Opposite **uninterested**

> **! Common mistake: interested**
>
> The correct preposition to use after **interested** is **in**.
>
> Don't say 'interested on/about/by something', say **interested in something**:
>
> ~~*I am very interested on the job you advertised.*~~
>
> **Remember:** when **interested in** is followed by a verb, the verb is in the **-ing** form:
>
> *I am interested in applying for this post.*

LEGAL RIGHT ▷ **2** relating to a person or group who have a connection with a particular situation, event, business, etc.: *All interested* ***parties*** *(= people who are involved) are advised to contact this office.*

ˈinterest ˌgroup noun [C] a group or organization with particular aims and ideas which tries to influence the government: *There's too much lobbying of MPs by special interest groups.*

interesting /ˈɪn.trəs.tɪŋ/ (US) /-trɪs-/ adj **1** (A1) Someone or something that is interesting keeps your attention because they are unusual, exciting, or have a lot of ideas: *She's quite an interesting woman.* ◦ *She's got some very interesting things to say on the subject.* ◦ ***It*** *is always interesting* ***to*** *hear other people's point of view.* ◦ *Oh, I didn't know they were married – that's interesting.* **2** humorous strange or different: *That's an interesting looking hat you're wearing, Neil!*

! Common mistake: interesting

Warning: Check your spelling!

Interesting is one of the 50 words most often spelled wrongly by learners. Remember: the correct spelling has an 'e' between the 't' and the 'r'.

! Common mistake: interesting or interested?

Warning: Choose the right word!

To talk about someone wanting to give their attention to something, don't say 'interesting', say **interested**:

~~*I am interesting in applying for the job.*~~

I am interested in applying for the job.

Remember: the correct preposition to use after **interested** is **in**.

+ Other ways of saying interesting

You can use **absorbing**, **gripping**, or **riveting** to describe a game, book, film, etc. that is so interesting that it keeps your attention completely:

I found the book absolutely ***gripping*** *– I couldn't put it down.*

It was a very ***absorbing*** *movie.*

The performance was ***riveting****.*

A game, book, TV programme, etc. that is so interesting that you cannot stop playing, reading, or watching it may be described as **compelling**:

It was a ***compelling*** *story.*

Fascinating is often used to describe someone or something you have seen or heard that you have found extremely interesting:

The history of the place was absolutely ***fascinating****.*

He's ***fascinating*** *on the subject.*

If something or someone is interesting and seems mysterious in a way that makes you want to know more about that thing or person, you can use the word **intriguing**:

It's a very ***intriguing*** *situation.*

interestingly /ˈɪn.trəs.tɪŋ.li/ (US) /-trɪs-/ adv used to introduce a piece of information that the speaker thinks is strange or interesting: *Interestingly (****enough****), he never actually said that he was innocent.*

ˈinterest ˌrate noun [C] the interest percent that a bank or other financial company charges you when you borrow money, or the interest percent it pays you when you keep money in an account: ***high/low*** *interest rates* ◦ *The bank has plans to* ***cut/raise*** *interest rates.*

interface /ˈɪn.tə.feɪs/ (US) /-t̬ɚ-/ noun; verb

▸**noun** [C] **1** a connection between two pieces of electronic equipment, or between a person and a computer: *My computer has a network interface, which allows me to get to other computers.* ◦ *The new version of the program comes with a much better* ***user*** *interface (= way of showing information to a user) than the original.* **2** a situation, way, or place where two things come together and affect each other: *the interface* ***between*** *technology and tradition* ◦ *We need a clearer interface* ***between*** *management and the workforce.*

▸**verb 1** [T] specialized to connect two or more pieces of equipment, such as computers: *The computers must be properly interfaced.* **2** [I] to communicate with someone, especially in a work-related situation: *We use email to interface* ***with*** *our customers.*

interfaith /ˌɪn.təˈfeɪθ/ (US) /-t̬ɚ-/ adj relating to activities involving members of different religions: *interfaith prayers/services/relations*

interfere /ˌɪn.təˈfɪəʳ/ (US) /-t̬ɚˈfɪr/ verb [I] (B2) to involve yourself in a situation when your involvement is not wanted or is not helpful: *It's their problem and I'm not going to interfere.* ◦ *I'd never interfere* ***between*** *(US* ***with****) a husband and wife.* ◦ *Interfering* ***in*** *other people's relationships is always a mistake.*

PHRASAL VERBS **interfere with sth 1** (C1) to prevent something from working effectively or from developing successfully: *Even a low level of noise interferes with my concentration.* **2** If something interferes with radio or television signals, it stops you from getting good sound or pictures. • **interfere with sb** UK disapproving to touch a child in a sexual manner: *He was sent to prison for interfering with little boys.*

interference /ˌɪn.təˈfɪə.rᵊns/ (US) /-t̬ɚˈfɪr.ᵊns/ noun [U] **1** (C1) an occasion when someone tries to interfere in a situation: *She seems to regard any advice or help from me as interference.* ◦ *The government's interference* ***in*** *the strike has been widely criticized.* **2** (C2) noise or other electronic signals that stop you from getting good pictures or sound on a television or radio

interfering /ˌɪn.təˈfɪə.rɪŋ/ (US) /-t̬ɚˈfɪr.ɪŋ/ adj [before noun] describes someone who gets involved in other people's lives in an unwanted and annoying way: *He's an interfering* ***old busybody*** *– who I go out with is none of his business!*

interferon /ˌɪn.təˈfɪə.rɒn/ (US) /-t̬ɚˈfɪr.ɑːn/ noun [C or U] specialized one of several PROTEINS in the body that are produced by cells as a reaction to infection by a virus

intergalactic /ˌɪn.tə.gəˈlæk.tɪk/ (US) /-t̬ɚ-/ adj [before noun] between GALAXIES (= large groups of stars and other matter): *intergalactic space*

interim /ˈɪn.tᵊr.ɪm/ (US) /-t̬ɚ-/ adj; noun

▸**adj** [before noun] **1** (C2) temporary and intended to be used or accepted until something permanent exists: *an interim solution* ◦ *An interim* ***government*** *was set up for the period before the country's first free election.* **2** used to describe part of a company's business year, rather than the whole year: *Directors declared an interim dividend of 30 cents.*

▸**noun in the interim** in the time between two particular periods or events: *The new secretary starts in June, but in the interim we're having to type our own letters.*

interior /ɪnˈtɪə.ri.əʳ/ (US) /-ˈtɪr.i.ɚ/ noun; adj

▸**noun 1** (B2) [C] the inside part of something: *The estate agent had pictures of the house from the outside but none of its interior.* ◦ *The car's interior is very impressive – wonderful leather seats and a wooden dashboard.* → Compare **exterior 2** [S] the land that is furthest away from the outside or coast of a country or continent: *the African interior* **3 the interior** in some countries, the government department that deals with subjects and events that are important in the country itself instead of events in other countries: *the Ministry of the Interior* ◦ *officials of the US Interior Department*

▸**adj** [before noun] **1** inside: *The interior walls have patches of damp on them.* ◦ *The paintwork on the interior doors (= those not in the outside wall of a building) is in good condition.* **2** relating to the government department in some countries that deals with subjects and events that are important in that country instead of events in other countries: *France's interior minister*

in,terior 'decorator noun [C] a person whose job is either planning the decoration of the inside of a building such as a house or office or doing the decoration themselves

in,terior de'sign noun [U] the art of planning the decoration of the inside of a building such as a house or office • **in,terior de'signer noun** [C]

interject /ˌɪn.tə'dʒekt/ ⓤⓢ /-t̬ɚ-/ **verb** [I or T] formal to say something while another person is speaking: [+ speech] *'That's absolutely ridiculous!' Mary interjected.* → Synonym **interrupt**

interjection /ˌɪn.tə'dʒek.ʃən/ ⓤⓢ /-t̬ɚ-/ **noun** formal **1** [C or U] an occasion when someone interrupts someone else, or the interruptions themselves: *Her controversial speech was punctuated with noisy interjections from the audience.* **2** [C] In grammar, an interjection is a word that is used to show a short sudden expression of emotion: *'Hey!' is an interjection.*

interlace /ˌɪn.tə'leɪs/ ⓤⓢ /-t̬ɚ-/ **verb** [T] to join different parts together to make a whole, especially by crossing one thing over another or fitting one part into another: *In her latest book, she interlaces historical events* ***with*** *her own childhood memories.*

interlink /ˌɪn.tə'lɪŋk/ ⓤⓢ /-t̬ɚ-/ **verb** [I or T] to cause to join or connect together, with the parts joined often having an effect on each other: *Police forces across Europe have begun to interlink their databases on stolen cars.* • **interlinked** /-'lɪŋkt/ **adj** *The circuits are interlinked* ***with*** *each other and the main power supply.* ◦ *It's clear that unemployment and crime are all interlinked.* • **interlinking** /-'lɪŋ.kɪŋ/ **adj**

interlock /ˌɪn.tə'lɒk/ ⓤⓢ /-t̬ɚ'lɑːk/ **verb** [I or T] to fit together firmly: *The edges interlock to form a tight seal.*

interlocking /ˌɪn.tə'lɒk.ɪŋ/ ⓤⓢ /-t̬ɚ'lɑː.kɪŋ/ **adj** firmly joined together, especially by one part fitting into another: *This jigsaw puzzle has 1,000 interlocking pieces.*

interlocutor /ˌɪn.tə'lɒk.jʊ.təʳ/ ⓤⓢ /-t̬ɚ'lɑː.kjə.t̬ɚ/ **noun** [C] formal **1** someone who is involved in a conversation **2** someone who is involved in a conversation and who is representing someone else

interloper /'ɪn.təˌləʊ.pəʳ/ ⓤⓢ /-t̬ɚˌloʊ.pɚ/ **noun** [C] disapproving someone who becomes involved in an activity or a social group without being asked, or enters a place without permission: *Security did not prevent an interloper from getting onto the stage at the opening ceremony.*

interlude /'ɪn.tə.luːd/ ⓤⓢ /-t̬ɚ-/ **noun** [C] a short period when a situation or activity is different from what comes before and after it: *Except for a brief Christian interlude at the beginning of the 11th century, Istanbul has been a Muslim city for almost 1,300 years.* ◦ *The musical interludes don't really fit in with the rest of the play.*

intermarriage /ˌɪn.tə'mær.ɪdʒ/ ⓤⓢ /-t̬ɚ'mer-/ **noun** [U] marriage between people who are from different social groups, races, or religions, or who are from the same family: *Have ethnic tensions in the area been reduced by intermarriage?* ◦ *Intermarriage* ***between*** *close relatives is prohibited in most societies.* • **intermarry** /-i/ **verb** [I] *Many of the immigrants have intermarried* ***with*** *the island's original inhabitants.*

intermediary /ˌɪn.tə'miː.di.ə.ri/ ⓤⓢ /-t̬ɚ-/ **noun** [C] someone who carries messages between people who are unwilling or unable to meet: *The police negotiated with the gunman* ***through*** *an intermediary.* ◦ *The former president has agreed to act as an intermediary* ***between*** *the government and the rebels.*

intermediate /ˌɪn.tə'miː.di.ət/ ⓤⓢ /-t̬ɚ-/ **adj** Ⓑ1 being between two other related things, levels, or points: *There are three levels of difficulty in this game: low, intermediate and high.* ◦ *This novel is too difficult for intermediate students of English.*

inter'mediate ,school noun [C] in the US, a school for students who are twelve to 14 years old, or ten to twelve years old

interment /ɪn'tɜː.mənt/ ⓤⓢ /-'tɝː-/ **noun** [C or U] formal the act of burying a dead body

intermezzo /ˌɪn.tə'met.səʊ/ ⓤⓢ /-t̬ɚ'met.soʊ/ **noun** [C] (plural **intermezzi** or **intermezzos**) a short piece of music written to be played on its own or as part of a longer piece

interminable /ɪn'tɜː.mɪ.nə.bl̩/ ⓤⓢ /-'tɝː-/ **adj** continuing for too long and therefore boring or annoying: *an interminable delay* ◦ *his interminable stories* • **interminably** /-bli/ **adv**

intermingle /ˌɪn.tə'mɪŋ.gl̩/ ⓤⓢ /-t̬ɚ-/ **verb** [I] to become mixed together: *The flavours intermingle to produce a very unusual taste.* ◦ *Fact is intermingled* ***with*** *fiction throughout the book.*

intermission /ˌɪn.tə'mɪʃ.ən/ ⓤⓢ /-t̬ɚ-/ **noun** [C or U] US (UK **interval**) **1** Ⓑ1 a short period between the parts of a play, film, CONCERT, etc. **2** US a period between parts of a game when the players rest and people watching can leave their seats: *The Sonics led by only two points at intermission.*

intermittent /ˌɪn.tə'mɪt.ənt/ ⓤⓢ /-t̬ɚ-/ **adj** not happening regularly or continuously; stopping and starting repeatedly or with periods in between: *intermittent rain* ◦ *an intermittent noise* ◦ *Although she made intermittent movie appearances, she was essentially a stage actress.* • **intermittently** /-li/ **adv** *We've discussed this problem intermittently, but so far we've failed to come up with a solution.*

intern verb; noun

▸**verb** [T often passive] /ɪn'tɜːn/ ⓤⓢ /-'tɝːn/ to put someone in prison for political or military reasons, especially during a war: *Many foreigners were interned for the duration of the war.*

▸**noun** [C] /'ɪn.tɜːn/ ⓤⓢ /-tɝːn/ **MEDICAL** ▷ **1** US a **houseman STUDENT** ▷ **2** mainly US someone who is finishing their training for a skilled job especially by getting practical experience of the work involved: *She worked in the White House as an intern.*

internal /ɪn'tɜː.nəl/ ⓤⓢ /-'tɝː-/ **adj** Ⓑ2 existing or happening inside a person, object, organization, place, or country: *He sustained injuries to his arms, legs, and several internal* ***organs.*** ◦ *The bank conducted its own internal investigation into the robbery.* ◦ *The government warned its neighbours not to interfere in its internal* ***affairs.*** → See also **interior** • **internally** /-i/ **adv** Ⓒ1 *This medicine is for external use only and should not be taken internally.*

in,ternal com'bustion ,engine noun [C] an engine which produces energy by burning fuel within itself

internalize formal (UK usually **internalise**) /ɪnˈtɜː.nəl.aɪz/ (US) /-ˈtɝː-/ **verb** [T] **1** to accept or absorb an idea, opinion, belief, etc. so that it becomes part of your character: *He had not expected the people so readily to internalize the values of democracy.* **2** If you internalize your emotions or feelings, you do not allow them to show although you think about them: *Women tend to internalize all their anxiety and distress – men hit out.* • **internalization** (UK usually **internalisation**) /ɪnˌtɜː.nəl.aɪˈzeɪ.ʃən/ (US) /ɪnˌtɝː.nəl.əˈ-/ **noun** [U]

inˌternal ˈmedicine **noun** [U] US the part of medical science that is involved in the discovery of diseases inside the body and the treatment of them without cutting the body open

the Inˌternal ˈRevenue ˌService **noun** (abbreviation **the IRS**) US the government department that collects most national taxes in the US

international /ˌɪn.təˈnæʃ.ən.əl/ (US) /-t̬ɚ-/ **adj; noun**

▸**adj** A2 involving more than one country: *international politics* • **internationally** /-i/ **adv**

▸**noun** [C] UK a sports event involving more than one country, or a person who competes in it: *a one-day international* ◦ *Six rugby internationals (= players) were charged with taking drugs to improve their performance.*

the Interˌnational Baccaˈlaureate **noun** [S] (abbreviation **IB**) trademark a set of exams in several subjects taken by students around the age of 18 or 19 in many different countries as a qualification for going to university

the interˌnational comˈmunity **noun** [S] countries of the world considered or acting together as a group: *Any taking of hostages is unacceptable and must be firmly opposed by the international community.*

Interˌnational ˈDate Line **noun** [S] The International Date Line is an imaginary line between the most northern and southern points on the Earth which goes through the Pacific Ocean. The date on the west side of the line is one day earlier than the date on the east side of the line.

the Internationale /ˌɪn.təˌnæʃ.əˈnɑːl/ (US) /-t̬ɚ-/ **noun** [S] a song that is sung by people who believe in COMMUNISM or SOCIALISM

internationalism /ˌɪn.təˈnæʃ.ən.əl.ɪ.zəm/ (US) /-t̬ɚ-/ **noun** [U] **1** the state of being international, or happening in and between many countries: *the increasing internationalism of criminals* **2** the belief that countries can achieve more advantages by working together and trying to understand each other than by arguing and fighting wars with each other • **internationalist** /-ɪst/ **noun** [C]

internationalize (UK usually **internationalise**) /ˌɪn.təˈnæʃ.ən.əl.aɪz/ (US) /-t̬ɚ-/ **verb** [T] to make something become international: *Bob Marley internationalized reggae, making it known throughout the world.* • **internationalization** (UK usually **internationalisation**) /ˌɪn.təˌnæʃ.ən.əl.aɪˈzeɪ.ʃən/ (US) /-t̬ɚˌnæʃ.ən.əl.əˈ-/ **noun** [U]

interˌnational ˈlaw **noun** [U] the set of rules that most countries obey when dealing with other countries

internecine /ˌɪn.təˈniː.saɪn/ (US) /-t̬ɚˈniː.sɪn/ **adj** formal Internecine war or fighting happens between members of the same group, religion, or country: *internecine* ***war/warfare***

internee /ˌɪn.tɜːˈniː/ (US) /-tɝː-/ **noun** [C] a person who has been put in prison for political or military reasons, especially during a war

the internet /ˈɪn.tə.net/ (US) /-t̬ɚ-/ **noun** [S] (informal **the Net**) A1 the large system of connected computers around the world that allows people to share information and communicate with each other: *I found out about the bombings* ***from/on*** *the internet.*

> **!** Common mistake: **internet**
>
> To talk about the large system of connected computers in general, remember to use **the**.
>
> Don't say 'internet', say **the internet**:
>
> ~~*Many companies use internet to advertise their products.*~~
>
> *Many companies use the internet to advertise their products.*

> Word partners for **the internet**
>
> *browse/surf* the internet • *post* sth **on** the internet • *download* sth **from** the internet • *on* the internet • internet *access* • an internet *chatroom/site* • an internet *provider/service provider* • an internet *account/address*

ˌinternet ˈbanking **noun** [U] the system that allows you to put in or take out money from a bank account by using the internet

ˌinternet ˈcafé **noun** [C] a small, informal restaurant where you can pay to use the internet

ˌinternet ˈdating **noun** [U] a way to meet people for possible romantic relationships, in which you look at descriptions of people on the internet and arrange to meet them if you like them

internist /ˈɪn.tɜː.nɪst/ (US) /-ˈtɝː-/ **noun** [C] US a doctor who specializes in IDENTIFYING and treating diseases which do not need SURGERY (= cutting into the body)

internment /ɪnˈtɜːn.mənt/ (US) /-ˈtɝːn-/ **noun** [U] the act of putting someone in prison for political or military reasons, especially during a war: *an internment* ***camp***

internship /ˈɪn.tɜːn.ʃɪp/ (US) /-tɝːn-/ **noun** [C] US **IN A HOSPITAL** ▷ **1** a period of training spent in a hospital by a young doctor in order to finish their medical qualification: *He served his internship at Garfield Hospital.* **IN a COMPANY** ▷ **2** a period of time during which someone works for a company or organization in order to get experience of a particular type of work: *Jane has a* ***summer*** *internship at a local TV station.*

interpersonal /ˌɪn.təˈpɜː.sən.əl/ (US) /-t̬ɚˈpɝː-/ **adj** connected with relationships between people: *The successful applicant will have excellent interpersonal* ***skills.***

interplanetary /ˌɪn.təˈplæn.ɪ.tər.i/ (US) /-ter.i/ **adj** [before noun] between planets: *interplanetary space*

interplay /ˈɪn.tə.pleɪ/ (US) /-t̬ɚ-/ **noun** [U] the effect that two or more things have on each other: *Our personalities result from the complex interplay* ***between*** *our genes and our environment.*

Interpol /ˈɪn.tə.pɒl/ (US) /-t̬ɚ.pɑːl/ **noun** [+ sing/pl verb] an international police organization that helps national police forces to work together to catch criminals

interpolate /ɪnˈtɜː.pə.leɪt/ (US) /-ˈtɝː-/ **verb** [T] formal **1** to add words to a text **2** to interrupt someone by saying something • **interpolation** /ɪnˌtɜː.pəˈleɪ.ʃən/ (US) /-ˌtɝː-/ **noun** [C or U]

interpose /ˌɪn.təˈpəʊz/ (US) /-t̬ɚˈpoʊz/ **verb** [T] formal **PUT BETWEEN** ▷ **1** to put yourself or something between two things, people, or groups, especially in order to stop them doing something: *The teacher interposed* ***herself between*** *the two snarling boys.* **INTERRUPT** ▷ **2** to interrupt someone: [+ speech] *'I can't agree with you, Mr Heath,' he interposed.* • **interposition** /-pəˈzɪʃ.ən/ **noun** [C or U]

interpret /ɪnˈtɜː.prɪt/ US /-ˈtɝː-/ verb **FIND MEANING** ▷ **1** C1 [T] to decide what the intended meaning of something is: *It's difficult to interpret these statistics without knowing how they were obtained.* ◦ *A jury should not interpret the silence of a defendant* ***as*** *a sign of guilt.* **EXPRESS** ▷ **2** [T] to express your own ideas about the intended meaning of a play or a piece of music when performing it: *If Shakespeare's plays are to reach a large audience they need to be interpreted in a modern style.* **BETWEEN LANGUAGES** ▷ **3** B2 [I or T] to change what someone is saying into another language: *We had to ask our guide to interpret for us.* → Compare **translate**

interpretation /ɪnˌtɜː.prɪˈteɪ.ʃən/ US /-ˌtɝː.prɪˈt̬eɪ-/ noun [C or U] **EXPLANATION** ▷ **1** C2 an explanation or opinion of what something means: *The dispute is based on two widely differing interpretations of the law.* ◦ *The rules are vague and* ***open to*** *interpretation.* ◦ *It is difficult for many people to accept a* ***literal*** *interpretation of the Bible.* **WAY OF PERFORMING** ▷ **2** C2 a particular way of performing a piece of music, a part in a play, etc.: *Her interpretation of Juliet was one of the best performances I have ever seen.*

interpreter /ɪnˈtɜː.prɪ.təʳ/ US /-ˈtɝː.prɪ.t̬ɚ/ noun [C] **BETWEEN LANGUAGES** ▷ **1** someone whose job is to change what someone else is saying into another language: *She works as an interpreter in Brussels.* ◦ ***Speaking through an*** *interpreter, the president said the terms of the ceasefire were completely unacceptable.* **COMPUTER PROGRAM** ▷ **2** specialized a computer program that changes the instructions in another program into a form that can be easily understood by a computer **EXPRESSING** ▷ **3** someone who performs a piece of music or a part in a play, etc. in a way that expresses their own ideas about its meaning: *He's a noted interpreter of traditional Irish music.*

interpretive /ɪnˈtɜː.prɪ.tɪv/ US /-ˈtɝː.prə.t̬ə.t̬ɪv/ adj (also **interpretative**) related to explaining or understanding the meaning of something: *an interpretive display/centre*

interracial /ˌɪn.təˈreɪ.ʃəl/ US /-t̬ɚ-/ adj involving different human races: *an interracial marriage/relationship*

interregnum /ˌɪn.təˈreg.nəm/ US /-t̬ɚ-/ noun [C usually singular] formal a period when a country or organization does not have a leader

interrelate /ˌɪn.tə.rɪˈleɪt/ US /-t̬ɚ-/ verb [I] to be connected in such a way that each thing has an effect on or depends on the other: *Children need to be educated about the way that diet and health interrelate.* • **interrelated** /-ˈleɪ.tɪd/ US /-ˈleɪ.t̬ɪd/ adj *interrelated problems/issues/activities*

interrelationship /ˌɪn.tə.rɪˈleɪ.ʃən.ʃɪp/ US /-t̬ɚ-/ noun [C or U] (also **interrelation**) the way in which two or more things or people are connected and affect one another: *the interrelationship* ***between*** *smoking and respiratory disease*

interrogate /ɪnˈter.ə.geɪt/ verb [T] **1** to ask someone a lot of questions for a long time in order to get information, sometimes using threats or violence: *Thousands of dissidents have been interrogated or imprisoned in recent weeks.* **2** specialized to get information from a computer • **interrogation** /ɪnˌter.əˈgeɪ.ʃən/ noun [C or U] *One by one they were taken for interrogation.* ◦ *She was* ***subjected to*** *torture and lengthy interrogations.* • **interrogator** /-geɪ.təʳ/ US /-geɪ.t̬ɚ/ noun [C] a person who interrogates someone

interrogative /ˌɪn.təˈrɒg.ə.tɪv/ US /-t̬əˈrɑː.gə.t̬ɪv/ noun; adj

▸**noun** specialized **1** [C] a word or sentence used when asking a question: *'Who' and 'why' are interrogatives.* **2 the interrogative** the form of a sentence that is used for asking questions

▸**adj** in the form of a question, or used in questions: *an interrogative adverb*

interrupt /ˌɪn.təˈrʌpt/ US /-t̬ə-/ verb **STOP SPEAKING** ▷ **1** B1 [I or T] to stop a person from speaking for a short period by something you say or do: *She tried to explain what had happened but he kept interrupting her.* ◦ *I wish you'd stop interrupting.* **STOP HAPPENING** ▷ **2** B2 [T] to stop something from happening for a short period: *We had to interrupt our trip when we heard John's mother had had an accident.*

interruption /ˌɪn.təˈrʌp.ʃən/ US /-t̬ə-/ noun [C or U] B2 an occasion when someone or something stops something from happening for a short period: *a brief interruption* ◦ *I worked all morning without interruption.*

interscholastic /ˌɪn.tə.skəˈlæs.tɪk/ US /-t̬ɚ.skə-/ adj [before noun] US involving two or more schools: *an interscholastic competition/debate*

intersect /ˌɪn.təˈsekt/ US /-t̬ɚ-/ verb **1** [I or T] (of lines, roads, etc.) to cross one another: *The roads intersect near the bridge.* **2** [T] to divide an area into smaller parts by crossing it with straight lines: *The gardens are intersected by gravel paths.*

intersection /ˌɪn.təˈsek.ʃən/ US /-t̬ɚ-/ noun **LINES** ▷ **1** [C or U] an occasion when two lines cross, or the point where this happens: *The intersection of the lines on the graph marks the point where we start to make a profit.* **ROADS** ▷ **2** [C] mainly US the place where two or more roads join or cross each other: *a busy intersection* ◦ *Turn right at the next intersection.*

intersperse /ˌɪn.təˈspɜːs/ US /-t̬ɚˈspɝːs/ verb [T] to mix one thing in with another in a way that is not regular: *The documentary intersperses graphical animations* ***with*** *film clips of the actual event.* ◦ *Her handwritten notes were interspersed* ***throughout*** *the text.*

interspersed /ˌɪn.təˈspɜːs/ US /-t̬ɚˈspɝːs/ adj **interspersed with sth** having something in several places among something else: *forests interspersed with meadows and lakes*

interstate adj; noun

▸**adj** [before noun] /ˌɪn.təˈsteɪt/ US /ˈɪn.t̬ɚ.steɪt/ involving two or more of the states into which some countries such as the US are divided: *the interstate highway system* ◦ *interstate banking legislation*

▸**noun** [C] /ˈɪn.tə.steɪt/ US /ˈɪn.t̬ɚ-/ a fast, wide road that goes between states and connects important cities in the US

interstellar /ˌɪn.təˈstel.əʳ/ US /-t̬ɚˈstel.ɚ/ adj [before noun] between the stars: *interstellar* ***space***

interstice /ɪnˈtɜː.stɪs/ US /-ˈtɝː-/ noun [C usually plural] formal a very small CRACK or space: *The wall was old and crumbling with plants growing in the interstices* ***between/in/of*** *the bricks.*

intertwine /ˌɪn.təˈtwaɪn/ US /-t̬ɚ-/ verb [I or T] to twist or be twisted together, or to be connected so as to be difficult to separate: *The town's prosperity is* ***inextricably*** *intertwined* ***with*** *the fortunes of the factory.* ◦ *The trees' branches intertwined to form a dark roof over the path.*

interval /ˈɪn.tə.vəl/ US /-t̬ɚ-/ noun [C] **TIME/DISTANCE** ▷ **1** C2 a period between two events or times, or the space between two points: *We see each other at* ***regular*** *intervals – usually about once a month.* ◦ *There's often a long interval* ***between*** *an author completing a book and it appearing in the shops.* **2** B1 UK (US **intermission**) a short period between the parts of a performance or a sports event: *There will be two 20-minute intervals during the opera.* ◦ *He scored his first goal of the match three minutes after the interval.* **3 at intervals** repeated after a particular period of time or a particular distance: *In the event of fire, the alarm will sound at 15-second intervals/at intervals **of** 15 seconds.* **MUSIC** ▷ **4** specialized the amount by which one note is higher or lower than another: *an interval of a fifth* (= *between one note and another one four notes higher*)

intervene /ˌɪn.təˈviːn/ (US) /-t̬ɚ-/ verb [I] **GET INVOLVED** ▷ **1** (C2) to intentionally become involved in a difficult situation in order to improve it or prevent it from getting worse: *The Central Bank intervened **in** the currency markets today to try to stabilize the exchange rate.* ◦ [+ to infinitive] *The minister intervened personally **to** stop the museum being closed.* **COME BETWEEN** ▷ **2** to happen between two times or between other events or activities: *Two decades intervened **between** the completion of the design and the opening of the theatre.* • **intervention** /-ˈven.ʃən/ noun [C or U] (C2) *Half the people questioned said they were opposed to **military** intervention (**in** the civil war).* ◦ *Repeated interventions on the currency markets have failed to prevent the value of the currency falling.*

intervening /ˌɪn.təˈviː.nɪŋ/ (US) /-t̬ɚ-/ adj [before noun] happening between two times or between other events or activities: *It was a long time since my last visit to Berlin, and it had changed dramatically in the intervening **period/years**.*

interventionist /ˌɪn.təˈven.ʃən.ɪst/ (US) /-t̬ɚ-/ adj (of a government or their actions) often becoming involved, either in the problems of another country, or in the economy of one's own country: *an interventionist role* ◦ *interventionist economic policy* • **interventionism** /-ɪ.zəm/ noun [U] *UN interventionism*

interview /ˈɪn.tə.vjuː/ (US) /-t̬ɚ-/ noun; verb

▸noun [C] **1** (B1) a meeting in which someone asks you questions to see if you are suitable for a job or course: *a job interview* ◦ *I **had** an interview **for** a job with a publishing firm.* **2** (B1) a meeting in which someone is asked questions about themselves for a newspaper article, television show, etc.: *an exclusive interview **with** Johnny Depp* ◦ ***In** a television interview last night she denied she had any intention of resigning.* **3** a meeting in which the police ask someone questions to see if they have committed a crime

> Word partners for **interview** noun
>
> *get/have* an interview • *conduct/do* an interview • *during/in* an interview • an interview *for* sth • *give* an interview (to sb) • a *brief/exclusive/frank/in-depth* interview • be *available* for interview

▸verb [T] (B1) to ask someone questions in an interview: *We've had 200 applicants for the job, but we only plan to interview about 20 of them.* ◦ *Who's the most famous person you've ever interviewed on TV?* ◦ *Police are interviewing a 43-year-old man in connection with the murder.*

interviewee /ˌɪn.tə.vjuˈiː/ (US) /-t̬ɚ-/ noun [C] the person who answers the questions during an interview

interviewer /ˈɪn.tə.vjuː.əʳ/ (US) /-t̬ɚ.vjuː.ɚ/ noun [C] the person who asks the questions during an interview

interweave /ˌɪn.təˈwiːv/ (US) /-t̬ɚ-/ verb [T] (**interwove, interwoven**) to twist together or combine two or more things so that they cannot be separated easily: *She has created an intriguing story by skilfully interweaving fictional and historical events.*

intestate /ɪnˈtes.teɪt/ adj [after verb] specialized describes someone who has died without leaving instructions about who should be given their property: *Many people **die** intestate because they thought they were too young to make a will.*

intesˌtinal ˈfortitude noun [U] US courage and determination: *The fact that he's still trying for the championship is a tribute to his intestinal fortitude.*

intestine /ɪnˈtes.tɪn/ noun [C usually plural] (either of the two parts of) a long tube through which food travels from the stomach and out of the body while it is being digested • **intestinal** /-tɪ.nəl/ adj *intestinal surgery*

intimacy /ˈɪn.tɪ.mə.si/ (US) /-t̬ə-/ noun **1** [U] a situation in which you have a close friendship or sexual relationship with someone: *Intimacy between teachers and students is not recommended.* **2** [C usually plural] things that are said or done only by people who have a close relationship with each other: *It was obvious from their witty intimacies that they had been good friends for many years.*

intimate[1] /ˈɪn.tɪ.mət/ (US) /-t̬ə-/ adj; noun

▸adj **PERSONAL** ▷ **1** (C2) having, or being likely to cause, a very close friendship or personal or sexual relationship: *intimate relationships* ◦ *The restaurant has a very intimate **atmosphere**.* ◦ *He's become very intimate **with** an actress.* **EXPERT** ▷ **2** (C2) (of knowledge or understanding) detailed, and obtained from a lot of studying or experience: *She has an intimate **knowledge** of Tuscany, where she has lived for 20 years.* • **intimately** /-li/ adv *Well, I know who she is although I'm not intimately* (= *closely*) ***acquainted** with her.* ◦ *She's been intimately **involved** in the project since it began.*

▸noun [C] formal a friend you know very well: *Intimates of the star say that he has been upset by the personal attacks on him that have appeared in the press recently.*

intimate[2] /ˈɪn.tɪ.meɪt/ (US) /-t̬ə-/ verb [T] formal to make clear what you think or want without saying it directly: [+ (that)] *She has intimated **that** she will resign if she loses the vote.* • **intimation** /ˌɪn.tɪˈmeɪ.ʃən/ (US) /-t̬ə-/ noun [C] *His suicide attempt was the first intimation **that** he was seriously depressed.*

intimidate /ɪnˈtɪm.ɪ.deɪt/ verb [T] to frighten or threaten someone, usually in order to persuade them to do something that you want them to do: *They were intimidated **into** accepting a pay cut by the threat of losing their jobs.* • **intimidation** /ɪnˌtɪm.ɪˈdeɪ.ʃən/ noun [U] *The campaign of violence and intimidation **against** them intensifies daily.*

intimidated /ɪnˈtɪm.ɪ.deɪ.tɪd/ (US) /-t̬ɪd/ adj frightened or nervous because you are not confident in a situation: *Older people can feel very intimidated by computers.*

intimidating /ɪnˈtɪm.ɪ.deɪ.tɪŋ/ (US) /-t̬ɪŋ/ adj making you feel frightened or nervous: *an intimidating array of weapons* ◦ *an intimidating manner*

into /ˈɪn.tuː/ preposition **INSIDE** ▷ **1** (A1) to the inside or middle of a place, container, area, etc.: *Would you put the jar back into the cupboard for me, please?* ◦ *Shall we go into the garden?* ◦ *Stop running around and get into bed!* ◦ *I can't get into these trousers any more. They're far too small for me.* **CHANGE** ▷ **2** (A2) used to show when a person or thing is changing from one form or condition to another: *Peel the cucumber and chop it into small cubes.* ◦ *There was a series of explosions and the van burst into flames* (= *started to burn violently*). ◦ *Her novels have been translated into 19 languages.* ◦ *We're planning to turn the smallest bedroom into an office.* **TOUCHING FORCEFULLY** ▷ **3** (B1) used to show movement which involves something touching something else with a lot of force but without moving inside it: *He's always walking into things when he hasn't got his glasses on.* **TOWARDS** ▷ **4** B1 in the direction of something or someone: *She was looking straight into his eyes.* **ABOUT** ▷ **5** involving or about something: *an inquiry into the cause of the accident* **DIVISION** ▷ **6** used when referring to the division of one number by another number: *What's 5 into 125?* **INTERESTED** ▷ **7** B1 enthusiastic about or interested in: *Jackie's really into classical music.*

intolerable /ɪnˈtɒl.ər.ə.bl̩/ US /-ˈtɑː.lɚ-/ **adj** C2 too bad or unpleasant to deal with or accept: *The situation has become intolerable.* ◦ *The constant fighting made life at home intolerable.* ◦ *Three-quarters of the world's population live in conditions that people in the West would find intolerable.* • **intolerably** /-bli/ **adv**

intolerance /ɪnˈtɒl.ər.əns/ US /-ˈtɑː.lɚ-/ **noun 1** C2 [U] the fact of refusing to accept ideas, beliefs, or behaviour that are different from your own: *racial/religious intolerance* ◦ *One side-effect of the drug is intolerance **of** (= being unable to bear) bright light.* **2** [C or U] If you have a food intolerance, you cannot digest a particular food in a normal way and may feel ill if you eat it: *(a) **food** intolerance* ◦ *a wheat/lactose intolerance* ◦ *Amy has an intolerance **to** dairy products.*

intolerant /ɪnˈtɒl.ər.ənt/ US /-ˈtɑː.lɚ-/ **adj** disapproving C2 disapproving of or refusing to accept ideas or ways of behaving that are different from your own: *She can be very intolerant **of** students who don't understand what she's talking about.* • **intolerantly** /-li/ **adv**

intonation /ˌɪn.təˈneɪ.ʃən/ **noun 1** [C or U] the sound changes produced by the rise and fall of the voice when speaking, especially when this has an effect on the meaning of what is said: *The end of a sentence that is not a question is usually marked by falling intonation.* **2** [U] the degree to which the notes of a piece of music are played or sung correctly: *The violinist had good intonation, and a wonderful pure tone.*

intone /ɪnˈtəʊn/ US /-ˈtoʊn/ **verb** [T] formal to say something slowly and seriously in a voice which does not rise or fall much: [+ speech] *'Let us pray,' the priest intoned to his congregation.*

ˌin ˈtoto **adv** formal as a total or whole: *The available information amounts to very little in toto.*

intoxicant /ɪnˈtɒk.sɪ.kənt/ US /-ˈtɑːk-/ **noun** [C] specialized a substance such as alcohol that produces feelings of pleasure or happiness in a person

intoxicated /ɪnˈtɒk.sɪ.keɪ.tɪd/ US /-ˈtɑːk.sɪ.keɪ.t̬ɪd/ **adj 1** formal drunk: *She was charged with driving while intoxicated.* **2** excited, happy, and slightly out of control because of love, success, etc.: *She was understandably intoxicated by her success in the national competition.*

intoxicating /ɪnˈtɒk.sɪ.keɪ.tɪŋ/ US /-ˈtɑːk.sɪ.keɪ.t̬ɪŋ/ **adj 1** If a drink is intoxicating, it makes you drunk if you have too much: *intoxicating **liquor*** **2** An intoxicating experience or idea makes you feel excited and emotional: *an intoxicating thought*

intoxication /ɪnˌtɒk.sɪˈkeɪ.ʃən/ US /-ˌtɑːk-/ **noun** [U] **1** formal the condition of being drunk: *He used to claim that he had his best ideas after several days of intoxication.* **2** a strong feeling of excitement or happiness: *The feeling of intoxication that followed her victory was cut short by her father's sudden death.*

intra- /ɪn.trə-/ **prefix** used to form adjectives meaning 'within' (the stated place or group): *intra-EU trade* ◦ *intra-family disputes* → Compare **inter-**

intractable /ɪnˈtræk.tə.bl̩/ **adj** formal very difficult or impossible to control, manage, or solve: *We are facing an intractable **problem**.* • **intractably** /-bli/ **adv** *an intractably violent relationship* • **intractability** /ɪnˌtræk.təˈbɪl.ɪ.ti/ US /-ə.t̬i/ **noun** [U]

intramural /ˌɪn.trəˈmjʊə.rəl/ US /-ˈmjʊr.əl/ **adj** happening within or involving the members of one school, college, or university: *an intramural basketball competition*

intranet /ˈɪn.trə.net/ **noun** [C] a system of connected computers that works like the internet and allows people within an organization to communicate with each other and share information: *I'll post the agenda for next week's meeting on the intranet.*

intransigent /ɪnˈtræn.zɪ.dʒənt/, /-ˈtrɑːn-/ **adj** formal disapproving refusing to change your opinions or behaviour: *Unions claim that the management continues to maintain an intransigent position.* • **intransigently** /-li/ **adv** • **intransigence** /-dʒəns/ **noun** [U]

intransitive /ɪnˈtræn.sə.tɪv/, /-ˈtrɑːn-/, /-zə-/ US /-ˈtræn.sə.t̬ɪv/ /-zə-/ **adj** specialized B2 (of a verb) having or needing no object: *In the sentence 'I tried to persuade him, but he wouldn't come', 'come' is an intransitive verb.* ◦ *In this dictionary, verbs which are intransitive are marked [I].* → Compare **ditransitive, transitive** • **intransitively** /-li/ **adv** • **intransitive noun** [C]

intravenous /ˌɪn.trəˈviː.nəs/ **adj** (abbreviation **IV**) into or connected to a VEIN: *intravenous **feeding/fluids*** ◦ *an intravenous **drip/injection**.* ◦ *Intravenous **drug users** are at particular risk of contracting the disease.* • **intravenously** /-li/ **adv**

ˈin ˌtray **noun** [C] UK (US **inbox**) a flat, open container where letters and other documents are put when they arrive in a person's office and where they are kept until the person has time to deal with them: *Just put it **in** my in tray and I'll look at it later.*

intrepid /ɪnˈtrep.ɪd/ **adj** extremely brave and showing no fear of dangerous situations: *a team of intrepid **explorers*** • **intrepidly** /-li/ **adv**

intricacy /ˈɪn.trɪ.kə.si/ **noun 1** **intricacies** [plural] complicated details: *I enjoyed the film, but I couldn't follow all the intricacies **of** the plot.* **2** [U] the quality of having a lot of complicated small parts or details: *the intricacy **of** the needlework*

intricate /ˈɪn.trɪ.kət/ **adj** having a lot of small parts or details that are arranged in a complicated way and are therefore sometimes difficult to understand, solve, or produce: *The watch mechanism is extremely intricate and very difficult to repair.* ◦ *Police officers uncovered an intricate **web** of deceit.* • **intricately** /-li/ **adv** *an intricately engraved pendant*

intrigue **verb; noun**

▸**verb** [T] /ɪnˈtriːg/ to interest someone a lot, especially by being strange, unusual, or mysterious: *Throughout history, people have been intrigued by the question of whether there is intelligent life elsewhere in the universe.*

▸**noun** [C or U] /ˈɪn.triːg/ (the making of) a secret plan to do something, especially something that will harm another person: *a tale of **political** intrigue*

intriguing /ɪnˈtriː.gɪŋ/ **adj** C2 very interesting because of being unusual or mysterious: *an intriguing possibility/question* ◦ *She has a really intriguing personality.* • **intriguingly** /-li/ **adv**

intrinsic /ɪnˈtrɪn.zɪk/ **adj** C2 being an extremely important and basic characteristic of a person or thing: *works of little intrinsic value/interest* ◦ *Maths is an intrinsic part of the school curriculum.* • **intrinsically** /-zɪ.kəl.i/ **adv**

intro /ˈɪn.trəʊ/ US /-troʊ/ **noun** [C] (plural **intros**) informal an **introduction**: *This song has a brilliant* *piano intro.* ◦ *Would you mind doing the intros, Martha, while I pour some drinks?*

introduce /ˌɪn.trəˈdjuːs/ (US) /-ˈduːs/ **verb** [T] **PUT INTO USE** ▷ **1** (B2) to put something into use, operation, or a place for the first time: *The smaller ten pence coin was introduced in 1992.* ◦ *Such unpopular legislation is unlikely to be introduced before the next election.* ◦ specialized *The tube which carries the laser is introduced* ***into*** *the abdomen through a small cut in the skin.* **GIVE SB'S NAME** ▷ **2** (B1) to tell someone another person's name the first time that they meet: *I'd like to introduce my son, Mark.* ◦ *Have you two been introduced* (***to*** *each other*)? **BEGIN** ▷ **3** to be the beginning of something: *A haunting oboe solo introduces the third movement of the concerto.* **4** (C2) to speak or write before the beginning of a programme or book and give information about it: *The director will introduce the film personally at its premiere.* ◦ *This is the first official biography of her and it is introduced by her daughter.*

PHRASAL VERB **introduce sb to sth** to help someone experience something for the first time: *When were you first introduced to sailing?*

introduction /ˌɪn.trəˈdʌk.ʃən/ **noun** **PUT INTO USE** ▷ **1** (B2) [U] an occasion when something is put into use or brought to a place for the first time: *The introduction* ***of*** *new working practices has dramatically improved productivity.* ◦ *Within a year of its introduction, questions began to emerge about the safety of the drug.* ◦ specialized *The introduction* ***of*** *the tube into the artery is a very delicate procedure.* **GIVING SB'S NAME** ▷ **2** (B2) [C or U] the action of telling someone another person's name the first time that they meet: *You'll have to* ***do/make*** *the introductions – I don't know everyone's name.* ◦ *My next guest* ***needs no*** *introduction* (= *is already known to everyone*). **BEGINNING** ▷ **3** (B2) [C] the first part of something: *Have you read the introduction to the third edition?* ◦ *The song's great, but the introduction's a bit too long.* **FIRST EXPERIENCE** ▷ **4** (C1) [S] the first time someone experiences something: *That trip was my introduction to winter sports.* **BASIC KNOWLEDGE** ▷ **5** (B2) [C] a book or course that provides basic knowledge about a subject: *an introduction* ***to*** *psychology*

introductory /ˌɪn.trəˈdʌk.tər.i/ **adj** **FIRST TIME** ▷ **1** existing, used, or experienced for the first time: *an introductory* ***price/offer*** ◦ *an introductory course in design* (= *for people who have not done it before*) **BEGINNING** ▷ **2** written or said at the beginning: *an introductory chapter* ◦ *I'd like to make some introductory remarks before beginning the lecture properly.*

introspection /ˌɪn.trəˈspek.ʃən/ **noun** [U] examination of and attention to your own ideas, thoughts, and feelings: *His defeat in the world championship led to a long period of gloomy introspection.*

introspective /ˌɪn.trəˈspek.tɪv/ **adj** examining and considering your own ideas, thoughts, and feelings, instead of talking to other people about them • **introspectively** /-li/ **adv**

introvert /ˈɪn.trə.vɜːt/ (US) /-vɝːt/ **noun** [C] (C2) someone who is shy, quiet, and unable to make friends easily → Compare **extrovert** • **introverted** /ˌɪn.trəˈvɜː.tɪd/ (US) /-ˈvɝː.t̬ɪd/ **adj** (also **introvert**) *an introverted child* • **introversion** /ˌɪn.trəˈvɜː.ʃən/ (US) /-ˈvɝː-/ **noun** [U]

intrude /ɪnˈtruːd/ **verb** [I] (C2) to go into a place or situation in which you are not wanted or not expected to be: *I didn't realize your husband was here, Dr Jones – I hope I'm not intruding.* ◦ *Newspaper editors are being urged not to intrude* ***on/into*** *the grief of the families of missing servicemen.*

intruder /ɪnˈtruː.dər/ (US) /-dɚ/ **noun** [C] **1** (C2) someone who is in a place or situation where they are not wanted: *I feel like an intruder when I visit their home.* **2** (C2) someone who enters a place without permission in order to commit a crime: *Intruders had entered the house through a back window.*

intrusion /ɪnˈtruː.ʒən/ **noun** [C or U] (C2) an occasion when someone goes into a place or situation where they are not wanted or expected to be: *They complained about excessive government intrusion* (= *unwanted involvement*) ***into*** *their legitimate activities.* ◦ *His phone call was a* ***welcome*** *intrusion into an otherwise tedious morning.*

intrusive /ɪnˈtruː.sɪv/ **adj** affecting someone or something in a way that annoys them and makes them feel uncomfortable: *intrusive questioning* ◦ *intrusive lighting*

intuit /ɪnˈtjuː.ɪt/ (US) /ɪnˈtuː-/ **verb** [T] formal to know or understand something because of a feeling that you have rather than because of facts or what someone has told you: [+ that] *He intuited* ***that*** *I was worried about the situation.*

intuition /ˌɪn.tjuːˈɪʃ.ən/ (US) /-tuː-/ **noun** [C or U] (C2) (knowledge from) an ability to understand or know something immediately based on your feelings rather than facts: *Often there's no clear evidence one way or the other and you just have to base your judgment on intuition.* ◦ [+ (that)] *I can't explain how I knew – I just had an intuition* ***that*** *you'd been involved in an accident.*

intuitive /ɪnˈtjuː.ɪ.tɪv/ (US) /-ˈtuː.ɪ.t̬ɪv/ **adj** **1** based on feelings rather than facts or proof: *an intuitive* ***approach/judgment*** ◦ *Most people have an intuitive* ***sense*** *of right and wrong.* **2** able to know or understand something because of feelings rather than facts or proof: *Men are often regarded as less intuitive than women.* • **intuitively** /-li/ **adv** *I knew intuitively that something dreadful had happened to him.*

Inuit /ˈɪn.ju.ɪt/ **noun** **1** [C] (plural **Inuit**) a member of a Native American people who live in the cold northern areas of North America and Greenland → See note at **Eskimo** **2** [U] the language spoken by the Inuit people

inundate /ˈɪn.ʌn.deɪt/ **verb** [T] **TOO MUCH** ▷ **1** to give someone so much work or so many things that they cannot deal with them all: *We have been inundated* ***with*** *requests for help.* **FLOOD** ▷ **2** formal to flood an area with water: *If the dam breaks it will inundate large parts of the town.* • **inundation** /ˌɪn.ʌnˈdeɪ.ʃən/ **noun** [C or U] formal

inure /ɪnˈjʊər/ (US) /-ˈjʊr/ **verb**

PHRASAL VERB **inure sb to sth** formal If you become inured to something unpleasant, you become familiar with it and able to accept and bear it: *After spending some time on the island they became inured to the hardships.*

invade /ɪnˈveɪd/ **verb** **1** (B2) [I or T] to enter a country by force with large numbers of soldiers in order to take possession of it: *Concentrations of troops near the border look set to invade within the next few days.* **2** (C1) [I or T] to enter a place in large numbers, usually when unwanted and in order to take possession or do damage: *Hundreds of squatters have invaded waste land in the hope that they will be allowed to stay.* **3** [T] to enter an area of activity in a forceful and noticeable way: *Maria looks set to invade the music scene with her style and image.* **4** (C2) [T] to spoil a situation or quality for another person without thinking about their feelings: *Famous people often find their **privacy** is invaded by the press.*

invader /ɪnˈveɪ.dəʳ/ (US) /-dɚ/ **noun** [C] an army or country that uses force to enter and take control of another country: *The **foreign** invaders were finally defeated by allied forces.* ◦ figurative *Any new company is seen as an invader in an already competitive market.*

invalid¹ /ɪnˈvæl.ɪd/ **adj 1** An invalid document, ticket, law, etc. is not legally or officially acceptable: *I'm afraid your driving licence is invalid in Eastern Europe.* **2** An invalid opinion, argument, etc. is not correct, usually because it is not LOGICAL or not based on correct information: *an invalid argument* • **invalidly** /-li/ **adv**

invalid² /ˈɪn.və.lɪd/ **noun; verb**

▸**noun** [C] old-fashioned someone who is sick and unable to take care of themselves, especially for a long time: *Is the invalid in bed?*

▸**verb**

PHRASAL VERB **invalid sb out** If you are invalided out of a job, especially a military job, you are forced to leave because of injury or illness.

invalidate /ɪnˈvæl.ɪ.deɪt/ **verb** [T] **1** to officially stop a document, ticket, law, etc. being legally or officially acceptable **2** to prove that an opinion, argument, etc. is wrong • **invalidation** /ɪnˌvæl.ɪˈdeɪ.ʃən/ **noun** [U] *Premature disclosure of the test sites might lead to invalidation of the experiment.*

invalidity /ˌɪn.vəˈlɪd.ɪ.ti/ (US) /-ə.t̬i/ **noun** [U] **NOT OFFICIAL** ▷ **1** the condition of not being legally or officially acceptable **ILLNESS** ▷ **2** the condition of being too ill to work or care for yourself

invaluable /ɪnˈvæl.ju.bl̩/ **adj** (C1) extremely useful: *The new job will provide you with invaluable experience.* ◦ *Such data will prove invaluable **to/for** researchers.*

invariable /ɪnˈveə.ri.ə.bl̩/ **adj** formal staying the same and never changing: *The menu is invariable but the food is always good.*

invariably /ɪnˈveə.ri.ə.bli/ **adv** (C2) always: *The train is invariably late.*

invasion /ɪnˈveɪ.ʒən/ **noun** [C or U] **1** (B2) an occasion when an army or country uses force to enter and take control of another country: *They were planning to mount an invasion **of** the north of the country.* **2** (C2) an occasion when a large number of people or things come to a place in an annoying and unwanted way: *the annual invasion of foreign tourists* **3** (C2) an action or process which affects someone's life in an unpleasant and unwanted way: *an invasion **of** privacy*

invasive /ɪnˈveɪ.sɪv/ **adj** moving into all areas of something and difficult to stop: *an invasive disease* ◦ *They treated the cancer with **non**-invasive methods/surgery (= not cutting into the body).*

invective /ɪnˈvek.tɪv/ **noun** [U] formal criticism that is very forceful, unkind, and often rude: *A **stream of** invective from some sectors of the press continues to assail the government.*

inveigh /ɪnˈveɪ/ **verb**

PHRASAL VERB **inveigh against sb/sth** formal to strongly criticize something or someone: *There were politicians who inveighed against immigrants to get votes.*

inveigle /ɪnˈveɪ.gl̩/ **verb** [T] formal to persuade someone to do something in a clever and dishonest way, when they do not want to do it: *Her son tried to inveigle her **into** giving him the money for a car.*

invent /ɪnˈvent/ **verb** [T] **NEW DESIGN** ▷ **1** (B1) to design and/or create something that has never been made before: *The first safety razor was invented by company founder King C. Gillette in 1903.* **NOT TRUE** ▷ **2** (B2) to create a reason, excuse, story, etc. that is not true, usually to deceive someone: *But I didn't invent the story – everything I told you is true.*

invention /ɪnˈven.ʃən/ **noun** [C or U] **NEW DESIGN** ▷ **1** (B1) something that has never been made before, or the process of creating something that has never been made before: *The world changed rapidly after the invention of the phone.* ◦ *a most amazing invention* **NOT TRUE** ▷ **2** a story or excuse that is not true, or the act of creating a story or excuse that is not true: *All that gossip about Linda was just pure invention.* ◦ *Be careful what you believe – her **powers of** invention (= ability to think of excuses, etc.) are well known.*

inventive /ɪnˈven.tɪv/ (US) /-t̬ɪv/ **adj** approving very good at thinking of new and original ideas: *He is very inventive, always dreaming up new gadgets for the home.* • **inventively** /-li/ **adv** approving • **inventiveness** /-nəs/ **noun** [U]

inventor /ɪnˈven.təʳ/ (US) /-t̬ɚ/ **noun** [C] (B2) someone who has invented something or whose job is to invent things

inventory /ˈɪn.vən.tər.i/ (US) /-tɔːr.i/ **noun 1** [C] a detailed list of all the things in a place: *A set of 24 gilded chairs appear on the inventory of the house for 1736.* **2** [U] US the amount of goods a shop has, or the value of them: *Our inventory of used cars is the best in town.* **3** [U] US for **stocktaking**

inverse /ɪnˈvɜːs/ (US) /-ˈvɝːs/ **adj; noun**

▸**adj** [before noun] opposite in relation to something else: *Their generosity was **in** inverse **proportion/relation to** their income (= the more money they had the less generous they were).* • **inversely** /-li/ **adv** *Sometimes it seems that press coverage of an event is inversely **proportional** to its true importance (= the more important the event, the less attention is paid to it).*

▸**noun** [S] formal **the inverse** the opposite: *Dividing by two is the inverse **of** multiplying by two.*

inversion /ɪnˈvɜː.ʒən/ (US) /-ˈvɝː-/ **noun** [C or U] a situation in which something is changed so that it is the opposite of what it was before, or in which something is turned upside down: *Her account of the case was an inversion **of** the facts (= it said the opposite of what really happened).*

invert /ɪnˈvɜːt/ (US) /-ˈvɝːt/ **verb** [T] formal to turn something upside down or change the order of two things: *In some languages, the word order in questions is inverted (= the verb comes before the subject of the sentence).* • **inverted** /-ˈvɜː.tɪd/ (US) /-ˈvɝː.t̬ɪd/ **adj** *Cover the bowl with an inverted plate.*

invertebrate /ɪnˈvɜː.tɪ.brət/ (US) /-ˈvɝː.t̬ə-/ **noun** [C] specialized an animal with no SPINE: *Invertebrates, such as worms, are the main diet of these water birds.* → Compare **vertebrate** • **invertebrate adj**

inˌverted ˈcommas noun [plural] UK (B2) the symbols ' ' or " " that are put around a word or phrase to show that someone else has written or said it

IDIOM **in inverted commas** used in spoken English after a word or phrase to show that it has not been used accurately or that the opposite meaning is intended: *Sick prisoners in the camp were 'cared for', in inverted commas, by guards, not nurses.*

inˌverted ˈsnob noun [C] UK disapproving a person who makes it known that they do not like things related to high social position but approve of things related to low social position • **inˌverted ˈsnobbery noun** [U]

invest /ɪnˈvest/ **verb** [I or T] (B2) to put money, effort, time, etc. into something to make a profit or get an advantage: *The institute will invest five million* ***in*** *the project.* ◦ *He's not certain whether to invest* ***in*** *the property market.* ◦ *You have all invested significant amounts of time and energy* ***in*** ***making*** *this project the success that it is.*

PHRASAL VERBS **invest in sth** to buy something because you think it will be useful, even if you think it is expensive: *We've decided it's time to invest in a new computer.* • **invest sb with sth** formal to give authority or power to someone: *Our government has invested the minister for trade with all the necessary powers to resolve the dispute.* • **invest sb/sth with sth** literary to make someone or something seem to have a particular characteristic: *In his poems everyday reality is invested with a sense of wonder and delight.*

investigate /ɪnˈves.tɪ.ɡeɪt/ verb [T] B2 to examine a crime, problem, statement, etc. carefully, especially to discover the truth: *Police are investigating allegations of corruption involving senior executives.* ◦ [+ question word] *We are of course investigating* ***how*** *an error like this could have occurred.*

investigation /ɪnˌves.tɪˈɡeɪ.ʃən/ noun [C or U] B2 the act or process of examining a crime, problem, statement, etc. carefully, especially to discover the truth: *An investigation has been under way for several days* ***into*** *the disappearance of a 13-year-old boy.* ◦ *a* ***full/thorough*** *investigation of the incident* ◦ *Currently, the individuals who might have caused the accident are* ***subject to/under*** *investigation.*

investigative /ɪnˈves.tɪ.ɡə.tɪv/ US /-t̬ɪv/ adj (formal **investigatory** /ɪnˈves.tɪ.ɡə.tər.i/ US /-tɔːr-/) intended to examine a situation in order to discover the truth: *Children are encouraged to take an investigative approach to learning.* ◦ *the investigatory panel*

inˌvestigative ˈjournalism noun [U] a type of JOURNALISM that tries to discover information of public interest that someone is trying to hide • **inˌvestigative ˈjournalist** noun [C]

investigator /ɪnˈves.tɪ.ɡeɪ.tər/ US /-t̬ɚ/ noun [C] B2 a person whose job is to examine a crime, problem, statement, etc. in order to discover the truth: *Investigators have studied the possible effects of contamination.* ◦ *a private investigator*

investiture /ɪnˈves.tɪ.tʃər/ US /-tʃɚ/ noun [C] formal a ceremony in which someone is given an official rank, authority, power, etc.: *The investiture of the new president will take place this evening.*

investment /ɪnˈvest.mənt/ noun [C or U] B2 the act of putting money, effort, time, etc. into something to make a profit or get an advantage, or the money, effort, time, etc. used to do this: *Stocks are regarded as good long-term investments.* ◦ *The account requires a minimum investment of £1,000.* ◦ *There's been a significant investment of time and energy in order to make the project a success.*

inˈvestment ˌbank noun [C] a bank that helps companies sell and buy SHARES, or helps them to buy other companies or MERGE (= join together) with each other • **inˌvestment ˈbanking** noun [U] the business of operating an investment bank • **inˌvestment ˈbanker** noun [C] someone who has an important job in an investment bank

investor /ɪnˈves.tər/ US /-t̬ɚ/ noun [C] B2 a person who puts money into something in order to make a profit or get an advantage: *A New York investor offered to acquire the company's shares for $13 each.* ◦ ***Small*** *investors (= people who invest only a small amount of money) are hoping that the markets will improve.*

inveterate /ɪnˈvet.ər.ət/ US /-ˈvet̬.ɚ-/ adj usually disapproving **an inveterate liar, gambler, etc.** someone who does something very often and cannot stop doing it

invidious /ɪnˈvɪd.i.əs/ adj formal likely to cause unhappiness or be unpleasant, especially because unfair: *Such a difficult choice placed her in an invidious* ***position.*** • **invidiously** /-li/ adv • **invidiousness** /-nəs/ noun [U]

invigilate /ɪnˈvɪdʒ.ɪ.leɪt/ verb [I or T] UK (US **proctor**) to watch people taking an exam in order to check that they do not cheat: *Miss Jekyll will be invigilating (your chemistry exam) today.* • **invigilator** /-leɪ.tər/ US /-leɪ.t̬ɚ/ noun [C] a person whose job is to watch people taking an exam in order to check that they do not cheat: *If you need more paper, please ask the invigilator.*

invigorate /ɪnˈvɪɡ.ər.eɪt/ US /-ɚ-/ verb [T] to make someone feel fresher, healthier, and more energetic: *We were invigorated by our walk.* • **invigorating** /-eɪ.tɪŋ/ US /-eɪ.t̬ɪŋ/ adj *an invigorating swim/run*

invincible /ɪnˈvɪn.sɪ.bl̩/ adj impossible to defeat or prevent from doing what is intended: *Last year the company* ***seemed/looked*** *invincible but in recent weeks has begun to have problems.* • **invincibly** /-bli/ adv • **invincibility** /ɪnˌvɪn.sɪˈbɪl.ɪ.ti/ US /-ə.t̬i/ noun [U]

inviolable /ɪnˈvaɪə.lə.bl/ adj formal that must be respected and not removed or ignored: *Everyone has an inviolable* ***right*** *to protection by a fair legal system.* • **inviolability** /ɪnˌvaɪə.ləˈbɪl.ɪ.ti/ US /-ə.t̬i/ noun [U]

inviolate /ɪnˈvaɪə.lət/ adj [after verb] formal (that must be) not harmed or damaged: *For centuries the tomb lay inviolate until, by chance, it was discovered by two miners.*

invisible /ɪnˈvɪz.ɪ.bl̩/ adj **1** B2 impossible to see: *The aircraft is designed to be invisible* ***to*** *radar.* ◦ *These bacteria are invisible unless viewed with a microscope.* **2** [before noun] specialized describes money that is added to a country's economy by activities such as the service and financial industries rather than the production of goods in factories: *an increase in invisible* ***exports*** ◦ *Tourism brings in 40 percent of the island's invisible* ***earnings.*** • **invisibly** /-bli/ adv • **invisibility** /ɪnˌvɪz.əˈbɪl.ɪ.ti/ US /-ə.t̬i/ noun [U] *The bits of gold in the sand were small* ***to the point of*** *invisibility (= so small that they almost could not be seen).*

inˌvisible ˈink noun [U] ink which cannot be seen until it is treated with chemicals or heat: *It's a secret message written in invisible ink.*

invitation /ˌɪn.vɪˈteɪ.ʃən/ noun **ASK TO AN EVENT** ▷ **1** A2 [C or U] the act of inviting someone to go to an event: *Thanks for the invitation* ***to*** *your birthday party.* ◦ *I'm happy to* ***accept*** *your invitation.* ◦ *The first day of the exhibition will be* ***by*** *invitation (****only****) (= only those who have been invited can come).* **ENCOURAGEMENT** ▷ **2** C2 [S] an action which causes or encourages something to happen: *Leaving your house unlocked is an* ***open*** *(= clear) invitation* ***to*** *burglars.* **FORMAL REQUEST** ▷ **3** [C] an occasion when someone is formally asked to do something: [+ to infinitive] *This is a once in a lifetime invitation* ***to*** *invest in your dream home in the sun.* **PIECE OF PAPER** ▷ **4** a piece of paper or card that invites someone to an event: *I need to order the wedding invitations.*

invitational /ˌɪn.vɪˈteɪ.ʃən.əl/ noun [C] US a sports event that people can only go to if they have been invited • **invitational** adj *an invitational basketball tournament*

invite verb; noun

►verb [T] /ɪnˈvaɪt/ **ASK TO AN EVENT** ▷ **1** A1 to ask or request someone to go to an event: *We're invited* ***to***

Lola's party. ◦ *Candidates who are successful in the written test will be invited **for** an interview.* ◦ [+ obj + to infinitive] *Her family invited me **to** stay with them for a few weeks.*

> **! Common mistake: invite**
>
> The most usual preposition to use after the verb **invite** is **to**.
>
> Don't say 'invite someone for/at' an event, say **invite someone to** an event:
>
> ~~*She invited me for a party at her parents' house.*~~
>
> However, you can **invite someone for** a meal, or **for the weekend**:
>
> *They invited me for/to dinner.*

REQUEST FORMALLY ▷ **2** C1 to request something, especially formally or politely: *Offers in the region of £1,000,000 are invited **for** the property.* ◦ [+ obj + to infinitive] *The newspaper invited readers **to** write in with their views.* **ENCOURAGE** ▷ **3** C2 to act in a way that causes or encourages something to happen or someone to believe or feel something: *Behaving provocatively in class is just inviting **trouble**.* ◦ *Such a badly presented exhibition invites **criticism**.*

PHRASAL VERBS **invite sb in** to ask someone to come into your house: *The neighbours invited us in for coffee.* • **invite sb over** (UK also **invite sb round**) to invite someone to come to your house: *Let's invite some people over.*

▸**noun** [C] /ˈɪn.vaɪt/ informal an invitation: *I didn't get an invite to their wedding.*

inviting /ɪnˈvaɪ.tɪŋ/ US /-t̬ɪŋ/ **adj** If someone or something is inviting, they encourage you to feel welcome or attracted: *The room looked cosy and inviting.* ◦ *an inviting smile* • **invitingly** /-li/ **adv**

ˌin ˈvitro **adj** [before noun], **adv** happening outside the body in artificial conditions, often in a TEST TUBE: *Scientists are studying these cells in vitro.* ◦ *in vitro experiments*

in ˌvitro fertiliˈzation **noun** [U] (abbreviation **IVF**) a treatment for a woman who cannot become pregnant naturally, in which an egg is FERTILIZED outside her body and the resulting EMBRYO is put into her WOMB to develop into a baby

invoice /ˈɪn.vɔɪs/ **noun**; **verb**

▸**noun** [C] a list of things provided or work done together with their cost, for payment at a later time: *Invoices must be **submitted** by the 24th of every month.*

▸**verb** [T] to supply an invoice: *We'll invoice you **for** parts and labour.*

invoke /ɪnˈvəʊk/ US /-ˈvoʊk/ **verb** [T] formal **1** to request or use a power outside yourself, especially a law or a god, to help you when you want to improve a situation: *Police can invoke the law of trespass to regulate access to these places.* ◦ *Their sacred dance is performed to invoke ancient gods.* **2** to make someone have a particular feeling or remember something • **invocation** /ˌɪn.vəˈkeɪ.ʃən/ **noun** [C or U]

involuntary /ɪnˈvɒl.ən.tər.i/ US /-ˈvɑː.lən.ter.i/ **adj** not done by choice; done unwillingly, or without the decision or intention of the person involved: *A sharp tap on the knee usually causes an involuntary movement of the lower leg.* • **involuntarily** /-ˈter.əl.i/ **adv** *Arthur shivered involuntarily as he came out of the building.*

involve /ɪnˈvɒlv/ US /-ˈvɑːlv/ **verb** [T not continuous] B1 to include someone or something in something, or to make them take part in or feel part of it: *The second accident involved two cars and a lorry.* ◦ *I prefer teaching methods that actively involve students **in** learn**ing**.* ◦ [+ -ing verb] *The operation involves putt**ing** a small tube into your heart.* ◦ *Research involving the use of biological warfare agents will be used for defensive purposes.* ◦ *She's been involved **with** animal rights for many years.* ◦ *It would be difficult not to involve the child's father **in** the arrangements.*

involved /ɪnˈvɒlvd/ US /-ˈvɑːlvd/ **adj** **DIFFICULT** ▷ **1** not simple and therefore difficult to understand: *an involved reason/excuse/argument* → Synonym **complicated** **EMOTIONAL** ▷ **2** being in a close relationship with someone: *emotionally/romantically involved* ◦ *Try not to become too emotionally involved **with** the children in your care.*

involvement /ɪnˈvɒlv.mənt/ US /-ˈvɑːlv-/ **noun** [C or U] **1** B2 the act or process of taking part in something: *The team's continued involvement **in** the competition is uncertain.* ◦ *Being on the committee is one involvement I could do without.* **2** a romantic or sexual relationship: *She spoke openly about her involvement with the former prime minister.*

invulnerable /ɪnˈvʌl.nər.ə.bl̩/ US /-nɚ-/ **adj** impossible to damage or hurt in any way: *The command bunker is virtually invulnerable, even to a nuclear attack.* • **invulnerability** /ɪnˌvʌl.nər.əˈbɪl.ɪ.ti/ US /-nɚ.əˈbɪl.ə.t̬i/ **noun** [U]

inward /ˈɪn.wəd/ US /-wɚd/ **adj**; **adv**

▸**adj** **INSIDE** ▷ **1** on or towards the inside: *The force pushes the object in an inward **direction**.* → Compare **outward** **2** inside your mind and not expressed to other people: *inward feelings* **MONEY** ▷ **3** relating to money coming into a country rather than leaving it: *Inward **foreign investment** helped India achieve strong annual growth rates.*

▸**adv** (also **inwards**) towards the inside: *After the accident, her thoughts began to turn inward (= to her own interests or problems).* ◦ *Fold the outside edges inward.*

inwardly /ˈɪn.wəd.li/ US /-wɚd-/ **adv** inside your mind and not expressed to other people: *He was inwardly relieved that the test was cancelled.*

ˌin-your-ˈface (also **ˌin-yer-ˈface**) **adj** informal describes something done in a forceful way that intends to shock people: *in-your-face television advertising*

the IOC /ˌaɪ.əʊˈsiː/ US /-oʊ-/ **noun** abbreviation for the International Olympic Committee

iodide /ˈaɪ.əʊ.daɪd/ US /-ə-/ **noun** [C] specialized a chemical COMPOUND of iodine with another element: *potassium iodide*

iodine /ˈaɪ.ə.diːn/, /-daɪn/ **noun** [U] (symbol **I**) a chemical element that is found in small amounts in sea water and used to prevent infection

ˈiodine soˌlution **noun** [U] specialized iodine dissolved in a solution of POTASSIUM IODIDE, used in chemistry to test for STARCH

iodized salt /ˌaɪ.ə.daɪzdˈsɒlt/ US /-ˈsɑːlt/ **noun** [U] salt to which iodine has been added

ion /ˈaɪ.ɒn/ US /-ɑːn/ **noun** [C] specialized an atom or small group of atoms that has an electrical charge because it has added or lost one or more ELECTRONS → See also **the ionosphere** • **ionic** /aɪˈɒn.ɪk/ US /-ˈɑː.nɪk/ **adj** *ionic bonding*

-ion /-ən/ **suffix** (also **-ation**, also **-ition**) added to verbs to form nouns showing action or condition: *obsession* ◦ *restoration* ◦ *repetition*

Ionic /aɪˈɒn.ɪk/ US /-ˈɑː.nɪk/ **adj** of or copying a style of ancient Greek building that has only a small amount of decoration: *an Ionic column* → Compare **Corinthian**, **Doric**

iˌonic ˈbond **noun** [C] specialized a chemical BOND in which two ions are joined together because one has a positive charge and the other a negative charge

ionize specialized (UK usually **ionise**) /ˈaɪ.ə.naɪz/ verb [I or T] to (cause to) form an ion • **ionized** (UK usually **ionised**) /-naɪzd/ adj *Nebulae contain very large amounts of ionized gas.* • **ionization** (UK usually **ionisation**) /ˌaɪ.ə.naɪˈzeɪ.ʃən/ noun [U] *Widespread ionization occurs readily in the Earth's upper atmosphere.*

ionizer (UK usually **ioniser**) /ˈaɪ.əˌnaɪ.zə/ (US) /-zɚ/ noun [C] an electrical device which puts negative ions into the air in a room in order to make the air fresher and healthier

the ionosphere /aɪˈɒn.əˌsfɪəʳ/ (US) /-ˈɑːn.əˌsfɪr/ noun [S] part of the Earth's ATMOSPHERE, from about 60 kilometres to about 1,000 kilometres above the surface, in which there are many ions → Compare **the stratosphere** • **ionospheric** /aɪˌɒn.əˈsfer.ɪk/ (US) /-ˌɑːn.ə-/ adj

iota /aɪˈəʊ.tə/ (US) /-ˈoʊ.t̬ə/ noun [S] an extremely small amount: *I haven't seen **one** iota **of** evidence to support his claim.*

IOU /ˌaɪ.əʊˈjuː/ (US) /-oʊˈ-/ noun [C] abbreviation for I owe you: a written promise to pay back a debt: *Here's an IOU for the fiver you lent me. I'll pay you back on Monday.*

iow written abbreviation for in other words: used to introduce an explanation that is simpler than the one given earlier

IP /ˌaɪˈpiː/ noun [U] **INTERNET** ▷ **1** abbreviation for internet protocol: the technical rules that control communication on the internet: *an IP address* **LAW** ▷ **2** abbreviation for **intellectual property**

IPA /ˌaɪ.piːˈeɪ/ noun [S] abbreviation for the International Phonetic Alphabet: a system of symbols for showing how words are pronounced

IˈP adˌdress noun [C] (also **IˈP ˌnumber**) abbreviation for Internet Protocol Address: a number that is given to each computer when it is connected to the internet

IPO /ˌaɪ.piːˈəʊ/ (US) /-ˈoʊ/ noun [C usually singular] abbreviation for initial public offering: the first sale of a company's SHARES to the public

iPod /ˈaɪ.pɒd/ noun [C] trademark a type of MP3 PLAYER

ipso facto /ˌɪp.səʊˈfæk.təʊ/ (US) /-soʊˈfæk.toʊ/ adv formal used to say that it is reasonable to state or believe something based on facts that are already known: *You admit you fired the gun and we now know that the shot killed the victim so you are, ipso facto, responsible for his death.*

IQ /aɪˈkjuː/ noun [C or U] abbreviation for intelligence quotient: a measure of someone's intelligence found from special tests: *Children with very **low/high** IQs often have problems at school.* ◦ *IQ is just one measure of intelligence.*

the IRA /ˌaɪ.ɑːˈreɪ/ (US) /-ɑːrˈeɪ/ noun [+ sing/pl verb] abbreviation for the Irish Republican Army: an illegal organization that wants Northern Ireland to be politically independent of the UK and united with the Republic of Ireland

irascible /ɪˈræs.ə.bl/ adj formal made angry easily: *She's becoming more and more irascible as she grows older.* • **irascibly** /-bli/ adv • **irascibility** /ɪˌræs.əˈbɪl.ɪ.ti/ (US) /-ə.t̬i/ noun [U]

irate /aɪˈreɪt/ adj very angry: *We have received some irate phone calls from customers.*

ire /aɪəʳ/ (US) /aɪr/ noun [U] formal anger: *Petty restrictions easily **raised/aroused** the ire of such a creative artist.*

iridescent /ˌɪr.ɪˈdes.ənt/ adj showing many bright colours which change with movement • **iridescence** /-əns/ noun [U]

iridium /ɪˈrɪd.i.əm/ noun [U] a very hard yellowish-white metal

iris /ˈaɪ.rɪs/ noun [C] **FLOWER** ▷ **1** a tall plant that has blue, yellow, or white flowers and long, narrow leaves **EYE** ▷ **2** the coloured circular part of that eye that surrounds the black PUPIL (= central part)

Irish /ˈaɪə.rɪʃ/ adj; noun

▸adj coming from Ireland, or relating to Ireland or its language: *Irish whiskey* ◦ *The Irish contingent sang loudest at the show.*

▸noun [plural] **the Irish** the people of Ireland

ˌIrish Aˈmerican noun [C] a person who lives in the US but whose family originally came from Ireland • **ˌIrish-Aˈmerican** adj

ˌIrish ˈcoffee noun [U] hot coffee mixed with WHISKY and with thick cream on the top, usually served in a glass

Irishman /ˈaɪə.rɪʃ.mən/ noun [C] (plural **-men** /-mən/) a man who comes from Ireland

ˌIrish ˈstew noun [U] meat, often MUTTON (= meat from a sheep) cooked in water with onions, potatoes, etc.

Irishwoman /ˈaɪə.rɪʃˌwʊm.ən/ noun [C] (plural **-women** /-wɪmɪn/) a woman who comes from Ireland

irk /ɜːk/ (US) /ɝːk/ verb [T] formal to annoy someone: *The negative reply to my complaint really irked me.*

irksome /ˈɜːk.səm/ (US) /ˈɝːk-/ adj formal annoying: *The vibration can become irksome after a while.*

iron /aɪən/ (US) /aɪrn/ noun; verb; adj

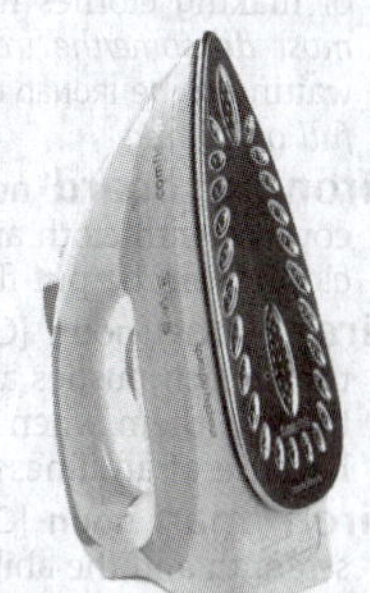
iron

▸noun **METAL** ▷ **1** B1 [U] (symbol **Fe**) a chemical element that is a common greyish-coloured metal. It is strong, used in making STEEL, and exists in very small amounts in blood: *Iron rusts easily.* ◦ *Liver is a particularly rich source of dietary iron.* ◦ *iron ore* ◦ *an iron deficiency* **FOR CLOTHES** ▷ **2** B1 [C] a piece of equipment for making clothes flat and smooth that has a handle and a flat base and is usually heated with electricity: *a steam iron* ◦ *a travel iron* **GOLF** ▷ **3** [C] a stick that has an iron or STEEL part at the end that is used to hit the ball in GOLF: *He'll probably use a 2 or 3 iron for the shot.* **CHAINS** ▷ **4 irons** [plural] literary chains tied around someone to prevent them from escaping or moving: *It was common practice for the prisoners to be **clapped in** irons (= tied with chains).*

IDIOM **have a few, several, etc. irons in the fire** to be involved with many activities or jobs at the same time or to make certain that there are always several possibilities available: *If that job application doesn't work out I've got a couple more irons in the fire.*

▸verb [I or T] B1 to make clothes flat and smooth using an iron: *It takes about five minutes to iron a shirt properly.*

PHRASAL VERB **iron sth out** to remove problems or find solutions: *We're still trying to iron out some problems with the computer system.* ◦ *We hope they can iron out their **differences** and get on with working together.*

▸**adj** [before noun] very strong physically, mentally, or emotionally: *I think you have to have an iron **will** to make some of these decisions.*

IDIOMS **an iron hand/fist in a velvet glove** used to describe someone who seems to be gentle but is in fact forceful and determined • **rule sth with an iron hand/fist** US to control a group of people very firmly, having complete power over everything they do

the ˈIron ˌAge noun [S] the period in early history starting about 1100 BC when iron was used for tools: *an Iron Age settlement* → Compare **the Bronze Age, the Stone Age**

ˈiron ˌbox noun [C] Indian English a piece of equipment for making clothes flat and smooth → See also **iron**

ironclad /ˈaɪən.klæd/ US /ˈaɪrn-/ **adj** [usually before noun] very certain and unlikely to be changed: *ironclad rules*

the ˌIron ˈCurtain noun [S] From 1946-1989 the Iron Curtain was the name of the border between Western Europe and the COMMUNIST countries of Eastern Europe, which made it very difficult to travel into or out of Eastern Europe.

ironic /aɪˈrɒn.ɪk/ US /aɪˈrɑː.nɪk/ **adj** (also **ironical** /aɪˈrɒn.ɪ.kəl/ US /-ˈrɑː.nɪ.kəl/) **1** C2 interesting, strange, or funny because of being very different from what you would usually expect: [+ that] ***It** is ironic **that** although many items are now cheaper to make, fewer people can afford to buy them.* **2** showing that you really mean the opposite of what you are saying: *an ironic comment/reply* • **ironically** /-ˈrɒn.ɪ.kəl.i/ US /-ˈrɑː.nɪ.kəl.i/ **adv**

ironing /ˈaɪə.nɪŋ/ US /ˈaɪr-/ noun [U] **1** B1 the activity of making clothes flat and smooth, using an IRON: *I must **do** some/the ironing tonight.* **2** clothes that are waiting to be IRONED or have just been IRONED: *a basket full of ironing*

ˈironing ˌboard noun [C] a narrow table, usually covered with cloth and having folding legs, on which clothes can be put flat to IRON them

ˌiron ˈlung noun [C] a machine with a large metal tube which pushes air in and out of someone's lungs to help them when they find it difficult to breathe because of an illness

ˌiron ˈman noun [C] US a person of great physical strength and the ability to continue doing something difficult for a long time

ironmonger /ˈaɪənˌmʌŋ.gər/ US /ˈaɪrnˌmʌŋ.gɚ/ noun [C] UK old-fashioned **1** someone who sells tools for use in homes and gardens **2 ironmonger's** (plural **ironmongers**) tools and equipment used in homes or gardens • **ironmongery** /-i/ noun [U] tools and equipment used in homes or gardens

ˌiron ˈrations noun [plural] old-fashioned a basic amount of food for a person to live on

ironwork /ˈaɪən.wɜːk/ US /ˈaɪrn.wɝːk/ noun [U] things made of iron such as gates, especially if made in a decorated way

ironworks /ˈaɪən.wɜːks/ US /ˈaɪrn.wɝːks/ noun [C, + sing/pl verb] (plural **ironworks**) a factory where iron is produced or iron objects are made

irony /ˈaɪ.rə.ni/ noun [U] OPPOSITE RESULT ▷ **1** C2 a situation in which something which was intended to have a particular result has the opposite or a very different result: *The irony (**of** it) is that the new tax system will burden those it was intended to help.* TYPE OF SPEECH ▷ **2** C2 the use of words that are the opposite of what you mean, as a way of being funny: *Her voice **heavy with** irony, Simone said, 'We're so pleased you were able to stay so long.'* (= *Her voice made it obvious they were not pleased.*) → Compare **sarcasm**

irradiate /ɪˈreɪ.di.eɪt/ verb [T] specialized to treat with light or other types of RADIATION: *The cells are irradiated so that they cannot reproduce.* • **irradiated** /-eɪ.tɪd/ US /-eɪt̬ɪd/ **adj** *irradiated fuel* ◦ *irradiated food* • **irradiation** /ɪˌreɪ.diˈeɪ.ʃən/ noun [U]

irrational /ɪˈræʃ.ən.əl/ **adj** C2 not using reason or clear thinking: *It's totally irrational, but I'm frightened of mice.* ◦ *His parents were worried by his increasingly irrational behaviour.* • **irrationally** /-i/ **adv** *People often behave irrationally when they are under stress.* • **irrationality** /ɪˌræʃ.ənˈæl.ə.ti/ US /-t̬i/ noun [U]

irreconcilable /ɪˌrek.ənˈsaɪ.lə.bl̩/ **adj** impossible to find agreement between or with, or impossible to deal with: *irreconcilable **differences** of opinion* ◦ *They have become irreconcilable, with both sides refusing to compromise any further.* • **irreconcilably** /-bli/ **adv**

irrecoverable /ˌɪr.ɪˈkʌv.ər.ə.bl̩/ **adj** impossible to get back: *irrecoverable financial losses* • **irrecoverably** /-bli/ **adv**

irredeemable /ˌɪr.ɪˈdiː.mə.bl̩/ **adj** formal impossible to correct, improve or change: *There are irredeemable flaws in the logic of the argument.* • **irredeemably** /-bli/ **adv** *The writing itself was irredeemably bad.*

irreducible /ˌɪr.ɪˈdjuː.sə.bl̩/ US /-ˈduː-/ **adj** formal impossible to make smaller or simpler: *A few simple shapes are the irreducible forms from which all of the patterns are generated.* • **irreducibly** /-bli/ **adv**

irrefutable /ˌɪr.ɪˈfjuː.tə.bl̩/ US /-t̬ə-/ **adj** formal impossible to prove wrong: *an irrefutable **argument*** ◦ *irrefutable **evidence** of health risks* • **irrefutably** /-bli/ **adv**

irregular /ɪˈreg.jə.lər/ US /-lɚ/ **adj; noun**

▸**adj** RULE ▷ **1** formal (of behaviour or actions) not according to usual rules or what is expected: *Releasing the goods without an invoice is **most** irregular.* **2** B1 In grammar, an irregular verb, noun, adjective, etc. does not obey the usual rules for words in the language. SHAPE ▷ **3** B2 not regular in shape or form; having parts of different shapes or sizes: *an irregular coastline* ◦ *irregular teeth* TIME/SPACE ▷ **4** B2 not happening at regular times or not with regular spaces in between: *an irregular heartbeat* ◦ *They met at irregular intervals.* **5** US informal not emptying your bowels as often as you would usually SOLDIER ▷ **6** (of a soldier) fighting for a country but not as a member of its official army • **irregularly** /-li/ **adv** *irregularly shaped*

▸**noun** [C] a soldier who is not a member of the official army of a country

irregularity /ɪˌreg.jəˈlær.ə.ti/ US /-ˈler.ə.t̬i/ noun SHAPE ▷ **1** [C or U] the quality of not being regular in shape or form, or an example of this: *The pictures showed cracks and other irregularities in otherwise perfectly regular crystals.* ◦ *The west of the island is famous for **the** irregularity **of** its coastline.* RULE ▷ **2** [C or U] something that is not correct or acceptable: *The inspectors found several irregularities **in** the business accounts.* ◦ ***The** irregularity **of** (= the lack of rules for) English spelling means that it is easy to make mistakes.* TIME/SPACE ▷ **3** [U] the fact that something does not happen at regular times

irrelevance /ɪˈrel.ɪ.vəns/ noun [C or U] (formal **irrelevancy** /-vən.si/) the fact that something is not related to what is being discussed or considered and therefore not important, or an example of this: *Sympathy is an irrelevance – we need practical help.* ◦ *Many of these problems may simply fade into irrelevance when the new rules come into force.* • **irrelevantly** /-li/ **adv**

irrelevant /ɪˈrel.ɪ.vᵊnt/ **adj** not related to what is being discussed or considered and therefore not important: *These documents are* ***largely*** *irrelevant* ***to*** *the present investigation.* ◦ *Making a large profit is irrelevant* ***to*** *us – the important thing is to make the book available to the largest possible audience.*

irreligious /ˌɪr.ɪˈlɪdʒ.əs/ **adj** formal disapproving having no interest in religion, or generally opposed to religion

irremediable /ˌɪr.ɪˈmiː.di.ə.bl̩/ **adj** formal impossible to correct or cure

irreparable /ɪˈrep.rə.bl̩/ **adj** impossible to repair or make right again: *Unless the oil spill is contained, irreparable* ***damage*** *will be done to the coastline.* • **irreparably** /-bli/ **adv** *The ship has been irreparably damaged.*

irreplaceable /ˌɪr.ɪˈpleɪ.sə.bl̩/ **adj** too special, unusual, or valuable to replace with something or someone else: *Most of the porcelain you see in the display cabinets is irreplaceable.* ◦ *No one's irreplaceable in the workplace.*

irrepressible /ˌɪr.ɪˈpres.ə.bl̩/ **adj** full of energy and enthusiasm; impossible to stop: *Even the rain failed to dampen his irrepressible* ***spirits.*** • **irrepressibly** /-bli/ **adv**

irreproachable /ˌɪr.ɪˈprəʊ.tʃə.bl̩/ (US) /-ˈproʊ-/ **adj** formal approving without fault and therefore impossible to criticize: *Her conduct throughout was irreproachable.* • **irreproachably** /-bli/ **adv**

irresistible /ˌɪr.ɪˈzɪs.tə.bl̩/ **adj** C2 impossible to refuse, oppose, or avoid because too pleasant, attractive, or strong: *an irresistible offer* ◦ *She gave me one of those irresistible smiles and I just had to agree.* • **irresistibly** /-bli/ **adv**

irresolute /ɪˈrez.ᵊl.uːt/ **adj** formal disapproving not able or willing to take decisions or actions: *an irresolute reply* • **irresolutely** /-li/ **adv** • **irresolution** /ɪˌrez.ᵊlˈuː.ʃᵊn/ **noun** [U]

irrespective /ˌɪr.ɪˈspek.tɪv/ **adv** C2 without considering; not needing to allow for: *The legislation must be applied irrespective* ***of*** *someone's ethnic origins.*

irresponsible /ˌɪr.ɪˈspɒn.sɪ.bl̩/ (US) /-ˈspɑːn-/ **adj** disapproving B2 not thinking enough or not worrying about the possible results of what you do: [+ to infinitive] ***It*** *would be irresponsible* ***to*** *ignore these warnings.* • **irresponsibly** /-bli/ **adv** *It's unlike you to behave so irresponsibly.* • **irresponsibility** /ˌɪr.ɪˌspɒn.səˈbɪl.ɪ.ti/ (US) /-ˌspɑːn.səˈbɪl.ə.t̬i/ **noun** [U] *It was an act of gross irresponsibility to leave someone who wasn't properly trained in charge of the machine.*

irretrievable /ˌɪr.ɪˈtriː.və.bl̩/ **adj** impossible to correct or return to a previously existing situation or condition: *I agree things look difficult, but the situation is far from irretrievable.* ◦ *The couple separated on the grounds of irretrievable* ***breakdown*** *(of their marriage).* • **irretrievably** /-bli/ **adv** *irretrievably damaged/lost*

irreverent /ɪˈrev.ᵊr.ᵊnt/ (US) /-ɚ-/ **adj** not showing the expected respect for official, important, or holy things: *an irreverent comment/approach/attitude* ◦ *irreverent thoughts* • **irreverently** /-li/ (US) /-ɚ-/ **adv** • **irreverence** /-ᵊns/ **noun** [U]

irreversible /ˌɪr.ɪˈvɜː.sɪ.bl̩/ (US) /-ˈvɝː-/ **adj** C2 not possible to change; impossible to return to a previous condition: *Smoking has caused irreversible damage to his lungs.* • **irreversibly** /-bli/ **adv**

irrevocable /ɪˈrev.ə.kə.bl̩/ **adj** impossible to change: *an irrevocable decision* • **irrevocably** /-bli/ **adv** *Closing the factory would irrevocably alter the character of the local community for the worse.*

irrigate /ˈɪr.ɪ.geɪt/ **verb** [T] **SUPPLY WATER** ▷ **1** to supply land with water so that crops and plants will grow: *irrigated land/fields* **WASH** ▷ **2** specialized to wash an injured part of a person's body, especially a cut, with a flow of liquid • **irrigation** /ˌɪr.ɪˈgeɪ.ʃᵊn/ **noun** [U]

irritable /ˈɪr.ɪ.tə.bl̩/ (US) /-t̬ə-/ **adj** C2 becoming annoyed very easily: *Be careful what you say – he's rather irritable today.* ◦ *'Don't disturb me again,' she said in an irritable (= angry) voice.* • **irritably** /-bli/ **adv** • **irritability** /ˌɪr.ɪ.təˈbɪl.ɪ.ti/ (US) /-t̬əˈbɪl.ə.t̬i/ **noun** [U]

ˌirritable ˈbowel ˌsyndrome **noun** [U] a condition that affects the bowels and causes stomach pain, and is often caused by worry or ANXIETY

irritant /ˈɪr.ɪ.tᵊnt/ (US) /-t̬ənt/ **noun** [C] **MAKING ANGRY** ▷ **1** something that causes trouble or makes you annoyed: *The report is bound to add a new irritant to international relations.* **MAKING SORE** ▷ **2** a substance that makes part of your body sore or painful: *Pollen is an irritant, causing red and sore eyes in sensitive people.*

irritate /ˈɪr.ɪ.teɪt/ **verb** [T] **MAKE ANGRY** ▷ **1** C1 to make someone angry or annoyed: *After a while her behaviour really began to irritate me.* **MAKE SORE** ▷ **2** to make a part of your body sore or painful: *At first my contact lenses irritated my eyes.*

irritated /ˈɪr.ɪ.teɪ.tɪd/ (US) /-t̬ɪd/ **adj** B2 annoyed: *Ben began to get increasingly irritated* ***by/at*** *her questions.*

irritating /ˈɪr.ɪ.teɪ.tɪŋ/ (US) /-t̬ɪŋ/ **adj** B2 making you feel annoyed: *an irritating habit* • **irritatingly** /-li/ **adv**

irritation /ˌɪr.ɪˈteɪ.ʃᵊn/ **noun** [C or U] **ANGER** ▷ **1** C2 the feeling of being angry or annoyed, or something that makes you feel like this: *That kind of behaviour is sure to cause irritation.* ◦ *Traffic noise is just one of several* ***minor*** *irritations (= small problems).* **SORE FEELING** ▷ **2** a painful or sore feeling in a part of the body: *It is an antiseptic cream suitable for minor* ***skin*** *irritations.* ◦ *The strap had rubbed against his skin and caused irritation.*

is strong /ɪz/ weak /z/ /s/ he/she/it form of **be**

ISA /ˈaɪ.sə/ **noun** [C] abbreviation for Individual Savings Account: a type of INVESTMENT account in the UK in which the tax on income is lower than usual, and there is no tax on profits made from an increase in the value of SHARES

ISBN /ˌaɪ.es.biːˈen/ **noun** [C] abbreviation for International Standard Book Number: a set of numbers used to IDENTIFY a particular book and show that it is different from other books

ISDN /ˌaɪ.es.diːˈen/ **noun** abbreviation for Integrated Services Digital Network: a system for sending voice, video, and information over phone wires very quickly

-ish /-ɪʃ/ **suffix** **FROM PLACE** ▷ **1** used to form adjectives and nouns which say what country or area a person, thing, or language comes from: *Spanish dancing* ◦ *Are you English?* ◦ *I've always liked the Irish (= people from Ireland).* ◦ *Do you speak Swedish?* **LIKE** ▷ **2** used to form adjectives which say what a person, thing, or action is like: *foolish* ◦ *childish* **QUITE** ▷ **3** used to form adjectives to give the meaning to some degree; fairly: *He had a sort of reddish beard.* ◦ *She was oldish – about 60, I'd say.* ◦ *We'll start at sevenish (= about seven o'clock).*

Islam /ˈɪz.lɑːm/, /-læm/ **noun** [U] the Muslim religion, and the people and countries who believe in it • **Islamic** /-ˈlæm.ɪk/, /-ˈlɑː.mɪk/ **adj** *Islamic culture/beliefs/art/law*

Islamist /ˈɪz.lə.mɪst/ **noun** [C] a person who believes strongly in Islam, especially one who believes that

Islam should influence political systems • **Islamist** adj • **Islamism** /-mɪ.zᵊm/ noun [U] *followers of Islamism*

island /ˈaɪ.lənd/ noun [C] **1** A2 a piece of land completely surrounded by water: *a desert island* ◦ *a Pacific island* ◦ *They live* ***on*** *the large Japanese island of Hokkaido.* **2 an island of peace, calm, sanity, etc.** **3** UK **traffic island**

> **Common mistake: island**
>
> **Remember:** use the correct preposition.
>
> Don't say 'in an island', say **on an island**:
>
> *We spent three days on a beautiful island.*

islander /ˈaɪ.lən.dəʳ/ US /-dɚ/ noun [C] someone who lives on an island: *Scottish islanders*

isle /aɪl/ noun [C] literary (used especially in place names) an island: *Explore the more remote Caribbean isles.* ◦ *the Isle of Skye*

I

ism /ˈɪz.ᵊm/ noun [C] informal mainly humorous a set of beliefs, especially ones that you disapprove of: *Thatcher is unique among her predecessors in having given the English language a brand new ism, created from her own name.*

-ism /-ɪ.zᵊm/ suffix **1** used to form nouns which describe social, political, or religious beliefs, studies or ways of behaving: *sexism* ◦ *feminism* ◦ *Buddhism* **2** an example of typical behaviour: *That expression was a real Taylor-ism (= an example of behaving or speaking like Taylor).*

isn't /ˈɪz.ᵊnt/ short form is not: *He isn't coming until tomorrow.*

isobar /ˈaɪ.sə.bɑːʳ/ US /-soʊ.bɑːr/ noun [C] specialized a line drawn on a weather map joining all the places that have the same air pressure

isolate /ˈaɪ.sə.leɪt/ verb [T] to separate something or someone from other things or people with which they are joined or mixed, or to keep them separate: *He was isolated* ***from*** *all the other prisoners.* ◦ *A high wall isolated the house* ***from*** *the rest of the village.* ◦ *They tried to isolate (= find) the cause of the problem.* ◦ specialized *Virus particles were eventually isolated* ***from*** *the tissue.*

isolated /ˈaɪ.sə.leɪ.tɪd/ US /-t̬ɪd/ adj **1** C1 not near to other places: *an isolated farm/village* **2** C2 happening or existing only once, separate: *There were only a few isolated cases of violent behaviour.* **3** C1 feeling unhappy because of not seeing or talking to other people: *Working at home was making her feel increasingly isolated.*

isolation /ˌaɪ.sᵊlˈeɪ.ʃᵊn/ noun [U] **1** C1 the condition of being alone, especially when this makes you feel unhappy: *The prisoner had been kept* ***in*** *isolation for three days.* ◦ *After all the visitors had left, she experienced a feeling of complete isolation.* **2** C2 the fact that something is separate and not connected to other things: *I can't think about it* ***in*** *isolation (= separately) – I need some examples of the problem.*

isolationism /ˌaɪ.sᵊlˈeɪ.ʃᵊn.ɪ.zᵊm/ noun [U] disapproving the political principle or practice of showing interest only in your own country and not being involved in international activities → Compare **globalism** • **isolationist** /-ɪst/ adj *an isolationist policy/nation/attitude*

isomer /ˈaɪ.sə.məʳ/ US /-soʊ.mɚ/ noun [C] specialized any one of a group of chemical substances which all have the same number and type of atoms but in which the arrangement of the atoms is slightly different between each substance: *structural/geometrical/optical isomers*

isosceles triangle /aɪˌsɒs.ᵊl.iːzˈtraɪ.æŋ.gl/ US /-ˌsɑː.sᵊl-/ noun [C] a triangle with two sides of equal length

isotherm /ˈaɪ.sə.θɜːm/ US /-soʊ.θɝːm/ noun [C] specialized a line drawn on a weather map joining all the places that have the same temperature

isotonic /aɪ.səˈtɒn.ɪk/ US /-ˈtɑː.nɪk/ adj describes a drink containing the liquid and minerals your body needs after physical exercise

isotope /ˈaɪ.sə.təʊp/ US /-toʊp/ noun [C] specialized a form of an atom that has a different ATOMIC WEIGHT from other forms of the same atom but the same chemical structure: *a radioactive isotope of hydrogen*

ISP /ˌaɪ.esˈpiː/ noun [C] abbreviation for Internet Service Provider: a company that provides use of the internet, allows you to use email, and gives you space on the internet to show documents: *Some ISPs are free and give you as many email addresses as you want.*

Israelite /ˈɪz.rə.laɪt/ noun [C] one of a race of people who lived in Israel in ancient times

issue /ˈɪʃ.uː/, /ˈɪs.juː/ noun; verb

▸noun [C] SUBJECT ▷ **1** B1 a subject or problem which people are thinking and talking about: *environmental/ethical/personal issues* ◦ *As employers we need to be seen to be* ***addressing*** *(= dealing with) these issues sympathetically.* ◦ *Don't worry about who will do it – that's just a* ***side*** *issue (= not the main problem).* **2 at issue** C2 most important in what is being discussed: *The point at issue is what is best for the child.* **3 make an issue of sth** disapproving to make something seem more important than it should be, or to argue about it: *Of course I'll help you, there's no need to make an issue of it.* **4 take issue with sth** C1 formal to disagree strongly: *I took issue with him* ***over*** *his interpretation of the instructions.* **5 have issues (with sb/sth)** to have difficulty or disagreement with someone or something: *All the people in the study had low self-esteem and had issues with their bodies.* ◦ *Anna has major issues with her employer.* PRODUCT ▷ **6** B2 a set of newspapers or magazines published at the same time or a single copy of a newspaper or magazine: *There's an article on motorbikes in the latest/next issue.* ◦ *An old issue of 'Homes and Gardens' lay on the table.* **7** An issue of SHARES is a time when a company gives people the chance to buy part of it or gives extra SHARES to people who already own some.

> **Word partners for issue noun**
>
> a *fundamental/important/key/major* issue • a *contentious/controversial/complex/thorny* issue • the *central/main* issue • *address/resolve/tackle* an issue • *discuss/raise* an issue • an issue *arises* • the issues *affecting/concerning/facing* sb • the issue *of* sth

IDIOM **without issue** old use or legal If someone dies without issue, they have no children.

▸verb [T] C2 to produce or provide something official: *The office will be issuing permits on Tuesday and Thursday mornings.* ◦ *The school issued a statement about its plans* ***to*** *the press./The school issued the press* ***with*** *a statement about its plans.*

PHRASAL VERB **issue from sth** literary If something issues from a place, it comes out of that place: *A terrible scream issued* ***from*** *the room.*

-ist /-ɪst/ suffix used to form adjectives and nouns which describe (a person with) a particular set of beliefs or way of behaving: *Marxist philosophy* ◦ *a feminist* ◦ *a sexist* → Compare **-ite**

-ista /-iː.stə/ **suffix** humorous used to describe someone who is a strong supporter of another person, when added to the name of that person: *Obamistas* ◦ *recessionistas*

isthmus /ˈɪsθ.məs/, /ˈɪs-/ **noun** [C] a narrow piece of land with water on each side which joins two larger areas of land: *the Isthmus of Panama*

it /ɪt/ **pronoun** THING ▷ **1** A1 used as the subject of a verb, or the object of a verb or preposition, to refer to a thing, animal, situation, or idea that has already been mentioned: *'Where's my pen? It was on my desk a minute ago.' 'You left it by the phone.'* ◦ *The company was losing money and it had to make people redundant.* ◦ *The argument was upsetting for us all – I don't want to talk about it.* ◦ *Children who stay away from school do it for different reasons.* SUBJECT/OBJECT ▷ **2** A1 used as the subject or object of a verb to represent a phrase at the end of the sentence: *It's unlikely that she'll arrive on time.* ◦ *It costs more if you travel before 9.00.* ◦ *I liked it in Scotland.* ◦ *I find it convenient to be able to do my banking by phone.* TIME/WEATHER ▷ **3** A2 used to talk about the time, date, weather, or distances: *What time is it?* ◦ *It was October, so it was quite cold.* ◦ *It rained all day.* ◦ *It's ten miles to Leeds.*

> **!** Common mistake: **it or there?**
>
> **Warning: it** cannot be used with a linking verb and a noun to say that something exists or is present.
>
> Don't say 'it is/was something', say **there is/was something**:
>
> ~~*It was no toilet on the coach.*~~
>
> *There was no toilet on the coach.*

it- /ɪt/ **prefix** informal used for describing things or people that are very fashionable, and everyone is interested in them, wants to have them, etc.: *The design of this bag makes it the 'it-bag' for this summer.*

IT /ˌaɪˈtiː/ **noun** [U] A2 abbreviation for **information technology**

italic /ɪˈtæl.ɪk/ **adj** printed or written in italics: *italic type/print/script*

italicize (UK usually **italicise**) /ɪˈtæl.ɪ.saɪz/ **verb** [T] to print or write something in italics: *Words are sometimes italicized for emphasis.*

italics /ɪˈtæl.ɪks/ **noun** [plural] a style of writing or printing in which the letters lean to the right: *This sentence is printed* ***in*** *italics.*

Italo- /ɪ.tæl.əʊ-/ (US) /-oʊ-/ **prefix** of or connected with Italy: *an Italo-German production*

itch /ɪtʃ/ **verb; noun**

▸**verb** [I] B2 to have or cause an uncomfortable feeling on the skin which makes you want to rub it with your nails: *I can't wear wool – it makes me itch.* • **itching** /ˈɪtʃ.ɪŋ/ **noun** [U] *This cream will reduce the itching.*

IDIOM **itch to do sth** (also **itch for sth**) C2 to want to do something very much and as soon as possible: *He was itching to hear the results.* ◦ *By four o'clock I was itching for the meeting to end.*

▸**noun** [C] an uncomfortable feeling on the skin which makes you want to rub it with your nails: *I've got an itch on the back of my neck.*

itchy /ˈɪtʃ.i/ **adj** having or causing an itch: *The sweater was itchy (= made me itch).* ◦ *The dust made me* ***feel*** *itchy all over.* • **itchiness** /-nəs/ **noun** [U]

IDIOM **get itchy feet** UK informal to start to want to travel or do something different: *After three years in the job she began to get itchy feet.*

it'd /ˈɪt.əd/ (US) /ˈɪt̬-/ **short form 1** it would: *It'd be better if we finished it off today.* **2** it had: *I found the radio – it'd been left in the shed all weekend.*

-ite /-aɪt/ **suffix** used for a person who supports particular beliefs, actions, or ideas, especially when added to the name of the person who is the origin of the ideas: *a Thatcherite* ◦ *a Reaganite*

item /ˈaɪ.təm/ (US) /-t̬əm/ **noun** [C] **1** B1 something that is part of a list or group of things: *the last item on the list* ◦ *The restaurant has a long menu of about 50 items.* ◦ *Several items* ***of clothing*** *(= clothes) lay on the floor.* **2** one of several subjects to be considered: *There are three items on the agenda.* **3** B2 a piece of news on television or radio, or in a newspaper: *There's an interesting item on the back page.* **4** **item by item** one thing at a time

IDIOM **be an item** informal If two people are an item, they are having a romantic relationship: *I saw Darren and Emma there. Are they an item?*

itemize (UK usually **itemise**) /ˈaɪ.tə.maɪz/ (US) /-t̬ə-/ **verb** [T] to list things separately, often including details about each thing: *We asked for an itemized* ***bill****, listing all our phone calls and how long they were.*

iteration /ˌɪt.ərˈeɪ.ʃən/ (US) /ˌɪt̬.əˈreɪ-/ **noun** [C or U] **1** formal the process of doing something again and again, usually to improve it, or one of the times you do it: *the repetition and iteration that goes on in designing something* ◦ *The software is on its fifth iteration.* **2** specialized an amount that you get when you use a mathematical rule several times

iterative /ˈɪt.ər.ə.tɪv/ (US) /ˈɪt̬.ə.reɪ.t̬ɪv/ **adj** formal or specialized doing something again and again, usually to improve it: *iterative processes*

itinerant /aɪˈtɪn.ər.ənt/ (US) /-ɚ-/ **adj** [before noun] travelling from one place to another, usually to work for a short period: *an itinerant journalist/labourer/preacher* • **itinerant noun** [C]

itinerary /aɪˈtɪn.ər.ər.i/ (US) /-ə.rer-/ **noun** [C] C1 a detailed plan or route of a journey: *The tour operator will arrange transport and plan your itinerary.*

it'll /ˈɪt.əl/ (US) /ˈɪt̬-/ **short form** it will: *It'll be hard to find someone to help.*

it's /ɪts/ **short form 1** it is: *It's my turn to do it.* **2** it has: *It's been a wonderful day – thank you.*

> **!** Common mistake: **its or it's?**
>
> **Remember: its** meaning 'of it' or 'belonging to it' does not have an apostrophe:
>
> ~~*The dog was chasing it's tail.*~~
>
> *The dog was chasing its tail.*
>
> **It's** is the short form of 'it is' or 'it has':
>
> *It's useful to listen to the radio in English.*
>
> *It's been very nice talking to you.*

its /ɪts/ **determiner** A1 belonging to or relating to something that has already been mentioned: *The dog hurt its paw.* ◦ *Their house has its own swimming pool.* ◦ *The company increased its profits.* ◦ *I prefer the second option – its advantages are simplicity and cheapness.*

itself /ɪtˈself/ **pronoun 1** A2 used when the subject of the verb is 'it' and the object is the same thing, animal, situation, or idea: *The cat licked itself all over.* ◦ *You have to do something about the problem – it isn't* just going to resolve itself. **2** (B1) used to emphasize the subject when it is a thing, animal, situation, or idea: *The shop itself (= only the shop and nothing else) started 15 years ago but the mail order side of the business is new.* **3 (all) by itself** alone or without help: *The animal had been left in the house by itself for a week.* ◦ *A cough will usually get better by itself.* **4 (all) to itself** for its use only: *The committee kept the results of the survey to itself (= did not tell anyone), fearing a bad public reaction.*

itsy-bitsy /ˌɪt.siˈbɪt.si/ **adj** [before noun] (US also **itty-bitty** /ˌɪt.iˈbɪt.i/ (US) /ˈɪt̬.iˈbɪt̬.i/) extremely small: *She has these itsy-bitsy little hands and feet.*

ITV /ˌaɪ.tiːˈviː/ **noun** abbreviation for Independent Television: a group of British television companies which earn most of their income from advertising: *There's a good film on ITV tonight.* → Compare **the BBC**

-ity /-ɪ.ti/ (US) /-ə.t̬i/ **suffix** added to adjectives to form nouns referring to a state or quality: *brutality* ◦ *legality*

IUD /ˌaɪ.juːˈdiː/ **noun** [C] abbreviation for intra-uterine device: a small object put by a doctor into the WOMB of a woman who wants to avoid becoming pregnant

IV /ˌaɪˈviː/ **adj; noun**

▸**adj** abbreviation for **intravenous**: *IV drug users*

▸**noun** [C] US for **drip**

-ive /-ɪv/ **suffix** (also **-ative**, also **-itive**, also **-tive**) added to verbs to form adjectives meaning showing the ability to perform the activity represented by the verb: *imaginative* ◦ *descriptive*

I've /aɪv/ **short form** I have: *I've been waiting an hour already.*

IVF /ˌaɪ.viːˈef/ **noun** [U] abbreviation for **in vitro fertilization**

ivied /ˈaɪ.vid/ **adj** literary covered with IVY: *these ancient ivied walls*

ivory /ˈaɪ.vᵊr.i/ (US) /-vɚ-/ **noun 1** [U] the hard yellowish-white substance that forms the TUSKS of some animals such as ELEPHANTS, used especially in the past to make decorative objects: *a ban on ivory trading* **2** [C usually plural] an object made from ivory: *a collection of Japanese ivories*

IDIOM **tickle the ivories** old-fashioned humorous to play the piano

ˌivory ˈtower noun [C] disapproving To live or be in an ivory tower is not to know about or to want to avoid the ordinary and unpleasant things that happen in people's lives: *Academics sitting **in** ivory towers have no understanding of what is important for ordinary people.*

ivy /ˈaɪ.vi/ **noun** [C or U] an EVERGREEN plant (= one that never loses its leaves) that often grows up trees or buildings: *Ivy covered the broken walls.*

ivy

the ˌIvy ˈLeague noun a group of eight respected colleges and universities in the northeast of the US: *an Ivy League education*

-ization (UK usually **-isation**) /-aɪˈzeɪ.ʃᵊn/ (US) /-əˈ-/ **suffix** used to form nouns from some verbs: *the modernization of the office*

-ize (UK usually **-ise**) /-aɪz/ **suffix** added to adjectives to form verbs meaning to cause to become: *to modernize (= to make modern)* ◦ *to centralize*

J

J, j /dʒeɪ/ noun [C or U] (plural **Js, J's** or **j's**) the tenth letter of the English alphabet

jab /dʒæb/ verb; noun

▸**verb (-bb-) 1** [I or T, usually + adv/prep] to push or hit something forcefully and quickly, often with a thin or sharp object: *The doctor jabbed the needle* ***into*** *the dog's leg.* ◦ *Watch out! You nearly jabbed me* ***in*** *the eye* ***with*** *your umbrella!* ◦ *He was jabbing a finger* ***at*** *(= towards) them and shouting angrily.* **2** [I] to make quick forceful hits with your FIST (= closed hand) when BOXING **3** [T] to kick a ball hard and quickly

▸**noun** [C] **1** a quick hard push or hit: *She gave me a sharp jab* ***in*** *the ribs with her elbow to stop me from saying any more.* ◦ *The boxer was floored by a punishing left jab.* **2** UK informal an **injection**: *a flu jab* ◦ *You'll need some jabs if you're going to Egypt.*

jabber /ˈdʒæb.əʳ/ (US) /-ɚ/ verb [I or T] disapproving to speak or say something quickly in a way that is difficult to understand: *The train was full of people jabbering (****away****) into their mobile phones.* ◦ *He jabbered (****out****) something about an accident further down the road.*

jack /dʒæk/ noun; verb

▸**noun** [C] **EQUIPMENT** ▷ **1** a piece of equipment that can be opened slowly under a heavy object such as a car in order to raise it off the ground: *You need a car jack in order to change a wheel.* **CARD** ▷ **2** (also **knave**) a playing card with a picture of a man on it. It has a lower value than the cards showing a king or queen: *the jack of clubs* **BALL** ▷ **3** a small ball towards which other balls are rolled or thrown in the games of BOWLS or BOULES **ELECTRICAL** ▷ **4** a connection between two pieces of electrical equipment

▸**verb**

PHRASAL VERBS **jack sth in** UK informal to stop doing something, often a job or something that you are not enjoying: *He's jacked in his job.* • **jack sth up LIFT** ▷ **1** to raise a heavy object such as a car off the ground with a jack **INCREASE** ▷ **2** informal disapproving to increase the price of something suddenly and by a large amount: *Once the tourists arrive, the restaurants jack up their prices.*

jackal /ˈdʒæk.əl/ noun [C] a wild animal like a dog that lives in Africa and southern Asia and eats animals that have died or been killed by others

jackaroo /dʒæk.əˈruː/ noun [C] (plural **jackaroos**) Australian English a man who is learning to work on a sheep or CATTLE farm → Compare **jillaroo**

jackass /ˈdʒæk.æs/ noun [C] **SILLY PERSON** ▷ **1** old-fashioned informal a person who behaves in a silly way **BIRD** ▷ **2** Australian English old-fashioned a **kookaburra**

jackboot /ˈdʒæk.buːt/ noun [C] a long boot which covers the leg up to the knee, especially as worn by NAZIS • **jackbooted** /-ˌbuː.tɪd/ (US) /-ˌbuː.t̬ɪd/ adj wearing jackboots: *a jackbooted thug*

jackdaw /ˈdʒæk.dɔː/ (US) /-dɑː/ noun [C] a black and grey bird of the CROW family, known for taking bright objects back to its nest

jacket /ˈdʒæk.ɪt/ noun [C] **CLOTHES** ▷ **1** (A1) a short coat: *a leather/denim/tweed jacket* ◦ *The keys are in my jacket pocket.* **BOOK** ▷ **2 dust jacket**

ˌjacket poˈtato noun [C] (plural **jacket potatoes**) UK for **baked potato**

ˌJack ˈFrost noun old-fashioned child's word very cold weather, when it is thought of as a person

jackhammer /ˈdʒækˌhæm.əʳ/ (US) /-ɚ/ noun [C] US for **pneumatic drill**

ˈjack-in-the-ˌbox noun [C] a children's toy consisting of a box with a model of a person inside it which jumps out and gives you a surprise when the top of the box is raised

jackknife /ˈdʒæk.naɪf/ verb; noun

▸**verb** [I] If a truck that has two parts jackknifes, one part moves around so far towards the other part that it cannot be driven: *The oil tanker jackknifed after skidding on the ice.*

▸**noun** [C] (plural **jackknives**) a large knife with a blade that folds into the handle

ˌjack-of-all-ˈtrades noun [C] someone who can do many different jobs

IDIOM **jack-of-all-trades, master of none** saying said about someone who is able to do many things, but is not an expert in any of them

jack-o'-lantern /ˌdʒæk.əˈlæn.tən/ (US) /-tɚn/ noun [C] US a light made from a hollow PUMPKIN with holes cut into the sides like the eyes and mouth of a person's face, inside which there is a candle

ˈjack ˌplug noun [C] UK (US **plug**) a metal pin at the end of a long wire joined to a piece of electrical equipment and used to connect it to another piece of electrical equipment

jackpot /ˈdʒæk.pɒt/ (US) /-pɑːt/ noun [C] the largest prize in a competition or game: *The jackpot was over $1 million.*

IDIOM **hit the jackpot 1** to win the largest prize in a competition or game **2** to have a big success or make a big profit, usually through luck: *He seems to have hit the jackpot with his new invention.*

jackrabbit /ˈdʒækˌræb.ɪt/ noun [C] a type of large North American RABBIT

Jack Robinson /ˌdʒækˈrɒb.ɪn.sən/ (US) /-ˈrɑː.bɪn-/ noun old-fashioned **before you can/could say Jack Robinson** done or happening very quickly: *I put the plate of food on the floor, and before you could say Jack Robinson, the dog had eaten it.*

jacks /dʒæks/ noun [U] a children's game in which you throw a ball into the air and try to pick up a number of small metal or plastic objects with the same hand before catching the ball again

ˌJack the ˈLad noun [C usually singular] UK old-fashioned a young man who behaves in a very confident way

Jacobean /ˌdʒæk.əˈbiː.ən/ adj relating to the period from 1603 to 1625 when James I was king of England

Jacuzzi /dʒəˈkuː.zi/ noun [C] trademark a bath or pool into which warm water flows through small holes, producing a pleasant bubbling effect

jade /dʒeɪd/ noun [U] a PRECIOUS green STONE from which jewellery and small models are made, especially in China and Japan: *jade earrings*

jaded /ˈdʒeɪ.dɪd/ adj not having interest or losing interest because something has been experienced too many times: *Flying is exciting the first time you do it, but you soon become jaded.* ◦ *Perhaps some caviar can tempt your jaded* ***palate****.*

jag /dʒæg/ noun [C] US informal a short period when

J

someone behaves in a particular way and finds it difficult to stop: *a crying/sneezing/coughing jag*

jagged /ˈdʒæɡ.ɪd/ **adj** rough and with sharp points: *a jagged cut/tear* ◦ *jagged rocks* ◦ *a jagged line/edge* • **jaggedly** /-li/ **adv**

jaguar /ˈdʒæɡ.ju.əʳ/ US /-juː.ɑːr/ **noun** [C] a large wild animal of the cat family which lives in Central and South America

jail /dʒeɪl/ **noun; verb**

▸**noun** [C or U] (UK old-fashioned **gaol**) B1 a place where criminals are kept to punish them for their crimes, or where people accused of crimes are kept while waiting for their trials: *the country's overcrowded jails* ◦ *a 13-year jail* ***sentence/term*** ◦ *The financier was* ***released from*** *jail last week.* ◦ *They spent ten years* ***in*** *jail* ***for*** *fraud.*

▸**verb** [T often passive] (UK old-fashioned **gaol**) to put someone in a jail: *He was jailed* ***for*** *three years.*

jailbird informal (UK old-fashioned **gaolbird**) /ˈdʒeɪl.bɜːd/ US /-bɝːd/ **noun** [C] a person who has been in prison

jailbreak (UK old-fashioned **gaolbreak**) /ˈdʒeɪl.breɪk/ **noun** [C] an escape from prison: *Three prisoners were involved in a dawn jailbreak today.*

jailer (UK old-fashioned **gaoler**) /ˈdʒeɪ.ləʳ/ US /-lɚ/ **noun** [C] a prison guard

jalapeño /ˌhæl.əˈpeɪ.njəʊ/ US /ˌhɑː.ləˈpeɪ.njoʊ/ **noun** [C] (also **jalapeño ˈpepper**) a medium-sized CHILLI, usually green, with a hot taste

jalopy /dʒəˈlɒp.i/ US /-ˈlɑː.pi/ **noun** [C] informal humorous an old car: *I've sold my old jalopy to my neighbour's son.*

jam /dʒæm/ **noun; verb**

▸**noun** **FOOD** ▷ **1** A2 [C or U] (US also **jelly**) a sweet, soft food made by cooking fruit with sugar to preserve it. It is eaten on bread or cakes: *strawberry/raspberry jam* ◦ *jam sandwiches* **ON A ROAD** ▷ **2** B2 [C] **traffic jam**: *We were stuck in a jam for two hours.* **BLOCK** ▷ **3** C1 [C] something that is stuck in a machine, or that prevents the parts of a machine from moving: *She fed the documents into the machine making sure that there were no paper jams.* **DIFFICULT SITUATION** ▷ **4** [S] informal a difficult situation: *I'm in a bit of a jam – could you lend me some money till next week?* ◦ *How are we going to get ourselves out of this jam?* **NO SPACE** ▷ **5** [S] a situation in which a lot of people are in a small space: *It's a real jam inside – it took me ten minutes to get to the bar.*

IDIOMS **jam tomorrow** UK something good that is promised but never happens: *As children we were always being promised jam tomorrow, if only we would be patient.* • **what more do you want – jam on it?** UK informal used to say that someone should be grateful for what they have or have been offered, and not demand something better: *They've given him a holiday in Italy. What more does he want – jam on it?*

▸**verb** (-mm-) **STICK** ▷ **1** C1 [I or T] to be, or make something, unable to move: *The door jammed behind me and I couldn't get out* ◦ [+ obj + adj] *He jammed the window open with a piece of wood.* **2** [T] to stop radio signals from reaching the people who want to receive them: *Foreign radio broadcasts were regularly jammed.* **MUSIC** ▷ **3** [I] to play JAZZ or ROCK MUSIC with other people informally without planning it or practising together **PUSH** ▷ **4** [T + adv/prep] to push something forcefully or with difficulty into something else: *He jammed the boxes* ***into*** *the back of the car.* **FILL** ▷ **5** C1 [T + adv/prep] to fill a place completely: *The centre of town was jammed* ***with*** *cars moving at a very slow pace.* ◦ *The motorway was jammed* ***solid*** (= the traffic could not move) *all morning.*

IDIOM **jam on the brakes** to use the BRAKES of a road vehicle suddenly and forcefully: *A motorbike appeared from nowhere and I had to jam on the brakes.*

jamb /dʒæm/ **noun** [C] the vertical part of a door or window frame: *She leaned against the door jamb.*

jamboree /ˌdʒæm.bəˈriː/ **noun** [C] a large organized event which many people go to, or a busy, noisy occasion or period: *The beer festival was a huge open-air jamboree with music, stalls and everyone enjoying themselves.*

jammed /dʒæmd/ **adj** **STUCK** ▷ **1** unable to move: *This drawer is jammed.* **FULL** ▷ **2** full of people: *Because the train was delayed, all the coaches were completely jammed.*

jammy /ˈdʒæm.i/ **adj** **LUCKY** ▷ **1** informal unfairly lucky: *He wasn't even trying to score – the ball just bounced off the jammy* ***beggar's/bastard's*** *head into the goal.* **EASY** ▷ **2** informal very easy: *It was a jammy assignment – more of a holiday really.* **FOOD** ▷ **3** containing or consisting of jam: *She left jammy fingermarks on the tablecloth.*

jam-ˈpacked **adj** full of people or things that are pushed closely together: *The streets were jam-packed* ***with*** *tourists.*

ˌjam ˈsandwich **noun** [C] two pieces of bread with jam between them, or a type of cake made in two parts with jam spread between

ˈjam ˌsession **noun** [C] an informal performance of JAZZ or ROCK MUSIC which the musicians have not planned or practised

Jane Doe /ˌdʒeɪnˈdəʊ/ US /-ˈdoʊ/ **noun** US a female JOHN DOE

jangle /ˈdʒæŋ.ɡl/ **verb** [I or T] to make a noise like metal hitting metal: *He jangled his keys in his pocket.*

IDIOM **jangle sb's nerves** to make someone feel annoyed or nervous: *The constant whine of the machinery jangled his nerves.*

jangling /ˈdʒæŋ.ɡlɪŋ/ **noun** [U] the noise of metal hitting metal: *the jangling of sleigh bells* ◦ *a loud jangling noise*

janitor /ˈdʒæn.ɪ.təʳ/ US /-t̬ɚ/ **noun** [C] C2 US or Scottish English for **caretaker**

January /ˈdʒæn.ju.ri/ US /-juː.er.i/ **noun** [C or U] (written abbreviation **Jan.**) A1 the first month of the year, after December and before February: *Her father died* ***in*** *January.* ◦ *His birthday is 25 January.* ◦ *We're going skiing* ***next*** *January.*

jape /dʒeɪp/ **noun** [C] old-fashioned or humorous an activity done to make someone laugh or to trick someone: *They put a frog in her boots for a jape.*

jar /dʒɑːʳ/ US /dʒɑːr/ **noun; verb**

▸**noun** [C] **CONTAINER** ▷ **1** B1 a glass or clay container with a wide opening at the top and sometimes a fitted lid, usually used for storing food: *a jar of coffee/pickled onions* ◦ *a jam jar* **2** UK informal a drink of beer: *We often* ***have*** *a jar or two at the pub after work.* **SHAKE** ▷ **3** a sudden forceful or unpleasant shake or movement: *With every jar of the carriage, the children shrieked with excitement.*

▸**verb** (-rr-) **SHAKE** ▷ **1** [I or T] to shake or move someone or something unpleasantly or violently: *The sudden movement jarred his injured ribs.* **NOT PLEASANT** ▷ **2** [I or T] If a sight, sound, or experience jars, it is so different or unexpected that it has a strong and unpleasant effect on something or someone: *The harsh colours jarred the eye.* ◦ *A screech of brakes jarred the silence.* **NOT RIGHT** ▷ **3** [I] to disagree or seem wrong or unsuitable: *This comment jars* ***with*** *the opinions we have heard expressed elsewhere.*

PHRASAL VERB **jar on sb** If something, especially a noise, jars on you, it annoys you: *His rather superior manner jars on me.* ◦ *That squeaky voice is beginning to jar on me.*

jarful /ˈdʒɑː.fʊl/ (US) /ˈdʒɑːr-/ **noun** [C] the amount that a jar can hold: *The recipe uses a whole jarful/two jarfuls of jam.*

jargon /ˈdʒɑː.gən/ (US) /ˈdʒɑːr-/ **noun** [U] usually disapproving (C1) special words and phrases that are used by particular groups of people, especially in their work: *military/legal/computer jargon* → Compare **terminology**

jarring /ˈdʒɑː.rɪŋ/ (US) /ˈdʒɑːr.ɪŋ/ **adj** **NOT PLEASANT** ▷ **1** a jarring sight, sound, or experience is so different or unexpected that it has a strong and unpleasant effect on something or someone: *a jarring cry/chord* ◦ *jarring colours* **NOT RIGHT** ▷ **2** wrong or unsuitable: *a jarring contrast* **SHAKE** ▷ **3** shaking or moving violently: *a jarring tackle/collision*

jasmine /ˈdʒæz.mɪn/ **noun** [C or U] a climbing plant. One type has white sweet-smelling flowers in summer and another type has yellow flowers in winter.

jaundice /ˈdʒɔːn.dɪs/ (US) /ˈdʒɑːn-/ **noun** [U] a serious disease in which substances not usually in the blood cause your skin and the white part of your eyes to turn yellow

jaundiced /ˈdʒɔːn.dɪst/ (US) /ˈdʒɑːn-/ **adj** formal **1** judging everything as bad because bad things have happened to you in the past: *He seems to* ***have/take*** *a very jaundiced* ***view*** *of life.* ◦ *I'm afraid I look on all travel companies' claims with a rather jaundiced* ***eye****, having been disappointed by them so often in the past.* **2** looking slightly yellow in colour because of having jaundice: *He was jaundiced from liver disease.*

jaunt /dʒɔːnt/ (US) /dʒɑːnt/ **noun; verb**

▸**noun** [C] a short journey for pleasure, sometimes including a stay: *a Sunday jaunt into the hills*

▸**verb** [I usually + adv/prep] to go on a jaunt: disapproving *He's always jaunting* ***off*** *around the world on business trips, leaving his wife to cope with the babies by herself.*

jaunty /ˈdʒɔːn.ti/ (US) /ˈdʒɑːn.t̬i/ **adj** showing that you are happy and confident: *a jaunty grin/step.* ◦ *When he came back his hat was at a jaunty angle and he was smiling.* • **jauntily** /-tɪ.li/ (US) /-t̬ɪ.li/ **adv** • **jauntiness** /-nəs/ **noun** [U]

Java /ˈdʒɑː.və/ **noun** [U] trademark a computer programming language that is often used on the internet

javelin /ˈdʒæv.lɪn/ **noun** [C] **1** a long stick with a pointed end that is thrown in sports competitions **2 the javelin** a competition in which javelins are thrown: *She was first in the javelin.*

javelin

jaw /dʒɔː/ (US) /dʒɑː/ **noun; verb**

▸**noun** **BODY PART** ▷ **1** (B2) [C] the lower part of your face which moves when you open your mouth: *a broken jaw* ◦ *a punch* ***on*** *(US* ***in****) the jaw* ◦ *He has a strong/square jaw.* **2** [C] either of the two bones in your mouth which hold your teeth: *upper/lower jaw* **3 jaws** [plural] **a** the mouth of a person or animal, especially a large and frightening animal: *The lion opened its jaws and roared.* **b** something which opens and closes like the upper and lower parts of a mouth: *His foot was caught in the jaws of the trap.* **DANGER** ▷ **4 jaws** [plural] something dangerous: *The rescuers snatched the children from the jaws* ***of death.*** **TALK** ▷ **5** [S] informal a talk: *I met Jane and we had a good jaw over lunch.*

IDIOM **sb's jaw drops (open)** If someone's jaw drops (open), they look very surprised: *My jaw dropped open when she told me how old she was.*

▸**verb** [I] informal to talk for a long time: *He was jawing* ***away to*** *his girlfriend for hours on the phone.*

jawbone /ˈdʒɔː.bəʊn/ (US) /ˈdʒɑː.boʊn/ **noun; verb**

▸**noun** [C] the bone that forms the shape of the lower part of the face

▸**verb** [I or T] US informal to talk to someone, especially to try to persuade them to do something: *Congresswoman Weintrob jawboned local officials* ***about*** *their responsibilities toward the immigrant community.*

jawbreaker /ˈdʒɔːˌbreɪ.kəʳ/ (US) /ˈdʒɑːˌbreɪ.kɚ/ **noun** [C] **SWEET** ▷ **1** US a large, hard, round sweet **LANGUAGE** ▷ **2** UK informal a **tongue-twister** **3** US and Australian English informal a word that is difficult to pronounce

ˈjaw-ˌdropping **adj** very surprising or shocking: *The jaw-dropping scale of the project has not defeated those involved.*

Jaws of ˈLife **noun** [plural] US trademark a piece of equipment that can cut through metal and is used to get people out of their vehicles after an accident

jay /dʒeɪ/ **noun** [C] a noisy, brightly coloured bird

jaywalk /ˈdʒeɪ.wɔːk/ (US) /-wɑːk/ **verb** [I] mainly US to walk across a road at a place where it is not allowed or without taking care to avoid the traffic • **jaywalker** /-wɔː.kəʳ/ (US) /-wɑː.kɚ/ **noun** [C]

jazz /dʒæz/ **noun; verb**

▸**noun** [U] (A2) a type of modern music developed by black people in the US, with a rhythm in which the strong notes often come before the beat. Jazz is usually IMPROVISED (= invented as it is played).

IDIOM **and all that jazz** informal used when speaking to mean 'and other similar things': *They sell televisions and radios and all that jazz.*

▸**verb**

PHRASAL VERB **jazz sth up** informal to make something more attractive or interesting: *Jazz the dress up* ***with*** *some bright accessories.* ◦ *He jazzed up the food* ***with*** *a spicy sauce.*

jazzy /ˈdʒæz.i/ **adj** **1** informal very bright and colourful: *a jazzy tie/dress* **2** in the style of jazz music

JCB /ˌdʒeɪ.siːˈbiː/ **noun** [C] UK trademark a machine used for digging and moving earth

ˈJ-cloth (also **ˈJeye cloth**) **noun** [C] UK trademark a cloth used for cleaning the home

jealous /ˈdʒel.əs/ **adj** **UNHAPPY** ▷ **1** (B1) upset and angry because someone that you love seems interested in another person: *a jealous husband/wife* ◦ *Anna says she* ***feels*** *jealous every time another woman looks at her boyfriend.* **2** (B2) unhappy and angry because someone has something that you want: *He had always been very jealous* ***of*** *his brother's good looks.* → Compare **envious** **CAREFUL** ▷ **3** extremely careful in protecting someone or something: *She is very jealous* ***of*** *her independence, and doesn't want to get married.* ◦ *Her parents used to keep a jealous* ***watch*** *over her when she was young.* • **jealously** /-li/ **adv** (B2) *The exact location of the hotel where the royal couple is staying is a jealously (= carefully)* ***guarded*** *secret.* ◦ *She eyed Gwen's engagement ring jealously.*

J

Other ways of saying jealous

Envious is a common alternative to 'jealous':
*She was very **envious** of her brother's success.*
You could also use the phrase be **green with envy**:
*You'll be **green with envy** when you meet her new boyfriend.*
Someone who is **possessive** is jealous because that person does not want to share someone's love and attention with anyone else:
*a **possessive** boyfriend*

jealousy /ˈdʒel.ə.si/ noun [C or U] C1 a feeling of unhappiness and anger because someone has something or someone that you want: *He broke his brother's new bike **in a fit of** jealousy.* ◦ *She was **consumed by/ eaten up with** jealousy (= she was very jealous) when she heard that he had been given a promotion.* ◦ *The team has performed very badly this season due to **petty** jealousies (= feelings of jealousy about unimportant things) among the players.* → Compare **envy**

jeans /dʒiːnz/ noun [plural] A1 trousers made of DENIM (= strong blue cotton cloth) that are worn informally: *jeans and a T-shirt* ◦ *I never wear jeans for work.*

Jeep /dʒiːp/ noun [C] trademark a small strong vehicle used for travelling over rough ground, especially by the army

jeepers (creepers) /ˌdʒiː.pəzˈkriː.pəz/ US /-pɚˈkriː.pɚz/ exclamation US old-fashioned an expression of surprise: *Jeepers, just look at the time! I'm going to be late!*

jeer /dʒɪəʳ/ US /dʒɪr/ verb [I or T] to laugh or shout insults at someone to show you have no respect for them: *The people at the back of the hall jeered **(at)** the speaker.* • **jeer** noun [C] *The news that the performance was being cancelled was greeted by **boos and** jeers from the audience.* • **jeering** /ˈdʒɪə.rɪŋ/ US /ˈdʒɪr.ɪŋ/ noun [U] *loud jeering from the opposition parties*

jeez /dʒiːz/ exclamation US slang an expression of surprise or strong emotion: *Jeez, don't yell at me – I'm just telling you what she said!*

jeggings /ˈdʒeg.ɪŋz/ noun [plural] informal very tight trousers made from a material that stretches easily, designed to look like JEANS: *a pair of jeggings* → Compare **leggings**

Jehovah /dʒɪˈhəʊ.və/ US /-ˈhoʊ-/ noun the name of God used in the OLD TESTAMENT of the Bible

Jeˌhovah's ˈWitness noun [C] a member of a religious organization which believes that the world will end soon and that only its members will be saved

jejune /dʒɪˈdʒuːn/ adj formal disapproving very simple or CHILDISH: *He made jejune generalizations about how all students were lazy and never did any work.*

Jekyll and Hyde /ˌdʒek.l̩.ᵊndˈhaɪd/ noun [S] disapproving a person with two very different sides to their personality, one good and the other evil: *The professor was a real Jekyll and Hyde – sometimes kind and charming, and at other times rude and obnoxious.*

jell /dʒel/ verb [I] to **gel**

jellied /ˈdʒel.id/ adj If meat or fish is jellied, it is cooked and then served in its own juices which become firm when cold: *jellied beef/eels*

ˈJell-O noun [U] US trademark **jelly**

jelly /ˈdʒel.i/ noun **1** [C or U] UK (US trademark **Jell-O**) a soft, sweet, usually brightly coloured food made from sugar, GELATINE, and fruit flavours, that shakes slightly when it is moved: *I've made a strawberry jelly for the children's tea.* ◦ *jelly and ice cream* **2** A2 US (UK **jam**) a sweet soft food made by cooking fruit with sugar to preserve it. It is eaten on bread or cakes: *a peanut butter and jelly sandwich* **3** [C or U] jam that is transparent and does not contain pieces of fruit: *apple jelly* **4** [U] any soft, slightly wet substance that shakes slightly when it is moved: *Frogs' eggs are covered in a sort of transparent jelly.*

IDIOM **turn to jelly** to suddenly feel weak because you are frightened, nervous, or ill: *As she knocked on the director's door, **her legs** turned to jelly.*

ˈjelly ˌbaby noun [C] UK a small soft sweet with a fruit flavour in the shape of a baby

ˈjelly ˌbean noun [C] a small sweet in the shape of a bean that is soft in the middle and covered with hard sugar

jellyfish

jellyfish /ˈdʒel.i.fɪʃ/ noun [C] (plural **jellyfish**) a sea creature with a soft, oval, almost transparent body

ˈjelly ˌroll noun [C] US for **Swiss roll**

jemmy /ˈdʒem.i/ noun; verb

▸noun [C] UK (US **jimmy**) a short, strong metal bar with a curved end, often used by thieves to force open windows or doors

▸verb [T] UK (US **jimmy**) to force a window or lock open with a jemmy

je ne sais quoi /ˌʒə.nə.seɪˈkwɑː/ noun [S] a pleasing quality which cannot be exactly named or described: *Although he's not conventionally attractive, he has **a certain** je ne sais quoi which makes him popular with the ladies.*

jeopardize (UK usually **jeopardise**) /ˈdʒep.ə.daɪz/ US /-ɚ-/ verb [T] to put something such as a plan or system in danger of being harmed or damaged: *She knew that by failing her exams she could jeopardize her whole future.*

jeopardy /ˈdʒep.ə.di/ US /-ɚ-/ noun **in jeopardy** in danger of being damaged or destroyed: *The lives of thousands of birds are in jeopardy as a result of the oil spillage.*

jerk /dʒɜːk/ US /dʒɝːk/ verb; noun

▸verb [I or T, usually + adv/prep] **1** to make a short sudden movement, or to cause someone or something to do this: *The car made a strange noise and then jerked **to a halt**.* ◦ *'What's wrong?' she asked, jerking her head up.* **2** to (force or cause someone or something to) suddenly behave differently, usually by understanding something or becoming active again: *The shock of losing his job jerked him **out of** his settled lifestyle.*

PHRASAL VERB **jerk off** offensive (of a man) to **masturbate**

▸noun [C] **MOVE** ▷ **1** a quick sudden movement: *She pulled the bush out of the ground **with** a sharp jerk.* ◦ *The alarm went off and he woke up **with** a jerk.* **PERSON** ▷ **2** (US also **ˈjerk-off**) a stupid person, usually a man: *You stupid jerk! You've just spilled beer all down my new shirt!*

jerkin /ˈdʒɜː.kɪn/ US /ˈdʒɝː-/ noun [C] a jacket with no sleeves or collar

jerkwater /ˈdʒɜːkˌwɔː.təʳ/ US /ˈdʒɝːkˌwɑː.t̬ɚ/ adj [before noun] US informal describes a place that is small, not important and a long way from other places: *I grew up in a jerkwater **town** in the middle of nowhere.* → Compare **backwater**

jerky /ˈdʒɜː.ki/ Ⓤⓢ /ˈdʒɝː-/ **noun; adj**
▸**noun** [U] US meat that has been cut into long thin strips and dried in the sun: *beef jerky*
▸**adj** quick and sudden: *The disease causes sudden jerky* ***movements*** *of the hands and legs.* • **jerkily** /-kɪ.li/ **adv** • **jerkiness** /-nəs/ **noun** [U]

jeroboam /ˌdʒer.əˈbəʊ.əm/ Ⓤⓢ /-ˈboʊ-/ **noun** [C] a very large wine bottle which contains four or six times the usual amount: *a jeroboam of champagne*

jerry-built /ˈdʒer.i.bɪlt/ **adj** informal disapproving built quickly and badly using cheap materials

jerrycan /ˈdʒer.iˌkæn/ **noun** [C] a large metal container with flat sides used for storing or carrying liquids such as fuel or water

jersey /ˈdʒɜː.zi/ Ⓤⓢ /ˈdʒɝː-/ **noun** **CLOTHING** ▷ **1** [C] a piece of clothing, made from wool or cotton and worn on the upper part of the body, that has sleeves and does not open at the front **2** [C] a shirt that is worn by a member of a sports team **CLOTH** ▷ **3** [U] soft thin cloth, usually made from wool, cotton, or SILK, that is used for making clothes: *100 percent cotton jersey*

Jersey /ˈdʒɜː.zi/ Ⓤⓢ /ˈdʒɝː-/ **noun** [C] a type of pale brown cow that produces milk that is rich in cream

Jerusalem artichoke /dʒəˌruː.sə.ləmˈɑː.tɪ.tʃəʊk/ Ⓤⓢ /-ˈɑːr.t̬ɪ.tʃoʊk/ **noun** [C] a root vegetable that looks like a potato

jest /dʒest/ **noun; verb**
▸**noun** formal **1** [C] something that is said or done in order to be funny: *His proposal was no jest – he was completely sincere.* **2 in jest** intended as a joke and not said seriously: *I only said it in jest – you're obviously not fat.*

IDIOM **many a true word is spoken in jest** saying said about humorous remarks that contain serious or true statements

▸**verb** [I] to say something intended to be funny: *Would I jest* ***about*** *something so important?*

jester /ˈdʒes.tər/ Ⓤⓢ /-tɚ/ **noun** [C] a man in the past whose job was to tell jokes and make people laugh: *a court jester*

Jesuit /ˈdʒez.ju.ɪt/ **noun** [C] a Roman Catholic priest who is a member of the Society of Jesus, a religious group begun in 1540: *a Jesuit* ***priest***

Jesus (Christ) /ˌdʒiː.zəsˈkraɪst/ **noun; exclamation**
▸**noun** (also **Christ**) (the title given to) the man who his religious FOLLOWERS believe is the son of God and on whose teachings and life Christianity is based
▸**exclamation** (also **Christ**) an expression of surprise, shock, or anger. Some people might consider this offensive: *Jesus, just look what a mess they've made!*

jet /dʒet/ **noun; verb**
▸**noun** **AIRCRAFT** ▷ **1** Ⓑ① [C] an aircraft with a jet engine that is able to fly very fast: *a jet plane* ◦ *a private jet* ◦ *We flew to New York* ***by*** *jet.* → See also **jetliner** **STREAM** ▷ **2** [C] a thin stream of something, such as water or gas, that is forced out of a small hole: *She turned on the hose and a jet* ***of*** *water sprayed across the garden.* **3** [C] a small hole in a piece of equipment through which gas or another fuel is forced before it is burned: *I think the* ***gas*** *jet must be blocked, because the oven won't light.* **STONE** ▷ **4** [U] a hard, black stone that shines when it is rubbed and is used to make jewellery and other decorative objects
▸**verb** [I + adv/prep] (**-tt-**) informal to travel somewhere by plane: *I'm jetting* ***off*** *to New Zealand next week.*

ˌjet ˈblack **noun** [U] a completely black colour • **jet-ˈblack adj**

ˈjet ˌengine **noun** [C] a very powerful engine. When fuel is burned inside the engine, hot air and gases are produced and then pushed out of the back of the engine at high speed and this forces the engine forward.

jetfoil /ˈdʒet.fɔɪl/ **noun** [C] a HYDROFOIL that is driven by water being sucked in from the sea and forced out at the back at great pressure

ˈjet ˌlag **noun** [U] the feeling of tiredness and confusion which people experience after making a long journey in an aircraft to a place where the time is different from the place they left: *Every time I fly to the States, I* ***get*** *really bad jet lag.* • **ˈjet-lagged adj**

jetliner /ˈdʒetˌlaɪ.nər/ Ⓤⓢ /-nɚ/ **noun** [C] a large JET aircraft that can carry a lot of passengers

ˌjet proˈpulsion **noun** [U] powerful forward movement produced by forcing gases backwards, as in a JET ENGINE

jetsam /ˈdʒet.səm/ **noun** [U] things that are thrown away from ships and float onto the land from the sea → See also **flotsam**

ˈjet-set **verb** [I] informal to travel around the world enjoying yourself: *She spends the summer jet-setting around the fashionable European resorts.* • **ˈjet-ˌsetting adj** [before noun] *a jet-setting millionaire*

the ˈjet ˌset **noun** [S, + sing/pl verb] informal rich, fashionable people who travel around the world enjoying themselves

ˈjet-ˌsetter **noun** [C] informal a member of the jet set

ˈjet ˌski **noun** [C] trademark a small vehicle for one or two people to ride on water that is moved forward by a fast stream of water being pushed out behind it • **ˈjet-ski verb** [I] • **ˈjet-ˌskiing noun** [U]

ˈjet ˌstream **noun** [C usually singular] a narrow current of strong winds high above the earth that move from west to east

jettison /ˈdʒet.ɪ.sən/ Ⓤⓢ /ˈdʒet̬-/ **verb** [T] **1** to get rid of something or someone that is not wanted or needed: *The station has jettisoned educational broadcasts.* **2** to decide not to use an idea or plan: *We've had to jettison our holiday plans because of David's accident.* **3** to throw goods, fuel, or equipment from a ship or aircraft to make it lighter: *The captain was forced to jettison the cargo and make an emergency landing.*

jetty /ˈdʒet.i/ Ⓤⓢ /ˈdʒet̬-/ **noun** [C] a wooden or stone structure built in the water at the edge of a sea or lake and used by people getting on and off boats

Jetway /ˈdʒet.weɪ/ **noun** [C] trademark a raised closed passage through which passengers walk from an airport building to an aircraft

Jew /dʒuː/ **noun** [C] a member of a people whose traditional religion is Judaism: *Although my family is Jewish, we're not* ***practising*** *Jews (= actively involved in the religion).* • **Jewish** /ˈdʒuː.ɪʃ/ **adj** *New York has one of the largest Jewish communities in the world.* • **Jewishness** /ˈdʒuː.ɪʃ.nəs/ **noun** [U]

jewel /ˈdʒuː.əl/ **noun** [C] **VALUABLE STONE** ▷ **1** Ⓑ② a PRECIOUS STONE that is used to decorate valuable objects: *She was wearing a large gold necklace set with jewels.* **2** specialized a small PRECIOUS stone or a piece of specially cut glass, used in the machinery of a watch **3 jewels** [plural] **jewellery** **BEAUTIFUL/IMPORTANT THING** ▷ **4** something that is very beautiful or valuable: *Many visitors consider the Sistine Chapel to be* ***the*** *jewel* ***of*** *the Vatican.* **PERSON** ▷ **5** old-fashioned a very kind or helpful person

IDIOM **the jewel in the crown** the best or most valuable part of something

ˈjewel ˌcase noun [C] a transparent plastic case in which a COMPACT DISC is kept

jewelled (US usually **jeweled**) /ˈdʒuː.əld/ **adj** decorated with jewels

jeweller (US usually **jeweler**) /ˈdʒuː.ə.ləʳ/ (US) /-lɚ/ **noun** [C] a person who sells and sometimes repairs jewellery and watches

jewellery UK (US **jewelry**) /ˈdʒuː.əl.ri/ **noun** [U] A2 decorative objects worn on your clothes or body that are usually made from valuable metals, such as gold and silver, and PRECIOUS STONES: *a jewellery box* ◦ *a piece of gold/silver jewellery*

ˈjewellery ˌbox UK (US **ˈjewelry ˌbox**) **noun** [C] a special box for keeping jewellery, often decorated and containing several separate parts

jewfish /ˈdʒuː.fɪʃ/ **noun** [C or U] (plural **jewfish**) a large fish which lives in warm or tropical seas

Jewry /ˈdʒʊə.ri/ (US) /ˈdʒuː-/ **noun** [U] formal all the Jews

Jew's ˈharp noun [C] a small musical instrument that is held between the teeth and played by hitting a metal strip with the finger

Jeye cloth noun [C] UK trademark a **J-cloth**

Jezebel /ˈdʒez.ə.bel/ **noun** [C] old-fashioned disapproving an IMMORAL woman who deceives people in order to get what she wants

J

jib /dʒɪb/ **noun; verb**

▸**noun** [C] specialized **BOAT** ▷ **1** a small sail in the shape of a triangle, positioned in front of the main sail on a boat **LIFTING TOOL** ▷ **2** a long horizontal frame that sticks out from a CRANE and from which the HOOK hangs

▸**verb** (**-bb-**)

PHRASAL VERB **jib at sth** old-fashioned **PERSON** ▷ **1** to be unwilling to do or continue with something: [+ -ing verb] *Although the tax is unpopular, the government has jibbed at abolish**ing** it completely.* **HORSE** ▷ **2** If a horse jibs at something, it stops suddenly in front of it and refuses to move forward.

jibe /dʒaɪb/ **noun; verb**

▸**noun** [C] (US usually **gibe**) an insulting remark that is intended to make someone look stupid: *Unlike many other politicians, he refuses to indulge in **cheap** jibes at other people's expense.*

▸**verb** [I] (US usually **gibe**) to make insulting remarks that are intended to make someone look stupid: *She jibed constantly **at** the way he ran his business.*

PHRASAL VERB **jibe with sth** (also **jive with sth**) US informal If one statement or opinion jibes with another, it is similar to it and matches it.

jiffy /ˈdʒɪf.i/ **noun** [S] informal a very short time: *I'll be with you **in a** jiffy.* ◦ *I've just got to fetch some books from upstairs – I **won't be a** jiffy* (= *I'll be very quick*).

ˈJiffy ˌbag noun [C] trademark a thick envelope for protecting objects that are easily damaged when they are sent through the post

jig /dʒɪg/ **noun; verb**

▸**noun** [C] **DANCE** ▷ **1** an energetic traditional dance of Great Britain and Ireland, or the music that is played for such a dance **TOOL** ▷ **2** specialized a piece of equipment for holding a tool or piece of wood, etc. firmly in position while you work with it

▸**verb** [I or T, usually + adv/prep] (**-gg-**) to move quickly up and down or from side to side, or to make someone or something do this: *Stop jigging **about**, Billy, and just stand still for a moment!*

jigger /ˈdʒɪg.əʳ/ (US) /-ɚ/ **noun; verb**

▸**noun** [C] US a small, round metal container used for measuring strong alcoholic drinks, or the amount of alcohol which this container holds

▸**verb** [T] US to change something, especially unfairly or illegally: *The ruling party jiggered the election results to stay in power.*

jiggery-pokery /ˌdʒɪg.əʳ.iˈpəʊ.kəʳ.i/ (US) /-ɚ.iˈpoʊ.kɚ-/ **noun** [U] old-fashioned informal secret or dishonest behaviour

jiggle /ˈdʒɪg.l̩/ **verb** [I or T] to move from side to side or up and down with quick short movements, or to make something do this: *If the door won't open, try jiggling the key in the lock.*

jigsaw /ˈdʒɪg.sɔː/ (US) /-sɑː/ **noun PICTURE GAME** ▷ **1** [C] (also **jigsaw puzzle**) a picture stuck onto wood or cardboard and cut into pieces of different shapes that must be joined together correctly to form the picture again: *We spent all evening **doing** a 1,000-piece jigsaw.* **MYSTERY** ▷ **2** [S] (also **jigsaw puzzle**) a complicated or mysterious problem that can only be solved or explained by connecting several pieces of information: *The police are trying to **piece together** the jigsaw of how the dead man spent his last hours.* **TOOL** ▷ **3** [C] a tool with an electric motor and a thin metal blade that is used for cutting curves in flat materials, such as wood or metal

jigsaw

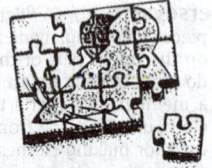

jihad /dʒɪˈhæd/ **noun** [C or U] a HOLY WAR fought by Muslims against people who are a threat to Islam

jihadi /dʒɪˈhæd.i/ **noun** [C] (also **jihadist** /-ɪst/) a Muslim who is fighting for Islam, especially a RADICAL (= someone with extreme views) who believes in using violence to achieve religious and political aims

jillaroo /ˌdʒɪl.əˈruː/ **noun** [C] (plural **jillaroos**) Australian English a woman who is learning to work on a sheep or CATTLE farm → Compare **jackaroo**

jilt /dʒɪlt/ **verb** [T] to finish a romantic relationship with someone suddenly and unkindly: *He jilted her **for** his best friend's sister.*

Jim Crow /ˌdʒɪmˈkrəʊ/ (US) /-ˈkroʊ/ **noun** [U] US old-fashioned disapproving the laws and policies once used in the US to treat black people unfairly and to keep them apart from white people

jim-dandy /ˌdʒɪmˈdæn.di/ **noun** [C] (plural **jim-dandies**) US old-fashioned informal something that is very pleasing or of excellent quality: *That new car you bought is a real jim-dandy.* • **jim-dandy adj** [before noun]

jimjams /ˈdʒɪm.dʒæmz/ **noun** [plural] UK child's word for **pyjamas** (= trousers and a shirt worn in bed)

jimmy /ˈdʒɪ.mi/ **noun, verb** US for **jemmy**

jingle /ˈdʒɪŋ.gl̩/ **verb; noun**

▸**verb** [I or T] to make a repeated gentle ringing sound, or to make things do this: *She waited for him by the car, jingling the keys in her hand.* ◦ *The coins jingled in her pocket as she walked along.*

▸**noun TUNE** ▷ **1** [C] a short simple tune, often with words, that is easy to remember and is used to advertise a product on the radio or television **RING** ▷ **2** [S] a repeated gentle ringing sound: *the jingle of sleigh bells*

jingoism /ˈdʒɪŋ.gəʊ.ɪ.zəm/ (US) /-goʊ-/ **noun** [U] disapproving the extreme belief that your own country is always best, often shown in enthusiastic support for a war against another country: *Patriotism can turn into jingoism and intolerance very quickly.*

jingoist /ˈdʒɪŋ.ɡəʊ.ɪst/ (US) /-ɡoʊ-/ **noun** [C] disapproving • **jingoistic** /ˌdʒɪŋ.ɡəʊˈɪs.tɪk/ (US) /-ɡoʊ-/ **adj**

jinx /dʒɪŋks/ **noun** [S] bad luck, or a person or thing that is believed to bring bad luck: *There's **a** jinx **on** this computer – it's gone wrong three times this morning!* • **jinxed** /dʒɪŋkst/ **adj** *I must be jinxed – whenever I wash a wine glass, it breaks.*

JIT /ˌdʒeɪ.aɪˈtiː/ **adj** [before noun] abbreviation for **just-in-time**

jitney /ˈdʒɪt.ni/ **noun** [C] US a small bus that follows a regular route

jitters /ˈdʒɪt.əz/ (US) /ˈdʒɪt̬.ɚz/ **noun** [plural] informal a feeling of nervousness which you experience before something important happens: *I always **get the** jitters the morning before an exam.* ◦ figurative *The collapse of the company has caused jitters in the financial markets.*

IDIOM **give sb the jitters** to make someone nervous or frightened: *Come away from that cliff edge! You're giving me the jitters!*

jittery /ˈdʒɪt.ər.i/ (US) /ˈdʒɪt̬.ɚ-/ **adj** informal **1** nervous: *He **felt** all jittery before the interview.* **2** shaking and slightly uncontrolled: *I **get** really jittery if I drink too much coffee.*

jiujitsu /ˌdʒuːˈdʒɪt.suː/ **noun** [U] **jujitsu**

jive /dʒaɪv/ **noun; verb**

▸**noun** DANCE ▷ **1** [S or U] a fast dance that was very popular with young people in the 1940s and 1950s: *My father taught me how to do **the** jive.* TALK ▷ **2** [U] US slang talk that has no meaning or is dishonest: *Don't believe a word he says, it's just **a bunch of** (= a lot of) jive!*

▸**verb** DANCE ▷ **1** [I] to dance a jive TALK ▷ **2** [T] US slang to try to make someone believe something that is untrue: *Quit jiving me and just tell me where you were!*

Jnr /ˈdʒuː.ni.əʳ/ (US) /-ɚ/ **adj** [after noun] UK (mainly US **Jr**) abbreviation for **junior**: used after a man's name to refer to the younger of two men in the same family who have the same name

job /dʒɒb/ (US) /dʒɑːb/ **noun** EMPLOYMENT ▷ **1** (A1) [C] the regular work that a person does to earn money: *a temporary/permanent job* ◦ *When she left college, she **got** a job **as** an editor in a publishing company.* ◦ *It's very difficult trying to bring up two children while **doing** a full-time job.* ◦ *He's never managed to **hold down** (= keep) a **steady** (= permanent) job.* ◦ *She's **applied for** a job **with** an insurance company.* ◦ *Are you going to **give up** your job when you have your baby?* ◦ *After a disastrous first month in office, many people are beginning to wonder if the new president is **up to** (= able to do) the job.* ◦ *Hundreds of workers could **lose** their jobs.* **2 out of a job** (C2) without a job: *How long have you been out of a job?* → Synonym **unemployed**

> **! Common mistake: job or work?**
>
> **Warning:** Choose the right word!
>
> **Job** is a countable noun and refers to a particular piece of work or the regular work that someone does to earn money:
>
> *Sarah is looking for a new job.*
>
> To talk about the activity that someone does in their job, don't say 'job', say **work**:
>
> *We need to improve the efficiency of our work.*

PIECE OF WORK ▷ **3** (A2) [C] a particular piece of work: *The builders are aiming to get the job done by the end of the month.* ◦ *He spent the afternoon **doing** jobs around the house.* RESPONSIBILITY ▷ **4** (B2) [S] something that is your responsibility: [+ to infinitive] *She believed her job as a politician was **to** represent the views of her party and the people who voted for her.* ◦ *I know it's not my job **to** tell you how to run your life, but I do think you've made a mistake.* PROBLEM ▷ **5** [S] informal a problem or an activity that is difficult: [+ -ing verb] *It was a real job gett**ing** the wheel off the bike.* ◦ *We were only given an hour to do the exam, and I **had a** job finish**ing** it.* EXAMPLE ▷ **6** [C] informal an example of a particular type: *It's an original, not one of those imitation jobs.* CRIME ▷ **7** [C] slang a crime in which money or goods are stolen, or an action or activity that is dishonest or unpleasant: *He was put in prison for five years for **doing** a **bank** job.* ◦ US *He really **did** a job **on** her, telling her that he would love her for ever and then moving to Fiji with someone else.* → See also **hatchet job**

> **Word partners for job (EMPLOYMENT)**
>
> a *full-time/part-time/permanent/temporary* job • a *dead-end/good/low-paid/well-paid* job • *have/hold down* a job • *find/get/land* a job • *apply for/look for* a job • *offer* sb a job • *lose/quit* your job • *create/provide* jobs • a job *as* sth

> **Word partners for job (PIECE OF WORK)**
>
> *do* a job • a *boring/difficult/hard/tough* job • the job *of* doing sth

> **Other ways of saying job**
>
> A more formal alternative is the noun **occupation**:
>
> *Please fill in your name, age, and **occupation**.*
>
> The nouns **post** and **position** are often used to talk about a particular job within an organization:
>
> *She's applied for a part-time teaching **position**.*
>
> The noun **career** is sometimes used to describe a job that a person does for a long period in their life:
>
> *She's had a very successful **career** in marketing.*
>
> An **internship** is a job that someone does for a short time in order to learn more about a particular kind of work:
>
> *She's got a year's **internship** before she can get her license to practice medicine.*

IDIOMS **be just the job** informal to be exactly what you want or need: *I've been looking for a new stereo system for my car, and this is just the job.* • **do a good/bad job** (B2) to do something well/badly: *You've done a great job – thank you Sam.* • **do the job** informal (C2) If something does the job, it performs the piece of work you want to be done and achieves the result you want: *Here, this knife should do the job.* • **do/make a good/bad job of sth** (C2) to do something well/badly: *I'm not going to let him repair my bike again because he made a really bad job of **it** last time.* ◦ *The dry cleaner's did a good job of remov**ing** that oil stain from my shirt.* • **it's more than my job's worth** something that you say in order to tell someone that you cannot do what they want you to do because you would lose your job • **job done** informal something you say when someone has achieved something, especially when it seems easier or quicker than you expected: *I just changed the fuse in the plug and the lamp worked, job done.* • **jobs for the boys** UK informal disapproving work that someone in an important position gives to their friends or relations • **just the man/woman for the job** a man/woman who has all the skills for a particular piece of work: *We need someone who has experience in marketing and teaching, and I think Alex is just the woman for*

J

the job. • **on-the-job** happening while you are working: *No formal qualifications are required for the work – you'll get on-the-job* ***training***.

ˈjob ˌaction noun [C usually singular] US a temporary show of DISSATISFACTION by a group of workers, often by doing their work more slowly, in order to make managers pay attention to their demands

jobbing /ˈdʒɒb.ɪŋ/ (US) /ˈdʒɑː.bɪŋ/ **adj** **a jobbing actor, builder, gardener, etc.** someone who does not work regularly for one person or organization but does small pieces of work for different people

ˈjob ˌcentre noun [C] UK a government office where unemployed people can go for advice and information about jobs that are available

ˈjob creˌation noun [U] the process of providing new jobs, especially for people who are unemployed: *the government's job creation strategy*

ˈjob desˌcription noun [C] a list of the responsibilities which you have and the duties which you are expected to perform in your work

ˈjob evaluˌation noun [C] UK the process of comparing a job with other jobs in an organization and deciding how much the person who is doing the job should be paid

J

jobless adj; noun

▸adj /ˈdʒɒb.ləs/ (US) /ˈdʒɑːb-/ unemployed: *He's been jobless for the past six months.* • **joblessness** /-nəs/ noun [U]

▸noun [plural] /ˈdʒɒb.ləs/ (US) /ˈdʒɑː.b.ləs/ mainly UK **the jobless** unemployed people: *The council has been running training schemes for the jobless.* ◦ *The jobless* ***total*** *(= the number of people unemployed) reached four million this week.*

ˌjob ˈlot noun [C] UK informal a collection of various objects that are bought or sold as a group, usually at a cheap price: *I bought a job lot* ***of*** *second-hand children's books.*

ˈjob satisˌfaction noun [U] the feeling of pleasure and achievement which you experience in your job when you know that your work is worth doing, or the degree to which your work gives you this feeling: *Many people are more interested in job satisfaction than in earning large amounts of money.*

ˈjob seˌcurity noun [U] If you have job security, your job is likely to be permanent.

jobseeker /ˈdʒɒbˌsiː.kər/ (US) /ˈdʒɑːbˌsiː.kɚ/ noun [C] UK someone who is trying to find a job

jobseeker's alˈlowance noun [U] (abbreviation **JSA**) in the UK, money that the government pays to unemployed people who are looking for a job

ˈjob-share verb [I] UK to divide the duties and the pay of one job between two people who work at different times during the day or week • **ˈjob-share** noun [C] • **ˈjob-ˌsharing** noun [U]

jobsworth /ˈdʒɒbz.wɜːθ/ (US) /ˈdʒɑːbz.wɝːθ/ noun [C] informal disapproving someone who always obeys all the rules of their job even when they cause problems for other people or when the rules are silly

jock /dʒɒk/ (US) /dʒɑːk/ noun **PERSON** ▷ **1** [C] US informal disapproving a person who is extremely enthusiastic about sport **UNDERWEAR** ▷ **2 jocks** [plural] Australian English informal a piece of underwear worn by men and boys which covers the area between the waist and the tops of the legs → Compare **underpants**

Jock /dʒɒk/ (US) /dʒɑːk/ noun [C] UK slang a man who comes from Scotland. This word is considered offensive by some people.

jockey /ˈdʒɒk.i/ (US) /ˈdʒɑː.ki/ noun; verb

▸noun [C] a person whose job is riding horses in races: *a champion jockey*

▸verb [I] to attempt to get power or get into a better position than other people using any methods you can: *Since the death of the president, opposition parties and the army have been jockeying* ***for*** *power.* ◦ *As the singer came on stage, the photographers jockeyed* ***for position*** *at the front of the hall.*

PHRASAL VERB **jockey sb into sth** to persuade someone to do what you want, often by deceiving them in a clever way: [+ -ing verb] *The bosses were eventually jockeyed into sign****ing*** *the union agreement.*

ˈjock ˌitch noun [U] US informal a skin infection that makes the GROIN and the top inside part of the legs sore and ITCHY

jockstrap /ˈdʒɒk.stræp/ (US) /ˈdʒɑːk-/ noun [C] (formal **athˌletic supˈport**) a tight piece of underwear worn by men to support and protect their sexual organs when playing sport

jocose /dʒəˈkəʊs/ (US) /dʒoʊˈkoʊs/ **adj** literary humorous or liking to play: *His jocose manner was unsuitable for such a solemn occasion.* • **jocosely** /-li/ adv

jocular /ˈdʒɒk.jʊ.lər/ (US) /ˈdʒɑː.kjə.lɚ/ **adj** formal **1** funny or intended to make someone laugh: *a jocular comment* **2** describes someone who is happy and likes to make jokes: *Michael was in a very jocular* ***mood*** *at the party.* • **jocularly** /-li/ adv • **jocularity** /ˌdʒɒk.jʊˈlær.ə.ti/ (US) /ˌdʒɑː.kjəˈler.ə.t̬i/ noun [U] formal

jodhpurs /ˈdʒɒd.pəz/ (US) /ˈdʒɑːd.pɚz/ noun [plural] trousers that are loose above the knees and tight below them, designed to be worn when riding a horse: *a new* ***pair of*** *jodhpurs*

Joe Bloggs /ˌdʒəʊˈblɒgz/ (US) /ˌdʒoʊˈblɑːgz/ noun [S] UK (US **Joe ˈBlow**) an average or typical man: *This stereo system is the most expensive in the range and is not the sort of thing that Joe Bloggs would buy.*

Joe Public /ˌdʒəʊˈpʌb.lɪk/ (US) /ˌdʒoʊ-/ noun UK informal (US informal **John Q. ˈPublic**) the general public: *The government's decision to tax gas and electricity has not been popular with Joe Public.*

joey /ˈdʒəʊ.i/ (US) /ˈdʒoʊ.i/ noun [C] a young KANGAROO

jog /dʒɒg/ (US) /dʒɑːg/ verb; noun

▸verb (-gg-) **RUN** ▷ **1** (B1) [I] to run at a slow, regular speed, especially as a form of exercise: *'What do you do to keep fit?' 'I jog and go swimming.'* ◦ *He was walking at a very quick pace and I had to jog to keep up with him.* **PUSH** ▷ **2** [T] to push or knock someone or something slightly, especially with your arm: *A man rushed past and jogged her* ***elbow****, making her drop the bag.*

IDIOM **jog sb's memory** to make someone remember something: *The police showed him a photo to try to jog his memory about what had happened on the night of the robbery.*

PHRASAL VERB **jog along** informal If something, such as your work, jogs along, it moves on at a slow but regular speed: *'How's your research going?' 'Oh, it's jogging along.'*

▸noun [S] (plural **-gg-**) a run that you do at a slow, regular speed, especially as a form of exercise: *I haven't done much exercise all week, so I think I'll* ***go for a*** *jog this morning.*

jogger /ˈdʒɒg.ər/ (US) /ˈdʒɑː.gɚ/ noun [C] someone who jogs as a form of exercise

jogging /ˈdʒɒg.ɪŋ/ (US) /ˈdʒɑː.gɪŋ/ noun [U] (B1) the activity of running at a slow, regular speed, especially as a form of exercise: *He usually* ***goes*** *jogging for half an hour before breakfast.*

ˈjogging ˌsuit noun [C] a loose shirt and loose

trousers, often made of thick cotton, that are worn informally or for running

joggle /ˈdʒɒg.l/ (US) /ˈdʒɑː.gl/ **verb** [T] to shake or move someone or something up and down in a gentle way

ˈjog trot noun [S] If you move at a jog trot, you run at a slow, regular speed.

john /dʒɒn/ (US) /dʒɑːn/ noun [C] **TOILET** ▷ **1** US informal a toilet: *I'm just **going to** the john – can you wait for me?* **PERSON** ▷ **2** US slang a man who is the customer of a PROSTITUTE (= a woman who charges men to have sex with her)

John ˈBull noun old-fashioned informal a character who represents a typical Englishman or the English people in general: *John Bull is traditionally depicted as a fat man wearing a waistcoat with the British flag on it.*

John ˈDoe noun **1** US legal a name used in a law court for a person whose real name is kept secret or is not known **2** [C] an average or typical person

John ˈDory noun [C or U] (plural **John Dory** or **John Dories**) a thin fish that can be eaten

John Hancock /ˌdʒɒnˈhæŋ.kɒk/ (US) /ˌdʒɑːnˈhæn.kɑːk/ noun [C] (also **John Henry** /ˌdʒɒnˈhen'ri/ (US) /ˌdʒɑːn-/) US informal a person's SIGNATURE: *Put your John Hancock at the bottom of the page.*

johnny /ˈdʒɒn.i/ (US) /ˈdʒɑː.ni/ noun [C] UK slang a **condom**

johnny-come-ˈlately noun [C] (plural **johnny-come-latelies** or **johnnies-come-lately**) disapproving someone who has only recently started a job or activity and has suddenly become very successful

John ˌQ. ˈPublic noun US informal (UK informal **ˌJoe ˈPublic**) the general public: *John Q. Public doesn't trust politicians.*

joie de vivre /ˌʒwɑː.dəˈviː.vrə/ noun [U] formal a feeling of great happiness and enjoyment of life

join /dʒɔɪn/ verb; noun

▸verb **CONNECT** ▷ **1** (B1) [T] to connect or fasten things together: *A long suspension bridge joins the two islands.* ◦ *Join the two pieces **together** using strong glue.* ◦ *The island is joined **to** the mainland by a road bridge.* ◦ *If you join (**up**) the dots on the paper, you'll get a picture.* **2** (B1) [I or T] If roads or rivers join, they meet at a particular point: *The A11 joins the M11 south of Cambridge.* ◦ *The River Murray and the River Darling join east of Adelaide.* **DO TOGETHER** ▷ **3** (A2) [I or T] to get involved in an activity or journey with another person or group: *I don't have time for a drink now, but I'll join you later.* ◦ *Why don't you ask your sister if she would like to join us **for** supper?* ◦ *We took the ferry across the Channel and then joined (= got on) the Paris train at Calais.* ◦ *If you're buying tickets, please join the **queue** (US **line**) (= stand at the end of it).* ◦ *I'm sure everyone will join me **in** wish**ing** you a very happy retirement (= everyone else will do this too).* ◦ *The police have joined **with** (= they have begun to work with) the drugs squad **in** try**ing** to catch major drug traffickers.* ◦ *The design company is planning to join **up with** a shoe manufacturer and create a new range of footwear.*

> **!** Common mistake: **join or attend?**
>
> **Warning:** choose the correct verb!
>
> To talk about going to an event, place, etc., don't say 'join', say **attend**:
>
> ~~*I joined a conference about global warming.*~~
>
> *I attended a conference about global warming.*
>
> **Remember: attend** is slightly formal. In more informal styles, say **go to**:
>
> *I went to a conference on global warming.*

BECOME A MEMBER ▷ **4** (A2) [I or T] to become a member of an organization: *I felt so unfit after Christmas that I decided to join a gym.* ◦ *It's a great club. Why don't you join?* **5 join the ranks** to become one of a particular large group of people: *When I leave school at the end of this month, I'll probably have to join the ranks **of** the unemployed.*

IDIOMS **be joined in marriage/matrimony** formal to become a married couple in an official ceremony • **join battle** formal If armies join battle, they start to fight. • **join duty** Indian English to return to work after a period of time away • **join hands** If two or more people join hands, they hold each other's hands, especially in order to do something: *The teacher asked us to form a circle and join hands.* • **join the club!** informal said in answer to something that someone has said, meaning that you are in the same bad situation as them: *'I've got no money till the end of this week.' 'Join the club!'*

PHRASAL VERBS **join in (sth)** (B1) to become involved in an activity with other people: *We only need one more player for this game – can you persuade your sister to join in?* ◦ *At the end of this verse, we'd like everyone to join in **with** the chorus.* • **join up** UK If you join up, you become a member of one of the armed forces.

▸noun [C] a place where two things meet or are fastened together: *She'd stitched the two pieces together really carefully so that you couldn't see the join.*

joined ˈup adj **1** mainly UK If writing is joined up, each letter in a word is connected to the next one: [before noun] *My daughter is just starting to learn how to do joined-up **writing** at school.* **2** UK If ideas, systems, or parts are joined up, they are combined in a useful and effective way.

joined-up ˈthinking noun [U] thinking about a complicated problem in an intelligent way that includes all the important facts: *This complex issue needs some joined-up thinking from ministers.*

joiner /ˈdʒɔɪ.nəʳ/ (US) /-nɚ/ noun [C] **WOOD WORKER** ▷ **1** a skilled worker who makes the wooden structures inside buildings, such as doors and window frames **TAKING PART** ▷ **2** someone who agrees to take part in an arrangement or become a member of an organization: *Recent joiners are in a worse position than existing members.* **3** informal a person who likes to get involved in activities with groups of people: *I don't think you'll persuade David to come along to tonight's meeting – he's not much of a joiner.*

joinery /ˈdʒɔɪ.nᵊr.i/ (US) /-nɚ-/ noun [U] the work of a joiner or the things made by a joiner

joint /dʒɔɪnt/ adj; noun; verb

▸adj (B2) belonging to or shared between two or more people: *a joint bank account* ◦ *The project was a joint effort between the two schools (= they worked on it together).* ◦ *The two Russian ice skaters came joint second (= they were both given second prize) in the world championships.* ◦ *In court, the parents were awarded joint **custody** of their son (= the right to care for him was shared between them).* • **jointly** /ˈdʒɔɪnt.li/ adv (C1) *The Channel Tunnel was jointly funded by the French and British.*

▸noun [C] **BODY** ▷ **1** (C2) a place in your body where two bones are connected: *an elbow/hip/knee joint* ◦ *As you become older, your joints get stiffer.* **2 put sth out of joint** to force a joint in the body out of its correct position by accident: *I put my shoulder out of joint last weekend lifting heavy boxes.* **CONNECTION** ▷ **3** a place where two things are fixed together: *Damp has* *penetrated the joints in the wood panelling.* **MEAT** ▷ **4** a large piece of meat that is cooked in one piece: *a joint of beef/pork* **5** a piece of meat for cooking, usually containing a bone: *Fry four chicken joints in a pan with some mushrooms and garlic.* **PLACE** ▷ **6** C1 informal a bar or restaurant that serves cheap food and drink: *We had lunch at a **hamburger** joint and then went to see a movie.* **DRUG** ▷ **7** slang a cigarette containing the drug CANNABIS

IDIOM **put sth out of joint** to prevent a plan from working correctly: *Our whole schedule was put out of joint by the designs arriving a week late.*

▸verb [T] to cut meat into large pieces ready for cooking

the ˌJoint ˌChiefs of ˈStaff noun [plural] the leaders of the US armed forces, who give military advice to the president

jointed /ˈdʒɔɪn.tɪd/ US /-t̬ɪd/ adj **BODY** ▷ **1** having joints and able to bend **CONNECTION** ▷ **2** having a place or places where two things are fixed together

ˌjoint ˈfamily noun [C] Indian English a family in which parents and their male children with their families live together and are considered as a single unit

ˌjoint ˈhonours noun [U or plural] UK a university degree in which two subjects are studied to an equally high level: *She has a joint honours degree in Philosophy and Psychology.*

ˌjoint resoˈlution noun [C usually singular] US a decision that is approved by both houses of the US Congress and becomes law when approved by the president

ˌjoint-stock ˈcompany noun [C] specialized a business that is owned by the group of people who have SHARES in the company

ˌjoint ˈventure noun [C] a business or business activity that two or more people or companies work on together: *The website was a joint venture between him and his partner.*

joist /dʒɔɪst/ noun [C] a long, thick piece of wood, metal, or concrete, used in buildings to support a floor or ceiling

jojoba /həˈhəʊ.bə/ US /-ˈhoʊ-/ noun [U] a large American plant with sharp leaves whose seeds contain a valuable oil that is used in beauty products: *jojoba oil*

joke /dʒəʊk/ US /dʒoʊk/ noun; verb

▸noun **FUNNY** ▷ **1** B1 [C] something, such as a funny story or trick, that is said or done in order to make people laugh: *Did I **tell** you the joke about the chicken crossing the road?* ◦ *She spent the evening **cracking** (= telling) jokes and telling funny stories.* ◦ *She tied his shoelaces together **for a** joke.* ◦ *I hope Rob doesn't tell any of his **dirty** jokes (= jokes about sex) when my mother's here.* ◦ *He tried to do a comedy routine, but all his jokes **fell flat** (= no one laughed at them).* ◦ *Don't you **get** (= understand) the joke?* **BAD/SILLY** ▷ **2** C1 [S] informal a person or thing that is so bad or silly that they do not deserve respect: *Our new teacher's a bit of a joke – he can't even control the class.* ◦ *The new software is a **complete** joke – it keeps going wrong.* ◦ *The exam was a joke (= was very easy) – everyone finished in less than an hour.*

IDIOMS **be no joke** informal to be serious or difficult: *It's no joke driving on icy roads.* • **get/go beyond a joke** to start to become annoying or worrying: *I don't mind helping her out occasionally, but this is getting beyond a joke.* • **the joke is on sb** informal If you say that the joke is on a particular person, you mean that they have tried to make someone else look silly but have made themselves look silly instead. • **make a joke of sth** to laugh at something although it is serious or important: *He tried to make a joke of the fact that he hadn't passed the exam.* • **take a joke** to laugh when someone says something funny about you and not be offended: *What's the matter? Can't you take a joke or something?*

▸verb [I] **1** B1 to say funny things: *They joked and laughed as they looked at the photos.* ◦ *It's more serious than you think, so please don't joke **about** it.* ◦ [+ speech] *'I didn't expect to be out so soon,' he joked, after spending nine months in hospital.* **2** B1 If you think that someone is joking when they say something, you think that they do not really mean it: *I thought he was joking when he said Helen was pregnant, but she really is.* ◦ *She wasn't joking (= she was serious) when she said she was going to move out of the house.*

IDIOMS **joking apart/aside** said when you want to start speaking seriously about something after making jokes and laughing about it: *Joking apart, will you be able to manage on your own?* • **only joking!** said when you mean that something you said was not intended to be serious: *Think I'll leave you with the kids while I go for a beer – only joking!* • **you must be joking** (also **you've got to be joking**) B1 said in answer to something that someone has said, meaning that you do not believe they said it seriously, or you think it is a stupid thing to say: *You've got to be joking if you think I'm going to stand in the rain watching you play rugby!* • **you're joking!** B1 something you say to show that you are surprised by what someone has said, or do not believe it is true: *'Hey, Maria's leaving.' 'You're joking!'*

joker /ˈdʒəʊ.kəʳ/ US /ˈdʒoʊ.kɚ/ noun [C] **CARD** ▷ **1** a special playing card that can be given any value and is used in some card games instead of any other card **FUNNY PERSON** ▷ **2** someone who likes telling funny stories or doing stupid things in order to make people laugh: *He's always been a bit of a joker and can't resist playing tricks on people.* **ANNOYING PERSON** ▷ **3** informal a person who has done something that annoys you: *Some joker keeps setting off the fire alarm.*

IDIOM **joker in the pack** the person or thing that could change the situation in an unexpected way

jokester /ˈdʒəʊ.kstəʳ/ US /ˈdʒoʊ.kstɚ/ noun [C] someone who likes telling funny stories or making people laugh

jokey /ˈdʒəʊ.ki/ US /ˈdʒoʊ-/ adj informal funny

jokingly /ˈdʒəʊ.kɪŋ.li/ US /ˈdʒoʊ-/ adv in a way that is intended to be funny: *She suggested **half**-jokingly that they should sell the family car and all buy bikes instead.*

jollies /ˈdʒɒl.iz/ US /ˈdʒɑː.liz/ noun informal **get your jollies** to get enjoyment from something, especially something unpleasant

jollification /ˌdʒɒl.ɪ.fɪˈkeɪ.ʃənz/ US /ˌdʒɑː.lə.fə-/ noun [C or U] old-fashioned an enjoyable activity or celebration

jolly /ˈdʒɒl.i/ US /ˈdʒɑː.li/ adj; adv; verb

▸adj **HAPPY** ▷ **1** happy and smiling: *a jolly smile/manner/mood* ◦ *She's a very jolly, upbeat sort of a person.* **ENJOYABLE** ▷ **2** old-fashioned enjoyable, energetic, and entertaining: *a jolly occasion* **ATTRACTIVE** ▷ **3** bright and attractive: *I love the bright yellow you've painted the children's room – it makes it look really jolly.*

IDIOM **jolly hockey sticks** UK humorous describes a woman or girl of a high social class who is enthusiastic in a way that annoys most people

▸adv UK old-fashioned informal very: *That's a jolly nice scarf you're wearing.*

IDIOMS **jolly good** old-fashioned used to express approval of something that someone has said or done, or to show that you have heard or understood what someone has said: *'I've left all the papers you need on your desk.' 'Oh, jolly good.'* • **jolly good show!** old-fashioned used to express admiration for what someone has said or done: *'We won!' 'Oh, jolly good show!'*

▸verb [T + adv/prep] informal to encourage someone to do something by putting them in a good mood and persuading them gently: *I'll try to jolly my parents* ***into*** *letting me borrow the car this weekend.* ◦ *She didn't really want to go to the party, so we had to jolly her* ***along*** *a bit.*

PHRASAL VERB **jolly sth up** UK informal to make something brighter and more attractive: *I thought I'd jolly the room up* ***with*** *some colourful curtains.*

the ˌJolly ˈRoger noun [S] the black flag with a picture of bones on it that was traditionally used on a ship belonging to PIRATES

ˈjolly ˌwell adv UK old-fashioned used to emphasize something you are saying, especially when you are angry or annoyed: *I'm going to jolly well tell her what I think of her!* ◦ *'Is she ready to leave yet?' 'I jolly well hope so!'*

jolt /dʒəʊlt/ US /dʒoʊlt/ verb; noun

▸verb **MOVE SUDDENLY** ▷ **1** [I or T, usually + adv/prep] to (cause something or someone to) move suddenly and violently: *The train stopped unexpectedly and we were jolted forwards.* ◦ *The truck jolted* ***along*** *the rough track through the field.* **SHOCK** ▷ **2** [T] to shock someone in order to change their behaviour or way of thinking: *The charity used photos of starving children in an attempt to jolt the public conscience (= make them feel guilty and take action).* **3 jolt sb into/out of sth** to give someone a sudden shock which forces them to act: *The news about Sam's illness jolted her into* ***action****.*

▸noun [C] **MOVEMENT** ▷ **1** a sudden violent movement: *As the plane touched the ground, there was a massive jolt and we were thrown forwards.* ◦ *I woke up* ***with a*** *jolt as I thought I heard my bedroom door being pushed open.* **SHOCK** ▷ **2** an unpleasant shock or surprise: *His self-confidence* ***took*** *a sudden jolt with the news that he had not been selected.*

jones /dʒəʊnz/ US /dʒoʊnz/ verb US informal **be jonesing for sth** to want something very much: *I'm jonesing for a coffee – can we take a break?*

josh /dʒɒʃ/ US /dʒɑːʃ/ verb [I or T] informal to joke, often in order to TEASE someone (= annoy them slightly in a humorous way): *They were always joshing him* ***about*** *his bald head.*

joss stick /ˈdʒɒsˌstɪk/ US /ˈdʒɑːs-/ noun [C] a thin wooden stick covered in a substance that is burned to produce a pleasant smell

jostle /ˈdʒɒs.l/ US /ˈdʒɑː.sl/ verb [I or T] to knock or push roughly against someone in order to move past them or get more space when you are in a crowd of people: *As we came into the arena, we were jostled by fans pushing their way towards the stage.* ◦ *Photographers jostled and shoved to get a better view of the royal couple.* • **jostling** /ˈdʒɒs.lɪŋ/ US /ˈdʒɑː.slɪŋ/ noun [U] • **jostling** /ˈdʒɒs.lɪŋ/ US /ˈdʒɑː.slɪŋ/ adj *a crowd of jostling reporters*

PHRASAL VERB **jostle for sth** If people jostle for something, they compete with each other in order to get what they want: *Since the fall of the government, the two opposition parties have been jostling for* ***position****.*

jot /dʒɒt/ US /dʒɑːt/ verb; noun

▸verb [T usually + adv/prep] (**-tt-**) to make a quick short note of something: *Could you jot your address and phone number* ***in*** *my address book?*

PHRASAL VERB **jot sth down** to write something quickly on a piece of paper so that you remember it: *I carry a notebook so that I can jot down any ideas.*

▸noun informal **not a/one jot** not at all or not even a small amount: *Don't listen to her! There's not a jot of truth (= there is no truth) in what she's saying.*

jotter /ˈdʒɒt.əʳ/ US /ˈdʒɑː.t̬ɚ/ noun [C] (also **ˈjotter ˌpad**) UK a small book used for writing in

jottings /ˈdʒɒt.ɪŋz/ US /ˈdʒɑː.t̬ɪŋz/ noun [plural] quickly written short notes: *She* ***made*** *some jottings in the margin of the book she was reading.*

joule /dʒuːl/ noun [C] (written abbreviation **J**) a unit of energy or work done

journal /ˈdʒɜː.nəl/ US /ˈdʒɝː-/ noun [C] **MAGAZINE** ▷ **1** C1 a serious magazine or newspaper that is published regularly about a particular subject: *a medical/trade journal* **DIARY** ▷ **2** C2 a written record of what you have done each day, sometimes including your private thoughts and feelings: *She* ***kept*** *a travel journal during her trip to South America.* → Synonym **diary**

journalese /ˌdʒɜː.nəˈliːz/ US /ˌdʒɝː-/ noun [U] disapproving a style of language considered typical of newspapers

journalism /ˈdʒɜː.nə.lɪ.zᵊm/ US /ˈdʒɝː-/ noun [U] B2 the work of collecting, writing, and publishing news stories and articles in newspapers and magazines or broadcasting them on the radio and television

journalist /ˈdʒɜː.nə.lɪst/ US /ˈdʒɝː-/ noun [C] B1 a person who writes news stories or articles for a newspaper or magazine or broadcasts them on radio or television: *a freelance political journalist* • **journalistic** /ˌdʒɜː.nəˈlɪs.tɪk/ US /ˌdʒɝː-/ adj *the decline of journalistic* ***standards***

journey /ˈdʒɜː.ni/ US /ˈdʒɝː-/ noun; verb

▸noun [C] A2 the act of travelling from one place to another, especially in a vehicle: *It's a two-hour train journey* ***from*** *York* ***to*** *London.* ◦ *I love* ***going on*** *long journeys.* ◦ *We* ***broke*** *our journey (= stopped for a short time) in Edinburgh before travelling on to Inverness the next day.* ◦ *Did you have a* ***good*** *journey?* ◦ *Have a* ***safe*** *journey!* ◦ figurative *He views his life as a* ***spiritual*** *journey towards a greater understanding of his faith.* → See note at **travel**

> **Word partners for journey**
>
> *go on/make* a journey • *begin/continue/complete* a journey • ***break*** your journey • an *arduous/epic/long/short* journey • a *wasted* journey • a *homeward/outward/return* journey • a journey *by* [train/road, etc.] • a *leg/part/stage* of a journey

▸verb [I usually + adv/prep] literary to travel somewhere: *As we journeyed south, the landscape became drier and rockier.*

journeyman /ˈdʒɜː.ni.mən/ US /ˈdʒɝː-/ noun [C] (plural **-men** /-mən/) **1** old-fashioned a worker who has a skill making them able to do a particular job, and who usually works for someone else **2** any worker who produces good but not excellent work

journo /ˈdʒɜː.nəʊ/ (US) /ˈdʒɝː.noʊ/ **noun** [C] informal for **journalist**

joust /dʒaʊst/ **verb** [I] **1** (in the past) to fight with a LANCE (= a long pointed weapon) while riding on a horse, especially as a sport **2** to compete, especially for power or control: *Manchester United and Liverpool are jousting **for** position at the top of the football league.*

Jove /dʒəʊv/ (US) /dʒoʊv/ **noun** **by Jove** old-fashioned used to express surprise or to emphasize a statement: *By Jove, I think he's won!*

jovial /ˈdʒəʊ.vi.əl/ (US) /ˈdʒoʊ-/ **adj** (of a person) friendly and in a good mood, or (of a situation) enjoyable because of being friendly and pleasant: *He seemed a very jovial chap.* ◦ *a jovial time/evening/chat* • **jovially** /-ə.li/ **adv** • **joviality** /ˌdʒəʊ.viˈæl.ə.ti/ (US) /ˌdʒoʊ.viˈæl.ə.t̬i/ **noun** [U]

jowl /dʒaʊl/ **noun** [C usually plural] the loose skin and flesh under the JAW: *a bloodhound with **heavy** jowls (= loose folds of skin and flesh on the lower parts of its face)* • **jowly** /ˈdʒaʊ.li/ **adj** *She's become increasingly jowly (= the skin and flesh on the lower part of her face has become looser) as she's got older.*

joy /dʒɔɪ/ **noun** **HAPPINESS** ▷ **1** (B2) [U] great happiness: *They were **filled with** joy when their first child was born.* ◦ *She **wept for** joy when she was told that her husband was still alive.* **2** (B2) [C] a person or thing which causes happiness: *Listening to music is one of his greatest joys.* ◦ *the joys of parenthood* ◦ [+ to infinitive] *Her singing is **a** joy **to** listen to.* **SUCCESS** ▷ **3** [U] UK informal success, action, or help: [+ -ing verb] *Did you **have** any joy finding that book you wanted?* ◦ *We tried asking local libraries for information, but **got no** joy **from** any of them.*

joyful /ˈdʒɔɪ.fəl/ **adj** very happy: *Christmas is such a joyful time of year.* ◦ *I don't have very much to feel joyful **about/over** at the moment.* • **joyfully** /-i/ **adv** • **joyfulness** /-nəs/ **noun** [U]

joyless /ˈdʒɔɪ.ləs/ **adj** unhappy: *Jane is trapped in a joyless marriage.* • **joylessly** /-li/ **adv** • **joylessness** /-nəs/ **noun** [U]

joyous /ˈdʒɔɪ.əs/ **adj** literary full of joy; very happy: *a joyous hymn/event/voice* • **joyously** /-li/ **adv** • **joyousness** /-nəs/ **noun** [U]

joypad /ˈdʒɔɪ.pæd/ **noun** [C] specialized a small device that you hold in your hand and use to move and control a machine or computer game

joyriding /ˈdʒɔɪˌraɪ.dɪŋ/ **noun** [U] UK the crime of stealing a vehicle and driving fast and dangerously for pleasure • **joyrider** /-dəʳ/ (US) /-dɚ/ **noun** [C] UK a person who steals a vehicle and drives it fast and dangerously for pleasure • **joyride** /ˈdʒɔɪ.raɪd/ **noun** [C]

joystick /ˈdʒɔɪ.stɪk/ **noun** [C] a vertical handle that can be moved forwards, backwards, and sideways to control the direction or height of an aircraft or to control a machine or computer game

JP /ˌdʒeɪˈpiː/ **noun** [C] abbreviation for **Justice of the Peace**

JPEG /ˈdʒeɪ.peg/ **noun** **1** [U] abbreviation for joint photographic experts group: a system for reducing the size of electronic image files: *JPEG can reduce files to five percent of their original size.* **2** [C] a type of computer file that contains pictures or photographs: *a JPEG file* ◦ *Sam sent me a JPEG of her family having Christmas dinner, but I can't open it.*

Jr /ˈdʒuː.ni.əʳ/ (US) /-ɚ/ **adj** [after noun] mainly US abbreviation for **junior**

JSA /ˌdʒeɪ.esˈeɪ/ **noun** [U] abbreviation for **jobseeker's allowance**

jubilant /ˈdʒuː.bɪ.lənt/ **adj** feeling or expressing great happiness, especially because of a success: *The fans were jubilant **at/about/over** England's victory over Germany.* • **jubilantly** /-li/ **adv**

jubilation /ˌdʒuː.bɪˈleɪ.ʃən/ **noun** [U] a feeling of great happiness, especially because of a success: *There was jubilation in the crowd as the winning goal was scored.*

jubilee /ˈdʒuː.bɪ.liː/, /ˌdʒuː.bɪˈliː/ **noun** [C] (the celebration of) the day on which an important event happened many years ago: *the Queen's silver jubilee*

Judaeo-Christian UK (US **Judeo-Christian**) /dʒuː-ˌdeɪ.əʊˈkrɪs.tʃən/ (US) /-oʊ-/ **adj** belonging to, shared by, or including both the Jewish and the Christian religion, or both Jewish and Christian people: *Judaeo-Christian tradition/values/fellowship*

Judaic /dʒuːˈdeɪ.ɪk/ **adj** belonging or relating to Judaism: *Judaic tradition*

Judaism /ˈdʒuː.deɪ.ɪ.zəm/ **noun** [U] the religion of the Jewish people, based on belief in one God and on the laws contained in the Torah and Talmud

Judas /ˈdʒuː.dəs/ **noun** [C] a person who is not loyal to a friend and helps the friend's enemies → Synonym **traitor**

judder /ˈdʒʌd.əʳ/ (US) /-ɚ/ **verb** [I] UK (US **shudder**) (especially of a vehicle) to shake violently: *The train juddered **to a halt**.* • **judder** **noun** [C] *The car gave **a** sudden judder, then stopped dead.*

judge /dʒʌdʒ/ **noun; verb**

▸**noun** [C] **PERSON** ▷ **1** (B2) a person who is in charge of a trial in a court and decides how a person who is guilty of a crime should be punished, or who makes decisions on legal matters: *a British high-court judge* ◦ *a US Supreme Court judge* **DECIDE** ▷ **2** (B1) the person who officially decides who is the winner of a competition: *a panel of judges* **3** (C2) a person who has the knowledge to give an opinion about something or is able to decide if someone or something is good or bad: *She's such a bad judge **of** character.* ◦ *'I really don't think you should have another drink.' 'I'll be/Let me be the judge **of** that (= I am able to make my own decision about that).'*

▸**verb** [I or T] **1** (B1) to form, give, or have as an opinion, or to decide about something or someone, especially after thinking carefully: *So far, he seems to be handling the job well, but it's really too soon to judge.* ◦ [+ question word] *It's difficult to judge **wh**ether the new system really is an improvement.* ◦ *The meeting was judged (**to** have been) a success.* ◦ *You shouldn't judge **by/on** appearances alone.* ◦ *I'm hopeless at judging **distance(s)** (= guessing how far it is between places).* **2** (C2) to express a bad opinion of someone's behaviour, often because you think you are better than them: *You have no right to judge other people because of what they look like or what they believe.* **3** (C1) to officially decide who will be the winner of a competition: *I've been asked to judge the fancy-dress competition.* **4** **judging by/from** (also **to judge by/from**) (B2) used to express the reasons why you have a particular opinion: *Judging by what he said, I think it's very unlikely that he'll be able to support your application.*

IDIOM **you can't judge a book by its cover** saying said to show that you cannot know what something or someone is like by looking only at their appearance

judgment (also **judgement**) /ˈdʒʌdʒ.mənt/ **noun** **DECIDE** ▷ **1** (C2) [U] the ability to form valuable opinions and make good decisions: *to show **good/sound/poor** judgment* ◦ *I don't think you have the right to **pass** judgment (**on** others) (= to say whether you think other people are good or bad).* ◦ *I'm going to **reserve** judgment (**on** the decision) (= not say whether I think it is good or bad) for the time being.* **2** B2 [C] a decision or opinion about someone or something that you form after thinking carefully: *It proved difficult to **come to/form/make** a judgment about how well the school was performing.* **3 in sb's judgment** according to someone's opinion: *In my judgment, we should let the solicitor deal with this.* LEGAL ▷ **4** [C or U] an official legal decision: *It is the judgment **of** this court that you are guilty of murder.* ◦ *We are still waiting for the court to **pass/pronounce** judgment (= give a decision) **on** the case.*

> Word partners for **judgment**
>
> *use* your judgment • *pass/reserve/suspend* judgment • *come to/form/make* a judgment • *affect/cloud/colour* sb's judgment • *question/trust* sb's judgment • *sit in/stand in* judgment **on** sb/sth • a *considered/harsh/subjective* judgment • *good/poor/sound* judgment • an *error/lapse* of judgment

IDIOM **against your better judgment** If something is against your better judgment, you think it would be wiser not to do it: *Against my better judgment, I gave him the job.*

judgmental (also **judgemental**) /dʒʌdʒˈmen.tᵊl/ US /-t̬ᵊl/ adj disapproving too quick to criticize people: *You must try not to be so judgmental **about** people.* • **judgmentally** /-i/ adv

ˈjudgment ˌcall noun [C] a decision someone has to make using their own ideas and opinions: *It's a judgment call – do we go by plane or risk taking the car to the conference?*

ˈJudgment ˌDay noun [U] (also **the ˌDay of ˈJudgment**) the time when some people believe the world will end and all the dead people will come back to life so that God can judge how everyone behaved when they were alive

judicature /ˈdʒuː.dɪ.kə.tʃəʳ/ US /-tʃɚ/ noun [U] specialized the legal system and the work it does

judicial /dʒuːˈdɪʃ.ᵊl/ adj involving a law court: *the judicial system* ◦ *a judicial **enquiry/review*** • **judicially** /-i/ adv

judiciary /dʒuːˈdɪʃ.ᵊr.i/ US /-ɚ-/ noun [C, + sing/pl verb] the part of a country's government that is responsible for its legal system, including all the judges in the country's courts: *a member of the judiciary*

judicious /dʒuːˈdɪʃ.əs/ adj having or showing reason and good judgment in making decisions: *We should make judicious use of the resources available to us.* • **judiciously** /-li/ adv *a judiciously worded statement*

judo /ˈdʒuː.dəʊ/ US /-doʊ/ noun [U] a sport in which two people fight using their arms and legs and hands and feet, and try to throw each other to the ground: *He's a black belt (= has the highest level of skill) **in/at** judo.*

jug /dʒʌg/ noun CONTAINER ▷ **1** B1 [C] UK (US **pitcher**) a container for holding liquids that has a handle and a shaped opening at the top for pouring: *a glass/plastic jug* ◦ *a milk/water jug* **2** [C] US a large round container for liquids that has a flat base, a handle and a very narrow raised opening at the top for pouring: *a whiskey jug* **3** [C] the amount of liquid that a jug holds: *a jug **of** milk* PRISON ▷ **4** [U] UK old-fashioned slang prison: *I always knew he'd end up **in** (**the**) jug.* • **jugful** /ˈdʒʌg.fʊl/ noun [C] the amount held by a jug: *There was a jugful of water on each table.*

jug

juggernaut /ˈdʒʌg.ə.nɔːt/ US /-ɚ.nɑːt/ noun [C] VEHICLE ▷ **1** UK (US **semitrailer**, **ˌtractor-ˈtrailer**) a very large, heavy truck: *The peace of the village has been shattered by juggernauts thundering through it.* POWERFUL FORCE ▷ **2** disapproving a large powerful force or organization that cannot be stopped

juggle /ˈdʒʌg.l̩/ verb ENTERTAIN ▷ **1** [I or T] to throw several objects up into the air, and then catch and throw them up repeatedly so that one or more stays in the air, usually in order to entertain people: *We all watched in amazement as he juggled **with** three flaming torches.* MANAGE ▷ **2** C2 [T] informal to succeed in arranging your life so that you have time to involve yourself in two or more different activities or groups of people: *Many parents find it hard to juggle children and a career.* CHANGE ▷ **3** [T] informal to change results or information recorded as numbers so that a situation seems to be better than it really is: *It won't matter if we juggle **the figures** – no one will know.*

juggler /ˈdʒʌg.ləʳ/ US /-lɚ/ noun [C] a person who juggles objects in order to entertain people • **juggling** /-lɪŋ/ noun [U]

ˈjuggling ˌact noun [S] a difficult task or situation that involves dealing with several different things at the same time: *Her life is a constant juggling act, coping with career, family, and home life single-handed.*

jugular (vein) /ˈdʒʌg.jʊ.ləˌveɪn/ US /-lɚ-/ noun [C] any of several large VEINS in the neck that carry blood from the head to the heart

IDIOM **go for the jugular** to make serious effort to defeat someone, usually by criticizing them or harming them in a cruel way: *Cunningham went **straight** for the jugular, telling him that his work was a complete disaster.*

juice /dʒuːs/ noun LIQUID ▷ **1** A1 [U] the liquid that comes from fruit or vegetables: *orange/lemon/grapefruit/carrot juice* ◦ *a carton of apple juice* **2 juices** the liquid in meat: *Fry the meat first to seal in the juices.* POWER ▷ **3** [U] US slang power or influence: *My cousin Gianni's got all the juice in this neighborhood.* ABILITY ▷ **4 juices** informal energy: *This early in the morning it's hard to **get the creative** juices **flowing** (= to start thinking of good ideas).*

juicer /ˈdʒuː.səʳ/ US /-sɚ/ noun [C] a machine for removing juice from fruit or vegetables

juicy /ˈdʒuː.si/ adj LIQUID ▷ **1** B1 Juicy foods contain a lot of juice, which makes them very enjoyable to eat: *a **nice** juicy orange/steak* GOOD ▷ **2** C2 [before noun] informal describes information that is especially interesting because it is shocking or personal: *I've got some really juicy **gossip** for you.* **3** [before noun] informal big, important, or of a high quality: *If sales continue like this, we should be showing a **nice** juicy **profit** at the end of the year.* • **juiciness** /-nəs/ noun [U]

jujitsu (also **jiujitsu**) /ˌdʒuːˈdʒɪt.suː/ noun [U] a type of SELF-DEFENCE from Japan that does not involve weapons and is done as a sport. Other similar sports such as JUDO and KARATE are based on it.

jukebox /ˈdʒuːk.bɒks/ US /-bɑːks/ noun [C] a machine in a bar, etc. which plays recorded music when a coin is put into it

juke joint /ˈdʒuːk.dʒɔɪnt/ noun [C] US informal a place

where people can dance to music, drink alcohol, and GAMBLE (= play games to win money), especially one run by and for African Americans in the southern US

July /dʒʊˈlaɪ/ noun [C or U] (written abbreviation **Jul.**) A1 the seventh month of the year, after June and before August: *The film festival is* ***in*** *July.* ◦ *My son's birthday is* ***on*** *29 July.* ◦ *They're getting married* ***next*** *July.*

jumble /ˈdʒʌm.bl/ noun; verb
▸noun **MIXTURE** ▷ **1** [S] an untidy and confused mixture of things, feelings, or ideas: *He rummaged through the jumble* ***of*** *papers on his desk.* ◦ *a jumble of thoughts/ideas* **OLD THINGS** ▷ **2** [U] UK things you no longer want that are sold at a jumble sale
▸verb [T] to mix things together untidily: *Her clothes were all jumbled up/together in the suitcase.*

ˈjumble ˌsale noun [C] UK (US **ˈrummage ˌsale**) a sale of a mixed collection of things that people no longer want, especially in order to make money for an organization

jumbo /ˈdʒʌm.bəʊ/ (US) /-boʊ/ adj [before noun] extremely large: *a jumbo bag of sweets* ◦ *a jumbo-****sized*** *packet*

J

jumbo ˈjet noun [C] (informal **jumbo**) a very large aircraft that can carry a lot of people

jump /dʒʌmp/ verb; noun
▸verb **IN THE AIR** ▷ **1** A2 [I] to push yourself suddenly off the ground and into the air using your legs: *The children were jumping* ***up and down*** *with excitement.* ◦ *She ran across the grass and jumped* ***into*** *the water.* ◦ *He had to jump* ***out of*** *an upstairs window to escape.* ◦ *Our cat is always jumping* ***up*** *on/onto the furniture.* **2** A2 [I or T] to push yourself suddenly off the ground in order to go over something: *Can you jump* ***over/across*** *this stream?* ◦ *All the horses are finding it difficult to jump the last fence.* **MOVE/ACT SUDDENLY** ▷ **3** B1 [I usually + adv/prep] to move or act suddenly or quickly: *He suddenly jumped* ***to his feet****/jumped* ***up*** *and left.* ◦ *She jumped* ***in/into*** *a taxi and rushed to the station.* **4** B2 [I] If a noise or action causes you to jump, your body makes a sudden sharp movement because of surprise or fear: *The loud explosion* ***made*** *everyone jump.* ◦ *I almost jumped* ***out of my skin*** *when I heard a loud crash downstairs.* **INCREASE** ▷ **5** [I] to increase suddenly by a large amount: *House prices have jumped* ***dramatically****.* ◦ *The cost of building the road has jumped* ***by*** *70 percent.* **SEQUENCE** ▷ **6** [I usually + adv/prep] If a story, film, play, etc. jumps, it moves suddenly between different parts of it: *The film is about his adult life, but it keeps jumping* (***back***) ***to*** *when he was a child.* ◦ *His talk was hard to follow because he kept jumping* ***from*** *one subject* ***to*** *another.* **AVOID** ▷ **7** [T] to avoid or leave out a point or stage from the correct order in a series: *You have to follow the instructions exactly, you can't just jump a few steps* ***ahead****.* **ATTACK** ▷ **8** [T] informal to attack someone suddenly: *They were just walking home when a bunch of guys jumped* (***on***) *them.* **MOVE ILLEGALLY** ▷ **9** [T] to go past or away from something illegally or wrongly: *The police video showed that she had jumped the* (***traffic***) ***lights****.* ◦ *Several sailors jumped* ***ship*** *(= left their ship without permission) in New York.* **10 jump bail** to fail to appear for a court trial after being released until the trial in exchange for payment **BUSY** ▷ **11 be jumping** old-fashioned informal If a place is jumping, it is crowded and full of life: *This joint (= place of entertainment) is really jumping tonight.*

IDIOMS **be jumping up and down** UK informal to be angry or annoyed: *Bill's jumping up and down because Mark didn't get his report finished in time.* • **go (and) jump in the lake** informal a rude way of telling someone to go away and stop annoying you • **jump down sb's throat** informal to react angrily to something that someone says or does: *I made the mildest of criticisms and he jumped down my throat.* • **jump for joy** to be extremely happy: *'So how did Robert take the news?' 'He didn't exactly jump for joy.'* • **jump in with both feet** informal to become involved in a situation too quickly without thinking about it first: *That's just like Julie – always jumping in with both feet before she knows the facts.* • **jump the gun** to do something too soon, especially without thinking carefully about it: *They've only just met – isn't it jumping the gun to be talking about marriage already?* • **jump rope** US to skip • **jump to conclusions** C2 to guess the facts about a situation without having enough information: *Don't jump to conclusions! Perhaps it was his daughter he was dancing with.* • **jump to it** informal used to tell someone to do something quickly: *I told you to tidy this room – now jump to it!* • **jump to sb's defence** to quickly defend someone: *Whenever anyone criticizes her husband, she immediately jumps to his defence.*

PHRASAL VERBS **jump at sth** C2 to accept something eagerly: *She jumped at the* ***chance*** *of a trip to Paris.* • **jump in** to interrupt when someone else is speaking: *I wish you'd stop jumping in and finishing my sentences for me all the time.* • **jump on sb** to criticize someone as soon as they have done something wrong or said something that you disagree with: *She jumps on her children instantly if they're disobedient.* • **jump out at sb** If something jumps out at you, you notice it immediately: *That's a very effective advertisement – it really jumps out at you.*

▸noun [C] **MOVEMENT** ▷ **1** B1 a sudden movement off the ground and into the air: *He won with a jump of 8.5 metres.* ◦ *a parachute jump* ◦ *Several horses fell at the last jump (= fence or other thing to be jumped over).* **2** a sudden sharp movement because of surprise or fear: *The door slammed and Rita woke up with a jump.* **INCREASE** ▷ **3** a sudden increase: *Interest rates are now at 6.75 – that's a jump of almost 2 percent.*

IDIOMS **be/stay/keep one jump ahead** to do something before other people do it: *The way to be successful in business is always to stay one jump ahead* ***of*** *your competitors.* • **get a jump on sb/sth** mainly US informal to start doing something before other people start, or before something happens, in order to win an advantage for yourself: *I like to leave work early on Fridays so I can get a jump on the traffic.*

jumped-ˈup adj [before noun] UK informal disapproving describes someone who behaves as if they are very important in their job or position, especially because they used to be in a much lower position: *He's just a jumped-up office boy (= he was once only an office boy).*

jumper /ˈdʒʌm.pər/ (US) /-pɚ/ noun [C] **CLOTHES** ▷ **1** A2 UK (US **sweater**) a piece of clothing, made from wool or cotton and worn on the upper part of the body, that has sleeves and does not open at the front: *a red woolly jumper* **2** US a dress which does not cover the arms and is usually worn over another piece of clothing which does cover the arms **IN THE AIR** ▷ **3** a person or animal that jumps

ˈjumper ˌleads noun [plural] Australian English a pair of thick wires for starting the engine of one vehicle with electricity from the BATTERY of another vehicle → Compare **jump leads**

jumping-ˈoff ˌpoint noun [C usually singular] a point from which to start a journey or activity

ˈjump ˌleads noun [plural] UK (US **ˈjumper ˌcables**) a pair of thick wires for starting the engine of one vehicle with electricity from the BATTERY of another vehicle

ˈjump ˌrope noun [C] US a **skipping rope**

ˈjump-start verb [T] CAR ▷ **1** to start a car engine by pushing the car or by using jump leads. → Compare **push-start** SITUATION ▷ **2** to improve a situation by taking a particular action: *Companies want lower interest rates to jump-start the nation's weak economy.* • **ˈjump-start** noun [C usually singular]

jumpsuit /ˈdʒʌmp.suːt/ noun [C] a piece of clothing which covers both the upper body and the legs

jumpy /ˈdʒʌm.pi/ adj informal nervous and worried, especially because you are frightened or guilty: *My mother gets very jumpy when she's alone in the house.*

junction /ˈdʒʌŋk.ʃən/ noun [C] (US usually **intersection**) a place where things, especially roads or railways, come together: *You should slow down as you approach the junction.* ◦ UK *There's a service station at the next* ***motorway*** *junction (= point from which you can leave the motorway).*

ˈjunction ˌbox noun [C] a box in which electrical wires can be safely joined together

juncture /ˈdʒʌŋk.tʃər/ (US) /-tʃɚ/ noun [C] formal a particular point in time: ***At*** *this juncture, it is impossible to say whether she will make a full recovery.*

June /dʒuːn/ noun [C or U] (written abbreviation **Jun.**) (A1) the sixth month of the year, after May and before July: *A lot of people get married* ***in*** *June.* ◦ *His birthday is* ***on*** *21 June.* ◦ ***Last*** *June we had a lot of rain.*

jungle /ˈdʒʌŋ.gl/ noun FOREST ▷ **1** (B1) [C or U] a tropical forest in which trees and plants grow very closely together: *Either side of the river is dense, impenetrable jungle.* UNTIDY PLACE ▷ **2** [S] an uncontrolled or confusing mass of things: *Our garden is a real jungle.* ◦ *a jungle* ***of*** *electronic equipment* SITUATION ▷ **3** [S] informal a situation in which it is difficult to succeed because a lot of people are competing against each other: *You've got to be determined in this life – it's a jungle out there, kid.* MUSIC ▷ **4** [U] a type of popular dance music with an extremely fast rhythm and a low range of musical notes

ˈjungle ˌgym noun [C] US FOR **climbing frame**

ˌjungle ˈwarfare noun [U] war fought in a tropical forest where it is difficult to see the enemy and they can attack unexpectedly

junior /ˈdʒuː.ni.ər/ (US) /-njɚ/ noun; adj

▸noun LOW RANK ▷ **1** [C] someone who has a job at a low level within an organization: *an office junior* STUDENT ▷ **2** [C] UK a student at a junior school **3** [C] US a student in the third year of a course that lasts for four years at a school or college **4 the juniors** UK **junior school**: *Lewis has just moved up to the juniors.* YOUNGER ▷ **5** [C] a young person below a particular age who is involved in an activity, especially sport: *Saturday morning sessions are for juniors only.* **6 three, eight, etc. years sb's junior** (C2) three, eight, etc. years younger than someone: *My brother is five years my junior.* ◦ *My sister is my junior* ***by*** *three years (= three years younger than me).* → Compare **senior** SON ▷ **7** [S] mainly US used to refer to your son: *Come on, Junior, time for bed.*

▸adj LOW RANK ▷ **1** (B2) low or lower in rank: *I object to being told what to do by someone junior* ***to*** *me.* ◦ *a junior doctor/partner* → Compare **senior** YOUNGER ▷ **2** (B2) connected with or involving young people below a particular age: *junior orchestra* ◦ *Junior members are not permitted to compete.* **3** (US written abbreviation **Jr**, mainly UK written abbreviation **Jnr**) used after a man's name to refer to the younger of two men in the same family who have the same name: *Sammy Davis, Jr*

junior ˈcollege noun [C or U] US a college in the US where students study for two years

junior ˈhigh (school) noun [C] a school in the US for children who are twelve to 15 years old

ˈjunior ˌschool noun [C] a school in the UK for children who are seven to eleven years old: *My son goes to the local junior school.*

juniper /ˈdʒuː.nɪ.pər/ (US) /-pɚ/ noun [C or U] a small EVERGREEN bush (= one that never loses its leaves) that has sharp leaves and small purple fruits that are used in medicine and in making GIN (= a type of strong alcoholic drink): *juniper berries*

junk /dʒʌŋk/ noun; verb

▸noun RUBBISH ▷ **1** (C1) [U] things that are considered to be of no use or value, or of low quality: *We ought to clear out this cupboard – it's full of junk.* ◦ *I can't stand watching the junk that's on TV these days.* DRUG ▷ **2** [U] mainly US slang a dangerous drug, especially HEROIN SHIP ▷ **3** [C] a Chinese ship with a flat bottom and square sails

▸verb [T] informal to get rid of something because it is of no use or value

junket /ˈdʒʌŋ.kɪt/ noun [C] disapproving a journey or visit made for pleasure by an official that is paid for by someone else or with public money

ˈjunk ˌfood noun [C or U] (B2) food that is unhealthy but is quick and easy to eat → Compare **health food**

junkie (also **junky**) /ˈdʒʌŋ.ki/ noun [C] informal **1** someone who cannot stop taking illegal drugs **2** someone who wants to have or do something all the time: *a computer/TV junkie* ◦ *a publicity junkie*

ˈjunk ˌmail noun [U] (C1) letters or emails, usually advertising products or services, that are sent to people although they have not asked to receive them

ˈjunk ˌshop noun [C] a shop which sells old furniture and other things of little value

junkyard /ˈdʒʌŋk.jɑːd/ (US) /-jɑːrd/ noun [C] mainly US a place to which people take large things such as old furniture or machines that they no longer want

junta /ˈdʒʌn.tə/, /ˈhʊn-/ noun [C, + sing/pl verb] a government, especially a military one, that has taken power in a country by force and not by election: *The* ***military*** *junta has/have today broadcast an appeal for calm.*

Jupiter /ˈdʒuː.pɪ.tər/ (US) /-t̬ɚ/ noun [S] the planet fifth in order of distance from the Sun, after Mars and before Saturn

Jurassic /dʒʊəˈræs.ɪk/ (US) /dʒʊ-/ adj specialized from or referring to the period of GEOLOGICAL time between around 208 and 146 million years ago, in which the first birds appeared and the single piece of land broke up into separate continents: *the Jurassic period* ◦ *Jurassic dinosaurs* • **the Jurassic** noun

jurisdiction /ˌdʒʊə.rɪsˈdɪk.ʃən/ (US) /ˌdʒʊr.ɪs-/ noun [U] the authority of an official organization to make and deal with especially legal decisions: *The court* ***has*** *no jurisdiction* ***in/over*** *cases of this kind.* ◦ *School admissions are not* ***under/within*** *our jurisdiction.*

jurisprudence /ˌdʒʊə.rɪsˈpruː.dəns/ (US) /ˌdʒʊr.ɪs-/ noun [U] specialized the study of law and the principles on which law is based • **jurisprudential** /-pruːˈden.ʃəl/ adj *Canada has a jurisprudential tradition of protecting human rights.*

jurist /ˈdʒʊə.rɪst/ (US) /ˈdʒʊr.ɪst/ noun [C] specialized an expert in law, especially a judge

J

juror (old-fashioned **juryman**) /ˈdʒʊə.rəʳ/ (US) /ˈdʒʊr.ɚ/ noun [C] a member of a jury

jury /ˈdʒʊə.ri/ (US) /ˈdʒʊr.i/ noun [C, + sing/pl verb] **1** B2 a group of people who have been chosen to listen to all the facts in a trial in a law court and to decide if a person is guilty or not guilty, or if a claim has been proved: *members of the jury* ◦ *The jury has/have been unable to return a verdict (= reach a decision).* ◦ *Police officers aren't usually allowed to* ***be/sit/serve on*** *a jury.* **2** C1 a group of people chosen to decide the winner of a competition

IDIOM **the jury is (still) out** C2 If the jury is (still) out on a subject, people do not yet know the answer or have not yet decided if it is good or bad: *The jury's still out* ***on*** *the safety of irradiated food.*

ˈjury ˌbox noun [C usually singular] the place in a court where the jury sits

ˈjury ˌservice noun [U] UK (US **ˈjury ˌduty**) a period of time when a person is a member of a jury: *I'm* ***on/doing*** *jury service next week.*

jus /ʒuː/ noun [C] a sauce: *pan-fried beef in a balsamic jus*

J

just /dʒʌst/ adv; adj; noun

▸adv NOW ▷ **1** A2 now, very soon, or very recently: *'Where are you, Jim?' 'I'm just coming.'* ◦ *I'll just finish this, then we can go.* ◦ *He'd just got into the bath when the phone rang.* ◦ *The children arrived at school just* ***as*** *(= at the same moment as) the bell was ringing.* ◦ *The doctor will be with you in just* ***a minute/moment/second*** *(= very soon).* ◦ *It's just after/past* (UK also *gone*) *ten o'clock.* **2 just now a** A2 a very short time ago: *Who was that at the door just now?* **b** at the present time: *John's in the bath just now – can he call you back?*

> **!** Common mistake: **just**
>
> **Warning:** check your word order!
>
> **Just** usually goes directly before the main verb in a sentence:
>
> ~~*I just have returned from a conference in Brighton.*~~
>
> *I have just returned from a conference in Brighton.*
>
> But if the main verb is **am/is/are/was/were**, **just** usually goes directly after it:
>
> ~~*I just was going to phone you.*~~
>
> *I was just going to phone you.*

EXACTLY ▷ **3** B1 exactly or equally: *This carpet would be just right for the dining room.* ◦ *The twins look just like each other.* ◦ *Things turned out just* ***as*** *I expected.* ◦ *You've got just* ***as*** *many toys* ***as*** *your brother.* ◦ *Thank you, it's just what I've always wanted.* ◦ *I can't help you just* ***now/yet***. ◦ *Just* ***then***, *the lights went out.* ◦ *I can just imagine Sophie as a police officer.* ◦ informal approving *That dress is just you (= suits you very well).* ONLY ▷ **4** B1 only; simply: *'Would you like another drink?' 'OK, just one more.'* ◦ *It was just a joke.* ◦ *His daughter's just a baby/just a few weeks old.* ◦ *We'll just have to (= the only thing we can do is) wait and see what happens.* ◦ *She lives just down the road (= very near).* ◦ *Just* ***because*** *you're older than me doesn't mean you can tell me what to do.* **5** B1 used to make a statement or order stronger: *He just won't do as he's told.* ◦ *It's just too expensive.* **6** used to reduce the force of a statement and to suggest that it is not very important: *Can I just borrow the scissors for a second?* ◦ *I just wanted to ask you if you're free this afternoon.* ALMOST ▷ **7** B1 almost not or almost: *We arrived at the airport just in time to catch the plane.* ◦ *This dress (****only****) just fits.* ◦ *'Can you see the stage?' 'Yes,* ***only*** *just/just* ***about***.*'* ◦ *I've just* ***about*** *finished painting the living room.* **8 be just possible** If something is just possible, there is a slight chance that it will happen: *It's just possible that we might be going away that weekend.* VERY ▷ **9** B1 very; completely: *It's just dreadful what happened to her.*

IDIOMS **isn't it/aren't they just?** informal used to strongly agree with what someone has said about someone or something: *'This is rather expensive.' 'Isn't it just?'* • **it's just one of those things** saying said about an event or situation that you cannot explain, or do not like but cannot change • **just a minute/moment/second 1** A2 used to ask someone to wait for a short period of time: *Just a second – I've nearly finished.* **2** mainly UK used to interrupt someone in order to ask them to explain something, to calm them, or to express disagreement: *Just a minute – can you tell me how to do that again?* • **(it's) just as well (that)** B2 it is a good thing: *It's beginning to rain – it's just as well that we brought our umbrellas.* • **just like that** disapproving suddenly and unexpectedly: *Their son went off and got married last week, just like that.* • **just my luck!** something that you say when something bad happens to you • **might just as well** If you might just as well do something, there are no reasons not to do it: *For the little extra it'll cost, we might just as well stay for another night.*

▸adj C2 fair; morally correct: *The judge's sentence was perfectly just in the circumstances.* ◦ *I don't really think he had just* ***cause*** *to complain.* • **justly** /ˈdʒʌst.li/ adv • **justness** /ˈdʒʌst.nəs/ noun [U]

IDIOM **get your just deserts** If you get your just deserts, something bad happens to you that you deserve because of something bad you have done.

▸noun **the just** formal people who behave in a morally correct way

justice /ˈdʒʌs.tɪs/ noun FAIRNESS ▷ **1** B2 [U] fairness in the way people are dealt with: *There's no justice in the world when people can be made to suffer like that.* ◦ *The winner has been disqualified for cheating, so justice has been* ***done*** *(= a fair situation has been achieved).* → Opposite **injustice** LAW ▷ **2** B2 [U] the system of laws in a country which judges and punishes people: *the justice system in this country consists of a series of law courts at different levels.* ◦ *The police are doing all they can to* ***bring*** *those responsible for the bombing* ***to*** *justice.* ◦ *They are victims of a* ***miscarriage of*** *justice (= when the law has been carried out wrongly).* ◦ *He has been accused of* ***obstructing the course of*** *justice (= preventing the law being put into action).* JUDGE ▷ **3** [C] US a judge in a law court: *The president is expected to name a new Supreme Court justice within the next few days.* ◦ *Justice Ben Overton* **4** [C] UK used before the name of a judge in the HIGH COURT: *Mr Justice Ellis*

IDIOMS **do justice to sb/sth** (also **do sb/sth justice**) C2 to treat someone or something in a way that is fair and shows their true qualities: *This postcard doesn't do justice to the wonderful scenery.* • **do justice to yourself** (also **do yourself justice**) to do something as well as you can in order to show your true qualities and ability: *She didn't really do justice to herself in the interview.*

ˌJustice of the ˈPeace noun [C] (abbreviation **JP**) a person who is not a lawyer but who acts as a judge in local law courts and, in the US, can marry people

justifiable /ˈdʒʌs.tɪ.faɪ.ə.bl/, /ˌdʒʌs.tɪˈfaɪ-/ adj C2 If something is justifiable, there is a good reason for it: *Her actions were quite justifiable in the circumstances.* • **justifiably** /-bli/ adv *He was justifiably proud of his achievements.*

justiˌfiable ˈhomicide noun [U] US an act of killing someone which the law allows because it considers that there is a good reason for it, for example if you are defending yourself

justification /ˌdʒʌs.tɪ.fɪˈkeɪ.ʃən/ noun [C or U] C2 a good reason or explanation for something: *There is no justification* ***for*** *treating people so badly.* ◦ *It can be said,* ***with*** *some justification, that she is one of the greatest actresses on the English stage today.*

justified /ˈdʒʌs.tɪ.faɪd/ adj C1 having a good reason for something: *I accept that the criticism is completely justified.* ◦ *I think you were quite justified* ***in*** *complaining.*

justify /ˈdʒʌs.tɪ.faɪ/ verb [T] **1** B2 to give or to be a good reason for: [+ -ing verb] *I can't really justify tak****ing*** *another day off work.* ◦ *Are you sure that these measures are justified?* **2 justify yourself** B2 If you justify yourself, you give a good reason for what you have done: *It was the only thing that I could do – I don't have to justify myself* ***to*** *anyone.*

ˌjust-in-ˈtime adj (also **JIT**) A just-in-time system of MANUFACTURING (= producing goods) is based on preventing waste by producing only the amount of goods needed at a particular time, and not paying to produce and store more goods than are needed.

jut /dʒʌt/ verb [I or T, usually + adv/prep] (**-tt-**) to (cause to) stick out, especially above or past the edge or surface of something: *The pier juts* ***(out) into*** *the sea.* ◦ *He jutted his* ***chin/jaw*** *(out) defiantly.* • **jutting** /ˈdʒʌt.ɪŋ/ US /ˈdʒʌt̬-/ adj [before noun] *jutting rocks*

jute /dʒuːt/ noun [U] a substance that comes from a Southeast Asian plant, used for making rope and cloth

juvenile /ˈdʒuː.vən.aɪl/ US /-nəl/ **adj; noun**

▸adj **1** C1 formal or legal relating to a young person who is not yet old enough to be considered an adult: *juvenile crime/offenders* **2** disapproving silly and typical of a child: *juvenile behaviour*

▸noun [C] a young person

ˌjuvenile deˈlinquent noun [C] a young person who commits crimes • **ˌjuvenile deˈlinquency** noun [U]

juxtapose /ˌdʒʌk.stəˈpəʊz/ US /-ˈpoʊz/ verb [T] to put things that are not similar next to each other: *The exhibition juxtaposes Picasso's early drawings* ***with*** *some of his later works.* • **juxtaposition** /ˌdʒʌk.stə.pəˈzɪʃ.ən/ **noun** [U] *the juxtaposition* ***of*** *two very different cultures*

J

K

K, k /keɪ/ **noun LETTER** ▷ **1** [C or U] (plural **Ks, K's** or **k's**) the eleventh letter of the English alphabet **COMPUTER** ▷ **2** [C] (plural **K**) abbreviation for **kilobyte**: *a computer with 256K **of** memory* **MONEY** ▷ **3** [C] (plural **K**) informal for 1,000, especially 1,000 pounds, dollars, etc.: *His car cost him £20K.* **TEMPERATURE** ▷ **4** [after noun] abbreviation for **kelvin**: *273°K*

kabaddi /ˈkʌb.ə.di/ **noun** [U] a sport originally from South Asia for teams of seven players. A player from one team runs around and tries to catch players from the other team, and must hold his or her breath while doing so.

kabuki /kəˈbuː.ki/ **noun** [U] a type of Japanese theatre which only uses male actors, who perform in a traditional and artificial manner

ka-ching /kəˈtʃɪŋ/ **noun or exclamation** slang used for talking about large amounts of money and wanting a lot of money: *Now it's time to count up the profits. Ka-ching!*

kaftan /ˈkæf.tæn/ **noun** [C] a long, loose piece of clothing with wide sleeves, of the type worn in the Middle East

K

kagoul **noun** [C] a **cagoule**

kaizen /ˈkaɪ.zen/ **noun** [U] a Japanese way of running a company by always trying to improve the way people work and what they do

Kalashnikov /kəˈlæʃ.nɪ.kɒf/ (US) /-kɑːf/ **noun** [C] a RIFLE that can fire bullets continuously, made in Russia

kale /keɪl/ **noun** [U] a type of CABBAGE with green or purple tightly curled leaves

kaleidoscope /kəˈlaɪ.də.skəʊp/ (US) /-skoʊp/ **noun** **1** [C] a toy in the shape of a tube, that you look through to see different patterns of light made by pieces of coloured glass and mirrors **2** [S] a changing and enjoyable mixture or pattern: *The street bazaar was a kaleidoscope **of** colours, smells, and sounds.*

kaleidoscopic /kəˌlaɪ.dəˈskɒp.ɪk/ (US) /-ˈskɑː.pɪk/ **adj** quickly changing from one thing to another • **kaleidoscopically** /-ˈskɒp.ɪ.kəl.i/ (US) /-ˈskɑː.pɪ.kəl.i/ **adv**

kameez /kəˈmiːz/ **noun** [C] a type of long shirt worn by people from South Asia, often with a SALWAR or CHURIDARS

kamikaze /ˌkæm.iˈkɑː.zi/ **adj** **1** [before noun] describes a sudden violent attack on an enemy, especially one in which the person or people attacking know that they will be killed: *a kamikaze attack/mission* **2** being willing to take risks and not worrying about safety: *kamikaze taxi drivers* ◦ *a kamikaze attitude*

kangaroo /ˌkæŋ.gərˈuː/ (US) /-gəˈruː/ **noun** [C] (plural **kangaroos** or specialized **kangaroo**) (B1) a large Australian mammal with a long stiff tail, short front legs and long powerful back legs on which it moves by jumping

ˌkangaroo ˈcourt **noun** [C] an unofficial court set up by a group of people, especially in a prison, TRADE UNION, or other organization, to deal with a disagreement or with a member of the group who is considered to have broken the rules

kanji /ˈkæn.dʒi/ **noun** [U] a Japanese writing system which uses Chinese symbols

kaolin /ˈkeɪə.lɪn/ **noun** [U] a white clay used in making PORCELAIN and some medicines

kapok /ˈkeɪ.pɒk/ (US) /-pɑːk/ **noun** [U] a soft white material that is used as the filling in soft toys and CUSHIONS or for making a thick warm layer in clothes

kaput /kəˈpʊt/ **adj** [after verb] informal not working correctly: *The radio's kaput.* → Synonym **broken**

karaoke /ˌkær.iˈəʊ.ki/ (US) /ˌker.iˈoʊ.ki/ **noun** [U] a form of entertainment, originally from Japan, in which recordings of the music but not the words of popular songs are played, so that people can sing the words themselves: *a karaoke bar/machine/night*

karat /ˈkær.ət/ (US) /ˈker-/ **noun** [C] US for **carat**

karate /kəˈrɑː.ti/ (US) /-t̬i/ **noun** [U] a sport, originally from Japan, in which people fight using their arms, legs, hands, and feet. The level of skill a person has is shown by what colour belt they wear.

karma /ˈkɑː.mə/ (US) /ˈkɑːr-/ **noun** [U] (in the Buddhist and Hindu religions) the force produced by a person's actions in one of their lives which influences what happens to them in their future lives

kayak /ˈkaɪ.æk/ **noun** [C] a light narrow CANOE with a covering over the top

kayaking /ˈkaɪ.æk.ɪŋ/ **noun** [U] the activity of travelling in a kayak

kazoo /kəˈzuː/ **noun** [C] (plural **kazoos**) a small musical instrument consisting of a plastic or metal tube with a small piece of paper inside which shakes when the player HUMS (= sings with closed mouth) into it, making a high sound

KC /ˌkeɪˈsiː/ **noun** [C] abbreviation for King's Counsel: a British lawyer of high rank who is allowed to represent a person in court, or the title given to such a lawyer when a king is ruling → Compare **QC**

kebab /kɪˈbæb/ (US) /-ˈbɑːb/ **noun** [C] **1** a **shish kebab** **2** UK a **döner kebab**

kedgeree /ˈkedʒ.ər.i/ (US) /-ɚ-/ **noun** [U] a dish consisting of rice, fish, and eggs mixed together

keel /kiːl/ **noun; verb**

▸**noun** [C] the long piece of wood or metal along the bottom of a boat that forms part of its structure and helps to keep the boat balanced in the water

▸**verb**

PHRASAL VERB **keel over** **PERSON** ▷ **1** to fall over suddenly: *He finished the bottle, stood up to leave, and keeled over.* **BOAT** ▷ **2** If a boat keels over, it turns upside down in the water.

keelhaul /ˈkiːl.hɔːl/ (US) /-hɑːl/ **verb** [T] old-fashioned informal to tell someone off severely

keen /kiːn/ **adj; verb**

▸**adj** **EAGER** ▷ **1** (B1) very interested, eager, or wanting (to do) something very much: *They were very keen **to** start work as soon as possible.* ◦ *Joan wanted to go to a movie but I wasn't keen (= I didn't want to go).* ◦ *She's a keen tennis player* ◦ *She's keen **on** (playing) tennis.* ◦ UK *My son's **mad** keen on cycling.* ◦ *He's rather keen **on** a girl in his school (= he is very attracted to her).* **STRONG** ▷ **2** extreme or very strong: *Many people are taking a keen **interest** (= a very great interest) in the result of the vote.* **3** (C1) very good or well developed: *a keen sense of smell* **SHARP** ▷ **4** literary very sharp: *a keen north wind* • **keenly** /ˈkiːn.li/ **adv** *They are keenly*

(= *extremely*) ***aware*** *that this will be their last chance to succeed.*

IDIOM **(as) keen as mustard** UK old-fashioned very eager and interested in everything

▸**verb** [I] literary to make a loud, long, sad sound, especially because someone has died • **keenness** /ˈkiːn.nəs/ **noun** [U] the quality of being keen

keen /kiːp/ verb; noun

▸**verb** (**kept, kept**) **CONTINUE TO HAVE** ▷ **1** (A2) [T] to have or continue to have in your possession: *Do you want this photograph back or can I keep it?* ◦ *Keep medicines in a locked cupboard (= store them there).* → See also **well kept** **2** [T] to own and manage a small shop: *My uncle kept a little tobacconist's in Gloucester.* **3** (B2) [T] If you keep animals, you own and take care of them, but not in your home as pets: *to keep pigs/goats/chickens* **4** [T] US to watch and care for someone's children while their parents are away: *Jody will keep the children while I shop.* **5 keep your promise/word** (B2) to do what you have told someone that you would do: *I made a promise to you and I intend to keep it.* **6 keep an appointment** to go to a meeting or event that has been arranged: *She phoned to say she couldn't keep her appointment.* **7 keep a diary, an account, a record, etc.** (B2) to make a regular record of events or other information so that you can refer to it later: *I've kept a diary for twelve years now.* ◦ *Keep an account of how much you're spending.* **8 keep a secret** (B1) to not tell anyone a secret that you know **9 keep goal** to be the player who defends your team's goal by trying to prevent players from the other team scoring goals **STAY** ▷ **10** (A2) [L only + adj, T] to (cause to) stay in a particular place or condition: *I wish you'd keep quiet.* ◦ *I like to keep busy.* ◦ *Keep left (= stay on the road to the left) at the traffic lights.* ◦ *Can you keep the dog outside, please?* ◦ [+ obj + adj] *Close the door to keep the room warm.* ◦ *The noise from their party kept me awake half the night.* **CONTINUE DOING** ▷ **11** (B1) [I + -ing verb] (also **keep on**) to continue doing something without stopping, or to do it repeatedly: *He keeps try**ing** to distract me.* ◦ *I keep on think**ing** I've seen her before somewhere.* ◦ *I kept hop**ing** that he'd phone me.* **DELAY** ▷ **12** (B1) [T] to delay someone or prevent them from doing something: *He's very late, what's keeping him?* ◦ [+ -ing verb] *I'm so sorry to keep you **waiting**.* ◦ *She kept me talk**ing** on the phone for half an hour.* ◦ *I hope I'm not keeping you **up** (= preventing you from going to bed).* **STAY FRESH** ▷ **13** (B2) [I] (of food) to stay fresh and in good condition: *Milk keeps much longer in a fridge.* **PROVIDE** ▷ **14** (C1) [T] to provide yourself or another person with food, clothing, a

> **+ Other ways of saying keep**
>
> If someone keeps something somewhere until it is needed, the verb **store** is sometimes used:
>
> *I've **stored** all Helen's books in the attic.*
>
> The verb **stash** is sometimes used if someone keeps a lot of something in a secret place:
>
> *His money was **stashed** in a cupboard.*
>
> The verb **save** is often used when someone keeps something to use in the future:
>
> *I have some really good chocolates that I've been **saving** for a special occasion.*
>
> The phrasal verbs **hang onto** and **hold onto** are also often used when someone keeps something that might be needed in the future:
>
> *You should **hang/hold onto** that picture – it might be worth something.*
>
> In formal situations, you can use the word **retain**:
>
> *You should **retain** a copy of the receipt.*

home, and other things necessary for basic living: *He wanted a job that would allow him to keep his family in comfort.*

IDIOMS **how are you keeping?** mainly UK old-fashioned used to ask if someone is well: *How's your mother keeping?* • **keep up appearances** to pretend to be happier, less poor, etc. than you really are, because you do not want people to know how bad your situation is: *They were very unhappily married but kept up appearances for the sake of their children.* • **keep up with the Joneses** disapproving to always want to own the same expensive objects and do the same things as your friends or NEIGHBOURS because you are worried about seeming less important socially than they are

PHRASAL VERBS **keep (sb) at it** (C2) to continue working hard at something difficult, or to make someone continue to work hard: *I kept at it and finally finished at three o'clock in the morning.* ◦ *We need to keep her at it if she's going to pass the exam.* • **keep (sb/sth) away** (B2) to not go somewhere or near something, or to prevent someone from going somewhere or near something: *Keep away from the edge of the cliff.* • **keep (sth/sb) back** (B2) to not go near something, or to prevent someone or something from going past a particular place: *Barriers were built to keep back the flood water.* • **keep sth back NOT USE ALL** ▷ **1** to not use the whole amount of something so that there is a small amount remaining for later **NOT TELL** ▷ **2** (C2) to not tell someone everything you know about a situation or an event that has happened: *I suspect she's keeping something back.* • **keep sth down FOOD** ▷ **1** to be able to eat or drink something without vomiting: *On the day after her operation she couldn't keep anything down.* **SIZE** ▷ **2** (B2) to control the size or number of something and prevent it from increasing: *We need to work hard to keep our prices down.* • **keep sb down** to prevent a person or group of people from having any power or freedom: *It's all part of a conspiracy to keep women down.* • **keep from doing sth** to manage to prevent yourself from doing something: *I couldn't keep from smil**ing** when she told me what she'd done.* • **keep sb/sth from sth** (C2) to prevent someone or something from doing something: [+ -ing verb] *Try to keep the children from throw**ing** food all over the floor.* ◦ *Am I keeping you from your work?* • **keep sth from sb** (C2) to not tell someone about something: *He says it's alright but I think he's keeping something from me.* • **keep sb in** (B1) to make a child stay inside as a punishment, or to make someone stay in hospital: *They kept her in overnight for observation.* • **keep in with sb** to continue to try to be friendly with someone, especially because they can help you: *I like to keep in with my ex-employer, you never know when you might need a reference.* • **keep (sb/sth) off sth** (B1) to not go onto an area, or to stop someone or something going onto an area: *There was a notice saying 'Keep off the grass'.* • **keep sth off (sb/sth)** (B2) to stop something touching or harming someone or something: *Put a cloth over the salad to keep the flies off.* ◦ *Wear a hat to keep the sun off (= to prevent it harming your skin).* • **keep (sb) off sth** to not eat, drink, or use something that can harm you, or to stop someone else from doing this: *The doctor told me to keep off fatty foods.* • **keep off sth** mainly UK If you keep off a particular subject, you avoid talking about it. • **keep on doing sth** (B1) to continue to do something, or to do something again and again: *She kept on asking me questions the whole time.* • **keep on** UK informal to continue to talk in an annoying way about something: *He kept on* ***at*** *me about the money, even though I told him I hadn't got it.* • **keep (sb/sth) out** B1 to not go in a place, or to stop someone or something from going into a place: *Building work in progress. Keep out!* • **keep (sb/sth) out of sth** to avoid becoming involved in something, or to stop someone or something becoming involved in something: *I prefer to keep* ***out of*** *arguments about money.* ◦ *Keep me out of this!* • **keep to somewhere** B2 to stay in one particular area: *Please keep to the footpaths.* • **keep sth to sth** If you keep something to a particular number or amount, you make certain it does not become larger than that. • **keep sth to yourself** C2 to keep something secret: *I don't want everyone to know, so if you could keep it to yourself I'd appreciate it.* • **keep yourself to yourself** to not talk to other people very much: *He's a very private person – he keeps himself to himself.* • **keep to sth** PLAN ▷ **1** B2 to do what you have promised or planned to do: *I think we should keep to our original plan.* SUBJECT ▷ **2** B2 If you keep to a particular subject, you only talk about that subject: *For heaven's sake let's keep to* ***the point*** *or we'll never reach any decisions.* • **keep sth up** B1 to make something continue at its present level and not allow it to fall: *You must eat to keep your strength up.* • **keep (sth) up** B1 to continue without stopping or changing, or to continue something without allowing it to stop or change: *Keep up the good work!* • **keep it up** used to encourage someone to continue doing something: *You're doing very well everybody. Keep it up!* • **keep up** B2 to be able to understand or deal with something that is happening or changing very fast: *I read the papers to keep up* ***with*** *what's happening in the outside world.* • **keep up (with sb/sth)** B2 If someone or something keeps up with someone or something else, they do whatever is necessary to stay level or equal with that person or thing: *He started to walk faster and the children had to run to keep up.* ◦ *Wages are failing to keep up with inflation.*

▸noun LIVING EXPENSES ▷ **1** [U] the cost of providing food, heating, and other necessary things for someone: *He's old enough now to* ***earn*** *his keep and stop living off his parents.* TOWER ▷ **2** [C] specialized the strong main tower of a castle

keeper /ˈkiː.pəʳ/ US /-pɚ/ noun [C] **1** B1 a person who takes care of animals or is in charge of valuable objects, a building, etc.: *a zoo keeper* ◦ *a lighthouse-keeper* **2** B1 UK informal a **goalkeeper**

ˌkeep-ˈfit noun [U] UK physical exercises to keep your body healthy, often done regularly with other people: *a keep-fit class*

keeping /ˈkiː.pɪŋ/ noun **1 in your keeping** If something is in your keeping, you are taking care of it: *I left my car in her keeping when I went abroad.* **2 in safe keeping** being carefully taken care of: *I left my son in safe keeping with my mother.*

IDIOM **in/out of keeping (with sth)** suitable or not suitable for a particular situation: *In keeping with tradition, they always have turkey on Christmas Day.* ◦ *The modern furniture was out of keeping with the old house.*

keepnet /ˈkiːp.net/ noun [C] a cone-shaped net that is put in a river and used for keeping fish alive after they have been caught

keeps /kiːps/ noun [plural] informal **for keeps** for ever: *'Do you want it back?' 'No it's yours, for keeps.'*

keepsake /ˈkiːp.seɪk/ noun [C] a small present, usually not expensive, that is given to you by someone so that you will remember that person

keg /keg/ noun [C] a small BARREL usually used for storing beer or other alcoholic drinks

ˈkeg ˌparty noun [C] US a party in which people drink beer that is poured from kegs rather than bottles or other containers

kelly green /ˌkel.iˈgriːn/ noun [U] US a bright, strong green colour • **ˌkelly-ˈgreen adj**

kelp /kelp/ noun [U] a large, brown plant that grows in the sea, used in some foods and medicines

kelvin /ˈkel.vɪn/ noun [C or U] (written abbreviation **K**) a standard unit of temperature. One degree kelvin is equal to one degree CELSIUS.

ken /ken/ noun; verb

▸noun old-fashioned **beyond your ken** not in your area of knowledge: *Financial matters are beyond my ken, I'm afraid.*

▸verb [I or T, not continuous] (-nn-) Scottish English to know someone or something

kennel /ˈken.əl/ noun [C] **1** (US usually **doghouse**) a small, usually wooden shelter for a dog to sleep in outside **2** US (UK **kennels**) a place where people leave their dogs to be taken care of while they are away, or a place where dogs are bred: *We left our dog* ***in*** *kennels when we went away.*

kennel

kept /kept/ verb; adj

▸verb past simple and past participle of **keep**

▸adj usually humorous **kept woman/man** someone who does not work but is instead given money and a place to live by the person she or he is having a sexual relationship with

keratin /ˈker.ə.tɪn/ noun [U] specialized a strong natural PROTEIN, the main substance that forms hair, nails, HOOFS, horns, feathers, etc.

kerb /kɜːb/ US /kɝːb/ noun [C] UK (US **curb**) the edge of a raised path nearest the road

ˈkerb-ˌcrawling noun [U] UK the activity of driving slowly along a road close to the path at the side in order to ask PROSTITUTES for sex

kerbside /ˈkɜːb.saɪd/ US /ˈkɝːb-/ noun [C usually singular] UK (US **curbside**) the area near where a road and the raised path next to it join

kerchief /ˈkɜː.tʃɪf/ US /ˈkɝː-/ noun [C] old use a square piece of cloth worn around the neck or on the head

kerfuffle /kəˈfʌf.l̩/ US /kɚ-/ noun [S] UK informal noise, excitement, and argument: *Her glasses were broken in the kerfuffle.*

kernel /ˈkɜː.nəl/ US /ˈkɝː-/ noun [C] PLANT PART ▷ **1** the part of a nut that is inside the shell and can be eaten **2** the whole seed of the MAIZE plant IMPORTANT PART ▷ **3** the most important part of something, although it might not always be easy to find: *There is often a kernel* ***of truth*** *in what they say.*

kerosene /ˈker.ə.siːn/ noun [U] mainly US for **paraffin**, especially when used as fuel in HEATERS and lights

kestrel /ˈkes.trəl/ noun [C] a type of small FALCON (= a bird that eats meat)

ketchup /ˈketʃ.ʌp/ noun [U] (UK **tomato ketchup**, US also **catsup**) a thick, cold, red sauce made from tomatoes: *Do you want some ketchup with your burger?*

ketone /ˈkiː.təʊn/ US /-toʊn/ noun [C] a type of chemical COMPOUND containing carbon, that is produced in the body when it burns fat

kettle /ˈket.l̩/ (US) /ˈket̬-/ **noun; verb**
▸**noun** [C] **EQUIPMENT** ▷ **1** a container for boiling water, that has a lid, handle, and SPOUT and is made from plastic or metal **2 put the kettle on** (B1) to start to boil water in a kettle **POLICE** ▷ **3** an occasion when police form lines around a crowd of people and prevent them from leaving a particular area

IDIOM **be another/a different kettle of fish** to be completely different from something or someone else that has been talked about: *Having knowledge is one thing but being able to communicate it to others is another kettle of fish.*

▸**verb** [T] If the police kettle a crowd of people, they form lines around them and prevent them from leaving a particular area.

kettledrum /ˈket.l̩.drʌm/ (US) /ˈket̬-/ **noun** [C] a very large drum with a round bottom that is played especially in an ORCHESTRA → See also **timpani**

kettling /ˈket.lɪŋ/ (US) /ˈket̬-/ **noun** [U] a method of controlling a crowd in which police form lines around the crowd and prevent them from leaving a particular area

key /kiː/ **noun; adj; verb**
▸**noun** [C] **LOCK** ▷ **1** (A1) a piece of metal that has been cut into a special shape and is used for opening or closing a lock, starting a car engine, etc.: *car/door keys* **PART** ▷ **2** (B2) any of the set of moving parts that you press with your fingers on a computer keyboard, or musical instrument to produce letters, numbers, symbols, or musical notes **MUSICAL NOTES** ▷ **3** a set of musical notes based on one particular note: *The song changes key halfway through.* ◦ *the key of C minor* **SYMBOLS** ▷ **4** a list of the symbols used in a map or book with explanations of what they mean **ANSWERS** ▷ **5** (A2) a list of the answers to the questions in an exercise or test: *See the key to test 3 on page 176.*

IDIOM **the key to sth** (B1) the best or only way to achieve something: *Hard work is the key to success.*

▸**adj** (B2) very important and having a lot of influence on other people or things: *She was a key figure in the international art world.* ◦ *a key factor in tackling the problem*
▸**verb**

PHRASAL VERBS **key sth in** (B2) to put information into a computer or a machine using a keyboard → Synonym **keyboard** • **key sth to sb** [usually passive] to arrange or plan something so that it is suitable for a particular person or situation

keyboard /ˈkiː.bɔːd/ (US) /-bɔːrd/ **noun; verb**
▸**noun** [C] **1** (A2) the set of keys on a computer or TYPEWRITER that you press in order to make it work, or the row of keys on a musical instrument such as a piano **2** (A2) an electronic musical instrument similar to a piano
▸**verb** [I or T] to put information into a computer using a keyboard

keyboarder /ˈkiːˌbɔː.dəʳ/ (US) /-ˌbɔːr.dɚ/ **noun** [C] someone whose job is to put information into a computer using a keyboard

keyboardist /ˈkiːˌbɔː.dɪst/ (US) /-ˌbɔːr-/ **noun** [C] a person who plays an electronic musical instrument that has a keyboard

keycard /ˈkiː.kɑːd/ (US) /-kɑːrd/ **noun** [C] a small, plastic electronic card that is used instead of a key to open a door

ˌkeyed ˈup **adj** [after verb] very excited or nervous, usually before an important event: *He always gets keyed up about exams.*

keyhole /ˈkiː.həʊl/ (US) /-hoʊl/ **noun** [C] a hole in a lock that you put a key into

ˌkeyhole ˈsurgery **noun** [U] (also **ˈkeyhole opeˈration** [C]) a medical operation in which a very small hole is made in a person's body to reach the organ or tissue inside

Keynesian /ˈkeɪn.zi.ən/ **adj** specialized relating to the economic principles of John Maynard Keynes, especially the importance of having government plans to create jobs and encourage spending: *a proponent of Keynesian* ***economics***

keynote /ˈkiː.nəʊt/ (US) /-noʊt/ **noun** [C] the most important or most emphasized part of something: *This issue has become the keynote of the election campaign.* ◦ *a keynote address/speech/speaker (= an important talk/speaker at a formal meeting)*

keypad /ˈkiː.pæd/ **noun** [C] a small set of keys with numbers on them used to operate a television, phone, CALCULATOR, etc., or the keys with numbers on them usually found on the right side of a computer keyboard

ˈkey ˌring **noun** [C] a metal or plastic ring used for keeping your keys together

key ring

ˈkey ˌsignature **noun** [C] the symbols at the beginning of a printed piece of music that show the SHARPS or FLATS to be played

keystone /ˈkiː.stəʊn/ (US) /-stoʊn/ **noun** [C] **STONE** ▷ **1** the middle stone in the top of an ARCH that has a special shape and holds all the other stones in position **IMPORTANT PART** ▷ **2** the most important part of a plan, idea, etc. on which everything else depends

keyword /ˈkiː.wɜːd/ (US) /-wɝːd/ **noun** [C] a word that you type into a computer so that the computer will find information that contains that word: *A quick search* ***by*** *keyword tracks down the book's title and author.*

kg written abbreviation for **kilogram**

khaki /ˈkɑː.ki/ **noun; adj**
▸**noun** [U] **1** dark, yellowish-green cloth, often worn by soldiers **2** a dark, yellowish-green colour, often worn by soldiers
▸**adj** of a dark, yellowish-green colour

kharif /kæˈriːf/ **noun** [U] Indian English a crop that is planted before the MONSOON (= the season of heavy rain during the summer) then cut and collected in autumn

kHz written abbreviation for **kilohertz**

kibbutz /kɪˈbʊts/ **noun** [C] (plural **kibbutzim**) a farm or factory in Israel where profits and duties are shared and all work is considered equally important: *to work* ***on*** *a kibbutz*

kibosh /ˈkaɪ.bɒʃ/ (US) /-bɑːʃ/ **noun** informal **put the kibosh on sth** to spoil or destroy an idea or plan: *The rain certainly put the kibosh on our plans for a picnic.*

kick /kɪk/ **verb; noun**
▸**verb 1** (A1) [I or T] to hit someone or something with the foot, or to move the feet and legs suddenly and violently: *I kicked the ball as hard as I could.* ◦ *He was accused of kicking a man* ***in*** *the face.* ◦ *She felt the baby kicking inside her.* **2** [I] If a gun kicks, it jumps back suddenly and with force when the gun is FIRED. **3 be kicking yourself/could have kicked yourself** (C2)

K

used to say that you are very annoyed with yourself because you have done something stupid or missed a chance: *When I realized what I'd done I could have kicked myself.* ◦ *They must be kicking themselves for selling their shares too early.*

IDIOMS **kick (some) ass** mainly US offensive to punish someone or to defeat someone with a lot of force: *We're gonna go in there and kick ass.* • **kick the bucket** (US **kick off**) to die • **kick the habit** informal to give up something harmful that you have done for a long time: *She used to be a heavy smoker but she kicked the habit last year.* • **kick your heels** UK informal to be forced to wait for a period of time • **kick sth into touch** UK informal to decide not to do what you had planned to do: *Our plans to buy a new car have had to be kicked into touch now Kev's lost his job.* • **kick over the traces** old-fashioned informal to behave badly and show no respect for authority • **kick the tires** US informal to try something or examine it carefully before you buy it: *Come and kick the tires on this latest version of the software.* • **kick up a fuss/row/stink** informal to show great anger about something, especially when this does not seem necessary: *He kicked up a tremendous fuss about having to wait.* • **kick up your heels** US informal to do things that you enjoy: *After the exams we kicked up our heels and had a really good party.* • **kick sb upstairs** to give someone a new job which seems more powerful but is really less powerful, usually in order to stop them causing trouble for you

K

PHRASAL VERBS **kick about/around** informal If something is kicking around a place, it is somewhere in that place, not being used: *There must be a copy of it kicking around the office somewhere.* • **kick against sth** UK informal to refuse to accept something and react strongly against it: *As a boy he always kicked against his father's authority.* • **kick sth around** informal If you kick ideas around, you talk about them informally in a group: *We need to get everyone together and kick a few **ideas** around* • **kick in** informal C1 to start to have an effect or to happen: *It takes half an hour for the tablets to kick in.* • **kick off** FOOTBALL ▷ **1** C1 If a game of football kicks off, it starts: *What time does the match kick off?* → See also **kick-off** COMPLAIN ▷ **2** informal to start to get angry or complain in a noisy way: *The children started to kick off so I couldn't stay.* • **kick (sth) off** C2 If you kick off a discussion or an activity, you start it: *I'd like to kick off the discussion **with** a few statistics.* ◦ *Right, any suggestions? Jim, you kick off.* • **kick sb out** informal C1 to force someone to leave a place or organization: *His wife kicked him out.* ◦ *She was kicked out of the squad.*

▸noun HIT ▷ **1** A2 [C] the action of kicking something: *He gave the ball a good kick.* STRONG FEELING ▷ **2** C2 [C] a strong feeling of excitement and pleasure: *I **get a** real kick **out of** winning a race.* ◦ *He decided to steal something from the shop, just **for** kicks (= because he thought it would be exciting).* **3** [C usually singular] informal the strong effect of an alcoholic drink: *Watch out for the fruit punch, it's got a **real** kick.* INTEREST ▷ **4** [C usually singular] informal a new interest, especially one that does not last long: *He's **on an** exercise kick (= he exercises a lot) at the moment.*

IDIOMS **kick in the teeth** informal If you describe the way someone treats you as a kick in the teeth, you mean that they treat you badly and unfairly, especially at a time when you need their support. • **a kick up the arse/backside** UK (US **a kick in the butt/pants**) If you give someone a kick up the arse, you do or say something to try to stop them being lazy.

kickabout /ˈkɪk.ə.baʊt/ noun [C usually singular] UK informal an occasion when a group of people kick a ball to each other for pleasure

ˈ**kick-ass** (also **kickass**) adj informal very exciting or forceful: *They play kick-ass rock and roll.*

kickback /ˈkɪk.bæk/ noun [C] an amount of money that is paid to someone illegally in exchange for secret help or work

kickboxing /ˈkɪk.bɒk.sɪŋ/ US /-bɑː-/ noun [U] a sport in which two competitors fight by hitting each other with their hands and kicking each other with their feet

ˈ**kick-off** (US **kickoff**) noun [C or U] **1** UK the time when a game of football starts, or when it begins again after it has stopped because of a goal, etc. → See also **kick off 2** informal the time when an activity starts

ˈ**kick-start** verb; noun

▸verb [T] MOTORCYCLE ▷ **1** to make the engine of a motorcycle start by forcefully pushing down a metal bar with your foot HELP ▷ **2** to make something start to happen: *Taxes were drastically cut in an attempt to kick-start the economy.*

▸noun [C] a metal bar that you push down forcefully with your foot to make the engine of a motorcycle start

kid /kɪd/ noun; verb

▸noun CHILD ▷ **1** B1 [C] informal a child: *He took the kids to the park while I was working.* **2** [C] informal a young person: *He was only 16, just a kid really.* ◦ [as form of address] *What's up, kid?* **3 sb's kid sister/brother** mainly US informal someone's younger sister or brother **4 be like a kid in a candy store** US and Australian English to be very happy and excited about the things around you, and often react to them in a way that is silly and not controlled: *You should have seen him when they arrived. He was like a kid in a candy store.*

> **!** Common mistake: **kid**
>
> **Remember: kid** is only used in informal English. In ordinary or more formal language, don't say 'kid', say **child**.

ANIMAL ▷ **5** [C] a young GOAT **6** [U] very soft leather made from the skin of a kid: *kid gloves*

IDIOM **handle/treat sb with kid gloves** to be very polite or kind to someone because you do not want to make them angry or upset

▸verb [I or T] (-dd-) informal **1** to say something as a joke, often making someone believe something that is not true: *Oh no, I've forgotten your birthday! Hey, **just/only** kidding!* ◦ *You won first prize? You're kidding!* (= *I'm really surprised.*) ◦ *I'm just kidding you!* **2 kid yourself** to believe something that is not true, usually because you want it to be true: *He says there's a good chance she'll come back to him but I think he's kidding himself.*

IDIOM **no kidding** (also **I kid you not**) used when you are surprised by what someone has just said: *Dean was there? No kidding!*

PHRASAL VERB **kid around** US informal to be silly or not serious: *Stop kidding around and listen to me!*

kiddie (also **kiddy**) /ˈkɪd.i/ noun [C] informal a young child

kidnap /ˈkɪd.næp/ verb; noun

▸verb [T] (-pp-) to take a person away illegally by force, usually in order to demand money in exchange for releasing them: *The wife of a businessman has been kidnapped from her home in Surrey.*

▸noun [C or U] the crime of taking someone away by force and demanding money in exchange for releasing them • **kidnapper** (US also **kidnaper**) /-əʳ/ (US) /-ɚ/ noun [C]

kidnapping /ˈkɪd.næp.ɪŋ/ **noun** [C or U] an occasion when someone is kidnapped

kidney /ˈkɪd.ni/ **noun** **1** C2 [C] either of a pair of small organs in the body which take away waste matter from the blood to produce urine: *kidney failure* **2** [C or U] these organs from an animal, used as food: *steak and kidney pie*

ˈkidney ˌbean **noun** [C usually plural] a small, dark red bean that has a curved shape like a kidney and can be eaten

ˈkidney maˌchine **noun** [C] a machine used to do the work of a human kidney for people whose kidneys have stopped working or have been removed → See also **dialysis**

ˈkidney ˌstone **noun** [C] a solid mass of hard material that can form in the kidney and cause pain

ˈkids' stuff **noun** [U] UK (US **ˈkid stuff**) an activity or piece of work that is very easy: *A five-mile bike ride? That's kids' stuff.*

kidult /ˈkɪd.ʌlt/ **noun** [C] informal an adult who likes doing or buying things that are intended for children

kike /kaɪk/ **noun** [C] US offensive a JEWISH person

kill /kɪl/ **verb; noun**

▸verb **DEATH** ▷ **1** A2 [I or T] to cause someone or something to die: *Her parents were killed in a plane crash.* ◦ *Smoking can kill.* ◦ *Food must be heated to a high temperature to kill harmful bacteria.* **FINISH** ▷ **2** C2 [T] to stop or destroy a relationship, activity, or experience: *Lack of romance can kill a marriage.* ◦ *They've given her some tablets to kill the pain.* ◦ *Kill your speed.* **3** [T] (also **kill off**) mainly US informal to drink all of something: *We killed off two six-packs watching the game.* **EFFORT** ▷ **4** C1 [T] informal to cause someone a lot of effort or difficulty: *It wouldn't kill you to apologize.* ◦ *He didn't exactly kill him**self** trying to get the work finished.* **HURT** ▷ **5** [T] informal to cause someone a lot of pain: *I must sit down, my feet are killing me!* **ANGER** ▷ **6** A2 [T] informal If you say that someone will kill you, you mean that they will be very angry with you: *My sister would kill me if she heard me say that.* **ENTERTAIN** ▷ **7** [T] mainly US informal to make someone laugh a lot: *That comedian kills me.* **8** **kill yourself** informal to laugh very much: *We were killing ourselves **laughing**.*

IDIOMS **kill sb with kindness** to be too kind to someone, harming them because you are helping or giving them too much • **kill the fatted calf** to have a special celebration for someone who has been away for a long time • **kill the goose that lays the golden egg** to destroy something that makes a lot of money for you • **kill time, an hour, etc.** B2 to do something that keeps you busy while you are waiting for something else to happen: *The train was late, so I killed an hour or so window-shopping.* • **kill two birds with one stone** to succeed in achieving two things in a single action: *I killed two birds with one stone and picked the kids up on the way to the station.*

PHRASAL VERB **kill sth off** to destroy something completely, usually over a period of time: *The use of pesticides is killing off wildlife.* ◦ figurative *Lack of funding is killing off small theatres.*

▸noun [C usually singular] an animal or bird that has been hunted and killed, or the action of killing: *The leopard seizes its kill and begins to eat.* ◦ *Like other birds of prey, it quickly **moves in for the** kill.*

IDIOMS **be in at the kill** to be present at the end of an unpleasant process • **kill or cure** UK a way of solving a problem that will either fail completely or be very successful: *Having a baby can be kill or cure for a troubled marriage.* • **move/go in for the kill** to prepare to defeat someone in an argument or competition when they are already in a weak position: *He asked her a couple of difficult questions and then went in for the kill.*

killer /ˈkɪl.əʳ/ (US) /-ɚ/ **noun** **DEATH** ▷ **1** B1 [C] someone who kills another person: *Police are still hoping to find the dead woman's killer.* **2** [C] something that kills people, especially a disease or other illness: *Cancer and heart disease are the UK's biggest killers.* **3** [C] something that destroys something: *This chemical is found in most weedkillers.* **EFFORT** ▷ **4** [S] informal something that is very difficult: *The last question was a real killer.* **AMUSEMENT** ▷ **5** [C] US and Australian English informal a very entertaining or skilful person, story, or performance: *Dizzy was a **real** killer on the trumpet.* • **killer** adj [before noun] *a killer disease* ◦ *killer bees*

ˌkiller ˈapp **noun** [C] (also **ˌkiller appliˈcation**) **1** a computer program that is much better than all others of its type **2** a use for a particular TECHNOLOGY that becomes extremely popular: *Many software companies and internet providers believe that e-learning is the next killer app.*

ˈkiller ˌinstinct **noun** [C usually singular] a way of behaving in order to achieve an advantage for yourself without considering or worrying if it hurts other people

ˈkiller ˌwhale **noun** [C] (also **orca**) a large, black and white sea mammal related to DOLPHINS

killing /ˈkɪl.ɪŋ/ **noun; adj**

▸noun [C] B1 an occasion when a person is murdered: *a series of brutal killings*

IDIOM **make a killing** informal to earn a lot of money in a short time and with little effort: *They made a killing with the sale of their London house.*

▸adj **EFFORT** ▷ **1** informal making you feel extremely tired **FUNNY** ▷ **2** old-fashioned extremely funny: *She told us a killing story about her driving test.*

killjoy /ˈkɪl.dʒɔɪ/ **noun** [C] disapproving a person who does not like other people enjoying themselves

kiln /kɪln/ **noun** [C] a type of large oven used for making bricks and clay objects hard after they have been shaped

kilo /ˈkiː.ləʊ/ (US) /-loʊ/ **noun** [C] (plural **kilos**) A2 a kilogram: *a 200 kilo block of concrete*

kilo- /kɪl.ə-/ **prefix** Kilo- means 1,000 times the stated unit of measurement: *kilowatt* ◦ *kilohertz*

kilobyte /ˈkɪl.ə.baɪt/ **noun** [C] (abbreviation **KB**) a unit of measurement of computer memory consisting of 1,024 BYTES: *a 20-kilobyte file*

kilogram /ˈkɪl.ə.græm/ **noun** [C] (written abbreviation **kg**) A2 a unit of mass equal to 1,000 grams

kilohertz /ˈkɪl.ə.hɜːts/ (US) /-hɝːts/ **noun** [C] (plural **kilohertz**) (written abbreviation **kHz**) a unit of measurement of radio waves that is equal to 1,000 HERTZ

kilojoule /ˈkɪl.əʊ.dʒuːl/ (US) /-oʊ-/ **noun** [C] (written abbreviation **kJ**) a unit of measurement equal to 1,000 JOULES (= measure of energy or work done)

kilometre UK (US **kilometer**) /ˈkɪl.əˌmiː.təʳ/ (US) /kɪˈlɑː.mə.t̬ɚ/ **noun** [C] (written abbreviation **km**) A2 a unit of measurement equal to 1,000 metres

K

kilowatt /ˈkɪl.ə.wɒt/ (US) /-wɑːt/ **noun** [C] (written abbreviation **kW**) a unit of power equal to 1,000 WATTS

kilt /kɪlt/ **noun** [C] a skirt with many folds, made from TARTAN cloth and traditionally worn by Scottish men and boys

kilter /ˈkɪl.təʳ/ (US) /-t̬ɚ/ **noun** informal **out of kilter** in a state of not working well: *Missing more than one night's sleep can throw your body out of kilter.*

kimono /kɪˈməʊ.nəʊ/ (US) /-ˈmoʊ.noʊ/ **noun** [C] (plural **kimonos**) a long loose piece of outer clothing with very wide sleeves, traditionally worn by the Japanese

kimono

kin /kɪn/ **noun** [plural] **1** old-fashioned family and relations **2 next of kin** formal your closest relation or relations: *We can't release his name until we have informed his next of kin.*

kinaesthesia UK (US **kinesthesia**) /ˌkɪn.iːsˈθiː.zi.ə/ **noun** [U] the ability to know where the parts of your body are and how they are moving • **kinaesthetic** (US **kinesthetic**) /-ˈθet.ɪk/ (US) /-ˈθet̬.ɪk/ **adj** *kinaesthetic sensations*

kind /kaɪnd/ **adj**; **noun**

▸**adj 1** (A2) generous, helpful, and thinking about other people's feelings: *She's a very kind and thoughtful person.* ◦ *It's really kind **of** you to help us.* ◦ *Please be kind **to** your sister!* ◦ formal *Would you be kind **enough** to/so kind **as** to close the door?* (= please would you do this) **2** not causing harm or damage: *kind to the environment* ◦ *This soap is kinder to the skin.*

> **Other ways of saying kind**
>
> The adjectives **nice** and **sweet** are common alternatives to 'kind':
>
> *It was really **nice** of you to come.*
>
> *Wasn't it **sweet** of Heidi to call?*
>
> If someone is **good to** you, that person does things to help you:
>
> *Jay's mother has been very **good to** us.*
>
> If someone is very willing to help, you can describe that person as **helpful**:
>
> *The staff here are very **helpful**.*
>
> Someone who is **caring** is kind to other people and tries to make them happy and well:
>
> *I've always thought of Jack as a very **caring** person.*
>
> You can describe someone who is kind and always thinks about other people's feelings as **thoughtful** or **considerate**:
>
> *Thank you for phoning when I was ill – it was very **thoughtful** of you.*
>
> *He's always very polite and **considerate**.*
>
> The expression **mean well** is sometimes used to describe a person who tries to be kind and help but who does not improve a situation:
>
> *I know my parents **mean well**, but I do wish they wouldn't interfere.*

▸**noun** [C] (A1) a group with similar characteristics, or a particular type: *Today's vehicles use two kinds **of** fuel – petrol and diesel.* ◦ *What kind **of** (a) job are you looking for?* ◦ *I just don't have that kind **of** money* (= I haven't got so much money). ◦ *The cupboard contained **all** kinds **of** strange things.* ◦ *Her travel company was the first **of its kind*** (= of others that are similar).

> **Common mistake: kind or kinds?**
>
> **Remember:** use the plural form, **kinds**, after plural words like 'all', 'these', and 'many'.
>
> Don't say 'all/these/many kind of sth', say **all/these/many kinds of sth**:
>
> ~~*I like listening to all kind of music.*~~
>
> *I like listening to all kinds of music.*

IDIOMS **in kind 1** (of payment) given in the form of goods or services and not money: *She wouldn't take any money but said I could pay her in kind by lending her the car.* **2** formal If you do something in kind, you do the same thing to someone that they have just done to you. • **kind of** informal used when you are trying to explain or describe something, but you cannot be exact: *It was kind of strange to see him again.* → See also **kinda** • **of a kind** (B2) used to describe something that exists but is not very good: *The school had a swimming pool of a kind, but it was too small for most classes to use.* • **of the kind** like or similar to what has been said: *'You said I was fat.' 'I didn't say anything of the kind!'*

kinda /ˈkaɪ.ndə/ **adv** not standard used in writing to represent an informal way of saying 'kind of': *I was kinda sorry to see him go.*

kindergarten /ˈkɪn.dəˌgɑː.tᵊn/ (US) /-dɚˌgɑːr-/ **noun** [C or U] **1** mainly US the first year of school, for children aged five **2** UK for **nursery school**

ˌkind-ˈhearted **adj** A kind-hearted person is one who likes other people a lot and always wants to help them. → Compare **hard-hearted**

kindle /ˈkɪn.dl̩/ **verb** FIRE ▷ **1** [T] to cause a fire to start burning by lighting paper, wood, etc. FEELING ▷ **2** [T often passive] literary to cause strong feelings or ideas in someone: *Her imagination was kindled by the exciting stories her grandmother told her.*

kindling /ˈkɪnd.lɪŋ/ **noun** [U] small dry sticks or other materials used to start a fire

kindly /ˈkaɪnd.li/ **adv**; **adj**

▸**adv 1** (B1) in a kind way: *Stella has very kindly offered to help out with the food for the party.* **2** old-fashioned formal used when asking someone to do something, especially when you are annoyed with them but still want to be polite: *You are kindly requested to leave the building.*

IDIOM **not take kindly to sth** (C2) to not like something: *After years of being looked after by his mother, he didn't take kindly to being told to cook for himself.*

▸**adj** old-fashioned A kindly person or action is a kind one: *a kindly old lady*

kindness /ˈkaɪnd.nəs/ **noun 1** (B2) [U] the quality of being kind: *love and kindness* **2** [C] a kind action: *I wanted to thank them for all their kindnesses.*

kindred spirit /ˌkɪn.drədˈspɪr.ɪt/ **noun** [C] old-fashioned a person who has the same opinions, feelings, and interests as you

kinetic /kɪˈnet.ɪk/ (US) /-ˈnet̬-/ **adj** [before noun] specialized involving or producing movement: *kinetic energy*

kinetics /kɪˈnet.ɪks/ (US) /-ˈnet̬-/ **noun** [U] specialized the scientific study of forces on things that are moving

kinfolk /ˈkɪn.fəʊk/ (US) /-foʊk/ **noun** [plural] (UK also **kinsfolk**) members of the same family

king /kɪŋ/ noun; adj

▸noun [C] MALE RULER ▷ **1** (A2) (the title of) a male ruler of a country, who holds this position because of his royal birth: *King Richard II* ◦ *the kings and queens of England* MOST IMPORTANT ▷ **2** (C1) the most important, best, or most respected member of a group of animals, things or people: *The lion is often called the king of the jungle.* ◦ *He's the new king of pop music.* GAMES ▷ **3** In the game of CHESS, the king is the most important piece on the board. It can move one square in any direction. **4** a card with a picture of a king on it, used in games: *the king of hearts*

IDIOM **a king's ransom** a large amount of money: *That diamond necklace must have cost a king's ransom.*

▸adj [before noun] used as part of the name of something that is larger than the ordinary type: *king prawns* ◦ *a king penguin*

kingdom /ˈkɪŋ.dəm/ noun [C] **1** (B2) a country ruled by a king or queen: *the United Kingdom of Great Britain and Northern Ireland* **2** an area that is controlled by a particular person or where a particular quality is important: *the kingdom of God/Heaven* **3** (C2) one of the groups that natural things can be divided into, depending on their type: *the animal/plant kingdom*

IDIOMS **blast/blow sb/sth to kingdom come** to destroy someone or something completely using a gun or bomb: *The bombs are capable of blasting a whole city to kingdom come.* • **till/until kingdom come** for ever: *I don't want to have to wait till kingdom come for you to make up your mind.*

kingfisher /ˈkɪŋˌfɪʃ.əʳ/ (US) /-ɚ/ noun [C] a small brightly coloured bird with a long pointed beak, which lives near rivers and lakes and eats fish

kingmaker /ˈkɪŋˌmeɪ.kəʳ/ (US) /-kɚ/ noun [C] a person who influences the choice of people for powerful positions within an organization

kingpin /ˈkɪŋ.pɪn/ noun [C] the most important person within a particular organization

ˌKing's ˈevidence noun [U] UK the phrase used for QUEEN'S EVIDENCE when a king is ruling the United Kingdom

kingship /ˈkɪŋ.ʃɪp/ noun [U] formal being a king: *the duties of kingship*

kingside /ˈkɪŋ.saɪd/ noun [U] specialized (in the game of CHESS) the side of the board where your king is at the start of the game • **kingside** adj

ˈking-size adj (also **ˈking-sized**) If something is king-size or king-sized, it is larger than the ordinary size: *a king-size bed/hamburger*

kink /kɪŋk/ noun [C] TWIST ▷ **1** an unwanted twist or bend in a wire, rope, pipe, etc. that is usually straight: *There must be a kink **in** the pipe.* **2** US a sore muscle, especially in the neck or back PROBLEM ▷ **3** something that is wrong: *Pete still needs to **iron out** a few kinks in his game.* HABIT ▷ **4** a strange habit

kinky /ˈkɪŋ.ki/ adj informal unusual, strange, and possibly exciting, especially in ways involving unusual sexual acts: *kinky ideas/behaviour*

kinship /ˈkɪn.ʃɪp/ noun [U] **1** the relationship between members of the same family: *Different ethnic groups have different systems of kinship.* **2** a feeling of being close or similar to other people or things: *He felt a real sense of kinship **with** his fellow soldiers.*

kinsman /ˈkɪnz.mən/ noun [C] (plural **-men** /-mən/) formal or old use someone who belongs to the same family

kinswoman /ˈkɪnzˌwʊm.ən/ noun [C] (plural **-women** /-wɪmɪn/) a female kinsman

kiosk /ˈkiː.ɒsk/ (US) /-ɑːsk/ noun [C] **1** a small building where things such as sweets, drinks, or newspapers are sold through an open window: *a station kiosk* **2** (also **telephone kiosk**) UK formal a **telephone box**

kip /kɪp/ verb; noun

▸verb [I usually + adv/prep] (**-pp-**) UK informal to sleep, especially in a place that is not your home: *You can have my bed and I'll kip (**down**) on the sofa.*

▸noun [S or U] UK informal sleep: *I must **get** some kip.* ◦ *I **had a** quick kip after lunch.*

kipper /ˈkɪp.əʳ/ (US) /-ɚ/ noun [C] a HERRING (= type of fish) that has been preserved by being treated with salt and then with smoke

kir /kɪəʳ/ (US) /kɪr/ noun [C or U] a drink consisting of a mixture of white wine and an alcoholic BLACKCURRANT drink

kirk /kɜːk/ (US) /kɝːk/ noun [C] **1** Scottish English a church **2 the Kirk** the Church of Scotland

kirpan /kɪəˈpɑːn/ (US) /kɪr-/ noun [C] a knife with a curved blade that some Sikh men wear as a sign of their religion

kirsch /kɪəʃ/ (US) /kɪrʃ/ noun [C or U] a strong alcoholic drink made from CHERRIES

kiss /kɪs/ verb; noun

▸verb **1** (A2) [I or T] to touch with your lips, especially as a greeting, or to press your mouth onto another person's mouth in a sexual way: *There was a young couple on the sofa, kissing passionately.* ◦ *She kissed him **on** the mouth.* ◦ [+ two objects] *He kissed the children **good night/goodbye*** (= kissed them as a part of saying good night/goodbye). **2** [T] literary to gently touch something: *The breeze/sun kissed her bare shoulders.* **3 kiss sth better** If you tell a child you will kiss a part of the body that hurts better, you mean you will make it feel better by kissing it: *'Mummy, I hurt my knee.' 'Come here, darling, and let me kiss it better.'*

IDIOMS **kiss and tell** to talk on television, in a newspaper, etc. about a sexual relationship you have had with a famous person, especially in order to get a lot of money → See also **kiss-and-tell** • **kiss sb's arse** UK (US **kiss sb's ass**) to be very nice to someone in order to get an advantage • **kiss ass** mainly US offensive to be very nice to someone in authority because you want them to help you • **kiss sth goodbye** (also **kiss goodbye to sth**) to accept that you have lost something or that you will not be able to have something: *If France lose this game, they can kiss their chances of winning the cup goodbye.* • **kiss my arse!** UK (US **kiss my ass!**) used to tell someone that you will not do what they want you to do

▸noun [C] (A2) an act of kissing someone: ***Give** your granny a kiss.* ◦ *a kiss **on** the lips*

IDIOMS **kiss of death** informal If you describe something as the kiss of death, you mean that it is certain to cause something else to fail: *Rain is the kiss of death for a barbecue.* • **the kiss of life** mainly UK informal **artificial respiration**

ˌkiss-and-ˈtell adj [before noun] A kiss-and-tell book, newspaper story, etc. is one in which someone talks about a sexual relationship they have had with a famous person, especially so they can get a lot of money: *She did a kiss-and-tell interview for a local newspaper.* • **ˌkiss-and-ˈtell** noun [C] a kiss-and-tell story, book, etc.: *She was upset by her last boyfriend's kiss-and-tell.*

ˈkiss ˌcurl noun [C] UK (US **ˈspit ˌcurl**) a curved piece of hair that hangs flat against the face on the cheek or FOREHEAD (= part of the face above the eyes)

K

kissogram (also **kissagram**) /ˈkɪs.ə.græm/ noun [C] a message brought by someone who kisses the person who is receiving it, especially one which other people have arranged to be sent as a surprise to that person on a day when they are celebrating something

kit /kɪt/ noun; verb

▸noun **1** B1 [C] a set of things, such as tools or clothes, used for a particular purpose or activity: *a first-aid/tool kit* ◦ *a pregnancy-testing kit* **2** [C] a set of parts sold ready to be put together: *He's making a model car from a kit.* **3** A2 [U] mainly UK the particular clothing worn by a sports team, or the particular clothing and small pieces of equipment worn and used by people such as soldiers and sailors: *football kit*

IDIOM **get your kit off** mainly UK slang humorous to take off your clothes: *Come on, get your kit off!*

▸verb (-tt-)

PHRASAL VERB **kit sb/sth out** mainly UK to supply someone or something with the clothes or equipment that are needed for a particular purpose: *They went shopping to get kitted out **for** the trip.*

kitbag /ˈkɪt.bæg/ noun [C] a long narrow bag used by soldiers, sailors, etc. for carrying their clothes and small pieces of equipment

kitchen /ˈkɪtʃ.ən/ noun [C] A1 a room where food is kept, prepared, and cooked and where the dishes are washed: *We usually eat breakfast in the kitchen.* ◦ *the kitchen table* ◦ *a new **fitted** kitchen (= cupboards that look the same fixed to the walls and floor in the kitchen)*

ˌkitchen ˈcabinet noun [C] a small unofficial group of people who give advice to a political leader

ˌkitchen ˈcounter noun [C] US for **worktop**

kitchenette /ˌkɪtʃ.ɪˈnet/ noun [C] a small room or area used as a kitchen

ˌkitchen ˈgarden noun [C] an area, especially a part of a large garden, where fruit, vegetables, and herbs are grown

ˈkitchen ˌpaper noun [U] UK **kitchen roll**

ˈkitchen ˌroll noun [U] (UK also **ˈkitchen ˌtowel**) soft, thick paper on a roll, from which square pieces are torn and used in the kitchen or other places, especially for removing liquid

ˌkitchen-ˈsink adj [before noun] UK describes plays, films, and NOVELS that are about ordinary people's lives: *a kitchen-sink drama*

ˈkitchen ˌtowel noun [C] US for **tea towel** → See also **kitchen roll**

kitchenware /ˈkɪtʃ.ən.weəʳ/ US /-wer/ noun [U] plates, bowls, knives, forks, spoons, etc. used in the kitchen

kite /kaɪt/ noun [C]

kite

FLYING OBJECT ▷ **1** A2 a frame covered with cloth or plastic and joined to a long string, that you fly in the air when the weather is windy: *to fly a kite* BIRD ▷ **2** a large bird that kills and eats small animals

ˈkite-ˌflying noun [U] the act of trying to find out what people's opinion about something new will be by informally spreading news of it: *These rumours of a new political party are obviously a kite-flying exercise.*

Kitemark /ˈkaɪt.mɑːk/ US /-mɑːrk/ noun [S] in the UK, a mark on goods that have been officially said to be of high quality

kith and kin /ˌkɪθ.ənˈkɪn/ noun [plural] old-fashioned people you are connected with, especially by family relationships

kitsch /kɪtʃ/ noun [U] art, decorative objects, or design considered by many people to be ugly, without style, or false but enjoyed by other people, often because they are funny • **kitschy** /ˈkɪtʃ.i/ adj

kitten /ˈkɪt.ən/ US /ˈkɪt̬-/ noun [C] B1 a very young cat

IDIOM **have kittens** (US **have a cow**) to be very worried, upset or angry about something: *My mother nearly had kittens when I said I was going to buy a motorbike.*

kittenish /ˈkɪt.ən.ɪʃ/ US /ˈkɪt̬-/ adj old-fashioned describes a woman who behaves in a humorous, silly way, especially as a way of attracting sexual attention • **kittenishly** /-li/ adv

kitty /ˈkɪ.ti/ US /-t̬i/ noun MONEY ▷ **1** [C usually singular] an amount of money that is made up of small amounts given by different people, used by them for an agreed purpose: *We all put £20 in/into the kitty to cover the cost of food.* CAT ▷ **2** [C] informal a cat or kitten

kiwi /ˈkiː.wiː/ noun [C] FRUIT ▷ **1** (also **kiwi fruit**, also **Chinese gooseberry**) an oval fruit with brown skin covered in hairs and bright green flesh BIRD ▷ **2** a New Zealand bird, with a long beak and feathers like hairs, which cannot fly and is the national symbol of New Zealand PERSON ▷ **3** informal a person from New Zealand

the KKK /ˌkeɪ.keɪˈkeɪ/ noun [S] abbreviation for **the Ku Klux Klan**

klaxon /ˈklæk.sən/ noun [C] trademark a very loud horn used, especially in the past on police cars and other emergency vehicles, as a way of warning other people

kleptocracy /ˌklepˈtɒk.rə.si/ US /-ˈtɑː.krə-/ noun [C] a society whose leaders make themselves rich and powerful by stealing from the rest of the people: *This was not a democracy; it was a kleptocracy.*

kleptomania /ˌklep.təˈmeɪ.ni.ə/ US /-toʊ-/ noun [U] a very strong wish to steal that you cannot control, especially without any need or purpose, usually considered to be a type of mental illness • **kleptomaniac** /-æk/ noun [C]

klutz /klʌts/ noun [C] mainly US slang a very silly or stupid person, or a person who moves awkwardly • **klutzy** /ˈklʌt.si/ adj

km written abbreviation for **kilometre**

knack /næk/ noun [S] a skill or an ability to do something easily and well: *a knack **for** remembering faces* ◦ *She **has** the knack **of** making people feel comfortable.* ◦ *There's **a** knack **to** using this corkscrew.*

knacker /ˈnæk.əʳ/ US /-ɚ/ verb [T] UK slang BREAK ▷ **1** to break something: *Careful or you'll knacker the gears!* MAKE TIRED ▷ **2** to make someone very tired: *Don't go too fast or you'll knacker yourself in the first hour.*

knackered /ˈnæk.əd/ US /-ɚd/ adj UK slang BROKEN ▷ **1** broken or too old to use: *My bike's knackered.* TIRED ▷ **2** [after verb] very tired: *I'm too knackered to go out this evening.*

knackering /ˈnæk.ər.ɪŋ/ US /-ɚ-/ adj UK slang making you feel very tired: *What a knackering day it's been!*

ˈknacker's ˌyard noun [C usually singular] a place where old or injured horses are killed: informal figurative *The state of the economy has led to many small businesses ending up in the knacker's yard (= failing completely).*

knapsack /ˈnæp.sæk/ noun [C] UK old-fashioned or US a bag carried on the back or over the shoulder, used especially by people who go walking or climbing for carrying food, clothes, etc.

knave /neɪv/ noun [C] old use **1** a dishonest man **2** a **jack**

knead /niːd/ verb [T] to press something, especially a mixture for making bread, firmly and repeatedly with the hands and fingers: *Knead the dough until smooth.*

knee /niː/ noun; verb

▸**noun** [C] **1** B1 the middle JOINT of the leg, which allows it to bend: *The baby was crawling around on its* ***hands and*** *knees.* ◦ *He got/went* ***down on*** *his knees (= got into a position where his knees were on the ground) in front of the altar.* ◦ *She took the child and sat it on her knee (= on the part of the leg above the knee when sitting down).* **2** the part of a piece of clothing that covers the knee: *She was wearing an old pair of trousers with rips at the knees.*

IDIOM **bring sb/sth to their knees** to destroy or defeat someone or something: *The strikes had brought the economy to its knees.*

▸**verb** [T] to hit someone with your knee: *She kneed him* ***in*** *the groin.*

kneecap /ˈniː.kæp/ noun; verb

▸**noun** [C] (specialized **patella**) the bone at the front of the knee JOINT

▸**verb** [T] (-pp-) to injure someone in the knee as a punishment, especially by shooting

ˌknee-ˈdeep adj **1** If you are knee-deep in a substance, it reaches up to your knees: *We walked through the field, knee-deep* ***in*** *mud.* **2** informal very involved in a difficult situation or large task: *I'm knee-deep* ***in*** *paperwork.*

ˌknee-ˈhigh adj tall enough to reach your knees: *knee-high grass/boots*

IDIOM **be knee-high to a grasshopper** informal humorous to be very small or young

ˈknee-jerk adj disapproving **knee-jerk reaction, response, etc.** a quick reaction that does not allow you time to consider something carefully

kneel /niːl/ verb [I] (**knelt** or **kneeled**, **knelt** or **kneeled**) B2 to go down into, or stay in, a position where one or both knees are on the ground: *She knelt* ***(down)*** *beside the child.* ◦ *He knelt in front of the altar and prayed.*

ˈknee-length adj Something that is knee-length is long enough to reach the knee: *knee-length socks* ◦ *a knee-length skirt*

ˈknees-up noun [C usually singular] UK informal an energetic, noisy party where people dance

knell /nel/ noun → See **death knell**

knew /njuː/ US /nuː/ past simple of **know**

ˌknickerˌbocker ˈglory noun [C] UK a sweet dish consisting of layers of ice cream, fruit, JELLY and cream, served in a tall glass

knickerbockers /ˈnɪk.əˌbɒk.əz/ US /-ɚˌbɑː.kɚz/ noun [plural] (US also **knickers**) short loose trousers that fit tightly below the knee, worn especially in the past or for ceremonies

knickers /ˈnɪk.əz/ US /-ɚz/ noun [plural] **1** B1 UK (US **panties**) a piece of underwear worn by women and girls covering the area between the waist and the tops of the legs: *a pair of black cotton knickers* **2** US for **knickerbockers**

IDIOM **get your knickers in a twist** UK informal humorous to become confused, worried, or annoyed about something

knick-knack (also **nick-nack**) /ˈnɪk.næk/ noun [C usually plural] a small, decorative object, especially in a house: *The shelves were covered with ornaments and useless knick-knacks.*

knife /naɪf/ noun; verb

▸**noun** [C] (plural **knives**) A1 a tool, usually with a metal blade and a handle, used for cutting and spreading food or other substances, or as a weapon: *a fish/butter/steak knife* ◦ *I prefer to use a knife* ***and fork.*** ◦ *He* ***drew/pulled*** *a knife and stabbed her.*

IDIOMS **go under the knife** to have a medical operation • **have your knife into sb** UK to try to upset or harm someone because you dislike them • **the knives are out** UK something you say which means that people are being unpleasant about someone, or trying to harm them: *The knives are out* ***for*** *the former president.* • **put/stick the knife into sb** (also **put/stick the knife in**) to be unpleasant about someone or try to harm them: *The reviewer in the magazine that I read really put the knife in.* • **twist/turn the knife (in the wound)** to make someone who is annoyed, worried, or upset feel even worse: *Just to turn the knife a little, he told me he'd seen my old girlfriend with her new man.* • **under the knife** while having a medical operation

▸**verb** [T] to attack someone using a knife: *He knifed her* ***in*** *the back.*

ˈknife edge noun **on a knife edge** in a difficult or worrying situation of which the result is very uncertain: *At the moment the election seems* ***balanced*** *on a knife edge.*

ˈknife-edge adj [before noun] **SHARP** ▷ **1** narrow and sharp: *We had to climb over a knife-edge mountain ridge.* **UNCERTAIN** ▷ **2** describes a situation where the result is very uncertain: *a knife-edge vote*

knight /naɪt/ noun; verb

▸**noun** [C] **1** a man given a rank of honour by a British king or queen because of his special achievements, and who has the right to be called 'Sir', or (in the past) a man of high social position trained to fight as a soldier on a horse: *He hopes to be made a knight for his work at the Bank of England.* ◦ *knights in black armour* **2** in the game of CHESS, a piece in the shape of a horse's head that moves two squares in one direction and then one square at an angle of 90°

IDIOM **a knight in shining armour** someone who saves you from a difficult or dangerous situation

▸**verb** [T] to give someone the rank of knight: *He was knighted by the Queen* ***for*** *his work with famine victims.*

ˌknight ˈerrant noun [C] (plural **knights errant**) literary a MEDIEVAL knight who travelled around doing brave things and helping people who were in trouble

knighthood /ˈnaɪt.hʊd/ noun [C or U] the rank of knight

knightly /ˈnaɪt.li/ adj literary of or suitable for a knight in the past, especially involving courage and honour

knit /nɪt/ verb **MAKE CLOTHES** ▷ **1** B1 [I or T] (present participle **knitting**, past tense **knitted** or **knit**, past participle **knitted** or **knit**) to make clothes, etc. by using two long needles to connect wool or another type of thread into joined rows: *She's forever knitting.* ◦ *She's busy knitting baby clothes.* ◦ [+ two objects] *My granny knitted me some gloves/knitted some gloves* ***for*** *me.* → See also **knitwear** **2** [T] (present participle **knitting**, past tense **knitted** or **knit**, past participle **knitted** or **knit**) specialized to do the most basic type of STITCH, when knitting something: *Knit one, purl one.* **JOIN** ▷ **3** [I or T] (present participle **knitting**, past tense **knit**, past participle **knit**) to join together: *The broken bone should begin to knit* ***(together)*** *in a few days.* **4 closely/tightly knit** (also **ˌclose/ˌtight-ˈknit**) closely connected: *a very close-knit family* ◦ *a tightly knit*

K

community ◦ *The two communities are closely knit by a common faith.*

IDIOM **knit your brow/brows** literary to FROWN (= move your eyebrows down and together) because you are thinking carefully, or because you are angry or worried: *He knitted his brow in concentration.*

knitted /ˈnɪt.ɪd/ US /ˈnɪt̬-/ **adj** (also **knit**) made using wool or thick cotton and two long needles: *a knitted jumper* ◦ *hand-knitted gloves*

knitter /ˈnɪt.əʳ/ US /ˈnɪt̬.ɚ/ **noun** [C] a person who knits

knitting /ˈnɪt.ɪŋ/ US /ˈnɪt̬-/ **noun** [U] the activity of knitting something, or a thing that is being knitted: *I'm hopeless at knitting.* ◦ *She takes her knitting with her everywhere.*

knitwear /ˈnɪt.weəʳ/ US /-wer/ **noun** [U] clothes made by connecting wool or another type of thread into joined rows

knob /nɒb/ US /nɑːb/ **noun** [C] **ROUND OBJECT** ▷ **1** C1 a round handle, or a small round device for controlling a machine or electrical equipment: *a brass door knob* ◦ *Turn/Twiddle the little knob to adjust the volume.* **2** a round LUMP on the surface or end of something **AMOUNT** ▷ **3** a small amount of something solid, especially butter: *Put a knob of butter in the frying pan.* **BODY PART** ▷ **4** UK offensive a PENIS

IDIOMS **and the same to you with (brass) knobs on** UK old-fashioned humorous used to return an insult forcefully to someone who has insulted you • **with (brass) knobs on** UK If you describe something as a particular thing with knobs on, you mean it has similar qualities to that thing but they are more extreme: *Disney World was like an ordinary amusement park with knobs on.*

knobbly /ˈnɒb.l̩.i/, /ˈ-bli/ US /ˈnɑː.bli/ **adj** (US **knobby**) having LUMPS (= raised areas) on the surface: *knobbly knees/elbows*

knock /nɒk/ US /nɑːk/ **verb; noun**

▸**verb MAKE NOISE** ▷ **1** B1 [I] to repeatedly hit something, producing a noise: *She knocked **on** the window to attract his attention.* ◦ *There's someone knocking **on/at** the door.* ◦ *Please knock before entering.* **2** [I] specialized If an engine is knocking, it is producing a repeated high sound either because the fuel is not burning correctly or because a small part is damaged and is therefore allowing another part to move in ways that it should not. **3** [I] If something such as a pipe knocks, it makes a repeated high sound. **HIT** ▷ **4** B1 [I + adv/prep, T] to hit, especially forcefully, and cause to move or fall: *He accidentally knocked the vase **off** the table.* ◦ *She knocked her head **against** the wall as she fell.* ◦ *Who knocked **over** that mug of coffee?* ◦ [+ obj + adj] *Some thug knocked him **unconscious/senseless**.* ◦ *She took a hammer and knocked **a hole in** the wall.* **5 knock into each other/knock through** If you knock two rooms into each other or knock two rooms through, you remove the wall between them so that they form one room. **CRITICIZE** ▷ **6** [T] UK informal to criticize, especially unfairly: *Don't knock him – he's doing his best.*

IDIOMS **be knocking (on) 60, 70, etc.** informal to have almost reached a particular, usually old, age • **knock sb's block off** informal If you say that you will knock someone's block off, you are threatening to hit them very hard, especially on the head: *I'll knock his block off if he tries anything with me!* • **knock sb off their pedestal** • **knock sth on the head** UK informal to prevent something from happening, or to finally finish something: *It's nearly done – another couple of hours should knock it on the head.* • **knock (some) sense into sb** informal to forcefully teach someone not to be silly: *A couple of years in the army will knock some sense into him.* • **knock sb sideways/for six** UK informal to shock or upset someone very much, or to make someone very ill: *That flu really knocked me sideways.* ◦ *The news of his death knocked me for six.* • **knock (on) wood** US for **touch wood** → See at **touch** • **knock 'em dead!** informal used to tell someone to perform or play as well as they can • **knock it off** informal used to tell someone to stop doing something that annoys you: *Oh, knock it off Alex, I'm really not in the mood for your jokes.* • **knock spots off sth** UK informal to be much better than something or someone else: *It knocks spots off that restaurant in Cotswold Street.* • **knock the bottom out of sth** to damage something severely, especially by destroying its support: *The rise in mortgage rates really knocked the bottom out of the housing market.*

PHRASAL VERBS **knock sb about/around** informal to behave violently towards someone and hit them: *Her husband used to knock her about.* • **knock about/around (sth)** informal to be in a place that is not exactly known or in various places especially over a long period of time: *I'm sure I've got a copy of 'Time's Arrow' knocking about somewhere.* ◦ *He spent years knocking around the Far East before the First World War.* • **knock around/about** informal **RELAX** ▷ **1** to spend time relaxing and doing very little: *I spent the weekend just knocking about the house.* **BE WITH SOMEONE** ▷ **2** to spend a lot of time with someone: *I used to knock around with him at school.* • **knock sb back (sth)** UK informal to cost someone a large amount of money: *I bet that computer knocked you back several hundred.* • **knock back (sth)** UK informal to quickly drink something, especially a lot of alcohol: *She was knocking back the champagne at Maria's party.* • **knock sb down** [M often passive] UK B1 to hit someone with a vehicle and injure or kill them: *She was knocked down by a bus.* • **knock sb/sth down HIT** ▷ **1** to cause someone or something to fall to the ground by hitting them **REDUCE PRICE** ▷ **2** informal to reduce a price, or to persuade someone to reduce the price of something they are selling: *She wanted £200 but I knocked her down **to** £175.* → See also **knock-down** • **knock sth down** B2 to destroy a building or part of a building: *The Council plans to knock the library down and replace it with a hotel complex.* ◦ figurative *She easily knocked down every argument he put up.* • **knock off (sth)** informal to stop working, usually at the end of the day: *I don't knock off until six.* ◦ *What time do you knock off work?* • **knock sth off (sth)** informal to take a particular amount away from a price: *The manager knocked £5 off because it was damaged.* • **knock sth off STEAL** ▷ **1** (US **knock sth over**) to steal something: *He has a stack of computer equipment he's knocked off **from** various shops.* ◦ *Terrorist groups are knocking off* (US also ***knocking over***) *banks to get money.* ◦ *He was caught selling knocked-off car radios in the pub.* **PRODUCE** ▷ **2** informal to produce something quickly and easily: *She can knock off (= write) a novel in a couple of weeks.* → See also **knock sth out** • **knock sb off MURDER** ▷ **1** slang to murder someone: *He hired a hit-man to knock off a business rival.* **HAVE SEX** ▷ **2** offensive old-fashioned to have sex with someone • **knock sb out MAKE UNCONSCIOUS** ▷ **1** B2 to hit someone so that they become unconscious: *His opponent knocked him out with one punch.* → See also **knockout MAKE SLEEP** ▷ **2** If a drug or alcohol knocks you out, it makes you go to sleep. **DEFEAT** ▷ **3** B2 to defeat a person or a team in a competition so that they can no longer take part in it: *The champion was unexpectedly knocked out* (**of** *the tournament) in the first round.* **IMPRESS** ▷ **4** old-fashioned slang to cause enjoyment or admiration in someone: *We were all really knocked out by the film.* • **knock yourself out** **1** to make yourself unconscious, usually by hitting your head: *She hit her head on the ceiling and knocked herself out.* **2** informal to make yourself ill with tiredness: *If you carry on working like this, you'll knock yourself out.* • **knock sth out** **PRODUCE** ▷ **1** informal to produce something quickly without spending time thinking about the details: *I've knocked out a first draft of the report that we can amend at a later date.* → See also **knock sth off** **DESTROY** ▷ **2** If something such as a piece of equipment is knocked out by something else, it stops working or is damaged or destroyed: *The surge in the power supply knocked out all the computers.* ◦ *Enemy aircraft have knocked out 25 tanks.* • **knock sth out of sb** If a quality is knocked out of someone, they lose that quality because the situation they are in does not allow it to exist: *Any creativity I had was soon knocked out of me at school.* • **knock sth over** US for **knock sth off** (= steal something) • **knock sb over** [M usually passive] to hit someone with a vehicle and injure or kill them: *She got knocked over by a taxi as she ran for the bus.* • **knock sth together/up** informal to make something quickly and without much care: *I could knock together a quick lunch if you like.* • **knock up** Players knock up before beginning a game of tennis or similar sport by hitting the ball to each other: *The players have a couple of minutes to knock up before the match starts.* • **knock sb up** **WAKE UP** ▷ **1** UK informal to wake someone up by knocking on the door of their house or bedroom: *I'm sorry to have to knock you up in the middle of the night.* **MAKE PREGNANT** ▷ **2** slang to make a woman pregnant: *You don't want to get knocked up by some guy you hardly know.*

▸**noun** [C] **NOISE** ▷ **1** a sudden short noise made when someone or something hits a surface: *There was a knock* **at/on** *the door.* **HIT** ▷ **2** the act of something hard hitting a person or thing: *He received a nasty knock* **on** *the head from a falling slate.*

IDIOM **take/have a knock** to be damaged because of a bad experience: *Her confidence took a* **hard** *knock when her application was rejected.*

knockabout /ˈnɒk.ə.baʊt/ (US) /ˈnɑːk-/ adj [before noun] (especially of a theatre performance) causing laughter by very silly behaviour → Compare **slapstick**

ˈknock-down adj [before noun] (of a price) extremely cheap: *They're selling jeans for ridiculous knock-down* **prices**. → See also **knock sb/sth down**

ˌknock-down-drag-ˈout adj [before noun] US a knock-down-drag-out fight or argument is very serious and continues for a long time: *Look, I don't want to get into a knock-down-drag-out fight with you over this, so let's forget it.*

knocker /ˈnɒk.əʳ/ (US) /ˈnɑː.kɚ/ noun [C] **METAL OBJECT** ▷ **1** (also **doorknocker**) a metal object fixed to a door which visitors use to hit the door in order to attract attention **CRITIC** ▷ **2** UK informal disapproving a person who is always criticizing someone or something **BREASTS** ▷ **3** **knockers** [plural] slang a woman's breasts. Some people consider this offensive.

ˈknocking ˌshop noun [C usually singular] UK humorous for **brothel**

ˌknock-ˈkneed adj If someone is knock-kneed, their knees bend towards each other.

ˈknock-off noun [C] informal a cheap copy of a popular product: *Is that the real thing or a knock-off?*

ˈknock-on eˌffect noun [C usually singular] mainly UK When an event or situation has a knock-on effect, it causes other events or situations, but not directly: *If one or two trains run late, it* **has** *a knock-on effect on the entire rail service.*

knockout /ˈnɒk.aʊt/ (US) /ˈnɑːk-/ noun; adj

▸**noun** [C] **UNCONSCIOUS** ▷ **1** in BOXING, the act of hitting the other fighter so that they fall to the ground and are unable to get up again within ten seconds: *a knockout punch/blow* → See also **knock sb out** **COMPETITION** ▷ **2** (US **elimination tournament**) a competition in which only the winners of each stage play in the next stage, until one competitor or team is the final winner: *The tournament is a straight knockout.* ◦ *a knockout competition/championship/match* **ATTRACTIVE** ▷ **3** informal a person or thing that looks, sounds, etc. extremely attractive: *Your sister's a real knockout!*

IDIOM **a knockout blow** an event or action that causes someone or something to fail: *Already out of training, the latest illness has dealt her hopes of a gold medal a knockout blow.*

▸**adj** informal extremely attractive: *She looked knockout in that dress.*

ˈknockout ˌdrops noun [plural] old-fashioned informal a drug, usually put secretly into your drink, that makes you sleep

ˈknock-up noun [C usually singular] a short time before the start of a game of tennis or a similar sport when players practise by hitting the ball to each other: *Shall we have a quick knock-up before the game?*

knoll /nəʊl/ (US) /noʊl/ noun [C] a small low hill with a rounded top: *a grassy knoll*

knot /nɒt/ (US) /nɑːt/ noun; verb

knot

▸**noun** [C] **FASTENING** ▷ **1** (C2) a join made by tying together the ends of a piece or pieces of string, rope, cloth, etc.: *to* **tie** *a knot* **MASS** ▷ **2** a tight mass, for example of hair or string: *Alice's hair is always full of knots and tangles.* **GROUP** ▷ **3** a small group of people standing close together: *Knots* **of** *anxious people stood waiting in the hall.* **WOOD** ▷ **4** a small hard area on a tree or piece of wood where a branch was joined to the tree **MEASUREMENT** ▷ **5** specialized a measure of the speed of ships, aircraft, or movements of water and air. One knot is one NAUTICAL MILE per hour: *a top speed of about 20 knots*

IDIOM **in knots** informal If your stomach is in knots, it feels tight and uncomfortable because you are nervous or excited.

▸**verb** (**-tt-**) **FASTEN** ▷ **1** [T] to tie in or with a knot: *He caught the rope and knotted it* **around** *a post.* **FORM MASS** ▷ **2** [I] to form a tight, hard, rounded mass: *His muscles knotted (= swelled) with the strain.* • **knotted** /ˈnɒt.ɪd/ (US) /ˈnɑː.t̬ɪd/ adj *a knotted rope*

IDIOM **get knotted!** UK old-fashioned slang a rude way of telling someone who is annoying you to go away

knotty /ˈnɒt.i/ (US) /ˈnɑː.t̬i/ adj **COMPLICATED** ▷ **1** informal (of a problem or difficulty) complicated and difficult to solve: *That's rather a knotty question.* **WOOD** ▷ **2** with a lot of knots: *a knotty piece of wood*

know /nəʊ/ (US) /noʊ/ verb; noun

▸**verb** (**knew, known**) **HAVE INFORMATION** ▷ **1** (A1) [I or T, not continuous] to have information in your mind: *'Where did he go?' 'I don't know.'* ◦ *'What does it cost?' 'Ask Kate. She'll know.'* ◦ *She knows the name of every kid in the school.* ◦ *I don't know anything* **about** *this.* ◦

[+ question word] *We don't know **wh**en he's arriving.* ◦ *I don't know (= understand) **wh**at all the fuss is about.* ◦ [+ (that)] *I just knew (**that**) it was going to be a disaster.* ◦ *She knew (= was aware) (**that**) something was wrong.* ◦ [+ obj + to infinitive] *Even small amounts of these substances are known **to** cause skin problems.* ◦ formal *The authorities know him **to** be (= know that he is) a cocaine dealer.* **2** A1 [T not continuous] used to ask someone to tell you a piece of information: *Do you know the time?* ◦ [+ question word] *Do you know **wh**ere the Post Office is?* **3** A2 [I or T, not continuous] to be certain: [+ (that)] *I know (**that**) she'll be really pleased to hear the news.* ◦ [+ question word] *I don't know **wh**ether I should tell her or not.* ◦ *The party is at Sarah's house **as/so far as** I know (= I think but I am not certain).*

> **! Common mistake: know or find out?**
>
> **Warning:** choose the correct verb!
>
> To talk about learning a fact or piece of information for the first time, don't say 'know', say **find out**:
>
> *~~I was shocked when I knew that I was pregnant.~~*
>
> *I was shocked when I found out I was pregnant.*

BE FAMILIAR WITH ▷ **4** B1 [T not continuous] to be familiar with or have experience and understanding of: *I've known Daniel since we were at school together.* ◦ *She grew up in Paris so she knows it well.* ◦ *I've seen the film 'Casablanca' so many times that I know a lot of it **by heart** (= I know it in my memory).* ◦ *Knowing Sarah (= from my experience of her in the past), she'll have done a good job.* ◦ formal *I have known (= experienced) great happiness in my life.* **5** B1 [I or T, not continuous] (also **know about**) If you know a subject, you are familiar with it and understand it: *Do you know **about** computers?* ◦ *She knows her subject **inside out*** (UK also ***backwards***) *(= very well).* **6** A2 [T not continuous] If you know a language, you can speak and understand it: *Do you know any French?* **7** [T not continuous] to recognize someone or something: *That's Peter alright – I'd know him anywhere!* ◦ *I know a bargain when I see one.* **8 know how to do sth** A2 to be able to do something because you have the necessary knowledge: *Do you know how to print on this computer?* **9 get to know sb/sth** B1 to spend time with someone or something so that you gradually learn more about them: *The first couple of meetings are for the doctor and patient to get to know each other.* ◦ *I'll need a few weeks to get to know the system.* **10 know sb by name** to have heard the name of a person but not seen or talked to them **11 know sb by sight** If you know someone by sight, their face is familiar to you, but they are not a friend of yours.

> **! Common mistake: know or get to know?**
>
> **Warning:** choose the correct verb!
>
> To talk about spending time with someone or something so that you learn more about them, don't say 'know', say **get to know**:
>
> *~~They organized a party so we could know other students.~~*
>
> *They organized a party so we could get to know the other students.*

IDIOMS **before you know it** C1 very soon: *We'll be on our way out again before you know it.* • **be known to be/do sth** C1 If something or someone is known to be or do something, people know that it is true or happens, or that someone is or does something: *A daily intake of 20 mg of vitamin C is known to be sufficient in most cases to ward off scurvy.* • **Goodness/God/Heaven/Christ knows** informal used to mean 'I don't know' or to emphasize a statement. Some people may find this offensive: *God **only** knows what'll happen next!* ◦ *Take your shirt off – Heaven knows it's hot enough today!* • **how was I to know?** informal used to say that something you did wrong was not your fault because you did not have enough information to have acted differently: *I just wanted to give her a surprise, how was I to know you'd already bought tickets?* • **I don't know** informal used to express that you do not understand or are angry at something that someone has done: *I don't know, however many notices I put up, people still park in my space.* • **I don't know how, what, why, etc.** informal used to add force to criticisms, expressions of surprise, etc.: *I don't know how you can eat that revolting stuff!* • **I know 1** B1 said when you suddenly think of a good idea, an answer or a solution: *I know – let's go to the beach!* **2** B2 said to show you agree with something someone has just said: *'But he's so awful.' 'I know – he's dreadful.'* • **know sth back to front** (also **know sth backwards**) to have very good and detailed knowledge of something: *She knows her part in the play back to front.* • **know sth like the back of your hand** informal to have very good and detailed knowledge of something: *I know this area like the back of my hand.* • **know your own mind** to be certain about what you believe or want • **know your place** to accept your position within society, an organization, your family, etc. and to not want to improve it: *I just get on with my job and do as I'm told – I know my place.* • **know your stuff** (old-fashioned **know your onions**) C2 to have good practical skills and knowledge in a particular activity or subject • **know your way around sth** (also **know the ropes**) to be familiar with a place or organization and able to act effectively within it • **know best** C2 to be the most suitable person to have responsibility and make important decisions: *When it comes to dealing with my own son, I think I know best.* • **know better (than to do sth)** C2 to be wise or moral enough not to do something: *Sure, she's only six, but she's **old enough to** know better than to run off without us.* ◦ *I'm surprised at you behaving so badly – you **ought to/should** know better.* • **know better (than sb)** to know more than someone else because you have more experience and more skill: *They thought the painting was a fake, but Shackleton knew better.* • **know the score** informal to know all the important facts in a situation, especially the unpleasant ones: *You know the score – no payment till after the article is published.* • **know what you are talking about** C1 to understand a subject because of your experience: *He doesn't know what he's talking about – he's never even been to Africa.* • **(you) know what I mean** informal used when you think that the person listening understands and so you do not need to say any more: *You've got to give him a chance, you know what I mean?* • **know what's what** informal If you know what's what, you have a lot of experience and can judge people and situations well: *Linda's been in the business for 30 years – she knows what's what.* • **know which side your bread is buttered (on)** informal to know who to be nice to and what to do in order to get an advantage • **sth knows no bounds** formal If someone has a quality that knows no bounds, it is extreme: *Her generosity knows no bounds.* • **not know sb from Adam** informal to have never met someone and not know anything about them: *Why should she lend me money? She doesn't know me from Adam.* • **not know the first thing about sth** to know nothing about a subject: *I'm afraid I don't know the first thing about car engines.* • **not**

know the meaning of the word If you are talking about a quality or an activity and you say that someone doesn't know the meaning of the word, you mean they do not have that quality or they have no experience of that activity: *Work? He doesn't know the meaning of the word!* ◦ *And the irony of Phil talking about ethics. He doesn't know the meaning of the word.* • **not know what has hit you** informal to be shocked and surprised because something unpleasant suddenly and unexpectedly happens to you: *You wait till he starts working for Michael – he won't know what's hit him!* • **not know where to put yourself** informal to feel very embarrassed: *And then he started to sing. Well, I didn't know where to put myself.* • **not know where/which way to turn** to not know what to do or who to ask for help: *When both her parents died, she didn't know which way to turn.* • **not know whether to laugh or cry** to not know how to react in a particular situation: *When she told me they were getting married I didn't know whether to laugh or cry.* • **not that I know of** used when answering a question to mean that, judging from the information you have, the answer is no: *'Is she especially unhappy at school?' 'Not that I know of.'* • **there's no knowing** If you say there's no knowing, you mean it is impossible to be certain about something: *There's no knowing what she'll do if she finds out about this.* • **(well) what do you know!** informal something you say when you are surprised by a piece of information. This phrase is often used humorously to mean the opposite: *So they're getting married, are they? Well, what do you know!* ◦ *Well, what do you know! The Raiders lost again!* • **wouldn't know sth if you fell over one/it** (also **wouldn't know sth if it hit you in the face**) used to say that someone would not recognize something even if it was obvious: *She wouldn't know a bargain if she fell over one!* • **you know** informal **1** B1 a phrase with little meaning, which you use while you are trying to think of what to say next: *Well I just thought, you know, I'd better agree to it.* ◦ *I'm not happy with the situation but, you know, there isn't much I can do about it.* **2** B1 used when trying to help someone remember something or when trying to explain something: *What's the name of that guy on TV – you know, the American one with the silly voice?* • **you know something?** (also **you know what?**) said before giving an opinion or a piece of information: *You know something? I don't think I like that man.* • **you never know** informal B2 said to mean there is a possibility that something good might happen, even if it is slight: *You never know, she might change her mind.*

PHRASAL VERBS **know sth from sth** to know the difference between two things and therefore be able to recognize either, used especially to mean that you have a good knowledge and understanding of a particular subject: *Computer expert? He doesn't know a mouse from a modem!* (= He knows nothing about computers.) • **know of sb/sth** mainly UK B2 to have heard of someone or something and be able to give a small amount of information about them: *Do you know of a good doctor?*

▸noun informal **be in the know** to have knowledge about something which most people do not have: *This resort is considered by those who are in the know to have the best downhill skiing in Europe.*

knowable /ˈnəʊ.ə.bl/ US /ˈnoʊ-/ adj able to be known

ˈknow-all noun [C] UK informal disapproving (US **ˈknow-it-all**) a person who thinks that they know much more than other people

ˈknow-how noun [U] informal practical knowledge and ability: *technical know-how*

knowing /ˈnəʊ.ɪŋ/ US /ˈnoʊ-/ adj showing that you know about something, even when it has not been talked about: *a knowing look/glance/smile*

knowingly /ˈnəʊ.ɪŋ.li/ US /ˈnoʊ-/ adv **1** C2 in a way that shows you know about something: *She smiled knowingly at him.* **2** C2 If you do something knowingly, you do it knowing what will be its likely effect: *I've never knowingly offended him.*

knowledge /ˈnɒl.ɪdʒ/ US /ˈnɑː.lɪdʒ/ noun **1** B1 [S or U] understanding of or information about a subject that you get by experience or study, either known by one person or by people generally: *Her knowledge **of** English grammar is very extensive.* ◦ *He has **a** limited knowledge **of** French.* ◦ *The details of the scandal are now **common** knowledge (= familiar to most people).* ◦ *She started to photograph the documents, safe **in the** knowledge **that** (= knowing that) she wouldn't be disturbed for at least an hour.* ◦ *In this town there are only a couple of restaurants that **to** my knowledge (= judging from my personal experience and information) serve good food.* **2** [U] the state of knowing about or being familiar with something: *The government **deny all** knowledge **of** the affair.* ◦ *It has **come/been brought** to our knowledge (= we have discovered) **that** several computers have gone missing.*

> **!** Common mistake: **knowledge**
>
> The correct preposition to use after **knowledge** is **of**.
> Don't say 'knowledge in/about/on something', say **knowledge of something**:
> ~~*This job requires knowledge about at least two foreign languages.*~~
> *This job requires knowledge of at least two foreign languages.*

> **!** Common mistake: **knowledge**
>
> **Knowledge** does not have a plural form.
> To talk about an amount of **knowledge**, do not say 'knowledges', say **knowledge**, **some knowledge**, or **a lot of knowledge**:
> ~~*I would like to improve my knowledges of English grammar.*~~
> *I would like to improve my knowledge of English grammar.*

> Word partners for **knowledge**
>
> *acquire/gain/have* knowledge • knowledge *of* sth • *detailed/in-depth/thorough* knowledge • *first-hand/intimate/personal* knowledge • *deny* (all) knowledge **of** sth • *background/general/specialist* knowledge • be/become *common/public* knowledge • a *thirst* for knowledge • (not) *to* sb's knowledge • *with/without* sb's knowledge • *in* the knowledge (that)

knowledgeable /ˈnɒl.ɪ.dʒə.bl/ US /ˈnɑː.lɪ-/ adj C1 knowing a lot: *He's very knowledgeable **about** German literature.* • **knowledgeably** /-bli/ adv

known /nəʊn/ US /noʊn/ adj **1** B2 describes something or someone that is familiar to or understood by people: *These people are known criminals.* ◦ *There is no known reason for the accident.* ◦ *He is known **to** the police because of his previous criminal record.* → See also **well known** **2** **known as sth** B1 If someone or something is known as a particular name, they are called by that name: *And this is Terry, **otherwise** known as 'Muscleman'.* **3** **make sth known** to tell people about something so that it becomes publicly known: *Local residents have made known their objec-*

tions to the proposals. ◦ I made **it** known **that** I was not happy with the decision.

IDIOM **make yourself known** to tell someone who you are: *Just go to the hotel reception and make yourself known (**to** the receptionist).*

knuckle /ˈnʌk.l̩/ noun; verb

▸**noun** [C] ⓒ2 one of the JOINTS in the hand where your fingers bend, especially where your fingers join on to the main part of your hand

IDIOM **near the knuckle** UK informal about sex and so likely to offend people: *Some of his jokes were a bit near the knuckle.*

▸**verb**

PHRASAL VERBS **knuckle down** informal to start working or studying hard • **knuckle under** informal to accept someone's power over you and do what they tell you to do

knuckleduster /ˈnʌk.l̩ˌdʌs.təʳ/ ⓤⓢ /-t̬ɚ/ noun [C] **1** UK (US **brass knuckles**) a metal weapon that is worn over the knuckles and is intended to increase the injuries caused when hitting a person **2** informal a large and noticeable ring

knucklehead /ˈnʌk.l̩.hed/ noun [C] US informal a stupid person

K

KO /ˌkeɪˈəʊ/ ⓤⓢ /-ˈoʊ/ verb [T] (present tense **KO'ing**, past tense and past participle **KO'd**) informal to make someone unconscious, especially in BOXING • **KO** noun [C] (**KOs**)

koala /kəʊˈɑː.lə/ ⓤⓢ /koʊ-/ noun [C] (also old-fashioned **koˈala ˌbear**) an Australian mammal with greyish fur. Koalas live in EUCALYPTUS trees and eat their leaves.

koala

kofta /ˈkɒf.tə/ ⓤⓢ /ˈkɑːf-/ noun [C or U] a South Asian dish of balls of meat, cheese, or vegetables mixed with spices, or one of these balls

kohl /kəʊl/ ⓤⓢ /koʊl/ noun [U] a dark substance which people put around their eyes, especially the edge of their EYELIDS, to make them more attractive: *a kohl pencil*

kombi (also **combi**) /ˈkɒm.bi/ ⓤⓢ /ˈkɑːm-/ noun [C] South African English a vehicle like a small bus that can carry about ten people

kook /kuːk/ noun [C] US informal a strange person

kookaburra /ˈkʊk.əˌbʌr.ə/ noun [C] a large Australian bird which lives in trees and makes a strange sound like laughter

kooky /ˈkuː.ki/ adj mainly US informal (especially of a person) strange in their appearance or behaviour, especially in a way that is interesting • **kookiness** /-nəs/ noun [U] mainly US informal

Koori (also **Koorie**) /ˈkʊə.ri/ noun [C], adj (an) **Aborigine**

the Koran (also **Qur'an**) /kɒrˈɑːn/ ⓤⓢ /kəˈrɑːn/ noun [S] the holy book of the Islamic religion

korma /ˈkɔː.mə/ ⓤⓢ /ˈkɔːr-/ noun [U] a South Asian dish that consists of meat, fish, or vegetables in a sauce made with cream or COCONUT: *chicken/vegetable korma*

koruna /kɒrˈuː.nə/ ⓤⓢ /ˈkɔːr.uː-/ noun [C] the standard unit of money used in the Czech Republic and in Slovakia

kosher /ˈkəʊ.ʃəʳ/ ⓤⓢ /ˈkoʊ.ʃɚ/ adj **1** (of food or places where food is sold, etc.) prepared or kept in conditions that follow the rules of Jewish law: *kosher food/meat ◦ a kosher restaurant/butcher/shop* **2** informal humorous legal, able to be trusted and therefore good

kowtow /ˌkaʊˈtaʊ/ verb [I] disapproving to show too much respect to someone in authority, always obeying them and changing what you do in order to please them

kph /ˌkeɪ.piːˈeɪtʃ/ abbreviation for kilometres per hour

KPI /ˌkeɪ.piːˈaɪ/ noun [C] specialized abbreviation for key performance indicator: a way of measuring a company's progress towards the aims it is trying to achieve

the Kremlin /ˈkrem.lɪn/ noun [S] a group of buildings in Moscow that is now the centre of government of Russia, or the government itself. In the past the Kremlin also meant the government of the Soviet Union.

krill /krɪl/ noun [U, + sing/pl verb] very small animals with a hard outer shell which live in the sea and are eaten in large numbers by some types of WHALE

Krishna /ˈkrɪʃ.nə/ noun one of the most important of the Hindu gods, considered to be one of the many ways that Vishnu appears

Kris Kringle /ˌkrɪsˈkrɪŋ.gl̩/ noun US for **Santa Claus**

krona /ˈkrəʊ.nə/ ⓤⓢ /ˈkroʊ-/ noun [C] the standard unit of money used in Sweden and Iceland

krone /ˈkrəʊ.nə/ ⓤⓢ /ˈkroʊ-/ noun [C] the standard unit of money used in Denmark and Norway

krypton /ˈkrɪp.tɒn/ ⓤⓢ /-tɑːn/ noun [U] (symbol **Kr**) a chemical element that is a gas which does not react with other elements and is used in some types of lights and LASERS

kudos /ˈkjuː.dɒs/ ⓤⓢ /ˈkuː.dɑːs/ noun [U] the public admiration that a person receives as a result of a particular achievement or position in society: *Being an actor has a certain amount of kudos attached to it.*

the Ku Klux Klan /ˌkuː.klʌksˈklæn/ noun [S, + sing/pl verb] (abbreviation **the KKK**) a secret US organization of white PROTESTANT Americans, especially in the south of the country, who oppose people of other races or religions

kumquat (Australian English usually **cumquat**) /ˈkʌm.kwɒt/ ⓤⓢ /-kwɑːt/ noun [C] a small, oval fruit that looks like an orange and has a sweet skin that can be eaten

kung fu /ˌkʌŋˈfuː/ noun [U] a Chinese method of fighting which involves using your hands and feet and not using weapons

Kurd /kɜːd/ ⓤⓢ /kɝːd/ noun [C] a member of a group of Middle-Eastern people who are not Arabs, who live mostly in an area called Kurdistan, and who speak the Kurdish language • **Kurdish** /ˈkɜː.dɪʃ/ ⓤⓢ /ˈkɝː-/ adj

kurta (also **kurtha**) /ˈkɜː.tə/ ⓤⓢ /ˈkɝː.t̬ə/ noun [C] a loose shirt without a collar, worn by women and men from South Asia

kurtha noun [C] a **kurta**

kvetch /kvetʃ/ verb [I] US informal to complain: *He was kvetching **about** the price.*

kW written abbreviation for **kilowatt**

Kwanzaa (also **Kwanza**) /ˈkwæn.zə/ ⓤⓢ /ˈkwɑːn.zɑː/ noun [U] US an African-American cultural celebration lasting from 26 December to 1 January

kwashiorkor /ˌkwæʃ.iˈɔː.kɔːʳ/ ⓤⓢ /ˌkwɑː.ʃiːˈɔːr.kɔːr/ noun [U] specialized a serious disease caused by eating too little PROTEIN, mainly found in children in parts of tropical Africa

L

L, l /el/ noun; adj noun (plural **Ls, L's** or **l's**) **LETTER** ▷ **1** [C or U] the twelfth letter of the English alphabet **NUMBER** ▷ **2** (also **l**) [C or U] the sign used in the Roman system for the number 50 **LAKE** ▷ **3** written abbreviation for lake: *L. Ontario*

l noun [C] **LINE OF PRINTING** ▷ **1** (plural **ll**) written abbreviation for line **LITRE** ▷ **2** written abbreviation for **litre**

l8r written abbreviation for later, used mainly in emails and text messages

la (also **lah**) /lɑː/ noun [S] the sixth note in the SOL-FA musical SCALE

lab /læb/ noun [C] informal B1 a **laboratory**: *a science lab* ◦ *a lab technician*

Lab. written abbreviation for **Labour**

label /ˈleɪ.bᵊl/ noun; verb

▸noun [C] **SIGN** ▷ **1** B1 a piece of paper or other material that gives you information about the object it is fixed to: *Remember to put some address labels on the suitcases.* ◦ *Washing instructions should be on the label.* **2** C2 a word or a phrase that is used to describe the characteristics or qualities of people, activities, or things, often in a way that is unfair: *He seems to be stuck with the label of 'troublemaker'.* **COMPANY** ▷ **3** B1 a company that produces goods for sale, the goods themselves, or the company's name or symbol: *Her favourite **designer** label (= maker of expensive clothes) is Armani.* ◦ *Their own-label vegetarian products have been a huge success.* ◦ *The group have just signed (= arranged to record) with a new **record** label.*

▸verb [T] (**-ll-** or US usually **-l-**) C1 to fasten a label to: [+ adj] *The parcel was **clearly** labelled 'Fragile'.* ◦ *If you spend any time in prison, you're labelled as a criminal for the rest of your life.*

labia /ˈleɪ.bi.ə/ noun [plural] specialized folds on the outside of the female sex organs

labial /ˈleɪ.bi.əl/ adj; noun

▸adj **1** specialized Labial sounds are consonant sounds made with the two lips: */m/ and /p/ are labial sounds.* **2** specialized relating to the lips: *labial surgery*

▸noun [C] specialized a consonant sound that is made with the two lips

labiodental /ˌleɪ.bi.əʊˈden.tᵊl/ US /-oʊˈden.tᵊl/ noun [C] specialized a consonant sound in which the lips touch the teeth: */f/ and /v/are labiodentals.*

Labor /ˈleɪ.bəʳ/ US /-bɚ/ noun [+ sing/pl verb] (abbreviation **ALP**) the Labor Party, an Australian political party that believes in social EQUALITY and the rights of workers → See also **Labour**

laboratory /ləˈbɒr.ə.tᵊr.i/ US /ˈlæb.rə.tɔːr.i/ noun [C] (informal **lab**) B1 a room or building with scientific equipment for doing scientific tests or for teaching science, or a place where chemicals or medicines are produced: *research laboratories* ◦ *a computer laboratory* ◦ *Laboratory tests suggest that the new drug may be used to treat cancer.*

ˈ**Labor** ˌ**Day** noun a US holiday on the first Monday in September, when people celebrate the achievements of workers and the workers' movement

laborious /ləˈbɔː.ri.əs/ US /-ˈbɔːr.i-/ adj needing a lot of time and effort: *a laborious task* • **laboriously** /-li/ adv

ˈ**labor** ˌ**union** noun [C] US for **trade union**

labour /ˈleɪ.bəʳ/ US /-bɚ/ noun; verb

▸noun UK (US **labor**) **WORK** ▷ **1** C1 [U] practical work, especially that which involves physical effort: *The car parts themselves are not expensive, it's the labour that costs the money.* ◦ ***manual** labour (= hard work using the hands)* **2** C1 [U] workers, especially people who do practical work with their hands: *skilled/unskilled labour* **3 labours** (US also **labors**) [plural] all the effort and hard work that have been involved in doing a particular piece of work: *Are you tired after your labours?* ◦ *West was paid very little for his labours.* ◦ *Retirement is the time to enjoy **the fruits of** your labours.* **BIRTH** ▷ **4** C2 [C or U] the last stage of pregnancy from the time when the muscles of the WOMB start to push the baby out of the body until the baby appears: *labour pains* ◦ *She **went into** (= started) labour at twelve o'clock last night.* ◦ *I was **in** labour for twelve hours with my first baby.* ◦ *No two labours are ever the same.*

IDIOM **labour of love** C2 a piece of hard work which you do because you enjoy it and not because you will receive money or praise for it, or because you need to do it: *He's always working on his car – it's a labour of love.*

▸verb UK (US **labor**) **1** [I] to do hard physical work: *He travelled around Europe labouring to pay his way.* ◦ [+ to infinitive] *Three hours after the explosion, rescue teams were still labouring **to** free those trapped.* **2** [I + adv/prep] to do something slowly with great physical or mental effort: *He laboured up the hill with his heavy load.* ◦ *She's been labouring over the same article for days.*

IDIOMS **labour the point** to try too hard to express an idea, feeling, or opinion, repeating it when this is not necessary: *Look, there's no need to labour the point – I made a mistake – I admit it!* • **labour under the delusion, illusion, misapprehension, etc.** to wrongly believe that something is true: *At the time I was still labouring under the delusion **that** the project might be a success.*

Labour /ˈleɪ.bəʳ/ US /-bɚ/ noun; adj

▸noun [+ sing/pl verb] the Labour Party, the political party in Britain that believes in social EQUALITY, a more equal sharing out of WEALTH, and the rights of workers: *Labour are sure to get in at the next election.* ◦ *I voted Labour in the last election.*

▸adj belonging or relating to the Labour Party: *the Labour **Party*** ◦ *Labour voters* ◦ *the Labour candidate*

ˈ**labour** ˌ**camp** UK (US ˈ**labor** ˌ**camp**) noun [C] a place in which people are kept as prisoners and forced to do hard physical work in bad conditions

ˈ**Labour** ˌ**Day** UK (US ˈ**Labor** ˌ**Day**) noun [C usually singular] a public holiday to celebrate working people: *1 May is Labour Day in a lot of countries.*

laboured UK (US **labored**) /ˈleɪ.bəd/ US /-bɚd/ adj needing a lot of effort, often because someone is tired: *Her breathing was heavy and laboured.* ◦ *a laboured joke*

labourer UK (US **laborer**) /ˈleɪ.bᵊr.əʳ/ US /-bɚ.ɚ/ noun [C] a person who does unskilled physical work, especially outside: *a farm labourer*

ˈ**labour** ˌ**force** UK (US ˈ**labor** ˌ**force**) noun [U] C2 all the people in a particular country who are of the right age to work, or all the people who work for a particular company

ˌ**labour-inˈtensive** UK (US ˌ**labor-inˈtensive**) adj

Industries and methods that are labour-intensive need a lot of workers

ˈlabour ˌmarket UK (US **ˈlabor ˌmarket**) **noun** [C] C1 the supply of people in a particular country or area who are able and willing to work: *More women are being encouraged into the labour market these days.*

ˈlabour reˌlations UK (US **ˈlabor reˌlations**) **noun** [plural] the relationships between employees and employers: *The firm prided itself on its good labour relations.*

ˈlabour-ˌsaving UK (US **ˈlabor-ˌsaving**) **adj** describes a device or method which saves a lot of effort and time

Labrador /ˈlæb.rə.dɔːʳ/ US /-dɔːr/ **noun** [C] a big yellow, black, or brown dog with short hair: *Labradors are used as guide dogs for blind people.*

laburnum /ləˈbɜː.nəm/ US /-ˈbɝː-/ **noun** [C or U] a small tree with groups of yellow flowers hanging down

labyrinth /ˈlæb.ə.rɪnθ/ **noun** [C] literary **1** a confusing set of connecting passages or paths in which it is easy to get lost: *Finally, through a labyrinth of corridors she found his office.* **2** something that is very confusing: *He was no stranger to the labyrinth **of** love.*

labyrinthine /ˌlæb.əˈrɪn.θaɪn/ **adj** literary describes something that has a lot of parts and is therefore confusing: *Beneath the city lies a labyrinthine network of tunnels.* ◦ *It takes a fair amount of concentration to follow the film's labyrinthine plot.*

L

lace /leɪs/ **noun; verb**

▸**noun MATERIAL** ▷ **1** [U] a decorative cloth made by twisting thin thread in delicate patterns with holes in them: *lace curtains* **STRING** ▷ **2** [C usually plural] a string which you use to fasten openings, especially in shoes, by putting it through two lines of small holes and tying the ends together: *Your **shoe** laces are undone.*

▸**verb** [T] **ADD ALCOHOL** ▷ **1** to add alcohol or drugs to food or drink, often secretly: *coffee laced **with** brandy* **STRING** ▷ **2** to put the lace of a shoe or boot through its holes, or to fasten a shoe or boot by tying a lace

PHRASAL VERB **lace sth up** to fasten shoes, boots, or a piece of clothing by tying the laces: *lace-up shoes*

lacerate /ˈlæs.ᵊr.eɪt/ US /-ə.reɪt/ **verb** [T] formal to cut or tear something, especially flesh: *The man's face was severely lacerated in the accident.*

laceration /ˌlæs.ᵊrˈeɪ.ʃᵊn/ US /-əˈreɪ-/ **noun** [C or U] formal a cut: *The boy had received horrific injuries in the attack, including lacerations **to** both arms.*

ˈlace-ups **noun** [plural] shoes or boots that are fastened using laces: *a pair of lace-ups*

lachrymose /ˈlæk.rɪ.məʊs/ US /-mous/ **adj** literary sad or likely to cry often and easily: *He is better known for his lachrymose ballads than hard rock numbers.*

lack /læk/ **noun; verb**

▸**noun lack of sth** B1 the fact that something is not available or that there is not enough of it: *Her only problem is a lack of confidence.* ◦ *Lack of sleep had made him irritable.* ◦ *If he fails it won't be **for/through** lack of effort (= he has certainly tried).* ◦ *We won't be going on holiday this year – lack of funds, I'm afraid.*

> **Word partners for lack noun**
>
> a *complete/distinct/marked/total* lack of sth • a *comparative/relative* lack of sth • an *apparent* lack of sth • *for* lack **of** sth

▸**verb** [T] B2 to not have or not have enough of something that is needed or wanted: *He just lacks a little confidence.* ◦ *What we lack in this house is space to store things.* ◦ *We are lacking three members of staff due to illness.*

> **Common mistake: lack**
>
> Remember that when **lack** is a verb it is never followed by 'of'.
>
> Don't say 'something lacks of something', say **something lacks something**:
>
> ~~*Our town lacks of a good shopping centre.*~~
>
> *Our town lacks a good shopping centre.*

lackadaisical /ˌlæk.əˈdeɪ.zɪ.kᵊl/ **adj** formal showing little enthusiasm and effort: *The food was nice enough but the service was rather lackadaisical.* • **lackadaisically** /-kᵊli/ **adv**

lackey /ˈlæk.i/ **noun** [C] disapproving a servant or someone who behaves like one by obeying someone else's orders or by doing all their unpleasant work for them: *He treats us all like his lackeys.*

lacking /ˈlæk.ɪŋ/ **adj** **1 be lacking** C2 If something that you need is lacking, you do not have enough of it: *Enthusiasm has been **sadly** lacking these past months at work.* **2 be lacking in sth** C1 to not have a quality: *He's totally lacking in charm.*

lacklustre UK (US **lackluster**) /ˈlækˌlʌs.təʳ/ US /-tɚ/ **adj** without energy and effort: *Britain's number-one tennis player gave a disappointingly lacklustre performance.*

laconic /ləˈkɒn.ɪk/ US /-ˈkɑː.nɪk/ **adj** formal using very few words to express what you mean: *She had a laconic wit.* • **laconically** /ləˈkɒn.ɪ.kᵊl.i/ US /-ˈkɑː.nɪ-/ **adv**

lacquer /ˈlæk.əʳ/ US /-ɚ/ **noun; verb**

▸**noun** [U] **WOOD/METAL** ▷ **1** a liquid that is painted on wood or metal and forms a hard, shiny surface when it dries **HAIR** ▷ **2** (also **hair lacquer**) UK for **hair spray**

▸**verb** [T] to paint wood or metal with lacquer

lacrosse /ləˈkrɒs/ US /-ˈkrɑːs/ **noun** [U] a game played by two teams in which the players each use a long stick with a net at the end to catch, carry, and throw a small ball, and try to get the ball in the other team's goal

lactate /lækˈteɪt/ US /ˈlæk.teɪt/ **verb** [I] specialized (of a woman or female mammal) to produce milk • **lactation** /lækˈteɪ.ʃᵊn/ **noun** [U]

lactic /ˈlæk.tɪk/ **adj** specialized relating to milk

ˌlactic ˈacid **noun** [U] an ACID that exists in sour milk and is produced in muscles after a lot of exercise

lactose /ˈlæk.təʊs/ US /-tous/ **noun** [U] specialized a type of sugar that is found in milk

ˌlactose inˈtolerance **noun** [U] the inability to digest lactose (= a substance in milk) • **ˌlactose-inˈtolerant adj**

lacto-vegetarian /ˌlæk.təʊ.vedʒ.ɪˈteə.ri.ən/ US /-tou.vedʒ.ɪˈter.i-/ **noun** [C] a person who does not eat meat, fish, or eggs but does drink milk and eat some foods made from milk: *As a lacto-vegetarian he eats cheese, as long as it does not contain animal products such as rennet.* • **lacto-vegetarian adj** *Lacto-vegetarian diets are common among Sikhs and Hindus.*

lacuna /ləˈkjuː.nə/ US /-ˈkuː-/ **noun** [C] (plural **lacunae** or **lacunas**) formal an absent part, especially in a book or other piece of writing

lacy /ˈleɪ.si/ **adj** made of or decorated with LACE (= decorative cloth): *lacy underwear*

lad /læd/ **noun** [C] a boy or young man: *A group of young lads were standing outside the shop.* ◦ *He's a nice lad.* ◦ *The prime minister's a **local** lad (= he was born and lived in this area).* ◦ *lads **and lasses** (= boys and* *girls)* ◦ [as form of address] *Come on, lads, let's get this job finished, shall we!*

IDIOMS **a bit of a lad** UK informal a young man who has sex with a lot of different women • **the lads** UK informal used to refer to the group of men that a young man spends time with socially, especially those who he drinks alcohol with or plays sport with: *I'm having a night out with the lads.*

ladder /ˈlæd.əʳ/ (US) /-ɚ/ noun; verb

▸noun **EQUIPMENT** ▷ **1** (B1) [C] a piece of equipment used for climbing up and down, which consists of two vertical bars or pieces of rope joined to each other by a set of horizontal steps: *She was **up** a ladder, cleaning the window.* **SERIES OF STAGES** ▷ **2** (C1) [S] a series of increasingly important jobs or stages in a particular type of work or process: *Once he started at Paramount in 1967, he moved rapidly up the corporate ladder.* ◦ *a first **rung/step on** the employment ladder* **HOLE** ▷ **3** [C] UK (US **run**) a long, vertical hole in a pair of TIGHTS or a STOCKING **COMPETITION** ▷ **4** [C] (also **ladder tournament**) mainly UK (in particular sports) a system in which all the players who play regularly are given a position in a list and can improve their position by beating other players in that list: *a squash ladder*

▸verb [I or T] UK If a pair of TIGHTS or a STOCKING ladder or if you ladder them, a long hole appears in them: *Damn! That's the second pair of tights I've laddered today!*

laddie /ˈlæd.i/ noun Scottish English informal for **lad**

laddish /ˈlæd.ɪʃ/ adj UK disapproving describes the noisy, energetic, and sometimes rude behaviour that some young men show in social groups • **laddishness** /-nəs/ noun [U]

laden /ˈleɪ.dᵊn/ adj carrying or holding a lot of something: *He always comes back from France laden **with** presents for everyone.* ◦ *The table, as always, was laden **with** food.*

ladette /lædˈet/ noun [C] informal a young woman who drinks a lot of alcohol, uses rude language, and behaves in a noisy way

la-di-da (also **lah-di-dah**) /ˌlɑː.dɪˈdɑː/ adj old-fashioned informal describes speech or behaviour that is not sincere because the person is pretending to belong to a higher social class

ˈladies' ˌfingers noun [plural] UK old-fashioned **okra**

ˈladies' ˌman noun [C usually singular] old-fashioned a man who gives women a lot of attention and likes to be with them: *John was always **a bit of a** ladies' man.*

ˈladies' ˌroom noun [S] US (UK **ladies**) a women's toilet in a public building such as a hotel or restaurant

ladle /ˈleɪ.dl/ noun; verb

▸noun [C] a very big spoon with a long handle and a deep cup-shaped part, used especially for serving soup: *a soup ladle*

▸verb [T] (also **ladle out**) to put soup or other liquid food into bowls to give to people, using a ladle

PHRASAL VERB **ladle sth out** informal to give money or goods in a (too) generous way to a lot of people: *In those days doctors ladled out antibiotics to patients.*

ˈlad ˌmag noun [C] informal a magazine for men

lady /ˈleɪ.di/ noun **1** (B1) [C] a polite or old-fashioned way of referring to or talking to a woman: *There's a young lady here to see you.* ◦ *Mind your language – there are ladies present!* ◦ *Say 'thank you' to the lady, children.* ◦ old-fashioned *Is the lady **of the house** (= the most important or only woman who lives in the house) at home?* **2** [C] old-fashioned a woman who behaves in a way that is traditionally considered to be suitable for a woman: *Of course I remember Mrs Connor – she was a real lady.* **3** [C] old-fashioned sometimes used before the name of a job done by a woman: *a lady doctor* **4** [as form of address] US used to talk to a woman in a way that is not polite and is considered offensive by many women: *Hey, lady, what's the rush?* **5 ladies** [S, + sing/pl verb] UK (US **ladies' room**) a women's toilet in a public place or building such as a hotel or restaurant: *I'm just going to the ladies.* ◦ *Is there a ladies on this floor?* **6 ladies and gentlemen** used to talk to the members of the audience when you are making a speech: *Good evening, ladies and gentlemen, and welcome to the Theatre Royal.*

Lady /ˈleɪ.di/ noun [C] a title given in the UK to a woman or girl who has the social rank of a PEER, or to the wife of a PEER or KNIGHT: *Lady Diana Spencer* → Compare **Lord**

ladybird /ˈleɪ.di.bɜːd/ (US) /-bɝːd/ noun [C] UK (US **ladybug** /ˈleɪ.di.bʌɡ/) a small, red BEETLE that is round and has black spots

ˌLady ˈBountiful noun [S] disapproving a woman who enjoys showing people how rich and kind she is by giving things to poor people

ˌlady-in-ˈwaiting noun [C] (plural **ladies-in-waiting**) a woman whose job is to help a queen or other woman of high social position

ˈlady-ˌkiller noun [C] old-fashioned a sexually attractive man who has sexual relationships with many women

ladylike /ˈleɪ.di.laɪk/ adj old-fashioned GRACEFUL, polite, and behaving in a way that is socially acceptable for a woman

ˌLady ˈMuck noun [S] UK informal disapproving a woman who thinks she is very important and should be treated better than everyone else: *Look at Lady Muck over there, expecting everyone to wait on her!*

ladyship /ˈleɪ.di.ʃɪp/ noun formal **her/your ladyship** a polite way of referring to or talking to a woman or girl who has the rank of a PEER OR KNIGHT without using her title: *We are honoured to welcome your ladyship (= you) here tonight.* → Compare **lordship**

lag /læɡ/ verb; noun

▸verb (-gg-) **MOVE SLOWLY** ▷ **1** [I] to move or make progress so slowly that you are behind other people or things: *He's lagging **behind** a bit – I think we'd better wait for him to catch us up.* ◦ *Sales are lagging at the moment.* **COVER** ▷ **2** [T] to cover something with a thick layer of material in order to stop heat from escaping or to stop water from freezing: *to lag pipes* **PRISON** ▷ **3** [T] Australian English informal to send someone to prison or to arrest someone

▸noun [C] **DELAY** ▷ **1** a delay between two things happening: *You have to allow for a time lag **between** order and delivery.* **PRISONER** ▷ **2** UK old-fashioned informal a prisoner or a person who has often been a prisoner in the past: *an **old** lag*

lager /ˈlɑː.ɡəʳ/ (US) /-ɡɚ/ noun [C or U] a type of beer that is pale in colour and usually contains a lot of bubbles: *Two pints of lager and a packet of crisps, please.*

L

ˈ**lager** ˌ**lout** noun [C usually plural] UK informal a young man whose behaviour is noisy, offensive, and often violent after drinking too much alcohol

laggard /ˈlæg.əd/ (US) /-ɚd/ noun [C] old-fashioned someone or something that is very slow

lagging /ˈlæg.ɪŋ/ noun [U] a thick layer of material used to cover pipes, water TANKS (= large containers), and other surfaces in order to stop heat from escaping or water from freezing

lagoon /ləˈguːn/ noun [C] an area of sea water separated from the sea by a REEF (= a line of rocks and sand): *a tropical lagoon*

lah /lɑː/ noun [S] the musical note **la**

lah-di-dah /ˌlɑː.dɪˈdɑː/ adj **la-di-da**

laid /leɪd/ verb past simple and past participle of **lay**

IDIOM **be laid up** to be forced to stay in bed because of an illness or accident: *She's been laid up in bed* ***with*** *flu for a week.*

ˌ**laid-**ˈ**back** adj informal C2 relaxed in manner and character; not usually worried about other people's behaviour or things that need to be done: *I've never seen her worried or anxious in any way – she's so laid-back.*

lain /leɪn/ verb past participle of **lie**

lair /leəʳ/ (US) /ler/ noun [C usually singular] a place where a wild animal lives, often underground and hidden, or a place where a person hides: *a fox's lair* ◦ *the thieves' lair*

L

laird /leəd/ (US) /lerd/ noun [C] a Scottish man who owns a large area of land

lairy /ˈleə.ri/ (US) /ˈle.ri/ adj UK slang behaving in a loud, excited manner, especially when you are enjoying yourself or drinking alcohol: *The bar was full of lairy, pint-swilling lads in football shirts.*

laissez-faire /ˌleɪ.seɪˈfeəʳ/ (US) /-ˈfer/ noun [U] **1** unwillingness to get involved in or influence other people's activities: *The problems began long before he became headteacher, but they worsened with his laissez-faire* ***approach/attitude***. **2** If a government is laissez-faire, it does not have many laws and rules which control the buying and selling of goods and services.

the laity /ˈleɪ.ə.ti/ (US) /-t̬i/ noun [S, + sing/pl verb] all the people who are involved with a Church but who are not priests

lake /leɪk/ noun [C] **1** A2 a large area of water surrounded by land and not connected to the sea except by rivers or streams: *We used to go boating on that lake.* ◦ *Lake Windermere* **2 milk, oil, wine, etc. lake** disapproving an amount of a liquid produced that is more than is needed, so that it has to be stored or wasted: *Overproduction caused butter mountains and wine lakes.*

lakeside /ˈleɪk.saɪd/ noun [S] the area at the edge of a lake: *a walk by the lakeside* ◦ *a lakeside chalet*

lakh /lɑːk/, /læk/ **number** Indian English the number 100,000: *The total cost of the project is around 50 lakh rupees.*

ˈ**la-la** ˌ**land** noun informal **be/live in la-la land** to think that things that are completely impossible might happen, rather than understanding how things really are

lam /læm/ noun US **on the lam** escaping, especially from the police: *The robbers were on the lam for several days before they were caught.*

lama /ˈlɑː.mə/ noun [C] a title given to a Tibetan Buddhist spiritual teacher → See also **the Dalai Lama**

Lamaism /ˈlɑː.mə.ɪ.zᵊm/ noun [U] Tibetan Buddhism

lamb /læm/ noun; verb

▸noun [C or U] B1 a young sheep, or the flesh of a young sheep eaten as meat: *lambs gambolling about in the fields* ◦ *lamb chops* ◦ *roast lamb* → See also **mutton**

IDIOM **like a lamb to the slaughter** If someone does something or goes somewhere like a lamb to the slaughter, they do it without knowing that something bad is going to happen and therefore act calmly and without fighting against the situation.

▸verb [I] (of a sheep) to give birth to lambs

lambada /læmˈbɑː.də/ noun [C] a dance, originally from Brazil, in which two people hold each other closely and move their hips at the same time

lambaste (also **lambast**) /læmˈbæst/ verb [T] to criticize someone or something severely: *His first novel was well and truly lambasted by the critics.*

lambent /ˈlæm.bᵊnt/ adj literary **1** shining gently: *a lambent glow* **2 lambent wit** the ability to use words in a clever and humorous way without being unkind

ˈ**lambing** ˌ**season** noun [C usually singular] the time in the year when sheep give birth to lambs

lambskin /ˈlæm.skɪn/ noun [U] leather made from the skin of a young sheep with the wool still joined to it

lambswool /ˈlæmz.wʊl/ noun [U] the soft wool from a young sheep, used especially to make clothes: *a lambswool sweater*

lame /leɪm/ adj **UNABLE TO WALK** ▷ **1** (especially of animals) not able to walk correctly because of physical injury to or weakness in the legs or feet **NOT SATISFACTORY** ▷ **2** (especially of an excuse or argument) weak and unsatisfactory: *a lame* ***excuse*** • **lamely** /-li/ adv • **lameness** /-nəs/ noun [U]

lamé /ˈlɑː.meɪ/ noun [U] a type of cloth with threads of gold or silver in it: *gold/silver lamé*

ˌ**lame** ˈ**duck** noun [C] **UNSUCCESSFUL** ▷ **1** an unsuccessful person or thing **POLITICS** ▷ **2** an elected official whose power is reduced because the person who will replace them has already been elected

lament /ləˈment/ verb; noun

▸verb [I or T] to express sadness and feeling sorry about something: *The poem opens by lamenting (****over****) the death of a young man.* ◦ *My grandmother, as usual, lamented the decline in moral standards in today's society.* ◦ *The* ***late*** *lamented (= dead and remembered with love) Frank Giotto used to live here.*

▸noun [C] formal a song, poem, or other piece of writing that expresses sadness about someone's death: *The whole play can be interpreted as a lament* ***for*** *lost youth.*

lamentable /ləˈmen.tə.bl̩/, /ˈlæm.ən-/ (US) /-t̬ə-/ adj formal deserving severe criticism; very bad: *the lamentable state of the economy* • **lamentably** /-bli/ adv *The government, says the report, have carried out lamentably few of their promises.*

lamentation /ˌlæm.enˈteɪ.ʃᵊn/ noun [C or U] formal sadness and feeling sorry, or something that expresses these feelings

laminate /ˈlæm.ɪ.nət/ noun [C or U] any material that is made by sticking several layers of the same material together: *laminate flooring*

laminated /ˈlæm.ɪ.neɪ.tɪd/ (US) /-t̬ɪd/ adj **1** covered with a thin layer of plastic to protect it: *The recipe cards are laminated so they can be wiped clean.* ◦ *a laminated menu/map/ID card* **2** consisting of several thin layers of wood, plastic, glass, etc. stuck together: *laminated kitchen worktops*

lamington /ˈlæm.ɪŋ.tən/ noun [C or U] Australian

English a cake covered with a chocolate layer and COCONUT

lamp /læmp/ noun [C] **1** A2 a device for giving light, especially one that has a covering or is contained within something: *an electric/oil/gas lamp* ◦ *a street lamp* ◦ *a table/bedside lamp* → See also **sunlamp** **2** any of various devices that produce particular types of light: *an infrared lamp*

lamplight /ˈlæmp.laɪt/ noun [U] literary light from a lamp, especially light that is not very bright and only shines over a small area: *She studied the pale skin of his face* ***in the*** *dim lamplight.*

lampoon /læmˈpuːn/ noun [C] a piece of writing, a drawing, etc. which criticizes in a humorous way a famous person or a public organization, allowing their bad qualities to be seen and making them seem stupid: *The magazine is famed for its merciless political lampoons.* • **lampoon** verb [T] *Many celebrities are lampooned on this satirical website.*

lamppost /ˈlæmp.pəʊst/ US /-poʊst/ noun [C] a tall post which holds a light at the side of roads and in other public places

lamprey /ˈlæm.pri/ noun [C] a long, snake-like fish which uses its sucking mouth to feed off the blood of other animals

lampshade /ˈlæmp.ʃeɪd/ noun [C] a decorative covering around an electric light which reduces its brightness or controls where it shines

lampstand /ˈlæmp.stænd/ noun [C] a heavy, often decorative, base for an electric light which stands on a table or the floor

LAN /læn/ noun [C] abbreviation for local area network: a system for connecting the computers of people who work in the same building → Compare **WAN**

lance /lɑːns/ US /læns/ noun; verb

▸noun [C] a long, thin pole with a sharp point which soldiers used in the past as a weapon when riding horses

▸verb [T] to cut the skin with a sharp tool in order to release infected matter that has collected under it: *She had a* ***boil*** *lanced at the doctor's this morning.*

ˌlance ˈcorporal noun [C] (also **Lance Corporal**) a soldier who has the second lowest rank in the British, Australian, or other army: *Lance Corporal Smith/Charlie Smith* ◦ [as form of address] *Thank you, Lance Corporal.*

lancer /ˈlɑːn.səʳ/ US /ˈlæn.sɚ/ noun [C] a soldier who belongs to the part of an army that used lances in the past: *the Queen's Royal Lancers*

lancet /ˈlɑːn.sɪt/ US /ˈlæn-/ noun [C] a small knife with two cutting edges and a sharp point that a doctor uses when cutting the skin

land /lænd/ noun; verb

▸noun DRY SURFACE ▷ **1** B2 [U] the surface of the Earth that is not covered by water: *It is cheaper to drill for oil* ***on*** *land than at sea.* ◦ *The treaty has led to a dramatic reduction in the number of land-****based*** *missiles in Europe.* ◦ *The military commanders won't deploy their land* ***forces*** *until they're satisfied that the air attacks have done their job.* **2** B1 [U] an area of ground, especially when used for a particular purpose such as farming or building: *This sort of land is no good for growing potatoes.* ◦ *I always prosecute people who trespass on my land.* ◦ *We want to buy* ***a plot of*** *land to build a house.* **3 the land** farms, farming, and the countryside: *Most of the families* ***lived off*** *the land* (= *grew their own food, etc.*). ◦ *My parents* ***worked*** (***on***) *the land.* COUNTRY ▷ **4** C2 [C] literary a country: *a land of ice and snow* ◦ *The group want to promote their ideas in schools* ***throughout*** *the land.* → See also **fatherland, homeland, motherland**

IDIOMS **be in the land of nod** old-fashioned informal to be sleeping: *Jamie's in the land of nod at last.* • **be in the land of the living** humorous to be awake or to be alive: *She was partying till the early hours, so I don't imagine she'll be in the land of the living before lunchtime.* • **find out/see how the land lies** to wait until you have all the available information about a situation before you take any action • **land of milk and honey** a country where living conditions are good and people have the opportunity to make a lot of money: *Many Mexicans regard the United States as a land of milk and honey.*

▸verb ARRIVE ▷ **1** B1 [I or T] to (cause to) arrive on the ground or other surface after moving down through the air: *We should land* ***in*** *Madrid at 7am.* ◦ *You can land a plane on water in an emergency.* ◦ *The bird landed on my finger.* ◦ figurative *The report first landed* ***on*** *my desk this morning.* **2** B1 [I] to arrive in a boat: *We landed at Port Said in the early evening.* UNLOAD ▷ **3** [T] to take goods or people off a ship or aircraft: *The general's plan involved landing troops behind enemy lines.* CATCH ▷ **4** [T] to catch a fish with a HOOK (= curved piece of wire) or net and remove it from the water: *He landed a huge salmon.* ACHIEVE ▷ **5** C2 [T] to get or achieve something good, especially in a way which seems easy or unexpected: *He's just landed a senior editorial job.*

IDIOM **land on your feet** to return to a good situation after experiencing problems, especially because of good luck rather than skill or hard work: *She's really landed on her feet with this new job.*

PHRASAL VERBS **land sb in sth** to cause someone to be in a difficult situation: *Revealing confidential information to a rival company could land you in serious trouble with your boss.* ◦ *The demonstration outside the embassy landed some of the protesters in jail overnight.* ◦ *He landed himself in* ***deep/hot water*** (= *in a very difficult or unpleasant situation*) *by lying to the tax office about his earnings.* • **land up** informal to finally be in a particular place, state, or situation, especially without having planned it: *When we accepted that lift in Paris, we never expected to land up* ***in*** *Athens.* ◦ *He'll land up* ***in*** *hospital if he carries on drinking like that.* • **land sb with sth** If someone or something lands you with something, they cause problems for you: *I hope you don't mind me landing you with the children at such short notice.* ◦ *Alan's gone off on holiday and I've been landed with the job of sorting out his mistakes.*

landbanking /ˈlænd.bæŋk.ɪŋ/ noun [U] a way of making a profit by buying fields and selling them at a much higher price to people who hope they can build houses on them in the future • **landbanker** /-əʳ/ US /-ɚ/ noun [C]

landed /ˈlæn.dɪd/ adj [before noun] describes people whose families have owned a lot of land for many GENERATIONS (= family age groups): *the landed* ***gentry***

landfall /ˈlænd.fɔːl/ US /-fɑːl/ noun [C or U] the first land that is reached or seen at the end of a journey across the sea or through the air, or the fact of arriving there: *Shannon Airport in Ireland was the first European landfall for planes flying from North America.* ◦ *After a long and gruelling flight, they finally* ***made*** *landfall in Florida.*

landfill /ˈlænd.fɪl/ noun [C or U] the process of getting rid of large amounts of rubbish by burying it, or a

L

place where rubbish is buried: *90 percent of American rubbish is dumped in landfill* ***sites***.

ˌland-grant uniˈversity noun [C] in the US, one of a group of universities that receive FEDERAL (= national government) money and that were originally created to educate members of the working classes in subjects relating to AGRICULTURE and science

landholding /ˈlændˌhəʊl.dɪŋ/ (US) /-ˌhoʊl-/ noun [C] an area of land that someone owns or rents • **landholder** /-dəʳ/ (US) /-dɚ/ noun [C]

landing /ˈlæn.dɪŋ/ noun [C] **PLANE/BOAT** ▷ **1** (B2) the fact of an aircraft arriving on the ground or a boat reaching land: *One person has died after the pilot of a light aircraft was forced to make a* ***crash/emergency*** *landing in a field.* **FLOOR** ▷ **2** an area of floor that joins two sets of stairs or that leads from the top of a set of stairs to rooms

ˈlanding ˌcraft noun [C] (plural **landing craft**) a small boat with a flat bottom that opens at one end and is used to take soldiers and their equipment from a ship onto land controlled by enemy forces

ˈlanding ˌgear noun [U] (UK also **undercarriage**) the set of wheels and other parts which support a plane when it is on the ground and make it possible to take off and land

ˈlanding ˌstage noun [C] a flat structure, often wooden and floating, that acts as a bridge with the land when taking goods on or off boats or ships

ˈlanding ˌstrip noun [C] a long flat area of ground that is used by aircraft with wings when taking off and landing

landlady /ˈlændˌleɪ.di/ noun [C] **OWNER** ▷ **1** (B2) a woman who is paid rent by people for the use of a room, building, or piece of land which she owns **BAR MANAGER** ▷ **2** a woman who is in charge of a pub or bar

landless /ˈlænd.ləs/ adj describes people who do not have any land for farming or who are prevented from owning the land that they farm by the economic system or by rich people who own a lot of land: *landless labourers/peasants*

landline /ˈlænd.laɪn/ noun [C] **1** a phone that is connected to the phone system by wires **2** a CABLE (= set of wires) that carries phone signals under the ground

landlocked /ˈlænd.lɒkt/ (US) /-lɑːkt/ adj surrounded by the land of other countries and having no sea coast

landlord /ˈlænd.lɔːd/ (US) /-lɔːrd/ noun [C] **OWNER** ▷ **1** (B2) a person or organization that owns a building or an area of land and is paid by other people for the use of it: *The landlord had promised to redecorate the bedrooms before we moved in.* ◦ *Housing associations are the biggest landlords in this area.* **BAR MANAGER** ▷ **2** UK a man who is in charge of a pub or bar

landlubber /ˈlændˌlʌb.əʳ/ (US) /-ɚ/ noun [C] old-fashioned a person who has little knowledge or experience of ships and travelling by sea

landmark /ˈlænd.mɑːk/ (US) /-mɑːrk/ noun [C] **OBJECT** ▷ **1** (C1) a building or place that is easily recognized, especially one which you can use to judge where you are: *The Rock of Gibraltar is one of Europe's most* ***famous*** *landmarks.* **STAGE** ▷ **2** (C2) an important stage in something's development: *The invention of the silicon chip was a landmark* ***in the history of*** *the computer.* ◦ *In a landmark* ***case/decision****, the governor pardoned a woman convicted of killing her husband, who had physically abused her.*

ˌlandmarked ˈbuilding noun [C] US for **listed building**

landmass /ˈlænd.mæs/ noun [C] specialized a large area of land that is in one piece and not broken up by seas

landmine /ˈlænd.maɪn/ noun [C] (also **mine**) a bomb that is put on or under the ground and explodes when a person steps on it or a vehicle drives over it

landowner /ˈlændˌəʊ.nəʳ/ (US) /-ˌoʊ.nɚ/ noun [C] someone who owns land, especially a large amount of land • **landowning** /-nɪŋ/ adj [before noun] *She was born into a wealthy landowning* ***family***.

ˈLand ˌRover noun [C] trademark a strong, powerful vehicle designed for travelling over rough or steep ground and used especially by people who work in the countryside

landscape /ˈlænd.skeɪp/ noun; verb; adj

▸**noun 1** (B1) [C] a large area of countryside, especially in relation to its appearance: *a rural/barren landscape* ◦ *The landscape is dotted with the tents of campers and hikers.* ◦ *The cathedral dominates the landscape for miles around.* **2** [C or U] a view or picture of the countryside, or the art of making such pictures: *a watercolour landscape.* ◦ *J.M.W. Turner is one of Britain's best-known landscape* ***painters***.

▸**verb** [T] to change the appearance of an area of land, especially next to a building or road so that it looks more like natural countryside

▸**adj** describes a document that is to be printed with the longer side of the paper at the top and bottom → Compare **portrait**

ˌlandscape ˈgardening noun [U] the art of making gardens, parks, and areas around buildings look more natural and attractive • **ˌlandscape ˈgardener** noun [C] (US also **landscaper**)

landslide /ˈlænd.slaɪd/ noun [C] **FALLING EARTH** ▷ **1** (also **landslip**) a mass of rock and earth moving suddenly and quickly down a steep slope **VICTORY** ▷ **2** the winning of an election with an extremely large number of votes: *The opinion polls are predicting a Labour landslide in next week's election.* ◦ *a landslide* ***victory***

ˈland ˌtenure noun [U] specialized the rules and arrangements connected with owning land, especially land that is used for farming

lane /leɪn/ noun [C] **ROAD** ▷ **1** (B2) a narrow road in the countryside or in a town: *He drives so fast along those narrow country lanes.* ◦ *I live at the end of Church Lane.* **STRIP** ▷ **2** (B2) a special strip of a road, sports track, or swimming pool that is used to keep vehicles or competitors separate: *a bus/cycle lane* ◦ *The northbound lane is closed because of an accident.* ◦ *I find driving in the* ***fast*** *lane rather stressful.* ◦ *The British runners/swimmers are in lanes 4 and 6.* **3** a route through the sea or the air which ships or aircraft regularly sail or fly along: *The English Channel is the busiest* ***shipping*** *lane in the world.*

langoustine /ˌlɑ̃ŋ.guˈstiːn/ noun [C] a sea creature with a shell and ten legs, like a large PRAWN or small LOBSTER, that can be eaten

language /ˈlæŋ.gwɪdʒ/ noun [C or U] (A1) a system of communication consisting of sounds, words, and grammar, or the system of communication used by people in a particular country or type of work: *She does research into how children acquire language.* ◦ *Do you* ***speak*** *any foreign languages?'* ◦ *I'm hopeless at learning languages.* ◦ *the English language* ◦ *legal/technical language* ◦ *the language of business* ◦ *Java and Perl are both important computer programming languages (= systems of writing instructions for computers).*

Word partners for language

learn/speak a language • a *foreign* language • *spoken/written* language • sb's *first/native/second* language • the *official* language • *abusive/bad/foul/strong* language

IDIOM **speak/talk the same language** to have similar ideas and similar ways of expressing them: *We come from similar backgrounds, so we speak the same language.*

ˈlanguage laˌboratory noun [C] (also **ˈlanguage ˌlab**) a room in a school or college in which students can use equipment to help them practise listening to and speaking a foreign language

languid /ˈlæŋ.gwɪd/ **adj** literary moving or speaking slowly with little energy, often in an attractive way: *a languid manner/voice* • **languidly** /-li/ **adv**

languish /ˈlæŋ.gwɪʃ/ **verb** [I] to exist in an unpleasant or unwanted situation, often for a long time: *After languishing* ***in obscurity*** *for many years, her early novels have recently been rediscovered.* ◦ *He has been languishing* ***in jail*** *for the past 20 years.* ◦ *The ruling party is languishing* ***in*** *third place in the opinion polls.*

languor /ˈlæŋ.gəʳ/ Ⓤⓢ /-gɚ/ **noun** [U] literary pleasant mental or physical tiredness or lack of activity: *She missed Spain and the languor of a siesta on a hot summer afternoon.* • **languorous** /-gə.rəs/ Ⓤⓢ /-gɚ.əs/ **adj** • **languorously** /-gə.rəs.li/ Ⓤⓢ /-gɚ.əs.li/ **adv**

la Niña /læˈniː.njə/ **noun** [S] the cooling of the water in the central and eastern Pacific Ocean that happens every few years and that affects the weather in many places

lank /læŋk/ **adj** Lank hair is not attractive because it is completely straight and thin: *His hair was lank and greasy and looked like it hadn't been washed for a month.* • **lankly** /-li/ **adv** • **lankness** /-nəs/ **noun** [U]

lanky /ˈlæŋ.ki/ **adj** tall and thin and often moving awkwardly as a result: *I was your typical lanky teenager.*

lanolin /ˈlæn.ə.lɪn/ **noun** [U] a substance containing a lot of fat that is obtained from wool and used in skin creams to make the skin feel soft

lantern /ˈlæn.tən/ Ⓤⓢ /-tɚn/ **noun** [C] a light inside a container which has a handle for holding it or hanging it up, or the container itself

lanthanide /ˈlæn.θə.naɪd/ **noun** [U] specialized any chemical element in the group of elements that have the ATOMIC NUMBERS 57 to 71 in the PERIODIC TABLE

lanyard /ˈlæn.jəd/ Ⓤⓢ /-jɚd/ **noun** [C] **1** a string worn around the neck on which a WHISTLE, key, knife, etc. is hung **2** a string that is used for fastening ropes on a ship

lap /læp/ **noun; verb**

▸**noun LEGS** ▷ **1** B2 [C usually singular] the top surface of the upper part of the legs of a person who is sitting down: *Come and sit* ***on*** *my lap and I'll read you a story.* **RACING** ▷ **2** B2 [C] a complete journey around a race track that is repeated several times during a competition: *He recorded the fastest lap in last weekend's Hungarian Grand Prix.* ◦ *After a strong start, she was passed by several runners* ***in/on*** *the final/last lap and finished ninth.* **3 lap of honour** UK (US **victory lap**) a journey around a track or sports field that is made by a winner of a race or a team that has won a game

IDIOMS **in the lap of luxury** living in very comfortable conditions because you have a lot of money • **in the lap of the gods** UK describes a situation that cannot be controlled and depends only on good luck: *The doctors have done everything possible for him, so his recovery now is in the lap of the gods.*

▸**verb** (**-pp-**) **IN RACING** ▷ **1** [T] to go past someone in a race who has been round the track one less time than you: *He finished last after being lapped twice by the leading runners.* **2** [I] to make one complete journey around a track **DRINK** ▷ **3** [T] (of an animal) to drink a liquid by taking it in small amounts into the mouth with a lot of short, quick movements of the tongue **HIT GENTLY** ▷ **4** [I or T] (of waves) to hit something gently, producing quiet sounds: *The water lapped* ***against*** *the side of the pool.* ◦ *The waves gently lapped the shore.*

PHRASAL VERB **lap sth up** to enjoy something very much: *We walked around the city, lapping up the atmosphere.* ◦ *Everyone clapped and cheered and you could see he was lapping it up.*

ˈlap ˌdancing noun [U] an activity in a bar or NIGHTCLUB in which a woman who is not wearing many clothes dances very close to a customer in exchange for money

lapdog /ˈlæp.dɒg/ Ⓤⓢ /-dɑːg/ **noun** [C] **DOG** ▷ **1** a small pet dog that is given a lot of attention by its owner **PERSON** ▷ **2** disapproving someone who is willing to do anything that a more important person tells them to do: *Opposition parties accuse the newspaper's editor of being a government lapdog.*

lapel /ləˈpel/ **noun** [C] a strip of cloth that is part of the front of a jacket or coat. It is joined to the collar and folded back onto the chest: *A flower was pinned* ***to/in*** *her lapel.*

lapse /læps/ **noun; verb**

▸**noun FAILURE** ▷ **1** [C] a temporary failure: *a lapse* ***of*** *concentration* ◦ *The management's decision to ignore the safety warnings demonstrated a remarkable lapse* ***of*** *judgment.* ◦ *a* ***memory*** *lapse* **PERIOD** ▷ **2** [C usually singular] a period of time passing between two things happening: *a time lapse/a lapse of time* ◦ *He turned up again after a lapse of two years.*

▸**verb** [I] to end legally or officially by not being continued or made effective for a longer period: *The association needs to win back former members who have allowed their subscriptions to lapse.*

PHRASAL VERB **lapse into sth LESS ACTIVE** ▷ **1** to start speaking or behaving in a less active or acceptable way: *No one could think of anything more to say, and the meeting lapsed into* ***silence***. **WORSE** ▷ **2** to gradually get into a worse state or condition: *He lapsed into* ***a coma*** *and died four days later.*

lapsed /læpst/ **adj** [before noun] **1** no longer involved in an activity or organization: *a lapsed Catholic* **2** no longer being continued or paid: *a lapsed subscription*

laptop /ˈlæp.tɒp/ Ⓤⓢ /-tɑːp/ **noun** [C] (also **ˌlaptop comˈputer**) A2 a computer that is small enough to be carried around easily and is flat when closed

lapwing /ˈlæp.wɪŋ/ **noun** [C] (also **peewit**) a small dark bird with a white chest and raised feathers on its head

larceny /ˈlɑː.sᵊn.i/ Ⓤⓢ /ˈlɑːr-/ **noun** [C or U] legal stealing, especially (in the US) the crime of taking something that does not belong to you, without getting illegally into a building to do so • **larcenous** /-əs/ **adj** US legal

larch /lɑːtʃ/ Ⓤⓢ /lɑːrtʃ/ **noun** [C] a tall tree which grows in cold northern countries and has leaves that are shaped like needles which it loses in winter

lard /lɑːd/ (US) /lɑːrd/ **noun; verb**
▸**noun** [U] a white substance made from pig fat and used in cooking
▸**verb**

PHRASAL VERB **lard sth with sth** If speech or a piece of writing is larded with a particular type of language, it has a lot of that type of language: *Her speech was larded with literary quotations.*

larder /ˈlɑː.dər/ (US) /ˈlɑːr.dɚ/ **noun** [C] a cupboard or small room used, especially in the past, for storing food in someone's home: *a well-stocked (= full of food) larder*

large /lɑːdʒ/ (US) /lɑːrdʒ/ **adj; noun; verb**
▸**adj** A2 big in size or amount: *a large house* ◦ *the world's largest computer manufacturer* ◦ *We need a larger car.* ◦ *We didn't expect such a large number of people to attend the concert.* ◦ *We've made good progress, but there's still a large amount of work to be done.* ◦ *There was a larger-than-expected fall in unemployment last month.* ◦ *Researchers have just completed the largest-ever survey of criminal behaviour in the UK.* ◦ *The population faces starvation this winter without large-scale emergency food aid.*

IDIOMS **by and large** C1 when everything about a situation is considered together: *There are a few small things that I don't like about my job, but by and large it's very enjoyable.* • **(as) large as life** used as a way of describing a person you see, and are surprised to see, in a particular place: *I looked up from my newspaper and there he was, as large as life, Tim Trotter!* • **larger than life** If someone is larger than life, they attract a lot of attention because they are more exciting or interesting than most people: *Most characters in his films are somewhat larger than life.*

▸**noun**

IDIOMS **at large** C2 generally: *This group is not representative of the population at large.* • **be at large** If someone dangerous is at large, they are free when they should not be: *Twelve prisoners are at large following a series of escapes.*

▸**verb** **larging it** informal enjoying yourself very much by dancing and drinking alcohol: *We were larging it at a club last night.*

ˌlarge inˈtestine **noun** [C usually singular] specialized the lower part of the bowels in which water is removed from digested food before it is passed out of the body as solid waste

largely /ˈlɑːdʒ.li/ (US) /ˈlɑːrdʒ-/ **adv** B2 almost completely: *a largely male company* ◦ *Their complaints have been largely ignored.* ◦ *Until recently the civil war had been largely unreported in the press.*

largesse (also **largess**) /lɑːˈʒes/ (US) /lɑːr-/ **noun** [U] formal willingness to give money, or money given to poor people by rich people: *The national theatre will be the main beneficiary of the millionaire's largesse.*

lark /lɑːk/ (US) /lɑːrk/ **noun; verb**
▸**noun** [C] **BIRD** ▷ **1** (also **skylark**) a small, brown bird that is known for its beautiful singing **ACTIVITY** ▷ **2** informal an activity done for a joke that is is not intended to cause serious harm or damage: *The kids hid their teacher's bike **for** a lark.* **3** **this ... lark** informal a way of referring to an activity or a situation that you do not take seriously: *I don't really think I'm suited to this marriage lark.* ◦ *I've had enough of this commuting lark.*

IDIOMS **be up with the lark** mainly UK to get out of bed very early in the morning • **bugger, sod, etc. this for a lark!** UK offensive used to show that you are extremely annoyed or bored with an activity and that you will not continue doing it: *I'd been waiting for him for an hour and I thought, sod this for a lark – I'm going home!*

▸**verb**

PHRASAL VERB **lark about/around** informal to behave in a silly way because you think it is funny: *We were just larking about – we didn't mean to do any damage.*

larva /ˈlɑː.və/ (US) /ˈlɑːr-/ **noun** [C] (plural **larvae** /-viː/) a form of an insect or an animal such as a FROG that has left its egg but is not yet completely developed • **larval** /-vəl/ **adj**

laryngitis /ˌlær.ɪnˈdʒaɪ.tɪs/ (US) /-t̬ɪs/ **noun** [U] a painful swelling of the larynx, usually caused by an infection

larynx /ˈlær.ɪŋks/ **noun** [C] (plural **larynxes** or specialized **larynges** /lærˈɪn.dʒiːz/) (informal **ˈvoice ˌbox**) an organ in humans and animals between the nose and the lungs that contains the muscles that move very quickly to create the voice or animal sounds

lasagne (US usually **lasagna**) /ləˈzæn.jə/ (US) /-ˈzɑː.njə/ **noun** [U] thin, wide sheets of PASTA, or a dish consisting of layers of this combined with two different sauces

lascivious /ləˈsɪv.i.əs/ **adj** formal disapproving expressing a strong DESIRE for sexual activity: *a lascivious smile* • **lasciviously** /-li/ **adv** • **lasciviousness** /-nəs/ **noun** [U]

laser /ˈleɪ.zər/ (US) /-zɚ/ **noun** [C] B2 (a device which produces) a powerful, narrow beam of light that can be used as a tool to cut metal, to perform medical operations, or to create patterns of light for entertainment: *laser beam*

ˌlaser-ˈguided **adj** [usually before noun] using lasers to help reach the target: *a laser-guided bomb/missile/weapon*

ˈlaser ˌprinter **noun** [C] a computer printer that produces very clear text and pictures by means of a laser beam • **ˈlaser ˌprinting** **noun** [U]

lash /læʃ/ **verb; noun**
▸**verb** **HIT** ▷ **1** [I or T] to hit with a lot of force: *The prisoners were regularly lashed with electric cable.* ◦ *The sound of the rain lashing **against** the windows was deafening.* → See also **lash out** **CRITICIZE** ▷ **2** [T] to criticize someone severely **TIE** ▷ **3** [T usually + adv/prep] to tie together tightly and firmly: *I've lashed your case **to** the roof rack.* ◦ *These poles will be easier to carry if we lash them **together** with a rope.*

PHRASAL VERBS **lash out (sth)** UK informal to spend a large amount of money in a way that is unnecessary or wastes it: *He lashed out £5,000 **on** his daughter's wedding.* • **lash out** to suddenly attack someone or something physically or criticize them in an angry way: *I was only teasing him and suddenly he lashed out (**at** me) and hit me in the face.* ◦ *Why's Tina in such a bad mood? She really lashed out **at** me when I was late for work.*

▸**noun** **HAIR** ▷ **1** [C usually plural] an **eyelash** **HIT** ▷ **2** [C or S] a thin strip of leather at the end of a WHIP, or a hit with this, especially as a form of punishment: *He received 30 lashes for the crime.* ◦ *The punishment for disobedience was **the** lash.* → See also **whiplash** **3** [C] a sudden, violent movement of something that can bend: *With a powerful lash of its tail, the fish jumped out of the net and back into the river.*

IDIOM **come/suffer under the lash** to be severely criticized: *The sales team came under the lash for poor results.*

lashing /ˈlæʃ.ɪŋ/ noun [C usually singular] **PUNISHMENT** ▷ **1** the punishment of being hit with a WHIP: *He was sentenced to receive a lashing.* → See also **a tongue lashing** **A LOT** ▷ **2 lashings** [plural] UK old-fashioned or humorous a lot of food or drink: *scones with lashings **of** cream ◦ lashings **of** ginger beer*

lass /læs/ noun [C] (also **lassie**) mainly Scottish English or Northern English a girl or young woman

lassi /ˈlæs.i/ noun [C or U] a South Asian drink made from YOGURT (= slightly sour liquid made from milk)

lassitude /ˈlæs.ɪ.tjuːd/ (US) /-tuːd/ noun [U] formal physical or mental tiredness: *Shareholders are blaming the company's problems on the lassitude of the managing director.*

lasso /læsˈuː/ noun; verb

▸noun [C] (plural **lassos** or US also **lassoes**) a rope, formed into a ring at one end, that can be tightened by pulling the other end: *Lassos are used particularly by cowboys to catch cattle and horses.*

▸verb [T] to catch an animal by throwing the ring of a lasso over its head and then tightening it around its neck

last /lɑːst/ (US) /læst/ **adj, adv, pronoun, noun; adj, pronoun, noun; adj, adv, pronoun; verb**

▸**adj, adv, pronoun, noun 1** (A2) (the person or thing) after everyone or everything else: [+ to infinitive] *I hate being **the** last one **to** arrive at a meeting. ◦ Our house is the last one on the left before the traffic lights. ◦ The Mets will surely finish the season in last **place** (= at the lowest rank of their division). ◦ I know Johnson finished last in the race, but who was **second to** last (= the one before the one at the end)? ◦ I don't know why he bothers to bet – his horses always come in last. ◦ **At** the last **moment** (= as late as possible) he changed his mind. ◦ He always leaves important decisions **to** the last (possible) **moment** (= as late as possible).* **2 at (long) last** (B1) finally: *I've finished my essay at last! ◦ At long last the government is starting to listen to our problems.* **3 the last person, thing, etc.** (B2) the least expected or wanted person or thing: *Three extra people to feed – that's the last thing I need! ◦ The last thing I wanted was to make you unhappy. ◦ Matthew is the last person I'd expect to be interested in dance. ◦ He's the last person I'd trust with my keys.* **4 last thing (at night)** at the latest time in the day: *I'll switch on the washing machine last thing so it'll be finished when I get up in the morning.* **5 the last time** If you say that it is the last time you will do something, you mean that you will never do it again: *He never even thanked me, so that's the last time I do him a favour.*

> **!** Common mistake: **last but not least**
>
> There is no preposition in this expression.
>
> Do not say 'at last but not least', just say **last but not least**:
>
> *I wrote to my mum and dad, my teacher and, last but not least, my best friend Rachel.*

> **!** Common mistake: **at last or finally?**
>
> **Warning:** choose the correct adverb!
>
> To introduce the last point or idea, usually at the beginning of a sentence, don't say 'at last', say **finally**:
>
> *~~At last, I would like to thank you all for listening.~~*
>
> *Finally, I would like to thank you all for listening.*

IDIOMS **have the last laugh** to finally get an advantage from an argument or disagreement, when it seemed that you would not • **last but not least** (B2) importantly, despite being mentioned after everyone else: *I would like to thank my publisher, my editor, and, last but not least, my husband.* • **the last but one** (US also **the next to last**) the one before the final one: *I'm almost finished – this is the last but one box to empty.* • **the last sb heard/saw of sb/sth** (C2) the last time someone heard anything about someone or something or the last time they saw them or it: *Then he went to Boston, and that was the last I saw of him.* • **to the last** formal **1** until something is complete or has been achieved: *I think my position is right, and I'll defend it to the last.* **2** until the end of someone's life: *She was a true patriot to the last.* • **(down) to the last ...** including all of the thing mentioned, used to emphasize what you are saying: *The model of the village is accurate down to the last detail. ◦ He has calculated the costs down to the last penny.* • **to the last (man)** until every person is dead: *Both sides have declared themselves ready to fight to the last man.*

▸**adj** [before noun], **pronoun, noun** [U] (B1) (being) the only one or part that is left: *Do you mind if I have the last chocolate? ◦ I'm down to my last 50p – could I borrow some money for lunch? ◦ I'm afraid Martha's eaten **the** last **of** the ice cream. ◦ She was **the** last **of** the great educational reformers.*

IDIOMS **as a last resort** (UK also **in the last resort**) if all other methods fail: *British police are supposed to use guns only as a last resort.* • **hear/see the last of sth** informal If you hear/see the last of something or someone unpleasant or difficult, they do not cause you trouble again: *I paid them £100 for the damage and I hope that's the last I'll hear of it. ◦ You haven't heard the last of this! – I'll see you in court. ◦ He's horrible – I really hope we've seen the last of him.* • **on your last legs** informal A person who is on their last legs is very tired or near to death: *We'd been out walking all day and I was on my last legs when we reached the hotel. ◦ It looks as though her grandfather's on his last legs.* • **on its last legs** informal Something that is on its last legs is in such bad condition that it will soon be unable to work as it should: *I've had the same TV for 15 years now and it's really on its last legs.*

▸**adj, adv, pronoun** (A1) (being) the most recent or the one before the present one: *Did you hear the storm last **night** (= during the previous night)? ◦ Did you see the news on TV last night (= yesterday evening)? ◦ They got married last November. ◦ When was the last time you had a cigarette? ◦ When did you last have a cigarette? ◦ She's been working there for the last month (= for the four weeks until now).* ◦ formal *Could you account for your whereabouts on Sunday last? ◦ The/These last five years have been very difficult for him. ◦ **The** last we heard of her, she was working as an English teacher in France. ◦ Each of her paintings has been better than **the** last.*

> **!** Common mistake: **last or latest?**
>
> **Warning:** choose the correct adjective!
>
> To talk about the newest or most recent or modern thing to be produced, don't say 'last', say **latest**:
>
> *She always wears the latest fashions.*

IDIOM **the week/month/year before last** (B2) during the week/month/year before the previous one: *We had lunch together the week before last.*

▸**verb** [I, L only + noun] **1** (B1) to continue to exist: *The meeting lasted two hours. ◦ The drought lasted **for** several months. ◦ They say the snow will last **until** the end of next week. ◦ I can't see the ceasefire lasting. ◦ They haven't had an argument for two weeks, but it's* *too good to* last (= they'll have an argument soon). ◦ I doubt their enthusiasm will last. ◦ He's working very efficiently at the moment, but it won't last. **2** (C1) to continue being good or suitable: *There's no point buying something that isn't going to last. ◦ The cheaper washing machines should last about five years. ◦ This pen should last (you) a lifetime if you look after it. ◦ Her previous secretary only lasted a month (= left after this period).*

IDIOM **not last long** (UK also **not last five minutes**) to fail or be unsuccessful very soon: *You won't last long in your job if you carry on being so rude to the customers. ◦ He wouldn't last five minutes in the police force – it's far too tough for him.*

PHRASAL VERB **last out** [L] to manage to stay alive: *How long can they last out without food? ◦ He won't last out the night.*

ˌlast-ˈditch adj (also **ˌlast-ˈgasp**) **last-ditch attempt/effort** an effort or attempt that is made at the end of a series of failures to solve a problem, and is not expected to succeed: *In a last-ditch attempt to save his party from electoral defeat, he resigned from the leadership.*

ˌlast hurˈrah noun [C usually singular] mainly US **1** Someone's last hurrah is their final effort after a long period of work: *Petersen has said that this season will be his last hurrah* ***as*** *a player.* **2** Someone or something's last hurrah is their last period of influence or power

lasting /ˈlɑː.stɪŋ/ (US) /ˈlæs.tɪŋ/ **adj** continuing to exist for a long time or for ever: *Few observers believe that the treaty will bring a lasting* ***peace*** *to the region. ◦ Did any of your teachers make a lasting* ***impression*** *on you? ◦ The tablets make you feel better for a while but the effect isn't (****long-****)lasting.*

the ˌlast ˈjudgment noun [S] **Judgment Day**

lastly /ˈlɑːst.li/ (US) /ˈlæst-/ adv (also **last**) (B2) used to show when something comes after all the other things in a list: *In accepting this award, I would like to thank the producer, the director, the scriptwriter, and, lastly, the film crew.*

the ˌlast ˈminute noun [S] (B2) the latest possible opportunity for doing something: *They only told me* ***at*** *the last minute that they couldn't come. ◦ Why do you always* ***leave*** *everything* ***till*** *the last minute?* • **last-ˈminute** adj [usually before noun] (B2) *a last-minute cancellation*

ˈlast ˌname noun [C] mainly US (A2) your family name, that you use in formal situations or with people you do not know well

ˌlast ˈorders noun [plural] in a British pub, the last drinks that customers are allowed to buy just before the bar closes: *Last orders, please!*

the ˌlast ˈpost noun [S] a tune that is played on a BUGLE at military funerals or when it is time for soldiers to go to bed

the ˌlast ˈrites noun [plural] a religious ceremony performed by a priest for a person who is dying

ˌlast will and ˈtestament noun [S] your written instructions about what should happen to your body and the things that you own after your death

ˌlast ˈword noun [S] the final remark in an argument or discussion: *You're not going, Helena, and that's my last word* ***on*** *the matter. ◦ She always has to* ***have the*** *last word (= win the argument).*

IDIOM **be the last word in sth** to be the best or most modern example of something: *It's a nice enough restaurant and it's very reasonably priced but it's not exactly the last word in style.*

lat. noun [U] written abbreviation for **latitude**

latch /lætʃ/ noun; verb

▸noun [C] **1** a device for keeping a door or gate closed, consisting of a metal bar that fits into a hole and is lifted by pushing down on another bar **2 on the latch** UK closed but not locked: *Don't forget to* ***leave*** *the front door on the latch if you go to bed before I get back.*

▸verb [I or T] to close a door, etc. with a latch

PHRASAL VERBS **latch on** UK informal to begin to understand something: *It took me ages to latch on* ***to*** *what she was talking about.* • **latch onto sth** BECOME CONNECTED ▷ **1** to become connected to something: *The antibodies work by latching onto proteins on the surfaces of the viruses and bacteria.* BECOME INTERESTED ▷ **2** informal to become interested in an idea, story, or activity, and to start to use it: *Unfortunately the press have already latched onto the story.* • **latch onto sb** informal to stay close to someone or spend a lot of time with them, usually when they do not want you with them: *She latched onto me as soon as she arrived, and I had to spend the rest of the evening talking to her.*

late /leɪt/ adj, adv; adj

▸adj, adv NEAR THE END ▷ **1** (A1) (happening or being) near the end of a period of time: *It was late at night. ◦ We talked late into the night. ◦ Is that the time? I'd no idea it was so late. ◦ It was late summer when it happened. ◦ It was built in the late 19th century. ◦ He's probably in his late twenties. ◦ As late (= as recently) as the 1980s they were still using horses on this farm.* AFTER EXPECTED TIME ▷ **2** (A1) (happening or arriving) after the planned, expected, usual, or necessary time: *This train is always late. ◦ You'll be late* ***for*** *your flight if you don't hurry up. ◦ Sorry I'm late. I was held up in the traffic. ◦ It's too late to start complaining now. ◦ We always have a late breakfast on Sunday mornings. ◦ Some late* ***news*** *(= news of something which happened after the news programme started) has just come in – a bomb has exploded in central London. ◦ Our ferry was two hours late because of the strike. ◦ Kathryn's just phoned to say she's working late this evening.* → See also **latecomer** • **lateness** /ˈleɪt.nəs/ noun [U] formal the fact of being late: *It was no great surprise that you were tired given the lateness* ***of the hour****.*

IDIOMS **late in the day** too late to be useful: *It's rather late in the day to start studying – your exams are next week.* • **of late** formal recently: *We haven't spoken of late.* • **too little, too late** not enough of something which should have been provided earlier: *A spokeswoman described the aid for the refugees as too little, too late.*

▸adj [before noun] (C2) describes someone who has died, especially recently: *She gave her late husband's clothes to charity.*

latecomer /ˈleɪtˌkʌm.əʳ/ (US) /-ɚ/ noun [C] a person who arrives late: *We regret that latecomers cannot be admitted until a suitable break in the performance.*

ˌlate deˈveloper noun [C] UK (US **ˌlate ˈbloomer**) someone who becomes good at something after people usually become good at it: *At school she was a late developer, and it wasn't until she went to university that her talents became apparent.*

lately /ˈleɪt.li/ adv (B1) recently: *I haven't been feeling so well lately. ◦ Have you been doing anything interesting lately?*

latent /ˈleɪ.tᵊnt/ adj present but needing particular conditions to become active, obvious, or completely developed: *Recent developments in the area have* brought latent ethnic tension out into the open. ◦ *We're trying to bring out the latent artistic talents that many people possess without realizing it.* • **latency** /-tᵊn.si/ noun [U] formal

ˈ**latent** ˌ**heat** noun [U] specialized the heat that is absorbed or released by a substance when it changes state, for example from a liquid to a gas, while the temperature of the substance does not change

later /ˈleɪ.təʳ/ (US) /-t̬ɚ/ **adv; adj; exclamation**
►adv **1** (A2) at a time in the future or after the time you have mentioned: *He'll be back later.* ◦ *We could always go later in the season.* ◦ *Police questioned him and he was later arrested.* **2 later on** (B1) at a time in the future, or after the time you have mentioned: *What are you doing later on this evening?* ◦ *Shall I go and fetch her later on?* ◦ *Later on, we could go and have a meal if you like.* **3 no/not later than** not after: *She said she'd prefer us to arrive no later than nine o'clock.*

IDIOM **see/catch you later!** informal (B1) a way of saying goodbye: *'Bye.' 'See you later.'*

►adj [before noun] **IN THE FUTURE** ▷ **1** (B2) happening at a time in the future, or after the time you have mentioned: *We could catch a later train.* ◦ *You can always change your password at a later date.* **TOWARDS THE END** ▷ **2** (C2) happening towards the end of a period of time or the end of someone's life: *He needed round-the-clock care in the later stages of his illness.* ◦ *During his later years, he lived in London.* **RECENT** ▷ **3** (C2) more modern or recent: *Later versions of the software are much better.* ◦ *Later models included a 2.5 litre engine.* ◦ *I prefer her earlier paintings to her later work.*
►exclamation (also **laters**) a way of saying goodbye: *Laters, Mike.*

lateral /ˈlæt.rᵊl/ (US) /ˈlæt̬.ɚ.ᵊl/ **adj 1** [before noun] specialized relating to the sides of an object or to sideways movement: *lateral movement* ◦ *Trim the lateral shoots of the flower* (= the ones that grow sideways from the main stem of a plant). **2** specialized refers to a consonant in which the flow of air is blocked in the middle, so the air flows to the side: *In English, /l/ is lateral.* • **laterally** /-i/ adv

ˌ**lateral** ˈ**thinking** noun [U] a way of solving a problem by thinking about it in a different and original way and not using traditional or expected methods

laterite /ˈlæt.ᵊr.aɪt/ (US) /ˈlæt̬.ə.raɪt/ **noun** [U] specialized a type of reddish clay soil containing iron and ALUMINIUM, found especially in tropical areas

latest /ˈleɪ.tɪst/ (US) /-t̬ɪst/ **adj; noun**
►adj [before noun] (A2) newest or most recent or modern: *Have you seen her latest movie?* ◦ *the latest fashions*
►noun **1 the latest** the most recent news or technical development: *Have you heard the latest* (= the most recent news) ***about*** *Jilly and Patrick – they're getting a divorce.* ◦ *This machine is the latest* ***in*** *LED technology.* **2 at the (very) latest** (C2) used to emphasize that something must happen or be done before a stated time or day: *I have to get this finished by Friday at the latest.*

latex /ˈleɪ.teks/ **noun** [U] a white liquid produced by many plants, especially rubber trees, or a rubber-like substance made from this or from plastic, used in making clothes, paint, glue, etc.: *a latex mask* ◦ *a pair of latex surgical gloves*

lath /lɑːθ/ (US) /læθ/ **noun** [C] a long, thin, flat strip of wood, used to make a structure to support PLASTER on walls or TILES on the roof of a building

lathe /leɪð/ **noun** [C] a machine for changing the shape of a piece of wood, metal, etc. which works by turning the material while a sharp tool is pressed against it

lather /ˈlɑː.ðəʳ/ (US) /ˈlæð.ɚ/ **noun; verb**
►noun **1** [S] a pale, usually white, mass of small bubbles produced especially when soap is mixed with water: *Wet the hair, apply shampoo, and massage into a rich lather.* **2** [U] small bubbles of SWEAT on a horse's skin, produced by physical effort • **lathery** /-i/ adj

IDIOMS **be in a lather** informal to be very worried or nervous about something: *She was in a lather when I left because she couldn't find her ticket.* • **get into a lather** informal *It's not worth getting into a lather over.*

►verb [I or T] to produce a lather from soap, or to cover something or someone in lather: *He stood under the shower lathering him****self*** *with the soap.*

lathi /ˈlɑː.ti/ **noun** [C] Indian English a long, heavy stick, especially one used as a weapon by police officers

lathi-charge /ˈlɑː.tiˌtʃɑːdʒ/ (US) /-ˌtʃɑːrdʒ/ **noun** [C] Indian English an occasion when a large group of police run forward in an attacking movement carrying their sticks

Latin /ˈlæt.ɪn/ (US) /ˈlæt̬-/ **noun; adj**
►noun [U] the language used by ancient Romans and as the language of educated people in many European countries in the past
►adj **1** written in Latin: *a Latin poem* **2** relating to (people or things in) countries that use a language that developed from Latin, such as French or Spanish: *his Latin good looks*

Latina /ˌlætˈiː.nə/ **noun** [C] US a woman or girl who lives in the US and who comes from, or whose family comes from, Latin America → See also **Latino**

ˌ**Latin Aˈmerican** adj from or relating to South America or Central America

Latino /ˌlætˈiː.nəʊ/ (US) /-noʊ/ **noun** [C] (plural **Latinos**) mainly US a person who lives in the US and who comes from, or whose family comes from, Latin America → See also **Latina**

latitude /ˈlæt.ɪ.tjuːd/ (US) /ˈlæt̬.ɪ.tuːd/ **noun POSITION** ▷ **1** [C or U] the position north or south of the EQUATOR measured from 0° to 90° → Compare **longitude** **2 latitudes** [plural] an area near to a particular latitude: *At these latitudes the sun does not rise at all on winter days.* **FREEDOM** ▷ **3** [U] formal freedom to behave, act, or think in the way you want to: *Courts can show a considerable degree of latitude when it comes to applying the law.* • **latitudinal** /ˌlæt.ɪˈtjuː.dɪ.nəl/ (US) /ˌlæt̬.ɪˈtuː-/ adj specialized

latrine /ləˈtriːn/ **noun** [C] **1** a simple toilet such as a hole in the ground, used in a military area or when staying in a tent **2** Indian English a toilet of any type

latte /ˈlæt.eɪ/ (US) /ˈlɑː.t̬eɪ/ **noun** [C or U] a hot drink made from ESPRESSO (= strong coffee) and warm milk

latter /ˈlæt.əʳ/ (US) /ˈlæt̬.ɚ/ **adj; noun**
►adj [before noun] (B2) near or towards the end of something: *Building of the new library should begin in the latter* ***part*** *of next year.* ◦ *In the latter stages of the fight he began to tire.*
►noun [S] **1 the latter** (B2) the second of two people, things, or groups previously mentioned: *She offered me more money or a car and I chose the latter.* → Compare **former** **2** not standard the last of more than two people, things, or groups previously mentioned

ˈ**latter-day** adj [before noun] describes a person or thing that is similar to someone or something that existed in the past: *the evil actions of a latter-day Caligula*

latterly /ˈlæt.ə.li/ (US) /ˈlæt̬.ɚ-/ adv formal recently

lattice /ˈlæt.ɪs/ (US) /ˈlæţ-/ **noun** [C] (also **latticework**) a structure made from strips of wood or other material which cross over each other with spaces between

ˌlattice ˈwindow noun [C] a window made from small pieces of glass that are held in place by metal strips

laud /lɔːd/ (US) /lɑːd/ **verb** [T] formal to praise: *The German leadership lauded the Russian initiative.*

laudable /ˈlɔː.də.bl/ (US) /ˈlɑː-/ **adj** formal (of actions and behaviour) deserving praise, even if there is little or no success: *a laudable aim/ambition* ◦ *The recycling programme is laudable, but does it save much money?* • **laudably** /-bli/ **adv**

laudatory /ˈlɔː.də.tᵊr.i/ (US) /ˈlɑː.də.tɔːr.i/ **adj** formal expressing praise

laugh /lɑːf/ (US) /læf/ **verb; noun**

▸**verb** [I] (A2) to smile while making sounds with your voice that show you think something is funny or you are happy: *They laughed **at** her jokes.* ◦ *I couldn't stop laughing.* ◦ *I said he'd have to give a talk and he laughed nervously.* ◦ *She's so funny – she really **makes** me laugh.* ◦ *It's very rare that a book is so good you actually laugh **out loud**.* ◦ *It was so funny, I **burst out** laughing (= laughed suddenly and loudly).* ◦ *I laughed **till I cried**.*

> **Other ways of saying laugh**
>
> If someone laughs quietly, the verb **chuckle** is sometimes used:
>
> *She was **chuckling** as she read the letter.*
>
> The verb **giggle** is often used when someone laughs in a quiet, childish way, often at something silly or rude, or because he or she is nervous:
>
> *The girls were **giggling** at the back of the classroom.*
>
> If someone laughs in a childish and unkind way, you can use the word **snigger** or in the US **snicker**:
>
> *They **sniggered** at what she was wearing.*
>
> **Chortle** can be used when someone laughs because of being pleased, especially at someone else's bad luck:
>
> *She **chortled** with glee at the news.*
>
> The phrasal verb **crack up** or the phrase **burst out laughing** can be used when someone suddenly starts laughing:
>
> *I just **cracked up** when I saw him in that hat.*
>
> *I fell over the chair and everyone **burst out laughing**.*
>
> If someone is laughing so much that they cannot stop, in informal situations you can use the phrase **in stitches**:
>
> *His jokes had us all **in stitches**.*

IDIOMS **be laughed out of court** to be considered as too silly or impossible to take seriously, especially in a law court: *The proposal will be laughed out of court.* • **be laughing** (also **will be laughing**) UK informal used to tell someone that they should not be worried by a particular situation, because they will get an advantage from it: *If the loan's approved you're laughing.* • **be laughing all the way to the bank** informal to be earning a lot of money easily: *We'll be laughing all the way to the bank if this deal works out.* • **be laughing on the other side of your face** UK (US **laugh out of the other side of your mouth**) used to tell someone that although they are pleased now, they will not be pleased later when things do not happen as they expected or planned: *She's pleased with her promotion but she'll be laughing on the other side of her face when she sees the extra work.* • **be no laughing matter** to be very serious: *It might seem funny but I tell you what, getting stuck up a tree is no laughing matter.* • **don't make me laugh!** informal said to someone to show that you cannot take their suggestion seriously: *You'll pay? Don't make me laugh!* • **he who laughs last, laughs longest/best** saying said to emphasize that the person who has control of a situation in the end is most successful, even if other people had seemed originally to have an advantage • **laugh your head off** (also **laugh yourself silly**) to laugh a lot, loudly: *You laughed your head off when I fell!* • **laugh in sb's face** to make it obvious to someone that you do not respect them: *They'd laugh in your face if you suggested me for the post.* • **laugh like a drain** UK informal to laugh a lot, very loudly • **laugh up your sleeve** to secretly find something funny: *They're very polite in your presence, but you get the feeling they're laughing up their sleeves.* • **you've got to laugh** (also **you have to laugh**) said when you can see something funny in a difficult situation

PHRASAL VERBS **laugh at sb/sth 1** (B1) to show that you think someone or something is stupid: *I can't go into work looking like this – everyone will laugh at me.* **2** (B1) to treat someone or something as if they are not important or do not deserve serious attention: *If you say that, people will just laugh at you.* • **laugh sth off** to make yourself laugh about something unpleasant in order to make it seem less important or serious: *She tried to laugh off their remarks, but I could see she was hurt.*

▸**noun** [C] **1** (B1) the act or sound of laughing: *a loud/nervous laugh* ◦ *I was embarrassed at the time, but I **had a good** laugh about it later.* **2** informal an enjoyable or funny activity: *'How was the party?' 'Oh, it was a laugh.'* **3** mainly UK informal someone who is funny: *You'd like Sharon – she's **a good** laugh.*

IDIOMS **for a laugh** informal If you do something for a laugh, you do it for enjoyment: *Just for a laugh, I pretended that I'd forgotten it was his birthday.* • **you're having a laugh** UK informal used to show that you think that what someone has just said is not reasonable or fair: *£500 to cut down a tree – you're having a laugh, mate!*

laughable /ˈlɑː.fə.bl̩/ (US) /ˈlæf.ə-/ **adj** silly and not deserving to be seriously considered: *Privately they thought the idea laughable.*

ˈlaughing ˌgas noun [U] informal **nitrous oxide**: a type of gas that is used as an ANAESTHETIC (= a substance that stops pain)

laughingly /ˈlɑː.fɪŋ.li/ (US) /ˈlæf.ɪŋ-/ **adv** **1** If you do something laughingly, you are laughing while you are doing it: *He laughingly pointed out our mistakes.* **2** disapproving If you say something is laughingly described in a particular way, you think this thing is so bad that it does not deserve the description: *It is only one of the absurd rules in the system of law laughingly known as British justice.*

ˈlaughing ˌstock noun [S] someone or something which seems stupid or silly, especially by trying to be serious or important and not succeeding: *Another performance like that and this team will be **the** laughing stock **of** the league.*

laughter /ˈlɑːf.təʳ/ (US) /ˈlæf.tɚ/ **noun** [U] the act or sound of laughing: *She **roared with** laughter (= laughed very loudly).* ◦ *As we approached the hall we could hear the sound of laughter.*

IDIOM **laughter is the best medicine** saying said to mean that trying to be happy is a good way to stop worrying

launch /lɔːntʃ/ (US) /lɑːntʃ/ noun; verb
▸noun [C] **EVENT** ▷ **1** (C1) an event to celebrate or introduce something new: *How much champagne will we need for the launch?* ◦ *Illness prevented her attending the launch **party** for her latest novel.* **LEAVE LAND** ▷ **2** (C1) an occasion when a ship is sent to sea, or a spacecraft into space, for the first time: *The launch of the space shuttle was delayed for 24 hours because of bad weather.* **BOAT** ▷ **3** a boat that has an engine and carries passengers for short distances, especially on a lake or a river, or from the land to a larger boat
▸verb **BEGIN** ▷ **1** (B2) [I or T] to begin something such as a plan or introduce something new such as a product: *The scheme was launched a year ago.* ◦ *The airline will launch its new transatlantic service next month.* ◦ *A devastating attack was launched **on** the rebel stronghold.* ◦ [+ adv/prep] UK *After working for the company for several years she decided to launch **out** on her own and set up in business.* **SEND** ▷ **2** (C1) [T] to send something out, such as a new ship to sea or a spacecraft into space: *A spokesman for the dockyard said they hoped to launch the first submarine within two years.* ◦ *to launch a missile* **3 launch yourself** mainly UK to jump with great force: *The defender launched himself **at** the attacking player, bringing him to the ground.*

PHRASAL VERB **launch into sth** to start saying something or criticizing something with a lot of energy or anger: *He launched into a verbal attack on her handling of the finances.*

launcher /ˈlɔːn.tʃəʳ/ (US) /ˈlɑːn.tʃɚ/ noun [C] a device that sends something such as a ROCKET or a MISSILE into the air with force: *a mobile **rocket** launcher*

ˈlaunch ˌpad noun [C] (UK also **ˈlaunching ˌpad**) a special area from which spacecraft or MISSILES are sent into the sky: *The rocket blew up on the launch pad.* ◦ figurative *Soap operas have long been a launch pad for film actors.*

launder /ˈlɔːn.dəʳ/ (US) /ˈlɑːn.dɚ/ verb [T] **CLOTHES** ▷ **1** to wash, dry, and IRON clothes, sheets, etc.: *freshly laundered sheets* **MONEY** ▷ **2** to move money that has been obtained illegally through banks and other businesses to make it seem to have been obtained legally: *Officials were accused of laundering the stolen funds overseas before returning them to the US.*

launderette (also **laundrette**) /ˌlɔːnˈdret/ (US) /ˌlɑːn-/ noun [C] mainly UK (US also trademark **laundromat**) a place where you pay to use the machines there which will wash and dry clothes

Laundromat /ˈlɔːn.drə.mæt/ (US) /ˈlɑːn.droʊ-/ noun [C] US trademark a **launderette**

laundry /ˈlɔːn.dri/ (US) /ˈlɑːn-/ noun **1** (B2) [U] the dirty clothes and sheets which need to be, are being, or have been washed: *I've got to **do** (= wash) my laundry.* **2** [C] a business which washes clothes, sheets, etc. for customers

IDIOM **a laundry list** mainly US a long list of subjects: *It wasn't much of a speech – just a laundry list of accusations against the government.*

ˈlaundry ˌbasket noun [C] (US also **hamper**) a large container in which dirty clothes are kept until they are washed

laureate /ˈlɒr.i.ət/ (US) /ˈlɑːr-/ noun [C] a person who has been given a very high honour because of their ability in a subject of study: *a Nobel laureate*

laurel /ˈlɒr.əl/ (US) /ˈlɑːr-/ noun [C or U] **TREE** ▷ **1** a small EVERGREEN tree (= one that never loses its leaves) that has shiny leaves and small, black fruit **PRAISE** ▷ **2 laurels** [plural] formal praise for a person because of something they have done, usually in sport, the arts, or politics: *The actors are very good, but when all is considered the laurels must surely go to the director of the play.*

ˈlaurel ˌwreath noun [C] a circle of leaves which, in the past, was worn on the head by an important person or the winner of a competition

lav /læv/ noun [C] UK informal for **lavatory** (= toilet)

lava /ˈlɑː.və/ noun [U] hot, liquid rock which comes out of the Earth through a VOLCANO, or the solid rock formed when it cools: *molten lava*

ˈlava ˌlamp noun [C] a decorative electric LAMP in which a brightly coloured amount of WAX moves up and down a container full of transparent liquid, forming new shapes as it does so

lavatorial /læv.əˈtɔː.ri.əl/ (US) /-tɔːr.i-/ adj UK disapproving describes jokes that refer to toilets or EXCRETION (= getting rid of waste from the body): *lavatorial humour*

lavatory /ˈlæv.ə.tərʳ.i/ (US) /-tɔːr.i/ noun [C] mainly UK formal a toilet

lavender /ˈlæv.ɪn.dəʳ/ (US) /-dɚ/ noun; adj
▸noun [U] **PLANT** ▷ **1** a plant that has grey-green leaves like needles and small, pale purple flowers with a strong smell, or its dried flowers and stems that have a pleasant smell: *a lavender bush* **COLOUR** ▷ **2** a pale purple colour
▸adj of a pale purple colour

ˈlavender ˌlanguage noun [U] informal special words and phrases that gay people use

lavish /ˈlæv.ɪʃ/ adj; verb
▸adj **1** (C2) large in quantity and expensive or impressive: *lavish gifts/promises/praise* ◦ *lavish spending* ◦ *lavish banquets* ◦ *The evening was a lavish affair with glorious food and an endless supply of champagne.* ◦ *The lavish production makes this musical truly memorable.* **2** very generous: *The critics were lavish **in** their praise for the paintings.* • **lavishly** /-li/ adv • **lavishness** /-nəs/ noun [U]
▸verb

PHRASAL VERB **lavish sth on sb/sth** to give someone a lot, or too much, of something such as money, presents, or attention: *She lavishes money on her grandchildren.* ◦ *The committee lavished praise on the project.*

law /lɔː/ (US) /lɑː/ noun **RULE** ▷ **1** (B1) [C or U] a rule, usually made by a government, that is used to order the way in which a society behaves, or the whole system of such rules: *There are laws **against** drinking in the street.* ◦ *The laws **governing** the possession of firearms are being reviewed.* ◦ *They led the fight to impose laws **on** smoking.* ◦ *They have to provide a contract **by** law.* ◦ *She's going to study law at university.* ◦ [or+ -ing verb + to infinitive] *Many doctors backed plans for a law bann**ing/to** ban all tobacco advertising.* → See also **bylaw, lawsuit, lawyer 2 the law a** (B2) the system of rules of a particular country: *What does the law say about having alcohol in the blood while driving?* ◦ *Of course robbery is **against** the law!* ◦ *The judge ruled that the directors had knowingly **broken** the law.* ◦ *You can't take that course of action and remain **within** the law.* **b** [S] informal the police: *The law was/were out in force at the demonstration.* **3 go to law** When someone goes to law about something, they ask a court to make a legal judgment about it. **PRINCIPLE** ▷ **4** (C2) [C] a general rule that states what always happens when the same conditions exist: *Newton's laws **of** motion* ◦ *the laws of nature/physics* ◦ humorous *The **first** law **of** (= the most*

L

important principle in) politics is – if you're going to lie, don't get found out! → See also **Murphy's law, Parkinson's law**

> **Word partners for law**
>
> *abolish/change/pass/propose* a law • a law *allows/bans/governs* sth • *become* law • a law *against* sth • *by* law

IDIOMS **be a law unto yourself** disapproving to behave in a way that is independent and does not follow the usual rules for a situation • **the law of averages** the belief that if something happens often then it will also happen regularly • **the law of the jungle** the idea that people who care only about themselves will be most likely to succeed in a society or organization • **take the law into your own hands** C2 to do something illegal and often violent in order to punish someone because you know the law will not punish that person: *One day, after years of violent abuse from her husband, she took the law into her own hands.*

ˈlaw-aˌbiding adj Someone who is law-abiding obeys the law: *Such actions against law-abiding* ***citizens*** *will not be tolerated.*

ˌlaw and ˈorder noun [U] C2 a situation in which the laws of a country are being obeyed, especially when the police or army are used to make certain of this: *a complete* ***breakdown in*** *law and order*

lawbreaker /ˈlɔː.breɪ.kəʳ/ US /ˈlɑː.breɪ.kɚ/ noun [C] a person who does not obey the law, especially intentionally and often

ˌlaw enˈforcement noun [U] mainly US the activity of making certain that the laws of an area are obeyed: *a law-enforcement officer*

lawful /ˈlɔː.fəl/ US /ˈlɑː-/ adj formal allowed by the law: *Judge Keenan concluded that the surveillance had been lawful.* ◦ *He said he was going about his lawful business as a journalist.* • **lawfully** /-i/ adv

lawless /ˈlɔː.ləs/ US /ˈlɑː-/ adj not controlled by laws, or illegal: *The film is set in a lawless city some time in the future.* • **lawlessly** /-li/ adv • **lawlessness** /-nəs/ noun [U]

lawmaker /ˈlɔːˌmeɪ.kəʳ/ US /ˈlɑːˌmeɪ.kɚ/ noun [C] someone, such as a politician, who is responsible for making and changing laws

lawn /lɔːn/ US /lɑːn/ noun [C or U] C1 an area of grass, especially near to a house or in a park, that is cut regularly to keep it short: *Will you* ***mow*** *the lawn at the weekend?*

ˈlawn ˌbowling noun [U] US for **bowls**.

lawnmower /ˈlɔːnˌməʊ.əʳ/ US /ˈlɑːnˌmoʊ.ɚ/ noun [C] a machine used for cutting grass

lawnmower

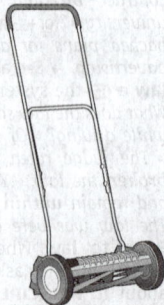

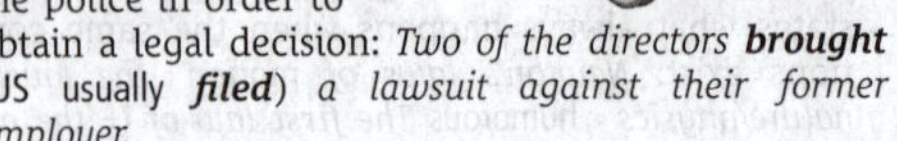

ˈlawn ˌparty noun [C] US for **garden party**

ˌlawn ˈtennis noun [U] formal or specialized **tennis**

lawsuit /ˈlɔː.suːt/, /-sjuːt/ US /ˈlɑː.suːt/ noun [C] (also **suit**) C2 a problem taken to a law court by an ordinary person or an organization rather than the police in order to obtain a legal decision: *Two of the directors* ***brought*** *(US usually* ***filed****) a lawsuit against their former employer.*

lawyer /ˈlɔɪ.əʳ/ US /ˈlɑː.jɚ/ noun [C] (US also **attorney**) B1 someone whose job is to give advice to people about the law and speak for them in court: *I want to see my lawyer before I say anything.*

> **Usage: lawyer, solicitor, barrister, and attorney**
>
> In the UK, **lawyers** are divided into two types: **solicitors** and **barristers. Solicitors** give you advice on legal subjects and discuss your case with you. They can also represent you and argue your case in the lower courts. **Barristers** give specialist legal advice and can represent you in both higher and lower courts. In the US, there is only one type of lawyer, who is sometimes called an **attorney**.

lax /læks/ adj **1** without much care, attention, or control: *The subcommittee contends that the authorities were lax* ***in*** *investigating most of the cases.* **2** not severe or strong enough: *He took a gun through baggage control to highlight the lax security.* **3** specialized (of a speech sound) made without much force → Compare **tense** • **laxity** /ˈlæk.sə.ti/ US /-t̬i/ noun [U] (also **laxness**) • **laxly** /ˈlæks.li/ adv

laxative /ˈlæk.sə.tɪv/ US /-t̬ɪv/ noun [C] a substance that makes the waste from someone's bowels come out

lay /leɪ/ verb; adj; noun

▸verb (**laid**) PUT DOWN ▷ **1** C1 [T usually + adv/prep] to put something in especially a flat or horizontal position, usually carefully or for a particular purpose: *She laid the baby on the bed.* ◦ *He laid the tray down on the table.* ◦ *She laid* ***aside*** *her book and went to answer the phone.* ◦ *We're having a new carpet laid in the hall next week.* ◦ *The plan is to lay (= build) the foundations for the new apartments in October.* **2** [T] to prepare a plan or a method of doing something: *Even the* ***best*** *laid plans go wrong sometimes.*

> **Common mistake: lay or lie?**
>
> **Warning:** do not confuse these two verbs!
>
> To talk about being in or moving into a horizontal position or being in a particular place, position, or direction, don't use the verb 'to lay', use the verb **to lie.**
>
> In the present tense, don't say 'lay' or 'lays', say **lie** or **lies**:
>
> *When I'm on holiday I lie on the beach all day and read.*
>
> In the -ing form, don't say 'laying', say **lying**:
>
> *He always leaves his clothes lying on the floor where he took them off.*
>
> Remember that the past simple of 'lie' is **lay**, not 'laid':
>
> *I lay down and went to sleep.*

LIE ▷ **3** past simple of **lie** PRODUCE EGGS ▷ **4** B2 [I or T] (of an animal or bird) to produce eggs from out of the body: *Thousands of turtles drag themselves onto the beach and lay their eggs in the sand.* HAVE SEX ▷ **5** [T] slang to have sex with someone: *So did you* ***get*** *laid (= find someone to have sex with)?* RISK MONEY ▷ **6** [T] to risk something, usually money, on the result of an event: *She won't get the job – I'd lay money* ***on*** *it!* EXPRESS ▷ **7** [T] to express a claim, legal statement, etc. in a serious or official way: *She can't accept she made a mistake and now she's trying to lay* ***the blame on*** *(= accuse) her assistant.* ◦ specialized *Do you understand the seriousness of the* ***charge*** *(= legal accusation) which has been laid* ***against*** *you?* **8 lay claim to sth** to say that you own something: *Two companies have laid claim to the design.*

IDIOMS **lay sth at sb's door** mainly UK to blame someone for something: *Blame for the accident has been laid at the government's door.* • **lay sb low** to cause someone to be unable to do what they usually do: *A kidney infection laid her low for a couple of months.* • **lay sth on the line 1** to risk harm to something: *I'd be laying my career/life on the line by giving you that information.* **2** informal to say very clearly that something is the case: *You're just going to have to lay it on the line and tell her that her work's not good enough.* • **lay yourself open to attack, criticism, ridicule, etc.** to make it easy for people to attack you, etc. *She lays herself open to criticism with such unashamedly extreme views.* • **lay sb to rest** to bury a dead person: *She was laid to rest next to her husband.* • **lay sth to rest** to end a worry or fear: *I hope what he said has laid your fears to rest.* • **lay sth to waste** (also **lay waste**) to completely destroy something: *The bomb laid the city centre to waste.* • **lay a finger on sb** to harm someone even slightly: *Don't you dare lay a finger on me.* • **lay a hand on sb** to harm someone: *I never laid a hand on her!* • **lay bare sth** to make something known: *It's been promoted as the biography that lays bare the truth behind the legend.* • **lay down the law** informal to forcefully make known what you think should happen: *She can't just come into this office and start laying down the law.* • **lay down your life for sth** to die for something you believe in strongly: *Today we remember those who laid down their lives for their country.* • **lay it on a bit thick** (also **lay it on with a trowel**) to praise someone too much: *She went on and on about how she admired his work – laid it on a bit thick, if you ask me.* • **lay the basis/foundations for sth** to prepare for or start an activity or task: *The initial negotiations are seen as laying the basis for more detailed talks.* • **lay the ghost of sth (to rest)** to finally stop being worried or upset about something that has worried or upset you for a long time: *With one stunning performance, Chelsea have laid to rest the ghost of their humiliating defeat at Old Trafford last season.* • **lay up trouble for yourself** to do something that will cause you trouble in the future: *You're laying up trouble for yourself if you ignore health problems now.*

PHRASAL VERBS **lay sth aside** STOP ▷ **1** to stop doing or thinking about something, usually for a short period of time: *He's temporarily laid aside some quite interesting projects to write the script.* MONEY ▷ **2** to keep something, usually money, for use in the future: *She's trying to lay something aside (= save some money) for her retirement.* • **lay sth down** WINE ▷ **1** specialized to store wine for drinking in the future WEAPONS ▷ **2** If someone lays down their weapons, they stop fighting: *They laid down their **weapons** and surrendered.* ◦ *Mediators have persuaded both sides to lay down their **arms**.* RULES ▷ **3** to officially establish a rule, or to officially say how something should be done: *This is in line with the policy laid down by the management.* • **lay sth in** to get a supply of something because you will probably need it in the future: *We'd better lay in plenty of food in case we're cut off when it snows.* • **lay into sb** informal to attack someone physically or to criticize them in an angry way: *In the middle of the meeting she suddenly laid into him for no apparent reason.* • **lay sb off** [M often passive] (B2) to stop employing someone, usually because there is no work for them to do: *Because of falling orders, the company has been forced to lay off several hundred workers.* • **lay off (sth/sb)** informal to stop using or doing something: *You'd better lay off alcohol for a while.* ◦ *Why can't you lay off (= stop criticizing or hurting) the kid for once!* • **lay sth on** PROVIDE ▷ **1** to provide something for a group of people: *They lay on free entertainment at the club every day.* ◦ *They laid on a wonderful buffet after the wedding.* TELL ▷ **2** mainly US slang to tell someone something they did not know: *I hate to be the one to lay this on you, but your girlfriend has just left with another guy.* • **lay sth out** ARRANGE ▷ **1** (C1) to arrange something on a flat surface: *Most of Manhattan is laid out **in/on** a grid pattern.* ◦ *We laid the pieces of the dress pattern out on the floor.* SPEND MONEY ▷ **2** (C2) informal to spend money, especially a large amount: *It's not every day you lay out £2,000 **on** a holiday.* → See also **outlay** EXPLAIN ▷ **3** (C1) to explain something clearly, usually in writing: *The code of practice lays out very clearly what the duties of the registrar are.* • **lay sb out** DEAD BODY ▷ **1** to prepare a dead person's body to be buried HIT ▷ **2** informal to hit someone so hard that they fall down and become unconscious

▸adj [before noun] NOT TRAINED ▷ **1** not trained in or not having a detailed knowledge of a particular subject: *From a lay viewpoint the questionnaire is virtually incomprehensible.* → See also **layman** CHURCH ▷ **2** having a position in a religious organization that is not a full-time job and is not paid: *a lay preacher* → See also **layman**

▸noun [C] slang used to describe how good someone is at sex, or how often they have sex: *She's a **good** lay (= sex with her is enjoyable).* ◦ *She got a reputation as an **easy** lay (= she was thought to have slept with a lot of people).*

layabout /ˈleɪ.əˌbaʊt/ noun [C] informal a person who is unwilling to work

layaway /ˈleɪ.ə.weɪ/ noun [U] US a system of paying for goods in small amounts and receiving the goods after the full amount has been paid, or goods bought in this way: *Could I **buy/put** the dress **on** layaway?*

ˈlay ˌbrother/ˌsister noun [C] someone who belongs to a religious group, especially a group living together in a MONASTERY or CONVENT, and who does simple work for the group, such as preparing food

ˈlay-by noun ROAD ▷ **1** [C] (plural **lay-bys**) UK a place at the side of a road where a vehicle can stop for a short time without interrupting other traffic: *We pulled into a lay-by to look at the map.* → See also **rest stop** PAYMENT ▷ **2** [U] Australian English a system of paying for goods in small amounts and receiving the goods after the full amount has been paid, or goods bought in this way → Compare **layaway**

layer /ˈleɪ.əʳ/ (US) /-ɚ/ noun; verb

▸noun [C] MATERIAL ▷ **1** (B2) a level of material, such as a type of rock or gas, that is different from the material above or below it, or a thin sheet of a substance: *the ozone layer* ◦ *A thick layer **of** clay lies over the sandstone.* ◦ *There was a thin layer **of** oil on the surface of the water.* ◦ *We stripped several layers **of** paint off the door.* PEOPLE ▷ **2** the group of people at a particular level in an organization: *We've cut the number of **management** layers from five to three.*

▸verb [T] to arrange something in layers: *Layer the pasta **with** slices of tomato.* ◦ *potatoes layered with onions* • **layered** /-əd/ (US) /-ɚd/ adj

ˈlayer ˌcake noun [C] US two or more soft cakes put on top of each other with jam, cream, ICING, etc. (= a sweet mixture made from sugar) between the cakes and covering the top and sides

layette /leɪˈet/ noun [C] old-fashioned a complete set of clothes, sheets, bed covers, and the other things needed for a new baby

layman /ˈleɪ.mən/ noun [C] (plural **-men** /-mən/) (also

L

layperson) CHURCH ▷ **1** someone who is part of a religious organization but who is not paid or specially trained NOT TRAINED ▷ **2** someone who is not trained in or does not have a detailed knowledge of a particular subject

layoff (also **'lay-off**) /'leɪ.ɒf/ (US) /-ɑːf/ **noun 1** [C often plural] an occasion when a company stops employing someone, sometimes temporarily, because the company does not have enough money or enough work: *The recent economic crisis has led to massive layoffs.* **2** [C usually singular] a period when someone is not working or playing sport

layout /'leɪ.aʊt/ **noun** [C] C1 the way that something is arranged: *I like the the layout of the house.* ◦ *Application forms vary greatly in layout and length.*

layover /'leɪˌəʊ.vəʳ/ (US) /-ˌoʊ.vɚ/ **noun** [C] US for **stopover** (= a short stay between parts of a journey, especially a plane journey): *We had a four-hour layover in Chicago.*

laywoman /'leɪˌwʊm.ən/ **noun** [C] (plural **-women** /-wɪmɪn/) a female layman

laze /leɪz/ **verb** [I + adv/prep] to relax and enjoy yourself, doing very little: *We spent the day lazing* ***around*** *in the garden.*

lazy /'leɪ.zi/ **adj 1** A2 disapproving not willing to work or use any effort: *Managers had complained that the workers were lazy and unreliable.* ◦ *Get out of bed, you lazy thing!* ◦ *He's too lazy to walk to work.* **2** B2 approving slow and relaxed: *We spent a lazy day on the beach sunbathing.* • **lazily** /-zɪ.li/ **adv** *Palm trees swayed lazily in the soft breeze.* • **laziness** /-nəs/ **noun** [U] B2 *I could go to the gym – it's just laziness that stops me.*

> **Other ways of saying lazy**
>
> If someone is lazy for a period of time because of being tired and lacking in energy, the adjective **lethargic** can be used:
>
> *I felt very* ***lethargic*** *after such a big lunch.*
>
> You can say that someone who shows no interest in things is **indolent**:
>
> *Some of my classmates are* ***indolent*** *in their health habits.*
>
> Someone who watches a lot of television and does not do much else can be described as a **couch potato** in informal English:
>
> *I was turning into a* ***couch potato****, watching TV and eating snacks all day.*

lazybones /'leɪ.zi.bəʊnz/ (US) /-boʊnz/ **noun** [C] (plural **lazybones**) informal disapproving someone who is lazy: [as form of address] *Hey lazybones, get up from the sofa and help me with the dishes!*

lb **noun** [C] (plural **lb**) written abbreviation for pound: *a 3 lb bag of flour* ◦ *I weighed 10 lb at birth.*

lbw /ˌel.biː'dʌb.l̩.juː/ **adj, adv** abbreviation for leg before wicket: in the game of cricket, the situation when your time as the person trying to hit the ball is ended because the ball has hit your leg when it should not have

LCD /ˌel.siː'diː/ **noun** [C] abbreviation for **liquid crystal display**

leach /liːtʃ/ **verb** [T] specialized to remove a substance from a material, especially from earth, by the process of water moving through the material, or to remove parts of a material using water: *The soil has been so heavily leached through intensive farming that it is no longer fertile.*

lead¹ /liːd/ **verb**; **noun**; **adj**

▸**verb** (**led**, **led** /led/) CONTROL ▷ **1** B2 [I or T] to control a group of people, a country, or a situation: *I think we've chosen the right person to lead the expedition.* ◦ *I've asked Gemma to lead the discussion.* BE WINNING ▷ **2** B2 [I or T] (especially in sport or other competitions) to be in front, to be first, or to be winning: *After 30 minutes the challengers were leading* ***by*** *two goals.* ◦ *With two laps to go Ngomo led* ***by*** *less than two seconds.* ◦ *The Lions are leading the Hawks 28–9.* INFLUENCE ▷ **3** C2 [T] to cause someone to do something, especially something bad: [+ to infinitive] *The brochure led me* ***to believe*** *that the price included home delivery.* ◦ *It's worrying that such a prominent politician is so* ***easily*** *led.* ◦ *He was a weak man, led* ***astray*** *by ambition.* SHOW WAY ▷ **4** B1 [I] to show the way to a group of people, animals, vehicles, etc. by going in front of them: *I don't know the way, so you'd better lead.* ◦ *If you lead in the jeep, we'll follow behind on the horses.* **5** [T] To lead a group of moving people or vehicles is to walk or drive in front of them: *The local youth band will lead the parade this weekend.* ◦ *A large black hearse led the funeral procession.* **6** B1 [T usually + adv/prep] to take someone somewhere, by going with them: *She led them down the hall.* ◦ *The waiter led us to our table.* ◦ *Our guide led us through the mountains.* **7** B1 [T usually + adv/prep] to take hold of a person or an animal, or of something fastened to them, and take them somewhere: *She took the child by the hand and led him upstairs to bed.* ◦ *He led the horse out of the stable.* **8** **lead the way a** to show the way by going in front: *You've been there before – why don't you lead the way?* **b** to make more progress than other people in the development of something: *The company has been leading the way* ***in*** *network applications for several years.* DIRECTION ▷ **9** B2 [I or T, usually + adv/prep] (especially of roads, paths, doors, signs, information, etc.) to go in a particular direction or have a particular result, or to allow or cause this: *There's a track that leads directly* ***to*** *the reservoir.* ◦ *The French windows lead* ***out onto*** *a wide, shady terrace.* ◦ *A narrow trail of blood led directly* ***into*** *the cave.* ◦ *This information led the police* ***to*** *a house near the harbour.* LIVE ▷ **10** **lead a busy, normal, quiet, etc. life** B2 to live a particular type of life: *He was able to lead a normal life, despite the illness.* ◦ *We certainly don't lead a life of luxury but we're not poor either.*

IDIOMS **lead sb a (merry) dance** informal to cause someone a lot of trouble, especially by getting them to do a lot of things that are not necessary • **lead sb by the nose** informal to control someone and make them do exactly what you want them to do • **lead sb up the garden path** informal to deceive someone: *It seems as if we've been led up the garden path about the position of our hotel – it's miles from the beach!* • **lead the field/pack/world** to be better than all other people or things: *Their scientists lead the world* ***in*** *nutrition research.*

PHRASAL VERBS **lead off** to begin to speak, usually as the first person to speak: *I want to lead off by thanking everyone for coming.* • **lead sb on** disapproving to persuade someone to believe something that is untrue: *All that time she'd been leading him on (= pretending she liked him), but she was only interested in his money.* • **lead to sth** B2 If an action or event leads to something, it causes that thing to happen or exist: *Reducing speed limits should lead to fewer deaths on the roads.* • **lead up to sth** HAPPEN ▷ **1** C2 If a period of time or series of events leads up to an event or activity, it happens until that event or activity begins: *The pilot had no recollection of the events leading up to the crash.* TALK ▷ **2** to prepare to talk about something by gradually mentioning the subject you want to talk about: *He started telling me about a wonderful new restaurant he'd been to and I wondered what he was leading up to.*

▸noun **WINNING POSITION** ▷ **1** B2 /liːd/ [S] a winning position during a race or other situation where people are competing: *For the first time in the race Harrison is* ***in*** *the lead.* ◦ *With a final burst of speed she* ***went/moved into*** *the lead.* ◦ *After last night's win Johnson has* ***taken*** *(****over****) the lead in the championship table.* ◦ *By the end of the day's play Davies had a lead* ***of*** *three points.* **SHOWING WAY** ▷ **2** C2 [C usually singular] the act of showing a person or group of people what to do: *We'll go through the dance routine again –* ***follow*** *my lead (= do what I do).* **INFORMATION** ▷ **3** [C] a piece of information which allows a discovery to be made or a solution to be found: *A lead from an informer enabled the police to make several arrests.* **ACTOR** ▷ **4 the lead** C2 [C] the main actor in a film or play **FOR ANIMAL** ▷ **5** [C] mainly UK (mainly US **leash**) a piece of rope, chain, etc. tied to an animal, especially to a dog at its collar when taking it for a walk: *Please keep your dog* ***on*** *a lead when on the beach.* **ELECTRICAL** ▷ **6** [C] (UK also **flex**, US also **cord**, **wire**) a wire covered in plastic and used to connect electrical equipment to the electricity supply

▸adj [before noun] B1 used to describe the main performer or part in a performance: *Who played the lead* ***role*** *in the movie?* ◦ *The lead guitarist was good.*

lead² /led/ noun [U] **1** [U] (symbol **Pb**) a chemical element that is a very heavy, soft, dark grey, poisonous metal, used especially in the past on roofs and for pipes and also for protection against RADIATION: *lead pipes* **2** [C or U] (the narrow strip of) coloured material, usually black and made of GRAPHITE, in the centre of a pencil

IDIOM **go down like a lead balloon** humorous If something that you say or show to people goes down like a lead balloon, they do not like it at all: *My joke about the alcoholic went down like a lead balloon.*

leaded /ˈled.ɪd/ adj describes petrol (= fuel) with small amounts of lead in it → See also **unleaded**

ˌleaded ˈwindow noun [C] a window made from small pieces of glass fixed together with lead strips

leaden /ˈled.ən/ adj **GREY** ▷ **1** literary dark grey: *leaden skies* **WITHOUT ENERGY** ▷ **2** disapproving without energy or feeling: *a leaden expression/performance*

leader /ˈliː.dər/ (US) /-dɚ/ noun [C] **CONTROLLING** ▷ **1** B1 a person in control of a group, country, or situation: *a religious leader* ◦ *The Russian leader wants to introduce further changes.* ◦ *He's a natural leader.* ◦ *She was elected as leader* ***of*** *the campaign group.* **WINNING** ▷ **2** C1 someone or something that is winning during a race or other situation where people are competing: *He's fallen two laps behind the leaders.* ◦ *Microsoft is a world leader in software design.* **NEWSPAPER** ▷ **3** UK **editorial** **MUSIC** ▷ **4** UK (US **concertmaster**) the most important VIOLIN player in an ORCHESTRA

leadership /ˈliː.də.ʃɪp/ (US) /-dɚ-/ noun [U] **1** C1 the set of characteristics that make a good leader: *What the company lacks is leadership.* ◦ *He lacks leadership qualities/skills.* **2** C1 the position or fact of being the leader: *The group flourished* ***under*** *her firm leadership.* ◦ *R&M gained* ***market*** *leadership (= sold more goods than other companies) by selling products that were of superior quality.* **3 the leadership** C1 the person or people in charge of an organization: *There is growing discontent with the leadership.* ◦ *The election for the leadership* ***of*** *the council will take place on Tuesday.*

ˈlead-in noun [C] something that introduces something else, such as the words and music that are used to introduce a television programme

leading¹ /ˈliː.dɪŋ/ adj [before noun] B2 very important or most important: *a leading* ***expert*** *on the country's ecology* ◦ *the world's leading manufacturer of audio equipment*

leading² /ˈled.ɪŋ/ noun [U] UK the LEAD (= type of metal) used to cover (parts of) a roof

ˌleading ˈarticle noun [C] UK **editorial**

ˌleading ˈedge noun [S] the most advanced position in an area of activity: *scientists* ***at*** *the leading edge of cancer research* • **ˌleading-ˈedge** adj [before noun]

ˌleading ˈhand noun [C usually singular] Australian English the most experienced person in a factory, etc.

ˌleading ˈlady noun [C] the female actor who has the most important part in a play or a film

ˌleading ˈlight noun [C] an important and respected person in a group or organization: *A leading light* ***in/of*** *the art world, she was a close friend of the director.*

ˌleading ˈman noun [C] the actor who has the most important part in a play or a film

ˌleading ˈquestion noun [C] a question that tricks someone into answering in a particular way

ˈlead-off adj first in a series of things: *Who swam the lead-off leg of the race?* ◦ *the lead-off topic/question*

ˌlead ˈsinger noun [C] the main singer in a musical group

leaf /liːf/ noun; verb

▸noun [C] (plural **leaves**) **PLANT** ▷ **1** B1 one of the flat, usually green parts of a plant that are joined at one end to the stem or branch: *a palm leaf* ◦ *autumn leaves* ◦ *He was sweeping up leaves in his garden.* **2 be in leaf/come into leaf** When a plant is in leaf or when it comes into leaf, it has or gets leaves on it: *The trees are in leaf early this year.* ◦ *The bushes are just coming into leaf.* **PAPER** ▷ **3** a thin sheet of paper **TABLE** ▷ **4** an extra part of a table that can be folded away when not being used

IDIOM **take a leaf out of sb's book** to copy something that someone else does because it will bring you advantages: *Maybe I should take a leaf out of Rick's book and start coming in at ten every morning.*

▸verb

PHRASAL VERB **leaf through sth** to quickly turn the pages of a book or a magazine, reading only a little of it: *The waiting room was full of people leafing through magazines.*

leaflet /ˈliː.flət/ noun; verb

▸noun [C] B2 a piece of paper which gives you information or advertises something: *Demonstrators handed out leaflets to passers-by.* ◦ *A leaflet about the new bus services came through the door today.*

▸verb [I or T] (-t- or UK also **-tt-**) to give out leaflets to people: *They leafleted the area two weeks before the event.*

ˈleaf ˌmould noun [U] UK (US **leaf mold**) a type of FERTILIZER (= substance that makes plants grow) made from leaves which fall from trees in the autumn

leafy /ˈliː.fi/ adj A leafy place is pleasant and has a lot of trees: *a leafy lane/suburb*

league /liːg/ noun [C] **SPORT** ▷ **1** B1 a group of teams playing a sport who take part in competitions between each other: *Who do you think will* ***win*** *the league championship this year?* ◦ *Liverpool were* ***top of*** *the Football League that year.* ◦ *They are currently* ***bottom of*** *the league.* **ORGANIZATION** ▷ **2** a group of people or countries who join together because they have the same interest: *the League of Nations*

IDIOMS **be in a different league** to be much better than something or someone else: *Our last hotel was quite good but this was in a different league.* • **be in league with sb** to be secretly working or planning something with someone, usually to do something bad • **be out of your league** to be too good or too expensive for you: *He was so good-looking and so popular that I felt he was out of my league.* • **not be in the same league** to be not as good as someone or something else: *Her latest film is quite watchable but it's not in the same league **as** her first two epics.*

leak /liːk/ verb; noun

▸**verb** [I or T] **LIQUID/GAS** ▷ **1** (B2) (of a liquid or gas) to escape from a hole or CRACK in a pipe or container or (of a container) to allow liquid or gas to escape: *Water was leaking **from** the pipe.* ◦ *Oil leaked **out** of the car.* ◦ *The tin was leaking.* ◦ *The car leaked oil all over the drive.* **INFORMATION** ▷ **2** (C2) to allow secret information to become generally known: *He leaked the names **to** the press.* ◦ *News of the pay cuts had somehow leaked **out**.*

IDIOM **leak like a sieve** informal to leak a lot

▸**noun** [C] **LIQUID/GAS** ▷ **1** (B2) a hole or CRACK through which a liquid or gas can flow out of a container, or the liquid or gas that comes out: *There's water on the floor – we must have a leak.* ◦ *If you suspect a **gas** leak, phone the emergency number.* **INFORMATION** ▷ **2** (C2) the origin of secret information which becomes known, or the act of making it known: *There have been several **security** leaks recently.* ◦ *They traced the leak to a secretary in the finance department.*

IDIOM **take a leak/have a leak** slang to urinate

leakage /ˈliː.kɪdʒ/ noun [C or U] **LIQUID/GAS** ▷ **1** the act of leaking or the leak itself: *The leakage was traced to an oil pipe in the cellar.* ◦ *A lot of water is wasted through leakage.* **INFORMATION** ▷ **2** making known secret information

leaky /ˈliː.ki/ adj Something that is leaky has a hole or CRACK in it that allows liquid or gas to get through: *leaky pipes* ◦ *a leaky valve*

lean /liːn/ verb; adj

▸**verb** [I or T, usually + adv/prep] (**leaned** or UK also **leant**, **leaned** or UK also **leant**) (B2) to (cause to) slope in one direction, or to move the top part of the body in a particular direction: *She leaned forward and whispered something in my ear.* ◦ *I sat down next to Bernard, who leaned over to me and said 'You're late.'* ◦ *Lean your head back a bit.* ◦ *That fence is leaning to the right.*

PHRASAL VERBS **lean (sth) against/on sth** (B2) to sit or stand with part of your body touching something as a support: *He leaned against the wall.* ◦ *She leaned her head on his shoulder.* • **lean sth against/on sth** (B2) to put something against a wall or other surface so that it is supported: *She leaned the brush against the wall.* • **lean on sb/sth** to use someone or something to help you, especially in a difficult situation: *He's always had his big brother to lean on.* • **lean on sb** informal (C2) to try to make someone do what you want by threatening or persuading them: *We may have to lean on them a bit if we want our money.*

▸**adj NO FAT** ▷ **1** describes meat that has little fat **2** thin and healthy: *lean and fit* **NOT ENOUGH** ▷ **3** If a period of time is lean, there is not enough of something, especially money or food, at that time: *It has been a particularly lean year for the education department.* **EFFICIENT** ▷ **4** approving A lean company or organization uses only a small number of people and a small amount of money, etc. so that there is no waste: *Nowadays even efficient, lean, well-run industries are failing.*

IDIOM **lean and hungry** showing a very strong and determined wish to get something: *He's got that lean and hungry look.*

leaning /ˈliː.nɪŋ/ noun [C usually plural] a particular set of beliefs, opinions, etc. that someone prefers: *I don't know what his political leanings are.*

ˈlean-to noun [C] **1** a building joined to one of the sides of a larger building with which it shares one wall: *a cottage with a lean-to garage* **2** US a shelter or simple building with a roof that slopes in one direction, used for sleeping in outside

leap /liːp/ verb; noun

▸**verb** [I + adv/prep] (**leaped** or **leapt**, **leaped** or **leapt**) **MOVE SUDDENLY** ▷ **1** (C2) to make a large jump or sudden movement, usually from one place to another: *He leaped out of his car and ran towards the house.* ◦ *I leaped up to answer the phone.* ◦ *The dog leaped over the gate into the field.* **HAPPEN SUDDENLY** ▷ **2** to provide help, protection, etc. very quickly: *He leaped **to** his friend's defence.* ◦ *Scott leapt **to** the rescue when he spotted the youngster in difficulty.* ◦ *Mr Davies leapt **in** to explain.* **3** to achieve something suddenly, usually FAME, power, or importance: *He leapt **to** fame after his appearance in a Broadway play.* **4** to increase, improve, or grow very quickly: *Shares in the company leapt 250 percent.*

PHRASAL VERBS **leap at sth** (C2) to eagerly accept the chance to do or have something: *When I offered her the job, she leapt at it.* • **leap out at sb** If something leaps out at you, you notice it immediately: *As I turned the page his picture leapt out at me.*

▸**noun** [C] **SUDDEN CHANGE** ▷ **1** (C2) a big change, increase, or improvement: *a leap in profits* ◦ *It takes quite a leap **of the imagination** to believe that it's the same person.* **MOVEMENT** ▷ **2** a large jump or sudden movement

IDIOMS **by/in leaps and bounds** (C2) If someone or something gets better by/in leaps and bounds, they improve very quickly: *Her Spanish has **come on** (= improved) in leaps and bounds this year.* • **a leap in the dark** something you do without being certain what will happen as a result: *I had very little information about the company, so writing to them was a bit of a leap in the dark.*

leapfrog /ˈliːp.frɒg/ (US) /-frɑːg/ noun; verb

▸**noun** [U] a children's game in which a number of children bend down and another child jumps over them one at a time

▸**verb** [I or T, usually + adv/prep] (**-gg-**) to improve your position by going past other people quickly or by missing out some stages: *They've leapfrogged from third to first place.* ◦ *She leapfrogged several older colleagues to get the manager's post.*

ˈleap ˌyear noun [C] a year that happens every four years and has an extra day on 29 February

learn /lɜːn/ (US) /lɝːn/ verb (**learned** or UK also **learnt**, **learned** or UK also **learnt**) **1** (A1) [I or T] to get knowledge or skill in a new subject or activity: *They learn Russian at school.* ◦ *'Can you drive?' 'I'm learning.'* ◦ *I've learned a lot **about** computers since I started work here.* ◦ [+ to infinitive] *I'm learning **to** play the piano.* ◦ [+ question word + to infinitive] *First you'll learn (**how**) **to** use this machine.* **2** (B1) [T] to make yourself remember a piece of writing by reading it or repeating it many times: *I don't know how actors manage to learn all those lines.* ◦ *We were told to learn Portia's speech* ***by heart*** *(= be able to say it from memory) for homework.* **3** B2 [I or T] to start to understand that you must change the way you behave: *She'll have to learn that she can't have everything she wants.* ◦ *She soon learned not* ***to*** *contradict him.* ◦ *He's not afraid to learn* ***from his mistakes.*** **4** B1 [I or T] to be told facts or information that you did not know: *We were all shocked to learn* ***of*** *his death.* ◦ [+ (that)] *I later learned (****that****) the message had never arrived.* ◦ *I only learned* ***about*** *the accident later.*

> **! Common mistake: learn or teach?**
>
> **Warning:** choose the right word!
>
> To talk about giving someone knowledge or instructing or training someone, don't say 'learn', say **teach**:
>
> ~~*Parents must learn their children the difference between right and wrong.*~~
>
> *Parents must teach their children the difference between right and wrong.*

> **+ Other ways of saying learn**
>
> See also: **study**
>
> You could use the verb **master** when someone learns how to do something well:
>
> *She lived in Italy for several years but never quite* ***mastered*** *the language.*
>
> If someone learns something by practising it rather than by being taught, you could use the phrasal verb **pick up**:
>
> *When you live in a country, you soon* ***pick up*** *the language.*
>
> When you learn about something or how to do something, you can say that you **familiarize** yourself with it:
>
> *He prepared for the interview by* ***familiarizing*** *himself with the company's work.*
>
> **Get the hang of** something is an informal phrase that means 'to learn how to do something, especially if it is not obvious or simple':
>
> *'I've never used this software before.' 'Don't worry, you'll soon* ***get the hang of*** *it.'*

IDIOMS **learn your lesson** B2 to suffer a bad experience and know not to do it again: *I got horribly drunk once at college and that was enough – I learned my lesson.* • **learn to live with sth** to accept a new but unpleasant situation that you cannot change

learned adj EDUCATED ▷ **1** /ˈlɜː.nɪd/ US /ˈlɝː-/ formal describes someone who has studied for a long time and has a lot of knowledge: *a learned professor* COPIED ▷ **2** /ˈlɜːnd/ US /ˈlɝːnd/ specialized describes behaviour that has been copied from others: *This sort of aggression is learned behaviour.*

learner /ˈlɜː.nəʳ/ US /ˈlɝː.nɚ/ noun [C] B2 a person who is still learning something: *He's a quick learner.* ◦ mainly UK *a learner driver*

learning /ˈlɜː.nɪŋ/ US /ˈlɝː-/ noun [U] **1** B2 the activity of obtaining knowledge: *This technique makes learning fun.* **2** knowledge obtained by study: *His friends praised his generosity, wit, and learning.*

ˈlearning ˌcurve noun [C] the rate of someone's progress in learning a new skill: *It's a* ***steep*** *learning curve when you're thrown into a job.*

ˈlearning ˌdifficulties noun [plural] mental problems which affect a person's ability to learn things

lease /liːs/ verb; noun

▸**verb** [T] to make a legal agreement by which money is paid in order to use land, a building, a vehicle, or a piece of equipment for an agreed period of time: *The estate contains 300 new homes, about a third of which are leased* ***to*** *the council.* ◦ [+ two objects] *It was agreed they would lease the flat* ***to*** *him/lease him the flat.*

▸**noun** [C] a legal agreement in which you pay money in order to use a building, piece of land, vehicle, etc. for a period: *He has the flat* ***on*** *a long lease.* ◦ *The lease runs out/expires in two years' time.* ◦ *We* ***signed*** *a three-year lease when we moved into the house.*

leaseback /ˈliːs.bæk/ noun [U] specialized a legal agreement by which the owner of a building, piece of land, vehicle, etc. allows the previous owner to continue to use it for a regular amount of money

leasehold /ˈliːs.həʊld/ US /-hoʊld/ noun [C or U] the legal right to live in or use a building or piece of land for an agreed period of time: *His family* ***held*** *the leasehold/****had*** *the property* ***on*** *leasehold.* → Compare **freehold** • **leasehold** adj *leasehold offices and shops*

leaseholder /ˈliːs.həʊl.dəʳ/ US /-hoʊl.dɚ/ noun [C] the person who pays the owner of a piece of land or a building in order to be able to use it

leash /liːʃ/ noun [C] mainly US for **lead**[1]

ˈleash ˌlaw noun [C] a law in many US cities and towns that says people must keep their dogs on a leash when they are outside their home

least /liːst/ adv, determiner, pronoun B1 less than anything or anyone else; the smallest amount or number: *This group is the least likely of the four to win.* ◦ *Disaster struck when we least expected it.* ◦ *It was the answer she least wanted to hear.* ◦ *I like the green one least of all.* ◦ *He's the relative I like (****the****) least.* ◦ *No one believed her, least* ***of all*** *(= especially not) the police.* ◦ *They refused to admit her,* ***not*** *least because (= there were several reasons but this was an important one) she hadn't got her membership card with her.*

IDIOMS **at least 1** A2 as much as, or more than, a number or amount: *It will cost at least $100.* ◦ *It will be £200 at* ***the very*** *least.* ◦ *You'll have to wait at least an hour.* **2** B2 used to reduce the effect of a statement: *I've met the president – at least, he shook my hand once.* → See also **leastways 3** B1 used to emphasize that something is good in a bad situation: *It's a small house but at least there's a garden.* **4** B1 used to say that someone should do something small, even if they do nothing else: *Even if she didn't want to send a present, she could at least have sent a card.* • **it's the least I can do** a polite answer to someone who thanks you, usually when you feel you should do more to help: *'Thanks for cleaning up' 'It's the least I can do, seeing as I'm staying here rent-free.'* • **not in the least** C2 not in any way: *'Are you dissatisfied with the results?' 'Not in the least.'* • **not the least** used for emphasis with nouns: *I haven't the least idea (= I do not know) who he was.* ◦ *She hasn't the least interest (= she has no interest) in the project.*

leastways /ˈliːst.weɪz/ adv US used to reduce the effect of a statement: *He said he'd be back later – leastways, I think he did.* → See also **at least**

leather /ˈleð.əʳ/ US /-ɚ/ noun [U] A2 animal skin treated in order to preserve it, and used to make shoes, bags, clothes, equipment, etc.: *a leather coat/belt/handbag*

leatherette /ˌleð.əˈret/ noun [U] an artificial material that is made to look like leather

leathery /ˈleð.ᵊr.i/ US /-ɚ-/ adj with the look and feel of leather: *leathery skin/hands*

L

leave /liːv/ verb; noun

▸verb (**left**, **left**) **GO AWAY** ▷ **1** (A1) [I or T] to go away from someone or something, for a short time or permanently: *I'll be leaving at five o'clock tomorrow.* ◦ *He left the house by the back door.* ◦ *She left the group of people she was with and came over to speak to us.* ◦ *The bus leaves in five minutes.*

> **!** Common mistake: **leave or live?**
>
> **Warning:** the verbs 'leave' and 'live' look and sound similar but have very different meanings. To talk about being alive or having a particular way of life, don't say 'leave', say **live**:
>
> ~~*The best way to improve your English is to leave with a family.*~~

> **!** Common mistake: **leave**
>
> **Warning:** choose the correct preposition!
>
> To talk about going away from somewhere to go somewhere else, don't say 'leave to' a place, say **leave for** a place:
>
> ~~*Trains leave to London every 30 minutes.*~~
>
> *Trains leave for London every 30 minutes.*

NOT TAKE ▷ **2** (A2) [T] to not take something or someone with you when you go, either intentionally or by accident: *Hey, you've left your keys on the table.* ◦ *Can I leave a message **for** Sue?* ◦ *Why don't you leave the kids **with** me on Friday?* **REMAIN** ▷ **3** (A2) If something leaves something else, a part or effect of it stays after it has gone or been used: *His shoes left muddy marks on the floor.* ◦ [+ two objects] *If I give you £10 that won't leave me enough cash to pay the bill.* ◦ [+ obj + adj] *Far from improving things the new law has left many people worse off (= they are now in a worse situation) than before.* **4** (B2) [T] If you leave something in a particular condition you do not touch it, move it, or act to change it in any way, so that it stays in the same condition: *Leave that chair where it is.* ◦ *He left most of his dinner (= did not eat much of it).* ◦ [+ obj + adj] *The family were left (= became and continued to be) homeless.* ◦ *I'll have to go back – I think I've left the iron on.* ◦ *You can leave the window open.* ◦ *Leave your sister alone (= stop annoying her).* **5** (C1) [T + obj + -ing verb] If you leave something or someone doing something, when you go away they are still doing it: *I left the children watch**ing** television.* ◦ *He left the engine runn**ing**.* **NOT USE ALL** ▷ **6** (A2) [T] to not eat or use all of something: *They'd eaten all the cake, but they'd left some sandwiches.* ◦ *Are there any cookies left?* ◦ *There's some food left **over** from the party.* ◦ *Make sure you leave enough hot water for the rest of us.* **STOP** ▷ **7** (A1) [T] to stop doing something, or to leave a place because you have finished an activity: *Many children leave school at 16.* ◦ *He left work in June for health reasons.* ◦ *She left **home** (= stopped living with her parents) at 18.* ◦ *Could we leave that subject (= stop discussing that subject) for the moment and go on to the next item on the agenda?* **END RELATIONSHIP** ▷ **8** (B1) [T] to end a relationship with a husband, wife, or partner and stop living with them: *I'll never leave you.* ◦ *She left her husband **for** a younger man.* **WAIT** ▷ **9** (C2) [T] If you leave (doing) something, you wait before you do it: *I'll leave these letters till Monday (= write them on Monday).* ◦ *Don't leave it too late (= don't wait too long to do it).* ◦ [+ -ing verb] *They left book**ing** their holiday **till/to** the last minute.* **AFTER DEATH** ▷ **10** [T] To leave a wife, husband, or other close family member is to die while these family members are still alive: *He left a wife and two children.* **11** (C2) [+ two objects] If you leave money or things that you own to someone, you say they should receive it or them when you die: *He left his nieces all his money./He left all his money **to** his nieces.* **GIVE RESPONSIBILITY** ▷ **12** [T] to allow someone to make a choice or decision about something, or to make someone responsible for something: *I left the decision (**up**) **to** her.* ◦ [+ to infinitive] *I left it to her **to** make the decision.* ◦ *Leave it (= the problem) **with** me, I'll see what I can do.* ◦ *I'll leave it **to chance** (= wait and see what happens without planning).*

IDIOMS **be left holding the baby** (US **be left holding the bag**) to suddenly have to deal with a difficult situation because others have decided that they do not want the responsibility: *The other investors pulled out of the project and we were left holding the baby.* • **leave sb be** to not worry someone, or to allow them to continue what they are doing: *She's only having a bit of fun – leave her be.* • **leave sb cold** to not make you feel interested or excited: *I'm afraid opera leaves me cold.* • **leave sb in the lurch** to leave someone at a time when they need you to stay and help them • **leave sb out in the cold** to not allow someone to become part of a group or an activity • **leave sb standing** (also **leave sb on the sidelines**) to be much better than other people or things of the same type: *Her voice is excellent – it leaves the others standing.* • **leave sb to their own devices** (C2) to allow someone to make their own decisions about what to do: *He seemed to be a responsible person, so I left him to his own devices.* • **leave a bad taste in sb's mouth** If an experience leaves a bad taste in your mouth, you have an unpleasant memory of it: *I think we all felt he'd been treated very unfairly and it left a bad taste in our mouths.* • **leave a lot to be desired** to be much worse than you would like: *Apparently, Meg's cooking leaves a lot to be desired.* • **leave go/hold of sth** informal to stop holding on to something: *Leave go of my arm!* • **leave it at that** to agree that there has been enough discussion, study, etc. and that it is time to stop: *Let's leave it at that for today and meet again tomorrow.* • **leave it out!** UK slang **1** stop doing or saying that: *Hey, leave it out! That hurt!* **2** I do not believe you: *'I tell you, he was driving a sports car.' 'Leave it out!'* • **leave no stone unturned** (C2) to do everything you can to achieve a good result, especially when looking for something: *He left no stone unturned in his search for his natural mother.* • **leave well alone** to allow something to stay as it is because doing more might make things worse: *It's going to get in a muddle if you carry on. I should just leave well alone if I were you.*

PHRASAL VERBS **leave sth aside** to not discuss one subject so that you can discuss a different subject: *Leaving aside the question of cost, how many people do we need on the job?* • **leave sth/sb behind** (B1) to leave a place without taking someone or something with you: *We left in a hurry and I must have left my keys behind.* ◦ *He was forced to leave the country, leaving behind his wife and children.* • **leave sth behind** to cause a situation to exist after you have left a place: *The army left a trail of destruction behind them.* • **leave sth for/to sb** to give someone responsibility for dealing with something: *I've left the paperwork for you.* ◦ *Leave it to me – I'll sort it out tomorrow.* • **leave sth/sb off sth** to not include something or someone on a list: *He left three people off the list by mistake.* • **leave off (sth/doing sth)** to stop, or to stop doing something: *This film begins where the other one leaves off.* ◦ *I've decided to leave off eating meat for a while.* • **leave off!** old-fashioned informal used to tell someone to stop being annoying: *Hey, leave off! I hate people* touching my hair. • **leave sb/sth out** B2 to not include someone or something: *You can leave the butter out of this recipe if you're on a low-fat diet.* ◦ *I've made a list of names – I hope I haven't left anyone out.* ◦ *None of the other children play with her, and I think she feels rather left out (= feels that no one wants to be her friend).*

▸**noun** HOLIDAY ▷ **1** C2 [U] time allowed away from work for holiday or illness: *How much* ***annual/paid*** *leave do you get?* ◦ *She's (****gone****)* ***on*** *leave (= holiday).* ◦ *I've asked if I can take a week's* ***unpaid*** *leave.* **2 leave of absence** formal permission to be away from work or studies PERMISSION ▷ **3** [U] formal permission or agreement: *He did it* ***without*** *(my) leave.* ◦ [+ to infinitive] *Did you* ***get*** *leave* ***to*** *do that?* GOODBYE ▷ **4 take leave** to say goodbye: *He decided the time had come to take leave* ***of*** *his home town.*

IDIOMS **take leave of your senses** to lose your good judgment: *You can't take the children out sailing in this weather! Have you completely taken leave of your senses?* • **without so much as a by-your-leave** old-fashioned disapproving without asking for permission: *That's twice now he's just walked in here without so much as a by-your-leave and picked a book off the shelf!*

leaven /ˈlev.ən/ **verb** [T] **1** to add a substance to bread or another food made with flour to make it get bigger when it is cooked **2** formal to make something less boring: *Even a speech on a serious subject should be leavened with a little humour.*

leaves /liːvz/ plural of **leaf**

ˈleave-ˌtaking **noun** [C] formal an act of saying goodbye

lech /letʃ/ **noun; verb**

▸**noun** [C] informal for **lecher**

▸**verb**

PHRASAL VERB **lech after sb** informal disapproving to show too much sexual interest in someone: *He's always leching after younger women.*

lecher /ˈletʃ.ər/ US /-ɚ/ **noun** [C] (informal **lech**, also **letch**) a lecherous person

lecherous /ˈletʃ.ər.əs/ US /-ɚ-/ **adj** disapproving (especially of men) showing a strong sexual interest in someone: *He gave her a lecherous look.* • **lechery** /-i/ **noun** [U] formal disapproving

lecithin /ˈles.ɪ.θɪn/ **noun** [U] a substance found in plant and animal tissue, often used in food products to help the different parts mix together well

lectern /ˈlek.tən/ US /-tɝːn/ **noun** [C] a piece of furniture with a sloping part on which a book or paper is put to be read from

lecture /ˈlek.tʃər/ US /-tʃɚ/ **noun; verb**

▸**noun** [C] **1** B1 a formal talk on a serious subject given to a group of people, especially students: *We went to a lecture* ***on*** *Italian art.* ◦ *Who's* ***giving*** *the lecture this afternoon?* → Compare **seminar** **2** an angry or serious talk given to someone in order to criticize their behaviour: *My dad* ***gave*** *me a lecture* ***on*** *the evils of alcohol last night.*

▸**verb** **1** C2 [I] to give a formal talk to a group of people, often at a university: *For ten years she lectured* ***in*** *law.* ◦ *She travelled widely in North America, lecturing* ***on*** *women's rights.* **2** [T] to talk angrily or seriously to someone in order to criticize their behaviour: *His parents used to lecture him* ***on*** *his table manners.*

> **!** Usage: **lecturer or teacher?**
>
> In American English, **lecturer** is formal. **Teacher** or **professor** is usually used instead.

lecturer /ˈlek.tʃər.ər/ US /-tʃɚ.ɚ/ **noun** [C] mainly UK B2 someone who teaches at a college or university: *a senior lecturer* ◦ *a lecturer in psychology*

lectureship /ˈlek.tʃə.ʃɪp/ US /-tʃɚ-/ **noun** [C] a teaching job in a British university at the lowest rank

led /led/ **verb** past simple and past participle of **lead**

-led /-led/ **suffix** planned or controlled by a particular person or thing: *child-led activities (= children deciding what to do)*

LED /ˌel.iːˈdiː/ **noun** [C] specialized abbreviation for light-emitting diode: a device which produces a light especially on electronic equipment

ˌLEˈD disˌplay **noun** [C] the letters or numbers shown in lights on a piece of electronic equipment

ledge /ledʒ/ **noun** [C] a narrow shelf which sticks out from a vertical surface

ledger /ˈledʒ.ər/ US /-ɚ/ **noun** [C] a book in which things are regularly recorded, especially business activities and money received or paid

lee /liː/ **noun** **1** [S] the side of hill, wall, etc. that provides shelter from the wind **2 the lees** [plural] the substance that is left at the bottom of a container of liquid, especially in a bottle of wine

leech /liːtʃ/ **noun** [C] **1** a fat creature which lives in wet places and fastens itself onto the bodies of humans and animals to take their blood **2** disapproving a person who gives attention to someone over a long period in order to get their money or support

leek /liːk/ **noun** [C] B2 a long, white vegetable with green leaves on top that tastes and smells like an onion

leer /lɪər/ US /lɪr/ **verb** [I] disapproving (especially of men) to look at someone in a sexually interested way: *He was always leering* ***at*** *female members of staff.* • **leer** **noun** [C] *a drunken leer*

leery /ˈlɪə.ri/ US /ˈlɪr.i/ **adj** [after verb] informal not trusting of someone or something and usually avoiding them if possible: *I've always been a bit leery* ***of*** *authority figures.* → Synonym **wary**

leet /liːt/ **noun** [U] (also **leetspeak** /ˈliːt.spiːk/) a way of writing used on the internet, in which words are deliberately spelled wrongly and numbers are used to replace some of the letters

leeward /ˈliː.wəd/ US /-wɚd/ **adj** specialized (on the side of a ship, etc.) facing away from the wind

leeway /ˈliː.weɪ/ **noun** [U] FREEDOM ▷ **1** freedom to act within particular limits: *Local councils will be* ***given*** *some leeway as to how they implement the legislation.* PERIOD OF TIME ▷ **2** UK an amount or period of time, which might be extra or wasted

left /left/ **adj, adv; noun; verb; adj**

▸**adj, adv** A2 on or towards the side of your body that is to the west when you are facing north: *His left eye was heavily bandaged.* ◦ ***Turn*** *left at the lights.* → Compare **right**

▸**noun** DIRECTION ▷ **1** A2 [S] the left side: *First I'll introduce the speaker sitting* ***on*** *my left.* ◦ *Take the first/second/third* ***on the*** *left.* ◦ *It's the shop to the left of the pub.* ◦ US *After the grocery store I made/took/*informal ***hung*** *a left (= turned into the next road on the left side).* POLITICS ▷ **2 the left** (also **the Left**) [S, + sing/pl verb] the political groups that believe WEALTH and power should be shared between all parts of society: *The war is generally opposed* ***on*** *the left.* → Compare **right**

▸**verb** past simple and past participle of **leave**

▸**adj** relating to political groups that believe WEALTH and power should be shared between all parts of society: *The left* ***wing*** *of the party is unhappy with the legislation.*

ˌleft-ˌclick verb [I] to press the button on the left of a computer mouse in order to make the computer do something

ˌleft ˈfield noun; adj

▸noun [S] the left part of the field in baseball

IDIOMS **be out in left field** US informal **1** to be completely wrong **2** to be very unusual or very different from other people or things: *She's kind of out in left field but she's fun.* • **come out of left field** US informal to be completely unexpected and often unusual: *Her comments came out of left field.*

▸adj (also **ˈleft-field**) unusual and different from what is normally seen, said, or done: *The festival aims to showcase left-field acts that are not often seen in mainstream theatres.*

ˌleft-hand adj [before noun] A2 on or to the left: *the left-hand side*

ˌleft-hand ˈdrive adj describes a vehicle that has the STEERING WHEEL on the left-hand side • **ˌleft-hand ˈdrive** noun [S] a vehicle that has the STEERING WHEEL on the left-hand side

ˌleft-ˈhanded adj **1** using your left hand to write and do most things: *Are you left-handed?* ◦ *a left-handed bowler* **2** designed to be used by a left-handed person: *left-handed scissors* **3** done using the left hand: *a left-handed stroke* • **ˌleft-ˈhanded** adv with the left hand • **left-handedness** /-nəs/ noun [U]

ˌleft-handed ˈcompliment noun [C] US (UK **ˌback-handed ˈcompliment**) a remark that seems to say something pleasant about a person but could also be an insult

left-hander /ˌleftˈhæn.dəʳ/ US /-dɚ/ noun [C] **1** someone who uses their left hand to write and do most things **2** (also **left**) a hit with the left hand

leftist /ˈlef.tɪst/ noun; adj

▸noun [C] a supporter of the political left

▸adj supporting the political left • **leftism** /-tɪ.zᵊm/ noun [U]

ˌleft-ˈluggage ˌoffice noun [C] UK (US **ˈbaggage ˌroom**) a place at a station, airport, hotel, etc. where you can put your bags for a short time until you need them → Compare **cloakroom**

ˌleft of ˈcentre UK (US **ˌleft of ˈcenter**) adj describes a political belief that contains some SOCIALIST ideas but is not extreme

leftover /ˈleftˌəʊ.vəʳ/ US /ˈlefˌt̬oʊ.vɚ/ adj; noun

▸adj [before noun] describes part of something that has not been used or eaten when the other parts have been: *some leftover curry from last night's meal*

▸noun **leftovers** [plural] food remaining after a meal: *This recipe can serve four easily, and the leftovers are just as good eaten cold.*

leftwards /ˈleft.wədz/ US /-wɚdz/ adv (mainly US **leftward**) towards the left in politics: *He accused the party leadership of moving leftwards.*

ˌleft-ˈwing adj C1 supporting the political left; relating to the belief that WEALTH and power should be shared between all parts of society: *Her views are fairly left-wing.*

the ˌleft ˈwing noun [S + sing/pl verb] the political LEFT: *He's* **on** *the left wing of the party.*

ˌleft-ˈwinger noun [C] someone who supports the beliefs of the political left

lefty /ˈlef.ti/ noun [C] (also **leftie**) informal disapproving a supporter of the political left

leg /leg/ noun; verb

▸noun [C] **BODY PART** ▷ **1** A1 one of the parts of the body of a human or animal that is used for standing or walking, or one of the thin vertical parts of an object that it stands on: *My legs were tired after so much walking.* ◦ *He broke his leg skiing.* ◦ *The horse broke its front leg in the fall.* ◦ *a chair/table leg* **2** the part of a piece of clothing that you put your leg in: *He rolled up his trouser legs and waded into the water.* **STAGE** ▷ **3** a particular stage of a journey, competition, or activity: *He has tickets for the* ***first*** *leg* ***of*** *the UEFA Cup tie.* ◦ *The* ***last*** *leg* ***of*** *the race was Paris to London.*

IDIOMS **get your leg over** UK slang (of a man) to have sex • **give sb a leg up** informal **1** to help someone to climb over something **2** to help someone to improve their situation, especially at work • **have a leg up on sb** US informal to have an advantage over someone • **have legs** informal **1** If a story in the news has legs, it will continue for a long time: *This latest scandal has legs – you'll probably still be reading about it in a year's time.* **2** If something has legs, it can continue to exist and be successful: *The business has legs.* • **leg before wicket** (abbreviation **lbw**) in the game of cricket, the situation when your time as the person trying to hit the ball is ended because the ball has hit your leg when it should not have • **not have a leg to stand on** to be in a situation where you cannot prove something: *If you haven't got a witness, you haven't got a leg to stand on.* • **pull sb's leg** informal to try to persuade someone to believe something that is not true as a joke: *Is it really your car or are you pulling my leg?*

▸verb UK informal **leg it** to run away in order to escape from something: *They legged it round the corner when they saw the police coming.*

legacy /ˈleg.ə.si/ noun [C] **1** C2 money or property that you receive from someone after they die: *An elderly cousin had* ***left*** *her a small legacy.* **2** C2 something that is a part of your history or which stays from an earlier time: *The Greeks have a rich legacy* ***of*** *literature.* ◦ *The war has left a legacy* ***of*** *hatred.*

legal /ˈliː.gᵊl/ adj **LAW** ▷ **1** B2 connected with the law: *legal advice* ◦ *a legal obligation/requirement* ◦ *legal status* ◦ *your legal rights* ◦ *legal action/proceedings* ◦ *my legal representatives (= my lawyers)* **2** B2 allowed by the law: *Is abortion legal in your country?* → Opposite **illegal** **PAPER** ▷ **3** US used to refer to a standard size of paper in the US, 8.5 inches by 14 inches: *Your poster should be on letter or legal size paper.*

IDIOM **make legal history** If you make legal history, the case you win in court or take to court is the first of its type and changes the way future cases will be dealt with.

ˌlegal ˈaid noun [U] a system of providing free advice about the law and practical help with legal matters for people who are too poor to pay for it: *Will we qualify for legal aid?*

legalese /ˌliː.gᵊlˈiːz/ noun [U] disapproving language used by lawyers and in legal documents that is difficult for ordinary people to understand

ˌlegal ˈhigh noun [C] a drug that is taken for pleasure and has the same effect as an illegal drug, but has not been made illegal: *Doctors have said that legal highs should be subject to more controls.*

legalistic /ˌliː.gᵊlˈɪs.tɪk/ adj disapproving giving too much attention to legal rules and details • **legalistically** /-tɪ.kᵊl.i/ adv

legality /liːˈgæl.ə.ti/ US /-t̬i/ noun [U] **1** the fact that something is allowed by the law: *Six journalists sought to challenge in court the legality* ***of*** *the ban on* *broadcasting.* **2 legalities** [plural] the things that are demanded by law: *I'm not sure about the legalities, but I suggest we go ahead with the plan and see what happens.*

legalize (UK usually **legalise**) /ˈliː.gəl.aɪz/ **verb** [T] to allow something by law: *The Irish government announced it was to legalize homosexuality.* • **legalization** (UK usually **legalisation**) /ˌliː.gəl.aɪˈzeɪ.ʃən/ **noun** [U] *the legalization of drugs*

legally /ˈliː.gəl.i/ **adv** B2 as stated by the law: *Children under 16 are not legally allowed to buy cigarettes.*

ˈlegal pad **noun** [C] US a book for writing in containing yellow paper with lines on it

ˌlegal ˈtender **noun** [U] the money that can be officially used in a country

legation /lɪˈɡeɪ.ʃən/ **noun** [C] specialized **1** a group of officials who represent their government in a foreign country but who have less importance than an EMBASSY: *Britain has sent a legation to discuss trade and tariffs.* **2** the office in which these officials work

legato /lɪˈɡɑː.təʊ/ (US) /-toʊ/ **adj**, **adv** specialized describes music that is played in a smooth, continuous way, or this way of playing music: *smooth legato phrasing*

legend /ˈledʒ.ənd/ **noun** **STORY** ▷ **1** B2 [C or U] a very old story or set of stories from ancient times, or the stories, not always true, that people tell about a famous event or person: *The dance was based on several Hindu legends.* ◦ *She is writing a thesis on Irish legend and mythology.* ◦ *Legend* ***has it*** *(= people say) that he always wore his boots in bed.* ◦ *This match will go into tennis legend (= it will always be remembered).* **PERSON** ▷ **2** C1 [C] someone very famous and admired, usually because of their ability in a particular area: *Jazz legend Ella Fitzgerald once sang in this bar.* **EXPLANATION** ▷ **3** [C] formal the words written on or next to a picture, map, coin, etc. that explain what it is about or what the symbols on it mean

legendary /ˈledʒ.ən.dri/ (US) /-der.i/ **adj** **FAMOUS** ▷ **1** C1 very famous and admired or spoken about: *He became editor of the legendary Irish journal 'The Bell'.* ◦ *The British are legendary (= well known)* ***for*** *their incompetence with languages.* **FROM A STORY** ▷ **2** C1 from a legend: *Was King Arthur a real or a legendary character?*

-legged /-leg.ɪd/ **suffix** having the number or type of legs mentioned: *a three-legged stool* ◦ *a six-legged creature*

leggings /ˈleg.ɪŋz/ **noun** [plural] very tight trousers made from a material that stretches easily, usually worn by women: *a pair of leggings*

leggy /ˈleg.i/ **adj** A leggy woman or girl has long legs: *She was a tall, leggy blonde.*

legible /ˈledʒ.ɪ.bl̩/ **adj** describes writing or print that can be read easily: *Her handwriting is barely legible.* → Opposite **illegible** • **legibly** /-bli/ **adv**

legion /ˈliː.dʒən/ **noun**; **adj**

▸**noun** [C] **SOLDIERS** ▷ **1** a large group of soldiers who form a part of an army, especially the ancient Roman army **MANY** ▷ **2 legions of sb** large numbers of people: *He failed to turn up for the concert, disappointing the legions of fans waiting outside.*

▸**adj** [after verb] formal very large in number: *The difficulties surrounding the court case are legion.*

legionnaires' disease /liː.dʒənˈeəz.dɪˌziːz/ (US) /-erz-/ **noun** [S] a serious and infectious disease of the lungs caused by bacteria in the air

legislate /ˈledʒ.ɪ.sleɪt/ **verb** [I] formal If a government legislates, it makes a new law: *They promised to legislate* ***against*** *cigarette advertising.* ◦ *It's hard to legislate* ***for*** *(= make a law that will protect) the ownership of an idea.*

legislation /ˌledʒ.ɪˈsleɪ.ʃən/ **noun** [U] C2 a law or set of laws suggested by a government and made official by a parliament: [+ to infinitive] *The government has promised to introduce legislation* ***to*** *limit fuel emissions from cars.*

legislative /ˈledʒ.ɪ.slə.tɪv/ (US) /-t̬ɪv/ **adj** formal relating to laws or the making of laws: *The European Parliament will have greater legislative powers (= ability to make laws).*

ˌlegislative asˈsembly **noun** [C usually singular] (US usually **assembly**) one of the two parts of the organization that makes laws in some American and Australian states, most Canadian PROVINCES and some countries

ˌlegislative ˈcouncil **noun** [C usually singular] one of the two parts of the organization which makes laws in some Australian and Indian states

legislator /ˈledʒ.ɪ.sleɪ.təʳ/ (US) /-t̬ɚ/ **noun** [C] formal a member of a group of people who together have the power to make laws

legislature /ˈledʒ.ɪ.slə.tʃʊəʳ/ (US) /-tʃɚ/ **noun** [C, + sing/pl verb] formal the group of people in a country or part of a country who have the power to make and change laws

legit /ləˈdʒɪt/ **adj** [after verb] informal **legitimate**: *I'm not getting involved in this fundraising scheme if it isn't legit.*

legitimacy /ləˈdʒɪt.ɪ.mə.si/ (US) /-ˈdʒɪt̬-/ **noun** [U] the quality of being legal or reasonable and acceptable: *The government expressed serious doubts about the legitimacy of military action.*

legitimate /ləˈdʒɪt.ɪ.mət/ (US) /-ˈdʒɪt̬-/ **adj** **1** C2 allowed by law: *The army must give power back to the legitimate government.* **2** C2 reasonable and acceptable: *He claimed that the restaurant bill was a legitimate business expense.* **3** A legitimate child is one whose parents are legally married at the time of his or her birth. • **legitimately** /-li/ **adv** *Most foreign visitors to Britain enter the country legitimately (= legally).*

legitimize (UK usually **legitimise**) /ləˈdʒɪt.ɪ.maɪz/ (US) /-ˈdʒɪt̬-/ **verb** [T] (US **legitimate**) to make something legal or acceptable: *The government fears that talking to terrorists might legitimize their violent actions.*

legless /ˈleg.ləs/ **adj** [after verb] UK slang extremely drunk

legroom /ˈleg.ruːm/ **noun** [U] the amount of space available for your legs when you are sitting behind another seat: *a car with plenty of legroom*

legume /ˈleg.juːm/ **noun** [C] specialized a plant that has its seeds in a POD, such as the bean or PEA • **leguminous** /ˌlegˈjuː.mɪ.nəs/ **adj** *leguminous plants*

legwarmers /ˈlegˌwɔː.məz/ (US) /-ˌwɔːr.mɚz/ **noun** [plural] long coverings for the legs, similar to socks but without feet, often worn by dancers to keep the lower leg muscles warm

legwork /ˈleg.wɜːk/ (US) /-wɝːk/ **noun** [U] informal the practical or boring work that needs to be done

leisure /ˈleʒ.əʳ/ (US) /ˈliː.ʒɚ/ **noun** [U] B1 the time when you are not working or doing other duties: *leisure activities* ◦ *Most people only have a limited amount of leisure* ***time.*** ◦ *The town lacks leisure* ***facilities*** *such as a swimming pool or squash courts.*

IDIOM **at (your) leisure** when you want to and when you have time to: *You can take the documents home and study them at (your) leisure.*

ˈleisure ˌcentre noun [C] UK a building containing a swimming pool and other places where you can play sports

leisurely /ˈleʒ.ə.li/ (US) /-ɚ-/ adj describes an action that is done in a relaxed way, without hurrying: *We enjoyed a leisurely picnic lunch on the lawn.*

ˈleisure ˌwear noun [U] clothes that are worn for relaxing in

leitmotiv /ˈlaɪt.məʊ.tiːf/ (US) /-moʊ.t̬iːf/ noun [C] (also **leitmotif**) a phrase or other feature that is repeated often in a work of art, literature, music and that tells you something important about it: *Death and renewal are leitmotivs running through the whole novel.*

lekker /ˈlek.əʳ/ (US) /-ɚ/ adj South African English tasting or smelling very good; very pleasant to eat

lemming /ˈlem.ɪŋ/ noun [C] an animal that looks like a large mouse and lives in cold northern areas. Lemmings MIGRATE (= move from one place to another) in large groups and are often, but wrongly, thought to jump off CLIFFS together.

IDIOM **like lemmings** in a silly way, without thinking, and in large numbers: *People rushed like lemmings to invest in the company.*

lemon /ˈlem.ən/ noun; adj

▸noun **FRUIT** ▷ **1** A2 [C or U] an oval fruit that has a thick, yellow skin and sour juice: *For this recipe you need the juice of two lemons.* ◦ *Would you like **a slice of** lemon in your tea?* ◦ *lemon juice* **2** [U] the juice of a lemon or a drink made from this juice **COLOUR** ▷ **3** [U] a pale yellow colour **STUPID PERSON/THING** ▷ **4** [C] UK informal a very silly person: *I felt such a lemon when I discovered I'd missed my appointment.* **5** [C] mainly US informal something that does not work: *Only one of his inventions turned out to be a lemon.*

▸adj of a pale yellow colour

lemonade /ˌlem.əˈneɪd/ noun [U] **1** A2 UK a cold, sweet FIZZY drink (= one with bubbles) with a lemon flavour **2** mainly US a drink made with the juice of lemons, water, and sugar

ˌlemon ˈcurd noun [U] mainly UK a thick, sweet substance made from lemons, sugar, eggs, and butter that you can spread on bread or cakes

ˈlemon ˌgrass noun [U] a tropical grass with a flavour like lemon, used especially in Southeast Asian cooking

ˌlemon ˈsole noun [C usually singular] a flat fish that can be cooked and eaten

lemur /ˈliː.məʳ/ (US) /-mɚ/ noun [C] a small animal similar to a monkey from Madagascar with thick fur and a long tail, which lives in trees and is active at night

lend /lend/ verb (**lent**, **lent**) **GIVE** ▷ **1** A2 [T] to give something to someone for a short period of time, expecting it to be given back: *She doesn't like lending her books.* ◦ [+ two objects] *If you need a coat I can lend you one/lend one **to** you.* **2** B2 [I or T] If a bank or other organization lends money, it gives money to someone who agrees that they will pay the money back in the future, usually with extra money added to the original amount: *The bank refuses to lend **to** students.* ◦ [+ two objects] *The bank agreed to lend him $5,000.* **ADD TO** ▷ **3** [T] If something lends a particular quality to something else, it adds that quality to it: [+ two objects] *Vases of flowers all around the room lent the place a cheerful look/lent a cheerful look **to** the place.* ◦ formal *These events lend support to the view that the law is inadequate.* **4 lend itself to sth** C2 formal If something lends itself to something else, it is suitable for that thing or can be considered in that way: *The novel's complex, imaginative style does not lend itself to translation.*

IDIOMS **lend your name to sth** to give something your support: *Some of the world's top dancers have lent their names to the project.* • **lend an ear** old-fashioned to listen to someone with sympathy: *Claire's always one to lend a sympathetic ear if you have problems.*

lender /ˈlen.dəʳ/ (US) /-dɚ/ noun [C] someone or something that lends money, especially a large financial organization such as a bank

ˈlending ˌlibrary noun [C] old-fashioned for **public library**

ˈlending ˌrate noun [C] (also **ˈinterest ˌrate**) mainly UK the amount that a bank charges on money that it lends: *Banks have raised their lending rates by two percent.*

length /leŋθ/ noun **DISTANCE** ▷ **1** B1 [C or U] the measurement of something from end to end or along its longest side: *The boat is ten metres **in** length.* ◦ *The length of the bay is approximately 200 miles.* ◦ *She planted rose bushes **(along) the** length **of** the garden (= the whole distance along it).* **2** [C] a piece of something such as string or pipe: *a length of rope* **3** [C] a unit used in describing the distance by which a horse or boat wins a race, equal to the measurement from one end of the horse or boat to the other: *We won by two lengths.* **4** [C] the distance from one end of a swimming pool to the other: *She swims 40 lengths a day.* **TIME** ▷ **5** B2 [C] the amount of time something lasts: *the length of a film/speech/play* ◦ *He is unable to concentrate on his work for any length **of time** (= for anything more than a short time).* **6** C1 [C or U] the amount of writing in a book or document: *He's written books of various lengths on the subject.* ◦ *All of your essays will be about the same length.* **7 at length a** C2 for a long time: *George went on at **great** length about his various illnesses.* **b** formal If something happens at length, it happens after a long period of time: *At length, the authorities allowed her to go home.*

> **Word partners for length**
>
> the length *of* sth • [20 m/3 cm] *in* length • *along/down* the length (of sth) • the *approximate/average/maximum* length • the *entire/full/overall/total* length

IDIOMS **go to great lengths** (also **go to any lengths**) to try very hard to achieve something: *Some people go to great lengths to make their homes attractive.* ◦ *He'll go to any lengths to get what he wants.* • **the length and breadth of somewhere** C2 If you travel the length and breadth of a place, you go to every part of it: *She travelled the length and breadth of Ireland looking for her missing brother.*

-length /-leŋθ/ suffix **DISTANCE** ▷ **1** long enough to reach the stated place: *a knee-length skirt* ◦ *shoulder-length hair* **TIME** ▷ **2** of the stated amount of time: *a full-length movie (= one which has not been shortened)*

lengthen /ˈleŋ.θən/ verb [I or T] **1** C1 to make something longer, or to become longer: *I'll have to lengthen this skirt.* ◦ *lengthening waiting lists* **2** If you lengthen something, or it lengthens, it takes longer to happen: *There is a plan to lengthen the three-year course to four years.* → Opposite **shorten**

lengthways /ˈleŋθ.weɪz/ adv (also **lengthwise**) in the direction of the longest side: *Cut the beans in half lengthways.*

lengthy /ˈleŋ.θi/ adj C1 continuing for a long time: *a* *lengthy discussion/process* ◦ *Many airline passengers face lengthy delays because of the strike.*

lenient /ˈliː.ni.ənt/ **adj** C2 not as severe or strong in punishment or judgment as would be expected: *They believe that judges are too lenient **with** terrorist suspects.* ◦ *In view of the quantity of drugs involved, 16 years was the most lenient **sentence** (= punishment) the judge could impose.* • **leniency** /-ən.si/ **noun** [U] • **leniently** /-li/ **adv**

Leninism /ˈlen.ɪ.nɪ.zᵊm/ **noun** [U] the social, political, and economic principles and theories developed from MARXISM by the Russian politician V. I. Lenin, supporting direct rule by workers • **Leninist** /-nɪst/ **noun** [C]

lenis /ˈliː.nɪs/ **adj** specialized (of a speech sound) made without a lot of force

lens /lenz/ **noun** [C] **GLASS** ▷ **1** a curved piece of glass, plastic, or other transparent material, used in cameras, glasses, and scientific equipment, that makes objects seem closer, larger, smaller, etc.: *a camera with a zoom lens* **2 contact lens EYE** ▷ **3** the part of the eye behind the PUPIL (= the black hole at the front of the eye) that helps you to see clearly by FOCUSING (= collecting) light onto the RETINA

lent /lent/ **verb** past simple and past participle of **lend**

Lent /lent/ **noun** [U] in the Christian religion, the 40 days before EASTER, a period during which, for religious reasons, some people stop doing particular things that they enjoy: *The children have promised to **give up** sweets **for** Lent.*

lentil /ˈlen.tᵊl/ US /-t̬ᵊl/ **noun** [C] a very small dried bean that is cooked and eaten: *lentil soup* ◦ *red/green/brown lentils*

Leo /ˈliː.əʊ/ US /-oʊ/ **noun** [C or U] (plural **Leos**) the fifth sign of the ZODIAC, relating to the period 23 July to 22 August, represented by a lion, or a person born during this period, or a particular group of stars

leonine /ˈliː.ə.naɪn/ **adj** formal (often of a person's head or hair) like a lion

leopard /ˈlep.əd/ US /-ɚd/ **noun** [C] B2 a large wild cat that has yellow fur with black spots on it and lives in Africa and southern Asia

IDIOM **a leopard can't/doesn't change its spots** saying something you say which means a person's character, especially if it is bad, will not change, even if they pretend it does

leotard /ˈliː.ə.tɑːd/ US /-tɑːrd/ **noun** [C] a tight piece of clothing that covers the body but not the legs, usually worn by female dancers or women doing physical exercise

leper /ˈlep.əʳ/ US /-ɚ/ **noun** [C] **1** a person who has leprosy **2** a person who is strongly disliked and avoided by other people because of something bad that he or she has done: *She claimed that the rumours had made her a **social** leper.*

leprechaun /ˈlep.rɪ.kɔːn/ US /-kɑːn/ **noun** [C] (in old Irish stories) a magical creature in the shape of a little old man who likes to cause trouble

leprosy /ˈlep.rə.si/ **noun** [U] an infectious disease that damages a person's nerves and skin

leptospirosis /ˌlep.təʊ.spɪˈrəʊ.sɪs/ US /-toʊ.spəˈroʊ-/ **noun** [U] specialized an infectious disease that damages the LIVER and KIDNEYS, found mainly in dogs and farm animals and caused by bacteria

lesbian /ˈlez.bi.ən/ **noun** [C] a woman who is sexually attracted to other women: *gays and lesbians* • **lesbian adj**

lesbianism /ˈlez.bi.ə.nɪ.zᵊm/ **noun** [U] the state of being a lesbian

lesion /ˈliː.ʒᵊn/ **noun** [C] specialized an injury to a person's body or to an organ inside their body: *skin/brain lesions*

less /les/ **determiner, pronoun, adv; preposition**

▸**determiner, pronoun, adv 1** A2 a smaller amount (of), or to a smaller degree: *We must try to spend less money.* ◦ *Exercise more and eat less.* ◦ *I eat less chocolate and fewer biscuits **than** I used to.* ◦ *Getting out of bed in summer is less difficult **than** in winter.* **2 less than ...** describes behaviour which does not have a stated characteristic that is good or attractive: *I think he was less than honest with me.* **3 less and less** If something happens less and less, it becomes gradually smaller in amount or happens less often: *He's less and less able to look after himself.*

> **Common mistake: less or fewer?**
>
> Use **less** to refer to uncountable nouns.
>
> Don't say 'less cars/facts/dollars', say **less traffic/information/money.**
>
> With nouns that have a plural form, don't use 'less', use **fewer**:
>
> ~~*There are less buses after 8 o'clock in the evening.*~~
>
> *There are fewer buses after 8 o'clock in the evening.*
>
> Warning: Many English speakers use 'less' before nouns that have a plural form, but some people consider this incorrect and it should not be used in exams.

IDIOMS **much/still less** formal used to make a negative statement stronger: *At the age of 14 I had never even been on a train, much less an aircraft.* • **no less** humorous used to show the importance of someone or something: *Who should arrive at the party but the prime minister, no less!* • **no less than** used to show your surprise at a large number: *There were no less than a thousand people there buying tickets.*

▸**preposition minus**: *The total is 30 pounds, less the five pounds deposit that you've paid.*

-less /-ləs/, /-lɪs/ **suffix** used to form adjectives meaning 'without (the thing mentioned)': *meaningless* ◦ *friendless*

lessee /lesˈiː/ **noun** [C] specialized a person who has the right to use something such as land, a building, or a piece of equipment, according to a LEASE (= legal agreement) → Compare **lessor**

lessen /ˈles.ᵊn/ **verb** [I or T] C1 If something lessens or is lessened, it becomes less strong: *A healthy diet can lessen the risk of heart disease.*

lesser /ˈles.əʳ/ US /-ɚ/ **adj; noun**

▸**adj** [before noun] used to describe something that is not as great in size, amount, or importance as something else: *A lesser **man** (= a man who was not as strong or brave) might have given up at that point.* ◦ *The charge of murder was altered to the lesser (= less serious) charge of manslaughter.* ◦ *Ethiopia and, **to a** lesser **extent/degree**, Kenya will be badly affected by the drought.*

▸**noun**

IDIOM **the lesser of two evils** the less unpleasant of two choices, neither of which is good: *But allowing a criminal to go free is perhaps the lesser of two evils if the alternative is imprisoning an innocent person.*

ˌlesser-ˈknown adj not as popular or famous as something else

lesson /ˈles.ᵊn/ **noun** [C] **1** A1 a period of time in which a person is taught about a subject or how to do

L

something: *How can we make science lessons more interesting?* ◦ *She has never* ***had/taken*** *any acting lessons.* ◦ *He* ***gives*** *French lessons.* **2** B2 an experience which teaches you how to behave better in a similar situation in the future: *There is a lesson for all parents* ***in*** *this tragic accident.* ◦ *My parents made me pay back all the money and it was a lesson I never forgot.* ◦ *We can* ***learn*** *important lessons (= gain new understanding)* ***from*** *this disaster.*

Word partners for lesson

have/take lessons • *give* sb a lesson • *prepare* a lesson • a lesson *in/on* sth • *during/in* a lesson

lessor /lesˈɔːr/ (US) /-ˈɔːr/ **noun** [C] specialized a person who allows someone to use something that they own, such as land, a building, or a piece of equipment, according to a LEASE (= legal agreement) → Compare **lessee**

lest /lest/ **conjunction** literary in order to prevent any possibility that something will happen: *They were afraid to complain about the noise lest they annoyed the neighbours.*

let /let/ **verb; adv; noun**

▸**verb** (present tense **letting**, past tense and past participle **let**) **ALLOW** ▷ **1** B1 [T + infinitive without to] to allow something to happen or someone to do something by not doing anything to stop an action or by giving your permission: *She wanted to go but her parents wouldn't let her.* ◦ *He decided to let his hair grow long.* ◦ *Let your shoes dry completely before putting them on.* ◦ *I'm letting you stay up late, just this once.* ◦ *Don't let it worry you.* ◦ *If he needs money, let him (= he should) earn it!* **2** [T + obj + infinitive without to, not in past tenses] used to show that you accept what is going to happen, although you do not like it: *Let it rain – it won't spoil our afternoon.*

Common mistake: let

Let is followed by a verb in the infinitive without 'to'.

Do not say 'let someone to do something', say **let someone do something**:

~~*My parents don't let me to watch television.*~~

My parents don't let me watch television.

Common mistake: let or leave?

Warning: Do not confuse 'let' and 'leave'.

To talk about not taking someone or something with you when you go, don't say 'let', say **leave**:

~~*People should let their cars at home and go to work by bus.*~~

People should leave their cars at home and go to work by bus.

SUGGEST ▷ **3 let's** (also formal **let us**) A2 used to express a suggestion or request which includes you and the other person or people: *Let's go out to dinner.* ◦ *Let us consider all the possibilities.* ◦ *Let's not* (UK also ***don't*** *let's*) *argue.* **RENT** ▷ **4** [T] mainly UK (mainly US **rent**) to allow your house or land to be lived in or used by someone else in exchange for a regular payment: *They are letting their house* (***out***) *for the summer.* ◦ *He's let his flat* ***to*** *a young couple.* ◦ *She has a room* ***to*** *let in her house.*

IDIOMS **let sb be** to stop criticizing or annoying someone • **let go 1** C2 to stop holding something: *Hold on tight and don't let go!* ◦ *Let go* ***of*** *my hand, you're hurting me!* **2** C2 to stop thinking about or being angry about the past or something that happened in the past: *She finds it hard to let go of a grudge.* ◦ *You need to let the past go and forgive those who have hurt you.* • **let sb go 1** to allow someone to be free: *He pleaded with them to let him go.* **2** to make someone leave their job: *The firm hired the staff to sell the stocks, then let most of them go only a few months after the crash.* • **let sth go/pass** to not correct or argue with something that a person says or does that is wrong: *I know what he said wasn't strictly accurate but I let it pass anyway.* • **let yourself go 1** informal to allow yourself to become less attractive or healthy: *It's easy to let yourself go when you've got small kids.* **2** to relax completely and enjoy yourself: *It's a party – let yourself go!* • **let your hair down** old-fashioned informal to allow yourself to behave much more freely than usual and enjoy yourself: *Oh let your hair down for once!* • **let sb have it** slang to attack someone with words or physically • **let sb in on a secret** to allow someone to know something that you have not told anyone else: *Shall I let you in on a little secret?* • **let sb know** A2 to tell someone something: *Let us know* ***when*** *you get there.* ◦ *Let me know if you need any help.* ◦ *Thank you for coming to the interview – we'll let you know (= tell you whether we are going to offer you a job) in the next week.* • **let sth slip** to tell people about something without intending to: *He let* ***it*** *slip* ***that*** *he hadn't actually read the report.* • **let sth go** to stop taking care of something such as a house or garden: *The garden was beautiful, but the new owners have just let it go.* • **let it all hang out** old-fashioned slang to behave freely without being shy or feeling worried about what other people will think of you • **let it be known** formal to make certain that people know something: *I let it be known* ***that*** *I was not happy about the decision that had been made.* • **let it lie** (also **let things lie**) to take no action about something: *Instead of going to the police they let things lie for a couple of months.* • **let rip/fly** informal to behave in an angry and emotional way: *She let rip about the state of the kitchen.* • **let the side down** mainly UK informal to behave in a way that embarrasses or disappoints a group of people that you are part of • **let's face it** C2 said before stating something that is unpleasant but true: *Let's face it, we're not going to win.* • **let's see** (also **let me see/think**) used when you want to think carefully about something or are trying to remember: *The last time I spoke to her was, now let me think, three weeks ago.*

PHRASAL VERBS **let sb down** B2 to disappoint someone by failing to do what you agreed to do or were expected to do: *You will be there tomorrow – you won't let me down, will you?* ◦ *When I was sent to prison, I really felt I had let my parents down.* • **let sth down CLOTHES** ▷ **1** If you let down a piece of clothing, you make it longer: *My trousers shrank in the wash so I let them down.* **AIR** ▷ **2** UK If you let down something filled with air, you cause the air to go out of it: *Someone let my tyres down while I was at the gym.* • **let sb/sth in** B2 to allow someone or something to enter: *She opened the door and let me in.* ◦ *These shoes are starting to let water in.* • **let yourself in for sth** to become involved in a difficult or unpleasant situation without intending to: *Do you realize how much extra work you're letting yourself in for?* • **let sb in on sth** to tell someone about something that is secret, or to allow someone to become involved in something which only very few people are involved in: *Debbie agreed to let me in on her plans.* • **let sb off** B2 to not punish someone who has committed a crime or done something wrong, or to not punish them severely: *Instead of a prison sentence they were let off* ***with*** *a fine.* ◦ *You won't be let off so* ***lightly*** *(= you will be* punished more severely) the next time. • **let sth off** to fire a gun or make something such as a bomb or FIREWORKS explode: *Don't let off fireworks near the house.* • **let on** informal to tell other people about something that you know, especially when it is a secret: *I suspect he knows more than he's letting on.* • **let sb/sth out** B2 to allow someone or something to leave a place, especially by opening a closed or locked door: *I heard a voice from the cupboard shouting 'Let me out!'* • **let sth out** ESCAPE ▷ **1** to cause something to come out: *He let the air out of the balloon.* ◦ *She let out a scream (= she made this noise).* CLOTHES ▷ **2** to make a piece of clothing wider by removing the sewing from the sides and sewing closer to the edge of the material: *These trousers are too tight – I'm going to have to let them out.* • **let out** US When something that people go to, such as school or a show, lets out, it ends and everyone leaves: *When does school let out for the summer?* • **let up** informal IMPROVE ▷ **1** If bad weather or an unpleasant situation lets up, it stops or improves: *When the rain lets up we'll go for a walk.* STOP ▷ **2** to stop doing something that you have been doing continuously or in a determined way: *Neil spent the entire evening moaning about his job – he just wouldn't let up.* ◦ *The police insist that they are not letting up **on** their campaign against drugs.*

▸adv **let alone** C1 used after a negative statement to emphasize how unlikely a situation is because something much more likely has never happened: *Some people never even read a newspaper, let alone a book.*

▸noun SPORT ▷ **1** [C] (in tennis or similar games) a situation in which the ball touches the net as it crosses it, so that you have to play the point again LAW ▷ **2 without let or hindrance** specialized without being prevented from doing something RENT ▷ **3** [C] UK the act of allowing someone to use your house, land, etc. in exchange for regular payments: *a five-year let **on** a flat*

-let /-lət/ suffix small, not very important: *piglet*

letch /letʃ/ noun [C] informal for **lecher**

letdown /ˈlet.daʊn/ noun [S] informal a disappointment: *After all I'd heard about the film, it turned out to be a bit of a letdown.*

lethal /ˈliː.θəl/ adj C2 able to cause or causing death; extremely dangerous: *Three minutes after the fire started, the house was full of lethal fumes.* ◦ *In the car the police found guns, knives, and other lethal **weapons** (= weapons which can kill).* ◦ *A 59-year-old man was executed by lethal **injection** (= by having a poisonous substance put into his body) this morning.* ◦ informal *That combination of tiredness and alcohol is lethal (= has a very bad effect).* • **lethally** /-i/ adv

lethargic /ləˈθɑː.dʒɪk/ US /-ˈθɑːr-/ adj having little energy; feeling unwilling and unable to do anything: *I was feeling tired and lethargic.* • **lethargy** /ˈleθ.ə.dʒi/ US /-ɚ-/ noun [U]

letter noun; adj

▸noun [C] /ˈlet.əʳ/ US /ˈleţ.ɚ/ MESSAGE ▷ **1** A1 a written message from one person to another, usually put in an envelope and sent by post: *I **got** a letter **from** the bank this morning.* SYMBOL ▷ **2** A2 any of the set of symbols used to write a language, representing a sound in the language: *the letter D* **3 the letter of the law** formal the exact words of the law and not its more important general meaning

IDIOM **to the letter** If you obey instructions or rules to the letter, you do exactly what you have been told to do, giving great attention to every detail: *I followed the instructions to the letter and it still went wrong.*

▸adj [before noun] US used to refer to a standard size of paper in the US, 8.5 inches by 11 inches: *Fliers are usually printed either on letter size or legal size paper.*

ˈletter ˌbomb noun [C] a small bomb that is put in an envelope or parcel and sent to someone by post

letterbox /ˈlet.ə.bɒks/ US /ˈleţ.ɚ.bɑːks/ noun [C] UK **1** (US **mail slot**) a rectangular hole in the door or in a wall near the entrance of a house or other building, through which letters, etc. are DELIVERED **2** (US **mailbox**) a large, metal container in a public place where you can post letters

ˈletter ˌcarrier noun [C] US for **postman**

letterhead /ˈlet.ə.hed/ US /ˈleţ.ɚ-/ noun [C] the top part of a piece of writing paper where the name and address of a person or business is printed

lettering /ˈlet.ər.ɪŋ/ US /ˈleţ.ɚ-/ noun [U] writing in a particular colour, style, etc.: *a black box with gold lettering*

ˌletter of ˈcredit noun [C] a letter from a bank allowing the person who has it to take a particular amount of money from a bank in another country

ˌletter-ˈperfect adj US for **word-perfect**

letting /ˈlet.ɪŋ/ US /ˈleţ-/ noun [C] UK a room or building that can be rented: *The town offers several holiday lettings.*

lettuce /ˈlet.ɪs/ US /ˈleţ-/ noun [C or U] B1 a plant with large, green leaves, eaten uncooked in salads

ˈlet-up noun [C usually singular] informal a pause or reduction in something, usually something bad: *The airline authorities are not expecting a let-up **in** delays (= are not expecting delays to stop) for the rest of the summer.*

leucocyte /ˈljuː.kə.saɪt/ US /ˈluː-/ noun [C] (US **leukocyte**) a **white blood cell**

leucotomy /luːˈkɒt.ə.mi/ US /-ˈkɑː.ţə-/ noun [C] UK for **lobotomy**

leukaemia (mainly US **leukemia**) /luːˈkiː.mi.ə/ noun [U] a serious disease in which the body produces too many white blood cells

the Levant /ləˈvænt/ noun the countries and islands of the eastern Mediterranean

levee /ˈlev.i/ noun [C] a wall made of land or other materials that is built next to a river to stop the river from OVERFLOWING (= coming out of a place because it is too full)

level /ˈlev.əl/ noun; adj; verb

▸noun [C] HEIGHT ▷ **1** B2 the height of something: *The water level in the lake is much higher after heavy rain.* **2** B2 the amount or number of something: *Inflation is going to rise two percent from its present level.* ◦ *Chess requires a very **high** level of concentration.* ◦ *There is some danger of **low** level (= a continuing small amount of) radiation.* ABILITY ▷ **3** A2 someone's ability compared to other people: *a course for advanced level students* ◦ *Students at this level require a lot of help.* ◦ *The exam can be taken at three levels.* FLOOR ▷ **4** a floor in a large building: *The library has three levels, with a conference centre **at** ground level.* ◦ *The exhibition is **on** level three of the building.* RANK ▷ **5** C1 a position within a system in which people are arranged according to their importance: *These are subjects for discussion at management level.* **6 at local/national level** relating to a particular area of the country/the whole of the country: *These sorts of policies are made at local level.*

IDIOMS **be on the level** to be acting or speaking honestly: *It seems too good to be true. Are you sure this guy's on the level?* • **find your own level** to find out how much ability you have and find a position that is

L

therefore suitable • **on one level...on another level** something that you say when you are speaking about two opposite ways of thinking about or reacting to a situation: *On one level I quite like the attention but on another level, I suppose I find it a bit disturbing.*

▸adj **AT SAME HEIGHT** ▷ **1** [after verb] at the same height: *The top of the tree is level **with** his bedroom window.* **FLAT** ▷ **2** B2 flat or horizontal: *Make sure the camera is level before you take the picture.* ◦ *Before I bang the nails in, would you say this picture was level?* **3 level spoonful/cupful** an amount of a liquid or substance that fills a spoon/cup but does not go above the edges, used as a measure in cooking **EQUAL** ▷ **4** having the same value, amount, number of points, etc.: *The unions are fighting to keep wages level* (US usually ***even***) ***with*** *inflation.* ◦ *Pieretti would have to win the next three stages in order to **draw** level **with*** (= *reach the same position as*) *Le Sage in the Tour de France.* **CONTROLLED** ▷ **5** [before noun] If you speak in a level voice or give someone a level look, you do it in a calm and controlled way: *In a level voice, he ordered the soldiers to aim and fire.* • **levelly** /-i/ adv *He looked levelly* (= *calmly and without excitement*) *across at me.*

IDIOMS **do your level best** to try as hard as you can: *Tickets are hard to come by but I'll do my level best to get you one.* • **level pegging** UK in an equal position in a competition or game: *Both teams are level pegging.* • **a level playing field** a situation in which everyone has the same chance of succeeding: *If the tax systems are different in each European country, how can industries start **on** a level playing field?*

▸verb [T] (**-ll-** or US usually **-l-**) **MAKE FLAT** ▷ **1** to make a surface flat: *Level the wet cement before it sets.* **DESTROY** ▷ **2** to completely destroy a building or area

PHRASAL VERBS **level sth against/at sb** to accuse someone in public of doing something wrong: *Criticism has been levelled at senior figures in the industry.* • **level sth at sb** to aim something such as a weapon at someone: *She picked up the gun and levelled it at me.* • **level off** If a rate or amount levels off, it stops rising or falling and stays at the same level: *House prices now seem to be levelling off after the steep rises of the last few years.* ◦ *Unemployment rose to ten percent and then levelled off.* • **level off/out** If an aircraft levels off/out, it starts to travel horizontally rather than going up or down: *The jet levelled off at 10,000 feet.* • **level with sb** informal to tell someone the truth about something: *I'll level with you – the salary's not particularly good, and there's little chance of promotion.*

ˌlevel ˈcrossing noun [C] UK (US **ˈgrade ˌcrossing**) a place where a railway and a road cross each other, usually with gates that stop the traffic while a train goes past

ˌlevel-ˈheaded adj calm and able to deal easily with difficult situations

leveller (US usually **leveler**) /ˈlev.əl.əʳ/ US /-ɚ/ noun [C usually singular] something, typically death, that affects people of every class and rank in the same way, making everyone seem equal: *death, the **great** leveller*

lever /ˈliː.vəʳ/ US /ˈlev.ɚ/ noun [C] **BAR/HANDLE** ▷ **1** a bar or handle which moves around a fixed point, so that one end of it can be pushed or pulled in order to control the operation of a machine or move a heavy or stiff object **ADVANTAGE** ▷ **2** something you use, often unfairly, to try to persuade someone to do what you want • **lever** verb [T usually + adv/prep] *She levered **up** the drain cover.*

leverage /ˈliː.vər.ɪdʒ/ US /ˈlev.ɚ.ɪdʒ/ noun; verb

▸noun [U] **ACTION** ▷ **1** the action or advantage of using a lever **POWER** ▷ **2** power to influence people and get the results you want: *If the United Nations had more troops in the area, it would have greater leverage.* **VALUE** ▷ **3** US (UK **gearing**) the relationship between the amount of money that a company owes to banks and the value of the company

▸verb [T] specialized to use borrowed money to buy a company • **leveraged** /-ɪdʒd/ adj *The company is highly leveraged and struggling with interest payments.*

ˌleveraged ˈbuyout noun [C] specialized an occasion when a small company buys a larger one using money borrowed against the value of the equipment, buildings, etc. of both companies

ˈlever ˌarch ˈfile noun [C] a type of large container used to hold paper, in which paper is held on two large, curved pieces of metal that are opened or closed using a metal bar

leviathan /ləˈvaɪə.θən/ noun [C] literary something or someone that is extremely large and powerful: *The US is seen as an economic leviathan.*

levitate /ˈlev.ɪ.teɪt/ verb [I or T] to (cause to) rise and float in the air without any physical support • **levitation** /ˌlev.ɪˈteɪ.ʃən/ noun [U]

levity /ˈlev.ɪ.ti/ US /-t̬i/ noun [U] formal humour or lack of seriousness, especially during a serious occasion: *a brief moment of levity amid the solemn proceedings*

levy /ˈlev.i/ noun [C] an amount of money, such as a tax, that you have to pay to a government or organization: *They **imposed** a five percent levy **on** alcohol.* • **levy** verb [T] *A new tax was levied **on** consumers of luxury goods.*

lewd /luːd/ adj disapproving (of behaviour, speech, dress, etc.) sexual in an obvious and rude way: *Ignore him – he's being lewd.* ◦ *a lewd suggestion* • **lewdly** /ˈluːd.li/ adv • **lewdness** /ˈluːd.nəs/ noun [U]

lexeme /ˈlek.siːm/ noun [C] specialized a unit of meaning in a language, consisting of a word or group of words

lexical /ˈlek.sɪ.kəl/ adj specialized relating to words

lexicographer /ˌlek.sɪˈkɒg.rə.fəʳ/ US /-ˈkɑː.grə.fɚ/ noun [C] a person whose job is to write dictionaries

lexicography /ˌlek.sɪˈkɒg.rə.fi/ US /-ˈkɑː.grə-/ noun [U] specialized the activity or job of writing dictionaries

lexicology /ˌlek.sɪˈkɒl.ə.dʒi/ US /-ˈkɑː.lə-/ noun [U] the study of words and their meaning and use

lexicon /ˈlek.sɪ.kən/ noun [C] specialized (a list of) all the words used in a particular language or subject, or a dictionary

lexis /ˈlek.sɪs/ noun [U] specialized all the words of a language

ley line /ˈleɪˌlaɪn/ noun [C] an imaginary line between some important places such as hills or very old churches in Britain, believed to be where there were very old paths

LGBT /ˌel.dʒiː.biːˈtiː/ adj abbreviation for lesbian, gay, bisexual, and transgender: *LGBT rights/organizations*

liability /ˌlaɪ.əˈbɪl.ɪ.ti/ US /-ə.t̬i/ noun **RESPONSIBILITY** ▷ **1** C1 [U] the fact that someone is legally responsible for something: *He denies any liability **for** the damage caused.* **2 liabilities** [plural] specialized debts: *The business has liabilities of £2 million.* → Compare **asset** **RISK** ▷ **3** C1 [S] something or someone that causes you a lot of trouble, often when they should be helping you: *After a certain age, a car's just a liability.* ◦ *Sue always manages to upset somebody when we go out – she's a real liability.*

liable /ˈlaɪ.ə.bl̩/ adj [after verb] **RESPONSIBLE** ▷ **1** C1 specialized having (legal) responsibility for something or someone: *The law holds parents liable if a child does not attend school.* ◦ *If we lose the case we may be liable* ***for*** *(= have to pay) the costs of the whole trial.* **LIKELY** ▷ **2** C2 very likely to happen: *The areas of town near the river are liable* ***to*** *flooding (= are often flooded).* ◦ [+ to infinitive] *He's liable* ***to*** *make a fuss if you wake him.*

liaise /liˈeɪz/ verb [I] to speak to people in other organizations in order to exchange information with them: *Our head office will liaise* ***with*** *the suppliers to ensure delivery.*

liaison /liˈeɪ.zɒn/ US /-zɑːn/ noun **LINK BETWEEN** ▷ **1** [S or U] communication between people or groups who work with each other: *He blamed the lack of liaison* ***between*** *the various government departments.* ◦ *The police have appointed a liaison* ***officer*** *to work with the local community.* **2** [C] mainly US someone who helps groups to work effectively with each other: *She served as a liaison between the different groups.* **RELATIONSHIP** ▷ **3** [C] formal a sexual relationship, especially between two people not married to each other: *He's had a number of liaisons.* **IN SPEECH** ▷ **4** [U] specialized the act of joining sounds together, for example pronouncing a consonant that is not usually pronounced at the end of a word, because the next word begins with a vowel sound

liar /ˈlaɪ.əʳ/ US /-ɚ/ noun [C] B2 someone who tells lies: *He's such a liar – you can't trust a word he says.* ◦ [as form of address] *You liar – I never touched it!*

lib /lɪb/ noun [U] **liberation**: used especially in informal names of organizations that try to remove the disadvantages experienced by particular groups within society: ***women's*** *lib* • **libber** /ˈlɪb.əʳ/ US /-ɚ/ noun [C] informal *She's a* ***women's*** *libber.*

Lib. /lɪb/ adj UK abbreviation for **liberal**

libation /laɪˈbeɪ.ʃən/ noun [C] formal an amount of alcoholic drink poured out or drunk in honour of a god or a dead relation

ˌLib ˈDem noun [C] UK informal a member of the LIBERAL DEMOCRATS

libel /ˈlaɪ.bəl/ noun [C or U] a piece of writing which contains bad and false things about a person: *She threatened to sue the magazine for libel.* → Compare **slander** • **libel** verb [T] (plural **-ll-** or US usually **-l-**) • **libellous** (US usually **libelous**) /-əs/ adj *libellous accusations*

liberal /ˈlɪb.ər.əl/ US /-ɚ-/ adj; noun

▸adj **SOCIETY** ▷ **1** C1 respecting and allowing many different types of beliefs or behaviour: *a liberal society/attitude* ◦ *Her parents were far more liberal than mine.* → Opposite **illiberal** **POLITICS** ▷ **2** C1 (of a political party or a country) believing in or allowing more personal freedom and a development towards a fairer sharing of WEALTH and power within society **GENEROUS** ▷ **3** formal giving or given in a generous way: *He was very liberal* ***with*** *the wine.* **NOT EXACT** ▷ **4** not exact; without attention to or interest in detail: *a liberal interpretation of the law* • **liberalism** /-ɪ.zəm/ noun [U] • **liberality** /ˌlɪb.əˈræl.ə.ti/ US /-t̬i/ noun [U] formal • **liberally** /-i/ adv formal *Apply the cream liberally to the affected area.*

▸noun [C] someone who respects many different types of beliefs or behaviour

ˌliberal ˈarts noun [plural] mainly US college or university subjects such as history, languages, and literature

ˌLiberal ˈDemocrats noun [plural] in the UK, a political party that believes in more power for local government, more personal freedom, and a gradual development towards a fairer sharing of WEALTH and power within society

liberalize (UK usually **liberalise**) /ˈlɪb.ər.əl.aɪz/ US /-ɚ-/ verb [T] to make laws, systems, or opinions less severe: *They have plans to liberalize the prison system.* • **liberalization** (UK usually **liberalisation**) /ˌlɪb.ər.əl.aɪˈzeɪ.ʃən/ US /-ɚ-/ noun [U] *Political reform and economic liberalization don't always go together.*

the ˈLiberal ˌParty noun [+ sing/pl verb] in the UK, a political party that joined with the SOCIAL DEMOCRATIC PARTY to become the 'Liberal Democrats'

liberate /ˈlɪb.ər.eɪt/ US /-ə.eɪt/ verb [T] **1** to help someone or something to be free: *They said they sent troops in to liberate the people/the country* ***from*** *a dictator.* **2** humorous to steal something: *She liberated those spoons from a restaurant last week.* • **liberator** /-eɪ.təʳ/ US /-eɪ.t̬ɚ/ noun [C] *People came out into the streets to welcome the liberators.*

liberated /ˈlɪb.ər.eɪ.tɪd/ US /-ə.eɪ.t̬ɪd/ adj not following traditional ways of behaving or old ideas: *She's chosen career advancement instead of having children – does that make her a liberated woman?*

liberating /ˈlɪb.ər.eɪ.tɪŋ/ US /-ə.eɪ.t̬ɪŋ/ adj making you feel free and able to behave as you like: *Taking all your clothes off can be a very liberating experience.*

liberation /ˌlɪb.əˈreɪ.ʃən/ noun [U] **1** C1 an occasion when something or someone is released or made free: *the liberation of France* ***from*** *Nazi occupation* ◦ *Leaving school was such a liberation for me.* **2** used to refer to activities connected with removing the disadvantages experienced by particular groups within society: *the women's liberation* (informal ***lib***) *movement* ◦ *animal liberation organizations*

libertarian /ˌlɪb.əˈteə.ri.ən/ US /-ɚˈter.i-/ noun [C] a person who believes that people should be free to think and behave as they want and should not have limits put on them by governments: ***Civil*** *libertarians are worried about what they see as government censorship.* • **libertarian** adj

libertine /ˈlɪb.ə.tiːn/ US /-ɚ-/ noun [C] formal disapproving a person, usually a man, who lives in a way that is not moral, having sexual relationships with many people

liberty /ˈlɪb.ə.ti/ US /-ɚ.t̬i/ noun **FREEDOM** ▷ **1** B2 [U] formal the freedom to live as you wish or go where you want: *For most citizens, liberty means the freedom to practise their religious or political beliefs.* ◦ *Hundreds of political prisoners are to be* ***given*** *their liberty (= released from prison).* ◦ *Of the ten men who escaped this morning from Dartmoor Prison, only two are still* ***at*** *liberty (= free or not yet caught).* **2 be at liberty to do sth** C2 formal to be allowed to do something: *I'm not at liberty to reveal any names.* **3 liberties** [plural] formal freedom to live as you wish or go where you want: *These laws will restrict our ancient rights and liberties.* **BAD BEHAVIOUR** ▷ **4** [C] an example of speech or behaviour that upsets other people because it shows little respect or does not follow what is thought to be polite or acceptable: ***What a*** *liberty, to refuse the invitation on your behalf, without even asking you!* **5 take liberties (with sth)** to change something, especially a piece of writing, in a way that people disagree with **6 take liberties (with sb)** old-fashioned to be too friendly with someone, usually in a sexual way: *Some of the younger women complained that he'd been taking liberties with them.*

IDIOM **take the liberty of doing sth** formal C1 to do something that will have an effect on someone else, without asking their permission: *I took the liberty of booking theatre seats for us.*

libidinous /lɪˈbɪd.ɪ.nəs/ **adj** formal having or showing strong sexual DESIRES

libido /lɪˈbiː.dəʊ/ (US) /-doʊ/ **noun** [C] (plural **libidos**) a person's sexual DESIRE: *Symptoms include weight gain, sleep disorders and loss of libido.*

Libra /ˈliː.brə/ **noun** [C or U] the seventh sign of the ZODIAC, relating to the period 23 September to 22 October, represented by a pair of measuring SCALES, or a person born during this period • **Libran** /-brən/ **noun** [C] a Libra

librarian /laɪˈbreə.ri.ən/ (US) /-ˈbrer.i-/ **noun** [C] a person who works in a library

library /ˈlaɪ.brər.i/, /-brer.i/ **noun** [C] **1** (A2) a building, room, or organization that has a collection, especially of books, for people to read or borrow usually without payment: *a public/university library* ◦ *a library book* **2** a collection or set of books, or other things, all produced in the same style or about the same subject: *the Penguin Shakespeare Library*

librettist /lɪˈbret.ɪst/ (US) /-ˈbreṭ-/ **noun** [C] specialized a person who writes the words for a musical work for the theatre

libretto /lɪˈbret.əʊ/ (US) /-ˈbreṭ.oʊ/ **noun** [C] (plural **libretti** or **librettos**) specialized the words that are sung or spoken in a musical work for the theatre

lice /laɪs/ plural of **louse**

licence UK (US **license**) /ˈlaɪ.sᵊns/ **noun** **1** (A2) [C] an official document which gives you permission to own, do, or use something, usually after you have paid money and/or taken a test: *a dog licence* ◦ *a driving licence* (US *driver's license*) ◦ *a TV licence* **2** [S or U] formal permission or freedom to do what you want: *As parents, they **allowed** their children very little licence.* ◦ [+ to infinitive] *He was **given** licence **to** reform the organization.* **3** **artistic/poetic licence** the freedom of artists, writers, etc. to change the facts of the real world when producing art **4** **under licence** with special permission from the person or company who has created a product: *It's a German product, made under licence in British factories.*

IDIOM **be a licence to print money** If a company or activity is a licence to print money, it causes people to become very rich without having to make any effort.

ˈlicence ˌplate UK (US **ˈlicense ˌplate**) **noun** [C] (UK also **ˈnumber ˌplate**) the sign on the front and back of a road vehicle that shows its REGISTRATION NUMBER

license /ˈlaɪ.sᵊns/ **verb; noun**

▸**verb** [T] to give someone official permission to do or have something: [+ to infinitive] *Several companies have been licensed **to** sell these products.* • **licensed** /-sᵊnst/ **adj** *a licensed pilot* ◦ *a licensed (= allowed to sell alcohol) restaurant*

▸**noun** US spelling of **licence**

ˌlicensed ˌpractical ˈnurse **noun** [C] a nurse in the US who has been trained to do practical NURSING but who is not allowed to give medicines without permission

licensee /ˌlaɪ.sᵊnˈsiː/ **noun** [C] formal a person who has official permission to do something, especially to sell alcoholic drinks

ˈlicensing ˌlaws **noun** [plural] in Britain, the laws which control when and where alcoholic drinks can be sold

licentious /laɪˈsen.ʃəs/ **adj** formal disapproving (especially of a person or their behaviour) sexual in an uncontrolled and socially unacceptable way • **licentiously** /-li/ **adv** • **licentiousness** /-nəs/ **noun** [U]

lichen /ˈlaɪ.kən/, /ˈlɪtʃ.ən/ **noun** [C or U] a grey, green, or yellow plant-like organism that grows on rocks, walls, and trees

lick /lɪk/ **verb; noun**

▸**verb** **MOVE TONGUE** ▷ **1** (B2) [T] to move the tongue across the surface of something: *He licked the chocolate off his fingers.* ◦ *She licked the stamps and stuck them on the parcel.* **2** [T, I + prep] If flames or waves lick something, they pass over it quickly or touch it lightly like a tongue: *Within a few seconds flames were licking **at** the curtains.* **DEFEAT** ▷ **3** [T] informal to defeat easily in a competition, fight, etc.: *We'll lick the other teams.*

IDIOMS **have (got) sth licked** informal to have solved a problem • **lick sb's boots** (offensive **lick sb's arse/ass**) to try very hard to please someone in authority, usually in order to get an advantage: *He needn't expect me to go licking his boots!* • **lick your lips** **1** to move your tongue along your lips: *She took a bite of doughnut and licked her lips.* **2** to feel pleasure at the thought of something: *He licked his lips at the thought of all that money.* • **lick your wounds** to spend time getting back your strength or happiness after a defeat or bad experience

▸**noun** **HIT** ▷ **1** [C] old-fashioned informal the act of hitting someone with something such as a WHIP **SPEED** ▷ **2** **at a fair, great, etc. lick** UK informal at a fast speed: *The trains go by at a hell of a lick.* **SMALL AMOUNT** ▷ **3** [C] informal a small amount or thin layer: *The living room could do with a lick **of paint**.* **MUSIC** ▷ **4** [C] specialized in JAZZ or ROCK MUSIC, a short series of notes played by one musician **TONGUE** ▷ **5** [C] the action of licking something: *Can I **have** a lick of your ice cream?*

IDIOM **a lick and a promise** old-fashioned informal a quick and careless cleaning or wash

lickety-split /ˌlɪk.ə.tiˈsplɪt/ (US) /-ṭi-/ **adv** old-fashioned informal very quickly

licking /ˈlɪk.ɪŋ/ **noun** [S] **DEFEAT** ▷ **1** informal a defeat in a competition: *The home team were **given** a good licking.* **PUNISHMENT** ▷ **2** old-fashioned informal the punishment of being hit

licorice /ˈlɪk.ᵊr.ɪs/, /-ɪʃ/ (US) /-ɚ-/ **noun** [U] mainly US for **liquorice**

lid /lɪd/ **noun** [C] **1** (B2) a cover on a container, that can be lifted up or removed: *Can you get the lid off this jar?* ◦ *Put a lid on the saucepan.* **2** an **eyelid** (= either of the two pieces of skin which can close over each eye): *She looked at him from under half-closed lids.*

IDIOMS **blow/take the lid off sth** (also **lift the lid on sth**) to cause something bad that was previously kept secret to be known by the public: *In 1989 they started an investigation that was to blow the lid off corruption in the police force.* • **keep the lid on sth** informal to control the level of something in order to stop it increasing: *The government have intervened to keep a lid on inflation.* • **put the lid on sth** UK old-fashioned If something that happens puts the lid on a plan, it causes the plan to fail: *Well, James' resignation just about puts the lid on **it**/the project.*

lido /ˈliː.dəʊ/, /ˈlaɪ-/ (US) /ˈliː.doʊ/ **noun** [C] (plural **lidos**) mainly UK a public swimming pool that is outside, or part of a beach where people can swim, lie in the sun, or do water sports

lie /laɪ/ **verb; noun**

▸**verb** **POSITION** ▷ **1** (A2) [I + adv/prep, L] (present participle **lying**, past tense **lay**, past participle **lain**) to be in or move into a horizontal position on a surface: *to lie in bed* ◦ *to lie on a beach* ◦ *to lie on your side* ◦ *A cat lay in* front of the fire. ◦ He lies **awake** at night, worrying. ◦ A pen lay on the desk. **2** B1 [I + adv/prep, L] (present participle **lying**, past tense **lay**, past participle **lain**) If something lies in a particular place, position, or direction, it is in that place, position, or direction: *There's an old pair of shoes of yours lying at/in the bottom of the wardrobe.* ◦ *The river lies 30 km to the south.* ◦ *Cambridge United are lying third in the league.* ◦ *Here lies the body of Mary Taylor (= this is where Mary Taylor is buried).* ◦ *There are several houses lying empty in the town.* ◦ *The town lay in ruins.* ◦ *The ship lies **off** (= is positioned near) the coast of Spain.* **3** [I + adv/prep] (present participle **lying**, past tense **lay**, past participle **lain**) to exist: *The hardest part of the competition still lies ahead of us.* **4** C2 [I usually + adv/prep] (present participle **lying**, past tense **lay**, past participle **lain**) If responsibility, blame, a decision, a choice, etc. lies with someone, they have responsibility, must make the decision, etc.: *Responsibility for the disaster must ultimately lie **with** the government.* ◦ *Where does the blame lie?* **5 lie in state** (present participle **lying**, past tense **lay**, past participle **lain**) When the dead body of an important person lies in state, it is arranged so that the public can see and honour it before it is buried. **SPEAK FALSELY** ▷ **6** B1 [I] (present participle **lying**, past tense **lied**, past participle **lied**) to say or write something that is not true in order to deceive someone: *Are you lying to me?* ◦ *Don't trust her – she's lying.* ◦ *I suspect he lies **about** his age.* → See also **liar**

IDIOMS **lie down on the job** mainly US disapproving to fail to work as hard or as well as you should • **lie low** informal to try not to be noticed: *I'd lie low if I were you till the trouble passes.* • **lie through your teeth** informal to tell someone something that you know is completely false: *He asked me how old I was and, lying through my teeth, I said '29'.* • **not take sth lying down** to refuse to be treated badly by someone: *He can't treat you like that! Surely you're not going to take that lying down!*

PHRASAL VERBS **lie about/around** If things are lying about/around, they are left in places where they should not be: *Has anyone seen my keys lying about?* ◦ *I wouldn't leave any money lying around the office if I were you.* • **lie around** to spend time lying down and doing very little: *I spent a week in Spain, lying around on the beach.* • **lie back** to move the top half of your body from a sitting to a lying position: *She lay back in the dentist's chair and tried to relax.* • **lie behind sth** If something lies behind something else, it is the hidden cause of it: *Do you know what lies behind their decision?* • **lie down** A2 to move into a position in which your body is flat, usually in order to sleep or rest: *He lay down on the bed and tried to relax.* • **lie in** UK to stay in bed later than usual in the morning: *It was a Sunday, so she could lie in till almost lunch time.* • **lie in sth** UK to exist or be found in something: *His skill lies in his ability to communicate quite complex ideas very simply.* ◦ *The play's interest lies in the questions it raises about sexuality.*

►**noun** [C] B1 something you say that you know is not true: *I **told** a lie when I said I liked her haircut.*

IDIOMS **be a pack of lies** (formal **be a tissue of lies**) to be completely untrue: *The whole report is a pack of lies.* • **give the lie to sth** to prove that something is not true • **I tell a lie** mainly UK something you say when you have just said something wrong and want to correct it: *Her name is Paula, no, I tell a lie (= I'm wrong) – it's Pauline.* • **the lie of the land** UK (US **the lay of the land**) the shape or height of the land

ˈlie deˌtector noun [C] (specialized **polygraph**) a piece of equipment used to try to discover if someone is telling lies: *Both men refused to take a lie detector test.*

ˌlie-ˈdown noun [S] mainly UK informal a short rest, usually in or on a bed: *I usually **have** a bit of a lie-down after lunch.* ◦ *She said she was going for a lie-down.*

ˌlie-ˈin noun [C usually singular] UK a time when you stay in bed later than usual in the morning: *I'm not working tomorrow so I can **have** a bit of a lie-in.*

lien /ˈliː.ən/ noun [C] legal an official order that allows someone to keep the property of a person who owes them money until it has been paid

lieu /ljuː/ /luː/ noun formal **in lieu (of)** instead (of): *The paintings were left to the nation by the Duke of Norfolk in lieu of inheritance taxes.*

Lieut. noun [before noun] written abbreviation for **lieutenant**

lieutenant /lefˈten.ənt/ US /luː-/ noun [C] (also **Lieutenant**) (the title of) an officer of middle rank in the armed forces: *first/second lieutenant* ◦ *He was promoted to the rank of lieutenant.* ◦ *Lieutenant Woods/Charles Woods* ◦ [as form of address] *Yes, Lieutenant.*

life /laɪf/ noun (plural **lives**) **1** A1 [C or U] the period between birth and death, or the experience or state of being alive: *Life's too short to worry about money!* ◦ *I'm not sure I want to **spend** the rest of my life with him.* ◦ *Unfortunately, accidents are **part of** life.* ◦ *He went mad towards the end of his life.* ◦ *Cats are supposed to have nine lives.* ◦ *He doesn't know what he really wants in/out of life.* ◦ *The accident changed my whole outlook on life.* ◦ *He **lost** his life (= died suddenly because of a violent event or accident) in the Great War.* ◦ *A simple mixture of glucose and water can **save** lives in many parts of the world.* ◦ *He ran off with her life **savings** (= all the money she had saved).* → See also **afterlife, pro-life** **2** B1 [C or U] a way of living or a particular part of someone's life: *her family/private/sex life* ◦ *my working life* ◦ *We interviewed senior politicians, famous writers, and others in **public** life.* ◦ *Drugs and violence are deeply rooted in American life.* ◦ *I left home at 16 to **see** life (= have different experiences with a lot of people in lots of places).* ◦ *Teaching has been her life (= the most important and enjoyable thing in her life).* **3** C2 [C usually singular] the period for which a machine or organization lasts: *The newer batteries have a much longer life.* ◦ *Careful use will prolong the life of your machine.* ◦ *The legislation won't be passed during the life of the present parliament.* **4** [U] the quality that makes people, animals, and plants different from objects, substances, and things that are dead: *The doctor could find no **sign of** life in the old man's body.* ◦ figurative *I looked through the window but I couldn't see any **signs of** life (= people moving).* **5** B2 [U] energy or enthusiasm: *She's so **full of** life.* **6** B1 [U] everything that is alive: *human/marine/plant life* **7** [U] specialized In art, if you work from life, you paint, draw, etc. real people or objects, usually while they are in front of you rather than from memory: *life drawing classes* **8** [C] informal especially in children's games, one of the limited number of times that you can lose, but still continue playing: *Every time the little man gets hit, you **lose** a life.* **9 bring sth to life** (also **come to life**) to make something more real or exciting, or to become more real or exciting: *It's always been an interesting period in history and this film really brought it to life.* **10 for life** C1 for the whole of a person's life: *I believe marriage is for life.* **11 give your life** (also **lay down your life**) to be willing to die in order to defend or support someone or something: *They were ready to give their lives **for** their country.* **12 life after death** If

L

you believe in life after death, you believe that people continue to exist in some form after they die. **13 start a new life** (also **make a new life for yourself**) to completely change how or where you live: *She decided to start a new life in Australia.*

> **! Common mistake: life**
>
> **Warning:** Irregular plural!
>
> If you want to form the plural of **life**, don't write 'lifes', write **lives**.

> **! Common mistake: life or live?**
>
> **Warning:** do not confuse the noun **life** with the verb **live**:
>
> ~~*There is a big library in the town where I life.*~~
>
> *There is a big library in the town where I live.*

> **! Common mistake: live or life?**
>
> **Warning:** do not confuse the verb **live** with the noun **life**:
>
> ~~*She moved to New Zealand to begin a new live.*~~
>
> *She moved to New Zealand to begin a new life.*

> **! Common mistake: life**
>
> **Remember:** it is not usual to use the definite article 'the' when talking in a general way about **life**:
>
> Don't say 'the life', just say **life**:
>
> ~~*We should take time to enjoy the life.*~~
>
> *We should take time to enjoy life.*
>
> ~~*The life is too short to spend all our time working.*~~
>
> *Life is too short to spend all our time working.*

> **Word partners for life**
>
> *have/lead/live* a (charmed/normal, etc.) life • *spend* your life (doing sth) • *affect/change/ruin* sb's life • *lose/risk* your life • *save* sb's life • *rebuild* your life • an *aspect/part* of sb's life • *all* sb's life

IDIOMS **be (all) part of life's rich tapestry/pageant** to be one of the difficult or bad experiences that is part of a full and interesting life • **be one/another of life's great mysteries** to be something that is very difficult to understand • **for the life of you** informal although you are trying very hard: *I can't **remember** her name for the life of me.* • **get a life!** informal something you say to a boring person when you want them to do more exciting things: *Don't tell me you're cleaning the house on a Saturday night? Get a life, Hannah!* • **give your life to sth** to continue to have a close involvement in a particular thing for the whole of your life: *She gave her life to cancer research.* • **how's life (treating you)?** said as an informal greeting • **lead/live the life of Riley** old-fashioned informal to live an easy and comfortable life, without any need to work hard • **the life and soul of the party** someone who is energetic and funny and at the centre of activity during social occasions • **the man/woman in sb's life** informal your romantic/sexual partner: *Who's the new man in your life, eh?* • **not on your life!** informal said as a way of strongly refusing someone's suggestion or request: *'So you're going to bring Kev, are you?' 'Not on your life!'* • **scare/frighten the life out of sb** to frighten someone very much • **take your (own) life** formal to kill yourself • **take sb's life** formal to kill someone • **take your life in your hands** to do something that is very dangerous, especially where you risk death: *Every time you go parachuting you're taking your life in your hands.* • **that's life!** informal said after something bad or unlucky has happened, to express your feeling that such events will sometimes happen and have to be accepted: *No, I didn't get the job but that's life, isn't it?* • **this is the life!** informal said to mean that you are very much enjoying the situation you are in

ˈlife-afˌfirming adj If you describe something as life-affirming, you mean that it makes you feel positive about life: *Such a warm, life-affirming film!*

ˌlife-and-ˈdeath adj [before noun] (also **ˌlife-or-ˈdeath**) **1** involving the possibility that someone will die: *We were now in a life-and-death situation.* **2** very important and serious: *a life-and-death matter*

lifebelt /ˈlaɪf.belt/ **noun** [C] (also **lifebuoy**) a piece of equipment, usually a ring filled with air or light material that floats, designed to help someone float if they fall into water

lifeblood /ˈlaɪf.blʌd/ **noun** [U] the thing that is most important to the continuing success and existence of something else: *Tourism is the lifeblood of Hawaii's economy.*

lifeboat /ˈlaɪf.bəʊt/ (US) /-boʊt/ **noun** [C] a large boat that is kept ready to go out to sea and save people who are in danger, or a smaller boat kept on a ship for people to leave in if the ship is not safe or might sink

ˈlife-ˌchanging adj having an effect that is strong enough to change someone's life: *a life-changing decision/moment*

ˈlife ˌcoach noun [C] someone who you pay to give you advice about how to improve your life

ˈlife ˌcycle noun [C usually singular] (also **ˈlife ˌhistory**) the series of changes that a living thing goes through from the beginning of its life until death

ˈlife ˌevent noun [C] a very important event in someone's life, such as marriage, the birth of a child, or the death of a family member: *Moving house can be a very stressful life event.*

ˈlife exˌpectancy noun [C usually singular] the length of time that a living thing, especially a human being, is likely to live: *Life expectancy in Europe increased greatly in the 20th century.*

ˈlife ˌform noun [C] any living thing: *They are searching for **intelligent** life forms in other solar systems.*

ˈlife-ˌgiving adj necessary for life or giving energy

lifeguard /ˈlaɪf.gɑːd/ (US) /-gɑːrd/ **noun** [C] a person on a beach or at a swimming pool whose job is to make certain that the swimmers are safe and save them if they are in danger

ˌlife ˈhistory noun [C] all the things that happen during the life of a living thing → See also **life story**

ˌlife imˈprisonment noun [U] (informal **life**) the punishment of being put in prison for a very long time without an arranged time for release or, in the US, until death → See also **life sentence**

ˈlife inˌsurance noun [U] (UK usually **ˈlife asˌsurance**) a system in which you make regular payments to an INSURANCE company in exchange for a fixed amount of money which will be paid to someone you have named, usually a member of your family, when you die

ˈlife ˌjacket noun [C] a piece of equipment, like a jacket without sleeves, that is filled with air or light material and is designed to help someone float if they fall into water

lifeless /ˈlaɪf.ləs/ **adj 1** dead: *His lifeless body lay on the floor.* **2** showing little energy or interest: *a lifeless performance* **3** not filled with or used by people: *The* *offices are still empty and lifeless.* • **lifelessly** /-li/ adv • **lifelessness** /-nəs/ noun [U]

lifelike /ˈlaɪf.laɪk/ adj describes something that appears real or very similar to what is real: *a lifelike portrait of the queen* ◦ *The mask was so lifelike it was quite frightening.*

lifeline /ˈlaɪf.laɪn/ noun [C] **1** something, especially a way of getting help, that you depend on to lead your life in a satisfactory way: *For many old people living on their own the phone is their lifeline **to** the outside world.* **2** a rope that is thrown to someone who is in the water, especially the sea, and is in danger

lifelong /ˈlaɪf.lɒŋ/ (US) /-lɑːŋ/ adj [before noun] C2 lasting for the whole of a person's life: *She was a lifelong member of the Labour party.* ◦ *a lifelong habit*

ˌlife ˈpeer noun [C] in the UK, a person who is given the honour of a title such as 'Lord' and a place in the House of Lords as a reward for the good things they have done for the country

ˈlife ˌpeerage noun [C] the honour and position of being a life peer

life preserver /ˈlaɪf.prɪˌzɜː.vəʳ/ (US) /-ˌzɝː.vɚ/ noun [C] US for **lifebelt** or **life jacket**

lifer /ˈlaɪ.fəʳ/ (US) /-fɚ/ noun [C] informal someone who has been punished by being put in prison for a very long time or, in the US, until they die

ˈlife ˌraft noun [C] a type of boat that is carried on a large ship and is used in emergencies, for example when the ship is sinking, to take people to safety

ˈlife-ˌsaver noun [C] **HELP** ▷ **1** someone or something that gives you a lot of help when you are in a very difficult situation: *When you're stuck in traffic, a mobile phone's an absolute life-saver.* **WATER** ▷ **2** Australian English a person on a beach or at a swimming pool whose job is to make certain that the swimmers are safe and save them if they are in danger → Compare **lifeguard**

ˈlife-ˌsaving adj; noun

▸adj (also **lifesaving**) done to prevent someone from dying: *She had a life-saving operation to remove a blood clot.* ◦ *the charity's life-saving work in Africa*

▸noun [U] actions that can save someone's life when they have fallen into water: *a certificate in life-saving*

ˈlife ˌscience noun [C usually plural] one of the types of science that deal with the structure and behaviour of living things, such as BOTANY, ZOOLOGY, BIOCHEMISTRY, and ANTHROPOLOGY

ˌlife ˈsentence noun [C] **1** (also informal **life**) the punishment of being put in prison for a very long time, or, in the US, until death → See also **life imprisonment, lifer 2** something that will make a person suffer for the rest of their life: *His life sentence was to have to live without her.*

ˈlife-size(d) adj describes a work of art or model that is the same size as the person or thing that it represents: *a life-size statue of the prime minister*

lifespan /ˈlaɪf.spæn/ noun [C] C2 the length of time for which a person, animal, or thing exists: *The **average** human lifespan in the developed countries has increased over the last hundred years.* ◦ *The project's lifespan is estimated at about five years.*

ˈlife ˌstory noun [C] everything that has happened to someone during their life: *The last time you sat me next to Alberto I had to hear his whole life story!*

lifestyle /ˈlaɪf.staɪl/ noun [C] B2 someone's way of living; the things that a person or particular group of people usually do: *He doesn't have a very healthy lifestyle.* ◦ *She needs a pretty high income to support her lifestyle.* ◦ *an alternative lifestyle*

> **! Common mistake: lifestyle**
>
> Remember that **lifestyle** is usually written as one word.
>
> Don't write 'life style', write **lifestyle**:
>
> ~~*Young people these days have a very unhealthy life style.*~~

ˈlifestyle ˌmanager noun [C] someone who you pay to give you advice about how to improve your life

ˈlife-suˌpport ˌsystem noun [C] **1** the equipment used to keep a person alive when they are very ill or injured: *He's been **on** a life-support system since the crash.* **2** the natural structures and systems that are necessary for living things, especially humans, to be able to live: *The lack of rain is threatening all the region's life-support systems* (= the Earth, trees and rivers).

ˈlife-ˌthreatening adj A life-threatening disease is a very serious one that can cause death: *life-threatening diseases such as cancer*

lifetime /ˈlaɪf.taɪm/ noun [C usually singular] B2 the period of time during which someone lives or something exists: *We'll see a tremendous lot of technological changes **during/in** our lifetime.* ◦ *Winners of the competition will receive the holiday **of a** lifetime (= the best holiday they will ever have).* ◦ *I've only been working here two days, but **it seems like a** lifetime.* ◦ *A watch of this quality should **last a** lifetime.* ◦ *Enter our competition and this **once-in-a-**lifetime experience could be yours!* ◦ *Marriage is no longer always seen as a lifetime commitment.* ◦ *You could win a lifetime's supply of toothpaste.*

lift /lɪft/ verb; noun

▸verb **RAISE** ▷ **1** B1 [T] to move something from a lower to a higher position: *Could you help me lift this table, please?* ◦ *Could you lift your chair a bit – I've got my bag caught under it.* ◦ *She lifted the cigarette (**up**) **to** her lips.* ◦ *He lifted his eyes (= looked up) from the paper and glared.* **2 lift a/the cup** to win a race or competition: *He is the hot favourite to lift the cup again next month.* **3** [T] specialized to dig underground vegetables or plants out of the ground: *They're lifting potatoes.* **TAKE HOLD** ▷ **4** [I or T, usually + adv/prep] to take hold of and raise something in order to remove, carry, or move it to a different position: *She lifted the baby out of her chair.* ◦ *He lifted the box carefully down from the shelf.* **MAKE LOUD** ▷ **5** [T] literary to make your voice louder, especially when performing **MAKE INTERESTING** ▷ **6** [T] informal to make something more interesting or enjoyable: *The article is informative enough, but it's a bit dull – we need something to lift it.* **MAKE HAPPY** ▷ **7 lift sb's spirits** informal to make someone happier: *Nothing – not even the prospect of dinner – could lift his spirits.* **GO AWAY** ▷ **8** [I] (of MIST or FOG) to go away until none is left: *The morning mist had lifted and the sun was starting to come through.* **END** ▷ **9** [T] to end a rule or law: *The restrictions on water usage have been lifted now that the river levels are normal.* ◦ *At last they've lifted the ban on jeans at the club.* **STEAL** ▷ **10** [T] informal to steal something **11** [T] informal to use someone else's writing, music, or idea, pretending that it is your own: *He'd lifted whole passages from a website.*

▸noun **CARRYING DEVICE** ▷ **1** A2 [C] UK (US **elevator**) a device like a box which moves up and down, carrying people or goods from one floor of a building to another or taking people up and down underground in a MINE: ***Take** the lift to the sixth floor.* **RAISE** ▷ **2** [C or U] an act of lifting or raising something **3** [U] specialized the force on the wing of a bird or aircraft that keeps it in the air as it moves forward **JOURNEY** ▷ **4** A2 [C usually singular] a free journey in another person's vehicle, especially a car: *I'll **give** you a lift **to** the station if you like.* ◦ *He **hitched** a lift (= stood by the road and made a signal asking a car to stop and take him) **to** Birmingham.* **MAKE HAPPY** ▷ **5 give sb a lift** to make someone happier: *She'd been feeling a bit low but hearing that she'd got the job gave her a lift.*

ˈlift-off noun [C or U] the action of a spacecraft or ROCKET leaving the ground: *We **have** lift-off.*

ligament /ˈlɪg.ə.mənt/ noun [C] any of the strong strips of tissue in the body that connect bones together, limiting movements in JOINTS (= places where two bones are connected) and supporting muscles and other tissue

ligature /ˈlɪg.ə.tʃəʳ/ US /-tʃɚ/ noun [C] specialized a thread or wire used for tying something, especially a BLOOD VESSEL: *Ligatures are used in surgery to stop the flow of a bleeding artery.*

light /laɪt/ noun; adj; verb

▸**noun BRIGHTNESS** ▷ **1** B1 [U] the brightness that comes from the sun, fire, etc. and from electrical devices, and that allows things to be seen: *a bright light* ◦ *fluorescent/ultraviolet light* ◦ *a beam/ray of light* ◦ *Light was streaming in through the open door.* ◦ *It's a north-facing room so it doesn't get much light (= brightness from the sun).* **2** A2 [C] a piece of equipment that produces light, such as a LAMP or a BULB: *Could you switch/turn the light **on/off**, please?* ◦ *She could see the city lights in the distance.* ◦ *As the lights went down, the audience grew quiet.* ◦ *My front bike light isn't working.* **FLAME** ▷ **3 a light** something that will produce a flame and cause burning, such as a match or a cigarette LIGHTER: *Have you got a light, please?* **4 set light to sth** UK to cause something to start burning: *The lamp caught fire and set light to the curtains.*

IDIOMS **cast/shed/throw light on sth** C2 Something or someone that casts/sheds/throws light on a situation provides an explanation for it or information that makes it easier to understand: *As an economist, he was able to shed some light on the problem.* • **come to light** (also **bring sth to light**) C2 If facts come to light or are brought to light, they become known: *Fresh evidence has recently come to light that suggests that he didn't in fact commit the murder.* • **go out like a light** informal to go to sleep very quickly or to become unconscious very quickly • **in the light of sth** (US usually **in light of**) C1 because of: *In the light of recent incidents, we are asking our customers to take particular care of their personal belongings.* • **light at the end of the tunnel** signs of improvement in a situation that has been bad for a long time, or signs that a long and difficult piece of work is almost finished: *As the exams approached, she felt that at last she could see the light at the end of the tunnel.* • **the light of your life** humorous the person you love most • **show someone in a bad light** to make someone seem to be a bad person: *He was concerned that the film had shown him in a bad light.*

▸**adj NOT HEAVY** ▷ **1** A2 not heavy: *Here, take this bag – it's quite light.* ◦ *He's a few pounds lighter than he used to be.* ◦ *How do you get your cakes so wonderfully light, Felicity?* ◦ *He has a very light (= gentle) **touch**, which is what is required in massage.* ◦ *She's very light **on her feet** (= she moves gracefully).* **2** A2 describes clothes that are made of thin material that allows you to be cool: *a light summer dress* **BRIGHT** ▷ **3** B1 lit by the natural light of the day: *The big windows make the room feel wonderfully light and airy.* ◦ *It gets light very early these summer mornings.* ◦ *Summer is coming and the evenings are getting lighter (= getting dark later).* **PALE** ▷ **4** A1 (of colours) pale: *light blue/green* → Opposite **dark** **NOT SERIOUS** ▷ **5** entertaining and easily understood, but not serious and not intended to make you think: *I want some light **reading** for the summer holidays – a romance or something.* ◦ *A lively argument between the two main speakers provided a bit of **light relief** (= something enjoyable or amusing) in an otherwise dull conference.* **6 make light of sth** C2 to behave as if a situation, especially a problem, is not serious or important: *It is easy to make light of other people's problems.* **NOT MUCH** ▷ **7** B1 not great in strength or amount: *A light wind was blowing.* ◦ *The traffic was quite light so we got through London quickly.* ◦ *It's only light rain – you don't need an umbrella.* **8 light eater/drinker/smoker** someone who eats/drinks/smokes only a little **9 light sleeper** someone who is easily woken up by noise, etc. **MEAL/DRINK** ▷ **10** A light meal is small and easy to digest: *I don't eat much for lunch – just a light snack.* **11** describes alcoholic drinks that are not strong in flavour: *It's described on the label as 'light, fruity wine'.* **NOT SEVERE** ▷ **12** needing only a very small amount of effort: *light exercise, such as walking* ◦ *a bit of light housework* **13** A light sentence in prison is a short one: *He got off with a fairly light sentence because it was his first conviction.* **14 make light work of sth/doing sth** to do something quickly and easily: *Heather made light work of painting the walls.* ◦ *You made light work of that chocolate cake (= you ate it quickly)!*

IDIOM **(as) light as a feather** very light

▸**verb (lit** or **lighted, lit** or **lighted) START FLAMES** ▷ **1** B1 [I or T] to start to burn or to make something start to burn: *to light a fire* ◦ *I can't get the cooker to light.* ◦ *He lit his fifth cigarette in half an hour.* **MAKE BRIGHT** ▷ **2** B2 [T] to produce light that makes an object or area bright or easy to see: *The stage had been lit with candles.* ◦ *Fireworks lit **up** the sky (= made the sky bright).*

PHRASAL VERBS **light on/upon sth** formal to find or think of something unexpectedly: *We lighted upon the solution entirely by accident.* • **light (sth) up EXPRESSION** ▷ **1** If your face or eyes light up, or if a smile lights up your face, you suddenly look happy: *Rosie's whole face lit up **with** excitement when she saw the presents.* **CIGARETTE** ▷ **2** to light a cigarette

ˌlight ˈaircraft noun [C] (plural **light aircraft**) a small plane suitable for carrying small LOADS

ˈlight ˌbulb noun [C] (also **bulb**) a rounded glass container with a thin thread of metal inside that produces light when an electric current goes through it

lighted /ˈlaɪ.tɪd/ US /-t̬ɪd/ adj [before noun] burning or starting to burn: *a lighted candle/match* ◦ *a lighted fuse*

lighten /ˈlaɪ.tᵊn/ US /-t̬ᵊn/ verb **BECOME BRIGHT** ▷ **1** [I] to become less dark: *The sky had lightened and there were breaks in the clouds.* → Opposite **darken** **MAKE LESS HEAVY** ▷ **2 lighten sb's burden, load, etc.** to make a difficult situation or responsibility easier: *Getting a new assistant will lighten (= reduce) the workload considerably.* **MAKE PALE** ▷ **3** [T] to make something lighter: *The sun always lightens my hair.* **MAKE/BECOME LESS SERIOUS** ▷ **4** [I or T] to (cause to) become happier and less worried: *His **mood** lightened after the phone call.* ◦ *He tried to lighten the atmosphere by telling a joke.*

PHRASAL VERBS **lighten sth up** to make a speech or piece of writing less serious: *I thought I'd slip in a few jokes to lighten up the talk.* • **lighten up** informal to become more relaxed and less serious: *Oh, lighten up! I was only joking!* ◦ *I wish she'd lighten up a bit.*

lighter /ˈlaɪ.təʳ/ (US) /-t̬ɚ/ noun [C] **B1** a small device for providing a flame for a cigarette, etc.: *a cigarette lighter*

ˌlight-ˈfingered adj informal If you describe someone as light-fingered, you mean that they have a habit of stealing things.

ˈlight ˌglobe noun [C] (also **globe**) Australian English a rounded glass container with a thin thread of metal inside which produces light when an electric current goes through it → Compare **light bulb**

ˌlight-ˈheaded adj If you feel light-headed, you feel weak and as if you are going to lose your balance: *She'd had a couple of glasses of champagne and was starting to feel light-headed.*

ˌlight-ˈhearted adj happy and not serious: *It was a fairly light-hearted discussion.*

ˌlight ˈheavyweight noun [C] a BOXER whose weight is between MIDDLEWEIGHT and HEAVYWEIGHT

lighthouse /ˈlaɪt.haʊs/ noun [C] a tall building by the sea with a flashing light at the top to warn ships of dangerous rocks

lighthouse

ˌlight ˈindustry noun [C or U] industry which makes small things and does not need to use large heavy machinery

lighting /ˈlaɪ.tɪŋ/ (US) /-t̬ɪŋ/ noun [U] **B2** the arrangement of lights used in a room, house, theatre, etc.

ˌlighting-ˈup ˌtime noun [C usually singular] UK the time in the afternoon or evening when the law states that vehicles must have their lights switched on

lightly /ˈlaɪt.li/ adv **GENTLY** ▷ **1** **B1** gently: *She patted him lightly on the shoulder.* **2** **C1** If food is lightly cooked, it is cooked for only a short time. **NOT SERIOUSLY** ▷ **3** If you say something lightly, you are not serious when you say it: *'Anyway, it won't affect me because I'm leaving,' she said lightly.* **4 not do sth lightly** **C2** If something is not said or treated lightly, it is said or treated in a serious way, after great thought: *Accusations like these from a top minister are not* ***made*** *lightly.* **NOT SEVERELY** ▷ **5 get off lightly; let sb off lightly** to be punished or to punish someone less severely than might have been expected: *I think he got off quite lightly considering it's his third driving offence.*

ˈlight ˌmeter noun [C] a device for measuring how much light there is, especially when taking a photograph

lightness /ˈlaɪt.nəs/ noun [U] the state of being light

lightning /ˈlaɪt.nɪŋ/ noun [U] **B1** a flash of bright light in the sky that is produced by electricity moving between clouds or from clouds to the ground: ***thunder and*** *lightning* ◦ *a* ***flash of*** *lightning* ◦ *That tree was* ***struck by*** *lightning.* ◦ *She changed her clothes* ***with*** *lightning* ***speed*** *(= extremely quickly).*

IDIOMS **lightning never strikes twice** saying said to show that it is unlikely that something bad or unusual will happen to the same person twice • **like lightning** extremely quickly

ˈlightning conˌductor noun [C] UK (US **ˈlightning ˌrod**) a strip of metal, going from the highest point of a building to the ground, that prevents lightning from damaging the building by taking the electricity to the ground before it can reach a dangerous level

ˈlightning ˌrod noun [C] US someone or something that takes all the blame for a situation, although other people or things are responsible too: *In a harsh economic climate, raises for teachers have become a lightning rod for criticism.*

ˈlightning ˌstrike noun [C] US for **wildcat strike**

ˈlight ˌpen noun [C] a pen-shaped device used for reading BAR CODES

ˌlight ˈrailway noun [C] a railway system for transporting people around a city

ˌlights-ˈout noun [U] (at a school where children live or in the army) the time in the evening when the lights are switched off in the room where people sleep: *No talking after lights-out!*

lightweight /ˈlaɪt.weɪt/ adj; noun

▸adj **NOT HEAVY** ▷ **1** weighing only a little or less than average: *I need a lightweight jacket for the summer evenings.* **NOT SERIOUS** ▷ **2** disapproving not showing deep understanding or knowledge of any subject: *She's the author of some fairly lightweight historical novels.*

▸noun [C] **SPORTS PERSON** ▷ **1** in some sports, including BOXING, a person whose weight is between FEATHERWEIGHT and WELTERWEIGHT → Compare **heavyweight** **NOT SERIOUS** ▷ **2** disapproving a person whose work in a particular area of activity does not show a deep understanding or knowledge of that subject: *In certain circles he has been dismissed as a literary lightweight.*

ˈlight ˌyear noun [C] the distance that light travels in one year (about 9,500,000,000,000 kilometres)

IDIOM **light years away** an extremely long time from now in the past or future: *It all happened when I was at college, which seems light years away now that I'm over 50.*

like /laɪk/ verb; preposition, conjunction; preposition; adv; noun; adj

▸verb [T] **ENJOY** ▷ **1** **A1** to enjoy or approve of something or someone: *I like your new haircut.* ◦ *Do you like fish?* ◦ *I like it when a book is so good that you can't put it down.* ◦ *I quite like wine but I could live without it.* ◦ *He's very* ***well****-liked (= popular) at work.* ◦ [+ -ing verb] *I don't like upsett****ing*** *people.* ◦ [+ to infinitive] *He likes* ***to*** *spend his evenings in front of the television.* ◦ [+ past participle] *He likes his steak well done.* **2** to be annoyed by something: *I like* ***the way*** *he just assumes we'll listen to him when he doesn't take in a word anyone else says!* **3** to show that you think something is good on a SOCIAL NETWORKING website by giving it a special symbol: *Like us on Facebook!* **WANT** ▷ **4 would like** (or formal **should like...**) **A1** used to say politely that you want something: *I think I'd like the soup for my starter.* ◦ *I'd like* ***to*** *go to Moscow.* ◦ *I would like* ***to*** *say a big thank you to everyone who's helped to make our wedding such a special occasion!* **5** **A1** used in requests: *I'd like one of the round loaves, please.* ◦ [+ to infinitive] *I'd like* ***to*** *book a seat for tonight's performance.* ◦ [+ obj + to infinitive] *I'd like you* ***to*** *send this for me, please.* ◦ [+ past participle] *I would like the whole lot finish****ed*** *by the weekend.*

IDIOMS **how do you like...?** **1** used when asking someone how they like their drinks made: *'How do you like your tea?' 'Milk and one sugar, please.'* **2** used when asking someone for an opinion: *How do you like*

! Common mistake: would like

When **would like** is followed by a verb, that verb cannot be in the infinitive without 'to'.
Do not say 'would like do something', say **would like to do something**:

~~*I would like recommend a restaurant for our meeting.*~~

I would like to recommend a restaurant for our meeting.

+ Other ways of saying like

If a person likes someone or something very much, you can use the verbs **love** and **adore**:

*I **adore/love** seafood.*

*Oliver **loves** animals.*

*Kate **adored** her grandfather.*

When a person likes someone very much, you could say that person **thinks the world of** someone or has a **soft spot for** someone:

*I've always had a **soft spot for** Rebecca ever since she was tiny.*

*Annabel's like a daughter to him – he **thinks the world of** her.*

The expression **be fond of** is sometimes used to talk about someone or something that you like:

*She's very **fond of** Chinese food.*

*I think she's very **fond of** you.*

The phrasal verbs **grow on**, **take to**, or **warm to** can be used when someone starts to like someone or something:

*I wasn't sure about the colour at first, but it's **growing on** me.*

*For some reason, I just didn't **take to/warm to** him.*

The expressions **take a shine to** or **take a liking to** are sometimes used when someone immediately likes someone or something:

*I think he's **taken a** bit of a **shine to** you.*

When someone likes something very much but knows it is not good to like it, you could say that the person has a **weakness** for it:

*I have a **weakness** for chocolate so I'm never going to lose weight.*

my new shoes? • **how would you like...?** informal said to suggest that someone would not like to be in a situation experienced by someone else: *I'm not surprised he shouted at you! How would you like to be pushed into a wall?* • **I'd like to see...** informal said to mean that you do not believe someone can do something: *He said women have an easier life than men, did he? – I'd like to see him bring up children and go to work at the same time.* • **if you like** Ⓐ2 used for asking if someone agrees with a suggestion: *We can leave now if you like.* ◦ *I'm not sure if I have the confidence, the nerve if you like (= if this phrase is suitable), to apply for the job.* • **like it or lump it** informal If you tell someone to like it or lump it, you mean they must accept a situation they do not like, because they cannot change it: *Like it or lump it, romantic fiction is read regularly by thousands.* • **would you like...?** Ⓐ1 used when offering something or inviting someone: *Would you like a drink?* ◦ *Would you like **to** join us for dinner tonight?*

▸**preposition, conjunction** **SIMILAR TO** ▷ **1** Ⓑ2 similar to; in the same way or manner as: *He **looks** like his brother.* ◦ *She's very much like her mother (= she is similar in appearance or character).* ◦ *Is Japanese food like Chinese?* ◦ *I've got a sweater **just** like that.* ◦ *Her hair was so soft it was like silk.* ◦ *You're acting like a complete idiot!* ◦ *She sings like an angel!* ◦ *Like I said (= as I have already said), I don't wear perfume.* ◦ *Like most people (= as most people would), I'd prefer to have enough money not to work.* ◦ *It **feels/seems** like (= it seems to me) ages since we last spoke.* ◦ *There's **nothing** like a good cup of coffee (= it's better than anything)!*

! Common mistake: like

Warning: choose the correct pronoun!
Don't say 'how is sb/sth like?' or 'how sb/sth is like', say **what is sb/sth like?** or **what sb/sth is like**:

~~*How is life like in England?*~~

What is life like in England?

I want to find out what life is like in England.

AS IF ▷ **2** Ⓑ1 in a way that suggests: *It **looks** like I'm going to be in the office until late tonight.* ◦ *It looks like rain (= I think it is going to rain).* ◦ *It **sounds** to me like you ought to change jobs.* ◦ *You look like you've just got out of bed!* ◦ not standard *She acts like she's stupid!*

IDIOMS **like two peas in a pod** very similar, especially in appearance: *The twins are like two peas in a pod.* • **what are you like?** (also **what is she/he like?**) UK informal used when someone has said or done something silly: *'Of course Emma's only worry was whether her lipstick had smudged.' 'Emma! What is she like?'* • **what is sb/sth like?** Ⓐ2 something you say to ask someone to describe someone or something: *You've met Ben's new girlfriend, haven't you? What's she like?* ◦ *I've never been to Bruges – what's it like?* ◦ *So what's it like, then, not having to work?*

▸**preposition** **TYPICAL OF** ▷ **1** Ⓑ2 typical or characteristic of: *That's just like Maisie to turn up half an hour late to her own party!* ◦ *It's not like you to be so quiet – are you all right, my love?* **SUCH AS** ▷ **2** Ⓑ1 such as: *She looks best in bright, vibrant colours, like red and pink.*

▸**adv** informal **FEELINGS/SPEECH** ▷ **1** used before you describe how you were feeling or what you said when something happened to you: *Then I saw how late it was and I'm like, so upset.* ◦ *He started shouting at me and I'm like, 'What's your problem? I'm on your side!'* **PAUSE** ▷ **2** used in conversation as a pause or to emphasize an adjective: *He's, like, really friendly – someone you can talk to.* ◦ *If there's nothing you can do to change the situation, it's like – why bother?*

▸**noun** **1** **the like of sb/sth; sb's/sth's like** a person, thing, or group similar in character or quality to the one mentioned: *He was a very great actor – we won't **see** his like again.* ◦ *He described a superlative meal, the like of which he'd never eaten.* **2** **and such like** (also **and the like**) and similar things: *There's a big sports hall for tennis and badminton and such like.* **3** **likes** Ⓑ2 [plural] the things that someone enjoys: *They can't expect me to accommodate all their silly little likes **and dislikes**.* **4** **not for the likes of sb** (also **like**) not for the type of people mentioned: *First-class travel is for posh people – it's not for the likes of us.*

▸**adj** **be like to do sth** old use to be likely to do something

IDIOM **be of like mind** formal When people are of like mind, they agree.

-like /-laɪk/ **suffix** like the thing mentioned: *The paper criticized what it described as the animal-like behaviour of the football fans.* ◦ *There was a large, ball-like structure on top of the building.* ◦ *childlike trust* ◦ *a cabbage-like vegetable*

likeable (US **likable**) /ˈlaɪ.kə.bl/ **adj** describes a person who is pleasant and easy to like: *He's a very likeable sort of bloke.*

likelihood /ˈlaɪ.kli.hʊd/ noun [U] **1** C2 the chance that something will happen: *This latest dispute greatly increases the likelihood* ***of*** *a strike.* ◦ [+ that] *There is* ***every*** *likelihood* ***that*** *more jobs will be lost later this year.* **2 in all likelihood** C2 almost certainly: *In all likelihood everything will go to plan.*

likely /ˈlaɪ.kli/ adj; adv

▸adj B1 describes something that will probably happen or is expected: *Do remind me because I'm likely* ***to*** *forget.* ◦ *What's the likely outcome of this whole business?* ◦ *I suppose that might happen but it's not very likely.* ◦ [+ that] *It's quite likely* ***that*** *we'll be in Spain this time next year.* → Opposite **unlikely**

IDIOM **(that's) a likely story!** informal said when you do not believe something: *'He said he bought them all very cheaply from some guy he knows.' 'That's a likely story!'*

▸adv **1 as likely as not** C1 probably: *As likely as not, she'll end up in court over this problem.* **2 most/very likely** C1 very probably: *Most likely he'll turn up late.* **3 not likely!** B1 informal certainly not!: *'Do you want to come running with me?' 'Not likely!'*

ˌlike-ˈminded adj People who are described as like-minded share the same opinions, ideas, or interests: *A dedicated football fan herself, she started the magazine for like-minded women.*

liken /ˈlaɪ.kən/ verb

PHRASAL VERB **liken sb/sth to sb/sth** [often passive] to say that someone is similar to or has the same qualities as someone else: *She's been likened to a young Elizabeth Taylor.*

likeness /ˈlaɪk.nəs/ noun [C or U] **1** being similar in appearance: *There's a definite* ***family*** *likeness around the eyes.* **2 a good, remarkable, etc. likeness** a painting or other image of a person that looks very like them

likewise /ˈlaɪk.waɪz/ adv C2 in the same way: *Just water these plants twice a week, and likewise the ones in the bedroom.* ◦ informal *'I haven't got time to spend hours preparing one dish!' 'Likewise (= it's the same for me).'*

liking /ˈlaɪ.kɪŋ/ noun [S] a feeling that you like someone or something: *She has a liking* ***for*** *fine wines.* ◦ *I'm developing quite a liking* ***for*** *jazz.* ◦ formal *Is the room* ***to*** *your liking, Sir (= are you satisfied with it)?* ◦ *The dessert was a bit sweet* ***for*** *my liking (= I like it less sweet).*

lilac /ˈlaɪ.lək/ noun; adj

▸noun [C or U] **PLANT** ▷ **1** a bush or small tree with sweet-smelling purple or white flowers: *The lilacs are in bloom.* **COLOUR** ▷ **2** a pale colour between pink and purple

▸adj having a pale colour between pink and purple

Lilliputian /ˌlɪl.ɪˈpjuː.ʃən/ adj mainly humorous extremely small

Li-lo /ˈlaɪ.ləʊ/ US /-loʊ/ noun [C] (plural **Li-los**) (also **ˈair ˌmattress**) UK trademark a type of plastic or rubber MATTRESS that you fill with air and use to lie on or to float on water

lilt /lɪlt/ noun [S] a gentle and pleasant rising and falling sound in a person's voice: *He's got that lovely Irish lilt in his voice.*

lilting /ˈlɪl.tɪŋ/ US /-t̬ɪŋ/ adj A lilting voice or tune gently rises and falls in a way that is pleasant to listen to.

lily /ˈlɪl.i/ noun [C] any of various plants with a large, bell-shaped flower on a long stem

ˌlily-ˈlivered adj literary **cowardly** (= not brave)

ˌlily of the ˈvalley noun [C/U] a small plant with large oval leaves and small bell-shaped white flowers which smell sweet

ˈlily ˌpad noun [C] the large, round-shaped leaf of the WATER LILY which floats on the surface of water

ˌlily-ˈwhite adj **COLOUR** ▷ **1** old-fashioned pure white **CHARACTER** ▷ **2** having a perfect character with no bad qualities

lima bean /ˌlaɪ.məˈbiːn/, /ˈliː-/ noun [C usually plural] US (UK **ˈbutter ˌbean**) a large, flat, pale yellow or pale green bean

limb /lɪm/ noun [C] an arm or leg of a person or animal, or a large branch of a tree: *The accident victims mostly had injuries to their lower limbs (= legs).* ◦ *an artificial limb*

IDIOM **out on a limb** having an opinion that is different from most people's and is unpopular: *She's* ***going*** *out on a limb in criticizing her own party leadership.*

limber /ˈlɪm.bər/ US /-bɚ/ adj; verb

▸adj (of a person) able to bend and move easily and smoothly

▸verb

PHRASAL VERB **limber up** to do gentle exercises to stretch the muscles in order to prepare the body for more active physical exercise: *The substitutes are beginning to limber up on the sidelines.*

limbo /ˈlɪm.bəʊ/ US /-boʊ/ noun **UNCERTAINTY** ▷ **1** [U] an uncertain situation that you cannot control and in which there is no progress or improvement: *Until we've got official permission to go ahead with the plans we're* ***in*** *limbo.* **DANCE** ▷ **2 the limbo** a dance from the West Indies in which the dancer bends backwards to go under a low bar that is made lower each time he or she goes under it

lime /laɪm/ noun; verb

▸noun **FRUIT** ▷ **1** [C or U] a round fruit containing a lot of juice that is sour like a lemon but smaller and green, or the small tree on which this fruit grows **TREE** ▷ **2** (also **lime tree**, US usually **linden**) a large tree with leaves shaped like a heart and pale yellow flowers **CHEMICAL** ▷ **3** [U] (also **quicklime**) a white substance that is used especially to spread on the land to improve the quality of earth so that crops grow better **4** [U] (also **limescale**, **scale**) white material that collects inside water pipes, KETTLES, etc. in areas where the water is HARD (= contains a lot of natural chemicals)

▸verb [T] to spread the substance lime on a piece of land

ˌlime ˈgreen noun [U] a light, bright, greenish-yellow colour • **ˌlime-ˈgreen adj**

the limelight /ˈlaɪm.laɪt/ noun [S] public attention and interest: *She's been* ***in*** *the limelight recently, following the release of her controversial new film.*

limerick /ˈlɪm.ər.ɪk/ US /-ɚ-/ noun [C] a humorous poem with five lines

limescale /ˈlaɪm.skeɪl/ noun [U] white material that collects inside water pipes, KETTLES, etc. in areas where water is HARD (= contains a lot of natural chemicals)

limestone /ˈlaɪm.stəʊn/ US /-stoʊn/ noun [U] a white or light grey rock that is used as a building material and in the making of CEMENT

Limey /ˈlaɪ.mi/ noun [C] US old-fashioned a British person

limit /ˈlɪm.ɪt/ **noun; verb**

▸**noun 1** B1 [C] the greatest amount, number, or level of something that is either possible or allowed: *Is there a limit* ***on*** *the amount of money you can claim?* ◦ *I think we ought to* ***put*** *a strict limit* ***on*** *the amount of time we can spend on the project.* ◦ *There's a limit* ***to*** *the number of times I can stop what I'm doing just so I can help him!* ◦ *We* ***set*** *a* ***time*** *limit* ***of*** *30 minutes for the test.* **2** [U] informal the amount of something that is enough and not too much: *Three cocktails are my limit.* ◦ *I won't have any more – I* ***know*** *my limit!* **3 the limit** old-fashioned informal something that is very annoying or not convenient: *And now you're cutting your toenails in bed! – That really is the limit!* **4** the largest amount of alcohol that is legally allowed to be present in the blood while a person is driving a vehicle: *She was definitely driving* ***over*** *the limit.* **5 limits** [plural] limit: *I'd like to play squash, but I'm 60 and I* ***know*** *my limits.* ◦ *His genius* ***knows no*** *limits.* ◦ *The pay rise was in excess of* ***spending*** *limits* ***imposed/set*** *by the government.*

> Word partners for **limit noun**
>
> *impose/put/set* a limit • *reach/exceed* a limit • an *age/height/speed/time* limit • a *lower/maximum/upper* limit • a *strict* limit • a limit *on/to* sth

IDIOM **within limits** C2 to some extent, but not allowing everything: *I'll pay for what you need – within limits.*

▸**verb** [T] B2 to control something so that it is not greater than a particular amount, number, or level: *I've been asked to limit my speech* ***to*** *ten minutes maximum.* ◦ *Having so little money to spend on an apartment does limit you in your choice.*

limitation /ˌlɪm.ɪˈteɪ.ʃən/ **noun 1** C1 [U] the act of controlling and especially reducing something: *the limitation of nuclear weapons* **2 limitations** C1 [plural] disapproving If someone or something has limitations, they are not as good as they could be: *Living in a flat is all right, but it* ***has its*** *limitations – for example, you don't have your own garden.* ◦ *Despite her limitations as an actress, she was a great entertainer.*

limited /ˈlɪm.ɪ.tɪd/ US /-t̬ɪd/ **adj 1** B1 small in amount or number: *a limited choice* ◦ *limited resources* **2** B2 kept within a particular size, range, time, etc.: *Places on the bus are limited* ***to*** *50 – so book early!* ◦ *The problem of stress is certainly not limited* ***to*** *people who work (= it exists for others too).* **3** (written abbreviation **Ltd**) used in the name of a limited company

ˌlimited ˈcompany noun [C] a company, especially one in the UK, whose owners only have to pay part of the money they owe if the company fails financially

ˌlimited eˈdition noun [C] one of a small set of books or pictures that were printed: *She's got some very valuable limited editions on her shelves.*

limiting /ˈlɪm.ɪ.tɪŋ/ US /-t̬ɪŋ/ **adj** preventing you from having much choice: *Not eating meat or fish can be very limiting when you go to a restaurant.*

limitless /ˈlɪm.ɪt.ləs/ **adj** without limit: *the limitless sky* ◦ *The minister said that the days of limitless spending were over.*

limousine /ˌlɪm.əˈziːn/ **noun** [C] (informal **limo** /ˈlɪm.əʊ/ US /-oʊ/) **1** a large, expensive car, often driven by a CHAUFFEUR (= a person employed to drive a car for someone else) **2** US a small bus to take people to and from an airport

limp /lɪmp/ **verb; adj; noun**

▸**verb** PERSON/ANIMAL ▷ **1** [I] to walk slowly and with difficulty because of having an injured or painful leg or foot: *Three minutes into the match, Jackson limped off the pitch with a serious ankle injury.* PROCESS/THING ▷ **2** [I + adv/prep] informal to move or develop slowly and with difficulty: *The little boat limped slowly towards the shore.* ◦ *After limping* ***along*** *for almost two years, the economy is starting to show signs of recovery.*

▸**adj** soft and neither firm nor stiff: *a limp lettuce leaf/salad* ◦ *a limp* ***handshake*** • **limply** /-li/ **adv** *She lay limply in his arms.* • **limpness** /-nəs/ **noun** [U]

▸**noun** [S] a way of walking slowly and with difficulty because of having an injured or painful leg or foot: *She* ***has*** *a slight limp.* ◦ *He* ***walks with*** *a limp.*

limpet /ˈlɪm.pɪt/ **noun** [C] a small sea creature with a cone-shaped shell that fixes itself to rocks

limpid /ˈlɪm.pɪd/ **adj 1** literary clear and transparent: *a limpid pool* **2** clearly expressed and easily understood: *limpid prose* • **limpidly** /-li/ **adv**

ˌlimp-ˈwristed adj **1** describes a man who does not behave in the strong and determined way traditionally expected in men **2** offensive describes a man who seems, by his manner, to be gay

limy /ˈlaɪ.mi/ **adj** describes land that has been covered with LIME or contains it naturally

linchpin (also **lynchpin**) /ˈlɪntʃ.pɪn/ **noun the linchpin of** the most important member of a group or part of a system, that holds together the other members or parts or makes it possible for them to operate as intended: *Woodford is the linchpin of the British athletics team.*

linctus /ˈlɪŋk.təs/ **noun** [U] UK a thick, sweet liquid medicine that is used to treat coughs and sore throats

linden /ˈlɪn.dən/ **noun** [C] US a **lime**

line /laɪn/ **noun; verb**

▸**noun** LONG MARK ▷ **1** A2 [C] a long thin, mark on the surface of something: *a straight line* ◦ *Sign your name on the dotted line.* ◦ *She was very old and her face was covered with lines.* ◦ *My legs felt all wobbly when I stood up and I couldn't walk* ***in a straight*** *line (= walk without moving to the side while moving forward).* ROW ▷ **2** C2 [C] a group of people or things arranged in a row: *a line of trees* ◦ *The prisoners formed a line against the wall.* **3** [C] US (UK **queue**) a group of people standing one behind the other who are waiting for something: *Just* ***get in*** *line and wait your turn like everyone else.* ◦ *I had to* ***wait/stand in*** *line for three hours to get tickets.* **4 a long line of** a series of people or things that follow each other in time: *She is the latest in a long line of controversial leaders.* ◦ *He comes from a long line of doctors (= a lot of his relatives were doctors before him).* DIVISION ▷ **5** C2 [C] a long, thin and sometimes imaginary mark that forms the edge, border, or limit of something: *That ball was definitely in! It was nowhere near the line!* ◦ *The police couldn't arrest him because he'd fled across the* ***state*** *line.* ◦ *For many television viewers the* ***dividing*** *line between fact and fiction is becoming increasingly blurred.* PHONE ▷ **6** B2 [C] a connection to a phone system: *I'm afraid your line's been disconnected because your last bill hasn't been paid.* ◦ *If you want to air your opinions live on the radio, the lines will be open (= you can phone) from eight o'clock.* ◦ *I've got Chris Foster* ***on*** *the line for you. Do you want to take it now or call her back later?* ◦ formal *Please* ***hold the*** *line (= wait). I'll see if she's available.* RAILWAY ▷ **7** B1 [C] (the route followed by) a railway track: *The train was delayed, apparently due to leaves on the line.* ◦ *The Northern Line is the worst on the London Underground.* ◦ ***Main*** *line services can be very quick, but travelling on the* ***branch*** *lines is much slower.* APPROACH TO SUBJECT ▷ **8** C2 [C] a way of dealing with or thinking about something or someone: *The government's* ***official*** *line has always been to refuse to negotiate with terrorists.* ◦ *The courts should* ***take*** *a tougher line* ***with*** *(= punish more severely) sex offenders.* ◦ *Several Labour MPs disagree with their party's line* ***on*** *taxation.* ◦ *What sort of line (= method of arguing) do you think we should* ***take*** *in the pay negotiations?* ◦ *The police are confident that this new line* ***of inquiry*** *will lead them to the murderer.* ◦ *It seems inevitable that the country will be* ***divided along*** *ethnic lines.* **9 line of reasoning, thinking, etc.** (C2) a way of thinking about a particular subject: *We cannot agree with their line of reasoning.* **MILITARY ▷ 10** (C2) [C] a row of positions used to defend against enemy attack, especially the ones closest to enemy positions: *They were taken prisoner while on a reconnaissance mission behind enemy lines.* ◦ figurative *In a game of football, the goalkeeper is the last line of defence.* **SHAPE ▷ 11** [C] the shape of something that has been designed or created: *They have a reputation for designing cars with elegant aerodynamic lines.* **SUPPORT ▷ 12** [C] a long, strong, thin piece of material, such as string, rope, or wire, used to support something: *I'd hung the washing out on the* ***clothes*** *line.* ◦ *Can you feel the fish tugging on the line?* **COMPANY ▷ 13** [C] a company that transports people or goods: *a shipping line* **REMARK ▷ 14** [C] a remark that is intended to entertain, persuade, or deceive: *a speech full of memorable lines* ◦ *He keeps giving me that line* ***about*** *not being able to do any work because his computer isn't working properly.* ◦ *Who was it who came up with that famous line about 'lies, damned lies and statistics'?* **WORDS ▷ 15** (B1) [C] a row of words that form part of a text: *We could get more lines on the page if we reduced the type size.* ◦ *The computer screen displays 80 characters per line.* **16** [C] a short series of musical notes **17** [C usually plural] the words that an actor speaks when performing in a film, play, etc.: *I only had two lines in the whole play.* ◦ *She hasn't* ***learned*** *her lines yet, and we've got our first rehearsal tomorrow.* ◦ *I'm terrified of* ***forgetting*** *my lines.* **18 lines** [plural] UK a punishment for school students in which a sentence has to be written repeatedly: *She got 200 lines for swearing at her teacher.* **JOB ▷ 19** [C usually singular] the type of job someone does: *You meet some very interesting people in my line* ***of*** *business.* **GOODS ▷ 20** (C1) [C] a range of similar things that are for sale: *There are discounts on many items from our older lines.* ◦ *I was shown all their new lines.*

IDIOMS **all along the line** ever since the beginning of a relationship or process: *The project's been plagued with financial problems all along the line.* • **along the lines of sth** (also **along those lines**) (C2) similar in type: *I was thinking of doing a meal along the lines of that dinner I did for Annie and Dave.* ◦ *They're campaigning for the electoral system to be reformed along the lines of (= so that it becomes similar to) the one in Germany.* • **be in line for sth** to be likely to get something, especially something good: *If anyone's in line for promotion, I should think it's Helen.* • **be in line to do sth** to have a very good chance of doing something: *Kim Bailey is* ***next*** *in line to replace Chris Finlay as managing director.* • **be in line to the throne** to be the person who will become king or queen after the present ruler: *Prince Charles is* ***first*** *in line to the British throne.* • **in line with sth** (C2) similar to, or at the same level as something: *The company's results are in line with stock market expectations.* ◦ *We're seeking a pay rise that's in line with inflation.* ◦ *The salaries of temporary employees ought to be* ***brought into*** *line with those of permanent staff.* • **be on the line** (C2) to be at risk: *Almost 3,000 jobs have been lost recently, and a further 3,000 are on the line.* • **be out of line with sth** to be different from something: *Their predictions were hopelessly out of line with the actual results.* • **get a line on sb** mainly US to find out information about someone that you do not know: *I've been trying to get a line on the guy they've nominated with no luck.* • **have a nice, good, etc. line in sth** UK informal to do something skilfully and successfully: *He has a good line in anecdotes.* • **in the line of duty** Something which happens to you in the line of duty happens when you are doing your job: *This year alone eight police officers have been killed in the line of duty.* • **put/lay sth on the line** to risk something: *Firefighters put their lives on the line every working day.* • **somewhere along the line** at some moment during a relationship or process: *I don't know what went wrong with our relationship, but somewhere along the line we just stopped loving each other.* • **step/be out of line** (C2) to behave in an unsuitable way

►verb [T] **FORM ROW ▷ 1** (C2) to form a row along the side of something: *Thousands of people lined the* ***streets*** *to watch the presidential procession pass by.* ◦ *Police lined the* ***route*** *of the demonstration.* ◦ *country lanes lined* ***with*** *trees* **COVER ▷ 2** to cover the inside surface of something: *I lined the drawers* ***with*** *old wallpaper.* ◦ *How much would it cost to have this jacket lined?* ◦ *Full-length mirrors lined each wall of the bathroom.*

IDIOM **line your pocket(s)** to earn money using dishonest or illegal methods: *Staff at the bank have apparently been lining their pockets* ***with*** *money from investors' accounts.*

PHRASAL VERBS **line (sb) up** (B2) to arrange people or things in a row or to stand in a row: *A fight broke out behind me as we lined up to receive our food rations.* ◦ *The soldiers lined us up against a wall and I thought they were going to shoot us.* • **line sth up** (C1) to prepare, organize, or arrange something: *Have you got anything exciting lined up* ***for*** *the weekend?* ◦ *I've lined up a meeting with them* ***for*** *tomorrow morning.* ◦ [+ to infinitive] *Have you got anyone lined up* ***to*** *do the catering at the Christmas party?*

lineage /ˈlɪn.i.ɪdʒ/ **noun** [C or U] formal the members of a person's family who are directly related to that person and who lived a long time before him or her: *She's very proud of her ancient royal lineage.* • **lineal** /-əl/ **adj** *She claims lineal descent from Henry VIII.* • **lineally** /-ə.li/ **adv**

linear /ˈlɪn.i.əʳ/ (US) /-ɚ/ **adj LINES ▷ 1** consisting of or to do with lines: *a linear diagram* **LENGTH ▷ 2** [before noun] relating to length, rather than area or volume: *linear measurement* **CONNECTION ▷ 3** involving a series of events or thoughts in which one follows another one directly: *These mental exercises are designed to break linear thinking habits and encourage creativity.* **4** describes a relationship between two things that is direct or clear: *Is there a linear relationship between salaries and productivity?*

linebacker /ˈlaɪnˌbæk.əʳ/ (US) /-ɚ/ **noun** [C] US a player in American football who tries to stop players from the other team from moving the ball along the field

lined /laɪnd/ **adj** (of paper) having lines printed across, or (of the skin on the face) having lines because of age: *lined paper* ◦ *His face was heavily lined.*

ˈline ˌdrawing noun [C] a pen or pencil drawing that consists only of lines

ˈline ˌitem noun [C] US specialized a single part of a

financial statement, especially one giving details of the accounts of a company or government

ˈline ˌmanager noun **1** **sb's line manager** mainly UK someone who is responsible for managing someone else in a company or business **2** one of the managers who are responsible for the most important activities of a large company, such as production

linen /ˈlɪn.ɪn/ noun [U] **1** C2 strong cloth made from the FIBRES of the FLAX plant: *a linen jacket* ◦ *the crumpled charm of linen* **2** C2 sheets, TABLECLOTHS, etc. made from linen or a similar material: ***bed** linen* ◦ ***table** linen*

ˈlinen ˌbasket noun [C] a container for clothes and sheets, etc. that need washing

ˌline of ˈscrimmage noun [C usually singular] US in American football, the line on which the ball is positioned at the beginning of PLAY (= a period of action)

lineout /ˈlaɪn.aʊt/ noun [C] UK a way of continuing a game of RUGBY after the ball has gone off the field, in which the attacking players from both teams form two parallel lines at the edge of the field and jump to catch the ball when it is thrown between the two lines

liner /ˈlaɪ.nəʳ/ US /-nɚ/ noun [C] a large ship for carrying passengers in great comfort on long journeys

ˈliner ˌnote noun [C] US information about a performer or a performance that is supplied with a sound recording

linesman /ˈlaɪnz.mən/ noun [C] (plural **-men** /-mən/) an official in some sports who is responsible for deciding when the ball has crossed the line that marks the edge of the playing area

ˈline-up noun [C] **1** UK a group of people that has been brought together to form a team or take part in an event: *Several important changes are expected in the line-up for Thursday's match against Scotland.* ◦ *We've got a star-studded line-up of guests on tonight's show.* **2** US for **identity parade** **3** US the order in which the players in a baseball team hit the ball

linger /ˈlɪŋ.gəʳ/ US /-gɚ/ verb [I] C2 to take a long time to leave or disappear: *After the play had finished, we lingered for a while in the bar hoping to catch sight of the actors.* ◦ *The smell from the fire still lingered days later.* ◦ *It's impossible to forget such horrific events – they linger **(on)** in the memory forever.* • **lingerer** /-əʳ/ US /-ɚ/ noun [C]

lingerie /ˈlɒn.ʒəʳr.i/ US /ˌlɑːn.ʒəˈreɪ/ noun [U] women's underwear

lingering /ˈlɪŋ.gəʳr.ɪŋ/ US /-gɚ.ɪŋ/ adj [before noun] lasting a long time: *She gave him a long, lingering kiss.* ◦ *She says she stopped seeing him, but I still have lingering doubts.* ◦ *The defeat ends any lingering hopes she might have had of winning the championship.* • **lingeringly** /-li/ adv

lingo /ˈlɪŋ.gəʊ/ US /-goʊ/ noun [C usually singular] (plural **lingos** or **lingoes**) informal **1** a foreign language: *In Italy, of course, Stef can speak the lingo.* **2** a type of language that contains a lot of unusual or technical expressions: *internet lingo*

lingua franca /ˌlɪŋ.gwəˈfræŋ.kə/ noun [C usually singular] a language used for communication between groups of people who speak different languages but not between members of the same group: *The international business community sees English as a lingua franca.*

linguine /lɪŋˈgwiː.nei/ noun [U] PASTA in the shape of long, thin strips

linguist /ˈlɪŋ.gwɪst/ noun [C] someone who studies foreign languages or can speak them very well, or someone who teaches or studies linguistics

linguistic /lɪŋˈgwɪs.tɪk/ adj C1 connected with language or the study of language: *I'm particularly interested in the linguistic development of young children.* • **linguistically** /-tɪ.kəl.i/ adv

linguistics /lɪŋˈgwɪs.tɪks/ noun [U] (also **linˌguistic ˈscience**) the scientific study of the structure and development of language in general or of particular languages

liniment /ˈlɪn.ə.mənt/ noun [U] old-fashioned a liquid, usually containing alcohol, that is rubbed into the skin to reduce pain or stiffness in a JOINT (= place where two bones are connected)

lining /ˈlaɪ.nɪŋ/ noun [C] a material or substance that covers the inside surface of something: *a coat/jacket lining* ◦ *the lining of the stomach*

link /lɪŋk/ noun; verb

▸**noun** [C] **CONNECTION** ▷ **1** B2 a connection between two people, things, or ideas: *There's a direct link **between** diet and heart disease.* ◦ *Their links **with** Britain are still strong.* ◦ *diplomatic links between the two countries* **2** B1 a connection between documents on the internet: *Click on this link to visit our online bookstore.* **CHAIN** ▷ **3** one of the rings in a chain

▸**verb** [T] B2 to make a connection between two or more people, things, or ideas: *The explosions are not thought to be linked in any way.* ◦ *The use of CFCs has been linked **to** the depletion of the ozone layer.*

PHRASAL VERB **link (sth) up** to form a connection, especially in order to work or operate together: *The organization's aim is to link up people from all over the country who are suffering from the disease.* ◦ *We offer advice to Polish companies who want to link up **with** Western businesses.*

linkage /ˈlɪŋ.kɪdʒ/ noun [C or U] the existence or forming of connections between things

ˈlinking ˌverb noun [C] specialized a verb which connects the qualities of an object or person to that object or person: *In the sentence 'My bags weigh 45 kg', 'weigh' is a linking verb.*

links /lɪŋks/ noun [C, + sing/pl verb] (plural **links**) (also **ˈgolf ˌlinks**) **1** a large area of hills covered with sand near the sea, used for playing GOLF **2** US any area of land that is used for playing GOLF

ˈlink-up noun [C] the act of connecting two things, organizations, etc., for example so that they can work together: *There are plans for a link-up between the two companies.* ◦ *a live satellite link-up*

linoleum /lɪˈnəʊ.li.əm/ US /-ˈnoʊ-/ noun [U] (UK also **lino**) a stiff, smooth material that is used for covering floors

linseed /ˈlɪn.siːd/ noun [U] a type of FLAX plant grown for its seeds, from which oil is made

ˈlinseed ˌoil noun [U] (also **ˈflaxseed ˌoil**) oil made from linseed, used for making linoleum, paint, and ink, and for protecting wood

lint /lɪnt/ noun [U] **FIBRES** ▷ **1** UK soft material made from cloth threads, used for protecting injuries **LOOSE MATERIAL** ▷ **2** mainly US for **fluff** (= small loose pieces of wool or other soft material)

lintel /ˈlɪn.təl/ US /-ţəl/ noun [C] a long piece of stone or wood at the top of a door or window frame which supports the wall above

lion /ˈlaɪ.ən/ noun [C] **1** A2 (female **lioness**) a large wild animal of the cat family with yellowish-brown fur that lives in Africa and southern Asia: *a pride (= group) of* lions **2** someone who is important, successful, or powerful: *a literary lion*

IDIOMS **the lion's den** a dangerous or threatening place or situation • **the lion's share** the largest part or most of something

ˌlion-ˈhearted adj literary very brave

lionize (UK usually **lionise**) /ˈlaɪ.ə.naɪz/ verb [T] to make someone famous, or to treat someone as if they were famous • **lionization** (UK usually **lionisation**) /ˌlaɪ.ə.naɪˈzeɪ.ʃən/ noun [U]

lip /lɪp/ noun **BODY PART** ▷ **1** B1 [C] one of the two soft, red edges of the mouth: *She kissed me on the lips.* ◦ *He licked his lips.* **EDGE** ▷ **2** [C] a part of an edge of a container that is shaped to allow liquid to be poured easily from the container **SPEECH** ▷ **3** [U] informal the act of arguing with someone in a way that is rude or does not show enough respect: *That's enough of your lip, young lady!*

IDIOMS **my lips are sealed** said when you are promising to keep a secret: *'Oh and please don't tell him you saw me here.' 'Don't worry. My lips are sealed.'* • **on everyone's lips** being talked about by a lot of people: *The question now on everyone's lips is 'Will the prime minister resign?'*

lipase /ˈlaɪ.peɪz/ US /ˈlɪp.eɪs/ noun [U] specialized a substance that is produced mainly in the PANCREAS and helps the body to digest lipids

ˈlip ˌbalm noun [U or C] **lipsalve**

ˈlip ˌgloss noun [C or U] a type of make-up that is put on the lips to make them look shiny → Compare **lipstick**

lipid /ˈlɪp.ɪd/ noun [C] specialized a substance such as a fat, oil, or WAX that dissolves in alcohol but not in water and is an important part of living cells

liposome /ˈlɪp.ə.səʊm/ US /-soʊm/ noun [C] specialized an extremely small SAC (= bag) made artificially from a type of lipid to carry a drug, VACCINE, or other substance to particular cells in the body

liposuction /ˈlɪp.əʊˌsʌk.ʃən/ US /ˈlaɪ.poʊ-/ noun [U] an operation in which fat is sucked out from under the skin

lippy /ˈlɪp.i/ adj; noun
▸adj informal showing no respect in the way that you talk to someone: *She can get a bit lippy with her parents.*
▸noun [U] informal UK **lipstick**

ˈlip-read verb [I or T] (**lip-read, lip-read**) to understand what someone is saying by watching the movements of their mouth • **ˈlip-ˌreading** noun [U]

lipsalve /ˈlɪp.sælv/ US /-sæv/ noun [U] UK a type of cream that is used to keep the lips soft or to help sore lips feel better → Synonym **lip balm**

ˈlip ˌservice noun **pay lip service to sth** to say that you agree with something but do nothing to support it: *She claims to be in favour of training, but so far she's only paid lip service to the idea.*

lipstick /ˈlɪp.stɪk/ noun [C or U] a coloured substance that women put on their lips to make them more attractive

lip-synch /ˈlɪp.sɪŋk/ verb [I] Performers who lip-synch songs pretend to be singing them when in fact they are just moving their lips.

liquefy (also **liquify**) /ˈlɪk.wɪ.faɪ/ verb [I or T] to (cause a gas or a solid to) change into a liquid form: *Gases liquefy under pressure.*

liqueur /lɪˈkjʊər/ US /-ˈkjʊr/ noun [C] a strong, sweet alcoholic drink that is usually drunk in small amounts at the end of a meal

liquid /ˈlɪk.wɪd/ noun; adj
▸noun [C or U] B1 a substance, such as water, that is not solid or a gas and that can be poured easily: *Mercury is a liquid at room temperature.*
▸adj **MONEY** ▷ **1** in the form of money, rather than INVESTMENTS or property, or able to be changed into money easily: *She has very few liquid **assets** as most of her wealth is tied up in stocks and shares.* **SUBSTANCE** ▷ **2** in the form of a liquid: *liquid hydrogen* • **liquidity** /lɪˈkwɪd.ɪ.ti/ US /-ə.t̬i/ noun [U]

liquidate /ˈlɪk.wɪ.deɪt/ verb **CLOSE** ▷ **1** [I or T] to cause a business to close, so that its ASSETS can be sold to pay its debts **KILL** ▷ **2** [T] to kill someone • **liquidation** /ˌlɪk.wɪˈdeɪ.ʃən/ noun [C or U] *After three years of heavy losses the company **went into** liquidation with debts totalling £100 million.*

liquidator /ˈlɪk.wɪ.deɪ.tər/ US /-t̬ɚ/ noun [C] one of the people in charge of closing a company

ˌliquid ˈcourage noun [U] US (UK **ˌDutch ˈcourage**) the confidence some people get from drinking alcohol before they do something that needs courage

ˌliquid crystal disˈplay noun [C] (abbreviation **LCD**) a screen for showing text or pictures which uses a liquid that becomes dark when an electric current flows across it

liquidize (UK usually **liquidise**) /ˈlɪk.wɪ.daɪz/ verb [T] to change food into a thick liquid using a BLENDER (= electric machine with blades that turn very quickly) → Compare **liquefy**

liquidizer (UK usually **liquidiser**) /ˈlɪk.wɪ.daɪ.zər/ US /-zɚ/ noun [C] UK for **blender** (= electric machine that changes food into a thick liquid)

ˌliquid ˈlunch noun [C] informal humorous a meal in the middle of the day that consists of drinks, usually alcoholic drinks, and no food, or not much food

ˌLiquid ˈPaper noun [U] trademark a white liquid for covering mistakes in a text or drawing so that they can be corrected

liquify /ˈlɪk.wɪ.faɪ/ verb to **liquefy**

liquor /ˈlɪk.ər/ US /-ɚ/ noun [U] US strong alcoholic drink

liquorice UK (US **licorice**) /ˈlɪk.ər.ɪs/, /-ɪʃ/ US /-ɚ-/ noun [U] **1** the dried root of a Mediterranean plant, used in medicines and to give flavour to food, especially sweets **2** a black sweet made from liquorice

ˈliquor ˌstore noun [C] US for **off-licence**

lira /ˈlɪə.rə/ US /ˈlɪr.ə/ noun [C] (plural **lira**) the standard unit of money used in Italy before the introduction of the euro, and also used in Malta and Turkey

lisp /lɪsp/ verb [I] to pronounce 's' and 'z' sounds like 'th' • **lisp** noun [C] *I was teased a lot at school because I spoke with a lisp.*

lissome (also **lissom**) /ˈlɪs.əm/ adj literary attractively thin and able to move quickly and smoothly

list /lɪst/ noun; verb
▸noun **RECORD** ▷ **1** A2 [C] a record of short pieces of information, such as people's names, usually written or printed with a single thing on each line and often ordered in a way that makes a particular thing easy to find: *a **shopping** list* ◦ *Is your name **on the** list?* ◦ *I've **made** a list of places I'd like to visit while we're in Paris.* **LEAN** ▷ **2** If a ship has a list, it leans to one side.

IDIOM **a list as long as your arm** informal a very long list: *I've got a list as long as my arm of the things we need to do before we go on holiday.*

▸verb **MAKE RECORD** ▷ **1** B2 [T] to make a list, or to include something in a list: *I've listed some useful reading material on the handout.* **LEAN** ▷ **2** [I] (of a ship) to lean to one side, especially as a result of damage: *The tanker is listing badly and liable to sink at any moment.* **COMPANY** ▷ **3** [T] to make a company's SHARES available on a particular financial market: *Last year, eight new companies were listed on the Lahore stock exchange.*

ˌlisted ˈbuilding noun [C] UK (US **ˌlandmarked ˈbuilding**) a building of great historical or artistic value that has official protection to prevent it from being changed or destroyed

ˌlisted ˈcompany noun [C] a company whose SHARES can be traded on a country's main STOCK MARKET

listen /ˈlɪs.ᵊn/ verb [I] A1 to give attention to someone or something in order to hear them: *What kind of music do you listen* ***to****? ◦ She does all the talking – I just sit and listen. ◦ You haven't listened to a word I've said! ◦ We listened in silence as the names of the dead were read out. ◦ Listen, we really need to sort out our insurance claim this weekend. ◦ Listen* ***to this****! You can win a holiday for two in the south of France just by answering three simple questions.* • **listen** noun [S] ***Have a*** *listen* ***to*** *this! I've never heard anything like it before.*

> **!** Common mistake: **listen**
>
> When **listen** is followed by a direct object, remember to use the preposition **to**.
>
> Don't say 'listen something', say **listen to something**:
>
> ~~*I often listen the radio while I am doing my homework.*~~
>
> *I often listen to the radio while I am doing my homework.*
>
> ~~*He never listens what I say.*~~
>
> *He never listens to what I say.*

> **!** Usage: **listen, listen to, or hear?**
>
> Use **hear** when you want to say that sounds, music, etc. come to your ears. You can **hear** something without wanting to:
>
> *I could hear his music through the wall.*
>
> *Can you hear me?*
>
> Use **listen** to say that you pay attention to sounds or try to hear something:
>
> *The audience listened carefully.*
>
> *Ssh! I'm listening!*
>
> Use **listen to** when you want to say what it is that you are trying to hear:
>
> *The audience listened to the speaker.*
>
> *Ssh! I'm listening to the radio!*

PHRASAL VERBS **listen in on sth** C2 If you listen in on a conversation, you listen to it, especially secretly, without saying anything: *I wish Dad would stop listening in on my phone conversations.* • **listen out for sth** to make an effort to hear a noise that you are expecting: *Would you listen out for the phone while I'm in the garden?* • **listen up** mainly US informal something you say to make people listen to you: *Okay everyone – listen up! I have an announcement to make.*

listener /ˈlɪs.ᵊn.əʳ/, /-nəʳ/ US /ˈlɪs.ᵊn.ɚ/ noun [C] C1 someone who listens: *We've received a lot of complaints about the changes from regular listeners* ***to*** *the programme.*

> **+** Other ways of saying **listen**
>
> **Hear** can sometimes be used instead of 'listen':
>
> *An audience gathered to* ***hear*** *him speak.*
>
> If someone listens to another person's conversation without them knowing, the verb **eavesdrop** or the phrasal verb **listen in on** is often used:
>
> *He was* ***eavesdropping*** *on our conversation.*
>
> *I wish my brother would stop* ***listening in on*** *my phone calls.*
>
> If you want someone to listen until you have said everything you want to say, you could use the phrasal verb **hear someone out**:
>
> *At least* ***hear me out*** *before you make up your mind.*
>
> If you suddenly start to listen to something carefully because you have heard something interesting, you could say that you **prick up your ears**:
>
> *I heard my name mentioned and I* ***pricked up my ears****.*

IDIOM **a good listener** someone who gives you a lot of attention when you are talking about your problems or things that worry you, and tries to understand and support you

listeria /lɪˈstɪə.ri.ə/ US /-ˈstɪr.i-/ noun [U] a bacterium which causes FOOD POISONING, found especially in cheese and other products made from milk

listeriosis /lɪˌstɪə.riˈəʊ.sɪs/ US /-ˈoʊ-/ noun [U] a serious type of food poisoning, caused by listeria

listings /ˈlɪs.tɪŋz/ noun [plural] information about different types of entertainment and activities that is published in newspapers and magazines, or on the internet: *I'll check the TV listings to see what's on tonight.*

listless /ˈlɪst.ləs/ adj having no energy and enthusiasm and unwilling to do anything needing effort: *He's been listless and a bit depressed ever since he got his exam results.* • **listlessly** /-li/ adv • **listlessness** /-nəs/ noun [U]

ˈlist ˌprice noun [C] specialized the price of something, suggested by the company that makes it

lit /lɪt/ verb; noun

▸verb past simple and past participle of **light**

▸noun [U] abbreviation for literature: *a degree in English Lit*

litany /ˈlɪt.ᵊn.i/ noun [C] **1** a long Christian prayer in which the priest speaks some parts and the other people at the ceremony speak other parts **2 a litany of sth** a long list of unpleasant things, especially things that are repeated: *The manufacturers are reported to have received a litany of complaints from dissatisfied customers.*

litchi /laɪˈtʃiː/ US /liː.tʃiː/ noun [C] a **lychee**

lit crit /lɪtˈkrɪt/ noun [U] abbreviation for **literary criticism**

lite /laɪt/ adj **FOOD** ▷ **1** used for describing food or drink that contains fewer CALORIES than usual and is therefore less likely to make you fat: *a lite yogurt* **NOT SERIOUS** ▷ **2** used for describing things that are not serious and that are easy to understand and enjoy: *lite news about celebrities* **3** [after noun] humorous or disapproving not as serious or as good quality as the real thing: *She described their relationship as 'marriage lite'.*

liter /ˈliː.təʳ/ US /-t̬ɚ/ noun [C] US for **litre**

literacy /ˈlɪt.ᵊr.ə.si/ US /ˈlɪt̬.ɚ-/ noun [U] **1** C1 the ability to read and write: *Far more resources are needed to improve adult literacy.* **2** knowledge of a particular subject, or a particular type of knowledge: ***Computer** literacy is becoming as essential as the ability to drive a car.*

literal /ˈlɪt.ər.əl/ ⓤⓢ /ˈlɪţ.ɚ-/ **adj** **C2** The literal meaning of a word is its original, basic meaning: *The literal meaning of 'television' is 'seeing from a distance'.* ◦ *You need to demonstrate to the examiners that you have more than a literal understanding of the text.* ◦ *Her translation is too literal (= done one word at a time), resulting in heavy, unnatural prose.* → Compare **figurative**

literally /ˈlɪt.ər.əl.i/, /-rə.li/ ⓤⓢ /ˈlɪţ.ɚ.əl.i/ **adv** **1** **B2** having the real or original meaning of a word or phrase: *They were responsible for literally millions of deaths.* ◦ *We live literally just round the corner from her.* ◦ *You'll lose marks if you translate too literally (= one word at a time).* **2** informal used to emphasize what you are saying: *He missed that kick literally by miles.* ◦ *I was literally bowled over by the news.* **3** informal simply or just: *Then you literally cut the sausage down the middle.*

literary /ˈlɪt.ər.ər.i/ ⓤⓢ /ˈlɪţ.ə.rer-/ **adj** **B2** connected with literature: *a literary critic* ◦ *literary prizes* ◦ *a literary style*

ˌliterary ˈcriticism **noun** [U] the formal study and discussion of works of literature, which involves judging and explaining their importance and meaning

literate /ˈlɪt.ər.ət/ ⓤⓢ /ˈlɪţ.ɚ-/ **adj** **1** **C2** able to read and write **2** having knowledge of a particular subject, or a particular type of knowledge: ***computer** literate*

literati /ˌlɪt.ərˈɑː.tiː/ ⓤⓢ /ˌlɪţ.əˈrɑː.ţiː/ **noun** [plural] people with a good education who know a lot about literature → Compare **glitterati**

literature /ˈlɪt.r.ɪ.tʃər/ ⓤⓢ /ˈlɪţ.ɚ.ɪ.tʃɚ/ **noun** [U] **WRITING** ▷ **1** **B1** written artistic works, especially those with a high and lasting artistic value: *classical/modern literature* ◦ *'Wuthering Heights' is a classic of English literature.* **SPECIALIST TEXTS** ▷ **2** all the information relating to a subject, especially information written by experts: *It's important to keep up-to-date with the literature in your field.* ◦ *There is very little literature **on** the disease.* **INFORMATION** ▷ **3** printed material published by a company that is intended to encourage people to buy that company's products or services: *Could you send me your literature **on/about** car insurance policies, please?*

lithe /laɪð/ **adj** young, healthy, attractive, and able to move and bend smoothly: *He had the lithe, athletic body of a ballet dancer.* • **lithely** /ˈlaɪð.li/ **adv**

lithium /ˈlɪθ.i.əm/ **noun** [U] (symbol **Li**) a chemical element that is a soft, silver-coloured metal

lithograph /ˈlɪθ.ə.grɑːf/ ⓤⓢ /-oʊ.græf/ **noun** [C] a picture printed using a stone or metal block on which an image has been drawn with a thick substance that attracts ink • **lithographic** /ˌlɪθ.əˈgræf.ɪk/ ⓤⓢ /-oʊ-/ **adj** • **lithography** /ˌlɪˈθɒg.rə.fi/ ⓤⓢ /-ˈθɑː.grə-/ **noun** [U]

litigant /ˈlɪt.ɪ.gənt/ ⓤⓢ /ˈlɪţ-/ **noun** [C] legal a person who is fighting a legal case

litigate /ˈlɪt.ɪ.geɪt/ ⓤⓢ /ˈlɪţ-/ **verb** [I or T] legal to cause an argument to be discussed in a law court so that a judgment can be made which must be accepted by both sides

litigation /ˌlɪt.ɪˈgeɪ.ʃən/ ⓤⓢ /ˌlɪţ-/ **noun** [U] legal the process of taking a case to a law court so that an official decision can be made: *The company has consistently denied responsibility, but it agreed to the settlement to avoid the expense of lengthy litigation.*

litigator /ˈlɪt.ɪ.geɪ.tər/ ⓤⓢ /ˈlɪţ.ɪ.geɪ.ţɚ/ **noun** [C] US legal a lawyer who specializes in taking legal action

against people and organizations: *a leading civil rights litigator*

litigious /lɪˈtɪdʒ.əs/ **adj** formal disapproving too often taking arguments to a law court for a decision: *The US is the most litigious society in the world.* • **litigiousness** /-nəs/ **noun** [U]

litmus /ˈlɪt.məs/ **noun** [U] a powder that is turned red by ACID and blue by ALKALI: *litmus paper* ◦ *a litmus test*

ˈlitmus ˌtest **noun** [C usually singular] someone's decision or opinion about something which suggests what they think about a wider range of related things: *The president's policy on abortion is regarded as a litmus test **of** his views on women's rights.*

litre UK (US usually **liter**) /ˈliː.tər/ ⓤⓢ /-ţɚ/ **noun** [C] (written abbreviation **l**) **A2** a unit for measuring the volume of a liquid or a gas: *The tax increase will add 4p to a litre of petrol.*

litter /ˈlɪt.ər/ ⓤⓢ /ˈlɪţ.ɚ/ **noun; verb**

▸**noun** **RUBBISH** ▷ **1** **B2** [U] small pieces of rubbish that have been left lying on the ground in public places **BABY ANIMALS** ▷ **2** [C, + sing/pl verb] a group of animals that are born at the same time and have the same mother: *a litter of kittens* **BED** ▷ **3** [U] dried grass or plant stems used by animals as a bed **ANIMAL TOILET** ▷ **4** [U] a substance that is put in a container to be used as a toilet by pets: *cat/pet litter*

▸**verb** **1** [T] to spread across an area or place untidily: *The park was littered **with** bottles and cans after the concert.* ◦ *Dirty clothes littered the floor of her bedroom.* **2 be littered with sth** A place, document, or other object that is littered with something has or contains a lot of that thing: *The newspaper has a reputation for being littered with spelling mistakes.* **3** [I] to drop rubbish on the ground in a public place: *People who litter often have no pride in the area.*

litterbug /ˈlɪt.ə.bʌg/ ⓤⓢ /ˈlɪţ.ɚ-/ **noun** [C] informal disapproving (UK also **ˈlitter ˌlout**) someone who drops rubbish on the ground in public places

little /ˈlɪt.l̩/ ⓤⓢ /ˈlɪţ-/ **adj; determiner; pronoun, noun; adv**

▸**adj** **SMALL** ▷ **1** **A1** small in size or amount: *It came in a little box.* ◦ *a little dog/nose/room* ◦ *A little old man came into the shop.* ◦ *He gave a little smile.* ◦ *It'll only take a little while to clear up the kitchen.* **2 a little something a** a small amount of food or drink: *I always like to have a little something around eleven o'clock in the morning.* **b** a present that is not of great value: *I want to buy a little something to give to Val when I visit her in hospital.* **YOUNG** ▷ **3** **A1** young: *When you were little your hair was really curly.* ◦ *She was my little (= younger) sister and I looked after her.* ◦ *Her little boy (= her young son) isn't well.* **EMPHASIZE** ▷ **4** **B2** [before noun] used to emphasize an opinion that is being given about something or someone: *That was a nice little suit she was wearing.* ◦ *It's not a bad little restaurant, this, is it?* ◦ *He's a nasty little man.* **UNIMPORTANT** ▷ **5** **B1** [before noun] not very important or serious: *I had a little problem with my car, but it's been fixed now.* ◦ *It's often the little things that count the most.* ◦ *Can I have a little word (= a short discussion about something not very important) with you?*

IDIOMS **a little bird told me** said if you know who gave you the information being discussed but will not say who it was: *'How did you know he was leaving?' 'Oh, let's just say a little bird told me.'* • **make little of sth** to not consider something to be very important: *He made little of his ordeal.*

▸**determiner** **NOT ENOUGH** ▷ **1** **B1** not much or enough: *There seems little hope of a ceasefire.* ◦ *They*

> **! Common mistake: little or small?**
>
> **Remember:** use **little** when you want to express an attitude or feeling such as disapproval or affection:
>
> *He is a nasty, selfish little man.*
>
> *They have a sweet little dog.*
>
> To just refer to the size of something without expressing your feelings, use **small**:
>
> ~~*Their house is quite little.*~~
>
> *Their house is quite small.*

have very little money. ◦ *There's so little choice.* **SMALL AMOUNT** ▷ **2 a little** B1 a small amount of something: *This sauce needs a little salt.* ◦ *With a little training she could do very well.*

▸**pronoun, noun SMALL AMOUNT** ▷ **1** B1 [S] a small amount: *I could only hear a little of what they were saying.* ◦ *He does as little as possible at work.* ◦ *There's not much flour left but you're welcome to the/what little there is.* **NOT ENOUGH** ▷ **2** B1 an amount that is not much or not enough: *We did* ***very*** *little on Sunday.* ◦ *Very little of what he said made any sense to me.* ◦ *Unfortunately, little* ***of*** *the artist's work has survived.* ◦ *The government has* ***done*** *little or nothing to help the poorest people in this country.* ◦ *The little we do know about the people who lived here suggests they had a very sophisticated society.*

▸**adv SMALL AMOUNT** ▷ **1 a little (bit)** A2 slightly: *I was a little bit worried by what she said.* ◦ *We'll wait a little longer and then I'll phone them.* ◦ *There's only a little further to go.* **2 little by little** B2 slowly or gradually: *Little by little she came to understand why he had behaved the way he did.* **NOT MUCH** ▷ **3** C1 not much: *She slept very little that night.* ◦ *a little-known fact* ◦ *Little* ***did he know*** *what lay in store for him.* **4 little more/better** C2 not much more or better: *The wine they gave us was little better than vinegar.*

ˌlittle ˈfinger noun [C] the smallest finger on each hand

ˈLittle ˌLeague noun [C or U] an organization in the US that organizes children's baseball teams and games

ˈlittle ˌone noun [C] informal a young child: *The little ones can play in the garden while we get lunch ready.*

ˈlittle ˌpeople noun [plural] (also **little folk**) small imaginary creatures, such as LEPRECHAUNS, that look like small humans

ˌlittle ˈtoe noun [C] the smallest toe on each foot

liturgy /ˈlɪt.ə.dʒi/ US /ˈlɪt̬.ɚ-/ noun [C or U] (a particular set of) the words, music, and actions used in ceremonies in some religions, especially Christianity • **liturgical** /lɪˈtɜː.dʒɪ.kəl/ US /-ˈtɝː-/ adj

livable /ˈlɪv.ə.bl̩/ adj **PLACE** ▷ **1** (UK **liveable**) (also **livable in**) If a building or place is livable, it is suitable or good for living in: *It's not a luxurious apartment by any means but it's livable in.* ◦ *It was rated the most livable city in the States.* **LIFE** ▷ **2** (also **liveable**) able to be lived: *These are the basic requirements that make life livable.*

live verb; adj; adv

▸**verb** /lɪv/ **BE ALIVE** ▷ **1** B1 [I] (to continue) to be alive or have life: *He only lived a few days after the accident.* ◦ [+ to infinitive] *I hope I live to see my grandchildren.* ◦ *Her granny lived* ***to*** *the ripe old age of 94.* ◦ *Can the right to live ever be denied to any human?* ◦ *She lived* ***on*** *well into her 90s.* **HAVE A HOME** ▷ **2 live in, at, etc.** A1 to have your home somewhere: *Where do you live?* ◦ *We live in London.* ◦ *Some students live on the University campus.* ◦ *He lives with four other people in a shared house.* **3** [I] informal to be kept usually in a particular place: *Where do the knives live in your kitchen?* **SPEND LIFE** ▷ **4** B1 [I usually + adv/prep, T] to spend your life in a particular way: *After a while you get used to living alone.* ◦ *When you retire, you want to live a comfortable life.* ◦ *So the couple got married and lived* ***happily ever after.*** ◦ *He simply wants to live* ***(out)*** *(= experience) the rest of his days in peace.* ◦ *The TV's broken – we'll just have to live* ***without*** *(= not have) it for a while.* ◦ *She certainly lived her life* ***to the full*** *(= was always doing something interesting).* ◦ figurative *The US is living* ***beyond*** *its* ***means*** *(= spending more than it earns).* **STAY ALIVE** ▷ **5** C2 [I] to stay alive, especially by getting enough money to pay for food, a place to stay, clothing, etc.: *For several years she lived* ***by*** *begging.* ◦ *She has an inheritance to live* ***off*** (US also *live* ***off of***) *so she doesn't need to work.* ◦ *He only agreed to marry her so he could live* ***off*** *her (money).* **CONTINUE** ▷ **6** [I] (of things that are not alive) to exist or continue to exist: *The memory of those terrible days lives* ***on.*** **INTERESTING LIFE** ▷ **7** [I] to have an interesting life: *I want to live* ***a bit*** *before I settle down.* ◦ *If you haven't seen Venice, you haven't lived.*

IDIOMS **live (on) in the memory** If something lives (on) in the memory, it has such an effect that it is remembered for a long time. • **live a lie** to live in a way that is dishonest because you are pretending to be something that you are not, to yourself or to other people: *She doesn't know you're married? You have to stop living a lie and tell her.* • **live and breathe sth** When a person lives and breathes something, it is extremely important to them: *He lives and breathes music.* • **live and let live** said to mean that people should accept the way other people live and behave, especially if they do things in a different way • **live by your wits** to make money in a clever and usually dishonest way • **live in sin** humorous to live with someone that you are having a sexual relationship with but are not married to: *Last I heard, they'd moved in together and were living in sin.* • **live it up** informal to have an exciting and very enjoyable time with parties, good food and drink, etc.: *He's alive and well and living it up in the Bahamas.* • **live like a king/lord** to have a LUXURIOUS (= spending a lot of money) way of life • **live to fight another day** to have another chance to fight in a competition: *We didn't win this time, but we live to fight another day.* • **live to tell the tale** to successfully deal with or continue to live despite a difficult situation or experience: *We had a horrific journey, but we lived to tell the tale.* • **lived in** regularly used and comfortable: *I like a room to look lived in.* • **never live sth down** to be unable to stop feeling embarrassed about something you have done: *I wish I'd never opened my mouth in the meeting – I'm never going to live it down!* • **within living memory** If something has happened within living memory, it can be remembered by some people who are still alive: *There is possibly less chance of another world war while the last one is within living memory.* • **you live and learn** said when you hear or discover something that is surprising: *I had no idea they were related. Oh well, you live and learn.*

PHRASAL VERBS **live for sth/sb** B2 to have something or someone as the most important thing in your life: *She just lives for music.* • **live off sb/sth** to use someone or something to provide the money or food that you need to live: *All his life he had lived off his father.* ◦ *They had learned to live off* ***the land*** *(= grow or find their own food).* • **live on sth MONEY** ▷ **1** B2 If you live on an amount of money, that is the money that you use to buy the things that you need: *We lived on very little when we first got married.* **FOOD** ▷ **2** B2 to only eat a particular type of food: *I more or less live on pasta.* • **live through sth** C2 to experience a difficult situation or event: *He could never know the pain and fear this child had lived through.* • **live together** B2 If two people live together, they share a house and have a sexual relationship but are not married: *Nowadays many young people live together before they get married.* • **live up to sth** B2 to be as good as something: *The concert was brilliant – it lived up to all our expectations.* • **live with sb** B2 to share a home with someone and have a sexual relationship with them although you are not married • **live with sth** to accept a difficult or unpleasant situation: *I can't change the situation so I'm going to have to learn to live with it.*

▸adj /laɪv/ **HAVING LIFE** ▷ **1** [before noun] having life: *Millions of live animals are shipped around the world each year.* ◦ *There was a tank of live lobsters in the restaurant.* **AS IT HAPPENS** ▷ **2** B1 (of a performance) broadcast, recorded, or seen while it is happening: *This evening there will be a live broadcast of the debate.* ◦ *a live recording* **ELECTRICITY** ▷ **3** (of a wire) carrying or charged with electricity: *a live wire* **ABLE TO EXPLODE** ▷ **4** able to explode: *live rounds of ammunition* ◦ *live shells* **BURNING** ▷ **5** (of a fire, coals, or a match) still burning or able to burn

▸adv **1** broadcast as it happens or performing in front of an audience: *I've got two tickets to see them (**perform**) live.* **2 go live** If a new system, especially a computer system, goes live, it starts to operate: *Our new payments system will go live at the beginning of next month.*

liveable /ˈlɪv.ə.bl̩/ adj **livable**

ˈlive-in adj [before noun] **RELATIONSHIP** ▷ **1** describes someone's sexual partner who lives in their home but is not married to them: *a live-in lover* **WORK** ▷ **2** describes a person who lives in the home where they work: *a live-in housekeeper/nanny*

livelihood /ˈlaɪv.li.hʊd/ noun [C or U] (the way someone earns) the money people need to pay for food, a place to live, clothing, etc.: *Many ship workers could **lose** their livelihoods because of falling orders for new ships.* ◦ *That farm is his livelihood.* → See also **living**

lively /ˈlaɪv.li/ adj **1** B1 having or showing a lot of energy and enthusiasm, or showing interesting and exciting thought: *It's hard work teaching a class of lively children.* ◦ *a lively city* ◦ *They take a lively interest in their grandchildren.* ◦ *There was some lively discussion at the meeting.* **2** describes colours that are bright and strong: *The room was painted a lively electric blue.* • **liveliness** /-nəs/ noun [U]

liven /ˈlaɪ.vᵊn/ verb

PHRASAL VERBS **liven (sth) up** to become more interesting and exciting, or to make something become like this: *A new coat of paint would liven the kitchen up.* ◦ *Liven up your meals with fresh herbs and spices.* ◦ *The party livened up as soon as Sally arrived.* • **liven (sb) up** to become more energetic or in a better mood, or to make someone feel this way: *She was a bit subdued to start with, but after a while she livened up.* ◦ *I'm going to liven my**self** up a bit by going for a run.*

liver /ˈlɪv.əʳ/ US /-ɚ/ noun [C or U] B2 a large organ in the body which cleans the blood and produces BILE, or this organ from an animal used as meat

liverish /ˈlɪv.ᵊr.ɪʃ/ US /-ɚ-/ adj UK old-fashioned feeling ill, usually because of having drunk or eaten too much

Liverpudlian /ˌlɪv.əˈpʌd.li.ən/ US /-ɚ-/ noun [C] a person from Liverpool, a city in northwest England • **Liverpudlian** adj *a Liverpudlian accent*

ˈliver ˌsausage noun [C or U] (US usually **liverwurst**) a type of cooked sausage which contains liver and is usually eaten cold on bread

livery /ˈlɪv.ᵊr.i/ US /-ɚ-/ noun **1** [C or U] a special uniform worn by servants or particular officials **2** [U] UK a special pattern or design that is put on the things that a company owns and sells

lives /laɪvz/ plural of **life**

livestock /ˈlaɪv.stɒk/ US /-stɑːk/ noun [plural] animals, such as cows and sheep, and birds, such as chickens, kept on a farm

ˈlive ˌwire noun [C] someone who is very quick and active, both mentally and physically

livid /ˈlɪv.ɪd/ adj **ANGRY** ▷ **1** extremely angry: *He was livid when he found out.* **COLOUR** ▷ **2** (especially of marks on the skin) of an unpleasant purple or dark blue colour: *He had a long, livid scar across his cheek.*

living /ˈlɪv.ɪŋ/ adj; noun

▸adj **HAVING LIFE** ▷ **1** B2 alive now: *living organisms* ◦ *He is probably the best-known living architect.* **CONTINUING** ▷ **2** still existing: *The pyramids are a living monument to the skill of their builders.*

▸noun **MONEY** ▷ **1** B2 [C] the money that you earn from your job: *What do you **do for a** living? (= What is your job?)* ◦ *I mean, I don't like my job but at least it's a living (= a way of earning money).* ◦ *You can make a **good** living (= earn a lot of money) in sales if you have the right attitude.* → See also **livelihood** **2** [C] old-fashioned in the Church of England, the job, given to a priest, of being in charge of a particular area **WAY OF LIFE** ▷ **3** [U] the way in which you live your life: *country/healthy living* → See also **cost of living** **PEOPLE** ▷ **4 the living** [plural] people who are still alive: *On this anniversary of the tragedy we remember the living as well as the dead.*

ˌliving ˈdeath noun [S] a life that is so full of suffering that it would be better to be dead: *She can't walk or feed herself and she can barely speak – it's a living death.*

ˈliving ˌroom noun [C] (UK also **ˈsitting ˌroom**) A1 the room in a house or apartment that is used for relaxing and entertaining guests

ˈliving room ˌsuite noun [C] US for **three-piece suite**

ˌliving ˈwage noun [S] enough money to buy the things that are necessary in order to live, such as food and clothes

ˌliving ˈwill noun [C usually singular] a written document in which a person says what type of medical treatment they would like if they become so ill that they are certain to die and are unable to communicate their wishes about their treatment

lizard /ˈlɪz.əd/ US /-ɚd/ noun [C] a small reptile that has a long body, four short legs, a long tail, and thick skin

'll /ᵊl/ short form of will: *I'll see you next week.*

llama /ˈlɑː.mə/ noun [C] a large South American animal with a long neck and long hair, often kept for its meat, milk, or fur and to carry heavy LOADS

LLB /ˌel.elˈbiː/ noun [C] (US also **BL**) abbreviation for Bachelor of Laws: a degree in law, or a person who has this degree

lo /ləʊ/ US /loʊ/ exclamation old use look

IDIOM **lo and behold** humorous something that you say when you tell someone about something surprising

L

that happened: *I was in Vienna sitting quietly in a café when, lo and behold, my cousin walked in.*

load /ləʊd/ (US) /loʊd/ **noun; verb**
▸noun **AMOUNT CARRIED** ▷ **1** B2 [C] the amount of weight carried, especially by a vehicle, a structure such as a bridge, or an animal: *The maximum load for this elevator is eight persons.* ◦ *One truck involved in the accident was **carrying** a heavy load **of** coal.* **2 a load** (also **loads**) B1 a lot: *I've got a load **of** work to get through before tomorrow.* ◦ *There were a load **of** people there.* ◦ *Have some more food – there's loads.* ◦ *She looks loads better with her new haircut.* **3** [C] specialized the amount of electrical power that is supplied **AMOUNT TO DO** ▷ **4** [C] the amount of work to be done by a person: *If we share the organization of the party, that will help spread the load a bit.* ◦ *I've got a **heavy/light** teaching load this term.* → See also **caseload, workload** **5** [S] a painful, difficult, or TIRING situation to deal with: *I wish I could do something to **lighten** your load (= make your situation easier).*

IDIOMS **get a load of that!** slang used to tell someone to pay attention to a person or thing that is interesting, surprising, or attractive: *Get a load of that, lads! Very nice.* • **a load of crap, nonsense, rubbish, etc.** UK informal something that is not true, or something of very bad quality: *Who said they were cheaper – what a load of rubbish!* ◦ *He liked the second series and I thought it was a load of crap.*

L

▸verb **CARRY** ▷ **1** B2 [I or T] to put a lot of things into a vehicle or machine: *How long will it take to load this sand **onto** the lorry?* ◦ *Let's load **up** the car and then we can go.* ◦ *to load the dishwasher/washing machine* → See also **overload** → Opposite **unload** **2 be loaded down with sth** to have too much to carry, or too much work to do: *I was loaded down with shopping.* **3 be loaded with sth** to contain a lot of something: *Most fast foods are loaded with fat.* **PUT INTO** ▷ **4** [T] to put film in a camera or bullets in a gun: *Do not load the film (= put it into the camera) in bright light.* **COMPUTER** ▷ **5** B2 [I or T] to put information or a program onto a computer: *You need to load this program onto your computer.* ◦ *The software is easy to load.*

-load /-ləʊd/ (US) /-loʊd/ **suffix** all the people or goods in the stated type of vehicle or container: *a coachload of football fans* ◦ *Busloads **of** tourists pour into this place in the summer.* ◦ *Truckloads of food and medical supplies arrived in the refugee camp.*

loaded /ˈləʊ.dɪd/ (US) /ˈloʊ-/ **adj** **FULL** ▷ **1** a loaded gun has bullets in it: *It's dangerous to leave a loaded **gun** lying around.* **NOT FAIR** ▷ **2** not fair, especially by being helpful to one person instead of another: *It seems that the report is loaded in favour of the developers.* **3 loaded question** a question that has particular words chosen to suggest the answer that is wanted: *A survey should avoid asking loaded questions.* → See also **leading question** **RICH** ▷ **4** [after verb] informal rich: *He inherited the family business – he must be loaded!* **DRUNK** ▷ **5** [after verb] mainly US slang drunk: *What a party – everyone was loaded!*

ˈ**loading** ˌ**bay** noun [C] UK (US ˈ**loading** ˌ**dock**) a space at the back of a ship where goods are put on or taken away

loaf /ləʊf/ (US) /loʊf/ **noun; verb**
▸noun (plural **loaves**) **BREAD** ▷ **1** B2 [C] bread that is shaped and baked in a single piece and can be sliced for eating: *two loaves of white bread* **FOOD** ▷ **2** [C or U] a dish made of meat or vegetables cut into small pieces then pressed together and cooked in a single solid piece: ***meat/nut** loaf*

IDIOM **use your loaf** UK old-fashioned used to tell someone in a slightly angry way that they should think more carefully about what they are doing

▸verb [I] informal to avoid activity, especially work: *Stop loafing (**about/around**) and get on with cleaning the windows!*

loafer /ˈləʊ.fər/ (US) /ˈloʊ.fɚ/ **noun** [C] **SHOE** ▷ **1** trademark a type of leather shoe with a wide strip across the top, which a person's foot slides into, without any way of fastening it to the foot **LAZY PERSON** ▷ **2** someone who avoids doing any work: *an idle loafer*

loam /ləʊm/ (US) /loʊm/ **noun** [U] high-quality earth that is a mixture of sand, clay, and decaying plant material • **loamy** /ˈləʊ.mi/ (US) /ˈloʊ.mi/ **adj**

loan /ləʊn/ (US) /loʊn/ **noun; verb**
▸noun **SUM** ▷ **1** B1 [C] an amount of money that is borrowed, often from a bank, and has to be paid back, usually together with an extra amount of money that you have to pay as a charge for borrowing: *She's trying to **get** a $50,000 loan to start her own business.* ◦ *We could **apply for/take out** a loan to buy a car.* **BORROW** ▷ **2** C1 [C or U] an act of borrowing or lending something: *Thank you very much for the loan **of** your bike.* ◦ *This exhibit is **on** loan (= being borrowed/lent) **from/to** another museum.*
▸verb [T] to lend: *This library loans books and CDs.* ◦ [+ two objects] *I'd loan you the money if I could./I'd loan the money **to** you if I could.*

ˈ**loan** ˌ**shark** noun [C] informal disapproving a person who charges very large amounts of money for lending money to someone

loanword /ˈləʊn.wɜːd/ (US) /ˈloʊn.wɝːd/ **noun** [C] a word taken from one language and used in another

loath (also **loth**) /ləʊθ/ (US) /loʊθ/ **adj** formal **be loath to do sth** to be unwilling to do something: *I'm loath to spend it all at once.*

loathe /ləʊð/ (US) /loʊð/ **verb** [T] C2 to hate someone or something: *From an early age the brothers have loathed each other.* ◦ [+ -ing verb] *I loathe **doing** housework.*

loathing /ˈləʊ.ðɪŋ/ (US) /ˈloʊ.ðɪŋ/ **noun** [S or U] formal C2 a strong feeling of hating someone or something: *The thought of him touching her filled her with deep loathing.* ◦ *He approached his rival with **fear and** loathing.*

loathsome /ˈləʊð.səm/ (US) /ˈloʊð-/ **adj** extremely unpleasant: *He's a loathsome man.* • **loathsomeness** /-nəs/ **noun** [U]

loaves /ləʊvz/ (US) /loʊvz/ plural of **loaf**

lob /lɒb/ (US) /lɑːb/ **verb; noun**
▸verb [T] (**-bb-**) to kick, hit, or throw something, especially a ball in a game, in a high curve: *Police started lobbing (= throwing) tear gas canisters **into** the crowd.*
▸noun [C] a high, curving hit of a ball: *Jones hit a beautiful lob over his opponent's head.*

lobby /ˈlɒb.i/ (US) /ˈlɑː.bi/ **verb; noun**
▸verb [I or T] C2 to try to persuade a politician, the government, or an official group that a particular thing should or should not happen, or that a law should be changed: *Small businesses have lobbied hard **for/against** changes in the tax laws.* ◦ [+ to infinitive] *Local residents lobbied **to** have the factory shut down.* ◦ [+ obj + to infinitive] *They have been lobbying Congress **to** change the legislation concerning guns.*
▸noun [C] **PRESSURE GROUP** ▷ **1** a group of people who try to persuade the government or an official group to do something: *the anti-smoking lobby* **ROOM** ▷ **2** B2

the (large) room into which the main entrance door opens in a hotel or other large building **3** in the British parliament, a room where someone meets a member of parliament who they have arranged to talk to, or one of the two passages which members of parliament walk through as a way of voting

lobbyist /ˈlɒb.i.ɪst/ (US) /ˈlɑː.bi-/ noun [C] someone who tries to persuade a politician or official group to do something: *Lobbyists for the tobacco industry have expressed concerns about the restriction of smoking in public places.*

lobe /ləʊb/ (US) /loʊb/ noun [C] **ORGAN** ▷ **1** specialized any part of an organ which seems to be separate in some way from the rest, especially one of the parts of the brain, lung, or LIVER **EAR** ▷ **2** an **earlobe** • **lobed** /ləʊbd/ (US) /loʊbd/ adj

lobotomy /ləˈbɒt.ə.mi/ (US) /-ˈbɑː.t̬ə-/ noun [C] (UK also **leucotomy**) a medical operation in which cuts are made in or near the front part of the brain, used in the past for the treatment of severe mental problems

lobster /ˈlɒb.stəʳ/ (US) /ˈlɑːb.stɚ/ noun [C or U] an animal which lives in the sea and has a long body covered with a hard shell, two large CLAWS, and eight legs, or its flesh when used as food

ˈlobster ˌpot noun [C] a type of box made of wire used for catching lobsters

local /ˈləʊ.kəl/ (US) /ˈloʊ-/ adj; noun

▸adj **1** (B1) from, existing in, serving, or responsible for a small area, especially of a country: *a local accent* ◦ *local issues* ◦ *a local newspaper/radio station* ◦ *Most of the local population depend on fishing for their income.* ◦ *Our children all go to the local school.* ◦ *Many local shops will be forced to close if the new supermarket is built.* **2** limited to a particular part of the body: *a local anaesthetic* ◦ *local swelling*

▸noun [C] **PERSON** ▷ **1** (C2) a person who lives in the particular small area which you are talking about: *The café is popular with both locals and visitors.* **PUB** ▷ **2** UK a pub near to where a person lives, especially if they often go there to drink: *The George is my local.* **VEHICLE** ▷ **3** US a train or bus which stops at all or most of the places on its route where passengers can get on or off: *the 12.24 local to Poughkeepsie* **ORGANIZATION** ▷ **4** US a division within an organization, especially a national workers' organization, representing people from a particular area

ˌlocal auˈthority noun [C, + sing/pl verb] UK the group of people who govern an area, especially a city

ˌlocal ˈcolour noun [U] the special or unusual features of a place, especially as described or shown in a story, picture, or film to make it seem more real

ˌlocal ˈderby noun [C] (also **derby**) UK a sports competition, especially a game of football, between two teams from the same city or area

locale /ləˈkɑːl/ noun [C] formal an area or place, especially one where something special happens, such as the action in a book or a film: *The book's locale is a seaside town in the summer of 1958.*

ˌlocal ˈgovernment noun [U] the control and organization of towns and small areas by people who are elected from them

locality /ləˈkæl.ə.ti/ (US) /loʊˈkæl.ə.t̬i/ noun [C] a particular area: *In 19th-century Britain, industries became concentrated in particular localities.*

localize (UK usually **localise**) /ˈləʊ.kəl.aɪz/ (US) /ˈloʊ-/ verb [T] **1** to limit something to a particular area: *Gravity has localized the swelling to the foot and ankle.* **2** formal to find the position of something: *Electricians worked through the night to localize the faulty switches.* **3** specialized to make a product or service more suitable for a particular area: *The TV station is continuing to localize content in order to maximize regional sales.*

localized (UK usually **localised**) /ˈləʊ.kəl.aɪzd/ (US) /ˈloʊ-/ adj happening in or limited to a particular area: *localized flooding*

locally /ˈləʊ.kəl.i/ (US) /ˈloʊ-/ adv in the particular small area which you are talking about: *The shopkeeper said all his fruit and vegetables are grown locally.* ◦ *Do they live locally?*

ˈlocal ˌtime noun [U] the official time in a country or an area

locate /ləʊˈkeɪt/ (US) /loʊ-/ verb **BE SITUATED** ▷ **1 be located in, near, on, etc.** (B1) to be in a particular place: *Our office is located in the city centre.* **FIND** ▷ **2** (B2) [T] to find or discover the exact position of something: *Police are still trying to locate the suspect.* **MOVE** ▷ **3** [I + adv/prep] US to move to a place to do business: *The company hopes to locate **in** its new offices by June.*

location /ləʊˈkeɪ.ʃən/ (US) /loʊ-/ noun **POSITION** ▷ **1** (B1) [C] a place or position: *The hotel is **in** a lovely location overlooking the lake.* ◦ *A map showing the location **of** the property will be sent to you.* **FILM** ▷ **2** (C1) [C or U] a place away from a STUDIO where all or part of a film or a television show is recorded: *The documentary was made **on** location in the Gobi desert.* **FINDING** ▷ **3** [U] formal the act of finding the exact position of something: *The latest navigational aids make the location of the airfield quite easy.*

locative /ˈlɒk.ə.tɪv/ (US) /ˈlɑː.kə.t̬ɪv/ noun [C or U] specialized (in some languages) the form of a noun, PRONOUN, or adjective that expresses the place where someone or something is • **locative** adj

loch /lɒk/ (US) /lɑːk/ noun [C] (plural **lochs**) in Scotland, a lake or INLET of the sea: *Loch Lomond*

loci /ˈləʊ.saɪ/ (US) /ˈloʊ-/ plural of **locus**

lock /lɒk/ (US) /lɑːk/ noun; verb

▸noun **FASTENER** ▷ **1** (B1) [C] a device that prevents something such as a door from being opened and can only be opened with a key: *I heard someone turn a key **in** the lock.* ◦ *safety locks* ◦ *Thieves got in by smashing the lock off the door.* → See also **padlock** **WATER** ▷ **2** [C] a length of water with gates at each end where the level of water can be changed to allow boats to move between parts of a CANAL or river that are at different heights **DEFINITE EVENT** ▷ **3** [C] US informal something that is certain to happen: *She's a lock **for** promotion this year.* **HAIR** ▷ **4** [C] a small group of hairs, especially a CURL: *There is a lock of Napoleon's hair in the display cabinet.* **5 locks** [plural] literary the hair on someone's head: *curly locks* ◦ *flowing golden locks* **WHEELS** ▷ **6** [U] UK the amount a road vehicle's front wheels can be turned from one side to the other by turning its STEERING WHEEL: *You need it **on full** lock (= with the wheel turned as much as possible).* **HOLD** ▷ **7** [C] a way of holding someone that you are fighting against so that they cannot move

IDIOMS **lock, stock, and barrel** including all or every part of something • **under lock and key 1** locked away safely: *Her jewellery is securely under lock and key at the bank.* **2** If a person, especially a criminal, is under lock and key, they are being kept in a place from which they cannot escape, usually a prison.

▸verb **MAKE SAFE** ▷ **1** (B2) [T usually + adv/prep] to put something in a safe place and fasten the lock: *He locked the confidential documents **in** his filing cabinet.* ◦ *You really should lock your car (**up**) or it'll get stolen.* **2** (B1) [I or T] to fasten something with a key, or be

L

fastened with a key: *Don't forget to lock the door when you go out.* ◦ *If you shut the door it will lock automatically.* **BECOME FIXED** ▷ **3** [I] to become fixed in one position: *I tried to move forwards but the wheels had locked.*

IDIOMS **be locked together** If people or animals are locked together, they are holding each other tightly so that neither one can move: *Sometimes, fighting stags become locked together by their antlers.* • **lock horns** to begin to argue or fight: *The mayor and her deputy locked horns **over** plans for the new road.*

PHRASAL VERBS **lock sth away** (B2) to put something in a safe place and lock the door in order that someone else cannot get it: *If you keep valuables in your house, lock them away somewhere safe.* • **lock in sth** to get and keep an advantage such as a low price: *People are jumping to purchase homes and lock in affordable mortgage rates before they increase.* • **lock sb in 1** (B2) to prevent someone from leaving a room or building by locking the door: *She stormed off to her bedroom and locked her**self** in.* ◦ *He was locked in his bedroom as a punishment.* **2** to prevent someone from ending or changing a financial arrangement: *Most phone contracts lock you in for a fixed period.* → See also **lock-in** • **be locked in sth 1** to be prevented from moving by something: *We were locked in traffic for over two hours on the way home.* **2** If you are locked in a situation or process, it is impossible for you to escape or make progress from it: *Both parties wish to avoid being locked in discussions that will resolve nothing.* • **lock sb into sth** to prevent a person or organization from ending or changing an agreement or financial arrangement: *The gas company is locked into long-term supply contracts.* • **lock sb out** **STOP ENTERING** ▷ **1** (B2) to prevent someone from entering a building or room by locking the door: *He had to break into the house because his girlfriend had locked him out.* **STOP WORKING** ▷ **2** usually disapproving to prevent workers from entering their place of work until they agree to particular conditions given by the employer: *Management has threatened to lock out the workforce if they do not accept the proposed changes in working methods.* • **lock sb out of sth** to prevent a person or organization from having or being able to take part in something: *The company risks being locked out of China's booming car market.* • **lock (sth) up** to lock all the doors and windows of a building when you leave it: *Sandra, will you lock up tonight when you go?* • **lock sb up** to put someone in a prison or a hospital for people who are mentally ill: *Murderers should be locked up for life.* ◦ *After what she did, they should lock her up **and throw away the key*** (= *lock her up until she dies*). → See also **lockup**

lockable /ˈlɒk.ə.bl̩/ (US) /lɑː.kə-/ **adj** that can be locked: *All our suitcases are lockable* (= *can be locked*).

locker /ˈlɒk.əʳ/ (US) /ˈlɑː.kɚ/ **noun** [C] a cupboard, often tall and made of metal, in which someone can keep their possessions, and leave them for a period of time: *We had several hours to wait for our train, so we left our bags in a* (***luggage***) *locker, and went to look around the town.*

locker

ˈlocker ˌroom **noun** [C usually singular] a room with lockers where people can keep clothes and other things, especially while doing sport

ˈlocker-room **adj** [before noun] describes the type of sexual jokes and remarks that men are thought to enjoy when they are together: *locker-room talk/jokes*

locket /ˈlɒk.ɪt/ (US) /ˈlɑː.kɪt/ **noun** [C] a small piece of jewellery which opens to show a small picture or piece of hair, usually worn on a chain around a person's neck

ˈlock-in **noun** [C] **FINANCIAL ARRANGEMENT** ▷ **1** a length of time during which you are not allowed to end or change a financial arrangement: *Your new mortgage may have a long lock-in **period**, particularly if you go for a fixed rate.* **PUB** ▷ **2** UK informal an occasion when a pub locks its doors and allows people to continue drinking illegally after the time when it should have closed: *There was a lock-in at my local last night.*

lockjaw /ˈlɒk.dʒɔː/ (US) /ˈlɑːk.dʒɑː/ **noun** [U] informal for **tetanus**

ˈlock-ˌkeeper **noun** [C] a person who controls a LOCK (= a body of water with gates) by opening or closing its gates

lockout /ˈlɒk.aʊt/ (US) /ˈlɑːk-/ **noun** [C or U] usually disapproving an occasion when an employer prevents workers from entering their place of work until they agree to particular conditions: *The General Strike in Britain in 1926 was caused by the lockout **of** coal miners.*

locksmith /ˈlɒk.smɪθ/ (US) /ˈlɑːk-/ **noun** [C] a person who repairs and/or makes locks and supplies keys

ˈlock-up **noun** [C] **1** a small room, used as a prison, usually in a small town, in which criminals can be kept for a short time **2** mainly UK a building where objects, especially a car, can be safely kept

loco /ˈləʊ.kəʊ/ (US) /ˈloʊ.koʊ/ **adj; noun**
▸**adj** [after verb] mainly US slang crazy: *Man, he just **went** loco and smashed the place up.*
▸**noun** [C] (plural **locos**) UK informal for **locomotive**

locomotion /ˌləʊ.kəˈməʊ.ʃᵊn/ (US) /ˌloʊ.kəˈmoʊ-/ **noun** [U] specialized the ability to move → Synonym **movement**

locomotive /ˌləʊ.kəˈməʊ.tɪv/ (US) /ˌloʊ.kəˈmoʊ.t̬ɪv/ **noun; adj**
▸**noun** [C] (UK informal **loco**) the engine of a train
▸**adj** relating to movement or the ability to move

locum /ˈləʊ.kəm/ (US) /ˈloʊ-/ **noun** [C] mainly UK a doctor who does the job of another doctor who is ill or on holiday

locus /ˈləʊ.kəs/ (US) /ˈloʊ.kəs/ **noun** [C] (plural **loci**) formal the place where something happens or the central area of interest in something being discussed: *The locus **of** decision-making is sometimes far from the government's offices.*

locust /ˈləʊ.kəst/ (US) /ˈloʊ-/ **noun** [C] a large insect found in hot areas which flies in large groups and destroys plants and crops: *a **swarm** of locusts*

lode /ləʊd/ (US) /loʊd/ **noun** [C] an amount of metal in its natural form

lodestar /ˈləʊd.stɑːʳ/ (US) /ˈloʊd.stɑːr/ **noun** [S] **1** a star, especially the POLE STAR, used to help find direction **2** literary an example or principle that people want to follow: *The party manifesto is no longer the lodestar it used to be.*

lodestone /ˈləʊd.stəʊn/ (US) /ˈloʊd.stoʊn/ **noun** [C or U] (a piece of) rock which contains a lot of iron and can therefore be used as a MAGNET (= an object that pulls metal objects towards it)

lodge /lɒdʒ/ (US) /lɑːdʒ/ verb; noun

▸verb **STAY** ▷ **1** [I usually + adv/prep] formal to pay rent to stay somewhere: *She lodged **with** Mrs Higgins when she first came to Cambridge.* **FIX** ▷ **2** [I or T, usually + adv/prep] to (cause to) become fixed in a place or position: *A fish bone had lodged **in** her throat.* **COMPLAIN** ▷ **3 lodge a claim, complaint, protest, etc.** to make an official complaint about something: *The US lodged a formal protest against the arrest of the foreign reporters.* ◦ *Lee's solicitor said that they would be lodging an appeal against the sentence.* **STORE** ▷ **4** [T usually + adv/prep] mainly UK formal to put something in a safe place: *You should lodge a copy of the letter **with** your solicitor.*

▸noun **SMALL BUILDING** ▷ **1** [C] a small house in the country used especially by people on holiday or taking part in sports, or one on land belonging to a large house: *a ski/hunting lodge* **2** [C] the place where a BEAVER lives **3** [C] US a **wigwam** **GROUP** ▷ **4** [C, + sing/pl verb] a local group of an organization such as the FREEMASONS: *a Masonic Lodge* **ROOM** ▷ **5** [C] UK the room used by a person whose job is to be at the entrance to a large building such as a hotel or college in order to help people: *the porter's lodge*

lodger /ˈlɒdʒ.əʳ/ (US) /ˈlɑː.dʒɚ/ noun [C] (US also **roomer**) someone who pays for a place to sleep, and usually for meals, in someone else's house: *She **takes in** lodgers to make a bit of extra money.*

lodging /ˈlɒdʒ.ɪŋ/ (US) /ˈlɑː.dʒɪŋ/ noun [U] **1** a temporary place to stay: *The price includes **board and** lodging (= meals and a room to sleep in).* **2 lodgings** [plural] (UK informal also **digs**) a room in someone's house that you pay money to live in

ˈlodging ˌhouse noun [C] (US also **ˈrooming ˌhouse**) a house with rooms that people can rent

loess /ˈləʊ.es/ (US) /ˈloʊ-/ noun [U] specialized a type of light brown or greyish soil, consisting of very small pieces of QUARTZ and clay, that is blown and left behind by the wind

loft /lɒft/ (US) /lɑːft/ noun; verb

▸noun [C] **1** (C2) a space at the top of a building under the roof used for storing things and usually entered by a LADDER, or sometimes made into a room: *The firm specializes in loft **conversions** (= making lofts into rooms).* **2** US an upper floor or room **3** an apartment in a large building that was previously used for industry

▸verb [T] to hit a ball high

lofty /ˈlɒf.ti/ (US) /ˈlɑː.f-/ adj **POSITION** ▷ **1** formal high: *a lofty ceiling/mountain/wall* **IDEAS** ▷ **2** formal Lofty ideas, etc. are of a high moral standard: *lofty sentiments/ideals* **3** disapproving If you have a lofty way of behaving or talking, etc., you act as if you think you are better than other people: *a lofty attitude/air/tone* • **loftily** /-tɪ.li/ adv disapproving • **loftiness** /-nəs/ noun [U]

log /lɒg/ (US) /lɑːg/ noun; verb

▸noun [C] **WOOD** ▷ **1** (C1) a thick piece of tree TRUNK or branch, especially one cut for burning on a fire **RECORD** ▷ **2** a full written record of a journey, a period of time, or an event: *the ship's log* **NUMBER** ▷ **3** informal for **logarithm**

▸verb (**-gg-**) **CUT WOOD** ▷ **1** [I or T] to cut down trees so that you can use their wood: *The forest has been so heavily logged that it is in danger of disappearing.* **RECORD** ▷ **2** [T] to officially record something: *The Police Complaints Authority has logged more than 90 complaints.* **3** [T] (UK also **log up**) to travel and record a particular distance

PHRASAL VERBS **log in/on** (B2) to connect a computer to a computer system by typing your name, so that you can start working: *Log on using your name and password.* • **log off/out** (B2) to stop a computer being connected to a computer system, usually when you want to stop working

loganberry /ˈləʊ.gᵊnˌbᵊr.i/ (US) /ˈloʊ.gənˌber-/ noun [C] a small, red fruit, similar to a RASPBERRY, or the tall plant on which it grows

logarithm /ˈlɒg.ə.rɪ.ðᵊm/ (US) /ˈlɑː.gə-/ noun [C] (informal **log**) the number which shows how many times a number, called the BASE, has to be multiplied by itself to produce another number. Adding or taking away logarithms can replace multiplying or dividing large numbers. • **logarithmic** /ˌlɒg.ᵊrˈɪð.mɪk/ (US) /ˌlɑː.gəˈrɪð-/ adj • **logarithmically** /ˌlɒg.ᵊrˈɪð.mɪ.kᵊl.i/ (US) /ˌlɑː.gəˈrɪð-/ adv

logbook /ˈlɒg.bʊk/ (US) /ˈlɑːg-/ noun [C] (also **regiˈstration ˌbook**) UK an official document that records information about a car and the people who have owned it

ˌlog ˈcabin noun [C] a small house made from tree TRUNKS

logger /ˈlɒg.əʳ/ (US) /ˈlɑː.gɚ/ noun [C] a person who cuts down trees for wood

loggerheads /ˈlɒg.ə.hedz/ (US) /ˈlɑː.gɚ-/ noun [plural] **be at loggerheads (with sb)** to strongly disagree (with someone): *The Chancellor is at loggerheads with the prime minister **over** public spending.*

logging /ˈlɒg.ɪŋ/ (US) /ˈlɑː.gɪŋ/ noun [U] the activity of cutting down trees for wood: *logging companies*

logic /ˈlɒdʒ.ɪk/ (US) /ˈlɑː.dʒɪk/ noun [U] **REASONABLE THINKING** ▷ **1** (C1) a particular way of thinking, especially one that is reasonable and based on good judgment: *I fail to see the logic behind his argument.* ◦ *If prices go up, wages will go up too – that's just logic.* ◦ *There's no logic in the decision to reduce staff when orders are the highest for years.* ◦ *The **internal** logic of her argument is undeniable.* **FORMAL THINKING** ▷ **2** a formal scientific method of examining or thinking about ideas: *a treatise on formal logic*

logical /ˈlɒdʒ.ɪ.kᵊl/ (US) /ˈlɑː.dʒɪ-/ adj (B2) using reason: *a logical choice/conclusion* ◦ *Students need the ability to construct a logical argument.* ◦ *It was the logical thing to do (= the decision was a reasonable one when all the facts were considered).* → Opposite **illogical** • **logically** /-i/ adv (C2) *Her ideas were clear and logically presented.*

logician /ləˈdʒɪʃ.ᵊn/ (US) /loʊˈdʒɪ-/ noun [C] someone who studies or is skilled in logic

login /ˈlɒg.ɪn/ (US) /ˈlɑːg-/ noun [C] specialized 'Login' often appears in an on-screen key that you CLICK (= press) with your mouse as part of the process to start using a computer that is connected to a computer system. → See also **log in/on**

logistics /ləˈdʒɪs.tɪks/ noun [plural] the careful organization of a complicated activity so that it happens in a successful and effective way: *We need to look at the logistics **of** the whole aid operation.* • **logistic** /-tɪk/ adj (also **logistical**) *logistic support/problems* • **logistically** /-tɪ.kᵊl.i/ adv

logjam /ˈlɒg.dʒæm/ (US) /ˈlɑːg-/ noun **1** [C usually singular] a situation in which neither group involved in an argument can win or get an advantage and no action can be taken: *This is the latest attempt to **break** the logjam in the peace process.* **2** [C] a mass of floating logs that block a river

logo /ˈləʊ.gəʊ/ (US) /ˈloʊ.goʊ/ noun [C] (plural **logos**) (B1) a design or symbol used by a company to advertise its products: *a corporate logo* ◦ *The players wore shirts with the sponsor's logo.*

loin /lɔɪn/ noun **1** [C or U] (a piece of) meat from the back of an animal near the tail or from the top part of the back legs → See also **sirloin (steak)** **2 loins** [plural] literary or humorous the part of the body that is above the legs and below the waist, especially the sexual organs: ***the fruit of*** *your loins* (= your child/children)

loincloth /ˈlɔɪn.klɒθ/ (US) /-klɑːθ/ **noun** [C] a piece of cloth that hangs down from around the waist, sometimes worn by men in hot countries

loiter /ˈlɔɪ.təʳ/ (US) /-t̬ɚ/ **verb** [I] **1** to move slowly around or stand especially in a public place without an obvious reason: *A gang of youths were loitering outside the cinema.* **2** to go slowly, stopping often: *Come straight home and don't loiter, Alan.* • **loiterer** /-əʳ/ (US) /-ɚ/ **noun** [C]

loitering /ˈlɔɪ.tᵊr.ɪŋ/ (US) /-t̬ɚ-/ **noun** [U] (US **ˌloitering with inˈtent**) the offence of waiting in a place, looking as if you are going to do something illegal

lol written abbreviation for laughing out loud: used, for example in emails and text messages, when you think something is very funny

Lolita /lɒlˈiː.tə/, /ləˈliː-/ (US) /loʊˈliː.t̬ə/ **noun** [C] a young girl who has a very sexual appearance or behaves in a very sexual way

loll /lɒl/ (US) /lɑːl/ **verb** [I usually + adv/prep] to lie, sit, or hang down in a relaxed, informal, or uncontrolled way: *I spent most of the weekend lolling* ***about/around*** *on the beach.* ◦ *a dog with its tongue lolling* ***out***

lollipop /ˈlɒl.i.pɒp/ (US) /ˈlɑː.li.pɑːp/ **noun** [C] a hard sweet on a stick

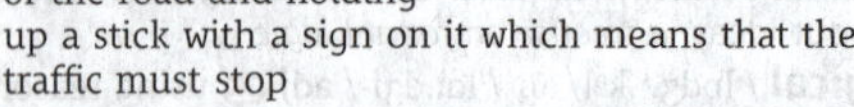
lollipop

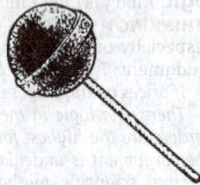

ˈlollipop ˌman/ˌlady **noun** [C] UK informal a person who helps children to cross the road near a school by standing in the middle of the road and holding up a stick with a sign on it which means that the traffic must stop

lollop /ˈlɒl.əp/ (US) /ˈlɑː.ləp/ **verb** [I usually + adv/prep] informal (of a person or especially a large animal) to move in an awkward, rolling way: *The dog lolloped along the beach.*

lolly /ˈlɒl.i/ (US) /ˈlɑː.li/ **noun** **SWEET** ▷ **1** [C] UK an **ice lolly** or a **lollipop** **2** [C] Australian English a wrapped sweet for sucking or CHEWING (= crushing with the teeth) **MONEY** ▷ **3** [U] UK old-fashioned slang for **money**

lone /ləʊn/ (US) /loʊn/ **adj** [before noun] **1** alone: *a lone survivor* ◦ *He was a lone* ***voice*** *(= the only person) arguing against a reduction in resources.* **2 lone parent/mother/father** someone who has children but no partner living with them

loneliness /ˈləʊn.li.nəs/ (US) /ˈloʊn-/ **noun** [U] C1 the state of being lonely

lonely /ˈləʊn.li/ (US) /ˈloʊn-/ **adj** **1** B1 unhappy because you are not with other people: *She gets lonely now that all the kids have left home.* ◦ *the lonely life of a farmer* **2** B2 A lonely place is a long way from where people live: *a lonely stretch of Arizona highway*

IDIOM **lonely hearts** (also **lonely hearts club/column, etc.**) a place or part of a magazine, etc. for people who would like to make new friends or meet a sexual partner

loner /ˈləʊ.nəʳ/ (US) /ˈloʊ.nɚ/ **noun** [C] a person who likes to do things on their own without other people: *He was always a bit of a loner at school.*

lonesome /ˈləʊn.səm/ (US) /ˈloʊn-/ **adj** US **1** → **lonely** **2 by/on your lonesome** alone: *I was just sitting here all by my lonesome.*

ˌlone ˈwolf **noun** [C usually singular] a **loner**

long /lɒŋ/ (US) /lɑːŋ/ **adj; adv; verb**

▸**adj** **TIME** ▷ **1** A1 continuing for a large amount of time: *a long film/meeting* ◦ *I've been waiting a long* ***time.*** ◦ *It's a long time since I worked there.* ◦ *Apparently the sessions are an hour long.*

> **! Common mistake: a long time**
>
> To talk about something continuing for a large amount of time, don't say 'long time', say **a long time**:
>
> ~~*I had to wait long time for the bus.*~~
>
> *I had to wait a long time for the bus.*

DISTANCE ▷ **2** A1 being a distance between two points that is more than average or usual: *long hair* ◦ *long legs* ◦ *a long dress* ◦ *There was a long queue at the post office.* ◦ *We're still a long way from the station.* **MANY WORDS** ▷ **3** A2 describes a piece of writing that has a lot of pages or words: *a long letter/book/report*

IDIOMS **be long in the tooth** informal to be old, often too old to do something: *He's a bit long in the tooth to be wearing jeans, don't you think?* • **before (very/too) long** (also **before much longer**) B2 soon: *They'll be home before very long.* • **go a long way** (also **go far**) If you say that someone will go a long way, you mean that they will be very successful. • **go a long way towards doing sth** to be very helpful: *The money raised will go a long way towards providing essential food and medicine.* • **go back a long way** If people go back a long way, they have known each other for a long time. • **have come a long way** to have advanced to an improved or more developed state: *Information technology has come a long way in the last 20 years.* • **it's a long story** something that you say when someone has asked you about something that has happened and you do not want to explain it to them because it would take too long: *'So why was Carlo knocking on your door at midnight?' 'It's a long story.'* • **the long arm of the law** literary the police: *You can't escape the long arm of the law (= the police will catch you if you have done something illegal).* • **(as) long as your arm** informal very long: *There was a list of complaints as long as your arm.* • **a long face** If you have a long face, you look sad: *'Why've you got such a long face?' 'My boyfriend doesn't want to see me any more.'* • **long live sb/sth!** said to show support for the person or thing mentioned: *Long live the president!* • **long on sth and short on sth** having too much of one quality and not enough of another: *I've always found his films long on style and short on content.* • **long story short** US C1 used when you do not tell all the details: *Long story short, I got fired.* • **long time no see** said when you meet someone who you haven't seen for a long period of time • **a long way to go** a lot of work to do or improvements to make: *He has a long way to go before he can present the scheme to the public.* • **no longer** (also **not any longer**) B1 in the past but not now: *The cinema is no longer used.* ◦ *She doesn't work here any longer.* • **not by a long chalk/shot** informal not in any way: *It wasn't as good as his first book – not by a long chalk.* • **not long for this world** old-fashioned If someone is not long for this world, they will die soon. • **so long** informal goodbye • **take a long, hard look at sth** to examine something very carefully in order to improve it in the future: *We need to take a long, hard look at the way we control gun ownership.* • **take the long view** to think about the effects that something will have in the future instead of in the present: *If you take the long* *view, of course, you can regard staff training as an investment for the company.*

▸adv **TIME** ▷ **1** A2 used to mean '(for) a long time', especially in questions and negative sentences: *Have you been waiting (**for**) long?* ◦ *I'm just writing a letter but it won't take long.* ◦ *How long have you been in England?* ◦ *Don't rush – take as long as you like.* ◦ *We've been walking all day long.* ◦ *I've known her longer than you have.* ◦ *I won't be staying much longer.* **2** C2 a long period of time before or after something: *She left the house long **before** I arrived.* ◦ *It wasn't long before he was back with his family.* ◦ *He did not join them until long **after** they had eaten.* **3** used with the past participle or the -ing form of the verb to mean that a state or activity has continued for a long time: *a long-awaited letter* ◦ *long-serving employees* **IF** ▷ **4 as/so long as** B1 used to say that something must happen before something else can happen: *I can come as long as I can leave by 4.00.* ◦ *Bring your friends by all means – just so long as I know how many are coming.*

▸verb formal **long for sth; long to do sth** C2 to want something very much: *She longed to see him again.* ◦ *I'm longing for news of him.*

IDIOM **the long and the short of it** informal said when you want to explain the general situation without giving details: *The long and the short of it is that they are willing to start the work in January.*

ˌlong-aˈwaited adj having been expected for a long time: *Last week the commission published its long-awaited report on the problem of teenage pregnancies.*

ˌlong-ˈdistance adj [before noun], adv B2 travelling a long way, or separated by a long distance: *a long-distance runner* ◦ *a long-distance phone call*

ˌlong diˈvision noun [C usually singular] in mathematics, a method of dividing one usually large number by another, which makes it necessary to write down each stage of the work

ˌlong-drawn-ˈout adj taking more time than is necessary: *a long-drawn-out process*

ˌlong ˈdrink noun [C] a cold drink served in a tall glass, often mixed with alcohol → Compare **short**

longevity /lɒnˈdʒev.ə.ti/ US /lɑːnˈdʒev.ə.t̬i/ noun [U] formal **1** C2 living for a long time: *To what do you attribute your longevity?* **2** remaining popular or useful for a long time: *For longevity in car design, you really need to keep it simple.*

ˌlong-grain ˈrice noun [U] a type of rice with long, thin seeds: *Indian curries are normally served with bread or long-grain rice.*

longhand /ˈlɒŋ.hænd/ US /ˈlɑːŋ-/ noun [U] ordinary writing by hand

ˈlong-haul adj [before noun] travelling a long distance: *a long-haul **flight***

longing /ˈlɒŋ.ɪŋ/ US /ˈlɑːŋ-/ noun [S or U] C2 a feeling of wanting something or someone very much: *He gazed at her, his eyes full of longing.* ◦ *a longing look* ◦ *a longing **for** his homeland* • **longingly** /-li/ adv *She gazed longingly at the cakes in the shop window.*

longish /ˈlɒŋ.ɪʃ/ US /ˈlɑːŋ-/ adj quite long

longitude /ˈlɒn.dʒɪ.tjuːd/, /ˈlɒŋ.gɪ-/ US /ˈlɑːn.dʒə.tuːd/ noun [C or U] (written abbreviation **long.**) the distance of a place east or west of an imaginary line from the top to the bottom of the Earth, measured in degrees → Compare **latitude** • **longitudinal** /ˌlɒn.dʒɪˈtjuː.dɪ.nəl/, /ˌlɒŋ.gɪ-/, /ˌlɒŋ.ɪ-/ US /ˌlɑːn.dʒəˈtuː-/ adj

longiˌtudinal ˈwave noun [C] specialized in physics, a wave moving in the same direction of travel as the VIBRATIONS (= fast movements backwards and forwards) of the PARTICLES of the substance through which it is travelling → Compare **transverse wave**

ˈlong ˌjohns noun [plural] underwear with long legs, worn under your outer clothes to keep you warm

the ˈlong ˌjump noun [S] (US also **the ˈbroad ˌjump**) a sports event in which a person runs up to a mark and then jumps as far forward as they can

ˌlong-ˈlasting adj C2 continuing for a long period of time: *a long-lasting friendship*

ˈlong-life adj [before noun] describes products that have been made or treated in such a way that they last for a long time: *long-life milk*

ˈlong-lost adj [before noun] describes a relation, friend, or object that you have not seen for a long time: *my long-lost cousin*

ˈlong-range adj [before noun] for a long time into the future, or across a long distance: *a long-range weather forecast* ◦ *long-range missiles/bombs*

ˈlong-running adj [before noun] C2 continuing for a long time: *a long-running musical* ◦ *their long-running dispute*

longshore drift /ˌlɒŋ.ʃɔːˈdrɪft/ US /ˌlɑːŋ.ʃɔːr-/ noun [U] specialized the movement of sand and small stones, etc. along the coast by waves travelling parallel or at an angle to the coast

longshoreman /ˈlɒŋ.ʃɔː.mən/ US /ˈlɑːŋ.ʃɔːr-/ noun [C] (plural **-men** /-mən/) US for **docker**

ˈlong ˌshot noun [C usually singular] something you try although it is unlikely to be successful: *It's a long shot, but you could try phoning him at home.*

ˌlong-ˈsighted adj (US **ˌfar-ˈsighted**) able to see things that are far away but not things that are near you

ˌlong-ˈstanding adj having existed for a long time: *a long-standing agreement*

ˌlong-ˈsuffering adj A long-suffering person is patient despite being annoyed or insulted regularly over a period of time.

ˌlong-ˈterm adj B2 continuing a long time into the future: *long-term unemployment* ◦ *long-term care for the seriously ill* ◦ *the long-term effects of the drug*

ˈlong-time adj [before noun] C1 describes someone who has been in a particular position for a long period: *A long-time **friend** of the chairman said she had expected the resignation.*

longueur /lɔ̃ˈgɜːr/ US /-ˈgɜː/ noun [C usually plural] literary a boring part of something, especially a book, film, etc.: *Despite the occasional longueurs, this is an impressive first novel.*

ˌlong vaˈcation noun [C] (informal **ˌlong ˈvac**) UK the three months in the summer when college and university students do not have classes

ˈlong ˌwave noun [U] (written abbreviation **LW**) a range of radio waves used for broadcasting and receiving with a FREQUENCY below 300 kHz

longways /ˈlɒŋ.weɪz/ US /ˈlɑːŋ-/ adv (US also **longwise**) along the length: *Fold the paper longways.* → See also **lengthways**

ˌlong weekˈend noun [C] Saturday and Sunday with at least one extra day of holiday added, either Friday or Monday: *We spent a long weekend with my parents.*

ˌlong-ˈwinded adj A long-winded speech, letter, article, etc. is too long, or uses too many words.

loo /luː/ noun [C] (plural **loos**) UK informal for toilet: *I'll just go to the loo.* ◦ *loo roll*

loofah /ˈluː.fə/ noun [C] a piece of a rough plant, used to rub the body when washing

L

look /lʊk/ verb; noun; exclamation

▸verb **SEE** ▷ **1** A1 [I] to direct your eyes in order to see: *Look! There's grandma.* ◦ *They looked* ***at*** *the picture and laughed.* ◦ *Look* ***at*** *all this rubbish on the floor.* ◦ *She looked* ***up*** *from her book and smiled at me.* ◦ *I looked out (of) the window.* ◦ *Look over there – there's a rainbow!*

! Common mistake: look

Remember: when **look** has an object, the correct preposition to use is **at**.

Don't say 'look something' or 'look to something', say **look at something**:

~~*She looked to the photo on her desk and smiled.*~~

She looked at the photo on her desk and smiled.

! Common mistake: look forward to

When **look forward to** is followed by a verb, that verb should be in the **-ing** form.

Do not say 'look forward to do something', say **look forward to doing something**:

~~*I look forward to meet you at the conference.*~~

I look forward to meeting you at the conference.

SEARCH ▷ **2** A1 [I] to try to find something or someone: *I'm looking* ***for*** *my keys.* ◦ *I've looked everywhere but I can't find my glasses.* ◦ *Have you looked in the dictionary?* ◦ *I looked down the list but couldn't see his name.* **SEEM** ▷ **3** A2 [L, I usually + adv/prep] to appear or seem: *You look well!* ◦ *The roads look very icy.* ◦ *That dress looks nice on you.* ◦ *He has started to look his age (= appear as old as he really is).* ◦ ***It's looking good*** *(= things are going well).* ◦ *He looked (****like****) a friendly sort of person.* ◦ *The twins look just* ***like*** *their mother.* ◦ *She looked* ***as if/though*** *she hadn't slept all night.* ◦ ***It*** *looks* ***like*** *rain (= as if it is going to rain).* **DIRECTION** ▷ **4** B2 [I usually + adv/prep] to face a particular direction: *The garden looks south.* ◦ *This window looks out onto the lake.* **WARNING** ▷ **5** [I] used when you are telling someone to be careful or to pay attention: [+ question word] *Look* ***where*** *you're going!* ◦ *Look at the time – we're late!* **HOPE** ▷ **6 be looking to do sth** C2 to plan to do something: *I'm looking to start my own business.*

IDIOMS **be looking for trouble** to be acting in a way that will certainly cause problems for you: *Parking outside the police station on double yellow lines is just looking for trouble.* • **be not much to look at** informal to not be attractive: *The house isn't much to look at but it's spacious.* • **I'm just looking** said to a person working in a shop when they offer to help you but you want to continue looking at the goods on your own • **look daggers at sb** informal to look angrily at someone • **look kindly on sb/sth** to have a good opinion of someone or something: *She had hoped the critics would look kindly on her first novel.* • **look lively/sharp!** UK old-fashioned used to tell someone to do something quickly: *Look lively – we haven't got all day!* • **look on the bright side** C1 to find good things in a bad situation: *Look on the bright side – no one was badly hurt.* • **look out for number one** informal to do what you think is best for yourself and not care about other people • **look straight/right through sb** UK to look at someone as if you cannot see them, either intentionally or because you are thinking about something else: *I said hello but she looked straight through me.* • **look to your laurels** to make an extra effort to succeed because there is more competition • **make sb look small** to show that someone is wrong in a way that makes them appear silly • **never look a gift horse in the mouth** saying said to advise someone not to refuse something good that is being offered • **never look back** to continue to be successful after doing something with a good result: *She never looked back after that first exhibition.* • **not look sb in the eye/face** If you cannot look someone in the eye/face, you are too ashamed to look at them directly and speak honestly to them.

+ Other ways of saying look

See also: **see**

Watch is used when someone looks at something for a period of time, especially something that is changing or moving:

I sat by the window and ***watched*** *people walking past.*

Glance is used when someone looks at a person or thing very quickly:

She ***glanced*** *around the room to see who was there.*

If you look very quickly and secretly, you can use the verbs **peep** or **peek**:

She ***peeped*** *through the curtains to see what was happening.*

He ***peeked*** *inside the box.*

The verb **stare** is used when someone looks for a long time, especially because of being surprised or frightened:

Don't ***stare*** *at people like that – it's rude.*

If you look at something or someone for a long time because you are admiring that thing or person or because you are thinking about something, you can use the verb **gaze**:

We sat there ***gazing*** *at the lake.*

Peer is used when someone looks at something with difficulty:

When no one answered the door, she ***peered*** *through the window.*

The verbs **examine**, **inspect**, or **scrutinize** are often used when someone looks at something very closely in order to find out more about it:

Police are ***examining*** *the house for clues.*

She ***inspected*** *the car for damage.*

He ***scrutinized*** *the woman's face to see if she was lying.*

PHRASAL VERBS **look after sb/sth** A2 to take care of or be in charge of someone or something: *We look after the neighbours' cat while they're away.* ◦ *If you look after your clothes they last a lot longer.* ◦ *Don't worry about Mia – she can look after her****self****.* • **look ahead** C2 to think about what will happen in the future and plan for these events: *We are trying to look ahead and see what our options are.* • **look at sth THINK** ▷ **1** B2 to think about a subject carefully so that you can make a decision about it: *Management is looking at ways of cutting costs.* **HAVE OPINION** ▷ **2** to consider something in a particular way: *If I'd had children I might have looked at things differently.* **READ** ▷ **3** B2 to read something in order to check it or form an opinion about it: *Can you look at my essay sometime?* **EXAMINE** ▷ **4** B2 If someone, usually an expert, looks at something, they examine it: *Did you get the doctor to look at your knee?* • **look back** B2 to think about something that happened in the past: *When I look back I can see where we went wrong.* ◦ *It wasn't such a bad experience when I look back* ***on*** *it.* • **look down on sb** (also **look down your nose at sb**) B2 to think that someone is less important than you: *She thinks they look down on her because she didn't go to university.* • **look forward to sth 1** B1 to feel pleased and excited about something that is going to happen: *I'm really looking forward to my holiday.* ◦ [+ -ing verb] *She was looking forward to seeing the grandchildren again.* ◦ *I'm not looking forward to Christmas this year.* **2** B2 [+ -ing verb] formal used at the end of a formal letter to say you hope to hear from or see someone soon, or that you expect something from them: *I look forward to **hearing from you**.* ◦ *In the circumstances, I look forward to **receiving** your client's cheque for the sum of £570 within the next seven days.* • **look in** informal to visit a person for a short time, usually when you are on your way somewhere else: *I thought I might look in **on** Bob on my way to the shops.* • **look into sth** B2 to examine the facts about a problem or situation: *We're looking into the possibility of merging the two departments.* • **look on** to watch something happen but not become involved in it: *A large crowd looked on as the band played.* → See also **onlooker** • **look on/upon sb/sth as sth** C1 to consider or think of someone or something as something: *We looked on her as a daughter.* ◦ *I've lived there so long I look on the town as my home.* • **look out 1** to watch what is happening and be careful: *The police have warned shopkeepers to look out **for** forged notes.* **2** B1 said or shouted in order to tell someone that they are in danger: *Look out! There's a car coming!* • **look sth out** UK to search for and find something: *I'll look out that recipe I told you about and send it to you.* • **look out for sb/sth** B2 to try to notice someone or something: *Look out for Anna while you're there.* • **look over sth** C2 to quickly examine something: *I had a few minutes before the meeting to look over what he'd written.* ◦ *Would you quickly look over these figures for me and see if there are any obvious mistakes?* • **look round (somewhere/sth)** B1 to visit a place and look at the things in it: *She spent the afternoon looking round the shops.* ◦ *When we went to Stratford, we only had a couple of hours to look round.* • **look through sth** B2 to read something quickly: *I've looked through some catalogues.* • **look to sb to do sth** to hope that someone will do something for you: *We're looking to you to advise us on how to proceed.* • **look to sb for sth** to hope that someone will provide something for you: *They looked to the government for additional support.* • **look up** informal C1 to become better: *I hope things will start to look up in the new year.* ◦ *Our financial situation is looking up at last.* • **look sth up** B1 to try to find a piece of information by looking in a book or on a computer: *If you don't know what the word means, look it up **in** a dictionary.* • **look sb up** informal to visit someone who you have not seen for a long time when you are visiting the place where they live: *Look me up next time you're in Los Angeles.* • **look up to sb** B2 to admire and respect someone: *He'd always looked up to his uncle.*

▸**noun** WITH EYES ▷ **1** B1 [C] the act of looking at someone or something: ***Take a (good) look at** this picture and see if you recognize anyone.* ◦ *Can I **have a look at** your dictionary?* SEARCH ▷ **2** B1 [C usually singular] the act of trying to find someone or something: *I **had** another look **for** the watch, but couldn't find it.* APPEARANCE ▷ **3** B2 [C] an expression on someone's face: *She had a worried look about her.* ◦ *She **gave** me a questioning look.* **4** C1 [C] a style or fashion: *The look this year will be relaxed and casual.* **5 the look of sb/sth** B2 the appearance of someone or something: *They liked the look of the hotel, but it was too expensive.* ◦ *I don't like the look of that fence* (= it appears to have something wrong with it). **6 sb's looks** C2 a person's appearance, especially how attractive they are: *I like her looks.* ◦ *He put on weight and started to **lose** his looks.*

IDIOMS **by the look(s) of things** (also **by the look of it**) judging by the information we have now: *By the look of things, we won't be able to take our holiday till the autumn.* • **if looks could kill...** saying said when you see someone look very angrily at someone else

▸**exclamation** used to express anger: *Look, I've already told you it's not possible.* ◦ old-fashioned *Look **here**, I've had enough of this.*

ˈlook-alike noun [C] someone or something that is similar in appearance to someone or something else: *She's a Marilyn Monroe look-alike.*

looker /ˈlʊk.əʳ/ US /ˈlʊk.ɚ/ noun [C] old-fashioned informal a physically attractive person, usually a woman: *Have you seen Karl's new girlfriend? She's a real looker!*

ˈlook-in noun UK informal **not get a look-in** to not have a chance to do something or to succeed: *There were so many children wanting a ride John didn't get a look-in.* ◦ *Our opponents were so good – we didn't get a look-in.*

ˈlooking ˌglass noun [C] old-fashioned a mirror

lookout /ˈlʊk.aʊt/ noun [C] **1** a person who watches for danger **2** a high place where a person can look at what is happening in the area around them, especially in order to watch for any danger **3** Australian English a place from where a person can look at something, especially at an area of natural beauty → Compare **viewpoint 4 be on the lookout for sth/sb** to search for something or someone: *I'm always on the lookout for interesting new recipes.* **5 keep a lookout for sth/sb** to continue to watch carefully for something or someone, especially in order to avoid danger: *Keep a lookout for small objects that a baby might swallow.*

IDIOM **it's your own lookout** UK informal said to someone in order to tell them that they are responsible for their own problems: *It's your own lookout if you're not properly insured.*

ˌlook-ˈsee noun [S] informal a quick look: *'Have they arrived yet?' 'I'll **take/have** a look-see.'*

loom /luːm/ verb; noun

▸**verb** [I] APPEAR ▷ **1** C2 to appear as a large, often frightening or UNCLEAR shape or object: *Dark storm clouds loomed **on the horizon**.* CAUSE WORRY ▷ **2** C2 If an unwanted or unpleasant event looms, it seems likely to happen soon and causes worry: *Her exams are looming.* ◦ *Here, too, the threat of unemployment has been looming **on the horizon**.* ◦ *The threat of closure looms **over** the workforce.*

IDIOM **loom large** C2 If something looms large, it becomes very important and often causes worry: *The issue of pay will loom large at this Easter's teacher conference.*

▸**noun** [C] a piece of equipment for WEAVING (= making thread into cloth)

looming /ˈluː.mɪŋ/ adj (of something unwanted or unpleasant) happening soon and causing worry: *the looming crisis*

loony /ˈluː.ni/ adj informal silly or stupid: *He had lots of loony ideas about education.*

ˈloony ˌbin noun [C] offensive or humorous a **psychiatric hospital**

loop /luːp/ noun; verb

▸**noun** [C] the curved shape made when something long and thin, such as a piece of string, bends until one part of it nearly touches or crosses another part of it: *belt loops* ◦ *a loop **of** string* ◦ *the loop **of** the* river ◦ *The tape ran in a continuous loop, repeating the same songs over and over.*

IDIOMS **be in the loop/be out of the loop** informal to have or not have the special knowledge or power that belongs to a particular group of people: *You can tell she's in the loop. She always knows about policy decisions before the rest of us.* ◦ *I've been out of the loop since I changed jobs. I didn't realize Wendy and Bob had got engaged.* • **knock/throw sb for a loop** US informal If something that happens knocks you for a loop, it upsets or confuses you because you do not expect it: *He knocked me for a loop when he said he was quitting his job.*

▸verb [I or T, usually + adv/prep] to make a loop or curve: *Loop the rope over the bar.* ◦ *Turn left where the road loops round the farm buildings.*

IDIOM **loop the loop** to fly in the shape of a loop in the sky

loophole /ˈluːp.həʊl/ US /-hoʊl/ noun [C] a small mistake in an agreement or law which gives someone the chance to avoid having to do something: *tax loopholes* ◦ *The company employed lawyers to find loopholes **in** environmental protection laws.*

loopy /ˈluː.pi/ adj informal strange, unusual, or silly: *He must have **gone** completely loopy to give up a job like that.*

loose /luːs/ adj; noun; verb

▸adj NOT FIXED ▷ **1** B2 not firmly fixed in place: *There were some loose wires hanging out of the wall.* ◦ *The nails in the bridge had **worked** them**selves** loose.* ◦ *The prisoners were so thin that their skin **hung** loose.* **2** B2 describes hair that is not tied back: *Her hair was **hanging** loose about her shoulders.* **3** describes things that are not fixed or held together or to anything else: *A few loose sheets of paper were lying around.* NOT TIGHT ▷ **4** B1 (of clothes) not fitting closely to the body: *Wear comfortable, loose clothing to your exercise class.* NOT EXACT ▷ **5** C2 not tightly controlled or not exact: *It's a fairly loose adaptation of the novel.* ◦ *It's only a loose translation of the poem.* IMMORAL ▷ **6** old-fashioned disapproving having low morals; sexually free: *a loose **woman***

IDIOMS **be at a loose end** informal to have nothing to do: *If you find yourself at a loose end, you could always clean the bathroom.* • **hang/stay loose** US informal to be calm and relaxed • **let sb loose** to allow someone to do what they want in a place: *You don't want to let Oliver loose in the kitchen.* • **let loose sth 1** If you let loose something such as bullets or bombs, you release a lot of them all together: *The allies let loose an intensive artillery bombardment over the border.* **2** to suddenly make a sound or speak in an uncontrolled way: *He turned round and let loose a torrent of abuse.* • **let/set sth loose** to allow an animal to run around freely after it has been tied up: *She let her horse loose in the field.*

▸noun

IDIOM **on the loose** If a dangerous person or animal is on the loose, they are free to move around a place and harm people: *Brewer escaped from prison last year and has been on the loose ever since.*

▸verb [T] to speak or express emotions very freely, especially in an uncontrolled way: *The minister loosed an angry tirade against the leader of the opposition.*

ˌloose ˈcannon noun [C] disapproving someone who behaves in an uncontrolled or unexpected way and is likely to cause problems for other people: *He's seen as something of a loose cannon by other team members.*

> **!** Common mistake: **loose or lose?**
>
> **Warning:** these two verbs look and sound similar but have very different meanings.
>
> To talk about no longer possessing something or having less of it, don't say 'loose', say **lose**:
>
> ~~*If we are not careful we will loose some of our best clients.*~~

ˌloose ˈchange noun [U] the coins that you have in your pocket or PURSE

ˌloose ˈends noun [plural] things that still need to be done or explained: *At the end of the film all the loose ends are neatly **tied up**.*

ˌloose-ˈfitting adj describes a piece of clothing that is quite large and does not fit tightly

ˌloose-ˈleaf adj [before noun] having pages that can easily be taken out and put back again: *a loose-leaf folder*

loosely /ˈluːs.li/ adv NOT FIXED ▷ **1** in a way that is not firmly fixed: *The parcel had only been loosely wrapped, and the paper had come off.* NOT EXACT ▷ **2** not exactly: *This phrase can be loosely translated as 'Go away'.* ◦ *The film is loosely based on the novel by Kundera.* NOT TIGHT ▷ **3** not tightly: *The jacket hung loosely on his thin body.*

loosen /ˈluː.sᵊn/ verb NOT FIXED ▷ **1** C2 [I or T] to (cause to) become loose: *The screws holding the bed together had loosened.* LESS TIGHT ▷ **2** [T] to make something less tight: *He loosened his tie.*

IDIOMS **loosen your grip** If you loosen your grip on an object, or your grip loosens, you hold something less tightly: *He held my hand very tightly at first but gradually his grip loosened.* • **loosen your grip/hold** If you loosen your grip/hold on a situation, or your grip/hold loosens, you decide to control it less. • **loosen sb's tongue** to make you speak more freely: *A couple of glasses of champagne had loosened my tongue and I said things that perhaps I shouldn't have.*

PHRASAL VERBS **loosen (sth) up** to prepare your muscles for a physical activity by stretching and doing simple exercises: *I do a few stretches to loosen up before I run.* • **loosen (sb) up** C2 to start to feel less embarrassed and to become more relaxed when you are with other people, or to make someone feel like this: *He seemed quite nervous at the beginning, but he soon loosened up.* ◦ *A gin and tonic will loosen you up.*

looseness /ˈluːs.nəs/ noun [U] NOT FIXED ▷ **1** the fact that something is not fixed NOT TIGHT ▷ **2** the fact that something is not tight

loot /luːt/ verb; noun

▸verb [I or T] **1** (usually of large numbers of people during a violent event) to steal from shops and houses: *During the riot shops were looted and cars damaged or set on fire.* **2** Indian English to steal something from a place or person: *Burglars looted cash and mobiles from a shop in Tagore Town.* ◦ *The passengers in the general compartment of Shramjivi Express were looted and robbed of their valuables.* • **looter** /ˈluː.təʳ/ US /-t̬ɚ/ noun [C]

▸noun [U] money and valuable objects that have been stolen, especially by an army from a defeated enemy

looting /ˈluː.tɪŋ/ US /-t̬ɪŋ/ noun [U] the activity of stealing from shops during a violent event: *There were reports of **widespread** looting as football hooligans stampeded through the city centre.*

lop /lɒp/ US /lɑːp/ verb (-pp-)

PHRASAL VERB **lop sth off** CUT ▷ **1** to cut something off in one quick movement: *I'll need to lop off the lower*

Focus on writing

Contents

Improving your writing

This writing guide will help you to write well in almost any situation. It gives you tips on style, grammar, punctuation, writing conventions, and the process of writing itself.

Most of all, it helps you to choose the words and phrases that will make your writing sound both impressive and natural. It does this both by suggesting words and phrases for specific situations and by providing sentences that act as models for what you want to write yourself.

The information in this section on improving your writing can be used for any type of writing. It will help you to use your dictionary effectively and produce writing that is clear, correct, and elegant.

Before you start

Before you start any piece of writing you should be able to answer three questions:

Who am I writing for?

What do I want to say?

Why do I want to say it?

Knowing **who** you are writing for will help you to use the appropriate tone, register, and style – a letter to a friend will be very different from a work report or a job application.

Knowing **what** you want to say will help you to be clear and include everything that you need to include.

Knowing **why** you want to say it will help to make sure that the writing achieves what you want it to. For instance, if you write a book review, it should be clear whether or not you recommend the book and why.

Planning

For longer pieces of writing, it is useful to plan before you start to write. This will help you to organize your work and make sure that you present it in a logical order. It will also help you to identify gaps in your own knowledge where you will need to find extra information.

Your planning can be done in whatever way suits you best. You could use **diagrams**, where you write the most important point of your writing in the centre of the page and work outwards from there, adding new ideas and details. Alternatively, you may like to produce a list of **headings** and use them to order your points and ideas.

Sometimes it can be useful to write a short **summary** of what your piece of writing is trying to achieve. This can help you to maintain focus in your writing and stop you from adding unnecessary detail that could weaken the impact of your main point or confuse your reader.

Research

For longer pieces of writing, particularly academic writing, you may need to do some research before you can start writing. If you are studying at a university or other educational institution, your teachers will be able to give you advice about reliable sources such as books, journals, and websites.

Remember that at university level your writing is assessed not just on the facts that you present, but also on your ability to engage with your subject and to present your arguments well. You may not use all your research in your finished writing, but the more you have done, the more solid the foundations of your writing will be.

Using the internet

Of course, a large amount of information is available on the internet, but it is important to be careful when using this. When you access a website, make sure you can answer the following questions:

- Who created the site? Does it come from a reliable source or might it have been written by an enthusiastic person who may not be completely accurate?
- Why is the site there? Are you sure that the information in it is not biased – for instance to try to persuade you to buy something or to try to convince you of a political or religious position?
- When was the site last updated? Is the information current?
- Does the site include any evidence for what it says, for instance a reference list?

Making notes

You will need to make notes while you are doing your research. Notes should be short, so you will need to summarize key points. This will help you to make sure you understand those points clearly.

If you have planned the structure of your writing, you may want to organize your notes in the same way. When you make notes, it is a good idea to distinguish between your own ideas, direct quotations, and summaries or paraphrases of sources, so that you will be able to add all necessary references and avoid plagiarism.

Ways to avoid errors

Spelling

Use the dictionary to check your spelling. If you have the CD-ROM version of the dictionary, you can look up words even if you are not sure of the spelling by typing * for the letters you do not know.

For instance, if you do not know how to spell *weird*, you can type in *w*rd*, and you will be shown a list of all words that start with *w* and end with *rd*.

Some words are spelled differently in **British and American English**. The dictionary will give you information about this. The labels UK and US indicate which spelling is used where:

favourite /ˈfeɪ.vᵊr.ɪt/ **adj; noun**
▸**adj** [before noun] UK (US **favorite**) A1 best liked or most enjoyed: *'What's your favourite colour?' 'Green.'* ◦ *my favourite restaurant/book/song*
▸**noun** [C] UK (US **favorite**) **1** B1 a thing that someone likes best or enjoys most: *How clever of you to buy chocolate chip cookies – they're my favourites.* **2** a person who is treated with special kindness by someone in authority: *the teacher's favourite* **3** C2 the person or animal most people expect to win a race or competition: *Great Gold is **the** favourite in the 2.00 race at Epsom.* ◦ [+ to infinitive] *Brazil are favourites **to** win this year's World Cup.*

Most verbs ending in *–ize*, such as *organize* or *realize*, are often spelled *–ise* in British English. For American English you should always use *–ize* spellings. For British English you can choose *–ize* or *–ise*, but make sure you are consistent throughout the whole piece of writing.

In general, American spellings of scientific words such as *estrogen* or *fetus* are used in academic writing.

Compound words

There are no strict rules about how to write **compound words** such as *frying pan, take-off* or *shoelace*. However, it is best to use the form that is listed in the dictionary.

When phrases or expressions consisting of more than one word are used before a noun, it is common practice to use hyphens to join the elements of the phrase or expression:

a well-trodden path (compare 'The path was well trodden.')

at-risk children (compare 'These children are at risk.')

second-year students (compare 'students who are in the second year')

However, a hyphen should not be used with an adverb ending in –ly:

a hastily assembled article

a critically acclaimed novel

a legally binding contract

Common spelling mistakes

Some spelling mistakes are particularly common. The dictionary shows the 50 words most often spelled wrongly by learners of English. This is the box for the word *accommodation*.

! Common mistake: **accommodation**

Warning: Check your spelling!

Accommodation is one of the 50 words most often spelled wrongly by learners. Remember: the correct spelling has 'cc' and 'mm'.

Grammar

Make sure you understand the grammar codes in the dictionary. There is an explanation for them at the front of the book. Look at the example sentences, because they will show you how the grammar works.

For instance, look at this entry for the word *haste*.

This word is uncountable. It cannot be made plural.

haste /heɪst/ **noun** [U] disapproving (too much) speed: *Unfortunately the report was prepared **in** haste and contained several inaccuracies.* ◦ [+ to infinitive] ***In** her haste **to** get up from the table, she knocked over a cup.*

IDIOMS **make haste** old-fashioned hurry up: *Make haste!* • **more haste, less speed** UK saying said to mean that if you try to do things too quickly, it will take you longer in the end

Haste is often followed by an infinitive verb.

Common grammar mistakes

This dictionary contains special boxes that warn against common mistakes. They are based on research done on many millions of words written by learners of English. This is the box for the word *explain*.

! Common mistake: **explain**

When **explain** is followed by an indirect object, remember to use the preposition **to**.

Don't say 'explain someone', say **explain to someone**:

~~*I had to explain him that I had lost his keys.*~~

I had to explain to him that I had lost his keys.

Make sure you read these boxes carefully so that you do not make the same mistakes.

Good style

Avoiding repetition

Try to avoid repeating words and phrases too much. Of course, if you are writing about a particular thing, you may have to refer to it many times, but in general, your writing will sound more interesting if you vary the language you use.

For some very common words, the dictionary has special boxes that give you other ways of saying a word. Look at this box for the word *ask*.

> **Other ways of saying ask**
>
> If someone is asking for information, the word **inquire** can be used:
>
> *She called to **inquire** when her car would be ready.*
>
> The verb **consult** is often used when you are asking for advice or information from someone who knows a lot because it is their job:
>
> ***Consult** your doctor if your symptoms don't improve.*
>
> If someone asks a lot of people in order to get information or help, you can use the phrasal verb **ask around**:
>
> *I'll **ask around** and see if anyone knows of a good carpenter.*
>
> The verb **question** is used in serious or official situations:
>
> *The police are **questioning** him about the robbery.*
>
> If someone asks a person questions for a television programme or newspaper article, the verb **interview** is often used:
>
> *After the race, she was **interviewed** by journalists.*

The CD-ROM version of the dictionary has a very useful feature called the SMARTthesaurus. For every sense of every word in the dictionary there is a button you can click that will give you a list of synonyms or other words in the same topic.

For instance, if you use the SMARTthesaurus on the word *sad*, you find words such as *depressed, distraught, glum, heartbroken*, and *miserable*.

Avoiding unnecessary words

If you use too many words, your message will not be as clear as it should be, and you risk boring or annoying your reader.

Of course, if you are producing a creative or descriptive piece of writing you may want to include a lot of detail, but in general, functional English, the simpler a sentence, the more effective it is likely to be.

Compare the following:

I have just had a message to tell me that there are various problems with the proposed wedding venue in terms of seating capacity and catering arrangements.

There are problems with seating and catering at the proposed wedding venue.

Avoiding ambiguity

If a sentence is ambiguous it can be understood in more than one way, and this can be confusing to your reader.

Be careful to make it clear who or what a pronoun refers to:

Peter spoke to John and then he left the room. (Who left the room, Peter or John?)

Peter spoke to John, who then left the room. (It is clear that John left the room.)

Remember that many words can have more than one meaning:

Suzie is very funny. (Does she make you laugh, or is she strange?)

If the meaning is not clear from the context, you may have to add another sentence, e.g. *She makes everyone laugh.*

Be careful to make it clear who or what an adjective refers to:

an unattractive man's coat (Is it the coat or the man who is unattractive?)

Be careful with sentence structure:

He told us about the accident that morning. (Did the accident happen that morning, or did we hear about it that morning?)

That morning, he told us about the accident. (We heard about it that morning.)

He told us about the accident that had happened that morning. (The accident happened that morning.)

Avoiding clichés

Clichés are words and phrases that have been used so often that they sound boring and unoriginal. It is particularly important to avoid clichés that do not add any meaning to your sentences. Phrases such as '*at the end of the day*' or '*in any way, shape, or form*' should not be used in writing at all.

Many idiomatic phrases (e.g. *reinvent the wheel, think outside the box*) have also become overused, and while they may be useful to convey an idea which will be easily understood, using too many of them would annoy your readers and give the impression that you do not have anything interesting to say. Think about what they actually mean, and try to express the same idea in a different way.

If English is not your first language, it can be quite difficult to distinguish between a cliché and a natural, useful phrase or idiom. For an important piece of writing, you may need to ask for advice on this. In academic writing, it is best to avoid idiomatic language altogether.

Collocation

Collocation is the way words go together in a way that sounds natural, for example *heavy rain* or *bitterly disappointed*. It is often difficult to guess which collocations to use, but collocation is one of the most important aspects of natural-sounding English.

This dictionary gives information about collocation in two ways. Some entries have 'Word partner' boxes that show their most important collocations:

> Word partners for **job** (**EMPLOYMENT**)
>
> a ***full-time/part-time/permanent/temporary*** job • a ***dead-end/good/low-paid/well-paid*** job • ***have/hold down*** a job • ***find/get/land*** a job • ***apply for/look for*** a job • ***offer*** sb a job • ***lose/quit*** your job • ***create/provide*** jobs • a job ***as*** sth

Other words have their collocations shown in **bold type** in the example sentences. For instance, in this entry for **music** you can see the collocations *piece of music, play music, make music*, and *put on some music*.

> **music** /ˈmjuː.zɪk/ noun [U] **1** A1 a pattern of sounds made by musical instruments, voices, or computers, or a combination of these, intended to give pleasure to people listening to it: *classical/pop/dance/rock music* ◦ *a beautiful **piece of** music* ◦ *What sort of music do you listen to?* ◦ *They **play** good music on this (radio) station.* ◦ *I just like **making** music (= playing an instrument or singing).* ◦ *Shall I **put on** some music (= play a recording)?* **2** the art or study of

Common collocations

Note the following common collocations, which are the ones which most frequently cause most problems for advanced students:

Verb + noun collocations

- ***have*** *an experience* (not ~~*make*~~)
- ***make*** *friends* (not ~~*find*~~)
- ***do*** *research* (not ~~*make*~~)
- ***do*** *your work* (not ~~*make*~~)
- ***make*** *mistakes* (not ~~*do*~~)
- ***carry out/do*** *a survey* (not ~~*make*~~)
- ***make*** *an effort* (not ~~*do*~~)
- ***have*** *children* (not ~~*get*~~)
- ***carry out/do*** *business* (not ~~*make*~~)
- ***make*** *changes* (not ~~*do*~~)

Adjective + noun collocations

- *a **large** number/amount/quantity* (not ~~*big*~~)
- *a **limited/narrow** choice* (not ~~*little*~~)
- *a **wide** range/variety/choice* (not ~~*big*~~)
- *a **loud** noise* (not ~~*big*~~)
- ***great/a lot of*** *pressure* (not ~~*high*~~)
- *of **great** importance* (not ~~*big*~~)
- *a **large** amount of money* (not ~~*big*~~)
- *a **tall** building/man* (not ~~*high*~~)
- *make **great/a lot of** progress* (not ~~*big*~~)
- *a **slight** decrease* (not ~~*little*~~)

Register and tone

The dictionary gives clear information about whether a word is formal or informal.

> **abhorrent** /əˈbɒr.ᵊnt/ US /æbˈhɔːr-/ adj formal morally very bad: *an abhorrent crime* ◦ *Racism of any kind is abhorrent **to** me.*
>
> **umpteen** /ʌmpˈtiːn/, /ˈʌmp.tiːn/ determiner, pronoun informal very many; a lot (of): *We've been there umpteen times and she still can't remember the way.* • **umpteenth** /ʌmpˈtiːnθ/, /ˈʌmp.tiːnθ/ determiner informal *I drank my umpteenth cup of coffee.* ◦ *For the umpteenth time, Anthony, knives and forks go in the middle drawer!*

It is important to use words that are appropriate to the audience. Formal words are not common in speech or in friendly emails, and informal words should be avoided in academic writing, formal letters, etc.

The *tone* of your writing is also important, because it shows your attitude towards the person or people you are writing for. Before you write, think about how you want to sound. For instance, if you want to ask your boss for something, you may want to sound persuasive yet respectful, while an email to your friend would probably be chatty, friendly, and perhaps humorous.

It can be easy, especially in quick communications such as emails or texts, to sound rude or angry without meaning to. In some cases, just a simple line of good wishes can be enough to make a letter or email sound more polite.

Think about how well you know the person you are writing for. If you do not know the person well, he or she may be offended by writing that is too informal or too brief. On the other hand, a friend could be offended by writing that seems too formal and unfriendly.

You should be aware that sometimes the words that you choose can show your attitude. The dictionary gives information about words that express approval or disapproval:

> **outgoing** adj **FRIENDLY** ▷ **1** C1 /ˌaʊtˈɡəʊ.ɪŋ/ US /ˈaʊt.ɡoʊ-/ approving (of a person) friendly and energetic and finding it easy and enjoyable to be with others: *Sales reps need to be outgoing, because they are constantly meeting customers.* ◦ *She has an outgoing personality.* **LEAVING** ▷ **2** C2 /ˈaʊtˌɡəʊ.ɪŋ/ US /-ˌɡoʊ-/ [before noun] leaving a place, or leaving a job: *Outgoing flights are booked until 15 January.* ◦ *the outgoing vice-president*
>
> **bumptious** /ˈbʌmp.ʃəs/ adj disapproving unpleasantly confident: *a bumptious young man* • **bumptiously** /-li/ adj • **bumptiousness** /-nəs/ noun [U]

Punctuation

It is important to use correct punctuation in order to make your writing clear and easy to read. Punctuation can change the meaning of a sentence. For instance, compare these sentences:

Shall we eat, Philip? (You are suggesting to Philip that you eat a meal together.)

Shall we eat Philip? (You are suggesting to someone else that you eat Philip.)

Punctuation marks

. full stop (UK) *or* **period (US)**

- at the end of a sentence: *I'm going for a walk.*
- sometimes after an abbreviation: *9 a.m.; Prof. Flavio Pernassi*
- in amounts of money: *£3.50; $19.99*
- as the decimal point in figures (said as '**point**'): *13.4*
- to separate parts of email and web addresses (said as '**dot**'): *http://dictionary.cambridge.org*

? question mark

- after a direct question: *What's your name?*
- to show doubt: *Sidney Morgan (?1898–1972)*

! exclamation mark

- at the end of a sentence, to show surprise, shock, excitement, anger, etc.: *I can't believe it! Go away!*
- to indicate a loud sound: *Bang!*

, comma

- between items on a list: *I need peas, butter, sugar, and eggs.* (Note that a comma is always used before the final item in American English, but not necessarily in British English.)
- to show a pause in a long sentence: *They didn't want to eat before I arrived, but I was an hour late.*
- when you want to add extra information: *The room, which was very small, was already full.*
- before names in speech when addressing someone: *'How are you, Emma?'*
- before question tags: *It's cold today, isn't it?*
- after words or phrases at the beginning of sentences: *Unfortunately, nobody had told him. In general, people were positive.*

' apostrophe

- to indicate missing letters: *I'll; they'd; don't*
- to show who or what something belongs to: *Noah's bike; the horses' hoofs; James's house; Archimedes' principle.* (Note that for plurals or classical names ending in *-s*, you do not need another *s* after the apostrophe.)

: colon

- to introduce a list: *You will need the following items: paint, brushes, water, cloths.*
- to introduce a quotation: *As the minister said: 'This is good news.'*
- in American English, after the greeting in a business letter: *Dear Mr Stein:*

; semicolon

- to separate two parts of a complex sentence: *I spoke to Linda; she can't come to the meeting tomorrow.*

- hyphen

- to join two words together: *blue-black*
- in some compound words: *number-crunching*
- in numbers between 21 and 99: *thirty-three, ninety-nine*
- to show that a word has been divided and continues on the next line.

– dash

- to add information to a sentence: *The house – like all our previous houses – was very large.*
- to add information that is surprising: *Guess where we're going on holiday – New York!*
- to add a phrase that summarizes what you have just written: *He loves football, tennis, swimming – any kind of sport.*
- to mean **to**: *The London–Edinburgh train.*

' ' " " quotation marks (UK & US) *or* **inverted commas (UK)**

- to show that words are spoken: *'I'm tired,' she said. 'Help!' he shouted.*
- to show that you are quoting someone: *He described the area as 'desirable'.*
- to show that you are using a word that may not be known to readers: *These are known as 'bucks parties' in Australia.*
- around titles of books, films, songs, etc.: *We watched 'Avatar'.*

( ) brackets (UK) *or* **parentheses (US or UK formal)**

- to add extra information or comments to a sentence: *The food (all cooked by Tom) was wonderful. Most of the data was collected by volunteers (see also 3.1, below). Haydn (1732–1809) was an Austrian composer.*

[ ] square brackets (UK) *or* **brackets (US)**

- around words that have been added to make a sentence correct or clear: *Taylor insisted that [the role] had been offered to him earlier.*
- around ellipses: *He described the book as 'intelligent and gripping [...] the best novel I have read this year.'*

/ slash *or* **oblique**

- to show alternatives: *Make sure you bring trainers and/or walking boots.*
- in email and web addresses. This is said as '**forward slash**': http://dictionary.cambridge.org/dictionary/english-spanish

... ellipsis *or* **dots**

- to show that words have been left out: *The show was described as 'stunning... a triumph.'*

Capital letters

In English, capital letters are used:

- at the beginning of sentences: *The milk is in the fridge.*
- for countries, nationalities, languages, religions, names of people, places, events, organizations, trademarks, days, months: *Portugal, Africa, the Sahara, Russian, Islam, Sarah White, the World Trade Fair, the Red Cross, Jaguar, Monday, June*
- for titles, when used with a person's name: *Mrs Murray, Doctor Levy, President Roosevelt* (compare *the president's aides*)
- for abbreviations: *BBC, WWF*
- In titles of books, films, songs, etc., the main words usually have a capital letter while words like *and* or *of* are written with lower-case letters, unless they are the first word: *Star of the Sea, Of Mice and Men.*

Italics

Italics are used:

- to emphasize a word or phrase: Please make sure that *all* windows and doors are closed.
- for titles of book, plays, newspapers, etc. She is a journalist for *The Times*.
- for foreign words and phrases: The policies demonstrate, *inter alia*, the rights and responsibilities of the individual. My daughter attends the *Hochschule*.

Speech

When you write the actual words that someone spoke, you use quotation marks (also called inverted commas). For American English, double quotation marks are usually used. For British English, either single or double quotation marks can be used.

The words spoken start with a capital letter, and there is a comma before the second quotation mark:

'The food is ready,' Ben said.

You can also begin the sentence with the reporting verb. In this case, the comma comes before the quotation mark:

Ben said, 'The food is ready.'

Question marks and exclamation marks also come inside the quotation marks:

'I was terrified!' she cried.

'Are you ready?' the teacher asked.

If the speech is broken by the reporting verb, the first comma comes after the quotation mark, and the second one before the second set of quotation marks. The second part of the speech starts with a lower case letter:

'I very much hope', said Julia, 'that you will be there.'

However, if a comma is thought to be a part of the original spoken sentence, it is put inside the first set of quotation marks:

'I invited all my friends,' said Ashley, 'but hardly anyone came.'

Writing dates and numbers

For British English, the following are possible:

18 August 2007; 18th August 2007; 18/08/07

Note that in American English the day and the month are the other way round:

August 18, 2007; 08/18/07

In general English, numbers can be written as words or figures. It is common to use words for numbers up to 10 or 12 and figures for larger numbers. In scientific or mathematical writing, figures are always used.

Very high numbers are often written like this:

30 million; 9 billion

Abbreviations

It is becoming less common to use a full stop after abbreviations, especially in British English:

the BBC; FM radio; Ms Smith; the US

However, for short forms of words, full stops are still usually used:

See fig. 7; I live at No.93.

If the short form has the last letter of the complete word, it is not necessary to use a full stop:

Dr Brown; Quickbuy Ltd

Formal writing

There are many situations in which formal writing is required, for example at work, to communicate with people you do not know well, or to communicate with banks, businesses, or governmental organizations.

Formal writing should be clear and objective. It can express emotion (for instance anger in a letter of complaint), but this must be done in a formal, factual way. It would not be usual to use any words labelled *informal* in this dictionary.

Letters

Starting a letter

A formal letter or email should begin *Dear x*.

If you do not know the person well enough to use their first name, make sure you use the correct title. For instance, do not write *Mr* or *Mrs* if the correct title is *Dr* or *Professor*. If the person you are writing to is a woman, use *Miss* (for unmarried women) or *Mrs* (for married women) if you know they prefer to be addressed this way. Otherwise use *Ms*, which is suitable for both married and unmarried women.

If you do not know the person's name, begin *Dear Sir or Madam*. Most people no longer consider *Dear Sir/s* to be suitable unless you know you are writing to men only.

A polite way to check whether someone minds you using their first name is:

Dear Max (if I may),

Ending a letter

It is usual to end a formal letter with a sentence like this:

If you have any queries, please do not hesitate to contact me.

I look forward to hearing from you soon.

I look forward to your earliest response.

I look forward to meeting you then.

Before your name, it is usual to add a short phrase:

Yours sincerely,
(This should be used if you have used the person's name at the beginning of the letter.)

Yours faithfully,
(This should be used if you have use Dear Sir or Madam at the beginning of the letter.)

Yours,
(This can be used for a short note.)

Kind regards,
Best wishes,
(These sound slightly more friendly.)

The main part of the letter

In a formal letter such as a business letter, it is common to have a heading, usually in **bold type**, before the letter starts, to make it easy to see what the letter is about, particularly if it refers to something such as a bill or a bank account.

Your letter should start with a clear explanation of what it is about:

This letter is to inform you…

I regret to inform you that…

I am writing to enquire/complain about…

Thank you for your letter of 1 June concerning…

Could you please send me some information about…?

You may want to end the main section with a sentence that sums up the purpose of the letter:

I will therefore arrange for a refund to be made to your account.

The payment will be made by 8 Jan.

Thank you again for all your hard work on this project.

I am therefore cancelling my subscription to your magazine.

If you want something to happen as a result of your letter, that should be clearly stated:

I hope that you will be able to clarify the situation as soon as possible.

I look forward to discussing this with you at the earliest opportunity.

I therefore hope to receive a refund from you as soon as possible.

Please would you let me know if this solution is acceptable to you?

Layout

There are several possible ways to present a formal letter, but the one shown opposite is generally acceptable.

13, Weaver's Court 1
Frimpton
FR27 7UP

16 July 2013 2

Mr A Wilkins 3
Windows4you
Unit 4
Bosforth Business Park
CL4 9AL

Dear Mr Wilkins

Invoice Ref. P64/007/69 4

I am writing in response to the above invoice, which I received this morning. 5

Please refer to my letter of July 10th, in which I detailed my complaints about the work done by your company.

Although work has subsequently been carried out to repair the locking mechanisms on the downstairs windows, problems with damaged frames and poor fitting still remain.

I would like an assurance from you that these difficulties will be resolved as a matter of urgency.

Until then, you will not receive payment from me. 5

I hope that this matter will be dealt with as soon as possible,

Yours sincerely

Monica Guttman 6

Ms Monica Guttman 7

1 Your address.

2 The date the letter is written.

3 The name and address of the person you are writing to.

4 A heading that says what the letter is about or gives a specific reference.

5 A clear statement of what you want to happen as a result of your letter.

6 Your signature, to be written by hand.

7 Your name and title.

Emails and instant messaging

Emails tend to be slightly more informal than letters, but you will need to judge what is appropriate. To a customer or a senior colleague, for instance, it may be best to write your email in a very similar way to a formal letter, as described above. To a colleague at the same level, or perhaps to a tutor you know well, a more informal tone is probably fine:

This mail is to let you know...

I wondered if you would have time to meet some time next week?

Try to use the subject line of the email to give a clear indication of what your message is about.

If you are using a form of instant messaging, it is not necessary to include a greeting with your messages.

Starting and ending emails

If your email is formal, it is best to use the same ways of starting and ending it as for a letter (see above). However, if it is less formal, for instance between colleagues who know each other, you could start the email:

Hi Gemma,

Hello Gemma,

If your email is part of a series between you and someone else, it is not necessary to write a greeting for each message – after the first one, you can just start the main part of the message straight away.

To end a slightly less formal email, you could use phrases such as the following:

Thanks,

Thanks again,

Many thanks,

I'll let you know as soon as possible,

See you on Monday,

Have a good weekend,

All the best,

Reports

Reports present facts, analyse information. and often make recommendations. Many of the phrases in the section on academic writing are also suitable for reports. As with academic writing, you should avoid informal and slang words and contractions such as *don't* and *they're*.

Your writing should be factual and unemotional. Avoid words such as *terrible*, *ridiculous*, and *fantastic*. Even if you want to express that idea, it is better to use less emotional words to do so. Compare the following, for example:

Sales results have been absolutely awful this year.

Sales results have been significantly below target this year.

Before you start writing, you should be clear about what you want to say and what you want your report to achieve. Is it mainly to inform others? In that case, what are the key things they need to know? Is it to try to convince others to take a particular course of action? In that case, have you presented your arguments effectively?

Structure

The structure of your report will depend on what you are writing about, but a common structure is as follows:

- **Title page** This includes the title of the report, your name, and the date the report was presented. If relevant, it may also include the name of the person or organization the report was written for.
- **Contents list** A list of sections and subheadings with their page numbers.
- **Executive summary** This is a short summary of the main points of the report. As a rough guide, there should be one sentence for each main part of the report.
- **Introduction** This should include any necessary background information, a statement of the purpose of the report, and a summary of what the report will cover.
- **Main part**
- **Conclusion** This clearly presents the conclusions you have reached in the report. There should be no new information in this section.
- **Recommendations** Many reports have a section where you make recommendations based on the findings of the report.
- **Appendices** In your report, you may want to refer to information that is too detailed or long to go in the body of the report, for instance tables of figures. Such information can be included in appendices.

Lists and bullet points

Numbered lists or lists with bullet points can often be a clear way of presenting information.

Make the style of lists consistent, for example by deciding whether or not each item begins with a capital and ends with a full stop.

For lists of items, a common phrase to use is *the following:*

Please ensure you bring the following items:
a recent photograph
a form of identification, such as a passport
a letter of recommendation from your teacher

If you introduce a list with a phrase, remember that you must be able to add each point to the phrase to make a sentence:

In future, all staff will be required to:

- *update their time sheets daily.*
- *take at least half an hour's break for lunch.*
- *attend regular health and safety briefings.*

Explaining graphs and charts

Diagrams such as graphs and charts can be a useful way to show comparisons, patterns, and trends. They can be placed either in the body of the text or in appendices. They should always be numbered and labelled.

Remember to make sure that diagrams include all the information necessary to understand them. For instance, it must be clear what units are being used on the axes of a graph. This can be explained in a key if the information is difficult to incorporate into the graph itself.

To refer to diagrams in your text or in the appendices, use phrases such as these:

***As shown** in table 1, ..*

***As can be seen from** the diagram...*

***According to** the graph...*

These are ways of talking about **increases** in numbers or amounts:

*These figures **show a rise in** sales from March...*

*Sales were **higher** in March.*

*The number of infections **rose** sharply...*

*There was **a** slight **increase in**...*

*Cases **reached a peak** in 2012...*

*This level **went up** slightly...*

*Numbers are **up** by...*

These are ways of talking about **decreases** in numbers or amounts:

*The period from May saw **a fall/decrease of**...*

*This **dip in** production was caused by...*

*There was **a drop** in temperatures...*

*The number **fell/declined** rapidly.*

*Our market share **shrank** by 5%.*

*There has been **a reduction in**...*

*Levels have since **come down**.*

*Numbers are **down** by...*

These are ways of talking about numbers or amounts that have **not changed**:

*There has been **little/no change** in this level since...*

*Prices have **remained** stable/constant...*

*Cases **continued at the same level**....*

When you talk about changes in numbers or amounts, you will often need to say **how much** they have changed by:

*Numbers rose/fell **by** 9%.*

*These methods produced an increase **of** more than 500 per month.*

*There has been a **small/huge** drop in reported cases.*

*This difference is **not statistically significant**.*

*Consumption of the drug **more than doubled** in this period.*

*Death rates from the disease have **almost halved**.*

*Since then, we have seen **a threefold increase/decrease** in accidents.*

*Sales have declined **at a steady rate** since then.*

Useful adverbs to talk about significant change: considerably, rapidly, sharply, significantly, steeply, suddenly

Making predictions

To talk about what might happen in the future, use phrases like these:

*This could **lead to**...*

*These problems are **likely to**...*

*It is **highly likely** that...*

*It is therefore **possible that**...*

*We must be prepared for **the possibility that**...*

*Current figures suggest that we **may see** a drop in revenue...*

Making recommendations

Recommendations may be presented in a block, with a heading: *Recommendations* or *Key recommendations.* They could be shown with bullet points or in a numbered list.

Alternatively, recommendations can be incorporated into the text with phrases like these:

I therefore recommend that...

It will be necessary for the organization to...

Procedures should therefore be reviewed.

The purchase of a new security system is strongly recommended.

Note that although the use of personal pronouns should usually be avoided in reports, they may sometimes be used in recommendations:

***I therefore recommend** the immediate cancellation of this project.*

***We are strongly opposed to** any changes in staffing levels.*

*In order to guarantee success, **we will have to**...*

Applying for jobs

CVs (UK) / Résumés (US)

A CV (curriculum vitae) sets out information about your education, work experience, and personal details in a clear way. It should be:

- **clear to read and attractively presented.** Remember that the person reading it may have to read many other applications. They must be able to find the information they need quickly and easily. Even with the best qualifications and experience, you are much less likely to get an interview if your CV is poorly presented or contains errors of spelling or grammar.
- **relevant.** Extra information is distracting and may give the impression that you are not committed to the particular job you are applying for.

In the UK, it is usual for a CV to be about 2–3 A4 pages. In the US, a single page (210 x 297 mm) is preferred, especially for new graduates. Use a clear typeface in 10 pt or 12 pt.

There are many different ways of setting out a CV. This is an example for someone who is applying for a job as a support worker in a charity for the homeless.

Serena Johansson CV

Address 5 Denson Court, Cambridge, CB1 3AM

Telephone 01223 539840

Email smason44@btnet.com **1**

Personal Profile 2 I am a lively and friendly person who loves working with people of all ages. I have a lot of volunteering experience, and am a hardworking team member.

Education 3

2009–2012 BSc (hons) Psychology. Anglia Ruskin University. 2:1

2007–2009 Hills Rd Sixth Form College
3 A-levels (Psychology A, Chemistry B, Maths C)

2001–2007 Parkside Academy
11 GCSEs (grades A-C, including maths and English) **4**

Work Experience 5

2012–present Volunteer English teacher, Southern India. I teach large classes of children using locally produced materials and assist in extracurricular activities such as sport and theatre. I have set up a new drama club at the school.

2008–2012 Volunteer, Re-Home (charity which supports the homeless). I supported clients in running a community café.

2009–2012 Weekend work in a local café – waitressing and food preparation.

2007 Two weeks work experience at local newspaper, shadowing news reporter.

Other skills and interests 6

Full, clean driving licence.

I am very computer-literate, and have experience of setting up and maintaining websites.

I play hockey and have a great interest in the theatre.

References 7

Dr J Khan (tutor)	Mrs M Mulholland (volunteer co-ordinator)
Anglia Ruskin University	Re-Home
East Rd	13 Water Lane
Cambridge	Lanston
CB1 1PT	LS9 3PQ

1 It is not necessary to give your age, gender, marital status, or religion.

2 This section should summarize your skills and qualities in a way that shows why you are suitable for the job. Try to write specific things that you can link to your experience rather than general statements about your personality. Use phrases such as these:

good communication skills

work well in a team

keen to take on new challenges

able to work independently

remain calm under pressure

understand the importance of meeting deadlines

Useful adjectives: accurate, creative, hard-working, effective, efficient, flexible, innovative, loyal, meticulous, numerate, organized, practical

3 Start with your most recent qualifications first. If you have had one or more full-time jobs, it is usual to put the Work Experience section before Education.

4 If you have higher qualifications, it is not necessary to give full detail of lower school qualifications, unless they are particularly relevant to the job, or are a specific requirement of the job.

5 This section should start with the most recent experience first. For each job, you should explain your main responsibilities, stressing any that are relevant to the job you are applying for. Give more detail for the most recent experience. Use phrases such as these:

was responsible for…

lead a team of six…

assisted in all aspects of…

worked at a senior level in…

introduced new systems for…

gained extensive experience of…

6 Include any skills that may be relevant to the job you are applying for. Try to include one or two interests to give some idea of the sort of person you are.

Full, clean driving licence.

Fluent French.

Familiar with QuickBooks and other accounting packages.

Trained lifeguard.

Voluntary literacy tutor.

7 Choose referees who can say something relevant about you if asked. You should try to include at least one referee who has worked with you, preferably as your manager. You may also choose one personal referee who can talk about your character. It is often considered acceptable to write: 'References available on request.' You may do this if you do not wish to ask someone to be a referee until a later stage in the application process.

Covering letters (UK) / Cover letters (US)

When you send a CV or other job application, it is usual to enclose a covering letter. This letter should summarize the reasons why you think you would be suitable for the position, and include any extra information you want to give, for example about your own career objectives or about your current personal circumstances.

The tone of the letter should be formal. Here is an example of a covering letter to accompany the CV on the previous page, sent to apply for a job as a support worker in a charity for the homeless.

5 Denson Court
Cambridge
CB1 3AM

19 July 2013

Dear Ms Park **1**

Support worker, Ely 2

I am writing in response to your advertisement in *The Big Issue* magazine on July 3rd for a support worker based at your Ely premises. **3**

I enclose my CV, from which you will see that I have a long-standing interest and involvement in the area of homelessness. For almost the whole of my time at university, I was a volunteer at the homeless charity Re-Home, where I undertook a variety of tasks connected with running a small, client-led café.

My experience at Re-Home confirmed my desire to work in the charitable sector. I believe that my academic training in psychology would be valuable in this job, where psychological issues are such an important aspect of many homeless people's lives. As part of my final-year dissertation, I conducted in-depth interviews with several homeless people. **4**

I am a good team member and I am quick to learn new skills. I love working with people from all kinds of backgrounds, and am friendly and cheerful. **5**

After almost 18 months of volunteering in India, I am now looking for a permanent position. **6** I plan to visit my parents at the above address in the near future, and could arrange the time to coincide with an interview date. Please use that address for any correspondence. **7**

I very much hope that you will consider me for this post **8**, and look forward to hearing from you soon.

Yours truly,

Serena Johansson

Serena Johansson

Enc. CV **9**

1 You should address your letter to a specific person. If the job advert does not contain a name, phone the company and find out.

2 Write the title of the job your are applying for at the beginning of the letter.

3 Say how you found out about the post.

4 Give the main points of your experience that make you suitable for the post.

5 Explain the personal qualities that make you suitable for the post.

6 If you are already in a job, it is usual to explain why you want to leave. Phrases such as the following may be used:

I now feel ready to move to a more challenging position.

I am looking for a post with more responsibility.

I feel that this post would make better use of my experience and qualifications.

I am no longer able to undertake the travel that my current post requires.

I have recently moved to this area in order to support my elderly parents.

7 Make sure you include any practical information about your address, availability for interview, etc.

8 In a formal job application, it is common to use the words *post* or *position* rather than 'job'.

9 If you have enclosed any documents with your letter, state this after your signature.

Literary criticism

Literary criticism is the analysis and discussion of different forms of literature: novels, stories, poetry, and plays. To write about them, you will need some specialist terms.

Styles of text

There are many different textual styles.

Stream of consciousness is a style that aims to represent a character's feelings and thoughts as they experience them, using long continuous pieces of text without obvious organization or structure. James Joyce's *Ulysses* is an example of this style.

A **coming-of-age** novel, also known as a **Bildungsroman** is a novel about the psychological development of a person entering adulthood. J.D. Salinger's *The Catcher in the Rye* is an example of this.

An **epistolary novel** is written in the form of letters. An example of this is *The Woman in White* by Wilkie Collins.

Plays are often categorized as **comedy, tragedy**, or **farce** (a humorous play where characters become involved in unlikely situations). A play or book that is both humorous and tragic is a **tragicomedy**. In a **melodrama**, characters show particularly strong emotions.

A play or part of a book or play where one character speaks for a long time is a **monologue**, while in a play, a speech in which a character speaks their thoughts is a **soliloquy**.

Some plays and novels have an extra meaning that is not obvious from its literal meaning. In an **allegory**, the characters and events represent particular qualities or ideas, related to morals, religion, or politics. *Animal Farm* by George Orwell is an **allegorical novella** (short novel).

A **pastiche** is a piece of writing that intentionally copies the style of someone else's work, while a **parody** copies but exaggerates the style of someone else's work for comic effect. **Satire** is writing that is intended to criticize people or ideas in a humorous way.

Aspects of novels, stories, and plays

What happens in a story is its **narrative**, and the way a story progresses is known as the **narrative drive**. The story can also be called the **plot**, and other, more minor stories within a text are the **subplots**. The end of a story, usually where everything is explained, is known as the **denoument**. An artificial or very unlikely end to a story or event, which solves or removes any problems too easily, is known as a **deus ex machina**.

Many works of fiction have both **major** and **minor characters**, and the way they are shown is known as **characterization**. The main character is sometimes called the **protagonist**. A character may be included to act as a **foil** for another character (to make the second character's qualities more obvious).

The person telling the story is the **narrator**. If the story is told by the main character in the book, using the pronoun *I*, this is a **first-person narrator**. An **omniscient narrator** writes about all the characters, using *he* and *she*. We say that this type of text is written **in the third person**. Some novels have an **unreliable narrator**. In these novels, an example of which is Kazuo Ishiguro's *The Remains of the Day*, it is clear to the reader that the narrator misunderstands or misrepresents what is happening.

Linguistic and literary devices

Literary techniques are often known as **rhetorical devices**.

There are many linguistic and literary devices that involve words used to represent something other than their literal meaning.

For example, a **figurative** use of *nightmare* means 'a bad situation'. We often call longer figurative expressions **figures of speech**. When people use **irony**, they mean the opposite of what they say. The phrase **dramatic irony** is used to describe a situation in which the reader understands more than the characters about what is happening, for example when characters do not know they are in danger. **Imagery** is the use of words to suggest ideas, emotions, or situations.

Metonymy is when something is referred to by a word that is closely connected with is, for example 'the crown' to refer to royalty, and **euphemism** is the use of a bland word to avoid using a word that is unpleasant or offensive.

When a writer or poet uses words that give human feelings or qualities to objects, nature, or animals, for example by referring to the 'cruel sea', this is known as **pathetic fallacy**. **Personification** is when human characteristics are given to inanimate objects or abstract ideas.

A **simile** is where one thing is compared to another, for example in the phrase 'as light as air', while a **metaphor** describes a person or object by referring to something that is considered to have similar characteristics, as for example in the phrase 'The mind is an ocean'.

Hyperbole is a way of writing that exaggerates what is said. In plays, a character may display **hubris**, an exaggerated sense of pride, usually to emphasize their subsequent downfall.

An **oxymoron** is a phrase composed of two seemingly contradictory words or phrases, used for emphasis, as in the phrase 'a deafening silence'. Similarly, a **paradox** is when two seemingly opposite ideas are used together, for example in the phrase 'You have to be cruel to be kind'.

Sounds of language

A unit of speech, either a whole word or one of the parts into which a word can be separated, is a **syllable**.

Alliteration is the use of the same sound or sounds, especially consonants, at the beginning of several words that are close together, while **assonance** is the use of similar sounds anywhere in a group of words.

Onomatopoeia is the use of words that have a similar sound to the things they describe, for example *splash*.

Poetry

Traditional forms of poetry have **rhyming** verses, but many more modern poets use **free verse**, where there is no pattern. **Blank verse** does not rhyme, but the lines usually have ten syllables. The arrangement of syllables in a poem's lines is its **metre** (UK)/**meter** (US). When a line of a poem has a number of beats which fits with the other lines, it is said to **scan**. This kind of regular rhythm is called **scansion**.

Two lines of poetry are a **couplet**, and if they rhyme, they are a **rhyming couplet**. A group of lines is a **stanza** or a **verse**.

A **foot** is a unit of division of a line of poetry containing one strong beat and one or two weaker ones. An **iambic** rhythm is one in which each short syllable that is not stressed is followed by a long or stressed syllable. An **iambic pentameter** is a rhythm in which each line is made of five iambic pairs.

Narrative poetry tells a story, often with characters speaking, and **dramatic poetry** takes the form of a play. Long narrative poems, often about heroic deeds are **epic poetry**, while **lyric poetry** expresses feelings and emotions.

An **elegy** is a sad poem, often about someone who has died. An **ode** expresses thoughts or feelings about a particular subject, and a **sonnet** is a 14-line poem with a particular pattern of rhyme.

Book and movie reviews

Reviews are to give your opinion about a book or a movie, and to provide a recommendation to the reader. This section will give you useful words and phrases for writing reviews.

As with most writing, a review should have an introduction, a main part, and a conclusion. The introduction should give the most important information about the book or movie, such as its name, its author, its genre, or the actors performing in it. It is usual to talk about the plot, but you should remember not to spoil the story for your readers. The conclusion should make your own opinion of the book or movie clear.

Introduction

Your introduction should make it clear what kind of book or movie you are reviewing. You can use common words for genres, such as *science fiction, romance, thriller, autobiography, historical novel*, or you could use a more descriptive phrase that gives a flavour of the style:

a gripping psychological thriller

this fascinating account of the life of Dickens

an authoritative guide to the birds of Britain

a gritty courtroom drama

a gentle comedy

the novel take a wry look at relationships

a fly-on-the-wall documentary

Useful adjectives for interesting books and movies: compelling, engrossing, intriguing, original, thought-provoking

Useful adjectives for uninteresting books and movies: banal, clichéd, corny, derivative, formulaic, hackneyed, mundane, unoriginal

The introduction should also give any basic background information:

an autobiographical/semi-autobiographical novel

an adaptation of Alan Hollinghurst's novel

the sequel to her best-selling novel

the second book in her trilogy about x

In the case of films, it should also name the main actors:

the new rom com ***starring*** *Natalie Portman and Ashton Kutcher*

Sylvester Stallone leads an ***all-star cast*** *in 'Expendables 2'.*

... in which Kate Winslet ***plays*** *a disaffected housewife...*

Viola Davis ***stars*** *alongside Maggie Gyllenhaal in...*

... in which Clooney is ***cast as*** *a hatchet man...*

Pitt, along with ***co-stars*** *Jonah Hill and Chris Pratt...*

The ***lead role*** *is taken by Mia Sarah.*

Plot

In a review, it is usual to describe the plot, without giving away the ending. The present tense is usually used:

When a young takes a job in Chicago, he gets caught up in a world of crime.

Newlyweds Chuck and Donna decide to take the holiday of a lifetime.

Useful adjectives: action-packed, fast-moving, pacy, slow-paced

Background

The review should talk about the background and setting:

... set against a backdrop of the civil war...

... set in 1914...

... written in the immediate aftermath of the 9/11 attacks.

Most of the action takes place aboard Clifford's yacht.

The novel follows the lives of two 18th-century scientists.

Features

You should mention any particular features or techniques. For movies, they may include the following:

*The movie was **shot on location** in Africa.*

The movie is shot in black and white.

*Look out for the amazing **special effects**.*

*The movie is available **in 3-D**.*

*The movie features a **soundtrack** by Nick Cave.*

*The film is remarkable for its 1960s **period details**.*

*The director has taken pains to ensure **historical accuracy**.*

For books, these phrases may be suitable:

*His **use of language** is highly original.*

The book is beautifully written.

*There are large stretches of **dialogue** in the novel.*

Acting

If you are reviewing a movie, you need to comment on the performances of the actors.

*I **found her performance** stale/electrifying.*

*She was **unconvincing** in the role of Jill.*

*His **portrayal** of a repentant villain was **masterful/mesmerizing**.*

*George Clooney **gives a fine performance as** a struggling dad.*

*There isn't much **on-screen chemistry** between the two stars.*

Recommendation

By the end of a review, the reader should know whether the reviewer recommends the book or movie or not. The conclusion of the piece usually makes this clear:

I could not put this book down.

A perfect holiday read!

A must-read volume for anyone interested in Russian history.

The movie had me on the edge of my seat all the way through.

This is a story that will stay with you for a long time.

Tremain is at the height of her powers in this engrossing book.

As a pleasant way to pass a couple of hours, this movie fits the bill, but it is hardly likely to become a classic.

Despite the leaden prose, this book contains much that is of interest.

A biased and inaccurate account of what could have been a fascinating subject.

This book would have benefited from being about half as long.

This latest volume gives the impression of being rushed out far too quickly.

Ultimately, the movie fails to engage its audience.

Academic writing

This section will give you general advice on academic writing. However, before you start any piece of academic writing (for example an essay, dissertation, or academic paper), check whether your institution or department has guidelines that they expect you to follow.

Style and structure

Style

Academic writing is formal in style, and has several important characteristics. These are some of the ways in which it is different from other forms of writing:

- **Avoidance of the first person**
  It is not usual to use *I* or *my* in academic writing. *We* and *our* are also much less common than in other forms of writing. Passive forms are often used instead.
- **Avoidance of contractions**
  Academic writing does not use contractions such as *won't, he's,* or *haven't.*
- **Use of nouns**
  Academic writing often uses nouns where other forms of writing would be more likely to use verbs, e.g. *the* ***spread*** *of diseases; the* ***measurement*** *of iron levels; an* ***analysis*** *of the data.*
- **Use of the passive**
  Passive forms are used frequently to talk about evidence and research methods, e.g. *It* ***has been shown*** *that… Reasearch* ***has been done****… The samples* ***were stored*** *in a sterile unit…*
- **Complex sentences**
  Academic writing often contains quite complex sentences using linking words like *furthermore* or *similarly.*
- **Avoidance of idiomatic language**
  Idioms are not usually appropriate for academic writing.
- **Avoidance of slang and informal language**
  Words and phrases labelled *informal* or *slang* in this dictionary are unlikely to be suitable.
- **Objectivity**
  It is important that academic writing is objective, and that what is written is supported by evidence rather than merely describing the writer's opinion.

Structure

Any piece of academic writing must have an introduction, a main part, and a conclusion. Longer pieces of writing often include an abstract, which is a short summary of the contents. See below for more detail about these sections.

Remember to use clear paragraphs, rather than long stretches of text. In general, each paragraph should contain one main point.

Headings

Academic texts often have headings and subheadings, especially if they are long. Making a draft of the structure of your piece of writing can help you organize your material.

Unless your institution has its own guidelines, you can use whatever numbering system you prefer, but make sure the structure is logical and consistent, for example by using the same font and size for the same type of heading, deciding how to use capital letters, and deciding whether or not to use full stops.

A common numbering system is as follows:

1. Main heading

1.1 Subheading

1.1.1 Sub-subheading

It is best not to use too many headings – usually not more than two or three per page. Make them as specific as you can.

Titles and abstracts

The title

You may be given a title, or you may make up a title of your own. In either case, pay particular attention to the verbs in the title, and make sure that the piece of writing does what the title says it will.

The following verbs are often used in essay titles:

analyse discuss illustrate assess evaluate outline compare explain summarize contrast identify

Writing an abstract

Long pieces of writing, especially academic papers, need an abstract. This is a short summary of what is in your paper. It follows roughly the same structure as the paper itself. The length of your abstract may vary, but would typically be around 200–300 words.

The introduction

Introducing topic and purpose

For talking about the topic and purpose of a piece of academic writing, we often use the future formed with *will* or the present simple:

This paper ***will look at*** *the question of…*

This report ***analyses*** *recent research in the field of…*

Useful verbs: assess, consider, deal with, discuss, examine, explore, evaluate, focus on, look at

Putting the writing into context

Your introduction should explain the reason for your work by explaining why it is important and placing it in a wider context:

It has long been believed that…

There has been a recent surge of interest in…

As more and more people use mobile phones, it is necessary to question…

The issue of public health resources is one that affects everybody.

Previous studies have shown conflicting results.

The internet was one of the most important developments of the 20th century.

Defining your terms

It is important that your readers understand exactly what you mean by the words you use in your writing, especially if you are using them in a technical or restricted way.

In this essay, x is defined as…

x is usually defined as…

The National Cancer Institute defines x as…

By 'x', the authors mean…

The term 'x' describes…

Throughout this paper, the term 'x' will refer to…

Explaining the structure

The introduction should explain how the piece is organized.

This paper is in three main parts.

Additional information is supplied in the appendices.

The first part of the essay deals with…

The first part of the essay will look at…

The essay begins by discussing…

The paper then goes on to discuss…

Some problems with the research will then be examined.

The essay concludes by…

The final part of the paper makes several recommendations for…

The main part of the text

Some of the words and phrases in the section on Formal Writing may also be useful for academic writing.

Presenting evidence

You will need to present evidence to back up the points you are making:

Research shows…

A recent report/survey showed…

There is a body of evidence to suggest…

The latest findings support the hypothesis that…

Our results confirmed that…

The latest/most recent figures suggest that…

Studies indicate that…

Useful verbs: confirm, demonstrate, establish, indicate, prove, reveal, show, suggest

Useful nouns: analysis, data, experiment, figures, findings, hypothesis, proof, research, study

You may also want to point out where there is little or no evidence:

Little is known about…

More research is needed into…

There are still gaps in the data.

A question remains whether…

Previous research fails to take account of…

If different sources of evidence are inconsistent, you can use phrases like these:

The findings of Smith (2001) and Jones (2007) appear to be contradictory.

However, other studies suggest…

These findings have not been replicated in other studies.

Methods

If you are describing research, you will need to talk about the methods you used. It is common to use passive forms for this:

The mice were fed three times a day.

Questionnaires were sent to over 1,000 households.

Useful verbs: analyse, calculate, carry out, check, collect, estimate, examine, implement, introduce, measure, obtain, test

It is important to be clear about the order of processes:

First/Firstly*, a questionnaire was produced.*

Secondly*, a pilot study was carried out.*

After *examining the tissue,….*

Next*, the team repeated the experiment.*

Finally*, all participants were informed of the results.*

You may want to explain the reasons behind the methods you have used:

In constructing the experiment in this way, ***our aim was to****...*

Participants were interviewed ***in order to*** *check...*

Measurements were taken ***for the purpose of...***

A second test was carried out ***so that****...*

Talking about accuracy

These are ways of talking about the accuracy of research methods:

To ***ensure accuracy****, each experiment is performed twice.*

The sensor measures blood sugar levels ***with great precision****.*

There was ***little margin for error****.*

Information was taken only from ***reliable*** *sources.*

Useful adjectives and adverbs: accurate/ly, authoritative/ly, exact/ly, precise/ly, rigorous/ly, scrupulous/ly, specific/ally, strict/ly

Opinions

In academic writing, your own opinions must always be supported by evidence. It is therefore rare to use general phrases such as *In my opinion*. However, for facts that are generally accepted it is permissible to use phrases such as the following:

It is certainly true that...,

It has long been the case that...

Few people would argue that...,

You will often want to talk about the views of other people.

Smith asserts that...

In Smith's opinion...

According to Smith,...

Many/some people argue that...

As Smith (2007) says,...

In his latest paper, Smith challenges the idea that...

Useful verbs: argue, assert, believe, claim, comment, maintain, point out

Referring to the work of others

(see also *Quoting and copyright, References and footnotes*)

Some pieces of academic writing include a **literature review**, which looks at material that is relevant to your writing. It puts your own work into context. The amount of literature you review will depend on the length of the piece you are writing: the longer your piece, the more detailed your literature review will be. For the literature review, the most important and relevant points of each article you describe must be summarized to one or two sentences:

Smith (2008) found no link between x and y.

Several studies (e.g. Taylor 2004, Jones 2008) have provided further evidence of this.

You may refer to other people's work in order to strengthen your own argument. In this case, you will present their work in a positive or a neutral way:

As Brown (2011) says,....

Smith (2007) gives several examples of this phenomenon.

In her 2009 article, White points out that...

Khan's studies lend weight to the idea that...

Criticizing the work of others

You may want to be critical of the work of others, for instance to show that further research is needed or to justify a contradictory position. Remember that you must always criticize the research, never the researcher:

Their research ***failed to take account of*** *other variables, such as....*

This argument ***overlooks/ignores the fact that****...*

Our own research ***found little evidence to support*** *this claim.*

Further studies have ***cast doubt on*** *these findings.*

The research methods were ***flawed****.*

The results were ***distorted*** *by...*

Describing cause and effect

To talk about the reasons for something, use phrases such as these:

This may be ***a result of****...*

A further ***consequence*** *of this was...*

This ***had the effect of****...The drop in numbers was* ***due to****...*

Contamination may have been ***a factor in*** *this result.*

The variation may be ***attributable to****...*

We often use adverbs or adverbial phrases to express cause:

Because of this,...

As a result,...

Consequently,...

The trials were ***therefore*** *carried out anonymously.*

Useful adverbs: accordingly, consequently, hence, therefore, thus

We often use *-ing verbs* to talk about changes that cause a particular result:

Employment levels fell, ***leading*** *to a decrease in non-essential spending.*

*Water became contaminated, **resulting** in a further spread of the disease.*

Useful verbs: bring about, cause, contribute to, ensure, generate, lead to, produce, yield

To add a more important reason:

More importantly,...

More significantly,...

Comparing and contrasting

To talk about things that are similar, use words and phrases such as these:

*There are some **similarities between** the two substances.*

*We can see **parallels between** the groups.*

*The results were **remarkably similar**.*

*The situations are **directly comparable**.*

*A battery is **analogous to** a pump in a water circuit.*

Useful adjectives: alike, analogous, comparable, equivalent, identical, similar

To talk about differences, use the following:

*These findings **differed from** those of the previous study.*

***This contrasts with** the effects seen under water.*

*Younger participants found this task simple, **whereas** older participants had some problems.*

We often emphasize differences by adding an adjective:

This was in marked/stark/sharp contrast to...

We found a clear distinction between...

There was a significant/considerable difference between...

We often begin a sentence with an adverb or an adverb phrase to show that what follows contrasts with what came before:

***On the other hand**, compounds are formed of two or more elements.*

***By contrast**, men were found to be less likely to eat these foodstuffs.*

***On the contrary**, life expectancy was shown to increase.*

***By comparison**, this technique proved more reliable.*

Useful adverbs: alternatively, conversely, however

We often modify comparatives using words such as *much, far,* and *slightly:*

The results were slightly less conclusive.

The experiment was repeated at far higher temperatures.

These participants were not quite as experienced as the previous group.

Classifying

In academic writing, it is often necessary to group things according to some form of classification:

There are two types/categories/classes/varieties of...

The x may be categorized on the basis of...

The x may be grouped into three categories...

These plants belong to the genus 'Sarracenia'.

His work falls into the genre of 'fantasy'.

Expressing degrees of truth

The following are ways of talking about things that often exist or are usually true:

***Most of** the cells of the lower epidermis resemble those of the upper epidermis.*

***The majority of** respondents were aged between 20 and 40.*

*The demand upon a resource **tends to** expand to match the supply of the resource.*

We often start a sentence with an adverb or an adverb phrase to show that things are usually true:

***In general**, people in group 1 were more successful.*

***In most cases**, the patients did not need drugs.*

***As a general rule**, the biggest eruptions come from magmas with high gas levels.*

***For the most part**, respondents agreed with this statement.*

***On the whole**, the experiments were successful.*

Adverbs are also used within sentences:

*Such symptoms are not **typically** associated with this disease.*

*These children **often** have behavioural problems.*

Useful adverbs: frequently, generally, mostly, normally, often, predominantly, typically, usually

To talk about things that sometimes exist or are sometimes true, you can use the following:

***Some/several of** the samples were found to be contaminated.*

***A number of** methods were trialled.*

*This phenomenon can **sometimes** be observed.*

***From time to time**, new dates were added.*

***Occasional** exceptions were noted.*

To talk about things that rarely exist or are rarely true, you can use the following:

*These creatures **hardly ever** live for more than a few months.*

*The disease is **rarely** found in children.*

*The report claims that mammograms **only occasionally** save lives.*

*This type of vehicle is **seldom** found outside Scandinavia.*

***Only a small minority** of partially sighted people have no useful sight.*

These are ways of talking about things that are partly true:

*The reasons are at least **partly** to do with age.*

***In some respects**, it is very similar to the process of mitosis.*

*All flat maps distort the size of the continents **to a certain degree**.*

*The disease can be alleviated **to some extent** by diet.*

*The numbers remained **relatively** stable.*

You may also want to say that something is almost certainly not true:

It seems unlikely that...

Most scientists do not believe that...

Talking about degrees of certainty

Words like *always* and *never* show that what you are saying is certain:

*These atoms **never** bind to one another.*

*Bats **always** try to avoid contact with humans.*

There are many adjectives and adverbs that express certainty:

*Discrimination has **undoubtedly** been the cause of suffering for many.*

*It was **evident** that current theories could not explain this.*

Useful adjectives and adverbs: categorical/ly, certain/ly, clear/ly, clear-cut, conclusive/ly, concrete, definite/ly, evident/ly, incontrovertible/ibly, undoubted/ly

There are many ways of showing that something is not certain:

It is not necessarily the case that...

The probable cause of the accident was...

The team made the assumption that...

One theory is that...

They worked on the hypothesis that...

It is likely that...

The data seems to be accurate.

The drugs are thought to work by reducing high pressure in arteries.

From these results, scientists inferred...

The side effects of the drugs are arguably worse than the disease.

Modal verbs are often used to express uncertainty:

*It **may** be the case that...*

*This **could** be the result of...*

*These drugs **might** have a greater effect if...*

*It **can** be difficult to measure...*

Talking about approximate numbers

Sometimes it is not possible to be exact. In these cases, use words like these:

*The test took **approximately** 10 minutes.*

*The survey was completed by **around/about** 80 students.*

***An estimated** 3,000 people took part in the trial.*

*The area is **roughly** equivalent to the size of Europe.*

Emphasizing

One way of emphasizing is to add an emphatic adverb or adverb phrase that links with something you said in the previous sentence:

***Indeed**, the increase was even greater than had been anticipated.*

*The students **actually** performed better without the aids.*

Another way is to add an emphatic adverb before an adjective.

*The studies were **deeply** flawed.*

*The results are **highly** significant.*

*This point has been **greatly** exaggerated.*

We often use adverbs or adverbial phrases for emphasis:

*Many people, **particularly/notably** those living in the south, benefited from these changes.*

***In particular**, the study has been useful in identifying areas for further research.*

*Some staff, **chiefly/especially** those working in the retail sector, have suffered from this.*

Giving examples

These words and phrases are used for giving examples:

*This occurs, **for example**, in patients with dehydration.*

*There were several non-text elements, **e.g.** images and graphs.*

***For instance**, some respondents felt that taxes were already too high.*

***One example of this** is the cochlear implants used to help deaf people hear again.*

*Cooling methods **such as** fanning were used.*

*Our example of the tomato is **a good illustration of** this.*

To highlight the importance of one particular example, use adverbs such as these:

*Some people, **particularly** those living in the south...*

*The novel enjoyed some success, **in particular** with young girls.*

Several universities, ***notably*** *Oxford and Cambridge,...*

Most found work, ***chiefly*** *in the construction industry.*

Adding further information

Another point is *that letter placement within words is not random.*

A related point is *the need to create clear categories.*

A further reason *for these claims is...*

To strengthen a point you have made, you can use an adverb or an adverb phrase to link the next sentence:

In addition, *there was a small administration charge.*

Additionally, *the women were asked to record their food intake.*

Furthermore, *some aspects of society are outside the domain of government.*

The samples were ***also*** *analysed.*

Moreover, *materials for classroom use must be carefully written.*

These adverbs are used to talk about a similar situation:

These techniques were ***equally*** *effective.*

Similarly, *further tests demonstrated the effect of colour on mood.*

Sometimes you will need to give information that may be surprising after what you have said before:

Despite this, *scientists have found...*

While this may be the case, *it is still true to say...*

Even so, *some improvement was recorded.*

Nevertheless, *many people still felt that the actions were unethical.*

Referring forwards and backwards

To talk about something that has been written earlier in the piece, use *above*, and to talk about something later in the piece, use *below:*

As discussed above...

See also Fig. 13, below.

Conclusion and references

References and footnotes

According to the length of your piece of writing, full references to works discussed in the text might be in a footnote or in a separate bibliography section. There are several different ways of showing references, and you will need to check which one you are expected to use.

To reference books to which you have referred, or to create a bibliography, a common method is: Author's family name, initial, (year of publication) *Title of book,* City of publication: Publisher:

Sinclair, J. (1991) *Corpus, Concordance, Collocation,* Oxford: OUP.

For books with more than one author:

Daunton, M. and Hilton, M. (2001) *The Politics of Consumption,* Oxford: Berg.

For books with chapters written by different authors, it is usual to reference the editor:

Smith, M. (ed.) (1999) *Thinking through the Environment,* London: Routledge.

However, if you want specifically to reference one of the authors in a multi-author volume, you start with that author but reference the editor too:

Brieger, G. (1993) 'The historiography of medicine' in Bynum, W.G. and Porter, R. (eds) *Companion Encyclopedia of the History of Medicine,* London: Routledge, 24-44.

Note that names of chapters are usually written in roman type, whereas names of books are usually italic. The page numbers of the chapter are shown at the end of the reference.

Papers or articles in journals are often referenced like this:

Vilpula, M. (1995) 'The Sun and the Definition of Day', in *International Journal of Lexicography* 8.1, 29-38.

You must also provide references for quotations from material found on the internet:

Seidelhofer, B. (2005) *English as a Lingua Franca.* Available at: < http://people.ufpr.br/~clarissa/pdfs/ELF_Seidlhofer2005.pdf > [Accessed on 15.07.2012].

The conclusion

The last part of your essay, dissertation, etc. brings together the evidence you have presented and draws conclusions from it.

Depending on the type of writing, your conclusion may do the following:

- Summarize facts that you have presented in the writing.
- State your opinion, based on the evidence you have given in the writing.
- Show that you have done what was asked for in the title.

You should explain the significance of your conclusions.

In conclusion...

We can therefore conclude that...

It is therefore clear that ...

It was not possible to reach any conclusions regarding...

The key findings of the research can be summarized thus:...

Quoting and copyright

Quotations and copying

Quotations can be useful to support your ideas or to show different opinions. Be careful not to use too many quotes – you should focus on your own work. If you use a quote, make sure it is there for a good reason.

If you refer to the work of others, you must *always* acknowledge it. Using other people's work without acknowledgment is called plagiarism, and is not allowed in academic writing. In some cases, it may even be illegal.

If you are a student, it can be tempting to use online essay banks, but you should be aware that most universities and exam boards now use sophisticated programs that can spot text that has been copied from the internet. Essay banks may be of poor quality, so it is best not to use them at all, even for research and planning – it is much better to use material that comes from a reliable source or has been recommended by your teachers.

Direct quotes

If you use a **direct quote**, you must give a full reference for the source (see below). It is essential that the words you use are identical to the original. However, if you want to leave out parts of the original, you can indicate that you have done so by writing [...].

Here are some ways of including direct quotes in your writing:

> *According to Tomalin (2002), 'On Pepys' side, the disapproval and scorn for the king expressed in the Diary appear to melt away.'*

> *As Todd Sandler (1997) points out: 'Nations are loathe to empower a supranational body with the authority to collect taxes.'*

In these quotes, the full reference must be given in a footnote or a bibliography. If you are not intending to include a section for references, a full reference can be incorporated into the main text:

> *In her 2002 biography of Samuel Pepys, Claire Tomalin says, 'On Pepys' side, the disapproval and scorn for the king expressed in the Diary appear to melt away.'*

If the quote you want to use is more than two or three lines long, it should go in a separate paragraph that is contrasted with the rest of your piece, for instance by being indented further from the margins or by being in a separate font. In this case, it is not necessary to use quotation marks.

You can also quote just a few words as part of a sentence:

> *The authors also suggest that such methods may be 'open to abuse'.*

Indirect quotes

Indirect quotes are when you put other people's ideas and research into your own words. This is fine, but you must still acknowledge your source, and you must make sure that your version is an accurate representation of the original.

> *Research by Mullin (2008) indicated that the problem is not restricted to low-income families.*

> *In her book 'Living with Depression', the author also argued that exercise may be beneficial in some cases.*

Copyright

In academic writing it is permissible to use short quotations as shown above. This is known as 'fair use'. However, you should be aware that using large amounts of someone else's text may be illegal if you do not have permission, even if you have acknowledged the source. The same is true for images such as drawings or photographs.

If you want to use copyright material that is outside the scope of 'fair use', you must get permission from the author, publisher, artist, photographer, etc. You may sometimes be asked to pay a fee for this.

For instance, if you wanted to make a published glossary using definitions from this dictionary, you would need to seek permission from Cambridge University Press.

Presentations

Giving a good presentation

Although a presentation is a spoken activity rather than a written one, you will almost certainly need to write at least notes to help you plan. Even if you only write down notes, the language shown in the section below will help you to be able to speak to those notes in a confident and natural way.

Many presenters also use notes to help them while they are giving the presentation. You could write down some of the phrases given here to use at particular points. However, you should never read a presentation word for word – this is very boring for the audience.

As with all longer types of writing, the key to a good presentation is being absolutely clear about your message and the best way to present it to your audience.

Think very carefully about how much your audience already knows about the subject.

If the audience is likely to include people whose first language is not the language of your presentation, you will need to think even more carefully about the language you use.

Remember that, unlike with a written document, they cannot re-read sections or look words up. You may want to make more use of the section on repeating and clarifying, below, and you should be very careful about the use of idiomatic language.

Style and structure

A presentation is a formal event, but you will be speaking and you need to hold the interest of your audience. In many presentations it will be acceptable to use a reasonably informal style and to include anecdotes and possibly jokes that would be out of place in a written report.

It is common in spoken presentations to introduce points with a question:

> *So, how does this relate to our work?*
>
> *What can we learn from these studies?*
>
> *How much is this likely to cost?*
>
> *How can we make this happen?*

The structure of a presentation is very like that of a piece of academic writing (see above). It should have a clear introduction, a main part, and a conclusion.

The best presentations start and finish with something very memorable.

Give extra thought to these sections. For example, you may wish to introduce your subject by relating it to a personal experience or something that is very topical at the time. You might conclude by showing how your audience could use the information given in your presentation in practice.

In some circumstances it may be possible to use humour, but you should always consider your audience's sensitivities and avoid giving offence of any kind.

Visuals

When referring to your slides and handouts, you will be able to use many of the phrases in the section on Explaining Graphs and Charts, above. You can introduce them by saying something such as:

> *As you can see from this chart…*
>
> *I'd like you to take a moment to look at this graph…*
>
> *Have a look at these figures.*
>
> *What we can see from this table is…*

Handouts

More detailed information can be provided in handouts if necessary.

Sometimes it can be a good idea to give out handouts *after* the presentation so that the audience is not distracted by reading them. This is particularly the case where your presentation is more interactive – you may, for example, ask the audience to come up with ideas or comments about a particular issue, an activity that loses its point if they already have the answers on a handout in front of them.

Slides

It is common to use computer slides when giving a presentation. These can give a professional touch to your presentation, but it is important not to let the features that such programs offer become too dominant and distract from your message.

Use contrasting colours for your text and background, generally a dark colour against a white or pale-coloured background. You should use no more than two colours for the text (it can be attractive to have a different colour and a larger font size for the main heading).

It is generally preferable to use a plain font such as Arial. To be sure that your text will be legible to people at the back of the room, you should generally use font sizes no smaller than 28 point.

Use short bullet points instead of continuous text, which can be difficult for your audience to

Computer slides
• Use contrasting colours
• Use a plain font, minimum 28 point
• Use short bullet points
• Use visual aids
• Avoid animation and sound effects

concentrate on. These bullet points can act as prompts to help you remember what you want to say. It can be helpful to reveal your points one by one, to avoid your audience reading ahead.

Think about using visual aids such as graphs, diagrams, and images, which can help to keep your audience's attention.

Animation and sound effects should either be avoided or kept as simple as possible. If you have bullet points appearing one by one, be consistent in the type of effect you use. Having text simply appear on the screen is easier for your audience to follow than text that flies in from the side.

Above is an example of a simple slide.

The language of presentations

Introducing yourself and your talk

These are general phrases that people often use to start a presentation:

It's great to see so many people here today.

Thank you for inviting me here today.

You may want to tell them more about who you are and why you are giving the presentation:

First, I'd like to tell you a bit about myself.

To give you a bit of background…

I'm here today to talk about…

You will probably want to explain the structure and content of your presentation:

I'm going to start off by…

First, I'll be talking about…

Just to give you a brief outline of what I hope to cover today…

I aim to cover three main areas.

I'm going to start off by explaining…

Then I'll be moving on to…

The second part of this talk deals with…

After that, we'll take a look at…

And I'll be finishing with…

It is often a good idea to say clearly how you want to deal with questions:

I'm happy to take questions as we go along.

There will be time for questions at the end.

Involving your audience

During the presentation, you will be very aware of your audience, and will probably want to acknowledge their presence. One way of doing this is to find ways of relating their own experiences to what you are saying:

How many of you have had a similar experience?

If you're anything like me, you probably find it hard to switch off from work.

Using question tags is another way to involve the audience. You are not really asking for a response, but the question acknowledges their presence:

We all know that this is a problem, don't we?

To show that you are aware that they may already know something about your subject you could say something like:

As you know,…

As you may be aware…

Some of you may already have seen…

As I'm sure many of you will know…

To show that you are aware of their probable reaction to what you are saying, you could say:

I know what you're thinking, but…

You may be wondering…

You're probably asking yourselves…

You can also check occasionally that your audience has understood what you have said:

Does that make sense?

Do you see what I mean?

Changing the subject

These are ways of moving onto a different part of your presentation:

Now I'd like to move on to…

Let's move on now to the subject of…

Let's turn now to…

This brings/leads us on to…

To return to an earlier point, you can say:

As I said before,…

This relates to my previous point about…

You'll remember that I said…

Earlier we saw that…

Going back to what I said earlier…

To refer to later parts of the presentation, you can say:

I'm coming on to that in a moment.

I'll be discussing that in more detail later.

Later, I'll be explaining a bit more about…

Talking about the future

In a presentation, you will often want to talk about what is going to happen in the future:

In the short/medium/long term,…

Looking a bit further ahead,…

Over the next few months,…

So, where do we go from here?

To discuss possibilities for future action, use phrases such as the following:

One option would be…

Another possible approach is…

At this stage, we're not ruling out…

Repeating and clarifying

In a written report, the reader can hesitate over an important or difficult point and can read it several times if necessary. This is not the case with a spoken presentation. For this reason, you may want to repeat the same point, or add extra explanation:

***In other words**, to do nothing is not an option.*

***Put more simply**, there is a lot of money involved.*

***To put it another way,** only 2.6 percent of applicants tested positive for illegal drugs.*

*Works of music are repeatable, **that is to say** you can listen to them again and again.*

Adding more detail

To add more information to a point you are discussing, use phrases like these:

One other thing I'd like to say about this is…

I'd like to say a little more about this issue.

While we're on this subject, it's also worth noting that…

Let's take a moment to look at this in a little more detail.

Finishing the presentation

To finish your presentation, use phrases like these:

I'd like to conclude by…

So, just to sum up…

What I hope you will go away with from today is…

If you take just one thing from this talk, I hope it will be…

This last slide is a summary of the main points that I've made…

I think that just about covers everything I wanted to say.

Does anyone have any questions or comments?

Responding to questions

Polite ways of acknowledging questions are:

I'm glad you asked me that.

That's an interesting question. Thank you.

Let me deal with the second part of your question first.

If you do not know the answer to a question, you might use phrases like these:

I'm afraid I don't have the figures to hand.

I'm afraid I don't know off the top of my head.

I'll have to come back to you on that.

Actually, I think Serge may be better able to answer that question.

If you do not understand the question, you can say:

I'm sorry, I don't think I quite understand what you're asking.

Sorry, could you repeat that, please? I didn't understand your question.

Are you asking… ?

Informal writing

Style and grammar

Informal writing uses a relaxed style and is often similar to speech. For instance, it is fine to use contractions such as *won't, he's*, or *haven't*.

You can choose your language according to who you are writing to. It would be unusual to use words and phrases that are labelled *formal* in the dictionary.

In informal writing, you can express your own emotions in a way that is usually inappropriate in formal writing, for instance by using forms of punctuation such as exclamation marks or dots at the ends of sentences.

I'm sooooo worried about my exam!!!
Guess what? I'm getting married NEXT WEEK!

Emails, letters, texts, and blogs

Informal emails are very similar to informal letters, but can also include some features of texts, such as smileys (also called emoticons), for example ☺ and ☹, to make it clear how you are feeling about what you have written.

Because emails are so quick, it is more common than with letters to end them with something that refers to the present or the near future:

Have a nice weekend!
See you on Saturday,

It is common in informal emails to use abbreviations such as those listed in the section on texts, below.

Here is an example of an informal email.

```
To: Emma Brown
From: Lauren Fisher
Subject: Party!!!
Attachments: 📎invite.doc (36KB) 1

Hi Em, 2

Hope u cn 3 come to my party next week - invite attached!

Paul and Charlotte are coming ☺ but Ethan is in France at the moment ☹. 4
Still, as long as Paul comes, you'll be happy, won't you?? ;-) 5

BTW, 6 my bro is in a new band called Ragbags - check them out!!!
http://www.youtube.com/Ragbags 7
(don't worry, they're not playing at my party!!!)

Have a fun weekend 8

Hugs and kisses 9
Lauren, xxxx
```

1 You can attach an electronic document to an email.

2 It is common to use *Hi* or *Hello* to start an informal email.

3 It is common to abbreviate words in a very informal email, just as in a text

4 Smileys make it clear how you are feeling about what you have written.

5 It can be particularly useful to use a smiley to show that you are joking.

6 It is common in informal emails to use abbreviations such as those listed in the section on texts, below.

7 You can include links to websites in your email.

8 Because emails are so quick, it is more common than with letters to end them with something that refers to the present or the near future.

9 In a letter it would be normal to have a comma here, but in emails people often pay much less attention to punctuation, capital letters, etc.

Letters

Letters are increasingly rare between friends and family, but sometimes a card or a letter seems more appropriate than a phone call, for example to thank someone you have stayed with or to send good wishes to someone who is ill.

Informal letters usually start with *Dear x*, though *Hi x* is often used between friends.

These are some general ways of starting an informal letter:

Just a quick note to say…

I thought I'd drop you a line to say…

I hope you are well.

Sorry I haven't been in touch for a while.

You may want to begin your letter with something more specific:

So sorry to hear you're ill.

It was lovely to get your letter.

Thank you so much for the lovely present.

Common ways of ending an informal letter include:

Please give my love to Peter.

Hope to hear from you soon.

Before your name, the most common ending is *Love, Love from,* or – if you are very fond of the person – *Lots of love from,* or *Much love,*.

In some cases, you may want a friendly ending that does not include the word *love*. Slightly formal options are *Best wishes,* or *Regards. All the best* is more informal.

Here is an example of an informal letter:

Cambridge **1**
9th December 2012 **2**

Hi Sarah,

Just a quick line to let you know that Max and I will be in Edinburgh at the beginning of Jan, and it would be great to meet up with you guys if you're around. **3**

We're off to visit my sister in New York for Christmas – I've just been out buying lots of warm clothes!

I guess you'll be entertaining huge numbers of guests as usual? (Make sure they all help you with the cooking and washing-up!) **4**

Anyway, do let me know about meeting up – I'm working on the 10th and 11th, but we don't have any plans for the weekend, so we're happy to go along with anything you suggest.

Hope to see you then!! **5**

Love and kisses

Lizzie, xx **6**

PS Did you hear that Mickey is getting married??!! **7**

1 You do not have to give your full address if the person you are writing to already knows it. You can either just put the town or city, or leave it out altogether.

2 It is common to put the date, even when writing to friends.

3 It is fine to use informal language, such as 'a line' and 'you guys'.

4 Informal letters may include humour and sometimes use punctuation such as exclamation marks to show that you are joking.

5 In quick letters and notes, personal pronouns are often omitted.

6 An x after your name indicates a kiss.

7 If you want to add something else when you have finished your letter, write PS. This stands for *postscript*. For a second added part, put PPS.

Texts

Texts are usually as short as possible. It is not necessary to use capital letters or punctuation unless the message is unclear without it.

Abbreviations are often used. All of these can be spelled using upper and lower-case letters. Here are some of the most common ones.

2	to, too
2moro	tomorrow
2nite	tonight
4	for
AFAIK	as far as I know
BFF	best friends forever
BRB	be right back
BTW	by the way
C	see
F2F	face to face
FWIW	for what it's worth
FYI	for your information
GR8	great
GTG	got to go
HMU	hit me up (= contact me)
HTH	hope that helps
IDK	I don't know
IIRC	if I remember/recall correctly
IMHO	in my humble opinion
IMO	in my opinion
KK	OK
L8R	later
LOL	laughing out loud (used to show that you find something funny)
NP	no problem
OIC	Oh, I see
OMG	Oh my god! (used as an expression of surprise, horror, etc.)
ROFL	rolling on the floor laughing (used to show that you find something funny)
THX	thanks
TTYL	talk to you later
U	you
UR	your
WBU	What about you?
WDYMBT	What do you mean by that?
WUU2	What (are) you up to?
YOLO	You only live once. (used to justify an extravagance or to encourage someone to do something)

Blogs

The style of writing used for a blog will depend on its subject matter. Some blogs are rather formal and technical, but most are written in an informal, conversational style. As well as text, blogs often contain images and links to other websites.

As with all writing, it is important to be clear about what you want to say and who your audience is likely to be.

A blog is personal. It is fine to use *I*, and you are free to write your own opinions. Your blog will probably be more interesting if you allow your own personality to show through the writing.

Most people do not have much time to read blogs, so make them fairly short and make sure that they look easy to read, for example by using short paragraphs or by using clear bullet points or lists.

If your blog is more than a few paragraphs long, it may be useful to add headings to guide the reader around its content.

Microblogging

Microblogging sites such as Twitter allow you to share information, opinions, images, and stories that you have found on the Web, etc. quickly and easily.

There are important conventions to bear in mind when you are tweeting. The most important is that your message must be no longer than 140 characters, so abbreviations are commonly used. Other conventions include the use of the hashtag, #, to indicate a topic of discussion so that people can find it easily, and the @ symbol to indicate that you are mentioning a particular person, business, etc.

Remember that, when you are microblogging, you are publishing what you write. This means that it can potentially be read by a large number of people, including people that you did not intend to read it, and may also be subject to laws regarding libel and copyright. For this reason you should avoid writing anything that might be offensive, or that you do not have the right to publish.

Body shapes

To talk about a person's size and shape, we use the words **build** or (usually for women) **figure**. If we are thinking about the structure of bones, we say **frame**, and for people such as athletes, we say **physique**.

Small builds: petite, slight

Large builds: broad, heavy-set, stocky, stout, well built

Thin: slender, slim, skinny, lanky

Fat: chubby, obese, overweight, paunchy, plump, potbellied

Strong: beefy, muscular, wiry

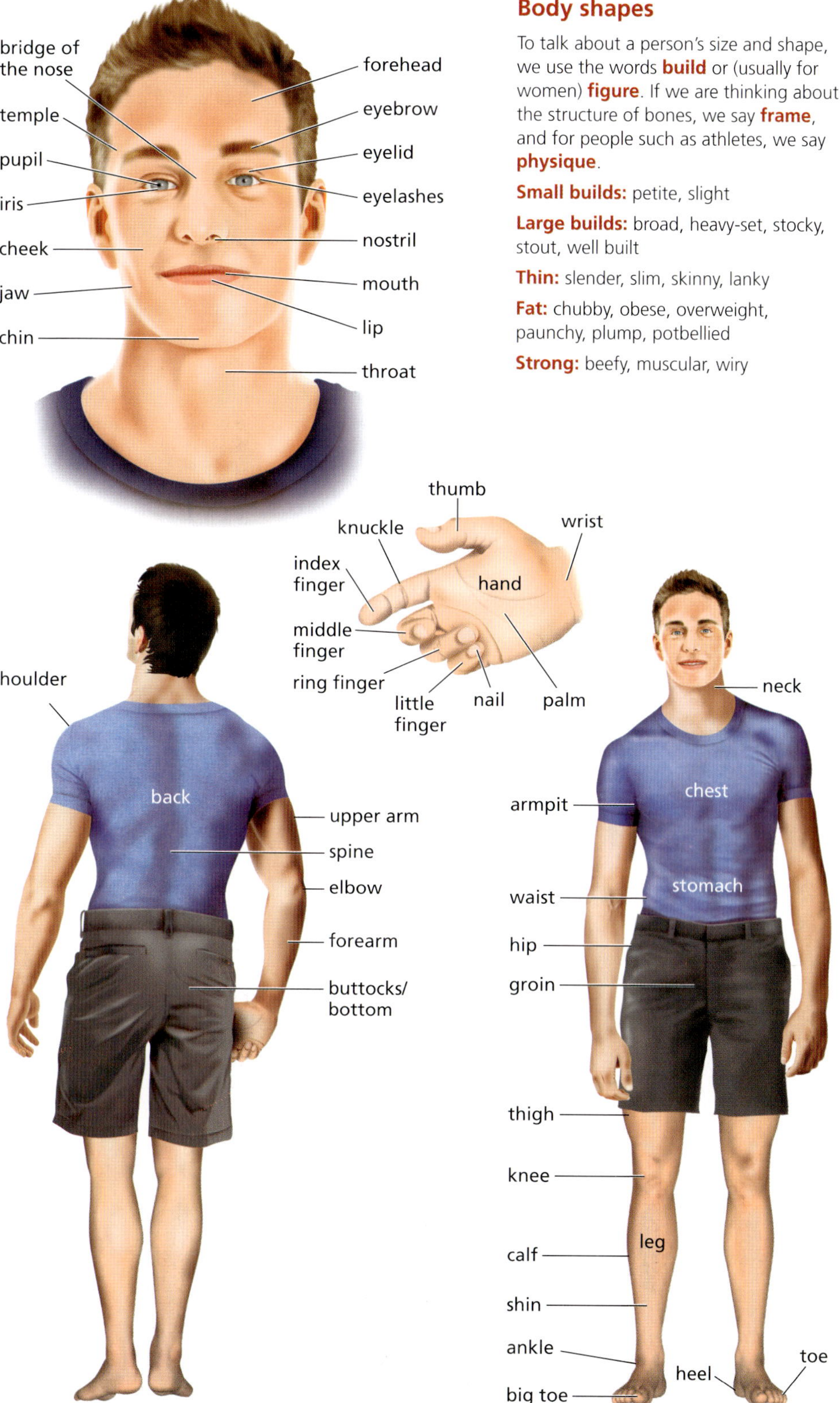

stretch
up to the
ceiling
stand on tiptoe(s)
balance
on one leg
crawl across
the floor
get down on all fours
squat (down)
kneel
on the
ground
go down
on bended
knee
crouch (down)
hunch
your
shoulders
fold your
arms
slouch

stand **arm in arm**

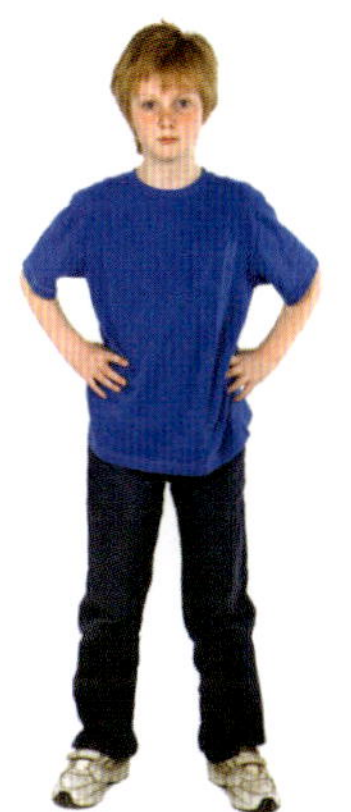
have your **hands on your hips**

hold hands

sprawl on a chair

perch on a stool

recline in a seat

sit **cross-legged**

slump forwards

curl up in a **foetal position** (UK)/ **fetal position** (US)

lie **spreadeagled**

lie **supine**

lie **prone**

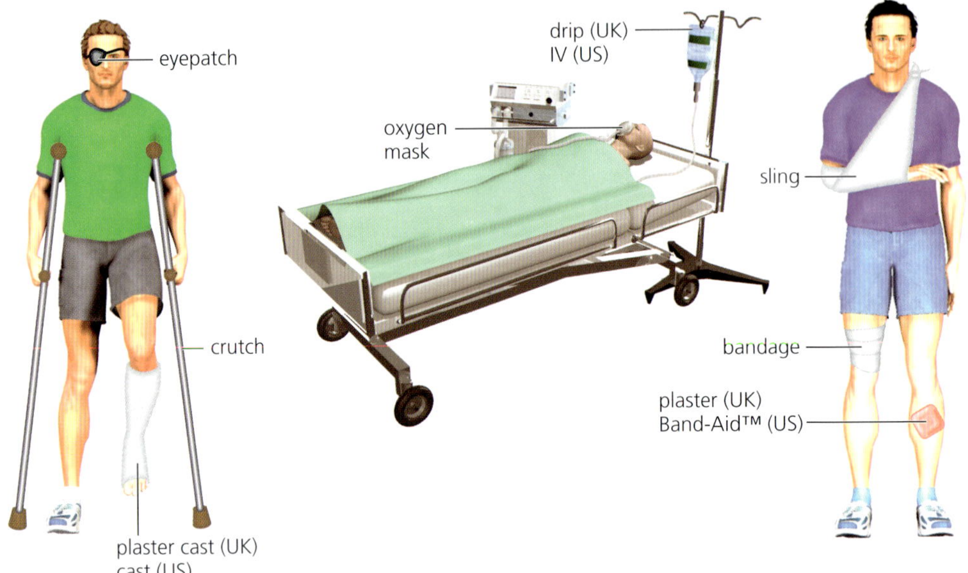

Types of medicine

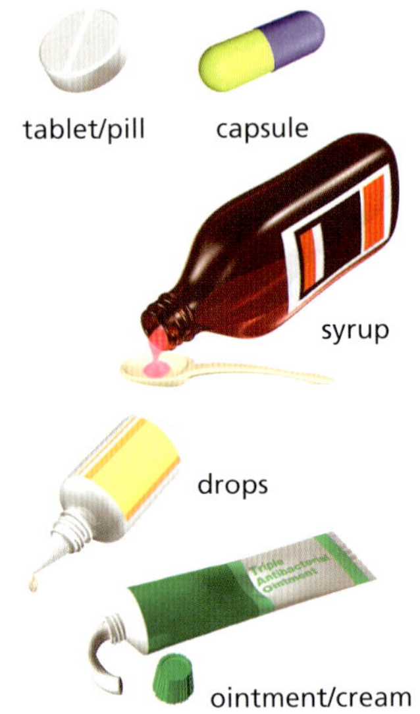

for pain: painkillers, for example aspirin, paracetamol (UK), ibuprofen, acetaminophen (US), Tylenol™ (US)

for coughs and colds: decongestant, cough medicine/mixture, cough sweet (UK) cough drop (US)

for allergies: antihistamines

for indigestion: antacid, indigestion tablets

for infections: antibiotics

for diabetes: insulin

for anxiety: tranquillizers (UK)/tranquilizers (US), sedatives

for depression: antidepressants

Taking medicine

if you are ill, your doctor may give you a **prescription** to take to a **pharmacist**. You may need to take a **dose** of medicine before each meal. If the medicine is not working, you may need to **increase the dose**. Always finish the **course** of medicine. If you experience any **side effects**, tell your doctor. If your **symptoms persist**, go back to your doctor. If you have a long-term illness or condition, you may need a **repeat prescription**.

Verbs to use with illness

I **caught** a cold.
He **contracted** malaria.
She **fell** ill.

I've **picked up** a bug.
He **suffers from** arthritis.
She was **diagnosed with** cancer.

Things medical staff do

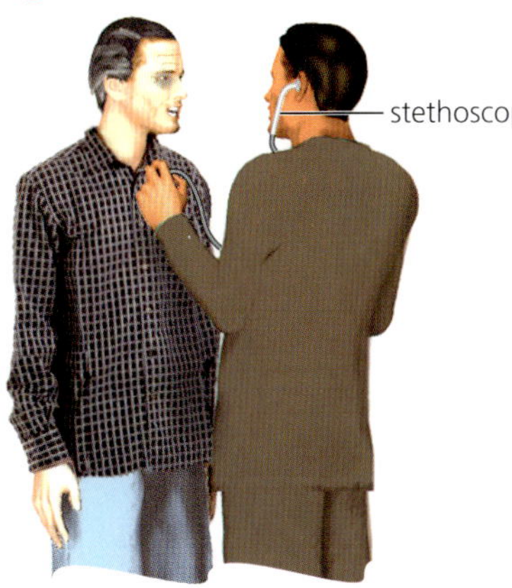

listen to your heart

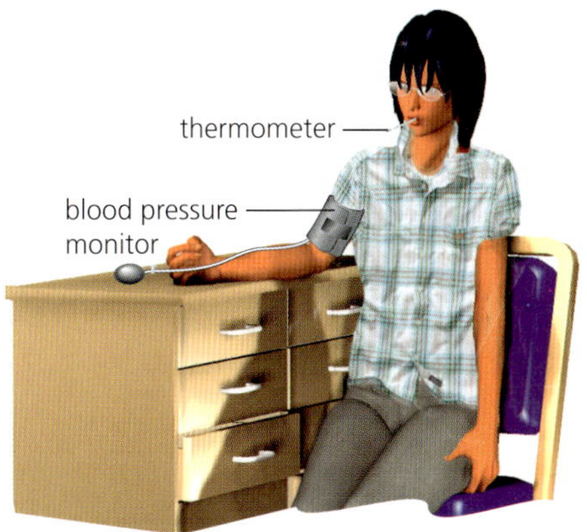

take your temperature and take your blood pressure

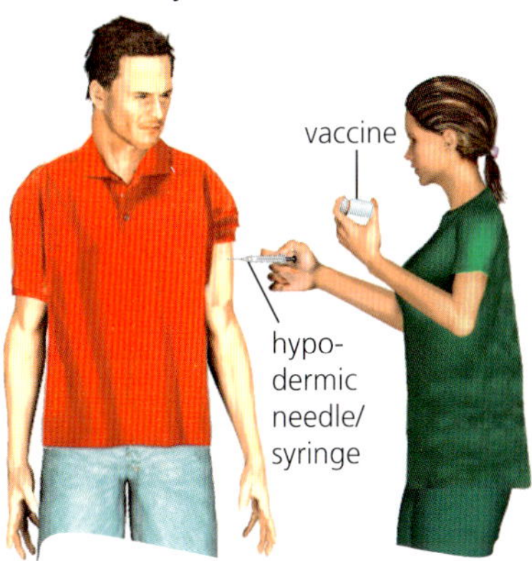

give you an injection/vaccinate you against a disease

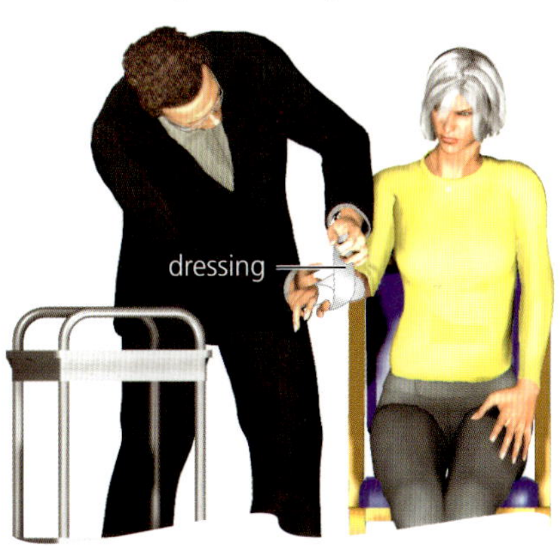

dress your wound

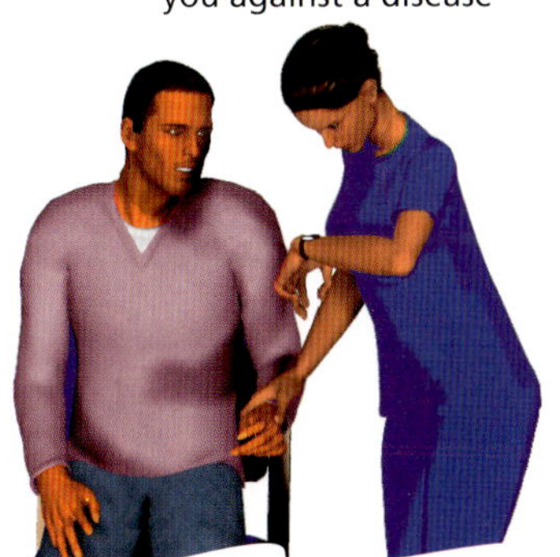
take your pulse

put in/take out your stitches

Places where you have medical treatment

hospital: a place where people who are ill or injured are treated and cared for by doctors and nurses
casualty (UK)/emergency room (US): the part of a hospital where people who are hurt in accidents or suddenly become ill are taken for urgent treatment
outpatients: the part of a hospital where people go to for treatment but do not stay for the night
clinic: a building, often part of a hospital, to which people can go for medical care or advice relating to a particular condition
ward: one of the parts or large rooms into which a hospital is divided, usually with beds for patients
operating theatre (UK)/operating room (US): a special room in which people are operated on in hospital

Bread

loaf

roll/ bread roll

baguette *UK also* French stick

bagel

sandwich

croissant

bap (UK) bun (US)

wrap

pitta (bread) (UK) pita (bread) (US)

Types of bread

Different kinds of bread are made using different kinds of flour. Some of the most common types are listed below.

white
uses white flour

brown
uses brown flour, often made from whole grain

wholemeal
(US mainly whole wheat)
uses flour made with whole grain

Granary™ (UK)
(US **whole wheat**)
uses flour containing whole grain that is not crushed

rye
uses dark brown flour made with rye

Describing food

Flavours bitter, bland, eggy, fiery, fishy, fruity, game, hot, mild, peppery, pickled, salty, savoury, sharp, sour, spicy, strong, sweet, tart

Textures al dente, chewy, creamy, crisp, crunchy, crusty, doughy, dry, fatty, gristly, jellied, mashed, mealy, mushy, smooth, starchy, sticky, stodgy, tender, tough

Meat

steak

chops

joint of pork

mince (UK) ground beef (US)

sausages

rasher of bacon

burger hamburger (US)

drumstick

meatballs

About meat

Meat from cows, pigs, or sheep is called red meat. Meat from birds is called white meat or dark meat, depending on which part of the bird the meat comes from.

cow
types: beef, corned beef, jerky, pastrami, veal
pieces: brisket, chuck steak, oxtail, porterhouse (steak) (US), schnitzel, silverside, T-bone (steak)

pig
types: pork, gammon, ham, prosciutto
pieces: bacon, brawn (UK) headcheese (US), chop, crackling, spare ribs, trotter

sheep
types: lamb, mutton
pieces: chop, cutlet, leg

birds
types: chicken, duck, goose, guinea fowl, turkey, partridge, pheasant, quail, squab
pieces: breast, dark meat, drumstick, giblets, gizzard, leg, thigh, white meat, wing

Cakes

sponge cake

Swiss roll (UK)
jelly roll (US)

cheesecake

fairy cake (UK)
cupcake (US)

tart

doughnut
US also donut

Danish pastry
US usually Danish

mince pie

hot cross bun

Describing food

The five basic tastes of food are: bitter, salty, sour, sweet, and umami.

Food that tastes good is: appetizing, delicious, flavourful (UK)/flavorful (US), juicy, lip-smacking, luscious, moreish, mouth-watering, palatable, scrummy, scrumptious, succulent, tangy, tasty, tempting, toothsome, yummy

Food that tastes bad is: bitter, bland, inedible, insipid, rancid, sharp, stodgy, tasteless, unpalatable

Food that tastes old is: bad, curdled, mouldy (UK)/moldy (US), off, overripe, rotten, sour, stale

Amounts of food

a **spoonful** of sugar

a **pinch** of salt

a **drop** of olive oil

a **blob** of cream

a **sprinkling** of chocolate

a **dash** of milk

a **hunk** of cheese

chunks of vegetables

a **bunch** of grapes

a **bar** of chocolate

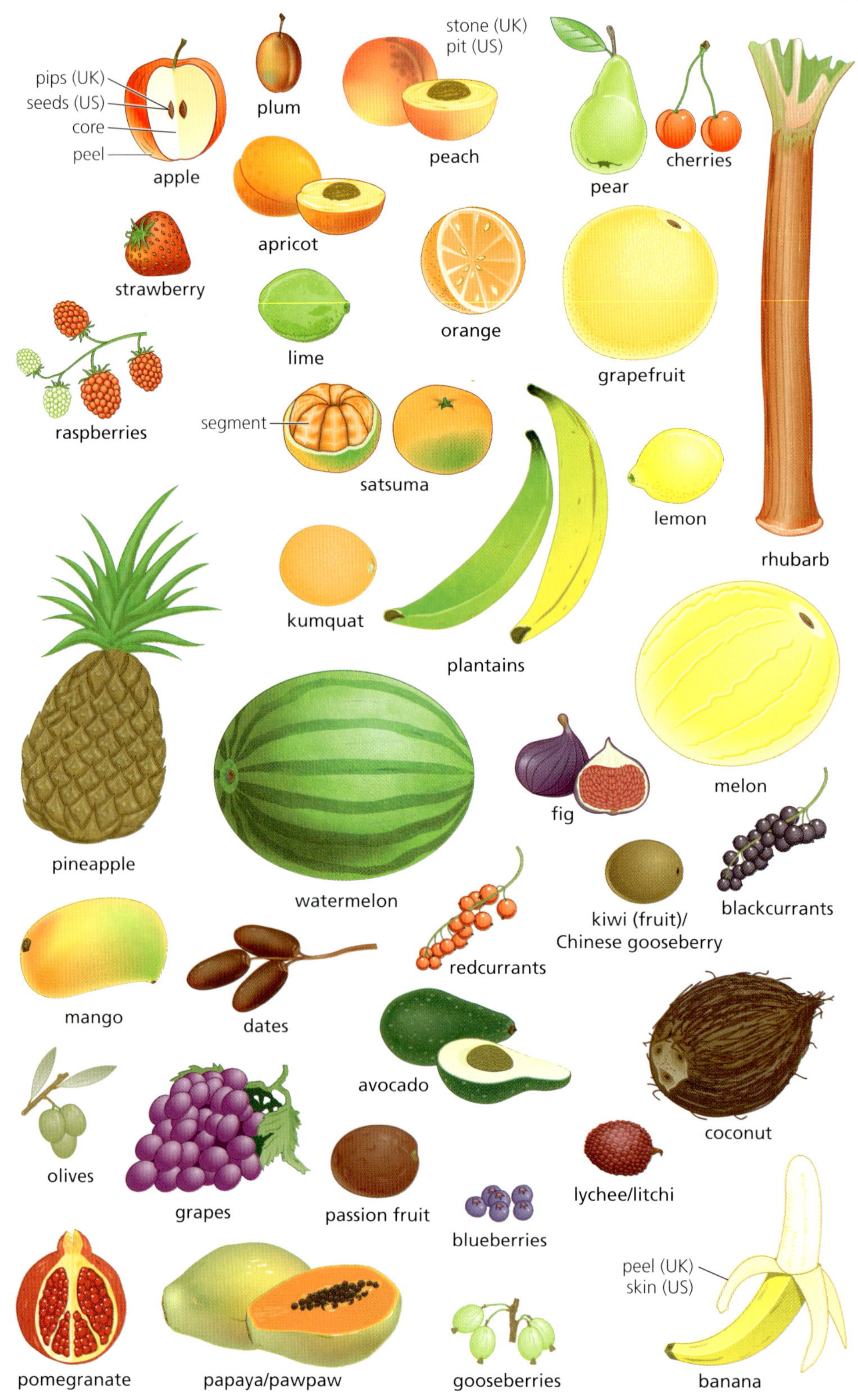
pips (UK)
seeds (US)
core
peel
apple
plum
stone (UK)
pit (US)
peach
pear
cherries
apricot
strawberry
orange
grapefruit
lime
raspberries
segment
satsuma
lemon
rhubarb
kumquat
plantains
melon
pineapple
watermelon
fig
blackcurrants
kiwi (fruit)/
Chinese gooseberry
redcurrants
mango
dates
coconut
avocado
olives
grapes
passion fruit
lychee/litchi
blueberries
peel (UK)
skin (US)
pomegranate
papaya/pawpaw
gooseberries
banana

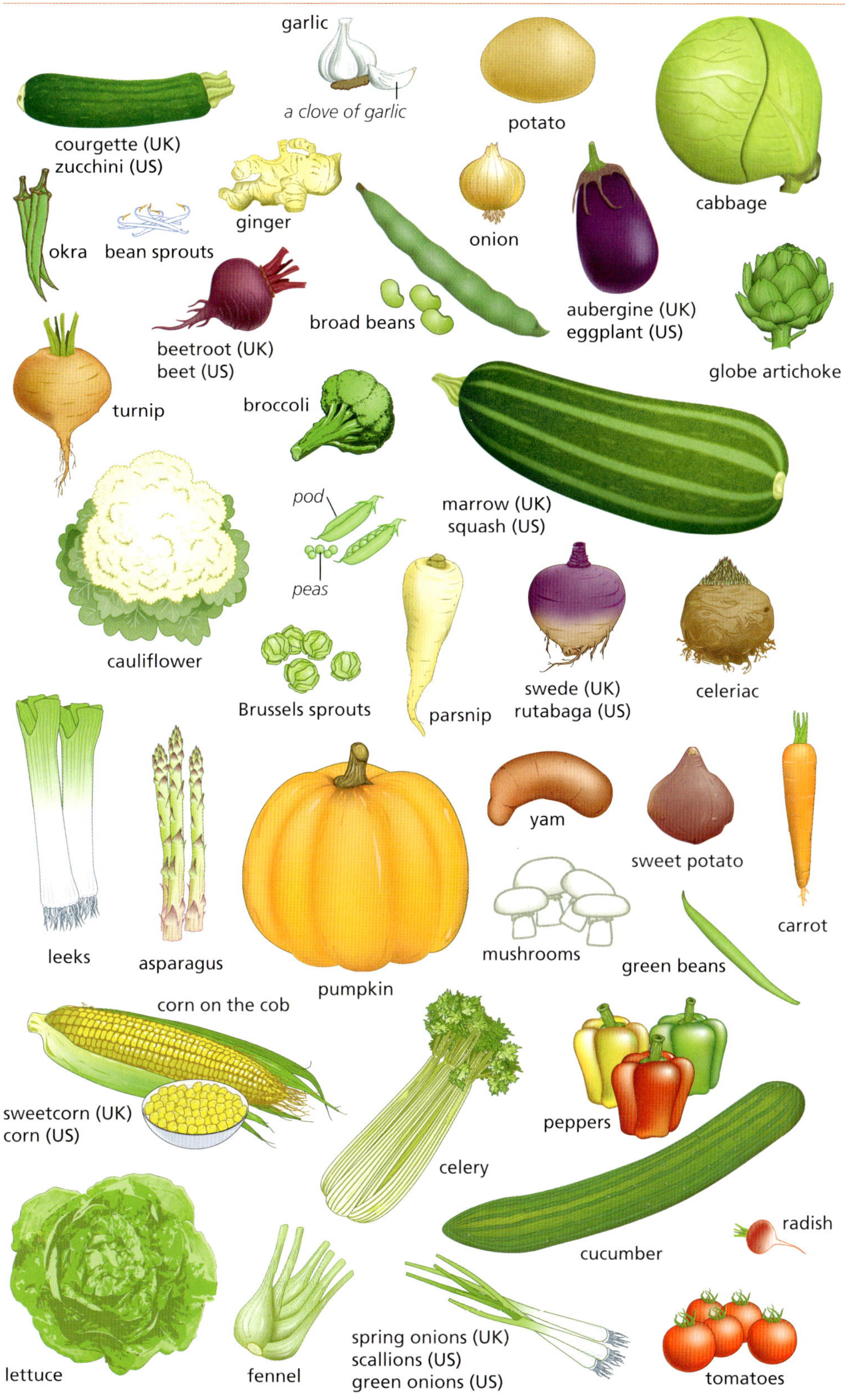
garlic
a clove of garlic
potato
courgette (UK)
zucchini (US)
cabbage
ginger
onion
okra
bean sprouts
beetroot (UK)
beet (US)
broad beans
aubergine (UK)
eggplant (US)
globe artichoke
turnip
broccoli
pod
marrow (UK)
squash (US)
peas
cauliflower
Brussels sprouts
parsnip
swede (UK)
rutabaga (US)
celeriac
yam
sweet potato
carrot
leeks
asparagus
pumpkin
mushrooms
green beans
corn on the cob
sweetcorn (UK)
corn (US)
peppers
celery
radish
cucumber
lettuce
fennel
spring onions (UK)
scallions (US)
green onions (US)
tomatoes

Trousers

Parts of clothes

Types of clothing material

cloth made from cotton: calico, chenille, corduroy, denim, flannel, gingham, linen, moleskin, muslin, oilskin, poplin, seersucker, twill

cloth from other plants: hemp, jute

clothing materials made from the hair or skin of animals: alpaca, angora, astrakhan, camel, cashmere, felt, fleece, gabardine, jersey, lambswool, leather, mohair, sealskin, wool, worsted

cloth made from silk: crepe, chiffon, gauze, satin, taffeta

man-made clothing materials: lamé, Lurex™, Lycra™, nylon, polyester, rayon, sharkskin, Spandex™, velour, viscose

Fasteners

belt

button

cufflink

zip (UK) zipper (US)

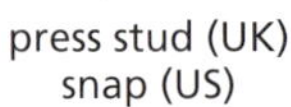

press stud (UK) snap (US)

toggle

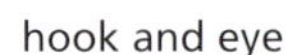

hook and eye

Velcro™

Necklines

Styles of clothing

Describing clothes

You can say somebody's clothes are:
baggy, clingy, fitted, loose-fitting, revealing. scanty, skimpy, skintight, tailored, tight, voluminous

To describe somebody's clothes in a positive way, you might say they are:
chic, dapper, elegant, exquisite, fashionable, fetching, flattering, glamorous, gorgeous, magnificent, presentable, resplendent, sharp, slinky, smart, snazzy, striking, stunning, stylish, trendy, beautifully/well/nicely turned out, well dressed

To describe somebody's cloths in a negative way, you might say they are:
creased, crumpled, frumpy, grungy, ill-fitting, mumsy, naff, outdated, outmoded, uncool, unflattering

Patterns on clothing

brocade, candy-striped, checked, Fair Isle, fishnet, floral, flowery, herringbone, paisley, pinstriped, plaid

Underwear

Hats

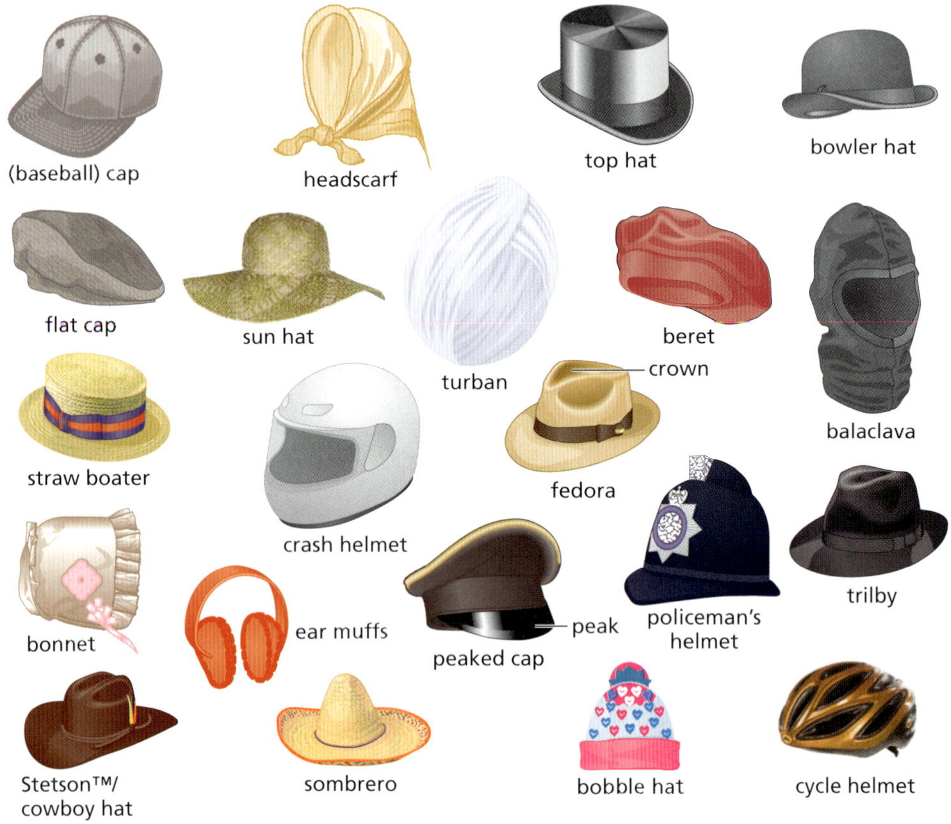

(baseball) cap
headscarf
top hat
bowler hat
flat cap
sun hat
turban
beret
balaclava
crown
straw boater
crash helmet
fedora
bonnet
ear muffs
peaked cap
peak
policeman's helmet
trilby
Stetson™/ cowboy hat
sombrero
bobble hat
cycle helmet

Shoes

flats
stilettos
high heels
sandals
wellington boots (UK) rubber boots (US)
trainers/training shoes (UK) sneakers (US)
slippers
flip-flops
boots
brogues
ankle boots
cowboy boots
mules

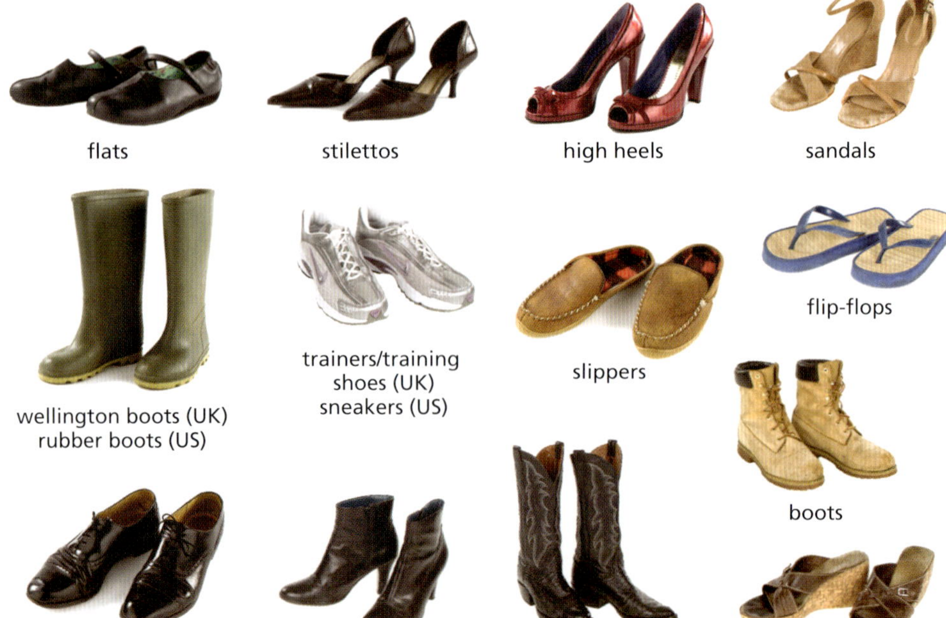

Hair

Talking about hair

To describe hair colour: ash-blonde, auburn, chestnut, flaxen, ginger, golden, greying (UK)/graying (US), mousy, pepper-and-salt (UK)/salt-and-pepper (US), platinum blonde, raven, sandy, strawberry blonde

Verbs for things you can do to hair: backcomb, blow-dry, brush, comb, condition, dye, highlight, part, perm, rinse, shampoo, style, tint, trim

To describe hair texture: bouffant, coarse, frizzy, matted, thin, silky, sleek, wispy

Using computers

To start using a computer, you **log in/on** using your name and a **password**. If you **double-click** on an **icon**, you can open or close a **program**. You may need to **install** some new **software**, or **uninstall** a program that you don't want. While you work, you may **copy and paste** information from one **file** into another, or **drag and drop** a file into a new **folder**. When you write an **email**, you may need to add an **attachment**. It's a good idea to **save** documents frequently, and to make a **backup** of your work before you finish and **log off/out**.

Making presentations

Office equipment

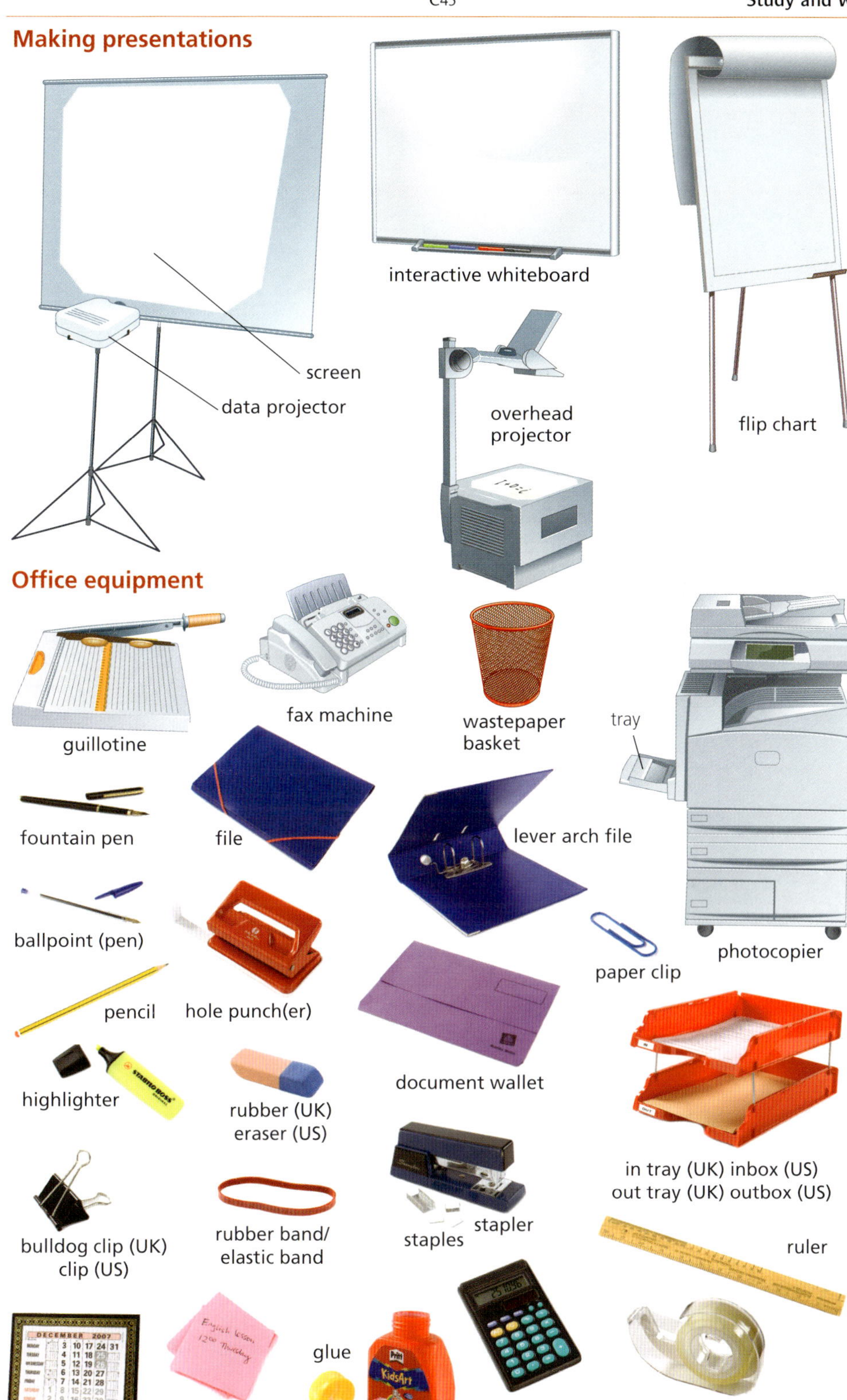
screen
data projector
interactive whiteboard
overhead projector
flip chart
guillotine
fax machine
wastepaper basket
tray
photocopier
fountain pen
file
lever arch file
ballpoint (pen)
hole punch(er)
paper clip
pencil
document wallet
highlighter
rubber (UK)
eraser (US)
in tray (UK) inbox (US)
out tray (UK) outbox (US)
bulldog clip (UK)
clip (US)
rubber band/
elastic band
staples
stapler
ruler
calendar
Post-it™ (note)
glue
calculator
Sellotape™ (UK)
Scotch tape™ (US)

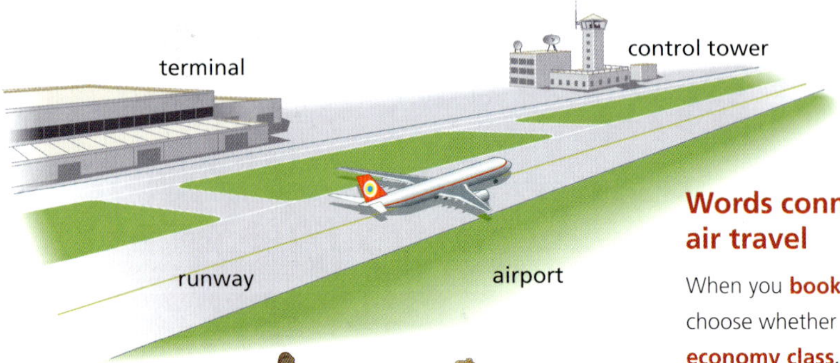

terminal

control tower

runway

airport

carousel

trolley

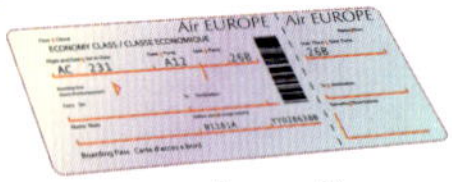

boarding card (UK)
boarding pass (US)

check-in (desk)

passport

Words connected with air travel

When you **book** a flight, you can choose whether you travel in **economy class**, **business class** or **first class**. When you arrive at the **airport terminal**, you will go to the **check-in desk** to get your **boarding card** or use a **self-service check-in** machine. After check-in, you'll show your **passport** at **security**. You may have time for some **duty-free** shopping, before going to the **departure lounge** to **board** your flight and **take off**. When you **land** at your **destination** and **disembark**, you collect your bags from the **carousel**.

platform

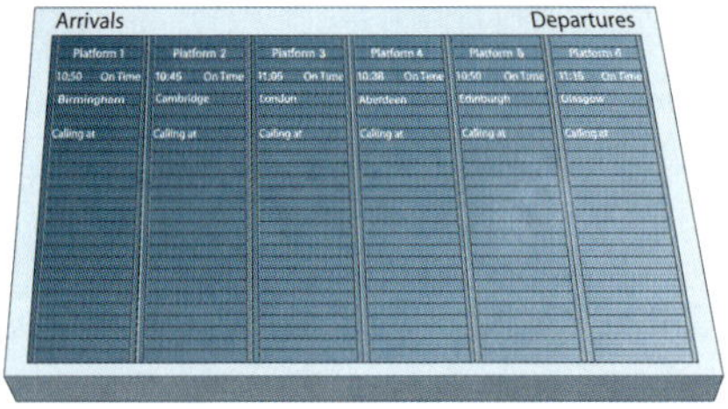

arrivals/departures board

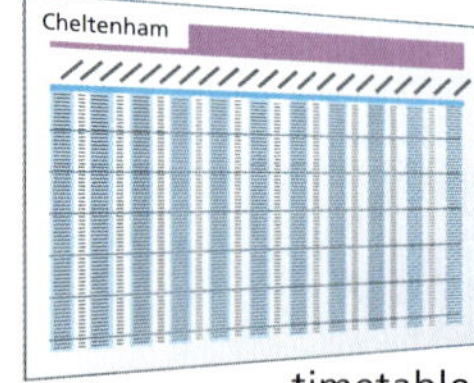

timetable

Words connected with rail travel

Millions of people use **commuter trains** each day to travel between their homes and work or school. They may use a **season ticket** if they travel every day. People also use **intercity** trains to travel longer distances for work or holidays. A **sleeper** train has **sleeping cars** or **couchettes** for overnight travel.

When you arrive at a **railway station**, check the **departures board** to see what **platform** your train is on. You can wait in the **waiting room** until you **board** the train and **set off** on your journey.

waiting room

rotor
helicopter
stealth fighter
transport plane
jumbo jet
glider
cockpit
fuselage
plane, airplane
engine
wing
landing gear
fighter
propellor
biplane
seaplane
microlight
trawler
tanker
warship
hovercraft
funnel
canoe
cruise ship/liner
mast
lifeboat
deck
paddle
anchor
ferry
submarine
periscope
sails
yacht
rowing boat (UK)
rowboat (US)
oars
motorboat

aerial (UK)
antenna (US)
rear window
boot (UK)
trunk (US)
bonnet (UK)
hood (US)
number plate (UK)
license plate (US)
wing (UK)
fender (US)
rear light (UK)
tail light (US)
indicator (UK)
turn signal (US)
exhaust pipe (UK)
tailpipe (US)
tyre (UK)
tire (US)

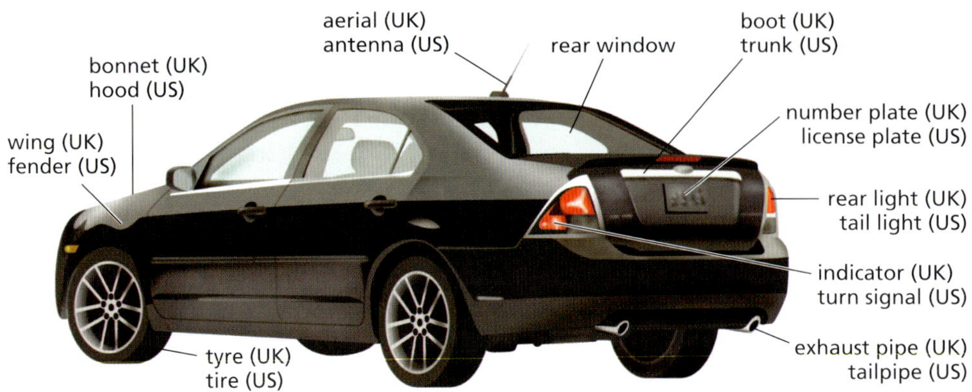

Driving

Someone who is driving is **behind the wheel**. Someone whose job is to drive someone else is a **driver** or a **chauffeur**. The distance your car has driven is its **mileage**. If you **run out of petrol** (UK)/**run out of gas** (US), you will need to **fill up** at a **petrol station** (UK)/**gas station** (US). You use the **pump** by putting the **nozzle** into your **petrol tank** (UK)/**gas tank** (US) and pressing the handle.

Verbs to use for driving

accelerate, back (up), brake, change gear (UK)/shift gear (US), change down (UK)/downshift (US), dip your headlights (UK), give way (UK)/yield (US), indicate (UK), manoeuvre (UK)/maneuver (US), overtake (UK)/ pass (US), park, pull out/away/over, etc., rev, skid, steer, swerve

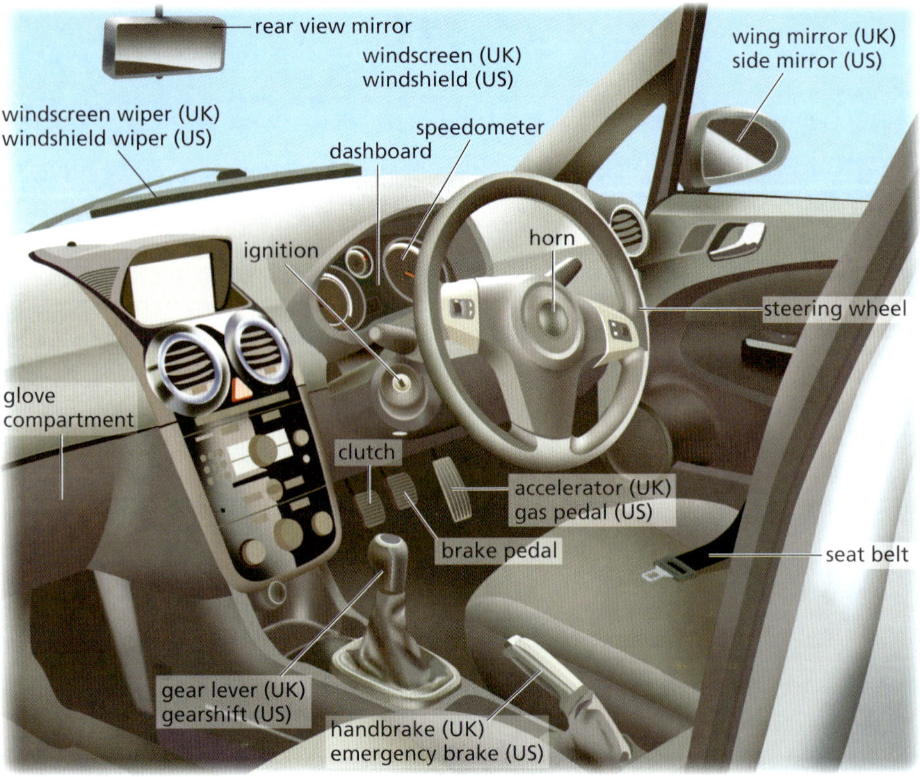

rear view mirror
windscreen (UK)
windshield (US)
wing mirror (UK)
side mirror (US)
windscreen wiper (UK)
windshield wiper (US)
speedometer
dashboard
ignition
horn
steering wheel
glove
compartment
clutch
accelerator (UK)
gas pedal (US)
brake pedal
seat belt
gear lever (UK)
gearshift (US)
handbrake (UK)
emergency brake (US)

estate (car) (UK)
station wagon (US)

hotrod

Jeep™

saloon (UK)/sedan (US)

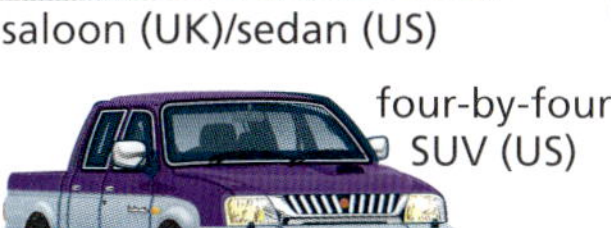

four-by-four
SUV (US)

fire engine

tow truck
breakdown truck (UK)

coach (UK)
bus (US)

tractor

buggy

limousine/limo

motorbike (UK)
motorcycle

van

convertible

tanker

truck
lorry (UK)

dumper truck (UK)
dump truck (US)

RV/motor home/Winnebago™

school bus

police car

people carrier/
MPV

caravan (UK)
trailer (US)

racing car

pickup (truck)

hearse

sports car

dustcart (UK)
garbage truck (US)

articulated lorry (UK)
semi (US)

forklift
truck

bus

chimney
gable
eaves
gutter
balcony
conservatory
shutters
sash window
windowsill /
window ledge
patio
French windows
window box
drainpipe
porch
bay window
bungalow
block of flats (UK)
apartment building (US)
terraced houses (UK)
row houses (US)
end-of-terrace
mobile home (UK)
trailer (US)
thatched roof
semi-detached house
cottage
log cabin
garage
detached house

cafetière
coffee machine
colander
sieve
kettle
bread bin (UK)
breadbox (US)
tin opener (UK)
can opener(US)
grater
scales (UK)
scale (US)
toaster
teapot
oven glove (UK)
oven mitt (US)
extractor fan
cupboard
fridge/refrigerator
hob (UK)
stove (US)
sink
tap (UK)
faucet (US)
grill
draining board
freezer
dishwasher
oven
washing machine
grate
peel
slice
spread
chop
mash
grill
fry
boil

The Orchestra

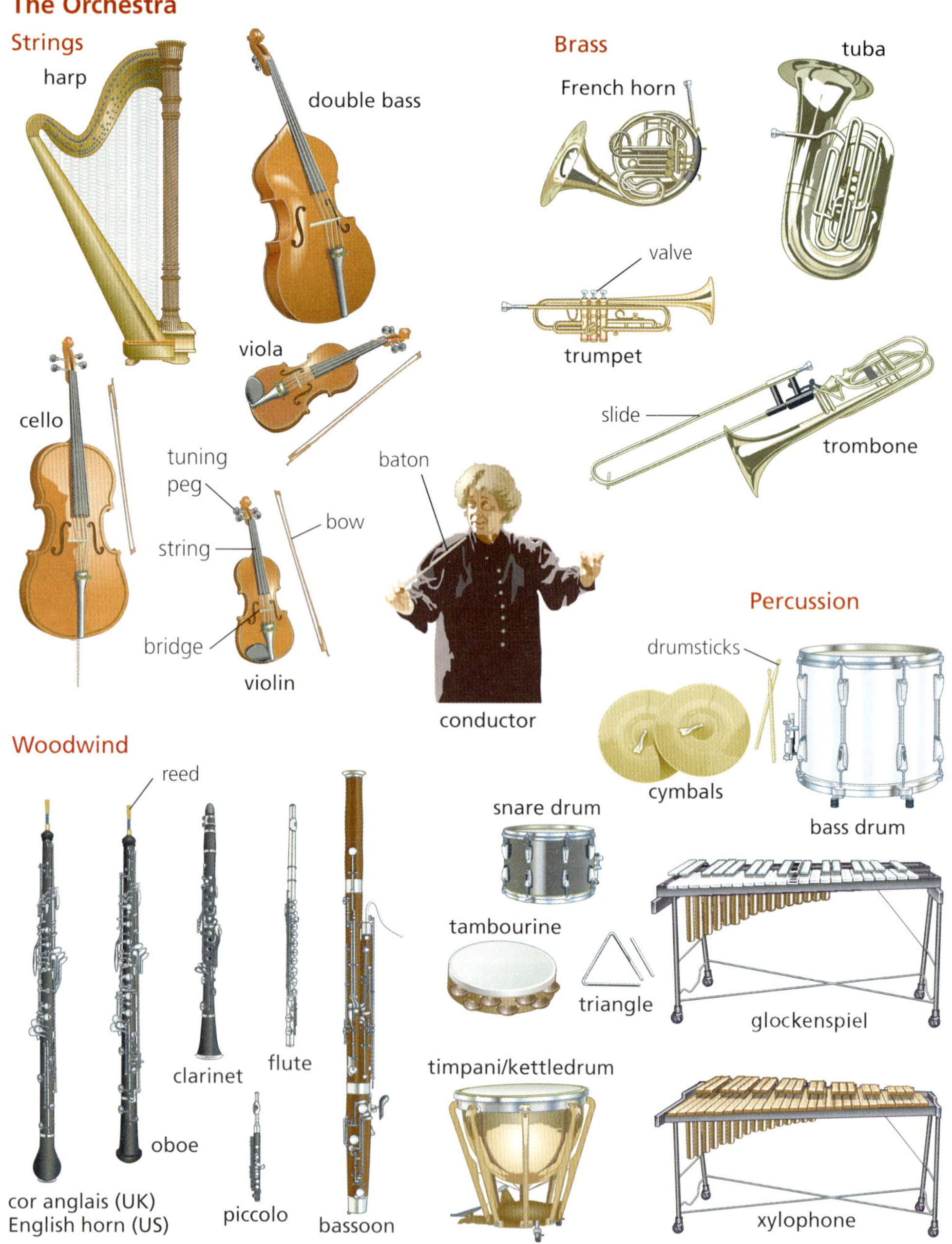

Musicians

Players: The names of many musicians are formed by adding –ist to the name of the instrument they play: bassist, bassoonist, cellist, clarinettist, flautist, guitarist, harpist, oboist, percussionist, pianist, timpanist, trombonist, saxophonist, violinist.

A couple are formed with –er: drummer, trumpeter.

For other, usually rarer, instruments, use the name of the instrument + *player*, piccolo player, recorder player, tuba player.

Classical singers: From lowest to highest, the male voices are bass, baritone, tenor, countertenor. Female voices are: contralto, mezzo-soprano, soprano. Boys' voices are: alto, treble.

Other instruments

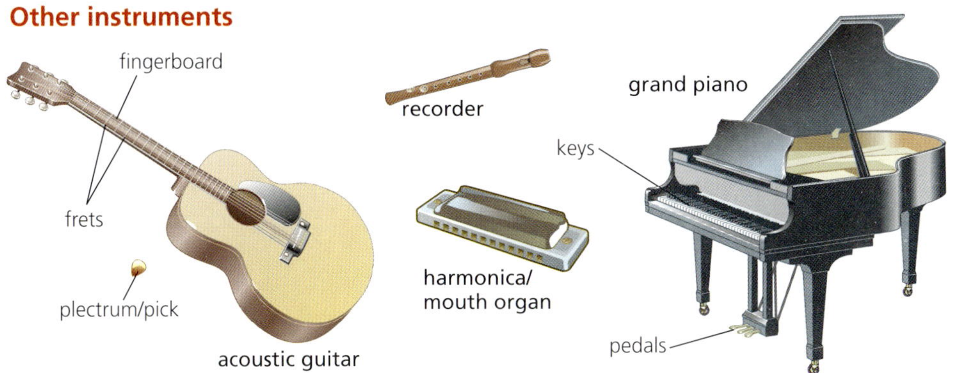

Playing music

A **soloist** plays the most important part of the music on their own, though they may be **accompanied** by other musicians. Jazz musicians often **improvise**, making up music as they play. When musicians play written music for the first time, they **sight-read** it, and if they have to play it in a different key, they **transpose** it.

Musicians often **tune** their instruments before they start to play, to make sure they are **in tune**. If they are not at the right **pitch**, they are **out of tune**. If they are too high, they are **sharp**, and if they are too low, they are **flat**.

Reading music

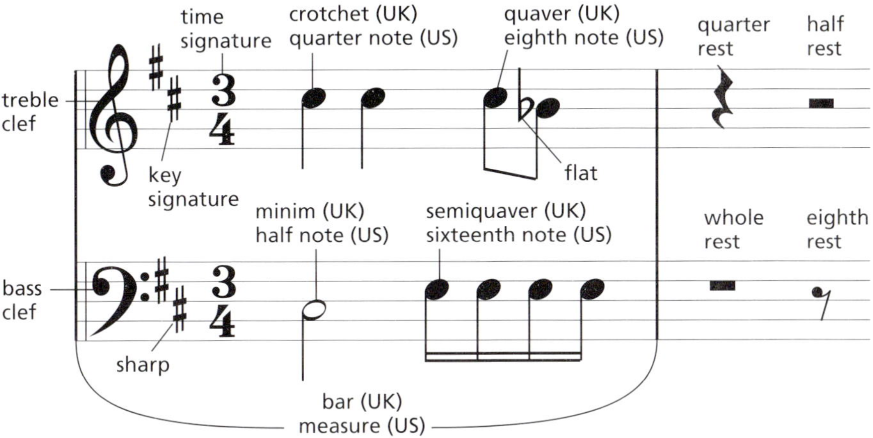

Listening to music

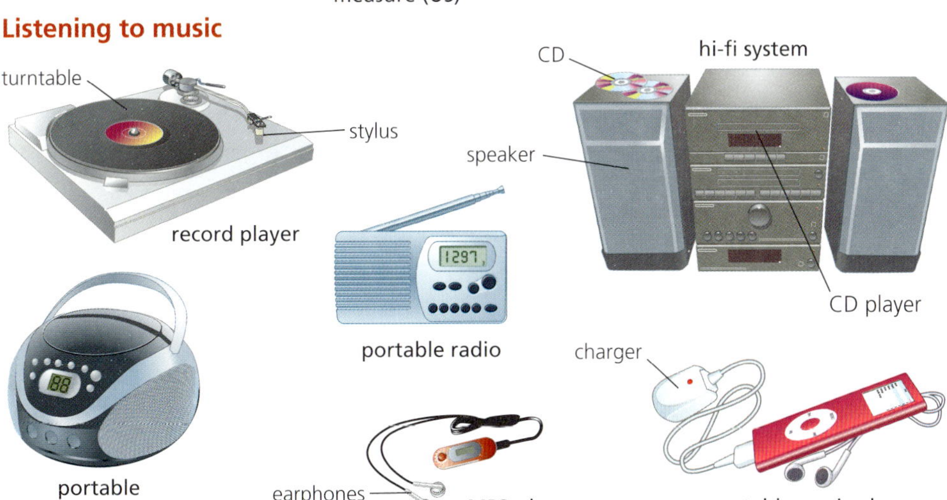

football (UK)
soccer (US)
American football (UK)
football (US)
racket
tennis
stumps
cricket
flag
caddie
club
golf
hole
basketball
hockey (UK)
field hockey (US)
batter
pitcher
diamond
baseball
glove/mitt
table tennis/Ping-Pong™
puck
ice hockey (UK)
hockey (US)
skiing
swimming
hurdles
posts
scrum
rugby
tape
running
discus
athletics (UK)
track and field (US)
long jump

bow
arrow
target
archery
judo
boxing
gloves
ring
boxing
wrestling
karate
gymnastics
rider
reins
saddle
skateboard
skateboarding
jockey
horseriding (UK)
horseback
riding (US)
horse racing
surfboard
surfing
in-line skates
in-line skating
bungee jumping
whitewater rafting
rope
climbing

rat
mouse
chimpanzee
monkey
leopard
cheetah
bison
US also buffalo
buffalo
wapiti
US also elk
moose
UK also elk
rabbit
hare
porpoise
dolphin
turtle
tortoise
alligator
crocodile
frog
toad
trout
salmon
moth
butterflv
bee
wasp
slug
snail

pansy
clover
dandelion
nettle
buttercup
chrysanthemum
hyacinth
orchid
fuchsia
daisy
thistle
tulip
sunflower
honeysuckle
geranium
snowdrop
carnation
daffodil
rose
bluebell
hollyhock
poppy
foxglove
lily
lupin

UNITED KINGDOM
GREAT BRITAIN
Scotland
Northern Ireland
Wales
ENGLAND
Shetland Islands
60°N
2°W
Fair Isle
Orkney Islands
Pentland Firth
Duncansby Head
John o' Groats
Cape Wrath
10°W
5°W
0°
Lewis
Harris
N. Uist
S. Uist
Outer Hebrides
Skye
North West Highlands
Moray Firth
Inverness
Loch Ness
Spey
Cairngorms
Ben Macdhui 1309
Aberdeen
Aberdeen
SCOTLAND
Grampian Mts.
Ben Nevis 1343
Mull
Dundee
Fife Ness
Loch Lomond
Dunfermline
Firth of Forth
Greenock
Glasgow
Glasgow
Edinburgh
Edinburgh
Paisley
Islay
Arran
Kintyre
Ayr
Nith
Tweed
Southern Uplands
Cheviot Hills
Newcastle
Tyne
Newcastle upon Tyne
Sunderland
Carlisle
Eden
Durham
Hartlepool
Middlesbrough
Solway Firth
Malin Head
Bloody Foreland
City of Derry
Londonderry
NORTHERN
Belfast
Belfast
Malinmore
ATLANTIC
OCEAN
North
Sea
55°N
55°N

REPUBLIC OF IRELAND
Dublin
Cork
Galway
Shannon
Knock International
Kerry County
Waterford
Valentia
Cape Clear
Mine Head
Clew Bay
Galway Bay
L. Conn
L. Mask
L. Corrib
Lough Derg
Shannon
Liffey
Suir
Wicklow Mts.
Mourne Mts.
Irish Sea
Isle of Man
Douglas
Anglesey
Snowdon 1085
Cardigan Bay
St. George's Channel
St. David's Head
WALES
Wrexham
Swansea
Newport
Cardiff
Teifi
Tywi
Dee
Bristol Channel
ENGLAND
LONDON
Barrow-in-Furness
Lancaster
Blackpool
Preston
Liverpool
Birkenhead
Chester
Crewe
Stoke-on-Trent
Shrewsbury
Wolverhampton
Birmingham
Coventry
Rugby
Worcester
Gloucester
Harrogate
York
Leeds
Bradford
Manchester
Sheffield
Peak District
Chesterfield
Derby
Nottingham
Grantham
Leicester
Lincoln
Boston
Bridlington
Kingston upon Hull
Spurn Head
Grimsby
The Wash
Kings Lynn
Norfolk Broads
Norwich
Great Yarmouth
Waveney
Ouse
Peterborough
Northampton
Bedford
Cambridge
Ipswich
The Naze
Colchester
Southend-on-Sea
Luton
Oxford
Chiltern Hills
Cotswolds
Swindon
Reading
Bristol
Bath
Avon
Salisbury Plain
Salisbury
Southampton
Portsmouth
Bournemouth
Poole
Isle of Wight
Guildford
Thames
The Weald
Brighton
Maidstone
Strait of Dover
Exmoor
Hartland Point
Exeter
Exe
Tamar
Dartmoor
Torquay
Plymouth
Start Point
Portland Bill
Land's End
Lizard Point
Isles of Scilly
English Channel
Channel Islands
Alderney
Sark
Guernsey
Jersey
FRANCE
Cherbourg
Baie de la Seine
Le Havre
Rouen
Caen
Seine
Calais
Boulogne
Leeds Bradford
Liverpool
Manchester
East Midlands
Birmingham
London Stansted
London Luton
London Heathrow
London City
London Gatwick
Southampton
Bournemouth
Bristol
Cardiff
Exeter
50°N
10°W
5°W
0°
International boundary
National boundary
Airport
Peak (metres)
7439
0 25 50 75 100 Miles
0 50 100 150 Kms
Conical Orthomorphic Projection
© Oxford Cartographers/97619
+44 (0) 1993 705 394
E & OE

THE USA, CANADA AND THE CARIBBEAN
ARCTIC OCEAN
Beaufort Sea
Kalaallit Nunaat (Greenland) (Denmark)
Mt. Forel 3360
Denmark Strait
ICELAND
Arctic Circle
Baffin Bay
Melville Bay
Davis Strait
Nunap Isua (Cape Farewell)
Queen Elizabeth Islands
Sverdrup Islands
Axel Heiberg Island
Ellesmere Island
Devon Island
Parry Islands
Melville Island
Prince Patrick I.
McClure Strait
Banks Island
Viscount Melville Sound
Lancaster Sound
Bylot Island
Somerset Island
Prince of Wales Island
Victoria Island
Cape Bathurst
Amundsen Gulf
Mackenzie Bay
Boothia Peninsula
Gulf of Boothia
King William I.
Qikiqtaaluk (Baffin Island)
Melville Peninsula
Prince Charles Island
Foxe Basin
Cumberland Sound
Southampton Island
Hudson Strait
Resolution I.
Cape Chidley
Ungava Bay
Ungava Peninsula
NUNAVUT
NORTHWEST TERRITORIES
Great Bear Lake
Great Slave Lake
Back
Garry Lake
Mackenzie
Mackenzie Mountains
YUKON TERRITORY
Mt. Logan 5959
ALASKA (U.S.A.)
Brooks Range
Yukon
Alaska Range
Mt. McKinley 6194
Anchorage
Seward Peninsula
Bering Strait
St. Lawrence I. (U.S.A.)
Bering Sea
Nunivak Island
Norton Sound
Kodiak I.
Gulf of Alaska
Alexander Archipelago
Prince of Wales I.
Queen Charlotte Islands
Queen Charlotte Sound
Vancouver Island
Vancouver
Mt. Waddington 4042
BRITISH COLUMBIA
Coast Mts
Rocky Mountains
Mt. Robson 3954
Mt. Columbia 3747
Columbia
ALBERTA
Edmonton
Calgary
Peace
Lake Athabasca
SASKATCHEWAN
Saskatchewan
Reindeer Lake
MANITOBA
Nelson
Lake Winnipeg
Winnipeg
Lake of the Woods
CANADA
Hudson Bay
Ottawa Islands
Belcher Islands
James Bay
Severn
Albany
ONTARIO
Lake Superior
GREAT
QUEBEC
Lake Sakami
Lac Mistassini
Smallwood Res.
NEWFOUNDLAND & LABRADOR
Newfoundland
C. Race
Gulf of Saint Lawrence
St. Lawrence
Gaspé Peninsula
NEW BRUNSWICK
PRINCE EDWARD I.
Cape Breton I.
Halifax
NOVA SCOTIA
Bay of Fundy
Québec
Montréal
MAINE
Great Plains
WASHINGTON
Seattle
Portland
Columbia
OREGON
IDAHO
Bitterroot Range
MONTANA
Fort Peck Lake
Yellowstone
NORTH DAKOTA
170°E
180°
170°W
160°W
145°W
140°W
130°W
110°W
90°W
70°W
50°W
40°W
35°W
30°W
25°W
20°W
10°W
65°N
60°N
55°N
50°N
45°N
40°N

UNITED STATES OF AMERICA
MEXICO
ATLANTIC OCEAN
PACIFIC OCEAN
Gulf of Mexico
Caribbean Sea
Greater Antilles
HAWAII
Honolulu
Nihoa
Kauai
Niihau
Oahu
Maui
Hawaii
4205
Miller Projection
0 200 400 Miles
0 200 400 600 Kms
Ice Cap
Metres
5000
3000
2000
1000
500
300
200
100
Sea level
Land depression
International boundary
Internal boundary
Airport
Peak (metres)
7439
Marsh
0 100 200 300 400 500 Miles
0 200 400 600 800 Kms
Zenithal Equal Area Projection
© Oxford Cartographers/97619
+44 (0) 1993 705 394
E & OE
Tropic of Cancer
San Francisco
Oakland
San Jose
Los Angeles
San Diego
Point Conception
Las Vegas
Salt Lake City
Phoenix
Denver
Kansas City
St. Louis
Oklahoma City
Dallas
Houston
San Antonio
New Orleans
Memphis
Chicago
Milwaukee
Detroit
Toronto
Buffalo
Cleveland
Indianapolis
Columbus
Cincinnati
Pittsburgh
Baltimore
Washington D.C.
Philadelphia
Newark
New York
Hartford
Boston
Norfolk
Charlotte
Atlanta
Tampa
Miami
Nassau
Havana
Kingston
Port-au-Prince
Santo Domingo
San Juan
Hamilton
Bermuda (U.K.)
Monterrey
Guadalajara
Mexico City
Puebla
Pico de Orizaba 5610
Belmopan
Guatemala City
San Salvador
Tegucigalpa
Managua
San José
Panama City
Barranquilla
Maracaibo
Valencia
Caracas
NEVADA
CALIFORNIA
UTAH
ARIZONA
COLORADO
NEW MEXICO
NEBRASKA
KANSAS
OKLAHOMA
TEXAS
IOWA
MISSOURI
ARKANSAS
LOUISIANA
ILLINOIS
INDIANA
OHIO
KENTUCKY
TENNESSEE
MISSISSIPPI
ALABAMA
GEORGIA
FLORIDA
SOUTH CAROLINA
NORTH CAROLINA
VIRGINIA
WEST VIRGINIA
PENNSYLVANIA
NEW JERSEY
MD.
DEL.
YORK
CONN.
R.I.
MASS.
DAKOTA
WISCONSIN
THE BAHAMAS
CUBA
JAMAICA
HAITI
DOMINICAN REP.
Hispaniola
BELIZE
GUATEMALA
HONDURAS
EL SALVADOR
NICARAGUA
COSTA RICA
PANAMA
COLOMBIA
VENEZUELA
Great Basin
Sierra Nevada
Grand Canyon
Colorado Plateau
Uinta Mts.
Great Salt Lake
Edwards Plateau
Ozark Plateau
Appalachian Mts.
Sierra Madre Occidental
Sierra Madre Oriental
Sierra Madre del Sur
Baja California
Gulf of California
Bay of Campeche
Yucatan Peninsula
Yucatan Channel
Gulf of Honduras
Gulf of Tehuantepec
Gulf of Mosquitos
Gulf of Darien
Panama Canal
Straits of Florida
Florida Keys
The Everglades
Cape Hatteras
Great Abaco Island
Eleuthera Island
Andros Island
Gt. Inagua Island
Turks & Caicos Is. (U.K.)
Cayman Is. (U.K.)
Islas de la Juventud (Pinos)
Cozumel I.
Cape Catoche
Turneffe Is.
Bay Is.
L. Caratasca
Cape Gracias a Dios
Lake Nicaragua
Puerto Rico (U.S.A.)
Virgin Is. (U.K.)
Aruba (Neth.)
Netherlands Antilles
Pta. Gallinas
Pico Cristóbal Colón 5775
Pico Bolívar 5007
Guadalupe (Mexico)
Pt. Eugenia
C. San Lucas
I. Marías
Revilla Gigedo Is. (Mexico)
Mississippi
Missouri
Arkansas
Red
Ohio
Pecos
Rio Grande
Colorado
Balsas
Lake Michigan
Lake Erie
Ontario
35°N
30°N
25°N
20°N
15°N
10°N
5°N
40°N
115°W
110°W
105°W
100°W
95°W
90°W
85°W
75°W
70°W
160°W
20°N

AUSTRALIA AND NEW ZEALAND

branches of the tree. **REDUCE ▷ 2** informal to reduce a price or the amount of time taken to do something by a particular amount: *He lopped eight seconds off the record.*

lope /ləʊp/ ⓤⓢ /loʊp/ verb [I] (of a person or animal) to run taking long, relaxed steps: *The lion loped across the grass.* • **lope** noun [S]

lopsided /ˌlɒpˈsaɪd.ɪd/ ⓤⓢ /ˌlɑːp-/ adj with one side bigger, higher, etc. than the other; not equally balanced: *a charming, lopsided grin*

loquacious /ləˈkweɪ.ʃəs/ ⓤⓢ /loʊˈkweɪ-/ adj formal describes someone who talks a lot • **loquaciously** /-li/ adv

lord /lɔːd/ ⓤⓢ /lɔːrd/ noun; verb

▸noun [C] **1** a male PEER **2** informal a man who has a lot of power in a particular area of activity: *Several alleged **drug** lords are to be put on trial.*

IDIOM **your lord and master** humorous a person who has authority over you, or your husband

▸verb informal **lord it over sb** to behave as if you are better than someone and have the right to tell them what to do: *He likes to lord it over his little sister.*

Lord /lɔːd/ ⓤⓢ /lɔːrd/ noun **TITLE ▷ 1** [U] a title used in front of the names of male PEERS and officials of very high rank: *Lord Longford ◦ the Lord Chancellor* → Compare **Lady 2 the Lords** [+ sing/pl verb] **the House of Lords 3 my Lord** in Britain, used to address a judge or PEER **GOD ▷ 4** (in the Christian religion) God or Jesus Christ: *Praise **the** Lord!* ◦ [as form of address] *Lord, hear our prayer.*

IDIOMS **(oh) Lord** (also **Good Lord**) used to express surprise, shock, or worry: *Oh Lord! I've forgotten the tickets! ◦ Good Lord! Is that the time?* • **Lord knows** informal used to say that you do not know: *Lord knows where we're going to get the money from.*

lordly /ˈlɔːd.li/ ⓤⓢ /ˈlɔːrd-/ adj describes someone who behaves as if they are better than other people: *a lordly air*

lordship /ˈlɔːd.ʃɪp/ ⓤⓢ /ˈlɔːrd-/ noun formal **your/his lordship** a polite way of referring to or talking to a male PEER without using his title: *It is a great pleasure to welcome your lordship this evening.* → Compare **ladyship**

the ˌLord's ˈPrayer noun [S] in the Christian religion, the prayer taught by Jesus Christ to his DISCIPLES (= the first men who believed in him)

the ˌLord's ˈSupper noun [S] → **Communion**

lore /lɔːr/ ⓤⓢ /lɔːr/ noun [U] traditional knowledge and stories about a subject: *According to local lore, the water has healing properties.* → See also **folklore**

lo-res (also **low-res**) /ləʊˈrez/ ⓤⓢ /loʊ-/ adj abbreviation for **low-resolution**

lorgnette /lɔːˈnjet/ ⓤⓢ /lɔːr-/ noun [C] a very old-fashioned pair of glasses with a long handle that you hold in front of your eyes

lorikeet /ˌlɒr.ɪˈkiːt/ ⓤⓢ /ˌlɑː.rɪ-/ noun [C] a small, brightly coloured PARROT found in Australia and Southeast Asia

lorn /lɔːn/ ⓤⓢ /lɔːrn/ adj literary alone and unhappy; left alone and not cared for

lorry /ˈlɒr.i/ ⓤⓢ /ˈlɔːr-/ noun [C] UK (US **truck**) **B1** a large vehicle used for transporting goods

lose /luːz/ verb (**lost, lost**) **NOT HAVE ▷ 1 A2** [T] to no longer have something because you do not know where it is, or because it has been taken away from you: *I've lost my ticket. ◦ He's always losing his car keys. ◦ At least 600 staff will lose their jobs if the firm closes. ◦ He lost his leg in a car accident. ◦ She lost her mother (= her mother died) last year.* → See Note **loose 2 B2** [T] to stop feeling something: *to lose confidence/faith ◦ I lost interest halfway through the book. ◦ He kept on crying and I lost my patience.* **3 B1** [T] to have less of something than you had before: *I'm trying to lose weight. ◦ He's losing his hair. ◦ She lost a lot of blood in the accident. ◦ to lose your memory/sight* **4 B2** [T] If you lose time, you waste it: *Four million hours were lost last year through stress-related illnesses. ◦ We lost valuable time stuck in traffic.* **5** [T] If a clock loses time, it goes more slowly than it should: *My watch loses ten minutes every day.* **6** [T] informal to get rid of something: *Lose the belt and let's see how the dress looks.* **7 lose money, pounds, dollars, etc. C1** A business that is losing money is spending more money than it is receiving: *Banks will lose millions of pounds because of new legislation.* **BE DEFEATED ▷ 8 B1** [I or T] to fail to succeed in a game, competition, etc.: *If we lose this game, we're out of the championship. ◦ They're losing 3–1. ◦ They lost **to** Arsenal. ◦ Everyone hates losing an argument. ◦ They hadn't lost an election in 15 years.*

IDIOMS **be losing it** informal to start to become crazy: *That's the third time this week I've lost my keys – I think I must be losing it.* • **lose your head** informal **C1** to lose control and not act in a calm way • **lose your heart to sb** literary to fall in love with someone • **lose your life B2** to die suddenly because of an accident or violent event: *Many people lost their lives in the floods.* • **lose your marbles** informal humorous to become crazy • **lose your mind** informal to become mentally ill, or to start behaving in a silly or strange way • **lose your rag** informal to suddenly become very angry: *He said one too many stupid things and I just lost my rag.* • **lose your shirt** US informal to lose a lot of money, especially as a result of a BET (= money risked when you guess the result of something) • **lose your touch** If you lose your touch, you can no longer do something as well as you could before: *It's good to see their goalkeeper's not losing his touch.* • **lose your way** to become lost • **lose ground C1** to become less popular or to be given less support: *Do you agree that left-wing politics are losing ground among the working classes?* • **lose heart C2** to stop believing that you can succeed: *Don't lose heart, there'll be plenty more chances for promotion.* • **lose it** informal to stop being able to control your emotions and suddenly start to shout, cry, or laugh: *I'd been trying so hard to stay calm but in the end I just lost it.* • **lose sight of sth C2** to forget about an important idea or fact because you are thinking too much about other things: *I'm worried that we're losing sight of our original objectives.* • **lose sleep over/about sth C2** to worry about something: *I wouldn't lose any sleep over what happened.* • **lose the plot** informal to behave in a strange or silly way: *I can't believe Stuart did that – he must be losing the plot.* • **you've got nothing to lose** (also **what have you got to lose?**) used to tell someone that they cannot cause any disadvantages for themselves by doing a particular thing: *Why don't you take the job? You've got nothing to lose.*

PHRASAL VERB **lose out** to not have an advantage that other people have: *The new tax means that the vast majority of pensioners will lose out.*

loser /ˈluː.zər/ ⓤⓢ /-zɚ/ noun [C] **DOES NOT WIN ▷ 1** a person or team that does not win a game or competition: *The losers of both games will play each other for third place. ◦ He's a **good/bad** loser (= he behaves well/badly when he is defeated).* **IS NOT SUCCESSFUL ▷ 2** informal a person who is always unsuccessful at everything they do: *He's a **born** loser.* **GETS WORSE** ▷ **3** someone or something that is in a worse position or has less value at the end of a process: *The latest price rises mean that the real loser, as usual, is the consumer.* ◦ *On the London Stock Exchange, losers beat gainers 1,353 to 823.*

loss /lɒs/ (US) /lɑːs/ **noun 1** (B2) [C or U] the fact that you no longer have something or have less of something: *Many parents feel a sense of loss when their children leave home.* ◦ *He suffered a gradual loss of memory.* ◦ *There will be substantial **job** losses if the factory closes down.* ◦ *blood/hair/weight loss* **2** (C2) [S] a disadvantage caused by someone leaving an organization: *It would be a great loss **to** the department if you left.* **3** (B2) [C or U] the death of a person: *They never got over the loss of their son.* **4** (C1) [C] a situation in which a business spends more money than it earns: *The company announced a pre-tax loss of three million pounds.* **5 loss of life** an occasion when a number of people die: *The plane crashed with serious loss of life.*

IDIOM **be at a loss** (C2) not to know what to do or say: *I'm at a loss to know how I can help you.* ◦ *It was unlike him to be at a loss for words.*

loss adjuster /ˈlɒs.əˌdʒʌs.təʳ/ (US) /ˈlɑːs.əˌdʒʌs.t̬ɚ/ **noun** [C] a person who works for an INSURANCE company and decides how much money should be paid out in each case of something having been damaged or lost

ˈloss ˌleader noun [C] an article that is sold cheaply in order to attract the public and make them buy other, more expensive things

ˈloss-ˌmaking adj not making a profit: *loss-making businesses/companies*

lost /lɒst/ (US) /lɑːst/ **adj PLACE UNKNOWN** ▷ **1** (A2) not knowing where you are and how to get to a place: *I **got** lost in the London Underground.* ◦ *You look lost – can I help you?* **2** (B1) If something is lost, no one knows where it is: *Things tend to **get** lost when you move house.* ◦ *Lost: black cat with white paws.* ◦ *Mikey turned up with the lost book.*

> **!** Common mistake: **lost or loss?**
> **Warning:** do not confuse the adjective **lost** with the noun **loss**:
> ~~*I am still upset about the lost of my diary.*~~
> *I am still upset about the loss of my diary.*

CONFUSED ▷ **3** (C1) not knowing what to do in a new situation: *It was his first day in the office and he seemed a bit lost.* **ATTENTION** ▷ **4** giving so much attention to what you are doing that you are not conscious of anything else that is happening around you: *Ann was completely lost **in** her book.*

IDIOMS **be lost for words** to be so shocked, surprised, full of admiration, etc. that you cannot speak: *Mary was lost for words when she was awarded the prize.* • **be lost on sb** If a joke or remark is lost on someone, they do not understand it. • **be lost without sb/sth** (C1) to be unable to live or work without someone or something: *I'm lost without my computer.* ◦ *I'd be lost without you.* • **get lost!** informal used to tell someone forcefully and quite rudely to go away: *Tell him to get lost!* • **lost in the shuffle** US and Australian English If something or someone gets lost in the shuffle, they do not get the attention they deserve: *Refugee children in the big camps just get lost in the shuffle and are sometimes left without food.*

ˌlost ˈcause noun [C usually singular] someone or something that has no chance of succeeding: *I used to try to get him to do some exercise but then decided he was a lost cause.*

ˌlost ˈproperty noun [U] UK personal objects that have been left by accident in public places

ˌlost ˈproperty ˌoffice noun [C usually singular] UK (US **ˌlost-and-ˈfound**) a place in a public building where lost things are stored

lot /lɒt/ (US) /lɑːt/ **noun; noun**

▸**noun LARGE AMOUNT** ▷ **1 a lot (of)** informal (A1) **lots (of)** a large amount or number of people or things: *She eats lots of fruit.* ◦ *There were a lot of people there.* ◦ *He does a lot of travelling in his job.* ◦ *I've got a lot to do today.* ◦ *He earns lots of money.* ◦ *There's lots of food.* **2 a lot** (A1) very much or very often: *Your sister looks a lot like you.* ◦ *I'm feeling a lot better today.* ◦ *He looks a lot older than his wife.* ◦ *We used to go there a lot.* **3 have a lot to answer for** to be the main cause of a problem or an unpleasant situation: *People who sell drugs to kids have a lot to answer for.* **4 the lot** UK informal everything: *I made enough curry for three people and he ate the lot.* ◦ *Have I got everything? Is that the lot?* ◦ *I'll sell you the **whole** lot for only £50.* ◦ *I'm sick of the lot **of** them.*

> **!** Common mistake: **a lot**
> Remember that **a lot** is always written as two words.
> Don't write 'alot', write **a lot**:
> ~~*I have heard alot of good things about that college.*~~
> *I have heard a lot of good things about that college.*

> **!** Common mistake: **a lot**
> **Warning:** check your word order!
> When **a lot** is used with a verb, it does not usually come between the verb and its object.
> Don't say 'do a lot something', say **do something a lot**:
> ~~*I enjoy a lot visiting my grandmother.*~~
> *I enjoy visiting my grandmother a lot.*

> **!** Common mistake: **a lot of and lots of**
> **Remember:** when **lot** is in the singular, a determiner always comes before it.
> Don't say 'lot of' something, say **a lot of** or **lots of** something:
> ~~*There are lot of places to visit in Dorset.*~~
> *There are a lot of places to visit in Dorset.*
> *There are lots of places to visit in Dorset.*

GROUP ▷ **5** [C] UK an amount or set of things, especially when there are several of these amounts: *I've already done one lot of washing.* ◦ *Another lot of visitors will be here this afternoon.* **SALE** ▷ **6** [C] in an AUCTION (= public sale), an object or set of objects that are being sold: *Lot number 134 is a fine old walnut bureau.* → See also **job lot** **LAND** ▷ **7** [C] mainly US an area of land: *an empty lot* ◦ *a parking lot* ◦ *They're planning to build a house on a vacant lot on 35th Street.* **8** [C] US a film STUDIO and the land around it **LIFE** ▷ **9 sb's lot/the lot of sb** the quality of someone's life and the experiences that they have: *They should do something to improve the lot of the lowest-paid workers.* ◦ *Do you think he's happy with his lot?* **CHANCE** ▷ **10 draw lots** to make a decision by choosing from a set of objects such as pieces of paper or sticks that are all the same except for one: *We drew lots to decide who would go.*

IDIOM **there's a lot of it about** humorous said to mean that the stated thing is very common

▸**noun** [plural] UK informal a group of people: *You're an ignorant lot!* ◦ *Are you lot coming to lunch?* ◦ *My lot (= children and family generally) won't eat spinach.*

loth /ləʊθ/ US /loʊθ/ **adj** → **loath**

lotion /ˈləʊ.ʃᵊn/ US /ˈloʊ-/ **noun** [C or U] a liquid that you put on your skin in order to protect it, improve its condition, or make it smell pleasant: ***suntan** lotion*

lottery /ˈlɒt.ᵊr.i/ US /ˈlɑː.t̬ɚ-/ **noun 1** B1 [C] a game, often organized by the state or a CHARITY in order to make money, in which tickets with numbers are sold to people who then have a chance of winning a prize if their number is chosen **2** [S] disapproving something that depends only on luck and is not fair: *Education in England is something of a lottery.*

lotus /ˈləʊ.təs/ US /ˈloʊ.t̬əs/ **noun** [C] a type of tropical WATER LILY (= a plant with large flat leaves which float on the surface of lakes and pools)

ˈlotus-ˌeater noun [C] someone who has a very comfortable, lazy life and does not worry about anything

ˈlotus poˌsition noun [S] a way of sitting with your legs crossed and your feet resting on your THIGHS (= part of the leg above the knee), used especially in YOGA

loud /laʊd/ **adj, adv; adj**

▸**adj, adv** A2 making a lot of noise: *a loud explosion/noise/voice* ◦ *I heard a loud bang and then saw black smoke.* ◦ *Could you speak a little louder, please?*

IDIOMS **loud and clear** very clear and easy to understand: *I can hear you loud and clear.* ◦ *The message from management came through loud and clear: things would have to change.* • **out loud** B1 If you say or read something out loud, you say or read it so that other people can hear you: *I had to read the essay out loud in front of the whole school.*

▸**adj** disapproving (of clothes) having unpleasantly bright colours or too strong patterns, or (of a person) demanding attention and talking and laughing loudly: *You shouldn't wear anything too loud to a job interview.* ◦ *The men at the bar were loud and obnoxious.* • **loudness** /-nəs/ **noun** [U]

> **Other ways of saying loud**
>
> An alternative to 'loud' is **noisy**:
> *Our neighbours are very **noisy**.*
>
> If something is extremely loud, you can use the words **deafening** or **thunderous**:
> *The music was **deafening**.*
> ***Thunderous** cheers erupted from the fans during the final seconds of the game.*
>
> A sound that is loud, unpleasant, and high can be described as **piercing** or **shrill**:
> *a **piercing** scream*
> *a **shrill** whistle*

loudhailer /ˌlaʊdˈheɪ.ləʳ/ US /-lɚ/ **noun** [C] UK for **megaphone**

loudly /ˈlaʊd.li/ **adv** B1 making a lot of noise: *She spoke very loudly.*

loudmouth /ˈlaʊd.maʊθ/ **noun** [C] informal a person who talks a lot, especially in an offensive or stupid way

loudspeaker /ˌlaʊdˈspiː.kəʳ/ US /ˈlaʊdˌspiː.kɚ/ **noun** [C] a piece of equipment that changes electrical signals into sounds, especially used in public places so that large numbers of people can hear someone speaking or music playing → See also **speaker**

lough /lɒk/ US /lɑːk/ **noun** [C] a lake in Ireland, or an INLET of the sea

lounge /laʊndʒ/ **noun; verb**

▸**noun** [C] **1** UK the room in a house or apartment that is used for relaxing and entertaining guests, but not usually for eating: *All the family were sitting in the lounge watching television.* **2** C1 a room in a hotel, airport, theatre, etc. where people can relax or wait: *an airport lounge* ◦ *a cocktail lounge*

▸**verb**

PHRASAL VERB **lounge about/around (sth)** to spend your time in a relaxed way, sitting or lying somewhere and doing very little: *We spent our days lounging around the pool.*

ˈlounge ˌbar noun [C] UK a room in a pub that is more comfortable than the other rooms in the pub

lounger /ˈlaʊn.dʒəʳ/ US /-dʒɚ/ **noun** [C] a comfortable chair on which people can sit or lie in order to relax, especially outside in hot weather: *a sun lounger*

ˈlounge ˌroom noun [C] Australian English a **living room**

ˈlounge ˌsuit noun [C] UK old-fashioned a man's suit worn for work or on quite formal occasions during the day

louse /laʊs/ **noun; verb**

▸**noun** [C] (plural **lice**) a very small insect that lives on the bodies or in the hair of people and animals

▸**verb**

PHRASAL VERB **louse (sth) up** mainly US informal to spoil something or cause it to fail: *This is a great opportunity, so don't louse it up.*

lousy /ˈlaʊ.zi/ **adj** informal very bad: *lousy food/service* ◦ *a lousy film* ◦ *I had a lousy weekend.* ◦ *I feel lousy (= very ill) – I'm going home.* ◦ *All he offered me was a lousy £20 (= a small amount of money)!*

lout /laʊt/ **noun** [C] a young man who behaves in a very rude, offensive, and sometimes violent way: *Teenage louts roam the streets at night.* • **loutish** /ˈlaʊ.tɪʃ/ US /-t̬ɪʃ/ **adj** informal *loutish behaviour* • **loutishness** /ˈlaʊ.tɪʃ.nəs/ US /-t̬ɪʃ-/ **noun** [U] rude, offensive behaviour

louvre /ˈluː.vəʳ/ US /-vɚ/ **noun** [C] UK (US **louver**) a door or window with flat sloping pieces of wood, metal, or glass across it to allow light and air to come in while keeping rain out • **louvred** (US **louvered**) /-vəd/ US /-vɚd/ **adj** *a louvred door/window*

lovable (also **loveable**) /ˈlʌv.ə.bl̩/ **adj** having qualities which make a person or animal easy to love: *a lovable child* ◦ *a lovable **rogue***

love /lʌv/ **verb; noun**

▸**verb** [T] **LIKE SOMEONE** ▷ **1** A1 to like another adult very much and be romantically and sexually attracted to them, or to have strong feelings of liking a friend or person in your family: *I love you.* ◦ *Last night he told me he loved me.* ◦ *I'm sure he loves his kids.* **LIKE SOMETHING** ▷ **2** A1 to like something very much: *She loves animals.* ◦ *I absolutely love chocolate.* ◦ *He really loves his job.* ◦ [+ -ing verb] *I love skiing.* ◦ *Love it or hate it, reality TV is here to stay.* **3 would love** A2 used, often in requests, to say that you would very much like something: *I'd love a cup of coffee if you're making one.* ◦ [+ to infinitive] *She would dearly love **to** start her own business.* ◦ *I'd love you **to** come to dinner some night.* ◦ US *I'd love **for** you **to** come to dinner tonight.*

IDIOM **love sb to bits** UK informal to love someone very much: *He's my old man and I love him to bits but I can't spend too much time with him.*

Other ways of saying love

A deep love that does not involve romantic feelings can be described as **adoration**:

*She described her complete **adoration** of her brother.*

The words **romance** or **passion** can be used when the love involves physical attraction:

*The **romance/passion** had gone out of their relationship.*

Infatuation is used when someone has a strong feeling of love which does not last very long:

*No one expected their **infatuation** with each other to last.*

If someone is very much in love, you can say that person is **head over heels (in love)**:

*He fell **head over heels in love** with his best friend's sister.*

Love between two people who are very young, which often disappears as they get older, can be described as **puppy love**:

*It won't last, it's just **puppy love**.*

▸noun **LIKING SOMEONE** ▷ **1** B1 [U] the feeling of liking another adult very much and being romantically and sexually attracted to them, or strong feelings of liking a friend or person in your family: *'I've been seeing him over a year now.' 'Is it love?'* ◦ *Children need to be shown lots of love.* ◦ *'I'm seeing Laura next week.' 'Oh, please **give** her my love'* (= tell her I am thinking about her with affection). ◦ informal *How's your love **life*** (= *your romantic and/or sexual relationships*) *these days?* **2** B1 [C] a person that you love and feel attracted to: *He was the love **of my life**.* ◦ *She was my **first** love.* **3** [as form of address] UK informal used as a friendly form of address: *You look tired, love.* ◦ *That'll be four pounds exactly, love.* **4** A2 [U] (also **love from**, **all my love**) informal used before your name at the end of letters, cards, etc. to friends or family: *See you at Christmas. Love, Kate.* **5 be in love** B1 to love someone in a romantic and sexual way: *I'm in love for the first time and it's wonderful.* ◦ *They're still **madly** in love (**with** each other).* **6 fall in love (with sb)** B1 to start to love someone romantically and sexually: *I was 20 when I first fell in love.* **LIKING SOMETHING** ▷ **7** B2 [U] strong liking for: *I don't share my boyfriend's love **of** sport.* **8** B2 [C] something that you like very much: *Music is one of her greatest loves.* **TENNIS** ▷ **9** [U] (in tennis) the state of having no points: *The score now stands at 40–love.*

Word partners for love noun

declare/express/show love • *find* love • *give/send* your love (to sb) • *brotherly/romantic/unconditional* love • *eternal/everlasting/true/undying* love • *unrequited* love • be *unlucky in* love • sb's *first* love • the love *of* sb's *life*

IDIOMS **be no/little love lost between** If there is no/little love lost between two people, they do not like each other. • **for love nor money** If you cannot get something, or if someone will not do something, for love nor money, it is impossible to get it or to persuade them to do it. • **make love** to have sex: *That night they made love for the first time.* • **make love to sb** old use to speak romantically and give attention to someone, especially in order to make them love you: *Mr Jackson, I do believe you are making love to me.*

ˈlove afˌfair noun **1** [C] a romantic and sexual relationship between two people who are not married to each other **2** [S] a strong liking for a particular activity or place: *Her love affair **with** ballet began when she was ten.*

lovebirds /ˈlʌv.bɜːdz/ (US) /-bɝːdz/ noun [plural] humorous two people who are obviously very much in love with each other: *Look at those two lovebirds holding hands and gazing into each other's eyes.*

ˈlove ˌbite noun [C] UK (US **hickey**) a temporary red mark on someone's skin, often their neck, where someone has sucked or bitten it as a sexual act

ˈlove ˌchild noun [C] old-fashioned a child whose parents are not married to each other

ˈloved ˌone noun [C usually plural] a person that you love, usually a member of your family: *People, naturally enough, want to know that their loved ones are out of danger.*

ˌloved ˈup adj slang feeling very happy, loved by other people, and loving other people, sometimes after taking drugs such as ECSTASY: [before noun] *loved-up kids*

ˈlove ˌhandles noun [plural] humorous the layer of fat around the middle of a person's body

ˌlove-hate reˈlationship noun [C] strong feelings about someone or something that are a mixture of love and hate: *He had a love-hate relationship **with** London.*

ˈlove-in noun [C] informal a situation where two or more people praise each other a lot, especially when the praise is more than they deserve: *The awards ceremony, as usual, was a love-in.*

loveless /ˈlʌv.ləs/ adj without love: *She was trapped in a loveless **marriage**.*

ˈlove ˌletter noun [C] a letter that you write to someone that you are having a romantic relationship with

ˈlove ˌlife noun [C] the romantic relationships in a person's life: *How's your love life these days?*

lovelorn /ˈlʌv.lɔːn/ (US) /-lɔːrn/ adj literary sad because the person you love does not love you

lovely /ˈlʌv.li/ adj; noun

▸adj **ENJOYABLE** ▷ **1** A2 mainly UK pleasant or enjoyable: *a lovely meal/evening* ◦ *We had a lovely time with them.* **BEAUTIFUL** ▷ **2** A2 mainly UK beautiful: *She has lovely eyes.* ◦ *You look lovely in that dress.* ◦ *Thank you for the lovely present.* **KIND** ▷ **3** describes a person who is kind, friendly, and pleasant to be with: *He's a lovely bloke.* • **loveliness** /-nəs/ noun [U] *She was **a vision of** loveliness in her wedding dress.*

▸noun [C] old-fashioned a sexually attractive woman: *Simon was there with the usual bevy of lovelies.*

ˈlove-ˌmaking noun [U] sexual activity

ˈlove ˌmatch noun [C] informal a marriage or relationship between two people who love each other very much

lover /ˈlʌv.əʳ/ (US) /-ɚ/ noun [C] **1** B1 the person you are having a sexual relationship with, but are not married to: *They were friends before they became lovers.* ◦ *She had a string of lovers before her marriage finally broke up.* **2** B1 someone with a strong liking for something: *an opera lover* ◦ *nature lovers*

ˈlove rat noun [C] UK informal a man who has had a secret sexual relationship with someone he is not married to or who is not his regular sexual partner. This word is usually used in popular newspapers.

lovesick /ˈlʌv.sɪk/ adj sad because the person you love does not love you: *He was moping around like a lovesick teenager.*

ˈlove-ˌstruck adj so in love with someone that it is difficult to behave as usual or even think of anything else except the person you love: *Look at me, I'm behaving like a love-struck teenager!*

lovey-dovey /ˈlʌv.iˌdʌv.i/ adj informal disapproving If two people in a romantic relationship are lovey-dovey, they show their love for each other in public by touching each other and saying loving things.

loving /ˈlʌv.ɪŋ/ adj showing a lot of love towards someone: *a loving relationship* ◦ *He's a very loving child.* ◦ *She's very loving.* • **lovingly** /-li/ adv *The table had been lovingly (= with great pleasure and care) restored.*

low /ləʊ/ US /loʊ/ **adj, adv; adj; verb; noun; adv**

▸adj, adv B1 not measuring much from the base to the top, or close to the ground or the bottom of something: *a low fence* ◦ *a low ceiling.* ◦ *When we went skiing, I only went on the lower slopes.* ◦ *The planes fly low across enemy territory.*

IDIOM **the low man on the totem pole** US someone who has the least important position in an organization: *He started as the low man on the totem pole and worked his way up to be manager.*

▸adj **LEVEL** ▷ **1** A2 below the usual level: *Temperatures are very low for the time of year.* ◦ *The big supermarket offers the lowest prices in town.* ◦ *These people are living on relatively low incomes.* ◦ *There is a tremendous need for more low-**cost** housing.* ◦ *a low-**fat** diet* ◦ *low-**alcohol** beer* ◦ *Vegetables are generally low **in** (= do not contain many) calories.* **2** A2 producing only a small amount of sound, heat, or light: *They spoke in low voices so I would not hear what they were saying.* ◦ *Turn the oven to a low heat.* ◦ *Soft music was playing and the lights were low.* **3** B2 of bad quality, especially when referring to something that is not as good as it should be: *low standards* ◦ *I have rather a low opinion of him.* ◦ *She has very low self-esteem.* **4 be/get/run low (on sth)** to have nearly finished a supply of something: *We're running low on milk – could you buy some more?* ◦ *The radio batteries are running low.* **NOT IMPORTANT** ▷ **5** C1 not important because of being at or near the bottom of a range of things, especially jobs or social positions: *low status jobs* ◦ *a low priority task* **NOT HONEST** ▷ **6** not honest or fair: *How low can you get?* ◦ *That was a pretty low trick to play.* **SOUND** ▷ **7** B2 (of a sound or voice) near or at the bottom of the range of sounds: *He has a very low voice.* ◦ *Those low notes are played by the double bass.* **SAD** ▷ **8** C1 unhappy: *Illness of any sort can leave you feeling low.* ◦ *He seemed in low spirits.*

▸verb [I] literary to make the deep, long sound of a cow

▸noun **1** a bad time in someone's life: *the **highs and lows** of an acting career* **2 a new/record/all-time low** the lowest level: *The dollar has hit an all-time low against the Japanese yen.*

IDIOM **the lowest of the low** people who have no moral standards and no personal qualities

▸adv B1 at or to a low level: *low-paid workers* ◦ *Turn the oven on low.*

ˌlow-ˈalcohol adj A low-alcohol drink has less alcohol in it than the normal type: *low-alcohol beer*

lowbrow /ˈləʊ.braʊ/ US /ˈloʊ-/ adj mainly disapproving (of entertainment) not complicated or demanding much intelligence to be understood: *He regards the sort of books I read as very lowbrow.* ◦ *I like a lowbrow action movie once in a while.* → Compare **highbrow, middlebrow**

ˌlow-ˈcalorie adj (also **low-cal, lo-cal** /ˌləʊˈkæl/ US /ˌloʊ-/) containing fewer CALORIES (= units for measuring the amount of energy a food provides) than normal: *low-calorie drinks/snacks*

ˌLow ˈChurch adj related to the part of the Church of England that does not consider ceremonies and RITUALS to be an important part of the religion → Compare **High Church**

ˌlow-ˈcost adj cheap: *The 1990s saw a huge increase in the numbers of low-cost airlines.*

ˌlow-ˈcut adj describes a piece of clothing that does not cover a woman's neck and the top part of her chest: *a low-cut dress*

ˈlow-down adj [before noun] informal describes a person or action that is very dishonest and unfair: *That was a low-down thing to do.*

the lowdown /ˈləʊ.daʊn/ US /ˈloʊ-/ noun [S] the most important facts and information about something: *Our fashion editor **gives** you the lowdown **on** winter coats for this season.*

ˈlow-end adj **1** Low-end products are the cheapest in a group of products: *a low-end model* **2** intended for people who do not have a lot of money to spend: *a low-end supermarket*

ˌlow-ˈenergy adj [before noun] using less electricity or other fuel than other similar things: *low-energy light bulbs/lighting*

lower /ˈləʊ.əʳ/ US /ˈloʊ.ɚ/ **verb; adj**

▸verb [T] **MOVE** ▷ **1** B2 to move something into a low position: *They lowered the coffin into the grave.* ◦ *Heavily pregnant by now, she lowered her**self** carefully into the chair.* ◦ *He lowered his eyes (= looked down) in embarrassment when he saw me.* **REDUCE** ▷ **2** B2 to reduce something: *Interest rates have been lowered again.* ◦ *Boil for five minutes, then lower the heat and simmer for half an hour.* ◦ *Please lower your voice (= speak more quietly).* **3** to make something worse than it was before: *a lowering of standards* ◦ humorous *Dale lowered **the tone of** the evening (= made it less socially acceptable) by telling a dirty joke.* **BEHAVE BADLY** ▷ **4 lower yourself** to behave in a way that makes people lose respect for you: [+ to infinitive] *I wouldn't lower myself **to** respond to his insults if I were you.*

▸adj positioned below one or more similar things, or of the bottom part of something: *the lower deck of a ship* ◦ *Her lower lip trembled as if she was about to cry.* ◦ *I've got a pain in my lower (= the bottom part of my) back.* → Opposite **upper**

ˌlower ˈcase noun [U] letters of the alphabet that are not written as capital letters, for example a, b, c → Compare **upper case** • **lower-ˈcase** adj *lower-case letters*

ˌlower ˈclass adj old-fashioned describes people who belong to the social class that has the lowest position in society and the least money → Compare **upper class, middle class, working class** • **the ˌlower ˈclasses** noun [plural]

ˌlower ˈhouse noun [C usually singular] (also **ˌlower ˈchamber**) one of the two parts that some parliaments are divided into, usually the one with more political power → Compare **upper house**

lowering /ˈlaʊə.rɪŋ/ US /ˈlaʊɚ.ɪŋ/ adj literary describes the sky when it is very dark and it looks as if it is about to rain: *The street party took place under lowering skies.*

ˌlowest common deˈnominator noun **NUMBER** ▷ **1** [U] specialized the smallest number that can be exactly divided by all the bottom numbers in a group of FRACTIONS **POPULAR** ▷ **2 the lowest common denominator** [S] the large number of people in society who will accept low-quality products and entertainment: *The problem with so much television is that it is aimed at the lowest common denominator.*

L

ˌlow-ˈfat adj containing only a small amount of fat: *a low-fat diet ◦ low-fat yogurt/cheese/spreads*

low-fi /ˈləʊ.faɪ/ (US) /ˈloʊ-/ **adj 1** abbreviation for low fidelity: the production by electrical equipment of poor-quality sound that has noises which should not be there **2** A low-fi website is a simple one for people who have an old computer or a slow connection to the internet.

ˌlow-ˈkey adj describes an event that is quiet and without a great show of excitement: *The wedding was a low-key affair, with fewer than 30 people attending.*

lowland /ˈləʊ.lənd/ (US) /ˈloʊ-/ **noun** [C usually plural] flat land that is at the same level as the sea: *From the lowlands of the south to the rugged peaks in the north, Derbyshire has something for everyone. ◦ These plants are mainly found in lowland areas/regions.*

ˈlow ˌlife noun [U] people who exist by criminal activities or have a way of life that most people disapprove of: *He started mixing with drug dealers, pimps, and other low life.*

lowly /ˈləʊ.li/ (US) /ˈloʊ-/ **adj** low in position and importance, or not respected: *He took a lowly job in an insurance firm. ◦ His first job in the hotel was as a lowly porter.*

ˌlow-ˈlying adj describes land that is at or near the level of the sea: *People living in low-lying areas were evacuated because of the floods.*

ˌlow-ˈpitched adj describes a sound that is at the bottom of the range of sounds: *He gave a low-pitched whistle.*

ˌlow-ˈrent adj mainly US disapproving cheap and not of good quality

ˌlow-resoˈlution adj (also informal **lo-res**) used to describe something such as a screen or photograph that does not show an image clearly: *All we had was a blurry low-resolution image.*

ˈlow-rise adj **BUILDING** ▷ **1** A low-rise building is one with only one or two floors. **TROUSERS** ▷ **2** low-rise trousers have the top part ending lower than the waist

ˈlow ˌseason noun [U] the period in the year when the fewest people visit a place and when the prices are at their lowest level → Compare **high season**

ˌlow-ˈspirited adj unhappy and having little hope

ˌlow-ˈtech adj not using the most recent equipment or methods: *a low-tech economy* → Compare **high-tech**

ˌlow ˈtide noun [C usually singular] the time when the sea has reached its lowest level

ˌlow-ˈwater ˌmark noun [C usually singular] a mark that shows the lowest point on a beach that is reached by the sea

lox /lɒks/ (US) /lɑːks/ noun [U] US **salmon** (= a type of fish) that has been preserved with smoke

loyal /ˈlɔɪ.əl/ adj (B2) firm and not changing in your friendship with or support for a person or an organization, or in your belief in your principles: *Jack has been a loyal worker in this company for almost 50 years. ◦ When all her other friends deserted her, Steve remained loyal. ◦ She's very loyal* ***to*** *her friends.* → Opposite **disloyal** • **loyally** /-ə.li/ adv

loyalist /ˈlɔɪ.ə.lɪst/ noun [C] a person or group that strongly supports the government or ruler in power: *The rebel forces have been repeatedly attacked by loyalist troops.*

Loyalist /ˈlɔɪ.ə.lɪst/ **noun** [C] in Northern Ireland, a person who believes that Northern Ireland should continue to be part of the UK

loyalty /ˈlɔɪ.əl.ti/ (US) /-t̬i/ **noun 1** (B2) [U] the quality of being loyal: *His loyalty was never in question. ◦ Her loyalty* ***to*** *the cause is impressive.* **2 loyalties** [plural] your feelings of support or duty towards someone or something: *My loyalties* ***to*** *my family come before anything else. ◦* ***divided*** *loyalties (= feelings of support for two different and opposing people or things)*

ˈloyalty ˌcard noun [C] UK a card that is given to a customer by a business, used by the business to record information about what the customer buys and to reward them for buying goods or services

lozenge /ˈlɒz.ɪndʒ/ (US) /ˈlɑː.zəndʒ/ **noun** [C] a small, flat sweet which you suck to make your throat feel better: *a cough lozenge*

LP /ˌelˈpiː/ **noun** [C] abbreviation for long-playing record: a record that is played at 33⅓ RPM

LPG /ˌel.piːˈdʒiː/ **noun** [U] abbreviation for liquefied petroleum gas: a type of fuel used for heating, cooking, and in some vehicles

ˈL-plate noun [C usually plural] UK a square, white sign with a red letter L on it, fixed to the back and the front of a vehicle that is being driven by a person learning to drive

LPN /ˌel.piːˈen/ **noun** [C] US abbreviation for **licensed practical nurse**

LSD /ˌel.esˈdiː/ **noun** [U] (slang **acid**) an illegal drug which causes people who use it to see the world differently from the way it really is or to see things that do not really exist

Lt noun [before noun] written abbreviation for **lieutenant**

Ltd adj [after noun] UK written abbreviation for limited liability company: used in the name of a company whose owners have limited responsibility for the money that it owes: *Smith and Jones Ltd*

luau /ˈluː.aʊ/ noun [C] a Hawaiian party or celebration

lubricant /ˈluː.brɪ.kənt/ noun [C or U] (informal **lube**) a liquid such as oil that is used to make the parts of an engine move easily together, or a substance put on any surface to help it move more easily against another one

lubricate /ˈluː.brɪ.keɪt/ **verb** [T] to use a substance such as oil to make a machine operate more easily, or to prevent something sticking or rubbing: *A car engine needs to be well lubricated with oil.* • **lubrication** /ˌluː.brɪˈkeɪ.ʃən/ noun [U] (informal **lube**)

lubricious /luːˈbrɪʃ.əs/ **adj** formal having or showing too great an interest in sex, especially in an unpleasant way • **lubriciously** /-li/ **adv** • **lubriciousness** /-nəs/ **noun** [U]

lucid /ˈluː.sɪd/ **adj** clearly expressed and easy to understand, or (of a person) thinking or speaking clearly: *She gave a clear and lucid account of her plans for the company's future. ◦ The drugs she's taking make her drowsy and confused, but there are times when she's quite lucid.* • **lucidity** /luːˈsɪd.ɪ.ti/ (US) /-ə.t̬i/ **noun** [U] (also **lucidness** /-nəs/) • **lucidly** /-li/ adv

Lucifer /ˈluː.sɪ.fəʳ/ (US) /-fɚ/ **noun** another name for SATAN (= a powerful evil force and the enemy of God)

Lucite /ˈluː.saɪt/ **noun** [U] US trademark a type of transparent plastic used to make paints and decorative objects such as picture frames

luck /lʌk/ **noun; verb**

▸**noun** [U] **1** (A2) the force that causes things, especially good things, to happen to you by chance and not as a result of your own efforts or abilities: *It was just luck that I asked for a job at the right time. ◦ Then I met this gorgeous woman and I couldn't believe my luck. ◦ She wears a charm that she thinks brings her* ***good*** *luck. ◦ He seems to have had a lot of* ***bad*** *luck in his life. ◦ So your interview's tomorrow? Good luck! ◦ The best of* luck *in/with* your exams! **2** B2 success: *Have you* ***had*** *any luck* ***with*** *booking your flight?* ◦ *He tried to get into teacher training college but with no luck.*

Word partners for luck

bad/good/rotten luck • *beginner's* luck • *pure/ sheer* luck • a *matter/stroke* of luck • *wish* sb luck • *bring* (sb) luck • *curse* your luck • not *have* any/ much luck • luck *in/with* sth

IDIOMS **as luck would have it** by chance: *We ran out of petrol on the way home, but as luck would have it, we were very near a garage.* • **bad/hard/tough luck!** said to express sympathy with someone when something bad has happened to them: *'They've just run out of tickets.' 'Oh, bad luck!'* • **be bad luck on sb** mainly UK to be a bad thing that happened to someone by chance: *It was bad luck on Alex that he was ill on his birthday.* • **be down on your luck** to be experiencing a bad situation or to have very little money: *He's been a bit down on his luck recently.* • **be in/out of luck** informal C1 to be able/unable to have or do what you want: *'Do you have any tuna sandwiches?' 'You're in luck – there's one left.'* • **be the luck of the draw** to be the result of chance and something that you have no control over: *You can't choose who you play against – it's just the luck of the draw.* • **for (good) luck** to bring good luck: *We have a horseshoe hanging on our wall for good luck.* • **for luck** usually humorous used to describe something extra which you take, especially in order to bring you good luck: *There's two spoonsful of sugar, and* ***one*** *for luck.* • **more by luck than judgment** UK by chance and not because of any special skill: *'You did amazingly well to get the ball in.' 'Oh, it was more by luck than judgment.'* • **no such luck** informal said after an event or result that would be very good has been suggested, to show disappointment that it cannot or did not happen: *I was rather hoping it would rain today and I wouldn't have to go on the walk, but no such luck.* • **with any luck** (also **with a bit of luck**) used before describing an event or a result that you are hoping for: *With any luck (= I hope that) we should get to Newcastle by early evening.* • **your luck's in!** UK humorous used to tell someone that they have been lucky or successful

▸verb

PHRASAL VERBS **luck into sth** US informal to get something that you want by chance: *We lucked into tickets for the World Cup finals.* • **luck out** US informal to be very lucky: *The Giants really lucked out in last night's game.*

luckily /ˈlʌk.əl.i/ adv B1 because of good luck: *Luckily, I had some money with me.*

luckless /ˈlʌk.ləs/ adj literary describes someone who has a lot of bad luck: *The luckless defender, Mark Emery, sustained his third injury of the season.*

lucky /ˈlʌk.i/ adj **1** A2 having good things happen to you by chance: *'I'm going on holiday.' 'Lucky you!'* ◦ *The lucky winner will be able to choose from three different holidays.* ◦ [+ to infinitive] *They're lucky* ***to*** *have such a nice office to work in.* ◦ *He's lucky* ***that*** *he wasn't fired.* ◦ *It sounds as if you had a lucky* ***escape*** *(= by good chance you were able to avoid something dangerous or unpleasant).* ◦ *We'll be lucky if we get there by midnight at this rate (= we might get there by midnight or it might be later).* **2** B1 bringing good luck: *a lucky charm* ◦ *Six is my lucky number.*

IDIOMS **get lucky** informal to meet someone you can have a sexual or romantic relationship with: *Why don't you come to the party? You never know, you might get lucky.* • **you'll be lucky!** (also **you should be so**

Other ways of saying lucky

Fortunate is a common, slightly more formal alternative to 'lucky':

It was ***fortunate*** *that he wasn't injured in the accident.*

If you want to say something is lucky, you could use the phrase **it's a good thing** or **it's a good job**:

It's a good thing *they didn't go camping this weekend – the weather's been awful.*

In informal US English, the phrasal verb **luck out** can be used to say that someone is lucky:

The Giants really ***lucked out*** *in last night's game.*

People who are lucky, especially after not being lucky, could be said to **land on** *their* **feet**:

She's really ***landed on her feet*** *with that job.*

lucky!) UK informal said in order to tell someone that it is very unlikely that they will get what they want: *'She's going to ask for a salary increase.' 'She'll be lucky!'*

lucrative /ˈluː.krə.tɪv/ US /-t̬ɪv/ adj C2 (especially of a business, job, or activity) producing a lot of money: *The merger proved to be very lucrative for both companies.* • **lucratively** /-li/ adv • **lucrativeness** /-nəs/ noun [U]

lucre /ˈluː.kəʳ/ US /-kɚ/ noun [U] old-fashioned disapproving or humorous money or profit: ***filthy*** *lucre*

Luddite /ˈlʌd.aɪt/ noun [C] usually disapproving a person who is opposed to the introduction of new working methods, especially new machines

ludicrous /ˈluː.dɪ.krəs/ adj stupid or unreasonable and deserving to be laughed at: *a ludicrous idea/ suggestion* ◦ *He looked ludicrous in that suit!* • **ludicrously** /-li/ adv • **ludicrousness** /-nəs/ noun [U]

lug /lʌg/ verb; noun

▸verb [T usually + adv/prep] (**-gg-**) informal to carry or pull something with effort or difficulty because it is heavy: *I'm exhausted after lugging these suitcases all the way across London.* ◦ *I don't want to lug these shopping bags* ***around*** *with me all day.*

▸noun [C] informal **EAR** ▷ **1** UK a **lughole** (= ear) **PERSON** ▷ **2** US an awkward or stupid man **3** US a way of talking to a man you like: *Come over here and give me a kiss, you* ***big*** *lug.*

luge /luːʒ/ noun **1** [C] a SLEDGE used for racing on ice. The person using it lies on their back with their feet pointing forward. **2 the luge** [S] the sport or event of using a luge to race down a track made of ice

luggage /ˈlʌg.ɪdʒ/ noun [U] (mainly US **baggage**) A2 the bags, cases, etc. which contain your possessions and that you take with you when you are travelling: *Never leave your luggage unattended.* ◦ ***hand*** *luggage (= small bags that you take with you onto the plane)*

ˈluggage ˌlabel noun [C] UK (US **ˈluggage ˌtag**) a small piece of card or plastic with your name and address written on it that you fasten to a bag or case to show that it belongs to you

luggage rack

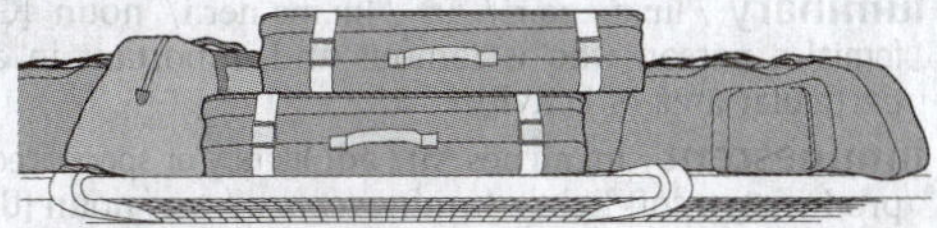

ˈluggage ˌrack noun [C] mainly UK a shelf on a train or a bus on which you can put your bags and cases

ˈluggage ˌvan noun [C] UK (US **ˈbaggage ˌcar**) a train CARRIAGE in which large bags are transported

lughole /ˈlʌg.həʊl/ (US) /-hoʊl/ noun [C] (also **lug**) UK informal humorous an ear: *You'll get a clip round the lughole if you're not careful.*

lugubrious /luːˈguː.bri.əs/ adj literary sad and serious: *a lugubrious face* • **lugubriously** /-li/ adv • **lugubriousness** /-nəs/ noun [U]

lukewarm /ˌluːkˈwɔːm/, /ˈluːk.wɔːm/ (US) /ˈluːk.wɔːrm/ adj **TEMPERATURE** ▷ **1** mainly disapproving (especially of a liquid) only slightly warm: *This coffee's lukewarm.* **REACTION** ▷ **2** disapproving not enthusiastic or interested: *Her proposals got a lukewarm **response**.*

lull /lʌl/ verb; noun

▸verb [T] to cause someone to feel calm or to feel as if they want to sleep: *The motion of the car almost lulled her **to sleep**.*

PHRASAL VERB **lull sb into sth** to make someone feel safe in order to trick them: *Most exercise classes start gently, lulling you into thinking that you're fit.* ◦ *Their promises lulled us **into a false sense of security** (= made us feel safe, when in fact we were not).*

▸noun [C] a short period of calm in which little happens: *There has been a lull **in** the fighting.* ◦ *a lull in the conversation/traffic*

IDIOM **the lull before the storm** a time that seems quiet but will very soon be followed by something unpleasant happening: *Things seem quiet in the office right now, but this is just the lull before the storm.*

L

lullaby /ˈlʌl.ə.baɪ/ noun [C] a quiet song that is sung to children to help them go to sleep

lumbago /lʌmˈbeɪ.gəʊ/ (US) /-goʊ/ noun [U] general pain in the lower part of the back

lumbar /ˈlʌm.bəʳ/ (US) /-bɚ/ adj [before noun] specialized in or of the lower part of the back

lumber /ˈlʌm.bəʳ/ (US) /-bɚ/ verb; noun

▸verb [I usually + adv/prep] to move slowly and awkwardly: *In the distance, we could see a herd of elephants lumbering across the plain.*

PHRASAL VERB **lumber sb with sth** mainly UK informal If you are/get lumbered with something, you have to deal with something or someone that you do not want to: *I always seem to get lumbered with the job of clearing up after a party.*

▸noun [U] mainly US (C2) wood that has been prepared for building

lumberjack /ˈlʌm.bə.dʒæk/ (US) /-bɚ-/ noun [C] (also **lumberman**) (especially in the US and Canada) a person whose job is to cut down trees that will be used for building, etc. or to transport trees that have been cut down

ˈlumber ˌjacket noun [C] a warm. short coat, often with a brightly coloured pattern of squares on it

lumberman /ˈlʌm.bə.mæn/ (US) /-bɚ-/ noun [C] (plural **-men** /-men/) a **lumberjack**

lumberyard /ˈlʌm.bə.jɑːd/ (US) /ˈlʌm.bɚ.jɑːrd/ noun [C] US an outside area where wood for building is stored and sold

luminary /ˈluː.mɪ.nə.ri/ (US) /ˈluː.mə.ner.i/ noun [C] formal a person who is famous and important in a particular area of activity

luminescent /ˌluː.mɪˈnes.ᵊnt/ adj literary or specialized producing a soft light • **luminescence** /-ᵊns/ noun [U]

luminous /ˈluː.mɪ.nəs/ adj producing or reflecting bright light (especially in the dark): *luminous clothing* • **luminosity** /ˌluː.mɪˈnɒs.ə.ti/ (US) /-ˈnɑː.sə.t̬i/ noun [U] • **luminously** /-li/ adv

lummox /ˈlʌm.əks/ noun [C] informal a stupid or awkward person: *Be careful, you big lummox, you just stamped on my foot!*

lump /lʌmp/ noun; verb

▸noun [C] **PIECE** ▷ **1** (C2) a piece of a solid substance, usually with no particular shape: *a lump **of** coal* ◦ *a sugar lump* ◦ *You don't want lumps in the sauce.* **2** informal a separate large amount: *I'll be getting the insurance money in two lumps.* **IN THE BODY** ▷ **3** a hard SWELLING found in or on the body, especially because of illness or injury: *She found a lump in her breast.* **PERSON** ▷ **4** informal a heavy, awkward, stupid person: *Come on, you **great** lump, get up from in front of that television and do some work.*

IDIOMS **bring a lump to sb's throat** (C2) to give someone a tight feeling in their throat because they want to cry: *It was quite a moving speech – it almost brought a lump to my throat.* • **take your lumps** US old-fashioned informal to be criticized or beaten as a punishment

▸verb informal **lump it** to accept a situation or decision although you do not like it: *The decision has been made, so if Tom doesn't like it, he **can** lump it.*

PHRASAL VERB **lump sb/sth together** to put different groups together and think about them or deal with them in the same way: *All the children are lumped together in one class, regardless of their ability.*

lumpectomy /lʌmˈpek.tə.mi/ noun [C] a medical operation to remove a lump from the breast

lumpen /ˈlʌm.pən/ adj **PERSON** ▷ **1** informal disapproving describes people who are not clever or well educated, and who are not interested in changing or improving their situation: *the lumpen **proletariat** (= unskilled working people)* **OBJECT** ▷ **2** disapproving heavy and awkward

lumpish /ˈlʌm.pɪʃ/ adj awkward and stupid

ˌlump ˈsum noun [C usually singular] an amount of money that is paid in one large amount on one occasion: *Her divorce settlement included a lump sum **of** $2 million.*

lumpy /ˈlʌm.pi/ adj covered with or containing lumps: *a lumpy bed/pillow* ◦ *a lumpy sauce*

lunacy /ˈluː.nə.si/ noun [U] **1** stupid behaviour that will have bad results: *It would be lunacy to try to climb the mountain in this weather.* ◦ *It was sheer lunacy spending all that money.* **2** old-fashioned mental illness

lunar /ˈluː.nəʳ/ (US) /-nɚ/ adj of or relating to the moon: *the lunar surface*

ˌlunar ˈmonth noun [C] the period of time (about 29.5 days) which the moon takes to go round the Earth → Compare **calendar month**

lunatic /ˈluː.nə.tɪk/ (US) /-t̬ɪk/ noun; adj

▸noun [C] **1** someone who behaves in a silly or dangerous way: *He drives like a lunatic.* **2** offensive old-fashioned a person who is mentally ill

▸adj silly in a dangerous way

IDIOM **the lunatic fringe** disapproving or humorous people who have very strong opinions that are outside the usual range

ˈlunatic aˌsylum noun [C] old-fashioned a hospital for mentally ill people

lunch /lʌntʃ/ noun; verb

▸noun [C or U] (A1) a meal that is eaten in the middle of the day: *What's for lunch?* ◦ UK *We had a **pub** lunch.* ◦ *I'm sorry, Joanna isn't here at the moment, she's* (*gone*) *out to/gone to lunch.* ◦ *We must* ***do*** *lunch sometime (= have lunch together).*

IDIOM **be out to lunch** informal to be crazy: *So do I take this guy seriously or is he out to lunch?*

▸verb [I] to eat lunch: *I'm lunching* ***with*** *Giles.*

lunchbox /ˈlʌntʃ.bɒks/ ⓤⓢ /-bɑːks/ noun [C] a box in which your lunch can be carried to work, school, etc.

luncheon /ˈlʌn.tʃən/ noun [C or U] formal for **lunch**

luncheonette /ˌlʌn.tʃəˈnet/ noun [C] US a small restaurant serving simple, light meals

ˈluncheon ˌvoucher noun [C] UK (US **ˈmeal ˌticket**) a type of ticket given to people by their employer that they can use instead of money for buying meals in some restaurants

ˈlunch ˌhome noun [C] Indian English a restaurant

ˈlunch ˌhour noun [C] (also **ˈlunch ˌbreak**) the period in the middle of the day when people stop work to have lunch

lunchroom /ˈlʌntʃ.ruːm/, /-rʊm/ noun [C usually singular] US (UK **ˈdining ˌhall**) a large room in a school where children can sit down to eat

lunchtime /ˈlʌntʃ.taɪm/ noun [C or U] A2 the time in the middle of the day when most people eat a meal: *What are you doing* ***at*** *lunchtime?*

> **!** Common mistake: **lunchtime**
>
> Remember that **lunchtime** is usually written as one word.
>
> Don't write 'lunch time', write **lunchtime**:
>
> ~~*I like to go for a walk at lunch time.*~~

lung /lʌŋ/ noun [C] B2 either of the two organs in the chest with which people and some animals breathe

IDIOM **have a good/healthy pair of lungs** You say that a baby has a good/healthy pair of lungs when it cries loudly.

lunge /lʌndʒ/ verb [I usually + adv/prep] to move forward suddenly and with force, especially in order to attack someone: *He suddenly lunged* ***at*** *her* ***with*** *a broken bottle.* • **lunge** noun [C]

lungi /ˈlʊŋ.giː/ noun [C] Indian English a piece of clothing consisting of a piece of cloth wrapped around the waist and worn by men and women from South Asia

lupin (US usually **lupine**) /ˈluː.pɪn/ noun [C] a garden plant with a long, pointed flower of various colours

lupus /ˈluː.pəs/ noun [U] specialized a general name for various serious skin diseases which also affect the INTERNAL organs and bones

lurch /lɜːtʃ/ ⓤⓢ /lɝːtʃ/ verb; noun

▸verb **1** [I] to move in a way that is not regular or normal, especially making sudden movements backwards or forwards or from side to side: *The train lurched* ***forward*** *and some of the people standing fell over.* **2** [I + adv/prep] to act or continue in away that is uncontrolled and not regular, often with sudden changes: *We seem to lurch* ***from*** *crisis* ***to*** *crisis.* ◦ *She just lurches* ***from*** *one bad relationship* ***to*** *another.*

▸noun [C] a sudden movement or change that is not smooth or normal: *The truck gave a sudden lurch as it was hit by a strong gust of wind.* ◦ *The party's lurch (= sudden change)* ***to*** *the left will lose it a lot of support.*

lure /ljʊəʳ/ ⓤⓢ /lʊr/ noun; verb

▸noun **1** C2 [C usually singular] the quality or power that something or someone has that makes them attractive: *the lure of fame/power/money* **2** [C] an artificial insect or other small animal that is put on the end of a fishing line to attract fish

▸verb [T] C2 to persuade someone to do something or go somewhere by offering them something exciting: *She was lured* ***into*** *the job by the offer of a high salary.* ◦ *He had lured his victim* ***to*** *a deserted house.* ◦ *Supermarket chains try to lure customers with price discounts.*

Lurex /ˈlʊə.reks/ ⓤⓢ /ˈlʊr.eks/ noun [U] trademark (cloth made from) a type of thread that looks shiny, like metal: *a gold/silver Lurex top*

lurgy /ˈlɜː.gi/ ⓤⓢ /ˈlɝː-/ noun [S] UK humorous an illness or disease, especially one that is not serious: *He's got* ***the dreaded*** *lurgy.*

lurid /ˈljʊə.rɪd/ ⓤⓢ /ˈlʊr.ɪd/ adj disapproving SHOCKING ▷ **1** (especially of a description) shocking because involving violence, sex, or IMMORAL activity: *You can read all the lurid* ***details*** *of the affair in today's paper.* COLOUR ▷ **2** too brightly coloured: *That's a very lurid shade of lipstick she's wearing.* • **luridly** /-li/ adv • **luridness** /-nəs/ noun [U]

lurk /lɜːk/ ⓤⓢ /lɝːk/ verb **1** [I usually + adv/prep] to wait or move in a secret way so that you cannot be seen, especially because you are about to attack someone or do something wrong: *Someone was lurking* ***in*** *the shadows.* ◦ *Why are you lurking* ***about*** *in the corridor?* **2** [I usually + adv/prep] (of an unpleasant feeling or quality) to exist although it is not always noticeable: ***Danger*** *lurks around every corner.* ◦ *It seems that old prejudices are still lurking* ***beneath*** *the surface.* **3** [I] informal to enter a CHAT ROOM and read other people's messages without taking part • **lurking** /ˈlɜː.kɪŋ/ ⓤⓢ /ˈlɝː-/ adj *I have some lurking* ***doubts*** *(= doubts which will not go completely away) about whether Simon is really capable of doing this job.* ◦ *She said she had a lurking* ***suspicion*** *(= she had a very slight feeling) that he wasn't telling the truth.*

lurker /ˈlɜː.kəʳ/ ⓤⓢ /ˈlɝː.kɚ/ noun [C] someone who reads the messages in a CHAT ROOM without taking part

lurve /lɜːv/ noun [U] UK not standard humorous love: *They spend every evening together – I think it might be lurve.* • **lurve** verb [T]

luscious /ˈlʌʃ.əs/ adj TASTY ▷ **1** having a pleasant sweet taste or containing a lot of juice: *luscious ripe figs* ATTRACTIVE ▷ **2** informal (of a woman) very sexually attractive **3** (of an area of countryside) very green and attractive • **lusciously** /-li/ adv • **lusciousness** /-nəs/ noun [U]

lush /lʌʃ/ adj; noun

▸adj PLANTS ▷ **1** A lush area has a lot of green, healthy plants, grass, and trees: *lush green valleys* LUXURIOUS ▷ **2** (of places, furniture, decoration, etc.) expensive and LUXURIOUS: *a lush carpet* ATTRACTIVE ▷ **3** informal very attractive to look at, taste, smell, etc.: *He's so lush.* • **lushly** /ˈlʌʃ.li/ adv • **lushness** /ˈlʌʃ.nəs/ noun [U]

▸noun [C] slang a person who regularly drinks too much alcohol: *She's a bit of a lush by all accounts.*

lust /lʌst/ noun; verb

▸noun DESIRE ▷ **1** [U] a very strong sexual DESIRE: *I don't think it's love so much as lust.* WISH ▷ **2** [C or U] a very powerful feeling of wanting something: *her lust* ***for*** *power* ◦ *It's wonderful to see the children's lust* ***for*** *life (= how enthusiastic they are about life).* • **lustful** /-fᵊl/ adj *lustful thoughts* • **lustfully** /-fᵊl.i/ adv • **lustfulness** /-fᵊl.nəs/ noun [U]

▸verb

PHRASAL VERBS **lust after sb** to feel sexual DESIRE for someone you are not having a sexual relationship with: *She's been lusting after Dave for months.* • **lust after/for sth** to want something very much: *I've been lusting after one of their silk shirts for ages.*

L

lustre UK (US **luster**) /ˈlʌs.təʳ/ (US) /-tɚ/ **noun 1** [S or U] the brightness that a shiny surface has: *a treatment for restoring the lustre to dull hair* ◦ *the rich lustre of well-polished furniture* **2** [U] a very special, attractive quality that people admire: *The dancing of the principal ballerina* ***added*** *lustre* ***to*** *an otherwise unimpressive production of 'Giselle'.*

lustrous /ˈlʌs.trəs/ **adj** very shiny: *long, lustrous hair* • **lustrously** /-li/ **adv**

lusty /ˈlʌs.ti/ **adj** healthy, energetic, and full of strength and power: *a baby's lusty cry* ◦ *We could hear the lusty singing of the church choir.* • **lustily** /-tɪ.li/ **adv** *The baby cried lustily the moment he was born.* • **lustiness** /-nəs/ **noun** [U]

lute /luːt/ **noun** [C] a musical instrument that has a body with a round back and a flat top, a long neck, and strings that are played with the fingers

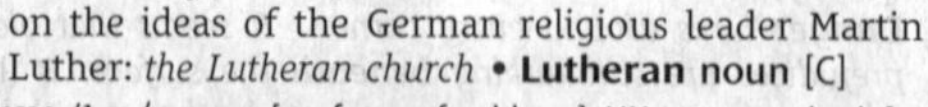
lute

Lutheran /ˈluː.θəʳ.ən/ (US) /-θɚ-/ **adj** of or relating to the part of Protestant Christianity that is based on the ideas of the German religious leader Martin Luther: *the Lutheran church* • **Lutheran noun** [C]

luv /lʌv/ **noun** [as form of address] UK not standard for love: *Can I get you a drink, luv?*

luvvy /ˈlʌv.i/ **noun** [C] (also **luvvie**) an actor who speaks and acts in a very artificial and noticeable way

lux /lʌks/ **noun** [C] (plural **lux**) specialized a measure of the amount of light produced by something

luxuriant /lʌgˈʒʊə.ri.ənt/ (US) /-ˈʒʊr.i-/ **adj 1** growing thickly, strongly, and well: *Tall, luxuriant plants grew along the river bank.* ◦ *This stretch of land was once covered with luxuriant forest, but is now bare.* ◦ *Her luxuriant hair fell around her shoulders.* **2** pleasantly thick or full: *We've bought a wonderfully luxuriant carpet for our bedroom.* ◦ *a luxuriant style of writing* • **luxuriance** /-əns/ **noun** [U] • **luxuriantly** /-li/ **adv**

luxuriate /lʌgˈʒʊə.ri.eɪt/ (US) /-ʒʊr.i-/ **verb**

PHRASAL VERB **luxuriate in sth** formal to get great pleasure from something, especially because it provides physical comfort: *There's nothing better after a hard day's work than to luxuriate in a hot bath.*

luxurious /lʌgˈʒʊə.ri.əs/ (US) /-ˈʒʊr.i-/ **adj 1** (C1) very comfortable and expensive: *They have a very luxurious house.* ◦ *We spent a luxurious weekend at a country hotel.* **2** giving great pleasure: *The cat gave a long, luxurious stretch.* • **luxuriously** /-li/ **adv**

luxury /ˈlʌk.ʃəʳr.i/ (US) /-ʃɚ-/ **noun 1** (B1) [U] great comfort, especially as provided by expensive and beautiful things: *to live in luxury* ◦ *a luxury cruise* ◦ *a luxury hotel* **2** (C1) [C] something expensive that is pleasant to have but is not necessary: *luxuries, such as champagne and chocolate* ◦ *I like to buy myself* ***little*** *luxuries from time to time.* **3** (B2) [S or U] something that gives you a lot of pleasure but cannot be done often: *A day off work is such a luxury.*

ˌluxury ˈgoods noun [plural] expensive things, such as jewellery and make-up, that are pleasant to have but are not necessary: *The government will pay for the new schools by increasing the tax on luxury goods.*

LW noun [U] written abbreviation for **long wave**

-ly /-li/ suffix **ADVERB** ▷ **1** in the stated way: *quickly* ◦ *carefully* ◦ *angrily* ◦ *loudly* **2** when considered in the stated way: *Personally (= in my opinion), I don't think animals should be killed for their fur.* ◦ *This is an environmentally (= in relation to the environment) disastrous proposal.* **3** regularly after the stated period of time: *a weekly/monthly meeting* **ADJECTIVE** ▷ **4** like the stated person or thing: *fatherly advice* ◦ *priestly duties* ◦ *cowardly behaviour* **5** describes one of a series of events which happen with the stated regular period of time between each: *a daily shower* ◦ *a weekly meeting* ◦ *a yearly check-up*

lycée /ˈliː.seɪ/ **noun** [C] a French school for older children, either in France or for French children living in other countries

lychee (also **litchi**) /ˈlaɪ.tʃiː/ (US) /ˈliː.tʃiː/ **noun** [C] a fruit with a rough, brown shell and sweet, white flesh around a large, shiny, brown seed, or the EVERGREEN tree (= one that never loses its leaves) on which this fruit grows

lychgate /ˈlɪtʃ.geɪt/ **noun** [C] a small gate with a small sloping roof over it which leads into the area around a church

lycopene /ˈlaɪ.kə.piːn/ (US) /-koʊ-/ **noun** [U] a substance in tomatoes and some other red fruits that may prevent some types of CANCER

Lycra /ˈlaɪ.krə/ **noun** [U] trademark a type of material that stretches, used especially for making clothes that fit very tightly: *a Lycra swimsuit* ◦ *Lycra leggings*

lye /laɪ/ **noun** [U] a highly ALKALINE substance, usually either SODIUM HYDROXIDE or POTASSIUM HYDROXIDE, that can cause severe damage or burns and is used in making cleaning products

lying /ˈlaɪ.ɪŋ/ **verb** present participle of **lie**

lymph /lɪmf/ **noun** [U] a clear liquid that transports useful substances around the body, and carries waste matter, such as unwanted bacteria, away from body tissue in order to prevent infection • **lymphatic** /lɪmˈfæt.ɪk/ (US) /-fæṭ-/ **adj** *the lymphatic system*

ˈlymph ˌgland noun [C] (also **ˈlymph ˌnode**) one of many small organs in the body that produce the white blood cells needed for the body to fight infection

lymphocyte /ˈlɪm.fə.saɪt/ **noun** [C] specialized a type of WHITE BLOOD CELL involved in fighting disease and infection in the body, some of which produce ANTIBODIES (= PROTEINS that attack and kill harmful bacteria)

ˈlymph ˌvessel noun [C] (also **lymˌphatic ˈvessel**) any of the thin tubes in the body through which lymph flows, and along which lymph glands are found

lynch /lɪntʃ/ **verb** [T] If a crowd of people lynch someone who they believe is guilty of a crime, they kill them without a legal trial, usually by HANGING (= killing using a rope round the neck). • **lynching** /ˈlɪnt.ʃɪŋ/ **noun** [C or U]

ˈlynch ˌmob noun [C] a group of people who want to attack someone who they think has committed a serious crime

lynchpin /ˈlɪntʃ.pɪn/ **noun** [C] a **linchpin**

lynx /lɪŋks/ **noun** [C] (plural **lynxes** or **lynx**) a wild animal of the cat family that has brown hair, sometimes with dark spots on it, pointed ears, and a short tail

lyre /laɪəʳ/ (US) /laɪr/ **noun** [C] an ancient musical instrument consisting of a U-shaped frame with strings fixed to it

lyrebird /ˈlaɪə.bɜːd/ (US) /ˈlaɪr.bɝːd/ **noun** [C] an Australian bird with long legs. The male has a tail that it can spread out into the shape of a lyre.

lyric /ˈlɪr.ɪk/ **noun; adj**

▸**noun 1 lyrics** (B2) [plural] the words of a song, especially a pop song: *Paul Simon writes the lyrics* *for most of his songs.* **2** [C] a short poem which expresses the personal thoughts and feelings of the person who wrote it

▸**adj** (especially of poetry and songs) expressing personal thoughts and feelings: *William Wordsworth wrote lyric poetry/was a lyric poet.*

lyrical /ˈlɪr.ɪ.kl̩/ **adj 1** expressing personal thoughts and feelings in a beautiful way: *The book contains lyrical descriptions of the author's childhood.* **2 wax lyrical** to talk about something with a lot of interest or excitement: *I recall Rosie waxing lyrical about the flatness of his stomach.* • **lyrically** /-kəl.i/ **adv**

lyricism /ˈlɪr.ɪ.sɪ.zəm/ **noun** [U] the beautiful expression of personal thoughts and feelings in writing or music

lyricist /ˈlɪr.ɪ.sɪst/ **noun** [C] someone who writes words for songs, especially pop songs

M

M, m /em/ **noun; adj**

▸**noun** (plural **Ms, M's** or **m's**) **LETTER** ▷ **1** [C or U] the 13th letter of the English alphabet **NUMBER** ▷ **2** (also **m**) [C] the sign used in the Roman system for the number 1,000 **ROAD** ▷ **3** [U] (in the UK and Ireland) abbreviation for **motorway**: *The M4 goes from London to Bristol.*

▸**adj** (plural **M's** or **Ms**) written abbreviation for **medium**: used on clothes to show that they are of medium size

'm /ᵊm/ **short form of** am, used in spoken and informal written English: *I'm sorry I'm late.*

m noun; adj

▸**noun AMOUNT** ▷ **1** [C] (plural **m**) written abbreviation for **million**: *The new library cost £5 m to build.* **LENGTH** ▷ **2** [C] (plural **m**) written abbreviation for **metre**: *Jeff is 1.8 m tall.* ◦ *She's the women's 1500 m champion (= the winner of a race run over that distance).* **DISTANCE** ▷ **3** written abbreviation for **mile**

▸**adj** written abbreviation for **male** (especially on forms)

ma /mɑː/ **noun** [C] **1** informal old-fashioned a mother: *As my old ma used to say, you can't spend what you ain't got.* ◦ [as form of address] *What's wrong, Ma?* **2** mainly US a title for an old woman: *Ma Johnson always used to bake the best cookies.*

MA /ˌemˈeɪ/ **noun** [C] abbreviation for **Master of Arts**: *Julia Richards, MA* ◦ *My brother has an MA **in** linguistics.* ◦ *She's **studying for/doing** an MA **in** French literature.*

M

ma'am /mɑːm/ **noun** [as form of address] **1** B1 a polite way of talking to a woman: *How can I help you, ma'am?* **2** in Britain, used to address the Queen, or a woman of high rank in particular organizations, such as the army or the police **3** in the past, used when talking to a woman of higher social class

mac (also **mack**) /mæk/ **noun** [C] UK a WATERPROOF coat (= one that does not allow rain to pass through): *a **plastic** mac*

macabre /məˈkɑː.brə/ **adj** describes something that is very strange and unpleasant because it is connected with death or violence: *Even the police were horrified at the macabre nature of the killings.* ◦ *She has a rather macabre sense of humour.*

macadamia /ˌmæk.əˈdeɪ.mi.ə/ **noun** [C] a round, white nut that grows on an Australian tropical tree

macaroni /ˌmæk.ᵊrˈəʊ.ni/ US /-əˈroʊ-/ **noun** [U] a type of PASTA in the shape of small tubes

macaˌroni ˈcheese noun [U] UK (US **macaˌroni and ˈcheese**) a dish made from macaroni and cheese sauce

macaroon /ˌmæk.ᵊrˈuːn/ US /-əˈruːn/ **noun** [C] a small, light biscuit made from eggs, sugar, and ALMONDS or COCONUT

macaw /məˈkɔː/ US /-ˈkɑː/ **noun** [C] a brightly coloured bird of the PARROT family found in Central and South America

macchiato /ˌmæk.iˈɑː.təʊ/ US /mɑːk.iˈɑː.t̬oʊ/ **noun** [C or U] strong coffee with a little warm milk that has bubbles in it, or a cup of this

mace /meɪs/ **noun SPICE** ▷ **1** [U] a spice made from the dried shell of NUTMEG **ROD** ▷ **2** [C] a decorated rod that is carried by or put in front of particular public officials as a symbol of their authority

Mace /meɪs/ **noun** [U] trademark a chemical in a container which, when SPRAYED (= forced out in small drops) into a person's face, causes pain in the eyes and tears to be produced

macerate /ˈmæs.ə.reɪt/ **verb** [I or T] specialized to leave food in a liquid so that it absorbs the liquid and becomes soft, or to become soft in this way: *Mix together all the ingredients and leave them to macerate in the fridge overnight.*

Mach /mɑːk/, /mæk/ **noun** [U] a measurement of speed that is calculated by dividing the speed of an object, especially an aircraft, by the speed of sound

machete /məˈʃet.i/ US /-ˈʃet̬-/ **noun** [C] a large knife with a wide blade, used for cutting trees and plants or as a weapon

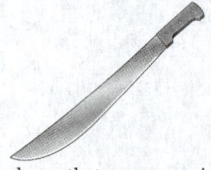

machete

Machiavellian /ˌmæk.i.əˈvel.i.ən/ **adj** using clever but often dishonest methods which deceive people so that you can win power or control

machinate /ˈmæʃ.ɪ.neɪt/, /ˈmæk-/ **verb** [I or T] to make secret plans in order to get an advantage

machinations /ˌmæʃ.ɪˈneɪ.ʃᵊnz/, /ˌmæk-/ **noun** [plural] complicated and secret plans to get power or control

machine /məˈʃiːn/ **noun; verb**

▸**noun** [C] **PIECE OF EQUIPMENT** ▷ **1** A2 a piece of equipment with several moving parts which uses power to do a particular type of work: *Eggs are sorted into different sizes by a machine.* ◦ *Don't forget to put the towels in the machine (= washing machine) before you go out.* ◦ *I got some chocolate from a **vending** machine.* **COMPUTER** ▷ **2** specialized a computer: *You'll need a powerful machine for editing videos.* **VEHICLE** ▷ **3** informal a vehicle, often a motorcycle: approving *That's a **mean** (= powerful) machine you've got there, Bill.* **GROUP OF PEOPLE** ▷ **4** a group of people who control and organize something: *Churchill's **war** machine* ◦ *The **party** machine has swung into action with its preparation for the election.* ◦ *It's now up to the government's **propaganda** machine to restore the prime minister's image.*

> **Word partners for machine**
>
> *operate/use* a machine • *switch on/turn on* a machine • *switch off/turn off* a machine • *install/service* a machine • do sth *by* machine • a machine *for* doing sth

▸**verb** [T] to sew cloth with a sewing machine: *I've almost finished making the curtains – I just have to machine the hem.*

maˈchine ˌcode noun [U] specialized a set of numbers that gives instructions to a computer

maˈchine ˌgun noun [C] an automatic gun that can fire a lot of bullets one after the other very quickly: *Several journalists were caught in machine-gun **fire**.*

maˈchine-gun verb [T] to shoot someone with a machine gun: *The raiders machine-gunned everyone in the bank before escaping in a van.*

maˌchine-ˈreadable adj specialized able to be understood by a computer: *a machine-readable book/dictionary*

machinery /məˈʃiː.nə.ri/ US /-nɚ.i/ **noun** [U] **MA-**

CHINES ▷ **1** Ⓒ1 a group of large machines or the parts of a machine which make it work: *industrial/farm machinery* ◦ *His hand was injured when he got it caught in the machinery.* **PROCESS/ORGANIZATION** ▷ **2** the structure and systems of an organization or process: *bureaucratic/political/decision-making machinery* ◦ *the machinery of government*

maˈchine ˌtool noun [C] a tool which uses power to cut and shape metal or other strong materials: *The car industry uses machine tools for cutting car body parts.*

maˌchine transˈlation noun [U] specialized the process of changing text from one language into another language using a computer

machinist /məˈʃiː.nɪst/ noun [C] a person whose job is operating a machine: *She works as a machinist in a clothing factory.*

machismo /məˈtʃɪz.məʊ/ Ⓤⓢ /məˈtʃiːz.moʊ/ noun [U] often disapproving male behaviour that is strong and forceful, and shows very traditional ideas about how men and women should behave

macho /ˈmætʃ.əʊ/ Ⓤⓢ /ˈmɑː.tʃoʊ/ adj informal mainly disapproving behaving forcefully or showing no emotion in a way traditionally thought to be typical of a man: *He's too macho to admit he was hurt when his girlfriend left him.* ◦ *I can't stand macho men.*

mackerel /ˈmæk.rəl/ noun [C or U] (plural **mackerel** or **mackerels**) a sea fish that can be eaten with a strong taste: ***smoked*** *mackerel*

mackintosh /ˈmæk.ɪn.tɒʃ/ Ⓤⓢ /-tɑːʃ/ noun [C] UK old-fashioned a **mac** (= a coat that does not allow rain through)

macramé /məˈkrɑː.meɪ/ noun [U] the art of joining pieces of string together in knots to form a decorative pattern, or something made this way: *a macramé wall-hanging*

macro /ˈmæk.rəʊ/ Ⓤⓢ /-roʊ/ noun [C] (plural **macros**) specialized a single instruction given to a computer which produces a set of instructions for the computer to perform a particular piece of work: *I've created a macro to spell check all the files at the same time.*

macro- /mæk.rəʊ-/, /-rə-/ Ⓤⓢ /-roʊ-/ prefix large; relating to the whole of something, rather than its parts: *macroscopic (= large enough to be seen by the human eye)* ◦ *macroeconomics (= the study of financial systems at a national level)* → Compare **micro-**

macrobiotic /ˌmæk.rəʊ.baɪˈɒt.ɪk/ Ⓤⓢ /-roʊ.baɪˈɑː.t̬ɪk/ adj describes food that is arranged into groups according to special principles, grown without chemicals, and thought to be very healthy: *A macrobiotic diet consists mainly of whole grains and certain kinds of vegetables.*

macrocosm /ˈmæk.rəʊˌkɒz.ᵊm/ Ⓤⓢ /-roʊˌkɑː.zᵊm/ noun [C] **1** any large organized system considered as a whole, rather than as a group of smaller systems → Compare **microcosm 2 the macrocosm** the universe

macroeconomics /ˌmæk.rəʊˌiː.kəˈnɒm.ɪks/ Ⓤⓢ /-roʊ-/ noun [U] the study of financial systems at a national level

mad /mæd/ adj (**madder** or **maddest**) **MENTALLY ILL** ▷ **1** Ⓑ1 mentally ill, or unable to behave in a reasonable way: *I think I must be* ***going*** *mad.* ◦ *Do I look like some mad old woman in this hat?* → Compare **insane SILLY** ▷ **2** Ⓑ1 mainly UK informal (US usually **crazy**) extremely silly or stupid: [+ to infinitive] *You're mad* ***to*** *walk home alone at this time of night.* ◦ *He must be mad spending all that money on a coat.* ◦ *Some of the things she does are* ***completely*** *mad.* → See also **madcap ANGRY** ▷ **3** Ⓐ2 [after verb] informal very angry or annoyed: *He's always complaining and it* ***makes*** *me so mad.* ◦ mainly US *Are you still mad* ***at*** *me?* ◦ mainly UK *Kerry got really mad* ***with*** *Richard for not doing the washing up.* ◦ *Bill's untidiness* ***drives*** *me mad.* **HURRYING** ▷ **4** [before noun] hurrying or excited and not having time to think or plan: *We made a mad* ***dash*** *for the train.* ◦ *I was in a mad* ***panic/rush*** *trying to get everything ready.* **ENTHUSIASTIC** ▷ **5 be mad about sb/sth** Ⓑ1 informal to love someone or something: *He's mad about football.* **6 be mad for sb/sth** UK informal to want someone or something very much, or to be very interested in them: *Everyone's mad for him and I just don't see the attraction.*

IDIOMS **(as) mad as a hatter/March hare** extremely silly or stupid • **don't get mad, get even** something that you say in order to tell someone not to be angry when someone has upset them, but to do something that will upset them as much: *This is my advice to wives whose husbands have left them for a younger woman – don't get mad, get even!* • **like mad** informal Ⓑ2 If you do something like mad, you do it very enthusiastically, quickly, or a lot: *She's been saving like mad because she wants to buy a car.*

-mad /-mæd/ suffix UK **car-mad, clothes-mad, sex-mad, etc.** extremely interested in cars, clothes, sex, etc.: *She's 16 and clothes-mad.*

madam /ˈmæd.əm/ noun **WOMAN** ▷ **1** Ⓑ1 (usually **Madam**) [as form of address] a formal and polite way of speaking to a woman: *May I carry your cases for you, Madam?* **2 Dear Madam** Ⓑ2 the usual way of beginning a formal letter to a woman whose name you do not know **3** [S] disapproving a young girl who behaves like an older woman, expecting others to obey her: *She's turning into* ***a proper little*** *madam.* **SEX** ▷ **4** [C] a woman who is in charge of a group of PROSTITUTES who live or work in the same house

madcap /ˈmæd.kæp/ adj [before noun] old-fashioned describes silly behaviour or a plan that is very silly and unlikely to succeed: *the madcap* ***antics*** *of the clowns*

ˌmad ˈcow disˌease noun [U] UK informal another name for BSE

madden /ˈmæd.ᵊn/ verb [T] to make someone very angry or annoyed: *It maddens me to see how unfairly Jon has been treated.* • **maddened** /-ᵊnd/ adj literary *He was standing in the path of the maddened bull.*

maddening /ˈmæd.ᵊn.ɪŋ/ adj making you angry: *She has a maddening* ***habit*** *of interrupting me when I'm talking to her.* • **maddeningly** /-li/ adv

made /meɪd/ verb past simple and past participle of **make**: *He was wearing a suit made* ***from*** *pure silk.* ◦ *The house was made* ***of*** *wood with an iron roof.*

IDIOM **have (got) it made** informal to be certain to be successful and have a good life, often without much effort: *With his father at the head of the firm, he's got it made.*

-made /-meɪd/ suffix produced in the stated way or place: *On the bottom of the watch it said 'Swiss-made'.*

ˌmade-to-ˈmeasure adj made specially to fit a particular person, room, etc.: *made-to-measure curtains*

ˌmade ˈup adj **APPEARANCE** ▷ **1** [after verb] wearing make-up: *She's always very* ***heavily*** *made up (= wearing a lot of make-up).* → See **make-up INVENTED** ▷ **2** describes a story or report that has been invented and is untrue **HAPPY** ▷ **3** [after verb] Northern English informal very happy about something good that has happened: *I was made up when she offered me the job.*

M

madhouse /ˈmæd.haʊs/ **noun 1** [S] informal disapproving a place where there is no order and control: *With four small children running around, the place is a madhouse.* ◦ *He called the government's policy 'the economics of the madhouse'.* **2** [C] old use a **mental hospital**

madly /ˈmæd.li/ **adv** QUICKLY ▷ **1** If you do something madly, you do it very quickly because you have little time: *I was rushing around madly tidying up the flat before they arrived.* ENTHUSIASTICALLY ▷ **2** with a lot of energy and enthusiasm: *We cheered madly as the team came out onto the field.* ◦ *She's madly (= extremely)* ***in love*** *with David.*

madman /ˈmæd.mən/, /-mæn/ **noun** [C] (plural **-men** /-mən/) STRANGE/DANGEROUS MAN ▷ **1** disapproving a man who behaves in a very strange and uncontrolled or dangerous way: *I drove* ***like a*** *madman to get there in time.* MENTALLY ILL ▷ **2** old use or offensive a man who is mentally ill

madness /ˈmæd.nəs/ **noun** [U] STUPID BEHAVIOUR ▷ **1** stupid or dangerous behaviour: *To begin a war would be sheer madness.* MENTAL ILLNESS ▷ **2** the state of being mentally ill, or unable to behave in a reasonable way: *She felt as if she were sliding into madness.*

Madonna /məˈdɒn.ə/ (US) /-ˈdɑː-/ **noun 1 the Madonna** [S] Mary, the mother of Jesus Christ: *a picture of the Madonna* **2** [C] a picture or model that represents Mary

madrasa (also **madrasah**) /məˈdræs.ə/ **noun** [C] a school where people go to learn about the religion of Islam

madrigal /ˈmæd.rɪ.gᵊl/ **noun** [C] a song performed without musical instruments in which several singers sing different notes at the same time

madwoman /ˈmædˌwʊm.ən/ **noun** [C] (plural **-women** /-wɪmɪn/) STRANGE WOMAN ▷ **1** disapproving a woman who behaves in a very strange and uncontrolled or dangerous way MENTALLY ILL ▷ **2** old use or offensive a woman who is mentally ill

maelstrom /ˈmeɪl.strɒm/ (US) /-strəm/ **noun** SITUATION ▷ **1** [C usually singular] a situation in which there is great confusion, violence, and destruction: *The country is gradually being sucked into the maelstrom* ***of*** *civil war.* WATER ▷ **2** [C] an area of water that moves with a very strong circular movement and sucks in anything that goes past

maestro /ˈmaɪ.strəʊ/ (US) /-stroʊ/ **noun** [C] (plural **maestros** or **maestri**) a man who is very skilled at playing or CONDUCTING (= directing the performance of) music

mafia /ˈmæf.i.ə/ (US) /ˈmɑː.fi.ə/ **noun** [+ sing/pl verb] **1 the Mafia** a criminal organization which began in Sicily and is active in Italy and the US **2** [C] a close group of people who are involved in similar activities and who help and protect each other, sometimes to the disadvantage of others

mafioso /ˌmæf.iˈəʊ.səʊ/ (US) /ˌmɑː.fiˈoʊ.soʊ/ **noun** [C] (plural **mafiosi**) a member of the Mafia

magazine /ˌmæg.əˈziːn/ **noun** [C] BOOK ▷ **1** A2 (informal **mag**) a type of thin book with large pages and a paper cover that contains articles and photographs and is published every week or month: *She has written articles for several* ***women's*** *magazines.* ◦ *a* ***glossy*** *magazine* ◦ ***men's*** *mags* ◦ *a magazine rack* GUN PART ▷ **2** a part of a gun in which CARTRIDGES are stored, or a building in which explosives, weapons, and supplies are kept

magenta /məˈdʒen.tə/ **noun** [U] a reddish-purple colour, one of the main colours that are used in colour printing and photography • **magenta adj** of a reddish-purple colour

maggot /ˈmæg.ət/ **noun** [C] a creature like a very small WORM which later develops into a fly and is found in decaying meat and other foods

the Magi /ˈmeɪ.dʒaɪ/ **noun** [plural] in the Bible, the three men, thought to be kings or ASTROLOGERS, who followed a star to visit Jesus Christ when he was a baby and give him presents. They are also called the Three Kings or the Three Wise Men.

magic /ˈmædʒ.ɪk/ **noun; adj; exclamation**

▸**noun** [U] SPECIAL POWER ▷ **1** A2 the use of special powers to make things happen which would usually be impossible, such as in stories for children: *The group are known for their belief in witchcraft and magic.* ◦ ***As if by*** *magic/****Like*** *magic, the car changes into a boat when it hits the water.* **2** A2 the skill of performing tricks to entertain people, such as making things appear and disappear and pretending to cut someone in half: *He's a comedian who also does magic.* SPECIAL QUALITY ▷ **3** B2 a special and exciting quality that makes something seem different from ordinary things: *Although the film was made 50 years ago, it has lost none of its magic.* ◦ *No one could fail to be charmed by the magic* ***of*** *this beautiful city.*

▸**adj 1** A2 with special powers: *The witch put a magic* ***spell*** *on the prince and turned him into a frog.* ◦ *I'll show you a magic* ***trick****.* **2** B1 happening in an unusual or unexpected way, or easily or quickly: *There's no magic* ***solution*** *to the problem.* ◦ *There's no magic* ***formula*** *for winning – just lots of hard work.*

IDIOM **a magic touch** a special ability to do something very well: *The film's great success will no doubt please the 46-year-old director, who was rumoured to have lost his magic touch.*

▸**exclamation** UK old-fashioned informal used when you think something is very good and you like it a lot: *'Kate's having a party on Saturday night.' 'Magic!'*

magical /ˈmædʒ.ɪ.kᵊl/ **adj** OF MAGIC ▷ **1** B2 produced by or using magic: *Diamonds were once thought to have magical* ***powers****.* SPECIAL/EXCITING ▷ **2** B2 describes something with a special and exciting quality: *We walked home arm-in-arm in the magical moonlight.* • **magically** /-kᵊl.i/ **adv**

ˌmagic ˈcarpet noun [C] in children's stories, a special carpet that you can sit on as it flies through the air

magician /məˈdʒɪʃ.ᵊn/ **noun** [C] a person who has magic powers in stories, or who performs tricks for entertainment: *Merlin was the magician in the stories of King Arthur and the Knights of the Round Table.* ◦ *There'll be a magician at the kids' Christmas party.*

ˌmagic ˈwand noun [C] **1** a small stick used by people who perform tricks for entertainment: *He* ***waved*** *his magic wand and a rabbit appeared.* **2** a quick and easy solution: *She warned that she had no magic wand to solve the problem.*

ˌmagic ˈword noun [C usually singular] a word said by someone performing a trick to help it work successfully: *I'll just say the magic word and the rabbit will disappear – Abracadabra!*

IDIOM **what's the magic word?** said to a child who has not said 'please' when asking for something: *'Can I have another chocolate?' 'What's the magic word?' 'Please.'*

magisterial /ˌmædʒ.ɪˈstɪə.ri.əl/ (US) /-ˈstɪr.i-/ **adj** formal having or seeming to have complete authority: *his magisterial presence* ◦ *Jenkins's magisterial biography of Gladstone*

magistracy /ˈmædʒ.ɪ.strə.si/ **noun** specialized **1** [U] the position of being a magistrate **2 the magistracy** [S, + sing/pl verb] magistrates considered as a group

magistrate /ˈmædʒ.ɪ.streɪt/, /-strət/ **noun** [C] C1 a person who acts as a judge in a law court that deals with crimes that are not serious: *He will **appear before** the magistrates tomorrow.* ◦ *Greenway appeared at Bow Street Magistrates' **Court** to face seven charges of accepting bribes.*

magma /ˈmæg.mə/ **noun** [U] hot liquid rock found just below the surface of the Earth

magnanimous /mægˈnæn.ɪ.məs/ **adj** formal very kind and generous towards an enemy or someone you have defeated: *Arsenal's manager was magnanimous in victory, and praised the losing team.* • **magnanimity** /ˌmæg.nəˈnɪm.ɪ.ti/ US /-ə.t̬i/ **noun** [U] • **magnanimously** /-li/ **adv**

magnate /ˈmæg.nət/ **noun** [C] a person who is very rich and successful in business or industry: *a well-known **shipping** magnate*

magnesia /mægˈniː.ʒə/ **noun** [U] a white substance used in stomach medicines

magnesium /mægˈniː.zi.əm/ **noun** [U] (symbol **Mg**) a chemical element that is a silver-white metal. Magnesium burns very brightly and is used in making FIREWORKS.

magnet /ˈmæg.nət/ **noun** [C] **OBJECT** ▷ **1** an object that is able both to attract iron and STEEL objects and also push them away **ATTRACTION** ▷ **2** a person, place, or thing that other people feel strongly attracted to: *The United States has always acted as a magnet **for** people seeking fame and fortune.*

magnet

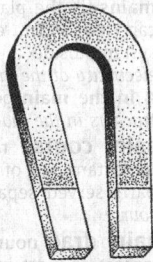

magnetic /mægˈnet.ɪk/ US /-ˈnet̬-/ **adj** **OBJECT** ▷ **1** C1 with the power of a magnet **ATTRACTIVE** ▷ **2** C1 describes someone whose personality attracts a lot of people

magˌnetic ˈfield **noun** [C] an area around a magnet or something magnetic, in which its power to attract objects to itself can be felt

magˌnetic ˈhead **noun** [C] a **head**

magˌnetic ˈnorth/ˈsouth **noun** [U] the direction towards north/south which the needle of a COMPASS shows

magˌnetic ˈpole **noun** [C] a point on the Earth near the NORTH POLE or the SOUTH POLE that a COMPASS shows as north or south

magˌnetic ˈresonance ˌimaging **noun** [U] specialized **MRI**

magˌnetic ˈtape **noun** [U] a plastic strip covered with a MAGNETIC substance on which sound, images, or computer information can be recorded

magnetism /ˈmæg.nə.tɪ.zᵊm/ US /-t̬ɪ-/ **noun** [U] **ATTRACTIVE QUALITY** ▷ **1** a quality that makes someone very attractive to other people: *The actress has a personal magnetism that is rare in someone so young.* **OBJECT** ▷ **2** the power of being able to attract iron and STEEL objects and also push them away

magnetize (UK usually **magnetise**) /ˈmæg.nə.taɪz/ **verb** [T] to make an object MAGNETIC: *Each worker has to carry a magnetized plastic entry card.*

magneto /mægˈniː.təʊ/ US /-ˈniː.t̬oʊ/ **noun** [C] an electrical GENERATOR that uses MAGNETS to produce electricity

magnification /ˌmæg.nɪ.fɪˈkeɪ.ʃᵊn/ **noun** [U] the process of making something look bigger than it is, for example by using a magnifying glass: *Magnification of the leaf allows us to see it in detail.* ◦ *These binoculars have x10 magnification (= they magnify ten times).*

magnificent /mægˈnɪf.ɪ.sᵊnt/ **adj** B1 very good, beautiful, or deserving to be admired: *a magnificent view* ◦ *a magnificent piece of writing* ◦ *They live in a magnificent Tudor house.* • **magnificence** /-sᵊns/ **noun** [U] • **magnificently** /-li/ **adv** C1 *I thought she coped magnificently.*

magnify /ˈmæg.nɪ.faɪ/ **verb** [T] **1** to make something look larger than it is, especially by looking at it through a specially cut piece of glass: *Although our skin looks smooth, when magnified it is full of bumps and holes.* **2** to make a problem bigger and more important: *The hot summer magnified the racial tensions in the community.*

ˈmagnifying ˌglass **noun** [C] a piece of curved glass which makes objects look larger than they are: *He uses a magnifying glass to read tiny print.*

magnifying glass

magnitude /ˈmæg.nɪ.tjuːd/ US /-tuːd/ **noun** [U] the large size or importance of something: *They don't seem to grasp the magnitude **of the problem**.*

magnolia /mægˈnəʊ.li.ə/ US /-ˈnoʊ-/ **noun; adj**
▸**noun** **TREE** ▷ **1** [C] a type of tree with large, usually white or pink flowers **COLOUR** ▷ **2** [U] UK a pale cream colour
▸**adj** UK of a pale cream colour

magnum /ˈmæg.nəm/ **noun** [C] **WINE** ▷ **1** 1.5 litres of wine, or a bottle containing this: *She won a magnum **of champagne**.* **GUN** ▷ **2** trademark a type of gun with bullets that are FIRED with more power than is usual for a gun of that size

ˌmagnum ˈopus **noun** [S] formal the most important piece of work done by a writer or artist: *Picasso's Guernica is considered by many to be his magnum opus.*

magpie /ˈmæg.paɪ/ **noun** [C] **1** a bird with black and white feathers and a long tail: *Magpies are attracted to small, shiny objects which they carry away to their nests.* **2** someone who likes to collect many different types of objects, or use many different styles

maharaja (also **maharajah**) /ˌmɑː.həˈrɑː.dʒə/ **noun** [C] in the past, the male ruler of an Indian state

maharani /ˌmɑː.həˈrɑː.ni/ **noun** [C] a female maharaja or the wife of a maharaja

mah-jong (also **mah-jongg**) /ˌmɑːˈdʒɒŋ/ US /-ˈdʒɑːŋ/ **noun** [U] a Chinese game in which players pick up and put down small painted pieces of wood or other material until they have the combination they need in order to win

mahogany /məˈhɒg.ᵊn.i/ US /-ˈhɑː.gᵊn-/ **noun** [U] a dark red-brown wood used to make furniture: *a handsome mahogany desk*

maid /meɪd/ **noun** [C] **SERVANT** ▷ **1** a woman who works as a servant in a hotel or in someone's home: *In the beach resort, the apartments and villas have daily maid **service**.* ◦ *In California many illegal immigrants work as maids and gardeners.* **GIRL** ▷ **2** old use a girl or young woman who is not married, or has not had sex

M

maiden /ˈmeɪ.dᵊn/ **noun; adj**
▸**noun** [C] WOMAN ▷ **1** literary a girl or young woman: *In the story, the prince woos and wins the **fair** maiden.* CRICKET ▷ **2** (also **maiden over**) an OVER in cricket in which no runs are scored
▸**adj** [before noun] of or about the first of its type: *The Titanic sank on her maiden **voyage**.*

ˌmaiden ˈaunt noun [C] old-fashioned an aunt who is not married and is no longer young

maidenhead /ˈmeɪ.dᵊn.hed/ noun [U] old use or literary a woman's VIRGINITY

ˈmaiden ˌname noun [C] A woman's maiden name is the family name she has before she gets married.

ˌmaiden ˈspeech noun [C] the first formal speech made by a British Member of Parliament in the House of Commons or by a member of the House of Lords

ˌmaid of ˈhonour noun [C] mainly US the most important BRIDESMAID at a marriage ceremony

mail /meɪl/ **noun; verb**
▸**noun** POST ▷ **1** A2 [S or U] (mainly UK **post**) the letters and parcels that are sent by post, or the system for sending letters and parcels from place to place: *She spent the morning reading and answering her mail.* ◦ *All of our customers will be contacted **by** mail.* ◦ *The book came **in** yesterday's mail.* ◦ *Some strange things get sent **through the** mail.* EMAIL ▷ **2** A2 [C or U] email: *I had almost 50 unread mails in my inbox.* ◦ *You have mail.* COVERING ▷ **3** [U] **chain mail**
▸**verb** [T] mainly US (mainly UK **post**) to send a letter or parcel or to email something: *She mailed it last week but it still hasn't arrived.* ◦ [+ two objects] *I promised to mail him the article/mail the article **to** him.*

Mail /meɪl/ **noun** used in the name of some newspapers: *the Daily Mail* ◦ *the Hull Mail*

mailbag /ˈmeɪl.bæg/ **noun 1** [C] (UK also **postbag**) a large, strong bag used by the post office for transporting and carrying letters and parcels **2** [C usually singular] the number of letters, emails, etc. received at one time or on one subject: *Since the controversial programme was broadcast, the BBC's mailbag has been bulging.*

mailbox /ˈmeɪl.bɒks/ ⓤⓢ /-bɑːks/ **noun** [C] **1** in the US, a box outside a person's house where letters are put, or a POSTBOX **2** the place on a computer screen which shows new emails that have arrived: *Look out for our emails in your **electronic** mailbox.*

ˈmail ˌcarrier noun [C] (also **ˈletter ˌcarrier**) US for **postman**

ˈmailing ˌlist noun [C usually singular] a list of names and addresses kept by an organization so that it can send information and advertisements to the people on the list: *I asked to be **put on** their mailing list.*

mailman /ˈmeɪl.mæn/ **noun** [C] (plural **-men** /-men/) (also **ˈmail ˌcarrier**) US for **postman**

ˈmail ˌmerge noun [C or U] specialized the use of a computer to produce many copies of a letter, each copy with a different name and address stored on file, or a computer program that does this

ˈmail ˌorder noun [U] a way of buying goods in which you choose what you want, usually from a CATALOGUE, and it is sent to you: *I often buy clothes **by** mail order.* ◦ *a mail-order **catalogue/company***

mailshot /ˈmeɪl.ʃɒt/ ⓤⓢ /-ʃɑːt/ **noun** [C] mainly UK (US usually **ˌmass ˈmailing**) the posting of advertising or similar material to a lot of people at one time

ˈmail ˌslot noun [C] US (UK **letterbox**) a rectangular hole in the door or in a wall near the entrance of a house or other building, through which letters, etc. are put

maim /meɪm/ **verb** [I or T] to injure a person so severely that a part of their body will no longer work as it should: *Many children have been maimed **for life** by these bombs.*

main /meɪn/ **adj; noun**
▸**adj** [before noun] B1 larger, more important, or having more influence than others of the same type: *The main **thing** is not to worry.* ◦ *One of the main **reasons** I came to England was to study the language.* ◦ *You'll find the main **points** of my proposal in the report.* ◦ *Our main **aim/objective** is to improve the company's productivity.* ◦ *The main **problem** in the health service is lack of resources.* ◦ *My main **concern** about moving to London is the cost of housing.*

IDIOM **be sb's main squeeze** US informal to be the person that someone has a romantic or sexual relationship with

▸**noun** PIPE ▷ **1** [C] a large pipe which carries water or gas, or a wire carrying electricity, from one place to another, to which a house can be connected: *a **gas** main* ◦ *The severe cold caused a **water** main to burst and flood the street.* **2 mains** [plural] UK the system of pipes or wires which carry water or electricity into a house, or the pipes which carry SEWAGE away from a house: *The house isn't **on** the mains.* ◦ *They bought a house with no mains **supply**.* ◦ *mains **electricity*** **3 the mains** UK the place at which outside pipes or wires carrying water, electricity, etc. connect with the system inside a house or building: *Switch off the electricity at the mains before starting work.* MOSTLY ▷ **4 in the main** generally or mostly: *Her friends are teachers in the main.*

ˌmain ˈcourse noun [C] A2 the largest or most important part of a meal in which there are different parts served separately: *I had salmon for my main course.*

ˌmain ˈdrag noun [C usually singular] US informal the largest or most important road in a town: *There's a great little restaurant just off the main drag.*

mainframe /ˈmeɪn.freɪm/ **noun** [C] specialized a very large, powerful computer with a lot of memory which many people can use at the same time

the mainland /ˈmeɪn.lænd/ **noun** [S] the main part of a country or continent, not including the islands around it: *He lives on an island off Scotland, but travels to the mainland once a month.* • **mainland** adj [before noun] *mainland Europe*

mainline /ˈmeɪn.laɪn/ **adj; verb**
▸**adj** COMMON ▷ **1** usually US involving beliefs, methods, etc. that are most common: *mainline churches* ◦ *the rivalry between catalog companies and mainline stores* RAILWAY ▷ **2** relating to an important railway route between large towns or cities
▸**verb** [I or T] slang to INJECT (= put into the body through a needle) drugs directly into the blood: *Several of her friends were mainlining heroin.* ◦ *By now she was mainlining.*

ˌmain ˈline noun [C] an important railway route between large towns or cities: *the main line **between** Belfast and Dublin*

mainly /ˈmeɪn.li/ **adv** B1 usually or to a large degree: *I mainly go to bed around midnight.* ◦ *The group is made up of mainly young people.* ◦ *They argued that the tax will mainly benefit the rich.*

ˌmain ˈroad noun [C] a large road which goes from one town to another: *Stick to the main roads and you won't get lost.* ◦ *They live on the main road out of town.*

mainspring /ˈmeɪn.sprɪŋ/ **noun** [C usually singular]

formal the most important reason for something; the thing that makes something else happen: *Work was **the** mainspring **of** his life.*

mainstay /ˈmeɪn.steɪ/ **noun the mainstay of sth** the most important part of something, providing support for everything else: *Cattle farming is the mainstay of the country's economy.*

mainstream /ˈmeɪn.striːm/ **adj; noun; verb**
▸**adj** C2 considered normal, and having or using ideas, beliefs, etc. that are accepted by most people: *This is the director's first mainstream Hollywood film.*
▸**noun the mainstream** the way of life or set of beliefs accepted by most people: *The new law should allow more disabled people to enter the mainstream **of** American life.*
▸**verb** [T] US to teach children with physical or mental problems in the same class as children without problems

ˌmain ˈstreet noun [C] US for **high street**

maintain /meɪnˈteɪn/ verb [T] **CONTINUE TO HAVE** ▷ **1** B2 to continue to have; to keep in existence, or not allow to become less: *The army has been brought in to maintain **order** in the region.* ◦ *We have **standards** to maintain.* ◦ *Despite living in different countries, the two families have maintained close **links**.* ◦ *The film has maintained its position as the critics' favourite for another year.* **KEEP IN GOOD CONDITION** ▷ **2** B2 to keep a road, machine, building, etc. in good condition: *A large house costs a lot to maintain.* ◦ *The roads around the town have been very poorly maintained.* **EXPRESS** ▷ **3** C2 to express firmly your belief that something is true: *Throughout his prison sentence Dunn has always maintained his **innocence**.* ◦ [+ that] *He maintains **that** he has never seen the woman before.* **PROVIDE** ▷ **4** to provide someone with food and whatever is necessary for them to live on: *They barely earn enough to maintain themselves and their four children.*

maintenance /ˈmeɪn.tɪ.nəns/ noun [U] **WORK** ▷ **1** B2 the work needed to keep a road, building, machine, etc. in good condition: *Old houses need a lot of maintenance.* ◦ *There are thorough maintenance **checks** on each plane before take-off.* ◦ *The magazine offers tips on cutting your house maintenance costs.* **MONEY** ▷ **2** money that a person must pay regularly by law in order to support their child or previous marriage partner after a DIVORCE (= official end to a marriage): *He refused to **pay** maintenance for his three children.* **CONTINUED EXISTENCE** ▷ **3** a situation in which something continues to exist or is not allowed to become less: *the maintenance of living standards*

ˈmaintenance ˌorder noun [C] UK an order made by a law court that a person must pay maintenance

ˌmain ˈverb noun [C] in a clause, the verb that contains the meaning, compared with any AUXILIARY VERBS that go with it: *In 'I should have been studying', 'studying' is the main verb.*

maisonette /ˌmeɪ.zᵊnˈet/ noun [C] UK a small apartment on two levels that is part of a larger building but has its own entrance

maître d' /ˌmeɪt.rəˈdiː/ Ⓤⓢ /ˌmeɪ.t̬ɚ-/ noun [C] (plural **maître d's**) (formal **maître d'hôtel** /ˌmeɪt.rə.dəʊˈtel/ Ⓤⓢ /ˌmeɪ.t̬ɚ.doʊ-/ (plural **maîtres d'hôtel**)) the person in charge of a restaurant or of the people who bring food to your table in a restaurant

maize /meɪz/ noun [U] UK (US **corn**) a tall plant grown in many parts of the world for its yellow seeds, which are eaten as food, made into flour, or fed to animals

majestic /məˈdʒes.tɪk/ adj beautiful, powerful, or causing great admiration and respect: *The majestic Montana scenery will leave you breathless.* • **majestically** /-tɪ.kᵊl.i/ adv *The white cliffs rise majestically from the sea.*

majesty /ˈmædʒ.ə.sti/ noun [U] If something has majesty, it causes admiration and respect for its beauty: *This music has majesty, power, and passion.* ◦ *The photograph captures the sunset **in all** its majesty.*

Majesty /ˈmædʒ.ə.sti/ noun [C] **1** the title used to speak to or about a king or queen: *I was invited to tea with **Her** Majesty the Queen.* ◦ ***their** Majesties, the King and Queen of Spain* ◦ [as form of address] *The performance begins at eight o'clock, (**Your**) Majesty.* **2 at Her/His Majesty's pleasure** UK **a** used to describe a prison SENTENCE (= time in prison) that does not have a fixed length: *She was sentenced to be detained at Her Majesty's pleasure.* **b** informal used to mean 'in prison': *He has had several spells at Her Majesty's pleasure.*

major /ˈmeɪ.dʒəʳ/ Ⓤⓢ /-dʒɚ/ **adj; noun; verb**
▸**adj IMPORTANT** ▷ **1** B2 [before noun] more important, bigger, or more serious than others of the same type: *All of her major plays have been translated into English.* ◦ *Sugar is a major cause of tooth decay.* ◦ *There are two problems with this situation, one major, one minor.* ◦ *Citrus fruits are a major source of vitamin C.* ◦ *There has been a major change in attitudes recently.* ◦ *The United States is a major influence in the United Nations.* → Compare **minor MUSIC** ▷ **2** [after noun] specialized belonging or relating to a musical SCALE that is generally thought to have a happy sound: *the key of C major* ◦ *a concerto in A major* → Compare **minor**
▸**noun** [C] **OFFICER** ▷ **1** (also **Major**) an officer of middle rank in the British, US, and many other armed forces: *Her father was a major in the Scots Guards.* ◦ *Major Winters/Richard Winters* ◦ [as form of address] *Thank you, Major.* **SPECIAL SUBJECT** ▷ **2** US the most important subject that a college or university student is studying, or the student himself or herself: *What is your major, English or French?* ◦ *She was a philosophy major at an Ivy League college.*
▸**verb major in sth** US to study something as your main subject at university: *She majored in philosophy at Harvard.*

majordomo /ˌmeɪ.dʒəˈdəʊ.məʊ/ Ⓤⓢ /-dʒɚˈdoʊ.moʊ/ noun [C] (plural **majordomos**) **1** old use the most important servant in a house, in charge of the other servants **2** US a person whose job is to make arrangements or organize things for other people: *Can you ask the majordomo in the hotel to get tickets for the tennis match?*

majorette /ˌmeɪ.dʒᵊrˈet/ Ⓤⓢ /-dʒəˈret/ noun [C] (also **ˌdrum majoˈrette**) a young woman or girl who wears a uniform and makes a pattern of movements with a BATON (= stick) by turning it and throwing it into the air, as part of a group of girls who do this or as the leader of a musical group

ˌmajor ˈgeneral noun [C] an officer of high rank in the British Army, the US Army and many other armed forces

majority /məˈdʒɒr.ə.ti/ Ⓤⓢ /-ˈdʒɑːr.ə.t̬i/ noun **NUMBER** ▷ **1** B2 [S] the larger number or part of something: *The majority **of** the employees have university degrees.* ◦ *A large majority **of** people approve of the death sentence.* ◦ *In Britain women are **in the/a** majority.* → Compare **minority 2** [C] in an election, the difference in the number of votes between the winning person or group and the one that comes second: *The Socialists won by a **narrow/large** majority.* **AGE** ▷ **3** [U] specialized the age when you legally become an adult: *the **age of** majority* ◦ *She will inherit her father's estate when she **reaches** her majority.*

M

> **Word partners for majority**
>
> a *large/overwhelming/substantial/vast* majority • a *clear/large/overall/outright* majority • a *narrow/slim/small/tiny* majority • *have/need* a majority • *secure/win* a majority • the majority *of* sth • be *in* the majority

maˈjority ˌrule noun [U] the system of giving the largest group in a particular place or area the power to make decisions for everyone: *Government by majority rule can be a threat to minority rights.*

ˌmajor ˈleague noun [C] in the US, the LEAGUE of professional sports teams at the highest level, especially in baseball

ˌmajor-ˈleague adj **1** belonging or relating to sport in a major league in the US: *major-league baseball* **2** important and having a lot of influence: *The directors all have major-league business experience.*

majorly /ˈmeɪ.dʒə.li/ (US) /-dʒɚ-/ adv mainly US informal very or extremely: *Have you seen Chrissie's new leather jacket? It's majorly cool.*

make /meɪk/ verb; noun

▸verb (**made**, **made**) **PRODUCE** ▷ **1** (A1) [T] to produce something, often using a particular substance or material: *Shall I make some coffee?* ◦ *He'd made a chocolate cake.* ◦ *She makes all her own clothes.* ◦ [+ two objects] *He made us some coffee./He made some coffee **for** us.* ◦ *The pot is made **to** withstand high temperatures.* ◦ *He works for a company that makes garden furniture.* ◦ *The label on the box said 'made in Taiwan'.* ◦ *Butter is made **out of/from** milk.* ◦ *earrings made **of** gold* ◦ *Her new trainer has promised to make an Olympic athlete **of** her.* **2** (A1) [T] To make a film or television programme is to DIRECT it, PRODUCE it, or act in it: *John Huston made some great films.* ◦ *The film was made by Goldcrest Productions.* ◦ *So why didn't Garbo make any films after 1941?* **CAUSE** ▷ **3** (B1) [T] to cause something: *The kids made such a mess in the kitchen.* ◦ *The bullet made a hole right through his chest.* ◦ [+ infinitive without to] *The wind is making my eyes water.* ◦ *What made you change your mind?* ◦ *Just seeing Woody Allen's face is enough to make me laugh.* ◦ *The photograph makes me look about 80!* **CAUSE TO BE** ▷ **4** [T] to cause to be, to become, or to appear as: [+ noun] *It's the good weather that makes Spain such a popular tourist destination.* ◦ [+ past participle] *She had to shout to make herself heard above the sound of the music.* ◦ *I can make myself understood in French, but I'm not fluent.* ◦ *They went up to the Ambassador and made themselves known (to her).* ◦ [+ adj] *The company accounts have not yet been made public.* ◦ *The book's advertised as 'navigation made **easy**'.* ◦ *The president has made Henry Paulson his Secretary of the Treasury.* ◦ *I'll have a steak – no, make **that** chicken.* **5 make certain/sure** (A2) to take action so that you are certain that something happens, is true, etc.: *I'll just make sure I've turned the oven off.* ◦ *Make certain (**that**) we have enough drink for the party.* ◦ *Make sure you're home by midnight.* ◦ *Jones made sure of his place in the side with three fine goals.* ◦ *I think I locked the door but I'll go back and check **just** to make sure.* **PERFORM** ▷ **6** (A2) [T] to perform an action: *I must make a phone call.* ◦ *Somebody has made a donation of £1 million to Oxfam.* ◦ *I need to make a trip to the shops.* ◦ *On foot they could only make about 20 miles a day.* ◦ *We must make a **decision** by tomorrow.* ◦ *You're not making any **effort**.* ◦ *Someone has made **a mistake/an error**.* ◦ *We're making good **progress**.* ◦ *She has made a **request** for a new car.* ◦ *We made an **offer** of £150,000 for the house.* ◦ *She made a short **speech**.* ◦ *Shall we make **a start** on the work?* ◦ *Can I make a **suggestion**?* ◦ *We made good **time** getting across town.* ◦ *There's a drunk at the door making **trouble**.* **7 make room/space/way** (C2) If you make room/space/way for something or someone, you move or move other things, so that there is space for them. **FORCE** ▷ **8 make sb do sth** (B1) to force someone or something to do something: *You can't make him go if he doesn't want to.* ◦ *The vet put something down the dog's throat to make it vomit.* **9 be made to do sth** to be forced to do something: *The prisoners are made to dig holes and fill them in again.*

> **Common mistake: make sb do sth**
>
> When **make** has the meaning 'to force', it is followed by a verb in the infinitive without 'to'.
> Do not say 'make someone to do something', say **make someone do something**:
>
> ~~*They made us to pay extra for the drinks.*~~
>
> *They made us pay extra for the drinks.*
>
> **Warning:** in passive sentences, use the infinitive with 'to'. Don't say 'be made do something', say **be made to do something**.

BE/BECOME ▷ **10** (C1) [L only + noun] to be or become something, usually by having the necessary characteristics: *I don't think he will ever make a (good) lawyer.* ◦ *He's a competent enough officer, but I doubt he'll ever make general.* ◦ *It's a story that would make a great film.* ◦ *She decided the back room would make a good study.* ◦ *Champagne and caviar make a wonderful combination.* ◦ *The story makes fascinating reading.* **11** [T] If people or things make a particular pattern, they are arranged in that way: *Let's make a circle.* ◦ *Those seven bright stars make the shape of a saucepan.* **TOTAL** ▷ **12** [L only + noun, T] to produce a total when added together: *12 and 12 make 24.* ◦ *Today's earthquake makes five since the beginning of the year.* ◦ [+ obj + noun] *I've got 29 different teapots in my collection – if I buy this one that'll make it 30.* **CALCULATE** ▷ **13** [T + obj + noun] to calculate as: *How much do you make the total?* ◦ *I make the answer (**to be**) 105.6.* ◦ *What do you make the time?/What time do you make it?* **EARN/GET** ▷ **14** (B2) [T] to earn or get: *She makes $100,000 a year as a doctor.* ◦ *How do you make **a living** as a painter?* ◦ *The company has made huge profits/losses.* ◦ *He's very good at making new friends.* **ARRIVE** ▷ **15** (B1) [T] informal to arrive at or reach, especially successfully: *She made **it to** the airport just in time to catch her plane.* ◦ *He made **it to** the bed and then collapsed.* ◦ *Could you make a meeting at 8 a.m.?/Could you make 8 a.m. for the meeting?* **PERFECT** ▷ **16** [T] informal to cause to be perfect: *Those little bows round the neck **really** make the dress!*

IDIOMS **be made for sb/sth** to be exactly suitable for someone or something: *Paul and Ann were **made for each other**.* ◦ *This wallpaper's just made for my bedroom.* • **be made of money** to be rich: *No you can't have another bike – I'm not made of money!* • **do you want to make something/anything of it?** informal something that you say to someone as a way of threatening or offering to fight them when they disagree with you • **make sth up as you go along** to invent a story or a tune without having thought before about how it will end • **make a day/night/evening/weekend of it** to make an activity longer or combine a series of activities so that they last for the whole of that particular period of time: *Let's make an evening of it and catch the last train home.* ◦ *We don't get out often so we thought we'd make a day of it.* • **make as if to do sth** If you make as if to do something, you seem as if that is what you are

Other ways of saying make

Produce is an alternative to 'make':

*California **produces** a lot of grapes.*

*Red blood cells are **produced** in the bone marrow.*

The verb **create** is used when someone makes something new, especially something original:

*Leonardo da Vinci **created** the masterpiece we know as 'Mona Lisa'.*

The verb **manufacture** is used when something is made in a factory:

*The product is **manufactured** in Germany.*

You can use the verbs **build** or **construct** when someone makes things by putting things together:

*The bird **built** its nest in a tree.*

*The walls are **constructed** of concrete.*

going to do: *He made as if to speak.* • **make do** C2 to manage to live without things that you would like to have or with things of a worse quality than you would like: *We didn't have cupboards so we made do **with** boxes.* • **make it (to the top)** C1 to be very successful: *She's very ambitious but I doubt she'll ever make it to the top.* • **make it up to sb** to do something good for someone you have upset, in order to become friends with them again: *I'm sorry we can't take you with us, but I promise I'll make it up to you somehow.* • **make it with sb** US informal to have sex with someone • **make like** US to pretend: *She made like she was about to leave, but then stayed for hours.* ◦ *Stop making like you know everything, OK?* • **make much/a lot of sb** informal to treat someone very well: *His mother used to make much of him when he went home for holidays.* • **make or break sth** to make something a success or a failure: *Recognition by this organization can make or break a career.* • **be make or break for sb/sth** to make someone or something a success or a failure: *The Milan show will be make or break for his new designs.* • **make time** C1 to make certain you have some time when you are not busy in order to do something you think you should do: *It's important to make time to read **to** your children.* ◦ *In a relationship you have to make time **for** each other.* • **make to do sth** formal If you make to do something, you are just going to do it when something interrupts you: *I made to leave but she called me back.* • **make up for lost time** to enjoy an experience as much as possible because you did not have the opportunity to do it earlier in life • **what sb is (really) made of** how strong, clever, or brave someone is: *The race next week will be a chance for her to show what she's made of.*

PHRASAL VERBS **make for somewhere/sth** B2 to go in the direction of a place or thing: *They made for the centre of town.* → See also **make towards sth/sb** • **make for sth** to result in or make possible: *Having faster computers would make for a more efficient system.* • **make sth into sth** B2 to change something into something else: *They've made the spare room into an office.* • **make of sth/sb** C2 If you ask someone what they make of someone or something, you want to know their opinion about that person or thing, often because there is something strange about them: *Can you make anything of this information?* ◦ *What do you make of the new boss?* ◦ *I don't know what to make of it.* • **make sth of sth make enough, much, more, etc. of sth** to give a particular level of value or importance to something: *You should make more of your IT skills on the application form.* ◦ *I think we make **too much** of the benefits of Western society.* → Compare **make light of sth** • **make off** informal to leave quickly, usually in order to escape: *The burglars made off before the police arrived.* • **make off with sth** informal to steal something: *Somebody broke into the shop and made off with several TVs.* • **make sth/sb out** B2 to see, hear, or understand something or someone with difficulty: *The numbers are too small – I can't make them out at all.* ◦ *I can't make out your writing.* ◦ *She's a strange person – I can't make her out at all.* ◦ [+ question word] *Nobody can make out **why** you should have been attacked.* • **make sth out** to write all the necessary information on an official document: *I made a cheque out **for** £20 **to** 'Henry's Supermarket'.* • **make out sth** informal to say, usually falsely, that something is true: [+ to infinitive] *He made himself out **to** be a millionaire.* ◦ [+ to be] *The British weather is not always as bad as it is made out **to be**.* ◦ [+ (that)] *He made out (**that**) he had been living in Paris all year.* • **make out** US informal SUCCEED ▷ **1** to deal with a situation, usually in a successful way: *How is Frances making out **in** her new job?* ◦ *The business made out better than expected and profits were slightly up.* HAVE SEX ▷ **2** to kiss and touch in a sexual way, or to succeed in having sex with someone: *Boys at that age are only interested in making out **with** girls.* • **make sth over to sb** to give something, such as money or land, to someone so that they legally own it: *Just before her death, she had made over $100,000 to her new husband.* • **make towards sth/sb** mainly UK to go in the direction of something or someone: *He made towards the door, but stopped and turned to face me.* → See also **make for somewhere/sth** • **make sth up** INVENT ▷ **1** B2 to invent something, such as an excuse or a story, often in order to deceive: *I made up an **excuse** about having to look after the kids.* ◦ *My dad was always really good at making up **stories**.* PREPARE ▷ **2** to prepare or arrange something by putting different things together: *Could you make up a list of all the things that need to be done?* ◦ *He asked the man behind the counter to make up a box with a mixed selection of chocolates.* ◦ *The maid will make up your room later.* **3** specialized to produce or prepare something from cloth: *We could use the rest of the material to make up some curtains.* **4** specialized If you make up a page, book, or newspaper, you arrange the text and pictures in the form in which they will be printed. **5** If you make up a bed for someone, you put sheets and covers on a bed so that they have a place to sleep in your home. **6** UK If you make up a fire, you prepare it or put more wood or coal on it when it is burning. COMPLETE ▷ **7** to make an amount of something complete or correct: *I have £20,000 and I need £25,000 but my parents have promised to make up **the difference**.* ◦ UK *I suspect we were only invited to make up **numbers*** (= to provide enough people). REPLACE ▷ **8** to reduce or replace something, usually an amount of time or work, that has been lost: *We're hoping to make up **time** on the return journey by not stopping at night.* ◦ *You'll have to make up the work you've missed while you were away.* • **make (sb/sth) up** to put make-up on your face, or on another person's face, to improve or change its appearance: *She takes ages to make up in the mornings.* ◦ *For the film, they made him up **as** an Indian.* • **make up sth** to form a particular thing, amount, or number as a whole: *Road accident victims make up almost a quarter of the hospital's patients.* ◦ *The book is made up of a number of different articles.* • **make up** (also **make it up**) to forgive someone and be friendly with them again after an argument or disagreement: *They **kissed and** made up, as usual.* ◦ *We often quarrel but we always make it up soon after.* • **make up for sth** B2 to take the place of something

M

lost or damaged or to COMPENSATE for something bad with something good: *No amount of money can make up for the death of a child.* ◦ *This year's good harvest will make up for last year's bad one.* ◦ [+ -ing verb] *He bought me dinner to make up for being so late the day before.* • **make up to sb** UK disapproving to be too friendly to someone or to praise them in order to get advantages: *Have you seen the disgusting way she makes up to the boss?* • **make with sth** US old-fashioned slang to give, bring, or do something: *He pointed a gun and said 'Make with the money bags, baby!'*

▸**noun** [C] a type of product or the name of the company which made it: *What make is your laptop?*

IDIOM **be on the make** disapproving to be trying very hard to get more money and power

ˈmake-beˌlieve noun [U] disapproving believing or imagining things that appear to be attractive or exciting, but are not real: *The ideal of a perfectly fair society is just make-believe.* ◦ *He lives in a* ***world of*** *make-believe/make-believe* ***world***.

ˌmake-or-ˈbreak adj describes a situation that will bring great success or complete failure

makeover /ˈmeɪkˌəʊ.vəʳ/ (US) /-ˌoʊ.vɚ/ noun [C] a set of changes that are intended to make a person or place more attractive: *One of the prizes was a makeover at a top beauty salon.*

maker /ˈmeɪ.kəʳ/ (US) /-kɚ/ noun [C] **1** (B2) the people or company that make something: *They're the biggest maker of fast-food products in the UK.* ◦ *The makers of the film will want to see a decent return on their investment.* **2 your Maker** God: humorous *He's gone to* ***meet*** *his Maker (= he has died).* **3** a person or machine which makes the stated thing: *a film maker* ◦ *a dressmaker* ◦ *policy makers* ◦ *a coffee/tea maker* → See also **bookmaker, holidaymaker, homemaker, ice-maker, kingmaker, matchmaker, pacemaker, peacemaker, troublemaker**

makeshift /ˈmeɪk.ʃɪft/ adj temporary and of low quality, but used because of a sudden need: *Thousands of refugees are living in makeshift* ***camps***.

ˈmake-up noun [U] FOR FACE ▷ **1** (A2) coloured substances used on your face to improve or change your appearance: *I* ***put on*** *a little eye make-up.* ◦ *She* ***wears*** *a lot of make-up.* PARTS ▷ **2** The make-up of something or someone is the combination of things that form it: *They argue that the membership of the Council does not reflect the racial make-up of the city.* ◦ *Organizational ability is not one of the most obvious parts of his make-up.*

makeweight /ˈmeɪk.weɪt/ noun [C] something or someone, without much value of its own, that is added so that there is the correct amount or number: *She may be the youngest member of the team, but she's no makeweight.*

making /ˈmeɪ.kɪŋ/ noun [U] the activity or process of producing something: *the art of film making* ◦ *There's an article on* ***the*** *making* ***of*** *the series.*

IDIOMS **be an actor, cook, etc. in the making** to have the ability and interest to become an actor, cook, etc. in the future • **be the making of sb** If something is the making of someone, it develops in them good qualities and characteristics which might not have developed without it: *Five years in the army – that'll be the making of him!* • **have (all) the makings of sth** to seem likely to develop into something: *She has the makings of a great violinist.* • **in the making** If something was a period of time in the making, it took that amount of time to make: *The film was several years in the making.* • **of your own making** your own fault: *Any problems she has with that child are of her own making.*

mal- /mæl-/ prefix formal badly or wrongly: *The disease rubella can cause pregnant women to have malformed babies.*

malachite /ˈmæl.ə.kaɪt/ noun [U] a green stone used in jewellery and decoration

maladjusted /ˌmæl.əˈdʒʌs.tɪd/ adj describes a person, usually a child, who has been raised in a way that does not prepare them well for the demands of life, which often leads to problems with behaviour in the future: *a residential school for disturbed and maladjusted children* • **maladjustment** /-mənt/ noun [U]

maladministration /ˌmæl.ədˌmɪn.ɪˈstreɪ.ʃən/ noun [U] formal lack of care, judgment, or honesty in the management of something: *Thousands of refugees are dying because of the incompetence and maladministration of local officials.*

maladroit /ˌmæl.əˈdrɔɪt/ adj formal awkward in movement or unskilled in behaviour or action: *She can be a little maladroit in social situations.* • **maladroitly** /-li/ adv • **maladroitness** /-nəs/ noun [U]

malady /ˈmæl.ə.di/ noun [C] formal DISEASE ▷ **1** a disease: *All the rose bushes seem to be suffering from the same mysterious malady.* PROBLEM ▷ **2** a problem within a system or organization: *Apathy is one of the maladies of modern society.*

malaise /mælˈeɪz/ noun [S or U] formal a general feeling of being ill or having no energy, or an uncomfortable feeling that something is wrong, especially with society, and that you cannot change the situation: *They claim it is a symptom of a deeper and more* ***general*** *malaise in society.* ◦ *We were discussing the roots of the current* ***economic*** *malaise.*

malapropism /ˈmæl.ə.prɒp.ɪ.zəm/ (US) /-prɑː.pɪ-/ noun [C] the wrong use of one word instead of another word because they sound similar to each other, with results that are unintentionally funny

malaria /məˈleə.ri.ə/ (US) /-ˈler.i-/ noun [U] a disease that you can get from the bite of a particular type of MOSQUITO (= a small flying insect) which causes periods of fever and makes you feel very cold and shake. It is common in many hotter parts of the world.

malarkey /məˈlɑː.ki/ (US) /-ˈlɑːr-/ noun [U] informal silly behaviour or nonsense: *I like the socializing but I can't be bothered with the dressing up and* ***all that*** *malarkey.*

malcontent /ˈmæl.kən.tent/ noun [C] literary a person who is not satisfied with the way things are, and who complains a lot and is unreasonable and difficult to deal with

male /meɪl/ adj; noun

▸**adj** SEX ▷ **1** (B1) describes men or boys, or the sex that FERTILIZES eggs, and does not produce babies or eggs itself: *male students* ◦ *a male giraffe* ◦ *IT is very much a male-dominated industry.* ◦ *What percentage of the adult male population is unemployed?* ◦ *The male parts of the flower are the stamens and the anthers.* → See also **masculine** CONNECTING PART ▷ **2** specialized describes a piece of equipment that has a part which sticks out and can be fitted into a hollow part in another piece of equipment: *a male plug* → Compare **female** • **maleness** /-nəs/ noun [U]

▸**noun** [C] (B2) a boy, man, or male animal: *The male of the species is less aggressive.* ◦ *Among the bodies are two unidentified British males.*

ˌmale ˈbonding noun [U] the forming of close friendships between men

ˌmale ˈchauvinist noun [C] disapproving a man who

believes that women are naturally less important, intelligent, or able than men, and so does not treat men and women equally: *She called him a male chauvinist **pig**.* • ˌ**male ˈchauvinism** noun [U] *a bastion of male chauvinism*

malefactor /ˈmæl.ɪ.fæk.təʳ/ (US) /-tɚ/ **noun** [C] formal a person who does bad or illegal things

ˌ**male ˈorgan** noun [C] polite expression for PENIS

malevolent /məˈlev.əl.ənt/ **adj** literary causing or wanting to cause harm or evil: *The central character is a malevolent witch out for revenge.* ◦ *I could feel his malevolent gaze as I walked away.* • **malevolence** /-əns/ **noun** [U] *It was an act of great malevolence.* • **malevolently** /-li/ **adv**

malfeasance /mælˈfiː.zəns/ **noun** [U] legal an example of dishonest and illegal behaviour, especially by a person in authority: *Several cases of malpractice and malfeasance in the financial world are currently being investigated.*

malformation /ˌmæl.fəˈmeɪ.ʃən/ (US) /-fɚ-/ **noun** [C or U] the condition of being wrongly formed, or a part of something, such as part of the body, that is wrongly formed: *She was born critically ill with a severe malformation of the heart.* • **malformed** /-ˈfɔːmd/ (US) /-fɔːrmd/ **adj**

malfunction /ˌmælˈfʌŋk.ʃən/ **verb; noun**
▸**verb** [I] formal to fail to work or operate correctly
▸**noun** [C] formal a failure to work or operate correctly: *Shortly before the crash the pilot had reported a malfunction of the aircraft's navigation system.*

malice /ˈmæl.ɪs/ **noun** [U] **1** the wish to harm or upset other people: *There certainly wasn't any malice in her comments.* ◦ formal *I **bear** him no malice (= do not want to harm or upset him).* **2 with malice aforethought** legal To illegally harm someone with malice aforethought is to have thought about it and planned it before acting.

malicious /məˈlɪʃ.əs/ **adj** **1** (C2) intended to harm or upset other people: *malicious gossip* ◦ *a malicious look in his eyes* ◦ *He complained that he'd been receiving malicious phone calls.* ◦ legal *He was charged with malicious **wounding**.* **2** intended to cause damage to a computer system, or to steal private information from a computer system: *protection against malicious **software/code*** • **maliciously** /-li/ **adv**

malign /məˈlaɪn/ **adj; verb**
▸**adj** formal causing or intending to cause harm or evil: *Foreign domination had a malign **influence** on local politics.* • **malignity** /məˈlɪg.nə.ti/ (US) /-t̬i/ **noun** [U]
▸**verb** [T often passive] to say false and unpleasant things about someone or to unfairly criticize them: *She has recently been maligned in the gossip columns of several newspapers.* ◦ ***Much**-maligned for their derivative style, the band are nevertheless enduringly popular.*

malignancy /məˈlɪg.nən.si/ **noun** [C or U] specialized a growth that is likely to get worse and lead to death, or the state of being malignant: *Tests revealed a malignancy that had to be removed.*

malignant /məˈlɪg.nənt/ **adj** DISEASE ▷ **1** describes a disease or a growth that is likely to get worse and lead to death: *The process by which malignant cancer cells multiply isn't fully understood.* ◦ *Is the tumour malignant or benign?* → Compare **benign** EVIL ▷ **2** formal having a strong wish to do harm: *He developed a malignant hatred for the land of his birth.* • **malignantly** /-li/ **adv**

malinger /məˈlɪŋ.gəʳ/ (US) /-gɚ/ **verb** [I] disapproving to pretend to be ill in order to avoid having to work: *And is he really ill or just malingering?* • **malingerer** /-əʳ/ (US) /-ɚ/ **noun** [C] *I'm sure she thinks I'm a malingerer.*

mall /mɔːl/ (US) /mɑːl/ **noun** [C] (also ˈ**shopping** ˌ**mall**) (B1) a large, usually covered, shopping area where cars are not allowed: *There are plans to build a new mall in the middle of town.*

mallard /ˈmæl.ɑːd/ (US) /-ɑːrd/ **noun** [C] (plural **mallard** or **mallards**) a wild DUCK that is common in Europe and North America: *The male mallard has a green head and reddish-brown chest.*

malleable /ˈmæl.i.ə.bl̩/ **adj** **1** describes a substance that is easily changed into a new shape: *Lead and tin are malleable metals.* **2** easily influenced, trained, or controlled: *He had an actor's typically malleable features.* ◦ *Europe saw its colonies as a source of raw material and a malleable workforce.* • **malleability** /ˌmæl.i.əˈbɪl.ɪ.ti/ (US) /-ə.t̬i/ **noun** [U]

mallet /ˈmæl.ɪt/ **noun** [C] a tool like a hammer with a large flat end made of wood or rubber, or a wooden hammer with a long handle used in sports such as CROQUET and POLO → See also **hammer**

mallet

malleus /ˈmæl.i.əs/ **noun** [C usually sing] (plural **mallei**) specialized one of three very small bones that carry sound from the EARDRUM to the INNER EAR → See also **incus, stapes**

ˈ**mall** ˌ**rat** noun [C] US slang a young person who goes to shopping MALLS (= large covered shopping areas) to spend time with their friends

malnourished /ˌmælˈnʌr.ɪʃt/ (US) /-ˈnɝː-/ **adj** weak and in bad health because of having too little food or too little of the types of food necessary for good health

malnutrition /ˌmæl.njuːˈtrɪ.ʃən/ (US) /-nuː-/ **noun** [U] physical weakness and bad health caused by having too little food, or too little of the types of food necessary for good health: *Many of the refugees are **suffering from** severe malnutrition.*

malodorous /ˌmælˈəʊ.dər.əs/ (US) /-ˈoʊ.dɚ-/ **adj** formal having an unpleasant smell: *The town is built on a malodorous swamp.*

malpractice /ˌmælˈpræk.tɪs/ **noun** [U] specialized failure to act correctly or legally when doing your job, often causing injury or loss: *They are accused of medical/financial/electoral malpractice.*

malt /mɒlt/ (US) /mɑːlt/ **noun** [U] grain, usually BARLEY, that has been left in water until it starts to grow and is then dried. It is used in the making of alcoholic drinks such as beer and WHISKY • **malt verb** [T]

ˌ**malted ˈmilk** noun [U] a drink made from milk and malt

ˌ**Maltese ˈcross** noun [C] a cross with four equal parts that get wider further from the centre

ˌ**malt ˈextract** noun [U] a sweet, dark, sticky substance made from malt, used in food

maltose /ˈmɔːl.təʊz/ (US) /-toʊz/ **noun** [U] specialized a type of sugar made in the body from STARCH by ENZYMES (= substances that cause chemical change)

maltreat /ˌmælˈtriːt/ **verb** [T] formal to treat someone cruelly or violently: *He had been badly maltreated as a child.* • **maltreatment** /-mənt/ **noun** [U]

ˌ**malt ˈwhisky** noun [C or U] (also **malt**) WHISKY made using MALT rather than ordinary grain: *a fine Highland malt*

malware /ˈmæl.weəʳ/ (US) /-wer/ **noun** [U] computer

software that is designed to damage the way a computer works

mam /mæm/ noun [C] Northern English informal for **mum**

mama /mə'mɑː/ (US) /'mɑː.mə/ noun [C] **1** UK old-fashioned or US informal a mother: [as form of address] *Can I have some more, Mama?* ◦ *Where's your mama?* **2** US slang a woman, especially an attractive one: *There's a good-looking mama sitting at the bar.*

'mama's ˌboy noun [C] US for **mummy's boy**

mamba /'mæm.bə/ noun [C] a very poisonous snake that lives mainly in caves or trees in parts of Africa

mammal /'mæm.əl/ noun [C] C1 any animal of which the female feeds her young on milk from her own body. Most mammals give birth to LIVE young, not eggs: *Humans, dogs, elephants, and dolphins are all mammals, but birds, fish, and crocodiles are not.* • **mammalian** /mə'meɪ.li.ən/ adj specialized *mammalian evolution* ◦ *mammalian species*

mammary /'mæm.ər.i/ (US) /-ɚ-/ adj specialized relating to the breasts or milk organs

'mammary ˌgland noun [C] specialized an organ in a woman's breast that produces milk to feed a baby, or a similar organ in a female animal

mammogram /'mæm.ə.græm/ noun [C] (also **mammograph**) an X-RAY photograph of the breasts

mammography /mə'mɒg.rə.fi/ (US) /-'mɑː.grə-/ noun [U] the use of X-RAY photographs of the breasts to help discover possible cancers

Mammon /'mæm.ən/ noun [U] literary the force which makes people try to become as rich as possible and the belief that this is the most important thing in life

M

mammoth /'mæm.əθ/ adj; noun

▸adj extremely large: *Cleaning up the city-wide mess is going to be a mammoth* ***task***. ◦ *It's a mammoth* ***undertaking*** *– are you sure you have the resources to cope?*

▸noun [C] a type of large ELEPHANT, no longer in existence, that was covered in hair and had TUSKS

mammy /'mæm.i/ noun [C] **1** mainly US or Irish child's word mother **2** US offensive old-fashioned a black woman whose job is to take care of white children

man /mæn/ noun; verb; exclamation

▸noun (plural **men** /men/) **MALE** ▷ **1** A1 [C] an adult male human being: *a young/tall man* ◦ *men and women* ◦ *the man in the green jacket* ◦ *the men's champion in the 400 metres* ◦ *Steve can solve anything – the man's a genius.* **2** [C] a male employee, without particular rank or title: *The gas company said they would send some men to fix the heating system.* ◦ *The man* ***from*** *the BBC wrote some positive things about the movie.* ◦ *The military expedition was made up of 100 officers and men.* ◦ *Our man in Washington sent us the news by fax yesterday.* ◦ old-fashioned *My man (= male servant) will show you to the door.* **3 a marketing, advertising, etc. man** a man typical of or involved in marketing, advertising, etc. **4** [C] informal a husband or male sexual partner: *I hear she's got a new man.* ◦ *Is there a man in her life?* **5** mainly US informal used when talking to someone, especially a man: *Hey, man, how are you doing?* **6 man and wife** old-fashioned If a man and a woman are man and wife, they are married to each other. **7 the man** [S] US slang a person or group that has power or authority, for example the police **PEOPLE** ▷ **8** B2 [U] the human race: *Man is still far more intelligent than the cleverest robot.* ◦ *Man is rapidly destroying the Earth.* ◦ *This is one of the most dangerous substances* ***known to*** *man.* ◦ *Try to imagine what life must have been like for Neolithic man 10,000 years ago.* **9** [C] literary or old-fashioned a person of either sex: *All men are equal in the sight of the law.* **OBJECT** ▷ **10** [C] any of the objects that are moved or played with in games such as CHESS

IDIOMS **as one man** formal If a group of people do something as one man, they do it together at exactly the same time: *As one man, the delegates made for the exit.* • **it's every man for himself** something that you say that means that everyone in a particular situation is trying to do what is best for themselves and no one is trying to help anyone else: *It might be a civilized place to shop at other times but come the January sales, it's every man for himself.* • **make a man (out) of sb** to cause a young man or boy to act like an adult and take responsibility: *A couple of years in the army should make a man of him.* • **man and boy** UK old-fashioned all a man's life: *From 1910 to 1970 he worked in that factory, man and boy.* • **be man enough to do sth** to be brave enough to do something: *He was man enough to admit he had made a mistake.* • **the man in the moon** (in children's stories) the human face that you can imagine you see when you look at the moon • **(as) man to man** If two men talk (as) man to man, they talk seriously and honestly together on an equal level. • **man's best friend** a dog • **man's inhumanity to man** the cruel behaviour that people show to each other: *Man's inhumanity to man never fails to shock me.* • **a man's man** a man who enjoys men's activities and being with other men: *Terry's what you'd call a man's man – I don't expect you'd find him at the ballet too many nights a week.* • **to a man** every person in a group: *There were 400 people at the meeting and they all, to a man, voted for the motion.* • **you the man!** US not standard used to praise a person who has done something well

▸verb [T] (-nn-) To man something such as a machine or vehicle is to be present in order to operate it: *The phones are manned 24 hours a day.* ◦ *Barricades were erected against the advancing government troops and they were manned throughout the night.* ◦ *Man the pumps!* → See also **overmanned, undermanned, unmanned**

> **! Note:**
> Many people find this use sexist and prefer to use other verbs such as 'operate' or 'staff'.

PHRASAL VERB **man up** informal used to tell someone that they should deal with something more bravely: *You need to man up and go get want you want.*

▸**exclamation** informal used to express a strong emotion: *Man, we had a good time – we drank all through the night!*

-man /-mæn/, /-mən/ **suffix** having the nationality or job mentioned, or (of a group or vehicle) containing the number of people mentioned: *an Irishman* ◦ *a policeman* ◦ *businessmen* ◦ *a five-man team* ◦ *a two-man helicopter*

ˌman-about-'town noun [S] a man who spends a lot of time in fashionable places, doing fashionable things

manacle /'mæn.ə.kl̩/ verb [T] to put manacles around a person's legs or arms: *They had manacled her legs* ***together***. ◦ *His arm was manacled* ***to*** *a ring on the wall.*

manacles /'mæn.ə.kl̩z/ noun [plural] two metal rings joined by a chain, used to prevent a prisoner from escaping by fastening the legs or arms

manage /'mæn.ɪdʒ/ verb **SUCCEED** ▷ **1** B1 [I or T] to succeed in doing something, especially something difficult: [+ to infinitive] *Did you manage* ***to*** *get any* bread? ◦ *I* ***only just*** *managed* ***to*** *finish on time.* ◦ *A small dog had* ***somehow*** *managed* ***to*** *survive the fire.* ◦ *I can't manage all this work on my own.* ◦ *Don't worry about us – we'll manage!* ◦ *Can you manage dinner on Saturday? (= Will you be able to come to dinner?)* ◦ mainly UK *I'm afraid I can't manage the time (= I'm too busy) to see you at the moment.* **2** [I] to succeed in living on a small amount of money: *After she lost her job, they had to manage* ***on*** *his salary.* **CONTROL** ▷ **3** **B1** [T] to be responsible for controlling or organizing someone or something, especially a business or employees: *Has she had any experience of managing large projects?* ◦ *He's not very good at managing people.* ◦ *His job involved managing large investment funds.* ◦ *When you have a job as well as children to look after, you have to learn how to manage your time.* → See also **mismanage**

manageable /ˈmæn.ɪ.dʒə.bl/ **adj** easy or possible to deal with: *The work has been divided into smaller, more manageable sections.*

management /ˈmæn.ɪdʒ.mənt/ **noun** **1** **B2** [U] the control and organization of something: *The company has suffered from several years of bad management.* ◦ *There is a need for stricter financial management.* ◦ *a management training scheme* **2** [C, + sing/pl verb] the group of people responsible for controlling and organizing a company: *Management has/have offered staff a three percent pay increase.*

ˌmanagement conˈsultancy **noun** **1** [U] the job of being a management consultant **2** [C] a company that offers other companies advice about the best way of managing and improving their businesses

ˌmanagement conˈsultant **noun** [C] someone whose job is to give advice to companies about the best way of managing and improving their businesses

manager /ˈmæn.ɪ.dʒəʳ/ US /-dʒɚ/ **noun** [C] **1** **A2** the person who is responsible for managing an organization: *a bank manager* ◦ *a station manager* ◦ *the production manager* ◦ *I wish to speak to the manager.* **2** **A2** the person whose job is to organize and sometimes train a sports team: *a football manager* **3** **A2** The manager of a singer, actor, or other performer is a person whose job is to arrange the business part of their work.

manageress /ˌmæn.ɪ.dʒəˈres/ US /-dʒə.res/ **noun** [C] old-fashioned a female manager

managerial /ˌmæn.əˈdʒɪə.ri.əl/ US /-ˈdʒɪr.i-/ **adj** relating to a manager or management: *managerial* ***responsibilities/decisions/skills***

ˌmanaging diˈrector **noun** [C] (abbreviation **MD**) UK the person in charge of a company

mañana /mænˈjɑː.nə/ **adv** informal some time in the future; later: *'When will you do it?' 'Oh, mañana!'*

ˈman ˌbag **noun** [C] informal a bag that a man uses for carrying his money, keys, mobile phone, etc.

ˈman ˌbreasts **noun** [plural] informal fat on a man's chest that looks like a woman's breasts

Mancunian /mæŋˈkjuː.ni.ən/ **noun** [C] a person from Manchester, a city in the north of England • **Mancunian adj**

mandarin /ˈmæn.dᵊr.ɪn/ US /-dɚ-/ **noun** [C] **FRUIT** ▷ **1** (also **mandarin orange**) a small, sweet type of orange but with a thinner, looser skin **OFFICIAL** ▷ **2** mainly disapproving a person who has a very important job in the government, and who is sometimes considered to be too powerful: *It often seems that true power lies with the Civil Service mandarins, rather than MPs and cabinet ministers.*

Mandarin (Chinese) /ˌmæn.dᵊr.ɪn.tʃaɪˈniːz/ **noun** [U] one of the two main types of the Chinese language and the official language in China and Taiwan

mandate /ˈmæn.deɪt/ **noun; verb**

▸**noun** [C usually singular] **AUTHORITY** ▷ **1** the authority given to an elected group of people, such as a government, to perform an action or govern a country: *At the forthcoming elections, the government will be seeking a fresh mandate* ***from*** *the people.* ◦ [+ to infinitive] *The president secured the Congressional mandate* ***to*** *go to war by three votes.* **AREA NAME** ▷ **2** specialized the name of an area of land that has been given to a country by the UN, following or as part of a peace agreement

▸**verb** [T] **GIVE PERMISSION** ▷ **1** to give official permission for something to happen: *The UN rush to mandate war totally ruled out any alternatives.* **ORDER** ▷ **2** mainly US to order someone to do something: [+ to infinitive] *Our delegates have been mandated* ***to*** *vote against the proposal at the conference.*

mandatory /ˈmæn.də.tᵊr.i/ US /-tɔːr.i/ **adj** formal describes something that must be done, or is demanded by law: *The minister is calling for mandatory prison sentences for people who assault police officers.* ◦ *Athletes must undergo a mandatory drugs test before competing in the championship.* ◦ *In 1991, the British government made it mandatory to wear rear seat belts in cars.*

mandible /ˈmæn.dɪ.bᵊl/ **noun** [C] specialized **1** in a person or animal, the lower JAW bone **2** in insects, one of the two parts of the mouth used for biting and cutting food

mandolin /ˌmæn.dəˈlɪn/ **noun** [C] a musical instrument with four pairs of metal strings and a round back

mandrake /ˈmæn.dreɪk/ **noun** [C] a plant with purple flowers and a root that is divided into two parts

mandrill /ˈmæn.drɪl/ **noun** [C] a large West African monkey that has a red and blue face and a very short tail

mane /meɪn/ **noun** [C] **1** the long, thick hair that grows along the top of a horse's neck or around the face and neck of a lion **2** thick, long hair on a person's head: *The painting depicts a beautiful young man with a flowing mane* ***of*** *red hair.*

ˈman-ˌeater **noun** [C] **WOMAN** ▷ **1** humorous a woman who uses men to have a series of sexual relationships without loving them **ANIMAL** ▷ **2** an animal that can kill and eat a person • **ˈman-ˌeating adj** [before noun] *a man-eating tiger*

maneuver /məˈnuː.vəʳ/ US /-vɚ/ **noun** [C], **verb** [I or T] US for **manoeuvre**

ˈman ˌflu **noun** [U] humorous an illness such as a cold that is not serious, but that the person who has it treats as more serious, usually when this person is a man: *John's got a touch of man flu and he won't get out of bed.*

ˌman ˈFriday **noun** [C usually singular] a man who helps someone with their work and is loyal and can be trusted

manfully /ˈmæn.fᵊl.i/ **adv** with determination and courage, despite great problems: *The actors* ***struggled*** *manfully with some of the worst lines of dialogue ever written.*

manga /ˈmæŋ.gə/ **noun** [C or U] Japanese COMIC BOOKS that tell stories in pictures

manganese /ˈmæŋ.gə.niːz/ **noun** [U] (symbol **Mn**) a

M

chemical element that is a grey-white metal, used in the process of making STEEL

mange /meɪndʒ/ **noun** [U] an infectious disease in animals that have hair, such as dogs and cats, which makes hair fall out and causes areas of rough skin

manger /ˈmeɪn.dʒəʳ/ (US) /-dʒɚ/ **noun** [C] an open box from which CATTLE and horses feed

mangetout /ˌmɑːnʒˈtuː/ **noun** [C usually plural] UK (US ˈ**snow** ˌ**pea**) the sweet, flat PODS of a type of PEA, picked and eaten whole

mangle /ˈmæŋ.gl/ **verb; noun**

▸**verb** **1** [T often passive] to destroy something by twisting it with force or tearing it into pieces so that its original form is completely changed: *My sweater got mangled in the washing machine.* ◦ *His arm was mangled in the machine.* **2** [T] If you mangle a speech or a piece of written work, you make so many mistakes that you completely spoil it: *As he read the poem out loud, he mangled the rhythm so badly that it scarcely made any sense.* • **mangled** /-gld/ **adj** *All that remains of yesterday's car crash is a pile of mangled metal.*

▸**noun** [C] (also **wringer**) a machine used for pressing water out of clothes by putting the clothes between two heavy, smooth, round bars

mango /ˈmæŋ.gəʊ/ (US) /-goʊ/ **noun** [C or U] (plural **mangoes** or **mangos**) (A2) an oval tropical fruit with a smooth skin, orange-yellow flesh, and a large, hard seed in the middle

ˌ**mango** ˈ**chutney** **noun** [U] a sweet PICKLE eaten with South Asian food

M

mangrove /ˈmæŋ.grəʊv/ (US) /-groʊv/ **noun** [C] a tropical tree, found near water, whose twisted roots grow partly above ground: *a mangrove* ***swamp***

mangy /ˈmeɪn.dʒi/ **adj** **ANIMAL** ▷ **1** suffering from MANGE: *a thin, mangy dog* **OLD/DIRTY** ▷ **2** informal describes something that is old and dirty and has been used a lot: *We need to get rid of that mangy old carpet in the bedroom.*

manhandle /ˌmænˈhæn.dəl/ **verb** [T] **HANDLE ROUGHLY** ▷ **1** to touch or hold someone roughly and with force, often when taking them somewhere: *There were complaints that the police had manhandled some of the demonstrators.* **MOVE** ▷ **2** to move something using the physical strength of the body: *Several pieces of heavy equipment had to be manhandled into the lorry.*

manhattan /mænˈhæt.ən/ (US) /-ˈhæṭ-/ **noun** [C] a type of alcoholic drink: *A manhattan contains whisky and vermouth.*

manhole /ˈmæn.həʊl/ (US) /-hoʊl/ **noun** [C] a covered opening in a road which a worker can enter in order to reach underground pipes, wires, or DRAINS which need to be examined or repaired: *a manhole* ***cover***

manhole

manhood /ˈmæn.hʊd/ **noun** **1** [U] the state of being a man: *The story is seen through the eyes of a boy on the verge of manhood.* ◦ *A celebration is held for the boy at the age when he is considered to have reached manhood.* **2** [U] the qualities that are considered typical of a man: *Tall and handsome, this young actor is Hollywood's ideal of manhood.* **3** [U] literary men, especially all the men of a particular country: *The* ***flower of the nation's*** *manhood (= the best young men in the country) was killed in the war.* **4** [U] a man's ability to express or experience sexual feelings: *Why do you think he needs to have so many women around him – is it just a way of* ***proving*** *his manhood?* **5** [S] humorous PENIS: *Careful you don't trap your manhood in your zip!*

ˈ**man-hour** **noun** [C] (also ˈ**person-**ˌ**hour**) the amount of work done by one person in one hour: *Just think how many man-hours we could save if we computerized the system.*

manhunt /ˈmæn.hʌnt/ **noun** [C] an organized search for a person, especially a criminal: *The police have* ***launched*** *a manhunt after the body of a six-year-old boy was found last night.*

mania /ˈmeɪ.ni.ə/ **noun** [C or U] **STRONG INTEREST** ▷ **1** disapproving a very strong interest in something which fills a person's mind or uses up all their time: *So why your sudden mania* ***for*** *exercise?* ◦ *The article describes the* ***religious*** *mania which is sweeping the US.* **MENTAL ILLNESS** ▷ **2** a state in which someone directs all their attention to one particular thing: *Van Gogh suffered from acute persecution mania.* ◦ *She's always cleaning – it's like a mania with her.* **3** specialized a state of extreme physical and mental activity, often involving a loss of judgment and periods of EUPHORIA

-mania /-meɪ.ni.ə/ **suffix** a very strong interest in the stated thing, especially among a large group of people: *Beatle-mania swept Britain in the 1960s.* → See also **kleptomania, nymphomania, pyromania**

maniac /ˈmeɪ.ni.æk/ **noun** [C] **INTERESTED** ▷ **1** informal a person who has a very strong interest in a particular activity: *a football/sex maniac* **MENTALLY ILL** ▷ **2** a person who behaves in an uncontrolled way, not worrying about risks or danger: *Some maniac was running down the street waving a massive metal bar.* ◦ informal *I won't get in the car with Richard – he drives* ***like a*** *maniac!*

IDIOM **like a maniac** If someone works or exercises like a maniac, they work or exercise extremely hard.

maniacal /məˈnaɪə.kəl/ **adj** describes a cry or laugh that is loud and wild: *He suddenly exploded into maniacal* ***laughter.***

manic /ˈmæn.ɪk/ **adj** very excited or ANXIOUS (= worried and nervous) in a way that causes you to be very physically active: *He's a bit manic – I wish he'd calm down.*

ˌ**manic de**ˈ**pression** **noun** [U] → **bipolar disorder**: *He* ***suffers from*** *manic depression.*

ˌ**manic de**ˈ**pressive** **noun** [C] a person who has manic depression

manicure /ˈmæn.ɪ.kjʊəʳ/ (US) /-kjʊr/ **noun** [C or U] a treatment for the hands which involves making the skin feel softer and making the nails look better by cutting, smoothing, and painting them → Compare **pedicure** • **manicure verb** [T]

manicured /ˈmæn.ɪ.kjʊəd/ (US) /-kjʊrd/ **adj** **HANDS** ▷ **1** having had a manicure: *He has very* ***well-****manicured hands.* **TIDY** ▷ **2** If something, such as a garden, is manicured, it is well cared for and looks very tidy: *The hotel is surrounded by perfectly manicured gardens.*

ˈ**manicure** ˌ**set** **noun** [C] a set of small tools that are used for cutting and smoothing the nails

manicurist /ˈmæn.ɪ.kjʊə.rɪst/ (US) /-kjʊ.rɪst/ **noun** [C] a person whose job is to give people manicures

manifest /ˈmæn.ɪ.fest/ **verb; adj; noun**

▸**verb** [T] formal to show something clearly, through signs or actions: *The workers chose to manifest their* *dissatisfaction* ***in*** *a series of strikes.* ◦ *The illness first manifested* ***itself in/as*** *severe stomach pains.* ◦ *Lack of confidence in the company manifested* ***itself in*** *a fall in the share price.*

▸**adj** formal easily noticed or obvious: *manifest relief* ◦ *manifest lack of interest*

▸**noun** [C] formal a list of people and goods carried on a ship or plane: *He had been listed on the manifest for the flight but it could not be confirmed if he had boarded.*

manifestation /ˌmæn.ɪ.fesˈteɪ.ʃᵊn/ **noun** formal **1** [C] a sign of something existing or happening: *She claimed that the rise in unemployment was just a further manifestation* ***of*** *the government's incompetence.* **2** [U] appearance: *Unlike acid rain or deforestation, global warming has no visible manifestation.*

manifestly /ˈmæn.ɪ.fest.li/ **adv** formal very obviously: *He claims that he is completely committed to the project and yet this is manifestly* ***untrue.*** ◦ *The government has manifestly* ***failed*** *to raise educational standards, despite its commitment to do so.*

manifesto /ˌmæn.ɪˈfes.təʊ/ (US) /-toʊ/ **noun** [C] (plural **manifestos** or **manifestoes**) a written statement of the beliefs, aims, and policies of an organization, especially a political party: *In their election manifesto, the Liberal Democrats proposed increasing taxes to pay for improvements in education.*

manifold /ˈmæn.ɪ.fəʊld/ (US) /-foʊld/ **adj; noun**

▸**adj** formal many and of several different types: *Despite her manifold faults, she was a strong leader.*

▸**noun** [C] specialized a pipe or closed space in a machine that has several openings, allowing liquids and gases to enter and leave

manikin (also **mannikin**) /ˈmæn.ə.kɪn/ **noun** [C] **MODEL** ▷ **1** a model of the human body, used for teaching medical or art students **MAN** ▷ **2** old-fashioned a very short man: *Manikins often appear in children's stories.*

manila (also **manilla**) /məˈnɪl.ə/ **adj** made of strong brown paper: *manila* ***envelopes***

manipulate /məˈnɪp.jʊ.leɪt/ **verb** [T] **INFLUENCE** ▷ **1** mainly disapproving to control something or someone to your advantage, often unfairly or dishonestly: *Throughout her career she has very successfully manipulated the media.* ◦ *The opposition leader accused government ministers of manipulating the statistics to suit themselves.* **USE HANDS** ▷ **2** to control something using the hands: *The wheelchair is designed so that it is easy to manipulate.* **3** to treat a part of the body, using the hands to push back bones into the correct position and put pressure on muscles: *The doctor manipulated the base of my spine and the pain disappeared completely.*

manipulation /məˌnɪp.jʊˈleɪ.ʃᵊn/ **noun** [C or U] **INFLUENCE** ▷ **1** mainly disapproving controlling someone or something to your own advantage, often unfairly or dishonestly: *They have been accused of fraud and stock market manipulations.* ◦ *There's been so much* ***media*** *manipulation of the facts that nobody knows the truth of the matter.* ◦ *The opposition party claims the president returned to power through* ***political*** *manipulation.* **BODY TREATMENT** ▷ **2** treatment of a part of the body using the hands: *Osteopathy involves massage and manipulation of the bones and joints.*

manipulative /məˈnɪp.jʊ.lə.tɪv/ (US) /-t̬ɪv/ **adj** disapproving describes someone who tries to control people to their advantage: *Even as a child she was manipulative and knew how to get her own way.*

manipulator /məˈnɪp.jʊ.leɪ.tər/ (US) /-t̬ɚ/ **noun** [C] mainly disapproving a person who controls people to their own advantage, often unfairly or dishonestly: *She was, said the judge, a ruthless and scheming manipulator.*

mankind /mænˈkaɪnd/ **noun** [U] (also **humankind**) (B2) the whole of the human race, including both men and women: *Mankind has always been obsessed by power.* → Compare **womankind**

manky /ˈmæŋ.ki/ **adj** UK informal describes an object that is unpleasantly dirty, usually because it is old or has been used a lot: *a manky tissue* ◦ *manky old carpets*

manly /ˈmæn.li/ **adj** approving having the qualities which people think a man should have: *He has such a manly voice.* ◦ *My mother used to tell me it wasn't manly for little boys to cry.* • **manliness** /-nəs/ **noun** [U]

ˌman-ˈmade **adj** artificial rather than natural: *man-made fibres* ◦ *It's a man-made lake.*

manna /ˈmæn.ə/ **noun** [U] (in the Bible) a food which dropped from heaven and prevented Moses and his people from dying of hunger in the desert

IDIOM **manna from heaven** help that you get when you need it but are not expecting it

mannequin /ˈmæn.ə.kɪn/ **noun** [C] **1** a large model of a human being, used to show clothes in the window of a shop **2** old-fashioned for **model**

manner /ˈmæn.ər/ (US) /-ɚ/ **noun** **WAY** ▷ **1** (B2) [S] the way in which something is done: *She stared at me* ***in*** *an accusing manner.* ◦ *He was elected* ***in*** *the normal manner.* ◦ *It was the manner* ***of*** *her death that stuck in the public's mind.* **2 in the manner of sth** in the style of something: *Her latest film is a suspense thriller very much in the manner of Hitchcock.* **BEHAVIOUR** ▷ **3** (B2) [S] the usual way in which you behave towards other people, or the way you behave on a particular occasion: *She has a rather cold, unfriendly manner.* ◦ *As soon as he realized that we weren't going to buy anything, his whole manner changed.* **POLITE BEHAVIOUR** ▷ **4 manners** (B2) [plural] polite ways of treating other people and behaving in public: *He needs to be* ***taught*** *some manners.* ◦ *It's* ***bad*** *manners to eat with your mouth open.* ◦ *It's considered* ***good*** *manners in some societies to leave a little food on your plate.* **TYPE** ▷ **5** [U] formal a type: *Very little is known about the new candidate – what manner* ***of*** *man is he?*

IDIOMS **all manner of sth** a lot of different types: *There are all manner of architectural styles in the capital.* • **as (if) to the manner born** formal If you do something as (if) to the manner born, you do it very well and very naturally as if it is usual and easy for you. • **in a manner of speaking** formal used for saying that something is partly true: *She's his partner, in a manner of speaking.* • **not by any manner of means** UK old-fashioned not in any way: *I'm not satisfied with his excuse – not by any manner of means.*

mannered /ˈmæn.əd/ (US) /-ɚd/ **adj** disapproving describes a style of speech or behaviour that is artificial, or intended to achieve a particular effect: *His performance as Hamlet was criticized for being very mannered.*

-mannered /-mæn.əd/ (US) /-ɚd/ **suffix** describes a person with the behaviour or character of the stated type: *a* ***bad****-mannered boy* ◦ *He was a* ***mild****-mannered (= gentle and calm) young man.* ◦ *I noticed how* ***well****-mannered her children were.*

mannerism /ˈmæn.ᵊr.ɪ.zᵊm/ (US) /-ɚ-/ **noun** [C] something that a person does repeatedly with their face, hands, or voice, and that they may not realize they are doing: *He's got some very strange mannerisms.*

mannikin /ˈmæn.ɪ.kɪn/ **noun** [C] a **manikin**

M

mannish /ˈmæn.ɪʃ/ adj disapproving If you describe a woman as mannish, you mean that her appearance or behaviour are too much like a man's: *her mannish voice* ◦ *She wondered if short hair made her look a bit mannish.*

mano a mano /ˌmæn.əʊ.æˈmæn.əʊ/ Ⓤⓢ /ˌmɑː.noʊ.ɑːˈmɑː.noʊ/ noun; adv

▸**noun** [C] mainly US **1** a **bullfight** (= fight between men and male cows) in which two people each fight several BULLS **2** a competition, argument, or fight between two people: *a mano a mano between the two presidential candidates*

▸**adv** If someone goes mano a mano, they compete, argue, or fight with someone: *a loudmouthed woman* ***going*** *mano a mano with officials*

manoeuvrable UK (US **maneuverable**) /məˈnuː.vrə.bl̩/ adj easy to move and direct: *The new missile is faster and more manoeuvrable than previous models.* • **manoeuvrability** UK (US **maneuverability**) /məˌnuː.vrəˈbɪl.ɪ.ti/ Ⓤⓢ /-ə.t̬i/ noun [U] *Power-assisted steering improves a car's manoeuvrability.*

manoeuvre /məˈnuː.vəʳ/ Ⓤⓢ /-vɚ/ noun; verb

▸**noun** UK (US **maneuver**) **MOVEMENT** ▷ **1** [C] a movement or set of movements needing skill and care: *Reversing round a corner is one of the manoeuvres you are required to* ***perform*** *in a driving test.* **MILITARY OPERATION** ▷ **2** [C usually plural] a planned and controlled movement or operation by the armed forces for training purposes and in war: ***military****/naval manoeuvres* ◦ *We saw the army* ***on*** *manoeuvres in the mountains.* **CLEVER ACTION** ▷ **3** [C] a cleverly planned action that is intended to get an advantage: *A series of impressive manoeuvres by the chairman had secured a lucrative contract for the company.*

IDIOM **room for manoeuvre** the opportunity to change your plans or choose between different ways of doing something: *The law in this area is very strict and doesn't allow us much room for manoeuvre.*

▸**verb** UK (US **maneuver**) **MOVE** ▷ **1** [I or T] to turn and direct an object: *Loaded supermarket trolleys are often difficult to manoeuvre.* ◦ *This car manoeuvres well at high speed.* **MAKE SB DO STH** ▷ **2** [T] to try to make someone act in a particular way: *The other directors are trying to manoeuvre her* ***into*** *resigning.*

manoeuvring UK (US **maneuvering**) /məˈnuː.vᵊr.ɪŋ/ Ⓤⓢ /-vɚ-/ noun **CLEVER ACTION** ▷ **1** [C or U] the action of cleverly planning something to get an advantage: *He claimed he knew nothing about the political manoeuvrings which had got him into power.* **MOVEMENT** ▷ **2** [U] the action of moving, or of moving something, with skill and care: *With some careful manoeuvring, I was able to get the car into the narrow space.*

ˌman of ˈGod noun [C] (also **ˌman of the ˈcloth**) mainly humorous a priest

ˌman of ˈletters noun [C] formal a man, usually a writer, who knows a lot about literature

manometer /mænˈɒm.ɪ.təʳ/ Ⓤⓢ /məˈnɑː.mə.t̬ɚ/ noun [C] a device for measuring the pressure of gases and liquids

manor /ˈmæn.əʳ/ Ⓤⓢ /-ɚ/ noun **LARGE HOUSE** ▷ **1** [C] (also **manor house**) a large old house in the country with land belonging to it **AREA** ▷ **2** [C usually singular] UK slang the area in which a person works or which they are responsible for

manpower /ˈmæn.paʊəʳ/ Ⓤⓢ /-paʊr/ noun [U] the supply of people who are able to work: *The industry has suffered from a lack of manpower.* ◦ *manpower* ***shortages***

manqué /mɒŋˈkeɪ/ adj formal **an artist, poet, writer, etc. manqué** someone who has not had the opportunity to do a particular job, despite having the ability to do it

mansard roof /ˌmæn.sɑːdˈruːf/ Ⓤⓢ /-sɑːrd-/ noun [C] (also **mansard**) a type of roof with four sides that each have two slopes, the lower one steeper than the upper one

manservant /ˈmænˌsɜː.vᵊnt/ Ⓤⓢ /-ˌsɝː-/ noun [C] old-fashioned a male servant with responsibility for the personal needs of his employer, such as preparing his food and clothes

mansion /ˈmæn.ʃᵊn/ noun [C] **C1** a very large, expensive house: *The street is lined with enormous mansions where the rich and famous live.*

Mansions /ˈmæn.ʃᵊnz/ noun [plural] UK used in the name of some buildings that contain apartments: *Her new address is 12 Warwickshire Mansions.*

ˈman-sized adj [before noun] old-fashioned big: *man-sized tissues*

manslaughter /ˈmænˌslɔː.təʳ/ Ⓤⓢ /-ˌslɑː.t̬ɚ/ noun [U] legal the crime of killing a person when the killer did not intend to do it or cannot be responsible for his or her actions: *She was sentenced to five years' imprisonment for manslaughter.* ◦ *He denies murder but admits manslaughter on the grounds of diminished responsibility.* → Compare **murder, suicide**

manta ray /ˈmæn.təˌreɪ/ noun [C] a very large, flat sea fish with wing-shaped FINS

mantelpiece /ˈmæn.tᵊl.piːs/ Ⓤⓢ /-t̬ᵊl-/ noun [C] (US also **mantel**) a shelf above a FIREPLACE, usually part of a frame which surrounds the FIREPLACE: *She's got photographs of all her grandchildren on the mantelpiece.*

mantis /ˈmæn.tɪs/ Ⓤⓢ /-t̬ɪs/ noun [C] a **praying mantis**

mantle /ˈmæn.tl/ Ⓤⓢ /-t̬l/ noun **RESPONSIBILITY** ▷ **1** [S] formal the responsibilities of an important position or job, especially as given from the person who had the job to the person who replaces them: *She unsuccessfully attempted to* ***assume*** *the mantle of presidency.* ◦ *He has been asked to* ***take on*** *the mantle of managing director in the New York office.* **LAYER** ▷ **2** [C] literary a layer of something which covers a surface: *A thick mantle* ***of*** *snow lay on the ground.* ◦ *We watched the building vanish under a mantle* ***of*** *thick smoke as the fire swiftly moved through it.* **3** [C] specialized the part of the Earth that surrounds the central CORE **4** [C] in the past, a piece of clothing without sleeves which was worn over other clothes

ˌman-to-ˈman adj [before noun], adv describes an honest and direct conversation between two men: *a man-to-man discussion* ◦ *We* ***talked*** *man-to-man.*

mantra /ˈmæn.trə/ noun [C] **1** (especially in Hinduism and Buddhism) a word or sound that is believed to have a special spiritual power: *A personal mantra is sometimes* ***repeated*** *as an aid to meditation or prayer.* **2** a word or phrase that is often repeated and expresses a particular strong belief: *The crowds chanted that familiar football mantra: 'Here we go, here we go, here we go…'*

manual /ˈmæn.ju.əl/ adj; noun

▸**adj 1** **B2** done with the hands: *the manual sorting of letters* ◦ *She tried to cure the pain in my knee by putting manual pressure on the joint.* **2** describes a machine that is operated with the hands rather than by electricity or a motor: *He still works on an old manual typewriter.* **3** **B2** involving physical work

rather than mental work: *unskilled manual* ***labour*** ◦ *750 manual* ***workers*** *will lose their jobs as a result of company cutbacks.* ◦ *Computer-controlled robots are taking over manual* ***jobs*** *in many industries.*
▸noun [C] B2 a book which gives you practical instructions on how to do something or how to use something, such as a machine: *a DIY manual* ◦ *The computer comes with a 600-page* ***instruction*** *manual.*

ˌmanual dexˈterity noun [U] someone's ability to perform a difficult action with the hands skilfully and quickly so that it looks easy

manually /ˈmæn.ju.ə.li/ adv by hand: *Few of the machines are* ***operated*** *manually.*

ˌmanual transˈmission noun [U] If a car has manual transmission, the GEARS are changed by the driver. → Compare **automatic transmission**

manufacture /ˌmæn.jʊˈfæk.tʃəʳ/ US /-tʃɚ/ **verb; noun**
▸verb [T] **PRODUCE** ▷ **1** B2 to produce goods in large numbers, usually in a factory using machines: *He works for a company that manufactures car parts.* ◦ *The report notes a rapid decline in manufactured* ***goods.*** **INVENT** ▷ **2** to invent something, such as an excuse or story, in order to deceive someone: *She insisted that every scandalous detail of the story had been manufactured.*
▸noun [U] the process of producing goods: *Oil is used in the manufacture of a number of fabrics.* ◦ *The amount of recycled glass used in manufacture doubled in five years.*

manufacturer /ˌmæn.jʊˈfæk.tʃᵊr.əʳ/ US /-tʃɚ.ɚ/ **noun** B2 [C] a company that produces goods in large numbers: *Germany is a major manufacturer of motor cars.* ◦ *Our kettle was leaking, so we had to send it back to the manufacturers.*

manufacturing /ˌmæn.jʊˈfæk.tʃə.rɪŋ/ US /-tʃɚ-/ **noun** [U] B2 the business of producing goods in large numbers: *car manufacturing* ◦ *the manufacturing of military equipment*

manuka honey /məˌnuːkəˈhʌn.i/ **noun** [U] a type of HONEY that is thought to be good for your health, made by BEES that feed on the manuka plant in New Zealand

manure /məˈnjʊəʳ/ US /-ˈnʊr/ **noun** [U] solid waste from animals, especially horses, that is spread on the land in order to make plants grow well

manuscript /ˈmæn.jʊ.skrɪpt/ **noun** [C] **1** the original copy of a book or article before it is printed: *He sent the 400-page manuscript to his publisher.* **2** an old document or book written by hand in the times before printing was invented

Manx /mæŋks/ **adj** of the Isle of Man, the people who live there, or their language

ˌManx ˈcat noun [C] a type of cat with no tail

many /ˈmen.i/ **determiner, pronoun** A1 used mainly in negative sentences and questions to mean 'a large number of': *I don't have many clothes.* ◦ ***Not*** *many people have heard of him.* ◦ *There* ***aren't*** *very many weekends between now and Christmas.* ◦ *Were there many cars on the road?* ◦ ***How*** *many students are there in each class?* ◦ *Many people would disagree with your ideas.* ◦ *Rachel was at the party with her many admirers.* ◦ *I've met him* ***so*** *many times and I still can't remember his name!* ◦ *There are* ***too*** *many people chasing too few jobs.* ◦ *If there are only five of us going to the concert, then I've booked one too many seats.* ◦ *If there were* ***as*** *many women as there are men in parliament, the situation would be very different.* ◦ ***As*** *many* ***as*** *(= the surprisingly large number of) 6,000 people may have been infected with the disease.* ◦ *There are already twelve bottles of wine, so if I buy* ***as many again*** *(= another twelve bottles) we'll have enough.* ◦ *A* ***good/great*** *many people who voted for her in the last election will not be doing so this time.* ◦ *She'd had five children* ***in as many*** *(= in the same number of) years and decided it was enough.*

IDIOMS **in so many words** directly, or in a way that makes it very clear what you mean: *'Did he say he was unhappy with Anna?' 'Well, not in so many words but that was certainly the impression I got.'* ◦ *I told her, in so many words, to stop interfering.* • **many a time** many times: *I've told you many a time not to ride your bike on the pavement.* • **many happy returns (of the day)** said to mean 'Happy Birthday' • **many's the** used to show something has happened many times or for long periods of time: *Many's the hour I've spent by the phone just waiting in case he called.* • **one too many** informal If you have had one too many, you have drunk too much alcohol.

ˌmany-ˈsided adj [before noun] having many sides or a lot of different features or characteristics: *a many-sided object* ◦ *A many-sided character, he wrote poetry and was a keen cricketer and cook.*

Maoism /ˈmaʊ.ɪ.zᵊm/ **noun** [U] the type of COMMUNISM introduced in China by Mao Zedong • **Maoist** /-ɪst/ **noun** [C], **adj**

Maori /ˈmaʊ.ri/ **noun; adj**
▸noun [C] (plural **Maori** or **Maoris**) one of the original people of New Zealand and the Cook Islands: *The Maori arrived in New Zealand from Polynesia over 1,000 years before the Europeans.*
▸adj related to the culture, people, or language of the Maori: *The Maori language is now officially encouraged.* ◦ *Before a rugby match the New Zealand team perform a Maori war dance.*

map /mæp/ **noun; verb**
▸noun [C] **1** A2 a drawing of the Earth's surface, or part of that surface, showing the shape and position of different countries, political borders, natural features such as rivers and mountains, and artificial features such as roads and buildings: *a map* ***of*** *the world* ◦ *a map of Paris* ◦ *a* ***road*** *map* ◦ *We need a large-scale map showing all the footpaths that we can walk along.* ◦ *I'm hopeless at map* ***reading*** *(= understanding maps).* **2** something which shows the position of stars in the sky or the features on the surface of planets: *a celestial map* ◦ *a map of Mars* **3** a very simple plan which shows a direction of travel between one place and another: *I'll* ***draw*** *you a quick map if you're worried about finding the hotel.*

IDIOMS **blow, bomb, wipe, etc. sth off the map** to destroy a place or thing completely, especially with bombs • **put sth/sb on the map** to make a thing, person, or place famous: *The governor has managed to put this sleepy southern state in America on the map.*

▸verb [T] (-pp-) to represent an area of land in the form of a map: *Parts of the mountainous region in the north of the country have still not been mapped.*

PHRASAL VERB **map sth out** to plan something in detail: *The government has issued a new document mapping out its policies on education.* ◦ *His future is all mapped out ahead of him.*

maple /ˈmeɪ.pl̩/ **noun** [C or U] a type of large tree which grows in northern areas of the world, or the wood of this tree: *a maple* ***leaf*** ◦ *maple trees*

ˌmaple ˈsyrup noun [U] a thick, sweet liquid produced from the maple tree, eaten with or used in making food: *pancakes with maple syrup*

M

mar /mɑːʳ/ (US) /mɑːr/ **verb** [T] **(-rr-)** formal to spoil something, making it less good or less enjoyable: *Sadly, the text is marred by careless errors.* ◦ *It was a really nice day, marred* ***only*** *by a little argument in the car on the way home.* ◦ *I hope the fact that Louise isn't coming won't mar* ***your enjoyment of*** *the evening.*

maracas /məˈræk.əz/ **noun** [plural] a musical instrument consisting of two hollow containers filled with beans or small stones. They are shaken to provide the rhythm for some types of music.

maracas

maraschino /ˌmær.əˈskiː.nəʊ/, /-ˈʃiː-/ (US) /-noʊ/ **noun** [U] slightly bitter LIQUEUR made from a particular type of CHERRY

ˌmaraˌschino ˈcherry **noun** [C usually plural] a CHERRY that is preserved in maraschino or a similar drink and used to decorate drinks and food

marathon /ˈmær.ə.θən/ (US) /-θɑːn/ **noun; adj**

▸**noun** [C] **RACE** ▷ **1** B2 a running race of slightly over 26 miles (42.195 kilometres): *the London/New York marathon* ◦ *She* ***did/ran*** *her first marathon in just under three hours.* **LONG ACTIVITY** ▷ **2** an activity which takes a long time and makes you very tired: *The election broadcast, a nine-hour marathon, lasts until seven o'clock in the morning.*

▸**adj** [before noun] **RACE** ▷ **1** related to marathons (= running races): *a marathon* ***runner*** **LONG TIME** ▷ **2** describes something which takes a very long time and makes you very tired: *I had a marathon* ***session*** *marking 55 exam papers yesterday.*

marauder /məˈrɔː.dəʳ/ (US) /-ˈrɑː.dɚ/ **noun** [C] a person or animal that goes from one place to another looking for people to kill or things to steal or destroy

marauding /məˈrɔː.dɪŋ/ (US) /-ˈrɑː-/ **adj** [before noun] going from one place to another killing or using violence, stealing, and destroying: *Witnesses reported gangs of marauding soldiers breaking into people's houses and setting fire to them.*

marble /ˈmɑː.bl̩/ (US) /ˈmɑːr-/ **noun** **ROCK** ▷ **1** [U] a type of very hard rock that has a pattern of lines going through it, feels cold, and can be POLISHED to become smooth and shiny: *a marble* ***floor/statue*** **GLASS BALL** ▷ **2** [C] a small ball, usually made of coloured or transparent glass, that is used in children's games **3 marbles** [U] a children's game in which small, round glass balls are rolled along the floor

marbled /ˈmɑː.bl̩d/ (US) /ˈmɑːr-/ **adj** decorated with a delicate pattern consisting of lines and areas of colour: *The church has an ornate black and white marbled interior.* ◦ *The plant has green leaves marbled* ***with*** *brownish-purple.* ◦ *The steak was just how he liked – pink, juicy, and marbled* ***with*** *fat.*

marcasite /ˈmɑː.kə.saɪt/ (US) /ˈmɑːr-/ **noun** [U] a mineral that can be cut and made to look like PRECIOUS STONES and is used to make jewellery

march /mɑːtʃ/ (US) /mɑːrtʃ/ **noun; verb**

▸**noun** **PUBLIC EVENT** ▷ **1** C1 [C] an event in which a large number of people walk through a public place to express their support for something, or their disagreement with or disapproval of something: *She's* ***going on*** *a march on Saturday in protest over the closure of the hospital.* **MUSIC** ▷ **2** [C] a piece of music with a strong, regular beat, written for marching to: *a funeral march* ◦ *Mendelssohn's Wedding March* **SOLDIERS' WALK** ▷ **3** [C or U] a walk, especially by a group of soldiers all walking with the same movement and speed: *It had been a long march and the soldiers were weary.* ◦ *The border was within a day's march (= distance measured in time taken to walk it).* **4 on the march** If soldiers are on the march, they have started marching to a place. **CONTINUOUS DEVELOPMENT** ▷ **5** [S] the continuous development of a state, activity. or idea: *It is impossible to stop the forward march of progress/time.* ◦ *The island is being destroyed by the relentless march of tourism.*

▸**verb** **WALK** ▷ **1** C2 [I] to walk somewhere quickly and in a determined way, often because you are angry: *She marched into my office demanding to know why I hadn't written my report.* **2** C1 [I] to walk through a public place as part of a public event to express support for something, or disagreement with or disapproval of something: *Over four thousand people marched through London today to protest against the proposed new law.* **3** C1 [I or T] to walk with regular steps keeping the body stiff, usually in a formal group of people who are all walking in the same way: *The band marched through the streets.* ◦ *The soldiers marched 90 miles in three days.* **TAKE FORCEFULLY** ▷ **4** [T + adv/prep] to forcefully make someone go somewhere by taking hold of them and pulling them there or going there with them: *Without saying a word, she took hold of my arm and marched me* ***off*** *to the headmaster's office.* ◦ *The police marched a gang of youths* ***out of*** *the building.* → See also **frogmarch**

IDIOM **quick march!** an order given to soldiers to make them start marching

March /mɑːtʃ/ (US) /mɑːrtʃ/ **noun** [C or U] (written abbreviation **Mar.**) A1 the third month of the year, after February and before April: *The next meeting will be* ***in*** *March.* ◦ *He left* ***on*** *26 March.* ◦ *She is retiring* ***next*** *March.*

marcher /ˈmɑː.tʃəʳ/ (US) /ˈmɑːr.tʃɚ/ **noun** [C] a person marching through a public place as part of a public event: *The marchers stopped outside the American embassy, chanting slogans and waving banners.*

ˈmarching ˌorders **noun** [plural] (US usually **ˈwalking ˌpapers**) If you give someone their marching orders, you ask them to leave a place or a job because they have done something wrong: *She was called into the boss's office and* ***given*** *her marching orders.*

ˈmarch-past **noun** [C usually singular] a march of the armed forces past an officer of high rank or a king or queen

Mardi Gras /ˌmɑː.diˈgrɑː/ (US) /ˌmɑːr-/ **noun** [C usually singular] the day before the beginning of LENT, celebrated in some countries with a lot of music, colourful COSTUMES, and dancing in the streets → Compare **Shrove Tuesday**

mare /meəʳ/ (US) /mer/ **noun** [C] an adult female horse → Compare **stallion**

margarine /ˌmɑː.dʒəˈriːn/ (US) /ˈmɑːr.dʒɚ-/ **noun** [U] (UK informal **marge**) a food used for cooking and spreading on bread, similar to butter but softer and usually made from vegetable fat

margarita /ˌmɑː.gəʳˈiː.tə/ (US) /-gəˈriː.t̬ə/ **noun** [C] a type of alcoholic drink: *A margarita is made with tequila, an orange liqueur, and lime or lemon juice.*

margin /ˈmɑː.dʒɪn/ (US) /ˈmɑːr-/ **noun** **DIFFERENCE** ▷ **1** C2 [C] the amount by which one thing is different from another: *The Senate approved the use of military force by a margin of 52 votes to 47.* ◦ *The poll shows that the government is leading by the* ***narrowest*** *of margins.* **PROFIT** ▷ **2** C2 [C or U] the profit made on a product or service: *Our increased profits are due to* ***improved*** *margins and successful cost control.* ◦ *Using cheap labour increases* ***profit*** *margin.* **OUTER PART** ▷ **3** C2

[C] the empty space to the side of the text on a page, sometimes separated from the rest of the page by a vertical line: *If I have any comments to make, I'll write them* ***in*** *the margin.* **4** [C] the outer edge of an area: *The plant tends to grow in the lighter margins of woodland areas.* **5 on the margins of sth** If someone is on the margins of a group of people, they are part of that group, but different in important ways, and if someone is on the margins of an activity, they are only slightly involved: *The government needs to reach out to those on the margins of* ***society****.* **POSSIBILITY** ▷ **6** [C or U] something that makes a particular thing possible, such as an extra amount of money, time, etc. allowed which makes it possible to deal with an emergency: *There is not much margin* ***for*** *creativity in a job like this.* ◦ *They allow an additional* ***safety*** *margin of five minutes between planes taking off.*

marginal /ˈmɑː.dʒɪ.nəl/ (US) /ˈmɑːr-/ **adj; noun**
▸**adj SMALL** ▷ **1** (C2) very small in amount or effect: *The report suggests that there has only been a marginal improvement in women's pay over the past few years.* **2 of marginal interest** of interest to only a few people: *programmes about subjects of marginal interest* **POLITICS** ▷ **3** describes a political area or position in parliament that can be won by only a small number of votes because support for the main parties is equally divided among the people voting: *The marginal Tory* ***constituency*** *was held by 2,200 votes.*
▸**noun** [C] UK a marginal political area or position in parliament: *Labour lost two of the* ***key*** *marginals in London.* ◦ *The minister's own seat is a Tory marginal.*

marginalize (UK usually **marginalise**) /ˈmɑː.dʒɪ.nə.laɪz/ (US) /ˈmɑːr-/ **verb** [T often passive] to treat someone or something as if they are not important: *Now that English has taken over as the main language, the country's native language has been marginalized.* • **marginalization** (UK usually **marginalisation**) /ˌmɑː.dʒɪ.nə.laɪˈzeɪ.ʃᵊn/ (US) /ˌmɑːr.dʒɪ.nə.lə-/ **noun** [U] *The marginalization* ***of*** *certain groups within the community may lead to social unrest.*

ˌ**marginal** ˈ**land** **noun** [U] land that is found on the edge of CULTIVATED areas and is often difficult to grow crops on

marginally /ˈmɑː.dʒɪ.nə.li/ (US) /ˈmɑːr-/ **adv** slightly: *marginally more expensive*

ˌ**margin of** ˈ**error** **noun** [C] (C2) an extra amount of something, such as time or money, which you allow because there might be a mistake in your calculations: *When archaeologists date objects that are thousands of years old, they allow a margin of error of several hundred years.* ◦ *The government estimates that its borrowing requirement this year could reach £150 billion, subject to a* ***wide*** *margin of error.*

marigold /ˈmær.ɪ.gəʊld/ (US) /-goʊld/ **noun** [C] a plant with bright yellow or orange flowers

marijuana (also **marihuana**) /ˌmær.əˈwɑː.nə/ **noun** [U] a usually illegal drug made from the dried leaves and flowers of the HEMP plant, which produces a pleasant feeling of being relaxed if smoked or eaten

marimba /məˈrɪm.bə/ **noun** [C] specialized an instrument like a XYLOPHONE but with a lower sound, having a row of wooden bars fixed along a frame that you hit with sticks

marina /məˈriː.nə/ **noun** [C] a small port that is used for pleasure rather than trade, often with hotels, restaurants, and bars

marinade /ˌmær.ɪˈneɪd/ **noun** [C] a mixture, usually containing oil, wine or VINEGAR, and herbs and spices, which you pour over fish or meat before it is cooked, in order to add flavour to it or make it TENDER: *Pour the marinade over the beef and leave it for 24 hours.*
• **marinate** /-neɪt/ **verb** [T] to pour a marinade over meat or fish: *Marinate the chicken in white wine for a couple of hours before frying.*

marine /məˈriːn/ **adj; noun**
▸**adj** [before noun] related to the sea or sea transport: *The oil slick seriously threatens marine* ***life*** *around the islands.* ◦ *The Central harbour area will be closed to all marine traffic from 3.45 p.m. to 4.30 p.m.* → See also **maritime**
▸**noun** [C] a soldier who works closely with the navy and is trained especially for military operations on land which begin from the sea

the ˈ**Marine** ˌ**Corps** **noun** [+ sing/pl verb] a part of the US military forces that consists of soldiers who operate on land and at sea

mariner /ˈmær.ɪ.nəʳ/ (US) /-nɚ/ **noun** [C] literary or old-fashioned a sailor: *Many a mariner lost his life on these rocks.*

Marines /məˈriːnz/ **noun** [plural] a part of a country's military forces which takes part especially in operations on land which begin from the sea: *He's in* ***the*** *Royal Marines.*

IDIOM **tell that/it to the Marines!** US saying said when you do not believe something

marionette /ˌmær.i.əˈnet/ **noun** [C] a small model of a person or animal with parts of the body that are moved with strings

marital /ˈmær.ɪ.tᵊl/ (US) /-t̬ᵊl/ **adj** formal connected with marriage: *They've been having marital* ***problems****, apparently.* ◦ humorous *You can't expect to live in a state of marital* ***bliss****.* ◦ *marital* ***breakdown***

ˌ**marital** ˈ**aid** **noun** [C] old-fashioned for **sex toy**

ˌ**marital** ˈ**status** **noun** [U] the fact of someone being married or not: *Could I ask you about your marital status?*

maritime /ˈmær.ɪ.taɪm/ **adj** formal **1** connected with human activity at sea: *Amalfi and Venice were important maritime powers.* ◦ *Make sure you visit the maritime* ***museum*** *if you're interested in anything to do with ships or seafaring.* **2** near the sea or coast: *The temperature change in winter is less pronounced in maritime areas.*

marjoram /ˈmɑː.dʒᵊr.əm/ (US) /ˈmɑːr.dʒɚ-/ **noun** [U] a sweet Mediterranean herb used to flavour food

mark /mɑːk/ (US) /mɑːrk/ **noun; verb**
▸**noun DIFFERENT AREA** ▷ **1** (B2) [C] a small area on the surface of something that is damaged, dirty, or different in some way: *There were* ***dirty*** *marks on her trousers where she had wiped her hands.* ◦ *His fingers had* ***left*** *marks on the table's polished surface.* ◦ *She had a red mark on her arm where she'd burned herself.* **2** [C] a typical feature or one that allows you to recognize someone or something: *Did your attacker have any* ***distinguishing*** *marks, such as a scar or a birthmark?* ◦ *You can tell which puppy is which from the marks (also* ***markings****) on their fur.* **SYMBOL** ▷ **3** (C1) [C] a symbol that is used for giving information: *I've put a mark on the map where I think we should go for a picnic.* ◦ *What do those marks in the middle of the road mean?* **4** [C] a written or printed symbol: *a question mark* ◦ *an exclamation mark* ◦ *punctuation marks* **FOR SCHOOL WORK** ▷ **5** (A2) [C] mainly UK a judgment, expressed as a number or letter, about the quality of a piece of work done at school, college, or university: *What mark did you* ***get*** *in the biology exam?* ◦ *Matilda's had very* ***good*** *marks in/for English throughout the year.* ◦ UK *You scored* ***full*** *marks in the test – ten out of ten!* **LEVEL** ▷ **6** [S] the level intended or wanted: *Sales have*

M

already **passed** the million mark. **REPRESENTATION** ▷ **7** Ⓒ2 [C] an action that is understood to represent or show a characteristic of a person or thing or feeling: *He took off his hat as a mark* ***of respect*** *for her dead husband.* ◦ *It's the mark* ***of*** *a gentleman to stand up when someone enters the room.* ◦ *I'd like to give this bottle of wine as a mark* ***of*** *appreciation for all the work you've done for us.* **MONEY** ▷ **8** [C] a **Deutschmark**

> **Other ways of saying mark**
>
> If a dirty mark is difficult to remove, you could use the word **stain**:
>
> *She had grass* ***stains*** *on her white jeans.*
>
> **Smear** or **smudge** can be used for marks which look like someone has rubbed something dirty on a surface:
>
> *He had* ***smears*** *of tomato ketchup on his shirt.*
>
> A mark which has an irregular shape, especially on someone's skin, is often called a **blotch**:
>
> *He had* ***blotches*** *all over his face.*
>
> A very small mark can be called a **speck** or **fleck**:
>
> *There were a few* ***specks/flecks*** *of paint on the window.*
>
> **Spot** can be used for a mark which is round:
>
> *He had some grease* ***spots*** *on his tie.*
>
> **Streak** can be used for long thin marks:
>
> *There was a* ***streak*** *of dirt on her arm.*
>
> If a mark has been made by blood, you could use the word **bloodstain**:
>
> ***Bloodstains*** *are difficult to get out of fabric.*

M

IDIOMS **be off the mark** If something someone says or writes is off the mark, it is not correct: *His criticisms are* ***way*** *off the mark.* ◦ *Bedini and Curzi were probably* ***not far*** *off the mark in their analysis.* • **be quick/slow off the mark** to be quick/slow to act or react to an event or a situation: *The police were certainly quick off the mark reaching the scene of the accident.* • **be up to the mark** to be good enough: *Her latest batch of work just isn't up to the mark.* • **leave your/its mark on sb/sth** Ⓒ2 to have an effect that changes someone or something, usually in a bad way: *The experience had left its mark on her.* • **make a/your mark (on sth)** Ⓒ2 to have an important effect on something: *Daniel didn't work here for very long, but he definitely made his mark on the place.* • **on your marks, get set, go!** (US also **on your mark, get set, go**) something called out to competitors at the beginning of a running race

▸verb **PIECE OF WORK** ▷ **1** Ⓑ2 [T] to correct mistakes in and give points for a piece of work: *I was up half the night marking* ***exam papers.*** ◦ UK *You'll be marked* ***down*** *(= given a lower mark) for poor spelling and punctuation.* **DAMAGE/MAKE DIRTY** ▷ **2** Ⓒ1 [I or T] to make a mark on something or someone: *Make sure you don't mark the paintwork while you're moving the furniture around.* ◦ *A dark carpet won't mark as easily as a light one.* **REPRESENT** ▷ **3** [T] to represent or show a characteristic of a person or thing or feeling: *The band's songs have always been marked by controversial lyrics.* ◦ *The signing of the treaty marked a major milestone on the road to European union.* **4** [T] to show respect for or COMMEMORATE: *Tomorrow's parade will mark the 50th* ***anniversary*** *of the battle.* **INDICATE** ▷ **5** Ⓑ2 [T] to show where something is by drawing or putting something somewhere: *I've marked the route around the one-way system on the town plan.* ◦ *I'd like everyone to mark their progress on the chart every week.* ◦ *X marks* ***the spot*** *where the treasure is buried.* **SPORT** ▷ **6** [T] UK (US **cover**) to prevent a member of the opposing team from taking control of the ball by staying close to them all the time

IDIOMS **be marked out as sth** UK (US **be marked as sth**) to be shown to be different because of a certain characteristic: *I can't speak a word of French so I'm marked out as a foreigner as soon as I arrive in France.* • **(you) mark my words!** old-fashioned something that you say when you tell someone about something that you are certain will happen in the future: *He'll cause trouble – you mark my words!* • **mark time 1** to march in one place without moving forward **2** to do little while waiting for something that is going to happen: *She's just marking time until she goes off to university.*

PHRASAL VERBS **mark sth down** **REDUCE** ▷ **1** to reduce the price of something, usually in order to encourage people to buy it: *Low consumer demand has forced us to mark down a wide range of goods, sometimes* ***by*** *as much as 30 percent.* ◦ *Shares in the electricity companies were marked down following the announcement of the new energy tax.* **RECORD** ▷ **2** to write something on a piece of paper in order to make a record of it: *I've marked down the number of each item sold.* ◦ *Look carefully at these questions and mark your answers down in the right-hand column.* • **mark sb down as sth** to consider someone as a particular type of person: *I'd marked her down* ***as*** *a Labour Party supporter, but I was completely wrong.* • **mark sth/sb off** If you mark off things or people that are on a list, you record that you have dealt with them: *As I complete each task I mark it off.* • **mark sth off** to separate an area by putting something around it: *Police had marked off* ***the area*** *where the body was found.* • **mark sth out** to show the shape or position of something by drawing a line around it: *He'd marked out a volleyball court on the beach with a stick.* • **mark sth up** to increase the price of something: *They buy paintings at auctions, mark them up, and then resell them at a vast profit to collectors.* ◦ *In the days of hyperinflation, we would rush to the market as soon as we were paid and buy our weekly groceries before they were marked up.* ◦ *Shares in retail businesses were marked up on the news that consumer spending rose last month.*

Mark /mɑːk/ Ⓤⓢ /mɑːrk/ **noun 1** used before a number to describe a particular version of a machine, especially one that is an improvement on the original version: *The car has enjoyed modest success since its launch, but the Mark 2 version is expected to be far more popular.* **2** used before a number to show what temperature you should use for cooking something in a gas oven: *Cook at Mark 5 for 20 minutes.*

markdown /ˈmɑːk.daʊn/ Ⓤⓢ /ˈmɑːrk-/ **noun** [C] a reduction in the price of something: *We're offering a ten percent markdown on selected items.*

marked /mɑːkt/ Ⓤⓢ /mɑːrkt/ **adj** describes a change or difference in behaviour or in a situation that is very obvious or noticeable: *There was a marked* ***improvement*** *in my health when I gave up smoking.* ◦ *Unemployment has fallen again, although the change is less marked than last month.* ◦ *The president spoke with passion for an hour,* ***in*** *marked* ***contrast*** *to his subdued address to the parliament yesterday.* • **markedly** /ˈmɑː.kɪd.li/ Ⓤⓢ /ˈmɑːr-/ **adv** *Eye-witness accounts of the fighting* ***differ*** *markedly from police reports of what happened.*

ˌmarked ˈman/ˈwoman **noun** [C usually singular] someone who is at risk of being harmed by someone: *He is still free to travel the world, but he knows that he is a marked man.*

marker /ˈmɑː.kəʳ/ Ⓤⓢ /ˈmɑːr.kɚ/ **noun** [C] **SYMBOL** ▷ **1** a sign which shows where something is: *I've put in* *some markers where I planted the seeds.* **PEN** ▷ **2** (also **marker pen**) a thick pen for writing or drawing

market /ˈmɑː.kɪt/ (US) /ˈmɑːr-/ **noun; verb**

▸**noun** [C] **BUYING AND SELLING** ▷ **1** (C1) the people who might want to buy something, or a part of the world where something is sold: *Are you sure there's a market **for** the product?* ◦ *We estimate the potential market **for** the new phones to be around one million people in this country alone.* ◦ *The **domestic** market is still depressed, but demand abroad is picking up.* ◦ *They've increased their **share of** the market by ten percent over the past year.* **2** (C2) the business or trade in a particular product, including financial products: *the coffee market* ◦ *the economic market* ◦ *the **commodities** market* ◦ *the **stock** market* ◦ *the **job** market* ◦ *the **housing** market* **3 in the market for sth** interested in buying something: *Thanks for the offer, but I'm not in the market for another car at the moment.* **4 on the market** available for sale: *We **put** our house on the market as soon as house prices started to rise.* ◦ *This is one of the best televisions on the market.* ◦ *The pictures would sell for half a million on the **open** market (= if offered for sale without a fixed price).* **PLACE** ▷ **5** (A2) a place or event at which people meet in order to buy and sell things: *Fruit and vegetables are much cheaper from/**in/on** the market than in the supermarket.* ◦ *She runs a stall in/on the market.* ◦ *The **indoor** flower market is a big tourist attraction.* ◦ *a craft market* ◦ *The town's always busy on market **day**.* → See also **marketplace** **SHOP** ▷ **6** US a shop that sells mainly food → See also **hypermarket, supermarket**

▸**verb** [T] to make goods available to buyers in a planned way which encourages people to buy more of them, for example by advertising: *Their products are very cleverly marketed.* • **marketer** /-kɪ.təʳ/ (US) /-kɪ.t̬ɚ/ **noun** [C]

marketable /ˈmɑː.kɪ.tə.bl̩/ (US) /ˈmɑːr.kɪ.t̬ə-/ **adj** Marketable products or skills are easy to sell because a lot of people want them: *This is a highly marketable product.* • **marketability** /ˌmɑː.kɪ.təˈbɪl.ɪ.ti/ (US) /ˌmɑːr.kɪ.t̬əˈbɪl.ə.t̬i/ **noun** [U]

marketeer /ˌmɑː.kɪˈtɪəʳ/ (US) /ˌmɑːr.kəˈtɪr/ **noun** [C] someone who works in or supports a particular market system: *Under the old regime **black** marketeers would buy almost anything from Western tourists and resell it at an enormous profit.* ◦ ***Free** marketeers are vehemently opposed to the new safety regulations.*

ˌmarket ˈforces **noun** [plural] the forces that decide price levels in an economy or trading system whose activities are not influenced or limited by government: *The action of market forces means that the cost of something rises if demand for it rises and the amount available remains constant.*

ˌmarket ˈgarden **noun** [C] UK (US **ˈtruck ˌfarm**) a small farm where fruit and vegetables are grown for selling to the public • **ˌmarket ˈgardener** **noun** [C] (US **truck farmer**) *Farmers and market gardeners have been badly affected by the drought.* • **ˌmarket ˈgardening** **noun** [U] (US **truck farming**)

marketing /ˈmɑː.kɪ.tɪŋ/ (US) /ˈmɑːr.kɪ.t̬ɪŋ/ **noun** [U] **JOB** ▷ **1** (B2) a job that involves encouraging people to buy a product or service: *a career in marketing* ◦ *Our marketing people have come up with a great idea for the launch of the new model.* **SHOPPING** ▷ **2** US or Indian English shopping: *We like to get the marketing done on Thursdays so we can have the weekend free.*

marketplace /ˈmɑː.kɪt.pleɪs/ (US) /ˈmɑːr-/ **noun** [C] **PLACE** ▷ **1** a small outside area in a town where there is a market: *I'll meet you in the marketplace next to the fountain.* **BUSINESS CONDITIONS** ▷ **2** a set of trading conditions or the business environment: *To remain competitive the company has to be able to adapt to the **changing** marketplace.* ◦ *It's essential that we maintain our position **in** the marketplace (= keep our share of business activity).*

ˌmarket ˈprice **noun** [S] a price that is likely to be paid for something: *They're asking £400,000 for their flat, but the market price is nearer £350,000.*

ˌmarket reˈsearch **noun** [U] the collection and examination of information about things that people buy or might buy and their feelings about things that they have bought: *Market research shows that demand for small cars will continue to grow.* • **ˌmarket reˈsearcher** **noun** [C] someone whose job is doing market research

ˈmarket ˌshare **noun** [U] the number of things that a company sells compared with the number of things of the same type that other companies sell: *The company has **increased** its market share.*

ˈmarket ˌtown **noun** [C] a small town in the countryside that has a regular market and acts as a business centre for surrounding farms and villages

marking /ˈmɑː.kɪŋ/ (US) /ˈmɑːr-/ **noun** [C usually plural] a mark which makes it possible to recognize something: *There are a couple of fish with blue markings, and a few more with gold stripes down the side.* ◦ *The army said the relief flight would be too dangerous as none of its helicopters had Red Cross markings.*

markka /ˈmɑː.kɑː/ (US) /ˈmɑːr-/ **noun** [C] the standard unit of money used in Finland before the introduction of the euro

marksman /ˈmɑːks.mən/ (US) /ˈmɑːrks-/ **noun** [C] (plural **-men** /-mən/) someone who can shoot a gun very accurately: ***Police** marksmen were called to the scene.*

marksmanship /ˈmɑːks.mən.ʃɪp/ (US) /ˈmɑːrks-/ **noun** [U] skill in shooting

markup /ˈmɑːk.ʌp/ (US) /ˈmɑːrk-/ **noun** [C] the amount by which the price of something is increased before it is sold again: *The usual markup **on** clothes is about 20 percent.*

marmalade /ˈmɑː.mə.leɪd/ (US) /ˈmɑːr-/ **noun** [U] a soft substance with a sweet but slightly bitter taste, made by cooking fruit such as oranges with sugar to preserve it. It is eaten on bread, usually for breakfast.

marmoset /ˈmɑː.mə.set/ (US) /ˈmɑːr-/ **noun** [C] a very small monkey from the tropical forests of South and Central America that has large eyes, thick fur, a long tail covered in hair, and long nails

maroon /məˈruːn/ **noun** [U] a dark reddish-purple colour • **maroon adj** of a dark reddish-purple colour

marooned /məˈruːnd/ **adj** left in a place from which you cannot escape: *What would you miss most if you found yourself marooned on a desert island?* ◦ *The police are advising motorists marooned by the blizzards to stay in their cars until the rescue services can reach them.* • **maroon** /-ˈruːn/ **verb** [T]

marque /mɑːk/ (US) /mɑːrk/ **noun** [C] a name of a range of cars that is sometimes different from the name of the company that produces them

marquee /mɑːˈkiː/ (US) /mɑːr-/ **noun; adj**

▸**noun** [C] **TENT** ▷ **1** UK a large tent used for eating and drinking in at events held mainly outside that involve a lot of people: *We're planning to hold the wedding reception in a marquee in the garden.* **ROOF** ▷ **2** US a roof-like structure which sticks out over the entrance to a public building, especially a theatre, and on which there is usually a sign

▸**adj** [before noun] US being the main performer or

M

sports person in a show, film, sports event, etc. or being the performer, etc. whose name will attract most people to the show, film, etc.: *The studio chiefs wanted a marquee **name** in the lead role, not some unknown.*

marquetry /ˈmɑː.kɪ.tri/ (US) /ˈmɑːr-/ **noun** [U] a decorative pattern on a piece of furniture which consists of thin sheets of very shiny wood of different colours fixed on the surface of the furniture

marquis (also **marquess**) /ˈmɑː.kwɪs/ (US) /ˈmɑːr-/ **noun** [C] (the title of) a British man of high social rank, between a DUKE and an EARL: ***the** Marquis **of** Blandford*

marriage /ˈmær.ɪdʒ/ (US) /ˈmer-/ **noun** **TWO PEOPLE** ▷ **1** (B1) [C or U] a legally accepted relationship between two people in which they live together, or the official ceremony that results in this: *They had a long and **happy** marriage.* ◦ *She went to live abroad after the break-up of her marriage.* ◦ *She has two daughters by her first marriage.* ◦ *the marriage ceremony* **2 marriage of convenience** a marriage in which the partners have married, not because they love each other, but in order to get an advantage, such as the right to live in the other partner's country **COMBINATION** ▷ **3** [C] a combination of two or more things: *His music is a marriage **of** jazz, blues, and pop.*

marriageable /ˈmær.ɪ.dʒə.bl/ (US) /ˈmer-/ **adj** old-fashioned suitable for marriage: *a wealthy man of marriageable age*

ˈmarriage ˌbureau **noun** [C] UK old-fashioned an organization that people join in order to find a partner, usually one that they can get married to

ˈmarriage cerˌtificate **noun** [C] the document that shows two people are legally married

ˌmarriage ˈguidance **noun** [U] UK (US **ˈmarriage ˌcounseling**) advice given by a trained person to people who are trying to find solutions to problems with their marriage: *a marriage guidance **counsellor***

married /ˈmær.id/ (US) /ˈmer-/ **adj** **1** (A2) having a wife or husband: *a married **couple*** ◦ *We've been **happily** married for five years.* ◦ *Please state whether you are single, cohabiting, married, separated, divorced or widowed.* ◦ *PC Smith was married with two children.* ◦ *So how are you enjoying married **life**?* ◦ *She had an affair with a married **man**.* ◦ *The survey reveals that two-thirds of married **women** earn less than their husbands.* ◦ *So how long have you been married **to** Nicky?* ◦ figurative *Rachel seems to be married **to** (= very involved with) her new job at the moment, so we hardly ever see her.* **2 get married** (A2) to begin a legal relationship with someone as their husband or wife: *When are you getting married?* ◦ *Chris and Debbie got married last summer.* ◦ *Jamie's getting married **to** Laura.*

ˈmarried ˌname **noun** [C usually singular] A woman's married name is the family name she takes after getting married: *She used to be Rachel Elliot – I think her married name is Cartwright.*

marrow /ˈmær.əʊ/ (US) /-oʊ/ **noun** **TISSUE** ▷ **1** [U] (also **bone marrow**) soft tissue containing a lot of fat in the centre of a bone **VEGETABLE** ▷ **2** [C or U] UK (mainly US **squash**) a long round vegetable with a thick green or yellow skin, white flesh, and a lot of seeds at its centre

IDIOM **be chilled/frozen to the marrow** mainly UK to be extremely cold

marrowbone /ˈmær.əʊ.bəʊn/ **noun** [C] a bone containing marrow that can be eaten, used in cooking, for example to flavour soups

marrowfat pea /ˌmær.əʊ.fæt'piː/ (US) /-oʊ-/ **noun** [C] a large PEA (= a round, green seed that is eaten as a vegetable)

marry /ˈmær.i/ (US) /ˈmer-/ **verb** **MAN AND WOMAN** ▷ **1** (B1) [I or T] to become the legally accepted husband or wife of someone in an official or religious ceremony: *Men tend to marry later than women.* ◦ *Paul married Lucy four years ago.* ◦ *They don't have any plans to marry at present.* **2** [T] to perform the ceremony of marriage as a priest or official: *The couple were married by the Archbishop of Canterbury.* **COMBINE** ▷ **3** to combine two different qualities: *a design which marries fun **with** function*

IDIOMS **marry beneath you** to marry someone people think is not good enough for you because he or she is from a lower social class • **not be the marrying kind** humorous If a man is not the marrying kind, he does not want to be married. People sometimes use this phrase to mean that the man is gay.

PHRASAL VERBS **marry sb off** to make certain that someone, especially a female member of your family, gets married, or that they marry the person you have chosen: *She was married off **to** the local doctor by the age of 16.* • **marry up (sth)** If two things marry up or if you marry them up, they match or join together: *We need to marry up the names on your list with those on my list and see what the overlap is.*

Mars /mɑːz/ (US) /mɑːrz/ **noun** [S] the planet fourth in order of distance from the Sun, after the Earth and before Jupiter: *Mars is sometimes called the Red Planet because of its distinctive colour.* ◦ *So is there **life on** Mars?* • **Martian** /ˈmɑː.ʃən/ (US) /ˈmɑːr-/ **adj**

Marsala /mɑːˈsɑː.lə/ (US) /mɑːrˈsɑː.lɑː/ **noun** [U] a strong, dark wine that is drunk when eating sweet dishes and is used in cooking

marsh /mɑːʃ/ (US) /mɑːrʃ/ **noun** **1** [C or U] ground near a lake, a river, or the sea that often floods and is always wet: *At the mouth of the river is a large area of marsh.* **2 marshes** [plural] a large area of marsh: *At low tide in the estuary, cows graze on the marshes.*

marshal /ˈmɑː.ʃəl/ (US) /ˈmɑːr-/ **verb; noun**

▸**verb** [T] (-**ll**- or US usually -**l**-) to bring together or organize people or things in order to achieve a particular aim: *The fighting in the city followed reports of the rebels marshalling their **forces** in the countryside.* ◦ *The company is marshalling its **forces/resources** for a long court case.* ◦ *They had marshalled an armada of 1,000 boats to help clear up the oil.* ◦ *It is unlikely that the rebels will be able to marshal as much firepower as the government troops.*

▸**noun** [C] **OFFICIAL** ▷ **1** an official who is involved in the organization of a public event: *Marshals struggled in vain to prevent spectators rushing onto the racetrack.* ◦ US *The parade's **grand** marshal (= the person leading it) carried an elaborately carved staff.* **LAW** ▷ **2** US a government official who is responsible for putting the decisions of a law court into action: *US marshals specialize in finding fugitives and escapees.* **OFFICER** ▷ **3** (also **Marshal**) a title used for important officers in the armed forces of some countries: *a **field** marshal/ **air vice** marshal* ◦ *Marshal Pétain* ◦ [as form of address] *Yes, Marshal.* **4** (also **Marshal**) a title used for police or fire officers in some parts of the US: [as form of address] *Thank you, Marshal.*

ˌMarshal of the ˌRoyal ˈAir ˌForce **noun** [C] the highest rank in the British air force

ˈmarsh ˌgas **noun** [U] a gas produced in a MARSH (= an area of very wet ground) by decaying plants that are covered by water

marshland /ˈmɑː.ʃ.lænd/ (US) /ˈmɑːrʃ-/ **noun** [C or U] an area of marsh

marshmallow /ˈmɑːʃˈmæl.əʊ/ (US) /ˈmɑːrʃˌmæl.oʊ/ **noun** SWEET ▷ **1** [C or U] a soft, sweet, pink or white food: *Why don't we toast some marshmallows over the fire?* COWARD ▷ **2** [C] informal humorous a person who is not strong, brave, or confident: *The situation called for someone tough, and I was a complete marshmallow.*

marshy /ˈmɑː.ʃi/ (US) /ˈmɑːr-/ **adj** describes an area of land that is always wet; like a MARSH: *This area was very marshy before the drainage system was installed.*

marsupial /mɑːˈsuː.pi.əl/ (US) /mɑːr-/ **noun** [C] a type of mammal from Australasia or South or Central America that is not completely developed when it is born and is carried around in a pocket on the mother's body, where it is fed and protected until it is completely developed: *Marsupials include koalas, possums, and kangaroos.*

mart /mɑːt/ (US) /mɑːrt/ **noun** [C] mainly US and Irish English a market or shopping centre: *Remember to get some bananas at the mart.* ◦ *discount marts*

martial /ˈmɑː.ʃəl/ (US) /ˈmɑːr-/ **adj** relating to soldiers, war, or life in the armed forces

ˌmartial ˈart **noun** [C usually plural] B2 a sport that is a traditional Japanese or Chinese form of fighting or defending yourself: *Kung fu and karate are martial arts.*

ˌmartial ˈlaw **noun** [U] the control of a city, country, etc. by an army instead of by its usual leaders: *Renegade forces captured the capital and **declared/imposed** martial law.*

Martian /ˈmɑː.ʃən/ (US) /ˈmɑːr-/ **noun** [C] a creature, usually appearing in films and books, who is believed to come from Mars

martin /ˈmɑː.tɪn/ (US) /ˈmɑːr.t̬ən/ **noun** [C] a small bird like a SWALLOW but with a shorter tail

martinet /ˌmɑː.tɪˈnet/ (US) /ˌmɑːr.t̬ɪ-/ **noun** [C] formal disapproving someone who demands that rules and orders always be obeyed, even when it is unnecessary or unreasonable to do so

martini /mɑːˈtiː.ni/ (US) /mɑːr-/ **noun** [C] an alcoholic drink which combines GIN and VERMOUTH

Martini /mɑːˈtiː.ni/ (US) /mɑːr-/ **noun** [U] trademark a type of **vermouth**

martyr /ˈmɑː.təʳ/ (US) /ˈmɑːr.t̬ɚ/ **noun; verb**

▸**noun** [C] **1** a person who suffers very much or is killed because of their political or religious beliefs, and is often admired because of it: *a Christian/Islamic/religious martyr* ◦ *She fought against racism all her life and died a martyr **to the cause**.* **2** disapproving someone who tries to get sympathy from others when they have a problem or too much work, usually having caused the problem or chosen to do the work themselves: *She offers to do extra work, then **plays the martyr**!*

IDIOM **be a martyr to sth** humorous to often suffer from an illness: *She's a martyr to migraine!*

▸**verb** [T often passive] to kill someone because of their religious or political beliefs

martyrdom /ˈmɑː.tə.dəm/ (US) /ˈmɑːr.t̬ɚ-/ **noun** [U] an occasion when someone suffers or is killed for their beliefs

martyred /ˈmɑː.təd/ (US) /ˈmɑːr.t̬ɚd/ **adj** **1** A martyred person has been killed because of their religious or political beliefs: *a martyred saint* ◦ *a martyred civil rights activist* **2** disapproving showing that you are suffering so that people will have sympathy for you: *She was wearing a martyred **expression**.*

marvel /ˈmɑː.vəl/ (US) /ˈmɑːr-/ **verb; noun**

▸**verb** [I] (-ll- or US usually -l-) to show or experience great surprise or admiration: *We paused to marvel **at** the view.* ◦ [+ that] *I often marvel **that** humans can treat each other so badly.* ◦ [+ speech] *'Just look at that waterfall! Isn't it amazing?' she marvelled.*

▸**noun** [C] a thing or person that is very surprising or causes a lot of admiration: *This miniature TV is the latest technological marvel from Japan.* ◦ ***It's** a marvel **(to me) how** they've managed to build the tunnel so quickly.*

marvellous UK UK (US **marvelous**) /ˈmɑː.vəl.əs/ (US) /ˈmɑːr-/ **adj** B1 extremely good: *He's done a marvellous job of the decorating.* ◦ *It took me ages to get it right, but it was a marvellous feeling when I did.* ◦ *It's marvellous how everyone's tried to help.* ◦ *He was a truly marvellous storyteller.* ◦ *We've achieved some marvellous results with this new drug.* • **marvellously** (US **marvelously**) /-li/ **adv** *We've had a few arguments over the years, but in general we get on marvellously.*

Marxism /ˈmɑː.k.sɪ.zəm/ (US) /ˈmɑːrk-/ **noun** [U] a social, political, and economic theory that is based on the writings of Karl Marx • **Marxist** /-sɪst/ **noun** [C], **adj** *a Marxist government*

ˌMarxist-ˈLeninist **adj** [before noun], **noun** [C] relating to the type of Marxism that was developed by Lenin before the political changes in Russia in 1917, or someone who follows this • **ˌMarxism-ˈLeninism** **noun** [U]

marzipan /ˈmɑː.zɪ.pæn/ (US) /ˈmɑːr-/ **noun** [U] a soft, yellow or white food made from ALMONDS, sugar, and eggs, used for decorating cakes and making sweets

masala (also **massala**) /məˈsɑː.lə/ **noun** [C or U] Indian English **1** in South Asian cooking, a mixture of spices **2** a South Asian dish made with a sauce containing a mixture of spices: *chicken tikka masala*

masc. **adj** written abbreviation for **masculine**

mascara /mæsˈkɑː.rə/ (US) /-ˈkær.ə/ **noun** [C or U] a thick dark liquid make-up that is used to make EYELASHES dark and make them appear thicker and longer • **mascaraed** /-ˈkɑː.rəd/ (US) /-ˈkær.əd/ **adj** *long mascaraed lashes*

mascarpone /ˌmæs.kɑːˈpəʊ.neɪ/ (US) /ˌmɑːs.kɑːrˈpoʊ-/ **noun** [U] a soft, white Italian cheese

mascot /ˈmæs.kɒt/ (US) /-kɑːt/ **noun** [C] a person, animal, or object that is believed to bring good luck, or one that represents an organization: *a **team** mascot* ◦ *The Olympic Games always have an **official** mascot.*

masculine /ˈmæs.kjʊ.lɪn/ **adj** MALE ▷ **1** C1 having characteristics that are traditionally thought to be typical of or suitable for men: *a masculine appearance/voice* → Compare **feminine** GRAMMAR ▷ **2** (written abbreviation **masc.**, **m**) belonging to the group of nouns, PRONOUNS, etc. that are not FEMININE or NEUTER: *The French word for 'sun' is masculine – 'le soleil', but the German word is feminine – 'die Sonne'.*

masculinity /ˌmæs.kjʊˈlɪn.ɪ.ti/ (US) /-ə.t̬i/ **noun** [U] the characteristics that are traditionally thought to be typical of or suitable for men

mash /mæʃ/ **verb; noun**

▸**verb** [T] **1** to crush food, usually after cooking it, so that it forms a soft mass: *Mash the potatoes and then mix in the butter and herbs.* **2** mainly US informal to violently crush part of a body or an object: *His face was badly mashed **up** in the accident.*

M

PHRASAL VERB **mash up sth** to crush something, especially food: *He always mashes up his peas before he eats them.*

▸noun [U] UK informal **mashed potatoes**: *sausage and mash*

mashed /mæʃt/ adj crushed: *mashed potatoes* (UK also *mashed potato*)

ˌmashed poˈtatoes noun [U] (UK also **ˌmashed poˈtato**) potatoes that have been boiled and crushed until they are smooth

masher /ˈmæʃ.əʳ/ (US) /-ɚ/ noun [C] a kitchen tool for mashing potatoes and other vegetables: *a* ***potato*** *masher*

mashup (also **ˈmash-up**) /ˈmæʃ.ʌp/ noun [C] **1** a type of recorded music or video that consists of parts of different songs or images that have been combined: *They created a mashup of all the artists who had performed on the show.* **2** a website or APPLICATION that uses information or technology from different websites

mask /mɑːsk/ (US) /mæsk/ noun; verb

▸noun [C] FACE COVER ▷ **1** B2 a covering for all or part of the face which protects, hides, or decorates the person wearing it: *a* ***gas*** *mask* ◦ *a* ***surgical*** *mask* ◦ *The bank robbers wore masks throughout the raid.* APPEARANCE/BEHAVIOUR ▷ **2** appearance or behaviour that hides the truth: *The newspaper revealed the sordid truth behind his mask* ***of*** *respectability.*

masks

IDIOM **sb's mask slips** If someone's mask slips, they do something which suddenly shows their real character, when they have been pretending to be a different, usually nicer, type of person.

▸verb [T] to prevent something from being seen or noticed: *I've put some flowers in there to mask the smell.*

masked /mɑːskt/ (US) /mæskt/ adj wearing a mask: *Suddenly two masked* ***gunmen*** *burst into the shop and demanded all the cash in the till.*

ˌmasked ˈball noun [C] a formal dance where masks are worn

ˈmasking ˌtape noun [U] sticky paper in a long roll that is used especially when painting to protect the edges of an area that you do not want to be painted

masochism /ˈmæs.ə.kɪ.zᵊm/ noun [U] **1** the activity of getting sexual pleasure from being hurt or controlled by another person → Compare **sadism 2** informal the enjoyment of an activity or situation that most people would find very unpleasant: *I reckon you need to be into masochism to run marathons.* → Compare **sadism** • **masochist** /-kɪst/ noun [C] • **masochistic** /ˌmæs.əˈkɪs.tɪk/ adj *masochistic behaviour/pleasure/fantasies*

mason /ˈmeɪ.sᵊn/ noun [C] **1** a **stonemason** (= person who cuts stone) **2** US a **bricklayer**

Mason /ˈmeɪ.sᵊn/ noun [C] a **Freemason** • **Masonic** /məˈsɒn.ɪk/ (US) /-ˈsɑː.nɪk/ adj • **Masonry** /ˈmeɪ.sᵊn.ri/ noun [U] **Freemasonry**

the Mason-Dixon Line /ˌmeɪ.sᵊnˈdɪk.sᵊnˌlaɪn/ noun [S] the border between the states of Maryland and Pennsylvania in the US, traditionally considered to mark the division between the north and south of the US

masonry /ˈmeɪ.sᵊn.ri/ noun [U] **1** the bricks and pieces of stone that are used to make a building: *Several of the firefighters were injured by falling masonry.* **2** the skill of building with brick and stone

masque /mɑːsk/ (US) /mæsk/ noun [C] a type of theatre entertainment including poetry, singing, and dancing, performed in England in the 16th and 17th centuries, especially at a royal COURT (= the official home of a king or queen)

masquerade /ˌmæs.kᵊrˈeɪd/ (US) /-kəˈreɪd/ noun; verb

▸noun [C or U] behaviour that is intended to prevent the truth about something unpleasant or not wanted from becoming known: *They kept up the masquerade of being happily married for over 30 years.*

▸verb

PHRASAL VERB **masquerade as sb/sth** to pretend or appear to be someone or something: *Hooligans masquerading as football fans have once again caused disturbances.*

mass /mæs/ adj; noun; verb

▸adj [before noun] C1 having an effect on or involving a large number of people or forming a large amount: *weapons of mass* ***destruction*** ◦ *a mass* ***murderer*** ◦ *mass* ***starvation*** ◦ *Opposition groups plan to stage mass* ***demonstrations*** *all over the country.*

▸noun LARGE AMOUNT ▷ **1** B2 [S] a large amount of something that has no particular shape or arrangement: *The explosion reduced the church to* ***a*** *mass* ***of*** *rubble.* ◦ *The forest is* ***a*** *mass* ***of*** *colour in autumn.* **2** (also **Mass**) [C or U] a religious ceremony in some Christian Churches based on Jesus' last meal with his DISCIPLES, or music written for parts of this ceremony: *to go to Mass* → See also **Communion 3 masses** [plural] mainly UK informal B2 a lot: [+ to infinitive] *I've got masses* ***to*** *do at the weekend.* ◦ *There were masses* ***of*** *people in town today.* **4 the mass of sth** most of something: *The mass of the people support the government's reforms.* SOLID LUMP ▷ **5** [C] a solid LUMP with no clear shape: *The sauce was now a sticky mass at the bottom of the pan.* ORDINARY PEOPLE ▷ **6 the masses** the ordinary people who form the largest group in a society PHYSICS ▷ **7** [C] specialized (in physics) the amount of matter in any solid object or in any volume of liquid or gas: *The acceleration of a body equals the force exerted on it divided by its mass.*

▸verb [I] to come together in large numbers: *Thousands of troops have massed along the border in preparation for an invasion.*

massacre /ˈmæs.ə.kəʳ/ (US) /-kɚ/ noun; verb

▸noun [C] **1** C2 an act of killing a lot of people: *He ordered the massacre of 2,000 women and children.* **2** informal a bad defeat, especially in sport: *The changes to the team come after their 7–2 massacre in the final.*

▸verb [T] **1** to kill many people in a short period of time: *Hundreds of civilians were massacred in the raid.* **2** informal to defeat an opponent very badly in a competition or election: *England was massacred 5–0 by France in the semifinal.*

massage /ˈmæs.ɑːʒ/ (US) /məˈsɑːʒ/ verb; noun

▸verb [T] BODY ▷ **1** to rub and press someone's body with regular repeated movements, in order to relax them or to reduce stiffness or pain in their JOINTS (= places where two bones are connected) or muscles: *Would you massage my shoulders?* FACTS/NUMBERS ▷ **2** to try to make facts or numbers appear better than they really are in order to deceive someone: *Television companies have been massaging their viewing* ***figures*** *in order to attract more advertising revenue.*

IDIOM **massage sb's ego** to praise someone in order to make them think they are better than they are

▸**noun** [C or U] the activity of rubbing or pressing parts of someone's body in order to make them relax or to stop their muscles hurting: *a back/foot/head massage* ◦ *a qualified massage therapist* ◦ *She **gave** me a massage.*

ˈmassage ˌparlour UK (US **ˈmassage ˌparlor**) **noun** [C] FOR TREATMENT ▷ **1** a place where you can pay someone to give you a massage FOR SEX ▷ **2** a place where a person can pay to have sex

massed /mæst/ **adj** [before noun] brought together in large numbers: *Every day, massed **ranks** of tourists pass slowly through the rooms of the palace.*

masseur /mæsˈɜːʳ/ Ⓤⓢ /-ˈɝː/ **noun** [C] a person whose job it is to give massages to people

masseuse /mæˈsɜːz/ Ⓤⓢ /-ˈsɝːz/ **noun** [C] a female masseur

massif /mæsˈiːf/ **noun** [C] specialized a group or area of mountains

massive /ˈmæs.ɪv/ **adj** B2 very large in size, amount, or number: *They've got a massive house.* ◦ *She died after taking a massive overdose of drugs.* ◦ *If the drought continues, deaths will occur on a massive scale.* • **massively** /-li/ **adv** *The film is a massively (= very) ambitious project.* • **massiveness** /-nəs/ **noun** [U]

ˌmass ˈmailing **noun** [C] US for **mailshot**

ˌmass ˈmarket **noun** [C usually singular] A product that is designed for the mass market is intended to be bought by as many people as possible, not just by people with a lot of money or a special interest: *Advances in technology have made these cameras affordable to the mass market.*

the ˌmass ˈmedia **noun** [plural, + sing/pl verb] newspapers, television, radio, and the internet: *The mass media has become one of the main instruments of political change.*

ˌmass-proˈduce **verb** [T] to produce a lot of goods cheaply using machines in a factory • **ˌmass proˈduction** **noun** [U] • **ˌmass-proˈduced** **adj** *mass-produced souvenirs*

ˌmass ˈtransit **noun** [U] US for **public transport**

mast /mɑːst/ Ⓤⓢ /mæst/ **noun** [C] BOAT ▷ **1** a tall pole on a boat or ship that supports its sails RADIO/TELEVISION ▷ **2** a tall metal pole used to support an AERIAL for radio or television signals: *a television/radio mast* FLAG ▷ **3** a pole that holds a flag

mastectomy /mæsˈtek.tə.mi/ **noun** [C] a medical operation to remove a woman's breast: *a **partial** mastectomy (= when part of the breast is removed)* ◦ *a **double** mastectomy (= when both breasts are removed)*

master /ˈmɑː.stəʳ/ Ⓤⓢ /ˈmæs.tɚ/ **noun; verb; adj**

▸**noun** [C] CONTROLLER ▷ **1** B2 a person who has control over or responsibility for someone or something, or who is the most important or INFLUENTIAL (= having most influence) person in a situation or organization: old-fashioned *a slave and his master* ◦ *With careful training, a dog will obey its master completely.* ◦ UK *The Master of St. John's College will be launching the appeal.* SKILLED PERSON ▷ **2** C2 a person who is very skilled in a particular job or activity: *He was **a** master **of** disguise.* **3** a famous and very skilled painter: *This painting is clearly the work of a master.* TEACHER ▷ **4** UK old-fashioned a male school teacher: *Mr Wells was my Latin master at school.* → See also **headmaster** COPY ▷ **5** an original version of something from which copies can be made: *I sent her a copy and kept the master.* ◦ *You should keep the master **copy** (= the original) in a safe place.*

IDIOM **be your own master** to be independent and able to make your own decisions

▸**verb** [T] CONTROL ▷ **1** to learn to control an emotion or feeling: *I finally mastered my fear of flying.* LEARN ▷ **2** to learn how to do something well: *to master a **technique*** ◦ *She lived in Italy for several years but never quite mastered the **language**.* ◦ *He quickly mastered **the art of** interviewing people.*

▸**adj** [before noun] extremely skilled: *a master craftsman* ◦ *a master chef*

ˈmaster ˌbedroom **noun** [C] the largest bedroom in a house

masterclass /ˈmɑː.stə.klɑːs/ Ⓤⓢ /ˈmæs.tɚ.klæs/ **noun** [C] a class taught by someone who has an expert knowledge or skill in a particular area, especially in music

masterful /ˈmɑː.stə.fəl/ Ⓤⓢ /ˈmæs.tɚ-/ **adj** ABLE TO CONTROL ▷ **1** able to control people and situations in a confident way: *Once she became a prosecutor, she quickly established herself as a masterful trial lawyer.* ◦ *He has a deep, masterful voice.* SKILFUL ▷ **2** If an action is masterful, it is very skilful: *a masterful **performance*** • **masterfully** /-i/ **adv**

ˈmaster ˌkey **noun** [C] a key that can be used to open any of several different locks

masterly /ˈmɑː.stə.li/ Ⓤⓢ /ˈmæs.tɚ-/ **adj** done extremely well: *She gave a masterly **performance** as Kate in 'The Taming of the Shrew'.*

mastermind /ˈmɑː.stə.maɪnd/ Ⓤⓢ /ˈmæs.tɚ-/ **verb** [T] to plan a difficult activity, often a crime, in detail and make certain that it happens successfully: *He's believed to have masterminded the attacks.* • **mastermind** **noun** [C] *a criminal mastermind*

ˌMaster of ˈArts **noun** [C] (abbreviation **MA**) an advanced college or university degree in a subject such as literature, language, history, or social science, or a person who has this degree

ˌmaster of ˈceremonies **noun** [C] (abbreviation **MC**) a person who makes certain that official events happen correctly, for example by introducing performers at the right time

ˌMaster of ˈPhilosophy **noun** [C] (abbreviation **MPhil**) in the UK, an advanced college or university degree in any subject, or a person who has this degree

ˌMaster of ˈScience **noun** [C] (UK abbreviation **MSc**, US abbreviation **MS**) an advanced college or university degree in a scientific subject, or a person who has this degree

masterpiece /ˈmɑː.stə.piːs/ Ⓤⓢ /ˈmæs.tɚ-/ **noun** [C] **1** C2 (also **masterwork**) a work of art such as a painting, film, or book that is made with great skill: *Leonardo's 'Last Supper' is widely regarded as a masterpiece.* → See also **chef-d'oeuvre** **2** a skilful or clever example of something: *Her press conference was a masterpiece **of** media manipulation.*

ˈmaster ˌplan **noun** [C] an organized set of decisions made by one person or a team of people about how to do something in the future

ˌMaster's deˈgree **noun** [C] (informal **Master's**) C1 an advanced college or university degree: *An MA and an MSc are both Master's degrees.*

ˈmaster stroke **noun** [C usually singular] mainly UK an action that is very clever and produces success: *His decision to change the team's formation for the final match was a master stroke.*

M

ˈmaster ˌswitch noun [C] a switch that can be used to turn on or off power to all the lights or machines in a building

mastery /ˈmɑː.stᵊr.i/ (US) /ˈmæs.tɚ-/ noun [U] **CONTROL** ▷ **1** complete control of something: *her mastery **of** the situation* **SKILL** ▷ **2** If someone has a mastery of something, they are extremely skilled at it: *her mastery **of** the violin*

masthead /ˈmɑːst.hed/ (US) /ˈmæst-/ noun [C] **ON NEWSPAPER** ▷ **1** the title of a newspaper or magazine that is printed at the top of the front page **2** US a list of the names of the most important people involved in producing and writing for a magazine or newspaper: *Hirth, listed on the masthead as publisher, wrote several articles in each issue.* **ON WEBSITE** ▷ **3** the name of a person, company, or organization that is displayed on the HOME PAGE of their website **ON LETTERS/EMAILS** ▷ **4** the name and information that is printed at the top of an organization's official letters or emails **ON SHIP** ▷ **5** the top part of a ship's MAST

masticate /ˈmæs.tɪ.keɪt/ verb [I or T] formal to CHEW (= crush with the teeth) food • **mastication** /ˌmæs.tɪˈkeɪ.ʃᵊn/ noun [U]

mastiff /ˈmæs.tɪf/ noun [C] a large, strong dog with short hair

mastitis /mæsˈtaɪ.tɪs/ (US) /-t̬ɪs/ noun [U] specialized painful swelling of the breast or the UDDER (= the part of a cow which produces milk), usually because of an infection

M

masturbate /ˈmæs.tə.beɪt/ (US) /-tɚ-/ verb **1** [I] to touch or rub your sexual organs in order to give yourself sexual pleasure **2** [T] to touch or rub someone's sexual organs in order to give them sexual pleasure • **masturbation** /ˌmæs.təˈbeɪ.ʃᵊn/ (US) /-tɚ-/ noun [U] • **masturbatory** /ˌmæs.təˈbeɪ.tᵊr.i/ (US) /-t̬ɚˈbeɪ.tɔːr.i/ adj *masturbatory fantasies*

mat /mæt/ noun [C] **FLOOR** ▷ **1** (C1) a small piece of strong material that covers and protects part of a floor: *Wipe your feet on the mat before you come inside.* → See also **doormat** **TABLE** ▷ **2** a small piece of cloth, cardboard, or plastic that is put on a surface such as a table to protect it: *a beer mat* ◦ *a place mat* **SPORT** ▷ **3** a piece of thick rubber or other soft material used in some sports for people to lie or fall on: *Please remember to bring a mat and a towel with you to the next aerobics class.* **LAYER** ▷ **4** a thick layer of something, such as grass or hair, that is twisted together untidily: *The top few buttons on his shirt were open, revealing a mat **of** dark hair on his chest.*

matador /ˈmæt.ə.dɔːʳ/ (US) /ˈmæt̬.ə.dɔːr/ noun [C] a man who fights and kills BULLS (= male cows) at a BULLFIGHT → Compare **picador, toreador**

match /mætʃ/ noun; verb

▸noun **COMPETITION** ▷ **1** (A2) [C] mainly UK (US usually **game**) a sports competition or event in which two people or teams compete against each other: *a football/cricket/tennis match* ◦ *We won/lost the match.* ◦ *Liverpool have a match **with** (= against) Blackburn next week.* **2 the man/woman of the match** mainly UK the person who has scored the most points or played the best in a match **STICK** ▷ **3** (B2) [C] a short, thin stick made of wood or cardboard and covered with a special chemical at one end that burns when rubbed firmly against a rough surface: *a **box** of matches* ◦ *You should always **strike** a match away from you.* **4 put a match to sth** UK to make something burn **EQUAL** ▷ **5** [S] a person or thing that is equal to another person or thing in strength, speed, or quality **6 be no match for sth/sb** (C2) to be less powerful or effective than someone or something else: *Gibson ran well but was no match for the young Italian.* **SUITABLE** ▷ **7** (C2) [S] something that is similar to or combines well with something else: *The curtains look great – they're **a perfect match for** the sofa.* **8** [S] If two people who are having a relationship are a good match, they are very suitable for each other: *Theirs is a match **made in heaven** (= a very good relationship).*

▸verb **EQUAL** ▷ **1** (C1) [T] to be as good as someone or something else: *It would be difficult to match the service this airline gives its customers.* **LOOK SIMILAR** ▷ **2** (B1) [I or T] If two colours, designs, or objects match, they are similar or look attractive together: *Do you think these two colours match?* ◦ *Does this shirt match these trousers?* ◦ *a sofa with curtains **to** match* **CHOOSE** ▷ **3** (B1) [T] to choose someone or something that is suitable for a particular person, activity, or purpose: *In the first exercise you have to match each capital city to its country.*

PHRASAL VERBS **match sb against sb** If one team or player is matched against another team or player, they are made to compete against each other. • **match up** **BE THE SAME** ▷ **1** If two pieces of information match up, they are the same: *Their accounts of what happened that evening don't match up.* **BE SIMILAR** ▷ **2** If two things match up, they are similar and are designed to connect or to work together: *If the teeth on the cogs don't match up properly (= if they are not in the correct place), the mechanism will jam.* **BE EQUALLY GOOD** ▷ **3** UK to be as good as another thing, person, or experience: *There was so much hype beforehand that it would have been difficult for the film to match up **to/with** our expectations of it.* • **match sth up** If you match up a design or material, you look for something that would look good with it and be similar to it: *I'm trying to match up this wallpaper **with** some suitable curtain material.* • **match sth/sb up** to find a similarity or connection between two things or people: *Can you match up these songs **with** the bands who sang them?*

matchbox /ˈmætʃ.bɒks/ (US) /-bɑːks/ noun [C] a small box containing matches

-matched /mætʃt/ suffix **well-matched/ill-matched** similar and suitable for each other/different and not suitable for each other: *an ill-matched couple*

ˈmatch-ˌfixing noun [U] dishonest activity to make sure that one team wins a particular sports match

matching /ˈmætʃ.ɪŋ/ adj [before noun] having the same colour or pattern as something else: *a green dress with matching green handbag*

matchless /ˈmætʃ.ləs/ adj of a very high standard or quality and better than everything else: *her matchless beauty* ◦ *matchless prose* • **matchlessly** /-li/ adv

matchmaker /ˈmætʃˌmeɪ.kəʳ/ (US) /-kɚ/ noun [C] a person who tries to arrange marriages or romantic relationships between people • **matchmaking** /-kɪŋ/ noun [U]

ˌmatch ˈpoint noun [C] a situation in a game such as tennis when the player who is winning will win the match if they get the next point

matchstick /ˈmætʃ.stɪk/ noun [C] the short wooden stick of a MATCH, or the match itself: *He likes making models out of matchsticks.*

ˈmatchstick ˌfigure noun [C] a **stick figure**

matchwood /ˈmætʃ.wʊd/ noun [U] UK the very small pieces of wood that are left after something wooden has been destroyed

mate /meɪt/ noun; verb

▸noun [C] **SEXUAL PARTNER** ▷ **1** an animal's sexual

partner: *Peacocks use their beautiful tails to attract mates.* **FRIEND** ▷ **2** B1 UK informal a friend: *We've been mates since our school days.* ◦ *I usually play football with some of my mates from the office on Saturdays.* ◦ *She's my* ***best*** *mate.* **3** [as form of address] UK informal used as a friendly way of talking to someone, especially a man: *Have you got the time, mate?* **HELPER** ▷ **4** UK a person who is employed to help a skilled worker: *a carpenter's/plumber's mate* **SHIP** ▷ **5** a type of officer on a trading ship rather than a military ship: *He had worked as a ship's mate for ten years.*
▸**verb** [I or T] to have sex and produce young, or to make animals do this: *Tigers mate repeatedly over a period of several days.* ◦ *Mating a horse with a donkey produces a mule.*

IDIOM **mate for life** If animals mate for life, they keep the same sexual partner for their whole life.

-mate /-meɪt/ **suffix** used to show that two people share a space or are involved in the same activity: *flat mate* ◦ *team-mate* ◦ *workmate*

mater /ˈmeɪ.təʳ/ US /-t̬ɚ/ **noun** [C] UK old-fashioned or humorous mother

material /məˈtɪə.ri.əl/ US /-ˈtɪr.i-/ **noun; adj**
▸**noun** **PHYSICAL SUBSTANCE** ▷ **1** B2 [C] a physical substance that things can be made from: ***building*** *materials, such as stone* ◦ *Crude oil is used as the* ***raw*** *(= basic) material for making plastics.* **INFORMATION** ▷ **2** B1 [C or U] information used when writing something such as a book, or information produced in various forms to help people or to advertise products: *I'm in the process of* ***collecting*** *material for an article that I'm writing.* **CLOTH** ▷ **3** B1 [C or U] cloth that can be used to make things such as clothes: *How much material will you need to make the skirt?* **EQUIPMENT** ▷ **4** **materials** B1 [plural] equipment that you need for a particular activity: *'Do we need any writing materials?' 'Only a pen and a pencil.'* ◦ ***teaching*** *materials*
▸**adj** **PHYSICAL** ▷ **1** relating to physical objects or money rather than emotions or the spiritual world: *the material* ***world*** ◦ *Material* ***wealth*** *never interested her.* **IMPORTANT** ▷ **2** formal important or having an important effect: *If you have any information that is material* ***to*** *the investigation, you should state it now.*

materialism /məˈtɪə.ri.ə.lɪ.zəm/ US /-ˈtɪr.i-/ **noun** [U] **MONEY** ▷ **1** C2 the belief that having money and possessions is the most important thing in life **PHYSICAL** ▷ **2** specialized the belief that only physical matter exists and the spiritual world does not

materialist /məˈtɪə.ri.ə.lɪst/ US /-ˈtɪr.i-/ **noun; adj**
▸**noun** [C] **MONEY** ▷ **1** C2 someone who believes that having money and possessions is the most important thing in life **PHYSICAL** ▷ **2** specialized someone who believes that only physical matter exists and the spiritual world does not
▸**adj** specialized relating to the belief that only physical matter exists

materialistic /məˌtɪə.ri.əˈlɪs.tɪk/ US /-ˌtɪr.i-/ **adj** C2 believing that having money and possessions is the most important thing in life

materialize (UK usually **materialise**) /məˈtɪə.ri.ə.laɪz/ US /-ˈtɪr.i-/ **verb** [I] **1** If an object materializes, it appears suddenly: *Suddenly a lorry appeared in front of her – it seemed to materialize out of nowhere.* **2** If an idea or hope materializes, it becomes real: *Her hopes of becoming a painter never materialized.* • **materialization** (UK usually **materialisation**) /məˌtɪə.ri.əl.aɪˈzeɪ.ʃən/ US /-ˌtɪr.i-/ **noun** [C or U]

materially /məˈtɪə.ri.ə.li/ US /-ˈtɪr.i-/ **adv** **MONEY** ▷ **1** in a way that relates to money and possessions: *Materially, of course, we're better off.* **IMPORTANTLY** ▷ **2** formal in an important or noticeable way: *Even if mistakes were made in the counting, they wouldn't have materially* ***affected*** *the results.*

maternal /məˈtɜː.nəl/ US /-ˈtɝː-/ **adj** **1** behaving or feeling in the way that a mother does towards her child, especially in a kind, loving way: *maternal* ***instincts*** ◦ *She is very maternal* ***towards*** *her staff.* → Compare **paternal** **2** related to a mother's side of the family: *Her maternal grandmother (= mother's mother) is still alive.* • **maternally** /-i/ **adv**

maternity /məˈtɜː.nə.ti/ US /-ˈtɝː.nə.t̬i/ **noun; adj**
▸**noun** [U] formal the state of being a mother
▸**adj** [before noun] related to pregnancy and birth: *maternity* ***clothes***

maˈternity ˌleave **noun** [U] a period in which a woman is legally allowed to be absent from work in the weeks before and after she gives birth

maˈternity ˌward **noun** [C] the part of a hospital in which women give birth and where they are taken care of after giving birth

ˈmates' ˌrate **noun** [C] informal a cheaper price than normal because the buyer is a friend

matey /ˈmeɪ.ti/ US /-t̬i/ **adj; noun**
▸**adj** (**matier**, **matiest**) UK informal friendly: *They've been very matey since they started working together.* • **mateyness** /-nəs/ **noun** [U]
▸**noun** [C] UK informal used as an informal form of address: *Are you all right, matey?*

mathematician /ˌmæθ.mə ˈtɪʃ.ən/ **noun** [C] someone who studies, teaches, or is an expert in mathematics

mathematics /ˌmæθˈmæt.ɪks/ US /-ˈmæt̬-/ **noun** [U] (UK informal **maths**, US informal **math**) A2 the study of numbers, shapes, and space using reason and usually a special system of symbols and rules for organizing them → See also **algebra, arithmetic, geometry** • **mathematical** /ˌmæθˈmæt.ɪ.kəl/ US /-ˈmæt̬-/ **adj** B2 *a mathematical formula* • **mathematically** /ˌmæθˈmæt.ɪ.kəl.i/ US /-ˈmæt̬-/ **adv**

matinee /ˈmæt.ɪ.neɪ/ US /ˌmæt̬.ənˈeɪ/ **noun** [C] a film shown or a play performed during the day, especially in the afternoon

ˈmatinee ˌidol **noun** [C] old-fashioned a male actor, especially in films of the 1930s and 1940s, who was very attractive to women

matins /ˈmæt.ɪnz/ US /ˈmæt̬-/ **noun** [U] the morning ceremony in some Christian Churches

matriarch /ˈmeɪ.tri.ɑːk/ US /-ɑːrk/ **noun** [C] an old and powerful woman in a family, or the female leader of a society in which power passes from mother to daughter → Compare **patriarch** • **matriarchal** /-ˈɑː.kəl/ US /-ˈɑːr.kəl/ **adj** *a matriarchal* ***society*** → Compare **patriarchal**

matriarchy /ˈmeɪ.tri.ɑː.ki/ US /-ɑːr-/ **noun** [C or U] a type of society in which women have most of the authority and power, or a society in which property belongs to women and is given to children by women rather than men → Compare **patriarchy**

matricide /ˈmæt.rɪ.saɪd/, /ˈmeɪ.trɪ-/ **noun** [U] a crime in which a person kills their mother → Compare **parricide, patricide**

matriculate /məˈtrɪk.jʊ.leɪt/ **verb** [I] formal to be formally admitted to study at a university or college • **matriculation** /məˌtrɪk.jʊˈleɪ.ʃən/ **noun** [C or U]

matrimonial /ˌmæt.rɪˈməʊ.ni.əl/ US /-ˈmoʊ-/ **adj** formal related to marriage or people who are married

matrimony /ˈmæt.rɪ.mə.ni/ **noun** [U] formal the state of being married

matrix /ˈmeɪ.trɪks/ **noun** (plural **matrices** or **matrixes**)

M

DEVELOPMENT ▷ **1** [C] formal the set of conditions that provides a system in which something grows or develops **MATHEMATICS** ▷ **2** [C] specialized a group of numbers or other symbols arranged in a rectangle that can be used together as a single unit to solve particular mathematical problems **SUBSTANCE** ▷ **3** [C or U] specialized a substance in which other things are fixed, buried, etc.: *The fossils lie embedded in a matrix of shale and sandstone.*

matron /ˈmeɪ.trən/ **noun** [C] **SCHOOL** ▷ **1** UK old-fashioned a female nurse in a school **HOSPITAL** ▷ **2** UK old-fashioned for **senior nursing officer** **PRISON** ▷ **3** US a woman who is in charge of female prisoners **MARRIED WOMAN** ▷ **4** US a married woman, especially one who is old or a WIDOW (= a woman whose husband has died)

matronly /ˈmeɪ.trən.li/ **adj** often disapproving describes a woman, usually one who is not young, who is fat and does not dress in a fashionable way

matt UK (US **matte**) /mæt/ **adj** describes a surface or colour or paint that is not shiny: *The paint is available in matt or gloss finish.* → Compare **emulsion, gloss**

matted /ˈmæt.ɪd/ Ⓤⓢ /ˈmæţ-/ **adj** twisted into a firm, untidy mass: *Her hair was matted* ***with*** *mud and rain.*

matter /ˈmæt.əʳ/ Ⓤⓢ /ˈmæţ.ɚ/ **noun; verb**

▸**noun** **SITUATION** ▷ **1** B2 [C] a situation or subject that is being dealt with or considered: *Could I talk to you about a personal matter?* ◦ *Alois denied any knowledge of the matter.* ◦ *Will you phone me back – it's a matter* ***of*** *some importance.* ◦ *Talking about the world's problems is one thing, but solving them is* ***another*** *matter* ***altogether*** (= is completely different). **2 matters** [plural] the situation being dealt with or being discussed: *Her resignation is not going to* ***help*** *matters.* **3 to make matters worse** B2 used to say that something has made a bad or difficult situation worse: *Three of our players were ill, and to make matters worse, our main scorer had broken his ankle.* **4 be a matter of confidence, luck, waiting, etc.** C2 If something is a matter of confidence, luck, waiting, etc. that is all you need for it to happen: *Baking a cake isn't difficult – it's just a matter of following the recipe.* **5 be no laughing matter** C2 to be very serious and not a situation that people should joke about: *Being arrested by the police is no laughing matter.* **PROBLEM** ▷ **6 the matter** A2 [S] the reason for pain, worry, or a problem: ***What's*** *the matter? Why are you crying?* ◦ *What's the matter* ***with*** *your hand? It's bleeding.* ◦ *Is anything the matter?* ◦ *I don't know what the matter is* ***with*** *the car, but it won't start.* **SUBSTANCE** ▷ **7** [U] physical substance in the universe: *Some scientists believe that there is about ten times as much matter in the universe as astronomers have observed.* **TYPE** ▷ **8** C2 [U] a substance or things of a particular type: *advertising/****printed*** *matter* ◦ *Do you find the* ***subject*** *matter of the book (= the subject that the book deals with) interesting?* **SMALL AMOUNT** ▷ **9** C2 [S] used in expressions describing how small an amount or period of time is: *The interview was over* ***in a*** *matter* ***of*** *minutes.* ◦ *She complained he had short-changed her, but it was only* ***a*** *matter* ***of*** *a few pence.*

IDIOMS **as a matter of course** C1 If something is done as a matter of course, it is a usual part of the way in which things are done and is not special: *Safety precautions are observed as a matter of course.* • **be (only) a matter of time** C1 If it is (only) a matter of time until something happens, it is certain to happen but you do not know when it will happen: *It's only a matter of time before he's forced to resign.* • **be a matter of life and/or death** C2 to be very serious: *And if you miss the bus, well, it's not a matter of life and death.* • **be a matter of opinion** If something is a matter of opinion, different people have different opinions about it: *Both performances were excellent, it's simply a matter of opinion as to whose was better.* • **be a matter of record** If a fact is a matter of record, it is generally known to be true. • **for that matter** used to show that a statement is true in another situation: *Ming's never been to Spain, or to any European country for that matter.* • **the matter in hand** UK (US **the matter at hand**) the subject or situation being considered: *Do these figures have any bearing on the matter in hand?* • **no matter** mainly UK it is not a problem: *'I haven't got that form with me.' 'No matter – here's another.'* • **no matter what, when, why, etc.** B2 used to emphasize that something is always true or that someone must do something: *I never seem to lose any weight, no matter how hard I try.* ◦ *Anyway, we've got to get to the airport on time, no matter what.* • **take matters into your own hands** to deal with a problem yourself because the people who should have dealt with it have failed to do so: *When the police failed to catch her son's murderer, she decided to take matters into her own hands.* • **that's a matter of opinion** said to show that you do not agree with something that has just been said: *'Anyway, she's a wonderful mother.' 'That's a matter of opinion.'*

▸**verb** [I] B2 to be important, or to affect what happens: *We were late but it didn't seem to matter.* ◦ *'What did you say?' 'Oh,* ***it doesn't*** *matter.'* ◦ [+ question word] ***It*** *doesn't matter* ***wh****at you wear – just as long as you come.* ◦ [+ that] ***It*** *didn't matter* ***that*** *our best player was injured after ten minutes – we still won.* ◦ *I know Charles doesn't think this project is important, but it matters* ***to*** *me.*

ˌmatter-of-ˈfact **adj** not showing feelings or emotion, especially in a situation when emotion would be expected: *He spoke in a very matter-of-fact way about the accident.* • **matter-of-factly** /-li/ **adv** • **matter-of-factness** /-nəs/ **noun** [U]

matting /ˈmæt.ɪŋ/ Ⓤⓢ /ˈmæţ-/ **noun** [U] strong, rough material that is used to cover floors: *straw/coconut matting*

mattress /ˈmæt.rəs/ **noun** [C] the part of a bed, made of a strong cloth cover filled with firm material, which makes the bed comfortable to lie on

maturation /ˌmæt.jʊəˈreɪ.ʃən/ Ⓤⓢ /-jʊ-/ **noun** [U] formal **GROWTH** ▷ **1** the process of becoming completely developed mentally or emotionally **2** the process of becoming completely grown physically **BUSINESS** ▷ **3** specialized the process of a market, industry, etc. no longer growing as fast as it did when it was new: *Some experts believe we are now seeing the maturation of the computer industry.*

mature **adj; verb**

▸**adj** /məˈtjʊəʳ/ Ⓤⓢ /-ˈtʊr/ **LIKE AN ADULT** ▷ **1** B2 Mature people behave like adults in a way that shows they are well developed emotionally: *He's very mature for his age.* **2** A mature decision is one that is made after a lot of careful thought: *Upon mature reflection, we find the accused guilty.* **PHYSICALLY GROWN** ▷ **3** completely grown physically: *a mature* ***adult*** ◦ ***sexually*** *mature* ◦ *Mature male gorillas have silver-grey hairs on their backs.* ◦ *mature oak trees* **FOOD** ▷ **4** having a flavour that is completely developed: *Do you prefer mild or mature cheddar?* **FINANCE** ▷ **5** specialized A mature INVESTMENT is ready to be paid.

▸**verb** /məˈtjʊəʳ/ Ⓤⓢ /-ˈtʊr/ /məˈtjʊəʳ/ Ⓤⓢ /-ˈtʊr/ **DEVELOP MENTALLY** ▷ **1** [I or T] to become more developed mentally and emotionally and behave in a responsible way: *Girls are said to mature faster than boys.* ◦ *He matured a lot while he was at college.* **2** [I] If ideas, opinions, etc. mature, they reach an advanced or developed state: *It took several years for her ideas to mature.* **GROW PHYSICALLY** ▷ **3** [I] to become completely grown physically: *Humans take longer to mature than most other animals.* **FOOD** ▷ **4** [I or T] to make food and wine old enough for the flavour to have developed completely: *The wine has been matured in oak vats.* ◦ *The cheese is left to mature for two years.* **FINANCE** ▷ **5** [I] specialized If an INSURANCE agreement or an INVESTMENT matures, it becomes ready to be paid: *The policy matures after 15 years.*

maˌture age ˈstudent noun [C] Australian a student at a college or university who is older than the usual age → See also **mature student**

maturely /məˈtjʊə.li/ US /-ˈtʊr-/ adv in a mature and responsible way

maˌture ˈstudent noun [C] UK (US **ˈolder ˌstudent**) a student at a college or university who is older than the usual age

maturity /məˈtjʊə.rɪ.ti/ US /-ˈtʊr.ə.t̬i/ noun [U] **MENTAL DEVELOPMENT** ▷ **1** the quality of behaving mentally and emotionally like an adult **2** a very advanced or developed form or state **FULL GROWTH** ▷ **3** the state of being completely grown physically: *How long does it take for the chicks to grow to maturity?* **FINANCE** ▷ **4** specialized the time when an INSURANCE agreement or INVESTMENT becomes ready to be paid: *The investment **reaches** maturity after ten years.*

maudlin /ˈmɔː.d.lɪn/ US /ˈmɑːd-/ adj feeling sad and sorry for yourself, especially after you have drunk a lot of alcohol

maul /mɔːl/ US /mɑːl/ verb [T often passive] **ANIMAL** ▷ **1** If an animal mauls someone, it attacks them and injures them with its teeth or CLAWS (= long sharp nails): *A small boy had been mauled by the neighbour's dog.* **CRITICIZE** ▷ **2** to criticize something or someone severely: *Both films were mauled by the critics.*

mauling /ˈmɔː.lɪŋ/ US /ˈmɑː-/ noun [S or U] severe criticism of someone or something: *Her latest novel **got** a real mauling in the review that I read.*

mausoleum /ˌmɔː.zəˈliː.əm/ US /ˌmɑː-/ noun [C] a building in which the bodies of dead people are buried

mauve /məʊv/ US /moʊv/ noun [U] a pale purple colour • **mauve** adj having a pale purple colour

maven /ˈmeɪ.vᵊn/ noun [C] US informal a person with good knowledge or understanding of a subject

maverick /ˈmæv.ᵊr.ɪk/ US /-ɚ-/ noun [C] a person who thinks and acts in an independent way, often behaving differently from the expected or usual way: *a **political** maverick*

maw /mɔː/ US /mɑː/ noun [C] literary **1** the mouth of a FIERCE (= frightening) animal: *the lion's maw* **2** something that seems to surround and absorb everything near it: *She fears that the matter will simply be swallowed up by the maw of bureaucracy.*

mawkish /ˈmɔː.kɪʃ/ US /ˈmɑː-/ adj showing emotion or love in an awkward or silly way: *The film lapses into mawkish sentimentality near the end.* • **mawkishly** /-li/ adv • **mawkishness** /-nəs/ noun [U]

max /mæks/ adj; noun; verb
▸adj informal for **maximum**, often used after an amount: *'How much will the trip cost?' '£40 max.'*
▸noun **to the max** US informal as much as possible: *These athletes push their bodies to the max.*
▸verb
PHRASAL VERB **max sth out** informal to use all that is available of something, especially money: *We maxed out all our credit cards.*

maxi- /mæk.sɪ-/ prefix most, very large: *maximum*

maxi dress /ˈmæk.si.dres/ noun [C] a long dress that covers the legs

maxim /ˈmæk.sɪm/ noun [C] a short statement of a general truth, principle, or rule for behaviour

maximal /ˈmæk.sɪ.məl/ adj specialized largest or greatest: *40 degrees centigrade is the maximal temperature at which this chemical reaction will occur.* → Compare **minimal**

maximize (UK usually **maximise**) /ˈmæk.sɪ.maɪz/ verb [T] C2 to make something as great in amount, size, or importance as possible: *Some airlines have cancelled less popular routes in an effort to maximize **profits**.* → Compare **minimize** • **maximization** (UK usually **maximisation**) /ˌmæk.sɪ.maɪˈzeɪ.ʃᵊn/ noun [U]

maximum /ˈmæk.sɪ.məm/ adj; noun
▸adj B1 being the largest amount or number allowed or possible: *maximum speed/effort/temperature* ◦ *The bomb was designed to cause the maximum **amount** of damage.*
▸noun [C usually singular] (plural **maxima** or **maximums**) B1 the largest amount allowed or possible: *The temperature will reach **a** maximum **of** 27°C today.* → Compare **minimum**

may /meɪ/ modal verb; noun
▸modal verb **POSSIBILITY** ▷ **1** A2 used to express possibility: *There may be other problems that we don't know about.* ◦ *I may see you tomorrow before I leave.* ◦ *The cause of the accident may never be discovered.* ◦ *The explosion may have been caused by a faulty electrical connection.* ◦ *We'd better not interfere – she may not like it.* ◦ *There may be some evidence to suggest she's guilty, **but** it's hardly conclusive.* → Compare **might**

> **! Common mistake: may**
> **May** is followed by an infinitive verb without 'to'.
> Don't say 'may does something', say **may do something**:
> ~~*It may sounds strange but it works!*~~
> *It may sound strange but it works!*

> **! Common mistake: may be or maybe?**
> **May** and **be** appear together as two separate words when they are both used as verbs:
> *I may be late for dinner tonight.*
> **Remember:** the adverb **maybe** is always written as one word:
> *Maybe you should leave work earlier?*

> **! Common mistake: may or can?**
> **Warning:** Choose the correct verb!
> To talk about the possibility that something will happen when you are not certain, use **may**:
> *Rory may be late again. The traffic is very heavy.*
> When you are certain that something is possible, don't say 'may', say **can**:
> ~~*You may get to my house by bus or by train.*~~
> *You can get to my house by bus or by train.*

PERMISSION ▷ **2** B1 formal used to ask or give permission: *A reader may borrow up to six books at any one time.* ◦ *'May I help myself to some more food?'*

M

'Yes, of course.' ◦ *Hi, my name's Tiffany. How may I help you?* → Compare **might** **WISH** ▷ **3** formal used to introduce a wish or a hope: *May you have a long and fruitful marriage.*

IDIOMS **be that as it may** formal used to mean that you accept that a piece of information is true but it does not change your opinion of the subject you are discussing: *Building a new children's home will cost a lot of money but, be that as it may, there is an urgent need for the facility.* • **may I ask** used in questions to show disapproval: *What, may I ask, was the point of repeating the tests?* • **may well** B2 If you say that something may well happen, you mean that it is likely to happen: *She may well not want to travel alone.*

▸noun [U] (also **may blossom**) the flowers of the HAWTHORN tree

May /meɪ/ noun [C or U] A1 the fifth month of the year, after April and before June: *My mother's birthday is **in** May.* ◦ *They got married **on** 12 May.* ◦ *We're supposed to be moving into new offices **next** May.*

maybe /ˈmeɪ.bi/ adv **1** A2 used to show that something is possible or that something might be true: *Maybe they'll come tomorrow.* ◦ *Maybe you were right after all.* **2** informal used to show that a number or amount is approximate: *There were 200, maybe 300, refugees on the boat.* **3** A2 used to politely suggest or ask for something: *Maybe Ted would like to go.* ◦ *Maybe we should start again.* **4** used to avoid giving a clear or certain answer to a question: *'Are you coming to Kelly's party?' 'Maybe.'* **5** used to mean that something is a possible explanation for why something else happened: *'Why were you chosen for the team and not me?' 'Maybe it's because I've been to more practice sessions than you.'*

Mayday /ˈmeɪ.deɪ/ noun [S], **exclamation** a special radio signal sent from a ship or an aircraft when it needs help

ˈMay ˌDay noun [C usually singular] the first day of May, a holiday in many countries. It traditionally celebrates spring but now it is often used to honour workers.

mayfly /ˈmeɪ.flaɪ/ noun [C] an insect which lives near water and only lives for a very short time as an adult

mayhem /ˈmeɪ.hem/ noun [U] a situation in which there is little or no order or control: *With 20 kids running around and only two adults to supervise, it was complete mayhem.*

mayonnaise /ˌmeɪ.əˈneɪz/ US /ˈmeɪ.ə.neɪz/ noun [U] (informal **mayo**) a thick, white sauce made from oil, VINEGAR, and the yellow part of eggs, usually eaten cold

mayor /meəʳ/ US /mer/ noun [C] B2 a person who is elected or chosen to be the leader of the group who governs a town or city • **mayoral** /ˈmeə.rəl/ US /ˈmeɪ.ɔːr.əl/ adj *mayoral duties*

mayoralty /ˈmeə.rəl.ti/ US /ˈmeɪ.ɔːr.əl-/ noun [U] the office of being a mayor, or the period of time for which someone is a mayor

mayoress /ˌmeəˈres/ US /ˈmer.ɪs/ noun [C] a female mayor, or the wife of a mayor

maypole /ˈmeɪ.pəʊl/ US /-poʊl/ noun [C] a tall pole with long RIBBONS (= narrow strips of cloth) fixed to the top of it, the ends of which people hold as they dance around the pole on the first of May

maze /meɪz/ noun [C] **PLACE** ▷ **1** a complicated system of paths or passages which people try to find their way through for entertainment **2** an area in which you can get easily lost because there are so many similar streets or passages: *The old part of the town was a maze of narrow passages.* **RULES/IDEAS** ▷ **3** a complicated set of rules, ideas, or subjects which you find difficult to deal with or understand: *It's almost impossible to get through the maze **of** bureaucracy.*

MB /ˌemˈbiː/ noun [C] **QUALIFICATION** ▷ **1** UK (US **BM**) abbreviation for Bachelor of Medicine: a degree in medicine, or a person who has this degree **COMPUTING** ▷ **2** written abbreviation for megabyte: a unit used in measuring the amount of information a computer can store, which has the value 1,048,576 BYTES

MBA /ˌem.biːˈeɪ/ noun [C] abbreviation for Master of Business Administration: an advanced degree in business, or a person who has this degree

MBE /ˌem.biːˈiː/ noun [C] abbreviation for Member of the Order of the British Empire: a British honour given to a person by the Queen for a particular achievement

MC /ˌemˈsiː/ noun [C] abbreviation for **master of ceremonies**

MD /ˌemˈdiː/ noun [C] **DOCTOR** ▷ **1** US abbreviation for Doctor of Medicine: a degree which someone must have to work as a doctor: *Steven Tay, MD* **MANAGER** ▷ **2** UK abbreviation for **managing director**: *You should talk to the MD about your proposal.* **RECORDING** ▷ **3** abbreviation for **MiniDisc**

MDF /ˌem.diːˈef/ noun [U] abbreviation for medium-density fibreboard: a type of board made from very small pieces of wood that have been pressed and stuck together, used for making furniture

me pronoun; noun

▸pronoun /miː/, /mi/ A1 used, usually as the object of a verb or preposition, to refer to the person speaking or writing: *Is there one for me?* ◦ *She gave me some money.* ◦ *Could you pass me that book?* ◦ *It wasn't me who offered to go, it was Charlotte.* → See also **I**

> **! Usage: me or I?**
>
> **Me** is used after 'than', 'as', or 'to be'. It would be wrong or would sound very formal if you used **I**:
>
> *She's taller than me.*
> *David is not as tall as me.*
> *'Who's there?' 'It's me.'*
>
> Sometimes **me** is used with another noun as the subject of a sentence, especially in informal English:
>
> *Jane and me went to the cinema yesterday.* (informal)
> *Jane and I went to the cinema yesterday.*

▸noun [S] /miː/ /miː/ [S] the musical note **mi**

ME /ˌemˈiː/ noun [U] UK abbreviation for myalgic encephalomyelitis: an illness, sometimes lasting for several years, in which a person's muscles and JOINTS (= places where two bones are connected) hurt and they are generally very tired → See also **chronic fatigue syndrome**

mea culpa /ˌmeɪ.əˈkʊl.pə/ **exclamation** humorous used to admit that something was your fault

mead /miːd/ noun [U] an alcoholic drink made from HONEY that was drunk in the past

meadow /ˈmed.əʊ/ US /-oʊ/ noun [C or U] a field with grass and often wild flowers in it

meagre UK (US **meager**) /ˈmiː.gəʳ/ US /-gɚ/ adj (of amounts or numbers) very small or not enough: *a meagre **salary*** ◦ *The prisoners existed on a meagre **diet**.*

meal /mɪəl/ noun **FOOD** ▷ **1** A1 [C] an occasion when food is eaten, or the food that is eaten on such an occasion: *a **hot** meal ◦ a three-course meal ◦ a **heavy** (= large) meal ◦ a **light** (= small) meal ◦ I have my **main** meal at midday. ◦ You must come round for a meal sometime.* **POWDER** ▷ **2** [U] a substance that has been crushed to make a rough powder, especially plant seeds crushed to make flour or for animal food: *bone meal ◦ soya meal*

IDIOM **make a meal (out) of sth** UK disapproving to spend more time or energy doing something than is necessary: *I only asked for a summary of the main points but she's making a real meal out of it.*

ˌmeals on ˈwheels noun [U] a service which takes hot meals to the homes of old and ill people, either for free or for a small payment

ˈmeal ˌticket noun **FOOD** ▷ **1** [C] US for **luncheon voucher** **MONEY** ▷ **2** [C usually singular] someone or something that you use as a way of getting regular amounts of money: *Gone are the days when a university degree was a meal ticket for life.*

mealtime /ˈmɪəl.taɪm/ noun [C usually plural] a time at which a meal is eaten: *The only time our family gets together is **at** mealtimes.*

mealy /ˈmiː.li/ adj dry and like a powder: *mealy potatoes ◦ a mealy apple*

ˌmealy-ˈmouthed adj disapproving not brave enough to say what you mean directly and honestly: *mealy-mouthed excuses ◦ a mealy-mouthed spokesperson*

mean /miːn/ verb; adj; noun

▸verb (**meant**, **meant**) **EXPRESS** ▷ **1** A2 [T] to express or represent something such as an idea, thought, or fact: *What does this word mean?* ◦ [+ that] *These figures mean **that** almost six percent of the working population is unemployed. ◦ What do you mean **by** that remark? ◦ She's quite odd though. Do you know what I mean?* **2** [T] used to add emphasis to what you are saying: *I want you home by midnight. **And I** mean midnight. ◦ Give it back now! I mean **it**.* **HAVE RESULT** ▷ **3** B1 [T] to have a particular result: *Lower costs mean lower prices.* ◦ [+ that] *Advances in electronics mean **that** the technology is already available.* ◦ [+ -ing verb] *If we want to catch the 7.30 train, that will mean leav**ing** the house at 6.00.* **INTEND** ▷ **4** B1 [I or T] to intend: *I'm sorry if I offended you – I didn't mean **any harm**. ◦ The books with large print are meant **for** our partially sighted readers.* ◦ [+ to infinitive] *I've been meaning **to** phone you all week. ◦ Do you think she meant **to** say 9 a.m. instead of 9 p.m.?* ◦ [+ obj + to infinitive] *This exercise isn't meant to be difficult. ◦ They didn't mean **for** her **to** read the letter.* **HAVE IMPORTANCE** ▷ **5** B1 [T] to have an important emotional effect on someone: *It wasn't a valuable picture but it meant a lot **to** me. ◦ Possessions mean nothing **to** him.*

IDIOMS **be meant for each other** If you say two people are meant for each other, you think they suit each other as romantic partners. • **I mean 1** A2 used to correct what you have just said or to add more information: *I really do love him – as a friend, I mean.* **2** something that people often say before they start or continue their sentence: *I mean, he's a good teacher, but I just don't like him.* • **mean business** informal to want very much to achieve something • **mean well** C2 to do what you think will be helpful, although by doing it you might cause problems without intending to: *I know he means well, but he just gets in the way.* → See also **well meaning** • **what do you mean?** used to show that you are annoyed or that you disagree: *What do you mean, it was my fault?*

▸adj **NOT GENEROUS** ▷ **1** B2 mainly UK not willing to give or share things, especially money: *He's too mean to buy her a ring. ◦ My landlord's very mean **with** the heating – it's only on for two hours each day.* **NOT KIND** ▷ **2** B2 unkind or unpleasant: *Stop being so mean **to** me! ◦ She just said it to be mean.* **VIOLENT** ▷ **3** mainly US frightening and likely to become violent: *a mean and angry mob ◦ a mean-looking youth* **GOOD** ▷ **4** [before noun] informal very good: *She's a mean piano player. ◦ She plays a mean piano (= she plays very well).* **MATHEMATICS** ▷ **5** C2 [before noun] specialized (in mathematics) a mean number is an average number: *a mean value ◦ Their mean weight was 76.4 kilos.*

IDIOMS **no mean** used to say a person is very good at a certain activity: *He's no mean cook.* • **no mean achievement/feat** a great achievement: *Getting the job finished on time was no mean achievement.*

▸noun [S] **MATHEMATICS** ▷ **1** (also **the arithmetic mean**) (in mathematics) the result you get by adding two or more amounts together and dividing the total by the number of amounts: ***The** mean **of** 5, 4, 10, and 15 is 8.5.* → Compare **average** **METHOD** ▷ **2** formal a quality or way of doing something that is in the middle of two completely different qualities or ways of doing something: *We need to find **a** mean **between** exam questions that are too difficult and those that are too easy.*

meander /miˈæn.dəʳ/ US /-dɚ/ verb; noun

▸verb **RIVER/ROAD** ▷ **1** [I] If a river, stream, or road meanders, it follows a route that is not straight or direct. **WALK** ▷ **2** [I usually + adv/prep] to walk slowly without any clear direction: *We spent the afternoon meandering **around** the streets of the old town.* **NO PURPOSE** ▷ **3** [I] If a text, process, or activity meanders, it has no clear direction: *The film meanders **along** with no particular story line.*

▸noun [C] **RIVER** ▷ **1** a curve of a river or stream **JOURNEY** ▷ **2** a journey that has no particular direction: *The TV series continues its haphazard meander **around** the globe – this week in Portugal.*

meandering /miˈæn.dəʳ.ɪŋ/ US /-dɚ-/ adj moving slowly in no particular direction or with no clear purpose: *a meandering **river** ◦ a long meandering **speech***

meanderings /miˈæn.dəʳ.ɪŋz/ US /-dɚ-/ noun [plural] talk that continues for a longer time than is necessary and is not interesting

meanie (also **meany**) /ˈmiː.ni/ noun [C] child's word someone who is unkind: *Don't be such a meanie!*

meaning /ˈmiː.nɪŋ/ noun **OF WORD/WRITING/SIGN, ETC.** ▷ **1** B1 [C or U] The meaning of something is what it expresses or represents: *The word 'flight' has two different meanings: a plane journey, and the act of running away. ◦ The meaning of his gesture was clear. ◦ His novels often have (a) **hidden** meaning.* **IMPORTANCE** ▷ **2** B2 [U] importance or value: *The birth of her first grandchild gave new meaning to her life. ◦ Education had no great meaning **for** him until much later in his life.*

> Word partners for **meaning** (**OF WORD, WRITING, SIGN, ETC.**)
>
> *grasp/understand* the meaning • *convey/express* the meaning • *clarify/explain* the meaning • a *different/hidden* meaning • the *exact/precise/real/true* meaning • the meaning *behind/of* sth

> Word partners for **meaning** (**IMPORTANCE**)
>
> *give* meaning *to* sth • *lose* (its) meaning • be *without* meaning

meaningful /ˈmiː.nɪŋ.fəl/ adj **EXPRESSING STH** ▷ **1** B2 intended to show meaning, often secretly: *a meaningful look* **IMPORTANT/SERIOUS** ▷ **2** B2 useful, serious, or important: *She seems to find it difficult to form meaningful relationships.* ◦ *Having the opportunity to work would make retirement more meaningful **for** many pensioners.* • **meaningfully** /-i/ adv • **meaningfulness** /-nəs/ noun [U]

meaningless /ˈmiː.nɪŋ.ləs/ adj **NO MEANING** ▷ **1** having no meaning: *a meaningless phrase* **NOT IMPORTANT** ▷ **2** having no importance or value: *a meaningless gesture* • **meaninglessly** /-li/ adv • **meaninglessness** /-nəs/ noun [U]

meanly /ˈmiːn.li/ adv showing that you are not willing to give or share things, especially money

meanness /ˈmiːn.nəs/ noun [U] the quality of being unwilling to give or share things, especially money

means /miːnz/ noun (plural **means**) **METHOD** ▷ **1** B2 [C] a method or way of doing something: *They had no means **of** communication.* ◦ *We need to find some other means **of** transportation.* ◦ *We must use every means at our disposal.* ◦ *She tried to explain **by** means **of** sign language.* ◦ *There is no means **of** tracing the debt at all.* ◦ *The family **had** no means **of** support (= way of getting money).* **MONEY** ▷ **2** C2 [plural] money, for example from an income, that allows you to buy things: [+ to infinitive] *He **has** the means **to** buy half the houses in the street if he wanted to.* **3 live beyond your means** to spend more money than you receive as income **4 live within your means** to spend less money than you receive as income **5 a man/woman of means** a rich man/woman

M

> **! Common mistake: means**
>
> **Warning: Means**, meaning 'method', always has an s. Don't write 'mean', write **means**:
>
> ~~*The bicycle is a convenient mean of transport.*~~
>
> *The bicycle is a convenient means of transport.*

IDIOMS **by all means** C2 used to give permission: *'May I borrow this book?' 'By all means.'* • **by no means** (also **not by any means**) C1 not at all: *It is by no means certain that we'll finish the project by June.* ◦ *This isn't the last we'll hear of it by any means.* • **a means to an end** C2 something that you do because it will help you to achieve something else: *I didn't particularly like the job – it was just a means to an end.*

ˈmeans-ˌtesting noun [U] UK the official process of measuring how much income a person has in order to decide if they should receive money from the government • **ˈmeans ˌtest** noun [C] • **ˈmeans-ˌtest** verb [T] *People who apply for housing benefit must be means-tested.* • **ˈmeans-ˌtested** adj *means-tested benefits*

meantime /ˈmiːn.taɪm/ noun **in the meantime** B2 until something expected happens, or while something else is happening: *Your computer won't arrive till Thursday. In the meantime, you can use Jude's.*

meanwhile /ˈmiːn.waɪl/ adv B1 until something expected happens, or while something else is happening: *Carl's starting college in September. Meanwhile, he's travelling around Europe.*

meany /ˈmiː.ni/ noun [C] a **meanie**

measles /ˈmiː.zlz/ noun [U] an infectious disease which produces small red spots all over the body

measly /ˈmiːz.li/ adj informal too small in size or amount, or not enough: *a measly amount of money* ◦ *a measly little present* • **measliness** /-nəs/ noun [U]

measurable /ˈmeʒ.ər.ə.bl/ US /-ɚ-/ adj able to be measured, or large enough to be noticed: *The service produces clear, measurable benefits to people's health.* • **measurably** /-bli/ adv

measure /ˈmeʒ.ər/ US /-ɚ/ verb; noun

▸verb **SIZE** ▷ **1** B2 [L only + noun, T] to discover the exact size or amount of something, or to be of a particular size: *'Will the table fit in here?' 'I don't know – let's measure it.'* ◦ *This machine measures your heart rate.* ◦ *He measured the flour into the bowl.* ◦ *The area, measuring/which measures five kilometres by three kilometres, has been purchased by the army.* **JUDGE** ▷ **2** C2 [T] to judge the quality, effect, importance, or value of something: *There is no way of measuring the damage done to morale.*

PHRASAL VERBS **measure sb/sth against sb/sth** to judge someone or something by comparing them against someone or something else: *She measured the shoe **against** the footprint, but it was smaller.* • **measure sth out** to weigh or measure a small amount of something from a larger amount of something: *Measure out 250 grams of flour and sift it into a large mixing bowl.* • **measure up** to be good enough, or as good as someone or something else: *She could never measure up **to** her mother's expectations.* • **measure sth/sb up** to discover what size something or someone is by measuring them

▸noun **METHOD** ▷ **1** B2 [C usually plural] a way of achieving something, or a method for dealing with a situation: *What further measures can we **take** to avoid terrorism?* ◦ *These measures were designed to improve car safety.* ◦ [+ to infinitive] *Emergency measures **to** help the refugees are badly needed.* **SIZE** ▷ **2** [C or U] a unit used for stating the size, weight, etc. of something, or a way of measuring: *weights and measures* ◦ *The sample's density is a measure of its purity.* **3** C2 [C or U] formal amount: *There was **a** large measure **of** agreement between the candidates.* ◦ *His success was **in** some measure due to his being in the right place at the right time.* **4** C2 [C] an exact amount, especially of alcohol: *One unit of alcohol is equal to half a pint of beer or a standard measure of spirits.* **5** [C] US for **bar** **WAY OF JUDGING** ▷ **6** C2 [C] a way of judging something: *Record sales are not always **a** measure **of** a singer's popularity.* ◦ *We have no accurate measure **of** the damage.*

IDIOM **have the measure of sb/sth** formal to understand what someone or something is like and to know how to deal with them: *I don't think she's under any illusions about her husband – she's got the measure of him.*

measured /ˈmeʒ.əd/ US /-ɚd/ adj careful and controlled, or not fast: *Her response to their criticism was calm and measured.*

measurement /ˈmeʒ.ə.mənt/ US /-ɚ-/ noun **1** C2 [C or U] the act or process of measuring: *The test is based on the measurement of blood levels.* ◦ *The machine makes thousands of measurements every day.* **2** B2 [C] the size, shape, quality, etc. of something, which you discover by measuring it: *The measurements **of** both rooms were identical.* ◦ *What is your inside leg measurement?* **3 measurements** [plural] Your measurements are the sizes of various parts of your body, especially your chest, waist, and hips, which you refer to when you want to buy clothes.

ˈmeasuring ˌjug noun [C] UK (US **ˈmeasuring ˌcup**) a container used for measuring liquids with lines printed on the side showing how much it contains

meat /miːt/ noun **FOOD** ▷ **1** A1 [U] the flesh of an animal when it is used for food: *I don't eat meat.*

◦ **raw** meat ◦ **red/white** meat **2** [C] a type of meat: *a buffet of* ***cold*** *meats and cheeses* **INTEREST** ▷ **3** [U] important, valuable, or interesting ideas or information: *It was a nicely written article and quite amusing but there wasn't much meat to it.*

IDIOMS **be meat and drink to sb** If a difficult or unpleasant activity is meat and drink to someone, they enjoy doing it very much and find it easy. • **one man's meat is another man's poison** saying said to emphasize that people like different things

ˌmeat-and-poˈtatoes adj [before noun] US more basic or important than other things: *For many unions, the meat-and-potatoes issue is no longer pay increases but job security.*

meatball /ˈmiːt.bɔːl/ (US) /-bɑːl/ noun [C] one of several small balls of meat that are eaten hot with a sauce: *spaghetti and meatballs*

ˌmeat ˈloaf noun [C or U] meat cut into extremely small pieces, mixed with other things, cooked in a container, and then cut into slices to be eaten

meaty /ˈmiː.ti/ (US) /-t̬i/ adj **FOOD** ▷ **1** full of meat or tasting a lot of meat: *a good meaty stew* **2** large and having a lot of flesh: *meaty tomatoes* **INTERESTING** ▷ **3** having a lot of important or interesting ideas: *a meaty book/letter/report* ◦ *She has written some wonderfully meaty parts for older actresses.* • **meatiness** /-nəs/ noun [U]

Mecca /ˈmek.ə/ noun **1** the holy city of Islam in Saudi Arabia **2** [C usually singular] a place to which many people are attracted: *His Indiana bookstore became a Mecca* ***for*** *writers and artists.* ◦ *The scheme would transform the park into a tourist Mecca.*

mechanic /məˈkæn.ɪk/ noun **JOB** ▷ **1** A2 [C] someone whose job is repairing the engines of vehicles and other machines: *a car/garage/motor mechanic* **STUDY** ▷ **2 mechanics** [U] the study of the effect of physical forces on objects and their movement **WAY OF WORKING** ▷ **3 the mechanics** [plural] informal the way something works or happens: *He knows a lot about the mechanics* ***of*** *running a school.*

mechanical /məˈkæn.ɪ.kəl/ adj **MACHINES** ▷ **1** B2 describes machines or their parts: *a mechanical* ***device*** ◦ *The company produces mechanical* ***parts*** *for airplane engines.* ◦ *The plane appeared to have crashed because of a mechanical* ***problem.*** **WITHOUT THOUGHT** ▷ **2** C2 (also **mechanistic**) without thinking about what you are doing, especially because you do something often: *I was taught to read in a mechanical way.*

meˌchanical enginˈeering noun [U] the study of the design and production of machines

mechanically /məˈkæn.ɪ.kəl.i/ adv **MACHINES** ▷ **1** using or relating to machines: *Most crops are harvested mechanically.* ◦ *I'm not very mechanically* ***minded*** *(= do not understand how machines work).* **WITHOUT THOUGHT** ▷ **2** (also **mechanistically**) without thinking about what you are doing, especially because you do something often

mechanism /ˈmek.ə.nɪ.zəm/ noun [C] **MACHINE PART** ▷ **1** C1 a part of a machine, or a set of parts that work together: *These automatic cameras have a special focusing mechanism.* **SYSTEM** ▷ **2** C1 a way of doing something that is planned or part of a system: *The mechanism* ***for*** *collecting taxes needs revising.* **BEHAVIOUR** ▷ **3** a part of your behaviour that helps you to deal with a difficult situation: *She's actually rather insecure, and her rudeness is just a* ***defence*** *mechanism.*

mechanistic /ˌmek.əˈnɪs.tɪk/ adj thinking of living things as if they were machines: *According to mechanistic views of behaviour, human action can be explained in terms of cause and effect.*

mechanize (UK usually **mechanise**) /ˈmek.ə.naɪz/ verb [T] to use a machine to do something that used to be done by hand: *Farming has been mechanized, reducing the need for labour.* • **mechanization** (UK usually **mechanisation**) /ˌmek.ə.naɪˈzeɪ.ʃən/ (US) /-nəˈ-/ noun [U] • **mechanized** (UK usually **mechanised**) adj

med /med/ adj mainly US informal **medical**: *med* ***school*** ◦ *a med* ***student***

the Med /ˈmed/ noun UK informal the Mediterranean sea or the countries near it: *They're going on a cruise round the Med.*

medal /ˈmed.əl/ noun; verb

▸noun [C] B2 a small metal disc, with words or a picture on it, given as a reward for a brave action, for winning a competition, or to remember a special event: *He was* ***awarded*** *a medal* ***for*** *bravery.* ◦ *She* ***won*** *three Olympic gold medals.*

▸verb [I] (-ll- or -l-) to win a medal in a sports competition: *She's medalled in both the heptathlon and the long jump.*

medallion /məˈdæl.jən/ noun [C] **METAL DISC** ▷ **1** a metal disc that is worn for decoration on a chain or string around the neck **MEAT** ▷ **2** a flat circular piece of meat without bones: *medallions of pork*

medallist UK (US **medalist**) /ˈmed.əl.ɪst/ noun [C] a person who has won a medal in sport: *She's a bronze medallist* ***in*** *judo.*

meddle /ˈmed.l/ verb [I] disapproving to try to change or have an influence on things that are not your responsibility, especially by criticizing in a damaging or annoying way: *My sister's always meddling* ***in*** *other people's* ***affairs.*** ◦ *People shouldn't meddle* ***with*** *things they don't understand.* • **meddler** /-əʳ/ (US) /-ɚ/ noun [C] • **meddling** /ˈmed.l̩.ɪŋ/, /-lɪŋ/ noun [U]

meddlesome /ˈmed.l̩.səm/ adj disapproving often getting involved in situations where you are not wanted, especially by criticizing in a damaging or annoying way

media /ˈmiː.di.ə/ noun **NEWSPAPERS** ▷ **1 the media** B2 [S, + sing/pl verb] the internet, newspapers, magazines, television, etc., considered as a group: *the* ***local/national*** *media* ◦ *media* ***attention/coverage/hype/reports*** ◦ *The issue has been much discussed* ***in*** *the media.* → See also **multimedia** **MEDIUM** ▷ **2** plural of **medium**

mediaeval /ˌmed.iˈiː.vəl/ adj **medieval**

median /ˈmiː.di.ən/ adj specialized describes the value that is the middle one in a set of values arranged in order of size: *Median household income fell last year.* • **median** noun [C]

ˈmedian ˌstrip noun [C usually singular] US and Australian English the narrow piece of land between the two halves of a large road → Compare **central reservation**

mediate /ˈmiː.di.eɪt/ verb [I or T] to talk to two separate people or groups involved in a disagreement to try to help them to agree or find a solution to their problems: *Negotiators were called in to mediate* ***between*** *the two sides.* ◦ *The two envoys have succeeded in mediating an end to the war.* • **mediation** /ˌmiː.diˈeɪ.ʃən/ noun [U] *Last-minute attempts at mediation failed.* • **mediator** /-eɪ.təʳ/ (US) /-eɪ.t̬ɚ/ noun [C]

medic /ˈmed.ɪk/ noun [C] **1** UK informal a medical student or doctor **2** US someone who does medical work in the military

Medicaid /ˈmed.ɪ.keɪd/ noun a government service in the US which allows poor people to receive medical treatment both in and out of hospitals → Compare **Medicare**

medical /ˈmed.ɪ.kəl/ **adj; noun**

▸**adj** B2 related to the treatment of illness and injuries: *medical advice* ◦ *medical books* ◦ *a medical team* ◦ *medical workers* • **medically** /-i/ **adv** C2 *The doctor declared her medically **fit** (= she had no illness or injury).*

▸**noun** [C] mainly UK (mainly US **physical**) an examination of your body by a doctor to find out if you are healthy: *The insurance company wanted me to have a medical.*

ˈ**medical** ˌ**hall** **noun** [C] Indian English a shop where you can buy medicines; a **pharmacy**

Medicare /ˈmed.ɪ.keəʳ/ US /-ker/ **noun** **1** a government service in the US that allows people aged 65 and over to receive medical treatment both in and out of hospitals → Compare **Medicaid** **2** a government service in Australia that allows people to receive medical treatment, paid for through taxes

medicated /ˈmed.ɪ.keɪ.tɪd/ US /-t̬ɪd/ **adj** containing a medical substance: *medicated lotion/shampoo/tissues*

medication /ˌmed.ɪˈkeɪ.ʃən/ **noun** [C or U] C2 a medicine, or a set of medicines or drugs, used to improve a particular condition or illness: *He is currently **on/taking** medication **for** his heart.* ◦ *In the study, patients were taken off their usual medications.*

medicinal /məˈdɪs.ɪ.nəl/ **adj** Medicinal substances are used to cure illnesses: *I keep a bottle of brandy purely **for** medicinal **purposes**.* • **medicinally** /-i/ **adv**

M

medicine /ˈmed.ɪ.sən/, /ˈmed.sən/ **noun** **TREATMENT** ▷ **1** B1 [U] treatment for illness or injury, or the study of this: *paediatric/preventative medicine* ◦ *orthodox/Western medicine* ◦ *a career **in** medicine* ◦ *She is a doctor, but is unable to **practise** medicine (= work as a doctor) in her own country.* **SUBSTANCE** ▷ **2** A2 [C or U] a substance, especially in the form of a liquid or a pill, that is a treatment for illness or injury: *cough medicine* ◦ ***Take** two spoonfuls of medicine at mealtimes.* ◦ *She knows quite a lot about herbal medicines.*

> Word partners for **medicine** (**TREATMENT**)
>
> *practise* medicine • *study* medicine • a *branch* of medicine • (advances/a career) *in* medicine

> Word partners for **medicine** (**SUBSTANCE**)
>
> *take* medicine • *prescribe* (sb) a medicine • medicine *for* sth • medicine *to* do sth • a *dose of* medicine

> Other ways of saying **medicine**
>
> A common alternative to 'medicine' is **drug**:
>
> *The new **drug** has been shown to eliminate tumours.*
>
> **Medication** is a medicine or set of medicines for a particular illness or condition:
>
> *He's currently on **medication** for his heart.*
>
> A small solid piece of medicine is a **pill** or **tablet**:
>
> *He takes a sleeping **pill** at night.*
>
> *Do you take any vitamin **tablets**?*
>
> **Ointment** is medicine in the form of a cream that you rub into your skin:
>
> *Apply the **ointment** to the sore area.*
>
> **Drops** are a type of liquid medicine that you put into your eyes, ears, or nose in small amounts:
>
> *These eye **drops** should clear up the infection.*

IDIOM **give sb a dose/taste of their own medicine** to treat someone as badly as they have treated you

medico /ˈmed.ɪ.kəʊ/ US /-koʊ/ **noun** [C] (plural **medicos**) UK informal a doctor

medieval (also **mediaeval**) /ˌmed.iˈiː.vəl/ **adj** B2 related to the MIDDLE AGES (= the period in European history from about 600 AD to 1500 AD): *a medieval building/painting/town* ◦ *a medieval manuscript*

mediocre /ˌmiː.diˈəʊ.kəʳ/ US /-ˈoʊ.kɚ/ **adj** disapproving C2 not very good: *The film's plot is predictable and the acting is mediocre.* ◦ *Parents don't want their children going to mediocre schools.*

mediocrity /ˌmiː.diˈɒk.rə.ti/ US /-ˈɑː.krə.t̬i/ **noun** **1** C2 [U] the quality of being not very good: *A goal just before half-time rescued the match from mediocrity.* **2** [C] a person who is not very good at something: *These people are just mediocrities (= people who do not have much skill or ability at anything).*

meditate /ˈmed.ɪ.teɪt/ **verb** [I] **1** to think calm thoughts in order to relax or as a religious activity: *Sophie meditates for 20 minutes every day.* **2** to think seriously about something for a long time: *He meditated **on** the consequences of his decision.*

meditation /ˌmed.ɪˈteɪ.ʃən/ **noun** **1** the act of giving your attention to only one thing, either as a religious activity or as a way of becoming calm and relaxed: *prayer and meditation* ◦ *She practises meditation.* **2** [C or U] serious thought or study, or the product of this activity: *Let us spend a few moments **in** quiet meditation.* ◦ *I left him deep in meditation.* ◦ *The book is a meditation **on** the morality of art.* • **meditative** /ˈmed.ɪ.tə.tɪv/ US /-t̬ɪv/ **adj** formal

Mediterranean /ˌmed.ɪ.təˈreɪ.ni.ən/ **noun; adj**

▸**noun** **the Mediterranean** **a** (also **the Mediterranean Sea**, informal **the Med**) the sea surrounded by southern Europe, northern Africa, and the Middle East **b** the countries next to the Mediterranean Sea

▸**adj** relating to the Mediterranean Sea or the countries around it: *a Mediterranean climate* ◦ *The Mediterranean diet is famously healthy including, as it does, olive oil and fresh fruit and vegetables.*

medium /ˈmiː.di.əm/ **adj; noun**

▸**adj** **MIDDLE** ▷ **1** B1 being in the middle between an upper and lower amount, size, degree, or value: *a girl of medium height* ◦ *a medium-sized book* **MEAT** ▷ **2** (of meat) cooked so that it is no longer red in the middle: *Would you like your steak rare, medium, or well-done?*

▸**noun** [C] **METHOD** ▷ **1** C2 (plural **media** or **mediums**) a method or way of expressing something: *the broadcasting/print medium* ◦ *They told the story **through** the medium **of** dance.* **PERSON** ▷ **2** (plural **mediums**) a person who says that they can receive messages from people who are dead **SUBSTANCE** ▷ **3** a substance that something grows in, lives in, or moves through

ˌ**medium** ˈ**rare** **adj** (of meat) cooked so that it is still slightly red in the middle: *I'd like my steak medium rare, please.* → Compare **medium, rare, well done**

ˈ**medium** ˌ**wave** **noun** [U] (written abbreviation **MW**) a range of radio waves with a frequency between 300 kHz and 3MHz

ˌ**medium-**ˈ**well** **adj** (of meat) cooked so that it has a small amount of pink in the centre

medley /ˈmed.li/ **noun** [C] **MIXTURE** ▷ **1** a mixture of different things, especially tunes put together to form a longer piece of music: *a medley **of** popular tunes* ◦ *The menu described the dessert as 'a medley **of** exotic fruits'.* **SWIMMING COMPETITION** ▷ **2** a swimming competition in which each of four swimmers in a team uses a different method of swimming

meds /medz/ **noun** [plural] mainly US informal a

medicine or a set of medicines that someone takes regularly: *Has he taken his meds today?*

medulla oblongata /meˌdʌl.ə.ɒb.lɒŋˈgɑː.tə/ (US) /mɪˈdʌl.ə.ɑːb.lɑːŋˈgɑː.t̬ə/ noun [C usually sing] (plural **medullae oblongatae** or **medulla oblongatas**) specialized the lowest part of the brain, positioned at the top of the SPINAL CORD, that controls activities such as HEARTBEAT, BLOOD PRESSURE, and breathing

meek /miːk/ adj quiet, gentle, and not willing to argue or express your opinions in a forceful way: *She seemed so very meek and mild.* • **meekly** /ˈmiː.kli/ adv • **meekness** /ˈmiːk.nəs/ noun [U]

meerkat /ˈmɪə.kæt/ (US) /ˈmɪr-/ noun [C] a small, grey, southern African animal that sometimes sits up on its back legs

meet /miːt/ verb; noun

▸verb (**met**, **met**) **FOR THE FIRST TIME** ▷ **1** (A1) [T or I] to see and speak to someone for the first time: *They met at work.* ◦ *I met her in Hawaii.* ◦ *Would you like to meet my sister?* ◦ *Come and meet (= be introduced to) my friend Laura.* **COME TOGETHER** ▷ **2** (A1) [I or T] to come together with someone intentionally: *Lorraine and I meet for lunch once a month.* ◦ *We agreed to meet on Tuesday to discuss the project.* ◦ *The children's club meets every Thursday afternoon.* ◦ *They're meeting* ***with*** *their advisers to work out a new plan.* ◦ *The president met the UK prime minister in London yesterday.* **3** (A1) [T or I] to come together with someone without intending to: *It's always awkward when you meet someone you know, but you can't remember their name.* ◦ *Guess who I met in town today.* ◦ *We met our old neighbours at an auction last Saturday.* **SATISFY** ▷ **4** (C1) [T] to FULFIL, satisfy, or achieve: *The workers' demands for higher pay were not met by the management.* ◦ *We haven't yet been able to find a house that meets our* ***needs/requirements****.* ◦ *They will only agree to sign the contract if certain* ***conditions*** *are met.* ◦ *Do you think we will be able to meet our* ***deadline/target****?* **5** [T] to pay: *The company has agreed to meet all our expenses.* **PLACE** ▷ **6** (B1) [T] to wait at a place for someone or something to arrive: *Will you meet me at the airport (= be there when the aircraft arrives)?* **TOUCH** ▷ **7** [I or T] to touch or join something: *There's a large crack where the ceiling meets the wall.* ◦ *The curtains don't quite meet.* ◦ *Turn left where the lane meets the main road.* **EXPERIENCE** ▷ **8** [T] to experience something: *I've never met that kind of problem/system before.* ◦ *He met his death (= he died) in the icy waters of the South Atlantic.*

IDIOMS **be more to this than meets the eye** If there is more to something than meets the eye, it is more difficult to understand or involves more things than you thought at the beginning. • **eyes meet** If people's eyes meet, they look at each other at the same time: *Their eyes met across a crowded room.* • **meet sb's eye** to look at someone directly while they are looking at you: *I tried to avoid meeting his eye.* • **meet sb halfway** to do some of the things that someone wants you to do, in order to show that you want to reach an agreement or improve your relationship with them • **meet your maker** humorous to die • **meet your match** to compete unsuccessfully with someone: *He was a good player, but he met his match* ***in*** *Peter.* • **meet your Waterloo** to be defeated by someone who is too strong for you or by a problem that is too difficult for you

PHRASAL VERBS **meet up PEOPLE** ▷ **1** to meet another person in order to do something together: *They suggested we meet up at Mustafa's.* **ROADS** ▷ **2** If roads or paths meet up, they join at a particular place. • **meet with sth EXPERIENCE** ▷ **1** formal to experience something, usually something unpleasant: *I heard she'd met with* ***an accident****.* ◦ *If you meet with any difficulties, just let me know.* **REACTION** ▷ **2** to cause a particular reaction or result: *At the time the decision was met with a barrage of criticism.* ◦ *I trust the arrangements meet with* ***your approval****.*

▸noun [C] **1** US a sports event: *a track/swim meet* ◦ *the first meet of the season* **2** UK an occasion when people go FOX HUNTING

ˌmeet-and-ˈgreet adj A meet-and-greet event is one that has been arranged so that a famous person can meet and talk to people: *The president took a short meet-and-greet walk to the restaurant.* • **ˌmeet-and-ˈgreet** noun [C] a meet-and-greet event

meeting /ˈmiː.tɪŋ/ (US) /-t̬ɪŋ/ noun [C] **1** (A2) an occasion when people come together intentionally or not intentionally: *We're* ***having*** *a meeting on Thursday to discuss the problem.* ◦ *I'm afraid she's* ***in*** *a meeting – I'll ask her to call you back later.* ◦ *A* ***chance*** *(= not intended) meeting with a publisher on an airplane had launched his career.* ◦ *I liked him from our first meeting.* **2** a group of people who have met for a particular purpose: *The meeting wants to look at the proposal again.* **3** UK a sports competition

> **Word partners for meeting**
>
> *have/hold* a meeting • *attend/go to* a meeting • *call/convene/organize/set up* a meeting • an *emergency/face-to-face/private/special* meeting • be *in* a meeting • a meeting *between* [two people] • a meeting *of* [a group of people] • a meeting *with* sb

IDIOM **a meeting of minds** a situation when two or more people have the same opinions about something

ˈmeeting ˌhouse noun [C usually singular] a building used by Quakers (= a Christian group) as their place of worship: *The Friends' (= Quakers') Meeting House*

ˈmeeting ˌpoint noun [C] an area in a large public place, such as an airport or station, where people can arrange to meet

meg /meg/ noun [C] informal for megabyte: used when talking about how much information a computer can store

mega /ˈme.gə/ adj slang very good or very big: *She's got a mega voice.*

mega- /meg.ə-/ prefix **NUMBER** ▷ **1** 1,000,000 times the stated unit: *a megawatt* ◦ *a megabyte* **BIG/GOOD** ▷ **2** informal large in amount or size: *He's mega-rich.* ◦ *They're earning megabucks (= a lot of money).*

megabyte /ˈmeg.ə.baɪt/ noun [C] (written abbreviation **MB**) a unit used in measuring the amount of information a computer can store, which has the value 1,048,576 BYTES

megacity /ˈmeg.ə.sɪt.i/ (US) /-sɪt̬.i/ noun [C] a very large city, especially one with more than 10 million people living in it

megahertz /ˈmeg.ə.hɜːts/ (US) /-hɝːts/ noun [C] (plural **megahertz**) (written abbreviation **MHz**) a million HERTZ

megalith /ˈmeg.ə.lɪθ/ noun [C] a large stone, sometimes forming part of a group or circle, thought to have been important to people in the Stone Age for social or religious reasons • **megalithic** /ˌmeg.əˈlɪθ.ɪk/ adj *megalithic monuments* ◦ *megalithic times (= the period when megaliths were important)*

megalomania /ˌmeg.əl.əˈmeɪ.ni.ə/ noun [U] an unnaturally strong wish for power and control, or

M

the belief that you are very much more important and powerful than you really are • **megalomaniac** /-æk/ noun [C] a person with megalomania • **megalomaniac** adj [before noun] (also **megalomaniacal**)

megaphone /ˈmeg.ə.fəʊn/ (US) /-foʊn/ noun [C] a cone-shaped device which makes your voice louder when you speak into it, so that people can hear you although they are not near to you

megaphone

megapixel /ˈmeg.ə.pɪk.səl/ noun [C] one million PIXELS (= small points that form part of the image on a computer screen), used to measure the amount of detail in images made by a DIGITAL camera, computer screen, etc.

megaplex /ˈme.gə.pleks/ noun [C] a very large cinema where a lot of films are shown at the same time: *a twelve-screen megaplex*

megastar /ˈmeg.ə.stɑːr/ (US) /-stɑːr/ noun [C] a very famous person, especially an actor or pop star

megastore /ˈmeg.ə.stɔːr/ (US) /-stɔːr/ noun [C] a very large shop: *a furniture megastore*

megaton /ˈmeg.ə.tʌn/ noun [C] a unit that has the same value as the force produced by 1,000,000 TONS of TNT (= an explosive), used for measuring the power of explosions, especially nuclear explosions

M

megawatt /ˈmeg.ə.wɒt/ (US) /-wɑːt/ noun [C] a unit for measuring electric power, which has the value of 1,000,000 WATTS

meh /me/ exclamation; adj
▸**exclamation** informal used to show that you are not interested in someone or something or do not care about them or it: *'Hurry up, or you'll be late for school.' 'Meh.'*
▸**adj** informal not very interesting or special: *The trip was kind of meh.*

meiosis /maɪˈəʊ.sɪs/ (US) /-ˈoʊ-/ noun [U] specialized the type of cell division that happens as part of REPRODUCTION (= the process of producing young animals or plants), in which one cell divides into four GAMETES (= reproductive cells), each with a different mixture of CHROMOSOMES and half the number contained in the original cell → Compare **mitosis**

-meister /-maɪ.stər/ (US) /-stɚ/ suffix informal used in a description showing what someone is famous for doing or what someone does very well: *funkmeister* ◦ *the horror-meister, Stephen King*

mela /ˈmeɪ.lə/ noun [C] Indian English a public event that is organized to celebrate a special occasion or an event where goods can be bought and sold

melancholia /ˌmel.əŋˈkəʊ.li.ə/ (US) /-ˈkoʊ-/ noun [U] old-fashioned or literary the condition of feeling unhappy or sad for no obvious reason

melancholic /ˌmel.əŋˈkɒl.ɪk/ (US) /-ˈkɑː.lɪk/ adj formal expressing feelings of sadness: *a melancholic expression* ◦ *melancholic songs*

melancholy /ˈmel.əŋ.kɒl.i/ (US) /-kɑː.li/ adj; noun
▸**adj** sad: *melancholy autumn days* ◦ *a melancholy piece of music*
▸**noun** [U] formal sadness which lasts for a long period of time, often without any obvious reason

mélange /meɪˈlɑ̃ːʒ/ noun [C usually singular] formal a mixture, or a group of different things or people: *Her book presents an interesting mélange **of** ideas.*

melanin /ˈmel.ə.nɪn/ noun [U] a dark brown PIGMENT (= substance that gives colour), found in eyes, skin, hair, feathers, etc. It helps to protect the skin against harmful light from the sun.

melanoma /ˌmel.əˈnəʊ.mə/ (US) /-ˈnoʊ-/ noun [C] specialized a type of skin CANCER that appears as a coloured mark or growth on the skin

melatonin /mel.əˈtəʊ.nɪn/ (US) /-ˈtoʊ-/ noun [U] specialized a **hormone** in the body that produces changes in skin colour and is involved in continuing BIORHYTHMS such as our sleep pattern

meld /meld/ verb [I or T] to (cause something to) combine with something else: *Several problems had melded **together**.* ◦ *He took folk music and melded it **with** pop.*

melee /ˈmel.eɪ/ noun [C usually singular] literary a large noisy uncontrolled crowd, in which people are moving in different directions and sometimes fighting with each other: *We lost sight of each other **in** the melee.*

mellifluous /melˈɪf.lu.əs/ adj formal having a pleasant and flowing sound: *a deep mellifluous voice* ◦ *the mellifluous sound of the cello*

mellow /ˈmel.əʊ/ (US) /-oʊ/ adj; verb
▸**adj** SMOOTH ▷ **1** smooth and soft, or not too sharp, bright, new, or rough: *mellow flavours* ◦ *mellow sounds* ◦ *mellow autumn sunlight* RELAXED ▷ **2** relaxed and pleasant or not severe: *a mellow mood/atmosphere* ◦ *After a few drinks, he became very mellow.*
▸**verb** BECOME SOFTER ▷ **1** [I] to become softer and more developed in a pleasing way: *The brickwork will mellow over the years so that it blends with the surroundings.* BECOME RELAXED ▷ **2** [I or T] to become more relaxed: *She used to be very impatient, but she's mellowed over time.* ◦ *The years have mellowed her.* ◦ US informal *Oh don't be so tough on yourself, Bill – mellow **out*** (= become more relaxed and less severe).

melodic /məˈlɒd.ɪk/ (US) /-ˈlɑː.dɪk/ adj **1** very pleasant to listen to **2** relating to the tune in a piece of music

melodious /məˈləʊ.di.əs/ (US) /-ˈloʊ-/ adj formal very pleasant to listen to

melodrama /ˈmel.əˌdrɑː.mə/ (US) /-ˌdræm.ə/ noun [C or U] a story, play, or film in which the characters show stronger emotions than real people usually do: *a television melodrama* ◦ mainly UK *The car's hardly damaged – there's no need to **make** a melodrama **out of** it* (= make the situation more important than it is).

melodramatic /ˌmel.ə.drəˈmæt.ɪk/ (US) /-ˈmæt̬-/ adj showing much stronger emotions than are necessary or usual for a situation: *a melodramatic speech* • **melodramatically** /-ɪ.kəl.i/ adv *'Life is not worth living,' she declared melodramatically.*

melody /ˈmel.ə.di/ noun [C or U] (C2) a tune, often forming part of a larger piece of music: *He played a few well-known melodies.* ◦ *His songs are always strong on melody.*

melon /ˈmel.ən/ noun [C or U] (A2) a large, round fruit with hard yellow or green skin, sweet flesh, and a lot of seeds

melt /melt/ verb; noun
▸**verb** BECOME LIQUID ▷ **1** (B2) [I or T] to turn from something solid into something soft or liquid, or to cause something to do this: *The snow usually melts by mid March.* ◦ *Melt the chocolate slowly so that it doesn't burn.* ◦ *The meat's beautifully cooked – it melts **in your mouth*** (= is so pleasantly soft that you do not need to

chew it). **FEEL LOVE** ▷ **2** [I] to start to feel love or sympathy, especially after feeling angry: *He only has to look at her, and she melts.* ◦ *He'd been going to refuse but his* ***heart*** *melted when he saw the children's faces.*

PHRASAL VERBS **melt away 1** to disappear slowly: *As the police sirens were heard, the crowd started to melt away.* **2** If a strong feeling melts away, you feel it less strongly and it disappears: *Her anger melted away when she read the letter.* • **melt sth down** to heat a metal object until it turns to liquid, because you want to use the metal rather than the object • **melt (away) into sth** to look so similar to something else all around you, or to be so much a part of it, that people do not see or notice you: *The security men just melted into the background until they were needed.*

▸**noun** [C] mainly US a sandwich containing melted cheese: *a* ***tuna*** *melt*

meltdown /ˈmelt.daʊn/ **noun NUCLEAR** ▷ **1** [C or U] an extremely dangerous situation in a nuclear power station in which the nuclear fuel becomes very hot and melts through its container and escapes into the environment **FAILURE** ▷ **2** [U] a complete failure, especially in financial matters: *financial/economic/market meltdown* ◦ *The last few months have seen the progressive meltdown* ***of*** *the country's political system.* **3** [C or U] informal an occasion when a person becomes extremely upset and is not able to deal with life

melted /ˈmel.tɪd/ US /-t̬ɪd/ **adj** having turned soft or into a liquid: *melted butter/chocolate/cheese*

melting /ˈmel.tɪŋ/ US /-t̬ɪŋ/ **adj** describes a look or voice which makes you feel sympathy or love

ˈmelting ˌpoint noun [C usually singular] the temperature at which a substance melts

ˈmelting ˌpot noun [C usually singular] a place where many different people and ideas exist together, often mixing and producing something new: *a* ***cultural*** *melting pot* ◦ *New Orleans is one of the great melting pots of America.*

member /ˈmem.bəʳ/ US /-bɚ/ **noun** [C] **PERSON** ▷ **1** A2 a person, animal, or thing that is part of a group: *a family member* ◦ *a member of the older generation* ◦ *male and female members of the group* ◦ *The lion is a member* ***of*** *the cat family.* ◦ *Representatives of the member states will be meeting next week.* **2** A2 a person who joins a group to take part in a particular activity: *a new club member* ◦ *Car parking facilities are for members only.* ◦ *Michael is a member* ***of*** *the Royal Society for the Protection of Birds.* **BODY PART** ▷ **3** formal a leg or arm **4** formal a PENIS: *the* ***male*** *member*

ˌMember of ˈParliament noun [C] (abbreviation **MP**) a person who has been elected to the parliament of a country

membership /ˈmem.bə.ʃɪp/ US /-bɚ-/ **noun 1** B1 [U] the state of belonging to an organization: *You have to* ***apply for*** *membership* ***of*** *(US* ***in****) the sports club.* ◦ *a membership* ***fee/card*** ◦ ***Annual*** *membership (= the amount you have to pay to join a particular organization for one year) is £25.* **2** C1 [C, + sing/pl verb] all the people who belong to an organization: *Our membership is/are divided on the issue.* ◦ *The society has* ***a*** *very large membership (= number of members).*

membrane /ˈmem.breɪn/ **noun** [C or U] specialized **1** a thin piece of skin that covers or connects parts of a person's or animal's body: *The cornea is the transparent membrane that covers the front of the eye.* **2** a very thin piece of material that covers an opening **3** the outer covering of a cell: *a cell membrane*

memento /məˈmen.təʊ/ US /-toʊ/ **noun** [C] (plural **mementos** or **mementoes**) an object that you keep to remember a person, place, or event: *I keep a stone as a memento* ***of*** *our holiday.*

memo /ˈmem.əʊ/ US /-oʊ/ **noun** [C] (plural **memos**) (formal **memorandum**) C1 a message or other information in writing sent by one person or department to another in the same business organization: *Did you get my memo about the meeting?*

IDIOM **get the memo** US informal to know something that everyone else knows: *I see everyone is wearing green today – I didn't get the memo.*

memoir /ˈmem.wɑːʳ/ US /-wɑːr/ **noun 1** [C] a book or other piece of writing based on the writer's personal knowledge of famous people, places, or events: *She has written a memoir of her encounters with W.H. Auden over the years.* **2 memoirs** [plural] (US also **memoir**) a written record of a usually famous person's own life and experiences: *She plans to* ***write*** *her memoirs.* ◦ *Waugh's first volume of memoirs dealt with his childhood and youth.*

memorabilia /ˌmem.ər.əˈbɪl.i.ə/ **noun** [plural] objects that are collected because they are connected with a person or event that is thought to be very interesting: *an auction of* ***pop*** *memorabilia* ◦ *Beatles memorabilia*

memorable /ˈmem.ər.ə.bl̩/ **adj** B2 likely to be remembered or worth remembering: *a memorable performance* ◦ *a memorable tune* ◦ *I haven't seen them since that memorable evening when the boat capsized.* • **memorably** /-bli/ **adv** *The book includes a range of memorably eccentric characters.*

memorandum /ˌmem.əˈræn.dəm/ **noun** [C] (plural **memoranda** or **memorandums**) **DOCUMENT** ▷ **1** specialized a short written report prepared specially for a person or group of people which contains information about a particular matter: *Michael Davis has prepared a memorandum outlining our need for an additional warehouse.* **2** legal an informal legal agreement: *The three countries have signed a memorandum pledging to work together.* **MESSAGE** ▷ **3** formal a **memo**

memorial /məˈmɔː.ri.əl/ US /-ˈmɔːr.i-/ **noun; adj**

▸**noun** [C] C2 an object, often large and made of stone, which has been built to honour a famous person or event: *a* ***war*** *memorial* ◦ *The statue was erected as a memorial* ***to*** *those who died in the war.*

▸**adj** [before noun] A memorial event or object is a way of remembering a person or people who have died: *Hundreds of people came to Professor Conner's memorial* ***service****.*

Meˈmorial ˌDay noun a US holiday on the last Monday in May when people remember men and women who have died, especially those who have died fighting for their country in wars

memorize (UK usually **memorise**) /ˈmem.ə.raɪz/ **verb** [T] to learn something so that you will remember it exactly: *When I was at school, we were required to memorize a poem every week.*

memory /ˈmem.ər.i/ US /-ɚ-/ **noun ABILITY TO REMEMBER** ▷ **1** B1 [C or U] the ability to remember information, experiences, and people: *a* ***good/bad*** *memory* ◦ *After the accident he suffered from* ***loss of*** *memory/memory* ***loss****.* ◦ *She has* ***an*** *excellent memory* ***for*** *names (= she can remember names easily).* **EVENT REMEMBERED** ▷ **2** B1 [C] something that you remember from the past: *I have* ***vivid*** *memories* ***of*** *that evening.* ◦ *That tune really* ***brings back*** *memories (= makes me remember past events).* ◦ *School is just a* ***dim/distant*** *memory for me now (= something I cannot remember very well).* **COMPUTER** ▷ **3** A2 [C usually singular, U] the part of a computer in which information or programs are stored either permanently or temporarily, or the amount of space available on it for storing information: *My computer has a gigabyte of memory.*

> Word partners for **memory (ABILITY TO REMEMBER)**
>
> *have* a *bad/good* memory • *have* a *long/short* memory • *have* a *selective* memory • *lose* your memory • sth *fades from* memory • sth *lingers in/remains in* the memory • memory *impairment/loss* • a memory *lapse*

> Word partners for **memory (EVENT REMEMBERED)**
>
> *bad/bitter/painful/unhappy* memories • *fond/good/happy* memories • a *clear/vivid* memory • a *hazy/vague* memory • a *childhood* memory • sth *brings back/rekindles/revives* memories • memories *come flooding back* • a memory *of* sth

IDIOMS **from memory** If you say something, such as a poem, or sing a song from memory, you speak or sing without looking at any words or music. • **have a memory like an elephant** to be able to remember things easily and for a long period of time • **in memory of sb** C2 as a way of remembering someone who has died: *A service was held in memory of those who had died in the fighting.* • **take a stroll/trip/walk down memory lane** C2 to remember happy times in the past • **within your memory** at a time that you are able to remember: *Women had gained the vote within my grandmother's memory.*

ˈMemory ˌStick noun [C] (also **flash drive**, **pen drive**) trademark a small piece of equipment that you connect to a computer or other piece of electronic equipment to copy and store information

men /men/ plural of **man**

menace /ˈmen.ɪs/ noun; verb

▸noun **1** [C usually singular] something that is likely to cause harm: *Drunk drivers are a menace* ***to*** *everyone.* ◦ *Dogs running loose are a* ***public*** *menace.* ◦ *the menace of industrial pollution* **2** [U] a dangerous quality that makes you think someone is going to do something bad: *He had a slight* ***air of*** *menace which I found unsettling.* ◦ *He spoke with a hint of menace.* **3** [C] a person, especially a child, who is very annoying **4 demand money with menaces** UK legal to demand money using threats: *He was accused of unlawfully demanding money with menaces.*

▸verb [T] formal If someone or something menaces a person or thing, they threaten seriously to harm it: *Hurricane Hugo menaced the US coast for a week.*

menacing /ˈmen.ɪ.sɪŋ/ adj making you think that someone is going to do something bad: *a menacing look/gesture* • **menacingly** /-li/ adv

ménage /meɪˈnɑːʒ/ noun [usually S, + sing/pl verb] formal a group of people living together in the same house

ménage à trois /meɪnˌɑːʒ.ɑːˈtrwɑː/ noun [C] an arrangement in which three people live together and have sexual relationships with each other

menagerie /məˈnædʒ.ər.i/ US /-ɚ-/ noun [C] a collection of wild animals that are kept privately or to show to the public

mend /mend/ verb; noun

▸verb [T] mainly UK B1 to repair something that is broken or damaged: *Could you mend this hole in my shirt?* ◦ *I've left my watch at the jeweller's to be mended.* ◦ *The plumber came to mend the burst pipe.* ◦ *The country's president is seeking to mend relations with the United States.*

IDIOMS **mend your fences** to try to be friendly again with someone after an argument • **mend your ways** to begin to behave well, having until now behaved badly

▸noun [C] mainly UK a place in a piece of clothing where a repair has been made

IDIOM **be on the mend** informal to be getting better after an illness or injury: *She's been ill with flu but she's on the mend now.*

mendacious /menˈdeɪ.ʃəs/ adj formal not telling the truth: *Some of these statements are misleading and some downright mendacious.*

mendacity /menˈdæs.ə.ti/ US /-t̬i/ noun [U] formal the act of not telling the truth: *Politicians are often accused of mendacity.*

mendicant /ˈmen.dɪ.kənt/ noun [C] formal someone who lives by asking people they do not know for money, especially for religious reasons • **mendicant** adj

mending /ˈmen.dɪŋ/ noun [U] old-fashioned clothes that need to be MENDED: *I have a pile of mending to do.*

menfolk /ˈmen.fəʊk/ US /-foʊk/ noun [plural] old-fashioned the men in a family or society

menial /ˈmiː.ni.əl/ adj disapproving describes work that is boring, makes you feel tired, and is given a low social value: *It's fairly menial* ***work****, such as washing dishes and cleaning floors.* ◦ *a menial* ***job/task***

meningitis /ˌmen.ɪnˈdʒaɪ.tɪs/ US /-t̬ɪs/ noun [U] a serious infectious disease that causes the tissues around the brain and SPINAL CORD to swell

meniscus /məˈnɪs.kəs/ noun [C] (plural **menisci** or **meniscuses**) specialized **BODY PART** ▷ **1** a curved piece of CARTILAGE inside a JOINT (= place where two bones are connected) of the body such as the knee **LIQUID** ▷ **2** on a liquid, a surface that curves either out or in as a result of SURFACE TENSION

menopause /ˈmen.ə.pɔːz/ US /-pɑːz/ noun [U] (informal **the change (of life)**) the time in a woman's life when she gradually stops having PERIODS (= blood flow from her WOMB each month): *Most women* ***go through*** *menopause* (UK also *the menopause*) *between the ages of 45 and 55.* • **menopausal** /-zəl/ adj *menopausal women/symptoms*

menorah /məˈnɔː.rə/ noun [C or S] in the Jewish religion, an object that holds seven or nine candles, used in religious celebrations

ˈmen's room noun [C usually singular] US (UK **the ˈgents**) a toilet for men in a public building such as a hotel or restaurant

menstrual /ˈmen.strəl/ adj connected with the time when a woman menstruates: *menstrual pain* ◦ *the menstrual* ***cycle*** → See also **premenstrual**

menstruate /ˈmen.stru.eɪt/ verb [I] formal When a woman menstruates, blood flows from her WOMB for a few days every month.

menstruation /ˌmen.struˈeɪ.ʃən/ noun [U] formal an occasion when a woman menstruates: *the onset of menstruation*

menswear /ˈmenz.weər/ US /-wer/ noun [U] **1** clothing for men **2** the part of a large shop where you find men's clothing

-ment /-mənt/ suffix used to form nouns which refer to an action or process or its result: *a great achievement* ◦ *successful management* ◦ *a disappointment*

mental /ˈmen.tᵊl/ (US) /-t̬ᵊl/ adj **1** (B2) [before noun] relating to the mind, or involving the process of thinking: *The family has a history of mental disorder.* ◦ *A doctor was asked about the mental state of the prisoner.* ◦ *She had a mental* ***picture*** *(= a picture in her mind) of how the house would look when they finished decorating it.* → Compare **physical 2** UK slang crazy

ˌmental ˈage noun [C usually singular] A person's mental age is a measurement of their ability to think when compared to the average person's ability at that age: *Although Andrew is 25, he has a mental age of six.*

ˌmental aˈrithmetic noun [U] calculations that you do in your mind, without writing down any numbers

ˌmental ˈblock noun [C] If you have a mental block about something, you cannot understand it or do it because something in your mind prevents you: *He's got a mental block* ***about*** *names – he just can't remember them.*

ˌmental ˈcruelty noun [U] behaviour that causes extreme suffering to another person but does not involve physical violence: *She divorced her husband on the grounds of mental cruelty.*

ˌmental ˈhandicap noun [C usually singular] old-fashioned for **learning difficulties**

ˌmental ˈhealth noun [U] the condition of someone's mind and the fact that they are suffering from any mental illness or not: *Laughing is good for your mental health.* ◦ *mental health disorders*

ˈmental ˌhospital noun [C] old-fashioned for **psychiatric hospital**

ˌmental ˈillness noun [C or U] an illness that affects the mind

mentality /menˈtæl.ə.ti/ (US) /-t̬i/ noun [C usually singular] (C1) a person's particular way of thinking about things: *I can't understand the mentality of people who hurt defenceless animals.*

mentally /ˈmen.tᵊl.i/ (US) /-t̬ᵊl-/ adv (B2) connected with or related to the mind: *mentally* ***ill*** ◦ *It's going to be a tough competition but I'm mentally* ***prepared*** *for it.*

ˌmental ˈnote noun **make a mental note of sth** to make an effort to remember something: *I made a mental note of her address.*

menthol /ˈmen.θᵊl/ (US) /-θɑːl/ noun [U] a solid, white natural substance that smells and tastes like MINT: *Menthol can help to clear your nose when you have a cold.*

mentholated /ˈmen.θᵊl.eɪ.tɪd/ (US) /-t̬ɪd/ adj containing menthol as a flavour

mention /ˈmen.ʃᵊn/ verb; noun

▸verb [T] **1** (B1) to speak about something quickly, giving little detail or using few words: *I'll mention your ideas to Jacinta.* ◦ [+ (that)] *He casually mentioned (****that****) he was leaving his job.* ◦ [+ -ing verb] *My wife mentioned see****ing*** *you the other day.* ◦ [+ question word] *Did she happen to mention* ***wh****ether she would be coming?* **2** (B1) to refer to something or someone: *I promised never to mention the incident again.* ◦ *Did she mention me in her letter?*

> **!** Common mistake: **mention**
>
> Remember that **mention** is not followed by 'about'.
>
> Don't say 'mention about something', say **mention something**:
>
> ~~*The advert didn't mention about the price.*~~
>
> *The advert didn't mention the price.*

IDIOMS **don't mention it!** said to be polite after someone has thanked you: *'Thanks for your help.' 'Don't mention it.'* • **not to mention** (B2) used when you want to emphasize something that you are adding to a list: *He's one of the kindest and most intelligent, not to mention handsome, men I know.*

▸noun **1** (B2) [C] a short remark or written statement: *The story didn't even* ***get*** *a mention in the newspaper.* ◦ *When I ordered the catalogue, there was no mention* ***of*** *any payment.* **2** [S] an occasion when something or someone is mentioned: *Even the mention* ***of*** *her name makes him blush.* **3** [C] an occasion when a person is publicly praised for having done something, such as their job, extremely well: *At the awards ceremony, Chrissie Scott* ***got/received*** *a special mention for her reporting of the conflict.*

mentor /ˈmen.tɔːʳ/ (US) /-tɔːr/ noun; verb

▸noun [C] a person who gives another person help and advice over a period of time and often also teaches them how to do their job → Compare **protégé**

▸verb [T] to help and give advice to someone who has less experience than you, especially in your job • **mentoring** noun [U]

menu /ˈmen.juː/ noun [C] FOOD ▷ **1** (A2) a list of the food that you can eat in a restaurant: *The waiter brought the menu and the wine list.* ◦ *What's* ***on*** *the menu today?* COMPUTING ▷ **2** (A2) a list of choices that can be made to appear on a computer screen: *Select the 'Edit' menu and then choose 'Copy'.*

ˈmenu ˌbar noun [C] a long, narrow area, usually at the top of a computer screen, that contains lists of instructions to the computer. These lists are kept out of view until you choose to see them: *Click 'File' in the menu bar, then click 'Exit'.*

ˈmenu-ˌdriven adj specialized A computer that is menu-driven is operated by making choices from different menus rather than by giving separate instructions on a keyboard.

ˈmenu ˌoption noun [C] one of the choices available in a computer menu

meow /ˌmiːˈaʊ/ noun [C], verb [I] US for **miaow**

MEP /ˌem.iːˈpiː/ noun [C] abbreviation for Member of the European Parliament: a person who represents an area of a European country in the European Parliament

mephedrone /ˈmef.ə.drəʊn/ (US) /-droʊn/ noun [U] (also informal **miˈaow miˌaow**) a drug, illegal in many countries, that is a STIMULANT (= a substance that makes the mind or body more active)

Mephistopheles /ˌmef.ɪˈstɒf.ᵊl.iːz/ (US) /-ˈstɑː.fə.liːz/ noun literary **the devil**

mercantile /ˈmɜː.kᵊn.taɪl/ (US) /ˈmɝː-/ adj formal related to trade or business

mercenary /ˈmɜː.sᵊn.ri/ (US) /ˈmɝː-/ adj; noun

▸adj disapproving interested only in the amount of money that you can get from a situation: *He had some mercenary scheme to marry a wealthy widow.*

▸noun [C] a soldier who fights for any country or group that pays them

merchandise noun; verb

▸noun [U] /ˈmɜː.tʃᵊn.daɪs/ (US) /ˈmɝː-/ formal goods that are bought and sold: *Japan exported $117 billion in merchandise to the US in 1999.*

▸verb [T] /ˈmɜː.tʃᵊn.daɪz/ (US) /ˈmɝː-/ US specialized to encourage the sale of goods by advertising them or by making certain that they are noticed: *She had to merchandise the new product line.*

merchandising /ˈmɜː.tʃᵊn.daɪ.zɪŋ/ (US) /ˈmɝː-/ noun [U] products connected with a popular film, singer, event, etc., or the selling of these products

merchant /ˈmɜː.tʃᵊnt/ (US) /ˈmɝː-/ noun [C] **1** formal a

M

person whose job is to buy and sell products in large amounts, especially by trading with other countries: *a wine/grain merchant* **2** UK informal disapproving someone who is involved in or enjoys something that is unpleasant or annoying to others: *a gossip merchant (= someone who enjoys talking about people's private lives)* ◦ *a speed merchant (= someone who drives too fast)*

IDIOM **merchant of doom/gloom** UK disapproving someone who is always saying that bad things are going to happen: *With exports rising and unemployment falling, the merchants of gloom are having to revise their opinions of the economy.*

ˌmerchant ˈbank noun [C] a bank which does business with companies rather than with people • **ˌmerchant ˈbanker** noun [C]

the ˌmerchant ˈnavy noun [S] UK (US **the ˌmerchant ˈmarine**) the ships of a country that are used for trading and not for fighting

ˌmerchant ˈseaman noun [C] a sailor who works on a trading ship

merciful /ˈmɜː.sɪ.fəl/ (US) /ˈmɝː-/ adj approving **PERSON** ▷ **1** (C2) someone who is merciful is willing to be kind to and forgive people who are in their power: *'God is merciful,' said the priest.* ◦ *a merciful ruler* **EVENT/SITUATION** ▷ **2** describes an event or situation which you are grateful for because it stops something unpleasant: *After such a long illness, her death came as a merciful **release**.* • **mercifully** /-i/ adv approving *His illness was mercifully **brief**.*

M

merciless /ˈmɜː.sɪ.ləs/ (US) /ˈmɝː-/ adj disapproving (C2) having or showing no MERCY: *There are reports of merciless attacks on innocent civilians.* ◦ *There was no shelter from the merciless (= very strong) heat.* • **mercilessly** /-li/ adv *Louis was teased mercilessly by his schoolmates.*

mercurial /mɜːˈkjʊə.ri.əl/ (US) /mɝːrˈkjʊr.i-/ adj literary **1** changing suddenly and often: *a mercurial temperament* ◦ *She was entertaining but unpredictable, with mercurial mood swings.* **2** intelligent, enthusiastic, and quick: *a mercurial **mind/wit***

mercury /ˈmɜː.kjʊ.ri/ (US) /ˈmɝː-/ noun [U] (old use **quicksilver**) (symbol **Hg**) a chemical element that is a heavy, silver-coloured metal, liquid at normal temperatures: *Mercury is used in batteries, pesticides, and thermometers.*

IDIOM **the mercury** old-fashioned informal the temperature: *With the mercury climbing to 40 degrees, beaches and pools will be crowded this afternoon.*

Mercury /ˈmɜː.kjʊ.ri/ (US) /ˈmɝː-/ noun [S] the planet closest in distance to the Sun

mercy /ˈmɜː.si/ (US) /ˈmɝː-/ noun **KINDNESS** ▷ **1** (C2) [U] kindness that makes you forgive someone, usually someone that you have authority over: *She appealed to the judge to **have** mercy **on** her husband.* ◦ *The prisoners **pleaded for** mercy.* ◦ *The gunmen **showed** no mercy, killing innocent men and women.* **2 be at the mercy of sb/sth** (C2) to be in a situation where someone or something has complete power over you: *Poor people are increasingly at the mercy of money-lenders.* **EVENT/SITUATION** ▷ **3** [S] an event or situation which you are grateful for because it stops something unpleasant: *After months of suffering, his death was a mercy.* ◦ *They were on a mercy **mission** to take food to the refugees when they were attacked.*

ˈmercy ˌkilling noun [C or U] the act of killing someone who is very ill or very old so that they do not suffer any more

mere /mɪəʳ/ (US) /mɪr/ adj [before noun] (B2) used to emphasize that something is not large or important: *It cost a mere 20 dollars.* ◦ *The mere **thought** of it makes me ill.*

merely /ˈmɪə.li/ (US) /ˈmɪr-/ adv **ONLY** ▷ **1** (B2) used to emphasize that you mean exactly what you are saying and nothing more: *I wasn't complaining, I merely **said** that I was tired.* ◦ *I didn't say that you had to go – I merely suggested that you might like to go.* **NOT LARGE/IMPORTANT** ▷ **2** (C2) used to emphasize that something is not large, important, or effective when compared to something else: *The medicine won't cure her – it merely stops the pain.*

merest /ˈmɪə.rɪst/ (US) /ˈmɪr.ɪst/ adj **the merest** (C2) used to emphasize the surprising or strong effect of a very small action or event: *The merest **mention** of seafood makes her feel sick.* ◦ *The merest **hint** of criticism makes him defensive.*

meretricious /ˌmer.ɪˈtrɪʃ.əs/ adj formal seeming attractive but really false or of little value: *He claims that a lot of journalism is meretricious and superficial.*

merge /mɜːdʒ/ (US) /mɝːdʒ/ verb **1** (C2) [I or T] to combine or join together, or to cause things to do this: *They decided to merge the two companies into one.* ◦ *The country's two biggest banks are planning to merge.* ◦ *After a while the narrow track merges **with** a wider path.* **2** [I] US for **filter in**

merger /ˈmɜː.dʒəʳ/ (US) /ˈmɝː.dʒɚ/ noun [C] (C2) an occasion when two or more companies join together: *She's an attorney who advises companies about mergers and takeovers.* ◦ *The merger of these two companies would create the world's biggest accounting firm.*

meridian /məˈrɪd.i.ən/ noun [C] an imaginary line from the North Pole to the South Pole, drawn on maps to help to show the position of a place

meringue /məˈræŋ/ noun [C or U] a very light, sweet cake made by mixing sugar with egg WHITE (= the clear part) and baking it: *lemon meringue pie*

merino /məˈriː.nəʊ/ (US) /-noʊ/ noun [C] a breed of sheep which produces soft, good-quality wool: *merino **wool***

merit /ˈmer.ɪt/ noun; verb

▸noun [C or U] **1** (C1) formal the quality of being good and deserving praise: *an entertaining film with little **artistic** merit* ◦ *Her ideas have merit.* ◦ *Brierley's book has the merit of being both informative and readable.* **2 the merits of sth** the advantages something has compared to something else: *We discussed the merits of herbal tea.* **3 on your (own) merits** according to the qualities you have or have shown, without considering any other information or comparing you to someone else: *The committee say they will **consider/judge** each applicant on his or her own merits.*

▸verb [T] formal (C2) If something merits a particular treatment, it deserves or is considered important enough to be treated in that way: *This plan merits careful attention.* ◦ *The accident merited only a small paragraph in the local paper.*

meritocracy /ˌmer.ɪˈtɒk.rə.si/ (US) /-ˈtɑː.krə-/ noun [C or U] a social system or society in which people have power because of their abilities, not because of their money or social position: *The prime minister claims he wants to create a classless meritocracy in Britain.*

meritorious /ˌmer.ɪˈtɔː.ri.əs/ (US) /-ˈtɔːr.i-/ adj formal deserving great praise: *an award for meritorious service*

mermaid /ˈmɜː.meɪd/ (US) /ˈmɝː-/ noun [C] an imaginary creature described in stories, with the upper body of a woman and the tail of a fish

merrily /ˈmer.ɪ.li/ adv **1** showing happiness or

enjoyment: *Her eyes sparkled merrily.* **2** informal without thinking about the result of what you are doing or about the problems it might cause: *The factory has been merrily pumping chemical waste into the river for the past ten years.*

merriment /ˈmer.i.mənt/ **noun** [U] an occasion when people laugh or have an enjoyable time together: *Sounds of merriment came from the kitchen.* ◦ *His unusual name has long been a source of merriment among his friends.*

merry /ˈmer.i/ **adj** HAPPY ▷ **1** old-fashioned happy or showing enjoyment: *the merry sound of laughter* ◦ *She's a merry little soul.* DRUNK ▷ **2** polite word for slightly drunk: *You **got** a bit merry last night, didn't you Cath?*

IDIOM **merry Christmas!** said at Christmas to wish people a pleasant Christmas period: *Hello, Phoebe. Merry Christmas!* ◦ *The shop assistant **wished** me a merry Christmas.*

ˈmerry-go-ˌround noun [C] FOR CHILDREN ▷ **1** (UK also **roundabout**, US also **carousel**) a large machine at a fair that turns round and has wooden or plastic animals or vehicles on which children ride: *The girls wanted the merry-go-round to go faster.* SEVERAL ACTIVITIES ▷ **2** a series of similar activities, which can often seem boring: *With his first book came the endless merry-go-round **of** publicity and interviews.*

merrymaking /ˈmer.iˌmeɪ.kɪŋ/ **noun** [U] literary the act of celebrating and having an enjoyable time: *The eating, drinking, and merrymaking went on late into the night.*

mescaline /ˈmes.kəl.iːn/ **noun** [U] (UK also **mescalin** /-ɪn/) a drug obtained from PEYOTE (= a type of desert plant) that makes you HALLUCINATE (= see things that do not exist)

mesh /meʃ/ **noun; verb**

▸**noun** [C or U] (a piece of) material like a net with spaces in it, made from wire, plastic, or thread: *a sieve with a fine/large mesh* ◦ *a wire mesh fence*

▸**verb** [I] SUIT ▷ **1** When different things or people mesh, they suit each other or work well together: *The members of the team just didn't mesh.* ◦ *Whether the new personal pension works will depend much on how well it meshes **with** employers' schemes.* JOIN ▷ **2** specialized to join together in the correct position: *The car's gears aren't meshing properly.*

mesmeric /mezˈmer.ɪk/ **adj** literary making you give your attention completely so that you cannot think of anything else

mesmerize (UK usually **mesmerise**) /ˈmez.mə.raɪz/ **verb** **1** [T often passive] to have someone's attention completely so that they cannot think of anything else: *I was completely mesmerized by the performance.* **2** [T] old-fashioned for **hypnotize**

mesmerizing (UK usually **mesmerising**) /ˈmez.mə.raɪ.zɪŋ/ **adj** very attractive, in a mysterious way, making you want to keep looking: *He had the most mesmerizing blue eyes.*

mesophyll /ˈmes.əʊ.fɪl/ (US) /ˈmez.oʊ-/ **noun** [U] specialized the part of a leaf between the two thin surface layers, containing the cells responsible for PHOTOSYNTHESIS

the mesosphere /ˈmes.əʊ.sfɪəʳ/ (US) /ˈmez.oʊ.sfɪr/ **noun** [S] specialized the layer of gases surrounding the Earth at a height of between 50 and 100 kilometres → Compare **the stratosphere, the troposphere**

mess /mes/ **noun; verb**

▸**noun** DIRT/UNTIDINESS ▷ **1** (B1) [S or U] Something or someone that is a mess, or is in a mess, looks dirty or untidy: *He **makes a** terrible mess when he's cooking.* ◦ *Jem's house is always **in a** mess.* ◦ *Go and **clear up** that mess in the kitchen.* ◦ *Ian can't stand mess.* ◦ *I **look a** mess – I can't go out like this!* ◦ *My hair's such a mess today!* **2** [C] an animal's solid waste: *Fido left another mess on the carpet.* PROBLEMS ▷ **3** (B2) [S] a situation that is full of problems: *She said that her life was a mess.* ◦ *I **got** myself **into a** mess by telling a lie.* ◦ *The company's finances are **in a** mess.* **4** [S] a person whose life is full of problems they cannot deal with: *After the divorce he was a real mess and drinking too much.* **5 make a mess of sth** (also **mess sth up**) to do something badly or spoil something: *I've made a real mess of my exams.* ROOM ▷ **6** [C] (US also **mess hall**) a room or building in which members of the armed forces have their meals or spend their free time: *The group captain was having breakfast in the mess hall.* ◦ *They spent their evenings in the **officers'** mess, drinking and playing cards.* **7** [C] Indian English a large public room where people have their meals; a DINING HALL

▸**verb** **1** [T] mainly US (UK **mess up**) to make something untidy: *Don't you dare mess my hair!* **2** [I] to leave solid waste somewhere: *Next door's dog has messed on our steps again!*

IDIOM **(and) no messing** UK informal said to emphasize that you want something to be done: *I want you both in bed by nine o'clock, no messing!*

PHRASAL VERBS **mess sb about/around** UK to treat someone badly: *I'm tired of being messed around by my bank.* ◦ *Don't mess me about!* • **mess around** (UK also **mess about**) SPEND TIME ▷ **1** (C1) informal to spend time doing various things that are not important, without any particular purpose or plan: *They spend their weekends messing around on their boat.* ◦ *My brother likes messing around **with** computers.* ◦ *He spent the day with friends, just messing about.* ACT STUPIDLY ▷ **2** to behave in a stupid or annoying way: *Stop messing about and listen to me!* • **mess around with sth** (UK also **mess about with sth**) (C2) to use or treat something in a careless or harmful way: *I don't want him coming in here and messing around with our computers.* ◦ *Never mess around **with** scissors.* • **mess around with sb** mainly US informal If a married man or woman messes around with someone, they have a sexual relationship with someone who is not their wife or husband. • **mess sth up** to make something untidy or dirty: *Who's messed up the bookshelf?* • **mess (sth) up** informal (B2) to spoil or damage something, or to do something wrong or badly: *I feel I've messed up my chances of becoming a great singer.* ◦ *He says that his divorce has really messed his life up.* ◦ *You've really messed up this time.* • **mess sb up** CAUSE PROBLEMS ▷ **1** to cause someone to suffer emotional and mental problems: *Drugs can really mess you up.* INJURE ▷ **2** US slang to hit someone repeatedly so that they are badly injured • **mess with sth/sb** informal to use or become involved with something or someone dangerous: *You shouldn't mess with drugs.* • **mess with sth** mainly US to try to change or repair something, but not carefully and usually without success: *He was messing with his bike and then he couldn't fit the parts back together.* • **mess with sb** informal to treat someone in a bad, rude, or annoying way, or to start an argument with them: *I've warned you already, don't mess with me!*

message /ˈmes.ɪdʒ/ **noun; verb**

▸**noun** [C] INFORMATION ▷ **1** (A1) a short piece of information that you give to a person when you cannot speak to them directly: *If I'm not there when you phone, **leave** a message.* ◦ [+ that] *I **got** a message **that** she'll be late.* IDEA ▷ **2** (B2) the most important

M

idea in a book, film, or play: *The film's message is that rich and poor are alike.* **3 get the message** informal to understand what someone is trying to tell you, even if they are not expressing themselves directly: *I never answer his calls, so you'd think he'd get the message.* **4 get the message across** to make someone understand: *We need to get the message across **that** too much sun is dangerous.*

▸verb [T] to send someone a text message: *I messaged him yesterday but haven't had a reply.*

ˈmessage ˌboard noun [C] B1 a place on a website where you can leave messages for other people to read

ˌmessed ˈup adj slang unhappy and emotionally confused: *She was really messed up as a teenager.* ◦ [before noun] *messed-up kids*

messenger /ˈmes.ɪn.dʒəʳ/ US /-dʒɚ/ noun [C] someone who takes a message or documents from one person to another: *The documents were delivered by special messenger.* ◦ *a messenger boy*

messiah /məˈsaɪ.ə/ noun [S] a leader who is believed to have the power to solve the world's problems: *An ordinary priest, he was hailed by thousands as the new messiah.*

the Mesˈsiah noun [S] **1** in the Christian religion, Jesus Christ **2** in the Jewish religion, the King of the Jews who will be sent by God

messianic /ˌmes.iˈæn.ɪk/ adj **1** formal relating or belonging to a messiah: *He announced the imminent arrival of a messianic **leader**.* **2** describes a religious group that believes that a leader will or has come who has the power to change the world and bring peace: *a messianic cult/movement/sect* **3** describes a speech or style that is very determined and full of emotion: *She talks about her work with a messianic **zeal**.*

Messrs /ˈmes.əz/ US /-ɚz/ formal plural of **Mr** (= title used before a man's name) used before the names of two or more people, usually in the title of a company: *Messrs Wood and Laurence, solicitors*

messy /ˈmes.i/ adj DIRTY/UNTIDY ▷ **1** B1 untidy: *a messy kitchen* ◦ *messy hands/hair* ◦ *His bedroom's always messy.* **2** producing or causing dirt and untidiness: *Eating spaghetti can be a messy business.* ◦ *Vicky cooks really well but she's rather messy.* SITUATION ▷ **3** describes a situation that is confused and unpleasant: *A war will be a long and messy **business**.* ◦ *They had a bitter, messy divorce.* • **messily** /-ɪ.li/ adv

met /met/ verb; adj

▸verb past simple and past participle of **meet**

▸adj [before noun] (usually **Met**) mainly UK informal for **meteorological**: *the Met Office*

the Met /ˈmet/ noun [+ sing/pl verb] abbreviation for **the Metropolitan Police**

meta- /ˈmet.ə/ US /ˈmeţ.ə/ prefix **1** involving change: *metamorphose* (= *to change into a completely different form*) ◦ *metabolism* (= *the processes in the body that change food into energy*) **2** outside the normal limits of something: *metalanguage* (= *a specialized form of language used for describing a language*)

metabolism /məˈtæb.əl.ɪ.zəm/ noun [C] specialized all the chemical processes in your body, especially those that cause food to be used for energy and growth: *Exercise is supposed to speed up your metabolism.* • **metabolic** /ˌmet.əˈbɒl.ɪk/ US /ˌmeţ.əˈbɑː.lɪk/ adj specialized *The athletes had taken pills to stimulate their metabolic **rate*** (= *the speed at which their bodies used energy*).

metal /ˈmet.əl/ US /ˈmeţ-/ noun [C or U] B1 a chemical element, such as iron or gold, or a mixture of such elements, such as STEEL, that is generally hard and strong, and through which electricity and heat can travel: *Metal, paper, and glass can be recycled.* ◦ *Silver, gold, and platinum are **precious** metals.* ◦ *The wooden beam is reinforced with a metal plate.*

metalanguage /ˈmet.əˌlæŋ.gwɪdʒ/ US /ˈmeţ-/ noun [C] specialized a specialized form of language or set of symbols used when discussing or describing the structure of a language

ˈmetal deˌtector noun [C] a machine that you move over the ground or a surface to discover if there is metal there: *He goes round fields and beaches with his metal detector, hoping to find buried treasure.*

ˈmetal faˌtigue noun [U] a weakness that develops in metal structures that are used repeatedly

metalled /ˈmet.əld/ US /ˈmeţ-/ adj UK specialized describes a road covered with small or crushed stones

metallic /məˈtæl.ɪk/ adj **1** describes a sound, appearance, or taste that is like metal: *a dull, metallic sound* ◦ *Beer from a can often has a metallic **taste**.* ◦ *Our new car is metallic blue.* **2** specialized consisting of, or partly consisting of, metal: *Brass is a metallic alloy of copper and zinc.*

metalloid /ˈmet.əl.ɔɪd/ US /ˈmeţ-/ noun [C] specialized a chemical element with some of the properties of a metal and some of a NON-METAL, for example SILICON and ARSENIC

metallurgist /məˈtæl.ə.dʒɪst/ US /ˈmeţ.əl.ɜːr-/ noun [C] a person who studies or knows about metals

metallurgy /məˈtæl.ə.dʒi/ US /ˈmeţ.əl.ɜːr-/ noun [U] the scientific study of the structures and uses of metals: *She has a doctorate in metallurgy from the University of Utah.* • **metallurgical** /ˌmet.əlˈɜː.dʒɪ.kəl/ US /ˌmeţ.əlˈɜːr-/ adj *a metallurgical process* ◦ *the metallurgical industry*

metalwork /ˈmet.əl.wɜːk/ US /ˈmeţ.əl.wɜːrk/ noun [U] **1** the activity of making metal objects: *Her favourite subject at school is metalwork.* **2** the metal part of something: *Rust has damaged the metalwork of the bicycle.*

metamorphic /ˌmet.əˈmɔː.fɪk/ US /ˌmeţ.əˈmɔːr-/ adj specialized (of rock) changed into a new form and structure by very great heat and pressure: *Slate and gneiss are metamorphic rocks.* → Compare **igneous, sedimentary**

metamorphose /ˌmet.əˈmɔː.fəʊz/ US /ˌmeţ.əˈmɔːr.foʊz/ verb [I] formal to change into a completely different form or type: *The awkward boy I knew had metamorphosed **into** a tall, confident man.*

metamorphosis /ˌmet.əˈmɔː.fə.sɪs/ US /ˌmeţ.əˈmɔːr-/ noun (plural **metamorphoses**) **1** [C] a complete change: *Under the new editor, the magazine has **undergone** a metamorphosis.* **2** [U] specialized the process by which the young form of insects and some animals, such as FROGS, develops into the adult form

metaphor /ˈmet.ə.fɔːʳ/ US /ˈmeţ.ə.fɔːr/ noun [C or U] C2 an expression, often found in literature, that describes a person or object by referring to something that is considered to have similar characteristics to that person or object: *'The mind is an ocean' and 'the city is a jungle' are both metaphors.* ◦ *Metaphor and simile are the most commonly used figures of speech in everyday language.*

IDIOM **a metaphor for sth** a symbol which represents a particular thing: *The author uses disease as a metaphor for the corruption in society.* ◦ *In the film, the city is a metaphor for confusion and loneliness.*

metaphorical /ˌmet.əˈfɒr.ɪ.kəl/ (US) /ˌmet̬.əˈfɑːr-/ **adj** (also **metaphoric**) **1** describes language which contains metaphors: *Her second novel is written in a very metaphorical style.* **2** not having real existence but representing some truth about a situation or other subject: *A metaphorical ocean (= extremely large area of disagreement) lies between the two groups.* • **metaphorically** /-kəl.i/ **adv** *The phrase 'born again' is used metaphorically to mean that someone has suddenly become very religious.* ◦ *By leaving school without any qualifications, she has, metaphorically* ***speaking****, shot herself in the foot (= harmed her chances of success).*

metaphysics /ˌmet.əˈfɪz.ɪks/ (US) /ˌmet̬-/ **noun** [U] the part of PHILOSOPHY that is about understanding existence and knowledge • **metaphysical** /-ɪ.kəl/ **adj** *Most teenagers ask themselves metaphysical questions such as 'What is love?' and 'What is death?'*

metastasize specialized (UK usually **metastasise**) /metˈæs.tə.saɪz/ **verb** [I] If CANCER cells metastasize, they spread to other parts of the body and cause TUMOURS to grow there. • **metastasis** /-sɪs/ **noun** [U] specialized an occasion when CANCER cells metastasize

metatarsal /ˌmet.əˈtɑː.səl/ (US) /ˌmet̬.əˈtɑːr-/ **noun** [C] specialized one of the bones in your foot between your ANKLE and your toes

mete /miːt/ **verb** (present tense **meting**, past tense and past participle **meted**)

PHRASAL VERB **mete sth out** [M often passive] formal to give or order a punishment or make someone receive cruel or unfair treatment: *Victorian schoolteachers regularly meted out physical punishment to their pupils.*

meteor /ˈmiː.ti.ɔːr/ (US) /-t̬i.ɔːr/ **noun** [C] specialized a piece of rock or other matter from space that produces a bright light as it travels through the Earth's ATMOSPHERE → See also **shooting star, falling star**

meteoric /ˌmiː.tiˈɒr.ɪk/ (US) /-t̬iˈɑːr-/ **adj** **OF A ROCK** ▷ **1** relating to or caused by a meteor: *The sudden flash of light in the night sky was caused by a meteoric fireball.* **VERY FAST** ▷ **2** describes something which develops very fast and attracts a lot of attention: *The group had a meteoric* ***rise*** *to fame in the 70s.* ◦ *Her parliamentary* ***career*** *has been meteoric.*

meteorite /ˈmiː.ti.ər.aɪt/ (US) /-t̬i.ə.raɪt/ **noun** [C] a piece of rock or other matter from space that has landed on Earth

meteorological /ˌmiː.ti.ər.əˈlɒdʒ.ɪ.kəl/ (US) /-t̬i.ɚ.əˈlɑː.dʒɪ-/ **adj** (informal **met**) relating to weather conditions: *Accurate meteorological records began 100 years ago.*

meteorologist /ˌmiː.ti.ərˈɒl.ə.dʒɪst/ (US) /-t̬i.əˈrɑːl-/ **noun** [C] someone who studies meteorology

meteorology /ˌmiː.ti.ərˈɒl.ə.dʒi/ (US) /-t̬i.əˈrɑː.lə-/ **noun** [U] the scientific study of the processes that cause particular weather conditions

meter /ˈmiː.tər/ (US) /-t̬ɚ/ **noun; verb**

▸**noun** [C] **DEVICE** ▷ **1** a device that measures the amount of something that is used: *The* ***electricity*** *meter is under the stairs.* ◦ *You'll need some change for the* ***parking*** *meter.* ◦ *The man from the gas board came to* ***read*** *the meter (= see how much gas had been used).* **2** the device in a taxi that measures the distance or the amount of time spent travelling and shows how much you have to pay: *The taxi driver left the meter* ***running*** *while I helped Mum to her front door.* **MEASUREMENT** ▷ **3** US for **metre**

▸**verb** [T] to use meters to measure how much gas, electricity, or water is used: *Britain's water companies are planning to meter water consumption.*

methadone /ˈmeθ.ə.dəʊn/ (US) /-doʊn/ **noun** [U] a drug that is often given to people who are trying to stop using HEROIN

methamphetamine /ˌmeθ.æmˈfet.ə.miːn/ (US) /-fet̬-/ **noun** [U] (also slang **crystal meth, meth**) a drug that makes your mind and body more active. It is ADDICTIVE (= you cannot stop taking it when you have started) and some people take it illegally.

methane /ˈmiː.θeɪn/ **noun** [U] a gas with no smell or colour, often used as a fuel: *Methane is the main constituent of natural gas.*

methanol /ˈmeθ.ə.nɒl/ (US) /-nɑːl/ **noun** [U] a poisonous chemical substance that is the simplest type of alcohol

methinks /mɪˈθɪŋks/ old use or humorous for I think: *There's more to this than meets the eye, methinks.*

metho /ˈmeθ.əʊ/ (US) /-oʊ/ **noun** [U] Australian English informal for **methylated spirits**

method /ˈmeθ.əd/ **noun** [C] (B1) a particular way of doing something: *Travelling by train is still one of the safest methods of transport.* ◦ *The new teaching methods encourage children to think for themselves.*

> **Word partners for method**
>
> an *alternative/different/new/traditional* method • an *effective/reliable/simple* method • *develop/devise/find* a method • *adopt/use* a method • a method *of* sth/doing sth

IDIOM **have method in your madness** (US usually **have a method to your madness**) to have a good reason for what you are doing, although you seem to be behaving strangely

methodical /məˈθɒd.ɪ.kəl/ (US) /-ˈθɑː.dɪ-/ **adj** describes people who do things in a very ordered, careful way: *Tom is a very methodical person and writes lists for everything.* • **methodically** /-i/ **adv**

Methodism /ˈmeθ.ə.dɪ.zəm/ **noun** [U] the beliefs and activities of a Christian group which follows the teachings of John Wesley • **Methodist** /-dɪst/ **noun** [C], **adj** *Her parents were staunch Methodists.* ◦ *the Methodist church* ◦ *a Methodist minister*

methodology /ˌmeθ.əˈdɒl.ə.dʒi/ (US) /-ˈdɑː.lə-/ **noun** [C or U] a system of ways of doing, teaching, or studying something: *The methodology and findings of the research team have been criticized.* • **methodological** /ˌmeθ.ə.dəlˈɒdʒ.ɪ.kəl/ (US) /-ˈɑː.dʒɪ-/ **adj**

meths /meθs/ **noun** [U] UK informal for **methylated spirits**

Methuselah /məˈθjuː.zəl.ə/ **noun** in the Bible, a man who was said to have lived for 969 years

IDIOM **as old as Methuselah** humorous describes an extremely old person

methylated spirits /ˌmeθ.ɪ.leɪ.tɪdˈspɪr.ɪts/ (US) /-t̬ɪd-/ **noun** [U] (informal **meths**) UK a liquid made from alcohol and other chemicals, used to remove dirty marks and as a fuel in small HEATERS and lights

meticulous /məˈtɪk.jʊ.ləs/ **adj** approving (C2) very careful and with great attention to every detail: *Many hours of meticulous preparation have gone into writing the book.* • **meticulously** /-li/ **adv** *The entire project was meticulously planned.* • **meticulousness** /-nəs/ **noun** [U]

métier /ˈmet.ɪ.eɪ/ (US) /ˈmet̬-/ **noun** [C] formal the type of work that you have a natural ability to do well: *Rose tried painting but found her métier in music.*

ˈme ˌtime **noun** [U] time when you can do what you

M

want to do: *All mothers of young children should try to find some me time.*

the ˈMet ˌOffice noun the British government department that studies weather conditions and says what is expected to happen with the weather: *The Met Office says that the heatwave will continue for most of the week.* ◦ *a Met Office forecast/spokesman*

metonymy /metˈɒn.ə.mi/ (US) /məˈtɑː.nə-/ **noun** [U] specialized the act of referring to something using a word that describes one of its qualities or features • **metonym** /ˈmet.ə.nɪm/ (US) /ˈmet̬-/ **noun** [C] • **metonymic** /ˌmetˈɒn.ə.mɪk/ (US) /ˌməˈtɑː.nə-/ **adj**

ˌme-ˈtoo adj [before noun] informal A company's me-too product is one that is designed to be similar to a very popular product made by another company.

metre UK (US **meter**) /ˈmiː.təʳ/ (US) /-t̬ɚ/ **noun** **MEASUREMENT** ▷ **1** (A2) [C] (written abbreviation **m**) a unit of measurement equal to 100 centimetres: *The bomb shelter has concrete walls that are three metres thick.* ◦ *a 15-metre yacht* ◦ *She won the 100 metres (= a race run over this distance) at the Olympics.* ◦ *He is 1 m 75 tall.* ◦ *The price of water rose to 48p per* ***cubic*** *metre (= a unit of volume equal to 1,000 litres).* ◦ *The room is six metres square.* **POETRY** ▷ **2** [C or U] specialized the regular arrangement of syllables in poetry according to the number and type of beats in a line: *He composes poems in a classical style and in strict metre.* ◦ *Many hymns have a firm, regular metre.*

metric /ˈmet.rɪk/ **adj** mainly UK using or relating to a system of measurement that uses metres, centimetres, litres, etc.: *The recipe is given in both metric and imperial measures.* ◦ *Most high-tech industry has been metric for decades.*

metrication /ˌmet.rɪˈkeɪ.ʃᵊn/ **noun** [U] the process of changing from measuring things in IMPERIAL units to using metric units

ˌmetric ˈton noun [C] a unit of weight equal to 1,000 kilograms

metro noun; adj

▸**noun** /ˈmet.rəʊ/ (US) /-roʊ/ **UNDERGROUND RAILWAY** ▷ **1** [U] an underground electric railway system in some cities, especially in France: *Let's* ***go by*** *Metro.* ◦ *a metro* ***station*** ◦ *the Paris metro* **CITY** ▷ **2** [C] Indian English a large city: *Our company has developed commercial properties across the four metros in India.*

> **Usage: metro, subway or underground?**
>
> All these words mean an underground railway system in a large city. **Underground** is the usual word in British English. **Subway** is the usual word in American English:
>
> *the Paris metro*
> *the London underground*
> *the New York subway*

▸**adj** [before noun] /ˈmet.rəʊ/ (US) /ˈmet.roʊ/ US relating to a large city and the area surrounding it: *This guidebook includes a map of the Phoenix metro area.*

metronome /ˈmet.rə.nəʊm/ (US) /-noʊm/ **noun** [C] a device that produces a regular repeated sound like a clock, to help musicians play music at a particular speed

metropolis /məˈtrɒp.ᵊl.ɪs/ (US) /-ˈtrɑː.pᵊl-/ **noun** [C] formal a very large city, often the most important city in a large area or country: *Soon afterwards he left to begin his career in the metropolis.* ◦ *a sprawling/bustling/modern metropolis*

metropolitan /ˌmet.rəˈpɒl.ɪ.tᵊn/ (US) /-ˈpɑː.lɪ-/ **adj** relating to a large city: *the Metropolitan Museum of Art in New York* ◦ *He was drawn to the metropolitan glamour and excitement of Paris.* ◦ *a metropolitan area/council*

metronome

the Metroˌpolitan Poˈlice noun [plural] (informal **the Met**) UK the police responsible for London

metrosexual /ˌmet.rəʊˈsek.sjʊəl/ (US) /-oʊ-/ **noun** [C] a man who is attracted to women sexually but who is also interested in fashion and his appearance

mettle /ˈmet.l̩/ (US) /ˈmet̬-/ **noun** [U] ability and determination when competing or doing something difficult: *The German athletes* ***showed/proved*** *their mettle in the final round.* ◦ *The real test of her political mettle came in the May elections.*

IDIOM **on your mettle** ready to do something as well as you can in a difficult situation: *Both players were on their mettle in the final round.* ◦ *Cooking for such important people really* ***puts*** *you on your mettle.*

mew /mjuː/ noun; verb

▸**noun** [C] the soft crying sound that a cat makes → Compare **miaow, purr**

▸**verb** [I] When a cat mews, it makes a soft crying sound.

mews /mjuːz/ **noun** [C] (plural **mews**) mainly UK **1** a building which was used in the past for keeping horses and is now used as a house: *They bought a converted mews.* ◦ *a tiny mews house* **2** a short, narrow road where these buildings are found: *Their new address is 6 Gloucester Mews.*

ˌMexican ˈwave noun [C usually singular] UK (US **the Wave**) a wave-like movement made by a crowd watching a sports game, when everyone stands and lifts up their arms and then sits down again one after another: *The crowd did a Mexican wave.*

mezzanine /ˈmet.sə.niːn/, /ˈmez.ə-/ **noun** [C] **1** a small extra floor between one floor of a building and the next floor up: *You can look down from the mezzanine into the ground floor lobby.* ◦ *The shoe department is on the mezzanine floor.* **2** US the front few rows of seats of the level above ground, or all of the level above ground, in a place such as a theatre or sports STADIUM

mezzo-soprano /ˌmet.səʊ.ʃəˈprɑː.nəʊ/ (US) /-soʊ.səˈpræn.oʊ/ **noun** [C or U] (plural **mezzo-sopranos**) (informal **mezzo**) a voice or musical part lower than SOPRANO but higher than CONTRALTO, or a singer with this type of voice: *She's the country's leading mezzo-soprano.*

mg written abbreviation for **milligram**

MHz written abbreviation for **megahertz**

mi noun **MILE** ▷ **1** written abbreviation for **mile**: *a radius of 5 mi* **MUSIC** ▷ **2** /miː/ (also **me**) [S] the third note in the SOL-FA musical SCALE

MI5 /ˌem.aɪˈfaɪv/ **noun** [+ sing/pl verb] the official British organization that is responsible for protecting military and political secrets

MI6 /ˌem.aɪˈsɪks/ **noun** [+ sing/pl verb] the official British organization that is responsible for discovering foreign military and political secrets

miaow (US usually **meow**) /ˌmiˈaʊ/ **noun** [C] the high crying sound of a cat → Compare **mew, purr** • **miaow verb** [I] *A cat was miaowing pitifully outside the door.*

miˈaow miˌaow (also **meow meow**) noun [U] UK informal for **mephedrone**

miasma /miˈæz.mə/ noun [C] literary **FOG** ▷ **1** an unpleasant FOG that smells bad: *A miasma **of** pollution hung in the air above Mexico City.* **UNPLEASANT FEELING** ▷ **2** a very unpleasant general feeling or character of a situation or place: *After he lost his job, he sank into a miasma **of** poverty and despair.*

mic /maɪk/ noun informal for **microphone**

mica /ˈmaɪ.kə/ noun [U] a natural substance like glass that breaks easily into thin layers and is not damaged by heat, often used in electrical equipment

mice /maɪs/ plural of **mouse**

mickey /ˈmɪk.i/ noun **MAKE FUN** ▷ **1 take the mickey/mick (out of someone)** UK informal to laugh at someone and make them seem silly, by copying their behaviour or tricking them in a funny or unkind way **DRUG** ▷ **2** [C] (also **Mickey Finn**) a drug added to a drink, especially an alcoholic drink, in order to make the person who drinks it unconscious: *He must have **slipped** the guard a mickey.*

ˌMickey ˈMouse adj [before noun] informal disapproving describes something such as an organization, machine, or course of study that you think is not as good or serious as it should be: *He works for some Mickey Mouse **outfit** (= company) in Oklahoma.*

micro /ˈmaɪ.krəʊ/ (US) /-kroʊ/ noun; adj
▸noun [C] (plural **micros**) informal for **microcomputer**
▸adj describes something that is very small: *The company has a 20 percent share in the market for mini or micro cars.*

micro- /maɪ.krəʊ-/, /-rə-/ (US) /-kroʊ-/ prefix **SMALL** ▷ **1** very small: *a microorganism ◦ microbiology* → Compare **macro-** **MEASUREMENT** ▷ **2** 1,000,000th of the stated unit: *a micrometre ◦ a microgram*

microbe /ˈmaɪ.krəʊb/ (US) /-kroʊb/ noun [C] a very small living thing, especially one that causes disease, that can only be seen with a MICROSCOPE

microbiology /ˌmaɪ.krəʊ.baɪˈɒl.ə.dʒi/ (US) /-kroʊ.baɪˈɑː.lə-/ noun [U] the study of very small living things, such as bacteria • **microbiological** /-ˌbaɪ.əˈlɒdʒ.ɪ.kᵊl/ (US) /-ˌbaɪ.əˈlɑː.dʒɪ.kᵊl/ adj • **microbiologist** /-ˈɒl.ə.dʒɪst/ (US) /-kroʊ.baɪˈɑː.lə..dʒɪst/ noun [C]

microblog /ˈmaɪ.krəˌblɒg/ (US) /-kroʊˌblɑːg/ noun [C] a BLOG in the form of a short message for anyone to read, sent especially from a mobile phone: *Microblogs, for example on Twitter, can be for anything from 'what I'm doing now' to coverage of serious political events.*

microblogging /ˈmaɪ.krəˌblɒg.ɪŋ/ (US) /-kroʊˌblɑː.gɪŋ/ noun [U] the activity of writing microblogs

microbrewery /ˈmaɪ.krəʊˌbruː.ᵊr.i/ (US) /-kroʊˌbruː.ɚ.i/ noun [C] mainly US a small company that makes beer, usually using traditional methods, and often has a restaurant where its beer is served: *Redhook was one of the first microbreweries in Seattle, Washington.*

microchip /ˈmaɪ.krəʊ.tʃɪp/ (US) /-kroʊ-/ noun [C] a **chip**

microcircuit /ˈmaɪ.krəʊˌsɜː.kɪt/ (US) /-kroʊˌsɝː-/ noun an **integrated circuit**

microclimate /ˈmaɪ.krəʊ.klaɪ.mɪt/ (US) /-kroʊˌ-/ noun [C] an area in which the weather is usually different from the areas around it

microcomputer /ˈmaɪ.krəʊ.kəmˌpjuː.təʳ/ (US) /-kroʊ.kəmˌpjuː.t̬ɚ/ noun [C] (informal **micro**) a small computer containing a MICROPROCESSOR (= part which controls operations)

microcosm /ˈmaɪ.krəʊˌkɒz.ᵊm/ (US) /-kroʊˌkɑː.zᵊm/ noun [C or U] a small place, society, or situation that has the same characteristics as something much larger: *The audience was selected to create a microcosm **of** American society.* → Compare **macrocosm**

microelectronics /ˌmaɪ.krəʊˌɪl.ekˈtrɒn.ɪks/ (US) /-kroʊ.ɪˌlekˈtrɑː.nɪks/ noun [U] the science and technology involved in the making and using of very small electronic parts

microfiche /ˈmaɪ.krə.fiːʃ/ (US) /-kroʊ-/ noun [C or U] (also **fiche**) a small, rectangular sheet of film on which information is photographed in a reduced size: *The information is now available **on** microfiche.*

microfilm /ˈmaɪ.krəʊ.fɪlm/ (US) /-kroʊ-/ noun [C or U] film that is used for photographing information in a reduced size, or a piece of this film • **microfilm** verb [T] *The paper records were microfilmed to save storage space.*

microgram /ˈmaɪ.krəʊ.græm/ (US) /-kroʊ-/ noun [C] one millionth of a gram

microlight /ˈmaɪ.krəʊ.laɪt/ (US) /-kroʊ-/ noun [C] UK (US **ultralight**) an extremely light and small aircraft with a very small engine, which carries only one or two people

micromanage /ˈmaɪ.krəʊˌmæn.ɪdʒ/ (US) /-kroʊˌ-/ verb [T] often disapproving to control every part of a situation, even small details: *The senator was criticized for micromanaging his presidential campaign.* • **micromanagement** /-mənt/ noun [U] • **micromanager** /-əʳ/ (US) /-ɚ/ noun [C]

micrometer /maɪˈkrɒm.ɪ.təʳ/ (US) /ˈkrɑː.mɪ.t̬ɚ/ noun [C] a device used for making very exact measurements or for measuring very small things

micrometre UK (US **micrometer**) /ˈmaɪ.krəʊˌmiː.təʳ/ (US) /-kroʊˌmiː.t̬ɚ/ noun [C] a **micron**

micron /ˈmaɪ.krɒn/ (US) /-krɑːn/ noun [C] one millionth of a metre

microorganism /ˌmaɪ.krəʊˈɔː.gᵊn.ɪ.zᵊm/ (US) /-kroʊˈɔːr-/ noun [C] a living thing which on its own is too small to be seen without a MICROSCOPE

microphone /ˈmaɪ.krə.fəʊn/ (US) /-foʊn/ noun [C] (informal **mike**, **mic**) B2 a piece of equipment that you speak into to make your voice louder, or to record your voice or other sounds: *The interviewer asked her to **speak into/use** the microphone.*

micropower /ˈmaɪ.krəʊˌpaʊəʳ/ (US) /-kroʊˌpaʊɚ/ noun [U] (also **microgeneration**) the use of your own equipment and the sun, wind, etc. to produce all the heat and power that you need: *Micropower could eventually fuel most homes.*

microprocessor /ˌmaɪ.krəʊˈprəʊ.ses.əʳ/ (US) /-kroʊˈprɑː.ses.ɚ/ noun [C] a part of a computer that controls its main operations

microscope /ˈmaɪ.krə.skəʊp/ (US) /-skoʊp/ noun [C] a device that uses LENSES to make very small objects look larger, so that they can be scientifically examined and studied: *They looked at the blood samples **under** the microscope.*

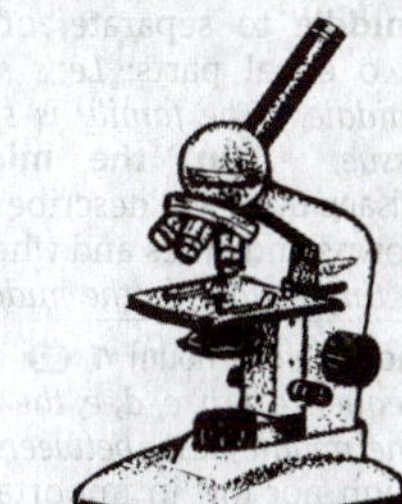
microscope

IDIOM **put sth under the microscope** to examine or think about a situation very carefully: *The investigation put the company's financial accounts under the microscope*

microscopic /ˌmaɪ.krəˈskɒp.ɪk/ (US) /-ˈskɑː.pɪk/ adj

M

1 informal humorous extremely small: *The helpings you get in the office canteen are microscopic!* **2** specialized very small and only able to be seen with a microscope: *microscopic algae* • **microscopically** /ˈskɒp.ɪ.kəl.i/ (US) /-ˈskɑː.pɪ.kəl.i/ **adv** informal or specialized *microscopically small*

microsecond /ˈmaɪ.krəʊˌsek.ənd/ (US) /-kroʊ-/ **noun** [C] one millionth of a second

microsite /ˈmaɪ.krəˌsaɪt/ **noun** [C] a small website, usually one advertising a particular product or service for a company: *She built a microsite, linked to the firm's main website, that targeted job seekers.*

microsurgery /ˌmaɪ.krəʊˈsɜː.dʒər.i/ (US) /-kroʊˈsɝː.dʒɚ-/ **noun** [U] operations on very small areas of a body, for example nerve FIBRES (= structures like threads) or the small tubes that carry blood: *She underwent microsurgery to re-attach her severed fingers.*

microwave /ˈmaɪ.krə.weɪv/ (US) /-kroʊ-/ **noun** [C] **1** (also **microwave oven**) an electric oven that uses waves of energy to cook or heat food quickly: ***Put** the fish **in** the microwave and it'll only take five minutes.* **2** a very short ELECTROMAGNETIC wave used for cooking food or for sending information by radio or RADAR • **microwave verb** [T] to cook something in a microwave: *Shall I microwave something for dinner?* • **microwaveable** (US **microwavable**) /-weɪ.və.bl̩/ **adj** *microwaveable frozen chips*

mid /mɪd/ **preposition** old-fashioned literary among or in the middle of

mid- /mɪd-/ **prefix** the middle of: *mid-March* ◦ *mid-afternoon* ◦ US *the Mideast* ◦ *He's in his mid-thirties.* ◦ *He stopped (in) mid-sentence.*

ˌmid-ˈair noun [U] a point in the air, not on the ground: *She caught the ball **in** mid-air.* • **ˌmid-ˈair adj** *a mid-air **collision***

Midas /ˈmaɪ.dəs/ **noun the Midas touch** If someone has the Midas touch, they are financially successful in everything they do.

midday /ˌmɪdˈdeɪ/ **noun** [U] (A2) twelve o'clock in the middle of the day: *I just have a sandwich **at** midday/for my midday meal.*

middle /ˈmɪd.l̩/ **noun; adj**

▸**noun 1** (A2) [S] the central point, position, or part: *This is my class photo – I'm the one **in the** middle.* ◦ *He was standing in **the** middle **of** the road.* ◦ *The noise woke us up **in the** middle **of** the night.* **2** [C usually singular] informal waist: *Those trousers look a bit tight around your middle.*

IDIOMS **be in the middle of sth** (B1) to be busy with an activity: *Someone phoned when I was in the middle of bathing the baby.* • **divide/split (sth) down the middle** to separate, or to divide something, into two equal parts: *Let's split the cost right down the middle.* ◦ *The family is split down the middle on this issue.* • **(in) the middle of nowhere** informal disapproving (B2) describes a place far away from any towns and cities and where few people live: *He lives in a tiny cottage in the middle of nowhere.*

▸**adj** [before noun] **1** (B2) in a central position: *In the sequence a, b, c, d, e, the middle letter is c.* ◦ *Jane sits at the middle desk, between Sue and Karen.* **2** (C1) neither high nor low in importance, amount, or size: *middle **income** families* ◦ *a middle-**sized** (= average-sized) sheepdog* **3** describes a child who has the same number of older brothers and sisters as younger brothers and sisters: *She's the middle child of three.* **4** describes a form of a particular language which existed between its origin and its present form: *14th-century Middle English*

IDIOM **follow/steer/take the middle course/way/path** to act in a way that is not extreme and that you consider will cause least harm: *Most parents steer a middle course between strict discipline and letting their kids run wild.*

ˌmiddle ˈage noun [U] the period of your life, usually considered to be from about 45 to 60 years old, when you are no longer young, but are not yet old: *Once you reach middle age, you have to be sensible with your health.*

ˌmiddle-ˈaged adj 1 (B1) in middle age: *They're a middle-aged couple, with grown-up children.* **2** disapproving too careful and not showing the enthusiasm, energy, or style of someone young: *What a conventional, middle-aged attitude he has to life!*

the ˈMiddle ˌAges noun [plural] a period in European history, between about 1000 AD and 1500 AD, when the power of kings, people of high rank, and the Christian Church was strong

ˌmiddle-age ˈspread noun [U] humorous fat around the waist that some people get as they grow older

ˌMiddle Amˈerica noun [U] the part of American society that is neither rich nor poor and has traditional political and religious opinions

middlebrow /ˈmɪd.l̩.braʊ/ **adj** mainly disapproving describes music, literature, art, or film that is of good quality, interesting, and often popular, but can be understood quite easily → Compare **highbrow, lowbrow**

ˌmiddle ˈC noun [C usually singular] specialized the musical note C near the middle of the keyboard on a piano

ˌmiddle ˈclass noun [S, + sing/pl verb] (also **the ˌmiddle ˈclasses**) a social group that consists of well-educated people, such as doctors, lawyers, and teachers, who have good jobs and are neither very rich nor very poor: *The **upper** middle class tend to go into business or the professions, becoming, for example, lawyers, doctors, or accountants.* → Compare **lower class, upper class, working class** • **ˌmiddle-ˈclass adj** *a middle-class suburb of New York*

ˌmiddle-ˈdistance adj [before noun] describes a race that is run over a medium distance, especially 800 or 1500 metres: *a middle-distance event/runner*

the ˌmiddle ˈdistance noun [S] the part of a picture or a view that is neither very near nor very far away: *From the top of the hill we could see the ocean far away and, in the middle distance, the village.* → Compare **background, foreground**

ˌmiddle ˈear noun [S] the central part of the ear, behind the EARDRUM, through which sound travels

the ˌMiddle ˈEast noun (US also **the Mideast** /ˌmɪdˈiːst/) the area from the eastern Mediterranean to Iran, including Syria, Jordan, Israel, Lebanon, Saudi Arabia, Iran, and Iraq, and sometimes also Egypt: *He worked in the Middle East for ten years.* → Compare **the Far East** • **ˌMiddle ˈEastern adj** *Middle Eastern capitals include Baghdad and Tel Aviv.*

ˌMiddle ˈEngland noun [U] a way of referring to middle-class people who live in England but not in London and who are considered to have traditional views about society and politics: *They knew that the policy would not be popular with Middle England.*

ˌmiddle ˈfinger noun [C] the longest finger on the hand

ˌmiddle ˈground noun [U] a position between two opposite opinions in an argument, or between two

M

descriptions: *The UN peace envoy has failed to find any middle ground between the government and the opposition parties.* ◦ *He can be magical, he can be comical, but only rarely does he* ***occupy*** *the middle ground.*

middleman /ˈmɪd.l̩.mæn/ noun [C] (plural **-men** /-men/) **1** a person who buys goods from the company that has produced them and makes a profit by selling them to a shop or a user: *You can lower the price by* ***cutting out*** *(= avoiding the use of) the middleman and buying directly from the factory.* **2** someone who communicates or makes arrangements between two people or groups who are unwilling or unable to meet or deal directly with each other

ˌmiddle ˈmanagement noun [U, + sing/pl verb] the people within a company who are in charge of departments or groups, but who are below those in charge of the whole company: *He cut hundreds of jobs in middle management.* • **ˌmiddle ˈmanager** noun [C]

ˌmiddle ˈname noun [C] the name some people have between their first name and their last name

IDIOM **be sb's middle name** informal to be a quality that is an important part of someone's character: *Don't worry, I won't tell anyone. Discretion is my middle name.*

ˌmiddle-of-the-ˈroad adj describes a person, organization, opinion, or type of entertainment that is not extreme and is acceptable to or liked by most people: *middle-of-the-road pop music* ◦ *They adopted a sensible, middle-of-the-road policy on defence spending.*

ˈmiddle ˌschool noun [C] in parts of the UK and the US, a school for children between the ages of about nine and 14

middleweight /ˈmɪd.l̩.weɪt/ noun [C] a **boxer** whose weight is between LIGHT HEAVYWEIGHT and WELTERWEIGHT

the ˌMiddle ˈWest noun **the Midwest**

middling /ˈmɪd.l̩.ɪŋ/, /-lɪŋ/ adj informal medium or average; neither very good nor very bad: *a man of about middling height* ◦ *a middling performance*

middy /ˈmɪd.i/ noun [C] Australian English a beer glass of medium size, containing 285 ml

midfield /ˈmɪd.fiəld/ noun [C or U] the central area of a sports field, or a central structure of a sports team: *Simon's a defender, but I always play* ***in*** *midfield.* ◦ *Arsenal's defence were strong, but their midfield fell apart in the first five minutes of the match.* ◦ *a midfield player* • **midfielder** /ˌmɪdˈfiəl.dəʳ/ (US) /-dɚ/ noun [C]

midge /mɪdʒ/ noun [C] a small fly which flies in groups, and often bites

midget /ˈmɪdʒ.ɪt/ noun; adj

▸noun [C] offensive a very small person

▸adj [before noun] describes an object that is much smaller than usual: *a midget submarine/car*

ˈmidi ˌsystem noun [C] a piece of high-quality electronic equipment of medium size for playing music → Compare **mini system**

the ˈMidlands noun [+ sing/pl verb] the central part of England, including the cities of Birmingham, Coventry, Nottingham, and Derby • **Midland** /-lənd/ adj *He's got a real Midland accent.*

midlife crisis /ˌmɪd.laɪfˈkraɪ.sɪs/ noun [C] (plural **midlife crises**) feelings of unhappiness, worry, and disappointment that some people experience at about 40 years old and that can sometimes lead them to make important changes in their life → See also **menopause, male menopause**

midnight /ˈmɪd.naɪt/ noun [U] (A2) twelve o'clock in the middle of the night: *There's a great film on TV* ***at*** *midnight.* ◦ *It was after midnight when we got home.*

ˌmidnight ˈfeast noun [C] UK a meal eaten late at night, often in secret: *The children raided the fridge for a midnight feast.*

the ˌmidnight ˈsun noun [S] the sun when seen in the middle of the night in summer in the ARCTIC or ANTARCTIC (= the parts of the world furthest to the north and the south)

midpoint /ˈmɪd.pɔɪnt/ noun [C usually singular] DISTANCE ▷ **1** a point half the distance along something such as a line: *The driveway is 20 metres long, so the midpoint must be at 10 metres.* TIME ▷ **2** a point in the middle of a period of time: *the midpoint of the football season*

midriff /ˈmɪd.rɪf/ noun [C] (US also **midsection**) the part of the human body between the chest and the waist: *She wore a short T-shirt that revealed her midriff.*

midshipman /ˈmɪdˌʃɪp.mən/ noun [C] (plural **-men** /-mən/) a person training to become an officer in a navy

midsize /ˈmɪd.saɪz/ adj (also **midsized** /-saɪzd/) mainly US describes something such as an organization or vehicle that is neither large nor small: *a midsize family car*

midst /mɪdst/, /mɪtst/ noun; preposition

▸noun [U] formal **1** the middle of a group of people or things: *She caught sight of Johnny* ***in*** *their midst (= among them), laughing and talking.* **2 in the midst of sth** in the middle of an event, situation, or activity: *I'm afraid I'm too busy – I'm in the midst of writing up a report.* ◦ *The country is in the midst of an economic crisis.*

▸preposition literary among: *The summit of the mountain appeared midst the clouds.*

midstream /ˌmɪdˈstriːm/ noun [U] the middle of a river where the water flows fastest: *They slowly paddled the boat into midstream.*

IDIOM **(in) midstream** in the middle of an activity, often one that is interrupted: *She interrupted him in midstream to ask a question.*

midsummer /ˌmɪdˈsʌm.əʳ/ (US) /-ɚ/ noun [U] **1** the period in the middle of summer: *I don't normally take my holiday in midsummer.* ◦ *a midsummer evening* **2** the summer SOLSTICE, the day of the year on which it is light for the longest period of time (21 June in northern parts of the world, 22 December in southern parts of the world)

ˌMidsummer('s) ˈDay noun [U] UK 24 June

midterm /ˈmɪd.tɜːm/ (US) /-tɝːm/ adj; noun

▸adj in the middle of the period when a government is in office: *The governing party usually does badly in midterm by-elections.*

▸noun [U] US for **half-term**

midway /ˌmɪdˈweɪ/ adv **1** half the distance between two places: *Leeds is midway* ***between*** *London and Edinburgh.* **2** in the middle of a process or period of time: *She stopped working midway* ***through*** *her pregnancy.*

midweek /ˌmɪdˈwiːk/ noun [U] the middle of the week, usually from Tuesday to Thursday: *By midweek, the situation had become worrying.* • **midweek** adj • **midweek** adv *The magazine comes out midweek.*

the Midwest /ˌmɪdˈwest/ noun an area in the US that includes Ohio, Indiana, Michigan, Illinois, Wisconsin, Iowa, Minnesota, Nebraska, Missouri, and Kansas

M

Midwestern /ˌmɪdˈwes.tən/ (US) /-tɚn/ **adj** relating to the Midwest: *a Midwestern city/state*

midwife /ˈmɪd.waɪf/ **noun** [C] (plural **midwives**) a person, usually a woman, who is trained to help women when they are giving birth • **midwifery** /mɪdˈwɪf.ər.i/ (US) /ˈ-ɚ-/ **noun** [U] *At nursing college, she specialized in midwifery.*

midwinter /ˌmɪdˈwɪn.tər/ (US) /-t̬ɚ/ **noun** [U] **1** the middle of the winter: *Temperatures can drop well below freezing in midwinter.* **2** the winter SOLSTICE, the particular day of the year on which it is light for the shortest period of time (22 December in northern parts of the world, 21 June in southern parts of the world): *They celebrate midwinter by lighting candles.*

mielie /ˈmiː.li/ **noun** [C] South African English an EAR (= part containing the yellow grains) of the MAIZE plant

ˈmielie ˌmeal **noun** [U] South African English **1** flour made from the grains of the MAIZE plant **2** a soft food made from MAIZE flour

mien /miːn/ **noun** [C] literary a person's appearance, especially the typical expression on their face: *His aristocratic mien and smart clothes singled him out.*

miffed /mɪft/ **adj** informal annoyed at someone's behaviour towards you: *She hadn't phoned for a week and I was getting quite miffed.*

might /maɪt/ **modal verb; noun**

▸**modal verb MAY** ▷ **1** past simple of the verb MAY, used especially when reporting what someone has said, thought, asked, etc.: *I brought him some sandwiches because I thought he might be hungry.* ◦ *Very politely the little boy asked if he might have another piece of cake (= he said 'May I have another piece of cake, please?').* **POSSIBILITY** ▷ **2** (A2) used to express the possibility that something will happen or be done, or that something is true although not very likely: *I might come and visit you in America next year, if I can save enough money.* ◦ *Don't go any closer – it might be dangerous/it mightn't be safe.* ◦ *Driving so fast, he might **have** had a nasty accident (= it could have happened but it did not).* ◦ *The rain might **have** stopped by now.* **PERMISSION** ▷ **3** UK formal used as a more polite form of may when asking for permission: *Might I ask a question?* ◦ *I wonder if I might have a quick look at your newspaper?* **SUGGESTION** ▷ **4** (C1) used to make a suggestion or suggest a possibility in a polite way: *You might like to try a little more basil in the sauce next time.* ◦ *I thought you might like to join me for dinner.* **SHOULD** ▷ **5** used to suggest, especially angrily, what someone should do to be pleasant, correct, polite, etc.: *You might at least try to look like you're enjoying yourself!* ◦ *'I've asked the boss to dinner tonight.' 'Well, you might **have** warned me!'* **INTRODUCE** ▷ **6** (also **may**) used to introduce a statement that is very different from the statement you really want to make, in order to compare the two: *Leeds might be an excellent team, **but** today they played appallingly.*

> **! Common mistake: might**
>
> **Might** is followed by an infinitive verb without 'to'.
>
> Don't say 'might does something', say **might do something**:
>
> ~~*This year's group might includes several vegetarians.*~~
>
> *This year's group might include several vegetarians.*

IDIOMS **I might have known** disapproving said when you are not surprised at a situation or someone's behaviour, because you expected it: *I might have known (**that**) he'd still be in bed at noon.* • **might I ask/inquire/know** UK formal used in questions to show disapproval by being more polite than is expected: *And what are you doing in there, might I ask?*

▸**noun** [U] power, strength, or force: *Pizarro defeated the might of the Inca Empire with only a few hundred men.* ◦ *She struggled **with all** her might to get free.*

mightily /ˈmaɪ.tɪ.li/ (US) /-t̬ɪ-/ **adv** formal with great effort: *He spent ten years struggling mightily with the bureaucracy.*

mightn't /ˈmaɪ.tənt/ short form of might not: *Don't panic – it mightn't be true.*

might've /ˈmaɪ.təv/ (US) /-t̬əv/ short form of might have: *She might've taken it with her to read on the train.*

mighty /ˈmaɪ.ti/ (US) /-t̬i/ **adj; adv**

▸**adj** literary (C2) very large, powerful, or important: *the mighty River Po*

▸**adv** mainly US informal very: *They offered to raise salaries by 15 percent – that's a mighty generous deal.*

migraine /ˈmiː.ɡreɪn/, /ˈmaɪ-/ (US) /ˈmaɪ-/ **noun** [C or U] severe continuous pain in the head, often with vomiting and difficulty in seeing: *Do you suffer from migraine?* ◦ *Considering the amount of stress she's under, it's not surprising she keeps **getting** migraines.* ◦ *a migraine headache*

migrant /ˈmaɪ.ɡrənt/ **noun** [C] a person or animal that travels from one place to another: *These birds are winter migrants from Scandinavia.* ◦ *The cities are full of migrants looking for work.* ◦ *migrant **workers*** ◦ *a migrant population*

migrate /maɪˈɡreɪt/ (US) /ˈmaɪ.ɡreɪt/ **verb TRAVEL/MOVE** ▷ **1** [I] When an animal migrates, it travels to a different place, usually when the season changes: *These animals migrate annually in search of food.* ◦ *In September, these birds migrate 2,000 miles south **to** a warmer climate.* **2** [I] If people migrate, they travel in large numbers to a new place to live temporarily: *Mexican farm workers migrate **into** the US each year to find work at harvest time.* **3** [I] to move from one place to another: *Trade is migrating **from** local shops **to** the larger out-of-town stores.* **COMPUTING** ▷ **4** [I or T] specialized to begin using a new computer system, or to move information from one type of system to another: *Migrating **to** Windows XP shouldn't cause you any problems.* • **migration** /maɪˈɡreɪ.ʃən/ **noun** [C or U] (C1) *There was a **mass** migration of poverty-struck farmers **into** the cities.* → Compare **immigration, emigration (emigrate)** • **migratory** /ˈmaɪ.ɡrə.tər.i/, /maɪˈɡreɪ-/ (US) /-tɔːr-/ **adj** *migratory **birds***

mike (also **mic**) /maɪk/ **noun** [C] informal for **microphone**

mild /maɪld/ **adj; noun**

▸**adj SLIGHT** ▷ **1** (C1) not violent, severe, or extreme: *She can't accept even mild criticism of her work.* ◦ *He has suffered a mild heart attack – nothing too serious.* **WEATHER** ▷ **2** (B1) describes weather that is not very cold or not as cold as usual: *We've had a mild winter this year.* **FOOD** ▷ **3** (B2) describes food or a food flavour that is not very strong: *He doesn't like a hot curry – he prefers a mild one.* ◦ *a mild chilli sauce* **GENTLE** ▷ **4** gentle and calm: *a shy, mild sort of guy* • **mildness** /ˈmaɪld.nəs/ **noun** [U] *mildness of manner*

▸**noun** [U] a dark beer that does not have a very strong or bitter taste → Compare **bitter**

mildew /ˈmɪl.djuː/ (US) /-duː/ **noun** [U] a black, green, or whitish area caused by a FUNGUS that grows on things such as plants, paper, cloth, or buildings, usually if the conditions are warm and wet: *There are* *patches of mildew on the walls.* • **mildewed** /-djuːd/ (US) /-duːd/ **adj** *mildewed rose bushes*

mildly /ˈmaɪld.li/ **adv** **1** slightly: *I was mildly* ***surprised*** *to see him here.* **2** in a gentle way: *'I think you've made a mistake,' he said mildly.*

IDIOM **to put it mildly** used for saying that something is much more extreme than your words suggest: *It has been a remarkable day, to put it mildly.*

ˌmild-ˈmannered **adj** describes a person who is gentle and does not show extreme emotions: *a mild-mannered philosophy professor*

mile /maɪl/ **noun** **1** B1 [C] a unit of distance equal to 1,760 YARDS or 1.6 kilometres: *a ten-mile drive* ◦ *The nearest town is ten miles away.* ◦ *The speed limit is 30 miles* ***an/per*** *hour.* **2 miles** C1 [plural] a very long way: *From the top, we could see for miles in every direction.* ◦ *He lives miles* ***away*** *on the other side of town.*

IDIOMS **be miles away** mainly UK to not be conscious of what is happening around you because you are thinking about something else: *You could tell by the expression on her face that she was miles away, thinking about home.* • **a mile a minute** very quickly: *Mike was very excited,* ***talking a mile a minute.*** • **a mile off** If you can see or realize something a mile off, you notice it easily and quickly: *She's lying – you can tell it a mile off.* • **(by) miles** informal used to say something is much greater or better than something else: *British restaurant food is* ***better*** *by miles/miles* ***better*** *than it used to be 20 years ago.* • **miles from anywhere/nowhere** a long distance from other houses or a town: *They live miles from nowhere, in the middle of the countryside.* • **miles too big, small, expensive, etc.** informal very much bigger, smaller, more expensive, etc. than you would like: *This tea is miles too sweet!* • **stand/stick out a mile** to be very obvious or easy to see: *His lack of experience sticks out a mile.*

mileage /ˈmaɪ.lɪdʒ/ **noun** [U] **DISTANCE TRAVELLED** ▷ **1** the distance that a vehicle has travelled or the distance that it can travel using a particular amount of fuel: *'What's the mileage on your car?' 'Oh, about 40,000.'* ◦ *Smaller cars have better mileage and so cost less to run.* **MONEY FOR TRAVEL** ▷ **2** (also **mileage allowance**) the amount of money that you are paid or that you must pay for each mile you travel: *The car costs £30 a day to rent, but you* ***get*** *unlimited mileage (= no charge for the miles travelled).* **ADVANTAGE** ▷ **3** informal the advantage that you can get from a situation: *There's no mileage* ***in*** *complaining to the Director – she'll just ignore you.* ◦ *political mileage*

milestone /ˈmaɪl.stəʊn/ (US) /-stoʊn/ **noun** [C] (UK also **milepost**) **STONE/POST** ▷ **1** a stone or post at the side of the road that shows the distance to various places, especially to the nearest large town **IMPORTANT EVENT** ▷ **2** an important event in the development or history of something or in someone's life: *He felt that moving out from his parents' home was a real milestone in his life.*

milieu /mɪˈljɜː/ (US) /miːlˈjɜː/ **noun** [C] (plural **milieux** or **milieus**) formal the people, physical, and social conditions and events that provide the environment in which someone acts or lives: *It is a study of the social and cultural milieu in which Michelangelo lived and worked.*

militant /ˈmɪl.ɪ.tᵊnt/ **adj** active, determined, and often willing to use force: *militant union extremists* ◦ *The group has taken a militant position on the abortion issue and is refusing to compromise.* • **militancy** /-tᵊn.si/ **noun** [U] • **militant** **noun** [C] *Militants within the party are demanding radical reforms.* • **militantly** /-li/ **adv**

militarism /ˈmɪl.ɪ.tᵊr.ɪ.zᵊm/ (US) /-t̬ɚ-/ **noun** [U] disapproving the belief that it is necessary to have strong armed forces and that they should be used in order to win political or economic advantages

militarist /ˈmɪl.ɪ.tᵊr.ɪst/ (US) /-t̬ɚ.ɪst/ **noun** [C] disapproving a person who wants more powerful armed forces in their country • **militaristic** /ˌmɪl.ɪ.tᵊrˈɪs.tɪk/ (US) /-t̬əˈrɪs-/ **adj** *a militaristic policy/government*

militarized (UK usually **militarised**) /ˈmɪl.ɪ.tᵊr.aɪzd/ (US) /-t̬ə.raɪzd/ **adj** describes an area, country, or organization that has a large, strong army and other armed forces and many weapons: *North Korea is said to be the world's most heavily militarized country, with over one million men in the armed forces.*

military **adj; noun**

▸**adj** /ˈmɪl.ɪ.tᵊr.i/ (US) /-ter-/ **1** B2 relating to or belonging to the armed forces: *foreign military* ***intervention*** ◦ *military* ***targets/forces*** ◦ *military uniform* **2** describes a characteristic that is typical of the armed forces: *military* ***precision*** • **militarily** /ˌmɪl.ɪˈter.ɪ.li/ **adv**

▸**noun** /ˈmɪl.ɪ.tᵊr.i/ (US) /-ter.i/ **the military** C1 the armed forces: *The military has opposed any cuts in defence spending.*

ˌmilitary aˈcademy **noun** [C] **1** a place where soldiers are trained to become officers **2** a private school in the US that expects students to obey the rules, has uniforms, and is generally run like the armed forces

ˌmilitary ˈband **noun** [C] a group of musicians within the armed forces who play marching and military music

ˌmilitary ˈhonours **noun** [plural] ceremonies performed by soldiers to honour a king, queen, or other important person, or to honour someone important who has died: *The Colonel was buried with* ***full*** *military honours.*

the ˌmilitary poˈlice **noun** [plural] (abbreviation **MP**) the police force within the armed forces, responsible for dealing with members of the armed forces who break the law

ˌmilitary poˈliceman **noun** [C] (abbreviation **MP**) a member of the military police

ˌmilitary ˈservice **noun** [U] army training that young people must do in some countries: *He has to* ***do*** *his military service before going to university.*

militate /ˈmɪl.ɪ.teɪt/ **verb**

PHRASAL VERB **militate against sth** formal to make something less likely to happen or succeed: *The complexity and costliness of the judicial system militate against justice for the individual.*

militia /mɪˈlɪʃ.ə/ **noun** [C, + sing/pl verb] a military force which only operates for some of the time and whose members often have other jobs: *A UN force was sent in to stop fighting between three rival militias.* ◦ *The government* ***called out*** *the militia to help cope with the rioting.*

militiaman /mɪˈlɪʃ.ə.mən/, /-mæn/ **noun** [C] (plural **-men** /-mən/, /-men/) a member of a militia

milk /mɪlk/ **noun; verb**

▸**noun** [U] **1** A1 the white liquid produced by cows, goats, and sheep and used by humans as a drink or for making butter, cheese, etc.: *a* ***glass/carton of*** *milk* ◦ *cow's/goat's milk* ◦ ***skimmed/pasteurized*** *milk* ◦ *a milk* ***bottle*** **2** the white liquid produced by women and other female mammals as food for their young: ***Breast/Mother's** milk is the best nourishment for a baby.* **3** the white liquid produced by some plants and trees: *coconut milk*

IDIOM **the milk of human kindness** good, kind qualities: *She's **full of** the milk of human kindness.*

▸verb GET MILK ▷ **1** [I or T] to get milk from an animal: *Milking a cow by hand is a skilled process.* ◦ *Some goats seem to milk (= produce milk) better than others.* GET MONEY/INFORMATION ▷ **2** [T] disapproving to get as much money or information out of someone or something as possible, often in an unfair or dishonest way: [+ obj + adj] *The newspapers milked the story **dry**.* ◦ *The directors milked the company **of** several million pounds.*

ˈmilk ˌbar noun [C] mainly Australian English a shop that sells milk products, bread, and sweets

ˌmilk ˈchocolate noun [C or U] sweet, light brown chocolate made with milk

ˈmilk ˌfloat noun [C] UK a vehicle, usually with an electric motor, used to take milk to people's houses in the UK

ˈmilking maˌchine noun [C] a machine used to take milk from cows

milkman /ˈmɪlk.mən/ noun [C] (plural **-men** /-mən/) a man whose job is to bring milk to your home in the early morning

ˌMilk of Magˈnesia noun [U] trademark a white liquid medicine containing MAGNESIUM, taken to cure slight stomach problems

M

ˈmilk ˌround noun **1** [C] a route that a milkman takes regularly or every day to take milk to the homes of customers: *Dad had a milk round and used to get up really early.* **2 the milk round** [S] UK informal the series of visits made at a particular time of the year by large companies to colleges to discuss giving jobs to students after they have finished their education

ˈmilk ˌrun noun [C usually singular] a journey that you make often, especially one including several stops

milkshake /ˈmɪlk.ʃeɪk/ noun [C or U] a drink made of milk and usually ice cream and a flavour such as fruit or chocolate, mixed quickly together until it is full of bubbles: *a chocolate milkshake*

ˈmilk ˌtooth noun [C] a **baby tooth**

milky /ˈmɪl.ki/ adj **1** describes a liquid containing milk or made with a lot of milk: *a cup of milky coffee* ◦ *Having a milky **drink** before bed helps me sleep.* **2** white, pale, or not transparent: *milky skin* ◦ *a milky white/blue*

the ˌMilky ˈWay noun [S] the GALAXY (= star system) that includes the Earth, seen at night as a pale strip across the sky

mill /mɪl/ noun; verb

▸noun [C] **1** a building where grain is crushed into flour **2** a small machine for crushing things into powder: *a pepper/coffee mill* **3** a factory where a particular substance is produced: *a cotton/paper/steel mill*

IDIOM **put sb through the mill** informal to cause someone to have a difficult and unpleasant experience, especially by asking them a lot of difficult questions: *I had the interview this morning – they really put me through the mill.*

▸verb [T] **1** to crush grain into flour or another substance into powder: *The grain is still milled locally.* **2** specialized to shape metal by removing parts from it using a special machine

PHRASAL VERB **mill around** (UK also **mill about**) If a group of people mill around, they move about with no particular purpose or in no fixed direction, sometimes while waiting for someone: *In the village square, people were milling about in the sunshine.*

millennium /mɪˈlen.i.əm/ noun [C] (plural **millennia** or **millenniums**) C2 a period of 1,000 years, or the time when a period of 1,000 years ends: *The corpse had lain preserved in the soil for almost two millennia.* → Compare **century** • **millennial** /-əl/ adj

millepede /ˈmɪl.ɪ.piːd/ noun [C] a **millipede**

miller /ˈmɪl.əʳ/ US /-ɚ/ noun [C] a person, especially in the past, who owned or was in charge of a mill

millet /ˈmɪl.ɪt/ noun [U] a plant that is similar to grass, or the small seeds from this plant that can be eaten

milli- /mɪl.ɪ-/ prefix 0.001 of the stated unit: *milliamp* ◦ *millijoule*

milliard /ˈmɪl.i.əd/ number South African English the number 1,000,000,000 → See also **billion**

millibar /ˈmɪl.ɪ.bɑːʳ/ US /-bɑːr/ noun [C] (written abbreviation **mb**) a unit of air pressure: *an anticyclone of 1,030 millibars*

milligram (UK also **milligramme**) /ˈmɪl.ɪ.græm/ noun [C] (written abbreviation **mg**) a unit of mass that is equal to 0.001 grams

millilitre UK (US **milliliter**) /ˈmɪl.ɪˌliː.təʳ/ US /-t̬ɚ/ noun [C] (written abbreviation **ml**) a unit of volume that is equal to 0.001 litres

millimetre UK (US **millimeter**) /ˈmɪl.ɪˌmiː.təʳ/ US /-t̬ɚ/ noun [C] (written abbreviation **mm**) B1 a unit of length that is equal to 0.001 metres

milliner /ˈmɪl.ɪ.nəʳ/ US /-nɚ/ noun [C] a person who makes or sells women's hats

millinery /ˈmɪl.ɪ.nər.i/ US /-ner-/ noun [U] the hats and other goods that are sold by a milliner

million /ˈmɪl.jən/ number (plural **million** or **millions**) **1** A2 [C] the number 1,000,000: *The city has a population of almost a/one million.* ◦ *She got eight million dollars for appearing in that film.* ◦ *His business is worth millions **of** euros.* **2 a million/millions of sth** informal B2 a large number: *I must have told you a million times to close the windows when you leave the house.* **3 the millions** numbers between 1,000,000 and 1,000,000,000: *In wealthy parts of the country, homes cost from £750,000 into the millions.*

> **! Common mistake: millions or million?**
>
> When **million** is used after a particular number, it is used in the singular form and without 'of'.
>
> Don't say 'five/ten/fifteen millions of sth', say five/ten/fifteen **million** sth:
>
> ~~*The house cost 2 millions of dollars.*~~
>
> *The house cost 2 million dollars.*
>
> When **million** is used without a particular number, it is used in the plural form and is sometimes followed by 'of':
>
> *The house cost millions (of dollars).*

IDIOMS **be one in a million** approving to be a very special person: *Thanks again – you're one in a million!* • **one in a million** describes a chance that is extremely unlikely: *Don't worry – the chances of anything going wrong are one in a million.* • **look/feel (like) a million dollars** (US **look/feel (like) a million bucks**) to look or feel extremely good, often because you are experiencing something that costs a lot of money: *'You look a million dollars in that dress,* *honey!'* • **thanks a million** informal thank you very much: *'I've done what you asked.' 'Thanks a million!'*

millionaire /ˌmɪl.jəˈneəʳ/ (US) /-ˈner/ noun [C] (female also **millionairess**) a person who has money, property, etc. that is worth at least 1,000,000 dollars, pounds, euros, etc.: *You want me to buy you a new car – do you think I'm a millionaire or something?*

millionth /ˈmɪl.jənθ/ ordinal number; noun
▸**ordinal number** 1,000,000th written as a word: *Coventry City football club counted their millionth supporter through the gates last Saturday.* ◦ informal *They're showing 'High Noon' on TV for the millionth time (= having already shown it a lot of times).*
▸**noun** [C] one of a million equal parts of something: *a/one millionth* ***of*** *a second*

millipede (also **millepede**) /ˈmɪl.ɪ.piːd/ noun [C] a small creature with a long body consisting of many parts, each part having two pairs of legs

millisecond /ˈmɪl.ɪˌsek.ənd/ noun [C or] (written abbreviation **ms, msec.**) a unit of time equal to 0.001 seconds

millpond /ˈmɪl.pɒnd/ (US) /-pɑːnd/ noun [C] a pool of water which provides the power to make the wheel of a MILL turn: *The sea that day was like a millpond (= very calm and not moving).*

millstone /ˈmɪl.stəʊn/ (US) /-stoʊn/ noun [C] one of a pair of large, circular, flat stones used, especially in the past, to crush grain to make flour

IDIOM **be (like) a millstone around/round your neck** to be a responsibility that is difficult to bear and causes you trouble: *The mortgage on his house had become a millstone around his neck.*

milometer UK (UK also **mileometer**) /maɪˈlɒm.ɪ.təʳ/ (US) /-ˈlɑː.mɪ.t̬ɚ/ noun [C] (US **odometer**) a device in a vehicle that measures and shows the distance it travels

mime /maɪm/ noun; verb
▸**noun 1** [U] the act of using movements of your hands and body, and expressions on your face, without speech, to communicate emotions and actions or to tell a story: *The first scene was performed in mime.* **2** [C] a short play without speech
▸**verb** [I or T] **1** to act or tell a story in mime: *The whole of the banquet scene is mimed.* **2** to pretend to sing, play, or say something without making any sound: *Most of the bands that appear on the show just mime* ***to*** *a recording of their songs.* ◦ *He was miming something at me across the pub.*

ˈmime ˌartist noun [C] a person who performs mime in a theatre or film

mimetic /mɪˈmet.ɪk/ (US) /-ˈmet̬-/ adj specialized using mime: *The actors have to rely on their mimetic skills.* • **mimetically** /mɪˈmet.ɪ.kəl.i/ (US) /-met̬-/ adv

mimic /ˈmɪm.ɪk/ verb; noun
▸**verb** [T] (present tense **mimicking**, past tense and past participle **mimicked**) to copy the way in which a particular person usually speaks and moves, usually in order to make people laugh
▸**noun** [C] a person who can copy the sounds or movements of other people: *She's a brilliant mimic.* • **mimicry** /-ɪ.kri/ noun [U]

mimosa /mɪˈməʊ.sə/ (US) /-moʊ-/ noun [C] US for **Buck's Fizz**

min. noun **TIME** ▷ **1** [C] written abbreviation for **minute**: *Cooking time required: 30–35 mins.* **SMALLEST** ▷ **2** [C usually singular] written abbreviation for **minimum**, used in notices, advertisements, etc.: *Holiday cottage: min. stay three days.*

minaret /ˌmɪn.əˈret/ noun [C] a tall, thin tower on or near a MOSQUE (= a Muslim holy building) from which Muslims are called to pray

minaret

mince /mɪns/ noun; verb
▸**noun** [U] UK (US ˌ**ground ˈbeef**) meat, usually BEEF, that has been cut up into very small pieces
▸**verb WALK** ▷ **1** [I] to walk in an artificial way, with small, delicate steps: *He minced across the room in a pair of tight pink trousers.* **MEAT** ▷ **2** [T] to cut meat, or other food, into very small pieces, sometimes using a special machine: *Mince two pounds of chicken finely.*

IDIOM **not mince (your) words** to say what you mean clearly and directly, even if you upset people by doing this: *The report does not mince words, describing the situation as 'ludicrous'.*

minced /mɪnst/ adj (US usually **ground**) (especially of meat) having been cut up into very small pieces: *minced beef/lamb/onions*

mincemeat /ˈmɪns.miːt/ noun [U] a sweet, spicy mixture of small pieces of apple, dried fruit, and nuts (but not meat), often eaten at Christmas in mince pies

IDIOM **make mincemeat of sb** informal to defeat someone very easily in an argument, competition, or fight: *A decent lawyer would have made mincemeat of them in court.*

ˌmince ˈpie noun [C] a covered pastry case filled with mincemeat

mincer /ˈmɪn.səʳ/ (US) /-sɚ/ noun [C] UK (US usually ˈ**meat ˌgrinder**) a machine for cutting food, especially meat, into small pieces

mincing /ˈmɪn.sɪŋ/ adj **WALK** ▷ describes an artificial way of walking with small, delicate steps: *He took short, mincing steps.*

mind /maɪnd/ noun; verb
▸**noun** [C] **1** (B1) the part of a person that makes it possible for him or her to think, feel emotions, and understand things: *Her mind was full of what had happened the night before, and she just wasn't concentrating.* ◦ *Of course I'm telling the truth – you've got such a suspicious mind!* ◦ *I just said the first thing that* ***came into*** *my mind.* ◦ *I'm not quite clear in my mind about what I'm doing.* **2** a very clever person: *She was one of the most brilliant minds of the last century.* **3 all in the/your mind** describes a problem that does not exist and is only imagined: *His doctor tried to convince him that he wasn't really ill and that it was all in the mind.* **4 bear/keep sth in mind** (B2) to remember a piece of information when you are making a decision or thinking about a matter: *Bearing in mind how young she is, I thought she did really well.* ◦ *Of course, repair work is expensive and you have to keep that in mind.* **5 go over sth in your mind** (also **turn sth over in your mind**) to think repeatedly about an event that has happened

IDIOMS **be bored, drunk, etc. out of your mind** informal to be extremely bored, drunk, etc. • **be of sound/unsound mind** legal not to be mentally ill/to be mentally ill • **be of the same mind** (also **be of one mind**) to have the same opinion: *We're of the same mind on most political issues.* • **bring/call sth to mind**

M

to remember something: *I can see his face, but I just can't bring his name to mind.* • **get your mind round something** to succeed in understanding something difficult or strange: *I find it hard to get my mind round such complex issues.* • **get sth out of your mind** to make yourself stop thinking about something: *I can't get that dreadful moment/image out of my mind.* • **have sth on your mind** C2 to be worrying about something: *Paul's got a lot on his mind at the moment.* • **have a mind of its own** mainly humorous A machine or other object can be said to have a mind of its own if it seems to be controlling the way it behaves or moves, independently of the person using it: *This shopping trolley has a mind of its own.* • **have half a mind/a good mind to do sth** to think that you might do something, often because something has annoyed you: *I've a good mind to go without him if he's going to be such a bore!* • **have something in mind** to have a plan or intention: *Did you have anything in mind for Helen's present?* • **in your mind's eye** C2 in your imagination or memory: *In my mind's eye, she remains a little girl of six although she's actually a grown woman.* • **a load/weight off your mind** an occasion when a problem that has been worrying you stops or is dealt with: *I'm so relieved that I don't have to make a speech – it's such a weight off my mind!* • **make up your mind** (also **make your mind up**) B1 to decide: *I haven't made up my mind where to go yet.* • **your mind is a blank/goes blank** When your mind is a blank/goes blank, you cannot remember a particular thing, or you cannot remember anything: *I tried to remember her name, but my mind went a* ***complete*** *blank.* • **your mind is on sth** When your mind is on something, you think about it or give attention to it: *I couldn't concentrate on my work – my mind was on other things.* ◦ *My mind wasn't on what he was saying, so I'm afraid I missed half of it.* • **mind over matter** the power of the mind to control and influence the body and the physical world generally: *He announced what he called 'the ultimate test of mind over matter' – a woman walking over hot coals.* • **out of your mind** **1** unable to behave or deal with things normally because something has made you very worried, unhappy, or angry: *She was out of her mind* ***with*** *grief.* ◦ *I'd* ***go*** *out of my mind if I had to do her job all day!* **2** informal extremely stupid or mentally ill: *You must* ***be*** *out of your mind paying £200 for one night in a hotel!* • **put sb in mind of sth** to cause someone to remember something: *The mention of skiing holidays put me in mind of a travelogue that I saw last week.* • **put sth out of your mind** to force yourself not to think about something: *It's over, put it out of your mind.* • **set/put sb's mind at rest/ease** C1 to stop someone from worrying about something: *Chris phoned to say they'd arrived safely, so that really put my mind at rest.* • **set/put your mind to sth** C1 to decide you are going to do something and to put a lot of effort into doing it: *If you'd just put your mind to it, I'm sure you could do it.* • **sb's state/frame of mind** the way someone feels about their life or situation at the moment: *He's in a much more positive state/frame of mind these days.* • **take sb's mind off sth** to stop you from worrying or thinking about a problem or pain, often by forcing you to think about other things: *The good thing about running is that it takes my mind off any problems I've got.* • **to my mind** B2 in my opinion: *He's got pink walls and a green carpet, which to my mind looks all wrong.*

▸verb **BE ANNOYED** ▷ **1** A2 [I or T] (used in questions and negatives) to be annoyed or worried by something: *Do you think he'd mind if I borrowed his book?* ◦ [+ -ing verb] *I don't mind hav****ing*** *a dog in the house so long as it's clean.* ◦ informal *I wouldn't mind (= I would like) something to eat, actually.* ◦ *Would you mind turn****ing*** *(= please turn) your radio down a little please?* ◦ *Do you mind* ***if*** *I (= may I) put the TV on?* ◦ [+ obj + -ing verb] *Do you mind me smok****ing****?* ◦ [+ question word] *I don't mind* ***wh****at you wear so long as it's not that awful pink shirt.* ◦ *I'd prefer to stay in tonight, if you don't mind.* ◦ mainly UK *'Would you like tea or coffee?' 'I don't mind – either.'* **2 do you mind?** said to someone when you feel annoyed with them for what they have just done or said: *Do you mind? That's my seat you're sitting on!*

! Common mistake: mind

Remember: mind is usually followed by a verb in the **-ing** form.

Don't say 'mind to do something', say **mind doing something**:

~~*Would you mind to send me an up-to-date catalogue?*~~

Would you mind sending me an up-to-date catalogue?

BE CAREFUL ▷ **3** B1 [T] mainly UK to be careful of, or give attention to something: [+ (that)] *Mind that box – the bottom isn't very strong.* ◦ *Mind (****that****) you don't bang your head on the shelf when you stand up.* ◦ *Mind (= make certain that) you take enough money with you.* ◦ old-fashioned *Mind your language (= don't use swear words), young lady!* **4 mind (out)!** mainly UK used to tell someone to move or be careful, or to warn them of danger: *Mind out! We're coming through with the stretcher.* ◦ *'Hey, mind!' he said when she trod on his foot.* ◦ *Mind out* ***for*** *falling rocks on this part of the trail.* **5 mind how you go** mainly UK informal said when you say goodbye to someone, meaning 'take care' **TAKE CARE OF** ▷ **6** [T] to take care of someone or something: *She asked me if I'd mind the children for an hour while she went shopping.* ◦ *Could you mind my bag for a moment while I go to the toilet?*

IDIOMS **don't mind me** said to tell someone who is in the same room as you not to pay any attention to you, because you do not want to interrupt what they are doing: *Don't mind me – I'm just sorting out some files here.* • **I don't mind if I do** said to politely accept an offer of food or drink: *'There's plenty more cake if you'd like another piece.' 'I don't mind if I do.'* • **if you don't mind me saying** used as a polite way to begin a criticism: *If you don't mind me saying (so), I think the curry could be a little hotter next time.* • **mind (you)** C2 used when you want to make what you have just said sound less strong: *He's very untidy about the house; mind you, I'm not much better.* ◦ *I know I'm lazy – I did go swimming yesterday, mind.* • **mind your own business** informal mainly humorous C2 used to tell someone in a rude way that you do not want them to ask about something private: *'Where have you been?' 'Mind your own business!'* → See also **myob** • **mind your p's and q's** old-fashioned to make an effort to be especially polite in a particular situation: *I have to mind my p's and q's when I'm with my grandmother.*

ˈmind-ˌaltering adj describes a drug that has a strong influence on a person's mental state, causing feelings of extreme happiness and making people consider things in an unusual way

ˈmind-ˌblowing adj informal extremely exciting or surprising: *The special effects in this film are pretty mind-blowing.*

ˈmind-ˌboggling adj informal extremely surprising and difficult to understand or imagine: *She was paid*

the mind-boggling sum of ten million pounds for that film.

-minded /-maɪn.dɪd/ **suffix** having a particular character, interest, or way of thinking about things: *She's very strong/independent-minded (= she has a very strong/independent character).* ◦ *I don't imagine that he's very politically-minded (= interested in politics).*

minder /ˈmaɪn.dəʳ/ (US) /-dɚ/ **noun** [C] someone who protects another person, often a famous person, from danger and unwanted public attention

mindful /ˈmaɪnd.fəl/ **adj** formal careful not to forget about something: *Mindful **of** the poor road conditions, she reduced her speed to 30 mph.* ◦ *Politicians are increasingly mindful **that** young voters are turning away from traditional parties.*

mindless /ˈmaɪnd.ləs/ **adj** disapproving **1** stupid and meaning nothing: *The film is full of mindless **violence**.* ◦ *pop songs with mindless lyrics* **2** not needing much mental effort: *I'm afraid it's fairly mindless **work** – opening mail and keying data into a computer.* • **mindlessly** /-li/ **adv** *Some children started mindlessly hurling stones at passing vehicles.* • **mindlessness** /-nəs/ **noun** [U]

ˈmind-ˌnumbing **adj** extremely boring: *a mind-numbing task* • **mind-numbingly** /-li/ **adv** *mind-numbingly **boring***

ˈmind ˌreader **noun** [C] mainly humorous a person who knows another person's thoughts without being told them: *Why didn't you tell me you weren't happy with the situation? – I'm not a mind reader, you know!*

mindset /ˈmaɪnd.set/ **noun** [U] a person's way of thinking and their opinions: *to have a different/the same mindset* ◦ *It's extraordinary how hard it is to **change** the mindset of the public and the press.*

mine /maɪn/ **pronoun; noun; verb**

▸**pronoun** (A2) the one(s) belonging to or connected with me: *'Whose bag is this?' 'It's mine.'* ◦ *Your son is the same age as mine.* ◦ *She's an old friend **of** mine.* ◦ *Mine is the silver car, the convertible.*

▸**noun** [C] **HOLE** ▷ **1** (B2) a hole or system of holes in the ground where substances such as coal, metal, and salt are removed: *a **coal/salt/gold** mine* ◦ *a mine **shaft*** ◦ *My grandfather used to work **in** (UK also **down**) the mines.* **BOMB** ▷ **2** a type of bomb put below the earth or in the sea which explodes when vehicles, ships, or people go over it: *He was killed when his tank **ran over** a mine.* ◦ *The US forces were **clearing** the surrounding area of mines.* → See also **landmine**

IDIOM **a mine of information** someone who has a lot of knowledge

▸**verb** **DIG** ▷ **1** [I or T] to dig coal or another substance out of the ground: *They're mining **for** salt.* ◦ *They mine a lot of copper around these parts.* **BOMB** ▷ **2** [T often passive] to place or hide mines in an area of land or sea: *The desert was **heavily** mined.*

ˈmine deˌtector **noun** [C] a device used to discover if there are mines (= bombs) in a particular area

minefield /ˈmaɪn.fiːld/ **noun** [C] **BOMBS** ▷ **1** an area of land or water that contains mines (= bombs) **PROBLEMS** ▷ **2** a situation or subject that is very complicated and full of hidden problems and dangers: *a **legal** minefield*

miner /ˈmaɪ.nəʳ/ (US) /-nɚ/ **noun** [C] (C1) a person who works in a mine: *a **coal** miner*

mineral /ˈmɪn.ər.əl/ **noun; adj**

▸**noun** **SUBSTANCE** ▷ **1** [C] a valuable or useful chemical substance that is formed naturally in the ground **2** [C] a chemical substance that your body needs to stay healthy: *A healthy diet should supply all necessary vitamins and minerals.* ◦ *a mineral supplement* **DRINK** ▷ **3** **minerals** [plural] UK old-fashioned cold sweet FIZZY drinks (= ones with bubbles) without alcohol

▸**adj** being or consisting of a mineral or minerals: *a mineral **deposit** (= substance or layer that is left)* ◦ *The speaker emphasized that much of South Africa's importance lay in its mineral wealth.*

mineralogist /ˌmɪn.əˈræl.ə.dʒɪst/ **noun** [C] someone who studies minerals

mineralogy /ˌmɪn.əˈræl.ə.dʒi/ **noun** [U] the scientific study of minerals

ˈmineral ˌwater **noun** [U] (also **ˌbottled ˈwater**) (A2) natural water from underground, containing dissolved minerals that are believed to be good for your health: *still/carbonated mineral water*

minestrone /ˌmɪn.ɪˈstrəʊ.ni/ (US) /-ˈstroʊ-/ **noun** [C or U] (also **ˌminestrone ˈsoup**) a type of Italian soup containing a mixture of vegetables and PASTA

minesweeper /ˈmaɪnˌswiː.pəʳ/ (US) /-pɚ/ **noun** [C] a ship that is used to discover if MINES (= bombs) are present and to remove them from the sea

minger /ˈmɪŋ.əʳ/ (US) /-ɚ/ **noun** [C] UK slang an ugly person, especially a woman

minging /ˈmɪŋ.ɪŋ/ **adj** UK slang **SMELLING** ▷ **1** smelling bad: *You're minging, mate! Go and take a shower.* **UGLY** ▷ **2** ugly: *Man, she was minging!*

mingle /ˈmɪŋ.gl/ **verb** **MIX** ▷ **1** (C2) [I or T] to mix or combine, or be mixed or combined: *The excitement of starting a new job is always mingled **with** a certain apprehension.* ◦ *The two flavours mingle well.* **BE WITH** ▷ **2** (C1) [I] to move around and talk to other people at a social event: *You've been talking to Roger all evening – you really ought to be mingling **with** the other guests.*

mingy /ˈmɪn.dʒi/ **adj** informal **1** not generous and unwilling to give money: *I only gave five dollars towards his present – do you think that was a bit mingy?* **2** describes an amount that is smaller than you would like: *I hate that restaurant – they give you really mingy portions.*

mini /ˈmɪn.i/ **noun** [C] a **miniskirt**

mini- /mɪn.i-/ **prefix** smaller or less important than a normal example of the same thing: *There's a mini-library in each classroom, as well as the central library.* ◦ *We took the kids to play mini-golf.*

miniature /ˈmɪn.ɪ.tʃəʳ/ (US) /-tʃɚ/ **adj; noun**

▸**adj** [before noun] (C2) describes something that is a very small copy of an object: *I bought some miniature furniture for my niece's dolls' house.*

▸**noun** [C] **PAINTING** ▷ **1** a very small painting, usually of a person **ALCOHOLIC DRINK** ▷ **2** a very small bottle of alcoholic drink **3** **in miniature** (C2) smaller than usual: *He's made a model of our village, with all the buildings and roads in miniature.*

miniaturization (UK usually **miniaturisation**) /ˌmɪn.ɪ.tʃər.aɪˈzeɪ.ʃən/ (US) /-tʃɚ.əˈ-/ **noun** [U] the process of making something very small using modern technology: *The silicon chip is a classic example of the benefits of miniaturization.* • **miniaturized** (UK usually **miniaturised**) /ˈmɪn.ɪ.tʃər.aɪzd/ (US) /-tʃɚ-/ **adj** *a miniaturized electronic circuit*

minibar /ˈmɪn.i.bɑːʳ/ (US) /-bɑːr/ **noun** [C] a small fridge in a hotel bedroom, with drinks inside

ˈmini-break **noun** [C] a very short holiday: *Winners of the competition will win a three-night mini-break in Paris.*

minibus /ˈmɪn.i.bʌs/ noun [C] a small bus in which there are seats for about ten people

minibus

minicab /ˈmɪn.i.kæb/ noun [C] UK a taxi that can only be ordered by phone and does not stop to collect passengers in the street

minicam /ˈmɪn.i.kæm/ noun [C] mainly US a type of small VIDEO CAMERA often used by television news REPORTERS

MiniDisc /ˈmɪn.i.dɪsk/ noun [C] trademark a very small plastic disc on which music or information can be stored

minim /ˈmɪn.ɪm/ noun [C] UK specialized (US usually ˈ**half** ˌ**note**) a musical note with a time value equal to two CROCHETS or half a SEMIBREVE

minimal /ˈmɪn.ɪ.məl/ adj C1 very small in amount: *There were no injuries and damage to the building was minimal.* • **minimally** /-i/ adv *minimally affected/involved/successful*

minimalist /ˈmɪn.ɪ.mə.lɪst/ adj; noun
▸adj **SIMPLE** ▷ **1** belonging or relating to a style in art, design, and theatre that uses the smallest range of materials and colours possible, and only very simple shapes or forms: *The set for the ballet is minimalist – white walls and a chair.* **NOT DOING MUCH** ▷ **2** taking or showing as little action and involvement in a situation as possible: *the party's minimalist* ***approach*** *to economic policy* • **minimalism** /-lɪ.zəm/ noun [U]
▸noun [C] an artist or DESIGNER who uses a minimalist style

M

minimize (UK usually **minimise**) /ˈmɪn.ɪ.maɪz/ verb [T] **1** C1 to reduce something to the least possible level or amount: *We must minimize* ***the risk of*** *infection.* ◦ *Environmentalists are doing everything within their power to minimize the impact of the oil spill.* → Opposite **maximize** **2** to make something seem less important or smaller than it really is: *She accused the government of minimizing the suffering of thousands of people.* ◦ *It's important to focus on your strengths and to minimize your weaknesses.* • **minimization** /ˌmɪn.ɪ.maɪˈzeɪ.ʃən/ US /-mə-/ noun [U]

minimum /ˈmɪn.ɪ.məm/ noun; adj; adv
▸noun [C usually singular] (plural **minimums** or specialized **minima**) (written abbreviation **min.**) B1 the smallest amount or number allowed or possible: *Wage increases are being* ***kept to a*** *minimum because of the recession.* ◦ *Pat hoped that her 80th birthday would pass with the minimum* ***of*** *fuss.* ◦ *We need a minimum* ***of*** *ten people to play this game.* → Opposite **maximum**
▸adj (written abbreviation **min.**) B1 describes something that is the smallest or least allowed or possible: *This certificate is the minimum qualification required to teach English in most language schools.* ◦ *18 is the minimum* ***age*** *for entering most nightclubs.*
▸adv (written abbreviation **min.**) at the least: *She reckons that you should do three exercise classes a week minimum to get any of the benefits.*

the ˌ**minimum** ˈ**wage** noun [S] the smallest amount of money that an employer is legally allowed to pay someone who works for them

mining /ˈmaɪ.nɪŋ/ noun [U] C1 the industry or activity of removing substances such as coal or metal from the ground by digging: ***coal/salt*** *mining*

minion /ˈmɪn.jən/ noun [C] usually disapproving a person who only exists in order to do what another person orders them to do: *He sent one of his minions to do something about it.*

minipill /ˈmɪn.i.pɪl/ noun [C] a type of pill containing only PROGESTERONE which women can take every day to prevent them from becoming pregnant when they have sex

miniseries /ˈmɪn.iˌsɪə.riːz/ US /-ˌsɪr.iːz/ noun [C] (plural **miniseries**) a programme or play divided into several different parts that is broadcast on television over a short period of time

miniskirt /ˈmɪn.iˌskɜːt/ US /-skɝːt/ noun [C] (also **mini**) a very short skirt

minister /ˈmɪn.ɪ.stər/ US /-stɚ/ noun; verb
▸noun [C] **POLITICIAN** ▷ **1** B2 a member of the government in Britain and many other countries who is in charge of a particular department or has an important position in it: *the foreign/health minister* ◦ *the Minister* ***of/for*** *Education* **PRIEST** ▷ **2** a priest in certain Churches: *a minister at the local Baptist church* **COUNTRY'S REPRESENTATIVE** ▷ **3** specialized a person below the rank of AMBASSADOR whose job is to represent his or her country in a foreign country: *the Belgian minister in Madrid*
▸verb

PHRASAL VERB **minister to sb** to give help to or care for someone, for example someone who is ill: formal *The priest ministers to his flock (= the people who go to his church).* ◦ humorous *I spent most of the morning ministering to my sick husband.*

ministerial /ˌmɪn.ɪˈstɪə.ri.əl/ US /-ˈstɪr.i-/ adj **POLITICIAN** ▷ **1** relating to or involving a minister (= an important member the government) **COUNTRY'S REPRESENTATIVE** ▷ **2** relating to or involving a minister who represents his or her country in another country: *He reached ministerial level in the Diplomatic Service.*

ministrations /ˌmɪn.ɪˈstreɪ.ʃənz/ noun [plural] formal acts of helping or taking care of people or providing for their needs: *In her last difficult years, she relied on the careful ministrations of her beloved husband.* ◦ humorous *That plant seems to be dying in spite of all my ministrations.*

ministry /ˈmɪn.ɪ.stri/ noun **GOVERNMENT DEPARTMENT** ▷ **1** C1 [C] a department of the government led by a minister: *the Ministry* ***of*** *Defence/Agriculture* **PRIEST'S WORK** ▷ **2** [U] work as a minister: *He practised a preaching and teaching ministry there for over 40 years.* **3 the ministry** the job of being a priest: *In 1985 he decided to* ***go into/leave*** *the ministry.*

mini ˌ**system** noun [C] a very small set of electronic equipment for playing recorded sound

minivan /ˈmɪn.i.væn/ noun [C] US (UK ˌ**people** ˈ**carrier**) a large, high car that can carry more people than a normal car

mink /mɪŋk/ noun [C or U] a small animal with valuable fur that is used to make expensive coats, or the fur from this animal: *a mink* ***coat***

minnow /ˈmɪn.əʊ/ US /-oʊ/ noun [C] **FISH** ▷ **1** a very small fish found in lakes and rivers **PERSON/ORGANIZATION** ▷ **2** an organization or person that is not important and has little influence or power

minor /ˈmaɪ.nər/ US /-nɚ/ adj; noun
▸adj **UNIMPORTANT** ▷ **1** B2 having little importance, influence, or effect, especially when compared with other things of the same type: *a minor* ***operation*** ◦ *It's only a minor* ***problem.*** ◦ *There's been an increase in minor* ***offences,*** *such as traffic violations and petty theft.* ◦ *She suffered only minor* ***injuries.*** ◦ *It requires a few minor adjustments.* ◦ *a minor poet of the 16th century* → Compare **major** **MUSIC** ▷ **2** belonging

or relating to a musical SCALE that is generally thought to have a sad sound: *The piece is written in a minor **key**. ◦ Mozart's Piano Concerto No. 20 **in** D minor.* → Compare **major**

▸noun [C] legal someone who is too young to have the legal responsibilities of an adult: *He was accused of having sex with a minor.*

minority /maɪˈnɒr.ɪ.ti/ (US) /-ˈnɑːr.ə.t̬i/ noun **SMALL PART** ▷ **1** (B2) [S] a smaller number or part: *It's only a tiny minority **of** people who are causing the problem. ◦ Children with single parents at my school were very much **in the** minority (= there were very few). ◦ This section of the bookstore caters for minority **interests** (= subjects that interest only a few people).* → Opposite **majority** **PEOPLE** ▷ **2** (C1) [C] any small group in society that is different from the rest because of their race, religion, or political beliefs, or a person who belongs to such a group: ***ethnic/religious** minorities ◦ The plan was designed to help women and minorities overcome discrimination in the workplace.*

IDIOM **be in a minority of one** to be the only person who has a particular opinion

minster /ˈmɪn.stəʳ/ (US) /-stɚ/ noun [C] used in Britain in the name of a large or important church: *York Minster*

minstrel /ˈmɪn.strəl/ noun [C] a travelling musician and singer common between the 11th and 15th centuries

mint /mɪnt/ noun; adj; verb

▸noun **PLANT** ▷ **1** (B2) [U] a herb whose leaves have a strong, fresh smell and taste and are used for giving flavour to food: *a sprig of mint ◦ mint-flavoured gum/toothpaste* **2** [C] a sweet with a mint flavour: *a packet of extra-strong mints ◦ after-dinner chocolate mints* **MONEY** ▷ **3** [C] a place where the new coins of a country are made **4** [S] informal an extremely large amount of money: *If his books sell in the States, he'll **make a** mint.*

▸adj [before noun] **1** describes stamps and coins, etc. that have not been used: *A collector would pay $500 for a mint copy.* **2 in mint condition** perfect, as if new: *CD player, in mint condition – £50.*

▸verb [T] **COIN** ▷ **1** to produce a coin for the government **NEW THING** ▷ **2** to produce something new, especially to invent a new phrase or word: *a freshly minted slogan/phrase ◦ newly minted college graduates*

ˌmint ˈsauce noun [U] mainly UK (US usually **ˌmint ˈjelly**) a sauce that is often served with LAMB, made of VINEGAR, sugar, and mint

minus /ˈmaɪ.nəs/ preposition; noun; adj

▸preposition **1** (A2) reduced by a stated number: *What is 57 minus 39? ◦ That will be £1,500, minus the deposit of £150 that you have already paid.* → Compare **plus** **2** informal without, or lacking: *We're minus a chair for Ian – could you get one from the other room?*

▸noun [C] (plural **minuses**) **DISADVANTAGE** ▷ **1** a disadvantage or a bad feature: *Having to travel such a long way to work is a definite minus.* **SUBTRACTION** ▷ **2** (also **minus sign**) the (-) sign, written between two numbers to show that the second number should be taken away from the first, or in front of one number to show that it has a value of less than 0

▸adj **SUBTRACTION** ▷ **1** [before noun] A minus number or amount is less than zero. → See also **negative** **2** [before noun] used to show that temperatures are less than zero: *Temperatures could fall to minus eight tonight.* **3** [after noun] used after a mark given to written work to mean that it is of a slightly lower standard than that mark: *I got A minus for my English homework.* **DISADVANTAGE** ▷ **4** [before noun] describes a disadvantage or bad point: *One of the minus **points** of working at home is not having social contact with colleagues.*

minuscule /ˈmɪn.ɪ.skjuːl/ adj extremely small: *All she gave him to eat was two minuscule pieces of toast.*

minute¹ /ˈmɪn.ɪt/ noun; verb

▸noun **TIME** ▷ **1** (A1) [C] (written abbreviation **min.**) any of the 60 parts which an hour is divided into, consisting of 60 seconds: *a 20-minute bus ride ◦ It takes me 20 minutes to get to work. ◦ The train leaves at three minutes to eight, so we'd better get there a few minutes before then.* **2** (A2) [C] used in spoken English to mean a very short time: ***Hang on/Wait a** minute – I'll just get my bag. ◦ **Just a** minute – I'll be with you when I've finished this. ◦ I **won't be a** minute (= I will be ready soon). ◦ When you've **got a** minute, I'd like a brief word with you.* **MESSAGE** ▷ **3** [C] mainly UK formal an official message from one person to another in an organization: *I've just received a minute from Jeremy authorizing the purchase of six more computers.* **4 the minutes** [plural] the written record of what was said at a meeting: *Could you **take/do** (= write) **the** minutes, Daniel? ◦ The minutes of the last meeting were approved unanimously (= everyone agreed that they were correct).* **ANGLE** ▷ **5** [C] specialized any of the 60 parts that the degrees of any angle are divided into

IDIOMS **the minute (that)** (C2) at the exact or first moment when: *The minute I saw him, I knew something was wrong.* • **not for a minute** certainly not: *I'm not suggesting for a minute that she meant to cause any trouble.* • **this minute** now or a very short time ago: *It doesn't have to be done this minute, but at some point this week please. ◦ She's **just** this minute left the office.* • **up-to-the-minute** **1** modern: *up-to-the-minute fashion* **2** containing all the most recent information: *up-to-the-minute news*

▸verb [T] to make a written record of what is said at a meeting: *The chairman is minuted as having said that profits had fallen to an all-time low.*

minute² /maɪˈnjuːt/ (US) /-ˈnuːt/ adj (C2) extremely small: *a minute amount/quantity ◦ I've never seen a man with such tiny hands – they're minute! ◦ The documentary showed an eye operation **in** minute **detail** (= showing every small detail).*

ˈminute ˌhand noun [C usually singular] the part on a clock or watch which points to the minutes and is longer than the HOUR HAND and thicker than the SECOND HAND

minutely /maɪˈnjuːt.li/ (US) /-ˈnuːt-/ adv very carefully, or looking at every small detail: *to **examine** something minutely*

ˈminute ˌsteak noun [C or U] a thin slice of STEAK (= a type of meat especially from cows) that can be cooked very quickly

the minutiae /mɪˈnuː.ʃi.aɪ/ noun [plural] small and often not important details: *The committee studied the minutiae of the report for hours.*

minx /mɪŋks/ noun [C] old-fashioned usually humorous a girl or young woman who knows how to control other people to her advantage

miracle /ˈmɪr.ɪ.kl̩/ noun [C] (B2) an unusual and mysterious event that is thought to have been caused by a god, or any very surprising and unexpected event: [+ (that)] *Looking at the state of his car, it's a miracle (**that**) he wasn't killed! ◦ I can't promise a miracle **cure**, but I think we can improve things.*

M

IDIOM **perform/work miracles/a miracle** informal to be extremely effective in improving a situation: *You've performed a miracle on this kitchen – I've never seen it so clean!*

miraculous /mɪˈræk.jʊ.ləs/ **adj** very effective or surprising, or difficult to believe: *The diet promised miraculous weight loss.* ◦ *Well, you've made a miraculous* ***recovery*** *since last night!* • **miraculously** /-li/ **adv**

mirage /mɪˈrɑːʒ/ **noun** [C] **1** an image, produced by very hot air, of something which seems to be far away but does not really exist **2** literary a hope or wish that has no chance of being achieved: *Electoral victory is just a distant mirage.*

mire /maɪəʳ/ (US) /maɪr/ **noun** **WET EARTH** ▷ **1** [C usually singular] an area of deep, wet, sticky earth **BAD SITUATION** ▷ **2** [S] literary an unpleasant situation that is difficult to escape: *We must not be drawn* ***into*** *the mire of civil war.*

mired /maɪəd/ (US) /maɪrd/ **adj** **be/become mired (down) in sth** to be involved in a difficult situation, especially for a long period of time: *The peace talks are mired in bureaucracy.*

mirror /ˈmɪr.əʳ/ (US) /-ɚ/ **noun; verb**

►**noun** **GLASS** ▷ **1** (A2) [C] a piece of glass with a shiny, metal-covered back that reflects light, producing an image of whatever is in front of it: *the bathroom mirror* ◦ *She was looking at her reflection* ***in*** *the mirror.* **REPRESENT** ▷ **2** **be a mirror of sth** to represent or show something honestly: *The movie is a mirror* ***of*** *daily life in wartime Britain.*

►**verb** [T] **1** to represent something honestly: *Our newspaper aims to mirror the opinions of ordinary people.* **2** to be very similar to something: *Her on-screen romances seem to mirror her experiences in her private life.*

ˌmirror ˈimage **noun** [C] **1** something that looks exactly the same as another thing but with its left and right sides in opposite positions: *His home is two terraced houses knocked together, each the mirror image of the other.* **2** a person or object that is very similar to another: *The current economic situation is a mirror image of the situation in France a few years ago.*

ˈmirror ˌsite **noun** [C] a website that is an exact copy of another website, but with a different address, allowing more people to be able to see and use it

mirth /mɜːθ/ (US) /mɝːθ/ **noun** [U] literary laughter, humour, or happiness: *Her impersonations of our teachers were a source of considerable mirth.*

mirthless /ˈmɜː.θ.ləs/ (US) /ˈmɝːθ-/ **adj** literary not showing real enjoyment or happiness: *a mirthless* ***laugh****/smile* • **mirthlessly** /-li/ **adv**

mis- /mɪs-/ **prefix** added to the beginning of a verb or word formed from a verb, to show that the action referred to by the verb has been done wrongly or badly: *I never said that! You must have misheard me.* ◦ *His misbehaviour eventually led to him being expelled from school.*

misadventure /ˌmɪs.ədˈven.tʃəʳ/ (US) /-tʃɚ/ **noun** [C] literary **1** an accident or bad luck **2** **death by misadventure** UK legal the official expression used in court for a death that happens by accident: *The coroner recorded a verdict of death by misadventure.*

misalign /ˌmɪs.əˈlaɪn/ **verb** [T] to arrange parts of a machine or system badly, with the result that they do not work well together: *If the wheels are misaligned, it can cause excessive wear on your tyres.* • **misalignment** /-mənt/ **noun** [U]

misanthrope /ˈmɪs.ən.θrəʊp/ (US) /-θroʊp/ **noun** [C] (also **misanthropist**) someone who dislikes other people and avoids involvement with society

misanthropic /ˌmɪs.ənˈθrɒp.ɪk/ (US) /-ˈθrɑː.pɪk/ **adj** not liking other people • **misanthropy** /mɪˈsæn.θrə.pi/ **noun** [U]

misapply /ˌmɪs.əˈplaɪ/ **verb** [T] to use something badly, wrongly, or in a way that was not intended: *It will be impossible to recover all the misapplied charity money.* • **misapplication** /-æp.lɪˈkeɪ.ʃən/ **noun** [C or U] *The inquiry found evidence of serious misapplication* ***of*** *funds.*

misapprehension /ˌmɪs.æp.rɪˈhen.ʃən/ **noun** [C or U] a failure to understand something, or an understanding or belief about something that is not correct: [+ that] *Most industrialists* ***labour under*** *a misapprehension (= wrongly believe)* ***that*** *unrestrained economic growth can be achieved without damaging the environment.*

misappropriate /ˌmɪs.əˈprəʊ.pri.eɪt/ (US) /-ˈproʊ-/ **verb** [T] formal to steal something that you have been trusted to take care of and use it for your own good: *He is accused of misappropriating $30,000 to pay off gambling debts.* • **misappropriation** /ˌmɪs.əˌprəʊ.priˈeɪ.ʃən/ (US) /-ˌproʊ-/ **noun** [U] *He was charged with embezzlement and misappropriation* ***of*** *union funds.*

misbegotten /ˌmɪs.bɪˈɡɒt.ən/ (US) /-ˈɡɑː.t̬ən/ **adj** **BADLY PLANNED** ▷ **1** formal badly or stupidly planned or designed: *a misbegotten belief/idea* ◦ *misbegotten social and economic policies* **NOT RESPECTED** ▷ **2** [before noun] old-fashioned formal not deserving to be respected or thought valuable: *Her misbegotten father spent most of his adult life in prison.*

misbehave /ˌmɪs.bɪˈheɪv/ **verb** [I] **PERSON** ▷ (C1) to behave badly: *I was always getting in trouble for misbehaving at school.* • **misbehaviour** UK (US **misbehavior**) /-ˈheɪ.vjəʳ/ (US) /-ˈheɪ.vjɚ/ **noun** [U] *The school expelled him for persistent misbehaviour.*

misc. written abbreviation for **miscellaneous**

miscalculate /mɪˈskæl.kjʊ.leɪt/ **verb** [I or T] **1** to calculate an amount wrongly: [+ question word] *We had a lot of food left over from the party because I'd miscalculated* ***how*** *much people would eat.* **2** to judge a situation badly: *He miscalculated badly when he underestimated the response of the international community to the invasion.* • **miscalculation** /ˌmɪs.kæl.kjʊˈleɪ.ʃən/ **noun** [C or U] *The conspirators' plot failed because they* ***made*** *two fatal miscalculations.*

miscarriage /ˈmɪsˌkær.ɪdʒ/ (US) /-ˌker-/ **noun** [C or U] an early, unintentional end to a pregnancy when the baby is born too early and dies because it has not developed enough: *The amniocentesis test carries a significant risk of miscarriage.* ◦ *I* ***had*** *two miscarriages before I gave birth to my daughter.* → Compare **abortion, stillbirth** • **miscarry** /-i/ **verb** [I] *Sadly, she miscarried eight weeks into the pregnancy.*

misˌcarriage of ˈjustice **noun** [C] a situation in which someone is punished by the law courts for a crime that they have not committed

miscast /ˌmɪsˈkɑːst/ (US) /-ˈkæst/ **verb** [T] (**miscast, miscast**) to choose someone to act in a film or play in a ROLE for which they are unsuitable: *Tom Hanks was miscast as the arrogant city high-flyer.*

miscellaneous /ˌmɪs.əlˈeɪ.ni.əs/ **adj** consisting of a mixture of various things that are not usually connected with each other: *miscellaneous household items*

miscellany /mɪˈsel.ə.ni/ **noun** [S] **MIXTURE** ▷ a mixture of different things: *The museum houses a fascinating miscellany of nautical treasures.*

mischance /ˌmɪsˈtʃɑːns/ (US) /-ˈtʃæns/ **noun** [C or U] formal bad luck or an unlucky event: ***By** an unfortunate mischance, the hospital had been built immediately beside a large ammunition dump.*

mischief /ˈmɪs.tʃɪf/ **noun 1** [U] behaviour, especially a child's, that is slightly bad but is not intended to cause serious harm or damage: *He needs a hobby to keep him busy and stop him from **getting into** mischief.* ◦ *Perhaps a new bike would **keep** him **out of** mischief.* ◦ *I hope you haven't been **up to** any mischief while I was away.* **2** [C] a mischievous child **3** [U] informal damage or harm: *criminal mischief*

IDIOMS **do sb/yourself a mischief** UK informal to hurt someone or yourself: *You'll do yourself a mischief if you're not careful with that knife.* • **make mischief** old-fashioned to say something which causes other people to be upset or annoyed with each other: *My children often try to make mischief **between** me and my new husband.*

ˈmischief-ˌmaking noun [U] the activity of intentionally causing problems for people: *He accused Mr James of mischief-making by raising allegations against Mr Aitken.*

mischievous /ˈmɪs.tʃɪ.vəs/ **adj 1** behaving in a way, or describing behaviour, that is slightly bad but is not intended to cause serious harm or damage: *She has a mischievous sense of humour.* ◦ *a book about the mischievous antics of his ten-year-old daughter* **2** expressing or suggesting mischief: *a mischievous **grin*** **3** describes behaviour or words that are intended to cause harm or trouble: *I think these rumours are mischievous.* • **mischievously** /-li/ **adv** *to grin mischievously* • **mischievousness** /-nəs/ **noun** [U]

miscible /ˈmɪs.ɪ.bəl/ **adj** specialized A miscible liquid can be mixed with another liquid without separating from it: *Alcohol is miscible **with/in** water.* → Compare **immiscible**

misconceived /ˌmɪs.kənˈsiːvd/ **adj** badly planned because of a failure to understand a situation and therefore unsuitable or unlikely to succeed: *The plan to build the road through the forest is wholly misconceived.*

misconception /ˌmɪs.kənˈsep.ʃən/ **noun** [C] an idea that is wrong because it has been based on a failure to understand a situation: *We hope our work will help to change **popular** misconceptions **about** disabled people.* ◦ [+ that] *I'd like to clear up the **common** misconception **that** American society is based on money.*

misconduct noun; verb

▸**noun** [U] /ˌmɪsˈkɒn.dʌkt/ (US) /-ˈkɑːn-/ **BEHAVIOUR** ▷ **1** unacceptable or bad behaviour by someone in a position of authority or responsibility: *The psychiatrist was found guilty of gross (= unacceptable) **professional** misconduct.* ◦ *The former priest denied allegations of **sexual** misconduct.* **BAD MANAGEMENT** ▷ **2** the fact that the activities of an organization are badly managed: *financial misconduct*

▸**verb** [T] /ˌmɪs.kənˈdʌkt/ to manage the activities of an organization badly: *The aid programme was misconducted, resulting in large quantities of food failing to reach the famine victims.*

misconstrue /ˌmɪs.kənˈstruː/ **verb** [T] formal to form a false understanding of the meaning or intention of something that someone does or says: *She said Harris had misconstrued her comments.* ◦ *Their caution was misconstrued **as** cowardice.*

miscount /ˌmɪsˈkaʊnt/ **verb** [I or T] to reach a total that is not correct when counting: *I thought we had enough plates for the party, but perhaps I miscounted.* • **miscount** /ˈmɪsˌkaʊnt/ **noun** [C]

miscreant /ˈmɪs.kri.ənt/ **noun** [C] formal **1** someone who behaves badly or does not obey rules **2** mainly Indian English a criminal

misdeed /ˌmɪsˈdiːd/ **noun** [C] formal an act that is criminal or bad: *She's been making up for her past misdeeds by doing a lot of voluntary work.*

misdemeanor /ˌmɪs.dɪˈmiː.nər/ (US) /-nɚ/ **noun** [C] US legal a crime considered to be one of the less serious types of crime

misdemeanour UK (US **misdemeanor**) /ˌmɪs.dɪˈmiː.nər/ (US) /-nɚ/ **noun** [C] an action that is slightly bad or breaks a rule but is not a crime: *sexual/youthful misdemeanours* ◦ *Every week, as children, we were beaten for some **minor** misdemeanour.*

misdirect /ˌmɪs.daɪˈrekt/, /-dɪˈ-/ **verb** [T] **1** to send something to the wrong place or aim something in the wrong direction: *My luggage was misdirected **to** a different airport.* ◦ *Vilas misdirected the shot, and the ball went over the net.* **2** to use something in a way that is not suitable or right: *The report accuses the charity of misdirecting large quantities of aid.* **3** to be wrong in how you feel or act in a situation: *The public's admiration is misdirected, as he has done nothing to deserve it.* • **misdirection** /-ˈrek.ʃən/ **noun** [U] *the misdirection **of** financial resources*

miser /ˈmaɪ.zər/ (US) /-zɚ/ **noun** [C] disapproving someone who has a strong wish to have money and hates to spend it

miserable /ˈmɪz.ər.ə.bl/ (US) /-ɚ-/ **adj UNHAPPY** ▷ **1** (B1) very unhappy: *She's miserable living on her own.* **2** (B2) unpleasant and causing unhappiness: *miserable weather* ◦ *What a miserable existence! How could anyone live in such dreadful conditions.* **OF LOW VALUE** ▷ **3** (C2) [before noun] having little value or quality: informal *She only offered me a miserable £20 for my old computer.* ◦ slang *Some miserable bastard went and vandalized my car.*

miserably /ˈmɪz.ər.ə.bli/ (US) /-ɚ-/ **adv UNHAPPILY** ▷ **1** causing or showing unhappiness: *'I'm so unhappy,' sobbed Chris, miserably.* ◦ *It's been miserably wet (= raining a lot) all week.* **LOW VALUE** ▷ **2** having little value, in a way that is disappointing: *to **fail** miserably (= completely fail)* ◦ *miserably low wages*

miserly /ˈmaɪ.zəl.i/ (US) /-zɚ.li/ **adj** disapproving **PERSON** ▷ **1** like or typical of a miser: *a miserly person* **AMOUNT** ▷ **2** describes an amount that is extremely small: *a miserly 75p a week rise in the state pension* • **miserliness** /-nəs/ **noun** [U]

misery /ˈmɪz.ər.i/ (US) /-ɚ-/ **noun UNHAPPY FEELING** ▷ (B2) [C or U] great unhappiness: *We have witnessed the most appalling scenes of **human** misery.* ◦ *Ten years of marriage to him have **made her life a** misery.*

IDIOMS **put sth out of its misery** to kill an animal because it is in great pain, so that it does not have to suffer any more • **put sb out of their misery** informal to stop someone worrying, usually by giving them information that they have been waiting for: *We try to put our students out of their misery and give them their exam results as early as possible.*

misfire /ˌmɪsˈfaɪər/ (US) /-ˈfaɪr/ **verb** [I] **GUN** ▷ **1** If a gun misfires, the bullet fails to come out. **ENGINE** ▷ **2** When an engine misfires, the fuel inside it starts to burn at the wrong moment: *There was a loud bang, like the sound of an engine misfiring.* **PLAN** ▷ **3** If a plan misfires, it does not have the result that was intended: *The boy's death was the result of a practical joke that misfired.*

misfit /ˈmɪs.fɪt/ **noun** [C] someone who is not suited to a situation or who is not accepted by other people because their behaviour is strange or unusual: *I didn't really know anyone at the party, so I felt a bit of a misfit.* ◦ *I was a bit of a* ***social*** *misfit at college because I didn't like going out in the evenings.*

misfortune /ˌmɪsˈfɔː.tʃuːn/ (US) /-ˈfɔːr.tʃən/ **noun** [C or U] C1 bad luck, or an unlucky event: [+ to infinitive] *That was the worst film I've ever had the misfortune* ***to*** *see.* ◦ *She's suffered a good deal of misfortune over the years.* ◦ *It's unfair to take advantage of other people's misfortunes.*

misgiving /ˌmɪsˈɡɪv.ɪŋ/ **noun** [C or U] a feeling of doubt or worry about a future event: *Many teachers expressed serious misgivings* ***about*** *the new exams.* ◦ *My only misgiving is that we might not have enough time to do the job properly.*

misguided /ˌmɪsˈɡaɪ.dɪd/ **adj** unreasonable or unsuitable because of being based on bad judgment or on wrong information or beliefs: *He was shot as he made a misguided* ***attempt*** *to stop the robbers single-handed.* ◦ *The company blamed its disappointing performance on a misguided business plan.* • **misguidedly** /-li/ **adv**

mishandle /ˌmɪsˈhæn.dəl/ **verb** [T] to deal with something without the necessary care or skill: *The police were accused of mishandling the investigation.* • **mishandling** /-ɪŋ/ **noun** [U] *Who do you blame for the mishandling* ***of*** *the economy?*

mishap /ˈmɪs.hæp/ **noun** [C or U] C2 bad luck, or an unlucky event or accident: *The parade was very well organized and passed* ***without*** *mishap.* ◦ *A* ***series of*** *mishaps led to the nuclear power plant blowing up.*

M

mishear /ˌmɪsˈhɪər/ (US) /-ˈhɪr/ **verb** [I or T] (**misheard, misheard**) to fail to hear someone's words correctly or in the way that was intended and to think that something different was said: *I'm sure I never said that! You must have misheard (me).*

mishmash /ˈmɪʃ.mæʃ/ **noun** [S] informal a confused mixture: *The new housing development is* ***a*** *mishmash* ***of*** *different architectural styles.*

misinform /ˌmɪs.ɪnˈfɔːm/ (US) /-ˈfɔːrm/ **verb** [T] C1 to tell someone information that is not correct: *I was told she would be at the meeting, but clearly I was misinformed.*

misinformation /ˌmɪs.ɪn.fəˈmeɪ.ʃən/ (US) /-fɚ-/ **noun** [U] **1** wrong information, or the fact that people are misinformed: *There's a lot of misinformation* ***about*** *AIDS that needs to be corrected.* **2** information intended to deceive: *His election campaign was based on misinformation* ***about*** *the rival candidates.*

misinterpret /ˌmɪs.ɪnˈtɜː.prɪt/ (US) /-ˈtɝː-/ **verb** [T] C2 to form an understanding that is not correct of something that is said or done: *My speech has been misinterpreted by the press.* ◦ *When we re-examined the regulations, we realized that we had misinterpreted them.* • **misinterpretation** /ˌmɪs.ɪnˌtɜː.prɪˈteɪ.ʃən/ (US) /-ˌtɝː-/ **noun** [C or U] C2 *The minister's statement is unclear and* ***open to*** *misinterpretation (= could easily be misinterpreted).*

misjudge /ˌmɪsˈdʒʌdʒ/ **verb** [T] **1** to form an opinion or idea about someone or something that is unfair or wrong: *I thought he wasn't going to support me, but I misjudged him.* ◦ *Sophie totally misjudged the situation and behaved quite inappropriately.* **2** to guess an amount or distance wrongly • **misjudgment** (also **misjudgement**) /-mənt/ **noun** [C or U] *Their decision to sell the house was a disastrous misjudgment.*

mislay /ˌmɪsˈleɪ/ **verb** [T] (**mislaid, mislaid**) to lose something temporarily by forgetting where you have put it: *Could I borrow a pen? I seem to have mislaid mine.*

mislead /ˌmɪsˈliːd/ **verb** [T] (**misled, misled**) C1 to cause someone to believe something that is not true: *He has admitted misleading the police* ***about*** *his movements on the night of the murder.*

misleading /ˌmɪsˈliː.dɪŋ/ **adj** B2 causing someone to believe something that is not true: *Adverts must not create a misleading* ***impression.*** • **misleadingly** /-li/ **adv** *A large sign misleadingly states: 'Escalator Works'.*

mismanage /ˌmɪsˈmæn.ɪdʒ/ **verb** [T] to organize or control something badly: *The restaurant was hopelessly mismanaged by a former rock musician with no business experience.* • **mismanagement** /-mənt/ **noun** [U] *mismanagement* ***of*** *the economy/economic mismanagement* ◦ *allegations of fraud and mismanagement*

mismatch **verb; noun**

▸**verb** [T] /ˌmɪsˈmætʃ/ to put together people or things that are unsuitable for each other: *I always thought Chris and Monique were mismatched, so I wasn't surprised when they got divorced.*

▸**noun** [C] /ˈmɪs.mætʃ/, /ˈmɪsˌmætʃ/ an occasion when people or things are put together that are not suitable for each other: *There is a mismatch* ***between*** *the capacity of the airport and the large number of people wanting to fly from it.*

misnomer /ˌmɪsˈnəʊ.məʳ/ (US) /-ˈnoʊ.mɚ/ **noun** [C] a name that does not suit what it refers to, or the use of such a name: *It was the scruffiest place I've ever stayed in, so 'Hotel Royal' was* ***a bit of a*** *misnomer.* ◦ *It's* ***something of a*** *misnomer to refer to these inexperienced boys as soldiers.*

miso /ˈmiː.səʊ/ (US) /-soʊ/ **noun** [U] a thick substance made from SOYA beans and salt, used in Japanese cooking

misogynist /mɪˈsɒdʒ.ɪ.nɪst/ (US) /-ˈsɑː.dʒɪ-/ **noun; adj**

▸**noun** [C] a man who hates women or believes that men are much better than women

▸**adj** (also **misogynistic**) showing feelings of hating women or a belief that men are much better than women: *She left the Church because of its misogynist teachings on women and their position in society.* ◦ *a misogynistic attitude/writer*

misogyny /mɪˈsɒdʒ.ɪ.ni/ (US) /-ˈsɑː.dʒɪ-/ **noun** [U] feelings of hating women, or the belief that men are much better than women

misplace /ˌmɪsˈpleɪs/ **verb** [T] C2 to lose something temporarily by forgetting where you have put it: *She misplaced her keys so often that her secretary used to carry spare ones for her.*

misplaced /ˌmɪsˈpleɪst/ **adj** directed towards someone or something wrongly or in a way that does not show good judgment: *misplaced* ***loyalty/trust*** ◦ *I'm afraid your confidence in my abilities is misplaced.*

misprint /ˈmɪs.prɪnt/ **noun** [C] a mistake, such as a word that is spelled wrong, in a printed text: *We can't publish the newsletter like this – it's full of misprints.*

mispronounce /ˌmɪs.prəˈnaʊns/ **verb** [T] to pronounce a word or sound wrongly: *French learners of English often mispronounce 'ch'* ***as*** *'sh'.* • **mispronunciation** /-ˌnʌn.siˈeɪ.ʃən/ **noun** [C or U] *Mispronunciation can be a serious obstacle to making yourself understood in a foreign language.*

misquote /ˌmɪsˈkwəʊt/ (US) /-ˈkwoʊt/ **verb** [T] to repeat something someone has said in a way that is not accurate: *Her promise was deliberately misquoted by her opponents, who then used it against her.* ◦ *I never said that at all – the press misquoted me.* • **misquotation** /ˌmɪs.kwəʊˈteɪ.ʃən/ (US) /-kwoʊ-/ **noun** [C or U] *That was a deliberate misquotation of what I said.*

misread /ˌmɪsˈriːd/ verb [T] (misread) READ WRONGLY ▷ **1** to make a mistake in the way that you read something: *I was given the wrong tablets when the chemist misread my prescription.* JUDGE WRONGLY ▷ **2** to judge a situation wrongly: *I thought he fancied me, but I'd completely misread the signals.* • **misreading** /-ˈriː.dɪŋ/ noun [C] *His misreading **of** the situation could have serious consequences.*

misreport /ˌmɪs.rɪˈpɔːt/ (US) /-ˈpɔːrt/ verb [T] to make known information that is not completely true or correct: *The magazine misreported its sales figures in order to boost advertising revenue.*

misrepresent /ˌmɪs.rep.rɪˈzent/ verb [T] to describe falsely an idea, opinion, or situation, often in order to get an advantage: *She accused her opponents of deliberately misrepresenting her **as** an extremist.* ◦ *I've grown used to my **views** being misrepresented in the press.*

misrepresentation /ˌmɪs.rep.rɪ.zenˈteɪ.ʃᵊn/ noun [C or U] something which misrepresents an idea, situation, or opinion, or the fact of something being misrepresented: *The documentary was a misrepresentation **of** the truth and bore little resemblance to actual events.* ◦ *The MP laughed off the remarks as media misrepresentation.*

misrule /ˌmɪsˈruːl/ noun [U] bad government that shows no JUSTICE or fairness: *She blames her country's economic collapse on 40 years of communist misrule.*

miss /mɪs/ verb; noun

▸verb NOT DO ▷ **1** B1 [T] to fail to do or experience something, often something planned or expected, or to avoid doing or experiencing something: *I missed the start of the exam because my bus was late.* ◦ *Often I miss (= do not eat) breakfast and have an early lunch instead.* ◦ *You should leave early if you want to miss the rush hour.* ◦ [+ -ing verb] *I only just missed be**ing** run over by a bus this morning.* **2** A2 [T] to arrive too late to get on a bus, train, or aircraft: *You'll miss your train if you don't hurry up.* **3** A2 [T] to not go to something: *You'll fall behind in your studies if you keep missing school.* ◦ *I'm trying to find an excuse for missing the office party.* **4** B1 [T] to not see or hear something or someone: *I missed the beginning of the film.* ◦ *Her latest movie is **too good to** miss (= it certainly should be seen).* ◦ *I was sorry I missed you at Pat's party – I must have arrived after you left.* **5** [T] to not notice someone or something: *You don't miss much, do you? Nobody else noticed that mistake.* ◦ *My office is first on the right with a bright red door. You **can't** miss **it** (= it is very easy to find).* FEEL SAD ▷ **6** A2 [T] to feel sad that a person or thing is not present: *I really missed her when she went away.* ◦ *She will be sadly missed by all who knew her.* ◦ *I still miss my old car.* ◦ *What did you miss most **about** England when you were living in France?* ◦ [+ -ing verb] *I haven't missed smok**ing** like I'd expected to.* NOT HIT ▷ **7** B2 [I or T] to fail to hit something or to avoid hitting something: *The bullet missed his heart by a couple of centimetres.* ◦ *I swerved to avoid the other car and only just missed a tree.* ◦ *He threw a book at me, but he/it missed.* NOTICE ▷ **8** [T] to notice that something is lost or absent: *He didn't miss his wallet until the waiter brought the bill.*

IDIOMS **miss a chance/opportunity** B1 to not use an opportunity to do something: *She missed the chance of promotion when she turned down the job of assistant manager.* • **miss the boat** C2 to lose an opportunity to do something by being slow to act: *There were tickets available last week, but he missed the boat by waiting till today to try to buy some.* • **miss the mark** to fail to achieve the result that was intended: *Her speech missed the mark and failed to generate the public support she had been hoping for.* • **miss the point** to not understand something correctly or what is important about it: *What you say is true, but you've missed the point **of** my argument.* • **not miss a trick** said about someone who never fails to notice and take advantage of a good opportunity: *Jonathan doesn't miss a trick! If there's a bargain to be had at the market, he'll find it.* • **not miss much** informal said when something you failed to see or experience was not important or special: *'I didn't manage to see that programme.' 'Don't worry, you didn't miss much.'*

PHRASAL VERBS **miss sb/sth out** UK to fail to include someone or something that should be included: *You've missed out your address on the form.* ◦ *Oh I'm sorry, Tina, I've missed you out. What would you like to drink?* • **miss out** B2 to fail to use an opportunity to enjoy or get an advantage from something: *Don't miss out **on** the fantastic bargains in our summer sale.* ◦ *We didn't have a TV at home when I was young, and I felt as though I missed out.*

▸noun NOT DO ▷ **1 give sth a miss** C1 UK informal to avoid or not do something: *We usually go to France in the summer, but we've decided to give it a miss this year.* ◦ *The restaurant's very good for fish, but I'd give their vegetarian options a miss.* NOT HIT ▷ **2** [C] an occasion when something or someone fails to hit something or avoids hitting something: *Well done! You scored eight hits and only two misses.* → See also **near miss** GIRL ▷ **3** [C] a girl or young woman, especially one who behaves rudely or shows no respect: *You're a cheeky little miss! Apologize at once.*

Miss /mɪs/ noun **1** A1 a title used before the family name or full name of a single woman who has no other title: *Dr White will see you now, Miss Carter.* ◦ *Miss Helena Lewis* → Compare **Ms, Mrs** **2** [as form of address] old-fashioned used as a form of address for a girl or young woman who does not appear to be married: *Excuse me, Miss, could you tell me the way to the station?* **3** [as form of address] mainly UK sometimes used by children to address or refer to teachers who are women: *Can I go to the toilet, Miss?* **4** a title given to a woman who wins a BEAUTY CONTEST, combined with the name of the place that she represents: *Miss India/UK* ◦ *the Miss World contest*

misshapen /ˌmɪsˈʃeɪ.pᵊn/, /mɪʃ-/ adj having an unusual shape or a shape that is not natural: *The drug caused some babies to be born with misshapen limbs.*

missile /ˈmɪs.aɪl/ (US) /-ᵊl/ noun [C] **1** C2 a flying weapon that has its own engine so that it can travel a long distance before exploding at the place that it has been aimed at: *a missile **launcher*** ◦ *Missile **attacks** on the capital resumed at dawn.* **2** formal any object that is thrown with the intention of causing injury or damage: *Stones, bottles, and other missiles were thrown at the police.*

missing /ˈmɪs.ɪŋ/ adj **1** A2 Someone who is missing has disappeared: *Her father has been missing since September 1992.* ◦ UK *The girl **went** missing during a family outing to Mount Snowdon.* **2** B1 describes something that cannot be found because it is not where it should be: *The burglars have been arrested but the jewellery is still missing.* ◦ *When did you realize that the money was missing **from** your account?* **3** describes soldiers or military vehicles that have not returned from fighting in a war but are not known completely certainly to be dead or destroyed: *He was **listed as** missing **in action**.*

ˌmissing ˈlink noun [S] **1** something that is necessary to complete a series or solve a problem: *Those documents provided the missing link, and the police were able to make an arrest soon after they discovered them.* **2 the missing link** an animal which no longer exists or might never have existed and is thought to explain how humans developed from APES

ˌmissing ˈperson noun [C] someone who has disappeared and is no longer in communication with their family and friends

mission /ˈmɪʃ.ən/ noun **JOB** ▷ **1** C2 [C] an important job, especially a military one, that someone is sent somewhere to do: *Your mission is to isolate the enemy by destroying all the bridges across the river.* ◦ *a* ***peace/rescue/fact-finding*** *mission* **2** B2 [C] any work that someone believes it is their duty to do: *My mission* ***in life*** *is to educate the rich about the suffering of the poor.* ◦ *She's a woman* ***with a*** *mission and she's absolutely determined to finish the project.* **3 mission accomplished** something that you say when you have finished doing something that you were told to do: *Mission accomplished. I've got everything you asked for on the list.* **PEOPLE** ▷ **4** [C, + sing/pl verb] a group of people whose job is to increase what is known about their country, organization, or religion in another country or area, or the place where such people are based: *More funds are needed to establish* ***trade*** *missions in eastern Europe.* ◦ *The Methodist mission is situated in one of the poorest parts of the city.*

missionary /ˈmɪʃ.ən.ri/ US /-er.i/ noun [C] a person who has been sent to a foreign country to teach their religion to the people who live there

M

ˈmissionary poˌsition noun [S] a position for having sex in which a woman lies on her back and her partner is above and facing her

ˌmissionary ˈzeal noun [U] extreme enthusiasm

ˌmission conˈtrol noun [U] the place on Earth from which a journey into space is controlled: *For a few tense minutes, the astronauts lost radio contact with mission control.*

ˈmission ˌcreep noun [U] disapproving doing a much larger job for a longer time than was originally expected, especially in a military operation

ˌmission-ˈcritical adj extremely important or necessary for a company, activity, etc. to operate successfully: *mission-critical* ***applications/systems/software***

ˈmission ˌstatement noun [C] a short written description of the aims of a business, CHARITY, government department, or public organization

missive /ˈmɪs.ɪv/ noun [C] an official, formal, or long letter: *She sent a ten-page missive to the council, detailing her objections.*

misspeak /ˌmɪsˈspiːk/ verb [I] (present participle **misspeaking**, past tense **misspoke**, past participle **misspoken**) mainly US to say something that is not correct, by mistake: *The Secretary denied lying, but said that he misspoke.*

misspell /ˌmɪsˈspel/ verb [T] (**misspelled** or UK **misspelt**, **misspelled** or UK **misspelt**) UK to fail to spell a word correctly • **misspelling** /-ɪŋ/ noun [C or U] *This essay is full of misspellings.*

misspend /ˌmɪsˈspend/ verb [T] (**misspent**) to use time or money in a way that wastes it or is not wise: *We must stop public money being misspent in this way.* ◦ *Being a good pool player is usually a sign of a misspent* ***youth***.

missus /ˈmɪs.ɪz/ noun [S] informal wife: *Me and* ***the*** *missus (= my wife) are going to our daughter's for Christmas.* ◦ *Have you met Jack's new missus?*

mist /mɪst/ noun; verb

▸noun [C or U] **1** B2 thin FOG produced by very small drops of water collecting in the air just above an area of ground or water: *The mountain villages seem to be permanently* ***shrouded in*** *mist.* ◦ *The early-morning mist soon* ***lifted/cleared***. **2** a thin layer of liquid on the surface of something which makes it difficult to see: UK *There's always a mist on the bathroom mirror/windows when I've had a shower.* ◦ *Through a mist* ***of*** *tears, I watched his train pull out of the station.*

IDIOM **the mists of time** used to show that something happened a very long time ago and is difficult to remember clearly: *The precise details of what happened have been* ***lost in*** *the mists of time.*

▸verb

PHRASAL VERB **mist (sth) over/up 1** mainly UK If something that you can see through mists over/up, it becomes covered with a thin layer of liquid so that it is more difficult to see through: *Open the window when you have a shower to stop the mirror misting over.* ◦ *The steam from the kettle misted up her glasses.* → See also **steam (sth) up 2** If your eyes mist over/up, they fill with tears.

mistake /mɪˈsteɪk/ noun; verb

▸noun [C] **1** A2 an action, decision, or judgment which produces an unwanted or unintentional result: *I'm not blaming you – we all* ***make*** *mistakes.* ◦ [+ to infinitive] *It was a mistake for us* ***to*** *come here tonight.* ◦ *This letter's full of* ***spelling*** *mistakes.* ◦ *I've discovered a few mistakes* ***in*** *your calculations.* ◦ *Why am I under arrest? There must be* ***some*** *mistake.* **2 by mistake** B1 by accident: *I've paid this bill twice by mistake.*

> **!** Common mistake: **mistake**
>
> **Warning:** Choose the right verb!
>
> Don't say 'do a mistake', say **make a mistake**:
>
> ~~I never do mistakes in my essays.~~
>
> *I never make mistakes in my essays.*

> Word partners for **mistake noun**
>
> *make* a mistake • *learn from* a mistake • *admit/realize* your mistake • *avoid/correct/repeat* a mistake • a *big/costly/fatal/terrible* mistake • a *genuine/honest* mistake • a *silly* mistake • a mistake *in* sth

IDIOMS **and no mistake** mainly UK old-fashioned added to the end of something you say to emphasize it: *He's a strange bloke and no mistake.* • **make no mistake about it** used to show that you are certain about something: *Make no mistake about it, this decision is going to cause you a lot of problems.*

▸verb [T] (**mistook**, **mistaken**) to be wrong about or to fail to recognize something or someone: *You can't mistake their house – it's got a bright yellow front door.* ◦ formal *I mistook your signature and thought the letter was from someone else.* • **mistakable** (UK also **mistakeable**) /-ˈsteɪ.kə.bl/ adj *She's* ***easily*** *mistakeable* ***for*** *a man when she wears that suit and hat.*

IDIOM **be no mistaking sth** When there's no mistaking something, it is impossible not to recognize it: *There's no mistaking a painting by Picasso.*

PHRASAL VERB **mistake sb/sth for sb/sth** to confuse someone or something with a different person or thing: *I often mistake her* ***for*** *her mother on the phone.*

mistaken /mɪˈsteɪ.kən/ adj C1 wrong in what you believe, or based on a belief that is wrong: *If you think you can carry on drinking so much without damaging your health, then you're mistaken.* ◦ *I'm afraid I was*

Other ways of saying mistake

A common alternative is the noun **error**:

*He admitted that he'd made an **error**.*

*The letter contained a number of typing **errors**.*

A stupid mistake is sometimes described as a **blunder**:

*The company was struggling after a series of financial **blunders**.*

A small mistake can be described as a **slip**:

*It was an understandable **slip**.*

A mistake which causes confusion is often described as a **mix-up**:

*There was a **mix-up** with the bags at the airport.*

An embarrassing mistake that someone makes when talking is sometimes described as a **gaffe**:

*I made a real **gaffe** by calling her 'Emma', which is the name of his previous girlfriend.*

The noun **oversight** is sometimes used to describe a mistake which someone makes by forgetting to do something:

*The payment was delayed because of an **oversight** in the accounting department.*

A mistake in which you say something that you did not intend to say is described as **a slip of the tongue**:

*It was **a slip of the tongue** – I meant to say 'painless' not 'painful'.*

A mistake in printed text is called a **misprint** or **typo**:

*The newspaper article was full of **misprints**.*

*mistaken **about** how much it would cost.* ◦ *The negotiations continued **in the** mistaken **belief** that a peaceful agreement could be reached.* ◦ *a case of mistaken **identity*** • **mistakenly** /-li/ **adv** *She mistakenly **believed** that she could get away with not paying her taxes.*

mister /ˈmɪs.təʳ/ (US) /-tɚ/ **noun 1** the complete form of the title **Mr 2** an informal and often rude form of address for a man whose name you do not know: *Listen to me, mister, I don't ever wanna see you in this bar again.*

mistime /ˌmɪsˈtaɪm/ **verb** [T] to do something at the wrong moment with the result that it is unsuccessful or has an unwanted effect: *She mistimed her stroke and the ball went into the net.*

mistletoe /ˈmɪs.l̩.təʊ/ (US) /-toʊ/ **noun** [U] an EVERGREEN plant (= one that never loses its leaves) with small, white fruits and pale yellow flowers that grows on trees, often used as a Christmas decoration: *They were kissing **under** the mistletoe at the office party.*

the mistral /mɪˈstrɑːl/ **noun** [S] a strong, cold, dry wind that blows south through France to the Mediterranean

mistreat /ˌmɪsˈtriːt/ **verb** [T] to treat a person or animal badly, cruelly, or unfairly: *Both parents have denied charges of mistreating their children.* ◦ *I think people who mistreat their pets should be banned from keeping them.* • **mistreatment** /-mənt/ **noun** [U] *She suffered years of mistreatment from her violent husband.*

mistress /ˈmɪs.trəs/ **noun WOMAN IN CONTROL** ▷ **1** [S or U] old-fashioned a woman who has control over or responsibility for someone or something: *I'll inform **the** mistress (**of** the house) of your arrival, madam.* ◦ *She intends to remain mistress **of** (= in charge of) her own life when she gets married.* **2** [C] UK old-fashioned a female school teacher: *She got a good report from her German mistress.* **3** [C] old-fashioned a female owner of a dog **SEXUAL PARTNER** ▷ **4** [C] a woman who is having a sexual relationship with a married man: *Edward VII and his mistress, Lillie Langtry*

mistrial /ˈmɪs.traɪəl/ **noun** [C] **1** a trial during which a mistake has been made, causing the judgment to have no legal value **2** US a trial in which it cannot be decided if a person is guilty or not

mistrust /ˌmɪsˈtrʌst/ **verb** [T] to have doubts about the honesty or abilities of someone: *I've always mistrusted politicians.* • **mistrust noun** [U] *There is still considerable mistrust **between** the management and the workforce.* • **mistrustful** /-fəl/ **adj** *Voters are bound to be mistrustful **of** a government that has broken so many promises.* • **mistrustfully** /-fəl.i/ **adv**

misty /ˈmɪs.ti/ **adj WEATHER** ▷ **1** (B2) In misty weather, there is mist in the air which makes it difficult to see into the distance: *The morning will start off misty.* **GLASS** ▷ **2** describes glass or a similar surface that is covered with a mist which makes it difficult to see through: *The windscreen is all misty.* • **mistily** /-tɪ.li/ **adv** • **mistiness** /-nəs/ **noun** [U]

ˌmisty-ˈeyed adj looking as if you are going to cry because you feel emotional about something: *He goes all misty-eyed whenever he hears that song.*

misunderstand /ˌmɪs.ʌn.dəˈstænd/ (US) /-dɚ-/ **verb** [I or T] (**misunderstood**, **misunderstood**) **1** (B2) to think you have understood someone or something when you have not: *If you think that these transport problems can be solved by building more roads, you completely misunderstand the nature of the problem.* ◦ *I told him I'd meet him here, but perhaps he misunderstood and went straight to the pub.* **2 be misunderstood** (C2) If someone is misunderstood, other people do not understand that they have good qualities: *In her teens she felt frustrated and misunderstood.*

misunderstanding /ˌmɪs.ʌn.dəˈstæn.dɪŋ/ (US) /-dɚ-/ **noun 1** (B2) [C or U] an occasion when someone does not understand something correctly: *There must be some misunderstanding. I never asked for these chairs to be delivered.* ◦ *His ridiculous comments showed a complete misunderstanding **of** the situation.* **2** [C] informal a disagreement, argument, or fight: often humorous *'How did you get your black eye?' 'Oh, I had a little misunderstanding **with** someone at the football match.'*

misuse verb; noun

▸**verb** [T] /ˌmɪsˈjuːz/ (C1) to use something in an unsuitable way or in a way that was not intended: *She was accused of misusing company funds.*

▸**noun** [C or U] /ˌmɪsˈjuːs/ (C1) an occasion when something is used in an unsuitable way or in a way that was not intended: *This new computer system is completely unnecessary and a misuse **of** taxpayers' money.* ◦ *the misuse of power/drugs*

mite /maɪt/ **noun ANIMAL** ▷ **1** [C] a very small animal similar to a SPIDER: *a red spider mite* **CHILD** ▷ **2** [C] mainly UK informal a young child, especially one deserving sympathy because they are ill or hungry: *Poor little mite, he looks so tired.* **SMALL AMOUNT** ▷ **3** [S] old-fashioned a very small amount: *I couldn't eat another mite.* **4 a mite** old-fashioned informal slightly: *He seemed a mite embarrassed.*

mitigate /ˈmɪt.ɪ.ɡeɪt/ (US) /ˈmɪt̬-/ **verb** [T] formal to make something less harmful, unpleasant, or bad: *It is unclear how to mitigate **the effects** of tourism on the island.*

mitigating /ˈmɪt.ɪ.ɡeɪ.tɪŋ/ (US) /ˈmɪt̬.ɪ.ɡeɪ.t̬ɪŋ/ **adj 1** formal making something less harmful, unpleasant or bad: *Are there any mitigating **circumstances/***

M

factors which might help explain her appalling behaviour? → Compare **unmitigated** **2** legal causing you to judge a crime to be less serious or to make the punishment less severe: *The jury must take into account any mitigating* ***circumstances*** *presented by the defence, such as previous good character.* • **mitigation** /ˌmɪt.ɪˈgeɪ.ʃᵊn/ (US) /ˌmɪţ-/ noun [U] formal *'I was very young at the time,' he said* ***in*** *mitigation.*

mitochondrion /ˌmaɪ.təˈkɒn.dri.ən/ (US) /-ţoʊˈkɑːn-/ noun [C] (plural **mitochondria**) specialized in a cell, a long or round piece found in the CYTOPLASM (= a substance surrounding the NUCLEUS) that produces energy for the cell by breaking down food

mitre (US also **miter**) /ˈmaɪ.təʳ/ (US) /-ţɚ/ noun [C] **HAT** ▷ **1** a tall, pointed hat worn by BISHOPS in official ceremonies **WOOD JOINT** ▷ **2** (also **mitre joint**) a JOINT made by two pieces of wood that have both been cut at an angle of 45° at the joining ends

mitt /mɪt/ noun **1** [C] a special type of GLOVE for protecting a person's hand, especially a thick leather glove used for catching a baseball: *a* ***catcher's*** *mitt* ◦ ***oven*** *mitts* **2** [C usually plural] a **mitten**: *baby/woollen mitts* **3** [C usually plural] slang a person's hand: *Get your filthy mitts off my sandwich!*

mitten /ˈmɪt.ᵊn/ (US) /ˈmɪţ-/ noun [C] (also **mitt**) a type of GLOVE with a single part for all the fingers and a separate part for the thumb → Compare **glove**

mittens

M

mix /mɪks/ verb; noun

▸verb **COMBINE** ▷ **1** (A2) [I or T] to (cause different substances to) combine, so that the result cannot easily be separated into its parts: *Oil and water don't mix. Even if you shake them together they separate into two layers.* ◦ *Radioactive material was mixed* ***in/up*** *(with) the effluent.* ◦ *Mix the eggs* ***into*** *the flour.* ◦ *In a large bowl, mix* ***together*** *the sugar and raisins.* ◦ [+ two objects] *Shall I mix (= make) you a cocktail?* **2** (B1) [T] to have or do two or more things, such as activities or qualities, at the same time: *Some people are happy to mix business* ***with/and*** *pleasure, but I'm not one of them.* **BE WITH PEOPLE** ▷ **3** (B2) [I] to be with or communicate well with other people: *I suppose you mix* ***with*** *a wide variety of people in your job.* ◦ *She mixes very well – perhaps that's why she's so popular.* **RECORD MUSIC** ▷ **4** [T] specialized to control the amounts of various sounds that are combined on a recording

IDIOMS **be mixed up with/in sth** usually disapproving to be connected with a bad or unpleasant person or thing: *Please don't get mixed up with him. You'll regret it if you do.* ◦ *I knew someone who was mixed up in that corruption scandal.* • **mix it** (US **mix it up**) to fight or argue with people: *Don't take any notice of Sally – she just likes to mix it.*

PHRASAL VERBS **mix sb/sth up** (B2) to fail to recognize two people or things correctly by thinking that one person or thing is the other person or thing: *People often mix us up because we look so similar.* ◦ *I think you're mixing me up* ***with*** *my sister.* • **mix sb up** to confuse, worry, or upset someone: *The roadworks mixed me up and I went the wrong way.* • **mix sth up** to make a group of things untidy or badly organized, or to move them into the wrong order: *Don't mix up the bottles – you'll have to repeat the experiment if you do.* ◦ *Your jigsaw puzzles and games are all mixed up* ***together*** *in that box.*

▸noun **COMBINE** ▷ **1** (B1) [C usually sing] a combination: *There was an odd mix* ***of*** *people at Patrick's party.* ◦ *'She's studying physics and philosophy.' 'That's an interesting mix.'* **2** [C or U] something that is sold in the form of a powder to which a liquid, such as water, can be added later: *cake/cement mix* **RECORD MUSIC** ▷ **3** [C] a version of a recorded piece of music: *A new mix of their hit single is due to be released early next month.*

mixed /mɪkst/ adj **1** showing a mixture of different feelings or opinions: *There has been a mixed* ***reaction*** *to the changes.* **2** for both sexes: *Our children go to a mixed* ***school.*** ◦ *Some of his jokes were too rude for mixed* ***company*** *(= a group where both males and females are present).* **3** combining people of a different religion or race: *a mixed* ***marriage***

ˌmixed-aˈbility adj involving students of different levels of ability: *mixed-ability* ***teaching/classes***

ˌmixed ˈbag noun [S] a range of different things or people: *There's a real mixed bag* ***of*** *people on the course.*

ˌmixed ˈblessing noun [S] something that has advantages and disadvantages: *Getting into the team is a mixed blessing – it's good to have the place, but I'll have to spend a lot of time training.*

ˌmixed ˈdoubles noun [U] a game, for example a tennis game, in which each team consists of one female and one male player

ˌmixed eˈconomy noun [C] an economic system in which some industries are controlled privately and some by the government

ˌmixed ˈfarming noun [U] a method of farming in which crops are grown and animals are kept on the same farm

ˌmixed ˈfeelings noun [plural] If you have mixed feelings about something, you feel both pleased and not pleased about it at the same time: *I had mixed feelings about leaving home. I was excited but at the same time, I knew I would miss my family.*

ˌmixed ˈgrill noun [C] a meal in which several types of meat are served together which have been cooked under a GRILL (= a hot surface which you cook food under)

ˌmixed ˈmedia noun [U] **1** different methods for producing art: *Modern art has encouraged the use of mixed media.* **2** different methods for advertising products and services, such as newspapers, TV, radio, and the internet: *mixed-media advertising campaigns*

ˌmixed-ˈrace adj **1** describes a person whose parents are of different RACES (= the groups that people are divided into according to their physical characteristics) **2** involving people of different RACES: *mixed-race marriages*

ˌmixed ˈup adj upset, worried, and confused, especially because of personal problems: [before noun] *He's just a mixed-up* ***kid.***

mixer /ˈmɪk.səʳ/ (US) /-sɚ/ noun **MACHINE** ▷ **1** [C] a machine that mixes substances: *a cement mixer* ◦ *an electric (food) mixer* **DRINK** ▷ **2** [C] a drink that does not contain alcohol and can be mixed with an alcoholic drink, especially a SPIRIT (= strong alcoholic drink): *We have ginger ale, tonic water, and various other mixers.* **SOCIALIZE** ▷ **3 a good/bad mixer** someone who is good/bad at meeting new people and talking to them: *You get to know lots of people at college if you're a good mixer.*

ˈmixer ˌtap noun [C] UK (US **ˈmixer ˌfaucet**) a device for controlling the flow of water, so that hot and cold water come out of the same pipe, but the flow of each is controlled separately so that the temperature of the water coming out can be changed

mixture /ˈmɪks.tʃəʳ/ (US) /-tʃɚ/ **noun 1** (B2) [C] a substance made from a combination of different substances, or any combination of different things: *The mixture **of** flour, water, and yeast is then left in a warm place for four hours.* ◦ *Their latest CD is a mixture **of** new and old songs.* **2** [U] the process of mixing **3** [U] a type of medicine that has to be shaken before being used: ***cough** mixture*

ˈmix-up noun [C] a mistake that causes confusion: *There was a mix-up at the office and we all received the wrong forms.*

Mk written abbreviation for **Mark**: *She was driving a bright yellow Mk XI Lotus two-seater.*

ml noun written abbreviation for **millilitre**: *a 7 ml bottle of perfume*

mm noun [C] (plural **mm**) written abbreviation for **millimetre**: *a 6 mm (diameter) drill*

MMR /ˌemˌemˈɑːʳ/ (US) /-ˈɑːr/ **noun** [S] an INJECTION given to young children to protect them against the illnesses MEASLES, MUMPS, and RUBELLA

mnemonic /nɪˈmɒn.ɪk/ (US) /-ˈmɑː.nɪk/ **noun** [C] something such as a very short poem or a special word used to help a person remember something: *The musical notes on the lines go EGBDF – use the mnemonic 'every good boy deserves fun'.* • **mnemonic** adj

mo /məʊ/ (US) /moʊ/ **noun** [S] informal a short period of time; a moment: *'Come on! We're going to be late.' 'Hang on **a** mo! I'll just get my wallet.'* ◦ *I'll be with you **in a** mo (= very soon).*

MO /ˌemˈəʊ/ (US) /-ˈoʊ/ **noun** [C] (plural **MOs**) **OFFICER** ▷ abbreviation for medical officer

moan /məʊn/ (US) /moʊn/ **verb; noun**

▸**verb** [I] **SOUND** ▷ **1** (C2) to make a long, low sound of pain, suffering, or another strong emotion: *He moaned **with** pain before losing consciousness.* ◦ *'Let me die,' he moaned.* **COMPLAIN** ▷ **2** (C2) informal disapproving to make a complaint in an unhappy voice, usually about something which does not seem important to other people: *Thelma's always moaning (**about** something), and forgets how lucky she actually is.* ◦ [+ speech] *'I don't like potatoes,' he moaned.* ◦ [+ (that)] *First she moans (**that**) she's too hot, and then that she's too cold.* • **moaner** /ˈməʊ.nəʳ/ (US) /ˈmoʊ.nɚ/ noun [C]

▸**noun** [C] **SOUND** ▷ **1** a long, low sound of pain, suffering, or another strong emotion: *We could hear the moans of someone trapped under the rubble.* ◦ *moans **of** ecstasy/agony* **COMPLAINT** ▷ **2** informal disapproving the act of complaining about something, or a complaint: *Apart from a slight moan about the waiter, he seemed to enjoy the meal.*

moaning minnie /ˌməʊ.nɪŋˈmɪn.i/ (US) /ˌmoʊ-/ **noun** [C] UK informal someone who annoys other people by complaining all the time: *Oh stop being such a moaning minnie!*

moat /məʊt/ (US) /moʊt/ **noun** [C] a long, wide hole that is dug all the way around a place such as a castle and usually filled with water, to make it more difficult to attack

moated /ˈməʊ.tɪd/ (US) /ˈmoʊ.t̬ɪd/ **adj** surrounded by a moat: *a moated house/castle*

mob /mɒb/ (US) /mɑːb/ **noun; verb**

▸**noun** [+ sing/pl verb] **1** [C] usually disapproving a large, angry crowd, especially one which could easily become violent: *The **angry** mob outside the jail was/were ready to riot.* ◦ *a **lynch** mob* ◦ *50 people were killed in three days of mob **violence**.* **2** [C] informal a group of people who are friends or who are similar in some way: *The usual mob were/was hanging out at the bar.* **3** [S] informal an organization of criminals: *a New York mob leader* → See also **mobster**

▸**verb** [T] (**-bb-**) **1** [T usually passive] to come together around someone in a crowd to express admiration, interest, or anger: *They were mobbed **by** fans when they arrived at the theatre.* ◦ *Let's not go to the Old Town tonight – it's always mobbed (= there are always a lot of people there) on Fridays.* **2** [I or T] When birds or small animals mob a bigger or more frightening bird or animal that is hunting them, they attack it together and force it to go away.

mobile /ˈməʊ.baɪl/ (US) /ˈmoʊ.bəl/ **adj; noun**

▸**adj** **MOVING** ▷ **1** able to move freely or be easily moved: *You've broken your ankle but you'll be fully mobile (= able to walk as usual) within a couple of months.* **PHONE SERVICE** ▷ **2** used to describe a service available on a mobile phone, PDA, etc.: *mobile computing*

▸**noun** [C] **PHONE** ▷ **1** (A1) mainly UK (US usually **cell phone**) a **mobile phone 2** a **mobile number**: *My mobile's 07796 10253.* **DECORATION** ▷ **3** a decoration or work of art that has many parts that move freely in the air, for example hanging from threads

ˌmobile deˈvice noun [C] any piece of electronic equipment such as a mobile phone or small computer that you can use in different places

ˌmobile ˈhome noun [C] a type of building that people live in, usually staying in one place, but able to be moved using a vehicle or sometimes its own engine

ˌmobile ˈlibrary noun [C] UK (US **bookmobile**) a large road vehicle which travels around, especially in the countryside, carrying books for people to borrow

ˈmobile ˌnumber noun [C] the number for your mobile phone

ˌmobile ˈphone noun [C] mainly UK (US usually **ˈcell phone**) (A1) a phone that is connected to the phone system by radio instead of by a wire, and can be used anywhere its signals can be received

mobility /məʊˈbɪl.ɪ.ti/ (US) /moʊˈbɪl.ə.t̬i/ **noun** [U] **MOVING** ▷ **1** the ability to move freely or be easily moved: *Some neck injuries cause total loss of mobility below the point of injury.* ◦ *I prefer the mobility of a hand-held camera.* → See also **ˌupward moˈbility** **OF SERVICES** ▷ **2** the ability to have particular services available on a mobile phone, PDA, etc.: *Consumers are demanding mobility, so that they can have access to information in places where it's not available today.*

mobilize (UK usually **mobilise**) /ˈməʊ.bɪ.laɪz/ (US) /ˈmoʊ-/ **verb 1** [T] to organize or prepare something, such as a group of people, for a purpose: *Representatives for all the main candidates are trying to mobilize voter **support**.* **2** [I or T] to prepare to fight, especially in a war: *The government has mobilized several of the army's top combat units.* ◦ *Troops have been mobilizing for the past three weeks.* • **mobilization** (UK also **mobilisation**) /ˌməʊ.bɪ.laɪˈzeɪ.ʃən/ (US) /ˌmoʊ.bɪ.lə-/ noun [U]

mobster /ˈmɒb.stəʳ/ (US) /ˈmɑːb.stɚ/ **noun** [C] mainly US for **gangster**

moccasin /ˈmɒk.ə.sɪn/ (US) /ˈmɑː.kə-/ **noun** [C] a soft leather shoe that you slide onto your foot and do not fasten, that has STITCHES around the top at the front

mocha /ˈmɒk.ə/ (US) /ˈmoʊ.kə/ **noun** [U] **1** a type of coffee of good quality, or a FLAVOURING which tastes of this **2** a mixture of coffee and chocolate

mock /mɒk/ (US) /mɑːk/ **verb; adj; noun**

▸**verb** [T] **1** formal to laugh at someone, often by

copying them in a funny but unkind way: *They were mocking him because he kept falling off his bike.* ◦ *She made fun of him by mocking his limp.* **2** to make something appear stupid or not effective: *The wind mocked their attempts to reach the shore by pushing the boat further and further out to sea.*

PHRASAL VERB **mock sth up** to make a model of something in order to show people what it will look like or how it will work

▸**adj** [before noun] not real but appearing or pretending to be exactly like something: *mock cream* ◦ *mock leather* ◦ *mock surprise*

▸**noun** [C] UK an exam taken at school for practice before a real exam: *You will have your mocks during the first two weeks of March.*

mockers /ˈmɒk.əz/ (US) /ˈmɑː.kɚz/ **noun** [plural] UK informal **put the mockers on sth** old-fashioned to spoil something or stop it from happening: *It rained, so that rather put the mockers on the barbecue.*

mockery /ˈmɒk.ər.i/ (US) /ˈmɑː.kɚ-/ **noun 1** [U] the act of mocking someone or something **2** [S] an action or event that is a failure and makes the people involved in or affected by it appear silly: *The trial was* ***a*** *mockery – the judge had decided the verdict before it began.*

IDIOM **make a mockery of sth** to make something seem stupid or without value: *The fact that he sent his children to private school makes a mockery of his socialist principles.*

mocking /ˈmɒk.ɪŋ/ (US) /ˈmɑː.kɪŋ/ **adj** mocking behaviour involves laughing at someone or something in an unkind way: *a mocking* ***voice*** ◦ *mocking humour/laughter* • **mockingly** /-li/ **adv**

mockingbird /ˈmɒk.ɪŋ.bɜːd/ (US) /ˈmɑː.kɪŋ.bɝːd/ **noun** [C] any of the types of North American or Australian birds which copy the sounds made by other birds

mockney /ˈmɒk.ni/ (US) /ˈmɑːk.ni/ **noun** [U] informal disapproving pronunciation of English by someone who pretends to speak like a COCKNEY, in order to seem as if they are from a lower social class

ˌmock ˈturtleneck noun [C] US for a **turtleneck**

mockumentary /ˌmɒk.jʊˈmen.tər.i/ (US) /ˌmɑː.kjə-ˈmen.t̬ɚ-/ **noun** [C] a film or television show made in the style of a DOCUMENTARY to make invented events seem real

ˈmock-up noun [C] a full-size model of something large that has not yet been built, showing how it will look or operate: *She showed us a mock-up of what the car will look like when it goes into production.*

mod /mɒd/ (US) /mɑːd/ **noun** [C] a member of a group of young people, especially in Britain in the 1960s, who wore stylish clothes and rode SCOOTERS (= small motorcycles): *mods and rockers*

the MOD /ˌem.əʊˈdiː/ (US) /-oʊ-/ **noun** abbreviation for the Ministry of Defence: the British government department that is responsible for defence, military activities, and the armed forces

modal /ˈməʊ.dəl/ (US) /ˈmoʊ.dəl/ **noun** [C] (also **ˌmodal ˈverb**) specialized (B1) a verb, such as 'can', 'might', and 'must', that is used with another verb to express an idea such as possibility that is not expressed by the main verb of a sentence

modality /məʊˈdæl.ə.ti/ (US) /moʊˈdæl.ə.t̬i/ **noun 1** [C] formal a particular way of doing or experiencing something: *A variety of modalities of communication can be used to transmit health warnings to the public.* **2** [U] specialized the meaning expressed by modal verbs

ˌmod ˈcons noun [plural] UK informal the machines and devices, such as washing machines and fridges, which make the ordinary jobs in a home easier: *The kitchen of this delightful cottage is fully equipped with all mod cons including a dishwasher.*

mode /məʊd/ (US) /moʊd/ **noun WAY** ▷ **1** (C1) [C] formal a way of operating, living, or behaving: *Each department in the company has its own mode* ***of*** *operation.* ◦ *Railways are the most important mode* ***of*** *transport for the economy.* **MATHS** ▷ **2** [C] specialized the number or value which appears most often in a particular set **FASHION** ▷ **3 be the mode** formal (especially of clothes) to be fashionable at a particular time: *Miniskirts were very much the mode in the 60s.* → See also **à la mode**

model /ˈmɒd.əl/ (US) /ˈmɑː.dəl/ **noun; verb**

▸**noun** [C] **COPY** ▷ **1** (C2) something that a copy can be based on because it is an extremely good example of its type: *The educational system was a model for those of many other countries.* ◦ *The council plans to build a model town on the site.* ◦ *Some groups want to set up an Islamic state* ***on the*** *Iranian model.* ◦ *Even Chris,* ***the very*** *model* ***of*** *calmness (= someone who is usually extremely calm), was angered by having to work such long hours.* ◦ *She really is a model (= perfect) student.* **PERSON** ▷ **2** (B1) a person who wears clothes so that they can be photographed or shown to possible buyers, or a person who is employed to be photographed or painted: *a fashion/nude model* ◦ *She's going out with a* ***male*** *model.* ◦ *I worked as an artist's model when I was a student.* → See also **supermodel** **MACHINE** ▷ **3** (A2) a particular type of machine, especially a car, that is slightly different from machines of the same type: *a* ***luxury/new*** *model* ◦ *the* ***latest*** *model* **REPRESENTATION** ▷ **4** (A2) something that represents another thing, either as a physical object that is usually smaller than the real object, or as a simple description that can be used in calculations: *a plastic model aircraft* ◦ *By looking at this model you can get a better idea of how the bridge will look.* ◦ *to construct a statistical/theoretical/mathematical model* ◦ *No computer model* ***of*** *the economy can predict when the next recession will be.*

▸**verb** (-ll- or US usually -l-) **CLOTHES** ▷ **1** [I or T] to wear fashionable clothes, jewellery, etc. in order to advertise them: *Tatjana is modelling a Versace design.* ◦ *I used to model when I was younger.* **MAKE A MODEL** ▷ **2** [T] to make a model of something: *to model animals out of clay* ◦ *to model clay into animal shapes* ◦ *The whole car can be modelled on a computer before a single component is made.*

PHRASAL VERB **model yourself on sb** to try to make yourself very similar to someone else: *Lots of young singers modelled themselves on Madonna.*

modelling UK (US usually **modeling**) /ˈmɒd.əl.ɪŋ/ (US) /ˈmɑː.dəl-/ **noun** [U] the job of wearing clothes, jewellery, etc. in order to advertise them: *Ashley's always wanted to go into modelling.* ◦ *a modelling contract*

modem /ˈməʊ.dem/ (US) /ˈmoʊ.dəm/ **noun** [C] an electronic device that allows one computer to send information to another through standard phone lines and therefore over long distances

moderate adj; noun; verb

▸**adj** /ˈmɒd.ər.ət/ (US) /ˈmɑː.dɚ-/ **MEDIUM-SIZED** ▷ **1** (C1) neither small nor large but between the two; clearly within the limits of a range of possibilities: *moderate growth/inflation* ◦ *He's a moderate drinker.* ◦ *The cabin is of moderate size – just right for a small family.*

◦ *Imposing sanctions is a moderate action when you consider that the alternative is military intervention.* ◦ *There has been a moderate improvement in her health since she began the treatment.* ◦ *We have had moderate success in changing people's attitudes.* **OPINIONS** ▷ **2** describes opinions, especially political ones, that are not extreme and are therefore acceptable to a large number of people: *The party leader is an extreme left-winger, but her deputy is more moderate in her views.* • **moderately** /-li/ **adv** C2 *There's very little moderately priced housing in this area.* ◦ *The company remains moderately profitable, but it is not making as much money as it should.*

▸**noun** [C] /ˈmɒd.ər.ət/ US /ˈmɑː.dɚ-/ a person whose opinions, especially their political ones, are not extreme and are therefore acceptable to a large number of people: *He is well-known as a moderate in the party.*

▸**verb** [I or T] /ˈmɒd.ər.eɪt/ US /ˈmɑː.də.reɪt/ C2 to (cause to) become less in size, strength, or force; to reduce something: *There have been repeated calls for the president to moderate his stance on contraception.* ◦ *Weather conditions have moderated, making a rescue attempt possible.*

moderation /ˌmɒd.ərˈeɪ.ʃən/ US /ˌmɑː.dəˈreɪ-/ **noun** [U] **REASONABLE LIMITS** ▷ **1** C1 the quality of doing something within reasonable limits: *You can eat whatever you like as long as it's* ***in*** *moderation.* ◦ *All parties will have to show great moderation during these very difficult negotiations.* **REDUCTION** ▷ **2** formal the fact that something becomes less in size, strength, or force: *We can't sail until there is some moderation of the storm.*

moderator /ˈmɒd.ər.eɪ.təʳ/ US /ˈmɑː.də.reɪ.t̬ɚ/ **noun** [C] **1** (US usually **mediator**) someone who tries to help other people come to an agreement: *An independent moderator should be appointed to oversee the negotiations.* **2** US someone who makes certain that a formal discussion happens without problems and follows the rules: *He challenged the president to a series of TV debates. Just the two of them, with no moderator.* **3** UK specialized someone who makes certain that all the people marking an exam use the same standards: *The final marks awarded for coursework will depend upon the moderator.* **4** someone who makes sure that the rules of an internet discussion are not broken, for example by removing any threatening or offensive messages

modern /ˈmɒd.ən/ US /ˈmɑː.dɚn/ **adj MOST RECENT** ▷ **1** A2 designed and made using the most recent ideas and methods: *modern technology/architecture/medicine/art* ◦ *We're in the very modern-looking building opposite the station.* ◦ approving *My grandpa's attitudes are very modern, considering his age.* **PRESENT** ▷ **2** B1 of the present or recent times, especially the period of history since around 1500: *What do you think is the role of religion in the modern* ***world****?*

ˌmodern ˈdance **noun** [U] a style of dance usually performed in a theatre, which expresses the dancer's feelings and does not have many rules about the dancer's movements

ˈmodern-day **adj** relating to people or things from modern times and not from a time in the past: *Modern-day engines are so much more efficient.*

modernism /ˈmɒd.ən.ɪ.zəm/ US /ˈmɑː.dɚ.nɪ-/ **noun** [U] **1** modern thinking or methods: *Modernism seeks to find new forms of expression and rejects traditional or accepted ideas.* **2** specialized the ideas and methods of modern art, especially from the 1920s until now

modernistic /ˌmɒd.ənˈɪs.tɪk/ US /ˌmɑː.dɚˈnɪs-/ **adj** designed in a way that is obviously modern

> **+ Other ways of saying modern**
>
> Another way of saying 'modern' is **up-to-date**:
>
> *The hospital has some of the most* ***up-to-date*** *equipment in the country.*
>
> **Latest** is a way of saying that something is the most modern:
>
> *She always wears the* ***latest*** *fashions.*
>
> The words **cutting-edge**, **high-tech**, or **state-of-the-art** can be used for things which use the most modern ideas, materials, features, etc.:
>
> *Computers have brought* ***cutting-edge*** *technology into the classroom.*
>
> *Divers with* ***high-tech*** *equipment discovered the wreck of the ship.*
>
> *They've got a new* ***state-of-the-art*** *kitchen.*
>
> Someone or something which uses modern ideas and systems to encourage change can be described as **progressive**:
>
> *It's a very* ***progressive*** *school.*
>
> The word **contemporary** is used for art, literature, music, etc. that is modern:
>
> *The music was written a hundred years ago, but it still has a* ***contemporary*** *feel to it.*
>
> If something is modern but you do not like it, you can use the adjective **newfangled**:
>
> *I can't cope with all this* ***newfangled*** *technology.*

modernity /mɒdˈɜː.nə.ti/ US /mɑːˈdɝː.nə.t̬i/ **noun** [U] the condition of being modern: *There is a stark contrast between tradition and modernity.*

modernize (UK usually **modernise**) /ˈmɒd.ən.aɪz/ US /ˈmɑː.dɚ.naɪz/ **verb** [I or T] to make something more modern: *Much of the house has been modernized.* ◦ *There has been a lot of opposition to modernizing working practices.* ◦ *If they want to increase output from the factory, they'll have to modernize.* • **modernization** (UK usually **modernisation**) /ˌmɒd.ən.aɪˈzeɪ.ʃən/ US /ˈmɑː.dɚ.naɪ-/ **noun** [U] *The modernization of the 100-year-old sewage and water systems will cost millions of pounds.*

ˌmodern ˈjazz **noun** [U] a type of JAZZ that began in the 1940s

ˌmodern ˈlanguages **noun** [plural] mainly UK languages that are spoken at the present time, especially European languages such as French, German, and Spanish

modest /ˈmɒd.ɪst/ US /ˈmɑː.dɪst/ **adj NOT LARGE** ▷ **1** B2 not large in size or amount, or not expensive: *They live in a fairly modest house, considering their wealth.* ◦ *There has been a modest improvement/recovery in housing conditions for the poor.* ◦ *The party made modest gains in the elections, but nothing like the huge gains that were predicted.* ◦ *Just a modest portion for me, please.* **QUIETLY SUCCESSFUL** ▷ **2** C1 approving not usually talking about or making obvious your own abilities and achievements: *He's very modest* ***about*** *his achievements.* **CLOTHES/BEHAVIOUR** ▷ **3** old-fashioned describes something, such as a woman's clothes or behaviour, that is intended to avoid attracting sexual interest: *a modest walk/manner* • **modestly** /-li/ **adv** C1 *At just £9, the training DVD is very modestly* ***priced****.* ◦ *She was dressed modestly.*

modesty /ˈmɒd.ɪ.sti/ US /ˈmɑː.dɪ-/ **noun** [U] **QUIET SUCCESS** ▷ **1** approving the quality of not talking about or not trying to make people notice your abilities and achievements: *She does a lot of work for charities, but her modesty* ***forbids*** *her from talking about it.* **2 in all**

M

modesty approving said when you want to say something good about yourself, but do not want to seem to think you are too important: *Quite frankly, and in all modesty, we'd probably have lost the game if I hadn't been playing.* **CLOTHES/BEHAVIOUR** ▷ **3** old-fashioned the quality, in women, of dressing or behaving in a way that is intended to avoid attracting sexual interest

modicum /ˈmɒd.ɪ.kəm/ (US) /ˈmɑː.dɪ-/ **noun** [S] formal a small amount of something good such as truth or honesty: *There's not even **a** modicum **of** truth in her statement.* ◦ *Anyone with **a** modicum **of** common sense could have seen that the plan wouldn't work.*

modification /ˌmɒd.ɪ.fɪˈkeɪ.ʃən/ (US) /ˌmɑː.dɪ-/ **noun** **CHANGE** ▷ **1** (C1) [C or U] a change to something, usually to improve it: *Modification of the engine to run on lead-free fuel is fairly simple.* ◦ *A couple of modifications and the speech will be perfect.* **LANGUAGE** ▷ **2** [U] specialized the fact of a word acting as a modifier of another

ˈmodified Aˌmerican ˌplan **noun** [U] (abbreviation **MAP**) US for **half board**

modifier /ˈmɒd.ɪ.faɪ.əʳ/ (US) /ˈmɑː.dɪ.faɪ.ɚ/ **noun** [C] specialized a word or phrase that is used with another word or phrase to limit or add to its meaning: *In 'safety barrier', the noun 'safety' is being used as a modifier.*

modify /ˈmɒd.ɪ.faɪ/ (US) /ˈmɑː.dɪ-/ **verb** [T] **CHANGE** ▷ **1** (C1) to change something such as a plan, opinion, law, or way of behaviour slightly, usually to improve it or make it more acceptable: *Instead of simply punishing them, the system encourages offenders to modify their behaviour.* ◦ *The proposals were unpopular and were only accepted in a modified form.* **LANGUAGE** ▷ **2** specialized If a word or phrase modifies another word or phrase used with it, it limits or adds to its meaning: *In the sentence 'She ran quickly', the adverb 'quickly' modifies the verb 'ran'.*

modish /ˈməʊ.dɪʃ/ (US) /ˈmoʊ-/ **adj** formal fashionable • **modishly** /-li/ **adv** formal

modulate /ˈmɒd.jʊ.leɪt/ (US) /ˈmɑː.dʒə-/ **verb** [T] **SOUND** ▷ **1** [I or T] to change the style, loudness, etc. of something such as your voice in order to achieve an effect or express an emotion: *His gentle introductory tone modulates into a football coach's pre-game pep talk.* **2** [I] specialized to change from one musical KEY to another: *Here we modulate **from** G major **to** A minor.* • **modulation** /ˌmɒd.jʊˈleɪ.ʃən/ (US) /ˌmɑː.dʒə-/ **noun** [C or U]

module /ˈmɒd.juːl/ (US) /ˈmɑː.dʒuːl/ **noun** [C] **1** one of a set of separate parts that, when combined, form a complete whole: *The emergency building is transported in individual modules, such as bedrooms and a kitchen, which are put together on site.* ◦ *The full computer program is made up of several modules (= small programs) which should be individually tested before being integrated.* **2** one of the units that together make a complete course taught especially at a college or university **3** a part of a spacecraft that can operate independently of the other parts, especially when separate from them: *a lunar landing module* • **modular** /ˈmɒd.jʊ.ləʳ/ (US) /ˈmɑː.dʒə.lɚ/ **adj** *Many colleges and universities now offer modular degree courses.*

modus operandi /ˌməʊ.dəsˌɒp.əˈræn.diː/ (US) /ˌmoʊ.dəsˌoʊ.pəˈrɑːn.di/ **noun** [S] formal a particular way of doing something

modus vivendi /ˌməʊ.dəs.vɪˈven.diː/ (US) /ˌmoʊ.dəs.viːˈven.di/ **noun** [S] formal an arrangement allowing people or groups of people who have different opinions or beliefs to work or live together: *Our two countries must put aside the memory of war and seek a modus vivendi.*

moggy /ˈmɒg.i/ (US) /ˈmɑː.gi/ **noun** [C] (also **moggie**) UK informal a cat, especially one that is ordinary or has an untidy appearance

mogul /ˈməʊ.gəl/ (US) /ˈmoʊ-/ **noun** [C] **PERSON** ▷ **1** an important person who is very rich or powerful: ***movie/media/industry** moguls* **SNOW** ▷ **2** specialized a small pile of hard snow on the side of a hill or mountain used for skiing, created to add interest and difficulty to the sport

mohair /ˈməʊ.heəʳ/ (US) /ˈmoʊ.her/ **noun** [U] a soft wool or cloth made from the outer hair of ANGORA goats (= goats with long soft hair): *a mohair jumper*

Mohammed /məˈhæm.ɪd/ (US) /moʊ-/ **noun** the Arab holy man on whose life and teaching Islam is based

Mohican /məʊˈhiː.kən/ (US) /moʊ-/ **noun** [C] UK (US **Mohawk**) a sometimes brightly coloured hairstyle, often worn in PUNK fashion, in which the hair is removed from the sides of the head and a central strip is made to point out from the head

moi /mwɑː/ **pronoun** humorous used instead of 'me', to express false surprise about something that you have been accused of: *Extravagant, moi?*

moist /mɔɪst/ **adj** slightly wet, especially in a good way: *Keep the soil in the pot moist, but not too wet.* ◦ approving *This cake is lovely and moist!* → See also **damp** • **moistness** /ˈmɔɪst.nəs/ **noun** [U]

moisten /ˈmɔɪ.sən/ **verb** [I or T] to make something slightly wet or to become slightly wet: *Moisten the cloth before using it to clean glass.*

moisture /ˈmɔɪs.tʃəʳ/ (US) /-tʃɚ/ **noun** [U] a liquid such as water in the form of very small drops, either in the air, in a substance, or on a surface: *These plants need a rich soil which **retains** moisture.*

moisturizer (UK usually **moisturiser**) /ˈmɔɪs.tʃər.aɪ.zəʳ/ (US) /-tʃɚ.aɪ.zɚ/ **noun** [C or U] a cream that you put on your skin to stop it from becoming dry: *I use (a) moisturizer every night.* • **moisturize** (UK usually **moisturise**) /-aɪz/ **verb** [I or T] *You should tone and moisturize (your skin) every day.*

mojito /məˈhiː.təʊ/ (US) /-t̬oʊ/ **noun** [C or U] (plural **mojitos**) an alcoholic drink made with RUM, LIME juice, sugar, and MINT

mojo /ˈməʊ.dʒəʊ/ (US) /ˈmoʊ.dʒoʊ/ **noun** [U] informal a quality that attracts people to you and makes you successful and full of energy: *He's definitely **lost** his mojo.* ◦ *He needs to **get** his mojo **working** if he's going to win the election.*

molar /ˈməʊ.ləʳ/ (US) /ˈmoʊ.lɚ/ **noun** [C] one of the large teeth at the back of the mouth in humans and some other animals used for crushing and CHEWING food → Compare **canine, incisor**

molasses /məˈlæs.ɪz/ **noun** [U] a thick, dark brown liquid that is produced during the process of making sugar, used in cooking

mold /məʊld/ (US) /moʊld/ **noun, verb** US for **mould**

molder /ˈməʊl.dəʳ/ (US) /ˈmoʊl.dɚ/ **verb** [I] US for **moulder**

mole /məʊl/ (US) /moʊl/ **noun** [C] **ANIMAL** ▷ **1** a small mammal that is nearly blind, has dark fur, and lives in passages that it digs underground **SPOT** ▷ **2** a small, dark spot or LUMP (= raised area) on a person's skin → Compare **freckle** **PERSON** ▷ **3** a person who works for an organization or government and secretly gives information to its competitor or enemy: *A mole inside the Department of Transport had leaked secret proposals to the press.* → Compare **spy**

moˌlecular biˈology noun [U] specialized the study of the structure and action of the molecules that make up living things

moˌlecular ˈweight noun [U] specialized another term for **relative molecular mass**

molecule /ˈmɒl.ɪ.kjuːl/ (US) /ˈmɑː.lɪ-/ noun [C] the simplest unit of a chemical substance, usually a group of two or more atoms • **molecular** /məˈlek.jʊ.ləʳ/ (US) /-lɚ/ adj

molehill /ˈməʊl.hɪl/ (US) /ˈmoʊl-/ noun [C] a small pile of earth pushed up to the surface of the ground by the digging of a MOLE (= a mammal that lives underground)

moleskin /ˈməʊl.skɪn/ (US) /ˈmoʊl-/ noun [U] a type of strong cotton cloth with a surface that feels like very short hairs: *moleskin trousers*

molest /məˈlest/ verb [T] **ATTACK SEXUALLY** ▷ **1** to touch or attack someone in a sexual way against their wishes: *The girl had been molested frequently by her stepfather from the age of eight.* ◦ *The man had previously been arrested several times for molesting young boys.* **ATTACK** ▷ **2** formal to touch, push, etc. someone violently: *United Nations premises were looted and personnel were molested by demonstrators.* • **molestation** /ˌmɒl.esˈteɪ.ʃᵊn/ (US) /ˌmɑː.les-/ noun [U] *sexual molestation* • **molester** /məˈles.təʳ/ (US) /-tɚ/ noun [C] *a **child** molester*

moll /mɒl/ (US) /mɑːl/ noun [C] **1** US slang a female COMPANION of a GANGSTER (= violent criminal) **2** Australian English a female COMPANION of a member of a group of people who ride motorcycles or SURF together

mollify /ˈmɒl.ɪ.faɪ/ (US) /ˈmɑː.lɪ-/ verb [T] to make someone less angry or upset: *I tried to mollify her by giving her flowers.*

mollusc (US also **mollusk**) /ˈmɒl.əsk/ (US) /ˈmɑː.ləsk/ noun [C] any animal that has a soft body, no SPINE, and is often covered with a shell. Many molluscs live in water: *Oysters are molluscs, as are snails and cuttlefish.*

mollycoddle /ˈmɒl.iˌkɒd.l̩/ (US) /ˈmɑː.liˌkɑː.dl̩/ verb [T] informal mainly disapproving to give someone too much care or protection: *You're not helping the children by mollycoddling them – they have to grow up sometime.*

Molotov cocktail /ˌmɒl.ə.tɒfˈkɒk.teɪl/ (US) /ˌmɑː.lə.tɑːfˈkɑːk-/ noun [C] old-fashioned a type of **petrol bomb**

molt /məʊlt/ (US) /moʊlt/ noun, verb US for **moult**

molten /ˈməʊl.tᵊn/ (US) /ˈmoʊl-/ adj describes metal or rock that is in a liquid state because of great heat: *molten glass/lava/lead*

molybdenum /mɒlˈɪb.dɪ.nəm/ (US) /mɑːˈlɪb-/ noun [U] (symbol **Mo**) a chemical element that is a very hard, silver-coloured metal, used especially to make STEEL stronger

mom /mɒm/ (US) /mɑːm/ noun [C] US (A1) mother: *I miss my mom and dad a lot.* ◦ [as form of address] *Aw, Mom, why can't I go?*

ˌmom-and-ˈpop adj [before noun] US informal used to describe a small business that is owned and operated by members of the same family: *a mom-and-pop business/store*

moment /ˈməʊ.mənt/ (US) /ˈmoʊ-/ noun **SHORT TIME** ▷ **1** (A2) [C] a very short period of time: *Can you wait **a** moment?* ◦ *I'll be ready **in** just **a** moment.* ◦ *A car drew up outside and **a few** moments later the doorbell rang.* ◦ *I'm expecting her to come **at any** moment (= very soon).* ◦ *Have you **got a** moment (= are you busy or have you got time to speak to me)?* **OCCASION** ▷ **2** (B1) [C] a particular time or occasion: *When would be **the** best moment to tell the family?* ◦ *Don't leave it to/till **the last** moment (= the latest time possible).* ◦ *If you want a private conversation with her you'll have to **choose** your moment (= find a suitable time).* ◦ ***The** moment (**that**) (= as soon as) I get the money I'll send the ticket.* **3 at the moment** (A2) now: *I'm afraid she's not here at the moment.* **4 for the moment** (B2) If you do something for the moment, you are doing it now, but might do something different in the future: *Let's carry on with what we agreed for the moment.* **5 at this moment in time** formal now: *I can give no information at this precise moment in time.* **IMPORTANCE** ▷ **6 of (great) moment** formal very important: *a decision of great moment* → See also **momentous**

IDIOMS **be having a moment 1** informal to not be acting as normal for a short time, for example because you are not thinking about what you are doing, or because you are feeling a strong emotion: *He was staring out of the window and he didn't answer me – I think he was just having a moment.* **2** informal to be very popular or fashionable at a particular time: *Right now, oversized sweaters are having a moment.* • **have your/its moments** to be sometimes very good or successful: *This album may not be as good as their last one but it has its moments.* • **the moment of truth** an occasion when something important happens that tests someone or something and that will have an effect on the future: *Lift-off is always the moment of truth for a new rocket.* • **not a moment too soon** used to say that something happened when it was almost too late: *Help arrived – and not a moment too soon.* • **not for a moment** used to say that you do not think or do something at all: *I don't believe that story for a moment.*

momentarily /ˌməʊ.mənˈter.ɪ.li/ (US) /ˌmoʊ-/ adv **1** for a very short time: *She was momentarily confused by the foreign road signs.* **2** US very soon: *I'll be ready to leave momentarily.*

momentary /ˈməʊ.mən.tᵊr.i/ (US) /ˈmoʊ-/ adj lasting for a very short time: *a momentary hesitation*

momentous /məˈmen.təs/ (US) /-t̬əs/ adj very important because of effects on future events: *Whether or not to move overseas was a momentous **decision** for the family.* • **momentously** /-li/ adv • **momentousness** /-nəs/ noun [U]

momentum /məˈmen.təm/ (US) /-t̬əm/ noun [U] (C2) the force that keeps an object moving or keeps an event developing after it has started: *Once you push it, it keeps going **under** its own momentum.* ◦ *The spacecraft will fly round the Earth to **gain/gather** momentum for its trip to Jupiter.* ◦ *The play **loses** momentum (= becomes less interesting, energetic, etc.) by its half way stage.* ◦ *In an attempt to **give** new momentum to their plans, the committee set a date for starting detailed discussions.*

momma /ˈmɒm.ə/ (US) /ˈmɑː.mə/ noun [C] US informal for **mother**

mommy /ˈmɒm.i/ (US) /ˈmɑː.mi/ noun [C] US child's word for mother: *I want my mommy.* ◦ [as form of address] *I'm thirsty, Mommy.*

Mon. written abbreviation for Monday

monarch /ˈmɒn.ək/ (US) /ˈmɑː.nɚk/ noun [C] a king or queen: *a **hereditary** monarch* ◦ *Britain's head of state is a **constitutional** monarch (= only has very limited powers).* • **monarchic** /məˈnɑː.kɪk/ (US) /-ˈnɑːr-/ adj (also **monarchical**)

monarchist /ˈmɒn.ə.kɪst/ (US) /ˈmɑː.nɚ-/ noun [C] a person who supports the system of having a king or queen

M

monarchy /ˈmɒn.ə.ki/ (US) /ˈmɑː.nɚ-/ **noun 1** [C] a country that has a king or queen **2** [U] the system of having a king or queen: *Is monarchy relevant in the modern world or should it be abolished?*

monastery /ˈmɒn.ə.stri/ (US) /ˈmɑː.nə.ster.i/ **noun** [C] a building in which MONKS live and worship → Compare **convent, nunnery**

monastic /məˈnæs.tɪk/ **adj 1** connected with MONKS or monasteries **2** describes a simple way of living with few possessions and no people near you: *a monastic life*

monasticism /məˈnæs.tɪ.sɪ.zᵊm/ **noun** [U] the way MONKS live

Monday /ˈmʌn.deɪ/ **noun** [C or U] (written abbreviation **Mon.**) A1 the day of the week after Sunday and before Tuesday: *I start my new job **on** Monday.* ◦ *Don't you hate going back to school **on** Mondays?* ◦ *I'll see you **next** Monday.* ◦ *He was late for work **last** Monday.* ◦ *The baby was born **on** a Monday.* ◦ *Monday **morning/afternoon/evening/night***

IDIOMS **(that) Monday morning feeling** (Australian English **Mondayitis**) the way people feel after the weekend when they do not want to go to work or school: *I've got **that** Monday morning feeling.* • **Monday-morning quarterback** US someone who says how an event or problem should have been dealt with by others after it has already been dealt with

monetarism /ˈmʌn.ɪ.tᵊr.ɪ.zᵊm/ (US) /-t̬ɚ.ɪ-/ **noun** [U] a system of controlling a country's economy by limiting how much money is in use at a particular time • **monetarist** /-ɪst/ (US) /-t̬ɚ-/ **noun** [C], **adj** *She's a convinced monetarist.* ◦ *monetarist policies*

monetary /ˈmʌn.ɪ.tri/ **adj** C2 relating to the money in a country: *monetary **policy*** ◦ *monetary **control*** ◦ *The monetary unit of the UK is the pound.*

ˌ**monetary** ˌ**system** **noun** [C] the system used by a country to provide money and to control the exchange of money

> **Word partners for money**
>
> *earn/make/raise* money • *invest/pay/spend* money • *cost* money • *save* money • *borrow/lend/owe* money • *put* money *into* sth • an *amount/sum* of money • a *waste* of money

money /ˈmʌn.i/ **noun** [U] **1** A1 coins or notes that are used to buy things, or the amount of these that one person has: *'How much money have you got on you?' '£10 in notes and a few coins.'* ◦ *We invested the money in a high-interest bank account.* ◦ *I wanted to buy it but it **cost** too much money (= was too expensive).* ◦ *We **spent** so much money redecorating the house that we didn't have any left over for a holiday.* ◦ *You can't pay in English money. You'll have to **change** some money (= buy some foreign money) at the bank.* ◦ *How much money do you **earn**?* ◦ *He enjoyed acting but he wasn't **making** (= earning) much money.* ◦ *Her investments haven't **made** (= produced as profit) much money this year.* ◦ *They **made** their money (= became rich) in the fashion business.* ◦ *He tried to persuade me to **put** money **into** the company (= invest in the company).* ◦ *We need to **raise** (= collect) money for a new school pool from the parents.* ◦ *Try to **save** (= keep) some money for your holiday.* ◦ *We're **saving** (= not spending as much) money by using volunteers.* ◦ *I didn't like the job, but **the** money (= amount of pay) was good.* ◦ *Money is **tight/short** (= we haven't got much money) at the moment.* ◦ *I had some very expensive dental treatment recently, but it was money **well spent** – it'll save me problems in the future.* **2 money in sth** If you say that there is money in something, you mean that the activity will produce a profit: *There's money in sport these days.* ◦ *There's money in it for you.*

IDIOMS **be in the money** to suddenly have a lot of money • **be made of money** to be very rich: *No you can't have a new computer game. I'm not made of money, you know.* • **for my money** in my opinion: *For my money, Sunday is the best day to travel because the roads are quiet.* • **get/have your money's worth** to receive good value from something you have paid for: *He's had his money's worth out of that suit – he's been wearing it for years.* • **have money** to be rich: *I believe her family has money.* • **have money to burn** to spend a lot of money on things that are not necessary: *I don't know what her job is but she certainly seems to have money to burn.* • **marry money** to marry a rich person: *One way to get rich is to marry money.* • **money doesn't grow on trees** saying said to warn someone that they have to be careful how much money they spend, because there is only a limited amount • **money for old rope** (also **money for jam**) UK money you get for doing something very easy: *Babysitting is money for old rope if the children don't wake up.* • **money talks** saying said about people or organizations that are rich, and can therefore get or do what they want • **put (your) money on sb/sth 1** to risk money on someone or something winning a race or competition: *He put some money on a horse in the five o'clock race.* **2** to strongly believe that someone will do something or that something will happen: *Chris will be promoted – I'd put money on it.* • **put your money where your mouth is** informal to show by your actions and not just your words that you support or believe in something • **you pays your money and you takes your chance/choice** informal humorous saying said to someone who must decide between different things and accept the results of their decision

moneybags /ˈmʌn.i.bægz/ **noun** [C] (plural **moneybags**) informal disapproving a rich person

ˈ**money** ˌ**box** **noun** [C] mainly UK a closed container in which money is kept, especially one with a hole in the top through which coins can be pushed

moneyed /ˈmʌn.id/ **adj** formal rich: *a moneyed family*

ˈ**money**-ˌ**grubbing** **adj** disapproving Someone or something that is money-grubbing has money as their main interest and does anything they can to get a lot of it.

ˈ**money** ˌ**laundering** **noun** [U] the crime of moving money that has been obtained illegally through banks and other businesses to make it seem as if the money has been obtained legally

moneylender /ˈmʌn.iˌlen.dəʳ/ (US) /-dɚ/ **noun** [C] mainly disapproving a person or organization whose job is to lend money to people in return for payment: *Families with money problems often fall into the hands of the moneylenders and get further into debt.*

moneymaker /ˈmʌn.iˌmeɪ.kəʳ/ (US) /-kɚ/ **noun** [C] (also ˈ**money-spinner**) a product or activity that produces a lot of money

ˈ**money** ˌ**market** **noun** [C or U] the system in which banks and other similar organizations buy and sell money from each other

ˈ**money**-ˌ**minded** **adj** interested in money and good at getting or saving it: *I've never been very money-minded – I leave all my business affairs to my financial adviser.*

ˈ**money** ˌ**order** **noun** [C] US (UK ˈ**postal** ˌ**order**) an official piece of paper with an amount of money written on it, which you send through the post to someone, who can then exchange it for the same amount of money at a post office

ˈmoney suˌpply noun [C usually singular] all the money that is in use in a country

-monger /-mʌŋ.gəʳ/ (US) /-gɚ/ suffix mainly disapproving a person who encourages a particular activity, especially one which causes trouble: *They're nothing but a bunch of war-mongers.* → See also **ironmonger, fishmonger** • **-mongering** /-ɪŋ/ suffix *They accused him of rumour-mongering/scandal-mongering.*

mongol /ˈmɒŋ.gəl/ (US) /ˈmɑːŋ-/ noun [C] offensive old-fashioned (US also **mongoloid**) a person who has DOWN'S SYNDROME

mongolism /ˈmɒŋ.gəl.ɪ.zəm/ (US) /ˈmɑːŋ-/ noun [U] offensive old-fashioned **Down's syndrome**

mongoose /ˈmɒŋ.guːs/ (US) /ˈmɑːŋ-/ noun [C] (plural **mongooses**) a small tropical animal with a long tail which eats snakes, RATS, and birds' eggs

mongrel /ˈmʌŋ.grəl/ noun [C] (US informal also **mutt**) a dog whose parents are of different breeds

monies (also **moneys**) /ˈmʌn.iz/ noun [plural] formal amounts of money: *Any monies received from this interest will be treated as capital.*

moniker (also **monicker**) /ˈmɒn.ɪ.kəʳ/ (US) /ˈmɑː.nɪ.kɚ/ noun [C] humorous a name or NICKNAME

monitor /ˈmɒn.ɪ.təʳ/ (US) /ˈmɑː.nɪ.t̬ɚ/ noun; verb

▸noun [C] **PERSON WHO WATCHES** ▷ **1** a person who has the job of watching or noticing particular things: *United Nations monitors were not allowed to enter the area.* **TESTING MACHINE** ▷ **2** a machine which regularly tests something: *a radiation monitor* **SCREEN** ▷ **3** (B2) a device with a screen on which words or pictures can be shown: *a computer monitor* ◦ *a TV monitor* ◦ *Doctors watched the old man's heartbeat on a monitor.* **AT SCHOOL** ▷ **4** a child in school who has special jobs to do: *the library monitor*

▸verb [T] (C1) to watch and check a situation carefully for a period of time in order to discover something about it: *The new findings suggest that women ought to monitor their cholesterol levels.* ◦ *The CIA were monitoring (= secretly listening to) his phone calls.*

monk /mʌŋk/ noun [C] a member of a group of religious men who do not marry and usually live together in a MONASTERY

monk

monkey /ˈmʌŋ.ki/ noun; verb

▸noun [C] **ANIMAL** ▷ **1** (A2) an animal that lives in hot countries, has a long tail, and climbs trees. Monkeys are PRIMATES (= the group of animals that are most like humans). **CHILD** ▷ **2** informal a child who behaves badly: *They ate all the cakes, the monkeys.* ◦ [as form of address] *Hey, put that down, you little monkey!*

IDIOMS **I'll be a monkey's uncle!** old-fashioned used to show you are very surprised • **make a monkey out of sb** to make someone appear stupid • **not give a monkey's** UK slang If you don't/couldn't give a monkey's about something, you are not at all worried by it: *'Chrissie won't like it.' 'I don't give a monkey's.'*

▸verb [T] US informal to copy or MIMIC someone

PHRASAL VERB **monkey about/around (with sth)** informal disapproving to behave, or to use or move things, in a silly and careless way

ˈmonkey ˌbusiness noun [U] behaviour that is not acceptable or is dishonest: *The teacher suspected that there had been some monkey business going on in the class.*

ˈmonkey-ˌpuzzle noun [C] a type of large EVERGREEN tree (= one that never loses its leaves) with stiff branches that spread out at the side and dark green, sharp leaves

ˈmonkey ˌwrench noun [C] mainly US a tool that has parts that can be moved to tighten or unfasten any size of NUT and BOLT

mono /ˈmɒn.əʊ/ (US) /ˈmɑː.noʊ/ noun; adj

▸noun [U] **SOUND** ▷ **1** recorded or broadcast sound that comes from a single direction: *The recording was available **in** mono or stereo.* **DISEASE** ▷ **2** US informal for **mononucleosis**

▸adj describes recorded or broadcast sound that comes from a single direction: *an old mono record player* → Compare **stereo, quadraphonic**

mono- /mɒn.əʊ-/ (US) /mɑː.noʊ-/ prefix one; single: *monolingual* ◦ *a monorail*

monochrome /ˈmɒn.ə.krəʊm/ (US) /ˈmɑː.nə.kroʊm/ adj **COLOUR** ▷ **1** using only black, white, and grey, or using only one colour: *Kodak still produces monochrome film.* ◦ *The park in winter is a depressing monochrome brown.* **BORING** ▷ **2** mainly UK not interesting or exciting: *a monochrome, dreary existence* • **monochromatic** /ˌmɒn.əʊ.krəˈmæt.ɪk/ (US) /ˌmɑː.noʊ.krəˈmæt̬-/ adj

monocle /ˈmɒn.ə.kl̩/ (US) /ˈmɑː.nə-/ noun [C] a round piece of glass worn, especially in the past, in front of one eye in order to help you to see more clearly

monocotyledon /ˌmɒn.əʊˌkɒt.ɪˈliː.dən/ (US) /ˌmɑː.nəˌkɑː.t̬əlˈiː-/ noun [C] specialized a type of plant that produces flowers and has only one COTYLEDON (= leaf part inside the seed). Monocotyledons include DAFFODILS and grasses.

monogamy /məˈnɒg.ə.mi/ (US) /məˈnɑː.gə-/ noun [U] the fact or custom of having a sexual relationship or marriage with only one other person at a time → Compare **bigamy, polygamy** • **monogamous** /-məs/ adj *a monogamous relationship*

monogram /ˈmɒn.ə.græm/ (US) /ˈmɑː.nə-/ noun [C] a symbol, usually formed from the first letters of a person's names joined together, that is sewn or printed on clothes or other possessions: *handkerchiefs/towels with his monogram in the corner* • **monogrammed** /-græmd/ adj *monogrammed envelopes*

monograph /ˈmɒn.ə.grɑːf/, /-græf/ (US) /ˈmɑː.nə.græf/ noun [C] a long article or a short book on a particular subject: *a monograph **on** Beethoven's symphonies*

monolingual /ˌmɒn.əʊˈlɪŋ.gwəl/ (US) /ˌmɑː.noʊ-/ adj speaking or using only one language: *This is a monolingual dictionary.* → Compare **bilingual, multilingual**

monolith /ˈmɒn.ə.lɪθ/ (US) /ˈmɑː.nə-/ noun [C] a large block of stone standing by itself which was put up by people in the DISTANT past (= a long time ago)

monolithic /ˌmɒn.əˈlɪθ.ɪk/ (US) /ˌmɑː.nə-/ adj disapproving too large, too regular, or without interesting differences, and unwilling or unable to be changed: *monolithic state-run organizations*

monologue /ˈmɒn.əl.ɒg/ (US) /ˈmɑː.nə.lɑːg/ noun [C] **1** a long speech by one person: disapproving *He* subjected me to a monologue **on** his last stay in hospital. **2** a short play for one actor: *Alan Bennett wrote a series of monologues called 'Talking Heads'.*

monomania /ˌmɒn.əʊˈmeɪ.ni.ə/ (US) /ˌmɑː.noʊ-/ **noun** [C or U] a condition in which someone is extremely interested in one thing, in a way that is not normal • **monomaniac** /-æk/ **adj, noun** • **monomaniacal** /-məˈnaɪə.kəl/ **adj**

mononucleosis /ˌmɒn.əʊˌnjuː.kliˈəʊ.sɪs/ (US) /ˌmɑː.noʊˌnuː.kliˈoʊ-/ **noun** [U] (informal **mono**) mainly US for **glandular fever** (= an infectious disease which makes you feel weak and ill for a long time)

monophthong /ˈmɒn.əf.θɒŋ/ (US) /ˈmɑː.nəf.θɑːŋ/ **noun** [C] specialized a vowel sound in which the tongue stays in one position → Compare **diphthong, triphthong**

monoplane /ˈmɒn.ə.pleɪn/ (US) /ˈmɑː.nə-/ **noun** [C] an aircraft with a single pair of wings → Compare **biplane**

monopolize (UK usually **monopolise**) /məˈnɒp.əl.aɪz/ (US) /-ˈnɑː.pə.laɪz/ **verb** [T] **BUSINESS** ▷ **1** in business, to control something completely and to prevent other people having any effect on what happens: *The company had monopolized the photography market for so many decades that they didn't worry about competition from other companies.* **PERSON/CONVERSATION** ▷ **2** If someone monopolizes a person or a conversation, they talk a lot or stop other people being involved: *She completely monopolized the conversation at lunch.* • **monopolization** (UK usually **monopolisation**) /məˌnɒp.əl.aɪˈzeɪ.ʃən/ (US) /-ˌnɑː.pəl-/ **noun** [U]

M

monopoly /məˈnɒp.əl.i/ (US) /-ˈnɑː.pəl-/ **noun** [C or S] **C2** (an organization or group that has) complete control of something, especially an area of business, so that others have no share: *The government is determined to protect its tobacco monopoly.* ◦ *Is Microsoft a monopoly?* ◦ *The drafting of a new constitution cannot be **a** monopoly **of** the white minority regime (= other people should do it too).* ◦ *He does not **have a/the** monopoly **on** (= he is not the only one who has) good looks.* • **monopolistic** /məˌnɒp.əlˈɪs.tɪk/ (US) /-ˌnɑː.pəˈlɪs-/ **adj** usually disapproving

monorail /ˈmɒn.ə.reɪl/ (US) /ˈmɑː.nə-/ **noun** [C] a railway system that has a single RAIL (= long metal bar on which the train travels) often above ground level, or the train that travels along it

monosaccharide /ˌmɒn.əʊˈsæk.ər.aɪd/ (US) /ˌmɑː.noʊˈsæk.ə.raɪd/ **noun** [C] specialized a simple type of CARBOHYDRATE, such as GLUCOSE and FRUCTOSE, formed of MOLECULES that cannot be broken down into any simpler form → Compare **polysaccharide**

monosodium glutamate /ˌmɒn.əˌsəʊ.di.əmˈgluː.tə.meɪt/ (US) /ˌmɑː.nəˌsoʊ.di.əmˈgluː.t̬ə-/ **noun** [U] (abbreviation **MSG**) a chemical that is sometimes added to food to improve the taste

monosyllabic /ˌmɒn.ə.sɪˈlæb.ɪk/ (US) /ˌmɑː.noʊ-/ **adj** **PERSON** ▷ **1** disapproving saying very little in a way that is rude or unfriendly: *He grunted a monosyllabic reply.* **WORD** ▷ **2** specialized containing only one syllable • **monosyllabically** /-ɪ.kəl.i/ **adv** disapproving

monosyllable /ˈmɒn.əˌsɪl.ə.bl̩/ (US) /ˈmɑː.noʊ-/ **noun** [C] specialized a word which contains only one syllable: *'Jump', 'buy', and 'heat' are monosyllables.*

monotheism /ˌmɒn.əʊˈθiː.ɪ.zəm/ (US) /ˌmɑː.noʊ-/ **noun** [U] the belief that there is only one god • **monotheistic** /-θiːˈɪs.tɪk/ **adj** *The three monotheistic religions with the most followers are Christianity, Judaism, and Islam.*

monotone /ˈmɒn.ə.təʊn/ (US) /ˈmɑː.nə.toʊn/ **noun** [U] a sound which stays on the same note without going higher or lower: disapproving *He spoke in a boring monotone.*

monotonous /məˈnɒt.ən.əs/ (US) /-ˈnɑː.t̬ən-/ **adj** **C1** not changing and therefore boring: *a monotonous job* ◦ *a monotonous voice* ◦ *The music became monotonous after a while.* • **monotonously** /-li/ **adv**

monotony /məˈnɒt.ən.i/ (US) /-ˈnɑː.t̬ən-/ **noun** [U] (also **monotonousness**) a situation in which something stays the same and is therefore boring: *The monotony of motorway driving causes many accidents.* ◦ *The routine was the same every day, with nothing to **break/relieve** the monotony.*

monounsaturated /ˌmɒn.əʊ.ʌnˈsætʃ.ər.eɪ.tɪd/ (US) /ˌmɑː.noʊ.ʌnˈsætʃ.ə.reɪ.t̬ɪd/ **adj** specialized refers to a fat or oil such as OLIVE OIL that is thought to be healthier than SATURATED FAT because its chemical structure contains one DOUBLE BOND → Compare **polyunsaturated**

monozygotic /ˌmɒn.əʊ.zaɪˈgɒt.ɪk/ (US) /ˌmɑː.noʊ.zaɪˈgɑː.t̬ɪk/ **adj** specialized If TWINS are monozygotic, they develop from just one egg and are commonly described as IDENTICAL TWINS. → Compare **dizygotic**

Monsignor /ˌmɒnˈsiː.njər/ (US) /ˌmɑːnˈsiː.njɚ/ **noun** (written abbreviation **Msgr**) a title used with the name of a Roman Catholic priest of high rank: *Monsignor Healey* ◦ [as form of address] *This way please, Monsignor.*

monsoon /mɒnˈsuːn/ (US) /mɑːn-/ **noun** [C] the season of heavy rain during the summer in hot Asian countries: *The failure of **the** monsoon would destroy harvests on which a billion people rely.*

monster /ˈmɒn.stər/ (US) /ˈmɑːn.stɚ/ **noun; adj; verb**

▸**noun** [C] **CREATURE** ▷ **1** **B1** any imaginary frightening creature, especially one that is large and strange: *a sea monster* ◦ *prehistoric monsters* ◦ *the Loch Ness monster* **PERSON** ▷ **2** **C2** a cruel and frightening person: *You'd have to be a monster to hit a child like that.* **LARGE** ▷ **3** informal something that is very big, or too big: *You should have seen the onions he grew for the competition – they were monsters!*

▸**adj** [before noun] informal very big: *a monster housing development*

▸**verb** [T] informal to criticize someone severely: *Andy Smith has been monstered by the media.*

monstrosity /mɒnˈstrɒs.ə.ti/ (US) /mɑːnˈstrɑː.sə.t̬i/ **noun** [C] something that is very ugly and usually large: *The new office building is a real monstrosity.*

monstrous /ˈmɒn.strəs/ (US) /ˈmɑːn-/ **adj** **BAD** ▷ **1** very cruel: *a monstrous crime* ◦ *monstrous cruelty* ◦ *But that's monstrous – he can't be allowed to get away with it!* **CREATURE** ▷ **2** like a monster: *The illustrations show monstrous beasts with bodies like bears and heads like tigers.*

monstrously /ˈmɒn.strəs.li/ (US) /ˈmɑːn-/ **adv** in a very cruel way: *monstrously unfair*

montage /ˈmɒn.tɑːʒ/ (US) /ˈmɑːn-/ **noun** [C or U] a piece of work produced by combining smaller parts, or the process of making such a work: *The ads feature a montage **of** images – people surfing, playing football and basketball.*

month /mʌnθ/ **noun** [C] **A1** a period of about four weeks, especially one of the twelve periods into which a year is divided: *I'll be away for a month from mid-June to mid-July.* ◦ *February is the shortest month.* ◦ *a two-month-old puppy* ◦ *The project will be finished **in** the next few months (= quite soon).* ◦ *They haven't been in contact with me **for** months (= a long time).* ◦ *She has two months' holiday every year.*

IDIOM **not in a month of Sundays** If you say that something will not happen in a month of Sundays, you mean that it is very unlikely to happen: *He's never going to get that finished in a month of Sundays!*

monthly /ˈmʌn.θli/ **adj, adv; noun**
▸**adj, adv** B1 happening or produced once a month: *monthly payments* ◦ *Most of these people are paid monthly.*
▸**noun** [C] a magazine that is published once a month

monument /ˈmɒn.jʊ.mənt/ US /ˈmɑːn-/ **noun** [C] **1** B2 a structure or building that is built to honour a special person or event: *In the square in front of the hotel stands a monument **to** all the people killed in the war.* **2 ancient/historic monument** B1 an old building or place that is an important part of a country's history: *Parts of the Berlin wall are being allowed to stand as **historic** monuments.*

IDIOM **be a monument to sth** to be an important and permanent result of an action or characteristic: *The annual arts festival is a monument to her vision and hard work.* ◦ *Protesters have called the building a monument to corporate greed.*

monumental /ˌmɒn.jʊˈmen.təl/ US /ˌmɑːn.jʊˈmen.t̬əl/ **adj** very big: *a monumental task* ◦ *a monumental waste of time* • **monumentally** /-i/ **adv** *monumentally dull*

moo /muː/ **noun** [C] (plural **moos**) (especially in children's books) the noise that a cow makes • **moo verb** [I]

moobs /muːbz/ **noun** [plural] slang fat on a man's chest that makes it look as if he has a woman's breasts

mooch /muːtʃ/ **verb; noun**
▸**verb** MOVE ▷ **1** [I usually + adv/prep] informal to walk or act slowly and without much purpose: disapproving *Stop mooching (**about/around**) in your room and do something useful!* GET ▷ **2** [I or T] US slang to get something without paying or working for it, or to borrow something without intending to return it: *You're old enough to get a job and stop mooching **off** your family.* ◦ *He mooched a ten **off** me, and I knew right then I'd never see it again.*
▸**noun** [S] informal a period of time spent walking around slowly and without much purpose: *I'm going for a mooch **round** the shops (= to look at what is there, not to buy a particular thing).*

mood /muːd/ **noun** [C] B1 the way you feel at a particular time: *She's **in a good/bad** mood.* ◦ *Her mood seemed to change during the course of the conversation.* ◦ *The drink had **put** him **in** an amiable mood.* ◦ *The public mood changed dramatically after the bombing.* ◦ *The mood of the crowd suddenly turned (= the crowd suddenly became) aggressive.*

IDIOMS **be in a mood** informal B2 to not be friendly to other people because you are feeling angry: *Ignore him – he's in a mood.* • **be in no mood for sth/to do sth** to not want to do something, often because you are angry: *I was in no mood for chatting.* • **be in one of your moods** informal If a person is in one of their moods, they are being unfriendly and angry in a way that is typical of them: *Tim's in one of his moods so I'm keeping out of his way.* • **be in the mood** C2 to feel like doing or having something: *I'm not really in the mood **for** shopping.*

moody /ˈmuː.di/ **adj** If someone is moody, they are often unfriendly because they feel angry or unhappy: *a moody teenager* ◦ *He can be quite moody.* • **moodily** /-dɪ.li/ **adv** • **moodiness** /-nəs/ **noun** [U]

moon /muːn/ **noun; verb**
▸**noun 1 the moon** [S] A2 the round object which moves in the sky around the Earth and can be seen at night: *What time does the moon **rise/set** (= appear/disappear in the sky)?* **2** [S or U] the shape made by the amount of the moon that you can see at a particular time: *There's no moon (= you cannot see the moon) tonight.* ◦ *a crescent/full/new moon* **3** [C] a similar round object that moves around another planet: *Jupiter has at least 16 moons.*

IDIOMS **be over the moon** B2 to be very pleased: *She was over the moon **about/with** her new bike.* • **many moons ago** old-fashioned a long time ago

▸**verb** [I usually + adv/prep] to move or spend time in a way which shows little interest and no clear purpose: *She was mooning **about/around** the house all weekend.* ◦ *He's been mooning **over** (= looking foolishly at) those holiday photos all afternoon.*

moonbeam /ˈmuːn.biːm/ **noun** [C] a beam or line of light which comes from the moon

Moonie /ˈmuː.ni/ **noun** [C] a member of the Unification Church, a religious group whose members must obey its rules and teachings completely: *He has joined the Moonies.*

mooning /ˈmuː.nɪŋ/ **noun** [U] slang the act of showing your naked bottom as a joke or as a protest

moonless /ˈmuːn.ləs/ **adj** without light from the moon: *a dark moonless night*

moonlight /ˈmuːn.laɪt/ **noun; verb**
▸**noun** [U] B2 the pale light of the moon: *The young lovers sat in the moonlight.*

IDIOM **do a moonlight flit** UK informal to leave secretly, especially to avoid paying money that you owe: *When he discovered the police were after him, he did a moonlight flit.*

▸**verb** [I] (**moonlighted**) to work at an extra job, especially without telling your main employer: *A qualified teacher, he moonlighted **as** a cabbie in the evenings to pay the rent.* • **moonlighting** /-laɪ.tɪŋ/ US /-laɪ.t̬ɪŋ/ **noun** [U]

moonlit /ˈmuːn.lɪt/ **adj** [before noun] able to be seen because of the light of the moon: *a bright, moonlit night*

moonshine /ˈmuːn.ʃaɪn/ **noun** [U] ALCOHOL ▷ **1** mainly US alcoholic drink made illegally SPEECH ▷ **2** informal silly talk or ideas → Synonym **nonsense**

moor /mɔːr/, /mʊər/ US /mʊr/ **noun; verb**
▸**noun** [C] an open area of hills covered with rough grass
▸**verb** [I or T] to tie a boat so that it stays in the same place: *We moored further up the river.* ◦ *We moored the boat **to** a large tree root.*

moorhen /ˈmɔː.hen/, /ˈmʊə-/ US /ˈmʊr-/ **noun** [C] a small, black bird which lives near water

mooring /ˈmɔː.rɪŋ/, /ˈmʊə-/ US /ˈmʊr.ɪŋ/ **noun 1** [C] a place to tie a boat: *We rented a mooring.* **2 moorings** [plural] the ropes or chains which keep a boat from moving away from a particular place

Moorish /ˈmʊə.rɪʃ/ US /ˈmʊr.ɪʃ/ **adj** of the Muslim people who were the rulers of Spain from 711 to 1492: *Moorish architecture*

moorland /ˈmɔː.lənd/, /ˈmʊə-/ US /ˈmʊr-/ **noun** [C or U] an area of MOOR

moose /muːs/ **noun** [C] (plural **moose**) (UK also **elk**) a type of large DEER with large, flat horns and a long nose that lives in the forests of North America, northern Europe, and Asia

moot /muːt/ **verb; adj; noun**
▸**verb** [T] formal to suggest something for discussion: *The idea was first mooted as long ago as the 1840s.*
▸**adj** DISCUSSION ▷ **1** often discussed or argued about

M

and having no real answer: *It's **a** moot **point** whether building more roads reduces traffic congestion.* **LEGAL CASE** ▷ **2** mainly US legal having no practical use or meaning: *The district attorney said if his conviction was upheld on appeal, the state prosecution would become moot.*

▸**noun** [C] specialized a trial or discussion dealing with an imaginary legal case, performed by students as part of their legal training but in exactly the same way as a real one: *a moot court*

mop /mɒp/ (US) /mɑːp/ **noun**; **verb**

▸**noun** [C] a stick with soft material fixed at one end, especially used for washing floors or dishes: *a floor mop* ∘ *a dish mop*

▸**verb** [T] (**-pp-**) **1** to use a mop to wash something: *He mopped the bathroom **floor**.* **2** to use a cloth to remove SWEAT from the face: *He kept pausing to mop his **brow**.*

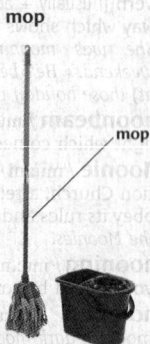

PHRASAL VERB **mop sth up** **CLEAN** ▷ **1** to use a cloth or a mop to remove liquid from the surface of something: *There's milk on the floor over there – could you get a cloth and mop it up?* **FINISH** ▷ **2** informal to finish dealing with something: *It took a week to mop up the last of the enemy soldiers (= defeat them).*

mope /məʊp/ (US) /moʊp/ **verb** [I] disapproving to be unhappy and unwilling to think or act in a positive way, especially because of a disappointment: *There's no point in sitting at home and moping – get out there and find yourself another job!*

PHRASAL VERB **mope about/around (somewhere)** to move about without any particular purpose or energy because you are unhappy or disappointed: *He was driving me mad, moping about the house all day.*

moped /ˈməʊ.ped/ (US) /ˈmoʊ-/ **noun** [C] a small motorcycle that has PEDALS (= parts that you press with your feet to move forward) that can be used when starting it or travelling up a hill

mopoke /ˈməʊ.pəʊk/ (US) /ˈmoʊ.poʊk/ **noun** [C] **BIRD** ▷ **1** a type of Australian and New Zealand OWL whose call sounds like its name **PERSON** ▷ **2** Australian English informal someone who is stupid or looks very unhappy

moppet /ˈmɒp.ɪt/ (US) /ˈmɑː.pɪt/ **noun** [C] informal an attractive young child, especially a girl: *a curly-haired moppet*

moral /ˈmɒr.əl/ (US) /ˈmɔːr-/ **adj**; **noun**

▸**adj** **1** (B2) relating to the standards of good or bad behaviour, fairness, honesty, etc. which each person believes in, rather than to laws: *It's her moral **obligation** to tell the police what she knows.* ∘ *It is not part of a novelist's job to make a moral **judgment**.* ∘ *She was the only politician to condemn the proposed law on moral grounds (= for moral reasons).* ∘ *The Democrats are attempting to **capture the** moral **high ground** (= are trying to appear more honest and good than the other political parties).* → Compare **amoral, immoral** **2** (C1) behaving in ways considered by most people to be correct and honest: *She's a very moral woman.* ∘ *Oh, stop being so moral!* ∘ *Is TV responsible for weakening people's moral **fibre** (= ability to behave well and honestly and work hard)?*

▸**noun** **STANDARDS** ▷ **1 morals** (C2) [plural] standards for good or bad character and behaviour: *public/private morals* ∘ old-fashioned disapproving *a person of **loose** morals (= whose character or sexual behaviour is considered unacceptable)* **MESSAGE** ▷ **2** [C] The moral of a story, event, or experience is the message which you understand from it about how you should or should not behave: *And the moral **of/to** the story is that honesty is always the best policy.*

ˌmoral ˈcompass **noun** [C] a natural feeling that makes people know what is right and wrong and how they should behave: *Some people believe that the increase in crime shows that society is losing its moral compass.*

morale /məˈrɑːl/ **noun** [U] (C2) the amount of confidence felt by a person or group of people, especially when in a dangerous or difficult situation: *A couple of victories would improve the team's morale enormously.* ∘ *There have been a lot of recent redundancies so morale is fairly low.*

moralist /ˈmɒr.əl.ɪst/ (US) /ˈmɔːr-/ **noun** [C] disapproving a person who tries to force or teach other people to behave in ways he or she considers to be most correct and honest

moralistic /ˌmɒr.əlˈɪs.tɪk/ (US) /ˌmɔːr-/ **adj** disapproving Someone or something that is moralistic judges people by fixed and possibly unfair standards of right and wrong and tries to force or teach them to behave according to these standards: *Drug addicts need sympathetic, not moralistic, treatment.*

morality /məˈræl.ə.ti/ (US) /mɔːˈræl.ə.t̬i/ **noun** [C or U] a personal or social set of standards for good or bad behaviour and character, or the quality of being right, honest, or acceptable: *They argued for a new morality based on self-sacrifice and honesty.* ∘ *I have to question the morality **of** forcing poor people to pay for their medical treatment.*

moralize disapproving (UK usually **moralise**) /ˈmɒr.əl.aɪz/ (US) /ˈmɔːr-/ **verb** [I] to express judgments about what is morally right and wrong: *his parents' self-righteous moralizing*

morally /ˈmɒr.əl.i/ (US) /ˈmɔːr-/ **adv** (B2) based on principles that you or people in general consider to be right, honest, or acceptable: *Morally, you're right, but in practice I don't think it would work.* ∘ *For a teacher to hit a child is not just morally **wrong** but also illegal.* ∘ *She thinks she's morally superior to the rest of us.*

ˌmoral maˈjority **noun** [S] those people in a society, especially the US in the 20th century, who support severe and old-fashioned Christian standards of behaviour

ˌmoral supˈport **noun** [U] If you give someone moral support, you encourage them and show that you approve of what they are doing, rather than giving them practical help.

ˌmoral ˈvictory **noun** [C] an occasion when you prove that your beliefs are right, although you lose an argument

morass /məˈræs/ **noun** [C usually singular] **COMPLICATED SITUATION** ▷ **1** something that is extremely complicated and difficult to deal with and makes any progress almost impossible: *The morass **of** rules and regulations is delaying the start of the project.* **WET GROUND** ▷ **2** literary an area of soft, wet ground in which it is easy to get stuck

moratorium /ˌmɒr.əˈtɔː.ri.əm/ (US) /ˌmɔːr.əˈtɔːr.i-/

noun [C] (plural **moratoriums** or **moratoria**) formal a stopping of an activity for an agreed amount of time: *a five-year worldwide moratorium* ***on*** *nuclear weapons testing*

morbid /ˈmɔː.bɪd/ (US) /ˈmɔːr-/ **adj** disapproving too interested in unpleasant subjects, especially death: *a morbid* ***fascination*** *with death* • **morbidity** /ˌmɔːˈbɪd.ɪ.ti/ (US) /ˌmɔːrˈbɪd.ə.t̬i/ **noun** [U] • **morbidly** /-li/ **adv**

mordant /ˈmɔː.dənt/ (US) /ˈmɔːr-/ **adj** formal (especially of humour) cruel and criticizing in a humorous way: *mordant* ***wit/humour*** ◦ *a mordant remark* → Synonym **biting** • **mordantly** /-li/ **adv**

more /mɔːʳ/ (US) /mɔːr/ **determiner, pronoun, adv 1** (A1) a larger or extra number or amount: *Would you like some more food?* ◦ *The doctors can't cope with* ***any*** *more patients.* ◦ *Add some more cream to the sauce.* ◦ *You need to listen more and talk less!* ◦ *More people live in the capital* ***than*** *in the whole of the rest of the country.* ◦ *We spent more time on the last job* ***than*** *usual.* ◦ *The noise was more* ***than*** *I could bear.* ◦ *It was a hundred times more fun* ***than*** *I'd expected.* ◦ *She's more* ***of a*** *poet* ***than*** *a novelist.* ◦ *Bring as much food as you can –* ***the*** *more,* ***the better.*** **2** (A1) used to form the COMPARATIVE of many adjectives and adverbs: *She couldn't be more beautiful.* ◦ *Let's find a more sensible way of doing it.* ◦ *You couldn't be more wrong.* ◦ *He finds physics* ***far/much*** *more difficult* ***than*** *other science subjects.* ◦ *Play that last section more passionately.* **3** used to emphasize the large size of something: *More* ***than*** *20,000 demonstrators crowded into the square.* **4 more and more** (B2) increasingly: *It gets more and more difficult to understand what is going on.* **5 the more...the more/less** used to say that when an action or event continues, there will be a particular result: *The more he drank, the more violent he became.* ◦ *The more he insisted he was innocent, the less they seemed to believe him.*

> **!** Common mistake: **more**
>
> **Warning:** do not use **more** before the **-er** form of an adjective.
> Don't say 'more happier/easier/better', just say **happier/easier/better**:
> ~~*Having a computer at home would make my life more easier.*~~

> **!** Usage: **more**
>
> The opposite of **more** is **fewer** for countable nouns and **less** for uncountable nouns:
> *He takes more exercise now.*
> *He takes less exercise now.*
> *He smokes fewer cigarettes.*

IDIOMS **all the more** even more than before: *Several publishers rejected her book, but that just made her all the more determined.* • **any more** (A2) If you do not do something or something does not happen any more, you have stopped doing it or it does not now happen: *I don't do yoga any more.* • **couldn't agree/disagree more** formal If you say that you couldn't agree/disagree more, you mean that you agree/disagree completely. • **more often than not** most of the time: *More often than not, a student will come up with the right answer.* • **more or less 1** mostly: *The project was more or less a success.* **2** (B2) approximately: *It's 500 kilos, more or less.* **3** (B2) very nearly: *He more or less admitted he'd done it.* • **more than** very: *It's more than* ***likely*** *that there's oil here under the ground.* ◦ *I was more than a little (= I was very) curious about the whole business.* ◦ formal *We will be more than glad/happy/willing to help you in any way we can.* • **the more the merrier** used to say an occasion will be more enjoyable if a lot of people are there: *'Do you mind if I bring a couple of friends to your party?' 'Not at all – the more the merrier!'* • **not/no more than** used to emphasize how small an amount is: *There are beautiful mountains not more than ten minutes' drive away.* • **that's more like it!** informal used to show that you think something or someone has improved

moreish /ˈmɔː.rɪʃ/ (US) /ˈmɔːr.ɪʃ/ **adj** UK informal approving (of food) having a very pleasant taste and making you want to eat more: *These peanuts are very moreish, aren't they?*

moreover /ˌmɔːˈrəʊ.vəʳ/ (US) /ˌmɔːrˈoʊ.vɚ/ **adv** formal (B2) (used to add information) also and more importantly: *The whole report is badly written. Moreover, it's inaccurate.*

mores /ˈmɔː.reɪz/ (US) /ˈmɔːr.eɪz/ **noun** [plural] formal the traditional customs and ways of behaving that are typical of a particular (part of) society: *middle-class mores* ◦ *the mores and culture of the Japanese*

morgue /mɔːg/ (US) /mɔːrg/ **noun** [C] mainly US for **mortuary** (= place where dead bodies are kept)

moribund /ˈmɒr.ɪ.bʌnd/ (US) /ˈmɔːr-/ **adj** formal disapproving (especially of an organization or business) not active or successful: *How can the Trade Department be revived from its present moribund state?*

Mormon /ˈmɔː.mən/ (US) /ˈmɔːr-/ **noun** [C] a member of a religious group called the Church of Jesus Christ of Latter-Day Saints, which began in the US in 1830

morn /mɔːn/ (US) /mɔːrn/ **noun** [C] literary a morning: *Yonder breaks a new and glorious morn.*

morning /ˈmɔː.nɪŋ/ (US) /ˈmɔːr-/ **noun; exclamation**

▸**noun** [C or U] **1** (A1) the part of the day from the time when the sun rises or you wake up until the middle of the day or LUNCH time: *a beautiful/sunny/wet morning* ◦ *I work three mornings a week at the bookshop.* ◦ *She only works* ***in the*** *mornings.* ◦ *What's our schedule for* ***this*** *morning?* ◦ *I'd like an appointment for* ***tomorrow*** *morning, please.* ◦ *I'll see you* ***on*** *Saturday morning.* ◦ *I had too much to drink at Sarah's party, and I felt terrible* ***the*** *morning* ***after.*** **2 in the morning a** (A1) during the early part of the day: *I listen to the radio in the morning.* **b** (B1) at some time between twelve o'clock at night and twelve o'clock in the middle of the day: *The murder took place* ***at*** *four in the morning.* **c** (B1) the next morning: *She said she would see you in the morning.*

IDIOM **morning, noon, and night** all the time: *Our neighbour's baby cries morning, noon, and night.*

▸**exclamation** informal a friendly way of greeting someone when you meet them in the morning: *Morning, Sue! How are you today?* → Compare **good morning**

ˌmorning-ˈafter ˌpill **noun** [C usually singular] a pill containing a drug which prevents a woman from getting pregnant if it is taken after she has had sex

ˈmorning ˌdress **noun** [U] (also **ˈmorning ˌsuit**) a very formal set of clothes worn by some men on occasions such as marriage ceremonies, including a long black or grey coat, STRIPED trousers, and a TOP HAT

ˈmorning ˌperson **noun** [C] informal someone who feels awake and full of energy in the mornings: *He's not really a morning person – he doesn't speak until about eleven o'clock!*

mornings /ˈmɔː.nɪŋz/ (US) /ˈmɔːr-/ **adv** mainly US every morning: *Mornings we go running in the park.*

ˈmorning ˌsickness **noun** [U] the feeling of wanting

M

to vomit experienced by some women during the first months of pregnancy

the ˌmorning ˈstar noun [S] a planet, especially Venus, that can be seen shining brightly in the east just before or as the sun rises

moron /ˈmɔː.rɒn/ ⓤⓢ /ˈmɔːr.ɑːn/ noun [C] informal a very stupid person: *Some moron smashed into the back of my car yesterday.* ◦ [as form of address] *You moron!*

moronic /məˈrɒn.ɪk/ ⓤⓢ /mɔːˈrɑː.nɪk/ adj informal disapproving very stupid: *a moronic grin* ◦ *some really moronic suggestions*

morose /məˈrəʊs/ ⓤⓢ /-ˈroʊs/ adj unhappy, annoyed, and unwilling to speak or smile: *a morose expression* ◦ *Why are you so morose these days?* → Synonym **sullen** • **morosely** /-li/ adv • **moroseness** /-nəs/ noun [U]

morph /mɔːf/ ⓤⓢ /mɔːrf/ verb [I or T] to change one image into another, or combine them, using a computer program: *The video showed a man morphing* ***into*** *a tiger.*

morpheme /ˈmɔː.fiːm/ ⓤⓢ /ˈmɔːr-/ noun [C] specialized the smallest unit of language that has its own meaning, either a word or a part of a word: *'Worker' contains two morphemes – 'work' and '-er'.*

morphine /ˈmɔː.fiːn/ ⓤⓢ /ˈmɔːr-/ noun [U] a drug made from OPIUM, used to stop people from feeling pain or to make people feel calmer

morphology /mɔːˈfɒl.ə.dʒi/ ⓤⓢ /mɔːrˈfɑː.lə-/ noun [U] specialized the scientific study of the structure and form of either animals and plants or words and phrases • **morphological** /ˌmɔː.fəˈlɒdʒ.ɪ.kəl/ ⓤⓢ /ˌmɔːr.fəˈlɑː.dʒɪ-/ adj

M

morris dancing /ˈmɒr.ɪsˌdɑːn.sɪŋ/ ⓤⓢ /ˈmɔːr.ɪsˌdæn-/ noun [U] a type of traditional English dancing in which a group of people, especially men, dance together, wearing special clothes decorated with little bells • **morris dance** /-ˌdɑːns/ ⓤⓢ /-ˌdæns/ noun [C] • **morris dancer** /-ˌdɑːn.səʳ/ ⓤⓢ /-ˌdæn.sɚ/ noun [C]

morrow /ˈmɒr.əʊ/ ⓤⓢ /ˈmɑːr.oʊ/ noun [S] literary the next day, or TOMORROW: *They arranged to meet* ***on the*** *morrow.*

Morse code /ˌmɔːsˈkəʊd/ ⓤⓢ /ˌmɔːrsˈkoʊd/ noun [U] a system used for sending messages, in which letters and numbers are represented by short and long marks, sounds, or flashes of light

morsel /ˈmɔː.səl/ ⓤⓢ /ˈmɔːr-/ noun [C] **1** a very small piece of food: *a morsel* ***of*** *cheese* ◦ *The prisoners ate every last morsel.* **2** a very small piece or amount: *a morsel* ***of*** *good news*

mortal /ˈmɔː.təl/ ⓤⓢ /ˈmɔːr.t̬əl/ adj; noun

►adj literary **1** (of living things, especially people) unable to continue living for ever; having to die: *For all men are mortal.* → Compare **immortal** **2** causing death: *a mortal injury/illness* ◦ *men engaged in mortal* ***combat*** *(= fighting until one of them dies)* ◦ figurative *New computing technology dealt a mortal* ***blow*** *to the power of the old printing unions.* → Compare **lethal** **3 mortal dread/fear/terror** extreme ANXIETY about or fear of someone or something: *We live in mortal dread of further attacks.* **4 mortal enemy, danger, threat, etc.** a very serious and dangerous enemy, danger, threat, etc.

►noun [C] mainly humorous an ordinary person, rather than a god or a special, important, or powerful person: *The police officers guarding the door let in the celebrities, but they prevented us* ***lesser/mere*** *mortals from going inside.*

mortality /mɔːˈtæl.ə.ti/ ⓤⓢ /mɔːrˈtæl.ə.t̬i/ noun [U] formal **1** the way that people do not live for ever: *Her death made him more aware of his own mortality.* → Compare **immortality** **2** ⓒ the number of deaths within a particular society and within a particular period of time: *the mortality* ***rate*** ◦ ***Infant*** *mortality is much higher in the poorest areas of the city.*

mortally /ˈmɔː.təl.i/ ⓤⓢ /ˈmɔːr.t̬əl-/ adv **1** so severe that death is likely: *mortally* ***wounded*** **2** extremely: *Apparently he was mortally* ***offended****.*

ˌmortal ˈsin noun [C usually singular] in the Roman Catholic religion, an action that is so bad that you will be punished for ever after your death if you do not ask God to forgive you

mortar /ˈmɔː.təʳ/ ⓤⓢ /ˈmɔːr.t̬ɚ/ noun **MIXTURE** ▷ **1** [U] a mixture of sand, water, and CEMENT or LIME that is used to fix bricks or stones to each other when building walls **GUN** ▷ **2** [C] a large gun with a short, wide BARREL (= part shaped like a tube) which fires bombs or other explosives very high into the air, or an explosive device shot from such a gun **BOWL** ▷ **3** [C] a hard, strong bowl in which substances are crushed into a powder by hitting or rubbing them with a PESTLE (= heavy tool): *Use a* ***pestle and*** *mortar to crush the spices.*

mortarboard /ˈmɔː.tə.bɔːd/ ⓤⓢ /ˈmɔːr.t̬ɚ.bɔːrd/ noun [C] a black hat with a square, flat top, worn on formal occasions by some teachers and students at college or university, and in the past by some school teachers

mortgage /ˈmɔː.gɪdʒ/ ⓤⓢ /ˈmɔːr-/ noun; verb

►noun [C] an agreement which allows you to borrow money from a bank or similar organization, especially in order to buy a house or apartment, or the amount of money itself: *They* ***took out*** *a £40,000 mortgage (= they borrowed £40,000) to buy the house.* ◦ *a monthly mortgage* ***payment***

►verb [T] to borrow money to buy a house or apartment: *The house was mortgaged* ***up to the hilt*** *(= the full value of the house had been borrowed).*

mortgagee /ˌmɔː.gɪˈdʒiː/ ⓤⓢ /ˌmɔːr-/ noun [C] specialized a bank or similar organization which gives mortgages to people, especially so that they can buy a house or apartment

mortician /mɔːˈtɪʃ.ən/ ⓤⓢ /mɔːr-/ noun [C] US for **undertaker**

mortification /ˌmɔː.tɪ.fɪˈkeɪ.ʃən/ ⓤⓢ /ˌmɔːr.t̬ə.fɪ-/ noun [U] a feeling of being very embarrassed: ***To the*** *mortification* ***of*** *the show's organizers, the top performer withdrew at the last minute.*

mortified /ˈmɔː.tɪ.faɪd/ ⓤⓢ /ˈmɔːr.t̬ə-/ adj very embarrassed: [+ to infinitive] *She was absolutely mortified to hear her son swearing at the teacher.*

mortify /ˈmɔː.tɪ.faɪ/ ⓤⓢ /ˈmɔːr.t̬ə-/ verb [T] to make someone very embarrassed: *The thought of the incident still mortified her.*

mortifying /ˈmɔː.tɪ.faɪ.ɪŋ/ ⓤⓢ /ˈmɔːr.t̬ə-/ adj very embarrassing: *Catching head lice from your kids is a mortifying experience.*

mortise (also **mortice**) /ˈmɔː.tɪs/ ⓤⓢ /ˈmɔːr.t̬ɪs/ noun [C] specialized a rectangular hole in a piece of wood, stone, etc. into which another piece is fixed, so that they form a JOINT

ˈmortise ˌlock UK (US **ˈmortice ˌlock**) noun [C] a lock that is inside the edge of a door, so that it cannot be seen or removed when the door is closed

mortuary /ˈmɔː.tjʊ.ri/ ⓤⓢ /ˈmɔːr.tʃu.er.i/ noun [C] **1** UK (US **morgue**) a building, or a room in a hospital, where dead bodies are kept so that they can be examined before the funeral **2** US for **funeral parlour**

mosaic /məʊˈzeɪ.ɪk/ (US) /moʊ-/ **noun** [C] a pattern or picture made using many small pieces of coloured stone or glass: *a beautiful tenth-century mosaic* ◦ figurative *The country is now a cultural and social mosaic (= mixture) due to the influx of different ethnic groups.*

mosey /ˈməʊ.zi/ (US) /ˈmoʊ-/ **verb** [I usually + adv/prep] informal to walk or go slowly, usually without a special purpose: *I'll just mosey **on down** to the beach for a while.*

mosh /mɒʃ/ (US) /mɑːʃ/ **verb** [I] informal to dance energetically and violently at a rock CONCERT • **mosher** /ˈmɒʃ.əʳ/ (US) /ˈmɑː.ʃɚ/ **noun** [C]

ˈmosh ˌpit **noun** [C or S] informal the area in front of the stage at a rock CONCERT where members of the audience dance energetically and violently

Moslem /ˈmʊz.lɪm/ (US) /ˈmɑːz.lem/ **noun, adj** **Muslim**

mosque /mɒsk/ (US) /mɑːsk/ **noun** [C] (A2) a building for Islamic religious activities and worship

mosquito /məˈskiː.təʊ/ (US) /-t̬oʊ/ **noun** [C] (plural **mosquitoes** or **mosquitos**) (UK informal **mossie**, **mozzie**) (B1) a small flying insect that bites people and animals and sucks their blood: *Some types of mosquito transmit malaria to humans.*

mosˈquito ˌnet **noun** [C] a net that hangs over and around a bed to keep insects away from someone who is sleeping

moss /mɒs/ (US) /mɑːs/ **noun** [C or U] a very small, green or yellow plant that grows especially in wet earth or on rocks, walls, and tree TRUNKS: *The rocks near the river were covered with moss.* • **mossy** /ˈmɒs.i/ (US) /ˈmɑː.si/ **adj** *a mossy tree/rock/lawn*

> **! Common mistake: most of or most?**
>
> Use **most of** before a plural noun that has a determiner or pronoun in front of it:
>
> *Most of the students live with host families.*
>
> Before a plural noun that does not have a determiner or pronoun in front of it, don't say 'most of', just say **most**:
>
> ~~*Most of students live with host families.*~~
>
> *Most students live with host families.*
>
> **Warning:** To talk about almost all of something, do not use 'the' before **most** or **most of**:
>
> ~~*The most of the students live with host families.*~~

most /məʊst/ (US) /moʊst/ **determiner, pronoun, adv** **1** (A2) the biggest number or amount of; more than anything or anyone else: *What's **the** most you've ever won at cards?* ◦ *Which of you earns **the** most money?* ◦ *He wanted to do **the** most good he could with the £200, so he gave it to charity.* ◦ *The kids loved the fair, but they enjoyed the bumper cars most **of all**.* **2** (A2) used to form the SUPERLATIVE of many adjectives and adverbs: *Joanne is **the** most intelligent person I know.* ◦ *The department needs three more computers in order to work most effectively (= to work as effectively as possible).* **3** (A2) almost all: *I don't eat meat, but I like most types of fish.* ◦ *In this school, most **of** the children are from the Chinese community.* **4** formal very: *It was a most beautiful morning.* **5** mainly US informal almost: *You'll find her in the bar most **every** evening about six o'clock.* **6 make the most of sth** (B2) to take full advantage of something because it may not last long: *It's a lovely day – we must make the most of **it**.*

-most /-məʊst/ (US) /-moʊst/ **suffix** used to mean 'furthest': *Dunnet Head is the northernmost part of the British mainland (= the part that is farther to the north than any other part).*

mostly /ˈməʊst.li/ (US) /ˈmoʊst-/ **adv** (B1) mainly: *In the smaller villages, it's mostly (= usually) very quiet at nights.* ◦ *The band are mostly (= most of them are) teenagers.*

MOT /ˌem.əʊˈtiː/ (US) /-oʊ-/ **noun** [C] a test which all British road vehicles more than three years old have to pass each year in order to prove that they are safe to drive: *The car will fail its MOT if we don't get the brakes fixed.* ◦ *an MOT certificate* • **MOT** **verb** [T] (**MOTing**, **MOT'd**, **MOT'd**) *I want to **get/have** the car MOT'd before we drive to France.*

mote /məʊt/ (US) /moʊt/ **noun** [C] literary something, especially a piece of dust, that is so small it is almost impossible to see

motel /məʊˈtel/ (US) /moʊ-/ **noun** [C] (US also **ˈmotor ˌinn/lodge**) a hotel by the side of a road, usually with spaces for cars next to each room

moth /mɒθ/ (US) /mɑːθ/ **noun** [C] an insect with wings that is similar to a BUTTERFLY, usually flies at night, and is attracted to light: *Some types of moth eat holes in clothes.*

mothball /ˈmɒθ.bɔːl/ (US) /ˈmɑːθ.bɑːl/ **verb** [T] to stop work on an idea, plan, or job, but leaving it in such a way that you can start on it again at some point in the future: *Six coal pits were mothballed in the hope that they could be reopened in a time of better economic conditions.*

ˈmoth-ˌeaten **adj** If clothing or furniture is moth-eaten, it looks old and has holes in it: *I found some moth-eaten old sweaters in the back of the wardrobe.*

mother /ˈmʌð.əʳ/ (US) /-ɚ/ **noun; verb**

▸**noun** [C] **PARENT** ▷ **1** (A1) a female parent: *My mother was 21 when she got married.* ◦ *All the mothers **and fathers** had been invited to the end-of-term concert.* ◦ *The little kittens and their mother were all curled up asleep in the same basket.* ◦ [as form of address] formal or old-fashioned *May I borrow your car, Mother?* **RELIGIOUS WOMAN** ▷ **2** (also **Mother**) the title of a woman who is in charge of, or who has a high rank within, a CONVENT (= house of religious women): *Mother Theresa* ◦ *a mother **superior*** ◦ [as form of address] *Good morning, Mother.* **SLANG** ▷ **3** offensive mainly US **motherfucker**

IDIOMS **at your mother's knee** literary If you learned something at your mother's knee, you learned it when you were a child: *I learned to sew at my mother's knee.* • **the mother of all sth** informal an extreme example of something: *We got caught in the mother of all storms.*

▸**verb** [T] often disapproving to treat a person with great kindness and love and to try to protect them from anything dangerous or difficult: *Stop mothering her – she's 40 years old and can take care of herself.*

motherboard /ˈmʌð.ə.bɔːd/ (US) /-ɚ.bɔːrd/ **noun** [C] specialized the main PRINTED CIRCUIT BOARD that contains the CPU of a computer and makes it possible for the other parts of a computer to communicate with each other

ˈmother ˌcountry noun [S] the country where you were born or which you feel is your original home: *Even though she hasn't lived in Spain for 50 years, she still calls it her mother country.*

ˈmother ˌfigure noun [C] a woman who you feel you can ask for help, support, or advice

motherfucker /ˈmʌð.əˌfʌk.əʳ/ (US) /-ɚˌfʌk.ɚ/ **noun** [C] (also **mother**) **1** mainly US offensive an extremely insulting name for someone you hate or for someone who has made you angry: *If that motherfucker touches my car again, I'll break his fingers!* **2** US offensive an extremely unpleasant thing: *That was a motherfucker of an exam.* • **motherfucking** /-ɪŋ/ **adj** US offensive *He's a motherfucking son of a bitch.*

motherhood /ˈmʌð.ə.hʊd/ (US) /-ɚ-/ **noun** [U] the state or time of being a mother: *I don't feel ready for motherhood yet.*

mothering /ˈmʌð.ər.ɪŋ/ **noun** [U] the process of caring for children as their mother or of caring for people in the way that a mother does: *He did not receive good mothering as a child.* ◦ *a woman's mothering instinct*

ˈmother-in-law noun [C] (plural **mothers-in-law**) B2 the mother of your husband or wife

motherland /ˈmʌð.ə.lænd/ (US) /-ɚ-/ **noun** [U] **fatherland**

motherless /ˈmʌð.ə.ləs/ (US) /-ɚ-/ **adj** without a mother: *a poor motherless* ***child***

motherly /ˈmʌð.əl.i/ (US) /-ɚ.li/ **adj** usually approving describes a woman who treats other people with a lot of kindness and love and tries to make certain they are happy

ˌMother ˈNature noun [U] often humorous nature, especially when considered as a force that controls the weather and all living things

ˌmother-of-ˈpearl noun [U] a smooth, hard substance forming a layer inside the shells of some sea creatures. It is white but also seems to shine with different colours, and is used to make buttons and for decoration.

ˈMother's ˌDay noun [C usually singular] (UK also **ˈMothering ˌSunday**) a day each year when people give a card or present to their mother or do something special for her

ˌmother-to-ˈbe noun [C] a woman who is pregnant

ˌmother ˈtongue noun [C usually singular] B2 the first language that you learn when you are a baby, rather than a language learned at school or as an adult

motif /məʊˈtiːf/ (US) /moʊ-/ **noun** [C] **PATTERN** ▷ **1** a pattern or design: *We chose some curtains with a flower motif.* **IDEA** ▷ **2** an idea that is used many times in a piece of writing or music: *The motif* ***of*** *betrayal is crucial in all these stories.*

motile /ˈməʊ.taɪl/ (US) /ˈmoʊ.t̬əl/ **adj** specialized (especially of plants, organisms, and very small forms of life) able to move by itself • **motility** /məʊˈtɪl.ə.ti/ (US) /moʊˈtɪl.ə.t̬i/ **noun** [U] *sperm motility*

motion /ˈməʊ.ʃən/ (US) /ˈmoʊ-/ **noun; verb**

▸**noun MOVEMENT** ▷ **1** C2 [C or U] the act or process of moving, or a particular action or movement: *The violent motion of the ship upset his stomach.* ◦ *He rocked the cradle with a gentle backwards and forwards motion.* ◦ *They showed the goal again* ***in slow*** *motion (= at a slower speed so that the action could be more clearly seen).* **2** [C] UK a polite way of referring to the process of getting rid of solid waste from the body, or the waste itself: *The nurse asked if her motions were regular.* **SUGGESTION** ▷ **3** C2 [C] a formal suggestion made, discussed, and voted on at a meeting: [+ to infinitive] *Someone* ***proposed*** *a motion* ***to*** *increase the membership fee to £500 a year.* ◦ *The motion was* ***accepted/passed/defeated/rejected.***

IDIOMS **go through the motions** informal disapproving C2 to do something without thinking it is very important or having much interest in it: *He says he's been investigating my complaint, but I feel he's just going through the motions.* • **put/set sth in motion** to start a machine or process: *Once the printing processes have been put in motion, they're not so easy to stop.* ◦ *We wrote to the passport office to set the whole process in motion.*

▸**verb** [I or T, usually + adv/prep] to make a signal to someone, usually with your hand or head: *I saw him motion* ***to*** *the man at the door, who quietly left.* ◦ *Her attendants all gathered round her, but she motioned them away.* ◦ [+ obj + to infinitive] *He motioned me* ***to*** *sit down.*

motionless /ˈməʊ.ʃən.ləs/ (US) /ˈmoʊ-/ **adj** without moving: *The horse lay motionless on the ground, as if dead.*

ˈmotion ˌpicture noun [C] US formal for **movie**

ˈmotion ˌsickness noun [U] **travel sickness**

motivate /ˈməʊ.tɪ.veɪt/ (US) /ˈmoʊ.t̬ɪ-/ **verb** **1** C1 [T often passive] to cause someone to behave in a particular way: *Like so many people, he's motivated by greed.* ◦ *He is genuinely motivated by a desire to help people.* **2** C1 [T] to make someone want to do something well: [+ to infinitive] *Teaching is all about motivating people* ***to*** *learn.* • **motivated** /-veɪ.tɪd/ (US) /-veɪ.t̬ɪd/ **adj** B2 *a racially motivated murder* ◦ *Our staff are hard-working and* ***highly*** *motivated (= enthusiastic).*

motivation /ˌməʊ.tɪˈveɪ.ʃən/ (US) /ˌmoʊ.t̬ɪ-/ **noun** **ENTHUSIASM** ▷ **1** B2 [U] enthusiasm for doing something: *He's a bright enough student – he just lacks motivation.* ◦ *There seems to be a lack of motivation among the staff.* **REASON** ▷ **2** C1 [C] the need or reason for doing something: *What was the motivation* ***for*** *the attack?* ◦ *The motivation* ***behind*** *the decision is the desire to improve our service to our customers.*

motivational /ˌməʊ.tɪˈveɪ.ʃən.əl/ (US) /ˌmoʊ.t̬ɪ-/ **adj** [before noun] giving you motivation (= enthusiasm): *a motivational* ***speaker***

motive /ˈməʊ.tɪv/ (US) /ˈmoʊ.t̬ɪv/ **noun; adj**

▸**noun** [C] B2 a reason for doing something: *Why would she have killed him? She has no motive.* ◦ *Does he have a motive* ***for*** *lying about where he was?* ◦ *What is the motive* ***behind*** *(= the reason for) the bombing?* ◦ *I think you should* ***examine/question*** *their motives* ***in*** *offering to lend you the money.* ◦ *She denies that she has an* ***ulterior*** *(= secret) motive for making the donation.*

▸**adj** [before noun] specialized (of power or force) causing movement or action

motiveless /ˈməʊ.tɪv.ləs/ (US) /ˈmoʊ.t̬ɪv-/ **adj** without a motive: *an apparently motiveless murder*

mot juste /ˌməʊˈʒuːst/ (US) /ˌmoʊ-/ **noun** [C usually singular] (plural **mots justes**) formal the word or phrase that is exactly right in a particular situation

motley /ˈmɒt.li/ (US) /ˈmɑːt-/ **adj** [before noun] consisting of many different types and therefore appearing strange or of low quality: *There's a motley* ***assortment/collection*** *of old furniture in the house we're renting at the moment.* ◦ *The people who turned up to the meeting were a motley* ***crew*** *(= a group consisting of many different types of people).*

motocross /ˈməʊ.tə.krɒs/ (US) /ˈmoʊ.t̬ə.krɑːs/ **noun** [U] (also **scrambling**) the sport of racing over rough ground on special motorcycles

motor /ˈməʊ.tər/ (US) /ˈmoʊ.t̬ɚ/ noun; adj; verb

▸noun [C] DEVICE ▷ **1** (B2) a device that changes electricity or fuel into movement and makes a machine work: *The pump is powered by a small* ***electric*** *motor.* ◦ *Our washing machine needs a new motor.* ◦ mainly US *I've had a new motor (= engine) put in my car.* CAR ▷ **2** mainly UK old-fashioned a car: *Do you know anyone who's looking for a second-hand motor?*

▸adj [before noun] CAR ▷ **1** mainly UK connected with cars or other vehicles that have engines and use roads: *This has been a difficult year for the motor* ***industry/trade***. ◦ *motor* ***insurance*** MUSCLES ▷ **2** specialized relating to muscles that produce movement, or the nerves and parts of the brain that control these muscles: *He has poor motor* ***control/functions***.

▸verb [I] **1** UK old-fashioned to drive: *I was just motoring* ***along***, *minding my own business, when suddenly I was stopped by the police.* **2** informal to move or increase very quickly: *Shares have motored* ***ahead*** *as profits have risen.*

motorbike /ˈməʊ.tə.baɪk/ (US) /ˈmoʊ.t̬ɚ-/ noun [C] **1** (A2) UK a **motorcycle**: *She jumped on her motorbike and raced off down the road.* **2** US a bicycle with a small engine

motorboat /ˈməʊ.tə.bəʊt/ (US) /ˈmoʊ.t̬ɚ.boʊt/ noun [C] a small, fast boat that is powered by an engine

motorcade /ˈməʊ.tə.keɪd/ (US) /ˈmoʊ.t̬ɚ-/ noun [C] (US also **autocade**) a series of cars and other motor vehicles which moves slowly along a road carrying someone important, especially during an official ceremony

ˈmotor ˌcar noun [C] UK formal or old-fashioned a car

motorcycle /ˈməʊ.təˌsaɪ.kl/ (US) /ˈmoʊ.t̬ɚ-/ noun [C] (also **motorbike**) (A2) a vehicle with two wheels and an engine

motorcyclist /ˈməʊ.təˌsaɪ.klɪst/ (US) /ˈmoʊ.t̬ɚ-/ noun [C] a person who rides a motorcycle

ˈmotor home noun [C] a large motor vehicle that is designed to be lived in while travelling. It contains cooking equipment, one or more beds, and sometimes a toilet.

motoring /ˈməʊ.tər.ɪŋ/ (US) /ˈmoʊ.t̬ɚ-/ adj [before noun] mainly UK relating to driving: *motoring* ***costs*** ◦ *It was the first time he'd been convicted of a motoring* ***offence***.

ˈmotor ˌinn noun [C] US for **motel**

motorist /ˈməʊ.tər.ɪst/ (US) /ˈmoʊ.t̬ɚ-/ noun [C] (B2) a person who drives a car

motorized (UK usually **motorised**) /ˈməʊ.tər.aɪzd/ (US) /ˈmoʊ.t̬ə.raɪzd/ adj WITH AN ENGINE ▷ **1** specially fitted with an engine or motor: *a motorized wheelchair* SOLDIERS ▷ **2** Soldiers who are motorized are provided with wheeled vehicles that have engines: *motorized infantry*

ˈmotor ˌlodge noun [C] US for **motel**

motorman /ˈməʊ.tə.mən/ (US) /ˈmoʊ.t̬ɚ.mæn/ noun [C] (plural **-men** /-mən/, /-men/) US a driver of an underground train

motormouth /ˈməʊ.tə.maʊθ/ (US) /ˈmoʊ.t̬ɚ-/ noun [C] informal disapproving a person who talks quickly and continuously, often without considering what they are saying

ˈmotor ˌmower noun [C] a machine for cutting grass that has a motor

ˌmotor ˈneurone diˌsease noun [U] a disease which causes the muscles to become weak and results in death

ˈmotor ˌracing noun [U] the sport of racing extremely fast and powerful cars around a track

ˈmotor ˌscooter noun [C] a very light motorcycle with small wheels

ˈmotor ˌvehicle noun [C] formal or legal a vehicle that has an engine: *The council has forbidden motor vehicles from entering the city centre.*

motorway /ˈməʊ.tə.weɪ/ (US) /ˈmoʊ.t̬ɚ-/ noun [C] (A2) a wide road for fast-moving traffic, especially in the UK, Ireland, and some other countries, with a limited number of places at which drivers can enter and leave it: *Because of the bad weather, motorway (driving) conditions are expected to be hazardous tonight.* → Compare **expressway**, **freeway**

mottled /ˈmɒt.ld/ (US) /ˈmɑː.t̬ld/ adj covered with areas of different colours which do not form a regular pattern: *mottled skin*

motto /ˈmɒt.əʊ/ (US) /ˈmɑː.t̬oʊ/ noun [C] (plural **mottos** or **mottoes**) a short sentence or phrase that expresses a belief or purpose: *Her motto is 'Work hard, play hard'.*

mould /məʊld/ (US) /moʊld/ noun; verb

▸noun UK (US **mold**) SUBSTANCE ▷ **1** [U] a soft, green or grey growth which develops on old food or on objects that have been left for too long in warm, wet air: *There was mould on the cheese.* SHAPE ▷ **2** [C] a hollow container with a particular shape into which soft or liquid substances are poured, so that when the substance becomes hard it takes the shape of the container: *a cake/jelly mould* TYPE OF PERSON ▷ **3** [S] If someone is from or in a particular mould, they have the characteristics typical of a certain type of person: *He's* ***cast in*** *a very different mould from his brother.* ◦ *He's a player in the Federer mould.*

▸verb UK (US **mold**) **1** [T] to make a soft substance a particular shape: *This plastic is going to be moulded* ***into*** *plates.* ◦ *The children moulded little pots* ***out of/from*** *(= made them by shaping) clay.* **2** [T] to try to change or influence someone: *He kept trying to mould me* ***into*** *something he wanted me to be.* **3** [I usually + adv/prep] to fit the body very closely: *She was wearing an extremely tight costume which moulded* ***to/round*** *the contours of her body.*

moulder UK (US **molder**) /ˈməʊl.dər/ (US) /ˈmoʊl.dɚ/ verb [I] **1** to decay slowly: *I found these apples mouldering in the cupboard.* → Synonym **rot 2** to be left somewhere and not used or cared for: *There's an old bike that's been mouldering* ***away*** *in the shed for years.*

moulding UK (US **molding**) /ˈməʊl.dɪŋ/ (US) /ˈmoʊl-/ noun [C or U] a piece of wood, plastic, stone, etc. that has been made into a particular shape to decorate the top or bottom of a wall, or a door, window, or piece of furniture

mouldy UK (US **moldy**) /ˈməʊl.di/ (US) /ˈmoʊl-/ adj HAVING MOULD ▷ **1** covered with mould: *mouldy* ***bread/cheese*** BAD ▷ **2** [before noun] UK old-fashioned slang of little value; unpleasant: *All he gave me was a mouldy* ***old*** *50p.* **3** not modern or interesting: *The city's museums are filled with mouldy* ***old*** *collections.*

moult UK (US usually **molt**) /məʊlt/ (US) /moʊlt/ verb [I] (of a bird or animal) to lose feathers, skin, or hair as a natural process at a particular time of year so that new feathers, skin, or hair can grow

mound /maʊnd/ noun [C] PILE ▷ **1** a large pile of earth, stones, etc. like a small hill: *a* ***burial*** *mound (= a place where people were buried in ancient times)* **2** a large pile of something: *a mound* ***of*** *potatoes/papers* BASEBALL ▷ **3** US the raised area in baseball from which the PITCHER throws the ball

M

mount /maʊnt/ verb; noun

▸verb **INCREASE** ▷ **1** [I] to gradually increase, rise, or get bigger: *The children's excitement is mounting as Christmas gets nearer.* **GET ON** ▷ **2** [I or T] to get on a horse, bicycle, etc.. in order to ride: *She mounted her horse and rode off.* **GO UP** ▷ **3** [T] to go up or onto: *He mounted the platform and began to speak to the assembled crowd.* ◦ formal *Queen Elizabeth II mounted **the throne** (= became queen) in 1952.* **ORGANIZE** ▷ **4** [T] to organize and begin an activity or event: *to mount an attack/campaign/challenge/protest* ◦ *to mount an exhibition/display* **FIX** ▷ **5** [T] to fix something on a wall, in a frame, etc., so that it can be looked at or used: *The children's work has been mounted **on** cards and put up on the walls of the classroom.* ◦ *The CCTV camera is mounted above the main door.* **GUARD** ▷ **6** [T] to place someone on guard: *Sentries are mounted outside the palace at all times.* **7 mount guard (on/over sb)** to guard someone

PHRASAL VERB **mount up** to gradually become a large amount: *It isn't a good idea to let bills mount up.*

▸noun [C] **HORSE** ▷ **1** formal a horse: *an excellent mount for a child* **FOR A PICTURE, ETC.** ▷ **2** something, such as a piece of card, that you put something on to show it: *I'm looking for a piece of card I can use as a mount **for** this picture.*

Mount /maʊnt/ noun (written abbreviation **Mt**) used as part of the name of a mountain: *Mount Everest* ◦ *Mount Hood*

mountain /ˈmaʊn.tɪn/ (US) /-tᵊn/ noun [C] **VERY LARGE HILL** ▷ **1** (A2) a raised part of the Earth's surface, much larger than a hill, the top of which might be covered in snow: *The Matterhorn is one of the biggest mountains in Europe.* ◦ *The Rockies are a mountain **chain/range** in the western USA.* ◦ *I'd love to go mountain-**climbing**.* ◦ *We're going to the mountains (= an area where there are mountains) for our holiday.* **LARGE AMOUNT** ▷ **2** UK a large amount of food that is stored instead of being sold, so that prices for it do not fall: *a grain mountain* **3 a mountain of sth** a large amount of something: *I've got a mountain of work to do.*

IDIOM **make a mountain out of a molehill** to make a slight difficulty seem like a serious problem: *You're making a mountain out of a molehill. You wrote one bad essay – it doesn't mean you're going to fail your exam.*

ˌmountain ˌbike noun [C] a bicycle with thick tyres and a lot of GEARS, originally made for riding on hills and rough ground, but now often used on roads

mountainboarding /ˈmaʊn.tɪnˌbɔː.dɪŋ/ (US) /-tᵊnˌbɔːr-/ noun [U] the sport of riding down hills or mountains on a board with small wheels

mountaineer /ˌmaʊn.tɪˈnɪəʳ/ (US) /-tᵊnˈɪr/ noun [C] a person who climbs mountains as a sport or job

mountaineering /ˌmaʊn.tɪˈnɪə.rɪŋ/ (US) /-tᵊnˈɪr.ɪŋ/ noun [U] the sport or activity of climbing mountains

ˌmountain ˈlion noun [C] US for **puma**

mountainous /ˈmaʊn.tɪ.nəs/ (US) /-tᵊn.əs/ adj **1** having a lot of mountains: *a mountainous region* **2** very big: *mountainous waves*

mountainside /ˈmaʊn.tɪnˌsaɪd/ (US) /-tᵊn-/ noun [C usually singular] the side or slope of a mountain: *Can you see those goats high up **on** the mountainside?*

mountaintop /ˌmaʊn.tɪnˈtɒp/ (US) /-tᵊnˈtɑːp/ noun [C] the top of a mountain → See also **peak, summit**

mounted /ˈmaʊn.tɪd/ (US) /-t̬ɪd/ adj [before noun] describes soldiers or police officers who ride horses while on duty: *mounted police officers*

Mountie /ˈmaʊn.ti/ (US) /-t̬i/ noun [C] informal a member of the Royal Canadian Mounted Police

mounting /ˈmaʊn.tɪŋ/ (US) /-t̬ɪŋ/ adj gradually increasing: *mounting anxiety/**excitement*** ◦ *mounting **debts***

mourn /mɔːn/ (US) /mɔːrn/ verb [I or T] to feel or express great sadness, especially because of someone's death: *Queen Victoria mourned Prince Albert/Prince Albert's death for 40 years.* ◦ *She was still mourning **for** her brother.* ◦ *They mourned the **passing of** traditional folk dancing (= felt sad because it had stopped existing).*

mourner /ˈmɔː.nəʳ/ (US) /ˈmɔːr.nɚ/ noun [C] a person at a funeral: *The dead man's wife and children were the chief mourners.*

mournful /ˈmɔːn.fᵊl/ (US) /ˈmɔːrn-/ adj very sad: *a mournful **expression*** ◦ *mournful music* • **mournfully** /-i/ (US) /ˈmɔːrn-/ adv • **mournfulness** /-nəs/ (US) /ˈmɔːrn-/ noun [U]

mourning /ˈmɔː.nɪŋ/ (US) /ˈmɔːr-/ noun [U] **1** great sadness felt because someone has died: *Shops will be closed today as a sign of mourning **for** the king.* ◦ *He was **in** mourning **for** his wife.* **2** the usually black clothes that are worn in some countries as an expression of sadness about someone's death

mouse /maʊs/ noun; verb

▸noun (plural **mice**) **ANIMAL** ▷ **1** (A2) [C] a small mammal with short fur, a pointed face, and a long tail: *a field mouse* ◦ *a pet mouse* **COMPUTER** ▷ **2** (A2) [C] a small device that you move across a surface in order to move a CURSOR on your computer screen **PERSON** ▷ **3** [C usually singular] a shy, quiet, nervous person

▸verb

PHRASAL VERB **mouse over sth** to use a computer mouse to move the CURSOR over a particular part of the screen: *The pictures become bigger when you mouse over them.*

ˈmouse ˌmat noun [C] UK (US **ˈmouse ˌpad**) the special flat piece of material on which you move the mouse of a computer

ˈmouse poˌtato noun [C] humorous a person who spends a lot of time on their computer and does not have an active style of life

mouser /ˈmaʊ.səʳ/ (US) /-sɚ/ noun [C] a cat that catches mice: *She's a good mouser.*

mousetrap /ˈmaʊs.træp/ noun [C] a small device that is used in houses and other buildings for catching and killing mice

mousetrap

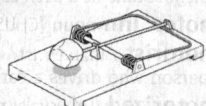

moussaka /muːˈsɑː.kə/ noun [U] a dish, originally from Greece, consisting of meat, tomato, and AUBERGINE (= a large, purple vegetable) with cheese on top

mousse /muːs/ noun [C or U] **FOOD** ▷ **1** a light cold food made from eggs mixed with cream: *chocolate mousse* ◦ *salmon mousse* **HAIR/SKIN** ▷ **2** a light substance that is put on the hair or skin to improve its appearance or condition: *styling mousse*

moustache (US usually **mustache**) /məˈstɑːʃ/ (US) /ˈmʌs.tæʃ/ noun [C] (B1) hair which a man grows above his upper lip: *Groucho Marx had a thick, black moustache.*

mousy /ˈmaʊ.si/ adj (**mousier**, **mousiest**) (also **mousey**) **HAIR** ▷ **1** describes hair that is brown and not special or attractive **PERSON** ▷ **2** shy and nervous and having few interesting qualities: *A mousy-looking woman accompanied him.*

mouth noun; verb

▸noun /maʊθ/ **BODY PART** ▷ **1** (A1) [C] the opening in

the face of a person or animal, consisting of the lips and the space between them, or the space behind containing the teeth and the tongue: ***Open** your mouth wide and say 'Ah'.* ◦ *You shouldn't put so much food in your mouth at once.* **OPENING** ▷ **2** C1 [C usually singular] the opening of a narrow container, the opening of a hole or cave, or the place where a river flows into the sea: *Quebec is at the mouth **of** the St Lawrence River.*

IDIOMS **be all mouth** (UK also **be all mouth and no trousers**) to talk a lot about doing something but never do it: *He says he's going to complain to the manager, but I reckon he's all mouth.* • **be down in the mouth** informal to be sad • **keep your mouth shut** informal B2 to not talk about something: *I don't know whether to tell him what I know or keep my mouth shut.* • **make sb's mouth water** If the smell or sight of food makes your mouth water, it makes you want to eat it. • **a mouth to feed** someone, especially a newborn baby, who you must provide food for: *They've got three kids and the husband's just lost his job – the last thing they need is **another** mouth to feed.*

▸verb [T] /maʊð/ to form words with the lips without making any sound: *It looks to me as if the singers are only mouthing the words.* ◦ [+ speech] *'Can we go?' mouthed Mary.* ◦ *I don't want to stand here listening to you mouthing (= saying in a way that is not sincere) excuses.* → See also **bad-mouth**

PHRASAL VERBS **mouth off (about sth)** informal disapproving to express your opinions too loudly and publicly: *I had to listen to Michael mouthing off about the government all through lunch.* • **mouth off (to/at sb)** informal disapproving to speak in a rude or offensive way to someone: *She's a typical teenager, coming home late at night and mouthing off to her parents.*

-mouthed /-maʊðd/ suffix having a mouth or way of talking of the stated type: *a loud-mouthed teenager (= talking very loudly, especially to attract attention)* ◦ *a **foul**-mouthed drunk (= often swearing)* ◦ *We stared **open**-mouthed (= in surprise) as the elephant walked slowly down Fairview Close.*

mouthful /ˈmaʊθ.fʊl/ noun **AMOUNT** ▷ **1** [C] an amount of food or drink which fills your mouth, or which you put into your mouth at one time: *He only ate a few mouthfuls of meat.* **WORD** ▷ **2** [S] informal a word or phrase that is difficult to pronounce or that has a lot of syllables: *I've always called myself 'Henny' because it's less of a mouthful than 'Henrietta'.*

IDIOM **give someone a mouthful** mainly UK informal to shout something angry at someone, usually using offensive language: *A taxi driver wound down his window and gave the cyclist a mouthful.*

ˈmouth ˌorgan noun [C] a **harmonica**

mouthpiece /ˈmaʊθ.piːs/ noun [C] **PIECE OF EQUIPMENT** ▷ **1** the part of a phone, musical instrument, or other device that goes near or between the lips: *To play the recorder, blow gently **into** the mouthpiece.* **PERSON/NEWSPAPER** ▷ **2** disapproving a person or a newspaper that only expresses the opinions of one particular organization: *This newspaper is just a Republican mouthpiece.*

ˌmouth-to-ˈmouth noun [U] (also **ˌmouth-to-mouth reˌsusciˈtation**) **artificial respiration**

mouthwash /ˈmaʊθ.wɒʃ/ US /-wɑːʃ/ noun [C or U] a liquid used for keeping the mouth clean and smelling fresh

ˈmouth-ˌwatering adj describes food that looks as if it will taste good: *Look at those mouth-watering cakes.*

mouthy /ˈmaʊ.ði/ adj (**mouthier**, **mouthiest**) informal

talking and expressing your opinions a lot, especially in a rude way: *a mouthy teenager*

movable (also **moveable**) /ˈmuː.və.bl̩/ adj able to be moved: *a chair with movable armrests*

ˌmovable ˈfeast noun [C] **1** a religious holiday that is not on the same day every year: *Easter is a movable feast.* **2** informal something that can happen at any time that suits people: *Lunch is officially from 12.30 to 1.00, although it tends to be a movable feast.*

move /muːv/ verb; noun

▸verb **CHANGE POSITION** ▷ **1** A2 [I or T] to (cause to) change position: *I'm so cold I can't move my fingers.* ◦ *Will you help me move this table to the back room?* ◦ *Can we move (= change the time of) the meeting **from** 2 p.m. **to** 3.30 p.m. ?* ◦ *Don't move! Stay right where you are.* ◦ *I thought I could hear someone moving **about/around** upstairs.* ◦ *If you move **along/over/up** (= go further to the side, back or front) a bit, Tess can sit next to me.* ◦ *Police officers at the scene of the accident were asking passers-by to move **along/on** (= to go to a different place).* ◦ *Come on, it's time we were moving (= time for us to leave).* ◦ *Let's stay here tonight, then move **on** (= continue our journey) tomorrow morning.* **2** [I or T] to change the position of one of the pieces used in a BOARD GAME: *In chess, the pieces can only move in certain directions.* **CHANGE PLACE** ▷ **3** B1 [I] to go to a different place to live or work: *We're moving **to** Paris.* ◦ *They've bought a new house, but it will need a lot of work before they can move **into** it/move **in**.* ◦ *I hear Paula has moved in **with** her boyfriend (= gone to live in his house).* ◦ *The couple next door moved **away** (= went to live somewhere else) last year.* ◦ *A lot of businesses are moving **out of** London because it's too expensive.* **4 move house** B1 UK to leave your home in order to live in a new one: *We're moving house next week.* **PROGRESS** ▷ **5** [I or T] to (cause to) progress, change, or happen in a particular way or direction: *The judge's decision will allow the case to move **forward**.* ◦ *If you want to move **ahead** in your career, you'll have to work harder.* ◦ *Share prices moved **up/down** slowly yesterday.* ◦ *Sophie has been moved **up/down** a grade at school.* ◦ *It's time this company moved **into** (= started to take advantage of the benefits of) the computer age.* **CAUSE** ▷ **6** [T] to cause someone to take action: [+ obj + to infinitive] formal *I can't imagine what could have moved him **to** say such a thing.* **CHANGE OPINION** ▷ **7** [I or T] to (cause to) change an opinion or the way in which you live or work: *He's made up his mind, and nothing you can say will move him **on** the issue.* ◦ *More and more people are moving **away from/towards** vegetarianism.* **FEELINGS** ▷ **8** B2 [T] to cause someone to have strong feelings, such as sadness, sympathy, happiness, or admiration: *She said that she was **deeply** moved by all the letters of sympathy she had received.* ◦ *It was such a sad film that it moved him **to tears** (= made him cry).* **SELL** ▷ **9** [I or T] informal to sell: *No one wants to buy these toys – we just can't move them.* **BE WITH PEOPLE** ▷ **10** [I + adv/prep] to spend time with people: *She moves **in/among** a very small circle of people.* **SUGGEST** ▷ **11** [I or T] specialized to suggest something, especially formally at a meeting or in a law court: *A vote was just about to be taken when someone stood up and said that they wished to move an amendment.* ◦ [+ that] *I should like to move **that** the proposal be accepted.* ◦ *Your Honour, we wish to move **for** dismissal of the charges.* **PASS** ▷ **12** [I or T] polite word (used especially by doctors and nurses) to pass the contents of the bowels out of the body: *The doctor asked him if he'd moved **his bowels** that day.*

M

IDIOMS **move heaven and earth** to do everything you can to achieve something: *He'll move heaven and earth to get it done on time.* • **move it!** informal used to tell someone to hurry: *Come on, Phil, move it!* • **move on to higher/better things** humorous to get a better job or improve your life in some way: *I hear you're leaving and moving on to higher things.* • **not move a muscle** to stay completely still: *She sat without moving a muscle as the nurse put the needle in.*

PHRASAL VERBS **move sb/sth in** If the police, army, or any group of people in authority move in, or if someone moves them in, they take control or attack, in order to deal with a difficult or dangerous situation: *When a company goes out of business, officials usually move in to take control.* ◦ *The decision has been made to move UN troops in to try and stop the fighting.* • **move in on sth/sb** If you move in on a person or place, you come close or closer to them in order to attack or take control of them: *Government troops are moving in on the rebel stronghold.* • **move off sth/on (to sth)** C1 to change from one subject to another when talking or writing: *Let's move off this subject now, shall we?* ◦ *Can we move on **to** the next item for discussion, please?* • **move on** NEW PLACE ▷ **1** C1 to leave the place where you are staying and go somewhere else: *I've been in Paris long enough – it's time to move on.* NEW ACTIVITY ▷ **2** C1 to start a new activity: *I'd done the same job for years and felt it was time to move on.* • **move out** B1 to stop living in a particular home: *Her landlord has given her a week to move out.*

▸noun CHANGE OF POSITION ▷ **1** C2 [S] an act of moving: *She held the gun to his head and said, 'One move and you're dead!'* ◦ *I hate the way my boss **watches my every** move (= watches everything I do).* **2** [C] in some BOARD GAMES, a change of the position of one of the pieces used to play the game, or a change of position that is allowed by the rules, or a player's turn to move their piece: *It takes a long time to learn all the moves in chess.* ◦ *It's your move.* CHANGE OF PLACE ▷ **3** C1 [C] an occasion when you go to live or work in a different place: *We've had four moves in three years.* ACTION ▷ **4** C1 [C] an action taken to achieve something: *Buying those shares was a **good** move.* ◦ *This move **towards** improving childcare facilities has been widely welcomed.* ◦ [+ to infinitive] *The council is **making** a move **to** ban traffic in some parts of the city.* **5 make the first move a** to be the first to take action: *Neither side seems prepared to make the first move towards reaching a peace agreement.* **b** informal to start a romantic or sexual relationship with someone: *She's liked him for ages, but doesn't want to make the first move.*

IDIOMS **be on the move** informal **1** to be physically active: *I've been on the move all day and I'm really tired.* **2** to be travelling: *We're going to be on the move all next week, but we'll call you when we get to Edinburgh.* • **get a move on** informal C2 to hurry: *Come on, you two, get a move on!* ◦ *We need to get a move on if we're going to catch that train.* • **make a move** UK (US **be on the move**) to leave a place: *It's late – I think it's time we made a move.*

moved /muːvd/ **adj** having strong feelings of sadness or sympathy, because of something someone has said or done: *When she told me about her daughter's death, I was too moved even to speak.*

movement /ˈmuːv.mənt/ **noun** POSITION CHANGE ▷ **1** B2 [C or U] a change of position: *He **made** a sudden movement and frightened the bird away.* ◦ *For a long time after the accident, he had no movement **in** (= was unable to move) his legs.* ◦ *Her movements were rather clumsy.* **2 sb's movements** what someone is doing during a particular period: *I don't know his movements this week.* GROUP OF PEOPLE ▷ **3** C1 [C, + sing/pl verb] a group of people with a particular set of aims: *The suffragette movement campaigned for votes for women.* ◦ [+ to infinitive] *a movement **to** stop animals being killed for their fur* CHANGE OPINION ▷ **4** [C or U] a situation in which people change their opinion or the way that they live or work: *There has been a movement **towards** more women going back to work while their children are still small.* ◦ *Recently there has been some movement **away from** traditional methods of teaching.* PROGRESS ▷ **5** [U] an occasion when something develops, changes, or happens in a particular way or direction: *There has been little movement in the dollar (= it has not changed in value very much) today.* MUSIC ▷ **6** [C] one of the main parts of a piece of CLASSICAL music: *Beethoven's fifth symphony has four movements.* CLOCK/WATCH ▷ **7** [C] the part of a clock or watch which turns the HANDS (= thin sticks) that point to the time EXCRETE ▷ **8** [C] polite word (used especially by doctors and nurses) an act of emptying the bowels: *When did you last **have** a (**bowel**) movement?*

mover /ˈmuː.vər/ US /-vɚ/ **noun** [C] MOVE POSSESSIONS ▷ **1** US (UK **remover**) someone who helps people move their possessions to a different place to live or work DANCER ▷ **2** old-fashioned used in descriptions of how someone dances: *He's a great mover.* SELL ▷ **3** informal a product which sells very well SUGGEST ▷ **4** specialized a person who formally makes a suggestion during a formal meeting or discussion PRICE CHANGE ▷ **5** specialized a company's SHARES which change in value during a particular period of time: *Among movers today, brewer Bavaria fell 1.5 percent to 3,250 pesos.*

ˌmovers and ˈshakers **noun** [plural] people with a lot of power and influence: *It's a play that's attracted the attention of the Broadway movers and shakers.*

movie /ˈmuː.vi/ **noun 1** A1 [C] mainly US for a cinema film: *My favourite movie is 'Casablanca'.* **2 the movies** [plural] mainly US a cinema or group of cinemas: *What's **on/showing at** the movies this week?* ◦ *Shall we go to the movies tonight?*

moviegoer /ˈmuː.viˌɡəʊ.ər/ US /-ˌɡoʊ.ɚ/ **noun** [C] US (UK **filmgoer/cinemagoer**) a person who regularly goes to watch films at the cinema • **moviegoing** /-ɪŋ/ **noun** [U], **adj** [before noun] mainly US (mainly UK **filmgoing/cinemagoing**) *the moviegoing **public***

moviemaker /ˈmuː.viˌmeɪ.kər/ US /-kɚ/ **noun** [C] someone who is in charge of making a movie • **moviemaking** /ˈmuː.viˌmeɪ.kɪŋ/ **noun** [U]

ˈmovie ˌstar **noun** [C] mainly US (mainly UK **ˈfilm ˌstar**) a very popular and successful movie actor: *She dated several of the big movie stars of the time.* ◦ *Who's your favourite movie star?*

ˈmovie ˌtheater **noun** [C] US A1 a cinema: *There's a season of Bergman films on at our local movie theater.*

moving /ˈmuː.vɪŋ/ **adj; noun**

▸adj CHANGING POSITION ▷ **1** [before noun] A moving object is one that moves: *a moving target* ◦ *moving **parts** in a machine* FEELINGS ▷ **2** B2 causing strong feelings of sadness or sympathy: *a very moving story* ◦ *I find some of Brahms's music **deeply** moving.* CAUSING ACTION ▷ **3** [before noun] causing someone to take action: *Local parents were the moving **force/spirit** behind the safety improvements at the playground (= they were the people who made them happen).*

▸noun [U] the action of going to a different place to live or work: *I hate moving.*

movingly /ˈmuː.vɪŋ.li/ **adv** in a way that causes strong feelings of sadness or sympathy: *He* ***spoke*** *movingly about his wife's death.*

ˈmoving ˌvan noun [C] US for **removal van**

mow /məʊ/ ⓤⓢ /moʊ/ verb [I or T] (**mowed**, **mown** or **mowed**) to cut plants, such as grass or WHEAT, which have long thin stems and grow close together: *You can't mow the* ***grass/lawn*** *if it's wet.* ◦ *I love the smell of* ***new****-mown hay.*

PHRASAL VERB **mow sb down** to kill people, usually in large numbers, by shooting them or driving a vehicle into them: *Three shoppers were mown down this afternoon when a drunken driver lost control of his car.*

mower /ˈməʊ.əʳ/ ⓤⓢ /ˈmoʊ.ɚ/ **noun** [C] a machine for cutting grass → See also **lawnmower**

mozzarella /ˌmɒt.səˈrel.ə/ ⓤⓢ /ˌmɑːt-/ **noun** [U] a soft white Italian cheese

MP /ˌemˈpiː/ **noun** [C] abbreviation for **Member of Parliament**: *Robert Smith MP* ◦ *Who is the MP* ***for*** *Cambridge?*

MP3 /ˌem.piːˈθriː/ **noun** [C or U] trademark a computer FILE which stores high-quality sound in a small amount of space, or the TECHNOLOGY that makes this possible: *I downloaded their latest album on MP3.*

MPˈ3 ˌplayer noun [C] A2 an electronic device or a computer program for playing music that has been stored as MP3 files

mpg /ˌem.piːˈdʒiː/ abbreviation for miles per gallon: the number of miles a vehicle travels using one GALLON of fuel: *My car* ***does*** *about 40 mpg.* ◦ *How many mpg do you* ***get*** *from your car?*

mph /ˌem.piːˈeɪtʃ/ abbreviation for miles per hour: *My car won't* ***do/go*** *more than 70 mph.* ◦ *She was caught driving* ***at*** *120 mph.*

MPhil /ˌemˈfɪl/ **noun** [C] UK abbreviation for **Master of Philosophy**: *Alison Wells, MPhil* ◦ *He has/is doing an MPhil* ***in*** *psychology.*

MPV /ˌem.piːˈviː/ **noun** [C] abbreviation for multi-purpose vehicle: a **people carrier**

Mr /ˈmɪs.təʳ/ ⓤⓢ /-tɚ/ **noun** **1** A1 a title used before the family name or full name of a man who has no other title, or when talking to man who holds a particular official position: *Mr Jones/Mr David Jones* ◦ [as form of address] *Good afternoon, Mr Dawson.* ◦ *We're looking for a Mr (= a man called) George Smith.* ◦ *It's an honour to have you here today, Mr President.* → Compare **Miss, Mrs, Ms** → See also **Messrs** **2** used when expressing the idea that a man is typical of or represents a quality, activity or place: *She's still hoping to meet Mr Right (= the perfect man).* ◦ *He thinks he's Mr Big (= someone very important).*

IDIOM **no more Mr Nice Guy** informal something that is said when someone has decided to stop thinking about the wishes and feelings of other people: *I've had enough of people taking advantage of me. From now on it's no more Mr Nice Guy.*

MRI /ˌem.ɑːrˈaɪ/ **noun** [U] abbreviation for magnetic resonance imaging: a system for producing electronic pictures of the organs inside a person's body, using radio waves and a strong MAGNETIC field

Mrs /ˈmɪs.ɪz/ **noun** **1** A1 a title used before the family name or full name of a married woman who has no other title: *Mrs Wood/Mrs Jean Wood* ◦ [as form of address] *Hello, Mrs Grant, how are you today?* → Compare **madam, Miss, Mr, Ms** **2** used when expressing the idea that a woman is typical of or represents a quality, activity, or place: *Mrs Average (= a woman who is typical of an ordinary woman)*

MRSA /ˌem.ɑːr.esˈeɪ/ **noun** [U] specialized methicillin-resistant Staphylococcus aureus: a type of BACTERIUM (= an extremely small organism) that cannot be treated by most ANTIBIOTICS

ms noun [C] (plural **mss**) written abbreviation for **manuscript**

Ms /məz/, /mɪz/ **noun** A2 a title used before the family name or full name of a woman, used to avoid saying if she is married or not: *Ms Hill/Ms Paula Hill* ◦ [as form of address] *What can I do for you, Ms Wood?* → Compare **Miss, Mr, Mrs**

MS /ˌemˈes/ **noun** [U] abbreviation for **multiple sclerosis**

MSc /ˌem.esˈsiː/ **noun** [C] UK UK (US **MS**) abbreviation for **Master of Science**: *Lynn Kramer MSc* ◦ *Phil has/is doing/is studying for an MSc* ***in*** *biochemistry.*

msec. written abbreviation for **millisecond**

MSG /ˌem.esˈdʒiː/ **noun** [U] abbreviation for **monosodium glutamate**

Msgr noun [before noun] written abbreviation for **Monsignor**

MSP /ˌem.esˈpiː/ **noun** [C] abbreviation for Member of the Scottish Parliament

Mt noun written abbreviation for **Mount** or **mountain**: *Mt Everest*

MTV /ˌem.tiːˈviː/ **noun** [U, + sing/pl verb] trademark abbreviation for Music Television: a company that broadcasts pop music videos and programmes popular with young people

much /mʌtʃ/ **determiner; pronoun, adv**

▸**determiner** (**more**, **most**) **1** A1 a large amount or to a large degree: *I don't earn much money.* ◦ *You haven't said much, Joan – what do you think?* ◦ *I like her very much.* ◦ *I don't think there's much to be gained by catching an earlier train.* ◦ *The children never eat (****very****) much, but they seem quite healthy.* ◦ *'Is there any wine left?'* ***'Not*** *much.'* ◦ *There's* ***not/nothing*** *much to do around here.* ◦ ***How*** *much (= what amount of) sugar do you take in your coffee?* ◦ ***How*** *much do these shoes cost?* ◦ *I spend* ***too*** *much on clothes.* ◦ *I don't have* ***as*** *much time* ***as*** *(= I have less time than) I would like for visiting my friends.* ◦ *Because of the rain, we weren't able to spend much* ***of*** *the day on the beach.* ◦ *Have you* ***seen/heard*** *much* ***of*** *Polly (= often seen or heard about her) recently?* ◦ *I'd* ***very*** *much like to visit them sometime.* ◦ *One day I hope I'll be able to do* ***as*** *much (= the same amount) for you* ***as*** *you've done for me.* ◦ *Things around here are much* ***as always/usual/ever*** *(= have not changed a lot).* ◦ *The two schools are much* ***the same*** *(= very similar).* ◦ *Much* ***to*** *our surprise, (= we were very surprised that) they accepted our offer.* ◦ *I'm* ***not*** *much* ***good at*** *knitting (= do not do it very well).* ◦ *This is a much (= often) discussed issue.* ◦ *Brian's become a much (= greatly) changed person since his car accident.* ◦ *I've been feeling much health****ier*** *(= a lot more healthy) since I became a vegetarian.* ◦ *The repairs to our car cost much* ***more than*** *we were expecting.* ◦ *I'm* ***very*** *much aware of the problem.* ◦ *She's much* ***the*** *best person for the job (= she is certainly better than everyone else).* ◦ *I* ***would*** *much* ***rather*** *have my baby at home than in hospital.* ◦ *She is as much a friend to me as a mother (= although she is my mother, she is also a friend).* **2** informal humorous used at the end of a sentence to emphasize what you have just said: *When he saw all the food on my plate, he said 'Hungry much?'* **3 much too much** a far larger amount of something than you want or need: *You've drunk much too much to* *drive.* **4 too much** A2 more than someone can deal with: *I can't look after six children at my age – it's too much.* **5 a bit much** unreasonable and unfair: *I think it's a bit much for you to expect me to do all the cleaning.*

! Common mistake: much or many?

Much and **many** are used in formal positive sentences. Use **much** to refer to uncountable nouns.
Don't say 'much cars/facts/dollars', say **much traffic/information/money**.
With nouns that have a plural form, don't use 'much', use **many**:
~~*There are much interesting places to visit in Venice.*~~
There are many interesting places to visit in Venice.
In less formal sentences and in negative sentences, you can use **a lot of** with both countable and uncountable nouns:
I don't have a lot of money.
We visited a lot of interesting places.

! Common mistake: very much

Warning: do not use **very much** between the verb and the object in a sentence.
Don't say 'do very much something', say **do something very much** or **very much do something**:
~~*I enjoyed very much my stay in England.*~~
I enjoyed my stay in England very much.
I very much enjoyed my stay in England.

M

IDIOMS **as much 1** If you say that you thought/expected/said as much, it means that something bad that you thought/expected/said would happen has happened: *I knew he'd fail – I said as much at the time.* **2** the same: *Go on, lend me the money – you know I'd do as much for you.* • **as much again** UK the same amount again: *My fare was nearly £10, and it was almost as much again for the children.* • **as much as** almost: *He as much as admitted that it was his fault.* • **as much as you can do** UK If you say something is as much as you can do, you manage to do it, but with great difficulty: *I felt so ill this morning, it was as much as I could do to get out of bed.* • **much as** although: *Much as I would like to help you, I'm afraid I'm simply too busy at the moment.* • **much less** and certainly not: *Tony can barely boil an egg, much less cook dinner.* • **not go much on sth** UK informal to dislike something: *I don't go much on white wine.* • **not so much sth as sth** If you say that something is not so much one thing as something else, you mean it is more the second thing: *They're not so much lovers as friends.* ◦ *I don't feel angry so much as sad.* • **so much** a particular amount: *By the time you've paid so much for the ferry and so much for the train fare, it would be cheaper to go by plane.* • **so much for sth** C2 used to express disappointment at the fact that a situation is not as you thought it was: *The car's broken down again. So much for our trip to the seaside.*

▸**pronoun, adv** C1 (something) of good quality: *He's **not** much **to look at**, but he has a wonderful personality.* ◦ *I've never been much **of** a dancer (= good at dancing, or interested in doing it).* ◦ *There's **not/nothing** much on TV tonight.*

muchness /ˈmʌtʃ.nəs/ noun UK informal **be much of a muchness** to be very similar and usually of low quality: *The songs you hear on the radio these days all sound much of a muchness.*

muck /mʌk/ noun; verb

▸**noun** [U] **1** dirt or solid animal waste: *You're treading muck into the carpet with your dirty shoes!* ◦ *a pile of **dog** muck* **2** something you consider very unpleasant or very low quality: *I'm not eating that muck!*

IDIOMS **make a muck of sth** informal to spoil something or do something very badly • **where there's muck there's brass** UK saying said to mean that a lot of money can be made from business activities that are dirty or unpleasant

▸**verb**

PHRASAL VERBS **muck sb/sth about/around** mainly UK informal to behave in a silly way, or to treat someone or something in a careless way: *Stop mucking about **with** those ornaments, you'll break something!* ◦ *I'm fed up with them mucking me about and cancelling our arrangements.* • **muck in** UK informal to share the work that needs to be done: *She doesn't mind mucking in **with** the rest of us when there's work to be done.* • **muck (sth) out** to clean a place where a large animal lives, especially a STABLE, by removing the waste products and old STRAW: *She'd spent all morning mucking out the horses.* • **muck sth up** informal to spoil something completely, or do something very badly: *I really prepared for the interview because I didn't want to muck it up.* ◦ *I mucked up the whole exam!*

muckraking /ˈmʌkˌreɪ.kɪŋ/ noun [U] disapproving the activity, especially by newspapers and REPORTERS, of trying to find out information about people or organizations in order to make it public: *There was so much muckraking about his family life that he decided not to stand for election.* • **muckraker** /-kəʳ/ US /-kɚ/ noun [C]

ˈmuck-up noun [C] informal a mistake that completely spoils something: *They **made** a muck-up of our order – it won't be ready till next week now.*

mucky /ˈmʌk.i/ adj **1** informal dirty: *Don't walk all over my clean floor in your mucky boots.* **2** UK informal related to or describing sex in an offensive way: *a mucky magazine*

mucous membrane /ˌmjuː.kəsˈmem.breɪn/ noun [C] specialized the thin skin that covers the inside surface of parts of the body such as the nose and mouth and produces mucus to protect them

mucus /ˈmjuː.kəs/ noun [U] a thick liquid produced inside the nose and other parts of the body: *This drug reduces mucus production in the gut.*

mud /mʌd/ noun [U] B2 earth that has become wet and sticky: *The vehicles got bogged down **in the** heavy mud.* ◦ *Modern houses have replaced the one-room mud **huts** with grass roofs that had been home to generations of peasants.*

IDIOMS **hurl/throw/sling mud at sb** to say insulting or unfair things about someone, especially to try to damage their reputation → See also **mudslinging** • **mud sticks** UK saying said to mean that people are likely to believe something bad that is said about someone, even if it is not true

muddle /ˈmʌd.l/ noun; verb

▸**noun** [S or U] C2 an untidy or confused state: *The documents were **in a** muddle.* ◦ *Whenever I go abroad I get **in a** muddle **about/over** (= become confused about) money.*

▸**verb**

PHRASAL VERBS **muddle along** to continue doing something with no clear purpose or plan: *Decide what you want in life – don't just muddle along.* • **muddle through** to manage to do something although you are not organized and do not know how to do it: *I'm afraid I can't help you – you'll just have to muddle through on your own.* • **muddle sth up** (C2) to arrange things in the wrong order: *I've arranged the books alphabetically so don't muddle them up.* • **muddle sb/sth up** (C2) to think that a person or thing is someone or something else because they are very similar: *I often muddle up Richard **with** his brother.* ◦ *It's easy to muddle up some Spanish and Italian words.*

muddled /ˈmʌd.l̩d/ adj **THINGS** ▷ **1** Things that are muddled are badly organized: *He left his clothes in a muddled pile in the corner.* **PERSON** ▷ **2** A person who is muddled is confused: *He became increasingly muddled as he grew older.*

ˌmuddle-ˈheaded adj not thinking clearly or in an organized way

muddy /ˈmʌd.i/ adj; verb
▸adj **DIRTY** ▷ **1** (B2) covered by or containing MUD (= wet, sticky earth): *Don't bring those muddy boots inside!* ◦ *muddy water* **COLOURS** ▷ **2** describes colours that are dark and not bright: *The sitting-room has been painted in muddy browns and greens.*
▸verb [T] to put MUD (= wet, sticky earth) into something or cover something with mud: *Industrial activity has muddied the river.*

IDIOM **muddy the waters** to make a situation more confused and less easy to understand or deal with

mudflap /ˈmʌd.flæp/ noun [C] UK (US ˈ**splash** ˌ**guard**) one of the pieces of rubber fixed to a vehicle behind the wheels to prevent dirt and small objects from being thrown up

mudflat /ˈmʌd.flæt/ noun [C] a flat area of very wet soil near the sea that is covered at HIGH TIDE (= the time when the sea reaches its highest level)

mudguard /ˈmʌd.gɑːd/ (US) /-gɑːrd/ noun [C] (US usually **fender**) a curved piece of metal or plastic above the wheels of a bicycle or motorcycle that prevents dirt from getting on the rider

mudpack /ˈmʌd.pæk/ noun [C] a special substance that you put on your face and leave for a short time to improve your skin

ˌmud ˈpie noun [C] a small round shape made of mud by children playing

mudslide /ˈmʌd.slaɪd/ noun [C] a mass of MUD (= wet earth) moving suddenly and quickly down a steep slope

mudslinging /ˈmʌdˌslɪŋ.ɪŋ/ noun [U] the act of saying insulting or unfair things about someone, especially to try to damage their reputation: *political mud-slinging*

muesli /ˈmjuːzli/ noun [U] a mixture of uncooked grains, dried fruit, and nuts that is eaten with milk as part of the first meal of the day → Compare **granola**

muezzin /muːˈez.ɪn/ noun [C] a man who calls Muslims to prayer from the tower of a MOSQUE (= a Muslim holy building)

muff /mʌf/ noun; verb
▸noun [C] a short tube of fur or warm cloth, into which women in the past put their hands in cold weather in order to keep them warm
▸verb [T] informal to spoil an opportunity or do something badly: *I only had two lines in the whole play and I muffed them.*

muffin /ˈmʌf.ɪn/ noun [C] **CAKE** ▷ **1** a small sweet cake that often has fruit inside it: *blueberry muffins* **BREAD** ▷ **2** UK (US **English muffin**) a small round flat type of bread, usually sliced in two and eaten hot with butter

ˈmuffin ˌtop noun [C or U] informal fat flesh that shows over the top of someone's trousers, especially because these are too tight

muffle /ˈmʌf.l̩/ verb [T] **MAKE LESS CLEAR** ▷ **1** to make a sound quieter and less clear: *The house's windows are double-glazed to muffle the **noise** of aircraft.* **KEEP WARM** ▷ **2** to wear thick warm clothes in order to keep warm: *I was muffled **up** against the cold in a scarf and hat.*

muffled /ˈmʌf.l̩d/ adj describes a sound that is quiet or not clear: *I could hear muffled **voices** next door but couldn't make out any words.*

muffler /ˈmʌf.ləʳ/ (US) /-lɚ/ noun [C] **CAR** ▷ **1** US and Australian English a part of a vehicle that reduces noise from the engine → See also **silencer** **CLOTHES** ▷ **2** old-fashioned a thick SCARF (= long piece of cloth worn around the neck)

mufti /ˈmʌf.ti/ noun [U] old-fashioned ordinary clothes worn by people who usually wear uniforms, especially soldiers: *The admiral arrived **in** mufti.*

mug /mʌg/ noun; verb
▸noun [C] **CUP** ▷ **1** (A2) a large cup with straight sides used for hot drinks: *I made myself a large mug **of** cocoa (= enough to fill a mug) and went to bed.* **2** **beer mug** mainly US a heavy glass with a handle and usually with patterns cut into its side, out of which you drink beer **STUPID PERSON** ▷ **3** mainly UK informal a person who is stupid and easily deceived: *He's such a mug, he believes everything she tells him.* **FACE** ▷ **4** informal mainly disapproving someone's face: *his **ugly** mug*

mug

IDIOM **a mug's game** UK informal an activity that will not make you happy or successful: *She decided that freelancing was a mug's game.*

▸verb [T] (-gg-) to attack a person in a public place and steal their money: *He was mugged in broad daylight.*

PHRASAL VERB **mug (sth) up** UK informal to study a subject quickly before taking an exam: *I've got to mug up (**on**) my History before tomorrow's exam.*

mugger /ˈmʌg.əʳ/ (US) /-ɚ/ noun [C] a person who attacks people in order to steal their money

mugging /ˈmʌg.ɪŋ/ noun [C or U] an act of attacking someone and stealing their money: *Police are concerned that mugging is on the increase.*

muggins /ˈmʌg.ɪnz/ noun [S] UK humorous a stupid person: often used to describe yourself when you have done something silly or when you feel you are being treated unfairly: *I suppose muggins **here** will have to look after the cat when they go on holiday (= I will have to do it but I don't want to).*

muggy /ˈmʌg.i/ adj When the weather is muggy, it is unpleasantly warm and the air contains a lot of water.

mugshot /ˈmʌgˌʃɒt/ (US) /-ʃɑːt/ noun [C] slang a photograph taken by the police of a person who has been charged with a crime: *A poster with mugshots of wanted men was on the wall.*

mujahideen (also **mujahedin**) /ˌmʌ.dʒə.həˈdiːn/ noun [plural] Muslims who are fighting in support of Islam

mulatto /məˈlæt.əʊ/, /mjuː-/ (US) /-ˈlæ.t̬oʊ/ noun [C] offensive an offensive word for someone with one black parent and one white parent

M

mulberry /ˈmʌl.bᵊr.i/ US /-ber-/ **noun** [C] a small soft purple fruit, or the tree that has these fruit

mulch /mʌltʃ/ **noun; verb**
▸**noun** [C or U] a covering of decaying leaves that is spread over the soil in order to keep water in it or to improve it
▸**verb** [I or T] to put mulch on or around something: [+ adv/prep] *Mulch* ***around*** *the base of the roses.* ◦ *Mulch the roses.*

mule /mju:l/ **noun** [C] **ANIMAL** ▷ **1** an animal whose mother is a horse and whose father is a DONKEY, used especially for transporting goods **PERSON** ▷ **2** a person who agrees to carry illegal drugs into another country in return for payment by the person selling the drugs: *These very poor women who are used as mules by drug barons often get long prison sentences.* **SHOE** ▷ **3** a woman's shoe or SLIPPER that has no back

mulish /ˈmju:.lɪʃ/ **adj** describes someone who is very determined and refuses to change their plans for anyone else

mull /mʌl/ **verb** [T] to heat wine or beer with added sugar and spices: *mulled* ***wine***

PHRASAL VERB **mull sth over** to think carefully about something for a long time: *I need a few days to mull things over before I decide if I'm taking the job.*

mullah /ˈmʊl.ə/ **noun** [C] an Islamic religious teacher or leader

mullered /ˈmʌl.əd/ **adj** UK slang drunk

mullet /ˈmʌl.ɪt/ **noun** [C] **FISH** ▷ **1** a small sea fish that can be cooked and eaten: *red mullet* **HAIR** ▷ **2** informal a men's hairstyle, popular in the 1980's, in which the hair on top and at the sides of the head is short and the hair at the back is long

mulligatawny /ˌmʌl.ɪ.gəˈtɔː.ni/ US /-ˈtɑː-/ **noun** [U] a spicy soup that has CURRY POWDER in it

mullioned /ˈmʌl.i.ənd/ **adj** A mullioned window has vertical parts, usually made of stone, separating the glass parts.

multi- /mʌl.ti-/ US /-t̬i-/ **prefix** having many: *a multi-coloured skirt (= a skirt with many colours)* ◦ *a multi-vitamin tablet (= a pill which contains several vitamins)*

multicellular /ˌmʌl.tiˈsel.jə.ləʳ/ US /-t̬iˈsel.jə.lɚ/ **adj** specialized A multicellular organism is made of many cells: *Some green algae are multicellular.* → Compare **unicellular**

multicultural /ˌmʌl.tiˈkʌl.tʃᵊr.ᵊl/ US /-t̬iˈkʌl.tʃɚ-/ **adj** including people who have many different customs and beliefs: *Britain is increasingly a multicultural* ***society***.

multiculturalism /ˌmʌl.tiˈkʌl.tʃᵊr.ᵊl.ɪ.zᵊm/ US /-t̬iˈkʌl.tʃɚ-/ **noun** [U] the belief that different cultures within a society should all be given importance

multidisciplinary /ˌmʌl.ti.dɪs.əˈplɪn.ᵊr.i/ US /-t̬i.dɪs.əˈplɪ.ner-/ **adj** involving different subjects of study in one activity: *a multidisciplinary course*

ˌmulti-ˈethnic **adj** consisting of, or relating to various different races: *Britain is a multi-ethnic* ***society****, with many black and Asian people.*

multifaceted /ˌmʌl.tiˈfæs.ɪ.tɪd/ US /-t̬iˈfæs.ɪ.t̬ɪd/ **adj** having many different parts: *It's a multifaceted business, offering a range of services.*

multifarious /ˌmʌl.tɪˈfeə.ri.əs/ US /-t̬ɪˈfer.i-/ **adj** formal of many different types: *The newspaper report detailed the fraudster's multifarious business activities.*

multigym /ˈmʌl.ti.dʒɪm/ US /-t̬i-/ **noun** [C] UK a machine on which you can do several different exercises to keep your body fit, or a room in which several different exercise machines can be used

multilateral /ˌmʌl.tiˈlæt.ᵊr.ᵊl/ US /-t̬iˈlæt̬.ɚ-/ **adj** involving more than two groups or countries: *Seven countries are taking part in the multilateral talks.* → Compare **bilateral, unilateral** • **multilaterally** /-i/ **adv**

multilingual /ˌmʌl.tiˈlɪŋ.gwəl/ US /-t̬i-/ **adj** (of people or groups) able to use more than two languages for communication, or (of a thing) written or spoken in more than two different languages: *a multilingual online dictionary* → Compare **bilingual, monolingual**

multimedia /ˌmʌl.tiˈmiː.di.ə/ US /-t̬i-/ **adj** [before noun] using a combination of moving and still pictures, sound, music, and words, especially in computers or entertainment: *multimedia software* • **multimedia noun** [U]

multimillionaire /ˌmʌl.tiˌmɪl.jəˈneəʳ/ US /-t̬iˌmɪl.jəˈner/ **noun** [C] a person who has money and property worth several million pounds, dollars, etc.

multinational /ˌmʌl.tiˈnæʃ.ᵊn.ᵊl/ US /-t̬i-/ **adj; noun**
▸**adj** involving several different countries, or (of a business) producing and selling goods in several different countries: *The UN has sent a multinational peace-keeping force.* ◦ *a major multinational food company*
▸**noun** [C] a large and powerful company that produces and sells goods in many different countries: *Are multinationals now more powerful than governments?*

multiple /ˈmʌl.tɪ.pl̩/ US /-t̬ɪ-/ **adj; noun**
▸**adj** C1 very many of the same type, or of different types: *The youth died of multiple burns.* ◦ *We made multiple copies of the report.*
▸**noun** [C] **NUMBER** ▷ **1** a number that can be divided by a smaller number an exact number of times: *18 is a multiple* ***of*** *3, because 18 = 3 × 6.* **LARGE COMPANY** ▷ **2** a large company that has shops in many towns

ˌmultiple ˈbirth **noun** [C] an occasion when more than two babies are born to the same woman at the same time

ˌmultiple-ˈchoice **adj** [before noun] describes an exam or question in which you are given a list of answers and you have to choose the correct one: *a multiple-choice test*

ˌmultiple scleˈrosis **noun** [U] (abbreviation **MS**) a disease in which the covering of the nerves gradually becomes destroyed, damaging a person's speech and sight and ability to move

multiplex /ˈmʌl.tɪ.pleks/ US /-t̬ɪ-/ **noun** [C] a very large cinema building that has a lot of separate cinemas inside it

multipliˈcation ˌtable **noun** [C] a list that shows the results of multiplying one number by a set of other numbers, usually from one to twelve, used especially by children at school

multiplicity /ˌmʌl.tɪˈplɪs.ɪ.ti/ US /-təˈplɪs.ə.t̬i/ **noun** [U] formal a large number or wide range (of something): *There is a multiplicity* ***of*** *fashion magazines to choose from.*

multiply /ˈmʌl.tɪ.plaɪ/ US /-t̬ɪ-/ **verb** [I or T] to increase very much in number, or (in mathematics) to add a number to itself a particular number of times: *In warm weather these germs multiply rapidly.* ◦ *If you multiply seven* ***by*** *15 you get 105.* → Compare **add, divide, subtract** • **multiplication** /ˌmʌl.tɪ.plɪˈkeɪ.ʃᵊn/ US /-t̬ɪ-/ **noun** [U]

multipurpose /ˌmʌl.tiˈpɜː.pəs/ US /-t̬iˈpɜː-/ **adj**

describes a tool, etc. that can be used in several different ways: *a multipurpose hall*

multiracial /ˌmʌl.tiˈreɪ.ʃəl/ (US) /-t̬i-/ **adj** involving people of several different races: *a multiracial school*

multistorey /ˌmʌl.tiˈstɔː.ri/ (US) /-t̬iˈstɔːr.i/ **adj; noun**
▸**adj** (US **multistory**) describes a building with several floors: *a multistorey car park* ∘ US *a multistory apartment block*
▸**noun** [C] UK a multistorey car park: *I left the car in the multistorey.*

multitasking /ˌmʌl.tiˈtɑːs.kɪŋ/ (US) /-t̬iˈtæs-/ **noun** [U] **PERSON** ▷ **1** a person's ability to do more than one thing at a time: *Women are often very good at multitasking.* **COMPUTER** ▷ **2** the ability of a computer to operate several programs at one time: *The machine allows multitasking without the need to buy extra hardware.* • **multitask** /-ˈtɑːsk/ (US) /-ˈtæsk/ **verb** [I]

multitude /ˈmʌl.tɪ.tjuːd/ (US) /-t̬ə.tuːd/ **noun** formal **1 a multitude of** a large number of people or things: *The city has a multitude of problems, from homelessness to drugs and murder.* ∘ *This case has raised a multitude of questions.* **2 the multitude** a large crowd of people: *He stepped out onto the balcony to address the multitude below.* **3 the multitudes** [plural] large numbers of people: *the multitudes using the internet* **4 the multitude** the ordinary people who form the largest group in a society

IDIOM **cover/hide a multitude of sins** humorous to prevent people from seeing or discovering something bad: *Large sweaters are warm and practical and hide a multitude of sins.*

mum /mʌm/ **noun; adj**
▸**noun** [C] UK informal (US **mom**) (A1) a mother: [as form of address] *Happy birthday, Mum.* ∘ *All the mums **and dads** are invited to the school play at the end of the year.* ∘ *She loves being a mum.*

IDIOM **mum's the word** saying old-fashioned said when you tell someone, or agree with someone, to keep something a secret: *'I'm not telling people generally yet.' 'OK, mum's the word!'*

▸**adj** informal **keep mum** to say nothing about a subject: *It's not official yet so keep mum.*

mumble /ˈmʌm.bl̩/ **verb** [I or T] (B2) to speak quietly and in a way that is not clear so that the words are difficult to understand: *She mumbled **something** about being too busy.* ∘ [+ speech] *'I'm sorry,' he mumbled.*

mumbo jumbo /ˌmʌm.bəʊˈdʒʌm.bəʊ/ (US) /-boʊˈdʒʌm.boʊ/ **noun** [U] informal words or activities that seem complicated or mysterious but have no real meaning: *You don't believe in horoscopes and all that mumbo jumbo, do you?*

mummify /ˈmʌm.ɪ.faɪ/ **verb** [T] to preserve a dead body as a mummy

mummy /ˈmʌm.i/ **noun** [C] **MOTHER** ▷ **1** UK (US **mommy**) child's word for mother: [as form of address] *I want to go home, Mummy.* ∘ *Could I speak to your mummy please, Phoebe?* **BODY** ▷ **2** (especially in ancient Egypt) a dead body that is prevented from decaying by being treated with special substances before being wrapped in cloth

ˈ**mummy's** ˌ**boy** **noun** [C usually singular] disapproving UK (US ˈ**mama's** ˌ**boy**) a boy or man who appears to do whatever his mother tells him to

mumps /mʌmps/ **noun** [U] an infectious disease that causes painful swelling in the neck and slight fever

mumsy /ˈmʌm.zi/ **adj** UK informal disapproving describes a woman with an old-fashioned appearance, like that of a traditional mother: *As she became more successful, she changed her mumsy hairstyle for something more glamorous.*

munch /mʌntʃ/ **verb; noun**
▸**verb** [I or T] to eat something, especially noisily: *He was munching **on** an apple.* ∘ *We watched her munch her way through two packets of peanuts.*
▸**noun** [U] UK informal food: *Shall we get some munch, then?*

Munchausen's Syndrome /ˈmʌn.tʃaʊ.zənzˌsɪn.drəʊm/ (US) /-droʊm/ **noun** [U] a mental condition in which someone pretends to be ill or deliberately tries to make themselves ill in order to get attention and treatment from doctors or other medical workers

munchies /ˈmʌn.tʃiz/ **noun** [plural] **1** mainly US informal small light things to eat: *We need a few munchies – some peanuts and crackers.* **2 the munchies** informal feelings of hunger: *I've got the munchies.*

mundane /mʌnˈdeɪn/ **adj** (C1) very ordinary and therefore not interesting: *Mundane matters such as paying bills and shopping for food do not interest her.*

mung bean /ˈmʌŋˌbiːn/ **noun** [C] a small bean that is often used in Chinese cooking and is eaten when it has grown long SHOOTS

municipal /mjuːˈnɪs.ɪ.pəl/ **adj** (C1) of or belonging to a town or city: *municipal authorities* ∘ *municipal tennis courts*

municipality /mjuːˌnɪs.ɪˈpæl.ə.ti/ (US) /-t̬i/ **noun** [C] a city or town with its own local government, or the local government itself: *The municipality provides services such as water and rubbish collection.*

munificent /mjuːˈnɪf.ɪ.sənt/ **adj** formal very generous with money: *A former student has donated a munificent sum of money to the college.* • **munificence** /-səns/ **noun** [U] *I thanked them for their munificence.*

munitions /mjuːˈnɪʃ.ənz/ **noun** [plural] military weapons such as guns and bombs: *The army used precision-guided munitions to blow up enemy targets.* ∘ *a munitions **depot***

Munro-bagging /mʌnˈrəʊˌbæg.ɪŋ/ (US) /ˈroʊ-/ **noun** [U] the activity of walking or climbing to the top of as many high Scottish mountains, known as Munros, as you can. Munros are Scottish mountains that are higher than 3,000 feet.

muppet /ˈmʌp.ɪt/ **noun** [C] UK informal a stupid person

mural /ˈmjʊə.rəl/ (US) /ˈmjʊr.əl/ **noun** [C] a large picture that has been painted on the wall of a room or building

murder /ˈmɜː.dər/ (US) /ˈmɝː.dɚ/ **noun; verb**
▸**noun** [C or U] (B1) the crime of intentionally killing a person: *Two sisters have been **charged with** (= officially accused of) murder.* ∘ *There were three murders in the town last year.* ∘ *The three were **convicted of** (= proved guilty of) murder.* ∘ *a murder **weapon** (= a weapon used to commit a murder)* → Compare **manslaughter, suicide**

IDIOM **be murder** informal to be very difficult to do: *It's murder find**ing** a parking space in town.*

▸**verb** [T] **1** (B1) to commit the crime of intentionally killing a person: *Her husband was murdered by gunmen as she watched.* ∘ *In the last year, terrorists have murdered several local journalists.* **2** UK informal If you say you will or could murder someone, you mean you are very angry with them: *If he's late again, I'll murder him!*

IDIOM **could murder sth** UK informal If you say you could murder a type of food or drink, it means you

M

would like very much to have it now: *I could murder a cup of tea!*

murderer /ˈmɜː.dər.ər/ (US) /ˈmɝː.dɚ.ɚ/ **noun** [C] (old-fashioned female **murderess**) (B1) someone who illegally and intentionally kills another person: *A* ***convicted*** *murderer was executed in North Carolina yesterday.* ◦ *a* ***mass*** *murderer (= someone who has killed a large number of people illegally)*

murderous /ˈmɜː.dər.əs/ (US) /ˈmɝː.dɚ-/ **adj** **1** extremely dangerous and likely to commit murder: *He was a murderous gangster.* ◦ *She gave me a look of murderous hatred.* **2** informal extremely unpleasant: *The traffic was murderous today.*

murk /mɜːk/ (US) /mɝːk/ **noun** [U] darkness or thick cloud, preventing you from seeing clearly: *It was foggy and the sun shone feebly through the murk.*

murky /ˈmɜː.ki/ (US) /ˈmɝː-/ **adj** **DARK/DIRTY** ▷ **1** dark and dirty or difficult to see through: *The river was brown and murky after the storm.* **UNPLEASANT SITUATION** ▷ **2** describes a situation that is complicated and unpleasant, and about which many facts are not clear: *He became involved in the murky* ***world*** *of international drug-dealing.* ◦ *I don't want to get into the murky* ***waters*** *of family arguments.*

murmur /ˈmɜː.məʳ/ (US) /ˈmɝː.mɚ/ **verb; noun**

▸verb **SPEAK QUIETLY** ▷ **1** (C2) [I or T] to speak or say something very quietly: [+ speech] *'I love you,' she murmured.* ◦ *He was murmuring* ***to himself***. ◦ humorous *He murmured* ***sweet nothings*** *(= romantic talk) in her ear.* **COMPLAIN** ▷ **2** [I] to complain about something that you disagree with or dislike, but not in a public way: *They were murmuring* ***about*** *the boss's nephew getting the job.*

▸noun **SOUND** ▷ **1** (C2) [C] the sound of something being said very quietly: *A murmur* ***of*** *agreement came from the crowd.* **2** [S] a soft continuous sound: *The murmur of the waves on the beach lulled me to sleep.* **COMPLAINT** ▷ **3** [C] a complaint that is expressed privately: *After the report was published, there were murmurs* ***of discontent*** *round the office.*

IDIOM **without a murmur** without even a small complaint: *For once the children went to bed without a murmur.*

Murphy's law /ˌmɜː.fizˈlɔː/ (US) /ˌmɝː.fizˈlɑː/ **noun** [U] (UK offensive also ˌ**Sod's** ˈ**law**) the principle that if it is possible for something to go wrong, it will go wrong: *The bus is always late but today when I was late it came on time – that's Murphy's law I suppose!*

muscle /ˈmʌs.l̩/ **noun; verb**

▸noun **BODY PART** ▷ **1** (B2) [C or U] one of many tissues in the body that can tighten and relax to produce movement: *neck/back/leg/stomach muscles* ◦ *facial muscles* ◦ ***bulging/rippling*** *(= large and clear to see) muscles* ◦ *He* ***flexed*** *his muscles (= tightened them to make them look large and strong) so that everyone could admire them.* ◦ *These exercises build muscle and increase stamina.* ◦ *a muscle* ***spasm*** *(= a sudden uncontrollable tightening movement)* **2 pull a muscle** (C1) to injure a muscle by stretching it too far so that it is very painful: *Russell pulled a back muscle early in the game.* **POWER** ▷ **3** [U] the power to do difficult things or to make people behave in a certain way: *This magazine has considerable financial muscle and can afford to pay top journalists.* ◦ *The company lacks the marketing muscle to compete with drug giants.*

▸verb

PHRASAL VERB **muscle in** informal to force your way into a situation and make certain you are included, although you are not wanted: *I hear Mark's muscled in* ***on*** *our meeting.*

ˈ**muscle-bound** **adj** disapproving describes someone who has very large muscles which make it difficult to move normally

ˈ**muscle-**ˌ**flexing** **noun** [U] a public show of military or political power that is intended to worry an opponent: *Opposition groups fear violence, after weeks of military muscle-flexing from the government.*

muscleman /ˈmʌs.l̩.mæn/ **noun** [C] (plural **-men** /-men/) a man who has very large muscles as a result of doing special exercises to improve them

muscly /ˈmʌs.li/ **adj** informal having a lot of well-developed muscles: *She's got big, muscly legs.*

Muscovite /ˈmʌs.kə.vaɪt/ **noun** [C] a person from Moscow

muscular /ˈmʌs.kjʊ.ləʳ/ (US) /-lɚ/ **adj** **BODY** ▷ **1** related to muscles: *muscular* ***contractions*** ◦ *muscular pain* **2** having well-developed muscles: *muscular arms/legs* ◦ *He wished he was more muscular.*

muscular dystrophy /ˌmʌs.kjʊ.ləˈdɪs.trə.fi/ (US) /-lɚ-/ **noun** [U] a serious disease in which a person's muscles gradually become weaker until walking is no longer possible

musculature /ˈmʌs.kjʊ.lə.tʃəʳ/ (US) /-tʃɚ/ **noun** [U] the position and structure of the muscles: *By looking at the bones of this animal, we can discover quite a lot about its musculature.*

muse /mjuːz/ **verb; noun**

▸verb [I] formal to think about something carefully and for a long time: *I began to muse* ***about/on*** *the possibility of starting my own business.*

▸noun [C] literary an imaginary being, person, or force that gives someone ideas and helps them to write, paint, or make music: *The muse has left me – I haven't written any poetry for months!* ◦ *Juliet was not only the painter's best model but also his muse.*

Muse /mjuːz/ **noun** [C] literary in ancient Greek and Roman stories, one of the nine GODDESSES who were believed to give encouragement in different areas of literature, art, and music

museum /mjuːˈziː.əm/ **noun** [C] (A1) a building where objects of historical, scientific, or artistic interest are kept: *a museum of modern art* ◦ *the Natural History Museum*

muˈ**seum** ˌ**piece** **noun** [C] humorous something that is very old-fashioned and should no longer be used: *That old car is a museum piece – you should get a new one.*

mush /mʌʃ/ **noun** [U] **SOFT SUBSTANCE** ▷ **1** informal any unpleasant thick soft substance, such as food that has been cooked for too long: *If you overcook the cabbage it'll* ***turn to*** *mush.* **2** If you say your brain has turned to mush, it means you cannot think clearly. **BOOK/FILM** ▷ **3** informal If you describe something such as a book or film as mush, you mean that it is too emotional: *The film was just romantic mush.*

mushroom /ˈmʌʃ.ruːm/, /-rʊm/ **noun; verb**

▸noun [C] (A2) a **fungus** with a round top and short stem. Some types of mushroom can be eaten: ***wild/*** *cultivated mushrooms* ◦ ***button*** *(= very small) mushrooms* ◦ *dried/grilled/stuffed/sliced mushrooms* ◦ *cream of mushroom soup* ◦ *For this recipe choose mushrooms with large caps (= top parts).* ◦ *Unfortunately some poisonous mushrooms look like* ***edible*** *mushrooms.* → Compare **toadstool**

▸verb [I] to increase very quickly: *The number of computers in schools has mushroomed in recent years.*

ˈ**mushroom** ˌ**cloud** **noun** [C usually singular] a very large cloud of dust that rises into the air in the shape of a large mushroom, especially after a nuclear explosion

mushy /ˈmʌʃ.i/ adj **SOFT** ▷ **1** soft and having no firm shape: *Cook the lentils until they are mushy.* ◦ disapproving *The meat was mushy and tasteless.* **EMOTIONAL** ▷ **2** informal disapproving too emotional: *I hate those mushy love stories.*

ˌ**mushy** ˈ**peas** noun [plural] UK soft, cooked MARROWFAT PEAS (= a type of large pea)

music /ˈmjuː.zɪk/ noun [U] **1** A1 a pattern of sounds made by musical instruments, voices, or computers, or a combination of these, intended to give pleasure to people listening to it: *classical/pop/dance/rock music* ◦ *a beautiful* ***piece of*** *music* ◦ *What sort of music do you listen to?* ◦ *They* ***play*** *good music on this (radio) station.* ◦ *I just like* ***making*** *music (= playing an instrument or singing).* ◦ *Shall I* ***put on*** *some music (= play a recording)?* **2** the art or study of music: *I studied music at college.* ◦ *the music business/industry* ◦ *music lessons* **3** the written system of symbols representing musical notes: *Can you* ***read*** *music?*

IDIOM **be music to sb's ears** to be something that you are very pleased to hear: *The rattle of the letterbox was music to my ears – the letter had arrived at last.*

musical /ˈmjuː.zɪ.kəl/ adj; noun

▸adj **1** A2 related to or connected with music: *musical* ***instruments*** ◦ *Mozart's musical compositions include symphonies and operas.* **2** C1 If you are musical, you have a skill in or great liking for music: *The family all play instruments – they're all very musical.* • **musically** /-i/ adv C2 *It's a school for musically* ***gifted*** *children (= those who are very good at playing a musical instrument or singing).* ◦ *Musically speaking (= referring to the music they produce), this band has a lot of talent.*

▸noun [C] B2 a play or film in which part of the story is sung to music

ˈ**musical** ˌ**box** noun [C] UK (mainly US ˈ**music** ˌ**box**) a decorative box with a device inside it that plays a tune when you open the lid

ˌ**musical** ˈ**chairs** noun [plural] a game in which children walk around a group of chairs while music plays. When the music stops they have to sit quickly on a chair, but because there is always one fewer chairs than children, the child that is left standing must leave the game: figurative *It's a game of musical chairs (= a situation in which people change jobs often) as editors move from one newspaper to another.*

musicality /mjuː.zɪˈkæl.ə.ti/ US /-t̬i/ noun [U] skill and good judgment in playing music: *Her natural musicality made this one of the most enjoyable concerts of the year.*

ˈ**music** ˌ**box** noun [C] US for **musical box**

ˈ**music** ˌ**hall** noun [C or U] UK (US also **vaudeville**) a type of theatre entertainment in the 1800s and 1900s that included music, dancing, and jokes, or the building used for this entertainment

musician /mjuːˈzɪʃ.ən/ noun [C] B1 someone who is skilled in playing music, usually as their job: *The concert features dancers and musicians of all nationalities.*

musicianship /mjuːˈzɪʃ.ən.ʃɪp/ noun [U] a person's skill in playing a musical instrument or singing: *The sheer musicianship of this young woman is breathtaking.*

ˈ**music-**ˌ**making** noun [U] the playing or writing of music: *His compositions were influenced by the great tradition of music-making in that country.*

musicology /ˌmjuː.zɪˈkɒl.ə.dʒi/ US /-ˈkɑː.lə-/ noun [U] the study of the history, theory, and science of music

• **musicologist** /-dʒɪst/ noun [C] *Arvinda is a respected musicologist.*

musk /mʌsk/ noun [U] a substance with a strong sweet smell, used in making PERFUMES • **musky** /ˈmʌs.ki/ adj *Her skin had a warm musky odour.*

musket /ˈmʌs.kɪt/ noun [C] a gun with a long BARREL, used in the past

Muslim /ˈmʊz.lɪm/ US /ˈmɑːz.lem/ noun; adj

▸noun [C] (also **Moslem**) a person who follows the religion of Islam

▸adj describes people who follow the religion of Islam: *a Muslim country/state* ◦ *a Muslim family*

muslin /ˈmʌz.lɪn/ noun [U] a very thin cotton material: *A 19th-century painting of a girl in a muslin dress hung on the wall.* ◦ *The soured milk is strained through muslin to leave a soft ball of cheese.*

muso /ˈmjuː.zəʊ/ US /-zoʊ/ noun [C] UK informal someone who likes popular music very much and knows a lot about it, often having a lot of musical equipment

muss /mʌs/ verb; noun

▸verb [T] mainly US to make untidy: *The wind is mussing (up) my hair.*

▸noun US **no muss, no fuss** used to say that something can be done without a lot of difficulty: *If we pack tonight, we can leave first thing in the morning – no muss, no fuss.*

mussel /ˈmʌs.əl/ noun [C] a small, orange sea creature that lives inside a black shell with two parts that close tightly together. Mussels can be eaten.

must strong /mʌst/ weak /məst/ /məs/ modal verb; noun

▸modal verb **NECESSARY** ▷ **1** A2 used to show that it is necessary or very important that something happens in the present or future: *Meat must be cooked thoroughly.* ◦ *I must get some sleep.* ◦ *You mustn't show this letter to anyone else.* ◦ *Luggage must not be left unattended (= it is against the rules).* ◦ formal *Must you leave so soon?* ◦ formal *'Must I sign this?' 'Yes, you must.'* **2** If you say that you must do something, you mean that you strongly intend to do something in the future: *I must phone my sister.* ◦ *We must get someone to fix that wheel.* ◦ *I mustn't bite my nails.* **3** used for emphasis: *I must* ***say****, you're looking extremely well.* ◦ *I must* ***admit****, I wasn't looking forward to it.* **4** B1 If you tell someone else that they must do something pleasant, you are emphasizing that you think it is a good idea for them to do that: *You must come and stay with us for the weekend.* ◦ *We must meet for lunch soon.*

> **!** Common mistake: **must**
>
> **Must** is followed by an infinitive verb without 'to'.
> Don't say 'must to do something', say **must do something**:
>
> ~~*You must to pay attention to your pronunciation.*~~
> *You must pay attention to your pronunciation.*

PROBABLY ▷ **5** B2 used to show that something is very likely, probable, or certain to be true: *Harry's been driving all day – he must be tired.* ◦ *There's no food left – we must have eaten it all.* ◦ *When you got lost in the forest you must have been very frightened.* ◦ *'You must know Frank.' 'No, I don't.'*

▸noun [C] informal something that is necessary: *If you live in the country a car is* ***a*** *must.*

must- /mʌst-/ prefix informal **a must-do, must-have, must-see, etc.** something that is so good, you must do it, have it, or see it: *The cashmere scarf is this season's must-have.*

mustache /mʊˈstɑːʃ/ (US) /ˈmʌs.tæʃ/ **noun** [C] US for moustache

mustachioed /məˈstæʃ.i.əʊd/ (US) /-oʊd/ **adj** mainly humorous having a large MOUSTACHE (= a line of hair above the upper lip): *a mustachioed gentleman*

mustang /ˈmʌs.tæŋ/ **noun** [C] an American wild horse

mustard /ˈmʌs.təd/ (US) /-tɚd/ **noun** [U] C1 a thick yellow or brown sauce that tastes spicy and is eaten cold in small amounts, especially with meat

ˈmustard ˌgas **noun** [U] a very poisonous gas, used as a weapon, that burns the skin, damages organs inside the body, and can kill

muster /ˈmʌs.təʳ/ (US) /-tɚ/ **verb; noun**
▸**verb** [I or T] **PRODUCE** ▷ **1** to produce or encourage something such as an emotion or support: *She managed to muster the* ***courage*** *to ask him to the cinema.* ◦ *The team will need all the* ***strength*** *they can muster to win this game.* ◦ *Opponents are unlikely to be able to muster enough* ***votes*** *to override the veto.* **COME TOGETHER** ▷ **2** (especially of soldiers) to come together, especially in preparation for fighting, or to cause to do this: *The twelfth division mustered on the hill.* ◦ *The general mustered his* ***troops****.*

PHRASAL VERB **muster sth up** If you muster up a feeling of courage or energy, you try hard to find that quality in yourself because you need it in order to do something: [+ to infinitive] *She finally mustered up the courage to ask him for more money.*

▸**noun** [C] a group of people, especially soldiers, who have been brought together

ˈmuster ˌpoint **noun** [C] (also **ˈmuster ˌstation**) UK a place where everyone in an area or on a boat is ordered to go when there is an emergency

ˈmust-have **adj** [before noun] A must-have object is something that many people want to own: *The iPod quickly established itself as a must-have device.*

mustn't /ˈmʌs.ᵊnt/ **short form** must not: *You mustn't worry too much about this.*

musty /ˈmʌs.ti/ **adj** smelling unpleasantly old and slightly wet: *musty old books* ◦ *a musty* ***smell*** ◦ *a musty room*

mutant /ˈmjuː.tᵊnt/ (US) /-t̬ᵊnt/ **noun** [C] **1** an organism that is different from others of its type because of a permanent change in its GENES: *These mutants lack a vital protein which gives them immunity to the disease.* ◦ *This mutant* ***gene*** *is thought to cause cancer.* ◦ figurative humorous *I'm convinced he's a mutant – he's not a bit like the rest of our family!* **2** disapproving an unpleasant and frightening thing: *The result of these experiments will be a nightmarish world filled with two-headed monsters and other mutants.*

mutate /mjuːˈteɪt/ **verb** [I] to develop new physical characteristics because of a permanent change in the GENES. These changes can happen naturally or can be produced by the use of chemicals or RADIATION: *These bacteria have mutated* ***into*** *forms that are resistant to certain drugs.*

mutation /mjuːˈteɪ.ʃᵊn/ **noun** **1** [U] the way in which GENES change and produce permanent differences: *It is well known that radiation can cause mutation.* **2** [C] a permanent change in an organism, or the changed organism itself: *Environmental pressures encourage genes with certain mutations to persist and others to die out.* ◦ *These plants* ***carry*** *the mutation* ***for*** *red flowers.*

mute /mjuːt/ **adj; noun; verb**
▸**adj** (of a person) unable or unwilling to speak, or (of an activity) silent: *a mute child* ◦ *The president has* ***remained*** *mute about plans to curtail the number of immigrants.* ◦ *I gazed at her in mute admiration.*
▸**noun** [C] **1** a button or other device on a musical instrument that can be fixed in order to make it quieter **2** old-fashioned offensive a person who is not able to speak
▸**verb** [T] If you mute a noise, you do something to make it less loud: *Double glazing muted the noise of the traffic.*

muted /ˈmjuː.tɪd/ (US) /-t̬ɪd/ **adj** **NOT LOUD** ▷ **1** not loud: *There was polite, muted* ***applause*** *when I finished speaking.* **NOT ENTHUSIASTIC** ▷ **2** showing little enthusiasm: *The idea received a muted response.* **NOT BRIGHT** ▷ **3** describes a colour that is not bright: *She was dressed in muted shades of blue.*

ˌmute ˈswan **noun** [C] the largest type of SWAN, which does not make as much noise as other SWANS when it flies

muti /ˈmuː.ti/ (US) /-t̬i/ **noun** [U] South African English **1** medicine **2** African traditional medicine, for example magic objects or medicines prepared from plants or animals

mutilate /ˈmjuː.tɪ.leɪt/ (US) /-tᵊl.eɪt/ **verb** [T] **1** to damage something severely, especially by violently removing a part: *Her body had been mutilated beyond recognition.* **2** to destroy an idea or a piece of art or entertainment: *They have mutilated a beautiful film by making these changes.* • **mutilation** /ˌmjuː.tɪˈleɪ.ʃᵊn/ (US) /-tᵊlˈeɪ-/ **noun** [C or U] *He admitted to the murder and mutilation of 16 young men.*

mutineer /ˌmjuː.tɪˈnɪəʳ/ (US) /-t̬ɪˈnɪr/ **noun** [C] someone who takes part in a mutiny

mutiny /ˈmjuː.tɪ.ni/ (US) /-t̬ɪ-/ **noun; verb**
▸**noun** [C or U] an occasion when a group of people, especially soldiers or sailors, refuses to obey orders and/or attempts to take control from people in authority: *Conditions on the ship were often very bad, and crews were on the point of mutiny.* ◦ *There were rumours of mutiny* ***among*** *the troops.* ◦ *Soldiers crushed mutinies in three jails.* • **mutinous** /-nəs/ **adj** *The mutinous sailors took control of the ship.*
▸**verb** [I] to take part in a mutiny: *The crew mutinied and murdered the ship's captain.* ◦ *The troops mutinied* ***against*** *their officers.*

mutt /mʌt/ **noun** [C] mainly US **PERSON** ▷ **1** informal a person who behaves in a silly or careless way: *Come on you mutts, play harder!* **DOG** ▷ **2** a **mongrel**

mutter /ˈmʌt.əʳ/ (US) /ˈmʌt̬.ɚ/ **verb; noun**
▸**verb** [I or T] B2 to speak quietly and in a low voice that is not easy to hear, often when you are worried or complaining about something: *Stop muttering and speak up!* ◦ *He was muttering* (***away***) ***to*** *himself.* ◦ *Laurence muttered something* ***about*** *his wife and left.* ◦ *He muttered something* ***under*** *his* ***breath*** *to the person next to him.*
▸**noun** **QUIET WORDS** ▷ **1** [S] (the sound of) words being said very quietly: *I heard the soft mutter of voices in the next room.* **COMPLAINT** ▷ **2** [C] a complaint that is made to only a few people: *There were mutters* ***that*** *other departments received more money than ours.*

mutterings /ˈmʌt.ə.rɪŋz/ (US) /ˈmʌt̬.ɚ-/ **noun** [plural] complaints that are made to only a few people: *There are mutterings* ***of discontent*** *among the staff.*

mutton /ˈmʌt.ᵊn/ (US) /ˈmʌt̬-/ **noun** [U] **1** the meat from an adult sheep eaten as food **2** Indian English the meat from a GOAT or sheep eaten as food

IDIOM **mutton dressed as lamb** UK informal disapproving a way of describing an older woman who is dressed in a style that is more suitable for a younger

M

woman: *Do you think this dress is too young-looking for me? – I don't want to look like mutton dressed as lamb.*

muttonchops /ˈmʌt.ən.tʃɒps/ (US) /ˈmʌt̬.ən.tʃɑːps/ noun [plural] (also ˌ**muttonchop** ˈ**whiskers**) long hair growing down each side of a man's face, fashionable especially in Europe and America in the 19th century

mutual /ˈmjuː.tʃu.əl/ **adj; noun**

▸**adj** C1 (of two or more people or groups) feeling the same emotion, or doing the same thing to or for each other: *Theirs was a partnership based on mutual respect, trust and understanding.* ◦ *The agreement was terminated by mutual consent.*

▸**noun** [C] (also ˌ**mutual** ˈ**company**) a financial organization such as a BUILDING SOCIETY that is owned by its members, rather than by SHAREHOLDERS

ˌ**mutual** ˈ**friend** noun [C] C1 a person who is the friend of two people who may or may not know each other: *Lynn and Phil* ***met through*** *a mutual friend.*

ˈ**mutual** ˌ**fund** noun [C usually singular] US for **unit trust**

mutually /ˈmjuː.tʃu.ə.li/ **adv** felt or done by two or more people or groups in the same way: *It will be a mutually* ***beneficial*** *project.* ◦ *Being rich and being a Socialist are not mutually* ***exclusive*** *(= they can exist together at the same time).*

Muzak /ˈmjuː.zæk/ **noun** [U] trademark recorded music that is played quietly and continuously in public places, such as airports, hotels, and shops, to make people feel relaxed

muzzle /ˈmʌz.l̩/ **noun; verb**

▸**noun** [C] **ANIMAL** ▷ **1** the mouth and nose of an animal, especially a dog, or a covering put over this in order to prevent the animal from biting **GUN** ▷ **2** the end of a gun BARREL, where the bullets come out

▸**verb** [T] **ANIMAL** ▷ **1** to put a muzzle on an animal: *Dangerous dogs should be muzzled.* **STOP OPINIONS** ▷ **2** to stop a person or organization from expressing independent opinions: *The new Secrecy Act will muzzle the media and the opposition.*

muzzy /ˈmʌz.i/ **adj** UK (of a person) confused and unable to think clearly because of tiredness, illness, alcohol or drugs, or (of a situation, plans, etc.) not clear or well explained: *Feeling muzzy from the blow on his head, he got up very slowly.* ◦ *Until a week ago, the group's objectives were slightly muzzy.* • **muzzily** /-ɪ.li/ **adv** • **muzziness** /-nəs/ **noun** [U]

MW **noun** [U] written abbreviation for **medium wave**

MWA /ˌem.dʌbl.juːˈeɪ/ **noun** [C] abbreviation for Member of the Welsh Assembly

my /maɪ/ **determiner; exclamation**

▸**determiner** **1** A1 of or belonging to me (= the speaker or writer): *my parents* ◦ *my feet* ◦ *my name* ◦ *my jacket* ◦ *It wasn't my fault.* ◦ formal *She was rather surprised at my ask****ing*** *(= that I asked) for the book to be returned.* → See also **I, me, mine** **2** **my own** used to emphasize that something belongs to or is connected with me and no one else: *I want my own car.* ◦ *It was my own decision.* ◦ *This cake is* ***all*** *my own* ***work*** *(= I made it without help).* **3** used in front of a noun as a way of expressing love or as a polite or humorous form of address: *My darling!* ◦ *Do you want any help, my dear?* **4** relating to a part of some websites where you can choose to see only the information that is important to you

▸**exclamation** old-fashioned used to express surprise or pleasure: *My, what delicious food!* ◦ *My, oh, my, what a busy day!*

myalgic encephalomyelitis /maɪˌæl.dʒɪk.enˌsef.ə.ləʊ.maɪ.əˈlaɪ.tɪs/ (US) /-loʊ.maɪ.əˈlaɪ.t̬əs/ **noun** [U] UK specialized for **chronic fatigue syndrome**

mycology /maɪˈkɒl.ə.dʒi/ (US) /-ˈkɑː.lə-/ **noun** [U] the scientific study of FUNGI • **mycologist** /-dʒɪst/ **noun** [C]

myelin /ˈmaɪə.lɪn/ **noun** [U] specialized a substance containing a lot of fat that forms a covering around nerves, especially those in the brain, protecting them and helping them to send signals effectively: *The myelin* ***sheath*** *around the neuron is damaged.*

mynah /ˈmaɪ.nə/ **noun** [C] (also ˈ**mynah** ˌ**bird**, Australian English ˌ**Indian** ˈ**mynah**) a black or dark brown bird from Asia that can copy human speech

myob written abbreviation for mind your own business: used in emails and text messages to say that you do not want to talk about something

myopia /maɪˈəʊ.pi.ə/ (US) /-ˈoʊ-/ **noun** [U] specialized a condition in which someone cannot clearly see things that are far away

myopic /maɪˈɒp.ɪk/ (US) /-ˈɑː.pɪk/ **adj** **1** specialized not able to see clearly things that are far away **2** disapproving unable to understand a situation or the way actions will affect it in the future: *Their myopic refusal to act now will undoubtedly cause problems in the future.*

myriad /ˈmɪr.i.əd/ **noun** [C] literary a very large number of something: *a myriad* ***of*** *choices* ◦ *And now myriads* ***of*** *bars and hotels are opening up along the coast.* • **myriad adj** *They offered no solution for all our myriad problems.*

myrrh /mɜːʳ/ (US) /mɝː/ **noun** [U] a sticky brown substance with a strong smell that is used in making PERFUME and INCENSE (= a substance burned to produce a sweet smell, for example in a religious ceremony)

myrtle /ˈmɜː.tl̩/ (US) /ˈmɝː.t̬l̩/ **noun** [C] a small tree with shiny green leaves, pleasant-smelling white flowers and blue-black fruit

myself /maɪˈself/ **pronoun** **1** A2 used when the subject of the verb is 'I' and the object is the same person: *I've bought myself a new coat.* ◦ *I caught sight of myself in the mirror.* ◦ *Yes, I thought to myself, it's time to take a holiday.* **2** B2 used to emphasize 'I' as the subject of a sentence: *I myself don't like a heavy meal at lunchtime.* ◦ *I don't like a heavy meal at lunchtime myself.* **3** used instead of 'I' or 'me': *My husband and myself were delighted with the gift.* **4** **(all) by myself** alone or without help from anyone else: *I live by myself.* ◦ *I had to do the whole job all by myself.* **5** **(all) to myself** for my use only: *I never get an hour to myself.* **6** **not be/seem/feel myself** not to be, seem, or feel as happy or as healthy as usual: *I went to see the doctor because I haven't been feeling myself lately.* **7** **in myself** UK informal used when describing your state of mind when you are physically ill: *I'm well enough in myself (= happy) – I've just got this nagging headache.*

> **! Common mistake: myself**
>
> Remember that **myself** is written as one word.
>
> Don't write 'my self', write **myself**:
>
> ~~*I enjoyed my self so much at the concert.*~~

IDIOM **keep (myself) to myself** to spend time alone, not talking to other people very much: *I don't see friends very often. I prefer to keep myself to myself.*

mysterious /mɪˈstɪə.ri.əs/ (US) /-ˈstɪr.i-/ **adj** B2 strange, not known, or not understood: *She's an actress whose inner life has remained mysterious, despite the many interviews she has given.* ◦ *He died in mysterious* ***circumstances****, and there is still a possibility that it was murder.* • **mysteriously** /-li/ **adv** C1 *'Perhaps, and perhaps not,' she said mysteriously.* ◦ *Mysteriously, the light came on, although no one was near the switch.*

mystery /ˈmɪs.tᵊr.i/ Ⓤⓢ /-tɚ-/ **noun** **STRANGE/UNKNOWN THING** ▷ **1** Ⓑ① [C or U] something strange or not known that has not yet been explained or understood: *How the massive stones were brought here from hundreds of miles away* ***is/remains*** *a mystery.* ◦ *The mystery was* ***solved*** *when the police discovered the murder weapon.* ◦ *The book tries to explain some of the mysteries* ***of*** *life.* ◦ *The details of the scandal remain* ***cloaked/shrouded/wrapped in*** *mystery.* ◦ *It's* ***a complete*** *mystery* (***to*** *me*) ***that/why*** (= *I do not understand why*) *she married him at all!* **BOOK/FILM/PLAY** ▷ **2** [C] a book, film, or play, especially about a crime or a murder, with a surprise ending that explains all the strange events that have happened: *I really enjoy* ***murder*** *mysteries.* ◦ *a mystery* ***writer***

ˈmystery ˌplay noun [C] a religious play based on stories from the Bible and performed especially in Europe between the 11th and 14th centuries

ˌmystery ˈshopper noun [C] (US also **ˌsecret ˈshopper**) someone employed to test the service in shops and businesses by pretending to be a normal customer

ˈmystery ˌtour noun [C] UK a short journey, especially with a group of other people in a bus, to visit places that are kept secret from you until you get there

mystic /ˈmɪs.tɪk/ **noun** [C] someone who attempts to be united with God through prayer • **mystical** /-tɪ.kᵊl/ **adj** (also **mystic**) *a mystical religion*

mysticism /ˈmɪs.tɪ.sɪ.zᵊm/ **noun** [U] the belief that there is hidden meaning in life or that each human being can unite with God

mystification /ˌmɪs.tɪ.fɪˈkeɪ.ʃᵊn/ **noun** [U] the state of feeling very confused because someone or something is impossible to understand: *And then, to the audience's mystification, the band suddenly stopped playing.*

mystify /ˈmɪs.tɪ.faɪ/ **verb** [T often passive] to confuse someone by being or doing something very strange or impossible to explain: *I was mystified by her decision.* ◦ *Most Americans seem totally mystified by cricket.* • **mystifying** /-ɪŋ/ **adj** *After ten years her mystifying disappearance was still unexplained.* • **mystifyingly** /-ɪŋ.li/ **adv**

mystique /mɪˈstiːk/ **noun** [U] formal a quality of being special in a mysterious and attractive way: *There's great mystique* ***attached to/surrounding*** *the life of a movie star.*

myth /mɪθ/ **noun** **ANCIENT STORY** ▷ **1** Ⓑ② [C or U] an ancient story or set of stories, especially explaining the early history of a group of people or about natural events and facts: ***ancient*** *myths* ◦ *The children enjoyed the stories about the gods and goddesses of* ***Greek*** *and* ***Roman*** *myth.* ◦ *Most societies have their own creation myths.* **FALSE IDEA** ▷ **2** Ⓒ① [C + that] disapproving a commonly believed but false idea: *Statistics* ***disprove*** *the myth* ***that*** *women are worse drivers than men.*

mythical /ˈmɪθ.ɪ.kᵊl/ **adj** (also **mythic** /ˈmɪθ.ɪ.k/) **1** existing only in stories: *the mythical island of Atlantis* ◦ *dragons and other mythical creatures* **2** imaginary or not real: *Start living life here and now instead of waiting for that mythical day when you'll be slim.*

mythological /ˌmɪθ.ᵊlˈɒdʒ.ɪ.kᵊl/ Ⓤⓢ /-əˈlɑː.dʒɪ-/ **adj** connected with myths: *a mythological hero/creature*

mythologize mainly US (UK usually **mythologise**) /mɪˈθɒl.ə.dʒaɪz/ Ⓤⓢ /mɪˈθɑː.lə-/ **verb** [I or T] to create a false picture of a situation: *People tend to mythologize* (***about***) *their youth/the past.*

mythology /mɪˈθɒl.ə.dʒi/ Ⓤⓢ /-ˈθɑː.lə-/ **noun** [U] **ANCIENT STORIES** ▷ **1** myths in general: *She's fascinated by the stories of* ***classical*** *mythology* (= *ancient Greek and Roman myths*). **POPULAR BELIEF** ▷ **2** a popular belief that is probably not true: *It's just a piece of* ***popular*** *mythology that people always get sacked when they are away.*

myxomatosis /ˌmɪk.sə.məˈtəʊ.sɪs/ Ⓤⓢ /-ˈtoʊ-/ **noun** [U] an infectious disease of RABBITS that usually kills them

N, n /en/ **noun; adj**
▸**noun** (plural **Ns, N's** or **n's**) **LETTER** ▷ **1** [C or U] the 14th letter of the English alphabet **NORTH** ▷ **2** [U] written abbreviation for **north**
▸**adj** written abbreviation for **north** or **northern**

'n' /-ən-/ **conjunction** not standard used in writing to mean 'and': *fish 'n' chips* ◦ *rock 'n' roll*

n /en/ **noun MATHEMATICS** ▷ **1** [U] used in mathematics to mean a number whose value is not known or not stated: *If 3n = 12, what is the value of n?* **2** [U] used more generally to represent a number that is not known or exact **GRAMMAR** ▷ **3** written abbreviation for **noun**

n/a (also **N/A**) written abbreviation for not applicable: used on a form when you cannot give a RELEVANT (= that answers the question) answer to a question

naan noun [C or U] **nan**

nab /næb/ **verb** [T] (**-bb-**) informal to take something suddenly, or to catch or arrest a criminal: *Undercover police officers nabbed the men at the airport.* ◦ *Someone nabbed my apple when I wasn't looking!*

nabob /ˈneɪ.bɒb/ (US) /-bɑːb/ **noun** [C] old-fashioned a rich or powerful person

nachos /ˈnɑː.tʃəʊz/ (US) /-tʃoʊz/ **noun** [plural] small pieces of fried TORTILLA (= flat bread made from MAIZE flour) covered with melted cheese, beans, and a spicy sauce

nadir /ˈneɪ.dɪəʳ/ (US) /-dɚ/ **noun** [S] formal the worst moment, or the moment of least hope and least achievement: *The defeat was **the** nadir **of** her career.* → Compare **zenith**

nads /nædz/ **noun** [plural] slang for **testicle**

nae /neɪ/ **adv** Scottish English or Northern English for **no** or **not**

naff /næf/ **adj; verb**
▸**adj** UK slang not stylish or fashionable: *His haircut was a bit naff.*
▸**verb**

PHRASAL VERB **naff off** UK slang old-fashioned used to rudely tell someone to go away because they are annoying you

nag /næg/ **verb; noun**
▸**verb** [I or T] (**-gg-**) to criticize or complain often in an annoying way: [+ obj + to infinitive] *My mum's always nagging me **to** get my hair cut.* ◦ *If she'd only stop nagging **at** me, I might actually help.* ◦ *I'm always nagging him **about** his diet.*

PHRASAL VERB **nag (away) at sb** If doubts or WORRIES nag (away) at you, you think about them all the time.

▸**noun** [C] old-fashioned informal a horse, especially one that is too old to be useful

nagging /ˈnæg.ɪŋ/ **adj; noun**
▸**adj 1** complaining or criticizing: *a nagging voice* **2** describes an unpleasant feeling that continues for a long period of time: *nagging doubts/pain*
▸**noun** [U] complaining and criticizing: *I got sick of her constant nagging.*

nah /næː/ **adv** slang for **no**

nail /neɪl/ **noun; verb**
▸**noun** [C] **METAL** ▷ **1** (B2) a small, thin piece of metal with one pointed end and one flat end which you hit into something with a hammer, especially in order to fasten or join it to something else: *a three-inch nail* ◦ *I stepped on a nail sticking out of the floorboards.* ◦ ***Hammer** a nail into the wall and we'll hang the mirror from it.* **BODY PART** ▷ **2** (B2) a thin, hard area that covers the upper side of the end of each finger and each toe: *Stop **biting** your nails!* ◦ *nail clippers* ◦ *a nail file* → See also **fingernail, toenail**

IDIOMS **another/the final nail in the coffin** an event which causes the failure of something that had already started to fail: *Each successive revelation of incompetence is another nail in the chairman's coffin.* • **hard/tough as nails** not feeling or showing any emotions such as sympathy, fear, or worry

▸**verb FASTEN** ▷ **1** [T + adv/prep] to fasten something with nails: *She had nailed a small shelf **to** the door.* ◦ *A notice had been nailed **up** on the wall.* ◦ *The lid of the box had been nailed **down**.* **CATCH** ▷ **2** [T] slang to catch someone, especially when they are doing something wrong, or to make it clear that they are guilty: *The police had been trying to nail those guys for months.*

IDIOMS **nail your colours to the mast** UK to make it obvious what your opinions or plans are • **nailing jelly to the wall** trying to give exact details for something that it is not possible to know about exactly: *Writing the history of this period is like nailing jelly to the wall.*

PHRASAL VERBS **nail sb down** informal to make someone give you exact details or a firm decision about something: *They nailed him down **to** a specific time and place.* • **nail sth down DECISION** ▷ **1** informal If you nail down an arrangement or decision, you fix and agree to the details of it: *After a five-hour meeting, we finally nailed down a deal.* **UNDERSTAND** ▷ **2** US informal to understand something completely, or to describe something correctly: *We haven't been able to nail down the cause of the fire yet.*

nail-biter /ˈneɪlˌbaɪ.təʳ/ (US) /-tɚ/ **noun** [C] a sports event or a film that is exciting because you do not know how it will end: *Saturday's semifinal was a real nail-biter.*

ˈnail-ˌbiting adj [before noun] describes a situation that is very exciting or worrying because you do not know how it will end: *Germany won the championship after a nail-biting final.*

nailbrush /ˈneɪl.brʌʃ/ **noun** [C] a small, stiff brush used for cleaning your nails and your hands

ˈnail ˌfile noun [C] a small strip of metal or paper with a rough surface used for making the edges of your nails smooth and curved

ˈnail ˌpolish noun [C or U] (UK also **ˈnail ˌvarnish**) a coloured liquid that is painted on FINGERNAILS or TOENAILS

ˈnail ˌscissors noun [plural] a small pair of curved SCISSORS used to cut your nails

naive (also **naïve**) /naɪˈiːv/ **adj** mainly disapproving (C1) too willing to believe that someone is telling the truth, that people's intentions in general are good, or that life is simple and fair. People are often naive because they are young and/or have not had much experience of life: *She was very naive to believe that he'd stay with her.* ◦ *They make the naive assumption that because it's popular it must be good.* ◦ ***It** was a little naive **of** you **to** think that they would listen to your suggestions.* • **naively** (also **naïvely**) /-li/ **adv** *I, perhaps naively, believed he was telling the truth.*

N

naivety (also **naiveté**) /naɪˈiː.vɪ.ti/ (US) /-və.t̬i/ **noun** [U] trust based on not having much experience: disapproving *He demonstrated a worrying naivety about political issues.* ◦ approving *I think her naivety is charming – she's so unspoilt and fresh.*

naked /ˈneɪ.kɪd/ **adj** NOT COVERED ▷ **1** B2 not covered by clothes: *a naked man* ◦ *naked bodies* ◦ ***stark** naked (= completely naked)* ◦ US informal *buck/butt naked (= completely naked)* ◦ *He was naked **to** the waist (= not wearing clothes above his waist).* ◦ *The children were **half** naked (= partly naked).* ◦ *They **stripped** naked (= took off their clothes) and ran into the sea.* **2** Something that is naked does not have its usual covering: *a naked flame/light bulb (= one with nothing surrounding or covering it)* ◦ *a naked hillside (= one without trees or plants)* NOT HIDDEN ▷ **3** C1 [before noun] A naked feeling or quality is not hidden, although it is bad: *naked aggression/greed*

IDIOM **the naked eye** C2 If something can be seen with the naked eye, it can be seen without the help of an instrument: *This organism is too small to be seen **with** the naked eye.* ◦ *The police found traces of blood on his jacket that were **invisible to** the naked eye.*

nakedly /ˈneɪ.kɪd.li/ **adv** in a way that is obvious and unpleasant: *a nakedly racist organization*

nakedness /ˈneɪ.kɪd.nəs/ **noun** [U] the state of being naked

namaskar /ˌnʌm.əsˈkɑːʳ/ (US) /-ˈkɑːr/ **noun; exclamation**

▸**noun** [U] Indian English a traditional way of greeting someone in which you put the insides of your hands together in front of your face or chest and bend your head forwards

▸**exclamation** Indian English said as a greeting while you put the insides of your hands together in front of your face or chest and bend your head forwards

namby-pamby /ˌnæm.biˈpæm.bi/ **adj** informal disapproving weak, silly, or emotional: *She probably regarded us as a bunch of namby-pamby liberals.*

name /neɪm/ **noun; verb**

▸**noun 1** A1 [C] the word or words that a person, thing, or place is known by: *'Hi, what's your name?' 'My name's Diane.'* ◦ *Please write your **full** (= complete) name **and address** on the form.* ◦ *What's the name of that mountain in the distance?* ◦ *We finally agreed on the name Luca for our son.* ◦ *The students were listed **by** name and by country of origin.* **2** B2 [C usually singular] the opinion or reputation that someone or something has: *She went to court to **clear** her name (= prove that the bad things said about her were not true).* ◦ *Their actions **gave** British football a **bad** name in Europe at that time.* ◦ *They're trying to restore the **good** name of the manufacturer.* **3** [C] someone who is famous or has a good reputation: *It seemed like all the **big** names in football were there.* **4 by the name of sth** formal called: *I've got to talk to a professor by the name of Bin Said.* **5 go by the name of sth** to give yourself a name that is not your real name: *In the business world he goes by the name of J. Walter Fortune.* **6 in the name of sb** (also **in sb's name**) for someone or belonging to someone: *I've come to collect my tickets – I reserved them by phone yesterday in the name of Tremin.* ◦ *The house is in my wife's name.*

IDIOMS **be a name to conjure with** UK to be a very important name, or an interesting name that gives you a mental picture of something pleasant or exciting: *In those days Churchill was still a name to conjure with.* ◦ *The House of the Blue Lagoon – now there's a name to conjure with!* • **in all but name** existing as a fact but not officially described that way: *She is vice-president in all but name.* • **in God's/heaven's name** (also **in the name of God/heaven**) used to add force to something that is said. Some people might find the use of 'God' offensive: *What in God's name caused that outburst?* • **in name only** If a situation exists in name only, it is officially described that way, although that description is not completely accurate: *A large percentage of the population is Catholic, though many are so in name only.* • **in the name of sth** (also **in sth's name**) C2 (said or done) in order to help a particular thing succeed: *Much blood has been spilled in the name of religion.* • **in the name of sb/sth** (also **in sb's/sth's name**) representing someone or something: *In old movies the police shouted 'Open up in the name of the law' before they broke the door down.* ◦ *They were arrested in the name of the king.* ◦ *As members of the union, we have the right to know what action the union is taking in our name.* • **make a name for yourself** C2 to become famous or respected by a lot of people: *He's made a name for himself **as** a talented journalist.* • **your name is mud** informal If your name is mud, other people are angry with you because of something you have said or done: *If he doesn't turn up tonight, his name will be mud.* • **the name of the game** informal the most important part of an activity, or the quality that you most need for that activity: *People say that in politics the name of the game is making the right friends.* • **take sb's name in vain** UK humorous to criticize someone or talk about someone without respect, especially when they are not there • **to your name** If you have nothing or very little to your name, you own very little or have no money: *He had arrived in America without a cent to his name.* • **under the name of** using the false name of: *Her detective stories were written under the name of Kramer.*

▸**verb** [T] GIVE/SAY NAME ▷ **1** B1 to give someone or something a name: [+ two objects] *We named our dogs 'Shandy' and 'Belle'.* ◦ *A man named Dennis answered the door.* **2** B1 to say what something or someone's name is: *In the first question you had to name three types of monkey.* ◦ *He couldn't name his attacker.* CHOOSE ▷ **3** B2 to choose someone or something: *Just name the time and I'll be there.* ◦ *Name your conditions/terms/price.* ◦ *Ms Martinez has been named **(as)** the new Democratic candidate.*

IDIOMS **name and shame** UK to publicly say that a person, group, or business has done something wrong: *The report names and shames companies that are not doing enough to fight industrial pollution.* • **name names** to tell someone in authority the names of people involved in a secret or illegal activity • **name the day** to decide the date on which you are going to get married: *When are you going to name the day?* • **you name it** C2 used to say there are many things to choose from: *Gin, vodka, whisky, beer – you name it, I've got it.*

PHRASAL VERB **name sb/sth after sb/sth** (US also **name sb/sth for sb/sth**) to give someone or something the same name as another person or thing: *Paul was named after his grandad.* ◦ *She told us about his brother, Apollo, born in 1969 and named for the US astronauts' mission to the moon.*

ˈname-ˌcalling **noun** [U] the act of insulting someone by calling them rude names

ˈname-dropping **noun** [U] disapproving the act of talking about famous people that you have met, often pretending that you know them better than you really do, in order to appear more important and special: *I find her name-dropping very irritating.* • ˈ**name-ˌdrop verb** [I] • ˈ**name-ˌdropper noun** [C]

nameless /ˈneɪm.ləs/ **adj** having no name, or having a name that is not known: *a nameless soldier* ◦ *the nameless author of a medieval text*

IDIOM **who shall remain nameless** humorous used when you are telling people about a bad thing that someone else has done: *One boy, who shall remain nameless, has been late every day this week.*

namely /ˈneɪm.li/ **adv** C1 used when you want to give more detail or be more exact about something you have just said: *We need to get more teachers into the classrooms where they're most needed, namely in high poverty areas.* ◦ *I learned an important lesson when I lost my job, namely that nothing is a hundred percent guaranteed.*

nameplate /ˈneɪm.pleɪt/ **noun** [C] a piece of metal or plastic fastened onto something to show who owns it, who has made it, or who lives or works there: *There was a brass nameplate outside the door saying Dr A. Aslan.*

namesake /ˈneɪm.seɪk/ **noun** [C] a person or thing having the same name as another person or thing

nan[1] /næn/ **noun** [C] UK informal child's word for a grandmother: *The kids love staying with their nan at the weekend.* ◦ [as form of address] *Happy birthday, Nan.*

nan[2] (also **naan**) /nɑːn/ **noun** [C or U] (also ˈ**nan ˌbread**, ˈ**naan ˌbread**) a flat bread, typically eaten with South Asian food

nana /ˈnæn.ə/ **noun** [C] informal child's word for a grandmother: [as form of address] *Will you read me a story, Nana?*

nandrolone /ˈnæn.drə.ləʊn/ US /-loʊn/ **noun** [U] a substance that can improve someone's physical strength and STAMINA (= the ability to do something for a long period). It is not allowed in most sports competitions.

nanny /ˈnæn.i/ **noun** [C] **JOB** ▷ **1** a woman whose job is to take care of a particular family's children **GRANDMOTHER** ▷ **2** UK informal child's word for a grandmother: [as form of address] *Can I have a drink, Nanny?*

ˈ**nanny ˌgoat noun** [C] a female GOAT

ˌ**nanny** ˈ**state noun** [C] disapproving a government which tries to give too much advice or make too many laws about how people should live their lives, especially about eating, smoking, or drinking alcohol: *The government was accused of trying to create a nanny state when it announced new guidelines on healthy eating.*

nano- /næn.əʊ-/ US /næn.oʊ-/ **prefix 1** one BILLIONTH: *a nanosecond* **2** extremely small: *nanotechnology*

nanocomputer /ˈnæn.əʊ.kəmˌpjuː.təʳ/ US /-oʊ.kəm-ˌpjuː.t̬ɚ/ **noun** [C] a computer with electronic parts that are so small that they can only be seen using a MICROSCOPE

nanometre /ˈnæn.əʊˌmiː.təʳ/ US /-oʊˌmiː.t̬ɚ/ **noun** [C] UK (US **nanometer**) 0.000,000,001 of a metre

nanosecond /ˈnæn.əʊˌsek.ənd/ US /-oʊ-/ **noun** [C] 0.000,000,001 seconds

nanotechnology /ˌnæn.əʊ.tekˈnɒl.ə.dʒi/ US /-oʊ.tekˈnɑː.lə-/ **noun** [U] an area of science which deals with developing and producing extremely small tools and machines by controlling the arrangement of separate atoms

nap /næp/ **noun; verb**

▸**noun SLEEP** ▷ **1** C1 [C] a short sleep, especially during the day: *Grandpa usually* ***has/takes a*** *nap after lunch.* **CLOTH** ▷ **2** [S] the surface of a piece of cloth such as VELVET, consisting of short threads that have been brushed in one direction

▸**verb** [I] (**-pp-**) to sleep for a short time, especially during the day: *He likes to nap for an hour when he gets home from work.*

napalm /ˈneɪ.pɑːm/ **noun** [U] a substance containing petrol which burns strongly and is used in bombs, especially to destroy areas of plants so that enemy soldiers cannot hide

nape /neɪp/ **noun** [C usually singular] the back of the neck: *She kissed* ***the*** *nape* ***of*** *his* ***neck***.

napkin /ˈnæp.kɪn/ **noun** [C] (UK also **serviette**) B2 a small square piece of cloth or paper used while you are eating for protecting your clothes or to clean your mouth or fingers

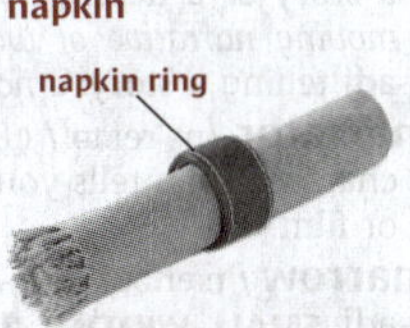

ˈ**napkin ˌring noun** [C] a small ring which holds a particular person's cloth napkin between meals when they are not using it

nappy /ˈnæp.i/ **noun** [C] UK (US **diaper**) a square of thick soft paper or cloth that is fastened around a baby's bottom and between its legs to absorb its urine and solid waste: *disposable/reusable nappies* ◦ *nappy cream* ◦ *She was* ***changing*** *the baby's nappy.* ◦ *I knew William when he was still* ***in*** *nappies (= when he was a baby).*

ˈ**nappy ˌrash noun** [U] UK (US ˈ**diaper ˌrash**) a red, painful area of skin on a baby's bottom caused by a wet nappy

narcissism /ˈnɑː.sɪ.sɪ.zəm/ US /ˈnɑːr.sə-/ **noun** [U] disapproving too much interest in and admiration for your own physical appearance and/or your own abilities

narcissist /ˈnɑː.sɪ.sɪst/ US /ˈnɑːr.sə-/ **noun** [C] someone who has too much admiration for themselves • **narcissistic** /ˌnɑː.sɪˈsɪs.tɪk/ US /ˌnɑːr.sə-/ **adj**

narcissus /nɑːˈsɪs.əs/ US /nɑːr-/ **noun** [C] (plural **narcissi**, **narcissuses** or **narcissus**) a yellow, white, or orange flower, similar to a DAFFODIL

narcolepsy /ˈnɑː.kə.lep.si/ US /ˈnɑːr.kə-/ **noun** [U] a medical condition which makes you go to sleep suddenly and when you do not expect it • **narcoleptic** /ˌnɑː.kəˈlep.tɪk/ US /ˌnɑːr.kə-/ **noun** [C], **adj**

narcotic /nɑːˈkɒt.ɪk/ US /nɑːrˈkɑː.t̬-/ **noun; adj**

▸**noun** [C] **1** mainly US an illegal drug such as HEROIN or COCAINE: *He faces three years in jail for selling narcotics.* **2** specialized a drug which makes you want to sleep and prevents you feeling pain: *Morphine is a narcotic.*

▸**adj** relating to drugs which make you want to sleep and prevent pain: *narcotic drugs* ◦ *a narcotic effect*

nark /nɑːk/ US /nɑːrk/ **verb; noun**

▸**verb ANNOY** ▷ **1** [T usually passive] UK slang old-fashioned to annoy someone: *I was a bit narked by David's comment.* **TELL POLICE** ▷ **2** [I] US slang to secretly tell the police or someone in authority about something bad or illegal that someone has done

▸**noun** [C] **CRIMINAL** ▷ **1** UK old-fashioned slang a person, especially a criminal, who gives the police information about other criminals: *a* ***coppers'*** *nark* **POLICE OFFICER** ▷ **2** (also **narc**) US slang a police officer whose job is to catch people who produce, sell, or use illegal drugs **ANNOYING PERSON** ▷ **3** Australian English a person who complains and spoils other people's enjoyment

narky /ˈnɑː.ki/ US /ˈnɑːr-/ **adj** UK slang old-fashioned easily annoyed: *You were a bit narky with me.*

N

narrate /nəˈreɪt/, /ˈnær.eɪt/ **verb** [T] to tell a story, often by reading aloud from a text, or to describe events as they happen: *Documentaries are often narrated by well-known actors.* ◦ *One by one the witnesses narrated the sequence of events which led up to the disaster.*

narration /nəˈreɪ.ʃᵊn/ (US) /nærˈeɪ-/ **noun** **1** [U] the act of telling a story **2** [C or U] a spoken description of events given during a film or television programme: *Dame Judi Dench did the narration for the documentary.*

narrative /ˈnær.ə.tɪv/ (US) /-t̬ɪv/ **noun** [C or U] formal C2 a story or a description of a series of events: *It's a moving narrative of wartime adventure.* • **narrative** adj telling a story: *a narrative poem*

narrator /nəˈreɪ.təʳ/ (US) /ˈnær.eɪ.t̬ɚ/ **noun** [C] C2 the character who tells you what is happening in a book or film

narrow /ˈnær.əʊ/ (US) /-oʊ/ **adj; verb**

▸adj **SMALL WIDTH** ▷ **1** B1 having a small distance from one side to the other, especially in comparison with the length: *a narrow bridge/passage/gap* ◦ *a narrow face* ◦ *narrow feet* ◦ *The little village has very narrow **streets**.* **LIMITED** ▷ **2** C2 mainly disapproving limited to a small area of interest, activity, or thought: *They are unable to see beyond the narrow world of the theatre.* ◦ *It was regarded as a very narrow interpretation of the law.* → See also **narrow-minded** **ONLY JUST** ▷ **3** A narrow result is one that could easily have been different because the amount by which someone failed or succeeded was very small: *The election was won by the very narrow **margin** of only 185 votes.* ◦ *The opposition had a narrow **defeat**.* ◦ *We won a narrow **victory**.* **4** **a narrow escape** C2 a situation in which you only just avoid danger: *We got out in time but it was a narrow escape.* • **narrowness** /-nəs/ **noun** [U]

IDIOM **a narrow squeak** UK informal a success that was almost a failure: *We caught the ferry but it was a narrow squeak.*

▸verb **LESS WIDE** ▷ **1** C1 [I or T] to become less wide or to make something less wide: *The road narrows after the bridge.* ◦ *He narrowed his **eyes** in suspicion.* ◦ *They have narrowed the focus of the investigation, to concentrate on younger adults.* ◦ figurative *We must strive to narrow the gap between rich and poor.* **LESS** ▷ **2** C2 [I] to become less: *The retailer's loss narrowed **to** $3 million **from** $10 million a year earlier.*

PHRASAL VERB **narrow sth down** C2 to make a number or list of things smaller, by removing the things that are least important, necessary, or suitable: *We narrowed the list of candidates down **from** ten **to** three.*

narrowboat /ˈnær.əʊ.bəʊt/ (US) /-oʊboʊt/ **noun** [C] UK a **canal boat** → Compare **barge**

ˌ**narrow-ˈgauge** adj [before noun] describes a railway with metal tracks that are closer together than the standard British and American distance of 56.5 INCHES

narrowly /ˈnær.əʊ.li/ (US) /-oʊ-/ **adv** **1** B2 only by a small amount: *She narrowly missed winning an Oscar.* **2** in a limited way: *a narrowly interpreted law* **3** formal carefully or in a way that shows doubt: *The officer looked at him narrowly through half-closed eyes.*

ˌ**narrow-ˈminded** adj disapproving C1 not willing to accept ideas or ways of behaving that are different from your own: *narrow-minded opinions/views* ◦ *a narrow-minded person* → Compare **broad-minded** • ˌ**narrow-ˈmindedness** noun [U] *He wanted to escape from the narrow-mindedness of people in the village.*

narrows /ˈnær.əʊz/ (US) /-oʊz/ **noun** [plural] **1** a narrow CHANNEL that connects two large areas of water **2** US a narrow part of a lake or river

NASA /ˈnæs.ə/ **noun** [+ sing/pl verb] abbreviation for National Aeronautics and Space Administration: the US government organization that is responsible for space travel and the scientific study of space

nasal /ˈneɪ.zᵊl/ **adj** **1** related to the nose: *nasal passages* ◦ *nasal congestion* ◦ *the nasal cavity* ◦ *a nasal spray* **2** usually disapproving If a person's voice is nasal, it has a particular sound because air is going through their nose when they speak: *a nasal accent* • **nasally** /-i/ **adv**

ˌ**nasal ˈconsonant** noun [C] specialized a consonant in which air escapes only through the nose: *In English, 'm' and 'n' are nasal consonants.*

nasalization (UK usually **nasalisation**) /ˌneɪ.zᵊl.aɪˈzeɪ.ʃᵊn/ **noun** [U] specialized the effect on a speech sound when air escapes through the nose

ˌ**nasal ˈvowel** noun [C] specialized a vowel sound in which some air escapes through the nose

NASCAR /ˈnæs.kɑːr/ **noun** abbreviation for National Association for Stock Car Auto Racing: the organization that controls the sport of STOCK CAR RACING (= in which ordinary cars are made stronger and faster for races) in the US

nascent /ˈnæs.ᵊnt/, /ˈneɪ.sᵊnt/ **adj** formal only recently formed or started, but likely to grow larger quickly: *a nascent political party* ◦ *a nascent problem*

nasturtium /nəˈstɜː.ʃᵊm/ (US) /-ˈstɜː-/ **noun** [C] a plant with yellow, red, or orange flowers and round leaves

nasty /ˈnɑː.sti/ (US) /ˈnæs.ti/ **adj** **1** B1 bad or very unpleasant: *a nasty shock/surprise* ◦ *There's a nasty smell in here.* ◦ *He had a nasty cut above the eye.* ◦ *She has a nasty **habit** of picking on people in meetings.* **2** B1 unkind: *Don't be so nasty **to** your brother – he's four years younger than you!* **3** B2 dangerous or violent: *In an emergency you could get out through a window, but it would be a nasty drop.* ◦ *The situation could **turn** (= become) nasty at any moment.* **4** rude or offensive: *She said some quite nasty things about him.* **5** **have a nasty feeling** to think that something bad is likely to happen or to be true: *I've got a nasty feeling **that** I forgot to tell Joe I couldn't come.* • **nastily** /ˈnɑː.stɪ.li/ (US) /ˈnæs.tɪ-/ **adv** *He laughed nastily (= unkindly) and walked away.* • **nastiness** /-nəs/ **noun** [U]

IDIOM **a nasty piece of work** informal a very unpleasant person

natch /nætʃ/ **adv** humorous informal naturally; as you would expect: *We're flying – by private plane, natch.*

nation /ˈneɪ.ʃᵊn/ **noun** **1** B2 [C] a country, especially when thought of as a large group of people living in one area with their own government, language, traditions, etc.: *All the nations of the world will be represented at the conference.* ◦ *The Germans, as a nation, are often thought to be well organized.* ◦ *Practically the whole nation watched the ceremony on television.* **2** [S] a large group of people of the same race who share the same language, traditions, and history, but who might not all live in one area: *the Navajo nation*

> **Word partners for nation**
> a *developing/independent/industrialized/powerful* nation • *govern/lead* a nation • *across* the nation

national /ˈnæʃ.ᵊn.ᵊl/, /ˈnæʃ.nəl/ **adj; noun**

▸adj A2 relating to or typical of a whole country and its people, rather than to part of that country or to other countries: *a national holiday* ◦ *Britain has more than ten national newspapers.* ◦ *The company's national*

headquarters is in Rome. ◦ *The children were wearing traditional national* ***costume/dress.*** ◦ *The government's view is that raising taxes now would not be in the national* ***interest*** *(= would not be good for the country).*
▸**noun** [C usually plural] someone who officially belongs to a particular country: *30 people, including six UK nationals, were killed in yesterday's plane crash.* ◦ *All* ***foreign*** *nationals were advised to leave the country following the outbreak of civil war.*

ˌnational ˈanthem noun [C] a country's official song, played and/or sung on public occasions

the ˌnational curˈriculum noun [S] in some countries, the set of subjects that children must study

ˌnational ˈdebt noun [C usually singular] (US also **ˌpublic ˈdebt**) the total amount of money that is owed by a country's government

the ˌNational ˈFront noun (abbreviation **NF**) a small British political party that is opposed to IMMIGRATION

ˌnational ˈgrid noun [S] UK a system of special wires that take electricity from POWER STATIONS (= places where electricity is made) to all parts of a country

the ˌNational ˈHealth ˌService noun (abbreviation **the NHS**) the service in the UK that provides free or cheap medical treatment for everyone and is paid for through taxes: *Can you get acupuncture* ***on*** *(= paid for by) the National Health Service?* • **National ˈHealth adj** (also **NHS**) *Is your dentist private or NHS?*

ˌnational ˈholiday noun [C] (US also **ˌfederal ˈholiday**) a day when most people in a country do not have to work

ˌNational Inˈsurance noun [U] a system in the UK in which the government collects money from companies and workers and makes payments to people who are too old or ill to work or who have no job

nationalism /ˈnæʃ.ən.əl.ɪ.zəm/, /ˈnæʃ.nə.lɪ-/ **noun** [U] **1** a nation's wish and attempt to be politically independent **2** a great or too great love of your own country: *The book documents the rise of the political right with its accompanying strands of nationalism and racism.*

nationalist /ˈnæʃ.ən.əl.ɪst/, /ˈnæʃ.nə.lɪst/ **noun; adj**
▸**noun** [C] a person who wants their country to be politically independent
▸**adj** wanting your country to be politically independent

nationalistic /ˌnæʃ.ən.əlˈɪs.tɪk/, /ˌnæʃ.nəˈlɪs-/ **adj** mainly disapproving being too proud of your own country: *a nationalistic viewpoint*

nationality /ˌnæʃ.ənˈæl.ə.ti/, /ˌnæʃˈnæl-/ (US) /-t̬i/ **noun** **1** A1 [C or U] the official right to belong to a particular country: *She* ***has*** *British nationality.* ◦ *What nationality are you?* **2** [C] a group of people of the same race, religion, traditions, etc.: *At the International School they have pupils of 46 different nationalities.*

nationalize (UK usually **nationalise**) /ˈnæʃ.ən.əl.aɪz/, /ˈnæʃ.nə.laɪz/ **verb** [T] (of a government) to take control of a business or industry: *The government recently nationalized the railways.* → Opposite **privatize**, or **denationalize** • **nationalization** (UK usually **nationalisation**) /ˌnæʃ.ən.əl.aɪˈzeɪ.ʃən/, /ˌnæʃ.nə.laɪ-/ **noun** [U] *Nationalization of agriculture is on the government's agenda.*

nationally /ˈnæʃ.ən.əl.i/, /ˈnæʃ.nə.li/ **adv** by or to everyone in a nation: *She's a nationally known columnist.*

ˌnational ˈpark noun [C] an area of a country that is protected by the government because of its natural beauty or because it has a special history

ˌnational ˈservice noun [U] UK the system by which young people, especially men, are ordered by law to spend a period of time in the armed forces: *In some countries, everyone* ***does*** *two years' national service after leaving school.* → Compare **selective service**

ˌNational ˈSocialism noun [U] **Nazism**

ˌnational ˈtreasure noun [C] someone or something of which a particular country is very proud: *The veteran actress has become something of a national treasure in Britain.*

the ˌNational ˈTrust noun an organization in the UK which owns and takes care of many beautiful and old buildings and beautiful and important areas of countryside

ˌnation-ˈstate noun [C] an independent country, especially when thought of as consisting of a single large group of people all sharing the same language, traditions, and history

nationwide /ˌneɪ.ʃənˈwaɪd/ **adj** B2 existing or happening in all parts of a particular country: *a nationwide network/chain of shops* ◦ *a nationwide survey/referendum* • **nationwide adv** B2 *Schools nationwide are experiencing a shortage of teachers.*

native /ˈneɪ.tɪv/ (US) /-t̬ɪv/ **adj; noun**
▸**adj** **1** B2 [before noun] relating to or describing someone's country or place of birth or someone who was born in a particular country or place: *She returned to live and work in her native Japan.* ◦ *She's a native Californian.* **2** C2 describes plants and animals which grow naturally in a place, and have not been brought there from somewhere else: *Henderson Island in the Pacific has more than 55 species of native flowering plants.* ◦ *The horse is not native* ***to*** *America – it was introduced by the Spanish.* **3** B2 [before noun] relating to the first people to live in an area: *The Aborigines are the native inhabitants of Australia.* ◦ *the native population* ◦ *native customs and traditions* → See also **indigenous** **4 your native language/tongue** B2 the first language that you learn: *French is his native tongue.* **5** [before noun] A native ability or characteristic is one that a person or thing has naturally and is part of their basic character: *his native wit* → See also **innate**

IDIOM **go native** disapproving or humorous If a person who is in a foreign country goes native, they begin to live and/or dress like the people who live there.

▸**noun** [C] **1** a person who was born in a particular place, or a plant or animal that lives or grows naturally in a place and has not been brought from somewhere else: *a native* ***of*** *Monaco* ◦ *The red squirrel is a native* ***of*** *Britain.* **2** offensive old-fashioned someone who lived in a country, especially in Africa, before Europeans went there

! Common mistake: native

Warning: one of the meanings of the noun **native** is offensive and old-fashioned.
To talk about the people who live in a particular place, don't say 'natives', say **local people**:
~~*The best way to learn the language is to get to know the natives.*~~
The best way to learn the language is to get to know the local people.

ˌNative Aˈmerican noun [C] a member of one of the races who were living in North and South America before Europeans arrived • **ˌNative Aˈmerican adj**

ˌnative ˈplace noun [C] Indian English the town or city or area that a person is from, especially the one in which they were born and lived while young

N

ˌ**native ˈspeaker** noun [C] B2 someone who has spoken a particular language since they were a baby, rather than having learned it as a child or adult: *All our teachers are native speakers of English.* ◦ *a native-speaker dictionary*

nativism /ˈneɪ.tɪ.vɪ.zᵊm/ US /-t̬ɪ-/ noun [U] the political idea that people who were born in a country are more important than IMMIGRANTS (= people who have come to live in the country from somewhere else) • **nativist** /-vɪst/ adj *nativist policies*

the Nativity /nəˈtɪv.ɪ.ti/ US /-ə.t̬i/ noun [S] the birth of Jesus Christ, celebrated by Christians at Christmas

nativity play /nəˈtɪv.ɪ.tiˌpleɪ/ US /-ə.t̬i-/ noun [C] a play which tells the story of Jesus Christ's birth, usually performed by children at Christmas time

NATO (also **Nato**) /ˈneɪ.təʊ/ US /-t̬oʊ/ noun [+ sing/pl verb] abbreviation for North Atlantic Treaty Organization: an international military organization consisting of the US, Canada, and many European countries

natter /ˈnæt.əʳ/ US /ˈnæt̬.ɚ/ verb [I] informal to talk continuously for a long time without any particular purpose: *Once he starts nattering you just can't stop him.* ◦ *My mother and her friends natter* ***away*** *on the phone all evening.* • **natter** noun [C] *We* ***had*** *a long natter over coffee.*

natty /ˈnæt.i/ US /ˈnæt̬-/ adj old-fashioned informal stylish and tidy in every detail: *He's always been a natty* ***dresser***. • **nattily** /-ɪ.li/ adv

natural /ˈnætʃ.ᵊr.ᵊl/ US /-ɚ-/ adj; noun

▸adj NOT ARTIFICIAL ▷ **1** B1 as found in nature and not involving anything made or done by people: *a natural substance* ◦ *People say that breast-feeding is better than bottle-feeding because it's more natural.* ◦ *He died from natural* ***causes*** *(= because he was old or ill).* ◦ *Floods and earthquakes are natural* ***disasters***. **2** C1 describes an ability or characteristic that you were born with: *natural beauty* ◦ *a natural talent for sports* ◦ *She's a natural blonde (= her real hair colour is blonde).* **3** describes food or drink that is pure and has no chemical substances added to it and is therefore thought to be healthy: *natural mineral water* ◦ *natural ingredients* **4 sb's natural mother/father/parent** a parent who caused someone to be born, although they might not be their legal parent or the parent who raised them EXPECTED ▷ **5** B2 normal or expected: *Of course you're upset – it's only natural.* ◦ ***It's*** *natural* ***that*** *you should feel anxious when you first leave home.* ◦ ***It's*** *quite natural* ***to*** *experience a few doubts just before you get married.* MUSIC ▷ **6** [after noun] (of a musical note) not SHARP or FLAT: *E natural*

▸noun [C] informal someone who was born with the right characteristics or abilities for doing a particular thing: *She won't have any troubles learning to ride a horse – you can see she's a natural.*

ˌ**natural ˈchildbirth** noun [U] a method of giving birth in which special preparation and breathing exercises are used to make the birth easier, instead of drugs

ˌ**natural ˈgas** noun [U] gas, found underground, that is used as a fuel

ˌ**natural ˈhistory** noun [U] the study of plants, animals, rocks, etc.: *We went to see the dinosaur skeletons in the Natural History Museum.*

naturalism /ˈnætʃ.ᵊr.ᵊl.ɪ.zᵊm/ US /-ɚ-/ noun [U] (in art and literature) showing people and experiences as they really are, instead of suggesting that they are better than they really are or representing them in a fixed style: *Ibsen and Chekhov are a few of the dramatists who were influenced by naturalism.*

naturalist /ˈnætʃ.ᵊr.ᵊl.ɪst/ US /-ɚ-/ noun [C] **1** a person who writes, paints, etc. in the style of naturalism **2** a person who studies and knows a lot about plants and animals

naturalistic /ˌnætʃ.ᵊr.ᵊlˈɪs.tɪk/ US /-ɚ.rəˈlɪs.t̬ɪk/ adj **1** Naturalistic art, literature, acting, etc. shows things as they really are. **2** similar to what exists in nature: *Most zoos try to exhibit animals in naturalistic settings.*

naturalize (UK usually **naturalise**) /ˈnætʃ.ᵊr.ᵊl.aɪz/ US /-ɚ.rə.laɪz/ verb [T] to make someone a legal CITIZEN of a country that they were not born in: *a naturalized US citizen* ◦ *She has lived in Australia for a long time, and recently she was naturalized.* • **naturalization** (UK usually **naturalisation**) /ˌnætʃ.ᵊr.ᵊl.aɪˈzeɪ.ʃᵊn/ US /-ɚ.rə.lə-/ noun [U]

ˌ**natural ˈlanguage** noun [U] specialized language that has developed in the usual way as a method of communicating between people, rather than language that has been created, for example for computers: *Computers are increasingly being used for natural language* ***processing***.

naturally /ˈnætʃ.ᵊr.ᵊl.i/ US /-ɚ-/ adv LIFE ▷ **1** C1 happening or existing as part of nature and not made or done by people: *A healthy body will be able to fight off the illness naturally without the use of medicine.* **2** C2 having an ability or characteristic from birth: *He's naturally funny – he doesn't even have to try.* **3 come naturally (to sb)** C1 If a particular skill comes naturally (to you), you are able to do it easily, with little effort or learning. EXPECTED ▷ **4** B2 as you would expect: *Naturally we want to see as few job losses in the industry as possible.* ◦ *'You will be polite, won't you?' 'Naturally.' (= Yes, obviously.)* NORMALLY ▷ **5** B2 in a normal way: *Relax and try to behave naturally.*

naturalness /ˈnætʃ.ᵊr.ᵊl.nəs/ US /-ɚ-/ noun [U] the quality of being real and not influenced by other people: *the naturalness of children* ◦ *Her performance was noted for its naturalness.*

ˌ**natural reˈsources** noun [plural] things such as minerals, forests, coal, etc. which exist in a place and can be used by people: *Some natural resources, such as natural gas and fossil fuel, cannot be replaced.*

the ˌ**natural ˈsciences** noun [plural] subjects such as biology, physics, and chemistry in which things that can be seen in nature are studied

ˌ**natural seˈlection** noun [U] the process that results in the continued existence of only the types of animals and plants that are best able to produce young or new plants in the conditions in which they live

ˌ**natural ˈwastage** noun [U] UK (US **attrition**) a reduction in the number of people who work for an organization that is achieved by not replacing those people who leave

> **! Common mistake: nature**
>
> **Remember:** do not use the definite article, 'the', when using **nature** to talk about life and living things.
>
> Don't say 'the nature', just say **nature**:
>
> ~~*Children learn a lot about the nature by visiting zoos.*~~

nature /ˈneɪ.tʃəʳ/ US /-tʃɚ/ noun LIFE ▷ **1** A2 [U] all the animals, plants, rocks, etc. in the world and all the features, forces, and processes that happen or exist independently of people, such as the weather, the sea, mountains, the production of young animals or plants, and growth: *her love of nature* ◦ *This new technique of artificially growing cells copies what actually happens* ***in*** *nature.* ◦ *a nature article/book/programme* **2 Nature** the force that is responsible for physical life and that is sometimes spoken of as a person: *Feeling tired-out is Nature's* ***way*** *of telling you to rest.* ◦ *Nature gave these tiny creatures the ability to reproduce quickly when food is abundant.*

> **!** Usage: **nature, the environment, and the countryside**
>
> **Nature** means all the things in the world which exist naturally and were not created by people:
>
> *He's fascinated by wildlife and anything to do with nature.*
>
> **The environment** means the land, water, and air that animals and plants live in. It is usually used when talking about the way people use or damage the natural world:
>
> *The government has introduced new policies to protect the environment.*
>
> **Countryside** means land where there are no towns or cities:
>
> *I love walking in the countryside.*

TYPE ▷ **3** Ⓒ1 [S or U] the type or main characteristic of something: *What was the nature* ***of*** *his inquiry?* ◦ *Motor-racing is* ***by*** *nature a dangerous sport.* **4 be in the nature of things** to be usual and expected: *There are problems in every relationship – it's in the nature of things.* **CHARACTER** ▷ **5** Ⓑ2 [C or U] Someone's nature is their character: *As a child Juliana had a lovely nature – everyone liked her.* ◦ [+ to infinitive] ***It's*** *not really* ***in*** *her nature* ***to*** *be aggressive.* ◦ *He is* ***by*** *nature inclined to be rather lazy.*

> Word partners for **nature** (LIFE)
>
> the *forces of/laws of* nature • a nature *lover* • be *found in* nature • *in* nature • nature *conservation*

> Word partners for **nature** (TYPE)
>
> the nature *of* sth • [different/temporary] *in* nature • *of* a [confidential/similar] nature • the *exact/precise/true* nature of sth • the *changing/complex/political/serious* nature of sth • *alter/change/reflect* the nature of sth

IDIOMS **be the nature of the beast** to be what something is like or what it involves: *Owning a car involves a lot of expense – that's the nature of the beast.* • **go/get back to nature** to start living a more simple life, often in the country • **let nature take its course** to allow someone or something to live or die naturally: *He could be kept alive artificially, but I think it would be kinder to let nature take its course.*

-natured /-neɪ.tʃəd/ Ⓤ /-tʃɚd/ **suffix** having this type of character: *He's such a good-natured/sweet-natured little boy.*

ˈnature reˌserve noun [C] an area of land that is protected in order to keep safe the animals and plants that live there, often because they are rare

ˈnature ˌstrip noun [C] Australian English a strip of grass, and often trees and other plants, that separates a path used by people walking from the part of a road used by vehicles

ˈnature ˌtrail noun [C] a path through an area of the countryside that is intended to attract the walker's attention to interesting plants, animals, and other features

naturist /ˈneɪ.tʃər.ɪst/ Ⓤ /-tʃɚ-/ noun [C] formal a NUDIST (= a person who likes to be naked and believes that people should not have to wear clothes) • **naturism** /-ɪ.zəm/ noun [U]

naturopath /ˈneɪ.tʃər.ə.pæθ/ Ⓤ /ˈneɪ.tʃɚ.ə-/ noun [C] a person who treats sick people using naturopathy

naturopathy /ˌneɪ.tʃərˈɒp.ə.θi/ Ⓤ /-tʃəˈrɑː.pə-/ noun [U] a system of treating diseases using natural methods such as controlling what a person eats, exercise, and treatments such as HOMEOPATHY and ACUPUNCTURE • **naturopathic** /-əˈpæθ.ɪk/ adj *naturopathic doctors/remedies*

naught /nɔːt/ Ⓤ /nɑːt/ number **NOTHING** ▷ **1** (also **nought**) old use or literary nothing: *All our efforts were* ***for*** *naught.* ◦ *All their plans* ***came to*** *naught (= did not achieve anything).* **ZERO** ▷ **2** US for **nought**

naughty /ˈnɔː.ti/ Ⓤ /ˈnɑː.t̬i/ adj **BADLY BEHAVED** ▷ **1** Ⓑ2 When children are naughty, or their behaviour is naughty, they behave badly or do not do what they are told to do: *Now that's naughty – you mustn't throw food on the floor!* ◦ *Our boss treats us all like naughty schoolchildren.* **2** used slightly humorously to describe an adult who has behaved badly or an adult's bad action: *'I'm afraid I borrowed your car without asking.' 'Yes, that was very naughty of you – I needed it at the weekend!'* **SEXUAL** ▷ **3** informal humorous involving or suggesting sex: *He always buys her naughty underwear for her birthday.* • **naughtily** /-tɪ.li/ Ⓤ /-t̬ɪ.li/ adv • **naughtiness** /-nəs/ noun [U]

nausea /ˈnɔː.zi.ə/, /-ʒə/ Ⓤ /ˈnɑː-/ noun [U] the feeling that you are going to vomit: *Signs of the illness include fever, nausea, and vomiting.*

nauseate /ˈnɔː.zi.eɪt/ Ⓤ /ˈnɑː-/ verb [T often passive] formal to cause someone to feel as if they are going to vomit: *He's nauseated by the smell of meat cooking.*

nauseating /ˈnɔː.zi.eɪ.tɪŋ/ Ⓤ /ˈnɑː.zi.eɪ.t̬ɪŋ/ adj **1** making you feel as if you are going to vomit: *the nauseating smell of rotting food* **2** If someone's opinions or behaviour are nauseating, you dislike and disapprove of them: *Her strongest criticism was reserved for the prime minister whom she accused of 'nauseating hypocrisy'.* ◦ humorous *She's good at everything she does – it's quite nauseating!*

nauseatingly /ˈnɔː.zi.eɪ.tɪŋ.li/ Ⓤ /ˈnɑː.zi.eɪ.t̬ɪŋ-/ adv **1** in a way that makes you feel as if you want to vomit **2** in a way that you dislike and disapprove of: *I detest the sort of ads that use nauseatingly cute children and animals.*

nauseous /ˈnɔː.zi.əs/, /-ʒəs/ Ⓤ /ˈnɑː.ʃəs/ adj **1** feeling as if you might vomit: *Roller coasters make me* ***feel*** *nauseous.* **2** formal making you feel as if you might vomit: *the nauseous smell of rotting flesh* ◦ humorous *The bride's mother was wearing a nauseous (= extremely unattractive) combination of green and yellow.*

nautical /ˈnɔː.tɪ.kəl/ Ⓤ /ˈnɑː.t̬ɪ-/ adj relating to ships, sailing, or sailors: *nautical equipment* ◦ *You're looking very nautical in your navy blue sweater.* • **nautically** /-kəl.i/ adv

ˌnautical ˈmile noun [C] (also **ˈsea ˌmile**) a unit of distance used at sea that is equal to 1,852 metres → Compare **mile**

naval /ˈneɪ.vəl/ adj Ⓒ2 belonging to a country's navy, or relating to military ships: *a naval officer* ◦ *naval forces*

nave /neɪv/ noun [C] the long central part of a church, often with AISLES (= long passages) on both sides

navel /ˈneɪ.vəl/ noun [C] (informal **ˈbelly ˌbutton**) the small round part in the middle of the stomach that is

N

left after the UMBILICAL CORD (= the long tube of flesh joining the baby to its mother) has been cut at birth

IDIOM **gaze at/contemplate your navel** humorous to spend too much time thinking about yourself and your own problems

ˈnavel-ˌgazing noun [U] humorous disapproving the activity of spending too much time considering your own thoughts, feelings, or problems

ˌnavel ˈorange noun [C] a type of orange that is sweet and usually without seeds

navigable /ˈnæv.ɪ.ɡə.bl/ adj (of an area of water) deep, wide, or safe enough for a boat to go through: *That stretch of river is too shallow to be navigable.* • **navigability** /ˌnæv.ɪ.ɡəˈbɪl.ɪ.ti/ (US) /-ə.t̬i/ noun [U]

navigate /ˈnæv.ɪ.ɡeɪt/ verb [I or T] **1** to direct the way that a ship, aircraft, etc. will travel, or to find a direction across, along, or over an area of water or land, often by using a map: *Sailors have special equipment to help them navigate.* ◦ *Even ancient ships were able to navigate large stretches of open water.* ◦ *Some migrating birds can navigate by the moon (= using the moon as a guide).* ◦ *There weren't any road signs to help us navigate through the maze of one-way streets.* ◦ *We had to navigate several flights of stairs to find his office.* **2** to move around a website or computer screen, or between websites or screens: *Their website is fairly plain, but very easy to navigate.*

navigation /ˌnæv.ɪˈɡeɪ.ʃən/ noun [U] **1** the act of directing a ship, aircraft, etc. from one place to another, or the science of finding a way from one place to another: *In the past, navigation depended on a knowledge of the positions of the stars.* ◦ *Mechanics discovered problems with the plane's navigation system.* **2** the act of moving around a website or computer screen, or between websites or screens: *We have streamlined our website for easier navigation.* • **navigational** /-əl/ adj *navigational errors*

N

naviˈgation ˌbar noun [C] a long narrow area on a computer screen that contains buttons or names you can choose to move to different parts of a website or window

navigator /ˈnæv.ɪ.ɡeɪ.təʳ/ (US) /-t̬ɚ/ noun [C] a person in a vehicle who decides on the direction in which the vehicle travels

navvy /ˈnæv.i/ noun [C] UK old-fashioned informal a man who is employed to do unskilled physical work, usually building or making roads

navy /ˈneɪ.vi/ noun; adj

▸noun SEA FORCE ▷ **1** (B2) [S, + sing/pl verb] the part of a country's armed forces that is trained to operate at sea: *My brother is an officer **in** the Navy.* ◦ *Gabriel **joined** the navy in 1997.* ◦ *a navy ship/vessel* COLOUR ▷ **2** (B1) [U] (also **ˌnavy ˈblue**) dark blue

▸adj (also **ˌnavy ˈblue**) dark blue: *He was wearing a navy sweater.*

nay /neɪ/ adv EVEN MORE ▷ **1** formal used to introduce a second and more extreme phrase in a sentence when the first phrase was not strong enough: *It is my pleasure, nay (my) privilege, to introduce tonight's guest speaker.* NO ▷ **2** Northern for **no**: *Nay lass, don't cry.*

Nazi /ˈnɑːt.si/ noun; adj

▸noun [C] **1** a member of the National Socialist Party, led by Adolf Hitler, which controlled Germany from 1933 to 1945 **2** disapproving a person who is cruel or demands that people obey them completely, or who has extreme and unreasonable beliefs about race

▸adj belonging to or connected with the National Socialist (Workers') Party which controlled Germany from 1933 to 1945: *a Nazi officer* ◦ *Nazi Germany* • **Nazism** /-sɪ.zəm/ noun [U]

NB /ˌenˈbiː/ formal written before a piece of important information to make readers notice it: *NB Applications received after the closing date will not be accepted.*

NBC /ˌen.biːˈsiː/ noun [+ sing/pl verb] abbreviation for National Broadcasting Company: a company that broadcasts television programmes in the US

NC-17 /ˌen.si.sev.ənˈtiːn/ adj used officially in the US to refer to a film that is not considered suitable for children under the age of 17 to watch because it contains sex or violence: *This movie is **rated** NC-17.* → Compare **G, PG, U, X**

NCO /ˌen.siːˈəʊ/ (US) /-ˈoʊ/ noun [C] (plural **NCOs**) abbreviation for non-commissioned officer: a member of the armed forces who has achieved the rank of officer by rising from the lower ranks rather than by receiving a COMMISSION → Compare **commissioned officer**

NE noun [U], adj written abbreviation for **northeast** or **northeastern**

neanderthal /niːˈæn.dəˌtɑːl/ (US) /-dɚ-/ adj **1** (of people or beliefs) very old-fashioned and not willing to change: *He criticized what he described as the 'neanderthal tendencies' of the right wing of the party.* **2** disapproving (of people) rude or offensive

Neanderthal /niːˈæn.dəˌtɑːl/ (US) /-dɚ-/ adj relating to a type of PRIMITIVE people who lived in Europe and Asia from about 150,000 to 30,000 years ago: *Neanderthal man* • **Neanderthal** noun [C]

near /nɪəʳ/ (US) /nɪr/ adv, preposition; adj; verb

▸adv, preposition **1** (A1) not far away in distance: *Is there a train station near here?* ◦ *I'd like to sit near a window, please.* ◦ *Don't come too near me – you might catch my cold.* ◦ *The hotel is near the airport.* ◦ *Which bus stop is nearest **(to)** your house?* ◦ *I was standing just near enough to hear what they were saying.* **2** (B2) not far away in time: *As the date of his operation **drew** near, he became more and more anxious.* ◦ *Her birthday was getting nearer and I still hadn't bought her a present.* ◦ UK *We can decide which route to take nearer the time.* **3** (C2) almost in a particular state or condition: *The runners looked near exhaustion.* ◦ *I was near **(to)** tears (= almost cried) at one point during the film.* **4 nowhere near** (C1) not close in distance, time, amount, or quality: *The house was nowhere near the sea.* ◦ *It's nowhere near time for us to leave yet.* ◦ *I'm nowhere near finishing the book – I'm only half-way through it.* ◦ *He's nowhere near as tall as his sister.* **5 near enough** informal almost: *They're the same age or near enough.*

▸adj [before noun] **1** (B1) not far away in distance, time, characteristics, or quality: *Where's the nearest post office?* ◦ *My pocket knife is **the** nearest **thing** (= the most similar thing) **to** a weapon that I have.* ◦ *I couldn't get any cream cheese so I bought the nearest equivalent (= the most similar thing) that I could find.* **2** UK Your near RELATIVES are people who are closely related to you, such as your parents, brothers, or sisters. **3 in the near future** (B2) at a time that is not far away: *All our computer equipment will be replaced in the near future.* • **nearness** /-nəs/ noun [U] *I bought my house because of its nearness **to** the office where I work.*

IDIOM **your nearest and dearest** humorous your family, especially those that you live with or are very involved with

▸verb [I or T] to get close to something in distance, time, or state: *I'm pleased to say the project is nearing completion.* ◦ *As the wedding day neared, I started to have second thoughts about getting married.* ◦ *The captain switched on the seat belt sign as we neared the airport.*

near- /nɪəʳ-/ (US) /nɪr-/ **prefix** combines with adjectives and nouns to mean 'almost': *We had a near-disaster this morning in the car!* ◦ *She was near-hysterical by the time I arrived there.*

nearby /ˌnɪəˈbaɪ/ (US) /ˌnɪr-/ **adv, adj** (B1) not far away: *If there's a café nearby, we could stop for a snack.* ◦ *I noticed a policeman standing nearby.* ◦ *We stopped at some nearby shops to buy some food.*

ˌnear-ˈdeath exˌperience **noun** [C] an experience described by some people who have been close to death, in which the person feels as if they have left their body and are watching themselves from above

nearly /ˈnɪə.li/ (US) /ˈnɪr-/ **adv 1** (A2) almost, or not completely: *It's been nearly three months since my last haircut.* ◦ *I've nearly finished that book you lent me.* ◦ *She's nearly as tall as her father now.* ◦ *They'd eaten nearly everything.* ◦ *It was so funny – we nearly died laughing.* **2 not nearly as/so** (C1) a lot less: *She's not nearly as beautiful as you said she was.* **3 not nearly enough** much less than you want or need: *There's not nearly enough food for all these people!*

ˌnear ˈmiss **noun** [C usually singular] **HIT** ▷ **1** (also **near thing**) a situation in which something almost hits something else: *A Boeing 747 was involved in a near miss with a private aircraft just south of San Francisco.* ◦ *That was a near miss – we must have come within an inch of that lorry!* **HAPPEN** ▷ **2** an attempt to do or achieve something which fails although it almost succeeds

nearside /ˈnɪə.saɪd/ (US) /ˈnɪr-/ **adj** [before noun] (also **near**) UK on the left side of something, especially a vehicle or road: *A car pulled out from the nearside lane without signalling.*

nearsighted /ˌnɪəˈsaɪ.tɪd/ (US) /ˌnɪrˈsaɪ.t̬ɪd/ **adj** US (UK **shortsighted**) (B2) Someone who is nearsighted cannot see objects clearly when they are far away. • **nearsightedness** /-nəs/ **noun** [U]

ˌnear ˈthing **noun** [S] UK a situation in which you almost failed to achieve something and only just succeeded: *We beat them but it was a near thing.* → See also **near miss**

neat /niːt/ **adj** **TIDY** ▷ **1** (B1) tidy, with everything in its place: *Your house is always so neat – how do you manage it with three children?* ◦ *She likes everything neat **and** tidy.* ◦ *You've got such neat handwriting.* ◦ *They did a very neat job stitching up your knee – there's hardly a scar there.* **2** A neat person likes to keep themselves, their house, and their possessions tidy and in good order: *Hassan is the neatest child I've ever met – even his shoes are clean!* ◦ *I try to be neat, but my husband is a slob.* **GOOD** ▷ **3** mainly US informal good: *That video game is really neat!* ◦ *Kyle has the neatest mom – she lets him stay up late on the weekends.* **CLEVER** ▷ **4** clever and simple: *It would be a neat solution to the problem.* **NOTHING ADDED** ▷ **5** (of a strong alcoholic drink) without anything, such as water or ice or another drink, added to it: *I'll have a neat gin, please.*

neaten /ˈniː.tᵊn/ (US) /-t̬ᵊn/ **verb** [T] to make something tidy: *She's careful to neaten her desk before she leaves in the evening.* ◦ *Could you neaten **up** those bookshelves, please?*

'neath /niːθ/ **preposition** literary **beneath**: *'Neath stars and sun we wandered*

neatly /ˈniːt.li/ **adv** **TIDY** ▷ **1** (C1) in a tidy way: *His clothes are all neatly folded in their drawers.* **CLEVER** ▷ **2** in a clever and simple way: *The announcement was neatly timed to coincide with the release of their new album.*

neatness /ˈniːt.nəs/ **noun** [U] the quality of being tidy, with everything in its place: *When writing your homework, remember that neatness counts.*

nebula /ˈneb.jʊ.lə/ **noun** [C] (plural **nebulae** or **nebulas**) specialized a cloud of gas or dust in space, appearing either bright or dark • **nebular** /-ləʳ/ (US) /-lɚ/ **adj**

nebulous /ˈneb.jʊ.ləs/ **adj** (especially of ideas) not clear and having no form: *She has a few nebulous ideas about what she might like to do in the future, but nothing definite.* • **nebulousness** /-nəs/ **noun** [U]

necessaries /ˈnes.ə.ser.iz/ **noun** [plural] the things that are needed, especially for a particular purpose: *He packed drinks, a map, and a compass – all the necessaries for a day's walking in the countryside.*

necessarily /ˈnes.ə.ser.ɪl.i/ **adv** (B2) used in negatives to mean 'in every case' or 'therefore': *The fact that something is cheap doesn't necessarily mean it's of low quality.* ◦ *You may love someone without necessarily wanting to marry them.* ◦ *That's **not** necessarily true.*

necessary /ˈnes.ə.ser.i/ **adj 1** (B1) needed in order to achieve a particular result: *He lacks the necessary skills for the job.* ◦ *I don't have much time so I won't be staying any longer than necessary.* ◦ *Just do what's necessary and then leave.* ◦ ***If** necessary, we can always change the dates of our trip.* ◦ *Is **it** necessary **for** all of us **to** be present at the meeting this afternoon?* ◦ *We don't want to take any more luggage with us than is **strictly** necessary.* **2** used in negatives and questions to show that you disapprove of something and do not think it should be used or done: *I really don't think that sort of language is necessary on television.* ◦ *Was **it** really necessary **for** you **to** say that?*

> **!** Common mistake: **necessary**
>
> **Warning:** Check your spelling!
> **Necessary** is one of the 50 words most often spelled wrongly by learners. Remember: the correct spelling has 'c' and 'ss'.

> **+** Other ways of saying **necessary**
>
> The verbs **need** and **require** and the modal verb **must** are very commonly used to show that something is necessary:
> *The meat **must** be cooked thoroughly.*
> *Does she have the skills **needed/required** for work of that sort?*
> If something is very important and necessary, you can use adjectives such as **essential**, **fundamental**, and **indispensable**:
> *Some understanding of grammar is **essential/fundamental** to learning a language.*
> *This book is an **indispensable** resource for teachers.*
> The expression **be a must** is sometimes used in informal situations to describe things that are very necessary to have or do:
> *This book **is a must** for anyone who loves history.*

ˌnecessary ˈevil **noun** [C] something that you do not like but must accept: *I think he regards work as a necessary evil.*

necessitate /nəˈses.ɪ.teɪt/ **verb** [T] formal to cause something to be needed, or to make something necessary: *Reduction in government spending will necessitate further cuts in public services.* ◦ [+ -ing

N

verb] *An important meeting necessitates my being in London on Friday.*

necessity /nə'ses.ɪ.ti/ (US) /-ə.t̬i/ **noun 1** C1 [U] the need for something: *You can come early if you want to, but there's no necessity* ***for*** *it.* ◦ [+ to infinitive] *Is there any necessity* ***to*** *reply to her letter?* ◦ *The report stresses the necessity* ***of*** *eat****ing*** *plenty of fresh fruit and vegetables.* ◦ *With a personal fortune of six million pounds, she certainly doesn't work* ***out of*** *necessity (= because she needs to).* ◦ *We'll employ extra staff to help out as and when the necessity* ***arises*** *(= when we need to).* **2** C1 [C] something that you need, especially in order to live: *We brought only the* ***bare*** *necessities with us.* ◦ *He regarded music as one of life's necessities.*

neck /nek/ **noun; verb**

▸**noun** [C] **BODY PART** ▷ **1** A2 the part of the body that joins the head to the shoulders: *He had the thickest neck I'd ever seen.* ◦ *She wore a gold chain around her neck.* **2** C2 the part of a piece of clothing that goes around a person's neck: *This sweater's too tight at the neck.* ◦ *He wasn't wearing a tie and his shirt was open at the neck.* ◦ *a low-neck dress* **TOP PART** ▷ **3** part of a hollow object that is at the top and is narrower than the part below it: *the neck of a bottle/guitar* → See also **bottleneck, halterneck, redneck, roughneck, turtleneck**

IDIOMS **be up to your neck (in sth)** informal to be very busy: *I'd like to help, but I'm up to my neck at the moment.* • **be up to your neck in sth** informal to be very involved in a situation, or to have too much of the thing stated: *She's up to her neck in debt/problems/work.* • **get it in the neck** UK informal to be punished or severely criticized for something that you have done: *Poor old Bob got it in the neck* ***for*** *being late.* • **neck and neck** C2 If two competitors are neck and neck, they are level with each other and have an equal chance of winning. • **this, our, etc. neck of the woods** informal this, our, etc. part of a particular area: *We don't often see you in this neck of the woods.* • **put your neck on the line** to do something that you know might fail and spoil other people's opinion of you or cause you to lose money: *There's a lot of money at stake here and none of the directors wants to put his neck on the line.* ◦ *No one wants to put their neck on the line and predict an outcome.*

▸**verb** [I] old-fashioned informal to kiss and hold a person in a sexual way

neckband /'nek.bænd/ **noun** [C] a narrow strip which goes round the neck of a piece of clothing: *I can't get this sweater over my head – the neckband's too tight.*

-necked /-nekt/ **suffix** refers to the type of neck someone or something has, or to the style of a piece of clothing around the neck or the way that it is worn: *a stocky, stiff-necked little man* ◦ *a round-necked jumper* ◦ *an open-necked shirt*

neckerchief /'nek.ə.tʃiːf/ (US) /-ɚ-/ **noun** [C] (plural **neckerchiefs** or **neckerchieves**) a piece of square cloth folded and worn around the neck, especially in the past

necklace /'nek.ləs/ **noun; verb**

▸**noun** [C] A2 a piece of jewellery worn around the neck, such as a chain or a string of decorative stones, BEADS, etc.: *a gold/silver/pearl necklace*

▸**verb** [T] to kill someone by putting a burning rubber tyre around their neck • **necklacing** /-lə.sɪŋ/ **noun** [C]

neckline /'nek.laɪn/ **noun** [C] the shape made by the edge of a dress or shirt at the front of the neck or on the chest: *She wore a dress with a* ***plunging*** *neckline (= one showing part of her breasts).*

necktie /'nek.taɪ/ **noun** [C] C2 mainly US for a TIE (= long piece of material worn under a shirt collar)

necromancy /'nek.rə.mæn.si/ **noun** [U] the act of communicating with the dead in order to discover what is going to happen in the future, or BLACK MAGIC (= magic used for bad purposes) • **necromancer** /-səʳ/ (US) /-sɚ/ **noun** [C]

necrophilia /ˌnek.rə'fɪl.i.ə/ **noun** [U] being sexually attracted to dead bodies, or sexual activity with dead bodies

necrophiliac /ˌnek.rə'fɪl.i.æk/ **noun** [C] a person who is sexually attracted to or has sex with dead bodies • **necrophiliac adj**

necropolis /nek'rɒp.əl.ɪs/ (US) /nek'rɑː-/ **noun** [C] an ancient CEMETERY (= piece of ground where people are buried)

nectar /'nek.təʳ/ (US) /-tɚ/ **noun** [U] **1** a sweet liquid produced by flowers and collected by bees and other insects: *The bee turns nectar into honey.* **2** in ancient Greek and Roman stories, the drink of the gods: *This wine tastes like nectar (= tastes excellent).*

nectarine /'nek.tᵊr.iːn/ (US) /ˌnek.tə'riːn/ **noun** [C] a type of sweet JUICY fruit like a PEACH but with a smooth skin

née /neɪ/ **adj** used after a woman's married name to introduce the family name by which she was known before she married: *Elaine Gibson (née Gillett)*

> **!** Common mistake: **need**
>
> **Warning:** when it is used to say that someone must do something, **need** must be followed by the infinitive with **to**.
>
> Don't say 'need do something', say **need to do something:**
>
> *~~Dave needs improve his French.~~*
>
> *Dave needs to improve his French.*

need /niːd/ **verb; noun**

▸**verb MUST HAVE** ▷ **1** A1 [T] to have to have something, or to want something very much: *Babies need constant care.* ◦ *The doctor said I needed an operation.* ◦ [+ to infinitive] *I need* ***to*** *go to the toilet.* ◦ *Most people need* ***to*** *feel loved.* ◦ [+ obj + to infinitive] *I need you* ***to*** *help me choose an outfit.* ◦ *I* ***badly*** *need (= strongly want) a rest from all this.* ◦ informal *I don't need all this hassle.* **2** B1 [T] If you say that someone or something needs something else, you mean that they should have it, or would get an advantage from having it: *What you need is a nice hot bowl of soup.* ◦ [+ -ing verb] *This room needs brighten****ing*** *up a bit.* ◦ [+ past participle] *She needs her hair wash****ed***. **MUST DO** ▷ **3** A1 [+ to infinitive or + infinitive without to] to have (to): [+ to infinitive] *He needs* ***to*** *lose a bit of weight.* ◦ *I need* ***to*** *do some shopping on my way home from work.* ◦ ***There*** *needs* ***to be*** *more effort from everyone.* ◦ [+ infinitive without to] *I don't think we need ask him.* ◦ *Nothing need be done about this till next week.* ◦ formal *'Need we take your mother?' 'No, we needn't.'* **4 sb/sth needn't do sth** UK A2 there is no reason for someone or something to do a particular thing: *You needn't worry – I'm not going to mention it to anyone.* ◦ *It's a wonderful way of getting to see Italy, and it needn't cost very much.* **5 sb needn't do sth** mainly UK used, often when you are angry with someone, to say that they should not do a particular thing or that they have no right to do it: *He needn't think I'm driving him all the way there!* ◦ *You needn't laugh! It'll be your turn next!* **6 sb didn't need to** used to say either that someone did a particular thing although they did not have to, or that they did not do it because they did not have to: *I gave her some extra money – I know I didn't need to but I thought it would be kind.* ◦ *'Did you* *ask Sophia to help?' 'I didn't need to – I managed perfectly well on my own.'* **7 sb needn't have done sth** mainly UK it was not necessary for someone to have done a particular thing, although they did do it: *You needn't have washed all those dishes, you know – I'd have done them myself when I got home.* ◦ *You needn't have worried about the dinner – it was delicious!*

IDIOMS **I need hardly do sth** formal used to say that what you are going to say is obvious: *I need hardly* ***say*** *what a pleasure it is to introduce our speaker.* ◦ *I need hardly* ***remind*** *you of the seriousness of the situation.* • **need you ask!** used to say that the person asking you something already knows the answer, because it is expected: *'Did he upset a lot of people at the meeting?' 'Need you ask!'* • **need I say** obviously: *Need I say, I'm extremely sorry to hear the news about your father.* • **need I say more?** humorous said after a statement when you expect that someone can guess the result of what you have just said: *Tom was doing the cooking – need I say more?* • **need your head examined/examining** (or **need your head testing**) humorous UK If you tell someone they need their head examining, you think that they are crazy because they have done something stupid or strange: *You need your head examined if you're willing to spend £120 on a pair of jeans.* • **who needs...?** mainly humorous used to mean that the thing referred to is not necessary or useful, or causes trouble: *Men! Who needs them?*

▸noun **1** B2 [S or U] the state of having to have something that you do not have, especially something that you must have so that you can have a satisfactory life: *Are you* ***in*** *need* ***of*** *help?* ◦ *There's* ***a*** *growing need* ***for*** *cheap housing in the larger cities.* **2 needs** B2 [plural] the things that a person must have in order to have a satisfactory life: *Housing and education are* ***basic*** *needs.* ◦ *They don't have enough food to* ***meet*** *their needs.* **3** B2 [C or U] a feeling or state of strongly wanting something: [+ to infinitive] *He seems to have* ***a*** *desperate need* ***to*** *be loved by everyone.* ◦ *I don't know about you but I'm* ***in*** *need* ***of*** *a drink.* ◦ formal *We* ***have*** *no need* ***of*** *your sympathy.* **4 in need** not having enough money or food: *You just hope that the money goes to those who are most in need.* **5** [U] the state of being necessary: *Help yourself to stationery as the need* ***arises***. ◦ ***If*** *need/needs* ***be*** (= *if necessary*), *we can take a second car to fit everyone in.* ◦ *I don't think there's any need* ***for*** *all of us* ***to*** *attend the meeting.* **6 be no need to do sth** B2 If there is no need to do something, it is not necessary or it is wrong: *There's no need to go to the shops – there's plenty of food in the fridge.* ◦ *I understand why she was angry but there was no need to be so rude to him.* ◦ *There's no need to shout, for goodness' sake! Just calm down.*

> **! Common mistake: need**
>
> **Warning:** do not confuse **in need of sth** with **a/the need for sth**:
>
> Don't say 'a/the need of sth', say **a/the need for sth**:
>
> ~~*I cannot see the need of a new supermarket.*~~
>
> *I cannot see the need for a new supermarket.*
>
> Don't say 'in need for sth', say **in need of sth**:
>
> ~~*This town is in need for a new supermarket.*~~
>
> *This town is in need of a new supermarket.*

ˈ**need-blind** adj mainly US not considering a person's ability to pay when making a decision, especially when making a decision about giving someone a place to study at university: *An institution with a need-blind admissions policy needs to be able to provide financial aid.*

needed /ˈniː.dɪd/ adj necessary or wanted: *After six hours work in the garden, we sat down for a* ***much-needed*** *rest.* ◦ *Most people like to feel needed.*

needle /ˈniː.dl̩/ noun; verb

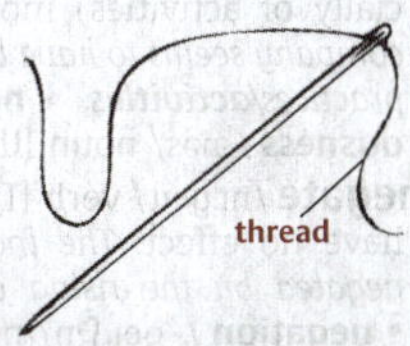

▸noun [C] **SEWING TOOL** ▷ **1** B2 a thin metal pin, used in sewing, that is pointed at one end and has a hole called an EYE at the other end for thread: *a needle and thread* ◦ *Here, your eyes are better than mine – could you* ***thread*** (= *put thread through*) *this needle for me?* → See also **needlework 2** a long thin metal stick used with another of the same type to KNIT: *a* ***knitting*** *needle* **MEDICAL TOOL** ▷ **3** C2 (also **hypodermic needle**) a very thin, hollow, pointed piece of metal that is connected to a SYRINGE and used to take blood from the body or to put drugs or medicine in **POINTER** ▷ **4** on a COMPASS or measuring device, the thin moving part that points in a particular direction or points to a particular measurement: *The needle on a compass always points to magnetic north.* **LEAF** ▷ **5** a thin hard pointed leaf of a PINE tree: *pine needles* **MUSIC** ▷ **6** the part of a RECORD PLAYER that touches the record as it turns round, usually made of a very hard material, such as a DIAMOND

IDIOM **a needle in a haystack** something that is impossible or extremely difficult to find, especially because the area you have to search is too large: *Finding the piece of paper I need in this huge pile of documents is like* ***looking for/trying to find*** *a needle in a haystack*

▸verb [T] informal to annoy someone, especially by repeated criticism: *His mother was always needling him* ***about*** *getting a job.*

needlepoint /ˈniː.dl̩.pɔɪnt/ noun [U] the activity of making a picture by sewing onto a piece of cloth

needless /ˈniːd.ləs/ adj C2 completely unnecessary: *needless worrying*

IDIOM **needless to say** C1 as you would expect; added to, or used to introduce, a remark giving information that is expected and not surprising: *Needless to say, he'll be off work for a while.*

needlessly /ˈniːd.ləs.li/ adv in a way that is not necessary: *She'd worried quite needlessly about whether there would be enough food.*

needlework /ˈniː.dl̩.wɜːk/ US /-wɝːk/ noun [U] sewing, especially decorative sewing, done by hand with needle and thread

needn't /ˈniː.dᵊnt/ short form of need not: *You needn't come until later.*

needy /ˈniː.di/ adj; noun

▸adj **1** poor and not having enough food, clothes, etc.: *The proceeds from the sale go to help needy people in the area.* **2** wanting too much attention and love: *Sybil was very insecure and needy.*

▸noun [plural] **the needy** poor people: *Let us pray for those who are not so fortunate as ourselves – the sick, the old and the needy.*

ne'er /neəʳ/ US /ner/ adv literary never: *Ne'er the night passes without my dreaming of you.*

ˈ**ne'er-do-well** noun [C] old-fashioned someone who is lazy or not willing to act in a responsible way

NEET (also **neet**) /niːt/ noun [C] UK abbreviation for not in education, employment, or training: used by the

N

government to describe a young person who is no longer in school and does not have a job or is not training to do a job

nefarious /nəˈfeə.ri.əs/ (US) /-ˈfer.i-/ **adj** formal (especially of activities) morally bad: *The director of the company seems to have been involved in some nefarious practices/**activities**.* • **nefariously** /-li/ **adv** • **nefariousness** /-nəs/ **noun** [U]

negate /nɪˈgeɪt/ **verb** [T] formal to cause something to have no effect: *The increase in our profits has been negated by the rising costs of running the business.* • **negation** /-ˈgeɪ.ʃən/ **noun** [U]

negative /ˈneg.ə.tɪv/ (US) /-t̬ɪv/ **adj; noun**

▸**adj** **NO** ▷ **1** B2 expressing 'no': *We received a negative answer to our request.* → Opposite **affirmative** **2** A2 A negative sentence or phrase is one that contains a word such as 'not', 'no', 'never', or 'nothing': *'I've never seen him in my life' is a negative sentence.* ◦ *'Don't' and 'do not' are negative forms of 'do'.* **WITHOUT HOPE** ▷ **3** B1 not expecting good things, or likely to consider only the bad side of a situation: *a negative attitude* ◦ *You're so negative about everything!* → Compare **positive** **BAD** ▷ **4** B2 bad or harmful: *The poor weather has had a very negative **effect/impact** on tourism.* **ELECTRICITY** ▷ **5** of the type of electrical charge that is carried by ELECTRONS → Opposite **positive** **TEST RESULTS** ▷ **6** (of a medical test) showing that the patient does not have the disease or condition for which he or she has been tested: *a negative pregnancy test* ◦ *The results of his HIV test were negative.* → Opposite **positive** **BELOW ZERO** ▷ **7** (of a number or amount) less than zero: *negative numbers* → Opposite **positive** **BLOOD TYPE** ▷ **8** not having the RHESUS FACTOR in the blood: *Her blood type is O negative.* → Opposite **positive** • **negatively** /-li/ **adv**

N

▸**noun** **PHOTOGRAPH** ▷ **1** [C] (informal **neg**) a piece of film from which a photograph can be produced, and in which light and dark areas appear the opposite way round to the way in which they appear in the photograph: *black-and-white/colour negatives* **NO** ▷ **2** [C or U] a word or statement that expresses 'no': *I didn't hear your answer, Edward – was that a negative?* ◦ *I'm afraid the reply was definitely **in the** negative (= was 'no').* → Compare **affirmative** **BAD THING** ▷ **3** [C] a bad feature or characteristic: *He always looks for the negatives in any situation.*

ˌnegative ˈequity **noun** [U] UK a situation in which the value of a house has become less than the amount of money its owner borrowed in order to buy it

ˌnegative ˈpole **noun** [C] specialized the part of a BATTERY that releases ELECTRONS

negativism /ˈneg.ə.tɪ.vɪ.zəm/ (US) /-t̬ɪ-/ **noun** [U] (also **negativity**) the feeling of not expecting good things, or considering only the bad side of a situation: *There's a real attitude of negativism among the team at the moment.*

neglect /nɪˈglekt/ **verb; noun**

▸**verb** [T] **1** C1 to not give enough care or attention to people or things that are your responsibility: *to neglect your appearance/the garden* ◦ *He neglects that poor dog – he never takes him for walks or gives him any attention.* ◦ *I'm afraid I've rather neglected my studies this week.* **2** **neglect to do sth** C2 to not do something, often because you forget: *I'd neglected to give him the name of the hotel where I'd be staying.* ◦ *He neglected to mention the fact that we could lose money on the deal.*

▸**noun** [U] C1 a situation in which you do not give enough care or attention to someone or something, or the state of not receiving enough care or attention: *Both parents were found guilty of neglect and their child was taken away from them.* ◦ *Over the years the church has fallen into a state of neglect.*

neglected /nɪˈglek.tɪd/ **adj** not receiving enough care or attention: *She was distressed at how neglected the children looked.*

neglectful /nɪˈglekt.fəl/ **adj** not giving enough care and attention to something or someone: *I'm sure my boss thinks I've been neglectful **of** my duties recently.*

negligée /ˈneg.lɪ.ʒeɪ/ (US) /ˌneg.lɪˈʒeɪ/ **noun** [C] (also **negligee**) a woman's decorative DRESSING GOWN (= a loose coat worn inside the house) made of light material

negligence /ˈneg.lɪ.dʒəns/ **noun** [U] C2 the fact of not giving enough care or attention to someone or something: *medical negligence*

negligent /ˈneg.lɪ.dʒənt/ **adj** C2 not being careful or giving enough attention to people or things that are your responsibility: *The judge said that the teacher had been negligent **in** allowing the children to swim in dangerous water.* • **negligently** /-li/ **adv**

negligible /ˈneg.lɪ.dʒə.bl̩/ **adj** C2 too slight or small in amount to be of importance: *The difference between the two products is negligible.* ◦ *My knowledge of German is negligible.* • **negligibly** /-bli/ **adv**

negotiable /nəˈgəʊ.ʃə.bl̩/ (US) /-ˈgoʊ.ʃi.ə-/ **adj** **DISCUSSED** ▷ **1** able to be discussed or changed in order to reach an agreement: *Everything is negotiable at this stage – I'm ruling nothing out.* **CHEQUE** ▷ **2** specialized A CHEQUE that is not negotiable cannot be exchanged for money and must be paid into a bank account → See also **non-negotiable** **FINANCIAL PRODUCT** ▷ **3** specialized A negotiable financial product is one that can be bought and sold: *Yamaichi will sell some negotiable **securities** to raise money.* → Compare **non-negotiable**

negotiate /nəˈgəʊ.ʃi.eɪt/ (US) /-ˈgoʊ-/ **verb** **DISCUSS** ▷ **1** C1 [I or T] to have formal discussions with someone in order to reach an agreement with them: *The government has refused to negotiate **with** the strikers.* ◦ *I'm negotiating **for** a new contract.* ◦ *I've managed to negotiate (= get by discussion) a five percent pay increase **with** my boss.* **MANAGE TO DO** ▷ **2** [T] to manage to travel along a difficult route: *The only way to negotiate the muddy hillside is on foot.* **3** [T] to deal with something difficult: *The company's had some tricky problems to negotiate in its first year in business.* **EXCHANGE** ▷ **4** [T] specialized to get or give an amount of money in exchange for a financial document of the same value

negotiation /nəˌgəʊ.ʃiˈeɪ.ʃən/ (US) /-ˌgoʊ-/ **noun** [C or U] C1 the process of discussing something with someone in order to reach an agreement with them, or the discussions themselves: *The agreement was reached after a series of difficult negotiations.* ◦ *The exact details of the agreement are still **under** negotiation.*

negotiator /nɪˈgəʊ.ʃi.eɪ.tər/ (US) /-ˈgoʊ.ʃi.eɪ.t̬ɚ/ **noun** [C] someone who tries to help two groups who disagree to reach an agreement with each other, usually as a job: *Some very skilful negotiators will be needed to settle this dispute.*

Negress (also **negress**) /ˈniː.grəs/ (US) /-grɪs/ **noun** [C] offensive old-fashioned a black woman

Negro /ˈniː.grəʊ/ (US) /-groʊ/ **noun** [C] (plural **Negroes**) offensive old-fashioned a black man

negroid /ˈniː.grɔɪd/ **adj** offensive old-fashioned specialized having the physical features of a black person from Africa

neigh /neɪ/ **noun** [C] a long, loud, high call that is produced by a horse when it is excited or frightened • **neigh** verb [I]

neighbour (US **neighbor**) /ˈneɪ.bər/ (US) /-bɚ/ noun [C] **1** A2 UK someone who lives very near to you: *Some of the neighbours have complained about the noise from our party.* ◦ *Have you met Pat, my **next-door** neighbour?* **2** B1 A country's neighbour is one that is next to it: *The relationship between Scotland and its southern neighbour has not always been peaceful.*

neighbourhood UK (US **neighborhood**) /ˈneɪ.bə.hʊd/ (US) /-bɚ-/ noun [C] B1 the area of a town that surrounds someone's home, or the people who live in this area: *There were lots of kids in my neighbourhood when I was growing up.* ◦ *They live in a wealthy/poor/friendly neighbourhood.* ◦ *I wouldn't like to live **in the** neighbourhood **of** (= in the area around) an airport.*

IDIOM **in the neighbourhood of sth** approximately: *We're hoping to get somewhere in the neighbourhood of £70,000 for our house.*

ˌneighbourhood ˈwatch UK (US **ˌneighborhood ˈwatch**) noun [C or U] a way of reducing crime by organizing the people who live in an area to watch each other's property and tell the police about possible criminals

neighbouring UK (US **neighboring**) /ˈneɪ.bər.ɪŋ/ (US) /-bɚ-/ adj [before noun] B2 Neighbouring places are next to or near each other: *neighbouring **countries/states*** ◦ *She married a man from the neighbouring village.*

neighbourly UK (US **neighborly**) /ˈneɪ.bəl.i/ (US) /-bɚ.li/ adj friendly or helpful: *It was very neighbourly **of** you to do her shopping for her.* • **neighbourliness** (US **neighborliness**) /-nəs/ noun [U]

neither /ˈnaɪ.ðər/, /ˈniː-/ (US) /-ðɚ/ **determiner, pronoun, conjunction, adv** **1** B2 not either of two things or people: *We've got two TVs, but neither works properly.* ◦ *Neither **of** my parents likes my boyfriend.* ◦ *Neither one **of** us is particularly interested in gardening.* ◦ *'Which one would you choose?' 'Neither. They're both terrible.'* ◦ *If she doesn't agree to the plan, neither will Tom (= he will also not).* ◦ *Chris wasn't at the meeting and neither was her assistant.* ◦ informal *'I don't feel like going out this evening.' 'Me neither.'* ◦ *On two occasions she was accused of stealing money from the company, but **in** neither **case** was there any evidence to support the claims.* **2 neither ... nor** B2 used when you want to say that two or more things are not true: *Neither my mother nor my father went to university.* ◦ *They speak neither French nor German, but a curious mixture of the two.* ◦ *I neither know nor care what's happened to him.*

> **!** Common mistake: **neither or either?**
>
> **Warning:** it is not usual to use two negative words in the same sentence.
>
> When using **not** in a sentence, don't say 'neither', say **either**:
>
> ~~*The air conditioning did not work neither.*~~
>
> *The air conditioning did not work either.*

> **!** Usage: **neither... nor**
>
> This is used with a singular verb:
>
> *Neither Jack nor Philip likes football.*

IDIOMS **be neither here nor there** to not be important: *It's essential that she has this medicine, and the cost is neither here nor there.* • **be neither one thing nor the other** to be a mixture of two different things, often things that do not combine well: *I prefer a book to be either fact or fiction – this one is neither one thing nor the other!*

nelly /ˈnel.i/ noun UK old-fashioned humorous **not on your nelly** there is no possibility of that: *'Perhaps you could take Simon to the party.' 'Not on your nelly!'*

nemesis /ˈnem.ə.sɪs/ noun [C] (plural **nemeses**) literary **1** Someone's nemesis is a person or thing that is very difficult for them to defeat. **2** (a cause of) punishment or defeat that is deserved and cannot be avoided: *The tax increases proved to be the president's political nemesis at the following election.*

neo- /niː.əʊ-/ (US) /-oʊ-/ **prefix** new or recent, or in a modern form: *neo-fascist* ◦ *neo-Nazi* ◦ *neo-realist cinema*

neoclassical /ˌniː.əʊˈklæs.ɪ.kəl/ (US) /-oʊ-/ adj specialized made in a style that is based on the art and building designs of ancient Greece and Rome • **neoclassicism** /-sɪ.zəm/ noun [U]

neocolonialism /ˌniː.əʊ.kəˈləʊ.ni.əl.ɪ.zəm/ (US) /-oʊ.kəˈloʊ-/ noun [U] political control by a rich country of a poorer country that should be independent and free to govern itself • **neocolonialist** /-ɪst/ adj

neocon /ˈniː.əʊ.kɒn/ (US) /-oʊ.kɑːn/ noun [C] informal abbreviation for neo-conservative: in the US, someone who is a Republican and thinks that the US should use its military power

neolithic /ˌniː.əˈlɪθ.ɪk/ (US) /-oʊ-/ adj belonging to the period when humans used tools and weapons made of stone and had just developed farming: *neolithic tools/artefacts/settlements* ◦ *The neolithic **period** is sometimes called the new stone age.* → Compare **palaeolithic**

neologism /niˈɒl.ə.dʒɪ.zəm/ (US) /-ˈɑː.lə-/ noun [C] formal a new word or expression, or a new meaning for an existing word

neon /ˈniː.ɒn/ (US) /-ɑːn/ noun [U] (symbol **Ne**) a chemical element that is a gas with no smell or colour, does not react with other chemicals, and shines red when an electric current goes through it: *a neon **light/sign***

neonatal /ˌniː.əʊˈneɪ.təl/ (US) /-oʊˈneɪ.t̬əl/ adj [before noun] of or for babies that were born recently: *Their baby is still in the hospital's neonatal **unit**.*

neophyte /ˈniː.ə.faɪt/ (US) /-oʊ-/ noun [C] formal someone who has recently become involved in an activity and is still learning about it

neoprene /ˈniː.ə.priːn/ (US) /-oʊ-/ noun [U] a type of SYNTHETIC rubber (= made by a chemical process rather than natural) that is strong and keeps its shape well: *He wore a tight-fitting neoprene wetsuit.*

nephew /ˈnef.juː/, /ˈnev-/ noun [C] B1 a son of your sister or brother, or a son of the sister or brother of your husband or wife → Compare **niece**

nepotism /ˈnep.ə.tɪ.zəm/ noun [U] disapproving the act of using your power or influence to get good jobs or unfair advantages for members of your own family: *He was guilty of nepotism and corruption.* • **nepotistic** /ˌnep.əˈtɪs.tɪk/ adj

Neptune /ˈnep.tjuːn/ (US) /-tuːn/ noun [S] the planet eighth in order of distance and farthest from the Sun, after Uranus: *Neptune was discovered in 1846.*

nerd /nɜːd/ (US) /nɝːd/ noun [C] informal disapproving **1** a person, especially a man, who is not attractive and is awkward or socially embarrassing: *He was a real nerd in high school – I can't believe he's so handsome now.* **2** a person who is extremely interested in one subject, especially computers, and knows a lot of facts about it: *I'm a real grammar nerd.* • **nerdy** /ˈnɜː.di/ (US) /ˈnɝː-/

N

adj informal disapproving *He's nice, but kind of nerdy.* ◦ *These glasses make me **look/feel** nerdy.*

nerve /nɜːv/ US /nɝːv/ **noun; verb**

▸**noun** **BODY** ▷ **1** C2 [C] a group of long thin FIBRES (= structures like threads) that carry information or instructions between the brain and other parts of the body: *the optic nerve* ◦ *a spinal nerve* ◦ *nerve **damage*** ◦ *nerve fibres* **COURAGE** ▷ **2** C2 [U] the courage or confidence necessary to do something difficult, unpleasant, or rude: *It takes a lot of nerve to be a bomb disposal expert.* ◦ *I wanted to ask her out, but I **lost** my nerve and couldn't go through with it.* ◦ [+ to infinitive] *I didn't have **the** nerve **to** tell him what I really thought of his suggestion.* **WORRY** ▷ **3 nerves** [plural] B2 worry or ANXIETY about something that is going to happen: *I never suffer from nerves when I'm speaking in public.* ◦ *She was **a bundle of** nerves (= very nervous) before the audition.* ◦ *I always have a cigarette to **calm/steady** my nerves (= make me less nervous) before I go on stage.* **4 get on sb's nerves** B2 to annoy someone a lot: *We really got on each other's nerves when we were living together.* ◦ *Please stop making that noise! It really gets on my nerves.* **5 steady/strong nerves** B2 the ability to be calm in difficult situations: *You need a cool head and steady nerves for this job.* **RUDENESS** ▷ **6** C2 [S or U] the rudeness to do something that you know will upset other people: [+ to infinitive] *She's late for work every day, but she still has **the** nerve **to** lecture me about punctuality.* ◦ *That man has such a nerve! He's always blaming me for things that are his fault.* ◦ *She drove the car into a tree and then told me it was my fault for not concentrating, **of all the** nerve!*

IDIOMS **have nerves of steel** to be very brave: *You need to have nerves of steel to be a fighter pilot.* • **hit/touch a (raw) nerve** C2 to upset someone: *She touched a raw nerve when she mentioned that job he didn't get.*

▸**verb** **nerve yourself** UK to make yourself brave enough to do something: [+ to infinitive] *It took her several months before she eventually nerved herself (**up**) **to** invite him to her house.*

ˈ**nerve** ˌ**cell** noun [C] a **neuron**

ˈ**nerve** ˌ**centre** UK (US ˈ**nerve** ˌ**center**) noun [C] a place from which an organization or activity is controlled or managed: *The Pentagon is the nerve centre of the US Armed Forces.*

ˈ**nerve** ˌ**gas** noun [U] a poisonous gas, often used as a weapon, that damages the nerves

nerve-ˌ**racking** (also ˈ**nerve-**ˌ**wracking**) adj describes something that is difficult to do and causes a lot of worry for the person involved in it: *My wedding was the most nerve-racking thing I've ever experienced.*

nervous /ˈnɜː.vəs/ US /ˈnɝː-/ adj **WORRIED** ▷ **1** B1 worried and ANXIOUS: *Do you **feel/get** nervous during exams?* ◦ *I was too nervous to speak.* ◦ *She's always been nervous **around** dogs.* ◦ *I was very nervous **about** driving again after the accident.* ◦ *He had/was of **a** nervous **disposition**.*

> **!** Common mistake: **nervous**
>
> **Warning:** check the meaning!
>
> To talk about someone often becoming annoyed, don't say 'nervous', say **irritable** or **bad-tempered**:
>
> ~~*The noise of the traffic makes him tired and nervous.*~~
>
> *The noise of the traffic makes him tired and irritable.*

BODY ▷ **2** relating to the nerves: *He suffers from a nervous **disorder**.*

ˌ**nervous** ˈ**breakdown** noun [C usually singular] a period of mental illness, usually without a physical cause, which results in ANXIETY, difficulty in sleeping and thinking clearly, a loss of confidence and hope, and a feeling of great sadness: *He **suffered** a nervous breakdown in his twenties.*

nervously /ˈnɜː.vəs.li/ US /ˈnɝː-/ adv B2 feeling or showing that you are worried and ANXIOUS: *He looked nervously over his shoulder, making sure no one else was listening.*

nervousness /ˈnɜː.vəs.nəs/ US /ˈnɝː-/ noun [U] C1 a feeling of worry and ANXIETY: *There is growing nervousness **about** the possibility of a war.*

ˈ**nervous** ˌ**system** noun [C usually singular] An animal's or person's nervous system consists of its brain and all the nerves in its body which together make movement and feeling possible by sending messages around the body.

nervy /ˈnɜː.vi/ US /ˈnɝː-/ adj UK worried: *I'm always nervy before an exam.*

-ness /-nəs/ **suffix** added to adjectives to form nouns which refer to a quality or a condition: *happiness* ◦ *sadness* ◦ *nervousness* ◦ *selfishness* ◦ *kindness*

nest /nest/ **noun; verb**

▸**noun** [C] **HOME** ▷ **1** C2 a structure built by birds or insects to leave their eggs in to develop, and by some other animals to give birth or live in: *a bird's nest* ◦ *a wasps'/hornets' nest* ◦ *a rat's nest* ◦ *Cuckoos are famous for laying their eggs in the nests of other birds.* ◦ *The alligators build their nests out of grass near the water's edge.* **2** a comfortable home: *One day the children grow up and **leave the** nest.* **3** a place where something unpleasant or unwanted has developed: *The diplomats have been sent home because their embassy has become a nest **of** spies.* **SET** ▷ **4** a set of things that are similar but different in size and have been designed to fit inside each other: *I'd like a nest **of** tables for the living room.*

▸**verb** [I] C2 to build a nest, or live in a nest: *We've got some swallows nesting in our roof at the moment.* ◦ *Stone farm buildings are ideal nesting **sites** for barn owls.*

ˌ**nest** ˌ**egg** noun [C] C2 an amount of money that has been saved or kept for a special purpose: *Regular investment of small amounts of money is an excellent way of building a nest egg.*

nesting /ˈnes.tɪŋ/ adj fitting inside each other: *a set of nesting **dolls***

ˈ**nesting** ˌ**box** noun [C] UK (US **birdhouse**) a box for birds to nest in

nestle /ˈnes.l̩/ verb [I or T, + adv/prep] **1** to rest yourself or part of your body in a warm, comfortable, and protected position: *She nestled (her head) **against** his shoulder.* **2** to be in, or put something in, a protected position, with bigger things around it: *Bregenz is a pretty Austrian town that nestles **between** the Alps and Lake Constance.*

nestling /ˈnest.lɪŋ/ noun [C] a young bird that has not yet learned to fly and still lives in the nest built by its parents

net /net/ **noun; verb; adj**

▸**noun** (plural **-tt-**) **MATERIAL** ▷ **1** B1 [C or U] material made of threads of rope, string, wire, or plastic with spaces between them, allowing gas, liquid, or small objects to go through, or an object made with this material that is used to limit the movement of something: *a fishing net* ◦ *a butterfly net* ◦ *Dolphins often get tangled in the nets that are used to catch tuna fish.* ◦ *The living-room windows have net **curtains** that let in sunlight but stop passers-by looking in from the street.* **SPORT** ▷ **2** B1 [C] a rectangular piece of material made from string, used to separate the two sides in various sports: *If the ball touches the net during a service in a game of tennis, you have to serve again.* **3** B1 [C] the area surrounded by a piece of material made from string into which a ball or PUCK is put in order to score points in various sports: *His penalty kick placed the ball decisively in the back of the net.* ◦ *a basketball net*

▸verb [T] (-tt-) **CATCH** ▷ **1** to catch something using a net: *How many fish did you net this afternoon?* **2** to get something good or to earn a lot of money from something: [+ two objects] *She netted herself a fortune when she sold her company.* ◦ *Mark's netted himself a top job with an advertising company.* ◦ *She netted £10 million (**for** herself) from the sale of her company.* **SCORE** ▷ **3** If you net the ball during a game such as football, you score a goal: *He secured a dramatic victory for England by netting the ball half a minute before the end of the game.*

▸adj [before or after noun] (-tt-) (UK also **nett**) left when there is nothing else to be taken away: *I earn £25,000 gross, but my net **income** (= income that is left after tax has been paid) is about £18,000.* ◦ *The net **weight** of something excludes the weight of the material that it is packed in.* → Compare **gross**

the ˈNet noun [S] A2 abbreviation for **the internet**: *I've found a really useful website about allergies on the Net.*

netball /ˈnet.bɔːl/ US /-bɑːl/ noun [U] UK a sport played by two teams of seven players, usually women or girls, in which goals are scored by throwing a ball through a net hanging from a ring at the top of a pole

netbook /ˈnet.bʊk/ noun [C] a small LAPTOP computer designed mainly for using the internet

nethead /ˈnet.hed/ noun [C] informal someone who is very interested in the internet

nether /ˈneð.əʳ/ US /-ɚ/ adj [before noun] literary or humorous in a lower position: *The boiler room is somewhere down in the building's nether **regions**.*

netherworld /ˈneð.ə.wɜːld/ US /-ɚ.wɝːld/ noun [S] a place, situation, or part of society that is hidden, and often unpleasant: *The film shows us a netherworld of drugs and crime.*

netiquette /ˈne.tɪ.ket/ noun [U] specialized the set of rules about behaviour that is acceptable on the internet: *It's considered bad netiquette to use capital letters in an email because it looks like YOU ARE SHOUTING.*

netizen /ˈne.tɪ.zən/ noun [C] informal a person who uses the internet

ˌnet reˈsult noun [S] the situation that exists at the end of a series of events: *The net result of the changes will be increased fares and reduced services.*

netspeak /ˈnet.spiːk/ noun [U] informal the words, abbreviations, etc. that people use when communicating on the internet

netting /ˈnet.ɪŋ/ US /ˈneţ-/ noun [U] material in the form of a net: *Safety netting was put up around the playing field.*

nettle /ˈnet.l/ US /ˈneţ-/ **noun; verb**

▸noun [C] a wild plant with heart-shaped leaves that are covered in hairs that STING (= cause a painful reaction when touched): ***stinging** nettles* ◦ *nettle soup/tea*

▸verb [T often passive] mainly UK to make someone annoyed or slightly angry: *She looked up at me sharply, clearly nettled by the interruption.*

nettlerash /ˈnet.l.ræʃ/ US /ˈneţ-/ noun [U] UK a condition that causes slightly raised red or white spots to appear on the skin

network /ˈnet.wɜːk/ US /-wɝːk/ **noun; verb**

▸noun [C] B2 a large system consisting of many similar parts that are connected together to allow movement or communication between or along the parts or between the parts and a control centre: *a television network* ◦ *a road/rail network* ◦ *a computer network* ◦ *Massive investment is needed to modernize the country's **phone** network.* ◦ *We could reduce our costs by developing a more efficient **distribution** network.* ◦ *a network of spies/a spy network*

▸verb **COMPUTERS** ▷ **1** [T] to connect computers together so that they can share information: *Our computer system consists of about 20 personal computers networked **to** a powerful file-server.* **MEET PEOPLE** ▷ **2** [I] to meet people who might be useful to know, especially in your job: *I don't really enjoy these conferences, but they're a good opportunity to network.*

neur(o)- /njʊə.rəʊ-/ US /nʊr.oʊ-/ **prefix** relating to nerves: *neuroscience*

neural /ˈnjʊə.rəl/ US /ˈnʊr.əl/ **adj** [before noun] involving a nerve or the system of nerves that includes the brain: *Some people suffered severe neural damage as a result of the vaccination.*

neuralgia /njʊəˈræl.dʒə/ US /nʊrˈæl-/ noun [U] short, severe pains felt suddenly along a nerve, especially in the neck or head • **neuralgic** /-dʒɪk/ adj

neurolinguistics /ˌnjʊə.rəʊ.lɪŋˈgwɪs.tɪks/ US /ˌnʊr.oʊ-/ noun [U] the study of the relationship between language and the brain

neurological /ˌnjʊə.rəˈlɒdʒ.ɪ.kəl/ US /ˌnʊr.əˈlɑː.dʒɪ-/ **adj** relating to nerves: *neurological disease/damage* ◦ *Alzheimer's disease is a neurological **disorder**.*

neurologist /njʊəˈrɒl.ə.dʒɪst/ US /nʊrˈɑː.lə-/ noun [C] a doctor who studies and treats diseases of the nerves

neurology /njʊəˈrɒl.ə.dʒi/ US /nʊrˈɑː.lə-/ noun [U] the study of the structure and diseases of the brain and all the nerves in the body

neuron /ˈnjʊə.rɒn/ US /ˈnʊr.ɑːn/ noun [C] (UK also **neurone**) a nerve cell that carries information between the brain and other parts of the body

neurosis /njʊəˈrəʊ.sɪs/ US /nʊrˈoʊ-/ noun [C or U] (plural **neuroses**) a mental illness resulting in high levels of ANXIETY, unreasonable fears and behaviour and, often, a need to repeat actions for no reason: *If you want my opinion, I think she's suffering from some form of neurosis.* ◦ *She's obsessively clean – it's almost become a neurosis with her.*

neurosurgeon /ˈnjʊə.rəʊˌsɜː.dʒən/ US /ˈnʊr.oʊˌsɝː-/ noun [C] a doctor who performs operations involving the brain or nerves • **neurosurgery** /-dʒər.i/ US /-dʒɚ.i/ noun [U]

neurotic /njʊəˈrɒt.ɪk/ US /nʊrˈɑː.ţɪk/ **adj; noun**

▸adj behaving strangely or in an ANXIOUS (= worried and nervous) way, often because you have a mental illness: *neurotic behaviour/tendencies* ◦ *She's neurotic **about** her weight – she weighs herself three times a day.* • **neurotically** /njʊəˈrɒt.ɪ.kəl.i/ US /nʊrˈɑː.ţɪ-/ adv

▸noun [C] someone who behaves strangely, often because they have a mental illness

neurotransmitter /ˌnjʊə.rəʊ.trænzˈmɪt.əʳ/ (US) /ˌnʊr.oʊ.trænsˈmɪţ.ɚ/ noun [C] a chemical that carries messages between NEURONS or between NEURONS and muscles

neuter /ˈnjuː.təʳ/ (US) /ˈnuː.ţɚ/ adj; verb
▸**adj** specialized relating to a particular GENDER (= class of nouns) in some languages: *The German word for 'book', 'Buch', is neuter.* → Compare **masculine, feminine**
▸**verb** [T] **1** to remove part of an animal's sexual organs, so that it cannot produce young animals: *Has your dog been neutered?* **2** to take the power away from something

neutral /ˈnjuː.trəl/ (US) /ˈnuː-/ adj; noun
▸**adj** NO OPINION ▷ **1** (C1) not saying or doing anything that would encourage or help any of the groups involved in an argument or war: *If there's an argument between my daughter and her mother, it's important that I* ***remain*** *neutral.* ◦ *The peace conference would have to be held in a neutral* ***country****.* ◦ *I'd rather meet on neutral* ***ground/territory*** *(= somewhere not controlled by or connected to either of us) rather than in his apartment.* NOT NOTICEABLE ▷ **2** (C1) having features or characteristics that are not easily noticed: *Huw wants dark red walls, but I'd rather a more neutral* ***colour*** *like cream.* SCIENCE ▷ **3** describes a chemical substance that is neither an ACID nor an ALKALI: *Pure water is neutral and has a pH of 7.* **4** describes an object in physics that has no electrical charge: *Atoms consist of positively-charged protons, negatively-charged electrons and neutral particles called neutrons.*
▸**noun** NO MOVEMENT ▷ **1** [U] the position of the GEARS in a vehicle when they are not connected to the engine: *You're supposed to put your car* ***into*** *neutral whenever you stop at a junction.* **2** [U] a state of no activity or development: *After two years* ***in*** *neutral, the economy is finally moving forward again.* NO OPINION ▷ **3** [C] a neutral person or thing: *Sweden and Switzerland were neutrals during the war.*

neutrality /njuːˈtræl.ə.ti/ (US) /nuːˈtræl.ə.ţi/ noun [U] a neutral position, especially in a war: *Sweden isn't likely ever to abandon its traditional neutrality.* ◦ *The Queen has maintained* ***political*** *neutrality throughout her reign.*

neutralize /ˈnjuː.trə.laɪz/ (US) /ˈnuː-/ verb [T] STOP EFFECT ▷ **1** (UK usually **neutralise**) to stop something from having an effect: *to neutralize an acid/odour* ◦ *The aerial bombardments have neutralized the threat of artillery attacks on allied ground forces.* CHEMISTRY/ELECTRICITY ▷ **2** (UK usually **neutralise**) to make something neutral: *Acidity in soil can be neutralized by spreading lime on it.* • **neutralization** (UK also **neutralisation**) /ˌnjuː.trə.laɪˈzeɪ.ʃən/ (US) /ˌnuː.trə.ləˈ-/ noun [U]

neutron /ˈnjuː.trɒn/ (US) /ˈnuː.trɑːn/ noun [C] a part of an atom that has no electrical charge → Compare **electron, proton**

ˈneutron ˌbomb noun [C] a nuclear weapon used across short distances that is designed to kill people rather than destroy buildings or vehicles: *Neutron bombs release lethal radiation instead of exploding with a lot of heat and wind.*

never /ˈnev.əʳ/ (US) /-ɚ/ adv (A1) not at any time or not on any occasion: *We've never been to Australia.* ◦ *I've never heard anything so ridiculous.* ◦ *Let us never forget those who gave their lives for their country.* ◦ *Wars never solve anything.* ◦ *He threatened to shoot, but I never thought (= did not think) he would.* ◦ *I never realized you knew my brother.* ◦ *It's never* ***too late*** *to start eating a healthy diet.* ◦ UK informal *'He's never 61! (= it's difficult to believe he's 61!) He looks so young.'* ◦ UK not standard *'You stole my drink!' 'No, I never (= I didn't).'*

> **! Common mistake: never**
>
> **Warning:** check your word order!
>
> **Never** usually goes directly before the main verb in a sentence.
>
> Don't say 'never someone does something', say **someone never does something**:
>
> ~~*Never he tells me where he is going.*~~
>
> *He never tells me where he is going.*
>
> But if the main verb is **am/is/are/was/were**, **never** usually goes directly after it:
>
> ~~*He never is here before 8 p.m.*~~
>
> *He is never here before 8 p.m.*

> **! Common mistake: never or ever?**
>
> **Warning:** it is not usual to use two negative words in the same sentence.
>
> When using **never** in a sentence, don't say 'not':
>
> ~~*You should not never give up studying.*~~
>
> *You should never give up studying.*
>
> When using 'not' in a sentence, don't say 'never', say **ever**:
>
> *You should not ever give up studying.*

IDIOMS **as never before** in a way that has never been possible before: *Satellite technology offers the opportunity, as never before, for continuous television coverage of major international events.* • **never fear!** old-fashioned or humorous do not worry: *Never fear! I'll have that leak fixed in a few moments.* • **never mind 1** (A2) used to tell someone not to worry about something because it is not important: *'I'm afraid I've lost that wallet you gave me.' 'Well, never mind, I can easily buy you another one.'* **2 never mind sth** used as a way of emphasizing that, although a particular thing is true, the one you have just mentioned is more important or interesting: *This is one of the best restaurants in the country, never mind Cambridge.* • **never mind that** informal despite the fact that: *He's going on holiday for the third time this year, never mind that he has hardly any money left.* • **that will never do** old-fashioned said when you think that something is unacceptable: *'He promised to pay me back last week, but he didn't.' 'Dear me, that will never do!'* • **well, I never (did)!** old-fashioned said when you are very surprised at something: *'Sophie's brother's been married seven times.' 'Well, I never (did)!'*

ˌnever-ˈending adj (C1) describes something that never ends or seems as if it will never end: *Writing a dictionary is a never-ending task.*

the ˌnever-ˈnever UK informal **on the never-never** using a system of payment in which part of the cost of something is paid immediately and then small regular payments are made until the debt is reduced to nothing: *I don't like* ***buying*** *things on the never-never because they charge you such a lot in interest.*

ˌnever-ˈnever ˌland noun [U] an imaginary place where everything is pleasant or perfect in a way that is impossible to achieve in real life: *If he thinks we can get this done by next week, he's* ***living*** *in never-never land.*

nevertheless /ˌnev.ə.ðəˈles/ (US) /-ɚ-/ adv (also **nonetheless**) (B2) despite what has just been said or referred to: *I knew a lot about the subject already, but her talk was interesting nevertheless.*

new /njuː/ (US) /nuː/ adj; noun
▸**adj** RECENTLY CREATED ▷ **1** (A1) recently created or having started to exist recently: *a new car* ◦ *She's very*

creative and always coming up with new ideas. ◦ *What have they decided to call their new baby?* ◦ *What's new in the fashion world?* ◦ *We have to invest in new technology if we are to remain competitive.* → See also **brand new** **DIFFERENT** ▷ **2** A1 [before noun] different to one that existed earlier: *Have you met the new secretary?* ◦ *She's looking for a new job.* ◦ *Have you seen Ann's new house (= where she has just started living)?* ◦ *They've just launched a new generation of computers that are much more powerful than earlier models.* **NOT FAMILIAR** ▷ **3** B1 [after verb] not yet familiar or experienced: *to be new* ***to*** *the area* ◦ *She's new* ***to*** *the job so you can't expect her to know everything yet.* **NOT USED** ▷ **4** not previously used or owned: *Used car sales have risen because of the increased cost of new cars.* ◦ *Did you buy your bike new or second-hand?* → See also **brand new** **RECENTLY DISCOVERED** ▷ **5** A1 recently discovered or made known: *This new cancer treatment offers hope to many sufferers.* ◦ *A retrial can only take place when new evidence has emerged.* • **newness** /ˈnjuː.nəs/ US /ˈnuː-/ **noun** [U]

> **+ Other ways of saying new**
>
> If something is completely new and has not been used, you can describe it as **brand new**:
>
> *How can he afford to buy a* ***brand new*** *car?*
>
> **Fresh** can be used when something is new and therefore interesting or exciting:
>
> *We need a* ***fresh*** *approach to the problem of crime.*
>
> The adjectives **novel** or **innovative** can be used when something involves new and unusual ideas or methods:
>
> *The bank has introduced a* ***novel*** *way of detecting fraud.*
>
> *The project uses* ***innovative*** *ideas for recycling.*

IDIOMS **be the new sth** used to say that something is now more popular or fashionable than the thing that it replaces: *This season fashion designers have declared that brown is the new black.* • **feel like a new woman/man** to feel very much better: *That holiday did me the world of good – I feel like a whole new woman since I came back.* • **the new kid on the block** informal someone who is new in a place or organization and has many things to learn about it: *Realizing I was the new kid on the block in this job, I was determined to prove myself.* • **a new lease of life** UK (US **a new lease on life**) **1** an occasion when you become more energetic and active than before: *His grandchildren have* ***given*** *him a new lease of life.* **2** an increase in the period for which something can be used or continued: *The project suddenly* ***got*** *a new lease of life when the developers agreed to provide some more funding.* • **that's a new one on me.** informal said when someone has just told you a surprising fact that you did not know before: *'Sian and Richard are getting married.' 'Really! That's a new one on me!'*

▸**noun** [U] **the new** new things: *Out with the old and in with the new.*

new- /njuː-/ US /nuː-/ **prefix** recent or recently: *The government's new-****found*** *enthusiasm for green issues has been welcomed by environmentalists.*

ˌNew ˈAge **noun** [U] a way of life and thinking that developed in the late 1980s, based on ideas that existed before modern scientific and economic theories: *Astrology and alternative medicine are part of the New Age* ***movement.*** • **New-Ager** /ˌnjuːˈeɪ.dʒəʳ/ US /ˌnuːˈeɪ.dʒɚ/ **noun** [C]

ˌNew Age ˈmusic **noun** [U] a type of music that is intended to produce a calm and peaceful state of mind: *My massage therapist always plays New Age music to help me relax.*

newbie /ˈnjuː.bi/ US /ˈnuː.bi/ **noun** [C] informal someone who has just started doing an activity, a job, etc.: *The guide helps newbies understand the internet.*

ˌnew ˈblood **noun** [U] people with a lot of energy or fresh ideas who are brought into an organization in order to improve it: *The new blood in the team should improve our chances of victory in next week's match.*

newborn /ˈnjuː.bɔːn/ US /ˈnuː.bɔːrn/ **adj** [before noun] recently born: *Breast-feeding is extremely beneficial to the health of newborn* ***babies.*** ◦ figurative *the newborn democracies of the world*

newbuild /ˈnjuːˌbɪld/ US /ˈnuː-/ **noun** [C] a house or other building that has been built recently

newcomer /ˈnjuːˌkʌm.əʳ/ US /ˈnuːˌkʌm.ɚ/ **noun** [C] someone who has recently arrived in a place or recently become involved in an activity: *We're* ***relative*** *newcomers* ***to*** *the village.* ◦ *The newcomer* ***on the*** *radio* ***scene*** *is a commercial station devoted to classical music.*

newfangled /ˌnjuːˈfæŋ.gl̩d/ US /ˌnuː-/ **adj** recently made for the first time, but not always an improvement on what existed before: *I really don't understand these newfangled computer games that my children are always playing.*

newfound /ˈnjuː.faʊnd/ US /ˈnuː-/ **adj** a newfound quality or ability has started recently: *This success is a reflection of their newfound confidence.*

ˈnew ˌgirl/ˌboy **noun** [C] mainly UK **1** a child who has recently started going to a school **2** someone who has recently become involved with an activity or organization: *Mark Kennedy is the new boy in the government.*

newish /ˈnjuː.ɪʃ/ US /ˈnuː.ɪʃ/ **adj** informal slightly new: *They have a four-bedroom house on a newish estate.*

newly /ˈnjuː.li/ US /ˈnuː.li/ **adv** B2 recently: *the newly formed residents' association* ◦ *Newly-discovered documents cast doubt on the guilt of the two men.*

newlywed /ˈnjuː.li.wed/ US /ˈnuː-/ **noun** [C usually plural] someone who has recently got married: *The hotel has a special discount rate for newlyweds.*

ˌnew ˈman **noun** [C] mainly UK a man who believes that women and men are equal and should be free to do the same things, and who does tasks and shows emotions that were traditionally considered only suitable for women

ˌnew ˈmedia **noun** [plural] products and services that provide information or entertainment using computers or the internet, and not by traditional methods such as television and newspapers: *We must embrace the opportunities presented by new media.*

ˌnew ˈmoon **noun** [C usually singular, U] the moon when it is shaped like a CRESCENT, or a time when it is shaped like this: *It was dark now and the sliver of a new moon could be seen overhead.*

ˌnew poˈtatoes **noun** [plural] small potatoes that are taken out of the ground earlier than the others in the crop

news /njuːz/ US /nuːz/ **noun** [U] **1** A2 information or reports about recent events: *That's the best (****piece of****) news I've heard for a long time!* ◦ *We've had no news* ***of*** *them since they left for Australia.* ◦ *Have you heard the news* ***about*** *Tina and Tom? They're getting divorced.* ◦ *Do write and tell us all your news.* ◦ [+ that] *The news* ***that*** *Madge had resigned took everyone by surprise.* ◦ *We've got some* ***good*** *news for you. We're getting* *married.* **2 the news** B1 a television or radio programme consisting of reports about recent events: *I usually watch the **early evening/late night** news.* ◦ *Was there anything interesting **on** the news this evening?* **3 break the news** to tell someone about something bad that has just happened and may have an effect on them: *I was devastated when the doctor broke the news **to** me.* ◦ *Where were you when the news of Kennedy's assassination **broke** (= became known)?* **4 be good/bad news** C1 to be someone or something that will affect a person or situation well/badly: *He's bad news **for** the company. He should never have been given the job.* **5 be in the news** to be reported about: *They've been in the news a lot recently because of their marital problems.*

> **Word partners for news**
>
> *hear* the news • *give/tell* sb the news • *welcome* the news • news *spreads/travels* • *bad/good/great/sad* news • the *latest* news • a *piece* of news • news *about/of* sb/sth

IDIOMS **be news to sb** informal C2 to be information that someone did not know before: *'I hear you and Phil are going to Paris for the weekend.' 'Really? That's news to me.'* • **have news for sb** used to say that someone is going to be unpleasantly surprised because something will not be as they want it to be: *I've got news for him, if he thinks he can carry on living here free of charge.* • **no news is good news** saying said to make someone feel less worried when they have not received information about someone or something, because if something bad had happened, they would have been told about it: *We haven't heard anything from the hospital today, but I suppose no news is good news.*

N

ˈnews ˌagency noun [C] an organization which supplies reports to newspapers, magazines, and television and radio companies

newsagent /ˈnjuːzˌeɪ.dʒᵊnt/ US /ˈnuːz-/ **noun** [C] UK **1** (also **newsagent's**) a shop that sells newspapers and magazines, as well as some foods and things that people often buy such as cigarettes: *Do you want anything from the newsagent's apart from a paper?* **2** a person who owns or manages a newsagent's

newscast /ˈnjuːz.kɑːst/ US /ˈnuːz.kæst/ **noun** [C] mainly US a radio or television programme that consists of news reports

newscaster /ˈnjuːzˌkɑː.stəʳ/ US /ˈnuːzˌkæs.tɚ/ **noun** [C] (UK also **newsreader**) someone who reads out the reports on a television or radio news programme

ˈnews ˌconference noun [C] mainly US a meeting in which someone makes a statement to REPORTERS or answers questions from them: *She **called** a news conference to give her side of the story.* → See also **press conference**

newsflash /ˈnjuːz.flæʃ/ US /ˈnuːz-/ **noun** [C] a short news report on radio or television, giving the most recent information about an important or unexpected event

newsgroup /ˈnjuːz.gruːp/ US /ˈnuːz.gruːp/ **noun** [C] a collection of messages that are shown on the internet and have been written by people interested in a particular subject: *If you want to read discussions on the latest films, subscribe to a newsgroup.*

newsletter /ˈnjuːzˌlet.əʳ/ US /ˈnuːzˌleţ.ɚ/ **noun** [C] C1 a printed or electronic document containing information about the recent activities of an organization, sent regularly to the organization's members: *a **monthly** newsletter*

newspaper /ˈnjuːzˌpeɪ.pəʳ/ US /ˈnuːzˌpeɪ.pɚ/ **noun** **1** A1 [C] a regularly printed document consisting of large sheets of paper that are folded together, or a website, containing news reports, articles, photographs, and advertisements: *Which newspaper do you read regularly?* ◦ *a **daily/Sunday** newspaper* **2** [C] an organization that publishes a newspaper: *He wants to work for a newspaper when he leaves school.* **3** A2 [U] old newspapers: *You'd better wrap that mirror up in newspaper before you put it in the car.*

> **! Common mistake: newspaper**
>
> **Remember:** use the correct preposition.
>
> Don't say 'on the newspaper', say **in the newspaper**:
>
> ~~*I read an interesting article on the newspaper.*~~
>
> *I read an interesting article in the newspaper.*

newsprint /ˈnjuːz.prɪnt/ US /ˈnuːz-/ **noun** [U] cheap, low quality paper that newspapers are printed on

newsreader /ˈnjuːzˌriː.dəʳ/ US /ˈnuːzˌriː.dɚ/ **noun** [C] UK for **newscaster**

newsreel /ˈnjuːz.riːl/ US /ˈnuːz-/ **noun** [C] a short film that consists of news reports, usually one that was made in the past for showing in a cinema: *The movie contains some recently discovered newsreel **footage** of the war.*

newsroom /ˈnjuːz.rʊm/, /-ruːm/ US /ˈnuːz-/ **noun** [C] an office at a television or radio station or a newspaper where news is collected and reports are prepared for broadcasting or publishing

newsstand /ˈnjuːz.stænd/ US /ˈnuːz-/ **noun** [C] a table or temporary structure used as a small shop for selling newspapers and magazines outside in public places

newsvendor /ˈnjuːzˌven.dəʳ/ US /ˈnuːzˌven.dɚ/ **noun** [C] someone who sells newspapers

newsworthy /ˈnjuːzˌwɜː.ði/ US /ˈnuːzˌwɝː-/ **adj** interesting enough to be described in a news report: *Nothing newsworthy ever happens around here. It's so boring.*

newsy /ˈnjuː.zi/ US /ˈnuː-/ **adj** informal containing a lot of news that is personal or not very serious: *I got a lovely, newsy email from Marion.*

newt /njuːt/ US /nuːt/ **noun** [C] a small animal that has a long thin body and tail and short legs, and lives both on land and in water

the ˌNew ˈTestament noun [S] the second of the two main parts of the Christian Bible, containing the books written after the birth of Jesus Christ: *the New Testament reading* → Compare **the Old Testament**

newton /ˈnjuː.tᵊn/, /ˈnuː-/ **noun** [C] (written abbreviation **N**) a unit used to measure force, equal to the force which moves a mass of one kilogram one metre in one second

ˈnew ˌtown noun [C] a British town which did not develop gradually but was planned and created by the government

ˌnew ˈwave noun **FASHION** ▷ **1** [S or U] a fashion in something, such as art, music, cinema, or politics, that is intentionally different from traditional ideas in that subject or activity: *new-wave music* **PEOPLE** ▷ **2** [S, + sing/pl verb] people who are doing activities in a new and different way: *the new wave **of** wine producers*

the ˌNew ˈWorld noun North, Central, and South America → Compare **the Old World**

ˌNew ˈYear (also **ˌnew ˈyear**) noun [C usually singular] the beginning of the year that is about to begin or has just begun: *I'm spending New Year (= the first days* *of the new year) in Scotland with my parents.* ◦ *We'll have to wait until* ***the*** *new year before we can make any definite plans.* ◦ *Best wishes for Christmas and a* ***Happy*** *New Year.*

ˌNew ˌYear('s) ˌresoˈlution noun [C] a promise that you make to yourself to start doing something good or stop doing something bad on the first day of the year: *'Have you* ***made*** *any New Year's resolutions?' 'Yes, I'm going to eat more healthily and give up smoking.'*

ˌNew ˌYear's ˈDay noun [U] (US **ˌNew ˈYear's**) the first day of the year, a public holiday in many countries

ˌNew ˌYear's ˈEve noun [U] the last day of the year: *Are you having a New Year's Eve party?* → See also **Hogmanay**

next /nekst/ adj, pronoun; adv

▸adj, pronoun A1 being the first one after the present one or after the one just mentioned: *Who works in the office next* ***to*** *yours?* ◦ *Take the next turning on the right.* ◦ *Who do you think will be the next president?* ◦ *Nothing really changes around here. One day is pretty much like* ***the*** *next.* ◦ *(The) next time you want to borrow something, please ask me first.* ◦ *I'm so busy it's hard to remember what I'm supposed to be doing* ***from one moment to the*** *next.* ◦ *She's on holiday for the next few days.* ◦ *You'll have to wait until your next birthday for a new bike.* ◦ *Can we arrange a meeting for the week after next?* ◦ *What do you think you'll be doing this time next year?* ◦ *We had a dreadful argument, but he phoned me* ***the*** *next* ***day*** *(= the day after) to apologize.* ◦ *Excuse me, it's my turn to be served – I was next.*

> **!** Common mistake: **next or the next?**
>
> Use **next** to talk about the moment or period of time that will be the first one after the present:
>
> *I look forward to seeing you next week/Tuesday/Christmas.*
>
> To talk about a moment or period of time in the past that immediately followed the moment or period of time just mentioned, don't say 'next', say **the next**:
>
> ~~*I went to Greece next year, but that was the last time.*~~
>
> *I went to Greece the next year, but that was the last time.*

IDIOMS **as much as the next person** as much as anyone would: *I enjoy winning awards as much as the next guy, but other things are more important to me.* • **the next best thing** C1 the thing that is best, if you cannot have or do the thing you really want: *I really wanted to work in television but I ended up in radio, which is the next best thing.* • **the next thing I knew** informal C2 used to talk about part of a story that happens in a sudden and surprising way: *A car came speeding round the corner, and the next thing I knew I was lying on the ground.*

▸adv **1** A2 immediately after: *So what happened next?* ◦ *What would you like next?* ◦ *First, fry the garlic. Next, add the ginger.* **2** B1 The time when you next do something is the first time you do it again: [+ -ing verb] *When are you next go**ing** to London?* **3 next to a** A2 used when describing two people or things that are very close to each other with nothing between them: *Can I* ***sit*** *next to the window?* ◦ *There was a really strange man standing next to me at the station.* **b** used to mean 'after' when making a choice or a comparison: *Cheese is my favourite food and, next to that, chocolate. (= Cheese is the only food that I like more than chocolate.)* **c** almost: *They pay me next to* ***nothing*** *(= very little) but I really enjoy the work.* ◦ *It's next to* ***impossible*** *(= extremely difficult) to find somewhere cheap to live in the city centre.* ◦ *We got home in next to* ***no time*** *(= very little time).* **4 next up** next in order to appear or happen, often in some form of entertainment: *Next up on Channel 4 is the first episode of a new medical drama.*

next ˈdoor adv; noun; adv, adj

▸adv very close: *Would you want to live next door to a nuclear power station?*

▸noun [U] UK informal the person or people living in the next room, house, or building: *Next door's having a party next week, did you know?*

▸adv, adj (also **ˌnext-ˈdoor**) B1 in the next room, house, or building: *A Russian couple have just moved in next door.* ◦ *Who lives next door* ***to*** *you?* ◦ *Margot is our next-door* ***neighbour.***

IDIOM **the boy/girl next door** used to describe someone who is completely ordinary, not rich, famous, etc.: *We couldn't believe it when he got a record deal. To us, he was just the boy next door.*

ˌnext of ˈkin noun [C] (plural **next of kin**) the person or group of people you are most closely related to: *We cannot release the names of the soldiers who were killed until we have informed their next of kin.*

ˌnext to ˈlast adj describes the person or thing before the last one: *I was next to last in the steeplechase.* ◦ *He injured himself on the next-to-last day of his vacation.*

nexus /ˈnek.səs/ noun [C usually singular] formal an important connection between the parts of a system or a group of things: *Times Square is the nexus of the New York subway.*

NGO /ˌen.dʒiːˈəʊ/ US /-ˈoʊ/ noun [C] abbreviation for non-governmental organization: an organization that tries to achieve social or political aims but is not controlled by a government

the NHS /ˌen.eɪtʃˈes/ noun abbreviation for **the National Health Service**: *Many forms of cosmetic surgery are not* ***available on*** *(= paid for by) the NHS.* • **NHS** adj *an NHS hospital*

niacin /ˈnaɪə.sɪn/ noun [U] specialized one of the VITAMIN B COMPLEX found in foods such as WHEAT, BEEF, chicken, and milk, important for producing energy from food and for keeping the DIGESTION and NERVOUS SYSTEM healthy

nib /nɪb/ noun [C] a pointed metal part at one end of a pen, which the ink flows through when you write or draw → Compare **ballpoint, felt-tip**

nibble /ˈnɪb.l̩/ verb; noun

▸verb **1** [I or T] to eat something by taking a lot of small bites: *Have you got some peanuts for us to nibble while the party warms up?* ◦ *A mouse has nibbled through the computer cables.* ◦ *Jenny's hamster's nibbled a hole* ***in*** *the sofa.* **2** [T] to bite something gently and repeatedly: *She nibbled his ear.*

PHRASAL VERB **nibble (away) at sth** to slowly reduce something: *Even when inflation is low, it nibbles away at people's savings, reducing their value considerably over several years.*

▸noun **1** [C] an act of nibbling something: *Just* ***take/have*** *a nibble to see if you like the taste.* **2 nibbles** [plural] UK informal small pieces of food that are eaten between or before meals, often with alcoholic drinks: *I bought some crisps and nuts and other nibbles.* **3** [S] an expression of interest in something: *Our house was on the market for six months and there wasn't a single nibble.*

N

nibs /nɪbz/ noun old-fashioned informal **his nibs** a man who is in a position of authority or who thinks he is more important than he really is: *Did his nibs say when he would be back in the office?*

NiCad /ˈnaɪ.kæd/ noun [C] trademark a type of BATTERY that can be RECHARGED (= filled with electricity again and again), used in electronic equipment

nice /naɪs/ adj **PLEASANT** ▷ **1** A1 pleasant, enjoyable, or satisfactory: *Did you have a nice holiday?* ◦ *Have a nice day/time!* ◦ *This milk doesn't smell very nice.* ◦ *Thanks for ringing – **it**'s been nice talking to you.* ◦ *Wasn't **it** nice **of** them **to** invite us?* **2 nice and...** B1 informal pleasantly: *This orange is nice and juicy.* **KIND** ▷ **3** A1 kind, friendly, or polite: *Jane's new boyfriend is a really nice guy.* ◦ *I wish you'd be nice **to** your brother.* ◦ ***It** was very nice **of** her **to** drive you home.* ◦ *It's not nice to talk with your mouth full.* **SLIGHTLY DIFFERENT** ▷ **4** [before noun] formal based on very slight differences: *I wasn't convinced by the minister's nice **distinction** between a lie and an untruth.*

Other ways of saying nice

If people are nice because they are generous and helpful to other people, you can say that they are **kind** or **sweet**:

*She's a very **kind** person.*

*Thank you so much for the card – it was very **sweet** of you!*

If something that you do is nice, you can describe it as **fun**, **enjoyable**, or **lovely**:

*We had a really **lovely** day at the beach.*

*You'd have liked the party – it was **fun**.*

If something is nice to look at, then adjectives such as **attractive**, **beautiful**, **pleasant**, **lovely**, and **pretty** are often used:

*There's some **beautiful** mountain scenery in Idaho.*

*That's a **pretty** dress you're wearing.*

If food tastes nice, you can say that it is **delicious** or **tasty**:

*This chicken soup is absolutely **delicious**.*

IDIOMS **nice one!** UK informal something that you say when you have just heard that someone has done something you think is good: *'Graham's brought some champagne along to mark the occasion.' 'Oh, nice one, Graham!'* • **nice work if you can get it** something you say about an easy way of earning money which you would like to do if you could: *She got one million dollars for appearing on television for five minutes – (that's) nice work if you can get it!*

ˌnice-ˈlooking adj attractive: *Isn't Gill's husband nice-looking?*

nicely /ˈnaɪs.li/ adv **PLEASANT** ▷ **1** B2 well, pleasantly, or in a satisfactory way: *Those trousers fit you nicely.* ◦ *You've painted the woodwork very nicely.* ◦ *Bake the mixture for 35 to 40 minutes until the cake is nicely browned.* ◦ *They said the baby was **doing** nicely (= was healthy) and would soon be back at home.* **KIND** ▷ **2** B2 in a kind, friendly, or polite way: *Well, I like her – she's always treated me very nicely.*

IDIOMS **do nicely** informal to make a large profit: *They did very nicely **from** the sale of their company.* • **that'll do nicely** used to say that something is satisfactory: *That'll do nicely, thank you.*

nicety /ˈnaɪ.sə.ti/ US /-t̬i/ noun **1** [C] a detail or small difference that is only obvious after careful thought: *They spent a lot of time arguing about **legal** niceties.* ◦ *We don't bother with all the **social** niceties here.* **2** [U] formal the fact that something is based on very slight differences

niche /niːʃ/ US /nɪtʃ/ noun [C] **POSITION** ▷ **1** a job or position that is very suitable for someone, especially one that they like: *Lloyd has **carved/made** a niche for himself as a professional tennis player.* **2** an area or position that is exactly suitable for a small group of the same type: *an ecological niche.* **HOLLOW** ▷ **3** a hollow in a wall, especially one made to put a STATUE (= artistic object) in so that it can be seen

ˈniche ˌmarket noun [C] a small area of trade within the economy, often involving specialized products: *Lotus make luxury cars for a small but significant niche market.*

nick /nɪk/ noun; verb

▸noun **CUT** ▷ **1** [C] a small cut in a surface or an edge: *Apart from a few nicks in the varnish, the guitar is in very good condition.* **PRISON** ▷ **2 the nick** [S] UK slang prison: *He's been **in** the nick half his life.* **CONDITION** ▷ **3** [U] UK slang a stated condition, especially of health: *He's **in** pretty good nick for a man of his age.* ◦ *The car really is **in** excellent nick.*

IDIOM **in the nick of time** at the last possible moment: *We got there just in the nick of time.*

▸verb [T] **STEAL** ▷ **1** UK informal to steal something: *I've had my bike nicked again.* ◦ *All right, who's nicked my ruler?* **CATCH** ▷ **2** UK slang If the police nick someone, they catch them for committing a crime: *They nicked him **for** driving at 70 in a 50 speed limit area.* **CUT** ▷ **3** to make a small cut in a surface or an edge: *Paintwork on the corner of a stairway tends to get nicked and scratched.*

nickel /ˈnɪk.l̩/ noun **METAL** ▷ **1** [U] (symbol **Ni**) a chemical element that is a silver-white metal: *a nickel alloy* **COIN** ▷ **2** [C] a US or Canadian coin worth five CENTS

ˌnickel-and-ˈdime adj US informal describes something that is not important, usually because it does not involve much money: *a nickel-and-dime dispute*

nick-nack /ˈnɪk.næk/ noun [C] a **knick-knack**

nickname /ˈnɪk.neɪm/ noun [C] B1 an informal name for someone or something, especially a name which you are called by your friends or family, usually based on your real name or your character: *We always use the nickname Beth for our daughter Elizabeth.* ◦ *'Darwin' was the nickname he was given at high school, because of his interest in science.* • **nickname** verb [T + obj + noun] *The campsite has been nicknamed 'tent city' by visiting reporters.*

nicotine /ˈnɪk.ə.tiːn/ US /-t̬iːn/ noun [U] a poisonous chemical found in tobacco which makes people who breathe it in regularly want more of it

ˈnicotine ˌpatch noun [C] a small piece of material with nicotine on it which a person can stick onto their skin to help them stop smoking

niece /niːs/ noun [C] B1 a daughter of your brother or sister, or a daughter of your husband's or wife's brother or sister → Compare **nephew**

niff /nɪf/ noun [C usually singular] UK informal an unpleasant smell: *a nasty niff* • **niffy** /ˈnɪf.i/ adj

nifty /ˈnɪf.ti/ adj informal good, pleasing, or effective: *a nifty piece of work/footwork* ◦ *a nifty little gadget*

niggardly /ˈnɪɡ.əd.li/ US /-ɚd-/ adj disapproving slight in amount, quality, or effort: *a niggardly donation/amount*

nigger /ˈnɪɡ.əʳ/ US /-ɚ/ noun [C] offensive an extremely offensive word for a black person

niggle /ˈnɪɡ.l/ verb; noun

▸verb [I or T] **WORRY** ▷ **1** to worry someone slightly, usually for a long time: *I just can't remember his name – it's been niggling me for a couple of weeks.* ◦ *One thought kept niggling **at** her.* **CRITICIZE** ▷ **2** to criticize someone about small details or give too much attention to details: *She niggles endlessly **over** the exact pronunciation.* ◦ *The accounts department is niggling me for ten cents they say I owe them.*

▸noun [C] **WORRY** ▷ **1** a small doubt or worry: *Don't you feel even a slight niggle about the morality of your experiments?* **CRITICISM** ▷ **2** a small criticism: *I do have a few minor niggles about the book, but generally it's very good.* • **niggling** /-l̩.ɪŋ/, /-lɪŋ/ **adj** [before noun] *a niggling doubt/fear* ◦ *a niggling comment/criticism*

nigh /naɪ/ **adv, preposition** old-fashioned or literary near: *She must have written nigh **on** (= nearly but not quite) 50 books.* ◦ ***The time is** nigh (= it is nearly time) for us to make a decision.*

night /naɪt/ noun; exclamation

▸noun **DARK PERIOD** ▷ **1** (A1) [C or U] the part of every 24-hour period when it is dark because there is very little light from the sun: *It gets cold **at** night.* ◦ *I slept really badly **last** night.* ◦ *I **spent** the night at Ted's.* ◦ *He took the night ferry/train.* **EVENING** ▷ **2** (A1) [C or U] the period of time between the late afternoon and going to bed; the evening: *Shall we go dancing on Saturday night?* ◦ *We've been out every night this week.* ◦ *She's a singer in a bar **by** night and a secretary by day.* **3** [S] the evening on which a special event happens: *When's the **last** night of your show?* ◦ *The **first/opening** night of her new film was a great success.* **4 night-night** child's expression used as another way of saying GOOD NIGHT, usually by or to children **5 the other night** on one evening recently: *I saw Naomi at the club the other night.* **6 a night out** an evening spent at a restaurant, theatre, etc. rather than staying at home: *Let's **have** a night out together on Saturday – we could go dancing.*

IDIOMS **night after night** **1** every night: *The howling of wild animals kept him awake night after night.* **2** every evening: *She stayed in night after night, waiting for him to call.* • **night and day** (also **day and night**) all the time: *They've worked night and day to publicize their campaign.* • **a night on the town** an evening when you go to various places and enjoy entertainment such as dancing, eating in a restaurant, or drinking in a bar: *Let's **have/go for** a night on the town to celebrate.*

▸**exclamation** informal a friendly way of saying goodbye when you leave someone in the evening or before going to bed or to sleep: *Night, darling! Sleep well!* → Compare **good night**

nightcap /ˈnaɪt.kæp/ noun [C] **DRINK** ▷ **1** a drink, often an alcoholic drink, which someone has just before they go to bed **HAT** ▷ **2** a type of hat made from soft cloth and worn in bed, especially in the past

nightclothes /ˈnaɪt.kləʊðz/ (US) /-kloʊðz/ noun [plural] clothes that are worn in bed

nightclub /ˈnaɪt.klʌb/ noun [C] (informal **nightspot**) (B1) a place that is open late into the night, where people can go to drink and dance and often see some type of entertainment

nightclubbing /ˈnaɪtˌklʌb.ɪŋ/ noun [U] old-fashioned for the activity of going to nightclubs for enjoyment: *to **go** nightclubbing* → Compare **clubbing**

nightdress /ˈnaɪt.dres/ noun [C] UK (US **nightgown**) a comfortable piece of clothing like a loose dress worn by a woman or a girl in bed

nightfall /ˈnaɪt.fɔːl/ (US) /-fɑːl/ noun [U] the time in the evening when it becomes dark

nightgown /ˈnaɪt.ɡaʊn/ noun [C] US for **nightdress**

nightie /ˈnaɪ.ti/ (US) /-t̬i/ noun [C] informal for **nightdress**

nightingale /ˈnaɪ.tɪŋ.ɡeɪl/ (US) /-t̬ɪŋ-/ noun [C] a small, brown European bird known especially for the beautiful song of the male, usually heard during the night

nightlife /ˈnaɪt.laɪf/ noun [U] (B1) entertainment and social activities which happen in the evening in bars and CLUBS

nightlight /ˈnaɪt.laɪt/ noun [C] a light that is not bright that can be left on through the night, especially for a child

nightlong /ˌnaɪtˈlɒŋ/ (US) /-ˈlɑːŋ/ **adj, adv** literary through the night

nightly /ˈnaɪt.li/ **adj, adv** **DARK PERIOD** ▷ **1** (happening) every night: *Nightly bombardment of the city looks set to continue.* **EVENING** ▷ **2** (happening) every evening: *They're appearing/performing twice nightly at the Playhouse Theatre.* ◦ *a nightly visit/news broadcast*

nightmare /ˈnaɪt.meəʳ/ (US) /-mer/ noun [C] **1** (B1) a very upsetting or frightening dream: *a terrifying nightmare* ◦ *I shouldn't have watched that movie – it'll give me nightmares.* **2** (B1) an extremely unpleasant event or experience or possible event or experience: *The whole journey was a nightmare – we lost our luggage and we arrived two days late.* ◦ *Being trapped underwater is my **worst** nightmare.* • **nightmarish** /-meə.rɪʃ/ (US) /-mer.ɪʃ/ **adj** • **nightmarishly** /-meə.rɪʃ.li/ (US) /-mer.ɪʃ.li/ **adv**

ˈnight ˌowl noun [C] informal a person who prefers to be awake and active at night

nights /naɪts/ **adv** at night, especially every night: *Because she's a nurse she often has to **work** nights.* ◦ US *I like to go out nights and sleep during the day.*

ˈnight ˌschool noun [C] classes held in the evening especially for adults who work during the day

ˈnight ˌshift noun **1** [C] a period in the night during which a particular group of people work: *People who work (**on**) the night shift are paid more.* **2** [S, + sing/pl verb] the group of workers who work for a period during the night

nightshirt /ˈnaɪt.ʃɜːt/ (US) /-ʃɝːt/ noun [C] a comfortable piece of clothing like a long loose shirt worn in bed, especially in the past by a man or boy

nightspot /ˈnaɪt.spɒt/ (US) /-spɑːt/ noun [C] a **nightclub**

nightstand /ˈnaɪt.stænd/ noun [C] (also **ˈnight ˌtable**) US for **bedside table**

nightstick /ˈnaɪt.stɪk/ noun [C] US (UK **truncheon**) a thick heavy stick used as a weapon by police officers

nighttime /ˈnaɪt.taɪm/ noun [U] the time in every 24-hour period when it is dark: *It's pretty noisy at nighttime.* ◦ *a nighttime curfew*

ˈnight ˌvision noun; adj

▸noun [U] the ability to see when it is dark: *Children have better night vision than adults.*

▸adj [before noun] (also **ˈnight-ˌvision**) used to describe a piece of equipment that helps you to see when it is dark: *The troops were slowly advancing through the fields using night vision goggles.* ◦ *night-vision cameras/equipment/technology*

ˌnight ˈwatchman noun [C] a person who guards a building at night

nightwear /ˈnaɪt.weəʳ/ (US) /-wer/ noun [U] clothes worn in bed or while preparing to go to bed

nigiri /nɪˈɡɪ.ri/ noun [U] a Japanese food made with

rice pressed into an oval shape and fish or vegetables on top

nihilism /ˈnaɪ.ə.lɪ.zᵊm/ noun [U] specialized a belief that all political and religious organizations are bad, or a system of thought that says that there are no principles or beliefs that have any meaning or can be true • **nihilist** /-lɪst/ noun [C] • **nihilistic** /ˌnaɪ.əˈlɪs.tɪk/ adj

the Nikkei (index) /ˌnɪk.eɪˈɪn.deks/ (US) /ˌniː.keɪ-/, /nɪˌkeɪ-/ noun [S] a list that gives the price of SHARES in the most important Japanese companies → Compare **Dow Jones, the FTSE 100**

nil /nɪl/ noun [U] nothing: *She claims that the operating risks are virtually nil.* ◦ UK *The challengers lost the game seven-nil (= zero).*

nimble /ˈnɪm.bl̩/ adj usually approving quick and exact either in movement or thoughts: *nimble fingers/feet* ◦ *His nimble mind calculated the answer before I could key the numbers into my computer.* • **nimbleness** /-nəs/ noun [U] • **nimbly** /-bli/ adv *She hopped nimbly over the fence.*

nimbostratus /nɪm.bəʊˈstrɑː.təs/ (US) /-oʊˈstræţ.əs/ noun [U] specialized a type of STRATUS (= flat grey cloud) formed in a wide thick layer at a low level and usually carrying rain → Compare **altostratus, cirrostratus**

nimbus /ˈnɪm.bəs/ noun [U] specialized dark grey cloud which often produces rain or snow → Compare **cirrus, cumulus, stratus**

nimby /ˈnɪm.bi/ noun [C] disapproving abbreviation for not in my back yard: a person who does not want something unpleasant to be built or done near where they live: *The spokeswoman said that nimby attitudes were delaying development of the site.* • **nimbyism** /-ɪsm/ noun [U] disapproving *Residents were accused of nimbyism when they tried to stop the new superstore development.*

N

nincompoop /ˈnɪŋ.kəm.puːp/ noun [C] informal a silly or stupid person

nine /naɪn/ number **1** (A1) the number 9: *The children go to bed at nine (o'clock).* ◦ *a nine-month prison sentence* **2 nine to five** describing or relating to work that begins at nine o'clock in the morning and finishes at five, the hours worked in many offices from Monday to Friday: *a nine-to-five routine* ◦ *She's tired of **working** nine to five.*

IDIOMS **be a nine days' wonder** UK old-fashioned to be a cause of great excitement or interest for a short time but then quickly forgotten • **done/dressed (up) to the nines** informal wearing very stylish and fashionable clothes, often for a particular purpose or occasion: *The doorbell rang and there was Chris, all dressed up to the nines.* • **go the whole nine yards** informal mainly US to continue doing something dangerous or difficult until it is finished: *The weather was terrible but I wanted to go the whole nine yards and get to the top of the mountain.* • **nine times out of ten** (also **ninety-nine times out of a hundred**) almost always: *Nine times out of ten, you can fix it.*

ninepins /ˈnaɪn.pɪnz/ noun [plural] UK **go down/fall like ninepins** to fall, break, or be damaged in large numbers: *Trees were going down like ninepins in the strong wind.*

nineteen /ˌnaɪnˈtiːn/ number (A1) the number 19: *Simson, aged nineteen, was convicted on two charges of burglary.* ◦ *It's nineteen miles to the nearest town.*

nineteenth /ˌnaɪnˈtiːnθ/ ordinal number 19th written as a word: *The new term starts on **the** nineteenth (**of** September).*

IDIOM **the nineteenth hole** informal the bar at a GOLF COURSE where people go to have drinks and talk after they have finished playing

nineties /ˈnaɪn.tiz/ (US) /-ţiz/ noun [plural] **1** (B2) A person's nineties are the period in which they are aged between 90 and 99: *She was well **into** her nineties when she died.* **2 the nineties** the range of temperature between 90° and 99°: *Today it's supposed to get very hot – maybe up **into** the nineties.* **3** (B2) the DECADE (= period of ten years) between 90 and 99 in any century, usually 1990–1999: *Bill Clinton was US president **in/during** the nineties.*

ninetieth /ˈnaɪn.ti.əθ/ (US) /-ţi-/ ordinal number 90th written as a word

ninety /ˈnaɪn.ti/ (US) /-ţi/ number (A2) the number 90: *eighty-nine, ninety, ninety-one* ◦ *Ninety percent of the people surveyed were in favour.*

IDIOM **ninety-nine times out of a hundred** (also **nine times out of ten**) almost always: *Ninety-nine times out of a hundred everything's fine, but now and then there's a problem.*

ninja /ˈnɪn.dʒə/ noun [C] a Japanese fighter, especially in the past, who moves and acts without being seen and usually carries a short SWORD

ninny /ˈnɪn.i/ noun [C] old-fashioned informal a silly person

ninth /naɪnθ/ ordinal number; noun

▸**ordinal number** (A2) 9th written as a word: *The ninth letter of the alphabet is I.* ◦ *The school term ends on **the** ninth (**of** July).* ◦ *She **was/came** ninth in the national finals.*

▸**noun** [C] one of nine equal parts of something: *A ninth of 27 is 3.*

nip /nɪp/ verb; noun

▸**verb** (-pp-) **GO QUICKLY** ▷ **1** [I usually + adv/prep] UK informal to go somewhere quickly or be somewhere for only a short time: *Can you nip **out/round/down** to the shop for me?* ◦ *Shall we nip **in** to the café for a bite to eat?* **PRESS QUICKLY** ▷ **2** [I or T] to press something quickly and quite hard between two objects, especially sharp objects such as teeth or nails: *Josie's hamster nipped me.* ◦ *When he dropped the crate he nipped his hand.*

IDIOM **nip sth in the bud** to stop something before it has an opportunity to become established: *Many serious illnesses can be nipped in the bud if they are detected early enough.*

▸**noun COLD** ▷ **1 a nip (in the air)** informal If there is a nip in the air, the air outside is quite cold: *You can tell winter's on its way – there's a real nip in the air in the mornings.* **QUICK PRESS** ▷ **2** an occasion when something nips a person or thing: *I gave my thumb a painful nip with the pliers.* **DRINK** ▷ **3** [C] UK informal a small amount of strong alcoholic drink: *a nip of gin/brandy*

IDIOMS **a nip (here) and a tuck (there)** US informal a series of small reductions: *The department made a nip here and a tuck there, but they were still way over budget.* • **a nip and tuck** informal **plastic surgery**: *I suspect she's had a nip and tuck to look like that at her age.* • **nip and tuck** mainly US If a competition is nip and tuck, first one side seems to be winning and then the other, so that the result is not certain: *It was nip and tuck as to who would win the playoffs.*

Nip /nɪp/ noun [C] old-fashioned offensive an offensive word for a Japanese person

nipper /ˈnɪp.ər/ (US) /-ɚ/ noun [C] informal a young child

nipple /ˈnɪp.l̩/ noun [C] **1** the dark part of the skin which sticks out from the breast of a mammal and through which milk is supplied to the young **2** US for **teat**

nippy /ˈnɪp.i/ adj QUICK ▷ **1** UK informal able to change speed and direction easily: *a nippy little car* COLD ▷ **2** informal describes weather or air that is quite cold: *It's a bit nippy today – you might need a coat.*

niqab /nɪk.æb/ noun [C] a piece of cloth worn by some Muslim women to cover the face

nirvana /nɪəˈvɑː.nə/ (US) /nɚ-/ noun [U] **1** a state of freedom from all suffering which Buddhists believe can be achieved by removing all personal wishes **2** a state of being perfect

Nissen hut /ˈnɪs.ən,hʌt/ noun [C] a building shaped like a tube cut in half along the middle, made from CORRUGATED iron sheets

nit /nɪt/ noun PERSON ▷ **1** [C] UK informal disapproving a **nitwit** EGG ▷ **2** [C usually plural] the egg of a LOUSE, which sticks to the fur of an animal or the hair of a person: *A few of the children have **got** nits.*

nite /naɪt/ noun [C] not standard for **night**. This word is sometimes used in advertisements.

nitpick /ˈnɪt.pɪk/ verb [I] informal disapproving to find faults in details that are not important: *Must you nitpick all the time?* • **nitpicker** /-ər/ (US) /-ɚ/ noun [C]

nitpicking /ˈnɪt,pɪk.ɪŋ/ noun [U] informal disapproving giving too much attention to details that are not important, especially as a way of criticizing: *If you spent less time nitpicking, you'd get more work done.* • **nitpicking** adj *a nitpicking attitude*

nitrate /ˈnaɪ.treɪt/ noun [C or U] a chemical that includes NITROGEN and OXYGEN, often used as a FERTILIZER (= a substance that helps plants grow): *potassium/sodium nitrate*

nitric acid /,naɪ.trɪkˈæs.ɪd/ noun [U] a clear liquid that is used in making many chemicals, especially explosives and FERTILIZERS (= substances that help plants grow)

nitrification /,naɪ.trɪ.fɪˈkeɪ.ʃən/ noun [U] specialized the process in which bacteria in the soil use OXYGEN to change COMPOUNDS of NITROGEN in dead plant material into NITRATES which plants can then absorb as food

nitrify /ˈnaɪ.trɪ.faɪ/ verb [T] specialized to add nitrogen or one of its COMPOUNDS to something, for example to soil in order to make it produce healthier plants

nitrogen /ˈnaɪ.trə.dʒən/ noun [U] (symbol **N**) a chemical element that is a gas with no colour or taste, forms about 78% of the Earth's ATMOSPHERE, and is a part of all living things

,nitrogen diˈoxide noun [U] specialized a poisonous brown gas, formed when some metals dissolve in NITRIC ACID

nitroglycerine /,naɪ.trəʊˈglɪs.ər.iːn/ (US) /-troʊˈglɪs.ɚ-/ noun [U] (US also **nitroglycerin**) a very powerful liquid explosive

nitrous oxide /,naɪ.trəsˈɒk.saɪd/ (US) /-ˈɑːk-/ noun [U] (informal **ˈlaughing ,gas**) specialized a type of gas with a sweet smell that is used as a weak ANAESTHETIC (= substance that stops pain), especially by dentists

the nitty-gritty /,nɪt.iˈgrɪt.i/ (US) /,nɪţ.iˈgrɪţ-/ noun [S] informal the basic facts of a situation: *Let's **get down to** the nitty-gritty – how much will it cost?*

nitwit /ˈnɪt.wɪt/ noun [C] (also **nit**) informal disapproving a silly or stupid person

nix /nɪks/ verb; noun, adv

▸verb [T] US informal to stop, prevent, or refuse to accept something: *The film studio nixed her plans to make a sequel.*

▸noun [U], adv US informal nothing or no: *All that effort for nix.* ◦ *I suppose mom will say nix to us going to the movies.*

no. noun [before noun] (plural **nos**) **1** written abbreviation for number: *They live at No. 17.* ◦ *The answers to nos 13–20 are on page 21.* **2** **No. 10** written abbreviation for **Number Ten**

no /nəʊ/ (US) /noʊ/ determiner; adv; noun

▸determiner **1** (A1) not any; not one; not a: *There's no butter left.* ◦ *There are no pockets in these trousers.* ◦ *That's my kind of holiday – no email, no phone, and no worries.* ◦ *There's no chance (= no possibility) of us getting there by eight.* **2** (A2) used in signs and on notices to show that something is not allowed: *No smoking/fishing.*

IDIOM **there's no knowing/telling/saying** informal it is not possible to know what will happen: *She's very unpredictable so there's no knowing how she'll react to the news.*

▸adv NEGATIVE ANSWER ▷ **1** (A1) used to give negative answers: *'Did you go to the shops?' 'No, I forgot.'* ◦ *'Would you like any more cake?' 'No thank you.'* ◦ *'Have you got any homework tonight?' 'No.'* NOT ▷ **2** (B1) not; not any: *The exam is no more difficult than the tests you've been doing in class.* ◦ *The issues are of no great interest (= only a little interest) to me.*

> **! Common mistake: no or not?**
>
> **Warning:** Choose the correct adverb!
>
> You can use **no** before the -er form of an adjective to make comparisons:
>
> *Their house is no bigger than ours.*
>
> Before other forms of adjectives, don't say 'no', say **not**:
>
> ~~*Their house is no big.*~~
>
> *Their house is not big.*
>
> **Remember:** before a determiner like 'many', 'much', or 'enough', don't say 'no', say **not**:
>
> ~~*There was no enough legroom on the coach.*~~
>
> *There was not enough legroom on the coach.*

▸noun [C] (plural **noes**) **1** a negative answer or reaction: *'Have you had any replies about the camping weekend?' 'So far I've had two yeses, a no, and a maybe.'* **2** a vote against a suggestion, idea, law, etc., or a person who votes 'no': *14 ayes to 169 noes – the noes have it.* → Compare **aye**

ˈno-a,ccount adj [before noun] US informal describes a person of little use or importance: *She left her no-account second husband and moved to Oregon.*

nob /nɒb/ (US) /nɑːb/ noun [C] UK old-fashioned informal disapproving a rich person whose family has been important for a long time

,no-ˈball noun [C] an occasion when the ball is BOWLED (= thrown) in cricket and some other games in a way that is not allowed by the rules

nobble /ˈnɒb.l̩/ (US) /ˈnɑː-/ verb [T] UK slang CAUSE TO FAIL ▷ **1** to make something fail, especially to make a horse in a race fail by giving it drugs PERSUADE ▷ **2** to persuade someone to do what you want them to do, especially by using money or threats: *The jury who convicted him were suspected of being nobbled.* CATCH ATTENTION ▷ **3** to intentionally catch the attention of someone so that you can talk to them: *He nobbled her in the corridor to sign the invoice.*

Nobel prize /,nəʊ.belˈpraɪz/ (US) /,noʊ-/ noun [C] any of the six international prizes that are given each year to people who make important discoveries or progress in chemistry, physics, medicine, literature, peace, and economics: *the Nobel prize for literature*

nobility /nəʊˈbɪl.ə.ti/, /nə'-/ (US) /noʊˈbɪl.ə.t̬i/ **noun** MORAL ▷ **1** [U] honesty, courage, and kindness: *nobility of spirit/purpose* HIGH RANK ▷ **2 the nobility** [S, + sing/pl verb] the people of the highest social rank in a society, considered as a group: *members of the nobility*

noble /ˈnəʊ.bl̩/ (US) /ˈnoʊ-/ **adj; noun**
▸**adj** MORAL ▷ **1** C1 moral in an honest, brave, and kind way: *a noble gesture* ◦ *His followers believe they are fighting for a noble cause.* HIGH RANK ▷ **2** C1 belonging to a high social rank in a society, especially by birth: *a noble family* CAUSING ADMIRATION ▷ **3** causing admiration because of a particular appearance or quality: *a noble bearing/gesture* ◦ *a building with a noble façade* • **nobly** /-bli/ **adv**
▸**noun** [C] a person of the highest social group in some countries

ˌnoble ˈgas noun [C] specialized any of a group of gases, such as HELIUM and NEON, that do not react with other chemicals

nobleman /ˈnəʊ.bl̩.mən/ (US) /ˈnoʊ-/ **noun** [C] (plural **-men** /-mən/) a member of the NOBILITY (= the highest social rank in a society)

noblesse oblige /nəʊˌbles.əʊˈbliːʒ/ (US) /noʊˌbles.oʊ-/ **noun** [U] formal the idea that someone with power and influence should use their social position to help other people

noblewoman /ˈnəʊ.bl̩ˌwʊm.ən/ (US) /ˈnoʊ-/ **noun** [C] (plural **-women** /-wɪmɪn/) a female member of the NOBILITY (= the highest social rank in a society)

nobody /ˈnəʊ.bə.di/, /-bɒd.i/ (US) /ˈnoʊ.bɑː.di/ **pronoun; noun**
▸**pronoun** (also ˈ**no one**) A2 not anyone: *Is there nobody here who can answer my question?* ◦ *I saw nobody all morning.* ◦ *Nobody agreed with me.*
▸**noun** [C] someone who is not important: *He's just some nobody trying to get noticed by the press.*

no-brainer /ˌnəʊˈbreɪ.nəʳ/ (US) /ˌnoʊˈbreɪ.nɚ/ **noun** [S] slang something such as a decision that is very easy or obvious

ˌno-claims ˈbonus noun [C] (also **ˌno-claims ˈdiscount**) UK an amount by which someone's payment for INSURANCE is reduced, especially for a motor vehicle, because they have not made any claims for a particular period

nocturnal /nɒkˈtɜː.nəl/ (US) /nɑːkˈtɝː-/ **adj** formal happening in or active during the night, or relating to the night: *nocturnal wanderings* ◦ *nocturnal light* ◦ *Most bats are nocturnal.* → Compare **diurnal** • **nocturnally** /-i/ **adv**

nocturne /ˈnɒk.tɜːn/ (US) /ˈnɑːk.tɝːn/ **noun** [C] a gentle piece of CLASSICAL music

nod /nɒd/ (US) /nɑːd/ **verb; noun**
▸**verb** [I or T] (**-dd-**) B2 to move your head down and then up, sometimes several times, especially to show agreement, approval, or greeting, or to show something by doing this: *Many people in the audience nodded* ***in*** *agreement.* ◦ *When I suggested a walk, Elena nodded enthusiastically.* ◦ *She looked up and nodded for me to come in.* → Compare **shake**

IDIOM **have a nodding acquaintance with sb/sth** to know someone slightly or have a slight knowledge of a subject: *She has only a nodding acquaintance with the issues involved.*

PHRASAL VERB **nod off** informal to begin sleeping, especially not intentionally: *After our busy day we both sat and nodded off in front of the TV.*

▸**noun** [C usually singular] (plural **-dd-**) a movement up and down with the head: *Chen* ***gave*** *her a nod of recognition across the crowded room.*

IDIOM **on the nod** UK informal If a suggestion is approved on the nod, it is accepted without discussion: *The new proposal* ***went through*** *on the nod.*

node /nəʊd/ (US) /noʊd/ **noun** [C] specialized LUMP ▷ **1** a LUMP (= raised area) or swelling on or in a living object JOIN ▷ **2** a place where things such as lines join, or where a leaf and stem join on a plant: *a leaf node* • **nodal** /ˈnəʊ.dəl/ (US) /ˈnoʊ-/ **adj** *a nodal point*

nodule /ˈnɒd.juːl/ (US) /ˈnɑː.djuːl/ **noun** [C] specialized a small raised area or swelling: *There was a soft nodule on my vocal cord.* • **nodular** /ˈnɒd.jʊ.ləʳ/ (US) /ˈnɑː.djə.lɚ/ **adj**

Noel (also **Noël**) /nəʊˈel/ (US) /noʊ-/ **noun** [U] Christmas

noes /nəʊz/ (US) /noʊz/ plural of **no**

ˌno-ˈfault adj [before noun] legal describes an agreement or system in which blame does not have to be proved before action can be taken, especially before money can be paid: *a no-fault divorce*

ˌno-ˈfly ˌzone noun [C] an area above a country which aircraft from other countries may not enter without risking attack: *Aircraft will enforce the no-fly zone to protect UN forces on the ground.*

ˌno-ˈfrills adj [before noun] describes a product or a service that is basic and has no extra or unnecessary details: *It's a no-frills shop supplying only basic goods at affordable prices.* ◦ *a no-frills airline*

ˌno-ˈgo ˌarea noun [C] informal an area, especially in a town, where it is very dangerous to go, usually because a group of people who have weapons prevent the police, army, and other people from entering

ˌno-ˈgood adj [before noun] US slang disapproving describes someone who does nothing useful or helpful and is therefore considered to be of little value: *a no-good* ***son of a bitch***

ˌno-holds-ˈbarred adj without any limits or controls: *a no-holds-barred interview/account*

no-hoper /ˌnəʊˈhəʊp.əʳ/ (US) /ˌnoʊˈhoʊ.pɚ/ **noun** [C] UK someone or something which will fail: *He's a* ***real/total*** *no-hoper – he'll never achieve anything.*

noir /nwɑːʳ/ (US) /nwɑːr/ **adj** used for describing films or literature that show the world as being unpleasant, strange, or cruel: *a noir thriller* → See also **film noir** • **noirish** /ˈnwɑː.rɪʃ/ **adj**

noise /nɔɪz/ **noun** SOUND ▷ **1** A1 [C or U] a sound or sounds, especially when unwanted, unpleasant, or loud: *The noise out in the street was deafening.* ◦ *I heard a loud noise and ran to the window.* ◦ *traffic/background noise* ◦ *dangerously high noise* ***levels*** SIGNAL ▷ **2** [U] specialized any bad change in a signal, especially in a signal produced by an electronic device: *Using a single chip reduces (the) noise on the output signal by 90 percent.*

> **Word partners for noise**
>
> *hear/make* a noise • *reduce* noise • a *deafening/loud/slight/strange* noise • *background* noise • [talk/shout/hear sb] *over* the noise • noise *levels*

IDIOMS **make (all) the right, correct, etc. noises** UK to say the things you are expected to say, sometimes when you do not mean them: *He made all the right noises about my audition but I couldn't tell if he was genuinely impressed.* • **make a noise about sth** informal to talk about or complain about something a lot: *She's been making a lot of noise about moving to a new house.* • **make noises** UK informal **1** to show what you think or feel by what you say, without stating it directly: *She made very positive noises at the interview about me getting the job.* **2** (also **make a noise**) to complain or make trouble: *If things start going badly again, our members are sure to make noises.*

noiseless /ˈnɔɪz.ləs/ adj silent: *Above them an eagle circled in noiseless flight.* • **noiselessly** /-li/ adv

ˈnoise polˌlution noun [U] noise, such as that from traffic, which upsets people where they live or work and is considered to be unhealthy for them: *to tackle/ease/reduce noise pollution*

noisome /ˈnɔɪ.səm/ adj literary very unpleasant and offensive: *a noisome stench*

noisy /ˈnɔɪ.zi/ adj **SOUND** ▷ **1** (A2) making a lot of noise: *a noisy crowd of fans* ◦ *noisy neighbours* **SIGNAL** ▷ **2** specialized having an unwanted change in signal, especially of an electronic device: *a noisy signal* • **noisily** /-zɪ.li/ adv • **noisiness** /-nəs/ noun [U]

nomad /ˈnəʊ.mæd/ (US) /ˈnoʊ-/ noun [C] a member of a group of people who move from one place to another rather than living in one place all of the time: *a tribe of Somalian desert nomads* • **nomadic** /nəʊˈmæd.ɪk/ (US) /noʊ-/ adj *nomadic people/herdsmen* ◦ *a nomadic life/existence*

ˈno-man's-land noun **1** [S or U] an area or strip of land that no one owns or controls, such as a strip of land between two countries' borders, especially in a war: *to be lost/stranded/stuck in no-man's-land* ◦ *They found themselves trapped in the no-man's-land between the two warring factions.* **2** [S] a situation or area of activity where there are no rules or which no one understands or controls because it belongs neither to one type nor another: *The families of people who die in custody are in a legal no-man's-land when they try to discover what went wrong.*

nom de plume /ˌnɒm.dəˈpluːm/ (US) /ˌnɑːm-/ noun [C] (plural **noms de plume**) a **pen name**

nomenclature /nəʊˈmeŋ.klə.tʃəʳ/ (US) /ˈnoʊ.men.kleɪ.tʃɚ/ noun [C or U] specialized a system for naming things, especially in a particular area of science: *(the) nomenclature of organic chemicals*

nominal /ˈnɒm.ɪ.nəl/ (US) /ˈnɑː.mə-/ adj **NOT REALLY** ▷ **1** in name or thought but not in fact or not as things really are: *She's the nominal head of our college – the real work is done by her deputy.* **SMALL** ▷ **2** describes an amount of money that is very small compared to an expected price or value: *a nominal sum/charge* **GRAMMAR** ▷ **3** relating to a noun • **nominally** /-i/ adv *The province is nominally independent.*

nominalization specialized (UK usually **nominalisation**) /ˈnɒm.ɪ.nəl.aɪˈzeɪ.ʃən/ (US) /ˈnɑː.mə-/ noun [U] the process of making a noun from a verb or adjective

nominate /ˈnɒm.ɪ.neɪt/ (US) /ˈnɑː.mə-/ verb [T] **SUGGEST** ▷ **1** (C1) to officially suggest someone for an election, job, position, or honour: *He's been nominated by the Green Party as their candidate in the next election.* ◦ *Would you like to nominate anyone **for/as** director?* **2** (C1) to say officially that a film, song, programme, etc. will be included in a competition for a prize: *The film was nominated **for** an Academy Award.* **CHOOSE** ▷ **3** to officially choose someone for a job or to do something: *She was nominated **as** the delegation's official interpreter.* ◦ [+ to infinitive] *President Yeltsin nominated acting prime minister Sergei Kiriyenko to head the government.*

nomination /ˌnɒm.ɪˈneɪ.ʃən/ (US) /ˌnɑː.mə-/ noun [C or U] **SUGGESTION** ▷ **1** (C1) the act of officially suggesting someone or something for a job, position, or prize: *There have been two nominations for the new job.* **CHOICE** ▷ **2** the act of officially choosing someone for a job or position: *The nomination **of** Judge Watkins as head of the inquiry was a surprise.*

nominative /ˌnɒm.ɪ.nə.tɪv/ (US) /ˌnɑː.mə.nə.t̬ɪv/ noun, adj specialized (being) a particular form of a noun in some languages that shows the noun is the subject of a verb

nominee /ˌnɒm.ɪˈniː/ (US) /ˌnɑː.mə-/ noun [C] **SUGGESTION** ▷ **1** someone who has been nominated for something: *All nominees for Treasurer will be considered.* **CHOICE** ▷ **2** a person who is officially chosen for a position or job

non- /nɒn-/ (US) /nɑːn-/ prefix used to add the meaning 'not' or 'the opposite of' to adjectives and nouns: *non-sexist* ◦ *non-racist* → Compare **dis-, in-, un-**

ˌnon-adˈdictive adj describes a drug that does not make people who take it want to take more of it regularly

nonagenarian /ˌnɒn.ə.dʒəˈneə.ri.ən/ (US) /ˌnɑː.nə.dʒəˈner.i-/ noun [C] a person who is between 90 and 99 years old • **nonagenarian adj**

ˌnon-agˈgression noun [U] formal a situation in which countries or groups avoid fighting each other: *a non-aggression pact*

ˌnon-alcoˈholic adj describes a drink that does not contain alcohol: *non-alcoholic beer*

ˌnon-aˈligned adj If a country is non-aligned, it does not support or depend on any powerful country or group of countries.

ˌnon-aˈlignment noun [U] the condition or principle of being non-aligned

ˌnon-beˈliever noun [C] a person who has no religious beliefs

ˌnon-ˈbio adj (also **ˌnon-bioˈlogical**) UK describes a washing powder or liquid that does not contain ENZYMES (= special chemical substances) to help clean clothes

nonce /nɒns/ (US) /nɑːns/ noun [C] slang a person who commits a crime involving sex, especially sex with a child

ˈnonce ˌword noun [C] a word invented for a particular occasion or situation

nonchalant /ˈnɒn.ʃəl.ənt/ (US) /ˌnɑːn.ʃəˈlɑːnt/ adj behaving in a calm manner, often in a way which suggests you are not interested or do not care: *a nonchalant manner/shrug* • **nonchalance** /ˈnɒn.ʃəl.əns/ (US) /ˌnɑːn.ʃəˈlɑːns/ noun [U] • **nonchalantly** /-li/ adv

ˌnon-ˈcombatant noun [C] a person, especially in the armed forces, who does not fight in a war, for example a priest or a doctor • **ˌnon-ˈcombatant adj** [before noun] *non-combatant troops/ships*

noncommittal /ˌnɒn.kəˈmɪt.əl/ (US) /ˌnɑːn.kəˈmɪt̬-/ adj not expressing an opinion or decision: *The ambassador was typically noncommittal when asked whether further sanctions would be introduced.* • **noncommittally** /-i/ adv

non compos mentis /ˌnɒnˌkɒm.pəsˈmen.tɪs/ (US) /ˌnɑːnˌkɑːm.poʊsˈmen-/ adj [after verb] describes someone who is unable to think clearly, especially because of mental illness, and therefore not responsible for their actions

nonconformist /ˌnɒn.kənˈfɔː.mɪst/ (US) /ˌnɑːn.kənˈfɔːr-/ noun [C] **1** someone who lives and thinks in a way that is different from other people **2** (also **Nonconformist**) a member of a Christian group

N

that is Protestant but does not belong to the Church of England • **nonconformist** adj *nonconformist behaviour ◦ a Nonconformist minister* • **nonconformity** /-mə.ti/ (US) /-mə.t̬i/ noun [U] (also **nonconformism** /-mɪ.zᵊm/) *Her clothes were an immediate signal of her nonconformity.*

ˌnon-conˈtributory adj refers to a financial plan or agreement for an employee that is completely paid for by the employer: *a non-contributory insurance policy ◦ a non-contributory pension plan*

ˌnon-ˈdairy adj containing nothing that is made from cow's milk: *non-dairy drinks made from soya milk ◦ non-dairy recipes*

ˌnon-deˌnomiˈnational adj not connected with a particular religious DENOMINATION → Opposite **denominational**

nondescript /ˈnɒn.dɪ.skrɪpt/ (US) /ˈnɑːn-/ adj very ordinary, or having no interesting or exciting features or qualities: *The meteorological bureau is in a nondescript building on the outskirts of town.*

none /nʌn/ pronoun B1 not one (of a group of people or things), or not any: *None **of** my children has/have blonde hair. ◦ 'I'd like some more cheese.' 'I'm sorry there's none left'. ◦ 'Have you any idea how much this cost?' 'None **at all**/None **whatsoever**.' ◦ She went to the shop to get some oranges but they had none.*

IDIOMS **have none of sth** formal to refuse to accept, agree with, or support something: *She tried to persuade him to retire, but he would have none of **it**.* • **none other than sb/sth** formal said when you want to show that someone or something is a surprising or exciting choice or example: *The first speech was given by none other than Clint Eastwood.* • **none the worse, better, richer, etc.** C2 not any worse, better, richer, etc. than before: *Luckily, the horse seemed none the worse **for** his fall. ◦ Small investors like myself are probably none the richer after handing over their financial affairs to professional advisers.* • **none too** formal C2 not very: *He seemed none too **happy/pleased** at the prospect of meeting the family.*

nonentity /ˌnɒnˈen.tɪ.ti/ (US) /ˌnɑːˈnen.t̬ə.t̬i/ noun **1** [C] disapproving a person without strong character, ideas, or influence: *She was once a political nonentity, but has since won a formidable reputation as a determined campaigner.* **2** [U] the fact that something or someone is not known about because of not having any strong character, ideas, or influence: *This collection of essays is saved from nonentity by the stature of the contributors.*

nonetheless /ˌnʌn.ðəˈles/ adv (also **nevertheless**) C1 despite what has just been said or done: *There are serious problems in our country. Nonetheless, we feel this is a good time to return.*

ˌnon-eˈvent noun [C usually singular] informal a disappointing occasion which was not interesting, especially one which was expected to be exciting and important: *The party turned out to be a bit of a non-event – hardly anybody turned up.*

ˌnon-eˈxistent adj C1 describes something that does not exist or is not present in a particular place: *Government funding of alternative healthcare is virtually non-existent.*

ˌnon-ˈfat adj Non-fat food contains no fat: *non-fat milk/yogurt*

ˌnon-ˈfiction noun [U] writing that is about real events and facts, rather than stories that have been invented → Compare **fiction**

ˌnon-ˈflammable adj describes something that cannot burn or is very difficult to burn

ˌnon-interˈvention noun [U] the practice of refusing to get involved in a situation, especially in a disagreement between countries or within a country: *a policy of non-intervention*

ˌnon-neˈgotiable adj NOT DISCUSSED ▷ **1** Something that is non-negotiable cannot be changed by discussion: *The terms of this agreement are non-negotiable.* CHEQUE ▷ **2** specialized A non-negotiable CHEQUE cannot be exchanged for money and must be paid into a bank account. FINANCIAL PRODUCT ▷ **3** specialized A non-negotiable financial product cannot be bought and sold: *Time deposits are non-negotiable **deposits** that are maintained in a bank for a specified period of time.*

ˈno-no noun [C usually singular] informal something that is thought to be unsuitable or unacceptable: *Total nudity is still a definite no-no on most of Europe's beaches.*

ˌno-ˈnonsense adj [before noun] practical and serious, and only interested in doing what is necessary or achieving what is intended, without silly ideas or methods: *a no-nonsense manner/leader ◦ a no-nonsense approach to child-rearing*

ˌnon-ˈpayment noun [U] a failure to pay money that is owed: *non-payment of taxes*

nonplussed /ˌnɒnˈplʌst/ (US) /ˌnɑːn-/ adj surprised, confused, and not certain how to react: *I was completely nonplussed by his reply.*

ˌnon-ˈprofit adj; noun
▸adj [before noun] not intended to make a profit, but to make money for a social or political purpose or to provide a service that people need: *We are a non-profit organization dedicated to the conservation of ocean mammals.*
▸noun [C] an organization whose aim is to make money for a social or political purpose or to provide a service that people need, rather than to make a profit

ˌnon-ˈprofit-ˌmaking adj **non-profit**

ˌnon-prolifeˈration noun [U] the controlling of the spread and/or amount of something, especially nuclear or chemical weapons: *a non-proliferation treaty*

ˌnon-ˈresident noun [C] a person who is not staying or living in or at a place: *The hotel bar is open to non-residents.* • **non-ˈresident** adj *During the summer the town has a large non-resident population of holidaymakers.*

ˌnon-reˈturnable adj describes something which cannot be returned: *a non-returnable deposit ◦ These bottles are non-returnable.*

nonsense /ˈnɒn.sᵊns/ (US) /ˈnɑːn.sens/ noun **1** B2 [S or U] an idea, something said or written, or behaviour that is silly or stupid: *This report is nonsense and nothing but a waste of paper. ◦ The accusations are (**absolute/complete/utter**) nonsense. ◦ Nonsense/Don't **talk** nonsense! She's far too ill to return to work! ◦ You mustn't upset your sister with any more nonsense about ghosts.* ◦ [+ to infinitive] ***It's** (a) nonsense **to** say that he's too old for the job.* **2** [U] language which cannot be understood because it does not mean anything: *The translation of the instructions was so poor they were just nonsense.*

IDIOMS **make (a) nonsense of sth** UK C2 to make something appear stupid or wrong, or to spoil something: *His repeated lack of promotion makes nonsense of the theory that if you work hard you'll be successful.* • **not stand any nonsense** (UK also **stand** no nonsense) to refuse to accept bad or silly behaviour: *The new teacher won't stand any nonsense.*

nonsensical /nɒnˈsen.sɪ.kl/ (US) /nɑːn-/ adj silly or stupid: *It's nonsensical to blame all the world's troubles on one man.* ◦ *Their methods of assessment produce nonsensical results.*

non sequitur /ˌnɒnˈsek.wɪ.təʳ/ (US) /ˌnɑːnˈsek.wɪ.t̬ɚ/ noun [C] a statement which does not correctly follow from the meaning of the previous statement

ˌnon-ˈslip adj designed to prevent sliding, especially by being made of sticky material or having a surface with a special TEXTURE: *a non-slip surface/grip*

ˌnon-ˈsmoker noun [C] a person who does not smoke

ˌnon-ˈsmoking adj **1** B2 [before noun] describes a person who does not smoke: *non-smoking passengers* **2** (also **ˌno-ˈsmoking**) describes a place where people are not allowed to smoke: *Let's get a table in the no-smoking area.* ◦ *a non-smoking flight*

ˌnon-ˈstandard adj **NOT USUAL** ▷ **1** not normal or usual: *The keyboard was fitted with a non-standard plug.* **LANGUAGE** ▷ **2** describes a word or phrase that is not considered correct by educated speakers of the language

ˌnon-ˈstarter noun [C] informal an idea, plan, or person with no chance of success: *The proposal was a non-starter from the beginning because there was no possibility of funding.*

ˌnon-ˈstick adj describes a cooking pan or tool that has a special surface which prevents food from sticking to it: *a non-stick frying pan*

ˌnon-ˈstop adj, adv without stopping or without interruptions: *a non-stop flight* ◦ *It felt like we travelled non-stop for the entire week.*

ˌnon-ˈunion adj describes a company or organization that does not employ workers who belong to a UNION, or a person who does not belong to a UNION: *non-union employers/employees*

ˌnon-vegeˈtarian adj refers to a meal that contains meat, or a person who eats meat

ˌnon-ˈverbal adj not using spoken language: *Body language is a potent form of non-verbal* ***communication.***

ˌnon-ˈviolence noun [U] a situation in which someone avoids fighting or using physical force, especially when trying to make political change: *The Dalai Lama has always counselled non-violence.* • **ˌnon-ˈviolent** adj *Gandhi was an exponent of non-violent protest.*

ˌnon-ˈwhite noun [C] a person who is not white: *Non-whites were not welcome in the club.* • **ˌnon-ˈwhite** adj

noob /nuːb/ noun [C] informal someone who has just started doing something, especially playing a computer game or using a type of software, and so does not know much about it → See also **newbie**

noodle /ˈnuː.dl/ noun **FOOD** ▷ [C usually plural] a food in the form of long thin strips made from flour or rice, water, and often egg, cooked in boiling liquid: *egg/rice noodles* ◦ *instant/crispy noodles*

nook /nʊk/ noun [C] literary a small space that is hidden or partly sheltered: *a cosy/sheltered/quiet nook*

IDIOMS **every nook and cranny** every part of a place: *Every nook and cranny of the house was stuffed with souvenirs of their trips abroad.* • **every nook and corner** Indian English **every nook and cranny**

nooky (also **nookie**) /ˈnʊk.i/ noun [U] slang sex

noon /nuːn/ noun [U] A2 twelve o'clock in the middle of the day, or about that time: *We used to ski before noon then take a long lunch.* ◦ *By noon, we had had ten phone calls.*

ˈno one pronoun (also **nobody**) A2 no person: *At first I thought there was no one in the room.* ◦ *'Who was that on the phone?' 'No one you would know.'* ◦ *I'd like to go to the concert but no one* ***else*** *(= no other person) wants to.* ◦ *No one told me she was ill.*

> **! Common mistake: no one**
>
> **Remember: no one** is not written as one word.
>
> Don't write 'noone', write **no one:**
>
> ~~*I opened the door but there was noone there.*~~
>
> *I opened the door but there was no one there.*

noose /nuːs/ noun **1** [C] one end of a rope tied to form a circle that can be tightened round something such as a person's neck to HANG (= kill) them: *They put him on the back of a horse and looped a noose around his neck.* **2** [S] a serious problem or limit: *The noose of poverty was* ***tightening*** *(= becoming more serious) daily.*

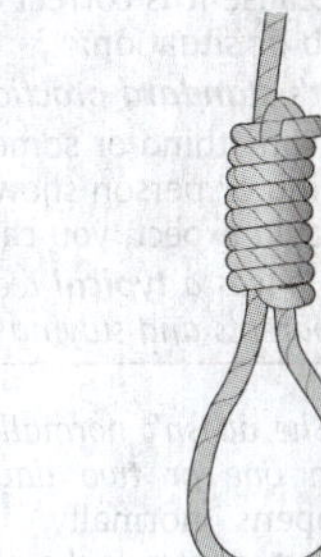
noose

nope /nəʊp/ (US) /noʊp/ adv slang no: *'Are you going out tonight?' 'Nope.'*

noplace /ˈnəʊ.pleɪs/ (US) /ˈnoʊ-/ adv US informal for **nowhere**: *Soon there would be noplace for them to go for help.*

nor /nɔːʳ/ (US) /nɔːr/ conjunction **1** used before the second or last of a set of negative possibilities, usually after 'neither': *We can neither change nor improve it.* ◦ *Strangely, neither Carlo nor Juan saw what had happened.* **2** B2 mainly UK neither: *'I've never been to Iceland.' 'Nor have I.'* ◦ *I can't be at the meeting and nor can Andrew.*

Nordic /ˈnɔː.dɪk/ (US) /ˈnɔːr-/ adj from or relating to the people of Scandinavia, Finland, or Iceland: *He's a classic Nordic type – tall with blond hair and blue eyes.*

norm /nɔːm/ (US) /nɔːrm/ noun [C usually plural] **1** C1 an accepted standard or a way of behaving or doing things that most people agree with: *Europe's varied cultural, political and ethical norms* ◦ *accepted social norms* **2 the norm** C1 a situation or type of behaviour that is expected and considered to be typical: *One child per family is fast becoming the norm in some countries.*

normal /ˈnɔː.məl/ (US) /ˈnɔːr-/ adj A2 ordinary or usual; the same as would be expected: *a normal working day* ◦ *Lively behaviour is normal for a four-year-old child.* ◦ ***It's*** *normal for couples* ***to*** *argue now and then.* ◦ *They were selling the goods at half the normal cost.* ◦ *The temperature was* ***above/below*** *normal for the time of year.* ◦ *Things are* ***back to*** *normal now that we've paid off all our debts.*

normality /nɔːˈmæl.ə.ti/ (US) /nɔːrˈmæl.ə.t̬i/ noun [U] (US also **normalcy**) C2 the state of being normal: *Now that the civil war is over, relative normality has returned to the south of the country.*

normalize (UK usually **normalise**) /ˈnɔː.mə.laɪz/ (US) /ˈnɔːr-/ verb **SITUATION** ▷ [I or T] to return to the normal or usual situation: *They claim that the new drug normalizes blood pressure.* ◦ *Relations between the two countries are gradually normalizing.*

normally /ˈnɔː.mə.li/ (US) /ˈnɔːr-/ adv **1** B1 If you normally do something, you usually or regularly do

Other ways of saying normal

The word **natural** can be used instead of 'normal' when talking about feelings:

*It's completely **natural** to feel anxious on your first day at a new school.*

If you are talking about what is normal because it happens most often, you can use the word **usual**:

*I went to bed at my **usual** time.*

If someone or something is normal because that person or thing is not different in any way, the word **ordinary** can be used:

*The magazine has stories about **ordinary** people rather than celebrities.*

Standard describes something that is normal because it is correct or acceptable in a particular job or situation:

*It's **standard** practice for surgeons to wear gloves.*

If something or someone is normal because that thing or person shows the characteristics you would expect, you can use the word **typical**:

*He was a **typical** teenager – arguing with his parents and staying out late.*

it: *She doesn't normally arrive until ten.* ◦ *Normally, I plan one or two days ahead.* **2** B2 If something happens normally, it happens in the usual or expected way: *Is the phone working normally again?*

Norman /ˈnɔː.mən/ US /ˈnɔːr-/ **adj** belonging or relating to the people from northern France, especially those who INVADED (= used force to enter) England in 1066 and became its rulers, or to the buildings which were made during their rule: *the Norman invasion/conquest* ◦ *a Norman castle/church/cathedral* • **Norman noun** [C] *The Anglo-Saxons were defeated by the Normans.*

normative /ˈnɔː.mə.tɪv/ US /ˈnɔːr.mə.t̬ɪv/ **adj** formal relating to rules, or making people obey rules, especially rules of behaviour

norovirus /ˈnɔː.rəʊˌvaɪə.rəs/ US /ˈnɔː.rəˌvaɪ-/ **noun** [S] a very infectious virus that makes people vomit and have diarrhoea (= solid waste from the body that is more liquid than usual)

Norse /nɔːs/ US /nɔːrs/ **adj** belonging or relating to the people who lived in Scandinavia in the past, especially the VIKINGS: *Norse mythology* ◦ *a Norse god/warrior*

north /nɔːθ/ US /nɔːrθ/ **noun; adj; adv**

▸**noun** [U] (also **North**) (written abbreviation **N**, UK also **Nth**, US also **No.**) **1** A2 the direction that goes towards the part of the Earth above the EQUATOR, opposite to the south, or the part of an area or country that is in this direction: *The points of the compass are north, south, east, and west.* ◦ *The countryside is more mountainous **in the** north (**of** the country).* ◦ *Cambridge **is/lies to the** north **of** London.* ◦ *a north-**facing** window* **2 the North a** the rich industrial countries of the world, most of which are above the EQUATOR **b** the northern states of the middle and eastern part of the US: *The North defeated the South in the American Civil War.*

IDIOM **north of sth** used to say that an amount is more than the stated amount: *The share price is expected to rise north of $20.*

▸**adj** (also **North**) (written abbreviation **N**, UK also **Nth**, US also **No**) **1** A2 in or forming the north part of something: *North America/Africa* ◦ *the north coast of Iceland* ◦ *Our farm is a few miles north of the village.* **2 north wind** a wind coming from the north

▸**adv** (also **North**) (written abbreviation **N**, UK also **Nth**, US also **No**) **1** A2 towards the north: *Go **due** (= directly) north for two miles.* ◦ *The garden **faces** north and doesn't get much sun in winter.* **2 up north** informal to or in the north of the country or region: *I live in Cambridge, but my relatives live up north in Manchester.*

ˌNorth Aˈmerica noun the continent that is to the north of South America, to the west of the Atlantic Ocean and to the east of the Pacific Ocean; → See table of **Geographical names**

ˌNorth Aˈmerican noun [C], **adj** → See table of **Geographical names.**

northbound /ˈnɔːθ.baʊnd/ US /ˈnɔːrθ-/ **adj, adv** going or leading towards the north: *northbound traffic* ◦ *The accident happened on the M1 northbound, just after Junction 18.*

northeast /ˌnɔːˈθiːst/ US /ˌnɔːrθ-/ **noun; adj, adv**

▸**noun** [U] (written abbreviation **NE**) **1** B1 the direction that is between north and east: *We live in **the** northeast **of** Spain.* **2 the Northeast** the area in the northeast of England, the US, or another country: *Newcastle is one of the largest cities **in** the Northeast.*

▸**adj, adv 1** B1 in or towards the northeast: *Go northeast for about five miles.* ◦ *The town **is/lies** roughly northeast **of** here.* ◦ *the northeast corner of the field* **2 northeast wind** a wind that comes from the northeast

northeasterly /ˌnɔːˈθiː.stə.li/ US /ˌnɔːrˈθiː.stɚ-/ **adj; noun**

▸**adj 1** towards the northeast: *a northeasterly direction* **2 northeasterly wind** a wind that comes from the northeast

▸**noun** [C] a wind that comes from the northeast

northeastern /ˌnɔːˈθiː.stən/ US /ˌnɔːrˈθiː.stɚn/ **adj** (written abbreviation **NE**) in or from the northeast: *the northeastern states* ◦ *Northeastern China*

northeastward /ˌnɔːθˈiːs.twəd/ US /ˌnɔːrθˈiːs.twɚd/ **adv; adj**

▸**adv** (also **northeastwards**) towards the northeast: *We travelled northeastward for about 250 kilometres.*

▸**adj** towards the northeast: *They went in a northeastward **direction**.*

northerly /ˈnɔː.ðəl.i/ US /ˈnɔːr.ðɚ.li/ **adj; noun**

▸**adj 1** towards or in the north: *They walked in a northerly direction across the desert.* ◦ *There are plans to build a hotel on the most northerly point of the island.* **2 northerly wind** a wind that comes from the north

▸**noun** [C] a wind that comes from the north

northern (also **Northern**) /ˈnɔː.ðən/ US /ˈnɔːr.ðɚn/ **adj** (written abbreviation **N**, US also **No**) B1 in or from the north part of an area: *northern Europe* ◦ *the Northern Hemisphere*

northerner (also **Northerner**) /ˈnɔː.ðən.ər/ US /ˈnɔːr.ðɚ.nɚ/ **noun** [C] a person who comes from the north of a country: *He lives in London now, but his family are all northerners.*

the ˌNorthern ˈLights noun [plural] **the aurora borealis**

northernmost /ˈnɔː.ðən.məʊst/ US /ˈnɔːr.ðɚn.moʊst/ **adj** furthest towards the north of an area: *Cape Columbia is the northernmost **point** of Canada.*

the ˌNorth ˈPole noun the point on the Earth's surface that is furthest north

the ˌNorth-ˌSouth diˈvide noun [S] **1** the difference in WEALTH between the rich countries of the world in the North and the poor countries in the South **2** in the UK, the difference in conditions, especially economic, between the poorer areas in the north and the richer areas in the south of the country

northward /ˈnɔːθ.wəd/ (US) /ˈnɔːrθ.wɚd/ adv; adj
▸adv (also **northwards**) towards the north: *The dust from the volcano spread northward.* ◦ *The plane turned northwards.*
▸adj towards the north

northwest /ˌnɔːθˈwest/ (US) /ˌnɔːrθ-/ noun; adj, adv
▸noun [U] (written abbreviation **NW**) **1** (B1) the direction that is between north and west: *We live in* ***the*** *northwest* ***of*** *the city.* **2 the Northwest** the area in the northwest of England, the US, or another country: *The Lake District is a very beautiful region* ***in*** *the Northwest.*
▸adj, adv **1** (B1) in or towards the northwest: *the sale of the company's northwest division* ◦ *Turn northwest.* ◦ *The town* ***is/lies*** *about 100 miles northwest* ***of*** *Las Vegas.* **2 northwest wind** a wind that comes from the northwest

northwesterly /ˌnɔːθˈwes.təl.i/ (US) /ˌnɔːrθˈwes.t̬ɚ.li/ adj; noun
▸adj **1** towards the northwest: *a northwesterly direction* **2 northwesterly wind** a wind that comes from the northwest
▸noun [C] a wind that comes from the northwest

northwestern /ˌnɔːθˈwes.tən/ (US) /ˌnɔːrθˈwes.t̬ɚn/ adj (written abbreviation **NW**) in or from the northwest: *northwestern Mexico*

northwestward /ˌnɔːθˈwes.twəd/ (US) /ˌnɔːrθˈwes.twɚd/ adv; adj
▸adv (also **northwestwards**) towards the northwest: *The road went northwestward over the hills.*
▸adj towards the northwest: *They were moving in a northwestward* ***direction.***

nos. plural of **no.**

nose /nəʊz/ (US) /noʊz/ noun; verb
▸noun [C] **BODY PART** ▷ **1** (A1) the part of the face that sticks out above the mouth, through which you breathe and smell: *a large/long/pointed nose* ◦ *I've got a sore throat and a* ***runny*** *nose (= liquid coming out of the nose).* ◦ *Come on now, stop crying –* ***blow*** *your nose on my hanky.* → See also **nasal 2** specialized the particular smell of a wine: *a wine praised for its smoky nose* **VEHICLE** ▷ **3** the front of a vehicle, especially an aircraft: *The symbol was painted on each side of the plane's nose.*

IDIOMS **be (right) under your nose** to be in a place that you can clearly see: *I spent ages looking for the book and it was right under my nose all the time.* ◦ *She shoved the letter under her boss's nose (= made certain he saw it).* • **by a nose** If a person or animal wins a race or competition by a nose, they win it by only very little: *My horse won but only by a nose. It was a very exciting finish.* • **get up sb's nose** mainly UK informal to annoy someone: *People who drive like that really get up my nose.* • **have your nose in a book** to be reading: *She's always got her nose in a book.* • **have a (good) nose for sth** informal to be good at finding things of the stated type: *She's got a good nose for a bargain.* ◦ *As a reporter, he had a nose for a good story.* • **keep your nose clean** informal to avoid getting into trouble: *I'd only been out of prison three months so I was trying to keep my nose clean.* • **keep your nose out of sth** informal to not become involved in other people's activities or relationships: *She can't keep her nose out of other people's business.* • **keep/put your nose to the grindstone** informal to work very hard for a long time: *She kept her nose to the grindstone all year and got the exam results she wanted.* • **nose in the air** describes the way someone behaves when they think they are better than other people and do not want to speak to them: *She walked past me* ***with*** *her nose in the air.* • **nose to tail** one closely behind the other: *The cars were parked nose to tail down the street.* • **on the nose** exactly right, often an exact amount of money or time: *Her description of the play was really on the nose.* • **poke/stick your nose into sth** informal (C2) to try to discover things that are not really related to you: *I wish he'd stop poking his nose into my personal life!* • **put sb's nose out of joint** informal to offend or upset someone, especially by getting something that they wanted for themselves: *John's nose was really put out of joint when Jane was promoted and he wasn't.* • **(from) under your nose** (US also **(out from) under your nose**) (C2) used about something bad that happens in an obvious way but in a way that you do not notice or cannot prevent: *She stole the shoes from right under the assistant's nose.*

▸verb **SEARCH** ▷ **1** [I usually + adv/prep] informal to look around or search in order to discover something, especially something that other people do not want you to find: *There were some journalists nosing* ***about/around.*** ◦ *The police came in and started nosing* ***into*** *drawers and looking through papers.* **VEHICLE** ▷ **2** [I or T, + adv/prep] to (make a vehicle) move forwards slowly and carefully: *The car nosed* ***out*** *of the side street, its driver peering anxiously around.* ◦ *He carefully nosed his lorry* ***into*** *the small gap.*

PHRASAL VERB **nose sth out** informal to discover something by searching carefully: *He soon nosed out the details of the accident by chatting innocently to people and making some phone calls.*

nosebag /ˈnəʊz.bæg/ (US) /ˈnoʊz-/ noun [C] UK (US **feedbag**) a bag for holding food that is hung around a horse's head

nosebleed /ˈnəʊz.bliːd/ (US) /ˈnoʊz-/ noun [C] an occasion when blood comes out of a person's nose: *She* ***gets/has*** *a lot of nosebleeds.*

ˈnose ˌcone noun [C] the front part of a spacecraft, aircraft, or MISSILE (= flying weapon)

-nosed /-nəʊzd/ (US) /-noʊzd/ suffix having a nose of the type mentioned: *sharp/snub/hook-nosed* ◦ *a blunt-nosed missile*

nosedive /ˈnəʊz.daɪv/ (US) /ˈnoʊz-/ noun; verb
▸noun [C usually singular] **1** a fast and sudden fall to the ground with the front pointing down: *The plane roared overhead and* ***went into*** *a nosedive.* **2** a sudden fast fall in prices, value, etc.: *There was alarm in the markets when the dollar* ***took*** *a nosedive.*
▸verb [I] **1** to suddenly fall to the ground with the front pointing down: *Spectators in the crowd watched in horror as the plane nosedived.* **2** to suddenly fall in value, quickly and by a large amount: *House prices nosedived without warning.*

ˈnose ˌjob noun informal **have a nose job** to have an operation to change the shape of your nose

nosh /nɒʃ/ (US) /nɑːʃ/ noun; verb
▸noun **1** [C or U] UK old-fashioned slang food or a meal: *They serve good nosh in the cafeteria.* **2** [U] US informal a small amount of food eaten between meals or as a meal: *I'll just have a little nosh at lunchtime, perhaps a hot dog.*
▸verb [I] informal to eat: US *We noshed* ***on*** *a burger before the match.*

ˌno-ˈshow noun [C] a person who is expected but does not arrive: *Two important witnesses were no-shows.* ◦ *a no-show passenger*

ˈnosh-up noun [C] UK informal a big, enjoyable meal: *We had some good nosh-ups on holiday.*

nostalgia /nɒsˈtæl.dʒə/ (US) /nɑːˈstæl-/ noun [U] (C2) a feeling of pleasure and also slight sadness when you

N

think about things that happened in the past: *Some people feel nostalgia **for** their schooldays.* ◦ *Hearing that tune again **filled** him **with** nostalgia.* ◦ *a **wave** (= sudden strong feeling) **of** nostalgia*

nostalgic /nɒsˈtæl.dʒɪk/ Ⓤⓢ /nɑːˈstæl-/ **adj** C2 feeling happy and also slightly sad when you think about things that happened in the past: *Talking about our old family holidays has made me feel quite nostalgic.* ◦ *We'll take a nostalgic look at the musical hits of the '60s.* • **nostalgically** /-dʒɪ.kəl.i/ **adv**

nostril /ˈnɒs.trəl/ Ⓤⓢ /ˈnɑː.strəl/ **noun** [C] C2 either of the two openings in the nose through which air moves when you breathe: *The horses came to a halt, steam streaming from their nostrils.*

nosy (**nosier**, **nosiest**) (also **nosey**) /ˈnəʊ.zi/ Ⓤⓢ /ˈnoʊ-/ **adj** disapproving C2 too interested in what other people are doing and wanting to discover too much about them: *She was complaining about her nosy parents.* • **nosily** /-zɪ.li/ **adv** *'Who was that on the phone?' she asked nosily.* • **nosiness** /-nəs/ **noun** [U]

nosy parker /ˌnəʊ.ziˈpɑː.kəʳ/ Ⓤⓢ /ˌnoʊ.ziˈpɑːr.kɚ/ **noun** [C] informal a person who is nosy

not /nɒt/ Ⓤⓢ /nɑːt/ **adv** **1** A1 used to form a negative phrase after verbs like 'be', 'can', 'have', 'will', 'must', etc., usually used in the short form 'n't' in speech: *He's not fat!* ◦ *I won't tell her.* ◦ *I can't go.* ◦ *Don't you like her?* ◦ *It isn't difficult (= it is easy).* ◦ *I'm just not interested.* ◦ *He's not bad-looking (= he is quite attractive).* ◦ *He's not **as** tall as his father.* **2** A1 used to give the next word or group of words a negative meaning: *I told you not to do that.* ◦ *I like most vegetables but not cabbage.* ◦ *'Come and play football, Dad.' 'Not now, Jamie.'* ◦ *It was Yuko who said that, not Richard.* **3** A2 used after verbs like 'be afraid', 'hope', 'suspect', etc. in short, negative replies: *'Is he coming with us?' 'I hope not.'* ◦ *'Have you finished?' 'I'm afraid not.'* **4** **if not** A2 used to say what the situation will be if something does not happen: *I hope to see you there but, if not, I'll call you.* **5** **or not** A2 used to express the possibility that something might not happen: *Are you going to reply or not?* ◦ *I still don't know whether she's coming or not.* **6** humorous sometimes used at the end of a statement to show that you did not mean what you have said: *That was the best meal I've ever had – not!*

IDIOMS **not all that** informal not very: *I'm not all that keen on swimming.* • **not at all** **1** B1 used as a polite reply after someone has thanked you: *'Thanks for helping.' 'Not at all.'* **2** B2 used to say 'no' or 'not' strongly: *'Was he a nuisance?' 'No, not at all.'* ◦ *I'm not at all happy about it.* • **not be up to much** informal to not be of good quality: *The food wasn't up to much.* • **not that** **1** used to say you are not suggesting something: *She wouldn't tell me how much it cost – not that I was really interested.* **2** used to say you do not think something is important: *Not that I mind, but why didn't you phone yesterday?*

notable /ˈnəʊ.tə.bl/ Ⓤⓢ /ˈnoʊ.t̬ə-/ **adj; noun**

▸**adj** C1 important and deserving attention, because of being very good or interesting: *a notable collection of rare plants* ◦ *Getting both sides to agree was a notable achievement.* ◦ *This attractive building is particularly notable **for** its garden setting.*

▸**noun** [C] literary an important or famous person: *Other notables among his pupils were the kings of Saudi Arabia and Thailand.*

notably /ˈnəʊ.tə.bli/ Ⓤⓢ /ˈnoʊ.t̬ə-/ **adv** **1** C1 especially or most importantly: *They have begun attracting investors, most notably big Japanese banks.* **2** to an important degree, or in a way that can or should be noticed: *The newspapers are notably biased.*

notarize US (UK usually **notarise**) /ˈnəʊ.tər.aɪz/ /ˈnoʊ.t̬ə.raɪz/ **verb** [T] If a letter or other document is notarized, it is signed by a notary public: *a notarized affidavit* ◦ *The airline requires children travelling alone to have a notarized letter of consent from one or both parents.*

notary /ˈnəʊ.tər.i/ Ⓤⓢ /ˈnoʊ.t̬ɚ.i/ **noun** [C] (also ˌ**notary** ˈ**public**) legal an official who has the legal authority to say that documents are correctly signed or true or to make an OATH (= promise) official: *This agreement was drawn up and verified by a notary.*

notation /nəʊˈteɪ.ʃən/ Ⓤⓢ /noʊ-/ **noun** [C or U] a system of written symbols used especially in mathematics or to represent musical notes: *musical/scientific notation* ◦ *Did you write things out in **standard** notation?*

notch /nɒtʃ/ Ⓤⓢ /nɑːtʃ/ **noun; verb**

▸**noun** [C] **CUT** ▷ **1** a V-shaped cut in a hard surface: *The stick has two notches, one at each end.* **POSITION** ▷ **2** an imaginary point or position in a system of comparing values, where a higher position is better and a lower position is worse: *Among current players, she is rated a notch **above** (= is better than) the rest.*

▸**verb** [T] to cut a notch in something

PHRASAL VERB **notch sth up** informal to achieve something: *She has recently notched up her third win at a major tennis tournament.*

note /nəʊt/ Ⓤⓢ /noʊt/ **noun; verb**

▸**noun** **WRITING** ▷ **1** A1 [C] a short piece of writing: *He left a note to say he would be home late.* ◦ *There's a note pinned to the door saying when the shop will open again.* **2** B2 [C] a short explanation or an extra piece of information that is given at the bottom of a page, at the back of a book, etc.: *For a further explanation see Note 3.* → See also **footnote** **3** **notes** A2 [plural] information written on paper: *The wind blew my notes all over the room.* ◦ *The journalist **took** notes throughout the interview.* **SOUND** ▷ **4** C2 [C] a single sound at a particular level, usually in music, or a written symbol that represents this sound: *high/low notes* ◦ *She played three long notes on the piano.* ◦ *The engine noise suddenly **changed** its note and rose to a whine.* **WAY OF EXPRESSING** ▷ **5** C1 [S] an emotion or a way of expressing something: *There was **a** note **of** caution in her letter.* ◦ *His speech **struck** just the right note.* ◦ *The meeting ended on an optimistic note.* **MONEY** ▷ **6** B1 [C] mainly UK (US usually **bill**) a piece of paper money: *a £20 note* ◦ *He took a wad of notes from his pocket.* **IMPORTANCE** ▷ **7** C2 [U] formal importance, or the fact that something deserves attention: *There was nothing **of** note in the latest report.*

IDIOMS **make/take a note** C1 to write something down or remember it carefully: *I'll just take a note **of** your name and address.* ◦ *She made a **mental** note **of** the title.* ◦ *Make a note **to** phone again next week.* • **take note of sth** C1 to give attention to something, especially because it is important: *You should take careful note of what she tells you because she knows their strategy well.*

▸**verb** [T] formal **1** B1 to notice something: *They noted the consumers' growing demand for quicker service.* ◦ [+ (that)] *Please note (**that**) we will be closed on Saturday.* ◦ [+ question word] *Note **how** easy it is to release the catch quickly.* **2** to give your attention to something by discussing it or making a written record of it: [+ that] *He said the weather was beyond our control, noting **that** last summer was one of the* hottest on record. ◦ In the article, she notes several cases of medical incompetence.

PHRASAL VERB **note sth down** B2 to write something so that you do not forget it: *I noted down his phone number.*

notebook /ˈnəʊt.bʊk/ US /ˈnoʊt-/ noun [C] PAPER ▷ **1** A2 a book of plain paper or paper with lines, for writing on: *She was jotting things down in a little notebook.* COMPUTER ▷ **2** (also **notebook computer**) a very small computer which you can carry easily → See also **laptop, palmtop**

noted /ˈnəʊ.tɪd/ US /ˈnoʊ.t̬ɪd/ adj known by many people, especially because of particular qualities: *Summerhill school was noted **for** its progressive policies.* ◦ *She's not noted **for** her patience (= she is not a patient person).*

notelet /ˈnəʊt.lət/ US /ˈnoʊt-/ noun [C] UK a small folded sheet of paper or card, usually with a picture on the front, inside which you write a short letter: *a box of notelets*

notepad /ˈnəʊt.pæd/ US /ˈnoʊt-/ noun [C] PAPER ▷ **1** a set of sheets of plain or LINED paper, joined at the top edge, for writing on: *a plain/ruled notepad* ◦ *a reporter's notepad* COMPUTER ▷ **2** (also **notepad computer**) a very small computer which you can carry easily

notepaper /ˈnəʊtˌpeɪ.pəʳ/ US /ˈnoʊtˌpeɪ.pɚ/ noun [U] plain paper for writing letters on: *three sheets/pieces of notepaper* ◦ *headed notepaper*

noteworthy /ˈnəʊtˌwɜː.ði/ US /ˈnoʊtˌwɝː-/ adj formal deserving attention because of being important or interesting: *a noteworthy example/event* ◦ *It is noteworthy **that** one third of students do not pay any tuition fees.* ◦ *King Darius I is noteworthy **for** his administrative reforms, military conquests, and religious toleration.*

ˌnot-for-ˈprofit adj [before noun] not intended to make a profit, but to make money for a social or political purpose or to provide a service that people need: *Credit unions are not-for-profit organizations that provide loans and other banking services.* → Compare **non-profit**

nothing /ˈnʌθ.ɪŋ/ pronoun; adv; noun

▸pronoun **1** A2 not anything: *There's nothing in the drawer – I took everything out.* ◦ *Nothing I could say would cheer her up.* ◦ *I have nothing new to tell you.* ◦ *There's nothing **else** (= no other thing) we can do to help.* ◦ *There's nothing **much** (= not very much) to do in our village.* ◦ *The story was nothing **but** (= only) lies.* ◦ US *The score is Yankees three, Red Sox nothing (= no points).* **2 be/have nothing to do with sb/sth** B2 to have no connection or influence with someone or something: *We are nothing to do with the firm which has the offices next door.* ◦ *In the evening he likes to read books and articles which have/are nothing to do with his work.* **3 be/mean nothing** to have no importance or value: *Money is nothing **to** him.* **4 be/have nothing to do with sb** B2 to be a matter or subject which someone has no good reason to know about or be involved with: *I wish he wouldn't offer advice on my marriage – it's nothing to do with him.* **5 for nothing a** free or without paying: *I got this picture for nothing from a friend.* **b** B2 with no good result or for no purpose: *He queued for two hours and (**all**) for nothing – there were no seats left.* ◦ *Let us make sure that these brave men did not die for nothing.* **6 nothing on a** no clothes on your body: *She sleeps **with** nothing on.* ◦ *I couldn't come to the door – I **had** nothing on!* **b** no arrangements for a stated period: *I've looked in her diary and she **has** nothing on on Tuesday afternoon.*

IDIOMS **all or nothing** relates to doing something either completely or not at all: *She either loves you or hates you – it's all or nothing with her.* ◦ *The government has rejected the all-or-nothing **approach** in favour of a compromise solution.* • **be nothing for it** used to emphasize you will have to do a particular thing to solve a problem: *There's nothing for it **but to** get some extra help.* • **be nothing if not generous, honest, helpful, etc.** C2 used to emphasize that someone or something is extremely generous, honest, helpful, etc.: *He's nothing if not charming.* • **be nothing less than sth** used to emphasize how important, special, or attractive something is: *Their dream to bring computers and ordinary people together was nothing less than revolutionary.* • **be nothing short of...** used to emphasize a situation, quality, or type of behaviour: *The party was nothing short of a disaster.* ◦ *Her behaviour was nothing short of rude.* ◦ *His achievements as a political reformer have been nothing short of miraculous.* • **be nothing special** to not be excellent or not be beautiful: *She's nothing special.* • **be nothing to it** used to say something is very easy: *Windsurfing is easy – there's nothing to it.* • **it is/was nothing** informal used to tell someone not to worry about, or place special value on, what you are doing or have done: *'You seem very upset.' 'No, no, it's nothing, I'm OK.'* ◦ *'It was very kind of you to look after the baby all day.' 'Oh, it was nothing, I enjoyed it.'* • **like nothing on Earth** informal very strange, unusual, or unpleasant in appearance, sound, or taste: *It looked nice, but it tasted like nothing on Earth.* • **nothing doing** informal used to mean 'no', especially when said in answer to a request: *We asked if she'd come over and help us, but she said, 'Nothing doing'.* • **nothing more than** disapproving only: *He dismissed Bryan as nothing more than an amateur.* • **nothing of the sort/kind** C1 used to emphasize a negative statement: *I told him nothing of the sort (= I did not tell him anything like that).* • **there's nothing in sth** used for saying that something you have been told is not true: *I heard a rumour that she's leaving, but apparently there's nothing in it.*

▸adv in no way: mainly UK *He had two letters of refusal but, nothing **daunted** (= not discouraged), he tried again.*

▸noun [C] informal someone of no value or importance: *He's a nothing, a low-down, useless nobody.*

nothingness /ˈnʌθ.ɪŋ.nəs/ noun [U] a state where nothing is present, or where nothing exists that is important or gives meaning to life

notice /ˈnəʊ.tɪs/ US /ˈnoʊ.t̬ɪs/ verb; noun

▸verb B1 [I or T] to see or become conscious of something or someone: *I noticed a crack in the ceiling.* ◦ *Mary waved at the man but he didn't seem to notice.* ◦ [+ (that)] *He noticed (**that**) the woman was staring at him.* ◦ [+ question word] *Did you notice **how** she did that?*

▸noun INFORMATION ▷ **1** A2 [C] (a board, piece of paper, etc. containing) information or instructions: *There was a large notice on the wall saying 'No Parking'.* ◦ *I saw a notice in the paper announcing their marriage.* **2 notices** [plural] printed statements of opinion in the newspapers about plays, films, books, etc.: *The musical has received wonderful notices.* WARNING ▷ **3** B1 [U] information or a warning given about something that is going to happen in the future: *The next time you visit, can you **give** me more notice?* ◦ *The emergency services are ready to spring into action **at a moment's** notice.* ◦ *The building is closed **until further** notice (= until another official announcement is made).* **4** [U] a letter or statement from an employer or from an employee saying that

N

they will leave their job after a particular period of time, or this period of time: *Do I have to work out my notice?* **5 give sb notice** to ask someone who works for you to leave their job, usually after a particular period of time: *My boss gave me a month's notice.* **6 hand/give in your notice** C2 to tell your employer that you intend to leave your job after a particular period of time: *I handed in my notice yesterday.* **ATTENTION** ▷ **7** B1 [U] attention: *It has **come to/been brought to** my notice (= I have been told) that you have been late for work every day this week.* **8 take notice** to give attention to something: *I asked him to drive more slowly, but he didn't take any notice.* ◦ *Don't take any notice of/Take no notice of what your mother says – she's just in a bad mood.*

IDIOM **at short notice** UK (US **on short notice**) C1 only a short time before something happens: *I can't cancel my arrangements at such short notice.*

noticeable /ˈnəʊ.tɪ.sə.bl/ US /ˈnoʊ.t̬ɪ-/ **adj** C1 easy to see or recognize: *There has been a noticeable improvement in Tim's cooking.* • **noticeably** /-bli/ **adv** *Fiona had become noticeably thinner.*

noticeboard /ˈnəʊ.tɪs.bɔːd/ US /ˈnoʊ.t̬ɪs.bɔːrd/ **noun** [C] UK (US ˈ**bulletin** ˌ**board**) B1 a board on a wall on which notices can be fixed: *I've put the list of players up on the noticeboard.*

notifiable /ˈnəʊ.tɪ.faɪ.ə.bl/ US /ˈnoʊ.t̬ə-/ **adj** describes a disease or offence that must be reported to public health or legal organizations: *If the animals have died from a notifiable **disease**, their bodies must be burned.*

notification /ˌnəʊ.tɪ.fɪˈkeɪ.ʃən/ US /ˌnoʊ.t̬ə-/ **noun** [C or U] the act of telling someone officially about something, or a document that does this: *You must give the bank (a) written notification if you wish to close your account.*

N

notify /ˈnəʊ.tɪ.faɪ/ US /ˈnoʊ.t̬ə-/ **verb** [T] C1 to tell someone officially about something: *The school is required to notify parents if their children fail to come to school.* ◦ *Has everyone been notified **of** the decision?* ◦ [+ that] *We notified the police **that** the bicycle had been stolen.*

notion /ˈnəʊ.ʃən/ US /ˈnoʊ-/ **noun** [C or U] C1 a belief or idea: [+ that] *The programme makers reject the notion **that** seeing violence on television has a harmful effect on children.* ◦ *I have only a **vague** notion **of** what she does for a living.*

IDIOM **have/take a notion to do sth** old-fashioned to suddenly want to do something: *I had a notion to write them a letter.*

notional /ˈnəʊ.ʃən.əl/ US /ˈnoʊ-/ **adj** formal existing only as an idea, not as something real: *Almost everyone will have to pay a higher tax bill than the notional amount suggested by the government.*

notoriety /ˌnəʊ.tərˈaɪ.ə.ti/ US /ˌnoʊ.t̬əˈraɪ.ə.t̬i/ **noun** [U] the state of being famous for something bad: *He **achieved/gained** notoriety **for** being difficult to work with as an actor.*

notorious /nəʊˈtɔː.ri.əs/, /nəˈ-/ US /noʊˈtɔːr.i-/ **adj** C1 famous for something bad: *one of Britain's most notorious **criminals*** ◦ *The company is notorious **for** paying its bills late.* • **notoriously** /-li/ **adv** *The game is notoriously (= famous as being) **difficult** to play.*

notwithstanding /ˌnɒt.wɪðˈstæn.dɪŋ/ US /ˌnɑːt-/ **preposition, adv** formal C1 despite the fact or thing mentioned: *Notwithstanding some members' objections, I think we must go ahead with the plan.* ◦ *Injuries notwithstanding, he won the semifinal match.*

nougat /ˈnuː.ɡɑː/ US /ˈnuː.ɡət/ **noun** [U] a hard CHEWY white or pink sweet food, usually containing nuts

nought /nɔːt/ US /nɑːt/ **number** **ZERO** ▷ **1** [C] mainly UK (US usually **naught**) the number 0 or zero: *He said it was only worth £10, but really you could add a couple of noughts to that (= it is really worth £1,000).* **NOTHING** ▷ **2** [U] **naught**

noughties /ˈnɔː.tiz/ US /ˈnɑː.t̬iz/ **noun** [plural] the period of years between 00 and 10 in any century, usually 2000–2010: *They were born **in** the noughties and grew up completely at ease with computer technology.*

ˌ**noughts and** ˈ**crosses** **noun** [U] UK (US ˌ**tick-tack-**ˈ**toe**) a game played on a piece of paper in which two players write either O or X in a pattern of nine squares. It is won by the first player who places three noughts or three crosses in a straight line.

noun /naʊn/ **noun** [C] A2 a word that refers to a person, place, thing, event, substance, or quality: *'Doctor', 'tree', 'party', 'coal' and 'beauty' are all nouns.*

ˈ**noun** ˌ**phrase** **noun** [C] a group of words in a sentence which together behave as a noun: *In the sentences 'We took the night train' and 'Do you know the man sitting in the corner', 'the night train' and 'the man sitting in the corner' are noun phrases.*

nourish /ˈnʌr.ɪʃ/ US /ˈnɝː-/ **verb** [T] **1** to provide people or living things with food in order to make them grow and keep them healthy: *Children need plenty of good fresh food to nourish them.* ◦ *She looks happy and well nourished.* ◦ *This cream is supposed to help nourish your skin.* **2** formal If you nourish a feeling, belief, or plan, you think about it a lot and encourage it: *Lisa has long nourished the hope of becoming a famous writer.*

nourishing /ˈnʌr.ɪ.ʃɪŋ/ US /ˈnɝː-/ **adj** A nourishing drink or food makes you healthy and strong: *Sweets aren't very nourishing.*

nourishment /ˈnʌr.ɪʃ.mənt/ US /ˈnɝː-/ **noun** [U] food that someone needs to make them grow and keep them healthy: *Young babies obtain all the nourishment they need from their mother's milk.*

nous /naʊs/ **noun** [U] UK informal good judgment and practical ability: *Anyone with a bit of nous would have known what to do.*

nouveau riche /ˌnuː.vəʊˈriːʃ/ US /-voʊ-/ **adj** disapproving describes people from a low social class who have recently become very rich and like to show this publicly by spending a lot of money • **the** ˌ**nouveau** ˈ**riche** **noun** [plural] *The restaurant is popular with the city's nouveau riche.*

nouvelle cuisine /ˌnuː.vel.kwɪˈziːn/ **noun** [U] a style of cooking in which food is lightly cooked and served in attractive patterns on the plate in small amounts

nova /ˈnəʊ.və/ US /ˈnoʊ-/ **noun** [C] (plural **novae**) specialized a type of star that shines much more brightly for a few months as a result of a nuclear explosion

novel /ˈnɒv.əl/ US /ˈnɑː.vəl/ **noun; adj**

▸**noun** [C] B1 a long printed story about imaginary characters and events: *a paperback novel* ◦ ***historical/romantic** novels* ◦ *Have you read any of Jane Austen's novels?* ◦ *His latest novel is selling really well.*

▸**adj** new and original, not like anything seen before: *a novel idea/suggestion* ◦ *Keeping a sheep in the garden is a novel way of keeping the grass short!*

novelist /ˈnɒv.əl.ɪst/ US /ˈnɑː.və-/ **noun** [C] B2 a person who writes novels

novella /nəʊˈvel.ə/ US /noʊ-/ **noun** [C] a short novel

novelty /ˈnɒv.əl.ti/ US /ˈnɑː.vəl.t̬i/ **noun** **1** C2 [U] the quality of being new and unusual: *The novelty of these* *toys soon* ***wore off*** *and the children became bored with them.* ◦ *In Britain in the 1950s, television had a novelty* ***value.*** **2** C2 [C] something that has not been experienced before and so is interesting: *Tourists are still a novelty on this remote island.* **3** [C] a cheap unusual object such as a small toy, often given as a present: *A Christmas cracker usually contains a paper hat, a joke, and a novelty.*

November /nəʊˈvem.bəʳ/, /nəˈ-/ US /noʊˈvem.bɚ/ **noun** [C or U] (written abbreviation **Nov.**) A1 the eleventh month of the year, after October and before December: *He's starting his new job* ***in*** *November.* ◦ *The next meeting is* ***on*** *2 November.* ◦ *The factory opened* ***last*** *November.*

novice /ˈnɒv.ɪs/ US /ˈnɑː.vɪs/ **noun** [C] **1** a person who is not experienced in a job or situation: *I've never driven a car before – I'm a complete novice.* ◦ *This is quite a difficult plant for novice gardeners to grow.* **2** a person who is training to be a MONK or a NUN

novocaine /ˈnəʊ.və.keɪn/ US /ˈnoʊ-/ **noun** [U] a drug given to people to stop them feeling pain, especially during an operation on their teeth

now /naʊ/ **adv; noun; conjunction**

▸**adv** AT PRESENT ▷ **1** A1 at the present time, not in the past or future: *She used to be a teacher, but now she works in publishing.* ◦ *I may eat something later, but I'm not hungry now.* ◦ *Many people now own a smartphone.* **2** A2 immediately: *I don't want to wait until tomorrow, I want it now!* **3** B2 used to express how long something has been happening, from when it began to the present time: *She's been a vegetarian* ***for*** *ten years now.* **4** used in stories or reports of past events to describe a new situation or event: *It was getting dark now and we were tired.* **5** used when describing a situation that is the result of what someone just said or did: *Oh yes, now I know who you mean.* **6 any minute/moment/second/time now** B2 very soon: *Our guests will be arriving any moment now and the house is still a mess.* **7 now for ...** informal used to introduce a new subject: *And now for what we're going to do tomorrow.* IN SPEECH ▷ **8** used in statements and questions to introduce or give emphasis to what you are saying: *Now, where did I put my hat?* ◦ *There was a knock at the door. Now Jan knew her mother had promised to visit, so she assumed it was her.* ◦ *Hurry, now, or you'll miss the bus!* ◦ *Sorry, I can't today. Now if you'd asked me yesterday, I would have said yes.*

IDIOMS **it's now or never** saying said when you must do something immediately, especially because you will not get another chance • **(every) now and then/again** B2 sometimes, but not very often: *We meet up for lunch now and then, but not as often as we used to.* • **now then** said to attract attention to what you are going to ask or suggest: *Now then, what's all this fuss about?* • **now you're talking** saying said when someone makes a suggestion or offer that is better than one that they have already made • **now, now** said when you want to make someone feel better or give them a gentle warning: *Now, now, don't cry.* ◦ *Now, now, children, stop fighting!*

▸**noun** [U] **1** the present moment or time: *Now isn't a good time to speak to him.* ◦ *I thought you'd have finished* ***by*** *now.* ◦ *You should have mentioned it before* ***now.*** ◦ *That's all* ***for*** *now (= until a future point in time).* **2 from now on/as from now** from this moment and always in the future: *From now on the gates will be locked at midnight.*

▸**conjunction now (that)...** B2 used to give an explanation of a new situation: *Now I've got a car, I don't get as much exercise as I used to.* ◦ *She's enjoying the job now that she's got more responsibility.*

nowadays /ˈnaʊ.ə.deɪz/ **adv** B1 at the present time, in comparison to the past: *Who remembers those films nowadays?* ◦ *Nowadays, I bake my own bread rather than buy it.*

> **!** Common mistake: **nowadays**
>
> **Warning:** Check your spelling!
> **Nowadays** is one of the 50 words most often spelled wrongly by learners. Remember: the correct spelling has 'a' between 'now' and 'days'.

nowhere /ˈnəʊ.weəʳ/ US /ˈnoʊ.wer/ **adv 1** B1 in, at, or to no place; not anywhere: *These young people have nowhere* ***(else)*** *to go.* ◦ *Nowhere does the article mention the names of the people involved.* **2** not in a successful or winning position: *The horse I bet on finished nowhere.*

IDIOMS **from/out of nowhere** B2 very suddenly and unexpectedly: *She said her attacker seemed to* ***come*** *out of nowhere.* ◦ figurative *The team has* ***come*** *from nowhere (= from a very bad position) to win football's biggest prize.* • **go/get/head nowhere** C2 to not have any success or achieve anything: *I'm trying to persuade her to come, but I'm* ***getting*** *nowhere.* ◦ *Bad manners will get you nowhere (= will not help you to succeed).* • **nowhere to be found** impossible to see or find: *We looked for her everywhere, but she was nowhere to be found.*

no-ˈwin adj [before noun] informal describes a set of conditions in which whatever happens there will be an unhappy and unsuccessful result: *to be in a no-win* ***situation***

nowt /naʊt/ **pronoun** Northern nothing: *That's got nowt to do with it!* → Compare **owt**

noxious /ˈnɒk.ʃəs/ US /ˈnɑːk-/ **adj** formal **1** describes something, especially a gas or other substance, that is poisonous or very harmful: *They died from inhaling noxious fumes.* **2** harmful and unpleasant: *a noxious smell/influence*

nozzle /ˈnɒz.l̩/ US /ˈnɑː.zl̩/ **noun** [C] a narrow piece fixed to the end of a tube so that the liquid or air that comes out can be directed in a particular way: *Attach the nozzle to the garden hose before turning on the water.*

nr written abbreviation for **near**, when used as part of an address: *Bray, nr Dublin*

NRI /ˌen.ɑːrˈaɪ/ **noun** [C] Indian English abbreviation for Non-Resident Indian: a person from India who is living in a different country

n't /-ənt/ **short form of** not: *didn't* ◦ *mustn't*

nth /enθ/ **adj** [before noun] informal used to describe the most recent in a long series of things, when you do not know how many there are: *I glanced at my watch* ***for*** *the nth* ***time*** *that morning.*

IDIOM **to the nth degree** as much or as far as possible: *We were questioned to the nth degree.*

nuance /ˈnjuː.ɑːns/ US /ˈnuː-/ **noun** [C] a very slight difference in appearance, meaning, sound, etc.: *The painter has managed to capture every nuance* ***of*** *the woman's expression.* ◦ *Linguists explore the nuances* ***of*** *language.*

nuanced /ˈnjuː.ɑːnst/ US /ˈnuː-/ **adj** made slightly different in appearance, meaning, sound, etc.: *His London accent is very slightly nuanced by an occasional Russian pronunciation.*

nub /nʌb/ **noun** [S] the most important or basic part

N

of something: *What do you think is the nub* ***of*** *the problem?*

nubile /ˈnjuː.baɪl/ Ⓤⓢ /ˈnuː-/ **adj** describes a woman who is young and sexually attractive: *Rich old men often like to be surrounded by nubile young women.*

nuclear /ˈnjuː.klɪəʳ/ Ⓤⓢ /ˈnuː.kliː.ɚ/ **adj** **POWER** ▷ **1** B2 being or using the power produced when the NUCLEUS of an atom is divided or joined to another nucleus: *nuclear energy/power* ◦ *a nuclear power plant* ◦ *the nuclear industry* **2** B2 relating to weapons, or the use of weapons, which use the power produced when the nucleus of an atom is divided or joined to another nucleus: *a nuclear war/attack* ◦ *nuclear disarmament* ◦ *How many nations have a nuclear* ***capability*** *(= have nuclear weapons)?* **PHYSICS** ▷ **3** specialized relating to the nucleus of an atom: *nuclear fission/fusion/physics*

ˌnuclear ˈfamily noun [C] specialized a family consisting of two parents and their children, but not including aunts, uncles, grandparents, etc. → Compare **extended family**

ˌnuclear ˈfission noun [U] specialized **fission**

ˌnuclear-ˈfree adj describes an area in which nuclear weapons and nuclear energy are not allowed: *The city has declared itself a nuclear-free* ***zone****.*

ˌnuclear ˈfusion noun [U] specialized the process of joining two NUCLEI to produce energy

ˌnuclear reˈactor noun [C] a large machine which uses nuclear fuel to produce power

ˌnuclear ˈwaste noun [U] unwanted, dangerously RADIOACTIVE material that is made when producing nuclear power: *to dump/dispose of nuclear waste*

N

nucleic acid /njuːˌkleɪ.ɪkˈæs.ɪd/ Ⓤⓢ /nuː-/ **noun** [C or U] specialized a type of ACID that exists in all living cells: *DNA and RNA are both nucleic acids.*

nucleotide /ˈnjʊ.kli.ə.taɪd/ Ⓤⓢ /ˈnuː.kli.oʊ-/ **noun** [C] specialized one of a group of chemical COMPOUNDS found in living cells in nucleic acids such as DNA and RNA

nucleus /ˈnjuː.kli.əs/ Ⓤⓢ /ˈnuː-/ **noun** [C] (plural **nuclei** or **nucleuses**) **1** specialized the central part of an atom, usually made up of PROTONS and NEUTRONS **2** specialized the part of a cell that controls its growth: *DNA is stored in the nucleus of a cell.* **3 the nucleus of sth** the group of people or things that are the most important part of something: *These three players will* ***form*** *the nucleus of a revised and stronger team.*

nude /njuːd/ Ⓤⓢ /nuːd/ **adj; noun**

▸**adj 1** not wearing any clothes: *She once posed nude for a magazine.* ◦ *Nude sunbathing is only allowed on certain beaches.* → Compare **naked 2** being the colour of skin: *nude lipstick*

▸**noun** [C] **1** a picture or other piece of art showing a person who is not wearing any clothes: *The exhibition includes several superb nudes.* **2 in the nude** not wearing any clothes: *The children were running around the garden in the nude.*

nudge /nʌdʒ/ **verb; noun**

▸**verb 1** [T] to push something or someone gently, especially to push someone with your ELBOW (= the middle part of your arm where it bends) to attract their attention: *The children were giggling and nudging each other.* ◦ *He nudged the cat off the sofa so that he could sit down.* **2** [I + adv/prep, T] to move slowly and almost reach a higher point or level: *Oil prices continue to nudge higher.* ◦ *Peter must be nudging 40 now.*

IDIOM **nudge nudge (wink wink)** UK informal something you say when you want to suggest that there is a sexual meaning in something that has just been said

▸**noun** [C] the act of nudging someone or something: *I gave him a nudge to wake him up.*

nudism /ˈnjuː.dɪ.zᵊm/ Ⓤⓢ /ˈnuː-/ **noun** [U] the activity of wearing no clothes because you believe that wearing no clothes is healthy

nudist /ˈnjuː.dɪst/ Ⓤⓢ /ˈnuː-/ **noun** [C] someone who practises nudism: *The whole family are committed nudists.* ◦ *a nudist beach (= beach for nudists)*

nudity /ˈnjuː.dɪ.ti/ Ⓤⓢ /ˈnuː.də.t̬i/ **noun** [U] the fact that people are not wearing clothes: *The film was criticized for its excessive violence and nudity.*

nugget /ˈnʌg.ɪt/ **noun** [C] **SMALL PIECE** ▷ **1** a small roughly shaped piece, especially of gold **2** a small piece of chicken or fish that has been covered in BREADCRUMBS and fried: *She won't eat anything except* ***chicken*** *nuggets and chips.* **INFORMATION** ▷ **3** something that a person has said or written that is very true or very wise: *a nugget* ***of*** *information/truth* ◦ humorous *What other astonishing nuggets* ***of*** *wisdom do you have for us?*

nuisance /ˈnjuː.sᵊns/ Ⓤⓢ /ˈnuː-/ **noun** [C or U] **1** B2 something or someone that annoys you or causes trouble for you: *I've forgotten my umbrella –* ***what a*** *nuisance!* ◦ [+ -ing verb] ***It's*** *such a nuisance hav****ing*** *to rewrite those letters.* ◦ *I hate to be a nuisance, but could you help me?* ◦ *Local residents claimed that the noise was causing a* ***public*** *nuisance.* **2 make a nuisance of yourself** to cause trouble or to annoy other people

nuke /njuːk/ Ⓤⓢ /nuːk/ **verb; noun**

▸**verb** [T] **1** informal to bomb somewhere with nuclear weapons: *The two countries were threatening to nuke each other.* **2** mainly US informal to heat or cook something in a MICROWAVE OVEN

▸**noun** [C] informal a nuclear weapon: *'No nukes here!' the banner read.*

null and void /ˌnʌl.əndˈvɔɪd/ **adj** [after verb] legal having no legal force: *The election was declared null and void.*

nullify /ˈnʌl.ɪ.faɪ/ **verb** [T] **1** formal to make a legal agreement or decision have no legal force: *The state death penalty law was nullified in 1977.* **2** to cause something to have no value or effect: *All my hard work was nullified when I lost my notes.*

numb /nʌm/ **adj; verb**

▸**adj 1** If a part of your body is numb, you are unable to feel it, usually for a short time: *I had been lying awkwardly and my leg had* ***gone*** *numb.* ◦ *My fingers were numb* ***with*** *cold.* **2** not able to feel any emotions or to think clearly, because you are so shocked or frightened, etc.: *When she first heard the news, she was numb* ***with*** *disbelief.* ◦ *Ever since his girlfriend left him he has* ***felt*** *numb.*

▸**verb** [T] to make something or someone feel numb: *The extreme cold numbed her face and hands.* ◦ *The children are still numbed by their father's death.*

• **numbly** /-li/ **adv**

number /ˈnʌm.bəʳ/ Ⓤⓢ /-bɚ/ **noun; verb**

▸**noun SYMBOL** ▷ **1** A1 [C] (a sign or symbol representing) a unit which forms part of the system of counting and calculating: *25, 300, and a billion are all numbers.* ◦ *She's very good with numbers (= good at adding, subtracting, etc.).* **2** A1 [C] (written abbreviation **no.**) a number that is used to mark a particular example of something: *They live at number 34 Orchard*

Street. ◦ *Please write your credit card number on this form.* ◦ *What's our flight number?* **3** A1 [C] (written abbreviation **no.**) a phone number: *I gave him my number.*

! Common mistake: number or figure?

To talk about a set of numbers or an amount expressed in numbers, the usual word is **figures**.

Don't say 'unemployment/sales/tax numbers', say **unemployment/sales/tax figures**:

~~*Our sales numbers were better this year than last year.*~~

Our sales figures were better this year than last year.

AMOUNT ▷ **4** B1 [S, + sing/pl verb] an amount or total: *The number **of** people killed in road accidents fell last month.* ◦ *There has been **an** increasing number **of** cases of the disease.* ◦ ***A** small number **of** children are educated at home.* ◦ ***A** large number **of** invitations has been sent.* ◦ *Letters of complaint were surprisingly few **in** number (= there were not many of them).* **5 numbers** [plural] a number of a particular description: ***Small** numbers **of** children are educated at home.* ◦ ***Large** numbers **of** invitations were sent.* ◦ *Newspapers are produced **in** vast numbers.* **6 a number of things** B2 several of a particular type of thing: *I decided not to go, for a number of reasons.* **7** [S, + sing/pl verb] a group of people: *On the trip, one **of** our number fell ill.* **PARTICULAR THING** ▷ **8** [C] a particular example of something **9** [C] a particular copy of a magazine: *Have you got last week's number **of** the New Yorker?* ◦ *He's got all the **back** numbers (= previous copies) **of** the magazine.* **10** [C] informal a piece of clothing, especially a dress, that you admire: *She was wearing a stylish Dior number.* **11** [C] US slang a person with a particular characteristic: *He's a real sexy number, don't you think?* **12** [C] a short tune or song: *Sing one of those romantic numbers.* **13** [C usually singular] mainly US slang something that is often said: *He tried the usual/that old number about how his wife didn't understand him.*

IDIOMS **any number of things** a lot of a particular thing: *His shop stocks any number of different kinds of pasta.* • **beyond/without number** literary too many to count: *An earthquake in the city could result in deaths beyond number.* • **by (sheer) force/weight of numbers** because the number of people or things was so great: *The crowd managed to force its way in by sheer weight of numbers.* • **by numbers** UK (US **by the numbers**) done according to a plan that has been decided previously, without using your own imagination and ideas: *This is painting by numbers – there's nothing original here.* • **do a number on sb** US slang to hurt, defeat, or embarrass someone: *She really did a number on her old boyfriend, making him beg her to come back and then turning him down.* • **have sb's number** slang to know a lot about someone and so have an advantage over them: *Don't worry, I've got his number, he doesn't fool me.* • **your number is up** slang When your number is up, you are going to die: *When the plane started to shake, I just thought my number was up.* • **a numbers game** a situation in which the most important factor is how many of a particular thing there are, especially when you disapprove of this: *To me, business is more than just a numbers game.*

▸verb **WRITE SYMBOL** ▷ **1** C1 [T] to give something a number in a series and usually to write this number on it: *All the folders have been carefully numbered and filed away.* ◦ *Number the pages **from** one **to** ten.* **AMOUNT** ▷ **2** C2 [L only + noun] If people or things number a particular amount, there are this many of them: *After the hurricane the homeless numbered over 200,000.*

PHRASAL VERB **number sb/sth among sb/sth** formal If you are numbered among a particular group, you belong to that group: *At one time, the club numbered an archbishop among its members.*

ˈnumber-ˌcrunching noun [U] mathematical work performed by people or computers that is often quite simple but takes a long time • **ˈnumber-ˌcruncher** noun [C] *I'm only a number-cruncher in the accounts department.*

numberless /ˈnʌm.bəl.əs/ ⓤⓢ /-bɚ.ləs/ adj literary too many to be counted: *numberless stars*

ˌnumber ˈone noun [U] **YOURSELF** ▷ **1** (US also **numero uno**) yourself and no one else: *Frank is completely selfish – he only cares about number one.* ◦ *I'm going to **look out for** number one (= take care of myself only).* **THE BEST** ▷ **2** the most important, best, most noticeable or most famous person or organization in a particular area of activity: *She's still the world number one in tennis.* ◦ *I'm your number one fan.*

ˈnumber ˌplate noun [C] UK (US **ˈlicense ˌplate**) the sign on the front and back of a road vehicle that shows its REGISTRATION NUMBER

ˌNumber ˈTen noun [S, + sing/pl verb] (written abbreviation **No. 10**) the official home of the British prime minister in Downing Street, London, or the people who work for or represent the prime minister: *Number Ten announced tonight that the election will be on 6 April.*

numbness /ˈnʌm.nəs/ noun [U] lack of physical or emotional feeling

numbskull /ˈnʌm.skʌl/ noun [C] a **numskull**

numeracy /ˈnjuː.mə.rə.si/ ⓤⓢ /ˈnuː-/ noun [U] ability to do basic mathematics

numeral /ˈnjuː.mə.rəl/ ⓤⓢ /ˈnuː-/ noun [C] a symbol that represents a number

numerate /ˈnjuː.mə.rət/ ⓤⓢ /ˈnuː-/ adj specialized able to add, multiply, etc.: *Geography graduates are literate and numerate and have very good IT skills.*

numerator /ˈnjuː.mə.reɪ.təʳ/ ⓤⓢ /ˈnuː.mə.reɪ.t̬ɚ/ noun [C] specialized the number above the line in a FRACTION: *In the fraction ¾, 3 is the numerator.* → Compare **denominator**

numerical /njuːˈmer.ɪ.kəl/ ⓤⓢ /nuː-/ adj involving or expressed in numbers: *a numerical calculation* ◦ *numerical skill/ability* ◦ *Keep your files in numerical **order**.* ◦ *The UN forces have a numerical superiority over the rebels (= there are more of the UN forces).* • **numerically** /-kəl.i/ adv *to be numerically superior*

numerous /ˈnjuː.mə.rəs/ ⓤⓢ /ˈnuː-/ adj C1 many: *We have discussed these plans on numerous occasions.* ◦ *Shops of this type, once rare, are now numerous.*

numismatics /ˌnjuː.mɪzˈmæt.ɪks/ ⓤⓢ /ˌnuː.mɪzˈmæt̬.ɪks/ noun [U] specialized the study or collecting of coins, paper money, and MEDALS

numskull (also **numbskull**) /ˈnʌm.skʌl/ noun [C] informal a very stupid or silly person: *You've spilled my coffee, you numskull!*

nun /nʌn/ noun [C] a member of a female religious group which lives in a CONVENT: *a convent school run by Catholic nuns*

nunchuk /ˈnʌn.tʃʌk/ noun [C] **1** a weapon used in traditional Japanese MARTIAL ARTS, that consists of two sticks joined at one end by a chain or rope **2** an

N

electronic device that is held in the hand and used to control movement in computer games

nunnery /ˈnʌn.ər.i/ (US) /-ɚ-/ noun [C] literary a **convent** → Compare **monastery**

nuptial /ˈnʌp.ʃəl/ adj formal belonging or relating to a marriage or to the state of being married: *nuptial vows/promises* ◦ *the nuptial bed*

nuptials /ˈnʌp.ʃəlz/ noun [plural] formal a person's marriage and marriage celebrations: *Sadly we weren't able to attend the nuptials.*

nurse /nɜːs/ (US) /nɝːs/ noun; verb
▸noun [C] **1** (A2) (the title given to) a person whose job is to care for people who are ill or injured, especially in a hospital: *He worked as a nurse in a psychiatric hospital.* ◦ *Nurse Millard will be with you shortly.* ◦ [as form of address] *Thank you, Nurse.* **2** old-fashioned a woman employed to take care of a young child or children
▸verb [T] **TAKE CARE OF** ▷ **1** (C2) to care for a person or an animal while they are ill: *He gave up his job so that he could nurse his mother at home.* ◦ *They found an injured cat and carefully nursed it* ***back to health*** *(= until it was well again).* **2** to spend a lot of time taking care of something as it grows or develops: *These young trees were carefully nursed by the head gardener.* ◦ *The project will have to be nursed* ***through*** *its first few months.* **3** If you nurse an illness or injury, you rest until it gets better: *Robert's in bed nursing a back injury.* **4** to hold a small child in your arms as a way of making them feel better: *She nursed the crying child on her lap.* **FEED** ▷ **5** When a woman nurses a baby, she feeds it with milk from her breasts. **FEEL EMOTION** ▷ **6** to have a strong feeling or an emotion for a long time: *She had long nursed a passion for Japanese art.* **HOLD** ▷ **7** to hold a drink for a long time without drinking it: *Mark was sitting in the corner nursing an almost empty pint glass.*

N

nursemaid /ˈnɜːs.meɪd/ (US) /ˈnɝːs-/ noun [C] old-fashioned a woman who takes care of someone else's young children: *I'm not going to be a nursemaid to you – make your own bed!*

nursery /ˈnɜː.sər.i/ (US) /ˈnɝː.sɚ-/ noun; adj
▸noun [C] **FOR CHILDREN** ▷ **1** (B2) a place where young children and babies are taken care of while their parents are at work: *Does Jake go to a nursery or a childminder?* **2** a room in a house where small children sleep and play **FOR PLANTS** ▷ **3** a place where plants and trees are grown, especially for sale
▸adj [before noun] relating to the teaching of children who are between the ages of two or three to five years old: *Do you think the state should provide free nursery* ***education****?*

ˈnursery ˌnurse noun [C] UK a person who has been trained to take care of young children

ˈnursery ˌrhyme noun [C] a short and usually very old poem or song for young children: *a book of nursery rhymes*

ˈnursery ˌschool noun [C] (US also **preschool**) a school for children between the ages of two and five

ˈnursery ˌslope noun [C] UK (US **ˈbunny ˌslope**) a gentle slope on a mountain used by people learning to ski

ˌnurse's ˈaide noun [C] US for **auxiliary nurse**

nursing /ˈnɜː.sɪŋ/ (US) /ˈnɝː-/ adj; noun
▸adj [before noun] describes a woman who is feeding her baby with her own breast milk: *Nursing* ***mothers*** *are advised to eat plenty of leafy green vegetables.*
▸noun [U] the job of being a nurse: *She studied nursing at Garfield Hospital.*

ˈnursing ˌaid noun [C] Australian English someone whose job is to help nurses to take care of people → Compare **auxiliary nurse**

ˈnursing auˌxiliary noun [C] UK an **auxiliary nurse**

ˈnursing ˌhome noun [C] a place where very old people who are ill live and receive medical treatment and care

nurture /ˈnɜː.tʃər/ (US) /ˈnɝː.tʃɚ/ verb; noun
▸verb [T] formal **HELP DEVELOP** ▷ **1** to take care of, feed, and protect someone or something, especially young children or plants, and help them to develop: *She wants to stay at home and nurture her children.* ◦ *a carefully nurtured garden* **2** to help a plan or a person to develop and be successful: *As a record company director, his job is to nurture young* ***talent****.* **FOR A LONG TIME** ▷ **3** to have a particular emotion, plan, or idea for a long time: *Winifred nurtured ambitions for her daughter to be a surgeon.*
▸noun [U] the way in which children are treated as they are growing, especially as compared with the characteristics they are born with: *Which do you believe has the strongest influence on how children develop –* ***nature or*** *nurture?*

nut /nʌt/ noun; verb
▸noun **FOOD** ▷ **1** (B2) [C] the dry fruit of particular trees which grows in a hard shell and can often be eaten: *a Brazil/cashew nut* **METAL OBJECT** ▷ **2** [C] a small piece of metal with a hole in it through which you put a BOLT: *Nuts and bolts are used to hold pieces of machinery together.* **PERSON** ▷ **3** [C] informal or offensive a person who behaves in a very silly, stupid, or strange way or an offensive term for a person who is mentally ill: *What kind of nut would leave a car on a railway track?* **4** [C] informal someone who is extremely enthusiastic about a particular activity or thing: *Ian's a tennis nut – he plays every day.* → See also **nuts** **HEAD** ▷ **5** [C] slang a person's head: *Come on,* ***use*** *your nut (= think clearly)!*

IDIOMS **be off your nut** slang to be very silly or stupid: *You can't do that! Are you off your nut?* • **do your nut** UK slang to become extremely angry: *She'll do her nut when she sees the mess.* • **a hard/tough nut to crack** a problem that is very difficult to solve or a person who is very difficult to understand • **the nuts and bolts** the practical facts about a particular thing, rather than theories or ideas about it: *When it came to the nuts and bolts* ***of*** *running a business, he was clearly unable to cope.* • **a tough/hard nut** someone who is very unpleasant and difficult to deal with: *As a teenager, Jack was a real hard nut, always getting into fights.*

▸verb [T] informal to hit someone or something with your head: *The guy turned round and nutted him.*

nutcase /ˈnʌt.keɪs/ noun [C] informal or offensive someone who behaves in an extremely silly way or an offensive term for someone who is mentally ill

nutcracker /ˈnʌtˌkræk.ər/ (US) /-ɚ/ noun [C] (UK also **nutcrackers**) a tool for breaking the shell of a nut, so that you can remove and eat the softer part inside

nutcracker

nuthouse /ˈnʌt.haʊs/ noun [C] offensive a **psychiatric hospital**

nutmeg /ˈnʌt.meg/ noun; verb
▸noun **SPICE** ▷ **1** [C or U] the hard fruit of a tropical tree, or a brown powder made from this, used as a spice to add flavour to food: ***Grate*** *some nutmeg on top of the pudding.* **FOOTBALL** ▷ **2** [C] informal in

football, an occasion when a player kicks the ball through an opponent's legs
▸**verb** [T] (**-gg-**) mainly UK informal in football, to kick the ball through an opponent's legs: *Roberts added the second goal five minutes into the second half when he nutmegged Evans.*

nutraceutical /ˌnjuː.trəˈsuː.tɪ.kəl/ ⓤⓢ /ˌnuː.trə.suː.t̬ɪ-/ noun [C] (also **ˈfunctional ˌfood**) a food to which VITAMINS, minerals, or drugs have been added to make it healthier

nutrient /ˈnjuː.tri.ənt/ ⓤⓢ /ˈnuː-/ **noun** [C] specialized any substance which plants or animals need in order to live and grow: *It's good soil – full of nutrients.* ◦ *A healthy diet should provide all your essential nutrients.*

nutrition /njuːˈtrɪʃ.ən/ ⓤⓢ /nuː-/ **noun** [U] **1** C1 the substances that you take into your body as food and the way that they influence your health: ***Good** nutrition is essential if patients are to make a quick recovery.* ◦ *improvements in nutrition* **2** the process of taking in and using food, or the scientific study of this

nutritional /njuːˈtrɪʃ.ən.əl/ ⓤⓢ /nuː-/ **adj** (also **nutritive**) C1 relating to nutrition: *Chemical sweeteners have no nutritional **value**.*

nutritionist /njuːˈtrɪʃ.ən.ɪst/ ⓤⓢ /nuː-/ **noun** [C] an expert on the subject of nutrition

nutritious /njuːˈtrɪʃ.əs/ ⓤⓢ /nuː-/ **adj** C1 containing many of the substances needed for life and growth: *a nutritious diet* ◦ *Raw spinach is especially nutritious.*

nuts /nʌts/ **noun; adj**
▸**noun** [plural] offensive for **testicle**
▸**adj** [after verb] informal silly, stupid, or strange: [+ to infinitive] *You must be nuts **to** go climbing mountains in winter.*

IDIOMS **be nuts about/over sth/sb** informal to be very enthusiastic about an object, activity, or person: *Sophie's nuts about dinosaurs.* ◦ *I'm nuts over this band.* • **go nuts** informal to become extremely angry: *My sister will go nuts when she finds out I've wrecked her car.*

nutshell /ˈnʌt.ʃel/ **noun in a nutshell** C1 using as few words as possible: *Well, to **put it** in a nutshell, we're lost.*

nutter /ˈnʌt.əʳ/ ⓤⓢ /ˈnʌt̬.ɚ/ **noun** [C] UK informal someone who is crazy, silly, or strange: *He's a bit of a nutter.*

nutty /ˈnʌt.i/ ⓤⓢ /ˈnʌt̬.i/ **adj** FOOD ▷ **1** containing or tasting of nuts PERSON ▷ **2** informal crazy, silly, or strange: *She's got some nutty idea about setting up a school for cats.* • **nuttiness** /-nəs/ **noun** [U]

IDIOM **be (as) nutty as a fruitcake** informal to be a very strange or crazy person

nuzzle /ˈnʌz.l/ **verb** [I + adv/prep, T] to touch, rub, or press something or someone gently and/or in a way that shows your love, especially with the head or nose, usually with small repeated movements: *My dog came and nuzzled my foot to try and cheer me up.* ◦ *The kittens like to nuzzle **up against/up to** their mother.*

NVQ /ˌen.viːˈkjuː/ **noun** [C] abbreviation for National Vocational Qualification: a British qualification in a technical or practical subject which shows that a person has a range of skills useful for work

NW **noun** [U], **adj** written abbreviation for **northwest** or **northwestern**

NY **noun** (also **NYC**) written abbreviation for New York (City)

nylon /ˈnaɪ.lɒn/ ⓤⓢ /-lɑːn/ **noun** [U] **1** an artificial substance used especially to make clothes, ropes, and brushes: *These covers are 100 percent nylon.* ◦ *a nylon shirt/bag* **2 nylons** [plural] old-fashioned women's nylon TIGHTS or STOCKINGS (= leg coverings)

nymph /nɪmf/ **noun** [C] (in ancient Greek and Roman traditional stories) a GODDESS or spirit in the form of a young woman, living in a tree, river, mountain, etc.

nymphet /nɪmˈfet/ ⓤⓢ /ˈnɪm.fət/ **noun** [C] usually humorous a young girl considered to be sexually attractive

nymphomaniac /ˌnɪm.fəˈmeɪ.ni.æk/ ⓤⓢ /-foʊ-/ **noun** [C] (informal **nympho**) a woman who likes to have sex very often, especially with a lot of different men • **nymphomania** /-ə/ **noun** [U]

NZ **noun** written abbreviation for New Zealand

N

O

O, o /əʊ/ Ⓤⓢ /oʊ/ **noun; exclamation**
▸**noun** [C or U] (plural **Os, O's** or **o's**) **LETTER** ▷ **1** the 15th letter of the English alphabet **ZERO** ▷ **2** (also **o**, also **oh**) used in speech to mean zero: *My phone number is three, one, o, five, one, double o (= 3105100).* ◦ *The year 1705 is usually pronounced seventeen o five.*
▸**exclamation** old use or literary used when talking to someone or something, or expressing something in an emotional or formal way: *O Zeus! Hear my prayer.* → Compare **oh**

o' /ə/ **preposition** used in writing to represent 'of' when the f is not pronounced: *a bottle o' beer*

oaf /əʊf/ Ⓤⓢ /oʊf/ **noun** [C] old-fashioned a stupid, rude, or awkward person, especially a man: *a drunken/insensitive/stupid oaf* ◦ *You clumsy oaf! You've broken it!*

oafish /ˈəʊ.fɪʃ/ Ⓤⓢ /ˈoʊ-/ **adj** old-fashioned stupid, rude, or awkward: *oafish behaviour* ◦ *an oafish young man* • **oafishness** /-nəs/ **noun** [U] informal disapproving

oak /əʊk/ Ⓤⓢ /oʊk/ **noun** [C or U] B2 a large tree that is common in northern countries, or the hard wood of this tree: *a mighty oak* ◦ *The timbers of those old sailing ships were mainly oak.* ◦ *an oak table/cupboard*

oaky /ˈəʊ.ki/ Ⓤⓢ /ˈoʊ-/ **adj** describes wine that has a slight flavour of wood, especially because it has been left to develop in a container made of oak: *a deliciously oaky red wine*

OAP /ˌəʊ.eɪˈpiː/ Ⓤⓢ /ˌoʊ-/ **noun** [C] UK abbreviation for **old age pensioner**: *OAPs get cheaper bus and train tickets.*

oar /ɔːʳ/ Ⓤⓢ /ɔːr/ **noun** [C] a long pole with a wide, flat part at one end, used for ROWING a boat: *a pair of oars* ◦ *She dipped her oars into the water and pulled.* → Compare **paddle**

IDIOM **put/stick your oar in** informal disapproving to say or do something which annoys other people because they have not asked you to join their conversation or activity: *No one asked him to help – he's always sticking his oar in.*

oarlock /ˈɔː.lɒk/ Ⓤⓢ /ˈɔːr.lɑːk/ **noun** [C] US for **rowlock**

oarsman /ˈɔːz.mən/ Ⓤⓢ /ˈɔːrz-/ **noun** [C] (plural **-men** /-mən/) a person who rows a boat, especially in competitions

oarswoman /ˈɔːzˌwʊm.ən/ Ⓤⓢ /ˈɔːrz-/ **noun** [C] (plural **-women** /-wɪmɪn/) a woman who rows a boat

oasis /əʊˈeɪ.sɪs/ Ⓤⓢ /oʊ-/ **noun** (plural **oases**) **1** [C] a place in a desert where there is water and therefore plants and trees and sometimes a village or town **2** [S] a calm, pleasant place in the middle of somewhere busy and unpleasant: *Her office was an oasis **of** peace and sanity amid the surrounding chaos.*

oat /əʊt/ Ⓤⓢ /oʊt/ **adj** [before noun] made of or from OATS: *oat biscuits* ◦ *oat bran/cereal*

oatcake /ˈəʊt.keɪk/ Ⓤⓢ /ˈoʊt-/ **noun** [C] a thin SAVOURY (= not sweet) biscuit made from oats, often made in Scotland

oath /əʊθ/ Ⓤⓢ /oʊθ/ **noun** [C] **PROMISE** ▷ **1** a promise, especially that you will tell the truth in a law court: *Medieval knights **took** an oath **of** allegiance/loyalty to their lord.* ◦ *The witness placed her hand on the Bible and **took the** oath (= promised to tell the truth).* **2 be under/on oath** to have formally promised to tell the truth: *The judge reminded the witness that she was under oath.* **SWEAR WORD** ▷ **3** old-fashioned an offensive word, especially one that uses a name for God: *muttering/mouthing oaths*

oatmeal /ˈəʊt.miːl/ Ⓤⓢ /ˈoʊt-/ **noun** [U] **1** a type of flour made from oats: *oatmeal porridge* **2** US for **porridge**

oats /əʊts/ Ⓤⓢ /oʊts/ **noun** [plural] a plant that is a type of grass, or its grain used in baking and cooking or to feed animals: *a field of oats* ◦ ***rolled** oats (= oats that have been pressed flat)* ◦ *porridge oats*

OB /ˌəʊˈbiː/ Ⓤⓢ /ˌoʊ-/ **noun** [C] US informal for **obstetrician**

obdurate /ˈɒb.djʊ.rət/ Ⓤⓢ /ˈɑːb.dʊr.ɪt/ **adj** formal disapproving extremely determined to act in a particular way and not to change despite what anyone else says: *The president remains obdurate **on** the question of tax cuts.*

obedience /əˈbiː.di.əns/ Ⓤⓢ /oʊ-/ **noun** [U] the fact that people or animals do what they are told to do: *He demands unquestioning obedience from his soldiers.*

obedient /əˈbiː.di.ənt/ Ⓤⓢ /oʊ-/ **adj** doing, or willing to do, what you have been told to do by someone in authority: *Students are expected to be quiet and obedient in the classroom.* ◦ *an obedient dog* → See also **obey** → Opposite **disobedient** • **obediently** /-li/ **adv**

obeisance /əʊˈbeɪ.sᵊns/ Ⓤⓢ /oʊ-/ **noun** [C or U] formal the fact of obeying or respecting someone, or something you do that expresses this: *One by one the noblemen **made** their obeisances (= bent at the waist) **to** the Queen.*

obelisk /ˈɒb.ᵊl.ɪsk/ Ⓤⓢ /ˈɑː.bᵊl-/ **noun** [C] a tall stone column with four sloping sides and a pointed top, made in honour of an important person or event

obese /əʊˈbiːs/ Ⓤⓢ /oʊ-/ **adj** C1 extremely fat • **obesity** /-ˈbiː.sɪ.ti/ Ⓤⓢ /-ˈbiː.sə.t̬i/ **noun** [U] C1 ***childhood** obesity* ◦ *A diet that is high in fat can lead to obesity.*

obey /əʊˈbeɪ/, /əˈ-/ Ⓤⓢ /oʊ-/ **verb** B2 [I or T] to act according to what you have been asked or ordered to do by someone in authority, or to behave according to a rule, law, or instruction: *The soldiers refused to obey (**orders**).* ◦ *to obey the **rules** of international law* ◦ *Falling objects obey the **law** of gravity.* → See also **obedient**

> **+ Other ways of saying obey**
>
> **Follow** can sometimes be used instead of 'obey':
> *All religions guide youths to **follow** the teachings of elders and parents.*
>
> **Comply** can be used in formal English when someone obeys an order, rule, or request:
> *There are serious penalties for failure to **comply** with the regulations.*
>
> **Observe** is often used in formal English when someone obeys a law or custom:
> *People must **observe** the law.*
>
> If someone continues to obey a rule, you could use the phrasal verb **adhere to**:
> *They failed to **adhere to** the terms of the agreement.*
>
> **Abide by** can be used when someone accepts and obeys a decision, agreement, etc.:
> *Players must **abide by** the referee's decision.*

obfuscate /ˈɒb.fʌs.keɪt/ (US) /ˈɑːb.fə.skeɪt/ **verb** [T] formal to make something less clear and harder to understand, especially intentionally: *She was criticized for using arguments that obfuscated the main issue.* • **obfuscation** /ˌɒb.fʌsˈkeɪ.ʃən/ (US) /ˌɑːb.fəˈskeɪ-/ **noun** [U] *They accused the White House of obstruction and obfuscation.*

ob-gyn /ˌəʊ.bi.dʒi.waɪˈen/ (US) /ˌoʊ-/ **noun** [C] US informal abbreviation for obstetrician-gynecologist: a doctor who specializes in pregnancy, birth, and diseases affecting women's REPRODUCTIVE organs

obituary /əˈbɪtʃ.ʊə.ri/ (US) /oʊˈbɪtʃ.u.er.i/ **noun** [C] (informal **obit**) a report, especially in a newspaper, which gives the news of someone's death and details about their life

object **noun**; **verb**

▸**noun** /ˈɒb.dʒɪkt/ (US) /ˈɑːb-/ **THING** ▷ **1** B1 [C] a thing that you can see or touch but that is not usually a living animal, plant or person: *a solid/material/physical object* ◦ *a collection of precious objects* ◦ *Look, there's a strange object in the sky!* **GRAMMAR** ▷ **2** B1 [C] (written abbreviation **obj**) specialized a noun or noun phrase that is affected by the action of a verb or that follows a preposition: *In the sentence 'I like ice cream', 'ice cream' is the object **of** the verb 'like'.* **PURPOSE** ▷ **3** C1 [C usually singular] a reason for doing something, or the result you wish to achieve by doing it: *The object **of** their expedition was to discover the source of the River Nile.* **4 the object of the exercise** the result that is wanted from an activity: *In today's session, the object of the exercise is to improve your interpersonal skills.* **CAUSE** ▷ **5** [C usually singular] someone or something that causes particular feelings in or actions by others: *He became an object **of** ridicule among the other workers.*

IDIOM **be no object** If something valuable, such as money, is no object, it does not need to be considered as a problem, because you have a lot of it: *For a millionaire like him, **money** is no object.*

▸**verb** [I] /əbˈdʒekt/ B2 to feel or express opposition to or dislike of something or someone: *Would anyone object **if** we started the meeting now?* ◦ *He objects **to** the label 'magician' which he is often given.* ◦ *No one objected when the boss said it was time to go home.*

objectification /ɒbˌdʒek.tɪ.fɪˈkeɪ.ʃən/ (US) /ɑːbˌdʒek.t̬ɪ-/ **noun** [U] specialized treating people like tools or toys, as if they had no feelings, opinions, or rights of their own: *Pornography is often an example of the objectification of women by men.*

objection /əbˈdʒek.ʃən/ **noun** [C] B2 the act of expressing or feeling OPPOSITION to or dislike of something or someone: *Her objection **to/against** the plan is based on incorrect facts.* ◦ *A couple of people **raised/voiced** objections to the proposal.* ◦ [+ that] *I **have no** objection except **that** it may cost more than expected.*

objectionable /əbˈdʒek.ʃən.ə.bl̩/ **adj** formal describes people or things that you dislike or oppose because they are so unpleasant or wrong: *an objectionable smell* ◦ *I **found** the violence in that film really objectionable.*

objective /əbˈdʒek.tɪv/ **noun**; **adj**

▸**noun** [C] B2 something which you plan to do or achieve: *Her **main/prime** objective now is simply to stay in power.* ◦ *Can the sales force **achieve/meet** its financial objectives?*

▸**adj** B2 based on real facts and not influenced by personal beliefs or feelings: *an objective and impartial report* ◦ *I can't really be objective when I'm judging my daughter's work.* → Opposite **subjective** • **objectively** /-li/ **adv** C1 *Judges must weigh the evidence logically and objectively.* • **objectivity** /ˌɒb.dʒekˈtɪv.ɪ.ti/ (US) /ˌɑːb.dʒekˈtɪv.ə.t̬i/ **noun** [U] *Surely true objectivity in a critic is impossible?*

ˈobject ˌlesson **noun** [C] approving an action or story which teaches you how or how not to act, or which clearly shows the facts of a situation, usually a bad one: *The disaster was an object lesson **in** how not to run a ship.*

objector /əbˈdʒek.tər/ (US) /-tɚ/ **noun** [C] someone who objects to something or someone: *a **conscientious** objector*

ˌobject-ˈoriented **adj** specialized in computing, refers to something based on groups of information and their effects on each other, rather than on a series of instructions: *C++ is a common object-oriented **programming** language.*

objet d'art /ˌɒb.ʒeɪˈdɑːr/ (US) /ˌɑːb.ʒeɪˈdɑːr/ **noun** [C] (plural **objets d'art**) an object, usually a small object, considered to have some worth or value as art

obligation /ˌɒb.lɪˈgeɪ.ʃən/ (US) /ˌɑː.blə-/ **noun** **1** B2 [C or U] the fact that you are obliged to do something: [+ to infinitive] *If you have not signed a contract, you are **under** no obligation **to** (= it is not necessary to) pay them any money.* ◦ *You have a **legal** obligation **to** (= the law says you must) ensure your child receives a proper education.* **2** [C] something that you must do: *I haven't got time to do his work for him – I've got too many obligations as it is.*

obligatory /əˈblɪg.ə.tər.i/ (US) /-tɔːr-/ **adj** **1** C1 describes something you must do because of a rule or law, etc.: *The medical examination before you start work is obligatory.* ◦ [+ to infinitive] *The statute made it obligatory **for** all fit males between 14 and 60 **to** work.* **2** C2 expected because it usually happens: *Some secret service agents turned up, all wearing the obligatory raincoat and hat.*

oblige /əˈblaɪdʒ/ **verb** **FORCE** ▷ **1** [T + obj + to infinitive] (mainly US or formal **obligate**) to force someone to do something, or to make it necessary for someone to do something: *The law obliges companies **to** pay decent wages to their employees.* **HELP** ▷ **2** C1 [I or T] to please or help someone, especially by doing something they have asked you to do: *We only went to the party to oblige some old friends who especially asked us to be there.* ◦ *We needed a guide and he was only too **happy to** oblige.*

PHRASAL VERB **oblige sb with sth** formal to help someone by giving them something: *Could you oblige me with a pen and a piece of paper, please?*

obliged /əˈblaɪdʒd/ **adj** [after verb] (mainly US or formal **obligated**) **FORCED** ▷ **1 be, feel, etc. obliged** B2 [+ to infinitive] to be forced to do something or feel that you must do something: *Doctors are legally obliged **to** take certain precautions.* ◦ *She feels obliged **to** be nice to Jack because he's her boss.* **GRATEFUL** ▷ **2 (be) much obliged** formal used to thank someone and say that you are grateful: *'Here's the information you requested.' 'Oh, (I'm) much obliged (to you).'* **3 be obliged if** formal used to ask someone politely to do something: *I'd be obliged if you would complete and return the form as soon as possible.*

obliging /əˈblaɪ.dʒɪŋ/ **adj** approving willing or eager to help: *He found an obliging doctor who gave him the drugs he needed.* • **obligingly** /-li/ **adv**

oblique /əˈbliːk/ (US) /oʊ-/ **adj**; **noun**

▸**adj** **ANGLE** ▷ **1** having a sloping direction, angle, or position: *Through the window came the last few oblique rays of evening sunshine.* ◦ *He gave her an oblique*

O

glance. **2** specialized (of an angle) either more or less than 90° **NOT DIRECT** ▷ **3** describes remarks that are not direct, so that the real meaning is not immediately clear: *She made several oblique **references** to the current financial situation.* • **obliquely** /-li/ adv

▸**noun** [C] (also **oˌblique ˈstroke**) UK for a **slash**: *Fractions can be written with an oblique, for example 2/3.*

obliterate /əˈblɪt.ər.eɪt/ (US) /-ˈblɪt̬.ə.reɪt/ verb **1** [T often passive] to remove all signs of something, either by destroying it or by covering it so that it cannot be seen: *The missile strike was devastating – the target was totally obliterated.* ◦ *All of a sudden the view was obliterated by the fog.* **2** [T] to make an idea or feeling disappear completely: *Perhaps she gets drunk to obliterate painful memories.* • **obliteration** /əˌblɪt.ərˈeɪ.ʃən/ (US) /-ˌblɪt̬.əˈreɪ-/ noun [U]

oblivion /əˈblɪv.i.ən/ noun [U] **NO MEMORY** ▷ **1** the state of being completely forgotten: *He was another minor poet, perhaps unfairly **consigned to** oblivion.* ◦ *These toys will be around for a year or two, then fade/slide/sink **into** oblivion.* **2** the state of being completely destroyed: *The planes bombed the city **into** oblivion.* **UNCONSCIOUS** ▷ **3** the state of being unconscious: *He sought oblivion in a bottle of whisky.*

oblivious /əˈblɪv.i.əs/ adj not conscious of something, especially what is happening around you: *Absorbed in her work, she was totally oblivious **of** her surroundings.* ◦ *The government seems oblivious **to** the likely effects of the new legislation.* • **obliviously** /-li/ adv • **obliviousness** /-nəs/ noun [U]

oblong /ˈɒb.lɒŋ/ (US) /ˈɑː.blɑːŋ/ noun [C] an object or shape that is longer than it is wide, especially a flat shape with four sides and four angles of 90° and opposite sides of equal length → Compare **square** • **oblong** adj *an oblong box*

O

obnoxious /əbˈnɒk.ʃəs/ (US) /-ˈnɑːk-/ adj disapproving very unpleasant or rude: *Some of his colleagues say that he's loud and obnoxious.* ◦ *When she's in a bad mood she's obnoxious **to** everyone.* • **obnoxiously** /-li/ adv *obnoxiously arrogant/drunk* • **obnoxiousness** /-nəs/ noun [U]

obo noun US written abbreviation for or best offer: used in advertisements for possessions that people are trying to sell, to show that they will accept slightly less money than the price they are asking for: *Exercise bike for sale – $40 obo.*

oboe /ˈəʊ.bəʊ/ (US) /ˈoʊ.boʊ/ noun [C] a tube-shaped musical instrument, played by blowing through a double REED at the top

oboist /ˈəʊ.bəʊ.ɪst/ (US) /ˈoʊ.boʊ-/ noun [C] someone who plays the oboe

obscene /əbˈsiːn/ adj **1** (C2) offensive, rude, or shocking, usually because of being too obviously related to sex or showing sex: *In the raid, police found several boxes of obscene DVDs.* ◦ *He was jailed for making obscene **phone calls** (= ones in which unwanted sexual suggestions were made to the listener).* ◦ *obscene language/graffiti* **2** (C2) morally wrong, often describing something that is wrong because it is too large: *to make obscene profits* ◦ *The salaries some company directors earn are obscene.* • **obscenely** /-li/ adv *He's obscenely rich/fat/cruel.*

obscenity /əbˈsen.ɪ.ti/ (US) /-ə.t̬i/ noun **1** [C or U] the fact that something is obscene: *The people who made that film could be prosecuted for obscenity.* ◦ *Such deliberate destruction of the environment is an obscenity (= offensive and shocking).* ◦ *obscenity laws* **2** [C usually plural] a very offensive or sexually shocking word or sentence: *He was shouting and screaming obscenities.*

obscure /əbˈskjʊər/ (US) /-ˈskjʊr/ adj; verb

▸**adj NOT KNOWN** ▷ **1** not known to many people: *an obscure island in the Pacific* ◦ *an obscure 12th-century mystic* **NOT CLEAR** ▷ **2** not clear and difficult to understand or see: *Official policy has changed, for reasons that remain obscure.* ◦ *His answers were obscure and confusing.*

▸**verb** [T] **1** to prevent something from being seen or heard: *Two new skyscrapers had sprung up, obscuring the view from her window.* ◦ *The sun was obscured by clouds.* **2** to make something difficult to discover and understand: *Managers deliberately obscured the real situation **from** federal investigators.* • **obscurely** /-li/ adv *The minister's statement was obscurely worded.*

obscurity /əbˈskjʊə.rɪ.ti/ (US) /-ˈskjʊr.ə.t̬i/ noun [U] **NOT KNOWN** ▷ **1** the state of not being known to many people: *He was briefly famous in his twenties but then **sank into** obscurity.* ◦ *He rose from relative obscurity to worldwide recognition.* **NOT CLEAR** ▷ **2** the state of being not clear and difficult to understand or see: *The story is convoluted and opaque, often to the point of total obscurity.*

obsequious /əbˈsiː.kwi.əs/ adj formal disapproving too eager to praise or obey someone: *She is almost embarrassingly obsequious to anyone in authority.*

observance /əbˈzɜː.vəns/ (US) /-ˈzɝː-/ noun [C or U] formal the act of obeying a law or following a religious custom: *religious observances such as fasting*

observant /əbˈzɜː.vənt/ (US) /-ˈzɝː-/ adj approving (C2) good or quick at noticing things: *'That's a new dress, isn't it?' 'Yes, you are observant!'*

observation /ˌɒb.zəˈveɪ.ʃən/ (US) /ˌɑːb.zɚ-/ noun **WATCHING** ▷ **1** (B2) [U] the act of observing something or someone: ***close** observation of nature/human nature/animal behaviour* ◦ *The police are keeping the suspect **under** observation.* ◦ *She was admitted to hospital **for** observation (= so that doctors could watch her and see if anything was wrong with her).* **NOTICING** ▷ **2** (B2) [U] the fact that you notice or see something: *She has remarkable **powers of** observation (= is very good at noticing things).* **3** (C1) [C] formal a remark about something that you have noticed: *The book is full of interesting observations **on/about** the nature of musical composition.* ◦ *May I **make** an observation?*

obserˈvation ˌpost noun [C] a place or building from which you can watch someone, especially an enemy

observatory /əbˈzɜː.və.tər.i/ (US) /-ˈzɝː.və.tɔːr.i/ noun [C] a building from which scientists can watch the planets, the stars, the weather, etc.

observe /əbˈzɜːv/ (US) /-ˈzɝːv/ verb [T] **WATCH** ▷ **1** (B2) formal to watch carefully the way something happens or the way someone does something, especially in order to learn more about it: *The role of scientists is to observe and describe the world, not to try to control it.* ◦ [+ question word] *He spent a year in the jungle, observing **how** deforestation is affecting local tribes.* **NOTICE** ▷ **2** (C1) formal to notice or see: *Jack observed a look of anxiety on his brother's face.* ◦ [+ question word] *The guards failed to observe **who** delivered the package.* ◦ [+ that] *In all these films one observes **that** directors are taking a new interest in Native American culture.* ◦ [+ infinitive without to] *A teacher observed her climb over the gate.* **SAY** ▷ **3** formal to make a remark about something: [+ speech] *'I've always found German cars very reliable,' he observed.* ◦ [+ that] *She observed **that** it would soon be time to stop for lunch.* **OBEY** ▷ **4** (C2) formal to obey a law, rule, or custom: *People must observe the law. Nobody should be an exception.* ◦ *The* *old people in the village still observe the local traditions.* • **observable** /-ˈzɜː.və.bl̩/ (US) /-ˈzɝː.və.bl̩/ **adj** *There's no observable connection between the two events.* • **observably** /-ˈzɜː.və.bli/ (US) /-ˈzɝː.və.bli/ **adv**

observer /əbˈzɜː.vəʳ/ (US) /-ˈzɝː.vɚ/ **noun** [C] **C2** a person who watches what happens but has no active part in it: *observers of the political situation/political observers* ◦ *UN observers are monitoring the ceasefire.*

obsess /əbˈses/ **verb** [I or T] If something or someone obsesses you, or if you obsess about something or someone, you think about them all the time: *The whole relationship obsessed me for years.* ◦ *She used to obsess* ***about*** *her weight.*

obsessed /əbˈsest/ **adj** **B2** unable to stop thinking about something; too interested in or worried about something: *Why are people so obsessed* ***with*** *money?* ◦ *As a society we're obsessed* ***by*** *sex.*

obsession /əbˈseʃ.ən/ **noun** [C or U] **B2** something or someone that you think about all the time: *an unhealthy obsession* ***with*** *death* ◦ *her chocolate obsession* ◦ *He's always wanted to find his natural mother but recently it's* ***become an*** *obsession.*

obsessive /əbˈses.ɪv/ **adj**; **noun**
▸**adj** (also **obsessional**) **1** **C2** thinking about something or someone, or doing something, too much or all the time: *He's obsessive* ***about*** *punctuality.* **2** like, typical of, or caused by an obsession: *obsessive secrecy* ◦ *obsessional behaviour* • **obsessively** /-li/ **adv** (also **obsessionally**)
▸**noun** [C] specialized an obsessive person

obˌsessive-comˈpulsive disˌorder **noun** [C or U] (abbreviation **OCD**) a mental illness which causes a person to do something repeatedly for no reason • **obˌsessive-comˈpulsive adj**

obsidian /ɒbˈsɪd.i.ən/ (US) /ɑːb-/ **noun** [U] a type of almost black rock that is like glass

obsolescence /ˌɒb.səˈles.əns/ (US) /ˌɑːb-/ **noun** [U] **1** the quality of being obsolete: *Mobile phone technology is developing so quickly that many customers are concerned about obsolescence.* **2** **built-in/planned obsolescence** the fact that a product is intentionally designed and made so that it will not last for a long time

obsolescent /ˌɒb.səˈles.ənt/ (US) /ˌɑːb-/ **adj** formal becoming obsolete: *Much of our existing military hardware is obsolescent.*

obsolete /ˌɒb.səlˈiːt/ (US) /ˌɑːb-/ **adj** **C1** not in use any more, having been replaced by something newer and better or more fashionable: *Gas lamps became obsolete when electric lighting was invented.*

obstacle /ˈɒb.stɪ.kl̩/ (US) /ˈɑːb-/ **noun** [C] **C1** something that blocks you so that movement, going forward, or action is prevented or made more difficult: *The biggest obstacle in our way was a tree trunk in the road.* ◦ *This decision has removed the last obstacle* ***to*** *the hostages' release.*

ˈobstacle ˌcourse **noun** [C] **1** a race in which runners have to climb over, under, or through a series of obstacles **2** a series of problems that you have to solve in order to achieve something

obstetrician /ˌɒb.stəˈtrɪʃ.ən/ (US) /ˌɑːb-/ **noun** [C] (US informal **OB**) a doctor with special training in how to care for pregnant women and help in the birth of babies

obstetrics /ɒbˈstet.rɪks/ (US) /ɑːb-/ **noun** [U] specialized the area of medicine which deals with pregnancy and the birth of babies: *obstetrics and gynaecology* • **obstetric** /-rɪk/ **adj** *an obstetric nurse*

obstinate /ˈɒb.stɪ.nət/ (US) /ˈɑː.bstə-/ **adj** **1** unreasonably determined, especially to act in a particular way and not to change at all, despite what anyone else says: *He can be very obstinate at times.* ◦ *her obstinate refusal to compromise* **2** [before noun] describes a problem, situation, or thing that is difficult to deal with, remove, or defeat: *obstinate weeds* ◦ *Invading troops met with obstinate resistance by guerrilla forces.* • **obstinacy** /-nə.si/ **noun** [U] • **obstinately** /-li/ **adv**

obstreperous /əbˈstrep.ər.əs/ (US) /ɑːbˈstrep.ɚ.əs/ **adj** formal difficult to deal with and noisy: *obstreperous customers* • **obstreperousness** /-nəs/ **noun** [U]

obstruct /əbˈstrʌkt/ **verb** [T] **1** to block a road, passage, entrance, etc. so that nothing can go along it, or to prevent something from happening correctly by putting difficulties in its way: *After the earthquake many roads were obstructed by collapsed buildings.* ◦ *Her view of the stage was obstructed by a pillar.* **2** to try to stop something from happening or developing: *to obstruct a police investigation* ◦ *He got five years in prison for withholding evidence and obstructing the course of justice.*

obstruction /əbˈstrʌk.ʃən/ **noun** **1** [C or U] something that blocks a road, passage, entrance, etc. so that nothing can go along it, or the act of blocking something in this way: *There's some sort of obstruction on the railway tracks.* **2** [U] behaviour or actions that prevent something from happening or working correctly: *They were charged with obstruction of the police/of justice (= preventing the police/law courts from doing their jobs).* **3** [U] in sport, an occasion when one player gets in the way of another and so prevents them from moving freely: *The referee said it was obstruction.*

obstructionism /əbˈstrʌk.ʃən.ɪ.zəm/ **noun** [U] disapproving the act of intentionally stopping or slowing down an official process • **obstructionist** /-ɪst/ **adj**

obstructive /əbˈstrʌk.tɪv/ **adj** disapproving trying to stop someone from doing something by causing problems for them: *We'd have made a decision by now if Jean hadn't been so obstructive.* • **obstructively** /-li/ **adv** • **obstructiveness** /-nəs/ **noun** [U]

obtain /əbˈteɪn/ **verb** formal **GET** ▷ **1** **B2** [T] to get something, especially by asking for it, buying it, working for it, or producing it from something else: *to obtain permission* ◦ *First editions of these books are now almost impossible to obtain.* ◦ *In the second experiment they obtained a very clear result.* ◦ *Sugar is obtained* ***by*** *crushing and processing sugar cane.* **EXIST** ▷ **2** [I not continuous] (especially of a situation) to exist: *Conditions of extreme poverty now obtain in many parts of the country.*

obtainable /əbˈteɪ.nə.bl̩/ **adj** able to be obtained: *Information on the subject is easily obtainable on the internet.* → Opposite **unobtainable**

obtrude /əbˈtruːd/ **verb** [I or T] formal (especially of something unwanted) to make something or to become too noticeable, especially by interrupting: *I don't want to obtrude* ***upon/on*** *her privacy.*

obtrusive /əbˈtruː.sɪv/ **adj** too noticeable: *The logo was still visible but less obtrusive this time in beige.* ◦ *The soldiers were in civilian clothes, to make their presence less obtrusive.* → Opposite **unobtrusive** • **obtrusively** /-li/ **adv** • **obtrusiveness** /-nəs/ **noun** [U]

obtuse /əbˈtjuːs/ (US) /ɑːbˈtuːs/ **adj** **ANGLE** ▷ **1** specialized (of an angle) more than 90° and less than 180° → Compare **acute, reflex** **STUPID** ▷ **2** formal stupid and slow to understand, or unwilling to try to understand: *Surely the answer's obvious – or are you being deliberately obtuse?* • **obtusely** /-li/ **adv** formal • **obtuseness** /-nəs/ **noun** [U] formal

O

obverse /ˈɒb.vɜːs/ US /ɑːbˈvɝːs/ **noun** [U] formal **1** the other side of something: *False humility and its obverse, arrogance, are equally unpleasant.* ◦ *Of course, **the** obverse **of** the theory may also be true.* → Synonym **opposite** **2 the obverse** specialized the front side of a coin which has the main picture on it

obviate /ˈɒb.vi.eɪt/ US /ˈɑːb-/ **verb** [T] formal to remove a difficulty, especially so that action to deal with it becomes unnecessary: *A peaceful solution would obviate **the need** to send a UN military force.*

obvious /ˈɒb.vi.əs/ US /ˈɑːb-/ **adj** B1 easy to see, recognize, or understand: [+ (that)] ***It's** obvious **(that)** she doesn't like him.* ◦ *They have a small child so **for** obvious **reasons** they need money.* ◦ *I know you don't like her, but do you have to **make** it so obvious?* ◦ *Am I **stating the** obvious (= saying what everyone already knows)?* ◦ *There is no obvious **solution**.*

> **Other ways of saying obvious**
>
> **Clear**, **apparent**, and **plain** are common alternatives to 'obvious':
>
> *It was **clear** that he was unhappy.*
> *Her joy was **apparent** to everyone.*
> *His disappointment was **plain** to see.*
>
> A more formal way of saying 'obvious' is by using the words **evident** or **manifest**:
>
> *The company president was impressed by her **evident** ambition.*
> *His **manifest** lack of interest has provoked severe criticism.*
>
> An obvious change can be described as **marked**:
>
> *There has been a **marked** improvement in his behaviour.*
>
> If someone or something is very different from everything or everyone else, you can describe them as **conspicuous**:
>
> *I felt very **conspicuous** in a suit when everyone else was in jeans.*
>
> When something is very obvious and bad, you can describe it as **blatant** or **glaring**:
>
> *It was a **blatant** attempt to gain publicity.*
> *They made some **glaring** errors.*

obviously /ˈɒb.vi.əs.li/ US /ˈɑːb-/ **adv** B1 in a way that is easy to understand or see: *He was in tears and obviously very upset.* ◦ *Obviously the school cannot function without teachers.*

> **Common mistake: occasion**
>
> **Remember:** the most usual preposition to use with **occasion** is **on.**
>
> Don't say 'in/at an occasion', say **on an occasion:**
>
> ~~*I have met him in several occasions.*~~
> *I have met him on several occasions.*

occasion /əˈkeɪ.ʒən/ **noun; verb**

▸**noun** [C] **1** B2 a particular time, especially when something happens or has happened: *We met on several occasions to discuss the issue.* ◦ *I've heard him be rude to her on a number of occasions.* ◦ *I seem to remember that **on** that occasion he was with his wife.* **2** B1 a special or formal event: *Sara's party was **quite an** occasion – there were over a hundred people there.* ◦ *At the wedding he sang a song specially written **for** the occasion.* ◦ *I have a suit but I only wear it **on special** occasions.* ◦ *The coronation of a new king is, of course, a **historic** occasion.* ◦ *Congratulations **on the** occasion **of** your wedding anniversary.* **3** formal an opportunity or reason for doing something or for something to happen: *The 200th anniversary of Mozart's death was the occasion **for** hundreds of special films, books and concerts.* ◦ *An occasion may **arise** when you can use your knowledge of French.* ◦ *The bride **took/used** the occasion to make a short speech.* **4 on occasion** C2 sometimes, but not often: *He has, on occasion, made a small mistake.*

IDIOM **have occasion to do sth** formal to need to do something: *Of course, as a teacher I had authority, but rarely did I have occasion to use it.*

▸**verb** [T] formal to cause something: *Her refusal occasioned a lot of trouble.* ◦ [+ two objects] *The case occasioned the authorities a lot of worry/The authorities were occasioned a lot of worry **by** the case.*

occasional /əˈkeɪ.ʒən.əl/, /-ˈkeɪʒ.nəl/ **adj** C1 not happening or done often or regularly: *I play the occasional game of football.* ◦ *He has the occasional cigar after dinner.*

occasionally /əˈkeɪ.ʒən.əl.i/, /-ˈkeɪʒ.nəl-/ **adv** B2 sometimes but not often: *I see him occasionally in town.*

the Occident /ˈɒk.sɪ.dənt/ US /ˈɑːk.sə-/ **noun** formal the western part of the world, especially the countries of Europe and America → Compare **the Orient** • **occidental** /ˌɒk.sɪˈden.təl/ US /ˌɑːk.səˈden.t̬əl/ **adj** *occidental cultures* → Compare **oriental (the Orient)**

occlude /əˈkluːd/ **verb** [T] specialized to block something: *Veins can get occluded by blood clots.*

occlusion /əˈkluː.ʒən/ **noun** specialized BLOCK ▷ **1** [C or U] in medicine, something that blocks a tube or opening in the body, or when something is blocked or closed TEETH ▷ **2** [U] in DENTISTRY, the way in which your upper and lower teeth meet WEATHER ▷ **3** [C] (also **occluded front**) a situation in the weather when two masses of air meet, especially when a mass of cold air reaches warm air and pushes the warm air up off the Earth's surface

occult /əˈkʌlt/ /ˈɒk.ʌlt/ US /ˈɑː.kʌlt/ **adj; noun**

▸**adj** relating to magical powers and activities, such as those of WITCHCRAFT and ASTROLOGY: *She claims to have occult **powers**, given to her by some mysterious spirit.*

▸**noun the occult** [S] the study of magic or mysterious powers

occupancy /ˈɒk.jʊ.pən.si/ US /ˈɑː.kjə-/ **noun** [U] formal **1** someone's use of a room or building for the purposes of living or working: *The family's occupancy of the apartment lasted only six months.* **2** the number of things, such as hotel rooms, that are being used, in relation to the total number available: *Average occupancy at Florida hospitals is now 49 percent.*

occupant /ˈɒk.jʊ.pənt/ US /ˈɑː.kjə-/ **noun** [C] formal **1** a person who lives or works in a room or building: *The previous occupants were an Italian family.* **2** a person who is in a car, room, seat, place, or position: *One of the occupants of the car was slightly injured.*

occupation /ˌɒk.jʊˈpeɪ.ʃən/ US /ˌɑː.kjə-/ **noun** JOB ▷ **1** A2 [C] a person's job: *In the space marked 'occupation' she wrote 'police officer'.* ACTIVITY ▷ **2** C1 [C] a regular activity or hobby: *It seems to me his favourite occupation is eating.* CONTROL ▷ **3** C2 [U] a situation in which an army or group of people moves into and takes control of a place: *the Italian occupation **of** Ethiopia*

occupational /ˌɒk.jʊˈpeɪ.ʃən.əl/ US /ˌɑː.kjə-/ **adj** [before noun] relating to or caused by your job: *Back problems are an occupational **hazard** (= a risk that you take in a job) for any desk-bound office worker.* ◦ *an occupational **disease***

occuˌpational ˈtherapy **noun** [U] a way of treating mentally or physically ill people by getting them to do special activities • occu̦pational ˈtherapist noun [C]

occupied /ˈɒk.jʊ.paɪd/ (US) /ˈɑː.kjʊ-/ **adj** describes a place that is being controlled by an army or group of people that has moved into it: *occupied territory* ◦ *She spent two years in occupied Paris (= Paris when it was under foreign control) during the war.*

occupier /ˈɒk.jʊ.paɪ.əʳ/ (US) /ˈɑː.kjə.paɪ.ɚ/ noun LIVING ▷ **1** [C] UK someone who lives or works in a particular room, building, or piece of land, or someone who is using it: *The envelope was simply addressed to 'The Occupier'.* CONTROLLING ▷ **2** [C usually plural] someone who has moved into a place and taken control of it: *The occupiers were driven out after fierce street fighting.*

occupy /ˈɒk.jʊ.paɪ/ (US) /ˈɑː.kjʊ-/ verb [T] FILL ▷ **1** (B2) to fill, exist in, or use a place or period of time: *The bathroom's occupied – I think John's in there.* ◦ *The rest of the time was occupied **with** writing a report.* ◦ *The house hasn't been occupied (= lived in) **by** anyone for a few months.* ◦ formal *A large picture of the battle of Waterloo occupied the space above the fireplace.* **2** (B2) to keep someone busy or interested: *On long car journeys I occupy my**self** with solving maths puzzles.* ◦ *All the new toys **kept** the kids occupied for hours.* TAKE CONTROL ▷ **3** (C1) (of an army or group of people) to move into and take control and/or possession of a place: *Troops quickly occupied the city.* ◦ *Protesting students occupied the university office for two weeks.* ◦ *the occupying forces*

occur /əˈkɜːʳ/ (US) /-ˈkɝː/ verb (-rr-) HAPPEN ▷ **1** (B2) [I] (especially of accidents and other unexpected events) to happen: *An accident involving over ten vehicles has occurred in the east-bound lane.* ◦ *If any of these symptoms occur while you are taking the medicine, consult your doctor immediately.* EXIST ▷ **2** [I + adv/prep] to exist or be present in, among, etc.: *Violence of some sort seems to occur in every society.* ◦ *Minerals occur naturally in the Earth's crust.*

> **! Common mistake: occur**
>
> **Warning:** Check your verb endings!
> Many learners make mistakes when using **occur** in the past tense.The past simple and past participle have 'rr'. Don't write 'occured', write occurred.The **-ing** form is occurring.

PHRASAL VERB **occur to sb** If a thought or idea occurs to you, it comes into your mind: *The thought did occur to me.* ◦ [+ that] ***It** never even occurred to us **that** he hadn't been invited.* ◦ *Does **it** never occur to you **that** I might like to be on my own occasionally?*

occurrence /əˈkʌr.ənts/ (US) /-ˈkɝː-/ noun HAPPENING ▷ **1** (C1) [C] something that happens: *Street-fights are an **everyday** occurrence in this area of the city.* EXISTING ▷ **2** (C1) [U] the fact of something existing, or how much of it exists: *The study compares the occurrence of heart disease in various countries.*

ocean /ˈəʊ.ʃən/ (US) /ˈoʊ-/ noun **1** (A2) [S] a very large area of sea: *These mysterious creatures live at the bottom of **the** ocean.* **2** [C] used in the name of each of the world's five main areas of sea: *the Atlantic/Pacific/Indian/Arctic/Antarctic Ocean*

IDIOM **oceans of sth** old-fashioned a lot of something: *We've got oceans of time.*

ˈocean-ˌgoing adj (also **seagoing**) (of a ship, boat, etc.) designed for travelling across large areas of sea: *an ocean-going vessel*

Oceania /əʊ.ʃiˈɑː.ni.ə/ (US) /oʊ-/ noun the region of the world that consists of the islands of the Pacific Ocean and the seas around them

oceanic /ˌəʊ.ʃiˈæn.ɪk/ (US) /ˌoʊ-/ adj specialized relating to oceans: *oceanic crust/plates*

oceanography /ˌəʊ.ʃəˈnɒg.rə.fi/ (US) /ˌoʊ.ʃəˈnɑː.grə-/ noun [U] the scientific study of the sea

ochre (US also **ocher**) /ˈəʊ.kəʳ/ (US) /ˈoʊ.kɚ/ noun [U] a yellowish-orange colour, or a substance obtained from the Earth that is used for giving this colour to paints • **ochre** adj having a yellowish-orange colour

ocker (also **okker**) /ˈɒk.əʳ/ (US) /ˈɑː.kɚ/ noun [C] Australian English informal an Australian who is not well educated and does not behave in a polite way

o'clock /əˈklɒk/ (US) /-ˈklɑːk/ adv (A1) used after a number from one to twelve to say the time when it is exactly that hour: *It's two o'clock.* ◦ *He rang me at four o'clock in the morning.*

OCR /ˌəʊ.siːˈɑːʳ/ (US) /ˌoʊ.siːˈɑːr/ noun [U] abbreviation for optical character recognition: the process by which an electronic device recognizes printed or written letters or numbers

octagon /ˈɒk.tə.gən/ (US) /ˈɑː.k.tə.gɑːn/ noun [C] a flat shape with eight sides • **octagonal** /ɒkˈtæg.ən.əl/ (US) /ɑːk-/ adj *an octagonal (= with eight sides) tower*

octahedron /ˌɒk.təˈhiː.drən/ (US) /ˌɑːk-/ noun [C] (plural **octahedrons** or **octahedra** /-drə/) specialized a solid shape whose eight sides are triangles of equal size

octane /ˈɒk.teɪn/ (US) /ˈɑːk-/ noun [U] a chemical in petrol

-octane /-ɒk.teɪn/ (US) /-ɑːk-/ suffix having the stated quality in relation to power or (of petrol, etc.) octane number: *Racing cars use a **high**-octane (= powerful) fuel.*

ˈoctane ˌnumber noun [C] (also **ˈoctane ˌrating**) a number showing the quality of petrol by representing how well and with how much power it can make an engine work

octave /ˈɒk.tɪv/ (US) /ˈɑːk-/ noun [C] specialized the distance between two musical notes that are eight notes apart: *Her remarkable vocal range spanned three and a half octaves.*

octet /ɒkˈtet/ (US) /ɑːk-/ noun **1** [C, + sing/pl verb] a group of eight singers or musicians performing together **2** [C] a piece of music written for eight people

October /ɒkˈtəʊ.bəʳ/ (US) /ɑːkˈtoʊ.bɚ/ noun [C or U] (written abbreviation **Oct.**) (A1) the tenth month of the year, after September and before November: *We have an open evening **in** October which you are welcome to attend.* ◦ *Hallowe'en is **on** 31 October.* ◦ *We're going to Madrid **next** October.*

octogenarian /ˌɒk.təʊ.dʒəˈneə.ri.ən/ (US) /ˌɑːk.toʊ.dʒɪˈner.i-/ noun [C] a person who is between 80 and 89 years old

octopus

octopus /ˈɒk.tə.pəs/ (US) /ˈɑːk-/ noun [C] a sea creature with a soft, oval body and eight TENTACLES (= long parts like arms)

octroi /ˈɒk.trwɑː/ (US) /ˈɑːk.trɔɪ/ noun [U] (in some countries) tax that you pay on goods when you bring them into a particular local area

ocular /ˈɒk.jʊ.ləʳ/ (US) /ˈɑː.kjə.lɚ/ adj specialized

O

of or related to the eyes or sight

oculist /ˈɒk.jʊ.lɪst/ (US) /ˈɑː.kjə-/ **noun** [C] old-fashioned for **ophthalmologist**

OD /ˌəʊˈdiː/ (US) /ˌoʊ-/ **verb** [I] (present tense **OD's**, present participle **OD'ing**, past tense and past participle **OD'd**) **1** slang to take an OVERDOSE (= too much) of a drug: *She OD'd* ***on*** *heroin and died.* **2** informal humorous to have too much of something, often food: *Nothing more for me, thanks. I think I OD'd* ***on*** *chocolate cake.* • **OD noun** [C] (plural **OD's**) mainly US slang

odd /ɒd/ (US) /ɑːd/ **adj** STRANGE ▷ **1** B2 strange or unexpected: *Her father was an odd man.* ◦ *What an odd thing to say.* ◦ *The skirt and jacket looked a bit odd together.* ◦ *That's odd – I'm sure I put my keys in this drawer and yet they're not here.* ◦ ***It's*** *odd* ***that*** *no one's seen him.* ◦ ***It*** *must be odd* ***to*** *live on the 43rd floor.* NOT OFTEN ▷ **2** C2 [before noun] not happening often: *She does* ***the*** *odd teaching* ***job*** *but nothing permanent.* ◦ *You get* ***the*** *odd person who's rude to you but they're generally quite helpful.* NUMBERS ▷ **3** (of numbers) not able to be divided exactly by two: *3, 5, and 7 are all odd numbers.* ◦ *The houses on this side of the street have all got odd numbers.* → Opposite **even** SEPARATED ▷ **4** [before noun] (of something that should be in a pair or set) separated from its pair or set: *He's got a whole drawer full of odd socks.* ◦ *I'd got a few odd (= I had various) balls of wool left over.*

IDIOM **the odd one out** (also **the odd man out**) a person or thing that is different from or kept apart from others that form a group or set: *Guess which number of the following sequence is the odd one out.* ◦ *She was always the odd one out at school – she didn't have many friends.*

-odd /-ɒd/ (US) /-ɑːd/ **suffix** informal used after a number, especially a number that can be divided by ten, to show that the exact number is not known: *I'd say Robert's about 40-odd – maybe 45.*

oddball /ˈɒd.bɔːl/ (US) /ˈɑːd.bɑːl/ **noun** [C] informal a person whose behaviour is unusual and strange • **oddball adj** [before noun] *The oddball superstar's habits include watching TV with his chimpanzee.*

oddity /ˈɒd.ɪ.ti/ (US) /ˈɑː.də.t̬i/ **noun** [C] someone or something that is strange and unusual: *Even today a man who stays at home to look after the children is regarded as something of an oddity.*

ˌodd-ˈjob man noun [C] (also **ˌodd-ˈjobber**) a man who is paid to do different types of jobs, especially in the house or garden

oddly /ˈɒd.li/ (US) /ˈɑːd-/ **adv** C2 in a strange or surprising way: *Didn't you think she was behaving rather oddly at the party yesterday?* ◦ *Oddly* ***enough*** *(= this is strange/surprising), she didn't mention anything about the fact that she was getting married.*

oddments /ˈɒd.mənts/ (US) /ˈɑːd-/ **noun** [plural] mainly UK small pieces, usually of cloth, that have been cut from larger pieces: *a few oddments* ***of*** *fabric*

oddness /ˈɒd.nəs/ (US) /ˈɑːd-/ **noun** [U] the quality of being strange or unexpected

odds /ɒdz/ (US) /ɑːdz/ **noun** [plural] **1** C1 the PROBABILITY (= how likely it is) that a particular thing will or will not happen: *If you drive a car all your life, the odds* ***are*** *that you'll have an accident at some point.* ◦ *There are heavy odds* ***against*** *people succeeding in such a bad economic climate.* ◦ *What are the odds* ***on*** *him being (= do you think he will be) re-elected?* ◦ *The odds* ***are stacked against*** *a woman succeeding (= it is not likely that a woman will succeed) in the business.* **2** in GAMBLING (= the activity of risking money guessing the result of something), a PROBABILITY expressed as a number: *The odds* ***against*** *my horse winning (= that it will not win)/****on*** *my horse winning (= that it will win) are a hundred to one.* ◦ *The odds* ***that*** *the US entrant will win the race are ten to one.*

IDIOMS **against (all) the odds/against all odds** C2 If you do or achieve something against (all) the odds/against all odds, you do or achieve it although there were a lot of problems and you were not likely to succeed: *Against all the odds, he recovered.* • **be at odds** C2 to disagree: *They're at odds* ***over*** *the funding of the project.* ◦ *Her version of events was at odds* ***with*** *(= very different from) the police report.* • **make no odds** mainly UK informal to not be important, or to not change a situation or result: *I don't mind whether you come or not – it makes no odds* ***to*** *me.* • **over the odds** UK informal more than something is really worth: *It's a nice enough car but I'm sure she paid over the odds for it.*

ˌodds and ˈends noun [plural] (UK informal **ˌodds and ˈsods**) C2 various things of different types, usually small and not important, or of little value: *I've taken most of the big things to the new house, but there are a few odds and ends left to collect.*

ˌodds-ˈon adj very probable: *It's odds-on she'll be late and I've rushed for no reason!* ◦ *The odds-on* ***favourite*** *to win in the 3.30 race is Killjoy.*

ode /əʊd/ (US) /oʊd/ **noun** [C] a poem expressing the writer's thoughts and feelings about a particular person or subject, usually written to that person or subject: *'Ode* ***to*** *a Nightingale' and 'Ode* ***on*** *a Grecian Urn' are poems by Keats.*

odious /ˈəʊ.di.əs/ (US) /ˈoʊ-/ **adj** formal extremely unpleasant and causing or deserving hate: *an odious crime* ◦ *an odious little man*

odium /ˈəʊ.di.əm/ (US) /ˈoʊ-/ **noun** [U] formal hate and strong disapproval

odometer /əʊˈdɒm.ɪ.tər/ (US) /oʊˈdɑː.mə.t̬ɚ/ **noun** [C] mainly US for **milometer**

odour UK formal (US **odor**) /ˈəʊ.dər/ (US) /ˈoʊ.dɚ/ **noun** [C or U] C2 a smell, often one that is unpleasant: *Inside the room there was the unmistakable odour* ***of*** *sweaty feet.* ◦ figurative *The odour* ***of*** *hypocrisy hung about everything she said.*

odourless UK formal (US **odorless**) /ˈəʊ.də.ləs/ (US) /ˈoʊ.dɚ-/ **adj** without a smell: *an odourless gas*

odyssey /ˈɒd.ɪ.si/ (US) /ˈɑː.dɪ-/ **noun** [C usually singular] literary a long exciting journey: *The film follows one man's odyssey to find the mother from whom he was separated at birth.* ◦ figurative *a spiritual odyssey*

oedema /ɪˈdiː.mə/ **noun** [U] UK (US **edema**) an unhealthy condition in which liquid collects in the body tissues between the cells

Oedipal /ˈiː.dɪ.pəl/ (US) /ˈe-/ **adj** belonging or relating to an Oedipus complex: *Freud argued that all people go through an Oedipal* ***phase*** *of sexual development.* ◦ *Oedipal fantasies*

Oedipus complex /ˌiː.dɪ.pəsˈkɒm.pleks/ (US) /-ˈkɑːm-/ **noun** [C usually singular] in PSYCHOLOGY (= the study of the human mind), a child's sexual DESIRE for their parent of the opposite sex, especially that of a boy for his mother

oenophile /ˈiː.nə.faɪl/ **noun** [C] specialized a person who loves wine and knows a lot about it

o'er /əʊər/ (US) /ɔːr/ **preposition** literary over: *O'er land and sea they sped.*

oesophagus (plural **oesophagi** or **oesophaguses**) UK specialized (US **esophagus**) /ɪˈsɒf.ə.gəs/ (US) /ɪˈsɑː.fə-/

noun [C] the tube in the body which takes food from the mouth to the stomach

oestrogen (mainly US **estrogen**) /ˈiː.strə.dʒən/ (US) /ˈes.trə-/ **noun** [U] a female HORMONE that causes development and change in the REPRODUCTIVE organs (= organs involved in producing babies)

oeuvre /ˈɜː.vrə/ **noun** [C usually singular] literary the complete works of a writer, painter, or other artist: *Sadly, I'm not familiar with his oeuvre.*

of weak /əv/ strong /ɒv/ (US) /ɑːv/ **preposition** **POSSESSION** ▷ **1** (A1) used to show possession, belonging, or origin: *a friend of mine* ◦ *the president of the United States* ◦ *employees of the company* ◦ *the colour of his hair* ◦ *a habit of mine* ◦ *that revolting dog of hers* ◦ *the love of a good woman* ◦ *the complete plays of (= written by) Lorca* **AMOUNT** ▷ **2** (A1) used after words or phrases expressing amount, number, or a particular unit: *a kilo of apples* ◦ *loads of food* ◦ *hundreds of people* ◦ *most of them* ◦ *none of them* ◦ *both of us* ◦ *a third of all people* ◦ *a speck of dust* ◦ *a drop of rain* **CONTAINING** ▷ **3** (A1) containing: *a bag of sweets* ◦ *a bottle of beer* ◦ *a book of short stories* ◦ *sacks of rubbish* ◦ *a class of idiots* **POSITION** ▷ **4** (A2) used in expressions showing position: *the top of his head* ◦ *the back of your dress* ◦ *on the corner of the street* ◦ *the front of the queue* ◦ *I've never been north of Edinburgh.* **TYPICAL** ▷ **5** typical or characteristic of: *She has the face of an angel.* ◦ *That man's got the brain of a donkey!* **DAYS** ▷ **6** (A1) used to refer to a particular date in a month: *the eleventh of March* ◦ *the first of the month* **MADE OF** ▷ **7** made or consisting of; having: *dresses of lace and silk* ◦ *plates of gold and silver* ◦ *a land of ice and snow* ◦ *a woman of great charm* ◦ *a subject of very little interest* **WITH ADJECTIVES/VERBS** ▷ **8** used to connect particular adjectives and verbs with nouns: *fond of swimming* ◦ *sick of his excuses* ◦ *frightened of spiders* **JUDGMENT** ▷ **9** (B2) used after an adjective when judging someone's behaviour: *It was a bit unkind of you* ***to*** *mention her weight.* **RELATING TO** ▷ **10** (C1) about; relating to: *Speaking of Elizabeth, here she is.* ◦ *One of the advantages of travelling by train is being able to read.* ◦ *Let us consider the events of the last five months.* ◦ *Of her childhood we know very little.* ◦ *And what of (= tell me about) young Adrian? How is he?* **THAT IS/ARE** ▷ **11** that is/are: *the problem of homelessness* ◦ *a rise of two percent in inflation* ◦ *the skill of negotiating* ◦ *the difficulty of bringing up twins* ◦ *the pain of separation* ◦ *At the age of six she could read a newspaper.* **DONE TO** ▷ **12** done to: *the massacre of hundreds of innocent people* ◦ *the oppression of a nation* ◦ *the destruction of the rain forest* **FELT BY** ▷ **13** felt or experienced by: *the suffering of millions* ◦ *the anguish of the murdered child's parents* **THROUGH** ▷ **14** (B1) through; having as the cause: *He died of cancer.* ◦ *I didn't have to go there – I did it of my own free will.* **COMPARING** ▷ **15** (A2) used when comparing related things: *I liked the green one best of all.* ◦ *He's the best looking of the three brothers.* ◦ *I think that of all his films it's my favourite.* **TIME** ▷ **16** US used in saying what the time is: *It's ten (minutes) of five (= ten minutes before five o'clock).* **SEPARATE FROM** ▷ **17** used in expressions showing distance from something in place or time: *We live within a mile of the city centre.* ◦ *She came within two seconds of beating the world record.* **LOSS** ▷ **18** used in expressions showing loss: *They were robbed of all their savings.* ◦ *I feel I've been deprived of your company.* **DURING** ▷ **19** old-fashioned during: *I like to relax with a pipe of an evening.*

IDIOM **of all people/things/places** used to express the idea that a particular person/thing/place is unlikely or surprising: *Stella, of all people, is the last one I'd expect to see at the club.* ◦ *And why did you choose Iceland for a holiday, of all places?*

off /ɒf/ (US) /ɑːf/ **adv; preposition; adj; noun; verb**

▸**adv** **AWAY FROM** ▷ **1** (B1) away from a place or position, especially the present place, position, or time: *He drove off at the most incredible speed.* ◦ *Keep the dog on the lead or he'll just run off.* ◦ *Someone's run off with (= taken) my pen.* ◦ *I'm just going off to the shops.* ◦ *If we can get off (= leave) early tomorrow morning we'll avoid most of the traffic.* ◦ *I'm off now – see you tomorrow.* ◦ *She's off* ***to*** *Canada next week.* ◦ *I saw her off (= said goodbye) at the station.* ◦ *The exams are so* ***far*** *off that I'm not even thinking about them yet.* **REMOVED** ▷ **2** (A2) used with actions in which something is removed or removes itself from another thing: *Take your jacket off.* ◦ *One of my buttons has come off.* ◦ *She's had all her hair cut off.* **NOT OPERATING** ▷ **3** (A2) (especially of machines, electrical devices, lights, etc.) not operating because of not being switched on: *Make sure the computers are all off before you go home.* ◦ ***Turn/Switch*** *the light/engine/television off.* **LESS MONEY** ▷ **4** (B1) (of money) taken away from the original price: *You can get some money off if you pay cash.* ◦ *There's 40 percent off this week on all winter coats.* ◦ *There was $40 or $50 off most jackets in the store.* **NOT AT WORK** ▷ **5** (A2) not at work; at home or on holiday: *I'm going to* ***take/have*** *some time off to work on my house.* ◦ *She was off* ***sick*** *last week.* ◦ *He's off at the moment – can I get him to ring you back?* **SEPARATED** ▷ **6** in such a way as to be separated: *The police have* ***shut/closed*** *off all streets leading to the city.* ◦ *The area in the park where the kids play is fenced off for safety reasons.* **COMPLETELY** ▷ **7** in such a way as to be completely absent, especially because of having been used or killed: *It says on the bottle that it* ***kills*** *off all known germs.* ◦ *It'll take some time before she manages to* ***pay*** *off all her debts.* ◦ *The good thing about exercise is that it burns off calories.* ◦ *Between us we managed to* ***finish*** *off eight bottles of wine.* **GET RID OF** ▷ **8** in such a way as to get rid of something: *We went out for a while to* ***walk*** *off some of our dinner.* ◦ *He's gone to* ***sleep*** *off a headache.* ◦ *There's no point in getting upset about such remarks – you've just got to laugh them off.*

IDIOMS **be/go off on one** informal to suddenly start talking or shouting in an angry way: *He went off on one and started accusing me of stealing his girlfriend.* • **off with sth** used as a way of ordering someone to remove something: *Off with his head!* ◦ *Off with your jacket!*

▸**preposition** **AWAY FROM** ▷ **1** (B1) down or away from a place, position, or time, especially the present place, position, or time: *There was a 'Keep off the grass' sign.* ◦ *All the berries had dropped off the tree.* ◦ *He fell off his bike.* ◦ *We're still a long way off our target of £30,000.* ◦ *I hope she knows where to get off (= leave) the bus/train.* ◦ *How far off finishing the project are we? (= How much more is there to do?)* ◦ *We've been working on the flat for six months now but we're still* ***a long way*** *off finish****ing****.* ◦ *We're not far off (= we are quite near) London now.* **REMOVED** ▷ **2** (B1) used with actions in which something is removed or removes itself from another thing: *I can't get the lid off this jar.* ◦ *Has anyone taken a book off my desk?* ◦ *Could you cut me a small piece off that big white cheese?* ◦ *Take your feet off that seat, young man!* ◦ *I don't like taking money off you (= asking you for money)!* ◦ *Get off me! (= Stop touching me!)* ◦ not standard *I got the knife off of him before he ran away.* **NOT LIKING** ▷ **3** not liking or taking something or someone: *He's been off his food*

O

ever since he had the stomach upset. ◦ *I used to love coffee but I've* ***gone*** *off it (= stopped liking it) recently.* ◦ *She's well enough to be off the medicine now.* ◦ *The doctor says he can* ***come*** *off the tablets.* ◦ *She's been off drugs for a year now.* **NEAR TO** ▷ **4** B2 near to: *He lives* ***just*** *off the main road.* ◦ *It's an island off the east coast of Spain.*

▸adj **BAD** ▷ **1** B2 [after verb] (of food and drink) no longer fresh or good to eat or drink because of being too old: *This milk smells off.* ◦ *I'd better eat this cheese before it* ***goes*** *off.* **STOPPED** ▷ **2** C2 [after verb] (of an arranged event) stopped or given up: *The wedding's off – she's decided she's too young to settle down.* ◦ informal *It's all off (= the relationship is finished) between Philippa and Mike.* **PROVIDED FOR** ▷ **3** having a particular amount or number, especially of money: UK *How are you off* ***for*** *money? (= Have you got enough?)* ◦ *Andrew must be so* ***well****-off (= rich) by now.* ◦ *I think they're fairly* ***badly****-off (= poor) now that David has lost his job.* ◦ *I'm quite* ***well*** *off* ***for*** *(= have a lot of) sweaters.* **BELOW USUAL LEVEL** ▷ **4** below the usual standard or rate: *I'm having an off* ***day*** *today – I just can't seem to do anything right!* **NO LONGER SERVED** ▷ **5** [after verb] (of food in a restaurant) not available at that particular time: *I'm sorry, sir, the salmon is off.* **RUDE** ▷ **6** [after verb] mainly UK informal not thinking or worrying about other people's feelings; rude: *He didn't even ring her up on her birthday – I thought that was* ***a bit*** *off.*

▸noun [S] UK informal **the off** the act of leaving somewhere: *Are we* ***ready for*** *the off, then?*

▸verb [T] US slang to kill someone: *They offed him and dumped his body in the swamp.*

offal /ˈɒf.əl/ US /ˈɑː.fəl/ noun [U] (mainly US **vaˈriety ˌmeat**) the organs inside an animal, such as the brain, the heart, and the LIVER, eaten as food

ˌoff ˈbalance adj [after verb], adv **1** If someone or something is off balance, they are in a position where they are likely to fall or be knocked down: *A gust of wind* ***knocked/threw*** *her off balance and she fell.* **2** confused or uncertain about what to do next: *Many Republicans were* ***thrown*** *off balance by the Democrats' landslide at the polls.*

ˌoff ˈbeam adj [after verb] UK informal (US **ˌoff ˈbase**) wrong: *You're (****way****) off beam there.*

offbeat /ˌɒfˈbiːt/ US /ˌɑːfˈbiːt/ adj unusual and strange and therefore surprising or noticeable: *an offbeat sense of humour*

ˌoff-ˈcentre adj [after verb] UK (US **ˌoff-ˈcenter**) nearly, but not quite, in a central position

ˈoff ˌchance noun UK informal **on the off chance** hoping that something may be possible, although it is not likely: *I applied for the job on the off chance, but I didn't seriously expect to get it.*

ˌoff-ˈcolour UK (US **off-color**) adj **ILL** ▷ **1** [after verb] informal slightly ill: *I'm feeling a bit off-colour today.* **SEXUAL** ▷ **2** describes remarks or jokes about sex that are slightly shocking

ˌoff-ˈduty adj B2 When police officers, doctors, guards, etc. are off-duty, they are not working: *He looks completely different when he's off-duty and in his normal clothes.*

offence (US usually **offense**) /əˈfens/ noun **CRIME** ▷ **1** B2 [C] an illegal act; a crime: *a serious/minor offence* ◦ *a criminal/drink-driving offence* ◦ *Driving without a licence is an offence.* ◦ *He* ***committed*** *several serious offences.* ◦ *It's the third time that he's been* ***convicted of*** *a drug offence.* **UPSET FEELINGS** ▷ **2** B2 [U] upset and hurt or annoyed feelings, often because someone has been rude or shown no respect: *I really didn't mean (to* ***cause/give****) any offence (= did not intend to upset anyone) – I was just stating my opinion.* ◦ *Do you think he* ***took*** *offence (= was upset) at what I said about his hair?* ◦ informal *If you don't mind, I'd rather go on my own –* ***no*** *offence (intended), but I think it would be better.*

> **Word partners for offence (CRIME)**
>
> *commit* an offence • be *charged with/convicted of/ prosecuted for* an offence • a *lesser/minor/serious* offence • an offence *against* sb • the offence *of* sth

> **Word partners for offence (UPSET FEELINGS)**
>
> *take* offence (at sth) • *cause/give* offence (to sb) • *intend/mean* no offence • *grave* offence

offend /əˈfend/ verb **UPSET** ▷ **1** B2 [T] to make someone upset or angry: [+ that] *I think she was a bit offended* ***that*** *she hadn't been invited to the party.* ◦ *He looked a bit offended when you called him middle-aged.* ◦ *If the sight of a few dirty dishes offends you, then I think you've got problems!* **COMMIT CRIME** ▷ **2** [I] legal to commit a crime: *Obviously if a police officer offends it's a fairly serious matter.*

PHRASAL VERB **offend against sth** formal to break a rule or principle or not fit well with something that people consider to be correct: *Do you suppose it would be offending against good taste to wear a patterned tie with my striped shirt?*

offender /əˈfen.dər/ US /-dɚ/ noun [C] legal B2 a person who is guilty of a crime: *first-time offenders* ◦ ***sex*** *offenders* ◦ *young offenders*

ofˌfender ˈprofile noun [C] specialized a **psychological profile**

offending /əˈfen.dɪŋ/ adj [before noun] often humorous unwanted, often because unpleasant and causing problems: *'There's a hair in my soup!' 'Well, pass it over here and I'll remove the offending* ***article****.'*

offense /əˈfens/ noun **1** [C or U] US spelling of **offence** **2** [U] US the part of a game such as American football that involves trying to score points, or the players who try to score points

offensive /əˈfen.sɪv/ adj; noun

▸adj **UPSETTING** ▷ **1** B2 causing offence: *This programme contains language that some viewers might find offensive.* ◦ *He told some really offensive sexist jokes.* → Opposite **inoffensive** **2** unpleasant: *offensive smells* **ATTACKING** ▷ **3** used for attacking: *Since the other side had taken offensive action (= attacked), we had no choice but to defend ourselves.* ◦ *Knives of any sort are classed as offensive* ***weapons****.* • **offensively** /-li/ adv • **offensiveness** /-nəs/ noun [U]

▸noun [C] **1** a planned military attack: *They* ***launched*** *the land offensive in the middle of the night.* ◦ *UN troops have gone* ***on the*** *offensive (= started to attack).* **2 take the offensive** to attack first

offer /ˈɒf.ər/ US /ˈɑː.fɚ/ verb; noun

▸verb **AGREE TO GIVE** ▷ **1** A2 [I or T] to ask someone if they would like to have something or if they would like you to do something: [+ two objects] *I feel bad that I didn't offer them any food/offer any food* ***to*** *them.* ◦ *She was offered a job in Paris.* ◦ *Can I offer you (= would you like) a drink?* ◦ *'Would you sell me that painting?' 'What are you offering (= what will you pay)* ***for*** *it?'* ◦ [+ to infinitive] *My father's offered* ***to*** *take us to the airport.* ◦ [+ speech] *'I'll do the cooking,' he offered.* ◦ *'I could help.' 'No, it's all right, thanks.' 'Well, don't say I didn't offer.'* **2** [T] (also **offer up**) to say a prayer or make a SACRIFICE (= an act of killing or giving up

something) to a god: *Dear Lord, we offer up our prayers...* **PROVIDE** ▷ **3** B1 [T] to provide or supply something: *It's an organization that offers free legal advice to people on low incomes.* ◦ *It says in the guide that this area of the countryside offers some of the best walks in England.* ◦ [+ two objects] *We are now offering you the chance to buy the complete set of pans at half price.* ◦ *Did he offer any explanation for his strange behaviour?* ◦ *It doesn't* ***have much to*** *offer as a town – its shops are fairly poor and there's only one cinema.*
▸**noun** [C] **1** A2 the act of asking if someone would like to have something or if they would like you to do something: *'If you like I can do some shopping for you.' 'That's a very kind offer.'* ◦ *I must say the offer* ***of*** *a weekend in Barcelona quite tempts me.* ◦ informal *One day I'll* ***take*** *you* ***up on*** *(= accept) that offer.* **2 make an offer** C2 (also **put in an offer**) to say officially that you would like to buy something, especially a house, at a particular price: *They were asking £180,000 for the place, so I put in an offer of £170,000.* ◦ *I've made an offer* ***on*** *a house in the town centre.* **3** B1 a reduction in the usual price of sth, usually for a short period: *This superb offer is available until the end of the month.* **4 on offer** B2 available to be bought or used: *We were amazed at the range of products on offer.* **5 on (special) offer** B1 UK If goods in a shop are on (special) offer, they are being sold at a lower price than usual. **6 under offer** UK If a house is under offer, someone has already suggested a particular price at which they would be willing to buy it.

> **Word partners for offer noun**
> *accept/get/make/receive/refuse/turn down* an offer • a *generous/good/tempting* offer • be *open to* offers • be *on* offer

offering /ˈɒf.ər.ɪŋ/ US /ˈɑː.fɚ-/ **noun** [C] something that you give or offer to someone: *a peace offering* ◦ *a sacrificial offering*

ˌoff-ˈgrid adj, adv → **off-the-grid**

offhand /ˌɒfˈhænd/ US /ˌɑːf-/ **adj; adv**
▸**adj** (UK informal **offish**) not friendly, and showing little interest in other people in a way that seems slightly rude: *I hope I didn't appear offhand* ***with*** *her – it's just that I was in such a hurry.* • **offhandedly** /-ˈhæn.dɪd.li/ adv • **offhandedness** /-ˈhæn.dɪd.nəs/ noun [U]
▸**adv** without looking for information and without thinking carefully; immediately: *I can't quote the exact statistics for you offhand, but they're there for you to see in the report.*

office /ˈɒf.ɪs/ US /ˈɑː.fɪs/ **noun** **WORK PLACE** ▷ **1** A2 [C] a room or part of a building in which people work, especially sitting at tables with computers, phones, etc., usually as a part of a business or other organization: *the director's office* ◦ *I didn't leave the office until eight o'clock last night.* ◦ *office equipment* ◦ *office workers* **2** [C] a part of a company: *They have offices in Paris, London, and Madrid.* **3** [C] US (UK **surgery**) a place where you can go to ask advice from or receive treatment from a doctor or dentist: *The doctor does not make house calls – you will have to come to her office.* **RESPONSIBILITY** ▷ **4** C1 [C or U] a position of authority and responsibility in a government or other organization: *the office of vice president* ◦ *As chairman of the association, he* ***held*** *office for over 20 years.* ◦ *The Socialist party has been* ***in*** *office (= governing)/****out of*** *office (= not governing) for almost ten years.* ◦ *She's held various offices during her time as a minister.*

Office /ˈɒf.ɪs/ US /ˈɑː.fɪs/ **noun** [C] a department of the national government in Britain, or an official government organization: *the Home Office* ◦ *the Foreign Office* ◦ *the Office of Fair Trading*

ˈoffice ˌbuilding noun [C] (UK also **ˈoffice ˌblock**) a large building that contains offices

ˈoffice-ˌgoer noun [C] Indian English someone who travels each day to work in an office

ˌoffice ˈhours noun [plural] **1** the hours during the day when people who work in offices are usually at work: *I'll have to do it* ***outside/out of*** *(= before or after) office hours.* ◦ *Their phone lines are only open* ***during*** *office hours.* **2** US (UK **surgery** [U]) the times during the day when you can go to see a doctor or dentist at his or her office: *Many doctors have evening office hours.*

officer /ˈɒf.ɪ.səʳ/ US /ˈɑː.fɪ.sɚ/ **noun** [C] **1** B2 a person in the armed forces who has a position of authority: *a naval officer* ◦ *a top-ranking officer* **2** B1 a person who has a position of authority in an organization: *a careers/customs/personnel officer* **3** B1 a member of the police force: *There was an incident in the High Street and two of our officers attended the scene.* ◦ *Officer Clarke* ◦ [as form of address] *'Were you aware of the speed you were driving at, madam?' 'No, officer.'*

official /əˈfɪʃ.əl/ **adj; noun**
▸**adj** **1** C2 relating to a position of responsibility: *He visited China in his official capacity as America's trade representative.* ◦ *Number Ten Downing Street is the British prime minister's official residence.* → Opposite **unofficial** **2** B2 agreed to or arranged by people in positions of authority: *The official photos of the prime minister's tour of India are in the magazine.* ◦ *The queen will attend the official opening of the theatre in June.* ◦ *There is to be an official inquiry into the incident.* **3** C2 If a piece of information is official, it has been announced publicly with authority: *Their engagement is now official.* ◦ *Inflation has fallen below two percent, and that's official.*
▸**noun** [C] C2 a person who has a position of responsibility in an organization: *a government/trade-union/council official*

officialdom /əˈfɪʃ.əl.dəm/ **noun** [U] disapproving used to refer to those people who have a position of authority, especially in government, usually when they are preventing you from doing what you want to do or are slow or not effective

officialese /əˌfɪʃ.əlˈiːz/ **noun** [U] US the type of language, often used in government documents, that is formal and often difficult to understand

officially /əˈfɪʃ.əl.i/ **adv** **1** C1 formally and in a way agreed to or arranged by people in positions of authority: *The royal engagement was announced officially this morning.* **2** as stated or accepted by people publicly but not privately or as things really are: *Well, officially I am on holiday this week but I'm just catching up on some paperwork.* **3** in or relating to a position of responsibility that you hold: *He has not visited the country officially since his election, only in a private capacity.*

ofˌficial reˈceiver noun [C] UK a person who is ordered by the government to deal with the income and property of a company or a person after they have gone BANKRUPT (= are unable to pay their debts)

ofˌficial ˈsecret noun [C] UK a piece of information that is known only by the government and its employees: *She was accused of leaking (= telling) official secrets to the newspapers.*

the Ofˌficial ˈSecrets ˌAct noun [S] a law in the UK that prevents government workers from giving out particular information that could be used against the government: *She had to **sign** the Official Secrets Act when she started her new job.*

officiate /əˈfɪʃ.i.eɪt/ verb [I] formal to be in charge of or to lead a ceremony or other public event: *A priest officiated **at** the wedding.*

officious /əˈfɪʃ.əs/ adj disapproving too eager to tell people what to do and having too high an opinion of your own importance: *He's an officious little man and widely disliked in the company.* • **officiously** /-li/ adv • **officiousness** /-nəs/ noun [U]

offie /ˈɒf.i/ (US) /ˈɑː.fi/ noun [C] UK informal an **off-licence**

offing /ˈɒf.ɪŋ/ (US) /ˈɑː.fɪŋ/ noun **in the offing** likely to happen soon: *With an election in the offing, the prime minister is keen to maintain his popularity.*

offish /ˈɒf.ɪʃ/ (US) /ˈɑː.fɪʃ/ adj **1** UK **offhand 2** US **standoffish**

ˌoff-ˈkey adv If you sing or play music off-key, you produce notes that are slightly higher or lower than they should be.

ˈoff-ˌlicence noun [C] UK (US **ˈliquor ˌstore**) a shop that sells mainly alcoholic drinks to be taken away and drunk at home

ˌoff-ˈlimits adj [after verb] (C2) If an area of land is off-limits, you are not allowed to enter it.

offline (also **ˌoff-ˈline**) /ˌɒfˈlaɪn/ (US) /ˌɑːf-/ adj, adv (of a computer) not connected to or directly controlled by a central system, or not connected to the internet

offload /ˌɒfˈləʊd/ (US) /ˈɑːf.loʊd/ verb [T] to get rid of something that you do not want by giving it to someone else: *I've managed to offload some of our old furniture **onto** a friend who's just bought a house.*

ˌoff-ˈmessage adv [after verb], adj UK describes a politician who says things in public that are different from the official ideas of their political party: *He was criticized severely by party leaders for **going** off-message during the debate.* → Compare **on-message**

ˌoff-ˈpeak adj not at the most popular and expensive time: *off-peak phone calls*

ˌoff-ˈpiste adj, adv mainly UK refers to skiing that is done on areas of snow that have not been specially prepared for skiing on

ˌoff-ˈputting adj [after verb] (C2) slightly unpleasant or worrying so that you do not want to get involved in any way: *He's slightly aggressive, which a lot of people find a bit off-putting when they first meet him.*

ˈoff-ˌramp noun [C] US (UK **ˈslip ˌroad**) a short road on which vehicles join or leave a main road

ˈoff-season noun [S] **1** a period of the year when there is less activity in business: *We tend to go skiing during the off-season because it's cheaper.* ◦ *Off-season rates for a double room are about $50 a night.* **2** US (in sports) the period of the year during which games are not played, between the end of one SEASON and the start of the next • **off-ˈseason adj**

offset /ˌɒfˈset/ (US) /ˌɑːf-/ verb [T] (present tense **offsetting**, past tense and past participle **offset**) **1** (C2) to balance one influence against an opposing influence, so that there is no great difference as a result: *The extra cost of travelling to work is offset **by** the lower price of houses here.* ◦ UK *He keeps his petrol receipts because petrol is one of the expenses that he can offset **against tax** (= can show to the government as being a business cost, and so not pay tax).* **2** to pay for things that will reduce carbon in order to reduce the damage caused by carbon that you produce: *We offset all our long-haul flights.*

offshoot /ˈɒf.ʃuːt/ (US) /ˈɑːf-/ noun [C] something that has developed from something larger that already existed: *It's an offshoot **of** a much larger company based in Sydney.*

offshore /ˌɒfˈʃɔːʳ/ (US) /ˌɑːfˈʃɔːr/ adj, adv; adj
▸adj, adv away from or at a distance from the coast: *offshore engineering* ◦ *The wind was blowing offshore.*
▸adj (of companies and banks) based in a different country with different tax rules that cost less money: *offshore banking/funds* → Compare **onshore**

offshoring /ˌɒfˈʃɔːʳ.ɪŋ/ (US) /ˌɑːfˈʃɔːr-/ noun [U] the act of paying someone in another country to do part of a company's work

offside adj; noun
▸adj mainly UK **IN SPORTS** ▷ **1** /ˌɒfˈsaɪd/ (US) /ˌɑːf-/ (US also **offsides** /ˌɑːfˈsaɪdz/) (in particular sports, especially football and HOCKEY) in a position that is not allowed by the rules of the game, often in front of the ball: *the offside rule* **OF VEHICLE** ▷ **2** /ˈɒf.saɪd/ (US) /ˈɑːf-/ [before noun] on or relating to the side of a vehicle that is furthest from the edge of the road and closest to the centre of the road when you are driving: *The offside rear wheel needs replacing.* → Compare **nearside**
▸noun /ˌɒfˈsaɪd/ (US) /ˌɑːf-/ **IN SPORTS** ▷ **1** [U] (in sports such as football) an occasion when a player is offside: *Coventry had a goal disallowed for offside.* → Compare **onside VEHICLE/ROAD** ▷ **2 the offside** /ðiˈɒf.saɪd/ (US) /ðiˈɑːf-/ [S] the side of a vehicle that is furthest from the edge of the road and closest to the centre of the road when you are driving, i.e. (in the UK) the right side: *The car was scraped all along the offside.* → Compare **onside**

offspring /ˈɒf.sprɪŋ/ (US) /ˈɑːf-/ noun [C] (plural **offspring**) **1** (C2) the young of an animal: *In the case of the guinea pig, the number of offspring varies between two and five.* **2** (C2) humorous or formal a person's children: *Tom's sister came round on Saturday with her numerous offspring.*

offstage /ˌɒfˈsteɪdʒ/ (US) /ˌɑːf-/ adj **1** off the stage, or happening behind or at the side of the stage, so that people who are watching cannot see: *The main characters are offstage for most of the second act.* **2** describes a performer when they are not performing in a play or film, etc.: *Though best known for the funny and outspoken roles that she plays on screen, offstage she is shy and rather serious.* • **offstage adv** *He never actually appears in the second half of the play – you just hear his voice offstage.*

ˌoff-the-ˈgrid adj, adv (also **ˌoff-ˈgrid**) **1** not connected to the main electricity GRID (= system of connected wires and power stations): *Solar power is useful in off-the-grid areas.* **2** not connected to any of the main UTILITIES (= electricity, water, etc.) and having your own power and water supply: *We're interested in independent self-sufficient living, off-the-grid.*

ˌoff-the-ˈpeg adj [before noun] UK (US **ˌoff-the-ˈrack**, Australian English **ˌoff-the-ˈhook**) describes clothes that are made and bought in standard sizes and not made especially to fit a particular person: *an off-the-peg suit* → Compare **made-to-measure**

ˌoff ˈwhite noun [U] a white colour with a little grey or yellow in it: *The walls were painted off white.* • **ˌoff-ˈwhite adj**

oft /ɒft/ (US) /ɑːft/ adv old use or formal often: *that oft-**repeated** cliché, 'Time heals'*

often /ˈɒf.ən/, /ˈɒf.tən/ (US) /ˈɑːf-/ adv (A1) many times: *I often see him in the garden.* ◦ ***How** often do you wash your hair?* ◦ *I don't often drink spirits.* ◦ ***It's not** often that you meet someone who you're instantly attracted to.* ◦ *I don't see my parents **as** often **as** I'd like to.* ◦ *Christmas is often mild in this country.* → Synonym **frequently**

! Common mistake: often

Warning: check your word order!
Often usually goes directly before the main verb in a sentence.
Don't say 'do often something', say **often do something**:
~~*I forget often my phone number.*~~
I often forget my phone number.
But if the main verb is **am/is/are/was/were**, **often** usually goes directly after it:
~~*She often is late for meetings.*~~
She is often late for meetings.

IDIOM **as often as not** (also **more often than not**) usually: *As often as not when I make the effort to visit her, I wonder why I've even bothered.*

oftentimes /ˈɒf.ən.taɪmz/ (US) /ˈɑːf-/ **adv** mainly US on many occasions: *Oftentimes a company will contribute toward an employee's moving expenses.* ◦ *He would oftentimes prefer to be alone.* → Synonym **often**

ogle /ˈəʊ.gl̩/ (US) /ˈoʊ-/ **verb** [I or T] to look at someone with obvious sexual interest: *I saw you ogling the woman in the red dress!*

ogre /ˈəʊ.gəʳ/ (US) /ˈoʊ.gɚ/ **noun** [C] **1** a large frightening character in children's stories who eats children **2** informal a FIERCE and frightening person: *The headmaster at my junior school was a real ogre.*

oh /əʊ/ (US) /oʊ/ **exclamation; noun**
▸**exclamation 1** (A1) used to express different emotions, such as surprise, disappointment, and pleasure, often as a reaction to something someone has said: *'He's been married three times.' 'Oh, really? I didn't know that!'* ◦ *'I'm afraid I can't come to the party.' ' Oh, that's a shame.'* ◦ *Is that for me? Oh, you're so kind!* ◦ *'I'm sorry I forgot to ring you.' 'Oh, don't worry.'* **2** (A1) introduces an idea that you have just thought of, or something that you have just remembered: *Oh, I've just thought of a problem.* ◦ *Oh, and don't forget to lock the back door.* **3** (A1) used with other expressions of disappointment, sadness, anger, etc.: *Oh dear, what a mess!* ◦ *Oh no, I've left my umbrella behind!*
▸**noun** [C] (also **o**) sometimes used in writing for the number zero: *My phone number is five, double oh, seven, six, six.*

ohm /əʊm/ (US) /oʊm/ **noun** [C] specialized the standard unit of electrical RESISTANCE

-oholic /-ə.hɒl.ɪk/ (US) /-ə.hɑː.lɪk/ **suffix -aholic**

OHP /ˌəʊ.eɪtʃˈpiː/ (US) /ˌoʊ-/ **noun** [C] abbreviation for **overhead projector**

oic written abbreviation for Oh, I see: used, in emails for example, to show that you understand what someone has said

oik /ɔɪk/ **noun** [C] UK slang a rude and unpleasant man from a low social class: *In his latest film he plays a racist oik from the East End of London.*

oil /ɔɪl/ **noun; verb**
▸**noun FUEL** ▷ **1** (B1) [U] PETROLEUM (= the black oil obtained from under the Earth's surface from which petrol comes): *drilling for oil* ◦ *the oil industry* **2** (B1) [U] a thick liquid that comes from PETROLEUM, used as a fuel and for making parts of machines move easily: *diesel/lubricating oil* **FOR COOKING** ▷ **3** (A2) [C or U] a smooth thick liquid produced from plants or animals that is used in cooking: *olive/corn/vegetable/sunflower oil* **FOR BODY/HAIR** ▷ **4** [C or U] a smooth thick liquid that is used to improve the appearance or quality of the skin or hair: *bath oil* **PAINT** ▷ **5 oils** [plural] thick paints with an oil base, used for painting pictures: *Do you paint in oils or watercolours?*
▸**verb** [T] to put oil on something, especially a machine, usually to make it work more easily without sticking → See also **well oiled**

IDIOM **oil the wheels** informal to make it easier for something to happen: *An aid programme was established to oil the wheels of economic reform in the region.*

oilcan /ˈɔɪl.kæn/ **noun** [C] a container for oil, especially one with a long thin tube for putting oil on machinery

oilfield /ˈɔɪl.fiːld/ **noun** [C] (C2) an area under the Earth's surface where there is a large amount of oil: *the Saudi Arabian oilfields*

oil-fired **adj** describes a heating system that uses REFINED oil (= oil from which unwanted substances have been removed) as a fuel

oilman /ˈɔɪl.mən/ **noun** [C] (plural **-men** /-mən/) a man who owns or operates OIL WELLS or who buys and sells oil: *He started off his career as a Texas oilman.*

ˈoil ˌpaint **noun** [U] a thick type of paint with an oil base, used for painting pictures → See also **oil**

ˈoil ˌpainting **noun 1** [C] a picture painted with oil paints **2** [U] the art or process of painting with oil paints

IDIOM **be no oil painting** UK humorous to not be attractive: *She's no oil painting but she's got a lovely personality.*

ˈoil rig **noun** [C] a large structure with equipment for removing oil from under the ground, especially from under the sea

oil rig

oilseed /ˈɔɪl.siːd/ **noun** [U] any of various seeds from crops that are grown to provide oil: *oilseed rape*

oilskin /ˈɔɪl.skɪn/ **noun 1** [U] cotton cloth that has a thin layer of oil on it to make it WATERPROOF: *a hat made of oilskin* **2** [C usually plural] a piece of clothing made out of oilskin: *The fishermen were all wearing oilskins.*

ˈoil ˌslick **noun** [C] a layer of oil that is floating over a large area of the surface of the sea, usually because an accident has caused it to escape from a ship or container

ˈoil ˌtanker **noun** [C] a ship which carries a large amount of oil

ˈoil ˌwell **noun** [C] a hole that is made in the ground so that oil can be taken out of it

oily /ˈɔɪ.li/ **adj WITH OIL** ▷ **1** consisting of or similar to oil: *an oily liquid* **2** covered in oil or containing a lot of oil: *an oily rag* ◦ *oily fish* ◦ *I've got oily skin (= it produces a lot of oil).* **TOO FRIENDLY** ▷ **3** too friendly and polite in a way that is not sincere

oink /ɔɪŋk/ **noun** [C] informal (especially in children's books) used in writing to represent the noise that a pig makes

ointment /ˈɔɪnt.mənt/ **noun** [U] a thick substance, usually containing medicine, that is put on the skin where it is sore or where there is an injury, in order to cure it: *eye ointment*

OK /ˌəʊˈkeɪ/ (US) /ˌoʊ-/ **exclamation; adj; adv; verb; noun**
▸**exclamation** (also **okay**) **AGREEING** ▷ **1** (A1) used to show that you agree with something or agree to do something: *'I'll pay you back tomorrow.' 'OK, no*

O

problem.' ◦ *'Could you pick me up from the station?' 'OK, what time?'* ◦ *I mean, OK (= I accept that), I wasn't exactly polite to him, but I don't think I was that rude!* **UNDERSTAND** ▷ **2** A2 used to check that someone understands something or that they agree to something: *You need to add a bit more vinegar, OK?* ◦ *I'll see you at 6.30, okay?* **ACTION** ▷ **3** A2 informal used as a way of showing that you are going to take action or start something new: *Okay, let's go.* ◦ *Okay then, if you're ready we'll start.* **PAUSE** ▷ **4** not standard used in the middle of a sentence as a way of pausing: *We saw these guys, okay, so we went up to them and started talking.*

▸adj (also **okay**) informal **AGREED** ▷ **1** A2 agreed or acceptable: *Is it okay if I bring a friend to the party?* ◦ *If it's okay* ***by/with*** *you, I'll leave the shopping till tomorrow.* **ACCEPTABLE** ▷ **2** A1 in a satisfactory state or of a satisfactory quality: *How's Paula? Is she okay after her fall yesterday?* ◦ *Are you OK? You look a bit pale.* ◦ *'Is everything OK with you?' 'Yes, fine.'* ◦ *I'll just check that the car's okay – that was a bit of a bang!* → Synonym **all right** **3** A2 not bad but certainly not good: *'Did you have a good meal last night?' 'It was okay, though I've certainly had better.'* ◦ *Her voice is OK, but it's nothing special.*

▸adv (also **okay**) informal A2 in a satisfactory way: *Everything was going OK until the printer stopped working.* ◦ *Did you sleep okay?*

▸verb [T] (present tense **OK's**, present participle **OK'ing**, past tense and past participle **OK'd**) (also **okay** (present tense **okays**, present participle **okaying**, past tense and past participle **okayed**)) informal to agree to something: *Have the committee OK'd your proposal?*

▸noun (also **okay**) **the OK** (also **the okay**) [S] permission: *He's* ***got*** *the OK to go ahead with his project.*

O

okapi /əʊˈkɑː.pi/ US /oʊˈ-/ **noun** [C] (plural **okapis** or **okapi**) specialized an African animal, related to the GIRAFFE, that is mainly brown with stripes of black and white around its legs and back part

okey-doke /ˌəʊ.kiˈdəʊk/ US /ˌoʊ.kiˈdoʊk/ **exclamation** (also **okey-dokey** /-ˈdəʊ.ki/ US /-ˈdoʊ-/) informal for **OK**

okker /ˈɒk.əʳ/ US /ˈɑː.kɚ/ **noun** [C] an **ocker**

okra /ˈəʊ.krə/ US /ˈoʊ-/ **noun** [U] (US also **gumbo**) the small green PODS from a tropical plant eaten as a vegetable or used to make foods such as soup thicker, or the plant itself

old /əʊld/ US /oʊld/ **adj; noun**

▸adj **NOT YOUNG/NEW** ▷ **1** A1 having lived or existed for many years: *an old man* ◦ *We're all* ***getting*** *older.* ◦ *I was shocked by how old he looked.* ◦ *Now come on, you're old* ***enough*** *to tie your own shoelaces, Carlo.* ◦ *I'm too old* ***to*** *be out clubbing every night.* ◦ *a beautiful old farm house in the country* ◦ *a battered old car* ◦ *That's an old joke – I've heard it about a thousand times.* ◦ *I think this cheese is a bit old judging by the smell of it.* **2** **too old/a bit old** disapproving unsuitable because intended for older people: *Don't you think that book is a bit old for you?*

> **Usage: old or elderly?**
>
> **Elderly** is sometimes used instead of **old** when describing a person as it is considered more polite:
>
> *an elderly gentleman*

WHAT AGE ▷ **3** A1 used to describe or ask about someone's age: ***How*** *old is your father?* ◦ *Rosie's six years old now.* ◦ *It's not very dignified behaviour for a 54-year-old man.* ◦ *He's a couple of years older than me.*

> **Usage: old**
>
> You can give someone's age using **old** in two different ways. You can write the age as three separate words when you name the person first:
>
> *My daughter is three years old.*
>
> However, when you use **old** before naming the person then you should write the age as one word (e.g. **three-year-old**) with hyphens. Note that the word **year** does not become **years** when you use **old** like this:
>
> *I've got a three-year-old daughter.*

> **Other ways of saying old**
>
> When we are talking about old people, we can use the following words.
>
> **Elderly** is a polite way of describing someone who is old:
>
> *A large number of* ***elderly*** *people live alone.*
>
> **The elderly** is used to refer to the group of people who are old:
>
> *Many among* ***the elderly*** *cannot afford to pay their electricity bills.*
>
> **Aged** and **ageing** can be used to describe people who are old:
>
> *He has to look after his* ***aged*** *aunt.*
>
> *The* ***ageing*** *chairman was forced to retire.*
>
> An informal way of saying that someone is old is to use the phrase **be getting on**:
>
> *He's* ***getting on*** *in years. He'll soon be eighty.*
>
> **Geriatric** is used to talk about medicine, services, etc. for old people, and it is also an informal and disapproving way of describing someone who is old and weak:
>
> *She specializes in* ***geriatric*** *medicine.*
>
> *Who's going to elect a* ***geriatric*** *president?*
>
> If someone is too old to do something, in informal or humorous situations you can say the person is **over the hill**:
>
> *I'm only forty, you know. I'm not* ***over the hill*** *yet!*
>
> When talking about old things, you can use the following words.
>
> The word **ancient** can be used for things that have existed for a very long time:
>
> *We need to protect* ***ancient*** *monuments.*
>
> **Ancient** can also be used informally for anything that is old:
>
> *That computer's* ***ancient.***
>
> **Archaic** is used to describe things that are old and no longer used or existing:
>
> ***archaic*** *language*
>
> Something that is old and valuable, rare, or beautiful can be described as **antique**:
>
> *The shop sells* ***antique*** *furniture.*
>
> **Age-old** is a literary word for stories, beliefs, customs, etc. that are very old:
>
> *It's an* ***age-old*** *story of love and betrayal.*

FROM THE PAST ▷ **4** A2 [before noun] from a period in the past: *I saw my old English teacher last time I went home.* ◦ *He's bought me a smart new camera to replace my old one.* ◦ *She showed me her old school.* ◦ *I saw an old boyfriend of mine.* ◦ *In my old job I wasn't given sick-pay.* → Synonym **former** **LANGUAGE** ▷ **5** **Old English, French, etc.** describes a language when it was in an early stage in its development **VERY FAMILIAR** ▷ **6** A2 [before noun] (especially of a friend) known for a long time: *She's one of my oldest friends – we met at school.* **7** [before noun] informal used before someone's name when you are referring to or talking to them, to show that you know them well and like them: *There's old Sara working away in the corner.* ◦ *I hear* ***poor*** *old Frank's lost his job.*

IDIOMS **be (as) old as the hills** to be very old • **for old times' sake** If you do something for old times' sake, you do it in order to remember a happy time that you had in the past: *We should all meet up again – just for old times' sake.* • **of old 1** literary in or from the past: *in* ***days*** *of old* **2** mainly UK for a very long time: *I know him of old.* • **of the old school** traditional and old-fashioned • **the oldest profession (in the world)** humorous PROSTITUTION (= the job of having sex for money) • **the oldest trick in the book** a way of tricking someone that is still effective although it has been used a lot before: *It was the oldest trick in the book – one man distracted me while another stole my wallet.*

▸noun [plural] **the old** old people considered together as a group: *These cuts in services will particularly affect the old.*

ˌold ˈage noun [U] the period in a person's life when he or she is old: *She became very depressed* ***in*** *her old age.*

ˌold age ˈpension noun [C] UK a PENSION that is paid by the state to people who have stopped working because they have reached a particular age

ˌold age ˈpensioner noun [C] (abbreviation **OAP**) UK a person who receives an old age pension from the state

ˌold ˈboy noun **OLD MAN** ▷ **1** [C] mainly UK informal an old man: *the old boy next door* **2** [as form of address] old-fashioned a way that some men address male friends that they have known for many years: *Come on, old boy, drink up.* **STUDENT** ▷ **3** [C] UK An old boy of a particular school is a man who went to school there as a child

IDIOM **the old-boy network** UK the way in which men who have been to the same expensive school or university help each other to find good jobs: *The old-boy network still operates in some City banks.*

the ˈold ˌcountry noun [S] the country that a person or a person's family originally came from: *I've no plans to go back to the old country.*

olden /ˈəʊl.dᵊn/ (US) /ˈoʊl-/ adj [before noun] from a long time ago: *We didn't have things like televisions and computers* ***in the*** *olden* ***days.*** ◦ ***In*** *olden* ***times,*** *people rarely travelled.*

olde-worlde /ˌəʊl.diˈwɜːl.di/ (US) /ˌoʊl.diˈwɜːl-/ adj UK informal old in a very noticeable or artificial way, or made to look old in a way that seems false: *The village is a bit too olde-worlde and more of a museum than a thriving community.*

ˌold-ˈfashioned adj mainly disapproving (B1) not modern; belonging to or typical of a time in the past: *old-fashioned clothes/ideas/furniture* ◦ *She's a bit old-fashioned in her outlook.*

ˌold ˈflame noun [C] a person that you loved or had a sexual relationship with in the past

ˌold ˈgirl noun **OLD WOMAN** ▷ **1** [C] mainly UK informal an old woman: *The poor old girl doesn't get out much these days.* **2** [as form of address] old-fashioned informal a way that some men address female friends that they have known for many years: *Come on, old girl, we haven't got all day.* **STUDENT** ▷ **3** [C] UK An old girl of a particular school is a woman who went to school there as a child.

ˌold ˈgrowth noun [U] US trees that have been growing for a very long time

> **Other ways of saying old-fashioned**
>
> **Antiquated**, **dated**, and **outdated** are alternatives to 'old-fashioned':
>
> *The school wants to update its* ***antiquated*** *computer system.*
>
> *The hotel's decor is starting to look* ***dated.***
>
> *Many hospitals struggle with* ***outdated*** *equipment and facilities.*
>
> Something that is attractive because it is old-fashioned can be described as **quaint**:
>
> *The area is full of* ***quaint*** *little villages.*
>
> **Behind the times** is a phrase that can be used to describe a person or thing that is thought old-fashioned in modern society:
>
> *Her grandfather was* ***behind the times*** *and thought that women shouldn't work outside the home.*

the ˌold ˈguard noun [S, + sing/pl verb] disapproving those people in an organization or society who oppose change and whose beliefs and ideas belong to a period in the past: *Radical reform was, of course, opposed by the old guard.*

ˌold ˈhand noun [C] someone who is very experienced and skilled in a particular area of activity: *We should be able to trust Silva to negotiate a good deal for us – he's an old hand* ***at*** *the game.*

ˌold ˈhat adj [after verb] disapproving not modern or exciting: *He may be old hat among the trendy younger generation, but his shows draw more viewers than any other comedian.*

oldie /ˈəʊl.di/ (US) /ˈoʊl-/ noun [C] informal **SONG** ▷ **1** an old popular song: ***golden*** *oldies from the 60s* **PERSON** ▷ **2** an old person

oldish /ˈəʊl.dɪʃ/ (US) /ˈoʊl-/ adj quite old: *'Is she old?' 'Oldish – late sixties, maybe.'*

ˌold ˈlady noun [S] slang a man's wife: *I haven't seen your old lady for months, Bill.* ◦ *How's* ***the*** *old lady, then?*

ˌold ˈmaid noun [C] old-fashioned a woman who is not married or has not had a sexual relationship and is not now young

ˌold ˈman noun [S] slang someone's father or someone's husband: *Thought I'd take* ***the*** *old man out for a drink tonight.* ◦ *My old man's taking me on holiday.*

ˌold ˈmaster noun [C] a painting by a famous European artist of the past, especially from the 13th to the 17th century

ˈold ˌmoney noun [U] **PEOPLE** ▷ **1** used to refer to rich people whose families have been rich for a long time: *Much of big business is still controlled by old money.* **MONEY** ▷ **2** a type of money that is no longer used

ˌOld ˈNick noun [S] old-fashioned humorous the **devil** (= the main evil spirit in the Christian religion)

ˌold ˈpeople's ˌhome noun [C] a place where old people can live together and be cared for when they are too weak or ill to take care of themselves

ˈold-school adj old-fashioned: *old-school ideas/traditions* ◦ *He was very old-school in his approach to management.*

the ˌold school ˈtie noun [S] the way in which people who have been to the same expensive private school help each other to find good jobs: *The old school tie still has enormous power in such companies.*

ˈold-style adj [before noun] old-fashioned, or based on

ideas from the past: *old-style teaching methods ◦ old-style politics*

the ˌOld ˈTestament noun [S] the first of the two main parts of the Christian Bible, which records the history of the Jewish people before the birth of Jesus → Compare **the New Testament**

ˈold-time adj [before noun] mainly US describes things from a long time ago: *old-time dancing*

ˌold-ˈtimer noun [C] informal an old man, or someone who has been or worked in a place for a long time

ˌold ˈwives' ˌtale noun [C] a piece of advice or a theory, often related to matters of health, that was believed in the past but is now known to be wrong

ˌold ˈwoman noun [C] disapproving a man who worries about matters and details that are not important: *What an old woman Dave is – he nearly had a fit because he got mud on his shoes!*

ˈold-ˌworld adj [before noun] approving belonging to or typical of a period in the past: *Much of the town centre retains its old-world **charm**, with buildings dating from Shakespeare's day.* → Compare **olde-worlde**

the ˌOld ˈWorld noun Asia, Africa, and Europe

oleaginous /ˌəʊ.liˈædʒ.ɪ.nəs/ (US) /ˌoʊ-/ adj formal extremely polite, kind, or helpful in a false way that is intended to bring some advantage to yourself

oleander /ˌəʊ.liˈæn.dər/ (US) /ˌoʊ.liˈæn.dɚ/ noun [C or U] an EVERGREEN Mediterranean tree or bush (= one that never loses its leaves) with strong leaves and white, red, or pink flowers

olfactory /ɒlˈfæk.tər.i/ (US) /ɑːlˈfæk.ter.i/ adj [before noun] specialized connected with the ability to smell: *the olfactory nerve*

oligarch /ˈɒl.ɪ.gɑːk/ (US) /ˈɑː.lɪ.gɑːrk/ noun [C] one of the people in an oligarchy

oligarchy /ˈɒl.ɪ.gɑː.ki/ (US) /ˈɑː.lɪ.gɑːr-/ noun [C or U, + sing/pl verb] (government by) a small group of powerful people

O

oligopoly /ˌɒl.ɪˈgɒp.əl.i/ (US) /ˌɑː.lɪˈgɑː.pəl.i/ noun [C] a situation in which a small number of organizations or companies has control of an area of business, so that others have no share

olive /ˈɒl.ɪv/ (US) /ˈɑː.lɪv/ noun [C] (B1) a small bitter green or black fruit that is eaten or used to produce oil, or a Mediterranean tree on which this fruit grows: *olive **groves***

IDIOM **hold out/offer an olive branch** to do or say something in order to show that you want to end a disagreement with someone: *He held out an olive branch to the opposition by releasing 42 political prisoners.*

ˌolive ˈdrab noun [U] US a greyish-green colour that is often used for military uniforms

ˌolive ˈoil noun [U] a yellow or green oil, made by pressing olives

-ological /-ə.lɒdʒ.ɪ.kəl/ (US) /-lɑː.dʒɪ-/ suffix used to form adjectives; belonging or relating to a particular type of scientific study: *biological ◦ technological*

-ologist /-ɒl.ə.dʒɪst/ (US) /-ɑː.lə-/ suffix used to form nouns; an expert in a particular area of scientific study: *archaeologist*

-ology /-ɒl.ə.dʒi/ (US) /-ɑː.lə.dʒi/ suffix the scientific study of a particular subject: *geology ◦ climatology*

Olympiad /əˈlɪm.pi.æd/ (US) /oʊ-/ noun [C] an occasion on which the Olympic Games are held

Olympian /əˈlɪm.pi.ən/ (US) /oʊ-/ adj; noun

▸adj literary having the qualities of a god: *She has maintained an Olympian **detachment** from (= avoided being involved with and worried by) the everyday business of the office.*

▸noun [C] mainly US a competitor in the Olympic Games

Olympic /əˈlɪm.pɪk/ (US) /oʊ-/ adj [before noun] of or relating to the OLYMPICS: *the International Olympic Committee ◦ an Olympic gold medallist*

the Oˈlympics noun [plural] (also **the ˌOlympic ˈGames**) a set of international sports competitions that happen once every four years: *The Olympic Games are held in a different country on each occasion. ◦ the Summer/Winter Olympics*

ombudsman /ˈɒm.bʊdz.mən/ (US) /ˈɑːm.bədz-/ noun [C] (plural **-men** /-mən/) someone who works for a government or large organization and deals with the complaints made against it: *Complaints to the Banking Ombudsman grew by 50 percent last year.*

Omega-3 /ˌəʊ.mɪ.gəˈθriː/ (US) /ˌoʊ-/ noun [U] a substance in the oil from some fish such as TUNA and SALMON and in some seeds, thought to be good for your health

omelette (US also **omelet**) /ˈɒm.lət/ (US) /ˈɑː.mə.lət/ noun [C] (A2) a dish made by mixing eggs together and frying them, often with small pieces of other food such as cheese or vegetables: *a cheese/mushroom omelette*

IDIOM **you can't make an omelette without breaking eggs** saying it is hard to achieve something important without causing unpleasant effects

omen /ˈəʊ.mən/ (US) /ˈoʊ-/ noun [C] something that is considered to be a sign of how a future event will take place: *England's victory over France is a **good** omen **for** next week's match against Germany. ◦ a **bad** omen ◦ Many people believe that a broken mirror is an omen **of** bad luck.*

omg informal written abbreviation for Oh my God: used when someone is surprised or excited about something: *And then, omg, I saw Johnny Depp in Starbucks!*

ominous /ˈɒm.ɪ.nəs/ (US) /ˈɑː.mə-/ adj suggesting that something unpleasant is likely to happen: *There was an ominous **silence** when I asked whether my contract was going to be renewed. ◦ The engine had been making an ominous **sound** all the way from London. ◦ ominous dark clouds* • **ominously** /-li/ adv

omission /əʊˈmɪʃ.ən/, /əˈ-/ (US) /oʊ-/ noun [C or U] the act of not including something or someone that should have been included, or something or someone that has not been included when they should have been: *Measures to control child employment are a **glaring** (= very obvious) omission **from** new legislation to protect children. ◦ There are some serious errors and omissions in the book. ◦ Many of the fans believe that the omission **of** Heacock **from** the team cost England the match.*

omit /əʊˈmɪt/, /əˈ-/ (US) /oʊ-/ verb [T] (-tt-) (C1) to fail to include or do something: *She was omitted **from** the list of contributors to the report. ◦ The Prince's tour conveniently omitted the most deprived areas of the city.* ◦ [+ to infinitive] formal *She omitted **to** mention that she was going to Yorkshire next week.*

omni- /ɒm.ni-/ (US) /ɑːm.ni-/ prefix everywhere or everything: *omnipresent ◦ omniscient*

omnibus /ˈɒm.nɪ.bəs/ (US) /ˈɑːm-/ noun [C] **SEVERAL PARTS** ▷ **1** a book consisting of two or more parts that have already been published separately → Compare **anthology** **2** UK a programme consisting of two or more parts that have already been broadcast separately: *the omnibus **edition** of a soap opera* **TRANSPORT** ▷ **3** old use a bus

omnipotent /ɒmˈnɪp.ə.tənt/ (US) /ɑːmˈnɪp.ə.ţənt/ adj formal having unlimited power and able to do anything: *How can a loving, omnipotent God permit disease, war and suffering?* • **omnipotence** /-tᵊns/ (US) /-t̬ᵊns/ **noun** [U] *God's omnipotence*

omnipresent /ˌɒm.nɪˈprez.ᵊnt/ (US) /ˌɑːm-/ **adj** formal present or having an effect everywhere at the same time: *The singer became an omnipresent icon of style and beauty.* • **omnipresence** /-ᵊns/ **noun** [U] *the omnipresence of the secret police*

omniscient /ɒmˈnɪs.i.ənt/ (US) /ɑːmˈnɪʃ.ᵊnt/ **adj** formal having or seeming to have unlimited knowledge: *the omniscient narrator* • **omniscience** /-əns/ **noun** [U]

omnivore /ˈɒm.nɪ.vɔːʳ/ (US) /ˈɑːm.nɪ.vɔːr/ **noun** [C] an animal that is naturally able to eat both plants and meat → Compare **carnivore, herbivore**

omnivorous /ɒmˈnɪv.ᵊr.əs/ (US) /ɑːmˈnɪv.ɚ-/ **adj** **1** naturally able to eat both plants and meat: *Pigs are omnivorous animals.* → Compare **carnivorous (carnivore), herbivorous (herbivore)** **2** enthusiastic and interested in many different areas of a subject: *an omnivorous **reader***

on /ɒn/ (US) /ɑːn/ **preposition; adv**

▸**preposition** **ABOVE** ▷ **1** (A1) used to show that something is in a position above something else and touching it, or that something is moving into such a position: *Look at all the books on your desk!* ◦ *Ow, you're standing on my foot!* ◦ *Your suitcase is on top of the wardrobe.* ◦ *They live in that old farmhouse on the hill.* ◦ *I got on my bike and left.* **CONNECTED** ▷ **2** (A1) covering the surface of, being held by, or connected to something: *You've got blood on your shirt.* ◦ *Which finger do you wear your ring on?* ◦ *Can you stand on your head?* ◦ *We could hang this picture on the wall next to the door.* ◦ *Dogs should be kept on their leads at all times.* ◦ UK *We've just moved house and we're not on the phone (= not connected to the phone service) yet.* **TIME** ▷ **3** (A1) used to show when something happens: *Many shops don't open on Sundays.* ◦ *What are you doing on Friday?* ◦ *My birthday's on 30 May.* ◦ *Would you mind telling me what you were doing on the afternoon of Friday the 13th of March?* ◦ *Trains to London leave on **the** hour (= at exactly one o'clock, two o'clock, etc.).* ◦ *On a clear day you can see the mountains from here.* ◦ *She was dead on **arrival** (= dead when she arrived) at the hospital.* ◦ *Please hand in your keys at reception on your departure from (= when you leave) the hotel.* **WRITING** ▷ **4** (A2) used to show where something has been written, printed, or drawn: *Which page is that curry recipe on?* ◦ *His initials were engraved on the back of his watch.* ◦ *What's on the menu tonight? (= What food is available?)* **TRAVEL** ▷ **5** (A2) used for showing some methods of travelling: *I love travelling on trains.* ◦ *She'll be arriving on the 5.30 train.* ◦ *We went to France on the ferry.* ◦ *It'd be quicker to get there on **foot**.* ◦ *two figures on **horseback*** **PROCESS** ▷ **6** used to show that a condition or process is being experienced: *He accidentally set his bed on **fire**.* ◦ *Their flights to Paris are on special **offer** at the moment.* ◦ *Martin's on **holiday** this week.* ◦ *I'll be away on a training course next week.* ◦ *I often feel carsick when I'm on a long journey.* ◦ *Crime is on the increase (= is increasing) again.* **RECORDING** ▷ **7** (A2) used to show the form in which something is recorded or performed: *How much data can you store on the disk?* ◦ *When's the movie coming out on DVD?* ◦ *I was really embarrassed the first time I saw myself on film.* ◦ *What's on television tonight?* ◦ *I wish there was more jazz on the radio.* **PAIN** ▷ **8** (B2) used to show what causes pain or injury as a result of being touched: *I hit my head on the shelf as I was standing up.* ◦ *You'll cut yourself on that knife if you're not careful.* **TO** ▷ **9** (A2) to or towards: *Our house is the first on the left after the post office.* ◦ *The attack on the village lasted all night.* ◦ *I wish you wouldn't creep up on me like that!* **RELATING** ▷ **10** (B1) relating to: *a book on pregnancy* ◦ *Her thesis is on Italian women's literature.* ◦ *The minister has refused to comment on the allegations.* ◦ *Criticism has no effect on him.* ◦ *Have the police got anything on you (= have they got any information about you that can be used against you)?* **MONEY** ▷ **11** (A2) used to show something for which a payment is made: *He spent £80 on a hat.* ◦ *I've wasted a lot of money on this car.* ◦ *We made a big profit on that deal.* ◦ *How much interest are you paying on the loan?* **NECESSARY** ▷ **12** used to show a person or thing that is necessary for something to happen or that is the origin of something: *We're relying on you.* ◦ *I might come – it **depends** on Andrew.* ◦ *Most children remain dependent on their parents while at university.* ◦ *His latest movie is **based** on a fairy story.* **INVOLVEMENT** ▷ **13** used to show when someone is involved or taking part in something: *I'm working on a new book.* ◦ *'Where had we got up to?' 'We were on page 42.'* **FINANCIAL SUPPORT** ▷ **14** used to show what is providing financial support or an income: *I've only got £50 a week to **live** on at the moment.* ◦ *He retired on a generous pension from the company.* ◦ UK *She's on (= earning) £25,000 a year.* **FOOD/FUEL/DRUG** ▷ **15** (B2) used to show something that is used as food, fuel, or a drug: *What do mice **live** on?* ◦ *Does this radio **run** on batteries?* ◦ *Is he on drugs?* **NEXT TO** ▷ **16** (B1) next to or along the side of: *Cambridge is on the River Cam.* ◦ *Our house was on Sturton Street.* ◦ *Strasbourg is on the border of France and Germany.* **MEMBER** ▷ **17** (C1) used to show when someone is a member of a group or organization: *Have you ever served on a jury?* ◦ *There are no women on the committee.* ◦ *How many people are on your staff?* ◦ *She's a researcher on a women's magazine.* **TOOL** ▷ **18** (B1) used when referring to a tool, instrument, or system that is used to do something: *I do all my household accounts on computer.* ◦ *Chris is on drums and Mike's on bass guitar.* ◦ *I'm on (= talking on) the phone.* **AGAIN** ▷ **19** literary used to show when something is repeated one or more times: *The government suffered defeat on defeat in the local elections.* ◦ *Wave on wave of refugees has crossed the border to escape the fighting.* **COMPARISON** ▷ **20** used when making a comparison: *£950 is my final offer, and I can't improve on it.* ◦ *The productivity figures are **down/up** on last week's.* **POSSESSION** ▷ **21** (C2) [before pronoun] used to show when someone has something with them in their pocket or in a bag that they are carrying: *Have you got a spare pen on you?* ◦ *I haven't got my driving licence on me.* **AFTER** ▷ **22** happening after and usually because of: *Acting on information given to them anonymously, the police arrested him.* ◦ *He inherited a quarter of a million pounds on his mother's death.* ◦ *On their return they discovered that their house had been burgled.* **PAYMENT** ▷ **23** informal used to show who is paying for something: *This meal is on me.* ◦ *She had her operation done on the National Health Service.* **FAULTY** ▷ **24** used to show who suffers when something does not operate as it should: *The phone suddenly went dead on me.* ◦ *Their car broke down on them in the middle of the motorway.* **POINTS** ▷ **25** UK used to show the number of points a person or team has in a competition: *Clive's team is on five points while Joan's is on seven.*

IDIOM **on the go** **1** very busy: *I've been on the go all day and I'm really tired.* **2** UK in the process of being produced: *Did you know that she's got a new book on the go (= being written)?*

O

▸adv **CONNECTED** ▷ **1** (A2) on your body or someone's body: *It's very cold so* ***put*** *a jumper on.* ◦ *She wanders round the house with* ***nothing*** *on.* ◦ *Can you remember what he* ***had*** *on (= was wearing)?* ◦ *I* ***tried*** *on a few jackets, but none of them looked nice.* **2** covering the surface of something or connected to something: *Screw the lid on tightly.* ◦ *Make sure the top's on properly.* ◦ *Surgeons managed to sew the finger back on.* **OPERATING** ▷ **3** (B2) used to show when something is operating or starting to operate: *Could you* ***switch*** *on the radio?* ◦ *Would you* ***turn*** *the TV on?* ◦ *You* ***left*** *the bedroom light on.* **NOT STOPPING** ▷ **4** continuing or not stopping: *If her phone's engaged,* ***keep*** *on trying.* ◦ *Stop talking and* ***get*** *on with your work.* ◦ *If Elise would just* ***hang*** *on (= wait) a little longer she'd certainly get the promotion.* ◦ *The noise just* ***went*** *on* ***and on*** *(= continued for a long time) and I thought it would never stop.* **TRAVEL** ▷ **5** (B1) into a bus, train, plane, etc., or in the correct position to start using some other method of travelling: *The train suddenly started moving as I was getting on.* ◦ *Her horse galloped off as soon as she was on.* **PERFORMING** ▷ **6** (C2) performing: *Hurry up with the make-up – I'm on in ten minutes.* ◦ *The audience cheered as the band came on (= came onto the stage).* **MOVING FORWARD** ▷ **7** (B2) continuing forward in space or time: *You cycle on and I'll meet you there.* ◦ *Move on, please, and let the ambulance through.* ◦ *When you've finished reading it would you pass it on to Paul?* ◦ *They never spoke to each other* ***from that day*** *on (= after that day).* ◦ *What are you doing* ***later*** *on?* **HAPPENING** ▷ **8** (B2) happening or planned: *I'm busy tomorrow, but I've got nothing on the day after.* ◦ *I've got a lot on at the moment.* ◦ *Is the party still on* ***for*** *tomorrow?* ◦ *Food had to be rationed when the war was on.* ◦ *Are there any good films on (= being shown) at the cinema this week?* **POSITION** ▷ **9** used when talking about the position of one thing compared with the position of another: *It's amazing nobody was injured because the two buses collided* ***head*** *on (= the front parts of the buses hit each other).* ◦ UK *The bike hit our car* ***side*** *on (= hit the side of the car rather than the front or back).* ◦ UK *It would be easier to get the bookcase through the doorway if we turned it* ***sideways*** *on (= turned it so that one of its sides is at the front).*

IDIOMS **be not on** mainly UK Something that is not on is unacceptable and should not happen: *You can't be expected to work for nothing – it's not on.* • **be on about** UK informal If you ask someone what they are on about, you are asking them, often in a slightly annoyed way, what they mean: *I dunno what you're on about.* • **be/go on at sb** UK to complain to someone again and again about their behaviour or to ask them to do something: *My parents are always on at us* ***about*** *having a baby.* ◦ *She's been on at me* ***to*** *get my hair cut.* • **on and off** (also **off and on**) (C1) If something happens on and off during a period of time, it happens sometimes: *I've had toothache on and off for a couple of months.* • **you're on!** informal used as a way of expressing agreement to something happening: *'I'll give you £50 for your bike.' 'You're on!'*

ˈon-board adj [before noun] describes things that are carried by a vehicle and form part of it: *The car comes with an on-board satellite navigation device.*

once /wʌns/ adv; conjunction

▸adv **ONE TIME** ▷ **1** (A2) one single time: *I went sailing once, but I didn't like it.* ◦ *We have lunch together once a month.* **2 at once** (C1) at the same time: *They all started talking at once.* **3 for once** (B2) used when something happens that does not usually happen: *For once, the bus came on time.* **4 just this once** used to say that you will only do or request something on this particular occasion: *All right, I'll give you a lift – just this once.* **5 once again** (also **once more**) (B1) again, as has happened before: *Once again, racist attacks are increasing across Europe.* **6 once more a** (B1) one more time: *I'd like to visit the colleges once more before we leave.* **b** again, as has happened before: *I'm pleased that Daniel's working with us once more.* **7 once or twice** a few times: *I've seen him once or twice in town.* **8 (every) once in a while** (B2) sometimes but not often: *We meet for lunch once in a while.* **9 once and for all** (C2) completely and in a way that will finally solve a problem: *Our intention is to destroy their offensive capability once and for all.* **10 once in a lifetime** only likely to happen once in a person's life: *An opportunity as good as this arises once in a lifetime.* → See also **once-in-a-lifetime** **11 the once** on a single occasion: *I've only played rugby the once, and I never want to play it again.* **PAST** ▷ **12** (B1) in the past, but not now: *This house once belonged to my grandfather.* ◦ *Computers are much cheaper nowadays than they once were.* ◦ *Once-thriving villages stand deserted and in ruins.*

IDIOM **once upon a time 1** (B1) used at the beginning of children's stories to mean 'a long time ago': *Once upon a time there was an ugly duckling.* **2** used when referring to something that happened in the past, especially when showing that you feel sorry that it no longer happens: *Once upon a time people knew the difference between right and wrong, but nowadays nobody seems to care.*

▸conjunction **1** (B2) as soon as, or from the moment when: *Once I've found somewhere to live I'll send you my address.* ◦ *Remember that you won't be able to cancel the contract once you've signed.* **2 at once** (B1) immediately: *I knew at once that I'd like it here.*

IDIOMS **all at once** (C1) suddenly and unexpectedly: *All at once there was a loud crashing sound.* • **once bitten, twice shy** saying said when you are frightened to do something again because you had an unpleasant experience doing it the first time

ˌonce-in-a-ˈlifetime adj [before noun] describes an experience or opportunity that is very special because it is the only time you will be able to have it: *A tour of Australia is a once-in-a-lifetime experience.*

ˈonce-over noun informal **LOOKING** ▷ **1 give sth/sb the once-over** to look at and examine something or someone quickly **CLEANING** ▷ **2** [S] the act of quickly cleaning a place: *Would you mind* ***giving*** *the carpet a once-over* ***with*** *the vacuum cleaner?*

oncogene /ˈɒŋ.kəʊ.dʒiːn/ (US) /ˈɑːn.kə-/ noun [C] specialized a GENE that is present in every cell and causes a healthy cell to become CANCEROUS under particular conditions

oncology /ɒŋˈkɒl.ə.dʒi/ (US) /ɑːnˈkɑː.lə-/ noun [U] the study and treatment of TUMOURS (= masses of cells) in the body • **oncologist** /-dʒɪst/ noun [C]

oncoming /ˈɒnˌkʌm.ɪŋ/ (US) /ˈɑːn-/ adj [before noun] moving towards you or coming nearer: *The car veered onto the wrong side of the road and collided with an oncoming truck.* ◦ *There seemed to be no way of averting the oncoming crisis.*

one /wʌn/ number, determiner; pronoun

▸number, determiner **NUMBER** ▷ **1** (A1) the number 1: *You've got three bags and I've only got one.* ◦ *She'll be one year old tomorrow.* **MEMBER** ▷ **2 one of** (A2) a member of a group of people or things: *One of their daughters has just got married.* ◦ *EMI is one of the world's largest record companies.* ◦ *Finding a cure for* *cancer is one of the biggest challenges facing medical researchers.* ◦ *Our organization is just one of* ***many*** *charities that are providing famine relief in the region.*

! Common mistake: one of

Remember: when **one of** is followed by a noun, the noun should be in the plural form:

~~*One of my friend is in hospital.*~~

One of my friends is in hospital.

FUTURE TIME ▷ **3** B2 used to refer to a time in the future that is not yet decided: *Why don't we meet for lunch one day next week?* ◦ *I'd like to go skiing one Christmas.* **PARTICULAR OCCASION** ▷ **4** B2 used to refer to a particular occasion while avoiding stating the exact moment: *One night we stayed up talking till dawn.* ◦ *He was attacked as he was walking home from work late one afternoon.* ◦ *One moment he says he loves me, the next moment he's asking for a divorce.* ◦ *She never seems to know what she's doing from one minute to the next.* **SINGLE** ▷ **5** B2 a single thing; not two or more: *Do you think five of us will manage to squeeze into* ***the*** *one car?* ◦ *There's too much data to fit onto just* ***the*** *one disk.* ◦ *Eat them one* ***at a time*** *(= separately).* ◦ *I think we should paint the bedroom* ***all*** *one (= in a single) colour.* **6 (all) in one** C2 combined in a single person or object: *With this model you get a radio, CD player, and MP3 dock all in one.* **ONLY** ▷ **7** B2 used when saying there is no other person or thing: *He's* ***the*** *one person you can rely on in an emergency.* ◦ *This may be your one* ***and only*** *(= only ever) opportunity to meet her.* ◦ *My final guest on tonight's show needs no introduction. Please welcome* ***the*** *one* ***and only*** *Michael Jordan!* **UNKNOWN PERSON** ▷ **8** formal used before the name of someone who is not known: *Her solicitor is one John Wintersgill.* **EMPHASIS** ▷ **9** mainly US used to emphasize an adjective: *His mother is one (= a very) generous woman.* ◦ *That's one (= a very) big ice-cream you've got there.* ◦ *It was one hell of a (= a very great) shock to find out I'd lost my job.*

▸**pronoun 1** A2 used to refer to a particular thing or person within a group or range of things or people that are possible or available: *I've got a few books on Chinese food. You can borrow one if you like.* ◦ *Which one would you like?* ◦ *Please make a copy for everybody in the office and a few extra ones for the visitors.* ◦ *'Which cake would you like?' 'The one at the front.'* ◦ *French croissants are so much better than the English ones.* ◦ *There were lots of people standing watching, and not one of them offered to help.* ◦ *I've received no replies to my job applications – not a single one (= none).* ◦ *Chris is the one (= the person) with curly brown hair.* **2 not be one to do sth** informal to never do something: *I'm not one to criticize other people, as you know.* **3 be one for sth** informal to like something very much: *I've never been one for staying out late.* ◦ *He's a* ***great*** *one for the ladies.* **COMPARISON** ▷ **4** used to talk about one person or thing compared with other similar or related people or things: *They look so similar it's often difficult to distinguish one from the other.* ◦ *You may have one or the other, but not both.* ◦ *Crime and freedom are inseparable. You can't have one without the other.* **ANY PERSON** ▷ **5** C1 formal any person, but not a particular person: *One has an obligation to one's friends.* **I/ME** ▷ **6** formal the person speaking or writing: *Of course, one (= I) would be delighted to dine with the Queen.*

IDIOMS **be a one** UK old-fashioned informal to be funny in a slightly rude way or in a way that shows no respect: *'He told me I couldn't have the job and I told him I never really wanted it in the first place.' 'Ooh, you are a one.'* • **be at one** (also **be as one**) formal to agree: *We disagree on most things, but on this question we are at one (****with*** *each other).* • **be one of a kind** C2 to be very unusual and special: *He's one of a kind, he really is.* • **down in one** informal If you drink a glass of alcohol down in one, you drink the whole glass without stopping. • **for one** used to say that you think your opinion or action is right, even if others do not: *The rest of you may disagree, but I, for one, think we should proceed with the plan.* • **go off on one** UK informal to suddenly become very angry and start shouting or behaving violently: *He went off on one because he thought I was threatening his dog.* • **got it in one!** something that you say when someone has guessed something correctly: *'Don't tell me – is Anna pregnant again?' 'Got it in one!'* • **a hundred/thousand/million and one** very many: *I can't stand around chatting – I've got a hundred and one things to do this morning.* • **in ones and twos** in small numbers: *The replies came back in ones and twos.* • **one after another** (also **one after the other**) B2 many, in a series: *I'll eat chocolates one after the other until the box is finished.* • **one and all** literary everyone: *The news of his resignation came as a surprise to one and all.* • **one by one** B2 separately, one after the other: *One by one the old buildings in the city have been demolished and replaced with modern tower blocks.* ◦ *They entered the room one by one.* • **one day** B1 at some time in the future: *I'd like to go to Berlin again one day.* • **one or two** B1 a few: *I'd like to make one or two suggestions.* • **one way or another 1** B2 in some way that is not stated: *Everyone at the party was related (****in****) one way or another.* **2** B2 in any way that is possible: *These bills have to be paid one way or another.* ◦ *We have to make a decision one way or another about what needs to be done.* • **the one about** informal the joke about: *Have you heard the one about the Italian, the American and the Australian?*

one aˈnother pronoun each other

ˌone-armed ˈbandit noun [C] UK informal a type of SLOT MACHINE with a large metal pole on the side that you pull to make it work

ˌone-diˈmensional adj **MEASURE** ▷ **1** having height or width or length, but not two or all of these **BORING** ▷ **2** boring or showing few different qualities: *The characters in his novels tend to be rather one-dimensional.*

ˌone-ˈhanded adv, adj using just one hand: *He had injured his left hand and was typing one-handed.*

ˌone-hit ˈwonder noun [C] informal a performer of popular music who makes one successful recording but then no others

ˌone-horse ˈrace noun [C usually singular] a race or competition which only one of the competitors has a real chance of winning: *This election has been a one-horse race right from the start.*

ˌone-horse ˈtown noun [C] mainly US a town that is small and not important

ˌone-ˈliner noun [C] informal a joke or a clever and funny remark or answer that is usually one sentence long: *There are some very* ***witty*** *one-liners in the film.*

ˌone-man ˈband noun [C usually singular] a musician who performs alone, usually outside, carrying and playing several instruments at the same time: figurative *The organization seems to have become a one-man band with just one person making all the decisions.*

ˌone-night ˈstand noun [C] **SEX** ▷ **1** a sexual relationship which lasts for only one night, or a person who you have had this type of relationship with **PERFORMANCE** ▷ **2** a performance which happens only once in a particular place

O

ˌone-ˈoff noun; adj
▸noun [S] UK something that happens or is made or done only once: *Will you be doing more talks in the future or was that just a one-off?*
▸adj UK (US **ˌone-ˈshot**) happening only once: *They gave him a one-off payment to compensate for the extra hours that he had to work.*

ˌone-on-ˈone adj; adv; noun
▸adj [before noun] (UK also **ˌone-to-ˈone**) A one-on-one activity involves two people talking directly, usually with one teaching or giving information to the other: *Each employee has a one-on-one performance review with his or her boss.*
▸adv **1** (UK also **ˌone-to-ˈone**) If two people discuss something one-on-one, they discuss it directly, without involving anyone else: *It's best to talk with him about the problem one-on-one.* **2** US In sports, if something is done one-on-one, it means that each player from one team is matched to a single player from the other team.
▸noun [C] (plural **one-on-ones**) (UK also **ˌone-to-ˈone**) a discussion or meeting between two people, without anyone else involved: *As well as general meetings, the president had one-on-ones with the other leaders.*

ˌone-parent ˈfamily noun [C] (also **ˌsingle-parent ˈfamily**) a family which includes either a mother or a father but not both

ˌone-ˈperson adj [before noun] (also **ˌone-ˈman/ˈwoman**) describes a play or show that is a performance or show of artistic works by just one person: *This is the first time her one-woman show has been on television.*

ˈone-piece noun [C] (US usually **ˌone-piece ˈswimsuit**) a piece of women's clothing that is worn when swimming or on a beach and consists of a single piece of material rather than a separate top and bottom: *I'd prefer a one-piece to a bikini.*

O

onerous /ˈəʊ.nᵊr.əs/ (US) /ˈɑː.nɚ-/ adj formal difficult to do or needing a lot of effort: *the onerous* ***task*** *of finding a peaceful solution* ◦ *She found the duties of motherhood onerous.* • **onerousness** /-nəs/ noun [U]

oneself /ˌwʌnˈself/ pronoun formal C1 the REFLEXIVE form of the PRONOUN 'one' when it refers to people in general or to the person speaking: *One has to learn to control oneself.*

ˌone-ˈsided adj **1** If a competition is one-sided, one team or player is much better than the other: *a one-sided contest/game* **2** only considering one opinion in an argument in a way that is unfair: *They blamed their defeat on the media's one-sided reporting of the election.* • **one-sidedness** /-nəs/ noun [U]

ˌone-size-fits-ˈall adj **1** mainly US describes a piece of clothing that is designed to fit a person of any size **2** disapproving (intended to be) suitable for everyone or every purpose: *a one-size-fits-all approach to education*

ˌone-ˈstar adj describes a hotel or restaurant that is not especially good but has achieved the lowest acceptable standard in an official quality test

ˈone-stop adj describes activities that all happen in a single place: *We offer our customers one-stop banking services and investment advice.*

ˈone-time adj **a one-time teacher, doctor, cleaner, etc.** someone who was a teacher, doctor, cleaner, etc. in the past: *Duggan, a TV presenter and one-time journalist, made the announcement last week.*

ˌone-to-ˈone adj; adv; noun
▸adj CONNECTION ▷ **1** Something that is in a one-to-one relationship with another thing strongly influences the way that the other thing changes: *Is there a one-to-one* ***relationship*** *between pay levels and productivity?* SAME VALUE ▷ **2** used to describe something that has the same value as another thing: *The dollar was fixed to the peso at a one-to-one* ***rate***. TWO PEOPLE ▷ **3** [before noun] UK (US **ˌone-on-ˈone**) A one-to-one activity involves two people talking directly, usually with one teaching or giving information to the other: *These children have special educational needs and require one-to-one attention.*
▸adv UK (US **ˌone-on-ˈone**) If two people discuss something one-to-one, they discuss it directly, without involving anyone else: *It's best to talk to him about the problem one-to-one.*
▸noun [C] (plural **one-to-ones**) UK (US **ˌone-on-ˈone**) a discussion or activity that involves two people talking directly, usually with one teaching or giving information to the other: *I have regular one-to-ones with my manager.*

ˌone-track ˈmind noun **have a one-track mind** to think about one particular thing and nothing else: *And no, Bill, I wasn't talking about sex – you've got a one-track mind!*

ˌone-trick ˈpony noun [C] informal someone or something that is only good for one particular purpose, or at doing one particular thing

ˌone-ˈtwo ˌpunch noun [usually S] US two unpleasant things that happen together: *The weather delivered a one-two punch to gardeners with unseasonal freezing temperatures and strong winds.*

one-upmanship /ˌwʌnˈʌp.mən.ʃɪp/ noun [U] disapproving a situation in which someone does or says something in order to prove that they are better than someone else

ˌone-ˈway adj **1** [before noun] travelling or allowing travel in only one direction: *I drove the wrong way down a one-way* ***street***. ◦ *How much is a one-way* ***ticket*** *to New York?* **2 a one-way ticket to sth** If something is a one-way ticket to an unpleasant situation, it will cause that situation to happen: *A rejection of the peace deal would be a one-way ticket to disaster for the country.* **3** describes a relationship that is not fair because only one person or group of the two makes any effort

ongoing /ˈɒŋˌgəʊ.ɪŋ/, /ˌɒŋˈgəʊ-/ (US) /ˈɑːnˌgoʊ-/ adj C2 continuing to exist or develop, or happening at the present moment: *an ongoing investigation/process/project* ◦ *No agreement has yet been reached and the negotiations are still ongoing.*

onion /ˈʌn.jən/ noun [C or U] A2 a vegetable with a strong smell and flavour, made up of several layers surrounding each other tightly in a round shape, usually brown or red on the outside and white inside: *I always cry when I'm chopping onions.* ◦ *Fry the onion and garlic for about two minutes.*

online adj; adv
▸adj [before noun] /ˈɒn.laɪn/ (US) /ˈɑːn.laɪn/ A2 describes products, services, or information that can be bought or used on the internet: *an online newspaper/magazine/dictionary* ◦ *online banking/shopping*
▸adv /ˌɒnˈlaɪn/ (US) /ˌɑːnˈlaɪn/ INTERNET ▷ **1** A2 bought, used, etc. using the internet: *Have you ever bought anything online?* ◦ *This dictionary* ***went*** *online in 1999.* **2 be online** to be able to use email or the internet: *I'll send you my email address once I'm online.* CONNECTED ▷ **3** connected to a system: *The new power station is expected to be online by July.* ◦ *When will the new factory come online (= start production)?*

ˌonline ˈdating noun [U] a way of starting a

romantic relationship on the internet, by giving information about yourself or replying to someone else's information: *an online dating website*

onlooker /ˈɒnˌlʊk.əʳ/ (US) /ˈɑːnˌlʊk.ɚ/ **noun** [C] someone who watches something that is happening in a public place but is not involved in it: *A crowd of curious onlookers soon gathered to see what was happening.*

only /ˈəʊn.li/ (US) /ˈoʊn-/ **adj; adv; conjunction**

▸**adj** [before noun] A1 used to show that there is a single one or very few of something, or that there are no others: *I was the only person on the train.* ◦ *Is this really the only way to do it?* ◦ *The only thing that matters is that the baby is healthy.* ◦ *It was the only thing I could do under the circumstances.* ◦ *Rita was the only person to complain.*

▸**adv** NOT MORE ▷ **1** A1 used to show that something is limited to not more than, or is not anything other than, the people, things, amount, or activity stated: *At present these televisions are only available in Japan.* ◦ *Only Sue and Mark bothered to turn up for the meeting.* ◦ *This club is for members only.* ◦ *Only an idiot would do that.* ◦ *These shoes only cost £20.* ◦ *Don't worry – it's only a scratch.* ◦ *I was only joking.* ◦ *I was only trying to help.* ◦ *I only arrived half an hour ago.* ◦ *She spoke to me only a few minutes ago on the phone.* ◦ *It's only four o'clock and it's already getting dark.* ◦ *'Who's there?' 'It's only me (= it is not someone you should worry about). I've locked myself out.'* ◦ *It's only **natural** that you should worry about your children.* **2 only just a** B1 used to refer to something that happens almost immediately after something else: *People were leaving and I'd only just arrived.* ◦ *We'd only just set off when the car broke down.* **b** almost not: *There was only just enough food to go round.* ◦ *We arrived in time for our flight, but only just (= but we almost did not).* **3 not only … (but) also** B2 used to say that two related things are true or happened, especially when this is surprising or shocking: *Not only did he turn up late, he also forgot his books.* ◦ *If this project fails it will affect not only our department, but also the whole organization.* **4 have only (got) to** If you say you have only (got) to do something, you mean that it is all you need to do in order to achieve something else: *If you want any help, you have only to ask.* ◦ *You've only got to look at her face to see that she's not well.* BAD RESULT ▷ **5** used when saying that something unpleasant will happen as a result of an action or a failure to act: *If you don't do something about it now it will only get worse.* FEEL SORRY ▷ **6** used to show that you feel sorry about something that cannot happen when explaining why it cannot happen: *I'd love to go to Australia. I only wish I could afford to.* **7 I only hope/wish (that)** B2 used to emphasize what you are hoping or wishing for: *I only hope you know what you're doing.* ◦ *I only wish **that** they would keep in touch more regularly.* SILLY ▷ **8** informal used to show that you think someone has done something silly: *She's only locked herself out of her flat again!*

> **!** Common mistake: **only**
>
> **Warning:** check your word order!
>
> **Only** usually goes directly before the main verb in a sentence:
>
> ~~*I only will accept the job if you increase my salary.*~~
>
> *I will only accept the job if you increase my salary.*
>
> But if the main verb is **am/is/are/was/were, only** usually goes directly after it:
>
> ~~*The winner only was five years old.*~~
>
> *The winner was only five years old.*

IDIOMS **if only** B1 used when you want to say how doing something would make it possible to avoid something unpleasant: *If only she'd listen to what he's saying, I'm sure they could work it out.* • **only to do sth** used to show that something is surprising or unexpected: *He spent ages negotiating for a pay increase, only to resign from his job soon after he'd received it.*

▸**conjunction** C2 used to show what is the single or main reason why something mentioned in the first part of the sentence cannot be performed or is not completely true: *I'd invite Frances to the party, only (= but I will not because) I don't want her husband to come.* ◦ *I'd phone him myself, only (= but I cannot because) I've got to go out.* ◦ *I'd be happy to do it for you, only (= but) don't expect it to be done before next week.* ◦ *This fabric is similar to wool, only (= except that it is) cheaper.*

ˌonly ˈchild noun [C] (plural **only children**) a child who has no sisters or brothers

ˌon-ˈmessage adv [after verb], **adj** UK A politician who is on-message says things in public that support the official ideas of their political party. → Compare **off-message**

o.n.o. noun UK written abbreviation for or near(est) offer: used in advertisements for things that people are trying to sell to show that they will accept slightly less money than the price they are asking for: *Ladies' bike – excellent condition. £80 o.n.o.*

onomatopoeia /ˌɒn.əˌmæt.əˈpiː.ə/ (US) /ˌɑː.noʊˌmæt̬.oʊ-/ **noun** [U] specialized the act of creating or using words that include sounds that are similar to the noises the words refer to • **onomatopoeic** /-ɪk/ **adj** *'Pop', 'boom', and 'squelch' are onomatopoeic words.*

ˌon-ˈscreen adv [before noun], **adj** describes something or someone seen or appearing on a television or computer screen: *Her on-screen husband is also her partner in real life.* ◦ *You can use the device to scan the image and reproduce it on-screen in an electronic format.*

onset /ˈɒn.set/ (US) /ˈɑːn-/ **noun 1 the onset of sth** the moment at which something unpleasant begins: *the onset of winter* ◦ *The new treatment can **delay** the onset of the disease by several years.* **2** specialized the first part of a syllable → Compare **coda**

onshore /ˌɒnˈʃɔːʳ/ (US) /ˈɑːn.ʃɔːr/ **adj, adv** moving towards land from the sea, or on land rather than at sea: *onshore winds* ◦ *onshore oil reserves* → Compare **offshore**

onside /ˌɒnˈsaɪd/ (US) /ˌɑːn-/ **adj, adv** (in football and some other sports) in a position where you are allowed to kick, throw, or receive the ball or PUCK → Compare **offside**

ˌon-ˈsite adj, adv existing or happening in the place where people are working or involved in a particular activity: *on-site facilities* ◦ *We're meeting the builders on-site tomorrow.*

onslaught /ˈɒn.slɔːt/ (US) /ˈɑːn.slɑːt/ **noun** [C] a very powerful attack: *It is unlikely that his forces could withstand an allied onslaught for very long.* ◦ *Scotland's onslaught **on** Wales in the second half of the match earned them a 4–1 victory.*

onstage /ˌɒnˈsteɪdʒ/ (US) /ˈɑːn-/ **adv, adj** onto or on a stage for a performance: *The audience cheered as the band walked onstage for another encore.* ◦ *onstage dancers*

onto (also **on to**) /ˈɒn.tu/ (US) /ˈɑːn.tu/ **preposition** MOVEMENT ▷ **1** B1 used to show movement into or on a particular place: *I slipped as I stepped onto the platform.* ◦ *The sheep were loaded onto trucks.* **CHANGING SUBJECT** ▷ **2** B2 used about changing to, or starting to talk about, a different subject: *How did we **get** onto this subject?* ◦ *Can we **move** onto the next item on the agenda?* ◦ *I'd now like to **come** onto my next point.* **HOLDING** ▷ **3 hold, hang, grip, etc. onto** to keep holding something: *Hold onto my hand and you'll be perfectly safe.* **KNOWING** ▷ **4** knowing about someone or something that can be useful to you: *So how did you **get** onto this deal?* ◦ *David **put** me onto (= told me about) a really good restaurant.* ◦ *You're onto **a good thing** with this buy-one-get-one-free offer at the shop.* **5** knowing about something bad someone has done: *He knows we're onto him.* ◦ *Who **put** the police onto (= told the police about) her?* **ASKING** ▷ **6** UK If you are onto someone, you talk to them, especially to ask them to do something, or to complain to them: *I must **get** onto the plumber about the shower.* ◦ *Dad was onto her again about doing her homework.* **ADDING** ▷ **7** used about someone or something that is added to or joins a particular thing: *Imir's been voted onto the union committee.* ◦ *I've been having problems loading this software onto my computer.*

ontological /ɒn.tə'lɒdʒ.ɪ.kəl/ US /ɑːn.toʊ'lɑː.dʒɪ-/ **adj** relating to ontology: *the ontological argument for the existence of God*

ontology /ɒn'tɒl.ə.dʒi/ US /ɑːn'tɑː.lə-/ **noun** [U] the part of PHILOSOPHY that studies what it means to exist

ˌon-'trend **adj** informal very fashionable: *the best place to buy cheap on-trend party clothes*

the onus /'əʊ.nəs/ US /'oʊ-/ **noun** [S] formal the responsibility or duty to do something: [+ to infinitive] *The onus is **on** the landlord **to** ensure that the property is habitable.* ◦ *We are trying to shift the onus **for** passenger safety onto the government.*

onward /'ɒn.wəd/ US /'ɑːn.wəd/ **adj** [before noun] formal C1 moving forward to a later time or a more DISTANT (= farther away) place: *the onward march of time.* ◦ UK *If you are continuing on an onward **flight**, your bags will be transferred automatically.*

IDIOM **onward and upward** becoming more and more successful: *Her publishing career started as an editorial assistant on a women's magazine and it was onward and upward from there.*

onwards /'ɒn.wədz/ US /'ɑːn.wədz/ **adv** mainly UK (mainly US **onward**) **TIME** ▷ **1 from 6.30, March, the 1870s, etc. onwards** C2 beginning at a particular time and continuing after it: *I'm usually at home from five o'clock onwards.* **DIRECTION** ▷ **2** C2 If you move onwards, you continue to go forwards: *We sailed onwards in a westerly direction.*

onyx /'ɒn.ɪks/ US /'ɑː.nɪks/ **noun** [U] a valuable stone with white and grey stripes that is used in jewellery

oodles /'uː.dlz/ **noun** [plural] old-fashioned informal a very large amount of something pleasant: *She inherited oodles **of** money from her uncle.*

ooh /uː/ **exclamation; verb**

▸**exclamation** an expression of surprise, pleasure, approval, disapproval or pain: *Ooh, what a lovely dress!* ◦ *Ooh, yes, that would be nice!* ◦ *Ooh, that's a bit unkind!*

▸**verb** [I]

IDIOM **ooh and aah** informal to express admiration: *We watched the fireworks, oohing and aahing with everyone else.*

oomph /ʊmf/, /uːmf/ **noun** [U] informal power, strength, or energetic activity: *You want a car **with a bit of** oomph.* ◦ *It's important to have someone with a bit of oomph in charge of the department.*

oops /uːps/, /ʊps/ **exclamation** (also **whoops**) an expression of surprise or feeling sorry about a mistake or slight accident: *Oops! I've typed two L's by mistake.*

'oops-a-ˌdaisy **exclamation** (also **'ups-a-ˌdaisy**) something said to young children when they fall over

ooze /uːz/ **verb; noun**

▸**verb** [I + adv/prep, T] to flow slowly out of something through a small opening, or to slowly produce a thick sticky liquid: *Blood was still oozing **out of** the wound.* ◦ *She removed the bandage to reveal a red swollen wound oozing pus.* ◦ *The waiter brought her a massive pizza oozing (**with**) cheese.* ◦ figurative *He oozes (= has a lot of) charm/confidence.*

▸**noun** [U] a thick brown liquid made of earth and water, found at the bottom of a river or lake

op /ɒp/ US /ɑːp/ **noun** [C] **OPERATION** ▷ **1** UK informal a medical operation: *How long did you take to recover from your op?* **OPPORTUNITY** ▷ **2** an opportunity: *a **photo** op (= a chance for a politician, etc. to be photographed looking good or doing good things)*

Op. **noun** written abbreviation for **opus**: *Dvorak's Piano Concerto in G Minor, Op. 33*

opacity /əʊ'pæs.ə.ti/ US /oʊ'pæs.ə.t̬i/ **noun** [U] formal the state of being OPAQUE, or the degree to which something is opaque

opal /'əʊ.pəl/ US /'oʊ-/ **noun** [C or U] a PRECIOUS STONE whose colour changes when the position of the person looking at it changes

opalescent /ˌəʊ.pəl'es.ənt/ US /ˌoʊ-/ **adj** literary describes something that reflects light and changes colour like an opal: *the opalescent scales of a fish* • **opalescence** /-əns/ **noun** [U]

opaque /əʊ'peɪk/ US /oʊ-/ **adj** **1** preventing light from travelling through, and therefore not transparent or TRANSLUCENT: *opaque glass/tights* **2** formal describes writing or speech that is difficult to understand: *I find her poetry rather opaque.* • **opaquely** /-li/ **adv**

'op ˌart **noun** [U] a type of modern art which uses patterns that do not exist naturally in order to create images which appear to move or to be something that they are not

op. cit. /ˌɒp'sɪt/ US /ˌɑːp-/ **adv** formal abbreviation used by writers to avoid repeating the details of a book or article that has already been referred to: *Johnson (op. cit., page 53) calls this phenomenon 'the principle of minimal effort'.*

OPEC /'əʊ.pek/ US /'oʊ-/ **noun** abbreviation for Organization of Petroleum Exporting Countries: a group of countries which produce oil and decide together how much to produce

op-ed /ˌɒp'ed/ US /ˌɑːp-/ **adj** [before noun] US describes a piece of writing which expresses a personal opinion and is usually printed in a newspaper opposite the page on which the EDITORIAL is printed: *an op-ed article/column/page* • **op-ed** **noun** [C] *His rebuttal appeared in yesterday's op-ed.*

open /'əʊ.pən/ US /'oʊ-/ **adj; verb; noun**

▸**adj** **NOT CLOSED** ▷ **1** A2 not closed or fastened: *an open door/window* ◦ *An open suitcase lay on her bed.* ◦ *You left the packet open.* ◦ *Someone had left the window **wide** (= completely) open.* ◦ *He had several nasty open **wounds** (= those which had not begun to heal).* **READY** ▷ **2** A1 [after verb] ready to be used or ready to provide a service: *The supermarket is open till 8.00 p.m.* ◦ *The road is open now, but it is often blocked by snow in the winter.* ◦ *The new hospital was declared open by the mayor.* **NOT ENCLOSED** ▷ **3** B1 not closed in or covered: *From the garden there was a marvellous view over open* ***countryside***. ◦ *It's not a good idea to camp in the middle of an open* ***field*** *(= one which is not covered with trees, bushes, etc.).* ◦ *The survivors were adrift on the open* ***sea*** *(= far from land).* **COMPUTER** ▷ **4** If a computer document or program is open, it is ready to be read or used: *Make sure the file you're copying to is open before you click 'Paste'.* **AVAILABLE** ▷ **5** (C1) [after verb] available; not limited: *There are still several possibilities open* ***to*** *you.* ◦ *The competition is open* ***to*** *anyone over the age of 16.* ◦ *Is the library open* ***to*** *the general public?* ◦ *Their whole attitude to these negotiations is open* ***to*** *criticism (= can be criticized).* ◦ *I'd like to think I'm open* ***to*** *(= willing to consider) any reasonable suggestion.* ◦ *An accident would* ***lay*** *the whole issue of safety open (= cause it to be considered).* **NOT SECRET** ▷ **6** (C2) not secret: *There has been open hostility between them ever since they had that argument last summer.* **7** (C2) honest and not trying to keep things secret: *He's quite open about his weaknesses.* ◦ *I wish you'd be more open* ***with*** *me, and tell me what you're feeling.* ◦ *She has an honest, open face.* **NOT DECIDED** ▷ **8** not decided or certain: *We don't have to make a firm decision yet. Let's* ***leave it*** *open.* ◦ *We can leave our offer open for another week, but we must have your decision by then.* ◦ *I want to keep my* ***options*** *open, so I'm not committing myself yet.*

IDIOM **greet/welcome sb with open arms** to show someone that you are very pleased to see them

▸verb **BEGIN** ▷ **1** (B2) [I or T] to (cause to) begin: *I would like to open my talk by giving a brief background to the subject.* ◦ *I'm going to open an account with another bank.* ◦ *The Olympic Games open tomorrow.* ◦ *A new radio station is due to open (****up****) next month.* ◦ *The film opens (= will be shown for the first time) in New York and Los Angeles next week.* **NOT CLOSED** ▷ **2** (A1) [I or T] to move something to a position that is not closed, or to make something change to a position that is not closed: *Could you open the window, please?* ◦ *You can open your eyes now – here's your present.* ◦ *The flowers open (****out****) in the morning but close again in the afternoon.* ◦ *From the kitchen there is a door that opens (****out****)* ***into/onto*** *the garden.* ◦ informal *'Open* ***up*** *(= open the door) – it's the police!' shouted the police officer, banging on the door.* **3** (A2) [T] to remove or separate part of a container or parcel so that you can see or use what it contains: *Don't open a new bottle just for me.* ◦ *I couldn't wait to open the letter.* **READY** ▷ **4** (A2) [I or T] If a shop or office opens at a particular time of day, it starts to do business at that time: *The café opens at ten o'clock.* ◦ *He opens (****up****) his café at ten o'clock.* **5** (B2) [T] If someone, usually someone important, opens a building or place or event, they officially say that it is ready to be used or to start operating: *The new hospital will be* ***officially*** *opened by the mayor on Tuesday.*

> **!** Common mistake: **opened or open?**
>
> **Warning:** do not confuse the past tense of the verb 'open', **opened**, with the adjective **open**:
>
> ~~*The supermarket is opened until 9 p.m. on Thursday.*~~
>
> *The supermarket is open until 9 p.m. on Thursday.*

AVAILABLE ▷ **6** [T] to make something available: *This research opens (up) the possibility of being able to find a cure for the disease.* ◦ *The country is planning to open (up) its economy* ***to*** *foreign investment.* **COMPUTER** ▷ **7** (B1) [T] If you open a computer document or program, you make it ready to read or use: *To open a new document, click 'File', then click 'New'.*

IDIOMS **the earth/ground/floor opens** People say that they wish the earth/floor/ground would open (up) if they are so embarrassed that they want suddenly to disappear: *At that moment the boss walked in and I just wanted the ground to open up and swallow me.* • **open sb's eyes** to make someone realize something surprising or shocking, which they had not known about or understood before: *She really opened my eyes* ***to*** *how stupid I'd been.* • **open your heart to someone** to tell someone about your problems and secrets: *She's very understanding – you feel you can really open your heart to her.* • **open your mouth** to speak or start to speak: *Don't look at me – I never opened my mouth.* • **open the door to sth** to allow something new to start: *The ceasefire has opened the door to talks between the two sides.*

PHRASAL VERBS **open sth out/up** to make a space larger or less closed in: *We're going to open up our kitchen by knocking down a couple of walls.* • **open (sth) up** to open the lock on the door of a building: *The caretaker opens up the school every morning at seven.* • **open sth up SITUATION** ▷ **1** to improve a situation by making it less limited: *The government has announced plans to open up access to higher education.* **SHOW** ▷ **2** to show something that was hidden or not previously known: *The debate could open up sharp differences between the countries.* • **open sb up** informal to do a medical operation on someone to see inside their body: *When they opened her up, they couldn't find anything wrong with her.* • **open up** (C2) to start to talk more about yourself and your feelings: *I've never opened up* ***to*** *anyone like I do to you.*

▸noun [S] **NOT ENCLOSED** ▷ **1 the open** somewhere outside, rather than in a building: *It's good to be (****out****)* ***in*** *the open after being cooped up in an office all day.* **NOT SECRET** ▷ **2 bring sth out into the open** to tell people information that was secret: *It's time this issue was brought out into the open.*

ˌopen adˈmissions noun [U] (also **ˌopen enˈrollment**) US a system that allows students to go to a college without having any special qualifications for it

ˌopen aˈdoption noun [C] mainly US an arrangement by which children are legally ADOPTED by people who are not their natural parents, but still continue to communicate with their natural parents

ˌopen-ˈair adj [before noun] describes a place that does not have a roof, or an event which takes place outside: *an open-air concert/market*

ˌopen-and-ˈshut adj describes a problem or legal matter that is easy to prove or answer: *Our lawyer thinks that we have an open-and-shut* ***case***.

ˌopen ˈbook noun **be an open book** If someone is an open book, it is easy to know what they are thinking and feeling.

ˌopen-ˈcasket adj US used to describe a funeral at which the COFFIN is open and people can see the dead person's body: *an open-casket* ***funeral/service*** → Compare **closed-casket**

opencast /ˈəʊ.pᵊn.kɑːst/ (US) /ˈoʊ.pᵊn.kæst/ adj UK (US **ˈopen-cut**) describes a place where minerals, especially coal, are taken from the surface of the ground rather than from passages dug under it, or relating to this way of getting minerals: *opencast mine/mining*

ˌopen ˈclassroom noun [U] in the US, a system for educating young children in which classes and activities are informal and changed to suit each child

ˌopen-ˈcut adj US for **opencast**

ˌopen ˈday noun [C] UK (US **ˌopen ˈhouse**) a day when an organization such as a school, college, or factory allows members of the public to go in and see what happens there

ˌopen-ˈdoor adj [before noun] allowing people and goods to come freely into a place or country: *an open-door system* ◦ *open-door regulations*

ˌopen-ˈended adj An open-ended activity or situation does not have a planned ending, so it may develop in several ways: *We are not willing to enter into open-ended discussions.*

opener /ˈəʊ.pᵊn.əʳ/ (US) /ˈoʊ.pᵊn.ɚ/ noun **1 bottle, can, tin, etc. opener** [C] a device for opening closed containers **2 for openers** informal first: *Just for openers, I'd like to ask a question.*

ˌopen-faced ˈsandwich noun [C] US (UK **ˌopen ˈsandwich**) a single slice of bread with various types of food, such as cold fish or meat, on the top

ˌopen ˈfire noun [C] UK (US **ˌopen ˈfireplace**) a space in a wall of a building in which a fire can be lit, with a CHIMNEY to take the smoke away, or a fire that burns in such a space: *We roasted chestnuts on the open fire.*

ˌopen-ˈhanded adj generous: *open-handed assistance*

ˌopen-ˈhearted adj Someone who is open-hearted is kind, loving, and honest.

ˌopen-heart ˈsurgery noun [U] a medical operation in which the body is cut open and the heart is repaired, while the body's blood is kept flowing by a machine

ˌopen ˈhouse noun [U] **1** a situation in which people welcome visitors at any time: *We **keep** open house, so come and see us any time.* **2** US a time when a house or apartment that is being sold can be looked at by the public

opening /ˈəʊ.pᵊn.ɪŋ/ (US) /ˈoʊp.nɪŋ/ noun; adj

►noun **HOLE** ▷ **1** C2 [C] a hole or space that something or someone can pass through: *The children crawled through an opening **in** the fence.* **CEREMONY** ▷ **2** B2 [C usually singular] a ceremony at the beginning of an event or activity: *The **official** opening **of** the new school will take place next month.* **BEGINNING** ▷ **3** B2 [C usually singular] the beginning of something: *The opening of the novel is amazing.* **OPPORTUNITY** ▷ **4** [C] a job or an opportunity to do something: *There's **an** opening **for** an editorial assistant in our department.*

►adj [before noun] C1 happening at the beginning of an event or activity: *her opening remarks* ◦ *the opening night*

ˈopening ˌhours noun [plural] UK the times when a business, such as a bar, restaurant, shop or bank, is open for people to use it

ˈopening ˌnight noun [C usually singular] the first night that a play, film, etc. is performed or shown: *The ballet's opening night was a huge success.*

ˈopening ˌtime noun [C usually singular] UK the time at which a bar or pub opens

ˌopen ˈletter noun [C] a letter intended to be read by a lot of people, not just the person it is written to: *An open letter to the prime minister, signed by several MPs, appeared in today's papers.*

openly /ˈəʊ.pᵊn.li/ (US) /ˈoʊ-/ adv C1 without hiding any of your thoughts or feelings: *They were openly contemptuous of my suggestions.* ◦ *We discussed our reservations about the contract quite openly.*

ˌopen ˈmarket noun [S] a situation in which companies can trade freely without limits, and prices are changed according to the number of goods and how many people are buying them: *In the meantime, the shares will continue to trade **on** the open market.*

ˌopen ˈmarriage noun [C] a marriage in which both partners are free to have sexual relationships with other people

ˌopen ˈmind noun **have/keep an open mind** B2 to wait until you know all the facts before forming an opinion or making a judgment: *We should keep an open mind until all of the evidence is available.*

ˌopen-ˈminded adj C1 willing to consider ideas and opinions that are new or different to your own: *Doctors these days tend to be more open-minded **about** alternative medicine.* • **open-mindedness** /-nəs/ noun [U]

ˌopen-ˈmouthed adj with your mouth wide open, especially because you are surprised or shocked: *They stared open-mouthed at the extent of the damage.*

ˌopen-ˈnecked adj [before noun] refers to a shirt that is not fastened at the neck

openness /ˈəʊ.pᵊn.nəs/ (US) /ˈoʊ-/ noun [U] C2 honesty: *If these discussions are to succeed, we'll need openness from/on both sides.*

ˌopen-ˈplan adj describes a room or building that has few or no walls inside, so it is not divided into smaller rooms: *an open-plan office*

ˌopen ˈprison noun [C] UK (US **ˌminimum-seˈcurity prison**) a prison where prisoners are not kept inside because they are trusted not to escape

ˌopen ˈsandwich noun [C] UK (US **ˌopen-faced ˈsandwich**) a single slice of bread with various types of food, such as cold fish or meat, on the top

ˌopen ˈseason noun **1** [S or U] the period in the year when it is legal to hunt particular animals → Compare **close season 2** [U] a situation which allows or causes a particular group of people to be treated unfairly: *To pass this legislation would be to **declare** open season **on** homosexuals.*

ˌopen ˈsesame noun [C usually singular] something that makes it very easy to achieve a particular thing: *A science degree can be an open sesame **to** a job in almost any field.*

ˌopen-ˈsource adj specialized Open-source software is free to use, and the original program can be changed by anyone.

ˈopen-top adj [before noun] (also **ˈopen-topped**) an open-top car, bus, etc. does not have a roof, or has a roof that you can fold back

ˌOpen Uniˈversity noun [S] in the UK, a university that usually accepts students without formal qualifications and allows them to study from home, receiving and sending work by post, by email, or over the internet

ˌopen ˈverdict noun [C usually singular] UK legal a legal decision which records a death but does not state its cause

opera /ˈɒp.ᵊr.ə/, /ˈɒp.rə/ (US) /ˈɑː.pɚ.ə/ noun [C or U] A2 a musical play in which most of the words are sung, or plays and music of this type: *'Carmen' is my favourite opera.* ◦ *I've never been a huge fan of opera.* ◦ *He goes to **the** opera (= to see an opera) whenever he can.* ◦ *an opera singer* → Compare **operetta**

operable /ˈɒp.ᵊr.ə.bl/ (US) /ˈɑː.pɚ.ə-/ adj **WORKING** ▷ **1** able to be used: *There will be a delay before the modified machines are operable.* **MEDICINE** ▷ **2** able to be treated by an operation: *In about half of diagnosed cases, the condition is operable.* → Opposite **inoperable**

ˈopera ˌglasses noun [plural] small BINOCULARS that can be used in large theatres by people sitting far

O

from the stage, so that they can see the performers more clearly

opera glasses

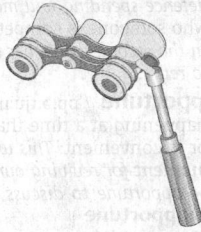

ˈ**opera ˌhouse** noun [C] a theatre that is specially designed for operas to be performed in: *the Royal Opera House, Covent Garden*

operate /ˈɒp.ᵊr.eɪt/ (US) /ˈɑː.pə.reɪt/ verb **WORK** ▷ **1** B2 [I or T] to (cause to) work, be in action or have an effect: *How do you operate the remote control unit?* ◦ *Does the company operate a pension scheme?* ◦ *For several years she operated a dating agency from her basement flat.* ◦ *Changes are being introduced to make the department operate more efficiently.* ◦ *Specially equipped troops are operating in the hills.* ◦ *We have representatives operating in most countries.* ◦ *Exchange rates are currently operating to the advantage of exporters.* **MEDICAL PROCESS** ▷ **2** B1 [I] to cut a body open for medical reasons in order to repair, remove, or replace an unhealthy or damaged part: *If the growth gets any bigger they'll have to operate.* ◦ *Are they going to operate **on** him?*

operatic /ˌɒp.ᵊrˈæt.ɪk/ (US) /ˌɑː.pəˈræt̬-/ adj of, for or relating to opera: *an operatic society* ◦ *operatic arias* • **operatically** /-ɪ.kᵊl.i/ adv

ˈ**operating ˌroom** noun [C] US for **operating theatre**

ˈ**operating ˌsystem** noun [C] a set of programs that control the way a computer system works, especially how its memory is used and how different programs work together

ˈ**operating ˌtable** noun [C] a special table that a patient lies on during an operation

ˈ**operating ˌtheatre** noun [C] UK (US ˈ**operating ˌroom**) a special room in which people are operated on in a hospital

operation /ˌɒp.ᵊrˈeɪ.ʃᵊn/ (US) /ˌɑː.pəˈreɪ-/ noun **WORK** ▷ **1** C1 [U] the fact of operating or being active: *There are several reactors of the type **in** operation (= working) at the moment.* ◦ *We expect the new scheme for assessing claims to **come into** operation (= start working) early next year.* **2** [U] the way that parts of a machine or system work together, or the process of making parts of a machine or system work together **3** C1 [C] a business organization: *Less profitable business operations will have difficulty in finding financial support.* **4** C1 [C] an activity that is planned to achieve something: *a military/peacekeeping operation.* ◦ *Following the earthquake, a large-scale **rescue** operation was **launched**.* ◦ [+ to infinitive] *The operation to fly in supplies will begin as soon as possible.* **MEDICAL PROCESS** ▷ **5** B1 [C] (UK informal **op**) an occasion when a doctor cuts a body for medical reasons in order to repair, remove, or replace an unhealthy or damaged part: *a major/minor/routine operation* ◦ *an abdominal/cataract/transplant operation* ◦ *He's got to **have** an operation **on** his shoulder.* ◦ [+ to infinitive] *We will know in a couple of days if the operation **to** restore her sight was **successful**.* **MATHEMATICS** ▷ **6** [C] specialized a mathematical process, such as addition, in which one set of numbers is produced from another

operational /ˌɒp.ᵊrˈeɪ.ʃᵊn.ᵊl/ (US) /ˌɑː.pəˈreɪ-/ adj **1** relating to a particular activity: *There are operational advantages in putting sales and admin in the same building.* **2** If a system is operational, it is working: *Repairs have already begun and we expect the factory to be **fully** operational again with six months.* • **operationally** /-i/ adv

opeˌrational reˈsearch noun [U] UK (US **opeˌrations reˈsearch**) work that is done to find the best ways to solve problems in business and industry

operative /ˈɒp.ᵊr.ə.tɪv/ (US) /ˈɑː.pɚ.ə.t̬ɪv/ **noun; adj**

▸**noun** [C] **1** formal a worker, especially one who is skilled in working with their hands: *a factory operative* **2** mainly US a person who works secretly for an organization: *a CIA operative*

▸**adj** formal working or being used: *The agreement will not become operative until all members have signed.* → Opposite **inoperative**

IDIOM **the operative word** the most important word in a phrase, which explains the truth of a situation: *He was a painter – 'was' being the operative word since he died last week.*

operator /ˈɒp.ᵊr.eɪ.təʳ/ (US) /ˈɑː.pə.reɪ.t̬ɚ/ noun [C] **1** B2 someone whose job is to use and control a machine or vehicle: *a computer operator* **2** B2 a company that does a particular type of business: *a tour operator* **3** a person who helps to connect people on a phone system **4 a smooth, clever, etc. operator** a person who deals with people or problems cleverly, especially for their own advantage: *He has shown himself to be a canny operator in wage negotiations.*

operetta /ˌɒp.ᵊrˈet.ə/ (US) /ˌɑː.pəˈret̬-/ noun [C or U] a humorous theatre piece with singing and sometimes dancing, or works of this type

ophˌthalmic opˈtician noun [C] UK for **optician**

ophthalmologist /ˌɒf.θælˈmɒl.ə.dʒɪst/ (US) /ˌɑːf.θælˈmɑː.lə-/ noun [C] a doctor who treats eye diseases → Compare **optician, optometrist**

ophthalmology /ˌɒf.θælˈmɒl.ə.dʒi/ (US) /ˌɑːf.θælˈmɑː.lə-/ noun [U] the scientific study of eyes and their diseases → Compare **optometry**

opiate /ˈəʊ.pi.ət/ (US) /ˈoʊ-/ noun [C] a drug which contains OPIUM, especially one which causes sleep

opine /əʊˈpaɪn/ (US) /oʊ-/ verb [T] formal to express an opinion: [+ speech] *Power grows from the barrel of a gun, opined Mao.* ◦ [+ that] *Ernest Rutherford opined **that** his work on radioactive substances would be of little or no practical use.*

opinion /əˈpɪn.jən/ noun **1** B1 [C] a thought or belief about something or someone: *What's your opinion **about/on** the matter?* ◦ *People tend to **have** strong opinions on capital punishment.* ◦ *He didn't **express/give** an opinion on the matter.* ◦ *Who, **in** your opinion, (= who do you think) is the best football player in the world today?* ◦ *He's very much **of the** opinion **that** alternative medicine is a waste of time.* **2** B2 [U] the thoughts or beliefs that a group of people have: *Eventually, the government will have to take notice of **public** opinion.* ◦ *There is a diverse range of opinion on the issue.* ◦ *There was a **difference of** opinion as to the desirability of the project.* ◦ *Opinion **is divided** as to whether the treatment actually works.* ◦ *Both performances were excellent, it's simply **a matter of** opinion as to whose was better.* **3** B1 [C] a judgment about someone or something: *Her opinion **of** Adam changed after he'd been so helpful at the wedding.* ◦ *She **has** a **good/high** opinion **of** his abilities (= thinks he is good).* ◦ *I **have** a rather **bad/low/poor** opinion **of** my sister's boyfriend (= I do not like or approve of him).* ◦ *He has a very **high** opinion **of himself** (= thinks he is very skilled/clever in a way that is annoying).* **4** B1 [C] a judgment made by an expert: *My doctor has referred*

O

me to a specialist for a **second** opinion on the results of my blood test.

! Common mistake: opinion

Warning: Check your spelling!

Opinion is one of the 50 words most often spelled wrongly by learners.

! Common mistake: opinion

Use **in my opinion** to introduce your own thoughts or beliefs about someone or something. Don't say 'to my opinion' or 'on my opinion', say **in my opinion**:

In my opinion, the school holidays are much too long.

Word partners for opinion

have/hold an opinion • *express/give/voice* an opinion • *conflicting/differing/strong* opinions • sb's *considered/personal* opinion • *in* sb's opinion • sb's opinion *about* sth • be *of* the opinion (that)

Other ways of saying opinion

The words **view**, **feeling**, and **thoughts** can be used instead of 'opinion':

*In my **view**, her criticisms were justified.*

*My **feeling** is that we should wait a while.*

*What are your **thoughts** on the matter?*

Point of view or **viewpoint** is used especially when someone's opinion depends on that person's situation:

*We interviewed a lot of people in order to get several **points of view**.*

*Try to understand my **viewpoint**.*

The word **attitude** is used especially when someone's opinion causes that person to behave in a particular way:

*It can be very difficult to change people's **attitudes**.*

If you want to talk about a person's or organization's official opinion, the words **position** or **stance** can be used:

*What's the company's **position** on recycling?*

*The president's **stance** on global warming has been criticized.*

opinionated /əˈpɪn.jə.neɪ.tɪd/ (US) /-t̬ɪd/ **adj** disapproving describes someone who is certain about what they think and believe, and who expresses their ideas strongly and often: *He was opinionated and selfish, but undeniably clever.*

oˈpinion ˌpoll **noun** [C] an occasion when people are asked questions to discover what they think about a subject: *The latest opinion poll shows that the president's popularity has declined.*

opium /ˈəʊ.pi.əm/ (US) /ˈoʊ-/ **noun** [U] a drug made from the seeds of a POPPY (= red flower) that is used to control pain or to help people sleep. It can make a person who takes it want more of it and is sometimes used by people as an illegal drug for pleasure: *an opium addict*

opossum /əˈpɒs.əm/ (US) /-ˈpɑː.səm/ **noun** [C] (also **possum**) US informal a small American MARSUPIAL that lives in trees and has thick fur, a long nose, and a tail without fur

opponent /əˈpəʊ.nənt/ (US) /-ˈpoʊ-/ **noun** [C] **1** (B2) a person who disagrees with something and speaks against it or tries to change it: *a political opponent* ◦ *Leading opponents **of** the proposed cuts in defence spending will meet later today.* **2** (B2) a person who someone is competing against in a sports event: *In the second game, her opponent hurt her leg and had to retire.*

opportune /ˈɒp.ə.tjuːn/ (US) /ˌɑː.pɚˈtuːn/ **adj** formal happening at a time that is likely to produce success or is convenient: *This would seem to be an opportune **moment** for reviving our development plan.* ◦ *Would **it** be opportune **to** discuss the contract now?* → Opposite **inopportune**

opportunism /ˌɒp.əˈtjuː.nɪ.zᵊm/ (US) /ˌɑː.pɚˈtuː-/ **noun** [U] behaviour in which you use every situation to try to get power or an advantage: *political opportunism*

opportunist /ˌɒp.əˈtjuː.nɪst/ (US) /ˌɑː.pɚˈtuː-/ **noun; adj**

▸**noun** [C] usually disapproving someone who tries to get power or an advantage in every situation: *He was portrayed as a ruthless opportunist who exploited the publicity at every opportunity.*

▸**adj** [usually before noun] usually disapproving using a situation to get power or an advantage: *The burglary was probably carried out by an opportunist thief who noticed the door was open.*

opportunistic /ˌɒp.ə.tjuːˈnɪs.tɪk/ (US) /ˌɑː.pɚ.tuː-/ **adj** usually disapproving using a situation to get power or an advantage • **opportunistically** /-tɪ.kᵊl.i/ **adv**

opportunity /ˌɒp.əˈtjuː.nə.ti/ (US) /ˌɑː.pɚˈtuː.nə.t̬i/ **noun** **1** (B1) [C or U] an occasion or situation which makes it possible to do something that you want to do or have to do, or the possibility of doing something: *Everyone will **have** an opportunity to comment.* ◦ *I was never given the opportunity **of** going to college.* ◦ [+ to infinitive] *The exhibition is a **unique** opportunity **to** see her later work.* ◦ *An ankle injury meant she **missed** the opportunity **to** run in the qualifying heat.* ◦ formal *Please contact us **at the earliest** opportunity (= as soon as possible).* ◦ *He goes fishing **at every** opportunity (= as often as possible).* ◦ *I used to enjoy going to the theatre, but I don't get much opportunity now.* ◦ *He had a **golden** (= an extremely good) opportunity to score in the first half but squandered it.* **2** (B2) [C] the chance to get a job: *employment/job opportunities* ◦ *opportunities **for young** graduates* ◦ *There are far more opportunities now **for** school-leavers than there were 50 years ago.*

! Common mistake: opportunity

Warning: Check your spelling! **Opportunity** is one of the 50 words most often spelled wrongly by learners. Remember: the correct spelling has 'pp'.

Word partners for opportunity

have/seize/take an opportunity • *give/provide/present* an opportunity • a *golden/great/ideal/perfect* opportunity • a *rare/unique* opportunity • a *lost/wasted* opportunity • *at/every/at the earliest/at the first* opportunity • an opportunity *for* sth

opporˈtunity ˌshop **noun** [C] (informal **ˈop-shop**) Australian English a shop in which a CHARITY sells all types of used goods that are given by the public, or in which they sell new goods, to make money for the work of the charity → Compare **charity shop**

oppose /əˈpəʊz/ (US) /-ˈpoʊz/ **verb** [T] (B2) to disagree with something or someone, often by speaking or fighting against them: *The proposed new exam system has been vigorously opposed by teachers.* ◦ *Most of the local residents opposed the closing of their hospital.* ◦ [+ -ing verb] *I would certainly oppose chang**ing** the system.*

Other ways of saying oppose

If someone opposes something, you can say that the person **objects**:

*No one **objected** to the decision.*

Defy can be used when someone opposes something by refusing to do it:

*A few workers **defied** the decision to strike and went in to work.*

If someone opposes something in a public way, you could use the phrase **speak out against**:

*More and more people are **speaking out against** this unpopular law.*

If someone opposes a particular thing, you can say that the person is **against** it or use the prefix **anti-**:

*His parents were completely **against** the idea.*

*A group of **anti**-war demonstrators were marching in the street.*

Hostile and **antagonistic** can be used when someone opposes something strongly in an angry way:

*Many people were **hostile** to the idea of change.*

*Management was **antagonistic** toward the workers' demands.*

opposed /əˈpəʊzd/ (US) /-ˈpoʊzd/ adj **DIFFERENT ▷ 1** completely different: *Two opposed interpretations of the facts have been presented.* ◦ *His view of the situation is **diametrically** (= very strongly) opposed **to** mine.* **2 as opposed to** (C2) rather than: *I'd prefer to go on holiday in May, as opposed to September.* **DISAGREE WITH ▷ 3 be opposed to sth** (C1) to disagree with a principle or plan: *She's opposed to religious education in schools.*

opposing /əˈpəʊ.zɪŋ/ (US) /-ˈpoʊ-/ adj [before noun] competing or fighting against each other: *Opposing **factions** on the committee are refusing to compromise.*

opposite /ˈɒp.ə.zɪt/ (US) /ˈɑː.pə-/ adj; preposition; noun; adv

▸adj **DIFFERENT ▷ 1** (B2) completely different: *You'd never know they're sisters – they're completely opposite **to** each other in every way.* ◦ *Police attempts to calm the violence had the opposite **effect**.* **FACING ▷ 2** (B1) being in a position on the other side; facing: *My brother and I live on opposite sides of London.* ◦ *The map on the opposite page shows where these birds commonly breed.* ◦ *They sat at opposite ends of the table (**to/from** each other), refusing to talk.* **3** facing the speaker or stated person or thing: *If you want to buy tickets, you need to go to the counter opposite.* ◦ *Who owns that shop opposite (= on the other side of the road)?*

▸preposition **1** (A2) in a position facing someone or something but on the other side: *We're in the building opposite the government offices.* ◦ *They sat opposite each other.* ◦ *Put a tick opposite (= next to) the answer that you think is correct.* **2 act/play/star opposite sb** to act a part in a film or play with someone as a partner: *Katharine Hepburn played opposite Henry Fonda in many films.*

▸noun [C often singular] (B1) something or someone that is completely different from another person or thing: *My father is a very calm person, but my mother is just **the** opposite.* ◦ *She's turned out to be **the exact** opposite of what everyone expected.* ◦ ***The** opposite **of** 'fast' is 'slow'.* ◦ *People say opposites **attract**.*

▸adv (B1) in a position facing someone or something but on the other side: *She asked the man sitting opposite whether he'd mind if she opened the window.* ◦ *The people who live opposite (= on the other side of the road) are always making a lot of noise.*

ˌopposite ˈnumber noun [C usually singular] a person who has a very similar job or rank to you but in a different organization

the ˌopposite ˈsex noun [S, + sing/pl verb] someone who is male if you are female, and female if you are male: *It's not always easy to meet **members of** the opposite sex.*

opposition /ˌɒp.əˈzɪʃ.ən/ (US) /ˌɑː.pə-/ noun **DISAGREEMENT ▷ 1** (C1) [U] strong disagreement: *There is a lot of opposition **to** the proposed changes.* ◦ *The unions are **in** opposition **to** the government over the issue of privatization.* **SPORT ▷ 2 the opposition** (C1) [S, + sing/pl verb] the team or person being played against in a sports competition: *The opposition has/have some good players so it should be a tough match.*

the ˌOppoˈsition noun [S, + sing/pl verb] in some political systems, the elected politicians who belong to the largest party that does not form the government: *the Leader of the Opposition* ◦ *The Opposition has/have condemned the government's proposed tax increases.*

oppress /əˈpres/ verb **RULE ▷ 1** [T often passive] to govern people in an unfair and cruel way and prevent them from having opportunities and freedom: *For years now, the people have been oppressed by a ruthless dictator.* **MAKE UNCOMFORTABLE ▷ 2** [T] to make a person feel uncomfortable or worried, and sometimes ill: *Strange dreams and nightmares oppressed him.*

oppressed /əˈprest/ adj **RULED ▷ 1** governed in an unfair and cruel way and prevented from having opportunities and freedom: *oppressed minorities* ◦ *the poor and the oppressed* **FEELINGS ▷ 2** worried and uncomfortable: *She felt oppressed and discouraged in such an unfriendly environment.*

oppression /əˈpreʃ.ən/ noun [U] **RULE ▷ 1** a situation in which people are governed in an unfair and cruel way and prevented from having opportunities and freedom: *Every human being has the right to freedom from oppression.* ◦ *War, famine and oppression have forced people in the region to flee from their homes.* ◦ *the oppression **of** women* **FEELINGS ▷ 2** a feeling of being very uncomfortable and worried: *Several people had experienced the same feeling of oppression when they slept in that room.*

oppressive /əˈpres.ɪv/ adj **CRUEL ▷ 1** cruel and unfair: *an oppressive government/military regime* **FEELINGS ▷ 2** causing people to feel worried and uncomfortable: *an oppressive silence* **3** If the weather or heat is oppressive, it is too hot and there is no wind: *We were unable to sleep because of the oppressive **heat**.* • **oppressively** /-li/ adv • **oppressiveness** /-nəs/ noun [U]

oppressor /əˈpres.əʳ/ (US) /-ɚ/ noun [C] someone who treats people in an unfair and cruel way and prevents them from having opportunities and freedom: *Sisters, we must rise up and defeat our oppressors.*

opprobrium /əˈprəʊ.bri.əm/ (US) /-ˈproʊ-/ noun [U] formal severe criticism and blame: *International opprobrium has been heaped on the country following its attack on its neighbours.* • **opprobrious** /-əs/ adj

ˈop-shop noun [C] Australian English informal for **opportunity shop**

opt /ɒpt/ (US) /ɑːpt/ verb [I] (C1) to make a choice, especially of one thing or possibility instead of others: *Mike opted **for** early retirement.* ◦ [+ to infinitive] *Most people opt **to** have the operation.*

PHRASAL VERBS **opt in** to choose to be part of an activity, arrangement, etc.: *Company policy is to leave*

O

new workers out of the pension scheme, unless they choose to opt in. • **opt out** to choose not to be part of an activity or to stop being involved in it: *Within any society, there will usually be people who decide to opt out (= choose not to live the way most people do).* ◦ *Employees can choose to opt out **of** the pension plan.*

optic /ˈɒp.tɪk/ (US) /ˈɑːp-/ **adj** [before noun] specialized relating to light or the eyes: *a fibre optic cable*

optical /ˈɒp.tɪ.kəl/ (US) /ˈɑːp-/ **adj** relating to light or the ability to see: *an optical effect* ◦ *an optical microscope* • **optically** /-i/ **adv**

ˌoptical ˈcharacter recogˌnition noun [U] (abbreviation **OCR**) the process by which an electronic device recognizes printed or written letters or numbers

ˌoptical ˈfibre noun [C] a long thin glass rod through which very large amounts of information can be sent in the form of light → See also **fibre optics**

ˌoptical ilˈlusion noun [C] something that tricks your eyes and makes you think you see something that is not really there, or see it differently from how it really is

optician /ɒpˈtɪʃ.ən/ (US) /ɑːp-/ **noun** [C] UK **1** (UK also **ophthalmic optician**, US **optometrist**) someone whose job is examining people's eyes and selling glasses or CONTACT LENSES to correct sight problems → Compare **ophthalmologist 2** US for **dispensing optician**

ˌoptic ˈnerve noun [C] specialized the group of nerve FIBRES (= structures like threads) that pass signals from the RETINA at the back of each eye to the brain

optics /ˈɒp.tɪks/ (US) /ˈɑːp-/ **noun** [U] the study of light and of instruments using light

optimism /ˈɒp.tɪ.mɪ.zəm/ (US) /ˈɑːp.tə-/ **noun** [U] (C2) the quality of being full of hope and emphasizing the good parts of a situation, or a belief that something good will happen: *There was a note of optimism in his voice as he spoke about the company's future.* ◦ *Judging from your exam results, I think you have cause/grounds/reason for **cautious** optimism about getting a university place.* → Opposite **pessimism**

O

optimist /ˈɒp.tɪ.mɪst/ (US) /ˈɑːp.tə-/ **noun** [C] (C1) someone who always believes that good things will happen: *She's a **born** optimist (= someone who has always been optimistic).*

optimistic /ˌɒp.tɪˈmɪs.tɪk/ (US) /ˌɑːp.tə-/ **adj** (B2) hoping or believing that good things will happen in the future: *She is optimistic **about** her chances of winning a gold medal.* • **optimistically** /-tɪ.kəl.i/ **adv**

optimization (UK usually **optimisation**) /ˌɒp.tɪ.maɪˈzeɪ.ʃən/ (US) /ˌɑːp.tə-/ **noun** [U] the act of making something as good as possible: *the optimization of chemical processes*

optimize (UK usually **optimise**) /ˈɒp.tɪ.maɪz/ (US) /ˈɑːp.tə-/ **verb** [T] to make something as good as possible: *We need to optimize our use of the existing technology.*

optimum /ˈɒp.tɪ.məm/ (US) /ˈɑːp-/ **adj** [before noun] (also **optimal**) best; most likely to bring success or advantage: *A mixture of selected funds is an optimum **choice** for future security and return on investment.*

ˈopt-in noun [C or U] the fact of choosing to take part in an activity, arrangement, etc. rather than being forced to take part: *The government operates an opt-in rather than an opt-out system, which means that permission must be sought on a case-by-case basis.*

option /ˈɒp.ʃən/ (US) /ˈɑːp-/ **noun 1** (B1) [C or U] one thing that can be chosen from a set of possibilities, or the freedom to make a choice: *The best option would be to cancel the trip altogether.* ◦ *There are various options **open** to someone who is willing to work hard.* ◦ *They didn't leave him much option – either he paid or they'd beat him up.* **2** [C] specialized the right to buy something in the future: *a share option* ◦ *The publishers decided not to take up their option **on** the paperback version.* **3 have no option (but to do something)** (C1) to have to do a particular thing because there is no possibility of doing anything else: *After her appalling behaviour, we had no option but to dismiss her.*

IDIOM **have/keep your options open** to wait before making a choice: *I'm going to keep my options open while I find out about college courses abroad.*

optional /ˈɒp.ʃən.əl/ (US) /ˈɑːp-/ **adj** (B2) If something is optional, you can choose if you want to do it, pay it, buy it, etc.: *English is compulsory for all students, but art and music are optional.*

optometrist /ɒpˈtɒm.ə.trɪst/ (US) /ɑːpˈtɑː.mə-/ **noun** [C] US (UK **optician**) someone whose job is examining people's eyes and selling glasses or CONTACT LENSES to correct sight problems → Compare **ophthalmologist** • **optometry** /-tri/ **noun** [U] mainly US

ˈopt-out noun [C] a situation in which some members of a group choose not to join or be involved in an activity: *Since the opt-out, the hospital has been responsible for its own budgeting.*

opulent /ˈɒp.jʊ.lənt/ (US) /ˈɑː.pjʊ-/ **adj** expensive and LUXURIOUS: *an opulent lifestyle* ◦ *an opulent hotel* • **opulence** /-ləns/ **noun** [U] • **opulently** /-li/ **adv**

opus /ˈəʊ.pəs/ (US) /ˈoʊ-/ **noun** [C] (plural **opuses** or specialized **opera**) specialized **1** (written abbreviation **Op.**) a piece of music written by a particular musician and given a number relating to the order in which it was published: *Carl Nielsen's Opus 43 quintet* **2** formal any work of art: *He showed us his latest opus, a rather awful painting of a vase of flowers.*

or strong /ɔːr/ (US) /ɔːr/ weak /ər/ (US) /ɚ/ **conjunction** POSSIBILITIES ▷ **1** (A1) used to connect different possibilities: *Is it Tuesday or Wednesday today?* ◦ *You can pay now or when you come back to pick up the paint.* ◦ *Are you listening to me or **not**?* ◦ *The patent was granted in (**either**) 1962 or 1963 – I can't quite remember which.* ◦ *It doesn't matter **whether** you win or lose – it's taking part that's important.* ◦ *There were ten or twelve (= approximately that number of) people in the room.* ◦ *He was only joking – or was he (= but it is possible that he was not)?* **2** (A2) used after a negative verb to mean not one thing and also not another: *The child never smiles or laughs.* → Compare **nor** IF NOT ▷ **3** (B1) if not: *You should eat more, or you'll make yourself ill.* EXPLAIN ▷ **4** (B2) used to show that a word or phrase means the same as, or explains, limits, or corrects, another word or phrase: *Rosalind, or Roz to her friends, took the initiative.* ◦ *Things have been going quite well recently. Or they were, up until two days ago.*

IDIOMS **or no** informal used to emphasize that the stated thing will not make any difference: *Extra pay or no extra pay, I'm not going to work late again tonight.* • **or so** informal (B1) approximately: *They raised two hundred pounds or so for charity.* • **or two** informal (C1) approximately or a little more than: *I'll be with you in **a** minute or two.*

OR /ˌəʊˈɑːr/ (US) /ˌoʊˈɑːr/ **noun** [C] US abbreviation for **operating room**

oracle /ˈɒr.ə.kl̩/ (US) /ˈɔːr-/ **noun** [C] **1** (especially in ancient Greece) a female priest who gave people wise but often mysterious advice from a god, or the advice given **2** someone who knows a lot about a subject and can give good advice: *Professor Ross is regarded as the oracle on eating disorders.*

oracular /ɒrˈæk.jʊ.ləʳ/ (US) /ɔːrˈæk.juː.lɚ/ **adj** formal mysterious and difficult to understand, but probably wise: *an oracular statement*

oral /ˈɔː.rəl/ (US) /ˈɔːr.əl/ **adj; noun**
▸**adj** SPOKEN ▷ **1** (B2) spoken and not written: *an oral agreement/exam* MOUTH ▷ **2** of, taken by, or done to the mouth: *oral hygiene* ◦ *oral contraceptives* ◦ *oral surgery* • **orally** /ˈɔː.rə.li/ (US) /ˈɔːr.ə-/ **adv** *This medicine is to be taken orally.*
▸**noun** [C] an exam, often a type of language exam, in which you give spoken and not written answers: *When do you have your Spanish oral (= exam in spoken Spanish)?*

ˌoral ˈhistory **noun** [U] information about a historical event or period that is told to you by people who experienced it

ˌoral ˈsex **noun** [U] the activity of using the tongue and lips to touch someone's sexual organs in order to give pleasure

orange /ˈɒr.ɪndʒ/ (US) /ˈɔːr-/ **noun; adj**
▸**noun** FRUIT ▷ **1** (A1) [C] a round sweet fruit that has a thick orange skin and an orange centre divided into many parts: *a glass of orange* ***juice*** COLOUR ▷ **2** [C or U] a colour between red and yellow: *Orange is her favourite colour.*
▸**adj** (A1) of a colour between red and yellow: *The setting sun filled the sky with a deep orange glow.* • **orangeness** /-nəs/ **noun** [U]

orangeade /ˌɒr.ɪndʒˈeɪd/ (US) /ˌɔːr-/ **noun** [U] **1** UK (US **orange soda**) a FIZZY sweet drink (= with bubbles), that tastes of oranges: *a can of orangeade* **2** US for **orange squash**

ˌorange ˈsquash **noun** [U] UK (US **orangeade**) a drink that tastes of oranges, made by adding water to very strong, sweet orange juice

orang-utan /əˈræŋ.uː.tæn/, /ɔːˌræŋ.uˈtæn/ (US) /ɔːˈræŋ.ə.tæn/ **noun** [C] (also **orang**) a large APE with reddish-brown hair and long arms that lives in the forests of Sumatra and Borneo

orang-utan

oration /ɔːˈreɪ.ʃən/, /ɒrˈeɪ-/ (US) /ɔːrˈeɪ-/ **noun** [C] formal a formal public speech about a serious subject

orator /ˈɒr.ə.təʳ/ (US) /ˈɔːr.ə.t̬ɚ/ **noun** [C] someone who is good at public speaking: *a skilled orator*

oratorio /ˌɒr.əˈtɔː.ri.əʊ/ (US) /ˌɔːr.əˈtɔːr.i.oʊ/ **noun** [C] (plural **oratorios**) a piece of music for ORCHESTRA and singers which tells a story, usually on a religious subject, without acting → Compare **cantata**

oratory /ˈɒr.ə.tər.i/ (US) /ˈɔːr.ə.tɔːr-/ **noun** [U] formal skilful and effective public speaking: *The prime minister has a reputation for powerful oratory.* • **oratorical** /ˌɒr.əˈtɒr.ɪ.kəl/ (US) /ˌɔːr.əˈtɔːr-/ **adj** *oratorical skill*

orb /ɔːb/ (US) /ɔːrb/ **noun** [C] literary something in the shape of a ball: *the glowing orb of the sun*

orbit /ˈɔː.bɪt/ (US) /ˈɔːr-/ **noun; verb**
▸**noun** [C or U] the curved path through which objects in space move around a planet or star: *The satellite is now* ***in*** *a stable orbit.* ◦ *Once in space, the spacecraft will* ***go into*** *orbit* ***around*** *the Earth.*

IDIOM **go into orbit** informal to increase or succeed very quickly or to be in a state of extreme activity: *Prices have gone into orbit this year.*

▸**verb** [I or T] to follow a curved path around a planet or star: *On this mission the Shuttle will orbit (the Earth) at a height of several hundred miles.* • **orbital** /-bɪ.təl/ (US) /-bɪ.t̬əl/ **adj** *an orbital space station*

ˈorbital ˌroad **noun** [C] UK a road which takes traffic around a city rather than through it

orchard /ˈɔː.tʃəd/ (US) /ˈɔːr.tʃɚd/ **noun** [C] an area of land where fruit trees (but not orange trees or other CITRUS trees) are grown: *an apple/cherry orchard*

orchestra /ˈɔː.kɪ.strə/ (US) /ˈɔːr-/ **noun** MUSIC ▷ **1** (B1) [C, + sing/pl verb] a large group of musicians who play many different instruments together and are led by a CONDUCTOR: *She's a cellist* ***in*** *the City of Birmingham Symphony Orchestra.* THEATRE ▷ **2 the orchestra** [S] US for **stall** • **orchestral** /ɔːˈkes.trəl/ (US) /ɔːr-/ **adj**

ˈorchestra ˌpit **noun** [usually S] the area of a theatre in which musicians play their instruments, usually in front of the stage

orchestrate /ˈɔː.kɪ.streɪt/ (US) /ˈɔːr-/ **verb** [T often passive] MUSIC ▷ **1** to arrange or write a piece of music so that it can be played by an ORCHESTRA ARRANGE ▷ **2** to arrange something carefully, and sometimes unfairly, so as to achieve a wanted result: *Their victory was largely a result of their brilliantly orchestrated election campaign.* • **orchestration** /ˌɔː.kɪˈstreɪ.ʃən/ (US) /ˌɔːr-/ **noun** [C or U]

orchid /ˈɔː.kɪd/ (US) /ˈɔːr-/ **noun** [C] a plant with beautifully coloured flowers that have an unusual shape

ordain /ɔːˈdeɪn/ (US) /ɔːr-/ **verb** CHURCH ▷ **1** [T often passive] to officially make someone a priest or other religious leader, in a religious ceremony: *He was ordained* ***(as)*** *a priest in Ely cathedral in 1987.* ORDER ▷ **2** [T] formal (of God or someone in authority) to order something to happen: *There is strong support here for the tough economic reforms ordained in the federal capital, Prague.* ◦ [+ that] humorous *The council, in its wisdom, has ordained* ***that*** *all the local libraries will close on Mondays.*

ordeal /ɔːˈdɪəl/ (US) /ɔːr-/ **noun** [C] (C2) a very unpleasant and painful or difficult experience: *The hostages' ordeal came to an end when soldiers stormed the building.*

order /ˈɔː.dəʳ/ (US) /ˈɔːr.dɚ/ **noun; verb**
▸**noun** REQUEST ▷ **1** (A2) [C] a request to make, supply, or DELIVER food or goods: *'Can I* ***take*** *your order now?' said the waiter.* ◦ *I would like to* ***place*** *(= make) an order for a large pine table.* **2** [C] a product or a meal that has been asked for by a customer: *The shop phoned to say your order has come in.* **3 be on order** If something is on order, you have asked for it but have not yet received it: *The new drilling equipment has been on order for several weeks.* **4 do/make sth to order** to do or make something especially for a person who has asked for it: *We make wedding cakes to order.* ARRANGEMENT ▷ **5** (B1) [U] the way in which people or things are arranged, either in relation to one another or according to a particular characteristic: *The children lined up* ***in*** *order* ***of*** *age/height.* ◦ *I can't find the file I need because they're all* ***out of*** *order (= they are no longer arranged in the correct way).* ◦ *Put the files in* ***alphabetical/chronological*** *order.* ◦ mainly UK *Here's the* ***running*** *order for the concert (= the order in which each item will happen).* INSTRUCTION ▷ **6** (B2) [C often plural] something that someone tells you you must do: *The soldiers fired as soon as their commander* ***gave*** *the order.* ◦ *Soldiers must* ***obey*** *orders.* ◦ *What are your orders?* ◦ *My orders are* ***to*** *search everyone's bag as they come in.* ◦ *The road was closed all day* ***by*** *order* ***of*** *the police.* ◦ *Clean up this room immediately – and*

O

that's an order! → Compare **request 7 be under orders** to have been told that you must do something by someone in authority: *We are under orders not to allow anyone into the building.* **8** [C] an official instruction telling someone what they can or cannot do, or a written instruction to a bank to pay money to a particular person **PURPOSE** ▷ **9 in order (for sb/sth) to do sth** (also **in order that sth**) (B1) with the aim of achieving something: *He came home early in order to see the children before they went to bed.* ◦ *I agreed to her suggestion in order **not** to upset her.* **TIDY** ▷ **10** (B2) [U] a situation in which everything is arranged in its correct place: *The house was so untidy that she spent the whole day trying to establish some sort of order.* **11 leave/put sth in order** to organize something well: *I try to leave my desk in order when I go home.* ◦ *He put his **affairs** in order (= made arrangements for his personal and business matters) before he went into hospital.* **STATE** ▷ **12** (B1) [U] the state of working correctly or of being suitable for use: *TV for sale **in** (**good**) **working** order.* ◦ *Are your immigration papers **in** order (= legally correct)?* ◦ *The coffee machine is **out of** order (= not working).* **CORRECT BEHAVIOUR** ▷ **13** (C2) [U] a situation in which rules are obeyed and people do what they are expected to do: *The teacher found it hard to **keep** her class **in** order.* ◦ *As the demonstration began to turn violent, the police were called in to **restore** order.* ◦ *After some heated discussion, the chair **called** the meeting **to** order (= told everyone to stop talking so that the meeting could continue).* ◦ UK *Is it **in** order (= allowed) for me to park my car outside the building?* **14 order!** formal an expression used in parliament or a formal meeting to get people's attention and make them stop talking, so that the meeting or discussion can start or continue **SYSTEM** ▷ **15** (C2) [C] a social or political system: *The collapse of Communism at the end of the 1980s encouraged hopes of a new world order.* **RELIGION** ▷ **16** [C, + sing/pl verb] a group of people who join together for religious or similar reasons and live according to particular rules: *religious/holy orders* ◦ *monks of the Cistercian/Franciscan Order* **HONOUR** ▷ **17** [S, + sing/pl verb] a group that people are made members of as a reward for services they have done for their country: *He was made a knight of the Order of the Garter.* **TYPE** ▷ **18** [U] the type or size of something: *These were problems of a completely different order from anything we had faced before.* ◦ formal *No successful business can be run without skills **of the highest** order (= great skills).* **19 of the order of** (UK also **in the order of**) approximately: *The cost will be something in the order of £500.* **BIOLOGY** ▷ **20** [C] specialized (used in the CLASSIFICATION of plants and animals) a group of related plants or animals: *An order is below a class and above a family.*

> **Word partners for order noun (INSTRUCTION)**
> *give/follow/ignore/issue/obey* orders • *clear/strict/written* orders • *act on/under* orders

IDIOMS **orders are orders** said when you have to do something because someone in authority has told you to, and usually when you do not really approve of it: *Nobody wants to do it, but orders are orders, so let's start.* • **out of order** informal If something someone says or does is out of order, it is unpleasant or not suitable and it is likely to upset or offend people: *His behaviour in the meeting was out of order.* • **the lower orders** UK old-fashioned disapproving the poorest social groups in society • **the order of the day 1** formal in parliament or in formal meetings, the list of matters to be discussed on a particular day **2** informal something that is very common or important: *On these TV channels, quiz shows and repeats are becoming the order of the day.*

▸verb **REQUEST** ▷ **1** (A2) [I or T] to ask for something to be made, supplied, or DELIVERED, especially in a restaurant or shop: *I ordered some pasta and a mixed salad.* ◦ [+ two objects] *There are no shirts left in this size but we could order one **for** you/order you one.* **INSTRUCT** ▷ **2** (B2) [T] If a person in authority orders someone to do something, or orders something to be done, they tell someone to do it: *The management has ordered a cutback in spending.* ◦ [+ speech] *'Wait over there,' she ordered.* ◦ [+ to infinitive] *They ordered him **to** leave the room.* **ARRANGE** ▷ **3** [T] to arrange a group of people or things in a list from first to last: *I've ordered the application forms **into** three groups.*

IDIOM **order your thoughts** to plan what you want to say or do: *Just give me a moment to order my thoughts, and then I'll explain the system to you.*

PHRASAL VERBS **order sb about/around** disapproving to tell someone what they should do in an unpleasant or forceful way, especially repeatedly: *You can't just come in here and start ordering people around.* • **order sth in** to order food that is ready to eat to be brought to your home or to the place where you work: *I think I'll stay home tonight, order in a pizza and watch a video.*

ˈorder ˌbook noun [C] a book in which a company or shop keeps a record of customers' orders

ordered /ˈɔː.dəd/ (US) /ˈɔːr.dɚd/ adj (also **ˌwell ˈordered**) carefully arranged or controlled

ˈorder ˌform noun [C] a printed form which a customer uses to request goods or a service

orderly /ˈɔː.dᵊl.i/ (US) /ˈɔːr.dɚ.li/ noun; adj

▸noun [C] **HOSPITAL WORKER** ▷ **1** a hospital worker who does jobs for which no training is necessary, such as helping the nurses or carrying heavy things: *He has a part-time job as a **hospital** orderly.* **SOLDIER** ▷ **2** a soldier who acts as an officer's servant

▸adj well arranged or organized: *She put the letters in three orderly piles.* ◦ *Form an orderly queue.* ◦ *During the bomb scare, the customers were asked to proceed **in an** orderly **fashion** out of the shop.*

ˌorder of ˈmagnitude noun [C usually singular] **1** the approximate size of something, especially a number: *The country's debt this year will be **of** the same order of magnitude as it was last year.* **2** specialized a level in a system used for measuring something in which each level is ten times larger than the one before: *These processor speeds have recently increased by two orders of magnitude (= by a hundred times).*

ˈorder ˌpaper noun [C] in parliament, a list which shows the order in which matters will be discussed on a particular day

ordinal /ˌɔː.dɪ.nəl/ (US) /ˌɔːr.dᵊn.ᵊl/ noun [C] (also **ˌordinal ˈnumber**) a number such as 1st, 2nd, 3rd, 4th, that shows the position of something in a list of things: *Ordinal numbers are used in these sentences: 'She was fifth in the race' and 'They celebrated the 200th anniversary of the university's foundation'.* → Compare **cardinal**

ordinance /ˈɔː.dɪ.nəns/ (US) /ˈɔːr.dᵊn.ᵊns/ noun [C] formal a law or rule made by a government or authority: *City Ordinance 126 forbids car parking in this area.*

ordinarily /ˈɔː.dɪ.nə.rə.li/, /ˌɔː.dᵊnˈer.ɪ-/ (US) /ˈɔːr.dᵊn.er-/ adv usually: *Ordinarily, we send a reminder about a month before payment is required.*

ordinary /ˈɔː.dɪ.nə.ri/ (US) /ˈɔːr.dᵊn.er-/ adj **1** (B1) not different or special or unexpected in any way; usual: *an ordinary neighbourhood* ◦ *Readers of the magazine said they wanted more stories about ordinary people and fewer stories about the rich and famous.* ◦ *Her last concert appearance in Britain was **no** ordinary (= a very special) performance.* **2 in the ordinary way** UK normally, or in the way that usually happens **3 out of the ordinary** C2 unusual: *For the police, the incident seemed **nothing** out of the ordinary/did not seem out of the ordinary.* • **ordinariness** /ˈɔː.dɪ.nə.ri.nəs/ US /ˌɔːr.dənˈer-/ noun [U] *She expected him to act like a star, but she was surprised at his ordinariness.*

ordination /ˌɔː.dɪˈneɪ.ʃən/ US /ˌɔːr.dənˈeɪ-/ noun [C or U] the act or ceremony of making someone a priest or other religious leader

ordnance /ˈɔː.d.nənts/ US /ˈɔːrd-/ noun [U] **1** military supplies, especially weapons and bombs **2** large guns on wheels

the Ordnance Survey /ˌɔːd.nənsˈsɜː.veɪ/ US /ˌɔːrd.nənsˈsɝː-/ noun [S] the government organization that makes detailed official maps of Britain and Northern Ireland

ore /ɔːr/ US /ɔːr/ noun [C or U] rock or soil from which metal can be obtained: *iron/copper ore*

oregano /ˌɒr.ɪˈgɑː.nəʊ/ US /ɔːˈreg.ə.noʊ/ noun [U] a herb whose dried leaves are used in cooking to add flavour, especially in Italian cooking

organ /ˈɔː.gən/ US /ˈɔːr-/ noun **BODY PART** ▷ **1** C1 [C] a part of the body of an animal or plant which performs a particular job: *an external/internal/reproductive organ* **INSTRUMENT** ▷ **2** C2 [C] a musical instrument with a keyboard in which sound is produced by air being forced through pipes of different sizes and lengths when you press the keys with your hands or feet, or in which sound is produced electronically: ***Electronic** organs are much smaller and cheaper than **pipe** organs.* **NEWSPAPER** ▷ **3 the organ of sth** formal a newspaper or broadcasting station produced by a particular organization and giving only the opinions of that organization: *The newspaper Pravda was the official organ of the Communist Party in the Soviet Union.*

organelle /ˌɔː.gənˈel/ US /ˌɔːr-/ noun [C] specialized any structure, such as a NUCLEUS or a CHLOROPLAST, that has a particular purpose inside a living cell

ˈorgan ˌgrinder noun [C] old-fashioned a person who earns money in the street by playing a type of organ that is operated by turning a handle

organic /ɔːˈgæn.ɪk/ US /ɔːr-/ adj **NO CHEMICALS** ▷ **1** B2 not using artificial chemicals in the growing of plants and animals for food and other products: *organic food/fruit/farms/farmers* **LIVING** ▷ **2** being or coming from living plants and animals: *A quarter of the contents of an average family's dustbin is organic **matter**.* → Opposite **inorganic 3** formal (of a disease or illness) producing a physical change in the structure of an organ or part of the body **CARBON** ▷ **4** specialized (of a chemical substance) containing carbon: *Organic chemicals are used in the manufacture of plastics, fibres, solvents and paints.* • **organically** /-ɪ.kəl.i/ adv *The wine is made from organically grown grapes.*

orˌganic ˈchemistry noun [U] the scientific study of chemical substances which contain carbon, including artificial substances such as plastics

organigram (also **organogram**) /ɔːˈgæn.ə.græm/ US /ɔːrˈgæn.ə-/ noun [C] a DIAGRAM (= simple plan) that shows the structure of the people in an organization, for example who has the highest rank

organism /ˈɔː.gən.ɪ.zəm/ US /ˈɔːr-/ noun [C] a single living plant, animal, virus, etc.: *Amoebae and bacteria are single-celled organisms.* → See also **microorganism**

organist /ˈɔː.gən.ɪst/ US /ˈɔːr-/ noun [C] a person who plays an organ, especially in a church or as a job

organization (UK usually **organisation**) /ˌɔː.gən.aɪˈzeɪ.ʃən/ US /ˌɔːr.gən.əˈ-/ noun **GROUP** ▷ **1** B1 [C] a group of people who work together in an organized way for a shared purpose: *the World Health Organization* ◦ *The article was about the international aid organizations.* **ARRANGEMENT** ▷ **2** B1 [U] the planning of an activity or event: *He didn't want to be involved in the organization **of/for** the conference, although he was willing to attend and speak.* **SYSTEM** ▷ **3** C1 [U] the way in which something is done or arranged • **organizational** (UK usually **organisational**) /-əl/ adj [before noun] *She is looking for a personal assistant with good organizational **skills**.*

> **Word partners for organization**
>
> *found/set up* an organization • *join* an organization • a *charitable/international/large/small* organization • be *in* an organization • an organization *for* sth

organize (UK usually **organise**) /ˈɔː.gən.aɪz/ US /ˈɔːr-/ verb [T] **ARRANGE** ▷ **1** B1 to make arrangements for something to happen: *They organized a meeting between the teachers and students.* ◦ [+ to infinitive] UK *She had organized a car **to** meet me at the airport.* **MAKE A SYSTEM** ▷ **2** B2 to do or arrange something according to a particular system: *The books were organized on the shelves **according to** their size.* ◦ informal *My mother is always trying to organize me (= make me do things in the way she likes).*

IDIOM **couldn't organize a piss-up in a brewery** UK offensive said about someone who is completely unable to organize things

O

organized (UK usually **organised**) /ˈɔː.gən.aɪzd/ US /ˈɔːr-/ adj **USING SYSTEM** ▷ **1** B2 arranged according to a particular system: *The letters had been placed in organized piles, one for each letter of the alphabet.* → Opposite **disorganized 2** B2 describes someone who is able to plan things carefully and keep things tidy: *She's not a very organized person and she always arrives late at meetings.* **PLANNED** ▷ **3** B2 (of travel, visits, activities, etc.) planned and arranged for you to do, especially as part of a group: *I don't like going on organized tours.*

ˌorganized ˈcrime noun [U] criminal organizations that plan and commit crime, or the crimes that are committed by such organizations: *The murders may have been linked to organized crime.*

organizer (UK usually **organiser**) /ˈɔː.gən.aɪ.zər/ US /ˈɔːr.gən.aɪ.zɚ/ noun [C] **1** B2 the person or group who plans and arranges an event or activity: *There aren't enough seats for all the guests – I must tell the organizers.* **2** a person who is able to plan things carefully: *We need someone who is a good organizer.*

organophosphate /ɔːˌgæn.əʊˈfɒs.feɪt/ US /ɔːrˌgæn.oʊˈfɑːs.feɪt/ noun [C] a chemical used for killing insects and small animals that damage crops: *organophosphate pesticides/poisoning*

orgasm /ˈɔː.gæz.əm/ US /ˈɔːr-/ noun [C or U] the moment of greatest pleasure and excitement in sexual activity: *to have an orgasm* ◦ *to achieve/reach orgasm* • **orgasm** verb [I]

orgasmic /ɔːˈgæz.mɪk/ US /ɔːr-/ adj **1** relating to orgasm **2** informal producing feelings of great pleasure or excitement: *Their chocolate mousse is simply orgasmic.*

orgiastic /ˌɔː.dʒiˈæs.tɪk/ (US) /ˌɔːr-/ **adj** formal describes an activity which involves wild uncontrolled behaviour and feelings of great pleasure and excitement

orgy /ˈɔː.dʒi/ (US) /ˈɔːr-/ **noun** [C] **1** an occasion when a group of people behave in a wild uncontrolled way, especially involving sex, alcohol or illegal drugs: *drunken orgies* **2 an orgy of sth** disapproving a period when there is too much of something, usually a bad or harmful activity: *The protest degenerated into an orgy of looting and shooting.* ◦ *When she got her first salary cheque, she indulged in an orgy of spending.*

the Orient /ˈɔː.ri.ənt/ (US) /ˈɔːr.i-/ **noun** old-fashioned the countries in the east and southeast of Asia → Compare **the Occident** • **oriental** /ˌɔː.riˈen.təl/ (US) /ˌɔːr.iˈen.t̬əl/ **adj** *oriental cuisine/fruits/plants* → Compare **occidental (the Occident)**

orientalist /ˌɔː.riˈen.təl.ɪst/ (US) /ˌɔːr.iˈen.t̬əl-/ **noun** [C] specialized a person who studies the languages and culture of countries in the east and southeast of Asia

orientate /ˈɔː.ri.ən.teɪt/ (US) /ˈɔːr.i-/ **verb** [T usually + adv/prep] UK (US **orient**) **AIM** ▷ **1** to aim something at someone or something, or make something suitable for a particular group of people: *It is essential that the public sector orientates **itself** more **towards** the consumer.* **FIND POSITION** ▷ **2 orientate yourself** UK (US **orient**) to discover your position in relation to what is around you: *If you get lost while you are out walking, try to use the sun to orientate yourself.*

orientated /ˌɔː.ri.ənˈteɪ.tɪd/ (US) /ˌɔːr.i.enˈteɪ.t̬ɪd/ **adj** UK (US **oriented**) directed towards or interested in something: *The industry is **heavily** orientated **towards** export markets.*

-orientated /-ɔː.ri.en.teɪ.tɪd/ (US) /-ɔːr.i.en.teɪ.t̬ɪd/ **suffix** UK (US **-oriented**) showing the direction in which something is aimed: *She wants to turn the company into a **profit**-orientated organization.*

orientation /ˌɔː.ri.enˈteɪ.ʃən/ (US) /ˌɔːr.i-/ **noun** [U] **PREFERENCES** ▷ **1** (C2) the particular things that a person prefers, believes, thinks, or usually does: *We employ people without regard to their **political** or **sexual** orientation.* **AIMS** ▷ **2** the particular interests, activities, or aims of an organization or business: *the company's new eco-friendly orientation* **TRAINING** ▷ **3** (C2) training or preparation for a new job or activity: *The department has arranged an orientation session.* **ARRANGEMENT** ▷ **4** (C1) formal arrangement or direction: *The building has an east-west orientation* (= it is built on a line between east and west).

orienteering /ˌɔː.ri.ənˈtɪə.rɪŋ/ (US) /ˌɔːr.i.enˈtɪr.ɪŋ/ **noun** [U] an activity in which you have to find your way to somewhere on foot as quickly as possible by using a map and a COMPASS

orifice /ˈɒr.ɪ.fɪs/ (US) /ˈɔːr.ə-/ **noun** [C] an opening or hole, especially one in the body, such as the mouth: humorous *I was stuffing cake into every available orifice.* ◦ formal *The driver was bleeding from every orifice.*

origami /ˌɒr.ɪˈɡɑː.mi/ (US) /ˌɔːr-/ **noun** [U] the art of making objects for decoration by folding sheets of paper into shapes: *Origami comes from Japan, where it is still widely practised.*

origin /ˈɒr.ɪ.dʒɪn/ (US) /ˈɔːr.ə-/ **noun** **1** (B2) [C] (also **origins**) the beginning or cause of something: *It's a book about the origin **of** the universe.* ◦ *Her unhappy childhood was the origin **of** her problems later in life.* ◦ *What's the origin **of** this saying?* (= Where did it come from?) **2 origins** [plural] used to describe the particular way in which something started to exist or someone started their life: *The story has obscure origins* (= no one knows how it started). ◦ *The president's family was **of** humble origins* (= they were poor people without a good position in society). **3** (C1) [U] where a person was born: *He is **of** North African origin.* ◦ *What is your **country of** origin?* **4** (B2) [U] where an object was made: *The furniture was French **in** origin.*

original /əˈrɪdʒ.ɪ.nəl/ **adj; noun**

▸**adj** **FIRST MADE** ▷ **1** (B1) [usually before noun] existing since the beginning, or being the earliest form of something: *Is this the original fireplace?* ◦ *The gardens have recently been restored to their original glory.* **2** (B2) [usually before noun] describes a piece of work, such as a painting, etc. produced by the artist and not a copy: *an original drawing/manuscript* ◦ *Is this an original Rembrandt?* (= Was it painted by him?) **DIFFERENT** ▷ **3** (B1) approving not the same as anything or anyone else and therefore special and interesting: *original ideas/suggestions/work* ◦ *She's a highly original young designer.* → Opposite **unoriginal**

▸**noun** [C] **1** (B2) the first one made and not a copy: *Can you let me have the original of your report? I can't read this photocopy.* **2** (B2) a piece of work by a famous artist or DESIGNER and not a copy by someone else: *If the painting is an original, it will be very valuable.* **3 in the original** If you read something in the original, you read it in the language in which it was first written.

originality /əˌrɪdʒ.ɪˈnæl.ə.ti/ (US) /-t̬i/ **noun** [U] approving the quality of being special and interesting and not the same as anything or anyone else: *We were impressed by the originality **of** the children's work.*

originally /əˈrɪdʒ.ɪ.nə.li/ **adv** (B2) first of all: *Originally it was a bedroom, but we turned it into a study.*

oˌriginal ˈsin **noun** [U] in the Christian religion, the idea that all humans are born with a TENDENCY to be evil

originate /əˈrɪdʒ.ɪ.neɪt/ **verb** **1** (C2) [I] to come from a particular place, time, situation, etc.: *Although the technology originated **in** the UK, it has been developed in the US.* ◦ *The game is thought to have originated **among** the native peoples of Alaska.* **2** [T] to start something or cause it to happen: *Who originated the saying 'Small is beautiful'?*

originator /əˈrɪdʒ.ɪ.neɪ.təʳ/ (US) /-t̬ɚ/ **noun** [C] the person who first thinks of something and causes it to happen: *He is best known as the originator of a long-running TV series.*

oriole /ˈɔː.ri.əʊl/ (US) /ˈɔːr.i.oʊl/ **noun** [C] a type of colourful European or North American bird

ornament **noun; verb**

▸**noun** /ˈɔː.nə.mənt/ (US) /ˈɔːr-/ **1** (C2) [C] an object that is beautiful rather than useful: *a glass ornament* ◦ *garden ornaments such as statues and fountains* **2** [U] formal decoration that is added to increase the beauty of something: *The building relies on clever design rather than on ornament for its impressive effect.*

▸**verb** [T] /ˈɔː.nə.ment/ (US) /ˈɔːr-/ formal to add decoration to something: *She ornamented her letters **with** little drawings in the margin.*

ornamental /ˌɔː.nəˈmen.təl/ (US) /ˌɔːr.nəˈmen.t̬əl/ **adj** beautiful rather than useful: *a bowl of ornamental china fruit* ◦ *The handles on each side of the box are purely ornamental* (= they are for decoration only).

ornamentation /ˌɔː.nə.menˈteɪ.ʃən/ (US) /ˌɔːr-/ **noun** [U] formal decoration: *a plain gold ring with no ornamentation*

ornate /ɔːˈneɪt/ (US) /ɔːr-/ **adj** having a lot of complicated decoration: *a room with an ornate ceiling and gold mirrors* • **ornately** /-li/ **adv**

ornery /ˈɔː.nə.ri/ ⓤⓢ /ˈɔːr-/ **adj** US likely to get angry and argue with people: *He had been in an ornery mood all day, rowing with his wife and his boss.*

ornithologist /ˌɔː.nɪˈθɒl.ə.dʒɪst/ ⓤⓢ /ˌɔːr.nəˈθɑː.lə-/ **noun** [C] specialized a person whose job is to study birds

ornithology /ˌɔː.nɪˈθɒl.ə.dʒi/ ⓤⓢ /ˌɔːr.nəˈθɑː.lə-/ **noun** [U] specialized the study of birds • **ornithological** /ˌɔː.nɪ.θəˈlɒdʒ.ɪ.kᵊl/ ⓤⓢ /ˌɔːr.nə.θəˈlɑː.dʒɪ-/ **adj** [before noun]

orographic /ˌɒr.əˈɡræf.ɪk/ ⓤⓢ /ˌɔːr.oʊˈ-/ **adj** specialized relating to mountains, their shape and how they were formed, etc.

orphan /ˈɔː.fᵊn/ ⓤⓢ /ˈɔːr-/ **noun; verb**
▸**noun** [C] ⓑ a child whose parents are dead: *The civil war is making orphans of many children.*
▸**verb** [T usually passive] to make someone an orphan: *He was orphaned **as** a baby (= his parents died when he was a baby).* ◦ *The children were orphaned by the war (= their parents were killed in the war).*

orphanage /ˈɔː.fᵊn.ɪdʒ/ ⓤⓢ /ˈɔːr-/ **noun** [C] a home for children whose parents are dead or unable to care for them

orthodontics /ˌɔː.θəˈdɒn.tɪks/ ⓤⓢ /ˌɔːr.θoʊˈdɑːn.t̬ɪks/ **noun** [U] specialized the job or activity of correcting the position of teeth and dealing with and preventing problems of the teeth • **orthodontic** /-tɪk/ ⓤⓢ /-t̬ɪk/ **adj** [before noun] *Does she need orthodontic **treatment** to have her teeth straightened?*

orthodontist /ˌɔː.θəˈdɒn.tɪst/ ⓤⓢ /ˌɔːr.θoʊˈdɑːn.t̬ɪst/ **noun** [C] specialized a person whose job is to correct the position of the teeth

orthodox /ˈɔː.θə.dɒks/ ⓤⓢ /ˈɔːr.θə.dɑːks/ **adj 1** ⓒ (of beliefs, ideas, or activities) considered traditional, normal, and acceptable by most people: *orthodox treatment/methods* ◦ *orthodox views/opinions* ◦ *We would prefer a more orthodox approach/solution to the problem.* → Compare **heterodox 2** ⓒ (of religious people) having more traditional beliefs than other people in the same religious group: *orthodox Christians/Jews/Muslims* **3 the (Greek/Russian/Eastern) Orthodox Church** a part of the Christian Church, with many members in Greece, Russia, and eastern Europe

ˌorthodox ˈmedicine **noun** [U] the use of drugs and operations to cure illness: *She is a cancer sufferer who has rejected orthodox medicine and turned instead to acupuncture and other forms of alternative medicine.*

orthodoxy /ˈɔː.θə.dɒk.si/ ⓤⓢ /ˈɔːr.θə.dɑːk-/ **noun 1** [C] the generally accepted beliefs of society at a particular time: *The current economic orthodoxy is of a free market and unregulated trade.* **2** [C or U] the traditional beliefs of a religious group or political party: *She is a strict defender of Catholic orthodoxy.* **3** [U] the degree to which someone believes in traditional religious or political ideas: *His orthodoxy began to be seriously questioned by his parish priest.*

orthogonal /ɔːˈθɒɡ.ᵊn.ᵊl/ ⓤⓢ /ɔːˈθɑː.ɡᵊn-/ **adj** specialized relating to an angle of 90 degrees, or forming an angle of 90 degrees

orthography /ɔːˈθɒɡ.rə.fi/ ⓤⓢ /ɔːˈθɑː.ɡrə-/ **noun** [U] specialized the accepted way of spelling and writing words • **orthographic** /ˌɔː.θəˈɡræf.ɪk/ ⓤⓢ /ˌɔːr.θə-/ **adj** [before noun] • **orthographically** /ˌɔː.θəˈɡræf.ɪ.kᵊl.i/ ⓤⓢ /ˌɔːr.θə-/ **adv**

orthopaedic UK specialized (mainly US **orthopedic**) /ˌɔː.θəˈpiː.dɪk/ ⓤⓢ /ˌɔːr.θə-/ **adj** [before noun] **1** relating to orthopaedics: *an orthopaedic surgeon/specialist/hospital* **2** designed to prevent or treat bone injuries: *an orthopaedic mattress* ◦ *orthopaedic shoes*

orthopaedics /ˌɔː.θəˈpiː.dɪks/ ⓤⓢ /ˌɔːr.θə-/ **noun** [plural] UK (mainly US **orthopedics**) the treatment or study of bones that have not grown correctly or that have been damaged

OS /ˌəʊˈes/ ⓤⓢ /ˌoʊ-/ **noun 1** [U] abbreviation for **the Ordnance Survey 2** [C] **operating system**

Oscar /ˈɒs.kər/ ⓤⓢ /ˈɑː.skɚ/ **noun** [C] trademark one of a set of prizes given each year in the US to the best film, the best male and female actor in any film, and to other people involved in the production of films: *The movie won Oscars **for** best costumes and best screenplay in this year's awards.* ◦ *The Oscar **ceremony** takes place in March every year.*

oscillate /ˈɒs.ɪ.leɪt/ ⓤⓢ /ˈɑː.sᵊl.eɪt/ **verb** [I] **1** to move repeatedly from one position to another: *The needle on the dial oscillated **between** 'full' and 'empty'.* **2** formal If you oscillate between feelings or opinions, you change repeatedly from one to the other: *My emotions oscillate **between** desperation and hope.* **3** specialized (of a wave or electric current) to change regularly in strength or direction • **oscillation** /ˌɒs.ɪˈleɪ.ʃᵊn/ ⓤⓢ /ˌɑː.sᵊlˈeɪ-/ **noun** [C or U] formal or specialized

oscilloscope /əˈsɪl.ə.skəʊp/ ⓤⓢ /-skoʊp/ **noun** [C] a device which represents a changing amount on a screen in the form of a line that moves up and down in curves

osmosis /ɒzˈməʊ.sɪs/ ⓤⓢ /ɑːzˈmoʊ-/ **noun** [U] specialized **LIQUID** ▷ **1** the process in plants and animals by which a liquid moves gradually from one part of the body or the plant to another through a MEMBRANE (= cell covering): *Fluid flows back into the tiny blood vessels **by** osmosis.* **IDEAS** ▷ **2** the way in which ideas and information gradually spread between people: *The children were never taught the songs, they just listened to other children singing them and learned them **by** osmosis.* ◦ *Reading is not picked up **by a process of** osmosis, but needs to be taught.* • **osmotic** /-ˈmɒt.ɪk/ ⓤⓢ /-ˈmɑː.t̬ɪk/ **adj** [before noun] *an osmotic process*

osprey /ˈɒs.preɪ/ ⓤⓢ /ˈɑː.spri/ **noun** [C] a large bird with black and white feathers that eats fish

ossify /ˈɒs.ɪ.faɪ/ ⓤⓢ /ˈɑː.sə-/ **verb** **IDEAS** ▷ **1** [I or T] formal disapproving If habits or ideas ossify, or if something ossifies them, they become fixed and unable to change: *Years of easy success had ossified the company's thinking and it never faced up to the challenge of the new technology.* **BODY** ▷ **2** [I] specialized If body tissue ossifies, it becomes hard and changes into bone. • **ossification** /ˌɒs.ɪ.fɪˈkeɪ.ʃᵊn/ ⓤⓢ /ˌɑː.sə-/ **noun** [U] • **ossified** /-faɪd/ **adj**

ostensible /ɒsˈten.sɪ.bl̩/ ⓤⓢ /ɑːˈsten-/ **adj** [before noun] formal appearing or claiming to be one thing when it is really something else: *Their ostensible goal was to clean up government corruption, but their real aim was to unseat the government.* • **ostensibly** /-bli/ **adv** *He has spent the past three months in Florida, ostensibly for medical treatment, but in actual fact to avoid prosecution.*

ostentation /ˌɒs.tenˈteɪ.ʃᵊn/ ⓤⓢ /ˌɑː.stən-/ **noun** [U] disapproving the quality of being ostentatious: *Her luxurious lifestyle and personal ostentation were both hated and envied.*

ostentatious /ˌɒs.tenˈteɪ.ʃəs/ ⓤⓢ /ˌɑː.stən-/ **adj** disapproving too obviously showing your money, possessions or power, in an attempt to make other people notice and admire you: *They criticized the ostentatious lifestyle of their leaders.* ◦ *an ostentatious gesture/manner* • **ostentatiously** /-li/ **adv** disapproving *The room was ostentatiously decorated in white and silver.* ◦ *He took out his gold watch and laid it ostentatiously*

(= *very obviously so everyone would notice*) *on the table in front of him.*

osteoarthritis /ˌɒs.ti.əʊ.ɑːˈθraɪ.tɪs/ ⓤⓢ /ˌɑː.sti.oʊ.ɑːrˈθraɪ.t̬əs/ **noun** [U] a disease which causes pain and stiffness in the JOINTS (= places where two bones are connected)

osteopath /ˈɒs.ti.ə.pæθ/ ⓤⓢ /ˈɑː.sti.oʊ-/ **noun** [C] a person who is trained to treat injuries to bones and muscles using pressure and movement

osteopathy /ˌɒs.tiˈɒp.ə.θi/ ⓤⓢ /ˌɑː.stiˈɑː.pə-/ **noun** [U] the treatment of injuries to bones and muscles using pressure and movement

osteoporosis /ˌɒs.ti.əʊ.pəˈrəʊ.sɪs/ ⓤⓢ /ˌɑː.sti.oʊ.pəˈroʊ-/ **noun** [U] a disease which causes the bones to become weaker and easily broken: *Osteoporosis afflicts many older women.*

ostracize (UK usually **ostracise**) /ˈɒs.trə.saɪz/ ⓤⓢ /ˈɑː.strə-/ **verb** [T] to avoid someone intentionally or to prevent them from taking part in the activities of a group: *His colleagues ostracized him after he criticized the company in public.* • **ostracism** /-sɪ.zᵊm/ **noun** [U] *AIDS patients often experience social ostracism and discrimination.*

ostrich /ˈɒs.trɪtʃ/ ⓤⓢ /ˈɑː.strɪtʃ/ **noun** [C] **BIRD** ▷ **1** a very large bird from Africa which cannot fly: *The ostrich is the fastest animal on two legs.* **PERSON** ▷ **2** informal someone who says that a problem does not exist, because they do not want to deal with it: *If you're an ostrich about your debts, you're only going to make matters worse.*

ostrich

OTE /ˌəʊ.tiːˈiː/ ⓤⓢ /ˌoʊ.t̬iː-/ **noun** UK abbreviation for on-target earnings: used in job advertisements to show how much money it is possible to earn if the person doing the job sells an amount of goods or services, or does an amount of work, stated by the employer

other /ˈʌð.əʳ/ ⓤⓢ /-ɚ/ **determiner; pronoun**

▸**determiner ADDITIONAL** ▷ **1** Ⓐ1 as well as the thing or person already mentioned: *The product has many other time-saving features.* ◦ *There is no other work available at the moment.* ◦ *There is only one other person who could help us.* ◦ *Are there any other people we should speak to?* ◦ *I've found one earring – do you know where **the** other **one** is?* → See also **another 2** Ⓐ1 used at the end of a list to show that there are more things, without being exact about what they are: *The plan has been opposed by schools, businesses and other local organizations.* ◦ *These two books will be especially useful for editors, journalists and other professional users of the language.* **OPPOSITE** ▷ **3 the other side/end (of sth)** Ⓑ1 the opposite side or end of something: *Put the chair at the other end of the desk.* ◦ *The man was waiting on the other side of the street.* **DIFFERENT** ▷ **4** Ⓑ1 different from the thing or person already mentioned: *I've no cash – is there no other way of paying?* ◦ *He likes travelling abroad and learning about other people's customs and traditions.* → See also **another 5 the other day, week, etc.** Ⓑ1 referring to a day, week, etc. in the recent past without saying exactly when it was: *I saw him just the other day/night.* **6 other than a** Ⓒ1 formal different from or except: *Holidays other than those in this brochure do not have free places for children.* ◦ *The form cannot be signed by anyone other than yourself.* **b** in a negative sentence, used to mean 'except': *There's nothing on TV tonight, other than rubbish.* **7 in other words** Ⓑ2 used to introduce an explanation that is simpler than the one given earlier: *He was economical with the truth – in other words, he was lying.* **8 or other** Ⓒ1 informal used when you cannot or do not want to be exact about the information you are giving: *The event was held in **some** park or other.* ◦ *We'll find **someone** or other to help us.*

▸**pronoun 1** Ⓐ2 the second of two things or people, or the thing or person that is left in a group or set of things: *Hold the racquet in one hand and the ball in **the** other.* ◦ *Some people prefer a vegetarian diet, while others prefer a meat-based diet.* ◦ *She gave me one book last week and promised to bring **the** others on Wednesday.* **2 others** [plural] **a** Ⓑ2 more ones: *I only know about this book, but there might be others* (= other books). **b** Ⓑ1 people in general, not including yourself: *You shouldn't expect others to do your work for you.*

> **! Common mistake: other**
>
> To talk about people in general, not including yourself, don't say 'the others', just say **others**:
>
> ~~*Parents must teach their children to respect the others.*~~
>
> *Parents must teach their children to respect others.*

> **! Common mistake: others or other?**
>
> **Warning:** do not confuse the pronoun 'others' with the determiner **other**.
>
> Before a plural noun, don't say 'others', say **other**:
>
> ~~*I would like to meet others people with the same hobby.*~~
>
> *I would like to meet other people with the same hobby.*
>
> **Remember:** before a singular noun, the correct determiner is **another**:
>
> *I met another person with the same hobby.*

ˌother ˈhalf **noun** [C usually singular] informal a person's husband, wife or usual partner: *Bring your other half next time you come.*

otherness /ˈʌð.ə.nəs/ ⓤⓢ /-ɚ-/ **noun** [U] formal being or feeling different in appearance or character from what is familiar, expected or generally accepted: *In the film, he is able to depict the sense of otherness and alienation that many teenagers feel.*

otherwise /ˈʌð.ə.waɪz/ ⓤⓢ /-ɚ-/ **conjunction; adv; adj**

▸**conjunction** Ⓑ1 used after an order or suggestion to show what the result will be if you do not follow that order or suggestion: *I'd better write it down, otherwise I'll forget it.* ◦ *Phone home, otherwise your parents will start to worry.*

▸**adv DIFFERENTLY** ▷ **1** differently, or in another way: *The police believe he is the thief, but all the evidence suggests otherwise* (= that he is not). ◦ *Under the Bill of Rights, a person is presumed innocent until proved otherwise* (= guilty). ◦ *Protestors were executed, jailed or otherwise persecuted.* ◦ *Marion Morrison, otherwise **known as** the film star John Wayne, was born in 1907.* ◦ formal *I can't meet you on Tuesday – I'm otherwise **engaged/occupied*** (= doing something else). **NOT INCLUDING** ▷ **2** Ⓑ2 except for what has just been referred to: *The bike needs a new saddle, **but** otherwise it's in good condition.* ◦ *The poor sound quality ruined an otherwise splendid film.*

IDIOM **or otherwise** used to refer to the opposite of the word which comes before it: *Hand in your exam papers, finished or otherwise* (= or not finished).

▸adj [after verb] formal used to show that something is completely different from what you think it is or from what was previously stated: *He might have told you he was a qualified electrician, but the truth is quite otherwise.*

otherworldly /ˌʌð.əˈwɜː.ld.li/ US /-ɚˈwɝːld-/ **adj** more closely connected to spiritual things than to the ordinary things of life: *The children in the picture look delicate and otherworldly, as though they had never run or shouted.*

otiose /ˈəʊ.ti.əʊs/, /-ʃi-/ US /ˈoʊ.t̬i.oʊs/ /-ʃi-/ **adj** formal describes a word or phrase, or sometimes an idea, that is unnecessary or has been used several times: *The use of the word 'recumbent' is surely otiose after the word 'recline'.*

otoh written abbreviation for on the other hand, used in emails, etc. → See **on the one hand … on the other hand**

OTT /ˌəʊ.tiːˈtiː/ US /ˌoʊ-/ **adj** UK abbreviation for **over the top** → See at **over the top**

otter /ˈɒt.əʳ/ US /ˈɑː.t̬ɚ/ **noun** [C] a mammal with four legs and short brown fur which swims well and eats fish

ottoman /ˈɒt.ə.mən/ US /ˈɑː.t̬ə.mən/ **noun** [C] **1** a piece of furniture like a long box with a soft top, that you can use to store things in or to sit on **2** US **pouf**

ouch /aʊtʃ/ **exclamation** **1** used to express sudden physical pain: *Ouch, you're hurting me!* **2** humorous used in answer to something unkind that someone says: *'I really think you're much too fat, Dorothy.' 'Ouch, that was a bit unkind.'*

ought /ɔːt/ US /ɑːt/ **modal verb** **DUTY** ▷ **1** B1 used to show when it is necessary or would be a good thing to perform the activity referred to by the following verb: [+ to infinitive] *You ought **to** be kinder to him.* ◦ *We ought not/oughtn't **to have** agreed without knowing what it would cost.* ◦ *'We ought **to** be getting ready now.' 'Yes, I suppose we ought (**to**).'* **PROBABLE** ▷ **2** B2 used to express something that you expect will happen: *He ought **to** be home by seven o'clock.* ◦ *They ought **to have** arrived at lunchtime but the flight was delayed.* ◦ *If you show the receipt, there ought not/oughtn't **to** be any difficulty getting your money back.*

oughtn't /ˈɔː.tᵊnt/ US /ˈɑː-/ **short form of** ought not: *He oughtn't to do that.*

Ouija board /ˈwiː.dʒəˌbɔːd/ US /-ˌbɔːrd/ **noun** [C] trademark a board printed with letters of the alphabet and numbers, which people use in the belief that it will help them receive messages from people who are dead

ounce /aʊns/ **noun** **1** C1 [C] (written abbreviation **oz**) a unit of weight equal to approximately 28 grams: *There are 16 ounces in one pound.* ◦ *a twelve-oz pack of bacon* **2** C2 [S] informal a very small amount: *She can eat as much as she wants and she never puts on an ounce (= her weight does not increase).* ◦ *If he's got an ounce of common sense, he'll realize that this project is bound to fail.*

our /aʊəʳ/, /ɑːʳ/ US /aʊɚ/ **determiner** A1 of or belonging to us: *We bought our house several years ago.* ◦ *He walked off and left us on our own.* ◦ *Drugs are one of the greatest threats in our society.* ◦ *There's no point in our buy**ing** a new car this year.*

ˌOur ˈFather **noun** [U] informal **the Lord's Prayer**

ˌOur ˈLady **noun** [S] (in some parts of the Christian religion) a name for Mary, the mother of Jesus

ours /aʊəz/, /ɑːz/ US /aʊɚz/ **pronoun** A2 the one(s) belonging to or connected with the person who is speaking and one or more other people: *Which table is ours?* ◦ *He's a cousin **of** ours.* ◦ *Ours is the red car parked over there.* ◦ *Ours is a huge country.*

ourselves /ˌaʊəˈselvz/, /ˌɑː-/ US /ˌaʊɚ-/ **pronoun** **1** A2 used when the subject of the verb is 'we' or the speaker and one or more others, and the object is the same group of people: *We went to get ourselves something to eat.* ◦ *John and I promised ourselves a good holiday this year.* **2** formal used to emphasize the subject 'we': *We ourselves realize that there are flaws in the scheme.* **3 (all) by ourselves** alone or without help from anyone else: *Nobody wanted to come with us, so we went by ourselves.* ◦ *It's a big garden, but we do all the gardening by ourselves.* **4 (all) to ourselves** for our use only: *The hotel was very quiet so we had the swimming pool all to ourselves.*

> **!** Common mistake: **ourselves**
>
> **Remember:** plural reflexive pronouns end in **-selves**.
>
> Don't write 'ourself', write **ourselves**:
>
> ~~*We had to carry our bags ourselfs.*~~
>
> *We had to carry our bags ourselves.*

-ous /-əs/ **suffix** added to nouns to form adjectives which refer to a quality or condition: *dangerous* ◦ *ambitious*

oust /aʊst/ **verb** [T] to force someone to leave a position of power, job, place or competition: *The president was ousted (**from power**) in a military coup in January 1987.* ◦ *Police are trying to oust drug dealers **from** the city centre.* ◦ *The champions were defeated by Arsenal and ousted **from** the League Cup.*

ouster /ˈaʊ.stəʳ/ US /-stɚ/ **noun** [C or U] US the process of removing someone from an important position or job: *The committee's chairperson is facing a possible ouster.*

out /aʊt/ **adv, preposition; verb; noun**

▸**adv, preposition** **AWAY FROM INSIDE** ▷ **1** B1 used to show movement away from the inside of a place or container: *She opened the window and stuck her head out.* ◦ *The bag burst and the apples fell out.* ◦ *I jumped out **of** bed and ran downstairs.* ◦ *He leaned out the window.* ◦ *He opened the drawer and took out a pair of socks.* ◦ *Get out!* ◦ *Out you go! (= Go out!)* ◦ *My secretary will **see** you out (= go with you to the door).* ◦ *Turn the trousers **inside** out (= put the inside on the outside).* **OUTSIDE** ▷ **2** outside a building or room: *Would you like to wait out here, and the doctor will come and fetch you in a minute?* ◦ *Danger! **Keep** out! (= Do not enter!)* ◦ *It's bitterly cold out, today.* **ABSENT** ▷ **3** A2 absent for a short time from the place where you live or work: *I came round to see you this morning, but you were out.* ◦ *Someone phoned for you while you were out.* **4** A2 used to refer to a period of time when someone goes away from home for a social activity: *I can't **go** out tonight – I've got work to do.* ◦ *Do you want to eat out (= eat in a restaurant) tonight?* ◦ *He's asked me out (= asked me to go with him) to the cinema next week.* **5** used to refer to a time when someone is away from the main office in order to do a particular job: *The thieves were spotted by a postman out **on his rounds** (= as he was delivering the post).* ◦ *The police were out **in force** (= there were a lot of police) at the demonstration.* **6** In a library, if a book is out, it has been borrowed by someone: *Both copies of 'Wuthering Heights' were out.* **DISAPPEAR** ▷ **7** B1 to the point where something is removed or disappears: *The stain won't come out.* ◦ *Cross out any words that are not on the list.* ◦ *Never use water to put out fires in electrical equipment.* ◦ *Our time/money/patience **ran** out.* **8 out**

of B2 used to say that no more of something is available: *We're nearly out of petrol.* ◦ *I'm* ***running*** *out of patience/time/money.* → See also **out of** DEFEATED ▷ **9** (in sport) no longer able to play because your turn has finished: *Two of the best players on the team were out after ten minutes.* ◦ *New Zealand were all out* ***for*** *246 (= the team finished with a score of 246).* **10** (in politics) no longer able to govern because you have lost an election: *The Social Democrats were voted out after 15 years in power.* GIVE ▷ **11** to many people: *The teacher* ***gave*** *out photocopies to all the children.* ◦ *Greenpeace* ***sent*** *a letter out to all its supporters.* MOVE AWAY ▷ **12** spreading out from a central point over a wider area: *The police search party* ***spread*** *out across the fields.* AVAILABLE ▷ **13** B1 When a book, magazine, film, or musical recording is out, it is available to the public: *Is her new book out yet?* ◦ *The new movie* ***comes*** *out in August.* APPEAR ▷ **14** B1 able to be seen: *The stars are out tonight.* ◦ *The rain stopped and the sun* ***came*** *out (= appeared).* ◦ *In spring all the flowers* ***came*** *out (= their petals opened).* VERY ▷ **15** used to make the meaning of a word stronger: *We walked all day and were tired out (= very tired) by the time we got home.* ◦ *It's up to you to* ***sort*** *this out (= solve it completely).* ◦ *Your room needs a good clean out.* LOUD ▷ **16** used with verbs describing sounds to emphasize the loudness of the sound: *He* ***cried*** *out in pain as he hit his head.* ◦ *Charlie Chaplin films always make me* ***laugh*** *out* ***loud***. FAR AWAY ▷ **17** C2 a long distance away from land, a town or your own country: *The fishing boats were out at sea for three days.* ◦ *They live out in the countryside, miles from anywhere.* ◦ *He lived out in Zambia for seven years.* ◦ mainly US *The weather's better out* ***west*** *(= a long distance away in the west of the country).* LIGHT/FIRE ▷ **18** B2 If a light or fire is out, it is no longer shining or burning: *When we got home, all the lights were out.* ◦ *Is that fire completely out?* COAST ▷ **19** away from the coast or beach: *Is the tide coming in or going out?* ◦ *You can only see the beach when the* ***tide*** *is out.* MADE PUBLIC ▷ **20** (of information) no longer kept secret: *You can't hide your gambling any longer – the secret's out.* **21** If a gay person comes out, they tell people that they are gay, and do not keep it a secret: *She came out three years ago.* ◦ *He hasn't* ***come*** *out* ***to*** *his family yet.* SPORT ▷ **22** (of a ball in a sport such as tennis) landing outside one of the lines that mark the area where the game is played: *He thought the ball had bounced on the line, but the umpire said it was out.* UNCONSCIOUS ▷ **23** unconscious or sleeping: *He* ***passes*** *out (= loses consciousness) at the sight of blood.* ◦ *I was hit on the head, and I must have been out* ***cold*** *(= completely unconscious) for about ten minutes.* NOT ACCURATE ▷ **24** C1 informal not accurate: *Our estimates were only out by a few dollars.* ◦ *You were 25 cm out in your measurements.* ◦ *Those sales figures were* ***way*** *out (= completely wrong).* ◦ US *I'm out $25 on this trip (= it cost me $25 more than expected).* EXISTING ▷ **25** informal (used with SUPERLATIVES) available or in existence: *This is the best automatic camera out.* ◦ *I think he's the greatest footballer out.* FINISHED ▷ **26** used to show that a period of time is finished: *I think I can finish this project before the month's out.* NOT ACCEPTABLE ▷ **27** informal not acceptable or not possible: *The option of taking on more staff is out at present.* NOT FASHIONABLE ▷ **28** informal no longer fashionable or popular: *Every month the magazine lists what's out and what's in (= fashionable).* ◦ *Trousers like that* ***went*** *out (= stopped being fashionable) in the 70s.* INTEND ▷ **29 out for sth/to do sth** informal doing something, or intending to do something, for an unpleasant reason or only because it is good for you and not others: *She doesn't usually help the charity – she's only out for the publicity.* ◦ [+ to infinitive] *He's always been out* ***to*** *cause trouble between us.* → See also **out of**

IDIOMS **out and about** active; doing the things you usually do: *The doctor says she's making a good recovery and she should be out and about in a few days' time.* • **out with it!** informal said to someone when you want them to tell you something which they do not want you to know: *What did he say, then? Come on, out with it!*

▸**verb** [T often passive] to publish the fact that a famous person is gay, especially when that person does not want it to be known: *Hardly a week went by without someone famous being outed.*

▸**noun 1** [C usually singular] informal an excuse or reason for avoiding an unpleasant situation: *We must arrange the negotiations so we have an out if we need it.* **2 on the outs** US informal People who are on the outs have argued and are not now friendly with each other: *Lizzie and Tyler are on the outs again.*

out- /aʊt-/ prefix NOT CENTRAL ▷ **1** used to add the meaning 'not central' to nouns and adjectives: *the outskirts of town (= the areas that form the edge of the town)* FURTHER ▷ **2** used to add the meaning 'going further' or 'being better than' to verbs: *She doesn't drink or smoke and I'm sure she'll outlive (= live longer than) us all.* AWAY FROM ▷ **3** used to add the meaning 'out of' or 'away from' to nouns and adjectives: *She turned away from their outstretched hands (= hands held out).*

outage /ˈaʊ.tɪdʒ/ US /-t̬ɪdʒ/ noun [C] US a period when a service, such as electricity, is not available: *The radio news reported* ***power*** *outages affecting 50 homes.*

ˌout-and-ˈout adj [before noun] complete or in every way; used to emphasize an unpleasant quality of a person or thing: *That's an out-and-out lie!* ◦ *The whole project was an out-and-out disaster.*

the outback /ˈaʊt.bæk/ noun [S] the areas of Australia that are far away from towns and cities, especially the desert areas in central Australia

outbid /ˌaʊtˈbɪd/ verb [T] (present tense **outbidding**, past tense and past participle **outbid**) to offer to pay a higher price for something than someone else, especially at an AUCTION (= public sale): *The retail group outbid all three competitors* ***for*** *space in the shopping centre.*

outboard motor /ˌaʊt.bɔːdˈməʊ.təʳ/ US /-bɔːrdˈmoʊ.t̬ɚ/ noun [C] **1** a motor with a PROPELLER, designed to be fixed to the back of a small boat **2** a boat with an outboard motor

outbound /ˈaʊt.baʊnd/ adj travelling away from a particular point: *There has been an increase in outbound* ***traffic*** *leaving London airport for the Mediterranean resorts.*

outbox /ˈaʊt.bɒks/ US /-bɑːks/ noun [C] **1** US for **out tray 2** a place on a computer where copies of email messages which you are going to send are kept

outbreak /ˈaʊt.breɪk/ noun [C] C2 a time when something suddenly begins, especially a disease or something else dangerous or unpleasant: *an outbreak* ***of*** *cholera/food poisoning/rioting/war* ◦ *Last weekend saw further thundery outbreaks.*

outbuilding /ˈaʊtˌbɪl.dɪŋ/ noun [C] a usually small building near to and on the same piece of land as a larger building: *The stables and other outbuildings were sold together with the main house.*

outburst /ˈaʊt.bɜːst/ US /-bɝːst/ noun [C] a sudden forceful expression of emotion, especially anger: *a* *violent outburst* ◦ *an outburst **of** creative activity* ◦ *Her comments provoked an outburst **of** anger from the boss.*

outcast /ˈaʊt.kɑːst/ (US) /-kæst/ **noun** [C] a person who has no place in their society or in a particular group, because the society or group refuses to accept them: *She has spent her life trying to help gypsies, beggars and other **social** outcasts.*

outclass /ˌaʊtˈklɑːs/ (US) /-ˈklæs/ **verb** [T] to be much better than someone or something: *The latest 500 cc road bike easily outclasses all the competition.*

outcome /ˈaʊt.kʌm/ **noun** [C usually singular] **C1** a result or effect of an action, situation, etc.: *It's too early to predict the outcome **of** the meeting.*

outcrop /ˈaʊt.krɒp/ (US) /-krɑːp/ **noun** [C] (US also **outcropping** /-ɪŋ/) a large rock or group of rocks that sticks out of the ground

outcry /ˈaʊt.kraɪ/ **noun** [C] a strong expression of anger and disapproval about something, made by a group of people or by the public: *The release from prison of two of the terrorists has provoked a **public** outcry.*

outdated /ˌaʊtˈdeɪ.tɪd/ (US) /-t̬ɪd/ **adj** old-fashioned and therefore not as good or as fashionable as something modern: *outdated weapons/ideas* → See also **out of date**

outdistance /ˌaʊtˈdɪs.tᵊns/ **verb** [T] to be faster in a race than other competitors, or (more generally) to be much better than someone: *The company outdistance their nearest business competitors **by** a long way.*

outdo /ˌaʊtˈduː/ **verb** [T] (**outdid**, **outdone**) to be, or do something, better than someone else: *He always tries to outdo everybody else in the class.*

IDIOM **not to be outdone** not wanting someone else to do something better than you: *Pat was wearing an outrageous purple dress, so, not to be outdone, I put on my new gold suit.*

outdoor /ˌaʊtˈdɔːʳ/ (US) /-ˌdɔːr/ **adj** [before noun] **1** **B1** existing, happening or done outside, rather than inside a building: *an outdoor swimming pool/festival* ◦ *outdoor clothes* **2** liking or relating to outdoor activities, such as walking and climbing: *Sara's not really the outdoor **type**.*

outdoors /ˌaʊtˈdɔːz/ (US) /-ˈdɔːrz/ **adv, noun** **B1** outside: *If the weather's good, we'll eat outdoors (= not in a building).* ◦ *Every year he takes a month off work to go trekking in **the great** outdoors (= in the countryside, far away from towns).* → See also **out of doors**

outer /ˈaʊ.təʳ/ (US) /-t̬ɚ/ **adj** [before noun] **B2** at a greater distance from the centre: *outer London* ◦ *the outer lane of the motorway*

outermost /ˈaʊ.tə.məʊst/ (US) /-t̬ɚ.moʊst/ **adj** [before noun] at the greatest distance from the centre: *These spacecraft may send back data about the outermost **reaches** of the solar system.*

ˌouter ˈring **noun** [C] US an area around the edges of a town or city where people live: *Big-box stores such as Ikea can be found in the outer ring.* • **ˌouter-ˈring adj** [before noun] *People are asking farmers in the outer-ring **suburbs** to sell a few acres so they can build big houses.* → Compare **inner ring**

ˌouter ˈspace **noun** [U] the part of space that is very far away from Earth

the outfield /ˈaʊt.fiːld/ **noun** [S] the part of a cricket or baseball field that is the longest distance away from the BATTER (= person trying to hit the ball) or the group of players there: *He can play **in** the outfield.* → Compare **the infield** • **outfielder** /ˈaʊtˌfiːl.dəʳ/ (US) /-dɚ/ **noun** [C] *He was a star outfielder for the Brooklyn Dodgers.*

outfight /ˌaʊtˈfaɪt/ **verb** [T] (past tense and past participle **outfought**) to fight better than someone: *The former heavyweight champion was outwitted and outfought.*

outfit /ˈaʊt.fɪt/ **noun; verb**

▸**noun** CLOTHES ▷ **1** [C] a set of clothes worn for a particular occasion or activity: *I've got a cowboy outfit for the fancy dress party.* GROUP ▷ **2** [C, + sing/pl verb] informal an organization, company, team, military unit, etc.: *He has recently set up his own research outfit.*

▸**verb** [T often passive] (present tense **outfitting**, past tense and past participle **outfitted**) to provide someone or something with equipment or clothes: *The ambulances have all been outfitted with new radios.*

outfitters /ˈaʊtˌfɪt.əz/ (US) /-ˌfɪt̬.ɚz/ **noun** [plural] old-fashioned a shop that sells a particular type of clothes, especially men's clothes or uniforms: *a gentlemen's outfitters*

outflank /ˌaʊtˈflæŋk/ **verb** [T] **1** to move forward past an enemy position in order to attack it from the side or from the back **2** to do better than an opponent by winning an advantage over him or her: *The government has outflanked the opposition by cutting taxes.*

outflow /ˈaʊt.fləʊ/ (US) /-floʊ/ **noun** [C] a movement away from a place: *I'm trying to measure the outflow **of** water/sewage from that pipe.* ◦ *The central bank has announced controls on **capital** outflows.*

outgoing **adj** FRIENDLY ▷ **1** **C1** /ˌaʊtˈgəʊ.ɪŋ/ (US) /ˈaʊt.goʊ-/ approving (of a person) friendly and energetic and finding it easy and enjoyable to be with others: *Sales reps need to be outgoing, because they are constantly meeting customers.* ◦ *She has an outgoing personality.* LEAVING ▷ **2** **C2** /ˈaʊtˌgəʊ.ɪŋ/ (US) /-ˌgoʊ-/ [before noun] leaving a place, or leaving a job: *Outgoing flights are booked until 15 January.* ◦ *the outgoing vice-president*

outgoings /ˈaʊtˌgəʊ.ɪŋz/ (US) /-ˌgoʊ-/ **noun** [plural] UK **C2** amounts of money that regularly have to be spent, for example to pay for heating or rent

outgrow /ˌaʊtˈgrəʊ/ (US) /-ˈgroʊ/ **verb** [T] (**outgrew**, **outgrown**) SIZE ▷ **1** to grow bigger than or too big for something: *My seven-year-old had new shoes in April and he's already outgrown them (= his feet have grown too large for them).* ◦ *The company outgrew (= became too large for) its office space.* AGE ▷ **2** to lose interest in an idea or activity as you get older: *He eventually outgrew his adolescent interest in war and guns.*

outgrowth /ˈaʊt.grəʊθ/ (US) /-groʊθ/ **noun** [C] **1** specialized a growth on the outside of an animal or plant: *Antlers are the bony outgrowths on the heads of deer.* **2** a result or development: *This policy is just an outgrowth of earlier decisions.*

outgun /ˌaʊtˈgʌn/ **verb** [T] (**-nn-**) **1** to win a war or fight by having more weapons than the other side: *Despite being heavily outgunned, the rebel forces seem to have held on to the south side of the city.* **2** to beat a person or team by using greater skill: *Arsenal were outgunned by Norwich in Saturday's game.*

outhouse /ˈaʊt.haʊs/ **noun** [C] **1** a small building joined to or near to a larger one **2** US a toilet in an OUTBUILDING

outing /ˈaʊ.tɪŋ/ (US) /-t̬ɪŋ/ **noun** JOURNEY ▷ **1** [C] a short journey made by a group of people, usually for pleasure or education: *Rosie's **going on** a class/school outing **to** the Museum of Modern Art.* MADE PUBLIC ▷ **2** [C or U] an occasion when it is made public that a famous person is gay when he or she wanted to keep

O

this information private: *There have been several outings of well-known movie stars recently.*

outlandish /ˌaʊtˈlæn.dɪʃ/ **adj** disapproving strange and unusual and difficult to accept or like: *an outlandish hairstyle/outfit* • **outlandishly** /-dɪʃ.li/ **adv** • **outlandishness** /-nəs/ **noun** [U]

outlast /ˌaʊtˈlɑːst/ (US) /-ˈlæst/ **verb** [T] to live or exist, or to stay energetic and determined, longer than another person or thing: *The queen outlasted all her children.* ◦ *The Orioles outlasted the Yankees, finally winning 10 to 9.*

outlaw /ˈaʊt.lɔː/ (US) /-lɑː/ **noun; verb**

▸**noun** [C] (especially in the past) a person who has broken the law and who lives separately from the other parts of society because they want to escape legal punishment: *Robin Hood was an outlaw who lived in the forest and stole from the rich to give to the poor.*

▸**verb** [T] to make something illegal or unacceptable: *The new law will outlaw smoking in public places.*

outlay /ˈaʊt.leɪ/ **noun** [C] an amount of money spent for a particular purpose, especially as a first INVESTMENT in something: *For an* ***initial*** *outlay* ***of*** *£2,000 to buy the equipment, you should be earning up to £500 a month if the product sells well.*

outlet /ˈaʊt.let/ **noun** [C] **WAY OUT** ▷ **1** a way, especially a pipe or hole, for liquid or gas to go out: *a waste water outlet* ◦ *an outlet pipe* **2** (C2) a way in which emotion or energy can be expressed or made use of: *Her work* ***provided*** *no outlet* ***for*** *her energies and talents.* ◦ *Writing poetry was his only form of emotional outlet.* **SHOP** ▷ **3** (C2) a shop that is one of many owned by a particular company and that sells the goods which the company has produced: *a fast-food outlet* ◦ *a retail outlet* **ELECTRICITY** ▷ **4** (C1) US for **power point**

O

ˈ**outlet** ˌ**mall** **noun** [C] US a large group of shops, usually outside a town or city, which sell clothes, goods, etc. for a reduced price: *In the last ten years, outlet malls have sprung up all over the country.*

outline /ˈaʊt.laɪn/ **noun; verb**

▸**noun** [C] **SHAPE** ▷ **1** (C2) the main shape or edge of something, without any details: *She drew the outline* ***of*** *the boat and then coloured it in.* **2 in outline** as a shape with an edge but without any details: *The mountain was visible only in outline as the light faded.* **DESCRIPTION** ▷ **3** (B2) a description of the main facts about something: *If you read the minutes of the meeting, they'll give you a broad outline* ***of*** *what was discussed.* ◦ *Some novelists start by writing an outline (= plan of the main points of the story).*

▸**verb** [T] **DRAW SHAPE** ▷ **1** to draw the main shape or edge of something: *The area we're interested in is outlined* ***in*** *red on the map.* **DESCRIBE** ▷ **2** (B2) to give the main facts about something: *At the interview she outlined what I would be doing.*

outlive /ˌaʊtˈlɪv/ **verb** [T] to live or exist longer than someone or something: *He outlived all of his brothers.*

IDIOM **outlive your usefulness** to no longer be useful: *This old system has outlived its usefulness.*

outlook /ˈaʊt.lʊk/ **noun** **FUTURE SITUATION** ▷ **1** (C1) [S] the likely future situation: *The outlook* ***for*** *the economy is bleak.* ◦ *The outlook* ***for*** *today is cloudy and dry at first with showers later.* **OPINION** ▷ **2** (C2) [C usually singular] a person's way of understanding and thinking about something: *He has a fairly positive outlook* ***on*** *life.* **VIEW** ▷ **3** [C usually singular] formal what you can see from a particular place

outlying /ˈaʊtˌlaɪ.ɪŋ/ **adj** [before noun] far away from main towns and cities, or far from the centre of a place: *Many of the pupils travel in by bus from outlying areas.*

outmanoeuvre UK (US **outmaneuver**) /ˌaʊt.məˈnuː.vəʳ/ (US) /-vɚ/ **verb** [T] to cleverly get an advantage over someone, especially a competitor: *In the negotiations, he outmanoeuvred his rivals by offering a higher price.*

outmoded /ˌaʊtˈməʊ.dɪd/ (US) /-ˈmoʊ-/ **adj** disapproving no longer modern, useful, or necessary: *Outmoded working practices are being phased out.* → Synonym **old-fashioned**

outnumber /ˌaʊtˈnʌm.bəʳ/ (US) /-bɚ/ **verb** [T] (C1) to be greater in number than someone or something: *In our office the women outnumber the men three to one.*

ˈ**out** ˌ**of** **preposition** **NO LONGER IN** ▷ **1 out of somewhere/sth** (A2) no longer in a stated place or condition: *An apple rolled out of the bag.* ◦ *Professor Aitchison is out of* ***town*** *this week.* ◦ *The patient is now out of* ***danger.*** ◦ *The coffee machine is out of* ***order*** *(= does not work).* ◦ *Both she and her husband are out of* ***work*** *(= no longer have jobs).* **MADE FROM** ▷ **2** (B1) (also **of**) used to show what something is made from: *The dress was made out of velvet.* **BECAUSE OF** ▷ **3** (B2) used to show the reason why someone does something: *I took the job out of* ***necessity*** *because we had no money left.* ◦ *You might like to come and see what we're doing out of* ***interest*** *(= because I think you might be interested).* **FROM AMONG** ▷ **4** (B1) from among an amount or number: *Nine out of ten people said they liked the product.* ◦ *No one got 20 out of 20 (= all the answers correct) in the test.* **ORIGIN** ▷ **5** used to describe where something came from or began: *She dresses like a character out of a 19th-century novel.* ◦ *I paid for the computer out of (= using some of) my savings.* **NOT INVOLVED** ▷ **6** [after verb] no longer involved in: *He missed two practice sessions so he's out of the team.* ◦ *I'm out of* ***the habit of*** *cycling to work.*

IDIOMS **out of your mind/head** informal extremely silly: *He must be out of his mind to have spent that much money on an old car!* • **out of it** informal **1** not conscious of where you are or what condition you are in as a result of taking alcohol or drugs: *She was lying on the sofa, totally out of it.* **2** unhappy because you are not included in what is happening: *I didn't know anyone at the party and I felt really out of it.*

ˌ**out-of-**ˈ**court** **adv** [before noun], **adj** agreed without involving a trial in a law court: *an out-of-court* ***settlement*** ◦ *My lawyer wants to* ***settle*** *out of court.*

ˌ**out of** ˈ**date** **adj** **FASHION** ▷ **1** (B1) If clothes, colours, styles, etc. are out of date, they are old and not fashionable: *That radio looks so out of date.* **INFORMATION** ▷ **2** (B1) If information is out of date, it is old and not useful or correct: *an out-of-date phone directory* ◦ *I have a map but I'm afraid it's out of date.* **FOOD** ▷ **3** (B1) If food is out of date, it is old and not now safe to eat.

ˌ**out-of-**ˌ**pocket ex**ˈ**penses** **noun** [plural] money that you spend on things such as food and travel while you are working for someone else: *All out-of-pocket expenses will be reimbursed by the company.*

ˌ**out-of-**ˈ**town** **adj** [before noun] **1** in a place outside the main part of a town: *an out-of-town shopping centre* **2** coming from outside a town or from another town: *an out-of-town visitor/businessman*

outpace /ˌaʊtˈpeɪs/ **verb** [T] to move or develop faster than someone or something else: *Bolt managed to outpace every other runner.* ◦ *The company has completely outpaced its rivals in the market.*

outpatient /ˈaʊt.peɪ.ʃᵊnt/ **noun** [C] a person who

goes to a hospital for treatment, but who does not stay any nights there: *an outpatient clinic* → Compare **inpatient**

outpatients /ˈaʊt.peɪ.ʃᵊnts/ **noun** [C or U] part of a hospital where people go for treatment but do not stay the night: *Can you tell me where outpatients is, please?*

outperform /ˌaʊt.pəˈfɔːm/ ⓤⓢ /-pɚˈfɔːrm/ **verb** [T] to do well in a particular job or activity compared to others of a similar type: *The Peugeot engine has consistently outperformed its rivals this season.*

outplay /ˌaʊtˈpleɪ/ **verb** [T] to play a game more cleverly and successfully than another person or team: *The French were completely outplayed by the Russian team.*

outpost /ˈaʊt.pəʊst/ ⓤⓢ /-poʊst/ **noun** [C] a place, especially a small group of buildings or a town, that represents the authority or business interests of a government or company that is far away: *a police/military/colonial outpost*

outpouring /ˈaʊtˌpɔː.rɪŋ/ ⓤⓢ /-ˌpɔːr.ɪŋ/ **noun** [C] **1** an expression of strong feeling that is difficult to control: *His death at the age of 35 has occasioned an outpouring **of** grief.* **2** mainly humorous a very large number of things produced at the same time: *Last year saw an outpouring **of** cookery books.*

output /ˈaʊt.pʊt/ **noun** [U] C2 an amount of something produced by a person, machine, factory, country, etc.: *Last year British manufacturing output fell by 14 percent.*

outrage /ˈaʊt.reɪdʒ/ **noun; verb**

▸**noun 1** [U] a feeling of anger and shock: *These murders have provoked outrage across the country.* ◦ *Many politicians and members of the public expressed outrage at the verdict.* **2** C2 [C] a shocking, morally unacceptable, and usually violent action: *The bomb, which killed 15 people, was the worst of a series of terrorist outrages.* ◦ [+ that] ***It's** an outrage (= it is shocking and morally unacceptable) **that** so much public money should have been wasted in this way.*

▸**verb** [T] (especially of an unfair action or statement) to cause someone to feel very angry, shocked or upset: *Local people were outraged **at** the bombing.* ◦ *A proposed five percent pay cut has outraged staff at the warehouse.* • **outraged** /-reɪdʒd/ **adj** feeling outrage: *Many outraged viewers wrote to the BBC to complain.*

outrageous /ˌaʊtˈreɪ.dʒəs/ **adj 1** B2 shocking and morally unacceptable: *The judge criticized the 'outrageous greed' of some of the bankers.* ◦ [+ that] ***It** is outrageous **that** these buildings remain empty while thousands of people have no homes.* ◦ *These prices are just outrageous (= much too high).* **2** describes something or someone that is shocking because they are unusual or strange: *outrageous clothes/behaviour* ◦ *an outrageous character* • **outrageously** /-li/ **adv** *outrageously high prices*

outran /ˌaʊtˈræn/ past simple of **outrun**

outrank /ˌaʊtˈræŋk/ **verb** [T] to have a higher rank than someone: *As a Chief Superintendent, she outranked all the other police officers in the room.*

outré /ˈuː.treɪ/ **adj** formal unusual, strange, and shocking, especially in a humorous way: *He wrote an outré comedy about Queen Victoria's childhood.*

outreach /ˈaʊt.riːtʃ/ **adj** [before noun] bringing medical or similar services to people at home or to where they spend time: *an outreach worker/centre* ◦ *An AIDS outreach program for prostitutes on the streets.*

outrider /ˈaʊtˌraɪ.dəʳ/ ⓤⓢ /-dɚ/ **noun** [C] a person, especially a police officer, who rides on a motorcycle next to or in front of an official vehicle

outright **adv; adj**

▸**adv** /ˌaʊtˈraɪt/ completely or immediately: *I think cigarette advertising should be banned outright.* ◦ *The driver and all three passengers were **killed** outright.*

▸**adj** [before noun] /ˈaʊt.raɪt/ complete: *Outsiders are regarded with outright hostility.* ◦ *There was no outright winner in the election.*

outrun /ˌaʊtˈrʌn/ **verb** [T] (present participle **outrunning**, past tense **outran**, past participle **outrun**) **1** to move faster or further than someone or something: *The thieves easily outran the policewoman who was chasing them.* **2** to develop faster or further than something: *In the future, demand for tungsten will outrun supply.*

outscore /ˌaʊtˈskɔːʳ/ ⓤⓢ /-ˈskɔːr/ **verb** [T] mainly US to score more points than another player or team in a competition: *Johnson outscored his nearest rival by 30 points.*

outsell /ˌaʊtˈsel/ **verb** [T] (**outsold**, **outsold**) (of a product) to be sold in greater numbers than another product: *MP3s soon began to outsell CDs.*

the outset /ˈaʊt.set/ **noun** [S] C2 the beginning: *I told him **at/from** the outset I wasn't interested.*

outshine /ˌaʊtˈʃaɪn/ **verb** [T] (**outshone**, **outshone**) to be much more skilful and successful than someone: *Ben Palmer easily outshone his rivals in the 200 metre freestyle.*

outside **adj, adv, preposition; adv, preposition; noun; adj**

▸**adj, adv, preposition** /ˌaʊtˈsaɪd/, /ˈaʊt.saɪd/ **1** A1 not inside a building: *It was a lovely day outside.* ◦ *Since it's such a nice day shall we eat/sit/go outside?* ◦ *an outside light/toilet* **2** C1 [before noun] coming from another place or organization: *The company has called in outside experts.* **3** **outside call/line** a phone call or connection going outside the place where you are **4** [before noun] the most that would be accepted or possible: *The outside limit/figure would be £350.*

IDIOM **the outside world** (also **the world outside**) things that are common in normal life but are not part of your experience: *An over-protected childhood meant that at the age of 22 she had no idea about the outside world.*

▸**adv, preposition** /ˌaʊtˈsaɪd/ **1** A2 not in a particular building or room, but near it: *She sat for two hours on the floor outside his room.* **2** A2 not in a particular place: *Nobody outside this room must ever know what we have discussed.* **3** not within or part of something: *I'm afraid that would be outside my job description.* **4** **outside of** mainly US except for: *Outside of us three, no one knows anything about the problem, yet.*

▸**noun** [C usually singular] /ˌaʊtˈsaɪd/, /ˈaʊt.saɪd/ **OUTER PART** ▷ **1** B2 the outer part or side of something: *The outside of the house needs painting.* ◦ *The house looks larger when looked at from **the** outside.* ◦ *The company needs to get help from outside (= from people who work for other organizations).* → Compare **inside** **LARGEST AMOUNT** ▷ **2** **at the outside** used to say that an amount is the most possible in a situation: *The job will take about ten days at the outside.*

▸**adj** [before noun] /ˈaʊt.saɪd/ slight: *There's still an outside **chance/possibility** that Scotland will get through into the World Cup.*

ˌoutside ˈbroadcast **noun** [C] (US **reˌmote ˈbroadcast**) a broadcast made away from the television or radio station

ˌoutside ˈlane **noun** **ROAD** ▷ **1** [S] (informal **outside**) UK the part of the road nearest the vehicles going in the opposite direction, used especially by faster vehicles: *She cruised by at 160 kilometres per hour* ***on*** *the outside/****in*** *the outside lane.* **2** [C] US the part of the road nearest the edge, especially used by slower vehicles **RACE TRACK** ▷ **3** [S] the part of a race track that is furthest from the centre

outsider /ˌaʊtˈsaɪ.dəʳ/ (US) /-dɚ/ **noun** [C] **NOT MEMBER** ▷ **1** a person who is not involved with a particular group of people or organization or who does not live in a particular place: *Outsiders have a glamorized idea of what it is like to work for the BBC.* **2** a person who is not liked or accepted as a member of a particular group, organization or society and who feels different from those people who are accepted as members: *As a child he was very much an outsider, never participating in the games other children played.* **UNLIKELY WINNER** ▷ **3** a person or animal with only a slight chance of winning: *The race was won by a* ***rank*** *outsider.*

outsize /ˈaʊt.saɪz/ **adj** [before noun] (especially of clothing) much larger than usual: *They specialize in outsize clothes.*

the outskirts /ˈaʊt.skɜːts/ (US) /-skɜːrts/ **noun** [plural] (B2) the areas that form the edge of a town or city: *The factory is* ***in/on*** *the outskirts* ***of*** *New Delhi.*

outsmart /ˌaʊtˈsmɑːt/ (US) /-ˈsmɑːrt/ **verb** [T] to **outwit**

outsold /ˌaʊtˈsəʊld/ (US) /-ˈsoʊld/ past simple and past participle of **outsell**

outsource /ˈaʊt.sɔːs/ (US) /-sɔːrs/ **verb** [I or T] If a company outsources, it pays to have part of its work done by another company: *Unions are fighting a plan by universities to outsource all non-academic services.* ◦ *Some companies outsource to cheaper locations to cut costs.* • **outsourcing** /ˈaʊtˌsɔː.sɪŋ/ (US) /-ˌsɑː-/ **noun** [U]

outspoken /ˌaʊtˈspəʊ.kᵊn/ (US) /-ˈspoʊ-/ **adj** expressing strong opinions very directly without worrying if other people are offended: *outspoken comments* ◦ *Mr Masack is an outspoken critic of the present government.*

outspread /ˌaʊtˈspred/ **adj** spread as far as possible: *a bronze statue of an angel with outspread wings*

outstanding /ˌaʊtˈstæn.dɪŋ/ **adj** **EXCELLENT** ▷ **1** (B2) clearly very much better than what is usual: *an outstanding performance/writer/novel/year* ◦ *It's an area of outstanding natural beauty.* → Synonym **excellent** **NOT FINISHED** ▷ **2** not yet paid, solved or done: *$450 million in outstanding debts* ◦ *There are still a couple of problems outstanding.* • **outstandingly** /-li/ **adv** *He was an outstandingly successful mayor from 1981 to 1984.*

outstation cheque /ˈaʊt.steɪ.ʃᵊnˌtʃek/ **noun** [C] Indian English a CHEQUE from a bank that is not local

outstay /ˌaʊtˈsteɪ/ **verb** **outstay your welcome** to continue to stay in a place although other people want you to leave: *They were busy so I left – I didn't want to outstay my welcome.*

outstretched /ˌaʊtˈstretʃt/ **adj** reaching out as far as possible: *He ran up to her, his arms outstretched.* ◦ *She put some pesos into the little girl's outstretched hand.*

outstrip /ˌaʊtˈstrɪp/ **verb** [T] (**-pp-**) to be or become greater in amount, degree or success than something or someone: *The demand for firewood now far outstrips supply.*

outta (also **outa**) /ˈaʊ.tə/ (US) /-t̬ə/ **preposition** mainly US informal out of: *We'd better get outta here, man!* ◦ *I'm outta here (= I'm leaving).*

outtake /ˈaʊt.teɪk/ **noun** [C] a short part of a film or television programme or music recording that was removed and not included, usually because it contains mistakes: *They showed a video of amusing outtakes from various movies.*

ˈout ˌtray **noun** [C] UK (US **outbox**) a flat, open container on a desk for letters and other documents that have already been dealt with and are waiting to be sent to someone else or put away: *The letter is* ***in*** *your out tray.*

outvote /ˌaʊtˈvəʊt/ (US) /-ˈvoʊt/ **verb** [T usually passive] to defeat someone by winning a greater number of votes: *The Democrats were outvoted, as usual.* ◦ informal *I suggested we should go for a pizza, but I was outvoted (= most people did not want to) so we went for a curry.*

outward /ˈaʊt.wəd/ (US) /-wɚd/ **adj** **ON OUTSIDE** ▷ **1** [before noun] relating to how people, situations or things seem to be, rather than how they are inside: *The outward* ***appearance*** *of the building has not changed at all in 200 years.* ◦ *If he is suffering, he certainly shows no outward* ***sign*** *of it.* ◦ ***To all*** *outward* ***appearances*** *everything was fine, but under the surface the marriage was very shaky.* → Compare **inward** **GOING AWAY** ▷ **2** away from the centre: *outward investment (= investment in other companies/countries)* ◦ *We have the chance to build an outward-****looking*** *Europe that lives up to its global responsibilities.* → Compare **inward** **3** [before noun] going towards a particular place, rather than returning from it: *The outward flight/journey took eight hours.* → Compare **return** • **outwardly** /-li/ **adv** *Outwardly, he seemed happy enough.*

ˌoutward-ˈbound **adj** [before noun] describes a ship or passenger going away from home: *At the port she managed to get a passage on an outward-bound ship.*

outwards /ˈaʊt.wədz/ (US) /-wɚdz/ **adv** (mainly US **outward**) going or pointing away from a particular place or towards the outside: *The door opens outwards.* ◦ *It's much healthier to direct your emotions outwards than to bottle them up inside you.* → Opposite **inward**

outweigh /ˌaʊtˈweɪ/ **verb** [T] (C1) to be greater or more important than something else: *The benefits of this treatment far outweigh any risks.*

outwit /ˌaʊtˈwɪt/ **verb** [T] (**-tt-**) (also **outsmart**) to get an advantage over someone by acting more cleverly and often by using a trick: *In the story, the cunning fox outwits the hunters.*

outwith /ˌaʊtˈwɪθ/ **adv, preposition** Scottish English outside: *22 percent of the students are from outwith Scotland.*

outworn /ˌaʊtˈwɔːn/ (US) /-ˈwɔːrn/ **adj** (especially of an idea or phrase) old-fashioned and used too often in the past, so no longer useful or important

ouzo /ˈuː.zəʊ/ (US) /-zoʊ/ **noun** [C or U] (plural **ouzos**) a Greek alcoholic drink with an ANISEED flavour, which turns white if mixed with water: *She ordered a couple of ouzos (= glasses of ouzo).*

ova /ˈəʊ.və/ (US) /ˈoʊ-/ plural of **ovum**

oval /ˈəʊ.vᵊl/ (US) /ˈoʊ-/ **adj** (B2) shaped like a circle that is FLATTENED so that it is like an egg or an ELLIPSE: *an oval mirror* ◦ *an oval face* • **oval noun** [C]

the ˌOval ˈOffice **noun** [S] the office of the US president, in Washington: *The president delivered his speech from the Oval Office.* ◦ figurative *It now seems unlikely that the Democratic nominee will reach the Oval Office (= become president).*

ovarian /əʊˈveə.ri.ən/ (US) /oʊˈver.i-/ **adj** of or relating to the ovaries or an ovary: *ovarian cancer* ◦ *an ovarian cyst*

ovary /ˈəʊ.vᵊr.i/ (US) /ˈoʊ-/ **noun** [C] either of the pair of organs in a woman's body which produce eggs, or the part of any female animal or plant that produces eggs or seeds

ovation /əʊˈveɪ.ʃən/ (US) /oʊ-/ **noun** [C] an occasion when a crowd of people expresses great enjoyment and/or approval of something with loud and long clapping: *She was given a* ***standing*** *ovation (= the crowd stood up while they clapped) at the end of her speech.*

oven /ˈʌv.ən/ **noun** [C] (B1) the part of a cooker with a door, used to bake or ROAST food: *a conventional/gas/fan-assisted oven ◦ a microwave oven ◦ a cool/medium/hot oven ◦ Place the cake* ***in*** *the oven at 200°C. ◦ Calcutta in summer is* ***like an*** *oven (= extremely and uncomfortably hot).*

ˈoven ˌgloves noun [C] UK (US **ˈoven ˌmitts**) thick coverings for the hands, used for taking hot things out of an oven

ovenproof /ˈʌv.ən.pruːf/ **adj** able to be used in an oven: *Is this dish ovenproof?*

ˌoven-ˈready **adj** sold already prepared for cooking: *an oven-ready chicken*

ovenware /ˈʌv.ən.weər/ (US) /-wer/ **noun** [U] containers in which food can be cooked inside an oven

over /ˈəʊ.vər/ (US) /ˈoʊ.vɚ/ **preposition; adv; noun**

▸**preposition HIGHER POSITION** ▷ **1** (B1) above or higher than something else, sometimes so that one thing covers the other; above: *The sign over the door said 'Exit'. ◦ She held the umbrella over both of us. ◦ Helicopters dropped leaflets over the city. ◦ I put my hands over my eyes/ears because I couldn't bear to watch/listen. ◦ I couldn't hear what she was saying over the noise of the planes taking off (= the aircraft were louder than her voice).* → Compare **under COVERING** ▷ **2** (A2) in a position that is covering something: *Put a clean cloth over the cakes while they cool. ◦ I put a shawl over my shoulders.* **ACROSS** ▷ **3** (B1) across from one side to the other, especially by going up and then down: *She jumped over the gate. ◦ The road goes over the mountains, not through a tunnel. ◦ She is always chatting with her neighbour over the garden wall. ◦ From the top of the tower you could see for miles over the city. ◦ Tanks travel over the most difficult ground.* **FALLING** ▷ **4** falling down from somewhere: *The coin rolled over the edge of the table. ◦ Harold jumped out of the car just before it went over the cliff.* **5** falling because of stepping on something: *She tripped over the rug.* **MORE THAN** ▷ **6** (A2) more than: *Most of the carpets cost/are over £100. ◦ Children over the age of twelve (= older than twelve) must pay the full price. ◦ I value quality of life over money.* **7** (A2) increasing to further than a particular limit or point: *They are already $25 million over budget.* **8 over and above** in addition to: *They receive extra money over and above the usual welfare payments.* **OTHER SIDE** ▷ **9** (B1) on the other side of: *There's a pub over the road we could go to. ◦ The story continues over the page.* **CONNECTED WITH** ▷ **10** (C2) (referring to a cause of interest, worry, discussion, etc.) connected with or about: *There's no point in arguing over something so unimportant. ◦ I need time to* ***talk/think*** *over your proposal (= to discuss/consider it carefully). ◦ The legal battle was over who should have custody of the child.* **DURING** ▷ **11** (B1) during something, or while doing something: *I was in Seattle over the summer. ◦ Shall we discuss it over lunch/over a drink? ◦ They took/spent an hour over lunch (= their meal lasted an hour). ◦ It's fascinating to watch how a baby changes and develops over* ***time*** *(= as time passes).* **FEELING BETTER** ▷ **12 be/get over sth** to feel physically or mentally better after an illness or an upsetting experience: *It takes you a while to get over an illness like that. ◦ His girlfriend finished with him last year and he's not over her yet. ◦ He's not fully recovered, but he's over* ***the worst*** *(= has experienced the worst stage of the illness and is now improving).* **CONTROL** ▷ **13** (C2) in control of or teaching someone or something: *A good teacher has an easy authority over a class. ◦ She's a sales manager but she has a regional sales director over (= with a higher rank than) her. ◦ The victory over the French at Waterloo was Wellington's greatest triumph.* **USING** ▷ **14** (B2) using: *They spoke over the phone. ◦ We heard the news over the radio.* **MATHS** ▷ **15** sometimes used when talking about a calculation in which one number is divided by another number: *40 over 7 is roughly 6.*

IDIOMS **all over somewhere** (B1) everywhere in a particular place: *Soon the news was all over town.* • **be all over sb** informal to be touching someone in a sexual way everywhere on their body: *She was all over him, kissing him and stroking him.*

▸**adv DOWN** ▷ **1** from a higher to a lower position; down: *The little boy* ***fell*** *over and started to cry. ◦ He was* ***run/knocked*** *over by a taxi.* **ACROSS** ▷ **2** (B1) across; from one side or place to another: *She leaned over and kissed me. ◦ A fighter plane flew over. ◦ Why don't you come over (= come to my house) for dinner on Thursday? ◦ I've got a friend over from Canada this week (= a friend came from Canada and is staying with me). ◦ Now we're going over to (= there will be a broadcast from) Wembley for commentary on the Cup Final. ◦ Come over* ***here*** *– it's warmer. ◦ Who's that man over* ***there****?* **3** (B2) describes the way an object moves or is moved so that a different part of it is facing up: *She turned another page over. ◦ The dog rolled over onto its back. ◦ The children rolled over* ***and over*** *(= turned over many times) down the gentle slope.* **4** changing or exchanging position: *Would you mind* ***changing/swapping*** *those plates over? ◦ She* ***changed*** *over* ***to*** *editing* ***from*** *marketing. ◦ Why should we* ***hand*** *over the money* ***to*** *them? ◦ I've done all I can – now it's over* ***to*** *you (= it's your turn to take action).* **HIGHER POSITION** ▷ **5** above or higher than something else, sometimes so that one thing covers the other: *A fighter plane flew over. ◦ A man came to paint over (= cover with paint) the cracks in the wall.* **MORE THAN** ▷ **6** (A2) more than a particular amount or level: *People who are 65 years old* ***and*** *over can get half-price tickets.* **FINISHED** ▷ **7** (B1) (especially of an event) finished: *I'll be glad when the competition is over. ◦ I used to have a thriving business and a happy marriage, but that's* ***all*** *over now.* **8 over and done with** (C2) completely finished: *She gets unpleasant tasks over and done with as quickly as possible.* **EXTRA** ▷ **9** extra; not used: *I have some American dollars* ***left*** *over from the last time I was there. ◦* UK *When all the guests had gone, we realized there was lots of food over.* **AGAIN** ▷ **10** US again or repeatedly: *You've ruined it – now I'll have to* ***do*** *it over!* **FINISHED TALKING** ▷ **11** said when you are talking to someone by radio, to mean that you have finished speaking and will wait for their answer: *'This is flight 595X. Do you read me? Over.'* **12 over and out** said when you are talking to someone by radio in order to end the conversation: *'Thank you, control tower. Over and out.'*

IDIOMS **over and over (again)** (B2) happening or done many times: *I read the article over and over till it made sense.* • **it isn't over until the fat lady sings** saying used for saying that it is still possible for a situation to change

▸**noun** [C] (in cricket) a set of six BOWLS (= throws) from the same end of the field

over- /əʊ.vər-/ (US) /oʊ.vɚ-/ **prefix TOO MUCH** ▷ **1** too much or more than usual: *The children got rather over-excited (= too excited).* **MORE THAN** ▷ **2** more than: *a club for the over-50s* **ACROSS** ▷ **3** across: *Of course, the overland route is much slower than going by air.* **HIGHER POSITION** ▷ **4** above: *She was knocked off her bicycle by an overhanging branch.*

overact /ˌəʊ.vəˈrækt/ (US) /ˌoʊ.vɚˈækt/ **verb** [I or T] disapproving to make your voice and movements express emotions too strongly when acting in a play

> **! Note:**
> Do not confuse with **overreact**.

overage /ˌəʊ.vəˈreɪdʒ/ (US) /ˌoʊ.vɚˈeɪdʒ/ **adj** older than a particular age and therefore no longer allowed to do or have particular things: *She lost her place on the youth team when the manager discovered she was overage.*

overall /ˌəʊ.vəˈrɔːl/ (US) /ˌoʊ.vɚˈɑːl/ **adv** [before noun], **adj** (B2) in general rather than in particular, or including all the people or things in a particular group or situation: *The overall situation is good, despite a few minor problems.* ◦ *Overall, it has been a good year.* ◦ *The overall winner, after ten games, will receive $250,000.*

overalls /ˈəʊ.vᵊr.ɔːlz/ (US) /ˈoʊ.vɚ.ɑːlz/ **noun** [plural] **1** UK (US **coveralls**) a piece of clothing that covers both the upper and lower parts of the body and is worn especially over other clothes to protect them: *She put on some overalls and got out a tin of paint.* **2** US for **dungarees**

overarching /ˌəʊ.vəˈrɑː.tʃɪŋ/ (US) /ˌoʊ.vɚˈɑːr-/ **adj** [before noun] formal most important, because of including or affecting all other areas: *a grand overarching strategy*

overarm /ˈəʊ.və.rɑːm/ (US) /ˈoʊ.vɚ.ɑːrm/ **adj, adv** (especially of a throw) made with the arm moving above the shoulder: *an overarm throw/serve* ◦ *Bowl it overarm.*

O

overate /ˌəʊ.vəˈret/, /-reɪt/ (US) /ˌoʊ.vɚˈeɪt/ past simple of **overeat**

overawe /ˌəʊ.vəˈrɔː/ (US) /ˌoʊ.vɚˈɑː/ **verb** [T usually passive] to cause someone to feel a mixture of respect and fear: *Some of the players were totally overawed by playing their first game at the national stadium.*

overbalance /ˌəʊ.vəˈbæl.ᵊns/ (US) /ˌoʊ-/ **verb** [I] to lose balance and therefore fall or nearly fall: *Halfway along the wall he overbalanced and fell.*

overbearing /ˌəʊ.vəˈbeə.rɪŋ/ (US) /ˌoʊ.vɚˈber.ɪŋ/ **adj** disapproving too confident and too determined to tell other people what to do, in a way that is unpleasant: *Milligan had a pompous, overbearing father.*

overbid /ˌəʊ.vəˈbɪd/ (US) /ˌoʊ.vɚ-/ **verb** [I or T] (present tense **overbidding**, past tense and past participle **overbid**) to offer more money than someone in an attempt to buy something, or to offer too much money in an attempt to buy something: *They were overbid by a Japanese firm.* ◦ *The Commission felt the company were overbidding and gave the franchise to their competitors instead.*

overblown /ˌəʊ.vəˈbləʊn/ (US) /ˌoʊ.vɚˈbloʊn/ **adj** disapproving bigger or more important than it should be: *an overblown news story* ◦ *Sir Neville's conducting is precise and delicate, never overblown.*

overboard /ˈəʊ.və.bɔːd/, /ˌəʊ.vəˈbɔːd/ (US) /ˈoʊ.vɚ.bɔːrd/ **adv** (C2) over the side of a boat or ship and into the water: *Someone had **fallen** overboard.*

IDIOMS **chuck/throw/toss sth/sb overboard** informal to get rid of something or someone: *She threw $2 million of energy shares overboard and bought computer shares instead.* • **go overboard** informal (C2) to do something too much, or to be too excited or eager about something: *I don't suppose there'll be more than six people eating so I wouldn't go overboard with the food.*

overbook /ˌəʊ.vəˈbʊk/ (US) /ˌoʊ.vɚ-/ **verb** [I or T] to sell more tickets or places for an aircraft, holiday, etc. than are available: *The hotel was overbooked.* ◦ *There was no seat for me on the plane, because the airline had overbooked.*

overburden /ˌəʊ.vəˈbɜː.dᵊn/ (US) /ˌoʊ.vɚˈbɝː-/ **verb** [T often passive] to make someone or something work too hard or carry, contain or deal with too much: *Insurance companies are already overburdened **with** similar claims.* ◦ *Now 5,000 new children will be attending the district's already overburdened school system.*

overcast /ˈəʊ.və.kɑːst/, /ˌəʊ.vəˈkɑːst/ (US) /ˈoʊ.vɚ.kæst/ **adj** with clouds in the sky and therefore not bright and SUNNY: *The sky/weather was overcast.* ◦ *a depressing, overcast winter morning*

overcharge /ˌəʊ.vəˈtʃɑːdʒ/ (US) /ˌoʊ.vɚˈtʃɑːrdʒ/ **verb** [I or T] to charge someone either more than the real price or more than the value of the product or service: *The shop overcharged me (**by** £10).* ◦ [+ two objects] *They overcharged her £45.*

overcoat /ˈəʊ.və.kəʊt/ (US) /ˈoʊ.vɚ.koʊt/ **noun** [C] a long thick coat worn in cold weather

overcome /ˌəʊ.vəˈkʌm/ (US) /ˌoʊ.vɚ-/ **verb** (**overcame, overcome**) **DEAL WITH** ▷ **1** (B2) [I or T] to defeat or succeed in controlling or dealing with something: *Juventus overcame Ajax in a thrilling match.* ◦ *to overcome **difficulties/obstacles/problems/resistance*** ◦ *Eventually she managed to overcome her shyness in class.* ◦ *20,000 demonstrators sang 'We shall overcome' as they marched through Washington.* **UNABLE TO ACT** ▷ **2** (C2) [T usually passive] to prevent someone from being able to act or think in the usual way: *They were overcome **by** fumes from the fire and had to be carried out of their houses.* ◦ *Overcome **with/by** emotion, she found herself unable to speak for a few minutes.*

overcompensate /ˌəʊ.vəˈkɒm.pən.seɪt/ (US) /ˌoʊ.vɚˈkɑːm-/ **verb** [I] to try too hard to correct a problem, therefore creating a new problem: *Chris is one of those small men who overcompensate **for** their lack of height **with** a larger than life personality.*

overcook /ˌəʊ.vəˈkʊk/ (US) /ˌoʊ.vɚ-/ **verb** [T often passive] to cook food for longer than necessary, reducing its quality as a result: *The chicken was overcooked and dry.*

overcrowded /ˌəʊ.vəˈkraʊ.dɪd/ (US) /ˌoʊ.vɚ-/ **adj** (C1) containing too many people or things: *overcrowded cities/prisons/schools* ◦ *The world market for telecommunications is already overcrowded **with** businesses.* • **overcrowd** /ˌəʊ.vəˈkraʊd/ (US) /ˌoʊ.vɚ-/ **verb** [T] • **overcrowding** /-ˈkraʊ.dɪŋ/ **noun** [U] *Investment in the railway network would reduce overcrowding on the roads.*

overdeveloped /ˌəʊ.və.dɪˈvel.əpt/ (US) /ˌoʊ.vɚ-/ **adj** having developed too much: *I don't like body builders who are so overdeveloped you can see the veins in their bulging muscles.*

overdo /ˌəʊ.vəˈduː/ (US) /ˌoʊ.vɚ-/ **verb** [T] (**overdid, overdone**) (C1) to do something in a way that is too extreme: *After a heart attack you have to be careful not to overdo **it/things** (= you have to work and live calmly).*

overdone /ˌəʊ.vəˈdʌn/ (US) /ˌoʊ.vɚ-/ **adj** (especially of meat) cooked too long: *The roast lamb was dry and overdone.*

overdose /ˈəʊ.və.dəʊs/ Ⓤⓢ /ˈoʊ.vɚ.doʊs/ **noun; verb**

▸**noun** [C] **1** (informal **OD**) too much of a drug taken or given at one time, either intentionally or by accident: *When he was 17 he* ***took*** *an overdose* ***of*** *sleeping pills and nearly died.* ◦ *Jimi Hendrix died of a* ***drug(s)*** *overdose.* **2** humorous too much of something: *After watching two operas, I was suffering from an overdose of culture.*

▸**verb** [I] **1** (informal **OD**) to take too much of a drug: *She overdosed* ***on*** *aspirin and died.* **2** humorous to have too much of something: *I think I've just overdosed* ***on*** *cheesecake!*

overdraft /ˈəʊ.və.drɑːft/ Ⓤⓢ /ˈoʊ.vɚ.dræft/ **noun** [C] **C1** an amount of money that a customer with a bank account is temporarily allowed to owe to the bank, or the agreement which allows this: *to* ***run up/pay off*** *an overdraft* ◦ *The bank offers overdraft* ***facilities.***

overdrawn /ˌəʊ.vəˈdrɔːn/ Ⓤⓢ /ˌoʊ.vɚˈdrɑːn/ **adj** **C1** having taken more money out of your bank account than the account contained, or (of a bank account) having had more money taken from it than was originally in it: *They were overdrawn* ***by*** *£150, so they couldn't write any cheques.* ◦ *The account was overdrawn.* • **overdraw** /-ˈdrɔː/ Ⓤⓢ /-ˈdrɑː/ **verb** [I or T] (**overdrew**, **overdrawn**) *I overdrew my account* ***by*** *£20.*

overdressed /ˌəʊ.vəˈdrest/ Ⓤⓢ /ˌoʊ.vɚ-/ **adj** wearing clothes that are too formal or special for a particular occasion: *Everyone else was wearing jeans so I felt a bit overdressed in my best suit.*

overdrive /ˈəʊ.və.draɪv/ Ⓤⓢ /ˈoʊ.vɚ-/ **noun** [U] a state of great activity, effort or hard work: *The official propaganda machine* ***went into*** *overdrive when war broke out.* ◦ *The cast were* ***in*** *overdrive, rehearsing for the first performance.*

overdue /ˌəʊ.vəˈdjuː/ Ⓤⓢ /ˌoʊ.vɚˈduː/ **adj** not done or happening when expected or when needed; late: *My library books are a week overdue.* ◦ *The baby is two weeks overdue (= the baby was expected to be born two weeks ago).* ◦ *Changes to the tax system are* ***long*** *overdue.* ◦ *She feels she's overdue* ***for*** *promotion.*

overeat /ˌəʊ.vəʳˈiːt/ Ⓤⓢ /ˌoʊ.vɚˈiːt/ **verb** [I] (**overate**, **overeaten**) to eat more food than your body needs, especially so that you feel uncomfortably full • **overeating** /-ˈiː.tɪŋ/ Ⓤⓢ /-ˈiː.t̬ɪŋ/ **noun** [U]

overestimate /ˌəʊ.vəˈres.tɪ.meɪt/ Ⓤⓢ /ˌoʊ.vɚˈes-/ **verb** [I or T] **C1** to think that something is or will be greater, more extreme or more important than it really is: *The benefits of nuclear technology, she said, had been grossly overestimated.* ◦ *They were forced to the conclusion that they had overestimated him/his abilities.* ◦ *I overestimated and there was a lot of food left over after the party.* • **overestimate** /ˌəʊ.vəˈres.tɪ.mət/ Ⓤⓢ /ˌoʊ.vɚˈes-/ **noun** [C]

overexpose /ˌəʊ.və.rɪkˈspəʊz/ Ⓤⓢ /ˌoʊ.vɚ.ɪkˈspoʊz/ **verb** [T usually passive] to give too much light to a piece of photographic film when taking a photograph: *Unfortunately the light was too bright and my photos were all overexposed.*

overfishing /ˌəʊ.vəˈfɪʃ.ɪŋ/ Ⓤⓢ /ˌoʊ.vɚ-/ **noun** [U] catching too many fish in an area of the sea so that there are not many fish left there: *low fish stocks caused by overfishing*

overflow **verb; noun**

▸**verb** /ˌəʊ.vəˈfləʊ/ Ⓤⓢ /ˌoʊ.vɚˈfloʊ/ **TOO FULL** ▷ **1** **C2** [I or T] When a liquid overflows, it flows over the edges of a container, etc. because there is too much of it: *The milk overflowed when I poured it into the jug.* ◦ *Because of heavy rain, the river may overflow its banks.* **2** [I or T] If a container or a place overflows, whatever is inside it starts coming out because it is too full: *Oh no, the bath is overflowing all over the floor.* ◦ *The bin was overflowing* ***with*** *rubbish.* **3** **C2** [I] When a place overflows, or people or things overflow from somewhere, some people or things have to come out because it cannot contain them all: *The bar was so full that people were overflowing* ***into/onto*** *the street.* ◦ *The train was* (***full to***) *overflowing (= so full that there was not space for any more passengers).* ◦ *His room is overflowing* ***with*** *books.* **4** **to overflowing** so that water or another substance is almost coming over the top: *Someone has filled the bath* (***full***) *to overflowing.* **EMOTIONS** ▷ **5** **C2** [I] If you overflow with thoughts or feelings, you express them strongly: *They were* (***full to***) *overflowing* ***with*** *emotion at the birth of their baby.* ◦ *Suddenly, her anger overflowed.*

▸**noun** /ˈəʊ.və.fləʊ/ Ⓤⓢ /ˈoʊ.vɚ.floʊ/ **AMOUNT** ▷ **1** [S or U] an amount of liquid or number of people that cannot fit in a space: *I put a bucket underneath to catch the overflow* ***from*** *the water tank.* ◦ *We can't cope with this overflow* ***of*** *patients* ***from*** *the other hospitals.* **PIPE** ▷ **2** [C] (also **overflow pipe**) a pipe that carries away water that is not needed

overgrown /ˌəʊ.vəˈgrəʊn/ Ⓤⓢ /ˌoʊ.vɚˈgroʊn/ **adj** **COVERED** ▷ **1** covered with plants that are growing thickly and in an uncontrolled way: *The field is overgrown* ***with*** *weeds.* **TOO LARGE** ▷ **2** disapproving describes something that has grown too large

IDIOM **overgrown schoolboy/schoolgirl** disapproving an adult who behaves like a child

overhand /ˈəʊ.və.hænd/ Ⓤⓢ /ˈoʊ.vɚ-/ **adj, adv** US for **overarm**

overhang **verb; noun**

▸**verb** [T] /ˌəʊ.vəˈhæŋ/ Ⓤⓢ /ˌoʊ.vɚ-/ (**overhung**, **overhung**) **STICK OUT** ▷ **1** to stick out over something at a lower level: *Several large trees overhang the path.* **AFFECT** ▷ **2** to have a negative effect on a situation: *Overhanging the controversy is the question of how much the government knew about the arms deal.*

▸**noun** [C] /ˈəʊ.və.hæŋ/ Ⓤⓢ /ˈoʊ.vɚ-/ **STICK OUT** ▷ **1** the part of a rock or roof that sticks out over something below: *The church is unsafe because it was built on an overhang.* **EFFECT** ▷ **2** something that has a negative effect on a situation: *Prices are unlikely to increase while there is an overhang* ***of*** *40,000 unsold new houses.* • **overhanging** /-ɪŋ/ **adj** *the overhanging branches of a tree*

overhaul /ˈəʊ.və.hɔːl/ Ⓤⓢ /ˈoʊ.vɚ.hɑːl/ **verb** [T] to repair or improve something so that every part of it works as it should: *I got the engine overhauled.* ◦ *The government plans to overhaul the health service.* • **overhaul** **noun** [C] *I took my motorbike in for an overhaul.*

overhead /ˈəʊ.və.hed/ Ⓤⓢ /ˈoʊ.vɚ-/ **adj, adv; adj; noun**

▸**adj, adv** above your head, usually in the sky: *overhead cables* ◦ *A flock of geese flew overhead.* ◦ *This room needs overhead lighting (= lights in the ceiling).*

▸**adj** [before noun] relating to the OVERHEADS of a business: *One way of increasing profit margins is to cut overhead costs.*

▸**noun** **TEXT/PICTURES** ▷ **1** [C] (also **ˌoverhead transˈparency**) a transparent sheet used for showing text or pictures with an OVERHEAD PROJECTOR **COSTS** ▷ **2** **overheads** [plural] UK (US **overhead** [C]) the regular and necessary costs, such as rent and heating, that are involved in operating a business: *We need to reduce* *our overheads.* ◦ *Many businesses are moving out of New York because the overhead there is so high.*

ˌ**overhead proˈjector** noun [C] (abbreviation **OHP**) a device which makes large images from a flat transparent sheet and shows them on a white screen or wall

overhear /ˌəʊ.vəˈhɪəʳ/ ⓤⓢ /ˌoʊ.vɚˈhɪr/ verb [I or T] (**overheard, overheard**) Ⓒ2 to hear what other people are saying without intending to and without their knowledge: *I overheard a very funny conversation on the bus this morning.* ◦ [+ obj + -ing verb] *He overheard his daughter telling her teddy not to be so naughty.* ◦ [+ obj + infinitive without to] *We overheard them say that they didn't really like the meal.* ◦ *I'm sorry, I couldn't help overhearing.*

overheat /ˌəʊ.vəˈhiːt/ ⓤⓢ /ˌoʊ.vɚ-/ verb **TEMPERATURE** ▷ **1** [I or T] to (cause to) become hotter than necessary or wanted: *I think the engine is overheating.* ◦ *It isn't healthy to overheat your house.* **ECONOMY** ▷ **2** [I] If an economy overheats, it grows very quickly, so that prices, etc. increase quickly.

overheated /ˌəʊ.vəˈhiː.tɪd/ ⓤⓢ /ˌoʊ.vɚˈhiː.t̬ɪd/ adj If a situation is/gets overheated, strong feelings, especially anger, are expressed: *Things got a bit overheated at the meeting.*

overhung /ˌəʊ.vəˈhʌŋ/ ⓤⓢ /ˌoʊ.vɚ-/ past simple and past participle of **overhang**

overindulge /ˌəʊ.və.rɪnˈdʌldʒ/ ⓤⓢ /ˌoʊ.vɚ.ɪn-/ verb [I or T] to allow yourself or someone else to have too much of something enjoyable, especially food or drink: *I wish I hadn't overindulged so much (= had so much to eat and drink) last night.* ◦ *It's not good for children to be overindulged (= always given what they want).* • **overindulgence** /-ˈdʌl.dʒᵊns/ noun [U] *For many Americans, Thanksgiving is a time of overindulgence (= eating and drinking too much).*

O

overjoyed /ˌəʊ.vəˈdʒɔɪd/ ⓤⓢ /ˌoʊ.vɚ-/ adj [after verb] extremely pleased and happy: *We're overjoyed **at** your news.* ◦ [+ to infinitive] *Helen was overjoyed **to** hear that she had got the job.* ◦ [+ that] *I'm overjoyed **that** you're coming to visit me.*

overkill /ˈəʊ.və.kɪl/ ⓤⓢ /ˈoʊ.vɚ-/ noun [U] disapproving much more of something than is needed, resulting in less effectiveness: *Should I add an explanation, or would that be overkill?*

overland /ˈəʊ.və.lænd/ ⓤⓢ /ˈoʊ.vɚ-/ adj, adv (of travel) across the land in a vehicle, on foot or on a horse; not by sea or air: *an overland trip across Australia* ◦ *We travelled overland.*

overlap verb; noun

▸verb /ˌəʊ.vəˈlæp/ ⓤⓢ /ˌoʊ.vɚ-/ (-pp-) **1** [I or T] to cover something partly by going over its edge; to cover part of the same space: *The fence is made of panels that overlap (each other).* **2** Ⓒ2 [I] If two or more activities, subjects or periods of time overlap, they have some parts that are the same: *My musical tastes don't overlap **with** my brother's at all.* • **overlapping** adj *The overlapping slates of the roofs in the mountain village resembled fish scales.* ◦ *The word has two separate but overlapping meanings (= parts of the meanings are the same).*

▸noun [C or U] /ˈəʊ.və.læp/ ⓤⓢ /ˈoʊ.vɚ-/ the amount by which two things or activities cover the same area: *The roof tiles will need an overlap **of** several centimetres.* ◦ *There are some overlaps **between** the products of the two companies.*

overlay verb; noun

▸verb [T often passive] /ˌəʊ.vəˈleɪ/ ⓤⓢ /ˌoʊ.vɚ-/ (**overlaid, overlaid**) **1** to cover something with a layer of something: *The foundation of the house is built from rubble overlaid **with** concrete.* **2 be overlaid with sth** literary something that is overlaid with something has a particular quality added to it that influences its character: *Her new novel is overlaid **with** political concerns.*

▸noun [C] /ˈəʊ.və.leɪ/ ⓤⓢ /ˈoʊ.vɚ-/ a thin covering of something: *The wood frame has a gold overlay.*

overleaf /ˌəʊ.vəˈliːf/ ⓤⓢ /ˌoʊ.vɚ-/ adv on the other side of the page: *See overleaf for a list of abbreviations.*

overload verb; noun

▸verb [T] /ˌəʊ.vəˈləʊd/ ⓤⓢ /ˌoʊ.vɚˈloʊd/ **1** Ⓒ1 to put too many things in or on something: *Don't overload the washing machine, or it won't work properly.* **2** to put too much electricity through an electrical system **3** Ⓒ2 to give someone more work or problems than they can deal with: *Try not to overload yourself **with** work.*

▸noun [C or U] /ˈəʊ.və.ləʊd/ ⓤⓢ /ˈoʊ.vɚ.loʊd/ Ⓒ2 the fact that something or someone is overloaded: *People today suffer from **information** overload (= being given too much information).* ◦ *There was an overload on the electrical circuit and the fuse blew.*

overloaded /ˌəʊ.vəˈləʊ.dɪd/ ⓤⓢ /ˌoʊ.vɚˈloʊ-/ adj having or supplied with too much of something: *The market is already overloaded **with** car magazines – why would anyone want to produce another one?*

overlong /ˌəʊ.vəˈlɒŋ/ ⓤⓢ /ˌoʊ.vɚˈlɑːŋ/ adj too long: *I enjoyed the film, but I thought it was overlong.*

overlook verb; noun

▸verb [T] /ˌəʊ.vəˈlʊk/ ⓤⓢ /ˌoʊ.vɚ-/ **VIEW** ▷ **1** Ⓑ2 to provide a view of, especially from above: *Our hotel room overlooked the harbour.* ◦ *The house is surrounded by trees, so it's not overlooked at all (= it cannot be seen from any other buildings).* **NOT NOTICE** ▷ **2** Ⓒ2 to fail to notice or consider something or someone: *I think there is one key fact that you have overlooked.* ◦ *No one will be overlooked in the selection of the team.* **FORGIVE** ▷ **3** to forgive or pretend not to notice something: *I'm prepared to overlook his behaviour this time.*

▸noun [C] /ˈəʊ.və.lʊk/ ⓤⓢ /ˈoʊ.vɚ-/ US a **viewpoint**: *There are lots of **scenic** overlooks along the road from New York to Montreal.*

overlord /ˈəʊ.və.lɔːd/ ⓤⓢ /ˈoʊ.vɚ.lɔːrd/ noun [C] a person in a position of power, especially in the past

overly /ˈəʊ.vᵊl.i/ ⓤⓢ /ˈoʊ.vɚ.li/ adv (also **over**) too; very: *Earlier sales forecasts were overly optimistic.* ◦ *His films have been criticized for being overly violent.*

overmanned /ˌəʊ.vəˈmænd/ ⓤⓢ /ˌoʊ.vɚ-/ adj having more employees than are needed → Synonym **overstaffed**

overmuch /ˌəʊ.vəˈmʌtʃ/ ⓤⓢ /ˌoʊ.vɚ-/ adv, adj (especially in negatives) too much or very much: *At least he didn't suffer overmuch before he died.* ◦ *I don't have overmuch confidence in Hal.*

overnight /ˌəʊ.vəˈnaɪt/ ⓤⓢ /ˌoʊ.vɚ-/ adj, adv **TIME OF DAY** ▷ **1** Ⓑ1 for or during the night: *an overnight stop in Paris* ◦ *You can stay overnight if you want to.* ◦ *Don't forget to pack an overnight **bag** (= a bag for things that you need when you stay away from home for a night).* **SUDDENLY** ▷ **2** Ⓒ2 suddenly and unexpectedly: *She became a star overnight.* ◦ *The book was an overnight success.*

overpass /ˈəʊ.və.pɑːs/ ⓤⓢ /ˈoʊ.vɚ.pæs/ noun [C] US for **flyover**

overpay /ˌəʊ.vəˈpeɪ/ ⓤⓢ /ˌoʊ.vɚ-/ verb [T often passive] (**overpaid, overpaid**) **1** to pay someone too much: *I felt I should tell my boss she'd overpaid me **by** £50.* ◦ disapproving *City bankers are grossly overpaid **for***

what they do. **2** to pay more than originally agreed when paying back a LOAN, in order to reduce the cost of the LOAN: *If you budget to overpay your mortgage on a regular basis, you can save a lot of money.* • **overpayment** /-mənt/ noun [C or U] *She did not notice that she had received a salary overpayment.*

overplay /ˌəʊ.vəˈpleɪ/ (US) /ˌoʊ.vɚ-/ verb [T] to make something seem more important than it really is: *I think she's overplaying the significance of his remarks.*

IDIOM **overplay your hand** to spoil your chance of success by saying or doing too much

overpopulated /ˌəʊ.vəˈpɒp.jʊ.leɪ.tɪd/ (US) /ˌoʊ.vɚˈpɑː.pjə.leɪ.t̬ɪd/ adj If a country or city, etc. is overpopulated, it has too many people for the amount of food, materials, and space available there. • **overpopulation** /-ˌpɒp.jʊˈleɪ.ʃən/ (US) /-ˌpɑː.pjəˈleɪ.ʃən/ noun [U]

overpower /ˌəʊ.vəˈpaʊəʳ/ (US) /ˌoʊ.vɚˈpaʊɚ/ verb [T] **1** to defeat someone by having greater strength or power: *The gunman was finally overpowered by three security guards.* **2** If a smell or feeling overpowers you, it is so strong that it makes you feel weak or ill: *The **heat/smell** of gas overpowered me as I went into the house.*

overpowering /ˌəʊ.vəˈpaʊə.rɪŋ/ (US) /ˌoʊ.vɚˈpaʊɚ.ɪŋ/ adj too strong: *Firefighters were driven back by the overpowering heat of the flames.* ◦ *There's an overpowering smell of garlic in the kitchen.* ◦ *He's suffering from overpowering feelings of guilt.*

overpriced /ˌəʊ.vəˈpraɪst/ (US) /ˌoʊ.vɚ-/ adj too expensive: *These shoes are very nice, but they're terribly overpriced.*

overproduce /ˌəʊ.və.prəˈdjuːs/ (US) /ˌoʊ.vɚ.prəˈduːs/ verb [I or T] to produce more of something than is needed, or to produce too much • **overproduction** /-prəˈdʌk.ʃən/ noun [C or U] *The company is in a bad financial position because of overproduction.*

overprotective /ˌəʊ.və.prəˈtek.tɪv/ (US) /ˌoʊ.vɚ-/ adj wishing to protect someone, especially a child, too much: *The children of overprotective parents are sometimes rather neurotic.*

overqualified /ˌəʊ.vəˈkwɒl.ɪ.faɪd/ (US) /ˌoʊ.vɚˈkwɑː.lɪ-/ adj having more knowledge, skill, and/or experience than is needed (for a particular job): *The problem with employing people who are overqualified **for** the job is that they often don't stay in it for long.*

overran /ˌəʊ.vəˈræn/ (US) /ˌoʊ.vɚ-/ past simple and past participle of **overrun**

overrate /ˌəʊ.vəˈreɪt/ (US) /ˌoʊ.vɚ-/ verb [T often passive] to have too good an opinion of something: *Be careful not to overrate the opposition.*

overrated /ˌəʊ.vəˈreɪ.tɪd/ (US) /ˌoʊ.vɚˈreɪ.t̬ɪd/ adj If something or someone is overrated, they are considered to be better or more important than they really are: *In my opinion, she's a hugely overrated singer.*

overreach /ˌəʊ.vəˈriːtʃ/ (US) /ˌoʊ.vɚ-/ verb **overreach yourself** to fail by trying to achieve, spend, or do more than you can manage: *Companies that overreach themselves soon find themselves in debt.*

overreact /ˌəʊ.və.riˈækt/ (US) /ˌoʊ.vɚ-/ verb [I] to react in an extreme, especially an angry or frightened, way: *You must learn not to overreact **to** criticism.* • **overreaction** /-ˈæk.ʃən/ noun [C or U]

override /ˌəʊ.vəˈraɪd/ (US) /ˌoʊ.vɚ-/ verb; noun
▸verb (**overrode, overridden**) **NOT ACCEPT** ▷ **1** [T] (of a person who has the necessary authority) to decide against or refuse to accept a previous decision, an order, a person, etc.: *Every time I make a suggestion at work, my boss overrides me/it.* ◦ *The president used his veto to override the committee's decision.* **2** [T] to operate an automatic machine by hand: *He overrode the autopilot when he realized it was malfunctioning.* **CONTROL** ▷ **3** [T] to take control over something, especially in order to change the way it operates: *The pills are designed to override your body's own hormones.* **MORE IMPORTANT** ▷ **4** [T] to be more important than something: *Parents' concern for their children's future often overrides all their other concerns.*
▸noun [C] **DEVICE** ▷ **1** a device that changes the control of a machine or system in special situations, especially from automatic to MANUAL: *The heating system has a manual override.* **POLITICS** ▷ **2** in American politics, an occasion when an elected group of people refuses to accept a decision made by an elected leader: *The vote fell short of the majority needed for an override **of** the Governor's veto.*

overriding /ˌəʊ.vəˈraɪ.dɪŋ/ (US) /ˌoʊ.vɚ-/ adj; noun
▸adj [before noun] more important than anything else: *The government's overriding **concern** is to reduce inflation.*
▸noun [U] travelling on public transport further than your ticket allows you to: *There is a penalty for overriding.*

overripe /ˌəʊ.vəˈraɪp/ (US) /ˌoʊ.vɚ-/ adj too RIPE and starting to decay

overrule /ˌəʊ.vəˈruːl/ (US) /ˌoʊ.vɚ-/ verb [T] formal (of a person who has official authority) to decide against a decision that has already been made: *In tennis, the umpire can overrule the line judge.*

overrun /ˌəʊ.vəˈrʌn/ (US) /ˌoʊ.vɚ-/ verb (present participle **overrunning**, past tense **overran**, past participle **overrun**) **FILL** ▷ **1** [T] If unwanted people or things overrun, they fill a place quickly and in large numbers: *Rebel soldiers overran the embassy last night.* ◦ *Our kitchen is overrun **with** cockroaches.* **GO PAST** ▷ **2** [I or T] to continue past an intended limit, especially a finishing time or a cost: *My evening class overran by ten minutes.* ◦ *It looks as if we're going to overrun our budget.* • **overrun** /ˌəʊ.vəˈrʌn/ (US) /ˌoʊ.vɚˈrʌn/ noun [C]

overseas /ˌəʊ.vəˈsiːz/ (US) /ˌoʊ.vɚ-/ adj, adv (B2) in, from or to other countries: *We need to open up overseas markets.* ◦ *There are a lot of overseas students in Cambridge.* ◦ *My brother is a student overseas.* ◦ *Many more people go/travel/live/work overseas these days.*

oversee /ˌəʊ.vəˈsiː/ (US) /ˌoʊ.vɚ-/ verb [T] (present participle **overseeing**, past tense **oversaw**, past participle **overseen**) to watch or organize a job or an activity to make certain that it is being done correctly: *As marketing manager, her job is to oversee all the company's advertising.*

overseer /ˈəʊ.vəˌsiː.əʳ/ (US) /ˈoʊ.vɚˌsiː.ɚ/ noun [C] old-fashioned a person whose job it is to make certain that employees are working or that an activity is being done correctly

oversell /ˌəʊ.vəˈsel/ (US) /ˌoʊ.vɚ-/ verb [T] (**oversold**) mainly US to sell more than is available: *The flight had been oversold.*

oversexed /ˌəʊ.vəˈsekst/ (US) /ˌoʊ.vɚ-/ adj wanting sex more often than is considered normal

overshadow /ˌəʊ.vəˈʃæd.əʊ/ (US) /ˌoʊ.vɚˈʃæd.oʊ/ verb [T often passive] **1** to cause someone or something to seem less important or less happy: *Karen has always felt overshadowed by her famous elder sister.* ◦ *My happiness was overshadowed by the bad news.* **2** (of a building) to be much taller than another building and therefore block the sun from it

O

overshoes /ˈəʊ.və.ʃuːz/ (US) /ˈoʊ.vɚ-/ **noun** [plural] (US also **galoshes**) WATERPROOF shoes, usually made of rubber, for wearing over an ordinary shoe in the rain or snow

overshoot /ˌəʊ.vəˈʃuːt/ (US) /ˌoʊ.vɚ-/ **verb** [T] (**overshot**, **overshot**) to go further than the end of or past something, without intending to: *The plane overshot the* ***runway*** *and finished up in the water.*

oversight /ˈəʊ.və.saɪt/ (US) /ˈoʊ.vɚ-/ **noun** MISTAKE ▷ **1** [C or U] a mistake made because of a failure to notice something: *They claimed it was simply (an) oversight.* RESPONSIBILITY ▷ **2** [U] responsibility for a job or activity and for making sure it is being done correctly: *Who has oversight of genetic testing?*

oversimplify /ˌəʊ.vəˈsɪm.plɪ.faɪ/ (US) /ˌoʊ.vɚˈsɪm.plə-/ **verb** [I or T] to describe or explain something in such a simple way that it is no longer correct or true: *The TV documentary grossly oversimplified the problem.* • **oversimplification** /ˌəʊ.vəˌsɪm.plɪ.fɪˈkeɪ.ʃən/ (US) /ˌoʊ.vɚˌsɪm.plə-/ **noun** [C or U]

oversize /ˈəʊ.və.saɪz/ (US) /ˈoʊ.vɚ-/ **adj** (also **oversized**) mainly US bigger than usual, or too big: *My daughter loves to wear oversize clothes.*

oversleep /ˌəʊ.vəˈsliːp/ (US) /ˌoʊ.vɚ-/ **verb** [I] (**overslept**, **overslept**) to sleep for longer than you intended to and so wake up late: *I missed the train this morning because I overslept again.*

oversold /ˌəʊ.vəˈsəʊld/ (US) /ˌoʊ.vɚˈsoʊld/ past simple and past participle of **oversell**

overspend verb; noun

▸**verb** [I or T] /ˌəʊ.vəˈspend/ (US) /ˌoʊ.vɚ-/ (**overspent**, **overspent**) to spend more money than you should: *The council seems likely to overspend this year.* ◦ *The hospital has already overspent (****on****) its drugs* ***budget****.* • **overspending** /-ˈspen.dɪŋ/ **noun** [U]

▸**noun** [S] /ˈəʊ.və.spend/ (US) /ˈoʊ.vɚ-/ UK an amount of extra money that is spent on something above the amount that should have been spent: *We're expecting to have a £5 million (****budget****) overspend this year.*

overspill /ˈəʊ.və.spɪl/ (US) /ˈoʊ.vɚ-/ **noun** [S or U] UK people who move out of a crowded city and into other towns or villages near the city: *the overspill* ***from*** *London/the London overspill* ◦ *an overspill housing estate.*

overstaffed /ˌəʊ.vəˈstɑːft/ (US) /ˌoʊ.vɚˈstæft/ **adj** (also **overmanned**) having more employees than are needed: *The department has been accused of being inefficient and hugely overstaffed.*

overstate /ˌəʊ.vəˈsteɪt/ (US) /ˌoʊ.vɚ-/ **verb** [T] to describe or explain something in a way that makes it seem more important or serious than it really is: *The impact of the new legislation has been greatly overstated.* ◦ *The shareholders seem to think that the executive board is overstating the* ***case*** *for a merger.* → Opposite **understate**

overstatement /ˌəʊ.vəˈsteɪt.mənt/, /ˈəʊ.vəˌsteɪt-/ (US) /ˌoʊ.vɚ-/ **noun** [C or U] the act of describing or explaining something in a way that makes it seem more important or more serious than it really is: *It would be an overstatement to say that she deserved to win the race.*

overstay /ˌəʊ.vəˈsteɪ/ (US) /ˌoʊ.vɚ-/ **verb** [I or T] to stay longer in a place than you are allowed or wanted: *Be careful not to overstay your visa.* ◦ *They left the party at 11 p.m., careful not to overstay* ***their welcome****.*

overstep /ˌəʊ.vəˈstep/ (US) /ˌoʊ.vɚ-/ **verb** [T] (**-pp-**) to go further than what is considered acceptable or correct: *The bad language in that play overstepped the* ***limits/boundaries*** *of what ought to be allowed on television.* ◦ *I think you're overstepping your authority.*

IDIOM **overstep the mark** to behave in a completely unacceptable way: *You've overstepped the mark this time, Simpson – you're fired!*

overstock **verb** [I or T] /ˌəʊ.vəˈstɒk/ (US) /ˌoʊ.vɚˈstɑːk/ to (cause to) have more goods or supplies than are needed: *The shop is overstocked (****with*** *shoes).*

overstretched /ˌəʊ.vəˈstretʃt/ (US) /ˌoʊ.vɚˈ-/ **adj** not having enough money, people, equipment, etc.: *Hospitals are overstretched, and patients are not getting the treatment they need.*

oversubscribed /ˌəʊ.və.səbˈskraɪbd/ (US) /ˌoʊ.vɚ-/ **adj** If something is oversubscribed, people still want to buy things, especially SHARES or tickets, although all of them are already sold: *The $400 million oil company share issue was three times oversubscribed.*

overt /əʊˈvɜːt/ (US) /oʊˈvɝːt/ **adj** done or shown publicly or in an obvious way and not secret: *overt criticism* ◦ *overt racism* ◦ *He shows no overt signs of his unhappiness.* → Compare **covert** • **overtly** /-li/ **adv** *It was an overtly sexual advertising campaign.*

overtake /ˌəʊ.vəˈteɪk/ (US) /ˌoʊ.vɚ-/ **verb** (**overtook**, **overtaken**) GO PAST ▷ **1** (C1) [T] to go past something by being a greater amount or degree: *Our US sales have now overtaken our sales in Europe.* ◦ *We'd planned to hold a meeting tomorrow, but* ***events*** *have overtaken us (= things have changed).* **2** (B2) [I or T] UK (US **pass**) to come from behind another vehicle or a person and move in front of them: *Always check your rear view mirror before you overtake (another car).* HAPPEN ▷ **3** [T] to happen to a person or a place suddenly and unexpectedly: *The family was overtaken by tragedy several years ago, and they still haven't recovered.*

overˈtaking ˌlane **noun** [C usually singular] UK (US **ˈpassing ˌlane**) the part of a main road that is used for passing other vehicles and is nearest the centre of the road

overtax /ˌəʊ.vəˈtæks/ (US) /ˌoʊ.vɚ-/ **verb** [T] MONEY ▷ **1** to demand too much tax from someone or to put too much tax on goods: *I've been overtaxed this month.* ◦ *Food should not be overtaxed.* DIFFICULTY ▷ **2** to cause to feel tired or confused as a result of doing too much or doing something too difficult: *Remember you've been ill, and don't overtax your****self****.*

ˌover-the-ˈcounter **adj** MEDICINE ▷ **1** an over-the-counter drug is bought from a shop without visiting a doctor first: *an over-the-counter medicine* SHARES ▷ **2** used to describe SHARES that are traded directly between DEALERS (= people and organizations that buy and sell for others), rather than on a STOCK MARKET: *Brokers can use the system to look up prices or enter quotes for over-the-counter* ***securities****.* • **ˌover the ˈcounter** **adv** *You can buy most cold remedies over the counter.*

overthrow verb; noun

▸**verb** (**overthrew**, **overthrown**) DEFEAT ▷ **1** /ˌəʊ.vəˈθrəʊ/ (US) /ˌoʊ.vɚˈθroʊ/ [T] to defeat or remove someone from power, using force: *He said that Allende's government in Chile was overthrown by the army and the CIA in 1973.* THROW ▷ **2** /ˈəʊ.və.θrəʊ/ (US) /ˈoʊ.vɚ.θroʊ/ /ˌəʊ.vəˈθrəʊ/ [I or T] US to throw a ball past the person or object you intended to throw to: *Joe Montana overthrew (the pass).*

▸**noun** /ˈəʊ.və.θrəʊ/ (US) /ˈoʊ.vɚ.θroʊ/ DEFEAT ▷ **1** [C usually singular] an occasion when someone or something is removed from power using force: *the overthrow* ***of*** *the monarchy* THROW ▷ **2** [C usually singular] the act of throwing a ball too far

overtime /ˈəʊ.və.taɪm/ US /ˈoʊ.vɚ-/ adv, noun; noun
▸**adv, noun** [U] **1** B2 (time spent working) after the usual time needed or expected in a job: *They're* ***doing/working*** *overtime to get the job finished on time.* ◦ *Everyone is* ***on*** *overtime (= being paid extra for working after the usual time) this weekend.* **2** US for **extra time**
▸**noun** [U] extra payment for working after the usual time: *You can earn some overtime by working after 6.00 p.m.*

overtired /ˌəʊ.vəˈtaɪəd/ US /ˌoʊ.vɚˈtaɪrd/ adj extremely tired, often so that you can not sleep

overtone /ˈəʊ.və.təʊn/ US /ˈoʊ.vɚ.toʊn/ noun [C usually plural] something that is suggested, but is not clearly stated: *The concert was supposed to be a charity event but it* ***had*** *strong political overtones.* ◦ *There was an overtone* ***of*** *regret in his farewell speech.*

overtook /ˌəʊ.vəˈtʊk/ US /ˌoʊ.vɚ-/ past simple of **overtake**

overture /ˈəʊ.və.tjʊəʳ/ US /ˈoʊ.vɚ.tʃɚ/ noun **MUSIC** ▷ **1** [C] a piece of music that is an introduction to a longer piece, especially a work for the theatre: *the overture* ***to*** *'The Magic Flute'* **COMMUNICATION** ▷ **2** [C usually plural] a communication made to someone in order to offer something: *overtures* ***of*** *friendship.* ◦ *Neither side in the conflict seems willing to* ***make*** *peace overtures.* ◦ informal *So he's been* ***making*** *overtures (= showing a sexual interest), has he?*

overturn /ˌəʊ.vəˈtɜːn/ US /ˌoʊ.vɚˈtɝːn/ verb **GO UPSIDE DOWN** ▷ **1** [I or T] to (cause to) turn over: *The car skidded off the road, hit a tree and overturned.* ◦ *The burglars had overturned all the furniture in the house.* **CHANGE** ▷ **2** [T] formal to change a legal decision: *The Court of Appeal overturned the earlier decision.*

overuse verb; noun
▸**verb** [T] /ˌəʊ.vəˈjuːz/ US /ˌoʊ.vɚ-/ to use something too often or too much: *I tend to overuse certain favourite expressions.*
▸**noun** [U] /ˌəʊ.vəˈjuːs/ US /ˌoʊ.vɚ-/ the fact that something is used too often or too much: *The overuse of X-rays may be causing 250 deaths each year.*

overvalue /ˌəʊ.vəˈvæl.juː/ US /ˌoʊ.vɚ-/ verb [T] to put too high a value on something: *The company is overvalued on the stock market.*

overview /ˈəʊ.və.vjuː/ US /ˈoʊ.vɚ-/ noun [C] C1 a short description of something that provides general information about it, but no details: *I'll* ***give*** *you a brief overview* ***of*** *what the job involves.*

overweening /ˌəʊ.vəˈwiː.nɪŋ/ US /ˌoʊ.vɚ-/ adj [before noun] formal disapproving being too proud or confident in yourself: *overweening pride/arrogance/vanity* • **overweeningly** /-li/ adv

overweight /ˌəʊ.vəˈweɪt/ US /ˌoʊ.vɚ-/ adj **1** B2 fat: *He used to be very overweight.* ◦ *I'm only a few kilos overweight, but I just can't seem to lose them.* ◦ *an overweight man/woman/child* → Opposite **underweight** **2** B2 heavier than is allowed: *If your luggage is overweight, you have to pay extra.*

overwhelm /ˌəʊ.vəˈwelm/ US /ˌoʊ.vɚ-/ verb **FORCE** ▷ **1** [T] to defeat someone or something by using a lot of force: *Government troops have overwhelmed the rebels and seized control of the capital.* **EMOTION** ▷ **2** C1 [T usually passive] to cause someone to feel sudden strong emotion: *They were overwhelmed* ***with/by*** *grief when their baby died.* ◦ *I was quite overwhelmed by all the flowers and letters of support I received.* **WATER** ▷ **3** [T] literary If water overwhelms a place, it covers it suddenly and completely.

overwhelming /ˌəʊ.vəˈwel.mɪŋ/ US /ˌoʊ.vɚ-/ adj **1** C1 difficult to fight against: *She felt an overwhelming* ***urge/desire/need*** *to tell someone about what had happened.* **2** C1 very great or very large: *She said how much she appreciated the overwhelming generosity of the public in responding to the appeal.* ◦ *An overwhelming* ***majority*** *have voted in favour of the proposal.*

overwhelmingly /ˌəʊ.vəˈwel.mɪŋ.li/ US /ˌoʊ.vɚ-/ adv strongly or completely; in an overwhelming way: *The team were overwhelmingly defeated in yesterday's game.*

overwork verb; noun
▸**verb** [I or T] /ˌəʊ.vəˈwɜːk/ US /ˌoʊ.vɚˈwɝːk/ to (cause someone to) work too much: *You look exhausted – I hope they're not overworking you.*
▸**noun** [U] /ˈəʊ.və.wɜːk/ US /ˈoʊ.vɚ.wɝːk/ doing too much work: *He was made ill by overwork.*

overworked /ˌəʊ.vəˈwɜːkt/ US /ˌoʊ.vɚˈwɝːkt/ adj **1** C1 having to work too much: *an overworked civil servant* ◦ *I'm overworked* ***and underpaid.*** **2** used to describe language that has been used too much and has lost its meaning: *The article was full of overworked expressions.*

overwrite /ˌəʊ.vəʳˈraɪt/ US /ˌoʊ.vɚ-/ verb (**overwrote**, **overwritten**) **REPLACE** ▷ **1** [T] If you overwrite a computer file, you replace it with a different one. **NOT SIMPLE** ▷ **2** [I or T] to write something in a way that is not clear and simple or is more detailed than it needs to be: *His new book is massively overwritten.* ◦ *She's one of those authors who has a tendency to overwrite.*

overwrought /ˌəʊ.vəʳˈrɔːt/ US /ˌoʊ.vɚˈrɑːt/ adj in a state of being upset, nervous, and worried: *She was so tired and overwrought that she burst into tears.* ◦ *He was in an overwrought* ***state/condition*** *for weeks after the accident.*

oviduct /ˈəʊ.vɪ.dʌkt/ US /ˈoʊ-/ noun [C] specialized a tube inside an animal that an egg passes through as it leaves the OVARY (= organ that produces eggs)

ovulate /ˈɒv.jʊ.leɪt/ US /ˈɑː.vjuː-/ verb [I] (of a woman or female animal) to produce an egg from which a baby can be formed: *Some women take drugs to help them ovulate.*

ovulation /ˌɒv.jʊˈleɪ.ʃᵊn/ US /ˌɑː.vjuː-/ noun [U] the time when a woman or female animal produces an egg

ovule /ˈɒv.juːl/ US /ˈɑːv-/ noun [C] specialized a part inside the OVARY (= organ that produces eggs) of a plant which contains the female sex cell and develops into a seed when that cell is FERTILIZED

ovum /ˈəʊ.vəm/ US /ˈoʊ-/ noun [C] (plural **ova**) specialized an egg cell produced by a woman or female animal: *If two ova are fertilized at the same time, the mother will have twins.*

ow /aʊ/ exclamation used to express sudden pain: *Ow, stop it, you're hurting me!* → See also **ouch**

owe /əʊ/ US /oʊ/ verb [T] **HAVE DEBTS** ▷ **1** B1 to need to pay or give something to someone because they have lent money to you, or in exchange for something they have done for you: [+ two objects] *I owe Janet £10.* ◦ *We still owe $1,000* ***on*** *our car (= we still need to pay $1,000 before we own our car).* ◦ *I owe you a drink* ***for*** *helping me move.* ◦ *I think you owe (= should give) me an* ***explanation/apology.*** → See also **IOU** **AS A RESULT** ▷ **2** C2 to have success, happiness, a job, etc. only because of what someone has given you or done for you or because of your own efforts: *I owe my success* ***to*** *my education.* ◦ *He owes his life* ***to*** *the staff at the hospital.* ◦ *I owe everything (= I am very grateful) to my parents.*

O

IDIOMS **I owe you (one)** informal said to thank someone for helping you and as a way of saying that you will do something for them in the future: *Thanks for the help, Bill – I owe you one.* • **owe sb a living** informal If you say that someone thinks that people owe him or her a living, you mean that that person thinks that he or she deserves to be paid without having to work hard for it: *He seems to think **the world** owes him a living.* • **owe it to yourself** to deserve and need to do something which will be good for you: *Take a few days off work – you owe it to yourself.*

owing /ˈəʊ.ɪŋ/ (US) /ˈoʊ-/ adj [after verb] UK still to be paid: *We have several hundred pounds owing **on** our car.*

ˈowing ˌto preposition B2 because of: *The concert has been cancelled owing to lack of support.*

owl /aʊl/ noun [C] **1** B2 a bird with a flat face, large eyes, and strong curved nails, which hunts small mammals at night **2** (also **night owl**) a person who likes to stay up late at night

owl

owlish /ˈaʊ.lɪʃ/ adj A person who is owlish looks serious and intelligent and usually wears glasses: *He was an owlish figure, sitting in the corner of the library.* • **owlishly** /-li/ adv *He peered owlishly over his glasses.*

own /əʊn/ (US) /oʊn/ **determiner, pronoun; verb**

▸**determiner, pronoun 1** A2 belonging to or done by a particular person or thing: *Each neighbourhood in New York has its own characteristics.* ◦ *I'd like to have my **very** own apartment.* ◦ *He wanted an apartment **of** his own.* ◦ *She makes **all** her own clothes.* ◦ *I'm going to be out tonight, so you'll have to get your own dinner (= prepare it yourself).* ◦ *Was that your own idea or did someone suggest it to you?* ◦ *You'll have to make up your own mind (= decide by yourself) what you want to do.* ◦ *I'd never have believed it if I hadn't **seen it with** my own **eyes/heard it with** my own **ears**.* ◦ *'Is that your mum's car?' 'No, it's my own (= it belongs to me).'* ◦ *James Joyce wrote in a style that was **all** his own (= that was not like that of anyone else).* ◦ *We like to take care of our own (= take care of people who are members of our family, or who work for us).* **2 (all) on your own a** B1 alone: *I like living on my own.* **b** B1 without any help: *I did my buttons up all on my own, Mummy.* **3 in your own time a** mainly UK If you do something in your own time, you do it at the speed at which you want to work. **b** UK (US **on your own time**) during the time when you are not officially working: *You may only use company computers to access the Web in your own time.*

IDIOMS **be your own person/woman/man** to be in control of your life and not allow other people to tell you what to do: *Nobody tells me how to live my life – I'm my own man.* • **come into your own** to be very useful or successful in a particular situation: *Eileen really comes into her own in a crisis.* • **for its own sake** If you do something for its own sake, you do it because it is interesting and enjoyable, and not because you have or need to do it: *I study for its own sake.* • **get your own back (on sb)** UK informal C2 to do something unpleasant to someone because they have done something unpleasant to you: *I'll get my own back on her one day.* • **get your own way** to persuade other people to allow you to do what you want: *My little brother always gets his own way.* • **make sth (all) your own** If you make a piece of music, etc. (all) your own, you make it famous by the way you perform it. • **on your own head be it** used to tell someone that they will have to take full responsibility for what they plan to do • **your own flesh and blood** your family or relations: *It's hard to believe that he could treat his own flesh and blood so badly.*

▸**verb HAVE LEGALLY** ▷ **1** B1 [T not continuous] to have something that legally belongs to you: *We own our house.* ◦ *I've never owned a suit in my life.* **ADMIT** ▷ **2** [I] old-fashioned to admit: [+ (that)] *I own (**that**) I was not very happy with the group's decision.*

IDIOM **as if you owned the place** UK (US **like you owned the place**) in a way that is too confident: *He walked into the office as if he owned the place.*

PHRASAL VERB **own up** C2 to admit that you have done something wrong: *No one has owned up **to** steal**ing** the money.*

ˌown ˈbrand noun [C] UK (US **ˈstore ˌbrand**) a product that has the name of the shop where you buy it, rather than the name of the company that made it: [before noun] *own-brand cosmetics*

-owned /-əʊnd/ (US) /-oʊnd/ **suffix** belonging to or controlled by: *a family-owned business*

owner /ˈəʊ.nəʳ/ (US) /ˈoʊ.nɚ/ noun [C] B1 someone who owns something: *Are you the owner **of** this car?* ◦ *We still haven't found the dog's owner.*

ˌowner-ˈoccupied adj UK describes houses or apartments that have been bought by the people who live in them • **ˌowner-ˈoccupier** noun [C]

ownership /ˈəʊ.nə.ʃɪp/ (US) /ˈoʊ.nɚ-/ noun [U] C1 the fact that you own something: *Do you have any proof of ownership **of/for** this car?* ◦ *Rates of home ownership have remained relatively constant.*

ˌown ˈgoal noun [C] UK **1** in sport, a point that a player scores by mistake against their own team: *Our team lost when we **scored** an own goal late in the second half.* **2** something that you do which gives you a disadvantage and helps someone else, even if this is the opposite of what you intended

owt /aʊt/ **pronoun** non standard Northern **anything**: *I haven't heard owt about it.* ◦ *Is there owt to drink?* → Compare **nowt**

ox /ɒks/ (US) /ɑːks/ noun [C] (plural **oxen**) a BULL (= male cow) that has had its REPRODUCTIVE organs removed, used in the past for pulling heavy things on farms, or, more generally, any adult of the CATTLE family

oxbow lake /ˌɒks.bəʊˈleɪk/ (US) /ˌɑːks.boʊ-/ noun [C] specialized a curved lake that was originally a bend in a river but became separated when the river took a new, straighter course

Oxbridge /ˈɒks.brɪdʒ/ (US) /ˈɑːks-/ **noun; adj**

▸**noun** [U] UK the universities of Oxford and Cambridge, considered as a unit separate from other universities in Britain: *Many members of the British government went to Oxbridge (= a college at either Oxford or Cambridge).*

▸**adj** belonging or relating to the universities of Oxford and Cambridge: *She's an Oxbridge student.* ◦ *He's very Oxbridge in his manner (= behaves as if he went to a college in Oxford or Cambridge).* → Compare **red-brick**

Oxfam /ˈɒks.fæm/ (US) /ˈɑːks-/ noun [+ sing/pl verb] a UK-based organization that works to help people who are extremely poor and suffering

Oxford /ˈɒks.fəd/ (US) /ˈɑːks.fɚd/ noun [C] (also **ˌOxford ˈshoe**) US a type of fairly formal man's shoe, usually made of leather, that fastens with LACES

ˌ**Oxford ˈshirt** noun [C] US a man's shirt made of a particular type of heavy cotton cloth

oxide /ˈɒk.saɪd/ (US) /ˈɑːk-/ **noun** [C or U] a chemical combination of OXYGEN and one other element: *iron oxide* ◦ *an oxide **of** copper*

oxidize (UK usually **oxidise**) /ˈɒk.sɪ.daɪz/ (US) /ˈɑːk-/ **verb** [I or T] **1** If a substance oxidizes, it combines with OXYGEN and loses HYDROGEN to form another substance, and if something oxidizes a substance, it causes it to do this: *Iron oxidizes to form rust.* ◦ *When you heat fat, it oxidizes easily.* **2** If a chemical element oxidizes, it loses ELECTRONS (= very small pieces of matter with negative electrical charge) and if you oxidize it, you cause it to do this. • **oxidization** (UK usually **oxidisation**) /ˌɒk.sɪ.daɪˈzeɪ.ʃən/ (US) /ˌɑːk-/ **noun** [U] (US usually **oxidation**)

oxtail /ˈɒks.teɪl/ (US) /ˈɑːks-/ **noun** [C or U] meat from the tail of an ox, or the tail itself: *oxtail **soup***

oxyacetylene /ˌɒk.si.əˈset.əl.iːn/ (US) /ˌɑːk.si.əˈset̬-/ **noun** [U] specialized a mixture of oxygen and ACETYLENE (= a gas) that produces a hot bright flame, and that can be used for cutting metal: *an oxyacetylene lamp/torch*

oxygen /ˈɒk.sɪ.dʒən/ (US) /ˈɑːk-/ **noun** [U] (symbol **O**) (B2) a chemical element that is a gas with no smell or colour. Oxygen forms a large part of the air on Earth, and is needed by animals and plants to live.

oxygenate /ˈɒk.sɪ.dʒə.neɪt/ (US) /ˈɑːk-/ **verb** [T] to add oxygen to something: *Fish tanks often have a pump which oxygenates the water.*

ˈ**oxygen ˌbar** noun [C] a place where you pay to breathe pure oxygen in order to improve your health and help you relax

ˈ**oxygen ˌmask** noun [C] a piece of equipment that can be put over a person's nose and mouth to supply them with oxygen

ˈ**oxygen ˌtank** noun [C] a container with oxygen inside it, used for helping people to breathe, for example when they are very ill, or when they are DIVING underwater

ˈ**oxygen ˌtent** noun [C] a clear covering put over the head and upper body of an ill person to provide oxygen to help them breathe

oxyhaemoglobin UK specialized (US **oxyhemoglobin**) /ˌɒk.siˌhiː.məˈgləʊ.bɪn/ (US) /ˌɑːk.siˌhiː.məˈgloʊ-/ **noun** [U] the bright red form of HAEMOGLOBIN (= substance in red blood cells) that contains oxygen

oxymoron /ˌɒk.sɪˈmɔː.rɒn/ (US) /ˌɑːk.sɪˈmɔːr.ɑːn/ **noun** [C] two words used together that have, or seem to have, opposite meanings

oyster /ˈɔɪ.stər/ (US) /-stɚ/ **noun** [C] a large flat sea creature that lives in a shell, some types of which can be eaten either cooked or uncooked, and other types of which produce PEARLS (= small round white precious stones)

ˈ**oyster ˌbed** noun [C] an area at the bottom of the sea where oysters live

oz noun [C] (plural **oz**) written abbreviation for **ounce**: *Add 8 oz **of** flour.*

Oz /ɒz/ (US) /ɑːz/ **noun** UK informal Australia

ozone /ˈəʊ.zəʊn/ (US) /ˈoʊ.zoʊn/ **noun** [U] **1** (C1) a poisonous form of OXYGEN **2** UK informal air that is clean and pleasant to breathe, especially near the sea

ozone-ˈfriendly adj describes a product that does not produce gases that are harmful to the OZONE LAYER: *ozone-friendly packaging*

the ˈozone ˌlayer noun [S] a layer of air containing ozone high above the Earth that prevents harmful ULTRAVIOLET light from the sun from reaching the Earth

O

P

P, p /piː/ **noun** (plural **Ps, P's** or **p's**) **LETTER** ▷ **1** [C or U] the 16th letter of the English alphabet **SIGN** ▷ **2** [U] UK written abbreviation for **parking**, used especially on road signs

p. PAGE ▷ (plural **pp.**) written abbreviation for **page**: *See p. 27.* ◦ *The references are on pp. 56–64.*

p /piː/ **noun** [C] **MONEY** ▷ UK abbreviation for **penny** or **pence**: *Could you lend me 50p?* ◦ *This packet of crisps costs 25p.* ◦ *I need a 1p/5p/20p* ***coin/piece***.

p.a. /ˌpiːˈeɪ/ **adv** abbreviation for PER ANNUM (= each year): *a salary of £20,000 p.a.*

pa /pɑː/ **noun** [C] informal old-fashioned a father: *I miss my pa.* ◦ [as form of address] *Thanks, Pa.* → Compare **ma**

PA /ˌpiːˈeɪ/ **noun JOB** ▷ **1** [C] UK abbreviation for personal assistant: someone whose job is helping someone in a higher position, especially by writing letters, arranging meetings, and making phone calls: *Chris works as a PA* ***to*** *the managing director.* **SOUND EQUIPMENT** ▷ **2** [C usually singular] (also **PA system**) abbreviation for **public address system** (= equipment for making sound, especially someone's voice, louder in a public place): *They've just announced* ***on*** *the PA that our flight's been delayed.*

paan (also **pan**) /pɑːn/ **noun** [U] Indian English leaves of the BETEL plant wrapped around tobacco, fruit, etc. and CHEWED , especially because they have a pleasant effect like a drug

pace /peɪs/ **noun; verb**

▸**noun SPEED** ▷ **1** (B2) [U] the speed at which someone or something moves, or with which something happens or changes: *a slow/fast pace* ◦ *When she thought she heard someone following her, she* ***quickened*** *her pace.* ◦ *Could you slow down a bit – I can't* ***keep*** *pace* ***with*** (= walk or run as fast as) *you.* ◦ *For many years this company has* ***set*** *the pace* (= has been the most successful company) *in the communications industry.* ◦ *These changes seem to me to be happening* ***at*** *too fast a pace.* ◦ *I don't like the pace* ***of*** *modern life.* → See also **pacemaker 2 force the pace** to make other people in a race go faster by going faster yourself **STEP** ▷ **3** [C] a single step, or the distance you move when you take a single step: *Take two paces forwards/backwards.* ◦ *The runner collapsed just a few paces from the finish.*

IDIOM **put sb/sth through their paces** to make someone show their skills or knowledge, or to make something show its good qualities

▸**verb SPEED** ▷ **1** [T] to get someone to run a race at a particular speed, for example by running with them **2 pace yourself** (C2) to be careful not to do something too quickly so that you do not get too tired to finish it: *No more soup, thank you. I'm pacing myself so that I have room for a dessert.* **STEP** ▷ **3** (C2) [I + adv/prep, T] to walk with regular steps in one direction and then back again, usually because you are worried or nervous: *He paced the room nervously.* ◦ *He paced* ***up and down****, waiting for the doctor to call.*

PHRASAL VERB **pace sth off/out** to measure a distance by taking steps of equal size across it and counting them: *You can get a rough idea of the size of the room by pacing it out.*

pacemaker /ˈpeɪsˌmeɪ.kəʳ/ (US) /-kɚ/ **noun** [C] **RUNNER** ▷ **1** (also **pacesetter** /-ˌset.əʳ/ (US) /-ˌset̬.ɚ/) the person or animal that establishes the speed in a race, or a person or organization that is an example for others by being successful **DEVICE** ▷ **2** a small device that is put inside someone's chest in order to help their heart beat at the correct speed

pachyderm /ˈpæk.ɪ.dɜːm/ (US) /-ə.dɝːm/ **noun** [C] old-fashioned a group of large mammals that includes ELEPHANTS, RHINOCEROSES, and HIPPOPOTAMUSES

pacific /pəˈsɪf.ɪk/ **adj** peaceful or helping to cause peace • **pacifically** /-ɪ.kəl.i/ **adv**

the ˌPacific ˈRim **noun** the countries on the edge of the Pacific Ocean such as Japan, Australia, and the West coast of the US: *We supply systems for clients* ***on*** *the Pacific Rim.*

pacifier /ˈpæs.ɪ.faɪ.əʳ/ (US) /-ɚ/ **noun** [C] **1** something that makes people calm when they are angry or upset **2** US for **dummy**

pacifism /ˈpæs.ɪ.fɪ.zəm/ **noun** [U] the belief that war is wrong, and therefore that to fight in a war is wrong

pacifist /ˈpæs.ɪ.fɪst/ **noun** [C] someone who believes in pacifism

pacify /ˈpæs.ɪ.faɪ/ **verb** [T] **CALM** ▷ **1** to cause someone who is angry or upset to be calm and satisfied: *He pacified his crying child* ***with*** *a bottle.* ◦ *It was difficult for the police to pacify the angry crowd.* **PEACE** ▷ **2** to bring peace to a place or end war in a place: *A UN force has been sent in to try and pacify the area worst affected by the civil war.* • **pacification** /ˌpæs.ɪ.fɪˈkeɪ.ʃən/ **noun** [U]

pack /pæk/ **verb; noun**

▸**verb PUT INTO** ▷ **1** (A2) [I or T] to put something into a bag, box, etc.: *We're leaving early tomorrow morning, so you'd better pack* (= put clothes and other possessions into a bag or bags) *tonight.* ◦ *She packed a small* ***suitcase*** *for the weekend.* ◦ *He just packed his* ***bags*** *and walked out on his wife and children.* ◦ *I haven't packed my clothes* (= put them into a bag, etc.) *yet.* ◦ [+ two objects] *Could you pack me a spare pair of shoes, please/pack a spare pair of shoes* ***for*** *me, please?* ◦ *These books need to be packed* ***in/into*** *a box.* **2** [T] to put a material around something before putting it into a bag, box, etc. so that it will not break or be damaged: *She packed the vase in tissue paper to protect it.* **FILL** ▷ **3** [I usually + adv/prep, T] to come or bring together in large numbers or to fill a space: *Thousands of fans are packing* ***into*** *the stadium.* ◦ *Fans packed the stadium to watch the final match.* ◦ *The people on the bus were packed* (***together***) ***like sardines*** (= there were many of them very close together). **MASS** ▷ **4** [I or T, usually + adv/prep] to (cause to) form into a solid mass: *The wind has packed the snow against the garage door.* ◦ *The snow has packed* ***down*** *tightly, making the streets dangerous to walk on.* **CARRY** ▷ **5** [T] US slang to carry something, especially a gun: *to pack a* ***gun*** ◦ *Each missile packs several warheads.* ◦ figurative *This gun packs* (= has) *a lot of firepower.*

IDIOM **pack a punch** informal to have a lot of force or a great effect: *His speech packed quite a punch.* ◦ *These cocktails taste quite innocent, but they really pack a punch!*

PHRASAL VERBS **pack sth away TIDY** ▷ **1** to put something into a bag or container, or to put something in the place where it is usually kept: *Come on, children, it's time to pack away your toys.* **EAT** ▷ **2** informal to eat a lot of food: *She's tiny but she can really pack away the biscuits.* • **pack sth in** informal **1** to stop doing something: *This course is really tough, – sometimes I feeling like packing* **it all** *in.* **2 pack it in!** UK informal said to rudely tell someone to stop doing something that is annoying you: *Pack it in, Julie – I'm trying to read.* • **pack sb in** END RELATIONSHIP ▷ **1** UK informal to end your relationship with someone, or to stop meeting or spending time with them: *'Is Emma still seeing Joe?' 'No, she's packed him in.'* BE POPULAR ▷ **2** If an entertainment or EXHIBITION packs people in, a large number of people come to see it: *Spielberg's new film is packing in the crowds.* • **pack sth/sb in** informal to manage to include a large number of things, activities, or people: *We were only there four days but we packed a lot in.* • **pack sth into sth** to manage to do a lot of activities in a limited period of time: *We packed a lot of sightseeing into our weekend in New York.* • **pack sb off** informal to send someone to another place: *We've packed the kids off for the weekend.* ◦ *I packed her off* **to** *my sister's.* • **pack sth/somewhere out** UK informal to make a place very full: *100,000 football supporters packed out Wembley Stadium to see the game.* • **pack up** UK informal If a machine packs up, it stops operating: *My camera has packed up.* • **pack up (sth)** UK informal to stop working or doing another regular activity: *She packed up her job, and went off to Australia.* ◦ [+ -ing verb] *It's time you packed up smoking.* • **pack (sth) up** B2 to collect all your things together when you have finished doing something: *I'm about to pack up my things and go home.*

▸noun [C] GROUP ▷ **1** B2 a group, set, or collection of something: *The* **information** *pack consists of a brochure and a map.* **2** C2 a group of animals, such as dogs, that live and/or hunt together: *a wolf pack* ◦ *a pack of wild dogs* **3** an organized group of children who are BROWNIES or CUBS: *My uncle was the leader of my Cub pack.* **4** (US also **deck**) a set of playing cards: *a pack of cards* **5** mainly disapproving a group of similar people, especially one that contains people whose activities you do not approve of: *a pack* **of** *thieves* ◦ *A pack* **of** *journalists was waiting outside the White House.* → See also **gang** CONTAINER ▷ **6** US for PACKET (= a paper or cardboard container): *a pack* **of** *cigarettes/gum* BAG ▷ **7** (US also **backpack**) a type of bag that you usually carry on your back when you are travelling MASS ▷ **8** a thick mass of a substance, often like clay, that is used as a beauty treatment for the face **9** a thick mass of cloth, etc. that can be put on an injury to stop any BLEEDING or swelling: *Hold this ice pack to your head to stop the bruising.* → See also **compress**

IDIOMS **a pack rat** US someone who collects things that they do not need: *For me there could be nothing worse than living with a pack rat.* • **be ahead of the pack** to be more successful than other people who are trying to achieve the same things as you: *At this stage in the campaign, the Democratic candidate is way ahead of the pack.*

-pack /-pæk/ **suffix** used in combination with an amount to show that that many of a particular type of goods have been wrapped and are being sold together: *a six-pack* **of** *beer* ◦ *a multi-pack* **of** *toilet paper*

package /ˈpæk.ɪdʒ/ **noun; verb**

▸noun [C] PAPER OBJECT ▷ **1** B2 (UK also **parcel**) an object or set of objects wrapped in paper, usually in order to be sent by post: *The postman has just delivered a package for you.* ◦ *The package was wrapped in plain brown paper.* **2** US (UK **packet**) a small paper or plastic container in which a number of small objects are sold: *a package* **of** *cookies* OFFERED TOGETHER ▷ **3** B2 a related group of things when they are offered together as a single unit: *The computer comes with a* **software** *package.* ◦ *The* **aid** *package for the earthquake-hit area will include emergency food and medical supplies.* **4** the pay and other rewards that a company manager receives: *He will receive a* **compensation** *package worth £15 million over three years.* ◦ *a total* **pay** *package valued at $59.5 million*

IDIOM **good things come in small packages** saying said to emphasize that something does not need to be big in order to be good

▸verb [T] **1** to put goods into boxes or containers to be sold: *These organic olives are packaged* **in** *recycled glass containers.* **2** to show someone or something in an attractive way so that people will like or buy them: *As a young film star, she was packaged* **as** *a sex symbol.*

packaged /ˈpæk.ɪdʒd/ **adj** sold already prepared in a container, usually one made of paper or cardboard: *packaged* **foods/cereals/soup**

ˈpackage ˌdeal noun [C] a set of arrangements that must be accepted together and not separately

ˈpackage ˌstore noun [C] US for **off-licence**

ˈpackage ˌtour noun [C] (UK also **ˌpackage ˈholiday**) a holiday at a fixed price in which the travel company arranges your travel, hotels, and sometimes meals for you: *We bought a cheap package tour to Spain and stayed in a big hotel by the sea.*

packaging /ˈpæk.ɪ.dʒɪŋ/ **noun** [U] the materials in which objects are wrapped before being sold: *All our packaging is biodegradable.*

ˈpack ˌanimal noun [C] an animal, such as a horse, that is used to transport things on its back

packed /pækt/ **adj** FILL ▷ **1** B2 completely full: *The train was so packed that I couldn't find a seat.* ◦ *This book is packed* **with** *useful information.* **2 packed out** very full of people: *The bar was packed out last night.* LUGGAGE ▷ **3 be packed** to have put your things into a bag or box, etc.: *Are you packed yet?* ◦ *I'm all packed and ready to go.*

-packed /-pækt/ **suffix** full of the thing described: *a fun-packed day* ◦ *an action-packed film*

ˌpacked ˈlunch noun [C] UK (US **ˈbox ˌlunch**) a light meal put in a container, usually to take with you somewhere to be eaten later

packer /ˈpæk.əʳ/ (US) /-ɚ/ **noun** [C] a person, company, or machine that puts goods into boxes or food into containers

packet /ˈpæk.ɪt/ **noun** [C] CONTAINER ▷ **1** B1 mainly UK a small paper or cardboard container in which a number of small objects are sold: *a packet* **of** *cereal/biscuits/crisps/peanuts* ◦ *a packet* **of** *chewing gum/cigarettes* ◦ *How many seeds are there in a packet?* → Compare **parcel** BODY PART ▷ **2** UK (US **package**) offensive for a man's sex organs MONEY ▷ **3 a packet** UK informal a large amount of money: *That house must have* **cost** *a packet!* ◦ *Someone's* **making** *a packet out of this business.*

ˈpack ˌice noun [U] a large mass of ice floating in the sea that has been formed by smaller pieces of ice being forced together

packing /ˈpæk.ɪŋ/ **noun** [U] **1** the act of putting things into cases, boxes, bags, etc.: *He always* **does** *his own packing.* → See also **postage and packing** **2** material that you put around something when it is put into a case, box, etc., to stop it from being damaged

ˈpacking ˌcase noun [C] UK (US **ˈpacking ˌcrate**) a large, strong box for transporting things: *I don't think we've got enough packing cases for all the equipment.*

P

pact /pækt/ **noun** [C] a formal agreement between two people or groups of people: *The United States and Canada have* ***signed*** *a free-trade pact.* ◦ [+ to infinitive] *The Liberal Democrats may* ***form*** *a pact* ***with*** *Labour* ***to*** *try to beat the Conservatives in the next election.*

pacy (**pacier**, **paciest**) (also **pacey**) /ˈpeɪ.si/ **adj** UK A pacy NOVEL, story, film, etc. contains a lot of action or events that happen quickly.

pad /pæd/ **noun; verb**

▸**noun** [C] **MATERIAL** ▷ **1** a piece of soft, thick cloth or rubber, used to protect a part of the body, give shape to something, or clean something: *a knee/shoulder pad* ◦ *Footballers often wear* ***shin*** *pads to protect their legs.* ◦ *In the 1980s,* ***shoulder*** *pads were very fashionable in women's clothes.* ◦ *She wiped her eye make-up off with a cotton wool pad.* **PAPER** ▷ **2** a number of pieces of paper that have been fastened together along one side, used for writing or drawing on: *I have a pad and pencil for taking notes.* ◦ *I always keep a pad* ***of paper*** *by the phone.* → See also **notepad** **FLAT SURFACE** ▷ **3** a hard flat area of ground where HELICOPTERS can take off and land, or from which ROCKETS are sent: *The hotel has its own helicopter pad.* **4** one of the large flat leaves of a WATER LILY: *a lily pad* **FOOT** ▷ **5** the soft part at the bottom of a cat or dog's PAW (= foot) **HOUSE** ▷ **6** old-fashioned slang a person's house or apartment: *a bachelor pad*

▸**verb** [T] (**-dd-**) to put pieces of soft material in something to make it soft, give it a different shape, or protect what is inside: *These walking boots are padded with shock-resistant foam.*

PHRASAL VERB **pad sth out** If you pad out a speech or piece of writing, you add unnecessary words or information to make it longer or to hide the fact that you are not saying anything very important.

padded /ˈpæd.ɪd/ **adj** containing a layer of soft material used for protection or to give shape: *It's a short jacket with padded* ***shoulders.*** ◦ *a padded* ***bra***

P

ˌpadded ˈcell **noun** [C usually singular] a room in a mental hospital that has very soft walls to stop a seriously mentally ill person from hurting themselves

padding /ˈpæd.ɪŋ/ **noun** [U] **1** the pieces of material used to protect something or give it shape **2** unnecessary words or information added to a speech or piece of writing

paddle

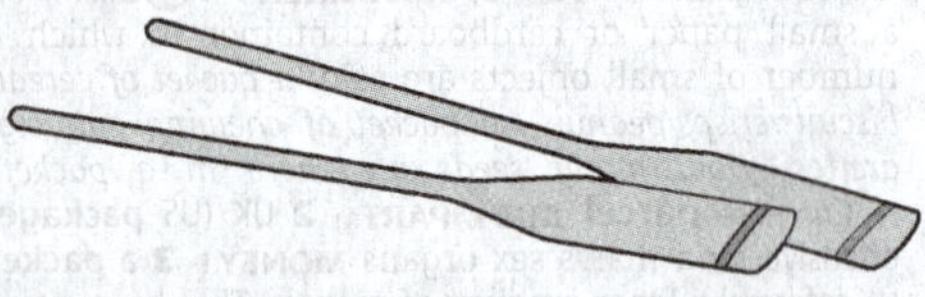

paddle /ˈpæd.l̩/ **noun; verb**

▸**noun** **POLE** ▷ **1** [C] a short pole with a wide, flat part at one end or both ends, used for moving a small boat or CANOE through the water **2** [C] a blade on a paddle wheel **WALK** ▷ **3** [C usually singular] UK (US **wade**) a walk through water that is not very deep, especially at the edge of the sea: *Shall we go for a paddle?*

▸**verb** **WALK** ▷ **1** [I] UK (US **wade**) to walk with no shoes or socks on through water that is not very deep, often at the edge of the sea: *We rolled up our trousers and paddled along the seashore.* **WITH POLE** ▷ **2** [I or T] to push a pole with a wide end through the water in order to make a boat move **3** [T] US to hit a child on the bottom with a short, wide piece of wood as a punishment **SWIM** ▷ **4** [I] to swim by moving your feet and hands up and down

ˈpaddle ˌsteamer **noun** [C] UK (US **ˈpaddle ˌwheeler**) a large boat that uses a paddle driven by steam to move through the water

ˈpaddle ˌwheel **noun** [C] a type of wheel with small flat blades fixed around the edge which makes a boat move through the water or which operates a piece of machinery

ˈpaddling ˌpool **noun** [C] UK (US **ˈwading ˌpool**) a pool that is not deep that small children can play in

paddock /ˈpæd.ək/ **noun** [C] **1** a small field where animals, especially horses, are kept **2** Australian English a field of any size that is used for farming **3** specialized an area surrounded by fences where horses or cars are kept and shown to the public before a race

paddy /ˈpæd.i/ **noun** [C usually singular] UK old-fashioned informal a very angry state: *There's no need to get* ***in/into*** *a paddy.*

Paddy /ˈpæd.i/ **noun** [C] offensive an offensive word for an Irish person

ˈpaddy ˌfield **noun** [C] UK (US **ˈrice ˌpaddy**) a field planted with rice growing in water

ˈpaddy ˌwagon **noun** [C] US a closed police vehicle used for transporting prisoners

padlock /ˈpæd.lɒk/ (US) /-lɑːk/ **noun; verb**

▸**noun** [C] a small metal lock with a U-shaped bar

▸**verb** [T] to fasten something using a padlock: *The box was securely padlocked and no one had the key.*

padlock

padre /ˈpɑː.dreɪ/ (US) /-dri/ **noun** [C] a Christian priest, especially in the armed forces

paean /ˈpiː.ən/ **noun** [C] literary a song, film, or piece of writing that praises someone or something very enthusiastically: *The song is a paean* ***to*** *solitude and independence.*

paederast /ˈped.ər.æst/ (US) /-dɚ-/ **noun** [C] UK old-fashioned for **pederast**

paediatric UK (US **pediatric**) /ˌpiː.diˈæt.rɪk/ **adj** relating to the medical care of children: *paediatric medicine* ◦ *a paediatric hospital*

paediatrician UK (US **pediatrician**) /ˌpiː.di.əˈtrɪʃ.ən/ **noun** [C] a doctor who has special training in medical care for children

paediatrics /ˌpiː.diːˈæt.rɪks/ **noun** [U] UK (US **pediatrics**) the science or study of medical care for children: *She specializes in paediatrics.*

paedo /ˈpiː.dəʊ/ (US) /ˈped.oʊ/ **noun** [C] (plural **paedos**) UK informal disapproving a paedophile

paedophile UK (US **pedophile**) /ˈpiː.də.faɪl/ (US) /ˈped.oʊ-/ **noun** [C] someone who is sexually interested in children • **paedophilia** (US **pedophilia**) /ˌpiː.dəˈfɪl.i.ə/ (US) /ˌped.oʊˈfiː.li-/ **noun** [U]

ˈpaedophile ˌring **noun** [C] a group of people who take part in illegal sexual activity involving children

paella /paɪˈel.ə/ (US) /pɑːˈjel-/ **noun** [C or U] a Spanish dish consisting of rice cooked with vegetables, fish, and chicken

pagan /ˈpeɪ.gən/ **adj; noun**

▸**adj** **1** belonging to a religion which worships many gods, especially one which existed before the main world religions: *a pagan religion* ◦ *The Easter egg has*

both pagan and Christian origins. **2** relating to religious beliefs that do not belong to any of the main religions of the world: *a pagan festival*
▸noun [C] **1** a person who has pagan beliefs **2** humorous a person who has no religious beliefs • **paganism** /-ɪ.zəm/ noun [U]

page /peɪdʒ/ noun; verb
▸noun [C] PAPER ▷ **1** A1 (written abbreviation **p.**) a side of one of the pieces of paper in a book, newspaper, or magazine, usually with a number printed on it: *For details on how to enter the competition, see page 134.* ◦ *The article appeared on the **front** page of the Guardian.* **2** one of the sheets of paper in a book, newspaper, or magazine: *Several pages have been torn out of this book.* COMPUTER ▷ **3** A2 (also **web page**) one part of a website → See also **home page** BOY ▷ **4** (in the past) a boy who worked as a servant for a KNIGHT and who was learning to become a KNIGHT → Compare **pageboy**

IDIOM **a page in/of history** literary an important part of the history of a place, time, or group of people: *The signing of the peace treaty will be seen as a glorious page in our country's history.*

▸verb [T] **1** to call a person using a LOUDSPEAKER (= an electric device for making sounds louder) in a public place: *He was paged at the airport and told to return home immediately.* **2** to send a message to someone's PAGER (= small piece of electronic equipment that receives signals): *Have you tried to page him?*

pageant /ˈpædʒ.ənt/ noun [C] **1** UK a show, usually performed outside, that consists of people wearing traditional clothing and acting out historical events: *Our youngest son is taking part in the school pageant.* **2** US a competition for young women in which they are judged on their beauty and other qualities: *a **beauty** pageant* **3** any colourful and impressive show or ceremony

pageantry /ˈpædʒ.ən.tri/ noun [U] impressive and colourful ceremonies: *She loved the pageantry and tradition of the monarchy.*

pageboy /ˈpeɪdʒ.bɔɪ/ noun [C] BOY ▷ **1** a young boy who is one of the people to go with the BRIDE (= the woman who is getting married) into the church: *The little pageboys were dressed in kilts and the bridesmaids in pink dresses.* → Compare **page** HAIR ▷ **2** a hairstyle, mainly for women, in which the hair is straight and quite short and turns under at the ends

pager /ˈpeɪ.dʒər/ US /-dʒɚ/ noun [C] (UK also **bleeper**, US also **beeper**) a small device that you carry or wear, which moves or makes a noise to tell you that someone wants you to phone them

ˌpage-ˈthree ˌgirl noun [C] UK a young woman who appears with naked breasts in photographs for some popular newspapers in the UK

page-turner /ˈpeɪ.dʒˌtɜː.nər/ US /-ˌtɝː.nɚ/ noun [C] informal a book that is so exciting that you want to read it quickly: *Her latest novel is a real page-turner.*

pagination /ˌpædʒ.ɪˈneɪ.ʃən/ US /-əˈneɪ-/ noun [U] specialized the way in which the pages of a book or document, etc. are given numbers

pagoda /pəˈgəʊ.də/ US /-ˈgoʊ-/ noun [C] a tall religious building in Asia with many levels, each of which has a curved roof

paid /peɪd/ verb; adj
▸verb past simple and past participle of **pay**
▸adj **1** being given money for something: *Are you looking for paid work or voluntary work?* ◦ *paid employment* ◦ *paid holiday* (US *vacation*) ◦ *paid leave* **2** used in combination to refer to the amount of money that someone is given for their work: ***low**-paid workers* ◦ *a **well**-paid job*

ˌpaid-ˈup adj [before noun] **1 paid-up member** someone who has paid the money necessary to be a member of a particular organization **2** UK informal describes someone who is a loyal and enthusiastic member of a group

pail /peɪl/ noun [C] mainly US a **bucket**: *Fill the pail with sand.* ◦ *It took several pails of water (= the amount a pail contains) to put out the fire.*

pain /peɪn/ noun; verb
▸noun [C or U] **1** A2 a feeling of physical suffering caused by injury or illness: *Her symptoms included abdominal pain and vomiting.* ◦ *Are you **in** (= suffering from) pain?* ◦ *She was in **constant** pain.* ◦ *These tablets should help to **ease** the pain.* ◦ *I felt a **sharp** pain **in** my foot.* ◦ *He's been suffering various **aches and** pains for years.* **2** B2 emotional or mental suffering: *It's a film about the pains and pleasures of parenthood.* ◦ *The parents are still in great pain **over** the death of their child.*

Word partners for pain noun

experience/feel/suffer pain • *have* a pain • *cause/inflict* pain • *alleviate/ease/relieve/soothe* pain • *excruciating/severe/unbearable* pain • a *nagging/sharps/hooting/stabbing* pain • *aches* and pains • be *in* pain • pain *relief*

Other ways of saying pain

Ache is used for a pain that is continuous and unpleasant but not very strong:

*I've got a dull (= slight) **ache** in my back.*

If you have a pain in a particular part of your body, you can say that it **hurts**:

*My leg **hurts**.*

Sore can be used when you feel pain because of an injury or infection:

*I've got a **sore** throat.*

If you feel pain when you touch a part of your body, you can use the word **tender**:

*The glands in my neck feel really **tender**.*

You can say that someone who is in extreme pain is in **agony**:

*He was lying on the floor in **agony**, clutching his stomach.*

In informal situations, if you feel a lot of pain in part of your body, you can say that it is **killing you**:

*I must take my shoes off. My feet are **killing me**.*

IDIOMS **on/under pain of death** formal If you have to do something on/under pain of death, you will be killed if you do not do it. • **a pain (in the neck)** informal B2 someone or something that is very annoying: *That child is a **real** pain in the neck.* • **a pain in the arse/backside** UK (US **pain in the ass/butt**) offensive someone or something that is very annoying: *The kids were a real pain in the arse.*

▸verb [T] formal If something pains you, it causes you to feel sad and upset: [+ to infinitive] ***It** pains me **to** see animals being mistreated.*

pained /peɪnd/ adj If you look or sound pained, you show that you are upset or offended: *a pained expression*

painful /ˈpeɪn.fəl/ adj **1** B1 causing emotional or physical pain: *The old photograph brought back painful memories.* ◦ *A painful injury forced her to withdraw*

P

from the game. **2** If something is painful to watch or listen to, it is so bad that it makes you feel embarrassed: *It was painful to listen to his pathetic excuses.*

painfully /ˈpeɪn.fəl.i/ **adv** **1** in a way that causes pain: *Without surgery, this animal will die slowly and painfully.* **2** used to emphasize a quality, action, or situation that is unpleasant or not wanted: *I am painfully aware that I have made mistakes.* ◦ *It was a painfully slow journey.*

painkiller /ˈpeɪnˌkɪl.əʳ/ (US) /-ɚ/ **noun** [C] medicine used to reduce or remove physical pain: *The body produces chemicals which are natural painkillers.* • **painkilling** /-ɪŋ/ **adj** [before noun] *This tiny capsule contains effective painkilling **ingredients**.*

painless /ˈpeɪn.ləs/ **adj** **1** causing no physical pain: *a painless medical procedure* **2** describes something that causes no problems: *a painless solution to a problem* • **painlessly** /-li/ **adv**

pains /peɪnz/ **noun** [plural] **1 be at pains to do sth** to try very hard to do something: *She is at pains to point out how much work she has done.* **2 go to/take great pains to do sth** to make a lot of effort to do something: *I went to great pains to select the best staff available.*

painstaking /ˈpeɪnzˌteɪ.kɪŋ/ **adj** extremely careful and correct, and using a lot of effort: *It took months of painstaking research to write the book.* ◦ *He was described by his colleagues as a painstaking journalist.*

painstakingly /ˈpeɪnzˌteɪ.kɪŋ.li/ **adv** in a way that shows you have taken a lot of care or made a lot of effort: *She painstakingly explained how the machine worked.*

paint /peɪnt/ **noun; verb**

▸**noun** [C or U] **1** (A1) a coloured liquid that is put on a surface such as a wall to decorate it: *a tin* (US *can*) *of paint* ◦ *This wall needs another **coat** of paint.* ◦ *The sign said 'Caution! Wet paint'.* ◦ *gloss paint* ◦ *matt* (US *matte*) *paint* **2 paints** [plural] tubes of paint or blocks of dried paint used for making pictures: *oil paints*

▸**verb** **1** (A2) [I or T] to cover a surface with paint: [+ obj + adj] *We've painted the bedroom blue.* ◦ *I've been painting all morning.* ◦ *I'll need to paint **over** (= cover with another layer of paint) these dirty marks on the wall.* **2** (A1) [I or T] to make a picture using paints: *All these pictures were painted by local artists.* **3** [T] If someone paints their nails or face, they put make-up on that part of their body: *She painted her nails bright red.*

paintball /ˈpeɪnt.bɔːl/ (US) /-bɑːl/ **noun** [U] a game in which people attempt to shoot each other with guns that fire paint rather than bullets

paintbox /ˈpeɪnt.bɒks/ (US) /-bɑːks/ **noun** [C] a box containing paints for making pictures

paintbrush /ˈpeɪnt.brʌʃ/ **noun** [C] a brush used for putting paint on a surface or on a picture

painter /ˈpeɪn.təʳ/ (US) /-t̬ɚ/ **noun** [C] **1** (A2) someone who paints pictures **2** someone whose job is to paint surfaces, such as walls and doors

painting /ˈpeɪn.tɪŋ/ (US) /-t̬ɪŋ/ **noun** **1** (A2) [C or U] a picture made using paint: *The walls are covered in oil paintings.* ◦ *an exhibition of 19th-century French painting* **2** (A2) [U] the skill or activity of making a picture or putting paint on a wall: *We were taught painting and drawing at art college.* ◦ *When we bought the house, we had to do a lot of painting and redecorating.*

ˈpaint ˌstripper **noun** [U] UK a liquid used to remove old paint from wooden surfaces

ˈpaint ˌthinner **noun** [U] a liquid that you add to paint to make it less thick or to remove paint from brushes

paintwork /ˈpeɪnt.wɜːk/ (US) /-wɝːk/ **noun** [U] the covering of paint on a surface: *The car's paintwork has been scratched.*

pair /peəʳ/ (US) /per/ **noun; verb**

▸**noun** [C] **1** (A2) two things of the same appearance and size that are intended to be used together, or something that consists of two parts joined together: *a pair **of** shoes/gloves* ◦ *a pair **of** scissors/glasses* ◦ *I can't find a matching pair of socks.* ◦ *He packed two pairs of trousers and four shirts.* ◦ *I'd like you to do this exercise **in** pairs (= in groups of two).* **2** two people who have a romantic relationship or are doing something together: *They seem a very happy pair.* ◦ *What have you pair been up to?* **3** two animals that come together to have sex and produce young

▸**verb**

PHRASAL VERBS **pair off** to begin a romantic or sexual relationship with someone: *All my friends seem to be pairing off and getting married.* ◦ *Ravens nest very early in the spring and they pair off in the late autumn.* • **pair sb off** to introduce two people to each other so that they will start a romantic relationship: *I managed to pair my best friend Sue off **with** Mike.* • **pair (sb) off** If a group of people pair off, they divide into pairs in order to do something, and if you pair them off, you divide them into pairs: *The students paired off to practise their conversational skills.* • **pair up** to join together temporarily with another person in order to do something: *Everyone should pair up for the next dance.*

paisa /ˈpaɪ.sɑː/ **noun** [C] (plural **paise** /ˈpaɪ.seɪ/) a unit of money in India, Pakistan, and Nepal worth one hundredth of a RUPEE, or a coin of this value

paisley /ˈpeɪz.li/ **noun** [C or U] a colourful pattern of curved shapes, usually on cloth: *a paisley tie*

pajamas /pɪˈdʒɑː.məz/ (US) /-ˈdʒæm.əz/ **noun** [plural] US for **pyjamas**

pak choi /ˌpæk.ˈtʃɔɪ/ (US) /ˌbɑːk-/ **noun** [U] a vegetable often used in Chinese cooking, which has dark green leaves on thick white stems

Paki /ˈpæk.i/ **noun** [C] offensive an offensive word for a person from Pakistan

pakora /pəˈkɔː.rə/ (US) /-ˈkɔːr.ə/ **noun** [C] a South Asian food consisting of small pieces of vegetable, meat, or fish that are covered in BATTER (= a mixture of flour and liquid) and fried

pal /pæl/ **noun; verb**

▸**noun** [C] informal **1** a friend: *You're my **best** pal.* ◦ *It's my **old** pal Pete!* **2** [as form of address] used when talking to a man, sometimes in a friendly way but more often to a man who is annoying you: *Look, pal, you're asking for trouble.*

▸**verb** (-ll-)

PHRASAL VERBS **pal around** US informal to spend time with someone that you are very friendly with: *He used to pal around **with** one of the president's sons.* • **pal up** UK old-fashioned to become friends with someone: *I've palled up **with** some people from work and we're going on holiday together.*

palace /ˈpæl.ɪs/ **noun** [C] **1** (B1) a large house that is the official home of a king, queen, or other person of high social rank: *a royal/presidential palace* ◦ *Buckingham Palace is open to the public.* **2** old-fashioned used in the names of large buildings, such as cinemas or places where people go dancing: *An old movie palace is being restored.*

the ˈPalace **noun** [S, + sing/pl verb] used when

P

referring to the people who live in a palace: *The Palace has issued a statement criticizing the newspaper report.* ◦ *A spokesman for the Palace has denied the accusation.*

ˌpalace ˈcoup noun [C] (also **ˌpalace revoˌlution**) a situation in which a leader is removed from power by the people who have worked with him or her: *A palace coup led by General Rodríguez has toppled the dictator.*

palaeo- (US also **paleo-**) /pæl.i.əʊ-/ (US) /peɪ.li.oʊ-/ prefix ancient; from a time before history was being recorded: *palaeobotany*

palaeolithic (US also **paleolithic**) /ˌpæl.i.əʊˈlɪθ.ɪk/ (US) /ˌpeɪ.li.oʊ-/ **adj** belonging to the period when humans used tools and weapons made of stone: *The Palaeolithic **Period** is sometimes called the Old Stone Age.* → Compare **neolithic**

palaeontology (US also **paleontology**) /ˌpæl.i.ɒnˈtɒl.ə.dʒi/ (US) /ˌpeɪ.li.ɑːnˈtɑː.lə-/ **noun** [U] the study of FOSSILS as a way of getting information about the history of life on Earth and the structure of rocks • **palaeontologist** (US also **paleontologist**) /-dʒɪst/ **noun** [C]

palatable /ˈpæl.ə.tə.bl̩/ (US) /-t̬ə-/ **adj** TASTE ▷ **1** formal describes food or drink that has a pleasant taste: *a very palatable wine* ◦ *The meal was barely palatable.* → Opposite **unpalatable** ACCEPTABLE ▷ **2** acceptable: *I'm afraid the members won't find all these changes very palatable.*

palatal /ˈpæl.ə.təl/ (US) /-t̬əl/ **adj** specialized (of a consonant) made by the tongue touching the highest part of the mouth

palate /ˈpæl.ət/ **noun 1** [C] the top part of the inside of your mouth **2** [C usually singular] a person's ability to taste and judge good food and wine: *a **discriminating** palate*

palatial /pəˈleɪ.ʃəl/ **adj** describes a house that is very large and beautiful

palato-alveolar /ˌpæl.ə.təʊ.æl.viˈəʊ.ləʳ/ (US) /ˌpæl.ə.toʊ.ælˈviː.ə.lɚ/ **adj** specialized (of a speech sound) made in the place between the top teeth and the highest part of the mouth

palaver /pəˈlɑː.vəʳ/ (US) /-ˈlæv.ɚ/ **noun** [S or U] informal unnecessary work and trouble: *Organizing the annual office lunch was such a palaver, I swore I'd never do it again.*

pale /peɪl/ **adj; verb**

▸**adj 1** (B2) describes someone's face or skin if it has less colour than usual, for example when they are ill or frightened, or if it has less colour than people generally have: *You're looking pale – do you feel ill?* ◦ *She has a naturally pale complexion and dark hair.* → See **beyond the pale 2** (A2) describes light or a colour that is not bright or strong: *She wore a pale blue hat.* ◦ *pale winter sunlight*

▸**verb** [I] If a person's face pales, it loses its usual colour: *His face paled and he looked as if he might faint.*

IDIOMS **pale in comparison** (also **pale beside sth/sb**) to seem much less serious or important when compared with someone or something else: *I thought I was badly treated but my experiences pale in comparison with yours.* • **pale into insignificance** to seem not important when compared with something else: *Everything else that happened in my life pales into insignificance beside that one event.*

ˌpale ˈale noun [C or U] a type of beer that does not contain much alcohol and is often sold in bottles

ˌpale imiˈtation noun [C] something that is similar to but not as good as something else: *Modern luxury ships are a pale imitation **of** the glamour and style of the early ocean liners.*

paleness /ˈpeɪl.nəs/ **noun** [U] the state of being pale

paleo- /pæl.i.əʊ-/ (US) /peɪ.li.oʊ-/ **prefix** another spelling of **palaeo-**

paleolithic /ˌpæl.i.əʊˈlɪθ.ɪk/ (US) /ˌpeɪ.li.oʊ-/ **adj** another spelling of **palaeolithic**

paleontology /ˌpæl.i.ənˈtɒl.ə.dʒi/ (US) /-ˈtɑː.lə-/ **noun** [U] another spelling of **palaeontology**

palette /ˈpæl.ət/ **noun 1** [C] a thin board with curved edges and a hole for your thumb, used by an artist to mix their paints on while they are painting **2** [C usually singular] specialized the range of colours that an artist usually paints with: *Matisse's palette typically consists of bright blues, greens and oranges.*

ˈpalette ˌknife noun [C] a knife with a wide thin blade, a rounded end and no sharp edge, used to mix paints together and also to spread soft substances when cooking

palindrome /ˈpæl.ɪn.drəʊm/ (US) /-droʊm/ **noun** [C] a word or group of words that is the same when you read it forwards from the beginning or backwards from the end: *'Refer' and 'level' are palindromes.*

paling /ˈpeɪ.lɪŋ/ **noun** [C] a fence made from long thin pieces of wood

palisade /ˌpæl.ɪˈseɪd/ (US) /ˈpæl.ɪ.seɪd/ **noun** [C] **1** a strong fence made out of wooden or iron poles that is used to protect people or a place from being attacked **2 palisades** [plural] US a line of CLIFFS by the sea or a river

palish /ˈpeɪ.lɪʃ/ **adj** quite pale: *The sky was a palish blue.*

pall /pɔːl/ (US) /pɑːl/ **noun; verb**

▸**noun** CLOUD ▷ **1** [C] a thick, dark cloud of smoke: *Palls **of** smoke obscured our view.* **2** [S] a negative feeling or mood: *The bad news **cast** a pall **over** the evening.* ◦ *A pall of embarrassment descended on the room.* CLOTH ▷ **3** [C] a cloth used to cover a COFFIN at a funeral **4** [C] US the COFFIN itself at a funeral

▸**verb** [I] to become less interesting or enjoyable: *The pleasure of not having to work quickly palled.*

pallbearer /ˈpɔːlˌbeə.rəʳ/ (US) /ˈpɑːlˌber.ɚ/ **noun** [C] a person who helps to carry a COFFIN at a funeral or who walks at the side of the people carrying it

pallet /ˈpæl.ɪt/ **noun** [C] a flat wooden structure that heavy goods are put onto so that they can be moved using a FORK-LIFT TRUCK (= a small vehicle with two strong bars of metal on the front that is used for lifting heavy goods)

palliative /ˈpæl.i.ə.tɪv/ (US) /-t̬ɪv/ **noun** [C] **1** specialized a drug or medical treatment that reduces pain without curing the cause of the pain **2** formal something that makes a problem seem less serious but does not solve the problem or make it disappear: *We want long-term solutions, not short-term palliatives.* • **palliative adj** specialized *palliative care*

pallid /ˈpæl.ɪd/ **adj 1** very pale, in a way that looks unhealthy and not attractive: *Next to his tanned face, hers seemed pallid and unhealthy.* **2** showing no enthusiasm or excitement

pallor /ˈpæl.əʳ/ (US) /-ɚ/ **noun** [U] the state of being very pale: *The **deathly** pallor of her skin was frightening.*

pally /ˈpæl.i/ **adj** informal friendly: *They've become very pally (**with** each other).* ◦ *Suddenly she started acting very pally **towards** me.*

palm /pɑːm/ **noun; verb**

▸**noun** [C] HAND ▷ **1** (C2) the inside part of your hand from your wrist to the base of your fingers: *This tiny device fits into **the** palm **of** your **hand**.* **2 read sb's**

P

palm to look at the lines on the inside of someone's hand and tell them what these lines say about their character and their future **TREE** ▷ **3** C1 (also **palm tree**) a tree that grows in hot countries and has a tall TRUNK with a mass of long pointed leaves at the top: *date palms* ◦ *palm **fronds*** ◦ *The island has long golden beaches fringed by palm trees.*

IDIOM **have sb in the palm of your hand** (also **have sb eating out of the palm of your hand**) to have complete control over someone and to be able to make them do anything you want them to: *He had the audience in the palm of his hand.*

▸**verb** [T] to make something seem to disappear by hiding it in the palm of your hand as part of a trick, or to steal something by picking it up in a way that will not be noticed: *I suspected that he had palmed a playing card.*

PHRASAL VERBS **palm sth off** to give away something, or persuade someone to accept something, because you do not want it and you know it has no value: *She tried to palm her old car off **on** me.* • **palm sb off with sth** to give someone an untrue or unsatisfactory answer, or to give them something that has no value in order to try to satisfy them and make them go away: *You're not going to palm me off with that feeble excuse.*

palmate /ˈpæl.meɪt/ **adj** specialized describes a type of COMPOUND LEAF with small leaves that all grow from the same point at the end of the stem → Compare **pinnate**

palmist /ˈpɑː.mɪst/ **noun** [C] (also **palm reader**) a person who looks at the lines on the palm of your hand and tells you what these lines say about your character and your future

palmistry /ˈpɑː.mɪ.stri/ **noun** [U] (also ˈ**palm ˌreading**) the ability that some people claim to have to see signs about your character and future from the lines on the inside of your hands

ˈ**palm ˌoil** **noun** [C or U] an oil from the nuts of some types of palm tree, used in some foods and to make soap

ˌ**Palm ˈSunday** **noun** [C or U] the Sunday before EASTER (= a Christian religious holiday) in Christian religions

palmtop /ˈpɑːm.tɒp/ (US) /-tɑːp/ **noun** [C] (also ˌ**palmtop comˈputer**) a type of computer that is small enough to hold with one hand

palomino (plural **palominos**) (also **palamino** (plural **palaminos**)) /ˌpæl.əˈmiː.nəʊ/ (US) /-noʊ/ **noun** [C] a horse that is gold in colour with a white MANE (= neck hair) and tail

palpable /ˈpæl.pə.bl̩/ **adj** so obvious that it can easily be seen or known, or (of a feeling) so strong that it seems as if it can be touched or physically felt: *a palpable **effect*** ◦ *Her joy was palpable.* • **palpably** /-bli/ **adv** *The system was palpably (= very obviously) unfair.*

palpitate /ˈpæl.pɪ.teɪt/ (US) /-pə-/ **verb** [I] (of the heart) to beat very fast and in a way that is not regular: *My heart was palpitating **with** fear.*

palpitations /ˌpæl.pɪˈteɪ.ʃənz/ (US) /-pə-/ **noun** [plural] **1** a condition in which your heart beats too quickly or not regularly: *He ended up in hospital with heart palpitations.* **2 have palpitations** humorous to be very shocked: *My mother will have palpitations when she sees my new boyfriend.*

paltry /ˈpɔːl.tri/ (US) /ˈpɑːl-/ **adj** **1** (of an amount of money) very small and of little or no value: *Student grants these days are paltry.* ◦ *The company offered Jeremy a paltry **sum** which he refused.* **2** low in quality: *She made some paltry **excuse** and left.*

pampas /ˈpæm.pəs/ **noun** [S or U, + sing/pl verb] the large, flat areas of land covered in grass in parts of South America

ˈ**pampas ˌgrass** **noun** [U] tall grass with silver-coloured flowers

pamper /ˈpæm.pəʳ/ (US) /-pɚ/ **verb** [T] to give someone special treatment, making them as comfortable as possible and giving them whatever they want: *She pampers her dog **with** the finest steak and salmon.* ◦ *Why not pamper yourself after a hard day **with** a hot bath scented with oils?* • **pampered** /-pəd/ (US) /-pɚd/ **adj** *He was a pampered rich kid who was driven to school in a limousine.*

pamphlet /ˈpæm.flət/ **noun** [C] a thin book with only a few pages which gives information or an opinion about something

pan /pæn/ **noun; verb**

▸**noun CONTAINER** ▷ **1** B1 [C] a metal container that is round and often has a long handle and a lid, used for cooking things on top of a cooker: *Heat the milk in a small pan.* ◦ *This dishwasher even washes **pots and pans** (= different types of pan).* **2** C2 [C] mainly US a metal container used for cooking things inside the cooker **TOILET** ▷ **3** [C] UK the bowl-shaped part of a toilet **BETEL LEAF** ▷ **4** [U] → **paan**

IDIOM **go down the pan** slang to fail or to be lost or destroyed: *We don't want to see our business go down the pan.*

▸**verb** (-nn-) **MOVE SLOWLY** ▷ **1** [I] (of a film camera) to move slowly from one side to another or up and down: *In the first scene, the camera pans slowly **across** the room.* **CRITICIZE** ▷ **2** [T] informal to criticize something severely: *The critics panned the film version of the novel.*

PHRASAL VERB **pan out** informal to develop in a particular way or in a successful way: *We'll have to see how things pan out.* ◦ *Their attempt to start a new business didn't pan out.*

pan- /pæn-/ **prefix** including or relating to all the places or people in a particular group: *a pan-American conference* ◦ *the Pan-African Congress*

panacea /ˌpæn.əˈsiː.ə/ **noun** [C usually singular] **1** disapproving something that will solve all problems: *Technology is not a panacea **for** all our problems.* **2** something that will cure all illnesses

panache /pəˈnæʃ/ **noun** [U] a stylish, original, and very confident way of doing things that makes people admire you: *The orchestra played with great panache.* ◦ *He dressed with panache.*

panama /ˈpæn.ə.mɑː/ **noun** [C] (also ˌ**panama ˈhat**) a man's hat made from STRAW and usually worn in hot weather

panatella /ˌpæn.əˈtel.ə/ **noun** [C] a long thin CIGAR

pancake /ˈpæn.keɪk/ **noun** [C] **1** B2 UK (mainly US **crepe**) a very thin flat round cake made from a mixture of flour, milk, and egg, fried on both sides: *Do you want a sweet pancake or a savoury one?* **2** US a sweet, thick, round cake made from flour, sugar, milk, and eggs, cooked in a pan and eaten with MAPLE SYRUP, usually for breakfast: *a **stack** of pancakes*

ˈ**Pancake ˌDay** **noun** [C usually singular] UK informal (also ˌ**Shrove ˈTuesday**, US informal ˌ**Pancake ˈTuesday**) the day before LENT (= a religious period in the Christian religion) starts, when pancakes are traditionally eaten

ˌ**pancake ˈlanding** **noun** [C] an occasion when an aircraft lands without using its wheels by dropping onto the ground from a low height, because it has a problem and cannot continue to fly

pancetta /pænˈtʃet.ə/ (US) /ˈtʃet̬-/ **noun** [U] an Italian type of BACON (= meat from a pig)

pancreas /ˈpæŋ.kri.əs/ **noun** [C] an organ in the body that produces INSULIN (= a chemical substance that controls the amount of sugar in the blood) and substances which help to digest food so that it can be used by the body • **pancreatic** /ˌpæŋ.kriˈæt.ɪk/ (US) /-ˈæt̬-/ **adj** *pancreatic cancer*

ˌpancreˌatic ˈduct **noun** [C usually sing] specialized in the human body, a tube that runs from the pancreas and joins the BILE DUCT, taking pancreatic juice into the SMALL INTESTINE

ˌpancreˌatic ˈjuice **noun** [U] specialized a liquid produced by the pancreas containing substances that digest food as it reaches the SMALL INTESTINE

panda /ˈpæn.də/ **noun** [C] (plural **pandas** or **panda**) (also **giant panda**) a large, black and white mammal that lives in forests in China. Pandas eat BAMBOO.

panda

pandemic /pænˈdem.ɪk/ **adj; noun**
▸**adj** specialized (of a disease) existing in almost all of an area or in almost all of a group of people, animals, or plants: *In some parts of the world malaria is still pandemic.*
▸**noun** [C] specialized a pandemic disease: *a pandemic* ***of*** *influenza* ◦ *an influenza pandemic*

pandemonium /ˌpæn.dəˈməʊ.ni.əm/ (US) /-ˈmoʊ-/ **noun** [U] a situation in which there is a lot of noise and confusion because people are excited, angry, or frightened: *Pandemonium reigned in the hall as the unbelievable election results were read out.* ◦ *the pandemonium of the school playground*

pander /ˈpæn.dəʳ/ (US) /-dɚ/ **verb**

PHRASAL VERB **pander to sb/sth** disapproving to do or provide exactly what a person or group wants, especially when it is not acceptable, reasonable, or approved of, usually in order to get some personal advantage: *It's not good the way she panders to his every whim.* ◦ *Political leaders almost inevitably pander to big business.*

pandit /ˈpæn.dɪt/ **noun** [C] (also **pundit** /ˈpʌn.dɪt/) Indian English **1** a Hindu priest **2** a teacher or wise man **3** someone who plays a musical instrument very well

Pandora's box /pænˌdɔː.rəzˈbɒks/ (US) /-ˌdɔːr.əzˈbɑːks/ **noun** [S] something which creates a lot of new problems that you did not expect: *Sadly, his reforms* ***opened up*** *a Pandora's box of domestic problems.*

p. and p. /ˌpiː.ənˈpiː/ **noun** [U] UK abbreviation for **postage and packing**: *The books cost £12.50 plus p. and p.*

pane /peɪn/ **noun** [C] a flat piece of glass, used in a window or door: *a window pane*

paneer (also **panir**) /pænˈɪəʳ/ (US) /-ˈɪr/ **noun** [U] a soft cheese from South Asia, often made in the home

panegyric /ˌpæn.əˈdʒɪr.ɪk/ **noun** [C] formal a speech or piece of writing that praises someone very much and does not mention anything bad about them: *She delivered a panegyric* ***on*** *the president-elect.*

panel /ˈpæn.əl/ **noun; verb**
▸**noun** **TEAM** ▷ **1** (C1) [C, + sing/pl verb] a small group of people chosen to give advice, make a decision, or publicly discuss their opinions as entertainment: *The competition will be judged by a panel* ***of*** *experts.* **PART** ▷ **2** (C2) [C] a flat, usually rectangular part, or piece of wood, metal, cloth, etc., that fits into or onto something larger: *a beautiful old door with oak panels* ◦ *White silk panels were inset into the sides of the dress.* ◦ *At the bottom of each page is a panel with grammatical information.* **CONTROL BOARD** ▷ **3** [C] a board or surface that has controls and other devices on it for operating an aircraft or other large machine: *a* ***control/instrument*** *panel*
▸**verb** [T usually passive] (**-ll-** or US usually **-l-**) to cover or decorate with flat, usually rectangular pieces of wood, metal, cloth, etc.: *The walls of the dining hall were panelled* ***in*** *oak.* ◦ *a panelled room/wall/door* • **panelling** UK (US usually **paneling**) /-ɪŋ/ **noun** [U] *wood panelling*

panellist (US **panelist**) /ˈpæn.əl.ɪst/ **noun** [C] a member of a panel

panettone /ˌpæn.əˈtəʊ.ni/ (US) /-ɪˈtoʊ-/ **noun** [C or U] an Italian Christmas cake containing dried fruit and nuts

ˈpan-fry **verb** [T] to cook food in a pan in a small amount of oil or fat: *pan-fried lobster*

pang /pæŋ/ **noun** [C] a sudden sharp feeling, especially of painful emotion: *a pang* ***of*** *jealousy* ◦ *We hadn't eaten since yesterday and the* ***hunger*** *pangs were getting harder to ignore.*

panhandle /ˈpænˌhæn.dəl/ **noun; verb**
▸**noun** [C] US a long thin piece of land joined to a larger area: *the Texas panhandle*
▸**verb** [I or T] US informal to ask people that you do not know for money, especially in a public place: *He was arrested for panhandling.* • **panhandler** /-ˌhænd.ləʳ/ (US) /-ˌhænd.lɚ/ **noun** [C] US

panic /ˈpæn.ɪk/ **noun; verb**
▸**noun** [C usually singular, U] (B2) a sudden strong feeling of fear that prevents reasonable thought and action: *a state of panic* ◦ *Panic* ***spread*** *through the crowd as the bullets started to fly.* ◦ *Carmel was* ***in*** *a panic about her exam.* ◦ *He* ***got in(to)*** *a panic that he would forget his lines on stage.*
▸**verb** [I or T] (present tense **panicking**, past tense and past participle **panicked**) (B2) to suddenly feel so worried or frightened that you cannot think or behave calmly or reasonably: *Don't panic! Everything will be okay.* ◦ *The sound of gunfire panicked the crowd.* ◦ *The boss always panics* ***over/about*** *the budget every month.*

ˈpanic atˌtack **noun** [C] a sudden period of severe ANXIETY in which your heart beats fast, you have trouble breathing and you feel as if something very bad is going to happen

ˈpanic ˌbutton **noun** [C usually singular] a device, usually a button, that is used to call for help by someone in a dangerous situation

IDIOM **hit/press/push the panic button** to do something quickly without thinking about it in order to deal with a difficult or worrying situation

ˈpanic ˌbuying **noun** [U] a situation in which many people suddenly buy as much food, fuel, etc. as they can because they are worried about something bad that may happen

panicky /ˈpæn.ɪ.ki/ **adj** informal feeling suddenly very worried or frightened: *a panicky feeling/expression/action* ◦ *Is he the panicky type?*

ˈpanic ˌselling **noun** [U] a situation in which many people suddenly start to sell company SHARES that they own, because they are worried their value is going to fall

ˈpanic ˌstations **noun** [plural] UK informal a situation in which people feel worried and nervous because things need to be done quickly: *Two weeks before an exam it's always panic stations as I realize how much I still have to do.*

ˈpanic-ˌstricken adj very frightened and worried about a situation, and therefore unable to think clearly or act reasonably: *The streets were full of panic-stricken people trying to escape the tear gas.*

panini /pəˈniː.ni/ noun [C] a small, flat LOAF of Italian bread that is often cut, filled with cheese, meat, or vegetables, and eaten warm

panir noun [U] Indian English **paneer**

pannier /ˈpæn.i.əʳ/ ⓤⓢ /-jɚ/ noun [C] a bag or similar container, especially one of a pair that hang on either side of a bicycle, motorcycle, or animal such as a horse or DONKEY

panoply /ˈpæn.ə.pli/ noun [S] formal a wide range or collection of different things: *There is a whole panoply **of** remedies and drugs available to the modern doctor.*

panorama /ˌpæn.ərˈɑː.mə/ ⓤⓢ /-əˈræm.ə/ noun [C] **1** a view of a wide area: *From the hotel roof you can enjoy a panorama of the whole city.* **2** a view, description, or study of events or activities: *The investigation revealed a panorama of corruption and illegal dealings.* • **panoramic** /ˌpæn.ərˈæm.ɪk/ ⓤⓢ /-əˈræm-/ adj *a wonderful panoramic **view** of the countryside*

panpipes /ˈpæn.paɪps/ noun [plural] a musical instrument made of short tubes of different lengths joined together, which you play by blowing across the open ends

panpipes

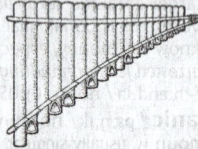

ˈpan ˌscourer noun [C] a **scouring pad**

pansy /ˈpæn.zi/ noun [C] **PLANT** ▷ **1** a small garden plant that has flowers of many different colours with rounded PETALS **PERSON** ▷ **2** offensive old-fashioned an offensive word for a man who behaves in a way that is considered to be more typical of a woman

pant /pænt/ verb [I] to breathe quickly and loudly through your mouth, usually because you have been doing something very energetic: *Matteo arrived at the top of the hill, panting and covered in sweat.* ◦ [+ speech] *'Hurry! They're almost here,' she panted.*

PHRASAL VERB **pant for/after sb/sth** UK to want someone or something very much: *The newspapers are panting for details of the scandal.*

pantechnicon /pænˈtek.nɪ.kən/ noun [C] formal a large vehicle used for carrying furniture and other things when you move to a different house

pantheism /ˈpæn.θi.ɪ.zəm/ noun [U] belief in many or all gods, or the belief that God exists in and is the same as all things, animals, and people within the universe • **pantheist** /-ɪst/ noun [C], adj • **pantheistic** /ˌpæn.θiˈɪs.tɪk/ adj (also **pantheist**)

pantheon /ˈpæn.θi.ən/ ⓤⓢ /-ɑːn/ noun [C usually singular] formal a small group of people who are the most famous, important, and admired in their particular area of activity: *Don't you agree that Malcolm X definitely has a place in **the** pantheon **of** black civil rights heroes?*

panther /ˈpæn.θəʳ/ ⓤⓢ /-θɚ/ noun [C] (plural **panthers** or **panther**) a black LEOPARD (= large wild cat)

panties /ˈpæn.tiz/ ⓤⓢ /-t̬iz/ noun [plural] (UK also **pants**) Ⓑ2 women's and girls' UNDERPANTS

pantomime /ˈpæn.tə.maɪm/ ⓤⓢ /-t̬ə-/ noun **1** [C] (UK informal **panto**) (in Britain) a funny musical play based on traditional children's stories, performed especially at Christmas **2** [C or U] **mime**

ˌpantomime ˈhorse noun [C] UK two people pretending humorously to be a horse by dressing in special clothes and standing one behind the other so that the front person appears as the horse's front half and the person behind forms the back part

pantry /ˈpæn.tri/ noun [C] a small room or large cupboard in a house where food is kept

pants /pænts/ noun; adj

▸noun [plural] **1** Ⓑ1 UK **underpants** **2** Ⓐ1 US for trousers: *a pair of pants*

IDIOMS **beat, bore, scare, etc. the pants off sb** informal to defeat, bore, frighten, etc. someone completely: *Sunbathing bores the pants off me.* • **piss/shit your pants** offensive to suddenly feel very frightened: *I shit my pants when all the lights went out.* • **wet your pants** to urinate in your clothes: *Tilly had wet her pants so I was looking for somewhere to change her.*

▸adj [after verb] UK slang not useful or of bad quality: *This music is pants.*

pantsuit /ˈpænt.suːt/ noun [C] US for **trouser suit**

pantyhose /ˈpæn.ti.həʊz/ ⓤⓢ /-t̬i.hoʊz/ noun [plural] Ⓑ1 US for **tights**

panty liner /ˈpæn.tiˌlaɪ.nəʳ/ ⓤⓢ /-t̬iˌlaɪ.nɚ/ noun [C] a small length of material that can be stuck to the inside of a woman's UNDERPANTS to absorb any liquid from the body

pap /pæp/ noun; verb

▸noun [U] informal disapproving **FOOD** ▷ **1** food that is soft and has little taste **ENTERTAINMENT** ▷ **2** television, cinema, or literature that is entertaining, but that has no artistic or educational value **PHOTOGRAPHER** ▷ **3** mainly UK a PAPARAZZI photographer who follows famous people in order to take photographs of them for newspapers and magazines → See also **paparazzi**

▸verb [T] (**-pp-**) informal mainly UK to take photographs of a famous person, usually after following them and without permission, for newspapers or magazines: *She didn't look happy about being papped without make-up.*

papa /pəˈpɑː/ ⓤⓢ /ˈpɑː.pə/ noun [C] UK old-fashioned formal or US informal father: [as form of address] *'Why is the sky blue, Papa?' she asked.*

the papacy /ˈpeɪ.pə.si/ noun [S] the position or authority of the POPE (= the leader of the Roman Catholic Church), or the length of time that a particular person is POPE

papal /ˈpeɪ.pəl/ adj connected with the position or authority of the POPE (= the leader of the Roman Catholic Church): *a papal messenger/announcement/election*

paparazzi /ˌpæp.ərˈæt.si/ ⓤⓢ /ˌpɑː.pɑːˈrɑːt.si/ noun [plural] the photographers who follow famous people everywhere they go in order to take photographs of them for newspapers and magazines

papaya /pəˈpaɪ.ə/ noun [C or U] (also **pawpaw**) a large oval fruit with a yellowish skin and sweet orange flesh, or the tropical tree on which this grows

paper /ˈpeɪ.pəʳ/ ⓤⓢ /-pɚ/ noun; verb

▸noun **MATERIAL** ▷ **1** Ⓐ1 [U] thin, flat material made from crushed wood or cloth, used for writing, printing, or drawing on: *a piece/sheet of paper* ◦ *a pack of **writing** paper* ◦ *Dictionaries are usually printed on thin paper.* ◦ *a paper bag* ◦ *This card is printed on **recycled** paper (= paper made from used paper).* ◦ *Get the idea **down on** paper (= write it) before you forget it.*

∘ *She works* **on** *paper* (= *writes things on paper*) *because she hates computers.* **DOCUMENT** ▷ **2** (B1) [C] a newspaper: *a daily/weekly/local/national paper* ∘ *The photo was on the front page of all the papers.* **3 papers** [plural] official documents, especially ones that show who you are: *The border guards stopped me and asked to see my papers.* **4** (A2) [C] UK a set of printed questions in an exam: *Candidates must answer two questions from each paper.* ∘ *The geography paper is not till next week.* **5** (C2) [C] a piece of writing on a particular subject written by an expert and usually published in a book or JOURNAL, or read aloud to other people: *He's giving a paper* **on** *thermodynamics at a conference at Manchester University.* **6** (B1) [C] US for **essay**: *Mr Jones thought my history paper was terrific.*

IDIOMS **sb couldn't act, argue, fight, etc. their way out of a paper bag** humorous said about someone you think has no energy or ability • **on paper** judging something by how it has been planned rather than how it really works in practice: *The design certainly* ***looks good*** *on paper.* ∘ *Several candidates seemed suitable on paper but failed the interview.* • **a paper chase** US and Australian English the activity of dealing with many different documents in order to achieve something: *To receive even the smallest amount of financial aid from a college, it's a real paper chase.*

▸**verb** [T] to cover a wall, room, etc. with WALLPAPER

IDIOM **paper over the cracks** to hide problems, especially arguments between people, in order to make a situation seem better than it really is: *She tried to paper over the cracks, but I could see that the relationship was failing.*

PHRASAL VERB **paper over sth** to hide an unpleasant situation, especially a problem or disagreement, in order to make people believe that it does not exist or is not serious: *He tried to paper over the country's deep-seated problems.*

paperback /ˈpeɪ.pə.bæk/ (US) /-pɚ-/ **noun** [C] a book with a cover made of thin card: *a best-selling paperback* ∘ *I'll buy some paperbacks at the airport.* ∘ *It will be published* **in** *paperback* (= *as a paperback*) *in March.* → Compare **hardback, softback**

paperbark /ˈpeɪ.pə.bɑːk/ (US) /-pɚ.bɑːrk/ **noun** [C] an Australian tree with thin BARK (= outer covering) that can be removed in large pieces

ˌpaper ˌclip noun [C] a small piece of bent wire used for holding pieces of paper together

ˈpaper ˌknife noun [C] UK (US **ˈletter ˌopener**) a knife for opening envelopes that is not sharp and is often decorative

ˌpaper ˈmoney noun [U] money in paper form, rather than coins

ˌpaper ˈprofit noun [C or U] a profit that is shown in financial records but has not yet been made by a company, especially because it is waiting for payments it is owed

ˈpaper ˌround noun [C] UK (US **ˈpaper ˌroute**) the job, often done by children, of taking newspapers to people's homes

ˈpaper ˌshop noun [C] UK a shop which sells newspapers

ˌpaper-ˈthin adj very thin: *paper-thin layers of pastry* ∘ *The walls were paper-thin and I could hear everything!*

ˌpaper ˈtiger noun [C] disapproving something, such as an enemy or foreign country, that seems very strong and dangerous but is really weak and not harmful: *The Soviet Union was suddenly revealed as a paper tiger.*

ˌpaper ˈtowel noun [C] a sheet of soft thick paper used for drying your hands, cleaning objects, absorbing liquids, etc.

ˈpaper ˌtrail noun [C usually singular] a series of documents that show a record of your activities

paperweight /ˈpeɪ.pə.weɪt/ (US) /-pɚ-/ **noun** [C] a small, heavy object that is put on top of pieces of paper to keep them in position

paperwork /ˈpeɪ.pə.wɜːk/ (US) /-pɚ.wɜːk/ **noun** [U] **1** (B2) the part of a job which involves writing letters and reports and keeping records **2** the written records connected with a particular job, deal, journey, etc.: *I've kept all the paperwork for the car.*

papery /ˈpeɪ.pᵊr.i/ (US) /-pɚ.i/ **adj** thin and dry like paper: *The skin on his hands was wrinkled and papery.*

papier mâché /ˌpæp.i.eɪˈmæʃ.eɪ/ (US) /ˌpeɪ.pɚ.məˈʃeɪ/ **noun** [U] pieces of paper mixed with glue or with flour and water, used to make decorative objects or models: *a papier mâché mask*

papist /ˈpeɪ.pɪst/ **noun** [C] offensive an offensive word for a Roman Catholic • **papist adj**

papoose /pəˈpuːs/ (US) /pæpˈuːs/ **noun** [C] old-fashioned a NATIVE AMERICAN baby or small child

pappy /ˈpæp.i/ **adj** **FOOD** ▷ **1** describes food that is unpleasantly soft or contains too much water: *pappy pasta* **ENTERTAINMENT** ▷ **2** informal disapproving entertaining but with no artistic or educational value: *It's just another pappy novel.*

paprika /ˈpæp.rɪ.kə/, /pəˈpriː-/ **noun** [U] a red powder used as a spice to give a slightly hot flavour to food, especially in meat dishes

ˈPap ˌsmear noun [C] US for **smear**

papyrus /pəˈpaɪ.rəs/ **noun** [C or U] (plural **papyruses** or **papyri**) a tall plant like a grass that grows in or near water, especially in North Africa, or paper made from this plant, especially by ancient Egyptians

par /pɑːʳ/ (US) /pɑːr/ **noun** **EQUAL** ▷ **1 on a par (with sb/sth)** the same as or equal to someone or something: *The regeneration of the city's downtown dock front will put it on a par with Nice or Cannes.* **STANDARD** ▷ **2** [U] the usual standard or condition **3** [U] the expected number of times in GOLF that a good player should have to hit the ball in order to get it into a hole or into all the holes: *Tiger Woods finished the round 10* ***below/under*** *par.* **4 par (value)** specialized the original value of a share in a business

IDIOMS **be par for the course** disapproving If a type of behaviour, event, or situation is par for the course, it is not good but it is normal or as you would expect: *The school budget is going to be cut again this year, but then that's par for the course.* • **be up to par** to be of the usual or expected standard: *Her work hasn't been up to par lately.* • **below/under par 1** ill: *Are you* ***feeling*** *a bit under par?* **2** worse than the usual or expected standard

para /ˈpær.ə/ (US) /ˈper.ə/ **noun** [C] **SOLDIER** ▷ **1** mainly UK informal for **paratrooper (paratroops)** **TEXT** ▷ **2** abbreviation for **paragraph**: *Paras 5 and 6 will have to be rewritten.*

para- /pær.ə-/ (US) /per.ə-/ **prefix** **FURTHER** ▷ **1** further than: *Parapsychology is the study of abilities that go beyond what is natural and normal.* ∘ *paranormal phenomena* **SIMILAR** ▷ **2** similar to, or helping to do a similar job: *a paramedic* ∘ *paramilitary*

parable /ˈpær.ə.bl̩/ (US) /ˈper-/ **noun** [C] a short simple story which teaches or explains an idea, especially a moral or religious idea

P

parabola /pəˈræb.əl.ə/ **noun** [C] specialized a type of curve such as that made by an object that is thrown up in the air and falls to the ground in a different place • **parabolic** /ˌpær.əˈbɒl.ɪk/ (US) /ˌper.əˈbɑː.lɪk/ **adj** *a parabolic curve/trajectory*

paracetamol /ˌpær.əˈsiː.tə.mɒl/ (US) /ˌper.əˈsiː.t̬ə.mɑːl/ **noun** [C or U] UK (US **acetaminophen**) a drug used to reduce pain

parachute /ˈpær.ə.ʃuːt/ (US) /ˈper-/ **noun; verb**

parachute

▸**noun** [C] B2 a piece of equipment made of a large piece of special cloth that is fastened to someone or something that is dropped from an aircraft, in order to make them fall slowly and safely to the ground

▸**verb**
1 [I usually + adv/prep] to jump from an aircraft using a parachute: *The plan is to parachute into the town.* **2** [T usually + adv/prep] to drop someone or something from an aircraft by parachute: [often passive] *Thousands of leaflets were parachuted behind enemy lines.*

parachutist /ˈpær.ə.ʃuː.tɪst/ (US) /ˈper.ə.ʃuː.t̬ɪst/ **noun** [C] someone who jumps out of an aircraft wearing a parachute on their back, especially as a sport or a military job

parade /pəˈreɪd/ **noun; verb**

▸**noun** [C] **LINE OF PEOPLE** ▷ **1** B2 a large number of people walking or in vehicles, all going in the same direction, usually as part of a public celebration of something: *a **victory** parade* **2** a series of people or things that appear one after the other: *For three hours a committee of state senators listened to a parade of local residents giving their opinions.* **3 on parade** When soldiers are on parade, they march and practise military movements in front of important officials or as part of a public celebration or ceremony: *The entire regiment was on parade.* **ROAD** ▷ **4** UK a row of shops **5 Parade** UK used in the names of some roads: *Park Parade*

▸**verb 1** [I or T, usually + adv/prep] (of a group) to walk or march somewhere, usually as part of a public celebration: *The Saint Patrick's Day marchers paraded up Fifth Avenue, past the cathedral.* ◦ *In ancient Rome, captured generals were paraded through the streets in chains.* **2** [I or T] to show something in an obvious way in order to be admired: *It's sickening the way he parades his wealth, his car and his expensive clothes.* ◦ *The children paraded **about/around** in their new clothes.*

paˈrade ˌground **noun** [C usually singular] a large flat area where soldiers march and practise military movements

paradigm /ˈpær.ə.daɪm/ (US) /ˈper-/ **noun** [C] formal C2 a model of something, or a very clear and typical example of something: *Some of these educators are hoping to produce a change in the current cultural paradigm.* • **paradigmatic** /ˌpær.ə.dɪgˈmæt.ɪk/ (US) /ˌper.ə.dɪgˈmæt̬-/ **adj**

ˈparadigm ˌshift **noun** [C] formal a time when the usual and accepted way of doing or thinking about something changes completely

paradise /ˈpær.ə.daɪs/ (US) /ˈper-/ **noun** [C usually singular, U] **1** C1 a place or condition of great happiness where everything is exactly as you would like it to be: *a tropical paradise* ◦ *His idea of paradise is to spend the day lying on the beach.* ◦ *This mall is a shopper's paradise.* **2 Paradise a** Heaven: *They believe they'll go to Paradise after they die.* **b** the GARDEN OF EDEN (= the place where Adam and Eve lived, in the Bible story)

paradox /ˈpær.ə.dɒks/ (US) /ˈper.ə.dɑːks/ **noun** [C or U] C2 a situation or statement which seems impossible or is difficult to understand because it contains two opposite facts or characteristics: [+ that] *It's a curious paradox **that** drinking a lot of water can often make you feel thirsty.* • **paradoxical** /ˌpær.əˈdɒk.sɪ.kəl/ (US) /ˌper.əˈdɑːk-/ **adj** C2 *It seems paradoxical to me, but if you drink a cup of hot tea it seems to cool you down.* • **paradoxically** /ˌpær.əˈdɒk.sɪ.kəl.i/ (US) /ˌper.əˈdɑːk-/ **adv**

paraffin /ˈpær.ə.fɪn/ (US) /ˈper-/ **noun** [U] **LIQUID** ▷ **1** UK (US **kerosene**) a clear liquid with a strong smell made from coal or PETROLEUM and used as a fuel, especially in HEATERS and lights **WAX** ▷ **2** (also **paraffin wax**) a white WAX made from PETROLEUM or coal, used especially to make candles

paragliding /ˈpær.əˌglaɪ.dɪŋ/ (US) /ˈper-/ **noun** [U] the sport of jumping out of an aircraft with a special PARACHUTE that allows you to travel a long horizontal distance before you land

paragon /ˈpær.ə.gən/ (US) /ˈper.ə.gɑːn/ **noun** [C] a person or thing that is perfect or has an extremely large amount of a particular good characteristic: *In the novel, Constanza is a paragon **of** virtue.*

paragraph /ˈpær.ə.grɑːf/ (US) /ˈper.ə.græf/ **noun** [C] (written abbreviation **para**) B1 a short part of a text, consisting of at least one sentence and beginning on a new line. It usually deals with a single event, description, idea, etc.

parakeet /ˌpær.əˈkiːt/, /ˈpær.ə.kiːt/ (US) /ˈper.ə.kiːt/ **noun** [C] a small PARROT with a long tail

paralegal /ˌpær.əˈliː.gəl/ (US) /ˌper.ə-/ **noun** [C] someone who works in a law company or a company's legal department and has some legal training, but does not have all the qualifications to be a lawyer

parallel /ˈpær.ə.lel/ (US) /ˈper-/ **adj; noun; verb; adv**

▸**adj** **POSITION** ▷ **1** If two or more lines, streets, etc. are parallel, the distance between them is the same all along their length: *Draw a pair of parallel lines.* ◦ *Hills Road is parallel **to** Mill Road.* **SIMILAR** ▷ **2** C2 describes an event or situation that happens at the same time as and/or is similar to another one: *a parallel example* ◦ *Parallel experiments are being conducted in Rome, Paris and London.*

▸**noun** **SIMILARITY** ▷ **1** C2 [C] something very similar to something else, or a similarity between two things: *I'm trying to see if there are any obvious parallels **between** the two cases.* ◦ *It would be easy to **draw** (= make) a parallel **between** the town's history and that of its football club.* **2 have no parallel** (also **be without parallel**) If something has no parallel or is without parallel, there is nothing similar to it or of the same high quality as it: *These beautiful African churches have no parallel in Europe.* **POSITION** ▷ **3 parallel (line)** a line that is always at the same distance from another line **4** one of a number of imaginary lines around the Earth always at the same distance from the EQUATOR: *Cambridge lies near the 52nd parallel.* **5 in parallel** specialized If two or more parts of an electrical system are in parallel, they are arranged in a way that means they both receive the same amount of electricity.

▸**verb** [T] to happen at the same time as something

else, or be similar or equal to something else: *The events of the last ten days in some ways parallel those before the 1978 election.* → Compare **unparalleled**

▸adv in a position that is always the same distance from something else: *It's a quiet street **running** (= positioned) parallel **to** the main road.*

the ˌparallel ˈbars noun [plural] a piece of equipment used in GYMNASTICS, consisting of two horizontal bars fastened to four poles and used for exercising and competing

ˌparallel ˈcircuit noun [C] specialized a CIRCUIT in which the electric current passes through two or more branches or connected parts at the same time before it combines again

parallelogram /ˌpær.əˈlel.ə.græm/ (US) /ˌper-/ noun [C] specialized a flat shape that has four sides. The two sets of opposite sides are parallel and of equal length to each other.

ˌparallel ˈparking noun [U] the act of parking a vehicle along or parallel to the side of the road, rather than facing into the side of the road

ˌparallel ˈport noun [C] specialized a part of a computer where wires from other pieces of equipment such as a printer can be connected to it, sending information eight BITS (= units of information), or one BYTE, at a time through a special wire → Compare **serial port**

ˌparallel ˈprocessing noun [U] specialized the ability of a computer to do two or more pieces of work at the same time

Paralympian /ˌpær.əˈlɪm.pi.ən/ (US) /ˌper-/ noun; adj

▸noun [C] someone who competes in the Paralympic Games

▸adj relating to the Paralympic Games

the Paralympics /ˌpær.əˈlɪm.pɪks/ (US) /ˌper-/ noun [plural] (also **the ˌParalympic ˈGames**) an international sports competition for people with physical DISABILITIES, which happens every four years immediately after the OLYMPICS • **Paralympic** /-pɪk/ adj [before noun]

paralyse UK (US **paralyze**) /ˈpær.əl.aɪz/ (US) /ˈper-/ verb [T] **1** to cause a person, animal, or part of the body to lose the ability to move or feel: *The drug paralyses the nerves so that there is no feeling or movement in the legs.* **2** to cause a person, group, or organization to stop working or acting normally: *A sudden snowstorm paralysed the city.*

paralysed UK (US **paralyzed**) /ˈpær.əl.aɪzd/ (US) /ˈper-/ adj unable to move or act: *The accident left her paralysed **from** the waist down.* ◦ *The government seems paralysed **by/with** indecision.* ◦ *She was paralysed **with** fear.*

paralysis /pəˈræl.ə.sɪs/ noun [C or U] (plural **paralyses**) **1** a condition in which you are unable to move all or part of your body because of illness or injury: *Some nervous disorders can produce paralysis.* **2** a situation in which you are unable to take action: *political paralysis*

paralytic /ˌpær.əˈlɪt.ɪk/ (US) /ˌper.əˈlɪt̬-/ adj **1** UK informal extremely drunk **2** related to or connected with paralysis: *a paralytic illness*

paramedic /ˌpær.əˈmed.ɪk/ (US) /ˌper.əˈmed-/ noun [C] a person who is trained to do medical work, especially in an emergency, but who is not a doctor or nurse

parameter /pəˈræm.ɪ.təʳ/ (US) /-ə.t̬ɚ/ noun [C usually plural] a set of facts or a fixed limit which establishes or limits how something can or must happen or be done: *The researchers must keep within the parameters of the experiment.* ◦ *The central office sets/establishes the parameters which guide policy at the local level.*

paramilitary /ˌpær.əˈmɪl.ɪ.tər.i/ (US) /ˌper.əˈmɪl.ə.ter.i/ adj; noun

▸adj **1** describes a group that is organized like an army but is not official and often not legal **2** connected with and helping the official armed forces

▸noun [C] a person who belongs to a paramilitary organization

paramount /ˈpær.ə.maʊnt/ (US) /ˈper-/ adj formal (C2) more important than anything else: *There are many priorities, but reducing the budget deficit is paramount/ is **of** paramount **importance**.*

paramour /ˈpær.ə.mɔːʳ/ (US) /ˈper.ə.mʊr/ noun [C] old use or literary the person you are having a romantic or sexual relationship with, but are not married to

paranoia /ˌpær.əˈnɔɪ.ə/ (US) /ˌper-/ noun **1** [C or U] an extreme and unreasonable feeling that other people do not like you or are going to harm or criticize you: *There's a lot of paranoia **about** crime at the moment.* **2** [U] specialized Someone who has paranoia has unreasonable false beliefs as a part of another mental illness, for example SCHIZOPHRENIA.

paranoiac /ˌpær.əˈnɔɪ.æk/ (US) /ˌper-/ noun [C] someone who is paranoid

paranoid /ˈpær.ən.ɔɪd/ (US) /ˈper.ə.nɔɪd/ adj **1** feeling extremely nervous and worried because you believe that other people do not like you or are trying to harm you: *He started feeling paranoid and was convinced his boss was going to fire him.* **2** specialized suffering from a mental illness in which you believe that other people are trying to harm you: *He was diagnosed as a paranoid **schizophrenic**.* ◦ *paranoid delusions*

paranormal /ˌpær.əˈnɔː.məl/ (US) /ˌper.əˈnɔːr-/ adj; noun

▸adj impossible to explain by known natural forces or by science: *paranormal powers/events/forces* ◦ *This book is about people who claim to have paranormal abilities such as ESP and mind-reading.*

▸noun **the paranormal** all the things that are impossible to explain by known natural forces or by science: *investigations into the paranormal*

parapet /ˈpær.ə.pet/ (US) /ˈper-/ noun [C] a low wall along the edge of a roof, bridge, etc.

IDIOM **put your head over/above the parapet** UK to be brave enough to state an opinion that might upset someone

paraphernalia /ˌpær.ə.fəˈneɪ.li.ə/ (US) /ˌper.ə.fɚˈneɪl.jə/ noun [U] all the objects needed for or connected with a particular activity: *We sell pots, gloves, seeds and other gardening paraphernalia.* ◦ *Bags of cocaine and all sorts of drug paraphernalia were seized at the airport.*

paraphrase /ˈpær.ə.freɪz/ (US) /ˈper-/ verb [I or T] to repeat something written or spoken using different words, often in a humorous form or in a simpler and shorter form that makes the original meaning clearer • **paraphrase** noun [C] *She gave us a quick paraphrase **of** what had been said.*

paraplegia /ˌpær.əˈpliː.dʒə/ (US) /ˌper-/ noun [U] specialized loss of the ability to move or feel in the legs and lower part of the body, usually because of a severe injury to the SPINE (= bones in the centre of the back)

paraplegic /ˌpær.əˈpliː.dʒɪk/ (US) /ˌper-/ adj, noun specialized (someone who is) unable to move or feel the legs or lower part of the body: *Is he paraplegic?* ◦ *She does a lot of work with paraplegics.*

parapsychology /ˌpær.ə.saɪˈkɒl.ə.dʒi/ (US) /ˌper.ə.

P

saɪˈkɑː.lə-/ **noun** [U] the study of mental abilities, such as knowing the future or TELEPATHY, which seem to go against or be outside the known laws of nature and science

paraquat /ˈpær.ə.kwɒt/ (US) /ˈper.ə.kwɑːt/ **noun** [U] a very strong liquid poison used to kill unwanted plants

parasailing /ˈpær.əˌseɪ.lɪŋ/ (US) /ˈper-/ **noun** [U] a sport in which you wear a PARACHUTE and are pulled behind a motor boat in order to sail through the air

parascending /ˈpær.əˌsen.dɪŋ/ (US) /ˈper-/ **noun** [U] a sport in which you wear a PARACHUTE and you are connected by a long rope to a car or boat which pulls you up into the air as it moves forward on the ground or on water

parasite /ˈpær.ə.saɪt/ (US) /ˈper / **noun** [C] **1** an animal or plant that lives on or in another animal or plant of a different type and feeds from it: *The older drugs didn't deal effectively with the malaria parasite.* **2** disapproving a person who is lazy and lives by other people working, giving them money, etc.: *Financial speculators are parasites* ***on*** *the national economy.*

parasitic /ˌpær.əˈsɪt.ɪk/ (US) /ˌper.əˈsɪţ-/ **adj** (also **parasitical**) caused by or connected with a parasite: *a parasitic disease* • **parasitism** /ˈpær.ə.saɪ.tɪ.zᵊm/ (US) /ˌper.əˈsɪţ-/ **noun** [U]

parasol /ˈpær.ə.sɒl/ (US) /ˈper.ə.sɑːl/ **noun** [C] a type of SUNSHADE (= round frame covered in cloth on a stick) carried especially by women in the past, to give protection from the sun

paratha /pəˈrɑː.tə/ **noun** [C or U] a type of South Asian flat bread that is fried in a pan or baked in a TANDOORI

parathyroid (gland) /ˌpær.əˈθaɪ.rɔɪdˌglænd/ (US) /ˌper.əˈθaɪ-/ **noun** [C] specialized any of four GLANDS (= small organs in the body) that control the amount of the chemicals CALCIUM and PHOSPHORUS in the body

paratroops /ˈpær.ə.truːps/ (US) /ˈper-/ **noun** [plural] (UK informal **paras**) (a military unit of) soldiers trained to be dropped from an aircraft with a PARACHUTE • **paratrooper** /-ˌtruː.pəʳ/ (US) /-ˌtruː.pɚ/ **noun** [C] (UK informal **para**) *Paratroopers were dropped behind enemy lines to capture key points on the roads into the city.*

parboil /ˈpɑː.bɔɪl/ (US) /ˈpɑːr-/ **verb** [T] to boil food for a short time until it is partly cooked

parcel /ˈpɑː.sᵊl/ (US) /ˈpɑːr-/ **noun; verb**

▸**noun** [C] **TO SEND** ▷ **1** (B1) mainly UK (mainly US **package**) an object or collection of objects wrapped in paper, especially so that it can be sent by post: *a food parcel* ◦ *The parcel was wrapped in plain brown paper.* **LAND** ▷ **2** mainly US specialized an area of land: *a 60-acre parcel*

▸**verb** (**-ll-** or US usually **-l-**)

PHRASAL VERBS **parcel sth out** [M often passive] to divide something and give the separate parts to different people: *The bigger farms were parcelled out after the revolution in 1973.* ◦ *She parcelled out the gifts* ***to*** *the other children.* • **parcel sth up** mainly UK to wrap something and make it into a parcel: *Parcel up the tins and we'll send them off tomorrow.*

ˈparcel ˌbomb **noun** [C] UK a bomb wrapped up as a parcel and sent by post

ˈparcel ˌpost **noun** [U] the system in which parcels are sent by post: *The cheapest way to send it would be by parcel post.*

parched /pɑːtʃt/ (US) /pɑːrtʃt/ **adj** **VERY DRY** ▷ **1** (especially of earth or crops) dried out because of too much heat and not enough rain: *parched earth/fields/corn* ◦ *It was the height of summer and the land was parched and brown.* **VERY THIRSTY** ▷ **2** informal extremely thirsty

parchment /ˈpɑːtʃ.mənt/ (US) /ˈpɑːrtʃ-/ **noun** **1** [U] the thin dried skin of some animals which was used in the past for writing on, or a high-quality paper made to look like this: *ancient parchment* ◦ *He'd been ill for a long time, and his skin was like parchment.* **2** [C] a document written on parchment: *A framed parchment hung on the wall.*

pardner /ˈpɑːd.nəʳ/ (US) /ˈpɑːrd.nɚ/ **noun** [C] US humorous used as an informal form of address, usually between men: ***Howdy*** *pardner!*

pardon /ˈpɑː.dᵊn/ (US) /ˈpɑːr-/ **verb; noun; exclamation**

▸**verb** [T] **1** to forgive someone for something they have said or done. This word is often used in polite expressions: *Pardon my ignorance, but what exactly is ergonomics?* ◦ [+ -ing verb] *Pardon me interrupt****ing****, but there's a client to see you.* **2** If someone who has committed a crime is pardoned, they are officially forgiven and their punishment is stopped: *Large numbers of political prisoners have been pardoned and released by the new president.*

IDIOMS **if you'll pardon the expression** said before or after using language which other people might consider shocking: *The man doesn't know his arse from his elbow, if you'll pardon the expression.* • **pardon (me)** (formal **I beg your pardon**) used to say that you are sorry for doing something wrong or for being rude • **pardon me for breathing/existing/living!** informal used to tell someone that you think they have just answered or spoken to you in an unreasonably CRITICAL or rude way: *'If you're going to get in my way, James, could you just leave the kitchen?' 'Oh, pardon me for breathing!'*

▸**noun** [C] an occasion when someone who has committed a crime is officially forgiven: *He had actively sought a pardon from the president.*

▸**exclamation** **1** (A2) (US also **pardon me**) used to politely ask someone to repeat something they have said because you have not heard it → See also **I beg your pardon** **2** (US also **pardon me**, formal or humorous **I beg your pardon**) used to show that someone has said something that offends you: *'Women tend to be fairly useless drivers, anyway.' 'I beg your pardon!'*

pardonable /ˈpɑː.dᵊn.ə.bl̩/ (US) /ˈpɑːr-/ **adj** able to be forgiven: *a pardonable mistake* • **pardonably** /-bli/ **adv**

pare /peəʳ/ (US) /per/ **verb** [T often + adv/prep] **1** to cut away the outer layer from something, especially a fruit or a vegetable: *He was busy paring apples in the kitchen.* ◦ *Pare* ***off*** *any bits of the carrots that don't look very nice.* **2** to reduce something, especially by a large amount: *The three-hour play has been pared (****down/back****) to two hours.*

IDIOM **pare sth (down) to the bone** to reduce something to a level at which only what is absolutely necessary is left

parent /ˈpeə.rənt/ (US) /ˈper.ᵊnt/ **noun** [C] **MOTHER/FATHER** ▷ **1** (A1) a mother or father of a person or an animal: *I'm going to meet Richard's parents for the first time this weekend.* **COMPANY** ▷ **2** (also **parent company**) a company that owns one or more other companies: *The subsidiary has issued shares that are guaranteed by its parent.* ◦ *The parent company is expected to spend $50 million in advertising this year.*

parentage /ˈpeə.rən.tɪdʒ/ (US) /ˈper.ᵊn.ţɪdʒ/ **noun** [U] When you refer to a person's parentage, you mean their parents and/or their parent's country and social class: *The novel starts when a child of unknown parentage is left at the house of the local priest.* ◦ *She is of mixed Australian and Japanese parentage.*

parental /pəˈren.təl/ US /-ţəl/ **adj** connected with parents or with being a parent: *parental advice/influence* ◦ *The government repeatedly stressed its support for parental* ***choice*** *in the selection of a child's school.*

paˌrental ˈleave noun [U] time that a parent is allowed to spend away from work to take care of their baby

ˌparent ˈcompany noun [C] a company which controls other smaller companies

parentheses /pəˈren.θə.siːz/ **noun** [plural] mainly US (UK usually **brackets**) the symbols ( ) that are put around a word, phrase, or sentence in a piece of writing to show that what is inside them should be considered as separate from the main part: *The students' first names are shown* ***in*** *parentheses, like this: Baker (Tina).*

parenthesis /pəˈren.θə.sɪs/ **noun** [C] (plural **parentheses**) **1** a remark that is added to a sentence, often to provide an explanation or extra information, that is separated from the main part of the sentence by COMMAS, BRACKETS, or DASHES **2 in parenthesis** If, while you are talking, you say something in parenthesis, you say it as something extra and then continue with the main part of the sentence: *Of his origins he said very little, merely mentioning in parenthesis that his background was poor.*

parenthetical /ˌpær.ənˈθet.ɪ.kəl/ US /ˌper.ənˈθeţ-/ **adj** (also **parenthetic**) describes a remark that is said in addition to the main part of what you are saying • **parenthetically** /-kəl.i/ **adv**

parenthood /ˈpeə.rənt.hʊd/ US /ˈper.ənt-/ **noun** [U] the state of being a parent: *The prospect of parenthood filled her with horror.*

parenting /ˈpeə.rən.tɪŋ/ US /ˈper.ən.ţɪŋ/ **noun** [U] the raising of children and all the responsibilities and activities that are involved in it

ˌparent-ˈteacher associˌation noun [C] (abbreviation **PTA**, US also **ˌparent-ˈteacher organiˌzation**) an organization run by teachers and the parents of children at a school that tries to help the school, especially by organizing activities that raise money for it

ˌpar ˈexcellence adj [after noun] You describe something as par excellence when it is the best example of its type

pariah /pəˈraɪə/ **noun** [C] a person who is not accepted by a social group, especially because he or she is not liked, respected, or trusted

paring /ˈpeə.rɪŋ/ US /ˈper.ɪŋ/ **noun** [C usually plural] a thin piece that has been cut away from something: *We feed most of our vegetable parings to the guinea pigs.*

ˈparing ˌknife noun [C] a small knife that is used to cut away a thin outer layer of something, especially fruit

parish /ˈpær.ɪʃ/ US /ˈper-/ **noun** [C] in some Churches, an area cared for by one priest with its own church, or (in England) the smallest unit of local government: *the parish church/magazine/priest/register* → See also **parochial**

ˌparish ˈclerk noun [C] an official whose duties are connected with a church

ˌparish ˈcouncil noun [C] a group of people who are elected to make decisions for their parish

parishioner /pəˈrɪʃ.ən.ər/ US /-ɚ/ **noun** [C] a member of a particular parish under the care of a priest, especially one who often goes to its church

parity /ˈpær.ə.ti/ US /ˈper.ə.ţi/ **noun** [U] EQUALITY, especially of pay or position: *British nurses would like to see pay parity* ***with*** *nurses in other major European countries.*

park /pɑːk/ US /pɑːrk/ **noun; verb**

▸**noun** [C] **1** A1 a large area of land with grass and trees surrounded by fences or walls, specially arranged so that people can walk in it for pleasure or children can play in it: *Central Park* ◦ *Hyde Park* ◦ *We watched the joggers in the park.* **2** UK an area of land around a large house in the countryside **3** US an area of land for playing sports

▸**verb 1** A2 [I or T] to put a vehicle in a place where it can stay for a period of time, usually while you leave it: *Where have you parked?* ◦ *Just park your car in the driveway.* **2** [T + adv/prep] informal to put yourself or something in a particular place for a long time, often annoying other people: *He parked him****self*** *in front of the TV and stayed there all afternoon.* ◦ *She's parked an enormous pile of papers on my desk and I haven't a clue what to do with them.*

parka /ˈpɑː.kə/ US /ˈpɑːr-/ **noun** [C] **1** a long jacket that comes down to the knees, often WATERPROOF, with a HOOD (= head cover) **2** US for **anorak**

ˌpark-and-ˈride noun **1** [C] a place in or near a town where you can park your car cheaply and take a bus or other form of public transport into the town centre: *It's easiest to leave your car in the park-and-ride.* **2** [U] the system of leaving your car in a park and ride area and taking public transport to the city centre: *Use park-and-ride wherever possible.* ◦ *the park-and-ride system*

parking /ˈpɑː.kɪŋ/ US /ˈpɑːr-/ **noun** [U] B1 leaving a vehicle in a particular place for a period of time: *a parking place/space* ◦ *He was fined for illegal parking.* ◦ *Parking* ***fines*** *are given for parking* ***offences/violations****.*

ˈparking ˌbrake noun [C usually singular] US for **handbrake**

ˈparking ˌgarage noun [C] US a building for parking cars: *an underground parking garage*

ˈparking ˌlight noun [C] US for **sidelight**

ˈparking ˌlot noun [C] US A2 an outside CAR PARK (= area of ground for parking cars)

ˈparking ˌmeter noun [C] a device at the side of the road that you put money into so that you can leave your vehicle there for a particular amount of time

ˈparking ˌticket noun [C] an official notice put on your vehicle when you have parked illegally that tells you that you must pay a FINE (= a punishment that involves paying an amount of money)

Parkinson's /ˈpɑː.kɪn.sənz/ US /ˈpɑːr-/ **noun** [U] (also **ˈParkinson's diˌsease**) a disease of the nervous system that makes the muscles become stiff and the body shake, and gradually gets worse as a person gets older

Parkinson's law /ˈpɑː.kɪn.sənzˌlɔː/ US /ˈpɑːr.kɪn.sənzˌlɑː/ **noun** [U] humorous the idea that any piece of work will increase to fill as much time as you have to do it in

park ˌkeeper noun [C] UK a person who is in charge of and takes care of a public park

parkland /ˈpɑːk.lænd/ US /ˈpɑːrk-/ **noun** [U] an area of open land with grass and trees: *The college is surrounded by 70 acres of parkland.*

parkour /pɑːˈkʊər/ US /ˈpɑːr.kʊr/ **noun** [U] **free running**

parkway /ˈpɑːk.weɪ/ US /ˈpɑːrk-/ **noun** [C] US a wide

P

road, usually divided, with an area of grass and trees on both sides and in the middle

parky /ˈpɑː.ki/ (US) /ˈpɑːr-/ **adj** [usually after verb] UK informal (of weather or the conditions in a room) quite cold: ***It's** a bit parky today, love – you'll want your coat!*

parlance /ˈpɑː.ləns/ (US) /ˈpɑːr-/ **noun** [U] formal a group of words or style of speaking used by a particular group of people: *Oral contraceptives are referred to in **common** parlance as 'the pill'.* ◦ *business/legal parlance*

parlay /ˈpɑː.li/ (US) /ˈpɑːr.leɪ/ **verb** [T] mainly US to use or develop money, skills, etc. in a way that makes more money or leads to success: *They parlayed a small inheritance **into** a vast fortune.*

parley /ˈpɑː.li/ (US) /ˈpɑːr-/ **noun** [C] old-fashioned or humorous a discussion between two groups of people, especially one that is intended to end an argument • **parley verb** [I] old-fashioned *After some serious parleying, both sides agreed to settle their differences.*

parliament /ˈpɑː.lɪ.mənt/ (US) /ˈpɑːr.lə-/ **noun** **1** B2 [C or U] in some countries, the group of (usually) elected politicians or other people who make the laws for their country: *On Tuesday the country's parliament voted to establish its own army.* ◦ *She was elected to Parliament in 1997.* **2** [C] a particular period of time during which a parliament is operating, between either holidays or elections

parliamentarian /ˌpɑː.lɪ.menˈteə.ri.ən/ (US) /ˌpɑːr.lə.menˈter.i-/ **noun** [C] **1** a member of a parliament, especially one who is respected for his or her experience and skill **2** US someone who is an expert on the rules and methods used by a group that makes laws or decisions

parliamentary /ˌpɑː.lɪˈmen.tᵊr.i/ (US) /ˌpɑːr.ləˈmen.t̬ɚ-/ **adj** of or relating to a parliament: *a parliamentary candidate/debate/election/session* ◦ *parliamentary procedures/rules*

parlour UK (US **parlor**) /ˈpɑː.ləʳ/ (US) /ˈpɑːr.lɚ/ **noun** [C] **SHOP** ▷ **1** a shop which provides a stated type of personal service or sells a stated product: *a beauty parlour* ◦ *an ice-cream/pizza parlour* **ROOM** ▷ **2** (especially in the past) a room in a private house used for relaxing, especially one which was kept tidy for entertaining guests: *the front parlour*

ˈparlour ˌgame UK (US **ˈparlor ˌgame**) **noun** [C] a game played inside a house, usually involving words or acting

parlous /ˈpɑː.ləs/ (US) /ˈpɑːr-/ **adj** formal very bad, dangerous, or uncertain: *Relations between the two countries have been in a parlous state for some time.* ◦ *I'd like to buy a new car, but my finances are in such a parlous **state** that I can't afford to.*

Parmesan /ˌpɑː.mɪˈzæn/ (US) /ˌpɑːr.məˈzɑːn/ **noun** [U] a hard, dry Italian cheese used especially in cooking: *grated Parmesan*

parochial /pəˈrəʊ.ki.əl/ (US) /-ˈroʊ-/ **adj** **OF A CHURCH** ▷ **1** connected with a PARISH (= an area that has its own church or priest): *parochial boundaries* **LIMITED** ▷ **2** disapproving showing interest only in a narrow range of matters, especially those that directly affect yourself, your town, or your country: *a parochial view/opinion* ◦ *Although it's just a local paper, it somehow manages not to be too parochial in its outlook.* • **parochialism** /-ə.lɪ.zᵊm/ **noun** [U] disapproving *political parochialism* • **parochially** /-ə.li/ **adv** disapproving

paˈrochial ˌschool **noun** [C] US a school controlled by a religious organization that usually receives no money from the government

parodist /ˈpær.ə.dɪst/ (US) /ˈper-/ **noun** [C] a person who writes parodies

parody /ˈpær.ə.di/ (US) /ˈper-/ **noun; verb**

▸**noun** **1** [C or U] writing, music, art, speech, etc. which intentionally copies the style of someone famous or copies a particular situation, making the features or qualities of the original more noticeable in a way that is humorous: *He was an 18th-century author who wrote parodies **of** other people's works.* ◦ *There is a hint of **self-parody** in his later paintings.* → Compare **travesty** **2** [C] disapproving something which so obviously fails to achieve the effect that was intended that it is stupid: *'It was a parody **of** a trial,' said one observer.*

▸**verb** [T] to copy the style of someone or something in a humorous way: *One of the papers is running a competition in which you've got to parody a well-known author.*

parole /pəˈrəʊl/ (US) /-ˈroʊl/ **noun** [U] permission for a prisoner to be released before their period in prison is finished, with the agreement that they will behave well: *He's been **released on** parole.* ◦ *She hopes to be **eligible for** parole in three years.* ◦ *Reynolds was sentenced to life **without** parole.* • **parole verb** [T]

paroxysm /ˈpær.ɒk.sɪ.zᵊm/ (US) /ˈper.ək-/ **noun** [C] a sudden and powerful expression of strong feeling, especially one that you cannot control: *In a sudden paroxysm **of** jealousy he threw her clothes out of the window.* ◦ *paroxysms of laughter*

parquet /ˈpɑː.keɪ/ (US) /pɑːrˈkeɪ/ **noun** [U] floor covering that consists of small rectangular blocks of wood arranged in a pattern → See also **woodblock**

parricide /ˈpær.ɪ.saɪd/ (US) /ˈper.ə-/ **noun** legal **1** [C or U] the crime of murdering a close relation, especially a parent → Compare **matricide, patricide** **2** [C] a person who has killed their father, mother, or another close relation

parrot /ˈpær.ət/ (US) /ˈper-/ **noun; verb**

▸**noun** [C] B1 a tropical bird with a curved beak, often kept as a pet and trained to copy the human voice

▸**verb** [T] disapproving to repeat exactly what someone else says, without understanding it or thinking about its meaning: *She doesn't have an original thought in her head – she just parrots anything that Sara says.*

ˈparrot-fashion **adv** UK If you learn or repeat a piece of text parrot-fashion, you learn or repeat the exact words, usually without understanding them.

parry /ˈpær.i/ (US) /ˈper-/ **verb** [T] **1** to defend yourself from a weapon or an attack by pushing the weapon away or by putting something between your body and the weapon **2** to manage cleverly to avoid dealing with a difficult question or some criticism: *Predictably the president parried enquiries about the arms scandal.* • **parry noun** [C]

parse /pɑːz/ (US) /pɑːrs/ **verb** [T] specialized to separate a sentence into grammatical parts, such as subject, verb, etc.

Parsi (also **Parsee**) /ˌpɑːˈsiː/ (US) /ˈpɑːr.siː/ **noun** [C] a member of a religious group found mainly in western India, whose religion, ZOROASTRIANISM, started in Persia (ancient Iran) • **Parsi adj**

parsimonious /ˌpɑː.sɪˈməʊ.ni.əs/ (US) /ˌpɑːr.səˈmoʊ-/ **adj** formal disapproving not willing to spend money or give something: *She's too parsimonious to heat the house properly.* • **parsimoniously** /-li/ **adv** • **parsimony** /ˈpɑː.sɪ.mə.ni/ (US) /ˈpɑːr.sə.moʊ-/ **noun** [U]

parsley /ˈpɑː.sli/ (US) /ˈpɑːr-/ **noun** [U] a herb with curly or flat leaves, used to add flavour to food and also to make it look attractive

parsnip /ˈpɑː.snɪp/ (US) /ˈpɑːr-/ **noun** [C or U] a long

P

cream-coloured root of a plant, eaten as a vegetable: *boiled/roasted parsnips*

parson /ˈpɑː.sᵊn/ (US) /ˈpɑːr-/ **noun** [C] old-fashioned or humorous any Christian priest

parsonage /ˈpɑː.sᵊn.ɪdʒ/ (US) /ˈpɑːr-/ **noun** [C] old-fashioned a house that was built for a parson

part /pɑːt/ (US) /pɑːrt/ **noun; verb; adv**

▸**noun SOME** ▷ **1** (A2) [U] some but not all of a thing: *Part **of** my steak isn't cooked properly.* ◦ *Part **of** this form seems to be missing.* ◦ *I think part **of** her problem is that she doesn't listen carefully enough to what other people say.* **2 in part** (C2) partly, or to some degree: *The deadline for applications is being extended, in part because of the postal strike.* **3 in (a) large part** to an important degree: *How quickly we can finish the project depends in (a) large part on when we get the payments through.* **4 for the most part** (C1) mostly or usually: *He was, for the most part, quite helpful.* **SEPARATE PIECE** ▷ **5** (A1) [C] a separate piece of something, or a piece which combines with other pieces to form the whole of something: *We learned about all the different parts **of** the digestive system.* ◦ *The lower part **of** her spine was crushed in the accident.* ◦ *I think there's always a part **of** you that doubts what you're doing.* ◦ *Fresh fruit and vegetables form an **essential/important** part **of** a healthy diet.* ◦ *There'll be snow **in** parts (= particular areas) **of** the Midlands tonight.* **6** (B2) [C] one of the pieces that together form a machine or some type of equipment: *He works for a company that makes aircraft parts.* **7** [C] a single broadcast of a series of television or radio programmes or a division of a story: *Next week we publish part three of 'The Diaries'.* ◦ *The programme will be shown in two parts.* **8** [C] one of two or more equal, or almost equal, measures of something: *Mix one part **of** the medicine with three parts water.* **9** (B1) [C] one of the characters in a film, play, or dance, or the words, actions, or movements that are said or done by that character: *He's got a small part in the school play.* ◦ *She **plays** the part of the sexy blonde waitress.* **10** [C] the music that a particular musician plays in a group **11 these parts** informal used to refer to an area of the country: *We don't see many foreigners **in** these parts.* **INVOLVEMENT** ▷ **12 take part** (B1) to be involved in an activity with other people: *She doesn't usually take part **in** any of the class activities.* **13** [U] involvement in or responsibility for an activity, or action: *He admitted his part **in** the robbery.* ◦ *I **want no** part **in/of** your crazy schemes!* **HAIR** ▷ **14** [C] US (UK **parting**) a line on someone's head made by brushing the hair in two different directions

IDIOMS **be part and parcel of sth** (C2) to be a necessary feature of a particular experience, which cannot be avoided: *Being recognized in the street is part and parcel of being a celebrity.* • **the best/better part of** (C2) most of: *I spent the better part of a day cleaning that kitchen!* • **dress/look/act the part** to look suitable or behave in a suitable way for a particular situation: *If you're going to be a high-powered businesswoman, you've got to look the part.* • **on the part of sb/on sb's part** (C2) done or experienced by someone: *This was a misjudgment on the part of the government.* ◦ *A little humility on her part would be appreciated.* • **part of the furniture** something or someone so familiar that you no longer notice them • **take sb's part** to support someone: *For once, my brother took my part **in** the argument.*

▸**verb 1** (C2) [I or T] to separate or cause something or someone to separate: *The curtains parted, revealing a darkened stage.* ◦ *To be parted **from** him even for two days made her sad.* **2** [T] If you part your hair, you arrange it so that it falls on either side of your head by separating it with a line down the middle or on one side. **3** (C2) [I] formal If two people part, they leave each other, often at the end of a relationship: *I'm afraid we parted on rather bad terms.*

IDIOMS **part company** If two people part company, they end their relationship: *The world's number one tennis player and his coach parted company earlier this month.* • **a parting of the ways** the point at which two people or organizations separate: *The parting of the ways came after a series of disagreements between the singer and his song-writer.*

PHRASAL VERB **part with sth** to give something to someone else, especially when you do not want to: *I was going to give away her old baby clothes, but I couldn't bring myself to part with them.*

▸**adv** partly: *He's part African – his father was born in Somalia.* ◦ *The exam is part spoken and part written.* • **part adj** [before noun] *He's (a) part **owner** of a racehorse (= he shares the ownership of it with other people).*

partake /pɑːˈteɪk/ (US) /pɑːr-/ **verb** [I] (**partook**, **partaken**) **EAT/DRINK** ▷ **1** old-fashioned or humorous to eat or drink: *Would you care to partake **of** a little wine with us?* **TAKE PART** ▷ **2** old-fashioned or formal to become involved with or take part in something: *She was happy to partake **in** the festivities.*

parted /ˈpɑː.tɪd/ (US) /ˈpɑːr.t̬ɪd/ **adj** separated: *He had neatly parted hair.*

ˌpart exˈchange **noun** [S or U] UK a way of paying for a new object that involves giving your old one as part of the payment: *I might offer them my old camera **in/as** part exchange for a new one.*

parthenogenesis /ˌpɑː.θə.nəʊˈdʒen.ə.sɪs/ (US) /ˌpɑːr.θə.noʊˈdʒen-/ **noun** [U] specialized a type of REPRODUCTION (= production of young plants or animals) in which living things develop from eggs that have not been FERTILIZED (= united with the male sexual cells)

partial /ˈpɑː.ʃᵊl/ (US) /ˈpɑːr-/ **adj NOT COMPLETE** ▷ **1** (B2) not complete: *The general has ordered a partial **withdrawal** of troops from the area.* **UNFAIR** ▷ **2** influenced by the fact that you personally prefer or approve of something, so that you do not judge fairly: *The reporting in the papers is entirely partial and makes no attempt to be objective.* → Opposite **impartial** **LIKING** ▷ **3** [after verb] old-fashioned or formal having a liking for something: *I'm rather partial **to** fish.*

partiality /ˌpɑː.ʃiˈæl.ə.ti/ (US) /ˌpɑːr.ʃiˈæl.ə.t̬i/ **noun** **UNFAIR** ▷ **1** [U] the fact of unfairly preferring or approving of something → Opposite **impartiality** **LIKING** ▷ **2** [C] old-fashioned or formal a liking: *He has a partiality **for** expensive suits.*

partially /ˈpɑː.ʃᵊl.i/ (US) /ˈpɑːr-/ **adv** (C1) not completely: *The meat was only partially cooked.*

ˌpartially ˈsighted **adj** People who are partially sighted are not completely blind but are able to see very little.

participant /pɑːˈtɪs.ɪ.pᵊnt/ (US) /pɑːrˈtɪs.ə-/ **noun** [C] (C1) a person who takes part in or becomes involved in a particular activity

> **! Common mistake: participate**
>
> When **participate** is followed by a direct object, remember to use the preposition **in**.
> Don't say 'participate something' or 'participate to something', say **participate in something:**
> ~~*She participates to a lot of sports activities.*~~
> *She participates in a lot of sports activities.*

P

participate /pɑːˈtɪs.ɪ.peɪt/ (US) /pɑːrˈtɪs.ə-/ **verb** [I] (B2) to take part in or become involved in an activity: *She never participates* ***in*** *any of our discussions, does she?* • **participatory** /pɑːˌtɪ.sɪˈpeɪ.tᵊr.i/ (US) /pɑːrˈtɪs.ə.pə-ˌtɔːr-/ adj

participation /pɑːˌtɪs.ɪˈpeɪ.ʃᵊn/ (US) /pɑːrˌtɪs.ə-/ **noun** [U] the fact that you take part or become involved in something

participle /pɑːˈtɪs.ɪ.pl̩/ (US) /ˈpɑːr.tɪ.sɪ-/ **noun** [C] the form of a verb that usually ends in 'ed' or 'ing' and is used as an adjective: *In the sentences 'He's sleeping' and 'I've already eaten', the words 'sleeping' and 'eaten' are both participles.*

particle /ˈpɑː.tɪ.kl̩/ (US) /ˈpɑːr.t̬ə-/ **noun** GRAMMAR ▷ **1** [C] a word or a part of a word that has a grammatical purpose but often has little or no meaning: *In the sentence 'I tidied up the room', the adverb 'up' is a particle.* SMALL PIECE ▷ **2** (C2) [C] an extremely small piece of matter: *Dust particles must have got into the motor.* ◦ *Electrons are atomic particles.*

ˈparticle acˌcelerator **noun** [C] in physics, a machine which makes extremely small pieces of matter travel at very high speeds, so that scientists can study the way they behave

particular /pəˈtɪk.jʊ.ləʳ/ (US) /pɚˈtɪk.jə.lɚ/ **adj; noun**
▸**adj** SPECIAL ▷ **1** (B2) [before noun] special, or this and not any other: *She wanted a particular type of cactus.* ◦ *He wouldn't take just any book – he had to have this particular one!* ◦ *'Why did you ask?' 'Oh, no particular reason, just making conversation.'* **2** **in particular** (B1) especially: *What in particular did you like about the last apartment that we saw?* ◦ *Are you looking for anything in particular?* NOT EASILY SATISFIED ▷ **3** (C1) [after verb] not easily satisfied and demanding that close attention should be given to every detail: *He's very particular* ***about*** *the kitchen – everything has to be perfectly clean and in its place.* ◦ *She's very particular* ***about*** *what she eats.*
▸**noun** **1** **particulars** [plural] details or information about a person or an event, especially when officially recorded: *There's a form for you to note down all your particulars.* **2** **the particular** formal If you are considering the particular, you are considering single examples rather than general matters or ideas: *The report focuses on the particular rather than the general and so doesn't draw any overall conclusions.*

particularity /pəˌtɪk.jʊˈlær.ə.ti/ (US) /pɚˌtɪk.jəˈler.ə.t̬i/ **noun** [U] formal **1** the quality of being exact or very detailed **2** **particularities** [plural] details: *The particularities* ***of*** *the case have not been revealed.*

particularly /pəˈtɪk.jʊ.lə.li/ (US) /pɚˈtɪk.jə.lɚ.li/ **adv** (B1) especially, or more than usual: *We're particularly interested to hear from people who speak two or more European languages.* ◦ *I didn't particularly want to go, but I had to.*

particulate /pəˈtɪ.kjuː.lət/ **noun** [C usually plural] specialized an extremely small piece of dirt, especially one produced by road vehicles, that causes POLLUTION

parting /ˈpɑː.tɪŋ/ (US) /ˈpɑːr.t̬ɪŋ/ **adj; noun**
▸**adj** [before noun] done while leaving or separating: *a parting glance/remark* → See also **parting shot**
▸**noun** SEPARATION ▷ **1** [C or U] a time when you are separated from another person, often for a long time: *They'd had an amicable parting.* ◦ *The pain of parting had lessened over the years.* HAIR ▷ **2** [C] UK (US **part**) a line on someone's head made by brushing the hair in two different directions: *a* ***centre/side*** *parting*

ˈparting ˌshot **noun** [C] a remark that you make when you are leaving, so that it has a stronger effect: *'And the dress that you bought me doesn't fit either!' was her parting shot.*

partisan /ˌpɑː.tɪˈzæn/, /ˈpɑː.tɪ.zæn/ (US) /ˈpɑːr.t̬ɪ.zən/ **adj; noun**
▸**adj** strongly supporting a person, principle, or political party, often without considering or judging the matter very carefully: *The audience was very partisan, and refused to listen to her speech.* ◦ *partisan politics* → See also **bipartisan**
▸**noun** [C] **1** (in a country that has been defeated) a member of a secret armed force whose aim is to fight against an enemy that is controlling the country **2** someone who supports a person, principle, or political party • **partisanship** /-ʃɪp/ **noun** [U] *There was a certain partisanship about the way that votes were cast.*

partition /pɑːˈtɪʃ.ᵊn/ (US) /pɑːr-/ **noun; verb**
▸**noun** DIVIDING STRUCTURE ▷ **1** [C] a vertical structure like a thin wall which separates one part of a room or building from another: *The partitions* ***between*** *the toilets were very thin.* NATIONAL DIVISION ▷ **2** [U] the dividing of a country into separate countries or areas of government: *The partition* ***of*** *India occurred in 1947.*
▸**verb** [T] DIVIDE ROOM ▷ **1** to divide one part of a room from another with a thin wall: *Why don't you partition that large room* ***into*** *a lounge and a dining-room?* DIVIDE COUNTRY ▷ **2** to divide a country into separate areas of government

partly /ˈpɑːt.li/ (US) /ˈpɑːrt-/ **adv** (B1) to some degree, but not completely: *His attractiveness is partly due to his self-confidence.* ◦ *The house is partly owned by her father.*

partner /ˈpɑːt.nəʳ/ (US) /ˈpɑːrt.nɚ/ **noun; verb**
▸**noun** [C] **1** a person or organization you are closely involved with in some way: *He gave up his job as a police officer after his partner was killed.* ◦ *The two companies are partners in a contract to build a new power station.* **2** (B2) one of the owners of a company: *He's a partner* ***in*** *an insurance company/a law firm.* **3** (B1) the person you are married to or living with as if you were married to them, or the person you are having a sexual relationship with: *I've invited David and his partner over for dinner.* **4** (A2) one of a pair of dancers or one of a pair who are playing a sport or a game together, especially when the pair are playing as a team
▸**verb** [T] If you partner someone in a sport, a game, or a dance, you act as their partner.

partnership /ˈpɑːt.nə.ʃɪp/ (US) /ˈpɑːrt.nɚ-/ **noun** **1** (B2) [C or U] the state of being a partner **2** [C] a company that is owned by two or more people: *the John Lewis Partnership*

ˌpart of ˈspeech **noun** [C] (specialized **ˈword ˌclass**) one of the grammatical groups, such as noun, verb, and adjective, into which words are divided depending on their use

partook /pɑːˈtʊk/ (US) /pɑːr-/ past simple of **partake**

partridge /ˈpɑː.trɪdʒ/ (US) /ˈpɑːr-/ **noun** [C] (plural **partridge** or **partridges**) a bird with a round body and a short tail that is sometimes hunted for food or for sport

ˌpart-ˈtime **adv, adj** (B1) If you work part-time or do part-time work, you work for only some of the day or the week: *a part-time job* ◦ *After my children were born I decided to* ***go*** *part-time.* → Compare **full-time**

ˌpart-ˈtimer **noun** [C] someone who works part-time

parturition /ˌpɑː.tjʊəˈrɪʃ.ᵊn/ (US) /ˌpɑːr.tuːˈrɪʃ-/ **noun** [U] specialized the act of giving birth

party /ˈpɑː.ti/ (US) /ˈpɑːr.t̬i/ **noun; verb**
▸**noun** CELEBRATION ▷ **1** (A1) [C] a social event where a

P

! Common mistake: party

Warning: Choose the right verb!

Don't say 'offer/make/prepare a party', say **throw/give/have a party**:

~~*I am making a surprise party for my sister.*~~

I am throwing a surprise party for my sister.

group of people meet to talk, eat, drink, dance, etc., often in order to celebrate a special occasion: *a birthday party* ◦ *a farewell party* ◦ *a dinner party* (= a small, sometimes formal party where a meal is eaten) ◦ *a **fancy-dress*** (US ***costume***) *party* (= a party where people wear clothes that make them look like someone or something else) ◦ *Peter **has/gives/throws** really wild parties.* **POLITICAL GROUP** ▷ **2** B1 [C, + sing/pl verb] an organization of people with particular political beliefs which competes in elections to try to win positions in local or national government: *the Democratic Party* ◦ *the Green party* ◦ *the Conservative party* ◦ *The party has/have just elected a new leader.* ◦ *He was elected as party **leader** in 2001.* ◦ *They contacted party **members** from across the nation to ask for their support.* **VISITING GROUP** ▷ **3** [C, + sing/pl verb] a group of people who are involved in an activity together, especially a visit: *a party of tourists* ◦ *Most museums give a discount to **school** parties.* **INVOLVEMENT** ▷ **4** [C] one of the people or groups of people involved in an official argument, arrangement, or similar situation: *The UN called on all parties **in** the conflict to take a positive stance towards the new peace initiative.* ◦ *It's often difficult to establish who the **guilty** party is following a road accident.*

Word partners for party noun (CELEBRATION)

have/give/go to/throw a party • a *birthday/Christmas/family/office* party • a *big/private/wild* party • *at* a party

Word partners for party noun (POLITICAL)

join/form/found/represent a party • a *political/left-wing/right-wing* party • the *governing/opposition/ruling* party • a party *activist/leader/member*

IDIOMS **be (a) party to sth** to be involved in something, especially something bad • **bring sth to the party** to have something such as a good quality to offer in a situation: *So what's Carter's involvement in all of this? What's he bringing to the party?*

▸verb [I] to enjoy yourself by drinking and dancing, especially at a party: *Let's party!*

ˈparty ˌanimal noun [C] informal someone who enjoys parties and party activities very much and goes to as many as possible

ˈparty ˌbag noun [C] (also **ˈgoody ˌbag**) a bag of small presents given to guests at a party

ˌparty ˈfaithful noun [plural] people who have been loyal members or supporters of a party for a long time: *This policy may appeal to the party faithful, but will it gain the support of uncommitted voters?*

ˈparty ˌfavor noun [C usually plural] US a small present given to guests, usually children, at a party: *He handed out the party favors as we were leaving.*

ˈparty ˌline noun [C] **POLITICS** ▷ **1 the party line** the official ideas and aims of a political party: *Her speech deviated little from the official party line.* **PHONE** ▷ **2** a phone connection that is shared by two or more customers with separate phones

ˈparty ˌpiece noun [C] UK humorous a short performance or an action done in public, especially one showing an unusual or humorous skill

ˈparty ˌplanner noun [C] someone whose job is to organize parties and social events for other people • **ˈparty ˌplanning** noun [U] *She runs a party planning business.*

ˌparty poˌlitical ˈbroadcast noun [C] UK (US **ˌpaid poˌlitical ˈbroadcast**) a short television or radio programme in which a politician talks about his or her party's ideas and plans in order to try to win more support

ˌparty ˈpolitics noun [plural] political activity and discussion within or relating to political parties rather than the whole country

party pooper /ˈpɑː.tiˌpuː.pəʳ/ US /ˈpɑːr.t̬iˌpuː.pɚ/ noun [C] humorous someone who spoils other people's enjoyment by disapproving of or not taking part in a particular activity

ˈparty ˌpopper noun [C] a small device, held in the hand, which makes a loud noise and produces many small strips of coloured paper when you pull the string on it

ˌparty ˈwall noun [C] UK (US **ˌcommon ˈwall**) a wall that divides two buildings that are joined together, and belongs to both of them

parvenu /ˈpɑː.və.nuː/ US /ˈpɑːr-/ noun [C] formal disapproving someone from a low social position who has suddenly become rich or successful

pas de deux /ˌpɑː.dəˈdɜː/ noun [C] (plural **pas-de-deux**) (in BALLET) a dance for two people, usually a man and a woman

pashmina /pæʃˈmiː.nə/ noun [C] a long piece of soft material such as wool that is worn by a woman around her shoulders. Some pashminas are made from the wool from a particular type of GOAT.

pass /pɑːs/ US /pæs/ verb; noun

▸verb **GO PAST** ▷ **1** B1 [I or T] to go past something or someone or move in relation to it or them: *I passed him on the stairs this morning.* ◦ *You should only pass a slower vehicle if it is safe to do so.* ◦ *I was just passing **by*** (= going past the place where you are), *so I thought I'd drop in for a chat.* ◦ *A momentary look of anxiety passed **across** his face.* ◦ *A cloud passed **over** the sun.* **2** [T] to go past a particular point in time: *Don't buy goods which have passed their sell-by date.* **3** C2 [T] to go past something by being greater in amount or degree: *The company's turnover is expected to pass **the** $10 million **mark** by the end of this year.* **4** C2 [I] If you say a state or feeling will pass, you mean it will disappear: *Don't worry, his depression is only temporary – it'll soon pass.* **SUCCEED** ▷ **5** A2 [I or T] to be successful in an exam, course, etc.: *Guess what? I've passed my driving test!* ◦ *The exam is so hard that only five percent of all applicants pass.* **GIVE** ▷ **6** B1 [T] to give something to someone: *Could you pass the salt please?* ◦ *I asked if I could see the letter, so she passed it **to** me reluctantly.* ◦ [+ two objects] *Gerald passed me the note./Gerald passed the note to me.* ◦ *Genes are the means by which parents' characteristics are passed **on to** their children.* **7** C2 [I or T] In sports, if you pass the ball, you kick, throw, or hit it to someone in your team. **8** [T] If you pass money, you give someone false or stolen money without telling them: [+ two objects] *I haven't trusted him since he passed me a forged £5 note.* ◦ *She was arrested for passing stolen cheques.* **TIME** ▷ **9** B1 [I] When time passes, it goes past: *Time seems to pass (**by**) so slowly when you're bored.* ◦ *I was a little worried about the party, but the evening passed without any great disasters.* **10** B2 [T] If you pass a period of

P

time, you do something to stop yourself being bored during that period: *The visitors pass their days swimming, windsurfing, and playing volleyball.* **APPROVE** ▷ **11** B2 [T] (of an official group of people) to give approval to something, especially by voting to make it law: *The government passed a law to restrict the sale of guns.* ◦ UK *The restaurant was serving meat that had not been passed **as** fit for human consumption.* **JUDGE** ▷ **12 pass judgment, comment, etc.** to express a judgment or opinion about something, especially someone else's behaviour: *As a convicted criminal, he's in no position to pass judgment (**on** the rest of us).* **13 pass sentence** to say officially, as a judge, what a criminal's official punishment will be **EXCRETE** ▷ **14** [T] formal to remove waste from the body: *to pass urine* **15 pass blood** formal to have blood in your urine or FAECES (= solid waste): *If you pass blood, you should go and see your doctor.* **NOT PLAY** ▷ **16** [I] to choose not to play in a part of a game or not to answer a question in a QUIZ **CHANGE** ▷ **17** [I usually + adv/prep] to change from one state to another: *Wax passes **from** solid **to** liquid when you heat it.*

IDIOMS **pass (all) belief** UK to be (extremely) difficult to believe: *It passes all belief **that** he could have been so selfish.* • **pass muster** to reach an acceptable standard: *New teams won't be admitted to the league if their stadiums don't pass muster.* • **pass the hat around/round** to try to collect money by asking people or organizations • **pass the time of day** to have a short informal conversation: *I was just passing the time of day **with** her.* • **pass water** polite expression for **urinate**

PHRASAL VERBS **pass sth around** B2 US for **pass sth round** • **pass as/for sth/sb** to appear to be someone or something else, or to cause people to believe that they are: *I really want to go and see the film, but I don't think I'd pass for 18.* ◦ *Do you think this jacket and trousers will pass as a suit? They're almost the same colour.* • **pass away/on** B2 polite expression for **die**: *She's terribly upset because her father passed away last week.* • **pass sb by** If an event or opportunity passes you by, you do not notice it, or get pleasure or an advantage from it: *Do you ever feel that life is passing you by?* • **pass sth down** [M often passive] to teach or give something to someone who will be alive after you have died: *His is a family trade, passed down **from** generation **to** generation.* • **pass off** [+ adverb] UK (US **come off**) to happen: *The pop festival passed off peacefully, despite the fears of local residents.* • **pass sth/sb off as sth/sb** to pretend that something or someone is a particular thing or person when they are not: *The dealer was trying to pass off fakes as valuable antiques.* • **pass sth on** **TELL** ▷ **1** B1 to tell someone something that another person has told you: *If he provided us with any information, no one passed it on **to** me.* **GIVE** ▷ **2** B1 to give someone something that another person has given you: *Could you pass it on to Laura when you've finished reading it?* **DISEASE** ▷ **3** to give a disease to another person: *It's possible to pass on the virus **to** others through physical contact.* • **pass out** **BECOME UNCONSCIOUS** ▷ **1** B2 to become unconscious for a short time, for example when ill, badly hurt or drunk: *I was hit on the head and passed out.* **LEAVE COLLEGE** ▷ **2** UK to leave a military college after successfully finishing the course: *The new officers passed out **from** Britannia Royal Naval College on Thursday 1 August .* • **pass sth out** US to give something to each person in a group of people: *The teacher passed out the test booklets.* • **pass sb/sth over** to ignore or not give attention to someone or something: *The woman alleges that her employers passed her over **for promotion** because she was pregnant.* • **pass sth round** UK (US **pass sth around**) B2 to offer something to each person in a group of people: *Could you do me a favour and pass these sandwiches round?* • **pass sth up** to fail to take advantage of an opportunity: *I can't believe she passed up the **chance** to go to South America.*

▸noun **EXAM RESULT** ▷ **1** B2 [C] UK a successful result in an exam: *Jon Hill achieved two grade A passes at A-level.* **2** [C] US a successful result in a course or exam for which the student will not be given a mark: *I got a pass in my Literature course.* **BALL** ▷ **3** C2 [C] a movement of the ball from one player to another member of the same team in a team sport **DOCUMENT** ▷ **4** B1 [C] an official document or ticket showing that you have the right to go somewhere or use a particular form of transport: *a bus pass* ◦ *a boarding pass* **PATH** ▷ **5** [C] a path or road between or over mountains: *a mountain pass* **BAD SITUATION** ▷ **6** [S] a difficult or unpleasant condition: *If I'd been aware things had **reached** such **a** pass, I'd have told the police.* ◦ UK *It's **come to a pretty** pass (= it's a bad situation) when you can't even have a few quiet drinks with some friends.* **SEXUAL ACTION** ▷ **7 make a pass at sb** informal to speak to or touch someone in a way that shows you would like to start a sexual relationship with them

passable /ˈpɑː.sə.bl/ (US) /ˈpæs.ə-/ adj **GO PAST** ▷ **1** possible to travel on: *Because of the heavy snow, roads were passable only with care in parts of Northern England.* **OKAY** ▷ **2** satisfactory but not excellent: *Mary can speak passable Russian.*

passably /ˈpɑː.sə.bli/ (US) /ˈpæs.ə-/ adv in a way that is satisfactory but not excellent

passage /ˈpæs.ɪdʒ/ noun **CONNECTING WAY** ▷ **1** B2 [C] (also **passageway**) a usually long and narrow part of a building with rooms on one or both sides, or a covered path that connects places: *A narrow passage led directly through the house into the garden.* ◦ *The bathroom's on the right at the end of the passage.* **2** [C] a hollow part of the body through which something goes: *the nasal passages* **PART** ▷ **3** B2 [C] a short piece of writing or music that is part of a larger piece of work: *Several passages **from** the book were printed in a national newspaper before it was published.* **TRAVEL** ▷ **4** [U] formal travel, especially as a way of escape: *The gunman demanded a plane and **safe** passage **to** an unspecified destination.* **5** [S] old-fashioned a journey, especially over the sea: *He had booked his passage **to** Rio de Janeiro.* **6 work your passage** old-fashioned to do work on a ship during your journey instead of paying for a ticket **MOVEMENT** ▷ **7** C2 [U] an act of moving through somewhere: *Many meteors disintegrate during their passage **through** the atmosphere.* ◦ *The government prohibits the passage of foreign troops and planes **across** its territory.* **TIME** ▷ **8 the passage of time** literary the process of time going past: *Memories fade **with** the passage of time.* **LAW** ▷ **9** [U] formal the official approval of something, especially a new law: *He again urged passage **of** a constitutional amendment outlawing abortion.*

passbook /ˈpɑːs.bʊk/ (US) /ˈpæs-/ noun [C] a small book that is used to officially record how much money is in a customer's bank account

ˈpass deˌgree noun [C] **DEGREE** ▷ **1** UK a degree given to university or college students who have passed their exams, but not well enough to get an HONOURS degree **DEGREE COURSE** ▷ **2** Australian English a degree course that is designed to be finished in three years instead of the usual four

passé /pɑːˈseɪ/ (US) /pæsˈeɪ/ **adj** disapproving no longer fashionable: *Wines from that region were quite popular for a while, but now they're rather passé.*

passenger /ˈpæs.ən.dʒər/ (US) /-dʒɚ/ **noun** [C] **1** (A2) a person who is travelling in a vehicle but is not driving it, flying it or working on it: *airline/rail/train/car passengers* **2 passenger train** a train carrying people rather than goods: *Two passenger trains were involved in the accident.*

passer-by /ˌpɑː.səˈbaɪ/ (US) /ˌpæs.ɚ-/ **noun** [C] (plural **passers-by**) someone who is going past a particular place, especially when something unusual happens: *The gunmen opened fire, killing a policeman and a passer-by.*

ˌpass-ˈfail adj mainly US If an exam or course is pass-fail, no mark is given for it, and the only thing the students are told about their performance is if they have passed.

passing /ˈpɑː.sɪŋ/ (US) /ˈpæs.ɪŋ/ **noun; adj**
▸noun **CONVERSATION** ▷ **1 in passing** If something is said in passing, it is said while talking about something else and is not the main subject of a conversation: *When asked if he had told the police about the incident, Mr Banks said he had* ***mentioned*** *it in passing to a detective.* **TIME** ▷ **2 the passing of time/the years** the process of time passing: *My parents seem to have mellowed* ***with*** *the passing of the years.* **3** [S] the death or end of someone or something: *Ten years after her death, the public still mourns her passing.* ◦ *the passing of the old year*
▸adj [before noun] **GOING PAST** ▷ **1** moving past: *A passing motorist stopped and gave her a lift to the nearby town.* **TIME** ▷ **2** lasting only for a short time and not important or complete: *I gave the restaurant a passing* ***glance*** *as I walked by, but I didn't notice who was in there.* ◦ *The matter is only of passing scientific interest.* **3** describes a period of time that is going past: *The situation seems to become more hopeless* ***with each/every*** *passing day.*

IDIOM **a passing resemblance** a slightly similar appearance: *He* ***bears*** *more than a passing resemblance* ***to*** *(= he is noticeably similar to) the young Marlon Brando.*

ˈpassing ˌlane noun [C usually singular] US for **overtaking lane**

ˌpassing-ˈout noun [S] UK the act of leaving a military college after successfully finishing the course: *His parents attended the passing-out ceremony.*

ˈpassing ˌshot noun [C] an occasion when you successfully hit the ball past the other player in tennis

passion /ˈpæʃ.ən/ **noun** [C or U] **1** (B2) a very powerful feeling, for example of sexual ATTRACTION, love, hate, anger, or other emotion: *Football* ***arouses*** *a good deal of passion among its supporters.* ◦ *At school, his early interest in music developed into an* ***abiding*** *passion.* ◦ *Politics and philosophy were his* ***lifelong*** *passions.* **2 a passion for sth** (C1) an extreme interest in or wish for doing something, such as a hobby, activity, etc.: *Anton has a* ***consuming*** *passion for science fiction.* **3 passions** [plural] very powerful feelings: *Touch a man's property and his passions are immediately aroused.*

IDIOM **passions run high** a way of describing a time when people feel strong emotions about a particular subject: *Passions run very high at election time.*

the ˈPassion noun [S] in Christianity, the suffering and death of Jesus Christ

passionate /ˈpæʃ.ən.ət/ (US) /-ə.nɪt/ **adj** (B2) having very strong feelings or emotions: *a passionate speech* ◦ *a passionate kiss/embrace* ◦ *The Italians are said to be the most passionate people in Europe.* ◦ *The child's mother made a passionate* ***plea*** *for help.* ◦ *Joe is passionate* ***about*** *baseball (= he likes it very much).* • **passionately** /-li/ (B2) *I walked into the room and found them kissing passionately.* ◦ *Ann has always believed passionately in women's rights.*

ˈpassion ˌflower noun [C] a tropical climbing plant with large colourful flowers and fruits called passion fruits

ˈpassion ˌfruit noun [C or U] a small fruit with thick purple or yellow skin and many seeds

passionless /ˈpæʃ.ən.ləs/ **adj** disapproving without any passion: *This music is passionless.*

ˈpassion ˌplay noun [C] a play that tells the story of the suffering and death of Jesus Christ

passive /ˈpæs.ɪv/ **adj; noun**
▸adj **BEHAVIOUR** ▷ **1** (B2) often disapproving not acting to influence or change a situation; allowing other people to be in control: *He's very passive in the relationship.* ◦ *Traditionally in the church women have been confined to more passive* ***roles.*** → See also **impassive GRAMMAR** ▷ **2** (B1) specialized describes the form of a verb used when the grammatical subject is the person or thing that experiences the effect of an action, rather than the person or thing that causes the effect: *'He was released from prison' is a passive sentence.* • **passively** /-li/ **adv** *He tends to wait passively for his boss to tell him what to do.*
▸noun [S] specialized **the passive** (B1) the form of a verb used when the grammatical subject is the person or thing which experiences the effect of an action, rather than the person or thing which causes the effect: *When changed into the passive, 'The dog chased the cat' becomes 'The cat was chased by the dog'.* → Compare **active**

ˌpassive-aˈggressive adj showing an unwillingness to be helpful or friendly, without expressing your anger openly: *passive-aggressive behaviour*

ˌpassive reˈsistance noun [U] the act of showing you oppose something in a peaceful way rather than using violence: *The Mahatma instigated several campaigns of passive resistance against the British government in India.*

ˌpassive ˈsmoking noun [U] the unwanted breathing in of other people's cigarette smoke, especially by people who do not smoke: *Doctors say passive smoking has caused his lung cancer.*

passivity /pæsˈɪv.ɪ.ti/ (US) /-ə.t̬i/ **noun** [U] the quality or state of being PASSIVE

passivize specialized (UK usually **passivise**) /ˈpæs.ɪ.vaɪz/ **verb** [T] to change a verb or sentence into the PASSIVE • **passivization** (UK usually **passivisation**) /ˌpæs.ɪ.vaɪˈzeɪ.ʃən/ (US) /-ɪ.vɪ-/ **noun** [U or C] the process of changing a verb or sentence into the PASSIVE

ˈpass key noun [C] a key for a door that is only given to people who are allowed to enter

ˈpass ˌmark noun [C] UK (US **ˈpassing ˌmark**) the number of points that must be achieved in order to be successful in an exam

Passover /ˈpɑːsˌəʊ.vər/ (US) /ˈpæsˌoʊ.vɚ/ **noun** [C or U] (also **Pesach**) a Jewish celebration in March or April every year to remember the escape of the Jews from Egypt

passport /ˈpɑːs.pɔːt/ (US) /ˈpæs.pɔːrt/ **noun** [C] **1** (A2) an official document containing personal information and usually a photograph which allows a person to

P

travel to foreign countries and to prove who they are: *Many refugees have arrived at the border without passports.* ◦ *He was a German, travelling* ***on*** *a Swiss passport.* ◦ *passport* ***control*** *(= the examining of travellers' passports)* ◦ *a passport* ***photo*** **2 a passport to sth** C2 a certain way of getting something you want: *Many students opt for business studies simply because it sounds like a passport to a good job.* ◦ *Beauty alone can be a passport to success.*

ˈpass ˌrate noun [C] the number of people, shown as a percent, who were successful in a particular exam

password /ˈpɑːs.wɜːd/ US /ˈpæs.wɝːd/ noun [C] B1 a secret word or combination of letters or numbers, used for communicating with another person or with a computer to prove who you are: *I can't let you in unless you* ***give*** *the password.* ◦ *You can't gain access to the computer system without* ***entering*** *your password.*

past /pɑːst/ US /pæst/ **preposition, adv; adj; noun**

▸**preposition, adv** **POSITION** ▷ **1** A2 in or to a position that is further than a particular point: *I live on Station Road, just past the post office.* ◦ *Three boys* ***went*** *past us on mountain bikes.* ◦ *Was that Peter who just jogged past in those bright pink shorts?* **TIME** ▷ **2** A1 used to say what the time is when it is a particular number of minutes after an hour: *It's* ***five/ten/a quarter/twenty/twenty-five/half*** *past three.* ◦ *I've got to leave at twenty past or I'll miss that train.* **3** B2 above a particular age or further than a particular point: *She's past the age where she needs a babysitter.* ◦ *Do what you want, I'm past* ***caring*** *(= I don't care any longer).*

IDIOMS **be past it** informal or humorous to be too old to do something: *Don't ask Andy to enter the race – he's past it!* • **be past your sell-by date** If someone is past their sell-by date, they are not wanted or useful any more because they are too old: *There's plenty of time to have a baby. I'm not past my sell-by date yet.* • **not put it past sb (to do sth)** informal to not be surprised if someone does something bad, because it is a typical thing for them to do: *Perhaps Helena told him – I wouldn't put it past her.*

P

▸**adj** **TIME BEFORE** ▷ **1** B1 [before noun] used to refer to a period of time before and until the present: *The average temperature worldwide has risen by about one degree Fahrenheit* ***in*** *the past 100 years.* ◦ *I've been walking three miles a day* ***for*** *the past 30 years.* ◦ *He was the fifth climber to die on these mountains* ***over*** *the past two days.* ◦ *In* ***centuries/years*** *past (= many centuries/years ago) even visiting the next village was considered a long journey.* **2** B1 [before noun] having happened or existed before now: *I know from past* ***experience*** *that you can't judge someone by their appearance.* ◦ *The prime minister's family have been instructed not to discuss his past* ***life*** *with the press.* **3** [after verb] finished: *I'm feeling much better now that the cold weather is past.* **GRAMMAR** ▷ **4** [before noun] of the past TENSE: *'Must' doesn't have a past form.*

▸**noun** [S] **TIME BEFORE** ▷ **1** B1 the period before and until, but not including, the present time: *Evolution can explain the past, but it can never predict the future.* ◦ ***In*** *the past, this sort of work was all done by hand.* ◦ *By winning the 1500 metres, he joins some of the great names* ***of*** *the past.* **2 a past** a part of someone's life in which they did unacceptable or dishonest things: *He's a man* ***with*** *a past.* **GRAMMAR** ▷ **3** A2 the form of a verb used to describe actions, events, or states that happened or existed before the present time: *The past of 'change' is 'changed'.*

pasta /ˈpæs.tə/ US /ˈpɑː.stə/ noun [U] A2 a food made from flour, water, and sometimes egg, that is cooked and usually served with a sauce. It is made in various shapes that have different names: *Spaghetti, lasagne, ravioli, and cannelloni are all types of pasta.*

the ˌpast conˈtinuous noun [S] (also **the ˌpast proˈgressive**) the grammatical form used for an action that someone was doing or an event that was happening at a particular time. It is made with 'was' or 'were' and the -ing form of a verb: *'I was cooking' is an example of the past continuous.*

paste /peɪst/ **noun; verb**

▸**noun** [U] **STICKY SUBSTANCE** ▷ **1** a thick soft sticky substance made by mixing a liquid with a powder, especially to make a type of glue: *flour-and-water paste* ◦ *wallpaper paste* **2** a thick soft substance made by crushing and mixing things such as fish, fruit, or vegetables for food: *tomato/anchovy/curry paste* **HARD MATERIAL** ▷ **3** specialized a hard type of glass used to make artificial JEWELS: *Are these real diamonds or paste?*

▸**verb** **STICK** ▷ **1** [T usually + adv/prep] to stick something to something, especially with paste: *You can make your own distorting mirror by pasting a sheet of kitchen foil* ***to*** *a piece of thin cardboard.* **COMPUTING** ▷ **2** [I or T] to move a piece of text to a particular place in a computer document: *Cut that paragraph and then paste it at the end of the page.*

pasteboard /ˈpeɪst.bɔːd/ US /-bɔːrd/ **noun** [U] a type of thick cardboard made from sheets of paper that have been stuck together with glue

pastel /ˈpæs.tᵊl/ US /pæsˈtel/ **noun; adj**

▸**noun** **MATERIAL** ▷ **1** [C or U] a soft, coloured substance, usually in the form of a small stick, that is used to draw pictures, or a picture made using this: *Do you like working with pastels/in pastel?* ◦ *The show includes 85 paintings, pastels, and sculptures.* **COLOUR** ▷ **2** [C] a colour that is pale and soft

▸**adj** [before noun] having a pale soft colour: *Their house is decorated in pastel* ***shades.***

ˈpaste-up noun [C] specialized a piece of paper to which text and pictures have been fixed while designing a magazine or book

pasteurize (UK usually **pasteurise**) /ˈpæs.tʃᵊr.aɪz/, /ˈpɑːs-/ US /ˈpæs.tʃə.raɪz/ **verb** [T] to heat something, especially milk, at a controlled temperature for a fixed period of time in order to kill bacteria: *pasteurized milk/cheese* ◦ *pasteurized beer* • **pasteurization** (UK usually **pasteurisation**) /ˌpæs.tʃᵊr.aɪˈzeɪ.ʃᵊn/, /ˌpɑːs-/ US /ˌpæs.tʃɚ.ɪ-/ **noun** [U]

pastiche /pæsˈtiːʃ/ US /pɑːˈstiːʃ/ **noun** [C or U] a piece of art, music, literature, etc. which intentionally copies the style of someone else's work or is intentionally in various styles, or the practice of making art in either of these ways: *The film is a skilful, witty pastiche* ***of*** *'Jaws'.*

pastille /ˈpæs.tᵊl/ US /pæˈstiːl/ **noun** [C] a type of small round sweet that can be sucked or CHEWED: *a throat pastille (= a sweet for people with a cough or a sore throat)*

pastime /ˈpɑːs.taɪm/ US /ˈpæs-/ **noun** [C] C2 an activity that is done for enjoyment: *Do-it-yourself is the nation's most popular pastime.* → Synonym **hobby**

pasting /ˈpeɪ.stɪŋ/ **noun** [S] mainly UK informal a severe beating, severe criticism, or a severe defeat in a game or competition: *The England team* ***got/took*** *a pasting in the semifinal.*

pastis /pæsˈtiːs/ **noun** [C or U] an alcoholic drink with an ANISEED flavour, or a glass of this

ˌpast ˈmaster noun [C] a person who is very skilled in a particular activity: *Joe is a past master* ***at*** *getting invitations to parties.*

pastor /ˈpɑː.stəʳ/ (US) /ˈpæs.tɚ/ noun [C] a religious leader in certain Protestant Churches

pastoral /ˈpɑː.stᵊr.ᵊl/ (US) /ˈpæs.tɚ-/ adj CARE ▷ **1** describes the part of the work of teachers and priests that involves giving help and advice about personal matters: *A priest's pastoral **duties** include helping the poor and sick.* ART ▷ **2** describes a piece of art, writing, or music that represents the pleasant and traditional features of the countryside: *The painting depicts an idyllic pastoral scene of shepherds watching over their grazing sheep.*

ˈpastoral ˌfarming noun [U] farming which involves keeping sheep, CATTLE, etc.

ˌpast ˈparticiple noun [C] the form of a verb, usually made by adding -ed, used in some grammatical structures such as the PASSIVE and the PRESENT PERFECT: *The past participle of 'cook' is 'cooked'.*

the ˌpast ˈperfect noun [S] the grammatical form used for an action that had already finished when another action happened. It is made with 'had' and a past participle: *'I had just cooked' is an example of the past perfect, and 'I had just been cooking' is an example of the past perfect **continuous**.*

pastrami /pæsˈtrɑː.mi/ (US) /pə-/ noun [U] spicy smoked BEEF usually cut in thin slices and eaten cold on bread

pastry /ˈpeɪ.stri/ noun **1** (C1) [U] a food made from a mixture of flour, fat, and water, rolled flat and wrapped round or put over or under other foods and baked: *shortcrust/puff/filo/choux/flaky pastry ∘ Ann makes delicious pastry – you should try her apple pie.* **2** (C1) [C] a type of sweet cake made of special pastry and usually containing something such as fruit or nuts: *We were offered a selection of cakes and pastries with our tea.* → See also **Danish pastry**

the ˌpast ˈsimple noun [S] (also **the ˌsimple ˈpast**) the form of a verb used to describe an action which happened before the present time and is no longer happening. It is usually made by adding -ed: *The past simple of 'cook' is 'cooked'.*

the ˌpast ˈtense noun [S] used to describe verb forms in many languages used for actions that have now finished. It is used by some people to refer to the past simple in English: *Add -ed to all these verbs to put them **in** the past tense. ∘ I think her husband must be dead – she always talks about him **in** the past tense.*

pasture /ˈpɑːs.tʃəʳ/ (US) /ˈpæs.tʃɚ/ noun [C or U] grass or similar plants suitable for animals such as cows and sheep to eat, or an area of land covered in this: *The sheep were grazing on the lush green pastures. ∘ Some fields are planted with crops for several years, and then returned to pasture for the cattle.*

IDIOMS **greener pastures** (UK also **pastures new**, US also **new pastures**) a new place or activity that offers new opportunities: *Many scientists working for the government have left for greener pastures in the private sector.* • **put sb out to pasture** informal to stop someone working in their job because they are too old to be useful

pasty noun; adj
▸noun [C] /ˈpæs.ti/ a piece of food made of pastry filled with meat, vegetables, or cheese: *a cheese-and-onion pasty*
▸adj /ˈpeɪ.sti/ disapproving (of someone's face or skin) very pale and unhealthy looking: *He's a rather unattractive man with long greasy hair and pasty skin.*

ˈpasty-ˌfaced adj looking pale and sick

PˈA ˌsystem noun [C usually singular] (also **PA**) a **public address system**

pat /pæt/ verb; noun; adj
▸verb [T] (-tt-) (C2) to touch someone or something gently and usually repeatedly with the hand flat: *He patted my head/patted me **on** the head affectionately. ∘ I bent down to pat the little puppy.*

IDIOM **pat sb on the back** to praise someone for doing something good

▸noun [C] TOUCH ▷ **1** the act of patting a person or animal: *I **gave** the little boy a pat **on** the head.* PIECE ▷ **2** a small flat piece, especially of butter

IDIOM **a pat on the back** praise: *I **got** a pat on the back **from** (= was praised by) my boss.*

▸adj usually disapproving describes an answer or remark that someone has previously prepared, so that they say it quickly and without any real thought: *The minister came out with a pat answer/response.*

IDIOM **have/know sth off pat** UK (US **have/know sth down pat**) to know something so well that you can say or do it without having to try or think: *I'd given the talk so many times I had it off pat.*

patch /pætʃ/ noun; verb
▸noun [C] AREA ▷ **1** (C2) a small area that is different in some way from the area that surrounds it: *Our dog has a black patch on his back. ∘ The hotel walls were covered in damp patches. ∘ There were lots of **icy** patches on the road this morning. ∘ This story is good **in** patches (= some parts are good), but I wouldn't really recommend it.* **2** informal a local area within which someone works: *He's been working as a policeman on the same patch for 20 years.* PIECE OF MATERIAL ▷ **3** (C2) a small piece of material fixed over something to cover it: *I'll have to sew a patch onto these jeans – they're ripped at the knee.* **4** a small piece of material that can be stuck to the skin, from which particular substances can be absorbed into the body: *Some people wear **nicotine** patches to help them give up smoking.* **5** an **eyepatch** COMPUTER ▷ **6** a small computer program that can be added to an existing program in order to make the existing program work as it should: *I downloaded a patch from their website.* → Compare **plug-in**

IDIOMS **go through a bad/difficult/rough/sticky patch** informal (C2) to experience a lot of problems in a period of your life: *Andy's going through a bit of a rough patch at the moment – his wife wants a divorce.* • **not be a patch on sth** UK informal to be much less good than something: *This new washing machine isn't a patch on our old one.*

▸verb CONNECT ▷ **1** [T usually + adv/prep] specialized to connect electronic or phone equipment to a system PIECE OF MATERIAL ▷ **2** (C2) [T] to put a patch on something

PHRASAL VERBS **patch sth together** to arrange something very quickly but not very carefully: *There is much disagreement, but the group of countries is trying to patch together a treaty on defence.* • **patch sth up** **1** (C2) to try to improve a relationship after there have been problems: *Jackie and Bill are still trying to patch up their marriage. ∘ Did you manage to patch **things** up **with** Jackie after your row?* **2** to repair something, especially in a simple and temporary way • **patch sb/sth up** to give basic medical care to someone that helps them temporarily: *If you've cut your hand, the first aider will patch you up.*

ˈpatch ˌpocket noun [C] a square of material sewn onto the outside of a piece of clothing for carrying things in: *a skirt with two patch pockets*

P

patchwork /ˈpætʃ.wɜːk/ (US) /-wɝːk/ **noun 1** [U] cloth made by sewing together a lot of smaller pieces of cloth with different patterns and colours, or the activity of doing this: *a patchwork quilt/jacket* ◦ *The old lady sat in the corner doing patchwork.* **2** [S] a mixture of different things: *We looked out of the aircraft window down onto the patchwork **of** fields below.*

patchy /ˈpætʃ.i/ **adj 1** only existing or happening in some parts: *The varnish is a bit patchy on this table.* ◦ *Southeast England will start with some patchy rain/patchy cloud at first.* **2** sometimes good and sometimes bad: *Matthew found the service extremely patchy.* • **patchily** /-ɪ.li/ **adv** • **patchiness** /-nəs/ **noun** [U]

pate /peɪt/ **noun** [C] old-fashioned or humorous the top of a person's head

pâté /ˈpæt.eɪ/ (US) /pætˈeɪ/ **noun** [C or U] a thick, smooth, soft mixture made from meat, fish, or vegetables: *liver/salmon/vegetarian pâté*

patella /pəˈtel.ə/ **noun** [C] (plural **patellae**) specialized a KNEECAP (= bone)

patent noun; verb; adj

▸**noun** /ˈpeɪ.tᵊnt/ (US) /ˈpæt.ᵊnt/ **LEGAL RIGHT** ▷ **1** [C] the official legal right to make or sell an INVENTION for a particular number of years: *In 1880 Alexander Graham Bell was granted a patent **on** an apparatus for signalling and communicating called a Photophone.* ◦ *The company **took out/filed** a patent **on** a genetically engineered tomato.* **LEATHER** ▷ **2** [U] **patent leather**

▸**verb** [T] /ˈpeɪ.tᵊnt/ (US) /ˈpæt.ᵊnt/ to get the official legal right to make or sell an INVENTION: *If you don't patent your invention, other people may make all the profit out of it.*

▸**adj OBVIOUS** ▷ **1** /ˈpeɪ.tᵊnt/ [before noun] formal very obvious: *a patent **lie*** ◦ *a patent disregard of the law* **LEGAL RIGHT** ▷ **2** /ˈpeɪ.tᵊnt/ (US) /ˈpæt.ᵊnt/ [before noun] A patent INVENTION is protected by law so that only particular people or companies have the right to make or sell it: *a patent screwdriver*

P

patentee /ˌpeɪ.tᵊnˈtiː/ (US) /ˌpæt.ᵊnˈtiː/ **noun** [C] specialized the person or organization that owns the legal right to make or sell something

ˌpatent ˈleather noun [U] (also **patent**) a type of leather that has a very smooth, shiny surface: *a purse made of glossy patent leather* ◦ *black patent shoes*

patently /ˈpeɪ.tᵊnt.li/ (US) /-tᵊnt-/ **adv** in a way that is clear: *She was patently lying.* ◦ *It's patently **obvious** that he doesn't care.*

ˌpatent ˈmedicine noun [C] a medicine, usually not very powerful, which you can buy from a shop without the written permission of a doctor

pater /ˈpeɪ.təʳ/, /ˈpɑː-/ (US) /ˈpɑː.t̬ɚ/ **noun** [C] UK old-fashioned formal father

paternal /pəˈtɜː.nᵊl/ (US) /-ˈtɝː-/ **adj** of or like a father: *He's very paternal (= showing the affectionate feelings of a father) – it's lovely to see him with the baby.* ◦ *My paternal grandparents (= my father's parents) were Irish.* → Compare **maternal** • **paternally** /-i/ **adv**

paternalism /pəˈtɜː.nə.lɪ.zᵊm/ (US) /-ˈtɝː-/ **noun** [U] usually disapproving thinking or behaviour by people in authority that results in them making decisions for other people which, although they may be to those people's advantage, prevent them from taking responsibility for their own lives • **paternalist** /-lɪst/ **noun** [C] • **paternalistic** /pəˌtɜː.nəˈlɪs.tɪk/ (US) /-ˌtɝː.nəˈlɪs-/ **adj**

paternity /pəˈtɜː.nɪ.ti/ (US) /-ˈtɝː.nə.t̬i/ **noun** [U] **1** the fact of being a father or connected with being a father: *Increasingly, the unmarried father of a child in Europe registers his paternity at the baby's birth.* **2** formal the origin of an idea or new product

paˈternity ˌleave noun [U] a period of time that a father is legally allowed to be away from his job so that he can spend time with his new baby

path /pɑːθ/ (US) /pæθ/ **noun** [C] **TRACK** ▷ **1** (A2) a route or track between one place and another, or the direction in which something is moving: *a garden path* ◦ *a concrete path* ◦ *a **well-trodden** path* ◦ *This is the path **to** the cliffs.* ◦ *It will be several days before snowploughs **clear** a path (**through**) to the village.* ◦ *They **followed** the path until they came to a gate.* ◦ *A fierce fire is still raging through the forest, burning everything in its path (= as it moves forward).* ◦ *The Weather Service issues warnings to people in the path **of** a hurricane (= in the area in which it is moving).* ◦ *The charged particles move in spiral paths.* ◦ figurative *His path through life was never easy.* **ACTIONS** ▷ **2** (B2) a set of actions, especially ones which lead to a goal or result: *The path **to** success is fraught with difficulties.*

IDIOM **paths cross** If two people's paths cross, they meet: *It was a pleasure meeting you – I hope our paths cross again.*

pathetic /pəˈθet.ɪk/ (US) /-ˈθet̬-/ **adj SAD** ▷ **1** (C2) causing feelings of sadness, sympathy, or sometimes lack of respect, especially because a person or an animal is suffering: *The refugees were a pathetic **sight** – starving, frightened and cold.* ◦ *After the accident he became a pathetic **figure**, a shadow of his former self.* → See also **pathos UNSUCCESSFUL** ▷ **2** (C2) disapproving making someone feel no respect, often because unsuccessful or showing no ability, effort, or bravery: *a pathetic attempt/joke/excuse* ◦ *Are you telling me you're frightened to speak to her? Don't be so pathetic!* • **pathetically** /-ɪ.kᵊl.i/ **adv** *Other former captives spoke of pathetically inadequate food rations.* ◦ *My parents' advice on sex was pathetically inadequate.*

paˌthetic ˈfallacy noun [U or S] specialized the use by a writer or poet of words that give human feelings or qualities to objects, nature, or animals, for example by referring to the 'cruel sea'

pathogen /ˈpæθ.ə.dʒən/ **noun** [C] any small organism, such as a VIRUS or a BACTERIUM that can cause disease: *a dangerous pathogen* • **pathogenic** /ˌpæθ.əˈdʒen.ɪk/ **adj**

pathological /ˌpæθ.əˈlɒdʒ.ɪ.kᵊl/ (US) /-ˈlɑː.dʒɪ-/ **adj NOT CONTROLLED** ▷ **1** informal (of a person) unable to control part of their behaviour; unreasonable: *I've got a pathological fear of heights.* ◦ *Anthony's a pathological **liar**.* **DISEASE** ▷ **2** relating to or caused by a disease: *a pathological condition/complaint* • **pathologically** /-kᵊl.i/ **adv**

pathologist /pəˈθɒl.ə.dʒɪst/ (US) /-ˈθɑː.lə-/ **noun** [C] an expert in the study of diseases, especially someone who examines a dead person's body and cuts it open to discover how they died

pathology /pəˈθɒl.ə.dʒi/ (US) /-ˈθɑː.lə-/ **noun** [U] the scientific study of disease

pathos /ˈpeɪ.θɒs/ (US) /-θɑːs/ **noun** [U] literary the power of a situation, piece of writing, work of art or person to cause feelings of sadness, especially because of sympathy: *There's a pathos in his performance which he never lets slide into sentimentality.*

pathway /ˈpɑːθ.weɪ/ (US) /ˈpæθ-/ **noun** [C] **1** a track which a person can walk along: *New pedestrian pathways are being built alongside the road.* **2** a PATH (= set of actions that you take in life): *Working your way up through a company is a difficult pathway.* **3** formal a set of connected chemical reactions in biology

patience /ˈpeɪ.ʃᵊns/ noun [U] **QUALITY** ▷ **1** (B2) the ability to wait, or to continue doing something despite difficulties, or to suffer without complaining or becoming annoyed: *You have to have such a lot of patience when you're dealing with kids.* ◦ *In the end I* ***lost*** *my patience and shouted at her.* ◦ *He's a good teacher, but he doesn't have much patience* ***with*** *the slower pupils.* ◦ *Making small-scale models* ***takes/ requires*** *a great deal of patience.* ◦ *Their youngest son was beginning to* ***try*** *my patience (= annoy me).* ◦ *Patience – they'll be here soon!* → Opposite **impatience** **CARD GAME** ▷ **2** UK (US **solitaire**) a game played with cards by one person

IDIOM **have the patience of a saint** to always be calm and never allow anything to upset you

patient /ˈpeɪ.ʃᵊnt/ noun; adj
▸noun [C] (B1) a person who is receiving medical care, or who is cared for by a particular doctor or dentist when necessary: *I'm a patient of Dr Stephens, please could I make an appointment to see her?*
▸adj (B1) having patience: *Dinner will be ready in half an hour – just be patient!* ◦ *Be patient* ***with*** *her – she's very young.* → Opposite **impatient** • **patiently** /-li/ adv (B2) *There was a queue of people* ***waiting*** *patiently for the bus to arrive.*

patina /ˈpæt.ɪ.nə/ (US) /ˈpæt̬.ᵊn.ə/ noun **1** [S] a thin surface layer which develops on something because of use, age, or chemical action: *His tomb was covered with* ***a*** *yellow patina* ***of*** *lichen.* **2** [S] formal something which makes someone or something seem to be something which they are not: *Beware their patina of civility, it's only an act.* **3** [U] specialized a blue-green layer that forms on COPPER, BRASS or BRONZE

patio /ˈpæt.i.əʊ/ (US) /ˈpæt̬.i.oʊ/ noun [C] (plural **patios**) an area outside a house with a solid floor but no roof, used in good weather for relaxing, eating, etc.: *In the summer we have breakfast out* ***on*** *the patio.*

patisserie /pəˈtiː.sə.ri/, /pætˈɪs.əʳ-/ noun **1** [U] cakes made in the French style **2** [C] a shop that sells these cakes

patois /ˈpæt.wɑː/ noun [C or U] (plural **patois**) the form of a language spoken by people in a particular area that is different from the standard language of the country: *the local patois*

patootie /pəˈtuː.ti/ (US) /-t̬i/ noun [C] informal mainly US an attractive woman

patriarch /ˈpeɪ.tri.ɑːk/ (US) /-ɑːrk/ noun [C] **RELIGION** ▷ **1** a BISHOP in certain Eastern Churches **SOCIETY** ▷ **2** the male leader of a family → Compare **matriarch**

patriarchal /ˌpeɪ.triˈɑː.kᵊl/ (US) /-ˈɑːr-/ adj ruled or controlled by men: *patriarchal structure* ◦ *a patriarchal society*

patriarchy /ˈpeɪ.tri.ɑː.ki/ (US) /-ɑːr-/ noun [C or U] a society in which the oldest male is the leader of the family, or a society controlled by men in which they use their power to their own advantage: *Patriarchy has not disappeared – it has merely changed form.* → Compare **matriarchy**

patrician /pəˈtrɪʃ.ᵊn/ adj formal of or like a person of high social rank • **patrician** noun [C]

patricide /ˈpæt.rɪ.saɪd/ (US) /-rə-/ noun [U] the crime of killing your own father → Compare **matricide, parricide**

patriot /ˈpæt.ri.ət/, /ˈpeɪ.tri-/ (US) /ˈpeɪ.tri.ɑːt/ noun [C] a person who loves their country and, if necessary, will fight for it

patriotic /ˌpæt.riˈɒt.ɪk/, /ˌpeɪ.tri-/ (US) /ˌpeɪ.triˈɑː.t̬ɪk/ adj showing love for your country and being proud of it: *patriotic fervour/pride* • **patriotically** /-kᵊl.i/ adv

patriotism /ˈpæt.ri.ə.tɪ.zᵊm/, /ˈpeɪ.tri-/ (US) /ˈpeɪ.tri-/ noun [U] the feeling of loving your country more than any others and being proud of it

patrol /pəˈtrəʊl/ (US) /-ˈtroʊl/ verb; noun
▸verb [I or T] (**-ll-**) (especially of soldiers or the police) to go around an area or a building to see if there is any trouble or danger: *The whole town is patrolled by police because of the possibility of riots.* ◦ *A security guard with a dog patrols the building site at night.* ◦ *Coastguards found a deserted boat while patrolling (along) the coast.*
▸noun **1** [C or U] the act of checking that there is no trouble or danger in a building or area: *a highway patrol* ◦ *Three reconnaissance aircraft are permanently* ***on*** *patrol.* **2** [C, + sing/pl verb] a small group of soldiers or military ships, aircraft, or vehicles, especially one which patrols an area: *Our forward patrol has/have spotted the enemy.*

paˈtrol ˌcar noun [C] an official car used by the police

paˈtrol ˌofficer noun [C] (male also **patrolman**) US a police officer who wears a uniform and patrols a particular area

paˈtrol ˌwagon noun [C] (also informal **ˈpaddy ˌwagon**) US a closed police vehicle used for transporting prisoners

patron /ˈpeɪ.trᵊn/ noun [C] **SUPPORTER** ▷ **1** a person or group that supports an activity or organization, especially by giving money: *The Princess Royal is a well-known patron* ***of*** *several charities.* **CUSTOMER** ▷ **2** formal a person who uses a particular shop, restaurant, hotel, etc., especially regularly: *Will patrons kindly note that this shop will be closed on 17 July .* → Synonym **customer**

patronage /ˈpæt.rə.nɪdʒ/, /ˈpeɪ.trᵊn.ɪdʒ/ noun [U] **SUPPORT** ▷ **1** the support given to an organization by someone: *The charity* ***enjoys*** *the patronage of many prominent local business people.* **2** mainly disapproving the power of a person to give someone an important job or position: *Patronage is a potent force if used politically.* **CUSTOMERS** ▷ **3** formal the business given to a shop or restaurant, etc. by its customers: *We would like to thank all of our customers for their patronage in the past.*

patronize /ˈpæt.rᵊn.aɪz/ (US) /ˈpeɪ.trᵊn-/ /ˈpæt.rᵊn-/ verb [T] **ACT SUPERIOR** ▷ **1** disapproving (UK usually **patronise**) to speak to or behave towards someone as if they are stupid or not important: *Stop patronizing me – I understand the play as well as you do.* **BE CUSTOMER** ▷ **2** formal (UK usually **patronise**) to be a regular customer of a shop or restaurant, etc.: *The restaurant was patronized by many artists and writers during the 1920s.*

patronizing (UK usually **patronising**) /ˈpæt.rə.naɪ.zɪŋ/ (US) /ˈpeɪ.trᵊn-/ /ˈpæt.rᵊn-/ adj speaking or behaving towards someone as if they are stupid or not important: *It's that patronizing tone of hers that I can't bear.*

ˌpatron ˈsaint noun [C] a Christian SAINT who is believed to give special help to a particular place, activity, person, or type of object: *St John Bosco is the patron saint* ***of*** *Turin.*

patsy /ˈpæt.si/ noun [C] US slang a person who it is easy to cheat or make suffer

patter /ˈpæt.əʳ/ (US) /ˈpæt̬.ə/ noun; verb
▸noun **SPEECH** ▷ **1** [U] continuous and sometimes funny speech or talk, especially used by someone trying to sell things or by an ENTERTAINER: *He should succeed – he dresses well and his* ***sales*** *patter is slick and convincing.* **SOUND** ▷ **2** [S] the sound of a lot of

P

things gently and repeatedly hitting a surface: *I find **the** patter **of** rain on the roof soothing.*

IDIOM **the patter(ing) of tiny feet** humorous something that you say which means that someone is going to have a baby: *Are you telling me we're going to be hearing the patter of tiny feet?*

▸**verb** [I usually + adv/prep] to make the sound of a lot of things gently and repeatedly hitting a surface: *I heard the rain patter **against/on** the window.* ◦ *We could hear mice pattering **about/around** looking for food.*

pattern /ˈpæt.ən/ Ⓤⓢ /ˈpæṭ.ɚn/ **noun; verb**

▸**noun WAY** ▷ **1** B2 [C] a particular way in which something is done, is organized, or happens: *The pattern of family life has been changing over recent years.* ◦ *A pattern is beginning to emerge from our analysis of the accident data.* ◦ *In this type of mental illness, the usual pattern is bouts of depression alternating with elation.* ◦ *Many **behaviour(al)** patterns have been identified in the chimp colony.* **ARRANGEMENT** ▷ **2** B1 [C] any regularly repeated arrangement, especially a design made from repeated lines, shapes, or colours on a surface: *Look, the frost has made a beautiful pattern on the window.* ◦ *The curtains had a **floral** pattern.* **EXAMPLE** ▷ **3** [C usually singular] something that is used as an example, especially to copy: *The design is so good it's sure to **set the** pattern for many others.* **DRAWING** ▷ **4** B2 [C] a drawing or shape used to show how to make something: *a knitting pattern* ◦ *a dress pattern* **PIECE** ▷ **5** [C] a small piece of cloth or paper taken from a usual-sized piece and used to show what it looks like: *a pattern book* → Synonym **sample**

> **Word partners for pattern (WAY)**
> *establish/fall into/follow* a pattern • *alter/change* the pattern (of sth) • a pattern *develops/emerges* • a pattern is *repeated* • a *familiar/general/normal/similar* pattern

> **Word partners for pattern (ARRANGEMENT)**
> *draw/make* a pattern • a *geometric/intricate/regular* pattern

▸**verb**

PHRASAL VERB **pattern yourself on sb/sth** to copy something or someone: *She patterns herself **on** her big sister.*

patterned /ˈpæt.ənd/ Ⓤⓢ /ˈpæṭ.ɚnd/ **adj** with a design made from repeated lines, shapes, or colours on the surface: *patterned textiles/wallpaper*

patty /ˈpæt.i/ Ⓤⓢ /ˈpæṭ-/ **noun** [C] a piece of food made into a disc shape that is then cooked: *minced meat patties/sweet corn patties*

paucity /ˈpɔː.sɪ.ti/ Ⓤⓢ /ˈpɑː.sə.ṭi/ **noun** [S] formal the fact that there is too little of something: *There is a paucity **of** information on the ingredients of many cosmetics.*

paunch /pɔːntʃ/ Ⓤⓢ /pɑːntʃ/ **noun** [C] a fat stomach, especially on a man • **paunchy** /ˈpɔːn.tʃi/ Ⓤⓢ /ˈpɑːn-/ **adj** • **paunchiness** /ˈpɔːn.tʃi.nəs/ Ⓤⓢ /ˈpɑːn-/ **noun** [U]

pauper /ˈpɔː.pər/ Ⓤⓢ /ˈpɑː.pɚ/ **noun** [C] a very poor person

pause /pɔːz/ Ⓤⓢ /pɑːz/ **noun; verb**

▸**noun** [C] B2 a short period in which something such as a sound or an activity is stopped before starting again: *There will be a brief pause **in** the proceedings while the piano is moved into place.* ◦ *After a long, awkward pause someone asked a question.* ◦ *She spoke for three quarters of an hour without so much as a pause.* ◦ *There followed a **pregnant** (= filled with meaning) pause in which neither of them knew what to say.*

IDIOM **give sb pause** formal to cause someone to stop and think about what they were doing or intending to do

▸**verb 1** [I] B1 to stop doing something for a short time: *He paused and thought for a moment.* ◦ *She paused to get her breath back and then carried on jogging.* **2** B2 [T, I] to make a recording stop for a short time by pressing a button: *Can you pause the movie there, please?*

pave /peɪv/ **verb** [T] to cover an area of ground with a hard, flat surface of pieces of stone, concrete, or bricks: *The area from the shops to the beach is paved **with** bricks set in patterns.*

IDIOMS **pave the way** C2 If something paves the way for/to something else, it makes the other thing possible: *Scientists hope that data from the probe will pave the way for a more detailed exploration of Mars.* • **paved with gold** used about a city to mean that it is easy to make money there: *Unemployed youngsters still come to London thinking that **the streets are** paved with gold.*

pavement /ˈpeɪv.mənt/ **noun** [C] **1** B1 UK (US **sidewalk**) a path with a hard surface on one or both sides of a road, that people walk on: *Keep to the pavement, Rosie, there's a good girl.* **2** B2 US the surface of a road when it has been covered with concrete or TARMAC

ˈ**pavement** ˌ**artist noun** [C] UK (US ˈ**sidewalk** ˌ**artist**) a person who draws pictures on a pavement using coloured CHALKS, especially so that people who walk past will give small amounts of money

pavilion /pəˈvɪl.jən/ **noun** [C] **BUILDING** ▷ **1** UK a building near a sports field, especially one where cricket is played, used by the players and sometimes by people watching the game **2** US one of a group of related buildings: *the West Pavilion of Central General Hospital* **3** US a large building in which sports or entertainment take place **TEMPORARY STRUCTURE** ▷ **4** a temporary structure, such as a large tent, especially used at public events or for shows

paving /ˈpeɪ.vɪŋ/ **noun** [U] a paved area, or material used to pave an area

ˈ**paving** ˌ**stone noun** [C] mainly UK a flat piece of stone, usually used in groups to cover a path or an area

pavlova /pævˈləʊ.və/ Ⓤⓢ /pɑːvˈloʊ-/ **noun** [C or U] a sweet cold dish consisting of a MERINGUE (= the transparent part of an egg cooked slowly with sugar) with a layer of fruit and cream on top

paw /pɔː/ Ⓤⓢ /pɑː/ **noun; verb**

▸**noun 1** B2 [C] the foot of an animal that has CLAWS or nails, such as a cat, dog, or BEAR: *I found paw **prints** in the kitchen.* → Compare **hoof 2** [C usually plural] informal humorous a human hand: *Take your filthy paws off my nice clean washing!*

▸**verb 1** [I or T] to touch something with a paw: *When their dog heard them it began pawing (**at**) the ground in excitement.* **2** [T] informal to feel or touch someone roughly with the hands, especially in an unpleasant sexual way

pawn /pɔːn/ Ⓤⓢ /pɑːn/ **noun; verb**

▸**noun GAME PIECE** ▷ **1** [C] any one of the eight least valuable pieces in the game of CHESS **2** [C] a person who does not have any real power but is used by others to achieve something: *The refugees are pawns **in** an international political dispute.* **MONEY** ▷ **3 in**

pawn left with a pawnbroker: *She had to put her ring in pawn to pay the bills.*
▸verb [T] to leave a possession with a pawnbroker in return for money, who can sell it if the money is not paid back within a certain time

pawnbroker /ˈpɔːnˌbrəʊ.kəʳ/ (US) /ˈpɑːnˌbroʊ.kɚ/ noun [C] a person who lends money in exchange for things which they can sell if the person leaving them does not pay an agreed amount of money in an agreed time

pawnshop /ˈpɔːn.ʃɒp/ (US) /ˈpɑːn.ʃɑːp/ **noun** [C] (also **pawnbroker's**) a shop where a pawnbroker operates their business

pawpaw /ˈpɔː.pɔː/ (US) /ˈpɑː.pɑː/ **noun** [C or U] **1** old-fashioned for **papaya** **2** (also **papaw**) US (the fruit of) a type of tree that grows in central and southern parts of the US

pay /peɪ/ verb; noun
▸verb (**paid, paid**) **BUY** ▷ **1** (A1) [I or T] to give money to someone for something you want to buy or for services provided: *How much did you pay* ***for*** *the tickets?* ◦ *I pay my taxes.* ◦ *Will you pay these cheques* ***into*** (US usually ***deposit*** *these checks* ***in***) *my account for me?* ◦ [+ two objects] *I'll pay you the fiver* ***back*** *tomorrow.* ◦ *I paid the driver* (***in/with***) *cash.* ◦ *Would you prefer to pay* ***with/by*** *cash, cheque or credit card?* ◦ [+ obj + to infinitive] *I think we'll need to pay a builder* ***to*** *take this wall down.* ◦ *Did Linda pay you* ***for*** *look****ing*** *after her cats while she was away?* ◦ *I paid* (***out***) *a lot of money to get the washing machine fixed and it still doesn't work!* **2 pay for itself** If something pays for itself, it works so well that it saves the same amount of money that it cost: *The advertising should pay for itself.*

> **! Common mistake: pay**
> When the direct object of **pay** is the thing that you buy, **pay** is always followed by 'for':
> ~~*You have to pay the tickets in advance.*~~
> *You have to pay for the tickets in advance.*
> In all other cases, **pay** is followed by the direct or indirect object only:
> *You have to pay the bill in advance.*
> *You have to pay £20 in advance.*
> *You have to pay the driver in advance.*

WORK ▷ **3** (B1) [I or T] to give money to someone for work which they have done: *The company pays £220 a week* ***for*** *people to act as couriers.* ◦ *Accountancy may be boring but at least it pays* ***well***. ◦ *Most of these women are very* ***poorly*** *paid and work in terrible conditions.* **PROFIT** ▷ **4** [I] to give a profit or advantage to someone or something: *It never pays* ***to*** *take risks where human safety is concerned.* **GIVE** ▷ **5** (C2) [T] to give or do something: *The commander paid* ***tribute to*** *the courage of his troops.* ◦ *It's always nice to be paid* ***a compliment***. ◦ *A crowd of mourners gathered to pay* ***their respects to*** *the dead man.* **6 pay attention (to sth)** (B1) to watch, listen to, or think about something carefully: *You weren't paying attention to what I was saying.* **7 pay (sb/sth) a call/visit** (B2) to visit a person or place, usually for a short time: *I'll pay you a call when I'm in the area.* ◦ *We thought we'd pay a visit to the museum while we were in Lisbon.*

> **! Common mistake: pay**
> **Warning:** Check your verb endings!
> Many learners make mistakes when using **pay** in the past tense. In the past simple and past participle, don't write 'paied' or 'payed', write **paid**.
> The **-ing** form is **paying**.

IDIOMS **he who pays the piper calls the tune.** saying said to emphasize that the person who is paying someone to do something can decide how it should be done • **pay your dues** to do something that you do not enjoy in order to have something that you want, or because you feel it is your duty • **pay your way** to pay for yourself rather than allowing someone else to pay • **pay dividends** If something you do pays dividends, it causes good results at a time in the future: *All that extra training is paying dividends.* • **pay the price** (C2) to experience the bad result of something you have done: *If you abuse your body now, you'll pay the price when you're older.* • **pay the ultimate price** to die because of something you have done, especially something you do for moral reasons: *These soldiers have paid the ultimate price for their country's freedom.* • **pay through the nose** informal to pay too much money for something: *We paid through the nose to get the car fixed and it still doesn't go properly.* • **pay top dollar** US to pay a lot of money for something • **put paid to sth** UK to finish or destroy something: *A knee injury has put paid to her chances of getting into the final.*

PHRASAL VERBS **pay sb/sth back** (B1) to pay someone the money that you owe them: *Can you lend me a fiver? I'll pay you/it back tomorrow.* • **pay sb back** to do something unpleasant to someone because they have done something unpleasant to you: *He swore he'd pay her back* ***for*** *all she'd done to him.* • **pay for sth** (C2) to be punished for doing something bad to someone else, or to suffer because of a mistake that you made: *We all pay for our mistakes in some way at some time.* ◦ *He tricked me and I'm going to make him pay for it!* • **pay sth in** (US usually **deposit**) to put money into a bank account: *If you go to the bank, will you pay these cheques in for me?* • **pay off** (B2) If something you have done pays off, it is successful: *All her hard work paid off in the end, and she finally passed the exam.* • **pay sth off** (B2) to pay back money that you owe: *We should be able to pay off the debt within two years.* • **pay sb off 1** If your employer pays you off, they pay you for the last time and then end your job, because they do not need you or could not pay you in the future. **2** informal to give someone money so that they will not do or say something, or so that they will go away: *There were rumours that key witnesses had been paid off to keep quiet.* • **pay (sth) out** to spend a lot of money on something, or to pay a lot of money to someone: *I've just paid out £500 on getting the car fixed.* • **pay sth out** to release a piece of rope or CABLE in a controlled way • **pay up** informal to give someone the money that you owe them, especially when you

> **! Usage: pay, wage, salary, or income?**
> **Pay** is a general word which means the money that you receive for working:
> *Doctors usually get more pay than teachers.*
> A **wage** is an amount of money you receive each day or week. It is often paid in **cash** (= notes and coins):
> *His weekly wage is $400.*
> A **salary** is the money you receive each month. A person's **salary** is often expressed as the total amount in a year:
> *His salary is £20,000.*
> Your **income** is the total amount of money that you get by working or other sources:
> *She has a monthly income of £1,400.*

P

do not want to: *Eventually they paid up, but only after receiving several reminders.*

▸**noun** [U] **1** B1 the money you receive for doing a job: UK *Any pay **rise*** (US usually ***raise***) *must be in line with inflation.* ◦ *It's a nice job but the pay is appalling.* **2 be in the pay of sb** to work for someone, especially secretly

payable /ˈpeɪ.ə.bl/ adj [after verb] **1** C1 that should be paid: *Interest payments are payable monthly.* **2** C1 If a CHEQUE is payable to a person or an organization, the money will be paid to them because their name is written on it: *Please make your cheque payable to WWF.*

ˌpay-as-you-ˈgo adj [before noun] describes a system in which you pay for a service before you use it and you cannot use more than you have paid for: *a pay-as-you-go mobile phone*

payback /ˈpeɪ.bæk/ noun [C or U] mainly US an advantage received from something, especially the profit from a financial INVESTMENT: *The payback for reorganization should be increased productivity.*

ˈpayback ˌperiod noun [C or U] the amount of time it takes to get back the amount of money originally INVESTED (= given to companies hoping to get more back) in something

ˈpay ˌchannel noun [C] a television CHANNEL (= a broadcasting company) that you pay money to watch

paycheck /ˈpeɪ.tʃek/ noun [C] US for **pay packet**

ˈpay ˌclaim noun [C] UK a demand for an increase in pay: *As expected, management said the workers' pay claim was too high.*

payday /ˈpeɪ.deɪ/ noun [U] the day on which a worker receives their pay

PAYE /ˌpiː.eɪ.waɪˈiː/ noun [U] UK abbreviation for Pay As You Earn: a system for collecting income tax in which a person's tax is taken away and sent to the government by their employer before they are paid

payee /peɪˈiː/ noun [C] specialized a person who money is paid to or should be paid to

payer /ˈpeɪ.əʳ/ US /ˈpeɪ.ɚ/ noun **1 good/bad payer** a person who usually pays on time/late **2** [C] used as a combining form meaning a person who pays something: *a tax payer*

payload /ˈpeɪ.ləʊd/ US /-loʊd/ noun [C] **1** the amount of goods or people that a vehicle, such as a truck or aircraft, can carry **2** the explosive that a MISSILE carries **3** the equipment carried in a spacecraft

paymaster /ˈpeɪˌmɑː.stəʳ/ US /-ˌmæs.tɚ/ noun [C] a person or an organization that pays for something to happen and therefore has or expects to have some control over it: *The government accused the opposition parties of being controlled by trade union paymasters.*

payment /ˈpeɪ.mənt/ noun **1** B2 [C or U] an amount of money paid: *Usually we ask for payment on receipt of the goods.* ◦ *We need a deposit of £165 followed by twelve monthly payments of £60.* ◦ *When is the first payment **due**?* **2** [S or U] reward: *Verbal abuse was hardly the payment I expected **for** my troubles.* **3 back payment** an amount of money received by an employee because of a pay rise at an earlier time

> Word partners for **payment**
>
> *make/receive* a payment • *demand/withhold* payment • an *advance/monthly/regular* payment • payment is *due* • a *form/method* of payment • payment *for/of* sth

payoff /ˈpeɪ.ɒf/ US /-ɑːf/ noun [C] **RESULT** ▷ **1** informal the result of a set of actions, or an explanation at the end of something: *The payoff for years of research is a microscope which performs better than all of its competitors.* **MONEY** ▷ **2** money paid to someone, especially so that they do not cause trouble or so that they will do what you want them to: *It has been alleged that the minister received a secret payoff from an arms dealer.*

payola /peɪˈəʊ.lə/ US /-ˈoʊ-/ noun [C or U] mainly US old-fashioned informal a secret payment to someone for doing an illegal business action

payout /ˈpeɪ.aʊt/ noun [C] a large amount of money that is paid to someone

ˈpay ˌpacket noun [C] UK (US **paycheck**) the amount of money a person earns

ˌpay-per-ˈview noun [U] (also **PPV**) a system for watching television in which people pay for the particular programmes that they watch: *pay-per-view television/channels* ◦ *We watched the boxing match **on** pay-per-view.*

payphone UK (US **ˈpay ˌphone**) /ˈpeɪ.fəʊn/ US /-foʊn/ noun [C] a public phone where you can make calls that you pay for using coins, a CREDIT CARD, or a PHONE CARD

ˈpay ˌrise noun [C] UK (US **ˈpay ˌraise**) C1 an increase in the amount of money you earn for doing your job

payroll /ˈpeɪ.rəʊl/ US /-roʊl/ noun **1** [C] a list of the people employed by a company showing how much each one earns: *a payroll tax* ◦ *McDermot Software is growing fast, adding another 100 employees to its payroll over the last year.* **2** [C usually singular] the total amount of money paid to the people employed by a particular company: *With debts of $4 million and a monthly payroll of $1.2 million, the venture is clearly heading for trouble.*

payslip /ˈpeɪ.slɪp/ noun [C] a piece of paper given to someone who is employed to show how much money they have earned and how much tax has been taken away

ˌpay TˈV noun [U] (also **ˌpay teleˈvision**) television stations that you must pay to watch: *Do you have pay TV?*

paywall /ˈpeɪ.wɔːl/ US /-wɑːl/ noun [C] a program that stops people who have not paid a SUBSCRIPTION from using a website

PBS /ˌpiː.biːˈes/ noun abbreviation for Public Broadcasting Service: a US organization broadcasting generally educational television programmes that is paid for by the people who watch it rather than from advertising

pc written abbreviation for **percent**: *an increase of 22 pc*

PC /ˌpiːˈsiː/ noun; adj

▸**noun** [C] **COMPUTER** ▷ **1** A2 abbreviation for **personal computer**: *The price of PCs has been tumbling recently.* **POLICE** ▷ **2** UK abbreviation for **police constable**: *PC Owens* → See also **WPC**

▸**adj** abbreviation for **politically correct**

PCB /ˌpiː.siːˈbiː/ noun [C or U] abbreviation for polychlorinated biphenyl: a harmful chemical that is used in industry

p.c.m. /ˌpiː.siːˈem/ adv (also **pcm**) UK abbreviation for **per calendar month**: *Fully furnished house to let, £650 p.c.m., quiet location.*

PDA /ˌpiː.diːˈeɪ/ noun [C] abbreviation for **personal digital assistant**: (= a small computer that you can carry with you)

PDF /ˌpiː.diːˈef/ noun [C or U] abbreviation for portable document format: a system for storing and sending documents between computers that does not allow the contents to be changed, or a document created using this system: *a PDF file*

PDQ /ˌpiː.diːˈkjuː/ adv informal pretty damn quick: very quickly or soon: *The phone bill's overdue – we need to pay it PDQ.*

PE /ˌpiːˈiː/ noun [U] abbreviation for **physical education**

pea /piː/ noun [C] **B1** a round, green seed, several of which grow in a POD, eaten as a vegetable: *frozen/dried peas* ◦ *pea soup*

peabrain /ˈpiː.breɪn/ noun [C] informal an extremely stupid person

peabrained /ˈpiː.breɪnd/ adj informal extremely stupid

peace /piːs/ noun [U] **NO VIOLENCE** ▷ **1** **B2** freedom from war and violence, especially when people live and work together happily without disagreements: *peace talks/proposals* ◦ *a peace conference/initiative* ◦ *Now that the war is over may there be **a lasting** peace between our nations.* ◦ *Peace lasted in Europe for just over 20 years after 1918 before war broke out again.* ◦ *She's very good at **keeping** (the) peace within the family.* ◦ *The police act on the public's behalf to **keep the** peace.* ◦ *Stop fighting you two – shake hands and **make** (your) peace (with each other)!* **CALM** ▷ **2** **B1** the state of not being interrupted or annoyed by worry, problems, noise, or unwanted actions: *You'll need peace **and quiet** to study.* ◦ *He says he's **at** peace when he's walking in the mountains.* ◦ *Go away and **leave** us to finish our dinner **in** peace.* ◦ *For everyone's peace **of mind** go back and check you locked the door.* ◦ *There'll be **no** peace until she gets what she wants.* ◦ *I didn't agree with what she said but I **held** my peace (= did not say anything).*

> **Word partners for peace**
>
> *bring about/establish/restore* peace • *make* peace *with* sb • a *fragile/lasting/uneasy* peace • a peace *agreement/initiative/treaty* • the peace *process* • peace *between* sb • be *at* peace

IDIOMS **at peace** a gentle way of saying that someone is dead: *Now she is at peace and her suffering is over.* • **be at peace with the world** to be feeling calm and happy because you are satisfied with your life

peaceable /ˈpiː.sə.bl/ adj **1** without violence; peaceful: *They believe only in peaceable, non-violent protest.* **2** avoiding arguments: *a peaceable person* • **peaceably** /-bli/ adv

the ˈPeace ˌCorps noun [+ sing/pl verb] an organization in the US that sends people to work as VOLUNTEERS (= people who work without being paid) in poor countries

ˈpeace ˌdividend noun [C usually singular] the money saved by a country when it no longer needs to make or buy weapons because the threat of war has grown less

peaceful /ˈpiːs.fᵊl/ adj **NO VIOLENCE** ▷ **1** **B2** without violence: *peaceful demonstrators* ◦ *She hoped the different ethnic groups in the area could live together in peaceful co-existence.* **CALM** ▷ **2** **B1** quiet and calm: *a peaceful afternoon/place* • **peacefully** /-i/ adv **B2** *He was back in her arms and she could once again sleep peacefully.* • **peacefulness** /-nəs/ noun [U]

peacekeeping /ˈpiːsˌkiː.pɪŋ/ noun [U] the activity of preventing war and violence, especially using armed forces not involved in a disagreement to prevent fighting: *a peacekeeping force/mission* • **peacekeeper** /-pəʳ/ (US) /-pɚ/ noun [C]

ˈpeace-ˌloving adj liking peace and trying to live and act in a way which will bring it: *a peace-loving people/nation*

peacemaker /ˈpiːsˌmeɪ.kəʳ/ (US) /-kɚ/ noun [C] a person who tries to stop people from arguing or fighting

ˈpeace ˌoffering noun [C] something said or given by a person to show that they want to be friendly, especially to someone they have argued with

ˈpeace ˌpipe noun [C] a decorated tobacco PIPE used by Native Americans at official events, especially as a sign of peace

ˈpeace ˌsign noun [C] a sign made with the hand by holding it with the PALM forward and the first two fingers in the shape of a V, used to express peace → See also **V-sign**

peacetime /ˈpiːs.taɪm/ noun [U] a period of time when a country is not at war → Compare **wartime**

peach /piːtʃ/ noun; adj

▸noun **FRUIT** ▷ **1** **B1** [C or U] a round fruit with sweet yellow flesh that has a lot of juice, a slightly FURRY red and yellow skin, and a large seed in its centre: *Would you like peaches **and cream** for dessert?* **EXCELLENT** ▷ **2** [S] informal someone or something that is excellent or very pleasing **COLOUR** ▷ **3** [U] a pale colour between pink and orange

▸adj having a pale colour between pink and orange

peach Melba /ˌpiːtʃˈmel.bə/ noun [C or U] a sweet food made from half a peach, ice cream, and pressed RASPBERRIES

peachy /ˈpiː.tʃi/ adj informal very good

peacock /ˈpiː.kɒk/ (US) /-kɑːk/ noun [C] **1** a large bird, the male of which has very long tail feathers that it can spread out to show bright colours and patterns shaped like eyes **2** old-fashioned disapproving a man is who is very proud of his appearance and gives a lot of attention to his clothes and the way he dresses

peacock

ˌpeacock ˈblue noun [U] a bright, slightly greenish-blue colour • **ˌpeacock-ˈblue** adj

ˌpea ˈgreen noun [U] a bright, yellowish-green colour • **ˌpea-ˈgreen** adj

peahen /ˈpiː.hen/ noun [C] a female PEACOCK

peak /piːk/ noun; adj; verb

▸noun [C] **HIGHEST POINT** ▷ **1** **B2** the highest, strongest, or best point, value, or level of skill: *Holiday flights **reach** a peak during August.* ◦ *Beat the egg whites until they are stiff enough to form firm peaks.* ◦ *We saw a victory by an athlete **at** the very peak of her fitness and career.* **MOUNTAIN** ▷ **2** **B1** the pointed top of a mountain, or the mountain itself: *It is one of the most difficult peaks to climb.* **HAT PART** ▷ **3** mainly UK (US usually **visor**) the flat curved part of a CAP which goes above the eyes of the person who is wearing it

▸adj [before noun] **1** peak times are the times when most people are using or doing something: *Traffic congestion is really bad at peak **periods** (= when it is most busy).* ◦ *It is most expensive to advertise at peak viewing times (= those with the most people watching).* ◦ *Don't go there in the peak (= busiest) **season** – it'll be hot and crowded.* **2** peak levels or rates are when they are at their highest: *peak rate electricity*

▸verb [I] to reach the highest, strongest, or best point, value, or level of skill: *Official figures show that unemployment peaked in November.*

peaked /piːkt/ adj **HAT PART** ▷ **1** describes a hat with a peak at the front: *a peaked cap* **HIGH POINT** ▷ **2** rising to a point **ILL** ▷ **3** US informal **peaky**

P

peaky /ˈpiː.ki/ adj mainly UK (US usually **peaked**) slightly ill, often looking pale: *You look **a bit** peaky, love, are you all right?*

peal /piːl/ verb; noun

▸verb [I] When bells peal, they ring with a loud sound: *After their wedding the bells pealed **out** from the tower.*

▸noun [C] **1** a long loud sound or series of sounds, especially of laughter or thunder: *Her suggestion was met with peals **of laughter**.* ◦ *A loud peal **of thunder** woke him from restless sleep.* **2** a long loud ring: *When we heard the peal of (the) bells, we knew a truce had been declared.*

peanut /ˈpiː.nʌt/ noun **NUT** ▷ **1** (B1) [C] (UK specialized also **groundnut**) an oval-shaped nut that grows underground in pairs inside a thin brown shell: *peanut/groundnut oil* ◦ *salted/dry-roast(ed) peanuts* **LITTLE MONEY** ▷ **2 peanuts** [plural] informal something so small it is not worth considering, especially an amount of money: *They **pay** people peanuts in that organization.*

ˌpeanut ˈbutter noun [U] (US **ˈpeanut ˌbutter**) a soft, pale brown substance made from crushed peanuts, often eaten spread on bread

pear /peəʳ/ (US) /per/ **noun** [C or U] (A2) a sweet fruit with a lot of juice and a green skin which has a round base and is slightly pointed towards the stem

pearl /pɜːl/ (US) /pɝːl/ **noun 1** [C or U] a small, round object, usually white, that forms around a grain of sand inside the shell of a sea creature, especially an OYSTER. Pearls are valuable and are used to make jewellery: *a string of pearls* ◦ *a pearl necklace* **2 pearls** [plural] jewellery made from pearls: *He gave her pearls for her birthday.* **3** [C] an artificially made pearl: *cultured pearls* **4** [C] literary a small drop of liquid: *There were pearls **of** dew on the grass.* **5** [U] the white shiny colour of pearl or a pale colour **6** [U] **mother-of-pearl**: *pearl buttons*

IDIOM **a pearl of great price** UK formal something that is very rare and is considered very important: *Inexhaustible patience is a pearl of great price.*

pearly /ˈpɜː.li/ (US) /ˈpɝː-/ **adj** white and shiny, like a pearl: *pearly white teeth*

the ˌpearly ˈgates noun [plural] humorous the imaginary entrance to heaven

ˈpear-shaped adj shaped like a pear: *a pear-shaped physique*

IDIOM **go pear-shaped** UK informal If a plan goes pear-shaped, it fails: *We'd planned to go away for the weekend, but it **all** went pear-shaped.*

peasant /ˈpez.ᵊnt/ noun [C] **1** (C1) a person who owns or rents a small piece of land and grows crops, keeps animals, etc. on it, especially one who has a low income, very little education and a low social position. This is usually used of someone who lived in the past or of someone in a poor country: *Tons of internationally donated food was distributed to the starving peasants.* ◦ *Most of the produce sold in the market is grown by peasant farmers.* **2** informal disapproving a person who is not well educated or is rude and does not behave well: *Joe's a real peasant.*

peasantry /ˈpez.ᵊn.tri/ **noun** [U] especially in the past, all the people who were peasants

peashooter /ˈpiː.ʃuː.təʳ/ (US) /-t̬ɚ/ **noun** [C] **1** a long, thin tube through which small objects, especially dried PEAS, can be blown in order to hit something **2** US a small weapon, especially a gun, that is not very effective

pea-souper /ˌpiːˈsuː.pəʳ/ (US) /-pɚ/ **noun** [C] UK old-fashioned informal (US **ˌpea ˈsoup**) a very thick FOG

peat /piːt/ **noun** [U] a dark brown substance like soil which was formed by plants dying and becoming buried. It is sometimes added to ordinary garden earth to improve it and is sometimes used as fuel.

ˈpeat ˌbog noun [C] an area of land from which peat is taken

peaty /ˈpiː.ti/ (US) /-t̬i/ **adj** of or like peat: *a dark peaty brown* ◦ *peaty soil*

pebble /ˈpeb.l/ **noun** [C] a small smooth round stone, especially one found on a beach or in a river: *This part of the coast has pebble beaches.* • **pebbled** /-ld/ **adj** (also **pebbly** /-li/)

pecan /piːˈkæn/ (US) /-ˈkɑːn/ **noun** [C] a type of long nut with a rough surface and a smooth reddish-brown shell: *chopped pecans* ◦ *pecan pie*

peccadillo /ˌpek.əˈdɪl.əʊ/ (US) /-oʊ/ **noun** [C] (plural **peccadillos** or **peccadilloes**) a small fault or a not very bad action: *a youthful peccadillo* ◦ *He dismissed what had happened as a mere peccadillo.*

peck /pek/ **verb; noun**

▸verb **1** [I or T] When a bird pecks, it bites, hits, or picks up something small with its beak: *The birds learn to peck holes in the milk bottle tops.* ◦ *Geese were pecking around for food.* ◦ *Chickens pecked **at** the seeds which covered the ground.* **2** [T] to give someone a quick kiss, especially on the side of the face: *He pecked his aunt **on the cheek**.*

PHRASAL VERB **peck at sth** to eat small quantities of something without any enthusiasm

▸noun [C] a quick kiss: *She gave me the usual peck **on the cheek**.*

pecker /ˈpek.əʳ/ (US) /-ɚ/ **noun PENIS** ▷ **1** [C] informal for PENIS **STAY HAPPY** ▷ **2 keep your pecker up** UK old-fashioned informal to try to stay happy when things are difficult

ˈpecking ˌorder noun [C usually singular] an informal social system in which some people or groups know they are more or less important than others: *He started as a clerk but gradually rose in the pecking order.*

peckish /ˈpek.ɪʃ/ **adj** UK slightly hungry: *By ten o'clock I was feeling rather peckish, even though I'd had a large breakfast.*

pectin /ˈpek.tɪn/ **noun** [U] a chemical found in some fruits which helps to make liquid firm when making jam

pectoral /ˈpek.tᵊr.ᵊl/ (US) /-tɔːr-/ **adj** specialized of the chest: *He flexed his pectoral **muscles**.*

ˈpectoral ˌfin noun [C] specialized the FIN on each side of a fish near the front of its body, used for controlling the direction the fish goes in and for slowing it down

pectorals /ˈpek.tᵊr.ᵊlz/ (US) /-tɔːr-/ **noun** [plural] (informal **pecs**) chest muscles

peculiar /pɪˈkjuː.li.əʳ/ (US) /-ˈkjuːl.jɚ/ **adj STRANGE** ▷ **1** (B2) unusual and strange, sometimes in an unpleasant way: *She has the most peculiar ideas.* ◦ *What a peculiar smell!* ◦ ***It's** peculiar **that** they didn't tell us they were going away.* ◦ UK *The video on road accidents made me **feel** rather peculiar (= ill).* **BELONGING TO** ▷ **2** (C2) belonging to, relating to or found in only particular people or things: *He gets on with things in his own peculiar way/manner/fashion.* ◦ *They noted that special manner of walking which was peculiar **to** her alone.* ◦ *This type of building is peculiar **to** the south of the country.*

peculiarity /pɪˌkjuː.liˈær.ə.ti/ (US) /-ˈer.ə.t̬i/ **noun STRANGE** ▷ **1** [C or U] the quality of being strange or unusual, or an unusual characteristic or habit: *You couldn't help but be aware of the peculiarity* ***of*** *the situation.* ◦ *Well, we all have our little peculiarities, don't we?* **BELONGING TO ▷ 2** [C] something that is typical of one person, group, or thing: *This technique is applicable to a wide variety of crops, but some modifications may be necessary to accommodate the peculiarities* ***of*** *each type.*

peculiarly /pɪˈkjuː.li.ə.li/ ⓤⓢ /-ˈkjuːl.jɚ-/ **adv STRANGELY ▷ 1** in a strange, and sometimes unpleasant, way: *He looked at me most peculiarly.* ◦ *The streets were peculiarly quiet for the time of day.* **VERY ▷ 2** old-fashioned or literary very or especially: *It's peculiarly painful where I burned my hand.* ◦ *She's a peculiarly attractive woman.*

pecuniary /pɪˈkjuː.njər.i/ ⓤⓢ /-ni.er-/ **adj** formal relating to money: *pecuniary interest/loss/benefit* ◦ *a pecuniary matter*

pedagogue /ˈped.ə.gɒg/ ⓤⓢ /-gɑːg/ **noun** [C] **1** disapproving a teacher who gives too much attention to formal rules and is not interesting **2** old use any teacher

pedagogy /ˈped.ə.gɒdʒ.i/ ⓤⓢ /-gɑː.dʒi/ **noun** [U] specialized the study of the methods and activities of teaching • **pedagogic** /ˌped.əˈgɒdʒ.ɪk/ ⓤⓢ /-ˈgɑː.dʒɪk/ **adj** (also **pedagogical**) • **pedagogically** /ˌped.əˈgɒdʒ.ɪ.kəl.i/ ⓤⓢ /-ˈgɑː.dʒɪ-/ **adv** *The minister's reforms are pedagogically questionable* (= not based on good teaching theory).

pedal /ˈped.əl/ **noun; adj; verb**

▸**noun** [C] **B2** a small part of a machine or object that is pushed down with the foot to operate or move the machine or object: *the brake/accelerator pedal* ◦ *This sewing machine is operated by a* ***foot*** *pedal.* ◦ *He stood up on the pedals of his bike to get extra power as he cycled up the hill.*

▸**adj** [before noun] operated by a pedal or pedals: *a pedal bike/boat/car* ◦ *She emptied the ashtray into the pedal bin.*

▸**verb** [I or T] (**-ll-** or US usually **-l-**) to push the pedals of a bicycle round with your feet: *He struggled to pedal his bicycle up the hill.* → See also **backpedal**

pedalo /ˈped.əl.əʊ/ ⓤⓢ /-oʊ/ **noun** [C] (plural **pedalos**) UK (US ˈ**pedal** ˌ**boat**) a small boat that is moved by pushing pedals with the feet

pedalo

ˈ**pedal** ˌ**power** **noun** [U] informal the activity of riding a bicycle: *The president showed he supported pedal power by turning up for work on a bike.*

pedant /ˈped.ənt/ **noun** [C] disapproving a person who is too interested in formal rules and small details that are not important • **pedantry** /-ən.tri/ **noun** [U] *There was a hint of pedantry in his elegant style of speaking.*

pedantic /pəˈdæn.tɪk/ ⓤⓢ /pedˈæn-/ **adj** disapproving giving too much attention to formal rules or small details: *They were being unnecessarily pedantic by insisting that Berry himself, and not his wife, should have made the announcement.* • **pedantically** /-tɪ.kəl.i/ **adv**

peddle /ˈped.l̩/ **verb** [T] mainly disapproving **1** to sell things, especially by taking them to different places: *These products are generally peddled (from) door to door.* ◦ *He travels around, peddling his* ***wares***. **2** If you peddle stories or information, you spread them by telling different people: *The organization has peddled the myth that they are supporting the local population.*

peddler /ˈped.lər/ ⓤⓢ /-lɚ/ **noun** [C] **1** (mainly UK **pedlar**) especially in the past, a person who travelled to different places to sell small goods, usually by going from house to house **2** (mainly UK **pedlar**) someone who gives ideas to other people: *a peddler of New Age philosophies* **3 (drug) peddler** old-fashioned someone who sells illegal drugs to people

pederast (UK old-fashioned **paederast**) /ˈped.ər.æst/ ⓤⓢ /-dɚ-/ **noun** [C] a man who has illegal sex with a young boy

pedestal /ˈped.ə.stəl/ **noun** [C] a long thin column which supports a STATUE, or a tall structure like a column on which something rests: *In the riot, the statues were toppled from their pedestals.*

IDIOMS **knock sb off their pedestal** to show people that someone is not as perfect as they seem to be: *This recent scandal has really knocked the president off his pedestal.* • **put sb on a pedestal** to believe that someone is perfect

pedestrian /pəˈdes.tri.ən/ **noun; adj**

▸**noun** [C] **B1** a person who is walking, especially in an area where vehicles go: *The death rate for pedestrians hit by cars is unacceptably high.*

▸**adj** formal disapproving not interesting; showing very little imagination: *Her books, with few exceptions, are workmanlike but pedestrian.* ◦ *His speech was long and pedestrian.* → Synonym **plodding**

peˌdestrian ˈcrossing **noun** [C] (US also **crosswalk**) a special place in a road where traffic must stop to allow people to walk across → Compare **pelican crossing, zebra crossing**

pedestrianize (UK usually **pedestrianise**) /pəˈdes.tri.ə.naɪz/ **verb** [T] to make an area into one where vehicles are not allowed to go: *They are pedestrianizing the town square.*

peˌdestrian ˈprecinct **noun** [C] (US usually **peˈdestrian ˌmall**) a covered area with shops where vehicles are not allowed

pediatrician /ˌpiː.di.əˈtrɪʃ.ən/ **noun** [C] mainly US for **paediatrician** • **pediatric** /-æt.rɪk/ **adj** mainly US

pedicure /ˈped.ɪ.kjʊər/ ⓤⓢ /-kjʊr/ **noun** [C or U] a beauty treatment for the feet which involves cutting and sometimes painting the nails, and MASSAGING (= rubbing) the skin or making it feel softer → Compare **manicure**

pedigree /ˈped.ɪ.griː/ **noun** **1** [C] a list of the parents and other relations of an animal: *The breeder showed us the dog's pedigree.* ◦ *He breeds pedigree poodles/cattle* (= ones whose parents and other relations are all of the same breed). **2** [C or U] a person's family history, education, and experience, or the history of an idea or activity: *His voice and manner suggested an aristocratic pedigree.* ◦ *Isolationism has a long and respectable pedigree in American history.*

pediment /ˈped.ɪ.mənt/ **noun** [C] specialized a TRIANGULAR part at the top of the front of a building that supports the roof and is often decorated

pedlar → See **peddler**

pedometer /peˈdɒm.ɪ.tər/ ⓤⓢ /pɪˈdɑː.mə.t̬ɚ/ **noun** [C] a device which measures how far someone has walked by counting the number of times the feet are raised and put down again

pedophile /ˈpiː.də.faɪl/ ⓤⓢ /ˈped.oʊ-/ **noun** [C] mainly US for **paedophile** • **pedophilia** /ˌpiː.dəˈfɪl.i.ə/ ⓤⓢ /ˌped.oʊˈfiː.li-/ **noun** [U] mainly US

pee /piː/ **verb; noun**

▸**verb** [I or T] informal for **urinate**

▸**noun** informal **1** [U] urine **2** [S] an act of URINATING: *I must go for/must have a pee.*

P

peek /piːk/ verb; noun
▸verb [I] **1** C2 to look, especially for a short time or while trying to avoid being seen: *Close your eyes. Don't peek. I've got a surprise for you.* ◦ *I peeked out the window to see who was there.* ◦ *The film peeks behind the scenes of a multinational corporation.* **2 peek out, through, etc.** to stick out slightly and be partly seen: *I could just see her petticoat peeking out from under her skirt.*
▸noun informal **have/take a peek** C1 to look at something for a short time: *If I'm passing by I might take a peek at the new premises.*

peekaboo /ˌpiːk.əˈbuː/ noun [U] (UK also **peep-bo** /ˈpiːp.bəʊ/ US /-ˈboʊ/) a game played with very young children in which you hide your face, especially with your hands, and then suddenly take your hands away saying 'peekaboo'

peel /piːl/ verb; noun
▸verb FOOD ▷ **1** B2 [T] to remove the skin of fruit and vegetables: *Peel, core and chop the apples.* COVERING ▷ **2** C2 [I or T, usually + adv/prep] If a layer or covering peels, it slowly comes off, and if you peel a layer or covering, you remove it slowly and carefully: *We peeled the wallpaper **off** the walls.* ◦ *Peel **off** the backing strip and press the label down firmly.* ◦ *The posters were peeling **away from** the damp walls.* ◦ *The new paint is already starting to crack and peel.* BODY ▷ **3** [I] If you peel, or part of your body or your skin peels, parts of the top layer of your skin comes off because you are burned from being in the sun: *My back is peeling.*

PHRASAL VERB **peel away/off** When vehicles, people, or animals peel away/off, they separate from the group or structure they were part of and move away in a different direction: *One motorbike peeled away **from** the formation and circled round behind the rest.*

▸noun [U] the skin of fruit and vegetables, especially after it has been removed: *apple peel* ◦ *potato peel* ◦ *The dessert was decorated with strips of lemon peel.*

peeler /ˈpiː.ləʳ/ US /-lɚ/ noun [C] a kitchen tool for removing the skin of fruit and vegetables: *a vegetable/potato peeler*

peelings /ˈpiː.lɪŋz/ noun [plural] the unwanted pieces of fruit or vegetable skin that have been taken off: *potato/apple peelings*

peep /piːp/ verb; noun
▸verb LOOK ▷ **1** C2 [I usually + adv/prep] to secretly look at something for a short time, usually through a hole: *I saw her peeping **through** the curtains/**into** the room.* APPEAR ▷ **2** [I usually + adv/prep] to appear slowly and not be completely seen: *A few early flowers had peeped up through the snow.* ◦ *The cat's tail was peeping **out** from under the bed.* NOISE ▷ **3** [I] to make a weak high noise
▸noun SOMETHING SAID ▷ **1** [S] informal a statement, answer, or complaint: *No one has **raised a** peep about this dreadful behaviour.* ◦ *One more peep **out of** you and there'll be no television tomorrow.* ◦ *There hasn't been **a** peep **out of** (= any form of communication from) my sister for a couple of weeks.* NOISE ▷ **2** [C] the weak high noise made by young birds LOOK ▷ **3** [S] a quick look: ***Take/Have a** peep **at** what it says in this letter.*

peephole /ˈpiːp.həʊl/ US /-hoʊl/ noun [C] (UK also **spyhole**) a small hole in a door or a wall through which you can look, especially without being seen: *I have a security peephole in my front door.*

ˌpeeping ˈTom noun [C] disapproving a man who tries to secretly watch women when they are wearing no clothes

peeps /piːps/ noun [plural] informal people or friends: *He's gone out with his peeps.*

peepshow /ˈpiːp.ʃəʊ/ US /-ʃoʊ/ noun [C] **1** a short, sexually exciting performance or film that someone pays to watch through a window in a small room **2** especially in the past, a sexually exciting picture or film, watched on a machine through a small hole

ˈpeep-toe adj used to describe shoes that show part of the big toe: *peep-toe sandals*

peer /pɪəʳ/ US /pɪr/ verb; noun
▸verb [I usually + adv/prep] C2 to look carefully or with difficulty: *When no one answered the door, she peered **through** the window to see if anyone was there.* ◦ *The driver was peering into the distance trying to read the road sign.*
▸noun [C] EQUAL ▷ **1** C1 a person who is the same age or has the same social position or the same abilities as other people in a group: *Do you think it's true that teenage girls are less self-confident than their male peers?* ◦ *He wasn't a great scholar, but as a teacher he had few peers (= not as many people had the same ability as him).* HIGH RANK ▷ **2** in Britain, a person who has a high social position and any of a range of titles, including BARON, EARL, and DUKE, or a LIFE PEER: *a hereditary peer* ◦ *a Conservative peer*

peerage /ˈpɪə.rɪdʒ/ US /ˈpɪr.ɪdʒ/ noun **1** [C usually singular] the position of being a peer: *She was given a peerage.* ◦ *He was **elevated to** the peerage after distinguished service in industry.* **2 the peerage** [S, + sing/pl verb] the group of people who are peers, either because of their families or because they are LIFE PEERS **3** [C] a book containing information about peers who are not LIFE PEERS and their family history

peeress /ˈpɪə.rəs/, /pɪəˈres/ US /ˈpɪr.ɪs/ noun [C] a female peer

ˈpeer ˌgroup noun [C usually singular, + sing/pl verb] the people who are approximately the same age as you and come from a similar social group: *These children scored significantly lower on intelligence tests than others in their peer group.*

peerless /ˈpɪə.ləs/ US /ˈpɪr-/ adj formal describes something that is better than any other of its type: *peerless beauty/ability*

ˌpeer of the ˈrealm noun [C] a member of the HOUSE OF LORDS (= the part of the UK parliament that is not elected) who is not a LIFE PEER

ˈpeer ˌpressure noun [U] (UK **ˈpeer group ˌpressure**) the strong influence of a group, especially of children, on members of that group to behave as everyone else does: *There is tremendous peer pressure to wear fashionable clothes.*

ˌpeer reˈview noun [U or C] the process of reading, checking, and giving your opinion about something that has been written by another scientist or expert working in the same subject area as you, or a piece of work in which this is done: *All these papers have been published after being subjected to peer review.* • **ˌpeer-reˈview** verb [T] *The results had been peer-reviewed by five independent scientists in the same field.* • **ˌpeer-reˈviewed** adj *peer-reviewed **journals/research/papers***

peeve /piːv/ verb [T] to annoy someone: *What peeved her most was his thoughtlessness.* ◦ [+ that] ***It** peeves me **that** she didn't bother to phone.*

peeved /piːvd/ adj informal annoyed: *He was peeved because we didn't ask him what he thought about the idea.*

peevish /ˈpiː.vɪʃ/ adj easily annoyed: *a peevish, bad-tempered person* • **peevishly** /-li/ adv *'I thought you might have helped,' she replied peevishly.*

peewit /ˈpiː.wɪt/ noun [C] a **lapwing**

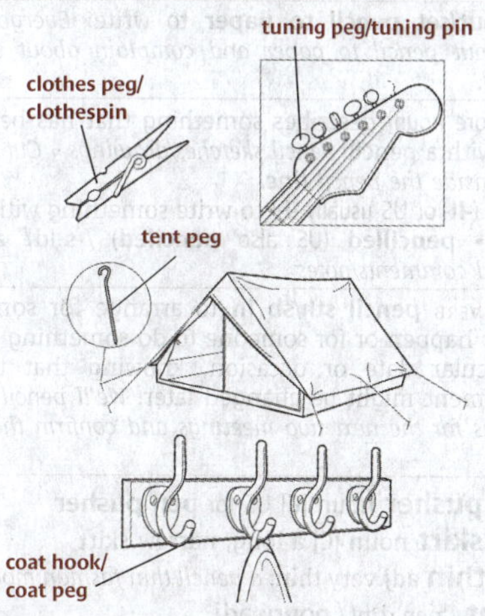

peg /peg/ noun; verb

▸noun **HOOK** ▷ **1** [C] a small stick or HOOK that sticks out from a surface and from which objects, especially clothes, can hang: *He took off his coat/hat and hung it* ***on*** *the peg.* **2** [S] a reason for discussing something further: *They decided to use the anniversary as the peg* ***for****/a peg* ***on which to hang*** *a TV documentary.* **FIXING DEVICE** ▷ **3** [C] a device used to fix something into a particular place: *There aren't enough pegs* (UK also ***clothes pegs***) (US ***clothespins***) *for all this washing.* ◦ *Hammer the* (***tent***) *pegs firmly into the ground.* **IN BASEBALL** ▷ **4** [C] US informal a low fast throw in baseball **LEVEL** ▷ **5** [C] an arrangement that fixes a price, CURRENCY, etc. at a particular level: *The government removed the currency from its peg* ***against*** *the dollar.*

IDIOM **bring/take sb down a peg (or two)** informal to show someone that they are not as important as they thought they were

▸verb (-gg-) **FIX** ▷ **1** [T usually + adv/prep] to fix something in place with pegs: *Make sure the tarpaulin is securely pegged* ***down***. ◦ *I'll peg* ***out*** *the clothes before I go to work.* **2** [T] to make a price, CURRENCY, etc. stay at a particular level: *The agreement works because member nations haven't tried to peg prices.* **THROW** ▷ **3** [T] US informal to throw a ball in baseball low and fast: *Mattingly pegged the ball to Stanley.*

PHRASAL VERBS **peg out** UK slang **1** to die **2** to stop working: *The car finally pegged out about 20 miles from home.* • **peg sth out** If you peg out an area, you mark the edges of it by hitting short sticks into the ground.

pejorative /pɪˈdʒɒr.ə.tɪv/ (US) /-ˈdʒɔːr.ə.t̬ɪv/ adj formal disapproving or suggesting that something is not good or is of no importance: *Make sure students realize that 'fat' is a pejorative word.*

Pekinese (plural **Pekinese** or UK **Pekineses**) (also **Pekingese**) /ˌpiː.kɪˈniːz/ noun [C] (also **peke**) a small dog with long, soft hair and a wide, flat nose

pelican

pelican /ˈpel.ɪ.kən/ noun [C] a large bird that catches fish and carries them in the lower part of its large, bag-shaped beak

ˌpelican ˈcrossing noun [C] UK a special place in the road in Britain, with a set of lights at the side of the road and a device which people can press to make the red light show and the traffic stop, allowing them to cross → Compare **pedestrian crossing, zebra crossing**

pellet /ˈpel.ət/ noun [C] **1** a small hard ball or tube-shaped piece of any substance: *iron/lead/wax/plastic/paper pellets* ◦ *food pellets* **2** the solid waste of particular animals: *rabbit/sheep pellets* **3** small metal objects that are shot from some types of gun: *airgun pellets* ◦ *shotgun pellets* ◦ *a pellet* ***gun***

pell-mell /ˌpelˈmel/ adv old-fashioned very fast and not organized: *At the sound of the alarm bell, the customers* ***ran*** *pell-mell for the doors.*

pelmet /ˈpel.mət/ noun [C] (US usually **valance**) a narrow strip of wood or cloth that is fixed above a window or door and hides the top of the curtains

peloton /ˈpel.ə.tɒn/ noun [C usually singular] in a bicycle race, the main or largest group of riders

pelt /pelt/ verb; noun

▸verb **THROW** ▷ **1** [T] to throw a number of things quickly at someone or something: *We saw rioters pelting police* ***with*** *bricks and bottles.* **RUN** ▷ **2** [I + adv/prep] informal to run fast: *The children pelted down the bank.*

IDIOM **pelt (down)** to rain heavily: *It's pelting down* (***with rain***).

▸noun **SKIN** ▷ **1** [C] the skin and fur of a dead animal, or the skin with the fur removed **RUN** ▷ **2 at full pelt** UK running as fast as possible

pelvis /ˈpel.vɪs/ noun [C] the bones which form a bowl-shaped structure in the area below the waist at the top of the legs, and to which the leg bones and SPINE are joined • **pelvic** /-vɪk/ adj *the pelvic region/area*

pen /pen/ noun; verb

▸noun [C] **FOR WRITING** ▷ **1** (A1) a long thin object used for writing or drawing with ink: *a fountain/ballpoint/felt-tip pen* ◦ *Don't write* ***in*** *pen (= using a pen), or you won't be able to rub out any mistakes you make.* **ENCLOSED SPACE** ▷ **2** a small area surrounded by a fence, especially one in which animals are kept: *a sheep/pig pen* → See also **playpen** **3** US slang for **penitentiary**: *He served nine years in the* ***state*** *pen.*

IDIOM **put/set pen to paper** to start to write: *It's time you put pen to paper and replied to that letter from your mother.*

▸verb [T] (-nn-) formal to write something: *She penned a note of thanks to her hostess.*

PHRASAL VERB **pen sb in/up** [often passive] to keep people or animals in a small area: *The sheep were penned in behind the barn.* ◦ *The soldiers were penned up in their barracks.*

penal /ˈpiː.nəl/ adj **PUNISHMENT** ▷ **1** [before noun] of or connected with punishment given by law: *Many people believe that execution has no place in the penal* ***system*** *of a civilized society.* ◦ *He had been in and out of penal institutions (= prison) from the age of 16.* **CAUSING DISADVANTAGE** ▷ **2** UK having a harmful effect; causing disadvantage: *They complained about the penal and counter-productive tax rates.*

ˈpenal ˌcode noun [C] the system of legal punishment of a country

ˈpenal ˌcolony noun [C] (also **ˈpenal ˌsettlement**) a type of prison, especially one that is far away from other people

P

penalize (UK usually **penalise**) /ˈpiː.nə.laɪz/ verb [T] CAUSE DISADVANTAGE ▷ **1** to cause someone a disadvantage: *The present tax system penalizes poor people.* ◦ *The scheme should ensure that borrowers are not penalized by sudden rises in mortgage rates.* PUNISH ▷ **2** to punish someone for breaking a rule: *He was penalized early in the match **for** dangerous play.*

ˌpenal reˈform noun [C or U] the attempt to improve the system of legal punishment

penalty /ˈpen.əl.ti/ (US) /-t̬i/ noun [C] PUNISHMENT ▷ **1** (B2) a punishment, or the usual punishment, for doing something that is against a law: *The law carries a penalty **of** up to three years in prison.* ◦ *They asked for the **maximum** penalty **for** hoax calls to be increased to one year.* ◦ *The protesters were told to clear the area around the building, **on** penalty **of** arrest (= or be arrested) if they did not.* **2** (B2) a type of punishment, often involving paying money, that is given to you if you break an agreement or do not follow rules: *Currently, ticket holders **pay** a penalty equal to 25 percent of the ticket price when they change their flight plans.* ◦ *There was a penalty **clause** which said you had to pay half the cost if you cancelled your booking.* **3** (B2) an advantage given in some sports to a team or player when the opposing team or player breaks a rule: *The referee **awarded** (= gave) a penalty **kick**.* ◦ *Hysen handled the ball and **conceded** the penalty that gave Manchester United the lead.* DISADVANTAGE ▷ **4** a disadvantage brought about as a result of a situation or action: *Loss of privacy is one of the penalties **of** success.* ◦ *She has **paid** a heavy penalty **for** speaking the truth.*

ˈpenalty ˌarea noun [C usually singular] (also **ˈpenalty ˌbox**) in football, the area surrounded by white lines in front of the goal

ˈpenalty ˌbox noun [C usually singular] in ICE HOCKEY, an area where players must sit when they are given a penalty

ˌpenalty ˈshootout noun [C] a way of deciding who will win a football game in which both teams finished with the same number of goals, by each team taking turns to have a set number of kicks at the goal

ˈpenalty ˌspot noun [S] in football, the place painted with a white spot from which a penalty kick is taken

penance /ˈpen.əns/ noun [C or U] an act which shows that you feel sorry about something that you have done, sometimes for religious reasons: *As a penance, she said she would buy them all a box of chocolates.* ◦ *They are **doing** penance **for** their sins.*

pence /pens/ (A2) plural of PENNY (= a unit of money) → See also **sixpence, tuppence**

penchant /ˈpɑ̃ːŋ.ʃɑ̃ːŋ/ (US) /ˈpen.tʃənt/ noun [C usually singular] a liking for, an enjoyment of, or a habit of doing something, especially something that other people might not like: *a penchant **for** melodrama/skiing/exotic clothes* ◦ *Her penchant **for** disappearing for days at a time worries her family.*

pencil /ˈpen.səl/ noun; adj; verb

▸noun [C or U] **1** (A1) a long, thin, usually wooden object for writing or drawing, with a sharp black or coloured point at one end: *a box of coloured pencils* ◦ *pens and pencils* ◦ *He sat with his pencil **poised**, ready to take notes.* ◦ *The pencil's **blunt** – you'd better **sharpen** it (= make its point sharp).* ◦ *Write your comments in the margin **in** (= using) pencil.* ◦ *a pencil sharpener* **2** the form of some types of make-up: *an eyebrow pencil* ◦ *a lip pencil* **3** literary a thin beam of light: *A pencil of light showed as the door opened slightly.*

IDIOM **put/set pencil to paper** to write: *Everyone should put pencil to paper and complain about the proposal.*

▸adj [before noun] describes something that has been drawn with a pencil: *pencil sketches/drawings* ◦ *Cut on or just inside the pencil **line**.*

▸verb [T] (-ll- or US usually -l-) to write something with a pencil • **pencilled** (US also **penciled**) /-səld/ adj *pencilled comments/notes*

PHRASAL VERB **pencil sth/sb in** to arrange for something to happen or for someone to do something on a particular date or occasion, knowing that the arrangement might be changed later: *We'll pencil in the dates for the next two meetings and confirm them later.*

ˈpencil ˌpusher noun [C] US for **pen pusher**

ˈpencil ˌskirt noun [C] a long, narrow skirt

ˌpencil-ˈthin adj very thin: *a pencil-thin fashion model*

pendant /ˈpen.dənt/ noun; adj

▸noun [C] a piece of jewellery worn around the neck, consisting of a long chain with an object hanging from it, or the object itself: *It was a necklace with a diamond pendant.*

▸adj **pendent**

pendent /ˈpen.dənt/ adj (also **pendant**) hanging from or over something: *pendent branches* ◦ *a pendent lampshade* → See also **pendant**

pending /ˈpen.dɪŋ/ adj; preposition

▸adj about to happen or waiting to happen: *There were whispers that a deal was pending.*

▸preposition formal used to say that one thing must wait until another thing happens: *The identity of the four people was not made public, pending (the) notification of relatives.* ◦ *Flights were suspended pending (an) investigation of the crash.*

ˈpen ˌdrive noun [C] (also **flash drive, Memory Stick**) a small piece of equipment that you connect to a computer or other piece of electronic equipment to copy and store information

pendulous /ˈpen.djʊ.ləs/ (US) /-dʒə.ləs/ adj formal hanging down loosely: *pendulous blossoms*

pendulum /ˈpen.djʊ.ləm/ (US) /-dʒə.ləm/ noun **1** [C] a device consisting of a weight on a stick or thread which moves from one side to the other, especially one which forms a part of some types of clocks: *The pendulum in the grandfather clock **swung** back and forth.* **2** [S] a change, especially from one opinion to an opposite one: *As so often in education, **the** pendulum has **swung back** to the other extreme and testing is popular again.*

penetrate /ˈpen.ɪ.treɪt/ verb MOVE INTO ▷ **1** [I or T] to move into or through something: *Amazingly, the bullet did not penetrate his brain.* ◦ *In a normal winter, the frost penetrates deeply enough to kill off insect eggs in the soil.* ◦ *The organization had been penetrated by a spy.* ◦ *The company has been successful in penetrating overseas markets this year.* **2** [T] If your eyes penetrate somewhere dark, you manage to see through it: *Our eyes couldn't penetrate the dark/**the gloom** of the inner cave.* UNDERSTAND ▷ **3** [I or T] to study or INVESTIGATE something in order to understand it: *It's hard to penetrate her mind.* ◦ *He penetrates deeper into the artist's life in the second volume of his autobiography.*

penetrating /ˈpen.ɪ.treɪ.tɪŋ/ (US) /-t̬ɪŋ/ adj LOUD ▷ **1** very loud: *I heard a penetrating scream.* ◦ *He has a very penetrating voice.* UNDERSTANDING ▷ **2** describes a way of looking at someone in which you seem to know what they are thinking **3 a penetrating mind** a mind which understands things quickly and well

penetration /ˌpen.ɪˈtreɪ.ʃən/ **noun** [U] **MOVEMENT INTO** ▷ **1** a movement into or through something or someone: *Sunscreens can help reduce the penetration of ultraviolet rays into the skin.* ◦ *The company is trying to increase its penetration of the market.* **2** the act of a man putting his PENIS into his partner's body during sex **UNDERSTANDING** ▷ **3** formal someone's ability to understand quickly and well

penetrative /ˈpen.ɪ.trə.tɪv/ (US) /-treɪ.t̬ɪv/ **adj** **MOVEMENT INTO** ▷ **1** involving movement into or through something or someone: *a penetrative thrust/attack* ◦ *penetrative sex* **UNDERSTANDING** ▷ **2** showing understanding: *a penetrative remark*

penfriend /ˈpen.frend/ **noun** [C] (also ˈ**pen** ˌ**pal**) (A2) someone who you write friendly letters to regularly, but you have never met

penguin /ˈpeŋ.gwɪn/ **noun** [C] (B1) a black and white bird which cannot fly but uses its small wings to help it swim

penicillin /ˌpen.əˈsɪl.ɪn/ **noun** [U] specialized a type of ANTIBIOTIC (= a medicine that kills bacteria)

penile /ˈpiː.naɪl/ **adj** specialized of the PENIS

peninsula /pəˈnɪn.sjʊ.lə/ (US) /-sə-/ **noun** [C] a long piece of land which sticks out from a larger area of land into the sea or into a lake: *the Korean/Arabian/Florida Peninsula*

penis /ˈpiː.nɪs/ **noun** [C] the part of a male's body that is used for urinating and for sex

penitent /ˈpen.ɪ.tənt/ **adj; noun**

▸**adj** formal showing that you are sorry for something you have done because you feel it was wrong: *'I'm sorry,' she said with a penitent smile.* ◦ *It was hard to be angry with him when he looked so penitent.* • **penitence** /-təns/ **noun** [U] • **penitently** /-li/ **adv**

▸**noun** [C] formal a person who is performing a formal religious act to show that they are sorry for something they have done wrong

penitentiary /ˌpen.ɪˈten.ʃər.i/, /-ə-/ (US) /-tʃə.riː/ **noun** [C] US for a PRISON (= building in which criminals are kept)

penknife /ˈpen.naɪf/ **noun** [C] (also **pocketknife**) a small knife which folds into a case and is usually carried in a pocket

penknife

ˈ**pen** ˌ**lid** **noun** [C] UK (US ˈ**pen** ˌ**cap**) a cover that goes over the top of a pen to stop the ink from escaping

penlight /ˈpen.laɪt/ **noun** [C] US a small TORCH about the size and shape of a pen

ˈ**pen** ˌ**name** **noun** [C] a name chosen by a writer to use instead of using their real name when publishing books

pennant /ˈpen.ənt/ **noun** [C] **1** a flag in the shape of a triangle **2** a flag that shows that a particular baseball team is the winner in its LEAGUE: *Divisional winners meet in the final to decide the pennant.*

penne /ˈpen.eɪ/ (US) /-i/ **noun** [U] a type of PASTA in the shape of tubes

penniless /ˈpen.i.ləs/ **adj** having no money: *She fell in love with a penniless artist.*

penny /ˈpen.i/ **noun** [C] (plural **pence**, **p** or **pennies**) **1** (B1) (abbreviation **p**) the smallest unit of money in Britain of which there are 100 in a pound, or a small coin worth this much. You use 'pence' or, more informally, 'p' when you are talking about the units of money and pennies when you are talking about the coins themselves: *Could you lend me 50 pence/50p please?* ◦ *I found a ten/twenty/fifty pence* **piece** *(= a coin of this value) on the floor.* ◦ *I keep pennies and other small coins in a jar.* **2** in the US and Canada, a CENT or a coin of this value **3** (also **old penny**, abbreviation **d**) in Britain before 1971, a large coin. There were twelve pennies in a SHILLING. **4** used when talking about the smallest amount of money possible: *Buy a TV now and it won't cost you a penny (= will cost nothing) for three months.* ◦ *It was an expensive meal but worth every penny.*

IDIOMS **be two/ten a penny** UK (US **be a dime a dozen**) to be very common: *Antique toy cars are ten a penny nowadays.* • **in for a penny (in for a pound)** UK saying something you say which means that since you have started something or are involved in it, you should complete the work although it has become more difficult or complicated than you had expected • **not have a penny to your name** (also **not have two pennies to rub together**) to be very poor • **the penny drops** UK informal If the penny drops, you suddenly understand something: *She looked confused for a moment, then suddenly the penny dropped.* • **(a) penny for your thoughts** said when you want to know what another person is thinking, usually because they have been quiet for a while

-penny /-pə.ni/ **suffix** UK used in the past with numbers to show how many pence something cost: *a fourpenny ice-cream*

ˈ**penny-**ˌ**ante** **adj** US of little value or importance: *He was proposing some penny-ante increase.*

ˌ**penny-**ˈ**farthing** **noun** [C] a type of bicycle used in the past that had a very large front wheel and a small back wheel

ˈ**penny-**ˌ**pinching** **adj** [before noun] unwilling to spend money: *I became tired of his penny-pinching friends.* • ˈ**penny-**ˌ**pinching** **noun** [U] *Local residents have accused the council of penny-pinching.*

ˌ**penny** ˈ**whistle** **noun** [C] a small cheap musical instrument shaped like a tube with holes along one side and a part for your mouth at one end that you blow into

pennyworth /ˈpen.i.wəθ/, /ˈpen.əθ/ (US) /ˈpen.i.wɝːθ/ **noun** [S] **1** (UK **penn'orth**) as much of something as could be bought for a penny **2** a small amount of something: *It won't make* **a** *pennyworth* **of** *difference to me.*

ˈ**pen** ˌ**pal** **noun** [C] (UK ˈ**pen** ˌ**friend**) (A2) someone who you exchange letters with as a hobby, but usually have not met: *I've got a pen pal in Australia.*

ˈ**pen** ˌ**pusher** **noun** [C] UK (US ˈ**pencil** ˌ**pusher**) a person who has an office job that is not interesting

pension /ˈpen.ʃən/ **noun; verb**

▸**noun** [C] (B2) an amount of money paid regularly by the government or a private company to a person who does not work any more because they are too old or they have become ill: *They find it hard to live on their* ***state pension****.* ◦ *He won't be able to* ***draw*** *(= receive) his pension until he's 65.*

▸**verb**

PHRASAL VERBS **pension sb off** [M often passive] mainly UK to make someone leave their job and give them a pension, usually when they have reached an age at which they can stop working: *Workers in the company are being pensioned off at 50.* • **pension sth off** to stop using something, usually a machine, because it is old and has been used too much: *After flying for 38 years, their Wessex helicopter is about to be pensioned off.*

pensionable /ˈpen.ʃən.ə.bl/ **adj** UK allowing someone to receive a pension: *She is **of** pensionable **age*** (= is old enough to claim a pension). ◦ *a pensionable job*

pensioner /ˈpen.ʃən.əʳ/ (US) /-ɚ/ **noun** [C] mainly UK (UK also ˌ**old age** ˈ**pensioner**) C1 a person who receives a pension, especially the government pension given to old people: *Students and pensioners are entitled to a discount.*

ˈ**pension** ˌ**fund** **noun** [C] money that employees of a company pay regularly, that is INVESTED to provide them with a pension when they are older

ˈ**pension** ˌ**plan** **noun** [C] (UK ˈ**pension** ˌ**scheme**) a financial plan that allows you to receive money after you or your employer have paid money into it for a number of years

pensive /ˈpen.sɪv/ **adj** thinking in a quiet way, often with a serious expression on your face: *She became withdrawn and pensive, hardly speaking to anyone.* • **pensively** /-li/ **adv** *He gazed pensively at the glass in front of him, lost in thought.*

pentagon /ˈpen.tə.gən/ (US) /-t̬ə.gɑːn/ **noun** [C] a shape with five sides and five angles

the ˈ**Pentagon** **noun** the building in Washington where the US Defense Department is based, or the US Defense Department itself: *The Pentagon is aiming to cut US forces by over 25 percent in the next five years.*

pentathlete /penˈtæθ.liːt/ **noun** [C] a person who competes in pentathlons

pentathlon /penˈtæθ.lɒn/ (US) /-lɑːn/ **noun** [C] a sports event in which ATHLETES compete in five different sports: *The pentathlon consists of running, swimming, riding, shooting, and fencing.* → Compare **biathlon, decathlon, heptathlon**

Pentecost /ˈpen.tɪ.kɒst/ (US) /-t̬ɪ.kɑːst/ **noun** **1** [C or U] in the Jewish religion, a holy day that comes 50 days after PASSOVER **2** [U] in the Christian religion, a holy day that is the seventh Sunday after EASTER

P

Pentecostalism /ˌpen.tɪˈkɒs.təl.ɪ.zəm/ (US) /-ˈkɑː.stəl-/ **noun** [U] a modern branch of the Christian religion which began in the US in 1901, whose members believe that everything written in the Bible is true • **Pentecostal** /-ˈkɒs.təl/ (US) /-ˈkɑː.stəl/ **adj, noun** [C]

penthouse /ˈpent.haʊs/ **noun** [C] an expensive apartment or set of rooms at the top of a hotel or tall building: *The singer is staying in a penthouse **suite*** (= set of rooms) *in the Hilton.*

pent-up /ˌpentˈʌp/ **adj** [before noun] Pent-up feelings are not allowed to be expressed or released: *Screaming at the top of your voice is a good way of venting pent-up frustration.*

penultimate /pəˈnʌl.tɪ.mət/ (US) /prˈnʌl.t̬ə.mət/ **adj** [before noun] formal second from the last: *It's the penultimate episode of the series tonight.*

penury /ˈpen.jʊ.ri/ (US) /-jʊr.i/ **noun** [U] formal the state of being extremely poor

peon /ˈpiː.ən/ **noun** [C] **1** a farm worker in South America, doing jobs that do not need any particular skill **2** US informal a person who does work that does not need any particular skill, often one who is not paid well or treated well: *The boss just never talked to peons like us. It was beneath her.* **3** Indian English someone whose job is to work in an office doing jobs that do not need any particular skill

peony /ˈpiː.ə.ni/ **noun** [C] a garden plant with large red, pink, or white flowers

people /ˈpiː.pl/ **noun; noun; verb**

▸**noun** [plural] **1** A1 men, women, and children: *Many people never take any exercise.* ◦ *We've invited 30 people to our party.* **2** used to refer to everyone, or informally to the group that you are speaking to: *People will think you've gone mad.* ◦ *People like to be made to feel important.* ◦ *Now that we've discussed our problems, are people happy with the decisions taken?* **3** men and women who are involved in a particular type of work: *We'll have to get the people from the tax office to look at these accounts.* ◦ *Most of her friends are media people.* **4 the people** C1 the large number of ordinary men and women who do not have positions of power in society: *She claims to be the voice of the people.* ◦ *The president has lost the support of the people.* **5 sb's people** informal the people someone is related to: *Her people come from Scotland originally.*

IDIOMS **man/woman of the people** a person, usually involved in politics, who is liked by a lot of ordinary people and seems to understand and like them • **of all people** used to show that you are especially surprised at a particular person's behaviour because it does not seem typical of them: *I thought that you, of all people, would believe me!*

▸**noun** [C, + sing/pl verb] **1** all the men, women, and children who live in a particular country: *The French are known as a food-loving people.* **2** a society: *Customs similar to this one are found among many peoples of the world.*

▸**verb**

PHRASAL VERB **people sth/somewhere by/with sb** If something or somewhere is peopled by/with a particular type of person, it is filled with them: *Her novels are peopled with the rich and beautiful.*

ˈ**people** ˌ**carrier** **noun** [C] a large, high car that can carry more people than a normal car

pep /pep/ **noun; verb**

▸**noun** [U] informal energy, or a willingness to be active

▸**verb** (-pp-)

PHRASAL VERB **pep sb/sth up** to make someone or something more energetic or interesting: *A good night's sleep will pep you up.* ◦ *The show needs to be pepped up with some decent songs.*

pepper /ˈpep.əʳ/ (US) /-ɚ/ **noun; verb**

▸**noun** POWDER ▷ **1** A2 [U] a grey or white powder produced by crushing dry peppercorns, used to give a spicy, hot taste to food: *freshly ground black pepper* ◦ ***salt and** pepper* VEGETABLE ▷ **2** B1 [C] a vegetable that is usually green, red, or yellow, has a rounded shape, and is hollow with seeds in the middle: *a red/green pepper* ◦ *Peppers are usually cooked with other vegetables or eaten raw in salads.*

▸**verb**

PHRASAL VERB **pepper sth with sth** HIT ▷ **1** to hit something repeatedly with small objects: *The city's walls were peppered with bullets.* INCLUDE ▷ **2** [often passive] If you pepper a speech or piece of writing with something, you include a lot of that particular thing: *The letter was peppered with exclamation marks.*

ˌ**pepper-and-**ˈ**salt** **adj** [before noun] UK (US ˌ**salt-and-**ˈ**pepper**) describes hair that is a mixture of dark hairs and grey or white hairs

peppercorn /ˈpep.ə.kɔːn/ (US) /-ɚ.kɔːrn/ **noun** [C] a small dried fruit that looks like a seed and is crushed to produce pepper

ˌ**peppercorn** ˈ**rent** **noun** [C] UK a very small amount of money that you pay as rent

ˈpepper ˌmill noun [C] a small device, the top part of which you turn by hand to crush the peppercorns inside it to produce pepper

pepper mill

peppermint /ˈpep.ə.mɪnt/ (US) /-ɚ-/ noun **1** [U] a strong fresh FLAVOURING from a type of MINT plant, used especially to give flavour to sweets: *She drinks peppermint-flavoured tea.* **2** [C] a hard white sweet that has the flavour of peppermint: *You can eat a peppermint as a breath freshener.*

pepperoni /ˌpep.əˈrəʊni/ (US) /-ˈroʊni/ noun [U] a spicy PORK OR BEEF sausage, used especially on PIZZA

ˈpepper ˌpot noun [C] UK (US **ˈpepper ˌshaker**) a small container with several holes in the top that contains pepper

peppery /ˈpep.ər.i/ (US) /-ɚ.i/ adj having a spicy flavour like pepper: *This salad has a sharp peppery flavour.*

pepsin /ˈpep.sɪn/ noun [U] specialized an ENZYME (= chemical substance made by living cells) that breaks down PROTEIN in food in the stomach and is produced by GLANDS there

ˈpep ˌtalk noun [C] a short speech intended to encourage people to work harder or try to win a game or competition: *The boss gave the staff a pep talk this morning in an attempt to boost sales.*

peptide /ˈpep.taɪd/ noun [C] specialized a chemical COMPOUND that is made of a small chain of two more more AMINO ACIDS

per strong /pɜːr/ (US) /pɜː/ weak /pər/ (US) /pɚ/ preposition A2 used when expressing rates, prices, or measurements to mean 'for each': *The meal will cost $20 per person.* ◦ *The car was travelling at 70 miles per hour (70 mph).* ◦ *There are more cafés per square mile here than anywhere else in the country.* → See also **percent**

IDIOMS **as per instructions** formal according to the instructions: *I had two spoonfuls after lunch, as per instructions.* • **as per usual/normal** as usual: *Carlo turned up without any money, as per usual.*

perambulator /pəˈræm.bjʊ.leɪ.tər/ (US) /-t̬ɚ/ noun [C] UK old-fashioned formal for **pram**

per ˈannum adv (written abbreviation **p.a.**) used in business when referring to an amount that is produced, sold, or spent each year: *The country exports goods worth $600 million per annum.*

per ˈcalendar ˌmonth adv (written abbreviation **pcm**) UK formal used in business when referring to an amount that is produced, sold, or spent each month: *The rent for this apartment is $600 per calendar month.*

per capita /pəˈkæp.ɪ.tə/ (US) /pɚˈkæp.ɪ.t̬ə/ adv, adj formal If you express an amount per capita, you mean that amount for each person: *France and Germany invest far more per capita in public transport than Britain.* ◦ *The per capita income in the country is very low.*

perceive /pəˈsiːv/ (US) /pɚ-/ verb [T] BELIEVE ▷ **1** C1 to come to an opinion about something, or have a belief about something: *How do the French perceive the British?* ◦ *Women's magazines are often perceived* ***to be*** *superficial.* SEE ▷ **2** C2 to see something or someone, or to notice something that is obvious: *Bill perceived a tiny figure in the distance.* ◦ *I perceived a note of unhappiness in her voice.* ◦ *Perceiving* ***that*** *he wasn't happy with the arrangements, I tried to book a different hotel.*

percent (also **per ˈcent**) /pəˈsent/ (US) /pɚ-/ adv B1 for or out of every 100, shown by the symbol %: *You got 20 percent* ***of*** *the answers right – that means one in every five.* ◦ *Only 40 percent of people bothered to vote in the election.*

percentage /pəˈsen.tɪdʒ/ (US) /pɚˈsen.t̬ɪdʒ/ noun AMOUNT ▷ **1** B2 [C] an amount of something, often expressed as a number out of 100: *What percentage of women return to work after having a baby?* ◦ *Interest rates have risen by two percentage* ***points***. ADVANTAGE ▷ **2** [U] US informal an advantage: *There's no percentage in working such long hours.*

percentile /pəˈsen.taɪl/ (US) /pɚ-/ noun [C] specialized one of the points into which a large range of numbers, results, etc. is divided to make 100 groups of the same size: *That score puts you on the 97th percentile.*

perceptible /pəˈsep.tə.bl/ (US) /pɚ-/ adj that can be seen, heard, or noticed: *There was a* ***barely*** *perceptible movement in his right arm.* ◦ *The past year has seen a perceptible improvement in working standards.* • **perceptibly** /-bli/ adv *The mood had changed perceptibly.*

perception /pəˈsep.ʃən/ (US) /pɚ-/ noun BELIEF ▷ **1** C2 [C] a belief or opinion, often held by many people and based on how things seem: *We have to change the public's perception that money is being wasted.* ◦ *These photographs will affect people's perceptions of war.* SIGHT ▷ **2** [U] the quality of being aware of things through the physical senses, especially sight: *Drugs can alter your perception of reality.* **3** [U] someone's ability to notice and understand things that are not obvious to other people: *She has extraordinary powers of perception for one so young.* ◦ *He's not known for his perception.*

perceptive /pəˈsep.tɪv/ (US) /pɚ-/ adj C2 very good at noticing and understanding things that many people do not notice: *Her books are full of perceptive insights into the human condition.* • **perceptively** /-li/ adv *He has spoken perceptively on many subjects.* • **perceptiveness** /-nəs/ noun [U]

perceptual /pəˈsep.tju.əl/ (US) /pɚ-/ adj specialized relating to the ability to notice something or come to an opinion about something using your senses: *Perceptual skills are particularly important in sports.*

perch /pɜːtʃ/ (US) /pɜːtʃ/ verb; noun

▸verb **1 perch in, on, etc. sth** to sit on or near the edge of something: *We perched on bar stools and had a beer.* ◦ *A blackbird was perching on the gate.* **2** [I or T] to be in a high position or in a position near the edge of something, or to put something in this position: *The village is perched on top of a high hill.*

▸noun FISH ▷ **1** [C or U] (plural **perch** or US also **perches**) a fish that lives in lakes and rivers and is eaten as food SEAT ▷ **2** [C] a place where a bird sits, especially a thin rod in a CAGE (= wire box) **3** [C] a seat or other place high up, often giving a good view of something below: *We watched the parade from our perch on the scaffolding.*

perchance /pəˈtʃɑːns/ (US) /pɚˈtʃæns/ adv old use by chance; possibly: *Do you know her, perchance?*

percipient /pəˈsɪp.i.ənt/ (US) /pɚ-/ adj formal good at noticing and understanding things

percolate /ˈpɜː.kəl.eɪt/ (US) /ˈpɜː-/ verb LIQUID ▷ **1** [I] If a liquid percolates, it moves slowly through a

P

substance with very small holes in it: *Sea water percolates down through the rocks.* **INFORMATION ▷ 2** [I] to spread slowly: *The news has begun to percolate* ***through*** *the staff.*

percolator /ˈpɜː.kəl.eɪ.təʳ/ (US) /ˈpɝː.kəl.eɪ.t̬ɚ/ **noun** [C] a device for making coffee in which hot water passes through crushed coffee beans into a container below

percussion /pəˈkʌʃ.ən/ (US) /pɚ-/ **noun** [U] musical instruments that you play by hitting them with your hand or an object such as a stick: *Drums, tambourines, and cymbals are all percussion instruments.* ◦ *Jean plays the guitar and her brother is* ***on*** *percussion (= plays percussion instruments).* → Compare **brass, woodwind**

percussionist /pəˈkʌʃ.ən.ɪst/ (US) /pɚ-/ **noun** [C] a person who plays percussion instruments

percussive /pəˈkʌs.ɪv/ (US) /pɚ-/ **adj** relating to percussion instruments

perdition /pəˈdɪʃ.ən/ (US) /pɚ-/ **noun** [U] literary a state of punishment which goes on for ever, suffered by evil people after death

peregrination /ˌper.ə.grɪˈneɪ.ʃən/ **noun** [C] formal a long journey in which you travel to various different places, especially on foot

peregrine falcon /ˌper.ə.grɪnˈfɒl.kən/ (US) /-ˈfɑːl-/ **noun** [C] a large bird with a dark back and wings and a lightly coloured front, which catches mice and other small animals

peremptory /pəˈremp.tər.i/ (US) /-tɚ-/ **adj** expecting to be obeyed immediately and without asking questions: *He started issuing peremptory instructions.* ◦ *She was highly critical of the insensitive and peremptory way in which the cases had been handled.*
• **peremptorily** /-trə.li/ **adv**

perennial /pəˈren.i.əl/ **adj; noun**
▸**adj** lasting a very long time, or happening repeatedly or all the time: *The film 'White Christmas' is a perennial favourite.* ◦ *We face the perennial problem of not having enough money.* → Compare **annual, biennial**
• **perennially** /-ə.li/ **adv** *She seems to be perennially short of money.*
▸**noun** [C] a plant that lives for several years: *Roses and geraniums are perennials, flowering year after year.* → Compare **annual**

perestroika /ˌper.əˈstrɔɪ.kə/ **noun** [U] the political, social, and economic changes that happened in the USSR during the late 1980s

perfect **adj; noun; verb**
▸**adj** /ˈpɜː.fekt/ (US) /ˈpɝː-/ **WITHOUT FAULT ▷ 1** (A2) complete and correct in every way, of the best possible type or without fault: *a perfect day* ◦ *What is your idea of perfect happiness?* ◦ *This church is a perfect example of medieval architecture.* ◦ *You have a perfect English accent.* ◦ *The car is five years old but is in almost perfect condition.* ◦ *She thought at last she'd found the perfect man.* **2** (C2) used to emphasize a noun: *It makes perfect sense.* ◦ *a perfect stranger* **3** (B1) exactly right for someone or something: *You'd be perfect* ***for*** *the job.* ◦ *The weather's just perfect for swimming.* **PAST TENSE ▷ 4** specialized of or relating to a verb indicating a completed action: *the present perfect tense*
▸**noun** [S] specialized **the perfect (tense)** (B2) the tense of a verb that shows action that has happened in the past or before another time or event: *In English, the perfect is formed with 'have' and the past participle of the verb.*
▸**verb** [T] /pəˈfekt/ (US) /pɝːˈ-/ (C2) to make something free from faults: *He is keen to perfect his golfing technique.*

perfection /pəˈfek.ʃən/ (US) /pɚ-/ **noun** [U] **1** (C1) the state of being complete and correct in every way: *In his quest for physical perfection, he spends hours in the gym.* **2 to perfection** extremely well: *The fish was cooked to perfection.*

> **+ Other ways of saying perfect**
>
> If something is perfect because it has no mistakes or anything bad, you can use adjectives such as **faultless, flawless, immaculate,** and **impeccable**:
> *They gave a* ***faultless*** *performance.*
> *The house was always in* ***immaculate*** *condition.*
> *His English is* ***impeccable.***
> *She has a* ***flawless*** *complexion.*
>
> The adjective **ideal** is sometimes used to describe something that is perfect for a particular purpose:
> *The book is* ***ideal*** *for children aged between four and six.*
>
> In informal situations, if you want to describe something such as a job, house, etc. that is perfect for you, you can describe it as a **dream** job, **dream** house, etc.:
> *A pretty cottage on the lake – that would be my* ***dream*** *home.*

perfectionism /pəˈfek.ʃən.ɪ.zəm/ (US) /pɚ-/ **noun** [U] the wish for everything to be correct: *Obsessive perfectionism can be very irritating.*

perfectionist /pəˈfek.ʃən.ɪst/ (US) /pɚ-/ **noun** [C] a person who wants everything to be perfect and demands the highest standards possible: *She's such a perfectionist that she notices even the tiniest mistakes.*

perfectly /ˈpɜː.fekt.li/ (US) /ˈpɝː-/ **adv** **1** (B1) in a perfect way: *The jacket fits perfectly, the skirt not so well.* ◦ *They're perfectly suited.* **2** (B2) used to emphasize the word that follows: *To be perfectly honest, I don't care any more.* ◦ *You know perfectly well what the matter is.* ◦ *I made it perfectly clear to him what I meant.* ◦ *I was perfectly happy on my own.*

ˌperfect ˈparticiple **noun** [C] another word for **past participle**

ˌperfect ˈstorm **noun** [C, usually singular] an extremely bad situation in which many bad things happen at the same time

perfidious /pəˈfɪd.i.əs/ (US) /pɚ-/ **adj** literary unable to be trusted, or showing no loyalty: *She described the new criminal bill as a perfidious attack on democracy.*

perfidy /ˈpɜː.fɪ.di/ (US) /ˈpɝː.fə-/ **noun** [U] literary behaviour that is not loyal

perforate /ˈpɜː.fər.eɪt/ (US) /ˈpɝː.fə.reɪt/ **verb** [T] to make a hole or holes in something: *He suffered from bruises and a perforated eardrum in the accident.*
• **perforation** /ˌpɜː.fərˈeɪ.ʃən/ (US) /ˌpɝː.fəˈreɪ-/ **noun** [C or U] *A tea bag is full of tiny perforations.*

perforated /ˈpɜː.fər.eɪ.tɪd/ (US) /ˈpɝː.fə.reɪ.t̬ɪd/ **adj** If paper or another material is perforated, it has a series of small holes made in it, often so that it will tear easily or allow light or air to enter: *The windows have been covered with perforated metal screens.*

perforce /pəˈfɔːs/ (US) /pɚˈfɔːrs/ **adv** old-fashioned formal because it is necessary

perform /pəˈfɔːm/ (US) /pɚˈfɔːrm/ **verb** **DO ▷ 1** (B2) [T] to do an action or piece of work: *Computers can perform a variety of tasks.* ◦ *The operation will be performed next week.* ◦ *Most of the students performed well in the exam.* **2 perform well/badly** to operate/not operate in a satisfactory way: *The equipment performed well during the tests.* ◦ *These tyres perform badly/poorly in hot weather.* **ENTERTAIN ▷ 3** (B1) [I or T] to entertain people by dancing, singing, acting, or playing music: *Thomas and Elisa performed a rousing duet for violin*

P

and piano. ◦ *A major Hollywood star will be performing on stage tonight.* ◦ *The council plans to ban circuses with performing animals.*

> **Word partners for performance (DO)**
> *improve* performance • *affect* sb's performance • *brilliant/disappointing/outstanding/poor* performance • *high* performance

performance /pəˈfɔː.mənts/ (US) /pɚˈfɔːr-/ noun **ACTIVITY** ▷ **1** (B2) [C or U] how well a person, machine, etc. does a piece of work or an activity: *Some athletes take drugs to improve their performance.* ◦ ***High-performance** cars (= those that are fast, powerful, and easy to control) are the most expensive.* ◦ *This was a very **impressive** performance by the young player, who scored 14 points within the first ten minutes.* **ENTERTAINMENT** ▷ **2** (B1) [C] the action of entertaining other people by dancing, singing, acting, or playing music: *a performance of Arthur Miller's play, 'The Crucible'* ◦ *She **gave** a superb performance as Lady Macbeth.* **3 a performance** mainly UK informal an action or type of behaviour that involves a lot of attention to detail or to small matters that are not important: *Cleaning the oven is such a performance.* ◦ *What a performance! Please stop shouting!* **4 a repeat performance** an occasion when an event or a situation happens again: *The police hope to avoid a repeat performance of last year, when the festivities turned into rioting.*

> **Word partners for performance**
> *give/put on* a performance • a *brilliant/fine/stunning/virtuoso* performance • sb's performance *in* [a play/flim/role, etc.]

perˈformance ˌart noun [C or U] a type of theatre entertainment in which the artist's personality and the way in which they create and develop their ideas form part of the show

perˈformance-enˌhancing adj used to describe drugs that are taken illegally by someone who plays sport to make them better at their sport

perˈformance-reˌlated adj used to describe money that someone earns that is directly to related to their success at doing their job: *Teachers have resisted the idea of performance-related **pay**.*

performer /pəˈfɔː.mər/ (US) /pɚˈfɔːr.mɚ/ noun [C] **ENTERTAIN** ▷ **1** (B1) a person who entertains people by acting, singing, dancing, or playing music: *He's a brilliant performer.* **DO** ▷ **2** If you are a particular type of performer, you are able to do the stated thing well or badly: *The British boat was the star performer in the race.*

the perˌforming ˈarts noun [plural] forms of entertainment such as acting, dancing, and playing music

perfume /ˈpɜː.fjuːm/ (US) /pɝːˈfjuːm/ noun **1** (A2) [C or U] a liquid with a pleasant smell, usually made from oils taken from flowers or spices and often used on the skin: *What perfume are you wearing?* ◦ *She adores French perfume.* **2** [U] a pleasant natural smell: *The perfume of the roses filled the room.* • **perfume** /ˈpɜː.fjuːm/ (US) /ˈpɝː-/ verb [T] *In the evening, the flowers perfume the air.*

perfumed /ˈpɜː.fjuːmd/ (US) /ˈpɝː-/ adj having a pleasant perfume: *perfumed bath oil* ◦ *expensively perfumed women*

perfunctory /pəˈfʌŋk.tᵊr.i/ (US) /pɚˈfʌŋk.tɚ.i/ adj done quickly, without taking care or interest: *His smile was perfunctory.* • **perfunctorily** /-ᵊl.i/ adv *The two heads of state shook hands perfunctorily for the photographers.*

pergola /ˈpɜː.gᵊl.ə/ (US) /ˈpɝː-/ noun [C] a structure in a garden that climbing plants can grow over and that people can walk through

perhaps /pəˈhæps/, /præps/ (US) /pɚˈhæps/ adv **1** (A2) used to show that something is possible or that you are not certain about something: *He hasn't written to me recently – perhaps he's lost my address.* ◦ *Perhaps the most important question has not been asked.* ◦ *We plan to travel to Europe – to Spain or Italy perhaps.* → See also **maybe** **2** used to show that a number or amount is approximate: *There were perhaps 500 people at the meeting.* **3** used when making polite requests or statements of opinion: *'I never remember people's birthdays.' 'Well, perhaps you should.'*

pericarp /ˈper.ɪ.kɑːp/ (US) /-kɑːrp/ noun [C usually sing] specialized the layer which develops from the OVARY wall around the seed of a plant after it is FERTILIZED and forms the skin and flesh of the fruit

peril /ˈper.ᵊl/ noun [C or U] formal **1** great danger, or something that is very dangerous: *I never felt that my life was **in** peril.* ◦ *The journey through the mountains was fraught with peril (= full of dangers).* ◦ *Teenagers must be warned about **the** perils **of** unsafe sex.* **2 do sth at your peril** to do something that might be very dangerous for you: *We underestimate the destructiveness of war at our peril.*

perilous /ˈper.ᵊl.əs/ adj formal extremely dangerous: *The country roads are quite perilous.* • **perilously** /-li/ adv *She **came** perilously **close** to getting herself killed in her attempt to break the world record.*

perimeter /pəˈrɪm.ɪ.tər/ (US) /-ˈrɪm.ə.t̬ɚ/ noun [C] **1** the outer edge of an area of land or the border around it: *Protesters cut a hole in the perimeter fence.* ◦ *A river runs along one side of the field's perimeter.* **2** specialized the length of the outer edge of a shape

period /ˈpɪə.ri.əd/ (US) /ˈpɪr.i-/ noun; adj

▸noun [C] **TIME** ▷ **1** (B1) a length of time: *Her work means that she spends long periods away from home.* ◦ *Unemployment in the first half of the year was 2.5 percent lower than **in** the same period the year before.* ◦ *15 people were killed **in/over** a period **of** four days.* ◦ *The study will be carried out **over** a six-month period.* **2** (B1) in school, a division of time in the day when a subject is taught: *We have six periods of science a week.* **3** a fixed time during the life of a person or in history: *Most teenagers go through a rebellious period.* ◦ *The house was built during the Elizabethan period.* **BLOOD** ▷ **4** the BLEEDING from a woman's WOMB that happens once a month when she is not pregnant: *period pains* ◦ *She'd missed a period and was worried.* **MARK** ▷ **5** mainly US for **full stop** **6** mainly US said at the end of a statement to show that you believe you have said all there is to say on a subject and you are not going to discuss it any more: *There will be no more shouting, period!*

▸adj **period costume/dress/furniture** the clothes or furniture of a particular time in history: *They performed 'Julius Caesar' in period dress.*

periodic /ˌpɪə.riˈɒd.ɪk/ (US) /ˌpɪr.iˈɑː.dɪk/ adj happening repeatedly over a period of time: *He suffers periodic mental breakdowns.*

periodical /ˌpɪə.riˈɒd.ɪ.kᵊl/ (US) /ˌpɪr.iˈɑː.dɪ-/ noun [C] a magazine or newspaper, especially on a serious subject, that is published regularly: *She has written for several legal periodicals.*

periodically /ˌpɪə.riˈɒd.ɪ.kᵊl.i/ (US) /ˌpɪr.iˈɑː.dɪ-/ adv in

P

a way that is repeated after a particular period of time: *The equipment should be tested periodically.*

the ˌperiodic ˈtable noun [S] specialized an arrangement of the symbols of chemical elements in rows and columns, showing similarities in chemical behaviour, especially between elements in the same columns

ˈperiod ˌpiece noun [C usually singular] something such as a book or a film that is very old-fashioned, often in a way that is funny to people now

peripatetic /ˌper.ɪ.pəˈtet.ɪk/ (US) /-ˈteţ-/ adj formal travelling around to different places, usually because you work in more than one place: *a peripatetic music teacher*

peripheral /pəˈrɪf.ər.əl/ (US) /-ˈrɪf.ɚ-/ **adj; noun**
▸**adj 1** describes something that is not as important as something else: *The book contains a great deal of peripheral detail.* **2** happening at the edge of something: *A figure came into my peripheral vision.*
▸**noun** [C] specialized a piece of equipment, such as a printer, that can be connected to a computer

periphery /pəˈrɪf.ər.i/ (US) /-ˈrɪf.ɚ-/ **noun** [C usually singular] **1** the outer edge of an area: *Houses have been built on the periphery of the factory site.* ◦ *The ring road runs around the periphery of the city centre.* **2** the less important part of a group or activity: *Many women feel they are being kept on the periphery of the armed forces.*

periscope /ˈper.ɪ.skəʊp/ (US) /-skoʊp/ **noun** [C] a long vertical tube containing a set of mirrors which gives you a view of what is above you when you look through the bottom of the tube: *Periscopes are used in submarines to allow you to look above the surface of the water.*

perish /ˈper.ɪʃ/ verb [I] **DIE** ▷ **1** to die, especially in an accident or by being killed, or to be destroyed: *Three hundred people perished in the earthquake.* ◦ *He believes that Europe must create closer ties or it will perish.* **DECAY** ▷ **2** UK If material such as rubber or leather perishes, it decays and starts to break into pieces: *Sunlight has caused the rubber to perish.*

P

IDIOM **perish the thought** humorous or informal said to show that you hope that something that has been suggested will never happen: *Me, get married? Perish the thought!*

perishable /ˈper.ɪ.ʃə.bl/ adj describes food that decays quickly: *It's important to store perishable food in a cool place.*

perishables /ˈper.ɪ.ʃə.bl̩z/ **noun** [plural] food products that decay quickly

perished /ˈper.ɪʃt/ adj [after verb] UK informal extremely cold: *Her hands were perished.* ◦ *I'm perished **with cold**.*

perisher /ˈper.ɪ.ʃər/ (US) /-ʃɚ/ **noun** [C] UK old-fashioned informal a child who is being annoying

perishing /ˈper.ɪ.ʃɪŋ/ adj **COLD** ▷ **1** UK informal extremely cold: *He's out there in the perishing **cold**.* **ANNOYED** ▷ **2** old-fashioned used to show your anger about something

peristalsis /ˌper.ɪˈstæl.sɪs/ (US) /-ˈstɑːl-/ **noun** [U] specialized the repeated movements made by the muscle walls in the DIGESTIVE TRACT tightening and then relaxing, which push food and waste through the body

peritonitis /ˌper.ɪ.təˈnaɪ.tɪs/ (US) /-ţəˈnaɪ.ţɪs/ **noun** [U] specialized a serious medical condition in which the inside wall of the ABDOMEN (= lower part of the body containing the stomach and other organs) becomes very sore and larger than its usual size, especially because of infection

periwinkle /ˈper.ɪˌwɪŋ.kl/ noun [C] **PLANT** ▷ **1** an EVERGREEN plant (= one that never loses its leaves) with small, blue flowers **SEA CREATURE** ▷ **2** US for **winkle**

perjure /ˈpɜː.dʒər/ (US) /ˈpɝː.dʒɚ/ verb legal **perjure yourself** to tell a lie in a law court, after promising formally to tell the truth: *The judge warned the witness not to perjure herself.* • **perjured** /-dʒəd/ (US) /-dʒɚd/ **adj** *a perjured testimony* • **perjurer** /-dʒər.ər/ (US) /-dʒɚ.ɚ/ **noun** [C]

perjury /ˈpɜː.dʒər.i/ (US) /ˈpɝː.dʒɚ-/ **noun** [U] legal the crime of telling lies in court when you have promised to tell the truth: *She was sentenced to two years in jail for **committing** perjury.*

perk /pɜːk/ (US) /pɝːk/ **noun; verb**
▸**noun** [C] **1** informal an advantage or extra thing, such as money or goods, which you are given because of your job: *A company car and a mobile phone are some of the perks that come with the job.* **2** an advantage: *Having such easy access to some of the best cinema and theatre is one of the perks of living in Sydney.*
▸**verb** [I or T] informal

PHRASAL VERBS **perk (sb) up** to become or cause someone to become happier, more energetic, or more active: *She perked up as soon as I mentioned that Charles was coming to dinner.* ◦ *He perked up **at** the news.* ◦ *Would you like a cup of coffee? It might perk you up a bit.* • **perk up** to improve or become more exciting: *Share prices perked up slightly before the close of trading.*

perky /ˈpɜː.ki/ (US) /ˈpɝː-/ **adj** happy and full of energy: *You look very perky this morning.* • **perkily** /-kɪ.li/ **adv** *'Does anyone want to come out jogging with me?' he said perkily.* • **perkiness** /-nəs/ **noun** [U]

perm /pɜːm/ (US) /pɝːm/ **noun** [C] (US or formal **permanent**, **permanent wave**) a chemical process that makes your hair curly, or a hairstyle that is created in this way: *Is your hair naturally curly or have you had a perm?* • **perm verb** [T] *I'm going to get my hair permed on Saturday.*

permafrost /ˈpɜː.mə.frɒst/ (US) /ˈpɝː.mə.frɑːst/ **noun** [U] specialized an area of land that is permanently frozen below the surface

permanence /ˈpɜː.mə.nəns/ (US) /ˈpɝː-/ **noun** [U] (formal **permanency**) staying the same or continuing for a long time: *A loving family environment gives children that sense of stability and permanence which they need.* → Opposite **impermanence**

permanent /ˈpɜː.mə.nənt/ (US) /ˈpɝː-/ **adj; noun**
▸**adj 1** (B1) lasting for a long time or for ever: *She is looking for a permanent place to stay.* ◦ *Are you looking for a temporary or a permanent job?* ◦ *The disease can cause permanent damage to the brain.* ◦ *A semi-permanent hair dye will wash out after about three months.* **2** describes something that exists or happens all the time: *Mont Blanc has a permanent snow cap.* ◦ *Our office is in a permanent state of chaos.*
▸**noun** [C] US for **perm**

permanently /ˈpɜː.mə.nənt.li/ (US) /ˈpɝː-/ **adv** (B2) always and for ever: *Smoking is likely to damage your health permanently.* ◦ *Michael and his family have settled permanently in the States.* ◦ *I seem to be permanently broke.*

ˌpermanent ˈsecretary noun [C] UK a government official who belongs to the CIVIL SERVICE (= the official departments responsible for putting government plans into action) rather than an elected government

ˌpermanent ˈwave noun [C] formal for **perm**

permeability /ˌpɜː.mi.əˈbɪl.ɪ.ti/ (US) /ˌpɝː.mi.əˈbɪl.ə.t̬i/ **noun** [U] formal the ability of a substance to allow gases or liquids to go through it: *Chalk has a **high** permeability (= liquids easily pass through it).*

permeable /ˈpɜː.mi.ə.bl̩/ (US) /ˈpɝː-/ **adj** formal If a substance is permeable, it allows liquids or gases to go through it: *Certain types of sandstone are permeable **to** water.* ◦ *The solvent passes through the permeable **membrane** to the solution.* ◦ *Soft and **gas**-permeable contact lenses are kinder to the eyes than hard lenses.* → Opposite **impermeable**

permeate /ˈpɜː.mi.eɪt/ (US) /ˈpɝː-/ **verb** [I usually + adv/prep, T] formal to spread through something and be present in every part of it: *Dissatisfaction with the government seems to have permeated every section of society.* ◦ *A foul smell of stale beer permeated the whole building.* ◦ *The table has a plastic coating which prevents liquids from permeating **into** the wood beneath.*

permissible /pəˈmɪs.ə.bl̩/ (US) /pɚ-/ **adj** formal allowed: [+ to infinitive] *Is **it** permissible **to** park my car here?* ◦ *a permissible level for vehicle exhaust emissions*

permission /pəˈmɪʃ.ᵊn/ (US) /pɚ-/ **noun** [U] **B1** If someone is given permission to do something, they are allowed to do it: [+ to infinitive] *You will need permission from your parents **to** go on the trip.* ◦ *Official permission has been **granted** for more building near the river.* ◦ *The authorities have **refused** permission for the demonstration to take place.* ◦ ***Planning** permission was refused for the hypermarket after a three-week inquiry.*

> **Word partners for permission**
>
> *ask for/request/seek* permission • *get/have/obtain* permission • *give/grant/refuse* permission • *special* permission • permission *for* sth • *with/without* (sb's) permission

permissive /pəˈmɪs.ɪv/ (US) /pɚ-/ **adj** A person or society that is permissive allows behaviour which other people might disapprove of: *It's a very permissive school where the children are allowed to do whatever they like.* ◦ *He claims that society has been far too permissive **towards** drug taking.*

permissiveness /pəˈmɪs.ɪv.nəs/ (US) /pɚ-/ **noun** [U] a situation in which behaviour that some people might disapprove of is allowed: *She attributed the social and economic problems of the 1980s to the permissiveness of the 1960s.* ◦ *He remembers his youth as being an era of **sexual** permissiveness.*

permit verb; noun

▸**verb** /pəˈmɪt/ (US) /pɚ-/ (-tt-) **1** **B1** [T] formal to allow something: *The regulations do not permit much flexibility.* ◦ [+ -ing verb] *The prison authorities permit visit**ing** only once a month.* ◦ [+ obj + to infinitive] *The security system will not permit you **to** enter without the correct password.* ◦ *As it was such a special occasion, she permitted herself a small glass of champagne.* ◦ formal *The law permits **of** no other interpretation.* **2** **C1** [I] formal to make something possible: *The Chancellor is looking to lower interest rates, when economic conditions permit.* ◦ *We have arranged to play tennis on Saturday, **weather** permitting (= if the weather is good enough).*

▸**noun** [C] /ˈpɜː.mɪt/ (US) /ˈpɝː-/ **C1** an official document that allows you to do something or go somewhere: *a work/travel/parking permit* ◦ *She has managed to obtain a temporary residence permit.* ◦ [+ to infinitive] *Do you need a permit **to** work here?*

permutation /ˌpɜː.mjuˈteɪ.ʃᵊn/ (US) /ˌpɝː.mjuː-/ **noun** **1** [C usually plural] formal any of the various ways in which a set of things can be ordered: *There are 120 permutations **of** the numbers 1, 2, 3, 4 and 5: for example, 1, 3, 2, 4, 5 or 5, 1, 4, 2, 3.* ◦ *He made six separate applications for a total of 39,000 shares, using permutations of his surname and Christian names.* **2** [C] one of several different forms: *The company has had five different names in its various permutations over the last few years.*

pernicious /pəˈnɪʃ.əs/ (US) /pɚ-/ **adj** formal having a very harmful effect or influence: *The cuts in government funding have had a pernicious effect on local health services.*

pernickety /pəˈnɪk.ɪ.ti/ (US) /pɚˈnɪk.ə.t̬i/ **adj** (US usually **persnickety**) giving too much attention to small details that are not important in a way that annoys other people: *As a writer, he is extremely pernickety about using words correctly.*

peroxide /pəˈrɒk.saɪd/ (US) /pəˈrɑːk-/ **noun** [C or U] a liquid chemical used to make hair very pale in colour or to kill bacteria: *Peroxide is a bleach and an antiseptic.*

perˌoxide ˈblonde **noun** [C] mainly disapproving a woman who has used peroxide to make her hair BLONDE

perpendicular /ˌpɜː.pᵊnˈdɪk.jʊ.ləʳ/ (US) /ˌpɝː.pənˈdɪk.juː.lɚ/ **adj; noun**

▸**adj** **1** formal at an angle of 90° to a horizontal line or surface: *We scrambled up the nearly perpendicular side of the mountain.* **2** specialized at an angle of 90° to another line or surface: *The wheel rotates about an axis which is perpendicular **to** the plane.* • **perpendicularly** /-li/ **adv** formal or specialized

▸**noun** [C] specialized **1** a perpendicular line: *Draw a perpendicular from the vertex of the triangle to its base.* **2** **the perpendicular** a perpendicular position or direction: *The wall was leaning at an angle of ten degrees to the perpendicular.*

perpetrate /ˈpɜː.pə.treɪt/ (US) /ˈpɝː-/ **verb** [T] formal to commit a crime or a violent or harmful act: *In Britain, half of all violent crime is perpetrated by people who have been drinking alcohol.* ◦ *Federal soldiers have been accused of perpetrating atrocities **against** innocent people.* • **perpetration** /ˌpɜː.pəˈtreɪ.ʃᵊn/ (US) /ˌpɝː-/ **noun** [U] *Human rights activists have accused the country's government of a systematic perpetration of violence **against** minority groups.*

perpetrator /ˈpɜː.pə.treɪ.təʳ/ (US) /ˈpɝː.pə.treɪ.t̬ɚ/ **noun** [C] (US old-fashioned slang **perp**) someone who has committed a crime or a violent or harmful act: *The perpetrators of the massacre must be brought to justice as war criminals.*

perpetual /pəˈpetʃ.u.əl/ (US) /pɚˈpetʃ-/ **adj** **1** continuing for ever in the same way: *They lived in perpetual fear of being discovered.* ◦ *He has hard, cold eyes and his mouth is set in a perpetual sneer.* ◦ *a perpetual student* **2** often repeated: *perpetual vandalism*

perpetually /pəˈpetʃ.u.ə.li/ (US) /pɚˈpetʃ-/ **adv** always or very often: *She's perpetually asking me for money.*

perpetuate /pəˈpetʃ.u.eɪt/ (US) /pɚˈpetʃ-/ **verb** [T] formal to cause something to continue: *Increasing the supply of weapons will only perpetuate the violence and anarchy.* ◦ *The aim of the association is to perpetuate the skills of traditional furniture design.* • **perpetuation** /pəˌpetʃ.uˈeɪ.ʃᵊn/ (US) /ˌpɚ.petʃ-/ **noun** [U] *The lack of military action from other countries has contributed to the perpetuation of the civil war.*

perpetuity /ˌpɜː.pəˈtjuː.ə.ti/ (US) /ˌpɝː.pəˈtuː.ə.t̬i/ **noun** formal **in perpetuity** for ever

perplex /pəˈpleks/ (US) /pɚ-/ **verb** [T] to confuse and

P

worry someone slightly by being difficult to understand or solve: *The disease has continued to perplex doctors.* • **perplexed** /pəˈplekst/ (US) /pɚ-/ **adj** *The students looked perplexed, so the teacher tried to explain once again.* • **perplexing** /pəˈplek.sɪŋ/ (US) /pɚ-/ **adj** *They find the company's attitude perplexing and unreasonable.*

perplexity /pəˈplek.sɪ.ti/ (US) /pɚˈplek.sə.t̬i/ **noun** [C or U] a state of confusion or a complicated and difficult situation or thing: *She stared at the instruction booklet **in** complete perplexity.* ◦ *the perplexities of life*

perp walk /ˈpɜːpˌwɔːk/ (US) /ˈpɝːpˌwɑːk/ **noun** [C] US informal an occasion when police officers take a person who has been arrested for a crime through a public area so he or she can be seen and photographed by the MEDIA

per se /ˌpɜːˈseɪ/ (US) /ˌpɝː-/ **adv** formal by or of itself: *Research shows that it is not divorce per se that harms children, but the continuing conflict between parents.*

persecute /ˈpɜː.sɪ.kjuːt/ (US) /ˈpɝː-/ **verb** [T] to treat someone unfairly or cruelly over a long period of time because of their race, religion, or political beliefs, or to annoy someone by refusing to leave them alone: *Religious minorities were persecuted and massacred during the ten-year regime.* ◦ *His latest film is about the experience of being persecuted **for** being gay.* ◦ *Ever since the news broke about her divorce, she has been persecuted by the tabloid press.*

persecution /ˌpɜː.sɪˈkjuː.ʃən/ (US) /ˌpɝː-/ **noun** [C or U] unfair or cruel treatment over a long period of time because of race, religion, or political beliefs: *refugees escaping from political persecution*

perseˈcution ˌcomplex **noun** [C] If someone has a persecution complex, they suffer from the feeling that other people are trying to harm them.

persecutor /ˈpɜː.sɪ.kjuː.təʳ/ (US) /ˈpɝː.sɪ.kjuː.t̬ɚ/ **noun** [C] someone who treats a particular group of people cruelly: *The country's native people rose up against their persecutors.* ◦ *The clergy were the main persecutors **of** witches in the Middle Ages.*

P

perseverance /ˌpɜː.sɪˈvɪə.rəns/ (US) /ˌpɝː.səˈvɪr.əns/ **noun** [U] approving (C2) continued effort and determination: *Through hard work and perseverance, he worked his way up from being a teacher in a village school to the headmaster of a large college.*

persevere /ˌpɜː.sɪˈvɪəʳ/ (US) /ˌpɝː.səˈvɪr/ **verb** [I] mainly approving to try to do or continue doing something in a determined way, despite having problems: *It looks as if the policy will be a success, providing that the government perseveres and does not give in to its critics.* ◦ *The education director is persevering **in** his attempt to obtain additional funding for the school.* ◦ *Despite receiving little support, the women are persevering **with** their crusade to fight crime.* • **persevering** /-ˈvɪə.rɪŋ/ (US) /-ˈvɪr.ɪŋ/ **adj** *She was persevering enough to reach the height of her ambition and become managing director.*

Persian cat /ˌpɜː.ʒənˈkæt/ (US) /ˌpɝː-/ **noun** [C] a type of cat with long hair, short legs, and a round face

persimmon /pəˈsɪm.ən/ (US) /pɚ-/ **noun** [C] a very sweet orange tropical fruit

persist /pəˈsɪst/ (US) /pɚ-/ **verb** [I] **1** (C2) If an unpleasant feeling or situation persists, it continues to exist: *If the pain persists, consult a doctor.* ◦ *The cold weather is set to persist throughout the week.* **2** (C2) to try to do or continue doing something in a determined but often unreasonable way: *If he persists **in** asking awkward questions, then send him to the boss.* ◦ *The government is persisting **with** its ambitious public works programme.*

persistence /pəˈsɪs.təns/ (US) /pɚ-/ **noun** [U] (C2) the fact that someone or something persists: *Most financial analysts have been surprised by the persistence **of** the recession.* ◦ *Her persistence and enthusiasm have helped the group to achieve its international success.*

persistent /pəˈsɪs.tənt/ (US) /pɚ-/ **adj** **1** lasting for a long time or difficult to get rid of: *a persistent smell/skin rash* ◦ *Symptoms of the illness include a high temperature and a persistent dry cough.* ◦ *There have been persistent **rumours** that the managing director might take early retirement.* **2** (C2) Someone who is persistent continues doing something or tries to do something in a determined but often unreasonable way: *Be persistent – don't give up.* ◦ *He has been a persistent critic of the president.* ◦ *She is a persistent **offender** and has been arrested five times this year for shoplifting.* • **persistently** /-li/ **adv** *They have persistently ignored our advice.*

perˌsistent ˌvegetative ˈstate **noun** [U] specialized a medical condition in which a person's brain shows no sign of activity and they have to be kept alive by drugs and machines

persnickety /pəˈsnɪk.ɪ.ti/ (US) /pɚˈsnɪk.ə.t̬i/ **adj** US for **pernickety**

person /ˈpɜː.sən/ (US) /ˈpɝː-/ **noun** [C] (plural **people** or formal **persons**) **HUMAN** ▷ **1** (A1) a man, woman, or child: *Who was the first person to swim the English Channel?* ◦ *A meal at the restaurant costs about $70 for two people.* ◦ legal *Four persons have been charged with the murder.* **2** used when describing someone and their particular type of character: *She's an extremely kind person.* ◦ *He's nice enough **as a** person, but he's not the right man for this job.* ◦ informal *I don't think of him as a book person (= a person who likes books).* **3 in person** (B2) If you do something or go somewhere in person, you do it or go there yourself: *If you can't be there in person, the next best thing is watching it on TV.*

> **! Common mistake: persons or people?**
>
> **Remember:** the plural of 'person' is usually **people**:
>
> ~~*There are twenty persons in my English class.*~~
>
> *There are twenty people in my English class.*
>
> **Persons** is usually used in official language, especially in public notices or legal documents:
>
> *Attention: This taxi is licensed to carry a maximum of 4 persons.*

GRAMMAR ▷ **4** specialized used in grammar to describe the verbs and PRONOUNS that refer to the different people in a conversation. The first person ('I' or 'we') refers to the person speaking, the second person ('you') refers to the person being spoken to and the third person ('he', 'she', 'it' or 'they') refers to another person or thing being spoken about or described: *The novel is written in the first person, so that the author and narrator seem to be the same.* ◦ *'Am' is the first person singular of the verb 'to be'.*

IDIOMS **in the person of sb** formal in the form of someone: *The editorial board has an expert with a world-wide reputation in the person of Professor Jameson.* • **on/about your person** formal in a pocket, bag, or something else that you are holding: *Do you have about your person such a thing as a lighter?*

-person /-pɜː.sən/ (US) /-pɝː-/ **suffix** used to combine with nouns to form new nouns referring to the particular job or duty that someone has. It is often used instead of -man or -woman to avoid making an unnecessary statement about the sex of the particular person: *spokesperson* ∘ *chairperson* ∘ *business people*

persona /pəˈsəʊ.nə/ (US) /pɚˈsoʊ-/ noun [C] (plural **personae** or **personas**) the particular type of character that a person seems to have and that is often different from their real or private character: *He had a shy, retiring side to his personality that was completely at odds with his* ***public*** *persona.*

personable /ˈpɜː.sᵊn.ə.bl̩/ (US) /ˈpɝː-/ adj formal having a pleasant appearance and character: *She is intelligent, hard-working and personable.*

personage /ˈpɜː.sᵊn.ɪdʒ/ (US) /ˈpɝː-/ noun [C] formal an important or famous person

personal /ˈpɜː.sᵊn.ᵊl/ (US) /ˈpɝː.sᵊn.ᵊl/ adj **1** (B1) relating or belonging to a single or particular person rather than to a group or an organization: *My personal* ***opinion/view*** *is that the students should be doing more work outside the classroom.* ∘ *Her uncle takes a personal interest in her progress.* ∘ *She has her own personal secretary/bodyguard/fitness instructor.* ∘ *Passengers are reminded to take all their personal* ***belongings*** *with them when they leave the plane.* **2** A personal action is one that is done by someone directly rather than getting another person to do it: *The health minister made a personal* ***appearance*** *at the hospital.* ∘ *I will give the matter my personal* ***attention.*** **3** (B1) private or relating to someone's private life: *The letter was marked 'Personal. Strictly confidential.'* ∘ *Do you mind if I ask you a personal question?* ∘ *His resignation was apparently for personal rather than professional reasons.* ∘ *For such a famous, wealthy man, his personal* ***life*** *was surprisingly simple and ordinary.* **4** (C1) relating to your body or appearance: *She is obsessed with personal* ***hygiene.*** **5 personal remark/comment** an intentionally offensive remark about someone's character or appearance: *Did you have to make such a personal remark about her new haircut?* **6 get personal** informal to start being rude to someone about their character or appearance: *As long as the criticism is honestly given and doesn't get personal, I can handle it.*

ˌpersonal ˈad noun [C] an advertisement that you put in a newspaper or magazine, often in order to find a sexual partner: *He placed/put a personal ad in The Times.*

ˌpersonal alˈlowance noun [C] UK specialized an amount of money that you can earn before you start to be taxed

ˈpersonal ˌcolumn noun [C] UK (US **the personals**) the part of a newspaper or magazine which contains short advertisements and private messages

ˌpersonal comˈputer noun [C] (abbreviation **PC**) a computer that is used mainly by people at home rather than by large organizations

ˌpersonal ˌdigital asˈsistant noun [C] (abbreviation **PDA**) a small computer that you can carry with you

ˌpersonal efˈfects noun [plural] formal things you own that you often carry with you, such as keys or clothing: *After she had identified the body of her husband, the police asked her to collect his personal effects.*

ˌpersonal identifiˈcation ˌnumber noun [C] formal for **PIN**

personality /ˌpɜː.sᵊnˈæl.ə.ti/ (US) /ˌpɝː.sᵊnˈæl.ə.t̬i/ noun CHARACTER ▷ **1** (B2) [C or U] the type of person you are, shown by the way you behave, feel, and think: *She has a very warm personality.* ∘ *He is well qualified for the job, but he does lack personality (= he is a boring person).* FAMOUS PERSON ▷ **2** (B2) [C] a famous person: *The show is hosted by a popular TV personality.*

> **Word partners for personality**
>
> *have* a [great/strong] personality • a *bubbly/forceful/outgoing/strong* personality • a personality *type* • personality *characteristics/traits*

personˈality ˌclash noun [C] a situation in which two or more people have very different characters and are unable to have a good relationship with each other: *There's a real personality clash between two of the directors.*

personˈality ˌcult noun [C] disapproving officially organized admiration and love for a particular person, especially a political leader

personalize (UK usually **personalise**) /ˈpɜː.sᵊn.ᵊl.aɪz/ (US) /ˈpɝː-/ verb [T] **1** If you personalize an object, you change it or add to it so that it is obvious that it belongs to or comes from you: *The computer allows you to personalize standard letters by adding a greeting to each one.* ∘ *She had done little to personalize her room, except hang a few posters on the walls.* **2** to make something suitable for the needs of a particular person: *She hired a trainer to create a personalized exercise schedule to get her into shape.* **3** If you personalize a subject, you make people feel more emotionally involved in it by giving examples about real people: *By telling people about her accident, she personalizes the numbing figure of road accidents that happen every year.* **4** disapproving If you personalize an argument or discussion, you start to criticize someone's bad qualities instead of discussing the facts.

personalized (UK usually **personalised**) /ˈpɜː.sᵊn.ᵊl.aɪz/ (US) /ˈpɝː-/ adj describes an object that has someone's name on it, or that has been made for a particular person: *His car has a personalized number plate* – TJ 1.

personally /ˈpɜː.sᵊn.ᵊl.i/ (US) /ˈpɝː.r.sᵊn.ᵊl.i/ adv **1** (B1) used when you give your opinion: *Personally (speaking), I think the show is going to be a great success.* **2** (B2) affecting you and not anyone else: *He believes that parents should be made personally responsible for their children's behaviour.* **3** (B2) done by you and not by someone else: *These figures should be correct because I've checked them personally.* **4 take sth personally** (C1) to think that someone is offending you when they are not: *These criticisms should not be taken personally (= they are not meant to criticize any one person in particular).*

> **Common mistake: personally**
>
> **Warning:** Common word-building error!
>
> If an adjective ends with 'l', add '-ly' to make an adverb. Don't write 'personaly', write **personally.**

ˌpersonal ˈorganizer noun [C] a small book or electronic device in which information is stored, such as names, addresses, phone numbers, and dates of meetings, used to help organize your time

ˌpersonal ˈpronoun noun [C] specialized in grammar, a word such as 'I', 'you' and 'they' which refers to a person in speech or in writing

ˌpersonal ˈproperty noun [U] legal the things you own which you can take with you, such as money, vehicles, or furniture

ˌpersonal ˈshopper noun [C] someone whose job is to find things for someone else to buy

ˌpersonal ˈstereo noun [C] a small electronic device that plays music and has HEADPHONES so that you can listen to music while you are doing other things

ˌpersonal ˈtrainer noun [C] someone whose job is to

P

help you become stronger and healthier by deciding which exercises you should do and showing you how to do them

persona non grata /pə,səʊ.nə,nɒŋ'grɑː.tə/ (US) /pɚ,soʊ.nə,nɑːn'grɑː.t̬ə/ **noun** [C not after the] (plural **personae non gratae**) **1** specialized a person who is not wanted or welcome in a particular country, because they are unacceptable to its government: *He was **declared** persona non grata and asked to leave the country within 48 hours.* **2** someone who is not popular or accepted by others: *From the look on their faces, I was obviously persona non grata.*

personify /pə'sɒn.ɪ.faɪ/ (US) /pɚ'sɑː.nɪ-/ **verb** [T] **1** to be a perfect example of something: *These louts personify all that is wrong with our society today.* **2** specialized to treat something as if it were in the form of a human being: *In Greek myth, love is personified by the goddess Aphrodite.* • **personification** /pə,sɒn.ɪ.fɪ'keɪ.ʃən/ (US) /pɚ,sɑː.nɪ-/ **noun** [C usually singular, U] *She played a character who was the personification **of** evil.* • **personified** /-faɪd/ **adj** [after noun] *She is charm personified.*

personnel /,pɜː.sən'el/ (US) /,pɝː-/ **noun** [U, + sing/pl verb] **1** (C1) the people who are employed in a company, organization, or one of the armed forces: *The new director is likely to make major changes in personnel.* ◦ *military personnel* **2** (C1) the department of a company or organization that deals with its employees when they first join, when they need training, or when they have any problems: *Personnel will help you find a flat to rent.* ◦ *For more information about the job, please contact the personnel **manager**.*

person'nel ,carrier **noun** [C] an armed transport vehicle used by the army

,person-to-'person **adj**; **adv**
▸**adj** US describes a phone call where you ask the OPERATOR (= a person who helps connect people on the phone) to allow you to speak directly to a particular person
▸**adv** mainly US If you talk to or meet someone person-to-person, you talk to or meet them directly.

P

perspective /pə'spek.tɪv/ (US) /pɚ'spek-/ **noun** **THOUGHT** ▷ **1** (C1) [C] a particular way of considering something: *Her attitude lends a fresh perspective to the subject.* ◦ *He writes **from** a Marxist perspective.* ◦ *Because of its geographical position, Germany's perspective **on** the situation in Eastern Europe is rather different from Britain's.* **2 get/keep sth in perspective** (C2) to think about a situation or problem in a wise and reasonable way: *You must keep things in perspective – the overall situation isn't really that bad.* **3 put sth in (to) perspective** (C2) to compare something to other things so that it can be accurately and fairly judged: *Total investments for this year reached £53 million, and, to put this into perspective, investments this year were double those made in 2011.* **ART** ▷ **4** [U] the way that objects appear smaller when they are further away and the way parallel lines appear to meet each other at a point in the distance **5 in perspective** An object or person that is in perspective has the correct size and position in comparison with other things in the picture. **6 out of perspective** An object or person that is out of perspective does not have the correct size or position in comparison with other things in the picture, and therefore does not look real or natural.

Perspex /'pɜː.speks/ (US) /'pɝː-/ **noun** [U] UK trademark (US trademark **Plexiglas**) a strong, transparent plastic that is sometimes used instead of glass

perspicacious /,pɜː.spɪ'keɪ.ʃəs/ (US) /,pɝː-/ **adj** formal approving quick in noticing, understanding, or judging things accurately: *His perspicacious grandfather had bought the land as an investment, guessing that there might be gold underground.*

perspicacity /,pɜː.spɪ'kæs.ə.ti/ (US) /,pɝː.spɪ'kæs.ə.t̬i/ **noun** [U] formal approving the ability to understand things quickly and make accurate judgments: *a woman of exceptional perspicacity*

perspiration /,pɜː.spər'eɪ.ʃən/ (US) /,pɝː.spə'reɪ-/ **noun** [U] polite word for SWEAT (= a clear liquid passed through the skin): *During the break between games, she had a drink of water and wiped the perspiration off her face and arms with a towel.* ◦ ***Beads** (= drops) of perspiration glistened on his brow.*

perspire /pə'spaɪər/ (US) /pɚ'spaɪɚ/ **verb** [I] formal or polite word for SWEAT (= to pass liquid through the skin): *He was perspiring in his thick woollen suit.* ◦ *The journalists and camera crews began to perspire in the heat as they stood waiting for the president to appear.*

persuade /pə'sweɪd/ (US) /pɚ-/ **verb** [T] (B1) to make someone do or believe something by giving them a good reason to do it or by talking to them and making them believe it: *If she doesn't want to go, nothing you can say will persuade her.* ◦ [+ (that)] *It's no use trying to persuade him (**that**) you're innocent.* ◦ [+ to infinitive] *He is trying to persuade local and foreign businesses **to** invest in the project.* ◦ *Using a bunch of bananas, the zoo-keeper persuaded the monkey back into its cage.* ◦ formal *The first priority is to persuade the management **of** the urgency of this matter.* ◦ *Her legal advisers persuaded her **into/out of** mentioning (= to mention/not to mention) the names of the people involved in the robbery.*

> **Other ways of saying persuade**
>
> The phrasal verb **talk someone into** doing something can be used instead of 'persuade':
>
> *She managed to **talk me into** going along.*
>
> The verbs **cajole** or **coax** are often used when someone persuades a person to do something by saying nice things to that person:
>
> *He really knows how to **cajole** people into doing what he wants.*
>
> *A mother was **coaxing** her reluctant child to get into the water.*
>
> If someone persuades a person that something is true, you could use the verb **convince**:
>
> *The lawyer **convinced** the jury of the man's innocence.*
>
> The verb **dissuade** means 'to persuade someone not to do something.':
>
> *I tried to **dissuade** her from leaving.*

persuasion /pə'sweɪ.ʒən/ (US) /pɚ-/ **noun** **CHANGING IDEAS** ▷ **1** (C2) [U] the action of persuading someone or of being persuaded: *It took a lot of persuasion to convince the committee of the advantages of the new scheme.* ◦ *She will help you – she just needs a bit of **gentle** persuasion.* ◦ *The occasion will be a test of the senator's **powers of** persuasion (= his ability to persuade people).* **BELIEFS** ▷ **2** [C] a particular set of beliefs, especially religious ones: *We need a society which welcomes people **of** all religious persuasions.*

persuasive /pə'sweɪ.sɪv/ (US) /pɚ-/ **adj** (C1) making you want to do or believe a particular thing: *a persuasive speaker/speech* ◦ *Your arguments are very persuasive.* ◦ *He can be very persuasive.* • **persuasively** /-li/ **adv** • **persuasiveness** /-nəs/ **noun** [U]

pert /pɜːt/ (US) /pɝːt/ **adj** **1** attractively small and firm, as a description of a part of the body: *a pert bottom/*

nose **2** describes behaviour or qualities, especially in a young woman, that are humorous because they do not show much respect: *a pert answer/glance/smile*

pertain /pɜːˈteɪn/ ⓤⓢ /pɝː-/ verb

PHRASAL VERB **pertain to sth** formal to be connected with a particular subject, event, or situation: *We are only interested in the parts of the proposals that pertain to local issues.*

pertinacious /ˌpɜː.tɪˈneɪ.ʃəs/ ⓤⓢ /ˌpɝː.tᵊnˈeɪ-/ **adj** formal very determined and refusing to be defeated by problems

pertinent /ˈpɜː.tɪ.nənt/ ⓤⓢ /ˈpɝː.tᵊn.ᵊnt/ **adj** formal relating directly to the subject being considered: *a pertinent question/remark* ◦ *Chapter One is pertinent* ***to*** *the post-war period.*

> **Note:**
> The opposite is **irrelevant.** Do not confuse with **impertinent** (= rude).

perturb /pəˈtɜːb/ ⓤⓢ /pɚˈtɝːb/ **verb** [T] formal to worry someone: *News of the arrest perturbed her greatly.*

perturbation /ˌpɜː.təˈbeɪ.ʃᵊn/ ⓤⓢ /ˌpɝː.t̬ɚ-/ **noun** **WORRY** ▷ **1** [U] formal worry **CHANGE** ▷ **2** [C or U] specialized a small change in the regular movement of an object: *Perturbations in the orbit of the planet Uranus led to the discovery of Neptune in 1846.*

perturbed /pəˈtɜːbd/ ⓤⓢ /pɚˈtɝːbd/ **adj** formal worried: *He didn't seem unduly/overly perturbed by the news.*

peruse /pəˈruːz/ **verb** [T] formal to read through something, especially in order to find the part you are interested in: *He opened a newspaper and began to peruse the personal ads.* • **perusal** /-ˈruː.zᵊl/ **noun** [S or U] formal *a brief perusal (= a quick read)* ◦ *He sent a copy of the report to the governors for their perusal (= for them to read).*

perv /pɜːv/ ⓤⓢ /pɝːv/ **noun** [C] UK informal for **pervert**

pervade /pəˈveɪd/ ⓤⓢ /pɚ-/ **verb** [T] formal When qualities, characteristics, or smells pervade a place or thing, they spread through it and are present in every part of it: *The film is a reflection of the violence that pervades our culture.*

pervasive /pəˈveɪ.sɪv/ ⓤⓢ /pɚ-/ **adj** formal present or noticeable in every part of a thing or place: *The influence of Freud is pervasive in her books.* ◦ *a pervasive smell of diesel* ◦ *Reforms are being undermined by the* ***all****-pervasive corruption in the country.* • **pervasively** /-li/ **adv** • **pervasiveness** /-nəs/ **noun** [U]

perverse /pəˈvɜːs/ ⓤⓢ /pɚˈvɝːs/ **adj** disapproving strange and not what most people would expect or enjoy: *Jack was being perverse and refusing to agree with anything we said.* ◦ *She took a perverse pleasure in hearing that her sister was getting divorced.* • **perversely** /-li/ **adv** *The best way to understand this book is to start, perversely, at the end.* • **perversity** /-ˈvɜː.sə.ti/ ⓤⓢ /-ˈvɝː.sə.t̬i/ **noun** [C or U] *The author of the book seems to be obsessed with* ***sexual*** *perversity.*

perversion /pəˈvɜː.ʒᵊn/ ⓤⓢ /pɚˈvɝː-/ **noun** [C or U] disapproving **1** sexual behaviour that is considered strange and unpleasant by most people: *The novels of the Marquis de Sade deal with sexual perversion.* **2** the changing of something so that it is not what it was or should be: *His testimony was clearly a perversion of the truth.*

pervert verb; noun

►**verb** [T] /pəˈvɜːt/ ⓤⓢ /pɚˈvɝːt/ disapproving **1** to change something so that it is not what it was or should be, or to influence someone in a harmful way: *Her ideas have been shamelessly perverted to serve the president's propaganda campaign.* **2 pervert the course of justice** legal to act illegally to avoid punishment or to get the wrong person punished: *The two police officers were charged with perverting the course of justice by fabricating evidence in the trial.*

►**noun** [C] /ˈpɜː.vɜːt/ ⓤⓢ /ˈpɝː.vɝːrt/ disapproving (UK informal **perv**) a person whose sexual behaviour is considered strange and unpleasant by most people

perverted /pəˈvɜː.tɪd/ ⓤⓢ /pɚˈvɝː.t̬ɪd/ **adj** disapproving considered strange and unpleasant by most people: *She told him he had a sick and perverted mind.* ◦ *He used a perverted form of socialism to incite racial hatred.*

pescetarian /ˌpes.kɪˈteə.ri.ən/ ⓤⓢ /-əˈteər.i-/ **noun** [C] (also **piscetarian** /ˌpɪs.kɪ-/ ⓤⓢ /ˌpɪs.kə-/) someone who eats fish but not meat • **pescetarian adj** (also **piscetarian**)

peseta /pəˈseɪ.tə/ ⓤⓢ /-t̬ə/ **noun** [C] the standard unit of money used in Spain before the introduction of the euro

pesky /ˈpes.ki/ **adj** [before noun] informal annoying or causing trouble: *Those pesky kids from next door have let down my car tyres again!*

peso /ˈpeɪ.səʊ/ ⓤⓢ /-soʊ/ **noun** [C] the standard unit of money used in Argentina, Mexico, and some other countries

pessimism /ˈpes.ɪ.mɪ.zᵊm/ **noun** [U] emphasizing or thinking of the bad part of a situation rather than the good part, or the feeling that bad things are more likely to happen than good things: *There is now a mood of deepening pessimism* ***about/over*** *the economy.* ◦ *An underlying pessimism infuses all her novels.* → Opposite **optimism** • **pessimist** /-mɪst/ **noun** [C] *Don't be such a pessimist!*

pessimistic /ˌpes.ɪˈmɪs.tɪk/ **adj** Ⓑ2 thinking that bad things are more likely to happen or emphasizing the bad part of a situation: *The tone of the meeting was very pessimistic.* ◦ *The doctors are pessimistic (= not hopeful)* ***about*** *his chances of recovery.* • **pessimistically** /-tɪ.kᵊl.i/ **adv**

pest /pest/ **noun** [C] **1** an insect or small animal that is harmful or damages crops: *common pests such as rats, mice, or cockroaches* **2** informal an annoying person, especially a child: *Put that back, you little pest!*

pester /ˈpes.təʳ/ ⓤⓢ /-tɚ/ **verb** [T] to behave in an annoying manner towards someone by doing or asking for something repeatedly: *At the frontier, there were people pestering tourists* ***for*** *cigarettes, food or alcohol.* ◦ [+ to infinitive] *John has been pestering her* ***to*** *go out with him all month.*

ˈpester ˌpower **noun** [U] informal the ability that children have to make their parents buy something, by asking for it many times until they get it: *Advertisers know how powerful pester power can be.*

pesticide /ˈpes.tɪ.saɪd/ ⓤⓢ /-t̬ə-/ **noun** [C or U] a chemical substance used to kill harmful insects, small animals, wild plants and other unwanted organisms: *The pesticides that farmers spray on their crops kill pests but they can also damage people's health.* → Compare **herbicide, insecticide**

pestilence /ˈpes.tɪ.ləns/ ⓤⓢ /-tᵊl.ᵊnts/ **noun** [C or U] formal any very serious infectious disease that spreads quickly and kills large numbers of people

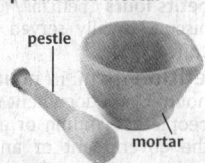

pestle and mortar

pestle

mortar

pestle /ˈpes.l̩/ **noun** [C] a heavy stick made of clay, stone, or metal with a thick, rounded end, used for crushing substances in a MORTAR (= a small strong bowl) by hitting or rubbing them

pesto /ˈpes.təʊ/ (US) /-toʊ/ **noun** [U] a green sauce used in Italian cooking, especially on PASTA

pet /pet/ **noun; verb; adj**

▸**noun** [C] **ANIMAL** ▷ **1** (A1) an animal that is kept in the home as a COMPANION and treated kindly: *They have several pets – a dog, two rabbits, and a guinea pig.* ◦ *a pet snake* **PERSON** ▷ **2 be sb's pet** disapproving to be the person that someone in authority likes best and treats better than anyone else: *The other children hated her because she was the* ***teacher's*** *pet.* **3** informal approving a kind person who is easy to like: *He's always sending me flowers – he's a real pet!* **4** UK informal a friendly way of talking to someone, especially a woman or a child: *Thank you, pet.*

▸**verb** (-tt-) **1** [T] If you pet an animal, child, etc., you touch it, him, or her gently and kindly with your hands: *Our dog loves to be petted and tickled behind the ears.* **2** [I] informal If two people are petting, they are kissing and touching each other in a sexual way. → See also **heavy petting**

▸**adj pet theory, subject, hate, etc.** a theory, subject, hate, etc. that is special and important to you: *Football is one of her pet hates.* ◦ US *My* ***pet peeve*** *(= pet hate) is cleaning the bathroom.*

petal /ˈpet.əl/ (US) /ˈpeţ-/ **noun** [C] **ON FLOWER** ▷ **1** any of the usually brightly coloured parts that together form most of a flower: *rose petals* **PERSON** ▷ **2** UK informal a friendly way of talking to someone, especially a woman or child: *What did you say, petal?*

-petalled (US usually **-petaled**) /-pet.əld/ (US) /-peţ-/ **suffix** having the number or colour of petals that is mentioned: *a five-petalled flower* ◦ *a white-petalled rose*

petard /petˈɑːd/ (US) /pɪˈtɑːrd/ **noun be hoist(ed) with/by your own petard** → See at **hoist**

peter /ˈpiː.təʳ/ (US) /-ţɚ/ **verb; noun**

▸**verb**

PHRASAL VERB **peter out** to gradually stop or disappear: *The fighting which started in the night had petered out by morning.* ◦ *The track petered out after a mile or so.*

▸**noun** [C] mainly US offensive a PENIS

petit bourgeois /ˌpet.iˈbɔː.ʒwɑː/ (US) /pəˌtiː.bʊrˈʒwɑː/ **adj** mainly disapproving (UK also ˌ**petty** ˈ**bourgeois**) belonging to the lower middle social class, or having the characteristics that are connected with this class, such as thinking money and possessions are more important than other things, and not trusting new or different ideas

petite /pəˈtiːt/ **adj 1** approving If a woman or girl is petite, she is small and thin in an attractive way: *She was dark and petite, as all his wives had been.* **2** of a clothing size that is for small women

the petite bourgeoisie (UK also **the** ˌ**petty** ˌ**bourgeoiˈsie**) /pəˌt.iːtˌbɔː.ʒwɑːˈziː/ (US) /-ˌbʊr-/ **noun** [S, + sing/pl verb] mainly disapproving the lower middle social class

petit four /ˌpet.iˈfɔːʳ/ (US) /ˌpeţ.iˈfɔːr/ **noun** [C] (plural **petits fours** /ˌpet.iˈfɔːʳ/ (US) /ˌpeţ.iˈfɔːr/) a small cake or biscuit, usually served at the end of a meal with coffee

petition /pəˈtɪʃ.ən/ **noun; verb**

▸**noun** [C] **1** a document signed by a large number of people demanding or asking for some action from the government or another authority: *I signed a petition* ***against*** *the proposed closure of the local hospital today.* **2** legal a formal letter to a law court asking for a particular legal action: *She's* ***filing*** *a petition* ***for*** *divorce.*

▸**verb** [I or T] to make a formal request for something, especially in a law court: *They're petitioning* ***for/about*** *better facilities for disabled people on public transport.* ◦ [+ obj + to infinitive] *I think we should petition the government* ***to*** *increase the grant for the project.* ◦ legal *She is petitioning* ***for*** *a re-trial.*

petitioner /pəˈtɪʃ.ən.əʳ/ (US) /-ɚ/ **noun** [C] **1** a person who organizes or signs a petition **2** legal a person who is asking for action from a law court

petits pois /ˌpet.iˈpwɑː/ (US) /pəˌtiː-/ **noun** [plural] mainly UK small PEAS (= round, green seeds that are eaten as a vegetable)

ˌ**pet** ˈ**name noun** [C] an informal name given to someone by their family or friends

petrel /ˈpet.rəl/ **noun** [C] a sea bird with a curved beak, which spends most of its life flying over the sea

Petri dish /ˈpet.riˌdɪʃ/ (US) /ˈpiː.tri-/ **noun** [C] a small, clear, round dish with a cover, used in scientific tests especially for growing bacteria

petrified /ˈpet.rə.faɪd/ **adj FRIGHTENED** ▷ **1** (B2) extremely frightened: *I stood petrified as the most enormous dog I've ever seen came bounding up to me.* ◦ *She's petrified* ***of*** *being on her own in the house at night.* **LIKE STONE** ▷ **2** having changed to a substance like stone: *a petrified tree/shell* **3** literary describes something that has stopped changing and developing, and often belongs to the past

petrify /ˈpet.rə.faɪ/ **verb FRIGHTEN** ▷ **1** [T] to frighten someone a lot, especially so that they are unable to move or speak: *I think you petrified poor Jeremy – he never said a word the whole time you were here.* **CHANGE TO STONE** ▷ **2** [I] If dead things petrify, they change to a substance like stone over a long period of time. • **petrifaction** /ˌpet.rɪˈfæk.ʃən/ **noun** [U] (also **petrification**)

petrochemical /ˌpet.rəʊˈkem.ɪ.kəl/ (US) /-roʊ-/ **noun** [C] any chemical substance obtained from PETROLEUM or natural gas: *the petrochemical industry*

petrodollar /ˈpet.rəʊˌdɒl.əʳ/ (US) /-roʊˌdɑː.lɚ/ **noun** [C] a unit of money earned by countries that produce PETROLEUM for sale to other countries: *Petrodollars have maintained Kuwait's wealth.*

petrol /ˈpet.rəl/ **noun** [U] UK (US **gas**) (A2) a liquid obtained from PETROLEUM, used especially as a fuel for cars, aircraft, and other vehicles: *a petrol tank/pump/station* ◦ *lead-free/unleaded/high-octane petrol* ◦ *I'm a bit* ***low on*** *(= I haven't got much) petrol.*

ˈ**petrol** ˌ**bomb noun** [C] a bottle filled with petrol or other liquid fuel with a piece of cloth in its top, that is set on fire and thrown: *The rioters were throwing petrol bombs.* • ˈ**petrol-bomb verb** [T]

ˈ**petrol** ˌ**bunk noun** [C] (also **bunk**) Indian English a place where fuel is sold for road vehicles

petroleum /pəˈtrəʊ.li.əm/ (US) /-ˈtroʊ-/ **noun** [U] a dark, thick oil obtained from under the ground, from which various substances including petrol, PARAFFIN, and DIESEL oil are produced

peˈtroleum-ˌbased adj containing petroleum: *petroleum-based fuels* ◦ *petroleum-based plastics*

peˌtroleum ˈ**jelly noun** [U] a clear substance made from petroleum, used as a base for medicines that are rubbed into the skin, and also for making parts in a machine move easily against each other

petrolhead /ˈpet.rəlˌhed/ **noun** [C] UK informal someone who likes and uses their car a lot, and does not want to use any other type of transport

ˈ**petrol** ˌ**station noun** [C] UK (US ˈ**gas** ˌ**station**) (A2) a place where fuel is sold for road vehicles, often with a small shop and public toilets

PET scan /ˈpet.skæn/ **noun** [C] abbreviation for positron emission tomography scan: a medical test that can produce an image of the brain or of another part of a person's body: *The researchers carried out a PET scan to monitor his brain activity.*

ˈpet-ˌsit verb [I or T] to take care of someone's pet while they are away from their home • **ˈpet-ˌsitter** noun [C] • **ˈpet-ˌsitting** noun [U]

petticoat /ˈpet.ɪ.kəʊt/ Ⓤⓢ /ˈpet̬.ɪ.koʊt/ **noun** [C] old-fashioned a **slip**

pettifogging /ˈpet.ɪˌfɒg.ɪŋ/ Ⓤⓢ /ˈpet̬.ɪˌfɑː.gɪŋ/ **adj** old-fashioned disapproving **1** Pettifogging people give too much attention to small details that are not important in a way that shows a limited mind: *pettifogging lawyers* **2** Pettifogging rules or details are too small and not important enough to give attention to.

ˈpetting ˌzoo noun [C] US an open area where small or young animals are kept that children can hold, touch, and sometimes feed

petty /ˈpet.i/ Ⓤⓢ /ˈpet̬-/ **adj** disapproving **1** C2 [before noun] not important and not worth giving attention to: *Prisoners complain that they are subjected to too many petty rules and restrictions.* **2** [after noun] complaining too much about things that are not important: *Don't be so petty!* • **pettiness** /-nəs/ **noun** [U] *It was the pettiness of their arguments that irritated her.*

ˌpetty ˈbourgeois adj UK for **petit bourgeois**

ˌpetty ˈcash noun [U] a small amount of money kept in an office for buying small things that are needed: *Take the money for stamps out of petty cash.*

ˌpetty ˈcrime noun [C or U] a type of crime that is not considered serious when compared with some other crimes: *petty crime such as shoplifting*

ˌpetty ˈofficer noun [C] (written abbreviation **PO**) a rank in a navy, below the officers but above the ordinary sailors: *Chief Petty Officer*

petulant /ˈpet.jʊ.lənt/ **adj** disapproving easily annoyed and complaining in a rude way like a child • **petulance** /-ləns/ **noun** [U] • **petulantly** /-li/ **adv** *'Well, he didn't invite me to his party so I'm certainly not inviting him to mine!' she said petulantly.*

petunia /pəˈtjuː.ni.ə/ Ⓤⓢ /-ˈtuː.njə/ **noun** [C] a garden plant grown for its white, pink, purple, or red bell-shaped flowers

pew /pjuː/ **noun** [C] a long wooden seat with a high back, which a row of people sit on in a church

IDIOM **take a pew!** UK humorous sit down!

pewter /ˈpjuː.təʳ/ Ⓤⓢ /-t̬ɚ/ **noun** [U] a bluish-grey metal that is a mixture of TIN and lead: *a pewter plate/tankard*

peyote /peɪˈəʊ.ti/ Ⓤⓢ /-ˈoʊ.t̬i/ **noun** [C] US a type of CACTUS (= a desert plant), part of which can be taken as a drug that makes you HALLUCINATE (= see things that do not exist) or the drug itself → See also **mescaline**

pfft /fʌt/ Ⓤⓢ /fət/ **exclamation** US for **phut**

PFI /ˌpiː.efˈaɪ/ **noun** [U] abbreviation for Private-Finance Initiative: a system where private companies build and sometimes manage large PROJECTS such as hospitals or roads, and then the government pays to use them

pg. noun [C] mainly US written abbreviation for **page**: *See pgs. 67–69.*

PG /ˌpiːˈdʒiː/ **adj, noun** abbreviation for parental guidance; refers to a film that contains slightly sexual or violent parts which parents might not consider suitable for young children: *Her latest film is classified/rated* ***(as)*** *PG.* ◦ *The film's a PG.* → Compare **G, NC-17, U, X**

PG-13 /ˌpiːˌdʒiː.θɜːˈtiːn/ Ⓤⓢ /-θɝː-/ **noun** [C] in the US, a symbol that marks a film that parents are strongly warned might not be suitable for children under the age of 13

PGCE /ˌpiː.dʒiː.siːˈiː/ **noun** [C usually singular] abbreviation for **Postgraduate Certificate in Education**

pH /ˌpiːˈeɪtʃ/ **noun** [C usually singular] a number which shows how strongly ACID or ALKALINE a substance is, in a range from 0 to 14: *Below pH 6.5 is acid, above pH 7.5 is alkaline.* ◦ *The soil in our garden has a* ***low/high*** *pH.*

phagocyte /ˈfæg.ə.saɪt/ Ⓤⓢ /-oʊ-/ **noun** [C] specialized a type of cell in the body that can surround things and swallow them, especially a white blood cell which protects the body against infection by destroying bacteria

phalanx /ˈfæl.æŋks/ Ⓤⓢ /ˈfeɪ.læŋks/ **noun** [C, + sing/pl verb] (plural **phalanxes** or **phalanges**) formal a large group of people standing very close to each other, usually for the purposes of defence or attack: *Bodyguards formed a solid phalanx around the singer so that photographers couldn't get close.*

phallic /ˈfæl.ɪk/ **adj** representing, shaped like, or related to the PENIS: *phallic symbolism/imagery*

phallocentric /ˌfæl.əʊˈsen.trɪk/ Ⓤⓢ /-oʊ-/ **adj** formal having the male, or male sexual feelings or activity, as the main subject of interest: *phallocentric eroticism/literature*

phallus /ˈfæl.əs/ **noun** [C] formal an image or a model of the PENIS, especially one representing the power of men to make women pregnant, or a PENIS

phantasm /ˈfæn.tæz.əm/ **noun** [C] literary something that is seen or imagined but is not real

phantasmagoria /ˌfæn.tæz.məˈgɔː.ri.ə/ Ⓤⓢ /-ˈgɔːr.i-/ **noun** [S] literary a confused group of real or imagined images which change quickly, one following the other as in a dream

phantom /ˈfæn.təm/ Ⓤⓢ /-t̬əm/ **noun; adj**

▸**noun** [C] a spirit of a dead person believed by some to visit the living as a pale, almost transparent form of a person, animal, or other object → Synonym **ghost**

▸**adj** [before noun] **1** like a GHOST: *A phantom coach is said to pass through the grounds of this house when there's a full moon.* ◦ humorous *The phantom wine-drinker has been around (= an unknown person has been drinking the wine)!* **2** describes something that you imagine exists or that appears to exist, although in fact it does not: *Although she had to have her leg amputated, she still feels as though she's got a phantom limb.* ◦ *They discovered it was a phantom organization set up for the processing of drug profits.*

pharaoh /ˈfeə.rəʊ/ Ⓤⓢ /ˈfer.oʊ/ **noun** [C] (the title of) a king of ancient Egypt

Pharisee /ˈfær.ɪ.siː/ Ⓤⓢ /ˈfer-/ **noun** [C] **1** a member of an ancient group of Jews, written about in the Bible, who believed in obeying religious laws very carefully and separated themselves from the ordinary people **2** disapproving a person who thinks they are very religious, but who does not care about others

pharmaceutical /ˌfɑː.məˈsuː.tɪ.kəl/ Ⓤⓢ /ˌfɑːr.məˈsuː.t̬ɪ-/ **adj; noun**

▸**adj** connected with the production of medicines: *the pharmaceutical industry* ◦ *a pharmaceutical company/product/journal*

▸**noun** [C usually plural] specialized a medicine

pharmacist /ˈfɑː.mə.sɪst/ Ⓤⓢ /ˈfɑːr-/ **noun** [C] B2 a

P

person who is trained to prepare medicines and who works in a hospital or shop

pharmacologist /ˌfɑː.məˈkɒl.ə.dʒɪst/ US /ˌfɑːr.mə-ˈkɑː.lə-/ **noun** [C] a person who has studied pharmacology

pharmacology /ˌfɑː.məˈkɒl.ə.dʒi/ US /ˌfɑːr.məˈkɑː.lə-/ **noun** [U] the study of medicines and drugs, including their action, their use, and their effects on the body

pharmacy /ˈfɑː.mə.si/ US /ˈfɑːr-/ **noun 1** B1 [C] a shop or part of a shop in which medicines are prepared and sold **2** [C] part of a hospital where medicines are prepared **3** [U] the activity or study of medicine preparation

pharyngeal /fəˈrɪn.dʒi.əl/ **adj** specialized (of a speech sound) made by making the muscles in the pharynx tighter so that air cannot flow freely

pharyngitis /ˌfær.ɪnˈdʒaɪ.tɪs/ US /ˌfer.ɪnˈdʒaɪ.t̬ɪs/ **noun** [U] specialized pain and swelling in the pharynx, often with a slight fever, usually caused by infection by a virus

pharynx /ˈfær.ɪŋks/ **noun** [C] (plural **pharynges** /færˈɪn.dʒiːz/ or **pharynxes**) specialized the soft part at the top of the throat which connects the mouth and nose to the OESOPHAGUS (= the tube which takes food to the stomach) and the LARYNX (= the hollow organ between the nose and lungs)

phase /feɪz/ **noun; verb**

▸**noun** [C] **1** B2 any stage in a series of events or in a process of development: *The project is only in the initial phase as yet, but it's looking quite promising.* ◦ *We're entering a new phase* ***in*** *international relations.* **2** B2 a period of strange or difficult behaviour, especially that a young child or person goes through, that will stop after a while: *When I was in my early teens I* ***went through*** *a phase of only ever wearing black.* **3** The phases of the moon are the regular changes in its shape as it appears to us on Earth.

P

IDIOM **in phase/out of phase** If two things are happening in/out of phase they are reaching the same or related stages at the same time/at different times.

▸**verb** [T often passive] to introduce something in stages over a particular period of time: *The reduction in armed forces will be phased over the next ten years.*

PHRASAL VERBS **phase sth in** to introduce something gradually or in stages: *They will phase the new healthcare system in over a period of five years.* • **phase sth out** to remove or stop using something gradually or in stages

phat /fæt/ **adj** slang very good: *The band has a really phat sound.*

PhD /ˌpiː.eɪtʃˈdiː/ **noun** [C] (also **DPhil**) abbreviation for doctor of philosophy: the highest college or university degree, or someone who has this: *a PhD student/thesis* ◦ *Susannah has a PhD* ***in*** *Italian literature.* ◦ *She's a PhD.*

pheasant /ˈfez.ənt/ **noun** [C or U] (plural **pheasants** or **pheasant**) a large bird with a rounded body and long tail, which spends a lot of time on the ground and is often shot for sport and food

phenom /fəˈnɒm/ US /-ˈnɑːm/ **noun** [C] US slang someone or something extremely successful, especially someone young in sports who achieves a lot very quickly: *In less than a year, the 21-year-old phenom has become the best player in baseball.*

phenomenal /fəˈnɒm.ɪ.nəl/ US /-ˈnɑː.mə-/ **adj** C2 extremely successful or special, especially in a surprising way: *Her rise to fame was quite phenomenal – in less than two years she was a household name.* • **phenomenally** /-i/ **adv** *His first novel was phenomenally successful.*

phenomenon /fəˈnɒm.ɪ.nən/ US /-ˈnɑː.mə.nɑːn/ **noun** [C] (plural **phenomena** /-ə/) **EXISTING THING** ▷ **1** C1 something that exists and can be seen, felt, tasted, etc., especially something unusual or interesting: *Gravity is a* ***natural*** *phenomenon.* ◦ *Do you believe in the paranormal and other psychic phenomena?* ◦ *There's evidence to suggest that child abuse is not just a recent phenomenon.* **SUCCESS** ▷ **2** someone or something that is extremely successful, often because of special qualities or abilities: *The Beatles were a phenomenon – nobody had heard anything like them before.*

phenotype /ˈfiː.nəʊ.taɪp/ US /-noʊ-/ **noun** [C] specialized the physical characteristics of something living, especially those characteristics that can be seen → Compare **genotype**

pheromone /ˈfer.ə.məʊn/ US /-moʊn/ **noun** [C] specialized a chemical substance which an animal releases that influences the behaviour of another creature of the same type, for example by attracting it sexually

phew! /fjuː/ **exclamation** informal mainly humorous used when you are happy that something difficult or dangerous has finished or is not going to happen, or when you are tired or hot: *Phew! I'm so glad I don't have to give that speech.* ◦ *Phew, it's boiling in here!*

phial /faɪəl/ **noun** [C] mainly UK old-fashioned (US usually **vial**) a small glass bottle, especially one containing liquid medicine: *a phial* ***of*** *opium/poison*

Phi Beta Kappa /ˌfaɪ biː.təˈkæp.ə/ US /-ˌbeɪ.t̬ə-/ **noun** [C or U] a national organization in the US whose members are elected because they have achieved a very high level in their studies at colleges or universities, or a member of this organization

philanderer /fɪˈlæn.dər.əʳ/ US /-dɚ.ɚ/ **noun** [C] old-fashioned disapproving a man who enjoys having sex with a lot of different women without becoming emotionally involved with any of them • **philandering** /-ɪŋ/ **adj, noun** [U]

philanthropic /ˌfɪl.ənˈθrɒp.ɪk/ US /-ænˈθrɑː.pɪk/ **adj** formal helping poor people, especially by giving them money

philanthropist /fɪˈlæn.θrə.pɪst/ **noun** [C] a person who helps the poor, especially by giving them money: *a donation from a wealthy 19th-century philanthropist* • **philanthropy** /-pi/ **noun** [U]

philatelist /fɪˈlæt.əl.ɪst/ US /-ˈlæt̬-/ **noun** [C] specialized a person who collects or studies stamps

philately /fɪˈlæt.əl.i/ US /-ˈlæt̬-/ **noun** [U] specialized the collecting or study of stamps as a hobby

-phile /-faɪl/ US /-fɪl/ **suffix** someone who enjoys a particular thing or has it as a hobby, or who likes a particular place: *A bibliophile likes books and an oenophile enjoys wine.* ◦ *An Anglophile likes England or Britain.*

philharmonic /ˌfɪl.hɑːˈmɒn.ɪk/ US /-hɑːrˈmɑː.nɪk/ **adj** [before noun] used in the names of musical groups, especially ORCHESTRAS: *the Vienna Philharmonic Orchestra.*

philistine /ˈfɪl.ɪ.staɪn/ US /-stiːn/ **noun** [C] disapproving a person who refuses to see the beauty or the value of art or culture: *I wouldn't have expected them to enjoy a film of that quality anyway – they're just a bunch of philistines!*

philology /fɪˈlɒl.ə.dʒi/ US /-ˈlɑː.lə-/ noun [U] old-fashioned the study of language, especially its history and development → See also **linguistics** • **philological** /ˌfɪl.əˈlɒdʒ.ɪ.kəl/ US /-ˈlɑː.dʒɪ-/ adj

philosopher /fɪˈlɒs.ə.fər/ US /-ˈlɑː.sə.fɚ/ noun [C] B2 someone who studies or writes about the meaning of life: *Plato was a Greek philosopher.*

philosophical /ˌfɪl.əˈsɒf.ɪ.kəl/ US /-ˈsɑː.fɪ-/ adj **1** C2 relating to the study or writing of philosophy: *philosophical writings/essays* **2** C2 If you are philosophical in your reaction to something that is not satisfactory, you accept it calmly and without anger, understanding that failure and disappointment are a part of life.

philosophically /ˌfɪl.əˈsɒf.ɪ.kəl.i/ US /-ˈsɑː.fɪ-/ adv calmly accepting a difficult situation

philosophize mainly disapproving (UK usually **philosophise**) /fɪˈlɒs.ə.faɪz/ US /-ˈlɑː.sə-/ verb [I] to talk for a long time about subjects such as the meaning of life

philosophy /fɪˈlɒs.ə.fi/ US /-ˈlɑː.sə-/ noun **1** B2 [U] the use of reason in understanding such things as the nature of the real world and existence, the use and limits of knowledge, and the principles of moral judgment: *René Descartes is regarded as the founder of modern philosophy.* → See also **PhD** **2** [C] a particular system of beliefs, values, and principles: *the Ancient Greek philosophy of Stoicism* **3** C1 [C usually singular] informal the way that someone thinks about life and deals with it: *Live now, pay later – that's my philosophy of life!*

phishing /ˈfɪʃ.ɪŋ/ noun [U] an attempt to trick someone into giving information over the internet or by email that would allow someone else to take money from them, for example by taking money out of their bank account • **phisher** /-ər/ US /-ɚ/ noun [C]

phlegm /flem/ noun [U] **SUBSTANCE** ▷ **1** a thick substance in your nose and throat that is produced when you have a cold **CALMNESS** ▷ **2** formal the ability to stay calm and not get emotional or excited about things even in a difficult or dangerous situation

phlegmatic /flegˈmæt.ɪk/ US /-ˈmæţ-/ adj formal describes someone who doesn't usually get emotional or excited about things: *As a footballer his great asset was his calm, phlegmatic manner.*

phloem /ˈfləʊ.em/ US /ˈfloʊ.em/ noun [U] specialized the type of plant tissue that transports food from the leaves to the other parts of the plant → Compare **xylem**

-phobe /-fəʊb/ US /-foʊb/ suffix someone who hates something: *An Anglophobe is a person who hates England or Britain.* ◦ *a commitment-phobe*

phobia /ˈfəʊ.bi.ə/ US /ˈfoʊ-/ noun [C] an extreme fear or dislike of a particular thing or situation, especially one that cannot be reasonably explained: *I've got a phobia* ***about/of*** *worms.* • **-phobia** suffix *Xenophobia means hatred of foreigners.*

phobic /ˈfəʊ.bɪk/ US /ˈfoʊ-/ adj informal having a strong dislike of something: *Why are so many companies phobic* ***about*** *employing fat people?* • **phobic** noun [C] *I wouldn't describe myself as a phobic but I don't like heights.*

phoenix /ˈfiː.nɪks/ noun [C usually singular] in ancient stories, an imaginary bird which set fire to itself every 500 years and was born again, rising from its ASHES (= the powder left after its body has been burned): *The town was bombed but was then rebuilt and rose from the ashes* ***like a/the*** *phoenix* (= *was just as good as before*).

phone /fəʊn/ US /foʊn/ noun; verb
▸noun **PHONE** ▷ **1** A1 [C or U] (formal **telephone**) a device that uses either a system of wires, along which electrical signals are sent, or a system of radio signals to make it possible for you to speak to someone in another place who has a similar device: *Just then, his phone* ***rang.*** ◦ *Could you* ***answer*** *the phone?* ◦ *We speak* ***on the/by*** *phone about twice a week.* ◦ *You had three phone* ***calls*** *this morning.* ◦ *If the phone* ***lines*** *are busy, please try again later.* ◦ *Could you* ***pick*** *the phone* ***up*** *for me – my hands are wet.* ◦ *I* ***left*** *the phone* ***off the hook,*** *so it wouldn't ring.* ◦ *I was so angry I just* ***put/slammed*** *the phone* ***down*** *(****on*** *her)* (= *replaced it before our conversation was finished*). **2 be on the phone a** to be using the phone: *That son of mine is on the phone all day!* **b** UK to have a LANDLINE (= fixed phone) in the home: *Are the Middletons on the phone, do you know?* **PHONETIC UNIT** ▷ **3** [C] specialized a unit of sound at the PHONETIC level, used when studying speech
▸verb [I or T] A1 to communicate with someone by phone: *She phoned just after lunch.* ◦ *He's phoned me* (***up***) *every day this week.*

> **! Common mistake: phone**
> Remember that **phone** is never followed by 'to'.
> Don't say 'phone to someone', say **phone someone:**
> ~~*Phone to me if you have any more questions.*~~
> *Phone me if you have any more questions.*

> **Word partners for phone noun**
> ***answer/pick up/put down*** the phone • the phone ***rings*** • ***on*** the phone • ***over*** the phone • ***by*** phone • a phone ***call/conversation*** • a ***public*** phone

PHRASAL VERBS **phone in** **WORK** ▷ **1** to phone the place where you work in order to tell your employer something: *She phoned in* ***sick*** (= *saying that she was ill*) *this morning.* **PROGRAMME** ▷ **2** to phone a television or radio programme in order to express your opinion on a matter: *Over three hundred people phoned in to complain.* • **phone in sth** informal often disapproving If someone phones in a performance, they do it without any effort: *The actor phoned in his performance without a hint of personality.*

ˈphone ˌbanking noun [U] the system of allowing customers to organize, examine, and make changes to their bank accounts using the phone

ˈphone ˌbook noun [C] informal a **telephone directory**: *Is he in the phone book?*

ˈphone ˌbooth noun [C] **1** UK a place in a public building, often with walls or parts of walls on three sides, where there is a public phone **2** US for **phone box**

ˈphone ˌbox noun [C] UK (US **ˈphone ˌbooth**) a small structure with a door, found outside in public places, containing a public phone

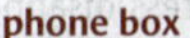
phone box

ˈphone ˌcall noun [C] an occasion when you use the phone: *Will you excuse me? I've got to* ***make a*** *phone call.*

ˈphone card noun [C] UK a small card that is used to pay for calls from a public phone

ˈphone ˌhacking noun [U] the activity of using someone else's phone system without permission, especially in order to listen to their spoken messages

ˈ**phone-in** noun [C] UK (US ˈ**call-in**) a television or radio programme in which members of the public phone to express their opinions or ask questions

phoneme /ˈfəʊ.niːm/ (US) /ˈfoʊ-/ **noun** [C] specialized one of the smallest units of speech that make one word different from another word: *The difference between 'pin' and 'pan' depends on the vowel, i.e. the different phonemes /ɪ/ and /æ/.*

phonemics /fəˈniː.m.ɪks/ (US) /foʊ-/ **noun** [U] the study of the phonemes of a language

ˈ**phone ˌnumber** noun [C] the number that you use to call a particular phone

ˈ**phone ˌsex** noun [U] the activity of talking on the phone with someone about sex in order to become sexually excited

ˈ**phone ˌtapping** noun [U] the activity of secretly fitting a special device to someone's phone in order to listen to their phone conversations without them knowing

phonetic /fəˈnet.ɪk/ (US) /foʊˈneţ-/ **adj** specialized **1** using special signs to represent the different sounds made by the voice in speech: *Pronunciations are shown in this dictionary using the International Phonetic Alphabet.* **2** A spelling system can be described as phonetic if you can understand how words are pronounced simply by looking at their spelling. • **phonetically** /-ɪ.kəl.i/ **adv** *She pronounced Leicester phonetically as 'Ley-ces-ter', but really we say 'Lester'.*

phonetics /fəˈnet.ɪks/ (US) /foʊˈneţ-/ **noun** [U] specialized the study of the sounds made by the human voice in speech

phoney (**phonier**, **phoniest**) informal disapproving (US also **phony**) /ˈfəʊ.ni/ (US) /ˈfoʊ-/ **adj** not sincere or not real: *All salespeople seem to have the same phoney smile.* ◦ *He gave the police a phoney address.* • **phoney noun** [C] *I don't trust him – I think he's a phoney.*

ˌ**phoney ˈwar** (also ˌ**phony ˈwar**) **noun** [C usually singular] UK a period during a war when there is no fighting and the situation appears calm

phonics /ˈfɒn.ɪks/ (US) /ˈfɑː.nɪks/ **noun** [U] a method of teaching people to read, based on learning the sounds that letters represent

phonograph /ˈfəʊ.nə.grɑːf/ (US) /ˈfoʊ.noʊ.græf/ **noun** [C] US old use for **record player**

phonology /fəˈnɒl.ə.dʒi/ (US) /fəˈnɑː.lə-/ **noun** [U] specialized the study of sounds in a particular language or in languages generally • **phonological** /ˌfɒn.əˈlɒdʒ.ɪ.kəl/ (US) /ˌfoʊ.nəˈlɑː.dʒɪ-/ **adj**

phooey /ˈfuː.i/ **exclamation** informal humorous used to express disappointment or to show you do not have much respect for something

phosphate /ˈfɒs.feɪt/ (US) /ˈfɑːs-/ **noun** [C] a chemical COMPOUND which contains PHOSPHORUS: *Most fertilizers contain nitrogen and phosphates.*

phosphorescent /ˌfɒs.fərˈes.ənt/ (US) /ˌfɑːs.fəˈres-/ **adj** specialized giving off light after RADIATION has hit it • **phosphorescence** /-əns/ **noun** [U]

phosphoric /fɒsˈfɒr.ɪk/ (US) /fɑːsˈfɔːr-/ **adj** (also **phosphorous**) of or containing phosphorus: *phosphoric acid*

phosphorus /ˈfɒs.fər.əs/ (US) /ˈfɑːs.fə.əs/ **noun** [U] (symbol **P**) a poisonous chemical element that is usually yellowish-white or sometimes red or black in colour, shines in the dark, and burns when in the air

photo /ˈfəʊ.təʊ/ (US) /ˈfoʊ.ţoʊ/ **noun** [C] (plural **photos**) informal (A1) a photograph: *She* ***took*** *a lot of photos* ***of*** *the kids.* ◦ *holiday/wedding photos*

photo- /fəʊ.təʊ-/ (US) /foʊ.ţoʊ-/ **prefix** LIGHT ▷ **1** connected with or produced by light: *photosynthesis* PHOTOGRAPH ▷ **2** connected with photography: *photojournalism*

ˈ**photo ˌalbum** noun [C] a type of book in which you keep photos

photocall /ˈfəʊ.təʊ.kɔːl/ (US) /ˈfoʊ.ţoʊ-/ **noun** [C] an occasion when people at a formal event are asked to have their photograph taken together, or when photographers are officially invited to take photographs of a famous person

photocell /ˈfəʊ.təʊ.sel/ (US) /ˈfoʊ.ţoʊ-/ **noun** [C] (also ˌ**photoelectric ˈcell**) an electrical device which produces a current or a VOLTAGE when light shines on it: *Photocells are used in burglar alarms.*

photochemical /ˌfəʊ.təʊˈkem.ɪ.kəl/ (US) /ˌfoʊ.ţoʊ-/ **adj** specialized relating to the effect of light on some chemicals

ˌ**photochemical ˈsmog** noun [C or U] a FOG caused by light from the sun shining on chemicals in the air produced by traffic and industry

photocopiable /ˌfəʊ.təʊˈkɒ.pɪ.ə.bəl/ (US) /ˌfoʊ.ţoʊˈkɑː.pɪ.ə.bəl/ **adj** If a page in a book is photocopiable, you can make copies of it legally.

photocopier /ˈfəʊ.təʊˌkɒp.i.ər/ (US) /ˈfoʊ.ţoʊˌkɑː.pi.ə/ **noun** [C] a machine which makes copies of documents using a photographic process

photocopy /ˈfəʊ.təʊˌkɒp.i/ (US) /ˈfoʊ.ţoʊˌkɑː.pi/ **noun** [C] (B1) a photographic copy of a document made on a photocopier: *I'll just* ***make*** *a photocopy* ***of*** *the agreement.* • **photocopy verb** [T] *Could you photocopy those three pages for me, please?*

photoelectric /ˌfəʊ.təʊ.ɪˈlek.trɪk/ (US) /ˌfoʊ.ţoʊ-/ **adj** of or using an electrical current or VOLTAGE that is produced because of light

ˌ**photoelectric ˈcell** noun [C] a **photocell**

ˌ**photo ˈfinish** noun [C] the end of a race when the competitors are so close that a photograph has to be examined in order to discover who has won

photofit (picture) /ˌfəʊ.təʊ.fɪtˈpɪk.tʃər/ (US) /ˈfoʊ.ţoʊ.fɪtˌpɪk.tʃə/ **noun** [C] UK a picture that represents as closely as possible a person's memory of a criminal's face, made by putting together photographs of eyes, nose, hair, etc. from a set showing different types of features → See also **Identikit**

ˈ**photo ˌframe** noun [C] a flat object with a clear front surface used to put a photograph in

photogenic /ˌfəʊ.təˈdʒen.ɪk/ (US) /ˌfoʊ.ţoʊ-/ **adj** having a face that looks attractive in photographs

photograph /ˈfəʊ.tə.grɑːf/ (US) /ˈfoʊ.ţoʊ.græf/ **noun; verb**

▸**noun** [C] (informal **photo**) (A2) a picture produced using a camera: *a* ***colour/black and white*** *photograph* ◦ *aerial photographs* ◦ *nude photographs* ◦ *My parents* ***took*** *a lot of photographs* ***of*** *us when we were small.*

▸**verb** [T] **1** (B2) to take a picture using a camera: *I prefer photographing people rather than places.* ◦ [+ obj + -ing verb] *MacKay was photographed leav****ing*** *the building.* **2 photograph well/badly** to appear attractive/unattractive in photographs

photographer /fəˈtɒg.rə.fər/ (US) /-ˈtɑː.grə.fə/ **noun** [C] (A2) a person who takes photographs, either as a job or hobby: *a fashion/press/amateur photographer*

photographic /ˌfəʊ.təˈgræf.ɪk/ (US) /ˌfoʊ.ţə-/ **adj** relating to, used for, or produced by photography: *photographic equipment/film/materials* ◦ *photographic skills* ◦ *Her paintings are almost photographic in their detail and accuracy.* • **photographically** /-ɪ.kəl.i/ **adv**

ˌ**photographic ˈmemory** noun [C usually singular] If

you have a photographic memory, you are able to remember things in exact detail.

photography /fəˈtɒg.rə.fi/ (US) /-ˈtɑː.grə-/ noun [U] A2 (the activity or job of taking) photographs or films: *She's doing an evening class in photography.* ◦ *The film won an award for its photography.*

photojournalism /ˌfəʊ.təʊˈdʒɜː.nəl.ɪ.zəm/ (US) /ˌfoʊ.t̬oʊˈdʒɝː-/ noun [U] the activity of creating news articles using mainly photographs or one of these articles • **photojournalist** /-ɪst/ noun [C]

photon /ˈfəʊ.tɒn/ (US) /ˈfoʊ.tɑːn/ noun [C] specialized a single unit of light

ˈphoto opporˌtunity noun [C] an occasion when a politician or famous person is photographed doing something that will make them popular with the public

photosensitive /ˌfəʊ.təʊˈsen.sɪ.tɪv/ (US) /ˌfoʊ.t̬oʊˈsen.sə-/ adj reacting to light: *a photosensitive lens/chemical/surface*

ˈphoto ˌsession noun [C] (also **ˈphoto ˌshoot**) an occasion arranged for newspaper photographers to take photographs of politicians or other famous people

photostat /ˈfəʊ.tə.stæt/ (US) /ˈfoʊ.t̬oʊ-/ noun [C] a machine used especially in the past to make photographic copies of documents, or a copy made by such a machine • **photostat** verb [T] (plural **-tt-**)

photosynthesis /ˌfəʊ.təʊˈsɪn.θə.sɪs/ (US) /ˌfoʊ.t̬oʊ-/ noun [U] the process by which a plant uses the energy from the light of the sun to produce its own food • **photosynthesize** (UK usually **photosynthesise**) /-saɪz/ verb [I or T]

phototropism /fəʊˈtɒt.rə.pɪ.zəm/, /foʊˈtɑː.trə-/ noun [U] specialized the growth or movement of a plant, or of a particular part of a plant, towards light or away from it

photovoltaic cell /ˌfəʊ.təʊ.vɒl.teɪ.ɪkˈsel/ (US) /ˌfoʊ.t̬oʊ.vɑːl-/ noun [C] specialized a type of PHOTOCELL that changes light from the sun into electricity, used in SOLAR PANELS, pocket CALCULATORS, etc.

phrasal verb /ˌfreɪ.zəlˈvɜːb/ (US) /-ˈvɝːb/ noun [C] B1 a phrase that consists of a verb with a preposition or adverb or both, the meaning of which is different from the meaning of its separate parts: *'Look after', 'work out' and 'make up for' are all phrasal verbs.*

phrase /freɪz/ noun; verb

▸noun [C] **GRAMMAR** ▷ **1** a group of words that is part of, rather than the whole of, a sentence **EXPRESSION** ▷ **2** B1 a short group of words that are often used together and have a particular meaning: *We are governed, in Lord Hailsham's famous phrase, by an 'elective dictatorship'.* → See also **phrase book** **MUSIC** ▷ **3** specialized a small group of notes forming a unit of a tune

▸verb [T usually + adv/prep] to express something with a particular choice of words: *The declaration was carefully/cleverly/tactfully, etc. phrased.*

ˈphrase book noun [C] a small book containing helpful groups of sentences and words in a particular foreign language, intended for use by travellers: *a Spanish phrase book*

phraseology /ˌfreɪ.ziˈɒl.ə.dʒi/ (US) /-ˈɑː.lə-/ noun [U] the way in which language is used, especially in the choice of words and expressions

phrasing /ˈfreɪ.zɪŋ/ noun [U] **WORDS** ▷ **1** the choice of words used to express something: *The phrasing of the contract is rather ambiguous.* **MUSIC** ▷ **2** specialized the way in which a singer or musician divides the tune into separate parts: *Her phrasing, as ever, is faultless.*

phut /fʌt/ (US) /fət/ noun UK informal **go phut** If a machine goes phut, it suddenly stops working.

phyllo pastry /ˌfiː.ləʊˈpeɪ.stri/ (US) /-loʊ-/ noun [U] US for **filo pastry**

phylum /ˈfai.ləm/ noun [C] specialized a main division in a TAXONOMIC (= scientific naming and organization system) relating to animals: *Members of the largest and most diverse phylum of animals (Arthropoda), have segmented bodies and an external skeleton.*

physical /ˈfɪz.ɪ.kəl/ adj; noun

▸adj **BODY** ▷ **1** B2 connected with the body: *physical exercise/fitness/strength/disabilities* ◦ *I'm not a very physical sort of person (= I don't enjoy physical activities).* **2** informal violent: *The referee stepped in because the game had started to get a bit physical.* **3** sexual: *There was obviously a great physical **attraction** between them.* **REAL** ▷ **4** C2 relating to things you can see or touch, or relating to the laws of nature: *the physical world* ◦ *All physical objects occupy space.* **5** connected with physics: *physical laws*

▸noun [C] (UK also **medical**) an examination of a person's body by a doctor in order to discover if that person is healthy, sometimes done before a person can be accepted for a particular job

ˌphysical eduˈcation noun [U] (abbreviation **PE**) classes at school in which children do exercise and learn to play sport, or the area of study relating to such classes

ˌphysical ˈgeography noun [U] the study of the natural features of the Earth, such as mountains and rivers

ˌphysical ˈjerks noun [plural] UK old-fashioned exercises that people do in order to be healthy

physically /ˈfɪz.ɪ.kəl.i/ adv **BODY** ▷ **1** in a way that relates to the body or someone's appearance: *Physically I find him very attractive.* ◦ *The protestors had to be physically removed from the room (= they were taken away).* ◦ *The work is physically **demanding** (= you have to work hard in a way that makes your body tired).* ◦ *Special holidays are available for physically **handicapped/disabled** people (= those lacking the full use of part of their body).* **REAL** ▷ **2** in a way that relates to things you can see or touch or the laws of nature: *No one could have climbed that wall – it's physically impossible.*

ˌphysical ˈsciences noun [plural] the sciences, such as physics, chemistry, and ASTRONOMY, that examine matter and energy and the way the universe behaves

ˌphysical ˈtherapy noun [U] US for **physiotherapy** • **ˌphysical ˈtherapist** noun [C]

physician /fɪˈzɪʃ.ən/ noun [C] mainly US or formal (UK usually **doctor**) a medical doctor, especially one who has general skill and is not a SURGEON

physicist /ˈfɪz.ɪ.sɪst/ noun [C] a person who studies physics or whose job is connected with physics

physics /ˈfɪz.ɪks/ noun [U] A2 the scientific study of matter and energy and the effect that they have on each other: *nuclear physics* ◦ *a physics lab*

physio /ˈfɪz.i.əʊ/ (US) /-oʊ/ noun (plural **physios**) **1** [C] UK informal for **physiotherapist** **2** [U] **physiotherapy**

physiognomy /ˌfɪz.iˈɒn.ə.mi/ (US) /-ˈɑː.nə-/ noun [U] formal the physical appearance of the face

physiologist /ˌfɪz.iˈɒl.ə.dʒɪst/ (US) /-ˈɑː.lə-/ noun [C] a person who studies physiology

physiology /ˌfɪz.iˈɒl.ə.dʒi/ (US) /-ˈɑː.lə-/ noun [U] (the scientific study of) the way in which the bodies of living things work • **physiological** /-əˈlɒdʒ.ɪ.kəl/ (US) /-əˈlɑː.dʒɪ.kəl/ adj

P

physiotherapist /ˌfɪz.i.əʊˈθer.ə.pɪst/ US /-oʊ-/ noun [C] UK (UK informal **physio**, US ˌ**physical** ˈ**therapist**) someone who treats people using physiotherapy

physiotherapy /ˌfɪz.i.əʊˈθer.ə.pi/ US /-oʊ-/ noun [U] UK (UK informal **physio**, US **physical therapy**) the treatment of muscle stiffness, pain, and injury, especially by rubbing and moving the sore parts

physique /fɪˈziːk/ noun [C] the shape and size of a human body: *He has a very powerful, muscular physique.*

pi (also π) /paɪ/ noun [U] a Greek letter, especially used in mathematics as a symbol for the number (approximately 3.14) used to calculate the size of circles

pianist /ˈpiː.ən.ɪst/ noun [C] someone who plays the piano: *a concert pianist* ◦ *a jazz pianist*

piano /piˈæn.əʊ/ US /-oʊ/ noun [C or U] (plural **pianos**) A2 a large musical instrument with a row of black and white keys that are pressed to play notes: *We're buying a new piano.* ◦ *I play* ***the*** *piano.* ◦ *She used to play piano in a jazz band.* ◦ *The music was written for piano.* ◦ *We all joined in the song, with Pat* ***at the*** *piano/***on** *piano.*

piˈano ˌstool noun [C] a type of chair without a back or sides that is used when playing the piano

piˈano ˌtuner noun [C] a person whose job is to make certain that a piano is producing the correct notes by testing it and changing the tightness of the strings

piazza /piˈæt.sə/ US /-ˈɑːt-/ noun [C] especially in Italy, an open area with a hard surface in a town, especially where there is no traffic → See also **square**

pic /pɪk/ noun [C] informal for **photograph**: *Would you like to see my holiday pics?*

picador /ˈpɪk.ə.dɔːʳ/ US /-dɔːr/ noun [C] someone, usually a man, who pushes sharp sticks into BULLS (= male cows) during a BULLFIGHT → Compare **matador, toreador**

P

picayune /ˌpɪk.əˈjuːn/, /ˈpɪk.ə.juːn/ adj US having little value or importance: *The misery suffered in this war makes your own problems seem pretty picayune.*

piccalilli /ˌpɪk.əˈlɪl.i/ US /ˈpɪk.ə.lɪl-/ noun [U] small pieces of different vegetables preserved in a MUSTARD sauce, usually eaten with cold meat

piccolo /ˈpɪk.ə.ləʊ/ US /-loʊ/ noun [C] (plural **piccolos**) a musical instrument, like a small FLUTE, which makes a high sound

pick /pɪk/ verb; noun

▸verb **CHOOSE** ▷ **1** B1 [T] to take some things and leave others: *Pick a card from the pack.* ◦ *One of my sisters has been picked* ***for*** *the Olympic team.* ◦ [+ obj + to infinitive] *She was picked* ***to*** *play for the team.* ◦ *The police asked him if he could pick (***out***) the killer from a series of photos.* ◦ *The fairest way to decide the winner is to pick a name* ***out of a hat/at random*** *(= without looking or choosing).* ◦ *They picked their* ***way*** *(= carefully chose a route) down the broken steps.* ◦ *He's brilliant at picking* ***winners*** *(= choosing what will be successful).* → Compare **choose 2 pick and choose** often disapproving to take some things but not others: *The richest universities can pick and choose which students they take.* **REMOVE** ▷ **3** B1 [I or T] to remove separate things or small pieces from something, especially with the fingers: *I picked a piece of fluff* ***off*** *my shiny black suit.* ◦ *The child continued picking (***at***) a sore on his leg (= trying to remove parts of it with his fingers).* ◦ [+ obj + adj] *The carcass had been picked* ***clean*** *(= all the flesh had been removed) by other animals and birds.* ◦ disapproving *He kept picking his* ***nose*** *(= removing mucus from it with his finger).* **4** B1 [T] When you pick flowers or fruit, you take them off a plant or tree: *They were picking strawberries for twelve hours a day.* ◦ *I picked some roses this morning.* ◦ *Machines pick the fruit (***from/off*** the trees).* **PLAY INSTRUMENT** ▷ **5** [T] When you pick a string on a guitar or similar instrument, you pull it quickly and release it suddenly with your fingers to produce a note.

IDIOMS **pick sb's brains** to ask someone who knows a lot about a subject for information or their opinion: *I was picking Simon's brains about which computer to buy.* • **pick sb's pocket** to steal small objects, especially money, from someone's pockets or bag → See also **pickpocket** • **pick yourself up off the floor** to make improvements to your life after a bad period • **pick a fight/quarrel/argument** to start a fight/QUARREL/argument with someone: *He'd had too much to drink and tried to pick a fight with the bartender.* • **pick holes in sth** disapproving to find mistakes in something someone has done or said, to show that it is not good or not correct • **pick 'n' mix** UK a system in a shop where you can choose a few of several different small things, especially sweets • **pick up the phone** informal to make a phone call to someone: *If you need me, you just have to pick up the phone.* • **pick up the bill/tab** (US also **pick up the check**) to pay for what has been bought, especially a meal in a restaurant • **pick up the pieces** C2 to try to return to a satisfactory situation: *The fire was a blow, but we were determined to pick up the pieces and get the business back on its feet.* • **pick up the thread(s)** to start again after an interruption: *Picking up the threads* ***of*** *our discussion, let's return to the topic of factory farming.*

PHRASAL VERBS **pick at *sth*** disapproving to eat only a small amount of your food, showing no interest or enjoyment while you eat it: *Charles picked at his food in a bored fashion.* → See also **picky** • **pick sb/sth off SHOOT** ▷ **1** to shoot at one particular person, animal, or vehicle that you have chosen from a group: *The snipers picked the soldiers off one by one as they ran for cover.* **TAKE THE BEST** ▷ **2** to take the best person or thing from a group: *It is relatively easy for newcomers to pick off the most lucrative business and ignore the rest.* • **pick on sb** B2 to criticize, punish, or be unkind to the same person often and unfairly: *He gets picked on by the other boys because he's so small.* ◦ *Why don't you pick on* ***someone your own size****?.* • **pick sb/sth out RECOGNIZE** ▷ **1** to recognize, find, or make a choice among different people or things in a group: *Can you pick out the three deliberate mistakes in this paragraph?* ◦ *The critics picked him out as the outstanding male dancer of the decade.* **EMPHASIZE** ▷ **2** to choose and emphasize, make clearer, or HIGHLIGHT someone or something: *The ship's name was picked out* ***in*** *bright gold letters along her stern.* • **pick sth out** If you pick out a tune, you play it slowly or with difficulty, note by note: *I can pick out a simple tune on the piano, but that's about it.* • **pick over sth** to look carefully at a group of things, choosing the ones you want or getting rid of the ones you do not want: *All the clothes at the sale had been thoroughly picked over and there was nothing nice left.* • **pick sb/sth up LIFT** ▷ **1** A2 to lift someone or something using your hands: *If she starts to cry, pick her up and give her a cuddle.* ◦ *I picked up the kids' clothes that were lying on the floor.* ◦ *I went to pick up the phone/receiver, but it had stopped ringing.* **COLLECT** ▷ **2** A2 to collect, or to go and get, someone or something: *When you're in town could you pick up the books I ordered?* ◦ *Whose turn is it to pick the children up after school?* ◦ *The crew of the* *sinking tanker were picked up (= saved from the sea) by helicopter.* • **pick sth up LEARN** ▷ **1** B2 to learn a new skill or language by practising it rather than being taught it: *Don't bother with the computer manual – you'll pick it up as you go along.* ◦ *When you live in a country you soon pick up the language.* **2** to learn interesting or useful information from someone or something: *The nurse had picked up the information from a conversation she overheard.* **BUY** ▷ **3** to buy something cheaply: *She picked up some real **bargains** in the sale.* **WIN** ▷ **4** to win or get a prize or something that gives you an advantage, such as votes or support: *The People's Front expect to pick up a lot more votes in this year's elections.* **SIGNAL** ▷ **5** (of a piece of electrical equipment) to receive a signal: *Can you pick up (= receive broadcasts from) Moscow **on** your radio?* **NOTICE** ▷ **6** to notice and react to something: *Police dogs picked up the scent of the two men from clothes they had left behind.* **ILLNESS** ▷ **7** to catch an illness from someone or something, caused by bacteria or a virus: *He picked up malaria when he was visiting the country on business.* • **pick (sth) up** to start something again after an interruption: *The author picks the same theme up again on page ten.* ◦ *After lunch shall we pick up **where** we **left off** yesterday?* • **pick sb up POLICE** ▷ **1** UK informal (of the police) to stop someone and take them to a police station in order to question them or arrest them: *He was picked up by the police **for** drug dealing.* ◦ *The police picked her up just outside Canterbury.* **MEET** ▷ **2** informal to start a sexual or romantic relationship with someone you do not know, by talking to them and giving them a lot of attention: *He said he'd picked the woman up in a bar.* • **pick up** [I or T] **INCREASE** ▷ **1** to increase or improve: *The truck picked up **speed** slowly.* ◦ *The wind always picks up in the evening.* ◦ *The number of applicants will pick up during the autumn.* ◦ *His spirits picked up when he got the good news.* ◦ *Her career only began to pick up when she was in her forties.* **PHONE** ▷ **2** to answer the phone: *I tried his home number but he didn't pick up.* • **pick sb up on sth** to criticize someone about something they have said: *'I want to pick you up on the point you made a few minutes ago about personal morality, Archbishop.'* ◦ *His teacher picked him up on his pronunciation.* • **pick up on sth RETURN** ▷ **1** to start talking again about something that someone said previously: *Can I just pick up on your first point again, please?* **NOTICE** ▷ **2** to notice something that other people have not noticed: *Only one newspaper picked up on the minister's statement.*

▸**noun CHOICE** ▷ **1** [U] choice: *You can have first pick of the cakes.* **2 have your pick** to have a large choice available: *The plane was fairly empty so we had our pick **of** seats.* **3 take your pick** to choose the one(s) you want from the different types available: *The shirts come in five different colours – just take your pick.* **TOOL** ▷ **4** [C] a **pickaxe**: *picks and shovels* **5** [C] especially in combinations, a sharp pointed tool: *a toothpick* **IN MUSIC** ▷ **6** [C] a **plectrum**

IDIOM **the pick of sth** (also **the pick of the bunch**) the best of a group of people or things: *The pick of this year's three-year-old race horses is Galileo.*

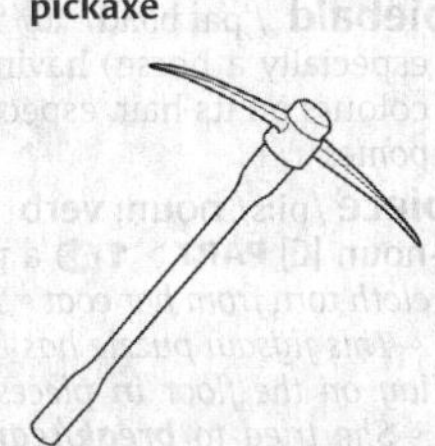

pickaxe (US **pickax**) /ˈpɪk.æks/ **noun** [C] (also **pick**) a tool for breaking hard surfaces, with a long wooden handle and a curved metal bar with a sharp point

picker /ˈpɪk.əʳ/ US /-ɚ/ **noun** [C] **CHOOSE** ▷ **1** mainly US a person who chooses a particular thing: *Traditional **stock** pickers (= people who choose companies in which others should invest) are being replaced by computer programs.* **REMOVE** ▷ **2** a person or a machine that picks crops

picket /ˈpɪk.ɪt/ **noun** [C] **1** a worker or group of workers who protest outside a building to prevent other workers from going inside, especially because they have a disagreement with their employers: *There were pickets outside the factory gates.* **2** an occasion on which a picket happens: *The union organized a month-long picket.* • **picket verb** [I or T] *They picketed the burger restaurant and handed out leaflets to potential customers.* • **picketing** /-ɪ.tɪŋ/ US /-ɪ.t̬ɪŋ/ **noun** [U] *The proposed new law would ban picketing.*

picketer /ˈpɪk.ɪ.təʳ/ US /-t̬ɚ/ **noun** [C] a person who stands outside a building as part of a picket

ˈpicket ˌfence noun [C] a low fence made of a row of flat sticks that are pointed at the top and often painted white

ˈpicket ˌline noun [C] a group of workers acting as pickets: *Journalists interviewed the union officials **on** the picket line.* ◦ *The van drivers refused to **cross** the picket line (= to go past the pickets).*

pickings /ˈpɪk.ɪŋz/ **noun** [plural] money that can be earned easily or dishonestly: *The street-sellers are lured to the town by the **rich/easy** pickings that are to be had from foreign tourists.*

pickle /ˈpɪk.l̩/ **noun; verb**

▸**noun 1** [C or U] vegetables or fruit that have been preserved in a VINEGAR sauce or salty water: *cheese and pickle sandwiches* ◦ *Have some pickles with your salad.* **2** [C] US a CUCUMBER that has been preserved in VINEGAR or salty water, or slices of this: *a sweet/sour pickle*

IDIOM **be in a (pretty/right) pickle** old-fashioned to be in a difficult situation

▸**verb** [T] to preserve vegetables or fruit in a VINEGAR sauce or salty water: *The onions had been pickled **in** brine.* • **pickling** /-l̩.ɪŋ/, /-lɪŋ/ **adj** [before noun] *pickling onions (= small onions of a type that are kept in vinegar)* ◦ *pickling spices (= used to give extra flavour to preserved vegetables)*

pickled /ˈpɪk.l̩d/ **adj 1** kept in VINEGAR: *pickled onions/gherkins/herring* **2** old-fashioned informal drunk: *I got really pickled at Pat's party.*

ˈpick-me-up noun [C] something which makes you feel better, often a drink or a TONIC (= a type of medicine): *It is traditional around here to drink brandy with coffee as a morning pick-me-up.*

pickpocket /ˈpɪkˌpɒk.ɪt/ US /-ˌpɑː.kɪt/ **noun** [C] a thief who steals things out of pockets or bags, especially in a crowd

pickup /ˈpɪk.ʌp/ **noun COLLECTION** ▷ **1** [C] the act of picking someone or something up, or the place where it happens: *The pickup **point** for the long-distance coaches is now in the new bus station.* **2** [C] informal a person who is picked up: *The taxi driver said I was the first pickup that he'd had all evening.* **SIGNAL** ▷ **3** [C] a device on an electrical musical instrument or a record player which causes sounds to be produced or made louder **INCREASE** ▷ **4** [S] an increase or improvement: *There's been a pickup in the share value.* **5 have good/bad pickup** US (of a car) to be able/unable to increase speed quickly

ˈpickup ˌtruck noun [C] a small vehicle with an open part at the back in which goods can be carried

picky /ˈpɪk.i/ **adj** informal disapproving describes

P

someone who is very careful about choosing only what they like: *The children are such picky* ***eaters***. ◦ *Big companies can afford to be picky about who they hire.*

ˌ**pick-your-ˈown** adj [before noun] (written abbreviation **PYO**) relating to the activity of picking fruit or vegetables yourself at a farm and then paying for the amount you have picked: *pick-your-own strawberries* ◦ *a pick-your-own farm*

picnic /ˈpɪk.nɪk/ **noun; verb**

▸**noun** [C] **A1** an occasion when you have an informal meal of sandwiches, etc. outside, or the food itself: *If the weather's nice we could* ***have*** *a picnic in the park.* ◦ *Why don't you* ***take*** *a picnic with you?* ◦ *a picnic area/lunch/table* ◦ *a picnic basket/hamper*

IDIOM **be no picnic** informal to be a difficult or unpleasant situation: *Being a single parent is no picnic, I can tell you.*

▸**verb** [I] (present tense **picnicking**, past tense and past participle **picnicked**) to have a picnic somewhere: *There were several families picnicking on the river bank.* • **picnicker** /-nɪ.kəʳ/ (US) /-nɪ.kɚ/ **noun** [C]

pictorial /pɪkˈtɔː.ri.əl/ (US) /-ˈtɔːr.i-/ **adj** shown in the form of a picture or photograph: *The exhibition is a pictorial history/record of the town in the 19th century.* • **pictorially** /-ə.li/ **adv**

picture /ˈpɪk.tʃəʳ/ (US) /-tʃɚ/ **noun; verb**

▸**noun IMAGE** ▷ **1** **A1** [C] a drawing, painting, photograph, etc.: *Freddy* ***drew/painted*** *a picture* ***of*** *my dog.* ◦ *We* ***took*** *a picture of (= photographed) the children on their new bicycles.* ◦ *I hate having my picture taken (= being photographed).* **2** **B2** [C] an image seen on a television or cinema screen: *We can't get a clear picture.* **3** **B1** [C] a film: *Could this be the first animated movie to win a best picture award?* **4 the pictures** [plural] old-fashioned the cinema: *Let's go to the pictures tonight.* **5** **B2** [C] something you produce in your mind, by using your imagination or memory: *I have a very* ***vivid*** *picture of the first time I met Erik.* **IDEA** ▷ **6** **B2** [S] (an idea of) a situation: *After watching the news, I had a clearer picture* ***of*** *what was happening.* ◦ *The picture emerging in reports from the battlefield is one of complete confusion.* **7** [S] a situation described in a particular way: figurative *The experts are* ***painting*** *a gloomy/brighter/rosy picture of the state of the economy.*

IDIOMS **be a picture** mainly UK to look beautiful: *The garden was a picture with all the roses in bloom.* • **be the picture of health, innocence, etc.** to look very healthy, innocent, etc.: *I can't believe there's anything seriously wrong with him – he's the picture of health.* • **every picture tells a story** saying said when what has really happened in a situation is clear because of the way that someone or something looks • **get the picture** **C2** to understand: *It's all right, don't say any more – I get the picture.* • **keep sb in the picture** **C1** to make sure someone knows all the facts about a changing situation: *I use the radio to keep me in the picture about what's happening abroad.* • **out of the picture 1** not important to or not involved in a situation: *He used to be in the team, but he's gradually drifted out of the picture.* **2** unnecessary in a particular situation: *The new systems* ***cut*** *humans out of the picture altogether.* • **put sb in the picture** **C1** to tell someone the facts about a situation • **sb's face is a picture** UK If someone's face is a picture, they look very surprised or angry: *Her face was a picture when I told her the price.*

▸**verb** [T] **C1** to imagine something: *Picture* ***the scene*** *– the crowds of people and animals, the noise, the dirt.* ◦ [+ -ing verb] *Try to picture yourself ly****ing*** *on a beach in the hot sun.* ◦ [+ question word] *Picture* ***to yourself how*** *terrible that day must have been.* ◦ formal *He was pictured (= an artist had painted him)* ***as*** *a soldier in full uniform.*

ˈ**picture** ˌ**book** noun [C] a book, especially for young children, that has a lot of pictures and not many words

ˈ**picture** ˌ**frame** noun [C] a frame into which a picture fits

ˈ**picture** ˌ**messaging** noun [U] sending and receiving pictures on a mobile phone

ˌ**picture** ˈ**postcard** noun [C] (also **postcard**) a POSTCARD with a picture, usually a photograph of a place, on one side

ˌ**picture-ˈpostcard** adj [before noun] describes a place that is extremely attractive: *a picture-postcard cottage/village* ◦ disapproving *I hate picture-postcard prettiness.*

picturesque /ˌpɪk.tʃəˈresk/ **adj** **B2** (especially of a place) attractive in appearance, especially in an old-fashioned way: *the picturesque narrow streets of the old city* • **picturesquely** /-li/ **adv** • **picturesqueness** /-nəs/ **noun** [U]

ˈ**picture** ˌ**window** noun [C] a large window positioned so that you can see an attractive view

picturize (UK usually **picturise**) /ˈpɪk.tʃər.aɪz/ **verb** [T] to make a picture of something, or to make a story, etc. into a film

piddle /ˈpɪd.l̩/ **noun; exclamation**

▸**noun** [S or U] informal urine, or an act of urinating: *There was piddle all over the floor.* ◦ *One minute – I just need a piddle.* • **piddle verb** [I]

▸**exclamation** informal an expression used when you are slightly annoyed: *Oh piddle! I've broken another glass.*

piddling /ˈpɪd.l̩.ɪŋ/, /ˈpɪd.lɪŋ/ **adj** informal disapproving very small or not important: *They are making piddling profits of less than £20,000.*

pidgin /ˈpɪdʒ.ɪn/ **noun** [C or U] **1** a language that has developed from a mixture of two languages. It is used as a way of communicating by people who do not speak each other's languages. **2 pidgin English, French, etc.** informal English, French, etc. when it is spoken in a simple way by someone who does not speak that language well: *'He come here?' he asked* ***in*** *pidgin English.*

pie /paɪ/ **noun** [C or U] **B1** a type of food made with meat, vegetables, or fruit covered in pastry and baked: *Would you like some more steak pie?* ◦ *a pecan pie*

pie

IDIOM **pie in the sky** something that you hope will happen but is very unlikely to happen: *Their plans to set up their own business are just pie in the sky.*

PIE /paɪ/, /ˌpiː.aɪˈiː/ **noun** [U] abbreviation for **Proto-Indo-European**

piebald /ˈpaɪ.bɔːld/ (US) /-bɑːld/ **adj** (of an animal, especially a horse) having a pattern of two different colours on its hair, especially black and white: *piebald ponies*

piece /piːs/ **noun; verb**

▸**noun** [C] **PART** ▷ **1** **A2** a part of something: *a piece* ***of*** *cloth torn from her coat* ◦ *He cut the cake into six pieces.* ◦ *This jigsaw puzzle has two pieces missing.* ◦ *The vase lay on the floor* ***in*** *pieces (= broken into small parts).* ◦ *She tried to* ***break/tear*** *a small piece* ***off*** *the edge.*

P

◦ *The building was taken apart and reassembled piece* ***by*** *piece (= one part after another).* **2 in one piece** as a single thing and not divided into smaller pieces: *We want to sell the business in one piece.* **3 come/fall to pieces** to break apart into smaller parts: *The glass must have been cracked – it just fell to pieces in my hand.* ◦ *His clothes were dirty and falling to pieces.* **THING ▷ 4** A2 a single object of a particular type: *a piece* ***of*** *furniture/clothing/equipment* ◦ *a piece of paper (= a whole sheet)* ◦ *a piece* ***of*** *china (= an object made of china)* ◦ *a piece* ***of*** *information/advice* **5** B2 something that has been created by an artist, musician, or writer: *an orchestral/piano/instrumental piece* ◦ *a skilful piece* ***of*** *work/research* ◦ *Did you read that piece (= article) in the newspaper?* **6** a single thing that forms part of a set: *a chess piece* **7** a coin with a stated value: *Could you swap me a 20p piece for two tens?* **GUN ▷ 8** old-fashioned a gun: *an artillery piece* ◦ US slang *He was carrying a piece when he was arrested.*

IDIOMS **come to pieces** UK If something comes to pieces, it has been designed so that it can be divided into smaller parts. • **give sb a piece of your mind** informal to speak angrily to someone about something they have done wrong: *I'm going to give that mechanic a piece of my mind if the car's not fixed this time.* • **go/fall to pieces 1** C2 If someone goes/falls to pieces, they become unable to think clearly and control their emotions because of something unpleasant or difficult that they have experienced: *She just goes (****all****) to pieces in exams.* **2** If a relationship, organization, or system goes/falls to pieces, it fails: *Their marriage began to fall to pieces after only a few months.* • **(all) in one piece** not damaged: *The radio had been stolen, but otherwise we got the car back (all) in one piece.* • **pick/pull sb/sth to pieces** informal to criticize someone or something severely: *The moment she left, the rest of the family started to pull her to pieces.* • **piece of ass** US offensive used to refer to a woman as a sexually attractive object • **piece of cake** informal B2 something that is very easy to do: *The exam was a piece of cake.* • **take sth to pieces** UK to separate something into smaller parts: *If you take the bookcase to pieces, it will fit in the back of your car.*

▸**verb**

PHRASAL VERB **piece sth together** to create something by joining the separate parts of it together or by joining different things together: *The ancient skull has been pieced together* ***from*** *fragments.* ◦ *The police are collecting clues in order to piece together the details of the day she died.*

-piece /-piːs/ suffix with the number of pieces mentioned: *a five-piece band (= with five players)*

pièce de résistance /piˌes.də.reɪ.zɪˈstɑ̃ːs/ noun [usually S] (plural **pièces de résistance** /piˌes-/) the best and most important or exciting thing, often the last in a series of things: *The pièce de résistance of his stage act was a brilliant Barbra Streisand impression.*

piecemeal /ˈpiːs.miːl/ adv, adj often disapproving not done according to a plan but done at different times in different ways: *Unfortunately, everything is being done piecemeal.*

ˌpieces of ˈeight noun [plural] (in the past) coins used in Spain

piecework /ˈpiːs.wɜːk/ (US) /-wɝːk/ noun [U] specialized work for which the amount of pay depends on the number of things finished rather than the time spent making them

ˈpie ˌchart noun [C] a way of showing information about how a total amount is divided up, consisting of a circle that is divided from its centre into several parts

ˈpie ˌcrust noun [C] the pastry on the bottom and sometimes covering a PIE

pied /paɪd/ adj [before noun] specialized (used especially in the names of birds) having fur or feathers of two or more colours, usually black and white: *pied kingfishers*

pied-à-terre /piˌeɪ.dætˈeəʳ/ (US) /-ˈer/ noun [C] (plural **pieds-à-terre**) a small house or apartment in a city that someone owns or rents in addition to their main home, where they stay when visiting that city for a short time

ˌpie-ˈeyed adj informal very drunk

pier /pɪəʳ/ (US) /pɪr/ noun [C] **PLATFORM ▷ 1** a long structure sticking out from the land over the sea, where people can walk or large boats can be tied, sometimes with restaurants and places of entertainment on it **2** a low structure built at the edge of water, used especially for getting into and out of boats **COLUMN ▷ 3** specialized a strong thick column used to support a wall, roof, or other structure

pier

pierce /pɪəs/ (US) /pɪrs/ verb **1** [I + adv/prep, T] to go into or through something, making a hole in it using a sharp point: *The needle pierces the fabric four times a second.* ◦ *I couldn't wear these earrings because my ears aren't pierced.* ◦ *The gun fires a shell capable of piercing the armour of an enemy tank.* ◦ *The hole they drilled pierces six kilometres* ***into*** *the Earth's crust.* **2** [T] (of a light, sound, etc.) to suddenly be seen or heard, despite darkness, noise, etc.: *A few rays of sunlight pierced the smoke.*

piercing /ˈpɪə.sɪŋ/ (US) /ˈpɪr-/ adj; noun

▸**adj 1** going through or into something: *Troops have been issued with new* ***armour****-piercing anti-tank grenades.* ◦ figurative *We shivered in the piercing wind.* **2** describes a sound that is high, loud, and unpleasant: *piercing screams* **3 a piercing criticism, question, remark, etc.** a criticism, question, remark, etc. that is unpleasant or uncomfortable because it is strong or it makes you think about or discuss something which you would prefer not to: *She hadn't really meant to lie, but their piercing questions had forced her to.* **4 piercing eyes, look, gaze, etc.** used to describe when a person looks very carefully at someone or something, especially when they are trying to discover something, often making people feel uncomfortable: *Sherlock Holmes gave him a piercing glance.* ◦ *He looked straight at me with his piercing blue eyes.* • **piercingly** /-li/ adv

▸**noun** [C or U] (also **ˈbody ˌpiercing**) a hole made in the body for wearing jewellery, or the process of making such a hole: *He has several tattoos and multiple piercings.*

pierhead /ˈpɪə.hed/ (US) /ˈpɪr-/ noun [C usually singular] the part of a pier that is furthest from the land

piety /ˈpaɪ.ə.ti/ (US) /ˈpaɪə.t̬i/ noun [U] (also **piousness**) formal strong belief in a religion that is shown in the way someone lives

piezoelectric /ˌpiː.zəʊ.ɪˈlek.trɪk/ (US) /piˌeɪ.zoʊ-/ adj specialized producing electrical power by putting pressure on particular types of stone

piffle /ˈpɪf.l̩/ noun [U] old-fashioned informal nonsense: *Jo really does talk a lot of piffle sometimes.*

piffling /ˈpɪf.l̩.ɪŋ/, /ˈpɪf.lɪŋ/ adj informal extremely small or not important: *piffling details* ◦ *a piffling amount*

P

pig /pɪɡ/ noun; verb

▸noun [C] **ANIMAL** ▷ **1** A1 (US also **hog**) a large pink, brown, or black farm animal with short legs and a curved tail, kept for its meat: *The meat produced from a pig is called pork, bacon, or ham.* ◦ *a pig farm* **UNPLEASANT PERSON/THING** ▷ **2** informal a person who is unpleasant and difficult to deal with: *He was an absolute pig to her.* ◦ *He's a real pig of a man.* **3 be a pig to do, play, etc.** UK informal to be very difficult or unpleasant to do, play, etc.: *It's a beautiful piece of music but it's a pig to play.* **EATS TOO MUCH** ▷ **4** informal a person who eats too much: *You **greedy** pig! You're not having another chocolate biscuit!* **POLICE** ▷ **5** offensive a police officer

IDIOMS **make a pig of yourself** disapproving to eat too much: *They made complete pigs of themselves at the dinner.* • **make a pig's ear of sth** UK informal to do something badly, wrongly, or awkwardly: *He's made a real pig's ear of that bookcase he was supposed to be making.* • **a pig in a poke** something that you buy or accept without first seeing it or finding out if it is good • **pigs might fly** humorous saying said when you think that there is no chance at all of something happening: *'I'll have finished it by tomorrow.' 'And pigs might fly!'*

▸verb (-gg-)

PHRASAL VERB **pig out** informal to eat a lot or too much: *We pigged out **on** all the lovely cakes and pastries.*

pigeon /ˈpɪdʒ.ən/ noun [C or U] a large, usually grey bird that is often seen in towns sitting on buildings in large groups, and is sometimes eaten as food

pigeon

IDIOM **be not sb's pigeon** UK old-fashioned to not be someone's responsibility: *Transport? That's not my pigeon – ask Danny.*

P

ˌpigeon-ˈchested adj (of a person) having a narrow chest that sticks out more than usual at the front

ˈpigeon ˌfancier noun [C] UK someone who keeps pigeons as pets

pigeonhole /ˈpɪdʒ.ən.həʊl/ US /-hoʊl/ noun; verb

▸noun [C] one of a set of small boxes, open at the front, in which letters and messages are left for different people: *Leave the report **in** my pigeonhole when you've read it.*

IDIOM **put sth/sb in a pigeonhole** usually disapproving to form a very fixed, often wrong, opinion about what type of person or thing someone or something is

▸verb [T] usually disapproving to have an often unfair idea of what type someone or something is: *He is a film producer who can't be conveniently pigeonholed.*

ˈpigeon-toed adj A person who is pigeon-toed bends their feet in towards each other when they walk.

piggy /ˈpɪɡ.i/ noun; adj

▸noun [C] child's word a pig: *Look at those lovely little piggies, James!*

▸adj informal disapproving like a pig: *He's got little piggy eyes.*

piggyback /ˈpɪɡ.i.bæk/ noun; adv; verb

▸noun [C] (also **ˈpiggyback ˌride**) a ride on someone's back with your arms round their neck and your legs round their waist: *I **gave** her a piggyback ride.*

▸adv on someone's back, or on the back of something: *Martha **rode** piggyback **on** her dad.* ◦ *Dom **carried** his daughter piggyback when she got too tired to walk.*

piggyback

▸verb [I] to use something that someone else has made or done in order to get an advantage: *Everyone wants to piggyback **on** the phenomenal success of the TV series.*

ˈpiggy ˌbank noun [C] a small container, sometimes in the shape of a pig, that is used by children for saving money

ˌpiggy in the ˈmiddle noun **1** [U] UK a game in which two people throw a ball to each other over the head of a person who stands between them and tries to catch it **2** [C usually singular] someone who is in a difficult situation because they know two people who are arguing and they do not want to become involved

pigheaded /ˌpɪɡˈhed.ɪd/ adj disapproving showing unreasonable support for an opinion or plan of action and refusing to change or listen to different opinions • **pigheadedly** /-li/ adv • **pigheadedness** /-nəs/ noun [U]

ˈpig ˌiron noun [U] a type of iron that is not pure

piglet /ˈpɪɡ.lət/ noun [C] a baby pig: *The sow had eight piglets.*

pigment /ˈpɪɡ.mənt/ noun [C or U] a substance which gives something a particular colour when it is present in it or is added to it: *Melanin is the dark brown pigment of the hair, skin and eyes which is present in varying amounts in every human being.* ◦ *Pigment is mixed into oil, glue, egg, etc. to make different types of paint.* • **pigmented** /pɪɡˈmen.tɪd/ US /ˈpɪɡ.mən.t̬ɪd/ adj *pigmented tissue/skin/areas*

pigmentation /ˌpɪɡ.mənˈteɪ.ʃən/ noun [U] the natural colour of something, usually a living thing

Pigmy /ˈpɪɡ.mi/ noun [C], adj **Pygmy**

pigskin /ˈpɪɡ.skɪn/ noun **1** [U] leather made from the skin of pigs: *pigskin gloves/shoes* **2** [C] US informal the ball used to play American football

pigsty /ˈpɪɡ.staɪ/ noun [C] (US also **pigpen**) **1** the building and closed area where pigs are kept **2** a dirty or untidy place: *Your bedroom's a pigsty!*

pigswill /ˈpɪɡ.swɪl/ noun [U] UK (US **swill**) **1** waste human food that is fed to pigs **2** informal bad or unpleasant food: *I can't eat this pigswill! Take it away!*

pigtail /ˈpɪɡ.teɪl/ noun [C] a length of hair that is tied at the back of the head or at each side of the head, sometimes in a PLAIT (= twist): *A little girl **in** pigtails presented the bouquet.*

pike /paɪk/ noun [C] **FISH** ▷ **1** (plural **pike**) a large fish which lives in lakes and rivers and eats other fish **ROAD** ▷ **2** (plural **pikes**) US for **turnpike**: *the Leesburg Pike* **WEAPON** ▷ **3** (plural **pikes**) a long sharp stick used in the past as a weapon by soldiers on foot: *A soldier with a pike could bring down a charging horse.* **HILL** ▷ **4** (plural **pikes**) Northern a hill in northern England with a pointed top

piker /ˈpaɪ.kər/ US /-kɚ/ noun [C] Australian English informal a person who avoids getting into difficult or dangerous situations

pikestaff /ˈpaɪk.stɑːf/ US /-stæf/ noun **be (as) plain as a pikestaff** → See at **plain**

Pilates /pəˈlɑː.tiːz/ noun [U] trademark a system of physical exercise involving controlled movements, stretching, and breathing

pilau /ˈpiː.laʊ/ (US) /pɪˈlɔː/ noun [C or U] (US usually **pilaf**) rice cooked in spicy liquid, often with vegetables or meat added: *a delicious mushroom pilau ◦ barbecued pork with pilau **rice***

pilchard /ˈpɪl.tʃəd/ (US) /-tʃɚd/ noun [C] a small fish you can eat that lives in the sea: *a **tin of** pilchards in tomato sauce*

pile /paɪl/ noun; verb

▸noun **AMOUNT** ▷ **1** (B1) [C] objects positioned one on top of another: *a large pile **of** sand ◦ a pile **of** books ◦ a pile **of** dirty clothes* **2 a pile of sth/piles of sth** informal a lot: *I've got piles/a pile of things to do today.* **COLUMN** ▷ **3** [C] a strong column or post of wood, metal, or concrete that is pushed into the ground to help support a building **SURFACE** ▷ **4** [S] the soft surface made by the ends of many short threads on a carpet or on cloth such as VELVET: *a luxurious **deep**-pile carpet* **BUILDING** ▷ **5** [C] mainly humorous a large building: *They've got a great big Victorian pile somewhere out in the country.* **MEDICAL** ▷ **6 piles** [plural] informal **haemorrhoids**

IDIOM **make a pile** informal to earn a large amount of money: *He made a pile selling computers and retired by the time he was 40.*

▸verb **OBJECTS** ▷ **1** [I or T, + adv/prep] (also **pile up**) to arrange objects into a pile: *We piled plenty of logs **up** next to the fire. ◦ Please pile your homework books neatly **on** the table as you leave. ◦ Her plate was piled (**high**) **with** salad. ◦ Snow had piled up against the walls.* **PEOPLE** ▷ **2** [I usually + adv/prep] informal (of a group of people) to move together, especially in an uncontrolled way: *As soon as the train stopped, they all piled **in/out**.*

IDIOMS **pile it high and sell it cheap** mainly UK to sell large amounts of a product at cheap prices • **pile it on** informal to say too much, especially giving too much emphasis: *You're really piling it on with the compliments tonight, Gareth, aren't you!* • **pile on the agony** UK informal to enjoy emphasizing how bad a situation is: *Okay, I'll give you some money – just stop piling on the agony.*

PHRASAL VERB **pile (sth) up FORM A PILE** ▷ **1** to form a pile, or to put a lot of things into a pile **INCREASE** ▷ **2** (B2) (of something bad) to increase: *Unpaid bills began to pile up alarmingly.*

piledriver /ˈpaɪlˌdraɪ.vəʳ/ (US) /-vɚ/ noun [C] a powerful machine that forces piles (= strong posts) into the ground

ˈpile-up noun [C] a traffic accident involving several vehicles which hit each other

pilfer /ˈpɪl.fəʳ/ (US) /-fɚ/ verb [I or T] to steal things of small value: *He was caught pilfering (sweets) **from** the shop.*

pilferage /ˈpɪl.fᵊr.ɪdʒ/ noun [U] the act of stealing things of small value: *Lockable cabinets provide protection against pilferage.*

pilgrim /ˈpɪl.grɪm/ noun [C] a person who makes a journey, often a long and difficult one, to a special place for religious reasons

pilgrimage /ˈpɪl.grɪ.mɪdʒ/ noun [C or U] **1** a special journey made by a pilgrim: *Muslims try to **make a** pilgrimage/**go on a** pilgrimage **to** Mecca at least once in their life.* **2** a visit to a place that is considered special, where you go to show your respect: *For many football fans, the national ground is **a place of** pilgrimage.*

the ˌPilgrim ˈFathers noun [plural] the group of English people who sailed to North America on the ship 'Mayflower', where they formed Plymouth Colony, Massachusetts in 1620

pill /pɪl/ noun; verb

▸noun [C] **MEDICINE** ▷ **1** (B1) a small solid piece of medicine that a person swallows without CHEWING (= crushing with the teeth): *a sleeping pill ◦ a vitamin pill ◦ My mother **takes** three or four pills a day. ◦ Jamie's always had trouble **swallowing** pills.* **2 the pill** a type of pill for women that is taken every day in order to prevent them from becoming pregnant: *Are you **on** the pill?* **PERSON** ▷ **3** US an annoying person: *Jennifer was being such a pill today.* **ON CLOTHING** ▷ **4** US (UK **bobble**) a small ball of threads that develops on the surface of clothes or material: *She sat there sulking and picking the pills off her sweater.*

IDIOM **sugar the pill** UK (US **sweeten the pill**) to make something bad seem less unpleasant: *Plans to improve public services are a way of sugaring the pill of increased taxation.*

▸verb [I] US (UK **bobble**) If a piece of clothing or material pills, it develops small balls of threads on its surface.

pillage /ˈpɪl.ɪdʒ/ verb [I or T] formal to steal something from a place or a person by using violence, especially during war: *Works of art were pillaged **from** many countries in the dark days of the Empire.* • **pillage** noun [U]

pillar /ˈpɪl.əʳ/ (US) /-ɚ/ noun [C] **1** a strong column made of stone, metal or wood which supports part of a building: *A row of reinforced concrete pillars supports the bridge.* ◦ figurative *a pillar **of** smoke/flame* **2 pillar of sth** a very important member or part of a group, organization, system, etc.: *Mrs Maple is a pillar of the local church. ◦ Equality is one of the pillars of socialism.*

IDIOM **from pillar to post** If someone goes from pillar to post, they are forced to keep moving from one place to another: *My parents were always on the move and so my childhood was spent being dragged from pillar to post.*

ˈpillar box noun [C] UK a tall, red box for posting letters

pillbox /ˈpɪl.bɒks/ (US) /-bɑːks/ noun [C] **CONTAINER** ▷ **1** a small container which pills are carried in **BUILDING** ▷ **2** a small, very strong building with narrow holes in the walls through which guns can be FIRED

pillion /ˈpɪl.i.ən/ (US) /-jən/ noun [C] UK a seat or place behind the person riding a motorcycle where a passenger can sit: *a pillion seat/passenger* • **pillion** adv *You get a bit uncomfortable after **riding** pillion for a couple of hours.*

pillock /ˈpɪl.ək/ noun [C] UK offensive a stupid or silly person: *You pillock, look what you've done!*

pillory /ˈpɪl.ᵊr.i/ (US) /-ɚ.i/ verb [T] to severely criticize someone, especially in a public way

pillow /ˈpɪl.əʊ/ (US) /-oʊ/ noun [C] **1** (A2) a rectangular cloth bag filled with soft material, such as feathers or artificial materials, used for resting your head on in bed: *Do you prefer a feather pillow or a foam pillow?* **2** (B1) US for CUSHION (= bag of soft material for sitting or leaning on)

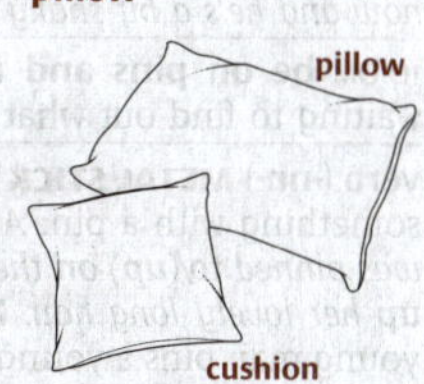

pillowcase /ˈpɪl.əʊ.keɪs/ (US) /-oʊ-/ noun [C] (also

P

pillowslip) a cloth cover for a pillow that can easily be removed and washed

ˈpillow ˌtalk noun [U] conversation between sexual partners in bed

ˈpill-ˌpopping noun [U] informal taking pills, especially when this is a habit or when the pills are illegal drugs

pilot /ˈpaɪ.lət/ noun; adj; verb

▸noun [C] AIRCRAFT ▷ **1** A2 a person who flies an aircraft: *a fighter/helicopter/bomber/airline pilot* SHIP ▷ **2** a person with detailed knowledge of an area of water, such as that around a port, who goes onto a ship to direct it safely TEST ▷ **3** a programme that is made to introduce a new radio or television series and test how popular it is: *If you'd seen the pilot, you'd know why they decided not to make a complete series of programmes!* FLAME ▷ **4** (also **pilot light**) a small flame that burns all the time in a gas device, such as a cooker or a device for heating water, and that starts the main flame burning when the gas is turned on

▸adj [before noun] describes a plan, product, or system that is used to test how good something is before introducing it: *If the pilot* ***scheme*** *(US pilot* ***program****) is successful, many more homes will be offered the new television service.*

▸verb AIRCRAFT ▷ **1** [T] to fly an aircraft: *She piloted the aircraft to safety after one of the engines failed.* TEST ▷ **2** [T] to test a new product before it is sold: *We shall pilot several new cosmetic products* ***to*** *selected potential purchasers.* INTRODUCE ▷ **3** [T usually + adv/prep] mainly UK to be responsible for introducing a new law or system and making certain it is established: *20 years ago he piloted a bill* ***through*** *Parliament on working conditions.* SHIP ▷ **4** [T] to direct a ship into a port or through an area of water

pimento /pɪˈmen.təʊ/ US /-toʊ/ noun [C or U] (plural **pimentos**) (US usually **pimiento**) a sweet red PEPPER

Pimm's /pɪmz/ noun [C or U] UK trademark a pink alcoholic drink usually drunk with ice in the summer

pimp /pɪmp/ noun [C] a man who controls PROSTITUTES, especially by finding customers for them, and takes some of the money that they earn • **pimp** verb [I]

pimple /ˈpɪm.pl̩/ noun [C] a small raised spot on the skin that is temporary

pimply /ˈpɪm.pəl.i/, /ˈ-pli/ adj (also **pimpled**) having pimples: *a pimply face ◦ a pimply adolescent boy*

pin /pɪn/ noun; verb

▸noun [C] METAL STICK ▷ **1** B1 a small thin piece of metal with a point at one end, especially used for temporarily holding pieces of cloth together: *I'll keep the trouser patch in place with pins while I sew it on.* **2** a thin piece of metal: *If you pull the pin out of a hand-grenade, it'll explode. ◦ Is it a two-pin plug or a three-pin plug? ◦ Doctors inserted a metal pin in his leg to hold the bones together.* **3** a decorative object, used as jewellery: *a hat/tie pin* **4** US for **brooch** LEG ▷ **5** [usually plural] old-fashioned humorous a leg: *Grandpa's very old now and he's a bit shaky on his pins.*

IDIOM **be on pins and needles** US to be nervously waiting to find out what is going to happen

▸verb (-nn-) METAL STICK ▷ **1** B1 [T + adv/prep] to fasten something with a pin: *A large picture of the president was pinned* ***to/(up) on*** *the office wall. ◦ She had pinned* ***up*** *her lovely long hair.* **2** [T] US old-fashioned When a young man pins a young woman, he gives her a piece of jewellery to show that they love each other. STOP MOVEMENT ▷ **3** [T + adv/prep] to force someone or something to stay in a particular place by putting weight on them: *She was pinned* ***(down) under*** *a pile of rubble. ◦ A guy leaped out at me and pinned me* ***(up) against*** *the wall.*

IDIOMS **pin back your ears** (also **pin your ears back**) UK informal to listen carefully • **pin your hopes on sth/sb** to hope very much that something or someone will help you to achieve what you want

PHRASAL VERBS **pin sb down** SURROUND ▷ **1** to stop someone from escaping by surrounding them and shooting at them if they try to escape: [often passive] *Government forces were pinned down by resistance fighters 30 miles north of the capital.* GET DETAILS ▷ **2** to make someone provide details about something or make a decision about something: *I've tried asking Stephanie, but she's proving difficult to pin down* ***to*** *a particular date.* • **pin sth down** to discover exact details about something: *We can't pin down where the leak came from.* • **pin sth on sb** (also **hang sth on sb**) to blame someone for something, especially for something they did not do: *You can't pin* ***the blame*** *on her – she wasn't even there when the accident happened.*

PIN /pɪn/ noun [C] (also **ˈPIN ˌnumber**) abbreviation for **personal identification number**: a secret number that a person uses together with a special card to get money from their bank account from a machine outside the bank

pinafore /ˈpɪn.ə.fɔːʳ/ US /-fɔːr/ noun [C] UK LOOSE CLOTHING ▷ **1** (informal **pinny**) a piece of clothing worn by women over the front of other clothes to keep them clean while doing something dirty, especially cooking DRESS ▷ **2** (US **jumper**) a loose dress with no sleeves, usually worn over other clothing such as a shirt

piñata /pɪnˈjɑː.tə/ US /-t̬ə/ noun [C] an object in the shape of an animal, etc. that contains sweets. It is hung up at parties and children hit it with sticks to break it open and release the sweets.

pinball /ˈpɪn.bɔːl/ US /-bɑːl/ noun [U] a game played on a special machine like a large box on legs in which the player keeps a small ball BOUNCING between devices to win points

ˈpinball maˌchine noun [C] a machine for playing pinball

pince-nez /ˌpæːnsˈneɪ/ noun [C] (plural **pince-nez**) (especially in the past) glasses held on a person's nose by a spring rather than by pieces which fit around their ears: *He wore* ***(a pair of)*** *pince-nez.*

pincer /ˈpɪn.səʳ/ US /-sɚ/ noun ANIMAL PART ▷ **1** [C usually plural] one of a pair of curved CLAWS of an animal such as a CRAB TOOL ▷ **2 pincers** [plural] a tool for holding or pulling something, made of two curved metal bars which move against each other so that when the handles are pushed together the other ends close tightly

ˈpincer ˌmovement noun [C usually singular] a type of attack in which two parts of an army follow curved paths towards each other in an attempt to surround and then defeat the enemy

pinch /pɪntʃ/ verb; noun

▸verb PRESS ▷ **1** [I or T] to press something, especially someone's skin, strongly between two hard things such as a finger and a thumb, usually causing pain: *Ouch! Stop pinching (me)! ◦ These shoes are too tight, they pinch (my feet).* **2 pinch yourself** informal You say that you have to pinch yourself if you cannot really believe something that has happened because it is so good or so strange: *I can't believe that he's back from Canada and he's mine – I keep having to pinch myself to* make sure I'm not dreaming. **STEAL** ▷ **3** [T] informal to steal something: *Right, who's pinched my chair?*

IDIOM **pinch pennies** (UK also **pinch and scrape**) to spend as little money as possible: *When we were first married we had to pinch pennies just to get by.*

▸noun **AMOUNT** ▷ **1** [C] a small amount of something, such as a powder, especially the amount which a person can hold between their first finger and thumb: *While the tomatoes are cooking add a pinch **of** salt/sugar/dried thyme.* ◦ figurative *Opinion polls on subjects like this should be **taken with** a pinch **of** scepticism.* **PRESS** ▷ **2** [C usually singular] the act of pinching something or someone: *She **gave** Emma a painful pinch **on** the arm.*

IDIOM **at a pinch** UK (US **in a pinch**) Something that you can do at a pinch can be done if it is really necessary, but it will be difficult, not perfect, or not what you would really like: *I need £2,000 to set up the business, but I suppose £1,500 would do at a pinch.*

pinched /pɪntʃt/ **adj** describes someone's face when it is thin and pale: *He had that pinched look which suggests poverty and lack of nourishment.*

ˈpinch-hit verb [I] US to do something for someone because they are suddenly unable to do it: *He was pinch-hitting **for** one of the regular TV sportscasters, and was a great success.*

ˈpin ˌcode noun [C] Indian English a short series of letters and numbers that is part of a postal address; a POSTCODE

pincushion /ˈpɪŋˌkʊʃ.ən/ (US) /ˈpɪn-/ **noun** [C] a small, soft object into which pins can be pushed to keep them safely until you need them

pindrop silence /ˌpɪn.drɒpˈsaɪ.ləns/ (US) /-drɑːp-/ **noun** [U] Indian English complete silence

pine /paɪn/ **noun; verb**

▸noun **1** (B2) [C or U] (also **pine tree**) an EVERGREEN tree (= one that never loses its leaves) that grows in cooler areas of the world: *a plantation of pines* ◦ *a pine forest* **2** [U] the wood of pine trees, usually pale in colour: *pine furniture* ◦ *Pine is a softwood.* • **piny** (also **piney**) /ˈpaɪ.ni/ **adj**

▸verb [I] to become increasingly thin and weak because of unhappiness, especially after the death of a loved person

PHRASAL VERB **pine for sth/sb** to want something or someone very much, usually when it is impossible to have them, or when they have gone away: *He's still pining for his ex-girlfriend.*

pineapple /ˈpaɪnˌæp.l̩/ **noun** [C or U] (B1) (the yellow flesh and juice of) a large tropical fruit with a rough orange or brown skin and pointed leaves on top: *tinned pineapples* ◦ *pineapple juice*

ˈpine ˌcone noun [C] the hard egg-shaped part of the pine tree which opens and releases seeds

ˈpine ˌneedle noun [C] the thin pointed leaf of a pine tree

ˈpine ˌnut noun [C] (UK also **ˈpine ˌkernel**) the white seed of the pine tree, often used in cooking

ping /pɪŋ/ **verb; noun**

▸verb [I] **1** to make a short, sharp sound: *We heard a small stone ping against our window.* **2** informal to send an email or text message: *Ping me an email.* **3** US for **pink** (= an engine noise)

▸noun [C] **1** a short, sharp sound **2** US for **pink** (= an engine noise)

ˈPing-Pong noun [U] informal trademark **table tennis**

pinhead /ˈpɪn.hed/ **noun** [C] **OF PIN** ▷ **1** the very small round end of a pin: *The fault was caused by a hole no larger than a pinhead.* **PERSON** ▷ **2** informal a stupid person

pinhole /ˈpɪn.həʊl/ (US) /-hoʊl/ **noun** [C] a very small hole made by or as if by a pin

pinion /ˈpɪn.jən/ **verb; noun**

▸verb [T] to hold someone, especially by the arms, to prevent them from moving: *He was pinioned **to** the wall by two men while another one repeatedly punched him.*

▸noun [C] a small wheel with teeth-like parts around its edge which fit against similar parts on a larger wheel or a RACK (= bar with teeth-like parts): *a rack-and-pinion assembly*

pink /pɪŋk/ **adj; noun; verb**

▸adj **COLOUR** ▷ **1** (A2) of a pale red colour: *pretty pink flowers* ◦ *Have you been in the sun? Your nose is a bit pink.* **POLITICS** ▷ **2** old-fashioned disapproving (slightly) supporting SOCIALIST ideas and principles **GAY** ▷ **3** connected with gay people: *the growth in the pink economy* • **pinkness** /ˈpɪŋk.nəs/ **noun** [U]

▸noun **COLOUR** ▷ **1** (A2) [C or U] a pale red colour: *She's very fond of pink.* **PLANT** ▷ **2** [C] a small garden plant with sweet-smelling pink, white, or red flowers and narrow, grey-green leaves, or one of its flowers

IDIOM **in the pink** old-fashioned informal in very good health

▸verb [I] UK (US **ping**) When a car engine pinks, it makes a high knocking sound because the fuel is not burning correctly.

ˌpink-ˈcollar adj mainly US describes a job that is traditionally done by a woman: *Until recently secretarial work and nursing were very much pink-collar professions.*

pinkie (also **pinky**) /ˈpɪŋ.ki/ **noun** [C] US informal or Scottish English for **little finger**: *a pinkie ring*

ˈpinking ˌshears noun [plural] special SCISSORS with V-shaped teeth along the blades, used to make V-shaped lines along the edges of cloth, so that threads do not easily come out

pinkish /ˈpɪŋ.kɪʃ/ **adj** slightly pink in colour: *a pinkish blue*

pinko /ˈpɪŋ.kəʊ/ (US) /-koʊ/ **noun** [C] (plural **pinkos** or **pinkoes**) old-fashioned disapproving a person who (slightly) supports SOCIALIST ideas and principles

the ˌpink ˈpound noun [S] UK (US **the ˌpink ˈdollar**) the money that all gay people together have available to spend: *Companies are becoming aware of the power of the pink pound.*

ˌpink ˈslip noun [C] US informal a document given to a person telling them that they do not have a job any more

ˌpink-ˈslip verb [T often passive] US informal to get rid of someone or something that is no longer needed

ˈpin ˌmoney noun [U] a small amount of extra money which a person earns to buy things they want but do not need

pinnacle /ˈpɪn.ə.kl̩/ **noun** **SUCCESS** ▷ **1** [C usually singular] the most successful or admired part of a system or achievement: *By the age of 32 she had **reached the** pinnacle **of** her career.* **TOP** ▷ **2** [C] a small pointed tower on top of a building, or the top part of a mountain: literary *The pinnacles of the Himalayas were visible above the clouds.*

pinnate /ˈpɪn.eɪt/ **adj** specialized describes a type of COMPOUND leaf that has a central stem with small leaves arranged on either side of it → Compare **palmate**

pinny /ˈpɪn.i/ **noun** [C] UK informal for **pinafore**

pinpoint /ˈpɪn.pɔɪnt/ (US) /ˈpɪn-/ **verb; noun; adj**
▸**verb** [T] **1** (C2) to find out or say the exact position in space or time of something: *It is not possible to pinpoint precisely the time of death.* **2** (C2) to discover or describe the exact facts about something: *Emergency workers at the site are still unable to pinpoint the cause of the explosion.*
▸**noun** [C] a very small spot of something: *a pinpoint* ***of*** *light*
▸**adj** [before noun] very exact: *The computer will calculate your position with pinpoint* ***accuracy.***

pinprick /ˈpɪn.prɪk/ (US) /ˈpɪn-/ **noun** [C usually plural] **HOLE/PAIN** ▷ **1** a very small hole in something where a pin or needle has been pushed into it, or a sudden pain where a pin or needle has been pushed into your skin: *There was a pinprick on his arm.* **SMALL AMOUNT** ▷ **2** a very small amount of something, especially light: *The darkness was broken by the odd pinprick of light.* **ANNOYING THING** ▷ **3** something that is slightly annoying for a short time: *You have to ignore the pinpricks and just get on with the job.*

ˌpins and ˈneedles noun [plural] If someone has pins and needles in a part of their body, they feel slight sharp pains in it, usually just after they have moved from being still in one position for a long time.

pinstripe /ˈpɪn.straɪp/ **noun 1** [U] a usually dark cloth with a pattern of narrow, usually pale, parallel lines: *He was wearing a pinstripe suit.* **2 pinstripes** [plural] suits made of pinstriped cloth: *She watched the businessmen walk past in their pinstripes.* • **pinstriped** /-straɪpt/ **adj**

pint /paɪnt/ **noun** [C] **1** (B2) a measure for liquid equal to about half a litre: *a pint* ***of milk*** ◦ *a pint* ***of beer*** **2** UK informal a pint of beer: *He usually goes out for a pint at lunchtime.*

pinta /ˈpaɪn.tə/ (US) /-t̬ə/ **noun** [C usually singular] UK old-fashioned informal a pint of milk

pinto bean /ˈpɪn.təʊˌbiːn/ (US) /-t̬oʊˌ-/ **noun** [C] a bean with small, brown marks on it, used in cooking

P

ˈpint-size(d) adj informal (of a person) small and not important: *Don't worry about him, he's just a pint-sized nobody.*

ˈpin-up noun [C] **1** a picture of a sexually attractive and usually famous person, especially someone wearing few clothes: *Every wall in her bedroom was covered with pin-ups of her favourite pop star.* **2** informal a person who is seen in pin-ups: *With his perfect college-boy looks, he's the latest teenage pin-up.*

pinwheel /ˈpɪn.wiːl/ **noun** [C] US for WINDMILL (= a child's toy)

pioneer /ˌpaɪəˈnɪəʳ/ (US) /-ˈnɪr/ **noun; verb**
▸**noun** [C] **1** (C2) a person who is one of the first people to do something: *one of the pioneers* ***of*** *modern science* ◦ *a pioneer heart surgeon* **2** a person who goes to an area and builds a house, begins a farm, etc.: *The pioneers went west across North America, cutting down forests and planting new crops.*
▸**verb** [T] to be one of the first people to do something: *It was universities that pioneered these new industries.*

pioneering /ˌpaɪəˈnɪə.rɪŋ/ (US) /-ˈnɪr.ɪŋ/ **adj** using ideas and methods that have never been used before: *pioneering techniques* ◦ *a pioneering surgeon*

pious /ˈpaɪ.əs/ **adj RELIGIOUS** ▷ **1** strongly believing in religion, and living in a way that shows this belief: *She is a pious follower of the faith, never missing her prayers.* **PRETENDING** ▷ **2** disapproving pretending to have sincere feelings: *Quit the pious apologies – I know you don't really care.* • **piously** /-li/ **adv**

pip /pɪp/ **noun; verb**
▸**noun SEED** ▷ **1** [C] UK (US **seed**) one of the small seeds of a fruit such as an apple or an orange → Compare **stone SOUND** ▷ **2** [C usually plural] mainly UK a short, high sound, especially one of a series: *She turned on the radio and heard the five o'clock pips.*
▸**verb** [T] (**-pp-**) UK informal to beat someone either by a very small amount or right at the end of a competition: *I got through to the final interview, but I was pipped* ***at the post*** *(= in the final stage) by a candidate with better qualifications.*

pipe /paɪp/ **noun; verb**
▸**noun** [C] **TUBE** ▷ **1** (B1) a tube inside which liquid or gas flows from one place to another: *a water/gas/sewer pipe* ◦ *a burst/fractured/leaking pipe* **FOR TOBACCO** ▷ **2** a short, narrow tube with a small container at one end, used for smoking tobacco: *I ordered some tea for myself and* ***lit*** *my pipe.* **INSTRUMENT** ▷ **3** a simple musical instrument made of a short, narrow tube that is played by blowing through it **4 pipes** [plural] another word for **bagpipes 5** one of the metal or wood tubes in an organ through which air is pushed to make sound **SYMBOL** ▷ **6** the | symbol on a computer keyboard

IDIOM **put/stick that in your pipe and smoke it!** old-fashioned or humorous a rude way of telling someone that they must accept what you have just said, even if they do not like it

▸**verb SPEAK** ▷ **1** [T] to speak or sing in a high voice **TUBE** ▷ **2** [T usually passive, + adv/prep] to transport something in a pipe: *Hot water is piped* ***to*** *all apartments from the central boiler room.* ◦ figurative *Music is piped throughout the hotel complex.*

PHRASAL VERBS **pipe down** informal to stop talking or making unnecessary noise: *Will you please pipe down, you two? I'm trying to read!* • **pipe up** informal to suddenly start to speak or make a noise: *In the silence that followed, a lone voice piped up from the back of the room.*

ˈpipe ˌcleaner noun [C] a piece of wire covered with soft threads that is used to clean a pipe

ˌpiped ˈmusic noun [U] often disapproving **Muzak**

ˈpipe ˌdream noun [C] an idea or plan that is impossible or very unlikely to happen: *Her plans are not realistic – they'll never be more than a pipe dream.*

pipeline /ˈpaɪp.laɪn/ **noun** [C] a very long, large tube, often underground, through which liquid or gas can flow for long distances

IDIOM **in the pipeline** being planned: *The theatre company has several new productions in the pipeline for next season.*

piper /ˈpaɪ.pəʳ/ (US) /-pɚ/ **noun** [C] someone who plays a pipe (= a short narrow tube played by blowing through it) or the BAGPIPES

pipette /pɪˈpet/ (US) /paɪ-/ **noun** [C] a thin glass tube used especially in biology and chemistry for measuring or moving a small amount of liquid

piping /ˈpaɪ.pɪŋ/ **noun DECORATION** ▷ **1** [C or U] a narrow strip of cloth used to decorate the edges of clothes or furniture **2** [U] UK (US **decoration**) a narrow line of ICING (= covering made with sugar) used to decorate a cake **TUBE** ▷ **3** [U] pipes in general or a particular system of pipes

ˌpiping ˈhot adj, adv usually approving describes very hot food or drinks

pipsqueak /ˈpɪp.skwiːk/ **noun** [C] informal someone who is not important and does not deserve respect: *You little pipsqueak!*

piquant /ˈpiː.kənt/ **adj INTERESTING** ▷ **1** formal interesting and exciting, especially because of being mysterious: *More piquant details of their private life* *were revealed.* **SPICY** ▷ **2** having a pleasant sharp or spicy taste: *a piquant mixture of spices* • **piquancy** /-kən.si/ **noun** [U] formal • **piquantly** /-li/ **adv** formal

pique /piːk/ **noun; verb**

▸**noun** [U] a feeling of anger, especially caused by damage to your feeling of being proud of yourself: *He stormed from the room* ***in a fit of*** *pique, shouting that he had been misunderstood.* • **piqued** /piːkt/ **adj**

▸**verb** [T]

IDIOM **pique sb's curiosity, interest, etc.** to make someone interested in something and want to know more about it: *The noise continued, piquing her curiosity.*

piracy /ˈpaɪ.rə.si/ (US) /ˈpaɪr.ə-/ **noun** [U] **SHIPS** ▷ **1** the act of attacking ships in order to steal from them: *Piracy is alive and flourishing on the world's commercial sea-lanes.* **COPYING** ▷ **2** the act of illegally copying a computer program, music, a film, etc. and selling it: *software/video piracy*

piranha /pɪˈrɑː.nə/ (US) /pəˈrɑː.njə/ **noun** [C] (plural **piranhas** or **piranha**) a fish which lives in South American rivers, has sharp teeth, and eats meat

pirate /ˈpaɪ.rət/ (US) /ˈpaɪr.ət/ **noun; verb**

▸**noun** [C] **SAILOR** ▷ **1** B1 a person who sails in a ship and attacks other ships in order to steal from them **COPYING** ▷ **2** a person who illegally copies music, films, computer programs, and sells them: *software pirates* **3 pirate radio station** a radio station that broadcasts without official permission • **piratical** /paɪˈræt.ɪ.kəl/ (US) /-ˈræṭ-/ **adj** formal

▸**verb** [T] to illegally copy a computer program, music, a film, etc. and sell it • **pirated** /ˈpaɪ.rə.tɪd/ (US) /ˈpaɪr.ə.ṭɪd/ **adj** *a pirated video*

pirouette /ˌpɪr.uːˈet/ **noun** [C] a fast turn of the body on the toes or the front part of the foot, performed especially by a BALLET dancer • **pirouette verb** [I]

Pisces /ˈpaɪ.siːz/ **noun** [C or U] the 12th sign of the ZODIAC, relating to the period 20 February to 20 March, represented by two fish, or a person born during this period • **Piscean** /-si.ən/ **noun** [C]

piss /pɪs/ **noun; verb**

▸**noun** [S or U] offensive urine: *There was piss all over the floor.* ◦ *I need* ***a*** *piss.* ◦ *He's* ***having a*** *piss.*

IDIOM **take the piss (out of) sb or sth** UK offensive to make a joke about someone or make them look silly

▸**verb** [I] offensive **1** to pass urine: *That dog keeps pissing* ***on*** *our fence.* **2 piss yourself** to urinate over yourself and the clothes you are wearing

IDIOMS **be pissing in the wind** to be trying to do something when there is no hope of succeeding: *You can try to change her mind if you like, but you'll be pissing in the wind.* • **piss yourself (laughing)** to laugh very much: *There I was writhing in agony on the floor and you lot were pissing yourselves laughing!*

PHRASAL VERBS **piss (sb) about/around** [I or T] UK offensive to behave in a stupid way or to treat someone badly: *Look, we haven't got much time so stop pissing about.* ◦ *Stop pissing me about and just tell me where they are.* • **piss sth away** to waste an opportunity: *This is your last chance to win the league so don't piss it away.* • **piss down** [I] UK offensive to rain heavily: ***It's*** *really pissing* (***it***) *down here at the moment.* • **piss off** UK offensive to leave or go away, used especially as a rude way of telling someone to go away: *Everyone just pissed off and left me to clean up.* ◦ *Why don't you just piss off – you've caused enough problems already!* • **piss sb off** (also **pee sb off**) to annoy someone: *He never does any washing-up and it's starting to piss me off.*

ˈ**piss ˌartist** **noun** [C] UK offensive **1** someone who does not do things correctly **2** someone who is often drunk

pissed /pɪst/ **adj** offensive **1** [after verb] UK drunk: *I can't remember – I was pissed at the time.* **2** US annoyed: *He's gonna be pissed when he finds out what happened.*

IDIOM **pissed as a newt/fart** (also **pissed out of your brain/head/mind**) UK very drunk

ˌ**pissed** ˈ**off** **adj** [after verb] UK offensive (US also **pissed**) annoyed: *He'd kept me waiting for an hour so I was pissed off to start with.* ◦ *She seemed a bit pissed off that she hadn't been invited.*

pisser /ˈpɪs.əʳ/ (US) /-ɚ/ **noun** [C] offensive **1** US something that is of very bad quality: *There was some pisser of a movie about a boy and his dog on TV last night.* **2** US something extremely good or humorous: *It was a pisser of a party!* **3** something that is very annoying or not convenient: *'I've got to work late tonight.' 'What a pisser!'*

pisshead /ˈpɪs.hed/ **noun** [C] UK offensive a person who drinks a lot of alcohol very often

ˈ**piss-poor** **adj** offensive **1** having very little money: *We were piss-poor.* **2** of very low quality: *a piss-poor film*

pisspot /ˈpɪs.pɒt/ (US) /-pɑːt/ **noun** [C] Australian English slang a person who drinks a lot of alcohol very often: *Patrick's a real pisspot.*

ˈ**piss-take** **noun** [C] UK offensive **1** an act of making someone or something look silly: *He told me I'd won and I thought it was just a piss-take.* **2** an act of copying someone else's behaviour and manner in a humorous way: *He* ***did*** *a piss-take* ***of*** *Fiona.*

ˈ**piss-up** **noun** [C] UK offensive an occasion when a lot of alcohol is drunk

pistachio (nut) /pɪˈstæʃ.i.əʊˌnʌt/ (US) /-oʊ-/ **noun** [C] a nut with a hard shell which contains a green seed that can be eaten

piste /piːst/ **noun** [C] a snow-covered area or track that is suitable for SKIING

pistil /ˈpɪs.tɪl/ **noun** [C] specialized the female REPRODUCTIVE part of a flower, consisting of one CARPEL or a group of carpels joined together

pistol /ˈpɪs.təl/ **noun** [C] a small gun that is held in and FIRED from one hand: *a loaded pistol* ◦ *an automatic pistol*

ˈ**pistol-whip** **verb** [T] US to hit someone with a pistol many times

piston /ˈpɪs.tən/ **noun** [C] a short solid piece of metal which moves up and down inside a cylinder in an engine to press the fuel into a small space and to send the power produced by it to the wheels

pit /pɪt/ **noun; verb**

▸**noun** [C] **PLACE/AREA** ▷ **1** C2 a large hole in the ground, or a slightly low area in any surface: *They'd dug a shallow pit and left the bodies in it.* ◦ *These pits in my skin are from when I had chickenpox.* → See also **armpit, sandpit** **2** a COAL MINE or an area of land from which a natural substance is taken by digging: *The coal-mining industry wants new pits to be opened.* ◦ *a gravel/chalk pit* **3** slang a very untidy or dirty place: *I'm afraid my room is a complete pit!* **4 the pit** [S] in a theatre, the seats at the lowest level, or the ORCHESTRA PIT **5 the pits** [plural] **a** informal something that is of extremely low quality: *The hotel we stayed in was the pits!* **b** the area next to a motor race track where the cars are given fuel or repaired during a race **SEED** ▷ **6** US for **stone**

IDIOM **pit of your stomach** the part of the body in which people say they feel fear or nervousness: *I got a* *sick feeling/a knot in the pit of my stomach when the news of the attack was announced.*

▸verb [T] (-tt-) US for **stone**

IDIOM **pit your wits against sb/sth** to see if you can be cleverer than someone or something: *Would you like to pit your wits against our quiz champion?*

PHRASAL VERB **pit sb/sth against sb/sth** to cause one person, group or thing to fight against or be in competition with another: *It was a bitter civil war, that pitted neighbour against neighbour.* ◦ *The climbers pitted themselves against the mountain.*

ˌpit bull ˈterrier noun [C] (also **ˈpit bull**) a type of dog that is often considered to be AGGRESSIVE and is used for fighting other dogs as entertainment

pitch /pɪtʃ/ noun; verb

▸noun **SPORTS FIELD** ▷ **1** B2 [C] UK (US **field**) an area painted with lines for playing particular sports, especially football: *a football/hockey/cricket pitch* ◦ *Supporters **invaded** (= ran onto) the pitch.* **LEVEL** ▷ **2** [C or U] the level or degree of something: *The piano and organ were tuned to the same pitch (= note).* ◦ *If you teach children and adults in the same class, it's difficult to get the pitch (= level of difficulty or interest) right.* **3** [S] the level of a feeling: *By this time their disagreement had reached **such a** pitch that there was no hope of an amicable conclusion.* ◦ *The children were **at fever** pitch (= very excited) the day before the party.* **PERSUASION** ▷ **4** [C] a speech or act that attempts to persuade someone to buy or do something: *The man in the shop gave me his (**sales**) pitch about quality and reliability.* ◦ *She **made** a pitch **for** the job but she didn't get it.* ◦ [+ to infinitive] *The city **made** a pitch **to** stage the Olympics.* **5** [C] UK a place in a public area where a person regularly sells goods or performs: *The flower seller was at his usual pitch outside the station.* **SLOPE** ▷ **6** [S] the amount of slope, especially of a roof: *This roof has a very **steep/high/gentle/low** pitch.* **BLACK SUBSTANCE** ▷ **7** [U] a thick black substance which was used in the past to make wooden ships and buildings WATERPROOF **BASEBALL** ▷ **8** [C] a throw in a baseball game: *a good/bad pitch* **TENT** ▷ **9** [C] UK (US **site**) the piece of ground on which you can put up a tent: *We chose a large level grassy pitch for our caravan.*

▸verb **MOVE** ▷ **1** [I or T, usually + adv/prep] to move or be moved suddenly, especially by throwing: *She pitched the stone **into** the river.* ◦ *He pitched the ball too short and the batsman hit it for six.* ◦ *The ball pitched (= landed) short.* ◦ *The bike hit a rut and I was pitched (**forward**) **onto** the road.* ◦ *The ship pitched **up and down/from side to side** in the rough seas.* **BASEBALL** ▷ **2** [I or T] in baseball, to throw a ball towards the player with the BAT in order for them to try to hit it: *Who will be pitching first for the White Sox this evening?* **TENT** ▷ **3** B2 [T] to put up a tent and fix it into position: *We pitched camp/our tent in the shade.* **LEVEL** ▷ **4** [T] to express or set something at a particular level: *The tune was pitched (= the notes in it were) too high for me to reach the top notes.* ◦ *A teacher's got to pitch a lesson **at** the right level for the students.* **PERSUADE** ▷ **5** [I or T] mainly US to try to persuade someone to do something: *She pitched her idea **to** me over a business lunch.* ◦ *They are pitching **for** business at the moment.* **SLOPE** ▷ **6** [I usually + adv/prep] to slope

IDIOM **be pitched into sth** to suddenly experience a bad feeling: *He was pitched (**headlong**) into despair by what happened to him in his final year at college.*

PHRASAL VERBS **pitch in** informal to start to do something as part of a group, especially something helpful: *If we all pitch in together, it shouldn't take too long.* ◦ [+ to infinitive] *When I bought this house, all my friends pitched in to help fix it up.* ◦ *My brother pitched in **with** an offer of transport.* ◦ *After we had seen the video everyone started pitching in **with** comments on its faults.* • **pitch into sb/sth** informal to criticize or attack someone or something forcefully: *He pitched into me as soon as I arrived, asking where the work was.* • **pitch up** informal to arrive in a place: *Gerald finally pitched up two hours late.*

ˌpitch-ˈdark adj C2 extremely dark: *a moonless, pitch-black night* • **ˌpitch-ˈdarkness** noun [U] (also **pitch-blackness**) *Suddenly the lights went out, and the house was left **in** pitch-darkness.*

pitched /pɪtʃt/ adj **ROOF** ▷ sloping and not flat: *The garage has a pitched roof, not a flat one.*

-pitched /-pɪtʃt/ suffix at the stated level or degree: *a high-pitched voice/scream*

ˌpitched ˈbattle noun [C] a large fight, or a BATTLE in which both sides stay in the same place

pitcher /ˈpɪtʃ.əʳ/ US /-ɚ/ noun [C] **CONTAINER** ▷ **1** UK a large container with a wide, round base, straight sides, and a narrow opening at the top, used in the past for holding water or another liquid: *an earthenware pitcher* **2** US for **jug**: *a pitcher **of** beer/water/lemonade* **IN BASEBALL** ▷ **3** a player who pitches the ball in a baseball game

pitchfork /ˈpɪtʃ.fɔːk/ US /-fɔːrk/ noun; verb

pitchfork

▸noun [C] a tool with a long handle and two or three large curved metal points used for moving HAY (= dried grass) or STRAW

▸verb

PHRASAL VERB **pitchfork sb into sth** to cause someone suddenly to be in a particular situation, usually a difficult one, especially when they are not ready: *Her father died when she was 22, and she was pitchforked into the running of the estate.*

piteous /ˈpɪt.i.əs/ US /ˈpɪt̬-/ adj causing you to feel sadness and sympathy: *The kitten gave a piteous cry.* • **piteously** /-li/ adv *She wept piteously.* • **piteousness** /-nəs/ noun [U]

pitfall /ˈpɪt.fɔːl/ US /-fɑːl/ noun [C usually plural] a likely mistake or problem in a situation: *The store **fell into** one of the major pitfalls of small business, borrowing from suppliers by paying bills late.* ◦ *There's a video that tells new students about pitfalls to **avoid**.*

pith /pɪθ/ noun [U] the white substance between the skin and the flesh of CITRUS fruits such as oranges, or the soft, white inside part of the stem of some plants

pithead /ˈpɪt.hed/ noun [C usually singular] mainly UK the area and buildings at the entrance to a MINE → See also **pit**

ˈpith ˌhelmet noun [C] (also **topee**) a large, hard, white hat worn to give protection from the sun. It was worn in the past by Europeans who were in hot countries.

pithy /ˈpɪθ.i/ adj **SHORT** ▷ **1** (of speech or writing) expressing an idea cleverly in a few words: *a pithy remark* **FRUIT** ▷ **2** with a lot of pith: *a pithy orange* • **pithily** /-ɪ.li/ adv

pitiable /ˈpɪt.i.ə.bl/ US /ˈpɪt̬-/ adj formal **pitiful** • **pitiably** /-bli/ adv formal **pitiful**

pitiful /ˈpɪt.i.fəl/ US /ˈpɪţ-/ adj **1** making people feel sympathy: *The refugees arriving at the camp had pitiful stories to tell.* **2** C2 describes something that you consider is bad or not satisfactory or not enough: *a pitiful state of affairs* ◦ *The amount of time and money being spent on researching this disease is pitiful.* • **pitifully** /-i/ adv • **pitifulness** /-nəs/ noun [U]

pitiless /ˈpɪt.i.ləs/ US /ˈpɪţ-/ adj **1** cruel and having no PITY: *the dictator's pitiless rule* ◦ *a pitiless critic* **2** severe and unpleasant: *Few people were out in the pitiless midday sun.* • **pitilessly** /-li/ adv • **pitilessness** /-nəs/ noun [U]

ˈpit ˌpony noun [C] a small horse used in the past to pull LOADS down MINES

ˈpit ˌstop noun [C] **1** an occasion when a driver in a motor race stops in the PITS (= area where cars are repaired): *to* ***make*** *a pit stop* **2** a short stop that you make during a long car journey in order to rest and eat: *We* ***made*** *a quick pit stop in York before continuing on our journey.*

pitta (US **pita**) /ˈpɪt.ə/ US /ˈpɪţ-/ noun [U or C] (also **ˈpitta ˌbread**, **ˈpita ˌbread**) flat, hollow bread in an oval shape

pittance /ˈpɪt.ənts/ US /ˈpɪţ-/ noun [C usually singular] disapproving a very small amount of money, especially money received as payment, income, or a present: *He works hard but he's* ***paid*** *a pittance.*

pitted /ˈpɪt.ɪd/ US /ˈpɪţ-/ adj **HOLES** ▷ **1** covered with holes or low areas: *He'd had bad acne as a youth and his face was pitted (= marked)* ***with*** *pockmarks.* **SEED** ▷ **2** US for STONED (= with the stone removed)

pitter-patter /ˈpɪt.əˌpæt.ər/ US /ˈpɪţ.əˌpæţ.ə/ noun [S] a quick, light knocking sound: *I heard* ***the*** *pitter-patter* ***of tiny feet*** *(= the noise of children running).* • **pitter-patter** verb [I + adv/prep] *The rain pitter-pattered on the roof.* • **pitter-patter** adv

pituitary (gland) /pɪˈtjuː.ɪ.tər.iˌglænd/ US /-ˈtuː.ə.ter-/ noun [C usually singular] specialized a small organ at the base of the brain which controls the growth and activity of the body by producing HORMONES

pity /ˈpɪt.i/ US /ˈpɪţ-/ noun; verb

▸noun **1** B2 [U] a feeling of sympathy and understanding for someone else's unhappiness or difficult situation: *The girl stood gazing* ***in/with*** *pity at the old lion in the cage.* ◦ *We* ***took*** *pity* ***on*** *(= felt sorry for and therefore helped) a couple of people waiting in the rain for a bus and gave them a lift.* → See also **self-pity** **2** A2 [S] If something is described as a pity, it is disappointing or not satisfactory: *'Can't you go to the party? Oh, that's (***such***)* ***a*** *pity.'* ◦ [+ (that)] *Pity (****that****) you didn't remember to give me the message.* ◦ [+ that] ***The*** *pity was* ***that*** *so few people bothered to come.* ◦ *We'll have to leave early,* ***more's the*** *pity (= and I am unhappy about it).* ◦ ***What a*** *pity you're ill!*

▸verb [T] C2 to feel sympathy for someone: *Pity (= feel sorry for) those on the street with no home to go to.*

pivot /ˈpɪv.ət/ noun [C] **1** a fixed point supporting something which turns or balances **2** the central or most important person or thing in a situation: *The former guerrilla leader has become the pivot on which the country's emerging political stability* ***turns/revolves*** *(= it depends on him).*

pivotal /ˈpɪv.ə.təl/ US /-ţəl/ adj central and important: *a pivotal figure/role/idea*

pixel /ˈpɪk.səl/ noun [C] specialized the smallest unit of an image on a television or computer screen

pixelated (also **pixellated**) /ˈpɪk.səl.eɪ.tɪd/ US /-ţɪd/ adj A pixelated image is made up of pixels.

pixie (also **pixy**) /ˈpɪk.si/ noun [C] (especially in children's stories) a small imaginary person

pizza /ˈpiːt.sə/ noun [C or U] (US old-fashioned also **ˌpizza ˈpie**) A1 a large circle of flat bread baked with cheese, tomatoes, and sometimes meat and vegetables spread on top: *a slice of pizza* ◦ *I like a lot of different pizza* ***toppings.*** ◦ *a* ***deep-pan*** *(US* ***deep-dish****) pizza*

ˈpizza ˌparlour UK (US **ˈpizza ˌparlor**) noun [C] a **pizzeria**

pizzazz /pɪˈzæz/ noun [U] informal approving the quality of noticeable and energetic excitement: *Their performance was full of pizzazz.*

pizzeria /ˌpiːt.səˈriː.ə/ noun [C] a restaurant that sells PIZZA

pizzicato /ˌpɪt.sɪˈkɑː.təʊ/ US /-ţoʊ/ adj, adv specialized played by PLUCKING the strings of a musical instrument such as a VIOLIN or CELLO with the fingers instead of using a BOW

pl. written abbreviation for **plural**

placard /ˈplæk.ɑːd/ US /-ɑːrd/ noun [C] a large piece of card, paper, etc. with a message written or printed on it, often carried in public places by people who are complaining about something: *Demonstrators marched past* ***holding/waving*** *placards that said, 'Send food, not missiles'.*

placate /pləˈkeɪt/ US /ˈpleɪ.keɪt/ verb [T] to stop someone from feeling angry: *Outraged minority groups will not be placated by promises of future improvements.*

placatory /pləˈkeɪ.tər.i/ US /ˈpleɪ.kə.tɔːr-/ adj formal trying to avoid making someone angry: *The tone of the letter was placatory.*

place /pleɪs/ noun; verb

▸noun **AREA** ▷ **1** A1 [C] an area, town, building, etc.: *Her garden was a cool pleasant place to sit.* ◦ *What was the name of that place we drove through on the way to New York?* ◦ *They decided to go to a pizza place.* ◦ *There are several places* ***of interest*** *to visit in the area.* ◦ *It's important to feel comfortable in your place* ***of work.*** **2** A2 [C] informal someone's home: *I'm looking for a place to live.* ◦ *We'll have the meeting at my place.* **3** [S] a suitable area, building, situation, or occasion: *University is a great place* ***for*** *making new friends.* ◦ [+ to infinitive] *This meeting* ***isn't*** *the place* ***to*** *discuss your problems, I'm afraid.*

> **! Common mistake: place or room?**
>
> **Warning:** choose the correct noun!
>
> To talk about the amount of space that someone or something needs, don't say 'place', say **room**:
>
> ~~*There is not enough place in the office for everyone.*~~
>
> *There is not enough room in the office for everyone.*

POSITION ▷ **4** [C] a position in relation to other things or people: *His leg was broken in two places.* ◦ *When you've finished, put the book back* ***in*** *its place on the shelf.* ◦ *This plant needs a warm, sunny place.* ◦ *Will you* ***keep*** *my place (****in*** *the queue) (= allow me to come back to the same position)?* ◦ *She spoke to me and I* ***lost*** *my place in the book (= I forgot where I had been reading).* → See also **decimal place** **5** B1 [C] the seat you will sit in on a particular occasion, or the seat where you usually sit, in the theatre, a class, a train, etc.: *My ticket says 6G but there's someone sitting in my place.* ◦ *The children collected their prizes and then went back to their places.* ◦ ***Save*** *me a place (= keep a seat for me until I arrive) near the front.* **6** [C] the space at a table where one person will sit and eat, usually with a plate

P

and knives, forks, and spoons arranged on it: *The waiter showed us to our places and gave us each a menu.* ◦ *He* ***laid*** *six places at the table.* **7** B1 [C] a position in an organization, a system, or a competition: *She's got a place* ***at*** *university* ◦ *She's got a place* ***on*** (US ***in***) *a fine-arts course.* ◦ *Our team finished* ***in*** *second place.* ◦ *He* ***took*** *third place* (UK also ***got a***) *third place* (= *was the third to finish*) *in the marathon last year.* **8** [C] US used after words such as 'any' and 'some' as a different way of saying 'anywhere', 'somewhere', etc.: *I know I left that book some place – now, where was it?* ◦ *That bar was like no place I'd ever been before.* **9 take place** B1 to happen: *The concert takes place next Thursday.* **10 out of place** C2 in the wrong place or looking wrong: *The boy looked uncomfortable and out of place among the adults.* **11 in place a** C2 If something is in place, it is in its usual or correct position: *The chairs are all in place.* ◦ *He screwed the shelf in place.* **b** C2 organized: *The arrangements are all in place for the concert next Thursday.* **12 in place of sb/sth** B2 instead of someone or something: *You can use margarine in place of butter in some recipes.* **13 take the place of sb/sth** B2 to be used instead of someone or something **DUTY** ▷ **14** [U] what a person should do or is allowed to do, especially according to the rules of society: [+ to infinitive] *It's not your place* ***to*** *tell me what to do.* ◦ *I'm not going to criticize his lordship – I* ***know*** *my place* (= *I know that I am of lower social rank*).

IDIOMS **all over the place 1** B2 put or left in a lot of different places in an untidy way: *There were dirty dishes and clothes all over the place.* **2** in every place: *You can buy T-shirts like this all over the place.* **3** informal not correct or suitable: *His drumming was all over the place.* • **go places** informal to be likely to be successful in the future: *They said that the group was clearly going places.* • **in the first/second place** B2 used to separate and emphasize reasons or opinions: *I don't want to go yet – in the first place I'm not ready, and in the second place it's raining.* • **a place in the sun** a good or lucky position: *He certainly earned his place in the sun.* • **put sb in their place** C2 to tell or show someone that they are less important than they thought they were: *When he tried to take charge, she soon put him in his place.* • **take first/second place** to be the most important thing/a less important thing: *Work takes second place.*

▸verb **POSITION** ▷ **1** B2 [I or T] to put something in a particular position: *She placed the letter in front of me.* ◦ *She placed her name on the list of volunteers.* ◦ *I'd place him among the ten most brilliant scientists of his age.* ◦ [+ obj + adj] *The horse was placed first/second/third in its first race* (= *finished the race in first/second/third position*). **2 place an advertisement, bet, order, etc.** C1 to arrange to have an advertisement, BET, order, etc.: *We placed the order for the furniture six weeks ago.* ◦ *They were placing bets* (= *gambling*) *on who would win.* **3 place emphasis, importance, etc. on sth** C2 to give something emphasis, importance, etc.: *She placed the emphasis on the word 'soon'.* ◦ *He placed importance on a comfortable lifestyle* (= *it was important to him*). **4** [T] to find someone a job: *The students are placed* ***in/with*** *companies for a period of work experience.* **RECOGNIZE** ▷ **5** [T] to recognize someone or remember where you have seen them or how you know them: *She looks familiar but I can't place her – did she use to work here?*

IDIOM **how are you placed for...?** UK informal used to ask someone if they have enough money, time, etc.: *How are you placed for money?* ◦ *How are you placed for Tuesday night?* (= *Are you busy then?*)

placebo /plə'siː.bəʊ/ US /-boʊ/ **noun** [C] (plural **placebos**) **1** a substance given to someone who is told that it is a particular medicine, either to make them feel as if they are getting better or to compare the effect of the particular medicine when given to others: *She was only given a placebo, but she claimed she got better – that's the placebo* ***effect.*** **2** something that is given to try to satisfy a person who has not been given the thing they really want: *These small concessions have been made as a placebo to stop the workers making further demands.*

'place ˌcard noun [C] a card with someone's name on it, put at the place at a table where they will sit, especially at a formal meal

placeholder /'pleɪs.həʊl.dəʳ/ US /-hoʊl.dɚ/ **noun** [C] specialized a symbol or piece of text in a mathematical expression or computer instruction that can be replaced by particular pieces of information

'place ˌmat noun [C] a decorative piece of card, cloth, wood, plastic, etc. on which someone's plate is put on a table

placement /'pleɪs.mənt/ **noun** **JOB** ▷ **1** [C or U] a temporary position or job in an organization: *I think we can* ***find*** *a placement for you in the accounts department.* ◦ *The trainee teachers* ***do*** *a school placement in the summer term.* **PLACE** ▷ **2** [U] the act of finding the right place for something: *The director gives instructions for the placement* ***of*** *the camera.*

'place ˌname noun [C] the official name of a town or an area: *York and Toledo are place names.*

placenta /plə'sen.tə/ US /-t̬ə/ **noun** [C] (plural **placentas** or **placentae** /-tiː/) specialized the temporary organ which feeds a FOETUS (= developing baby) inside its mother's WOMB

ˌplace of 'worship noun [C] a building for religious services, such as a church, TEMPLE, etc.

'place ˌsetting noun [C] the glasses, plates, knives and forks, etc. that one person needs for eating a meal, arranged on a table

placid /'plæs.ɪd/ **adj** having a calm appearance or characteristics: *a slow-moving and placid river* ◦ *the placid pace of village life* ◦ *She was a very placid* (= *calm and not easily excited*) *child who slept all night and hardly ever cried.* • **placidly** /-li/ **adv** • **placidness** /-nəs/ **noun** [U] (also **placidity**)

plagiarize (UK usually **plagiarise**) /'pleɪ.dʒəʳr.aɪz/ US /-dʒə.raɪz/ **verb** [I or T] to use another person's idea or a part of their work and pretend that it is your own: *The book contains numerous plagiarized passages.* ◦ *If you compare the two books side by side, it is clear that the author of the second has plagiarized* (***from*** *the first*). • **plagiarism** /-dʒəʳr.ɪ.zəm/ US /-dʒɚ.ɪ.zəm/ **noun** [U] • **plagiarist** /-dʒəʳr.ɪst/ US /-dʒɚ.ɪst/ **noun** [C]

plague /pleɪɡ/ **verb; noun**

▸verb [T] **1** C2 to cause worry, pain, or difficulty to someone or something over a period of time: *Financial problems have been plaguing their new business partners.* ◦ *My shoulder's been plaguing me all week.* **2** to annoy someone, especially by asking repeated questions: *The children plagued him* ***with*** *questions all through lunch.*

▸noun [C or U] **1** C2 **bubonic plague**, or any serious disease that kills many people **2 a plague of sth** a large number of things that are unpleasant or likely to cause damage: *a plague of insects* ◦ humorous *A plague of journalists descended on the town.*

plaice /pleɪs/ **noun** [C or U] (plural **plaice**) a sea fish with a flat, circular body, or its flesh eaten as food

plaid /plæd/ noun [U] mainly US for **tartan**

plain /pleɪn/ adj; noun; adv

▸adj **WITH NOTHING ADDED** ▷ **1** B1 not decorated in any way; with nothing added: *She wore a plain black dress.* ◦ *We've chosen a plain carpet (= one without a pattern) and patterned curtains.* ◦ *He prefers plain food – nothing too fancy.* ◦ *We're having plain blue walls in the dining room.* ◦ *a catalogue sent in a plain brown envelope* ◦ *a plain style of architecture* ◦ *plain yogurt (= with no added fruit or sugar)* **2 plain paper** paper that has no lines on it: *a letter written on plain paper* **CLEAR** ▷ **3** C2 obvious and clear to understand: *It's quite plain **that** they don't want to speak to us.* ◦ *The reason is perfectly plain.* ◦ *I **made it** quite plain (**that**) (= explained clearly that) I wasn't interested.* **COMPLETE** ▷ **4** [before noun] (used for emphasis) complete: *It was plain stupidity on Richard's part.* **NOT BEAUTIFUL** ▷ **5** C2 (especially of a woman or girl) not beautiful: *She had been a very plain child.* **6 a plain Jane** a woman or girl who is not attractive: *If she'd been a plain Jane, she wouldn't have had all the attention.* • **plainness** /-nəs/ noun [U]

IDIOMS **be (as) plain as the nose on your face** (also **be (as) plain as a pikestaff**) to be very obvious: *He's not happy here – that's as plain as the nose on your face.* • **be plain sailing** UK (US also **be smooth sailing**) to be easy and without problems: *The roads were busy as we drove out of town, but after that it was plain sailing.*

▸noun **LAND** ▷ **1** [C] (also **plains** [plural]) a large area of flat land: *the coastal plain* ◦ *High mountains rise above the plain.* **STITCH** ▷ **2** [U] a type of simple STITCH in KNITTING: *a row of plain and two rows of purl*

▸adv informal completely: *I mean, taking the wrong equipment with you – that's just plain **stupid**.*

ˌplain ˈchocolate noun [C or U] **1** UK for **dark chocolate** → Compare **milk chocolate** **2** Australian English **milk chocolate**

ˌplain ˈclothes noun [plural] ordinary clothes when worn by police when they are working: *There were police **in** plain clothes in the crowd.* • **ˌplain-ˈclothes** adj [before noun] *plain-clothes police officers/detectives*

ˌplain ˈEnglish noun [U] clear, simple language: *Why can't they write these instructions in plain English?*

ˌplain ˈflour noun [C or U] UK (US **ˌall-purpose ˈflour**) flour that contains no chemical to make cakes RISE (= become large when cooked) → Compare **self-raising flour**

plainly /ˈpleɪn.li/ adv **CLEARLY** ▷ **1** clearly or obviously: *This is plainly wrong.* ◦ *Every footstep could be plainly heard.* ◦ *The men had plainly lied.* ◦ *Plainly, a great deal of extra time will be needed for the security checks.* **WITH NOTHING ADDED** ▷ **2** simply and without a lot of decoration: *a plainly furnished room*

plainsong /ˈpleɪn.sɒŋ/ US /-sɑːŋ/ noun [U] (also **plainchant** /-tʃɑːnt/ US /-tʃænt/) a type of simple group singing without instruments, used in the Christian Church → Compare **Gregorian chant**

ˌplain ˈspeaking noun [U] the act of saying clearly and honestly what you think without trying to be polite: *It's time for some plain speaking.* • **ˌplain-ˈspoken** adj *He's very plain-spoken.*

plaintiff /ˈpleɪn.tɪf/ US /-t̬ɪf/ noun [C] legal someone who makes a legal complaint against someone else in court → Compare **defendant**

plaintive /ˈpleɪn.tɪv/ US /-t̬ɪv/ adj describes something which sounds slightly sad: *the plaintive sound of the bagpipes* ◦ *'What about me?' came a plaintive voice.* • **plaintively** /-li/ adv *'I've broken my glasses,' he said plaintively.* • **plaintiveness** /-nəs/ noun [U]

plait /plæt/ verb; noun

▸verb [I or T] (US usually **braid**) to join three or more pieces of hair or string-like material by putting them over each other in a special pattern: *She plaited the horse's tail.* ◦ *a plaited leather bracelet/belt*

▸noun [C] (US usually **braid**) a length of hair or other material that is divided into three parts that are then crossed over each other in a special pattern: *She usually wears her hair **in a** plait/**in** two plaits.*

plan /plæn/ noun; verb

▸noun **DECISION** ▷ **1** A2 [C] a set of decisions about how to do something in the future: *a company's business plan* ◦ *a negotiated peace plan* ◦ *a five-year plan* ◦ *holiday plans* ◦ *What are your plans **for** this weekend?* ◦ [+ to infinitive] *My plan is **to** hire a car when I arrive in America and travel about.* **2** [C] a type of arrangement for financial INVESTMENT: *a pension/savings plan* **3 go according to plan** to happen in the way you intend: *Events of this type rarely go according to plan.* **DRAWING** ▷ **4** B2 [C] a drawing of a building, town, area, vehicle, machine, etc. which only shows its shape from above, its size, and the position of important details: *a street plan (= a type of map of a town showing the roads)* ◦ *a seating plan (= a drawing which shows where each person will sit)* **5 plans** [plural] B2 drawings from which something is made or built: *The architect showed us the house plans that she had **drawn up**.* ◦ *I'll send a set of plans **for** the new machine.*

> **Word partners for plan noun**
>
> *have/make* a plan • *announce/outline/unveil* a plan • *approve/back/oppose/reject* a plan • *go ahead/press ahead* with a plan • *abandon/drop/shelve* a plan • an *ambitious/controversial/detailed/strategic* plan • a plan *of action* • a plan *for* sth

▸verb (-nn-) **DECIDE** ▷ **1** B1 [I + adv/prep, T] to think about and decide what you are going to do or how you are going to do something: *She helped them to plan their route.* ◦ *If we plan carefully, we should be able to stay within our budget.* ◦ [+ question word] *She's already planning **how** to spend her prize money.* **2** A2 [I or T] to intend to do something or that an event or result should happen: *Our meeting wasn't planned – it was completely accidental.* ◦ [+ to infinitive] *I'm not planning **to** stay here much longer.* ◦ [+ adv/prep] *We only planned **for** six guests, but then someone brought a friend.* **DESIGN** ▷ **3** [T] to design a building or structure: *The people who planned Britain's new towns had a vision of clean modern housing for everyone.*

> **! Common mistake: plan**
>
> **Warning:** Check your verb endings!
>
> Many learners make mistakes when using **plan** in the past tense. The past simple and past participle are plan**ned**. The **-ing** form is plan**ning**.

PHRASAL VERBS **plan on doing sth** to intend to do something: *We were planning on just having a snack and catching the early train.* • **plan on sb/sth doing sth** to realize that someone might do something or that something might happen and to make arrangements to deal with the situation: *They hadn't planned on the whole family coming.* • **plan sth out** to think about and decide what you are going to do or how you are going to do something: *I've planned out the day – train to town, some shopping, then a slap-up meal and a show.*

P

plane /pleɪn/ noun; verb; adj
▸**noun** [C] **AIRCRAFT** ▷ **1** A1 (UK also **aeroplane**, US also **airplane**) a vehicle designed for air travel, with wings and one or more engines: *a fighter/transport/passenger plane* ◦ *We'll be* ***boarding*** *the plane in about 20 minutes.* ◦ *He hates travelling* ***by*** *plane.* ◦ *a plane ticket* **SURFACE** ▷ **2** specialized in mathematics, a flat or level surface that continues in all directions: *an inclined plane* **LEVEL** ▷ **3** a particular level or standard: *The poet's treatment of the subject lifts it to a mystical plane.* ◦ *His work is* ***on*** *a completely different plane from (= is much better than) other writers.* **TOOL** ▷ **4** a tool used to make wooden surfaces and edges flat and smooth by removing small strips of the wood **TREE** ▷ **5** (also **plane tree**) a large tree with wide leaves and spreading branches that grows especially in towns
▸**verb** [T] to remove small strips of wood from a surface with a special tool: *You'll have to plane some more off the bottom of the door – it's still sticking.*
▸**adj** [before noun] specialized flat: *a plane edge/surface*

planet /ˈplæn.ɪt/ noun [C] B1 an extremely large, round mass of rock and metal, such as Earth, or of gas, such as Jupiter, that moves in a circular path around the sun or another star: *the planet Earth/Venus* ◦ *Might there be intelligent life on other planets?*

IDIOM **be on another planet** informal to not give attention to what is happening around you and to think differently from other people: *Some days that girl seems as if she's on another planet.*

planetarium /ˌplæn.ɪˈteə.ri.əm/ US /-ˈter.i-/ noun [C] (plural **planetariums** or **planetaria** /-ə/) a building in which moving images of the sky at night are shown using a special machine

planetary /ˈplæn.ɪ.tᵊr.i/ US /-ɪ.ter-/ adj relating to planets: *planetary science/motion* → See also **interplanetary**

plank /plæŋk/ noun [C] **FLAT PIECE** ▷ **1** a long, narrow, flat piece of wood or similar material, of the type used for making floors: *oak/concrete planks* ◦ *a plank of wood* ◦ *We used a plank to cross the ditch.* **PRINCIPLE** ▷ **2** literary an important principle on which the activities of a group, especially a political group, are based: *Educational reform was one of the main planks* ***of*** *their election campaign.*

planking /ˈplæŋ.kɪŋ/ noun [U] an area of planks used to form a surface: *rotten planking*

plankton /ˈplæŋk.tən/ noun [U] very small plants and animals that float on the surface of the sea and on which other sea creatures feed

planner /ˈplæn.əʳ/ US /-ɚ/ noun [C] **DECISIONS** ▷ **1** a person who makes decisions about how something will be done in the future: *a systems planner* **DESIGNS** ▷ **2** a person whose job is to decide how land in a particular area is to be used, what is to be built on it, etc. and who designs plans for it: *a town/urban/environmental/local planner* **DOCUMENT** ▷ **3** a document or software program that helps you plan something: *a wall planner*

planning /ˈplæn.ɪŋ/ noun [U] **DECIDING** ▷ **1** B2 the act of deciding how to do something: *Events like these take months of careful planning.* **DESIGNING** ▷ **2** C1 the process of deciding how land in a particular area will be used and designing plans for it: *town/environmental/urban planning* ◦ *the planning department of the local council*

ˈplanning perˌmission noun [U] UK (US **ˈbuilding ˌpermit**) an official agreement that something new can be built or an existing building can be changed

plant /plɑːnt/ US /plænt/ noun; verb
▸**noun** **LIVING THING** ▷ **1** A1 [C] a living thing that grows in earth, in water, or on other plants, usually has a stem, leaves, roots, and flowers, and produces seeds: *native plants and animals* ◦ *garden/greenhouse/indoor plants* ◦ *a tomato plant* → See also **houseplant** **BUILDING/MACHINES** ▷ **2** [U] machines used in industry: *The industry was accused of having invested little in plant or infrastructure.* **3** [C] a factory in which such machines are used: *Two more car-assembly plants were closed by the strike.* **4** [U] UK a large, heavy machine or vehicle used in industry, for building roads, etc.: *The sign by the roadworks said 'Slow – heavy plant crossing'.* ◦ *The firm's main business was plant* ***hire***. **PUT SECRETLY** ▷ **5** [C usually singular] something illegal or stolen that has been put secretly in a person's clothing or among the things that belong to them to make them seem guilty of a crime: *He insisted the money was a plant.*
▸**verb** **LIVING THING** ▷ **1** B1 [T] to put a plant into the ground or into a container of earth so that it will grow: *We planted trees and bushes* ***in*** *our new garden.* ◦ *Hyacinth bulbs planted in pots now will flower early in the spring.* **2** [T] If you plant a particular area, you put plants into the ground there: *The plot was surrounded by a stone wall and planted* ***with*** *flowering trees.* ◦ *a densely planted garden (= one in which the plants are close together)* **PUT** ▷ **3** [T + adv/prep] to put something firmly and strongly in a particular place: *My brother planted him****self*** *on the sofa in front of the television.* ◦ *He planted a kiss on her forehead/a blow on his opponent's jaw.* **4** C2 [T usually + adv/prep] to cause an idea or story to exist: *That incident planted* ***doubts*** *about him* ***in*** *my mind.* ◦ *Who planted these* ***rumours****?* **PUT SECRETLY** ▷ **5** B2 [T usually + adv/prep] informal to put something or someone in a position secretly, especially in order to deceive someone: *She insisted that the drugs had been planted* ***on*** *her without her knowledge.* ◦ *The bomb was planted in the station waiting room.* • **planting** /ˈplɑːn.tɪŋ/ US /ˈplæn.t̬ɪŋ/ noun [C or U] *Heavy rain delayed planting in parts of Indiana.*

PHRASAL VERB **plant sth out** to put a plant into the ground outside to continue growing: *Plant out the geraniums in early June.*

plantain /ˈplæn.tɪn/ noun [C or U] a tropical fruit similar to a BANANA with green skin, or the plant that produces this fruit

plantation /plænˈteɪ.ʃᵊn/, /plɑːn-/ US /plæn-/ noun [C] **1** a large farm, especially in a hot part of the world, on which a particular type of crop is grown: *a tea/cotton/rubber plantation* **2** an area where trees are grown for wood: *plantations of fast-growing conifers*

planter /ˈplɑːn.təʳ/ US /ˈplæn.t̬ɚ/ noun [C] **1** someone who grows a particular crop in a hot part of the world: *a tea/rubber planter* **2** a large container in which plants are grown for decoration **3** a machine used to plant crops: *a potato planter*

plaque /plɑːk/, /plæk/ US /plæk/ noun **FLAT OBJECT** ▷ **1** [C] a flat piece of metal, stone, wood, or plastic with writing on it that is fixed to a wall, door, or other object: *There was a* ***brass*** *plaque outside the surgery listing the various dentists' names.* ◦ *The First Lady* ***unveiled*** *a* ***commemorative*** *plaque.* → See also **plate** **2 blue plaque** UK a plaque on the wall of a house that shows that someone famous once lived there: *The blue plaque said 'Charles Darwin, biologist, lived here'.* **SUBSTANCE** ▷ **3** [U] a substance containing bacteria that forms on the surface of teeth

plasma /ˈplæz.mə/ noun [U] **BLOOD** ▷ **1** (also **blood plasma**) the pale yellow liquid that forms 55% of human blood and contains the blood cells **GAS** ▷ **2** a type of gas with almost no electrical CHARGE, found in the sun and other stars: *solar plasma* ◦ *plasma physics*

ˌplasma ˌscreen noun [C] a screen for showing very clear words or pictures which uses a type of gas pressed between two flat pieces of glass: *plasma screen TV*

plaster /ˈplɑː.stəʳ/ Ⓤⓢ /ˈplæs.tɚ/ **noun; verb**
▸noun **SUBSTANCE** ▷ **1** [U] a substance which becomes hard as it dries and is used especially for spreading on walls and ceilings in order to give a smooth surface: *The plaster on the walls was cracked and flaking.* → See also **plasterboard 2 in plaster** UK (US **in a cast**) If a part of your body is in plaster, it has a plaster cast around it to protect it while a broken bone repairs itself: *My leg was in plaster for about six weeks.* **STICKY MATERIAL** ▷ **3** [C or U] UK (UK also **sticking plaster**, US trademark **ˈBand-Aid**) a small piece of sticky material used to cover and protect a cut in the skin: *a box of waterproof plasters* ◦ ***Put*** *a plaster* ***on*** *it so that it doesn't get infected.*
▸verb **1** [T] to spread plaster on a surface **2** [T + adv/prep] to make something stick in a flat smooth layer: *The torrential rain had plastered her hair* ***to*** *her head.* **3** [T usually + adv/prep] informal to cover a surface or an object with something completely or thickly: *She had plastered her bedroom walls* ***with*** *photos of pop stars.* ◦ *The car was plastered* ***with*** *mud.* ◦ *The story was plastered* ***all over*** *(= printed so that it completely covered) the front page of the newspaper.* • **plastering** /ˈplɑː.stᵊr.ɪŋ/ Ⓤⓢ /ˈplæs.tɚ.ɪŋ/ **noun** [U] *There's only the plastering left to be done.*

plasterboard /ˈplɑː.stə.bɔːd/ Ⓤⓢ /ˈplæs.tɚ.bɔːrd/ **noun** [U] material consisting of two sheets of heavy paper with a layer of plaster between them, used to make walls and ceilings before putting on a top layer of plaster

ˌplaster ˈcast noun [C] **1** (also **cast**) a covering made of plaster of Paris that is put around part of someone's body, forming a hard case to protect them while a broken bone repairs itself **2** a copy of a STATUE or similar object, made of plaster of Paris

plastered /ˈplɑː.stəd/ Ⓤⓢ /ˈplæs.tɚd/ **adj** [after verb] informal extremely drunk: *They went out to the pub and* ***got*** *plastered.*

plasterer /ˈplɑː.stᵊr.əʳ/ Ⓤⓢ /ˈplæs.tɚ.ɚ/ **noun** [C] a person whose job is to cover walls and ceilings with plaster

plaster of Paris /ˌplɑː.stər.əvˈpær.ɪs/ Ⓤⓢ /ˌplæs.tɚ.əvˈper-/ **noun** [U] a mixture of a white powder and water which becomes hard quickly as it dries and is used especially to make plaster casts

plastic /ˈplæs.tɪk/ **noun; adj**
▸noun **SUBSTANCE** ▷ **1** Ⓐ2 [C or U] an artificial substance that can be shaped when soft into many different forms and has many different uses: *He put* ***a sheet of*** *plastic over the broken window.* ◦ *Those flowers aren't real – they're made of plastic.* **2 plastics** [U] the process or business of producing plastic: *The company has moved into plastics.* **MONEY** ▷ **3** [U] (also **plastic money**) CREDIT CARDS or DEBIT CARDS, rather than money in the form of notes, coins, or CHEQUES: *I'd prefer a restaurant where they take plastic.*
▸adj **SUBSTANCE** ▷ **1** Ⓐ2 made of plastic: *a plastic bag/box/cup* **FALSE** ▷ **2** disapproving artificial or false: *I hate the hostesses' false cheerfulness and plastic smiles.* **SOFT** ▷ **3** soft enough to be changed into a new shape: *Clay is a very plastic material.* ◦ *This metal is plastic at high temperatures.*

ˌplastic ˈbullet noun [C] a large bullet made of hard plastic that is intended to hurt but not kill people

ˌplastic exˈplosive noun [U] a soft explosive substance that is used to make bombs and can be easily formed into different shapes

Plasticine /ˈplæs.tə.siːn/, /ˈplɑː.stə-/ Ⓤⓢ /ˈplæs-/ **noun** [U] UK trademark a soft substance like clay produced in different colours, used especially by children to make shapes and models

plasticity /plæsˈtɪs.ɪ.ti/ Ⓤⓢ /plæsˈtɪs.ə.t̬i/ **noun** [U] the quality of being soft enough to be changed into a new shape

ˌplastic ˈsurgeon noun [C] a doctor who performs plastic surgery

ˌplastic ˈsurgery noun [U] a medical operation to bring a damaged area of skin, and sometimes bone, back to a usual appearance, or to improve a person's appearance: *Several of the crash victims had to have extensive plastic surgery.* ◦ *She had plastic surgery* ***on*** *her nose to straighten it.*

ˌplastic ˈwrap noun [U] US for **cling film**

plate /pleɪt/ **noun; verb**
▸noun **DISH** ▷ **1** Ⓐ1 [C] a flat, usually round dish with a slightly raised edge that you eat from or serve food from: *paper/plastic/china plates* ◦ *a dinner/salad plate* ◦ *clean/dirty plates* ◦ *There's still lots of food* ***on*** *your plate.* **2** [C] (also **plateful**) an amount of food on a plate: *Stephen ate three plates of spaghetti.* **FLAT PIECE** ▷ **3** [C] a flat piece of something that is hard and does not bend: *Thick* ***bony*** *plates protected the dinosaur against attack.* ◦ *The ship's deck is composed of* ***steel*** *plates.* → See also **licence plate, number plate 4** [C] specialized a flat piece of metal with words and/or pictures on it that can be printed **PICTURE** ▷ **5** [C] specialized a picture, especially in colour, in a book: *The three birds differ in small features (see Plate 4).* **IN BASEBALL** ▷ **6 the plate** [S] US informal for **home plate THIN LAYER** ▷ **7** [U] ordinary metal with a layer of another metal on top: *The knives and forks are* ***silver*** *plate.* **8** [U] objects, especially plates, dishes, and cups, completely made of a valuable metal such as gold or silver: *The thieves got away with a large quantity of church plate.*

IDIOMS **give/hand sth to sb on a plate** informal to allow someone to get or win something very easily: *They were handed the contract on a plate.* ◦ *Arsenal handed the game to them on a plate.* • **have sth on your plate** informal to have something, usually a large amount of important work, to deal with: *She's got* ***a lot*** *on her plate – especially with two new projects starting this week.* ◦ *The aid agencies have* ***(more than) enough*** *on their plate without having unnecessary visitors to look after.*

▸verb [T] to cover a metal object with a thin layer of another metal, especially gold or silver: *We normally plate the car handles* ***with*** *nickel and then chrome.* • **-plated** /-pleɪ.tɪd/ Ⓤⓢ /-t̬ɪd/ **suffix** ***Gold****-plated earrings are much cheaper than solid gold ones.* • **plating** /ˈpleɪ.tɪŋ/ Ⓤⓢ /-t̬ɪŋ/ **noun** [U] *gold/silver plating*

PHRASAL VERB **plate sth up** to put food onto plates, so that one plate of food can be served to each person in a group: *Will you collect the soup bowls while I plate up the main course?*

plateau /ˈplæt.əʊ/ Ⓤⓢ /plætˈoʊ/ **noun; verb**
▸noun [C] (plural UK **plateaux** /-z/ or US also **plateaus**) **FLAT LAND** ▷ **1** a large flat area of land that is high above sea level **NO CHANGE** ▷ **2** a period during which there are no large changes: *The US death rate* ***reached*** *a plateau in the 1960s, before declining suddenly.*
▸verb [I] to reach a particular level and then stay the

P

same: *The economic slowdown has caused our sales to plateau.*

plateful /ˈpleɪt.fʊl/ noun [C] all that there is on one plate: *I offered him a biscuit and he ate the* ***whole*** *plateful.*

ˌplate ˈglass noun [U] large sheets of glass used especially as windows and doors in shops and offices: *a plate-glass window*

platelet /ˈpleɪt.lət/ noun [C] specialized a very small cell in the blood that makes it thicker and more solid in order to stop BLEEDING caused by an injury

ˈplate ˌmeal noun [C] Indian English a meal that is served in a restaurant at a fixed price with little choice of dishes

plate tectonics /ˌpleɪt.tekˈtɒn.ɪks/ (US) /ˈtɑːn-/ noun [U] specialized the study of how the surface of the Earth is formed, how the separate pieces of it move, and the effects of this movement

platform /ˈplæt.fɔːm/ (US) /-fɔːrm/ noun **STRUCTURE** ▷ **1** B2 [C] a flat raised area or structure **2** A2 [C] a long, flat raised structure at a railway station, where people get on and off trains: *The train for Cambridge will depart from platform 9.* **3** [C] the raised part of the floor in a large room, from which you make a speech or give a musical performance: *Speaker after speaker* ***mounted/took the*** *platform to denounce the policy.* ◦ *This brilliant young violinist has appeared on* ***concert*** *platforms all round the world.* **4 the platform** UK **IDEAS** ▷ **5** C2 [C usually singular] an opportunity to make your ideas or beliefs known publicly: *By refusing to give us a grant to make this programme, they are denying us a platform.* **6** [S] all the things that a political party promises to do if they are elected: *We campaigned on a platform of low taxation.* **COMPUTING** ▷ **7** [C] the type of computer system you are using, in connection with the type of SOFTWARE (= computer programs) you can use on it: *This new personal banking software can be used with any Windows platform.*

IDIOM **share a platform** to give speeches or to perform at the same public event: *It was the first time a Green politician and a Labour minister had shared a platform.*

ˈplatform ˌshoes noun [plural] (also **platforms**) shoes with extremely thick SOLES which raise the feet from the ground more than usual

platinum /ˈplæt.ɪ.nəm/ (US) /ˈplæt.nəm/ noun [U] (symbol **Pt**) a chemical element that is an extremely valuable silver-coloured metal, used in jewellery and in industry: *a platinum wedding ring*

ˌplatinum ˈblonde adj describes hair that is so pale it is almost white • **ˌplatinum ˈblonde** noun [C] *She's a platinum blonde.*

ˌplatinum ˈdisc noun [C] a prize given to the performer(s) of a popular song, or a collection of popular songs, when a very large number of copies of the recording of it have been sold → Compare **gold disc**

platitude /ˈplæt.ɪ.tjuːd/ (US) /ˈplæţ.ə.tuːd/ noun [C] disapproving a remark or statement that may be true but is boring and has no meaning because it has been said so many times before: *He doesn't* ***mouth*** *platitudes about it not mattering who scores as long as the team wins.* • **platitudinous** /ˌplæt.ɪˈtjuː.dɪ.nəs/ (US) /ˌplæţ.əˈtuː.dən-/ adj formal disapproving

platonic /pləˈtɒn.ɪk/ (US) /-ˈtɑː.nɪk/ adj A platonic relationship or emotion is loving but not sexual: *She knew he fancied her, but preferred to keep their relationship platonic.*

platoon /pləˈtuːn/ noun [C, + sing/pl verb] a small group of about ten or twelve soldiers, with a LIEUTENANT in charge of it

platter /ˈplæt.əʳ/ (US) /ˈplæţ.ɚ/ noun [C] a large plate used for serving food or a meal with one type of food served on a large plate: *a fish platter*

IDIOM **give/hand sth to sb on a (silver) platter** to allow someone to get something very easily, without having to work for it: *If you sell your share in the company now, you're handing the ownership to him on a silver platter.*

platypus /ˈplæt.ɪ.pəs/ (US) /ˈplæţ-/ noun [C] (also **ˌduck-billed ˈplatypus**) an Australian river mammal with a wide beak whose young are born from eggs

plaudit /ˈplɔː.dɪt/ (US) /ˈplɑː-/ noun [C usually plural] formal praise: *She's received plaudits for her work with homeless people.* ◦ *The quality of his photography* ***earned/won*** *him plaudits from the experts.*

plausible /ˈplɔː.zə.bl̩/ (US) /ˈplɑː-/ adj **1** C2 seeming likely to be true, or able to be believed: *a plausible explanation/excuse* **2** disapproving describes someone who appears to be honest and telling the truth, even if they are not: *a plausible salesman* • **plausibility** /ˌplɔː.zəˈbɪl.ɪ.ti/ (US) /ˌplɑː.zəˈbɪl.ə.ţi/ noun [U] *In Chapter 2 she goes on to test the plausibility of these assumptions.* • **plausibly** /-bli/ adv *February's figures cannot plausibly be blamed on flukes or special factors.*

play /pleɪ/ verb; noun

▸verb **ENJOY** ▷ **1** A1 [I] When you play, especially as a child, you spend time doing an enjoyable and/or entertaining activity: *The children spent the afternoon playing in the garden.* ◦ *My daughter used to play* ***with*** *the kids next door.* **GAME** ▷ **2** A1 [I or T] to take part in a game or other organized activity: *Do you want to play cards/football (****with*** *us)?* ◦ *Irene won't be able to play* ***in*** *the match on Saturday.* ◦ *Which team do you play* ***for****?* ◦ *Luke plays centre-forward (= plays in that position within the team).* **3** B1 [T] to compete against a person or team in a game: *Who are Aston Villa playing next week?* **4** [T] to hit or kick a ball in a game: *He played the ball back* ***to*** *the goalkeeper.* ◦ *A good snooker player takes time deciding which shot to play.* **5** [T] to choose a card, in a card game, from the ones you are holding and put it down on the table: *She played the ace of spades.* **ACT** ▷ **6** B1 [I or T] to perform an entertainment or a particular character in a play, film, or other entertainment: *In the film version, Branagh played the hero.* ◦ *Scottish Opera played* ***to*** *full houses every night.* ◦ *I didn't realize that 'Macbeth' was playing (= being performed)* ***at*** *the Guildhall.* **7** [T] to behave or pretend in a particular way, especially in order to produce a particular effect or result: *to play dead/dumb* ◦ *Would you mind playing* ***host*** *(= entertaining the guests)?* **8 play a joke/trick** B2 to deceive someone to make them laugh or in order to get an advantage over them: *She loves playing practical jokes* ***on*** *her friends.* **9 play a part** B2 to help to achieve something: *My thanks to everyone who has played a part* ***in*** *saving the hospital.* **PRODUCE SOUNDS/PICTURES** ▷ **10** A2 [I or T] to perform music on an instrument or instruments: *He learned to play the clarinet at the age of ten.* ◦ [+ two objects] *Play us a song!/Play a song* ***for*** *us!* ◦ *On Radio London they play African and South American music as well as rock and pop.* ◦ *They could hear a jazz band playing in the distance.* ◦ *Play* ***up*** *a bit (= play louder) – I can hardly hear you!* **11** A2 [I or T] to (cause a machine to) produce sound or a picture: *Play the last few minutes of the video again.* → See also **playback** **MOVE** ▷ **12** [I or T] to direct or be directed over or onto something: *Firefighters played their* ***hoses onto*** *the base of the fire.* ◦ *A fountain was playing (= sending out water) in the courtyard outside.* **13** [I + adv/prep] (of something you see, such as light) to move quickly or be seen for a short time: *A smile played* ***across/over/on*** *his lips.* **RISK MONEY** ▷ **14** [T] to risk money, especially on the results of races or business DEALS, hoping to win more money: *He plays* ***the horses/the stock market****.*

IDIOMS **be playing at sth** UK If you ask what someone is playing at, you are angry because they are doing something stupid: *What on Earth/the hell were you playing at? – You could have got us all killed!* • **go play with yourself!** offensive a rude way of telling someone to go away and stop annoying you: *Oh, go play with yourself!* • **have sth to play with** informal If you have a particular amount of time or money to play with, that amount is available for you to use: *Having only £200 to play with, they bought a second-hand piano.* • **play sb at their own game** UK to try to get an advantage over someone by using the same methods as them: *If women want to succeed in business, they have to play men at their own game.* • **play your cards right** to behave in the right way so that you get an advantage or succeed in something: *If you play your cards right, you could make quite a lot of money out of this.* • **play (sth) by ear** ⓔ to play a piece of music by remembering the notes: *He did not need sheet music. He could play the piece by ear.* • **play it by ear** ⓔ to decide how to deal with a situation as it develops, rather than acting according to plans made earlier: *We can't make a decision yet. Let's just play it by ear.* • **play (merry) hell with sth** informal to seriously damage or confuse something: *The power cuts played hell with our computers.* • **play (it) safe** to be careful and not take risks: *To play safe, I'd allow an extra ten minutes, just in case.* • **play a joke/trick on sb** to confuse someone or cause problem for them: *I thought I heard something – my* ***ears*** *must have been playing tricks on me.* ◦ *Fate played a cruel trick on him when he was injured in his first game.* • **play ball** informal to agree to work with or help someone in the way they have suggested: *The family wanted him to be looked after at home, but the insurance company refused to play ball.* • **play both ends against the middle** to try to get opposing people or groups to fight or disagree so that you will get an advantage from the situation • **play fair** to act in a fair and honest way: *It wasn't really playing fair not to tell her the job was already filled.* • **play footsie** to touch someone's feet with your own under the table, usually in order to show sexual interest in them: *She kicked off her shoes and started playing footsie* ***with*** *him.* • **play for time** to delay until you are ready: *We can't sign the agreement yet – we'll have to play for time.* • **play games** ⓔ to try to deceive someone: *Don't play games* ***with*** *me!* • **play God** to act as if you are in total control of something: *Genetic engineers should not be allowed to play God, interfering with the basic patterns of Nature.* • **play hard to get** to pretend that you are less interested in someone than you really are as a way of making them more interested in you, especially at the start of a romantic relationship: *Why won't you call him back? Are you playing hard to get?* • **play hardball** mainly US informal to be firm and determined in order to get what you want: *He's a nice guy, but he can play hardball when he needs to.* • **play it cool** to behave in a calm, controlled way, often intentionally appearing not to be interested in the thing that you very much want to get: *Play it cool – don't let them know how much you need the money.* • **play second fiddle** to be less important or in a weaker position than someone else: *I'm not prepared to play second fiddle* ***to*** *Christina any more – I'm looking for another job!* • **play silly buggers** UK slang to behave in a silly, stupid, or annoying way: *There'll be a serious accident sooner or later if people don't stop playing silly buggers.* • **play the field** to hold an interest in a number of people or things, especially to become romantically or sexually involved with a number of partners: *Becky's not ready to settle down with one man – she enjoys playing the field too much.* • **play the game** to behave fairly: *You should have told them – it wasn't playing the game to keep it secret.* • **play to the gallery** to behave in a way intended to make people admire or support you: *Politicians these days are more interested in playing to the gallery than exercising real influence on world events.*

PHRASAL VERBS **play along** to do what someone asks you to do, for a limited period of time: *I know you don't like Jack's idea, but just play along* ***with*** *him for a while.* • **play around** **BE SILLY** ▷ **1** (UK also **play about**) to behave in a silly way: *Stop playing around and get on with your homework!* ◦ *I wish you wouldn't play about with that – you'll break it.* **SEX** ▷ **2** informal disapproving (UK also **play about**) If someone who is married or has a serious relationship plays around, they have sex with another person or people: *If she finds out he's been playing around* ***with*** *his secretary, there'll be trouble.* • **play around/about with sth** to try out different methods or different things, before deciding which one to choose: *We've been playing around with* ***ideas*** *for a new TV show.* ◦ *Why don't you play about with the different fonts on the computer and see which one you want to use?* • **play at sth 1** to pretend to be a particular person or to do a particular thing, usually as a game: *The children were playing at Batman and Robin.* **2** to do something for enjoyment or interest, or without much care and effort, not in a serious way or as a job: *She's only playing at being an actress – she's going off to law school next year.* • **play sth back** If you play back something that has been recorded, you put it through a machine so that you can listen to it or watch it: *The message I recorded for the answering machine sounded terrible when I played it back.* • **play sth down** to make something seem less important or less bad than it really is: *Military spokespeople tried to play down the seriousness of the disaster.* • **play off** to play a game, in a team sport, to decide which side will win: *United and Rangers are playing off for the championship.* • **play sb/sth off against sb/sth** to encourage one person or group to compete or argue with another, hoping to get some advantage from this situation: *Management policy seemed to be to play one department off against another.* • **play on/upon sth** If you play on/upon someone's feelings, you encourage and make unfair use of these feelings in order to get an advantage for yourself: *I hate marketing strategies that play on people's fears and prejudices.* • **play sth out** to pretend that an imaginary situation or event is really happening: *In the psychotherapy group, patients were free to play out their fantasies.* • **play itself out** If a situation plays itself out, it develops until nothing more can happen and it is no longer very important: *We were forced to stand back and let the crisis play itself out.* • **play out** mainly US When a situation plays out, it happens and develops: *The debate will play out in the media over the next week or two.* • **play sth up** to emphasize a particular quality or part of something, or make it seem more important than it really is, usually for your own advantage: *The official report plays up the*

P

likely benefits of the scheme, but glosses over the costs. • **play (sb) up** UK informal to cause someone pain: *His knee's been playing him up again.* ◦ *My stomach was playing up so I had to go home.* • **play up CHILD** ▷ **1** UK When children play up, they behave badly: *The boys have been playing up at school again.* **MACHINE** ▷ **2** If a machine plays up, it does not work as it should: *The starter motor was playing up again.* • **play up to sb** to try to make someone like you and treat you well by behaving in a way you think will please them: *Julia knows how to play up to the supervisors – she can always get time off work when she wants it.* • **play with sth IDEA** ▷ **1** to consider an idea or plan: *Patricia and I were playing* (***around***) *with the* ***idea/possibility*** *of moving to Glasgow.* **TOUCH** ▷ **2** disapproving to keep touching and moving something around with no purpose or interest: *Stop playing with your hair!* ◦ *She was just playing with her food – she didn't eat a mouthful.* • **play with yourself** offensive **masturbate**

▸**noun ACTING** ▷ **1** (A2) [C] a piece of writing that is intended to be acted in a theatre or on radio or television: *a radio play* ◦ *'Did you see the play (= the performance of the play) on Thursday?' 'No, I went on Wednesday night.'* **GAME** ▷ **2** [U] the activity of taking part in a sport or a game: *Rain stopped play during the final of the National Tennis Championship.* **3** [C] US a plan or a small set of actions in sport: *The new pitcher made a great play on that throw to first base.* **4 in/out of play** describes a ball that is/is not in a position where it can be hit, kicked,: *The ball had gone out of play.* ◦ *She managed to keep the ball in play.* **ENJOYMENT** ▷ **5** (B2) [U] activity that is not serious but done for enjoyment, especially when children enjoy themselves with toys and games: *The kids don't get much time for play in the evenings.* ◦ *We watched the children* ***at*** *play in the park.* **MOVEMENT** ▷ **6** [U] movement: *the play of moonlight* ***across*** *the water* ◦ *the play of emotion* ***across/on*** *his face* **7** [U] the fact that a rope or a structure is free to move, especially a small distance: *Aircraft wings are designed to have a certain amount of play in them.*

IDIOMS **come into play** (also **bring sth into play**) If something comes into play, it starts to have a use or an effect in a particular situation, and if it is brought into play, it is given a use or an effect: *In the summer months a different set of climatic factors come into play.* • **make a play for sth/sb** to try to get something, or start a relationship with someone, sometimes by using a plan: *I wouldn't have made a play for him if I'd known he was married.* • **play on words** a humorous use of a word with more than one meaning or that sounds like another word: *The name of the shop – 'Strata Various' – is a play on words, because it sounds like 'Stradivarius', the famous violin maker.*

playable /ˈpleɪ.ə.bl̩/ **adj** describes a piece of music that is not too difficult for someone to play

ˈplay-acting noun [U] an attempt to hide your feelings from other people, or to entertain people, by deliberately behaving in a way that does not represent your true feelings: *Don't take any notice of him – it's just play-acting.* • **ˈplay-act verb** [I]

playback /ˈpleɪ.bæk/ **noun** [C or U] the act of playing a recording again in order to hear or see something again: *Let's have a playback of those last few frames.* → See also **replay**

ˈplayback ˌsinger noun [C] (especially in connection with Indian films) a singer whose songs actors pretend to be singing when in fact they are just moving their lips

playbill /ˈpleɪ.bɪl/ **noun** [C] a piece of paper advertising a play and giving information about where and when it is being performed

playboy /ˈpleɪ.bɔɪ/ **noun** [C] a rich man who spends his time and money on expensive things and a life of pleasure

Play-Doh /ˈpleɪ.dəʊ/ (US) /-doʊ/ **noun** [U] trademark a soft substance produced in different colours, used especially by children to make shapes and models

ˌplayed ˈout adj informal tired and no longer having power or effectiveness: *I'm about played out, Jack – it's time I retired.* ◦ [before noun] figurative *They won't get people to vote for those played-out old policies.*

player /ˈpleɪ.əʳ/ (US) /-ɚ/ **noun** [C] **GAME** ▷ **1** (A1) someone who takes part in a game or sport: *Each player takes three cards.* ◦ *The team has many talented players.* **2** someone who is very involved in an activity or organization: *She was a* ***leading/key*** *player in the reorganization of the health service.* **ACTING** ▷ **3** old use an actor **4** used in the names of some theatre companies: *the Shakespeare Players* **SOUNDS/PICTURES** ▷ **5** (A2) a person who plays a musical instrument: *a recorder/piano player* **6** (A2) a machine for playing music, sound or pictures: *a CD/DVD player*

playful /ˈpleɪ.fəl/ **adj** funny and not serious: *a playful exchange of insults* ◦ *He was in a playful mood.* • **playfully** /-i/ **adv** • **playfulness** /-nəs/ **noun** [U]

playground /ˈpleɪ.graʊnd/ **noun 1** (A2) [C] an area designed for children to play in outside, especially at a school **2** [S] a place where a particular group of people enjoy themselves: *This area of the coast is the playground* ***of*** *the rich and famous.* **3** [C] US for **recreation ground**

playgroup /ˈpleɪ.gruːp/ **noun** [C] (also **playschool**) UK an organized group for children aged between three and five to play and learn together informally at regular times in a place outside their homes, run by parents or trained leaders

playhouse /ˈpleɪ.haʊs/ **noun** [C] **THEATRE** ▷ **1** a theatre. This is now only used in the names of theatres: *the La Jolla Playhouse in San Diego* ◦ *the Edinburgh Playhouse* **TOY HOUSE** ▷ **2** (UK also **Wendy house**) a small structure that looks like a house, for children to play in

ˈplaying ˌcard noun [C] one of a set of 52 small, rectangular pieces of stiff paper, each with a number and a design showing one of four suits printed on it, used in games

ˈplaying ˌfield noun [C] a large area of ground where sport is played: *The school playing fields were marked out for football and rugby.*

playlist /ˈpleɪ.lɪst/ **noun** [C] **1** a list of all the pieces of music chosen to be broadcast on a radio show or radio station **2** a list of pieces of music that someone has DOWNLOADED onto their computer, phone, etc.

playmate /ˈpleɪ.meɪt/ **noun** [C] a friend, especially another child, who a child often plays with: *We were childhood playmates.*

playoff /ˈpleɪ.ɒf/ (US) /-ɑːf/ **noun** [C usually singular] an extra game in a competition played between teams or competitors who have both got the same number of points, in order to decide who wins the competition

playpen /ˈpleɪ.pen/ **noun** [C] a small structure with bars or a net around the sides but open at the top, which you can put a baby in to play safely

playroom /ˈpleɪ.rʊm/, /-ruːm/ **noun** [C] a room intended for children to play in

playschool /ˈpleɪ.skuːl/ **noun** [C] UK a **playgroup**

PlayStation /ˈpleɪˌsteɪ.ʃən/ **noun** [C] trademark a

machine that you use to play games on your television

plaything /ˈpleɪ.θɪŋ/ **noun** [C] **1** an object used for pleasure or enjoyment, such as a child's toy: *I keep all the children's playthings in that big cupboard.* ◦ *'Limousines and yachts are the playthings of the rich,' he said dismissively.* **2** someone who is considered or treated without respect and forced to do things for someone else's pleasure or advantage: *These men's magazines just treat women as playthings.*

playtime /ˈpleɪ.taɪm/ **noun** [U] a period of time, especially during school hours, when children can play outside: *You'll have to stay in at playtime today, because it's raining.*

playwright /ˈpleɪ.raɪt/ **noun** [C] a person who writes plays

plaza /ˈplɑː.zə/ **noun** [C] **1** an open area or square in a town, especially in Spanish-speaking countries **2** a group of buildings including shops designed as a single development within a town

plc (also **PLC**) /ˌpiː.elˈsiː/ **noun** [C] abbreviation for public limited company: a British company whose SHARES can be bought and sold by the public and whose debts are limited if it fails financially: *J Sainsbury plc*

plea /pliː/ **noun** [C] **REQUEST** ▷ **1** C2 formal an urgent and emotional request: *He **made** a plea **for** help/mercy.* **STATEMENT** ▷ **2** legal the answer that a person gives in court when they have been accused of committing a crime: *Mr Wilson **entered** a plea **of** not guilty.*

ˈplea ˌbargaining noun [U] an agreement that someone accused of a crime will not be charged with a more serious crime if they admit that they are guilty of a less serious one

plead /pliːd/ **verb** (**pleaded** or US also **pled**, **pleaded** or US also **pled**) **REQUEST** ▷ **1** C2 [I] to make an urgent, emotional statement or request for something: *He was on his knees, pleading **for** mercy/forgiveness.* ◦ *She appeared on television to plead **with** the kidnappers.* ◦ [+ speech] *'Give us more time,' they pleaded.* **STATE** ▷ **2** C2 [I, L only + adj, T] formal to make a statement of what you believe to be true, especially in support of something or someone or when someone has been accused in a law court: legal *The defendant pleaded **not guilty/innocent** to robbery with violence.* ◦ legal *They paid a high-powered attorney to plead their **case** (= argue for them in court).* ◦ legal *The judge ruled her unfit to plead (= to answer a legal charge) on the grounds of insanity.* **EXCUSE** ▷ **3** C2 [T] to say something as an excuse or explanation: *She left early, pleading pressure of work.* **4 plead ignorance** formal to say that you do not know about something: *He pleaded ignorance when they found the package in his suitcase.* • **pleading** /ˈpliː.dɪŋ/ **adj** *a pleading tone of voice* • **pleadingly** /ˈpliː.dɪŋ.li/ **adv**

pleasant /ˈplez.ᵊnt/ **adj** A2 enjoyable, attractive, friendly, or easy to like: *a pleasant climate/smile/person* ◦ *a pleasant day/surprise* ◦ *Harold did his best to be pleasant **to** the old man.* ◦ ***It** was pleasant **to** sit down after standing for hours.* • **pleasantly** /-li/ **adv** B1 *They treated me pleasantly enough.* ◦ *Jacqui was pleasantly **surprised** to get a B for history.* • **pleasantness** /-nəs/ **noun** [U]

pleasantry /ˈplez.ᵊn.tri/ **noun** [C usually plural] formal a polite and often slightly humorous remark, usually made to help other people feel relaxed: *After **exchanging** pleasantries, the delegation revealed the purpose of their visit.*

please /pliːz/ **exclamation; verb**

▸**exclamation 1** A1 used to make a request more polite: *Could I have two cups of coffee and a tea, please?* ◦ *Please remember to close the windows before you leave.* **2** used to add force to a request or demand: *Please, David, put the knife down.* ◦ *Oh, please. Do shut up!* **3** UK used especially by children to a teacher or other adult in order to get their attention: *Please, Miss, I know the answer!* **4** A1 used when accepting something politely or enthusiastically: *'More potatoes?' 'Please.'* ◦ *'May I bring my husband?' 'Please do.'* ◦ mainly UK *'Oh, **yes** please,' shouted the children.*

▸**verb 1** B1 [I or T] to make someone feel happy or satisfied, or to give someone pleasure: *I only got married to please my parents.* ◦ *He was always a good boy, very friendly and eager to please.* ◦ [+ obj + to infinitive] ***It** always pleases me **to** see a well-designed book!* **2** C2 [I] to want, like, or choose, when used with words such as 'whatever', 'whoever' and 'anywhere': *She thinks she can just do **whatever/as** she pleases.* ◦ *I shall go out with whoever I please.* **3 if you please a** formal used to express surprise and anger: *They want £200, if you please, just to replace a couple of broken windows!* **b** old-fashioned or formal used to make a request more polite: *Take your seats, ladies and gentlemen, if you please.*

IDIOMS **please God** used to express a strong hope: *It'll be finished by Christmas, please God.* • **please yourself** informal to do whatever you choose to do, often used in a slightly rude way by someone who does not agree with or care about what you to do: *'I can't stand this place – I'm going home.' 'Please yourself.'*

pleased /pliːzd/ **adj 1** A2 happy or satisfied: *a pleased expression/smile* ◦ *Are you pleased **about** John's promotion?* ◦ *We're so pleased **that** you're able to come to the wedding.* ◦ *I'm really pleased **with** your work this term.* ◦ *I'm pleased **to** hear you're feeling better.* **2 be pleased to do sth** to be very willing to do something: *The personnel manager will be pleased to advise you.* ◦ *I'm **only too** (= very) pleased to help.*

IDIOMS **(as) pleased as Punch** old-fashioned very pleased: *She was as pleased as Punch about the news.* • **(I'm) pleased to meet you** A2 a polite way of greeting someone when you meet them for the first time • **pleased with yourself** happy and satisfied about something good that you have done or that has happened to you: *Simon's looking very pleased with himself today.*

pleasing /ˈpliː.zɪŋ/ **adj** formal giving a feeling of satisfaction or enjoyment: *a pleasing performance* ◦ *The music was very pleasing **to** the ear (= to listen to).* ◦ ***It** was pleasing **to** know that the presentation had gone so well.* • **pleasingly** /-li/ **adv** *pleasingly smooth/soft*

pleasurable /ˈpleʒ.ᵊr.ə.bl/ US /-ɚ.ə-/ **adj** C1 enjoyable: *a pleasurable evening/meal* ◦ *a pleasurable sensation*

> **Word partners for pleasure**
>
> *derive/get* pleasure **from** sth • *take* pleasure **in** (doing) sth • *afford/bring/give* pleasure • *have* the pleasure **of** sth • *enormous/great/real/sheer* pleasure • *genuine/pure* pleasure • *simple* pleasures • pleasure *at* sth • *for* pleasure

pleasure /ˈpleʒ.əʳ/ US /-ɚ/ **noun** [C or U] B1 enjoyment, happiness, or satisfaction, or something that gives this: *His visits **gave** his grandparents such pleasure.* ◦ *Why do so many boys **take** pleasure **in** torturing insects and small animals?* ◦ [+ to infinitive] ***It** was such a pleasure **to** meet you.* ◦ *He wrote an article*

P

on the pleasures and pains **of** camping. ◦ Smoking is one of my few pleasures.

IDIOMS **it's a pleasure** (also **it's my pleasure**) a polite way of replying to someone who has thanked you: *'It was so kind of you to give us a lift.' 'Don't mention it – it was a pleasure.'* • **with pleasure** formal **willing**: *'Would you mind holding the door open for me, please?' 'Oh, with pleasure.'*

pleat /pliːt/ **noun** [C] a narrow fold in a piece of cloth made by pressing or sewing two parts of the cloth together • **pleated** /ˈpliː.tɪd/ ⓤⓢ /-t̬ɪd/ **adj** *a pleated skirt*

pleb /pleb/ **noun** [C] informal disapproving a person of a low social class • **plebby** /ˈpleb.i/ **adj** *I can't bear her plebby friends.*

plebeian /pləˈbiː.ən/ **adj** formal disapproving belonging to a low social class: *He used to make fun of what he called her 'plebeian origins'.* ◦ *He retained a plebeian taste in food and drink.*

plebiscite /ˈpleb.ɪ.sɪt/ ⓤⓢ /-ə.saɪt/ **noun** formal a **referendum**

plectrum /ˈplek.trəm/ **noun** [C] (plural **plectrums** or **plectra** /-ə/) (informal **pick**) a small, thin piece of plastic, metal, etc. that is held between the fingers and thumb and used for playing instruments such as the guitar

pled /pled/ US or Scottish English past simple and past participle of **plead**

pledge /pledʒ/ **noun; verb**

▸**noun** [C] a serious or formal promise, especially one to give money or to be a friend, or something that you give as a sign that you will keep a promise: [+ to infinitive] *All the candidates have **given/made** pledges not **to** raise taxes if they are elected.* ◦ *Thousands of people **made** pledges (= promised to give money) to the charity campaign.* ◦ *I give you this ring as a pledge **of** my everlasting love for you.*

IDIOM **take/sign the pledge** UK old-fashioned or humorous to make a formal promise to stop drinking alcohol: *What's this then, you're only drinking orange juice – have you signed the pledge or something?*

▸**verb** [T] to make a serious or formal promise to give or do something: *We are asking people to pledge their **support** for our campaign.* ◦ *If you join the armed forces, you have to pledge **allegiance** to your country.* ◦ *So far, £50,000 has been pledged (= people have promised to pay this amount) in response to the appeal.* ◦ [+ to infinitive] *Both sides have pledged **to** end the fighting.* ◦ *I've been pledged **to** secrecy.*

plenary /ˈpliː.nə.ri/ ⓤⓢ /-nɚ.i/ **adj; noun**

▸**adj** specialized describes a meeting at which all the members of a group or organization are present, especially at a CONFERENCE: *a plenary **session** of the UN Security Council*

▸**noun** [C] specialized a plenary meeting

plenipotentiary /ˌplen.ɪ.pəˈten.ʃər.i/ ⓤⓢ /-poʊˈten.ʃi.er-/ **noun** [C] old-fashioned formal a person who has the authority to represent his or her country, especially in another country • **plenipotentiary adj** *a plenipotentiary diplomat/role*

plentiful /ˈplen.tɪ.fəl/ ⓤⓢ /-t̬ɪ-/ **adj** If something is plentiful, there is a lot of it available: *Strawberries are plentiful in the summer.* ◦ *I took a plentiful **supply** of games to keep the children amused.* • **plentifully** /-i/ **adv**

plenty /ˈplen.ti/ ⓤⓢ /-t̬i/ **pronoun, noun, adv** **B1** (the state of having) enough or more than enough, or a large amount: *'Would you like some more wine?' 'No thanks, I've had plenty.'* ◦ *Don't grab at the balloons, children – there are plenty **for** everyone.* ◦ *We've got plenty **of** time before we need to leave for the airport.* ◦ *They've always had plenty **of** money.* ◦ *There's plenty to do here.* ◦ US informal *This car cost me plenty (= a lot of money).* ◦ *There's plenty **more** beer in the fridge.*

IDIOM **be plenty more where sb/sth came from** informal to be a lot more things or people of the same type available: *Have another sandwich – there's plenty more where that came from.*

plethora /ˈpleθ.ər.ə/ ⓤⓢ /-ɚ.ə/ **noun** [S] formal **C2** a very large amount of something, especially a larger amount than you need, want or can deal with: *There's **a** plethora **of** books about the royal family.* ◦ *The plethora **of** regulations is both contradictory and confusing.*

pleurisy /ˈplʊə.rə.si/ ⓤⓢ /ˈplʊr.ə-/ **noun** [U] a serious illness in which the covering of the lungs becomes red and swollen, causing sharp pain when breathing

Plexiglas /ˈplek.si.glɑːs/ ⓤⓢ /-glæs/ **noun** [U] US trademark **Perspex**

pliable /ˈplaɪ.ə.bl/ **adj** **1** A pliable substance bends easily without breaking or CRACKING: *Some kinds of plastic become pliable if they're heated.* **2** often disapproving A pliable person is easily influenced and controlled by other people: *He wanted a sweet, pliable, obedient wife.* • **pliability** /ˌplaɪ.əˈbɪl.ɪ.ti/ ⓤⓢ /-ə.t̬i/ **noun** [U]

pliant /ˈplaɪ.ənt/ **adj** **PERSON** ▷ **1** Pliant people are easily influenced or controlled by other people: *I don't think it's a good thing for children to be too pliant.* **2** being able and willing to accept change or new ideas: *The management has adopted a more pliant position, and has agreed to listen to the staff's requests.* **SUBSTANCE** ▷ **3** able to bend easily without breaking: *These toys are made of pliant rubber, so they won't break.* • **pliancy** /-ən.si/ **noun** [U] • **pliantly** /-li/ **adv**

pliers /ˈplaɪ.əz/ ⓤⓢ /-ɚz/ **noun** [plural] a small tool with two handles for holding or pulling small things like nails, or for cutting wire: *Pass me that **pair of** pliers, please.*

pliers

plight /plaɪt/ **noun; verb**

▸**noun** [S] **C2** an unpleasant condition, especially a serious, sad, or difficult one: ***the** plight **of** the poor/homeless*

▸**verb** old use or humorous **plight your troth** to (promise to) marry

plimsoll /ˈplɪm.səl/ **noun** [C] UK old-fashioned a flat, light shoe made of heavy cloth with a rubber SOLE, worn especially for sports

ˈPlimsoll ˌline **noun** [C usually singular] (also **ˈPlimsoll ˌmark**) a line painted on the outside of a ship which shows how deep it is legally allowed to go down into the water when it is full

plinth /plɪnθ/ **noun** [C] a square block, especially of stone, on which a column or a STATUE stands

plod /plɒd/ ⓤⓢ /plɑːd/ **verb** [I + adv/prep] (**-dd-**) **WALK** ▷ **1** to walk taking slow steps, as if your feet are heavy: *We plodded through the mud.* ◦ *Despite the wind and the rain, they plodded **on** until they reached the cottage.* **WORK** ▷ **2** to work slowly and continuously, but without imagination, enthusiasm, or interest: *For years, he's plodded **away at** the same dull routine job.* ◦ *Alex is just plodding **along** at school, making very little progress.* • **plodder** /ˈplɒd.ər/ ⓤⓢ /ˈplɑː.dɚ/ **noun**

[C] *Dennis is a bit of a plodder, but he gets the job done in the end.* • **plodding** /ˈplɒd.ɪŋ/ (US) /ˈplɑː.dɪŋ/ **adj**

plonk /plɒŋk/ (US) /plɑːŋk/ **verb; noun; adv**

▸**verb** informal **PUT DOWN** ▷ **1** [I or T, usually + adv/prep] (US usually **plunk**) to put something down heavily and without taking care: *Just plonk the shopping (**down**) **on** the table, and come and have a cup of tea.* ◦ *Come in and plonk your**selves** (**down**) (= sit down) anywhere you like.* **INSTRUMENT** ▷ **2** [I usually + adv/prep] (US also **plunk**) to play a musical instrument, usually not very well but often loudly: *I really enjoy plonking **away on** the piano.*

▸**noun** [U] **SOUND** ▷ **1** (US also **plunk**) a hollow sound like that made when an object is dropped heavily onto a surface: *the plonk of a tennis ball* **WINE** ▷ **2** mainly UK informal cheap wine, especially wine that is not of good quality: *We had pizza and a bottle of plonk.*

▸**adv** (US also **plunk**) making a plonk sound: *I heard something go plonk.* ◦ *An apple landed plonk **on** the ground.*

plonker /ˈplɒŋ.kəʳ/ (US) /ˈplɑːŋ.kɚ/ **noun** [C] UK informal a silly or stupid person

plop /plɒp/ (US) /plɑːp/ **noun; verb**

▸**noun** [S] informal a soft sound like that of something solid dropping lightly into a liquid: *The stone fell into the water with **a** plop.* • **plop adv** *Her earring went plop into the soup.*

▸**verb** (**-pp-**) **PUT DOWN** ▷ **1** [I or T, + adv/prep] to sit down or land heavily or without taking care, or to put something down without taking care: *He came and plopped **down** next to me.* ◦ *Lynn plopped a paper cup **down** beside her.* **FALL** ▷ **2** [I usually + adv/prep] informal to fall with a soft sound: *I noticed drops of water plopping **onto** the carpet.*

plosive /ˈpləʊ.sɪv/ (US) /ˈploʊ-/ **noun** [C] specialized a consonant sound that is made by stopping air flowing out of the mouth, and then suddenly releasing it: */p/ and /d/ are examples of plosives.*

plot /plɒt/ (US) /plɑːt/ **noun; verb**

▸**noun** [C] **STORY** ▷ **1** (B2) the story of a book, film, play, etc.: *The film has a very simple plot.* ◦ *The plots **of** his books are basically all the same.* **PLAN** ▷ **2** a secret plan made by several people to do something that is wrong, harmful, or not legal, especially to do damage to a person or a government: *The plot was discovered before it was carried out.* ◦ [+ to infinitive] *The police have **foiled** a plot **to** assassinate the president.* **GROUND** ▷ **3** (C) a small piece of land that has been marked or measured for a particular purpose: *a vegetable plot* ◦ *There are several plots **of land** for sale.* **4** US for **ground plan**

IDIOM **the plot thickens** humorous said when a situation suddenly becomes more complicated or mysterious: *'Now there are two men phoning her up all the time.' 'The plot thickens!'*

▸**verb** (**-tt-**) **MARK** ▷ **1** [T] to mark or draw something on a piece of paper or a map **2** [T] to make marks to show the position, movement, or development of something, usually in the form of lines or curves between a series of points on a map or piece of paper: *Radar operators plotted the **course** of the incoming missile.* ◦ *We've plotted our projected costs for the coming year, and they show a big increase.* **PLAN** ▷ **3** [I or T] to make a secret plan to do something wrong, harmful, or illegal: *The army is plotting the overthrow of the government.* ◦ *I can't believe that he's plotting **against** his own father.* ◦ [+ to infinitive] *They're plotting (**together**) **to** take over the company.* **4** [T] humorous to make a secret plan to do something funny or enjoyable to or for someone: [+ to infinitive] *They're plotting **to** play a trick on their brother.* ◦ *He's plotting a surprise party for his wife's birthday.* **STORY** ▷ **5** [T] to write the plot for something: *So far I've only plotted (**out**) the story in a rough form.*

plotter /ˈplɒt.əʳ/ (US) /ˈplɑː.t̬ɚ/ **noun** [C] **PERSON** ▷ **1** someone who makes a secret plan to do something wrong, harmful, or illegal **EQUIPMENT** ▷ **2** a piece of equipment which marks things, such as the position of a ship or aircraft, on a map or piece of paper

plough /plaʊ/ **noun; verb**

▸**noun** [C] UK (US **plow**) **1** a large farming tool with blades which digs the earth in fields so that seeds can be planted → See also **snowplough 2 under the plough** formal describes land on which crops are grown: *These fields have been under the plough for centuries.*

▸**verb** [I or T] UK (US **plow**) to dig land with a plough: *Farmers start ploughing in the spring.* ◦ *We're going to plough the top field next week.* ◦ *Large areas of grazing land have been ploughed **up** to grow wheat.*

PHRASAL VERBS **plough sth back/in** to dig the roots and other remaining parts of a crop into the earth to make the soil more healthy • **plough sth back** to spend the money that a business has earned on improving that business: *All the profits are being ploughed back **into** the company.* • **plough into sth/sb** If a vehicle ploughs into something or someone, it hits the object or person with great force: *Many people were injured when the train came off the rails and ploughed into the bank.* • **plough sth into sth** informal to INVEST money (= give money hoping to get more back) in a business, especially to help make it successful or to make more money: *They ploughed all their savings into their daughter's business.* • **plough on** to continue doing something although it is difficult or boring: *He could see that she didn't like what he was saying, but he ploughed on (= continued talking) regardless.* ◦ *It would be a mistake to plough on **with** this scheme – it'll never work.* • **plough through sth** **1** informal to go through a substance or an area of something with difficulty: *We ploughed through the mud.* **2** to finish reading, eating, or dealing with something with difficulty: *I've got an enormous pile of papers to plough through.*

the ˈPlough **noun** [S] UK (US **the ˌBig ˈDipper**) a group of seven bright stars that can only be seen in the northern part of the world

ploughed UK (US **plowed**) /plaʊd/ **adj** dug ready for planting seeds: *You shouldn't walk over ploughed **fields**.*

ploughman (plural **-men** /-mən/) UK (US **plowman**) /ˈplaʊ.mən/ **noun** [C] a man whose job is to direct a plough by leading a horse or other animal that is pulling it

ˌploughman's ˈlunch **noun** [C] (also **ploughman's**) UK a small meal of bread, cheese, and PICKLE eaten in the middle of the day, especially served in a pub: *I had a ploughman's in the Eagle.*

ploughshare UK (US **plowshare**) /ˈplaʊ.ʃeəʳ/ (US) /-ʃer/ **noun** [C] the sharp blade of a plough

plover /ˈplʌv.əʳ/ (US) /-ɚ/ **noun** [C] (plural **plovers** or **plover**) a bird with a short tail and long legs that is found mainly by the sea or in areas covered with grass

ploy /plɔɪ/ **noun** [C] something that is done or said in order to get an advantage, often dishonestly: *There are various ploys we can **use** if necessary.* ◦ [+ to infinitive] *He only said he had a meeting as a ploy **to** get her to leave.*

P

pls written abbreviation for please

pluck /plʌk/ verb; noun

▸verb **REMOVE** ▷ **1** [T] to pull something, especially with a sudden movement, in order to remove it: *Caged birds sometimes pluck* ***out*** *their breast feathers.* ◦ *He plucked the letter* ***from/out of*** *my hand, and ran off with it.* ◦ *Do you pluck your* ***eyebrows*** *(= remove some of the hairs from them to give them a better shape)?* **2** [T] to remove the feathers from a chicken or other bird so that it can be cooked and eaten **3** [T usually passive] to remove someone suddenly from a situation that is ordinary: *He was plucked* ***from obscurity*** *to star in the film.* **4** [T] to remove someone quickly from a dangerous or difficult situation: *The last passengers were plucked* ***from*** *the ship just seconds before it sank.* **5** [T] Indian English to collect flowers by breaking or cutting their stems; PICK **MUSIC** ▷ **6** [I or T] (US also **pick**) to pull and then release the strings of a musical instrument with your finger to play notes: *He sat on the bed, idly plucking (****at****) the strings of his guitar.*

IDIOMS **pluck sth out of the air** to say something quickly, usually because a reply is expected, without having thought about it or made certain it is correct: *'Where did you get those figures from?' 'Oh, I just plucked them out of the air.'* • **pluck up your courage** (also **pluck up (the) courage to do sth**) C2 to force yourself to be brave enough to do something, although you are frightened or worried about it: *He finally plucked up courage to ask her to marry him.* ◦ *I'd love to do a parachute jump, but I can't pluck up the/enough courage.*

PHRASAL VERB **pluck at sth** to pull something with your fingers again and again, using quick, small movements: *I felt a small hand plucking at my jacket.*

▸noun [U] informal courage and a strong wish to succeed: *She* ***showed*** *a lot of pluck in standing up to her boss.*

P

plucky /ˈplʌk.i/ adj informal brave: *It was plucky of you to chase after the burglar.*

plug /plʌg/ noun; verb

▸noun [C] **ELECTRICAL** ▷ **1** B1 a small plastic or rubber object with two or three metal pins, fixed to the end of a wire on a piece of electrical equipment and pushed into a special opening in a wall to connect the equipment to a supply of electricity: *a three-pin/two-pin plug* ◦ *to fit/change a plug* ◦ *If a plug is wired incorrectly, it can be dangerous.* **2** mainly UK informal an electric SOCKET: *Is there a plug in the bedroom that I can use for my hairdryer?* **3** US for **jack plug 4** informal for **spark plug FOR HOLE** ▷ **5** B1 a small piece of rubber, plastic, wood, etc. that fits into a hole in order to close it → See also **earplug 6** B1 a round piece of rubber or plastic that fits into the hole in a sink or a bath: *a bath plug* ◦ *Put the plug in the sink and run some water.* **7** a small piece of plastic or wood that you put into a hole in a wall before putting a SCREW into it **8** a small piece of material such as COTTON WOOL, twisted or pressed tightly so it is firm **ADVERTISEMENT** ▷ **9** the act of telling people publicly about a product, event, etc.: *She never misses an opportunity to get in a plug* ***for*** *her new film.*

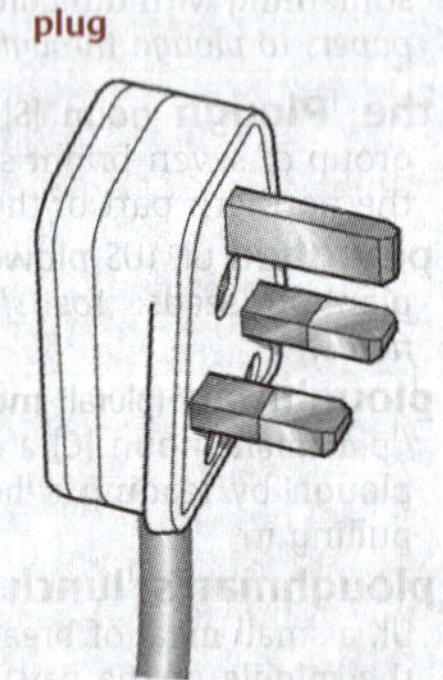
plug

▸verb [T] (-gg-) **ADVERTISE** ▷ **1** to advertise something by talking about it a lot or praising it, especially on the radio or television: *That interview was just a way for him to plug his new book.* **SHOOT** ▷ **2** US slang to shoot someone with a gun: *Sure, boss, we plugged the guy (****full of lead****).* **FILL HOLE** ▷ **3** to fill a hole with a piece of suitable material: *Have you plugged that leak (= stopped it by filling the hole) in the pipe?* ◦ *My nose was bleeding and I plugged it* ***with*** *cotton wool.*

PHRASAL VERBS **plug away** informal to work hard and in a determined way, especially at something that you find difficult: *Katie has been plugging away* ***at*** *her homework for hours.* • **plug (sth) in/plug (sth) into sth** B2 to connect an electrical device to an electrical system or device so that it can be used, by pushing its plug into a SOCKET: *Of course the radio isn't working – you haven't plugged it in!* ◦ *I want to plug the kettle into the right-hand socket.* ◦ *Can you show me where the microphone plugs into the tape recorder?* ◦ *The keyboard plugs in at the back of the computer.* • **plug (sth/sb) into sth** informal to make something or someone fit well or have good connections with something: *This new product line should be able to plug into our existing distribution* ***network****.*

ˌplug and ˈplay noun [U] a feature of a computer system which allows an electronic device to be used as soon as it is connected to a computer

plughole /ˈplʌg.həʊl/ US /-hoʊl/ noun [C] a hole in a bath, sink, etc. through which water flows away and into which you can put a plug

ˈplug-in noun [C] a small computer program that makes a larger one work faster or have more features → Compare **patch**

plum /plʌm/ noun; adj

▸noun [C or U] a small, round fruit with a thin, smooth, red, purple, or yellow skin, sweet, soft flesh, and a single large hard seed: *plum jam* ◦ *a plum tree*

▸adj **GOOD** ▷ **1** [before noun] (**plummer**, **plummest**) very good and worth having: *How did you manage to get such a plum* ***job****?* **COLOUR** ▷ **2** (also **ˈplum-ˌcoloured**) having a dark reddish-purple colour: *a plum-coloured dress*

plumage /ˈpluː.mɪdʒ/ noun [U] a bird's covering of feathers: *Male peacocks have beautiful plumage.*

plumb /plʌm/ verb; adv; adj

▸verb [T] **WATER** ▷ **1** to supply a building or a device with water pipes, or to connect a building or a device to a water pipe: *We've discovered that our house isn't plumbed properly.* ◦ *I think we can plumb the new bath* ***into*** *the existing pipes.* ◦ *Have you plumbed the dishwasher* ***in*** *yet?* **DEEP** ▷ **2** specialized to measure how deep something is, especially water **3** to understand or discover all about something: *Now that she had begun, she wanted to plumb her own childhood further.*

IDIOM **plumb the depths** to reach the lowest point: *Roy plumbed the depths* ***of*** *despair when his wife left him.* ◦ humorous *They must be really plumbing the depths (= must have been unable to find anyone better) if they're offering the job to her.*

▸adv **EXACTLY** ▷ **1** informal exactly: *The hotel is plumb in the middle of the town.* ◦ *He hit me plumb on the nose.* **COMPLETELY** ▷ **2** US informal completely: *I plumb forgot your birthday.*

▸adj [after verb] specialized **1** exactly straight, usually describing a vertical surface or line: *When you hang a door, you need to make sure that it is both level and plumb.* **2** **out of plumb** not straight vertically: *The external wall is out of plumb by half a metre.*

plumber /ˈplʌm.əʳ/ (US) /-ɚ/ noun [C] B2 a person whose job is to supply and connect or repair water pipes, baths, toilets, etc.: *When is the plumber coming to mend the burst pipe?*

plumbing /ˈplʌm.ɪŋ/ noun [U] **1** the water pipes and similar systems in a building: *There's something wrong with the plumbing.* **2** the work of connecting water and other pipes in a building: *We did all the plumbing (**work**) in our house ourselves.*

ˈplumb ˌline noun [C] a piece of string with a weight fixed to one end, used either to test if something vertical, such as a wall, is exactly straight, or to find the depth of water

plume /pluːm/ noun **1** [C usually plural] a large feather: *fans made of ostrich plumes* → See also **nom de plume** **2** [C] a decoration that looks like several large feathers tied together, worn by soldiers on their hats or attached to horses' heads: *The coffin was drawn by horses with black plumes.* **3 a plume of dust, smoke, etc.** a tall, thin mass of smoke, dust, or similar substance that rises up into the air: *After the explosion, a plume of smoke could be seen in the sky for miles around.* • **plumed** /pluːmd/ adj [before noun] *The dancers wore plumed headdresses (= with a decoration which looked like several large feathers tied together).*

plummet /ˈplʌm.ɪt/ verb [I] to fall very quickly and suddenly: *House prices have plummeted in recent months.* ◦ *Several large rocks were sent plummeting **down** the mountain.* ◦ *She plummeted **to** the ground.*

plummy /ˈplʌm.i/ adj **SPEECH** ▷ **1** describes a low voice or way of speaking using long vowels, of a type thought to be typical of the English upper social class: *a plummy voice* ◦ *a plummy accent* **FRUIT** ▷ **2** having the taste or dark reddish-purple colour of plums: *This wine has an almost plummy flavour.*

plump /plʌmp/ adj; verb

▸adj **1** C2 having a pleasantly soft, rounded body or shape: *a nice plump chicken* ◦ *plump juicy grapes* ◦ *a child with plump rosy cheeks* **2** C2 polite word for fat: *He's got rather plump since I last saw him.* • **plumpness** /ˈplʌmp.nəs/ noun [U]

▸verb [T] to shake and push something to make it round and soft: *My aunt was busy straightening furniture and plumping **cushions**.*

PHRASAL VERBS **plump (sb/sth) down** informal to sit down suddenly and heavily, or to put an object or child down suddenly and without taking care: *She plumped down next to me **on** the sofa.* ◦ *He rushed in and plumped him**self** down **in** a chair.* ◦ *Joan sat down at the front of the bus, and plumped her bags down beside her.* • **plump for sth/sb** UK informal to choose something or someone, especially after taking time for careful thought: *I'm going to plump for the vegetable curry.* ◦ *Which film did you plump for in the end?* • **plump sth up** to make something fuller or fatter: *She went round plumping up the cushions.* ◦ *Lips can be plumped up with injections.*

ˌplum ˈpudding noun [C or U] US or UK old-fashioned → **Christmas pudding**

plunder /ˈplʌn.dəʳ/ (US) /-dɚ/ verb; noun

▸verb **1** [I or T] to steal goods violently from a place, especially during a war: *After the president fled the country, the palace was plundered by soldiers.* ◦ *Tragically, the graves were plundered and the contents scattered.* **2** [T] to steal or remove something precious from something, in a way that does not consider moral laws or is more severe than it need be: *Someone has been plundering funds **from** the company.* ◦ *The future of our planet is in danger if we continue to plunder it as we do.* • **plunderer** /-əʳ/ (US) /-ɚ/ noun [C]

▸noun [U] **1** an occasion when goods are stolen from a place, especially violently or during a war, or these stolen goods: *Residents in the villages under attack have been unable to protect their homes from plunder.* ◦ *The thieves hid their plunder in the woodshed.* **2** a situation in which something is taken in a way that is not morally right or is too extreme: *We need to put a stop to the plunder **of** the rain forest.*

plunge /plʌndʒ/ verb; noun

▸verb **FALL** ▷ **1** C2 [I or T, usually + adv/prep] to (cause someone or something to) move or fall suddenly and often a long way forward, down, or into something: *We ran down to the beach and plunged **into** the sea.* ◦ *The car went out of control and plunged **over** the cliff.* ◦ *Cook the peas by plunging them **into** boiling water.* ◦ *Niagara Falls plunges 55.5 metres.* **BECOME LOWER** ▷ **2** C1 [I] to become lower in value or level very suddenly and quickly: *The fall in demand caused share prices to plunge.* ◦ *Our income has plunged dramatically.*

PHRASAL VERBS **plunge in/plunge into sth** C2 to suddenly start doing something actively or enthusiastically: *Two months before his exams, he suddenly plunged into his studies.* • **plunge (sb/sth) into sth** [often passive] to suddenly experience a bad situation or unhappiness, or to make someone or something suddenly experience a bad situation or unhappiness: *The country was plunged into recession.* ◦ *He was plunged into despair when his wife left him.*

▸noun [C] **MOVEMENT** ▷ **1** a sudden movement or fall forward, down, or into something: *I really enjoyed my plunge (= jumping in and swimming) **in** the pool.* **REDUCTION** ▷ **2** a sudden and large fall in value or level: *We are expecting a plunge **in** profits this year.*

IDIOM **take the plunge** C2 to make a decision to do something, especially after thinking about it for a long time: *They're finally taking the plunge and getting married.*

plunger /ˈplʌn.dʒəʳ/ (US) /-dʒɚ/ noun [C] **1** a SUCTION device consisting of a cup-shaped piece of rubber on the end of a stick, used to get rid of things that are blocking pipes **2** a part of a device which you push down into it: *He pressed down the plunger of his cafetière.*

plunging /ˈplʌn.dʒɪŋ/ adj describes something that drops suddenly or that has a shape which drops a long way down: *plunging sales figures* ◦ *a dress with a plunging **neckline** (= having a deep curve at the neck to show part of the breasts)*

plunk /plʌŋk/ noun, verb US for **plonk**

the pluperfect /ˌpluːˈpɜː.fekt/ (US) /ˈpluːˌpɝː-/ noun [S] specialized **the past perfect** • **pluperfect** adj *the pluperfect tense*

plural /ˈplʊə.rəl/ (US) /ˈplʊr.əl/ noun; adj

▸noun [C or U] (written abbreviation **pl.**) A2 a word or form which expresses more than one: *'Geese' is the plural **of** 'goose'.* ◦ *'Woman' **in the** plural is 'women'.* → Compare **singular**

▸adj **DIFFERENT** ▷ **1** consisting of a lot of different races or types of people or of different things: *We need to recognize that we are now living in a plural **society**.* **2** for or relating to more than one person or thing: *Very few countries allow people to have plural citizenship (= citizenship of more than one country).* **GRAMMAR** ▷ **3** of or relating to the form which expresses more than one: *'Cattle' and 'trousers' are both plural nouns.*

pluralism /ˈplʊə.rə.lɪ.zᵊm/ (US) /ˈplʊr.ᵊl.ɪ-/ **noun** [U] **1** the existence of different types of people, who have different beliefs and opinions, within the same society: *After years of state control, the country is now moving towards* ***political/religious/cultural*** *pluralism.* **2** the belief that the existence of different types of people within the same society is a good thing: *They are committed to human rights and pluralism.*

pluralist /ˈplʊə.rə.lɪst/ (US) /ˈplʊr.ᵊl.ɪst-/ **noun; adj**
▸**noun** [C] a person who believes that the existence of different types of people, beliefs, and opinions within a society is a good thing
▸**adj** (also **pluralistic** /ˌplʊə.rᵊlˈɪs.tɪk/ (US) /ˌplʊr.ᵊl-/) including or considering many different types of people, with different beliefs, opinions, and needs: *A pluralist society allows its members to express their beliefs freely.* ◦ *We need to take a pluralistic approach to education.*

plurality /plʊəˈræl.ə.ti/ (US) /plʊˈræl.ə.t̬i/ **noun** GRAMMAR ▷ **1** [U] the state of being plural DIFFERENT ▷ **2** [C usually sing] formal a large number of different types of something: *There was* ***a*** *marked plurality* ***of*** *opinions/views among the people attending the meeting.* **3 have/win a plurality** specialized to receive more votes in an election than any other person or party, but not more than the total number of votes which the other people or parties have received

pluralize (UK usually **pluralise**) /ˈplʊə.rᵊl.aɪz/ (US) /ˈplʊr.ᵊl.aɪz/ **verb** [T] to make a word into a form that expresses more than one: *Certain nouns, such as 'guilt', cannot be pluralized.*

plus /plʌs/ **preposition; preposition, conjunction; noun; adj**
▸**preposition** (A2) added to: *What is six plus four?* ◦ *The rent will be £75 a week, plus (= added to the cost of) gas and electricity.*
▸**preposition, conjunction** (B1) and also: *There will be two adults travelling, plus three children.* ◦ informal *Let's not go on holiday in August – it'll be too hot – plus it'll be more expensive.*
▸**noun** [C] ADVANTAGE ▷ **1** (B2) (plural **pluses** or **plusses**) informal an advantage or a good feature: *Your teaching experience will be a plus in this job.* ADDITION SIGN ▷ **2** (also **plus sign**) the (+) sign, written between two numbers to show that they should be added together
▸**adj** ADDITION ▷ **1** [before noun] describes a stated number or amount more than zero: *Plus 8 is eight more than zero.* ◦ *The temperature is expected to be no more than plus two (degrees).* **2** [after noun] more than the number or amount mentioned: *temperatures of 40 plus* ◦ *Those cars cost £15,000 plus.* **3** [after noun] used by teachers after a letter, such as B or C, to show that the standard of a piece of work is slightly higher than the stated mark: *I got C plus/C+ for my essay.* ADVANTAGE ▷ **4** [before noun] informal describing an advantage: *The house is near the sea, which is a plus* ***factor*** *for us.* ◦ UK *The fact that the flight goes from our nearest airport is a real plus* ***point***.

ˌplus ˈfours noun [plural] trousers with legs that are wide above the knee and end in a tightly-fitted strip just below the knee, sometimes worn by men playing GOLF

plush /plʌʃ/ **adj; noun**
▸**adj** informal expensive, comfortable, and of high quality: *He took me out to a really plush restaurant.* → Synonym **luxurious**
▸**noun** [U] thick, soft cloth, with a surface like short fur, used especially for covering furniture: *a plush(-covered) sofa* ◦ *two metres of dark red plush* ◦ *plush cushions/curtains*

Pluto /ˈpluː.təʊ/ (US) /-t̬oʊ/ **noun** [S] a DWARF PLANET that is farther away from the sun than Neptune, and is the second largest DWARF PLANET in the SOLAR SYSTEM

plutocracy /pluːˈtɒk.rə.si/ (US) /-ˈtɑː.krə-/ **noun 1** [U] a system of government in which the richest people in a country rule or have power: *It's time we put an end to plutocracy.* **2** [C] a country where the richest people have power **3** [S, + sing/pl verb] the richest people in a country who have power in it

plutocrat /ˈpluː.tə.kræt/ (US) /-t̬ə-/ **noun** [C] someone who becomes powerful because they are rich: *The country has long been run by plutocrats.* • **plutocratic** /ˌpluː.təˈkræt.ɪk/ (US) /-toʊˈkræt̬-/ **adj**

plutonium /pluːˈtəʊ.ni.əm/ (US) /-ˈtoʊ-/ **noun** [U] (symbol **Pu**) a chemical element that is a metal used in the production of nuclear power, and in nuclear weapons

ply /plaɪ/ **verb; noun**
▸**verb** WORK ▷ **1** [T] to sell or to work regularly at something, especially a job involving selling things: *Fishermen in small boats ply their* ***trade*** *up and down the coast.* ◦ *Dealers are openly plying drugs in school playgrounds.* ◦ *The market traders were loudly plying their* ***wares***. **2 ply for business, trade, etc.** to try to get customers for your business in a public place, for example, as a taxi driver, by driving around or waiting in a regular place: UK *There are never any taxis plying for trade/hire in our area.* ◦ *I noticed a couple of prostitutes plying for business on the corner.* TRAVEL ▷ **3** [I + adv/prep, T] old-fashioned When a boat, train, bus, etc. plies a particular route, it makes that journey regularly: *High-speed trains regularly ply* ***between*** *Paris and Lyons.* ◦ *This airline has been plying the transatlantic* ***route*** *for many years.*

PHRASAL VERB **ply sb with sth 1** to keep giving a person something, usually food or drink: *John's been plying me with drinks all evening.* **2** to keep giving someone work or forms to complete, or asking them questions: *We plied Charlie with questions about his trip round the world.*

▸**noun** [U] **1** the particular number of threads from which wool, rope, etc. is made, used as a measure of its thickness: *six balls of four-ply (wool)* ◦ *What ply do you need for that knitting pattern?* **2** the particular number of layers from which plywood or TISSUE is formed, used as a measure of its thickness: *Will* ***three-ply*** *(= wood made from three layers stuck together) be strong enough for making a shelf?*

plywood /ˈplaɪ.wʊd/ **noun** [U] wood that consists of several thin layers of wood stuck together: *a box made of plywood* ◦ *a cheap plywood door*

p.m. /ˌpiːˈem/ **abbreviation** (A1) used when referring to a time in the afternoon or evening or at night: *We'll be arriving at about 4.30 p.m.* ◦ *The 6 p.m. train is usually very crowded.* → Compare **a.m.**

PM /ˌpiːˈem/ **noun** [C] UK informal abbreviation for **prime minister**: *The PM wants to see you.*

PMS /ˌpiː.emˈes/ **noun** [U] abbreviation for **premenstrual syndrome**: (= a condition in which some women experience unpleasant physical and emotional feelings for a few days before their period)

PMT /ˌpiː.emˈtiː/ **noun** [U] UK abbreviation for premenstrual tension: another name for **PMS**: *She gets terrible PMT.* → See **premenstrual syndrome**

pneumatic /njuːˈmæt.ɪk/ (US) /nuːˈmæt̬-/ **adj 1** operated by air pressure: *Our car has pneumatic* ***brakes***. **2** containing air: *pneumatic* ***tyres*** • **pneumatically** /-ɪ.kᵊl.i/ **adv**

pneu͵matic ˈdrill noun [C] (US also **jackhammer**) a powerful tool that is held in the hand and operates by air pressure, used for breaking hard surfaces such as roads

pneumonia /njuːˈməʊ.ni.ə/ Ⓤⓢ /nuːˈmoʊ.njə/ noun [U] **1** a serious illness in which one or both lungs become red and swollen and filled with liquid **2 catch/get pneumonia** informal to make yourself ill by getting too cold: *She'll catch pneumonia going out without a coat in this weather!*

PO /ˌpiːˈəʊ/ Ⓤⓢ /-ˈoʊ/ noun **MAIL** ▷ **1** [S] abbreviation for **the Post Office** **ARMY** ▷ **2** written abbreviation for **petty officer**: *PO McLintock*

poach /pəʊtʃ/ Ⓤⓢ /poʊtʃ/ verb **COOK** ▷ **1** [T] to cook something such as a fish, or an egg with its shell removed, by putting it in gently boiling water or other liquid: *We had poached eggs for breakfast.* ◦ *Do you like pears poached in red wine?* **TAKE** ▷ **2** [I or T] to catch and kill animals without permission on someone else's land: *The farmer claimed that he shot the men because they were poaching on his land.* **3** [T] to take and use for yourself unfairly or dishonestly something, usually an idea, that belongs to someone else: *Jeff always poaches my **ideas**, and then pretends that they're his own.* **4** [T] disapproving to persuade someone who works for someone else to come and work for you: *They were furious when one of their best managers was poached by another company.*

poacher /ˈpəʊ.tʃəʳ/ Ⓤⓢ /ˈpoʊ.tʃɚ/ noun [C] someone who catches and kills animals illegally

IDIOM **poacher turned gamekeeper** someone who opposed people in authority in the past but who now has a position of authority themselves

ˈPO ˌbox noun [C] a box with a number in a POST OFFICE to which your letters and parcels can be sent and from which you can collect them: *Write to PO box 123.* ◦ *a PO box number*

pocket /ˈpɒk.ɪt/ Ⓤⓢ /ˈpɑː.kɪt/ noun; verb; adj

▸noun [C] **BAG** ▷ **1** Ⓐ② a small bag for carrying things in, made of cloth and sewn into the inside or onto the outside of a piece of clothing: *a jacket/trouser/coat pocket* ◦ *a hip/breast pocket* ◦ *She thrust her hands deep **in/into** her pockets.* ◦ *He took some coins **from/out of** his pocket.* **2** Ⓑ① a container, usually made of cloth, that is sewn into or onto a bag or fixed to a seat or door in a vehicle: *Sarah put her maps in the outside pocket of her rucksack.* ◦ *The safety instructions are in the pocket **of** the seat in front of you.* **3** one of several holes around the edge of a BILLIARD or SNOOKER table, into which balls are hit **4** Ⓒ② informal the amount of money that someone has for spending: *You need **deep** pockets (= a lot of money) if you're involved in a long law suit.* ◦ *I paid for my ticket **out of** my **own** pocket (= with my own money), but I can claim the cost of it back from my employer.* **GROUP/AREA** ▷ **5** a group, area, or mass of something that is separate and different from what surrounds it: *Among the staff there are some pockets **of** resistance to the planned changes (= some small groups of them are opposed).* ◦ *The pilot said that we were going to encounter a pocket **of** turbulence (= an area of violently moving air).*

IDIOMS **be/live in each other's pockets** disapproving to be with each other all the time and depend on each other: *I don't think it's healthy the way you two are always in each other's pockets.* • **have sth in your pocket** informal to be certain to win or succeed at something: *Last year's winners again have the championship firmly in their pocket.* • **in sb's pocket** disapproving in a situation where someone has power or control over you: *The head teacher **has** the school governors completely in her pocket/The school governors **are** completely in the head teacher's pocket.* • **in/out of pocket** UK having more/less money than you started with after an activity involving money: *Even when we've paid all our expenses, we should still be several hundred pounds in pocket.* ◦ *The last time I went to the pub with you, I ended up seriously out of pocket!*

▸verb [T] **1** to put something into your pocket: *He carefully pocketed his change.* **2** to hit a BILLIARD or SNOOKER ball into a pocket: *Davis pocketed the black to win the game.* **3** to take something for yourself, especially dishonestly: *I'll tell them I sold it for £20, not £25, then I can pocket the rest.*

▸adj [before noun] describes something that is small enough to put in your pocket, or that you regularly carry in your pocket: *a pocket dictionary* ◦ *a pocket diary* ◦ *a pocket calculator*

pocketbook /ˈpɒk.ɪt.bʊk/ Ⓤⓢ /ˈpɑː.kɪt-/ noun [C] US **1** a woman's HANDBAG: *I need a new pocketbook to go with these shoes.* **2 sb's pocketbook** the money that someone has or their ability to pay for things: *These new tax arrangements will hit everyone's pocketbook.*

pocketful /ˈpɒk.ɪt.fʊl/ Ⓤⓢ /ˈpɑː.kɪt-/ noun [C] as many or as much of something as a pocket will hold: *She always takes a pocketful **of** tissues with her when she takes the children out.* ◦ informal *They won pocketfuls (= a large amount) of money playing cards.*

ˌpocket ˈhandkerchief noun [C] (plural **pocket handkerchiefs** or UK also **pocket handkerchieves**) old-fashioned for **handkerchief**

pocketknife /ˈpɒk.ɪt.naɪf/ Ⓤⓢ /ˈpɑː.kɪt-/ noun [C] (plural **pocketknives**) a **penknife**

ˈpocket ˌmoney noun [U] **CHILD'S MONEY** ▷ **1** Ⓑ① mainly UK (US **allowance**) an amount of money which parents regularly give to their child to spend as they choose: *My mum gives me £5 a week pocket money.* **ADULT'S MONEY** ▷ **2** money for spending on your own personal things: *I make a little pocket money delivering catalogues.* **3** UK informal not enough money: *I work really hard at this job, and all I get paid is pocket money.*

ˈpocket-sized adj small enough to fit in your pocket: *pocket-sized dictionaries*

ˌpocket ˈveto noun [C usually singular] US a way that a government can stop a law from being introduced by deliberately failing to sign it before the government finishes its business for the year

pockmark /ˈpɒk.mɑːk/ Ⓤⓢ /ˈpɑːk.mɑːrk/ noun [C] a small hollow on your skin that is left after a spot caused by a disease, such as CHICKENPOX or SMALLPOX, has HEALED: *a face covered with pockmarks*

pockmarked /ˈpɒk.mɑːkt/ Ⓤⓢ /ˈpɑːk.mɑːrkt/ adj (also **pocked**) **1** marked with pockmarks: *a pockmarked face* **2** describes a surface with a lot of holes or low areas in it: *The houses in the village were pockmarked **with** bullet holes.*

pod /pɒd/ Ⓤⓢ /pɑːd/ noun [C] **PLANT** ▷ **1** a long, narrow, flat part of some plants, such as beans and PEAS, that contains the seeds and usually has a thick skin: *seed pods* ◦ *a pea/vanilla pod* **AIRCRAFT** ▷ **2** a long, narrow container that is fixed to an aircraft for carrying engines, weapons, extra fuel, etc.: *an escape/storage/accommodation pod* ◦ *a space pod* **WHALES/**

DOLPHINS ▷ **3** a group of sea mammals such as WHALES or DOLPHINS

podcast /ˈpɒd.kɑːst/ (US) /ˈpɑːd.kæst/ **noun** [C] a radio programme that is stored in a DIGITAL form (= one using signals in the form of numbers) that you can DOWNLOAD from the internet and play on a computer or on an MP3 PLAYER • **podcasting** /-kɑːst.ɪŋ/ (US) /-kæst.ɪŋ/ **noun** [U] the process of making DIGITAL recordings of radio programmes that people can DOWNLOAD from the internet

podgy /ˈpɒdʒ.i/ (US) /ˈpɑː.dʒi/ **adj** UK informal (mainly US **pudgy**) slightly fat: *a podgy face* ◦ *pudgy fingers* • **podginess** /-nəs/ **noun** [U] UK (mainly US **pudginess**)

podiatrist /pəˈdaɪ.ə.trɪst/ **noun** [C] mainly US for **chiropodist** • **podiatry** /-tri/ **noun** [U] mainly US

podium /ˈpəʊ.di.əm/ (US) /ˈpoʊ-/ **noun** [C] (plural **podiums** or **podia**) a raised area on which a person stands to speak to a large number of people, to CONDUCT music, or to receive a prize in a sports competition: *Tears ran down her face as she stood on the winner's podium.*

poem /ˈpəʊ.ɪm/ (US) /ˈpoʊ.əm/ **noun** [C] (B1) a piece of writing in which the words are arranged in separate lines, often ending in RHYME, and are chosen for their sound and for the images and ideas they suggest: *a book of love poems* ◦ *The poet recited some of her recent poems.*

poet /ˈpəʊ.ɪt/ (US) /ˈpoʊ.ət/ **noun** [C] (B1) a person who writes poems

poetic /pəʊˈet.ɪk/ (US) /poʊˈet̬-/ **adj** (also **poetical**) **1** (C2) like or relating to poetry or poets: *a collection of Dryden's poetical works (= poems)* ◦ *The story is written in richly poetic **language**.* **2** approving very beautiful or expressing emotion: *Deanne Sokolin creates abstract, mournfully poetic black-and-white images of wrapped objects.* • **poetically** /-ɪ.kəl.i/ **adv**

poˌetic ˈjustice **noun** [U] an occasion when something bad happens to a person who seems to deserve it, usually because of bad things that person has done: *What poetic justice that Brady has to go to court to plead to be allowed to die, just like his innocent victims pleaded to be allowed to live.*

poˌetic ˈlicence **noun** [U] the act by a writer or poet of changing facts or rules to make a story or poem more interesting or effective: *She used a fair amount of poetic licence when describing her life in rural France.*

ˌpoet ˈlaureate **noun** [C usually singular] in the UK, a poet given a special position by the king or queen, who is asked to write poems about important public occasions

poetry /ˈpəʊ.ɪ.tri/ (US) /ˈpoʊ.ə-/ **noun** [U] **1** (B1) poems in general as a form of literature: *contemporary poetry and prose* ◦ *She started writing poetry at a young age.* **2** a very beautiful or emotional quality: *This film **has** a savage poetry and brilliance.*

po-faced /ˌpəʊˈfeɪst/ (US) /ˌpoʊ-/ **adj** **1** UK informal disapproving too serious and disapproving: *Two po-faced men came to inspect the house.* ◦ *The film is serious but not po-faced.* **2** informal describes someone whose face shows a serious, disapproving, or empty expression: *She **remained** po-faced all evening, even when the rest of us were in stitches at Bob's jokes.*

pogo stick /ˈpəʊ.ɡəʊˌstɪk/ (US) /ˈpoʊ.ɡoʊ-/ **noun** [C] a children's toy made of a long metal stick with a bar to hold across the top, and a large spring and a bar for your feet at the bottom, used to BOUNCE around on

pogrom /ˈpɒɡ.rəm/ (US) /ˈpoʊ.ɡrəm/ **noun** [C] an act of organized cruel behaviour or killing that is done to a large group of people because of their race or religion

poignant /ˈpɔɪ.njənt/ **adj** causing or having a very sharp feeling of sadness: *The photograph awakens poignant memories of happier days.* ◦ ***It** is especially poignant **that** he died on the day before the wedding.* • **poignancy** /-njən.si/ **noun** [U] *The poem has **a** haunting poignancy.* • **poignantly** /-li/ **adv**

poinsettia /ˌpɔɪnˈset.i.ə/ (US) /-ˈset̬-/ **noun** [C] a tropical plant with groups of bright red leaves which look like flowers

point /pɔɪnt/ **noun; verb**

▸**noun** **IDEA EXPRESSED** ▷ **1** (B1) [C] an idea, opinion, or piece of information that is said or written: *I'd like to discuss the first point in your essay.* ◦ *You **made** some interesting points in your speech.* **2 the/sb's point** (B2) the meaning or most important part of what someone says or writes: *The point is, if you don't claim the money now you might never get it.* ◦ *I think you **missed** (= did not understand) the point of what she was saying.* ◦ *I **take** your point/Point **taken** (= I understand that what you are saying is important).* ◦ *Please **get to** the point (= say the thing that is most important to you).* ◦ *He hasn't got much money, but that's not the point (= that is not the important thing).* **3** (B1) [S] an opinion or fact that deserves to be considered seriously, or which other people agree is true: *Yes, I can **see** your point/you've **got** a point **there**.* ◦ *OK, you've **made** your point (= told us your opinion) – there's no need to go on about it.* **4 beside the point** not important or not related to the subject being discussed: *The fact that he doesn't want to come is beside the point – he should have been invited.* **5 that's a (good) point** (B2) said to show that what someone has just said is true or important: *'We'll take the bus.' 'But we haven't got any money for the fare.' 'That's a point.'* **TIME/PLACE** ▷ **6** (B2) [C] a particular time or stage reached in a process: ***At** that point, a soldier opened fire on the car.* ◦ *I was completely lost at one point.* ◦ [+ question word] *It was so confusing that eventually it **got to** the point **wh**ere no one knew what was going on.* ◦ *I said I'd tell her the bad news, but when **it came to the point** (= when I had to do it), I couldn't.* **7** [C] a particular place: *the point where the road bends* ◦ *This is a good point from which to watch the race.* **8 boiling, melting, freezing, etc. point** the temperature at which a substance boils, melts, freezes, etc. **PURPOSE** ▷ **9** (B2) [S or U] purpose or usefulness: [+ -ing verb] informal *There's no point argu**ing** about it – we're going and that's that.* ◦ *I'd like to write to him, but **what's the** point? He never writes back.* ◦ *I see little point **in** discuss**ing** this further.* **UNIT** ▷ **10** (B1) [C] a mark or unit for counting, especially how much a person or team has scored in a sport: *The youngest skier won the most points.* ◦ *He won the world heavyweight boxing championship **on** points (= as a result of the points that he had won).* ◦ *Interest rates have risen by two percentage points (= two percent).* **11** [C] specialized a unit used for measuring the size of printed letters, equal to about 0.3 mm: *The large letters are **in** 7.5 point type, and the small letters are **in** 6 point.* **SHARP END** ▷ **12** (B2) [C] the sharp end of something, such as a knife: *The knife landed with its point sticking into the floor.* ◦ *Be careful with that needle – it has a very sharp point.* → See also **gunpoint** **CHARACTERISTIC** ▷ **13** (B2) [C] a particular quality or characteristic of a person or thing: *There are various points to look out for when you're judging dogs in a competition.* ◦ *He's boring, but I suppose he has his **good** points.* ◦ *I think her kindness is one of her **strong** points (= one of her good qualities).* **PIECE OF LAND** ▷ **14** [C] a long, thin area of land that stretches out into the sea: *Spurn Point* **SIGN ▷ 15** B2 [C] a small, round spot that is used in numbers to separate whole numbers from parts of numbers: *One kilogram equals two point two (= 2.2) pounds.* ◦ *The error occurred when someone left out the **decimal** point.* **FEET ▷ 16 points** [plural] specialized the toes of a BALLET dancer's shoes: *She is learning how to dance on her points.* **ELECTRIC ▷ 17** [C] UK a SOCKET to which a wire from a piece of electrical equipment is connected in order to supply it with electricity or a radio, television, or other signal: *a TV antenna point* **18** [C] specialized in some car engines, either of two parts that allow or prevent the flow of electricity: *He checked the points and plugs and topped up the oil.* **RAILWAY ▷ 19 points** [plural] mainly UK (US usually **switches**) a place on a railway track where the RAILS (= metal bars on which the trains travel) can be moved to allow a train to change from one track to another: *The train rattled as it went over the points.* **MARK ▷ 20** [C] a small, round mark on a line, plan, or map to show the position of something: *Join the points A and B together on the diagram with a straight line.* **21** C2 [C] a mark on a COMPASS that shows direction, such as north, south, east, and west **22** [C] a very small, round light that you can see in the distance: *I could just make out the tiny points of a car's headlights far away.*

IDIOMS **be on the point of (doing) sth** B2 to be going to do something very soon: *As we were on the point of giving up hope, a letter arrived.* ◦ *She was so tired that she was on the point of collapse.* • **make a point of doing sth** C1 to always do something or to take particular care to do something: *She makes a point of keeping all her shopping receipts.* • **my point exactly** said in answer to something that someone has just said when you believe it yourself, or when you have said it yourself earlier: *'So even if we got the funding, we still couldn't get the project started.' 'My point exactly.'* • **to the point** C2 expressing something very important or suitable for the subject being discussed: *Her comments on my work were very apt and to the point.* • **up to a point** B2 partly, or to a limited degree: *Of course there is some truth in all this, but **only** up to a point.* ◦ *The new traffic scheme worked up to a point, but it had its problems.*

►**verb 1** A2 [I] to direct other people's attention to something by holding out your finger towards it: *'Look at that!' she said, pointing **at** the hole in the door.* ◦ *Small children are often told that it's rude to point.* **2** B1 [T] to hold something out in the direction of someone or something: *He said that the man had pointed a knife **at** him.* **3** B1 [I] If something points in a particular direction, it is turned towards that direction: *The road sign points left.* ◦ *All the cars were pointing in the same direction.* ◦ *There was an arrow pointing **to** the door.*

> **!** Common mistake: **point or point out?**
>
> **Warning:** choose the correct verb!
>
> To talk about making a person notice something, or telling someone about some information, don't say 'point', say **point out**:
>
> ~~*I would like to point a number of mistakes in your article.*~~
>
> *I would like to point out a number of mistakes in your article.*

PHRASAL VERBS **point (sth/sb) out** to make a person notice someone or something, usually by telling them where they are or by holding up one of your fingers towards them: *If you see her, please point her out **to** me.* ◦ *The tour guide pointed out the inscription that runs round the inside of the dome.* • **point sth out** B2 to tell someone about some information, often because you believe they do not know it or have forgotten it: [+ that] *He was planning to book a rock-climbing holiday, till I pointed out **that** Denis is afraid of heights.* ◦ [+ question word] *I feel I should point out **how** dangerous it is.* • **point to/towards sth** to make it seem likely that a particular fact is true or that a particular event will happen: *All the evidence points to suicide.* • **point sth up** formal to emphasize a problem or fact, so that people notice it more: *It was a badly researched documentary which glossed over important questions while pointing up trivial ones.*

ˌpoint-ˈblank adv [before noun], adj **CLOSE ▷ 1** describes shooting from a gun that is FIRED from extremely close to the target or when almost touching it: *Two bullets were **fired** into the car **at** point-blank **range**.* ◦ *a point-blank shot* **NOT POLITE ▷ 2** saying something very clearly in very few words, without trying to be polite or pleasant: *He asked me to work at the weekend, but I **refused** point-blank.*

pointed /ˈpɔɪn.tɪd/ US /-t̬ɪd/ adj **SHARP END ▷ 1** A pointed object has a thin, sharp end or becomes much narrower at one end: *He's got funny little pointed ears.* **CRITICISM ▷ 2** describes a remark, question, or manner that is intended as a criticism of the person it is directed to: *My aunt made a few pointed remarks about my taste in clothes.*

pointedly /ˈpɔɪn.tɪd.li/ US /-t̬ɪd-/ adv in a very obvious way, usually to express criticism or disapproval: *He pointedly ignored her after the show.*

pointer /ˈpɔɪn.təʳ/ US /-t̬ɚ/ noun [C] **STICK ▷ 1** something that is used for pointing at things, such as a long, thin stick that you hold to direct attention to a place on a map or words on a board, or a CURSOR **INFORMATION ▷ 2** a helpful piece of advice or information: *This booklet gives some useful pointers **on** what to expect when you arrive.* **3** something which shows you an existing or developing situation: *The performance of the car industry is a (good) pointer to the general economic health of the country.* **DOG ▷ 4** a hunting dog that has been trained to stand very still with its nose pointing towards the animals and birds that are being hunted

pointillism /ˈpɔɪn.tɪ.lɪ.zᵊm/, /ˈpwæn-/ US /ˈpwæn.tə.lɪ-/ noun [U] specialized a style of painting developed in France at the end of the 19th century in which a painting is created out of small spots of pure colour which seem to mix when seen from far away • **pointillist** /-lɪst/ adj, noun [C] specialized

pointless /ˈpɔɪnt.ləs/ adj C1 Something that is pointless has no purpose and it is a waste of time doing it: *This is a pointless **exercise**.* ◦ ***It** seemed pointless **to** continue.* ◦ informal ***It's** pointless argu**ing** with him.* • **pointlessly** /-li/ adv *Innocent lives were cruelly and pointlessly wiped out.* • **pointlessness** /-nəs/ noun [U] *a poem about the pointlessness of life*

ˌpoint of no reˈturn noun [S] the stage at which it is no longer possible to stop what you are doing and when its effects cannot now be avoided or prevented: *Russia, he said, had **reached** the point of no return on the road to reform and had to go forward.* ◦ *Scientists fear that global warming has gone beyond the point of no return.*

ˌpoint of ˈorder noun [C usually singular] formal an occasion on which a person in a formal meeting states their belief that a rule of the meeting has been broken: *I would like to **raise** a point of order.*

ˌpoint of ˈview noun [C] (plural **points of view**) **1** B2 a way of considering something: ***From** a purely*

P

practical point of view, the house is too small. ◦ From a medical point of view, there was no need for the operation. **2** B2 an opinion: *You have to be willing to* ***see*** *(= understand) other people's points of view. ◦ I appreciate that* ***from*** *your point of view it's an unwelcome development.*

> **! Common mistake: point of view**
>
> **Remember:** use the correct preposition.
>
> Don't say 'in someone's point of view', say **from someone's point of view:**
>
> *From my point of view, it would be better to start straightaway.*

pointy /ˈpɔɪn.ti/ US /-t̬i/ adj informal shaped into a point: *She was wearing a pointy hat.*

poise /pɔɪz/ noun [U] approving calm confidence in a person's way of behaving, or a quality of GRACE (= moving in an attractive way) and balance in the way a person holds or moves their body: *He looked embarrassed for a moment, then quickly regained his poise. ◦ Her confidence and poise show that she is a top model.*

poised /pɔɪzd/ adj **1** [after verb] describes an object or a part of your body that is completely still but ready to move at any moment: *My pencil was poised over the page, ready to take down her words.* **2** [after verb] ready to do a particular thing at any moment: [+ to infinitive] *The company is poised* ***to*** *launch its new advertising campaign. ◦ The military forces are poised* ***for*** *attack.* **3** approving showing very calm and controlled behaviour

poison /ˈpɔɪ.zən/ noun; verb

▸noun [C or U] B2 a substance that can make people or animals ill or kill them if they eat or drink it: *The pest control officer put bowls of rat poison in the attic. ◦ Her drink had been laced with a* ***deadly*** *poison.*

IDIOM **name your poison** (also **what's your poison?**) used to ask what type of alcoholic drink someone would like

P

▸verb [T] **ADD SUBSTANCE** ▷ **1** B2 to kill a person or animal or to make them very ill by giving them poison: *Four members of the family had been poisoned, but not fatally.* **2** B2 to put poison in someone's food or drink: *He said that someone had poisoned his coffee.* **3** B2 to add dangerous chemicals or other harmful substances to something such as water or air: *The chemical leak had poisoned the water supply.* **SPOIL** ▷ **4** to spoil a friendship or another situation, by making it very unpleasant: *The long dispute has poisoned relations between the two countries.*

IDIOM **poison sb's mind** disapproving to make someone believe unpleasant things about another person that are not true: *Don't listen to her lies – she's just trying to poison your mind* ***against*** *me.*

ˌpoisoned ˈchalice noun [S] something that seems very good when it is first received, but in fact does great harm to the person who receives it: *The leadership of the party turned out to be a poisoned chalice.*

poisoner /ˈpɔɪ.zən.əʳ/ US /-ɚ/ noun [C] a person who has killed or harmed someone using poison

ˌpoison ˈgas noun [U] a gas that is used to kill people, especially in a war

poisoning /ˈpɔɪ.zən.ɪŋ/ noun [U] an illness caused by eating, drinking, or breathing a dangerous substance: *alcohol/lead poisoning*

ˌpoison ˈivy noun [C or U] a North American plant which causes your skin to ITCH and turn red if you touch its leaves

poisonous /ˈpɔɪ.zən.əs/ adj **1** B2 very harmful and able to cause illness or death: *poisonous chemicals ◦ Can you tell the difference between poisonous mushrooms and edible varieties?* **2** B2 A poisonous animal or insect uses poison in order to defend itself: *a poisonous snake* **3** very unpleasant and unkind: *He said some poisonous things to me.*

ˌpoison-ˈpen ˌletter noun [C] a letter in which very unkind or unpleasant things are written about the person it is sent to, in order to offend or upset them

poke /pəʊk/ US /poʊk/ verb; noun

▸verb **PUSH** ▷ **1** [T] to push a finger or other pointed object quickly into someone or something: *You'll poke someone* ***in*** *the eye with that umbrella if you're not careful! ◦ Two kids were poking a stick* ***into*** *the drain.* **APPEAR** ▷ **2** [I or T, usually + adv/prep] to (cause something to) appear or stretch out from behind or through something else: *Cathy poked her head round the door to say hello. ◦ The first green shoots are poking* ***through*** *the soil/****up****.*

IDIOM **poke fun at sb** to make someone seem stupid by making jokes about them or laughing unkindly at them

PHRASAL VERB **poke around** (UK also **poke about**) to search for something by moving things about, usually not in a very careful or organized way: *I was poking about* ***in*** *the drawer, looking for the key, when I found this!*

▸noun [C] the act of poking someone or something: *She* ***gave*** *me a poke* ***in*** *the stomach.*

poker /ˈpəʊ.kəʳ/ US /ˈpoʊ.kɚ/ noun **GAME** ▷ **1** [U] a game played with cards in which people try to win money from each other **TOOL** ▷ **2** [C] a long, thin metal stick that you use to move around coal or wood in a fire so that it burns better

ˈpoker-ˌfaced adj describes someone whose face does not show what they are thinking or feeling: *She sat poker-faced all the way through the film.* • **ˈpoker ˌface** noun [C] *to wear/keep a poker face*

poky (**pokier**, **pokiest**) (also **pokey**) /ˈpəʊ.ki/ US /ˈpoʊ-/ adj **SMALL** ▷ **1** UK informal describes a room, house, or other place that is unpleasantly small and uncomfortable: *They live in a poky little flat.* **SLOW** ▷ **2** US informal slow: *I wish you wouldn't be so poky when you're getting ready.* **FAST** ▷ **3** UK informal (of a car) fast: *a poky two-litre petrol engine*

polar /ˈpəʊ.ləʳ/ US /ˈpoʊ.lɚ/ adj **PLACE** ▷ **1** relating to the North or South Pole or the areas around them: *the polar ice caps* **OPPOSITE** ▷ **2** Polar opposites are complete opposites: *The novel deals with the polar opposites of love and hate.*

ˌpolar ˈbear noun [C] B2 a BEAR with white fur that lives in the Arctic

polar bear

polarity /pəˈlær.ə.ti/ US /poʊˈler.ə.t̬i/ noun [U] **OPPOSITE** ▷ **1** the quality of being opposite: *The film is based on the polarity of the two main characters.* **PLACE** ▷ **2** the quality of having two poles: *reversed polarity*

polarize (UK usually **polarise**) /ˈpəʊ.lə.raɪz/ US /ˈpoʊ-/ verb [T] to cause something, especially something that contains different people or opinions, to divide into two completely opposing groups: *The debate is becoming polarized and there seems to be no middle ground.* • **polarization** (UK usually **polarisation**) /ˌpəʊ.lə.raɪˈzeɪ.ʃən/ US /ˌpoʊ.lɚ.ə-/ noun [U] *The polarization* of society **into** rich and poor can clearly be seen in the city centres.

Polaroid /ˈpəʊ.lər.ɔɪd/ US /ˈpoʊ.lə.rɔɪd/ **noun** **CAMERA** ▷ **1** [C] trademark a camera that takes a picture and prints it after a few seconds, or a photograph taken with this type of camera: *Did you take these with a Polaroid?* ◦ *Please send us your Polaroids and the best ones will be published.* **GLASSES** ▷ **2** **Polaroids** [plural] mainly UK trademark dark glasses that have been treated with a substance that reduces the amount of reflected light that reaches the eyes: *I always wear Polaroids when I'm driving.*

pole /pəʊl/ US /poʊl/ **noun** [C] **STICK** ▷ **1** C2 a long, thin stick of wood or metal, often used standing straight up in the ground to support things: *a telegraph/electricity pole* ◦ *A flag fluttered from a 40-foot pole.* **PLACE** ▷ **2** either of the two points at the most northern and most southern ends of the Earth, around which the Earth turns: *the North/South Pole* ◦ *Most weather satellites are stationed over the Equator or travel over the poles.* **OPPOSITE** ▷ **3** either of two completely opposite or different opinions, positions, or qualities: *These two men might be thought to represent the opposite poles of economic ideology.*

IDIOM **poles apart** C2 completely opposite: *My sister and I are poles apart in personality.*

poleaxe /ˈpəʊl.æks/ US /ˈpoʊl-/ **verb** [T] **1** to hit someone so hard that they fall down: *Blake was poleaxed by a missile thrown from the crowd.* **2** informal to give someone such a great shock that they do not know what to do: *He was completely poleaxed when his wife left him.*

polecat /ˈpəʊl.kæt/ US /ˈpoʊl-/ **noun** [C] a small, FIERCE wild animal that lives in Europe, Asia, and North Africa, with dark brown fur and a strong, unpleasant smell

polemic /pəˈlem.ɪk/ **noun** [C] formal a piece of writing or a speech in which a person strongly attacks or defends a particular opinion, person, idea, or set of beliefs: *She has published a fierce anti-war polemic.* • **polemical** /-ɪ.kəl/ **adj** *a polemical essay*

polenta /pəˈlen.tə/ US /poʊˈlen.t̬ə/ **noun** [U] **1** a yellow food made from MAIZE flour: *grilled polenta* **2** flour made from MAIZE, used in Italian cooking

ˈpole poˌsition **noun** [C or U] the starting position on the inside of the front row in a motor race or similar racing competition, considered to be best and given to the competitor with the fastest time in the previous race: *Alonso is* **in** *pole position for today's Monaco Grand Prix.*

the ˈPole ˌStar **noun** [S] a star that can be seen by people in the northern part of the world and always shows where north lies

ˈpole ˌvault **noun** [S] a sports competition in which you jump over a high bar using a long stick to push yourself off the ground: *She won silver in the pole vault for Australia.* ◦ *world pole vault champion* • **ˈpole-ˌvaulter** **noun** [C]

police /pəˈliːs/ **noun; verb**

▸**noun** [plural] **1** A2 the official organization that is responsible for protecting people and property, making people obey the law, finding out about and solving crime, and catching people who have committed a crime: *I think you should call* **the** *police.* ◦ **The** *police are investigating fraud allegations against him.* **2** members of this organization: *There should be more police patrolling the area on foot.*

▸**verb** [T] **1** to control or guard a public event or area by using members of the police or a similar force: *The march will be heavily policed by an anti-riot unit.* **2** to control the way in which a possibly dangerous substance is dealt with or a dangerous activity is done: *The use of these chemicals must be carefully policed.*

poˈlice ˌcar **noun** [C] an official car used by the police

poˌlice ˈconstable **noun** [C] (abbreviation **PC**) in the UK, a police officer of the lowest rank

poˈlice deˌpartment **noun** [C] US in the US, the police force in an area or city

poˈlice ˌforce **noun** [C, + sing/pl verb] the police in a country or area: *More young people are needed to* **join** *the police force.* ◦ *the Metropolitan Police Force*

policeman /pəˈliːs.mən/ **noun** [C] (plural **-men** /-mən/) A2 a male member of a police force

poˈlice ˌofficer **noun** [C] A2 a male or female member of the police force

poˈlice ˌstate **noun** [C usually singular] disapproving a country in which the government uses the police to severely limit people's freedom

poˈlice ˌstation **noun** [C] A2 the local office of the police in a town or part of a city: *He was taken to the police station for questioning.*

policewoman /pəˈliːsˌwʊm.ən/ **noun** [C] (plural **-women** /-wɪmɪn/) A2 a female member of a police force

policy /ˈpɒl.ə.si/ US /ˈpɑː.lə-/ **noun** [C] **PLAN** ▷ **1** B2 a set of ideas or a plan of what to do in particular situations that has been agreed officially by a group of people, a business organization, a government, or a political party: *They believe that the European Community needs a common foreign and security policy.* ◦ *What is your party's policy* **on** *immigration?* **DOCUMENT** ▷ **2** C1 a document showing an agreement you have made with an INSURANCE company: *You should check your policy to see if you're covered for flood damage.*

ˈpolicy-ˌmaking **noun** [U] the activity of deciding on new policies

polio /ˈpəʊ.li.əʊ/ US /ˈpoʊ.li.oʊ/ **noun** [U] (specialized **poliomyelitis**) a serious infectious disease that can cause permanent PARALYSIS (= being unable to move the body): *a polio vaccination programme*

polish /ˈpɒl.ɪʃ/ US /ˈpɑː.lɪʃ/ **verb; noun**

▸**verb** [T] to rub something using a piece of cloth or brush to clean it and make it shine: *to polish the furniture* ◦ *Polish your shoes regularly to protect the leather.*

PHRASAL VERBS **polish sth off** informal to finish something quickly and easily, especially a lot of food or work: *He polished off the whole pie.* ◦ *I polished off three essays in one week.* • **polish sth/sb off** informal to defeat a competitor easily: *Arsenal polished off Chelsea 5–0 in Saturday's match.* • **polish sb off** mainly US informal to kill someone: *He was accused of polishing off his former partner.* • **polish sth up** **OBJECT** ▷ **1** to rub or brush an object to make it shine, especially a metal or wooden object: *Robert was polishing up some old silver candlesticks.* **SKILL** ▷ **2** to improve a skill, especially when you have allowed it to become less good over a period of time: *I really must polish up my Japanese before we visit Japan next year.*

▸**noun** **CLEANING** ▷ **1** [S] the act of cleaning something by rubbing it: *I'll just* **give** *my shoes* **a** *quick polish.* **2** [C or U] a cream or other substance that you use to clean something: *shoe/furniture/silver polish* **SKILL** ▷ **3** [U] the quality of having been done in a way that shows skill and experience: *It's a lively, good-hearted film but*

P

it lacks a little polish. ◦ This is a musical with polish and wit.

polished /'pɒl.ɪʃt/ (US) /'pɑː.lɪʃt/ adj CLEAN ▷ **1** having been polished: *a highly polished floor* SKILLED ▷ **2** describes a person who has style and confidence: *He's suave, polished, and charming.* **3** showing great skill: *The dancers gave a polished performance.*

the politburo /'pɒl.ɪtˌbjʊə.rəʊ/ (US) /'pɑː.lɪtˌbjʊr.oʊ/ noun [S, + sing/pl verb] the main government group in a Communist country, which makes all the important decisions

polite /pə'laɪt/ adj **1** A2 behaving in a way that is socially correct and shows understanding of and care for other people's feelings: *I'm afraid I wasn't very polite to her.* ◦ *She sent me a polite letter thanking me for my invitation.* ◦ *He was too polite to point out my mistake.* **2** socially correct rather than friendly: *polite conversation* **3 polite society/company** old-fashioned or humorous people who have been taught how to behave in a socially correct way: *Sex never used to be discussed **in** polite society.* • **politeness** /-nəs/ noun [U]

Other ways of saying polite

The adjectives **courteous**, **respectful**, and **well mannered** are sometimes used when someone is polite and shows respect for other people:

*Although she often disagreed with me, she was always **courteous**.*

*They were quiet, **well-mannered** children.*

A man who is polite to a woman is sometimes described as **chivalrous**:

*He held open the door in that **chivalrous** way of his.*

Someone who is polite but in a formal and not very friendly way can be described as **civil**:

*Try to at least be **civil** toward him even if you don't like him.*

Conversation which is polite and calm is sometimes described as **civilized**:

*Let's discuss this in a **civilized** manner.*

politely /pə'laɪt.li/ adv **1** B1 in a polite way: *He told them politely to leave him in peace.* **2** without enthusiasm: *The audience clapped politely.*

politic /'pɒl.ɪ.tɪk/ (US) /'pɑː.lə-/ adj [+ to infinitive] formal wise and showing the ability to make the right decisions: ***It** would not be politic **for** you **to** be seen there.*

political /pə'lɪt.ɪ.kəl/ (US) /-'lɪt̬.ə-/ adj B1 relating to politics: *political leaders* ◦ *There are two political parties in the US – the Democratic Party and the Republican Party.* ◦ *Education is back at the top of the political **agenda** (= the matters that the government is considering).* • **politically** /-i/ adv C1 *to be politically naive*

IDIOM **a political football** a problem that politicians from different parties argue about and try to use in order to get an advantage for themselves: *We don't want the immigration issue to become a political football.*

poˌlitical a'sylum noun [U] the protection given by a government to foreign people who have left their own country because they disagree with their own government: *The number of people **seeking** political asylum in Britain has risen dramatically.*

poˌlitically cor'rect adj (abbreviation **PC**) **1** describes someone who believes that language and actions which could be offensive to others, especially those relating to sex and race, should be avoided **2** describes a word or expression that is used instead of another one to avoid being offensive: *Some people think that 'fireman' is a sexist term, and prefer the politically correct term 'firefighter'.* • **poˌlitical cor'rectness** noun [U] *We can't even use the word 'chairman'! It's just political correctness **gone mad**!*

poˌlitical 'prisoner noun [C] someone who is put in prison for expressing disapproval of their own government, or for belonging to an organization, race, or social group not approved of by that government

poˌlitical 'science noun [U] the study of how people get or compete for power and how it is used in governing a country

politician /ˌpɒl.ɪ'tɪʃ.ən/ (US) /ˌpɑː.lə-/ noun [C] B1 a member of a government or law-making organization: *a distinguished/disgraced politician*

politicize (UK usually **politicise**) /pə'lɪt.ɪ.saɪz/ (US) /-'lɪt̬.ə-/ verb [T often passive] to make something or someone political, or more involved in or conscious of political matters: *The whole issue has become increasingly politicized.* ◦ *a highly politicized debate*

politicking /'pɒl.ɪ.tɪ.kɪŋ/ (US) /'pɑː.lə-/ noun [U] mainly disapproving the activity of trying to persuade or even force others to vote for a particular political party or CANDIDATE

politics /'pɒl.ɪ.tɪks/ (US) /'pɑː.lə-/ noun **1** B1 [U] the activities of the government, members of law-making organizations, or people who try to influence the way a country is governed: *Joe is very active in left-wing politics.* **2** [U] the job of holding a position of power in the government: *The group is campaigning to get more women into politics.* ◦ *He is planning to retire from politics next year.* **3** [U]the study of the ways in which a country is governed: *She read politics at Leicester University.* **4** [plural] **sb's politics** someone's opinions about how a country should be governed: *Her politics have become more liberal over the past few years.* **5** [plural] the relationships within a group or organization which allow particular people to have power over others: *I don't like to get involved in **office** politics.*

Word partners for politics

enter/go into/be involved in politics • *discuss/talk* politics • *local/national/regional* politics

IDIOM **play politics** UK to use a situation or the relationships between people for your own advantage: *He accused councillors of playing politics **with** children's education.*

polity /'pɒl.ə.ti/ (US) /'pɑː.lə.t̬i/ noun [C] specialized a society or state considered as a political unit: *a democratic polity*

polka /'pɒl.kə/ (US) /'poʊl-/ noun [C] a fast, active dance that was popular in the 19th century, or a piece of music that can be used for this dance

'polka ˌdot noun [C usually plural] one of a large number of small, round spots that are printed in a regular pattern on cloth: *a shocking pink dress with white polka dots* ◦ *a polka-dot bikini/bow tie*

poll /pəʊl/ (US) /poʊl/ noun; verb

▸**noun 1** [C] a study in which people are asked for their opinions about a subject or person: *We're **carrying out/conducting** a poll to find out what people think about abortion.* ◦ *The latest **opinion** poll puts the Democrats in the lead.* **2 the polls** [plural] the places where people vote in a political election: *The TV stations agreed not to announce the projected winner until after the polls closed.* **3 go to the polls** to vote: *The country will go to the polls on 13 September.*

▸verb [T] **ELECTION** ▷ **1** When a person or a political party polls a particular number of votes in an election, they receive that number: *With nearly all the votes counted, Mr Soto had polled 67 percent of the vote.* **OPINION** ▷ **2** to ask a person for their opinion as part of a general study of what people think about a subject: *Half the people polled said they would pay more for environmentally friendly food.*

pollack /ˈpɒl.æk/ (US) /ˈpɑː.læk/ noun [C or U] a large sea fish that you can eat

pollen /ˈpɒl.ən/ (US) /ˈpɑː.lən/ noun [U] a powder produced by the male part of a flower that causes the female part of the same type of flower to produce seeds. It is carried by insects or the wind. • **pollinate** /ˈpɒl.ə.neɪt/ (US) /ˈpɑː.lə-/ verb [T] *Bees pollinate the plants by carrying the pollen from one flower to another.* • **pollination** /ˌpɒl.əˈneɪ.ʃən/ (US) /ˌpɑː.lə-/ noun [U]

ˈpollen ˌcount noun [C] a measurement of the amount of pollen in the air: *The pollen count is high today, which is bad news for hay fever sufferers.*

ˈpolling ˌbooth noun [C] UK a small area with walls on three sides in a polling station where you can vote in private

ˈpolling ˌday noun [U] mainly UK (US usually **eˈlection ˌday**) the day when people vote in an election

ˈpolling ˌstation noun [C] (US also **ˈpolling ˌplace**) a place where people go to vote in an election

pollster /ˈpəʊl.stəʳ/ (US) /ˈpoʊl.stɚ/ noun [C] a person who does opinion polls

pollutant /pəˈluː.tənt/ (US) /-t̬ənt/ noun [C] a substance that pollutes: *Sulphur dioxide is one of several pollutants that are released into the atmosphere by coal-fired power stations.*

pollute /pəˈluːt/ verb [T] (B2) to make an area or substance, usually air, water, or earth, dirty or harmful to people, animals, and plants, especially by adding harmful chemicals: *The pesticides used on many farms are polluting the water supply.* ◦ *We won't invest in any company that pollutes the environment.* ◦ figurative *Many complain that broadcasters pollute the airwaves with sensationalism and sleaze.*

polluter /pəˈluː.təʳ/ (US) /-t̬ɚ/ noun [C] a person or organization that pollutes

pollution /pəˈluː.ʃən/ noun [U] (B1) damage caused to water, air, etc. by harmful substances or waste: *air/water pollution* ◦ *The manifesto includes tough measures to tackle road congestion and* ***environmental*** *pollution.*

Pollyanna /ˌpɒl.iˈæn.ə/ (US) /ˌpɑː.li-/ noun [C] old-fashioned a person who believes that good things are more likely to happen than bad things, even when this is very unlikely

polo /ˈpəʊ.ləʊ/ (US) /ˈpoʊ.loʊ/ noun [U] a game played between two teams who ride horses and carry long wooden hammers with which they hit a small, hard ball, trying to score goals: *Prince Charles is a keen polo player.*

ˈpolo ˌneck noun [C] UK (US **turtleneck**) **1** a high, round collar that folds over on itself and covers the neck **2** a JUMPER or shirt with a polo neck: *Why don't you wear your black polo neck?* • **ˈpolo-necked** adj [before noun] *a polo-necked jumper*

polonium /pəˈləʊ.ni.əm/ (US) /-ˈloʊ-/ noun [U] (symbol **Po**) a RADIOACTIVE chemical element that is found in URANIUM ORE

ˈpolo ˌshirt noun [C] an informal style of cotton shirt, with short sleeves, a collar, and some buttons at the neck

poltergeist /ˈpɒl.tə.gaɪst/ (US) /ˈpoʊl.t̬ɚ-/ noun [C] a spirit or force that moves furniture and throws objects around in a house

poly /ˈpɒl.i/ (US) /ˈpɑː.li/ noun [C] (plural **polys**) informal for **polytechnic**

poly- /pɒl.i-/ (US) /pɑː.li-/ prefix many: *a polytheistic (= believing in many gods) society* ◦ *a polymath (= person who knows a lot about many different subjects.)*

polyester /ˌpɒl.iˈes.təʳ/ (US) /ˌpɑː.liˈes.tɚ/ noun [U] a type of artificial cloth: *a polyester shirt*

polyethylene /ˌpɒl.iˈeθ.ɪ.liːn/ (US) /ˌpɑː.liˈeθ.ə-/ noun [U] US for **polythene**

polygamy /pəˈlɪg.ə.mi/ noun [U] the fact or custom of being married to more than one person at the same time • **polygamist** /-mɪst/ noun [C] • **polygamous** /-məs/ adj *a polygamous society*

polyglot /ˈpɒl.ɪ.glɒt/ (US) /ˈpɑː.lɪ.glɑːt/ adj formal **1** speaking or using several different languages **2** containing people from many different and DISTANT places: *New York is an exciting polyglot city.* • **polyglot** noun [C] *My tutor's something of a polyglot – she speaks seven languages.*

polygon /ˈpɒl.ɪ.gɒn/ (US) /ˈpɑː.lɪ.gɑːn/ noun [C] specialized a flat shape with three or more straight sides: *Triangles and squares are polygons.*

polygraph /ˈpɒl.ɪ.grɑːf/ (US) /ˈpɑː.lɪ.græf/ noun [C] specialized a **lie detector**

polyhedron /ˌpɒl.iˈhiː.drən/ (US) /ˌpɑː.liˈhiː.drɑːn/ noun [C] (plural **polyhedrons** or **polyhedra** /-drə/) specialized a solid shape with four or more flat surfaces: *A cube is a polyhedron.*

polymath /ˈpɒl.ɪ.mæθ/ (US) /ˈpɑː.lɪ-/ noun [C] formal approving a person who knows a lot about many different subjects

polymer /ˈpɒl.ɪ.məʳ/ (US) /ˈpɑː.lɪ.mɚ/ noun [C] specialized a chemical substance consisting of large MOLECULES made from many smaller and simpler MOLECULES: *Many polymers, such as nylon, are artificial.* ◦ *Proteins and DNA are* ***natural*** *polymers.*

polymorphous /ˌpɒl.ɪˈmɔː.fəs/ (US) /ˌpɑː.lɪˈmɔːr-/ adj formal having or experiencing many different forms or stages of development: *Intelligence is a polymorphous concept.*

polyp /ˈpɒl.ɪp/ (US) /ˈpɑː.lɪp/ noun [C] **ANIMAL** ▷ **1** a small, simple, tube-shaped water animal **GROWTH** ▷ **2** specialized a small mass of cells that grows in the body, and is usually not harmful

polyphony /pəˈlɪf.ən.i/ noun [U] specialized music in which several different tunes are played or sung at the same time • **polyphonic** /ˌpɒl.ɪˈfɒn.ɪk/ (US) /ˌpɑː.lɪˈfɑː.nɪk/ adj specialized *polyphonic ring tones* ◦ *a 32-voice polyphonic synthesizer*

polysaccharide /ˌpɒl.ɪˈsæk.ər.aɪd/ (US) /ˈpɑː.lɪ-/ noun [C] specialized a COMPLEX type of CARBOHYDRATE, such as STARCH and CELLULOSE, formed of large MOLECULES → Compare **monosaccharide**

polysemous /pəˈlɪs.ɪ.məs/ (US) /ˌpɑː.lɪˈsiː-/ adj A polysemous word has more than one meaning: *a highly polysemous word such as 'play'* • **polysemy** /-mi/ noun [U] the fact of having more than one meaning

polystyrene /ˌpɒl.ɪˈstaɪ.riːn/ (US) /ˌpɑː.lɪˈstaɪ-/ noun [U] (US usually trademark **Styrofoam**) a light, usually white plastic used especially for putting around delicate objects inside containers to protect them from damage, or for putting around something to prevent it from losing heat: *polystyrene cups/*

P

plates ◦ The ceiling was covered with polystyrene insulation tiles.

polysyllabic /ˌpɒl.ɪ.sɪˈlæb.ɪk/ ⓤⓢ /ˌpɑː.lɪ.sɪ-/ **adj** specialized containing three or more syllables: *The word 'internationalism' is polysyllabic.*

polytechnic /ˌpɒl.ɪˈtek.nɪk/ ⓤⓢ /ˌpɑː.lɪ-/ **noun** [C] (informal **poly**) (especially in Britain before 1992) a college where students study for degrees, especially in technical subjects, or train for particular types of work: *a polytechnic student/course ◦ I considered applying to university, but I eventually decided to go to the local poly.* → Compare **university**

polytheism /ˈpɒl.ɪ.θiː.ɪ.zᵊm/, /ˌpɒl.ɪˈθiː-/ ⓤⓢ /ˈpɑː.lɪ-/ **noun** [U] specialized belief in many different gods • **polytheistic** /ˌpɒl.ɪ.θiˈɪs.tɪk/ ⓤⓢ /ˌpɑː.lɪ-/ **adj** *Ancient Egyptian society was polytheistic.*

polythene /ˈpɒl.ɪ.θiːn/ ⓤⓢ /ˈpɑː.lɪ-/ **noun** [U] (US also **polyethylene**) a light, usually thin, soft plastic, often used for making bags or for keeping things dry or fresh: *a polythene **bag** ◦ They covered the broken windows with sheets of polythene.*

polytunnel /ˈpɒl.iˌtʌn.ᵊl/ ⓤⓢ /ˈpɑː.li-/ **noun** [C] a long, curved plastic structure that plants are grown under in order to protect them from the weather

polyunsaturate /ˌpɒl.i.ʌnˈsæt.jʊ.rət/ ⓤⓢ /ˌpɑː.li-/ **noun** [C usually plural, U] a type of fat found in some vegetable oils that is thought to be healthier than SATURATES (= fat from meat, milk, and cheese): *This margarine is **high in** polyunsaturates.* → Compare **saturate**

polyunsaturated /ˌpɒl.i.ʌnˈsætʃ.ᵊr.eɪ.tɪd/ ⓤⓢ /ˌpɑː.li.ʌnˈsætʃ.ə.reɪ.t̬ɪd/ **adj** specialized describes a fat or oil that has a chemical structure that does not easily change into CHOLESTEROL (= a substance containing a lot of fat that can cause heart disease) because it contains several DOUBLE BONDS: *polyunsaturated margarine/vegetable oil* → See also **monounsaturated**

polyurethane /ˌpɒl.ɪˈjʊə.rə.θeɪn/ ⓤⓢ /ˌpɑː.lɪˈjʊr.ə-/ **noun** [U] a plastic used especially as a type of VARNISH or as a protection for delicate objects

pom /pɒm/ ⓤⓢ /pɑːm/ **noun** [C] (also **pommy**) Australian English informal disapproving an English person

pomander /pəˈmæn.dəʳ/ ⓤⓢ /ˈpoʊ.mæn.dɚ/ **noun** [C] an object containing dried herbs, spices, flowers, etc., used to make a room, drawer, or cupboard smell pleasant

pomegranate /ˈpɒm.ɪˌɡræn.ɪt/ ⓤⓢ /ˈpɑːmˌɡræn-/ **noun** [C] a round, thick-skinned fruit containing a mass of red seeds and a lot of juice

pommel /ˈpɒm.ᵊl/ ⓤⓢ /ˈpʌm-/ **noun** [C] **1** the usually rounded part that sticks up at the front of a SADDLE (= seat for sitting on a horse) **2** the rounded part on the end of a SWORD handle

ˈpommel ˌhorse **noun** [C] a piece of equipment used in GYMNASTICS, that stands on four legs, and has two handles on the top that you hold while moving your body and legs around

pomp /pɒmp/ ⓤⓢ /pɑːmp/ **noun** [U] **1** impressive and colourful ceremonies, especially traditional ceremonies on public occasions: *The prime minister was received with all the traditional pomp **and ceremony** that is laid on for visiting heads of government. ◦ Despite all the pomp **of** his office/position, he has only limited powers.* **2 pomp and circumstance** formal ceremonies

pompadour /ˈpɒm.pə.dɔːʳ/ ⓤⓢ /ˈpɑːm.pə.dɔːr/ **noun** [C] US for **quiff**

pompom /ˈpɒm.pɒm/ ⓤⓢ /ˈpɑːm.pɑːm/ **noun** [C] a small ball of wool or other material used as a decoration, especially on the top of a hat

pompous /ˈpɒm.pəs/ ⓤⓢ /ˈpɑːm-/ **adj** disapproving too serious and full of importance: *He's a pompous old prig who's totally incapable of taking a joke. ◦ He can sometimes **sound** a bit pompous when he talks about acting.* • **pomposity** /pɒmˈpɒs.ə.ti/ ⓤⓢ /pɑːmˈpɑː.sə.t̬i/ **noun** [U] (also **pompousness** /-nəs/) • **pompously** /-li/ **adv** *He strode around pompously, telling everyone what to do.*

ponce /pɒns/ ⓤⓢ /pɑːns/ **noun; verb**

▸**noun** [C] **CRIMINAL** ▷ **1** UK informal a man who controls PROSTITUTES and takes a large part of the money that they earn for himself **MAN** ▷ **2** UK informal disapproving a man who does not behave, dress, or speak in a traditionally male way, especially one who behaves in a very careful way: *Don't be such a ponce! Pick the spider up – it won't hurt you!* • **poncy** /ˈpɒn.si/ ⓤⓢ /ˈpɑːn-/ **adj** UK informal disapproving *a poncy flowery shirt*

▸**verb**

PHRASAL VERB **ponce about/around** **LIKE A WOMAN** ▷ **1** UK informal disapproving If a man ponces about/around, he behaves or dresses more like a woman than like a man: *He was poncing around in a pair of fluffy slippers/yellow silk dressing gown.* **NOT HELPFUL** ▷ **2** informal disapproving to waste time doing silly things that do not achieve anything or help anyone: *There's no time for poncing around – we've got to get these boxes packed by this evening.*

poncho /ˈpɒn.tʃəʊ/ ⓤⓢ /ˈpɑːn.tʃoʊ/ **noun** [C] (plural **ponchos**) a piece of clothing made of a single piece of material, with a hole in the middle through which you put your head

poncho

pond /pɒnd/ ⓤⓢ /pɑːnd/ **noun** [C] B2 an area of water smaller than a lake, often artificially made: *a duck pond*

ponder /ˈpɒn.dəʳ/ ⓤⓢ /ˈpɑːn.dɚ/ **verb** [I or T] formal C2 to think carefully about something, especially for a noticeable length of time: *She sat back for a minute to ponder her next move in the game.*

ponderous /ˈpɒn.dᵊr.əs/ ⓤⓢ /ˈpɑːn.dɚ-/ **adj** formal mainly disapproving **1** slow and awkward because of being very heavy or large: *He had a rather slow and ponderous manner.* **2** If a book, speech, or style of writing or speaking is ponderous, it is boring because it is too slow, long, or serious: *The ponderous reporting style makes the evening news dull viewing.* • **ponderously** /-li/ **adv**

pong /pɒŋ/ ⓤⓢ /pɑːŋ/ **noun** [C] UK humorous an unpleasant smell: *What a pong!* • **pong** **verb** [I] UK humorous *After a couple of days of continuous use, the costumes began to pong.*

pontiff /ˈpɒn.tɪf/ ⓤⓢ /ˈpɑːn.t̬ɪf/ **noun** [C] formal for POPE (= leader of the Roman Catholic Church)

pontificate **verb; noun**

▸**verb** [I] /pɒnˈtɪf.ɪ.keɪt/ ⓤⓢ /pɑːn-/ disapproving to speak or write and give your opinion about something as if you knew everything about it and as if only your opinion was correct: *I think it should be illegal for non-parents to pontificate **on/about** parenting.*

▸**noun** [C] /pɒnˈtɪf.ɪ.kət/ ⓤⓢ /pɑːn-/ formal the period of office of a POPE (= leader of the Roman Catholic Church): *The decision was made during the pontificate of Pope John XX.*

pontoon /pɒnˈtuːn/ (US) /pɑːn-/ noun **BRIDGE** ▷ **1** [C] a small, flat boat or a metal structure of a similar shape used especially to form or support a temporary floating bridge: *Military engineers hurriedly constructed a pontoon* ***bridge*** *across the river.* **GAME** ▷ **2** [U] UK for **blackjack**

pony /ˈpəʊ.ni/ (US) /ˈpoʊ-/ noun [C] **ANIMAL** ▷ **1** (C1) a small type of horse: *As a young girl, she spent every weekend riding her pony.* **HAIR** ▷ **2** a **ponytail**

ponytail /ˈpəʊ.ni.teɪl/ (US) /ˈpoʊ.ni.teɪl/ noun [C] a hairstyle in which the hair is tied up high at the back of the head so that it hangs down like a horse's tail → Compare **pigtail, plait**

ˈpony ˌtrekking noun [U] UK riding horses through the countryside, especially as a holiday activity: *How much does it cost to* ***go*** *pony trekking for an afternoon?*

Ponzi scheme /ˈpɒn.ziˌskiːm/ (US) /ˈpɑːn-/ noun [C] a way of deceiving INVESTORS (= people who give money to a company hoping to get more back) by using the money they give to pay interest to existing customers rather than INVESTING it

poo /puː/ noun [C or U] UK (US **poop**) (a piece of) solid waste from the body: *Ugh, it looks like poo!* ◦ *Have you* ***done*** *a poo, Ellie?* • **poo** verb [I] UK informal *Ten minutes after we'd left home, Anna announced that she needed to poo.*

pooch /puːtʃ/ noun [C] informal mainly humorous a dog: *a* ***pampered*** *pooch* ◦ *a big cuddly/cute little pooch*

poodle /ˈpuː.dl/ noun [C] a dog with curly hair that is usually cut short, except on its head, tail, and legs: *a miniature poodle*

IDIOM **be sb's poodle** UK humorous disapproving to be too willing to support or be controlled by someone in authority: *They accused the Labour party of being the unions' poodle.*

poof /pʊf/ noun; exclamation

▸noun [C] (also **pouf**) (also **poofter**) mainly UK offensive a gay man

▸exclamation used to show that something has happened suddenly or by magic: *He waved his hand over the empty box and – poof! – a dove appeared.*

pooh /puː/ exclamation informal said when you smell something unpleasant: *Pooh! Something stinks in here.*

ˌpooh-ˈpooh verb [T] informal to express an opinion that an idea or suggestion is silly or not worth considering: *The government has pooh-poohed the idea that primary schools will begin to select pupils.*

pool /puːl/ noun; verb

▸noun **LIQUID** ▷ **1** (B2) [C] a small area of usually still water: *We looked for crabs in the* ***rock*** *pools along the seashore.* **2** (B2) [C] a small amount of liquid on a surface: *a pool of blood/oil* ◦ figurative *a pool of light* **3** (A2) [C] a **swimming pool**: *I spent most of my holiday lying/sunbathing by the pool.* **COLLECTION** ▷ **4** [C] a number of people or a quantity of a particular thing, such as money, collected together for shared use by several people or organizations: *Patrick crashed a Ford that he'd borrowed from the* ***car*** *pool at work.* ◦ *As unemployment rises, the pool of cheap labour increases.* **MONEY** ▷ **5 the pools** [plural] (also **football pools**) UK a type of GAMBLING in which people risk a small amount of money and try to guess the results of football matches correctly and win a lot of money: *They* ***do*** *the pools every week.* **GAME** ▷ **6** (B1) [U] a game in which two people use CUES (= long thin poles) to hit 16 coloured balls into six holes around the edge of a large table covered in soft cloth: *a pool table/room/hall* ◦ mainly US informal *Do you want to* ***shoot*** *(= play) some pool?* → Compare **snooker**

▸verb [T] to collect something such as money in order for it to be used by several different people or groups: *Three schools in Putney have pooled their* ***resources/money*** *in order to buy an area of waste ground and turn it into a sports field.*

poop /puːp/ noun; verb

▸noun **SOLID WASTE** ▷ **1** [U] mainly US informal solid waste, especially from dogs and found on the ground in public places **INFORMATION** ▷ **2 the poop** US old-fashioned slang information: *Did you get the poop on all the candidates?*

▸verb **TIRED** ▷ **1 be pooped** US informal to be very tired: *I'm pooped! I must get some sleep.* **SOLID WASTE** ▷ **2** [I] mainly US informal to pass solid waste from the body: *Your puppy's just pooped right outside my front door.*

PHRASAL VERBS **poop out** US informal to become very tired and unable to continue working or operating: *I just poop out if I stay up too late.* • **poop sb out** US informal to make someone very tired: *All that dancing has really pooped me* ***out***.

pooper-scooper /ˈpuː.pəˌskuː.pər/ (US) /ˈpuː.pɚˌskuː.pɚ/ noun [C] (also **ˈpoop scoop**) a tool like a small SPADE, used for picking up and removing a dog's solid waste

Other ways of saying poor

Penniless and **impoverished** are more formal alternatives to 'poor':

I was a ***penniless*** *student.*

Benefits should be targeted at the most ***impoverished*** *families.*

In informal English, **broke** or the phrase **strapped (for cash)** are ways of saying that someone has very little money at a particular time:

I'm not going away this year. I'm ***broke***.

Most schools are pretty ***strapped for cash***.

Needy people are poor and do not have enough food, clothes, etc.:

Your donations will make a difference to ***needy*** *children all over the world.*

If a person or place is **poverty-stricken**, that person or place is suffering very badly from the effects of being poor:

He visited ***poverty-stricken*** *countries where people are starving.*

Destitute is used when someone is extremely poor and has no house or possessions:

The floods left thousands of people ***destitute***.

The adjectives **deprived** or **disadvantaged** are often used when people are poor and do not have the good living conditions and opportunities that other people have:

It's one of the most ***deprived*** *areas of the city.*

The scheme was set up to help ***disadvantaged*** *children.*

poor /pɔːr/ (US) /pʊr/ adj; noun

▸adj **NO MONEY** ▷ **1** (A1) having little money and/or few possessions: *Most of the world's poorest countries are in Africa.* ◦ *He came from a poor immigrant family.* → Opposite **rich** **2 be poor in sth** (B2) to have very little of a particular substance or quality: *Unfortunately, Iceland is poor in natural resources.* **BAD** ▷ **3** (B2) not good, being of a very low quality, quantity, or standard: *a poor harvest* ◦ *Last year's exam results were fairly poor.* ◦ *I was always very poor* ***at*** *maths at school.* ◦ *Dad had been in poor* ***health*** *for several years.*

P

◦ *At last month's meeting, attendance was poor.* **DESERVING SYMPATHY** ▷ **4** (A2) [before noun] deserving sympathy: *That cold sounds terrible, you poor thing!* ◦ *Look at that dog – the poor thing only has three legs.*

IDIOMS **be as poor as church mice** old-fashioned to be very poor: *When we first got married, we were as poor as church mice.* • **come/be a poor second, third, etc.** to be considered much lower in value, quality, or importance than the one, two, etc. other things or people mentioned: *For Jackie, I'm afraid, money is always of first importance and the children come a poor second.* • **poor relation** something or someone similar to but less important than another thing or person, and that people do not consider equally valuable: *The air force and navy were modernized but the army, very much **the** poor relation, was not.*

▸**noun** [plural] **the poor** (C1) poor people considered together as a group: *housing for the poor*

poorhouse /ˈpɔː.haʊs/ (US) /ˈpʊr-/ **noun** [C] in the past, a building in which extremely poor people could live and be fed, paid for by the public → Compare **workhouse**

poorly /ˈpɔː.li/ (US) /ˈpʊr-/ **adv; adj**

▸**adv** (C1) not well: *A business as poorly managed as that one doesn't deserve to succeed.*

IDIOM **think poorly of sb/sth** old-fashioned to have a low opinion of someone or something

▸**adj** [after verb] UK informal (C1) ill: *He says he's **feeling** poorly and he's going back to bed.*

ˌpoorly ˈoff adj [after verb] poor, having little money and/or few possessions

pootle /ˈpuː.tl̩/ (US) /-t̬l̩/ **verb** [I, + adv/prep] UK informal to move somewhere slowly and with no real purpose: *They were pootling along country roads in a very old car.* ◦ *Tom pootled off into the house.*

pop. /pɒp/ (US) /pɑːp/ abbreviation for **population**: *The village (pop. 3,915) is a bustling river port.*

P

pop /pɒp/ (US) /pɑːp/ **noun; verb**

▸**noun MUSIC** ▷ **1** (A2) [U] (formal **popular music**) modern popular music, usually with a strong beat, created with electrical or electronic equipment, and easy to listen to and remember: *pop music* ◦ *a pop concert/song* ◦ *The song reached No. 32 in the pop **charts**.* ◦ *She wants to be a pop **singer/star** like Madonna.* **SOUND** ▷ **2** [C] a short, sharp sound, like something exploding: *I heard a pop and the lights went out.* **FATHER** ▷ **3** mainly US informal a father: [as form of address] *Hey Pop, can I do anything to help?* **DRINK** ▷ **4** [U] old-fashioned informal (US usually **soda**) a sweet FIZZY drink (= with bubbles), usually with a fruit flavour: *a bottle of pop* **CRITICISM** ▷ **5 take a pop at sb** UK informal to criticize someone, especially in public: *She never expected anyone from her own family to take a pop at her.* **OCCASION/OBJECT** ▷ **6** [C usually singular] US informal each particular occasion or object in a series: *She gives lectures and gets paid $5,000 **a** pop.*

IDIOM **go pop** humorous to explode: *If I eat any more I'm going to go pop!*

▸**verb** (-pp-) **GO** ▷ **1** (B2) [I + adv/prep] mainly UK informal to go to a particular place: *I've just got to pop **into** the bank to get some money.* ◦ *Paula popped **out** for a minute.* ◦ *Would you pop **upstairs** and see if Grandad is okay?* ◦ *Why don't you pop **in/over** and see us this afternoon?* **SOUND** ▷ **2** (C2) [I or T] to (cause something to) make a short explosive sound, often by breaking something: *The kids were popping all the birthday balloons.* ◦ *The music played and champagne corks popped.* **3** [I] If your ears pop, you experience a strange noise and feeling in your ears as a result of a sudden change in air pressure: *My ears always pop as the plane comes in to land.* **MOVE** ▷ **4** [I + adv/prep] to move quickly and suddenly, especially from a closed space: *When you open the box, a clown pops **out**.* **PUT** ▷ **5** [T + adv/prep] informal to put or take something quickly: *If you pop the pizza **in** the oven now, it'll be ready in 15 minutes.* ◦ *He popped his head **into** the room/**round** the door and said 'Lunchtime!'* ◦ *Pop your shoes **on** and let's go.* **6 pop pills** informal to take pills regularly, especially ones containing an illegal drug: *A decade of heavy drinking and popping pills ruined her health.*

IDIOMS **your eyes pop out of your head** informal a way of describing the way you look when you are extremely surprised to see something or someone: *When she saw the amount written on the cheque, her eyes **nearly** popped out of her head.* • **pop your clogs** UK humorous to die: *I think I'll leave all my money to charity when I pop my clogs.* • **pop the question** to ask someone to marry you: *So did he pop the question, then?*

PHRASAL VERBS **pop off** humorous to die: *You're all just waiting till I pop off so you can get your hands on my money.* • **pop sb off** humorous to kill someone • **pop up** informal to appear or happen, especially suddenly or unexpectedly: *She's one of those film stars who pops up everywhere, on TV, in magazines, on Broadway.* ◦ *The words 'Hard disk failure – program aborted' popped up on the screen.*

POP3 /pɒpˈθriː/ (US) /pɑːp-/ specialized abbreviation for Post Office Protocol 3: a way of looking at and collecting emails from an Internet Service Provider

ˈpop ˌart noun [U] a type of modern art that started in the 1960s and uses images and objects from ordinary life: *Andy Warhol's pictures of soup cans are a famous example of pop art.*

popcorn /ˈpɒp.kɔːn/ (US) /ˈpɑːp.kɔːrn/ **noun** [U] (B1) seeds of MAIZE that are heated until they break open and become soft and light, usually FLAVOURED with salt, butter, or sugar: *a tub of popcorn*

ˌpop ˈculture noun [U] music, TV, cinema, literature, etc. that is popular and enjoyed by ordinary people, rather than experts or very educated people

pope /pəʊp/ (US) /poʊp/ **noun** [C] (the title of) the leader of the Roman Catholic Church: *Pope John Paul II* → See also **the papacy, pontiff**

IDIOM **is the Pope a Catholic?** saying humorous or offensive used to say that the answer to a question you have just been asked is obviously 'yes'

ˈpop-eyed adj informal having your eyes wide open with surprise or excitement: *The children were pop-eyed **with** excitement.*

ˈpop ˌgroup noun [C, + sing/pl verb] a small group of people who play and/or sing pop music together: *The Beatles will always be the world's most famous pop group.*

poplar /ˈpɒp.ləʳ/ (US) /ˈpɑː.plɚ/ **noun** [C] a tall tree with branches that form a thin pointed shape: *a tall row of poplars*

poplin /ˈpɒp.lɪn/ (US) /ˈpɑː.plɪn/ **noun** [U] a type of slightly shiny cotton cloth: *100 percent **cotton** poplin*

poppadom (also **poppadum**) /ˈpɒp.ə.dɒm/ (US) /ˈpɑː.pə-/ **noun** [C] a very thin, flat, circular South Asian bread that breaks easily into pieces

popper /ˈpɒp.əʳ/ (US) /ˈpɑː.pɚ/ **noun FASTENER** ▷ **1** [C] UK a **press stud DRUG** ▷ **2** [C usually plural] slang the drug AMYL NITRITE, usually in a small container

poppet /ˈpɒp.ɪt/ (US) /ˈpɑː.pɪt/ **noun** [C] UK informal a person, especially a child, that you like or love: [as form of address] *Come on, poppet, it's time for bed.* ◦ *Oh, Becky's a real poppet – such a sweet girl.*

ˌpop psyˈchology noun [U] theories and advice about people's behaviour that are easily understood and intended to help people improve their lives

poppy /ˈpɒp.i/ (US) /ˈpɑː.pi/ noun [C] a plant with large, delicate flowers that are typically red and have small, black seeds

poppycock /ˈpɒp.ɪ.kɒk/ (US) /ˈpɑː.pɪ.kɑːk/ noun [U] old-fashioned disapproving nonsense: *He dismissed the allegations as poppycock.*

Popsicle /ˈpɒp.sɪ.kl̩/ (US) /ˈpɑːp-/ noun [C] US trademark **ice lolly**

the populace /ˈpɒp.jʊ.ləs/ (US) /ˈpɑː.pjə-/ noun [S, + sing/pl verb] formal the ordinary people who live in a particular country or place: *Some studies show that workers in the nuclear industry are more likely than the* ***general*** *populace to get cancer.*

popular /ˈpɒp.jʊ.ləʳ/ (US) /ˈpɑː.pjə.lɚ/ adj **LIKED** ▷ **1** (A2) liked, enjoyed, or supported by many people: *She's the most popular teacher in school.* ◦ *That song was popular* ***with*** *people from my father's generation.* ◦ *Walking is a popular form of exercise in Britain.* ◦ *How popular is Madonna* ***among/with*** *teenagers?* ◦ informal *Jan wasn't very popular (= people were annoyed by her) when she opened all the windows on that cold day.* → Opposite **unpopular** **GENERAL** ▷ **2** (B2) [before noun] for or involving ordinary people rather than experts or very educated people: *popular music/entertainment/culture* ◦ *The issue was virtually ignored by the popular press.* ◦ *The popular myth is that air travel is more dangerous than travel by car or bus.* • **popularly** /-li/ adv *In Britain, BSE is popularly known as Mad Cow Disease.*

popularity /ˌpɒp.jʊˈlær.ə.ti/ (US) /ˌpɑː.pjəˈler.ə.t̬i/ noun [U] (B2) the fact that something or someone is liked, enjoyed, or supported by many people: *the increasing popularity of organic food*

popularize (UK usually **popularise**) /ˈpɒp.jʊ.lə.raɪz/ (US) /ˈpɑː.pjə-/ verb [T] **LIKED** ▷ **1** to make something become popular: *It was Pavarotti in the 1980s who really popularized opera.* **GENERAL** ▷ **2** to make something known and understood by ordinary people: *Television has an important role to play in popularizing new scientific ideas.* • **popularization** (UK usually **popularisation**) /ˌpɒp.jʊ.lə.raɪˈzeɪ.ʃən/ (US) /ˌpɑː.pjə.lɚ.ə-/ noun [U]

ˌpopular ˈmusic noun [U] formal for **pop**

populate /ˈpɒp.jʊ.leɪt/ (US) /ˈpɑː.pjə-/ verb [T] **1** (C1) If an area is populated by people or animals, they live in that area: *The inner cities are no longer densely populated.* ◦ *The river is populated mainly by smaller species of fish.* **2** to live in an area or place: *The settlers began to move inland and populate the river valleys.* **3** specialized to automatically add information to a list or TABLE on a computer: *There are several ways to populate the database.*

population /ˌpɒp.jʊˈleɪ.ʃən/ (US) /ˌpɑː.pjə-/ noun [C, + sing/pl verb] **1** (B1) all the people living in a particular country, area, or place: *Ten percent of* ***the*** *population lived in poverty.* ◦ *In 1992* ***the*** *population of Cairo was approximately 6,500,000.* ◦ *a growing/shrinking population* ◦ *Throughout the war, there were horrific casualties amongst the civilian populations of both countries.* ◦ *The UN is investigating new methods of population* ***control*** *(= limiting the growth of the number of people).* ◦ *The country is facing a population* ***explosion*** *(= sudden growth in the number of people).* **2** (B2) all the people or animals of a particular type or group who live in one country, area, or place: *There's been a nine percent rise in the prison population (= the number of people in prison).* ◦ *The dolphin population has been decimated by tuna fishing.*

> **Word partners for population**
>
> *have* a population **of** [50 million, etc.] • the population ***declines/decreases/falls/grows/increases*** • the population ***of*** [a place] • the ***adult/civilian/local/general*** population

populism /ˈpɒp.jʊ.lɪ.zəm/ (US) /ˈpɑː.pjə-/ noun [U] mainly disapproving political ideas and activities that are intended to represent ordinary people's needs and wishes: *Their ideas are simple populism – tax cuts and higher wages.*

populist /ˈpɒp.jʊ.lɪst/ (US) /ˈpɑː.pjə-/ adj representing or connected with the ideas and opinions of ordinary people: *a populist manifesto* ◦ *a populist leader* • **populist** noun [C]

populous /ˈpɒp.jʊ.ləs/ (US) /ˈpɑː.pjə-/ adj formal A populous country, area, or place has a lot of people living in it: *China is the world's most populous country.*

ˈpop-up adj; noun

▸adj **1** used to describe a machine, book, etc. that has parts that push out from a surface or from inside: *a pop-up children's book* ◦ *a pop-up toaster* **2** used to describe a shop, restaurant, etc. that operates temporarily and only for a short period when it is likely to get a lot of customers

▸noun [C] **COMPUTER** ▷ **1** (also **ˈpop-up ˌmenu**) a list of choices that is shown on a computer screen when the user requests it: *Select the option you want from the pop-up (menu).* **2** a new window that opens quickly on a computer screen in front of what you are working on: *software to block pop-ups* **BASEBALL** ▷ **3** (also **pop fly**) in baseball, a ball that is hit very high in the air but not very far **SHOP/STORE** ▷ **4** a shop, restaurant, etc. that operates only temporarily for a short period when it is likely to get a lot of customers

porcelain /ˈpɔː.səl.ɪn/ (US) /ˈpɔːr-/ noun [U] **1** a hard but delicate shiny white substance made by heating a special type of clay to a high temperature, used to make cups, plates, decorations, etc.: *a porcelain dish* ◦ *The tea cups are (made of) porcelain.* **2** cups, plates, and decorations, etc. made of porcelain: *He had a fine collection of Meissen porcelain.*

porch /pɔːtʃ/ (US) /pɔːrtʃ/ noun [C] **1** a covered structure in front of the entrance to a building **2** US a **veranda**: *We sat out on the porch to cool off.*

porcini /pɔːˈtʃiː.ni/ (US) /pɔːrˈ-/ noun [plural] a type of wild MUSHROOM, used in cooking

porcupine /ˈpɔː.kjʊ.paɪn/ (US) /ˈpɔːr-/ noun [C] an animal with a covering of long, sharp QUILLS (= stiff hairs like needles) on its back

porcupine

pore /pɔːʳ/ (US) /pɔːr/ noun; verb

▸noun [C] a very small hole in the skin of people or other animals, or a similar hole on the surface of plants or rocks: *Sweat passes through the pores and cools the body down.* ◦ *Pimples form when pores become blocked with dirt.*

▸verb

PHRASAL VERB **pore over sth** to look at and study something, usually a book or document, carefully: *She spends her evenings poring over textbooks.* ◦ *He pored over the letter searching for clues about the writer.*

pork /pɔːk/ (US) /pɔːrk/ **noun** [U] (B1) meat from a pig, eaten as food: *a pork chop* ◦ *pork sausages*

ˈpork-ˌbarrel **adj** [before noun] US slang disapproving involving spending large amounts of money in an area in order to make local people more likely to vote for a particular person or party: *pork-barrel projects/spending/politics*

porker /ˈpɔː.kəʳ/ (US) /ˈpɔːr.kɚ/ **noun** [C] a pig, especially one raised to produce meat

ˌpork ˈpie **noun** [C] **FOOD** ▷ **1** mainly UK a small, round pastry case filled with cooked pork, eaten cold **LIE** ▷ **2** UK humorous slang another word for **porky**

ˌpork ˈscratchings **noun** [plural] UK (US **ˈpork ˌrinds**) small, hard pieces of fried pork skin eaten cold and usually sold in bags

porky /ˈpɔː.ki/ (US) /ˈpɔːr-/ **adj; noun**

▸**adj** informal disapproving fat: *He's been looking a bit porky since he gave up smoking.*

▸**noun** [C usually plural] (also **ˌpork ˈpie**) UK humorous slang a lie: *Have you been **telling** porkies again?*

porn /pɔːn/ (US) /pɔːrn/ **noun; adj**

▸**noun** [U] informal for **pornography**: *Some of those photos they show in tabloid newspapers are nothing but porn.*

▸**adj** (also **porno**) informal for **pornographic**: *a porn shop* ◦ *porn movies*

pornographer /pɔːˈnɒg.rə.fəʳ/ (US) /pɔːrˈnɑː.grə.fɚ/ **noun** [C] disapproving a person who makes or sells pornography

pornography /pɔːˈnɒg.rə.fi/ (US) /pɔːrˈnɑː.grə-/ **noun** [U] (informal **porn**) books, magazines, films, etc. with no artistic value which describe or show sexual acts or naked people in a way that is intended to be sexually exciting: *a campaign against pornography* ◦ ***hard**(-**core**) (= very detailed) porn* ◦ ***soft**(-**core**) (= not very detailed) porn* • **pornographic** /ˌpɔː.nəˈgræf.ɪk/ (US) /ˌpɔːr-/ **adj** (informal **porn**, **porno**)

P

porosity /pɔːˈrɒs.ə.ti/ (US) /pɔːrˈɑː.sə.t̬i/ **noun** [U] specialized the state of being porous

porous /ˈpɔː.rəs/ (US) /ˈpɔːr.əs/ **adj** **1** describes something that has many small holes, so liquid or air can pass through, especially slowly: *porous soil with good drainage* ◦ *porous brick walls* ◦ *a porous polymer membrane* **2** not protected enough to stop people going through: *The border in this region is porous and many refugees have simply walked across.*

porpoise /ˈpɔː.pəs/ (US) /ˈpɔːr-/ **noun** [C] a mammal that lives in the sea, swims in groups, and looks similar to a DOLPHIN but has a shorter rounder nose

porridge /ˈpɒr.ɪdʒ/ (US) /ˈpɔːr-/ **noun** [U] **FOOD** ▷ **1** mainly UK (US usually **oatmeal**) a thick, soft food made from OATS boiled in milk or water, eaten hot for breakfast **PRISON** ▷ **2** UK slang a period of time spent in prison: *He **did** ten years porridge for armed robbery.*

port /pɔːt/ (US) /pɔːrt/ **noun** **TOWN** ▷ **1** (B1) [C or U] a town by the sea or by a river that has a HARBOUR, or the HARBOUR itself: *a naval/fishing/container port* ◦ *We had a good view of all the ships **coming into/leaving** port.* **CONNECTION** ▷ **2** [C] specialized a part of a computer where wires from other pieces of equipment, such as a printer, can be connected **LEFT** ▷ **3** [U] specialized the left side of a ship or aircraft → Opposite **starboard** **WINE** ▷ **4** [U] a strong sweet wine made in Portugal **BAG** ▷ **5** [C] Australian English a case or bag

portable /ˈpɔː.tə.bl/ (US) /ˈpɔːr.t̬ə-/ **adj** **1** (C1) light and small enough to be easily carried or moved: *a portable radio/phone/computer* **2** possible to take with you if you move to a different place or job: *They offer portable pensions, carried by employees from job to job.* ◦ *Your phone number is portable if you decide to move to a different home or office.* • **portability** /ˌpɔː.təˈbɪl.ɪ.ti/ (US) /ˌpɔːr.t̬əˈbɪl.ə.t̬i/ **noun** [U] *The advantage of the smaller model is its greater portability.*

Portakabin /ˈpɔː.təˌkæb.ɪn/ (US) /ˈpɔːr.t̬ə-/ **noun** [C] UK trademark a small building that is designed to be moved from place to place and is used as a temporary office, school, or home, especially when building work is being done

portal /ˈpɔː.tᵊl/ (US) /ˈpɔːr.t̬ᵊl/ **noun** specialized **1** [C] a page on the internet that allows people to get useful information, such as news and weather, and to find other websites **2** **portals** [plural] formal a large, important entrance to a building: *Passing through the portals of the BBC for the first time, she felt slightly nervous.*

ˈportal ˌvein **noun** [C usually sing] (also **heˌpatic ˈportal ˌvein**) the VEIN that carries blood, containing substances obtained from food, from the INTESTINES to the LIVER

portcullis /ˌpɔːtˈkʌl.ɪs/ (US) /ˌpɔːrt-/ **noun** [C] a strong gate made of bars with points at the bottom that hangs above the entrance to a castle and in the past was brought down to the ground in order to close the entrance against enemies

portend /pɔːˈtend/ (US) /pɔːr-/ **verb** [T] formal to be a sign that something bad is likely to happen in the future: *It was a deeply superstitious country, where earthquakes were commonly believed to portend the end of dynasties.* • **portent** /ˈpɔː.tent/ (US) /ˈpɔːr-/ **noun** [C] *Is it true that cows lying down in a field are a portent **of** rain?*

portentous /pɔːˈten.təs/ (US) /pɔːrˈten.t̬əs/ **adj** **1** formal disapproving too serious and trying to be very important: *The problem with the book is that it sometimes descends into portentous philosophizing.* **2** literary Portentous events, statements, or signs are important because they show that something unpleasant is very likely to happen: *The report contains numerous portentous references to a future environmental calamity.* • **portentously** /-li/ **adv** formal disapproving

porter /ˈpɔː.təʳ/ (US) /ˈpɔːr.t̬ɚ/ **noun** [C] **1** a person whose job is to carry things, especially travellers' bags at railway stations, airports, etc.: *There aren't any porters, so we'll have to find a trolley for the luggage.* **2** UK (US **doorman**) someone whose job is to take care of a building and be present at its entrance in order to help visitors: *The hotel porter opened the door for me and then called a taxi.* **3** US a person whose job is to help travellers who are spending the night on a train by arranging their bed, taking care of their bags, etc.

portfolio /ˌpɔːtˈfəʊ.li.əʊ/ (US) /ˌpɔːrtˈfoʊ.li.oʊ/ **noun** [C] (plural **portfolios**) **CASE** ▷ **1** a large, thin case used for carrying drawings, documents, etc. **2** a collection of drawings, documents, etc. that represent a person's, especially an artist's, work: *She's trying to build up a portfolio **of work** to show during job interviews.* **FINANCIAL** ▷ **3** specialized a collection of company SHARES and other INVESTMENTS that are owned by a particular person or organization **JOB** ▷ **4** UK specialized a particular job or area of responsibility of a member of a government: *The prime minister offered her the foreign affairs portfolio.* **5** **without portfolio** UK specialized In Britain, a MINISTER without portfolio is an important government official who is not in charge of a particular department, but who still takes part in the decisions of the government.

porthole /ˈpɔːt.həʊl/ (US) /ˈpɔːrt.hoʊl/ **noun** [C] a small, usually round window in the side of a ship or aircraft

portico /ˈpɔː.tɪ.kəʊ/ (US) /ˈpɔːr.t̬ɪ.koʊ/ **noun** [C] (plural **porticoes** or **porticos**) a covered entrance to a building, usually a large and impressive building, that is supported by columns

portion **noun**; **verb**

▸**noun** [C] /ˈpɔː.ʃən/ (US) /ˈpɔːr-/ **1** C1 a part or share of something larger: *A large/major portion* ***of*** *the company's profit goes straight back into new projects.* ◦ *I accept my portion* ***of*** *the blame.* **2** B2 the amount of a particular food that is served to one person, especially in a restaurant or a shop which sells food ready to be eaten: *The portions are very* ***generous*** *in this restaurant.*

▸**verb** /ˌpɔː.ʃən/ (US) /ˌpɔːr-/

PHRASAL VERB **portion sth out** to share something out: *We'll have to portion the money out* ***among/between*** *the six of us.* → See also **apportion**

portly /ˈpɔːt.li/ (US) /ˈpɔːrt-/ **adj** (especially of middle-aged or old men) fat and round: *He was a portly figure in a tight-fitting jacket and bow tie.*

portmanteau /pɔːtˈmæn.təʊ/ (US) /pɔːrtˈmæn.toʊ/ **noun**; **adj**

▸**noun** [C] (plural **portmanteaus** or **portmanteaux** /-təʊz/ (US) /-toʊz/) old-fashioned a large case for carrying clothes while travelling, especially one which opens out into two parts

▸**adj** [before noun] consisting of a wide range of things that are considered as a single thing: *The Official Secrets Act was described as a piece of portmanteau legislation, covering everything from nuclear weapons to army boots.*

portˈmanteau ˌword **noun** [C] a word formed by combining two other words: *'Jeggings' is a portmanteau word formed from 'jeans' and 'leggings'.*

ˌport of ˈcall **noun** [C] a place where you stop for a short time, especially on a journey

portrait /ˈpɔː.trət/, /-treɪt/ (US) /ˈpɔːr.trɪt/ **noun**; **adj**

▸**noun** [C] **1** B2 a painting, photograph, drawing, etc. of a person or, less commonly, of a group of people: *She's commissioned an artist to paint her portrait/paint a portrait* ***of*** *her.* ◦ *a portrait gallery* ◦ *a portrait painter* **2** A film or book that is a portrait of something describes or represents that thing in a detailed way: *Her latest novel paints a very vivid portrait* ***of*** *the aristocracy in the 1920s.*

▸**adj** describes a computer document that is to be printed with the shorter side of the paper at the top and bottom → Compare **landscape**

portraiture /ˈpɔː.trɪ.tʃər/ (US) /ˈpɔːr.trɪ.tʃɚ/ **noun** [U] specialized the act or art of making portraits

portray /pɔːˈtreɪ/ (US) /pɔːr-/ **verb** [T] **1** C2 to represent or describe someone or something in a painting, film, book, or other artistic work: *The painting portrays a beautiful young woman in a blue dress.* ◦ *The writer portrays life in a small village at the turn of the century.* **2** **portray sb as sth** If a person in a film, book, etc. is portrayed as a particular type of character, they are represented in that way: *The father in the film is portrayed as a fairly unpleasant character.* • **portrayal** /-əl/ **noun** [C] *His latest movie is a grim portrayal* ***of*** *wartime suffering.*

ˌport ˈwine ˌstain **noun** [C] a dark red BIRTHMARK (= mark on the skin that has been there since a person's birth)

pose /pəʊz/ (US) /poʊz/ **verb**; **noun**

▸**verb** CAUSE ▷ **1** C1 [T] to cause something, especially a problem or difficulty: *Nuclear weapons pose* ***a threat*** *to everyone.* ◦ *The mountain terrain poses particular problems for civil engineers.* ASK ▷ **2** C2 [T] to ask a question, especially in a formal situation such as a meeting: *Can we go back to the question that Helena posed earlier?* POSITION ▷ **3** C1 [I] to move into and stay in a particular position, in order to be photographed, painted, etc.: *We all posed* ***for*** *our photographs next to the Statue of Liberty.* PRETEND ▷ **4** [I] to pretend to be something that you are not or to have qualities that you do not have, in order to be admired or attract interest: *He doesn't really know a thing about the theatre – he's just posing!*

PHRASAL VERB **pose as sb** C2 If you pose as a particular person, you pretend to be that person in order to deceive people: *He's posing* ***as*** *her date, but he's really her bodyguard.*

▸**noun** POSITION ▷ **1** [C] a particular position in which a person stands, sits, etc. in order to be photographed, painted, etc.: *He* ***adopted/assumed/struck*** *(= moved into) an elegant pose.* PRETENDING ▷ **2** [C usually singular] an occasion when someone pretends to have qualities that they do not have: *She likes to appear as if she knows all about the latest films and art exhibitions, but it's all a pose (= she's pretending and it's not true).*

poser /ˈpəʊ.zər/ (US) /ˈpoʊ.zɚ/ **noun** [C] informal a problem or question that is difficult to solve or answer: *Who was the last woman to win three Olympic gold medals? That's quite a poser.*

poseur /ˈpəʊ.zər/ (US) /ˈpoʊ.zɚ/ **noun** [C] (also **poser**) someone who pretends to be something they are not, or to have qualities that they do not have: *You look like a real poseur in your fancy sports car!*

posey /ˈpəʊ.zi/ (US) /ˈpoʊ-/ **adj** (**posier**, **posiest**) UK informal disapproving expensive and fashionable, in a way that is intended to make other people feel admiration

posh /pɒʃ/ (US) /pɑːʃ/ **adj** **1** B2 informal (of places and things) expensive and of high quality: *He takes her to some really posh restaurants.* **2** C2 UK informal (of people and their voices) from a high social class: *A woman with a very posh accent phoned for him earlier.* **3** **too posh to push** informal humorous used for describing a woman who chooses to have a CAESAREAN SECTION (= a medical operation) when having her baby • **posh** **adv** UK not standard *She talks dead posh.*

posit /ˈpɒz.ɪt/ (US) /ˈpɑː.zɪt/ **verb** [T] formal to suggest something as a basic fact or principle from which a further idea is formed or developed: [+ that] *If we posit* ***that*** *wage rises cause inflation, it follows that we should try to minimize them.*

position /pəˈzɪʃ.ən/ **noun**; **verb**

▸**noun** PLACE ▷ **1** B1 [C] the place where something or someone is, often in relation to other things: *Well, I've found our position on the map if you want to see where we are.* ◦ *You've moved the furniture around – the sofa is* ***in*** *a different position.* ◦ *I didn't know you played hockey – what position (= place or job in the team) do you play?* **2** C1 [C or U] the place where people are sent in order to carry out a course of action: *The troops took up their battle positions at the front line.* ◦ *As soon as his officers were* ***in*** *position/had moved* ***into*** *position, the police commander walked up the path towards the house.* SITUATION ▷ **3** B1 [C usually singular] a situation: *My financial position is rather precarious at the moment.* ◦ *When two of your best friends argue it* ***puts*** *you* ***in*** *a very awkward position.* **4** **be in a position to do sth** C1 to be able to do something, usually because you have the necessary experience, authority, or money: *I'm not in a position to reveal any of the details of the project at present.* ◦ *I'm sure they'd like to help her out financially but they're not in a position to do so.*

P

RANK ▷ **5** B2 [C] a rank or level in a company, competition, or society: *Whether or not you're given a car depends on your position* ***in*** *the company.* ◦ UK *She finished the race* ***in*** *third position.* **6** B2 [C] a job: *She applied for a position in the firm that I work for.* **ARRANGEMENT** ▷ **7** B1 [C] the way in which something is arranged: *I go to sleep on my back but I always wake up in a different position.* ◦ *Keep the bottles in an upright position.* ◦ *This is not a very comfortable position.* **OPINION** ▷ **8** [C usually singular] formal an opinion: *What's the company's position* ***on*** *recycling?* ◦ *He* ***takes*** *the position (= believes) that individuals have a responsibility to look after themselves.*

▸**verb** [T usually + adv/prep] to put something or someone in a particular place: *The army had been positioned to the north and east of the city.* ◦ *When it came to seating people for dinner, I positioned my****self*** *as far away from him as possible.*

positional /pəˈzɪʃ.ən.əl/ **adj** relating to position, especially in sports: *The Brazilian side had made eight changes, six of them positional.*

positive /ˈpɒz.ə.tɪv/ US /ˈpɑː.zə.t̬ɪv/ **adj** **HOPEFUL** ▷ **1** B1 full of hope and confidence, or giving cause for hope and confidence: *a positive attitude* ◦ *On a more positive note, we're seeing signs that the housing market is picking up.* ◦ *The past ten years have seen some very positive developments in East-West relations.* ◦ *There was a very positive response to our new design – people seemed very pleased with it.* → Opposite **negative** **CERTAIN** ▷ **2** B2 certain and without any doubt: [+ (that)] *Are you positive (****that****) you saw me switch the iron off?* ◦ *'Are you sure it's okay for me to use your mother's car?' 'Positive.'* ◦ *'It was him – I saw him take it.' 'Are you positive* ***about*** *that?'* **TEST RESULTS** ▷ **3** C2 (of a medical test) showing that a person has the disease or condition for which they are being tested: *a positive pregnancy test* ◦ *He's HIV positive.* ◦ *She* ***tested*** *positive* ***for*** *hepatitis.* → Opposite **negative** **COMPLETE** ▷ **4** [before noun] (used to add force to an expression) complete: *Far from being a nuisance, she was a positive joy to have around.* **ABOVE ZERO** ▷ **5** (of a number or amount) more than zero: *Two is a positive number.* → Opposite **negative** **ELECTRICITY** ▷ **6** being the type of electrical charge that is carried by PROTONS → Opposite **negative** **BLOOD TYPE** ▷ **7** having the RHESUS FACTOR in the blood: *My blood type is O positive.* • **positiveness** /-nəs/ **noun** [U]

ˌpositive discrimiˈnation **noun** [U] UK the act of giving advantage to those groups in society that are often treated unfairly because of their race, sex, etc.

positively /ˈpɒz.ə.tɪv.li/ US /ˈpɑː.zə.t̬ɪv-/ **adv** **WELL** ▷ **1** B2 in a good or positive way: *I don't respond very positively to being bossed around – it just makes me angry.* **CERTAINLY** ▷ **2** certainly: *He said quite positively that he would come, so I've saved a place for him.* **COMPLETELY** ▷ **3** informal used to emphasize something, especially something that is unexpected: *That sales assistant was positively rude to me!*

ˌpositive ˈvetting **noun** [U] UK the detailed examination of a person's past, political beliefs, etc. in order to discover if they are suitable for a government job which might involve dealing with secret information

positron /ˈpɒz.ɪ.trɒn/ US /ˈpɑː.zɪ.trɑːn/ **noun** [C] specialized an extremely small piece of matter with a positive electrical charge, having the same mass as an ELECTRON

poss /pɒs/ US /pɑːs/ **adj** [after verb] UK informal for possible: *I want it done as soon as poss really.*

posse /ˈpɒs.i/ US /ˈpɑː.si/ **noun** [C, + sing/pl verb] **1** a group of people who have come together for the same purpose: *The disgraced minister walked swiftly from the car to his house pursued by a whole posse* ***of*** *reporters.* **2** in the past, a group of men in the US who were brought together to catch a criminal: *The sheriff rounded up a posse and went after the bank robbers.* **3** slang a group of friends: *I was hanging with my posse.*

possess /pəˈzes/ **verb** [T] **OWN** ▷ **1** C1 to have or own something, or to have a particular quality: *I don't possess a single DVD (= I don't have even one DVD).* ◦ *In the past the root of this plant was thought to possess magical powers.* **CONTROL** ▷ **2** (of a wish or an idea) to take control over a person's mind, making that person behave in a very strange way: [+ to infinitive] *Whatever possessed him* ***to*** *wear that appalling jacket!*

possessed /pəˈzest/ **adj** **OWNING** ▷ **1 be possessed of sth** formal to own something or have something as a quality: *He was possessed of a large fortune, but sadly no brains to speak of.* **CONTROL** ▷ **2** [after verb] Someone who is possessed is thought to be controlled by an evil spirit.

IDIOM **like a man/woman possessed** in a wild and uncontrolled way: *He's been running around the office this morning like a man possessed.*

possession /pəˈzeʃ.ən/ **noun** **1** C2 [U] the fact that you have or own something: *The possession of large amounts of money does not ensure happiness.* ◦ formal *I have* ***in*** *my possession a letter which may be of interest to you.* ◦ formal *He was found* ***in*** *possession* ***of*** *explosives.* **2** B2 [C usually plural] something that you own or that you are carrying with you at a particular time: *Please remember to take all your* ***personal*** *possessions with you when you leave the aircraft.* **3** [C usually plural] a country that is ruled by another country: *a former overseas possession* **4 get/take possession of sth** legal to start to use and control a building or piece of land that you may or may not own: *We've already bought the house but we won't take possession of it until May.*

possessive /pəˈzes.ɪv/ **adj** **PERSON** ▷ **1** If you are possessive about something that you own, you do not like lending it to other people or sharing it with other people: *He's a bit possessive* ***about*** *his iPod – I wouldn't dare ask to borrow it.* **2** C2 Someone who is possessive in his or her feelings and behaviour towards or about another person wants to have all of that person's love and attention and will not share it with anyone else: *a possessive mother* ◦ *Her boyfriend was getting too possessive so she finished with him.* **GRAMMAR** ▷ **3** B1 In grammar, a possessive word, form, etc. shows who or what something belongs to: *'Mine' and 'yours' are possessive* ***pronouns****.*

possessor /pəˈzes.əʳ/ US /-ɚ/ **noun** [C usually singular] formal or humorous someone who owns something: *I'm pleased to say that I'm now the* ***proud*** *possessor* ***of*** *a driving licence!*

> **!** Common mistake: **possibility or opportunity?**
>
> **Warning:** Choose the right word!
>
> To talk about an occasion or situation which makes it possible to do something, don't say 'possibility', say **opportunity**:
>
> ~~*Thank you for giving me the possibility to be here.*~~
>
> *Thank you for giving me the opportunity to be here.*

possibility /ˌpɒs.əˈbɪl.ɪ.ti/ US /ˌpɑː.səˈbɪl.ə.t̬i/ **noun** **1** B1 [C or U] a chance that something may happen or be true: *It's not likely to happen but I wouldn't* ***rule out***

> **! Common mistake: possibility**
>
> When **possibility** is followed by a verb, that verb cannot be in the infinitive with 'to'.
>
> Do not say 'possibility to do something', say **possibility of doing something**:
>
> ~~*There is no possibility to find a job in this town.*~~
>
> *There is no possibility of finding a job in this town.*

the possibility. ◦ *The forecast said that there's a possibility* ***of*** *snow tonight.* ◦ [+ (that)] *There's a distinct possibility (****that****) I'll be asked to give a speech.* ◦ *Is there any possibility (****that****) you could pick me up from the station?* → Opposite **impossibility** **2** B2 [C] something that you can choose to do in a particular situation: *We could take on extra staff – that's one possibility.* ◦ *'Have you decided what to do?' 'No, I'm still considering the various possibilities.'*

possible /ˈpɒs.ə.bl/ US /ˈpɑː.sə-/ adj **CAN ACHIEVE** ▷ **1** A1 able to be done or achieved, or able to exist: *I can't get it all done by Friday – it's just not possible.* ◦ *Is* ***it*** *possible* ***to*** *buy tickets in advance?* ◦ *They got as far as was* ***humanly*** *possible (= as far as anyone could have) before turning back.* → Opposite **impossible** **2 as much, quickly, soon, etc. as possible** A2 as much, quickly, soon, etc. as something can happen or be done: *Please take your seats as quickly as possible.* ◦ *I'll go as soon as possible.* **NOT CERTAIN** ▷ **3** B1 [+ (that)] that might or might not happen: ***It's*** *possible (****that****) Mira might turn up tonight.* ◦ *'Do you think he'll end up in prison?' 'It's very possible.'* ◦ *That's one possible solution to the problem.* → Compare **probable**

IDIOM **anything's possible** anything could happen: *Well, if your brother can find a woman who's willing to marry him then I suppose anything's possible.*

possibly /ˈpɒs.ə.bli/ US /ˈpɑː.sə-/ adv **NOT CERTAIN** ▷ **1** A2 used when something is not certain: *He may possibly decide not to come, in which case there's no problem.* **2** used to agree or disagree when some doubt is involved: *'Do you think this skirt might be too small for her?' '(Very) possibly – she has put on a bit of weight.'* ◦ *'Will he come?' 'Possibly not.'* **WITH CAN/COULD** ▷ **3** B2 used with 'can' or 'could' for emphasis: *He* ***can't*** *possibly have drunk all that on his own!* ◦ *We did all that we possibly* ***could*** *to persuade her to come.* **4** B1 used in polite requests: ***Could*** *I possibly ask you to move your chair a little?* **5** used when politely refusing offers: *'Have another chocolate.' 'No, really, I* ***couldn't*** *possibly.'*

possum /ˈpɒs.əm/ US /ˈpɑː.səm/ noun [C] **1** a small MARSUPIAL found in Australia and New Zealand that lives in trees and has thick fur and a long nose and tail **2** US informal an **opossum**

IDIOM **play possum** informal to pretend to be dead or unconscious, usually as a way of protecting yourself from attack

post /pəʊst/ US /poʊst/ noun; verb

▸noun **LETTERS** ▷ **1** A2 [U] mainly UK (US usually **mail**) letters and parcels that are DELIVERED to homes or places of work: *I'd been away for a few days so I had a lot of post waiting for me.* ◦ *Unless it's marked 'private', my secretary usually* ***opens*** *my post.* ◦ *Has the post* ***come/arrived*** *yet?* **2** A2 [U] mainly UK (US usually **mail**) the public system that exists for the collecting and DELIVERING of letters: *My letter must have got lost* ***in the post.*** ◦ *If you don't want to take it there, you can just send it* ***by*** *post.* **3** [S] UK the time during the day when letters, etc. are collected or DELIVERED: *I* ***missed*** *the post this morning.* ◦ *Did you manage to* ***catch*** *the post?* **JOB** ▷ **4** B2 [C] a job in a company or organization: *Teaching posts are advertised in Tuesday's edition of the paper.* ◦ *She's* ***held*** *the post for 13 years.* ◦ *They have several vacant posts.* **POLE** ▷ **5** [C] a vertical stick or pole fixed into the ground, usually to support something or show a position **6** [C] used as a combining form: *a lamppost* ◦ *a signpost* **7 the post a** in the sport of horse racing, the place where the race finishes or, less often, the place from which the race starts **b** in sports such as football, a GOALPOST (= either of two vertical posts showing the area in which the ball is kicked to score points) **PLACE** ▷ **8** [C] the particular place where someone works, especially where a soldier is told to be for military duty, usually as a guard: *The soldier was disciplined for* ***deserting*** *his post.* ◦ *I was ordered to remain at my post until the last customer had left.* **MESSAGE** ▷ **9** an electronic message that you send to a website in order to allow many people to see it → Compare **posting**

▸verb [T] **LETTERS** ▷ **1** A2 UK (US **mail**) to send a letter or parcel by post: *Did you remember to post my letter?* ◦ *I must post that parcel (****off****) or she won't get it in time for her birthday.* ◦ [+ two objects] *Could you post me the details/post the details* ***to*** *me?* **2** UK to put an object through a LETTERBOX (= special opening in a door): *Just post the key through the door after you've locked it.* **PLACE** ▷ **3** C2 to send someone to a particular place to work: *He's been posted* ***to*** *Pakistan for six months.* ◦ *Guards were posted* ***at*** *all the doors.* **MESSAGE** ▷ **4** to stick or pin a notice on a wall in order to make it publicly known: *Company announcements are usually posted (****up****)* ***on*** *the noticeboard.* **5** B1 to leave an electronic message on a website: *Somebody's been posting obscene messages in this chat room.* **PAY** ▷ **6** US to pay money, especially so that a person who has been accused of committing a crime can be free until their trial: *She has agreed to post* ***bail*** *for her brother.* **RESULTS** ▷ **7** to announce a company's financial results: *The oil company posted* ***profits*** *of $25.1 billion.*

post- /pəʊst-/ US /poʊst-/ prefix after or later than: *postgraduate* ◦ *postoperative* ◦ *He took a post-lunch nap.*

postage /ˈpəʊ.stɪdʒ/ US /ˈpoʊ-/ noun [U] the money that you pay for sending letters and parcels through the post: *Please enclose £15.99, plus £2 for postage.*

ˌpostage and ˈpacking noun [U] UK (US **ˌshipping and ˈhandling**) a charge for the cost of having something put into a container and then posted to you

ˈpostage ˌstamp noun [C] formal a **stamp**

postal /ˈpəʊ.stəl/ US /ˈpoʊ-/ adj C1 relating to post or to the public service that collects and DELIVERS the post: *postal charges* ◦ *the postal service* ◦ *a postal strike*

IDIOM **go postal** US informal to become very angry and do something violent: *The man went postal and shot twelve of his colleagues.*

ˈpostal ˌballot noun [C] UK (US **ˌabsentee ˈballot**) a system of voting in which people send their votes by post

ˈpostal ˌorder noun [C] UK (US **ˈmoney ˌorder**) an official piece of paper with an amount of money written on it, which you post to someone who can then exchange it for the same amount of money at a POST OFFICE

ˌpost-alˈveolar adj specialized (of a speech sound) made in the place between the top teeth and the highest part of the mouth

postbag /ˈpəʊst.bæg/ US /ˈpoʊst-/ noun UK (UK also and US **mailbag**) **1** [U] the number of letters received at one time or on one subject: *It was clear from our*

P

postbag that viewers were unhappy about the programme. **2** [C] a large strong bag used by the POST OFFICE for transporting and carrying letters and parcels

postbox /ˈpəʊst.bɒks/ (US) /ˈpoʊst.bɑːks/ **noun** [C] UK (US **mailbox**) a metal container in the street or other public place in which you can post letters. In the UK these are bright red.

postcard /ˈpəʊst.kɑːd/ (US) /ˈpoʊst.kɑːrd/ **noun** [C] (A2) a card, often with a photograph or picture on one side, which can be sent without an envelope

postcode /ˈpəʊst.kəʊd/ (US) /ˈpoʊst.koʊd/ **noun** [C] UK in Britain, a short series of letters and numbers that is part of an address, and shows exactly where a place is → See also **zip code**

ˈpostcode ˌlottery noun [C] in the UK, a situation in which the type of medical treatment you can have, the type of government services you receive, etc. depends on which part of the country you live in

postcoital /ˌpəʊstˈkɔɪ.təl/ (US) /ˌpoʊstˈkɔɪ.t̬əl/ **adj** [before noun] formal happening or existing after sexual INTERCOURSE

postdate /ˌpəʊstˈdeɪt/, /ˈpəʊst.deɪt/ (US) /ˌpoʊstˈdeɪt/ **verb** [T] **HAPPEN AFTER** ▷ **1** to happen or exist after something: *Most manuscripts postdate the stories which have circulated by word of mouth for centuries.* → Compare **backdate, predate** **WRITE DATE** ▷ **2** to write a date on a document, such as a CHEQUE or letter, that is later than the date on which you are writing it, usually to get some advantage: *Luckily, she let me postdate the cheque until the end of the month when I get paid.*

posted /ˈpəʊs.tɪd/ (US) /ˈpoʊs-/ **adj** [not before noun] **keep sb posted** (C1) to make sure that someone always knows what is happening: *Keep me posted* ***on*** *anything that happens while I'm away.*

poster /ˈpəʊ.stər/ (US) /ˈpoʊ.stɚ/ **noun** [C] (A2) a large printed picture, photograph, or notice which you stick or pin to a wall or board, usually for decoration or to advertise something: *The children* ***put up*** *posters on the classroom walls.* ◦ *We noticed a poster advertising a circus.* → See also **poster paint**

ˈposter ˌchild noun [C] (also **ˈposter ˌboy**, **ˈposter ˌgirl**) someone or something considered to represent a particular quality: *He is a poster boy for political corruption.*

poste restante /ˌpəʊstˈres.tɑːnt/, /-tɑ̃ːnt/ (US) /ˌpoʊst.resˈtɑːnt/ **noun** [U] UK (US **ˌgeneral ˈdelivery**) a system in which a POST OFFICE keeps someone's post until they can collect it, usually used by people who are travelling • **poste restante adv** *I don't know the name of her hotel, so I'm sending her mail poste restante.*

posterior /pɒsˈtɪə.ri.ər/ (US) /pɑːˈstɪr.i.ɚ/ **adj; noun**

▸**adj** [before noun] formal positioned at or towards the back, or later in time → Compare **anterior**

▸**noun** humorous **your posterior** your bottom: *If you would kindly move your posterior just a fraction to the right, I might get by.*

posterity /pɒsˈter.ə.ti/ (US) /pɑːˈster.ə.t̬i/ **noun** [U] formal the people who will exist in the future: *Every attempt is being made to ensure that these works of art are* ***preserved for*** *posterity.*

ˈposter ˌpaint noun [C or U] brightly coloured paint used for painting pictures → See also **poster**

ˌpost-ˈfree adv, adj (also **ˌpost-ˈpaid**) UK used when something is sent by post without any money having to be paid: *Send for an educational DVD post-free.* ◦ *The guidebook costs £10.95 post-free.*

postgrad /ˈpəʊst.græd/ (US) /ˈpoʊst-/ **noun** [C] a **postgraduate** • **postgrad adj** *a postgrad degree*

postgraduate /ˌpəʊstˈgrædʒ.u.ət/ (US) /ˌpoʊstˈgrædʒ.u-/ **noun; adj**

▸**noun** [C] (US usually **graduate**) a student who has already got one degree and is studying at a university for a more advanced qualification

▸**adj** [before noun] (mainly US **graduate**) describes university studies or students at a more advanced level than a first degree: *postgraduate studies/research* ◦ *a postgraduate degree* ***in*** *microbiology*

Postˌgraduate Cerˈtificate in Eduˈcation noun [C usually singular] (abbreviation **PGCE**) a British teaching qualification for people who already have a university degree: *It takes a year to do a PGCE and then you can teach in a primary or secondary school.*

posthaste /ˌpəʊstˈheɪst/ (US) /ˌpoʊst-/ **adv** old-fashioned formal as fast as possible: *They travelled posthaste to Rome to collect the award.*

posthumous /ˈpɒs.tjʊ.məs/ (US) /ˈpɑːs.tʃə-/ **adj** formal happening after a person's death: *a posthumous award* • **posthumously** /-li/ **adv** *His last novel was published posthumously.*

postie /ˈpəʊs.tiː/ (US) /ˈpoʊs-/ **noun** [C] UK informal for **postman**

ˌpost-inˈdustrial adj belonging or relating to an economy that is no longer based on heavy industry, such as the making of large machines

posting /ˈpəʊ.stɪŋ/ (US) /ˈpoʊ-/ **noun** [C] **JOB** ▷ **1** UK (US and Australian English usually **post**) a job, often within the same organization that you are working for, which involves going to a different country or town: *If you were offered an overseas posting, would you take it?* **MESSAGE** ▷ **2** an electronic message that you send to a website in order to allow many people to see it

ˈPost-it (ˌnote) noun [C] trademark a small, coloured piece of paper for short messages that can be stuck temporarily to something else

postman /ˈpəʊst.mən/ (US) /ˈpoʊst-/ **noun** [C] (plural **-men** /-mən/) UK (UK informal **postie**, US **mailman**) (B1) someone whose job is to DELIVER and collect letters and parcels that are sent by post

postmark /ˈpəʊst.mɑːk/ (US) /ˈpoʊst.mɑːrk/ **noun** [C] an official mark put on a letter or parcel, typically showing the place that it was sent from and the time or date that it was sent • **postmark verb** [T]

postmaster /ˈpəʊstˌmɑː.stər/ (US) /ˈpoʊstˌmæs.tɚ/ **noun** [C] a person who is in charge of a POST OFFICE

postmistress /ˈpəʊstˌmɪs.trəs/ (US) /ˈpoʊst-/ **noun** [C] a woman who is in charge of a POST OFFICE

postmodern /ˌpəʊstˈmɒd.ən/ (US) /ˌpoʊstˈmɑː.dɚn/ **adj** (also **postmodernist**) relating to POSTMODERNISM: *a postmodern building* ◦ *a postmodernist critique*

postmodernism /ˌpəʊstˈmɒd.ən.ɪ.zəm/ (US) /ˌpoʊstˈmɑː.dɚ.nɪ-/ **noun** [U] a style of art, writing, music, theatre, and especially ARCHITECTURE popular in the West in the 1980s and 90s, that includes features from several different periods in the past or from the present and past

post-mortem /ˌpəʊstˈmɔː.təm/ (US) /ˌpoʊstˈmɔːr.t̬əm/ **noun** [C] **1** a medical examination of a dead person's body in order to find out the cause of death: *to* ***conduct*** *a post-mortem* ***examination*** → Synonym **autopsy** **2** informal a discussion of an event after it has happened, especially of what was wrong with it or why it failed: *After we've played a match, there's usually a post-mortem over a few beers.*

postnatal /ˌpəʊstˈneɪ.təl/ (US) /ˌpoʊstˈneɪ.t̬əl/ **adj** relating to the period of time immediately after a baby has been born: *postnatal care* ◦ *postnatal depression* → Compare **antenatal, prenatal**

postnuptial /ˌpəʊstˈnʌp.ʃəl/ US /ˌpoʊst-/ **adj** formal done after marriage or relating to the period after marriage

ˈpost ˌoffice noun [C] A2 a place where stamps are sold and from where letters and parcels are sent

the ˈPost ˌOffice noun the organization in many countries, including the UK, that is in charge of collecting and delivering the post

ˌpost-ˈoperative adj specialized relating to the period of time which immediately follows a medical operation: *post-operative care* ◦ *post-operative infection*

postpartum /ˌpəʊstˈpɑː.təm/ US /ˌpoʊstˈpɑːr.ţəm/ **adj** specialized after giving birth: *postpartum depression*

postpone /pəʊstˈpəʊn/, /pəst-/ US /poʊstˈpoʊn/ **verb** [T] B1 to delay an event and plan or decide that it should happen at a later date or time: *They decided to postpone their holiday* ***until*** *next year.* ◦ [+ -ing verb] *We've had to postpone go****ing*** *to France because the children are ill.* • **postponement** /-mənt/ **noun** [C or U] *We were disappointed by yet another postponement of our trip.*

postprandial /ˌpəʊstˈpræn.di.əl/ US /ˌpoʊst-/ **adj** formal happening after LUNCH or DINNER: *He took the usual postprandial stroll around the grounds of his house.*

postscript /ˈpəʊst.skrɪpt/ US /ˈpoʊst-/ **noun** [C] **1** (abbreviation **PS**) a short remark or message added to the bottom of a letter after you have signed your name, usually introduced by the abbreviation PS: *There was the usual romantic postscript at the end of his letter – PS I love you.* **2** any written or spoken addition to something already finished: *As a postscript* ***to*** *that story I told you last week, it turned out that the woman was his sister-in-law.*

postseason /ˈpəʊstˌsiː.zən/ US /ˈpoʊst-/ **adj** mainly US describes games that are played after the end of the sports season • **postseason noun** [C] *The Indians have won three straight one-run games in the postseason.*

ˌpost-trauˌmatic ˈstress diˌsorder noun [U] (abbreviation **PTSD**) a mental condition in which a person suffers severe ANXIETY and DEPRESSION after a very frightening or shocking experience, such as an accident or a war

postulate verb; noun

▸**verb** [I or T] /ˈpɒs.tjʊ.leɪt/ US /ˈpɑː.stjə-/ formal to suggest a theory, idea, etc. as a basic principle from which a further idea is formed or developed: [+ that] *It was the Greek astronomer, Ptolemy, who postulated* ***that*** *the Earth was at the centre of the universe.*

▸**noun** [C] /ˈpɒs.tjʊ.lət/ US /ˈpɑː.stjə-/ formal an idea that is suggested or accepted as a basic principle before a further idea is formed or developed from it

posture /ˈpɒs.tʃər/ US /ˈpɑːs.tʃɚ/ **noun** POSITION OF BODY ▷ **1** C1 [C or U] the way in which someone usually holds their shoulders, neck, and back, or a particular position in which someone stands, sits, etc.: *She's got very good/bad posture.* ◦ *He always* ***adopts/assumes*** *(= moves into) the same posture for the cameras.* OPINION ▷ **2** [C usually singular] a way in which a government or other organization thinks about and/or deals with a particular matter: *For the third time this week the opposition has attacked the government's posture* ***on*** *defence.* ◦ *The tone of the feminist speakers suggested they were adopting a rather defensive posture.*

posturing /ˈpɒs.tʃər.ɪŋ/ US /ˈpɑːs.tʃɚ-/ **noun** [U] disapproving behaviour or speech that is intended to attract attention and interest, or to make people believe something that is not true: *His writing has been dismissed as mere intellectual posturing.* • **posture** /ˈpɒs.tʃər/ US /ˈpɑːs.tʃɚ/ **verb** [I]

postwar /ˈpəʊst.wɔː/ US /ˈpoʊst.wɔːr/ **adj** happening or existing in the period after a war, especially the First or Second World War: *postwar Europe* ◦ *the postwar period* → Compare **pre-war**

posy /ˈpəʊ.zi/ US /ˈpoʊ-/ **noun** [C] **1** UK and US a small BUNCH of cut flowers: *a posy of violets* **2** US a flower: *a delicate yellow posy*

pot /pɒt/ US /pɑːt/ **noun; verb**

▸**noun** CONTAINER ▷ **1** B1 [C] any of various types of container, usually round, especially one used for cooking food: *Fill a large pot with salted water and bring it to the boil.* ◦ *There's plenty of cupboard space in the kitchen for all your pots* ***and pans.*** → See also **teapot** **2** B1 [C] mainly UK any of different types of containers, with or without a lid, especially for storing food or liquids: *a pot of cream/jam/paint/ink* **3** B1 [C] a **flowerpot**: *a terracotta* ***plant*** *pot* ◦ *Most lilies grow well in pots.* **4** [C] the amount that is contained inside a pot: *I've just drunk a whole pot of tea!* ◦ *She'd made a large pot of chicken soup.* **5** [C] used in combination to refer to a container of a stated type: *a coffee pot* ◦ *a flowerpot* ◦ *a teapot* **6** [C] a dish, bowl, etc. made by hand out of clay **7 pots of sth** a large amount of something: *She's got pots of* ***money*** *(= she's very rich).* TOILET ▷ **8** [C] a POTTY (= bowl used by children as a toilet) DRUG ▷ **9** [U] US slang or UK slang **cannabis**: *a pot smoker* STOMACH ▷ **10** [C usually singular] mainly humorous a **potbelly** BAD STATE ▷ **11 go to pot** informal to be damaged or spoiled because people are not working hard on it or caring for it: *I'm afraid I've let the garden go to pot this summer.* HIT BALL ▷ **12** [C] UK an act of hitting a ball into a hole, especially in games such as SNOOKER: *Dawson made a difficult pot look very easy.*

IDIOMS **not have a pot to piss in** very informal to be very poor: *Any help we can offer them will be appreciated. They don't have a pot to piss in.* • **the pot calling the kettle black** something you say that means someone should not criticize another person for a fault that they have themselves: *Elliott accused me of being selfish. Talk about the pot calling the kettle black!*

▸**verb** (-tt-) SHOOT ▷ **1** [I or T] mainly UK to shoot birds or small animals for food, or to shoot (at) them without taking careful aim: *He strolled through the fields, potting* ***(at)*** *the occasional rabbit.* HIT BALL ▷ **2** [T] UK in games such as SNOOKER, to hit a ball so that it falls into one of the holes at the edge of the table PUT IN CONTAINER ▷ **3** [T] to put a plant into a container to grow: *I'm just going to pot* ***(up)*** *these seedlings.*

potable /ˈpəʊ.tə.bl̩/ US /ˈpoʊ.ţə-/ **adj** formal clean and safe to drink: *potable water*

potage /pəˈtɑːʒ/, /ˈpɒt.ɪdʒ/ US /ˈpɑː.ţɪdʒ/ **noun** [U] old use thick soup, especially one made from vegetables

potash /ˈpɒt.æʃ/ US /ˈpɑːt-/ **noun** [U] a white powder containing potassium that is put on the earth to make crops grow better

potassium /pəˈtæs.i.əm/ **noun** [U] (symbol **K**) a silver-white chemical element which, when combined with other elements, is used in the production of soap, glass, and FERTILIZERS (= substances which help plants to grow)

poˌtassium ˈiodide noun [U] specialized a white chemical COMPOUND similar to salt, which forms in CRYSTALS and has medical and photographic uses

P

potato /pəˈteɪ.təʊ/ US /-t̬oʊ/ **noun** [C or U] (plural **potatoes**) A1 a round vegetable which grows underground and has white flesh with light brown, red, or pink skin, or the plant on which these grow: *boiled/roasted/fried potatoes* ◦ *mashed potato/mashed potatoes*

poˈtato ˌchip noun [C] A2 US for **crisp**

poˌtato ˈsalad noun [C or U] small pieces of cooked potato mixed with MAYONNAISE (= a thick cold white sauce)

potbelly /ˌpɒtˈbel.i/ US /ˌpɑːt-/ **noun** [C] (also **pot**) a fat, round stomach: *After 20 years of heavy drinking, he has a massive potbelly.* • **potbellied** /-ˈbel.id/ **adj** *Who's that potbellied man sitting over there?*

potboiler /ˈpɒtˌbɔɪ.ləʳ/ US /ˈpɑːtˌbɔɪ.lɚ/ **noun** [C] disapproving an artistic work, usually of low quality, that has been created quickly just to earn money

ˈpot-bound adj UK (US **rootbound**) If a plant is pot-bound, its roots have filled the container it is growing in and it stops growing well.

potency /ˈpəʊ.tən.si/ US /ˈpoʊ.t̬ənt-/ **noun** [U] **1** strength, influence, or effectiveness: *This new drug's potency is not yet known.* ◦ *He owed his popular support to the potency of his propaganda machine.* **2** a man's ability to have sex: *Consuming large amounts of alcohol can significantly reduce a man's potency.* → Compare **impotence**

potent /ˈpəʊ.tənt/ US /ˈpoʊ.t̬ənt/ **adj** very powerful, forceful, or effective: *Surprise remains the terrorists' most potent **weapon**.* ◦ *The Berlin Wall was a potent **symbol** of the Cold War.* ◦ *This is a very potent **drug** and can have unpleasant side-effects.* • **potently** /-li/ **adv** *Her arguments were strong, and potently deployed.*

potentate /ˈpəʊ.tən.teɪt/ US /ˈpoʊ.t̬ən-/ **noun** [C] literary a ruler who has a lot of power, especially one whose power is not limited, for example by the existence of a parliament

potential /pəˈten.ʃəl/ US /poʊ-/ **adj; noun**

▸**adj** [before noun] B2 possible when the necessary conditions exist: *A number of potential **buyers** have expressed interest in the company.* ◦ *Many potential **customers** are waiting for a fall in prices before buying.* ◦ *The accident is a grim reminder of the potential **dangers** involved in North Sea oil production.*

▸**noun** [U] B2 someone's or something's ability to develop, achieve, or succeed: *The region has **enormous** potential **for** economic development.* ◦ *I don't feel I'm **achieving** my **full** potential in my present job.* ◦ [+ to infinitive] *You have the potential **to** reach the top of your profession.* ◦ *I think this room has got a lot of potential (= could be very good if some changes were made to it).*

poˌtential ˈenergy noun [U] specialized in physics, the energy stored by something because of its position (as when an object is raised), because of its condition (as when something is pulled or pushed out of shape), or in chemical form (as in fuel or an electric BATTERY)

potentiality /pəˌten.ʃiˈæl.ə.ti/ US /poʊˌten.ʃiˈæl.ə.t̬i/ **noun** [C or U] formal an ability for development, achievement, or success that is natural or has not been used: [+ to infinitive] *The army's potentiality **to** intervene in politics remains strong.*

potentially /pəˈten.ʃəl.i/ US /poʊ-/ **adv** B2 possibly: *Hepatitis is a potentially **fatal** disease.* ◦ *This crisis is potentially the most **serious** in the organization's history.*

pothead /ˈpɒt.hed/ US /ˈpɑːt-/ **noun** [C] informal someone who uses CANNABIS regularly

potholder /ˈpɒtˌhəʊl.dəʳ/ US /ˈpɑːtˌhoʊl.dɚ/ **noun** [C] mainly US a thick piece of material used for protecting your hands when removing hot dishes or pans from the cooker

pothole /ˈpɒt.həʊl/ US /ˈpɑːt.hoʊl/ **noun** [C] **HOLE** ▷ **1** a hole in a road surface which results from gradual damage caused by traffic and/or weather: *The car's suspension is so good that when you hit a pothole you hardly notice it.* **2** a deep hole formed underground in LIMESTONE areas by the gradual rubbing and dissolving action of water flowing through the stone **PROBLEM** ▷ **3** a problem: *The road to economic recovery is full of potholes.*

potholed /ˈpɒt.həʊld/ US /ˈpɑːt.hoʊld/ **adj** describes a road that contains a lot of potholes: *The cottage is situated in the middle of a wood at the end of a narrow potholed lane.*

potholing /ˈpɒtˌhəʊ.lɪŋ/ US /ˈpɑːtˌhoʊ-/ **noun** [U] UK (US **spelunking**) a sport which involves climbing into and around underground caves • **potholer** /-ləʳ/ US /-lɚ/ **noun** [C] (US **spelunker**)

potion /ˈpəʊ.ʃən/ US /ˈpoʊ-/ **noun** [C] **1** a liquid that is believed to have a magical effect on someone who drinks it: *a love/magic potion* **2** mainly disapproving a liquid or substance that is said to cure an illness or a condition, but is not a medicine: *Americans are said to spend more on pills and potions than any other nation.*

ˌpot ˈluck noun **1** [U] anything that is available or is found by chance, rather than something chosen, planned, or prepared: *We had no idea which hotel would be best, so we just **took** pot luck **with** the first one on the list.* ◦ *Mary's welcome to stay for dinner if she doesn't mind **taking** pot luck (= having whatever is available).* **2** [C] mainly US an informal meal where guests bring a different dish that is then shared with the other guests: *a pot luck **dinner*** ◦ *We're having a pot luck on Saturday.*

ˈpot ˌplant noun [C] **1** UK a **houseplant** **2** US informal a **cannabis** plant

potpourri /ˌpəʊ.pəˈriː/ US /ˌpoʊ-/ **noun** **1** [U] a mixture of dried PETALS and leaves from various flowers and plants that is used to give a room a pleasant smell: *a bowl of potpourri* **2** [S] an unusual or interesting mixture of things: *Her new TV show will be a potpourri **of** arts and media reports.*

ˈpot ˌroast noun [C] a piece of BEEF that is cooked slowly in a covered dish with a small amount of liquid and sometimes vegetables: *We usually have a pot roast for Sunday lunch.*

potshot /ˈpɒt.ʃɒt/ US /ˈpɑːt.ʃɑːt/ **noun** [C] **1** (UK also **pot**) a shot that is FIRED carelessly or with little preparation: *He was **taking** potshots **at** neighbourhood cats.* **2** a criticism: *The recent criticism of his leadership has included potshots from several leading political journalists.*

potted /ˈpɒt.ɪd/ US /ˈpɑː.t̬ɪd/ **adj** [before noun] **1 potted plant** a plant that is grown in a pot **FOOD** ▷ **2** UK describes cooked food, especially meat or fish, that is preserved in a closed container: *potted meat/shrimps* **SHORT FORM** ▷ **3** UK informal describes a form of a story or book that has been made shorter and simpler and contains only the main facts or features: *They publish a potted **version** of Shakespeare's plays especially for children.*

potter /ˈpɒt.əʳ/ US /ˈpɑː.t̬ɚ/ **verb; noun**

▸**verb** [I usually + adv/prep] mainly UK (US usually **putter**) to move about without hurrying, and in a relaxed and pleasant way: *I spent the afternoon pottering **around** the garden doing a few odd jobs.* ◦ *He doesn't drive very fast – he tends to potter **along**.*

▸**noun** **POT MAKER** ▷ **1** [C] a person who makes dishes, plates, and other objects from clay, usually by hand on a special wheel **WALK** ▷ **2** [S] UK a slow, relaxed walk around a place: *I'm just going into town for **a** potter **round** the shops.*

ˌpotter's ˈwheel noun [C usually singular] a machine with a horizontal spinning disc on which clay is shaped into decorative or useful objects

potter's wheel

pottery /ˈpɒt.ər.i/ ⓤⓈ /ˈpɑː.t̬ɚ-/ noun [U] **1** B2 the activity or skill of making clay objects by hand **2** B2 objects that are made out of clay by hand: *They sell pottery and other handmade goods.*

ˈpotting ˌshed noun [C] mainly UK a small building in a garden in which plant containers, young plants, seeds, tools, etc. are kept

potty /ˈpɒt.i/ ⓤⓈ /ˈpɑː.t̬i/ adj; noun

▸adj UK informal **1** silly or slightly crazy: *She must have been potty to sell that car so cheaply.* ◦ *I'd go potty if I had to work here all the time.* **2 be potty about sth/sb** to like something very much: *He's potty about old cars.* • **pottiness** /-nəs/ noun [U]

IDIOM **drive sb potty** to annoy someone a lot: *The noise from our next-door neighbours is driving us potty.*

▸noun [C] (also **pot**) mainly UK a bowl, sometimes with a handle, which young children sit on and use as a toilet: *Don't forget to sit Jamie on the potty before you take him to the zoo.*

ˈpotty ˌchair noun [C] a small chair with a hole in the seat and a bowl fixed under it for teaching young children to use the toilet

ˈpotty-trained (also **ˈtoilet-trained**) describes children who know how to use a potty or toilet and no longer need to wear NAPPIES: *By what age are children usually potty-trained?* • **ˈpotty-ˌtraining** noun [U] (also **ˈtoilet-ˌtraining**) the process of teaching a child to use a potty

pouch /paʊtʃ/ noun [C] **BAG** ▷ **1** a bag or soft container for a small object or a small amount of something: *All our electric shavers are supplied with a free travel pouch.* ◦ *Food sealed in foil pouches lasts for a long time.* **OF ANIMALS** ▷ **2** a pocket on the lower part of the body of some female animals in which their young are carried and protected after they are born: *Kangaroos carry their young in pouches.* **3** a bag formed from skin in the mouths of some animals, used for carrying and storing food

pouf noun [C] **SEAT** ▷ **1** (also **pouffe**) /puːf/ (US **ottoman**) a soft, round or square seat with no back or sides, used for sitting on or resting your feet on **PERSON** ▷ **2** /pʊf/ UK offensive a POOF (= gay man)

poultice /ˈpəʊl.tɪs/ ⓤⓈ /ˈpoʊl.t̬ɪs/ noun [C] a piece of cloth covered with a thick, often warm substance, wrapped around an injury to reduce pain or swelling

poultry /ˈpəʊl.tri/ ⓤⓈ /ˈpoʊl-/ noun; noun

▸noun [plural] birds, such as chickens, that are bred for their eggs and meat

▸noun [U] the meat from birds such as chickens

pounce /paʊns/ verb [I] to jump or move quickly in order to catch or take hold of something: *The cat sat in the tree ready to pounce **on** the ducks below.* ◦ *The police were waiting to pounce when he arrived at the airport.*

PHRASAL VERB **pounce on sth** **CRITICIZE** ▷ **1** to immediately criticize a mistake: *He knows that his critics are waiting to pounce on any slip that he makes.* **ACCEPT** ▷ **2** to accept something quickly and with enthusiasm: *I think if she were given the opportunity to work here, she'd pounce on it.*

pound /paʊnd/ noun; verb

▸noun [C] **MONEY** ▷ **1** A2 (symbol **£**) the standard unit of money used in the UK and some other countries: *a one-pound/two-pound coin* ◦ *There are one hundred pence in a pound.* ◦ *They stole jewellery valued at £50,000 (= 50,000 pounds).* ◦ *'Have you got any change?' 'Sorry, I've only got a five-pound **note**.* **2 the pound** (symbol **£**) the value of the UK pound, used in comparing the values of different types of money from around the world: *The devaluation of **the** pound will make British goods more competitive abroad.* ◦ *On the foreign exchanges the pound rose two cents against the dollar to $1.52.* **WEIGHT** ▷ **3** B2 (written abbreviation **lb**) a unit for measuring weight: *One pound is approximately equal to 454 grams.* ◦ *One kilogram is roughly the same as 2.2 lbs.* ◦ *There are 16 ounces in one pound.* ◦ *Ann's baby weighed eight and a half pounds at birth.*

IDIOM **pound of flesh** disapproving something that you have the right to receive but is unreasonable to demand from someone

▸verb [I or T] B2 to hit or beat repeatedly with a lot of force, or to crush something by hitting it repeatedly: *I could feel my heart pounding as I went on stage to collect the prize.* ◦ *Nearly 50 people are still missing after the storm pounded the coast.* ◦ *The city was pounded **to** rubble during the war.* ◦ *He pounded **on** the door demanding to be let in.* ◦ *She was pounding **away** on her typewriter until four in the morning.*

PHRASAL VERB **pound away at sth/sb** to criticize something or try to get someone to do something: *The campaigners have promised to **keep** pounding away at the council until the decision to build the road is reversed.*

-pounder /-paʊn.dər/ ⓤⓈ /-dɚ/ suffix informal weighing the number of pounds or FRACTION of a pound mentioned: *'What sort of burger do you want?' 'I think I'll have a **quarter**-pounder.'* ◦ mainly US *The newest member of the team is a 23-year-old 212-pounder from Miami.*

pounding /ˈpaʊn.dɪŋ/ noun [C or S] **DEFEAT** ▷ **1** a heavy attack or defeat: *The city received heavy poundings from the air every night last week.* **SOUND** ▷ **2** a regular sound of something hitting something else or of a loud noise: *the pounding of his heart*

IDIOM **take/get a pounding** to receive a lot of criticism: *The movie took quite a pounding from the critics.*

ˈpound ˌsign noun [C] the symbol £

ˌpound ˈsterling noun [C] (plural **pounds sterling**) the official name of the pound used as money in the UK

pour /pɔːr/ ⓤⓈ /pɔːr/ verb **CAUSE TO FLOW** ▷ **1** B1 [I or T] to make a substance flow from a container, especially into another container, by raising just one side of the container that the substance is in: *I spilled the juice while I was pouring it.* ◦ *Pour the honey **into** the bowl and mix it thoroughly with the other ingredients.* ◦ [+ two objects] *Would you like me to pour you some more wine?* ◦ *Would you like to pour (= pour a drink into a glass or cup) while I open some bags of nuts?* **FLOW QUICKLY** ▷ **2** B1 [I or T, usually + adv/prep] to

P

(cause to) flow quickly and in large amounts: *The bus was pouring* ***out*** *thick black exhaust fumes.* ◦ *The government has been pouring money* ***into*** *inefficient state-owned industries and the country can no longer afford it.* ◦ *I felt a sharp pain and looked down to see blood pouring* ***from*** *my leg.* ◦ *Refugees have been pouring* ***into*** *neighbouring countries to escape the civil war.* ◦ *The sweat was pouring* ***down*** *her face by the end of the race.* ◦ *It looks as though* ***it's*** *about to pour* (***with rain***). ◦ *I was standing in* ***the*** *pouring* ***rain*** *for an hour waiting for my bus.*

IDIOMS **pour your heart out** to tell someone your secret feelings and things that worry you, usually because you feel a strong need to talk about them: *I poured my heart out* ***to*** *him and then he told all his friends what I'd said.* • **pour oil on troubled waters** UK to do or say something in order to make people stop arguing and become calmer: *My husband's always arguing with my father, and I'm the one who has to pour oil on troubled waters.* • **pour scorn on sb/sth** to say a person or thing is stupid and not worth anything: *Critics of the president have been pouring scorn on the plan ever since it was first proposed.*

PHRASAL VERB **pour sth out** B2 to tell all your problems or feelings to someone, especially privately or secretly: *He spends every lunchtime pouring out his emotional problems to me and expects me to find a solution.*

pout /paʊt/ **verb** [I or T] to push the lower lip forward to show you are annoyed, or to push both lips forward in a sexually attractive way: *Vanessa always pouts if she doesn't get what she wants.* ◦ *Caroline pouts her lips when she's putting on lipstick.* • **pout noun** [C] *She didn't say anything but I could tell from her pout that she wasn't very pleased.*

poverty /ˈpɒv.ə.ti/ (US) /ˈpɑː.vɚ.t̬i/ **noun** [U] **1** B2 the condition of being extremely poor: *Two million people in the city live in* ***abject*** *(= very great) poverty.* ◦ *He emigrated to Australia to escape the* ***grinding*** *(= very great) poverty of his birthplace.* ◦ *Helping to alleviate poverty in developing countries also helps to reduce environmental destruction.* **2 a poverty of sth** formal a lack of something or when the quality of something is extremely low: *There is a disappointing poverty of creativity in their work.*

ˈpoverty ˌline noun [S] the official level of income that is needed to achieve a basic living standard with enough money for things such as food, clothing, and a place to live: *In 1991 almost 36 million Americans were* ***living below*** *the poverty line.*

ˈpoverty-ˌstricken adj describes a person or place suffering from the effects of being extremely poor: *Some beggars are neither poverty-stricken nor homeless.* ◦ *There are few jobs for the peasants who have flooded into the cities from the poverty-stricken countryside in search of work.*

ˈpoverty ˌtrap noun [S] UK a situation in which someone would be even poorer or not much richer if they had a job because they would no longer receive financial help from the government: *He's* ***caught in*** *the poverty trap and will only be five pounds a week better off if he accepts the job.*

pow /paʊ/ **exclamation** informal (especially in children's CARTOONS) a word which represents the noise of an explosion or a gun being shot: *When I shout 'Pow!' that means I've shot you and you've got to pretend to be dead.*

POW (UK also **PoW**) /ˌpiː.əʊˈdʌb.l̩.juː/ (US) /-oʊ-/ **noun** [C] abbreviation for **prisoner of war**: *He was a POW during the Vietnam war.* ◦ *a POW camp*

powder /ˈpaʊ.dəʳ/ (US) /-dɚ/ **noun; verb**

▸**noun 1** B1 [C or U] a solid substance that consists of extremely small pieces, is soft and easy to divide, and often has the same shape as the container that it is in: *curry/chilli powder* ◦ *talcum powder* ◦ *A packet of white powder was found and police scientists are analysing it.* ◦ *You'll get more flavour from the spices if you grind them into a powder.* ◦ UK *Why are there so many adverts for* ***washing*** *powders on TV?* ◦ *You can buy milk in powder form.* → See also **gunpowder 2** [U] a soft, dry substance that is spread over the skin of the face, in order to stop the skin from looking shiny: *face powder* ◦ *Dust the face lightly with powder.* **3** [U] fallen snow that is loose and dry and has not begun to melt: *I love skiing in deep powder.* • **powdery** /-i/ **adj** *The snow was fresh and powdery.*

▸**verb** [T] to put powder on someone's skin: *Powder the baby's bottom to stop it chafing.*

IDIOM **powder your nose** a polite or humorous way of saying that you are going to go to the toilet: *Would you get me another drink while I go and powder my nose?*

powdered /ˈpaʊ.dəd/ (US) /-dɚd/ **adj** in the form of a powder or covered with a powder: *Shall I put some powdered* ***milk*** *in your coffee?* ◦ *Her face was heavily powdered.*

ˌpowdered ˈsugar noun [U] US for **icing sugar**

ˈpowder ˌkeg noun [C] a situation or a place that could easily become extremely dangerous: *The new tax is a* ***political*** *powder keg which could result in widespread violence.*

ˈpowder ˌpuff noun [C] a round piece of soft material used for putting powder on the face or body

ˈpowder ˌroom noun [C usually singular] a polite word for a women's toilet in a public building, such as a restaurant, hotel, theatre, etc.

power /paʊəʳ/ (US) /paʊɚ/ **noun; verb**

▸**noun CONTROL** ▷ **1** B2 [U] ability to control people and events: *I've no power* ***over*** *him – he does what he wants to.* ◦ *Once nicotine has you* ***in*** *its power, it's very difficult to stop smoking.* ◦ *She has the power to charm any man she meets.* **2** C1 [U] the amount of political control a person or group has in a country: *Does the president have more power than the prime minister?* ◦ *How long has the Conservative Party been* ***in*** *power?* ◦ *The army* ***seized*** *power after five days of anti-government demonstrations.* **STRENGTH** ▷ **3** C1 [U] strength: *Our car doesn't have enough power to tow a trailer.* ◦ *Weightlifters have tremendous power in their arms and legs.* ◦ *Scientists are working to harness the power of the atom.* ◦ *The economic power of many Asian countries has grown dramatically in recent years.* **OFFICIAL RIGHT** ▷ **4** [U] an official or legal right to do something: [+ to infinitive] *I'd like to help but I don't have the power* ***to*** *intervene in this dispute.* ◦ *It's not* ***in*** *your power* ***to*** *cancel the order.* ◦ *I can't give you a refund – I'm afraid it's not* ***within*** *my power.* **5 powers** [plural] authority: *You were acting* ***beyond*** *your powers when you agreed to give her a pay rise.* ◦ *Visitors to the city are respectfully reminded of the council's powers* ***to*** *remove illegally parked vehicles.* **ELECTRICITY** ▷ **6** B1 [U] electricity, especially when considering its use or production: *You should disconnect the power before attempting to repair electrical equipment.* ◦ *Our building lost power (= the electricity was stopped) during the storm.* ◦ *power* ***cables/lines*** **ABILITY** ▷ **7 powers** [plural] abilities: *My mental powers aren't as good as they used to be.* **8** C1 [U] a natural skill or an ability to do something: *He was so shocked by what happened to* his parents that he lost the power **of** speech. ◦ [+ to infinitive] *The surgeon did everything* **in** *her power* **to** *save him.* **PERSON WITH CONTROL** ▷ **9** C1 [C] a person, organization, or country that has control over others, often because of WEALTH, importance, or great military strength: *Spain was an important* **military** *power in the 16th century.* ◦ *Germany is on its way to becoming a* **world** *power with a permanent seat on the UN Security Council.* ◦ *She is an increasingly important power* **in the** *company.* **ENERGY** ▷ **10** [U] the rate at which energy is used, or the ability to produce energy: *The ship was only slightly damaged in the collision and was able to sail into port under its own power.* ◦ specialized *The power* **rating** *of my amplifier is 40 watts per channel.* **IMAGE SIZE** ▷ **11** [U] the amount by which an image is increased by a device used for seeing things that are very small or a long distance away: *What's the magnification power of your binoculars?* ◦ *You'll need a very high-power microscope to see something as small as that.* ◦ *A low-power telescope is enough if you only want to look at the moon.* **MATHEMATICS** ▷ **12** [S] specialized the number of times that a number is to be multiplied by itself: *2* **to the** *fourth power is 2 times 2 times 2 times 2, which equals 16.* ◦ *3* **to the** *power 4 is usually written as* 3^4*.*

> Word partners for **power** (**CONTROL**)
>
> *come into/rise to* power • *assume/seize/take* power • *devolve/hand over* power • *considerable/enormous* power • a *position* of power • a power *struggle* • have power *over* sb • be *in* power

> Word partners for **power** (**ELECTRICITY**)
>
> *lose/restore* power • *switch off/turn off* the power • a power *cable/line/supply* • be *without* power

> Word partners for **power** (**ENERGY**)
>
> *generate/produce/provide/supply* power • *harness* power • *nuclear/solar/wind* power

IDIOMS **do sb a power of good** UK to be extremely good for someone: *He's been working too hard and some time off would do him a power of good.* • **more power to your elbow!** UK (US **more power to you!**) an expression of praise or admiration for someone's success or brave actions: *'I've decided to quit my job and set up my own business.' 'Well, good for you. More power to your elbow!'* • **the power behind the throne** someone who does not have an official position in a government or organization but who secretly controls it • **the powers that be** important people who have authority over others: *It's up to the powers that be to decide what should be done next.*

▸verb **ENERGY** ▷ **1** [T] to provide a machine with energy and the ability to operate: *Buses and trucks are usually powered by diesel engines.* ◦ *In the future electricity will be used to power road vehicles.* **STRENGTH** ▷ **2** [I usually + adv/prep] to act with great strength or in a forceful way: *Halfway through, she powered into the lead and went on to win the race.*

PHRASAL VERB **power (sth) up** mainly US If something that needs power or energy powers up, or if someone powers it up, it is turned on or prepared so that it is ready for use or action: *The computer takes a few seconds to power up after it's been switched on.* ◦ *College baseball teams across the country are powering up for the new season.*

ˌpower-asˌsisted ˈsteering noun [U] (ˈ**power ˌsteering**) a system for changing the direction in which a road vehicle is moving by using power from the engine to help the driver turn the vehicle

ˈpower ˌbase noun [C usually singular] an area of a country or a group of people on which someone's power depends: *The industrial cities are the Labour Party's traditional power base.*

powerboat /ˈpauə.bəut/ US /ˈpauɚ.bout/ noun [C] a small boat with a powerful engine that can travel very fast and is used in races

ˈpower ˌbreakfast/ˌlunch noun [C] humorous an occasion at which people eat while they are working and talking about business

ˈpower ˌbroker noun [C] someone who has a big influence on decisions about who should have political power

ˈpower ˌcut noun [C] UK (US ˈ**power ˌoutage**) B2 an interruption in the supply of electricity: *Storms caused power cuts in hundreds of homes last night.*

ˈpower ˌdressing noun [U] a style of dressing in which business people wear formal clothes to make them seem powerful

-powered /-pauəd/ US /-pauɚd/ suffix operated by the type of energy stated: *a battery-powered radio* ◦ *nuclear-powered submarines* ◦ *My calculator doesn't need batteries because it's* **solar***-powered* (= it obtains its energy from the sun).

powerful /ˈpauə.fəl/ US /ˈpauɚ-/ adj **CONTROL** ▷ **1** B1 having a lot of power to control people and events: *The president is more powerful than the prime minister.* ◦ *She's the most powerful person in the organization.* **STRENGTH** ▷ **2** B1 having a lot of strength or force: *She's an extremely powerful runner.* ◦ *The picture quality is bad because the TV signal isn't powerful enough.* **3** B2 having a very great effect: *a powerful drug* ◦ *Her speech about cruelty to children was very powerful.* **IMAGE SIZE** ▷ **4** having the power to increase the size of an image of something that is very small or far away many times: *You'd need an extremely powerful microscope to see something so small.* • **powerfully** /-i/ US /ˈpauɚ-/ adv B2 *He argued powerfully and persuasively against capital punishment.* ◦ *She kicked the ball so powerfully that it flew over the hedge.* ◦ *Klaus is a very powerfully* **built** *man* (= has a body with large strong muscles).

powerhouse /ˈpauə.haus/ US /ˈpaur-/ noun [C usually singular] a country, organization, or person with a lot of influence, power, or energy: *Germany is an economic powerhouse.* ◦ *She's a powerhouse* **of** *original ideas and solutions.*

powerless /ˈpauə.ləs/ US /ˈpauɚ-/ adj having no power: *The villagers are powerless* **against** *the armed invaders.* ◦ *The police seem to be powerless* (= unable) **to** *prevent these attacks.* • **powerlessness** /-nəs/ noun [U] *A significant cause of stress in the workplace is a sense of powerlessness and lack of control.*

ˈpower ˌnap noun [C] a short sleep that you have during the day: *Taking a 20-minute power nap can boost your energy levels.* • ˌ**power-ˌnap** verb [I] (-pp-)

ˌpower of ˈattorney noun [C or U] legal the legal right to act for someone else in their financial or business matters, or the document which gives someone this right

ˈpower ˌplant noun [C] US for **power station**

ˈpower ˌpoint noun [C] UK (US **eˌlectrical ˈoutlet**) a device to which a piece of electrical equipment can be connected in order to provide it with electricity

ˈpower ˌpolitics noun [plural] the threat or use of military force to end an international disagreement: *Woodrow Wilson hoped the League of Nations would replace power politics with international cooperation.*

P

ˈpower-sharing noun [U] a situation in which two people or groups share responsibility for running a government, organization, etc.: *a power-sharing arrangement/scheme*

the ˌpowers of ˈdarkness noun [plural] evil spiritual forces: *Throughout the play, Macbeth struggles with the powers of darkness.*

ˈpower ˌstation noun [C] (US also **ˈpower ˌplant**) a factory where electricity is produced

ˈpower ˌstructure noun [C] a way in which power is organized or shared in an organization or society: *The president has promised a new constitution and the creation of democratic power structures.*

ˈpower ˌstruggle noun [C] an unpleasant or violent competition for power

ˈpower ˌtool noun [C] a tool that operates with an electric motor

ˈpower ˌvacuum noun [C usually singular] a condition that exists when someone has lost control of something and no one has replaced them: *She was quick to* ***fill*** *the power vacuum that was left by the sudden death of the managing director.*

powwow /ˈpaʊ.waʊ/ noun **1** [C] a meeting of Native Americans for making decisions or for having spiritual ceremonies or celebrations **2** [C usually singular] humorous a meeting where something important is discussed: *My brother's getting divorced so I'm going home for a family powwow this weekend.*

the pox /ˈpɒks/ (US) /ˈpɑːks/ noun [S] old-fashioned informal for **syphilis** → See also **chickenpox, cowpox, smallpox**

poxy /ˈpɒk.si/ (US) /ˈpɑːk-/ adj UK informal having little value, importance, or influence: *She lives in a poxy little village in the middle of nowhere.*

pp. written abbreviation for pages: *This matter is discussed in more detail on pp. 101–123.*

pp (also **p.p.**) UK written abbreviation used to show when someone has signed a document for a person who is not available to sign it: *I hope to hear from you soon. Yours sincerely, Chris Smith, pp Rebecca Collings.*

PPS /ˌpiː.piːˈes/ adv used when an extra short message is added to the end of a letter after a message has already been added: *PS I forgot to invite you to our party next Sunday at six. PPS Please tell Ellis that he's welcome to come too.* → See also **PS**

PPV /piːpiːviː/ noun [U] abbreviation for **pay-per-view**

PR /ˌpiːˈɑːʳ/ (US) /-ˈɑːr/ noun [U] **ADVERTISING** ▷ **1** abbreviation for **public relations**: *The company's putting out a lot of PR about the new product line.* ◦ *They've decided to hire a PR* ***firm*** *to improve their public image.* ◦ *a PR exercise/campaign* **VOTING** ▷ **2** abbreviation for **proportional representation**: *Do you think a system of PR makes elections fairer?*

practicable /ˈpræk.tɪ.kə.bl̩/ adj formal able to be done or put into action: *The troops will be brought home as soon as practicable.* ◦ *It is not practicable* ***to*** *complete the tunnel before the end of the year.* → Opposite **impracticable** • **practicability** /ˌpræk.tɪ.kəˈbɪl.ɪ.ti/ (US) /-ə.t̬i/ noun [U] *Many people have expressed serious doubts about the practicability of the proposed schedule for next year.*

practical /ˈpræk.tɪ.kəl/ adj; noun

▸adj **EXPERIENCE** ▷ **1** (B2) relating to experience, real situations, or actions rather than ideas or imagination: *Qualifications are important but practical* ***experience*** *is always an advantage.* ◦ *The service offers young people practical* ***advice*** *on finding a job.* ◦ *What's the use of theoretical knowledge that has no practical* ***application****?* **2 for all practical purposes** in fact: *Dr Frampton is in charge, but for all practical purposes, her assistant runs the office.* **SUITABLE** ▷ **3** (C1) suitable for the situation in which something is used: *I tend to wear clothes that are practical rather than fashionable.* ◦ *Heavy boots aren't very practical for running.* → Opposite **impractical** **EFFECTIVE** ▷ **4** (C2) approving able to provide effective solutions to problems: *She has a lot of interesting ideas, but they're not very practical.* ◦ *We need someone practical who can cope with a crisis.* → Opposite **impractical** **POSSIBLE** ▷ **5** (C1) able to be done or put into action: [+ to infinitive] *It's simply not practical* ***to*** *divide the work between so many people.* → Opposite **impractical**

▸noun [C] a class or exam in a scientific or technical subject in which students do things rather than just write or talk about them: *We had to dissect a worm and a frog in our biology practical today.*

practicality /ˌpræk.tɪˈkæl.ɪ.ti/ (US) /-ə.t̬i/ noun [U] **SUITABLE** ▷ **1** [U] quality of being suitable for a particular occasion or use: *I bought these shoes for their practicality, not their appearance.* **EFFECTIVE** ▷ **2** [U] approving the quality of being able to provide effective solutions to problems: *Jonathan has demonstrated enormous practicality in his successful management of the shop.* **POSSIBLE** ▷ **3** [U] the possibility of being put into practice: *Your suggestion is appealing in theory, but it lacks practicality.* **REALLY** ▷ **4 practicalities** [plural] the conditions which result from an idea becoming a real situation: *The practicalities of having two young children and working full time meant we had to employ a nanny.* ◦ *It sounds like a good idea, but you ought to consider the practicalities before you put it into action.*

ˌpractical ˈjoke noun [C] a joke which makes someone seem silly and involves a physical action rather than words: *She glued her boss's cup and saucer together as a practical joke.* • **ˌpractical ˈjoker** noun [C]

practically /ˈpræk.tɪ.kəl.i/ adv **NEARLY** ▷ **1** (B2) almost or very nearly: *She blamed me for practically every mistake in the report.* ◦ *These changes would cost us practically* ***nothing****.* ◦ *It's practically* ***impossible*** *for me to get home in less than an hour.* ◦ *They used to argue all the time and now they've practically* ***stopped*** *talking to each other.* **REALLY** ▷ **2** in a way that relates to real situations and actions rather than ideas: *Many people have offered to help, but there is little they can do practically.* ◦ *Theoretically, it's a good idea to live without a car, but practically* ***speaking****, it would be difficult to manage without one.*

practice /ˈpræk.tɪs/ noun **ACTION** ▷ **1** (B2) [U] action rather than thought or ideas: *How do you intend to* ***put*** *these proposals* ***into*** *practice, Mohamed?* **2 in practice** (B2) used to describe what really happens as opposed to what you think will happen in a particular situation: *It seemed like a good idea before we started, but in practice it was a disaster.* ◦ *Officially, Robert's in charge, but in practice Hannah runs the office.* ◦ *I can't see how your plan is going to work in practice.* **REGULAR ACTIVITY** ▷ **3** (C2) [C or U] something that is usually or regularly done, often as a habit, tradition, or custom: *What can European companies learn from Japanese business practices?* ◦ *It's* ***common*** *practice in the States to tip the hairdresser.* ◦ *This is a cruel practice that should be banned immediately.* ◦ *What is* ***standard*** *practice (= what is usually done) in a situation like this?* ◦ *Newspaper editors have agreed a new* ***code of*** *practice on the invasion of privacy.* **4 make a practice of sth** UK old-fashioned to do something regularly: *I'll do your washing for you this time, but I'm not going to make a practice of it.* **TRAINING** ▷ **5** (A2) [C or U] the act of doing something regularly or repeatedly to improve your skill at doing it: *I need to get some more practice before I take my driving test.* ◦ *Are you coming to choir practice this evening?* ◦ *She's never at home because she spends all her free time at hockey practices.* ◦ *You'll gradually get better at it – it's just a question of practice.* ◦ *I'm a bit **out of** practice (= I haven't had any recent experience) but I'd love to play.* ◦ *Do you mind if I have a few practice shots before we start the game?* **WORK** ▷ **6** [C] a job or business that involves a lot of skill or training: *a dental/medical/veterinary/legal practice* ◦ *Our practice is responsible for about 5,000 patients.*

IDIOM **practice makes perfect** saying said to encourage someone to continue to do something many times, so that they will learn to do it very well

practise UK (US **practice**) /ˈpræk.tɪs/ verb **TRAINING** ▷ **1** A1 [I or T] to do or play something regularly or repeatedly in order to become skilled at it: *I'm quite good at tennis but I need to practise my serve.* ◦ *She practises the violin every day.* ◦ [+ -ing verb] *His written French is very good but he needs to practise speak**ing** it.* **WORK** ▷ **2** C1 [I or T] to work in an important skilled job for which a lot of training is necessary: *How long have you been practising **as** a dentist?* ◦ *She practised medicine for 20 years.* **REGULAR ACTIVITY** ▷ **3** [T] to do something regularly, often according to a custom, religion, or set of rules, or as a habit: *The new government has promised all citizens the right to practise their religion.* ◦ *Practising safe sex is an important way of avoiding HIV infection.* ◦ *The company denies that it has practised discrimination against any of its employees.*

IDIOM **practise what you preach** to do the things that you advise other people to do: *He's such a hypocrite! He never practises what he preaches.*

practised UK (US **practiced**) /ˈpræk.tɪst/ adj **1** very good at doing something because you have a lot of experience of doing it: *She is a confident and practised speaker who always impresses her audience.* ◦ *He is practised **in** the art of public debate.* ◦ *We need someone who is practised **at** negotiating business deals.* **2** formal describes a skill that has been obtained from a lot of practice: *She performed the song with practised skill.*

practising UK (US **practicing**) /ˈpræk.tɪ.sɪŋ/ adj [before noun] **RELIGION** ▷ **1** actively involved in a religion: *a practising Muslim/Jew/Christian* **WORK** ▷ **2** actively involved in a job: *a practising doctor/lawyer* ◦ *The number of practising doctors is falling even though more people are qualifying in medicine.*

practitioner /prækˈtɪʃ.ən.ər/ (US) /-ɚ/ noun [C] formal C2 someone involved in a skilled job or activity: *Elizabeth Quan is a London-based practitioner of traditional Chinese medicine.* ◦ *She was a **medical** practitioner (= a doctor) before she entered politics.* → See also **GP**

pragmatic /prægˈmæt.ɪk/ (US) /-ˈmæṭ-/ adj C2 solving problems in a sensible way that suits the conditions that really exist now, rather than obeying fixed theories, ideas, or rules: *In business, the pragmatic **approach** to problems is often more successful than an idealistic one.*

pragmatically /prægˈmæt.ɪ.kəl.i/ (US) /-ˈmæṭ-/ adv in a pragmatic way: *It is intended that these guidelines should be applied flexibly and pragmatically.*

pragmatism /ˈpræg.mə.tɪ.zəm/ noun [U] the quality of dealing with a problem in a sensible way that suits the conditions that really exist, rather than following fixed theories, ideas, or rules: *The council has operated much more effectively since pragmatism replaced political dogma.* • **pragmatist** /-tɪst/ noun [C] *She rose to power by being a political pragmatist who took advantage of every opportunity.*

prairie /ˈpreə.ri/ (US) /ˈprer.i/ noun [C or U] a wide area of flat land without trees in Canada and the northern US

ˈprairie ˌdog noun [C] a small wild mammal that lives on the prairies of Canada and the US

praise /preɪz/ verb; noun

▸verb [T] **SHOW APPROVAL** ▷ **1** B2 to express admiration or approval about the achievements or characteristics of a person or thing: *He should be praised **for** his honesty.* ◦ *My parents always praised me when I did well at school.* ◦ *He was **highly** praised for his research on heart disease.* **WORSHIP** ▷ **2** to honour, worship, and express admiration for a god: *They sang hymns praising God.*

> **Other ways of saying praise**
>
> If you **congratulate** someone, you praise that person and say that you are pleased for his or her success or because something special has happened:
>
> *I **congratulated** him on passing his driving test.*
>
> **Compliment** can be used when someone praises what someone has done or the way that person looks:
>
> *I was just **complimenting** Robert on the wonderful meal he has cooked.*
>
> If someone praises a person publicly or officially, you can use the verb **commend** or the phrase **pay tribute to**:
>
> *The judge **commended** her for her bravery.*
>
> *He **paid tribute to** the firefighters who had saved his daughter's life.*
>
> **Flatter** means 'to make someone feel important or attractive, or to praise someone in order to please him or her':
>
> *I knew he was only **flattering** me because he wanted to borrow some money.*
>
> In informal English, the verb **rave** is used when someone praises someone or something a lot:
>
> *Everyone's **raving** about the new band.*

▸noun [U] **APPROVAL** ▷ **1** C1 things that you say that express your admiration and approval for someone or something: *They deserve praise **for** all their hard work.* ◦ *His economic policies have **won** widespread praise for reducing government debt.* ◦ *Praise from Adrian is (high) praise **indeed**. (= praise from him is particularly special because he rarely praises anyone.)* **GOD** ▷ **2** formal an expression of respect and worship to a god: *As we **give** praise to God, let us remember those who are less fortunate than ourselves.*

praiseworthy /ˈpreɪzˌwɜː.ði/ (US) /-ˌwɜː-/ adj deserving praise: *His actions during the crisis were truly praiseworthy.*

praline /ˈprɑː.liːn/ (US) /ˈpreɪ-/ noun [C or U] a mixture of crushed nuts and burnt sugar that is used in sweet dishes and chocolates: *almond/hazelnut praline*

pram /præm/ noun [C] UK (US **ˈbaby ˌcarriage**) a vehicle for moving a baby around that consists of a small bed supported by a

pram

P

frame on four wheels: *I saw her **pushing** a pram down the street.*

prance /prɑːns/ Ⓤⓢ /præns/ **verb 1** [I + adv/prep] to walk in an energetic way and with more movement than necessary: *It's pathetic to see 50-year-old rock stars prancing **around** on stage as if they were still teenagers.* ◦ *She pranced into the office and demanded to speak to the manager.* **2** [I] When a horse prances, it takes small, quick steps and raises its legs higher than usual.

prang /præŋ/ **verb; noun**

▸**verb** [T] UK informal to damage a vehicle slightly in a road accident: *She pranged her mother's car a week after she passed her driving test.*

▸**noun** [C] UK (US ˈ**fender** ˌ**bender**) a road accident in which the vehicles involved are only slightly damaged

prank /præŋk/ **noun; verb**

▸**noun** [C] a trick that is intended to be funny but not to cause harm or damage: *When I was at school we were always **playing** pranks **on** our teachers.* ◦ *I've had enough of your **childish** pranks.*

▸**verb** [I or T] to play a trick on someone that is intended to be funny but not to cause harm or damage: *He finally realized he'd been pranked.* • **pranking** /ˈpræŋ.kɪŋ/ **noun** [U] *It was just harmless pranking.*

prankster /ˈpræŋk.stəʳ/ Ⓤⓢ /-stɚ/ **noun** [C] someone who plays pranks on people

prat /præt/ **noun; verb**

▸**noun** [C] UK informal someone who behaves stupidly or has little ability: *He looked a right prat in that pink suit.* ◦ *You've made me spill my drink, you prat!* ◦ *Occasionally I'll have a few too many drinks at a party and **make a** prat **of** my**self** (= behave stupidly).*

▸**verb** (-tt-)

PHRASAL VERB **prat about/around** UK informal to behave stupidly, especially when you should be behaving in a responsible way: *Stop pratting around and get on with your work!*

P

pratfall /ˈpræt.fɔːl/ Ⓤⓢ /-fɑːl/ **noun** [C] **1** mainly US a fall in which a person lands on their bottom, especially for a humorous effect in a play, film, etc. **2** an embarrassing defeat or failure: *Most of us get over the pratfalls of childhood.*

prattle /ˈpræt.l̩/ Ⓤⓢ /ˈpræţ-/ **verb** [I] to talk in a silly way or like a child for a long time about things that are not important or without saying anything important: *She'd have prattled **on about** her new job for the whole afternoon if I'd let her.* ◦ *Stop your prattling and go to sleep!* • **prattle noun** [U] *His speech contained nothing new and was full of political prattle and clichés.* • **prattler** /-l̩.əʳ/, /-ləʳ/ Ⓤⓢ /-l̩.ɚ/ **noun** [C]

prawn /prɔːn/ Ⓤⓢ /prɑːn/ **noun** [C] mainly UK (US usually **shrimp**) B2 a small sea creature with a shell and ten legs, that can be eaten: *Prawns are grey when they're raw, and turn pink when they're cooked.* ◦ *peeled prawns*

ˌ**prawn** ˈ**cocktail noun** [C or U] UK a salad made with prawns, LETTUCE, and tomatoes in a cold sauce, usually eaten as a STARTER (= small dish served before a main course) and often served in a glass → Compare **shrimp cocktail**

praxis /ˈpræk.sɪs/ **noun** [U] specialized the process of using a theory or something that you have learned in a practical way: *She is interested in both the theory and praxis of criminology.*

pray /preɪ/ **verb; adv**

▸**verb 1** A2 [I or T] to speak to a god either privately or in a religious ceremony in order to express love, admiration, or thanks or in order to ask for something: *She knelt and prayed silently.* ◦ *Let us pray **for** the victims of this terrible disaster.* ◦ [+ that] *We've been praying **to** God **that** your son will make a complete recovery.* ◦ formal *You must pray (= ask for) God's forgiveness for what you have done.* **2** B2 [I] to hope for something very much: *We're praying **for** good weather for tomorrow's cricket match.*

▸**adv** old use or formal a forceful way of saying 'please': *Pray tell your sister that I long to see her.* ◦ *And where have you been, pray **tell**?*

prayer /preəʳ/ Ⓤⓢ /prer/ **noun 1** B1 [C] the words that someone says or thinks when they are praying: *a prayer **of** thanks* ◦ *She always **says** her prayers (= prays) before she goes to sleep.* ◦ *We thought he'd been killed, but our prayers were **answered** when he arrived home unexpectedly.* ◦ *a prayer book* **2** [U] the act or ceremony in which someone prays: *I found her **kneeling in** prayer at the back of the church.* ◦ *The prisoners find their only solace in prayer.*

IDIOM **not have a prayer** to have no chance of succeeding: *She hasn't a prayer **of** winn**ing** the competition.*

ˈ**prayer** ˌ**mat noun** [C] a small piece of thick cloth on which a Muslim goes down on his knees and bends his body down to the ground when praying

ˌ**praying** ˈ**mantis noun** [C] (also **mantis**) a large, green insect that holds its front legs in a way that makes it look as if it is praying when it is waiting to catch another insect

pre- /priː-/ **prefix** before (a time or an event): *a pre-flight check* ◦ *a pre-lunch drink* ◦ *pre-industrial societies*

preach /priːtʃ/ **verb** IN CHURCH ▷ **1** [I or T] (especially of a priest in a church) to give a religious speech: *Father Martin preached **to** the assembled mourners.* ◦ *During the sermon, he preached about the need for forgiveness.* PERSUADE ▷ **2** [T] to try to persuade other people to believe in a particular belief or follow a particular way of life: *They preach the abolition of established systems but propose nothing to replace them.* ADVISE ▷ **3** [I] disapproving to give unwanted advice, especially about moral matters, in a boring way: *He's such a pain – he's always preaching **about** the virtues of working hard and getting up early.* ◦ *My mother's always preaching **at/to** me **about** keeping my room tidy.*

IDIOM **preach to the converted** (also **preach to the choir**) to try to persuade people to believe things which they already believe: *You needn't bother telling us how recycling helps the environment, because you're preaching to the converted.*

preacher /ˈpriː.tʃəʳ/ Ⓤⓢ /-tʃɚ/ **noun** [C] a person, usually a priest, who gives a religious speech

preachy /ˈpriː.tʃi/ **adj** informal sounding as if you want to give someone moral advice: *How do you address social issues without being preachy?*

preamble /ˈpriː.æm.bl̩/, /priˈæm-/ **noun 1** [C] specialized an introduction to a speech or piece of writing **2** [U] talk or activity not connected with the most important matter

prearranged /ˌpriː.əˈreɪndʒd/ **adj** arranged at an earlier time: *a prearranged visit* ◦ *At a prearranged **signal**, everyone started moving forwards.*

prebuilt /ˌpriːˈbɪlt/ **adj** US for **prefabricated**

Precambrian /ˌpriːˈkæm.bri.ən/ **adj** from or referring to the earliest period of GEOLOGICAL time, between about 4,600 and 543 million years ago, from when the Earth was formed until the first simple forms of life appeared: *the Precambrian era/period* ◦ *Precambrian rocks* • **the Precambrian noun** [S] the Precambrian period

precancerous /ˌpriːˈkæn.sᵊr.əs/ (US) /-sɚ.əs/ **adj** specialized (especially of cells) showing signs of developing into a CANCER: *a precancerous* ***growth***

precarious /prɪˈkeə.ri.əs/ (US) /-ˈker.i-/ **adj 1** in a dangerous state because not safe or firmly fixed: *The lorry was lodged in a very precarious way, with its front wheels hanging over the cliff.* **2** A precarious situation is likely to get worse: *Many borrowers now find themselves caught in a precarious financial position.* • **precariousness** /-nəs/ **noun** [U]

precariously /prɪˈkeə.ri.əs.li/ (US) /-ˈker.i-/ **adv** in a way that is likely to fall, be damaged, fail, etc.: *Her suitcase was precariously* ***balanced*** *on the tiny luggage rack above her head.* ◦ *He lived rather precariously from one day to the next, never knowing where his next meal was coming from.*

precast /ˌpriːˈkɑːst/ (US) /ˈpriː.kæst/ **adj** (especially of concrete) formed into a particular shape and allowed to become solid before being used: *precast concrete slabs*

precaution /prɪˈkɔː.ʃᵊn/ (US) /-ˈkɑː-/ **noun 1** C1 [C] an action that is done to prevent something unpleasant or dangerous happening: *Many people have been stockpiling food as a precaution* ***against*** *shortages.* ◦ *They failed to* ***take*** *the necessary precautions to avoid infection.* **2 precautions** [plural] a polite way of referring to CONTRACEPTION (= methods that prevent a woman becoming pregnant): *If you're going to have sex, make sure you* ***take*** *precautions.* • **precautionary** /-ᵊr.i/ (US) /-er.i/ **adj** *The company has withdrawn the drug as a precautionary* ***measure.***

precede /prɪˈsiːd/ (US) /priː-/ **verb** [T] C2 to be or go before something or someone in time or space: *Kofi Annan preceded Ban Ki-moon as the Secretary-General of the UN.* ◦ *It would be helpful if you were to precede the report* ***with*** *an introduction.*

precedence /ˈpres.ɪ.dᵊns/ (US) /-ə.dens/ **noun** [U] **1** the condition of being dealt with before other things or of being considered more important than other things: *Precedence must be* ***given*** *to the injured in the evacuation plans.* ◦ *Business people often think that fluency and communication* ***take*** *precedence* ***over*** *grammar when speaking.* **2** formal the order of importance given to people in particular societies, groups, or organizations

precedent /ˈpres.ɪ.dᵊnt/ (US) /-ə.dent/ **noun 1** C2 [C] an action, situation, or decision that has already happened and can be used as a reason why a similar action or decision should be performed or taken: *There are several precedents* ***for*** *promoting people who don't have formal qualifications.* ◦ *Some politicians fear that agreeing to the concession would* ***set*** *a dangerous precedent.* **2** [U] the way that something has been done in the past which therefore shows that it is the correct way: *Would it be* ***breaking with*** *precedent for the bride to make a speech?* **3** [C] legal a decision about a particular law case which makes it likely that other similar cases will be decided in the same way: *The judgment on pension rights has* ***established/set*** *a precedent.*

preceding /prɪˈsiː.dɪŋ/ (US) /priː-/ **adj** [before noun] existing or happening before someone or something: *The paintings are a development of ideas she explored in the preceding decade.* ◦ *In conclusion, I hope the preceding arguments have convinced you of the need for action.*

precept /ˈpriː.sept/ **noun** [C] formal a rule for action or behaviour, especially obtained from moral thought: *This policy goes against common precepts* ***of*** *decency.*

precinct /ˈpriː.sɪŋkt/ **noun SHOPPING AREA ▷ 1** [C] UK a part of a city or a town in which vehicles are not allowed, used for a special purpose, such as shopping: *a shopping precinct* ◦ *a pedestrian precinct* **AROUND BUILDING ▷ 2 precincts** [plural] (also **precinct** [C]) mainly UK formal the area that surrounds a building or place, especially one with a wall around it: *A tunnel entrance was found within* ***the*** *precincts* ***of*** *the prison camp.* **PART OF CITY ▷ 3** [C] US a division of a city or a town, especially an area protected by a particular unit of the police or a division used for voting purposes: *The voter turnout in most precincts is expected to be high.*

precious /ˈpreʃ.əs/ **adj; adv**

▸**adj VALUABLE ▷ 1** B2 of great value because of being rare, expensive, or important: *a precious gift* ◦ *a precious moment/memory* ◦ *Clean water is a precious commodity in many parts of the world.* ◦ *You're so precious* ***to*** *me.* **NOT NATURAL ▷ 2** mainly UK disapproving behaving in a very formal and unnatural way by giving too much attention to details that are not important and trying too hard to be perfect: *He's so precious* ***about*** *his work that he never gets anything done.* ◦ *Don't you hate the precious* ***way*** *she speaks, pronouncing each single consonant so precisely.* **SHOWING DISLIKE ▷ 3** [before noun] informal used to express dislike and/or anger: *You and your precious car – it's all you're interested in!* • **preciousness** /-nəs/ **noun** [U]

▸**adv** informal very: *A lot of people will start, but precious* ***few*** *will finish.* ◦ *Be careful – you'll be precious* ***little*** *help if you come back injured.*

preciously /ˈpreʃ.əs.li/ **adv** disapproving in a way that is too formal and unnatural: *He speaks too preciously for my liking.*

ˌprecious ˈmetal noun [C] a metal that is valuable and usually rare: *Platinum and gold are precious metals.*

ˌprecious ˈstone noun [C] (US also **ˌprecious ˈgem**) a valuable stone that is used in jewellery: *The crown, decorated with diamonds and other precious stones, was exhibited in a special case.*

precipice /ˈpres.ɪ.pɪs/ **noun** [C] **1** a very steep side of a CLIFF or a mountain: *The film opens with a shot of a climber dangling from a precipice.* **2** a dangerous situation which could lead to harm or failure: *This latest tax increase may push many small companies over the financial precipice.*

precipitate verb; noun; adj

▸**verb** /prɪˈsɪp.ɪ.teɪt/ **MAKE HAPPEN ▷ 1** [T] formal to make something happen suddenly or sooner than expected: *An invasion would certainly precipitate a political crisis.* ◦ *Fear of losing her job precipitated (= suddenly forced) her* ***into*** *action.* **THROW ▷ 2** [T usually + adv/prep] formal to throw someone or something from a height with great force **CHEMISTRY ▷ 3** [I or T] specialized If a liquid precipitates, substances in it become solid and separate from the liquid: *Cooling the beaker helps precipitate the compound.* ◦ *If any organic salt is formed, it will precipitate* ***(out)*** *immediately.*

▸**noun** [C or U] /prɪˈsɪp.ɪ.tət/ (US) /priːˈsɪp.ə.t̬ɪt/ specialized a solid substance that is produced from a liquid during a chemical process: *After filtration, the precipitate was dried at 90°C.*

▸**adj** /prɪˈsɪp.ɪ.tət/ (US) /priːˈsɪp.ə.t̬ɪt/ (also **precipitous**) If an action is precipitate, it is done sooner or faster than expected and without enough thought or preparation: *Don't be precipitate – think it through before you make a decision.*

precipitately /prɪˈsɪp.ɪ.tət.li/ (US) /priːˈsɪp.ə.t̬ɪt-/ **adv** formal in a way that is too sudden and done without thinking: *Scientists are annoyed that the research programme has been abandoned so precipitately.*

precipitation /prɪˌsɪp.ɪˈteɪ.ʃən/ (US) /priː-/ **noun** [U] **RAIN** ▷ **1** specialized water which falls from the clouds towards the ground, especially as rain or snow: *Hail and sleet are types of precipitation.* ◦ *The forecast is for dry, cloudy weather with no precipitation expected.* **QUICK ACTION** ▷ **2** formal a way of behaving too quickly and without thinking: *The prime minister has been accused of acting with precipitation over the crisis.* **IN CHEMISTRY** ▷ **3** specialized a chemical process in which a solid substance is produced from a liquid: *The compound is finally obtained by precipitation.*

precipitous /prɪˈsɪp.ɪ.təs/ (US) /priːˈsɪp.ɪ.t̬əs/ **adj** **1** If a slope is precipitous, it is very steep: *a precipitous mountain path* **2** If a reduction or increase is precipitous, it is fast or great: *Over the past 18 months, there has been a precipitous **fall** in car sales.* • **precipitously** /-li/ **adv**

précis /ˈpreɪ.si/ **noun** [C] a short form of a text which gives only the important parts: *You have all been given a précis **of** the report.* • **précis verb** [T] *If I may précis the president's words – 'This country will never give in to terrorism.'*

precise /prɪˈsaɪs/ (US) /prə-/ **adj** **EXACT** ▷ **1** (B2) exact and accurate: *The bunker's precise location is a closely guarded secret.* ◦ *He caught me at the precise **moment** that I fainted.* ◦ *There was a good turnout for the meeting – twelve of us **to be** precise.* **CAREFUL** ▷ **2** approving very careful and accurate, especially about small details: *Years of doing meticulous research had made her very precise in her working methods.*

precisely /prɪˈsaɪs.li/ (US) /prə-/ **adv** **EXACTLY** ▷ **1** (B2) exactly: *The fireworks begin at eight o'clock precisely.* ◦ *What do you think the problem is, precisely?* **2** (B2) used to emphasize what you are saying: *'You look tired – you should go home and rest.' 'I'm going to do precisely that.'* ◦ *But it's precisely because of the noise that they're thinking of moving.* **3** (C1) used to express complete agreement with someone or suggest that what they have said is obvious: *'It would be stupid to attempt the journey in the dark.' 'Precisely,' he answered.* **CAREFULLY** ▷ **4** approving carefully and accurately: *He works slowly and precisely whereas I tend to rush things and make mistakes.*

precision /prɪˈsɪʒ.ən/ (US) /prə-/ **noun** [U] **EXACT** ▷ **1** the quality of being exact: *Great precision is required to align the mirrors accurately.* ◦ *Precision **bombing** was used to destroy enemy airbases and armaments factories.* **CAREFUL** ▷ **2** approving the qualities of being careful and accurate: *His books are a pleasure to read because he writes with such clarity and precision.*

preˌcision ˈinstrument **noun** [C] (also **preˌcision ˈtool**) a tool that can be controlled very accurately so that it produces very accurate results

preclude /prɪˈkluːd/ (US) /prə-/ **verb** [T] formal to prevent something or make it impossible, or prevent someone from doing something: *His contract precludes him **from** discussing his work with anyone outside the company.* ◦ *The fact that your application was not successful this time does not preclude the possibility of you applying again next time.* • **preclusion** /-ˈkluː.ʒən/ **noun** [U] *Your age should not act as a preclusion **to** you being accepted on the course.*

precocious /prɪˈkəʊ.ʃəs/ (US) /prəˈkoʊ-/ **adj** **1** (especially of children) showing mental development or achievement much earlier than usual: *A precocious child, she went to university at the age of 15.* ◦ *She recorded her first CD at the precocious age of twelve.* **2** disapproving describes a child who behaves as if they are much older than they are: *a precocious little brat* • **precociousness** /-nəs/ **noun** [U] (formal **precocity** /-ˈkɒs.ɪ.ti/ (US) /-ˈkɑː.sə.t̬i/)

precociously /prɪˈkəʊ.ʃəs.li/ (US) /prə-/ **adv** in a way that is unnaturally advanced or developed

precognition /ˌpriː.kɒɡˈnɪʃ.ən/ (US) /-kɑːɡ-/ **noun** [U] specialized knowledge of a future event, especially when this comes from a direct message to the mind, such as in a dream, rather than by reason • **precognitive** /-ˈkɒɡ.nɪ.tɪv/ (US) /-ˈkɑːɡ.nɪ.t̬ɪv/ **adj** *She claims she has precognitive **abilities** and can foresee events.*

pre-Columbian /ˌpriː.kəˈlʌm.bi.ən/ **adj** related to or from America in the period before Columbus arrived in 1492

preconceived /ˌpriː.kənˈsiːvd/ **adj** (of an idea or an opinion) formed too early, especially without enough thought or knowledge: *You must judge each film on its own merits, without any preconceived **notions** about what it's like.*

preconception /ˌpriː.kənˈsep.ʃən/ **noun** [C] an idea or opinion formed before enough information is available to form it correctly: *Try to go into the meeting without too many preconceptions **about** what the other group want.*

precondition /ˌpriː.kənˈdɪʃ.ən/ **noun** [C] something which must happen or be true before it is possible for something else to happen: *A halt to the fighting is a precondition **for** negotiations.*

precook /ˌpriːˈkʊk/ **verb** [T] to cook food before it is needed so that it can be heated and then eaten at a later time • **precooked** /-ˈkʊkt/ **adj** *Sales of precooked **meals** have risen sharply over the past few years.*

precursor /ˌpriːˈkɜː.səʳ/ (US) /-ˈkɝː.sɚ/ **noun** [C] formal something which happened or existed before another thing, especially if it either developed into it or had an influence on it: *Sulphur dioxide is the main precursor **of** acid rain.* ◦ *Biological research has often been a precursor **to** medical breakthroughs.*

predate /ˌpriːˈdeɪt/ **verb** [T] to have existed or happened before another thing: *These cave paintings predate any others which are known.* → Compare **backdate**, **postdate**

predator /ˈpred.ə.təʳ/ (US) /-t̬ɚ/ **noun** [C] **1** (C1) an animal that hunts, kills, and eats other animals: *lions, wolves, and other predators* **2** disapproving someone who follows people in order to harm them or commit a crime against them: *a sexual predator* ◦ *In court, he was accused of being a merciless predator who had tricked his grandmother out of her savings.*

predatory /ˈpred.ə.tər.i/ (US) /-tɔːr-/ **adj** **1** A predatory animal kills and eats other animals: *The owl is a predatory bird which kills its prey with its claws.* **2** mainly disapproving A predatory person or organization tries to get something that belongs to someone else: *The company spent much effort in avoiding takeover bids from predatory competitors.* **3** disapproving describes someone who expresses sexual interest in a very obvious way: *I hate going to bars on my own because men look at you in such a predatory way.*

ˌpredatory ˈpricing **noun** [U] specialized a situation in which a company offers goods at such a low price that other companies cannot compete with it: *The* *airline has reduced its prices so sharply that it has been accused of predatory pricing.*

predecease /ˌpriː.dɪˈsiːs/ (US) /-diː-/ **verb** [T] formal or legal to die before someone else: *Her husband predeceased her by five years.*

predecessor /ˈpriː.dɪ.ses.əʳ/ (US) /ˈpred.ə.ses.ɚ/ **noun** [C] C2 someone who had a job or a position before someone else, or something which comes before another thing in time or in a series: *My predecessor worked in this job for twelve years.* ◦ *The latest Ferrari is not only faster than its predecessors but also more comfortable.*

predestination /ˌpriː.des.trˈneɪ.ʃən/ **noun** [U] the belief that people have no control over events because these things are controlled by God or by FATE

predestined /ˌpriːˈdes.tɪnd/ **adj** If an action or event is predestined, it is controlled by God or by FATE: *It seems the expedition is predestined **to** fail because there have been so many problems.*

predetermine /ˌpriː.dɪˈtɜː.mɪn/ (US) /-diːˈtɝː.mən/ **verb** [T] formal to decide or arrange something at an earlier time: *It's impossible to say how much a person's behaviour is predetermined by their genes.* • **predetermination** /-ˌtɜː.mɪˈneɪ.ʃən/ (US) /-ˌtɝː.məˈneɪ.ʃən/ **noun** [U] formal • **predetermined** /-mɪnd/ **adj** *At a predetermined **time**, we'll all shout 'Happy Birthday, Dave'.*

predeterminer /ˌpriː.dɪˈtɜː.mɪ.nəʳ/ (US) /-diːˈtɝː.mə.nɚ/ **noun** [C] specialized in grammar, a word that is sometimes used before a DETERMINER to give more information about a noun in a noun phrase: *In the phrases 'all these children' and 'once a day', the words 'all' and 'once' are predeterminers.*

predicament /prɪˈdɪk.ə.mənt/ (US) /prə-/ **noun** [C] formal an unpleasant situation that is difficult to get out of: *She is hoping to get a loan from her bank to help her out of her financial predicament.* ◦ *I'm in a bit of a predicament because I've accidentally accepted two invitations to dinner on the same night.*

predicate noun; verb

▸**noun** [C] /ˈpred.ɪ.kət/ (US) /-kɪt/ specialized in grammar, the part of a sentence which contains the verb and gives information about the subject: *In the sentence 'We went to the airport', 'went to the airport' is the predicate.*

▸**verb** [T] /ˈpred.ɪ.keɪt/ formal **1** to say that something is true: [+ that] *It would be unwise to predicate **that** the disease is caused by a virus before further tests have been carried out.* **2 be predicated on sth** If an idea or argument is predicated on something, it depends on the existence or truth of this thing: *The sales forecast is predicated on the assumption that the economy will grow by four percent.*

predicative /prɪˈdɪk.ə.tɪv/ (US) /ˈpred.ɪ.keɪ.t̬ɪv/ **adj** specialized (in grammar, especially of adjectives or phrases) following a verb: *In the sentence 'She is happy', 'happy' is a predicative adjective.* → Compare **attributive**

predict /prɪˈdɪkt/ **verb** [T] B1 to say that an event or action will happen in the future, especially as a result of knowledge or experience: *It's still not possible to accurately predict the occurrence of earthquakes.* ◦ [+ that] *Who could have predicted **that** within ten years he'd be in charge of the whole company?* ◦ [+ to infinitive] *The hurricane is predicted **to** reach the coast tomorrow morning.* ◦ [+ question word] *No one can predict **wh**en the disease will strike again.*

predictability /prɪˌdɪk.təˈbɪl.ɪ.ti/ (US) /-ə.t̬i/ **noun** [U] the state of knowing what something is like, when something will happen, etc.: *Although her job is boring and monotonous, she likes the sense of predictability and security that it gives her.*

predictable /prɪˈdɪk.tə.bl̩/ **adj** **1** B2 Something that is predictable happens in a way or at a time that you know about before it happens: *Comets appear at predictable times.* → Opposite **unpredictable** **2** disapproving happening or behaving in a way that you expect and not unusual or interesting: *The ending to the film was just so predictable.*

predictably /prɪˈdɪk.tə.bli/ **adv** as expected: *Predictably, after the initial media interest, the refugees now seem to have been forgotten.*

prediction /prɪˈdɪk.ʃən/ **noun** [C or U] B2 a statement about what you think will happen in the future: *Please don't ask me to **make** any predictions **about** tomorrow's meeting.* ◦ [+ that] *No one believed her prediction **that** the world would end on 12 November.*

predictive /prɪˈdɪk.tɪv/ **adj** formal relating to the ability to predict: *The predictive value of this new method of analysis has still to be proven.*

preˌdictive ˈtexting **noun** [U] a feature of a mobile phone in which words are suggested automatically while you are writing a TEXT MESSAGE

predigested /ˌpriː.daɪˈdʒes.tɪd/ **adj** disapproving (of information) made simpler or easier to understand, especially by removing any parts which would make a person have to think hard: *The booklet presents information about the project in a predigested form and explains things in an easy, non-technical way.*

predilection /ˌpriː.dɪˈlek.ʃən/ (US) /ˌpred.əlˈek-/ **noun** [C] formal If someone has a predilection for something, they like it a lot: *Ever since she was a child, she has had a predilection **for** spicy food.*

predispose /ˌpriː.dɪˈspəʊz/ (US) /-ˈspoʊz/ **verb**

PHRASAL VERB **predispose sb to/towards sth** formal to make someone more likely to behave in a particular way or to suffer from a particular illness or condition: *Smoking predisposes you to lung cancer.* ◦ *His family background predisposes him to support the Democrats.*

predisposed /ˌpriː.dɪˈspəʊzd/ (US) /-ˈspoʊzd/ **adj** **be predisposed to/towards sth** to be more likely than other people to have a medical condition or to behave in a particular way: *Researchers have discovered that the children of these patients are genetically predisposed to cancer.* ◦ *The president is predisposed towards negotiation and favours a peaceful way of resolving the crisis.*

predisposition /ˌpriː.dɪ.spəˈzɪʃ.ən/ **noun** [C] formal the state of being likely to behave in a particular way or to suffer from a particular disease: *She has an annoying predisposition **to** find fault.* ◦ *There is evidence that a predisposition **to(wards)** asthma runs in families.*

predominance /prɪˈdɒm.ɪ.nəns/ (US) /-ˈdɑː.mə-/ **noun** [U] **1** a situation in which one person or group of people has more importance or power than others **2 a predominance of sth** a situation in which one type of person or thing within a set is the largest in number: *There is a predominance of people with an arts degree on the board of governors.*

predominant /prɪˈdɒm.ɪ.nənt/ (US) /-ˈdɑː.mə-/ **adj** C2 more noticeable or important, or larger in number, than others: *Research forms the predominant part of my job.* ◦ *Dancers have a predominant role in this performance.*

predominantly /prɪˈdɒm.ɪ.nənt.li/ (US) /-ˈdɑː.mə-/ **adv** C2 mostly or mainly: *a predominantly Muslim community*

P

predominate /prɪˈdɒm.ɪ.neɪt/ (US) /-ˈdɑː.mə-/ **verb** [I] to be the largest in number or the most important: *In industrial areas, the dark-coloured variety of the moth now predominates.*

preemie /ˈpriː.mi/ **noun** [C] US informal a baby that is born earlier than expected

ˌpre-ˈeminent **adj** formal more important or better than others: *She is the pre-eminent authority in her subject.* • **ˌpre-ˈeminence noun** [U] *His pre-eminence in his subject is internationally recognized.*

ˌpre-ˈeminently **adv** formal mainly, or to a very great degree: *The arts festival is pre-eminently a festival of theatre.*

pre-empt /ˌpriːˈempt/ **verb** [T] **1** to do or say something before someone so that you make their words or actions unnecessary or not effective: *The minister held a press conference in order to pre-empt criticism in the newspapers.* **2** US to replace one television programme with another, usually more important one: *All the networks pre-empted their regular schedules to broadcast news of the hijacking.*

pre-emptive /ˌpriːˈemp.tɪv/ **adj** formal describes something that is done before other people can act, especially to prevent them from doing something else: *The Treasury has decided to raise interest rates as a pre-emptive **measure** against inflation.* ◦ *The prime minister authorized a pre-emptive air **strike** against the rebels.*

preen /priːn/ **verb** **TIDY** ▷ **1** [I or T] If a bird preens or preens itself, it cleans and arranges its feathers using its beak. **2** [I or T] disapproving to spend time making yourself look attractive: *Roald always spends ages preening (himself) before he goes out.* **FEEL PROUD** ▷ **3 preen yourself** to feel very proud or satisfied with yourself because of an action or quality: *The government is publicly preening itself **on** the latest trade figures.* ◦ *The company preened itself **for** having taken on so many new employees last year.*

P

ˌpre-eˈxist **verb** [I or T] formal to exist before something else: *Dinosaurs pre-existed human beings **by** many millions of years.* • **ˌpre-eˈxisting adj** *a pre-existing medical condition*

prefab /ˈpriː.fæb/ **noun** [C] informal a small house that can be built quickly from pieces that have been made in a factory: *After the Second World War lots of prefabs were put up to ease the housing crisis.*

prefabricated /ˌpriːˈfæb.rɪ.keɪ.tɪd/ (US) /-t̬ɪd/ **adj** (informal **prefab**) describes buildings or objects built from parts that have been made in a factory and can be put together quickly: *a prefabricated **house*** • **prefabrication** /-fæb.rɪˈkeɪ.ʃ(ə)n/ **noun** [U]

preface /ˈpref.ɪs/ **noun; verb**

▸**noun** [C] **1** an introduction at the beginning of a book explaining its aims: *In his preface, the author says that he took eight years to write the book.* **2 a preface to sth** an event which comes before something more important: *We're hoping these talks could be a preface to peace.*

▸**verb** [T] formal If you preface your words or actions with something else, you say or do this other thing first: *Each work is prefaced **by** a descriptive note and concludes with an author's note.* ◦ *I should like to preface my response **with** the following observation.*

prefatory /ˈpref.ə.t(ə)r.i/ (US) /-tɔːr-/ **adj** formal coming at the beginning of a piece of writing or a speech: *After a few prefatory **comments/remarks**, she began her speech.* → Synonym **introductory**

prefect /ˈpriː.fekt/ **noun** [C] **OFFICIAL** ▷ **1** (in some countries) a very important official in the government or the police: *He has been appointed Prefect of Bologna.* **STUDENT** ▷ **2** (in some British and Australian schools) an older student who is given some authority and helps to control the younger students

prefecture /ˈpriː.fek.tʃə(r)/ (US) /-tʃɚ/ **noun** [C] a political region or local government area in some countries, for example Japan, France, and Italy

prefer /prɪˈfɜː(r)/ (US) /-ˈfɝː/ **verb** [T] (**-rr-**) **CHOOSE** ▷ **1** (A2) to like, choose, or want one thing rather than another: *Do you prefer hot or cold weather?* ◦ *I prefer red wine **to** white.* ◦ [+ -ing verb] *He prefers watch**ing** rugby to play**ing** it.* ◦ [+ to infinitive] *I'd prefer not **to** discuss this issue.* ◦ formal *I'd prefer you not **to** smoke (= I would like it better if you did not smoke), please.* **ACCUSE** ▷ **2** UK legal to accuse someone officially: *The police have decided not to prefer **charges** against them because of insufficient evidence.*

> **!** Common mistake: **prefer**
>
> **Warning:** Check your spelling!
>
> **Prefer** is one of the 50 words most often spelled wrongly by learners.

> **!** Common mistake: **prefer**
>
> **Warning:** Check your verb endings!
>
> Many learners make mistakes when using **prefer** in the past tense. The past simple and past participle have 'rr'. Don't write 'prefered', write pre**rr**ed. The **-ing** form is prefe**rr**ing.

preferable /ˈpref.(ə)r.ə.bl̩/ (US) /-ɚ.ə-/ **adj** (B2) better or more suitable: *Surely a diplomatic solution is preferable **to** war.*

preferably /ˈpref.(ə)r.ə.bli/ (US) /-ɚ.ə-/ **adv** (B2) if possible: *Water the plants twice a week, preferably in the morning.*

preference /ˈpref.(ə)r.(ə)ns/ (US) /ˈ-ɚ-/ **noun** [C or U] **1** (B2) the fact that you like something or someone more than another thing or person: *Her preference is **for** comfortable rather than stylish clothes.* ◦ *I have a preference **for** sweet food over spicy.* ◦ *Choosing furniture is largely a matter of **personal** preference.* ◦ *It would be wrong to discriminate against a candidate because of their **sexual** preference (= the sex of the people they are sexually attracted to).* **2** an advantage that is given to a person or a group of people: *We give preference **to** those who have worked with us for a long time.* ◦ *Special preferences were offered initially to encourage investment.* **3 in preference to sth** If you choose one thing in preference to another thing, you choose it because you like or want it more than the other thing: *He studied chemistry in preference to physics at university.*

preferential /ˌpref.əˈren.ʃ(ə)l/ (US) /-əˈren-/ **adj** [before noun] describes something you are given that is better than what other people receive: *Inmates claimed that some prisoners had received preferential **treatment**.* ◦ *Single mothers have been given preferential access to council housing.* • **preferentially** /-i/ **adv**

preferred /prɪˈfɜːd/ (US) /-ˈfɝːd/ **adj** liked or wanted more than anything else: *The earlier train would be my preferred **option**.*

prefigure /priːˈfɪg.ə(r)/ (US) /-jɚ/ **verb** [T] formal to show or suggest that something will happen in the future: *His paintings prefigure the development of perspective in Renaissance art.*

prefix /ˈpriː.fɪks/ **noun** [C] **GRAMMAR** ▷ **1** (B2) a letter or group of letters added to the beginning of a word to make a new word: *In the word 'unimportant', 'un-' is* *a prefix.* → See also **affix** PHONE ▷ **2** UK a **dialling code**

preggers /ˈpre.gəz/ (US) /-ɚ/ **adj** informal pregnant

pregnancy /ˈpreg.nən.si/ **noun** [C or U] C1 the state of being pregnant: *Most women feel sick in the mornings during their first months of pregnancy.* ◦ *My first pregnancy was very straightforward – there were no complications.*

ˈ**pregnancy** ˌ**test** **noun** [C usually singular] a chemical test performed on a woman's urine which shows if she is pregnant or not

pregnant /ˈpreg.nənt/ **adj** FEMALE ▷ **1** B1 (of a woman and some female animals) having a baby or babies developing inside the WOMB: *She's five and a half months pregnant.* ◦ *My mother stopped smoking when she* ***became*** *pregnant.* ◦ *He believes that men who* ***get*** *(= make) young girls pregnant should be severely punished.* ◦ *My sister is pregnant* ***with*** *twins.* MEANING ▷ **2** filled with meaning or importance that has not yet been expressed or understood: *There followed a pregnant* ***pause*** *in which both knew what the other was thinking but neither knew what to say.*

preheat /ˌpriːˈhiːt/ **verb** [T] to heat a cooker to a particular temperature before putting food in it: *Preheat the oven to 180°C.* ◦ *a preheated oven*

prehensile /prɪˈhen.saɪl/ (US) /priːˈhen.sɪl/ **adj** specialized (of parts of the body) able to hold on to things, especially by curling around them: *a prehensile tail*

prehistoric /ˌpriː.hɪˈstɒr.ɪk/ (US) /-hɪˈstɔːr-/ **adj** **1** describing the period before there were written records: *prehistoric man/humans/animals* ◦ *Painting originated* ***in*** *prehistoric* ***times.*** **2** informal disapproving very old-fashioned: *He has prehistoric views about women who have careers.*

prehistory /priːˈhɪs.tᵊr.i/ (US) /-t̬ɚ.i/ **noun** [U] the period of human history before there were written records of events: *Human prehistory is divided into three successive periods: the Stone Age, the Bronze Age and the Iron Age.*

prejudge /ˌpriːˈdʒʌdʒ/ **verb** [T] disapproving to form an opinion about a situation or a person before knowing or considering all of the facts: *Let's not prejudge the situation – we need to hear both sides of the story first.* • **prejudgment** /-mənt/ **noun** [C or U] (also **prejudgement**) *You shouldn't make any sort of prejudgment about her before you've met her.*

prejudice /ˈpredʒ.ʊ.dɪs/ **noun; verb**

▸**noun** [C or U] **1** B2 an unfair and unreasonable opinion or feeling, especially when formed without enough thought or knowledge: *Laws against* ***racial*** *prejudice must be strictly enforced.* ◦ [+ that] *The campaign aims to dispel the prejudice* ***that*** *AIDS is confined to the homosexual community.* ◦ *He claims that prejudice* ***against*** *homosexuals would cease overnight if all the gay stars in the country were honest about their sexuality.* **2 without prejudice to sth** formal or legal If a decision or action is made without prejudice to a right or claim, it is made without having an effect on that right or claim: *My client accepts the formal apology without prejudice to any further legal action she may decide to take.*

▸**verb** [T] **1** Someone or something that prejudices you influences you unfairly so that you form an unreasonable opinion about something: *His comments may have prejudiced the voters* ***against*** *her.* **2** formal Something or someone that prejudices something else has a harmful influence on it: *The fact that you were late all this week may prejudice your chances of getting a promotion.*

prejudiced /ˈpredʒ.ʊ.dɪst/ **adj** disapproving C1 showing an unreasonable dislike for something or someone: *The media has been accused of presenting a prejudiced view of people with disabilities.* ◦ *Some companies are prejudiced* ***against*** *taking on employees who are over the age of 40.*

prejudicial /ˌpredʒ.ʊˈdɪʃ.ᵊl/ **adj** formal harmful or influencing people unfairly: *The judge decided that allowing the video as evidence would be prejudicial* ***to*** *the outcome of the trial.*

prelate /ˈprel.ɪt/ **noun** [C] an official of high rank in the Christian religion, such as a BISHOP or an ABBOT

prelim /ˈpriː.lɪm/, /prɪˈlɪm/ **noun** [C usually plural] informal a sports event or an exam that acts as a preparation for a more important event that will follow

preliminary /prɪˈlɪm.ɪ.nᵊr.i/ (US) /-ə.ner-/ **adj; noun**

▸**adj** [before noun] C1 coming before a more important action or event, especially introducing or preparing for it: *Preliminary results show that the vaccine is effective, but this has to be confirmed by further medical trials.* ◦ *We've decided to change the design based on our preliminary findings.*

▸**noun** [C usually plural] an event or action that introduces or prepares for something else: *After a few polite preliminaries (= introductions), we stated our main ideas and intentions.* ◦ *The French team finished first in the competition preliminaries (= the first part of the competition).*

preliterate /ˌpriːˈlɪt.ᵊr.ət/ (US) /-ˈlɪt̬.ɚ.ət/ **adj** specialized (of a society) not having a written language

prelude /ˈprel.juːd/ **noun** INTRODUCTION ▷ **1** [C usually singular] something that comes before a more important event or action which introduces or prepares for it: *The changes are seen as a prelude* ***to*** *wide-ranging reforms.* MUSIC ▷ **2** [C] specialized a short piece of music which introduces the main work **3** [C] specialized a short independent piece of music written especially for the piano

premarital /ˌpriːˈmær.ɪ.tᵊl/ (US) /-ˈmer.ə.t̬ᵊl/ **adj** [before noun] before marriage: *premarital* ***sex*** ◦ *premarital counselling*

premature /ˈprem.ə.tʃəʳ/, /-tjʊəʳ/, /ˌprem.əˈtjʊəʳ/ (US) /ˌpriː.məˈtʊr/ **adj** happening or done too soon, especially before the natural or suitable time: *premature birth/death* ◦ *a premature* ***baby*** ◦ *Their criticisms seem premature considering that the results aren't yet known.* • **prematurely** /-li/ **adv** *Their baby was born prematurely and weighed only one kilogram.* ◦ *His stressful job made him go prematurely grey (= made his hair turn grey at a young age).*

premeditated /ˌpriːˈmed.ɪ.teɪ.tɪd/ (US) /-t̬ɪd/ **adj** (especially of a crime or something unpleasant) done after being thought about or carefully planned: *premeditated murder* ◦ *a premeditated attack* ◦ *The assault was premeditated and particularly brutal.* → Opposite **unpremeditated** • **premeditation** /-med.ɪˈteɪ.ʃᵊn/ **noun** [U]

premenstrual /ˌpriːˈmen.stru.əl/ (US) /-strəl/ **adj** [before noun] of the time just before a woman's period

preˌ**menstrual** ˈ**syndrome** **noun** [U] (UK also **pre**ˌ**menstrual** ˈ**tension**) a condition in which some women experience pain and swelling in particular parts of their bodies, and feelings such as ANXIETY, anger, or unhappiness for a few days before their PERIOD (= flow of blood each month)

premier /ˈprem.i.əʳ/ (US) /prɪˈmɪr/ **adj; noun**

▸**adj** [before noun] best or most important: *He's one of the nation's premier scientists.*

▸**noun** [C] (especially used in news reports) the leader

of the government of a country, or of a large part of a country

premiere /ˈprem.i.eəʳ/ (US) /prɪˈmɪr/ **noun** [C] the first public performance of a play or any other type of entertainment: *The **world** premiere **of** the opera will be at the Metropolitan Opera House in New York.* • **premiere verb** [T] *The play was premiered in New York.*

premiership /ˈprem.i.ə.ʃɪp/ **noun** [C or U] the period when someone is PRIME MINISTER, or the job of being prime minister

the ˈPremiership noun [S] the group of the best English football teams who compete against each other

premise noun; verb

▸**noun** [C] /ˈprem.ɪs/ an idea or theory on which a statement or action is based: [+ that] *They had started with the premise **that** all men are created equal.* ◦ *The research project is based on the premise stated earlier.*

▸**verb** [T] /prɪˈmaɪz, ˈprem.ɪs/ formal to base a theory, argument, etc. on an idea, thought, or belief: *He premised his argument **on** several incorrect assumptions.*

premises /ˈprem.ɪ.sɪz/ **noun** [plural] (C1) the land and buildings owned by someone, especially by a company or organization: *The company is relocating to new premises.* ◦ *There is no smoking allowed anywhere on school premises.* ◦ *The ice cream is made **on the** premises (= in the building where it is sold).* ◦ *The security guards escorted the protesters **off** (= away from) the premises.*

premium /ˈpriː.mi.əm/ **noun; adj**

▸**noun EXTRA** ▷ **1** [C] an amount that is more than usual: *We're willing to pay a premium for the best location.* ◦ *Because of their location, these offices **attract** a premium.* ◦ *The modified cars are available **at** a premium **of** five percent **over** the original price.* ◦ *The busy shopper **puts** a premium **on** (= appreciates and will pay more for) finding everything in one big store.* **PAYMENT** ▷ **2** (C2) [C] an amount of money paid to get INSURANCE: *Car insurance premiums have increased this year.* ◦ *The premiums **for** healthcare plans are high.* **FUEL** ▷ **3** [U] (also **premium gas**) US for **four-star**

IDIOM **be at a premium** (C2) to be not common and therefore valuable: *Free time is at a premium for working parents.*

▸**adj** (C2) describes something that is of higher than usual quality: *premium ice cream* ◦ *The building is on a premium site.*

ˈPremium ˌBond noun [C] UK a government investment in which you do not receive interest but have the chance every month to win a prize of money

ˈpremium-ˌrate adj describes a phone number or service that costs more to call than a normal phone number: *a premium-rate number/line/service*

premmie /ˈprem.i/ **noun** [C] Australian English informal a baby that is born earlier than expected → Compare **preemie**

premolar /ˌpriːˈməʊ.ləʳ/ (US) /-ˈmoʊ.lɚ/ **noun** [C] specialized one of the two teeth immediately in front of the MOLARS on both sides of the upper and lower JAWS of humans and some other animals, used for GRINDING and CHEWING food (= crushing it with the teeth)

premonition /ˌprem.əˈnɪʃ.ən/, /ˌpriː.mə-/ **noun** [C] a feeling that something, especially something unpleasant, is going to happen: [+ that] *He had a premonition **that** his plane would crash, so he took the train.* ◦ *She had a **sudden** premonition **of** what the future might bring.*

prenatal /ˌpriːˈneɪ.təl/ (US) /-t̬əl/ **adj** [before noun] US for **antenatal**

prenuptial /ˌpriːˈnʌp.ʃəl/ **adj** before getting married

ˌprenuptial aˈgreement noun [C] (informal **prenup** /ˈpriː.nʌp/) an official document signed by two people before they get married that says what will happen to their possessions and/or children if they DIVORCE (= officially stop being married)

preoccupation /priːˌɒk.jʊˈpeɪ.ʃən/ (US) /-ˌɑː.kjuː-/ **noun 1** [C] an idea or subject that someone thinks about most of the time: *My main preoccupation now is trying to keep life normal for the sake of my two boys.* **2** [C or U] the state of being worried about or thinking about something most of the time: *Lately, his preoccupation **with** football had caused his marks at school to slip.*

preoccupied /ˌpriːˈɒk.jʊ.paɪd/ (US) /-ˈɑː.kjuː-/ **adj** thinking or worrying about something too much: *She's been very preoccupied recently because her mother has been very ill.* ◦ *Why is the media so preoccupied **with** the love lives of politicians?*

preoccupy /ˌpriːˈɒk.jʊ.paɪ/ (US) /-ˈɑː.kjuː-/ **verb** [T] to be the main thought in someone's mind, causing other things to be forgotten: *Economic concerns are preoccupying the voters in this election.*

preordain /ˌpriː.ɔːˈdeɪn/ (US) /-ɔːr-/ **verb** [T] formal (especially of a power thought to be greater than ordinary people) to decide or fix what will happen in a way that cannot be changed or controlled: [+ to infinitive] *Illness and suffering seemed (to be) preordained **to** be her lot.* ◦ *His life seems to have followed a preordained path/direction.*

prep /prep/ **noun SCHOOL WORK** ▷ **1** [U] UK school work that students, especially students at PRIVATE SCHOOL and PUBLIC SCHOOL, do at home or not during school time: *Have you got much prep tonight?* **GRAMMAR** ▷ **2** abbreviation for **preposition**

prepacked /ˌpriːˈpækt/ **adj** (US usually **prepackaged**) wrapped or put into a container before being sold: *The nails come prepacked in small boxes.*

prepaid /ˌpriːˈpeɪd/ **adj** paid for earlier: *Admission tickets are $20 prepaid, $25 at the door.*

preparation /ˌprep.ərˈeɪ.ʃən/ (US) /-əˈreɪ-/ **noun GETTING READY** ▷ **1** (B1) [U] the things that you do or the time that you spend preparing for something: *The teacher didn't seem to have **done** much preparation **for** the class.* ◦ *The team blamed injuries and lack of preparation for their failure to win.* ◦ *Yasmin assisted **in the** preparation **of** this article.* **2 preparations** (B2) [plural] plans or arrangements that you make to prepare for something: [+ to infinitive] *We are **making** preparations **to** fly Mr Goodall to the nearest hospital.* ◦ *Preparations **for** the opening ceremony are well under way.* **MIXTURE** ▷ **3** [C] a mixture of substances, often for use as a medicine: *a preparation for nappy rash*

> **Word partners for preparation**
>
> *begin/finalize/make/start* preparations • *adequate/careful/thorough* preparation • *advance/final/last-minute* preparations • preparations are *underway* • do sth *in* preparation (*for* sth) • be *in/under* preparation

preparatory /prɪˈpær.ə.tər.i/ (US) /-ˈper.ə.tɔːr-/ **adj** done in order to get ready for something: *preparatory work* ◦ *Differences over these issues narrowed during the preparatory meetings/talks.*

preˈparatory ˌschool noun [C] formal for **prep school**

prepare /prɪˈpeəʳ/ (US) /-ˈper/ **verb** [I or T] **1** A2 to make or get something or someone ready for something that will happen in the future: *Have you prepared **for** your interview?* ◦ *She'll prepare the food ahead of time and freeze it.* ◦ *This course aims to prepare students **for** middle and senior managerial positions.* ◦ [+ obj + to infinitive] *Are the players mentally and physically prepared **to** play a tough game?* ◦ *The meal took two hours to prepare.* **2** B1 to expect that something will happen and to be ready for it: [+ to infinitive] *It almost seems as if she is preparing **to** die.* ◦ *You need to prepare your**self for** a long wait.*

> **Common mistake: prepare**
>
> **Warning:** Check your spelling!
>
> **Prepare** is one of the 50 words most often spelled wrongly by learners.

IDIOM **prepare the ground** If you prepare the ground for an activity or a situation, you do something that will help it to happen: *The leaders of both countries are preparing the ground **for** negotiations which may lead to peace.*

prepared /prɪˈpeəd/ (US) /-ˈperd/ **adj 1** B1 ready to deal with a situation: *When she called on me, I wasn't prepared.* ◦ *They were prepared **for the worst**.* **2** B2 made earlier: *The spokesperson read a prepared statement.* **3 be prepared to do sth** B2 to be willing, or happy to agree to do something: *Would you be prepared to help me get things ready for the party?* ◦ *People are not really prepared to talk about these kinds of personal problems.*

preparedness /prɪˈpeəd.nəs/ (US) /-ˈperd-/ **noun** [U] formal the state of being prepared for a particular situation: *The army is in a state of preparedness **for** war.*

ˌpre-ˈpay **adj** [before noun] describes a mobile phone which you must pay to use before you can use it

preponderance /prɪˈpɒn.dᵊr.ᵊns/ (US) /-ˈpɑːn.dɚ-/ **noun** [S] formal the largest part or greatest amount: *The preponderance **of** evidence suggests that he's guilty.*

preponderant /prɪˈpɒn.dᵊr.ᵊnt/ (US) /-ˈpɑːn.dɚ-/ **adj** formal important or large: *Music does not play a very preponderant role in the school's teaching.* • **preponderate** /-eɪt/ **verb** [I] *Although it was a mixed class, girls preponderated.*

preponderantly /prɪˈpɒn.dᵊr.ᵊnt.li/ (US) /-ˈpɑːn.dɚ-/ **adv** formal mostly or mainly: *Industry is still a preponderantly male environment.*

prepone /priːˈpəʊn/ (US) /-ˈpoʊn/ **verb** [T] Indian English to do something at an earlier time than was planned or is usual: *The government might prepone these elections so we'd better be prepared.* → Opposite **postpone**

preposition /ˌprep.əˈzɪʃ.ᵊn/ **noun** [C] B1 in grammar, a word that is used before a noun, a NOUN PHRASE, or a PRONOUN, connecting it to another word: *In the sentences 'We jumped in the lake', and 'She drove slowly down the track', 'in' and 'down' are prepositions.* • **prepositional** /-ᵊl/ **adj** [before noun] *a prepositional phrase*

prepossessing /ˌpriː.pəˈzes.ɪŋ/ **adj** interesting, noticeable, or attractive: *He wasn't a very prepossessing sort of person.* ◦ *The box didn't look very prepossessing, but the necklace inside was beautiful.*

preposterous /prɪˈpɒs.tᵊr.əs/ (US) /-ˈpɑː.stɚ-/ **adj** formal very silly or stupid: *The very idea is preposterous!* ◦ *a preposterous suggestion*

preppy (also **preppie**) /ˈprep.i/ **noun** [C] mainly US a young person from a rich family who goes to an expensive school and who wears expensive, tidy clothes • **preppy adj** *preppy clothes*

ˈprep ˌschool **noun** [C] in the UK, a PRIVATE SCHOOL (= a school paid for by parents not the government) for children, especially boys, between the ages of seven and 13, who will then usually go to PUBLIC SCHOOL and in the US, a private school for children over the age of eleven that prepares them to go to college

ˈprep time **noun** [U] US a period when teachers are at school but do not teach, and are therefore able to prepare for later classes

prepubescent /ˌpriː.pjuːˈbe.sᵊnt/ **adj** relating to the period before children start to develop adult sexual characteristics: *prepubescent girls/boys/children*

prequel /ˈpriː.kwəl/ **noun** [C usually singular] a film, book, or play which develops the story of an earlier film, etc. by telling you what happened before the events in the first film, etc.: *Jean Rhys's novel 'Wide Sargasso Sea' is a prequel **to** Charlotte Bronte's 'Jane Eyre'.* → Compare **sequel**

Pre-Raphaelite /ˌpriːˈræf.ᵊl.aɪt/ (US) /ˌpriːˈræf.i.ᵊl-/ **noun; adj**

▸**noun** [C] a member of a 19th-century group of British painters who were influenced by the style of painting of the 14th and 15th centuries

▸**adj** belonging or relating to the Pre-Raphaelites, or typical of their style of painting: *a Pre-Raphaelite artist/painter* ◦ *She was a woman of Pre-Raphaelite beauty (= had pale skin and long wavy reddish-brown hair, like the women often painted by the Pre-Raphaelites).*

prerecord /ˌpriː.rɪˈkɔːd/ (US) /-ˈkɔːrd/ **verb** [T] to record something, especially music or speech, in order to use it at a later time: *Is this a live broadcast, or was it prerecorded?*

prerequisite /ˌpriːˈrek.wɪ.zɪt/ **noun** [C] formal something which must exist or happen before something else can exist or happen: *Passing a written exam is a prerequisite for taking the advanced course.* ◦ *Public support is a prerequisite **for/to** the success of this project.* ◦ *They had to agree to certain conditions as a prerequisite **of being** lent the money.*

prerogative /prɪˈrɒg.ə.tɪv/ (US) /-ˈrɑː.gə.t̬ɪv/ **noun** [C usually singular] formal something that certain people are able or allowed to do or have, but is not possible or allowed for everyone: *Alex makes all the big decisions – that's his prerogative as company director.* ◦ *Skiing used to be the prerogative **of** the rich, but now a far wider range of people do it.* ◦ ***the Royal** Prerogative (= the special rights of the ruling king or queen)*

Pres. **noun** written abbreviation for **president**

presage /ˈpres.ɪdʒ/, /prɪˈseɪdʒ/ **verb** [T] formal to show or suggest that something, often something unpleasant, will happen: *But still the economy is not showing signs of any of the excesses that normally presage a recession.*

Presbyterian /ˌprez.bɪˈtɪə.ri.ən/ (US) /-bɪˈtɪr.i-/ **adj** relating or belonging to a Christian group that has members especially in Scotland and the US • **Presbyterian noun** [C]

preschool /ˈpriː.skuːl/ **adj; noun**

▸**adj** [before noun] of or relating to children who have not yet gone to school, and their activities: *a preschool playgroup* ◦ *preschool children/toys*

▸**noun** [C or U] a school for children who are younger than five years old

preschooler /ˈpriːˌskuː.ləʳ/ (US) /-lɚ/ **noun** [C] a child

P

who is under five years old and therefore does not go to formal school

prescient /ˈpres.i.ənt/ adj formal knowing or suggesting correctly what will happen in the future: *a prescient warning* • **prescience** /-əns/ noun [U] *the prescience of her remarks*

prescribe /prɪˈskraɪb/ verb GIVE MEDICINE ▷ **1** C2 [T often passive] (of a doctor) to say what medical treatment someone should have: *The drug is often prescribed **for** ulcers.* ◦ [+ two objects] *I've been prescribed painkillers.* GIVE RULE ▷ **2** [T] formal to tell someone what they must have or do; to give something as a rule: *Penalties for not paying taxes are prescribed by law.* ◦ [+ that] *The law prescribes **that** all children must go to school.* ◦ [+ question word] *Grammatical rules prescribe **how** words may be used together.*

prescribed /prɪˈskraɪbd/ adj RULE ▷ **1** set by a rule or order: *The product will have to meet internationally prescribed (= demanded) standards.* MEDICINE ▷ **2** decided by a doctor as treatment: *The patient was taking a widely prescribed sedative.*

prescription /prɪˈskrɪp.ʃən/ noun MEDICINE ▷ **1** B1 [C] a piece of paper on which a doctor writes the details of the medicine or drugs that someone needs: *a doctor's prescription* ◦ *a prescription **for** sedatives* ◦ UK *The doctor should give you a **repeat** prescription (= another piece of paper allowing more of the same medicine to be given, often without the person seeing the doctor again).* ◦ *These drugs are only available **on** prescription (= with a prescription from a doctor).* ◦ *Prescription **charges** (= the standard amount of money you pay for any medicine prescribed by a doctor) are rising in June.* RULE ▷ **2** [C or U] formal the act of telling someone else what they must have or do: *So what is his prescription **for** success?*

preˈscription ˌdrug noun [C] a drug that can only be bought if a doctor orders it for you → Compare **over-the-counter**

P

prescriptive /prɪˈskrɪp.tɪv/ adj formal mainly disapproving saying exactly what must happen, especially by giving an instruction or making a rule: *Most teachers think the government's guidelines on homework are too prescriptive.*

preseason /ˈpriːˌsiː.zən/ adj; noun
▸**adj** [before noun] in sports, happening before the main period of competition: *a preseason match/game*
▸**noun** [C usually singular] in sports, a short period of competition before the main period: *Barkley suffered a strained thigh muscle late in the preseason.* ◦ *David Beckham had a great preseason.*

presence /ˈprez.əns/ noun **1** B2 [S] the fact that someone or something is in a place: *She was overawed by the presence **of** so many people.* ◦ *The presence **of** pollen in the atmosphere causes hay fever in some people.* ◦ *He's usually quite polite **in** my **presence**.* ◦ *The document was signed **in the presence of** two witnesses.* **2** C2 [C usually singular] a feeling that someone is still in a place although they are not there or are dead: *His daughter's presence seemed to fill her empty bedroom.* **3** C2 [S] a group of police or soldiers who are watching or controlling a situation: *The United Nations has maintained a presence in the region for some time.* ◦ *There was a strong police presence at the demonstration.* **4** C2 [U] approving a quality that makes people notice or admire you, even when you are not speaking: *stage presence* ◦ *He stood there in the corner of the room, a dark, **brooding** (= worrying) presence.*

IDIOM **make your presence felt** C2 to have a strong effect on other people or on a situation: *The new police chief has really made his presence felt.*

ˌpresence of ˈmind noun [U] approving C2 the ability to make good decisions and to act quickly and calmly in a difficult situation or an emergency: *When the gunmen came into the bank, she **had** the presence of mind to press the alarm.*

present noun; adj; verb
▸**noun** /ˈprez.ənt/ SOMETHING GIVEN ▷ **1** A2 [C] (UK informal **prezzie**, or **pressie**) something that you are given, without asking for it, on a special occasion, especially to show friendship, or to say thank you: *a birthday/Christmas/wedding present* ◦ *They gave me theatre tickets as a present.* NOW ▷ **2 the present** B1 [S] the period of time that is happening now, not the past or the future: *That's all for the present.* ◦ *The play is set **in** the present.* → See also **presently** **3 the present (tense)** A1 [S] the form of the verb that is used to show what happens or exists now: *All the verbs in this text are in the present.* **4 at present** B1 formal now: *'Are you busy?' 'Not at present.'* ◦ *At present she's working abroad.*
▸**adj** /ˈprez.ənt/ IN A PLACE ▷ **1** B1 [after verb] in a particular place: *The whole family was present.* ◦ *There were no children present.* NOW ▷ **2** [before noun] happening or existing now: *I don't have her present address.* ◦ *Please state your present occupation and salary.*

IDIOM **present company excepted** used to show that a criticism or a rude remark does not refer to the people you are talking to: *People here just don't know how to dress, present company excepted.*

▸**verb** [T] /prɪˈzent/ GIVE ▷ **1** B2 to give, provide, or make something known: *The winners were presented **with** medals.* ◦ *The letter presented the family **with** a **problem** that would be difficult to solve.* ◦ *The documentary presented us **with** a balanced view of the issue.* ◦ *He presented the report **to** his colleagues at the meeting.* ◦ *The classroom presented a cheerful busy atmosphere **to** the visitors (= appeared to them to have this).* ◦ *The school is presenting (= performing) 'West Side Story' as its end-of-term production.* INTRODUCE ▷ **2** B2 UK to introduce a television or radio show: *She presents the late-night news.* **3** formal to introduce a person: *May I present Professor Carter?* ◦ *Later on I'd like to present you **to** the headteacher.* **4 present yourself** to arrive somewhere and introduce yourself: *He presented himself at the doctor's at 9.30 a.m. as arranged.* **5 present itself** C2 If something presents itself, it happens: *An **opportunity** suddenly presented itself.*

presentable /prɪˈzen.tə.bl̩/ US /-t̬ə-/ adj looking suitable or good enough, especially in the way you are dressed: *Jeremy was **looking** quite presentable in a suit and tie.* ◦ *I've got to have a wash and **make** myself presentable for our guests.*

presentation /ˌprez.ənˈteɪ.ʃən/ noun EVENT ▷ **1** B1 [C] a talk giving information about something: *The speaker gave an interesting presentation on urban transport.* **2** B2 [C] an occasion when prizes, qualifications, etc. are formally given to those who have won or achieved them: *The presentation of prizes and certificates will take place in the main hall.* APPEARANCE ▷ **3** C2 [U] the way something looks when it is shown to other people, or the way someone looks: *Presentation is important if you want people to buy your products.*

the ˌpresent conˈtinuous noun [S] the verb form used for actions or events that are happening or developing now: *The sentences 'The children are watching television' and 'The weather is getting colder' are* ***in*** *the present continuous.*

ˌpresent-ˈday adj [before noun] existing now: *present-day attitudes*

presenteeism /prə.zənˈtiː.ɪzm/ noun [U] the act of staying at work longer than usual to show that you work hard and are important to your employer: *Job insecurity is making presenteeism increasingly common.*

presenter /prɪˈzen.təʳ/ (US) /-t̬ɚ/ noun [C] UK **B2** someone who introduces a television or radio show: *a news/sports presenter* ◦ *children's television presenters*

presentiment /prɪˈzen.tɪ.mənt/ noun [C] formal a feeling that something, especially something unpleasant, is going to happen: *She had had a presentiment* ***of*** *what might lie ahead.* → Synonym **premonition**

presently /ˈprez.ᵊnt.li/ adv **NOW** ▷ **1** **C1** mainly US formal now; at the present time: *Of 200 boats, only 20 are presently operational.* ◦ *Three sites are presently under consideration for the new hotel.* **SOON** ▷ **2** old-fashioned soon; not at the present time but in the future, after a short time: *The room was hot and presently her eyes grew heavy and she began to feel sleepy.*

ˌpresent ˈparticiple noun [C] a form of a verb that in English ends in '-ing' and comes after another verb to show continuous action. It is used to form the PRESENT CONTINUOUS.: *In the sentences 'The children are watching television', 'The weather is getting colder' and 'I heard him singing', 'watching', 'getting' and 'singing' are present participles.*

the ˌpresent ˈperfect noun [S] the form of the verb used for actions or events that have been completed or that have happened in a period of time up to now: *The sentences 'She has broken her leg' and 'I have never been to Australia' are all* ***in*** *the present perfect.*

the ˌpresent ˈsimple noun [S] the tense that is used to refer to events, actions, and conditions that are happening all the time, or exist now: *The sentences 'I live in Madrid', 'She doesn't like cheese' and 'I think you're wrong' are all* ***in*** *the present simple.*

preservation /ˌprez.əˈveɪ.ʃᵊn/ (US) /-ɚ-/ noun [U] **C1** the act of keeping something the same or of preventing it from being damaged: *building preservation* ◦ *wood preservation* ◦ *There is great public concern about some of the chemicals used in food preservation.* ◦ *The church is in a poor state of preservation (= has not been kept in good condition).* ◦ *The president has said that the government is committed to the preservation (= protection)* ***of*** *the country's national interests.* ◦ *She belongs to the Association for the Preservation of Civil War Sites* → See also **self-preservation**

preservationist /ˌprez.əˈveɪ.ʃᵊn.ɪst/ (US) /-ɚ-/ noun [C] mainly US someone who works to prevent old buildings and areas of the countryside from being destroyed or damaged

preserˈvation ˌorder noun [C] UK an official decision that a building or area has special value and must be kept in good condition: *This avenue of mature trees has a preservation order* ***on*** *it.*

preservative /prɪˈzɜː.və.tɪv/ (US) /-ˈzɝː.və.t̬ɪv/ noun **1** [C or U] a substance used to prevent decay in wood: *a timber/wood preservative* ◦ *The fence has been treated with preservative.* **2** [C] a chemical used to stop food from decaying: *This bread is completely free from* ***artificial*** *preservatives.* ◦ *No added preservatives.*

preserve /prɪˈzɜːv/ (US) /-ˈzɝːv/ verb; noun

▸verb [T] **1** **B2** to keep something as it is, especially in order to prevent it from decaying or being damaged or destroyed: *to preserve the environment* ◦ *We want to preserve the character of the town while improving the facilities.* ◦ *The agreement preserved our right to limit trade in endangered species.* ◦ *Putting varnish on wood is a way of preserving it.* ◦ *I need to get out of the house from time to time just to preserve (= prevent me from losing) my* ***sanity.*** → See also **well preserved** **2** to treat food in a particular way so that it can be kept for a long time without going bad: *preserved fruit* ◦ *oranges preserved* ***in*** *brandy*

▸noun **FOOD** ▷ **1** [C or U] a food made from fruit or vegetables boiled with sugar and water until it becomes like a firm sauce: *apricot preserve* ◦ *jars of preserves* → See also **conserve** **ACTIVITY** ▷ **2** [S] an activity which only one person or a particular type of person does or is responsible for: *Owning racehorses is the preserve* ***of*** *the rich.* ◦ *Sport used to be a male preserve.* **PLACE** ▷ **3** [C] US for RESERVE (= an area of land kept in its natural state, especially for wild animals to live in to be protected)

preset verb; adj

▸verb [T] /ˌpriːˈset/ (present tense **presetting**, past tense and past participle **preset**) to prepare a machine so it will operate or stop later, or to arrange for or agree to something: [+ to infinitive] *I'll preset the oven* ***to*** *come on at 5 p.m.* ◦ *The agenda for the meeting has been preset.*

▸adj /ˈpriː.set/ **1** arranged, agreed, or chosen earlier: *We have a device which switches the lights on at a preset time in the evening.* ◦ *The shares will be sold at a preset price.* **2** relating to part of a machine that is used to prepare it to operate or stop later: *a preset button*

preshrunk /ˌpriːˈʃrʌŋk/ adj (of clothes) SHRUNK (= made smaller) by washing before being sold: *preshrunk jeans*

preside /prɪˈzaɪd/ verb [I] to be in charge of a formal meeting or ceremony: *Who would be the best person to preside* ***at/over*** *the public enquiry?* • **presiding** /-ˈzaɪ.dɪŋ/ adj *the presiding judge*

PHRASAL VERB **preside over sth** to be in charge of a situation, especially a formal meeting or a trial: *Judge Langdale is to preside over the official enquiry into the case.* ◦ *This government has presided over some of the most significant changes in education this century.*

presidency /ˈprez.ɪ.dᵊn.si/ noun [C usually singular] **B2** the job of being president, or the period when someone is a president: *He has announced that he is running for the presidency.* ◦ *She* ***won*** *the presidency by a wide margin.*

president /ˈprez.ɪ.dᵊnt/ noun [C] **POLITICS** ▷ **1** **A2** (the title given to) the person who has the highest political position in a country that is a REPUBLIC and who, in some of these countries, is the leader of the government: *President Kennedy* ◦ *the president of France* ◦ [as form of address] *Thank you, Mr/Madam President.* **ORGANIZATION** ▷ **2** the person who has the highest position in an organization or, especially in the US, in a company: *a former president of the Royal Society* ◦ mainly US *She's a friend of the president* ***of*** *the bank.* • **presidential** /ˌprez.ɪˈden.ʃᵊl/ adj [before noun] **B2** *a presidential* ***candidate*** ◦ *'Art and the Community' was the theme of her presidential address to the annual meeting.*

ˈPresidents' ˌDay noun **Washington's Birthday**

press /pres/ verb; noun

▸verb **PUSH** ▷ **1** **B1** [I or T, usually + adv/prep] to push something firmly, often without causing it to move permanently further away from you: *Press the button* to start the machine. ◦ He pressed his face against the window. ◦ Can you press a bit harder on my shoulders, please? ◦ The crowd pressed against the locked doors trying to get into the building. ◦ Press **down** firmly on the lever. **2** [T] to make clothes smooth by IRONING them: *I'll just press these trousers.* **3** [T] to put a weight on fruit in order to remove the juice: *to press grapes* **4** [T] to make a CD, DVD, etc.: *Over 3,000 copies of the CD were pressed and sent out to college radio stations.* **5** [T] to make something flat and firm by putting it under something heavy: *The children pressed some flowers.* ◦ *pressed turkey breast* **PERSUADE** ▷ **6** C2 [T] to try hard to persuade someone to do something: [+ obj + to infinitive] *The committee pressed him **to** reveal more information.* ◦ *He's pressing me **for** an answer.* ◦ *Can I press you further **on** (= persuade you to say more about) this issue?* **7 press charges** C2 to complain officially about someone in a law court: *The family have decided not to press charges **against** him.* **8 press a case/claim** to continue to try to make people accept your demands: *Once again he tried to press his case **for** promotion.*

IDIOMS **press sth/sb into service** to use something or someone that is not completely suitable because nothing or no one more suitable is available: *The car's broken down so I've had to press my old bike back into service.* • **press home your advantage** to use an advantage that you already have in order to succeed • **press the flesh** informal to shake hands with a lot of people: *Politicians have to get out and about and press the flesh.*

PHRASAL VERBS **press on/ahead** C2 to start or continue doing something in a determined way, often despite problems: *It was pouring with rain, but we pressed on **regardless**.* ◦ *The government is pressing ahead **with** its plans to reorganize the penal system.* • **press sth on sb** to give something to someone and not allow them to refuse to accept it: *All the children had sweets and presents pressed on them by the visitors.*

▸noun **NEWSPAPERS** ▷ **1 the press** [S, + sing/pl verb] UK B2 newspapers and magazines, and those parts of television and radio that broadcast news, or REPORTERS and photographers who work for them: *The incident has been widely reported **in** the press.* ◦ *press reports/coverage* ◦ *press reporters/photographers* ◦ *the local/national press* ◦ *The charity invited the press (= reporters and photographers) to a presentation of its plans for the future.* ◦ *The press was out in force at the awards ceremony.* ◦ *The **freedom of** the press (= the right of newspapers to publish news and opinions without being controlled by the government) must be upheld.* **2** C1 [S or U] the judgment that is given of someone or something in the newspapers or on radio or television: *What kind of press did his play get?* ◦ UK *The play has **had a good/bad** press.* ◦ US *The play has **had good/bad** press.* **BOOKS** ▷ **3** [C] a business that prints and produces books and similar things: *Cambridge University Press* **PRINTING MACHINE** ▷ **4** [C] a machine that is used for printing: *a printing press* **5 go to press** to start to be printed: *The newspaper will go to press at midnight.* **PUSH** ▷ **6** [C usually singular] a firm push against something using the fingers: *To start the machine, just **give** this button a press.* **7** [S] the act of making cloth smooth with an IRON: *Can you **give** this shirt a quick press?* **8** [C] a piece of equipment that is used to put weight on something in order to crush it, remove liquid from it or to make it flat: *a garlic/trouser/wine press*

the ˈPress Associˌation noun (abbreviation **PA**) an organization that supplies news reports to newspapers, magazines, and broadcasting and internet companies

ˈpress ˌbaron noun [C] a person who owns several newspapers and sometimes controls what they publish

ˈpress ˌbox noun [C usually singular] a room or other area kept for REPORTERS to work in, especially at sports events

ˈpress ˌconference noun [C] a meeting at which a person or organization makes a public statement and REPORTERS can ask questions

ˈpress ˌcutting noun [C] a piece cut out of a newspaper

pressed /prest/ adj **be pressed for time, money, space, etc.** to be in a difficult situation because you do not have enough time, money, space, etc.: *I'm a bit pressed for time – could we meet later?*

ˈpress ˌgallery noun [C usually singular] in a parliament or other place where laws are made, the upper part of a room where REPORTERS sit to watch what is happening below

ˈpress-gang verb [T] informal to force or strongly persuade someone to do something they do not want to do: *I've been press-ganged **into** tak**ing** the kids swimming.*

pressing /ˈpres.ɪŋ/ adj; noun

▸adj urgent or needing to be dealt with immediately: *a pressing need for housing* ◦ *a pressing issue*

▸noun [C] a large number of CDs, records, etc. produced at one time

ˈpress ˌrelease noun [C] a public statement given to the press to publish if they wish

ˈpress ˌsecretary noun [C] someone who works for a political leader or organization and makes statements to the press or answers questions for them

ˈpress ˌstud noun [C] UK (US **snap**) a small piece of metal or plastic used to fasten clothes with two usually round parts, one of which is pushed into the other

press stud

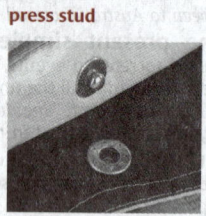

ˈpress-up noun [C] UK (US **ˈpush-up**) a physical exercise in which you lie flat with your face towards the floor, and try to push up your body with your arms, while keeping your legs and your back straight: *I do 20 press-ups every morning.*

pressure /ˈpreʃ.əʳ/ US /-ɚ/ noun; verb

▸noun **PUSHING** ▷ **1** C2 [U] the force you produce when you press something: *He put too much pressure on the door handle and it snapped.* ◦ *You can stop bleeding by **applying** pressure close to the injured area.* **2** C1 [C or U] the force that a liquid or gas produces when it presses against an area: *gas/water pressure* ◦ *The new material allows the company to make gas pipes which withstand higher pressures.* ◦ *The gas is stored **under** pressure (= in a container which keeps it at a higher pressure than it would usually have).* **PERSUADING** ▷ **3** B2 the act of trying to make someone else do something by arguing, persuading, etc.: *public/political pressure* ◦ *Teachers are **under** increasing pressure to work longer hours.* ◦ [+ to infinitive] *Pressure **to** abandon the new motorway is increasing.* ◦ *The government is facing pressure **from** environmental campaigners.* ◦ *He only asked her **under** pressure **from** his wife (= because his wife forced him to).* ◦ *She's **putting** pressure **on** him (= trying to persuade him) to get married.* ◦ formal *The international commu-*

*nity is trying to **bring** pressure **to bear** on the government (= trying to persuade them) to resolve the situation.* **4** B2 [C or U] a difficult situation that makes you feel worried or unhappy: *She's got a lot of pressure **on** her at work just now.* ◦ *Be nice to him – he's been **under** a lot of pressure recently.* ◦ *Can you work well **under** pressure?* ◦ *the pressures **of** work* **5 so no pressure then!** humorous something that you say when what someone has just said makes you feel that you must try very hard to do something: *'These exams are the most important of all.' 'Oh, so no pressure then!'*
▸verb [T] mainly US to strongly persuade someone to do something they do not want to do: *She was pressured **into** join**ing** the club.*

ˈpressure ˌcooker noun [C] a cooking pan with a tightly fitting lid which allows food to cook quickly in steam under pressure

ˈpressure ˌgroup noun [C] a group of people who work together to try to influence what other people or the government think about a particular subject, in order to achieve the things they want

ˈpressure ˌpoint noun [C] BODY ▷ **1** a place on the body where an ARTERY (= tube carrying blood from the heart) is close to the surface of the skin, where it can be pressed to partly stop the flow of blood SITUATION ▷ **2** a place or situation that is likely to cause trouble: *Hospitals are a pressure point for the entire health system.*

ˈpressure ˌwasher noun [C] a machine that sends out a strong stream of water, used for cleaning things

pressurization (UK usually **pressurisation**) /ˌpreʃ.ᵊr.aɪˈzeɪ.ʃᵊn/ US /-ɚ.ɪ-/ noun [U] the state in which something is pressurized

pressurize (UK usually **pressurise**) /ˈpreʃ.ᵊr.aɪz/ US /-ɚ-/ verb [T] (mainly US **pressure**) to strongly persuade someone to do something they do not want to do: *He was pressurized **into** sign**ing** the agreement.*

pressurized (UK usually **pressurised**) /ˈpreʃ.ᵊr.aɪzd/ US /-ə.raɪzd/ adj If a container is pressurized, the air pressure inside it is higher than the air pressure outside it: *a pressurized tank* ◦ *Aircraft cabins are pressurized.*

prestige /presˈtiːʒ/ noun; adj
▸noun [U] C1 respect and admiration given to someone or something, usually because of a reputation for high quality, success, or social influence: *The company has gained international prestige.* ◦ *Many people are attracted by the prestige **of** work**ing** for a top company.*
▸adj [before noun] causing admiration because of being connected with being rich or powerful: *a prestige address/car/job/label*

prestigious /presˈtɪdʒ.əs/ adj C1 very much respected and admired, usually because of being important: *a prestigious literary award* ◦ *a prestigious university*

prestressed /ˌpriːˈstrest/ adj describes concrete or a similar material that has been made stronger by having tightly stretched wires put inside it

presumably /prɪˈzjuː.mə.bli/ US /-ˈzuː-/ adv B2 used to say what you think is the likely situation: *They can presumably afford to buy a bigger apartment.* ◦ *Presumably he just forgot to send the letter.*

presume /prɪˈzjuːm/ US /-ˈzuːm/ verb BELIEVE ▷ **1** C1 [T] to believe something to be true because it is very likely, although you are not certain: [+ (that)] *I presume (**that**) they're not coming, since they haven't replied to the invitation.* ◦ [+ speech] *You are Dr Smith, I presume?* ◦ *'Are we walking to the hotel?' 'I presume **not/so**.'* ◦ [+ obj + adj] *The boat's captain is missing, presumed **dead** (= it is believed that he is dead).* ◦ *In British law, you are presumed innocent until you are proved guilty.* ◦ [+ obj + to infinitive] *The universe is presumed **to** contain many other planets with some form of life.* BE RUDE ▷ **2** [I] to do something although you know that you do not have a right to do it: [+ to infinitive] *I wouldn't presume **to** tell you how to do your job, but shouldn't this piece go there?* ◦ *I don't wish to presume (= make a suggestion although I have no right to), but don't you think you should apologize to her?* ◦ *He presumes **on** her good nature (= takes unfair advantage of it).*

presumption /prɪˈzʌmp.ʃᵊn/ noun [C or U] C1 the act of believing that something is true without having any proof: *The presumption of innocence is central to American law.* ◦ *There is no scientific evidence to support such presumptions.* ◦ [+ that] *The decision is based on the presumption **that** all information must be freely available.*

presumptive /prɪˈzʌmp.tɪv/ adj formal believed to be something, or likely to be true, based on the information that you have: *presumptive signs of pregnancy*

presumptuous /prɪˈzʌmp.tʃəs/ US /-ˈzʌmp.tʃuː.əs/ adj A person who is presumptuous shows little respect for others by doing things they have no right to do: *It would be presumptuous of me to comment on the matter.* • **presumptuously** /-li/ adv • **presumptuousness** /-nəs/ noun [U] (formal **presumption**)

presuppose /ˌpriː.səˈpəʊz/ US /-ˈpoʊz/ verb [T] **1** to accept that something is true before it has been proved: [+ that] *You're presupposing **that** he'll have told her – but he may not have.* **2** formal If an idea or situation presupposes something, that thing must be true for the idea or situation to work: *Investigative journalism presupposes some level of investigation.* ◦ [+ that] *All this presupposes **that** he'll get the job he wants.*

presupposition /ˌpriː.sʌp.əˈzɪʃ.ᵊn/ noun [C or U] something that you believe is true without having any proof: *Your actions are based on some false presuppositions.* ◦ *This is all presupposition – we must wait until we have some hard evidence.*

pretax /ˌpriːˈtæks/ adj before tax is paid: *She predicts pretax **earnings** of over $13 million for the company this year.* ◦ *pretax **profits/losses***

ˌpre-ˈteen noun [C] a boy or girl between the ages of nine and twelve: *a magazine for pre-teens* • **ˌpre-ˈteen** adj pre-teen fashions

pretence (US usually **pretense**) /prɪˈtens/ noun [U] a way of behaving that is intended to deceive people: *She **made** absolutely **no** pretence of being interested.* ◦ *They **kept up** (= continued) a pretence of normality as long as they could.* ◦ *The army has given up any pretence of neutrality in the war.*

pretend /prɪˈtend/ verb; adj
▸verb [I] **1** B2 to behave as if something is true when you know that it is not, especially in order to deceive people or as a game: [+ (that)] *He pretended (**that**) he didn't mind, but I knew that he did.* ◦ *The children pretended (**that**) they were dinosaurs.* ◦ [+ to infinitive] *Were you just pretending **to** be interested?* ◦ *She's not really hurt – she's only pretending.* ◦ *Of course I was angry – I can't pretend **otherwise**.* **2 not pretend to do sth** formal to not claim something that is false: *I don't pretend to be an expert on the subject.*
▸adj imaginary or not real: *'Do you want a cup of tea?'*

P

she asks, offering me a pretend cup. ◦ *They knew the argument was only pretend, but they still got upset.*

pretended /prɪˈten.dɪd/ **adj** [before noun] false: *his pretended enthusiasm/interest*

pretender /prɪˈten.dəʳ/ US /-dɚ/ **noun** [C] a person who states they have a right to the high position that someone else has, although other people disagree with this: *The rebel forces are led by the pretender **to** the throne (= person who wants to replace the present king or queen).*

pretension /prɪˈten.ʃən/ **noun** **1** [C usually plural] a claim or belief that you can succeed or that you are important or have serious value: *The Chronicle has pretensions **to** being a serious newspaper.* ◦ *The NY Giants' Super Bowl pretensions took a dent when they were beaten last week.* **2** [U] (also **pretentiousness**) the act of trying to appear or sound more important or clever than you are

pretentious /prɪˈten.ʃəs/ **adj** disapproving trying to appear or sound more important or clever than you are, especially in matters of art and literature: *a pretentious art critic* ◦ *The novel deals with grand themes, but is never heavy or pretentious.* • **pretentiously** /-li/ **adv** • **pretentiousness** /-nəs/ **noun** [U] (also **pretension**) *I couldn't believe the pretentiousness of the book.*

preternatural /ˌpriː.təˈnætʃ.ər.əl/ US /-t̬ɚˈnætʃ.ɚ-/ **adj** formal more than is usual or natural: *Anger gave me preternatural strength, and I managed to force the door open.* • **preternaturally** /-i/ **adv** *The house seemed preternaturally silent.*

pretext /ˈpriː.tekst/ **noun** [C] a pretended reason for doing something that is used to hide the real reason: *The border dispute was used as a pretext **for** military intervention.* ◦ *I called her **on the** pretext **of** needing more information.* ◦ *He came round to see her on some **flimsy** (= obviously false) pretext.*

prettify /ˈprɪt.ɪ.faɪ/ US /ˈprɪt̬-/ **verb** [T] often disapproving to make something pretty: *Everything in the town seems to have been prettified to within an inch of its life.*

prettily /ˈprɪt.ɪ.li/ US /ˈprɪt̬-/ **adv** in a pretty way: *The menus are printed on prettily illustrated cards.* ◦ *She danced prettily.*

pretty /ˈprɪt.i/ US /ˈprɪt̬-/ **adv; adj**

▸**adv** informal **1** B1 quite, but not extremely: *The house has four bedrooms, so it's pretty big.* ◦ *I'm pretty sure it was her.* ◦ *I've got a pretty good idea of how to get there.* **2 pretty much/well** B1 almost: *I've pretty much finished here.* ◦ *She knows pretty well everything there is to know on the subject.*

▸**adj** A2 pleasant to look at, or (especially of girls or women or things connected with them) attractive or pleasant in a delicate way: *That's a pretty hat you're wearing.* ◦ *The sofa was covered in very pretty flowery material.* ◦ *She's got such a pretty daughter.* • **prettiness** /-nəs/ **noun** [U]

IDIOMS **cost sb a pretty penny** to be very expensive: *That coat must have cost you a pretty penny!* • **not be a pretty sight** humorous to be ugly or unpleasant to look at: *I can tell you, first thing in the morning he's not a pretty sight.* • **not be just a pretty face** humorous If someone is not just a pretty face, they are not only attractive but also intelligent: *'How did you know that?' 'Well, I'm not just a pretty face, you know.'* • **a pretty pass** old-fashioned a bad situation: *Things **have come to** a pretty pass when a referee can no longer be trusted.*

ˌpretty-ˈpretty **adj** UK disapproving describes something that has had too much decoration added to it by someone trying too hard to make it pretty

pretzel /ˈpret.səl/ **noun** [C] a hard salty biscuit that has been baked especially in stick or knot shapes

prevail /prɪˈveɪl/ **verb** [I] formal **1** C2 to get control or influence: *I am sure that common sense will prevail in the end.* ◦ *And did reason prevail **over** (= become a more powerful influence than) emotion?* **2** to be common among a group of people or area at a particular time: *This attitude still prevails among the middle classes.*

PHRASAL VERB **prevail on/upon sb** [+ to infinitive] to persuade someone to do something that they do not want to do: *He was eventually prevailed upon to accept the appointment.*

prevailing /prɪˈveɪ.lɪŋ/ **adj** **1** existing in a particular place or at a particular time: *the prevailing attitude* ◦ *The prevailing mood is one of optimism.* **2 prevailing wind** a wind which usually blows in a particular place: *The town is kept cool by the prevailing westerly winds.*

prevalent /ˈprev.əl.ənt/ **adj** existing very commonly or happening often: *These diseases are more prevalent **among** young children.* ◦ *Trees are dying in areas where acid rain is most prevalent.* • **prevalence** /-əns/ **noun** [U] *the prevalence of smoking amongst teenagers*

prevaricate /prɪˈvær.ɪ.keɪt/ US /-ˈver-/ **verb** [I] formal to avoid telling the truth or saying exactly what you think • **prevarication** /prɪˌvær.ɪˈkeɪ.ʃən/ US /-ˌver-/ **noun** [U] *All my attempts to question the authorities on the subject were met by prevarication.*

prevent /prɪˈvent/ **verb** [T] B1 to stop something from happening or someone from doing something: *Label your suitcases to prevent confusion.* ◦ [+ -ing verb] *His disability prevents him **(from)** driving.*

> **Other ways of saying prevent**
>
> Two common alternatives to 'prevent' are **avoid** and **stop**:
>
> *Label the boxes to **avoid** confusion.*
>
> *This should **stop** any further trouble.*
>
> *They've put barriers up to **stop** people from getting through.*
>
> To talk about preventing something bad from happening, the verb **avert** can be used:
>
> *We had to act quickly to **avert** disaster.*
>
> If something prevents something else by making it impossible, you can use the verb **prohibit**:
>
> *Behavioural problems in the classroom **prohibit** learning.*
>
> **Check** can be used when something prevents another thing from continuing or increasing:
>
> *Children are being vaccinated in an attempt to **check** the spread of the disease.*
>
> The verbs **foil** and **thwart** mean to prevent someone or something from being successful:
>
> *The attempted kidnapping was **foiled** by some undercover police.*
>
> *My trip to London was **thwarted** by a pilots' strike.*

preventable /prɪˈven.tə.bl̩/ US /-t̬ə-/ **adj** able to be prevented: *preventable accidents/injuries*

prevention /prɪˈven.ʃən/ **noun** [U] B2 the act of stopping something from happening or of stopping someone from doing something: *crime prevention*

IDIOM **prevention is better than cure** UK (US **an ounce of prevention is worth a pound of cure**) It is better to stop something bad from happening than it is to deal with it after it has happened.

preventive /prɪˈven.tɪv/ (US) /-t̬ɪv/ **adj** [before noun] (also **preventative**) C2 intended to stop something before it happens: *In the past ten years, preventive* ***measures*** *have radically reduced levels of tooth decay in children.* ◦ *preventative* ***medicine***

preview /ˈpriː.vjuː/ **noun; verb**
▸**noun** [C] an opportunity to see something such as a film or a collection of works of art before it is shown to the public, or a description of something such as a television programme before it is shown to the public
▸**verb** [I or T] to be shown or to describe something before it officially begins: *Miller's new play is previewing (= being performed publicly before it officially opens) at the Theatre Royal tomorrow.* ◦ *On page 11, Sally Gaines previews next week's films on TV.*

previous /ˈpriː.vi.əs/ **adj** [before noun] B1 happening or existing before something or someone else: *The previous owner of the house had built an extension on the back.* ◦ *Training is provided, so no previous* ***experience*** *is required for the job.* ◦ *He has two daughters from a previous marriage.*

previously /ˈpriː.vi.əs.li/ **adv** B1 before the present time or the time referred to: *She was previously employed as a tour guide.* ◦ *I had posted the card two months previously.*

ˌpre-ˈwar adj happening before a war, especially the Second World War: *the pre-war years* → Compare **postwar**

prey /preɪ/ **noun; verb**
▸**noun** [U] C2 an animal that is hunted and killed for food by another animal: *A hawk hovered in the air before swooping on its prey.*

IDIOMS **be easy prey** to be easy to deceive or be taken advantage of: *Homeless young people are easy prey for drug-dealers and pimps.* • **be/fall prey to sth** C2 to be hurt or deceived by someone or something bad: *Small children are prey to all sorts of fears.*

▸**verb**

IDIOM **prey on sb's mind** If a problem preys on your mind, you think about it and worry about it a lot: *I lost my temper with her the other day and it's been preying on my mind ever since.*

PHRASAL VERBS **prey on sb** to hurt or deceive a group of people, especially people who are weak or can easily be hurt or deceived: *He would attack at night, preying on lone women in their twenties or thirties.* ◦ *It's particularly contemptible that these sort of people prey on the elderly.* • **prey on sth** If an animal preys on another animal, it catches and eats it: *The spider preys on small flies and other insects.*

prezzie /ˈprez.i/ **noun** [C] UK informal for **present**

priapic /praɪˈæp.ɪk/ **adj** mainly disapproving relating to male sexual activity and interests: *His latest film has been condemned as the priapic fantasies of an old man.*

> **Word partners for price noun**
> *charge/pay* a price • *increase/put up/raise* the price • *cut/lower/reduce/slash* the price • prices *fall/go down/go up/rise* • a price *cut/freeze/increase* • an *exorbitant/high/low/reasonable* price • the *average* price (of sth) • the price *of* sth

price /praɪs/ **noun; verb**
▸**noun** [C] **1** A2 [C] the amount of money for which something is sold: *The price of oil has risen sharply.* ◦ *House prices have been falling.* ◦ *We thought they were asking a very* ***high/low*** *price.* ◦ *The large supermarkets are offering big price* ***cuts***. **2** C1 [singular] the unpleasant results that you must accept or experience for getting or doing something: *Perhaps being unpopular is the price* ***of*** *success.* ◦ *An extra few minutes at the airport is* ***a small*** *price* ***to pay for*** *safe travel.*

IDIOMS **at any price** C2 If you want something at any price, you are willing to do anything in order to get it: *He wanted success at any price.* • **at/for a price** If you can buy or get something at/for a price, you either have to pay a lot of money or be involved in something unpleasant in order to get it: *You can buy the best of gourmet cuisine here, for a price.* • **not at any price** used to say that you would never do something: *I wouldn't invite her again at any price.* • **what price...?** said when you think it is possible that the admiration, success, etc. that has been achieved was not worth all the suffering it has caused: *What price victory when so many people have died in the struggle?*

▸**verb 1** C1 [T often passive] to say what the price of something is: *The car is priced* ***at*** *£28,000.* ◦ *There is a lack of reasonably priced housing for rent.* **2** [T] to discover how much something costs: *We went around all the travel agents pricing the different tours.*

IDIOM **price yourself out of the market** If a company prices itself out of the market, it charges so much for a product or service that no one wants to buy it.

ˈprice-ˌconscious adj knowing how much things cost and avoiding buying expensive things: *price-conscious shoppers*

priceless /ˈpraɪs.ləs/ **adj 1** B2 describes an object that has such a high value, especially because it is rare, that the price of it cannot be calculated: *A priceless collection of vases was destroyed.* ◦ figurative *Her knowledge and experience would make her a priceless (= extremely useful) asset to the team.* **2** informal extremely funny to see or hear: *You should have seen the look on her face when I told her – it was priceless!*

ˈprice-ˌsensitive adj describes a product whose sales are influenced by price rather than quality

ˈprice ˌtag noun [C] (also **ˈprice ˌticket**) a piece of paper with a price that is fixed to a product, or the amount that something costs: *How much is it? I can't find the price tag.* ◦ *These suits have designer names and a price ticket to match.*

ˈprice ˌwar noun [C] a situation in which different companies compete with each other by reducing prices: *A supermarket price war has led to lower profit margins.*

pricey (**pricier, priciest**) (also **pricy**) /ˈpraɪ.si/ **adj** informal expensive: *It's a bit pricey but the food is wonderful.*

prick /prɪk/ **verb; noun**
▸**verb** [T] to make a very small hole or holes in the surface of something, sometimes in a way which causes pain: *Prick the skin of the potatoes with a fork before baking them.* ◦ *She pricked the balloon with a pin and it burst with a loud bang.*

IDIOMS **prick sb's conscience** to make someone do something because they feel guilty: *Dan's mentioning Julia pricked my conscience and I gave her a call.* • **prick the bubble (of sth)** to make someone suddenly understand the unpleasant truth of a situation

PHRASAL VERB **prick (sth) up 1** When an animal pricks its ears up, or when its ears prick up, it puts its ears up straight because it is listening carefully to a small sound or one that is far away. **2** If you prick up your ears, or if your ears prick up, you suddenly begin to

P

listen very carefully because you have heard something interesting: *I overheard them mentioning my name and pricked up my ears.*

▸noun [C] offensive **BODY PART** ▷ **1** a PENIS **MAN** ▷ **2** a stupid man: *I'm not wearing that – I'd look a right prick.*

prickle /ˈprɪk.l̩/ **noun; verb**

▸noun [C] **1** one of several thin, sharp points that stick out of a plant or animal: *The fruit can be eaten once the prickles have been removed.* **2** a feeling as if a lot of little points are sticking into your body: *I felt a hot prickle of embarrassment spread across my cheeks.*

▸verb **1** [T] If thin, sharp objects prickle you, they cause slight pain by touching against your skin: *She lay on the grass and the stiff dry grass prickled the back of her legs.* **2** [I] If part of your body prickles, it feels as if a lot of sharp points are touching it because you are frightened or excited: *Turner started to be worried and felt the back of his neck prickle.*

prickly /ˈprɪk.l̩.i/, /-li/ **adj** **1** covered with prickles: *I find this sweater a bit prickly (= it makes the skin sore).* **2** informal unfriendly and slightly rude: *She was asked a couple of questions about her private life and got a bit prickly.*

ˌprickly ˈheat noun [U] **heat rash**

ˌprickly ˈpear noun [C] a type of CACTUS (= desert plant) that has oval fruit that can be eaten with sharp SPINES on them

ˈprick-tease noun [C] (also **ˈprick-teaser**) a woman who tries to make a man sexually excited but does not intend to have sex with him

pride /praɪd/ **noun; verb**

▸noun **SATISFACTION** ▷ **1** B2 [U] a feeling of pleasure and satisfaction that you get because you or people connected with you have done or got something good: *She felt a great sense of pride as she watched him accept the award.* ◦ *He felt such pride walking his little daughter down the street.* → See also **proud** **2** **take pride in sth/sb** to feel very pleased about something or someone that you are closely connected with: *If you don't take professional pride in your work, you're probably in the wrong job.* **RESPECT FOR YOURSELF** ▷ **3** B2 [U] your feelings of your own worth and respect for yourself: *She has too much pride to accept any help.* ◦ *The country's national pride has been damaged by its sporting failures.* **FEELING OF IMPORTANCE** ▷ **4** [U] disapproving the belief that you are better or more important than other people: *Pride was his downfall.* → See also **proud** **LIONS** ▷ **5** [C] a group of lions

IDIOMS **be your pride and joy** to be something or someone that is very important to you and that gives you a lot of pleasure: *He spends hours cleaning that motorcycle – it's his pride and joy.* • **be the pride of somewhere/sth** to be something or someone that a particular place or group of people is very proud of: *This village is the pride of East Sussex.* • **have/take pride of place** to have the most important position in a group of things: *A portrait of the earl takes pride of place in the entrance hall.* • **swallow your pride** C2 to decide to do something although it will make you feel embarrassed or ashamed: *He was forced to swallow his pride and ask if he could have his old job back.*

▸verb

PHRASAL VERB **pride yourself on sth** to value a skill or good quality that you have: *He prides himself on his loyalty to his friends.*

priest /priːst/ **noun** [C] B1 a person, usually a man, who has been trained to perform religious duties in the Christian Church, especially the Roman Catholic Church, or a person with particular duties in some other religions: *Father O'Dooley was ordained a priest in 1949.* ◦ *Many in the Anglican Church are still opposed to women priests.*

priestess /ˌpriːˈstes/ **noun** [C] a woman who performs religious duties in some religions that are not Christian

the priesthood /ˈpriːst.hʊd/ **noun** [S] the position of being a priest: *He left the priesthood to get married.*

priestly /ˈpriːst.li/ **adj** relating to or like a priest

prig /prɪg/ **noun** [C] disapproving a person who obeys the rules of correct behaviour and considers himself or herself to be morally better than other people

priggish /ˈprɪg.ɪʃ/ **adj** disapproving like a prig: *I found him priggish and cold.*

prim /prɪm/ **adj** (**primmer**, **primmest**) disapproving very formal and correct in behaviour and easily shocked by anything rude: *She's much too prim **and proper** to drink pints of beer.* • **primly** /ˈprɪm.li/ **adv** *primly dressed*

prima ballerina /ˌpriː.mə.bæl.əˈriː.nə/ US /-əˈiː-/ **noun** [C usually singular] the most important female dancer in a BALLET company

primacy /ˈpraɪ.mə.si/ **noun** [U] formal the state of being the most important thing: *The government insists on the primacy **of** citizens' rights.*

prima donna /ˌpriː.məˈdɒn.ə/ US /-ˈdɑː.nə/ **noun** [C usually singular] **1** the most important female singer in an OPERA company **2** disapproving someone who demands to be treated in a special way and is difficult to please: *I had to entertain visiting authors and some of them were real prima donnas.* • **prima donna-ish** /-ɪʃ/ **adj** disapproving *prima donna-ish behaviour*

primaeval → See **primeval**

prima facie /ˌpraɪ.məˈfeɪ.ʃi/ **adj** [before noun] formal or legal at first sight (= based on what seems to be the truth when first seen or heard): *There is prima facie **evidence** that he was involved in the fraud.* ◦ *For millions of Americans witnessing the event, it was a prima facie **case** of police brutality.*

primal /ˈpraɪ.məl/ **adj** [before noun] **1** relating to the time when human life on Earth began: *The universe evolved from a densely packed primal inferno.* **2** formal basic and connected with an early stage of development: *a primal urge to connect with nature* ◦ *primal fears*

primarily /praɪˈmer.ɪ.li/ **adv** B2 mainly: *We're primarily concerned with keeping expenditure down.* ◦ *Soccer is primarily a winter game.*

primary /ˈpraɪ.mə.ri/ US /-mɚ.i/ **adj; noun**

▸adj **MAIN** ▷ **1** B2 more important than anything else; main: *The Red Cross's primary concern is to preserve and protect human life.* ◦ *The primary responsibility lies with those who break the law.* **EDUCATION** ▷ **2** B1 [before noun] UK of or for the teaching of young children, especially those between five and eleven years old: *primary education* ◦ *a primary **school*** **EARLIEST** ▷ **3** happening first: *the primary stages of development*

▸noun [C] in the US, an election in which people who belong to a political party choose who will represent that party in an election for political office

ˌprimary ˈcare noun [U] medical treatment provided by local doctors or other health workers, rather than special treatment in a hospital

ˌprimary ˈcolour noun [C] one of the three colours, red, yellow, and blue, that can be mixed together in different ways to make any other colour

primate /ˈpraɪ.meɪt/, /-mət/ **noun** [C] specialized **ANIMAL** ▷ **1** a member of the most developed and intelligent group of mammals, including humans, monkeys, and APES **PRIEST** ▷ **2** a priest with the highest position in his country: *He was made the Roman Catholic Primate of All Ireland last year.*

prime /praɪm/ **adj; noun; verb**
▸**adj** [before noun] **1** C2 main or most important: *This is a prime **example** of 1930s architecture.* ◦ *the prime suspect in a murder investigation* ◦ *a prime source of evidence* ◦ *The president is a prime (= likely) **target** for the assassin's bullet.* **2** of the best quality: *prime beef* ◦ *The hotel is in a prime location in the city centre.*
▸**noun** [S] the period in your life when you are most active or successful: *This is a dancer **in** her prime.* ◦ *Middle age can be the prime **of life** if you have the right attitude.* ◦ *I suspect this cheese is **past its** prime.*
▸**verb** [T] **1** to tell someone something that will prepare them for a particular situation: *I'd been primed so I knew not to mention her son.* **2** to cover the surface of wood with a special paint before the main paint is put on **3** to make a bomb or gun ready to explode or fire

the ˌprime meˈridian **noun** [S] specialized the imaginary line from the North Pole to the South Pole that passes through Greenwich in England and marks 0° LONGITUDE, from which all other LONGITUDES are measured

ˌprime ˈminister **noun** [C usually singular] (UK informal abbreviation **PM**) B2 the leader of the government in some countries

ˌprime ˈmover **noun** [C usually singular] someone who has a lot of influence in starting something important: *He was a prime mover **in** developing a new style of customer-friendly bookshops in the UK.*

ˌprime ˈnumber **noun** [C] specialized a number that cannot be divided by any other number except itself and the number 1: *2, 3, and 7 are prime numbers.*

primer /ˈpraɪ.məʳ/ US /-mɚ/ **noun** **PAINT** ▷ **1** [C or U] a type of paint that you put on a wooden surface before the main paint is put on: *It's best to use a **coat of** primer before the top coat.* **BOOK** ▷ **2** [C] old-fashioned a small book containing basic facts about a subject, used especially when you are beginning to learn about that subject

ˈprime ˌtime **noun** [U] in television and radio broadcasting, the time when the largest number of people are watching or listening: *prime-time TV*

primeval (mainly UK **primaeval**) /praɪˈmiː.vəl/ **adj** ancient; existing at or from a very early time: *primeval forests*

primitive /ˈprɪm.ɪ.tɪv/ US /-t̬ɪv/ **adj** **1** C1 relating to human society at a very early stage of development, with people living in a simple way without machines or a writing system: *Primitive races colonized these islands 2,000 years ago.* ◦ *primitive man* ◦ *The spiny anteater is a mammal, although a very primitive one.* **2** C1 disapproving describes living conditions that are basic, unpleasant, and uncomfortable: *Early settlers had to cope with very primitive living conditions.*

primogeniture /ˌpraɪ.məʊˈdʒen.ɪ.tʃəʳ/ US /-moʊˈdʒen.ɪ.tʃɚ/ **noun** [U] specialized the custom by which all of a family's property goes to the oldest son when the father dies

primordial /praɪˈmɔː.di.əl/ US /-ˈmɔːr-/ **adj** formal **1** existing at or since the beginning of the world or the universe: *The planet Jupiter contains large amounts of the primordial gas and dust out of which the solar system was formed.* **2** basic and connected with an early stage of development

primrose /ˈprɪm.rəʊz/ US /-roʊz/ **noun** [C] a wild plant with pale yellow flowers

IDIOM **the primrose path** literary If you lead someone down the primrose path, you encourage them to live an easy life that is full of pleasure but bad for them: *Unable to enjoy his newly acquired wealth, he felt he was being **led down the primrose path** to destruction.*

primula /ˈprɪm.jʊ.lə/ **noun** [C] specialized any of a group of wild plants with white, yellow, pink, or purple flowers

Primus (stove) /ˈpraɪ.məsˌstəʊv/ US /-ˌstoʊv/ **noun** [C] trademark a small cooker that burns PARAFFIN

prince /prɪns/ **noun** [C] **1** B1 an important male member of a royal family, especially a son or GRANDSON of the king or queen: *Prince Edward* ◦ *Prince Juan Carlos of Spain became king in 1975.* **2** a male ruler of a country, usually a small country: *Prince Rainier is the ruling prince of Monaco.* **3 prince among/of sth** literary a man who is excellent at something: *that prince of flautists, William Bennett*

ˌPrince ˈCharming **noun** [S] humorous A woman's Prince Charming is her perfect partner: *How much time have you wasted sitting around waiting for Prince Charming to appear?*

ˌprince ˈconsort **noun** [C usually singular] the title sometimes given to the husband of a ruling queen

princely /ˈprɪns.li/ **adj** humorous **the princely sum of** used to refer to a surprisingly small amount of money: *She acquired the painting at a jumble sale for the princely sum of 25p.*

ˌPrince of ˈWales **noun** [C usually singular] in the UK, a title given to the oldest son of the king or queen

princess /prɪnˈses/, /ˈprɪn.ses/ **noun** [C] B1 an important female member of a royal family, especially a daughter or GRANDDAUGHTER of a king and queen, or the wife of a PRINCE

principal /ˈprɪn.sɪ.pəl/ **adj; noun**
▸**adj** [before noun] B1 first in order of importance: *Iraq's principal export is oil.* ◦ *He was principal dancer at the Dance Theatre of Harlem.* ◦ *That was my principal reason for moving.*
▸**noun** **PERSON** ▷ **1** A2 [C] US the person in charge of a school or college for children aged between approximately eleven and 18 **MONEY** ▷ **2** [C usually singular] specialized an amount of money which someone has INVESTED in a bank or lent to a person or organization so that they will receive interest on it from the bank, person, or organization: *She lives off the interest and tries to keep the principal intact.*

ˌprincipal ˈboy **noun** [C] UK the most important male character in a PANTOMIME (= musical play for children) played by a woman

principality /ˌprɪn.sɪˈpæl.ɪ.ti/ US /-ə.t̬i/ **noun** [C] a country ruled by a prince, or from which a prince takes his title: *Monaco is a principality.*

principally /ˈprɪn.sɪ.pəl.i/ **adv** mainly: *The advertising campaign is aimed principally at women.*

principle /ˈprɪn.sɪ.pl/ **noun** **IDEA** ▷ **1** C1 [C] a basic idea or rule that explains or controls how something happens or works: *the principles of the criminal justice system* ◦ *The country is run **on** socialist principles.* ◦ *The machine works according to the principle **of** electromagnetic conduction.* ◦ *The organization works **on the** principle **that** all members have the same rights.* → See also **first principles** **2 in principle** C2 If you agree with or believe something in principle, you agree with the idea in general, although you might not support it in reality or in every situation: *In principle I*

P

agree with the idea, but in practice it's not always possible. ◦ *They have approved the changes in principle.* RULE ▷ **3** Ⓒ2 [C or U] approving a moral rule or standard of good behaviour: *She doesn't have any principles.* ◦ *He was a man of principle.* ◦ *Anyway, I can't deceive him – it's* ***against*** *all my principles.* ◦ *I never gamble,* ***as a matter of*** *principle (= because I believe it is wrong).* ◦ *She'd never ask to borrow money,* ***on*** *principle.*

principled /ˈprɪn.sɪ.pl̩d/ adj formal **1** always behaving in an honest and moral way: *She was a very principled woman.* **2** based on moral rules: *The Church is taking a principled stand against the conflict.*

print /prɪnt/ noun; verb

▸noun TEXT ▷ **1** Ⓒ2 [U] letters, numbers, or symbols that have been produced on paper by a machine using ink: *The title is in bold print.* ◦ *This novel is available in large print for readers with poor eyesight.* ◦ *The book was rushed* ***into*** *print (= was produced and published) as quickly as possible.* ◦ *The print quality (= the quality of the text produced) of the new laser printer is excellent.* **2** [U] newspapers, books, and magazines: *The debate is still raging, both* ***in*** *print and online.* **3 in/out of print** Ⓒ2 If a book is in print, it is possible to buy a new copy of it, and if it is out of print, it is not now possible: *Is her work still in print?* ◦ *Classic literature never* ***goes*** *out of print.* PICTURE ▷ **4** Ⓒ1 [C] a photographic copy of a painting, or a picture made by pressing paper onto a special surface covered in ink, or a single photograph from a film: *a print of Van Gogh's 'Sunflowers'* ◦ *a signed Hockney print* PATTERN ▷ **5** [C] any type of pattern produced using ink on a piece of clothing: *a floral/paisley print* FINGERPRINT ▷ **6** [C] informal for **fingerprint**: *The burglar had left his prints all over the window.*

▸verb TEXT ▷ **1** Ⓐ2 [I or T] to produce writing or images on paper or other material with a machine: *The leaflets will be printed* ***on*** *recycled paper.* ◦ *I'm waiting for a document to print.* **2** Ⓑ2 [T] to include a piece of writing in a newspaper or magazine: *Some newspapers still refuse to print certain swear words.* ◦ *They printed his letter in Tuesday's paper.* **3** Ⓑ2 [T] to produce a newspaper, magazine or book in large quantities: *20,000 copies of the novel will be printed in hardback.* WRITE ▷ **4** [I or T] to write without joining the letters together: *Please print your name clearly below your signature.* PICTURE ▷ **5** [T] to produce a photograph on paper: *Photographs are better if they are printed* ***from*** *the original negative.* PATTERN ▷ **6** [T] to produce a pattern on material or paper: *The designs are printed onto the fabric by hand.*

PHRASAL VERB **print sth out** to produce a printed copy of a document that has been written on a computer: *Could you print out a copy of that letter for me?*

printable /ˈprɪn.tə.bl̩/ ⓊⓈ /-t̬ə-/ adj If something that you say is not printable, it is too rude or offensive to be included in a newspaper or magazine: *He let out a torrent of abuse, none of it printable in a respectable daily newspaper.*

printed /ˈprɪn.tɪd/ ⓊⓈ /-t̬ɪd/ adj **the printed word** information in the form of books, newspapers, and magazines: *Children who watch TV all the time have no real interest in the printed word.*

ˌ**printed** ˈ**circuit** (ˌ**board**) noun [C] a set of electrical connections made by thin lines of metal fixed onto a surface

ˈ**printed** ˌ**matter** noun [U] documents, letters, advertisements, etc. that are printed

printer /ˈprɪn.təʳ/ ⓊⓈ /-t̬ɚ/ noun [C] **1** Ⓐ2 a machine that is connected to a computer and prints onto paper using ink: *a bubble-jet/dot-matrix/laser printer* **2** a person whose job is to print books, newspapers, and magazines

printing /ˈprɪn.tɪŋ/ ⓊⓈ /-t̬ɪŋ/ noun **1** [U] the activity or business of producing writing or images on paper or other material with a machine: *She runs her own printing business.* **2** [C] the number of copies of a book which the publisher has produced: *The publishers produced a first printing of 2,500.*

ˈ**printing** ˌ**press** noun [C] a machine that prints books, newspapers, or magazines

printout /ˈprɪnt.aʊt/ noun [C] text produced by a computer printer: *There were pages of* ***computer*** *printout all over the desk.*

ˈ**print** ˌ**run** noun [C] the number of copies of a book produced at one time

prion /ˈpraɪ.ɒn/ ⓊⓈ /-ɑːn/ noun [C] specialized a small piece of PROTEIN that is thought to cause certain brain diseases, such as BSE and CJD

prior /praɪəʳ/ ⓊⓈ /praɪr/ adj; noun

▸adj [before noun] EARLIER ▷ **1** Ⓒ1 formal existing or happening before something else, or before a particular time: *The course required no prior knowledge of Spanish.* ◦ *They had to refuse the dinner invitation because of a prior* ***engagement*** *(= something already planned for that time).* **2 prior to sth** Ⓒ1 before a particular time or event: *the weeks prior to her death* MORE IMPORTANT ▷ **3** formal more important: *Mothers with young children have a prior* ***claim*** *on funds.*

▸noun [C] a man who is in charge of a priory or who is second in charge of an ABBEY

prioress /ˈpraɪə.res/ ⓊⓈ /ˈpraɪ-/ noun [C] a female prior

prioritize (UK usually **prioritise**) /praɪˈɒr.ɪ.taɪz/ ⓊⓈ /-ˈɔːr.ə-/ verb [I or T] to decide which of a group of things are the most important so that you can deal with them first: *You must learn to prioritize your work.*

priority /praɪˈɒr.ɪ.ti/ ⓊⓈ /-ˈɔːr.ə.t̬i/ noun [C or U] Ⓑ2 something that is very important and must be dealt with before other things: *The management did not seem to consider office safety to be a priority.* ◦ *My* ***first/top*** *priority is to find somewhere to live.* ◦ *You have to learn to* ***get*** *your priorities* ***right/straight*** *(= decide which are the most important jobs or problems and deal with them first).* ◦ *Mending the lights is a priority task (= more important than other jobs).* ◦ *Banks normally* ***give*** *priority* ***to*** *large businesses when deciding on loans (= they deal with them first because they consider them most important).* ◦ *Official business requirements obviously* ***take/have*** *priority* ***over*** *personal requests (= official business matters will be dealt with first).*

priory /ˈpraɪə.ri/ ⓊⓈ /praɪr.i/ noun [C] a building where MONKS or NUNS live, work, and pray

prise /praɪz/ verb [T] UK for **prize**

prism /ˈprɪz.əm/ noun [C] a transparent glass or plastic object which separates white light that passes through it into different colours

prison /ˈprɪz.ən/ noun **1** Ⓑ1 [C or U] a building where criminals are forced to live as a punishment: *Conditions in the prison are said to be appalling.* ◦ *He's spent a lot of time* ***in*** *prison.* ◦ *She* ***went to/was sent to*** *prison for six months.* ◦ *It was a* ***maximum-security*** *prison (= intended to be especially difficult to escape from).* ◦ *They should* ***put*** *him* ***in*** *prison and throw away the key!* ◦ *a prison cell/sentence/warder* **2** [U] the system of keeping people in prisons: *the prison service* ◦ *Do you think prison works?* ◦ *Prison (= the time he had spent in prison) hadn't changed him*

P

at all. **3** [C] a situation or relationship from which it is difficult to escape: *She felt that her marriage had become a prison.*

> **Word partners for prison**
> *go to/be sent to* prison • *put* sb *in* prison • *escape from/be released from* prison • a prison *cell/sentence* • *in/out of* prison

ˈprison ˌcamp noun [C] a place where people, usually prisoners of war or political prisoners, are forced to stay

prisoner /ˈprɪz.ən.əʳ/ (US) /-ə/ noun [C] **1** (B1) a person who is kept in prison as a punishment: *Prisoners climbed onto the prison roof to protest at the conditions inside the prison.* → See also **political prisoner** **2** **hold/keep/take sb prisoner** (C2) to catch someone and guard them so that they cannot escape: *Of 10,000 troops, 7,000 were killed, wounded or taken prisoner.* ◦ *The pilot and several passengers were held prisoner by the gunmen for 57 hours.*

IDIOM **take no prisoners** If someone takes no prisoners, when they try to achieve something they are very determined and do not care about other people's feelings: *When Eric's anger is aroused, he takes no prisoners.*

ˌprisoner of ˈconscience noun [C] someone kept in prison because their political or religious beliefs are different from those of the government

ˌprisoner of ˈwar noun [C] (abbreviation **POW**) a member of the armed forces who has been caught by enemy forces during a war: *a prisoner of war camp*

prissy /ˈprɪs.i/ adj disapproving always behaving and dressing in a way that is considered correct and that does not shock: *a prissy sort of a woman* • **prissily** /-ɪ.li/ adv

pristine /ˈprɪs.tiːn/ (US) /prɪˈstiːn/ adj formal approving new or almost new, and in very good condition: *pristine new offices* ◦ *Washing machine for sale – only two months old and* ***in*** *pristine* ***condition***.

privacy /ˈprɪv.ə.si/ (US) /ˈpraɪ.və-/ noun [U] **1** (B2) someone's right to keep their personal matters and relationships secret: *The new law is designed to protect people's privacy.* **2** the state of being alone: *I hate sharing a bedroom – I never get any privacy.*

private /ˈpraɪ.vət/ adj; noun

▸adj PERSONAL ▷ **1** (B1) only for one person or group and not for everyone: *She has a small office that is used for private discussions.* ◦ *I caught him looking through my private papers.* ◦ *The sign on the gate said 'Private* ***Property*** *– No Admittance.'* **2** describes activities that involve personal matters or relationships and are not connected with your work: *Apparently in interviews he refuses to talk about his private* ***life***. **3** (B1) describes thoughts and opinions that are secret and not discussed with other people: *Although I support the project in public, my private opinion is that it will fail.* ◦ *This is a private matter.* **4** describes a place that is quiet and where there are no other people to see or hear you: *Is there somewhere private where we can talk?* **5** describes someone who does not like to talk about their personal feelings and thoughts: *She's quite a private person.* **6** **in private** (B2) If you talk to someone or do something in private, you do it without other people being present: *Jamie wants to speak to me in private.* → Compare **in public** NOT OFFICIAL ▷ **7** (B2) controlled or paid for by a person or company and not by the government: *private education/healthcare* ◦ *a private doctor/dentist* ◦ *Banks should be supporting small private businesses.*

▸noun [C] (also **Private**) a soldier of the lowest rank in an army: *Private Murray/Sam Murray* ◦ [as form of address] *You're dismissed, Private.*

ˌprivate ˈcompany noun [C] a company with SHARES that are not traded on a STOCK MARKET: *EM.TV is a family-owned private company.* → Compare **public company**

ˌprivate deˈtective noun [C] (also **ˌprivate inˈvestigator**, informal **ˌprivate ˈeye**) a person whose job is discovering information about people. A private detective is not a government employee or a police officer: *She* ***hired*** *a private detective to find out if her husband was having an affair.*

ˌprivate ˈenterprise noun [U] industry and businesses owned by ordinary people, not by the government

privately /ˈpraɪ.vət.li/ adv PERSONAL ▷ **1** (B2) in secret, or with only one or two other people present: *She spoke privately with the manager.* ◦ *Despite his public support, privately (= secretly) he was worried.* NOT OFFICIAL ▷ **2** by a person or company and not by the government: *a privately owned business*

ˌprivate ˈmeans noun [plural] (UK also **ˌprivate ˈincome**) income that you receive from your family, INVESTMENTS, or land, and not from a job

ˌprivate ˈmember noun [C] UK a member of parliament who does not have a government job

ˌprivate ˈmember's ˌbill noun [C] UK a law that is officially suggested by a member of parliament who is not a government MINISTER

ˌprivate ˈparts noun [plural] (informal **privates**) polite word for sexual organs: *He grabbed a towel to cover his private parts.*

ˌprivate ˈpractice noun [U] the work of a PROFESSIONAL person such as a doctor or lawyer who has their own business and does not work for a company or the government

ˌprivate ˈschool noun [C] a school which does not receive financial support from the government

ˌprivate ˈsecretary noun [C] **1** a SECRETARY who works for someone, dealing with their personal affairs **2** someone whose job is to help a government MINISTER

the ˈprivate ˌsector noun [S] businesses and industries that are not owned or controlled by the government: *30 percent of graduates are working* ***in*** *the private sector.* ◦ *private sector employers*

privation /praɪˈveɪ.ʃən/ noun [C or U] formal a lack of the basic things that are necessary for an acceptable standard of living: *Economic privation is pushing the poor towards crime.* ◦ *Several villages* ***suffered*** *serious privations during their long isolation during the war.*

privatize (UK usually **privatise**) /ˈpraɪ.və.taɪz/ verb [T] (C1) If a government privatizes an industry, company, or service that it owns and controls, it sells it so that it becomes privately owned and controlled: *I bought shares in British Gas when it was privatized.* • **privatization** (UK usually **privatisation**) /ˌpraɪ.vɪ.taɪˈzeɪ.ʃən/ (US) /-t̬ə-/ noun [U]

privet /ˈprɪv.ɪt/ noun [C or U] an EVERGREEN bush (= one that never loses its leaves), often grown as a HEDGE around the edges of gardens

privilege /ˈprɪv.əl.ɪdʒ/ noun **1** (C1) [C or U] an advantage that only one person or group of people has, usually because of their position or because they are rich: *Healthcare should be a right, not a privilege.* ◦ *Senior management* ***enjoy*** *certain privileges, such as company cars and private healthcare.* **2** (C1) [S] an opportunity to do something special or enjoyable: *I* *had the privilege **of** interviewing Picasso in the 1960s.* ◦ ***It** was a real privilege **to** meet her.* **3** [U] the way in which rich people or people from a high social class have most of the advantages in society: *a life of privilege* **4** [C or U] specialized the special right that some people in authority have which allows them to do or say things that other people are not allowed to: *diplomatic/parliamentary privilege*

privileged /ˈprɪv.əl.ɪdʒd/ **adj** **1** C1 having a privilege: *As an ambassador, she enjoys a very privileged status.* ◦ [+ to infinitive] *I have been privileged **to** work with the pioneers of silicon technology.* **2** specialized describes information that is secret and does not have to be given even in a law court

privy /ˈprɪv.i/ **adj; noun**

▸**adj** formal **be privy to sth** to be told information that is not told to many people: *I was never privy to conversations between top management.*

▸**noun** [C] old use a toilet, especially in a very small building in the garden of a house

the ˌPrivy ˈCouncil **noun** [S] in the UK, a group of people of high rank in politics who sometimes advise the king or queen but who have little power • **ˌPrivy ˈCouncillor noun** [C]

prize /praɪz/ **noun; verb; adj**

▸**noun** [C] **1** A2 something valuable, such as an amount of money, that is given to someone who succeeds in a competition or game or that is given to someone as a reward for doing very good work: *The critics' prize **for** best film was won by Marc Abbott for 'Belly Laugh'.* ◦ *I **won** a prize in the raffle.* ◦ *The **first** (= main) prize is a weekend for two in Bruges.* ◦ *The prize **money** for literary competitions can be as high as £40,000.* **2** something important and valuable that is difficult to achieve or get: *The prize would be her hand in marriage.*

IDIOM **no prizes for guessing sth** something you say when it is very easy to guess something: *No prizes for guessing where Daniel is.*

P

▸**verb** LIFT ▷ **1** (UK also **prise**) [T + adv/prep] to move or lift something by pressing a tool against a fixed point: *I prized the lid **off** with a spoon.* ◦ *The window had been prized **open** with a jemmy.* REWARD ▷ **2** [T often passive] to think that someone or something is very valuable or important: *In parts of Asia this plant is prized **for** its medicinal qualities.* ◦ *I prize that intimacy above everything.*

PHRASAL VERB **prize sth out of sb** to get something from someone with difficulty, especially information or money: *He's so secretive – you'll have a hard time prizing any information out of him.*

▸**adj** [before noun] **1** A prize animal, flower, or vegetable is one that has won or deserves to win a prize in a competition because it is of very good quality: *a prize bull* ◦ *a prize marrow* **2** describes something that is a very good or important example of its type: *prize assets* ◦ *Some prize **idiot** (= extremely foolish person) forgot to lock the door.*

prized /praɪzd/ **adj** considered valuable and important: *The 1961 vintage is **highly** prized among wine connoisseurs.* ◦ *Her photograph is among my most prized **possessions**.*

prizefight /ˈpraɪz.faɪt/ **noun** [C] a BOXING competition in which people fight to win money

prizefighter /ˈpraɪzˌfaɪ.təʳ/ US /-t̬ɚ/ **noun** [C] a BOXER who fights to win money

prizewinning /ˈpraɪzˌwɪn.ɪŋ/ **adj** [before noun] having won a prize: *a prizewinning film/novel*

pro /prəʊ/ US /proʊ/ **noun; adj, preposition**

▸**noun** [C] (plural **pros**) ADVANTAGE ▷ **1** B2 an advantage or a reason for doing something: *One of the big pros **of** living in Madrid is the night life.* ◦ *We're just weighing up the pros **and cons** (= advantages and disadvantages) of moving to a bigger house.* SPORTSPERSON ▷ **2** informal a person who plays sport as a job rather than as a hobby: *a tennis pro* ◦ *a pro golfer*

▸**adj, preposition** supporting or agreeing with something: *Are you pro or anti the new bill (= do you support it or are you against it)?*

pro- /prəʊ-/ US /proʊ-/ **prefix** supporting or approving of something: *pro-American* ◦ *pro-democracy demonstrations* → Compare **anti-**

proactive /ˌprəʊˈæk.tɪv/ US /ˌproʊ-/ **adj** taking action by causing change and not only reacting to change when it happens: *Companies are going to have to be more proactive about environmental management.* ◦ *a proactive approach/role* • **proactively** /-li/ **adv**

pro-am /ˌprəʊˈæm/ US /ˌproʊ-/ **adj** [before noun] describes a competition in which the teams include PROFESSIONALS (= people who compete as a job) and AMATEURS (= people who compete for pleasure): *a pro-am golf competition*

probability /ˌprɒb.əˈbɪl.ɪ.ti/ US /ˌprɑː.bəˈbɪl.ə.t̬i/ **noun** [C or U] **1** C1 the level of possibility of something happening or being true: *What is the probability **of** winning?* ◦ *The probability **of** getting all the answers correct is about one in ten.* ◦ ***There's a high/strong** probability (**that**) (= it is very likely that) she'll be here.* ◦ *Until yesterday, the project was just a possibility, but now it has become a real probability (= it is likely to happen).* → Synonym **likelihood** **2** **in all probability** C2 used to mean that something is very likely: *She will, in all probability, have left before we arrive.*

probable /ˈprɒb.ə.bl/ US /ˈprɑː.bə-/ **adj** B2 likely to be true or likely to happen: *The probable cause of death was heart failure.* ◦ *An election in June seems increasingly probable.* ◦ [+ that] ***It** is probable **that** share prices will fall still further.* → Compare **possible** → Opposite **improbable**

probably /ˈprɒb.ə.bli/ US /ˈprɑː.bə-/ **adv** A2 used to mean that something is very likely: *I'll probably be home by midnight.* ◦ *I'm probably going – it depends on the weather.* ◦ *He probably didn't even notice.* ◦ *Probably the best thing to do is to call them before you go.*

> **!** Common mistake: **probably**
>
> **Warning:** check your word order!
>
> **Probably** usually goes directly before the main verb in a sentence:
>
> ~~*I probably will go to Greece this summer.*~~
>
> *I will probably go to Greece this summer.*
>
> But if the main verb is **am/is/are/was/were**, **probably** usually goes directly after it:
>
> ~~*She probably is tired after the journey.*~~
>
> *She is probably tired after the journey.*

probate /ˈprəʊ.beɪt/ US /ˈproʊ-/ **noun; verb**

▸**noun** [U] **1** legal the legal process of deciding if a person's will has been made correctly and if the information it contains is correct: *Before probate can be **granted**, all business assets have to be identified and valued.* **2** Australian English legal a tax paid on money or property you have received from someone who has died → Compare **inheritance tax**

▸**verb** [T] US legal to prove that a person's will has been made correctly and that the information it contains is correct

probation /prəˈbeɪ.ʃən/ US /proʊ-/ **noun** [U] **1** a

period of time when a criminal must behave well and not commit any more crimes in order to avoid being sent to prison: *He was fined and given two years' probation.* ◦ *The judge* ***put*** *him* ***on*** *probation for two years.* ◦ *He served a year in prison and was then* ***let out on*** *probation.* **2** a period of time at the start of a new job when you are watched and tested to see if you are suitable for the job: *a period of probation* **3** US a period of time in which a student who has behaved badly must improve their work or behaviour in order to stay in a school: *Gene's* ***on*** *probation this semester.* • **probationary** /-ər.i/ (US) /-er.i/ **adj** *a probationary period*

probationer /prəˈbeɪ.ʃən.əʳ/ (US) /proʊˈbeɪ.ʃən.ɚ/ **noun** [C] **1** a criminal on probation **2** a person such as a police officer or teacher who has recently passed his or her final exams and who is doing the first year of work

proˈbation ˌofficer **noun** [C] a person whose job is to regularly see people who have committed crimes and who are on probation, and to help them to avoid committing crimes again

probe /prəʊb/ (US) /proʊb/ **verb; noun**

▸**verb** [I or T] **1** to try to discover information that other people do not want you to know, by asking questions carefully and not directly: *The interviewer probed deep* ***into*** *her private life.* ◦ *Detectives questioned him for hours, probing* ***for*** *any inconsistencies in his story.* ◦ *The article probes (= tries to describe and explain) the mysteries of nationalism in modern Europe.* **2** to examine something with a tool, especially in order to find something that is hidden: *They probed* ***in/into*** *the mud with a special drill.*

▸**noun** [C] **1** an attempt to discover information by asking a lot of questions: *an FBI probe* ***into*** *corruption* ◦ *a Justice Department probe* ***into*** *the Democrats' fund raising* **2** specialized a long, thin metal tool used by doctors to examine inside someone **3** specialized a device that is put inside something to test or record information → See also **space probe**

probing /ˈprəʊ.bɪŋ/ (US) /ˈproʊ-/ **adj** intended to get information: *She asked me a few probing* ***questions.***

probiotic /ˌprəʊ.baɪˈɒt.ɪk/ (US) /ˌproʊ.baɪˈɑː.t̬ɪk/ **noun** [C] a food or pill that contains good bacteria which may keep you healthy • **probiotic adj** *probiotic yogurt*

probity /ˈprəʊ.bɪ.ti/ (US) /ˈproʊ.bə.t̬i/ **noun** [U] formal complete honesty

> **!** Common mistake: **problem**
>
> When **problem** is followed by a verb, that verb should be in the **-ing** form.
>
> Do not say 'have problems to do something', say **have problems doing something**:
>
> ~~*I had problems to learn English before I came to England.*~~
>
> *I had problems learning English before I came to England.*

problem /ˈprɒb.ləm/ (US) /ˈprɑː.bləm/ **noun** [C] **1** (A1) a situation, person, or thing that needs attention and needs to be dealt with or solved: *financial/health problems* ◦ *Our main problem is lack of cash.* ◦ *I'm* ***having*** *problems* ***with*** *my computer.* ◦ *No one has* ***solved*** *the problem* ***of*** *what to do with radioactive waste.* ◦ *The very high rate of inflation* ***poses/presents*** *(= is) a serious problem for the government.* ◦ *When is the government going to* ***tackle*** *(= deal with) the problem of poverty in the inner cities?* ◦ [+ -ing verb] *Did you have any problems (= difficulties)* ***getting*** *here?* ◦ *I'd love to come –* ***the only*** *problem* ***is*** *I've got friends staying that night.* **2** a question in mathematics which needs an answer: *We were given ten problems to solve.* **3 problem child, family, etc.** a child, etc. whose behaviour is bad

> Word partners for **problem**
>
> *experience/have* a problem • *cause/create/pose/present* a problem • a problem *faces* sb • *address/deal with/tackle* a problem • a problem *arises/comes up/occurs* • a *big/major/real/serious* problem • a problem *with* sth • the problem *of* sth

> **+** Other ways of saying **problem**
>
> The noun **difficulty** is a common alternative to 'problem':
>
> *The company is having some financial* ***difficulties*** *at the moment.*
>
> You can describe several problems as **trouble**:
>
> *We've had a lot of* ***trouble*** *with the new computer system.*
>
> A small, temporary problem may be described informally as a **hitch**:
>
> *The ceremony went without a* ***hitch.***
>
> A **glitch** is a problem that stops something from working properly:
>
> *We've had a few technical* ***glitches,*** *but I'm confident we'll be ready on time.*
>
> A **hurdle** or **obstacle** is a problem that you need to deal with so that you can continue to make progress:
>
> *Getting a work permit is only the first* ***hurdle.***
>
> *There may be too many* ***obstacles*** *in the way of progress.*
>
> A **pitfall** is a problem that is likely to happen in a particular situation:
>
> *It's just one of the* ***pitfalls*** *of buying a house.*
>
> A **setback** is a problem that makes something happen less quickly than it should:
>
> *The project has suffered a series of* ***setbacks*** *this year.*
>
> A **snag** is a small problem in something which is mostly good:
>
> *The only* ***snag*** *is the cost.*

IDIOMS **have a problem with sth/sb** informal to find something or someone annoying or offensive: *I have a real problem with people who use their mobile phones on the train.* ◦ *She can smoke – I don't have a problem with that.* • **no problem** informal **1** (A2) said to show that you will or can do what someone has asked you to: *'Can you get me to the station by 11.30?' 'No problem.'* **2** (A2) used as a friendly answer when someone thanks you for something you have done: *'Thanks for the lift.' 'No problem.'*

problematic /ˌprɒb.ləˈmæt.ɪk/ (US) /ˌprɑː.bləˈmæt̬-/ **adj** (also **problematical** /-ɪ.kəl/) (C1) full of problems or difficulties: *Getting everyone there on time might prove problematic.* • **problematically** /-ɪ.kəl.i/ **adv**

pro bono /ˌprəʊˈbəʊ.nəʊ/ (US) /ˌproʊˈboʊ.noʊ/ **adj, adv** (relating to work that is done, especially by a lawyer) without asking for payment: *pro bono cases/lawyers/work* ◦ *He takes on some charity cases pro bono.*

proboscis /prəˈbɒs.ɪs/ (US) /proʊˈbɑː.sɪs/ **noun** [C] (plural **probosces**) specialized the long nose of some animals, or the long tube-like mouth of some insects: *An elephant's trunk is a proboscis.*

probs /prɒbz/ (US) /prɑːbz/ **noun** [plural] UK informal **no probs** used to tell someone that you can do something or deal with a situation easily and without

P

problems: *Don't worry, I'll fix it or give you a new one. No probs!*

procedure /prəˈsiː.dʒəʳ/ US /-dʒɚ/ **noun** WAY TO DO ▷ **1** B2 [C or U] a set of actions that is the official or accepted way of doing something: *The company has new procedures **for** dealing with complaints.* ◦ *You must **follow** correct procedure at all times.* MEDICAL TREATMENT ▷ **2** [C] a medical operation: *It's a routine/standard surgical procedure.* COMPUTING ▷ **3** [C] specialized a part of a computer program that performs a particular job and is operated by the main part of the program when it is needed • **procedural** /-əl/ **adj** *procedural errors/matters*

proceed /prəˈsiːd/ US /proʊ-/ **verb** [I] **1** C1 to continue as planned: *His lawyers have decided not to proceed **with** the case.* ◦ *Preparations for the festival are now proceeding smoothly.* **2 proceed to do sth** C2 to do something after you have done something else: *She sat down and proceeded to tell me about her skiing holiday.* ◦ humorous *He told me he was on a diet and then proceeded to eat a plateful of chips!* **3** formal to move forward or travel in a particular direction: *Passengers for Madrid should proceed to gate 26 for boarding.*

PHRASAL VERB **proceed against sb** legal to start to take legal action against someone: *Lack of evidence meant that the Council could not proceed against Mr Naylor.*

proceedings /prəˈsiː.dɪŋz/ US /proʊ-/ **noun** [plural] EVENTS ▷ **1** a series of events that happen in a planned and controlled way: *Millions of people watched the proceedings on television.* ◦ *The Chairperson opened the proceedings with a short speech.* **2** a complete written record of what is said or done during a meeting → Compare **the minutes** LEGAL ACTION ▷ **3** C2 legal legal action: *Allegations of sexual harassment have led to **disciplinary** proceedings being taken **against** three naval officers.* ◦ *I **started/took legal** proceedings to try to have him taken away from his parents permanently.*

proceeds /ˈprəʊ.siːdz/ US /ˈproʊ-/ **noun** [plural] the amount of money received from a particular event or activity or when something is sold: ***The** proceeds **of** today's festival will go to several local charities.*

P

process **noun**; **verb**

▸**noun** [C] /ˈprəʊ.ses/ US /ˈprɑː-/ **1** B2 a series of actions that you take in order to achieve a result: *the peace process* ◦ *Increasing the number of women in top management jobs will be a slow process.* ◦ *This decision may delay the process **of** European unification.* ◦ *The party has begun the **painful** (= difficult) process of rethinking its policies and strategy.* ◦ *Going to court to obtain compensation is a long process.* ◦ *She arrived at the correct answer by a process **of elimination** (= by deciding against each answer that was unlikely to be correct until only one was left).* **2** B2 a series of changes that happen naturally: *the digestive process* ◦ *the ageing process* ◦ *It's all part of the learning process.* **3** a method of producing goods in a factory by treating natural substances: *They have developed a new process for extracting aluminium from bauxite.*

IDIOMS **be in the process of doing sth** C2 to have started doing something: *We're still in the process of decorating the house.* • **in the process** C2 If you are doing something, and you do something else in the process, the second thing happens as a result of doing the first thing: *I stood up to say hello and spilled my drink in the process.*

▸**verb** DEAL WITH ▷ **1** B2 /ˈprəʊ.ses/ US /ˈprɑː-/ [T] to deal with documents in an official way: *Visa applications take 28 days to process.* **2** /ˈprəʊ.ses/ US /ˈprɑː-/ [T] If a computer processes information, it performs a particular series of operations on the information, such as a set of calculations. **3** [T] to prepare, change, or treat food or natural substances as a part of an industrial operation: *a waste processing plant* **4** [T] to make pictures from photographic film: *I need to get those films processed.* WALK ▷ **5** /prəˈses/ [I + adv/prep] formal to walk slowly: *We watched them process down the aisle.* • **processing** /-ɪŋ/ **noun** [U] *data processing*

processed /ˈprəʊ.sest/ US /ˈprɑː-/ **adj** Processed food has had some sort of chemical or industrial treatment in order to cook it, preserve it, or improve its taste or appearance: *processed cheese/meat* ◦ *highly processed convenience foods*

procession /prəˈseʃ.ən/ **noun** **1** C2 [C] a line of people who are all walking or travelling in the same direction, especially in a formal way as part of a religious ceremony or public celebration: *a wedding/funeral procession* **2** [S] a series of people or things, one after the other: *My day has just been a never-ending procession **of** visitors.*

processional /prəˈseʃ.ən.əl/ **adj** [before noun] used in a procession: *There was tight security along the processional route.*

processor /ˈprəʊ.ses.əʳ/ US /ˈprɑː.ses.ɚ/ **noun** [C] the part of a computer that performs operations on the information that is put into it → See also **microprocessor**

ˌpro-ˈchoice **adj** supporting the belief that a pregnant woman should have the freedom to choose an ABORTION (= the intentional ending of pregnancy) if she does not want to have a baby: *pro-choice activists/demonstrators* → Compare **anti-choice**

proclaim /prəˈkleɪm/ US /proʊ-/ **verb** [T] ANNOUNCE ▷ **1** formal to announce something publicly or officially, especially something positive: *All the countries have proclaimed their loyalty to the alliance.* ◦ *Republican party members were confidently proclaiming victory even as the first few votes came in.* ◦ [+ that] *It was the famous speech in which he proclaimed **that** socialism was dead.* ◦ [+ two objects] *She was proclaimed Queen at the age of 13 after the sudden death of her father.* SHOW ▷ **2** literary to show something or make it clear: *Wearing scarves and hats which proclaimed their allegiance, the football fans flooded into the bar.*

proclamation /ˌprɒk.ləˈmeɪ.ʃən/ US /ˌprɑː.klə-/ **noun** [C or U] an official announcement: *to issue a proclamation* ◦ *A bloody civil war followed the proclamation of an independent state.*

proclivity /prəˈklɪv.ɪ.ti/ US /-ə.t̬i/ **noun** [C] formal the fact that someone likes something or likes to do something, especially something considered morally bad: *the **sexual** proclivities of celebrities* ◦ *his proclivity **for** shapely blondes*

procrastinate /prəˈkræs.tɪ.neɪt/ US /proʊ-/ **verb** [I] to keep delaying something that must be done, often because it is unpleasant or boring: *I know I've got to deal with the problem at some point – I'm just procrastinating.* • **procrastination** /-ˌkræs.tɪˈneɪ.ʃən/ **noun** [U]

procreate /ˈprəʊ.kri.eɪt/ US /ˈproʊ-/ **verb** [I] formal to produce young: *While priests were denied the right to marry and procreate, he said, their situation would remain impossible.* • **procreation** /ˌprəʊ.kriˈeɪ.ʃən/ US /ˌproʊ-/ **noun** [U] *Some people believe that sex should only be for the purpose of procreation.*

proctor /ˈprɒk.təʳ/ US /ˈprɑːk.t̬ɚ/ **verb** [I or T] US for **invigilate**

procure /prəˈkjʊəʳ/ (US) /-ˈkjʊr/ **verb** formal **1** [T] to get something, especially after an effort: *She's managed somehow to procure his phone number.* ◦ [+ two objects] *He'd procured us seats in the front row.* **2** [I or T] to get a PROSTITUTE for someone else to have sex with

procurement /prəˈkjʊə.mənt/ (US) /-ˈkjʊr-/ **noun** [U] formal the process of getting supplies: *a substantial budget for the procurement **of** military supplies*

procurer /prəˈkjʊə.rəʳ/ (US) /-ˈkjʊr.ɚ/ **noun** [C] formal a person who finds PROSTITUTES for people who want to have sex with them

prod /prɒd/ (US) /prɑːd/ **verb; noun**

▸**verb** (-dd-) **1** [I or T] to push something or someone with your finger or with a pointed object: *I prodded her in the back to get her attention.* ◦ *She prodded the cake with her fork to see if it was cooked.* ◦ *He prodded **at** the fish with his fork a few times, but he didn't eat a mouthful.* **2** [T] to encourage someone to take action, especially when they are being slow or unwilling: *He gets things done, but only after I've prodded him **into doing** them.*

▸**noun 1** [C] an act of pushing something or someone with your finger or with a pointed object: *He **gave** her a prod in the ribs.* **2** [S] encouragement to do something: *She hasn't ordered that book for me yet – I must **give** her a prod.*

prodigal /ˈprɒd.ɪ.gəl/ (US) /ˈprɑː.dɪ-/ **adj** formal spending large amounts of money without thinking of the future, in a way that is not wise: *There have been rumours that he has been prodigal **with** company funds.* • **prodigality** /ˌprɒd.ɪˈgæl.ɪ.ti/ (US) /ˌprɑː.dɪˈgæl.ə.ti/ **noun** [U] • **prodigally** /-gəli/ **adv**

ˌprodigal ˈson noun [C usually singular] a man or boy who has left his family in order to do something that the family disapprove of and has now returned home feeling sorry for what he has done: figurative *Manchester City football club sees the return of the prodigal son tonight with Black once again in the side after a season away.*

prodigious /prəˈdɪdʒ.əs/ **adj** formal extremely great in ability, amount or strength: *She wrote a truly prodigious number of novels.* ◦ *She was a prodigious musician.* ◦ *He had a prodigious appetite for both women and drink.* • **prodigiously** /-li/ **adv** *He was a prodigiously gifted artist.*

prodigy /ˈprɒd.ɪ.dʒi/ (US) /ˈprɑː.də-/ **noun** [C] someone with a very great ability which usually shows itself when that person is a young child: *The 16-year-old tennis prodigy is the youngest player ever to reach the Olympic finals.* ◦ *He read in the paper about a mathematical prodigy who was attending university at the age of twelve.* → See also **child prodigy**

produce verb; noun

▸**verb** [T] /prəˈdjuːs/ (US) /-ˈduːs/ MAKE ▷ **1** (B1) to make something or bring something into existence: *France produces a great deal of wine for export.* ◦ *Red blood cells are produced in the bone marrow.* ◦ *She works for a company that produces (= makes for sale) electrical goods.* ◦ *I was wondering whether I could produce a meal out of what's left in the fridge.* ◦ *She's asked me to produce a report on the state of the project.* **2** When animals produce young, they give birth to them: *Our cat produced four kittens during the course of the night.* ◦ humorous *All our friends seem to be busy producing offspring at the moment.* CAUSE ▷ **3** (B2) to cause a reaction or result: *The senator's speech produced an angry response from the opposition.* ◦ *Her remarks produced an awkward silence.* ◦ *If used on delicate skin, this cream may produce a stinging sensation.* FILM/MUSIC ▷ **4** to organize the practical and financial matters connected with the preparation of a film, play, or television or radio programme → Compare **direct 5** to be in charge of making a musical recording and to be responsible for the arrangement of the music, the combination of the different instruments or voices and the general sound of it BRING OUT ▷ **6** (C1) to bring something out from somewhere and show it: *He produced a letter **from** his desk that he asked me to read.* ◦ *One of the men suddenly produced a knife from his pocket.* RESULT IN ▷ **7** to result in or discover something, especially proof: *A lengthy police investigation failed to produce any evidence on which the suspect could be convicted.*

▸**noun** [U] /ˈprɒd.juːs/ (US) /ˈprɑː.djuːs/ (C2) food or any other substance or material that is grown or obtained through farming: *agricultural/dairy/fresh produce*

producer /prəˈdjuː.səʳ/ (US) /-ˈduː.sɚ/ **noun** [C] FILM/MUSIC ▷ **1** (B2) a person who makes the practical and financial arrangements needed to make a film, play, or television or radio programme: *a film/Hollywood/movie producer* → Compare **director 2** a person who makes the practical and financial arrangements needed to make a CD or other recording: *a record producer* MAKER ▷ **3** (C1) a company, country, or person that provides goods, especially those that are produced by an industrial process or grown or obtained through farming, usually in large amounts: *egg producers* ◦ *gas/oil producers* ◦ *Australia is one of the world's main producers **of** wool.*

product /ˈprɒd.ʌkt/ (US) /ˈprɑː.dʌkt/ **noun** THING MADE ▷ **1** (B1) [C or U] something that is made to be sold, usually something that is produced by an industrial process or, less commonly, something that is grown or obtained through farming: *They do a range of skin-care products.* ◦ *The product is so good it sells itself.* ◦ *I'm trying to cut down on **dairy** products.* → See also **by-product 2 a/the product of sth** a/the result of something: *A figure like that is usually the product of many hours spent in the gym.* ◦ *She had a very happy childhood, and I guess her confidence is a product of that.* IN MATHEMATICS ▷ **3** [C] specialized the result you get when two or more numbers are multiplied together: *The product of 6 and 3 is 18.*

P

> **Word partners for production**
>
> sth *goes into* production • *halt/increase/reduce* production • production *falls/grows* • *large-scale/mass* production • *annual/domestic/global* production • production *costs* • be *in* production • production *of* sth

production /prəˈdʌk.ʃən/ **noun** MAKING ▷ **1** (B2) [U] the process of making or growing goods to be sold: *Coke is used in the production of steel.* ◦ *We saw a quick film showing the various stages in the production of glass.* ◦ *The company's new model will be **going into** production early next year.* **2** (B2) [U] the amount of something that is made or grown by a country or a company: *Swedish industrial production has fallen steadily this year.* ◦ *Wheat production has risen over the years.* OF FILM/MUSIC ▷ **3** (B2) [C or U] the activity of organizing the practical and financial matters connected with the preparation of a film, play, or television or radio programme: *She's hoping to get into television production.* ◦ *Disney's latest production (= film) looks likely to be their most successful ever.* **4** [C] a particular series of performances of a theatre entertainment such as a play or OPERA: *They're doing a new production **of** Macbeth at the National Theatre.* **5** [U] the preparation and general quality of a musical recording's sound, showing the way in which the music was recorded rather than the quality of the singing and the music: *George Martin* ***did*** *the production* ***on*** *the Beatles records.* **BRINGING OUT ▷** **6** [U] formal the act of taking something out and showing it: *Entry to the club is only permitted* ***on*** *production (= the showing)* ***of*** *a membership card.*

IDIOM **make a production (out) of sth** to make something seem more difficult or complicated to do than it is: *If you ask Tom to do anything, he always makes such a production of it that you wish you'd just done it yourself.*

proˈduction ˌline noun [C] a line of machines and workers in a factory which a product moves along while it is being built or produced. Each machine or worker performs a particular job, which must be finished before the product moves to the next position in the line.

productive /prəˈdʌk.tɪv/ adj **1** B2 resulting in or providing a large amount or supply of something: *In order to turn the deserts into fertile and productive land, engineers built an 800-mile canal.* ◦ *He had an amazingly productive five years in which he managed to write four novels.* → Opposite **unproductive** **2** B2 having positive results: *We had a very productive meeting – I felt we sorted out a lot of problems.* • **productively** /-li/ adv *Their working system is based on the belief that people work more productively (= produce better results) in a team.*

productivity /ˌprɒd.ʌkˈtɪv.ɪ.ti/ US /ˌproʊ.dəkˈtɪv.ə.t̬i/ noun [U] C1 the rate at which a company or country makes goods, usually judged in connection with the number of people and the amount of materials necessary to produce the goods: *Studies show that if a working environment is pleasant, productivity increases.* ◦ *a productivity bonus/incentive* ◦ *Productivity in the steel industry improved by five percent last year.*

ˈproduct ˌplacement noun [C or U] a way of advertising a product by supplying it for use in films or television programmes

prof /prɒf/ US /prɑːf/ noun [C] informal a **professor**

Prof. noun [C] written abbreviation for **professor**: *Prof. Tina Pritchard*

profane /prəˈfeɪn/ adj formal **AGAINST RELIGION ▷** **1** showing no respect for a god or a religion, often through language: *profane language* ◦ *Funny, profane, and fearless, she has become one of America's biggest television celebrities.* **NOT SPIRITUAL ▷** **2** not connected with religion or spiritual matters → Synonym **secular**

profanity /prəˈfæn.ɪ.ti/ US /-ə.t̬i/ noun formal **1** [C or U] (an example of) showing no respect for a god or a religion, especially through language **2** [C] an offensive or OBSCENE word or phrase

profess /prəˈfes/ verb [T] to state something, sometimes in a way that is not sincere: [+ to infinitive] *She professes not* ***to*** *be interested in money.* ◦ *I don't profess* ***to*** *know all the details about the case.* ◦ *She professes ignorance of the whole affair, though I'm not sure I believe her.*

professed /prəˈfest/ adj [before noun] **1** describes a belief which someone has made known: *She is a professed monarchist.* **2** refers to a belief or feeling that someone says they have or feel, but is probably not sincere: *His professed love of women seems a little odd when you consider how he treats them.*

profession /prəˈfeʃ.ən/ noun **WORK ▷** **1** B1 [C, + sing/pl verb] any type of work that needs special training or a particular skill, often one that is respected because it involves a high level of education: *He left the teaching profession in 1965 to set up his own business.* ◦ *The report notes that 40 percent of lawyers* ***entering*** *the profession are women.* ◦ *Teaching as a profession is very underpaid.* ◦ *He's a doctor* ***by*** *profession.* **2** B2 [C, + sing/pl verb] the people who do a type of work, considered as a group: *There's a feeling among the nursing profession that their work is undervalued.* **3 the professions** jobs that need special training and skill, such as being a doctor or lawyer, but not work in business or industry **STATEMENT ▷** **4** [C] a statement about what someone feels, believes, or intends to do, often made publicly: *The government's professions* ***of*** *commitment to the environment seem less believable every day.* ◦ *his professions of love*

professional /prəˈfeʃ.ən.əl/ adj; noun

▸adj **1** B2 related to work that needs special training or education: *Chris, you're a nurse, so can I ask your professional* ***opinion*** *on bandaging ankles?* ◦ *Both doctors have been charged with professional* ***misconduct*** *(= bad or unacceptable behaviour in their work).* → Compare **amateur** **2** B1 approving having the qualities that you connect with trained and skilled people, such as effectiveness, skill, organization, and seriousness of manner: *It would look more professional if the letter was typed.* ◦ *She always looks very professional in her smart suits.* ◦ *You've done a very professional job stripping that floor!* **3** B1 describes someone who does a job that people usually do as a hobby: *She's a professional dancer/photographer.* ◦ *He's a runner who's just* ***turned*** *professional.* **4** having the type of job that is respected because it involves a high level of education and training: *Room for rent in shared house – would suit professional person.* ◦ *a bar full of young professional types in suits*

▸noun [C] **1** C1 a person who has the type of job that needs a high level of education and training: *health professionals* → Compare **amateur** **2** informal someone who has worked hard in the same type of job for a long time and has become skilled at dealing with any problem that might happen: *I thought the whole meeting was going to fall apart but you rescued it like a true professional!* ◦ *the consummate professional* **3** B2 a person who does a job that people usually do as a hobby: *He's only been playing football as a professional for two years.* **4** a person who plays sport, especially a GOLF or tennis player, who is employed by a CLUB to train its members in a particular sport

proˌfessional adˈvice noun [U] advice from a lawyer or an ACCOUNTANT (= someone who deals with money matters)

proˌfessional ˈfoul noun [C] in football, an intentional FOUL (= an act that breaks the rules), especially one that is intended to prevent the other team from scoring a goal

proˌfessional ˈhelp noun [U] polite phrase for help from a PSYCHIATRIST (= a doctor trained in treating mental illnesses): *Personally, I think he should get some professional help.*

professionalism /prəˈfeʃ.ən.əl.ɪ.zəm/ noun [U] the combination of all the qualities that are connected with trained and skilled people: *He praised her professionalism and dynamism.*

professionally /prəˈfeʃ.ən.əl.i/ adv **1** by people with particular skills or qualifications: *I think next time we need any decorating we'll get it done professionally.* **2** as a paid job, not as a hobby: *He started to sing professionally (= for money) after leaving college.* **3** as a person with a particular job: *Are you asking for my opinion of him personally or professionally?*

professor /prəˈfes.ər/ US /-ɚ/ noun [C] B1 a teacher of

the highest rank in a department of a British university, or a teacher of high rank in an American university or college: *Professor Stephen Hawking* ◦ *a professor of sociology* ◦ *a sociology professor* ◦ [as form of address] *Thank you, Professor.*

professorial /ˌprɒf.əˈsɔː.ri.əl/ (US) /ˌprɑː.fəˈsɔːr.i-/ **adj** formal of or like a professor: *He retains an almost professorial air.*

professorship /prəˈfes.ə.ʃɪp/ (US) /-ɚ-/ **noun** [C] the position of professor in a university

proffer /ˈprɒf.əʳ/ (US) /ˈprɑː.fɚ/ **verb** [T] formal to offer something by holding it out, or to offer advice or an opinion: *He shook the warmly proffered hand.* ◦ *I didn't think it wise to proffer an opinion.*

proficient /prəˈfɪʃ.ᵊnt/ **adj** skilled and experienced: *a proficient swimmer* ◦ *She's proficient **in** two languages.* ◦ *It takes a couple of years of regular driving before you become proficient **at** it.* • **proficiency** /-ᵊn.si/ **noun** [U] *The job ad said they wanted proficiency **in** at least two languages.*

profile /ˈprəʊ.faɪl/ (US) /ˈproʊ-/ **noun** [C] DESCRIPTION ▷ **1** (B2) a short description of someone's life, work, character, etc. ATTENTION ▷ **2** (C1) the amount of public attention and notice that something receives: *We need to increase our company's profile in Asia.* ◦ *There is a growing number of women in **high**-profile positions (= positions where they are noticed) in the government.* SIDE VIEW ▷ **3** a side view of a person's face: *Drawing profiles is somehow easier than drawing the full face.* ◦ *a strong profile* ◦ *The actor is photographed **in** profile, smoking a cigarette.* • **profile verb** [T] *Every week in the books section of the paper they profile a different author.*

IDIOM **keep a low profile** (C1) to avoid attracting attention to yourself: *He's been in a bit of trouble recently so he's trying to keep a low profile.*

profiling /ˈprəʊ.faɪ.lɪŋ/ (US) /ˈproʊ-/ **noun** [U] the activity of collecting information about someone, especially a criminal, in order to give a description of them → See also **psychological profile**

profit /ˈprɒf.ɪt/ (US) /ˈprɑː.fɪt/ **noun; verb**

▸**noun 1** (B2) [C or U] money that is earned in trade or business, especially after paying the costs of producing and selling goods and services: *She **makes** a big profit from selling waste material to textile companies.* ◦ *A year ago the Tokyo company had a **pretax** profit of 35 million yen.* ◦ *Company profits are down on last year's figures.* ◦ *You don't expect to make much profit within the first couple of years of setting up a company.* ◦ *He sold his house **at a** huge profit.* **2** [U] the good result or advantage that can be achieved by a particular action or activity: *There's no profit to be **gained** from endlessly discussing whose fault it was.*

> **Common mistake: profit**
>
> **Warning:** Choose the right verb!
>
> Don't say 'get a profit', say **make a profit**:
>
> ~~*The company will get a big profit from this investment.*~~
>
> *The company will make a big profit from this investment.*

> **Word partners for profit noun**
>
> *make* a profit • *boost/increase/maximize* profits • profits *drop/fall/increase/rise* • *report* a profit • a *drop/fall/increase/rise* in profits • *high/massive/record* profits • a *small* profit • a profit *of* [£2,000, $1 million, etc.]

▸**verb**

PHRASAL VERB **profit from sth 1** to earn money from something: *A lot of companies will profit from the fall in interest rates.* **2** to achieve an advantage from something: *I profited enormously from work**ing** with her.*

profitable /ˈprɒf.ɪ.tə.bl/ (US) /ˈprɑː.fɪ.t̬ə-/ **adj** (B2) resulting in or likely to result in a profit or an advantage: *Over the years it has developed into a highly profitable business.* ◦ *I made profitable use of my time (= used my time to get advantages or benefits), mixing with a lot of different people and practising my Spanish.* → Opposite **unprofitable** • **profitability** /ˌprɒf.ɪ.təˈbɪl.ɪ.ti/ (US) /ˌprɑː.fɪ.t̬əˈbɪl.ə.t̬i/ **noun** [U] *The company needs to return to profitability extremely soon.* • **profitably** /-bli/ **adv** *It was several months before the company started to trade profitably (= making money).* ◦ *Use your time profitably (= use it to get advantages or benefits).*

profiteer /ˌprɒf.ɪˈtɪəʳ/ (US) /ˌprɑː.fɪˈtɪr/ **noun** [C] disapproving a person who takes advantage of a situation in which other people are suffering to make a profit, often by selling goods that are difficult to get at a high price: *a war profiteer* • **profiteering** /-ɪŋ/ **noun** [U] *The pharmaceutical company has been charged with profiteering from the AIDS crisis.*

profiterole /prəˈfɪt.ᵊr.əʊl/ (US) /-ˈfɪt̬.ə.roʊl/ **noun** [C usually plural] a small pastry cake with a cream filling and a covering of chocolate sauce, usually served in a pile

ˈprofit ˌmargin noun [C] the difference between the total cost of making and selling something and the price it is sold for: *Many small companies operate on very **narrow** profit margins.*

ˈprofit ˌsharing noun [U] the system of sharing the profits that a company makes between all the people who work for it

profligate /ˈprɒf.lɪ.gət/ (US) /ˈprɑː.flɪ-/ **adj** formal spending money in a way that wastes it and is not wise: *She is well-known for her profligate spending habits.* • **profligacy** /-gə.si/ **noun** [U] *The profligacy of the West shocked him.*

pro forma /ˌprəʊˈfɔː.mə/ (US) /ˌproʊˈfɔːr-/ **adj, adv; noun**

▸**adj** [before noun], **adv** formal describes words or actions that are usual or done in the usual way: *a pro forma declaration of loyalty*

▸**noun** [C] (also **ˌpro forma ˈinvoice**) a list of things that have been ordered, sent with their prices to a customer so that the things can be paid for before they are DELIVERED

profound /prəˈfaʊnd/ **adj** EXTREME ▷ **1** (C2) felt or experienced very strongly or in an extreme way: *His mother's death when he was aged six had a very profound **effect** on him.* ◦ *The invention of the contraceptive pill brought about profound changes in the lives of women.* ◦ *Those two lines of poetry express perfectly the profound sadness of loss.* ◦ *My grandfather has a profound mistrust of anything new or foreign.* ◦ *There was a note of profound irritation in his voice.* SHOWING UNDERSTANDING ▷ **2** (C2) showing a clear and deep understanding of serious matters: *profound truths/wisdom* ◦ *The review that I read said that it was 'a thoughtful and profound film'.*

profoundly /prəˈfaʊnd.li/ **adv** (C2) deeply or extremely: *Society has changed so profoundly over the last 50 years.* ◦ *We are all profoundly grateful for your help and encouragement.*

profundity /prəˈfʌn.dɪ.ti/ (US) /-də.t̬i/ **noun** formal UNDERSTANDING ▷ **1** [U] the quality of showing a

P

clear and deep understanding of serious matters: *the profundity of his remarks* **2** [C usually plural] a remark or thought that shows, or is intended to show, great understanding **EXTREME QUALITY** ▷ **3** [U] the quality of being felt or experienced very strongly

profuse /prəˈfjuːs/ **adj** produced or given in large amounts: *She was admitted to St Mary's Hospital with profuse bleeding.* ◦ *The company accepted blame and sent us profuse* ***apologies.*** • **profusely** /-li/ **adv** *She apologized/thanked us profusely.* ◦ *He was bleeding/sweating profusely.*

profusion /prəˈfjuː.ʒən/ **noun** [S or U] formal an extremely large amount of something: *I was remarking on the recent profusion of books and articles on the matter.* ◦ *She'd never seen flowers so beautiful and* ***in*** *such profusion.*

progenitor /prəʊˈdʒen.ɪ.təʳ/ (US) /proʊˈdʒen.ɪ.t̬ɚ/ **noun** [C] formal a person who first thinks of something and causes it to happen: *Marx was the progenitor of communism.*

progeny /ˈprɒdʒ.ə.ni/ (US) /ˈprɑː.dʒə-/ **noun** [plural] formal the young or OFFSPRING of a person, animal, or plant: *His numerous progeny are scattered all over the country.*

progesterone /prəʊˈdʒes.tər.əʊn/ (US) /proʊˈdʒes.tə.roʊn/ **noun** [U] a female HORMONE which causes the WOMB to prepare for pregnancy

prognosis /prɒgˈnəʊ.sɪs/ (US) /prɑːgˈnoʊ-/ **noun** [C] (plural **prognoses**) **1** (also **prognostication**) a doctor's judgment of the likely or expected development of a disease or of the chances of getting better: *The prognosis after the operation was for a full recovery.* **2** a statement of what is judged likely to happen in the future, especially in connection with a particular situation: *I was reading a gloomy economic prognosis in the paper this morning.*

program /ˈprəʊ.græm/ (US) /ˈproʊ-/ **noun; verb**

▸**noun** [C] **1** (A2) a series of instructions that can be put into a computer in order to make it perform an operation: *a* ***computer*** *program* ◦ *She's* ***written*** *a program to find words that frequently occur together.* **2** (A2) US and Australian English a **programme**

▸**verb** [T] (-mm-) to write a series of instructions that make a computer perform a particular operation: [+ to infinitive] *She programmed the computer* ***to*** *calculate the rate of exchange in twelve currencies.*

programmable /prəʊˈgræm.ə.bl/, /ˈprəʊ.græm-/ (US) /ˈproʊ.græm.ə-/ **adj** able to be programmed

programme /ˈprəʊ.græm/ (US) /ˈproʊ-/ **noun; verb**

▸**noun** [C] UK (US **program**) **BROADCAST** ▷ **1** (A2) a broadcast on television or radio: *It's one of those arts programmes late at night.* ◦ *It's my favourite TV programme – I never miss an episode.* **BOOK** ▷ **2** a thin book or piece of paper giving information about a play or musical or sports event, usually bought at the theatre or place where the event happens: *I looked in the programme to find out the actor's name.* **PLAN** ▷ **3** (B2) a plan of activities to be done or things to be achieved: *The school offers an exciting and varied programme of social events.* ◦ *The rail system is to put 20 million pounds into its modernization programme.* ◦ *I'm running three mornings a week – it's all part of my fitness programme.*

IDIOM **get with the programme** informal to accept new ideas and give more attention to what is happening now: *They've been playing the same old music for ten years now – it's time to get with the programme.*

▸**verb** [T + obj + to infinitive] UK (US **program** (-mm-)) **1** to tell a device or system to operate in a particular way or at a particular time: *I've programmed the heating to come on at 6.00.* **2 be programmed to do sth** to always do or think a particular thing, although you do not try to: *I'm programmed to wake up at seven.*

programmer /ˈprəʊ.græm.əʳ/ (US) /ˈproʊ.græm.ɚ/ **noun** [C] (also **comˌputer ˈprogrammer**) (C1) a person whose job is to produce computer programs

programming /ˈprəʊ.græm.ɪŋ/ (US) /ˈproʊ-/ **noun** [U] (B2) the activity or job of writing computer programs

progress **noun; verb**

▸**noun** [U] /ˈprəʊ.gres/ (US) /ˈprɑː-/ **1** (B1) movement to an improved or more developed state, or to a forward position: *Technological progress has been so rapid over the last few years.* ◦ *I'm not* ***making*** *much progress with my Spanish.* ◦ *The doctor said that she was* ***making*** *good progress (= getting better after a medical operation or illness).* ◦ *The recent free elections mark the next step in the country's progress* ***towards*** *democracy.* ◦ *The yacht's crew said that they were* ***making*** *relatively slow progress.* **2 in progress** (B2) formal happening or being done now: *Repair work is in progress on the south-bound lane of the motorway and will continue until June.*

> **Word partners for progress noun**
>
> *make* progress • *follow/monitor* progress • *halt/hinder/impede/stop* progress • *considerable/good/rapid/real* progress • *slow/steady* progress • *lack of* progress • progress *in/on/towards* sth

▸**verb** [I] /prəˈgres/ **1** (B2) to improve or develop in skills, knowledge, etc.: *My Spanish never really progressed* ***beyond*** *the stage of being able to order drinks at the bar.* → Compare **regress** **2** (C2) to continue gradually: *As the war progressed more and more countries became involved.* ◦ *We started off talking about the weather and gradually the conversation progressed* ***to*** *politics.*

progression /prəˈgreʃ.ən/ **noun** [C or U] (C1) the act of changing to the next stage of development: *Drugs can slow down the progression of the disease.* ◦ *The novel follows the progression of a woman from youth to middle age.* ◦ *She'd always worked with old people so becoming a nurse was a* ***logical/natural*** *progression.*

progressive /prəˈgres.ɪv/ **adj; noun**

▸**adj** **GRADUAL** ▷ **1** (C1) developing or happening gradually: *There's been a progressive decline in the standard of living over the past few years.* ◦ *a progressive disease* **MODERN** ▷ **2** (B2) describes ideas or systems that are new and modern, encouraging change in society or in the way that things are done: *progressive ideas/attitudes* ◦ *The left of the party is pressing for a more progressive social policy.* ◦ *a progressive school* **TAX** ▷ **3** describes a tax system in which the rate of tax is higher on larger amounts of money **GRAMMAR** ▷ **4** describes the form of a verb that is used to show that the action is continuing. It is formed with the verb 'be' followed by the present participle (= -ing form of the verb): *'He's working hard at the moment' is an example of the* ***present*** *progressive form of the verb 'work'.* ◦ *'I was eating when the phone rang' is an example of the* ***past*** *progressive.*

▸**noun** [C] a person who supports new ideas and social change, especially one who belongs to a political party → Compare **reactionary**

progressively /prəˈgres.ɪv.li/ **adv** gradually: *My eyesight has got progressively worse over the years.*

prohibit /prəˈhɪb.ɪt/ **verb** **1** (B2) [T often passive] to officially refuse to allow something: *Motor vehicles are prohibited* ***from*** *driving in the town centre.* ◦ *The government introduced a law prohibiting tobacco advertisements on TV.* ◦ *Parking is* ***strictly*** *prohibited* between these gates. **2** [T] to prevent a particular activity by making it impossible: *The loudness of the music prohibits serious conversation in most nightclubs.*

prohibition /ˌprəʊ.ɪˈbɪʃ.ən/, /-hɪ-/ (US) /ˌproʊ-/ **noun** [C or U] the act of officially not allowing something, or an order that does this: *New York City has announced a prohibition* ***on*** *smoking on buses.* ◦ *The environmental group is demanding a complete prohibition* ***against*** *the hunting of whales.* ◦ *It's my feeling that the money spent on drug prohibition would be better spent on information and education.*

Prohibition /ˌprəʊ.ɪˈbɪʃ.ən/, /-hɪ-/ (US) /ˌproʊ-/ **noun** [U] the period from 1920 to 1933 when the production and sale of alcohol was not allowed in the US

prohibitive /prəˈhɪb.ɪ.tɪv/ (US) /-t̬ɪv/ **adj** If the cost of something is prohibitive, it is too expensive for most people. • **prohibitively** /-li/ **adv** *Property in the area tends to be prohibitively* ***expensive.***

project noun; verb

▸**noun** [C] /ˈprɒdʒ.ekt/ (US) /ˈprɑː.dʒekt/ **1** (B2) a piece of planned work or an activity that is finished over a period of time and intended to achieve a particular aim: *the Kings Cross housing project* ◦ *a scientific research project* ◦ *Her latest project is a film based on the life of a 19th-century music hall star.* ◦ *My next project is decorating the kitchen.* **2** (A2) a study of a particular subject done over a period of time, especially by students: *He's* ***doing*** *a class project* ***on*** *pollution.* ◦ *In our third year at college everyone had to do a special project.*

▸**verb** /prəˈdʒekt/ **CALCULATE** ▷ **1** [T usually passive] to calculate an amount or number expected in the future from information already known: [+ to infinitive] *Government spending is projected* ***to*** *rise by three percent next year.* **THROW** ▷ **2** [T] to throw or direct something forwards, with force: *90 percent of the projected missiles will hit their target.* **3 project your voice** to sing or speak loudly and clearly: *It's a big theatre so you really have to project your voice if you're going to be heard at the back.* **MAKE AN IMAGE** ▷ **4** [T] to cause a film, image, or light to appear on a screen or other surface: *Laser images were projected* ***onto*** *a screen.* **5** [T] specialized to wrongly imagine that someone else is feeling a particular emotion or DESIRE when in fact it is you who feels this way: *I suspect he's projecting his fears* ***onto*** *you.* **6** [T] If you project a particular quality, that quality is what most people notice about you: *Recently the president has sought to project a much tougher* ***image.*** **STICK OUT** ▷ **7** [I + adv/prep] to stick out over an edge or from a surface: *The hotel dining room projects out over the water.*

projected /prəˈdʒek.tɪd/ **adj** planned for the future or calculated based on information already known: *The projected extension to the motorway is going to cost over £4 million.*

projectile /prəˈdʒek.taɪl/ (US) /-təl/ **noun; adj**

▸**noun** [C] specialized an object that is thrown or shot forwards, especially from a weapon

▸**adj** [before noun] specialized describes things that are thrown or shot forwards with great force: *projectile weapons* ◦ *projectile vomiting*

projection /prəˈdʒek.ʃən/ **noun** **CALCULATION** ▷ **1** (C1) [C] a calculation or guess about the future based on information that you have: *The company has failed to achieve last year's sales projections by 30 percent.* **IMAGE** ▷ **2** (C1) [U] the act of projecting a film or an image onto a screen or wall **STICKING OUT** ▷ **3** [C] something that projects from a surface or above the edge of something **DRAWING** ▷ **4** [C] specialized a drawing that represents a solid shape or a line as seen from a particular direction

projectionist /prəˈdʒek.ʃən.ɪst/ **noun** [C] a person whose job is to operate a projector in a cinema

projector /prəˈdʒek.təʳ/ (US) /-tɚ/ **noun** [C] a device for showing films or images on a screen or other surface

prolapse /ˈprəʊ.læps/ (US) /ˈproʊ-/ **noun** [C] specialized a medical condition in which an organ has moved down out of its usual position: *a rectal prolapse/a prolapse of the rectum* • **prolapsed** /-læpst/ **adj** *a prolapsed womb*

prole /prəʊl/ (US) /proʊl/ **noun** [C] UK informal an insulting word for a person from a low social class; a short form of 'proletarian'

proletarian /ˌprəʊ.lɪˈteə.ri.ən/ (US) /ˌproʊ.ləˈter.i-/ **noun** [C] a member of the proletariat • **proletarian** **adj**

the proletariat /ˌprəʊ.lɪˈteə.ri.ət/, /ˌprɒl.ɪ-/ (US) /ˌproʊ.ləˈter.i-/ **noun** [S, + sing/pl verb] the class of people who do unskilled jobs in industry and own little or no property

ˌpro-ˈlife **adj** opposed to the belief that a pregnant woman should have the freedom to choose an ABORTION (= the intentional ending of pregnancy) if she does not want to have a baby → Compare **pro-choice**

proliferate /prəˈlɪf.ər.eɪt/ (US) /-ə.reɪt/ **verb** [I] formal to increase a lot and suddenly in number: *Small businesses have proliferated in the last ten years.* • **proliferation** /prəˌlɪf.əˈreɪ.ʃən/ (US) /-əˈreɪ-/ **noun** [U] *The past two years have seen the proliferation of TV channels.*

prolific /prəˈlɪf.ɪk/ **adj** producing a great number or amount of something: *He was probably the most prolific songwriter of his generation.* ◦ *Rabbits and other rodents are prolific (= have a lot of babies).*

prolix /ˈprəʊ.lɪks/ (US) /ˈproʊ-/ **adj** formal disapproving using too many words and therefore boring or difficult to read or listen to: *The author's prolix style has done nothing to encourage sales of the book.* → Synonym **verbose**

prologue /ˈprəʊ.lɒg/ (US) /ˈproʊ.lɑːg/ **noun** **1** [C] a part that comes at the beginning of a play, story, or long poem, often giving information about events that happened before the time when the play, story, or poem begins → Compare **epilogue** **2** [S] literary a series of events that happen before the main event and are related to it: informal *A series of internal struggles was the prologue* ***to*** *full-scale civil war.*

prolong /prəˈlɒŋ/ (US) /-ˈlɑːŋ/ **verb** [T] (C1) to make something last a longer time: *We were having such a good time that we decided to prolong our stay by another week.* ◦ *She chewed each delicious mouthful as slowly as she could, prolonging the pleasure.* • **prolongation** /ˌprəʊ.lɒŋˈgeɪ.ʃən/ (US) /ˌproʊ.lɑːŋ-/ **noun** [U]

prolonged /prəˈlɒŋd/ (US) /-ˈlɑːŋd/ **adj** (C1) continuing for a long time: *Prolonged use of the drug is known to have harmful side-effects.*

prom /prɒm/ (US) /prɑːm/ **noun** [C] **PARTY** ▷ **1** US a formal party held for older students at the end of the school year, at which there is dancing: *Who are you taking to the Senior Prom?* **PATH** ▷ **2** informal for **promenade**

promenade /ˌprɒm.əˈnɑːd/ (US) /ˌprɑː.məˈneɪd/ **noun; verb**

▸**noun** [C] (informal **prom**) a path for walking on, especially one built next to the sea: *We strolled along on the promenade eating ice creams.*

P

▸**verb** [I] old-fashioned to walk slowly along a road or path for pleasure

prominence /ˈprɒm.ɪ.nəns/ (US) /ˈprɑː.mə-/ **noun** [U] the state of being easily seen or well known: *Most of the papers **give** prominence **to** (= put in a noticeable position) the same story this morning.* ◦ *It's the first time that a lawyer of such prominence (= fame and importance) has been given the freedom to air his views on TV.* ◦ *Elton was one of the comedians who **came to/rose to/gained** prominence in the 1980s.*

prominent /ˈprɒm.ɪ.nənt/ (US) /ˈprɑː.mə-/ **adj** **FAMOUS** ▷ **1** (C1) very well known and important: *a prominent Democrat* ◦ *a prominent member of the Saudi royal family* ◦ *The government should be playing a more prominent role in promoting human rights.* **NOTICEABLE** ▷ **2** sticking out from a surface: *She has a rather prominent chin/nose.* **3** (C2) describes something that is in a position in which it is easily seen: *New books are displayed in a prominent **position** on tables at the front of the shop.* • **prominently** /-li/ **adv** *A photograph of her daughter was prominently displayed (= in a position where it could be seen) on her desk.*

promiscuity /ˌprɒm.ɪˈskjuː.ɪ.ti/ (US) /ˌprɑː.mɪˈskjuː.ə.t̬i/ **noun** [U] the fact of being promiscuous

promiscuous /prəˈmɪs.kju.əs/ **adj** disapproving (of a person) having a lot of different sexual partners or sexual relationships, or (of sexual habits) involving a lot of different partners: *I suppose I was quite promiscuous in my youth.* ◦ *It's a fallacy that gay men are more promiscuous than heterosexuals.* • **promiscuously** /-li/ **adv**

> **Other ways of saying promise**
>
> **Guarantee** is an alternative to 'promise':
>
> *I can't **guarantee** that the operation will be successful.*
>
> To **give someone** *your* **word** is a formal way of saying 'promise':
>
> *He **gave me his word** that the job would be finished on time.*
>
> If someone promises a person something in order to make that person feel less worried, the word **assure** is often used:
>
> *'Don't worry, your car will be ready tomorrow,' the mechanic **assured** him.*
>
> **Swear** can be used when someone promises in a strong way that he or she is telling the truth or will do something or behave in a particular way:
>
> *I didn't know what happened, I **swear**.*
>
> **Pledge** is used when someone formally promises to give or do something:
>
> *We are asking people to **pledge** their support for our campaign.*
>
> If you make a promise to yourself that you will do something, you can use the verbs **resolve** or **vow**:
>
> *I **vowed** I would never speak to him again.*
>
> *I have **resolved** to lose ten pounds.*

promise /ˈprɒm.ɪs/ (US) /ˈprɑː.mɪs/ **verb; noun**

▸**verb** **SAY CERTAINLY** ▷ **1** (B1) [I or T] to tell someone that you will certainly do something: [+ to infinitive] *He promised faithfully **to** call me every week.* ◦ [+ that] *The government have promised **that** they'll reduce taxes.* ◦ [+ (that)] *Promise me (**that**) you won't tell him.* ◦ *I'll have a look for some while I'm at the shops but I'm not promising anything.* ◦ *Can I have that book back when you've finished because I've promised it (= I have said I will give it) **to** Sara.* ◦ [+ two objects] *Her parents promised her a new car if she passed her exams.* ◦ *I've promised myself a long bath when I get through all this work.* ◦ [+ speech] *'I'll come round and see you every day,' she promised.* ◦ *'I won't do anything dangerous.' 'You promise?' 'I promise.'* ◦ *'I won't have time to take you shopping this afternoon.' 'But you promised!'* **BE EXPECTED** ▷ **2 promise to be good, exciting, etc.** (B2) to be expected to be good, exciting, etc.: *It promises to be a really exciting match.*

IDIOM **promise sb the earth/moon** informal to say that you will do much greater things than you will ever be able to achieve: *Like most governments in their first term of office, they promised the earth.*

▸**noun** **SAY CERTAINLY** ▷ **1** (B1) [C] the act of saying that you will certainly do something: *I'll tidy my things away tonight – and that's a promise!* ◦ *I'll try to get back in time, but I'm not **making** any promises.* **2 keep/break a promise** (B2) to do/not do what you said that you would do: *If I make a promise, I like to keep it.* **EXPECTED** ▷ **3** [U] the idea that someone or something is likely to develop successfully and that people expect this to happen: *His English teacher had written on his report that he **showed** great promise.* ◦ *As a child I was quite a good dancer, but I didn't fulfil my early promise.*

> **Word partners for promise noun**
>
> ***break/make/renege on*** a promise • ***fulfil/honour/keep*** a promise • ***give*** sb a promise • an ***empty/rash/solemn/vague*** promise • ***broken*** promises

IDIOM **promises, promises!** informal something that you say when someone says they will do something and you do not believe them: *'When I've got some time I'll show you everything.' 'Promises, promises!'*

ˈPromised ˌLand **noun** [S] in the Bible, the land of Canaan, promised by God to Abraham and his race: figurative *America was the Promised Land for many immigrant families.*

promising /ˈprɒm.ɪ.sɪŋ/ (US) /ˈprɑː.mɪ-/ **adj** (C1) Something that is promising shows signs that it is going to be successful or enjoyable: *They won the award for the most promising new band of the year.* ◦ *'How's your new venture going?' 'It's looking quite promising.'* ◦ *It's a great restaurant but it doesn't look at all promising from the outside.* → Opposite **unpromising** • **promisingly** /-li/ **adv** *The film starts promisingly enough but doesn't maintain the interest level.*

promissory note /ˈprɒm.ɪ.sər.i.ˌnəʊt/ (US) /ˈprɑː.mɪ.sɔːr.i.ˌnoʊt/ **noun** [C] specialized a document which contains a promise to pay a stated amount of money to a stated person either on a fixed date or when the money is demanded

promo /ˈprəʊ.məʊ/ (US) /ˈproʊ.moʊ/ **noun** [C] (plural **promos**) **1** informal a short film made to advertise a product, especially a pop song **2** US an advertisement, broadcast announcement, or discussion with a writer, film PRODUCER, actor, etc. that is designed to give attention to a book or film in order to increase sales

promontory /ˈprɒm.ən.tri/ (US) /ˈprɑː.mən.tɔːr-/ **noun** [C] (also **headland**) a narrow area of high land that sticks out into the sea

promote /prəˈməʊt/ (US) /-ˈmoʊt/ **verb** **ENCOURAGE** ▷ **1** (B2) [T] to encourage people to like, buy, use, do, or support something: *Advertising companies are always having to think up new ways to promote products.* ◦ *The Institute is intended to promote an understanding of the politics and culture of the Arab world.* ◦ *Greenpeace works to promote awareness of the dangers that threaten our planet today.* ◦ *It has long been known that regular exercise promotes all-round good health.*

RAISE ▷ **2** B1 [T often passive] to raise someone to a higher or more important position or rank: *If I'm not promoted within the next two years, I'm going to change jobs.* ◦ *She's just been promoted* ***to*** *senior sales rep.* ◦ *If Coventry City win this match, they'll be promoted* ***to*** *the Premier League.* → Opposite **demote** **3** [T often passive] US If a student is promoted, he or she goes up to the next level in school.

promoter /prəˈməʊ.təʳ/ US /-ˈmoʊ.t̬ɚ/ **noun** [C] **1** someone who tries to encourage something to happen or develop: *a promoter* ***of*** *peace/sexual equality* **2** a person who organizes and arranges FINANCE for sports and musical events: *a boxing/rock concert promoter*

promotion /prəˈməʊ.ʃən/ US /-ˈmoʊ-/ **noun** **ENCOURAGE** ▷ **1** B2 [C or U] activities to advertise something: *a* ***sales*** *promotion* ◦ *There was a promotion in the supermarket and they were giving away free glasses of wine.* ◦ *Obviously as sales manager he'll be very involved in the promotion and marketing of the product.* **2** C1 [U] the act of encouraging something to happen or develop: *the promotion of a healthy lifestyle* **RAISE** ▷ **3** B2 [C or U] the act of raising someone to a higher or more important position or rank: *Did Steve* ***get****/Was Steve* ***given*** *the promotion he wanted?* ◦ *The job offers excellent promotion* ***prospects****.* ◦ *River Plate's win last night has considerably increased their chances of promotion this season.*

promotional /prəˈməʊ.ʃən.əl/ US /-ˈmoʊ-/ **adj** intended to advertise something: *a promotional campaign/video*

prompt /prɒmpt/ US /prɑːmpt/ **verb; adj; noun; adv**

▸**verb** [T] **CAUSE** ▷ **1** to make something happen: *The bishop's speech has prompted an angry response from both political parties.* ◦ *Recent worries over the president's health have prompted speculation over his political future.* **2 prompt sb to do sth** C2 to make someone decide to say or do something: *What prompted you to say that?* ◦ *I don't know what prompted him to leave.* **HELP REMEMBER** ▷ **3** to help someone, especially an actor, to remember what they were going to say or do: *I forgot my line and had to be prompted.*

▸**adj** B2 (of an action) done quickly and without delay, or (of a person) acting quickly or arriving at the arranged time: *They've written back already – that was a very prompt reply.* ◦ *They're usually fairly prompt in dealing with enquiries.* ◦ *Try to be prompt because we'll be very short of time.*

▸**noun** [C] **COMPUTER** ▷ **1** a sign on a computer screen that shows that the computer is ready to receive your instructions **ACTOR'S HELP** ▷ **2** words that are spoken to an actor who has forgotten what he or she is going to say during the performance of a play **3** (also **prompter** /ˈprɒmptəʳ/ US /ˈprɑːmptɚ/) a person whose job is to help actors, during a performance, to remember words that they have forgotten

▸**adv** at the time stated and no later: *We'll be leaving at six o'clock prompt.*

prompting /ˈprɒmp.tɪŋ/ US /ˈprɑːmp-/ **noun** [C or U] the act of trying to make someone say something: [+ to infinitive] *Kids of that age really shouldn't need prompting* ***to*** *say thank you for things.* ◦ *Amazingly – without any prompting – my husband actually said how nice I looked in my new dress!*

promptly /ˈprɒmpt.li/ US /ˈprɑːmpt-/ **adv** B2 quickly, without delay, or at the arranged time: *We'll have to leave fairly promptly (= on time) if we want to catch that train.* ◦ *We try to answer readers' letters as promptly (= quickly) as we can.* ◦ *She promised she'd*

keep it secret and promptly (= immediately after) went and told Ben!

promulgate /ˈprɒm.əl.geɪt/ US /ˈprɑː.məl-/ **verb** [T] formal **SPREAD** ▷ **1** to spread beliefs or ideas among a lot of people **ANNOUNCE** ▷ **2** to announce something publicly, especially a new law: *The new law was finally promulgated in the autumn of last year.* • **promulgation** /ˌprɒm.əlˈgeɪ.ʃən/ US /ˌprɑː.məl-/ **noun** [U]

prone /prəʊn/ US /proʊn/ **adj** **TENDING** ▷ **1 be prone to sth/do sth** C2 likely to suffer from an illness or show a particular negative characteristic: *I've always been prone to headaches.* ◦ *He was prone to depression even as a teenager.* ◦ *She's prone to exaggerate, that's for sure.* **LYING DOWN** ▷ **2** formal lying on the front with the face down: *The photograph showed a man lying prone on the pavement, a puddle of blood about his head.*

-prone /-prəʊn/ US /-proʊn/ **suffix** C2 likely to experience a particular problem more often than is usual: *accident-prone* ◦ *injury-prone*

prong /prɒŋ/ US /prɑːŋ/ **noun** [C] one of two or more long, sharp points on an object, especially a fork

-pronged /-prɒŋd/ US /-prɑːŋd/ **suffix** **two-pronged, three-pronged, etc.** having the stated number of prongs: figurative *To tackle inflation the government have evolved a three-pronged strategy (= a plan that involves three ways of dealing with the problem).*

pronoun /ˈprəʊ.naʊn/ US /ˈproʊ-/ **noun** [C] B1 a word that is used instead of a noun or a noun phrase: *Pronouns are often used to refer to a noun that has already been mentioned.* ◦ *'She', 'it' and 'who' are all examples of pronouns.* • **pronominal** /prəʊˈnɒm.ɪ.nəl/ US /proʊˈnɑː.mə-/ **adj** specialized

pronounce /prəˈnaʊns/ **verb** [T] **MAKE SOUND** ▷ **1** B1 to say a word or a letter in a particular way: *How do you pronounce your surname?* ◦ *Sade, pronounced shah-day, is a singer.* **TO STATE** ▷ **2** formal to say something officially or certainly: [+ obj + noun/adj] *He was taken to the hospital where he was pronounced dead on arrival.* ◦ *The jury pronounced him guilty.* ◦ *He gazed vacantly while the verdict and sentence were pronounced.* ◦ *She surveyed the building and pronounced herself pleased with their work.* ◦ [+ that] *The government pronounced* ***that*** *they are no longer a nuclear state.* ◦ *'Have I met him?' 'You have indeed – I recall you pronounced the man (= said that he was) a fool.'* ◦ *The dessert was tried and pronounced delicious.*

PHRASAL VERB **pronounce on/upon sth** [T] formal to give a judgment or opinion about something: *I'd rather not go pronouncing on a subject that I know so little about.*

pronounced /prəˈnaʊnst/ **adj** very noticeable or certain: *I'm told I have a very pronounced English accent when I speak French.* ◦ *She's a woman of very pronounced views which she is not afraid to air.*

pronouncement /-mənt/ **noun** [C] formal an official announcement: *The treasurer has been taking a more optimistic view of economic recovery in his recent public pronouncements.*

pronto /ˈprɒn.təʊ/ US /ˈprɑːn.t̬oʊ/ **adv** informal quickly and without delay: *I'll send those off pronto, before I forget.*

pronunciation /prəˌnʌn.siˈeɪ.ʃən/ **noun** [C or U] B1 how words are pronounced: *English pronunciation is notoriously difficult.* ◦ *There are two different pronunciations of this word.*

proof /pruːf/ **noun; adj; verb**

▸**noun** **SHOWING TRUTH** ▷ **1** B2 [C or U] a fact or piece

P

of information that shows that something exists or is true: [+ that] *Do they have any proof* ***that*** *it was Hampson who stole the goods?* ◦ *I have a suspicion that he's having an affair, though I don't have any* ***concrete*** *(= definite) proof.* ◦ *If anyone needs proof* ***of*** *Andrew Davies' genius as a writer, this novel is it.* ◦ *'How old are you?' '21.' 'Have you got any proof on you?'* ◦ *Keep your receipt as proof* ***of*** *purchase.* **PRINTED COPY** ▷ **2** [C] a printed copy of something that is examined and corrected before the final copies are printed: *I was busy correcting proofs.*

IDIOM **the proof of the pudding (is in the eating)** saying said to mean that you can only judge the quality of something after you have tried, used, or experienced it

▸**adj** [after noun] **ALCOHOL** ▷ **1** of the stated alcoholic strength, a higher number meaning a greater amount of alcohol: *It says on the bottle that it's 60 percent proof.* **PROTECTED** ▷ **2** formal providing protection against something: *No household security devices are proof* ***against*** *(= protect completely against) the determined burglar.* ◦ *Her virtue would be proof* ***against*** *his charms.*

▸**verb** [T] to treat a surface with a substance that will protect it against something, especially water

-proof /-pruːf/ **suffix** protecting against, or not damaged by, a particular thing: *a bullet-proof vest* ◦ *a waterproof/wind-proof jacket* ◦ *frost-proof pots for the garden*

ˌproof ˈpositive **noun** [U] facts that cannot be doubted: *The strength of reaction to the article is proof positive that this is a very important issue.*

proofread /ˈpruːf.riːd/ **verb** [I or T] (**proofread**) to find and correct mistakes in text before it is printed or put online • **proofreading** /-ˌriː.dɪŋ/ **noun** [U] *Most of the errors were corrected at the proofreading stage.*

proofreader /ˈpruːfˌriː.dəʳ/ ⓤⓢ /-dɚ/ **noun** [C] a person whose job is to check text before it is printed or put online

P

prop /prɒp/ ⓤⓢ /prɑːp/ **verb; noun**

▸**verb** [T + adv/prep] (**-pp-**) to support something physically, often by leaning it against something else or putting something under it: *I propped my bike* ***(up) against*** *the wall.* ◦ *She was sitting at the desk with her chin propped* ***on*** *her hands.* ◦ *This window keeps on closing – I'll have to prop it* ***open*** *with something.*

PHRASAL VERB **prop sth up** **1** to lift and give support to something by putting something under it: *He was sitting upright in his hospital bed, propped up by pillows.* ◦ *There were the usual bunch of drinkers propped up at (= leaning against) the bar.* **2** to give support to something, especially a country or organization, so that it can continue to exist in a difficult situation: *How long is the government likely to survive without the US military force there to prop it up?*

▸**noun** **IN FILM/THEATRE** ▷ **1** [C usually plural] an object used by the actors performing in a play or film: *The set is minimal and the only props used in the show are a table, a chair and a glass of water.* **ON AIRCRAFT/SHIP** ▷ **2** [C] informal for **propeller** **SUPPORT** ▷ **3** [C] an object that is used to support something by holding it up: *I need some sort of a prop to keep the washing line up.* ◦ figurative *A lot of people use cigarettes as a sort of* ***social*** *prop (= to make them feel more confident).* **4** (also **prop forward**) a player in a RUGBY team who is large and strong, and who supports the SCRUM

propaganda /ˌprɒp.əˈgæn.də/ ⓤⓢ /ˌprɑː.pə-/ **noun** [U] mainly disapproving ⓒ information, ideas, opinions, or images, often only giving one part of an argument, that are broadcast, published, or in some other way spread with the intention of influencing people's opinions: *political/wartime propaganda* ◦ *At school we were fed communist/right-wing propaganda.* ◦ *One official dismissed the ceasefire as a mere propaganda exercise.* • **propagandize** formal mainly disapproving (UK usually **propagandise**) /-daɪz/ **verb** [I] to create or spread propaganda

propagandist /ˌprɒp.əˈgæn.dɪst/ ⓤⓢ /ˌprɑː.pə-/ **noun** [C] mainly disapproving someone who creates or spreads propaganda: *Communist/Nazi/Republican/right-wing propagandists* • **propagandist adj** *The papers were full of the most blatant propagandist nonsense.*

propagate /ˈprɒp.ə.geɪt/ ⓤⓢ /ˈprɑː.pə-/ **verb** **GROW** ▷ **1** [I or T] to produce a new plant from a parent plant: *Most house plants can be propagated from stem cuttings.* ◦ *Plants needs certain conditions to propagate.* **2** [I or T] formal (of a plant or animal) to produce young plants or animals **SPREAD** ▷ **3** [T] formal to spread opinions, lies, or religions among a lot of people: *Such lies are propagated in the media.* • **propagation** /ˌprɒp.əˈgeɪ.ʃən/ ⓤⓢ /ˌprɑː.pə-/ **noun** [U]

propagator /ˈprɒp.ə.geɪ.təʳ/ ⓤⓢ /ˈprɑː.pə.geɪ.t̬ɚ/ **noun** [C] specialized a box in which seeds or young plants are grown, that has a transparent cover and is sometimes heated

propane /ˈprəʊ.peɪn/ ⓤⓢ /ˈproʊ-/ **noun** [U] a gas used as fuel, especially in cooking and heating

propel /prəˈpel/ **verb** [T] (**-ll-**) **1** to push or move something somewhere, often with a lot of force: *a rocket propelled through space* ◦ *The Kon-Tiki sailed across the Pacific Ocean propelled by wind power.* **2 propel sb into/to/towards sth** to cause someone to do an activity or be in a situation: *The film propelled him to international stardom.*

propellant /prəˈpel.ənt/ **noun** [C or U] **1** an explosive substance or fuel that causes something to move forwards **2** a gas that is used in AEROSOLS to force the liquid out in very small drops

propeller /prəˈpel.əʳ/ ⓤⓢ /-ɚ/ **noun** [C] (informal **prop**) a device which causes a ship or aircraft to move, consisting of two or more blades which turn round at high speed

proˌpelling ˈpencil **noun** [C] UK (US **meˌchanical ˈpencil**) a pencil in which the LEAD is pushed out by turning or pressing a part of the pencil

propensity /prəˈpen.sɪ.ti/ ⓤⓢ /-sə.t̬i/ **noun** [S] formal the fact that someone is likely to behave in a particular way, especially a bad way: [+ to infinitive] *She's inherited from her father a propensity* ***to*** *talk too much.* ◦ *He's well-known for his natural propensity* ***for*** *indiscretion.*

proper /ˈprɒp.əʳ/ ⓤⓢ /ˈprɑː.pɚ/ **adj; adv**

▸**adj** **REAL** ▷ **1** Ⓑ1 [before noun] real, satisfactory, suitable, or correct: *This is Sara's first proper job – she usually does temporary work just for the money.* ◦ *If you're going to walk those sort of distances you need proper walking boots.* ◦ *I would have done the job myself but I didn't have the proper equipment.* ◦ *I've had sandwiches but I haven't eaten a proper meal.* ◦ *She likes everything to be in its proper place.* **SOCIALLY ACCEPTABLE** ▷ **2** showing standards of behaviour that are socially and morally acceptable: [+ to infinitive] *In those days* ***it*** *was considered not quite proper for young ladies* ***to*** *be seen talking to men in public.* ◦ *She was very proper, my grandmother – she'd never go out without wearing her hat and gloves.* **MAIN** ▷ **3** [after noun] belonging to the main, most important, or typical part: *It's a suburb of Manchester really – I wouldn't call it Manchester proper.* **COMPLETE** ▷

4 [before noun] UK informal complete: *I've got myself into a proper mess!*
▸**adv** UK not standard sometimes used instead of the adverb 'properly' to describe how someone speaks: *She was an educated lady so she* ***talked*** *proper.*

ˌproper ˈfraction noun [C] specialized a FRACTION in which the number below the line is larger than the number above it: *¾ and ⅝ are proper fractions.*

properly /ˈprɒp.əl.i/ (US) /ˈprɑː.pɚ.li/ adv **CORRECTLY** ▷ **1** correctly, or in a satisfactory way: *It's still not working properly.* ◦ *I'm not properly dressed for this sort of weather.* ◦ *I think you should take it somewhere to have it mended properly.* **SOCIALLY ACCEPTABLE** ▷ **2** formal in a socially and morally acceptable way: *Most vegetables should be eaten with a fork but asparagus can be properly eaten with the fingers.*

IDIOM **properly speaking** formal really: *It's not, properly speaking, champagne but it is very similar.*

ˈproper ˌnoun noun [C] specialized (B2) the name of a particular person, place or object that is spelled with a capital letter: *Examples of proper nouns in English are Joseph, Vienna, and the White House.* → Compare **common noun**

property /ˈprɒp.ə.ti/ (US) /ˈprɑː.pɚ.t̬i/ noun **THINGS OWNED** ▷ **1** (B1) [U] an object or objects that belong to someone: *The club does not accept responsibility for loss of or damage to club members'* ***personal*** *property.* ◦ *Both books have 'Property of Her Majesty's Government' stamped inside them.* ◦ *Children need to be taught to have respect for other people's property.* **2** (B2) [C or U] a building or area of land, or both together: *He owns a number of properties in the centre of London.* ◦ *The notice said 'Private Property, Keep Off'.* ◦ *Yes, I've bought my own house – I'm now a* ***man/woman of*** *property!* **3** [U] specialized the legal right to own and use something **QUALITY** ▷ **4** [C] a quality in a substance or material, especially one which means that it can be used in a particular way: *One of the properties of copper is that it conducts heat and electricity very well.* ◦ *We value herbs for their taste, but we forget that they also have medicinal properties.*

ˈproperty deˌveloper noun [C] a person whose job involves buying and selling buildings and land, and arranging for new buildings to be built

the ˈproperty ˌladder noun [S] a series of stages in owning houses in which you buy a small house or apartment first and then buy a bigger or more expensive house when you have enough money: *House prices are so high now it is hard for first-time buyers to* ***get on*** *the property ladder (= buy their first house).*

prophecy /ˈprɒf.ə.si/ (US) /ˈprɑː.fə-/ noun **1** [C] a statement that says what is going to happen in the future, especially one that is based on what you believe about a particular matter rather than existing facts: *The minister suggested that the dire prophecies of certain leading environmentalists were somewhat exaggerated.* ◦ *These doom and gloom prophecies are doing little to help the economy.* **2** [U] formal the ability to say what is going to happen in the future

prophesy /ˈprɒf.ə.saɪ/ (US) /ˈprɑː.fə-/ verb [I or T] to say that you believe something will happen in the future: *Few could have prophesied this war.* ◦ [+ that] *He prophesied* ***that*** *the present government would only stay four years in office.* ◦ [+ question word] *I wouldn't like to prophesy* ***wh****at will happen to that marriage!*

prophet /ˈprɒf.ɪt/ (US) /ˈprɑː.fɪt/ noun [C] **1** a person who is believed to have a special power which allows them to say what a god wishes to tell people, especially about things that will happen in the future: *an Old Testament prophet* ◦ *Let us hear the words of the prophet Isaiah on the coming of the Prince of Peace.* **2** a person who supports a new system of beliefs and principles: *Rousseau, that great prophet of the modern age* **3 the Prophet** Mohammed, the man who made Islam known to the world through the Koran

IDIOM **prophet of doom** disapproving someone who always expects bad things to happen: *The prophets of doom have been predicting the end of European cinema for the last ten years.*

prophetess /ˌprɒf.ɪˈtes/ (US) /ˈprɑː.fɪ.t̬əs/ noun [C] a female prophet

prophetic /prəˈfet.ɪk/ (US) /-ˈfet̬-/ adj saying correctly what will happen in the future: *Much of Orwell's writing now seems grimly prophetic.* • **prophetically** /-ɪ.kəl.i/ adv

prophylactic /ˌprɒf.ɪˈlæk.tɪk/ (US) /ˌprɑː.fɪ-/ adj; noun
▸**adj** specialized preventing disease: *Some dentists are convinced that the addition of fluoride in water is ineffective as a prophylactic treatment.*
▸**noun** [C] **1** specialized something that is intended to prevent disease **2** mainly US a **condom**

propitiate /prəˈpɪʃ.i.eɪt/ verb [T] formal to please and make calm a god or person who is annoyed with you: *In those days people might sacrifice a goat or sheep to propitiate an angry god.* ◦ *The radicals in the party were clearly sacked to propitiate the conservative core.* • **propitiation** /-ˌpɪʃ.iˈeɪ.ʃən/ noun [U]

propitiatory /prəˌpɪʃ.iˈeɪ.tər.i/ (US) /prəˈpɪʃ.i.ə.tɔːr-/ adj formal intended to please someone and make them calm: *a propitiatory gesture*

propitious /prəˈpɪʃ.əs/ adj formal likely to result in or showing signs of success: *With the economy in recession, it was not a propitious time to start a company.* • **propitiously** /-li/ adv

proponent /prəˈpəʊ.nənt/ (US) /-ˈpoʊ-/ noun [C] a person who speaks publicly in support of a particular idea or plan of action: *He is one of the leading proponents* ***of*** *capital punishment.* → Compare **opponent**

proportion /prəˈpɔː.ʃən/ (US) /-ˈpɔːr-/ noun **AMOUNT** ▷ **1** (C1) [C, + sing/pl verb] the number or amount of a group or part of something when compared to the whole: *Children make up a large proportion* ***of*** *the world's population.* ◦ *A higher proportion* ***of*** *women now smoke than used to be the case.* ◦ *The report shows that poor families spend a larger proportion* ***of*** *their income on food.* **2** (C2) [S or U] the number, amount, or level of one thing when compared to another: *The proportion* ***of*** *women* ***to*** *men at my college was about five to one.* ◦ *The chart shows how weight increases* ***in*** *proportion* ***to*** *height (= the increase in weight depends on the increase in height).* ◦ *The level of crime in an area is almost always* ***in direct*** *proportion* ***to*** *the number of unemployed.* **SIZE** ▷ **3** (C2) [C or U] the correct or most attractive relationship between the size of different parts of the same thing or between one thing and another: *Your legs are very much* ***in*** *proportion* ***to*** *(= the right size for) the rest of your body.* ◦ *His feet seem very small* ***in*** *proportion* ***to*** *his body.* ◦ *My head was much nearer the camera than the rest of me so I'm all* ***out of*** *proportion.* **4 proportions** [plural] the size, shape, or level of something: *a building of elegant proportions* ◦ *I'm not very good at drawing people – I can never get the proportions right.* ◦ humorous *She's a woman of generous proportions (= she is fat).* ◦ *A small worry in the back of your mind can for no apparent reason* ***assume/take on*** *massive proportions in the*

P

middle of the night. **IMPORTANCE** ▷ **5** [U] used in a number of phrases to mean importance and seriousness: *You've got to keep a* ***sense of*** *proportion (= the ability to understand what is important and what is not).* ◦ *I think a certain amount of worry about work is very natural, but you've got to* ***keep it in*** *proportion (= judge correctly its seriousness).*

IDIOM **blow sth out of proportion** to treat a particular event or problem far too seriously: *It's ridiculous – we have a tiny disagreement and you blow the whole thing out of proportion!* ◦ *Of course, when the papers get hold of a story, it's blown out of* ***all*** *proportion.*

proportional /prəˈpɔː.ʃᵊn.ᵊl/ (US) /-ˈpɔːr-/ **adj** (also **proportionate**) If two amounts are proportional, they change at the same rate so that the relationship between them does not change: *Weight is proportional* ***to*** *size.* • **proportionally** /-i/ **adv** (also **proportionately**) *Unemployment is proportionally much higher in the north of the country.*

pro͵portional represent͵ation **noun** [U] (abbreviation **PR**) a political system in which parties are represented in parliament according to the number of people who voted for them

proportioned /prəˈpɔː.ʃᵊnd/ (US) /-ˈpɔːr-/ **adj** having parts of the size or shape that is described: *We wandered through the beautifully proportioned rooms of the Winter Palace.* ◦ *She has the dancer's finely proportioned physique.* ◦ humorous *The* ***generously*** *proportioned (= fat) singer has to have all his garments specially made.*

proposal /prəˈpəʊ.zᵊl/ (US) /-ˈpoʊ-/ **noun** [C] **1** (B2) a suggestion, sometimes a written one: *Congress has rejected the latest economic proposal* ***put forward*** *by the president.* ◦ [+ to infinitive] *There has been an angry reaction to the government's proposal* ***to*** *reduce unemployment benefit.* ◦ *Have you read Steve's proposals for the new project?* ◦ [+ that] *There was anger at the proposal* ***that*** *a UN peacekeeping force should be sent to the area.* **2** (B2) an offer of marriage

propose /prəˈpəʊz/ (US) /-ˈpoʊz/ **verb** **SUGGEST** ▷ **1** (B2) [T] to offer or suggest a possible plan or action for other people to consider: [+ that] *I propose* ***that*** *we wait until the budget has been announced before committing ourselves to any expenditure.* ◦ [+ -ing verb] *He proposed deal****ing*** *directly with the suppliers.* ◦ *She proposed a boycott of the meeting.* ◦ *He proposed a* ***motion*** *that the chairman resign.* **2** [T] to suggest someone for a position or as a member of an organization: *To be nominated for union president you need one person to propose you and another to second you.* **3** (B2) [I] to ask someone to marry you: *I remember the night your father proposed* ***to*** *me.* **4** **propose a toast** to ask people at a formal social occasion to express their good wishes or respect for someone by holding up their glasses, usually of alcohol, at the same time and then drinking from them: *Now, if you'd all please raise your glasses, I'd like to propose a toast* ***to*** *the bride and groom.*

> **!** Common mistake: **propose or offer?**
>
> **Warning:** choose the correct verb!
>
> To talk about providing or supplying something such as an object or service, don't say 'propose', say **offer**:
>
> ~~*This school proposes individual tuition on demand.*~~
>
> *This school offers individual tuition on demand.*

INTEND ▷ **5** (B2) [T] formal to intend to do something: [+ to infinitive] *How do you propose* ***to*** *complete the project in such a short time scale?* ◦ [+ -ing verb] *How do you propose tackl****ing*** *this problem?* ◦ *I do not propose* ***to*** *reveal details at this stage.* ◦ *What we are proposing is a radical change in approach.* • **proposed** /-ˈpəʊzd/ (US) /-ˈpoʊzd/ **adj** (B2) *There have been huge demonstrations against the proposed factory closure.*

proposer /prəˈpəʊ.zəʳ/ (US) /-ˈpoʊ.zɚ/ **noun** [C] **1** a person who suggests a subject for discussion: *The proposer of the motion tonight is Jonathan Hesk.* **2** a person who suggests someone for a position or as a member of an organization

proposition /͵prɒp.əˈzɪʃ.ᵊn/ (US) /͵prɑː.pə-/ **noun; verb**

▸**noun** [C] **1** (C1) an offer or suggestion, usually in business: *He wrote to me last week regarding a business proposition he thought might interest me.* ◦ *I've* ***put*** *my proposition* ***to*** *the company director for his consideration.* **2** an idea or opinion: *They were debating the proposition that 'All people are created equal'.*

▸**verb** [T] to ask someone who you are not in a relationship with if they would like to have sex with you: *I was propositioned by a complete stranger.*

propound /prəˈpaʊnd/ **verb** [T] formal to suggest a theory, belief, or opinion for other people to consider: *It was Ptolemy who propounded the theory that the Earth was at the centre of the universe.*

proprietary /prəˈpraɪə.tᵊr.i/ (US) /-ter.i/ **adj** [before noun] **1** relating to owning something, or relating to or like an owner: *I just assumed he owned the place – he had a proprietary air about him.* **2** describes goods that are made and sent out by a particular company whose name is on the product: *proprietary medicines*

proprietor /prəˈpraɪə.təʳ/ (US) /-t̬ɚ/ **noun** [C] a person who owns a particular type of business, especially a hotel, a shop, or a company that makes newspapers: *a hotel/newspaper proprietor*

proprietorial /prə͵praɪəˈtɔː.ri.əl/ (US) /-ˈtɔːr.i-/ **adj** relating to or like an owner: *He put a proprietorial arm around her.*

proprietress /prəˈpraɪə.trəs/ **noun** [C] old-fashioned a woman who is a proprietor

propriety /prəˈpraɪə.ti/ (US) /-t̬i/ **noun** **1** [U] formal correct moral behaviour or actions: *The director insisted that there was no question as to the propriety of how the funds were raised.* ◦ *She was careful always to behave with propriety.* **2** **proprieties** [plural] formal the rules of polite social behaviour: *They'd invited us to dinner so we thought we'd better* ***observe*** *the proprieties and invite them back.*

propulsion /prəˈpʌl.ʃᵊn/ **noun** [U] a force that pushes something forward: *wind propulsion* ◦ *a propulsion system* → See also **jet propulsion**

pro rata /͵prəʊˈrɑː.tə/ (US) /͵proʊˈreɪ.t̬ə/ **adj, adv** formal calculated according to, or as a share of, the fixed rate for a larger total amount: *a pro rata payment/pay increase* ◦ *It's £20,000 pro rata, but I'm doing half the full number of hours, so I'll be getting £10,000.*

prorate /prəʊˈreɪt/ (US) /proʊ-/ **verb** [T] specialized to calculate a cost, payment, or price according to the amount of something that has been used, in relation to the fixed rate for a larger total amount: *The rental will be prorated if occupancy does not begin on the first day of the month.* • **prorated** /-ˈreɪ.tɪd/ **adj** specialized *Attendees joining the course later will pay a prorated fee.* → See also **pro rata**

prosaic /prəˈzeɪ.ɪk/ **adj** formal without interest, imagination, and excitement: *He asked if I'd got my black eye in a fight – I told him the prosaic truth that I'd banged my head on a door.*

prosciutto /prəˈʃuː.təʊ/ US /-t̬oʊ/ noun [U] Italian dried HAM (= meat from the leg or shoulder of a pig) served in very thin slices

proscribe /prəʊˈskraɪb/ US /proʊ-/ verb [T] formal (of a government or other authority) to not allow something: *The Broadcasting Act allows ministers to proscribe any channel that offends against good taste and decency.* ◦ *The Athletics Federation have banned the runner from future races for using proscribed drugs.* • **proscription** /prəʊˈskrɪp.ʃən/ US /proʊ-/ noun [U]

prose /prəʊz/ US /proʊz/ noun [U] written language in its ordinary form rather than poetry: *I've always preferred reading prose to poetry.* → Compare **verse**

prosecute /ˈprɒs.ɪ.kjuːt/ US /ˈprɑː.sɪ-/ verb LEGAL ▷ **1** C2 [I or T] to officially accuse someone of committing a crime in a law court, or (of a lawyer) to try to prove that a person accused of committing a crime is guilty of that crime: *Shoplifters will be prosecuted.* ◦ *He was prosecuted **for** fraud.* ◦ *Any manufacturer who does not conform to the standards could be prosecuted under the Consumers Protection Act, 1987.* ◦ *The victim has said that she will not prosecute.* → Compare **defend** CONTINUE ▷ **2** [T] formal to continue to take part in a planned group of activities, especially a war: *He seemed convinced that the US would prosecute the war to its end.*

prosecution /ˌprɒs.ɪˈkjuː.ʃən/ US /ˌprɑː.sɪ-/ noun LEGAL ▷ **1** C2 [C or U] the act of prosecuting someone: *A number of the cases have resulted in successful prosecution.* ◦ *Doctors guilty of neglect are **liable to** prosecution.* **2 the prosecution** [S, + sing/pl verb] UK C2 the lawyers in a trial who try to prove that a person accused of committing a crime is guilty of that crime: *The prosecution alleged that he lured the officer to his death by making an emergency call.* ACTIVITIES ▷ **3** [U] formal the act of taking part in a planned set of activities, especially a war

prosecutor /ˈprɒs.ɪ.kjuː.təʳ/ US /ˈprɑː.sɪ.kjuː.t̬ɚ/ noun [C] C2 a legal official who accuses someone of committing a crime, especially in a law court

proselytize disapproving formal (UK usually **proselytise**) /ˈprɒs.əl.ɪ.taɪz/ US /ˈprɑː.sə.lɪ-/ verb [I] to try to persuade someone to change their religious or political beliefs or their way of living to your own: *He was also remarkable for the proselytizing zeal with which he wrote his political pamphlets.* ◦ *The television has provided the evangelists with yet another platform for their proselytizing.* • **proselytizer** formal (UK usually **proselytiser**) /ˌprɒs.əl.ɪˈtaɪ.zəʳ/ US /ˌprɑː.səl.ɪ.taɪ.zɚ/ noun [C]

prosody /ˈprɒs.ə.di/ US /ˈprɑː.sə-/ noun [U] specialized **1** the pattern of rhythm and sound in poetry **2** the rhythm and INTONATION (= the way a speaker's voice rises and falls) of language

prospect /ˈprɒs.pekt/ US /ˈprɑː.spekt/ noun; verb
▸noun POSSIBILITY ▷ **1** B2 [C or U] the possibility that something good might happen in the future: *Is there any prospect **of** the weather improving?* ◦ *There seems little prospect **of** an end to the dispute.* ◦ [+ that] *There's not much prospect **that** this war will be over soon.* ◦ *There's **every** prospect **of** success.* **2 prospects** B2 [plural] the possibility of being successful, especially at work: *She's hoping the course will improve her **career** prospects.* ◦ *Prospects **of/for** (= opportunities for) employment remain bleak for most people in the area.* **3** C2 [S] the idea of something that will or might happen in the future: *The prospect **of** spend**ing** three whole days with her fills me with horror.* ◦ *I'm very excited **at the** prospect **of** see**ing** her again.* ◦ *We face the prospect of having to start all over again.* **4** [C] a person who might be chosen, for example as an employee: *We'll be interviewing four more prospects for the posts this afternoon.* VIEW ▷ **5** [C] formal a good view of a large land area or of a city: *From the restaurant there was a marvellous prospect **of/over** Siena and the countryside beyond.*
▸verb [I] to search for gold, oil, or other valuable substances on or under the surface of the earth: *to prospect **for** oil/gold* • **prospector** /prəˈspek.təʳ/ US /-t̬ɚ/ noun [C]

prospective /prəˈspek.tɪv/ adj **prospective buyers, employers, parents, etc.** C1 people who are expected to buy something, employ someone, become a parent, etc.: *We've had three sets of prospective buyers looking round the house.*

prospectus /prəˈspek.təs/ noun [C] a document giving details of a college, school, or business and its activities: *You will find details of all our courses in the prospectus.*

prosper /ˈprɒs.pəʳ/ US /ˈprɑː.spɚ/ verb [I] (of a person or a business) to be or become successful, especially financially: *A lot of microchip manufacturing companies prospered at that time.*

prosperity /prɒsˈper.ɪ.ti/ US /prɑːˈsper.ə.t̬i/ noun [U] C1 the state of being successful and having a lot of money: *A country's future prosperity depends, to an extent, upon the quality of education of its people.* ◦ *The war was followed by a long period of peace and prosperity.*

prosperous /ˈprɒs.pər.əs/ US /ˈprɑː.spɚ-/ adj C1 successful, usually by earning a lot of money: *In a prosperous country like this, no one should go hungry.* • **prosperously** /-li/ adv

prostate /ˈprɒs.teɪt/ US /ˈprɑː.steɪt/ noun [C] (also **ˈprostate ˌgland**) an organ near the PENIS in male mammals that produces a liquid that mixes with and carries SPERM: *He has prostate trouble.* ◦ *prostate cancer*

prosthesis /ˈprɒs.θiː.sɪs/ US /ˈprɑːs-/ noun [C] (plural **prostheses**) specialized an artificial body part, such as an arm, foot, or tooth, which replaces a missing part • **prosthetic** /prɒsˈθet.ɪk/ US /prɑːsˈθet̬-/ adj *a prosthetic hand*

prostitute /ˈprɒs.tɪ.tjuːt/ US /ˈprɑː.stɪ.tuːt/ noun; verb
▸noun [C] C1 a person who has sex with someone for money
▸verb [T] formal disapproving **1** to use yourself or your abilities or beliefs in a way which does not deserve respect, especially in order to get money: *Some critics say he prostituted his musical skills by going into pop rather than staying with classical music.* ◦ *He went to work in Hollywood and was accused of prostituting himself.* **2 prostitute yourself** formal to have sex for money

prostitution /ˌprɒs.tɪˈtjuː.ʃən/ US /ˌprɑː.stɪˈtuː-/ noun [U] the work of a prostitute: *Poverty drove her to prostitution.*

prostrate adj; verb
▸adj /ˈprɒs.treɪt/ US /ˈprɑː.streɪt/ LYING ▷ **1** lying with the face down and arms stretched out, especially as a sign of respect or worship VERY TIRED ▷ **2** (also **prostrated**) having lost all strength or all determination because of an illness or an extremely bad experience: *A woman, prostrate with grief, lay wailing on the ground.*
▸verb /prɒsˈtreɪt/ US /ˈprɑː.streɪt/ **prostrate yourself** to lie with the face down and arms stretched out, especially as a sign of respect or worship • **prostration** /prɒsˈtreɪ.ʃən/ US /prɑːˈstreɪ-/ noun [C or U]

prot(o)- /prəʊ.təʊ-/ US /proʊ.t̬oʊ-/ prefix first, especially from which other similar things develop; original: *protoplasm* ◦ *a prototype*

protagonist /prəˈtæg.ən.ɪst/ **noun** [C] SUPPORTER ▷ **1** an important supporter of an idea or political system: *Key protagonists* ***of*** *the revolution were hunted down and executed.* → Compare **antagonist** CHARACTER ▷ **2** C2 formal one of the main characters in a story or a play

protean /ˈprəʊ.ti:.ən/ US /ˈproʊ.t̬i-/ **adj** literary easily and continuously changing: *the protean talents of this comedian*

protease /ˈprəʊ.ti:.eɪz/ US /ˈproʊ.t̬i-/ **noun** [C] specialized an ENZYME which causes PROTEINS to break into smaller pieces

protease inhibitor /ˈprəʊ.ti.eɪz.ɪnˌhɪb.ɪ.təʳ/ US /ˈproʊ.t̬i.eɪz.ɪnˌhɪb.ɪ.t̬ɚ/ **noun** [C] a drug for treating HIV which works by preventing the virus from increasing

protect /prəˈtekt/ **verb** **1** B1 [I or T] to keep someone or something safe from injury, damage, or loss: *clothing that protects you* ***against*** *the cold* ◦ *It's important to protect your skin* ***from*** *the harmful effects of the sun.* ◦ *Surely the function of the law is to protect everyone's rights.* ◦ *Of course the company will act to protect its financial interests in the country if war begins.* ◦ *Patients' names have been changed to protect their privacy.* ◦ *Public pressure to protect the environment is strong and growing.* ◦ *Vitamin C may help protect* ***against*** *cancer.* **2** [T] If a government protects a part of its country's trade or industry, it helps it by taxing goods from other countries. **3** [T] to provide someone with INSURANCE against injury, damages, etc. • **protected** /-ˈtek.tɪd/ **adj** *This dolphin is a protected* ***species*** (= it is illegal to harm or kill them).

protection /prəˈtek.ʃən/ **noun** [U] **1** B2 the act of protecting or state of being protected: *Their flimsy tent* ***gave/offered*** *little protection* ***against*** *the severe storm.* ◦ *Round-the-clock police protection is given to all senior politicians.* ◦ *New legislation still does not offer adequate protection* ***for*** *many endangered species.* ◦ *Always wear goggles as a protection* ***for*** *your eyes when using the machines.* ◦ *The insurance policy provides protection* (= will make a financial payment) *in case of accidental loss of life or serious injury.* **2** informal for **protection money** **3** a CONDOM (= thin rubber covering for the PENIS) used as a way of preventing pregnancy or the spread of disease: *Did you use any protection?*

protectionism /prəˈtek.ʃən.ɪ.zəm/ **noun** [U] disapproving the actions of a government to help its country's trade or industry by taxing goods bought from other countries • **protectionist** /-ɪst/ **adj**

proˈtection ˌmoney **noun** [U] money that criminals take from people in exchange for agreeing not to hurt them or damage their property

protective /prəˈtek.tɪv/ **adj** **1** B2 giving protection: *protective clothing* ◦ *a protective mask and goggles* **2** C1 wanting to protect someone from criticism, hurt, danger, etc. because you like them very much: *It's easy to be too protective* ***towards/of*** *your children.* ◦ *She's fiercely protective* ***of*** *the man she married 29 years ago.* • **protectively** /-li/ **adv** *He put an arm around her shoulder protectively.* • **protectiveness** /-nəs/ **noun** [U]

proˌtective ˈcustody **noun** [U] a safe place, sometimes prison, where someone is kept by the police for their own safety

protector /prəˈtek.təʳ/ US /-tɚ/ **noun** [C] **1** someone who protects someone or something: *Philip II considered himself the protector of the Catholic Church.* **2** a piece of equipment that protects someone: *a back and chest protector*

protectorate /prəˈtek.tər.ət/ US /-tɚ-/ **noun** [C] a country that is generally controlled and defended by a more powerful country

protégé /ˈprɒt.ə.ʒeɪ/ US /ˈprɑ:.t̬ə-/ **noun** [C] a young person who is helped and taught by an older and usually famous person: *The young composer regarded himself as Berg's protégé.* → Compare **mentor**

protein /ˈprəʊ.ti:n/ US /ˈproʊ-/ **noun** [C or U] C1 one of the many substances found in food such as meat, cheese, fish, or eggs, that is necessary for the body to grow and be strong

pro tem /ˌprəʊˈtem/ US /ˌproʊ-/ **adv, adj** now and for only a short period: *Phil is taking over from David on a pro tem basis.* ◦ [after noun] US *mayor/president pro tem*

protest **noun; verb**

▸**noun** /ˈprəʊ.test/ US /proʊˈtest/ **1** [C or U] a strong complaint expressing disagreement, disapproval, or opposition: *Protests have been* ***made/registered*** *by many people who would be affected by the proposed changes.* ◦ *A formal protest was made by the German team* ***about*** *their disqualification from the relay final.* ◦ *Conservation groups have united* ***in*** *protest* ***against*** *the planned new road.* **2** B2 [C] an occasion when people show that they disagree with something by standing somewhere, shouting, carrying signs, etc.: *a public protest* ***against*** *the war* ◦ *a peaceful/violent protest* **3** **under protest** If something is done under protest, it is done unwillingly: *I only went to the meeting under protest.*

▸**verb** [I or T] /prəˈtest/ US /ˈproʊ.test/ **1** B2 to show that you disagree with something by standing somewhere, shouting, carrying signs, etc.: *A big crowd of demonstrators were protesting* ***against*** *cuts in health spending.* ◦ US *Outside, a group of students were protesting research cuts.* **2** B2 to say something forcefully or complain about something: *A lot of people protested* ***about*** *the new working hours.* ◦ *They protested bitterly* ***to*** *their employers, but to no avail.* ◦ [+ that] *A young girl was crying, protesting* ***that*** *she didn't want to leave her mother.* ◦ *All through the trial he protested his* ***innocence*** (= strongly said he was not guilty).

IDIOM **protest too much** to express an opinion or fact so strongly or so often that people start to doubt that you are telling the truth: *She keeps trying to impress on me how she doesn't fancy him but does she protest too much?*

Protestant /ˈprɒt.ɪ.stənt/ US /ˈprɑ:.t̬ɪ-/ **noun; adj**

▸**noun** [C] a member of the parts of the Christian Church which separated from the Roman Catholic Church during the 16th century

▸**adj** **1** of or relating to these parts of the Christian Church: *a Protestant minister* **2** **the Protestant work ethic** the belief that work is valuable as an activity, as well as for what it produces • **Protestantism** /-stən.tɪ.zəm/ **noun** [U]

protestation /ˌprɒt.esˈteɪ.ʃən/ US /ˌprɑ:.t̬esˈteɪ-/ **noun** [C usually plural] formal an act of saying something forcefully or complaining about something: *Ignoring my protestations, they went ahead and chopped the tree down.* ◦ *Their protestations* ***of*** *loyalty seem rather hollow in view of the way they behaved.*

protester (also **protestor**) /prəˈtes.təʳ/ US /-tɚ/ **noun** [C] someone who shows that they disagree with something by standing somewhere, shouting, carrying signs, etc.

ˈprotest ˌmarch **noun** [C] an occasion when people

show that they disagree with something by walking somewhere, often shouting and carrying signs, etc.

ˈprotest ˌsong noun [C] a song which expresses disapproval, usually about a political subject

protocol /ˈprəʊ.tə.kɒl/ (US) /ˈproʊ.t̬ə.kɑːl/ noun **RULES** ▷ **1** [U] the system of rules and acceptable behaviour used at official ceremonies and occasions: *a breach of Royal protocol* ◦ *diplomatic protocol* **AGREEMENT** ▷ **2** [C] a formal international agreement: *The Geneva Protocol of 1925 prohibits the use of poisonous gases in war.* **IN COMPUTING** ▷ **3** [C] specialized a computer language allowing computers that are connected to each other to communicate

proton /ˈprəʊ.tɒn/ (US) /ˈproʊ.t̬ɑːn/ noun [C] a type of ELEMENTARY PARTICLE (= very small piece of matter) that has a positive electrical charge and is found in the NUCLEUS of all atoms → Compare **electron, neutron**

protoplasm /ˈprəʊ.tə.plæz.əm/ (US) /ˈproʊ.t̬ə-/ noun [U] the transparent liquid that is inside all living cells

prototype /ˈprəʊ.tə.taɪp/ (US) /ˈproʊ.t̬ə-/ noun [C] the first example of something, such as a machine or other industrial product, from which all later forms are developed: *a prototype* ***for/of*** *a new car*

protozoan /ˌprəʊ.təˈzəʊ.ən/ (US) /ˌproʊ.t̬əˈzoʊ-/ noun [C] (also **protozoon** (plural **protozoa**)) any of various types of very small animals with one cell: *Amoebas are protozoans.* • **protozoan** adj

protracted /prəˈtræk.tɪd/ adj lasting for a long time or made to last longer: *protracted negotiations* ◦ *a protracted argument/discussion* • **protract** /-ˈtrækt/ verb [T] formal *I have no desire to protract the process.* • **protraction** /-ˈtræk.ʃən/ noun [U] formal

protractor /prəˈtræk.tər/ noun [C] a device used for measuring and drawing angles. It is usually in the form of half a circle made from transparent plastic with degrees printed on it.

protrude /prəˈtruːd/ verb [I] to stick out from or through something: *A rotting branch protruded* ***from*** *the swamp like a ghostly arm.* ◦ *protruding ears/teeth*

protrusion /prəˈtruː.ʒən/ noun [C or U] something that sticks out from a surface, or the act of doing this: *It has a series of protrusions along its back.* ◦ *The condition results in weight loss, rapid heart beat and protrusion of the eyes.*

protuberance /prəˈtjuː.bər.əns/ (US) /-ˈtuː-/ noun [C] formal something that sticks out from a surface: *If the plant has been infected you will see dark protuberances along the stems.*

protuberant /prəˈtjuː.bər.ənt/ (US) /-ˈtuː.bɚ-/ adj formal sticking out: *He stared at me with blue, slightly protuberant eyes.*

proud /praʊd/ adj; adj, adv

▸adj **SATISFIED** ▷ **1** (B1) feeling pleasure and satisfaction because you or people connected with you have done or got something good: *You must be very proud* ***of*** *your son.* ◦ *We're particularly proud* ***of*** *our company's environmental record.* ◦ *When she received her prize I think I was the proudest parent on the face of the earth.* ◦ [+ to infinitive] *I'm very proud* ***to*** *have been involved in this project.* ◦ [+ (that)] *I was so proud* ***(that)*** *my son had been chosen for the national team.* → See also **houseproud** **RESPECTING YOURSELF** ▷ **2** approving having or showing respect for yourself: *We Albanians are a proud people.* ◦ *He might be poor but he's also proud, and he won't be pushed around by anyone.* **FEELING IMPORTANT** ▷ **3** (B2) disapproving feeling that you are better and more important than other people: *Come on, admit you're wrong and don't be so proud.* ◦ *She knows she's lost, but she's* ***too*** *proud* ***to*** *admit it.*

IDIOM **do sb proud 1** UK old-fashioned to treat someone who is visiting you very well, especially by giving them a lot of food: *We had a lovely tea – Sheila did us proud.* **2** informal to make someone proud of you by doing something very well: *Once again, the armed forces have done us proud.*

▸adj, adv mainly UK specialized sticking out from the surrounding area: *Sand the surface with abrasive paper until no flakes of paint stand proud* ***of*** *the surface.*

proudly /ˈpraʊd.li/ adv (B2) in a proud way: *He proudly held out his trophy for us to admire.*

prove /pruːv/ verb (**proved**, **proved**, mainly US **proven**) **SHOW** ▷ **1** (B2) [T, L] to show a particular result after a period of time: *The operation proved a complete success.* ◦ *The dispute over the song rights proved impossible to resolve.* ◦ [L (+ to be)] *The new treatment has proved* ***to be*** *a disaster.* **2 prove yourself** (C2) to show that you are good at something: *I wish he'd stop trying to prove himself all the time.* **SHOWING TRUTH** ▷ **3** (B1) [T] to show that something is true: [+ that] *They suspected that she'd killed him but they could never actually prove* ***that*** *it was her.* ◦ [+ adj] *They proved him* ***innocent/guilty****.* ◦ *Under the present system, you're innocent until proven guilty.* ◦ [+ question word] *'I lost £30 in the bus.' 'That just* ***goes to*** *prove* ***what*** *an idiot you are!'* ◦ *Computers have been used to prove mathematical theorems.* ◦ *That theory was proved false.* ◦ *He's so aggressive – it's as if he's always trying to prove something.* • **proven** /ˈpruː.vən/, /ˈprəʊ-/ adj *You've got a proven work record, which gives you a big advantage.*

provenance /ˈprɒv.ən.əns/ (US) /ˈprɑː.vən-/ noun [S or U] formal the place of origin of something: *jewels of uncertain provenance* ◦ *This raised doubts about the provenance of the painting.* ◦ *I don't need to see a label to identify the provenance of a garment that someone is wearing.*

proverb /ˈprɒv.ɜːb/ (US) /ˈprɑː.vɝːb/ noun [C] (C2) a short sentence, etc., usually known by many people, stating something commonly experienced or giving advice: *The appetite, says the proverb, grows with eating.* ◦ [+ that] *There is an old Arab proverb* ***that*** *everything you write or speak should pass through three gates: Is this kind? Is this necessary? Is this true?*

proverbial /prəˈvɜː.bi.əl/ (US) /-ˈvɝː-/ adj **1** as used in a proverb or other phrase: *He's got to pull the proverbial finger out.* **2** well known: *his proverbial good humour* • **proverbially** /-ə.li/ adv

provide /prəˈvaɪd/ verb **SUPPLY** ▷ **1** (B1) [T] to give someone something that they need: *This booklet provides useful information about local services.* ◦ *All meals are provided throughout the course.* ◦ *The author provides no documentary references to support her assertions.* ◦ *We have concerns about whether the government will be able to provide viable social services* ***for*** *poorer families/provide poorer families* ***with*** *viable social services.* ◦ *Putting more police on patrol doesn't provide a real solution to the problem of increasing violence.*

LAW ▷ **2** [+ that] formal (of a law or decision) to say that something must happen if particular conditions exist: *Section 17 provides* ***that*** *all decisions must be circulated in writing.*

PHRASAL VERBS **provide against sth** formal to make plans in order to prevent or deal with a bad situation: *Beach operators do not have a legal obligation to provide against injury or drowning.* • **provide for sb** to

P

> **! Common mistake: provide**
>
> When **provide** is followed by an indirect object, remember to use the preposition **with**.
>
> Don't say 'provide someone something', say **provide someone with something**:
>
> ~~*Could you provide us a list of hotels in the area?*~~
>
> *Could you provide us with a list of hotels in the area?*

give someone the things they need such as money, food, or clothes: *He has a wife and two young children to provide for.* • **provide for sth 1** C2 to make plans in order to deal with a possible event in the future: *We must provide for depreciation when calculating the costs.* **2** formal If a law or agreement provides for something, it allows it to happen or exist: *Current legislation provides for the detention of those suspected of terrorism.*

proˈvided (that) conjunction (also **providing (that)**) B2 if, or only if: *He's welcome to come along, provided that he behaves himself.*

providence /ˈprɒv.ɪ.dᵊns/ US /ˈprɑː.və-/ noun [U] an influence that is not human in origin and is thought to control people's lives: *divine providence*

provident /ˈprɒv.ɪ.dᵊnt/ US /ˈprɑː.və-/ adj formal approving making arrangements for future needs, especially by saving money • **providently** /-li/ adv

providential /ˌprɒv.ɪˈden.ʃᵊl/ US /ˌprɑː.və-/ adj formal happening exactly when needed but without being planned: *a providential opportunity* • **providentially** /-i/ adv

provider /prəˈvaɪ.dəʳ/ US /-dɚ/ noun [C] C1 someone who provides something: *an internet service provider* ◦ *The bank is now a major provider of financial services to industry.* ◦ *Until her illness she was the main provider (= earned most of the money) in the family.*

province /ˈprɒv.ɪns/ US /ˈprɑː.vɪns/ noun REGION ▷ **1** C2 [C] an area that is governed as part of a country or an EMPIRE: *the Canadian province of Alberta* **2 the provinces** [plural] the parts of a country that are not the capital city SUBJECT ▷ **3 sb's province** formal a subject or activity of special interest, knowledge or responsibility: *Renaissance art is not really his province – he specializes in the modern period.* ◦ *Marketing is within the province **of** the sales department.*

provincial /prəˈvɪn.ʃᵊl/ noun; adj

▸noun [C] mainly disapproving a person who comes from somewhere in a country outside its capital city

▸adj **1** relating to an area that is governed as part of a country or an EMPIRE: *provincial governments* **2** C2 in or from the parts of the country that are not the capital city: *The majority of young professionals in the capital have moved there from provincial towns.* **3** disapproving having opinions and ideas that are old-fashioned and simple: *provincial attitudes* • **provincialism** /-ɪ.zᵊm/ noun [U] disapproving

ˈproving ˌground noun [C usually singular] a situation or place where something such as a new theory or machine can be tested

provision /prəˈvɪʒ.ᵊn/ noun; verb

▸noun SUPPLY ▷ **1** C1 [C or U] the act of providing something: ***The** provision **of** good public transport will be essential for developing the area.* ◦ *Of course there's provision in the plan **for** population increase.* ◦ *When designing buildings in this area, you have to **make** provision **against** earthquakes.* **2 provisions** [plural] supplies of food and other necessary things: *provisions for the journey* LAW ▷ **3** [C] a statement within an agreement or a law that a particular thing must happen or be done, especially before another can happen or be done: *We have inserted certain provisions into the treaty to safeguard foreign workers.* ◦ [+ that] *She accepted the job with the provision **that** she would be paid expenses for relocating.* FINANCE ▷ **4** in a company's ACCOUNTS (= financial records), an amount of money that is kept in case of a possible future loss: *The insurance company **made** a provision **against** claims over alleged pension fraud.* **5 make provision for sth** to make arrangements to deal with something, often financial arrangements: *He hasn't made any provision for his retirement yet.*

▸verb [T] formal to supply someone or something with food and other necessary things

provisional /prəˈvɪʒ.ᵊn.ᵊl/ adj for the present time but likely to change: *a provisional government* ◦ *These dates are only provisional.* • **provisionally** /-i/ adv *Club members have provisionally agreed to the changes.*

proˌvisional ˈlicence noun [C] UK (US **ˈlearner's ˌpermit**) an official document that a person has to have when they are learning to drive

proviso /prəˈvaɪ.zəʊ/ US /-zoʊ/ noun [C] (plural **provisos**) a statement in an agreement, saying that a particular thing must happen before another can: [+ that] *He was released from prison **with/on** the proviso **that** he doesn't leave the country.*

provocation /ˌprɒv.əˈkeɪ.ʃᵊn/ US /ˌprɑː.və-/ noun [C or U] C2 an action or statement that is intended to make someone angry: *He'd fly into a rage **at the slightest** provocation.*

provocative /prəˈvɒk.ə.tɪv/ US /-ˈvɑː.kə.t̬ɪv/ adj CAUSING THOUGHT ▷ **1** causing thought about interesting subjects: *The programme will take a detailed and provocative look at the problem of homelessness.* MAKE ANGRY ▷ **2** causing an angry reaction, usually intentionally: *a provocative question/remark* ◦ *In a deliberately provocative speech, she criticized the whole system of government.* SEXUAL ▷ **3** If behaviour or clothing is provocative, it is intended to cause sexual DESIRE: *She slowly leaned forward in a provocative way.* • **provocatively** /-li/ adv *She dresses very provocatively (= intending to cause sexual interest).*

provoke /prəˈvəʊk/ US /-ˈvoʊk/ verb [T] CAUSE REACTION ▷ **1** C2 to cause a reaction, especially a negative one: *The prospect of increased prices has already provoked an outcry.* MAKE ANGRY ▷ **2** C2 to make or try to make a person or an animal angry: *It was a vicious-looking dog and I didn't want to provoke it.* ◦ *He was clearly trying to get at me but I refused to be provoked.* ◦ *I was provoked **into** the argument.*

provost /ˈprɒv.əst/ US /ˈprɑː.vəst/ noun [C] **1** UK (in some universities) the person in charge of a particular college: *the Provost of King's College, Cambridge* **2** US an important official who helps to run a college or university

prow /praʊ/ noun [C] the front part of a boat or ship

prowess /ˈpraʊ.es/ noun [U] formal great ability or skill: *athletic/sporting prowess* ◦ *He's always boasting about his **sexual** prowess.*

prowl /praʊl/ verb; noun

▸verb [I or T] to move around quietly in a place trying not to be seen or heard, such as when hunting: *There have been reports of a masked man prowling in the neighbourhood.* ◦ *At night, adult scorpions prowl the desert **for** (= trying to catch) insects.* ◦ informal *Unable to sleep, he prowled (= walked without purpose) (**about/around**) the hotel corridors.*

▸noun **be on the prowl** to be moving around quietly in a place trying not to be seen or heard: *There was a fox on the prowl earlier.*

prowler /ˈpraʊ.ləʳ/ (US) /-lɚ/ noun [C] someone who moves around quietly in a place, trying not to be seen, often before committing a crime

proximity /prɒkˈsɪm.ɪ.ti/ (US) /prɑːkˈsɪm.ə.t̬i/ noun [U] formal C2 the state of being near in space or time: *The best thing about the location of the house is its proximity **to** the town centre.*

proxy /ˈprɒk.si/ (US) /ˈprɑːk-/ noun [C or U] authority given to a person to act for someone else, such as by voting for them in an election, or the person who this authority is given to: *a proxy vote* ◦ *My brother's voting for me **by** proxy in the club elections.* ◦ *Can I nominate someone as a proxy to sign for me?*

Prozac /ˈprəʊ.zæk/ (US) /ˈproʊ-/ noun [U] trademark a drug that is used to treat DEPRESSION (= a mental illness that makes you feel extremely unhappy) and ANXIETY (= a mental illness that makes you feel very worried)

prude /pruːd/ noun [C] disapproving a person who is easily shocked by rude things, especially those of a sexual type: *Don't be such a prude.* • **prudish** /ˈpruː.dɪʃ/ adj *I don't consider myself prudish but I do think the sex scenes in the film were a bit excessive.* • **prudishly** /ˈpruː.dɪʃ.li/ adv • **prudishness** /ˈpruː.dɪʃ.nəs/ noun [U] (also **prudery**)

prudent /ˈpruː.dᵊnt/ adj formal careful and avoiding risks: [+ to infinitive] ***It's** always prudent **to** read a contract properly before signing it.* → Synonym **cautious** → Opposite **imprudent** • **prudence** /-dᵊns/ noun [U] *The firm was commended for its financial prudence.* • **prudently** /-li/ adv

prune /pruːn/ verb; noun

▸verb [T] **1** to cut off branches from a tree, bush, or plant, especially so that it will grow better in future: *She spent the afternoon pruning roses.* **2** to reduce something by removing things that are not necessary: *Arco has reacted to the loss in revenue by pruning (**back**) its expansion plans.* ◦ *I felt his essay needed a little pruning.*

▸noun [C] a dried PLUM

ˈpruning ˌshears noun [plural] US SECATEURS (= a tool for cutting branches of a plant)

prurient /ˈprʊə.ri.ənt/ (US) /ˈprʊr.i-/ adj formal disapproving too interested in the details of another person's sexual behaviour • **prurience** /-əns/ noun [U] • **pruriently** /-li/ adv *Newspapers often delve pruriently into people's private lives.*

prussic acid /ˌprʌs.ɪkˈæs.ɪd/ noun [U] old-fashioned a very poisonous ACID that is a type of CYANIDE

pry /praɪ/ verb **ASK QUESTIONS** ▷ **1** [I] disapproving to try to find out private facts about a person: *As a reporter, I was paid to pry **into** other people's lives.* ◦ *I hope you don't think I'm prying, but has your boyfriend ever lived with anyone before?* ◦ *She wanted a private holiday **away from** prying **eyes** (= where no one would be trying to see her).* **OPEN** ▷ **2** [T] mainly US to move or lift something by pressing a tool against a fixed point: [+ adj] *The car trunk had been pried **open** and all her equipment was gone.*

PS /ˌpiːˈes/ noun [C] used when you want to add extra information at the end of a letter or email: *Love from Sophie. PS Say hi to Gemma.* ◦ *She **added** a PS asking for your address.*

psalm /sɑːm/ noun [C] a holy poem or song, especially one of the 150 collected together in the Bible

pseud /sjuːd/ (US) /suːd/ noun [C] UK informal disapproving a person who tries to seem to have detailed knowledge or excellent judgment of a subject, especially in art, literature, music, etc.: *He's such a pseud, with his talk of 'lambent harmonies' and 'melting arpeggios'.* • **pseudy** /ˈsjuː.di/ (US) /ˈsuː.di/ adj *I have to say, I don't have much time for the pseudy vocabulary of wine snobs.*

pseud(o)- /sjuː.dəʊ/ (US) /suː.doʊ/ prefix disapproving pretended and not real: *pseudo-religious*

pseudonym /ˈsjuː.də.nɪm/ (US) /ˈsuː.də.nɪm/ noun [C] a name which a person, such as a writer, uses instead of their real name, especially on their work: *She writes **under** a pseudonym.* ◦ *George Orwell was a pseudonym – his real name was Eric Blair.* • **pseudonymous** /sjuːˈdɒn.ɪ.məs/ (US) /suːˈdɑː.nɪ-/ adj specialized *pseudonymous literature*

ˈpseudo-science noun [C usually singular] a system of thought or a theory that is not formed in a scientific way

psoriasis /səˈraɪə.sɪs/ noun [U] a disease in which areas of skin turn red and are covered with small dry pieces of skin

psst /pst/ exclamation a sound made to get someone's attention, especially without other people noticing: *Psst, what's the time?*

psych /saɪk/ verb

PHRASAL VERBS **psych sb out** informal to behave in a very confident or forceful way in order to make a competitor, especially in a sports event, feel less confident: *Both athletes were trying to psych each other out before the race.* • **psych yourself up** informal to try to make yourself feel confident and ready to do something difficult

psych(o)- /saɪ.kəʊ/ (US) /-koʊ/ prefix of the mind or mental processes: *psychopharmacology (= the study of drugs which affect the mind)*

psyche /ˈsaɪ.ki/ noun [C usually singular] the mind, or the deepest thoughts, feelings, or beliefs of a person or group: *the male psyche* ◦ *Peru is a very traditional country, and embedded in its psyche is a love of ceremony.*

psychedelic /ˌsaɪ.kəˈdel.ɪk/ adj **1** (of a drug) causing effects on the mind, such as feelings of deep understanding or seeing strong images: *psychedelic drugs* **2** Psychedelic art or clothing has bright colours and strange patterns of a type which might be experienced by taking psychedelic drugs.

psychiatric /ˌsaɪ.kiˈæt.rɪk/ adj of or relating to the study of mental illness: *psychiatric treatment* ◦ *a psychiatric patient* ◦ *the hospital's psychiatric unit* • **psychiatrically** /-rɪ.kᵊl.i/ adv

psychiˈatric ˌhospital noun [C] a place where people who are mentally ill stay and receive treatment

psychiatrist /saɪˈkaɪə.trɪst/, /sɪ-/ noun [C] C2 a doctor who is also trained in psychiatry

psychiatry /saɪˈkaɪə.tri/ noun [U] the part of medicine which studies mental illness → Compare **psychology**

psychic /ˈsaɪ.kɪk/ adj; noun

▸adj **KNOWING** ▷ **1** having a special mental ability, for example so that you are able to know what will happen in the future or know what people are thinking: *psychic powers* **MENTAL** ▷ **2** (especially of an illness) of the mind rather than the body: *psychic problems* • **psychical** /-kɪ.kᵊl/ adj [before noun] *The Society for Psychical Research is investigating reports of a ghost at the old vicarage.* • **psychically** /-kɪ.kᵊl.i/ adv

▸noun [C] a person who has a special mental ability, for example being able to know what will happen in the future or what people are thinking: *a gifted psychic*

psycho /ˈsaɪ.kəʊ/ (US) /-koʊ/ noun [C] (plural **psychos**) informal someone who is crazy and frightening: *The man's a psycho.* • **psycho** adj informal *He suddenly **went** psycho and started shooting in all directions.*

psychoanalyse UK (US **psychoanalyze**) /ˌsaɪ.kəʊˈæn.əl.aɪz/ (US) /-koʊ-/ verb [T] to examine someone or treat them using psychoanalysis • **psychoanalyst** /-ɪst/ noun [C] (also **analyst**)

psychoanalysis /ˌsaɪ.kəʊ.əˈnæl.ə.sɪs/ (US) /-koʊ-/ noun [U] any of a number of the theories of the human personality, which attempt to examine a person's unconscious mind to discover the hidden causes of their mental problems: *Sigmund Freud is known as the father of psychoanalysis.*

psychoanalytic /ˌsaɪ.kəʊˈæn.əl.ɪ.tɪk/ (US) /-koʊˈæn.əl.ɪ.t̬ɪk/ adj relating to psychoanalysis

psychobabble /ˈsaɪ.kəʊˌbæb.l̩/ (US) /-koʊ-/ noun [U] informal disapproving language using a lot of words and expressions taken from PSYCHOLOGY (= the study of the human mind)

psychokinesis /ˌsaɪ.kəʊ.kɪˈniː.sɪs/ (US) /-koʊ-/ noun [U] changing the state or position of a physical object, using only the power of the mind • **psychokinetic** /-ˈnet.ɪk/ (US) /-ˈnet̬.ɪk/ adj

psychological /ˌsaɪ.kəlˈɒdʒ.ɪ.kəl/ (US) /-kəˈlɑː.dʒɪ-/ adj **1** B2 relating to the human mind and feelings: *psychological problems* ◦ *He claims that the constant aircraft noise has a bad psychological effect on the residents.* ◦ *We are concerned with the physical and psychological well-being of our employees.* **2** (of an illness or other physical problem) caused by worry or sadness: *I suspect his headaches are purely psychological.* • **psychologically** /-i/ adv B2 *psychologically disturbed*

psychoˌlogical ˈmoment noun [S] the time when something is most likely to be accepted: *They chose the right psychological moment to announce the plans.*

psychoˌlogical ˈprofile noun [C] (specialized **ofˌfender ˈprofile**) a description of the likely character, behaviour, and interests of a violent criminal that is based on EVIDENCE collected from the place where a crime was committed • **psychoˌlogical ˈprofiling** noun [U] (specialized **ofˌfender ˈprofiling**)

psychoˌlogical ˈwarfare noun [U] the use of activities which cause fear and ANXIETY in the people you want to influence without hurting them physically

psychologist /saɪˈkɒl.ə.dʒɪst/ (US) /-ˈkɑː.lə-/ noun [C] B2 someone who studies the human mind and human emotions and behaviour, and how different situations have an effect on them: *a child psychologist* ◦ *an educational psychologist* ◦ *She spent 15 years as a **clinical** psychologist.*

psychology /saɪˈkɒl.ə.dʒi/ (US) /-ˈkɑː.lə-/ noun [U] B2 the scientific study of the way the human mind works and how it influences behaviour, or the influence of a particular person's character on their behaviour: *She studied psychology at Harvard.* ◦ *a lecturer in psychology* ◦ *child psychology* ◦ *the psychology **of** the soldier* → Compare **psychiatry**

psychometric /ˌsaɪ.kəʊˈmet.rɪk/ (US) /-koʊ-/ adj specialized designed to show someone's personality, mental ability, opinions, etc.: *psychometric testing*

psychopath /ˈsaɪ.kə.pæθ/ noun [C] **1** specialized in PSYCHOLOGY (= the scientific study of the human mind), a person who has no feeling for other people, does not think about the future, and does not feel bad about anything they have done in the past **2** (informal **psycho**) someone who is very mentally ill and dangerous • **psychopathic** /-ˈpæθ.ɪk/ adj (informal **psycho**) *A series of unsolved murders on the island has raised fears that a psychopathic serial killer is on the loose.*

psychopathology /ˌsaɪ.kəʊ.pəˈθɒl.ə.dʒi/ (US) /-koʊ.pəˈθɑː.lə-/ noun [U] the study of mental diseases: *She's doing an MPhil in psychopathology.*

ˈpsych ops noun [plural or U] (also **psy ops** /ˈsaɪ.ɒps/ (US) /-ɑːps/) informal military activities that involve trying to influence the enemy's beliefs and state of mind

psychosis /saɪˈkəʊ.sɪs/ (US) /-ˈkoʊ-/ noun [C or U] (plural **psychoses**) any of a number of the more severe mental diseases that make you believe things that are not real: *She fell into a drug-induced psychosis.*

psychosomatic /ˌsaɪ.kəʊ.səˈmæt.ɪk/ (US) /-koʊ.soʊˈmæt̬-/ adj (of an illness) caused by ANXIETY and worry and not by an infection or injury: *a psychosomatic illness*

psychotherapist /ˌsaɪ.kəˈθer.ə.pɪst/ noun [C] someone who gives people psychotherapy: *He sees a psychotherapist twice a week.*

psychotherapy /ˌsaɪ.kəʊˈθer.ə.pi/ (US) /-koʊ-/ noun [U] the treatment of mental illness by discussing someone's problems with them, instead of using drugs or operations

psychotic /saɪˈkɒt.ɪk/ (US) /-ˈkɑː.t̬ɪk/ adj suffering from PSYCHOSIS (= severe mental disease): *a psychotic disorder* ◦ *His dislike of women bordered on the psychotic.*

pt noun [C] PART ▷ **1** written abbreviation for part, when referring to a part of a document: *See pt 3 for further details.* MEASUREMENT ▷ **2** written abbreviation for **pint**: *Add 1 pt of water and bring to the boil.* POINT ▷ **3** written abbreviation for **point**: *He needs a good high jump to score more than 9,000 pts.* PLACE ▷ **4** written abbreviation for **point**: *Spurn Pt*

PTA /ˌpiː.tiːˈeɪ/ noun [C] abbreviation for **parent-teacher association**: *a PTA meeting*

pterodactyl /ˌter.əˈdæk.tɪl/ (US) /-təl/ noun [C] a very large flying animal that lived many millions of years ago

PTO /ˌpiː.tiːˈəʊ/ (US) /-ˈoʊ/

▸abbreviation for please turn over: written at the bottom of a page to show that there is more information on the other side

▸noun [C] mainly US abbreviation for PARENT-TEACHER ORGANIZATION → See **parent-teacher association**

Pty adj [after noun] written abbreviation for **proprietary**, used in the names of private companies in Australia, New Zealand, and South Africa whose owners are responsible for only a limited amount of the companies' debts: *Mackenzie Investments Pty*

pub /pʌb/ noun [C] (formal **ˌpublic ˈhouse**) UK A2 a place in Britain and Ireland where alcoholic drinks can be bought and drunk and where food is often available: *Do you want to **go to** (informal **go down**) the pub after work?* ◦ *our local pub* ◦ *a pub lunch.* → See also **publican, local**

ˈpub ˌcrawl noun [C] UK informal a visit to several pubs, one after the other, having a drink or drinks at each one: *We **went on** a pub crawl on Saturday night.*

pube /pjuːb/ noun [C often plural] informal one of the short, curly hairs that grow around the sexual organs after puberty

puberty /ˈpjuː.bə.ti/ (US) /-bɚ.t̬i/ noun [U] the stage in a person's life when they develop from a child into an adult because of changes in their body that make them able to have children: ***At** puberty, pubic hair develops and girls begin to menstruate.*

pubescent /pjuːˈbes.ənt/ adj describes someone who is at the stage in their life when they are developing

P

from a child into an adult and becoming able to have children: *pubescent girls/boys*

ˈ**pub** ˌ**grub** noun [U] UK informal meals that are served in a pub

pubic /ˈpjuː.bɪk/ adj [before noun] of or near the sexual organs on the outside of a person's body: *pubic* ***hair***

public /ˈpʌb.lɪk/ adj; noun

▸adj **PEOPLE** ▷ **1** B2 relating to or involving people in general, rather than being limited to a particular group of people: *Public opinion (= the opinions of most people) has turned against him.* ◦ *Is it really* ***in the*** *public* ***interest*** *(= useful to people) to publish this information?* ◦ *We need to increase public* ***awareness*** *of the disease.* ◦ *Peaceful demonstrations that do not cause a public* ***nuisance*** *(= do not harm other people) are a fundamental right in any truly democratic country.* ◦ *The government has had to bow to public* ***pressure*** *on the issue.* ◦ *The information only became public after his death.* ◦ *The results will not be* ***made*** *public (= told to everyone) until tomorrow.* ◦ *We will not* ***go*** *public with (= tell people in general) the results until tomorrow.* **GOVERNMENT** ▷ **2** B1 provided by the government from taxes to be available to everyone: *public funds/services/spending* ◦ *public buildings* ◦ *a public library* ◦ *He is unlikely to* ***hold*** *public* ***office*** *(= have an important job in national or local government).* **PLACE** ▷ **3** describes a place where a lot of people are: *It's too public here – let's go back to my room to talk.*

IDIOMS **be in the public eye** C1 to be famous and written about in newspapers and magazines and seen on television • **public enemy number one/no. 1** someone or something that many people do not like or approve of

▸noun [U, + sing/pl verb] **1 the public** B1 all ordinary people: *The public has a right to know about this.* ◦ *The palace and its grounds are* ***open to*** *the public (= people can visit) during the summer months.* ◦ *When will the product be available to the* ***general*** *public (= all ordinary people)?* ◦ ***Members of*** *the public were asked about their shopping habits.* **2** the group of people who are involved with you or your organization, especially in a business relationship: *Newspapers publish these outrageous stories because they know what their public wants.* **3 in public** B2 in a place where people can see you: *I'd never behave like that in public.* → Compare **in private**

ˌ**public adˈdress** ˌ**system** noun [C] (abbreviation **PA**) equipment for making sound louder in a public place

publican /ˈpʌb.lɪ.kən/ noun [C] UK the manager of a pub

publication /ˌpʌb.lɪˈkeɪ.ʃən/ noun **1** B2 [U] the act of making information or stories available to people in a printed form: *The brochure will be ready for publication in September.* ◦ *Will you arrange the publication* ***of*** *the names of the winners?* ◦ *When is the publication* ***date****? (= When will the book be available to buy?)* **2** B2 [C] a book, magazine, newspaper, or document in which information or stories are published: *Our latest publication is a magazine for health enthusiasts.*

ˌ**public ˈbar** noun [C] a drinking room in a pub with plainer furniture and sometimes lower prices than in the other drinking rooms

ˌ**public ˈcompany** noun [C] a business that is owned by many people who have bought SHARES in it → Compare **private company**

ˌ**public conˈvenience** noun [C] mainly UK formal a building containing toilets that are available for everyone to use

ˌ**public ˈfigure** noun [C] someone who is famous because of what they do, and is written about in newspapers and magazines or is often on television or the radio

ˌ**public ˈholiday** noun [C] a day when almost everyone in a particular country does not have to go to work or school: *New Year's Day is a public holiday in many countries.*

ˌ**public ˈhouse** noun [C] UK formal for **pub**

ˌ**public ˈhousing** noun [U] US for **council housing**

publicist /ˈpʌb.lɪ.sɪst/ noun [C] someone who arranges publicity for a person or organization by giving information to REPORTERS and television and radio companies and arranging public meetings and special events

publicity /pʌbˈlɪs.ɪ.ti/ US /-ə.t̬i/ noun [U] B2 the activity of making certain that someone or something attracts a lot of interest or attention from many people, or the attention received as a result of this activity: *He attracted a lot of* ***adverse/bad*** *publicity with his speech about unmarried mothers.* ◦ *Her first novel was published last year* ***in a blaze of*** *(= with a lot of) publicity.* ◦ *We have planned an exciting publicity* ***campaign*** *with our advertisers.* ◦ *The publicity* ***generated*** *by the court case has given a welcome boost to our sales.* ◦ *The normally publicity-****shy*** *director will be making several public appearances for the launch of the movie.* ◦ *The enormous publicity surrounding the case will make it very difficult to hold a fair trial.* ◦ *The pop group's arrival by hot-air balloon was just a publicity* ***stunt*** *(= an unusual way of attracting the public's attention).*

publicize (UK usually **publicise**) /ˈpʌb.lɪ.saɪz/ verb [T] to make information about something generally available: *Attitudes seem to be changing as a result of recent* ***highly*** *publicized* ***cases*** *of sexual harassment.* ◦ *The event was* ***well*** *publicized all over town.* ◦ *The work of the charity has been* ***widely*** *publicized throughout the media.*

ˌ**public ˈlibrary** noun [C] a building where people can read or borrow books without having to pay

publicly /ˈpʌb.lɪ.kli/ adv **TO EVERYONE** ▷ **1** C1 If something is done publicly, it is done so that everyone can know about it: *The company publicly apologized and agreed to contribute some money to charity.* ◦ *publicly* ***humiliated*** **GOVERNMENT** ▷ **2** done, owned, or paid for by the government: *The new railway will not be publicly* ***funded****.*

ˌ**public ˈprosecutor** noun [C] legal a lawyer who acts for the government against a criminal in court

the ˌ**public ˈpurse** noun [S] mainly UK money from the government: *People should provide for their own retirement and not expect to be supported by the public purse.*

ˌ**public reˈlations** noun [U] (abbreviation **PR**) the activity of keeping good relationships between an organization and the people outside it: *Environmentalists attacked the company's ad as a public-relations* ***exercise****.*

> **!** Usage: **public schools**
>
> In England, schools provided by the government, where people do not have to pay, are called **state schools**. The term **public school** describes very expensive schools of a high academic standard which are for the children of very rich people, often of a high social class. **Private school** and **independent school** are more general terms for schools where people have to pay. In the US, Scotland, and Australia, **public schools** are free schools provided by the government.

P

ˌpublic ˈschool noun [C or U] **EXPENSIVE SCHOOL** ▷ **1** in England, an expensive type of PRIVATE SCHOOL (= school paid for by parents not by the government) **FREE SCHOOL** ▷ **2** US in Scotland, Australia, and the US, a free school provided by the government

the ˈpublic ˌsector noun [S] businesses and industries that are owned or controlled by the government: *Most doctors work in the public sector.* ◦ *public sector workers such as nurses or teachers*

ˌpublic ˈservant noun [C] a government employee

ˌpublic ˈservice noun **1** [C usually plural] a service provided by the government, such as hospitals, schools, or the police: *The prime minister wants to stop Italy's huge public debt growing, and to make its public services more efficient.* **2** [U] the government and the work that its departments do: *The Senator has worked in public service all his life.* ◦ [before noun] *Inner-city teaching has become a popular public-service job for new graduates.* **3** [C] something that is done or provided for the public because it is needed, and not in order to make a profit: [before noun] *The star has recorded public-service announcements for local TV on subjects including HIV and teen pregnancy.*

ˌpublic ˌservice ˈbroadcasting noun [U] television and radio programmes that are broadcast to provide information, advice, or entertainment to the public without trying to make a profit

ˌpublic-ˈspirited adj approving wanting to help people generally: *You pick litter up in the park? That's very public-spirited of you!*

ˌpublic ˈtransport noun [U] UK (US **ˌpublic transporˈtation**) B1 a system of vehicles such as buses and trains which operate at regular times on fixed routes and are used by the public: *Greater investment in public transport would keep more cars off the roads.*

ˌpublic uˈtility noun [C] an organization that supplies the public with water, gas, or electricity

P

publish /ˈpʌb.lɪʃ/ verb [T] B1 to make information available to people, especially in a book, magazine, or newspaper, or to produce and sell a book, magazine, or newspaper: *She's just had an article published in their weekend supplement.* ◦ *The government publishes figures every six months showing how many people are unemployed.* ◦ *The names of the winners of the competition will be published in June.* • **publishing** /-ɪŋ/ noun [U] *a career in publishing*

publisher /ˈpʌb.lɪ.ʃər/ (US) /-ʃɚ/ noun [C] **1** B2 an organization which prints text or music **2** an employee of a publishing company who has responsibility for deciding what is published

ˈpublishing ˌhouse noun [C] a company which publishes books

puce /pjuːs/ noun [U] a dark brownish-purple colour: *Her face turned puce with rage.* • **puce adj** being a dark brownish-purple colour

puck /pʌk/ noun [C] a small, hard rubber disc that is used instead of a ball in ICE HOCKEY (= a game played on ice)

pucker /ˈpʌk.ər/ (US) /-ɚ/ verb [I or T] (also **pucker up**) to tighten skin or cloth until small folds appear or (of skin or cloth) to form small folds: *He puckered his lips and kissed her.* ◦ *Her mouth puckered and I thought she was going to cry.* ◦ *puckered seams* • **pucker noun** [C]

puckish /ˈpʌk.ɪʃ/ adj literary liking to make jokes about other people and play silly tricks on them: *a puckish sense of humour* ◦ *a puckish grin*

pud /pʊd/ noun [C or U] UK informal for **pudding**: *What's for pud?*

pudding /ˈpʊd.ɪŋ/ noun **SWEET FOOD** ▷ **1** B2 [C or U] UK a sweet and usually hot dish made with pastry, flour, bread, or rice, and often fruit: *a sticky toffee/treacle pudding* ◦ *Is there any more rice pudding?* **2** [U] US a sweet, soft food made from milk, sugar, eggs, and FLAVOURING, eaten cold: *chocolate/vanilla/butterscotch pudding* **3** [U] (informal **pud**) UK the final part of a meal, when a sweet dish is eaten: ***What's for** pudding?* ◦ *I thought we'd **have** trifle **for** pudding.* → Synonym **dessert** **NON-SWEET FOOD** ▷ **4** [C or U] (informal **pud**) UK a hot dish made with pastry or flour that contains or is eaten with meat: *steak and kidney pudding*

IDIOMS **be in the pudding club** UK old-fashioned to be pregnant • **over-egg the pudding** UK to spoil something by trying too hard to improve it

ˈpudding ˌbasin noun [C] UK a large bowl that is used for making puddings

ˌpudding-ˌbasin ˈhaircut noun [C] UK a short hairstyle that is not fashionable and looks as if it has been created by putting a pudding basin over your head and cutting round the edge of it

puddle /ˈpʌd.l̩/ noun [C] a small pool of liquid on the ground, especially from rain

pudgy /ˈpʌdʒ.i/ adj mainly US short and fat: *I was a pudgy child.* • **pudginess** /-nəs/ noun [U]

puerile /ˈpjʊə.raɪl/ (US) /ˈpjʊr.ɪl/ adj disapproving behaving in a silly way, not like an adult: *I find his sense of humour rather puerile.* • **puerility** /pjʊəˈrɪl.ɪ.ti/ (US) /pjʊrˈɪl.ə.t̬i/ noun [U]

puff /pʌf/ verb; noun

▸verb **BREATHE** ▷ **1** [I] to breathe fast and with difficulty, usually because you have been doing exercise: *He came puffing up the stairs.* ◦ [+ speech] *'I ran all the way home,' she puffed (= said while puffing).* **2 puff and pant** to breathe fast and with difficulty, usually because you have been doing exercise **SMOKE** ▷ **3** [I or T] to smoke tobacco: *She was puffing **on** a cigarette at the time.* ◦ *He sat there, puffing **away at** a cigarette.* **BLOW** ▷ **4** [I or T] to blow out in clouds, or make steam or smoke do this: *The chimney was puffing **out** clouds of smoke.*

PHRASAL VERBS **puff sth out** to make your chest or your face become bigger by filling it with air: *He puffed out his cheeks and sat back in his chair.* • **puff up** If part of your body puffs up, it becomes bigger because it is infected or injured. • **puff sth up** to become larger or full of air, or to make something become larger in this way: *When the pastry is golden and puffed up, take the pie out of the oven.*

▸noun **SMALL AMOUNT** ▷ **1** [C] a small amount of smoke, air, or something that can rise into the air in a small cloud: *Sean blew a puff **of smoke** at his reflection in the mirror.* ◦ *He hit the ground with his stick and a puff **of** dust rose up into the air.* **FOOD** ▷ **2** [C] a piece of food made of PUFF PASTRY filled with something sweet or with food such as cheese: *a cream/jam puff* ◦ *cheese puffs* **PRAISE** ▷ **3** [C] informal mainly disapproving (US also **puff piece**) a piece of writing or speech which praises something too much **BREATHE** ▷ **4 be out of puff** informal to be breathing with difficulty because you have been doing physical exercise **SMOKING** ▷ **5** [C] an act of smoking: *She **took a** puff **on** her cigarette and thought for a moment.*

IDIOM **vanish/go up/disappear in a puff of smoke** informal to disappear suddenly and completely: *One moment he was standing behind me, the next he had vanished in a puff of smoke.* ◦ *All his hard work seemed to be going up in a puff of smoke.*

ˈpuff ˌadder noun [C] a poisonous African snake which swells to a larger size when it is attacked

puffball /ˈpʌf.bɔːl/ (US) /-bɑːl/ noun [C] **MUSHROOM** ▷ **1** a large, white, round FUNGUS that can be eaten **SKIRT** ▷ **2** (also **puffball skirt**) a skirt that has a rounded shape because it is GATHERED (= pulled together in folds) in at the bottom

ˌpuffed (ˈout) adj [after verb] UK (US **pooped**) breathing with difficulty because you have been doing physical exercise: *I can't walk any further – I'm puffed!*

puffer train /ˈpʌf.əˌtreɪn/ (US) /-ɚ-/ noun [C] child's word a steam train (= train driven by steam)

puffin /ˈpʌf.ɪn/ noun [C] a bird which lives near the sea in northern parts of the world and has a large, brightly coloured beak

puffin

ˌpuff ˈpastry noun [U] pastry with a lot of thin layers which swells to a larger size when cooked

ˌpuff(ed) ˈsleeve noun [C usually plural] a short sleeve which swells out into a ball shape

puffy /ˈpʌf.i/ adj If the skin around your eyes is puffy, it is slightly swollen: *His eyes were still puffy with sleep.*

pug /pʌg/ noun [C] a small dog with a flat face and a short, wide nose

pugnacious /pʌgˈneɪ.ʃəs/ adj formal wanting to start an argument or fight, or expressing an argument or opinion very forcefully: *I found him pugnacious and arrogant.* • **pugnacity** /pʌgˈnæs.ɪ.ti/ (US) /-ə.t̬i/ noun [U] (also **pugnaciousness** /-nəs/)

puke /pjuːk/ verb; noun

▸verb [I or T] slang to vomit: *The baby puked all down my shirt.* ◦ *She puked her dinner* **up** *again.*

IDIOM **it makes me (want to) puke** used to say that something makes you very upset or angry

▸noun [U] slang vomit: *The floor was covered with puke.*

pukka /ˈpʌk.ə/ adj **1** old-fashioned real: *a nice little Italian restaurant serving pukka pizzas and pasta* **2** slang of excellent quality: *I've had some pukka food there.* **3** extremely formal and educated: *He's not one of the pukka types she usually favours.*

pulchritude /ˈpʌl.krɪ.tjuːd/ (US) /-tuːd/ noun [U] formal beauty, especially a woman's beauty • **pulchritudinous** /ˌpʌl.krɪˈtjuː.dɪ.nəs/ (US) /-ˈtuː.d-/ adj

pull /pʊl/ verb; noun

▸verb **MOVE TOWARDS YOU** ▷ **1** (A2) [I or T] to move something towards yourself, sometimes with great physical effort: *Could you help me move this bookcase over there? You pull and I'll push.* ◦ *He pulled the chair away from the desk.* ◦ *He pulled the heavy box across the floor to the door.* ◦ [+ obj + adj] *He pulled the door open.* ◦ *The sun was so strong we had to pull* **down** *the blinds.* ◦ *She pulled* **out** *the drawer.* **REMOVE** ▷ **2** (B1) [T] to take something out of or away from a place, especially using physical effort: *He pulled* **off** *his sweater.* ◦ *The dentist pulled both teeth* **out**. ◦ *I spent the morning pulling* **up** *the weeds in the flowerbeds.* **3** [T] to remove or stop something that was going to be published or broadcast, especially because it is found to be offensive or not accurate: *When officials realized the cultural gaffe, the company pulled the ad and apologized.* **MOVE** ▷ **4** (B2) [I +adv/prep] to move in the stated direction: *During the last lap of the race one of the runners began to pull* **ahead**. ◦ *We waved as the train pulled* **out of** *the station.* ◦ *Our armies are pulling* **back** *on all fronts.* **5 pull yourself along, up, etc.** (B2) [T] to take hold of something and use effort to move your body forwards or up: *She pulled herself up the stairs, holding onto the rail.* ◦ *He put his hands on the side of the pool and pulled himself out of the water.* **ATTRACT** ▷ **6** [T] to attract a person or people: *The show has certainly pulled* **(in) the crowds**. **7** [I or T] UK informal to succeed in starting a sexual relationship with someone: *He certainly knows how to pull women.* ◦ *Did Tracy pull at the nightclub last night?* **INJURE** ▷ **8** (C2) [T] to injure a muscle by stretching it too much: *I pulled a muscle in my back lifting some drawers.* ◦ *He pulled a hamstring.* **DISHONEST** ▷ **9** [T] slang to perform a dishonest action: *The gang that pulled the bank robbery were all arrested.* ◦ *No one's gonna pull that kind of trick* **on** *me!* **INTERNET** ▷ **10** [T] specialized to get information from the internet, after asking or searching for it: *Companies should encourage customers to pull information from their website, thus putting the customer in control.* → Compare **push**

Other ways of saying pull

If someone is pulling something heavy, you could use the verbs **drag** or **haul**:

She ***dragged*** *the canoe down to the water.*

They ***hauled*** *the boat out of the water.*

If a vehicle is pulling another vehicle behind it, the word **tow** is used:

You shouldn't drive fast when your car is ***towing*** *a trailer.*

Yank is used in informal language when someone pulls something very quickly and hard:

She marched to the door and ***yanked*** *it open.*

You could use the verb **wrench** when someone pulls something violently from its position:

The phone had been ***wrenched*** *from the wall.*

If you pull something several times with your fingers, the verbs **pull at** or **pluck at** are often used. If you do it hard, you could use **tug at**:

The child ***pulled at*** *my sleeve to catch my attention.*

I felt a small hand ***plucking at*** *my jacket.*

Tom ***tugged at*** *the doorknob.*

IDIOMS **like pulling teeth** If you say that making someone do something was like pulling teeth, you mean it was very difficult and they did not want to do it: *Getting her to tell me about her childhood was like pulling teeth.* • **not pull any/your punches** to speak in an honest way without trying to be kind: *Her image is that of an investigative reporter who doesn't pull any punches.* • **pull sth out of the bag/hat** to do something unexpected that suddenly improves a bad situation • **pull your socks up** UK informal to make an effort to improve your work or behaviour because it is not good enough: *He's going to have to pull his socks up if he wants to stay in the team.* • **pull sb up short** to surprise someone, often so that they stop what they are doing: *Seeing her picture in the paper pulled me up short.* • **pull your weight** (C2) to work as hard as other people in a group: *The others had complained that Sarah wasn't pulling her weight.* • **pull a fast one** informal to successfully deceive someone: *It's never worth that much – I think he pulled a fast one* **on** *you.* • **pull a gun, knife, etc. on sb** to suddenly take out a weapon and threaten someone with it • **pull out all the stops** to do everything you can to make something successful: *They pulled out all the stops for their daughter's wedding.* • **pull rank** to use the power that your position gives you over someone in order to make them do what you want:

P

He doesn't have the authority to pull rank ***on*** *me.* • **pull strings** C2 to secretly use the influence you have over important people in order to get something or to help someone: *I may be able to pull a few strings if you need the document urgently.* • **pull the other leg/one (it's got bells on)!** UK informal humorous used when you do not believe what someone has just said: *Helen, mountain climbing? Pull the other one – she can't even climb a ladder without feeling sick!* • **pull the plug** to do something that prevents an activity from continuing, especially to stop giving money: *If the viewing figures drop much further, the TV network will probably pull the plug* ***on*** *the whole series.* • **pull the rug from under sb's feet** to suddenly take away help or support from someone, or to suddenly do something that causes many problems for them • **pull the strings** to be in control of an organization, often secretly: *I want to know who's pulling the strings around here.* • **pull up short** to stop suddenly in a vehicle: *A dog suddenly ran across the road and I had to pull up short.*

PHRASAL VERBS **pull sth/sb apart** to separate two things or people: *They went for each other with their fists and had to be pulled apart.* • **pull sth apart** **DESTROY** ▷ **1** to destroy something by tearing it into pieces **CRITICIZE** ▷ **2** to say that something, usually a piece of work, is very bad: *The last essay I gave him he completely pulled apart.* • **pull at sth** to pull something quickly and usually repeatedly: *The child pulled at his sleeve to get his attention.* ◦ *He pulled at his ear as he spoke.* • **pull away** **VEHICLE** ▷ **1** If a vehicle pulls away, it starts moving: *There was a roar and a cloud of smoke as the car pulled away from the traffic lights.* **PERSON** ▷ **2** If you pull away from someone who is holding you, you suddenly move your body backwards, away from them: *She pulled away just as he was about to kiss her.* • **pull back (from sth)** mainly US to decide not to do or involve yourself with something when you were previously going to: *The news is that the company intends to pull back from petrochemicals.* • **pull sth back** mainly UK If a team that is losing pulls a goal back or pulls points back, it scores a goal or wins some points. • **pull sth down** B2 to destroy a building: *They pulled down the warehouse to build a new supermarket.* • **pull down sth** US informal to earn a stated amount of money: *Between them they must be pulling down over $100,000 a year.* • **pull in/pull into somewhere** B2 If a vehicle pulls in or pulls into somewhere, it moves in that direction and stops there: *He pulled in at the side of the road.* ◦ *I pulled into the empty parking space.* • **pull sb in** mainly US informal If the police pull you in, they arrest you: *The police pulled in dozens of protesters during the demonstration.* • **pull sth off** informal to succeed in doing something difficult or unexpected: *The central bank has pulled off one of the biggest financial rescues of recent years.* • **pull off** UK If a vehicle pulls off, it starts moving: *The car pulled off and sped up the road.* • **pull sth on** to put on clothes quickly: *I pulled on my jeans and ran downstairs.* • **pull on** Indian English **1** to manage or deal with a situation: *Few of us can ever pull on with such meagre salaries.* **2** to have a friendly relationship with someone: *Radha and Rema come from different backgrounds but they pull on very well in office.* • **pull out** B2 If a vehicle pulls out, it starts moving onto a road or onto a different part of the road: *A car pulled right out in front of me.* • **pull (sb/sth) out** **AREA** ▷ **1** If soldiers or military forces pull out or are pulled out, they move out of an area because they have been ordered to. **ACTIVITY** ▷ **2** to stop being involved in an activity or agreement: *He pulled out* ***of*** *the deal at the last moment.* ◦ *They've pulled all their athletes out of the competition.* • **pull over** B2 If a vehicle pulls over, it moves to the side of the road and stops: *Just pull over here, and I'll get out and walk the rest of the way.* • **pull through (sth)** to become well again after a serious illness, especially when you might have died: *They said the operation had been successful and they expected his wife to pull through.* • **pull (sb) through (sth)** to succeed in dealing with a difficult period, or to help someone do this: *He'd never have managed on his own, but his colleagues have pulled him through.* ◦ *It was a crisis year for the company, but we have pulled through.* • **pull yourself together** to become calm and behave normally again after being angry or upset: *Just pull yourself together. There's no point crying about it.* • **pull together** to work hard as a group in order to achieve something: *We don't have much time but if we all pull together we should get the job done.* • **pull sb up** to tell someone that they have done something wrong: *She's always pulling me up* ***for/over*** *my bad spelling.* • **pull up** B2 When a car or someone driving a car pulls up, the driver stops the car, often for a short time: *A car pulled up outside my house.*

▸noun **MOVEMENT TOWARDS YOU** ▷ **1** [C usually singular] the act of pulling something towards yourself: ***Give*** *the rope a hard pull.* **2** [C] something that you pull to make something work or to open something: *a curtain pull* ◦ *a drawer pull* **ATTRACTION** ▷ **3** [C] something that attracts people: *'How can we persuade people to come to the meeting?' 'A glass of wine is quite a good pull.'* **4** [U] the physical or emotional power to attract something: *The greater the mass of an object, the greater its gravitational pull.* ◦ *The movie's all-star cast should give it a lot of pull.* **INFLUENCE** ▷ **5** [U] influence: *He's still got quite a bit of pull in the club – he could probably get you elected.*

IDIOM **be on the pull** UK informal to be trying to find someone to have sex with: *Michael was out on the pull again last night.*

ˈpull ˌdate noun [C] US for **sell-by date**

ˈpull-down ˌmenu noun [C] a list of instructions on a computer screen, which you cannot see until you choose to see it: *Click 'Tools', then select 'Options' from the pull-down menu.*

pulley /ˈpʊl.i/ noun [C] a piece of equipment for moving heavy objects up or down, consisting of a small wheel over which a rope or chain fixed to the object can be easily pulled or released slowly: *The blocks of stone had to be lifted into position with a system of pulleys.*

ˈpull-in noun [C] UK informal (US **ˈrest ˌstop**) a place at the side of a road where vehicles can stop and where it is sometimes possible to buy food and drinks

ˈpulling ˌpower noun [U] the ability to attract people: *Circuses don't seem to have much pulling power these days.*

Pullman /ˈpʊl.mən/ noun [C] (also **ˈPullman ˌcar**, **ˈPullman ˌcarriage**) a LUXURY (= expensive and comfortable) CARRIAGE of a train, especially one for sleeping or eating in: *The vehicle had brass and mahogany fittings, like a Pullman carriage.*

pullout /ˈpʊl.aʊt/ noun; adj

▸noun **PAGES** ▷ **1** [C] (also **pullout section**) in a magazine or newspaper, a set of pages that are intended to be taken out and used separately: *a 16-page pullout* **REMOVING** ▷ **2** [C usually singular] the process of removing soldiers from an area where there has been fighting

▸adj **pullout bed, table, etc.** a piece of furniture that

P

can be pulled into position when you want to use it and folded away when you do not

pullover /ˈpʊlˌəʊ.vəʳ/ US /-ˌoʊ.vɚ/ noun [C] mainly UK (US usually **sweater**) B1 a piece of clothing, usually made of a warm material such as wool and worn over the top part of the body, that has long sleeves and is put on by pulling it over your head

ˈ**pull-tab** noun [C] US for **ring pull**

pulmonary /ˈpʊl.mə.nə.ri/ US /-ner.i/ adj specialized relating to the LUNGS (= organs used for breathing): *the pulmonary artery*

pulp /pʌlp/ noun; verb

▸noun **WET SUBSTANCE** ▷ **1** [S or U] a soft, wet mass: *Mash the bananas* ***to a*** *pulp and then mix in the yogurt.* **2** [U] small pieces of paper, cloth, or wood mixed with water until they form a soft wet mass, used for making paper: *wood pulp* ◦ *a pulp mill* **BOOKS** ▷ **3** [U] disapproving books and magazines that are of low quality in the way they are produced and the stories and articles they contain: *pulp fiction*

IDIOM **beat sb to a pulp** informal to hit someone repeatedly until they are badly injured

▸verb [T] to make something into a pulp: *Old newspapers are pulped and recycled.*

pulpit /ˈpʊl.pɪt/ noun [C] a raised place in a church, with steps leading up to it, from which the priest speaks to the people during a religious ceremony

pulpit

pulsar /ˈpʌl.sɑːʳ/ US /-sɑːr/ noun [C] specialized a very small DENSE (= heavy in relation to its size) star that sends out radio waves

pulsate /pʌlˈseɪt/ US /ˈpʌl.seɪt/ verb [I] to beat or move with a strong, regular rhythm: *The whole room was pulsating* ***with*** *music.* • **pulsation** /pʌlˈseɪ.ʃən/ noun [C or U]

pulsating /pʌlˈseɪ.tɪŋ/ US /ˈpʌl.seɪ.t̬ɪŋ/ adj very interesting and exciting: *Rue St. Denis is the pulsating heart of French street life in Montreal.*

pulse /pʌls/ noun; verb

▸noun **REGULAR BEAT** ▷ **1** C1 [C] the regular beating of the heart, especially when it is felt at the wrist or side of the neck: *The child's pulse was* ***strong/weak.*** ◦ *Exercise increases your pulse* ***rate.*** **2 take sb's pulse** to hold someone's wrist and count how many times their heart beats in one minute **3** [C] a short period of energy that is repeated regularly, such as a short, loud sound or a short flash of light: *The data, normally transmitted electronically, can be changed into pulses of light.* **FOOD** ▷ **4 pulses** [plural] specialized seeds such as beans or PEAS that are cooked and eaten: *Pulses include peas, lentils, and chickpeas.*

IDIOMS **have/keep your finger on the pulse** C2 to be/stay familiar with the most recent changes or improvements: *The situation changes daily, so you've got to keep your finger on the pulse.* • **set your pulse racing** (also **quicken your pulse**) to make you excited: *This is a movie that will set your pulse racing.*

▸verb [I] to move or beat with a strong, regular rhythm: *I could feel the blood pulsing through my veins.*

pulverize (UK usually **pulverise**) /ˈpʌl.vᵊr.aɪz/ US /-və.raɪz/ verb [T] **1** to press or crush something until it becomes powder or a soft mass: *pulverized coal/bones* **2** informal to defeat someone easily • **pulverization** (UK usually **pulverisation**) /ˌpʌl.vᵊr.aɪˈzeɪ.ʃən/ US /-vɚ.ə-/ noun [U]

puma /ˈpjuː.mə/ US /ˈpuː.mə/ noun [C] mainly UK (mainly US **cougar**) a large, brown wild cat that lives in North and South America

pumice (stone) /ˈpʌm.ɪsˌstəʊn/ US /-ˌstoʊn/ noun [C or U] a type of grey, light stone that is used in pieces or as a powder for rubbing things to make them smooth: *Pumice is produced in volcanic eruptions.*

pummel /ˈpʌm.ᵊl/ verb [T] (-ll- or US usually -l-) **1** to hit someone or something repeatedly, especially with your FISTS (= closed hands): *The boxer had pummelled his opponent* ***into*** *submission by the end of the fourth round.* **2** informal to defeat someone easily at a sport: *They were pummelled in the second round.* • **pummelling** (US usually **pummeling**) /-ɪŋ/ noun [C]

pump /pʌmp/ noun; verb

▸noun [C] **DEVICE** ▷ **1** B1 a piece of equipment that is used to cause liquid, air, or gas to move from one place to another: *a water/bicycle/fuel pump* ◦ *a* ***petrol*** *(US* ***gas****) pump* **SHOE** ▷ **2** [usually plural] a type of flat shoe, like a BALLET dancer's shoe, worn by women **3** [usually plural] US (UK **court shoe**) a type of plain shoe with a raised HEEL and no way of fastening it to the foot, worn by women **4** [usually plural] UK a flat shoe made of heavy cloth, worn by children for doing sports

▸verb **LIQUID/GAS** ▷ **1** [T usually + adv/prep] to force liquid or gas to move somewhere: *Our latest machine can pump a hundred gallons a minute.* ◦ *The new wine is pumped* ***into*** *storage tanks.* ◦ *The heart pumps blood* ***through*** *the arteries/****round*** *the body.* **INFORMATION** ▷ **2** [T] informal to keep asking someone for information, especially in a way that is not direct: *She was pumping me* ***for*** *details of the new project.*

IDIOMS **pump sb's hand** to SHAKE someone's hand (= hold their hand and move it up and down, especially in order to greet them) • **pump iron** informal to lift heavy weights for exercise: *These days both men and women pump iron for fitness.*

PHRASAL VERBS **pump sth into sth** to spend a lot of money trying to make something operate successfully: *They had been pumping money into the business for some years without seeing any results.* • **pump sth out REMOVE** ▷ **1** to remove water or other liquid from something using a pump: *We took turns pumping out the boat.* **PRODUCE** ▷ **2** informal disapproving to produce words or loud music in a way that is repeated, forceful, and continuous: *The government keeps pumping out the same old propaganda.* ◦ *The car radio was pumping out music with a heavy beat.* • **pump out sth** If someone's stomach is pumped out, a poisonous substance is removed from it by being sucked through a tube: *She had to go to hospital to have her stomach pumped out.* • **pump sb up** informal to make someone feel more confident or excited: *He was offering them advice and trying to pump them up.* ◦ *The players were pumping them****selves*** *up by singing the national anthem before the game.* • **pump sth up 1** to fill something with air using a pump: *Have you pumped up the balloons yet?* ◦ *I must pump the tyres up on my bike.* **2** informal to increase something by a large amount: *The US was able to pump up exports.* ◦ *Let's pump up the volume a bit!*

ˈ**pump-action** adj [before noun] describes a device which operates by forcing something, especially air, in or out of a closed space or container: *a pump-action shotgun* ◦ *a pump-action toilet*

pumpernickel /ˈpʌm.pəˌnɪk.l̩/ US /-pɚ-/ noun [U] a

P

type of firm, dark brown bread made from RYE (= a type of grain)

pumpkin /ˈpʌmp.kɪn/ noun [C or U] a large, round vegetable with hard yellow or orange flesh: *pumpkin pie*

ˈpump-ˌpriming noun [U] specialized the activity of helping a business, programme, economy, etc. to develop by giving it money: *The government is awarding small, pump-priming grants to single mothers who are starting their own businesses.*

pun /pʌn/ noun; verb

▸noun [C] a humorous use of a word or phrase that has several meanings or that sounds like another word: *She **made** a couple of dreadful puns.* ◦ *This is a well-known joke based on a pun: 'What's black and white and red (= read) all over?' 'A newspaper.'*

▸verb [I] (**-nn-**) to make a pun

punch /pʌntʃ/ noun; verb

▸noun **HIT** ▷ **1** B2 [C] a forceful hit with a FIST (= closed hand): *She **gave** him a punch **on** (US **in**) the nose.* **EFFECT** ▷ **2** [U] the power to be interesting and have a strong effect on people: *I felt the performance/speech/presentation **lacked** punch.* **DRINK** ▷ **3** [C or U] a cold or hot drink made by mixing fruit juices, pieces of fruit, and often wine or other alcoholic drinks **TOOL** ▷ **4** [C] a piece of equipment which cuts holes in a material by pushing a piece of metal through it: *a ticket punch* ◦ *Have you seen the **hole** punch anywhere?*

▸verb [T] **HIT** ▷ **1** B2 to hit someone or something with your FIST (= closed hand): *He punched him **in** the stomach.* **2** mainly US to hit with your fingers the buttons on a phone or the keys on a keyboard **USE TOOL** ▷ **3** to make a hole in something with a special piece of equipment: *I was just punching holes in some sheets of paper.* ◦ *This belt's too big – I'll have to punch an extra hole in it.*

IDIOMS **punch sb's lights out** informal to hit someone repeatedly very hard • **punch the clock** US to put a card into a special machine to record the times you arrive at and leave work: *After 17 years of punching the clock, he just disappeared one morning and was never heard from again.*

Punch and Judy show /ˌpʌntʃ.ənˈdʒuː.diˌʃəʊ/ US /-ˌʃoʊ/ noun [C] a traditional children's entertainment in which a man, Mr Punch, argues with his wife, Judy. It was especially popular in the past as an entertainment in British towns by the sea in summer.

punchball /ˈpʌntʃ.bɔːl/ US /-bɑːl/ noun [C] UK (US **ˈpunching ˌbag**) a leather bag filled with air, hung from a frame or fixed to a stand and used by BOXERS for training or exercise

ˈpunch ˌbowl noun [C] a large bowl in which PUNCH (= a drink) is served

ˈpunch-drunk adj **INJURED** ▷ **1** describes a BOXER who behaves in a way that suggests his brain has been damaged as a result of being hit repeatedly on the head **TIRED** ▷ **2** tired and confused, especially after dealing with a difficult situation

punchline /ˈpʌntʃ.laɪn/ noun [C] the last part of a story or a joke that explains the meaning of what has happened previously or makes it funny

ˈpunch-up noun [C] mainly UK informal a fight: *There was a punch-up in the bar.*

punchy /ˈpʌn.tʃi/ adj expressing something effectively and with power: *a short punchy presentation/speech* ◦ *The article is written in his usual punchy style.*

punctilious /pʌŋkˈtɪl.i.əs/ adj formal very careful to behave correctly or to give attention to details: *He was always punctilious in his manners.* • **punctiliously** /-li/ adv • **punctiliousness** /-nəs/ noun [U]

punctual /ˈpʌŋk.tju.əl/ adj arriving, doing something, or happening at the expected, correct time; not late: *a punctual start to the meeting* ◦ *He's fairly punctual (= he usually arrives on time).* • **punctuality** /ˌpʌŋk.tjuˈæl.ɪ.ti/ US /-ə.t̬i/ noun [U] *Punctuality has never been his strong point.* • **punctually** /-ə.li/ adv *The meeting started punctually at 10.00 a.m.*

punctuate /ˈpʌŋk.tju.eɪt/ US /-tuː-/ verb [T] **1** formal to happen or cause something to happen repeatedly while something else is happening; to interrupt something repeatedly: *The president spoke at length in a speech punctuated **by** applause.* ◦ *He chatted freely, punctuating his remarks as often as possible **with** the interviewer's first name.* **2** to add PUNCTUATION MARKS (= symbols) to writing so that people can see when a sentence starts and finishes, see that something is a question, etc.

punctuation /ˌpʌŋk.tjuˈeɪ.ʃən/ noun [U] B1 (the use of) special symbols that you add to writing to separate phrases and sentences, to show that something is a question, etc.: *His letter was completely without punctuation.*

punctuˈation ˌmark noun [C] a symbol used in PUNCTUATION: *Full stops, commas, colons, and brackets are all different types of punctuation mark.*

puncture /ˈpʌŋk.tʃər/ US /-tʃɚ/ noun; verb

▸noun [C] a small hole made by a sharp object, especially in a tyre: *My bike has **had** two punctures in the last three weeks.* ◦ *I (= my car tyre) **had** a puncture when I was driving back from work.* ◦ *She had a puncture wound in her arm, from a wasp sting.*

▸verb **1** [I or T] to make a small hole in something, or to get a small hole in something: *She had used a screwdriver to puncture two holes in the lid of a paint tin.* ◦ *The knife went through his ribs and punctured his lung.* **2** [T] to suddenly make someone less confident or positive: *My positive mood was rather punctured by the news.*

pundit /ˈpʌn.dɪt/ noun [C] **1** a person who knows a lot about a particular subject and is therefore often asked to give an opinion about it: *a political/foreign-policy/sports pundit* **2** Indian English **pandit**

pungent /ˈpʌn.dʒənt/ adj **1** describes a very strong smell or taste, sometimes one that is unpleasantly strong: *the pungent whiff of a goat* ◦ *I sat down to a cup of wonderfully pungent Turkish coffee.* **2** literary describes speech or writing that is very strongly felt: *pungent criticism/commentary* • **pungency** /-dʒən.si/ noun [U] • **pungently** /-li/ adv

punish /ˈpʌn.ɪʃ/ verb [T] **CRIME** ▷ **1** B1 to cause someone who has done something wrong or committed a crime to suffer, by hurting them, forcing them to pay money, sending them to prison, etc.: *Those responsible for these crimes must be brought to court and punished.* ◦ *He punished the class **by** giving them extra work.* ◦ *The oil company was found guilty on ten counts of pollution, and was punished **with** a $250 million fine.* → See also **punitive 2** to punish anyone who commits a particular crime: *Drunken driving can be punished **with** a prison sentence.*

punishable /ˈpʌn.ɪ.ʃə.bl̩/ adj describes a crime that you can be punished for: *a punishable offence* ◦ *Drug dealing is punishable **by death** in some countries.*

punishing /ˈpʌn.ɪ.ʃɪŋ/ adj; noun

▸adj very difficult and making you feel tired: *Currently she has a punishing **schedule** of five presentations a day.* • **punishingly** /-li/ adv *a punishingly heavy workload (= a very large amount of work)*

▸noun informal **take a punishing** to be damaged because of rough treatment: *My tyres took quite a punishing on the rough terrain.*

punishment /ˈpʌn.ɪʃ.mənt/ noun **CRIME** ▷ **1** B2 [C or U] the act of punishing someone: *Many people think that the death penalty is too severe a punishment **for** any crime.* ◦ formal *It was always our father who **administered/meted** out punishments.* ◦ *Drink-driving is one case where severe punishment seems to work as a deterrent.* **BAD TREATMENT** ▷ **2** [U] rough treatment: *These trucks are designed to take a lot of punishment.*

> Word partners for **punishment**
>
> *deserve* punishment • *avoid/escape* punishment • *impose/inflict/mete out* punishment • *get/receive* a punishment • an *appropriate/cruel/harsh/severe* punishment • punishment *for* sth • do sth *as* a punishment • a *form* of punishment

punitive /ˈpjuː.nɪ.tɪv/ (US) /-t̬ɪv/ adj **1** formal intended as a punishment: *punitive action* ◦ *The UN has imposed punitive sanctions on the invading country.* ◦ legal *She is suing the newspaper for $5 million punitive **damages**, claiming they knew the article about her was untrue.* **2** used to describe costs that are so high they are difficult to pay: *The president has threatened to impose punitive import duties/tariffs on a range of foreign goods.* • **punitively** /-li/ adv

punk /pʌŋk/ noun; adj

▸noun **CULTURE** ▷ **1** [U] a culture popular among young people, especially in the late 1970s, involving opposition to authority expressed through shocking behaviour, clothes, and hair, and fast, loud music **2** [C] (also **punk rocker**) a person who wears punk clothes and likes punk music **CRIMINAL** ▷ **3** [C] mainly US slang a young man who fights and is involved in criminal activities: *Listen to me, you little punk – you do that again and I'm gonna break your neck.*

▸adj [before noun] of or relating to punk or punk rockers: *a punk band* ◦ *a punk hairstyle*

ˌpunk ˈrock noun [U] a type of fast, loud, often offensive music that was originally popular among young people in the late 1970s

punnet /ˈpʌn.ɪt/ noun [C] UK a small square or rectangular box in which particular types of fruit are sold: *a punnet **of** strawberries/raspberries*

punster /ˈpʌn.stəʳ/ (US) /-stɚ/ noun [C] a person who makes PUNS (= type of joke)

punt /pʌnt/ noun; verb

punt

▸noun [C] **BOAT** ▷ **1** a long, narrow boat with a flat bottom and a square area at each end, moved by a person standing on one of the square areas and pushing a long pole against the bottom of the river **KICK** ▷ **2** a way of kicking the ball in RUGBY or American football, by dropping it from your hands and kicking it before it hits the ground, or a powerful kick in football that causes the ball to go a long way **RISK** ▷ **3 take a punt on sth** to risk money by buying or supporting something, in the hope of making or winning more money: *It might be a good idea to take a punt on a few technology stocks.* **MONEY** ▷ **4** (also **Irish pound**) the standard unit of money used in Ireland before the introduction of the euro

▸verb **KICK** ▷ **1** [T] (in RUGBY or American football) to kick the ball after you have dropped it from your hands and before it touches the ground, or (in football) to kick the ball powerfully so that it goes a long way **2** [T] US informal If you punt something, you decide not to do or include it: *We were running out of time, so we decided to punt the sightseeing and just go shopping.* **BOAT** ▷ **3** [I or T] to travel in a punt: *We punted up the river.* ◦ *It's a lovely afternoon – let's **go** punting.*

PHRASAL VERB **punt on sth 1** informal to risk money by buying or supporting something, in the hope of making or winning more money: *Traders are punting on a big move on the stock markets next week.* **2** US informal If you punt on something, you decide not to do or include it: *We punted on a motion that makes no sense.*

punter /ˈpʌn.təʳ/ (US) /-t̬ɚ/ noun [C] **GAMBLER** ▷ **1** UK specialized a person who risks money guessing the result of something: *Bookmakers are offering punters odds of 6–1 on the horse Red Devil winning the race.* **CUSTOMER** ▷ **2** UK informal a customer; a user of services or buyer of goods: *Many hotels are offering discounts in an attempt to attract punters/pull in the punters.* **3** UK slang a person who uses the services of a PROSTITUTE **BOAT** ▷ **4** a person who travels in a PUNT

puny /ˈpjuː.ni/ adj small; weak; not effective: *a puny little man* ◦ *My car only has a puny little engine.* ◦ *The party's share of the vote rose from a puny 13 percent in the last election to 21 percent this time.*

pup /pʌp/ noun [C] a baby of particular animals, or a PUPPY: *a seal pup* ◦ *an otter pup*

pupa /ˈpjuː.pə/ noun [C] (plural **pupae** /-piː/) an insect in the stage of development that happens before it is completely developed, during which it is contained and protected by a hard covering called a COCOON and does not move: *a moth pupa* ◦ *mosquito pupae* → See also **chrysalis** • **pupal** /-pəl/ adj *the pupal **stage** of development*

pupil /ˈpjuː.pəl/ noun [C] **STUDENT** ▷ **1** A2 a person, especially a child at school, who is being taught: *a second-year pupil* ◦ *a primary-school pupil* ◦ *The school has over 400 pupils.* ◦ *There is a very relaxed atmosphere between staff and pupils at the school.* **2** someone who is being taught a skill, especially painting or music, by an expert: *The painting is believed to be by a pupil of Titian.* **EYE PART** ▷ **3** the circular black area in the centre of your eye, through which light enters: *Pupils contract in bright light, and dilate in darkness.*

puppet /ˈpʌp.ɪt/ noun [C] **1** a toy in the shape of a person or animal that you can move with strings or by putting your hand inside: *We took the children to a puppet **show/theatre**.* **2** disapproving a person or group whose actions are controlled by someone else: *Western powers have been accused of trying to establish a puppet **government/regime** in the divided country.*

puppeteer /ˌpʌp.ɪˈtɪəʳ/ (US) /-əˈtɪr/ noun [C] a person who entertains with puppets

puppy /ˈpʌp.i/ noun [C] (also **pup**) B1 a young dog: *Our dog has just had four puppies.* ◦ *a dalmatian puppy*

ˈpuppy ˌfat noun [U] UK (US **ˈbaby ˌfat**) fat that a child sometimes has that disappears as the child grows older: *He's a little overweight but it's just puppy fat.*

ˈpuppy ˌlove noun [U] romantic love that a young person feels for someone else, that usually disappears as the young person becomes older

ˈpup ˌtent noun [C] US a small tent for two people

purchase /ˈpɜː.tʃəs/ (US) /ˈpɝː-/ verb; noun

▸verb [T] formal B2 to buy something: *Tickets must be purchased two weeks in advance.* ◦ *Except under clearly defined circumstances, it is illegal in Britain for a company to purchase its own shares.* ◦ *She purchased her first house **with** the money.*

P

▸noun formal **BUYING** ▷ **1** B2 [C] something that you buy: *How do you wish to pay for your purchases?* ◦ *a major purchase* **2** B2 [C or U] the act of buying something: *New restrictions have been placed on the purchase **of** guns.* ◦ *A house is the most expensive purchase that most people ever **make**.* ◦ *No purchase is necessary for you to enter this competition.* ◦ *This product may be frozen. If required, freeze on day of purchase.* **HOLD** ▷ **3** [S or U] a firm hold which allows someone or something to be pulled or lifted without sliding or falling: *Dancers use a special powder on their shoes to help them **get** a better purchase **on** the floor.*

purchaser /ˈpɜː.tʃə.səʳ/ US /ˈpɝː.tʃə.sɚ/ noun [C] formal the person who buys something: *We haven't been able to find a purchaser **for** our house yet.*

ˈpurchasing ˌpower noun [U] **1** A person's purchasing power is their ability to buy goods: *The purchasing power **of** people living on investment income has fallen as interest rates have gone down.* **2** the value of money considered as the amount of goods it will buy: *The purchasing power **of** the average hourly wage has risen in the last five years.*

purdah /ˈpɜː.də/ US /ˈpɝː-/ noun [U] **1** (the condition of following) the custom, found in some Muslim and Hindu cultures, of women not allowing their faces to be seen by men they are not related to, either by staying in a special part of the house or by wearing a covering over their faces: *The women in the village live **in** (**strict**) purdah.* ◦ *In this region women seldom venture **out of** purdah.* **2** the state of not seeing or speaking to anyone: *Jeff has **gone into** purdah while he's preparing for his exams.*

pure /pjʊəʳ/ US /pjʊr/ adj **NOT MIXED** ▷ **1** B1 not mixed with anything else: *a pure cotton shirt* ◦ *pure orange juice* ◦ *pure English honey* ◦ *a pure Arab horse* **2** describes a colour that is not mixed with any other colour: *a swan's pure white plumage* **3** describes a sound that is clear and perfect: *the pure vocal tones of the choirboy* **4** B1 clean and free from harmful substances: *The mountain air was wonderfully pure.* ◦ *Tap water is never chemically pure.* → Opposite **impure** **COMPLETE** ▷ **5** B2 [before noun] complete; only: *It was pure coincidence/chance that we met.* ◦ *This last month has been pure hell.* ◦ *Her face had a look of pure delight.* ◦ *The minister dismissed the newspaper reports as pure speculation.* **6** [before noun] describes an area of study that is studied only for the purpose of developing theories about it, not for the purpose of using those theories in a practical way: *pure mathematics* ◦ *pure economics* **7 pure and simple** used after a noun to mean 'and nothing else': *He is motivated by greed, pure and simple.* **MORALLY GOOD** ▷ **8** behaving in a way that is morally completely good, or not having sex: *I'm trying to think only pure thoughts.* ◦ *He invited me up to his flat for coffee, but I didn't think that his motives were entirely pure.* ◦ *In many cultures, it is considered important for a woman to keep herself pure (= not to have sex) until she marries.* → Opposite **impure**

IDIOM **be as pure as the driven snow** to be morally completely good: *How dare he criticize me for having an affair? He's not exactly as pure as the driven snow himself.*

purebred /ˈpjʊə.bred/ US /ˈpjʊr-/ adj (of an animal or type of animal) with parents that are both of the same breed: *purebred cattle* ◦ *a purebred stallion* → See also **thoroughbred**

purée /ˈpjʊə.reɪ/ US /ˌpjʊˈreɪ/ verb; noun
▸verb [T] (past tense and past participle **puréeing**) to make fruit or vegetables into a thick, smooth sauce by crushing them, usually in a machine: *Purée the strawberries in the liquidizer and add the lightly whipped cream.* ◦ *The first solid food she gave her baby was puréed carrot.*
▸noun [C or U] a thick, smooth sauce made by crushing fruit or vegetables: *apple purée* ◦ *Add two tablespoonsful of tomato purée.*

purely /ˈpjʊə.li/ US /ˈpjʊr-/ adv **1** C1 only: *On a purely practical level, it is difficult to see how such proposals would work.* ◦ *We made this decision purely for financial reasons.* **2 purely and simply** for only one reason or purpose: *They decided to close the museum purely and simply because it cost too much to run.*

purgative /ˈpɜː.ɡə.tɪv/ US /ˈpɝː.ɡə.t̬ɪv/ noun [C] a substance that makes you empty your bowels → See also **laxative** • **purgative** adj *Prunes can have a purgative effect.*

purgatory /ˈpɜː.ɡə.tᵊr.i/ US /ˈpɝː.ɡə.tɔːr.i/ noun [U] **1** the place to which Roman Catholics believe that the spirits of dead people go and suffer for the evil acts that they did while they were alive, before they are able to go to heaven **2** humorous an extremely unpleasant experience that causes suffering: *I've been on a diet for two weeks now, and it's purgatory!*

purge /pɜːdʒ/ US /pɝːdʒ/ verb; noun
▸verb [T] **REMOVE PEOPLE** ▷ **1** to get rid of people from an organization because you do not agree with them: *Party leaders have undertaken to purge the party **of** extremists.* ◦ *Hard-liners are expected to be purged **from** the administration.* **REMOVE EVIL** ▷ **2** to make someone or something free of something evil or harmful: *Roman Catholics go to confession to purge their souls/them**selves** (**from/of** sin).* ◦ *The new state governor has promised to purge the police force **of** corruption.*
▸noun [C] the act of getting rid of people from an organization because you do not agree with them: *Between 1934 and 1938, Stalin mounted a massive purge **of** the Communist Party, the government and the armed forces in the Soviet Union.*

purification /ˌpjʊə.rɪ.fɪˈkeɪ.ʃᵊn/ US /ˌpjʊr-/ noun [U] **NOT MIXED** ▷ **1** the act of removing harmful substances from something: *a water purification plant* ◦ *an air purification system* **MORALLY GOOD** ▷ **2** in some religions, the act of removing from a person, usually by a ceremony, the bad effects that they are suffering because they have broken a religious or moral law

purifier /ˈpjʊə.rɪ.faɪ.əʳ/ US /ˈpjʊr.ɪ.faɪ.ɚ/ noun [C] a machine or a substance which removes harmful substances from something: *a water purifier*

purify /ˈpjʊə.rɪ.faɪ/ US /ˈpjʊr-/ verb [T] **NOT MIXED** ▷ **1** to remove bad substances from something to make it pure: *Plants help to purify the air.* ◦ *One of the functions of the kidneys is to purify the blood.* ◦ *water-purifying tablets* **MORALLY GOOD** ▷ **2** to remove IMMORAL thoughts or acts from something: *One of the main teachings of Buddhism is that you should try to purify your mind.*

purist /ˈpjʊə.rɪst/ US /ˈpjʊr.ɪst/ noun [C] someone who believes in and follows very traditional rules or ideas in a subject: *Although purists may object to split infinitives, like 'to boldly go', the fact is, they are commonly used.* ◦ *Purists eat smoked salmon with nothing more than lemon and black pepper.* • **purism** /ˈpjʊə.rɪ.zᵊm/ US /ˈpjʊr.ɪ-/ noun [U]

puritan /ˈpjʊə.rɪ.tᵊn/ US /ˈpjʊr.ɪ.t̬ᵊn/ noun [C] someone who believes that it is important to work hard and control yourself, and that pleasure is wrong or unnecessary: *Despite his apparent liberal views, he's really something of a puritan/he has a puritan streak.*

Puritan /ˈpjʊə.rɪ.tᵊn/ ⓤⓢ /ˈpjʊr.ɪ.t̬ᵊn/ **noun** [C] a member of an English religious group in the 16th and 17th centuries who wanted to make church ceremonies simpler, and who believed that it was important to work hard and control yourself and that pleasure was wrong or unnecessary: *During the 17th century the Puritans destroyed many decorations in English churches.*

puritanical /ˌpjʊə.rɪˈtæn.ɪ.kᵊl/ ⓤⓢ /ˌpjʊr.ɪ-/ **adj** believing or involving the belief that it is important to work hard and control yourself, and that pleasure is wrong or unnecessary: *He rebelled against his puritanical upbringing.* • **puritanically** /-i/ **adv**

puritanism /ˈpjʊə.rɪ.tᵊn.ɪ.zᵊm/ ⓤⓢ /ˈpjʊr.ɪ.t̬ᵊn-/ **noun** [U] **1** the belief that it is important to work hard and control yourself, and that pleasure is wrong or unnecessary **2 Puritanism** the beliefs and behaviour of a Puritan

purity /ˈpjʊə.rɪ.ti/ ⓤⓢ /ˈpjʊr.ə.t̬i/ **noun** [U] **NOT MIXED** ▷ **1** C1 the state of not being mixed with anything else: *the atrocities carried out in the name of ethnic/racial purity* **2** the clear and perfect quality of a sound: *the purity of her voice* **3** C1 the fact of being clean or free from harmful substances: *air/water purity* **MORALLY GOOD** ▷ **4** the quality of being morally good or the state of not having sex: *the purity and innocence of children* ◦ *For Christians, the Virgin Mary is a symbol of purity.*

purl /pɜːl/ ⓤⓢ /pɝːl/ **noun; verb**

▸**noun** [U] a type of STITCH that you make when you KNIT by putting the needle into the front of the first stitch on the other needle

▸**verb** [I or T] to KNIT a purl STITCH: *Knit one, purl one.*

purloin /pəˈlɔɪn/ ⓤⓢ /pɚ-/ **verb** [T] formal or humorous to steal something: *I was using a pen that I'd purloined **from** the office.*

purple /ˈpɜː.pl̩/ ⓤⓢ /ˈpɝː-/ **adj; noun**

▸**adj COLOUR** ▷ **1** A2 of a dark reddish-blue colour: *purple plums* ◦ *a dark purple bruise* **2 purple in the face/purple with rage** dark red in the face because of anger **STYLE** ▷ **3** UK describes a piece of writing that is complicated or sounds false because the writer has tried too hard to make the style interesting: *Despite occasional patches of purple **prose**, the book is mostly clear and incisive.* • **purpleness** /-nəs/ **noun** [U]

▸**noun** [C or U] A2 a dark reddish-blue colour: *Purple is my favourite colour.* ◦ *The evening sky was full of purples and reds.*

ˌPurple ˈHeart noun [C] an American MEDAL given to soldiers who have been injured in war

purplish /ˈpɜː.pl.ɪʃ/, /-plɪʃ/ ⓤⓢ /ˈpɝː-/ **adj** almost purple in colour: *He has a purplish birthmark on his cheek.*

purport verb; noun

▸**verb** [T + to infinitive] /pəˈpɔːt/ ⓤⓢ /pɝːˈpɔːrt/ formal to pretend to be or to do something, especially in a way that is not easy to believe: *They purport **to** represent the wishes of the majority of parents at the school.* ◦ *The study purports **to** show an increase in the incidence of the disease.*

▸**noun** [U] /ˈpɜː.pɔːt/ ⓤⓢ /ˈpɝː.pɔːrt/ formal the general meaning of someone's words or actions: *I didn't read it all but I think the purport of the letter was that he will not be returning for at least a year.*

purported /pəˈpɔː.tɪd/ ⓤⓢ /pɝːˈpɔːr.t̬ɪd/ **adj** [before noun] that has been stated to be true or to have happened, although this may not be the case: *A recent study into the purported health benefits of the drink was not conclusive.*

purportedly /pəˈpɔː.tɪd.li/ ⓤⓢ /pɝːˈpɔːr.t̬ɪd-/ **adv** in a way that is stated to be true, although this may not be the case: *The study purportedly found that men married to smart women live longer.*

purpose /ˈpɜː.pəs/ ⓤⓢ /ˈpɝː-/ **noun 1** B1 [C] why you do something or why something exists: *The purpose **of** the research is to try and find out more about the causes of the disease.* ◦ *His only purpose **in life** seems to be to enjoy himself.* ◦ *Her main/primary purpose **in suing** the newspaper for libel was to clear her name.* ◦ *I came to Brighton **for/with** the **express** purpose **of** seeing you.* ◦ *Letters whose **sole** purpose is to make a political point will not be published.* ◦ *She had the operation entirely **for** cosmetic purposes.* ◦ *a multi-purpose kitchen knife* ◦ *I can see no useful purpose in continuing this conversation.* ◦ *All my efforts were **to no** purpose (= failed).* ◦ *He gave her a sum of money which she used **to good** purpose (= well).* **2 on purpose** B1 If you do something on purpose, you do it intentionally, not by accident: *I didn't do it on purpose – it was an accident.* **3** C2 [U] determination or a feeling of having a reason for what you do: *I've always admired her for her strength of purpose.* ◦ *Parenthood would give him **a sense of** purpose.* **4** [C] a need: *We haven't yet managed to find new premises that are suitable for our purposes.* ◦ *The fabric I bought isn't exactly what I wanted, but it will **serve** my purposes (= fulfil my needs).* **5 serve a purpose** C2 to have a use: *These small village shops serve a very useful purpose.*

> **Word partners for purpose**
>
> *have* a purpose • the *main/primary/real* purpose • a *clear/practical/useful* purpose • a *variety* of purposes • the purpose *of* sth • *for* the purpose *of* sth • *for* [business/cosmetic/tax] purposes

ˌpurpose-ˈbuilt adj designed and built for a particular use: *The college was the first purpose-built teacher training college in the country.*

purposeful /ˈpɜː.pəs.fᵊl/ ⓤⓢ /ˈpɝː-/ **adj** showing that you know what you want to do: *He has a quiet, purposeful air.* • **purposefully** /-i/ **adv** *He strode purposefully into the room.* • **purposefulness** /-nəs/ **noun** [U]

purposeless /ˈpɜː.pəs.ləs/ ⓤⓢ /ˈpɝː-/ **adj** done without a clear intention: *a purposeless existence* ◦ *purposeless fighting* • **purposelessly** /-li/ **adv** • **purposelessness** /-nəs/ **noun** [U]

purposely /ˈpɜː.pəs.li/ ⓤⓢ /ˈpɝː-/ **adv** intentionally

purr /pɜː/ ⓤⓢ /pɝː/ **verb; noun**

▸**verb** [I] to make a quiet, continuous, soft sound: *The cat purred as I stroked its fur.* ◦ *We could hear the sound of a lawnmower purring in the back garden.* ◦ *A black limousine purred **up** (= drove up making a quiet, continuous, soft sound) outside the hotel.* ◦ [+ speech] *'I love it when you stroke my back,' she purred (= said with pleasure).*

▸**noun** [S] a purring noise: *I stroked the cat and it gave a low purr.* ◦ *I heard the gentle purr **of** an engine outside the house.*

purse /pɜːs/ ⓤⓢ /pɝːs/ **noun; verb**

▸**noun CONTAINER** ▷ **1** A2 [C] UK a small container for money, usually used by a woman: *a leather purse* → Compare **wallet 2** [C] US for **handbag AMOUNT TO SPEND** ▷ **3** [C usually singular] the total amount of money that an organization or government has available for spending: *Having a lot of people out of work places a large drain on the **public** purse.* **PRIZE** ▷ **4** [C] an amount of money that is offered as a prize in a sports competition: *The players in the golf tournament are competing for a purse **of** £525,000.*

IDIOM **the purse strings** the spending of money by a family, company or country: *A recent survey showed that in 53 percent of families, women **hold** (= control) the purse strings.*

▸verb [T] to bring your lips tightly together so that they form a rounded shape, usually as an expression of disapproval: *'I don't approve of that kind of language,' she said, pursing her lips.*

purser /ˈpɜː.səʳ/ (US) /ˈpɜː.sɚ/ noun [C] an officer on a ship who deals with the ship's accounts, or a person on a passenger ship or aircraft who is responsible for taking care of passengers

pursuance /pəˈsjuː.əns/ (US) /pɚˈsuː-/ noun [U] formal **the pursuance of something** the act of trying to achieve something: *She has devoted herself to the pursuance **of** justice for her son.* ◦ ***In** pursuance **of** his aims, he has decided to stand for parliament.*

pursuant /pəˈsjuː.ənt/ (US) /pɚˈsuː-/ adj [after verb] formal or legal according to: *The fact that a person acted pursuant **to** an order of his government does not relieve him from responsibility under international law.*

pursue /pəˈsjuː/ (US) /pɚˈsuː/ verb [T] **FOLLOW** ▷ **1** to follow someone or something, usually to try to catch or kill them: *The car was pursued by helicopters.* ◦ *The hunters spent hours pursuing their prey.* ◦ *He was killed by the driver of a stolen car who was being **hotly** pursued by the police.* **TRY TO GET** ▷ **2** to try very hard to persuade someone to accept a job: *The company has been pursuing Holton for some time, but so far he has rejected all their offers.* **3** to try to discover information about a subject: *We will not be pursuing this **matter** any further.* ◦ *The police are currently pursuing several lines of inquiry into the case.* ◦ *I don't think this idea is worth pursuing any further.* **4** to try very hard to persuade someone to have a relationship with you: *He's been pursuing her for months and yet she's so clearly not interested.* **TRY TO DO** ▷ **5** (C1) If you pursue a plan, activity, or situation, you try to do it or achieve it, usually over a long period of time: *He decided to pursue a career in television.* ◦ *Michael Evans is leaving the company to pursue his own business interests.* ◦ *She is ruthless in pursuing her goals.*

pursuer /pəˈsjuː.əʳ/ (US) /pɚˈsuː.ɚ/ noun [C] **FOLLOWING** ▷ **1** someone who is chasing you: *She made a sudden right turn off the road in order to escape her pursuers.* ◦ figurative *The team are ten points ahead of their closest pursuers in the league.* **ATTEMPT** ▷ **2** someone who is trying to achieve something: *He described himself as a pursuer **of** truth and justice.*

pursuit /pəˈsjuːt/ (US) /pɚˈsuːt/ noun **ACTIVITY** ▷ **1** [C usually plural] an activity that you spend time doing, usually when you are not working: *I enjoy **outdoor** pursuits, like hiking and riding.* ◦ *I don't have much opportunity for **leisure** pursuits these days.* **FOLLOWING** ▷ **2** [C or U] the act of following someone or something to try to catch them: *Three people have been killed in high-speed pursuits by the police recently.* ◦ *The robbers fled the scene of the crime, with the police **in** pursuit.* **ATTEMPT** ▷ **3** (C2) [U] the act of trying to achieve a plan, activity, or situation, usually over a long period of time: *the pursuit **of** happiness* ◦ *The company is ruthless **in** its pursuit **of** profit.* ◦ *The union is on strike **in** pursuit **of** (= trying to achieve) a ten percent pay increase.*

purvey /pəˈveɪ/ (US) /pɚ-/ verb [T] formal to provide goods or services as a business, or to provide information: *This company has purveyed clothing **to** the armed forces for generations.* ◦ *The prime minister's speech was intended to purvey a message of optimism.*

purveyor /pəˈveɪ.əʳ/ (US) /pɚˈveɪ.ɚ/ noun [C usually plural] formal a business which provides goods or services: *purveyors **of** seafood* ◦ UK *Purveyors of Jams and Marmalades to Her Majesty the Queen*

purview /ˈpɜː.vjuː/ (US) /ˈpɝː-/ noun [U] formal the limit of someone's responsibility, interest, or activity: *This case falls **outside** the purview **of** this particular court.* ◦ *Some of the bank's lending operations come **under/within** the purview **of** the deputy manager, and some are handled directly by the manager.*

pus /pʌs/ noun [U] thick, yellowish liquid that forms in and comes from an infected cut or injury in the body: *a pus-filled wound*

push /pʊʃ/ verb; noun

▸verb **USE PRESSURE** ▷ **1** (A2) [I or T] to use physical pressure or force, especially with your hands, in order to move something into a different position, usually one that is further away from you: *Can you help me move this table? You push and I'll pull.* ◦ *The window sticks – you have to push **hard** to open it.* ◦ *He helped me push my car off the road.* ◦ *He pushed his plate away from him, refusing to eat any more.* ◦ *She pushed her hair out of her eyes.* ◦ *I tried to push the door open but it was stuck.* ◦ *It isn't clear whether he fell off the balcony, or was pushed.* ◦ *To turn the television on, you just push (= press) this button.* ◦ *He pushed the money into my hand (= forcefully gave me the money), saying, 'Please take it.'* **MOVE WITH FORCE** ▷ **2** (B1) [I or T, usually + adv/prep] to move forcefully, especially in order to cause someone or something that is in your way to move, so that you can go through or past them: *Stop pushing – wait your turn.* ◦ *She pushed **through** the crowd.* ◦ *I'm sorry – I didn't mean to push in front of you.* ◦ *The minister pushed past the waiting journalists, refusing to speak to them.* ◦ *In the final lap of the race, he managed to push (= move strongly) **ahead**.* ◦ *Weeds push (= grow strongly) **up** through the cracks in the concrete.* ◦ *They pushed (= forcefully made) their **way** to the front.* **3** [I usually + adv/prep] When an army pushes in a particular direction, it moves forward there: *The invading troops have pushed further into the north of the country.* **PERSUADE WITH FORCE** ▷ **4** (B2) [T] to forcefully persuade or direct someone to do or achieve something: *Her parents pushed her **into** marry**ing** him.* ◦ *The school manages to push most of its students **through** their exams.* ◦ *If we want an answer from them by Friday, I think we're going to have to push them **for** it.* ◦ [+ to infinitive] *We had to push them **to** accept our terms, but they finally agreed to the deal.* ◦ *You'll never be successful if you don't push your**self** (= work) harder.* **ADVERTISE** ▷ **5** [T] informal to advertise something repeatedly in order to increase its sales: *They're really pushing their new car.* **SELL DRUGS** ▷ **6** [T] informal to sell illegal drugs: *He was arrested for pushing drugs **to** schoolchildren.* **INTERNET** ▷ **7** [T] specialized to send information over the internet without receiving a request for it first
→ Compare **pull**

IDIOMS **be pushing up (the) daisies** humorous to be dead: *I'll be pushing up the daisies long before it happens.* • **push your luck** (also **push it**) to try too hard to get a particular result and risk losing what you have achieved: *She's agreed to help on Saturday, but I think I'd be pushing my luck if I asked her to be here the whole weekend.* • **push the boat out** UK informal to spend a lot of money on celebrating something: *They really pushed the boat out for Annie's wedding.*

PHRASAL VERBS **push sb about/around** informal disapproving to tell someone what to do in a rude or threatening way: *If you think you can push me around like that, you're mistaken.* • **push ahead** to continue with an activity in a determined or enthusiastic way, especially when it is difficult or makes you feel tired: *They have decided to push ahead* ***with*** *the legal action.* • **push along** old-fashioned informal to leave: *Anyway, I'd better be pushing along now.* • **push sb/sth aside** to decide to forget about or ignore someone or something: *He claimed that he had been pushed aside (= not given a job) in favour of a younger person.* • **push for sth** to demand something repeatedly, or to take strong action to try to make it happen: *Local residents are pushing for the road to be made safer.* • **push (sth) forward** to continue doing something or making progress in something, with effort or enthusiasm: *Their research has pushed forward the frontiers of knowledge.* ◦ *An additional grant has enabled the team to push forward* ***with*** *research plans.* • **push yourself forward** to try to make other people notice and pay attention to you: *She always seemed to be pushing herself forward and not giving anyone else a chance.* • **push in** mainly UK to rudely join a line of people who are waiting for something, by moving in front of some of the people who are already there: *I was about to get on the bus when two men pushed in in front of me.* • **push off** **GO** ▷ **1** mainly UK slang used to rudely tell someone to go away: *He told me to push off.* **IN WATER** ▷ **2** to push against the side of a pool, lake, or river in order to move your body or a boat away from the side: *He pushed off* ***from*** *the side of the pool and swam slowly to the other side.* • **push on 1** to continue doing something, especially when this is difficult: *They are pushing on* ***with*** *their campaign for improved childcare facilities.* **2** to continue travelling somewhere: *'You've been driving for a long time – do you want to stop for a rest?' 'No, we're nearly there – let's push on.'* • **push sb out** to make someone leave a job or stop being involved in an activity by being unpleasant or unfair to them: *I felt I was being pushed out* ***of*** *the job.* • **push sb/sth over** to push someone or something so that they fall to the ground: *Daddy, Matthew pushed me over.* • **push sth through** to cause a plan or suggestion to be officially accepted or put into use: *We are trying to push this deal through as quickly as possible.* ◦ *The president is trying to push through various tax reforms.* • **push (sb) toward(s) sth** to try to do or achieve something, or to make someone more likely to do or achieve something: *It is hoped that these measures will push the nation towards recovery.* ◦ [+ -ing verb] *New employment laws are expected to push more women towards work****ing*** *full-time.* • **push sth up/down** to cause the amount, number, or value of something to increase or be reduced: *Rising demand tends to push prices up, and falling demand pushes them down.* ◦ *The rise in interest rates has pushed up the value of my investments.*

▸noun **PRESSURE** ▷ **1** (B1) [C] the act of moving someone or something by pressing them with your hands or body: *Get on the swing and I'll* ***give*** *you a push.* ◦ *I* ***gave*** *the door a hard push, but it still wouldn't open.* ◦ *I can order all these goods* ***at*** *the push* ***of*** *a button (= by pushing a button).* **STRONG MOVEMENT** ▷ **2** [C] a strong movement towards a place: *The army is continuing its push (= advance) towards the capital.* **ATTEMPT** ▷ **3** [C] a determined attempt to get an advantage over other companies in business: *The company plans to* ***make*** *a big push into the European market next spring.* ◦ [+ to infinitive] *The hotel is* ***making*** *a major push* ***to*** *attract customers.* **ENCOURAGEMENT** ▷ **4** (C1) [S] encouragement to make someone do something: *My mother had always wanted to learn how to paint – she just needed a gentle push.* **ADVERTISING** ▷ **5** [S] a lot of advertising: *This film is unlikely to attract large audiences unless it* ***gets****/it is* ***given*** *a big push in the media.*

IDIOMS **at a push** UK If you can do something at a push, you can do it but it will be difficult: *At a push I could be there by eight o'clock.* • **get the push** UK informal **1** to be told to leave your job: *Rick got the push a few weeks ago.* **2** to be told by someone that your relationship with them has ended: *She got the push from Martin last night.* • **give sb the push** UK informal **1** to tell someone to leave their job: *I heard he'd been given the push.* **2** to end a relationship with someone: *Oh, give him the push – he's a loser.* • **if/when push comes to shove** (C2) If something can be done if push comes to shove, it can be done if the situation becomes so bad that you have to do it: *If push comes to shove, we can always sell the car.*

pushbike /ˈpʊʃ.baɪk/ noun [C] UK old-fashioned a bicycle

ˈpush-button adj [before noun] describes an electronic object that you control by pushing buttons: *a push-button phone*

pushchair /ˈpʊʃ.tʃeəʳ/ (US) /-tʃer/ noun [C] UK (US **stroller**) a small folding chair on wheels that a baby or small child sits in and is pushed around in

pushed /pʊʃt/ adj **1 be pushed for time/money** mainly UK to not have enough time or money: *I'm a bit pushed for money this month.* **2 be (hard) pushed to do sth** to find it difficult to do something: *We'll be hard pushed to get to Brighton by six o'clock.*

pusher /ˈpʊʃ.əʳ/ (US) /-ɚ/ noun [C] (also **ˈdrug ˌpusher**) someone who sells illegal drugs

pushing /ˈpʊʃ.ɪŋ/ adv **be pushing 50, 60, etc.** to be almost 50, 60, etc. years old: *He looks great and yet he must be pushing 60 by now.*

ˌpush notifiˈcation noun [C or U] a message sent to a SMARTPHONE relating to one of its APPS, even when it is not running, or the act of sending such messages

pushover /ˈpʊʃˌəʊ.vəʳ/ (US) /-ˌoʊ.vɚ/ noun [C usually singular] informal something that is easy to do or to win, or someone who is easily persuaded or influenced or defeated: *The interview was an absolute pushover.* ◦ *Jean will look after Harry, I'm quite sure – she's a pushover* ***for*** *babies (= will do anything for them).*

pushpin /ˈpʊʃ.pɪn/ noun [C] US a small pin with a small ball-shaped piece of plastic on one end, used especially for fixing notices, pictures, etc. to a board or a wall

ˈpush-start verb [T] (also **ˈbump-start**) to push your car in order to make the engine start • **ˈpush ˌstart** noun [C] (also **ˈbump start**)

ˈpush-up noun [C] US (UK **ˈpress-up**) a physical exercise in which you lie flat with your face towards the floor and try to push up your body with your arms while keeping your legs and your back straight

pushy /ˈpʊʃ.i/ adj disapproving (C2) behaving in an

unpleasant way by trying too much to get something or to make someone do something: *a pushy salesman* • **pushiness** /-nəs/ **noun** [U]

pusillanimous /ˌpjuː.sɪˈlæn.ɪ.məs/ **adj** formal weak and COWARDLY (= not brave); frightened of taking risks: *He's too pusillanimous to stand up to his opponents.* • **pusillanimity** /ˌpjuː.sɪ.ləˈnɪm.ɪ.ti/ (US) /-ə.t̬i/ **noun** [U] • **pusillanimously** /-li/ **adv**

puss /pʊs/ **noun** [C] informal a cat: [as form of address] *Here, puss.*

pussy /ˈpʊs.i/ **noun** **CAT** ▷ **1** a **pussycat** **VAGINA** ▷ **2** [C] offensive a woman's VAGINA **3** [U] offensive sex with a woman

pussycat /ˈpʊs.i.kæt/ **noun** **ANIMAL** ▷ [C] (also **pussy**) a cat: *Look, Martha, a pussycat!*

pussyfoot /ˈpʊs.i.fʊt/ **verb** [I] informal disapproving to avoid making a decision or expressing an opinion because you are uncertain or frightened about doing so: *Stop pussyfooting **around/about** and tell me what you really think.*

ˌpussy ˈwillow **noun** [C or U] a tree with small, greyish flowers covered in fur in the spring, or the flowers themselves

pustule /ˈpʌs.tjuːl/ **noun** [C] specialized a small raised area on the skin which contains PUS (= thick liquid)

put /pʊt/ **verb** (present tense **putting**, past tense and past participle **put**) **MOVE** ▷ **1** (A1) [T + adv/prep] to move something or someone into the stated place, position, or direction: *Where have you put the keys?* ◦ *Put your clothes **in** the cupboard.* ◦ *He put salt **into** the sugar bowl by mistake.* ◦ *She put her bag **on** the table.* ◦ *She put her hands **over** her eyes.* ◦ *I put my arm **round** him to comfort him.* ◦ *We always put the cat **out** (= outside the house) at night.* ◦ *Every night, she puts **out** her clothes (= takes them from where they are kept so that they are ready) for the next day.* ◦ *If we put the chairs a bit closer **together** (= move them nearer to each other), we should be able to get another one round the table.* ◦ *If you put **together** (= mix) yellow and blue paint you get green.* ◦ *The prisoners were put **up against** (= moved into a position next to) a wall and shot.* **WRITE** ▷ **2** (A2) [T + adv/prep] to write something: *She puts her name **in** all her books.* ◦ *Put a cross **next to** the name of the candidate you want to vote for.* ◦ *I've put the date of the party **down** in my diary.* ◦ *He asked me to put my objections (**down**) **on paper**.* ◦ *It was an interesting article but I wish they'd put **in** more information (= included more information) about the costs.* **EXPRESS** ▷ **3** (C2) [T usually + adv/prep] to express something in words: *She wanted to tell him that she didn't want to see him any more, but she didn't know **how to** put **it**.* ◦ *We're going to have to work very hard, but **as** Chris so succinctly put **it**, there's no gain without pain.* ◦ *Why do you always have to put things so crudely?* ◦ *Has everyone had a chance to put their point of view?* **4** **put a price/value/figure on sth** to say what you think the price or value of something is: *The agent has put a price of £120,000 on our house.* ◦ *You can't put a value on friendship (= say what it is worth).* **5** **to put it bluntly, simply, mildly, etc.** used to describe the way you are expressing an event or opinion: *To put it bluntly, you're going to have to improve.* ◦ *He was annoyed, to put it mildly (= he was very annoyed).* **CONDITION** ▷ **6** (B2) [T] to cause someone or something to be in the stated condition or situation: *Are you prepared to put your children **at risk**?* ◦ *This puts me **in** a very difficult position.* ◦ *What has put you **in** such a bad mood?* ◦ *This election is a chance for the country to put a new government **in** (= elect a new government).* ◦ *It's broken into so many pieces, it'll be impossible to put it **back together** again (= repair it).* ◦ *Let's give her the chance to put her ideas into practice.* ◦ *The terrorists were put on trial (= their case was judged in a court of law) six years after the bombing.* ◦ *Wilson was put **out** (**of** the competition) (= was defeated) by Clarke in the second round.* ◦ [+ adj] *How much did it cost to have the television put **right** (= repaired)?* ◦ *I originally thought he was Australian, but he soon put me **straight** (= corrected me) and explained he was from New Zealand.* ◦ *I know she's gone forever, but I just can't put her out of my mind/head (= forget her).* ◦ *He's putting me under pressure to change my mind.* **OPERATION** ▷ **7** [T usually + adv/prep] to bring into operation; to cause to be used: *When the drugs failed to cure her, she put her **faith/trust in** herbal medicine.* ◦ *The school puts a lot of **emphasis on** teaching children to read and write.* ◦ *He's putting **pressure on** me to change my mind.* ◦ *The events of the last few weeks have put a real **strain on** him.* ◦ *In the story of Sleeping Beauty, the wicked fairy puts a **spell/curse** (US **hex**) on the baby princess.* ◦ *You know it was your fault, so don't try and put the **blame on** anyone else.* ◦ *The government is expected to put a new **tax on** cars.* ◦ *The new tax will put 15 percent **on** fuel prices (= increase them by 15 percent).* ◦ *She's never put **a bet/money on** a race before.* ◦ *He put everything he had **into** (= he used all his abilities and strength in) the final game.* ◦ *The more you put **into** something, the more you get out of it (= the harder you work at something, the more satisfying it is).* ◦ *They put (= invested) a lot of money **into** the family business.* ◦ *The president is trying to put **through** (= bring into operation) reforms of the country's economic system.* ◦ *They've got to put **an end to/a stop to** their fighting (= to stop fighting).* **JUDGE** ▷ **8** [T + adv/prep] to judge something or someone in comparison with other similar things or people: *I'd put him **among** the top six tennis players of all time.* ◦ *Drama critics have put her on a level/par with the great Shakespearean actresses.* ◦ *He always puts the needs of his family **first/last** (= they are the most/least important thing to him).* **SAIL** ▷ **9** [I + adv/prep] to travel in a boat or ship across the sea: *Our mast broke, so we had to put **about** (= turn round) and return to port.* ◦ *The ship put **in at** (= stopped at) Cape Town for fresh supplies.* ◦ *We put **to sea** (= began our sea journey) at dawn.*

IDIOMS **never put off until tomorrow what you can do today** saying said to emphasize that you should not delay doing something if you can do it immediately • **put your back into sth** to use a lot of physical effort to try to do something: *You could dig this plot in an afternoon if you really put your back into it.* • **put yourself in sb's place/position/shoes** to imagine how someone else feels in a difficult situation: *Put yourself in my place – what else could I have done?* • **put sb to sth** to cause someone to experience or do something: *Your generosity puts me to **shame**.* ◦ *I've put the children to **work** clearing the snow from the path.* ◦ *I hope we're not putting you to any **inconvenience**.* • **put it about** (also **put yourself about**) UK informal to have sex with a lot of different people: *Have you been putting it about recently, then?* • **put it there!** informal something that you say when you want someone to shake your hand to show that you have just made an agreement: *'So, do we have a deal?' 'Sure, put it there.'* • **put one over on sb** informal to trick someone: *He'd tried to put one over on the tax office and got found out.* • **put the shot** to throw a heavy metal ball as far as possible in a sports competition • **put the squeeze on sb** (US also **put the bite on sb**) to ask someone to give you money:

P

She put the squeeze on her mother ***for*** *a hundred bucks.* ◦ *The insurance company put the bite on me* ***for*** *a huge increase in my premium after I crashed the car.*

PHRASAL VERBS **put sth about/around** informal to tell a lot of people something that is not true: [+ that] *I'd like to know who put the rumour around* ***that*** *I'm pregnant.* ◦ *Someone's been putting* ***it*** *about* ***that*** *Dan is leaving.* • **put sth across/over sb** informal to cause a piece of false information to be believed by one or more people: *You didn't manage to put that story over* ***on*** *the tax people, did you?* • **put sth across** to express your ideas and opinions clearly so that people understand them easily: *It's an interesting idea and I thought he put it across well.* • **put yourself across** to express your ideas and opinions clearly so that people understand them and realize what you are like as a person: *I don't think I managed to put myself across very well in my interview.* • **put sth aside** **SAVE** ▷ **1** B2 to save something, usually time or money, for a special purpose: *I put aside a little every month for a deposit on a house.* ◦ *He tries to put some time aside every evening to read to the kids.* **IGNORE** ▷ **2** C2 If you put a disagreement or problem aside, you ignore it temporarily so that it does not prevent you doing what you want to do: *Let's put our differences aside and make a fresh start.* ◦ *Can we put that question aside for now, and come back to it later?* • **put sth at sth** to guess or roughly calculate that something will cost a particular amount, or that something is a particular size, number, or amount: *The value of the painting has been put at £1 million.* ◦ *I'd put her at (= guess that her age is) about 35.* • **put sth away** **STORE** ▷ **1** B1 to put something in the place or container where it is usually kept: *Put your toys away now.* **EAT** ▷ **2** informal to eat a large amount of food: *He put away a whole box of chocolates in one evening.* • **put sb away** **1** informal to move someone into a place where people live and are cared for together, such as a mental hospital or old people's home: *In the past, people who suffered from schizophrenia were often put away.* **2** slang to send someone to prison: *After what he did, he deserves to be put away for life.* • **put sth back** **REPLACE** ▷ **1** B1 to return an object to where it was before it was moved: *Will you put the books back when you've finished with them?* **DELAY** ▷ **2** UK to delay a planned event: *We had to put the meeting back a week.* **DRINK** ▷ **3** mainly UK informal to drink something quickly, especially a large amount of alcohol: *He regularly puts back six pints a night – I don't know how he does it.* **OF CLOCK** ▷ **4** to change a clock or watch to make it show an earlier time, for example because you are now in a part of the world where the time is different • **put sth before sb** **IMPORTANCE** ▷ **1** to give more attention to one thing than another because you think it is more important: *I'd never put my work before my family.* **TELL** ▷ **2** to formally tell or explain facts or ideas to a group of people in authority: *We've got to put our proposal before the committee.* • **put sth behind you** If you put an unpleasant experience behind you, you stop thinking about it, so that it does not affect your life: *Like any divorce, it was a painful business but I've put it all behind me now.* • **put sth by** to save an amount of money to use later: *I try to put by a few pounds every week.* • **put sth/sb down** **STOP HOLDING** ▷ **1** B1 to put an object that you are holding onto the floor or onto another surface, or to stop carrying someone: *I put my bags down while we spoke.* ◦ *Put me down, Daddy!* **2** B2 to write someone's name on a list or document, usually in order to include them in an event or activity: *Do you want me to put you down* ***for*** *the trip to London?* ◦ *I've put my****self*** *down* ***for*** *the office football team.* ◦ *If you want to get your children into that school, you have to put their* ***names*** *down at birth.* **not put sth down** If you cannot put a book down, you are unable to stop reading it until you reach the end: *It was so exciting from the first page I couldn't put it down.* • **put sth down** **PHONE** ▷ **1** B1 If you put the phone down, you place it or the RECEIVER back in the position you keep it in when it is not being used. **PAY** ▷ **2** to pay part of the cost and promise to pay the rest later: *I've put a deposit down* ***on*** *a new car.* • **put sb down** **INSULT** ▷ **1** informal to make someone feel silly or not important by criticizing them: *Why did you have to put me down in front of everybody like that?* **LAY DOWN** ▷ **2** to place and make a baby comfortable in the place where it sleeps: *I'd just put Jack down for his nap.* • **put sth down** **KILL** ▷ **1** to kill an animal that is old, sick, or injured, to prevent it from suffering: *If a horse breaks its leg, it usually has to be put down.* **STOP** ▷ **2** to stop or limit an opposing political event or group: *Police used tear gas to put the* ***riot*** *down.* ◦ *Thousands of troops were needed to put down the* ***uprising****.* **REDUCE** ▷ **3** UK (UK and US **bring sth down**) to reduce a price or a charge: *Shops are being forced to put their prices down in order to attract customers.* ◦ *It's time that the government put down interest rates.* • **put (sth) down (somewhere)** When an aircraft puts down, it lands, and when pilots put down their aircraft, they land: *She put down safely in the corner of the airfield.* • **put sb down somewhere** UK old-fashioned to stop a vehicle and allow someone to get out of it or off it: *Ask the taxi driver to put you down outside the church.* • **put sb down as sth** to think that someone is a particular type of person, especially when you do not know them very well: *I'd hate them to put me down as a snob.* • **put sb down for sth** to make a record that someone has promised to pay a particular amount of money as part of a collection to help people in need: *Put me down for a £10 donation.* • **put sth down to sth** to think that a problem or situation is caused by a particular thing: *I put the children's bad behaviour down to the fact that they were tired.* • **put sth/sb forward** (US **put sth/sb forth**) C1 to state an idea or opinion, or to suggest a plan or person, for other people to consider: *The* ***proposals*** *that you have put forward deserve serious consideration.* ◦ *I wasn't convinced by any of the* ***arguments*** *that he put forward.* ◦ *Many* ***suggestions*** *have been put forward, but a decision is unlikely until after next year's general election.* ◦ *The peace* ***plan*** *put forward last August has been revived for the latest round of negotiations.* ◦ *She has decided to put her* ***name****/put her****self*** *forward* ***as*** *a candidate.* • **put sth forward** to change a clock or watch to make it show a later time, especially an hour later: *Most European countries put the clocks forward in the spring.* • **put sth in** **FIX** ▷ **1** to fix a large piece of equipment or system into a room or building, ready to be used: *I've just had central heating/a new kitchen put in.* **OFFER** ▷ **2** to formally offer a particular thing to be considered: *They've put in a bid for the company/a bid to buy the company.* • **put sth in/put sth into sth** to spend a lot of time or effort doing something: *You've obviously put a lot of* ***work*** *in* ***on*** *your garden.* ◦ *If I put in some extra hours (= spend some extra hours working) today, I can have some time off tomorrow.* ◦ *We've put a lot of time and effort into mak****ing*** *the house look nice.* • **put (sth) in** to say something that adds to or interrupts what is already being said: [+ speech] *'But she's rather inexperienced for the job,' put in Jane.* • **put in for sth** to make an official request to have or do something: *I'm putting in for a job at the hospital.*

P

◦ *Richard's finally put in for his driving test.* • **put sth off** B1 to decide or arrange to delay an event or activity until a later time or date: *The meeting has been put off* ***for*** *a week.* ◦ [+ -ing verb] *I can't put off go****ing*** *to the dentist any longer.* • **put sb off** to tell someone that you cannot see them or do something for them, or stop them from doing something, until a later time: *I really don't want to go out with Helen and Greg tonight – can't we put them off?* ◦ *He keeps asking me out, and I keep putting him off.* • **put sb off (sth)** to take someone's attention away from what they want to be doing or should be doing: *Could you be quiet please – I'm trying to concentrate and you're putting me off.* ◦ *The sudden flash of the camera put the players off their game.* • **put sb off (sth/sb)** B2 to make someone dislike something or someone, or to DISCOURAGE someone from doing something: *The smell of hospitals always puts me off.* ◦ *You have to work long hours and that puts off a lot of people.* ◦ *His attitude put me* ***right*** *off him.* ◦ [+ -ing verb] *Personally, I didn't enjoy the film, but don't let that put you off go****ing****.* • **put sth on** **OPERATE** ▷ **1** A2 mainly UK to make a device operate, or to cause a device to play something, such as a CD or DVD, by pressing a switch: *Could you put the light on?* ◦ *Do you mind if I put the television/some music on?* ◦ *Don't forget to put the brake on.* **COVER BODY** ▷ **2** A2 to cover part of the body with clothes, shoes, make-up, or something similar: *Put your shoes on – we're going out.* ◦ *He put on his jacket.* ◦ *She puts face cream on every night.* **PRETEND** ▷ **3** to pretend to have a particular feeling or way of behaving that is not real or natural to you: *Why are you putting on that silly* ***voice****?* ◦ *There's no need to put on that injured expression – you know you're in the wrong.* ◦ *I can't tell whether he's really upset, or if he's just putting* ***it*** *on.* **PRODUCE** ▷ **4** mainly UK to produce or provide something, especially for the good of other people or for a special purpose: *She put on a wonderful meal for us.* ◦ *They've put on a late-night bus service for students.* **GET HEAVIER** ▷ **5** B1 If people or animals put weight on, they become heavier: *I'd expected to put* ***weight*** *on when I gave up smoking, but I didn't.* ◦ *He's put on ten pounds in the last month.* • **put sb on** mainly US informal to try to deceive someone into believing something that is not true: *She said she was planning to give her house to a charity for the homeless but I thought she was putting me on.* • **put sb onto sth** to introduce a person to something or someone that could bring them an advantage: *David put me onto a wonderful vegetarian cookery book.* ◦ *Can you put me onto (= tell me where to find) a good dentist?* • **put sth out** **LIGHT** ▷ **1** to make a light stop shining by pressing a switch: *Did you put the lights out downstairs?* ◦ *Put that torch out!* **STOP BURNING** ▷ **2** B1 to make something such as a fire or cigarette stop burning: *Firefighters have been called to put out the* ***fire*** *in the city centre.* ◦ *Would you mind putting your* ***cigarette*** *out, please?* • **put sb out** **1** to cause trouble or extra work for someone: *Would it put you out if we came tomorrow instead of today?* **2** [M usually passive] to annoy or upset someone, often by what you do or say to them: *She was rather put out when they turned up two hours late for dinner.* ◦ *He seemed a bit put out* ***at*** *not having been invited.* • **put yourself out** to make an effort to do something to help someone, even if it is not convenient: *Brian's always willing to put himself out* ***for*** *other people.* • **put sth out** **MOVE FORWARD** ▷ **1** to move forward part of your body, such as your hand or your tongue, from your body: *She put out her hand to shake mine.* ◦ *Don't put your tongue out – it's rude.* **INJURE** ▷ **2** informal to injure part of your body by causing it to be moved out of its correct position: *He put his knee out playing football.* **MAKE AVAILABLE** ▷ **3** to produce something in large quantities, so that it can be sold: *They put out millions of pairs of shoes a year.* **4** to produce information and make it available for everyone to read or hear: *Police have put out a warning to people living in the area.* **MAKE WRONG** ▷ **5** If a mistake puts out a set of mathematical calculations, it causes them to be wrong: *That one error put the figures out by several thousand pounds.* **GIVE WORK** ▷ **6** UK (US usually **contract sth out**) If you put work out, you employ someone outside your organization to do it: *The council has put the job of street-cleaning out* ***to*** *a private firm.* • **put out** US slang (especially of a woman) to agree to have sex: *I wasn't going to put out just because he'd paid for dinner.* • **put sth over/across** to express an idea clearly so that people understand it: *Did you feel that you managed to put over your point of view?* ◦ *She's not very good at putting across her ideas.* • **put sb through sth** **BAD EXPERIENCE** ▷ **1** to make someone experience something unpleasant or difficult: *I'm sorry to put you through this ordeal.* **EDUCATION** ▷ **2** to pay for someone to study at school, college, or university: *It's costing them a lot of money to put their children through school.* ◦ *She's putting her****self*** *through college.* • **put sb through** B1 to connect a person using a phone to the person they want to speak to: *Could you put me through* ***to*** *customer services, please?* • **put sth to sb** **1** to suggest an idea or plan to someone so that they can consider it or discuss it: *'Shall we all go out for a pizza tonight?' 'I don't know. I'll put* ***it*** *to Jim and see what he says.'* ◦ [+ that] formal *I put* ***it*** *to you (= I believe it to be true), Ms Dawson,* ***that*** *you were in the building at the time of the murder.* **2** to ask someone a question: *I have a question I want to put to you.* • **put sth together** **1** B2 to put the parts of something in the correct places and join them to each other: *I had to put the wardrobe together myself.* **2** C1 to prepare a piece of work by collecting several ideas and suggestions and organizing them: *The management are putting together a* ***plan/proposal/package*** *to rescue the company.* ◦ *It takes about three weeks to put the magazine together.* **3** **put together** said after a phrase that refers to a group of people or things to show that you are thinking of them as a group rather than separately: *The population of the US is bigger than that of Britain, France, and Germany put together.* • **put sth towards sth** to use an amount of money to pay part of the cost of something: *My grandma gave me some money to put towards a new coat.* • **put sth up** **RAISE** ▷ **1** B1 to raise something, or to fix something in a raised position: *Why don't you put up your hood/umbrella?* ◦ *I put my hand up to ask the teacher a question.* ◦ *I put my hair up (= fixed it into a position on the top of my head) for the wedding.* **BUILD** ▷ **2** B2 to build something: *They're planning to put a hotel up where the museum used to be.* ◦ *We're going to put up a new fence around our garden.* **FIX** ▷ **3** to fix an object to a vertical surface: *We've put up some new curtains in the living room.* ◦ *Posters advertising the concert have been put up all over the town.* **MONEY** ▷ **4** B1 mainly UK to increase the price or value of something: *I see they've put up the price of fuel again.* **5** to provide or lend an amount of money for a particular purpose: *The money for the new hospital was put up by an anonymous donor.* ◦ *His brother has agreed to put up* ***bail*** *for him.* • **put up sth** to show or express a particular type of opposition to something: *The villagers were unable to put up any* ***resistance*** *to the invading troops.* ◦ *We're not going to let them build a* *road here without putting up a **fight**.* • **put sth/sb up** to suggest an idea, or to make a person available, to be considered: *It was Bob who originally put up the idea of the exhibition.* ◦ *Each party is allowed to put up one **candidate**.* ◦ *William has been put up **as** a candidate for the committee.* ◦ *Is Chris willing to be put up **for** election?* • **put sb up** B2 to provide someone with a place to stay temporarily: *Sally is putting me up **for** the weekend.* • **put up 1** mainly UK to stay somewhere for the night: *We put up **at** a small hotel for the night.* **2 put up or shut up** informal If you say someone should put up or shut up, you mean that they should either take action in order to do what they have been talking about, or stop talking about it: *You keep saying you're going to ask her out. Well, put up or shut up.* • **put sb up to sth** to encourage someone to do something, usually something wrong: *I think he was put up to it by his friends.* • **put up with sth/sb** B2 to accept or continue to accept an unpleasant situation or experience, or someone who behaves unpleasantly: *I can put up with the house being untidy, but I hate it if it's not clean.* ◦ *He's so moody – I don't know why she puts up with him.* ◦ *They have a lot to put up with* (= *they have a lot of difficulties*). • **be put upon** informal to be treated badly by someone who takes advantage of your wish to be helpful: *I'm fed up with being put upon by my boss all the time.*

putative /ˈpjuː.tə.tɪv/ US /-t̬ə.t̬ɪv/ **adj** [before noun] formal generally thought to be or to exist, even if this may not really be true: *The putative leader of the terrorist cell was arrested yesterday.* • **putatively** /-li/ **adv**

ˈput-down noun [C] informal an unkind remark that makes someone seem silly

ˈput-on noun [C] US informal an attempt to deceive someone into believing something that is not true: *She's not really angry – it's just a put-on.*

putrefaction /ˌpjuː.trɪˈfæk.ʃən/ **noun** [U] formal the state of decaying

putrefy /ˈpjuː.trɪ.faɪ/ **verb** [I] to decay, producing a strong, unpleasant smell: *the smell of putrefying flesh*

putrid /ˈpjuː.trɪd/ **adj** DECAYED ▷ **1** decayed and having an unpleasant smell: *the putrid body of a dead fox* ◦ *What's that putrid **smell**?* UNPLEASANT ▷ **2** informal very unpleasant or ugly

putsch /pʊtʃ/ **noun** [C] an attempt to remove a government by force

putt /pʌt/ **verb; noun**

▸**verb** [I or T] to hit a GOLF BALL gently across an area of short and even grass towards or into a hole: *Palmer putted the ball straight into the hole.* ◦ *You need to use a special club for putting.*

▸**noun** [C] a gentle hit across short grass which sends a ball towards or into a hole: *She won the competition with an impressive six-metre putt.*

putter /ˈpʌt.əʳ/ US /ˈpʌt̬.ɚ/ **verb; noun**

▸**verb** MOVE ▷ **1** [I usually + adv/prep] US (UK **potter**) to move about without hurrying and in a relaxed and pleasant way: *He really enjoys puttering around in the garden.* MAKE NOISE ▷ **2** [I] If a machine putters, it makes a low sound repeatedly, showing that it is working slowly.

▸**noun** IN GOLF ▷ **1** [C] a GOLF CLUB (= stick for hitting a golf ball) with a short handle and metal end that is specially designed for putting **2** [C] someone who PUTTS: *He's a good putter.* WALK ▷ **3** [S] US (UK **potter**) a slow, relaxed walk around a place

ˈputting ˌgreen noun [C usually singular] a small area of short grass on which people can gently hit GOLF BALLS into a series of holes for entertainment or for practice

putty /ˈpʌt.i/ US /ˈpʌt̬-/ **noun** [U] a soft substance like clay that is used especially for fixing glass into window frames or for filling small holes in wood

IDIOM **be (like) putty in sb's hands** to be willing to do anything someone wants you to, because you like them so much

ˈput-up ˌjob noun [C usually singular] informal an attempt to trick or deceive someone

ˌput upon adj informal having to do more than is fair in order to allow other people to get what they want in a situation: *I don't mind helping them, but I can't help **feeling** a bit put upon.*

putz /pʌts/ **noun** [C] US slang a stupid person

puzzle /ˈpʌz.l̩/ **noun; verb**

▸**noun 1** C2 [S] a situation that is difficult to understand: *Scientists have been trying to **solve** this puzzle for years.* **2** A2 [C] a game or toy in which you have to fit separate pieces together, or a problem or question that you have to answer by using your skill or knowledge: *a jigsaw puzzle* ◦ *a crossword puzzle* ◦ *a puzzle book*

▸**verb** [I + adv/prep, T] C1 to cause someone to feel confused and slightly worried because they cannot understand something, or to think hard about something in order to understand it: *The findings of the survey puzzle me – they're not at all what I would have expected.* ◦ [+ question word] ***It** puzzles me **why** she said that.* ◦ *Management are still puzzling **about/over** how the accident could have happened.*

PHRASAL VERBS **puzzle sth out** to discover or understand something by thinking hard about it: [+ question word] *I still can't puzzle out **how** I managed to spend so much money last month.* • **puzzle over sth** to try to solve a problem or understand a situation by thinking carefully about it: *Scientists are puzzling over the results of the research on the drug.*

puzzled /ˈpʌz.l̩d/ **adj** B2 confused because you do not understand something: *He had a puzzled look on his face.* ◦ *I'm still puzzled as to why she said that.* ◦ *I'm a bit puzzled **that** I haven't heard from Liz for so long.*

puzzlement /ˈpʌz.l̩.mənt/ **noun** [U] formal a state of confusion because you do not understand something

puzzler /ˈpʌz.ləʳ/, /-l̩.əʳ/ US /-lɚ/ **noun** [C] informal something that is difficult to explain or understand: *I don't know what happened to the money – it's a real puzzler.*

puzzling /ˈpʌz.l̩.ɪŋ/, /ˈ-lɪŋ/ **adj** difficult to explain or understand: *It's a rather puzzling film.* ◦ *a puzzling situation*

PVC /ˌpiː.viːˈsiː/ **noun** [U] abbreviation for polyvinyl chloride: a type of plastic, used especially for making clothes, floor coverings, and bags

p.w. /ˌpiːˈdʌb.l̩.juː/ UK abbreviation for per week: *I am writing to inform you that your rent will be increased to £60 p.w. from 1 October.*

PWA /ˌpiː.dʌb.l̩.juːˈeɪ/ **noun** [C] abbreviation for person with AIDS (= a serious disease that destroys the body's ability to fight infection)

pwn /pəʊn/ US /poʊn/ **verb** [T] informal to defeat or take control of someone or something, usually in an internet video game: *You were just pwned!*

PWR /ˌpiː.dʌb.l̩.juːˈɑːʳ/ US /-ˈɑːr/ **noun** [C] specialized abbreviation for pressurized water reactor: a device for producing nuclear power which uses water at high pressure to control the production of heat

PX /ˌpiːˈeks/ **noun** [C] a shop at a place where American soldiers live and work

pygmy /ˈpɪɡ.mi/ **adj; noun**
▸**adj** [before noun] (also **pigmy**) describes an animal or bird that is one of a type that is smaller than animals or birds of that type usually are: *a pygmy hippopotamus* ◦ *a pygmy owl*
▸**noun** [C] (also **pigmy**) disapproving someone who is not important or who has little skill: *a political pygmy* ◦ *an intellectual pygmy*

Pygmy (also **Pigmy**) /ˈpɪɡ.mi/ **noun** [C] a member of one of several groups of very small people who live in central Africa: *Pygmies average about 1.5 metres in height.*

pyjama (US usually **pajama**) /pɪˈdʒɑː.mə/ **noun** [C] loose trousers that are tied around the waist and worn by men and women in some Asian countries

pyjamas (US usually **pajamas**) /pɪˈdʒɑː.məz/ **noun** [plural] B2 mainly UK soft, loose clothing that is worn in bed and consists of trousers and a type of shirt: *I need a new **pair of** pyjamas.* • **pyjama** mainly UK (US usually **pajama**) /-mə/ **adj** [before noun] *pyjama bottoms* (= *trousers*) ◦ *a pyjama top*

pylon /ˈpaɪ.lɒn/ US /-lɑːn/ **noun** [C] **1** a tall metal structure to which wires carrying electricity are fixed so that they are safely held high above the ground: *electricity pylons* **2** a tall tower or post which shows where aircraft should land

PYO /ˌpiː.waɪˈəʊ/ US /-ˈoʊ/ abbreviation for 'pick your own', used in signs outside farms where people can pick fruit and vegetables themselves and then pay for the amount they have picked: *PYO strawberries*

pyramid /ˈpɪr.ə.mɪd/ **noun** [C] **1** C1 a solid object with a square base and four TRIANGULAR sides that form a point at the top **2** a pile of things that has the shape of a pyramid: *The acrobats formed a pyramid by standing on each other's shoulders.* ◦ figurative *Many organizations have a pyramid **structure** (= there are fewer people at the top levels of them than there are at the bottom).*

pyramid

pyramidal /pɪˈræm.ɪ.dəl/ **adj** specialized having a pyramid shape

the ˈPyramids **noun** [plural] stone structures in Egypt of a PYRAMID shape that were built in ancient times as places to bury important people, especially kings and queens

ˈpyramid ˌscheme **noun** [C] US a way of deceiving INVESTORS (= people giving money to a company hoping to get more back) in which money that a company receives from new customers is not INVESTED to their advantage, but is used instead to pay debts owed to existing customers

ˈpyramid ˌselling **noun** [U] in business, the act of someone buying the right to sell a company's goods, and then selling the goods to other people. These people then sell the goods to other people.

pyre /paɪəʳ/ US /paɪr/ **noun** [C] a large pile of wood on which a dead body is burned in some parts of the world: *A traditional Hindu custom used to involve widows burning themselves alive on their husbands' **funeral** pyres.*

Pyrex /ˈpaɪ.reks/ **noun** [U] trademark a type of glass that does not break when it is heated, so it is used for making containers that are used for cooking: *a Pyrex dish/bowl*

pyrites /paɪˈraɪ.tiːz/ **noun** [U] specialized a shiny, yellow MINERAL containing SULPHUR and a metal, usually iron

pyromania /ˌpaɪ.rəˈmeɪ.ni.ə/ US /-roʊ-/ **noun** [U] a mental illness in which a person feels a strong wish to start fires

pyromaniac /ˌpaɪ.rəˈmeɪ.ni.æk/ US /-roʊ-/ **noun** [C] someone who suffers from PYROMANIA

pyrotechnics /ˌpaɪ.rəˈtek.nɪks/ US /-roʊ-/ **noun** [plural] **1** a public show of FIREWORKS **2** a show of great skill, especially by a musician or someone giving a speech: *His verbal pyrotechnics could hold an audience spellbound.* • **pyrotechnic** /-nɪk/ **adj** [before noun]

Pyrrhic victory /ˌpɪr.ɪkˈvɪk.tər.i/ US /-tə-/ **noun** [C usually singular] a VICTORY that is not worth winning because the winner has lost so much in winning it: *She won the court case, but it was a Pyrrhic victory because she had to pay so much in legal fees.*

python /ˈpaɪ.θən/ US /-θɑːn/ **noun** [C] (plural **pythons** or **python**) a very large snake that kills animals for food by wrapping itself around them and crushing them

pzazz /pəˈzæz/ **noun** [U] informal **pizzazz**

Q, q /kjuː/ **noun** (plural **Qs, Q's** or **q's**) **LETTER** ▷ **1** [C or U] the 17th letter of the English alphabet **QUESTION** ▷ **2** (also **q**) written abbreviation for **question** **PERIOD OF TIME** ▷ **3** abbreviation for quarter: a period of three months in a company's financial year: *Apple reports lower than expected Q3 profits.*

ˌQ and ˈA adj [before noun] mainly US abbreviation for question and answer: *The textbook has a Q and A section at the end of each chapter.*

QC /ˌkjuːˈsiː/ **noun** [C] abbreviation for Queen's Counsel: a British lawyer of high rank → Compare **KC**

QED /ˌkjuː.iːˈdiː/ specialized written after an argument in mathematics to show that you have proved something that you wanted to prove

QR code /kjuːˈɑː.kəʊd/ (US) /-ˈɑːr.koʊd/ **noun** [C] a pattern of black-and-white squares that is printed on something and that can be read by some types of mobile phone to give information to the user of the phone

qt written abbreviation for **quart**

ˈQ-Tip noun [C] US trademark **cotton bud**

qua /kwɑː/ **preposition** formal as a particular example of something, or the general idea of something: *Qua musician, he lacks skill, but his playing is lively and enthusiastic.*

quack /kwæk/ **verb; noun**
▸**verb** [I] to make the usual sound of a DUCK: *The ducks started quacking loudly when we threw them some bread.*
▸**noun** [C] **PERSON** ▷ **1** disapproving a person who dishonestly pretends to have medical skills or knowledge **2** UK informal often disapproving a doctor: *Have you seen a quack about that cough?* **SOUND** ▷ **3** [C] the sound that a DUCK makes

quackery /ˈkwæk.ᵊr.i/ (US) /-ɚ-/ **noun** [U] disapproving medical methods that do not work and are only intended to make money

quad /kwɒd/ (US) /kwɑːd/ **noun** [C] **PERSON** ▷ **1** informal for **quadruplet** **SQUARE** ▷ **2** (formal **quadrangle**) a square space outside, which has buildings on all four sides, especially in a school or college

ˈquad ˌbike noun [C] a motor vehicle similar to a motorcycle with four wheels

quad bike

quadrant /ˈkwɒd.rənt/ (US) /ˈkwɑː.drənt/ **noun** [C] **QUARTER** ▷ **1** specialized a quarter of a circle **DEVICE** ▷ **2** specialized a device for measuring the height of stars in the sky which was used in the past for calculating directions when travelling across the sea

quadraphonic (UK also **quadrophonic**) /ˌkwɒd.rəˈfɒn.ɪk/ (US) /ˌkwɑː.drəˈfɑː.nɪk/ **adj** (of an electronic system of recording, playing or receiving sound) having sound coming from four different directions → Compare **mono, stereo**

quadratic equation /kwɒdˌræt.ɪk.ɪˈkweɪ.ʒᵊn/ (US) /-ˌræṭ-/ **noun** [C] an EQUATION that includes an unknown value that is multiplied by itself only once, and does not include an unknown value multiplied by itself more than once: *In the quadratic equation,* $2y^2+3y=14$, $y=2$ *or* $y=-3\frac{1}{2}$.

quadrilateral /ˌkwɒd.rɪˈlæt.ᵊr.ᵊl/ (US) /ˌkwɑː.drɪˈlæṭ-/ **noun** [C] specialized a flat shape with four straight sides: *Squares and rectangles are quadrilaterals.*

quadriplegic (Australian English **quadruplegic**) /ˌkwɒd.rəˈpliː.dʒɪk/ (US) /ˌkwɑː.drə-/ **noun** [C] a person who is permanently unable to move any of their arms or legs, often because their back has been injured

quadruped /ˈkwɒd.rʊ.ped/ (US) /ˈkwɑː.drə-/ **noun** [C] specialized any animal that has four legs: *Horses, lions and dogs are quadrupeds, but humans are bipeds.* → Compare **biped**

quadruple **verb; adj, predeterminer**
▸**verb** [I or T] /kwɒdˈruː.pl̩/ (US) /kwɑːˈdruː-/ to become four times as big, or to multiply a number or amount by four: *The number of students at the college has quadrupled in the last ten years.* ◦ *We expect to quadruple our profits this year.*
▸**adj, predeterminer** /ˈkwɒd.rʊp.l̩/ (US) /kwɑːˈdruː.pl̩/ **1** four times as big: *a quadruple measure* ◦ *We have had quadruple the number of applicants we expected.* **2** involving four parts, people, places, etc.: *a quadruple fracture of his thumb*

quadruplegic noun [C] Australian English **quadriplegic**

quadruplet /kwɒdˈruː.plət/ (US) /kwɑːˈdruː-/ **noun** [C] (informal **quad**) any of four children who are born to the same mother at the same time

quaff /kwɒf/ (US) /kwæf/ **verb** [I or T] old-fashioned to drink something quickly or in large amounts

quaffable /ˈkwɒf.ə.bl̩/ (US) /ˈkwæf-/ **adj** humorous If an alcoholic drink is quaffable, it is easy and pleasant to drink a lot of it: *This wine is very quaffable, isn't it?*

quagmire /ˈkwɒg.maɪəʳ/ (US) /ˈkwæg.maɪr/ **noun** [C] **1** an area of soft, wet ground which you sink into if you try and walk on it: *At the end of the match, the pitch was a real quagmire.* **2** a difficult and dangerous situation: *Since the coup, the country has sunk deeper into a quagmire of violence and lawlessness.*

quail /kweɪl/ **noun; verb**
▸**noun** [C or U] (plural **quail** or **quails**) a small, brown bird that is shot for sport or food, or the meat of this bird: *Quails' eggs are considered to be a delicacy.*
▸**verb** [I] literary to feel or show fear; to want to be able to move away from something because you fear it: *Charlie quailed* **at** *the sound of his mother's angry voice.* ◦ *She quailed* **before** *her boss's anger.*

quaint /kweɪnt/ **adj** **1** (C2) attractive because of being unusual and especially old-fashioned: *a quaint old cottage* **2** Quaint can also be used to show that you do not approve of something, especially an opinion, belief or way of behaving, because it is strange or old-fashioned: *'What a quaint idea!' she said, laughing at him.* • **quaintly** /-li/ **adv** • **quaintness** /-nəs/ **noun** [U]

quake /kweɪk/ **verb; noun**
▸**verb** [I] to shake because you are very frightened or find something very funny, or to feel or show great fear: *Every time I get on a plane, I quake* **with fear**. ◦ *Charlie stood outside the head teacher's office, quaking* **in his boots/shoes** *(= feeling very frightened).*

◦ *The play was so funny, we were all quaking **with** laughter.*

▸noun [C] informal for **earthquake**

Quaker /ˈkweɪ.kəʳ/ (US) /-kɚ/ noun [C] (also **Friend**) a member of a Christian group, called the Society of Friends, that does not have formal ceremonies or a formal system of beliefs, and is strongly opposed to violence and war • **Quaker adj**

qualification /ˌkwɒl.ɪ.fɪˈkeɪ.ʃᵊn/ (US) /ˌkwɑː.lɪ-/ noun **TRAINING** ▷ **1** (B1) [C] an official record showing that you have finished a training course or have the necessary skills, etc.: *You'll never get a good job if you don't have any qualifications.* ◦ *Do you have any teaching/legal/medical/secretarial/academic qualifications?* **2** (B2) [C or U] an ability, characteristic or experience that makes you suitable for a particular job or activity: *Some nursing experience is a necessary qualification **for** this job.* ◦ [+ to infinitive] *One of the qualifications you need **to** work here is a sense of humour!* **COMPETITION** ▷ **3** (C1) [U] success in getting into a competition: *The win earned them qualification **for** the World Cup finals.* **LIMIT** ▷ **4** [C] a piece of information that you add which limits the effect of something: [+ that] *The doctor said I can leave hospital today, but with the qualification **that** I've got to come back every day to have the dressing changed.*

> **Word partners for qualification**
>
> *have/possess* a qualification • *get/gain/obtain* a qualification • *need/require* a qualification • *lack* qualifications • an *academic/basic/formal/recognized* qualification • a qualification *in* sth

qualified /ˈkwɒl.ɪ.faɪd/ (US) /ˈkwɑː.lɪ-/ adj **TRAINED** ▷ **1** (B1) having finished a training course, or having particular skills, etc.: *Tim is now a qualified architect.* ◦ *What makes you think that you are qualified **for** this job?* ◦ [+ to infinitive] *I'm not qualified **to** give advice on such matters.* **LIMITED** ▷ **2** limited: *There seems to be qualified support for the idea.*

qualifier /ˈkwɒl.ɪ.faɪ.əʳ/ (US) /ˈkwɑː.lɪ.faɪ.ɚ/ noun [C] **COMPETITION** ▷ **1** a team or person who has won part of a competition and is therefore competing in the next part of it: *The qualifiers from the first round will go into the quarter final.* **2** a game from which the winner will go on to compete in the next part of a competition: *Belgium and Italy are playing in tonight's qualifier.* **GRAMMAR** ▷ **3** specialized in grammar, a word or phrase which limits the meaning of another word or phrase, or makes it less general, such as an adjective or adverb

qualify /ˈkwɒl.ɪ.faɪ/ (US) /ˈkwɑː.lɪ-/ verb **FINISH TRAINING** ▷ **1** (B2) [I or T] to successfully finish a training course so that you are able to do a job; to have or achieve the necessary skills, etc.: *She hopes to qualify (**as** a lawyer) at the end of the year.* ◦ [+ obj + to infinitive] *This course qualifies you **to** teach in any secondary school.* **HAVE RIGHT** ▷ **2** (B2) [I or T] to have the legal right to have or do something because of the situation you are in, or to cause someone to have such a right: *She doesn't qualify **for** maternity leave because she hasn't been in her job long enough.* ◦ *To qualify **for** the competition you need to be over 18.* ◦ *Being a single parent qualifies you **for** extra benefits.* ◦ [+ obj + to infinitive] figurative *He thinks the fact that he's worked here longer than the rest of us qualifies him (= gives him the right) **to** tell us all what to do.* **GET INTO COMPETITION** ▷ **3** (B2) [I] to succeed in getting into a competition: *Nigeria was the first team to qualify **for** the World Cup.* ◦ *England has to win tonight's qualifying match to go through to the next round of the competition.* **LIMIT** ▷ **4** [T] to limit the strength or meaning of a statement: *I'd like to qualify my criticisms of the school's failings, by adding that it's a very happy place.* **5** [T] specialized In grammar, a word or phrase which qualifies another word or phrase limits it and makes it less general: *In the sentence 'He walked quickly along the road', 'quickly' and 'along the road' qualify 'walked'.*

qualitative /ˈkwɒl.ɪ.tə.tɪv/ (US) /ˈkwɑː.lɪ.teɪ.t̬ɪv/ adj formal **STANDARD** ▷ **1** relating to how good or bad something is: *Is there any qualitative difference between these two DVD players?* **CHARACTERISTIC** ▷ **2** relating to what something or someone is like: *There has been a qualitative change in the relationship between the public and the government.* → Compare **quantitative** • **qualitatively** /-li/ adv

quality /ˈkwɒl.ɪ.ti/ (US) /ˈkwɑː.lə.t̬i/ noun; adj

▸noun **STANDARD** ▷ **1** (B1) [C or U] how good or bad something is: *a shop advertising top quality electrical goods* ◦ *The food was of such **poor/low** quality.* ◦ *Their products are of very **high** quality.* ◦ *I only buy good-quality wine.* ◦ *The quality **of** the picture on our television isn't very good.* **2** (B1) [U] a high standard: *He's not interested in quality. All he cares about is making money.* **3 quality of life** the level of enjoyment, comfort, and health in someone's life: *My quality of life has improved tremendously since I moved to the country.* **CHARACTERISTIC** ▷ **4** (B2) [C] a characteristic or feature of someone or something: *leadership qualities* ◦ *He has a lot of good qualities but being organized isn't one of them.* ◦ [+ to infinitive] *I don't think he has the right qualities **to** be a teacher.* ◦ *This cheese has a rather rubbery quality **to** it (= it is like rubber).*

> **Word partners for quality (STANDARD)**
>
> *affect/impair* quality • *enhance/improve* quality • *maintain* quality • *excellent/good/high/top* quality • *low/inferior/poor/variable* quality • the quality *of* sth

> **Word partners for quality (CHARACTERISTIC)**
>
> *have/possess* a quality • an *essential/good/special/unique* quality • a quality *of* sth

▸adj **1** (B1) [before noun] of a high standard: *This is a quality product.* ◦ mainly UK *The story received little coverage in the quality **papers** (= more serious newspapers).* **2** [after verb] informal very good: *That gig was quality.*

ˈquality conˌtrol noun [C or U] the process of looking at goods when they are being produced to make certain that all the goods are of the intended standard

ˈquality ˌtime noun [U] time that you spend with someone, giving them your full attention because you value the relationship: *He makes sure he **spends** a few hours quality time **with** his children every day.*

qualm /kwɑːm/ noun [C usually plural] an uncomfortable feeling when you doubt if you are doing the right thing: *She **had** no qualms **about** lying to the police.*

quandary /ˈkwɒn.dri/ (US) /ˈkwɑːn-/ noun [C usually singular] a state of not being able to decide what to do about a situation in which you are involved: *I've had two job offers, and I'm **in** a real quandary **about/over** which one to accept.*

quango /ˈkwæŋ.ɡəʊ/ (US) /-ɡoʊ/ noun [C] (plural **quangos**) often disapproving an organization that is established by a government to consider a subject of public importance, but is independent from the government

quant /kwɒnt/ US /kwɑːnt/ **noun** [C] specialized someone in the financial industry who uses mathematical methods, for example to measure the risk of an INVESTMENT

quantifiable /ˈkwɒn.tɪ.faɪ.ə.bl/ US /ˈkwɑːn.t̬ə-/ **adj** able to be measured: *The benefits of the new policy are not easily quantifiable.*

quantifier /ˈkwɒn.tɪ.faɪ.əʳ/ US /ˈkwɑːn.t̬ə.faɪ.ɚ/ **noun** [C] specialized a word or phrase that is used before a noun to show the amount of it that is being considered: *'Some', 'many', 'a lot of' and 'a few' are examples of quantifiers.*

quantify /ˈkwɒn.tɪ.faɪ/ US /ˈkwɑːn.t̬ə-/ **verb** [T] to measure or judge the size or amount of something: *It's difficult to quantify how many people will be affected by the change.* • **quantification** /ˌkwɒn.tɪ.fɪˈkeɪ.ʃən/ US /ˌkwɑːn.t̬ə-/ **noun** [U]

quantitative /ˈkwɒn.tɪ.tə.tɪv/ US /ˈkwɑːn.t̬ə.teɪ.t̬ɪv/ **adj** specialized relating to numbers or amounts: *quantitative analysis* → Compare **qualitative** • **quantitatively** /-li/ **adv**

quantitative easing /ˌkwɒn.tɪ.tə.tɪvˈiːz.ɪŋ/ US /ˌkwɑːn.t̬ə.teɪ.t̬ɪv-/ **noun** [U] specialized the act of a country's central bank increasing the amount of money in the economy at a time when INTEREST RATES are very low as a way of increasing economic growth

quantity /ˈkwɒn.tə.ti/ US /ˈkwɑːn.t̬ə.t̬i/ **noun** [C or U] **B1** the amount or number of something, especially that can be measured or is fixed: *Police found a **large/small** quantity **of** drugs in his possession.* ◦ *We consumed **vast** quantities **of** food and drink that night.* ◦ *The (**sheer**) quantity (= large amount) **of** equipment needed for the trip is staggering.* ◦ *They are now developing ways to produce the vaccine **in** large quantities and cheaply.* ◦ *This recipe is only for four, so I usually do double the quantity if I'm cooking for my family.* ◦ *It's quality not quantity that really counts.*

> **Word partners for quantity**
>
> a *large/huge/small/vast* quantity • a *significant/substantial/sufficient* quantity • the *sheer* quantity of sth • *equal* quantities • *in* (big/large/small) quantities • a quantity *of* sth

ˈquantity surˌveyor **noun** [C] UK a person whose job is to calculate the cost of the materials and work needed for future building work

quantum /ˈkwɒn.təm/ US /ˈkwɑːn.t̬əm/ **noun** [C] (plural **quanta**) specialized the smallest amount or unit of something, especially energy: *quantum theory*

ˌquantum ˈleap **noun** [C usually singular] a great improvement or important development in something: *The appointment of a female director is a quantum leap for women's equality.*

ˌquantum meˈchanics **noun** [plural] specialized in physics, a theory that explains the behaviour of ELEMENTARY PARTICLES, both separately and in groups

quarantine /ˈkwɒr.ən.tiːn/ US /ˈkwɔːr-/ **noun; verb**

▸**noun** [U] a period of time during which an animal or person that might have a disease is kept away from other people or animals so that the disease cannot spread: *The horse had to spend several months **in** quarantine when it reached Britain.*

▸**verb** [T] to put an animal or person in quarantine

quark /kwɑːk/ US /kwɑːrk/ **noun** [C] specialized **PHYSICS** ▷ **1** in physics, one of the most basic forms of matter that make up the heavier ELEMENTARY PARTICLES: *Atoms are made up of smaller particles – protons, neutrons and electrons – some of which are made up of even smaller ones, called quarks.* **FOOD** ▷ **2** a type of soft white cheese

quarrel /ˈkwɒr.əl/ US /ˈkwɔːr-/ **noun; verb**

▸**noun** [C] **B2** an angry disagreement between two or more people or groups: *They **had** a bitter quarrel **about/over** some money three years ago and they haven't spoken to each other since.* ◦ *We have no quarrel **with** the people of your country (= we have no reason to disagree with or dislike them).* ◦ *They seem to have **patched up** their quarrel (= finished their disagreement and started to be friendly).*

▸**verb** [I] (**-ll-** or US usually **-l-**) **B2** to have an angry disagreement with someone: *What did you quarrel **about/over**?* ◦ *She quarrelled **with** everyone in the village.*

PHRASAL VERB **quarrel with sth** to think that something is wrong: *No one can quarrel with the improvements that have been made.*

quarrelsome /ˈkwɒr.əl.səm/ US /ˈkwɔːr-/ **adj** disapproving A quarrelsome person repeatedly argues with other people.

quarry /ˈkwɒr.i/ US /ˈkwɔːr-/ **noun; verb**

▸**noun** **HOLE** ▷ **1** [C] a large artificial hole in the ground where stone, sand, etc. is dug for use as building material: *a granite/limestone/marble/slate quarry* **IN HUNTING** ▷ **2** [S] a person or animal being hunted or looked for: *The dogs pursued their quarry into an empty warehouse.*

▸**verb** [T] to dig stone, etc. from a quarry

quart /kwɔːt/ US /kwɔːrt/ **noun** [C] (written abbreviation **qt**) a unit of measurement for liquids, equal to approximately 1.14 litres in Britain, or 0.95 litres in the US: *A quart is so called because it is a quarter of a gallon.*

quarter /ˈkwɔː.təʳ/ US /ˈkwɑː.t̬ɚ/ **noun; verb**

▸**noun** **FOURTH PART** ▷ **1** **A2** [C] one of four equal or almost equal parts of something; ¼: *He cut the orange into quarters.* ◦ *Under a quarter **of** people questioned said that they were happily married.* ◦ *My house is situated a mile and three-quarters from here.* **2 a quarter of an hour** 15 minutes: *I waited a quarter of an hour and then went home.* ◦ *I was there three-quarters of an hour.* ◦ *an hour and three-quarters* **3 a quarter to two, three, etc.** **A1** (also US **a quarter of two, three, etc.**) 15 minutes before two, three, etc.: *It was a quarter to six when I left.* **4 a quarter past two, three, etc.** **A1** (also US **a quarter after two, three, etc.**) 15 minutes after two, three, etc.: *I'll meet you at a quarter past five.* **5** [C] one of four periods of time into which a year is divided for financial calculations, such as for profits or taxes: *There was a fall in unemployment in the second quarter of the year.* ◦ *I get an electricity bill every quarter.* **6** [C] one of four periods in a game of American football and other ball sports **COIN** ▷ **7** **B2** [C] in the US and Canada, a coin worth 25 CENTS **AREA** ▷ **8** **C2** [C] an area of a town where a particular group of people live or work or where a particular activity happens: *This is the bustling commercial quarter of the city.* **PEOPLE** ▷ **9** [C] one or more people who provide help, information or a particular reaction to something but who are not usually named: *Help came from an unexpected quarter.* ◦ *There is a feeling **in certain/some** quarters (= some people consider) that a change is needed.* **PLACE TO LIVE** ▷ **10 quarters** [plural] a room or house that has been provided, especially for servants or soldiers and their families, to live in: *The army's **married** quarters are just outside the town.* **11** [C] Indian English a house or other place to live that has been provided by a

Q

company for an employee **FORGIVENESS** ▷ **12** [U] literary the fact of being kind towards or forgiving a person that you have defeated, especially by allowing them to live: *We can expect* ***no*** *quarter from our enemies.*

▸verb **CUT INTO FOUR** ▷ **1** [T often passive] to cut something into four parts **SOLDIER** ▷ **2** [T usually passive, + adv/prep] to send someone, especially soldiers, to live in a place: *The soldiers were quartered with (= they lived with) local villagers during the war.*

quarterback /ˈkwɔː.tə.bæk/ ⓤⓢ /ˈkwɑː.t̬ɚ-/ **noun** [C] mainly US (in American football) the player who receives the ball at the start of every play and tries to move it along the field

quarterdeck /ˈkwɔː.tə.dek/ ⓤⓢ /ˈkwɑː.t̬ɚ-/ **noun** [C] the highest part of the DECK at the back of a ship: *The quarterdeck is usually reserved for officers.*

ˌquarter-ˈfinal **noun** [C] any of the four games in a competition that decides which players or teams will play in the two SEMIFINALS

quarterly /ˈkwɔː.tᵊl.i/ ⓤⓢ /ˈkwɑː.t̬ɚ.li/ **adj, adv** done or produced four times a year: *a quarterly magazine ◦ The magazine will be published quarterly.*

ˈquarter ˌnote **noun** [C] US for **crotchet**

ˈquarter ˌplate **noun** [C] Indian English a small plate, for example one that you put your bread on when you are eating the main part of a meal

quartet /kwɔːˈtet/ ⓤⓢ /kwɔːr-/ **noun** **1** [C, + sing/pl verb] a group of four people who play musical instruments or sing as a group: *A string quartet was playing Mozart.* **2** [C] a piece of music written for four people

quartz /kwɔːts/ ⓤⓢ /kwɔːrts/ **noun** [U] a hard, transparent mineral substance, used in making electronic equipment and accurate watches and clocks

quasar /ˈkweɪ.zɑːʳ/ ⓤⓢ /-zɑːr/ **noun** [C] specialized the centre of a GALAXY (= group of stars) that is very far away, producing large amounts of energy

quash /kwɒʃ/ ⓤⓢ /kwɑːʃ/ **verb** [T] **REFUSE** ▷ **1** to say officially that something, especially an earlier official decision, is no longer to be accepted: *His* ***conviction*** *was quashed in March 1986 after his counsel argued that the police evidence was all lies.* **STOP** ▷ **2** to forcefully stop something that you do not want to happen: *The revolt was swiftly quashed by government troops. ◦ The company moved quickly to quash* ***rumours/speculation*** *that it is losing money.*

quasi- /kweɪ.zaɪ-/ **prefix** used to show that something is almost, but not completely, the thing described: *The school uniform is quasi-military in style.*

quatrain /ˈkwɒt.reɪn/ ⓤⓢ /ˈkwɑː.treɪn/ **noun** [C] specialized a group of four lines in a poem

quaver /ˈkweɪ.vəʳ/ ⓤⓢ /-vɚ/ **verb; noun**

▸verb [I] If a person's voice quavers, it shakes, usually because of emotion: *Her* ***voice*** *began to quaver and I thought she was going to cry.* • **quavery** /-i/ **adj** (also **quavering** /-ɪŋ/)

▸noun **MUSICAL NOTE** ▷ **1** [C] mainly UK (US usually **eighth note**) a musical note that is half as long as a CROTCHET **SHAKE** ▷ **2** [S] a slight shake in someone's voice, especially because of emotion: *There was a quaver in her voice as she thanked her staff for all their support.*

quay /kiː/ **noun** [C] a long structure, usually built of stone, where boats can be tied up to take on and off their goods

quayside /ˈkiː.saɪd/ **noun** [C usually singular] the edge of a quay, near the water: *The animals were unloaded* ***on/at*** *the quayside.*

queasy /ˈkwiː.zi/ **adj** likely to vomit: *I started to* ***feel*** *queasy as soon as the boat left the harbour. ◦ Just the thought of blood makes me queasy.* • **queasily** /-zɪ.li/ **adv** • **queasiness** /-nəs/ **noun** [U]

queen /kwiːn/ **noun** [C] **WOMAN** ▷ **1** Ⓐ② a woman who rules a country because she has been born into a royal family, or a woman who is married to a king: *How long did* ***Queen*** *Victoria* ***reign****? ◦ The Queen is meeting the prime minister today.* **2** any woman who is considered to be the best at what she does: *She's the* ***reigning queen of*** *crime writers.* **3** the most powerful piece on the board in the game of CHESS **4** in a group of insects, a single large female that produces eggs: *a* ***queen bee*** *◦ a* ***queen ant*** *◦ a* ***queen wasp*** **5** in a set of playing cards, a card with a picture of a queen on it. It is usually worth less than a king. **GAY MAN** ▷ **6** slang offensive a gay man, especially an older man, whose way of behaving is noticeable and artificial: *James is such an* ***old queen****.*

Queen Anne's lace /ˌkwiː.n.ænzˈleɪs/ **noun** [U] mainly US **cow parsley**

ˌqueen ˈmother **noun** [C usually singular] the mother of the king or queen who is ruling

ˌQueen's ˈevidence **noun** [U] legal **1** evidence from someone who has been accused of committing a crime, given against the people who were accused with them, in order to have their own punishment reduced → See also **King's evidence, state's evidence** **2** **turn Queen's evidence** to give EVIDENCE against someone else in this way

queenside /ˈkwiːn.saɪd/ **noun** [U] specialized in the game of CHESS, the side of the board where your queen is at the start of the game • **queenside adj**

ˈqueen-size **adj** (also **ˈqueen-sized**) US If something is queen-size or queen-sized, it is larger than the normal size but smaller than KING-SIZE: *a queen-size bed*

queer /kwɪəʳ/ ⓤⓢ /kwɪr/ **adj; noun; verb**

▸adj **GAY** ▷ **1** offensive (especially of a man) gay

> **Note:**
>
> Gay people sometimes use this word in a way that is not offensive.

STRANGE ▷ **2** old-fashioned strange, unusual, or not expected: *What a queer thing to say! ◦ I'm feeling rather queer (= ill), may I sit down?*

▸noun [C] offensive a gay person, especially a man

▸verb UK informal **queer sb's pitch** to spoil a chance or an opportunity for someone, often on purpose: *If she asks Ian for a pay rise before I do, it will probably queer my pitch.*

ˈqueer-ˌbashing **noun** [U] slang the act of physically attacking and hurting someone because they are gay

quell /kwel/ **verb** [T] to stop something, especially by using force: *Police in riot gear were called in to quell the* ***disturbances/unrest****. ◦ This latest setback will have done nothing to quell the growing* ***doubts*** *about the future of the club.*

quench /kwentʃ/ **verb** [T] **1** to drink liquid so that you stop being thirsty: *When it's hot, it's best to quench your* ***thirst*** *with water.* **2** literary to use water to put out a fire: *The flames were quenched by heavy rain.* **3** to satisfy a need or wish: *Her thirst for knowledge will never be quenched.*

querulous /ˈkwer.ʊ.ləs/ **adj** often complaining, especially in a weak high voice: *He became increasingly dissatisfied and querulous in his old age.* • **querulously** /-li/ **adv**

query /ˈkwɪə.ri/ (US) /ˈkwɪr.i/ **noun; verb**
▸**noun** [C] B2 a question, often expressing doubt about something or looking for an answer from an authority: *If you have any queries* ***about*** *your treatment, the doctor will* ***answer*** *them.*
▸**verb** [T] to ask questions, especially in order to check if something is true: *A few students have queried their marks.* ◦ [+ question word] *She queried* ***wh****ether three months was long enough.* ◦ [+ speech] *'Any chance of a cup of tea?' he queried hopefully.*

quest /kwest/ **noun** [C] literary C2 a long search for something that is difficult to find, or an attempt to achieve something difficult: *Nothing will stop them* ***in*** *their quest* ***for*** *truth.* ◦ *She went to India* ***on*** *a spiritual quest.* ◦ [+ to infinitive] *She does aerobics four times a week in her quest* ***to*** *achieve the perfect body.*

question /ˈkwes.tʃən/ **noun; verb**
▸**noun ASKING** ▷ **1** A1 [C] a sentence or phrase used to find out information: *The police* ***asked*** *me questions all day.* ◦ *Why won't you* ***answer*** *my question?* ◦ *'So where is the missing money?'* ***'That's a good*** *question.'* (= *I don't know the answer.*) ◦ *There will be a question-****and-answer session*** (= *a period when people can ask questions*) *at the end of the talk.* **2** A2 [C] in an exam, a problem that tests a person's knowledge or ability: ***Answer/Do*** *as many questions as you can.* **PROBLEM** ▷ **3** B2 [C] any matter that needs to be dealt with or considered: *This* ***raises*** *the question of teacher pay.* ◦ *What are your views on the Northern Irish question?* **4** B2 [U] doubt or confusion: *There's no question* ***about*** (= *it is certain*) *whose fault it is.* ◦ *Whether children are reading fewer books is* ***open to*** *question* (= *there is some doubt about it*). ◦ *Her loyalty is* ***beyond*** *question* (= *there is no doubt about it*). ◦ *There's no question that he's guilty.* **5 sb/sth in question** C2 formal the person or thing that is being discussed: *I stayed at home on the night in question.*

> **Word partners for question noun (ASKING)**
> *ask/have/pose* a question • *answer/reply to/respond to* a question • *address/put* a question to sb • *avoid/evade* a question • *bombard* sb **with** questions • an *awkward/difficult/embarrassing/tough* question • a question *about/on* sth

> **Word partners for question noun (PROBLEM)**
> *raise* questions about sth • *address* a question • a *basic/big/fundamental/important* question • the *whole* question of sth

IDIOMS **be a question of doing sth** C1 to be necessary to do a particular thing: *It's* ***simply/just*** *a question of working hard for a month and then you can relax.* • **be out of the question** (also **be no question of (doing) sth**) C2 to be an event which cannot possibly happen: *A trip to New Zealand is out of the question this year.* ◦ *There's no question of agree****ing*** *to the demands.*

▸**verb** [T] **1** B2 to ask a person about something, especially officially: *Several men were questioned by police yesterday about the burglary.* ◦ *68 percent of those questioned in the poll thought noise levels had increased.* **2** B2 to express doubts about the value or truth of something: *I questioned* ***the wisdom of*** *taking so many pills.* ◦ [+ question word] *Results from a study questioned* ***wh****ether treatment with the drug really improved survival.* ◦ *She gave me a questioning look* (= *as if she wanted an answer from me*).

questionable /ˈkwes.tʃə.nə.bl̩/ **adj** [+ question word] C2 not certain, or wrong in some way: ***It*** *is questionable* ***wh****ether this goal can be achieved.* ◦ *Much of late-night television is of questionable* ***value/taste.***

questioner /ˈkwes.tʃə.nəʳ/ (US) /-nɚ/ **noun** [C] a person who asks a question

questioning /ˈkwes.tʃə.nɪŋ/ **noun** [U] the situation in which the police ask someone questions about a crime: *Three suspects were* ***taken in for*** *questioning at Hereford police station.*

ˈquestion ˌmark noun [C] B1 the symbol ? used in writing at the end of a phrase or sentence to show that it is a question

IDIOM **a question mark over sth** an expression used when doubt exists about a particular thing: *A question mark* ***hangs*** *over the future of the company.*

questionnaire /ˌkwes.tʃəˈneəʳ/ (US) /-ˈner/ **noun** [C] B1 a list of questions that several people are asked so that information can be collected about something: *Visitors to the country have been asked to* ***fill in*** *a detailed questionnaire.*

ˈquestion ˌtag noun [C] a short phrase such as 'isn't it' or 'don't you' that is added to the end of a sentence to check information or to ask if someone agrees with you: *In the sentence, 'It's hot, isn't it?', 'isn't it' is a question tag.*

queue /kjuː/ **noun; verb**

queue

▸**noun** [C] UK (US **line**) **1** B1 a line of people, usually standing or in cars, waiting for something: *Are you* ***in*** *the queue* ***for*** *tickets?* ◦ *There was a* ***long*** *queue of traffic stretching down the road.* ◦ *If you want tickets you'll have to* ***join*** *the queue.* ◦ disapproving *It makes me mad when someone* ***jumps the*** *queue* (= *goes straight to the front*). **2** a lot of people wanting something: *There's a queue of companies wanting to sell the product.*
▸**verb** [I] UK (US **line**, US **line up**, also UK **queue up**) **1** B2 to wait in a line of people, often to buy something: *Dozens of people were queueing up* ***to*** *get tickets.* ◦ *We had to queue for three hours to get in.* **2** informal to want very much to do something: [+ to infinitive] *There are thousands of young women queueing up* ***to*** *be models.*

ˈqueue-jump verb [I] UK to unfairly go to the front of a queue • **ˈqueue-ˌjumping noun** [U] UK *Hey, no queue-jumping!*

quibble /ˈkwɪb.l̩/ **verb; noun**
▸**verb** [I] disapproving to argue about, or say you disapprove of, something that is not important: *There's no point quibbling* ***about/over*** *a couple of dollars.*
▸**noun** [C] disapproving a complaint or criticism about something that is not very important: *My only quibble is that the colour wasn't very nice.*

quiche /kiːʃ/ **noun** [C or U] an open pastry case, filled with a mixture of eggs, cream, and other SAVOURY (= not sweet) foods, that is baked and eaten hot or cold: *asparagus/broccoli quiche*

quick /kwɪk/ **adj; exclamation; noun**
▸**adj 1** A2 happening or done with great speed, or lasting only a short time: *It's a quick journey.* ◦ *I had a quick coffee and left the house.* ◦ *I only had time for a quick glance at the paper this morning.* ◦ *He scored three goals in quick* ***succession*** (= *one after the other in a short time*). ◦ *Could I have a quick* ***word*** (= *speak to you for a short time*)? ◦ ***Quick as lightning*** (= *very quickly*), *he snatched the book and ran out of the room.* **2** A1 doing something fast: *I tried to catch him but he was too quick for me.* **3 be quick to do sth** to do something fast, sometimes too fast: *She was quick to*

Q

point out that it wasn't her fault. **4** B1 describes someone who is clever and understands or notices things quickly: *She was quick* ***at*** *understand****ing*** *what we wanted her to do.* ◦ *He has a quick mind.* ◦ *Glyn's quick* ***thinking*** *(= ability to solve problems with speed) averted what could have been a disaster.* → See also **quick-witted 5 a quick study** US informal someone who is able to learn things quickly: *He's a quick study and easily grasps all the details of a discussion.*

Other ways of saying quick

A very common alternative is **fast**:

I tried to catch him, but he was too ***fast*** *for me.*

If something is done quickly, without waiting, you can use the adjectives **prompt, speedy**, or **swift**:

A ***prompt*** *reply would be very much appreciated.*

He made a ***speedy*** *recovery.*

His plea for aid resulted in a ***swift*** *response.*

If something is done too quickly, without thinking carefully, the adjectives **hasty** and **hurried** are often used:

I don't want to make a ***hasty*** *decision.*

We left early after a ***hurried*** *breakfast.*

A quick walk is often described as **brisk**:

We took a ***brisk*** *walk through the park.*

The adjective **rapid** is often used to describe quick growth or change:

The 1990s were a period of ***rapid*** *growth.*

▸**exclamation** used for telling someone to do something quickly: *Quick! Close the door before the cat comes in!*

▸**noun** [U] the area of flesh under your nails: *He's bitten his nails* ***to the*** *quick.*

quicken /ˈkwɪk.ən/ **verb** [I or T] **1** to become quicker, or to make something become quicker: *This is music that will make your pulse quicken.* ◦ *We'll have to quicken the pace if we want to keep up with him.* ◦ literary *Peter walked in the room and her heart quickened.* **2** If a feeling or quality quickens, it becomes more active, or to make a feeling or quality do this: *His interest quickened when he saw her.* ◦ *War quickens our awareness.*

Q

ˈ**quick-fire** **adj** [before noun] happening very quickly, one after another: *His quick-fire jokes were very popular with the audience.*

ˌ**quick** ˈ**fix** **noun** [C] informal disapproving something that seems to be a fast and easy solution to a problem but is in fact not very good or will not last long: *People are still looking for the quick fix.*

quickie /ˈkwɪk.i/ **noun** [C] informal something done or had quickly, especially sex or an alcoholic drink: *Shall we just* ***have*** *a quickie?* ◦ *a quickie* ***divorce***

quickly /ˈkwɪk.li/ **adv 1** A2 at a fast speed: *We'll have to walk quickly to get there on time.* ◦ *Quickly now, you two, daddy's waiting in the car!* **2** A2 after only a very short time: *He replied very quickly.* ◦ *He quickly realized that she wasn't telling the truth.*

ˈ**quick** ˌ**one** **noun** informal **have a quick one** to have a drink, usually an alcoholic drink, just before going somewhere: *Do we have time for a quick one before the train arrives?*

quicksand /ˈkwɪk.sænd/ **noun** [U] deep wet sand that sucks in anyone trying to walk across it

quicksilver /ˈkwɪkˌsɪl.vəʳ/ US /-vɚ/ **noun** old use **mercury**

quickstep /ˈkwɪk.step/ **noun** [C] a dance with a lot of quick steps, or a piece of music for this

ˌ**quick** ˈ**temper** **noun** **have a quick temper** to become angry very easily • ˌ**quick-**ˈ**tempered** **adj**

ˌ**quick-**ˈ**witted** **adj** able to reply in a clever or funny way without thinking for a long time

quid /kwɪd/ **noun** [C] (plural **quid**) UK informal a pound: *Could you lend me 20 quid (= £20), mate?*

IDIOM **be quids in** to be making a profit: *If this deal goes ahead, we'll be quids in.*

quid pro quo /ˌkwɪd.prəʊˈkwəʊ/ US /-proʊˈkwoʊ/ **noun** [C usually singular] (plural **quid pro quos**) formal something that is given to a person in return for something they have done: *The government has promised food aid* ***as a*** *quid pro quo* ***for*** *the stopping of violence.*

quiescent /kwiˈes.ənt/ **adj** formal temporarily quiet and not active: *The political situation was now relatively quiescent.*

quiet /kwaɪət/ **adj; noun**

▸**adj 1** A2 making very little noise: *She spoke in a quiet voice so as not to wake him.* ◦ *It's so quiet without the kids here.* ◦ *Please be quiet (= stop talking)!* ◦ *Could you* ***keep*** *quiet while I'm on the phone, please?* ◦ *She was* ***as quiet as a mouse*** *(= very quiet). I didn't even know she'd come in.*

Note:

Do not confuse with **quite**.

2 A2 having little activity or excitement and few people: *a quiet, peaceful little village* ◦ *It was a quiet wedding, with just a few friends and relations.* ◦ *Business is quiet during the holidays.* **3** B1 A quiet person is one who does not talk much: *He was a quiet, almost taciturn, young man.* **4 keep (sth) quiet** C2 to try to stop other people from finding out about a fact: *She managed to keep the operation quiet for a while.* ◦ *Davies kept quiet* ***about*** *the amount of money being spent.* • **quietness** /-nəs/ **noun** [U] *This luxury car offers comfort, quietness and speed.*

Other ways of saying quiet

If there is no noise or sound at all, the word **silent** is often used:

The stadium fell ***silent*** *after the goal was scored.*

Voices or sounds which are quiet can be described as **soft**:

'Come here!' he said in a ***soft*** *voice.*

The restaurant had nice ***soft*** *music playing in the background.*

If a sound is quiet and not clear you could describe it as **muffled**:

I could hear ***muffled*** *voices from the next room.*

If a sound is so quiet you can only just hear it, the adjective **faint** can be used:

There was the ***faint*** *sound of traffic in the distance.*

Hushed is usually used when people are quiet because they are afraid that someone might hear them or because they are waiting for something important to happen:

The judge delivered his decision to a crowded but ***hushed*** *courtroom.*

Quiet places where not much happens can be described as **peaceful, sleepy**, or **tranquil**:

He needed a ***peaceful*** *place to write his novels.*

They retired to a ***sleepy*** *little village.*

The hotel is in a ***tranquil*** *rural setting.*

A person who is quiet and does not often talk very much can be described as **taciturn**:

Her father was a shy, ***taciturn*** *man.*

▸**noun** [U] B2 the state of being silent: *Let's have **some** quiet!* ◦ *I go camping for some **peace and** quiet (= absence of activity and excitement).*

IDIOM **on the quiet** informal secretly: *His wife found out he'd been seeing someone on the quiet.*

quieten /ˈkwaɪə.tᵊn/ **verb** [I or T] UK (US **quiet**) to (cause someone to) become calmer or less noisy: *The barking dogs quietened (**down**) when they recognized me.*

quietism /ˈkwaɪə.tɪ.zᵊm/ **noun** [U] formal the belief that it is best to accept things in life and not try to change them

quietly /ˈkwaɪət.li/ **adv** **1** B1 without making much noise: *I slipped quietly out of the back door.* ◦ *He is a quietly spoken, thoughtful man.* **2** in a way that is not obvious to other people because you do not say much: *He is quietly **confident** that there will be no problems this time.*

quietude /ˈkwaɪə.tjuːd/ US /-tuːd/ **noun** [U] formal a state of being calm and peaceful: *In many of his poems the poet reflects on the quietude of the countryside.*

quiff /kwɪf/ **noun** [C] UK (US **pompadour**) a hairstyle, worn usually by men, in which the hair at the front of the head is brushed up

quill /kwɪl/ **noun** [C] **1** any of the long sharp pointed hairs on the body of a PORCUPINE **2** (also **quill pen**) a pen made from a bird's feather, used in the past

quilt /kwɪlt/ **noun** [C] **1** a decorative cover for a bed **2** UK a **duvet**

quilted /ˈkwɪl.tɪd/ US /-t̬ɪd/ **adj** (especially of clothes) filled with thick soft material that is sewn in place: *She wore a quilted satin jacket.*

quince /kwɪns/ **noun** [C or U] a hard fruit that looks like an apple and has a strong sweet smell: *quince jam*

quinine /ˈkwɪn.iːn/ US /ˈkwaɪ.naɪn/ **noun** [U] a drug used to treat fevers such as MALARIA

quinoa /kɪnˈwɑː/, /kɪˈnəʊə/ US /kɪnˈwɑː/ **noun** [U] the seeds of a South American plant that are cooked and eaten as food

quintessence /kwɪnˈtes.ᵊns/ **noun** [U] formal the most typical example: *An American football game is **the** quintessence **of** machismo.*

quintessential /ˌkwɪn.tɪˈsen.ʃᵊl/ **adj** formal being the most typical example or most important part of something: *Sheep's milk cheese is the quintessential Corsican cheese.* • **quintessentially** /ˌkwɪn.tɪˈsen.ʃᵊl.i/ **adv** *The painting is quintessentially British.*

quintet /kwɪnˈtet/ **noun** **1** [C, + sing/pl verb] a group of five people who play musical instruments or sing as a group **2** [C] a piece of music written for five people

quintuplet /kwɪnˈtuː.plət/, /ˈkwɪn.tjʊ-/ US /-ˈtuː.plɪt/ **noun** [C] (also **quin**) any of five children born at the same time to the same mother

quip /kwɪp/ **noun** [C] a humorous and clever remark: *It was Oscar Wilde who **made** the famous quip about life mimicking art.* • **quip verb** [I] (plural **-pp-**) [+ speech] *When asked earlier why he seemed to be so relaxed, Mr McCarthy quipped: 'It's the drugs'.*

quirk /kwɜːk/ US /kwɝːk/ **noun** [C] an unusual habit or part of someone's personality, or something that is strange and unexpected: *You have to get used to other people's quirks and foibles.* ◦ *There is a quirk in the rules that allows you to invest money without paying tax.* ◦ ***By** some strange quirk/**By** an odd quirk **of fate** (= unexpectedly), we ended up on the same train.*

quirky /ˈkwɜː.ki/ US /ˈkwɝː-/ **adj** unusual in an attractive and interesting way

quisling /ˈkwɪz.lɪŋ/ **noun** [C] a person who helps an

enemy that has taken control of his or her country → Synonym **collaborator**

quit /kwɪt/ **verb** [I or T] (present tense **quitting**, past tense and past participle **quit**) B1 to stop doing something or leave a job or a place: *Would you quit your job if you inherited lots of money?* ◦ [+ -ing verb] *I'm going to quit smok**ing**.* ◦ *Quit wast**ing** my time!* ◦ *Press Q to quit the program.*

quite /kwaɪt/ **adv, predeterminer; adv**

▸**adv, predeterminer** UK A2 a little or a lot but not completely: *I'm quite tired but I can certainly walk a little further.* ◦ *There was quite a lot of traffic today but yesterday was even busier.* ◦ *It was quite a difficult job.* ◦ *He's quite attractive but not what I'd call gorgeous.* ◦ *It would be quite a nuisance to write to everyone.*

> **!** Common mistake: **quite or quiet?**
>
> **Warning:** Choose the right word!
> These two words look similar, but they are spelled differently and have different meanings.

▸**adv** **1** B1 completely: *The two situations are quite different.* ◦ *Are you quite sure you want to go?* ◦ *The colours almost match but not quite.* ◦ *I enjoyed her new book though it's **not** quite as good as her last one.* ◦ *Quite **honestly/frankly**, the thought of it terrified me.* **2 not quite** B2 used to express that you are not certain about something: *I don't quite know what to say.* ◦ *I didn't quite catch what he said.* **3** UK used to show agreement with someone's opinion: *'You'd think he could spare some money – he's not exactly poor.' 'Quite.'* **4 quite the best, worst, etc.** formal used for emphasis: *It was quite the worst dinner I have ever had.*

quits /kwɪts/ **adj** informal **be quits** to not owe money to someone or to each other now: *I paid for the tickets and you bought dinner so we're quits, I reckon.* ◦ *Am I quits **with** you now?*

quitter /ˈkwɪt.əʳ/ US /ˈkwɪt̬.ɚ/ **noun** [C] disapproving a person who gives up easily instead of finishing something: *I'm no quitter.*

quiver /ˈkwɪv.əʳ/ US /-ɚ/ **verb; noun**

▸**verb** [I] to shake slightly, often because of strong emotion: *Lennie's bottom lip quivered and tears started in his eyes.*

▸**noun** [C] CONTAINER ▷ **1** a long thin container for carrying arrows SHAKE ▷ **2** a slight shake, often because of strong emotion: *The opening bars of the music sent **a** quiver **of** excitement through the crowd.*

quixotic /kwɪkˈsɒt.ɪk/ US /-ˈsɑː.t̬ɪk/ **adj** literary having or showing ideas that are different and unusual but not practical or likely to succeed • **quixotically** /kwɪkˈsɒt.ɪ.kᵊl.i/ US /-ˈsɑː.t̬ɪ-/ **adv**

quiz /kwɪz/ **noun; verb**

▸**noun** [C] (plural **quizzes**) **1** A2 a game or competition in which you answer questions: *a history/sport, etc. quiz* ◦ *There are so many inane television quiz **shows**.* ◦ UK *A lot of pubs have quiz **nights** once or twice a week.* **2** B1 mainly US a short informal test: *There was a **pop** (= surprise) quiz in history at school today.*

▸**verb** [T] (**-zz-**) to ask someone questions about something

quizzical /ˈkwɪz.ɪ.kᵊl/ **adj** seeming to ask a question without saying anything: *She gave me a quizzical **look/glance/smile**.* • **quizzically** /-i/ **adv**

quoits /kwɔɪts/, /kɔɪts/ **noun** [U] a game in which you throw rings over a small post, often played on ships

quokka /ˈkwɒk.ə/ US /ˈkwɑː.kə/ **noun** [C] a small WALLABY (= an animal with a long tail and strong legs for jumping with) which in the past existed in great numbers in Western Australia

Quonset hut /ˈkwɒn.sɪtˌhʌt/ (US) /ˈkwɑːn-/ noun [C] US trademark **Nissen hut**

quorate /ˈkwɔː.reɪt/ (US) /ˈkwɔːr.eɪt/ **adj** formal having the necessary number of people present for decisions to be allowed to be made: *a quorate meeting*

Quorn /ˈkwɔːn/ (US) /ˈkwɔːrn/ **noun** [U] trademark a substance made of vegetable PROTEIN that is used in cooking instead of meat

quorum /ˈkwɔː.rəm/ (US) /ˈkwɔːr.əm/ **noun** [S] formal the smallest number of people needed to be present at a meeting before it can officially begin and before official decisions can be taken

quota /ˈkwəʊ.tə/ (US) /ˈkwoʊ.t̬ə/ **noun** [C] a fixed, limited amount or number that is officially allowed: *The country now has a quota* ***on*** *immigration.* ◦ figurative *The class contains the usual quota (= number) of troublemakers.*

quotation /kwəʊˈteɪ.ʃᵊn/ (US) /kwoʊ-/ **noun** [C] (informal **quote**) **SAID** ▷ **1** (C2) a phrase or short piece of writing taken from a longer work of literature, poetry, etc. or what someone else has said: *At the beginning of the book there's a quotation* ***from*** *Abraham Lincoln.* **PRICE** ▷ **2** (C2) the price that a person says they will charge to do a piece of work: *I asked several builders to* ***give*** *me a quote for the work.* **SHARES** ▷ **3** mainly UK the fact that a company's SHARES are being traded on a particular STOCK MARKET: *Changes in the listing rules have reduced the advantage of obtaining a quotation on this stock market.*

quoˈtation ˌmarks noun [plural] (UK also **inˌverted ˈcommas**, informal **quotes**) the symbols ' ' or ' ' that are put around a word or phrase to show that someone else has written or said it

quote /kwəʊt/ (US) /kwoʊt/ **verb; noun**

▸verb **SAY** ▷ **1** (C1) [I or T] to repeat the words that someone else has said or written: *He's always quoting* ***from*** *the Bible.* ◦ *'If they're flexible, we're flexible', the official was quoted* ***as saying.*** ◦ *She worked,* ***to*** *quote her daughter, 'as if there was no tomorrow'.* ◦ *Can I quote you* ***on*** *that (= can I repeat to other people what you have just said)?* **2** (C1) [T] If you quote a fact or example, you refer to it in order to add emphasis to what you are saying: [+ two objects] *Quote me one organization that doesn't have some bad managers.* **GIVE PRICE** ▷ **3** (C2) [T] to give a price, especially one that will be charged for doing a piece of work: *The architect has quoted £40,000 to build an extension.*

IDIOM **quote...unquote** informal said to show that you are repeating someone else's words, especially if you do not agree with them: *She says they're, quote 'just good friends' unquote.*

▸noun **1** (C2) [C] informal for **quotation 2 quotes** [plural] informal for **quotation marks**: *Put the title of the article* ***in*** *quotes.*

quoth /kwəʊθ/ (US) /kwoʊθ/ **verb** [T] old use or humorous said: *'Point taken, Kingers,' quoth I.*

quotidian /kwəʊˈtɪd.i.ən/ (US) /kwoʊ-/ **adj** formal ordinary: *Television has become part of our quotidian existence.* → Synonym **everyday**

quotient /ˈkwəʊ.ʃᵊnt/ (US) /ˈkwoʊ-/ **noun** [C] **1** a particular degree or amount of something: *This is a car with a high head-turning quotient (= a lot of people turn to look at it).* **2** specialized the result of dividing one number by another

the Qur'an /kɒrˈɑːn/ (US) /kəˈrɑːn/ **noun** [S] another spelling of **the Koran**

qwerty /ˈkwɜː.ti/ (US) /ˈkwɜːr.t̬i/ **adj** with or relating to the usual arrangement of the keys on the KEYBOARD of a computer, in which the top line of letters begins with q, w, e, r, t, and y: *a qwerty* ***keyboard*** ◦ *qwerty layout*

R, r /ɑːʳ/ US /ɑːr/ noun; adj; adv
▸noun (plural **Rs**, **R's** or **r's**) **LETTER** ▷ **1** [C or U] the 18th letter of the English alphabet **RIVER** ▷ **2** written abbreviation for **river**, used in writing before or after the name of a river: *R Thames* **DIRECTION** ▷ **3** written abbreviation for **right** **ROYAL PERSON** ▷ **4** abbreviation for Rex (= king) or Regina (= queen), used after the name of a king or queen: *Elizabeth R*
▸adj **ROYAL** ▷ **1** written abbreviation for **royal**, used in the names of organizations: *He's an RAF officer.* **DIRECTION** ▷ **2** written abbreviation for **right**: *R eye: 3.20/L eye: 3.25* **FILM** ▷ **3** [C or U] US abbreviation for **restricted**: used to refer to a film that people under 17 years of age can see only if a parent or GUARDIAN is with them
▸adv written abbreviation for **right**

rabbi /ˈræb.aɪ/ noun [C] a religious leader and teacher in the Jewish religion: *Rabbi Jonathan Sacks* ◦ [as form of address] *Good morning, Rabbi.* • **rabbinical** /rəˈbɪn.ɪ.kəl/ adj relating to rabbis: *a rabbinical student/college*

rabbit /ˈræb.ɪt/ noun; verb
▸noun [C] A2 a small animal with long ears and large front teeth that moves by jumping on its long back legs → See also **bunny**
▸verb [I]

PHRASAL VERB **rabbit on** UK informal disapproving to continue talking about something that is not interesting to the person you are talking to: *He's always rabbiting on **about** his stamp collection.*

rabble /ˈræb.l̩/ noun [C usually singular, + sing/pl verb] disapproving **1** a large noisy uncontrolled group of people: *The defeated army returned home as a demoralized rabble.* ◦ *He views his opponents as a mindless rabble.* **2 the rabble** people of a low social position: *Her speech stirred the emotions of the rabble.*

rabble-rouser /ˈræb.lˌraʊ.zəʳ/ US /-zɚ/ noun [C] a person who makes speeches that make people excited or angry, especially in a way that causes them to act as the person wants them to: *Johnson was unpopular with the management because he was a well-known rabble-rouser.* • **ˈrabble-ˌrousing** adj [before noun] *a rabble-rousing speech*

rabi /ˈrʌb.i/ noun [U] Indian English the grain crop that is cut and collected in spring

rabid /ˈræb.ɪd/ adj **1** disapproving having and expressing extreme and unreasonable feelings: *The attack is believed to have been carried out by a group of rabid anti-semites.* ◦ *a rabid feminist* **2** suffering from rabies: *a rabid dog* • **rabidly** /-li/ adv disapproving in an extreme and unreasonable way

rabies /ˈreɪ.biːz/ noun [U] (specialized **hydrophobia**) a serious disease of the nervous system of dogs and other animals, which can also cause death in humans who are bitten by an animal with this disease: *Dogs, cats, foxes, and bats can all **carry** rabies.*

the RAC /ˌɑː.reɪˈsiː/ US /ˌɑːr.eɪ-/ noun [+ sing/pl verb] abbreviation for the Royal Automobile Club: a British organization that gives help and information to drivers who are members of it

raccoon (also **racoon**) /rækˈuːn/ noun [C] (mainly US informal **coon**) a small North American animal with black marks on its face and a long tail with black rings on it

race /reɪs/ noun; verb
▸noun **COMPETITION** ▷ **1** A2 [C] a competition in which all the competitors try to be the fastest and to finish first: *Do you know who **won/lost** the race?* ◦ *Let's **have** a swimming race.* ◦ *They're taking part in a race **to** the top of Ben Nevis.* **2** C1 [C] an attempt to be the first to do or to get something: *Kieran and Andrew are in a race **for** promotion.* ◦ [+ to infinitive] *Three newspapers are involved in a race **to** publish the story.* ◦ *Another candidate has now **entered** the presidential race (= attempted to be elected as president).* ◦ *Finishing this project by December is going to be a race **against time/the clock** (= an attempt to finish fast within a time limit).* **3 races** [plural] a series of horse races in a particular place on one day: *He often has **a day at** the races.* **PEOPLE** ▷ **4** C1 [C or U] a group, especially of people, with particular similar physical characteristics, who are considered as belonging to the same type, or the fact of belonging to such a group: *People of many different races were living side by side.* ◦ *Discrimination on grounds of race will not be tolerated.* ◦ *An increasing number of people in the country are of **mixed** race (= with parents of different races).* **5** [C, + sing/pl verb] a group of people who share the same language, history, characteristics, etc.: *The British are an island race.*

IDIOM **play the race card 1** UK disapproving to try to win an election by saying unfair things about people from another race **2** US disapproving to mention someone's race in order to influence the way people think about them

▸verb **COMPETITION** ▷ **1** B1 [I or T] to (cause to) compete in a race: *He has been racing for over ten years.* ◦ *I used to race (**against**) him when we were boys.* ◦ *He's racing three of his dogs on Saturday.* **HURRY** ▷ **2** C1 [I or T, usually + adv/prep] to move or go fast: *He raced down the street.* ◦ *The ambulance raced (= quickly took) the injured **to** a nearby hospital.* ◦ *The summer seems to have raced **by** (= passed very quickly).* ◦ *He raced the car engine (= made it work faster than it needed to) as he sat impatiently at the traffic lights.*

IDIOM **sb's heart/mind/pulse races** If your heart/mind/pulse races it works extremely fast because of excitement, drugs, illness, etc.: *A glimpse of his bare torso set my pulse racing.*

racecourse /ˈreɪs.kɔːs/ US /-kɔːrs/ noun [C] mainly UK (mainly US **racetrack**) a wide, usually circular, path with a grass surface, on which horses race, or the area that includes this path and buildings around it

racehorse /ˈreɪs.hɔːs/ US /-hɔːrs/ noun [C] a horse bred and trained for racing

ˈrace ˌmeeting noun [C] UK (US **ˈrace ˌmeet**) a series of horse, car, or running races that happen on one day in one place

racer /ˈreɪ.səʳ/ US /-sɚ/ noun [C] **1** a person or thing that races **2** a **racing bike**

ˌrace reˈlations noun [plural] the relationship between the members of different races

racetrack /ˈreɪs.træk/ noun [C] **1** a path or road, usually circular and with a hard surface, on which runners, cars, bicycles, etc. race, or the area that includes this path and buildings around it **2** mainly US for **racecourse**

racial /ˈreɪ.ʃəl/ adj **1** B2 happening between people of different races: *racial **discrimination/prejudice*** ◦ *He*

R

had a vision of a society living in racial harmony. **2** B2 connected with someone's race: *They are members of a racial* ***minority***. • **racially** /-i/ adv C1 *Racially* ***motivated*** *assaults on Asians are increasing.*

racing /ˈreɪ.sɪŋ/ noun [U] **1** competition in races: *I enjoy cycling, but I'm not interested in racing.* ◦ *I like watching* ***horse/motor*** *racing on television.* **2** horse races

ˈracing ˌbike noun [C] (also **racer**) a bicycle designed for speed with a light frame and HANDLEBARS which curve downwards so that the rider's back is parallel to the ground

ˈracing ˌcar noun [C] a low car with a powerful engine and wide wheels, designed for use in races

ˈracing ˌdriver noun [C] a driver of a racing car

ˈracing ˌpigeon noun [C] a PIGEON that takes part in races

ˌracing ˈstart noun [C usually singular] an advantage you have because you start more quickly than other people or things: *We* ***had*** *a racing start* ***over*** *our competitors.*

racism /ˈreɪ.sɪ.zᵊm/ noun [U] (UK old-fashioned **racialism**) B2 the belief that people's qualities are influenced by their race and that the members of other races are not as good as the members of your own, or the resulting unfair treatment of members of other races: *The authorities are taking steps to combat/fight/tackle racism in schools.* ◦ *The report made it plain that* ***institutional*** *racism (= racism in all parts of an organization) is deep-rooted in this country.*

racist /ˈreɪ.sɪst/ noun; adj

▸noun [C] (UK old-fashioned **racialist**) C2 someone who believes that other races are not as good as their own and therefore treats them unfairly: *Two of the killers are known to be racists.*

▸adj disapproving C2 believing that other races are not as good as your own and therefore treating them unfairly: *He furiously denied being racist.*

rack /ræk/ noun; verb

▸noun **FRAME** ▷ **1** [C] a frame or shelf, often formed of bars, that is used to hold things: *a vegetable rack* ◦ *a plate rack* ◦ *a luggage rack* **2** [C] US (UK **frame**) a wooden or plastic triangle used to arrange the balls at the start of a game of BILLIARDS, POOL, SNOOKER, etc. **3 the rack** in the past, a device to which people were tied that stretched their bodies by pulling their arms in one direction and their legs in the other direction, usually used as a way of forcing them to give information **MACHINE** ▷ **4** [C] a bar with tooth-like parts along one edge which fits into a PINION (= a wheel with tooth-like parts) allowing change between circular and straight-line movement **DECAY** ▷ **5 rack and ruin** (mainly US **wrack and ruin**) a state of decay: *The whole farm was* ***going to*** *rack and ruin.*

IDIOM **be on the rack** to be suffering great physical or mental pain

▸verb [T often passive] to cause physical or mental pain, or trouble, to someone or something: *Even at the end, when cancer racked his body, he was calm and cheerful.* ◦ *The dog was already racked* ***by/with*** *the pains of old age.* ◦ *He was racked* ***by/with*** *doubts/guilt.*

IDIOM **rack your brains** to think very hard: *I've been racking my brains all day but I can't remember her name.*

PHRASAL VERB **rack sth up 1** mainly US informal to gradually get more points, profits, etc.: *He has racked up 450 points in three months.* ◦ *Astronomical* ***profits/losses*** *were racked up by airlines last year.* → Synonym **accumulate 2** to increase something such as a rent or price, especially by an amount that is considered to be too much: *Our landlord racked up the rent by 15 percent this year.*

-racked /-rækt/ suffix showing or feeling the physical or mental pain, trouble, etc. mentioned: *a pain-racked gesture* ◦ *a guilt-racked society*

racket /ˈræk.ɪt/ noun

SPORT ▷ **1** A2 (also **racquet**) [C] an object used for hitting the ball in various sports, consisting of a net fixed tightly to a round frame with a long handle: *a tennis/squash/badminton racket* **NOISE** ▷ **2** C2 [S] informal an unpleasant loud continuous noise: *They were* ***making*** *such a racket outside that I couldn't get to sleep.* **CRIME** ▷ **3** [C usually singular] informal a dishonest or illegal activity that makes money: *They were jailed for* ***running*** *a protection/prostitution racket.* → See also **protection 4** [C usually singular] disapproving a way of making a large unfair profit: *Phone chat lines are a real racket.*

racketeering /ˌræk.əˈtɪə.rɪŋ/ US /-ˈtɪr.ɪŋ/ noun [U] disapproving making money from a dishonest or illegal activity: *They have been accused of racketeering.* • **racketeer** /-ˈtɪəʳ/ US /-ˈtɪr/ noun [C] disapproving someone who makes money from a dishonest or illegal activity

racking /ˈræk.ɪŋ/ adj very bad and very painful: *a racking cough/headache/toothache*

raconteur /ˌræk.ɒnˈtɜːʳ/ US /-ɑːnˈtɜː/ noun [C] someone who tells funny or interesting stories: *He was a brilliant raconteur.*

racoon /rækˈuːn/ noun [C] a **raccoon**

racy /ˈreɪ.si/ adj (of speech or writing) exciting, especially because of being about sex, or (of someone or something) having an exciting, interesting, and attractive appearance, sometimes in a sexual way: *a racy story* ◦ *a racy style* ◦ *a racy advertisement* ◦ *racy swimwear* ◦ *She is trying to create a racier image for herself.* • **racily** /-sɪ.li/ adv • **raciness** /-nəs/ noun [U]

rad /ræd/ adj slang extremely exciting or good: *a rad new computer game*

radar /ˈreɪ.dɑːʳ/ US /-dɑːr/ noun [U] a system which uses radio waves to find the position of objects which cannot be seen: *Other vessels in the area show up on the ship's radar (****screen****).*

IDIOM **fall off/drop off the radar** (also **drop beneath the/sb's radar**) to be forgotten or ignored, often because someone's attention is on something more important: *I was so busy at work, organizing a summer holiday just dropped off the radar.*

ˈradar ˌtrap noun [C] a system, using radar, which the police use to catch vehicles that are travelling too fast

raddled /ˈræd.ld/ adj UK looking tired or old

radial /ˈreɪ.di.əl/ adj; noun

▸adj spreading out from a central point: *a radial road system* • **radially** /-i/ adv

▸noun [C] (UK also **ˈradial ˈtyre**, US also **ˈradial ˈtire**) a tyre that has strings inside the rubber that go across the edge of the wheel at an angle of 90° rather than along it

radiance /ˈreɪ.di.əns/ noun [U] **HAPPINESS/BEAUTY** ▷ **1** happiness, beauty, or good health which you can

R

see in someone's face: *He was struck by the radiance of her smile.* **LIGHT/HEAT** ▷ **2** light or heat that comes from something: *We basked in the radiance of the African sun.*

radiant /ˈreɪ.di.ənt/ adj **HAPPY/BEAUTIFUL** ▷ **1** obviously very happy, or very beautiful: *He gave a radiant* ***smile*** *when he heard her news.* **HEAT/LIGHT** ▷ **2** [before noun] producing heat or light: *a radiant heater*

radiate /ˈreɪ.di.eɪt/ verb **PRODUCE HEAT/LIGHT** ▷ **1** [I or T] to produce heat and/or light, or (of heat or light) to be produced: *The planet Jupiter radiates twice as much heat from inside as it receives from the Sun.* ◦ *A single beam of light radiated* ***from*** *the lighthouse.* **EXPRESS** ▷ **2** [I or T] to show an emotion or quality, or (of an emotion or quality) to be shown or felt: *He was radiating joy and happiness.* ◦ *Enthusiasm was radiating* ***from*** *her.* **SPREAD** ▷ **3** [I + adv/prep] to spread out in all directions from a central point: *Flows of lava radiated* ***out from*** *the volcano's crater.* ◦ *Just before the breeding season, these birds radiate outwards to warmer climates.*

radiation /ˌreɪ.diˈeɪ.ʃᵊn/ noun [U] **1** C1 a form of energy that comes from a nuclear reaction and that can be very dangerous to health: *Many servicemen suffered radiation* ***sickness*** *after the early atomic tests.* **2** energy from heat or light that you cannot see: *microwave/ultraviolet/electromagnetic radiation*

radiator /ˈreɪ.di.eɪ.təʳ/ US /-t̬ɚ/ noun [C] a device, usually a container filled with water, that sends out heat, often as part of a heating or cooling system: *When we installed the central heating, we put a radiator in every room.* ◦ *My car engine overheated because the water had leaked out of the radiator.*

radical /ˈræd.ɪ.kᵊl/ adj; noun

▸adj **SUPPORTING CHANGE** ▷ **1** C2 believing or expressing the belief that there should be great or extreme social or political change: *He was known as a radical reformer/thinker/politician.* ◦ *These people have very radical views.* **VERY IMPORTANT** ▷ **2** C1 relating to the most important parts of something or someone; complete or extreme: *We need to make some radical* ***changes*** *to our operating procedures.* ◦ *She has had to undergo radical surgery (= aimed at removing the cause of a disease).* • **radically** /-i/ adv C1 *Barker introduced some radically new ideas.*

▸noun [C] C2 a person who supports great social and political change: *She was a radical all her life.* • **radicalism** /-ɪ.zᵊm/ noun [U]

radicchio /ræˈdɪ.ki.əʊ/ US /-oʊ/ noun [U] a type of plant with purple or red leaves that are eaten uncooked in salads: *Radicchio has a slightly bitter flavour.*

radii /ˈreɪ.di.aɪ/ plural of **radius**

radio /ˈreɪ.di.əʊ/ US /-oʊ/ noun; verb

▸noun (plural **radios**) **1** A1 [C] a piece of electronic equipment used for listening to radio broadcasts: *a car radio* ◦ *I switched on the radio.* **2** A1 [S or U] the programmes that you hear when you listen to the radio: *I heard a good programme* ***on the*** *radio last night.* ◦ *I don't listen to radio much.* **3** B1 [U] the system or work of broadcasting sound programmes for the public to listen to: *a local radio station* ◦ *She's got some kind of job in radio.* **4** [C or U] a piece of electronic equipment that can send and receive spoken messages or signals, or the messages or signals that are sent or received: *We sent a message over the radio/by radio.* ◦ *The children had radio-****controlled*** *toy cars for Christmas.*

▸verb [I or T] to send a message to someone by radio: *We'll have to radio for more supplies.*

radioactive /ˌreɪ.di.əʊˈæk.tɪv/ US /-oʊ-/ adj having or producing the energy which comes from the breaking up of atoms: *Uranium is a radioactive material.* ◦ *radioactive* ***waste***

radioactivity /ˌreɪ.di.əʊ.ækˈtɪv.ɪ.ti/ US /-oʊ.ækˈtɪv.ə.t̬i/ noun [U] **1** the quality that some atoms have of producing energy, which can be very harmful to health **2** the energy produced by atoms in this way: *A dangerous amount of radioactivity was* ***released*** *into the environment last month.*

ˌradio aˈlarm ˌclock noun [C] (also **ˌradio aˈlarm**, also **ˌclock ˈradio**) a radio that can be switched on by a clock at a particular time, usually to wake someone up

radiocarbon dating /ˌreɪ.di.əʊ.kɑː.bənˈdeɪ.tɪŋ/ US /-oʊ.kɑːr.bənˈdeɪ.t̬ɪŋ/ noun [U] specialized **carbon dating**

radiographer /ˌreɪ.diˈɒg.rə.fəʳ/ US /-ˈɑː.grə.fɚ/ noun [C] a person who operates a machine that uses RADIATION, especially X-RAYS, to take pictures of the inside of people or things, or for the treatment of disease

radiography /ˌreɪ.diˈɒg.rə.fi/ US /-ˈɑː.grə-/ noun [U] the use of RADIATION (= a form of energy), especially X-RAYS, either to produce a picture of the inside of people or objects, or for the treatment of disease

radiologist /ˌreɪ.diˈɒl.ə.dʒɪst/ US /-ˈɑː.lə-/ noun [C] a person who specializes in radiology

radiology /ˌreɪ.diˈɒl.ə.dʒi/ US /-ˈɑː.lə-/ noun [U] the scientific study of the medical use of RADIATION, especially X-RAYS

ˌradio ˈtelescope noun [C] a device for receiving, for scientific study, the ELECTROMAGNETIC waves sent out by objects in space such as stars

radiotherapy /ˌreɪ.di.əʊˈθer.ə.pi/ US /-oʊ-/ noun [U] the use of controlled amounts of RADIATION (= a form of energy) aimed at a particular part of the body, to treat disease

radish /ˈræd.ɪʃ/ noun [C] a small vegetable, usually red or white and round or shaped like a finger, which grows underground and is usually eaten uncooked in salads

radium /ˈreɪ.di.əm/ noun [U] (symbol **Ra**) a RADIOACTIVE chemical element that is used in the treatment of some diseases, especially CANCER

R

radius /ˈreɪ.di.əs/ noun [C] (plural **radii**) **DISTANCE** ▷ **1** (the length of) a straight line joining the centre of a circle to its edge or the centre of a SPHERE to its surface: *The radius of this wheel is 30 cm.* ◦ *This wheel* ***has*** *a radius* ***of*** *30 cm.* **2** a distance: *The station, shopping centre and school lie* ***within*** *a one-mile radius of the house.* **BONE** ▷ **3** specialized the thicker of the two bones in the lower arm

radon /ˈreɪ.dɒn/ US /-dɑːn/ noun [U] (symbol **Rn**) a chemical element that is a RADIOACTIVE gas formed when radium decays and found naturally in rock and soil: *Tests showed high radon levels.*

the RAF /ˌɑː.reɪˈef/ US /ˌɑːr.eɪ-/ /ræf/ noun [+ sing/pl verb] abbreviation for the Royal Air Force: the air force of the UK: *He was in the RAF for 30 years.* → See also **air force**

Rafferty's rules /ˈræf.ə.tizˌruːlz/ US /-ə.t̬iz-/ noun [plural] Australian informal (especially used when referring to a competition or an organization that is not well organized) no rules

raffia /ˈræf.i.ə/ noun [U] long narrow pieces of pale yellow dried leaf, especially from a type of PALM tree, used as string or for making hats, containers, etc.

Australian English informal an exciting or entertaining event involving a lot of activity: *The party was a rage.*

IDIOM **be (all) the rage** old-fashioned to be very popular at a particular time: *Long hair for men was all the rage in the 70s.*

raffish /ˈræf.ɪʃ/ **adj** not following usual social standards of behaviour or appearance, especially in a careless and attractive way: *He has a certain raffish elegance.* • **raffishness** /-nəs/ noun [U]

raffle /ˈræf.l̩/ **noun; verb**
▸noun [C] an activity in which people buy tickets with different numbers, some of which are later chosen to win prizes, that is organized in order to make money for a good social purpose: *a raffle* ***ticket****/prize* ◦ *I have never won anything* ***in*** *a raffle.*
▸verb [T] to offer something as a prize in a raffle: *We are going to raffle* ***off*** *a car for the hospital appeal.* → See also **draw**

raft /rɑːft/ (US) /ræft/ **noun; verb**

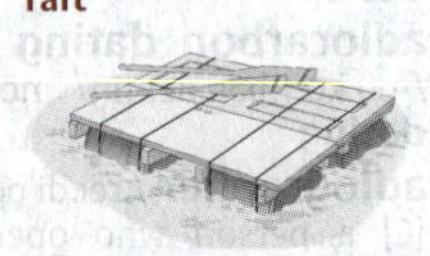
raft

▸noun **FLOATING STRUCTURE** ▷ **1** [C] a flat floating structure for travelling across water, often made of pieces of wood tied roughly together and moved along with a PADDLE (= pole with a flat end): *We lashed together anything that would float to make a raft.* **2** [C] a fixed flat floating structure which swimmers can use to land on or DIVE from **3** [C] a small rubber or plastic boat that can be filled with air: *a rubber raft* **MANY** ▷ **4** [C usually singular] a large number or range; a lot: *a raft* ***of*** *data* ◦ *We have designed* ***a whole*** *raft* ***of*** *measures to improve the transport system.*
▸verb [I or T] to travel or transport something on a raft: *They rafted their supplies down the river.* ◦ *We rafted through the rapids.* ◦ *Have you ever been* ***white water*** *rafting?*

rafter /ˈrɑːf.təʳ/ (US) /ˈræf.tɚ/ **noun** [C] any of the large sloping pieces of wood which support a roof

rag /ræg/ **noun; verb**
▸noun [C] **CLOTH** ▷ **1** a torn piece of old cloth: *I keep these rags for cleaning the car.* **2** US for **duster 3 rags** [plural] clothes that are old and torn: *an old man dressed* ***in*** *rags.* ◦ *Their clothes were* ***in*** *rags (= torn).* **NEWSPAPER** ▷ **4** informal a newspaper or magazine that is considered to be of bad quality: *He had his picture taken for some* ***local*** *rag.* **COLLEGE EVENT** ▷ **5** in Britain, a series of entertaining events and activities organized by college students once a year to collect money for CHARITY **MUSIC** ▷ **6** a piece of RAGTIME music
▸verb [T] **(-gg-)** old-fashioned informal to say things that are funny but a little unkind: *They ragged him* ***about*** *his girlfriend.*

R

raga /ˈrɑː.gə/ **noun** [C] a traditional pattern of notes in Indian music; a piece of music based on a particular pattern

ragamuffin /ˈræg.əˌmʌf.ɪn/ **noun** [C] old-fashioned informal a dirty untidy child in torn clothes

ˌrag-and-ˈbone man **noun** [C] UK (US **ragman**) in the past, a man who went round the streets of a town to buy old clothes, furniture, and other unwanted things cheaply

ragbag /ˈræg.bæg/ **noun** [C usually singular] a confused mixture of different types of things: *His book is just a ragbag* ***of*** *unsupported opinions.*

ˌrag ˈdoll **noun** [C] a soft child's toy, made from cloth, in the shape of a person

rage /reɪdʒ/ **noun; verb**
▸noun **ANGER** ▷ **1** (B2) [C or U] (a period of) extreme or violent anger: *Her sudden* ***towering*** *rages were terrifying.* ◦ *I was frightened because I had never seen him* ***in*** *such* ***a*** *rage before.* ◦ *He flew into* ***a fit of*** *rage over the smallest mistake.* **EVENT** ▷ **2** [C usually singular] Australian English informal an exciting or entertaining event involving a lot of activity: *The party was a rage.*

▸verb [I usually + adv/prep] **1** (C2) to speak very angrily to someone: *He raged* ***at*** *(= spoke angrily to) us for forgetting to order a replacement.* **2** (C2) to happen in a strong or violent way: *The storm raged outside.* ◦ *A flu epidemic is raging in/through local schools.* ◦ *The argument rages* ***on*** *(= continues strongly).*

-rage /-reɪdʒ/ **suffix** describes situations where people become extremely angry or violent: *road-rage* ◦ *trolley-rage* ◦ *air-rage*

ragga /ˈræg.ə/ **noun** [U] a type of music which combines elements of REGGAE, RAP and dance music, mostly played by Afro-Caribbean people

ragged /ˈræg.ɪd/ **adj** **1** (of clothes) torn and not in good condition: *The children were wearing dirty, ragged clothes.* **2** (of a person) untidy, dirty, and wearing old, torn clothes: *Two ragged children stood outside the station, begging for money.* **3** (especially of an edge) rough and not smooth: *The leaves of this plant have ragged edges.* ◦ *The patient's* ***breathing*** *was ragged (= not regular) and uneven.* ◦ *A ragged (= not straight) line of people were waiting at the bus stop.* **4** not performing well, because of not being organized: *The team was rather ragged in the first half of the match.* • **raggedly** /-li/ **adv** • **raggedness** /-nəs/ **noun** [U]

raging /ˈreɪ.dʒɪŋ/ **adj** **1** very severe or extreme: *a raging toothache* ◦ *a raging* ***thirst*** ◦ *He's got a raging (= high)* ***temperature****.* ◦ *a raging bore* **2** very strong or violent: *a raging temper* ◦ *The rains had turned the stream into a raging* ***torrent****.*

raglan /ˈræg.lən/ **adj** (of a sleeve) sewn in two straight lines out from the neck to a point under the arm: *a sweater with raglan* ***sleeves***

ragout /rægˈuː/ **noun** [C or U] a dish consisting of small pieces of meat or fish and vegetables cooked together

ˌrags-to-ˈriches **adj** [before noun] used to describe what happens to a person who was poor but becomes rich: *a rags-to-riches* ***story***

ragtag /ˈræg.tæg/ **adj** untidy and not similar or organized: *The village was guarded by a ragtag group of soldiers.* ◦ *He arrived with a ragtag collection of friends.*

ragtime /ˈræg.taɪm/ **noun** [U] a type of popular music, developed by black musicians in North America in the early 1900s, with tunes that are not on regular beats

the ˈrag ˌtrade **noun** [S] informal the clothes-making industry

ragù /rægˈuː/ **noun** [C or U] an Italian sauce made with meat and tomatoes, eaten with PASTA

raid /reɪd/ **noun; verb**
▸noun [C] **1** (C2) a short sudden attack, usually by a small group of people: *The commandos* ***made/staged/ carried out*** *a daring raid (****on*** *the enemy).* ◦ *planes on a* ***bombing*** *raid* **2** the act of entering a place by force in order to steal from it: *Millions of dollars were stolen in a* ***bank*** *raid last night.* **3** (C2) an occasion when the police enter a place suddenly in order to find someone or something: *The drugs were found during a police raid* ***on*** *the house.*
▸verb [T] **1** (C2) to attack a place suddenly: *The nomads raided the enemy camp and captured over 100 camels.* **2** to enter a place illegally and usually violently, and steal from it: *The post office was raided late at night.*

3 C2 (of the police) to enter a place suddenly in order to find someone or something: *Police officers from the organized crime branch have raided solicitors' offices in central London.* **4** informal to take something from a place, usually secretly: *I caught Toby raiding **the fridge**.*

raider /ˈreɪ.dəʳ/ US /-dɚ/ **noun** [C] someone who enters a place illegally and usually violently, and steals from it: *Armed raiders forced their way into the couple's home.*

rail /reɪl/ **noun; verb**

▸**noun** TRAINS ▷ **1** B1 [U] the system of transport that uses trains: *Environmentalists argue that more goods should be transported **by** rail.* **2** [C] one of the two metal bars fixed to the ground on which trains travel: *A train left/went off the rails and crashed into the bank, killing several passengers.* BAR ▷ **3** C2 [C] a horizontal bar fixed in position, especially to a wall or to vertical posts, used to close something off, as a support, or to hang things on: *Will spectators please stay behind the rail?* ◦ ***Hold onto** the rail so that you don't fall.* ◦ *The **(clothes)** rail in her wardrobe was crammed full of dresses.* ◦ *He folded the towels and hung them on the **towel** rail (US **towel** rack).*

IDIOM **go off the rails** informal to start behaving in a way that is not generally acceptable, especially dishonestly or illegally: *He went off the rails in his first year at university.*

▸**verb** [I + prep] formal to complain angrily: *He railed **against/at** the injustices of the system.*

PHRASAL VERB **rail sth off** to close something, especially using railings: *Part of the playing field had been railed off for use as a car park.*

railcard /ˈreɪl.kɑːd/ US /-kɑːrd/ **noun** [C] in Britain, a card which you can buy and then use to buy train tickets more cheaply: *a **young person's** railcard* ◦ *a **family** railcard*

railing /ˈreɪ.lɪŋ/ **noun** [C usually plural] a vertical post, usually metal or wooden, that is used together with other such posts to form a fence: *Tourists pressed their faces against the palace railings.*

raillery /ˈreɪ.lər.i/ US /-lɚ.i/ **noun** [U] formal joking or laughing at someone in a friendly way

railroad /ˈreɪl.rəʊd/ US /-roʊd/ **noun; verb**

▸**noun** [C] (written abbreviation **RR**) A2 US for **railway**

▸**verb** [T usually + adv/prep] to force something to happen or force someone to do something, especially quickly or unfairly: *We were railroaded **into** sign**ing** the agreement.*

ˈrailroad ˌtie **noun** [C] US for **sleeper**

railway /ˈreɪl.weɪ/ **noun** [C] UK (US **railroad**) **1** A2 the metal tracks on which trains run: *We live close to the railway **line**.* ◦ *She travelled across Siberia on the Trans-Siberian railway.* **2** A2 the system of tracks, stations, trains, etc.: *a railway station/timetable/siding, etc.* ◦ *Thomas Grant worked **on the** railway(s) for 50 years.*

raiment /ˈreɪ.mənt/ **noun** [U] old use clothes

rain /reɪn/ **noun; verb**

▸**noun** [U] **1** A1 drops of water from clouds: *Rain is forecast for tomorrow.* ◦ *Come inside out of **the** rain.* ◦ *We had **heavy/light** rain all day.* ◦ *We got caught in **pouring/torrential** (= a lot of) rain without either raincoats or umbrellas.* ◦ *There will be **showers of** rain/rain **showers** (= short periods of rain) in the east.* ◦ ***It looks like** rain (= as if rain is going to fall).* **2 the rains** [plural] the season of the year in tropical countries when there is a lot of rain: *Villagers are now waiting for the rains to **come** so that the rice will grow.* ◦ *This is the third year in a row that the rains have failed.*

IDIOM **come rain or shine** whatever happens: *Come rain or shine, I'll see you on Thursday.*

▸**verb** [I] A1 If it rains, water falls from the sky in small drops: *I think **it**'s starting to rain.* ◦ ***It**'s raining **hard/heavily** (= a large amount of rain is falling).*

IDIOMS **it never rains but it pours** UK (US **when it rains, it pours**) said when one bad thing happens, followed by a lot of other bad things, which make a bad situation worse • **it's raining cats and dogs!** old-fashioned something that you say when it is raining heavily • **rain on sb's parade** to do something that spoils someone's plans: *I'm sorry to rain on your parade but you're not allowed to have alcohol on the premises.*

PHRASAL VERBS **rain (sth) down** to fall in large amounts, or to direct something in large amounts, usually forcefully or violently: ***Bombs** rained down **on** the besieged city.* ◦ *Her attacker rained down **blows** on her.* • **rain sth off** UK (US **rain sth out**) If an event is rained off, it cannot start or continue because it is raining: *His hockey match was rained off.*

rainbow /ˈreɪn.bəʊ/ US /-boʊ/ **noun** [C] B2 an ARCH (= curved shape) of different colours seen in the sky when rain is falling and the sun is shining: *The tropical butterfly's wings were shimmering with **all the colours of the** rainbow.*

ˈrain ˌcheck **noun** [C] US **1** a piece of paper that you are given by a shop when something that is advertised for sale at a certain price is not available. This piece of paper allows you to buy the product at the advertised price when it becomes available. **2** a ticket that allows you to see an event at a later time if bad weather stops that event from happening

IDIOM **take a rain check (on sth)** informal used to tell someone that you cannot accept their invitation now, but would like to do so at a later time: *Mind if I take a rain check on that drink? I've got to work late tonight.*

raincoat /ˈreɪŋ.kəʊt/ US /-koʊt/ **noun** [C] A2 a coat which protects the wearer against rain: *a plastic raincoat*

raindrop /ˈreɪn.drɒp/ US /-drɑːp/ **noun** [C] a single drop of rain

rainfall /ˈreɪn.fɔːl/ US /-fɑːl/ **noun** [U] rain, or the amount of rain that falls: ***Heavy** rainfall ruined the match.* ◦ *The **average** annual rainfall in this region is 750 mm.*

rainforest /ˈreɪn.fɒr.ɪst/ US /-fɔːr-/ **noun** [C or U] B1 a forest in a tropical area which receives a lot of rain: *a **tropical** rainforest*

ˈrain ˌgauge **noun** [C] a device for measuring how much rain falls

rainstorm /ˈreɪn.stɔːm/ US /-stɔːrm/ **noun** [C] a weather condition with strong wind and heavy rain

rainwater /ˈreɪnˌwɔː.təʳ/ US /-ˌwɑː.t̬ɚ/ **noun** [U] water that has fallen as rain, rather than water that has come from a TAP

rainy /ˈreɪ.ni/ **adj** B1 raining a lot: *We had three rainy days on holiday, but otherwise it was sunny.*

IDIOM **save/keep money for a rainy day** to save money for a time when it might be needed unexpectedly: *Luckily she had saved some money for a rainy day.*

raise /reɪz/ **verb; noun**

▸**verb** [T] LIFT ▷ **1** B1 to lift something to a higher

R

position: *Would all those in favour please raise their **hands**?* ◦ *He raised the window and leaned out.* ◦ *Mary Quant was the first fashion designer to raise hemlines.* **INCREASE** ▷ **2** B1 to cause something to increase or become bigger, better, higher, etc.: *The government plan to raise **taxes**.* ◦ *I had to raise my **voice** (= speak more loudly) to make myself heard over the noise.* ◦ *The inspector said that **standards** at the school had to be raised.* ◦ *Our little chat has raised my **spirits** (= made me feel happier).* **EXIST** ▷ **3** B2 to cause to exist: *Her answers raised **doubts/fears/suspicions** in my mind.* ◦ *This discussion has raised many important **issues/problems**.* ◦ *The announcement raised a **cheer/laugh**.* ◦ *I want to raise (= talk about) two problems/questions **with** you.* ◦ *I want to start my own business if I can raise (= obtain) the **money/cash/capital/funds**.* ◦ formal *The chapel was raised (= built) as a memorial to her son.* **DEVELOP** ▷ **4** B2 to take care of a person, or an animal or plant, until they are completely grown: *Her parents died when she was a baby and she was raised by her grandparents.* ◦ *The lambs had to be raised **by hand** (= fed artificial milk by people) when their mother died.* ◦ *The farmer raises (= breeds) chickens and pigs.* ◦ *The soil around here isn't good enough for raising (= growing) crops.* **CARD GAMES** ▷ **5** If you raise another player in a game of cards, you risk more money than that player has risked: *I'll raise you.* ◦ [+ two objects] *I'll raise you $50.* **STOP** ▷ **6** formal to end or stop: *They agreed to raise the trade embargo if three conditions were met.* ◦ *After three weeks the siege was raised.* **COMMUNICATE** ▷ **7** to communicate with someone, especially by phone or radio: *I've been trying to raise Jack/Tokyo all day.*

IDIOMS **raise (a few) eyebrows** to cause surprise or shock: *Jemma's miniskirt raised a few eyebrows at the board meeting.* • **raise your game** to make an effort to improve the way that you do something: *They're going to have to raise their game if they want to stay in the Premiership this season.* • **raise your hand to/against sb** to hit someone: *Never raise your hand to a child.*

▸noun [C] US for RISE (= increase in pay): *She asked the boss for a raise.*

-raiser /-reɪ.zəʳ/ US /-zɚ/ **suffix** a person or thing that causes the stated thing to exist or to be obtained: *a money-raiser* ◦ *These new taxes are designed to be a revenue-raiser.*

raisin /ˈreɪ.zən/ **noun** [C] a dried black GRAPE

raison d'être /ˌrez.ɑ̃ːˈdet.rə/ US /ˌreɪ.zɑːn-/ **noun** [C usually singular] (plural **raisons d'être**) a reason for existence: *Her job is her raison d'être.*

raita /ˈraɪ.tə/ **noun** [U] a South Asian dish consisting of YOGURT with very small pieces of RAW (= not cooked) vegetables mixed in

the Raj /rɑːdʒ/, /rɑːʒ/ **noun** [S] the period of British rule in India: *the days of the Raj*

rajah /ˈrɑː.dʒə/ **noun** [C] a male Indian ruler → See also **rani**

rake /reɪk/ **noun; verb**

▸noun [C] **TOOL** ▷ **1** a garden tool with a long handle and long, pointed metal parts sticking out in a row at the bottom, used for making the earth level or for collecting leaves, etc. **MAN** ▷ **2** old-fashioned a man, especially one who is rich or with a high social position, who lives in an IMMORAL way, espe-cially having sex with a lot of women **SLOPE** ▷ **3** a slope

▸verb **SEARCH** ▷ **1** [I + adv/prep] to search in a container by moving the contents around quickly: *He raked **about in** the drawer looking for his passport.* ◦ *I've raked **through** the cupboard but I can't find my tennis racket.* **USE TOOL** ▷ **2** [I or T] to use a rake to make earth level or to collect leaves: *In the autumn I rake (**up**) the dead leaves.* ◦ *Rake (**over**) the soil before planting the seeds.*

PHRASAL VERBS **rake sth in** to earn or get a large amount of money: *He rakes in over £100,000 a year.* ◦ *She's really raking **it** in (= making a lot of money).* • **rake sth out** UK to look for something and find it, usually among various things you have stored: *I raked this old blanket out for camping.* • **rake over sth** to keep talking or thinking about an unpleasant event or experience: *He keeps on raking over his divorce, when really he should be getting on with his life.* • **rake sth up** to talk again about a past event or experience which should be forgotten, because it upsets or annoys someone else: *She's always raking up the past/that old quarrel.* • **rake sth/sb up** to get the things or people you need, with difficulty or by looking in various places: *I'm trying to rake up some people to play football on Saturday – do you want to come along?*

raked /reɪkt/ **adj** sloping: *a steeply raked stage, sloping down towards the audience* ◦ *raked wings* ◦ *a raked mast*

ˈrake-off noun [C] informal a dishonest or illegal share in profits that is given to someone who has been involved in making the profits

rakish /ˈreɪ.kɪʃ/ **adj** **1** confidently careless and informal: *He wore his hat at a rakish **angle**.* **2** old-fashioned describes a man, especially a rich man, who lives in an IMMORAL way, especially having sex with a lot of women: *He has a rakish air about him.* • **rakishly** /-li/ **adv** • **rakishness** /-nəs/ **noun** [U]

rally /ˈræl.i/ **noun; verb**

▸noun [C] **MEETING** ▷ **1** C2 a public meeting of a large group of people, especially supporters of a particular opinion: *5,000 people **held** an anti-nuclear rally.* ◦ *an **election/campaign** rally* **RACE** ▷ **2** C2 a car or motorcycle race, especially over long distances on public roads **SPORT** ▷ **3** a continuous exchange of hits between players in tennis, SQUASH or BADMINTON **IMPROVEMENT** ▷ **4** an improvement: *Share prices fell again today after yesterday's rally.*

▸verb **SUPPORT** ▷ **1** [I or T] to (cause to) come together in order to provide support or make a shared effort: *Supporters/Opponents of the new shopping development are trying to rally local people **in favour of/against** it.* ◦ *The prime minister has called on the public to rally **to/behind** the government.* ◦ [+ obj + to infinitive] *The general rallied his forces **to** defend the town.* ◦ *'Workers of the world unite' was their rallying **cry/call** (= a phrase said to encourage support).* **IMPROVE** ▷ **2** [I] to return to a better condition: *The nurse said my mother had rallied after a poor night.* ◦ *The team played badly in the first half of the match but rallied in the second.* ◦ *The pound rallied **against** the dollar in trading today.*

PHRASAL VERB **rally round (sb)** UK (US **rally around (sb)**) to help or support someone: *When I'm ill, my friends always rally round.*

ram /ræm/ **verb; noun**

▸verb [I or T] (**-mm-**) to hit or push something with force: *Someone rammed (**into**) my car while it was parked outside my house.* ◦ *He rammed the sweets/his pipe **into** his mouth.* ◦ *I rammed **down** the soil around the fence post.* ◦ *The prisoners who were being force-fed had tubes rammed **down** their throats.* ◦ *She slammed* the door and rammed **home** the bolt (= closed it forcefully and completely).

IDIOMS **ram sth down sb's throat** to force someone who disagrees with you to listen to your opinions • **ram sth home** to emphasize the importance of what you are saying in order to make certain people understand it: *He thumped the desk as he rammed his point home.*

PHRASAL VERB **ram sth into sb** to force someone to accept an idea, opinion or principle: *It's time someone rammed a bit of* ***sense*** *into you.*

▸noun [C] **SHEEP** ▷ **1** an adult male sheep that can breed **EQUIPMENT** ▷ **2** (also **battering ram**) a piece of equipment used to hit something and force it open or break it: *They used a ram to break down the door.* **3** a moving part in a machine that puts pressure or force on something

RAM /ræm/ noun [U] specialized abbreviation for random access memory: a type of computer memory that can be searched in any order and changed as necessary → Compare **ROM**

Ramadan /ˈræm.ə.dæn/ (US) /ˌræm.əˈdɑːn/ noun [U] the ninth month of the Muslim year, during which time Muslims have no food or drink during the day

ramble /ˈræm.bl̩/ verb; noun

▸verb **WALK** ▷ **1** [I usually + adv/prep] to walk for pleasure, especially in the countryside: *I love to ramble* ***through*** *the fields and lanes in this part of the country.* ◦ *Shall we* ***go*** *rambling tomorrow?* **TALK/WRITE** ▷ **2** [I] disapproving to talk or write in a confused way, often for a long time: *Sorry, I'm rambling (****on****) – let me get back to the point.* **SPREAD** ▷ **3** [I] (especially of a plant) to go in many different directions: *An old clematis rambles* ***over*** *the garden wall.*

▸noun [C] a long walk especially through the countryside: *We* ***go for a*** *ramble through the woods every Saturday.*

rambler /ˈræm.blər/ (US) /-blɚ/ noun [C] a person who enjoys long walks in the countryside

rambling /ˈræm.blɪŋ/ adj; noun

▸adj **TALK** ▷ **1** too long and confused: *a long rambling speech* **SPREADING** ▷ **2** large and spreading out in many different directions: *a rambling rose* ◦ *a rambling old* ***house***

▸noun [U] **WALKING** ▷ **1** the activity of going for long walks in the countryside **SPEECH/WRITING** ▷ **2 ramblings** [plural] long and confused speech or writing

Rambo /ˈræm.bəʊ/ (US) /-boʊ/ noun (plural **Rambos**) [C] someone who uses, or threatens to use, strong and violent methods against their enemies: *The Americans responded, Rambo-****style****/Rambo-****like****, by threatening to attack immediately if their conditions were not met.*

rambunctious /ræmˈbʌŋk.ʃəs/ adj mainly US full of energy and difficult to control: *rambunctious children* ◦ *a lively and rambunctious puppy*

ramekin /ˈræm.ə.kɪn/ noun [C] a small dish in which food for one person is baked and served

ramification /ˌræm.ɪ.fɪˈkeɪ.ʃənz/ noun [C usually plural] the possible results of an action: *Have you considered all the ramifications* ***of*** *your suggestion?*

ramp /ræmp/ noun; verb

▸noun [C] **1** an artificial slope: *I pushed the wheelchair up the ramp and into the supermarket.* **2** UK a raised strip built into a road to make vehicles drive more slowly **3** US for **slip road**

▸verb

PHRASAL VERB **ramp sth up 1** If a business ramps up its activity, it increases it: *The company announced plans to ramp up production to 10,000 units per month.* ◦ *To stay competitive, they'll have to ramp up product development as well as cutting prices.* **2** to increase the speed, power, or cost of something: *Announcement of the merger is expected to ramp up share prices over the next few days.* ◦ *Mitsubishi has ramped up the speed of its new micro-controllers.*

rampage verb; noun

▸verb [I] /ræmˈpeɪdʒ/ to go through an area making a lot of noise and causing damage: *The demonstrators rampaged* ***through*** *the town, smashing windows and setting fire to cars.*

▸noun [C or U] /ˈræm.peɪdʒ/ violent and usually wild behaviour: *Rioters* ***went on a/the*** *rampage through the city.*

rampant /ˈræm.pənt/ adj **INCREASING** ▷ **1** (of something bad) getting worse quickly and in an uncontrolled way: *rampant corruption* ◦ *Rampant inflation means that our wage increases soon become worth nothing.* ◦ *He said that he had encountered rampant prejudice in his attempts to get a job.* ◦ *Disease is rampant in the overcrowded city.* **STANDING** ▷ **2** [after noun] specialized (of an animal represented on a COAT OF ARMS) standing on its back legs with its front legs raised: *a lion rampant*

rampart /ˈræm.pɑːt/ (US) /-pɑːrt/ noun [C usually plural] a large wall built round a town, castle, etc. to protect it

ˈram-raiding noun [U] the act of driving a car, usually a stolen car, through the front window of a shop so that the contents of the shop can be stolen: *The police are increasing their efforts to prevent car thefts and subsequent ram-raiding.* • **ˈram-raid** noun [C] • **ˈram-raider** noun [C]

ramrod /ˈræm.rɒd/ (US) /-rɑːd/ noun [C] a long thin rod used for pushing explosives, bullets, etc. into old types of gun

IDIOM **(as) stiff/straight as a ramrod** very straight: *The old lady's back is still as straight as a ramrod.*

ramshackle /ˈræmˌʃæk.l̩/ adj **1** disapproving badly or untidily made and likely to break or fall down easily: *There's a ramshackle old shed at the bottom of the garden* **2** badly organized: *We need to reorganize this ramshackle system.*

ran /ræn/ past simple of **run**

ranch /rɑːntʃ/ (US) /ræntʃ/ noun [C] a very large farm on which animals are kept, especially in North and South America: *a* ***cattle*** *ranch* ◦ *a* ***sheep*** *ranch* ◦ *He went to work* ***on*** *a ranch.*

rancher /ˈrɑːn.tʃər/ (US) /ˈræn.tʃɚ/ noun [C] someone who owns or works on a ranch

ˈranch ˌhouse noun [C] (also **ˈranch-style ˌhouse**) US a house which usually has only one level, and a roof that does not slope much, either in a city or on a ranch

ranching /ˈrɑːn.tʃɪŋ/ (US) /ˈræn-/ noun [U] the activity of keeping animals on a ranch

rancid /ˈræn.sɪd/ adj (of butter, oil, etc.) tasting or smelling unpleasant because of not being fresh

rancour UK formal (US **rancor**) /ˈræŋ.kər/ (US) /-kɚ/ noun [U] a feeling of hate and continuing anger about something in the past: *They cheated me, but I feel no rancour* ***towards/against*** *them.* • **rancorous** /-əs/ adj formal *a rancorous dispute*

rand /rænd/ noun [C] (plural **rand**) the standard unit of money used in South Africa

R & B /ˌɑːr.ənˈbiː/ (US) /ˌɑːr-/ noun [U] abbreviation for **rhythm and blues**

R

ˌR and ˈD noun [U] abbreviation for research and development: the part of a business that tries to find ways to improve existing products, and to develop new ones: *If we want to get ahead of our competitors, we ought to invest more in R and D.*

random /ˈræn.dəm/ adj **1** C1 happening, done, or chosen by chance rather than according to a plan: *random **checks/tests**/attacks* ◦ *We asked a random **sample/selection** of people what they thought.* **2** informal strange or unusual: *I just saw Billy wearing a top hat – he's so random!* **3 at random** C1 by chance, or without being chosen intentionally: *The winning entry will be the first correct answer drawn at random.* • **randomly** /-li/ adv C1 *The books were randomly arranged on the shelves.*

random ˈbreath ˌtest noun [C] (abbreviation **RBT**) Australian English a test given by the police to drivers chosen by chance, to measure the amount of alcohol the drivers have in their blood

randomize /ˈræn.də.maɪz/ verb [T] (UK usually **randomise**) to make something random (= so that it happens or is chosen by chance), especially as a way of making a test fairer or more accurate: *In a proper randomized trial, patients who are given the drug and those given the placebo are chosen at random.*

ˌR and ˈR (also **R & R**) noun [U] abbreviation for rest and relaxation: a period of time when you stop working and rest: *He went to his parents' house in Florida for a little R & R.*

randy /ˈræn.di/ adj informal full of sexual DESIRE • **randiness** /-nəs/ noun [U]

ranee /ˈrɑː.niː/, /rɑːˈniː/ noun [C] a **rani**

rang /ræŋ/ past simple of **ring**

range /reɪndʒ/ noun; verb

▸noun **SET** ▷ **1** B1 [C] a set of similar things: *I offered her a range **of** options.* ◦ *There is a **wide/whole** range of opinions on this issue.* **2** B1 [C] (US also **line**) the goods made by one company or goods of one particular type that are sold in a shop: *We stock the **full** range **of** model railway accessories.* ◦ *This jacket is part of our autumn/spring range.* **3** B1 [C] a group of hills or mountains: *a **mountain** range* ◦ *the Pennine Range* ◦ *We could see a low range **of** hills in the distance.* **LIMIT** ▷ **4** B2 [S] the amount, number or type of something between an upper and a lower limit: *The price range is **from** $100 **to** $500.* ◦ *The product is aimed at young people **in** the 18–25 **age** range.* ◦ *The coat was **in/out of** my price range.* ◦ *This type of work is **outside/beyond/out of** my range (**of** experience).* **5** C2 [S or U] the distance within which you can see, hear or hit someone: *The ship was **in/out of** range of our guns.* ◦ *He was shot **at point blank/at close** range (= from very near).* **6** [S] the period of time in the future within which something is planned or expected to happen: *long-range plans* ◦ ***short-/medium-/long-range** weather forecasting* **7** [S] the distance that a vehicle or aircraft can travel without having to stop for more fuel: *short-/medium-/long-range airliners* **8** [C] all the musical notes that a singer can sing or a musical instrument is able to produce **WEAPONS AREA** ▷ **9** [C] an area where people can practise shooting or where bombs or other weapons can be tested: *The soldiers were practising on the **rifle/shooting** range.* ◦ *The bomb was tested on a missile range in the desert.* **LAND** ▷ **10** [C] US land for animals to feed on: *The cowboys were herding the cattle **on** the range.* **COOKER** ▷ **11** [C] (also **kitchen range**) UK an old type of cooker, with one or more ovens and cooking surfaces, that is heated with wood or coal and is kept hot all the time **12** [C] US a **cooker**

▸verb **LIMIT** ▷ **1** B2 [I usually + adv/prep] to have an upper and a lower limit in amount, number, etc.: *Dress sizes range **from** petite **to** extra large.* ◦ *Prices range **between** $50 **and** $250.* **POSITION** ▷ **2** [T usually + adv/prep] to position people or things together, especially in rows: *The crowd ranged it**self** along the route of the procession.* ◦ *The troops were ranged in front of the commanding officer.* → Synonym **arrange** **MOVE** ▷ **3** [I usually + adv/prep] to move or travel freely: *The hens range freely about/over the farm.* ◦ *The walkers ranged through/over the hills all day.* **4** [I usually + adv/prep] (of a piece of writing or speech) to deal with: *Our discussion ranged **over** many current issues.* ◦ *The findings of a **wide**-ranging (= including many subjects) survey of young people's attitudes are published today.*

PHRASAL VERB **range against/with sth/sb** [T often passive] to join together as a group to oppose/support a particular idea, plan or group: *Politicians from all parties are ranged against the new law.* ◦ *She ranged her**self** with my opponents.*

rangefinder /ˈreɪndʒˌfaɪn.dəʳ/ US /-dɚ/ noun [C] an instrument that you use for measuring the distance of an object when you are shooting at it or taking a photograph of it

ranger /ˈreɪn.dʒəʳ/ US /-dʒɚ/ noun [C] a person whose job is to protect a forest or natural park: *a **forest** ranger*

rani (also **ranee**) /ˈrɑː.niː/, /rɑːˈniː/ noun [C] a female Indian ruler or the wife of an Indian ruler

rank /ræŋk/ noun; adj; verb

▸noun **POSITION** ▷ **1** C1 [C or U] a position in an organization, such as the army, showing the importance of the person having it: *senior/high/junior/low rank* ◦ *He has just been promoted to the rank **of** captain.* ◦ *Ministers of cabinet rank receive a higher salary than other ministers.* ◦ *Having a large income is one of the advantages of rank (= high position).* **2** [C or U] a particular position, higher or lower than others: *He's **in the front/first** rank **of** (= one of the best) international tennis players.* ◦ *Consumer preferences were placed in rank **order** from 1 to 5.* **3 ranks** [plural] the members of a group or organization: ***Party** ranks have swelled by nearly 300,000.* ◦ *Marty has **joined the** ranks **of** the (= become) unemployed.* ◦ *The party leadership seems to be losing support in **the** ranks.* **4 rise from/through the ranks** to be moved up from a low level position in an organization to a higher one: *He rose through the ranks to become a general.* ◦ *He joined the company in 2008 and has been rising through the ranks ever since.* **ROW** ▷ **5** [C] a row, especially of people or things standing side by side: *The front rank **of** the riot squad raised their shields.* ◦ literary *We could see nothing for miles but **serried** ranks (= many close rows) of fir trees.* **6** [C] a place where taxis wait for passengers: *There were no taxis at the **taxi/cab** rank.*

▸adj **EXTREME** ▷ **1** [before noun] (especially of something bad) complete or extreme: *It was rank **stupidity** to drive so fast on an icy road.* ◦ *The horse that won the race was a rank **outsider**.* **GROWN** ▷ **2** describes plants that grow too fast or too thickly, or an area covered by these: *The abandoned garden was rank **with** weeds.* **SMELL** ▷ **3** smelling strong and unpleasant: *His clothes were rank **with** sweat.*

▸verb [I or T, usually + adv/prep] C1 to have a position higher or lower than others, or to be considered to have such a position: *A captain ranks (= has a position) **above** a lieutenant.* ◦ *My entry was ranked third in the* *flower show.* ◦ *She ranked the bottles* ***in order of*** *size along the shelf.* ◦ *In my opinion, he ranks* ***among*** *the theatre's greatest actors.* ◦ *2012 must rank* ***as*** *(= be) the most difficult year for Europe since the 30s.*

ˌrank and ˈfile noun [+ sing/pl verb] the ordinary workers in a company or the ordinary members of an organization, and not the leaders: *The* ***party's*** *rank and file are beginning to question the prime minister's choice of advisers.* ◦ [before noun] *rank-and-file police officers*

ranking /ˈræn.kɪŋ/ noun; adj
▸noun [C] a rank or level, for example in a competition: *Last year Wiseman rose from 266 to 35 in the tennis world rankings.* ◦ *The city's housing costs were enough to earn it a ranking* ***of*** *66th nationally.*
▸adj [before noun] US being the officer of highest rank present at a particular time: *General Steinberger was the ranking officer present at the meeting.*

rankle /ˈræŋ.kl̩/ verb [I] to make someone annoyed or angry for a long time: *The unkind way in which his girlfriend left him still rankled* ***with*** *him long after.* ◦ [+ that] ***It*** *still rankles* ***that*** *she got promoted, and I didn't.*

ˈrank outˌsider noun [C] someone who is not expected to win a race or competition: *He came from nowhere, this rank outsider, to beat a field of top-class athletes.*

ransack /ˈræn.sæk/ verb [T] to search a place or container in a violent and careless way: *The burglars ransacked the house but found nothing valuable.* ◦ *I ransacked the cupboard* ***for*** *my ski boots.*

ransom /ˈræn.səm/ noun; verb
▸noun [C or U] a large amount of money that is demanded in exchange for someone who has been taken prisoner, or sometimes for an animal: *a ransom* ***demand/note*** ◦ *They* ***demanded*** *a huge ransom* ***for*** *the return of the little girl whom they had kidnapped.* ◦ *The gang* ***held*** *the racehorse* ***to/for*** *ransom.*

IDIOM **hold sb to ransom** to force someone to do something by putting them in a situation where something bad will happen if they do not: *The government says it is being held to ransom by the actions of terrorist groups.*

▸verb [T] to pay money in order to set someone free: *Her father ransomed her* ***for*** *a million dollars.*

rant /rænt/ verb; noun
▸verb [I] to speak or shout in a loud, uncontrolled or angry way, often saying confused or silly things: *He's always ranting (****on****)* ***about*** *the government.* ◦ *I get fed up with my mother ranting* ***and raving*** *(****about*** *my clothes) all the time.*
▸noun [C] a long, angry, and confused speech: *The minister's speech descended into a rant* ***against*** *his political opponents.* • **ranting** /ˈræn.tɪŋ/ (US) /-t̬ɪŋ/ noun [U] (also **rantings**)

rap /ræp/ noun; verb
▸noun **MUSIC** ▷ **1** (A2) [U] a type of popular music with a strong rhythm in which the words are spoken, not sung: *a rap* ***artist****/star* **PUNISHMENT** ▷ **2** [C or U] mainly US slang a statement accusing someone of a crime, or the punishment that someone is given for a crime: *He always said he was jailed on a* ***bum*** *rap (= false accusation).* ◦ *The police caught him, but somehow he managed to* ***beat*** *the rap (= escape punishment).* ◦ *I'm not going to* ***take*** *the rap* ***for*** *you (= be punished for something you did).* **JUDGMENT** ▷ **3** [C] US slang a judgment or a reaction: *The new show got a* ***bum/bad*** *rap (= was severely criticized) in all the papers.* **HIT** ▷ **4** [C] a sudden short noise, especially one made by hitting a hard surface: *There was a series of raps* ***on*** *the window.*

IDIOM **a rap on/over the knuckles** the act of speaking to someone severely or angrily because of something they have done or failed to do: *I* ***got*** *a rap on the knuckles for not finishing my essay on time.*

▸verb (-pp-) **HIT** ▷ **1** [I or T] to hit or say something suddenly and forcefully: *She rapped (****on****) the table to get everyone's attention.* ◦ *The colonel rapped (****out****) an order to his men.* **2** [T] to criticize someone, especially officially: *The headline read 'Judge raps police'.* **MUSIC** ▷ **3** [I] to perform rap

IDIOM **rap sb over the knuckles** to speak officially to someone, in a severe or angry way, because you disapprove of their actions: *He was rapped over the knuckles by the management.*

rapacious /rəˈpeɪ.ʃəs/ adj formal having or showing a strong wish to take things for yourself, usually using unfair methods or force: *a rapacious landlord/businessman* ◦ *her rapacious appetite for fame* • **rapaciously** /-li/ adv • **rapaciousness** /-nəs/ noun [U] • **rapacity** /rəˈpæs.ə.ti/ (US) /-t̬i/ noun [U]

rape /reɪp/ verb; noun
▸verb [I or T] (B2) to force someone to have sex when they are unwilling, using violence or threatening behaviour: *She was pulled from the car and raped.* ◦ *It's difficult to understand what causes a man to rape.*
▸noun **SEX CRIME** ▷ **1** (B2) [C or U] (an example of) the crime of forcefully having sex with someone against their wish: *He had* ***committed*** *several rapes.* ◦ *He was convicted of rape.* **DESTRUCTION** ▷ **2** [U] destruction of the natural world, often for profit: *The road builders were accused of the rape* ***of*** *the countryside.* **PLANT** ▷ **3** [U] (also **oilseed rape, rapeseed**) a plant with yellow flowers from which oil and animal food are produced

rapid /ˈræp.ɪd/ adj (B2) fast or sudden: *The 1990s were a period of rapid* ***change/growth****.* ◦ *I was startled by a rapid movement to my left.* ◦ *His response to the accusation was rapid.* • **rapidity** /rəˈpɪd.ɪ.ti/ (US) /-ə.t̬i/ noun [U] formal • **rapidly** /-li/ adv

ˈrapid-fire adj [before noun] describes questions or jokes which come very quickly one after another

rapids /ˈræp.ɪdz/ noun [plural] a dangerous part of a river which flows very fast because it is steep and sometimes narrow: *They* ***shot*** *(= travelled through) the rapids in a canoe.*

ˌrapid-ˈtransit adj [before noun] describes a system of fast-moving trains in a city

rapier /ˈreɪ.pi.əʳ/ (US) /-ɚ/ noun; adj
▸noun [C] a SWORD with a long thin blade
▸adj [before noun] describes humour or a remark that is extremely clever and funny: *He is renowned for his rapier(****-like****)* ***wit****.*

rapist /ˈreɪ.pɪst/ noun [C] a person who forces someone to have sex with them: *The police have caught the rapist.*

rappel /ræˈpel/ verb [I] (-ll-) US for **abseil**

rapper /ˈræp.əʳ/ (US) /-ɚ/ noun [C] someone who performs RAP music

rapport /ræˈpɔːʳ/ (US) /-ˈpɔːr/ noun [S or U] a good understanding of someone and an ability to communicate well with them: *We'd worked together for years and developed a* ***close/good*** *rapport.* ◦ *She* ***has*** *an excellent rapport* ***with*** *her staff.*

rapprochement /ræˈprɒʃ.mɒ̃ŋ/ (US) /ˌræ.proʊʃˈmɑːŋ/ noun [C or U] formal an agreement reached by opposing groups or people: *There are signs of (a) rapprochement* ***between*** *the warring factions.*

R

ˈrap ˌsheet noun [C] US informal an official police document which lists the crimes that a particular person has committed → Compare **charge sheet**

rapt /ræpt/ adj giving complete attention, or showing complete involvement, or (of attention) complete: *She sat with a rapt expression reading her book.* ◦ *The children watched with rapt* ***attention***.

rapture /ˈræp.tʃəʳ/ US /-tʃɚ/ noun **1** [U] extreme pleasure and happiness or excitement: *The prime minister's supporters greeted her speech with rapture.* **2 raptures** [plural] an expression of extreme pleasure and happiness or excitement: *She* ***went into*** *raptures at the news of her success.* ◦ *She was* ***in*** *raptures about/over her first visit to Paris.*

rapturous /ˈræp.tʃər.əs/ US /-tʃɚ-/ adj [before noun] showing extreme pleasure and happiness or excitement: *The play was greeted with rapturous* ***applause***. ◦ *The team received a rapturous* ***welcome***. • **rapturously** /-li/ adv

rare /reəʳ/ US /rer/ adj **NOT COMMON** ▷ **1** B1 not common; very unusual: *a rare disease/species* ◦ *The museum is full of rare and precious treasures.* ◦ *a rare occasion/opportunity/visit/treat, etc.* ◦ [+ to infinitive] ***It's*** *very rare* ***to*** *find these birds in England in winter.* ◦ *It's very rare to find someone who combines such qualities.* **OF MEAT** ▷ **2** C1 (of meat) not cooked for very long and still red: *I'd like my steak rare, please.* → Compare **medium** **OF AIR** ▷ **3** describes the air at the top of a mountain, which contains less OXYGEN, making it harder to breathe → See also **rarefied**

IDIOMS **have a rare old time** **1** mainly UK old-fashioned to enjoy yourself very much: *We went on a tour of the city's bars and had a rare old time.* **2** UK old-fashioned to have difficulty: *We had a rare old time trying to get tickets.* • **rare bird** an unusual person: *He's that rare bird, a barman who doesn't drink alcohol.*

rarefied /ˈreə.rɪ.faɪd/ US /ˈrer.ə-/ adj **LITTLE OXYGEN** ▷ **1** (of air) with little OXYGEN **NOT ORDINARY** ▷ **2** describes a place or situation that does not have any of the problems of ordinary life: *the rarefied* ***atmosphere/circles*** *of college life*

rarely /ˈreə.li/ US /ˈrer-/ adv B1 not often: *We rarely see each other now.* ◦ *I rarely have time to read a newspaper.* ◦ formal *Rarely have I seen such a beautiful sunset.* → See also **seldom**

R

raring /ˈreə.rɪŋ/ US /ˈrer.ɪŋ/ adj **be raring to do sth** to be very enthusiastic about starting something: *I've bought all the paint for decorating the bedrooms and I'm raring to get started.* ◦ *I had been preparing for the exam for a year and now I was raring* ***to go*** *(= eager to start).*

rarity /ˈreə.rə.ti/ US /ˈrer.ə.t̬i/ noun [C or U] C1 something that is very unusual, or the quality of being very unusual: *Men who do the cooking are* ***something of a*** *rarity.* ◦ *Diamonds are valuable because of their rarity.*

rascal /ˈrɑː.skəl/ US /ˈræs.kəl/ noun [C] **1** a person, especially a child or a man, who does things that you disapprove of, but who you still like: *I caught those* ***little/young*** *rascals dressing up in my clothes.* ◦ *What's that* ***old*** *rascal been up to now?* **2** old-fashioned a dishonest person • **rascally** /-i/ adj

rash /ræʃ/ noun; adj

▸noun **SKIN CONDITION** ▷ **1** C2 [C or U] a lot of small red spots on the skin: *I've got an* ***itchy*** *rash all over my chest.* ◦ *He* ***came out/up in*** *a rash after he fell in a patch of nettles.* ◦ *If you stay in the sun too long you'll get (a)* ***heat*** *rash.* **LARGE NUMBER** ▷ **2 a rash of sth** a large number of unpleasant events of the same type: *There has been a rash of robberies/accidents/complaints in the last two months.*

▸adj C2 careless or unwise, without thought for what might happen or result: *That was a rash* ***decision*** *– you didn't think about the costs involved.* ◦ [+ to infinitive] *I think* ***it*** *was a bit rash* ***of*** *them* ***to*** *get married when they'd only known each other for a few weeks.* • **rashly** /ˈræʃ.li/ adv • **rashness** /ˈræʃ.nəs/ noun [U] ***In a moment of*** *rashness, I agreed to do a parachute jump for charity.*

rasher /ˈræʃ.əʳ/ US /-ɚ/ noun [C] a thin flat piece of BACON

rasp /rɑːsp/ US /ræsp/ noun; verb

▸noun **TOOL** ▷ **1** [C] a tool with a rough blade, used for shaping wood or metal **SOUND** ▷ **2** [S] a rough unpleasant noise, like metal being rubbed against metal: *There was* ***the*** *rasp* ***of*** *a bolt and the door suddenly opened.*

▸verb **MAKE SOUND** ▷ **1** [I or T] to make a rough unpleasant sound, especially while breathing or speaking: *I heard his breath rasping in his chest.* ◦ *The gunman rasped (****out****) an urgent order (= gave it in an unpleasant-sounding voice) to the other members of the gang.* **RUB** ▷ **2** [T] to rub something roughly: *The horse rasped my hand with his tongue as I fed him the apple.*

raspberry /ˈrɑːz.bər.i/ US /ˈræz.ber-/ noun **FRUIT** ▷ **1** [C or U] a small soft red fruit, or the bush on which it grows: *raspberries and ice cream* ◦ *raspberry jam* **SOUND** ▷ **2** [C] informal a rude sound made by sticking the tongue out and blowing: *The boy turned and* ***blew*** *a raspberry at the teacher before running off.*

raspy /ˈrɑː.sp.i/ US /ˈræsp-/ adj A raspy voice sounds unpleasantly rough.

Rastafarian /ˌræs.təˈfeə.ri.ən/ US /ˌrɑː.stəˈfɑːr.i.ən/ noun [C] (informal **Rasta** /ˈræs.tə/ US /ˈrɑː.stə/) a member of a religious group that began in Jamaica and worships Haile Selassie • **Rastafarian** adj • **Rastafarianism** /-ə.nɪ.zəm/ noun [U]

rasta roko /ˌrɑː.stəˈrəʊ.kəʊ/ US /-ˈroʊ.koʊ/ noun [C] Indian English an occasion when people put a temporary structure across a road to stop traffic in order to show that they disagree with something that a company or the government is doing

rat /ræt/ noun; verb

▸noun [C] **ANIMAL** ▷ **1** A2 a small RODENT, larger than a mouse, that has a long tail and is considered to be harmful: *Rats carry disease.* ◦ *I think we've* ***got*** *rats (= there are rats in our house).* **PERSON** ▷ **2** informal an unpleasant person who deceives others or is not loyal

▸verb slang disapproving

PHRASAL VERB **rat on sb/sth** to be not loyal to someone, especially by giving away secret information about them, or to fail to do something that you said you would do: *He ratted on us.* ◦ *They ratted on the deal.*

ˈrat-arsed adj UK (US **ˈrat-assed**) extremely drunk: *I got completely rat-arsed at Kate's party.*

ratatouille /ˌræt.əˈtuː.i/ US /ˌræt̬-/ noun [U] a dish made by cooking vegetables, such as tomatoes, AUBERGINES, and PEPPERS, in liquid at a low heat

ratbag /ˈræt.bæg/ noun [C] mainly UK informal an unpleasant person

ratchet /ˈrætʃ.ɪt/ noun; verb

▸noun [C] a part of a machine which allows movement in one direction only. It is usually a wheel with teeth-like parts which either slide over or lock against the free end of a bar.

▸verb

PHRASAL VERB **ratchet sth up/down** to increase/reduce something over a period of time: *The debate should* *ratchet up awareness of the problem among members of the general public.* ◦ *The government was accused of ratcheting up pressure on the health services.* ◦ *Costs have been ratcheted down by as much as 50 percent since 1999.*

Word partners for rate noun (MEASURE)

cut/increase/lower/raise the rate • an *alarming/high/rapid* rate • a *low/reduced/slow* rate • an *annual/average/current* rate • an *increase in/rise in* the rate • a *cut in/drop in/fall in* the rate • *at* a rate (of) • the rate *for/of*

rate /reɪt/ **noun; verb**

▸**noun** [C] **MEASURE** ▷ **1** B2 the speed at which something happens or changes, or the amount or number of times it happens or changes in a particular period: *Although she's recovering from her illness, her rate **of** progress is quite slow.* ◦ *I told my assistants to work **at** their **own** rate.* ◦ *The taxi was going **at** a tremendous rate.* ◦ *the growth/inflation/mortality/unemployment, etc. rate* ◦ *The drug has a high **success/failure** rate.* **PAYMENT** ▷ **2** B2 an amount or level of payment: *We agreed a rate with the painter before he started work.* ◦ *What's the **going** (= standard) rate **for** this type of work?* ◦ *Do you pay your mortgage on a **fixed** or **variable** rate?* **TAX** ▷ **3 rates** [plural] a local tax paid in Australia, and in Britain in the past, by the owners of houses and other buildings

Word partners for rate noun (PAYMENT)

an *annual/hourly/weekly* rate • the *going* rate • a *cheap/low/reduced/special* rate • a *basic/fixed/flat* rate • a *cut in/drop in/fall in* the rate • an *increase in/rise in* the rate • *at* a rate *of* sth

IDIOMS **at a rate of knots** UK If someone does something at a rate of knots, they do it very quickly: *She got through her work at a rate of knots.* • **at any rate 1** C2 whatever happens: *Well, I'm not going home on foot, at any rate.* **2** something you say to show that you are going to say something more exactly: *I don't think they liked my idea. At any rate, they weren't very enthusiastic about it.* • **at this rate** C2 if the situation stays as it is: *At this rate, we won't be home till midnight.*

▸**verb** [T] **JUDGE** ▷ **1** C1 to judge the value or character of someone or something: *How do you rate him **as** a footballer?* ◦ *She is rated very **highly** by the people she works for.* ◦ informal *'What do you think of her as a singer?' 'I don't really rate her (= I do not think that she is very good).'* ◦ *I rate cars **as** one of the worst polluters of the environment.* ◦ [+ obj + noun] *On a scale of one to ten, I'd rate his book a five.* ◦ *Car crashes are so frequent that they don't rate **a mention** (= are not considered to be worth reporting) in the newspaper unless a lot of people are killed.* → See also **underrate, overrate** **2 rate as sth** to be considered to be something of a particular quality: *That rates as the worst film I've ever seen.* **TAX** ▷ **3** UK In Britain in the past, a building was rated to decide how much local tax the owner should pay.

-rate /-reɪt/ **suffix** C1 used with words such as first, second, etc. to show how good you think something is: *His suggestions are always **first**-rate (= very good).* ◦ *This company produces **second/third**-rate (= not very good) goods.*

rateable value /ˌreɪ.tə.blˈvæl.juː/ US /-t̬ə-/ **noun** [C] an official value that used to be given to a building in the UK, based partly on its size and type, which decided the amount of local tax that the owner should pay

ˌrate of exˈchange noun [C] the **exchange rate**

rather adv; adv, predeterminer; exclamation

▸**adv** /ˈrɑː.ðəʳ/ US /ˈræð.ɚ/ **SMALL AMOUNT** ▷ **1** B1 quite; to a slight degree: *It's rather cold today, isn't it?* ◦ *That's rather **a** difficult book – here's an easier one for you.* ◦ *The train was rather too crowded for a comfortable journey.* ◦ *She answered the phone rather sleepily.* ◦ *I rather doubt I'll be able to come to your party.* **MORE EXACTLY** ▷ **2** B2 more accurately; more exactly: *She'll go to London on Thursday, **or** rather, she will if she has to.* ◦ *He's my sister's friend really, rather **than** mine.* **3** used to express an opposite opinion: *The ending of the war is not a cause for celebration, but rather for regret that it ever happened.* ◦ *No, I'm not tired. Rather the opposite in fact.* **PREFERENCE** ▷ **4 rather than** B1 instead of; used especially when you prefer one thing to another: *I think I'd like to stay at home this evening rather than go out.*

IDIOM **rather you than me** said by someone who does not want to do the thing that someone else is doing: *'I've got to have two teeth out next week.' 'Rather you than me.'*

▸**adv, predeterminer** /ˈrɑː.ðəʳ/ US /ˈræð.ɚ/ very; to a large degree: *Actually, I did rather well in my exams.* ◦ *I've got rather a lot of work to do at the moment.*

▸**exclamation** /ˌrɑːˈðɜːʳ/ US /ˌræðˈɝː/ mainly UK old-fashioned certainly; yes: *'Do you want to come out for dinner with us this evening?' 'Rather!'*

ratify /ˈræt.ɪ.faɪ/ US /ˈræt̬.ə-/ **verb** [T] formal (especially of governments or organizations) to make an agreement official: *Many countries have now ratified the UN convention on the rights of the child.* ◦ *The decision will have to be ratified (= approved) by the executive board.* • **ratification** /ˌræt.ɪ.fɪˈkeɪ.ʃᵊn/ US /ˌræt̬.ə-/ **noun** [U]

rating /ˈreɪ.tɪŋ/ US /-t̬ɪŋ/ **noun 1** C1 [C or U] a measurement of how good or popular someone or something is: *The government's **popularity** rating sank to an all-time low.* **2 ratings** C2 [plural] a list of television and radio programmes showing how popular they are: *Advertisers are interested in ratings.* ◦ *The serial has fallen in **the** ratings this week.*

ratio /ˈreɪ.ʃi.əʊ/ US /-oʊ/ **noun** [C] (plural **ratios**) C1 the relationship between two groups or amounts, which expresses how much bigger one is than the other: *The ratio **of** men **to** women at the conference was ten to one/10:1.* ◦ *The school is trying to improve its pupil-teacher ratio (= the number of teachers compared with the number of students).*

ration /ˈræʃ.ᵊn/ **noun; verb**

▸**noun** [C] **1** a limited amount of something which one person is allowed to have, especially when there is not much of it available: *During the war, no one was allowed more than their ration **of** food, clothing and fuel.* **2 rations** [plural] the total amount of food that is given to someone to be eaten during a particular activity and in a particular period of time, especially an amount given to soldiers when they are fighting **3** an amount of something that you would expect to have: *We've had more than our ration **of** problems recently.*

▸**verb** [T] to limit the amount of a particular thing that someone is allowed to have: *Do you remember when petrol was rationed **to** five gallons a week?* ◦ *My children would watch television all day long, but I ration it.*

PHRASAL VERB **ration sth out** to divide something between a group of people so that each person gets a small amount: *Ann rationed out the cake **between** the children.*

R

rational /ˈræʃ.ən.əl/ adj C1 showing clear thought or reason: *He was too upset to be rational.* ◦ *a rational course of action/argument/explanation* • **rationality** /ˌræʃ.ənˈæl.ɪ.ti/ US /-ə.t̬i/ noun [U]

rationale /ˌræʃ.əˈnɑːl/ US /-ˈnæl/ noun [C or U] formal the reasons or intentions for a particular set of thoughts or actions: *I don't understand the rationale **behind** the council's housing policy.*

rationalism /ˈræʃ.ən.əl.ɪ.zəm/ noun [U] the belief or principle that actions and opinions should be based on reason rather than on emotion or religion

rationalist /ˈræʃ.ən.əl.ɪst/ noun [C] someone whose actions and decisions are based on reason rather than emotions or beliefs • **rationalist** /ˈræʃ.ən.əl.ɪst/ adj (also **rationalistic**)

rationalize (UK usually **rationalise**) /ˈræʃ.ən.əl.aɪz/ verb **EXPLAIN** ▷ **1** [T] to try to find reasons to explain your behaviour, decisions, etc.: *She rationalized the expense by saying that the costly carpet she had bought would last longer than a cheaper one.* **CHANGE** ▷ **2** [I or T] to make a company, way of working, etc. more effective, usually by combining or stopping particular activities, or (of a company, way of working, etc.) to become more effective in this way: *We rationalized the production system so that one operator could control all three machines.* ◦ *The recession is forcing the company to rationalize.* • **rationalization** (UK usually **rationalisation**) /ˌræʃ.ən.əl.aɪˈzeɪ.ʃən/ US /-əˈ-/ noun [C or U]

rationally /ˈræʃ.ən.əl.i/ adv in a way based on reason rather than emotions: *Rationally, he knows that she won't go back to him, but emotionally he can't accept it.*

rationing /ˈræʃ.ən.ɪŋ/ noun [U] a system of limiting the amount of something that each person is allowed to have: *fuel rationing*

the ˈrat ˌrace noun [S] a way of life in modern society, in which people compete with each other for power and money: *He decided to get out of the rat race, and went to work on a farm.*

ˈrat ˌrun noun [C] UK a small road that is used by a lot of drivers who are trying to avoid traffic on larger roads: *The road through our village has become a rat run for commuters trying to avoid delays on the A14.*

R

rattan /rəˈtæn/ noun [U] specialized **1** a tropical climbing plant with thin, tough stems **2** these stems used as a material for making WICKER furniture, or furniture made from them

rattle /ˈræt.l/ US /ˈræt̬-/ noun; verb

▸**noun 1** [S] a sound similar to a series of quickly repeated knocks: *From across the town came the rattle **of** machine-gun fire.* **2** [C] a toy which makes a noise like a series of knocks: *The baby was waving around a plastic rattle.* **3** [C] a wooden device that when turned round and round produces a noise like a series of knocks **4** [C] the part of a rattlesnake's tail that produces a noise

▸**verb WORRY** ▷ **1** [T] to worry someone or make someone nervous: *The creaking upstairs was starting to rattle me.* **SOUND** ▷ **2** [I or T] to (cause something to) make a noise like a series of knocks: *The explosion rattled the cups on the table.* ◦ *The dying man's voice rattled in his throat.* ◦ [+ adv/prep] *The car rattled **over** the cobblestones.* ◦ *My car engine is making a strange rattling noise.*

PHRASAL VERBS **rattle sth off** informal to say or read aloud very quickly a list of names or things, or something you have learned: *She rattled off the names of the people who were coming to the party.* • **rattle on/away** informal to talk for a long time, especially about things that are not important: *She was on the phone for hours last night, just rattling on to her friends.* • **rattle through sth** informal to do or say something very quickly: *I'm going to rattle through my work today so that I can go home early.* ◦ *He rattled through the list of countries he had visited.*

rattlesnake /ˈræt.l̩.sneɪk/ US /ˈræt̬-/ noun [C] (informal **rattler**) a poisonous snake found in southern parts of the US which, when annoyed, produces a loud noise by shaking its tail

ratty /ˈræt.i/ US /ˈræt̬-/ adj informal feeling annoyed: *She was a bit ratty with me this morning.* → Synonym **irritable**

raucous /ˈrɔː.kəs/ US /ˈrɑː-/ adj loud and unpleasant: *I heard the raucous call of the crows.* ◦ *Raucous **laughter** came from the next room.* ◦ *The party was becoming rather raucous.* • **raucously** /-li/ adv • **raucousness** /-nəs/ noun [U]

raunchy /ˈrɔːn.tʃi/ US /ˈrɑːn-/ adj connected with sex in a very clear and obvious way: *a raunchy novel* • **raunchily** /-tʃɪ.li/ adv • **raunchiness** /-nəs/ noun [U]

ravage /ˈræv.ɪdʒ/ verb [T often passive] to cause great damage to something: *The area has been ravaged by drought/floods/war.*

ravages /ˈræv.ɪ.dʒɪz/ noun [plural] **the ravages of disease, time, war, etc.** the damage caused by disease, time, war, etc.: *The ravages of the fire showed in the splintered woodwork and blistered paint.*

rave /reɪv/ verb; adj; noun

▸**verb** [I] **SPEAK FOOLISHLY** ▷ **1** to speak in an uncontrolled way, usually because you are upset or angry, or because you are ill: *He's always raving **(on) about** the government.* ◦ *She was **ranting and** raving **about** some imagined insult.* **PRAISE** ▷ **2** informal to praise something very much: *She raved **about/over** the clothes she had seen at the Paris fashion shows.*

▸**adj** [before noun] informal admiring and giving a lot of praise: *The show has received rave **reviews/notices** in all the papers.*

▸**noun** [C] mainly UK informal an event where young people dance to modern electronic music and sometimes take illegal drugs: *an all-night/open-air rave* ◦ *rave music*

ravel /ˈræv.əl/ verb (**-ll-** or US usually **-l-**) formal **SEPARATE** ▷ **1** [T] (also **ravel sth out**) to separate a knot, mass of threads, etc. into a single thread or threads: *It took Daisy a long time to ravel out all the wool.* **CONFUSE** ▷ **2** [I or T] (also **ravel sth up**) to become or to make someone or something become more confused: *Mark's interference merely ravelled the situation further.*

raven /ˈreɪ.vən/ noun; adj

▸**noun** [C] the largest bird in the CROW family, with shiny black feathers

▸**adj** [before noun] literary (especially of hair) shiny and black: *Her pale face was framed by raven locks.*

ravening /ˈræv.ən.ɪŋ/ adj **1** literary (especially of wild animals) violently hunting for food: *ravening **wolves*** **2** describes a group of people who try to get what they want in a forceful way

ravenous /ˈræv.ən.əs/ adj extremely hungry: *I'm ravenous – where's supper?* ◦ *Growing boys have ravenous appetites.* • **ravenously** /-li/ adv *He looked ravenously at the buffet table.* ◦ *I'm ravenously **hungry**.*

raver /ˈreɪ.vər/ US /-vɚ/ noun [C] someone who goes to a rave (= an event where young people dance to modern electronic music and sometimes take illegal drugs)

ravine /rəˈviːn/ noun [C] a deep narrow valley with steep sides

raving /ˈreɪ.vɪŋ/ adj [before noun], adv informal complete or extreme, or completely or extremely: *He must be a raving **idiot/lunatic**.* ◦ *Her last book was a raving best-seller/**success**.* ◦ *She's no raving **beauty**.* ◦ *I think you're (**stark**) raving **mad** to agree to do all that extra work without being paid for it.*

ravings /ˈreɪ.vɪŋz/ noun [plural] crazy statements that have no meaning: *The things he said are simply the ravings of a disturbed mind.*

ravioli /ˌræv.iˈəʊ.li/ (US) /-ˈoʊ-/ noun [U] small, square cases of PASTA filled with meat or cheese, cooked in boiling water, and usually eaten with a sauce

ravish /ˈræv.ɪʃ/ verb **PLEASURE** ▷ **1** [T usually passive] literary to give great pleasure to someone: *I was utterly ravished by the way she smiled.* **FORCE** ▷ **2** [T] old use or literary to force a woman to have sex against her wishes

ravishing /ˈræv.ɪ.ʃɪŋ/ adj literary very beautiful: *She **looked** ravishing/She was a ravishing **sight** in her wedding dress.*

raw /rɔː/ (US) /rɑː/ adj; noun

▸adj **NOT COOKED** ▷ **1** (B1) (of food) not cooked: *raw fish* **NOT PROCESSED** ▷ **2** (B2) (of materials) in a natural state, without having been through any chemical or industrial process: *Oil is an important raw **material** that can be processed into many different products, including plastics.* ◦ *They claimed that raw **sewage** was being pumped into the sea.* **3** describes information that has been collected but has not yet been studied in detail: *raw **data**/evidence/figures* **4** describes a person who is not trained or is without experience: *I would prefer not to leave this job to John while he's still a raw **recruit**/beginner.* **5** Feelings or qualities that are raw are natural and difficult to control: *We were struck by the raw **energy/power** of the dancers' performances.* ◦ *Her emotions are still a bit raw after her painful divorce.* **6** A piece of writing that is raw is one that does not try to hide anything about its subject: *His new play is a raw drama about family life.* **PAINFUL** ▷ **7** sore or painful because of being rubbed or damaged: *The shoe had rubbed a raw place on her heel.* **COLD** ▷ **8** describes weather that is very cold: *a raw morning* ◦ *a raw wind* • **rawness** /-nəs/ noun [U]

IDIOMS **come the raw prawn** Australian English to try to deceive someone, especially by pretending that you have no knowledge of something: *Don't come the raw prawn **with** me – you know very well what I'm talking about.* • **a raw deal** bad or unfair treatment: *He said that many children in the city's schools were **getting/being given** a raw deal by being taught in classes that were too large.*

▸noun

IDIOM **in the raw 1** informal naked: *They sunbathed in the raw.* **2** in a plain and honest way, with nothing hidden: *The film really showed you prison life in the raw.*

ˌraw siˈenna noun [U] a brownish-yellow colour • **ˌraw siˈenna** adj

ray /reɪ/ noun **BEAM** ▷ **1** (B2) [C] a narrow beam of light, heat, etc. travelling in a straight line from its place of origin: *A ray **of** sunshine shone through a gap in the clouds.* ◦ *Light rays bend as they pass from air to water.* **SMALL AMOUNT** ▷ **2** (C2) [C] a small amount of a feeling that makes you feel happier or more full of hope: *There's still a ray **of hope** that the missing child will be found alive.* **FISH** ▷ **3** [C] a large flat sea fish with a long narrow tail

IDIOM **ray of sunshine** a happy person who makes others feel happy, especially in a difficult situation

ˈray ˌgun noun [C] in SCIENCE FICTION stories, a gun which produces rays that kill people or make them unable to move

rayon /ˈreɪ.ɒn/ (US) /-ɑːn/ noun [U] a smooth cloth used to make clothes

raze /reɪz/ verb [T] to completely destroy a city, building, etc.: *The town was razed **to the ground** in the bombing raid – not a building was left standing.*

razor /ˈreɪ.zəʳ/ (US) /-zɚ/ noun; verb

▸noun [C] (B2) a small device with a sharp blade for removing hair, especially from the face or legs: *Do you use an **electric** razor or the kind that you have to put a razor **blade** in?*

IDIOM **on a razor edge** in a very uncertain and dangerous situation: *Allegations of fraud have put the minister's career on a razor edge.*

▸verb [T] to cut something such as hair using a razor

ˈrazor ˌblade noun [C] a thin flat piece of metal with a sharp edge for cutting that can be used in a razor

ˈrazor ˌknife noun [C] US for **Stanley knife**

ˌrazor-ˈsharp adj **SHARP** ▷ **1** extremely sharp: *These animals have razor-sharp teeth.* **CLEVER** ▷ **2** If you describe someone or someone's mind as razor-sharp, you mean that they think very clearly and quickly: *She's got a razor-sharp **mind**.*

ˌrazor-ˈthin adj describes a difference in amount that is very small: *The president won the election by a razor-thin **margin**.*

ˈrazor ˌwire noun [U] wire with pieces of sharp metal fixed across it, often positioned on top of walls, such as those surrounding a prison, to stop people climbing over the walls

razzle /ˈræz.l/ noun UK informal **on the razzle** enjoying yourself, visiting bars and dancing, etc.: *I was (**out**) on the razzle last night, and I'm rather tired this morning.*

ˌrazzle-ˈdazzle noun [U] mainly US (confusion caused by) noisy and noticeable activity or very colourful appearance, intended to attract attention: *Amid all the razzle-dazzle of the party convention, it was easy to forget about the real political issues.*

razzmatazz /ˈræz.mə.tæz/ noun [U] (also **razzamatazz**) noisy and noticeable activity, intended to attract attention: *The new car was launched with great razzmatazz: champagne, food, free gifts and dancers.*

RBT /ˌɑː.biːˈtiː/ (US) /ˌɑːr-/ noun [C] Australian English abbreviation for **random breath test**

RC /ˌɑːˈsiː/ (US) /ˌɑːr-/ adj, noun [C] abbreviation for **Roman Catholic**

the RCMP /ˌɑː.siː.emˈpiː/ (US) /ˌɑːr-/ noun [+ sing/pl verb] abbreviation for the Royal Canadian Mounted Police

Rd written abbreviation for **road**: *Shaftesbury Rd*

RDA /ɑː.diːˈeɪ/ (US) /ɑːr-/ noun [C usually singular] abbreviation for **recommended daily allowance**

RDS /ˌɑː.diːˈes/ (US) /ˌɑːr-/ noun [U] abbreviation for Radio Data System: a system for automatically finding the strongest signal for a radio station, and for providing information about it on an electronic screen

R

're /ᵊr/ (US) /ɚ/ **short form of** are: *You're late.*

re- /riː-/, /ri-/, /rɪ-/ **prefix 1** used to add the meaning 'do again', especially to verbs: *rebuild* ◦ *remarry* ◦ *reusable* **2** returning something to its original state: *reafforestation* (= *planting new trees in an area where they were previously cut down*).

re¹ /riː/ **preposition** formal (especially in business letters) about; on the subject of: *Re your communication of 15 February...*

re² (also **ray**) /reɪ/ **noun** [S] the second note of the SOL-FA musical SCALE

reach /riːtʃ/ **verb; noun**

▸**verb ARRIVE ▷ 1** (B1) [T] to arrive at a place, especially after spending a long time or a lot of effort travelling: *We won't reach Miami till five or six o'clock.* ◦ *They finally reached the coast after five weeks sailing.* ◦ *News of his accident had only just reached us.* **2 reach a decision, agreement, conclusion, etc.** (B2) to make a decision, agreement, etc. about something: *She reached the conclusion that there was no more she could do.* ◦ *We'll inform you when a decision has been reached.* ◦ *The jury took four days to reach a verdict.*

> **! Common mistake: reach or achieve?**
>
> **Warning:** choose the right word!
>
> To talk about reaching an aim, especially after a lot of work or effort, don't say 'reach', say **achieve**:
>
> ~~*What are the qualities a person needs to reach success?*~~
>
> *What are the qualities a person needs to achieve success?*

LEVEL ▷ 3 (B2) [T] to get to a particular level, especially a high one: *The temperature is expected to reach 30°C today.* ◦ *He's just reached the grand old age of 95.* ◦ *I've reached the **point** where I'm not going to put up with her criticisms of me any more.* **STRETCH ▷ 4** (B2) [I or T] to stretch out your arm in order to get or touch something: *She's grown so tall that she can reach the door handle now.* ◦ *He reached **for** the phone and knocked over a glass.* ◦ *The child reached **down/out/over** and picked up the kitten.* ◦ *He reached his hand **out** for the money.* ◦ [+ two objects] UK *Can you reach me (**down**) that book?* **5** [I or T] If an object reaches something, the top or bottom of it touches that thing: *The ladder won't quite reach the top of the wall.* ◦ *She was wearing a dress that reached (**to**) her ankles.* **COMMUNICATE ▷ 6** (B2) [T] to communicate with someone in a different place, especially by phone or email: *I've been trying to reach you on the phone all day.* **7** [T] to understand and communicate with someone: *He's a strange child and his teachers find it difficult to reach him.*

R

> **! Common mistake: reach**
>
> Remember that in all meanings except 'stretch', **reach** is never followed by 'to'.
>
> Don't say 'reach to something', say **reach something**:
>
> ~~*Our income reached to $90 million in 1999.*~~
>
> *Our income reached $90 million in 1999.*

IDIOM **reach for the stars** to want or try to get something that is difficult or impossible to get

PHRASAL VERB **reach out to sb 1** to try to communicate with a person or a group of people, usually in order to help or involve them: *The new mayor is reaching out to the local community to involve them in his plans for the city.* **2** to offer help and support to someone: *She set up her charity to reach out to the thousands of homeless on the streets.*

▸**noun DISTANCE ▷ 1** (B2) [U] Someone's reach is the distance within which they can stretch out their arm and touch something: *I like to keep a notebook and pencil **within** (**arm's**) reach.* ◦ *The top shelf is **within/out of** (his) reach.* ◦ *Make sure that you keep all dangerous substances **out of** the reach **of** the children.* **2** (B2) [U] the distance that can be travelled, especially easily: *We live **within** (**easy**) reach of the station.* **3** [S] the length of your arm when you stretch it out: *You've got quite a long reach – can you get that box down from the top shelf for me?* **4** [C usually singular] an act of stretching out your arm: *He made a sudden reach **for** his gun.* **LIMIT ▷ 5** (C2) [S or U] the limit within which someone can achieve something: *An expensive trip like that would be completely **beyond/out of** (my) reach* (= *I would not have enough money to pay for it*). ◦ *After years of saving, the car was at last **within** (her) reach* (= *she had enough money to pay for it*). **PART ▷ 6 reaches** [plural] **a** a part of a river or part of an area of land: *The expedition set out for the **upper** reaches **of** the Amazon.* ◦ *There was little snow on the **lower** reaches **of** the ski run.* ◦ *We know very little about the **farthest/outermost** reaches **of** the universe.* **b** the highest or lowest levels of an organization: *The news has shocked **the upper** reaches **of** the government.*

IDIOM **a reach of the imagination** the act of trying very hard to imagine something: *It **takes** (quite) a reach of the imagination to believe that story.*

react /ri'ækt/ **verb** [I] (B2) to act in a particular way as a direct result of something else: *She slapped him and called him names, but he didn't react.* ◦ *The judge reacted angrily **to** the suggestion that it hadn't been a fair trial.* ◦ *Many people react (**badly**) **to*** (= *are made ill by*) *penicillin.* ◦ specialized *Potassium reacts* (= *changes when mixed*) ***with** water.*

PHRASAL VERB **react against sth** (C2) to intentionally do the opposite of what someone wants you to do because you do not like their rules or ideas: *He reacted against everything he had been taught.*

reactant /ri'æk.tᵊnt/ **noun** [C] specialized a substance that is part of a chemical reaction

> **Word partners for reaction**
>
> ***bring/provoke/produce*** a reaction • ***gauge/judge*** sb's reaction • an ***adverse/angry/negative*** reaction • a ***favourable/positive*** reaction • a ***lukewarm/mixed*** reaction • a ***knee-jerk*** reaction • sb's ***first/gut/immediate/initial*** reaction • a reaction ***against/to/towards*** sth

reaction /ri'æk.ʃᵊn/ **noun BEHAVIOUR ▷ 1** [C] behaviour, a feeling or an action that is a direct result of something else: *I love to watch people's reactions when I say who I am.* ◦ *There has been an immediate/widespread/hostile reaction **against** the government's proposed tax increases.* ◦ *Reactions **to** the proposal so far have been adverse/favourable/mixed.* **2 reactions** [plural] someone's ability to act quickly when something happens: *You need to have **quick** reactions to play these computer games.* **3** [C usually singular] a type of behaviour or opinion that is produced or held with the intention of being different from something else: *Her left-wing views are a reaction **against** the conservatism of her parents.* **UNPLEASANT EFFECT ▷ 4** [C] an unpleasant effect resulting from eating particular things or taking particular drugs: *Some people **have** an **allergic** reaction **to** shellfish.* **IN SCIENCE ▷ 5** [C or U] an occasion when two or more substances react with and change each other: *a*

***chemical** reaction* **NO CHANGE** ▷ **6** [U] disapproving the belief or principle that there should be no social or political change, and the attempt to stop such change from happening: *We must not allow reaction to stand in the way of progress.*

reactionary /riˈæk.ʃən.ər.i/ (US) /-er-/ noun [C] disapproving a person who is opposed to political or social change or new ideas: *Reactionaries are preventing reforms.* • **reactionary** adj *Reactionary **forces/elements** in the industry are preventing its progress towards greater efficiency.*

reactivate /riˈæk.tɪ.veɪt/ verb [I or T] to bring or come back into action or use: *The police file was reactivated because of new evidence.* ◦ *The virus can reactivate at any time.*

reactive /riˈæk.tɪv/ adj reacting to events or situations rather than acting first to change or prevent something: *Unfortunately, the police have dealt with the problem of car theft in a reactive rather than a proactive way.*

reactor /riˈæk.tər/ (US) /-tɚ/ noun [C] (also **ˌnuclear reˈactor**) a large machine in which atoms are either divided or joined in order to produce power

read /riːd/ verb; noun

►verb (**read, read** /red/) **UNDERSTAND** ▷ **1** (A1) [I or T] to look at words or symbols and understand what they mean: *He spent a pleasant afternoon reading (the newspaper/a book).* ◦ *I read **about** the family's success in the local paper.* ◦ *It was too dark to read our map and we took a wrong turning.* ◦ *Can you read music?* ◦ *Your handwriting is so untidy I can't read it.* ◦ [+ (that)] *I've read in the newspapers (**that**) there is a threat of war.* ◦ *Put your plastic card in the slot, and the machine will read it and identify who you are.* ◦ *Some children can read (= have learned the skill of reading) by the age of four.* **2** (A2) [I or T] to say the words that are printed or written: *She read (the poem) slowly and quietly.* ◦ [+ two objects] *Their teacher always reads them a story at the end of the day.* ◦ *Children love to have stories read (**aloud/out**) **to** them.* **3** (C2) [T] to understand and give a particular meaning to written information, a statement, a situation, etc.: *She missed the train because she read 18.30 p.m. **as** 8.30 p.m. instead of 6.30 p.m.* ◦ *On page 19, **for** 'Blitish', please read 'British'.* ◦ *If I've read the situation correctly, we should have some agreement on the contract by the end of the week.* **4** [I or T] How you read a piece of writing, or how it reads, is how it seems when you read it: *The letter reads **as if** (also non-standard **like**) it was written in a hurry.* ◦ *Her latest novel reads well (= is written in an attractive way).* **5** [T] (especially when communicating by radio), to hear and understand someone: *Do you read me?* ◦ *I read you loud and clear.* **6 read sb to sleep** to read aloud to someone until they go to sleep: *Every night when I was a child my father used to read me to sleep.* **STATE** ▷ **7** [L] (of something written or printed) to have or give the stated information or meaning: [+ speech] *The start of the American Constitution reads 'We, the people of the United States…'* ◦ *The thermometer is reading 40°C in the shade.* **STUDY** ▷ **8** [I or T] UK formal to study at university or to study for a specialized qualification: *They're both reading history at Cambridge.* ◦ legal *She's reading **for the Bar** (= studying to become a type of lawyer called a barrister).*

IDIOMS **read sb's lips** to follow the movements of someone's lips in order to understand what they are saying, especially if you are unable to hear them speak: *She read his lips across the busy conference hall – 'Time to go'.* → See also **lip-read** • **read sb's mind** (also **read sb's thoughts**) to know what someone is thinking without them telling you: humorous *'How about a drink, then?' 'Ah, you read my mind!'* • **read sb's palm** to look at the lines on a person's hand as a way of trying to find out what will happen to them in the future: *In a tent an old gypsy woman was reading palms.* • **read (sb) the riot act** to speak angrily to someone about something they have done and warn them that they will be punished if they do it again • **read between the lines** (C2) to try to understand someone's real feelings or intentions from what they say or write: *Reading between the lines, I'd say he isn't happy with the situation.* • **read my lips** informal a slightly rude way of telling someone to listen carefully to what you are saying: *Read my lips. No new taxes.* • **read the runes** UK literary to understand what will happen in the future, by looking at what is happening now: *He was the first of the Eastern leaders to read the runes and make political changes to stay in power.* • **take sth as read** UK to accept that something is true without making sure that it is: *I just took it as read that anyone who applied for the course would have the necessary qualifications.*

PHRASAL VERBS **read sth into sth** to believe that an action, remark or situation has a particular importance or meaning, often when this is not true: *Don't read **too much** into her leaving so suddenly – she probably just had a train to catch.* • **read sth out** (B2) to read something and say the words aloud so that other people can hear: *He read out the names of all the winners.* • **read sth over/through** (B2) to read something quickly from the beginning to the end, especially to find mistakes: *I read your proposal through last night and I think we'll agree to it.* ◦ *Always read over your work when you've finished.* • **read up (on/about) sth** (C1) to spend time reading in order to find out information about something: *It's a good idea to read up on a company before going for an interview.*

►noun [S] UK (C2) the act of reading something: *It's not brilliant but it's worth a read.* ◦ *The book is a **good/easy**, etc. read.* ◦ informal *Could I **have a** read **of** (= can I read) your newspaper?*

readable /ˈriː.də.bl/ adj easy and enjoyable to read: *It is an excellent and **highly** readable account of the army today.*

-readable /-riː.də.bl/ suffix **machine-/computer-readable** in a form that is able to be used by a computer: *Machine-readable passports will permit precise identity-checking.*

readdress /ˌriː.əˈdres/ verb [T] to write a different address on an envelope because the person it is intended for has moved to another place: *We re-addressed all his letters **to** Australia for years after he had emigrated.*

reader /ˈriː.dər/ (US) /-dɚ/ noun [C] **PERSON WHO READS** ▷ **1** someone who reads for pleasure, especially a person who reads a lot: *He's a **great/voracious** reader (= reads many books).* ◦ *She's an **avid** reader **of** historical novels.* **2** someone who reads a particular newspaper or magazine: *We asked our readers to write in and give us their views.* ◦ *She described him as a typical Guardian reader.* **3** specialized a person whose job is to advise a publishing company if a particular book should be published **SIMPLE BOOK** ▷ **4** a book containing a simple story that is designed for children who are learning to read or people who are learning a language: *There are readers at five different levels, from beginner to upper intermediate.* **TEACHER** ▷ **5** specialized a teacher, at British universities, just

R

under the rank of PROFESSOR: *Alan is a Reader* ***in*** *History at Dublin University.* **DEVICE** ▷ **6** a device that helps you to read very small writing, or a machine that can recognize printed material: *a microfilm/microfiche reader* ◦ *an optical character reader*

readership /ˈriː.də.ʃɪp/ (US) /-dɚ-/ **noun** [S, + sing/pl verb] (C1) the group of people who regularly read a particular newspaper, magazine, etc.: *The magazine has a readership* ***of*** *over 250,000.* ◦ *It's a newspaper with a large right-wing readership.*

the readies /ˈred.iz/ **noun** [plural] UK slang for money: *I'm a bit short of the readies.*

readily /ˈred.ɪ.li/ **adv** quickly, immediately, willingly, or without any problem: *He readily* ***agreed*** *to help.* ◦ *Larger sizes are readily* ***available****.*

readiness /ˈred.i.nəs/ **noun** [U] (C1) willingness or a state of being prepared for something: [+ to infinitive] *The company has declared its readiness* ***to*** *fight a challenge in the courts.* ◦ *The scaffolding has been put up* ***in*** *readiness* ***for*** *the repair work on the building.*

reading /ˈriː.dɪŋ/ **noun** **WRITTEN TEXT** ▷ **1** (A1) [U] the skill or activity of getting information from books: *Reading and tennis are my favourite pastimes.* ◦ *The diaries* ***make good*** *(****bedtime****) reading (= are good to read (in bed at night)).* ◦ *These books are* ***compulsory/required*** *reading for students of architecture.* **2** (C2) [C] an occasion when something written, especially a work of literature, is spoken to an audience: *The society often arranges* ***poetry*** *readings and musical evenings.* **UNDERSTANDING** ▷ **3** [C] the way in which you understand something: *My reading* ***of*** *the situation is that John wanted any excuse to resign.* **PARLIAMENT** ▷ **4** [C] In a parliament, a reading of a new law is one of the stages of discussion before it is approved: *The Housing Bill was* ***given*** *its second reading in Parliament today.* **MEASUREMENT** ▷ **5** [C] the number or amount that a piece of measuring equipment shows: *a thermometer reading*

ˈreading ˌknowledge **noun** [S or U] the ability to read a language, but not to speak it

ˈreading ˌlist **noun** [C] a list of books that students are expected to read as part of their course

ˈreading ˌroom **noun** [C] a room in a library, hotel, or other building where people can read quietly and conversation is not usually allowed

readjust /ˌriː.əˈdʒʌst/ **verb** [I or T] (C1) to change in order to fit a different situation, or to repair something slightly: *After living abroad for so long, he found it difficult to readjust* ***to*** *life at home.* ◦ *The clock automatically readjusts when you enter a new time zone.* ◦ *The machines were old and constantly needed readjusting.* • **readjustment** /-mənt/ **noun** [C or U]

readout /ˈriːd.aʊt/ **noun** [C usually singular] information produced by electronic equipment, shown in print, on a screen or by sound: *I got the computer to give a readout* ***of*** *the total figures.*

ready /ˈred.i/ **adj; noun**

▸**adj** **PREPARED** ▷ **1** prepared and suitable for fast activity: [+ to infinitive] *Are you ready* ***to*** *leave?* ◦ *Are you ready* ***to*** *order, Madam?* ◦ *Okay, Evie, ready* ***when you are*** *(= I am ready to do what we have arranged).* ◦ *Dinner's ready!* ◦ *Are you ready? Hurry up – we're late.* ◦ *We're leaving at eight o'clock, so you've got half an hour to* ***get*** *ready.* ◦ *The army are said to be ready* ***for*** *action.* ◦ *The concert hall was* ***made/got*** *ready (= prepared)* ***for*** *the performance.* **2 ready and waiting** waiting and prepared to act: *Secret information allowed the police to be ready and waiting when the robbers came out of the bank.* **QUICK** ▷ **3** [before noun] mainly approving quick with answers, jokes, solutions, etc.: *He had a ready reply to every question.* ◦ *He was charming, with a ready* ***wit*** *(= the ability to quickly say clever and funny things).*

IDIOMS **be ready to do sth** **1** informal to be going to do something immediately: *I should think you're about ready to collapse after all that walking.* **2** to be willing to do something: *These men are ready to die for their country.* • **be ready to roll** mainly US **1** to be going to start soon: *The new TV series from the West Wing team is ready to roll.* **2** to be going to leave soon: *Give me a call when you're ready to roll and I'll meet you outside.* • **ready to hand** UK close to you and therefore available for use when necessary: *The sheriff slept with his gun ready to hand under his pillow.* • **ready, steady, go!** UK said at the start of a race, especially one for children

▸**noun** **at the ready** prepared to be used or to act immediately: *He stood by the phone, pencil at the ready.*

ˌready-ˈmade **adj** bought or found in a finished form and available to use immediately: *a ready-made frozen meal* ◦ figurative *When she married Giles, she acquired a ready-made family – two teenage sons and a daughter.*

ˈready ˌmeal **noun** [C] UK a meal cooked and bought at a shop but taken somewhere else, often home, to be heated and eaten

ˌready ˈmoney **noun** [U] old-fashioned informal money that is available to be spent immediately → See also **the readies**

ˌready-to-ˈwear **adj** (of clothes) produced in standard sizes and not made to fit a particular person: *ready-to-wear suits*

reaffirm /ˌriː.əˈfɜːm/ (US) /-ˈfɝːm/ **verb** [T] to give your support to a person, plan, idea, etc. for a second time; to state something as true again: *The government yesterday reaffirmed its* ***commitment*** *to the current peace process.* ◦ *These events reaffirm my* ***belief*** *in the need for better information.*

reafforest /ˌriː.əˈfɒr.ɪst/ (US) /-ˈfɔːr.ɪst/ **verb** [T] UK for **reforest**

reafforestation /ˌriː.əˌfɒr.ɪˈsteɪ.ʃən/ (US) /-ˌfɔːr.ɪ-/ **noun** [U] UK for **reforestation**

reagent /riːˈeɪ.dʒənt/ **noun** [C] specialized a substance which acts on another in a chemical reaction

real /rɪəl/ (US) /riː.əl/ **adj; adv**

▸**adj** **NOT IMAGINARY** ▷ **1** existing in fact and not imaginary: *Assuring the patient that she has a real and not imaginary problem is the first step.* ◦ *There is a very real threat that he will lose his job.* **2 real earnings, income, etc.** the value of earnings, etc. after the effect of rising prices is considered: *Wages rose by 2.9 percent last year, but real earnings still fell by 1.3 percent.* **3 in real terms** existing in fact, despite what appears to be the situation: *Average earnings rose five percent in real terms after deducting income tax.* **NOT FALSE** ▷ **4** [before noun] being what it appears to be and not false: *real leather/fur* ◦ *Is that a toy gun or* ***the*** *real* ***thing****?* → Synonym **genuine** **5** [before noun] UK approving (especially of foods) produced using traditional methods and without artificial substances: *The pub sells several kinds of real* ***ale*** *(= traditional beer).* **6 for real** informal real, not pretended: *I thought it was just a fire practice but apparently it was for real.* **IMPORTANT** ▷ **7** [before noun] the most important; the main: *The real difficulty was the language, because my children don't speak English.* ◦ *Novelty value may be a part of it, but the real reason people like our paper is that it speaks the truth.* **VERY GREAT** ▷ **8** [before noun]

R

used to emphasize a noun: *He's a real gentleman.* ◦ *She was a real help.* ◦ *It's a real nuisance.*

IDIOMS **get real!** informal used for telling someone that they should try to understand the true facts of a situation and not hope for what is impossible: *Get real! He's never going to give you the money.* • **is he/she for real?** informal used when you think someone is silly or very surprising

▸**adv** mainly US informal very: *I like this homemade lemonade, it's real good!*

> **! Common mistake: real**
>
> **Remember: real** is used as an adverb in informal US English but not usually in UK English.
>
> In UK English, don't use 'real' as an adverb, say **really**:
>
> *I had a really good time at the barbecue.*

the ˌreal ˈdeal noun [S] informal **1** someone or something that is very good and has all the qualities that people say they have: *His performance proved he's the real deal.* **2** the facts about something: *The booklet gives you the real deal on smoking.*

ˈreal esˌtate noun [U] mainly US property in the form of land or buildings: *We're going to buy a piece of real estate.*

ˈreal estate ˌagent noun [C] US for **estate agent**

ˈreal estate ˌbroker noun [C] Australian English for **estate agent**

realia /riˈeɪ.li.ə/ **noun** [U] real objects or pieces of writing, used to help teach students in a class

realign /ˌriː.əˈlaɪn/ **verb** [T] **1** to put something into a new or correct position: *She realigned the books along the edge of the shelf.* **2 realign yourself (with sb/sth)** to change your ideas or policies so that they are the same as those of another person or group: *Several politicians left the party and realigned themselves with the opposition.* • **realignment** /-mənt/ **noun** [C or U] *This war will inevitably lead to a realignment **of/within** European politics.*

realism /ˈrɪə.lɪ.zəm/ (US) /ˈriː.ə-/ **noun** [U] **THOUGHT** ▷ **1** a way of thinking and acting based on facts and what is possible, rather than on hopes for things that are unlikely to happen: *His decision not to expand the business shows his down-to-earth realism.* → Compare **idealism 2** specialized in science and PHILOSOPHY, the belief that objects continue to exist in the world even when no one is there to see them **ART** ▷ **3** specialized paintings, films, books, etc. that try to represent life as it really is: *The anti-drugs adverts used handheld camera techniques to add to the **gritty** realism of the situations.*

realist /ˈrɪə.lɪst/ (US) /ˈriː.ə-/ **noun** [C] **THOUGHT** ▷ **1** someone who hopes for or accepts only what seems possible or likely, and does not hope for or expect more: *I'm a realist – I knew there was no way I could win, so I swam for a good finish, for points.* **ART** ▷ **2** specialized an artist, writer, etc. who represents life as it really is, rather than in an imagined way

realistic /ˌrɪəˈlɪs.tɪk/ (US) /ˌriː.ə-/ **adj** **1** (B2) accepting things as they are in fact and not making decisions based on unlikely hopes for the future: *Let's be realistic (**about** this) – I just can't afford to pay that much money.* ◦ ***It** isn't realistic **to** expect people to work for so little money.* → See also **Realpolitik 2** (B2) seeming to exist or be happening in fact: *The special effects were so realistic.*

realistically /ˌrɪəˈlɪs.tɪ.kəl.i/ (US) /ˌriː.ə-/ **adv** **1** (C2) according to the facts and what is possible: *Realistically speaking, he hadn't a hope, but that didn't stop him trying.* **2** (C1) in a way that seems as if it exists: *He was made up very realistically to look like an old woman.*

reality /riˈæl.ɪ.ti/ (US) /-ə.t̬i/ **noun** **1** (B2) [S or U] the state of things as they are, rather than as they are imagined to be: *The reality **of** the situation is that unless we find some new funding soon, the youth centre will have to close.* ◦ *He **escaped from** reality by going to the cinema every afternoon.* ◦ *He seemed very young, but he was **in** reality (= in fact) older than all of us.* **2** (B2) [C] a fact: *The book confronts the harsh social and political realities of the world today.* ◦ *Her childhood ambition **became a** reality (= happened in fact) when she was made a judge.*

reˈality ˌcheck noun [C usually singular] an occasion that causes you to consider the facts about a situation and not your opinions, ideas or beliefs: *The recent failure of so many internet businesses has provided a reality check for those who predicted huge profits.*

reˈality TˌV noun [U] television programmes about ordinary people who are filmed in real situations, rather than actors

realizable (UK usually **realisable**) /ˈrɪə.laɪ.zə.bl̩/ (US) /ˈriː.ə-/ **adj** **CAN ACHIEVE** ▷ **1** able to be achieved: *He doubted whether the plan was realizable in practice.* **MONEY** ▷ **2** legal able to be sold to get money: *realizable assets*

realization (UK usually **realisation**) /ˌrɪə.laɪˈzeɪ.ʃən/ (US) /ˌriː.ə.lə-/ **noun** **BECOMING AWARE** ▷ **1** (C1) [C usually singular] the fact or moment of starting to understand a situation: [+ that] *The realization was **dawning that** this was a major disaster.* **ACHIEVEMENT** ▷ **2** (C2) [U] the act or moment of achieving something you planned to do or hoped for: *To win the Olympic gold medal was the realization of his life's dream.* **MONEY** ▷ **3** [U] legal the act of getting money by selling something: *Even the realization of all his assets would not be enough to prevent financial ruin.*

realize (UK usually **realise**) /ˈrɪə.laɪz/ (US) /ˈriː.ə-/ **verb** **BECOME AWARE** ▷ **1** (B1) [I or T] to understand a situation, sometimes suddenly: *They didn't realize the danger they were in.* ◦ [+ (that)] *'Do you realize (**that**) this is the third time you've forgotten?' she said angrily.* ◦ [+ question word] *I realize **how** difficult it's going to be, but we must try.* ◦ *As he watched the TV drama, he **suddenly** realized (**that**) he'd seen it before.* ◦ *'You're standing on my foot.' 'Sorry, I didn't realize.'* **ACHIEVE** ▷ **2** (C1) [T] to achieve something you were hoping for: *Lots of money, a luxury house, a fast car – Danny had realized all his ambitions by the age of 25.* **3 sb's worst fears are realized** [T] used for saying that something that someone was worrying about really happened: *Ten years later her worst fears were realized.* **MONEY** ▷ **4** specialized to be sold for a particular amount of money: *The paintings are expected to realize £500,000 each.* **5 realize assets** legal to sell property in order to get some money: *He had to realize all his assets to pay off his debts.*

ˌreal ˈlife noun [U] what happens in human situations rather than in a story, film, etc.: ***In** real life the star of the film is a devoted husband and father.* ◦ [before noun] *a real-life **story***

really /ˈrɪə.li/ (US) /ˈriː.ə-/ **adv; exclamation**

▸**adv** **NOT IMAGINARY** ▷ **1** (B1) in fact: *He isn't really angry – he's just pretending.* ◦ *You don't really expect them to refuse, do you?* **2** (A2) used to say that something is certain: *Thank you, but I really couldn't eat another thing.* ◦ *He's really going to do it this time.* **VERY** ▷ **3** (A1) very or very much: *She's really nice.*

R

∘ *This room is really hot.* ∘ *That's really interesting.* ∘ *It's a really difficult decision.* ∘ *'Did you like it? **Not** really (= no).'*

> **!** Common mistake: **really**
>
> **Warning:** Common word-building error!
>
> If an adjective ends with 'l', add '-ly' to make an adverb. Don't write 'realy', write **really**.

▸**exclamation** (A2) used to express interest, surprise or anger: *'I'm getting married to Fred.' 'Really? When?'* ∘ *'She's agreed to do a parachute jump for charity.' 'Really? Do you think she'll do it?'* ∘ *'He hasn't brought the book back.' 'Oh, really! That's the second time I've asked him!'*

realm /relm/ noun [C] **AREA** ▷ **1** (C2) an area of interest or activity: *Her interests are **in** the realm **of** practical politics.* **COUNTRY** ▷ **2** formal a country ruled by a king or queen: *the defence of the realm* ∘ *The matter was hotly debated in all the towns of the realm.*

IDIOM **within the realms of possibility** possible: *A pay rise is not within the realms of possibility, I'm afraid.*

the real McCoy /ˌrɪəl məˈkɔɪ/ (US) /ˌriː.əl-/ noun [S] the original or best example of something: *The caviar was the real McCoy too – not the stuff we buy in the supermarket at home.*

Realpolitik /reɪˈɑːlˌpɒl.ɪ.tiːk/ (US) /-poʊ.lɪ-/ noun [U] practical politics, decided more by the urgent needs of the country, political party, etc., than by morals or principles

the ˌreal ˈthing noun [S] the original, best, or most typical example of something: *It's a synthetic material that looks like the real thing.*

ˈreal-time adj [before noun] describes computer systems that are able to deal with and use new information immediately and therefore influence or direct the actions of the objects supplying that information

realtor /ˈrɪəl.təʳ/ (US) /ˈriː.əl.tɔːr/ noun [C] US for **estate agent**

realty /ˈrɪəl.ti/ (US) /ˈriː.əl.t̬i/ noun [U] US for **real estate**: *a realty agent* ∘ *a realty company*

the ˌreal ˈworld noun [S] the set of situations most humans have to deal with in their lives, rather than what happens in stories, films, etc.: *Christine, the play's main character, wouldn't last a minute **in** the real world.* ∘ [before noun] *real-world **situations/experiences***

ream /riːm/ noun; verb

▸**noun 1** [C] specialized 500 sheets of paper **2** [C usually plural] informal a lot of something, especially writing: *She's written reams **of** poetry.*

▸**verb**

PHRASAL VERB **ream sb (out)** US slang to tell someone off severely because you strongly disapprove of their behaviour: *The boss reamed them out for sleeping on the job.*

reamer /ˈriː.məʳ/ (US) /-mɚ/ noun [C] specialized a tool used to make holes larger or an exact size

reap /riːp/ verb [I or T] to cut and collect a grain crop

IDIOMS **reap the benefit, reward, etc.** (C2) to get something good as a result of your own actions: *She studied every evening and reaped the benefit at exam time.* ∘ *We sold them most of their modern weapons and now we are reaping the bitter harvest.* • **reap what you have sown** to win or lose as a result of something you did in the past

reappear /ˌriː.əˈpɪəʳ/ (US) /-ˈpɪr/ verb [I] to appear again or return after a period of time: *Ten minutes later she reappeared from the storeroom holding the paint.* • **reappearance** /-ˈpɪə.rəns/ (US) /-ˈpɪr.əns/ noun [C]

reapply /ˌriː.əˈplaɪ/ verb **ASK** ▷ **1** [I] to officially ask again for something, for example for yourself to be considered for a job, especially by writing or sending in a form: *Mr Gubbay said yesterday that he will not be reapplying **for** the job.* **PUT ON** ▷ **2** [T] to put a substance on again: *She carefully reapplied her lipstick* **USE** ▷ **3** [T] to make use of something in a different way or use it for a different practical purpose: *to reapply principles/methods*

reappraisal /ˌriː.əˈpreɪ.zəl/ noun [C or U] the act of examining and judging something or someone again: *He'd like to see a fundamental reappraisal **of** the way unions operate.*

reappraise /ˌriː.əˈpreɪz/ verb [T] to examine and judge something or someone again: *We need to reappraise the situation in a year's time.*

rear /rɪəʳ/ (US) /rɪr/ adj; noun; verb

▸**adj** [before noun] (B2) at the back of something: *There's a sticker on the rear **door/window**.* ∘ *The horse had injured one of its rear **legs**.* → See also **rearguard**

▸**noun 1 the rear** (C1) the back part of something: *We walked round to the rear of the house.* ∘ *Two police motorcyclists **brought up** the rear (= formed the last part) of the demonstration.* **2** [C] (also **rear end**) old-fashioned informal a person's bottom

▸**verb CARE FOR** ▷ **1** (C1) [T] to care for young animals or children until they are able to care for themselves: *Some women make a deliberate choice to rear a **child** alone.* ∘ *He describes how these birds rear their **young**.* → See also **child-rearing** **RISE** ▷ **2** [I or T] to rise up or to lift something up: *The horse reared (**up**) (= suddenly rose onto its back legs) when it heard the gun shot.* ∘ *The lion slowly reared its head (= lifted it up) and looked around.*

IDIOM **rear its (ugly) head** (of something unpleasant) to appear: *The familiar spectre of drought and famine has reared its ugly head again.*

PHRASAL VERB **rear above/over sth/sb** literary to appear very tall and big in comparison with another thing or person: *The mountain reared above the village.*

ˌrear ˈadmiral noun [C] (also **Rear Admiral**) an officer of very high rank in the navy: *Rear Admiral Hopper/Grace Hopper* ∘ [as form of address] *Yes, Rear Admiral.*

ˈrear-end verb [T] US informal to hit the back of one car with another in an accident

rearguard /ˈrɪə.gɑːd/ (US) /ˈrɪr.gɑːrd/ noun [C] the people who are the last in a row or group, especially in a military situation

ˈrearguard ˌaction noun [C or U] a final attempt to prevent something from happening: *The unions were determined to **fight** a rearguard action **against** the government's plans to strip them of their powers.*

ˌrear ˈlight noun [C] UK (US **ˈtail ˌlight**) a red light at the back of a road vehicle that makes it possible for the vehicle to be seen in the dark

rearm /ˌriːˈɑːm/ (US) /-ˈɑːrm/ verb [I or T] to supply yourself or others with new weapons, especially in order to become a strong military power again • **rearmament** /riˈɑː.mə.mənt/ (US) /-ˈɑːr-/ noun [U]

rearmost /ˈrɪə.məʊst/ (US) /ˈrɪr.moʊst/ adj [before noun] formal furthest to the back or the last in a row: *the rearmost seats on the bus*

rearrange /ˌriː.əˈreɪndʒ/ verb [T] B2 to change the order, position or time of arrangements already made: *The new sofa was bigger than the old one, so they had to rearrange the rest of the furniture.* ◦ *I'm busy tomorrow – could we rearrange the meeting* ***for*** *Monday (= have it on Monday instead)?*

rearrangement /ˌriː.əˈreɪndʒ.mənt/ noun [C] the act of changing the order, position, or time of arrangements already made: *a rearrangement* ***of/to*** *our plans* ◦ *As students of chemistry know, even small rearrangements* ***of*** *a molecule's structure can produce a compound that acts differently.* ◦ *Going on a long trip always means lots of rearrangements* ***to*** *my schedule.*

ˌrearview ˈmirror noun [C] a mirror that allows a driver to see what is happening behind their car

ˌrear-wheel ˈdrive noun [U] If a car has rear-wheel drive, the engine provides power to the back wheels.

reason /ˈriː.zən/ noun; verb

▸noun **EXPLANATION** ▷ **1** A2 [C or U] the cause of an event or situation or something which provides an excuse or explanation: *The reason* ***for*** *the disaster was engine failure, not human error.* ◦ [+ question word] *The reason* ***why*** *grass is green was a mystery to the little boy.* ◦ [+ (that)] *The reason* ***(that)*** *I'm ringing is to ask a favour.* ◦ not standard *The reason I walked out was* ***because*** *I was bored.* ◦ [+ to infinitive] *The police* ***have*** *(****every good****) reason* ***to*** *believe that he is guilty.* ◦ *She was furious, and* ***with*** *reason (= with good cause).* ◦ ***For some*** *reason/****For*** *reasons* ***best known to*** *himself (= for reasons no one else knows about) he's decided to leave his job.* **2 by reason of** formal because of: *He's always asked to these occasions by reason of his position.*

> **! Common mistake: reason**
>
> The correct preposition to use after **reason** is **for**.
> Don't say 'the reason of something', say **the reason for something.**

JUDGMENT ▷ **3** [U] the ability of a healthy mind to think and make judgments, especially based on practical facts: *We humans believe that we are the only animals to have* ***the power of*** *reason.* ◦ mainly UK old-fashioned *He* ***lost*** *his reason (= became mentally ill) when both his parents were killed in the crash.* **4 within reason** C2 within the limits of what is acceptable and possible: *We can wear anything we like to the office, within reason.*

> **Word partners for reason noun**
>
> *give/have* a reason • a *compelling/good/major/obvious* reason • the *main/real/simple* reason • the reason *for* sth • the reason *why* • *for* reasons **of** sth • the reason *behind* sth

IDIOM **listen to reason** (also **see reason**) to listen to good advice and be influenced by it: *Friends tried to persuade them to change their minds, but neither man would listen to reason.*

▸verb [T] to try to understand and to make judgments based on practical facts: [+ (that)] *Newton reasoned* ***(that)*** *there must be a force such as gravity, when an apple fell on his head.* ◦ *I spent hours reasoning* ***out*** *the solution to the puzzle.*

PHRASAL VERB **reason with sb** to try to persuade someone to act in a wise way or to change their behaviour or a decision, by giving them good reasons: [+ to infinitive] *The police reasoned with the hijackers* ***to*** *at least let the children go free.*

reasonable /ˈriː.zən.ə.bl̩/ adj **1** B2 based on or using good judgment and therefore fair and practical: *If you tell him what happened, I'm sure he'll understand – he's a reasonable man.* ◦ *He went free because the jury decided there was a reasonable* ***doubt*** *about his guilt.* **2** B1 acceptable: *We had a reasonable journey.* ◦ *We have a strong team and a reasonable chance of winning the game.* **3** B1 not too expensive: *Tomatoes are very reasonable at this time of year.* • **reasonableness** /-nəs/ noun [U]

reasonably /ˈriː.zən.ə.bli/ adv **1** B2 using good judgment: *Stop shouting and let's discuss this reasonably.* **2** B2 in a satisfactory way: *She writes reasonably good children's books.* **3** B1 at a price that is not too expensive: *You can eat out very reasonably these days.* ◦ *I bought a reasonably* ***priced*** *radio.*

reasoned /ˈriː.zənd/ adj If an argument is (well) reasoned, it is clear and carefully considered.

reasoning /ˈriː.zən.ɪŋ/ noun [U] **1** C2 the process of thinking about something in order to make a decision: *The reasoning* ***behind*** *her conclusion is impossible to fault.* **2 be no reasoning with sb** If there is no reasoning with someone, it is impossible to persuade them to change their opinions or actions by arguing with them: *She's absolutely determined to go and* ***there's*** *just no reasoning with her.*

reassemble /ˌriː.əˈsem.bl̩/ verb **1** [I or T] to come together again, or bring something together again, in a single place: *After lunch, the class reassembled.* **2** [T] to make something again by joining its separate parts together: *Investigators have been reassembling the wreckage of the plane.*

reassess /ˌriː.əˈses/ verb [T] to think again about something in order to decide if you should change the way you feel about it or deal with it: *We need to reassess our values as a nation.* ◦ *The customer services department is reassessing its procedures for handling customer complaints.* ◦ *I've reassessed the situation and decided to stay.*

reassurance /ˌriː.əˈʃɔː.rəns/ (US) /-ˈʃʊr.əns/ noun [C or U] C2 words of advice and comfort intended to make someone feel less worried: *I felt I couldn't cope with the situation and was in desperate need of some reassurance.* ◦ *Despite her father's reassurances, she was still frightened of the dark.*

reassure /ˌriː.əˈʃɔːr/ (US) /-ˈʃʊr/ verb [T] C1 to comfort someone and stop them from worrying: [+ to infinitive] *I was nervous on my first day at college, but I was reassured* ***to*** *see some friendly faces.* ◦ [+ (that)] *He reassured me* ***(that)*** *my cheque would arrive soon.*

reassuring /ˌriː.əˈʃɔː.rɪŋ/ (US) /-ˈʃʊr.ɪŋ/ adj C1 making you feel less worried: *He smiled at me in a reassuring way.* • **reassuringly** /-li/ adv *'Don't worry,' he said reassuringly. 'Everything will be all right.'*

rebate /ˈriː.beɪt/ noun [C] an amount of money that is returned to you, especially by the government, for example when you have paid too much tax: *a* ***tax*** *rebate*

rebel noun; verb

▸noun [C] /ˈreb.əl/ B2 a person who is opposed to the political system in their country and tries to change it using force, or a person who shows their disagreement with the ideas of people in authority or of society by behaving differently: *The rebels took over the capital and set up a new government.* ◦ *He was a bit of a rebel when he was a teenager and dyed his hair pink.*

▸verb [I] /rɪˈbel/ (-ll-) **1** B2 to fight against the government or to refuse to obey rules, etc.: *The people rebelled* ***against*** *the harsh new government.* ◦ *Jacob rebelled* ***against*** *his parents' plans for him and left school at the age of 16.* **2** to react against a feeling,

R

action, plan, etc.: *My poor sick stomach rebelled* ***at*** *the idea of any more food.*

rebellion /rɪˈbel.i.ən/ noun [C or U] **1** C1 violent action organized by a group of people who are trying to change the political system in their country: *The government has brutally crushed the rebellion.* **2** action against those in authority, against the rules, or against normal and accepted ways of behaving: *a backbench rebellion* ***against*** *the new foreign policy ◦ her teenage rebellion*

rebellious /rɪˈbel.i.əs/ adj **1** If a group of people are rebellious, they oppose the ideas of the people in authority and plan to change the system, often using force: *rebellious groups of southern tribespeople* **2** C1 If someone is rebellious, they are difficult to control and do not behave in the way they are expected to: *Her teachers regard her as a rebellious, trouble-making girl.* • **rebelliously** /-li/ adv • **rebelliousness** /-nəs/ noun [U]

rebirth /ˌriːˈbɜːθ/ US /-ˈbɝːθ/ noun [S or U] a new period of growth of something, or a time when something that was popular in the past becomes popular again: *English drama has enjoyed a rebirth since the 1950s with writers like John Osborne, Harold Pinter and Tom Stoppard.*

reboot /ˌriːˈbuːt/ verb [I or T] When a computer reboots, it switches off and then starts again immediately, and when you reboot a computer, you make it do this.

rebound verb; noun

▸verb [I] /ˌriːˈbaʊnd/ **1** to BOUNCE back after hitting a hard surface **2** If an action rebounds on you, it does not have the effect you hoped for but has an unpleasant effect on you instead: *His continual demands for sympathy rebounded* ***on*** *him because his friends finally stopped listening.* **3** to rise in price after a fall: *Cotton rebounded from declines early in the day to end at a higher price.*

▸noun [C or U] /ˈriː.baʊnd/ the act of rebounding: *I hit the ball* ***on the*** *rebound (= after it had hit the wall or ground once).*

IDIOM **on the rebound** informal unhappy and confused because a close, romantic relationship of yours has recently finished: *Five months after Nick had left her, she married another man on the rebound.*

R

rebuff /rɪˈbʌf/ verb [T] formal to refuse to accept a helpful suggestion or offer from someone, often by answering in an unfriendly way: *She rebuffed all suggestions that she should resign.* • **rebuff** noun [C] *Her desperate request for help was met with a rebuff.*

rebuild /ˌriːˈbɪld/ verb [T] (**rebuilt**, **rebuilt**) **1** B1 to build something again that has been damaged or destroyed: *The cathedral was completely rebuilt in 1425 after it had been destroyed by fire.* **2** B2 If you rebuild a system or organization, you develop it so that it works effectively: *Before the election, the party claimed it would rebuild the country's economy.* **3 rebuild your life** B2 to try to return to the good situation that you were in before an unpleasant event happened to you: *Many people have difficulty in rebuilding their lives when they come out of prison.*

rebuke /rɪˈbjuːk/ verb [T] formal to speak angrily to someone because you disapprove of what they have said or done: *I was rebuked by my manager* ***for being*** *late.* • **rebuke** noun [C or U] *He received a* ***stern*** *rebuke from the manager.*

rebut /rɪˈbʌt/ verb [T] (**-tt-**) formal to argue that a statement or claim is not true: *She has rebutted charges that she has been involved in any financial malpractice.*

rebuttal /rɪˈbʌt.əl/ US /-ˈbʌt̬-/ noun [C] formal a statement which says that something is not true: *She issued a point-by-point rebuttal of the company's accusations.*

recalcitrant /rɪˈkæl.sɪ.trənt/ adj formal (of a person) unwilling to obey orders or to do what should be done, or (of an animal) refusing to be controlled • **recalcitrance** /-trəns/ noun [U]

recall /rɪˈkɔːl/ US /ˈriː.kɑːl/ verb; noun

▸verb REMEMBER ▷ **1** B2 [I or T] to bring the memory of a past event into your mind, and often to give a description of what you remember: *The old man recalled the city as it had been before the war. ◦ 'As I recall,' he said with some irritation, 'you still owe me £150.'* ◦ [+ (that)] *He recalled (****that****) he had sent the letter over a month ago.* ◦ [+ question word] *Can you recall* ***what*** *happened last night?* ◦ [+ -ing verb] *She recalled see****ing*** *him outside the shop on the night of the robbery.* **2** [T] to cause you to think of a particular event, situation or style: *His paintings recall the style of Picasso.* CALL BACK ▷ **3** [T] to order the return of a person who belongs to an organization or of products made by a company: *The ambassador was recalled when war broke out. ◦ The company recalled thousands of tins of baby food after a salmonella scare.*

▸noun REMEMBERING ▷ **1** [U] the ability to remember things: *Old people often have astonishing* ***powers of*** *recall. ◦ My brother has* ***total*** *recall (= he can remember every detail of past events).* CALLING BACK ▷ **2** [C usually singular] an occasion when someone orders the return of a person who belongs to an organization, or orders the return of products made by a company: *an emergency recall* ***of*** *Parliament ◦ The company issued a recall* ***of*** *all their latest antibiotics.*

recant /rɪˈkænt/ verb [I or T] formal to announce in public that your past beliefs or statements were wrong and that you no longer agree with them: *After a year spent in solitary confinement, he* ***publicly*** *recanted (his views).* • **recantation** /ˌriː.kænˈteɪ.ʃən/ noun [C or U]

recap /ˈriː.kæp/, /ˌriːˈkæp/ verb [I or T] (**-pp-**) to repeat the main points of an explanation or description: *Finally, the teacher recapped the main points of the lesson. ◦ To recap, our main aim is to increase sales by 15 percent this year.* • **recap** /ˈriː.kæp/ noun [S] *Could you give me a quick recap* ***on*** *what happened in the meeting?*

recapitulate /ˌriː.kəˈpɪt.jʊ.leɪt/ verb [I or T] formal for **recap**

recapitulation /ˌriː.kəˌpɪt.jʊˈleɪ.ʃən/ noun [S] formal for **recap**

recapture /ˌriːˈkæp.tʃər/ US /-tʃɚ/ verb [T] **1** to take something into your possession again, especially by force: *The army recaptured the town* ***from*** *the rebels.* **2** If something recaptures a previous emotion or style, it makes you experience that emotion again or it repeats that style.

recast /ˌriːˈkɑːst/ US /-ˈkæst/ verb [T] (**recast**, **recast**) to change the form of something, or to change an actor in a play or film: *She recast her novel* ***as*** *a musical comedy. ◦ In despair, the theatre director recast the leading role.*

recce /ˈrek.i/ noun [C] informal for **reconnaissance**

recede /rɪˈsiːd/ verb [I] to move further away into the distance, or to become less clear or less bright: *As the boat picked up speed, the coastline receded* ***into*** *the distance until finally it became invisible. ◦ The painful memories gradually receded in her mind.*

re͵ceding ˈhairline noun [C usually singular] If a man has a receding hairline, he is losing the hair from the front of his head.

receipt /rɪˈsiːt/ noun **PIECE OF PAPER** ▷ **1** A2 [C] (US also **sales slip**) a piece of paper which proves that money, goods or information have been received: *Make sure you are given a receipt* ***for*** *everything you buy.* **RECEIVING** ▷ **2** B2 [U] formal the act or state of receiving money or goods: *Goods will be delivered* ***on*** *receipt* ***of*** *payment (= after the money is received).* ◦ *You have been* ***in*** *receipt* ***of*** *unemployment benefit for two months.* **3 receipts** [plural] the amounts of money received during a particular period by a business: *The theatre's receipts* ***for*** *the winter were badly down.*

receive /rɪˈsiːv/ verb [T] **GET** ▷ **1** A2 to get or be given something: *Did you receive my letter?* ◦ *I received a phone call* ***from*** *your mother.* ◦ *They received a visit* ***from*** *the police.* ◦ *She died after receiving a blow to the head.* ◦ *Members of Parliament received a 4.2 percent pay increase this year.* **2** (of a radio or television) to change a signal into sounds and pictures → See also **reception 3** to be able to hear someone's voice when they are communicating with you by radio: *I'm receiving you* ***loud and clear.*** **WELCOME** ▷ **4** to formally welcome a visitor or guest: *She stood by the door to receive her guests as they arrived.* → See also **reception 5** Indian English to meet someone when they arrive somewhere: *My friend offered to receive me at the railway station.* **6** C1 to react to something or someone in a particular way that shows how you feel about it or them: *The prime minister's speech was well/warmly/coldly, etc. received by the conference delegates.* **7 be received into sth** formal to be made a member of an organization: *He was received into the church.*

> **! Common mistake: receive**
>
> **Warning:** Check your spelling!
>
> **Receive** is one of the 50 words most often spelled wrongly by learners. Remember: don't write 'ie', write **ei**.

IDIOM **be at/on the receiving end** If you are at/on the receiving end of something unpleasant that someone does, you suffer because of it: *Sales assistants are often at the receiving end of verbal abuse from customers.*

received /rɪˈsiːvd/ adj [before noun] formal generally accepted as being right or correct because it is based on authority: *According to received* ***wisdom****, exposure to low level radioactivity is harmless.*

Re͵ceived Pronunciˈation noun [U] (abbreviation **RP**) UK specialized the standard way in which middle-class speakers of southern British English pronounce words

receiver /rɪˈsiː.vəʳ/ US /-vɚ/ noun [C] **EQUIPMENT** ▷ **1** the part of a phone in two parts that you hold to your ear and mouth: *She picked up the receiver and dialled his number.* **2** a piece of equipment that changes radio and television signals into sounds and pictures **PERSON** ▷ **3** (UK also **official receiver**) a person who officially deals with the business matters of companies who cannot pay their debts: *The company went bankrupt and was* ***put into the hands of*** *the receivers.* **4** UK legal A receiver (of stolen goods) is a person who buys and sells property which they know has been stolen.

receivership /rɪˈsiː.və.ʃɪp/ US /-vɚ-/ noun [U] a situation in which a company is controlled by the receiver because it has no money: *Since January over a hundred companies have been forced* ***into*** *receivership.*

recent /ˈriː.sənt/ adj B1 happening or starting from a short time ago: *Is that a recent photo?* ◦ *Have you been following recent political events?* ◦ *In recent times/years/months, etc. there has been an increase in the amount of violence on television.*

recently /ˈriː.sənt.li/ adv B1 not long ago, or at a time that started not long ago: *Have you seen any good films recently?* ◦ *Until very recently he worked as a teacher and he still shudders at the memories.* ◦ *Recently, I've been feeling a bit depressed.*

receptacle /rɪˈsep.tə.kl/ noun [C] formal a container used for storing or putting objects in: *Householders are given four separate receptacles* ***for*** *their rubbish.*

reception /rɪˈsep.ʃən/ noun **WELCOME** ▷ **1** B2 [C] a formal party at which important people are welcomed: *The president* ***gave*** *a reception for the visiting heads of state.* **2** C1 [S] the way in which people react to something or someone: *Her first book* ***got*** *a wonderful/warm/frosty reception from the critics.* **3** [U] the act of welcoming someone or something: *The new hospital was ready for the reception* ***of*** *its first patients.* → See also **receive WELCOME** ▷ **4** B1 [U] the place in a hotel or office building where people go when they first arrive: *Ask for me at reception.* ◦ *I signed in at the reception* ***desk.*** **SCHOOL** ▷ **5** [U] UK the first year of infant school: *a reception class/teacher* **RADIO/TELEVISION** ▷ **6** [U] the degree to which radio or television sounds and pictures are clear: *We live on top of a hill and so we get excellent radio reception.* → See also **receive**

receptionist /rɪˈsep.ʃən.ɪst/ noun [C] A2 a person who works in a place such as a hotel, office, or hospital, who welcomes and helps visitors and answers the phone

reˈception ͵room noun [C] UK formal (especially in descriptions of houses for sale) a room in a house where people can sit together: *The house has two reception rooms – a living room and a dining room.*

receptive /rɪˈsep.tɪv/ adj C2 willing to listen to and accept new ideas and suggestions: *The government is not receptive* ***to*** *the idea of a Freedom of Information Act.* • **receptiveness** /-nəs/ noun [U] (also **receptivity**)

receptor /rɪˈsep.təʳ/ US /-tɚ/ noun [C] specialized a nerve ending that reacts to a change, such as heat or cold, in the body by sending a message to the CENTRAL NERVOUS SYSTEM

recess /rɪˈses/, /ˈriː-/ noun **PAUSE** ▷ **1** [C or U] a period of time in the year when the members of a parliament are not meeting **2** [U] US in school, a period of time between classes when children do not study **SPACE** ▷ **3** [C] a small area in a room that is formed by one part of a wall being set back further than other parts: *The room has a recess designed to hold bookshelves.* **4** [C usually plural] a secret or hidden place: *Psychoanalysts aim to explore the* ***deepest/innermost*** *recesses of the mind.*

recessed /rɪˈsest/ adj built in a space in a wall: *recessed* ***lights***

recession /rɪˈseʃ.ən/ noun [C or U] B2 a period when the economy of a country is not successful and conditions for business are bad: *The country is sliding into the depths of (a) recession.*

recessive /rɪˈses.ɪv/ adj specialized (of GENES and the physical qualities they control) only appearing in a child if both parents supply the controlling GENE

recharge /͵riːˈtʃɑːdʒ/ US /-ˈtʃɑːrdʒ/ verb [I or T] C1 If a BATTERY recharges, it becomes filled with electricity so that it can work again and if you recharge a BATTERY, you fill it with electricity.

R

IDIOM **recharge your batteries** C2 to rest and relax for a period of time so that you feel energetic again: *She took a trip to the South of France to recharge her batteries.*

rechargeable /riːˈtʃɑː.dʒə.bl/ US /-ˈtʃɑːr-/ **adj** able to be recharged: *a rechargeable* ***battery***

recherché /rəˈʃeə.ʃeɪ/ US /-ˈʃer-/ **adj** formal very unusual, not generally known about, and chosen with great care in order to make people admire your knowledge or style: *a recherché word/topic* ◦ *a recherché menu*

recidivist /rɪˈsɪd.ɪ.vɪst/ **noun** [C] specialized a criminal who continues to commit crimes even after they have been punished • **recidivism** /-vɪ.zəm/ **noun** [U]

recipe /ˈres.ɪ.pi/ **noun** [C] B1 a set of instructions telling you how to prepare and cook food, including a list of what food is needed for this: *For real South Asian food, just* ***follow*** *these recipes.* ◦ *Do you know a good recipe* ***for*** *wholemeal bread?*

IDIOM **be a recipe for disaster, trouble, success, etc.** C2 to be very likely to become a DISASTER, success, etc.: *All those children unsupervised sounds to me like a recipe for disaster.*

recipient /rɪˈsɪp.i.ənt/ **noun** [C] formal a person who receives something

reciprocal /rɪˈsɪp.rə.kəl/ **adj** formal A reciprocal action or arrangement involves two people or groups of people who behave in the same way or agree to help each other and give each other advantages. • **reciprocally** /-i/ **adv**

reciprocate /rɪˈsɪp.rə.keɪt/ **verb** **1** [I or T] formal to share the same feelings as someone else, or to behave in the same way as someone else: *Sadly, my feelings for him were not reciprocated.* ◦ *We invited them to dinner and a week later they reciprocated.* **2** specialized If a part of a machine reciprocates, it moves backwards and forwards: *Some electric razors have reciprocating heads.* • **reciprocation** /rɪˌsɪp.rəˈkeɪ.ʃən/ **noun** [U]

reciprocity /ˌres.ɪˈprɒs.ɪ.ti/ US /-ˈprɑː.sə.t̬i/ **noun** [U] formal behaviour in which two people or groups of people give each other help and advantages

recital /rɪˈsaɪ.təl/ US /-t̬əl/ **noun** [C] **1** a performance of music or poetry, usually given by one person or a small group of people: *I went to a violin recital today.* ◦ *He is* ***giving*** *a recital* ***of*** *Bach's sonatas.* **2** a detailed description of something or a list of things: *She gave us a long, boring recital* ***of*** *all her troubles.*

recitation /ˌres.ɪˈteɪ.ʃən/ **noun** [C] saying a piece of writing aloud from memory: *He gave a beautiful recitation* ***of*** *some poems by Blake.*

recitative /ˌres.ɪ.təˈtiːv/ **noun** [C or U] specialized in music, words that are sung as if they are being spoken

recite /rɪˈsaɪt/ **verb** [I or T] to say a piece of writing aloud from memory, or to publicly say a list of things: *She proudly recited the Oath of Allegiance.* ◦ *The opposition party recited a long list of the government's failings.*

reckless /ˈrek.ləs/ **adj** C2 doing something dangerous and not worrying about the risks and the possible results: *He was found guilty of reckless* ***driving***. • **recklessly** /-li/ **adv** • **recklessness** /-nəs/ **noun** [U]

reckon /ˈrek.ən/ **verb** THINK ▷ **1** B2 [I] informal to think or believe: *I reckon it's going to rain.* ◦ [+ (that)] *How much do you reckon* ***(that)*** *it's going to cost?* ◦ *'Can you fix my car today?' 'I reckon not/so (= probably not/probably).'*

> **!** Common mistake: **reckon**
>
> **Remember: reckon** meaning 'think' is only used in informal English. In ordinary or more formal language, don't say 'reckon', say **think** or **believe**.

CONSIDER ▷ **2** [T] to consider or have the opinion that something is as stated: *I don't reckon much* ***to*** *(US* ***of****) their chances of winning (= I do not think they will win).* ◦ *She was widely reckoned* ***(to be)*** *the best actress of her generation.* CALCULATE ▷ **3** [T] mainly UK to calculate an amount: *Angela quickly reckoned the amount on her fingers.* ◦ *The inflation rate is now reckoned* ***to be*** *ten percent.*

IDIOM **to be reckoned with** Someone or something to be reckoned with is difficult to deal with because they are strong or powerful: *Since the government limited their powers, the unions are no longer* ***a force*** *to be reckoned with (= they are no longer very strong).*

PHRASAL VERBS **reckon sth in** to include an amount in your calculations: *When you reckon in all my overtime, my total pay is quite good.* • **reckon on sth** C2 to feel that something is likely to happen and to make plans which depend upon it happening: [+ -ing verb] *We're reckoning on* ***having*** *sales of 2,000 cars a month.* ◦ *I'm reckoning on your continued support.* • **reckon sth up** to calculate the total amount of something: *She can reckon up a bill faster than any calculator.* • **reckon with sb/sth** informal C2 to deal with a difficult or powerful person or thing: *If you harm her, you're going to have the police to reckon with.* • **reckon without sth** UK to fail to think about something when you are making plans and therefore not be prepared to deal with it: *We'd expected a two-hour drive but had reckoned without the rain.*

reckoning /ˈrek.ən.ɪŋ/ **noun** [C or U] a calculation which you make: ***By my*** *reckoning, we should arrive in ten minutes.*

reclaim /rɪˈkleɪm/ **verb** [T] **1** to take back something that was yours: *You'll be able to reclaim the tax on all equipment that you buy.* ◦ *I reclaimed my suitcase* ***from*** *the left luggage office.* **2** to make land, such as desert or areas covered by water, suitable for farming or building **3** to treat waste materials in order to get useful materials, such as glass or paper, that can be used again

reclamation /ˌrek.ləˈmeɪ.ʃən/ **noun** [U] formal **1** the attempt to make land suitable for building or farming **2** the treatment of waste materials to get useful materials from them

recline /rɪˈklaɪn/ **verb** formal **1** [I or T] to lean or lie back with the upper part of your body in a nearly horizontal position: *She was reclining elegantly* ***on*** *the sofa.* ◦ *He reclined his head* ***against/on*** *my shoulder.* **2** [T] If you recline a chair, you change the position of its back so that it is in a leaning position. • **reclining** /-ɪŋ/ **adj** [before noun] *The coach has air conditioning and reclining* ***seats***.

recliner /rɪˈklaɪ.nər/ US /-nɚ/ **noun** [C] a chair in which you can lean back at different angles

recluse /rɪˈkluːs/ **noun** [C] a person who lives alone and avoids going outside or talking to other people • **reclusive** /-ˈkluː.sɪv/ **adj**

recognition /ˌrek.əɡˈnɪʃ.ən/ **noun** ACCEPTING ▷ **1** C2 [S or U] agreement that something is true or legal: *It's a new country, hoping for diplomatic recognition from the international community.* ◦ [+ that] *There's a growing recognition* ***that*** *this country can no longer afford to be a nuclear power.* **2** C2 [S or U] If you are

R

given recognition, people show admiration and respect for your achievements: *Ella complained that the company never gave her any recognition* ***for*** *her work.* ◦ *He was presented with a gold watch* ***in*** *recognition* ***of*** *(= to show respect for) his years as club secretary.* **KNOWING** ▷ **3** C2 [U] the fact of knowing someone or something because you have seen, heard, or experienced them before: *When he returned to his home town after the war, he found it had* ***changed out of all/beyond all*** *recognition (= it had changed so much that he no longer recognized it).*

recognizable (UK usually **recognisable**) /ˈrek.əg.naɪ.zə.bl̩/ **adj** easy to recognize: *The Eiffel Tower in Paris is an* ***instantly*** *recognizable landmark.* • **recognizably** (UK usually **recognisably**) /-bli/ **adv** *At seven weeks, an embryo is recognizably human.*

recognize (UK usually **recognise**) /ˈrek.əg.naɪz/ **verb** **KNOW** ▷ **1** B1 [T] to know someone or something because you have seen, heard or experienced them before: *I hadn't seen her for 20 years, but I recognized her immediately.* ◦ *Do you recognize this song?* ◦ *Doctors are trained to recognize the symptoms of different diseases.* **ACCEPT** ▷ **2** B2 [T] to accept that something is legal, true or important: *The international community has refused to recognize (= officially accept the existence of) the newly independent nation state.* ◦ [+ (that)] *He sadly recognized* ***(that)*** *he would die childless.* ◦ *You must recognize the seriousness of the problems we are facing.* **3** C1 [T often passive] If a person's achievements are recognized, official approval is shown for them: *The prime minister recognized her services to her country by awarding her an MBE.*

recognized /ˈrek.əg.naɪzd/ **adj** If someone or something is recognized, it is generally accepted that they have a particular position or quality: *Professor Jones is a recognized authority on ancient Egypt.* ◦ *Violence in schools is a recognized problem.*

recoil verb; noun

▸**verb** [I] /rɪˈkɔɪl/ **1** to move back because of fear or DISGUST (= dislike or disapproval): *He leaned forward to kiss her and she recoiled* ***in horror.*** ◦ *I recoiled* ***from*** *the smell and the filth.* **2** to refuse to accept an idea or principle, feeling strong dislike or disapproval: *She wondered how it would be to touch him and recoiled* ***at*** *the thought.*

▸**noun** [U] /ˈriː.kɔɪl/ the sudden backward movement that a gun makes when it is FIRED

recollect /ˌrek.əˈlekt/ **verb** [I or T] formal C2 to remember something: *Can you recollect his name?* ◦ *As far as I can recollect, his name is Edward.* ◦ [+ (that)] *She suddenly recollected* ***(that)*** *she had left her handbag in the restaurant.* ◦ [+ question word] *Do you recollect* ***where*** *she went?* ◦ [+ -ing verb] *He does not recollect see****ing*** *her at the party.*

recollection /ˌrek.əˈlek.ʃən/ **noun** formal **1** C2 [C] a memory of something: *I have many pleasant recollections* ***of*** *the time we spent together.* **2** C2 [U] the ability to remember things: *His powers of recollection are extraordinary.*

IDIOM **to the best of my recollection** from what my memory tells me: *To the best of my recollection I have never seen her before.*

recommend /ˌrek.əˈmend/ **verb** [T] B1 to suggest that someone or something would be good or suitable for a particular job or purpose, or to suggest that a particular action should be done: *I can recommend the chicken in mushroom sauce – it's delicious.* ◦ *She has been recommended* ***for*** *promotion.* ◦ *The headmistress agreed to recommend the teachers' proposals* ***to*** *the school governors.* ◦ [+ (that)] *The doctor recommended* ***(that)*** *I take more exercise.* ◦ [+ -ing verb] *I recommend writ****ing*** *your feelings down on paper.* ◦ *The city* ***has much/little to*** *recommend it (= many/few pleasant qualities).* • **recommended** /-ˈmen.dɪd/ **adj** *It is dangerous to take more than the recommended* ***dose*** *of this medicine.* ◦ *She is a* ***highly*** *recommended architect.*

> **!** Common mistake: **recommend**
>
> **Warning:** Check your spelling!
>
> **Recommend** is one of the 50 words most often spelled wrongly by learners. Remember: the correct spelling has 'c' and 'mm'.

> **!** Common mistake: **recommend**
>
> When **recommend** is followed directly by another verb, that verb cannot be in the infinitive with 'to'.
>
> Do not say 'recommend to do something', say **recommend doing something**:
>
> ~~*I recommend to take an umbrella in case it rains.*~~
>
> *I recommend taking an umbrella in case it rains.*
>
> You can also say **recommend someone does something**:
>
> *I recommend you take an umbrella in case it rains.*

recommendation /ˌrek.ə.menˈdeɪ.ʃən/ **noun** **1** B2 [C or U] a suggestion that something is good or suitable for a particular purpose or job: *I bought this computer* ***on*** *John's recommendation (= because John told me that it was good).* ◦ *I got the job* ***on*** *Sam's recommendation (= because she told her employers that I was suitable for the job).* **2** B2 [C] advice telling someone what the best thing to do is: [+ that] *The report* ***makes*** *the recommendation* ***that*** *no more prisons should be built.*

recomˌmended ˌdaily alˈlowance **noun** [C usually singular] (abbreviation **RDA**) the amount of a substance, such as a VITAMIN, that should be in your food every day

recompense /ˈrek.əm.pens/ **noun** [U] formal a present given to someone to thank them for their help, or payment given to someone because of slight problems or because of the loss of or damage to their property: *I received £500 from my neighbour* ***in*** *recompense* ***for*** *the damage to my garden.* • **recompense verb** [T] *The court awarded the women $100,000 each to recompense them* ***for*** *nine years of lost wages.*

recon /ˈriː.kɒn/ US /-kɑːn/ **noun** [C] US informal for **reconnaissance**

reconcile /ˈrek.ən.saɪl/ **verb** [T] **1** C2 to find a way in which two situations or beliefs that are opposed to each other can agree and exist together: *It is sometimes difficult to reconcile science and religion.* ◦ *It's difficult to reconcile such different points of view.* ◦ *How can you reconcile your fur coat* ***and/with*** *your love of animals?* **2 be reconciled** When two people are reconciled, they become friendly again after they have argued: *They were finally reconciled* ***with*** *each other, after not speaking for nearly five years.*

PHRASAL VERB **reconcile yourself to sth** C2 to accept a situation or fact although you do not like it: *She must reconcile herself to the fact that she must do some work if she wants to pass her exams.*

reconciliation /ˌrek.ənˌsɪl.iˈeɪ.ʃən/ **noun** **1** [C or U] a situation in which two people or groups of people become friendly again after they have argued: *It took hours of negotiations to bring about a reconciliation* *between* the two sides. **2** [U] the process of making two opposite beliefs, ideas, or situations agree

recondite /ˈrek.ᵊn.daɪt/ **adj** formal not known about by many people and difficult to understand: *We had to work from material that was both complex and recondite.*

recondition /ˌriː.kᵊnˈdɪʃ.ᵊn/ **verb** [T] to repair a machine or piece of equipment and return it to a good condition: *The shop sells reconditioned vacuum cleaners.*

reconnaissance /rɪˈkɒn.ɪ.sᵊns/ Ⓤⓢ /-ˈkɑː.nə-/ **noun** [U] (UK informal **recce**, US informal **recon**) the process of getting information about enemy forces or positions by sending out small groups of soldiers or by using aircraft, etc.: ***Aerial*** *reconnaissance* ***of*** *the enemy position showed they were ready to attack.*

reconnoitre specialized (US usually **reconnoiter**) /ˌrek.əˈnɔɪ.təʳ/ Ⓤⓢ /ˌriː.kəˈnɔɪ.t̬ɚ/ **verb** [I or T] (of soldiers or military aircraft) to get information about an area or the size and position of enemy forces

reconsider /ˌriː.kᵊnˈsɪd.əʳ/ Ⓤⓢ /-kɑːnˈsɪd.ɚ/ **verb** [I or T] **C1** to think again about a decision or opinion and decide if you want to change it: *He begged her to reconsider but she would not.* ◦ *We have reconsidered your proposals and we have decided to go ahead with the deal.* • **reconsideration** /-ˌsɪd.əˈreɪ.ʃᵊn/ **noun** [U]

reconstitute /ˌriːˈkɒn.stɪ.tjuːt/ Ⓤⓢ /-ˈkɑːn.stə.tuːt/ **verb** [T] **1** to change food that has been dried back into its original form by adding water: *The powdered milk/egg can be reconstituted by adding water.* **2** to change an organization so that it has a different form: *The Health Education Council has been reconstituted* ***as*** *the Health Education Authority.* • **reconstitution noun** [U] *the reconstitution of the Communist party*

reconstruct /ˌriː.kᵊnˈstrʌkt/ **verb** [T] **1 C1** to build or create again something that has been damaged or destroyed: *The post-war government had the enormous task of reconstructing the city.* **2** to change a system or organization completely, so that it works more effectively: *They were given the task of reconstructing the city's public transport system.* **3 C2** If you reconstruct something that has happened in the past, you combine a lot of information in order to get a complete description of what happened: *The police tried to reconstruct the crime using the statements of witnesses.*

R

reconstruction /ˌriː.kᵊnˈstrʌk.ʃᵊn/ **noun 1 C1** [U] the process of building or creating something again that has been damaged or destroyed: *Post-war economic reconstruction in the country must begin with the resumption of agricultural production.* **2 C2** [C] an attempt to get a complete description of an event using the information available, or an attempt to repeat what happened during the event: *A dramatized reconstruction of the robbery was shown on television to try to make people remember information that would help the police.*

reconstructive /ˌriː.kᵊnˈstrʌk.tɪv/ **adj** [before noun] describes medical treatment that involves changing the shape of part of a person's body, either because it has been badly damaged or to improve someone's appearance: *After the accident, he underwent reconstructive* ***surgery*** *to rebuild his face.*

record verb; noun; adj

▸**verb** [T] /rɪˈkɔːd/ Ⓤⓢ /-ˈkɔːrd/ **STORE ELECTRONICALLY** ▷ **1 A2** to store sounds or moving pictures using electronic equipment so that they can be heard or seen later: *Cliff Richard has recorded more number one hit songs than any other British pop star.* ◦ *We recorded their wedding* ***on*** *video.* ◦ *I tried to phone her, but all I got was a recorded message saying that she was away for the weekend.* ◦ *Was the concert live or was it recorded (= made before being broadcast)?* **STORE INFORMATION** ▷ **2 B2** to keep information for the future, by writing it down or storing it on a computer: *She records everything that happens to her in her diary.* ◦ *Unemployment is likely to reach the highest total that has ever been recorded.* ◦ [+ that] *In his journal, Captain Scott recorded* ***that*** *he and his companions were weakened by lack of food.* ◦ legal *The coroner recorded (= decided) a verdict of accidental death.* **3 C1** If a device records a measurement, it shows that measurement: *The thermometer recorded a temperature of 30 degrees Celsius.*

▸**noun** /ˈrek.ɔːd/ Ⓤⓢ /-ɚd/ **INFORMATION** ▷ **1 B2** [C or U] a piece of information or a description of an event that is written on paper or stored on a computer: *The weather centre* ***keeps*** *a record* ***of*** *the weather.* ◦ *This summer has been the hottest* ***on*** *record (= the hottest summer known about).* **2 B2** [C] information about someone or something that is stored by the police or by a doctor: *A person's* ***medical*** *records are confidential.* ◦ *He is well known to the police and has a long* ***criminal*** *record (= a list kept by the police of his previous crimes).* **3 C2** [C] the facts that are known about a person or a company and the actions they have done in the past: *I won't fly with an airline that has a bad* ***safety*** *record (= whose aircraft have often had accidents).* **4 for the record** something that you say before you tell someone something important that you want them to remember: *And, just for the record, we were never any more than good friends.* **MUSIC** ▷ **5 B1** [C] a flat plastic disc on which music is recorded: *Would you like to listen to some records?* **6 B1** [C] a song or music that has been recorded and is available for the public to buy: *The Beatles' first hit record was 'Love Me Do'.* **BEST** ▷ **7 B1** [C] the best or fastest ever done: *He ran the 100 metres in 9.79 seconds and* ***broke/smashed*** *the* ***world*** *record.* ◦ *She* ***set/established*** *a new European record in the high jump.*

> **Word partners for record noun (INFORMATION)**
>
> *have/keep* a record • *check/consult* records • *destroy/falsify* records • an *accurate/detailed/permanent* record • records *indicate/reveal/show* • a record *of* sth • [hottest/lowest, etc.] *on* record • record *keeping*

> **Word partners for record noun (MUSIC)**
>
> *make/release* a record • a *best-selling/hit* record • record *company/deal/industry/producer*

> **Word partners for record noun (BEST)**
>
> *establish/set* a record • *hold* a record • *beat/break/equal/smash* a record • an *all-time/unbeaten/unbroken* record • a *new/previous* record • the record *for* sth/doing sth • [world, British, etc.] record *holder*

IDIOMS **go on record** (also **be on record**) If you go on record or if you are on record as saying something, you say it publicly and officially and it is written down. • **off the record C1** If someone says something off the record, they do not want it to be publicly reported: *She made it clear that her comments were strictly off the record.* • **on the record** If you say something on the record, you state it publicly: *None of the company directors were prepared to comment on the record yesterday.* • **set/put the record straight C1** to write or say something in order to make the true facts known: *She's decided to write her memoirs to set the record straight once and for all.*

▸**adj** /ˈrek.ɔːd/ (US) /-ɚd/ at a higher level than ever achieved before: *The long hot summer has led to a record harvest this year.* ◦ *Inflation has reached record* ***levels***. ◦ *We finished the work* ***in*** *record* ***time*** *(= faster than had ever been done before).*

ˈrecord-ˌbreaking adj [before noun] better, bigger, longer, etc. than anything else before: *Company profits are rising and it looks as though this is going to be a record-breaking year.*

reˌcorded deˈlivery noun [C or U] UK (US ˌ**certified** ˈ**mail**) If a letter is sent by recorded delivery, the person who receives it must write their name in a book to show that they have received it.

recorder /rɪˈkɔː.dəʳ/ (US) /-ˈkɔːr.dɚ/ noun [C] **INSTRUMENT** ▷ **1** a musical instrument consisting of a wooden or plastic tube which you blow down while covering holes with your fingers **JUDGE** ▷ **2** UK a judge **DEVICE** ▷ **3** a **cassette recorder**, a **tape recorder**, or a **video recorder**

recording /rɪˈkɔː.dɪŋ/ (US) /-ˈkɔːr-/ noun **1** B1 [C] speech, music, or moving pictures that have been recorded to be listened to or watched later: *I bought a recording* ***of*** *Maria Callas singing Verdi.* **2** B2 [U] the process or business of storing sounds or moving pictures using electronic equipment: *a recording* ***studio***

ˈrecord ˌlabel noun [C] a company that records and sells music: *She's signed a three-album deal with a new record label.*

ˈrecord ˌplayer noun [C] a machine on which records can be played

recount¹ /rɪˈkaʊnt/ verb [T] formal **DESCRIBE** ▷ to describe how something happened, or to tell a story: *He recounted his adventures since he had left home.* ◦ [+ question word] *He was fond of recounting* ***how*** *he had played for Manchester United when he was 19.*

recount² verb; noun

▸**verb** [T] /ˌriːˈkaʊnt/ to count something again

▸**noun** [C] /ˈriː.kaʊnt/ another count, especially of the number of votes in an election: *to* ***demand*** *a recount*

recoup /rɪˈkuːp/ verb [T] to get back money that you have spent or lost: *It takes a while to recoup the initial* ***costs*** *of starting up a business.* ◦ *The gambler recouped his* ***losses*** *in the next game.*

recourse /rɪˈkɔːs/ (US) /ˈriː.kɔːrs/ noun [U] formal using something or someone as a way of getting help, especially in a difficult or dangerous situation: *It is hoped that the dispute will be settled* ***without*** *recourse* ***to*** *litigation.*

recover /rɪˈkʌv.əʳ/ (US) /-ɚ/ verb [I or T] B1 to get back something lost, especially health, ability, possessions, etc.: *It took her a long while to recover (= become completely well again)* ***from/after*** *her heart operation.* ◦ *He never really recovered* ***from*** *the shock of his wife dying (= he was never happy after his wife died).* ◦ *She went into a coma and died without recovering consciousness.* ◦ *She was astonished to see me, but she soon recovered her composure/****herself*** *(= soon gave the appearance of being calm).* ◦ *It took a long time for the economy to recover (= improve)* ***after*** *the slump.* ◦ *Police only recover (= get back) a very small percentage of stolen goods.* ◦ *The initial outlay of setting up a company is considerable and it takes a while to recover those* ***costs*** *(= get back what you have spent).*

recovery /rɪˈkʌv.ər.i/ (US) /-ɚ-/ noun [S or U] B2 the process of getting back something lost, especially health, ability, possessions, etc.: *Mira* ***made*** *a full/speedy, etc. recovery* ***from*** *the operation.* ◦ *At last the economy is showing* ***signs of*** *recovery (= is starting to improve).* ◦ *The police arranged the recovery (= the getting back)* ***of*** *her body from the river.*

recreate /ˌriː.kriˈeɪt/ verb [T] C1 to make something exist or happen again: *They plan to recreate a typical English village in Japan.* ◦ *Their work involves restoring and recreating wildlife habitats all across the country.*

recreation /ˌrek.riˈeɪ.ʃən/ noun [C or U] **ENJOYMENT** ▷ **1** B2 (a way of) enjoying yourself when you are not working: *His favourite recreations are golf and playing Scrabble.* ◦ *Emma's only* ***form of*** *recreation seems to be shopping.* **MAKE AGAIN** ▷ **2** the act of making something exist or happen again: *a recreation of one of the most famous events in history* • **recreational** /-əl/ adj C2 *recreational* ***activities/facilities/interests***

recreˌational ˈvehicle noun [C] (abbreviation **RV**) US for **motor home**

recreˈation ˌcenter noun [C] US a building that is open to the public where meetings are held, sports are played, and there are activities available for young and old people

recreˈation ˌground noun [C] a piece of publicly owned land used for sports and games

recrimination /rɪˌkrɪm.ɪˈneɪ.ʃən/ noun [U] (also **recriminations**) arguments between people who are blaming each other: *The peace talks broke down and ended in* ***bitter*** *mutual recrimination(s).* • **recriminatory** /rɪˈkrɪm.ɪ.nə.tər.i/ (US) /-ə.nə.tɔːr-/ adj formal involving recrimination

recrudescence /ˌriː.kruːˈdes.əns/ noun [U] formal a sudden new appearance and growth, especially of something dangerous and unpleasant

recruit /rɪˈkruːt/ verb; noun

▸**verb** [T] C1 to persuade someone to work for a company or become a new member of an organization, especially the army: *Charities such as Oxfam are always trying to recruit volunteers to help in their work.* ◦ *Even young boys are now being recruited* ***into*** *the army.*

▸**noun** [C] C2 a new member of an organization, especially the army: ***Raw*** *recruits (= completely new soldiers) were trained for six months and then sent to the war front.*

recruitment /rɪˈkruːt.mənt/ noun [U] C1 the process of finding people to work for a company or become a new member of an organization: *The recession has forced a lot of companies to cut down on graduate recruitment.* ◦ *It's all part of a recruitment* ***drive*** *intended to increase the party's falling numbers.*

rectangle /ˈrek.tæŋ.ɡl/ noun [C] C1 a flat shape with four 90° angles and four sides, with opposite sides of equal length

rectangular /rekˈtæŋ.ɡjʊ.ləʳ/ (US) /-ɡjə.lɚ/ adj B2 shaped like a rectangle

rectifier /ˈrek.tɪ.faɪ.əʳ/ (US) /-ɚ/ noun [C] specialized an electronic device for changing AC to DC

rectify /ˈrek.tɪ.faɪ/ verb [T] **CORRECT** ▷ **1** C1 formal to correct something or make something right: *I am determined to take whatever action is necessary to rectify the* ***situation***. ◦ *Every effort is made to rectify any* ***errors/mistakes*** *before the book is printed.* **MAKE PURE** ▷ **2** specialized in chemistry, to make a substance pure **ELECTRIC CURRENT** ▷ **3** specialized to change an electrical current from AC to DC • **rectification** /ˌrek.tɪ.fɪˈkeɪ.ʃən/ noun [C or U] formal

rectilinear /ˌrek.tɪˈlɪn.i.əʳ/ (US) /-təˈlɪn.i.ɚ/ adj formal

R

moving in or formed from straight lines: *a rectilinear street plan*

rectitude /ˈrek.tɪ.tjuːd/ US /-tə.tuːd/ **noun** [U] formal honesty and correct moral behaviour: *An austere man of unquestioned* ***moral*** *rectitude, Nava inspired deep devotion in those who worked for him.*

rector /ˈrek.təʳ/ US /-tɚ/ **noun** [C] **1** a priest in charge of a PARISH (= area) in the Church of England **2** an important official at some colleges in Scotland, elected by the students **3** US the person in charge of a university or school

rectory /ˈrek.tᵊr.i/ US /-tɚ-/ **noun** [C] the house in which a rector lives

rectum /ˈrek.təm/ **noun** [C] specialized the lowest end of the bowels, down which solid waste travels before leaving the body through the ANUS • **rectal** /-tᵊl/ **adj** relating to the rectum • **rectally** /-tᵊl.i/ **adv** *They took his temperature rectally.*

recumbent /rɪˈkʌm.bənt/ **adj** literary lying down: *She looked at Timothy's recumbent* ***form*** *beside her.*

recuperate /rɪˈkuː.pᵊr.eɪt/ **verb** [I] to become well again after an illness; to get back your strength, health, etc.: *She spent a month in the country recuperating* ***from/after*** *the operation.* • **recuperation** /rɪˌkuː.pᵊrˈeɪ.ʃᵊn/ **noun** [U]

recuperative /rɪˈkuː.pᵊr.ə.tɪv/ US /-ˈkuː.pɚ.ə.t̬ɪv/ **adj** formal helping you to become well again after illness: *the recuperative* ***power*** *of a good night's sleep*

recur /rɪˈkɜːʳ/ US /-ˈkɝː/ **verb** [I] **(-rr-)** C2 to happen many times or to happen again: *The theme of freedom recurs throughout her writing.* ◦ *If the pain/problem/trouble, etc. recurs, come and see me.* • **recurrence** /rɪˈkʌr.ᵊns/ US /-ˈkɝː-/ **noun** [C or U] *The doctor told him to go to the hospital if there was a recurrence* ***of*** *his symptoms.*

recurring /rɪˈkɜː.rɪŋ/ US /-ˈkɝː.ɪŋ/ **adj** (also **recurrent**) happening many times, or happening again: *The father-daughter relationship is a recurring* ***theme*** *in her novels.* ◦ *For much of his life he suffered from recurring bouts of depression.* ◦ *LeFanu suffered all his life from a recurrent* ***nightmare*** *that he was trapped in a falling house.*

reˌcurring ˈnumber **noun** [C] (specialized **reˌcurring ˈdecimal**) a number that repeats itself for ever following a DECIMAL POINT, such as 3.3333...

recursive /rɪˈkɜː.sɪv/ US /-ˈkɝː-/ **adj** specialized involving doing or saying the same thing several times in order to produce a particular result or effect

recyclable /ˌriːˈsaɪ.klə.bl/ **adj** able to be recycled

recycle /ˌriːˈsaɪ.kl/ **verb** [T] B1 to collect and treat rubbish in order to produce useful materials that can be used again: *The Japanese recycle more than half their waste paper.*

recycled /ˌriːˈsaɪ.kld/ **adj** B1 having been used before and then put through a process so that it can form a new product: *This newspaper is made of recycled* ***paper.***

recycling /ˌriːˈsaɪ.klɪŋ/ **noun** [U] **1** B1 the process of collecting and changing old paper, glass, plastic, etc. so that it can be used again: *ways to encourage recycling* ◦ *a recycling centre* **2** B2 materials such as paper, glass, and plastic that you collect to be recycled: *We put out our recycling for pickup on Tuesdays.* ◦ *Put this bottle with the recycling.*

red /red/ **adj; noun**

▸**adj (redder, reddest) 1** A1 of the colour of fresh blood: *red lipstick* ◦ *The dress was bright red.* **2** A2 describes hair that is an orange-brown colour **3 go/turn (bright) red** B2 If you go/turn red, your face becomes red because you are angry or embarrassed: *Look, you've embarrassed him – he's gone bright red!* **4** If your eyes are red, the white part of your eyes and the skin around your eyes is red, because of crying, tiredness, too much alcohol, etc. • **redness** /ˈred.nəs/ **noun** [U]

IDIOMS **be like a red rag to a bull** mainly UK to be certain to produce an angry or violent reaction: *Don't tell him you're a vegetarian – it's like a red rag to a bull.* • **not a red cent** US informal no money at all: *It turns out his paintings aren't worth a red cent.*

▸**noun** [C or U] A2 the colour of fresh blood: *She uses a lot of reds and pinks in her paintings.* ◦ *I've always worn a lot of red.* ◦ *She was dressed all* ***in*** *red.*

IDIOM **be in the red** informal C2 If you or your bank account are in the red, you owe money to the bank. → Compare **be in the black**

Red /red/ **noun** [C] mainly disapproving a person who has SOCIALIST or COMMUNIST political opinions • **Red** **adj**

redact /rɪˈdækt/ **verb** [T] formal to remove words or information from a text before it is printed or made available to the public: *Officers' names are routinely redacted* ***from*** *any publicly released reports.* ◦ *Some parts of secret files are available to the public, but heavily redacted.*

ˌred aˈlert **noun** [C] (the state of being ready to deal with) a sudden dangerous situation: *The army was* ***on*** *red alert against the possibility of an attack.*

the ˌRed ˈArmy **noun** in the past, the SOVIET army

ˌred ˈblood ˌcell **noun** [C] (specialized **ˌred ˈcorpuscle**) any of the cells that carry OXYGEN around the body

ˌred-ˈblooded **adj** describes someone who seems full of confidence or sexual energy: *He says he's a red-blooded American* ***male!***

ˈred-brick **adj** [before noun] describes any of the British universities built in the late 19th and early 20th centuries in cities such as Liverpool and Manchester, and not one of the older ones such as Oxford or Cambridge: *Ben chose to go to a red-brick* ***university.*** → Compare **Oxbridge**

ˌred ˈcard **noun** [C usually singular] in football, a small, red card that is shown by the REFEREE (= the official who is responsible for making certain that the rules are followed) to a player who has not obeyed a rule and who is therefore not allowed to continue playing

the ˌred ˈcarpet **noun** [S] a long, red floor covering that is put down for an important guest to walk on when he or she visits somewhere and receives a special official welcome, or a special welcome of this type: *We'll* ***roll out*** *the red carpet for the senator.* • **ˌred-ˈcarpet** **adj** *Although a celebrity may attend a red-carpet event without a tie, he always has to remain dressed up.* ◦ *The minister was given the red-carpet* ***treatment.***

the ˌRed ˈCrescent **noun** an international organization in Muslim countries that takes care of people who are suffering because of war, hunger, disease, or other problems

the ˌRed ˈCross **noun** an international organization that takes care of people who are suffering because of war, hunger, disease, or other problems: *The Red Cross is/are supplying medicine to the earthquake victims.*

redcurrant /ˈredˌkʌr.ᵊnt/ US /-ˌkɝː-/ **noun** [C] a very small, round, red fruit that can be eaten, or the bush which produces it: *redcurrant wine/jam/jelly*

ˌred ˈdeer **noun** [C] a DEER with brown fur that changes to a brownish-red colour in summer

redden /ˈred.ᵊn/ **verb** [I or T] If something reddens, it

R

becomes or is made more red than it was: *His face reddened with embarrassment.*

reddish /ˈred.ɪʃ/ **adj** slightly red in colour: *Nicky's got reddish-blond hair.*

redecorate /ˌriːˈdek.ə.reɪt/ **verb** [I or T] UK to paint the inside of a house or put paper on the inside walls when this has been done previously: *We're redecorating the kitchen.* • **redecoration** /ˌriː.dek.əˈreɪ.ʃᵊn/ **noun** [C or U]

redeem /rɪˈdiːm/ **verb** **IMPROVE** ▷ **1** [T] formal to make something or someone seem less bad: *A poor game was redeemed in the second half by a couple of superb goals from Anthony Edwards.* ◦ *He was an hour late, but he redeemed him****self*** *in her eyes by giving her a huge bunch of flowers.* ◦ *She took me to see a really dull film, the only redeeming* ***feature*** *of which (= the only thing which prevented it from being completely bad) was the soundtrack.* **GET BACK** ▷ **2** [T] to get something back: *She managed to save enough money to redeem her jewellery* ***from*** *the pawn shop.* **EXCHANGE** ▷ **3 redeem a coupon, voucher, etc.** to exchange a piece of paper representing a particular amount of money for that amount of money or for goods to this value **SATISFY** ▷ **4** [T] formal to carry out a promise or pay back a debt: *The amount required to redeem the mortgage was £358,587.* **RELIGION** ▷ **5** [T] (in Christianity) to free people from SIN: *'Jesus,' said the priest, 'saved and redeemed mankind by taking our sins upon himself.'*

the Redeemer /rɪˈdiː.məʳ/ (US) /-mɚ/ **noun** [S] (in Christianity) Jesus Christ

redefine /ˌriː.dɪˈfaɪn/ **verb** [T] to change the meaning of something or to make people think about something in a new or different way: *Social networking has redefined the meaning of 'friend'.* ◦ *We want to redefine the way people look at mental illness.*

redemption /rɪˈdemp.ʃᵊn/ **noun** **IMPROVEMENT** ▷ **1 be beyond/past redemption** to be too bad to be improved or saved by anyone **IN RELIGION** ▷ **2** [U] (especially in Christianity) an occasion when someone is saved from evil, suffering, etc. **EXCHANGE** ▷ **3** [C or U] the act of exchanging BONDS, SHARES, etc. for money: *The bonds will be redeemed at 100% of their principal amount, plus interest to the redemption* ***date***. • **redemptive** /-tɪv/ **adj** formal (especially in Christianity) giving someone redemption

redeploy /ˌriː.dɪˈplɔɪ/ **verb** [T] to move employees, soldiers, equipment, etc. to a different place or use them in a more effective way • **redeployment** /-mənt/ **noun** [C or U] *the redeployment of troops*

redevelop /ˌriː.dɪˈvel.əp/ **verb** [T] (C1) to change an area of a town by replacing old buildings, roads, etc. with new ones • **redevelopment** /-mənt/ **noun** [C or U]

ˌred-eye **noun** **FLIGHT** ▷ **1** [C] mainly US informal a flight taken at night: *We caught the red-eye from LA and got to New York at five this morning.* **IN PHOTOGRAPH** ▷ **2** [U] the red colour that a person's eyes seem to be in some photographs: *a flash which minimizes red-eye*

ˌred ˈflag **noun** [C] **1** a flag used as a sign of danger: *You're not allowed to swim when the red flag is flying.* **2** a flag used as a symbol of REVOLUTION

ˌred ˈgiant **noun** [C] specialized a very large cool star that gives out a reddish light

ˌred-ˈhanded **adj** **catch sb red-handed** to find someone in the act of doing something illegal

redhead /ˈred.hed/ **noun** [C] informal a person, especially a woman, whose hair is a colour between red, brown, and orange

ˌred ˈherring **noun** [C] a fact, idea, or subject that takes people's attention away from the central point being considered: *The police investigated many clues, but they were all red herrings.*

ˌred-ˈhot **adj** **1** extremely hot **2** extreme; extremely new, exciting, etc.: *red-hot news, straight from the war zone*

ˌRed ˈIndian **noun** [C] offensive old-fashioned for a **Native American**

redirect /ˌriː.daɪˈrekt/, /-dɪ-/ **verb** [T] to change the direction of something, especially to send a letter to a new address: *Resources must be redirected into the many under-funded areas of education.* ◦ *Please redirect any* ***mail*** *that arrives for me to my address in Ottawa.*

rediscover /ˌriː.dɪˈskʌv.əʳ/ (US) /-ɚ/ **verb** [T] to find something or someone again after losing or forgetting about them for a long time: *The athlete rediscovered her best form with a morale-boosting win in the triple jump.* ◦ *After her husband's death, she rediscovered the joys of bowling and golf.*

redistribute /ˌriː.dɪˈstrɪb.juːt/, /-strɪˈbjuːt/ **verb** [T] (C2) to share something out differently from before, especially in a fairer way: *As president he would redistribute the country's* ***wealth***. • **redistribution** /ˌriː.dɪ.strɪˈbjuː.ʃᵊn/ **noun** [U]

ˌred-letter ˌday **noun** [C usually singular] a special, happy, and important day that you will always remember: *The day I first set foot in America was a red-letter day for me.*

ˌred ˈlight **noun** [C] a red traffic signal that tells drivers to stop: *The police fined her for* ***driving through/jumping*** *a red light.*

ˌred-ˈlight ˌdistrict **noun** [C] a part of a city where people and businesses sell sex

ˌred ˈmeat **noun** [U] meat from mammals, especially BEEF and LAMB

redneck /ˈred.nek/ **noun** [C] mainly US informal a poor white person without education, especially one living in the countryside in the southern US, who has PREJUDICED (= unfair and unreasonable) ideas and beliefs

redo /riːˈduː/ **verb** [T] **1** to do something again: *These new measurements mean that I'll have to redo the calculations.* **2** If you redo a room or a building, you paint it, put new furniture in it, etc. to make it more attractive or useful: *We spent £2,000 redoing the kitchen.*

redolent /ˈred.ᵊl.ᵊnt/ **adj** [after verb] literary smelling strongly of something or having qualities (especially smells) that make you think of something else: *The album is a heartfelt cry, redolent* ***of*** *a time before radio and television.* ◦ *The mountain air was redolent* ***with*** *the scent of pine needles.*

redouble /ˌriːˈdʌb.l̩/ **verb** [T] to make something much more than before; to increase something: *The government, he said, must redouble their* ***efforts*** *to beat crime.*

redoubt /rɪˈdaʊt/ **noun** [C] **1** formal something which holds or defends a belief or a way of life, especially one that is disappearing or threatened: *He described British public schools as 'the* ***last*** *redoubt* ***of*** *upper-class privilege'.* **2** specialized a small, often hidden, building in which soldiers can hide themselves while they are fighting

redoubtable /rɪˈdaʊ.tə.bl̩/ (US) /-t̬ə-/ **adj** literary or humorous very strong, especially in character; producing respect and a little fear in others: *Tonight he faces the most redoubtable opponent of his boxing career.*

ˌred ˈpepper **noun** **1** [C] the red fruit of the CAPSICUM plant, eaten as a vegetable **2** [U] a red powder made from these fruits that gives a spicy taste to cooked food

redress /rɪˈdres/ verb; noun

▸verb [T] formal to put right a wrong or give payment for a wrong that has been done: *Most managers, politicians and bosses are men – how can women* ***redress the balance*** *(= make the situation fairer and more equal)?*

▸noun [U] formal money that someone has to pay to someone else because they have injured them or treated them badly: *He went to the industrial tribunal to* ***seek*** *redress for the way his employers had discriminated against him.*

redskin /ˈred.skɪn/ noun [C] offensive old-fashioned for a **Native American**

ˌred ˈtape noun [U] disapproving C2 official rules and processes that seem unnecessary and delay results: *We must* ***cut through*** *the red tape.*

reduce /rɪˈdjuːs/ US /-ˈduːs/ verb [I or T] B1 to make something smaller in size, amount, degree, importance, etc.: *Do nuclear weapons really reduce the risk of war? ◦ The plane reduced speed as it approached the airport. ◦ My weight reduces when I stop eating sugar. ◦ We bought a television that was reduced (****from*** *£500* ***to*** *£350) in the sales. ◦ To make a thicker sauce, reduce the ingredients by boiling for five minutes. ◦ I reduced the problem* ***to*** *a few simple questions.*

IDIOM **reduce, reuse, recycle** said to encourage people to waste less, by using less and using things again, in order to protect the environment

PHRASAL VERBS **reduce sb to sth 1** C2 to make someone unhappy or cause them to be in a bad state or situation: *His comments reduced her to* ***tears*** *(= made her cry). ◦ The sergeant was reduced* ***to the ranks*** *(= made an ordinary soldier) for his cowardice.* **2** C2 If you are reduced to doing something, you are forced to do it because you have no other choice: *I'd run out of cigarettes and was reduced to smoking the butts left in the ashtrays.* • **reduce sth to sth** C2 to cause something, especially a large structure, to be destroyed and broken into pieces: *Allied bombing reduced the city to* ***ruins/rubble****.*

reˌduced ˈcircumstances noun [plural] old-fashioned a polite way to describe a situation in which someone is poorer than they once were: *She claims she is a duchess* ***living in*** *reduced circumstances.*

reˌduced ˈtime noun [U] **short time**

reduction /rɪˈdʌk.ʃᵊn/ noun **1** B2 [C or U] the act of making something, or of something becoming, smaller in size, amount, degree, importance, etc.: *a reduction* ***in*** *traffic ◦ huge* ***price*** *reductions* **2** [C] a copy of a photograph, picture, etc. that is smaller than the original one

redundancy /rɪˈdʌn.dᵊn.si/ noun **NOT EMPLOYED** ▷ **1** C1 [C or U] UK a situation in which someone loses their job because their employer does not need them: *The economic downturn has meant 10,000 redundancies in the Northeast. ◦ She took* ***voluntary*** *redundancy.* **NOT NEEDED** ▷ **2** [U] a situation in which something is unnecessary because it is more than is needed

reˈdundancy ˌpayment noun [C] money that a company pays to workers who have lost their jobs because they are no longer needed

redundant /rɪˈdʌn.dᵊnt/ adj **NOT EMPLOYED** ▷ **1** B2 UK having lost your job because your employer no longer needs you: *To keep the company alive, half the workforce is being* ***made*** *redundant.* ◦ figurative *New technology often* ***makes*** *old skills and even whole communities redundant.* **NOT NEEDED** ▷ **2** C2 (especially of a word, phrase, etc.) unnecessary because it is more than is needed: *In the sentence* ***She is a single unmarried woman*** *the word 'unmarried' is redundant.*

ˌred ˈwine noun [C or U] wine with a dark red colour that is made from black GRAPES, including their skins: *red wines from Chile ◦ Would you like a glass of red wine?*

redwood /ˈred.wʊd/ noun [C or U] a CONIFEROUS tree of California that grows very tall, or the valuable wood of this tree

reed /riːd/ noun [C] **1** (the hollow stem of) any of various types of tall, stiff plants like grasses growing together in groups near water **2** a thin piece of wood or metal which shakes very quickly to produce sound when a musician blows over it

ˈreed ˌinstrument noun [C] a musical instrument such as the CLARINET or OBOE, which produces sound when a musician blows on the reed

reedy /ˈriː.di/ adj **PLANTS** ▷ **1** describes a place where there are many reeds (= tall plants like grass) growing: *the reedy river banks* **SOUND** ▷ **2** disapproving describes a sound, especially a voice, that is thin and high and not pleasant to listen to

reef /riːf/ noun [C] a line of rocks or sand just above or just below the surface of the sea, often dangerous to ships: *a dangerous offshore reef ◦ a* ***coral*** *reef*

reefer /ˈriː.fəʳ/ US /-fɚ/ noun [C] **CIGARETTE** ▷ **1** old-fashioned informal a cigarette that you roll yourself containing the drug CANNABIS **JACKET** ▷ **2** (also **reefer jacket**) a jacket made of thick material and often worn by sailors

ˈreef ˌknot noun [C] (US also **ˈsquare ˌknot**) a type of strong knot that is tied twice and cannot easily be unfastened

reek /riːk/ verb [I] informal to have a strong unpleasant smell: *Her breath reeked* ***of*** *garlic.* • **reek** noun [S] *The room was filled with the reek* ***of*** *stale beer.*

PHRASAL VERB **reek of sth** If an event or situation reeks of an unpleasant quality, it seems to be caused by or connected to that quality: *His promotion reeks of favouritism.*

reel /rɪəl/ noun; verb

▸noun [C] **HOLDER** ▷ **1** a round, wheel-shaped object on which sewing thread, fishing wire, film, etc. can be rolled, or the amount of thread, etc. stored on one of these **DANCE** ▷ **2** a fast Scottish or Irish dance, or the music for this

▸verb [I] **1** to walk, moving from side to side, looking like you are going to fall: *At closing time he reeled out of the bar and fell down on the pavement. ◦ She hit him so hard that he reeled backwards.* **2** If the place where you are reels, what you are looking at seems to go round and round in front of you: *A stone hit his head and the street reeled before his eyes.* **3** If you reel, or your mind or brain reels, you feel very confused or shocked and unable to act: *We were reeling (****in*** *amazement/shock/delight, etc.)* ***from/with*** *the news that we had won all that money.*

PHRASAL VERBS **reel sth in/out** to pull in a rope or an object on the end of a rope by turning a wheel round and round, or to release something in the same way: *Slowly the fisherman reeled in his line, bringing the fish ashore. ◦ The firemen reeled out the hoses from their fire engine.* • **reel sth off LIST** ▷ **1** informal to say a long list of things quickly and without stopping: *The old man reeled off the names of his 22 grandchildren.* **SPORT** ▷ **2** US informal to win several games or points one after the other in a sports competition

ˌre-eˈlect verb [T] to elect someone again to a particular position

ˌre-eˈlection noun [C or U] the act of electing someone again to the same position: *She's **standing for** (US **running for**) re-election (= she is trying to be re-elected).*

ˌre-eˈnact (also **reenact**) verb [T] If you re-enact an event, you try to make it happen again in exactly the same way that it happened the first time, often as an entertainment or as a way to help people remember certain facts about an event.

ˌre-eˈnactment noun [C] an occasion on which people re-enact an event: *a re-enactment **of** the battle of Gettysburg*

ref /ref/ noun [C] **SPORT** ▷ **1** informal abbreviation for **referee** **BUSINESS** ▷ **2** written abbreviation for **reference**

refectory /rɪˈfek.tᵊr.i/ (US) /-tɚ-/ noun [C] a large room in a MONASTERY, college, school, etc. where meals are eaten

refer /rɪˈfɜːʳ/ (US) /-ˈfɝː/ verb (-rr-)

> **! Common mistake: refer**
>
> **Warning:** Check your verb endings!
> Many learners make mistakes when using **refer** in the past tense. The past simple and past participle have 'rr'. Don't write 'refered', write **referred**. The **-ing** form is refe**rr**ing.

PHRASAL VERBS **refer to sb/sth** **1** (B2) to talk or write about someone or something, especially in only a few words: *In her autobiography she occasionally refers to her unhappy schooldays.* ◦ *He always refers to the house **as** his 'refuge'.* **2** (C1) If writing or information refers to someone or something, it relates to that person or thing: *The new salary scale only refers to company managers and directors.* • **refer sb to sth** (C2) to direct someone or something to a different place or person for information, help or action, often to a person or group with more knowledge or power: *My doctor referred me to a hospital specialist.* ◦ *The High Court has referred the **case** to the Court of Appeal.* • **refer (sb) to sth** (C2) to look at, or tell someone else to look at, a book or similar record in order to find information and help: *She spoke for an hour without once referring to her notes.* ◦ *He referred to a history book to find out the dates of the French Revolution.* ◦ *The reader is constantly referred **back** to the introduction.*

referee /ˌref.əˈriː/ noun; verb

▸noun [C] **JUDGE** ▷ **1** (B2) a person who is in charge of a sports game and who makes certain that the rules are followed: *Liverpool only lost the game because the referee was biased.* **2** a person or organization that helps to find a fair answer to a disagreement: *A senior judge is acting as referee in the pay dispute between the trade union and management.* **SUPPORTER** ▷ **3** (also **reference**) UK a person who knows you and who is willing to describe and, usually, praise you, in order to support you when you are trying to get a job, etc.: *She **gave** her college tutor **as** her referee to the interviewer.*

▸verb [I or T] to be a referee in a game: *They had to ask one of the spectators to referee (the match).*

reference /ˈref.ᵊr.ᵊns/ (US) /-ɚ-/ noun **MENTION** ▷ **1** (B2) [C or U] a mention of something: *Knowing what had happened, I avoided **making** any reference **to** (= mentioning) weddings.* ◦ formal *I am writing **with/in** reference **to** (= in connection with) your letter of 15 March.* **IN A PIECE OF WRITING** ▷ **2** (B2) [C] a writer or a book, article, etc. that is mentioned in a piece of writing, showing you where the person writing found their information **3** [C] (abbreviation **ref**) in a business letter, a number that tells you who to speak to or where to look for more information: *In all future letters on this subject, please use/quote our reference JW/155/C.* **LETTER** ▷ **4** (B2) [C] a letter that is written by someone who knows you, to describe you and say if you are suitable for a job, course, etc.: *My old headteacher said he would **write/give** me a glowing (= very good) reference.* **LOOK AT** ▷ **5** (C1) [U] a quick look at a book, piece of paper, etc. in order to find information and help: *He made the whole speech **without** reference **to** the notes in front of him.*

ˈreference ˌbook noun [C] a book of facts, such as a dictionary or an ENCYCLOPEDIA, which you look at to discover particular information

ˈreference ˌlibrary noun [C] (a place for looking at) a collection of books that must be read only where they are kept and not taken away

referendum /ˌref.əˈren.dəm/ noun [C] (plural **referendums** or formal **referenda**) (formal **plebiscite**) (C2) a vote in which all the people in a country or an area are asked to give their opinion about or decide an important political or social question: *Is it more democratic to **hold a** referendum, rather than let the government alone decide?*

referent /ˈref.ᵊr.ənt/ noun [C] specialized the person, thing, or idea that a word, phrase, or object refers to: *The obvious textual referent in this movie is Shakespeare's 'Hamlet'.*

referral /rɪˈfɜː.rəl/ (US) /-ˈfɝː.ᵊl/ noun [C or U] the act of directing someone to a different place or person for information, help, or action, often to a person or group with more knowledge or power: *The doctor gave him a referral **to** (= arranged for him to see) the consultant.*

refill noun; verb

▸noun [C] /ˈriː.fɪl/ (a container holding) an amount of some material needed to fill up again an object that has become empty: *My pen seems to be running out of ink – I need a refill.* ◦ informal *Chuck, you've nearly finished your drink – do you want a refill?*

▸verb [T] /ˈriː.fɪl/, /ˌriːˈfɪl/ to fill something again: *He got up and refilled their **glasses**.*

refine /rɪˈfaɪn/ verb [T] **1** to make something pure or improve something, especially by removing unwanted material: *Crude **oil** is industrially refined to purify it and separate out the different elements, such as benzene.* **2** (C2) to improve an idea, method, system, etc. by making small changes: *Engineers spent many months refining the software.*

refined /rɪˈfaɪnd/ adj **CHANGED** ▷ **1** A refined substance has been made pure by removing other substances from it: *refined **foods** such as white bread and white sugar* **2** (C2) improved because of many small changes that have been made: *highly refined theories* **POLITE** ▷ **3** (C2) very polite and showing knowledge of social rules

refinement /rɪˈfaɪn.mənt/ noun **CHANGE** ▷ **1** [U] the process of making a substance pure: *The refinement of raw opium yields other drugs, such as morphine.* **2** [C or U] a small change that improves something: *These refinements have increased the machine's accuracy by 25 percent.* ◦ *Clearly, the hypothesis does need some refinement, in the light of these surprising results.* **POLITENESS** ▷ **3** [U] a quality of politeness and education: *She's the personification of culture and refinement.*

refinery /rɪˈfaɪ.nᵊr.i/ (US) /-nɚ-/ noun [C] a factory where substances in their natural state, such as oil or

R

sugar, are made pure: *There were two huge* ***oil*** *refineries on the coast.*

refit /ˌriːˈfɪt/ verb [I or T] (**-tt-**) to put a ship or building back into good condition by repairing it or adding new parts: *The ship sailed into the dock to refit/to be refitted.* ◦ *The pubs will be refitted and re-branded by their new owner.* • **refit** /ˈriː.fɪt/ noun [C]

reflate /ˌriːˈfleɪt/ verb [I or T] specialized in economics, to increase the amount of money in use in a country's economy: *The government hopes to increase consumer demand and therefore industrial production by reflating (the economy).* • **reflation** /ˌriːˈfleɪ.ʃən/ noun [C or U] • **reflationary** /ˌriːˈfleɪ.ʃən.ər.i/ (US) /-er-/ adj

reflect /rɪˈflekt/ verb **RETURN** ▷ **1** (B2) [I or T] If a surface reflects light, heat, sound, or an image, it sends the light, etc. back and does not absorb it: *He saw himself reflected* ***in*** *the water/mirror/shop window.* ◦ *The light reflected* ***off*** *the surface of the water.* **SHOW** ▷ **2** (B2) [T] to show, express, or be a sign of something: *The statistics reflect a change in people's spending habits.* **THINK** ▷ **3** (B2) [I] formal to think carefully, especially about possibilities and opinions: *The manager demanded time to reflect (***on*** *what to do).* ◦ [+ that] *She reflected* ***that*** *this was probably the last time she would see him.*

PHRASAL VERB **reflect on sb/sth** to affect other people's opinion of someone or something, especially in a bad way: *When one player behaves disgracefully, it reflects (***badly***) on the whole team.* ◦ *The whole affair does not reflect well on the government.*

reˌflected ˈray noun [C] specialized a RAY (= beam of light) that is reflected from a surface → Compare **incident ray**

reflection /rɪˈflek.ʃən/ noun **IMAGE** ▷ **1** (B2) [C or U] the image of something in a mirror or on any reflective surface: *In Greek mythology, Narcissus fell in love with his own reflection* ***in*** *a pool of water.* **SIGN** ▷ **2** (C1) [C usually singular] a sign or result of something: *The fact that soldiers are on the streets is a reflection* ***of*** *how terrified the government is.* **THOUGHT** ▷ **3** (C2) [C or U] formal serious and careful thought: ***On*** *reflection (= after considering it), I decided I had been wrong.* ◦ *After 30 years as a judge, her reflections* ***on/about*** *justice were well worth listening to.* **4 a reflection on sb/sth** something that makes other people have a particular opinion about someone or something, especially a bad opinion: *Low test scores are a sad reflection on our school system.*

reflection

reflective /rɪˈflek.tɪv/ adj **SURFACE** ▷ **1** describes a surface that sends back most of the light that shines on it and can therefore be seen easily **THINKING** ▷ **2** formal thinking carefully and quietly: *After hearing the news they sat in a quiet, reflective silence.* • **reflectively** /-li/ adv

reflector /rɪˈflek.təʳ/ (US) /-tɚ/ noun **1** [C] an object on a bicycle, car, or other vehicle which reflects light and is intended to show the vehicle's position to other road users **2 reflectors** [plural] US for **cat's eyes**

reflex /ˈriː.fleks/ noun; adj

▸noun **1** [C] a physical reaction to something that you cannot control: *I'm sorry I punched him, it was a reflex* ***action/response****.* **2 reflexes** [plural] the ability to react quickly: *Fighter pilots need* ***good/fast*** *reflexes.*

▸adj specialized describes an angle that is more than 180° and less than 360° → Compare **acute, obtuse**

reflexive /rɪˈflek.sɪv/ adj **GRAMMAR** ▷ describes words that show that the person who does the action is also the person who is affected by it: *In the sentence* ***She prides herself on doing a good job****,* ***prides*** *is a reflexive* ***verb*** *and* ***herself*** *is a reflexive* ***pronoun****.*

reflexively /rɪˈflek.sɪv.li/ adv in a way that is caused by an uncontrolled physical reaction: *My arm went up reflexively.*

reflexology /ˌriː.flekˈsɒl.ə.dʒi/ (US) /-ˈsɑː.lə-/ noun [U] a treatment in which your feet are rubbed and pressed in a special way in order to improve blood flow and help you relax

reforest /ˌriːˈfɒr.ɪst/ (US) /-ˈfɔːr-/ verb [T] (mainly UK **reafforest**) to plant trees on an area of land that has become empty or spoiled • **reforestation** /ˌriː.fɒr.ɪˈsteɪ.ʃən/ (US) /-fɔːr.ɪ-/ noun [U] mainly US

reform /rɪˈfɔːm/ (US) /-ˈfɔːrm/ verb; noun

▸verb [I or T] (C2) to make an improvement, especially by changing a person's behaviour or the structure of something: *Who will reform Britain's unfair electoral system?* ◦ *For years I was an alcoholic, but I reformed when the doctors gave me six months to live.* • **reformation** /ˌref.əˈmeɪ.ʃən/ (US) /-ɚ-/ noun [C or U] *He's undergone something of a reformation – he's a changed man.*

▸noun [C or U] (C2) an improvement, especially in a person's behaviour or in the structure of something: *Some reforms* ***of/to*** *the system will be necessary.* ◦ *The education system in Britain was crying out for reform.*

the ˌReforˈmation noun [S] the 16th-century religious ideas and activity in Europe that were an attempt to change and improve the Catholic Church, and resulted in the Protestant Churches being established

reformed /rɪˈfɔːmd/ (US) /-ˈfɔːrmd/ adj [before noun] (especially of a person) changed and improved because of no longer doing something harmful: *a reformed* ***alcoholic/criminal***

reˌformed ˈcharacter noun [C] someone who has changed and become a much better person: *He was in trouble with the police a lot when he was younger, but now he's a reformed character.*

reformer /rɪˈfɔː.məʳ/ (US) /-ˈfɔːr.mɚ/ noun [C] someone who tries to improve a system or law by changing it: *a* ***social*** *reformer* • **reformist** /-mɪst/ adj *a reformist, rather than a revolutionary approach to progress*

refract /rɪˈfrækt/ verb [T] specialized When water or glass, etc. refracts light or sound, etc., it causes it to change direction or to separate when it travels through it: *The glass prism refracted the white light* ***into*** *the colours of the rainbow.* • **refraction** /-ˈfræk.ʃən/ noun [U] • **refractive** /-ˈfræk.tɪv/ adj

refractory /rɪˈfræk.tər.i/ adj **1** specialized not affected by a treatment, change, or process: *This is a chronic and disabling condition that is refractory* ***to*** *treatment.* **2** formal difficult to control; unwilling to obey: *a refractory child*

refrain /rɪˈfreɪn/ verb; noun

▸verb [I] formal (C2) to avoid doing or stop yourself from doing something: *We refrained* ***from*** *talk***ing** *until we knew that it was safe.* ◦ *The sign on the wall said 'Please refrain* ***from*** *smoking.'*

▸noun [C] **1** a short part of a song or poem that is repeated, especially between the VERSES (= the separate parts) **2** a phrase that is often repeated: *'Every vote counts' is a familiar refrain in politics.*

refresh /rɪˈfreʃ/ verb **FEEL BETTER** ▷ **1** (C1) [T] to make someone less hot or tired: *It was such a hot night that I had a cold shower to refresh myself.* COMPUTER SCREEN ▷ **2** [I or T] to make the most recent information on an internet page appear, usually by CLICKING a button on the computer screen

IDIOM **refresh sb's memory** to help someone remember something: *I looked the word up in the dictionary to refresh my memory* ***of*** *its exact meaning.*

refreshed /rɪˈfreʃt/ **adj** less hot or tired: *I feel so refreshed after that cup of tea.* ◦ *He felt refreshed (= more energetic and relaxed) after the holiday.*

refresher /rɪˈfreʃ.əʳ/ (US) /-ɚ/ **noun** [C] a course to practise and improve skills, especially because you have not used them for a long time: *I went on a refresher* ***course*** *on new techniques in design to bring myself up to date.*

refreshing /rɪˈfreʃ.ɪŋ/ **adj** **1** C1 making you feel less hot or tired: *There's nothing more refreshing on a hot day than a cold beer.* **2** C1 pleasantly different and interesting: *It's a refreshing* ***change*** *to see a losing team shaking hands and still smiling after a match.* • **refreshingly** /-li/ **adv** *refreshingly cold water* ◦ figurative *a woman with refreshingly original ideas*

refreshment /rɪˈfreʃ.mənt/ **noun** [C or U] (also **refreshments**) B1 (small amounts of) food and drink: *He stopped at a bar for a little refreshment.* ◦ ***Light*** *refreshments will be available at the back of the hall.*

refrigerate /rɪˈfrɪdʒ.ər.eɪt/ (US) /-ə.eɪt/ **verb** [T] to make or keep something, especially food or drink, cold so that it stays fresh, usually in a fridge • **refrigeration** /rɪˌfrɪdʒ.əˈreɪ.ʃən/ **noun** [U]

refrigerator /rɪˈfrɪdʒ.ər.eɪ.təʳ/ (US) /-ə.eɪ.t̬ɚ/ **noun** [C] A1 US or UK formal for **fridge**

reˌfrigerator-ˈfreezer **noun** [C] US for **fridge-freezer**

refuel /ˌriːˈfjʊəl/ **verb** [I or T] to put more fuel into an aircraft, ship, etc. so that it can continue its journey • **refuelling** /-ɪŋ/ **noun** [U]

refuge /ˈref.juːdʒ/ **noun** [C or U] C2 (a place which gives) protection or shelter from danger, trouble, unhappiness, etc.: *These people are* ***seeking/taking*** *refuge* ***from*** *persecution.* ◦ *The climbers slept in a mountain refuge.* ◦ *She had fled from her violent husband to a* ***women's*** *refuge.*

refugee /ˌref.jʊˈdʒiː/ **noun** [C] B2 a person who has escaped from their own country for political, religious, or economic reasons or because of a war: *Thousands of refugees* ***fled*** *across the border.*

refuˈgee ˌcamp **noun** [C] a place where people who have escaped their own country can live, usually in bad conditions and only expecting to stay for a limited time

refund **noun; verb**

▸**noun** [C] /ˈriː.fʌnd/ B1 an amount of money that is given back to you, especially because you are not happy with a product or service that you have bought: *I took the radio back to the shop and asked for/demanded/got/was given a refund.*

▸**verb** [T] /ˌriːˈfʌnd/ C1 to give someone a refund: *When I went on business to Peru, the office refunded my expenses.* ◦ [+ two objects] *The holiday was cancelled so the travel agency had to refund everybody the price of the tickets.* • **refundable** /ˌriːˈfʌn.də.bl/ **adj**

refurbish /ˌriːˈfɜː.bɪʃ/ (US) /-ˈfɝː-/ **verb** [T] formal to make a building look new and bright again: *The developers refurbished the house inside and out.* • **refurbished** /-bɪʃt/ **adj** [before noun] • **refurbishment** /-mənt/ **noun** [C or U]

refusal /rɪˈfjuː.zəl/ **noun** [C or U] C1 the act of refusing to do or accept something: *Our request for permission to travel* ***met with/received*** *a* ***flat/point-blank*** *(= complete) refusal from the authorities.* ◦ [+ to infinitive] *The government's refusal* ***to*** *see that the protection of the environment must be our first priority today is a great tragedy.*

refuse **verb; noun**

▸**verb** [I or T] /rɪˈfjuːz/ B1 to say that you will not do or accept something: *He asked me to give him another loan, but I refused.* ◦ *He's in trouble but he's refused all (my offers of) help.* ◦ [+ to infinitive] *On cold mornings the car always refuses* ***to*** *start.* ◦ [+ two objects] *The local council refused him planning permission to build an extra bedroom.*

▸**noun** [U] /ˈref.juːs/ formal unwanted waste material, especially material that is regularly thrown away from a house, factory, etc.: ***garden/kitchen*** *refuse*

ˈrefuse colˌlector **noun** [C] UK formal for **dustman**

ˈrefuse ˌdump **noun** [C] a place where a town's rubbish is put

refute /rɪˈfjuːt/ **verb** [T] formal to say or prove that a person, statement, opinion, etc. is wrong or false: *to refute a person/theory/argument/claim* • **refutation** /ˌref.jʊˈteɪ.ʃən/ **noun** [C or U]

reg /redʒ/ **noun** [C] informal for **registration**

regain /rɪˈɡeɪn/ **verb** [T] **1** B2 to take or get possession of something again: *The government has regained* ***control*** *of the capital* ***from*** *rebel forces.* ◦ *She made an effort to regain her self-control.* **2** literary to reach or return to a place, especially after difficulty or danger: *The swimmers struggled to regain the shore.*

regal /ˈriː.ɡəl/ **adj** very special and suitable for a king or queen: *a regal manner* ◦ *He made a regal entrance.* • **regally** /-i/ **adv**

regale /rɪˈɡeɪl/ **verb**

PHRASAL VERB **regale sb with sth** mainly humorous to entertain someone with stories, jokes, etc.

regalia /rɪˈɡeɪ.li.ə/ **noun** [U] **1** official and traditional special clothes and decorations, especially those worn or carried in formal ceremonies: *The queen's regalia at her coronation included her crown and sceptre.* **2** informal humorous any set of special clothes: *The biker was dressed* ***in full*** *regalia, with shiny black leather and lots of chains.*

regard /rɪˈɡɑːd/ (US) /-ˈɡɑːrd/ **verb; noun**

▸**verb** [T usually + adv/prep] **1** B2 to consider or have an opinion about something or someone: *Local people regard the idea of a motorway through their village* ***with*** *horror.* ◦ *Her parents always regarded her* ***as*** *the cleverest of their children.* **2** formal to look carefully at something or someone: *The bird regarded me* ***with*** *suspicion as I walked up to its nest.* **3 as regards** B2 formal in connection with: *There is no problem as regards the financial arrangements.*

▸**noun** [U] formal **1** C1 respect or admiration for someone or something: *The company* ***holds*** *her* ***in high*** *regard.* ◦ *He* ***has*** *no regard* ***for*** *other people's feelings.* **2 in/with regard to** B2 in connection with: *I am writing to you with regard to your letter of 15 March.* **3 in this/that regard** in this particular way: *The union is the largest in the country and in this/that regard is best placed to serve its members.* **4 regards** B1 [plural] formal greetings: *Please* ***give/send/convey*** *my regards to your mother if you see her.*

regarding /rɪˈɡɑː.dɪŋ/ (US) /-ˈɡɑːr-/ **preposition** formal B1 about: *The company is being questioned regarding its employment policy.*

R

! Common mistake: regarding

Remember that **regarding** is never followed by 'to'.

Don't say 'regarding to something', say **regarding something**:

~~*I am writing regarding to your letter of 31 May.*~~

I am writing regarding your letter of 31 May.

regardless /rɪˈɡɑː.dləs/ US /-ˈɡɑːrd-/ **adv** C1 despite; not being affected by something: *The plan for a new office tower went ahead regardless **of** local opposition.* ◦ *She knew it was dangerous to visit him except at night, but she set out regardless (**of the risk**).* ◦ *This job is open to all, regardless **of** previous experience.*

regatta /rɪˈɡæt.ə/ US /-ˈɡɑː.t̬ə/ **noun** [C] a sports event consisting of boat races

regency /ˈriː.dʒən.si/ **noun** [C] a period of time when a country is ruled by a regent

Regency /ˈriː.dʒən.si/ **adj** describes the style of buildings, furniture, literature, etc. popular in Britain from 1811 to 1820

regenerate /rɪˈdʒen.ər.eɪt/ US /-ə.eɪt/ **verb** **IMPROVE** ▷ **1** [T] to improve a place or system, especially by making it more active or successful **GROW** ▷ **2** [I or T] specialized to grow again: *Tissue regenerates after skin is scratched.* ◦ *A lizard can regenerate its tail.* • **regeneration** /rɪˌdʒen.əˈreɪ.ʃən/ US /-ə-/ **noun** [U] *The council is committed to a programme of **urban** regeneration.* • **regenerative** /-ə.tɪv/ US /-ə.t̬ɪv/ **adj**

regent /ˈriː.dʒənt/ **noun** [C] a person who rules a country only for a limited period, because the king or queen is absent or too young, too ill, etc. • **regent adj** [after noun] ***Prince** Regent*

reggae /ˈreɡ.eɪ/ **noun** [U] a type of popular music from Jamaica, with a strong second and fourth beat

regicide /ˈredʒ.ɪ.saɪd/ **noun** [C or U] formal a person who kills a king, or the act of killing a king

regime /reɪˈʒiːm/ **noun** [C] **MANAGEMENT** ▷ **1** C2 mainly disapproving a particular government or a system or method of government: *The old corrupt, totalitarian regime was overthrown.* **2** a particular way of operating or organizing a business, etc.: *The regime in this office is hard work and more hard work.* **RULES** ▷ **3** a **regimen**

reˈgime ˌchange **noun** [U] a complete change of government, especially one brought about by force

regimen /ˈredʒ.ɪ.mən/ **noun** [C] formal any set of rules about food and exercise that someone follows, especially in order to improve their health: *After his heart attack the doctor put him on a strict regimen.*

regiment /ˈredʒ.ɪ.mənt/ **noun** [C, + sing/pl verb] a large group of soldiers, or (more generally) any large number of things or people: *Regiments are usually commanded by a colonel and are sometimes made up of soldiers from a particular city or part of the country.* • **regimental** /ˌredʒ.ɪˈmen.təl/ US /-əˈmen.t̬əl/ **adj** *a regimental tie/uniform*

regimentation /ˌredʒ.ɪ.menˈteɪ.ʃən/ US /-ə.mən-/ **noun** [U] disapproving extreme organization and control of people

regimented /ˈredʒ.ɪ.men.tɪd/ US /-ə.men.t̬ɪd/ **adj** disapproving too organized and controlled: *a regimented school/society/lifestyle*

region /ˈriː.dʒən/ **noun** [C] **1** B1 a particular area or part of the world, or any of the large official areas into which a country is divided: *the semi-desert regions of Australia* ◦ *the Birmingham region* **2** a particular part of someone's body: *He said he had sharp pains **in** the stomach region/the region of the stomach.* **3 in the region of** C1 approximately: *They estimate that the temperature yesterday was (somewhere) in the region of -30°C.*

regional /ˈriː.dʒən.əl/ **adj** B2 relating to or coming from a particular part of a country: *a regional **accent/dialect**/newspaper* • **regionally** /-i/ **adv**

regionalism /ˈriː.dʒən.əl.ɪ.zəm/ **noun** **1** [U] a feeling of loyalty to a particular part of a country and a wish for it to be more politically independent **2** [C] a phrase, custom, etc. that is used or found only in a particular part of a country or area

register /ˈredʒ.ɪ.stər/ US /-stə/ **verb**; **noun**

▸verb **PUT ON LIST** ▷ **1** B1 [I or T] to put information, especially your name, into an official list or record: *I registered the car in my name.* ◦ *Within two weeks of arrival all foreigners had to register **with** the local police.* ◦ *Students have to register **for** the new course by the end of April.* **SHOW** ▷ **2** C2 [I or T] to record, show, or express something: *The Geiger counter registered a dangerous level of radioactivity.* ◦ *The earthquake was too small to register **on** the Richter scale.* ◦ formal *His face registered extreme disapproval of what he had witnessed.* **REALIZE** ▷ **3** [I or T] informal If something registers, someone realizes it and if someone registers something, they realize it: *I did mention the address but I'm not sure that it registered (**with** him).* ◦ *I scarcely registered the fact that he was there.* **MAIL** ▷ **4** [T] If you register a letter or parcel, you send it using a special POSTAL SERVICE, so that it will be dealt with in a special way and not be lost: *a registered **letter***

▸noun **LIST** ▷ **1** [C] a book or record containing a list of names: *Guests write their names in the (hotel) register.* ◦ *Is your name on the register **of** voters?* **2** [C] a book used to record if a child is present at school: *If a child is absent, the teacher notes it down in the (**class**) register.* **3** [U] in school, the period at the start of the morning and afternoon when a teacher records on an official list which children are present **LANGUAGE STYLE** ▷ **4** C1 [C or U] specialized the style of language, grammar, and words used for particular situations: *People chatting at a party will usually be talking in (an) informal register.* **SOUNDS** ▷ **5** [C] all the notes that a musical instrument or a person's voice can produce, from the highest to the lowest: *music written mainly for the **lower/higher** register of the clarinet* **MONEY** ▷ **6** [C] US for **till**: *a **cash** register*

registered /ˈredʒ.ɪ.stəd/ US /-stəd/ **adj** officially listed and accepted: *a registered nurse/charity/trademark*

ˌregistered ˈpost **noun** [U] UK (US **ˌregistered ˈmail**) a way of sending letters or parcels by using a service that deals with them in a special way and makes sure they do not get lost: *You'd better send the cheque (**by**) registered post.*

ˈregister ˌoffice **noun** [C] a **registry office**

registrar /ˌredʒ.ɪˈstrɑːr/ US /ˈredʒ.ɪ.strɑːr/ **noun** [C] **RECORD KEEPER** ▷ **1** an official whose job is to keep official records, especially of births, deaths, and marriages **2** at some colleges, an official in charge of exams, keeping records, and new students **DOCTOR** ▷ **3** UK a type of hospital doctor: *A hospital registrar is of a lower rank than a consultant.*

registration /ˌredʒ.ɪˈstreɪ.ʃən/ **noun** **LIST** ▷ **1** B1 [U] the act of recording a name or information on an official list: *voter registration* **CAR** ▷ **2** [C] (also **registration number**, UK informal **reg**, US usually **license plate number**) the official set of numbers and letters shown on the front and back of a road vehicle: *Police are looking for a small blue car with the registration number B34-ACS.*

registry /ˈredʒ.ɪ.stri/ noun [C] mainly UK a place where official records are kept: *a land/business/electoral registry*

ˈregistry ˌoffice noun [C] (also **ˈregister ˌoffice**) mainly UK a place where births, deaths, and marriages are officially recorded and where you can get officially married, without a religious ceremony

regress /rɪˈgres/ verb [I] formal to return to a previous and less advanced or worse state, condition, or way of behaving: *She suffered brain damage from the car accident and regressed **to** the mental age of a five-year-old.* → Compare **progress** • **regression** /-ˈgreʃ.ᵊn/ noun [U]

regressive /rɪˈgres.ɪv/ adj formal (of tax) lower on large amounts of money, so that the rich are less affected

regret /rɪˈgret/ noun; verb

▸noun [C or U] **1** B2 a feeling of sadness about something sad or wrong or about a mistake that you have made, and a wish that it could have been different and better: *I left school at 16, but I've had a great life and I **have no** regrets.* ◦ *The manager expressed deep regret **at/for** the number of staff reductions.* ◦ *We think, **much to** our regret (= and we are very sorry about this), that we will not be able to visit you next year.* **2 send (sb) your regrets** to send a polite message that you cannot go to a party, etc.: *We did have an invitation, but we had to send Graham our regrets.*

▸verb [T] (-tt-) B1 to feel sorry about a situation, especially something sad or wrong or a mistake that you have made: *Is there anything you've done in your life that you regret?* ◦ [+ -ing verb] *I have always regretted not hav**ing** studied harder at school.* ◦ [+ (that)] formal *The council regrets (**that**) the money to subsidize the youth club is no longer available.* ◦ [+ to infinitive] formal *British Airways regret **to** announce the cancellation of flight BA205 to Madrid.*

regretful /rɪˈgret.fᵊl/ adj showing that you feel sorry about something: *a regretful goodbye/glance/smile* • **regretfully** /-i/ adv

regrettable /rɪˈgret.ə.bl/ US /-ˈgreţ-/ adj formal making you feel sad and sorry about something: *a most/deeply regrettable mistake* • **regrettably** /-bli/ adv

regular /ˈreg.jʊ.ləʳ/ US /-lə/ adj; noun

▸adj **OFTEN** ▷ **1** B1 happening or doing something often: *a regular customer/churchgoer/reader/user* ◦ *Top footballers make regular appearances on TV.* **EVEN** ▷ **2** B2 existing or happening repeatedly in a fixed pattern, with equal or similar amounts of space or time between one and the next; even: *Her heartbeat was regular.* ◦ *The gardeners planted the trees at regular **intervals**.* ◦ *I suggest that we have regular meetings/meet **on a** regular **basis**.* **3** If you say someone is regular, you mean they pass the contents of their bowels out of their body often enough, or (of women) that their period is always at approximately the same time: *The doctor asked if I was regular/if my bowel movements were regular.* **USUAL** ▷ **4** A2 US usual or ordinary: *Her regular secretary was off sick for a week.* ◦ *I couldn't see my regular dentist.* ◦ mainly US *I bought a regular size T-shirt, rather than extra large.* **5** B1 specialized describes a verb, noun, or adjective which follows the usual rules in the structure of its various forms: *'To talk' is a regular verb but 'to be' is not.* **6 a regular guy** US a normal man who is liked and trusted **7 regular army, soldier, etc.** an army that exists all the time, or a soldier in such an army **SIMILAR** ▷ **8** the same on both or all sides: *He's very handsome, with regular features and deep brown eyes.* ◦ *A square is a regular quadrilateral.* **COMPLETE** ▷ **9** [before noun] informal real; complete: *The situation here now is becoming a regular disaster.* ◦ old-fashioned *That child is a regular charmer/little nuisance.* • **regularity** /ˌreg.jʊˈlær.ə.ti/ US /-ˈler.ə.ţi/ noun [U] *The same familiar faces reappear in the law courts **with** depressing regularity.* • **regularly** /-li/ adv B1 *Accidents regularly occur on this bend.*

IDIOM **(as) regular as clockwork** never late: *In this country the trains are regular as clockwork.*

▸noun [C] **CUSTOMER** ▷ **1** someone who often goes to a particular event or place, such as a shop or restaurant: *He's one of the regulars at the pub.* **SOLDIER** ▷ **2** a soldier whose permanent job is being a soldier

regularize (UK usually **regularise**) /ˈreg.jʊ.lᵊr.aɪz/ US /-lə-/ verb [T] to change a situation or system so that it obeys laws or is based on reason: *The position of our formerly illegal workers has now been regularized (= made legal and official).* ◦ *Some people want to regularize the English spelling system (= change it so that all words follow the same rules for spelling).* • **regularization** (UK usually **regularisation**) /ˌreg.jə.lə.raɪˈzeɪ.ʃᵊn/ US /-ə-/ noun [U]

regulate /ˈreg.jʊ.leɪt/ verb [T] C1 to control something, especially by making it work in a particular way: *You can regulate the temperature in the house by adjusting the thermostat.* ◦ [+ question word] *Her mother strictly regulates **how** much TV she can watch.*

regulation /ˌreg.jʊˈleɪ.ʃᵊn/ noun; adj

▸noun [C or U] B2 an official rule or the act of controlling something: *safety/health/traffic/fire/security regulations* ◦ *The correct procedure is laid down in the **rules and** regulations.* ◦ *government regulation **of** inflation*

▸adj according to the rules or the usual way of doing things: *businessmen in their regulation pinstripe suits* ◦ *It's regulation to wear suits at the office.*

regulator /ˈreg.jʊ.leɪ.təʳ/ US /-ţə/ noun [C] **1** a device used to control things such as the speed of a clock, the temperature in a room, etc. **2** an official who makes certain that the companies who operate a system, such as the national electricity supply, work effectively and fairly

regulatory /ˌreg.jʊˈleɪ.tᵊr.i/ US /ˈreg.jə.lə.tɔːr-/ adj formal controlling: *a regulatory **body/organization***

regurgitate /rɪˈgɜː.dʒɪ.teɪt/ US /-ˈgɜː.dʒə-/ verb **1** [I or T] to bring back swallowed food into the mouth: *Owls regurgitate partly digested food to feed their young.* **2** [T] disapproving If you regurgitate facts, you just repeat what you have heard without thinking about it: *Many students simply regurgitate what they hear in lectures.*

rehab /ˈriː.hæb/ noun [U] informal the process of helping someone to stop taking drugs or alcohol: *a rehab **clinic*** ◦ *After his arrest in 2011, he checked himself into rehab to get over his heroin addiction.*

rehabilitate /ˌriː.həˈbɪl.ɪ.teɪt/ verb [T] to return someone or something to a good or healthy condition, state, or way of living: *The prison service should try to rehabilitate prisoners so that they can lead normal lives when they leave prison.* ◦ *After 20 years in official disgrace, she's been rehabilitated (= given a positive public image again).* • **rehabilitation** /-ˌbɪl.ɪˈteɪ.ʃᵊn/ noun [U] *a drug rehabilitation **clinic*** ◦ *the rehabilitation of derelict buildings*

rehash /ˈriː.hæʃ/ noun [C] informal disapproving writing or speech that uses old ideas as if they were new: *His new book is just a rehash (**of** his previous ones).*

• **rehash** /ˌriːˈhæʃ/ verb [T] *Some students merely rehash what they've heard in lectures.*

rehearsal /rɪˈhɜː.səl/ (US) /-ˈhɝː-/ noun [C or U] (B2) a time when all the people involved in a play, dance, etc. practise in order to prepare for a performance: *They didn't have time for (a) rehearsal before the performance.* ◦ *He's a producer with three plays* ***in*** *rehearsal.*

rehearse /rɪˈhɜːs/ (US) /-ˈhɝːs/ verb **1** (C1) [I or T] to practise a play, a piece of music, etc. in order to prepare it for public performance: *The musicians rehearsed (the symphony) for the concert.* ◦ figurative *On her way to her interview she silently rehearsed what she would say.* **2** [T] formal When someone rehearses a story or an argument, they repeat it with all the details: *These are arguments that I've heard rehearsed at meetings many times before.*

rehouse /ˌriːˈhaʊz/ verb [T] to move someone to a new and usually better place to live: *The local residents demanded to be rehoused.*

rehydration /ˌriː.haɪˈdreɪ.ʃən/ noun [U] the process of putting water into someone's body when they are suffering from DEHYDRATION (= a lack of water)

the Reich /raɪk/, /raɪx/ noun (also **the ˌThird ˈReich**) Germany during the period of NAZI control from 1933 to 1945

reign /reɪn/ verb; noun

▸verb [I] **1** (C2) to be the king or queen of a country: *Queen Victoria reigned* ***over*** *Britain from 1837 to 1901.* **2** (C2) to be the main feeling or quality in a situation or person: *The bomb attacks produced a panic which reigned* ***over*** *the city.* ◦ *Love reigned supreme in her heart.*

▸noun [C] **1** (C1) the period of time when a king or queen rules a country: *the reign of Henry VIII* **2** a period when a particular person, feeling, or quality is very important or has a strong influence: *his successful reign as manager of the team*

IDIOM **a reign of terror** a period of time when a ruler controls people in a violent and cruel way

reigning /ˈreɪ.nɪŋ/ adj [before noun] being the most recent winner of a competition: *She's the reigning* ***champion*** *at Wimbledon.*

reiki /ˈreɪ.ki/ noun [U] a treatment that involves directing energy from your hands into someone's body to make them feel better

reimburse /ˌriː.ɪmˈbɜːs/ (US) /-ˈbɝːs/ verb [T] formal to pay back money to someone who has spent it for you or lost it because of you: *The airline reimbursed me* ***for*** *the amount they had overcharged me.* ◦ *She was reimbursed by the gas company* ***for*** *the damage to her house.* • **reimbursement** /-mənt/ noun [C or U]

rein /reɪn/ noun; verb

▸noun [C usually plural] **1** a long thin piece of material, especially leather, that helps you to control and direct a horse: *You pull on both reins to stop or slow a horse, but only the left rein to turn left.* **2** UK a strap that is put around a small child's body or wrist and held at the other end by an adult so that the adult can stop the child running away: *I always put my son* ***on*** *reins when we go shopping.*

IDIOMS **free rein** the freedom to do, say, or feel what you want: *The young film-makers were* ***given*** *free rein* ***to*** *experiment with new themes and techniques.* ◦ *He deliberately* ***gave*** *his emotions free rein as he played the sonata.* • **keep a tight rein on sb/sth** (also **keep sb/sth on a tight rein**) to have a lot of control over someone or something: *My father always kept us on a tight rein.* • **take over/up the reins** to take control of something, especially an organization or a country: *He took up the reins* ***of*** *government immediately after the coup.*

▸verb

PHRASAL VERB **rein sth in** **HORSE** ▷ **1** to make a horse go more slowly or stop by pulling on its reins **ACTIVITY** ▷ **2** (also **rein sth back**) to control an emotion, activity, or situation to prevent it from becoming too powerful: *We tried to rein in our excitement and curiosity.* ◦ *Reports today suggest consumers are already reining back spending.*

reincarnate /ˌriː.ɪn.kɑːˈneɪt/ (US) /-ˈkɑːr.neɪt/ verb [T always passive] If a dead person or animal is reincarnated as someone or something else, their spirit returns to life in that person or animal.

reincarnation /ˌriː.ɪn.kɑːˈneɪ.ʃən/ (US) /-kɑːr-/ noun **1** [U] the belief that a dead person's spirit returns to life in another body: *Hindus and Buddhists believe in reincarnation.* **2** [C] a person or animal in whose body a dead person's spirit returns to life: *He believes he's a reincarnation* ***of*** *Julius Caesar.*

reindeer /ˈreɪn.dɪər/ (US) /-dɪr/ noun [C] (plural **reindeer**) a type of DEER with large horns that lives in the northern parts of Europe, Asia, and America: *Father Christmas travels in a sleigh pulled by reindeer.*

reinforce /ˌriː.ɪnˈfɔːs/ (US) /-ˈfɔːrs/ verb [T] **1** (C2) to make something stronger: *The pockets on my jeans are reinforced* ***with*** *double stitching.* **2** (C1) If something reinforces an idea or opinion, it provides more proof or support for it and makes it seem true: *The final technical report into the accident reinforces the findings of initial investigations.* ◦ *His behaviour merely reinforced my dislike of him.* **3** to provide an army with more soldiers or weapons to make it stronger: *The garrison is to be reinforced* ***with/by*** *another two battalions of soldiers.*

ˌreinforced ˈconcrete noun [U] concrete that contains metal rods to make it stronger

reinforcement /ˌriː.ɪnˈfɔːs.mənt/ (US) /-ˈfɔːrs-/ noun **1** [U] the act of making something stronger: *The harbour walls need urgent reinforcement.* **2** **reinforcements** [plural] soldiers sent to join an army to make it stronger

reinstate /ˌriː.ɪnˈsteɪt/ verb [T] formal to give someone back their previous job or position, or to cause something to exist again: *A month after being unfairly dismissed, he was reinstated* ***in*** *his job.* ◦ *The Supreme Court reinstated the death penalty in 1976.*

reinstatement /ˌriː.ɪnˈsteɪt.mənt/ noun [U] formal the act of giving someone back their job or making something exist again: *The union demanded the immediate reinstatement* ***of*** *all the workers who'd been sacked.* ◦ *Reinstatement* ***of*** *the tax would be a disaster.*

reinvent /ˌriː.ɪnˈvent/ verb [T] **1** to produce something new that is based on something that already exists: *The story of Romeo and Juliet was reinvented as a Los Angeles gangster movie.* **2** **reinvent yourself** to change your job and/or the way you look and behave so that you seem very different: *He's one of those sportsmen who reinvent themselves* ***as*** *TV presenters.*

IDIOM **reinvent the wheel** to waste time trying to create something that someone else has already created

reinvigorate /ˌriː.ɪnˈvɪg.ər.eɪt/ (US) /-ə.reɪt/ verb [T] PERSON ▷ **1** to make someone feel healthier, and more energetic again: *His beliefs, both political and religious, seem to reinvigorate him.* ACTIVITY ▷ **2** to make something stronger, or more exciting or successful again: *Lower interest rates could reinvigorate consumer spending and the struggling housing market.*

reissue /ˌriːˈɪʃ.uː/ verb [T] to print or produce something again: *The recording has been reissued to celebrate the conductor's 80th birthday.* • **reissue** noun [C]

reiterate /riˈɪt.ər.eɪt/ (US) /-ˈɪt̬.ə.eɪt/ verb [T] formal to say something again, once or several times: *The government has reiterated its refusal to compromise with terrorists.* ◦ [+ that] *She reiterated* ***that*** *she had never seen him before.* • **reiteration** /riˌɪt.ərˈeɪ.ʃən/ (US) /-ˌɪt̬.əˈreɪ-/ noun [C or U]

reject verb; noun

▸verb [T] /rɪˈdʒekt/ **1** (B2) to refuse to accept, use, or believe something or someone: *The appeal was rejected by the High Court.* ◦ *Coin-operated machines in England reject euros.* ◦ *The prime minister rejected the suggestion that it was time for him to resign.* ◦ *I applied for a job as a mechanic in a local garage, but I was rejected (= I was not offered the job).* ◦ *The football coach rejected him* ***for*** *the first team (= he was not offered a place).* **2** (B2) to not give someone the love and attention they want and are expecting from you: *When she was sent to boarding school, she felt as though her parents had rejected her.* **3** specialized If your body rejects an organ that has been put in during a medical operation, it fails to accept it and tries to attack and destroy it.

▸noun [C] /ˈriː.dʒekt/ **1** a product that is damaged or not perfectly made **2** a person who has not been accepted by an organization or by society: *He considered himself as one of life's rejects.*

rejection /rɪˈdʒek.ʃən/ noun **1** (C2) [C or U] the act of refusing to accept, use, or believe someone or something: *The government's rejection* ***of*** *the plans is a setback for us.* **2** (C2) [C] a letter, etc. that tells you that you have not been successful in getting a job, a place on a course of study, etc.: *I've applied for ten jobs, but I've only had rejections/rejection letters.* **3** (C2) [U] the act of not giving someone the love and attention they want and expect: *He never asked her to marry him out of fear of rejection.*

ˈreject ˌshop noun [C] a shop that sells damaged or not perfect products that cannot be sold at the full price

rejig /ˌriːˈdʒɪg/ verb [T] (-gg-) UK informal (US usually **rejigger**) to change and improve the arrangement of something: *We'll have to rejig the shed in order to get the extra chairs in.*

rejoice /rɪˈdʒɔɪs/ verb [I] formal to feel or show great happiness about something: *Everyone rejoiced* ***at*** *the news of his safe return.* ◦ *She rejoiced* ***in*** *her good fortune.* ◦ [+ to infinitive] *I rejoiced* ***to*** *see that she had made such a quick recovery.*

rejoicing /rɪˈdʒɔɪ.sɪŋ/ noun [U] formal the act or feeling of showing great happiness about something: *There was much rejoicing* ***at/over*** *the good news.*

rejoin verb RETURN ▷ **1** /ˌriːˈdʒɔɪn/ [T] to return to someone or something: *She rejoined her husband in Toronto, after her holiday in Paris.* ANSWER QUICKLY ▷ **2** /rɪˈdʒɔɪn/ [+ speech] formal to give a quick answer to what someone has said, in an angry or humorous way: *'No, I do not have time to help you,' he rejoined impatiently.*

rejoinder /rɪˈdʒɔɪn.dər/ (US) /-dɚ/ noun [C] formal a quick and often angry or humorous answer: *She always has a witty rejoinder* ***to/for*** *any question.*

rejuvenate /rɪˈdʒuː.vən.eɪt/ verb [T] **1** to make someone look or feel young and energetic again: *She felt rejuvenated by her fortnight in the Bahamas.* **2** to make an organization or system more effective by introducing new methods, ideas, or people: *He has decided to rejuvenate the team by bringing in a lot of new, young players.* • **rejuvenation** /rɪˌdʒuː.vənˈeɪ.ʃən/ noun [U]

rekindle /ˌriːˈkɪn.dl̩/ verb [T] to make someone have a feeling that they had in the past: *The holiday was a last chance to rekindle their love.*

relapse verb; noun

▸verb [I] /rɪˈlæps/ formal to become ill or start behaving badly again, after making an improvement: *She managed to stop using drugs for a month, but then relapsed.* ◦ *He looked happy for a brief while, before relapsing* ***into*** *silent misery.*

▸noun [C] /ˈriː.læps/ formal If someone who is getting better after an illness has a relapse, they become ill again: *She was looking quite healthy on Friday, but she* ***had/suffered*** *a relapse over the weekend and was taken back into hospital.*

relate /rɪˈleɪt/ verb [T] CONNECT ▷ **1** (C2) to find or show the connection between two or more things: *Researchers are trying to relate low exam results* ***and/to/with*** *large class sizes.* TELL ▷ **2** (C2) formal to tell a story or describe a series of events: *She related the events of the previous week* ***to*** *the police.* ◦ [+ question word] *He relates* ***how*** *at the age of 23 he was interned in a prison camp.*

PHRASAL VERBS **relate to sb/sth 1** (C1) to be connected to, or to be about someone or something: *Chapter nine relates to the effects of inflation on consumers.* **2 relating to** connected with something: *Anything relating to maths is a complete mystery to me.* • **relate to sb** (C1) to understand someone and be able to have a friendly relationship with them: *Many parents find it hard to relate to their children when they are teenagers.* • **relate to sth** to understand a situation or someone's feelings because you have experienced a similar situation or similar feelings: *The culture that he describes is so different from mine that I sometimes find it hard to relate to.*

related /rɪˈleɪ.tɪd/ (US) /-t̬ɪd/ adj CONNECTED ▷ **1** (B2) connected: *We discussed unemployment and related issues.* ◦ *Experts believe that the large number of cancer cases in the area are* ***directly*** *related* ***to*** *the new nuclear power station.* FAMILY ▷ **2** (B2) If people are related, they belong to the same family: *She claims she is related* ***to*** *royalty.* ◦ *Jim and I are related* ***by marriage.*** **3** If different types of animal are related, they come from the same type of animal: *The cat and the lion are related species.*

relation /rɪˈleɪ.ʃən/ noun FRIENDSHIP ▷ **1 relations** [plural] (B2) the way in which two people or groups of people feel and behave towards each other: *Relations* ***between*** *him and his new wife are rather strained.* ◦ formal *Britain* ***enjoys*** *friendly relations* ***with*** *Canada.*

> **!** Common mistake: **relation or relationship?**
>
> **Warning:** Choose the right word!
>
> To talk in the singular about the way in which people feel and behave towards each other, don't say 'a relation', say **a relationship**:
>
> ~~*He has a very good relation with his colleagues.*~~
>
> *He has a very good relationship with his colleagues.*

R

CONNECTION ▷ **2** B2 [U] the connection or similarity between two things: *The relation* ***between*** *the original book* ***and*** *this new film is very faint.* ◦ *She* ***bears*** *no relation* ***to*** (= she is not similar to) *her brother.* **3 in/with relation to sth** B2 in connection with something: *She used the map to discover where she was in relation to her surroundings.* **FAMILY MEMBER** ▷ **4** B1 [C] a member of your family: *The funeral was attended by friends and relations.* ◦ *She's a relation* ***by marriage*** *because she married my cousin.*

IDIOM **have (sexual) relations (with sb)** formal to have sex or a sexual relationship with someone

relationship /rɪˈleɪ.ʃən.ʃɪp/ noun [C] **CONNECTION** ▷ **1** B2 the way in which two things are connected: *Scientists have established the relationship* ***between*** *lung cancer* ***and*** *smoking.* **FRIENDSHIP** ▷ **2** B1 the way in which two or more people feel and behave towards each other: *He has a very good relationship* ***with*** *his uncle.* **3** B1 a close romantic friendship between two people, often a sexual one: *Have you had any serious relationships in the past year?* **4 a love/hate relationship** a relationship in which you have feelings of love and hate for someone or something

> **!** Common mistake: **relationship**
>
> **Warning:** choose the correct preposition!
>
> Don't say 'someone's relationship to someone', say **someone's relationship with someone**:
>
> ~~*I have a good relationship to my parents.*~~
>
> *I have a good relationship with my parents.*

FAMILY CONNECTION ▷ **5** the family connection between people: *The judge asked the witness what the relationship was between her and the victim.*

> Word partners for **relationship**
>
> *have/maintain* a relationship • *end/establish/form* a relationship • a relationship *breaks down* • a *close/good/personal/special/strong* relationship • a *long-term/serious/stable* relationship • a relationship *with* sb • a relationship *between* sb/sth and sb/sth • be *in* a relationship

relative /ˈrel.ə.tɪv/ US /-t̬ɪv/ **noun; adj**

▸**noun** [C] B1 a member of your family: *I haven't got many* ***blood*** *relatives* (= people related to me by birth rather than by marriage). ◦ *All her* ***close/distant*** *relatives came to the wedding.*

▸**adj** formal **COMPARING** ▷ **1** C1 being judged or measured in comparison with something else: *We weighed up the relative advantages of driving there or going by train.* **2** true to a particular degree when compared with other things: *Since I got a job, I've been living in relative comfort* (= more comfort than before). **CONNECTED** ▷ **3 relative to a** C2 If something is relative to something else, it changes according to the speed or level of the other thing: *The amount of petrol a car uses is relative to its speed.* **b** If something is relative to a particular subject, it is connected with it: *Are these documents relative to the discussion?*

ˌrelative aˌtomic ˈmass noun [C or U] (also **aˌtomic ˈweight**) the mass of an atom of a particular chemical element, usually expressed in ATOMIC MASS UNITS → Compare **atomic mass**

ˌrelative ˈclause noun [C] specialized part of a sentence that cannot exist independently and describes a noun that comes before it in the main part of the sentence: *In the sentence 'The woman who I met was wearing a brown hat', 'who I met' is a relative clause.*

ˌrelative ˈdensity noun [C] specialized the mass of a particular volume of a substance when compared with the mass of an equal volume of water at 4°C

ˌrelative huˈmidity noun [S] The relative humidity of the air is the amount of water that is present in the air compared to the greatest amount it would be possible for the air to hold at that temperature.

relatively /ˈrel.ə.tɪv.li/ US /-t̬ɪv-/ **adv 1 relatively good, bad, etc.** B2 quite good, bad, etc. in comparison with other similar things or with what you expect: *He's a relatively good squash player.* ◦ *There was relatively little violence.* **2 relatively speaking** said when you are judging one thing in comparison with other things: *Relatively speaking, it's a fairly poor country.*

ˌrelative moˌlecular ˈmass noun [U] (also **moˌlecular ˈweight**) specialized the total of the RELATIVE ATOMIC MASSES of the atoms in a particular MOLECULE

ˌrelative ˈpronoun noun [C] specialized a PRONOUN such as which, who, or that, used to begin a RELATIVE CLAUSE: *In the sentence 'The woman who I met was wearing a brown hat', 'who' is a relative pronoun.*

relativity /ˌrel.əˈtɪv.ɪ.ti/ US /-ə.t̬i/ **noun** [U] specialized either of two theories of physics giving the relationship between space, time, and energy, especially for two objects moving in different ways

> **!** Common mistake: **relax or relaxed?**
>
> **Warning:** do not confuse the verb **relax** with the adjective **relaxed**:
>
> ~~*The atmosphere was very friendly and relax.*~~
>
> *The atmosphere was very friendly and relaxed.*

> **+** Other ways of saying **relax**
>
> The phrasal verb **chill out** is a common informal way of saying 'relax':
>
> *We spent the whole week* ***chilling out*** *on the beach.*
>
> The verb **unwind** means 'to start to relax after working or doing something difficult':
>
> *Music helps me to* ***unwind****.*
>
> If a person relaxes and doesn't use much energy, the expression **take it easy** is often used:
>
> *You'll need to spend a few days* ***taking it easy*** *after the operation.*
>
> The fixed expression **put your feet up** is also often used to mean 'sit down and relax':
>
> *I'm going to make myself a cup of coffee and* ***put my feet up*** *for half an hour.*

relax /rɪˈlæks/ **verb PERSON** ▷ **1** B1 [I or T] to (cause someone to) become less active and more calm and happy, or to (cause a part of the body to) become less stiff: *After work she relaxed* ***with*** *a cup of tea and the newspaper.* ◦ *A good massage will relax your tired muscles.* ◦ *He relaxed his* ***grip*** *on my arm* (= he began to hold it less tightly). **RULE** ▷ **2** [T] to make a rule or control less severe: *Two weeks after the police relaxed security at the airports, there was a bomb attack.*

IDIOM **relax your grip/hold** to start to control something less: *The Mafia has relaxed its grip on local businesses.*

relaxation /ˌriː.lækˈseɪ.ʃən/ **noun FEELING** ▷ **1** B1 [U] the feeling of being relaxed: *I go fishing* ***for*** *relaxation.* **2** [C] a pleasant activity which makes you become calm and less worried: *Yoga is one of my favourite relaxations.* **RULE** ▷ **3** [U] the act of making rules or the control of something less severe: *I cannot allow any relaxation* ***in/of*** *the rules.*

relaxed /rɪˈlækst/ **adj 1** B1 feeling happy and

R

comfortable because nothing is worrying you: *She seemed relaxed and in control of the situation.* **2** B2 A relaxed situation or place is comfortable and informal: *It's a very friendly bar with a nice relaxed atmosphere.* **3** If someone is relaxed about something, they are not worried about it: *My parents are fairly relaxed **about** me staying out late.*

relaxing /rɪˈlæk.sɪŋ/ **adj** B1 making you feel relaxed: *a relaxing holiday* ◦ *I find swimming so relaxing.*

relay verb; noun

▸verb [T] /ˌrɪˈleɪ/, /ˈriː.leɪ/ to repeat something you have heard, or to broadcast a signal, message, or programme on television or radio: *I was told the news first and then I relayed it **to** the others.* ◦ *TV pictures of the war were relayed around the world by satellite.*

▸noun [C] /ˈriː.leɪ/ **TEAM** ▷ **1** a group of people who continue an activity that others from the same team or organization have been doing previously: *Relays of workers kept the machines going through the night.* ◦ *After the landslide, volunteers worked **in** relays to rescue people buried under the rubble.* **2** (also **relay race**) a running or swimming race between two or more teams in which each person in the team runs or swims part of the race **EQUIPMENT** ▷ **3** a device that reacts to a small change in an electrical current by moving switches or other devices in an electrical CIRCUIT

release /rɪˈliːs/ verb; noun

▸verb [T] **MAKE FREE** ▷ **1** B2 to give freedom or free movement to someone or something: *He was released **from** prison after serving two years of a five-year sentence.* ◦ *She was arrested for shoplifting but was released **on bail** (= after paying a sum of money to the law court).* ◦ figurative *The operation released him from years of pain.* **2** to move a device from a fixed position to allow it to move freely: *He released the handbrake and the car jumped forwards.* **3** to fire a bomb or a MISSILE (= flying weapon), or to allow it to fall: *The plane released its bombs at 10,000 feet.* **4** C1 to allow a substance to flow out from somewhere: *Coal power stations release sulphur dioxide **into** the atmosphere.* ◦ *Hormones are released **from** glands **into** the bloodstream.* **5** to express a feeling which you have been trying not to show: *He punched the pillow in an effort to release his anger.* **MAKE PUBLIC** ▷ **6** C1 to allow something to be shown in public or to be available for use: *Police have released a picture of the man they want to question.* ◦ *The minister has released a statement explaining the reasons for his resignation.* **7** B2 If a company releases a film or musical recording, it allows the film to be shown in cinemas, or makes the musical recording available for the public to buy: *The band's latest album will be released next week.* **8** Indian English to make a product, for example a book, available for the public to buy, often with a celebration; LAUNCH: *The new edition of the dictionary will be released by the education minister later this month.*

▸noun **MAKING FREE** ▷ **1** C1 [S or U] an occasion when someone is allowed to leave prison, etc.: *Her early release **from** prison led to a demonstration.* **2** C1 [U] the act of flowing out from somewhere: *The accident caused the release **of** radioactivity **into** the atmosphere.* **3** [S or U] a feeling that you are free from something unpleasant: *I noticed a release **of** tension when he left the room.* ◦ *After years of suffering, his death came as a merciful release.* **MAKING PUBLIC** ▷ **4** [U] the act of making something public or available for use: *There are strict rules on the release **of** official information.* **5** [C] a written statement which gives information to be broadcast or published: *The Department of Transport has issued a **press** release about the proposals for the new motorway.* **6** B2 [C] a musical recording that is made available for the public to buy: *Her latest release, a song about doomed love, she wrote herself.* **7 on general release** If a film is on/in general release, it is available to be shown in cinemas: *The latest film from Disney goes on general release next month.*

relegate /ˈrel.ɪ.ɡeɪt/ **verb** [T] **1** to put someone or something into a lower or less important rank or position: *She resigned when she was relegated **to** a desk job.* ◦ *The story was relegated **to** the middle pages of the paper.* **2** UK If a football team is relegated, it is moved down to a lower division: *If Southampton lose again they may be relegated **from** the Premier League **to** the First Division.* → Compare **promote**

relegation /ˌrel.ɪˈɡeɪ.ʃən/ **noun** [U] UK the act of moving a football team to a lower division: *Southampton **face** relegation if they lose again.*

relent /rɪˈlent/ **verb** [I] to act in a less severe way towards someone and allow something that you had refused to allow before: *Her parents eventually relented and let her go to the party.*

relentless /rɪˈlent.ləs/ **adj** C2 continuing in a severe or extreme way: *relentless criticism/pressure* ◦ *relentless heat* • **relentlessly** /-li/ **adv** C2 *She has campaigned relentlessly for her husband's release from prison.*

relevance /ˈrel.ə.vəns/ **noun** [U] (also **relevancy**) C1 the degree to which something is related or useful to what is happening or being talked about: *What relevance does that point have **to** the discussion?* → Opposite **irrelevance**

relevant /ˈrel.ə.vənt/ **adj** **1** B2 connected with what is happening or being discussed: *Education should be relevant **to** the child's needs.* ◦ *For further information, please refer to the relevant leaflet.* ◦ *The point is highly relevant **to** this discussion.* ◦ *I'm sorry but your personal wishes are not relevant (= important) in this case.* → Opposite **irrelevant** **2** correct or suitable for a particular purpose: *plans to make schooling more relevant **to** life beyond school*

> **!** Common mistake: **relevant**
>
> **Warning:** choose the correct adjective!
>
> To say that something has great effect or influence, don't say 'relevant', say **important**:
>
> ~~*Childhood is the most relevant period in a person's life.*~~
>
> *Childhood is the most important period in a person's life.*

reliable /rɪˈlaɪə.bl̩/ **adj** B1 Something or someone that is reliable can be trusted or believed because they work or behave well in the way you expect: *Is your watch reliable?* ◦ *reliable information* ◦ *Gideon is very reliable – if he says he'll do something, he'll do it.* → Opposite **unreliable** • **reliability** /rɪˌlaɪəˈbɪl.ɪ.ti/ US /-ə.t̬i/ **noun** [U] C1 *Rolls-Royce cars are famous for their quality and reliability.* • **reliably** /-bli/ **adv** *I am reliably **informed** that you have been talking about resigning from the company.*

reliance /rɪˈlaɪ.əns/ **noun** [U] C2 the state of depending on or trusting in something or someone: *The region's reliance **on** tourism is unwise.* ◦ *You **place** too much reliance **on** her ideas and expertise.* • **reliant** /rɪˈlaɪ.ənt/ **adj** C2 *He's completely reliant **on** his wheelchair to get about.* → See also **self-reliant**

relic /ˈrel.ɪk/ **noun** [C] **1** an object, tradition, or system from the past which continues to exist: *During the dig, the archaeological team found some relics **from** the Stone Age.* ◦ *The country's employment system is a relic **of** the 1960s when jobs were scarce.* **2** a part of the body

R

or something that belonged to a holy person: *These bones are the relics **of** a 12th-century saint.*

relief /rɪˈliːf/ noun **HAPPINESS** ▷ **1** B2 [S or U] a feeling of happiness that something unpleasant has not happened or has ended: [+ to infinitive] ***It** was such **a** relief **to** hear that Marta was found safe and well.* ◦ *After the exam, I felt an incredible **sense of** relief.* ◦ *'James can't come tonight.' 'Well, **that's a** relief!'* ◦ *to seek/find/provide relief **from** the heat/cold/pain/noise* **HELP** ▷ **2** C2 [C or U] food, money, or services which provide help for people in need: *an international relief **operation*** ◦ *relief **agencies/supplies*** ◦ *Pop stars have raised millions of pounds for **famine** relief in Africa.* **RAISED AREA** ▷ **3** [U] a method of raising shapes above a flat surface so that they appear to stand out slightly from it: *Coins have pictures on them **in** relief.* **4** [C] specialized a SCULPTURE made from a flat surface in which the forms are raised above the surface: *stone reliefs*

> Word partners for **relief** (**HAPPINESS**)
>
> a *big/great/tremendous* relief • a *blessed/welcome* relief • relief *from* sth • *in/with* relief • *to* sb's relief • a *sense of* relief • a *sigh of* relief

> Word partners for **relief** (**HELP**)
>
> relief *agency/operation/organization/services* • relief *worker* • relief *effort/flight/measure* • relief *supplies* • *give/provide/send* relief

IDIOMS **be on relief** US informal to be receiving money from the government because you are poor • **stand (out) in relief** to appear or show very clearly and obviously: *The mountain stood out in **sharp** relief against the evening sky.*

reˈlief ˌmap noun [C] a map that shows the hills, valleys, and mountains of a particular area or country

reˈlief ˌroad noun [C] UK a road that drivers can use to avoid driving on a very busy main road

relieve /rɪˈliːv/ verb **MAKE BETTER** ▷ **1** C2 [T] to make an unpleasant feeling, such as pain or worry, less strong: *She was given a shot of morphine to relieve the **pain**.* ◦ *She relieved her boredom at home by learning how to type.* **2** [T] to improve an unpleasant situation: *The council is considering banning vehicles from the town centre to relieve congestion.* **HELP** ▷ **3** [T] to provide relief for a bad situation or for people in need: *emergency food aid to help relieve the famine* **4** [T] to take the place of someone and continue doing their job or duties: *I'm on duty until 2 p.m. and then Peter is coming to relieve me.* **5** [T] formal to free a place that has been surrounded by an enemy army by military force: *An armoured battalion was sent to relieve the besieged town.* **URINATE** ▷ **6 relieve yourself** polite word for **urinate**: *He proceeded to relieve himself against a tree.*

PHRASAL VERB **relieve sb of sth TAKE** ▷ **1** C2 formal to take from a person something that they are carrying, in a helpful or polite way: *May I relieve you of that heavy bag?* **2** humorous to steal something from someone: *The pickpocket delicately relieved him of his wallet.* **END JOB** ▷ **3** C2 [usually passive] formal to remove someone from their job or position because they have done something wrong: *Following the scandal, he was relieved of his post as deputy finance minister.* ◦ *The committee's chairperson is to be relieved of her **duties**.* ◦ *The general was relieved of his command in 1941.*

relieved /rɪˈliːvd/ adj B2 happy that something unpleasant has not happened or has ended: [+ to infinitive] *I'm so relieved **to** find you – I thought you'd already gone.* ◦ *He was relieved **to** see Jeannie reach the other side of the river safely.* ◦ [+ (that)] *I'm relieved (**that**) you didn't tell her.*

religion /rɪˈlɪdʒ.ən/ noun **1** B1 [C or U] the belief in and worship of a god or gods, or any such system of belief and worship: *the Christian religion* **2** [C] informal an activity which someone is extremely enthusiastic about and does regularly: *Football is a religion **for** these people.*

IDIOM **get religion** humorous **1** to become very religious: *He suddenly got religion when he went to college.* **2** US to start doing something in a serious and careful way: *I get religion each time I do my income tax – I always wonder why I didn't keep better records.*

religious /rɪˈlɪdʒ.əs/ adj **1** B2 relating to religion: *religious education* **2** B2 having a strong belief in a god or gods: *He's **deeply** religious and goes to church twice a week.*

religiously /rɪˈlɪdʒ.əs.li/ adv **1** in ways or subjects relating to religion: *India is quite diverse, both politically and religiously.* **2** informal If you do something religiously, you do it regularly: *He visits his mother religiously every week.*

relinquish /rɪˈlɪŋ.kwɪʃ/ verb [T] formal **1** to give up something such as a responsibility or claim: *He has relinquished his **claim** to the throne.* ◦ *She relinquished **control** of the family investments **to** her son.* **2** to unwillingly stop holding or keeping something: *She relinquished her **hold/grip** on the steering wheel.*

relish /ˈrel.ɪʃ/ verb; noun

▸verb [T] formal **1** C2 to like or enjoy something: *I always relish a challenge.* ◦ [+ -ing verb] *I don't relish tell**ing** her that her son has been arrested.* **2** If you relish the idea or thought of something, you feel pleasure that it is going to happen: *She's relishing the prospect of studying in Bologna for six months.*

▸noun **SAUCE** ▷ **1** C2 [C or U] a type of sauce that is eaten with food to add flavour to it: *tomato and onion relish* ◦ *Would you like relish on your burger?* **ENJOYMENT** ▷ **2** C2 [U] formal the enjoyment you get from doing something: *She ate her cake slowly and **with** relish.* ◦ *I have no relish **for** hunt**ing** and kill**ing** animals.*

relive /ˌriːˈlɪv/ verb [T] to remember clearly an experience that happened in the past: *Whenever I smell burning, I relive the final moments of the crash.*

rellie /ˈrel.i/ noun [C] (also **rello** /ˈrel.əʊ/ (US) /-oʊ/) Australian English informal for **relative**

reload /ˌriːˈləʊd/ (US) /-ˈloʊd/ verb [I or T] to put more bullets in a gun: *to reload a gun/rifle/pistol*

relocate /ˌriː.ləʊˈkeɪt/ (US) /-ˈloʊ.keɪt/ verb [I or T] C1 to (cause a person or company to) move to a new place: *The company has relocated **to** Liverpool.* ◦ *My company relocated me **to** Paris.* • **relocation** /ˌriː.ləʊˈkeɪ.ʃən/ (US) /-ˈloʊ.keɪ-/ noun [U] *relocation costs*

reluctance /rɪˈlʌk.təns/ noun [S or U] an unwillingness to do something: *I accepted his resignation with great reluctance.* ◦ [+ to infinitive] *Her reluctance **to** talk to the press was quite understandable.*

reluctant /rɪˈlʌk.tənt/ adj C1 not willing to do something and therefore slow to do it: [+ to infinitive] *I was having such a good time I was reluctant **to** leave.* ◦ *Many parents feel reluctant **to** talk openly with their children.* ◦ *She persuaded her reluctant husband to take a trip to Florida with her.* • **reluctantly** /-li/ adv C1 *She reluctantly **agreed** to step down as managing director.*

PHRASAL VERB **rely on sb/sth** **1** B2 to need a particular thing or the help and support of someone or something in order to continue, to work correctly, or to succeed: [+ -ing verb] *The success of this project relies on everyone making an effort.* ◦ *I rely on you **for** good advice.* ◦ [+ to infinitive] *I'm relying on the garage **to** fix the car by tomorrow.* **2** B2 to trust someone or something or to expect them to behave in a particular way: *British weather can never be relied on – it's always changing.* ◦ [+ -ing verb] *Don't rely on finding me here when you get back (= I might have gone).*

REM /rem, ˌɑːr.iːˈem/ **noun** [U] abbreviation for rapid eye movement: quick movements of the eyes that happen at certain times while you are sleeping and dreaming: *REM sleep*

remade /ˌriːˈmeɪd/ past simple and past participle of **remake**

remain /rɪˈmeɪn/ **verb** **1** B1 [I or L] formal to stay in the same place or in the same condition: *The doctor ordered him to remain in bed for a few days.* ◦ *Most commentators expect the basic rate of tax to remain at 25 percent.* ◦ [+ to infinitive] *A great many things remain **to** be done (= have not yet been done).* ◦ *He remained silent.* ◦ *It remains a secret.* ◦ *The bank will remain open while renovations are carried out.* **2** B2 [I] to continue to exist when other parts or other things no longer exist: *After the flood, nothing remained of the village.* ◦ *Only a few hundred of these animals remain today.*

IDIOMS **the fact remains** it is still true: *I know you're sorry now, but the fact remains **that** you hit your sister.* • **it remains to be seen** it is not yet certain: *It remains to be seen **who** will win.*

remainder /rɪˈmeɪn.dəʳ/ US /-dɚ/ **noun; verb**

▸**noun** PART LEFT ▷ **1** **the remainder** [S] the part of something that is left after the other parts have gone, been used, or been taken away: *I ate most of it and gave the remainder to the dog.* ◦ *It rained the first day but the remainder **of** the trip was lovely.* MATHEMATICS ▷ **2** [U] specialized in mathematics, the amount that is left when one number cannot be exactly divided by another: *9 divided by 4 is 2, remainder 1.*

▸**verb** [T] to sell a book cheaply because it has not sold well and no more copies of it will be produced: *His autobiography never sold very well and was soon remaindered.*

remaining /rɪˈmeɪ.nɪŋ/ **adj** [before noun] B2 continuing to exist or be left after other parts or things have been used or taken away: *Bernstein's remaining lecture will take place on 22 January.* ◦ *Mix in half the butter and keep the remaining 50 g for later.*

remains /rɪˈmeɪnz/ **noun** [plural] **1** B2 pieces or parts of something which continue to exist when most of it has been used, destroyed, or taken away: *The remains **of** lunch were still on the table.* ◦ *We visited the remains **of** a twelfth-century monastery.* **2** **human/sb's remains** formal someone's dead body or the remaining parts of it: *50 years after he died, his remains were returned to his homeland.* ◦ *Human remains were found in the woods.*

remake /ˌriːˈmeɪk/ **verb** [T] (**remade, remade**) to make a new film that has a story and title similar to an old one: *The French film 'Trois Hommes et un Couffin' was remade in Hollywood **as** 'Three Men and a Baby'.* • **remake** /ˈriː.meɪk/ **noun** [C] *Do you prefer **the** remake **of** 'King Kong' to the original?*

remand /rɪˈmɑːnd/ US /-ˈmænd/ **verb; noun**

▸**verb** [T often passive] legal **1** to send someone accused of committing a crime away from court until their trial begins: *He was remanded **on** theft charges.* ◦ *The accused was remanded **in custody** (= kept in prison before the trial began) for a week.* **2** **be remanded on bail** to be allowed to leave a law court after you have been accused of committing a crime to go to a particular place, usually your home, to wait until the trial begins, after paying an amount of money to the court which will not be given back if you do not appear at the trial

▸**noun** [U] **1** legal the state of being remanded **2** **on remand** UK legal in prison until a court trial begins: *He was **held** on remand in Brixton prison for 18 months.*

reˈmand ˌcentre **noun** [C] UK a place where young people accused of committing a crime are sent to wait until their trial begins

remark /rɪˈmɑːk/ US /-ˈmɑːrk/ **verb; noun**

▸**verb** [T] B2 to give a spoken statement of an opinion or thought: [+ (that)] *Dr Johnson once remarked (**that**) 'When a man is tired of London, he is tired of life.'* ◦ [+ that] *He remarked **that** she was looking thin.*

PHRASAL VERB **remark on sth** B2 to notice something and make a remark about it: *All his friends remarked on the change in him since his marriage.*

▸**noun** [C] B2 something that you say, giving your opinion about something or stating a fact: *Her remarks **on** the employment question led to a heated discussion.* ◦ *The children **made** rude remarks **about** the old man.*

> **Word partners for remark noun**
>
> *make* a remark • *withdraw* a remark • a *critical/disparaging/scathing/snide* remark • an *obscene/offensive/rude/suggestive* remark • a *casual/chance/offhand/passing* remark • a remark *about/concerning/on* sth

remarkable /rɪˈmɑː.kə.bl̩/ US /-ˈmɑːr-/ **adj** B2 unusual or special and therefore surprising and worth mentioning: *Nelson Mandela is a truly remarkable man.* ◦ *Meeting you here in Rome is a remarkable coincidence.* ◦ *The 20th century was remarkable **for** its inventions.*

remarkably /rɪˈmɑː.kə.bli/ US /-ˈmɑːr-/ **adv** C1 used for emphasizing how surprising or unusual something is: *It is a remarkably noisy and crowded city.* ◦ *Remarkably, she wasn't hurt in the crash.*

remarry /ˌriːˈmær.i/ US /-ˈmer-/ **verb** [I or T] to marry again: *After a lengthy and painful divorce, she vowed never to remarry.*

remaster /ˌriːˈmɑː.stəʳ/ US /-ˈmæs.tɚ/ **verb** [T often passive] to make a new MASTER (= a recording from which all copies are made) of an earlier recording, usually in order to produce copies with better sound quality: *The soundtrack of 'The Godfather' was digitally remastered and transformed from mono to stereo.*

remedial /rɪˈmiː.di.əl/ **adj** TO IMPROVE ▷ **1** formal describes an action intended to correct something that is wrong or to improve a bad situation: *to take urgent/immediate remedial **action*** ◦ *The bill requires owners to undertake remedial **work** on dilapidated buildings.* **2** formal describes exercises that are intended to improve someone's health when they are ill EDUCATION ▷ **3** [before noun] UK describing or relating to teaching that is intended to help people who have difficulties in reading or writing: *remedial classes/courses* ◦ *She is a teacher of remedial English.*

remediate /rɪˈmiː.di.eɪt/ **verb** [T] formal to correct something that is wrong or damaged or to improve a

R

bad situation: *It's a problem that we will need to continue to monitor and remediate.*

remedy /ˈrem.ə.di/ **noun; verb**
▸**noun** [C] **1** B2 a successful way of curing an illness or dealing with a problem or difficulty: *an effective herbal remedy* ***for*** *headaches* ◦ *The best remedy* ***for*** *grief is hard work.* **2 legal remedy** legal a way of solving a problem or ordering someone to make a payment for harm or damage they have caused, using a decision made in a law court: *We have exhausted all possible legal remedies* ***for*** *this injustice.*
▸**verb** [T] formal to do something to correct or improve something that is wrong: *This mistake must be remedied immediately.*

> **Other ways of saying remember**
>
> More formal alternatives are verbs such as **recall** and **recollect**:
>
> *I don't* ***recall*** *arranging a time to meet.*
>
> *I didn't* ***recollect*** *having seen him.*
>
> **Remind** means 'to make someone remember something', or 'to make someone remember to do something':
>
> *Every time we meet he* ***reminds*** *me about the money he lent me.*
>
> *Will you* ***remind*** *me to buy some eggs?*
>
> The phrasal verb **come back** is often used when someone suddenly remembers something:
>
> *I forgot his name but it's just* ***come back*** *to me.*
>
> To **reminisce** is to remember and talk about pleasant things that happened in the past:
>
> *We were just* ***reminiscing*** *about our school days.*
>
> To **keep/bear** something **in mind** is to remember someone or something that may be useful in the future:
>
> *When you book your flight,* ***keep/bear in mind*** *that the holidays are the busiest period.*
>
> If something **sticks in your mind**, you can remember it easily, often because it is strange or exciting:
>
> *His name* ***stuck in my mind*** *because it was very unusual.*

R

remember /rɪˈmem.bəʳ/ US /-bɚ/ **verb 1** A1 [I or T] to be able to bring back a piece of information into your mind, or to keep a piece of information in your memory: *'Where did you park the car?' 'I can't remember.'* ◦ *I can remember people's faces, but not their names.* ◦ [+ (that)] *She suddenly remembered* ***(that)*** *her keys were in her other bag.* ◦ [+ -ing verb] *I don't remember sign****ing*** *a contract.* ◦ [+ question word] *Can you remember* ***wh****at her phone number is?* ◦ *I remember him* ***as*** *(= I thought he was) a rather annoying man.* **2 remember to do sth** A2 to not forget to do something: *Did you remember to do the shopping?* **3 be remembered for sth** to be kept in people's memories because of a particular action or quality: *She will be remembered for her courage.* **4 you remember** informal said when you are talking to someone about something that they used to know but may have forgotten: *We went and had tea in that little café – you remember, the one next to the bookshop.* **5** [T] to hold a special ceremony to honour a past event or someone who has died: *On 11 November, the British remember those who died in the two World Wars.* **6** [T] to give a present or money to someone you love or who has provided good service to you: *My Granny always remembers me (= sends me a present) on my birthday.* ◦ *My cousin remembered me in her will.*

PHRASAL VERB **remember sb to sb** formal to ask someone to say hello to another person for you: *Please remember me to your parents.*

remembrance /rɪˈmem.brᵊns/ **noun** formal **1** [U] the act of remembering and showing respect for someone who has died or a past event: *A church service was held* ***in*** *remembrance* ***of*** *the victims.* **2** [C usually plural] a memory of something that happened in the past: *fond/sweet/personal remembrances*

Reˈmembrance ˌDay noun [C usually singular] (also **Reˌmembrance ˈSunday**) in Britain, 11 November or the closest Sunday to that date, when people honour those who were killed in wars, especially the two World Wars

remind /rɪˈmaɪnd/ **verb** [T] B1 to make someone think of something they have forgotten or might have forgotten: *Could you remind Paul* ***about*** *dinner on Saturday?* ◦ [+ to infinitive] *Please remind me* ***to*** *post this letter.* ◦ [+ (that)] *I rang Jill and reminded her* ***(that)*** *the conference had been cancelled.*

> **Common mistake: remind**
>
> When **remind** meaning 'make someone think of someone or something' is followed by an indirect object, remember to use the preposition **of**.
>
> Don't say 'remind somebody something', say **remind someone of something**:
>
> ~~*The smell of roses reminds me my grandmother.*~~
>
> *The smell of roses reminds me of my grandmother.*

PHRASAL VERB **remind sb of sth/sb** B1 to be similar to, and make someone think of, something or someone else: *Your hair and eyes remind me of your mother.*

reminder /rɪˈmaɪn.dəʳ/ US /-dɚ/ **noun 1** C1 [C] a written or spoken message which reminds someone to do something: *If he forgot to pay his rent, his landlady would send him a reminder.* ◦ [+ to infinitive] *Mum sent me off with a final reminder* ***to*** *be back before 11 p.m.* **2 a reminder of sb/sth** C1 a person or thing which makes you remember a particular person, event, or situation: [+ question word] *Alison's story is a reminder of* ***how*** *vulnerable women can be in what is still essentially a man's world.*

reminisce /ˌrem.ɪˈnɪs/ **verb** [I] formal to talk or write about past experiences which you remember with pleasure: *My grandfather used to reminisce* ***about*** *his years in the navy.*

reminiscence /ˌrem.ɪˈnɪs.ᵊns/ **noun** formal **1** [U] the act of remembering events and experiences from the past **2 reminiscences** [plural] Your reminiscences are the experiences you remember from the past, often written in a book: *The novel contains endless reminiscences* ***of/about*** *the author's youth.*

reminiscent /ˌrem.ɪˈnɪs.ᵊnt/ **adj** formal **reminiscent of sb/sth** making you remember a particular person, event, or thing: *That song is so reminiscent of my adolescence.*

remiss /rɪˈmɪs/ **adj** [after verb] formal careless and not doing a duty well enough: *You have been remiss* ***in*** *your duties.* ◦ [+ to infinitive] ***It*** *was remiss* ***of*** *me* ***to*** *forget to give you the message.*

remission /rɪˈmɪʃ.ᵊn/ **noun OF ILLNESS** ▷ **1** [C or U] formal a period of time when an illness is less severe: *Her cancer has been* ***in*** *remission for several years.* **REDUCTION** ▷ **2** [U] UK legal a reduction of the time that a person has to stay in prison: *He was given three months' remission for good behaviour.* **IN RELIGION** ▷ **3** [U] formal the fact of being forgiven for breaking religious laws or rules: *He believes that redemption is based on remission* ***of*** *sins.*

remit verb; noun
▸verb [T] /rɪˈmɪt/ (-tt-) REDUCE ▷ **1** UK legal to reduce a period of time that someone must spend in prison: *She has had part of her sentence remitted.* SEND ▷ **2** formal to send money to someone: *He worked as a builder in Chicago and remitted half his monthly wage* ***to*** *his family in the Philippines.* **3** formal to refer a matter to someone in authority to deal with: *She remitted the case* ***to*** *a new tribunal for reconsideration.*
▸noun [C usually singular] /ˈriː.mɪt/ the area which a person or group of people in authority has responsibility for or control over: *The remit* ***of*** *this official inquiry is to investigate the reasons for the accident.*

remittance /rɪˈmɪt.ᵊns/ (US) /-ˈmɪṭ-/ noun formal **1** [C] an amount of money which you send to someone: *She sends a small remittance home to her parents each month.* **2** [U] the act of sending payment to someone: *remittance advice/information*

remix verb; noun
▸verb [T] /ˌriːˈmɪks/ to use a machine or computer to change or improve the different parts of an existing music recording to make a new recording
▸noun [C] /ˌriːˈmɪks/, /ˈriː.mɪks/ a piece of music that has been remixed

remnant /ˈrem.nənt/ noun [C usually plural] a small piece or amount of something that is left from a larger original piece or amount: *the remnants* ***of*** *last night's meal* ◦ *remnants* ***of*** *the city's former glory* ◦ *a carpet remnant*

remodel /ˌriːˈmɒd.ᵊl/ (US) /-ˈmɑː.dᵊl/ verb [T] (-ll- or US usually -l-) to give a new shape or form to something: *We've completely remodelled the kitchen.*

remonstrate /ˈrem.ᵊn.streɪt/ (US) /rɪˈmɑːn-/ verb [I] formal to complain to someone or about something: *I went to the boss to remonstrate* ***against*** *the new rules.* ◦ *The barrister remonstrated* ***with*** *the judge* ***about*** *the amount of the fine.* • **remonstrance** /rɪˈmɒn.strᵊns/ (US) /-ˈmɑːn-/ noun [C or U]

remorse /rɪˈmɔːs/ (US) /-ˈmɔːrs/ noun [U] formal C2 a feeling of sadness and being sorry for something you have done: *He felt no remorse* ***for*** *the murders he had committed.* ◦ *After the argument, she was* ***filled with*** *remorse.*

remorseful /rɪˈmɔː.sfᵊl/ (US) /-ˈmɔːr-/ adj formal feeling sad and guilty • **remorsefully** /-i/ adv

remorseless /rɪˈmɔːs.ləs/ (US) /-ˈmɔːrs-/ adj formal **1** severe and showing no sadness or GUILT: *remorseless cruelty/violence* ◦ *a remorseless judge* **2** never stopping or impossible to stop: *the hurricane's remorseless approach* ◦ *remorseless pressure to succeed* • **remorselessly** /-li/ adv

remortgage /ˌriːˈmɔː.gɪdʒ/ (US) /-ˈmɔːr-/ verb [I or T] to arrange a second MORTGAGE (= an agreement with a bank or similar organization in which you borrow money to buy property) or increase the first MORTGAGE, especially in order to get more money: *Robin decided to remortgage his house to pay off his debts.* • **remortgage** /ˈriː.mɔː.gɪdʒ/ (US) /-mɔːr-/ noun [C] *The building society will arrange a remortgage for a fee of £100.*

remote /rɪˈməʊt/ (US) /-ˈmoʊt/ adj; noun
▸adj DISTANT ▷ **1** B2 far away in distance or time, or not closely related: *remote galaxies* ◦ *It happened in the remote* ***past****, so no one worries about it any more.* ◦ *They take little interest in a conflict far from their homes and remote* ***from*** *their everyday problems.* **2** B2 describes an area, house, or village that is a long way from any towns or cities: *a remote mountain village* **3** specialized remote computer systems are available to users in another part of a building or in another place, for example through a NETWORK: *a remote server* SLIGHT ▷ **4** C2 slight: *a remote possibility* ◦ *The chances of a visit by Martians to the Earth are remote.* NOT FRIENDLY ▷ **5** not very friendly or showing little interest in other people: *Her manner was remote and cool.* • **remoteness** /-nəs/ noun [U]

IDIOM **not have the remotest idea** to not know at all: *'Who's that?' 'I haven't the remotest idea.'*

▸noun [C] a **remote control**

reˌmote conˈtrol noun **1** [U] a system for controlling something such as a machine or vehicle from a distance, by using electrical or radio signals: *The bomb was detonated* ***by*** *remote control.* **2** B1 [C] (also **remote**) a piece of equipment that you hold in your hand and use to control a television, DVD player, etc.: *Have you seen the remote for the TV anywhere?* • **reˌmote-conˈtrolled** adj *a remote-controlled model aircraft*

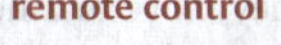
remote control

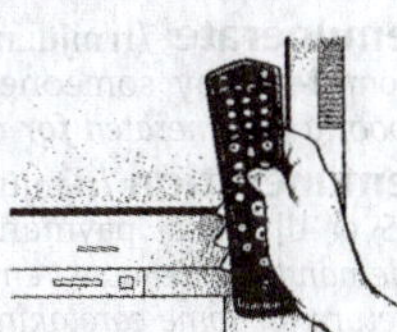

remotely /rɪˈməʊt.li/ (US) /-ˈmoʊt-/ adv FAR AWAY ▷ **1** in a remote place: *a remotely situated farmhouse* FROM DISTANCE ▷ **2** from a distance: *Most of our employees work remotely (= from home, using email and the phone).* SLIGHTLY ▷ **3** in a remote or very slight way: *I'm afraid we're* ***not*** *remotely* ***interested*** *in your proposal.*

remould /ˈriː.məʊld/ (US) /-moʊld/ verb, noun UK for **retread**

removable /rɪˈmuː.və.bl̩/ adj able to be removed: *This jacket has removable sleeves/a removable collar.*

removal /rɪˈmuː.vᵊl/ noun [U] TAKING AWAY ▷ **1** the act of taking something or someone away from somewhere or something: *stain removal* ◦ *furniture removal* **2 removals** [plural] the business of transporting furniture and other possessions when people move to a new home: *Does your firm do removals?* ENDING JOB ▷ **3** formal the act of forcing someone to leave an important position or job: *There have been calls for the president's removal.*

removalist /rɪˈmuː.vᵊl.ɪst/ noun [C] Australian English someone who helps people move their possessions to a different place to live or work → Compare **mover**

reˈmoval ˌvan noun [C] UK (US **ˈmoving ˌvan**) a vehicle used to transport furniture and other possessions when people move to a new home

remove /rɪˈmuːv/ verb; noun
▸verb [T] TAKE AWAY ▷ **1** B1 to take something or someone away from somewhere, or off something: *The men came to remove the rubbish* ***from*** *the backyard.* ◦ *This detergent will remove even old stains.* ◦ *It got so hot that he removed his tie and jacket.* ◦ *They decided to remove their son from the school.* **2** to make a negative feeling disappear: *Hearing your opinion has removed my last doubts/suspicions about her.* END JOB ▷ **3** C2 formal to force someone to leave an important job or a position of power because they have behaved badly or not in a way you approve of: *The company's shareholders have voted to remove the executive board.* ◦ *Several opposition groups are fighting to remove the president* ***from power****.* ◦ *She has been removed* ***from*** *her* ***post/position*** *as director.*

IDIOM **be far removed from sth** formal C2 to be very different from something: *It's a wonderful experience but it's far removed from reality.*

▸noun [C] formal a stage in a process or development: *We are* ***at one*** *remove* ***from*** *(= very close to) war.*

removed /rɪˈmuːvd/ adj formal **once, twice, etc. removed** describes a COUSIN (= a relation) separated from you by one, two, etc. GENERATIONS (= same family age groups): *She's my first cousin once removed.*

remover /rɪˈmuː.vəʳ/ (US) /-vɚ/ noun [C or U] **1** a substance which removes something: *Do you have any nail-varnish remover?* **2 (furniture) remover** (US **(furniture) mover**) a person or company who helps people to move their furniture and other possessions when they move to a new home

remunerate /rɪˈmjuː.nəʳ.eɪt/ (US) /-nə.reɪt/ verb [T] formal to pay someone for work or services: *He is poorly remunerated **for** all the work he does.*

remuneration /rɪˌmjuː.nəʳˈeɪ.ʃən/ (US) /-nəˈreɪ-/ noun [S or U] formal payment for work or services: *They demanded adequate remuneration **for** their work.* ◦ *In return for some caretaking duties, we are offering a free flat and a small remuneration.* ◦ *a remuneration package*

remunerative /rɪˈmjuː.nəʳ.ə.tɪv/ (US) /-nə.reɪ.t̬ɪv/ adj formal providing payment for work: *a highly remunerative (= well paid) job* ◦ *Charity work is not very remunerative.*

renaissance /rəˈneɪ.sənts/ (US) /ˈren.ə.sɑːnts/ noun [S] a new growth of activity or interest in something, especially art, literature, or music: *Opera in Britain is enjoying a long-awaited renaissance.*

the Reˈnaissance noun [S] the period of new growth of interest and activity in the areas of art, literature, and ideas in Europe during the 15th and 16th centuries • **Renaissance** adj [before noun] *Renaissance art/painting/architecture*

renal /ˈriː.nəl/ adj specialized relating to the KIDNEYS (= body organs): *a renal unit* ◦ *renal dialysis*

rename /ˌriːˈneɪm/ verb [T] to give something a new name: *You must rename the file before you save it.* ◦ *The ship was sold, painted and renamed the 'Suez Star'.*

rend /rend/ verb [T] (**rent** or US also **rended**, **rent** or US also **rended**) old use or literary to tear or break something violently: *With one stroke of his sword, he rent his enemy's helmet **in** two.* ◦ [+ adj] *Firemen had to rend him **free** of (= pull him out of) the burning car.* ◦ figurative *A terrifying scream rent **the air**.*

R

render /ˈren.dəʳ/ (US) /-dɚ/ verb [T] **CAUSE** ▷ **1** (C2) formal to cause someone or something to be in a particular state: [+ adj] *His rudeness rendered me **speechless**.* ◦ *New technology has rendered my old computer obsolete.* **2** formal to change words into a different language or form: *She is rendering the book **into** English from French.* **GIVE** ▷ **3** (C1) formal to give something such as a service, a personal opinion or expression, or a performance of a song or poem, etc. to people: *The singers rendered the song with enthusiasm.* ◦ *We see that freight railroads make good profits while rendering excellent **service**.* **BUILDING** ▷ **4** specialized to put a first layer of PLASTER or CEMENT on a wall

PHRASAL VERB **render sth down 1** specialized to melt fat in order to make it purer **2** to prepare or treat the bodies of dead animals in order to take out the fat and other substances that can be used in other products: *to render down animal carcasses*

rendering /ˈren.dəʳr.ɪŋ/ (US) /-dɚ-/ noun **PERFORMANCE** ▷ **1** [C] (also **rendition**) the way that something is performed, written, drawn, etc.: *Her rendering **of** the song was delightful.* **TRANSLATION** ▷ **2** [C] a TRANSLATION of a book or piece of writing into a different language or a different style: *a new rendering of the Bible **into** modern English* **IN BUILDING** ▷ **3** [U] specialized a layer of PLASTER or CEMENT on a wall: *The rendering on two sides of the house needed to be removed.* **OF DEAD ANIMALS** ▷ **4** [U] the process of preparing or treating the bodies of dead animals in order to take out the fat and other substances that can be used in other products: *the rendering of beef products* ◦ *a rendering plant*

rendezvous /ˈrɒn.deɪ.vuː/ (US) /ˈrɑːn-/ noun [C] (plural **rendezvous**) **1** an arrangement to meet someone, especially secretly, at a particular place and time, or the place itself: *We have a rendezvous **for** next week, don't we?* ◦ *The lovers met at a secret rendezvous in the park.* **2** a place where a particular group of people often go or meet, by arrangement or habit: *This restaurant is a popular rendezvous **for** local artists.* • **rendezvous** verb [I] *The police arranged to rendezvous **with** their informant at a disused warehouse.*

rendition /renˈdɪʃ.ən/ noun **PERFORMANCE** ▷ **1** [C] a particular way of performing a song, piece of music, or poem: *She ended the concert with a powerful rendition of 'I Will Always Love You'.* **OF PRISONERS** ▷ **2** [U] **extraordinary rendition**

renegade /ˈren.ɪ.geɪd/ noun [C] formal disapproving a person who has changed their feelings of support and duty from one political, religious, national, etc. group to a new one: *A band of renegades had captured the prince and were holding him to ransom.* • **renegade** adj [before noun] *a renegade soldier/priest*

renege /rɪˈneɪg/ verb [I] formal to fail to keep a promise or an agreement, etc.: *If you renege **on** the deal now, I'll fight you in the courts.*

renew /rɪˈnjuː/ (US) /-ˈnuː/ verb [T] **MAKE NEW** ▷ **1** (B2) to increase the life of or replace something old: *Every year I renew my **membership** of the sports club.* ◦ *I forgot to renew my season **ticket**.* ◦ *I'll use this material to renew the chair covers.* **REPEAT** ▷ **2** to begin doing something again: *The kidnappers renewed their **threats**.* ◦ *She renewed her **efforts** to escape.* • **renewal** /-əl/ noun [C or U] *Do you deal with season-ticket renewals here?* • **renewed** /-ˈnjuːd/ (US) /-ˈnuːd/ adj *renewed **interest/enthusiasm***

renewable /rɪˈnjuː.ə.bl̩/ (US) /-ˈnuː-/ adj **1** (C1) describes a form of energy that can be produced as quickly as it is used: *renewable **energy** sources such as wind and wave power* **2** (C2) If an official document is renewable, its use can be continued for an extra period of time: *a renewable passport/**contract***

renewables /rɪˈnjuː.ə.blz/ (US) /-ˈnuː-/ noun [plural] types of energy such as wind power and power from the sun that can be replaced as quickly as they are used

renminbi /ˈren.mɪn.bi/ noun [S] the CURRENCY of the People's Republic of China → Compare **yuan**

rennet /ˈren.ɪt/ noun [U] (US also **rennin**) a substance used for making milk thicker, especially to make cheese

renounce /rɪˈnaʊnts/ verb [T] formal to say formally or publicly that you no longer own, support, believe in, or have a connection with something: *Her ex-husband renounced his **claim** to the family house.* ◦ *Gandhi renounced the use of violence.*

renovate /ˈren.ə.veɪt/ verb [T] (C1) to repair and improve something, especially a building: *He renovates old houses and sells them at a profit.* • **renovation** /ˌren.əˈveɪ.ʃən/ noun [C or U] (C1) *The museum is closed for renovation.* ◦ *Extensive renovations were carried out on the property.*

renown /rɪˈnaʊn/ noun [U] formal the state of being

famous: *a woman of great renown* ◦ *Her renown spread across the country.*

renowned /rɪˈnaʊnd/ **adj** C2 famous for something: *The region is renowned **for** its outstanding natural beauty.* ◦ *Marco Polo is a renowned explorer/is renowned **as** an explorer.*

rent /rent/ **noun; verb**

▸**noun** PAYMENT ▷ **1** A2 [C or U] a fixed amount of money that you pay regularly for the use of a room, house, car, television, etc. that someone else owns: *I pay a higher rent/more rent than the other tenants because my room is bigger.* ◦ *Rents here are ridiculously **high/low**.* **2 for rent** offered by the owner for someone else to use in exchange for money HOLE ▷ **3** [C] formal a large hole torn in a piece of material

▸**verb** PAY TO USE ▷ **1** A2 [T] to pay or receive a fixed amount of money for the use of a room, house, car, television, etc.: *I rented a car **from** a garage so that I could get about.* ◦ [+ two objects] *The old lady rented us her spare bedroom **for** £55 a week.* ◦ *My Dad has a cottage which he rents (**out**) **to** tourists.*

> **!** Usage: **rent or hire?**
>
> In British English you usually **rent** something for a long time:
>
> *I rent a two-bedroom flat.*
>
> In British English you **hire** something for a short time:
>
> *We hired a car for the weekend.*
>
> In American English the word **rent** is used in both situations:
>
> *I rent a two-bedroom apartment.*
>
> *We rented a car for the weekend.*

TORN ▷ **2** past simple and past participle of **rend**

rent-a- /ren.tə-/ **prefix** UK disapproving used when a person, thing, or group of people seems to have been rented for a particular purpose and is not sincere: *Most of the people on the protest seemed to be rent-a-mob, not real supporters.* ◦ humorous *Old rent-a-quote is always turning up on TV to give his opinions.*

rental /ˈren.təl/ US /-t̬əl/ **noun** [C or U] an arrangement to rent something, or the amount of money that you pay to rent something: *Property rental is quite expensive here.* ◦ *DVD rentals have decreased this year.* ◦ *a car rental **company***

ˈrent ˌboy **noun** [C] UK informal a young male PROSTITUTE (= someone who has sex for money) used by other men

rented /ˈren.tɪd/ **adj** describes something that you rent: *rented **accommodation***

renter /ˈren.tər/ US /-t̬ɚ/ **noun** [C] US someone who pays money to live in a house or an apartment that someone else owns

ˌrent-ˈfree **adj, adv** If a house is rent-free or if you are living or staying rent-free, the owner is not asking for payment.

ˈrent ˌstrike **noun** [C] an act of refusing to pay rent, especially by all the people living in a particular house or houses

renunciation /rɪˌnʌn.siˈeɪ.ʃən/ **noun** [S or U] the formal announcement that someone no longer owns, supports, believes in, or has a connection with something: *the renunciation **of** violence*

reopen /ˌriːˈəʊ.pən/ US /-ˈoʊ-/ **verb** [I or T] **1** If a place or business, etc. reopens or is reopened, it begins to operate, or it becomes open for people to use, after being closed for a period of time: *The museum has reopened after nearly two years of reconstruction.* ◦ *He hung a sign on the door of the shop which said it would reopen at 11.00.* **2** If a formal process or activity reopens or is reopened, it begins again or starts to be dealt with again after a period of time: *to reopen an **enquiry/investigation*** ◦ *to reopen a debate/discussion* ◦ *to reopen a legal case/file*

reorganize (UK usually **reorganise**) /riːˈɔː.gən.aɪz/ US /-ˈɔːr-/ **verb** [I or T] C1 to organize something again in order to improve it: *I've reorganized my files so that I can easily find what I'm looking for.* ◦ *The new managing director plans to completely reorganize this department.* • **reorganization** /riːˌɔː.gən.aɪˈzeɪ.ʃən/ US /-ˌɔːr-/ **noun** [C or U]

rep /rep/ **noun** BUSINESS ▷ **1** [C] informal a **sales rep** THEATRE ▷ **2** [U] informal for **repertory**

Rep. 1 abbreviation for **Republican 2** abbreviation for **representative**

repaid /rɪˈpeɪd/ past simple and past participle of **repay**

repair /rɪˈpeər/ US /-ˈper/ **verb; noun**

▸**verb** [T] **1** A2 to put something that is damaged, broken, or not working correctly, back into good condition or make it work again: *to repair (the surface of) the road* ◦ *to repair a roof after a storm* ◦ *The garage said the car was so old it wasn't worth repairing.* ◦ *I really must **get** my bike repair**ed** this weekend.* **2** C2 If you repair something wrong or harmful that has been done, you do something to make it right: *to repair a broken friendship* ◦ *Is it too late to repair the **damage** we have done to our planet?*

> **+** Other ways of saying **repair**
>
> The verbs **fix** and **mend** are common alternatives:
>
> *I must get my bike **fixed**.*
>
> *Can you **mend** that hole in my trousers?*
>
> The phrasal verb **do up** is often used when someone repairs something and improves it:
>
> *Nick loves **doing up** old cars.*
>
> The verb **service** is often used when examining and repairing cars or other machines:
>
> *I'm taking the car to the garage to have it **serviced** this afternoon.*
>
> The verb **patch** can be used when someone fixes something in a basic and temporary way:
>
> *We managed to **patch** the hole in the roof.*

PHRASAL VERB **repair to somewhere** formal to go to another place, usually in a group of people: *After dinner, we repaired to the lounge for coffee.*

▸**noun** [C or U] B1 the act of fixing something that is broken or damaged: *My car is in the garage for repairs.* ◦ *The repairs **to** the roof will be expensive.* ◦ *The mechanic pointed out the repair (= repaired place) on the front of my car.*

IDIOMS **in good, bad, etc. repair** (also **in a good, bad, etc. state of repair**) C2 in good, bad, etc. condition: *The house is in very good repair.* • **under repair** being repaired: *This section of motorway will be under repair until January.*

R

repairable /rɪˈpeə.rə.bl̩/ US /-ˈper.ə-/ **adj** able to be repaired

reparation /ˌrep.əˈreɪ.ʃən/ **noun** [C or U] formal payment for harm or damage: *The company had to **make** reparation **to** those who suffered ill health as a result of chemical pollution.*

repartee /ˌrep.ɑːˈtiː/ US /-ɑːr-/ **noun** [U] quick and usually funny answers and remarks in conversation: *Oscar Wilde's plays are full of **witty** repartee.*

repast /rɪˈpɑːst/ US /-ˈpæst/ **noun** [C] literary a meal: *Yet that simple repast was fit for a king.*

repatriate /ˌriːˈpæt.ri.eɪt/ (US) /-ˈpeɪ.tri-/ **verb** [T] to send or bring someone, or sometimes money or other property, back to their own country: *The government repatriated him because he had no visa.* • **re·patriation** /ˌriː.pæt.riˈeɪ.ʃən/ (US) /rɪˌpeɪ.tri-/ **noun** [U]

repay /rɪˈpeɪ/ **verb** [T] (**repaid**, **repaid**) B2 to pay back or to reward someone or something: *He had to sell his car to repay the bank **loan**.* ◦ *She repaid the loan **to** her mother.* ◦ [+ two objects] *She repaid her mother the loan.* ◦ *How can I ever repay you **for** all your kindness?*

repayable /rɪˈpeɪ.ə.bl̩/ **adj** If something is repayable, you must pay it back: *The loan is repayable over six months.*

repayment /rɪˈpeɪ.mənt/ **noun** [C or U] the act of repaying someone or something: ***mortgage** repayments* ◦ *The bank demanded immediate repayment.*

repeal /rɪˈpiːl/ **verb** [T] If a government repeals a law, it causes that law no longer to have any legal force. • **repeal noun** [S or U] *We're campaigning for a/the repeal **of** the abortion laws.*

repeat /rɪˈpiːt/ **verb; noun**

▸**verb 1** A2 [T] to say or tell people something more than once: *Would you mind repeating what you just said?* ◦ *Please don't repeat what I've just told you **to** anyone else.* ◦ [+ that] *She repeated **that** she had no intention of standing for president.* **2** A2 [I or T] to happen, or to do something, more than once: *The test must be repeated several times.* ◦ *This is an offer never to be repeated.* ◦ *Johnny had to repeat a year/class at school.* ◦ *Some historians think that history repeats **itself**.* **3 repeat yourself** to say the same thing again, or the same things again and again: *His speech was dreadful – he just kept repeating himself.*

PHRASAL VERB **repeat on sb** When food repeats on you, the taste of it comes up again into your mouth: *Cucumber always repeats on me.*

▸**noun** [C] **1** a situation in which something happens or is done more than once: *All this is a repeat/a repeat **performance** of what happened last year.* **2** a television or radio programme that is broadcast again: *There's nothing but repeats on television these days.*

repeated /rɪˈpiː.tɪd/ (US) /-t̬ɪd/ **adj** C2 happening again and again: *repeated **attempts/mistakes/warnings***

repeatedly /rɪˈpiː.tɪd.li/ (US) /-t̬ɪd-/ **adv** C1 many times: *He phoned repeatedly, begging her to return.*

repel /rɪˈpel/ **verb** [T] (-ll-) FORCE AWAY ▷ **1** to force something or someone to move away or stop attacking you: *This coat has a special surface that repels moisture.* ◦ formal *The defenders repelled the attack without losing any men.* **2** specialized to have a MAGNETIC FIELD which pushes away something with a similar magnetic field: *Similar poles of magnets repel each other, and opposite poles attract.* CAUSE STRONG DISLIKE ▷ **3** People or things that repel you make you feel strongly that you do not want to be near, see, or think about them: *She was repelled by his ugliness.* ◦ *Her arrogance repels many people.*

repellent /rɪˈpel.ənt/ **noun; adj**

▸**noun** [C or U] a substance used to repel something: ***insect/mosquito** repellent*

▸**adj** making you feel strong disapproval and that you do not want to be involved with someone or something: *repellent behaviour/beliefs* ◦ *I find any cruelty to children utterly repellent.*

repent /rɪˈpent/ **verb** [I] formal to be very sorry for something bad you have done in the past and wish that you had not done it: *He repented (**of** his sins) just hours before he died.* • **repentance** /-ˈpen.təns/ **noun** [U] *This was an extremely violent crime, for which the boy showed no repentance.*

repentant /rɪˈpen.tənt/ **adj** formal feeling sorry for something that you have done → Opposite **unrepentant**

repercussion /ˌriː.pəˈkʌʃ.ən/ (US) /-pɚ-/ **noun** [C usually plural] the effect that an action, event or decision has on something, especially a bad effect: *Any decrease in tourism could have **serious** repercussions for the local economy.*

repertoire /ˈrep.ə.twɑːr/ (US) /-ɚ.twɑːr/ **noun** [C] all the music or plays, etc. that you can do or perform or that you know: *The Royal Shakespeare Company also have many modern plays **in** their repertoire.* ◦ *There is an extensive repertoire of music written for the flute.*

repertory /ˈrep.ə.tər.i/ (US) /-ɚ.tɔːr-/ **noun** [U] (informal **rep**) **1** the repeated performance of several plays one after the other by one company of actors: *a repertory **company/group/theatre*** **2 in repertory a** If a play is in repertory, it is one of several different plays being performed on particular days by the same company of actors: *'Macbeth' is in repertory at the Royal Shakespeare Company.* **b** If an actor is in repertory, they are working with a repertory theatre group.

repetition /ˌrep.ɪˈtɪʃ.ən/ **noun 1** C2 [U] the act of doing or saying something again: *His books are full of repetition.* **2** [C] something that happens in the same way as something which happened before: *We want to prevent a repetition of last summer's fires which destroyed more than 500,000 acres of land.*

repetitive /rɪˈpet.ə.tɪv/ (US) /-ˈpet̬.ə.t̬ɪv/ **adj** (also **repetitious**) C1 involving doing or saying the same thing several times, especially in a way that is boring: *a repetitive **job/task*** • **repetitively** /-li/ **adv**

reˌpetitive ˈstrain ˌinjury noun [U] (abbreviation **RSI**) a painful medical condition that can cause damage to the hands, wrists, upper arms, and backs, especially of people who use computers and other forms of KEYBOARD

rephrase /ˌriːˈfreɪz/ **verb** [T] to say or write something again in a different and usually clearer way: *Could you rephrase your question, please?*

replace /rɪˈpleɪs/ **verb** [T] CHANGE FOR ▷ **1** B1 to take the place of something, or to put something or someone in the place of something or someone else: *The factory replaced most of its workers **with** robots.* ◦ *Tourism has replaced agriculture as the nation's main industry.* **2** B1 If you replace something broken, damaged, or lost, you provide a new one: *I promised to replace the plate that I'd dropped.* PUT BACK ▷ **3** C2 to put something back where it was before: *The librarian replaced the books correctly on the shelves.* • **replaceable** /-ˈpleɪ.sə.bl̩/ **adj** *Don't worry – all that stolen stuff is replaceable.*

replacement /rɪˈpleɪs.mənt/ **noun 1** C1 [U] the process of replacing something with something else: *the replacement of existing computer equipment* ◦ *replacement windows* **2** B2 [C] someone who does a job instead of someone else, or something which you use instead of something else: *The agency sent a replacement **for** the secretary who resigned.*

replay /ˌriːˈpleɪ/ **verb** [T] COMPETITION ▷ **1** to play a game, especially a football game, again that neither team won the first time RECORDING ▷ **2** to play something again, especially music or film recorded already: *The police replayed the video of the robbery in court.* • **replay** /ˈriː.pleɪ/ **noun** [C] *The semifinal replay will be on Saturday.* ◦ *a slow-motion replay*

replenish /rɪˈplen.ɪʃ/ **verb** [T] formal to fill something up again: *Food stocks were replenished **by/with** imports from the US.* ◦ *Does your glass need replenishing?* • **replenishment** /-mənt/ **noun** [U]

replete /rɪˈpliːt/ **adj** [after verb] formal **1** full, especially with food: *After two helpings of dessert, Sergio was at last replete.* **2** well supplied: *This car has an engine replete **with** the latest technology.*

replica /ˈrep.lɪ.kə/ **noun** [C] an exact copy of an object: *The ship is an **exact** replica **of** the original Golden Hind.*

replicate /ˈrep.lɪ.keɪt/ **verb 1** [T] formal to make or do something again in exactly the same way: *Researchers tried many times to replicate the original experiment.* **2** [I or T] specialized If organisms and GENETIC or other structures replicate, they make exact copies of themselves: *Chromosomes replicate before cells divide and multiply.* ◦ *Computer viruses replicate them**selves** and are passed along from user to user.* • **replication** /ˌrep.lɪˈkeɪ.ʃən/ **noun** [C or U] formal

reply /rɪˈplaɪ/ **verb; noun**

▸**verb** [I] **1** B1 to answer: [+ speech] *'Where are you going?' I asked. 'Home,' he replied.* ◦ [+ that] *I replied **that** it was twelve o'clock.* ◦ *I try to reply **to** letters the day I receive them.* **2** to react to an action by someone else: *She replied **to** the threats by going to the police.* ◦ *France took an early lead before Spain replied **with** three goals in 14 minutes.*

▸**noun** [C or U] B1 an answer: *I asked why, but he **made/gave** no reply.* ◦ *There were very few replies **to** our advertisement.* ◦ ***In** reply **to** their questions, she just shrugged.*

> Word partners for **reply noun**
>
> *give/make/send* a reply • *get/have/receive* a reply • a reply *comes* • a *brief/immediate/monosyllabic/personal* reply • a reply *to* sth • *in* reply

reˌply-ˈpaid **adj** [before noun] UK A reply-paid envelope has had the cost of posting it already paid for, usually by the person it is sent to.

report /rɪˈpɔːt/ (US) /-ˈpɔːrt/ **verb; noun**

▸**verb** TELL ▷ **1** B1 [I or T] to give a description of something or information about it to someone: *We rang the insurance company to report the theft.* ◦ *The assassination was reported in all the newspapers.* ◦ *I want you to report (**to** me) **on** progress (= on what you have done) every Friday.* ◦ [+ -ing verb] *Spies reported see**ing** a build-up of soldiers.* ◦ [+ obj + adj] *He was reported missing in action.* ◦ *The inquiry reports (= will officially make its results known) next week.* **2 be reported to be/do sth** to be described by people as being or doing a particular thing although there is no real proof: *The storm is reported to have killed five people.* **3** [T] to make a complaint to a person in authority about something or someone: *My neighbours reported me **to** the police **for** firing my rifle in the garden.* GO ▷ **4** [I usually + adv/prep] to go to a place or a person and say that you are there: *I report **for** (= am ready for and at) work/duty at 8 a.m. every morning.*

PHRASAL VERBS **report back** to bring information to someone in authority: *Find out their names and report back **to** me tomorrow.* • **report to sb** Someone you report to at work is the person in authority over you who gives you tasks and checks that you do them: *You will report directly to the boss.*

▸**noun** [C] DESCRIPTION ▷ **1** A2 (also **school report**, US also **report card**) a teacher's written statement to parents about a child's ability and performance at school **2** B1 a description of an event or situation: *a news/weather report* ◦ *a company's financial/annual report* ◦ *I gave/made/submitted a report **of** the theft to the insurance company.* ◦ *She sent in weekly reports **on** the situation.* **3 reports** [plural] stories for which you do not yet have real proof: *According to reports, ten pupils were expelled.* ◦ *We're **getting** reports **of** a plane crash in Paris.* NOISE ▷ **4** formal the loud noise of a shot: *We heard the loud/sharp report of a rifle.*

reportage /ˌrep.ɔːˈtɑːʒ/ (US) /rɪˈpɔːr.t̬ɪdʒ/ **noun** [U] formal the activity of, or style of, reporting events in newspapers or broadcasting them on television or radio

reported /rɪˈpɔː.tɪd/ (US) /-ˈpɔːr.t̬ɪd/ **adj** [before noun] **1** described by people although there is no proof yet: *There has been a reported hijack in Tel Aviv this morning.* **2** formally mentioned to someone in authority, for example the police: *The number of reported crimes has increased.* ◦ *There are over 55,000 reported cases of food poisoning every year.*

reportedly /rɪˈpɔː.tɪd.li/ (US) /-ˈpɔːr.t̬ɪd-/ **adv** C2 according to what many people say: *New York is reportedly a very exciting place to live.*

reˌported ˈspeech **noun** [U] specialized **indirect speech**

reporter /rɪˈpɔː.təʳ/ (US) /-ˈpɔːr.t̬ɚ/ **noun** [C] B1 a person whose job is to discover information about news events and describe them for a newspaper or magazine or for radio or television

repose /rɪˈpəʊz/ (US) /-ˈpoʊz/ **verb; noun**

▸**verb** [I usually + adv/prep] formal to rest or lie: *She reposed on the sofa.*

▸**noun** [U] formal the state of resting or lying down: *Your face is so beautiful **in** repose.*

repository /rɪˈpɒz.ɪ.tər.i/ (US) /-ˈpɑː.zɪ.tɔːr-/ **noun 1** [C] formal a place where things are stored and can be found **2** [C usually singular] a person who has, or a book that contains, a lot of information or detailed knowledge: *She's a repository **of** knowledge about our family history.*

repossess /ˌriː.pəˈzes/ **verb** [T] to take back possession of something, especially property that has not been completely paid for: *I couldn't make my mortgage repayments so the building society repossessed my house.*

repossession /ˌriː.pəˈzeʃ.ən/ **noun** [C or U] the act of taking something back, or the thing that is taken back

reprehensible /ˌrep.rɪˈhen.sə.bl/ **adj** formal If someone's behaviour is reprehensible, it is extremely bad or unacceptable: *reprehensible conduct/actions* • **reprehensibly** /-bli/ **adv**

represent /ˌrep.rɪˈzent/ **verb** ACT FOR ▷ **1** C2 [T] to speak, act, or be present officially for another person or people: *They chose a famous barrister to represent them in court.* ◦ *Union officials representing the teachers met the government today.* ◦ *I sent my husband to represent me at the funeral.* ◦ *Women were **well/poorly** represented at the conference (= there were many/few present).* **2** [T] to be the Member of Parliament, or of Congress, etc. for a particular area: *Ed Smythe represents Barnet.* **3** C2 [T] to be the person from a country, school, etc. that is in a competition: *She was chosen to represent France at the Olympics.* **4** formal to express or complain about something, to a person in authority: *We represented our grievances/demands **to** the boss.* DESCRIBE ▷ **5** C2 [T] to show or describe something or someone: [+ -ing verb] *The statue represents St. George kill**ing** the dragon.* ◦ *This new report represents the current situation in our schools.* ◦ *He represents himself **as** an expert, but he knows*

R

nothing. **6** B2 [T] to be a sign or symbol of something: *To many people the Queen represents the former glory of Britain.* **BE ▷ 7** B2 [L only + noun] to be the result of something, or to be something: *This book represents ten years of thought and research.* ◦ *The new offer represented an increase of ten percent on the previous one.*

representation /ˌrep.rɪ.zenˈteɪ.ʃən/ **noun ACTING FOR ▷ 1** C2 [U] a person or organization that speaks, acts, or is present officially for someone else: *Can he afford **legal** representation?* **DESCRIPTION ▷ 2** C2 [U] the way that someone or something is shown or described: *He gave a talk on the representation of women in 19th-century art.* **3** [C] a sign, picture, model, etc. of something: *This statue is a representation of Hercules.*

IDIOM **make representations/a representation to sb/sth** formal to complain officially to a person or organization: *We made representations to the boss **about** the long working hours.*

representational /ˌrep.rɪ.zenˈteɪ.ʃən.əl/ **adj** showing things as they are normally seen: *representational art/pictures*

representative /ˌrep.rɪˈzen.tə.tɪv/ US /-t̬ə.t̬ɪv/ **noun; adj**

▸**noun** [C] **1** B2 someone who speaks or does something officially for another person or group of people: *The firm has two representatives in every European city.* **2 Representative** someone who has been elected to the US House of Representatives

▸**adj TYPICAL ▷ 1** typical of, or the same as, others in a larger group of people or things: *Are your views/opinions representative **of** all the workers here?* ◦ *a representative **sample/cross-section/selection*** **ACTING FOR ▷ 2** A representative system of government is one in which people vote for politicians to represent them.

repress /rɪˈpres/ **verb** [T] **1** to not allow something, especially feelings, to be expressed: *He repressed a sudden desire to cry.* **2** to control what people do, especially by using force

repressed /rɪˈprest/ **adj** having feelings which you do not express: *repressed **anger/sexuality*** ◦ *English people are notoriously repressed and don't talk about their feelings.*

repression /rɪˈpreʃ.ən/ **noun** [U] **1** the use of force or violence to control a group of people: *The political repression in this country is enforced by terror.* **2** the process and effect of keeping particular thoughts and wishes out of your conscious mind in order to defend or protect it: *an attitude of unhealthy **sexual** repression*

repressive /rɪˈpres.ɪv/ **adj 1** controlling what people do, especially by using force: *a repressive military **regime*** **2** preventing people from expressing their feelings • **repressiveness** /-nəs/ **noun** [U]

reprieve /rɪˈpriːv/ **noun; verb**

▸**noun** [C] **1** an official order that stops or delays the punishment, especially by death, of a prisoner: *He was sentenced to death but was **granted** a last-minute reprieve.* **2** an escape from a bad situation or experience: *The injection provided a temporary reprieve **from** the pain.*

▸**verb** [T] **1** to stop or delay the punishment, especially by death, of a prisoner **2** to provide something or someone with an escape from a bad situation or experience, especially to delay or stop plans to close or end something: *The threatened hospitals could now be reprieved.*

reprimand /ˈrep.rɪ.mɑːnd/ US /-rə.mænd/ **verb** [T] formal to express to someone your strong official disapproval of them: *She was reprimanded by her teacher **for** biting another girl.* • **reprimand noun** [C] *His boss **gave** him a severe reprimand **for** being late.*

reprint verb; noun

▸**verb** [I or T] /ˌriːˈprɪnt/ to print a book again, or to be printed again: *The first edition sold out so we are reprinting it/it is reprinting.*

▸**noun** [C] /ˈriː.prɪnt/ the act of printing a book again, or a book that has been reprinted

reprisal /rɪˈpraɪ.zəl/ **noun** [C or U] (an example of) activity against another person, especially as a punishment by military forces or a political group: ***economic/military** reprisals* ◦ *They promised that individuals could live freely **without fear of** reprisal from the military.* ◦ *The attack was **in** reprisal **for** the kidnapping of their leaders.*

reprise /rɪˈpriːz/ **noun** [C] specialized a repeat of something or part of something, especially a piece of music

reproach /rɪˈprəʊtʃ/ US /-ˈproʊtʃ/ **verb; noun**

▸**verb** [T] C2 to criticize someone, especially for not being successful or not doing what is expected: *His mother reproached him **for** not eating all his dinner.* ◦ *You have nothing to reproach your**self for/with**.*

▸**noun** [C or U] C2 something that you say or do to criticize someone, especially for not being successful or for not doing what is expected: *The look of reproach on his face made her feel guilty.* ◦ *Your reproaches are useless – what's done is done.*

IDIOMS **be a reproach to sb/sth** to be something that should make a person or organization feel ashamed: *His immaculate garden was a reproach to all his less organized neighbours.* • **be above/beyond reproach** to not deserve any blame: *Your behaviour today has been above reproach.*

reproachful /rɪˈprəʊtʃ.fəl/ US /-ˈproʊtʃ-/ **adj** expressing criticism: *reproachful **looks**/words* • **reproachfully** /-i/ **adv**

reprobate /ˈrep.rə.beɪt/ **noun** [C] formal or humorous a person of bad character and habits: *Every time I see you, you're drunk, you old reprobate!*

reprocess /ˌriːˈprəʊ.ses/ US /-ˈprɑː-/ **verb** [T] to put a material that has been used through another industrial process to change it so that it can be used again: *to reprocess nuclear waste* • **reprocessing** /-ɪŋ/ **noun** [U] *waste/plutonium reprocessing*

reproduce /ˌriː.prəˈdjuːs/ US /-ˈduːs/ **verb COPY ▷ 1** C1 [I or T] to produce a copy of something, or to be copied in a production process: *His work was reproduced on leaflets and magazines.* ◦ *They said the printing was too faint to reproduce well.* **2** [T] to show or do something again: *The new design unfortunately reproduced some of the problems of the earlier model.* **PRODUCE YOUNG ▷ 3** C2 [I or T] When living things reproduce, they produce young plants, animals, etc.: *These plants can reproduce sexually and asexually.* ◦ *Some creatures were better at surviving and reproducing them**selves** than others.*

reproduction /ˌriː.prəˈdʌk.ʃən/ **noun PRODUCING YOUNG ▷ 1** C2 [U] the process of having babies, producing young, or producing new plants: *human/**sexual** reproduction* ◦ *We are researching reproduction **in** elephants/**the** reproduction **of** elephants.* **COPY ▷ 2** C1 [C or U] a copy of something, especially a painting, or the process of copying something: *The book contains excellent colour reproductions of Monet's paintings.* ◦ *This system has excellent sound reproduction.*

ˌreproduction ˈfurniture noun [U] copies of ANTIQUE (= old) furniture

reproductive /ˌriː.prəˈdʌk.tɪv/ adj relating to the process of reproduction: *reproductive* ***organs***

reproof /rɪˈpruːf/ noun [C or U] formal something that you say or do to show that you disapprove of someone's bad or silly behaviour: *She got a sharp reproof* ***for*** *being late.* ◦ *He picked up the broken vase without a word of reproof to his son.*

reprove /rɪˈpruːv/ verb [T] formal to tell someone that you disapprove of their bad or silly behaviour: *The teacher gently reproved the boys* ***for*** *not paying attention.* • **reproving** /-ˈpruː.vɪŋ/ adj *She threw him an angry and reproving look/glance.*

reptile /ˈrep.taɪl/ noun [C] C1 an animal which produces eggs and uses the heat of the sun to keep its blood warm

reptilian /repˈtɪl.i.ən/ adj **1** specialized belonging to or like a reptile: *reptilian skin/eyes* **2** disapproving describes an unpleasantly strange and unfriendly person or type of behaviour: *He turned a cold, reptilian gaze on me.*

republic /rɪˈpʌb.lɪk/ noun [C] C1 a country without a king or queen, usually governed by elected REPRESENTATIVES of the people and a president: *the People's Republic of China*

republican /rɪˈpʌb.lɪ.kən/ noun; adj

▸noun [C] a supporter of government by elected REPRESENTATIVES of the people rather than government by a king or queen

▸adj relating to a republic: *a republican system of government* • **republicanism** /-kə.nɪ.zᵊm/ noun [U]

Republican /rɪˈpʌb.lɪ.kən/ noun [C] (written abbreviation **Rep.**) **1** a member of the Republican Party in the US **2** a person who believes that Northern Ireland belongs to the Irish Republic

the Reˈpublican ˌParty noun [+ sing/pl verb] one of the two largest political parties in the US

repudiate /rɪˈpjuː.di.eɪt/ verb [T] formal to refuse to accept something or someone as true, good, or reasonable: *He repudiated the allegation/charge/claim that he had tried to deceive them.* ◦ *I utterly repudiate those remarks.* • **repudiation** /rɪˌpjuː.diˈeɪ.ʃᵊn/ noun [U] *They were surprised by his sudden repudiation* ***of*** *all his former beliefs.*

repugnant /rɪˈpʌg.nənt/ adj formal If behaviour or beliefs, etc. are repugnant, they are very unpleasant, causing a feeling of DISGUST: *a repugnant smell* ◦ *I* ***find*** *your attitude towards these women quite repugnant.* ◦ *The idea of cheating in an exam is morally repugnant* ***to*** *me.* • **repugnance** /-nəns/ noun [U] *The thought of eating meat fills me* ***with*** *repugnance.*

repulse /rɪˈpʌls/ verb; noun

▸verb formal PUSH AWAY ▷ **1** [T] to push away or refuse something or someone unwanted, especially to successfully stop a physical attack against you: *The enemy attack was quickly repulsed.* DISLIKE ▷ **2** [T often passive] If something repulses you, it causes you to have a strong feeling of dislike, disapproval, or DISGUST: *The tourists were repulsed* ***by*** *the filthy conditions.*

▸noun [S or U] formal or old-fashioned the act of pushing someone or something unwanted away or of refusing them

repulsion /rɪˈpʌl.ʃᵊn/ noun [U] DISLIKE ▷ **1** strong dislike or disapproval: *to feel repulsion* ◦ *A look of repulsion flashed across her face.* → Synonym **disgust** PUSHING AWAY ▷ **2** specialized the force in physics that pushes two objects apart: *magnetic repulsion*

repulsive /rɪˈpʌl.sɪv/ adj extremely unpleasant or unacceptable: *What a repulsive old man!* ◦ *I think rats and snakes are repulsive.*

repurpose /ˌriːˈpɜː.pəs/ US /-ˈpɝː-/ verb [I or T] to find a new use for an idea, product, or building: *The company's role is to repurpose print data for use on the Web.* ◦ *Movie theaters are harder to repurpose than ordinary stores in a shopping mall.*

reputable /ˈrep.jʊ.tə.bḷ/ US /-t̬ə-/ adj C1 having a good reputation and able to be trusted: *I insured my property with an established, reputable company.* → Opposite **disreputable** • **reputably** /-bli/ adv

reputation /ˌrep.jʊˈteɪ.ʃᵊn/ noun [C usually singular, U] B2 the opinion that people in general have about someone or something, or how much respect or admiration someone or something receives, based on past behaviour or character: *The company has a worldwide reputation* ***for*** *quality.* ◦ *She has the reputation* ***of*** *being a good doctor.* ◦ *His reputation was destroyed when he was caught stealing some money.* ◦ *The hotel has a* ***bad/good*** *reputation.* ◦ *He* ***earned/established/gained/acquired*** *a reputation* ***as*** *an entertaining speaker.*

> **Word partners for reputation**
>
> *enjoy/have* a reputation • *acquire/establish/gain/get* a reputation • *damage/destroy/ruin* your reputation • *enhance/protect* your reputation • an *international/national/worldwide* reputation • an *enviable/fearsome/good/growing* reputation • a *bad/poor/unsavoury* reputation • a reputation *for* sth • a reputation *as* a sth

IDIOM **by reputation** not directly, by hearing what other people say: *The two men know each other only by reputation.*

repute /rɪˈpjuːt/ noun formal **ill, good, etc. repute** a bad, good, etc. reputation: *a place* ***of*** *ill repute*

IDIOM **hold sb in high/low repute** to respect someone very much/very little: *My father was held in high repute by his colleagues.*

reputed /rɪˈpjuː.tɪd/ US /-t̬ɪd/ adj BELIEVED ▷ **1** said to be the true situation although this is not known to be certain and may not be likely: *She is reputed* ***to*** *be 25 years younger than her husband.* ◦ *They employed him because of his reputed skill in dealing with the press.* FAMOUS ▷ **2** famous and with a good reputation: *These comments were provided by reputed experts on the subject.* • **reputedly** /-li/ adv *He's reputedly (= is said to be) the strongest man in Britain.*

request /rɪˈkwest/ noun; verb

▸noun **1** B1 [C or U] the act of politely or officially asking for something: *They received hundreds of requests* ***for*** *more information.* ◦ [+ to infinitive] *The boss refused our request* ***to*** *leave work early.* ◦ *The clause was added to the contract* ***at*** *Carlos's request (= because Carlos asked for this).* ◦ *An application form will be sent to you* ***on*** *request (= if you ask).* → Compare **order 2** [C] a song or something similar which someone has asked to be included in a show or on the radio: *The next song is a request* ***from/for*** *Roz in Oxford.*

▸verb [T] formal B1 to ask for something politely or officially: [+ that] *We requested* ***that*** *the next meeting be held on a Friday.* ◦ [+ obj + to infinitive] *Visitors are requested not* ***to*** *walk on the grass.* ◦ *I requested a taxi for eight o'clock.*

requiem (mass) /ˌrek.wi.əmˈmæs/ noun [C] **1** a MASS (= a Christian ceremony) at which people honour and pray for a dead person **2** a piece of music written for this ceremony: *Mozart's/Verdi's Requiem*

R

require /rɪˈkwaɪəʳ/ US /-ˈkwaɪr/ **verb** [T] B1 to need something or make something necessary: *Please phone this number if you require any further information.* ◦ *Skiing at 80 miles per hour requires total concentration.* ◦ [+ obj + to infinitive] *Bringing up children often requires you* ***to*** *put their needs first.* ◦ *You are required by law to stop your car after an accident.* ◦ [+ that] *The rules require* ***that*** *you bring only one guest to the dinner.*

> **!** Common mistake: **require or request?**
>
> **Warning:** choose the right word!
>
> To say that someone has politely or officially asked for something, don't use 'require', use **request**:
>
> ~~*I am sending you the information you required in your letter.*~~
>
> *I am sending you the information you requested in your letter.*

requirement /rɪˈkwaɪə.mənt/ US /-ˈkwaɪr-/ **noun** [C] B2 something that you must do, or something you need: *A good degree is a minimum requirement* ***for*** *many jobs.* ◦ [+ that] *It is a legal requirement* ***that*** *you have insurance for your car.* ◦ *Students who fail to* ***meet*** *the requirements (****of*** *the course) will fail.*

requisite /ˈrek.wɪ.zɪt/ **adj; noun**

▸**adj** [before noun] formal necessary or needed for a particular purpose: *He lacked the requisite* ***skills*** *for the job.* ◦ *The requisite* ***number*** *of countries have now ratified the convention.*

▸**noun** [C usually plural] formal an important necessary thing: *A good book is a requisite* ***for*** *long journeys.* ◦ *Self-esteem, self-judgment and self-will are said to be the three requisites* ***of*** *independence.*

requisition /ˌrek.wɪˈzɪʃ.ən/ **verb; noun**

▸**verb** [T] to officially request or take something: *The army requisitioned all the cars and trucks they could find.*

▸**noun** [C or U] the act of officially asking for or taking something: *The staff* ***made a*** *requisition* ***for*** *new chairs and desks.*

requite /rɪˈkwaɪt/ **verb** [T] formal to give or do something in return for something given to you or done for you: *Requited* ***love*** *is not enough to sustain a long-term relationship.*

rerelease /ˌriː.rɪˈliːs/ **verb; noun**

▸**verb** [T] to make a record or film available for people to buy or see for a second time: *There are plans to rerelease all the band's albums on download.*

▸**noun 1** [C or U] the act of rereleasing a record or film: *After a recent rerelease, sales of the album increased to more than 20,000.* **2** [C] a record or film that has been rereleased: *I went to see the rerelease of 'The Jungle Book'.*

reroute /ˌriːˈruːt/ US /-ˈraʊt/ **verb** [T] to change the route of something: *The plan entails rerouting* ***traffic*** *through a tunnel to create a vast pedestrian area around Al-Azhar.*

rerun **verb; noun**

▸**verb** [T] /ˌriːˈrʌn/ (present participle **rerunning**, past tense **reran**, past participle **rerun**) to show a television programme, film, etc. again: *The James Bond films are always being rerun on television.*

▸**noun** /ˈriː.rʌn/ **1** [C] a programme or film that has already been shown before on television: *This week's films are all reruns.* **2** [C usually singular] something that happens or is done again: *The Popular Party is demanding a rerun* ***of*** *last week's presidential poll.*

resat /ˌriːˈsæt/ past simple and past participle of **resit**

reschedule /ˌriːˈʃed.juːl/ US /-ˈskedʒ.uːl/ **verb** [T] **1** to agree a new and later date for something to happen: *I rescheduled my doctor's appointment* ***for*** *later in the week.* **2** specialized to agree that money owed can be paid back at a later date: *Banks have rescheduled the* ***debts*** *of many Third-World countries.*

rescind /rɪˈsɪnd/ **verb** [T] formal to make a law, agreement, order, or decision no longer have any (legal) power

rescission /rɪˈsɪʒ.ən/ **noun** [C or U] specialized the act of officially ending a law, taking back a decision, or saying that an agreement no longer exists

rescue /ˈres.kjuː/ **verb; noun**

▸**verb** [T] B1 to help someone or something out of a dangerous, harmful, or unpleasant situation: *The lifeboat rescued the sailors* ***from*** *the sinking boat.* ◦ *The government has refused to rescue the company* ***from*** *bankruptcy.* • **rescuer** /-əʳ/ US /-ɚ/ **noun** [C] *Two of the rescuers died in a second earthquake.*

▸**noun** [C or U] B1 the act of helping someone out of a dangerous or unpleasant situation: *Lifeboats carry out many rescues every month.* ◦ *We huddled together on the cliff ledge, waiting for rescue.* ◦ *I didn't know anybody at the party, but the hostess* ***came to*** *my rescue (= helped me out of a difficult situation) by introducing me to a few people.*

> Word partners for **rescue noun**
>
> a rescue ***attempt/effort/mission/operation*** • a rescue ***boat/helicopter*** • a rescue ***team/worker*** • the rescue ***of*** sb/sth

research **noun; verb**

▸**noun** [U, plural] /rɪˈsɜːtʃ/, /ˈriː.sɜːtʃ/ US /ˈriː.sɝːtʃ/ (also **researches**) B1 a detailed study of a subject, especially in order to discover (new) information or reach a (new) understanding: *scientific/medical research* ◦ *a research student/assistant/laboratory* ◦ *They are* ***carrying out/conducting/doing*** *some fascinating research* ***into/on*** *the language of dolphins.* ◦ *His researches in the field of disease prevention produced unexpected results.*

> **!** Common mistake: **research**
>
> **Warning:** Choose the right verb!
>
> Don't say 'make research', say **do/carry out/conduct research**:
>
> ~~*The company makes research into alternative energy sources.*~~
>
> *The company does research into alternative energy sources.*

> **!** Common mistake: **research**
>
> In its main meaning, **research** cannot be used with **a** or **an**.
>
> To talk about an amount of **research**, do not say 'a research', say **research**, **some research**, or **a lot of research**:
>
> ~~*He has done an interesting research into animal behaviour.*~~
>
> *He has done some interesting research into animal behaviour.*
>
> To talk about **research** in the singular, you can say **a piece of research**:
>
> *I read a very interesting piece of research on the environment.*

▸**verb** [I or T] /rɪˈsɜːtʃ/ US /-ˈsɝːtʃ/ B2 to study a subject in detail, especially in order to discover new information or reach a new understanding: *She's researching* ***into*** *possible cures for AIDS.* ◦ *Journalists were frantically researching the new prime minister's background,*

> **Word partners for research noun**
>
> *carry out/conduct/do* research • research *indicates/proves/reveals/suggests* sth • research *focuses on* sth • *detailed/extensive/in-depth* research • *current/the latest/new/recent* research • research *into/on* sth • *according to* research • a research *assistant/grant/project/programme* • research *findings*

family, and interests. • **researcher** /-ˈsɜː.tʃəʳ/ (US) /-ˈsɝː.tʃɚ/ **noun** [C] B2 *a television/political researcher*

reˌsearch and deˈvelopment **noun** [U] (abbreviation ˌ**R and ˈD**) the part of a business that tries to find ways to improve existing products, and to develop new ones: *All our profits are re-invested in research and development.*

resell /ˌriːˈsel/ **verb** [T] (**resold**) to sell something which you previously bought: *He buys up run-down properties, fixes them up and resells them.*

resemblance /rɪˈzem.bləns/ **noun** [C or U] C2 the fact that two people or things look like each other or are similar in some other way: *There was a clear* ***family*** *resemblance* ***between*** *all the brothers.* ◦ *These prices* ***bear*** *no resemblance* ***to*** *(= are completely different from) the ones I saw printed in the newspaper.*

resemble /rɪˈzem.bl̩/ **verb** [T] C1 to look like or be like someone or something: *You resemble your mother very closely.* ◦ *After the earthquake, the city resembled a battlefield.*

resent /rɪˈzent/ **verb** [T] C2 to feel angry because you have been forced to accept someone or something that you do not like: *She bitterly resented her father's new wife.* ◦ [+ -ing verb] *He resents hav****ing*** *to explain his work to other people.* • **resentment** /-mənt/ **noun** [C or U] C2 *He feels/harbours (a) deep resentment* ***against/towards*** *his parents for his miserable childhood.*

resentful /rɪˈzent.fᵊl/ **adj** feeling angry because you have been forced to accept someone or something that you do not like: *a resentful look* ◦ *She was resentful* ***of*** *anybody's attempts to interfere in her work.* • **resentfully** /-i/ **adv** • **resentfulness** /-nəs/ **noun** [U]

reservation /ˌrez.əˈveɪ.ʃən/ (US) /-ɚ-/ **noun** THING KEPT ▷ **1** B1 [C or U] an arrangement in which something such as a seat on an aircraft or a table at a restaurant is kept for you: *I'd like to* ***make*** *a table reservation* ***for*** *two people* ***for*** *nine o'clock.* ◦ *Please* ***confirm*** *your reservation in writing by Friday.* **2** [C] an area of land made available for a particular group of people to live in: *The family lives* ***on*** *a Native American reservation.* **3** [C] (also **reserve**, US also **preserve**) an area of land in which wild animals are protected: *He's the chief warden of a big-game reservation.* DOUBT ▷ **4** C2 [C usually plural, U] a doubt or feeling of not being able to agree with or accept something completely: *Workers and employees shared deep reservations* ***about*** *the wisdom of the government's plans for the industry.* ◦ *He accepted my advice* ***without*** *reservation.*

reserve /rɪˈzɜːv/ (US) /-ˈzɝːv/ **verb; noun**

▸**verb** [T] **1** B1 to keep something for a particular purpose or time: *I reserve Mondays* ***for*** *tidying my desk and answering letters.* ◦ *These seats are reserved* ***for*** *the elderly and women with babies.* ◦ *I reserve* ***judgment*** *on this issue (= I won't give an opinion on it now) until we have more information.* **2** B1 If you reserve something such as a seat on an aircraft or a table at a restaurant, you arrange for it to be kept for your use: *I reserved a double room at the Lamb Hotel.* ◦ [+ two objects] *If you get there early, reserve me a seat/reserve a seat* ***for*** *me.*

▸**noun** SHY BEHAVIOUR ▷ **1** [U] the habit of not showing your feelings or thoughts: *I took her out for a drink and tried to break through her reserve.* KEEPING ▷ **2** C2 [C or U] the act of keeping something or a supply of something until it is needed, or a supply that you keep: *She keeps a little money* ***in*** *reserve (= for use if and when needed).* ◦ *The librarian has put the book* ***on*** *reserve* ***for*** *me (= will keep it for me when it becomes available).* ◦ *We still have a reserve of food/food reserves in case of emergency.* AREA OF LAND ▷ **3** B2 [C] (also **reservation**, US also **preserve**) an area of land kept in its natural state, especially for wild animals to live in and be protected: *a* ***nature/game/wildlife*** *reserve* EXTRA PERSON ▷ **4** [C] in sports, an extra player who is ready to play if needed: *We had two reserves in case anyone was injured.* **5 the reserves** [plural] a group of people who are not permanently in the armed forces but are used only if needed: *They will* ***call up*** *the reserves.* DOUBT ▷ **6** [U] formal a feeling of doubt about someone or something: *I can recommend him to you* ***without*** *reserve.* LOWEST PRICE ▷ **7** [C usually singular] (also **reserve price**) the lowest amount of money the owners will accept for something being sold, especially at AUCTION (= public sale): *A rare Stradivarius violin failed to* ***reach*** *its reserve price (= no one offered to pay it) when put up for auction on Tuesday.* ◦ *We set/put a reserve* ***of*** *£50* ***on*** *the picture.*

reserved /rɪˈzɜːvd/ (US) /-ˈzɝːvd/ **adj** PERSON ▷ **1** B2 describes people who do not often talk about or show their feelings or thoughts: *a quiet, reserved woman* KEPT ▷ **2** Reserved tickets, seats, etc. are ones which someone has arranged to be kept for them: *May I sit here, or is this seat/table reserved?*

reservist /rɪˈzɜː.vɪst/ (US) /-ˈzɝː-/ **noun** [C] a person who is trained as a soldier and is ready to fight in the army if needed

reservoir /ˈrez.ə.vwɑːʳ/ (US) /-ɚ.vwɑːr/ **noun** [C] **1** a place for storing liquid, especially a natural or artificial lake providing water for a city or other area **2** a large supply of something: *The universities constitute a reservoir* ***of*** *expert knowledge.*

ˈreset (ˌbutton) **noun** [C] a button or switch on a computer that allows you to turn the computer off and then on again when a program does not work correctly

resettle /ˌriːˈset.l̩/ (US) /-ˈset̬-/ **verb** [I or T] to (be helped or forced to) move to another place to live: *His family originally came from Ireland, but resettled* ***in*** *the US in the 19th century.* ◦ *The US government forcibly resettled the Native Americans* ***in*** *reservations.* • **resettlement** /-mənt/ **noun** [U] *the resettlement of refugees*

reshape /ˌriːˈʃeɪp/ **verb** [T] to shape something again or differently

reshuffle **noun; verb**

▸**noun** [C] /ˈriːˌʃʌf.l̩/ an occasion when the positions of people or things within a particular group are changed: *They expect a Cabinet reshuffle in the summer.* ◦ *a* ***government/management*** *reshuffle*

▸**verb** [T] /ˌriːˈʃʌf.l̩/ to change the positions of people or things within a particular group: *to reshuffle the deck/cards* ◦ *The prime minister is expected to reshuffle his ministerial team next month.*

reside /rɪˈzaɪd/ **verb** [I usually + adv/prep] formal to live, have your home, or stay in a place: *The family now resides in southern France.*

PHRASAL VERB **reside in sth/sb** If a power or quality resides in someone or something, they have that

R

power or quality: *The power to sack employees resides in the Board of Directors.*

residence /ˈrez.ɪ.dᵊns/ **noun** [C] formal **1** C2 a home: *the Governor's* ***official*** *residence* **2 in residence** officially staying or living somewhere: *The Queen is in residence at the Palace this week.* **3 author/poet/artist in residence** an AUTHOR (= writer), poet, or artist who is employed at a school or college, etc. for a short period **4 take up residence/residency somewhere** to go to live somewhere: *She took up residence* ***in*** *Canada.* ◦ *She took up permanent residency abroad.*

residency /ˈrez.ɪ.dᵊn.si/ **noun** [U] formal the fact of living in a place: *There is a residency requirement for obtaining citizenship.*

resident /ˈrez.ɪ.dᵊnt/ **noun; adj**

▸**noun** [C] **HOME** ▷ **1** B2 a person who lives or has their home in a place: *a resident of the UK/Australia* ◦ *The* ***local*** *residents were angry at the lack of parking spaces.* ◦ *The hotel bar was only* ***open to*** *residents (= to people staying at the hotel).* **MEDICAL** ▷ **2** US Austalian a doctor who is still training, and who works in a hospital: *She's a first-year resident in oncology at Boston General Hospital.* → See also **houseman**

▸**adj 1** C1 living or staying in a place: *She's resident abroad/in Moscow.* **2** [before noun] describes someone who has a special skill or quality in a group or organization: *She is the university's resident* ***expert*** *on Italian literature.* ◦ humorous *Tony is the company's resident clown.*

residential /ˌrez.ɪˈden.ʃᵊl/ **adj 1** B2 A residential road, area, etc. has only private houses, not offices and factories. **2** C2 A residential job, position, course, etc. is one for which you live at the same place where you work or study. **3** relating to where you live or have lived: *You must satisfy the residential qualifications to get a work permit.*

residual /rɪˈzɪd.ju.əl/ US /-ˈzɪdʒ-/ **adj** remaining after most of something has gone: *I still felt some residual bitterness ten years after my divorce.*

residue /ˈrez.ɪ.djuː/ US /-ə.duː/ **noun** [C usually singular] **1** formal the part that is left after the main part has gone or been taken away, or a substance that remains after a chemical process such as EVAPORATION: *She cut off the best meat and threw away the residue.* ◦ *The white residue* ***in/on*** *the kettle is a result of minerals in the water.* **2** legal the part of a dead person's money and property that is left after taxes, debts, etc. have been paid: *The residue (****of*** *the estate) went to her granddaughter.*

R

resign /rɪˈzaɪn/ **verb** [I or T] B2 to give up a job or position by telling your employer that you are leaving: *He resigned* ***from*** *the company in order to take a more challenging job.* ◦ *She resigned* ***as*** *director.* ◦ *She resigned the directorship.*

IDIOM **be resigned to sth** If you are resigned to something unpleasant, you calmly accept that it will happen: *She seems resigned to los****ing*** *the race.*

PHRASAL VERB **resign yourself to sth** C2 to make yourself accept something that you do not like because you cannot change it: [+ -ing verb] *He resigned himself to liv****ing*** *alone.*

resignation /ˌrez.ɪɡˈneɪ.ʃᵊn/ **noun JOB** ▷ **1** C2 [C or U] the act of telling your employer that you are leaving your job: *There have been calls for his resignation.* ◦ *I* ***handed in/gave in/sent in*** *my resignation this morning.* **ACCEPTING** ▷ **2** C2 [U] a sad feeling of accepting something that you do not like because you cannot easily change it: *They received the news* ***with*** *resignation.*

resigned /rɪˈzaɪnd/ **adj** accepting that something you do not like will happen because you cannot change it: *a resigned look/expression/tone* • **resignedly** /-li/ **adv** *'We're going to be late again,' he said resignedly.*

resilient /rɪˈzɪl.i.ənt/ **adj** C2 able to quickly return to a previous good condition: *This rubber ball is very resilient and immediately springs back into shape.* ◦ *She's a resilient girl – she won't be unhappy for long.* • **resilience** /-əns/ **noun** [U] (formal **resiliency**)

resin /ˈrez.ɪn/ **noun** [U] a thick, sticky substance that is produced by some trees and that becomes yellow and hard after it is collected, or any of various similar substances produced by a chemical process for use in industry: *pine resin* • **resinous** /-ɪ.nəs/ **adj**

resist /rɪˈzɪst/ **verb 1** C1 [I or T] to fight against something or someone that is attacking you: *The soldiers resisted (the enemy attacks) for two days.* **2** [T] to refuse to accept or be changed by something: *The party leader resisted* ***demands*** *for his resignation.* ◦ *He tried to run away from the police and was charged with resisting* ***arrest***. ◦ *The new hybrid crops are much better at resisting* ***disease***. **3** B2 [T] to stop yourself from doing something that you want to do: *I can never resist temptation/chocolate/****the urge*** *to laugh.* ◦ [+ -ing verb] *She couldn't resist laugh****ing*** *at him in those clothes.*

resistance /rɪˈzɪs.tᵊns/ **noun 1** C2 [U] the act of fighting against something that is attacking you, or refusing to accept something: *resistance* ***to*** *disease* ◦ *Government troops* ***offered*** *no resistance (****to*** *the rebels).* ◦ *There's a lot of resistance (= opposition)* ***to*** *the idea of a united Europe.* **2** [U] a force that acts to stop the progress of something or make it slower: *The car's speed was reduced by* ***air/wind*** *resistance.* **3** [C or U] specialized the degree to which a substance prevents the flow of an electric current through it: *Copper has (a) low resistance.*

IDIOM **the path of least resistance** (UK usually **the line of least resistance**) the easiest way to continue: *I* ***took*** *the path of least resistance and agreed with the others.*

the Reˈsistance noun an organization that secretly fights against an enemy that has taken control of its country

reˈsistance ˌtraining noun [U] the activity of lifting heavy objects for exercise, especially to improve the strength of the muscles

resistant /rɪˈzɪs.tᵊnt/ **adj NOT ACCEPTING** ▷ **1** not wanting to accept something, especially changes or new ideas: *Why are you so resistant* ***to*** *change?* **NOT AFFECTED** ▷ **2** not harmed or affected by something: *a stain-resistant carpet* ◦ *a disease-resistant variety of tomato*

resistor /rɪˈzɪs.təʳ/ US /-tɚ/ **noun** [C] specialized a part of an electrical CIRCUIT designed to produce a particular amount of resistance to the flow of current

resit /ˌriːˈsɪt/ **verb** [T] (present tense **resitting**, past tense and past participle **resat**) mainly UK to take an exam again: *If you fail these exams, you can resit them next year.* • **resit** /ˈriː.sɪt/ **noun** [C] *She's got to do resits* ***in*** *French and German.*

reskill /ˌriːˈskɪl/ **verb 1** [I] to learn new skills so that you can do a different job: *Many unemployed people are forced to reskill.* **2** [T] to train people to do a different job: *The company plans to reskill 300 of its engineers.*

resolute /ˈrez.ə.luːt/ **adj** formal determined in character, action, or ideas: *Their resolute opposition to new* *working methods was difficult to overcome.* ◦ *She's utterly resolute* ***in*** *her refusal to apologize.* • **resolutely** /-li/ **adv** *She resolutely refused to learn about computers.*

resolution /ˌrez.əˈluː.ʃən/ noun **DECISION** ▷ **1** Ⓒ2 [C] an official decision that is made after a group or organization have voted: *to* ***approve/adopt*** *a resolution* ◦ [+ to infinitive] *The United Nations* ***passed*** *(= voted to support) a resolution* ***to*** *increase aid to the Third World.* **2** Ⓒ2 [C] a promise to yourself to do or to not do something: [+ to infinitive] *I* ***made*** *a resolution* ***to*** *give up chocolate.* **DETERMINATION** ▷ **3** [U] (also **resoluteness**) formal approving determination: *He showed great resolution* ***in*** *facing the robbers.* **SOLVING** ▷ **4** Ⓒ2 [S or U] formal the act of solving or ending a problem or difficulty: *a successful resolution* ***to*** *the crisis* **DETAIL** ▷ **5** [U] specialized the ability of a MICROSCOPE, or a television or computer screen, to show things clearly and with a lot of detail: *a* ***high/low*** *resolution image* **SEPARATION** ▷ **6** [U] specialized the act of separating or being separated into clearly different parts: *the resolution of oil* ***into*** *bitumen and tar*

resolve /rɪˈzɒlv/ Ⓤⓢ /-ˈzɑːlv/ verb; noun

▸verb **SOLVE** ▷ **1** Ⓒ1 [T] to solve or end a problem or difficulty: *Have you resolved the* ***problem*** *of transport yet?* ◦ *The couple resolved their* ***differences*** *and made an effort to get along.* **DECIDE** ▷ **2** [I] formal to make a decision formally or with determination: [+ that] *She resolved* ***that*** *she would never speak to him again.* ◦ [+ adv/prep] *After hours of argument, they resolved* ***against*** *taking legal action.* ◦ [+ to infinitive] *The company resolved* ***to*** *take no further action against the thieves.* → See also **resolute**

PHRASAL VERB **resolve sth into sth** specialized to separate something into different parts: *There was a blur of sound, which slowly resolved it****self*** *into different words.*

▸noun [U] formal Ⓒ2 strong determination: *to* ***weaken/strengthen/test*** *someone's resolve*

resolved /rɪˈzɒlvd/ Ⓤⓢ /-ˈzɑːlvd/ adj [after verb] formal determined: [+ to infinitive] *He was resolved* ***to*** *ask her to marry him the next day.*

resonance /ˈrez.ən.əns/ noun **SOUND** ▷ **1** [U] the quality of being loud and clear **2** [C or U] specialized the production of a sound as a result of VIBRATION (= shaking) of another object: *magnetic resonance* **QUALITY** ▷ **3** [C or U] a feeling, thought, memory, etc. that a piece of writing or music makes you have, or the quality in a piece of writing, etc. which makes this happen: *This poem has many resonances* ***for*** *me.*

resonant /ˈrez.ən.ənt/ adj **SOUND** ▷ **1** clear and loud, or causing sounds to be clear and loud: *a deep, resonant voice* ◦ *a resonant concert hall* → See also **resound** **QUALITY** ▷ **2** making you think of a similar experience or memory: *We felt privileged to be the first group of Western visitors to enter the historic palace, resonant* ***with*** *past conflicts.*

resonate /ˈrez.ən.eɪt/ verb [I] **MAKE SOUND** ▷ **1** to produce, increase, or fill with sound, by VIBRATING (= shaking) objects that are near: *His voice resonated in the empty church.* ◦ *The noise of the bell resonated* ***through*** *the building.* → Compare **resound** **HAVE QUALITY/EFFECT** ▷ **2** to be filled with a particular quality: *The building resonates* ***with*** *historic significance.* **3** to continue to have a powerful effect or value: *The significance of those great stories resonates down the centuries.* **4** If an experience or memory resonates, it makes you think of another similar one: *Her* ***experiences*** *resonate powerfully* ***with*** *me, living, as I do, in a similar family situation.*

resonator /ˈrez.ən.eɪ.təʳ/ Ⓤⓢ /-t̬ɚ/ noun [C] specialized a device, for example in a musical instrument, which makes sounds resonate

resort /rɪˈzɔːt/ Ⓤⓢ /-ˈzɔːrt/ noun; verb

▸noun **PLACE** ▷ **1** Ⓑ1 [C] a place where many people go for rest, sport, or another stated purpose: *a* ***tourist*** *resort* ◦ *a* ***holiday*** (US ***vacation***) *resort* ◦ *a* ***seaside/beach*** *resort* ◦ *a* ***ski*** *resort* **ACTION** ▷ **2** [U] the fact that you have to do something because there is no other way of achieving something: *He got hold of the money legally, without resort* ***to*** *violence.*

IDIOM **be your last resort** Ⓒ2 to be the only person or thing that might be able to help you, when every other person or possibility has failed

▸verb

PHRASAL VERB **resort to sth** Ⓒ2 to do something that you do not want to do because you cannot find any other way of achieving something: *I had to resort to violence/threats to get my money.* ◦ [+ -ing verb] *When she didn't answer the phone, I resorted to calling up to her from the street.*

resound /rɪˈzaʊnd/ verb [I] to sound loudly or for a long time, or (of a place) to be filled with sound: *The noise of the fire alarm resounded* ***through/throughout*** *the building.* ◦ *The concert hall resounded* ***with*** *cheers and applause.* → See also **resonate**

resounding /rɪˈzaʊn.dɪŋ/ adj [before noun] **LOUD** ▷ **1** loud: *Supporters gave the team three resounding cheers.* **GREAT** ▷ **2** very great: *The plan was a resounding* ***success****/failure.* • **resoundingly** /-li/ adv

resource /rɪˈzɔːs/, /ˈriː.sɔːs/ Ⓤⓢ /ˈriː.sɔːrs/ noun; verb

▸noun **1** Ⓑ2 [C usually plural] a useful or valuable possession or quality of a country, organization, or person: *The country's greatest resource is the dedication of its workers.* ◦ *Britain's mineral resources include coal and gas deposits.* **2** [U] formal for **resourcefulness**

IDIOM **have inner resources** to have the ability to help yourself manage or achieve something: *He can't cope with difficult situations on his own – he has no inner resources.*

▸verb [T] to provide an organization or department with money or equipment: *The school must be properly resourced* ***with*** *musical instruments and audio equipment.* • **resourced** /rɪˈzɔːst/, /ˈriː.sɔːst/ Ⓤⓢ /ˈriː.sɔːrst/ **adj** *It is widely acknowledged that the welfare system is* ***under****-resourced.*

resourceful /rɪˈzɔː.sfəl/ Ⓤⓢ /-ˈsɔːr-/ adj approving Ⓒ2 skilled at solving problems and making decisions on your own: *She's a very resourceful manager.* • **resourcefully** /-i/ adv

resourcefulness /rɪˈzɔː.sfəl.nəs/ Ⓤⓢ /-ˈsɔːr-/ noun [U] (formal **resource**) the ability to make decisions and act on your own: *This film reveals their resourcefulness* ***in*** *overcom****ing*** *appalling weather and treacherous terrain.*

respect /rɪˈspekt/ noun; verb

▸noun **ADMIRATION** ▷ **1** Ⓑ1 [U] admiration felt or shown for someone or something that you believe has good ideas or qualities: *I* ***have*** *great/the greatest respect* ***for*** *his ideas, although I don't agree with them.* ◦ *She is a formidable figure who* ***commands*** *a great deal of respect (= who is greatly admired by others).* ◦ *New teachers have to* ***earn/gain*** *the respect* ***of*** *their students.* → See also **self-respect** **HONOUR** ▷ **2** Ⓑ1 [U] politeness, honour, and care shown towards someone or something that is considered important: *You really should treat your parents with more respect.* ◦ *She* ***has*** *no respect* ***for*** *other people's property (= she does not treat it carefully).* **3** [U] a feeling that something is right or important and you should not attempt to

R

change it or harm it: *In their senseless killing of innocent people, the terrorists have **shown** their lack of respect **for** human life.* ◦ *She grumbled that young people today **have/show** no respect **for** the **law**.* **4** [U] the feeling you show when you accept that different customs or cultures are different from your own and behave towards them in a way which would not cause offence: *She teaches the students to **have** respect **for** different races and appreciate the diversity of other cultures.* **5 sb's respects** formal polite formal greetings: *Please **convey/give** my respects **to** your parents.* FEATURE ▷ **6** B2 [C] a particular feature or detail: *This proposal differs from the last one **in** many important respects/one important respect.* ◦ ***In most** respects, the new film is better than the original.*

IDIOMS **in respect of sth** (also **with respect to sth**) B2 in connection with something: *I am writing with respect to your letter of 15 June.* • **pay your respects** formal **1** to visit someone in order to welcome them or talk to them: *We went to pay our respects **to** our new neighbours.* **2** (also **pay your last respects**) to honour someone after their death, usually by going to their funeral: *Friends and relatives came to pay their last respects **to** Mr Clarke.* • **with (all due) respect** (also **with (the greatest) respect**) used to express polite disagreement in a formal situation: *With all due respect, Minister, I cannot agree with your last statement.*

▸verb [T] ADMIRE ▷ **1** B1 to feel or show admiration for someone or something that you believe has good ideas or qualities: *I deeply respect David **for** what he has achieved.* **2 respect yourself** to be proud of your own qualities or achievements HONOUR ▷ **3** to treat something or someone with kindness and care: *to respect someone's feelings* ◦ *We should respect the environment and not pollute it.* **4** B2 to accept the importance of someone's rights or customs and to do nothing that would harm them or cause them offence: *The agreement will respect the rights of both nations.* ◦ *I would appreciate it if you would respect my **privacy**.* **5** to accept that something is right or important and not to attempt to change it or harm it: *The president pledged to respect the existing frontiers between the two countries.* **6** to think that it is important to obey a law or rule: *I was always taught to respect the law.* **7 respect sb's wishes** B2 to do what someone has asked to have done: *His children respected his **last** wishes and held a simple funeral for him.*

respectability /rɪˌspek.təˈbɪl.ɪ.ti/ (US) /-ə.t̬i/ noun [U] the quality of being considered socially acceptable: *an attempt to **gain** international respectability* ◦ *The company operates out of modern offices to create an **air of** respectability.*

respectable /rɪˈspek.tə.bl̩/ adj **1** B2 considered to be socially acceptable because of your good character, appearance or behaviour: *a respectable young woman from a good family* ◦ *This part of the city has become quite respectable in the last ten years.* **2** C2 describes an amount or quality that it is large enough or of a good enough standard to be acceptable: *She earns a respectable salary.* ◦ *The final score was a respectable 2–1.*

IDIOM **make yourself respectable** humorous to put on clothes so that you are in a suitable state to meet someone: *Could you wait a minute while I make myself respectable?*

respectably /rɪˈspek.tə.bli/ adv **1** in a respectable way **2** in a way which achieves a reasonable result: *The car performs respectably on the motorway, although it is slightly noisy.* ◦ *It is a small-budget film, but it has done respectably at the box office.*

respected /rɪˈspek.tɪd/ adj B2 admired by many people for your qualities or achievements: *a highly respected figure/politician/doctor* ◦ *the country's most respected daily newspaper* ◦ *He is very **well** respected in the business world.*

respecter /rɪˈspek.təʳ/ (US) /-tɚ/ noun [C] **1** someone who thinks that something is very important: *He is a great respecter **of** tradition.* **2 be no respecter of sth** to treat or affect everyone in the same way: *Air pollution is **no** respecter **of** national frontiers.*

respectful /rɪˈspekt.fᵊl/ adj ADMIRATION ▷ **1** C1 showing admiration for someone or something: *'We're so pleased to meet you at last,' he said in a respectful tone of voice.* → Opposite **disrespectful** HONOUR ▷ **2** C1 showing politeness or honour to someone or something: *There was a respectful two-minute silence as we remembered the soldiers who had died in the war.* **3 be respectful of sth** to accept that something is important and not to try to change it or cause offence: *He taught his children to be respectful of other cultures.*

respectfully /rɪˈspekt.fᵊl.i/ adv POLITE ▷ **1** C2 in a way that shows you want to be polite or honour someone: *When she was asked if she had any ambition to become prime minister, she respectfully (= politely) declined to answer the question.* ◦ *As the body was carried through the crowd, people drew back respectfully (= to show their respect).* ADMIRATION ▷ **2** C2 in a way that shows you admire someone or something

IDIOM **Respectfully yours** a very formal and polite way of ending a letter

respective /rɪˈspek.tɪv/ adj [before noun] C1 relating or belonging to each of the separate people or things you have just mentioned: *Everyone would go into the hall for assembly and then afterwards we'd go to our respective classes.* • **respectively** /-li/ adv *In the 200 metres, Lizzy and Sarah came first and third respectively (= Lizzy won the race and Sarah was third).*

respiration /ˌres.pɪˈreɪ.ʃᵊn/ noun [U] formal or specialized breathing: *Her respiration was slow and difficult.* ◦ *The diaphragm is the principal muscle of respiration.* → See also **artificial respiration**

respirator /ˈres.pɪ.reɪ.təʳ/ (US) /-tɚ/ noun [C] **1** artificial breathing equipment: *Doctors put the patient **on** a respirator.* **2** a device worn over the mouth and nose to prevent harmful substances from being breathed in: *The firefighters wore respirators to help them breathe in the smoke-filled house.*

respiratory /rɪˈspɪr.ə.tᵊr.i/ (US) /ˈres.pɚ.ə.tɔːr.i/ adj [before noun] formal or specialized relating to breathing: *Smoking can cause respiratory **diseases**.*

reˈspiratory ˌsystem noun [C usually singular] the organs which make it possible for you to breathe

respire /rɪˈspaɪəʳ/ (US) /-ˈspaɪr/ verb [I] specialized to breathe

respite /ˈres.paɪt/ noun formal **1** [U] a pause or rest from something difficult or unpleasant: *We worked for hours without respite.* **2** [S] a useful delay before something unpleasant happens: *Their teacher was away, so they had a day's respite before their essays were due.*

resplendent /rɪˈsplen.dᵊnt/ adj literary having a very bright or beautiful appearance: *the queen's resplendent purple robes* ◦ *I saw Anna at the other end of the room, resplendent **in** a red cocktail dress.* • **resplendence** /-dᵊns/ noun [U] • **resplendently** /-li/ adv

respond /rɪˈspɒnd/ (US) /-ˈspɑːnd/ verb [I] **1** B2 to say or

R

do something as a reaction to something that has been said or done: [+ speech] *To every question, he responded 'I don't know.'* ◦ *I asked her what the time was, but she didn't respond.* ◦ *He responded* **by** *marching off and slamming the door behind him.* ◦ *How did she respond* **to** *the news?* ◦ [+ that] *When the tax office wrote to me demanding unpaid income tax, I responded* **that** *I had been working abroad since 1998.* ◦ *The police respond* **to** *emergencies (= arrive and are ready to deal with emergencies) in just a few minutes.* **2 respond to sth** If diseases or patients respond to treatment, the treatment begins to cure them: *It remains to be seen whether the cancer will respond to treatment.* ◦ *For patients who do not respond to drug treatment, surgery is a possible option.*

respondent /rɪˈspɒn.dənt/ (US) /-ˈspɑːn-/ **noun** [C] **1** specialized a person who answers a request for information: *In a recent opinion poll, a majority of respondents were against nuclear weapons.* **2** legal in a court case, the person who a PETITION (= a formal letter to the court asking for a particular action) is made against, especially in a DIVORCE case: *She divorced the respondent on the grounds of unreasonable behaviour.* → Compare **co-respondent**

response /rɪˈspɒns/ (US) /-ˈspɑːns/ **noun 1** (B2) [C or U] an answer or reaction: *Responses* **to** *our advertisement have been disappointing.* ◦ *Her proposals met with an enthusiastic response.* ◦ *I looked in her face for some response, but she just stared at me blankly.* ◦ *Management have granted a ten percent pay rise* **in** *response* **to** *union pressure.* **2** [C] any of the parts sung or said, in some religious ceremonies, by the people in answer to the parts said or sung by the priest

> **Word partners for response**
>
> *draw/elicit/evoke/provoke* a response • *get/have/receive* a response • an *encouraging/favourable/good/positive* response • an *angry/negative/poor* response • a *direct/quick/rapid* response • sb's *immediate/initial/instinctive* response • sb's response *to* sth • *in* response **to** sth

reˈsponse ˌtime noun [C or U] the amount of time that a person or system takes to react or to deal with something: *The ambulance service is trying to reduce delays in response time.*

responsibility /rɪˌspɒn.sɪˈbɪl.ɪ.ti/ (US) /-ˌspɑːn.səˈbɪl.ə.t̬i/ **noun** DUTY ▷ **1** (B2) [C or U] something that it is your job or duty to deal with: [+ to infinitive] *It's her responsibility* **to** *ensure the project finishes on time.* ◦ *She takes her responsibilities as a nurse very seriously.* **2 have responsibility** to be in a position of authority over someone and to have a duty to make certain that particular things are done: *Who has responsibility here?* ◦ *Jenny, you have responsibility* **for** *clearing up the room after the class.* **3 have a responsibility to sb** to have a duty to work for or help someone who is in a position of authority over you: *The company says it cannot cut its prices any more because it has a responsibility to its shareholders.* BLAME ▷ **4** (B2) [U] blame for something that has happened: *Terrorists have* **claimed** *responsibility* **for** *(= stated that they caused) yesterday's bomb attack.* ◦ *The minister* **took/accepted** *full responsibility* **for** *(= admitted that he was to blame for) the disaster and resigned.* GOOD JUDGMENT ▷ **5** [U] good judgment and the ability to act correctly and make decisions on your own: *He has no sense of responsibility.* ◦ *The job* **carries** *a lot of responsibility (= it involves making important decisions).*

IDIOM **act/do sth on your own responsibility** formal to act without being told to by someone in authority

> **Common mistake: responsibility**
>
> **Warning:** Check your spelling!
>
> **Responsibility** is one of the 50 words most often spelled wrongly by learners.

> **Word partners for responsibility (DUTY)**
>
> *have* a responsibility • responsibility *falls on* sb • *share* responsibility • *abdicate/avoid/shirk* responsibility • a *big/heavy/huge* responsibility

> **Word partners for responsibility (BLAME)**
>
> *accept/bear/shoulder/take* responsibility • *admit/claim* responsibility • *full/total* responsibility • responsibility *for* sth

responsible /rɪˈspɒn.sɪ.bl̩/ (US) /-ˈspɑːn-/ **adj** DUTY ▷ **1 be responsible for sb/sth/doing sth** (B1) to have control and authority over something or someone and the duty of taking care of it or them: *Paul is directly responsible* **for** *the efficient running of the office.* ◦ *Her department is responsible* **for** *overseeing the councils.* **2 be responsible to sb/sth** to be controlled by someone or something: *In Australia, the prime minister and the Cabinet are responsible* **to** *the House of Representatives.*

> **Common mistake: responsible**
>
> The correct preposition to use after **responsible** is **for**.
>
> Don't say 'responsible of/about something', say **responsible for something**:
>
> ~~*We are all responsible of our own decisions.*~~
>
> *We are all responsible for our own decisions.*

BLAME ▷ **3 be responsible for sth/doing sth** (B2) to be the person who caused something to happen, especially something bad: *Who is responsible for this terrible mess?* ◦ *Last month's bad weather was responsible for the crop failure.* **4 hold sb/sth responsible** to blame someone or something: *He held me personally responsible whenever anything went wrong in the project.* **5 be responsible for your actions** to be in control of yourself so that you can fairly be blamed for your bad actions: *The defendant was depressed and therefore not fully responsible for her* **own** *actions.* GOOD JUDGMENT ▷ **6** (B2) having good judgment and the ability to act correctly and make decisions on your own: *a hard-working and responsible employee* ◦ *Let's stay calm and try to behave like responsible adults.* ◦ *Many big companies are now becoming more responsible* **about** *the way they operate.* → Opposite **irresponsible 7** (B2) A responsible job or position involves making important decisions or doing important things. • **responsibly** /-bli/ **adv**

> **Common mistake: responsible**
>
> **Warning:** Check your spelling!
>
> **Responsible** is one of the 50 words most often spelled wrongly by learners. Remember: the correct spelling ends in 'ible', and not 'able'.

responsive /rɪˈspɒn.sɪv/ (US) /-ˈspɑːn-/ **adj** making a positive and quick reaction to something or someone: *a responsive engine* ◦ *a responsive audience* ◦ *She wasn't responsive* **to** *questioning.* ◦ *The disease has proved responsive* **to** *the new treatment.* → Opposite **unresponsive** • **responsively** /-li/ **adv** • **responsiveness** /-nəs/ **noun** [U]

rest /rest/ **verb; noun**

▸**verb** STOP ▷ **1** (B1) [I or T] to (cause someone or

R

something to) stop doing a particular activity or stop being active for a period of time in order to relax and get back your strength: *The doctor told him that he should rest for a few days.* ◦ *He looked away from the computer screen to rest his eyes.* ◦ *She promised that she would not rest (= would not stop looking) until the murderer of her son was caught and imprisoned.* → See also **rest up** **2 be resting** informal to be an actor who does not have any work: *Over 90 percent of professional actors are resting at any given time.* **3 I rest my case** (also **my case rests**) said by lawyers in a law court when they have finished the explanation of their case SUPPORT ▷ **4** [I or T, usually + adv/prep] to lie or lean on something, or to put something on something else so that its weight is supported: *She rested her head **on** my shoulder.* ◦ *The bicycle was resting **against** the wall.* REMAIN ▷ **5** [I] formal to remain in a particular state or place: *We must talk to the council about the problem – the matter cannot be allowed to rest here (= further action must be taken).*

IDIOMS **let sth rest** informal to not talk about or mention a particular subject: *After he had told his friends he was writing a novel, they wouldn't let the subject rest.* • **rest easy** (also **rest assured**) used to tell someone not to worry and that you are in control of the situation: *'Rest assured, Mrs. Cooper' said the police officer. 'We will find your son for you.'* • **rest in peace** **1** said to express the hope that someone's spirit has found peace after they have died: *She was a decent and compassionate woman: **may** she rest in peace.* **2** (abbreviation **RIP**) often written on a GRAVESTONE • **rest on your laurels** to be satisfied with your achievements and not to make an effort to do anything else: *Just because you've got your degree doesn't mean you can rest on your laurels.*

PHRASAL VERBS **rest on sb/sth** If your eyes rest on something or someone when you are looking around an area, you start looking only at that particular object or person: *Her eyes rested on a small wooden box at the back of the shop.* • **rest on/upon sth** formal If something rests on a particular idea, belief, or fact, it is based on it or needs it in order for it to be true: *Christianity rests on the belief that Jesus was the son of God.* • **rest on/upon sb/sth** formal to depend on someone or something: *Our success rests on an increase in sales.* • **rest up** to relax in order to have strength for something: *Why don't you take a nap to rest up **for** the party?* • **rest with sb** formal If a responsibility or decision rests with someone, they are responsible for it: *The authority to call an emergency meeting rests with the president.* • **rest with sb/sth** to depend on someone or something: *Our hopes rest with you.*

R

▸noun OTHER PART ▷ **1 the rest** [S, + sing/pl verb] A2 the other things, people, or parts that remain or that have not been mentioned: *I've got two bright students, but the rest are average.* ◦ *I'll keep a third of the money and the rest is for you.* ◦ *Have you got anything planned for the rest **of** the day?* STOP ▷ **2** A2 [C or U] a period of time in which you relax, do not do anything active, or sleep: *After they had carried the piano up the stairs, they stopped for a rest.* ◦ *The doctor prescribed some pills and told her to **get/have** a week's rest.* **3** [C] specialized a period of silence between musical notes, or a symbol which represents this: *a minim rest* **4 at rest a** describes someone or something that is not doing anything active, or not moving: *Her heartbeat is only 55 at rest.* **b** used as a polite way to say that someone is dead: *Your father was a very troubled man, but he's at rest now.* **5 come to rest** to stop, usually in a particular place: *The car hit the kerb, rolled over and came to rest in a ditch.* SUPPORT ▷ **6** [C] an object which supports the weight of something: *I used a pile of books as a rest **for** my telescope.* → See also **headrest, armrest**

IDIOMS **(and) all the rest** informal used at the end of a phrase or list to refer to other things or people that belong to the same set or group and that you have not had time to mention: *June and Alison and all the rest are coming to dinner tonight.* • **for the rest** used when you have already mentioned the important parts of something and you now want to mention the other less important parts: *The salary in my new job is great, but (as) for the rest, I'm not impressed.* • **give it a rest** informal said when you want someone to stop talking about or doing something that is annoying you: *Oh, give it a rest, can't you?* • **the rest is history** everything which happened since then is well known: *The Beatles had their first hit record in 1962 and the rest is history.*

restart /ˌriːˈstɑːt/ US /-ˈstɑːrt/ **verb** [I or T] C1 to start something again: *Our car stalled and wouldn't restart.* ◦ *Please restart your computer to complete installation.*

restate /ˌriːˈsteɪt/ **verb** [T] to say something again or in a different way: *He restated his belief that the sanctions need more time to work.* • **restatement** /-mənt/ **noun** [C or U] *Her recent speech was merely a restatement **of** her widely publicized views.*

restaurant /ˈres.trɒnt/ US /-tə.rɑːnt/ **noun** [C] A1 a place where meals are prepared and served to customers

> **! Common mistake: restaurant**
>
> **Warning:** Check your spelling!
>
> **Restaurant** is one of the 50 words most often spelled wrongly by learners. Remember: the correct spelling has 'au' in the middle.

> **Word partners for restaurant**
>
> *go to* a restaurant • *manage/own/run* a restaurant • a restaurant *offers/serves/specializes in* sth • *at/in* a restaurant • a *cheap/expensive/good/posh* restaurant • a restaurant *manager/owner/worker* • the restaurant *business/industry*

ˈrestaurant ˌcar **noun** [C] UK (mainly US **ˈdining ˌcar**) a CARRIAGE of a train in which passengers are served meals

restaurateur /ˌres.tər.əˈtɜːr/ US /-tɚ.əˈtɝː/ **noun** [C] formal a person who owns and manages a restaurant

rested /ˈres.tɪd/ **adj** healthy and active after a period spent relaxing: *I came back from my trip to California **feeling** rested and rejuvenated.*

restful /ˈrest.fəl/ **adj** describes something that produces a feeling of being calm and relaxed: *I love the restful sound of the wind in the trees.* • **restfully** /-i/ **adv** • **restfulness** /-nəs/ **noun** [U] *She always thought of the house as being a place of great peace and restfulness.*

ˈrest ˌhome **noun** [C] a place where old people live and are cared for

ˈresting place **noun** [C usually singular] formal a place where someone is buried: *His **last/final** resting place was in the village where he was born.*

restitution /ˌres.tɪˈtjuː.ʃən/ US /-ˈtuː-/ **noun** [U] **1** formal the return of objects that were stolen or lost: *They are demanding the restitution **of** ancient treasures that were removed from the country in the 16th century.* **2** legal payment made for damage or loss: *The chemicals company promised to **make** full restitution **to** the victims **for** the injury to their health.*

restive /ˈres.tɪv/ **adj** formal unwilling to be controlled or be patient: *The audience was becoming restive as they waited for the performance to begin.* • **restively** /-li/ **adv** • **restiveness** /-nəs/ **noun** [U]

restless /ˈrest.ləs/ **adj** C1 unwilling or unable to stay still or to be quiet and calm, because you are worried or bored: *He's a restless type – he never stays in one country for long.* ◦ *She spent a restless night (= she did not sleep well), tossing and turning.* • **restlessly** /-li/ **adv** *She shifted restlessly in her chair.* • **restlessness** /-nəs/ **noun** [U]

restoration /ˌres.tᵊrˈeɪ.ʃᵊn/ US /-təˈreɪ-/ **noun** [C or U] the act or process of returning something to its earlier good condition or position: *The first task following the disaster was the restoration **of** clean water supplies.* ◦ *Restoration **work** on the Sistine Chapel ceiling is now complete.* ◦ *A large majority of the population is demanding the restoration **of** the former government.*

the Restoration /ˌres.tᵊrˈeɪ.ʃᵊn/ US /-təˈreɪ-/ **noun** [S] the event in British history when Charles II was made king in 1660 after a period in which there was no king or queen • **Restoration adj** [before noun] belonging to or popular during the Restoration: *Restoration comedy/architecture/art*

restorative /rɪˈstɒr.ə.tɪv/ US /-ˈstɔːr.ə.t̬ɪv/ **noun** [C] old-fashioned something which makes you feel better or more energetic if you are feeling tired or ill: *After a hard day at the office, a hot bath is a welcome restorative.* • **restorative adj** formal

restore /rɪˈstɔːʳ/ US /-ˈstɔːr/ **verb** [T] **1** B2 to return something or someone to an earlier good condition or position: *The badly neglected paintings have all been carefully restored.* ◦ *After a week in bed, she was fully restored **to** health (= she felt healthy again).* ◦ *The former leader was today restored **to** power in the first free elections for 20 years.* **2** C1 If you restore a quality or ability that someone has not had for a long time, you make it possible for them to have that quality or ability again: *Doctors have restored his sight.* ◦ *The government is trying to restore public **confidence** in its management of the economy.* **3** to bring back into use something that has been absent for a period of time: *Some people are in favour of restoring capital punishment for murderers.* **4** formal to give something that has been lost or stolen back to the person it belongs to: *The painting was restored **to** its **rightful owner**.*

restorer /rɪˈstɔː.rəʳ/ US /-ˈstɔːr.ɚ/ **noun** [C] a person who restores buildings, furniture, or paintings to their original condition: *She's a **furniture** restorer.*

restrain /rɪˈstreɪn/ **verb** [T] C1 to control the actions or behaviour of someone by force, especially in order to stop them from doing something, or to limit the growth or force of something: *When he started fighting, it took four police officers to restrain him.* ◦ *She was so angry that she could hardly restrain her**self**.* ◦ *You should try to restrain your ambitions and be more realistic.* ◦ *Growth in car ownership could be restrained by increasing taxes.*

restrained /rɪˈstreɪnd/ **adj** **1** acting in a calm and controlled way: *I was expecting him to be furious but he was very restrained.* **2** controlled: *a more restrained policy on mortgage lending* ◦ *The tone of his poetry is restrained and unemotional.*

reˈstraining ˌorder **noun** [C] legal a written instruction made by a court which FORBIDS (= does not allow) a particular action until a judge has made a decision about the matter: *She obtained a restraining order forbidding her partner from seeing their two children.*

restraint /rɪˈstreɪnt/ **noun** **1** [U] calm and controlled behaviour: *He showed admirable restraint, and refused to be provoked.* ◦ *The security forces **exercised** (= used) great restraint by not responding to hostile attacks and threats.* **2** [C or U] something which limits the freedom of someone or something, or which prevents something from growing or increasing: *government spending restraints* ◦ *Lack of space is the main restraint **on** the firm's expansion plans.* ◦ *During the recession, the government opted for a policy of pay/wage restraint rather than a reduction in public investment.* **3 keep/place sb under restraint** to keep a violent person in a way that prevents them from moving freely: *The two prisoners were kept under restraint while they were transported between prisons.*

restrict /rɪˈstrɪkt/ **verb** [T] C1 to limit the movements or actions of someone, or to limit something and reduce its size or prevent it from increasing: *measures to restrict the sale of alcohol* ◦ *The government has restricted freedom of movement into and out of the country.* ◦ *Having small children really restricts your social life.*

PHRASAL VERB **restrict yourself to sth** to limit yourself to one particular thing or activity: *If I'm driving, I restrict myself to one glass of wine.*

restricted /rɪˈstrɪk.tɪd/ **adj** **1** C1 limited, especially by official rules, laws, etc.: *Building in this area of town is restricted.* ◦ *Membership is restricted **to** (= it is only for) chief executive officers.* ◦ *Our view of the stage was restricted (= objects prevented us from seeing the whole stage).* **2** describes an area which you need official permission to enter because the police or the armed forces want to keep it secret, or because it is considered dangerous: *Wellington Barracks is a restricted area and anyone who enters should have identification.* **3** describes a document which you need official permission to read because the government wants to keep it secret

restriction /rɪˈstrɪk.ʃᵊn/ **noun** [C or U] C2 an official limit on something: *import/export/currency restrictions* ◦ ***speed/parking** restrictions* ◦ *At the turn of the century, Congress **imposed/placed** a height restriction of 13 storeys **on** all buildings in Washington.* ◦ *The president urged other countries to **lift** the trade restrictions.*

restrictive /rɪˈstrɪk.tɪv/ **adj** often disapproving C2 limiting the freedom of someone or preventing something from growing: *He is self-employed because he finds working for other people too restrictive.* ◦ *The college is not able to expand because of restrictive planning laws.*

reˌstrictive ˈpractice **noun** [C] UK specialized in industry or business, an action which limits the freedom of workers or employers: *Management accused the union of restrictive practices.*

reˌstrictive ˈtrade ˌpractice **noun** [C] specialized a business agreement between companies which controls prices or the areas in which goods are sold, preventing fair competition from other companies

restroom /ˈrest.ruːm/ **noun** [C] mainly US A2 a room with toilets that is in a public place, for example in a restaurant

restructure /ˌriːˈstrʌk.tʃəʳ/ US /-tʃɚ/ **verb** [T] C2 to organize a company, business, or system in a new way to make it operate more effectively: *The government restructured the coal industry before selling it to private owners.* • **restructuring** /-tʃᵊr.ɪŋ/ US /-tʃɚ.ɪŋ/ **noun** [C or U] *The company **underwent** restructuring and 1,500 workers lost their jobs.*

ˈrest ˌstop **noun** [C] (also **ˈrest ˌarea**) US an area next to

R

a road where people can park their vehicles, go to the toilet, eat, etc.

result /rɪˈzʌlt/ noun; verb

▸noun **EFFECT** ▷ **1** B1 [C or S] something that happens or exists because of something else: *The road has been widened, but **the** result is just more traffic.* ◦ *His broken leg is **the** direct result **of** his own carelessness.* ◦ *I tried to repaint the kitchen walls **with** disastrous results.* ◦ *To ensure **good/the best** results, use Italian tomatoes and fresh basil.* **2 as a result of sth** B2 because of something: *Profits have declined as a result of the recent drop in sales.* **3** [C usually plural] a good or pleasing effect: *We've spent a lot of money on advertising and we're beginning to see the results.* ◦ *She's an excellent coach who knows how to **get** results.* **OF TEST** ▷ **4** B1 [C] the information you get from something such as a scientific EXPERIMENT or medical test: *The results of the opinion poll showed that most women supported this action.* **5** B1 [C] the mark you receive after you have taken an exam or test: *I finished my exams yesterday, but I won't **know/get** the results until August.* **ANSWER** ▷ **6** [C] the answer to a calculation in mathematics: *We used different methods of calculation, but we both **got** the same result.* **IN COMPETITION** ▷ **7** B1 [C] the score or number of votes, showing the success or failure of the people involved, in a sports competition, election, etc.: *the results of the local elections* ◦ *the football results* ◦ *We were expecting to win, so a draw was a disappointing result for us.* **8** [C] UK informal a win in a sports competition: *The team needs a result to go through to the semifinals.* **COMPANY** ▷ **9 results** [plural] the amount of a company's sales, profit, etc. during a particular period: *Airlines reported significantly better **financial** results for the first quarter.*

> **Word partners for result noun**
>
> ***achieve/produce*** a result • ***disastrous/excellent/positive/satisfactory*** results • the ***desired*** result • the ***end/final*** result • the result ***of*** sth • ***with*** [catastrophic/disastrous] results

> **Other ways of saying result**
>
> The result of a particular influence is an **effect**:
>
> *The radiation leak has had a disastrous **effect** on the environment.*
>
> **Consequence** is used especially when the result of an action or situation is bad or inconvenient:
>
> *Failure to do proper safety checks may have serious **consequences**.*
>
> **Outcome** and **upshot** are alternatives to 'result':
>
> *It's too early to predict the **outcome** of the meeting.*
>
> *The **upshot** of the discussions is that there will be no layoffs.*
>
> The result of a process or series of events is the **end result**:
>
> *The **end result** of these changes should be a more efficient system for dealing with complaints.*
>
> **Fallout** is also used when a result is very bad:
>
> *The political **fallout** of the revelations was very damaging for the president.*
>
> A **by-product** is something unexpected that happens as a result of something else:
>
> *Unpleasant noises in the head can be a distressing **by-product** of some forms of deafness.*

▸verb [I] to happen or exist because something else has happened: *Teachers were not fully prepared for the major changes in the exam system, and chaos resulted.*

PHRASAL VERBS **result from sth** If a situation or problem results from a particular event or activity, it is caused by it: *His difficulty in walking results from a childhood illness.* • **result in sth** B2 to cause a particular situation to happen: *The fire resulted in damage to their property.* ◦ [+ -ing verb] *Icy road conditions in Teesdale resulted in two roads be**ing** closed.*

resulting /rɪˈzʌl.tɪŋ/ adj [before noun] (formal **resultant**) caused by the event or situation which you have just mentioned: *The tape was left near a magnetic source, and the resulting damage was considerable.*

resume /rɪˈzjuːm/ (US) /-ˈzuːm/ verb formal **1** C1 [I or T] If an activity resumes, or if you resume it, it starts again after a pause: *Normal services will be resumed in the spring.* ◦ [+ -ing verb] *He stopped to take a sip of water and then resumed speak**ing**.* ◦ *The talks are due to resume today.* → See also **resumption** **2** [T] If you resume a place or position that you have left for a period of time, you return to it: *to resume your post/job* ◦ *Please resume your seats, as the performance will continue in two minutes.*

résumé /ˈrez.juː.meɪ/ (US) /ˈrez.ʊ-/ noun [C] **1** a short statement of the important details of something: *She gave us a brief résumé **of** the project so far.* **2** US for **CV**

resumption /rɪˈzʌmp.ʃən/ noun [S or U] the start of something again after it has stopped: *The president called for an immediate ceasefire and **a** resumption **of** negotiations between the two sides.*

resurface /ˌriːˈsɜː.fɪs/ (US) /-ˈsɝː-/ verb **COVER** ▷ **1** [T] to put a new surface on a road: *Drivers will experience delays while stretches of the road are being resurfaced.* **APPEAR AGAIN** ▷ **2** [I] to rise to the surface of the water again: *When the divers did not resurface after an hour, three crew members dived down to look for them.* **3** [I] to appear again after being lost, stolen, or absent: *Please contact me if any of the stolen paintings resurface.* ◦ *Jill resurfaced last week, after spending the past few months doing research in the library.* **4** [I] If a memory resurfaces, you remember it again after you had forgotten about it: *Memories of his childhood resurfaced when he saw the photographs.*

resurgence /rɪˈsɜː.dʒəns/ (US) /-ˈsɝː-/ noun [S or U] formal a new increase of activity or interest in a particular subject or idea which had been forgotten for some time: *The creation of independent states has led to **a** resurgence **of** nationalism.* ◦ *resurgence **in** demand/popularity/interest*

resurgent /rɪˈsɜː.dʒənt/ (US) /-ˈsɝː-/ adj formal increasing again, or becoming popular again: *resurgent inflation* ◦ *Many people were critical of the resurgent militarism in the country.*

resurrect /ˌrez.ərˈekt/ (US) /-əˈrekt/ verb [T] **1** to bring someone back to life: *Almost all Christians believe that Jesus was resurrected **from** the dead.* **2** to bring back something into use or existence that had disappeared or ended: *Several members of the party have resurrected the idea of constitutional change.* ◦ *She has been busily trying to resurrect her Hollywood career.*

resurrection /ˌrez.ərˈek.ʃən/ (US) /-əˈrek-/ noun [U] the act of bringing something that had disappeared or ended back into use or existence

the Resurrection /ˌrez.ərˈek.ʃən/ (US) /-əˈrek-/ noun [S] In the Christian religion, the Resurrection is Jesus Christ's return to life on the third day after his death, or the return of all people to life at the end of the world.

resuscitate /rɪˈsʌs.ɪ.teɪt/ verb [T] to bring someone or something back to life or wake them: *Her heart had stopped, but the doctors successfully resuscitated her.*

resuscitation /rɪˌsʌs.ɪˈteɪ.ʃᵊn/ **noun** [U] the act of bringing someone or something back to life or waking them: *The patient suffered a cardiac arrest and died, despite an attempt at resuscitation.* → See also **mouth-to-mouth**

retail /ˈriː.teɪl/ **noun; verb**

▸**noun** [U] C1 the activity of selling goods to the public, usually in shops: *The job is open to applicants with over two years' experience in retail.* ◦ *The clothing company has six retail **outlets** (= shops) in Perth.* ◦ *$13 off the manufacturer's recommended retail **price*** → Compare **wholesale**

▸**verb** [T] **1** to sell goods to the public in shops, on the internet, etc.: *The company makes and retails moderately priced sportswear.* **2 retail at/for sth** to be sold at a particular price: *This model of computer is retailing at £650.* • **retail adv** *It's much cheaper to buy wholesale than retail.*

retailer /ˈriː.teɪ.ləʳ/ US /-lɚ/ **noun** [C] C2 a person, shop, or business that sells goods to the public: *a big electronics retailer*

ˈretail ˌpark noun [C] a shopping area on the edge of a town or city, where there are several large stores

ˌretail ˈprice ˌindex noun [S] (abbreviation **RPI**) UK a measurement of the changes in the cost of basic goods and services → Compare **consumer price index**

ˈretail ˌtherapy noun [U] humorous the act of buying special things for yourself in order to feel better when you are unhappy: *I needed a lot of retail therapy to help me get over my ex-boyfriend.*

retain /rɪˈteɪn/ **verb** [T] **1** C2 formal to keep or continue to have something: *She has lost her battle to retain **control** of the company.* ◦ *He managed to retain his dignity throughout the performance.* ◦ *She succeeded in retaining her lead in the second half of the race.* ◦ *I have a good memory and am able to retain (= remember) facts easily.* **2** formal If a substance retains something, such as heat or water, it continues to hold or contain it: *The sea retains the sun's warmth longer than the land.* → See also **retention 3** legal to get the services of a lawyer by paying them before you need them

retainer /rɪˈteɪ.nəʳ/ US /-nɚ/ **noun** [C] **1** specialized an amount of money which you pay to someone so as to be sure that they can work for you when you need them to **2** old-fashioned a servant who has usually been with the same family for a long time: *a faithful **old** retainer*

retake verb; noun

▸**verb** [T] /ˌriːˈteɪk/ (**retook, retaken**) EXAM ▷ **1** to take an exam again because you failed it the first time: *to retake your driving **test/final exams*** GET BACK ▷ **2** to take something such as a place or position into your possession again, often by force, after losing possession of it: *In the battle to retake the village, over 150 soldiers were killed.* ◦ *Finally, our team had a chance to retake the lead.* ◦ *The junta tried to retake power in 1999.* FILM ▷ **3** to take a photograph or film again

▸**noun** [C] /ˈriː.teɪk/ EXAM ▷ **1** an exam that you take again because you failed it the first time: *I'm **doing** my retakes next summer.* FILM ▷ **2** a part of a film that must be photographed again to change or improve it: *It **took** seven retakes to get the scene exactly right.*

retaliate /rɪˈtæl.i.eɪt/ **verb** [I] to hurt someone or do something harmful to them because they have done or said something harmful to you: *If someone insults you, don't retaliate as it only makes the situation worse.* ◦ *The demonstrators threw rocks at the police, who retaliated **by** firing blanks into the crowd.* ◦ *The terrorists retaliated **against** the government **with** a bomb attack.* • **retaliation** /rɪˌtæl.iˈeɪ.ʃᵊn/ **noun** [U] *The bomb attack was **in** retaliation **for** the recent arrest of two well-known terrorists.*

retaliatory /rɪˈtæl.i.ə.tᵊr.i/ US /-tɔːr.i/ **adj** describes an action that is harmful to someone who has done something to harm you: *retaliatory measures*

retard verb; noun

▸**verb** [T] /rɪˈtɑːd/ US /-ˈtɑːrd/ formal to make something slower: *A rise in interest rates would severely retard economic **growth**.*

▸**noun** [C] /ˈriː.tɑːd/ US /-tɑːrd/ offensive a stupid or mentally slow person

retardant /rɪˈtɑː.dᵊnt/ US /-ˈtɑːr-/ **noun** [C or U], **adj** (a substance) that makes the progress or growth of something slower: *Pot plants are commonly treated with (a) growth retardant so that they retain their shape.* ◦ ***fire/flame** retardant furniture (= furniture that does not burn easily)*

retardation /ˌriː.tɑːˈdeɪ.ʃᵊn/ US /-tɑːr-/ **noun** [U] formal slow development, or development that is slower than it should be: *Severe iron deficiency can cause developmental delay and growth retardation.*

retarded /rɪˈtɑː.dɪd/ US /-ˈtɑːr-/ **adj** offensive old-fashioned having had a slower mental development than other people of the same age: *mentally/emotionally retarded*

retch /retʃ/ **verb** [I] to react in a way as if you are vomiting: *The sight of blood makes him retch.*

retd adj [after noun] **1** written abbreviation for **retired 2** written abbreviation used after someone's name to show that they are no longer in one of the armed forces: *The meeting will be chaired by Colonel E. Smith (retd).*

retention /rɪˈten.ʃᵊn/ **noun** [U] formal C2 the continued use, existence, or possession of something or someone: *Two influential senators have argued for the retention of the unpopular tax.* ◦ *The retention of old technology has slowed the company's growth.* ◦ ***water/heat** retention*

retentive /rɪˈten.tɪv/ US /-t̬ɪv/ **adj** formal If you have a retentive memory or brain, you can remember things easily. → See also **anally retentive**

rethink /ˌriːˈθɪŋk/ **verb** [I or T] (**rethought, rethought**) C1 to think again about a plan, idea, or system in order to change or improve it: *Her family's disapproval made her rethink her plans.* ◦ [+ question word] *The European Commission is having to rethink **how** it can maintain farmers' incomes while cutting costs and excess production.* • **rethink** /ˈriː.θɪŋk/ **noun** [S] *This new information means we should **have a** rethink.*

reticent /ˈret.ɪ.sᵊnt/ US /ˈret̬.ə-/ **adj** formal unwilling to speak about your thoughts or feelings: *He is very reticent **about** his past.* ◦ *Most of the students were reticent **about** answering questions.* • **reticence** /-sᵊns/ **noun** [U] *His reticence **about** his past made them very suspicious.* • **reticently** /-li/ **adv**

reticulation /rɪˌtɪk.jʊˈleɪ.ʃᵊn/ **noun** [C] specialized a pattern like a net of lines and squares, or a structure of pipes or wires • **reticulated** /rɪˈtɪk.jʊ.leɪ.tɪd/ US /-t̬ɪd/ **adj** (also **reticulate**) *a reticulated pattern* ◦ *leaves with a reticulate vein structure*

retina /ˈret.ɪ.nə/ US /ˈret̬.ᵊn.ə/ **noun** [C] (plural **retinas** or **retinae**) the area at the back of the eye that receives light and sends pictures of what the eye sees to the brain • **retinal** /ˈret.ɪ.nəl/ US /ˈret̬.ᵊn.ᵊl/ **adj** *The disease can result in retinal damage and loss of vision.*

retinue /ˈret.ɪ.njuː/ US /ˈret̬.ᵊn.uː/ **noun** [C usually singular, + sing/pl verb] a group of people who travel

R

with an important person to help them: *The president travels with a large retinue of aides and bodyguards.*

retire /rɪˈtaɪəʳ/ US /-ˈtaɪr/ **verb** STOP WORKING ▷ **1** B1 [I] to leave your job or stop working because of old age or ill health: *Since retiring **from** the company, she has done voluntary work for a charity.* ◦ *He is due to retire **as** chief executive next year.* **2** [I] to stop taking part in a race or competition because of illness or injury: *She retired **from** the competition after pulling a leg muscle.* **3** [T often passive] If an employer retires an employee, they make that person leave their job, usually at a time when they are near to the age at which they would normally stop working, or because they are ill: *Following the merger, he was retired with a generous pension.* LEAVE A PLACE ▷ **4** [I] formal to leave a room or group of people and go somewhere quiet or private: *After dinner our host said, 'Shall we retire **to** the drawing room?'* **5** [I] formal or old-fashioned to go to bed: *It had been a long day, so I retired early.*

retired /rɪˈtaɪəd/ US /-ˈtaɪrd/ **adj** (written abbreviation **retd**) B2 If someone is retired, they have stopped working: *Both my parents are retired.* ◦ *He is a retired airline pilot.*

retiree /rɪˌtaɪəˈriː/ US /-ˈtaɪ.riː/ **noun** [C] US a person who has stopped working: *The neighborhood is a mixture of retirees and single professionals.*

retirement /rɪˈtaɪə.mənt/ US /-ˈtaɪr-/ **noun** [C or U] **1** B2 the act of leaving your job and stopping working, usually because you are old: *Many teachers over the age of 50 are **taking early** retirement.* ◦ *What is the normal retirement **age** in this country?* **2** B2 the period in someone's life after they have stopped working because they reached a particular age: *We wish you a long and happy retirement.*

retiring /rɪˈtaɪə.rɪŋ/ US /-ˈtaɪr.ɪŋ/ **adj** SHY ▷ **1** formal unwilling to be noticed or to be with other people: *to be **shy and** retiring* STOP WORKING ▷ **2** [before noun] describes someone who is planning to leave their job: *The match ended in disappointment for the retiring captain.*

reˈtiring ˌroom **noun** [C] Indian English a room in a bus station or railway station where a passenger can pay to stay for a few days

retort /rɪˈtɔːt/ US /-ˈtɔːrt/ **verb; noun**
▸**verb** [T] to answer someone quickly in an angry or funny way: [+ speech] *'That doesn't concern you!' she retorted.*
▸**noun** [C] a quick answer that is angry or funny: *'I'm going to tell him,' said Max. 'Just you try!' came the retort.*

retouch /ˌriːˈtʌtʃ/ **verb** [T] to make small changes to a picture, photograph, etc., especially in order to improve it: *We had the wedding photos retouched to make it seem like a sunny day.*

retrace /rɪˈtreɪs/ **verb** [T] to go back over something, for example a path or a series of past actions: *When he realized he had lost his keys, he retraced in his mind his movements that day.*

IDIOM **retrace your steps** C2 to go back to a place in the same way that you came: *She walked straight past her office and then had to retrace her steps.*

retract /rɪˈtrækt/ **verb** formal **1** [T] to take back an offer or statement, etc. or admit that a statement was false: *retract an invitation/confession/promise* ◦ *When questioned on TV, the minister retracted his **allegations**.* **2** [I or T] to pull something back or in: *The wheels retract after the aircraft takes off.* ◦ *The cat retracted its claws.* • **retractable** /-ˈtræk.tə.bl/ **adj** *Cats have retractable claws.* • **retraction** /-ˈtræk.ʃən/ **noun** [C] *The newspaper printed a retraction for their previous error.*

retrain /ˌriːˈtreɪn/ **verb** **1** [I] to learn new skills so you can do a different job: *Mark used to be an actor but now he's retraining **as** a teacher.* **2** [T] to teach someone a new skill so they can do a different job: *The programme retrains unemployed people.* • **retraining** /-ɪŋ/ **noun** [U]

retread /ˌriːˈtred/ **verb** [T] (UK also **remould**) to put a new rubber surface on the outer part of a worn tyre: *Your tyres need retreading.* • **retread** /ˈriː.tred/ **noun** [C] *Are those new tyres or retreads?*

retreat /rɪˈtriːt/ **verb; noun**
▸**verb** POSITION ▷ **1** C2 [I often + adv/prep] to go away from a place or person in order to escape from fighting or danger: *Attacks by enemy aircraft forced the tanks to retreat (**from** the city).* ◦ *When she came towards me shouting, I retreated (behind my desk).* **2** C2 [I] to go to a quiet safe place in order to avoid a difficult situation: *When he's done something wrong, he retreats **to** his bedroom.* DECISION ▷ **3** [I often + adv/prep] to decide not to do something, or to stop believing something, because it causes too many problems: *The government is retreating **from** its promises.* PRICE ▷ **4** [I] If a price retreats, it goes down after it has gone up: *Wheat prices retreated after a two-day increase.*
▸**noun** POSITION ▷ **1** C2 [C usually singular, U] a move back by soldiers or an army, either because they have been defeated or in order to avoid fighting: *the retreat **from** Dunkirk* ◦ *Enemy soldiers are now **in** (full) retreat.* **2** C2 [C] a private and safe place: *a country/mountain/lakeside retreat* **3** [C or U] a period of time used to pray and study quietly, or to think carefully, away from normal activities and duties: *We **went on** (a) retreat **at/to** a monastery in Wales.* DECISION ▷ **4** [C] a change from previous beliefs or behaviour: *The professor's speech marked/signalled a retreat **from** his usual extreme views.* PRICE ▷ **5** [S or U] a situation in which the price of something goes down: *Over the past few weeks we have seen the currency's big retreat from its historic high.*

retrench /rɪˈtrentʃ/ **verb** [I] formal If governments, companies, etc. retrench, they start spending less money, or reducing costs: *The company had to retrench because of falling orders.*

retrenchment /rɪˈtrentʃ.mənt/ **noun** [C or U] a situation in which a government, etc. spends less or reduces costs

retrial /ˈriː.traɪəl/ **noun** [C] a new trial of a law case: *The discovery of new evidence forced a retrial.*

retribution /ˌret.rɪˈbjuː.ʃən/ **noun** [U] formal deserved and severe punishment: *They fled because they feared retribution **for** the genocide.* ◦ *She was asked whether a civilian government should **seek** retribution **against** military officers involved in human rights abuses.* ◦ *Many saw her death as **divine** retribution (= punishment by God) **for** her crimes.* • **retributive** /rɪˈtrɪb.jʊ.tɪv/ US /-t̬ɪv/ **adj** [before noun] *retributive **action/justice***

retrieve /rɪˈtriːv/ **verb** [T] C2 to find and bring back something: *We taught our dog to retrieve a ball.* ◦ *Computers are used to store and retrieve **information** efficiently.* • **retrieval** /-ˈtriː.vəl/ **noun** [U] *the storage and retrieval of information*

retriever /rɪˈtriː.vəʳ/ US /-vɚ/ **noun** [C] a large dog with thick black or light brown fur

retro /ˈret.rəʊ/ US /-roʊ/ **adj** similar to styles, fashions, etc. from the past: *retro clothes/music* ◦ *a retro style* ◦ *Inside, the decor is very retro.*

retro- /ret.rəʊ-/ (US) /-roʊ-/ **prefix** BACKWARDS ▷ **1** going backwards PAST ▷ **2** looking at or copying the past: *retro-pop (= popular music from the past)*

retroactive /ˌret.rəʊˈæk.tɪv/ (US) /-roʊ-/ **adj** (also **retrospective**) If a law or decision, etc. is retroactive, it has effect from a date before it was approved: *the first British law to have retroactive effect* • **retroactively** /-li/ **adv**

retrofit verb; noun

▸verb [T] /ˈret.rəʊ.fɪt/ (US) /-rə-/ (**-tt-**) to provide a machine with a part, or a place with equipment, that it did not originally have when it was built: *A state program to retrofit engines with pollution controls has succeeded in reducing pollution from trains.*

▸noun [C] an occasion when a machine or place is retrofitted: *Many hospitals are struggling to pay for the retrofits.*

retroflex /ˈret.rə.fleks/ **adj** specialized (of a speech sound) made with the end of the tongue curling upwards and backwards

retrograde /ˈret.rə.greɪd/ **adj** formal returning to older and worse conditions, methods, ideas, etc.: *He said it would be a retrograde* ***step*** *to remove single parent benefit.*

retrogress /ˌret.rəˈgres/ (US) /ˈret.rə.gres/ **verb** [I] formal to return to an older and worse state • **retrogression** /ˌret.rəˈgreʃ.ən/ **noun** [U] • **retrogressive** /ˌret.rəˈgres.ɪv/ (US) /ˈret.rə.gres-/ **adj** *retrogressive and disastrous policies*

retrosexual /ˌret.rəʊˈsek.sjʊəl/ (US) /-rəˈ-/ **noun** [C] informal a HETEROSEXUAL man who does not spend much money on his appearance because he is not interested in the way he looks

retrospect /ˈret.rə.spekt/ **noun** **in retrospect** (C2) thinking now about something in the past: *In retrospect, I think my marriage was doomed from the beginning.* ◦ *I'm sure my university days seem happier in retrospect than they really were.* • **retrospection** /ˌret.rəˈspek.ʃən/ **noun** [U] *a time/mood of retrospection*

retrospective /ˌret.rəˈspek.tɪv/ **noun; adj**

▸noun [C] a show of the work an artist has done in their life so far: *a Hockney retrospective/a retrospective of Hockney's work*

▸adj relating to or thinking about the past • **retrospectively** /-li/ **adv** *Retrospectively, I can see where we went wrong.*

retrovirus /ˌret.rəʊˈvaɪ.rəs/ (US) /-rə-/ **noun** [C] specialized a type of virus that includes some CANCER viruses and HIV (= the virus that causes AIDS, a serious disease that destroys the body's ability to fight infection)

retsina /retˈsiː.nə/ **noun** [U] a Greek wine that tastes strongly of the RESIN of particular trees

return /rɪˈtɜːn/ (US) /-ˈtɝːn/ **verb; noun; adj**

▸verb GO BACK ▷ **1** (A2) [I] to come or go back to a previous place: *Odysseus returned home/returned* ***to*** *his home after many years of travelling.* ◦ *She left South Africa at the age of 15 and has never returned.* ◦ [+ to infinitive] *David returned (****from*** *work)* ***to*** *find his house had burned down.* **2 return to sth a** (C1) If people or things return to a previous condition, they go back to that condition: *Within a week, the situation had returned to normal.* **b** (B2) If you return to an activity or subject, you start doing it or talking about it again: *Gandhi urged Indians to return to spinning their own yarn.* ◦ *Every five minutes, he returned to the same subject.* EXCHANGE ▷ **3** (C1) [T] to give, do, or get something in exchange for something: *to return an invitation/greeting* ◦ *I returned his stare.* ◦ *I gave her a ride when her car broke down and now she is returning* ***the favour*** *(= doing something to help me in exchange).* ◦ *The terrorists started shooting and the police returned* ***fire*** *(= started shooting back).* **4** to give a particular amount of profit in exchange for an INVESTMENT: *My investments return a high rate of interest.* PUT BACK ▷ **5** (A2) [T] to send, take, give, put, etc. something back to where it came from: *The new TV broke so they returned it* ***to*** *the shop.* ◦ *He returned two books he had borrowed from me in 2003.* ◦ *She carefully returned the book* ***to*** *its place on the shelf.* **6** [T] in sports such as tennis, to hit the ball back to your opponent HAPPEN AGAIN ▷ **7** (B2) [I] to happen again: *You must go to the doctor if the pain returns.* DECIDE ▷ **8 return a verdict/sentence** legal to decide and say if you think someone is guilty or not guilty, or what punishment the person will be given in a court of law: *The jury returned a verdict* ***of*** *not guilty.* **9** [T] UK to elect someone to be a member of parliament, or to another political job • **returnable** /rɪˈtɜː.nə.bl̩/ (US) /-ˈtɝː-/ **adj** *a returnable bottle*

▸noun GOING BACK ▷ **1** (B1) [S] an occasion when someone goes or comes back to a place where they were before: *The whole town came out to celebrate his return (****from*** *the war).* ◦ ***On*** *her return, she went straight to the office.* **2** [S] an occasion when you start to do or have something again: *Some environmentalists argue for a return* ***to*** *a pre-industrial society.* ◦ *Most people have welcomed her return* ***to power/office***. **3** (B1) [C] UK (also **return ticket**, US **ˌround-ˈtrip ˌticket**) a ticket for travel to a place and back again: *May I have a return to Birmingham, please?* EXCHANGE ▷ **4 in return** (B2) in exchange: *America helped the rebels in return* ***for*** *their promise to support democracy.* **5** [C or U] the act of giving, doing, or receiving something in exchange for something: *Several soldiers were wounded in the return* ***of*** *fire.* **6** [C or U] the profit that you get from an INVESTMENT: *The return* ***on*** *the money we invested was very low.* HAPPENING AGAIN ▷ **7** [S] an occasion when something starts to happen or be used again: *Will we ever see the return* ***of****/a return* ***to*** *comfortable fashion clothes?* COMPUTER KEY ▷ **8** (B1) [U] the key on a computer keyboard that you press in order to say that the words or numbers on the screen are correct, or that an instruction should be performed, or in order to move down a line on the screen: *Press return/the return key twice to leave a blank line.* GIVING BACK ▷ **9** (C1) [S] the act of giving, putting, or sending something back: *the return of the stolen goods* **10** [C] the act of hitting the ball back to your opponent in sports such as tennis **11 returns** [plural] **a** goods that have been taken back to the shop where they were bought by customers because they are damaged or unsuitable **b** US the votes that are returned, or the results of the voting, in an election: *The* ***election*** *returns produced a confusing picture of gains and losses.* **12 by return (of post)** UK in the first post collection that leaves after you receive a letter: *She answered my letter by return.*

▸adj [before noun] describes the part of a journey in which you go back to the place where you started: *The return* ***journey*** *took longer because the train was rerouted.*

reˈturn ˌmatch **noun** [C] another game between the same teams or players: *We enjoyed the game so much that we arranged a return match for the next week.*

reˈturn ˌticket **noun** [C] **1** UK a ticket for travel to a place and back again: *May I have a return ticket to Birmingham, please?* **2** US a ticket for the return part of a journey

retweet /ˌriːˈtwiːt/ **noun; verb**

▸noun [C] (abbreviation **RT**) trademark a short remark or

R

piece of information that you have seen published on TWITTER™ and published again yourself
▸**verb** [I or T] (abbreviation **RT**) trademark to publish a short remark or piece of information that you have seen published on TWITTER™ again yourself

reunification /ˌriː.juː.nɪ.fɪˈkeɪ.ʃən/ **noun** [U] an occasion when a country that was temporarily divided into smaller countries is joined together again as one country

reunify /riːˈjuː.nɪ.faɪ/ **verb** [T] to join together into one country, parts of a country that were divided

reunion /ˌriːˈjuː.ni.ən/ (US) /ˈ-njən/ **noun** **1** (C2) [C] a social event for a group of people who have not seen each other for a long time: *We're having a* ***family*** *reunion next week.* ◦ *The college has an annual reunion for former students.* **2** (C2) [C or U] a situation when people meet again after they have not seen each other for a long time: *She had a tearful reunion with her parents at the airport.*

reunite /ˌriː.juːˈnaɪt/ **verb** [T] to bring people together again: *to reunite a divided family/country/world* ◦ *Sarah was finally reunited* ***with*** *her children at the airport.*

reuse /ˌriːˈjuːz/ **verb** [T] to use something again: *To conserve resources, please reuse this carrier bag.* • **reusable** /-ˈjuː.zə.bl/ **adj** *reusable* ***nappies/packaging***

rev /rev/ **noun**; **verb**
▸**noun** [C usually plural] informal a REVOLUTION (= one complete turn of a part in an engine): *Keep the revs* ***up*** (= *the engine parts turning quickly*) *or the engine will stall.* ◦ *a rev counter* → See also **rpm**
▸**verb** [I or T] (**-vv-**) to increase the operating speed of an engine while the vehicle is not moving, usually to warm it to the correct temperature: *The noise of the car engine revving* ***up*** *woke the whole neighbourhood.*

PHRASAL VERB **rev up (sb/sth)** to become more active, or to make someone or something become more active: *The hotel is revving up for the busy summer season.* ◦ *drugs which rev up your nervous system*

Rev. **noun** [before noun] (UK also **Revd**) written abbreviation for **Reverend**

revalue /ˌriːˈvæl.juː/ **verb** [T] to change the value of something or to consider it again: *to revalue a currency*

revamp /ˌriːˈvæmp/ **verb** [T] informal to change or arrange something again, in order to improve it: *We revamped the management system, but the business is doing no better than it was before.* • **revamp** /ˈriː.væmp/ **noun** [C usually singular] *The company has spent £5 million on a major revamp of its offices.*

Revd **noun** UK written abbreviation for **Reverend**

reveal /rɪˈviːl/ **verb** [T] **1** (B2) to make known or show something that is surprising or that was previously secret: *He was jailed for revealing* ***secrets*** *to the Russians.* ◦ [+ that] *Her biography revealed* ***that*** *she was not as rich as everyone thought.* ◦ [+ question word] *He would not reveal* ***where*** *he had hidden her chocolate eggs.* **2** (C2) to allow something to be seen that, until then, had been hidden: *A gap in the clouds revealed the Atlantic far below.*

revealing /rɪˈviː.lɪŋ/ **adj** **1** describes clothes which show more of the body than is usual: *a revealing dress/shirt* **2** showing something that was not previously known or seen: *A joke can be very revealing* ***about/of*** *what someone's really thinking.* • **revealingly** /-li/ **adv**

reveille /rɪˈvæl.i/ (US) /ˈrev.ə.li/ **noun** [S or U] a musical signal played to wake up soldiers in the morning, or the time when it is played

revel /ˈrev.əl/ **verb** [I] (**-ll-** or US usually **-l-**) literary to dance, drink, sing, etc. at a party or in public, especially in a noisy way • **reveller** UK (US **reveler**) /-əʳ/ (US) /-ɚ/ **noun** [C] *On New Year's Eve, thousands of revellers fill Trafalgar Square.*

PHRASAL VERB **revel in sth** to get great pleasure from a situation or an activity: *She's revelling in her newly found freedom.* ◦ *He revelled in his role as team manager.*

revelation /ˌrev.əˈleɪ.ʃən/ **noun** [C or U] **1** (C2) the act of making something known that was secret, or a fact that is made known: *a moment of revelation* ◦ [+ that] *His wife divorced him after the revelation* ***that*** *he was having an affair.* ◦ *Shocking revelations* ***about*** *their private life appeared in the papers.* **2** **come as/be a revelation** (C2) to be an extremely pleasant surprise: *This book came as a complete revelation* ***to*** *me.*

revelry /ˈrev.əl.ri/ **noun** [C usually plural, U] literary a situation in which people are drinking, dancing, singing, etc. at a party or in public, especially in a noisy way: *Sounds of revelry came from next door.* ◦ *The revelries next door kept me awake all night.*

revenge /rɪˈvendʒ/ **noun**; **verb**
▸**noun** [U] (B2) harm done to someone as a punishment for harm that they have done to someone else: *She* ***took/got/exacted*** *(her) revenge* ***on*** *him* ***for*** *leaving her by smashing up his car.* ◦ *He is believed to have been shot by a rival gang* ***in*** *revenge* ***for*** *the shootings last week.*

IDIOM **revenge is sweet** saying said when you feel satisfaction from harming someone who has harmed you

▸**verb** [T] to harm someone as a punishment for harm that they have done to you: *to revenge a death/defeat/injustice* ◦ *The red team revenged them****selves on*** *the blue team by winning the semifinal.*

revengeful /rɪˈvendʒ.fəl/ **adj** wanting revenge

revenue /ˈrev.ən.juː/ (US) /-ə.nuː/ **noun** [U] (also **revenues**) (C1) the income that a government or company receives regularly: *Taxes provide most of the government's revenue.* ◦ *Government revenues fell dramatically.*

reverberate /rɪˈvɜː.bər.eɪt/ (US) /-ˈvɝː.bə.eɪt/ **verb** **SOUND** ▷ **1** [I] literary If a loud, deep sound reverberates, it continues to be heard around an area, so that the area seems to shake: *The narrow street reverberated* ***with/to*** *the sound of the workmen's drills.* **EFFECT** ▷ **2** [I + adv/prep] If an event or idea reverberates somewhere, it has an effect on everyone or everything in a place or group: *News of the disaster reverberated* ***around*** *the organization.* ◦ *The surge in US share prices reverberated* ***across*** *the globe.*

reverberation /rɪˌvɜː.bərˈeɪ.ʃən/ (US) /-ˌvɝː.bəˈreɪ-/ **noun** **SOUND** ▷ **1** [C usually plural, U] literary a sound that lasts for a long time and makes things seem to shake: *She felt the reverberation(s) in her chest and cursed the drilling outside.* **EFFECTS** ▷ **2** **reverberations** [plural] effects which spread and affect a lot of people: *This move is likely to* ***have*** *reverberations throughout the health service.*

revere /rɪˈvɪəʳ/ (US) /-ˈvɪr/ **verb** [T] formal to very much respect and admire someone or something: *Nelson Mandela is revered* ***for*** *his brave fight against apartheid.*

reverence /ˈrev.ər.əns/ (US) /-ɚ.əns/ **noun** [U] a feeling of respect or admiration for someone or something: *She has/shows/feels great reverence* ***for*** *her professors.*

Reverend /ˈrev.ər.ənd/, /-rənd/ (US) /-ɚ.ənd/ **noun** (written abbreviation **Rev.**, **Revd**) a title for a priest of the Christian Church: *the Reverend H. Clark*

reverent /ˈrev.ər.ənt/ (US) /-ɚ.ənt/ **adj** showing great respect and admiration: *A reverent **silence** fell over the crowd.* → Opposite **irreverent** • **reverently** /-li/ **adv** *He laid the wreath reverently in front of the memorial.*

reverential /ˌrev.əˈren.ʃəl/ (US) /-əˈren-/ **adj** formal caused by, or full of respect and admiration: *He opened the ancient book with reverential care.* • **reverentially** /-i/ **adv**

reverie /ˈrev.ər.i/ (US) /-ɚ-/ **noun** [C or U] literary (a state of having) pleasant dream-like thoughts: *He was lost **in** reverie until he suddenly heard someone behind him.*

reversal /rɪˈvɜː.səl/ (US) /-ˈvɝː-/ **noun** [C] **1** (C2) the act of changing or making something change to its opposite: *He demanded a reversal **of** the previous decision/policy.* **2** a problem or failure: *We have suffered a couple of minor/temporary reversals.*

reverse /rɪˈvɜːs/ (US) /-ˈvɝːs/ **verb; noun**
▸**verb** CHANGE TO OPPOSITE ▷ **1** (C1) [T] to change the direction, order, position, result, etc. of something to its opposite: *The new manager hoped to reverse the decline in the company's fortunes.* ◦ *Now that you have a job and I don't, our situations are reversed.* ◦ *The Court of Appeal reversed the earlier judgment.* DRIVE BACKWARDS ▷ **2** (B2) [I or T] to drive a vehicle backwards: *He reversed **into** a lamppost and damaged the back of the car.* ◦ *She reversed the car into the parking space.* PHONE ▷ **3 reverse the charges** (US also **call collect**) to make a phone call that is paid for by the person receiving it
▸**noun 1 the reverse a** (C2) the opposite of what has been suggested: *The teachers say my son is slow, but I believe the reverse (is true).* **b** the back of a coin, MEDAL, etc.: *The English £1 coin has a royal coat of arms on the reverse.* **2 in reverse (order)** (C1) in the opposite order or way: *To stop the engine, you repeat the same procedures, but in reverse (order).* **3** (C2) [U] (also **reverse gear**) the method of controlling a vehicle that makes it go backwards: *To go backwards, you must **put** the car **in/into** reverse (gear).* **4** [C] formal a defeat or failure: *They suffered a serious military/political reverse.*

IDIOM **go into reverse** If a situation goes into reverse, it becomes the opposite of what it was before: *The trend towards home ownership has gone into reverse.*

reˌverse discrimiˈnation **noun** [U] (UK also **ˌpositive discrimiˈnation**) the act of giving advantage to those groups in society that are often treated unfairly, usually because of their race, sex, or SEXUALITY

reˌverse ˌengiˈneering **noun** [U] the act of copying the product of another company by looking carefully at how it is made

reˌverse psyˈchology **noun** [U] a method of trying to make someone do what you want by asking them to do the opposite and expecting them to disagree with you

reversible /rɪˈvɜː.sə.bl̩/ (US) /-ˈvɝː-/ **adj 1** (C2) If something is reversible, it can be changed back to what it was before. **2** (C2) describes clothes that can be worn so that the inside becomes the outside: *a reversible raincoat*

reversion /rɪˈvɜː.ʃən/ (US) /-ˈvɝː.ʒən/ **noun** [S or U] **1** formal a change back to a previous and often worse condition: *The new procedures are being seen as a reversion **to** old, inefficient ways of working.* **2** legal a return of something to its previous owner

revert /rɪˈvɜːt/ (US) /-ˈvɝːt/ **verb**

PHRASAL VERBS **revert to sth** (C2) to return to doing, using, being, or referring to something, usually something bad or less satisfactory: *Why does the conversation have to revert to money every five minutes?* ◦ [+ -ing verb] *When they divorced, she reverted to **using** her maiden name.* • **revert to sb** legal to become the property of a particular person again: *When I die, the house will revert to my sister.*

review /rɪˈvjuː/ **verb; noun**
▸**verb** [T] THINK AGAIN ▷ **1** (C1) to consider something in order to make changes to it, give an opinion on it or study it: *The committee is reviewing the current arrangement/situation.* ◦ *Let's review (= talk about) what has happened so far.* ◦ *He reviewed (= thought about) his options before making a final decision.* BOOK/FILM ▷ **2** (B2) If CRITICS review a book, play, film, etc. they write their opinion of it: *I only go to see films that are reviewed favourably.* MILITARY ▷ **3** When an important person reviews a large group of military forces, they formally visit and look at them: *The Queen reviewed the troops on her recent visit.* STUDY ▷ **4** US for **revise**
▸**noun** THINK AGAIN ▷ **1** (C2) [C or U] the act of considering something again in order to make changes to it, give an opinion of it or study it: *an annual review **of** company performance* ◦ *a review **of** the year's top news stories* ◦ *Salary levels are **under** review at the moment.* ◦ *Your licence will **come up for** review every July.* BOOK/FILM ▷ **2** (B1) [C] a report in a newspaper, magazine, or programme that gives an opinion about a new book, film, etc.: *Derek writes **film/theatre/book** reviews for the newspapers.* ◦ *The play **got** excellent reviews when it was first seen.* **3** [C usually singular] a (part of a) newspaper or magazine that has articles on films, books, travel, famous people, etc.: *Could you pass me the review (**section** of the paper), please?* MILITARY ▷ **4** [C] a formal military ceremony in which forces are reviewed by an important person: *Many diplomats attended a naval review to mark the anniversary of the end of the war.* THEATRE ▷ **5** [C] a **revue** STUDY ▷ **6** [C] US information or a practice exercise about a subject to be studied: *Their teacher distributed a review for the exam.*

reviewer /rɪˈvjuː.ər/ (US) /-ɚ/ **noun** [C] CRITIC ▷ **1** someone who writes articles expressing their opinion of a book, play, film, etc. OFFICIAL ▷ **2** someone who works for an official organization that controls a particular type of activity: *A Food and Drug Agency reviewer said the new treatment appears to be working effectively.*

revile /rɪˈvaɪl/ **verb** [T] formal to criticize someone strongly, or say unpleasant things to or about someone: *The judge was reviled in the newspapers **for** his opinions on rape.*

revise /rɪˈvaɪz/ **verb** CHANGE ▷ **1** (B2) [T] to look at or consider again an idea, piece of writing, etc. in order to correct or improve it: *His helpfulness today has made me revise my original **opinion**/impression of him.* ◦ *His publishers made him revise his manuscript three times.* STUDY ▷ **2** (B1) [I or T] UK (US **review**) to study again something you have already learned, in preparation for an exam: *We're revising (algebra) **for** the test tomorrow.*

revised /rɪˈvaɪzd/ **adj** changed in some ways: *a revised edition of a book*

revision /rɪˈvɪʒ.ən/ **noun** CHANGE ▷ **1** [C or U] a change that is made to something, or the process of doing this: *These proposals will need a lot of revision.*

R

◦ *He was forced to make several revisions* ***to*** *his speech.* **STUDY** ▷ **2** B1 [U] study of work you have done, in order to prepare for an exam: *She* ***did*** *no revision, but she still got a very high mark.*

revisionism /rɪˈvɪʒ.ən.ɪ.zəm/ **noun** [U] asking questions about, and trying to change, the existing beliefs of a political or religious system, especially the Marxist political system • **revisionist** /-ɪst/ **noun** [C] *revisionists within the Communist Party* • **revisionist adj** *revisionist ideas/history*

revisit /riːˈvɪz.ɪt/ **verb** [T] **PLACE** ▷ **1** to go to a place again: *I revisited Prague last month.* **SUBJECT** ▷ **2** to talk or think about something again, with the intention of improving it or changing it: *Gun laws need to be revisited.*

revitalize (UK usually **revitalise**) /ˌriːˈvaɪ.təl.aɪz/ US /-t̬əl-/ **verb** [T] to give new life, energy, activity or success to something: *Japanese investment has revitalized this part of Britain.*

revival /rɪˈvaɪ.vəl/ **noun 1** C2 [C or U] the process of becoming more active or popular again: *Recently, there has been some revival* ***of*** *(****interest in****) ancient music.* ◦ *An economic/artistic revival is sweeping the country.* **2** [C] a performance of a play that has not been seen for a long time: *We're* ***staging*** *a revival of a 1950s play.*

revive /rɪˈvaɪv/ **verb** [I or T] C2 to come or bring something back to life, health, existence, or use: *to revive someone's hopes/confidence/fortunes* ◦ *My plants revived as soon as I gave them some water.* ◦ *A hot shower and a cup of tea will revive you.* ◦ *Traditional skills are being revived.*

revivify /ˌriːˈvɪv.ɪ.faɪ/ **verb** [T] **formal** to give new energy and strength to an event or activity: *A leader with real charisma is needed to revivify the political party.*

revoke /rɪˈvəʊk/ US /-ˈvoʊk/ **verb** [T] **formal** to say officially that an agreement, permission, a law, etc. is no longer in effect: *The authorities have revoked their original decision to allow development of this rural area.* • **revocation** /re.vəˈkeɪ.ʃən/ **noun** [C or U]

revolt /rɪˈvəʊlt/, /-ˈvɒlt/ US /-ˈvoʊlt/ **verb; noun**

▸**verb PROTEST** ▷ **1** C2 [I] If a large number of people revolt, they refuse to be controlled or ruled, and take action against authority, often violent action: *The people revolted* ***against*** *foreign rule and established their own government.* **UNPLEASANT FEELING** ▷ **2** C2 [T] to make someone feel unpleasantly shocked or DISGUSTED: *We were revolted* ***by*** *the dirt and mess in her house.* ◦ *It revolts me to know that the world spends so much money on arms when millions are dying of hunger.* → See also **revulsion**

▸**noun** [C or U] an attempt to get rid of a government by using violence: *Troops were called in to crush/put down the revolt.* ◦ *The army is* ***in*** *revolt (****against*** *its commanders).* → See also **revolution**

revolting /rɪˈvəʊl.tɪŋ/ US /-ˈvoʊl-/ **adj** extremely unpleasant: *a revolting smell of rotting cabbage* ◦ *Picking your nose is a revolting habit.* → Synonym **disgusting** • **revoltingly** /-li/ **adv**

revolution /ˌrev.əˈluː.ʃən/ **noun POLITICS** ▷ **1** B2 [C or U] a change in the way a country is governed, usually to a different political system and often using violence or war: *The French Revolution changed France from a monarchy to a republic.* ◦ *The country seems to be heading towards revolution.* **CHANGE** ▷ **2** B2 [C] a very important change in the way that people do things: *a technological revolution* ◦ *Penicillin produced a revolution* ***in*** *medicine.* **CIRCULAR MOVEMENT** ▷ **3** [S] a circular movement: *The revolution of the Earth around the sun was proposed by Copernicus.* **4** [C] one complete circular movement of something, for example a wheel: *Engine speed can be measured in revolutions per minute* (abbreviation ***rpm***).

revolutionary /ˌrev.əˈluː.ʃən.ər.i/ US /-er-/ **adj; noun**

▸**adj IN POLITICS** ▷ **1** B2 involved in or relating to a revolution: *a revolutionary leader/movement* **NEW AND IMPORTANT** ▷ **2** B2 completely new and having a great effect: *Penicillin was a revolutionary drug.* ◦ *The 20th century brought about revolutionary* ***changes*** *in our lifestyles.*

▸**noun** [C] someone who tries to cause or take part in a revolution

revolutionize (UK usually **revolutionise**) /ˌrev.əˈluː.ʃən.aɪz/ **verb** [T] to completely change something so that it is much better: *Newton's discoveries revolutionized physics.*

revolve /rɪˈvɒlv/ US /-ˈvɑːlv/ **verb** [I or T] to move or cause something to move around a central point or line: *The Earth revolves around the sun.* ◦ *The gun turret revolved until the gun was aimed at the advancing soldiers.*

IDIOM **think the (whole) world revolves around you** disapproving to think you are extremely important

PHRASAL VERB **revolve around/round sb/sth** to have someone or something as the main or most important interest or subject: *The conversation revolved around childcare problems.* ◦ *His whole life revolves around football.*

revolver /rɪˈvɒl.vər/ US /-ˈvɑːl.vɚ/ **noun** [C] a type of small gun held in one hand that can be FIRED several times without putting more bullets in it

revolving /rɪˈvɒl.vɪŋ/ US /-ˈvɑːl-/ **adj** [before noun] describes something that revolves (= moves around a central point): *a revolving bookcase*

reˌvolving ˈdoor noun [C] a set of doors which you go through by pushing them round in a circle

revolving door

revue /rɪˈvjuː/ **noun** [C] (also **review**) a show with songs, dances, jokes, and short plays often about recent events

revulsion /rɪˈvʌl.ʃən/ **noun** [U] a strong, often sudden, feeling that something is extremely unpleasant: *I turned away* ***in*** *revulsion when they showed a close-up of the operation.* ◦ *She looked at him* ***with*** *revulsion.* ◦ *He expressed his revulsion* ***at/against/towards*** *the whale hunting.* → See also **revolt**

reward /rɪˈwɔːd/ US /-ˈwɔːrd/ **noun; verb**

▸**noun** [C] **1** B1 something given in exchange for good behaviour or good work, etc.: *There's a reward* ***for*** *whoever finishes first.* ◦ *The rewards of motherhood outweigh the anguish.* **2** B1 an amount of money given to someone who helps the police or who helps to return stolen property to its owner: *The police offered a reward* ***for*** *any information about the robbery.*

> Word partners for **reward noun**
>
> *get/receive* a reward • *reap* the rewards *of* sth • *bring/have/offer/promise* a reward • a *big/handsome/huge/substantial* reward • *poor/scant/small* reward • a reward *for* sth • *as a/in* reward • a reward *of* [$400, £300, etc.]

▸**verb** [T] B2 to give someone a reward: *The company*

*rewarded him **for** his years of service **with** a grand farewell party and several presents.* ◦ *All his hard work was rewarded (= was made worth it) when he saw his book in print.* ◦ formal *He rewarded their kindness **with** hostility and contempt.*

rewarding /rɪˈwɔː.dɪŋ/ (US) /-ˈwɔːr-/ **adj** giving a reward, especially by making you feel satisfied that you have done something important or useful, or done something well: *Is it a rewarding job?* ◦ *Textbook writing can be an intellectually and financially rewarding activity.*

rewind /ˌriːˈwaɪnd/ **verb** [T] (**rewound**) to put a tape recording back to the beginning: *Will you rewind the tape so we can hear it again?* • **rewind** /ˈriː.waɪnd/ **adj**

rewire /ˌriːˈwaɪəʳ/ (US) /-ˈwaɪr/ **verb** [T] to put a new system of electric wires into a building or machine: *You really should have the whole house rewired – the existing wiring isn't safe.*

reword /ˌriːˈwɜːd/ (US) /-ˈwɝːd/ **verb** [T] to write something again in different words: *She reworded sensitive areas of the report so that it wouldn't be so controversial.*

rework /ˌriːˈwɜːk/ (US) /-ˈwɝːk/ **verb** [T] to change a speech or a piece of writing in order to improve it or make it more suitable for a particular purpose: *She reworked her speech for a younger audience.* • **reworking** /riːˈwɜː.kɪŋ/ (US) /-ˈwɝː-/ **noun** [C] *His latest book is a reworking **of** material from his previous short stories.*

rewound /ˌriːˈwaʊnd/ past simple and past participle of **rewind**

rhapsodic /ræpˈsɒd.ɪk/ (US) /-ˈsɑːd-/ **adj** **1** in the form of a rhapsody, or expressing powerful feelings: *The slow movement is wonderfully moody and rhapsodic.* **2** formal expressing great enthusiasm about something

rhapsodize formal (UK usually **rhapsodise**) /ˈræp.sə.daɪz/ **verb** [I] to express great enthusiasm for something: *He's always rhapsodizing **about/over** the joys of having children.*

rhapsody /ˈræp.sə.di/ **noun** [C] **1** specialized a piece of music that has no formal structure and expresses powerful feelings: *Rachmaninov's 'Rhapsody on a Theme of Paganini'* **2** formal a speech or piece of writing that contains powerful feelings and enthusiasm

IDIOM **go into rhapsodies** to express very great enthusiasm and admiration for something: *She went into rhapsodies **over/about** the chocolate cake.*

rheostat /ˈriː.ə.stæt/ (US) /-oʊ-/ **noun** [C] specialized a device used to control and change the flow of electric current through a machine such as an electric light

rhesus factor /ˈriː.səsˌfæk.təʳ/ (US) /ˈriː.səsˌfæk.tɚ/ **noun** [S] (written abbreviation **Rh factor**) a substance in the red blood cells of most people which causes the production of ANTIBODIES in the blood: *People whose blood contains the rhesus factor are rhesus positive (Rh+) and those whose blood does not contain it are rhesus negative (Rh-).*

rhesus monkey /ˈriː.səsˌmʌŋ.ki/ **noun** [C] a monkey from northern India

rhetoric /ˈret.əʳ.ɪk/ (US) /ˈreţ.ɚ-/ **noun** [U] **1** speech or writing intended to be effective and influence people: *How far the president will be able to translate his campaign rhetoric into action remains to be seen.* ◦ *I was swayed by her rhetoric into donating all my savings to the charity.* **2** specialized the study of the ways of using language effectively **3** disapproving clever language that sounds good but is not sincere or has no real meaning: *In reply to the question, he just produced a lot of **empty** (= meaningless) rhetoric.*

rhetorical /rɪˈtɒr.ɪ.kəl/ (US) /-ˈtɔːr.ɪ-/ **adj** describes speech or writing that is intended to seem important or influence people: *repetition, that tedious rhetorical **device*** • **rhetorically** /-i/ **adv** *'You want to know what courage is?' he asked rhetorically.*

rheˌtorical ˈquestion **noun** [C] a question, asked in order to make a statement, that does not expect an answer: *'Why do these things always happen to me?' is a rhetorical question.*

rhetorician /ˌret.əˈrɪʃ.ən/ (US) /ˌreţ-/ **noun** [C] **1** formal a person who is good at speaking in public, especially someone who is able to influence people **2** specialized a person who teaches the skill of speaking and writing in an effective way which influences people

rheuˌmatic ˈfever **noun** [U] a serious disease that causes fever, swelling of the JOINTS (= places where two bones are connected), and possible heart damage

rheumatism /ˈruː.mə.tɪ.zəm/ **noun** [U] a medical condition that causes stiffness and pain in the JOINTS (= places where two bones are connected) or muscles of the body: *She suffers from rheumatism.* ◦ *I can't play the piano any more because I have rheumatism **in** my fingers.* • **rheumatic** /ruːˈmæt.ɪk/ (US) /-ˈmæţ-/ **adj** *She has a rheumatic hip.*

rheumatoid arthritis /ˌruː.mə.tɔɪd.ɑːˈθraɪ.tɪs/ (US) /-ɑːrˈθraɪ.ţəs/ **noun** [U] a disease that causes stiffness, swelling, and pain in the JOINTS (= places where two bones are connected) of the body

rheumy /ˈruː.mi/ **adj** rheumy eyes have a lot of water in them and are not clear: *The old man peered at him with rheumy eyes.*

Rh factor **noun** [C usually singular] written abbreviation for **rhesus factor**

rhinestone /ˈraɪn.stəʊn/ (US) /-stoʊn/ **noun** [C] a bright, transparent artificial JEWEL that looks like a DIAMOND and can be sewn onto clothes

rhino /ˈraɪ.nəʊ/ (US) /-noʊ/ **noun** [C] a **rhinoceros**

rhinoceros /raɪˈnɒs.əʳ.əs/ (US) /-ˈnɑː.sɚ-/ **noun** [C] (plural **rhinoceros** or **rhinoceroses**) (informal **rhino**) a very large thick-skinned animal from Africa or Asia, which has one or two horns on its nose: *a population of black/white rhinoceros*

rhinoceros

rhizome /ˈraɪ.zəʊm/ (US) /-zoʊm/ **noun** [C] specialized a stem of some plants that grows horizontally along or under the ground and produces roots and leaves

rhododendron /ˌrəʊ.dəˈden.drən/ (US) /ˌroʊ-/ **noun** [C] a large EVERGREEN bush (= one that never loses its leaves) with large, usually bright pink, purple, or white flowers: *a rhododendron bush*

rhomboid /ˈrɒm.bɔɪd/ (US) /ˈrɑːm-/ **noun** [C] specialized a type of flat shape with four sides in which the sides next to each other are not of equal length but the sides opposite each other are

rhombus /ˈrɒm.bəs/ (US) /ˈrɑːm-/ **noun** [C] (plural **rhombuses** or **rhombi**) specialized a flat shape that has four sides that are all of equal length

rhotic /ˈrəʊ.tɪk/ (US) /ˈroʊ.ţɪk/ **adj** specialized describes a type of English, in which an /r/ is pronounced in all situations where there is an 'r' in spelling: *In a rhotic accent, an /r/ is pronounced at the end of 'car'.*

rhubarb /ˈruː.bɑːb/ (US) /-bɑːrb/ **noun; exclamation**

▸**noun** FOOD ▷ [U] a plant that has long, sour-tasting

R

red and green stems that can be cooked and eaten as a fruit: *Have you ever eaten rhubarb crumble?*
▸**exclamation** a word that is repeated many times in order to produce the sound of people talking when the meaning of the word is not important: *We had to stand at the back of the stage saying 'rhubarb, rhubarb' in the crowd scenes.*

rhyme /raɪm/ verb; noun
▸**verb** [I or T] C2 Words that rhyme have the same last sound: *'Blue' and 'flew' rhyme.* ◦ *Can you think of a word that rhymes **with** 'orange'?*
▸**noun 1** [C] a word that has the same last sound as another word: *Can you think of a rhyme **for** 'orange'?* **2** C2 [C] a short poem, especially for young children: *a book of rhymes and songs* → See also **nursery rhyme** **3** C2 [U] the use of rhymes in poetry: *This poem is her first attempt at rhyme.* **4 in rhyme** C2 written as a poem so that the word at the end of a line has the same last sound as a word at the end of another line: *A lot of modern poetry is not written in rhyme.* **5** (also **rime**) [C] specialized the vowel in the middle of a syllable, and any sounds after it in the syllable

IDIOM **be no/without rhyme or reason** to be without any obvious reasonable explanation: *Government money was given out to some people and not to others, apparently without rhyme or reason.* ◦ *There is no rhyme or reason **to** her behaviour.*

ˌrhyming ˈslang noun [U] a type of slang in which certain words are used instead of other words that they RHYME with: *In **Cockney** rhyming slang, you say 'apples and pears' to mean 'stairs'.*

rhythm /ˈrɪð.ᵊm/ noun **1** B2 [C or U] a strong pattern of sounds, words, or musical notes that is used in music, poetry, and dancing: *He beat out a jazz rhythm on the drums.* ◦ *I've got no **sense of** rhythm, so I'm a terrible dancer.* **2** B2 [C or U] a regular movement or pattern of movements: *She was lulled to sleep by the gentle rhythm of the boat in the water.* ◦ *She hit the ball so hard that her opponent had no chance to establish any rhythm in her game.* **3** [C] a regular pattern of change, especially one that happens in nature: *the rhythm of the seasons* ◦ *Breathing and sleeping are examples of **biological** rhythms in humans.*

R

ˌrhythm and ˈblues noun [U] (also **R & B**) a type of popular music of the 1940s and 1950s

rhythmic /ˈrɪð.mɪk/ adj (also **rhythmical**) describes a sound with a regular movement or beat that is repeated: *the rhythmic **sound** of the train* • **rhythmically** /-mɪ.kᵊl.i/ adv *Try to breathe deeply and rhythmically.*

ˈrhythm ˌmethod noun [S] a way of preventing pregnancy, in which partners have sex on those days when the woman is unlikely to become pregnant

ˈrhythm ˌsection noun [C usually singular] the instruments in a dance or JAZZ group that give a strong beat to the music: *The drums and double bass usually form the rhythm section of a jazz group.*

rial /ˈraɪ.əl/, /riˈɑːl/ US /ˈriː.ɔːl/ noun [C] the standard unit of money used in Iran, Oman, and Yemen

rib /rɪb/ noun; verb
▸**noun BONE** ▷ **1** B2 [C] a bone that curves round from your back to your chest: *My son broke a rib when he fell off a ladder.* **2** [C or U] a piece of meat taken from this part of an animal: *He cooked rib of lamb for Sunday lunch.* → See also **spare ribs** **3** [C] one of the curved pieces of metal or wood which support the structure of a boat or roof **PATTERN** ▷ **4** [U] a method of KNITTING that makes a pattern of raised parallel lines → See also **ribbed**

IDIOM **poke/dig sb in the ribs** to push your finger quickly into someone's chest, usually to make them notice something or to stop them from doing or saying something

▸**verb** [T] (**-bb-**) informal to joke and laugh at someone in a friendly way about something: *His brothers ribbed him **about** his new girlfriend.* → See also **ribbing**

ribald /ˈrɪb.ᵊld/, /ˈraɪ.bᵊld/ US /ˈraɪ.bɔːld/ adj old-fashioned describes language that refers to sex in a rude but humorous way: *He entertained us with ribald stories.*

ribaldry /ˈrɪb.ᵊl.dri/, /ˈraɪ.bᵊl-/ US /ˈraɪ.bɔːl-/ noun [U] old-fashioned language that refers to sex in a rude but humorous way: *good-natured ribaldry*

ribbed /rɪbd/ adj made from KNITTED material that has a pattern of raised lines on it: *Do you prefer plain or ribbed tights?*

ribbing /ˈrɪb.ɪŋ/ noun **PATTERN** ▷ **1** [U] a pattern of raised lines on a piece of clothing made from wool: *He liked the ribbing on the cuffs of the sweater.* **JOKE** ▷ **2** [C usually singular] informal the act of laughing at someone in a friendly way as a joke: *They **gave** him a ribbing about his accent.*

ribbon /ˈrɪb.ᵊn/ noun **1** C2 [C or U] a long, narrow strip of material used to tie things together or as a decoration: *Sandra often wears a ribbon in her hair.* ◦ *He tied up the present with ribbon.* **2 a ribbon of sth** literary a long, narrow piece of something: *A ribbon of road stretched ahead of us across the desert.* **3** [C] a small piece of coloured material given to someone in the armed forces to show approval and admiration for their brave actions

IDIOMS **cut/tear sth/sb to ribbons** to destroy or badly damage something or someone by cutting or tearing them many times: *Our new kitten has torn the living room curtains to ribbons.* ◦ figurative *The attacking soldiers were cut to ribbons (= killed) by machine gun fire.* • **in ribbons** torn into narrow strips: *Her coat was in ribbons.* ◦ *His shirt hung in tattered ribbons.*

ˌribbon deˈvelopment noun [U] UK long rows of buildings built along main roads leading out of towns

ˈribbon ˌlake noun [C] specialized a long, narrow lake along a deep valley formed by a GLACIER

ribcage /ˈrɪb.keɪdʒ/ noun [C usually singular] the structure of RIBS that protects your heart and lungs in your chest

riboflavin /ˌraɪ.bəʊˈfleɪ.vɪn/ US /ˈraɪ.bə.fleɪ-/ noun [U] specialized **vitamin B_2**

ribonucleic acid /ˌraɪ.bəʊ.njuːˌkliː.ɪkˈæs.ɪd/ US /-boʊ.nuː.kliː-/ noun [U] (abbreviation **RNA**) an important chemical present in all living cells

ˈrib-tickling adj (also **ˌrib-ticklingly ˈfunny**) describes a story or joke that is very funny

rice /raɪs/ noun [U] **1** A1 the small seeds of a particular type of grass, cooked, and eaten as food: *boiled/steamed/fried rice* ◦ *long-grain rice* ◦ *Do you prefer brown rice or white rice?* **2** a grass that produces these seeds and grows in warm wet places

ˈrice ˌpaddy noun [C] a field full of water in which rice is grown

ˈrice ˌpaper noun [U] thin paper that can be eaten and is used in cooking and in painting

ˌrice ˈpudding noun [U] a sweet dish made by cooking rice in milk and sugar

rich /rɪtʃ/ adj; noun
▸**adj MONEY** ▷ **1** A2 having a lot of money or valuable

possessions: *He's the third richest man in Britain.* ◦ *They're one of the world's richest nations.* ◦ *He is determined to **get** rich quickly.* **HAVING A LOT OF STH** ▷ **2** B2 containing a large amount of a valuable natural substance such as coal, oil, or wood: *The region is rich **in** minerals and coal deposits.* ◦ *The country has vast oil reserves and rich deposits of other minerals.* **3 rich in sth** B2 containing a lot of something good or useful: *Pineapple juice is rich in vitamins A and B.* ◦ *The English language is rich in vocabulary.* **4** Rich land or soil contains a large amount of substances that help plants to grow: *the richest arable land in the country* **5** containing a lot of exciting events or experiences and therefore very interesting: *He has written a book about the island's rich **history**.* ◦ *She had a rich and varied life and met many famous and exciting people.* **6** If the style of something such as a piece of furniture or a building is rich, it contains a lot of decoration: *The temple is noted for its rich carvings.* **ATTRACTIVE** ▷ **7** A rich colour, sound, smell, or taste is strong in a pleasing or attractive way: *This lipstick gives long-lasting rich colour.* ◦ *She produced a rich, deep tone from her clarinet.* ◦ *The wine has a rich aromatic flavour.* **8** A rich material is very beautiful and valuable: *She wore a velvet skirt and a rich brocade jacket.* **FOOD** ▷ **9** B2 If food is rich, it contains a large amount of oil, butter, eggs, or cream: *This chocolate mousse is too rich for me.* **CRITICISM** ▷ **10** [after verb] used to describe someone's opinions when that person has the same bad qualities that they are criticizing: *The education minister's criticism of the new exam system seems rich, considering it was he who demanded the changes in the first place.* ◦ *'He said I was looking rather fat.' '**That's** a bit rich **coming from** him.'*

Other ways of saying rich

The adjectives **wealthy** and **well off** are common alternatives to 'rich':

*Oliver's parents are very **wealthy/well off**.*

If someone is very rich, in informal situations you can use the adjective **loaded**:

*They don't have any money worries – they're **loaded**.*

If someone is richer than he or she was previously, the adjective **better off** is often used:

*We're a lot **better off** now that Jane's working.*

The adjectives **affluent** and **prosperous** are sometimes used to describe areas where people are rich:

*It's a very **affluent** neighbourhood.*

*In a **prosperous** country like this, no one should go hungry.*

▸**noun** [plural] **the rich** C1 rich people considered together as a group: *The resort is frequented by the rich and famous.*

-rich /-rɪtʃ/ **suffix** containing a large amount of a valuable substance: *milk and other calcium-rich food* ◦ *an oil-rich country*

riches /ˈrɪtʃ.ɪz/ **noun** [plural] **1** C2 a large amount of money or valuable possessions: *She donated a sizeable portion of her riches to children's charities.* **2** a large quantity of a valuable natural substance: *The country has great oil/mineral riches.*

richly /ˈrɪtʃ.li/ **adv 1 richly decorated, furnished, etc.** having a lot of beautiful or expensive decoration, furniture, etc.: *The façade of the church is richly decorated in green and white marble.* **2** in a very special or valuable way, or in a way that is greater than usual: *The cake takes two hours to cook, but your patience will be richly **rewarded**.* ◦ *She finally obtained the recognition which she so richly **deserved**.*

richness /ˈrɪtʃ.nəs/ **noun** [U] **A LOT OF STH** ▷ **1** C1 the quality of having a lot of something that is valuable or interesting: *We were impressed by the great richness of detail in her painting.* **ATTRACTIVE** ▷ **2** C1 the quality of looking, sounding, smelling, or tasting strong in a pleasing or attractive way: *richness of flavour* ◦ *It's a wonderful painting – I love the richness of the colours.* **FOOD** ▷ **3** the fact that a food contains a large amount of butter, oil, eggs, or cream: *The richness of the food made him feel slightly ill.*

the Richter scale /ˈrɪk.tə.skeɪl/ US /-t̬ɚ-/ **noun** [S] a system used to measure the strength of an EARTHQUAKE: *The earthquake in Mexico City registered 7.1 on the Richter scale.*

ricin /ˈraɪ.sɪn/ **noun** [U] a poisonous powder obtained from the bean of the CASTOR OIL plant

rick /rɪk/ **noun; verb**

▸**noun** [C] (also **hayrick**) a large pile of STRAW or HAY (= dried grass) that has been built in a regular shape

▸**verb** [T] UK informal to twist a part of your body and hurt it: *I ricked my neck while I was playing squash.*

rickets /ˈrɪk.ɪts/ **noun** [U] a disease which children who do not have enough VITAMIN D can suffer from, in which the bones become soft and not shaped correctly

rickety /ˈrɪk.ɪ.ti/ US /-ə.t̬i/ **adj** in bad condition and therefore weak and likely to break: *Careful! That chair's a bit rickety.* ◦ *She slowly climbed the rickety wooden steps.* ◦ figurative *The recession put a lot of strain on an already rickety economic system.*

rickshaw (also **riksha**) /ˈrɪk.ʃɔː/ US /-ʃɑː/ **noun** [C] a small, covered passenger vehicle with two wheels that is usually pulled by one person

ricochet /ˈrɪk.ə.ʃeɪ/ **verb** [I] If a ball or bullet ricochets, it hits a surface and moves away from it at an angle: *The ball ricocheted **off** the goalkeeper and into the net.* • **ricochet noun** [C] *He was hit by a ricochet from a stray bullet.*

ricotta /rɪˈkɒt.ə/ US /-ˈkɑː.t̬ə/ **noun** [U] a soft, white Italian cheese which does not have a strong taste

rid /rɪd/ **adj; verb**

▸**adj 1 be rid of sth/sb** to not now have an unwanted or unpleasant task, object, or person: *I didn't enjoy marking those papers and I was glad to be rid of them.* **2 get rid of sth a** B1 to remove or throw away something unwanted: *That cream got rid of my skin rash.* ◦ *I used weedkiller to get rid of the weeds in the garden.* **b** B1 to sell an old or unwanted possession: *Have you managed to get rid of your old Volvo yet?* **3 get rid of sb** C1 to send away someone annoying or to persuade them to leave: *We got rid of our unwelcome guests by saying we had to go to bed.*

▸**verb** (present tense **ridding**, past tense and past participle **rid** or **ridded**)

PHRASAL VERB **rid sb/sth of sth/sb** to cause someone or something to be free of an unpleasant or harmful thing or person: *Our aim is to rid this government of corruption.*

riddance /ˈrɪd.ᵊns/ **noun** informal **good riddance (to bad rubbish)** said when you are pleased that a bad or unwanted thing or person, or something of poor quality, has gone: *We've got rid of the old computer system, and good riddance to bad rubbish is what I say.*

ridden /ˈrɪd.ᵊn/ past participle of **ride**

-ridden /-rɪd.ᵊn/ **suffix** full of something unpleasant or bad: *She was guilt-ridden when she discovered that the business had failed because of her.*

R

riddle /ˈrɪd.l̩/ noun; verb

▸noun QUESTION ▷ **1** [C] a type of question that describes something in a difficult and confusing way and has a clever or funny answer, often asked as a game **2** [C usually singular] something that is confusing, or a problem that is difficult to solve: *Scientists may have* ***solved*** *the riddle* ***of*** *Saturn's rings.*

IDIOM **talk/speak in riddles** to say things in a confusing way

▸verb [T] to make a lot of holes in something: *The anti-aircraft guns riddled the plane's wings* ***with*** *bullets.*

riddled /ˈrɪd.l̩d/ adj **riddled with holes** full of holes: *He wore an old jacket riddled with holes.*

IDIOM **be riddled with sth** If a plan or system, etc. is riddled with bad features, such as mistakes, it is full of them: *This article is riddled with errors.*

ride /raɪd/ verb; noun

▸verb (**rode, ridden**) **1** A1 [I or T] to sit on a horse or a bicycle and travel along on it controlling its movements: *I learned to ride a bike when I was six.* ◦ *I ride my bicycle to work.* ◦ *I ride to work* ***on*** *my bicycle.* ◦ *The hunters came riding* ***by/past*** *on their horses.* ◦ *He rides well/badly (= he can ride horses well/badly).* **2** A2 [I or T] to travel in a vehicle, such as a car, bus, or train: mainly US *We rode the train from Sydney to Perth.* ◦ *He doesn't have a car so he rides to work* ***on*** *the bus.*

IDIOMS **be riding for a fall** to be behaving in a way that is likely to lead you into trouble: *She spends far more than she earns and she's riding for a fall.* • **be riding high** to be very successful: *riding high* ***in*** *the polls/charts* • **let sth ride** informal to not take any action to stop something wrong or unpleasant, thinking that action may not be necessary or is not yet necessary: *Don't panic about the low sales – let it ride for a while till we see if business picks up.* • **ride (on) a wave of sth** If you ride (on) a wave of a feeling, you get an advantage from it: *The prime minister is riding (on) a wave of popularity.* • **ride herd on sb/sth** US to be responsible for controlling a group of people and their actions: *The new editor will ride herd on the staff, checking on the overall policy and tone of the paper.* • **ride (out) the storm** to manage not to be destroyed, harmed, or permanently affected by the difficult situation you experience: *The government seems confident that it will ride out the storm.* • **ride roughshod over sb/sth** to do what you want without giving any attention to other people or their wishes: *They accused the government of riding roughshod over parliamentary procedure.*

PHRASAL VERBS **ride on sth/sb** When something important, such as your reputation or money, rides on a particular person or thing, it will be won or achieved if that person or thing is successful: *The future of the company now rides on the new managing director.* ◦ *I have a lot of money riding on that horse (= I will win or lose a lot of money if that horse wins or loses the race).* • **ride sth out 1** to continue to exist during a difficult situation and until it ends, without serious harm: *Many companies did not manage to ride out the recession.* **2** If a ship rides out a period of bad weather, it continues to float during it, without serious damage: *The ship managed to ride out the storm.* • **ride up** If a piece of clothing rides up, it moves up out of position: *Your skirt has ridden up at the back.*

▸noun [C] **1** B1 a journey on a horse or bicycle, or in a vehicle: *It's a short bus ride to the airport.* ◦ *I went for a (horse) ride last Saturday.* ◦ *Do you want to come for a ride* ***on*** *my bike?* **2** B1 mainly US (UK usually **lift**) a free journey in a car to a place where you want to go: *He asked me for a ride into town.* **3** US a person who gives you a ride in their car: *Well, I have to go – my ride is here.* **4** US informal someone's car: *Hey, nice ride.* **5** B1 a machine in an AMUSEMENT PARK that people travel in or are moved around by for entertainment: *My favourite ride is the Ferris wheel.*

IDIOMS **a rough ride** C2 a difficult time: *Government plans to cut sick pay had a rough ride in the House of Commons.* ◦ *The construction industry is in for a rough ride this year.* • **take sb for a ride** informal to deceive or cheat someone: *Be careful or he'll take you for a ride.*

rider /ˈraɪ.dəʳ/ US /-dɚ/ noun [C] ON HORSE/BICYCLE ▷ **1** B1 a person who travels along on a horse or bicycle: *One of the riders was thrown off his horse.* EXTRA STATEMENT ▷ **2** formal a statement that is added to what has already been said or decided, or an addition to a government BILL (= a written plan for a law): *I should like to add a rider* ***to*** *the judgment of the court.*

riderless /ˈraɪ.də.ləs/ US /-dɚ-/ adj without a person riding: *a riderless horse*

ridge /rɪdʒ/ noun [C] **1** a long, narrow raised part of a surface, especially a high edge along a mountain: *We walked along the narrow mountain ridge.* ◦ figurative *A ridge (= narrow area) of high pressure will bring good weather this afternoon.* **2** the part of a roof where the sloping sides join at the top

ridicule /ˈrɪd.ɪ.kjuːl/ noun; verb

▸noun [U] unkind words or actions that make someone or something look stupid: *She was treated with scorn and ridicule by her colleagues when she applied for the job.* ◦ *He's become an* ***object of*** *ridicule (= a person that everyone thinks is stupid and criticizes or laughs at).*

IDIOMS **hold sb/sth up to ridicule** to laugh unkindly and publicly at someone or something, or make them seem stupid: *Her plans were held up to ridicule.* • **lay yourself open to ridicule** to make it easy for people to laugh unkindly at you: *You lay yourself open to ridicule wearing clothes like that.*

▸verb [T] to laugh at someone in an unkind way: *He was ridiculed* ***for*** *his ideas.*

ridiculous /rɪˈdɪk.jʊ.ləs/ adj B2 stupid or unreasonable and deserving to be laughed at: *Do I look ridiculous in this hat?* ◦ *Don't be so ridiculous! I can't possibly afford to go on holiday.* ◦ *It's ridiculous to expect a two-year-old to be able to read!* • **ridiculously** /-li/ adv *Hotel rooms in the city are ridiculously overpriced.*

riding /ˈraɪ.dɪŋ/ noun [U] the sport or activity of riding horses: *Have you ever been riding?* ◦ *She* ***goes*** *riding on Saturdays.* ◦ *riding* ***boots*** *and a riding* ***hat***

ˈriding ˌschool noun [C] a place where you can learn to ride horses

rife /raɪf/ adj [after verb] formal **1** If something unpleasant is rife, it is very common or happens a lot: *Dysentery and malaria are rife in the refugee camps.* **2 rife with sth** full of something unpleasant: *The office was rife with rumours.*

riff /rɪf/ noun [C] in JAZZ or popular music, a tune that continues or appears regularly in a piece of music while other parts change or are added: *The song is punctuated by long* ***guitar*** *riffs.*

riffle /ˈrɪ.fl̩/ verb [T] (also **riffle through**) to look quickly through the pages of a book, magazine, etc., or through a collection of things: *He riffled through the stack of papers on his desk.*

riff-raff /ˈrɪf.ræf/ noun [plural] disapproving people with a bad reputation or of a low social class: *She says that charging high prices will keep the riff-raff out.*

R

rifle /ˈraɪ.fl̩/ noun; verb

▸**noun** [C] a type of gun with a long BARREL (= part shaped like a tube), fired from the shoulder and designed to be accurate at long distances

▸**verb** [I or T] to search quickly through something, often in order to steal something: *The safe had been rifled and the diamonds were gone.* ◦ *He rifled* ***through*** *the papers on the desk, but couldn't find the photographs.*

ˈrifle ˌrange noun [C] a place where you can practise shooting with a rifle

rift /rɪft/ noun [C] **1** a large CRACK in the ground or in rock: *The stream had cut a deep rift* ***in*** *the rock.* **2** a serious disagreement which separates two people who have been friends and stops their friendship continuing: *The marriage caused a rift* ***between*** *the brothers and they didn't speak to each other for ten years.*

ˈrift ˌvalley noun [C] a valley with steep sides formed by movements of the Earth's surface

rig /rɪg/ verb; noun

▸**verb** [T] (**-gg-**) **DISHONESTLY ARRANGE** ▷ **1** to arrange dishonestly for the result of something, for example an election, to be changed: *Previous* ***elections*** *in the country have been rigged by the ruling party.* **FIX IN PLACE** ▷ **2** to fix a piece of equipment in place: *We rigged* ***up*** *a tent between two trees.* ◦ *The sailors rigged the ship* ***with*** *new sails.*

IDIOM **rig the market** to make the price of SHARES go up or down in order to make a profit

PHRASAL VERBS **rig sb out** informal to put a particular type of clothing on someone: *We rigged our****selves*** *out* ***in*** *tracksuits and running shoes for the race.* • **rig sth up** to quickly make a piece of equipment from any materials you can find: *I rigged up a temporary radio aerial from a coat hanger.*

▸**noun** [C] **STRUCTURE** ▷ **1** a large structure that is used for removing oil or gas from the ground or the bottom of the sea: *Safety precautions on* ***oil*** *rigs are designed to cope with fires and small-scale explosions.* **TRUCK** ▷ **2** mainly US a truck consisting of two or more parts that bend where they are joined so that the vehicle can turn corners more easily

rigatoni /ˌrɪg.əˈtəʊ.ni/ ⓤⓢ /-ˈtoʊ/ noun [U] a type of PASTA in the shape of tubes with lines on the outside

rigging /ˈrɪg.ɪŋ/ noun [U] **DISHONESTLY ARRANGE** ▷ **1** the act of arranging dishonestly for the result of something, for example an election, to be changed: ***ballot*** *rigging* ◦ *Opposition parties have protested over alleged* ***vote*** *rigging in the election.* **SHIP'S ROPES** ▷ **2** the ropes which support and control a ship's sails

right /raɪt/ adj, adv; noun; exclamation; adv; verb

▸**adj** **CORRECT** ▷ **1** (A1) correct: *You* ***got*** *three answers right and two wrong.* ◦ *I set the clock to the right time.* ◦ *'Is that Ms Kramer?' 'Yes,* ***that's*** *right.'* ◦ *Am I right* ***in*** *think****ing*** *(= is it true) that you will be at the conference?* ◦ *You're right* ***to*** *be annoyed – you've been treated very badly.* ◦ *You must* ***put*** *matters right (= make the situation better) by telling the truth.* → Compare **wrong** **2** (A1) If you are right about something or someone, you are correct in your judgment or statement about it or them: *You were right* ***about*** *Pete – he's a real troublemaker.*

> **Usage: right or true?**
>
> **Right** is usually used to say something is correct or to agree with something someone has said:
>
> *He gave the right answer.*
>
> *'That's right, they live in central London.'*
>
> **True** is usually used to say that something is based on facts:
>
> *Is it true that she's leaving?*
>
> *Everything I've told you is true.*

SUITABLE ▷ **3** (B1) suitable or correct, or as it should be: *He's the right person for the job.* ◦ *I think you've made the right decision.* ◦ *The temperature of the swimming pool was just right (= exactly as I wanted it).* ◦ *That hat looks just right on you.* ◦ *He thought the* ***time*** *was right* ***to*** *let his intentions be known.* → Compare **wrong** **4** describes a person who is considered to be socially important or a place that such people go to: *She knows all the right people.* ◦ *He likes to be seen in the right clubs and restaurants.* **5 the right way round/up** UK (US **the right way around/up**) in the correct position: *The lid has to go on the right way round or it won't fit.* ◦ *Keep the bottle the right way up.* **MORALLY ACCEPTABLE** ▷ **6** (B2) [after verb] considered fair or morally acceptable by most people: *I don't believe they should have put him in prison. It isn't right.* ◦ [+ to infinitive] ***It's*** *not right* ***to*** *criticize someone behind their back.* ◦ [+ that] ***It*** *is* ***only*** *(= completely) right* ***that*** *men and women should be paid the same for doing the same work.* → Compare **wrong** **HEALTHY** ▷ **7** healthy, or working correctly: *Since eating that food last night,I haven't felt quite right.* ◦ *Something isn't quite right* ***with*** *the brakes on your bike.* **COMPLETE** ▷ **8** [before noun] informal used for emphasizing when something is bad: *He's a right idiot.* ◦ *His house is a right mess.*

IDIOMS **be as right as rain** informal to be healthy, especially after having been ill for a period of time • **be not (quite) right in the head** informal to not have one or more of the mental abilities that most people have • **be not in your right mind** to be not thinking clearly or to be mentally ill: *My poor old granny isn't in her right mind half the time.* • **be on the right lines** If you are on the right lines, you are doing something in a way that will bring good results: *Do you think we're on the right lines with this project?* • **be on the right track** to be doing something in a way that will bring good results: *These results suggest that we are on the right track.* • **in the right place at the right time** in the best position or place to take advantage of an opportunity: *The key to success is to be in the right place at the right time.* • **press/push the right button(s)** to do exactly what is necessary to get the result that you want: *You have to know how to push all the right buttons if you want to be a successful diplomat.* • **put/set sb right** informal **1** to stop someone believing something that is not true, or to correct them by telling them the truth: *She thought she wouldn't have to work hard, but we soon put her right* ***on*** *that.* **2** to make someone feel better: *A good night's sleep will soon put you right.* • **a right one** informal someone or something that you think is very silly: *We've got a right one here, eh!*

▸**adj, adv** **DIRECTION** ▷ (A2) on or towards the side of your body that is to the east when you are facing north: *Most people write with their right hand.* ◦ ***Turn/ Go*** *right (= take the road on the right) at the first traffic lights.* → Compare **left**

IDIOMS **give your right arm** informal If you say that you would give your right arm to do or have something, you mean you would like it very much: *I would give my right arm **to** meet the president.* • **right, left, and centre** (US **right and left**) all the time or everywhere: *He spends money right, left, and centre.*

▸noun **DIRECTION** ▷ **1** A2 [S] the right side: *English is written and read from left to right.* ◦ *King's Avenue is the first right (= the first road on the right side).* ◦ US *I **took/made*** (informal ***hung***) *a right (= turned into the next road on the right side) after crossing the bridge.* ◦ *In this photo, my wife is the woman standing **on/to** my right.* **POLITICS** ▷ **2 the right** (also **the Right**) [S, + sing/pl verb] C2 political parties or people that have traditional opinions, and that believe in low taxes, property, and industry being privately owned, and less help for the poor: *In Britain, the right was/were in power after 1979.* ◦ *He's a man of the **far** (= extreme) right.* → Compare **left** **MORALLY ACCEPTABLE** ▷ **3** B2 [U] what is considered to be morally good or acceptable: *Your conscience should tell you the difference between right **and wrong**.* **4 in the right** If you are in the right, what you are doing is morally or legally correct. **5** B2 [C] the fact that a person or animal can expect to be treated in a fair, morally acceptable, or legal way, or to have the things that are necessary for life: *She campaigned for **women's** rights during the 1960s.* ◦ *Everyone has a right **to** education.* ◦ *She has no more right **to** a company car than I have (= she does not deserve one more than I do).* ◦ [+ to infinitive] *You're not my boss, so what right (= authority) have you got **to** criticize me?* ◦ *You have **every** right (= you have a good reason) **to** complain.* **6 within your rights** If you are within your rights to do something, you are legally allowed to do it: *I think I'm quite within my rights **to** demand a full refund.* **7 rights** [plural] **a** legal controls over who is allowed to use a book or film: *He has acquired the **film** rights to the book (= he is allowed to make a film of the book).* **b** new SHARES in a particular company that have become available for people to buy who already own SHARES: *The company made a rights **issue** of one new share for every four held.* **8 put/set sth to rights** to improve or correct something: *The company needs over a million dollars to set its finances to rights.*

IDIOMS **by right of** because of: *She spoke first, by right of her position as director.* • **by rights** if the situation was fair: *By rights, it should be my turn next.* • **in your own right** If someone has a position in their own right, they have earned it or got it by themselves and not because of anyone else: *She's a millionaire in her own right.* • **the rights and wrongs** the details of who or what is fair or unfair: *I don't care about the rights and wrongs of the matter – I just want you both to stop arguing.*

▸exclamation informal **AGREEMENT** ▷ **1** A2 used to express agreement with someone or to show that you have understood what someone has said: *'Johnny, you climb up first.' 'Right.'* **2** A2 said when you want to make a group of people notice you, especially so that you can start an activity: *Right, you lot. Could you all stop talking, and then we'll begin.* **3** said between parts of a story that you are telling, in order to make certain that people are paying attention and understanding: *So there I was right, middle of the night, right, and this guy came up to me…*

IDIOMS **right you are!** (also **righto!**) old-fashioned informal said to show that you understand and agree: *'Give me a shout when you're ready.' 'Right you are.'* • **too right** UK informal said when you agree completely: *'You can't do anything in this town if you haven't got any money.' 'Too right.'*

▸adv **EXACTLY** ▷ **1** B1 exactly or all the way: *I've got a pimple right on the end of my nose.* ◦ *They built a row of hotels right along the sea-front.* **2** used for emphasis: *The car ran right (= completely) out of fuel.* ◦ *She walked right (= all the way) past me without noticing me.* ◦ *I'll be right back/I'll be right with you (= I will return very soon).* **3 right away/now** B1 immediately: *You'd better leave right now.* **4 right now** at the present time: *We're very busy right now.* **IN TITLES** ▷ **5** used as part of the title of particular people, such as BISHOPS and some members of Parliament: *the Right Honourable Diane Abbott, MP* **CORRECTLY** ▷ **6** B2 correctly: *Why does he never do anything right?* **SUCCESSFULLY** ▷ **7 go right** If something goes right, it is successful or happens in a way that you hoped it would: *Things haven't been going right for me these past few months.*

IDIOM **right behind sb** If someone is right behind you, they give you their complete support: *My whole family are right behind me in this crisis.*

▸verb [T] **1** formal If you right a situation or a mistake, you make it better or correct it: *It's a terrible situation and we should right it as soon as possible.* **2** If a boat rights itself, it turns itself back to its correct position in the water: *The canoe will right itself if it capsizes.*

ˈright ˌangle noun [C] an angle of 90°: *A square has four right angles.*

right-angled ˈtriangle noun [C] UK (US **ˌright ˈtriangle**) a triangle that has one angle of 90°

ˈright-ˌclick verb [I] to press the button on the right of a computer mouse in order to make the computer do something: *Right-click on the Start button and then click on 'Explore'.*

righteous /ˈraɪ.tʃəs/ adj formal morally correct: *He was regarded as a righteous and holy man.* ◦ *an outburst of righteous anger* → See also **self-righteous** • **righteously** /-li/ adv • **righteousness** /-nəs/ noun [U]

ˌright ˈfield noun [U] the area of a baseball field outside the BASES (= places to which players run) and between first and second base

rightful /ˈraɪt.fəl/ adj A rightful position or claim is one that is morally or legally correct: *Don't forget that I am the rightful **owner** of this house.* • **rightfully** /-i/ adv *The furniture rightfully belongs to you.*

ˈright-hand adj [before noun] A2 on or to the right: *In North America, vehicles drive on the right-hand **side** of the road.*

right-hand ˈdrive adj A right-hand drive vehicle has the controls on the right side, and the vehicle is intended to be driven on the left side of the road. • **ˌright-hand ˈdrive** noun [C] a vehicle that is right-hand drive

ˌright-ˈhanded adj using your right hand to write with and do most things: *She's right-handed.*

right-hander /ˌraɪtˈhæn.dəʳ/ US /-dɚ/ noun [C] informal **1** someone who uses their right hand for writing and for doing most things **2** (also **right**) a hit made with the right hand

ˌright-hand ˈman noun [C usually singular] someone who helps and supports you the most, especially at work: *How will he cope without his right-hand man?*

rightist /ˈraɪ.tɪst/ US /-t̬ɪst/ noun; adj

▸noun [C] a politician who supports the beliefs of the political right

▸adj A rightist politician or government is one that supports the beliefs of the political right.

R

rightly /ˈraɪt.li/ adv **MORALLY ACCEPTABLE** ▷ **1** B2 behaving in a way that is suitable and acceptable: *They quite rightly complained to the manager.* **2 rightly or wrongly** used to mean that something may or may not be morally correct, but it is a fact: *Rightly or wrongly, she has been given the post of managing director.* **CORRECTLY** ▷ **3** B2 in a correct or exact way: *Many people rightly* ***believe*** *that the war is a sham.*

ˌright-ˈminded adj [before noun] (also **ˌright-ˈthinking**) having beliefs or opinions that most people think are reasonable and show good judgment: *Every right-minded person is against terrorism.*

rightness /ˈraɪt.nəs/ noun [U] the state of being morally or legally correct: *He is convinced of the rightness of his actions.*

ˌright of ˈway noun **RIGHT TO GO FIRST** ▷ **1** [C or U] the legal right to go first across a road, before other road users: *Pedestrians* ***have*** *right of way at this turning.* **ROAD/PATH** ▷ **2** [C] a path or road over private land which people are legally allowed to walk along

ˌright ˈon adj; exclamation
▸adj often disapproving having beliefs that are characteristic of someone who supports the political left
▸exclamation old-fashioned slang an expression of agreement or approval: *'D'you want to listen to some Jimi Hendrix?' 'Right on.'*

ˌright-ˈwing adj C2 supporting the political right: *She's extremely right-wing.*

the ˌright ˈwing noun [S + sing/pl verb] the political RIGHT: *He's* ***on*** *the right wing of the party.*

ˌright-ˈwinger noun [C] someone who supports the beliefs of the political right

rigid /ˈrɪdʒ.ɪd/ adj **1** C2 stiff or fixed; not able to be bent or moved: *a rigid steel and concrete structure* ◦ *I was rigid* ***with*** *(= stiff and unable to move because of) fear.* **2** not able to be changed or persuaded: disapproving *We were disappointed that they insisted on such a rigid interpretation of the rules.* • **rigidity** /rɪˈdʒɪd.ɪ.ti/ US /-ə.t̬i/ noun [U] • **rigidly** /-li/ adv mainly disapproving

rigmarole disapproving (US also **rigamarole**) /ˈrɪg.mə.rəʊl/ US /-roʊl/ noun [U] a long set of actions or words without any real purpose: *The customs officials made us* ***go through the*** *(****whole****) rigmarole of opening up our bags for inspection.*

rigor mortis /ˌrɪg.əˈmɔː.tɪs/ US /-ɚˈmɔːr.t̬ɪs/ noun [U] specialized the stiffness of the JOINTS (= places where two bones are connected) and muscles of a dead body: *Rigor mortis usually* ***sets in*** *between two and four hours after death.*

rigorous /ˈrɪg.ər.əs/ US /-ɚ-/ adj **CAREFUL** ▷ **1** approving careful to look at or consider every part of something to make certain it is correct or safe: *rigorous testing/checking/methods* **SEVERE** ▷ **2** controlling behaviour in a severe way: *the rigorous controls governing the sale of shares* • **rigorously** /-li/ adv

rigour UK (US **rigor**) /ˈrɪg.əʳ/ US /-ɚ/ noun [U] **FORCEFULNESS** ▷ **1** the fact that people are made to follow rules in a very severe way: *They were punished with unusual rigour.* **2 the rigours of sth** the unpleasant or severe conditions of something: *They survived the rigours of the winter.* **CARE** ▷ **3** formal approving the quality of being detailed, careful, and complete: *Her arguments lacked intellectual rigour.*

ˈrig-out noun [C] informal old-fashioned a set of clothes: *I want to get myself a new rig-out for the party.*

rile /raɪl/ verb [T] informal to make someone angry: *Don't let her rile you.*

rim /rɪm/ noun; verb
▸noun [C] the outer, often curved or circular, edge of something: *The rim of the cup was chipped and broken.* ◦ *My reading glasses have wire rims.* • **rimless** /-ləs/ adj *He's got new rimless reading* ***glasses****.*
▸verb [T] (**-mm-**) to be round or along the edge of something: *The martini glass was rimmed* ***with*** *sugar.* • **-rimmed** /-d/ suffix ***gold****-rimmed glasses*

rind /raɪnd/ noun [C or U] the hard outer layer or covering of particular fruits and foods: *lemon/orange rind* ◦ *bacon/cheese rind* → Compare **peel**

ring /rɪŋ/ noun; verb
▸noun **CIRCLE** ▷ **1** B2 [C] a circle of any material, or any group of things or people in a circular shape or arrangement: *The game involved throwing metal rings over a stick.* ◦ *The children sat in a ring around the teacher.* **2** A2 [C] a circular piece of jewellery worn especially on your finger: *He bought her a diamond/emerald, etc. ring (= a ring with a jewel fixed to it).* **3** [C] a group of people who help each other, often secretly and in a way that is to their advantage: *a drug ring* ◦ *a spy ring* → See also **ringleader 4** [C] (US usually **element**) a circular piece of material often made of metal that can be heated in order to be used for cooking: *a gas ring* ◦ *an electric ring* **5** [C] a special area where people perform or compete: *a boxing ring* ◦ *The horses trotted round the ring.* → See also **ringside 6 rings** [plural] two round handles at the ends of two long ropes that hang from the ceiling and are used in GYMNASTICS **PHONE** ▷ **7** A2 [S] mainly UK (US usually and UK also **call**) the act of making a phone call to someone: *I'll* ***give*** *you* ***a*** *ring tomorrow.* **SOUND** ▷ **8** B2 [C] the sound a bell makes: *There was a ring at the door.* ◦ *He gave a ring at the door.*

IDIOMS **familiar ring** If something has a familiar ring, you think you already know it, but you are not sure: *Her name had a familiar ring* ***to it****.* • **ring of truth** If something has a ring of truth, it seems to be true: *This story* ***has a/the*** *ring of truth.* • **run rings round sb** If someone runs rings round you, they are very much better, faster, or more successful at something than you are.

▸verb **PHONE** ▷ **1** A2 [I or T] (**rang, rung**) mainly UK (US usually and UK also **call**) to make a phone call to someone: *I ring home once a week to tell my parents I'm okay.* ◦ *There's been an accident – can you ring* ***for*** *an ambulance?* ◦ *The boss rang (****in****) to say he'll be back at 4.30.* ◦ UK *I rang* ***round*** *the airlines (= called many of them) to find out the cheapest price.* ◦ *Why don't you ring (****up****) Simon and ask him to the party?* **MAKE SOUND** ▷ **2** B1 [I or T] (**rang, rung**) to (cause to) make the sound of a bell: *The doorbell/phone rang.* ◦ *Anne's alarm clock rang for half an hour before she woke.* ◦ *I rang the bell but nobody came to the door.* ◦ *My head is/My ears are still ringing (= are full of a ringing noise) from the sound of the military band.* **CIRCLE** ▷ **3** [T] (**ringed, ringed**) to surround something: *Armed police ringed the hijacked plane.* ◦ *The harbour is dangerous – it's ringed* ***by/with*** *rocks and reefs.* **4** [T] (**ringed, ringed**) UK to draw a circle round something: *Students should ring the correct answers in pencil.* **5** [T] (**ringed, ringed**) to put a ring on something, especially an animal: *We ringed the birds (= put rings around their legs) so that we could identify them later.*

IDIOMS **ring a bell** (also **ring any bells**) C2 to sound familiar: *The name rang a bell but I couldn't remember where I had heard it before.* ◦ *No, I'm sorry, that description doesn't ring any bells* ***with*** *me.* • **ring the changes (on)** to do something in a different way in order to make it more interesting: *For variety, ring the changes on packed lunches using different types of*

R

bread and spicy fillings. • **ring true/false** to seem true/false: *Her explanations didn't ring true.*

PHRASAL VERBS **ring (sb) back** UK B1 to phone someone who phoned you earlier or to phone someone for a second time: *I'm a bit busy – can I ring you back later?* • **ring off** UK to end a phone conversation intentionally: *She said 'No, thank you' and rang off hurriedly.* • **ring out** When a sound rings out, it is loud and clear: *A cry of warning rang out.* ◦ *A shot rang out.* • **ring sb/sth up** B1 to make a phone call to someone: *She rang me up to say she couldn't come.* ◦ *He rang up the office and asked to speak to the manager.* • **ring sth up** to record the money that has been paid by a customer by pressing buttons on a CASH REGISTER: *I'm sorry, I've rung up the wrong amount.* • **ring with sth** If a place rings with a sound, it is full of it: *The room rang with his screams.*

ˈring ˌbinder noun [C] a piece of stiff folded cardboard with metal rings inside, used to keep loose pages in position

ˈring ˌfinger noun [C] the finger nearest to your LITTLE FINGER. In many Western cultures, people often wear a ring on their ring finger to show that they are married or are planning to get married. → See **engagement ring, wedding ring**

ˈring-in noun [C] Australian English informal a person included in an activity at a late stage

ringleader /ˈrɪŋˌliː.dəʳ/ US /-dɚ/ noun [C] the leader of a group of people who are doing something harmful or illegal

ringlet /ˈrɪŋ.lət/ US /-lɪt/ noun [C usually plural] a curled piece of long hair: *Her hair hung about her shoulders **in** ringlets.*

ringmaster /ˈrɪŋˌmɑː.stəʳ/ US /-ˌmæs.tɚ/ noun [C] the person who introduces the performers at a CIRCUS

ˈring ˌpull noun [C] UK (US **ˈpull-ˌtab**) a metal ring which must be lifted to open a closed metal container, especially of drink: *a ring pull can*

ˈring ˌroad noun [C] UK (US usually **beltway**) a main road that goes around the edge of a town, allowing traffic to avoid the town centre

ringside /ˈrɪŋ.saɪd/ noun [S] the edge of a special area where people compete or perform: *We managed to get ringside **seats** for the circus.*

R

ringtone /ˈrɪŋ.təʊn/ US /-toʊn/ noun [C] the sound that a phone makes, especially a mobile phone when someone is ringing it

ringtoss /ˈrɪŋ.tɒs/ US /-tɑːs/ noun [U] US for **hoopla**

ringworm /ˈrɪŋ.wɜːm/ US /-wɜːm/ noun [U] a disease that causes red rings on the skin

rink /rɪŋk/ noun [C] a large, flat surface, of ice or other hard material, for SKATING (= a sport using special boots to move along) or the area or building which contains this: *an ice rink* ◦ *a roller-skating rink*

rinky-dink /ˈrɪŋ.ki.dɪŋk/ adj US informal having little importance or influence, or old-fashioned or of poor quality: *Their family business is a rinky-dink operation.*

rinse /rɪns/ verb; noun

▸verb [I or T] **CLEAN** ▷ to use water to clean the soap or dirt from something: *First apply shampoo to hair and then rinse **thoroughly**.* ◦ *There was no soap, so I just rinsed my hands with water.*

PHRASAL VERB **rinse sth out** to quickly wash the inside of something with clean water: *I'll just rinse these glasses out and leave them to dry.* ◦ *She rinses out her mouth every morning to prevent bad breath.*

▸noun **1** [C] the process of using water to get rid of soap or dirt: *He **gave** the soapy dishes a rinse.* **2** [C or U] a substance that gives a temporary colour to the hair: *My grandmother had a blue rinse every month.*

Rioja /riːˈɒ.kə/ US /-ˈɑː-/ noun [C or U] a type of Spanish wine

riot /ˈraɪ.ət/ noun; verb

▸noun **1** C1 [C] a noisy, violent, and uncontrolled public meeting: *Inner-city riots **erupted** when a local man was shot by police.* **2** [S] old-fashioned informal a very funny or entertaining occasion or person: *'How was the party?' 'It was great – we **had** a riot.'* ◦ *I met Mike's brother for the first time – he's a riot.*

IDIOMS **a riot of colour** C2 extremely colourful and bright: *Jim's rose garden is a riot of colour.* • **run riot** **1** C2 If people run riot, they behave in a way that is not controlled, running in all directions or being noisy or violent: *I dread them coming round because they let their kids run riot.* **2** If your imagination runs riot, you have a lot of strange, exciting or surprising thoughts: *My imagination was running riot, thinking of all the ways that I could spend the money.*

▸verb [I] C2 to take part in a riot: *Students are rioting in the streets of the capital.* • **rioter** /ˈraɪ.ə.təʳ/ US /-t̬ɚ/ noun [C] *Police and rioters clashed violently.* • **rioting** /ˈraɪ.ə.tɪŋ/ US /-t̬ɪŋ/ noun [U] *The government is afraid of further serious rioting today.*

ˈriot ˌgear noun [U] the special clothes and equipment that the police use when they are dealing with a large violent group of people: *Police in riot gear broke up the protest.*

riotous /ˈraɪ.ə.təs/ US /-t̬əs/ adj very loud and uncontrolled, and full of energy: *We went to a riotous party and danced all night.* ◦ UK *Five students were arrested for riotous behaviour.* • **riotously** /-li/ adv • **riotousness** /-nəs/ noun [U]

ˈriot poˌlice noun [U] a special part of a police force trained to deal with noisy, violent groups

rip /rɪp/ verb; noun

▸verb (-pp-) **TEAR** ▷ **1** B2 [I or T] to pull apart; to tear or be torn violently and quickly: *His new trousers ripped when he bent down.* ◦ *I ripped my shirt on a nail.* ◦ [+ obj + adj] *She excitedly ripped the parcel **open**.* ◦ *The wind ripped the flag **to/into shreds** (= into little pieces).* **2** C1 [T + adv/prep] to remove something quickly, without being careful: *I wish the old fireplaces hadn't been ripped **out**.* ◦ *We ripped **up** the carpets and laid a new wooden floor.* **COPY** ▷ **3** [T] to copy pictures or sounds from a CD or DVD onto a computer: *How do I rip a DVD movie **to** my hard drive?*

PHRASAL VERBS **rip sb off** informal C2 to cheat someone by making them pay too much money for something: *Bob's tickets cost much less than ours – I think we've been ripped off.* • **rip sth off** **REMOVE** ▷ **1** to remove something very quickly and carelessly: *They ripped off their clothes and ran into the sea.* **STEAL** ▷ **2** slang to steal something: *He rips stuff off from supermarkets to pay for his heroin.* • **rip through sth** to move very powerfully through a place or building, destroying it quickly: *The explosion ripped through the hotel.* ◦ *A hurricane ripped through the Caribbean.* • **rip sth up** to tear something into small pieces: *She ripped up his letters and burned the pieces.*

▸noun [C] (plural **-pp-**) **TEAR** ▷ **1** a tear in a piece of cloth or paper: *Your sleeve has got a rip in it.* **COPY** ▷ **2** a copy of a CD or DVD that you make on a computer: *illegal rips of copyrighted music*

RIP /ˌɑː.raɪˈpiː/ US /ˌɑːr.aɪ-/ abbreviation for rest in peace → See at **rest**

ripcord /ˈrɪp.kɔːd/ (US) /-kɔːrd/ noun [C] a rope that you pull to open a PARACHUTE

ripe /raɪp/ adj **FRUIT/CROPS** ▷ **1** (B2) (of fruit or crops) completely developed and ready to be collected or eaten: *Those bananas aren't ripe yet – they're still green.* **CHEESE** ▷ **2** describes cheese that has developed a strong flavour: *This brie smells good and ripe.* **SMELL** ▷ **3** describes a smell that is strong and unpleasant: *There was a ripe **smell** from his socks.* **LANGUAGE** ▷ **4** old-fashioned humorous describes language that is rude: *a ripe joke* • **ripeness** /ˈraɪp.nəs/ noun [U]

IDIOMS **ripe for** (C2) developed to a suitable condition for something to happen: *The company is ripe for takeover.* ◦ ***The time** is ripe (= it is the right time) for investing in new technology.* • **ripe old age** approving old age: *My grandmother died at the ripe old age **of** 92.*

ripen /ˈraɪ.pᵊn/ verb **1** [I or T] to (cause to) become ripe: *The summer sunshine ripened the melons.* ◦ *These melons are ripening nicely.* **2** [I] to develop to a suitable condition for something to happen: *My plans are ripening – now all I need is official approval.*

ˈrip-off noun [C usually singular] something that is not worth what you pay for it: *$300 for that shirt? – That's a complete rip-off.*

riposte /rɪˈpɒst/ (US) /-ˈpoʊst/ noun [C] a quick and clever remark, often made in answer to a criticism: *She made a sharp/witty/neat riposte.* • **riposte** verb [I or T]

ripples

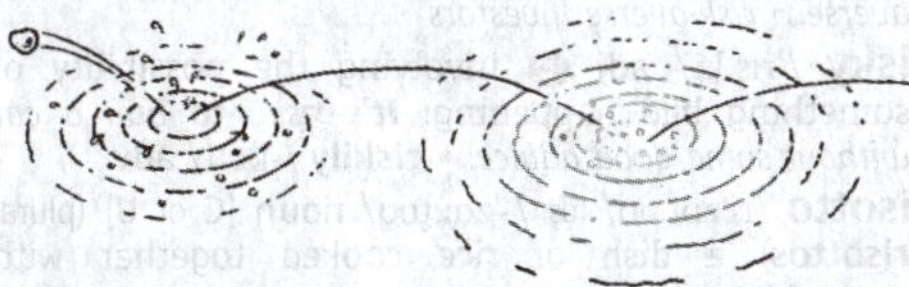

ripple /ˈrɪp.l̩/ noun; verb

▸**noun 1** [C] a small wave on the surface of water: *The stone she threw caused ripples to spread across the lake.* **2** [C] a sound or feeling that spreads through a person or group of people, gradually increasing and then becoming smaller: *A ripple **of laughter/applause, etc.** ran through the crowd.* ◦ *A ripple **of excitement/unease, etc.** flowed up her spine.* ◦ *News of the war hardly caused a ripple (= people showed little interest).* **3** [U] plain ice cream with thin lines of other flavours in it: *raspberry ripple*

▸**verb** [I or T] to (cause to) move in small waves: *The breeze rippled the water.* ◦ *His **muscles** rippled under his skin.*

ˈripple efˌfect noun [C usually singular] a situation in which one event produces effects which spread and produce further effects: *The bank crash has **had** a ripple effect **on** the whole community.*

ˌrip-ˈroaring adj [before noun] informal wild, noisy, and exciting: *The party was a rip-roaring, riotous **success**.*

rise /raɪz/ verb; noun

▸**verb** (**rose**, **risen**) **MOVE UP** ▷ **1** (B1) [I] to move upwards: *The balloon rose gently (**up**) into the air.* ◦ *At 6 a.m. we watched the sun rise (= appear and move upwards in the sky).* ◦ *When you put yeast in bread and bake the bread, it rises (= gets bigger).* ◦ *New buildings are rising (= being built) throughout the city.* ◦ *The River Cam rises (= first comes out of the ground) **in/at** a place called Ashwell.* ◦ figurative *Murmurs of disapproval rose **from** (= came from) the crowd.* **2** [I] to stand, especially after sitting: *She rose **from** her chair to welcome us.* ◦ *He rose **to** his **feet** to deliver his speech.* **3** [I] formal to get out of bed: *My grandfather rises at five every morning to do his exercises.* **INCREASE** ▷ **4** (B2) [I] to increase: *Inflation is rising at/by 2.1 percent a month.* ◦ *The wind/storm is rising (= beginning to get stronger).* **5** [I] When emotions, etc. rise, they start to increase: *Tempers are rising (= people are becoming angry).* ◦ *My spirits rise (= I feel happier) whenever I think of my friends.* ◦ *She felt panic and terror rise **in** her whenever she thought of the future.* ◦ *His voice rose (= became louder or higher) as he got angry.*

> **!** Common mistake: **rise up or rise?**
>
> To talk about something increasing in amount or strength, don't say 'rise up', say **rise**:
>
> ~~*Last year unemployment rose up dramatically.*~~
>
> *Last year unemployment rose dramatically.*

> **!** Common mistake: **rise or raise?**
>
> **Warning:** choose the right verb!
>
> To talk about causing something to increase in size or amount, don't say 'rise', say **raise**:
>
> ~~*If we rise their salaries the staff will be more motivated.*~~
>
> **Remember: rise** cannot be followed by a direct object.

BECOME SUCCESSFUL ▷ **6** (C2) [I] to become important, successful, or powerful: *After a long career with the company, she has risen **to** the position of chief executive.* ◦ *He rose **to power** as the country emerged from its financial crisis.* ◦ *She quickly rose **through the ranks** to become head of marketing.* ◦ *The singer has risen **from** humble origins to become one of the most successful entertainers of all time.* **BECOME HIGHER** ▷ **7** [I] to become higher: *The ground rises over there.* ◦ *The castle is built on rising ground (= ground higher than areas around it).* ◦ *You can see the Alps rising (= showing as a higher area) **in** the distance/**above** the clouds.* **BE OPPOSED TO** ▷ **8** [I usually + adv/prep] (of a group of people) to begin to oppose or fight a bad government or ruler: *The people rose (**up**) **against** the oppressor/tyrant/dictator.* **STOP WORK** ▷ **9** [I] formal If parliament or a court rises, it stops work: *Parliament/The court rose at 6 p.m.*

> **!** Common mistake: **rise**
>
> **Warning:** Check your verb endings!
>
> Many learners make mistakes when using **rise** in the past tense.The past simple is **rose**. Don't write 'rised', write **rose**. The past participle is **risen**.

IDIOMS **rise and shine!** humorous said to tell someone to wake up and get out of bed: *Wakey wakey, rise and shine!* • **rise from the dead/grave** to become alive again after having died • **rise to fame** to become famous: *He rose to fame in the 90s as a TV presenter.* • **rise to the bait** to accept an offer or suggestion that seems good but is really a trick: *They offered a good salary, but I didn't rise to the bait.* • **rise to the occasion/challenge** to show that you can deal with a difficult situation successfully: *In the exam she rose to the occasion and wrote a brilliant essay.*

PHRASAL VERB **rise above sth** to not allow something bad to affect your behaviour or upset you: *He rose above his pain/bad luck/difficulties.*

▸**noun INCREASE** ▷ **1** (B2) [C] an increase: *a sudden temperature rise* ◦ *a five percent rise **in** inflation* ◦ *August has seen a large rise in the number of unemployed.* **2 on the rise** increasing: *Police say that youth crime is on the rise again.* **MOVEMENT UP** ▷ **3** (C2) [S] the process of becoming very famous, powerful, or popular: *Her rapid rise **to***

R

Common mistake: rise

When you are talking about the thing that has risen, the most usual preposition to use after **rise** is **in**.

Don't say 'a rise of something', say **a rise in something**:

There has been a two percent rise in the rate of unemployment.

Remember: when **rise** is followed by an amount, the correct preposition is **of**:

There has been a rise of two percent.

Word partners for rise noun (INCREASE)

a *dramatic/huge/sharp/steep* rise • a *steady* rise • *cause/fuel/spark* a rise • a rise *in* sth

Word partners for rise noun (MOVEMENT UP)

a *meteoric/phenomenal/spectacular* rise • the riseof sth • sb/sth's rise *to* sth • *chart/chronicle* the rise of sb/sth

fame/power/popularity, etc. meant that she made many enemies. **SLOPE/HILL** ▷ **4** [C] a small hill or slope: *The castle is built on a slight rise above the town.*

IDIOMS **get a rise out of** (UK also **take a rise out of**) to annoy someone: *Steve always manages to get a rise out of me with his racist jokes.* • **give rise to** C2 to cause something: *International support has given rise to a new optimism in the company.*

riser /ˈraɪ.zəʳ/ US /-zɚ/ noun **PERSON** ▷ **1 early/late riser** a person who usually gets out of bed early/late in the morning **STEP** ▷ **2** [C] specialized the vertical part of a step **3 risers** [plural] US a group of steps on which people sit or stand to see or be seen better **PRICE** ▷ **4** [C] something such as a SHARE price or CURRENCY whose value has gone up during a particular period: *The day's sharpest riser was British Borneo, which put on 33p to 320p.*

risible /ˈrɪz.ə.bl̩/ adj formal disapproving not effective or useful: *She's been making risible attempts to learn the trumpet.*

rising /ˈraɪ.zɪŋ/ noun; preposition

▸noun [C] an **uprising**

▸**preposition** mainly UK about to become: *The school accepts children who are rising five years old.*

ˌrising ˈdamp noun [U] water that moves into the walls of buildings from the ground and damages them

ˌrising ˈstar noun [C] a person who is likely to be successful: *She's the rising star of the organization.*

risk /rɪsk/ noun; verb

▸**noun 1** B2 [C or U] the possibility of something bad happening: *In this business, the risks and the rewards are high.* ◦ *There's a high risk* ***of*** *another accident happening in this fog.* ◦ [+ (that)] *The risk (**that**) we might fail made us work twice as hard.* ◦ [+ -ing verb] *It's always a risk start**ing** up a new business.* ◦ *The company is quite a **good** risk (= safe to lend money to).* ◦ *We want clean rivers and lakes, where you can swim without risk **to** your health.* ◦ *It's a **low/high**-risk strategy (= one that is safe/not safe).* **2** C1 [C] something bad that might happen: *This wire is a **safety/fire** risk.* ◦ *His employers thought he was a **security** risk (= he might tell their secrets to a competitor).* **3 at risk** B2 in a dangerous situation: *All houses within 100 metres of the seas are at risk **of** flooding.* **4 at your own risk** C2 used to mean that you are responsible for any damage, loss, or difficulty: *Owners are reminded that they leave their cars here at their own risk.* **5 run/take a risk** B2 to do something you know might be dangerous: *Don't take any risks – just ring the police.*

Word partners for risk noun

increase/minimize/reduce a risk • *carry/pose* a risk • a *considerable/great/high/serious* risk • a *low/slight/small* risk • a risk *factor* • an *element of* risk • a risk *of* sth • a risk *to* sb/sth

IDIOMS **at the risk of doing sth** used before you say something that may seem offensive or stupid: *At the risk of seeming rude, I'm afraid I have to leave now.* ◦ *At the risk of sounding stupid, how do I send this email?* • **run the risk of doing sth** to do something although something bad might happen because of it: *If you tell him the truth, you run the risk of hurting his feelings.*

▸**verb** [T] **1** B2 to do something although there is a chance of a bad result: *'It's dangerous to cross here.' 'I'll just have to risk **it**.'* ◦ [+ -ing verb] *He risked los**ing** his house when his company went bankrupt.* **2** B2 If you risk something important, you cause it to be in a dangerous situation where you might lose it: *I'm not risking my **life*** (informal ***neck***) *in that old car.* ◦ *He risked **life and limb** to get the cat down from the tree.* ◦ *She was prepared to risk everything **on** a last throw of the dice.*

ˈrisk-aˌverse adj unwilling to take risks or wanting to avoid risks as much as possible: *He feels modern attitudes to children's play are too restrictive and risk-averse.* ◦ *risk-averse investors*

risky /ˈrɪs.ki/ adj B2 involving the possibility of something bad happening: ***It's** risky **to** buy a car without some good advice.* • **riskily** /-kɪ.li/ adv

risotto /rɪˈzɒt.əʊ/ US /-ˈzɑː.t̬oʊ/ noun [C or U] (plural **risottos**) a dish of rice cooked together with vegetables, meat, etc.

risqué /rɪˈskeɪ/ adj (of jokes or stories) slightly rude or shocking, especially because of being about sex

rissole /ˈrɪs.əʊl/ US /-oʊl/ noun [C] a type of food made from meat or vegetables cut into small pieces and then pressed together and cooked in fat: *chicken/lentil rissoles*

rite /raɪt/ noun [C usually plural] (a usually religious ceremony with) a set of fixed words and actions: *funeral/marriage/fertility rites* ◦ *You have to go through an initiation rite before you become a full member.*

ˌrite of ˈpassage noun [C] an official ceremony or informal activity which marks an important stage or occasion in a person's life, especially becoming an adult

ritual /ˈrɪt.ju.əl/ US /ˈrɪtʃ.u-/ noun [C or U] C2 a set of fixed actions and sometimes words performed regularly, especially as part of a ceremony: *Coffee and the newspaper are part of my morning ritual.* ◦ *The birds were performing a complex mating ritual.* • **ritualistic** /ˌrɪt.ju.əlˈɪs.tɪk/ US /ˌrɪtʃ.u-/ adj • **ritualistically** /ˌrɪt.ju.əlˈɪs.tɪ.kəl.i/ US /ˌrɪtʃ.u-/ adv

ritzy /ˈrɪt.si/ adj old-fashioned informal expensive and fashionable: *That's a ritzy dress.*

rival /ˈraɪ.vəl/ noun; verb

▸**noun** [C] C1 a person, group, etc. competing with others for the same thing or in the same area: *He beat his **closest/nearest** rival by 20 marks.* ◦ *The companies produce rival versions of the toy.*

▸**verb** [T] (**-ll-** or US usually **-l-**) C2 to be as good, clever, beautiful, etc. as someone or something else: *No computer can rival a human brain **for/in** complexity.* ◦ *The beauty of the country is only rivalled by (= is equal to) the violence of its politics.*

rivalry /ˈraɪ.vəl.ri/ **noun** [C or U] C2 a situation in which people, businesses, etc. compete with each other for the same thing: *There's such rivalry* ***among/between*** *my three sons.* ◦ *There's fierce rivalry* ***for*** *the job/****to*** *get the job.*

riven /ˈrɪv.ən/ **adj** [after verb] literary violently divided: *It was a community/nation/family riven* ***by*** *hatred.*

river /ˈrɪv.ər/ (US) /-ɚ/ **noun** [C] **1** A1 a natural wide flow of fresh water across the land into the sea, a lake, or another river: *We sailed slowly down the river.* **2** A1 (written abbreviation **R**) used usually before, sometimes after, the name of a river: *the River Thames* **3 up (the) river** in the opposite direction to the flow of water in the river: *We sailed up river.* **4 down (the) river** in the same direction as the flow of water in the river

IDIOM **rivers of sth** a large amount of a liquid: *Rivers of sweat ran down his back.* ◦ figurative *If there's a revolution, rivers of blood will flow.*

riverbank /ˈrɪvəˌbæŋk/ (US) /-ɚ-/ **noun** [C] (also **bank**) the land at either edge of a river: *We sat on the riverbank and had a picnic.*

riverbed /ˈrɪv.ə.bed/ **noun** [C] the ground over which a river usually flows: *a stony/muddy/dry riverbed*

riverboat /ˈrɪv.ə.bəʊt/ (US) /-ɚ.boʊt/ **noun** [C] a large passenger boat which travels up and down a river

riverside /ˈrɪv.ə.saɪd/ (US) /-ɚ-/ **noun** [S] the land along the edges of a river: *a riverside restaurant*

rivet /ˈrɪv.ɪt/ **noun; verb**

▸**noun** [C] a metal pin used to fasten flat pieces of metal or other thick materials such as leather

▸**verb** [T] **1** to fasten parts together with a rivet: *Many parts of an aircraft are riveted* ***together.*** **2 be riveted** to not be able to stop looking at something because it is so interesting or frightening: *It was an amazing film – I was absolutely riveted.* ◦ *His eyes were riveted* ***on*** *the television.* ◦ *He pulled out a gun and I was riveted* ***to the spot*** (= *so frightened that I could not move*).

riveting /ˈrɪv.ɪ.tɪŋ/ (US) /-t̬ɪŋ/ **adj** extremely interesting: *It was a riveting story.*

riviera /rɪ.viˈeə.rə/ (US) /-ˈer.ə/ **noun** [C] an area of coast, especially one where there are holiday towns with beaches: *the French/Italian/Cornish riviera*

rivulet /ˈrɪv.jʊ.lət/ (US) /-lɪt/ **noun** [C] literary a very small stream: figurative *Rivulets of sweat/rain/blood ran down his face.*

riyal /riˈɑːl/ (US) /riːˈjɑːl/ **noun** [C] the standard unit of money used in Saudi Arabia and Qatar

RN /ˌɑːrˈen/ **noun** abbreviation for Royal Navy: used especially after the names of officers in the navy: *Captain H. Doughty, RN*

RNA /ˌɑː.renˈeɪ/ (US) /ˌɑːr.en-/ **noun** [U] specialized abbreviation for **ribonucleic acid**: an important chemical present in all living cells

roach /rəʊtʃ/ (US) /roʊtʃ/ **noun** [C] **FISH** ▷ **1** (plural **roach**) a European fish that lives in fresh water **INSECT** ▷ **2** (plural **roaches**) US informal for **cockroach** **CIGARETTE** ▷ **3** (plural **roaches**) slang the end part of a CANNABIS cigarette that the smoke is breathed through

road /rəʊd/ (US) /roʊd/ **noun** [C or U] **1** A1 a long, hard surface built for vehicles to travel along: *We live on a busy/quiet road.* ◦ *Be careful when you cross a* ***main*** *road.* ◦ *There's a sweet shop on the other side of the road.* ◦ *The road* ***from*** *here* ***to*** *Adelaide runs/goes through some beautiful countryside.* ◦ *All roads* ***into/out of*** *the town were blocked by the snow.* ◦ *I hate flying so I go everywhere* ***by*** *road or rail.* ◦ *I live* ***in/on*** *Mill Road.* ◦ *My address is 82 Mill Road.* ◦ *Is this the Belfast road (= the road that goes to Belfast)?* ◦ *Most road* ***accidents*** *are caused by people driving too fast.* **2 on the road a** If a vehicle is on the road, it is working as it should and can be legally used: *My car was in the garage for a week, but it's now back on the road.* **b** C1 When you are on the road, you are driving or travelling, usually over a long distance: *After two days on the road, they reached the coast.* **c** If a group of actors or musicians are on the road, they are travelling to different places to perform: *Most rock groups spend two or three months a year on the road.*

IDIOMS **be on the road to sth** informal to be likely to achieve something: *The doctors say she's on the road to recovery.* • **come to the end of the road** to finish: *My relationship with Jeannie has come to the end of the road.* • **one for the road** informal an alcoholic drink just before leaving: *Before I went home, she persuaded me to have one for the road.* • **road to Damascus** Someone's road to Damascus is an experience they have that they consider to be very important and that changes their life.

roadblock /ˈrəʊd.blɒk/ (US) /ˈroʊd.blɑːk/ **noun** [C] a temporary structure put across a road to stop traffic: *Police put up/set up roadblocks on all roads out of the town in an effort to catch the bombers.*

ˈroad ˌhog **noun** [C] informal disapproving a driver who is dangerous because they do not think about other drivers

roadholding /ˈrəʊd.həʊl.dɪŋ/ (US) /ˈroʊd.hoʊl-/ **noun** [U] the degree to which a vehicle can travel quickly and safely on roads that are wet or have a lot of bends

roadhouse /ˈrəʊd.haʊs/ (US) /ˈroʊd-/ **noun** [C] mainly US old-fashioned a restaurant or bar on a main road leading out of a city

roadie /ˈrəʊ.di/ (US) /ˈroʊ-/ **noun** [C] informal someone who works for travelling performers, especially moving, arranging, and taking care of their equipment

ˈroad ˌkill **noun** [U] informal animals that are killed on roads by cars or other vehicles: *On average, two crocodiles a year end up as road kill on Florida's Highway 1.*

ˈroad ˌmap **noun** [C] a plan for how to achieve something: *A business plan is a road map* ***for*** *achieving a vision or goal.* ◦ *the road map* ***to*** *peace*

ˈroad ˌrage **noun** [U] anger or violence between drivers, often caused by difficult driving conditions: *Earlier today a man was arrested for attacking a motorist in a road rage* ***incident.***

roadrunner /ˈrəʊdˌrʌn.ər/ (US) /ˈroʊdˌrʌn.ɚ/ **noun** [C] a bird from the southwestern US and Mexico with a long tail and feathers that stand up on the top of its head, that runs very fast

ˈroad ˌsense **noun** [U] If you have good road sense, you have the ability to drive or walk carefully and safely through traffic.

roadshow /ˈrəʊd.ʃəʊ/ (US) /ˈroʊd.ʃoʊ/ **noun** [C] a series of shows or events that take place in different places around the country, for entertainment or in order to give the public information about a company, product, etc.: *To raise new capital in the US, the company organized an* ***investor*** *roadshow for three days in Boston and New York.*

roadside /ˈrəʊd.saɪd/ (US) /ˈroʊd-/ **noun** [S] the edge of a road: *The car pulled in* ***at/by/on*** *the roadside.* ◦ *We stopped at a roadside café for lunch.*

roadster /ˈrəʊd.stər/ (US) /ˈroʊd.stɚ/ **noun** [C] old-fashioned a car without a roof and with only two seats

ˈroad ˌtax **noun** [C or U] in the UK, a tax that you must pay on your vehicle to drive it on the roads

R

ˈroad ˌtest noun [C] **TEST OF CAR** ▷ **1** If you give a car a road test, you drive it to test its safety or how well it works. **TEST OF DRIVER** ▷ **2** US a test of a driver's ability to control a vehicle, which must be passed in order to get official permission to drive

ˈroad ˌtoll noun [C] Australian English the number of people who have died in road accidents

ˈroad ˌtrip noun [C] US If someone, especially a sports team, takes a road trip, they travel to other places to play games against other teams or for business reasons.

roadway /ˈrəʊd.weɪ/ Ⓤ /ˈroʊd-/ noun [S] the part of the road on which vehicles drive: *An overturned bus was blocking the roadway.*

roadworks /ˈrəʊd.wɜːks/ Ⓤ /ˈroʊd.wɝːks/ noun [plural] UK (US **roadwork**) building or repair work on a road: *There are delays on the M4 because of roadworks.*

roadworthy /ˈrəʊdˌwɜː.ði/ Ⓤ /ˈroʊdˌwɝː-/ adj (of a vehicle) in good enough condition to be driven without danger

roam /rəʊm/ Ⓤ /roʊm/ verb [I + adv/prep, T] to move about or travel, especially without a clear idea of what you are going to do: *After the pubs close, gangs of youths roam the city* ***streets***. ◦ *She roamed* ***around*** *America for a year, working in bars and restaurants.*

roaming /ˈrəʊ.mɪŋ/ Ⓤ /ˈroʊ-/ noun [U] using a mobile phone service that you can connect to when you cannot connect to the one that you normally use, for example if you are in another country: *You will face extra costs for roaming.* ◦ *Beware of roaming* ***charges*** *of up to $3 a minute.*

roan /rəʊn/ Ⓤ /roʊn/ noun [C] a horse that is red, black, or brown with a few white hairs

roar /rɔːʳ/ Ⓤ /rɔːr/ verb; noun

▸verb **1** C2 [I] to make a long, loud, deep sound: *We could hear the* ***lions*** *roaring at the other end of the zoo.* **2** [I] If a vehicle or aircraft roars somewhere, it moves there very quickly making a lot of noise: *She looked up as a plane roared overhead.* ◦ *The street was full of boys roaring up and down on their motorbikes.* **3** C2 [T] to shout loudly: [+ speech] *'Stop that!' he roared.*

PHRASAL VERB **roar with sth** to express an emotion, such as laughter or anger, noisily: *She roared with* ***laughter*** *when she saw what he was wearing.*

▸noun [C or S] C2 a loud, deep sound: *The lion* ***let out*** *a loud roar.* ◦ *His apartment was on a main road and there was* ***a*** *constant roar* ***of traffic***.

roaring /ˈrɔː.rɪŋ/ Ⓤ /ˈrɔːr.ɪŋ/ adj loud and powerful: *the roaring wind* ◦ *a roaring fire*

IDIOMS **do a roaring trade** informal to sell a lot of goods very quickly: *It was a hot sunny day and the ice cream sellers were doing a roaring trade.* • **roaring drunk** informal very drunk and noisy: *They came back from the pub roaring drunk.* • **a roaring success** informal something that is very successful: *The party was a roaring success.*

roast /rəʊst/ Ⓤ /roʊst/ verb; adj; noun

▸verb **COOK** ▷ **1** A2 [T or I] to cook food in an oven or over a fire: *Just roast the chicken in the oven and baste it in oil and lemon.* ◦ figurative *We lay on the beach and roasted (= got very hot) in the Mediterranean sun.* **2** [T or I] to heat nuts or coffee beans so that they become drier and browner **CRITICIZE** ▷ **3** [T] informal to criticize severely or speak angrily to someone

▸adj [before noun] (also **roasted**) A2 Roast meat or vegetables have been cooked in an oven or over a fire: *roast beef/chicken/potatoes* ◦ *roasted red pepper sauce*

▸noun [C] a large piece of roasted meat

roasting /ˈrəʊ.stɪŋ/ Ⓤ /ˈroʊ-/ adj; noun

▸adj (also **ˌroasting ˈhot**) very hot: *It was a roasting summer day.* ◦ *I'm roasting!*

▸noun [C usually singular] informal the act of criticizing someone in an angry way: *I got a roasting from Mum for being back late.*

rob /rɒb/ Ⓤ /rɑːb/ verb [T] (-bb-) **1** B1 to take money or property illegally from a place, organization, or person, often using violence: *The terrorists financed themselves by robbing banks.* ◦ *My wallet's gone! I've been robbed!* ◦ *They robbed the company* ***of*** *£2 million.* **2** C2 If someone is robbed of something they deserve or want, it is taken away from them: *A last-minute injury robbed me* ***of*** *my place on the team.*

IDIOM **rob Peter to pay Paul** to borrow money from one person to pay back money you borrowed from someone else

robber /ˈrɒb.əʳ/ Ⓤ /ˈrɑː.bɚ/ noun [C] someone who steals: *The robbers shot a policeman before making their getaway.*

robbery /ˈrɒb.ər.i/ Ⓤ /ˈrɑː.bɚ-/ noun [C or U] B2 the crime of stealing from somewhere or someone: *The gang admitted they had* ***committed*** *four recent bank robberies.* ◦ *He is in prison for* ***armed*** *robbery.*

robe /rəʊb/ Ⓤ /roʊb/ noun [C] **1** a long, loose piece of clothing worn especially on very formal occasions: *Judges wear black robes when they are in court.* **2** (also **bathrobe**) a loose piece of clothing that is worn before or after a bath or on top of clothing worn in bed: *He wrapped a robe around himself before answering the door.*

robed /rəʊbd/ Ⓤ /roʊbd/ adj formal **robed in** to be dressed in a particular way: *The judges were robed in scarlet.*

robin /ˈrɒb.ɪn/ Ⓤ /ˈrɑː.bɪn/ noun [C] (literary **robin redbreast** /ˌrɒb.ɪnˈred.brest/ Ⓤ /ˌrɑː.bɪn-/) a small, brown European bird with a red front, or a similar but slightly larger brown bird of North America: *Robins mostly appear in the winter and are commonly pictured on Christmas cards.*

robin

robot /ˈrəʊ.bɒt/ Ⓤ /ˈroʊ.bɑːt/ noun [C] **MACHINE** ▷ **1** B1 a machine controlled by a computer that is used to perform jobs automatically **PERSON** ▷ **2** disapproving someone who does things in a very quick and effective way but never shows their emotions **TRAFFIC LIGHT** ▷ **3** South African English a traffic light

robotic /rəʊˈbɒt.ɪk/ Ⓤ /roʊˈbɑː.t̬ɪk/ adj relating to or like a robot

robotics /rəʊˈbɒt.ɪks/ Ⓤ /roʊˈbɑː.t̬ɪks/ noun [U] the science of making and using robots

robust /rəʊˈbʌst/ Ⓤ /roʊ-/ adj (of a person or animal) strong and healthy, or (of an object or system) strong and unlikely to break or fail: *He looks robust and healthy enough.* ◦ *a robust pair of walking boots* ◦ *a robust economy* • **robustness** /-nəs/ noun [U]

robustly /rəˈbʌst.li/ adv If you do something robustly, you do it in a determined way: *Some of his colleagues felt he could have defended himself more robustly.*

rock /rɒk/ Ⓤ /rɑːk/ noun; verb

▸noun **STONE** ▷ **1** B1 [C or U] the dry solid part of the

Earth's surface, or any large piece of this that sticks up out of the ground or the sea: *Mountains and cliffs are formed from rock.* ◦ *The boat struck a rock outside the bay and sank.* **2** [C] a piece of rock or stone: *The demonstrators were hurling rocks at the police.* **3 rocks** [plural] a line of large stones sticking up from the sea: *The storm forced the ship onto the rocks.* **4** [C] slang for a valuable stone used in jewellery, especially a DIAMOND: *Have you seen the size of the rock he gave her for their anniversary?* **MUSIC** ▷ **5** A2 [U] a type of popular music with a strong, loud beat that is usually played with electric guitars and drums: *a rock* ***group*** ◦ *a rock* ***star***

IDIOMS **be (caught) between a rock and a hard place** to be in a very difficult situation and to have to make a hard decision • **be (as) solid as a rock** to be very strong: *You'd think her own marriage was solid as a rock.* • **get your rocks off** UK slang to have an ORGASM • **on the rocks 1** informal likely to fail soon: *I think their marriage is on the rocks.* **2** If you have an alcoholic drink on the rocks, you have it with pieces of ice: *I'll have a whisky on the rocks, please.*

▸**verb 1** C2 [I or T] to (cause someone or something to) move backwards and forwards or from side to side in a regular way: *He picked up the baby and gently rocked her* ***to sleep.*** ◦ *If you rock* ***back*** *on that chair, you're going to break it.* **2** [T] If a person or place is rocked by something such as an explosion, the force of it makes the person or place shake: *The explosion, which rocked the city, killed 300.* **3** [T] If an event rocks a group of people or society, it causes feelings of shock: *The managing director's resignation rocked the whole company.* **4** [T] slang to wear a particular style of clothing, etc. and look good or fashionable: *There are celebrities over 40 years old who can still rock a tattoo.*

IDIOMS **sb/sth rocks** slang used to show that you like or approve of someone or something a lot: *He rocks!* • **rock the boat** informal C2 If you rock the boat, you do or say something that will upset people or cause problems: *Don't rock the boat until the negotiations are finished.*

PHRASAL VERB **rock up** UK informal to arrive somewhere: *They rocked up two hours late, dressed in ball gowns.* → Synonym **turn up**

ˌrock and ˈroll (also **ˌrock 'n' ˈroll**) noun [U] a style of popular dance music that began in the 1950s in the US and has a strong, loud beat and simple repeated tunes

IDIOM **be the new rock and roll** UK informal If an activity is the new rock and roll, it has become very popular and many people are doing it and talking about it.

ˌrock ˈbottom noun [U] informal **LOW** ▷ **1** the lowest possible level: *Confidence in the government is* ***at*** *rock bottom.* ◦ *Prices have* ***reached*** *rock bottom.* ◦ *The prime minister's opinion poll ratings have* ***hit*** *rock bottom.* **UNHAPPY** ▷ **2** the most unhappy that someone has ever been in their life: *Ian had just left me and I was* ***at*** *rock bottom.* ◦ *Alcoholics often have to* ***reach/hit*** *rock bottom before they can recognize that they have a problem.*

ˈrock ˌcake noun [C] (also **ˈrock ˌbun**) UK a small cake with a rough surface, made with dried fruit

ˈrock ˌcandy noun [C or U] US large, clear, hard pieces of sugar, often on a string or a stick

ˈrock ˌchick noun [C] informal a woman who likes ROCK MUSIC

rocker /ˈrɒk.əʳ/ US /ˈrɑː.kɚ/ noun [C] **CHAIR** ▷ **1** one of the two curved pieces of wood under a ROCKING CHAIR that allow it to move backwards and forwards **2** a rocking chair **MUSIC** ▷ **3** a singer of ROCK MUSIC: *an* ***ageing*** *rocker* **4** US a rock song or a person who likes ROCK MUSIC **5** old-fashioned a young person, especially in Britain in the 1950s, who wore leather clothes, rode a motorcycle, and listened to ROCK AND ROLL music

IDIOM **off your rocker** informal If you say that someone is off their rocker, you mean that they are behaving in a very strange or silly way.

rockery /ˈrɒk.ər.i/ US /ˈrɑː.kɚ-/ noun [C] UK (US usually **ˈrock ˌgarden**) a garden or an area within a garden that has plants growing between piles of stones

rocket /ˈrɒk.ɪt/ US /ˈrɑː.kɪt/ noun; verb

▸**noun DEVICE** ▷ **1** B2 [C] a large cylinder-shaped object that moves very fast by forcing out burning gases, used for space travel or as a weapon: *They* ***launched*** *a rocket to the planet Venus.* ◦ *The rebels were* ***firing*** *anti-tank rockets.* **2** [C] (also **skyrocket**) a type of FIREWORK that flies up into the air before exploding **PLANT** ▷ **3** [U] UK (US **arugula**) a plant whose long green leaves are used in salads

IDIOM **give sb a rocket** UK informal If someone gives you a rocket, they criticize you severely: *Her Mum gave her a rocket for tearing her new jeans.*

▸**verb** [I often + adv/prep] (also **skyrocket**) to rise extremely quickly or make extremely quick progress towards success: *House prices in the north are rocketing* ***(up).*** ◦ *Their team rocketed* ***to*** *the top of the League.* ◦ *Sharon Stone rocketed* ***to*** *fame in the film 'Basic Instinct'.*

ˈrocket ˌscience noun [U] the scientific study of rockets • **ˈrocket ˌscientist** noun [C]

IDIOM **it's not rocket science** (also **it doesn't take a rocket scientist**) used to say that you do not think that something is very difficult to do or to understand: *Come on, it's only a crossword, it's not rocket science.* ◦ *Drugs equals crime. It doesn't take a rocket scientist* ***to*** *figure that one out.*

ˈrocket ˌship noun [C] US a spacecraft that is driven by a rocket

ˈrock ˌface noun [C] an area of vertical surface on a large rock or mountain: *The path down to the beach was a precarious one, tiny steps hewn out of the* ***sheer*** *rock face.*

rockfall /ˈrɒk.fɔːl/ US /ˈrɑːk.fɑːl/ noun [C] a mass of stones that is falling or has already fallen: *The road was blocked by a rockfall.*

ˈrock ˌgarden noun [C] a **rockery**

ˌrock-ˈhard adj extremely hard: *I can't eat this cake – it's rock-hard.*

ˈrocking ˌchair noun [C] (also **rocker**) a chair built on two pieces of curved wood so that it moves forwards and backwards when you are sitting in it

rocking chair

ˈrocking ˌhorse noun [C] a wooden toy horse that children can move backwards and forwards while sitting on it

rockmelon /ˈrɒkˌmel.ən/ US /ˈrɑːk-/ noun [C] Australian English a **cantaloupe**

ˈrock ˌpool noun [C] (US **ˈtide ˌpool**) a small area of sea water contained by the rocks around it

ˈrock ˌsalt noun [U] salt that is taken from the ground, not the sea

R

ˌrock-ˈsolid adj not likely to move or break: *I've fixed the table – it's rock-solid now.*

rocky /ˈrɒk.i/ US /ˈrɑː.ki/ adj **STONE** ▷ **1** C1 made of rock and therefore usually rough and difficult to travel along **UNSTEADY/UNCERTAIN** ▷ **2** unable to balance very well: *After two months in a hospital bed, I felt a bit rocky on my feet.* **3** uncertain and difficult and not likely to last long: *Their relationship got off to a rocky **start**.*

IDIOM **rocky road** If you are on a rocky road, you are experiencing a difficult period and have a lot of problems: *Bernanke predicts a rocky road ahead for the economy.*

rococo /rəˈkəʊ.kəʊ/ US /rəˈkoʊ.koʊ/ adj relating to the very decorated and detailed style in buildings, art, and furniture that was popular in Europe in the 18th century • **rococo** noun [U]

rod /rɒd/ US /rɑːd/ noun [C] a long, thin pole made of wood or metal: *He was given a **fishing** rod for his birthday.* ◦ *The concrete is strengthened with steel rods.*

IDIOM **make a rod for your own back** UK If you make a rod for your own back, you act in a way that creates more problems for yourself in the future: *By giving in to the terrorists' demands, the government will simply be making a rod for its own back.*

rode /rəʊd/ US /roʊd/ past simple of **ride**

rodent /ˈrəʊ.dənt/ US /ˈroʊ-/ noun [C] any of various small mammals with large, sharp front teeth, such as mice and RATS

rodeo /rəʊˈdeɪ.əʊ/, /ˈrəʊ.di-/ US /ˈroʊ.di.oʊ/ noun [C] (plural **rodeos**) in North America, a sport and public entertainment in which COWBOYS show different skills by riding wild horses and catching cows with ropes

roe /rəʊ/ US /roʊ/ noun [U] fish eggs, eaten as food

ˈroe ˌdeer noun [C] (plural **roe deer**) a small European and Asian DEER

roentgen (also **röntgen**) /ˈrɒnt.gən/ US /ˈrent-/ noun [C] specialized a unit of measurement for showing the amount of RADIATION received by a person over a period of time

rofl (also **rotfl**) written abbreviation for rolling on the floor laughing: used, for example in an internet CHAT ROOM, to show that you think something is very funny

R

rogan josh /ˌrəʊ.gənˈdʒəʊʃ/ US /ˌroʊ.gənˈdʒoʊʃ/ noun [C or U] a South Asian dish consisting of meat, especially LAMB, cooked in a sauce made of tomatoes

roger /ˈrɒdʒ.ər/ US /ˈrɑː.dʒɚ/ exclamation; verb

▸**exclamation** used in radio communications to mean that a message has been received and understood: *'You are clear to land.' 'Roger, I'm coming in to land now.'*

▸**verb** [T] UK offensive old-fashioned to have sex with someone

rogue /rəʊg/ US /roʊg/ adj; noun

▸**adj** [before noun] **1** behaving in ways that are not expected or not normal, often in a way that causes damage: *a rogue **state*** ◦ *rogue **cells*** **2** specialized A rogue animal is a dangerous wild animal that lives apart from the rest of its group.

▸**noun** [C] **1** old-fashioned humorous a person who behaves badly but who you still like: *'Come here, you little rogue!' chuckled my uncle.* ◦ *The women all think he's a **lovable** old rogue.* **2** old-fashioned a dishonest or bad man

ˌrogues' ˈgallery noun [C usually singular] a collection of photographs of criminals kept by the police: figurative *He occupies a prominent position in the rogues' gallery of the financial world.*

ˌrogue ˈstate noun [C] a nation that is considered very dangerous to other nations

ˌrogue ˈtrader noun [C] a STOCKBROKER (= someone who buys and sells SHARES for other people) who secretly loses a large amount of their employer's money after making a bad or illegal INVESTMENT

roguish /ˈrəʊ.gɪʃ/ US /ˈroʊ-/ adj (of a person) looking as if they are going to laugh because of slightly bad behaviour: *His eyes were bright blue with a roguish twinkle in them.* • **roguishly** /-li/ adv • **roguishness** /-nəs/ noun [U]

roil /rɔɪl/ verb [I or T] mainly US **TWIST** ▷ **1** to (cause to) move quickly in a twisting circular movement: *Fierce winds roiled the sea.* ◦ *A massive tower of smoke roiled skyward.* **UPSET** ▷ **2** to cause something to stop working in the usual or expected way: *Fears about Japan roiled world financial markets last week.* ◦ *The immigration debate has roiled the country for more than a year.* • **roiling** /ˈrɔɪl.ɪŋ/ adj *The rain turned a small creek into a roiling surge.* ◦ *The country faces a roiling financial crisis.*

role /rəʊl/ US /roʊl/ noun [C] **DUTY** ▷ **1** B2 the position or purpose that someone or something has in a situation, organization, society, or relationship: *What is his role **in** this project?* ◦ *Schools **play** an important role **in** society.* ◦ *Six people have been put on trial for their role (= involvement) **in** the anti-government demonstrations.* **ACTING** ▷ **2** B1 an actor's part in a film or play: *She's got a **leading/supporting** role in the school play.* ◦ *She **plays** the role **of** a crooked lawyer.*

ˈrole ˌmodel noun [C] C1 a person who someone admires and whose behaviour they try to copy: *Sports stars are role models for thousands of youngsters.*

ˈrole ˌplay noun [C or U] pretending to be someone else, especially as part of learning a new skill: *Role play is used in training courses, language-learning and psychotherapy.*

ˈrole reˌversal noun [C usually singular] a situation in which two people exchange their usual duties or positions

roll /rəʊl/ US /roʊl/ verb; phrasal verb; noun

▸**verb MOVE** ▷ **1** B2 [I or T, usually + adv/prep] to (cause something to) move somewhere by turning over and over or from side to side: *The vase rolled off the edge of the table and smashed.* ◦ *The dog rolled over onto its back.* ◦ *I rolled the wheel along the side of the road back to the car.* **2** B2 [I or T, usually + adv/prep] to move somewhere easily and without sudden movements: *A tear rolled down his cheek.* ◦ *A wave of cigarette smoke rolled towards me.* ◦ *The piano's on wheels, so we can roll it into the room.* **3** [I] If an aircraft or a ship rolls, it leans to one side and then to the other because of the wind or waves. **4** [I] If a machine is rolling, it is operating: *Just as the television **cameras** started rolling, it began to pour down with rain.* **5** C2 [T] If you roll your eyes, you move them so that you are looking up, to show that you consider someone or something stupid or silly: *When he suggested they should buy a new car, she rolled her eyes **in** disbelief.* **TURN OVER** ▷ **6** B1 [T usually + adv/prep] to (cause something to) turn over onto itself to form the shape of a ball or a tube: *He rolled the clay **into** a ball in his hands.* ◦ *As I got closer, the hedgehog rolled itself (**up**) **into** a ball.* **7** [T] to make a cigarette by wrapping a piece of paper around some tobacco **8** [I or T, + adv/prep] to fold over a piece of clothing or material to make it shorter: *We rolled **back** the carpet to see the floorboards.* **SMOOTH** ▷ **9** [T] to make something smooth and flat: [+ obj + adj] *She borrowed a garden* *roller to roll the grass flat.* ◦ *When you have rolled* (***out***) *the pastry, place it in a pie dish.* **SOUND** ▷ **10** [I] to make a continuous, repeated, deep sound: *The* ***drums*** *rolled as the acrobat walked along the tightrope.* **11** [T] If you roll your r's, you pronounce them with your tongue moving quickly and repeatedly against the top of the mouth: *The Italians roll their r's.*

IDIOMS **rolled into one** If someone or something has several qualities rolled into one, they have all of those qualities: *He is a father, sales manager, and athlete all rolled into one.* • **be rolling in it** (also **rolling in money**) to be extremely rich: *If they can afford a yacht, they must be rolling in it.* • **be rolling in the aisles** informal to laugh without being able stop: *The comedian had the audience rolling in the aisles.* • **roll on the weekend, five o'clock, etc.** UK informal said when you want time to go quickly because you are looking forward to something: *I can't wait to be finished with this project – roll on October!* • **roll up!** UK old-fashioned said, especially in the past, by someone who wanted people to come and pay to look at something unusual or interesting • **roll up your sleeves** informal to prepare for hard work: *There's a lot of work to do, so roll up your sleeves and get busy.* • **roll with the punches** informal to be able to deal with a series of difficult situations

PHRASAL VERBS **roll back sth** to limit or reduce the effects of a particular arrangement: *He wants to roll back laws designed to clean up the air, water and land.* • **roll sth back** to reduce the cost or price of something: *The furniture dealer is rolling back the prices on all beds for this week only.* • **roll by** literary If an amount of time rolls by, it passes: *The* ***years*** *rolled by, and I didn't see her again until she was married with two children.* • **roll in** informal to arrive in great numbers or amounts: *Once our business gets started, the* ***money*** *will be rolling in.* • **roll (sth) out** to make a new product, service or system available for the first time: *The government plans to roll out a series of tax cuts over the next few years.* • **roll (sth) over sth** If you roll over something on a computer screen, you move the mouse over an active place so that you can see information that is hidden under it: *If you roll your mouse over a word, its definition will appear.* • **roll sth up** to fold something around itself to make the shape of a ball, or to fold cloth around itself to make a piece of clothing shorter: *Could you roll up that string for me?* ◦ *I rolled up my sleeves and began to wash the dishes.* • **roll up** informal to arrive at a particular place or event, usually late: *They rolled up at the party two hours late and rather drunk.*

▸noun **TUBE** ▷ **1** B2 [C] a piece of film, paper, or cloth that is rolled into the shape of a tube: *a roll of carpet* ◦ *a toilet roll* (= *a roll of toilet paper*) **2** [C] If a person or animal has rolls of fat on their body, they are very fat: *The dog had rolls of fat along its neck.* **BREAD** ▷ **3** B1 [C] (also **bread roll**) a small LOAF of bread for one person: *Would you like a roll and butter with your soup?* ◦ UK *I bought a cheese roll* (US *cheese on a roll*) (= *a small piece of bread filled with cheese*) *for lunch.* **LIST** ▷ **4** [C] an official list of names: *Is your name on the* ***electoral*** *roll* (= *the list of people who can vote*)? **5 take/call the roll** mainly US If you take/call the roll, you read aloud the names of all the people on the list to make certain that they are present: *The teacher called the roll to see if any students were absent.* **MOVEMENT** ▷ **6** [C] an act of rolling on the ground: *The dog went for a roll in the grass.* **7 a roll in the hay** humorous sexual activity that is quick and enjoyable and does not involve serious feelings: *I wouldn't sacrifice my marriage for a roll in the hay with a waitress.* **8** [U] The roll of a ship or aircraft is its movement from side to side in the water or air. **SOUND** ▷ **9** [C usually singular] a continuous repeated deep sound: *a* ***drum*** *roll* ◦ *a deafening roll* ***of thunder***

IDIOM **be on a roll** informal to be having a successful or lucky period: *Pippa won five games in a row and it was obvious she was on a roll.*

rollaway /ˈrəʊl.ə.weɪ/ US /ˈroʊl-/ **adj** A rollaway piece of furniture is on wheels so you can move it very easily: *a rollaway* ***bed*** • **rollaway noun** [C] US a bed on wheels that you can move very easily

ˈroll ˌbar noun [C] a metal bar across the roof of a car, especially one used for racing, that protects the people inside if the car turns over

ˈroll ˌcall noun [C] If someone does a roll call, they read aloud the names of all the people on the list to make certain that they are present.

ˌrolled ˈgold noun [U] UK jewellery made of cheap metal covered with a thin layer of gold

ˌrolled ˈoats noun [plural] OATS that have had their outer covering removed and have been crushed

roller /ˈrəʊ.ləʳ/ US /ˈroʊ.lɚ/ **noun MACHINE/DEVICE** ▷ **1** [C] a tube-shaped object in a machine that turns over and over in order to carry things along or press them down or together: *As the hot metal passed between the huge rollers it was pressed into thin sheets.* **2** [C usually plural] a tube-shaped device, often heated, that women use to CURL their hair: *She answered the door with her rollers* ***in***. **3** [C] a heavy machine used to make surfaces smooth and flat: *The men used a roller to flatten the tarmac.* → See also **steamroller WAVE** ▷ **4** [C] a large, long wave on the sea

ˈroller ˌblind noun [C] UK (US **ˈwindow ˌshade**) a piece of material fixed onto a wooden or metal roller that can be pulled down to cover a window

ˈroller ˌcoaster noun 1 [C] an exciting entertainment in an AMUSEMENT PARK, like a fast train that goes up and down very steep slopes and around very sudden bends **2** [S] a situation which changes from one extreme to another, or in which a person's feelings change from one extreme to another: *He was* ***on*** *an emotional roller coaster for a while when he lost his job.*

ˈroller ˌderby noun [C] US a race around a circular track between two teams of people on roller skates

R

ˈroller ˌskate noun [C] a type of boot with four wheels on the bottom which you wear in order to travel along quickly for enjoyment • **ˈroller-ˌskating noun** [U] • **ˈroller-ˌskate verb** [I]

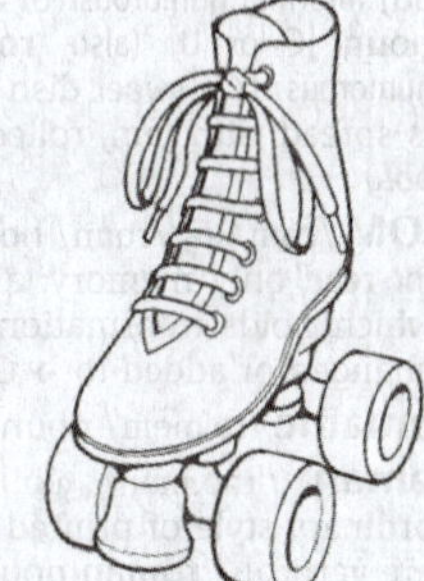

roller skate

ˈroller ˌtowel noun [C] a piece of cloth, joined at both ends, that is fixed onto a wooden or metal roller and is used for drying your hands

rollicking /ˈrɒl.ɪ.kɪŋ/ US /ˈrɑː-/ **adj; noun**

▸**adj** [before noun] old-fashioned happy, energetic, and often noisy: *The play is described as 'a rollicking tale about love and lust'.*

▸**noun** [C usually singular] UK informal an occasion when someone tells you in a very angry way that you have done something wrong: *We* ***got*** *a rollicking from the coach at half time.*

rolling /ˈrəʊ.lɪŋ/ US /ˈroʊ-/ **adj** [before noun] **GRAD-**

UAL ▷ **1** gradual: *The plan is for a rolling extension of the tax over the next ten years.* **OF HILLS** ▷ **2** (of hills) gently rising and falling: *The train journey took us through a valley past rolling hills.*

ˈrolling ˌmill noun [C] a factory or machine in which metal is rolled into flat pieces

ˈrolling ˌpin noun [C] a tube-shaped object that is used for making pastry flat and thin before cooking it

ˈrolling ˌstock noun [U] the engines and CARRIAGES that are used on a railway

rollmop /ˈrəʊl.mɒp/ (US) /ˈroʊl.mɑːp/ noun [C] UK a piece of HERRING with the bones removed that has been rolled up and kept in VINEGAR

ˈroll neck noun [C] UK a **polo neck**

ˌroll of ˈhonour noun [C usually singular] US (US **ˈhonor ˌroll**) a list of people who should be remembered for their brave actions

ˈroll-on noun [C] a small container with a moving ball at the top, used for storing and rubbing on DEODORANT (= a chemical substance that prevents or hides unpleasant body smells)

roll-ˌon roll-ˈoff adj [before noun] (informal **ro-ro** /ˈrəʊ.rəʊ/ (US) /ˈroʊ.roʊ/) UK describes a ship built so that vehicles can drive on at one end and off at the other: *a roll-on roll-off* ***ferry***

rollover /ˈrəʊl.əʊ.vəʳ/ (US) /ˈroʊl.oʊ.vɚ/ noun [C] a situation in which a prize has not been won in a competition and is added to the prize offered in the next competition: *a rollover week*

Rolls-Royce /ˌrəʊlzˈrɔɪs/ (US) /ˌroʊlz-/ noun [C] trademark a large and very expensive type of car made in the UK

IDIOM **the Rolls-Royce of sth** mainly UK the best type of a particular type of thing: *This model is the Rolls-Royce of lawnmowers.*

rolltop desk /ˌrəʊl.tɒpˈdesk/ (US) /ˌroʊl.tɑːp-/ noun [C] a type of writing table with a cover that you can push back or pull down

ˈroll-up noun [C] UK a cigarette that you make by wrapping a piece of paper around some tobacco

ˌroll-your-ˈown noun [C] Australian English a cigarette that you make by wrapping a piece of paper around some tobacco → Compare **roll-up**

roly-poly /ˌrəʊ.liˈpəʊ.li/ (US) /ˌroʊ.liˈpoʊ-/ adj; noun

▸adj informal humorous (of a person) short and round

▸noun [C or U] (also **ˌroly-ˌpoly ˈpudding**) informal humorous UK a sweet dish made with thick pastry that is spread with jam, rolled up, and cooked: *jam roly-poly*

ROM /rɒm/ (US) /rɑːm/ noun [U] specialized abbreviation for read only memory: a type of computer memory which holds information that can be used but not changed or added to → Compare **RAM**

romaine /rəˈmeɪn/ noun [C] US for **cos**

roman /ˈrəʊ.mən/ (US) /ˈroʊ-/ adj describes the ordinary style of printed writing in which the letters are vertical • **roman** noun [U] *In this book, definitions are printed* ***in*** *roman.*

Roman /ˈrəʊ.mən/ (US) /ˈroʊ-/ adj; noun

▸adj **1** relating to the city of Rome and its EMPIRE in ancient times **2** relating to the modern city of Rome

▸noun [C] **1** a person who lived in Rome or the Roman EMPIRE in ancient times: *The Romans ruled over most of Europe.* **2** a person who lives in the modern city of Rome

ˌRoman ˈalphabet noun [U] (also **ˌLatin ˈalphabet**) the alphabet used for writing most western European languages, including English

ˌRoman ˈcandle noun [C] a type of FIREWORK which produces brightly coloured stars when it explodes

ˌRoman ˈCatholic noun [C] (also **Catholic**) a member of the Roman Catholic Church • **ˌRoman ˈCatholic** adj

the ˌRoman ˌCatholic ˈChurch noun the part of the Christian religion that is ruled by the Pope in Rome

ˌRoman Caˈtholicism noun [U] the beliefs and activities of the Roman Catholic Church

romance /rəʊˈmæns/, /ˈrəʊ.mæns/ (US) /roʊˈmæns/ noun; verb

▸noun **1** (B1) [C] a close, usually short relationship of love between two people: *They got married last year after a* ***whirlwind*** *(= very short and unexpected) romance.* ◦ *It was just a* ***holiday*** *romance.* ◦ ***Office*** *romances are usually a bad idea.* **2** [U] the feelings and behaviour of two people who are in a loving and sexual relationship with each other: *I felt as though all the romance had gone out of my marriage.* **3** [U] the feeling of excitement or mystery that you have from a particular experience or event: *He loves the romance* ***of*** *travelling on a steam train.* **4** [C] a story about love: *a historical romance* ◦ *She loves reading romances.* **5** [C] a story of exciting events, especially one written or set in the past

▸verb **1** [I] to tell stories that are not true, or to describe an event in a way that makes it sound better than it was **2** [T] old-fashioned to try to persuade someone to love you

Romance /rəʊˈmæns/ (US) /roʊ-/ adj [before noun] specialized (of a language) developed from Latin: *French, Italian, and Spanish are all Romance languages.*

Romanesque /ˌrəʊ.məˈnesk/ (US) /ˌroʊ-/ adj specialized relating to the style of building which was common in Western and Southern Europe from the 10th to the 12th centuries • **Romanesque** noun [U]

ˌRoman ˈlaw noun [U] legal the system of laws of the ancient Romans, on which some modern legal systems are based

ˌRoman ˈnose noun [C] a nose that is higher than usual at the top

ˌRoman ˈnumeral noun [C usually plural] any of the letters that the ancient Romans used to write numbers, for example I (= 1), II (= 2), III (= 3) → Compare **Arabic numeral**

Romano- /rəˈmɑː.nəʊ-/ (US) /-ˈmæn.oʊ-/ prefix of or connected with Rome or Romans: *a tutor in Romano-British history*

romantic /rəʊˈmæn.tɪk/, /rəˈ-/ (US) /roʊˈmæn.t̬ɪk/ adj; noun

▸adj **1** (B1) relating to love or a close loving relationship: *a romantic* ***novel/comedy*** ◦ *You used to be so romantic, but now you never tell me that you love me.* ◦ *I suppose he is quite romantic – he sends me flowers on my birthday and tells me I'm looking beautiful and so on.* **2** exciting and mysterious and having a strong effect on your emotions: *We thought that Egypt was an incredibly romantic country.* **3** (C2) sometimes disapproving not practical and having a lot of ideas that are not related to real life: *She has a romantic* ***idea*** *of what it's like to be a struggling young artist.* • **romantically** /-tɪ.kəl.i/ adv

▸noun [C] mainly disapproving someone who is not practical and has ideas that are not related to real life: *You're a hopeless/incurable romantic.*

romanticism /rəʊˈmæn.tɪ.sɪ.zəm/, /rəˈ-/ (US) /roʊˈmæn.t̬ə-/ noun [U] describing things in a way that makes them sound more exciting or mysterious than they really are

Romanticism /rəʊˈmæn.tɪ.sɪ.zᵊm/, /rəˈ-/ (US) /roʊˈmæn.t̬ə-/ **noun** [U] specialized a style of art, music, and literature, popular in Europe in the late 18th and early 19th centuries, that deals with the beauty of nature and human emotions • **Romantic** /-tɪk/ (US) /-t̬ɪk/ **adj, noun** [C] *Beethoven, Schumann, and Chopin were leading Romantic composers.*

romanticize (UK usually **romanticise**) /rəʊˈmæn.tɪ.saɪz/, /rəˈ-/ (US) /roʊˈmæn.t̬ə-/ **verb** [I] to talk about something in a way that makes it sound better than it really is, or to believe that something is better than it really is: *Stop romanticizing! Nothing's that perfect.*

Romany /ˈrəʊ.mə.ni/ (US) /ˈrɑː-/ **noun** [C or U] a GYPSY, or the language of the GYPSY people

rom com /ˈrɒm.kɒm/ (US) /ˈrɑːm.kɑːm/ **noun** [C or U] abbreviation for romantic comedy: a film or television programme about love, that is intended to make you laugh

Rome /rəʊm/ (US) /roʊm/ **noun**

IDIOM **when in Rome (do as the Romans do)** something that you say which means that when you are visiting another country, you should behave like the people in that country: *I don't drink wine usually but on holiday, well, when in Rome…*

Romeo /ˈrəʊ.mi.əʊ/ (US) /ˈroʊ.mi.oʊ/ **noun** [C] (plural **Romeos**) humorous or disapproving a man who thinks he is attractive to women and has sexual relationships with many women

romp /rɒmp/ (US) /rɑːmp/ **verb; noun**

▸**verb** [I usually + adv/prep] to play in a rough, excited, and noisy way: *The children romped happily around/about in the garden.*

IDIOM **romp home/in** UK to win easily: *She is riding the fastest horse and is certain to romp home.*

PHRASAL VERB **romp through sth** informal to successfully do something, quickly and easily: *Rory expected to romp through the test and interviews.*

▸**noun** [C usually singular] a funny, energetic, and often sexual entertainment or situation: *The newspaper headline was 'Vicar Caught In Sex Romp'.*

rompers /ˈrɒm.pəz/ (US) /ˈrɑːm.pɚz/ **noun** [plural] (also ˈ**romper** ˌ**suit**) a single piece of clothing consisting of a top part and trousers worn by babies and very young children

rondo /ˈrɒn.dəʊ/ (US) /ˈrɑːn.doʊ/ **noun** [C] (plural **rondos**) specialized a piece of music that repeats the main tune several times and often forms part of a longer piece

röntgen /ˈrɒnt.gən/ (US) /ˈrent-/ **noun** [C] specialized **roentgen**

roo /ruː/ **noun** [C] (plural **roos**) Australian English informal for **kangaroo**

rood screen /ˈruːdˌskriːn/ **noun** [C] specialized a decorative wooden or stone wall that in some Christian churches separates the area near the ALTAR from the other parts of the church

roof /ruːf/ **noun; verb**

▸**noun** [C] **A2** the covering that forms the top of a building, vehicle, etc.: *The house has a sloping/flat/tiled/thatched, etc. roof.* ◦ *Put the luggage **on** the roof of the car.* ◦ *The roof (= upper surface) of the cave is 50 metres up.* ◦ *This cake is so dry that it sticks to the roof **of** your **mouth** (= upper surface of the mouth).*

IDIOMS **go through the roof 1 C2** to rise to a very high level: *Prices have gone through the roof.* **2 C2** (also **hit the roof**) to get very angry: *When I was expelled from school, my parents went through the roof.* • **raise the roof** to play/sing very loudly and enthusiastically: *With their last, triumphant piece, the musicians raised the roof.* • **a roof over your head C2** a place to live: *She gave him enough money to get a roof over his head.* • **under the same roof** in the same building: *I refuse to live under the same roof as that man.*

▸**verb** [T often passive] to put a roof on a building • **-roofed** /-t/ **suffix** *a slate-roofed house*

PHRASAL VERB **roof sth in/over** to put a roof over a place or area: *The council has decided to roof over the open-air swimming pool.*

roofer /ˈruː.fəʳ/ (US) /-fɚ/ **noun** [C] a person whose job is to put new roofs on buildings or to repair damaged roofs

ˈ**roof** ˌ**garden** **noun** [C] a garden on the roof of a building

roofing /ˈruː.fɪŋ/ **noun** [U] **1** material used for making roofs: *Slates, tiles, and shingles are roofing materials.* **2** the job or process of putting roofs on new buildings or repairing damaged roofs

roofless /ˈruːf.ləs/ **adj** without a roof

ˈ**roof** ˌ**rack** **noun** [C] a frame fixed on top of the roof of a vehicle, for carrying large objects

roof rack

rooftop /ˈruːf.tɒp/ (US) /-tɑːp/ **noun** [C usually plural] the outside surface of the roof of a building: *a magnificent view of the rooftops* ◦ *Police marksmen with rifles were stationed **on** the rooftops.*

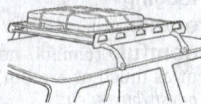

IDIOM **shout/proclaim sth from the rooftops** to say something publicly: *I'm so in love I want to shout your name from the rooftops.*

rooibos /ˈrɔɪ.bɒs/ (US) /-bɔːs/ **noun** [U] a type of tea that is made from a plant also called rooibos, found in South Africa

rook /rʊk/ **noun; verb**

▸**noun** [C] **BIRD** ▷ **1** a large black bird similar to a CROW **GAME PIECE** ▷ **2** (informal **castle**) in the game of CHESS, a piece that can move along any number of squares in straight lines parallel to the sides of the board

▸**verb** [T] old-fashioned informal to cheat someone out of some money

rookery /ˈrʊk.ᵊr.i/ (US) /-ɚ-/ **noun** [C] several rooks' nests, high up in the branches of a group of trees

rookie /ˈrʊk.i/ **noun** [C] mainly US informal a person who is new to an organization or an activity: *These rookie cops don't know anything yet.*

room /ruːm/, /rʊm/ **noun; verb**

▸**noun** **PLACE** ▷ **1 A1** [C] a part of the inside of a building that is separated from other parts by walls, floor, and ceiling: *She's waiting for you in the conference room upstairs.* ◦ *She's upstairs in her room (= her private room, where she sleeps).* ◦ figurative *The whole room (= all the people in the room) turned and looked at her.* **2** [C] Room is also used as a combining form: *a bedroom* ◦ *a bathroom* ◦ *a dining room* ◦ *a living room* ◦ *a hotel room* ◦ *He booked a **single/double** room (= a room for one person/two people in a hotel).* **3 rooms** [plural] UK old-fashioned a set of rented rooms, especially in a college or university **SPACE** ▷ **4 B1** [U] the amount of space that someone or something needs: *That sofa would **take up** too much room in the flat.* ◦ *James took the books off the little table to **make** room **for** the television.* ◦ *He's fainted!*

Don't crowd him – give him room. ◦ *Is there (enough/any) room* ***for*** *me* ***in*** *the car?* ◦ [+ to infinitive] *There's hardly room* ***to*** *move in here.* **5** [U] opportunity for doing something: *I feel the company has little room* ***for*** *manoeuvre.*

> **Word partners for room (SPACE)**
>
> *leave/make* room **for** sb/sth • *take up* room • *ample/enough/insufficient/sufficient* room • room *for* sb/sth

IDIOMS **no room for sth** If you say there is no room for a feeling or type of behaviour, you mean it is not acceptable: *In a small company like this, there is no room for lazy staff.* • **room for doubt** a possibility of something being true: *There is little room for doubt about what happened.* • **room for improvement** C1 a possibility or hope that someone or something will improve: *Her writing is better but there is still room for improvement.* • **no/not enough room to swing a cat** said about a place or space that is very small

▸verb [I usually + adv/prep] US to rent a room from someone, or share a rented room with someone: *At college he rooms* ***with*** *this guy from Nebraska.*

ˌroom and ˈboard noun [U] US for **board and lodging**

roomer /ˈruː.məʳ/ US /-mɚ/ noun [C] US for **lodger**

roomful /ˈruːm.fʊl/ noun [C usually singular] as many or as much as a room will hold: *a roomful* ***of*** *people/guests/boxes, etc.*

ˈroom ˌheater noun [C] a device, for example an electric fire, that heats a room

ˈrooming ˌhouse noun [C] US for **boarding house**

roommate /ˈrʊm.meɪt/, /ˈruːm-/ noun [C] **1** A2 a person who you share a room with for a period of time: *Jean was my roommate during our first year at university.* **2** B2 US (UK **housemate**, UK **flatmate**) a person who you share an apartment or house with

ˈroom ˌservice noun [U] in a hotel, the serving of food and drink to customers in their rooms, or the people who do this work

roomy /ˈruː.mi/ adj approving If something such as a house or car is roomy, it has a lot of space inside it.

R

roost /ruːst/ noun; verb

▸noun [C] a place, such as a branch of a tree, where birds rest or sleep

▸verb [I] When birds roost, they go somewhere to rest or sleep.

IDIOM **come back/home to roost** to return to cause problems: *All his earlier mistakes are coming home to roost.*

rooster /ˈruː.stəʳ/ US /-stɚ/ noun [C] US for **cock**

root /ruːt/ noun; verb

▸noun [C] **PLANT PART** ▷ **1** B2 the part of a plant that grows down into the earth to get water and food and holds the plant firm in the ground **CAUSE/ORIGIN** ▷ **2** C1 the cause or origin of something bad: *We must* ***get to the*** *root* ***of*** *(= discover the cause of) this problem.* ◦ *What* ***is/lies at*** *the root* ***of*** *the problem is their lack of interest.* ◦ *The high crime rate has its roots* ***in*** *unemployment and poverty.* ◦ *So what's the root* ***cause*** *of his anxiety?* **3 roots** B2 [plural] origins: *The city of Tours can* ***trace*** *its roots* ***back to*** *Roman times.* → See also **grassroots OF TOOTH/HAIR/NAIL** ▷ **4** the part of a hair, tooth, or nail that is under the skin **OF WORD** ▷ **5** specialized The root of a word is its most basic form, to which other parts, such as AFFIXES, can be added: *The root of the word 'sitting' is 'sit'.* **IN MATHEMATICS** ▷ **6** specialized a solution of some EQUATIONS (= mathematical statements) **7** specialized A root of a particular number is another number which, when multiplied by itself one or more times, reaches that number: *The* ***square*** *root of 64 is 8, and the* ***cube*** *root of 64 is 4.*

IDIOMS **put down roots** If you put down roots in a place where you have moved to live, you make new friends and join in new activities there so that you feel it is your home. • **root and branch** UK (US **roots and all**) completely: *Racism must be eliminated, root and branch.* • **take root** If an idea, belief, or system takes root somewhere, it starts to be accepted there: *Communism has never really taken root in England.*

▸verb **LOOK** ▷ **1** [I usually + adv/prep] to look for something by turning things over: *She rooted* ***through/among*** *the papers on her desk.* ◦ *The pigs rooted* ***for*** *acorns in the forest.* **PLANT** ▷ **2** [I] to grow roots

IDIOM **rooted to the spot** unable to move: *She was rooted to the spot with fear/amazement.*

PHRASAL VERBS **root about/around (somewhere)** informal to search for something, especially by looking through other things: *She was rooting around* ***in*** *her drawer for a pencil.* • **root for sb** informal to show support for someone who is in a competition or who is doing something difficult: *Most of the crowd were rooting for the home team.* ◦ *Good luck! We're all rooting for you.* • **root sth/sb out SEARCH FOR** ▷ **1** informal to search and find something or someone that is difficult to find: *I've rooted out an old pair of shoes that might fit you.* **GET RID OF** ▷ **2** to find and remove a person or thing that is causing a problem: *Ms Campbell has been appointed to root out inefficiency in this company.* • **root sth out/up** to remove a whole plant, including the roots, from the ground: *I suggest you root out those weeds before they take hold.*

ˈroot ˌbeer noun [C or U] a FIZZY (= with bubbles) brown drink without alcohol, that is FLAVOURED with the roots of various plants

rootbound /ˈruːt.baʊnd/ adj US for **pot-bound**

ˈroot ˌcellar noun [C] US an area, often underground, for storing root crops and vegetables

ˈroot ˌcrop noun [C] a plant such as potatoes that is grown because its roots are eaten

rootless /ˈruːt.ləs/ adj describes a person without a home to return to • **rootlessness** /-nəs/ noun [U]

rootstock /ˈruːt.stɒk/ US /-stɑːk/ noun [C] specialized a stem to which part of another plant is joined so that both parts can grow together and get an advantage from a good feature of the stem

rope /rəʊp/ US /roʊp/ noun; verb

▸noun **1** B2 [C or U] (a piece of) strong, thick string made of long twisted threads: *A sailor threw a rope ashore and we tied the boat to a post.* ◦ *a* ***coil of*** *rope* **2** [C] several of one type of object connected together on a string: *a rope* ***of*** *garlic* ◦ *a rope* ***of*** *pearls* **3 the ropes** [plural] thick rope which surrounds an area used for BOXING (= sport in which two people hit each other) or WRESTLING: *The middleweight boxing champion had his opponent up against the ropes.*

IDIOMS **learn/know the ropes** C2 to learn/know how to do a job or activity • **on the ropes** informal doing badly and likely to fail: *I think the business is finally on the ropes.* • **show/teach sb the ropes** to show someone how to do a job or activity: *Lynn spent an afternoon showing the new girl the ropes.*

▸verb [T usually + adv/prep] to tie things together with

rope: *I'll rope my horse* ***to*** *your car and pull you out of the ditch.* ◦ *The climbers roped themselves* ***together.***

PHRASAL VERBS **rope sb in** informal to persuade someone to do something for you: *At the last minute, we roped in a couple of spectators to complete the team.* • **rope sth/somewhere off** to surround an area or place with ropes in order to keep people out: *The police roped off the scene of the crime.*

ˌrope ˈbridge noun [C] a bridge made of long pieces of rope tied together with knots, and wooden boards for people to walk on, used especially in the past or for children's games

ˌrope ˈladder noun [C] a LADDER made of two long pieces of rope connected by short pieces of rope, metal, wood, etc.

ropy (**ropier, ropiest**) (also **ropey**) /ˈrəʊ.pi/ (US) /ˈroʊ-/ adj mainly UK informal in bad condition or of low quality: *Your tyres look a bit ropy, don't they?* ◦ *I usually feel rather ropy (= ill) the morning after a big party.*

Rorschach test /ˈrɔː.ʃɑːkˌtest/ (US) /ˈrɔːr-/ noun [S] (also **ˈinkblot ˌtest**) a PSYCHOLOGICAL test in which a person is shown spots of ink and asked what they look like, as a way of learning about the person's personality or feelings

rort /rɔːt/ (US) /rɔːrt/ verb; noun

▸verb [T] Australian English informal to take unfair advantage of a public service: *Gary's been rorting the system, getting both a student allowance and unemployment benefit.*

▸noun [C] Australian English informal a plan to take unfair advantage of a public service

rosary /ˈrəʊ.zər.i/ (US) /ˈroʊ.zɚ-/ noun [C] a string of BEADS (= little decorative balls) used especially by Roman Catholics and Buddhists to count prayers, or the prayers themselves: *She was* ***saying*** *the rosary.*

rose /rəʊz/ (US) /roʊz/ verb; noun; adj

▸verb past simple of **rise**

▸noun **PLANT** ▷ **1** (B1) [C] a garden plant with THORNS on its stems and pleasant-smelling flowers, or a flower from this plant: *a rose bush* ◦ *She sent him a bunch of red roses.* **FOR WATER CONTAINER** ▷ **2** [C] a circular object with small holes in it that is put on the end of a WATERING CAN (= a container used for pouring water on plants) **COLOUR** ▷ **3** [U] a pink colour: *The houses were painted various shades of rose.*

IDIOMS **coming up roses** If something is coming up roses, it is happening successfully. • **not all roses** (also **not a bed of roses**) If a situation is not all roses, there are unpleasant things to deal with as well as the pleasant ones: *Being in a relationship is not all roses, you know.* • **put the roses (back) into sb's cheeks** informal If something puts the roses back into your cheeks, it makes you look healthy, especially after an illness: *A brisk walk will put the roses back into your cheeks.*

▸adj having a pink colour

IDIOM **look at/see sth through rose-coloured/tinted glasses** (UK also **look at/see sth through rose-coloured/tinted spectacles**) to see only the pleasant things about a situation and not notice the things that are unpleasant: *She's always looked at life through rose-tinted glasses.*

rosé /ˈrəʊ.zeɪ/ (US) /roʊˈzeɪ/ noun [C or U] a pink wine

roseate /ˈrəʊ.zi.ət/ (US) /ˈroʊ.zi.ɪt/ adj literary pink

rosebud /ˈrəʊz.bʌd/ (US) /ˈroʊz-/ noun [C] the beginning stage of a rose flower

ˈrose ˌhip noun [C usually plural] a small, round, red fruit produced by a rose bush

rosella /rəʊˈzel.ə/ (US) /roʊ-/ noun [C] any of several brightly coloured PARROTS of eastern Australia

rosemary /ˈrəʊz.mə.ri/ (US) /ˈroʊz.mer.i/ noun [U] a bush whose leaves are used to add flavour in cooking and are used in some PERFUMES, or the leaves themselves

rosette /rəʊˈzet/ (US) /roʊ-/ noun [C] a flower-shaped decorative object cut into wood or stone, or one made of RIBBON (= narrow cloth strips) worn as a sign that you support a particular team or political party or that you have won a race, etc.: *The winning horse had a rosette fixed to its bridle.*

ˈrose ˌwater noun [U] a liquid with a pleasant smell made from ROSES (= type of sweet-smelling flower), used on the skin as a PERFUME or to add flavour to food

ˌrose ˈwindow noun [C] a round window, especially in a church, with coloured glass in it

rosewood /ˈrəʊz.wʊd/ (US) /ˈroʊz-/ noun [U] a hard dark wood used especially for making high-quality furniture

Rosh Hashanah (also **Rosh Hashana**) /ˌrɒʃ.hæʃˈɑː.nə/ (US) /ˌroʊʃ.həˈʃɔː.nə/ noun [U] the Jewish New Year holiday, held in September

roster /ˈrɒs.təʳ/ (US) /ˈrɑː.stɚ/ noun [C] mainly US a list of people's names, often with the jobs they have been given to do: *If you look on the* ***duty*** *roster, you'll see when you're working.*

rosti (also **rösti** /ˈrɜː.sti/) /ˈrɒ.sti/ (US) /ˈrɑː-/ noun [C or U] a dish, originally from Switzerland, consisting of small pieces of potato pressed together into a flat shape and cooked in oil

rostrum /ˈrɒs.trəm/ (US) /ˈrɑː.strəm/ noun [C] (plural **rostrums** or **rostra**) a raised surface on which a person making a speech or a music CONDUCTOR (= leader) stands

rosy /ˈrəʊ.zi/ (US) /ˈroʊ-/ adj **1** (C2) having a colour between pink and red: approving *Your rosy* ***cheeks*** *always make you look so healthy.* **2** (C2) If a situation is described as rosy, it gives hope of success or happiness: *Our financial position is rosy.*

rot /rɒt/ (US) /rɑːt/ verb; noun

▸verb [I or T] (-tt-) (C2) to (cause something to) decay: *The fruit had been left to rot on the trees.* ◦ *Rain has got in and rotted* ***(away)*** *the woodwork.* ◦ *the smell of rotting fruit*

IDIOM **rot in jail, prison, etc.** to stay in prison for a very long time: *Ruben Carter was* ***left*** *to rot in jail for most of his life.*

▸noun [U] **1** decay: *Rot has got into the furniture.* **2** old-fashioned informal nonsense: *Don't talk rot!*

IDIOMS **the rot sets in** informal (of a situation) to begin to go wrong: *The rot set in when his parents divorced and he started taking drugs.* • **stop the rot** to take action against something bad, before it spreads and becomes worse: *We must try to stop the rot before the whole school is corrupted.*

rota /ˈrəʊ.tə/ (US) /ˈroʊ.t̬ə/ noun [C] mainly UK (US usually **roster**) a list of things that have to be done and of the people who will do them: *a weekly rota*

rotary /ˈrəʊ.tər.i/ (US) /ˈroʊ.t̬ɚ-/ adj (of a machine) having a part that moves around in a circle: *a rotary engine*

rotate /rəʊˈteɪt/ (US) /ˈroʊ.teɪt/ verb **1** [I or T] to turn or cause something to turn in a circle, especially around a fixed point: *Rotate the handle by 180° to open the door.* ◦ *The wheel rotates* ***around*** *an axle.* ◦ *The satellite slowly rotates as it circles the Earth.* **2** [I or T] If a job

R

rotates or if a group of people rotate their jobs, the jobs are done at different times by different people. **3** [T] When farmers rotate crops, they regularly change which crops they grow in a particular field.

rotation /rəʊˈteɪ.ʃən/ (US) /roʊ-/ **noun 1** [U] movement in a circle around a fixed point: *the speed of rotation* **2** [C] a complete circular movement around a fixed point: *The Earth completes 366 rotations* ***about*** *its axis in every leap year.* **3** [C or U] the act by farmers of regularly changing which crops they grow in a field: ***crop*** *rotation* **4** [U] the act of different people doing the same job at different times: *the rotation of key positions such as that of chairman*

IDIOM **in rotation** one after the other, in a regular order: *There are ten employees and they do the various jobs in rotation.*

rote /rəʊt/ (US) /roʊt/ **noun** [U] usually disapproving **rote learning** learning something in order to be able to repeat it from memory, rather than in order to understand it

IDIOM **learn sth by rote** usually disapproving to learn something in order to be able to repeat it from memory, rather than in order to understand it

rotf written abbreviation for rolling on the floor: used, for example in an internet CHAT ROOM, to show that you think something is funny

rotfl (also **rofl**) written abbreviation for rolling on the floor laughing: used, for example in an internet CHAT ROOM, to show that you think something is very funny

rotflol written abbreviation for rolling on the floor laughing out loud: used, for example in an internet CHAT ROOM, to show that you think something is extremely funny

roti /ˈrəʊ.ti/ (US) /ˈroʊ.t̬i/ **noun** [C or U] a type of flat, round South Asian bread

rotisserie /rəʊˈtɪs.ər.i/ (US) /roʊˈtɪs.ɚ-/ **noun** [C] (a shop or restaurant which contains) a device for cooking meat, especially chicken, by turning it round slowly near a flame or cooker

rotor /ˈrəʊ.təʳ/ (US) /ˈroʊ.t̬ɚ/ **noun** [C] a part of a machine that SPINS, especially the device supporting the turning blades of a HELICOPTER

R

rotten /ˈrɒt.ən/ (US) /ˈrɑː.tən/ **adj 1** B2 decayed: *The room smelled of rotten vegetables.* **2** very bad: *rotten weather* ◦ old-fashioned ***It*** *was rotten* ***of*** *you* ***to*** *leave without saying goodbye.*

IDIOM **be rotten to the core** If a person or organization is rotten to the core, it behaves in a way that is not honest or moral: *The whole legal system is rotten to the core.*

rotter /ˈrɒt.əʳ/ (US) /ˈrɑː.t̬ɚ/ **noun** [C] mainly UK old-fashioned someone who is very unpleasant or does very unpleasant things

rottweiler /ˈrɒtˌwaɪ.ləʳ/, /-ˌvaɪ-/ (US) /ˈrɑːtˌwaɪ.lɚ/ **noun** [C] a large, frightening, and sometimes dangerous type of dog: figurative *Jenkins is one of the new breed of political rottweilers in his party.*

rotund /rəʊˈtʌnd/ (US) /roʊ-/ **adj** (especially of a person) round or rounded in shape

rotunda /rəʊˈtʌn.də/ (US) /roʊ-/ **noun** [C] a building, or part of one, that is round in shape, and often has a DOME (= rounded roof) on top

rouble (also **ruble**) /ˈruː.bl̩/ **noun** [C] the standard unit of money used in Belarus, Russia, and Tajikistan

rouge /ruːʒ/ **noun** [U] a red or pink powder put on the cheeks to make the face look more attractive

rough /rʌf/ **adj; verb; noun; adv**

▸**adj NOT EVEN** ▷ **1** B1 not even or smooth, often because of being in bad condition: *It was a rough mountain road, full of stones and huge holes.* **2** B1 If a surface such as paper or skin is rough, it does not feel smooth when you touch it: *My hands get very rough in the cold.* **3** Rough ground is ground that is not used for any particular purpose, is not even, and is full of wild plants. **NOT EXACT** ▷ **4** B1 [before noun] not exact or detailed: *The builder did a rough sketch of how the new stairs would look.* ◦ *This is only a rough guess.* ◦ *She made a rough* ***estimate****/calculation of the likely cost.* ◦ *The tests are a rough* ***guide*** *to students' progress.* → Synonym **approximate POOR QUALITY** ▷ **5** describes an alcoholic drink, especially wine, that tastes cheap and often strong **6** not made in a careful or expensive way: *I made a rough table out of some old boxes.* **SOUND** ▷ **7** A rough voice or sound is hard and loud. **8** If a machine sounds rough, it is making a noise because it is in bad condition. **VIOLENT** ▷ **9** B2 dangerous or violent; not calm or gentle: *a rough area of town* ◦ *The other boys were rough, always looking for a fight.* ◦ *I'm always seasick if the water/wind/sea/weather is rough* (= stormy). **DIFFICULT** ▷ **10** B2 difficult or unpleasant: *He's had a rough time/month/year, what with the divorce and then his father dying.* ◦ ***It*** *must be rough* ***to*** *have two kids and nowhere to live.* **ILL** ▷ **11** [after verb] UK ill: *You look a bit rough – how much did you have to drink last night?* • **roughness** /ˈrʌf.nəs/ **noun** [U]

IDIOMS **rough and ready 1** produced quickly, with little preparation **2** simple but good enough: *rough and ready accommodation* • **rough edges 1** If a piece of work or a performance has rough edges, some parts of it are not of very good quality: *He's a great footballer, but his game still has a few rough edges.* **2** If a person has rough edges, they do not always behave well and politely: *I knew him before he was successful, and he had a lot of rough edges back then.* • **rough justice/luck** something that happens to you that is severe or unfair: *It seems like rough justice that he should lose his house as well as his wife.*

▸**verb rough it** informal to live temporarily in basic and uncomfortable conditions: *While the house was being decorated we roughed it in a tent.*

PHRASAL VERBS **rough sth in** If you rough a drawing in, you draw the basic lines, without the detail. • **rough sth out** If you rough out a drawing, idea, or plan, you draw or write the main parts of it without giving its details. • **rough sb up** informal to hit and kick someone, usually to frighten or threaten them

▸**noun DRAWING** ▷ **1** [C] a first quick drawing of something **2 in rough** simple and without details: *His first plans were drawn up in rough.* **VIOLENT PERSON** ▷ **3** [C] a violent person **IN GOLF** ▷ **4 the rough** in GOLF, an area of ground with long grass: *My ball landed* ***in*** *the rough.*

IDIOMS **rough and tumble 1** fighting between children that is not serious: *It was just a bit of rough and tumble.* **2** a busy activity which people do in a very forceful way: *She enjoys* ***the*** *rough and tumble* ***of*** *politics.* • **take the rough with the smooth** to accept the unpleasant parts of a situation as well as the pleasant parts: *That's relationships for you – you have to take the rough with the smooth.*

▸**adv VIOLENTLY** ▷ **1** forcefully or violently: *The team had a bad reputation for playing rough.* **OUTSIDE** ▷ **2 live/sleep rough** to live outside not in a house, and sleep on the ground: *When we ran out of money, we slept rough for a week.*

roughage /ˈrʌf.ɪdʒ/ noun [U] → **fibre**

roughcast /ˈrʌf.kɑːst/ (US) /-kæst/ noun [U] specialized a mixture of water, sand, LIME, and small stones, used to cover the outside of buildings

ˌrough ˈcider noun [U] Australian English an alcoholic drink made from apples → Compare **cider**

ˌrough ˈdiamond noun [C] UK (US **ˌdiamond in the ˈrough**) a person who is kinder and more pleasant than they seem to be from their appearance and manner

roughen /ˈrʌf.ən/ verb [I or T] to (cause something to) become less smooth

ˌrough-ˈhewn adj describes a material, such as wood or stone, that has been shaped, but not given a smooth surface

roughhouse /ˈrʌf.haʊs/ verb; noun

▸verb [I or T] US or old-fashioned to fight in a way that is not serious: *A couple of boys were roughhousing (each other) in the park.*

▸noun [C usually singular] US or old-fashioned a fight between many people, without weapons

roughly /ˈrʌf.li/ adv **NOT EXACTLY** ▷ **1** (B2) approximately: *There has been an increase of roughly 2.25 million.* ◦ *Roughly* ***speaking****, it's 2.25 million.* ◦ *We have roughly similar tastes/roughly the same tastes.* **NOT EVENLY** ▷ **2** (C2) without taking a lot of care to make something perfect: *Roughly chop the tomatoes and add to the onions.* **VIOLENTLY** ▷ **3** (C2) in a violent or angry way: *He pushed the children roughly to one side.* ◦ *'And what's going on here?' he said roughly.*

roughneck /ˈrʌf.nek/ noun [C] **1** a worker on an OIL RIG (= a large piece of equipment for getting oil from underground) **2** mainly US and Australian English informal a person, usually a man, who is rough and rude

ˌrough ˈpaper noun [U] UK paper that is used for the first versions of a drawing, piece of writing, or calculation

ˌrough ˈtrade noun [U] slang male PROSTITUTES who have sex with other men and who give the appearance of being from a poor social class: *He went to the docks to pick up a bit of rough trade.*

roulette /ruːˈlet/ noun [U] a game of chance in which a small ball is dropped onto a wheel that is spinning and the players guess in which hole it will finally stop

round /raʊnd/ preposition, adv; adj; noun; verb

▸preposition, adv mainly UK (US usually **around**) **AROUND** ▷ **1** (A2) in a circular direction or position; around: *The Moon goes round the Earth.* ◦ *We ran round (the outside of the house) to the back, looking for the dog.* ◦ *The idea has been going round* ***and round*** *in my head all day (= I can't stop thinking about it).* ◦ *When one engine stopped, we had to* ***turn*** *round (= turn to face the opposite direction) and fly home.* → See also **theatre in the round IN ALL PARTS** ▷ **2** (B1) in every part of a place, or in various parts of a place: *The landlord showed me round (the house).* ◦ *I had to go* ***all*** *round town to find a hotel that was open.* ◦ *This virus has been going round (the school) (= many people have had it).* **SURROUNDING** ▷ **3** (A2) on all or some sides of something: *We sat round the fire.* ◦ *The house has trees* ***all*** *round.* ◦ *The pyramid is 50 metres high and 100 metres round (the base).* ◦ *Everyone for a mile round (= in the area) heard the explosion.* **DIRECTION** ▷ **4** (A2) in a particular direction: *The garden is round the back (of the house).* ◦ *I used to live round (= near) here when I was a child.* ◦ *You must come round (****to*** *my house) sometime soon.* ◦ UK not standard *We're going round (= to) the pub for a quick drink.*

IDIOMS **right/wrong way round** facing the right/wrong way: *He put the wheel on the right/wrong way round.* • **round about** approximately: *We'll be at your house at round about nine o'clock, okay?* • **round the corner** very near here: *There's a great restaurant* ***just*** *round the corner.* • **way round** a way of dealing with or avoiding a problem: *There's no way round this problem.*

▸adj **CIRCULAR** ▷ **1** (A2) shaped like a ball or circle, or curved: *Tennis balls and oranges are round.* ◦ *a round hole/stone/table/window* ◦ *a round face* **COMPLETE** ▷ **2** (of a number) whole or complete; given to the nearest 1, 10, 100, etc. and not as exact amounts: *2.8 to the nearest round* ***number*** *is 3.* ◦ *'I've got 95 bottles here for you.' 'Could you make it a round hundred, please?'*

▸noun [C] **GROUP** ▷ **1** (C2) a number of things or group of events: *Russia and America will hold another round* ***of*** *talks next month.* ◦ *When we were young life was just one long round of parties/pleasure.* **2** (C2) drinks that you buy for a group of people: *It's your turn to buy a round.* **3** UK a single slice of TOAST, or a sandwich **4** UK (US **route**) a set of regular visits that you make to a number of places or people, especially in order to take products as part of your job: *He has a* ***milk/paper*** *round.* **5** specialized a song for several singers, who begin singing one after the other at various points in the song **COMPETITION PART** ▷ **6** (B2) a part of a competition: *She was knocked out of the championship in the third round.* **7** one of the periods of time during a BOXING or WRESTLING match when the competitors are fighting **8** a complete game in GOLF **BULLET** ▷ **9** a bullet or other single piece of AMMUNITION: *The soldiers had only 20 rounds left.*

IDIOMS **the daily round** UK old-fashioned the tasks you have to do every day: *I get exhausted just by the daily round.* • **go the rounds** UK to go from person to person or place to place: *That story has gone the rounds in our office.* • **make/do the rounds** to talk to a lot of people: *I've made/done the rounds of all the agents, but nobody has any tickets left.* • **on your rounds** to be out on a regular visit: *The doctor's out on his rounds.* • **round of applause** (C2) a period of time during which people are clapping: *The singer got a big round of applause.*

▸verb [T] to go around something: *Colin rounded the corner at high speed.*

PHRASAL VERBS **round sth down** to reduce a number to the nearest whole or simple number • **round sth off SHAPE** ▷ **1** to make something that is pointed or sharp into a smooth, curved shape by rubbing it **COMPLETE** ▷ **2** to complete an event or activity in a pleasant or satisfactory way: *To round off her education, her father sent her to a Swiss finishing school.* ◦ *We rounded the meal off* ***with*** *a chocolate and rum cake.* • **round on sb/sth** If you round on someone or something, you suddenly turn and attack them: *The fox rounded on its pursuers.* ◦ figurative *The prime minister rounded on his critics with a very forceful speech.* • **round sth/sb up** to find and bring together a group of animals or people: *The cowboys rounded the cattle up.* ◦ *I'll just go and round up Andrew and Patrick for the meeting.* • **round sth up** to increase a number to the nearest whole or simple number

roundabout /ˈraʊnd.ə.baʊt/ noun; adj

▸noun [C] UK **ON ROAD** ▷ **1** (A2) (US **traffic circle**) a place where three or more roads join and traffic must go around a circular area in the middle, rather than straight across **PLAY EQUIPMENT** ▷ **2** (US **ˈmerry-go-ˌround**) a flat, round piece of equipment in play areas on which children sit or stand and are pushed round

R

and round **3** a MERRY-GO-ROUND (= machine with animals or vehicles for children to ride at a fair)
▸**adj** not in a simple, direct, or quick way: *We took a roundabout **route** to avoid the accident.* ◦ *He asked me, in a roundabout **way**, if he could have a salary increase.*

ˈround ˌbrackets noun [plural] UK for **parentheses**

rounded /ˈraʊn.dɪd/ adj round or curved: *The little boy stared at the pregnant woman's rounded belly.*

roundel /ˈraʊn.dəl/ noun [C] a circular decoration, especially a coloured circle on a military aircraft that shows its nationality

rounders /ˈraʊn.dəz/ (US) /-dɚz/ noun [U] a British game similar to baseball, in which you try to hit a ball and you score a point if you run round all four sides of a large square area

ˌround-ˈeyed adj [after verb] describes someone whose eyes are open very wide because they are surprised, shocked, or frightened: *She was round-eyed **with** amazement/terror.*

roundhouse kick /ˌraʊnd.haʊsˈkɪk/ noun [C] a type of kick used in some MARTIAL ARTS that involves lifting and moving your whole leg around your body before hitting someone with your foot

roundly /ˈraʊnd.li/ adv formal severely: *The government is being roundly **criticized** for its education policy.* ◦ *The home team were roundly **defeated**.*

ˌround ˈrobin noun [C] **LETTER** ▷ **1** UK a letter, usually of demands or complaints, that is signed by many people **2** UK a letter that you send to a lot of people, for example at Christmas, telling them what you have done that year **COMPETITION** ▷ **3** a competition in which all the players play against each other at least once

ˌround-ˈshouldered adj having shoulders that curve down and forward: *He had become round-shouldered from years of sitting in front of a computer.*

ˌround-ˈtable adj [before noun] A round-table discussion/meeting is one where people meet and talk in conditions of EQUALITY.

ˌround-the-ˈclock adj [before noun] (also **aˌround-the-ˈclock**) happening or done all day and all night: *He's very sick and needs round-the-clock **care**.* → See also **clock**

R

ˌround ˈtrip noun [C] If you make a round trip, you go on a journey and return to where you started from.

ˈround-up noun [C] **1** a bringing together of people, animals, things, etc.: *The president ordered the round-up and imprisonment of all opposition politicians.* → See also **round 2** a statement on the radio or television of the main points of the news

roundworm /ˈraʊnd.wɜːm/ (US) /-wɝːm/ noun [C] any of various types of creature with a round body that can live in the bowels of people and some animals, and often cause disease

rouse /raʊz/ verb [T] to wake someone up or make someone more active or excited: *He roused himself (**from** a pleasant daydream) and got back to work.* ◦ *The speaker attempted to rouse the crowd with a cry for action.*

rouseabout /ˈraʊz.ə.baʊt/ noun [C] Australian English a person whose job involves heavy unskilled work → Compare **roustabout**

rousing /ˈraʊ.zɪŋ/ adj making people feel excited and proud or ready to take action: *We sang a last rousing **chorus** of the national anthem.* ◦ *She delivered a rousing **speech** full of anger and passion.*

roustabout /ˈraʊst.ə.baʊt/ noun [C] US a person whose job involves heavy unskilled work

rout /raʊt/ verb; noun
▸**verb** [T] formal to defeat an enemy completely and force them to run away: figurative *The Russian chess team have routed all the rest.*

PHRASAL VERB **rout sb out** US to make someone come out of the place where they are: *His wife had to rout him out **of** the crowd.*

▸**noun** [C] a defeat: *The battle/election was a complete and utter rout.*

route /ruːt/ (US) /ruːt/ /raʊt/ noun; verb
▸**noun** [C] **1** (B1) a particular way or direction between places: *The route we had planned took us right across Greece.* ◦ *I live **on** a bus route so I can easily get to work.* **2** (C2) a method of achieving something: *A college education is often the best route **to** a good job.* **3** US (UK **round**) a set of regular visits that you make to a number of places or people, especially in order to take products as part of your job

> **Word partners for route noun**
> *follow/take* a route • *plan/work out* a route • sb/sth *lines* the route • the *best/fastest/preferred/shortest* route • a *circuitous/direct* route • a *main/major* route • a route *across/between/from/to* • *along/on* a route

▸**verb** [T usually + adv/prep] to send something somewhere: *Deliveries are routed via/by way of London.*

Route /ruːt/ (US) /ruːt/ /raʊt/ noun In the US, Route is used before the names of main roads between some cities: *Route 66*

ˈroute ˌmarch noun [C usually singular] a long, difficult walk, especially one done by soldiers as part of their training

router /ˈruː.təʳ/ (US) /ˈraʊ.t̬ɚ/ noun [C] a piece of electronic equipment that connects computer NETWORKS to each other, and sends information between networks

routine /ruːˈtiːn/ noun; adj
▸**noun 1** (B1) [C or U] a usual or fixed way of doing things: *There's no **set/fixed** routine at work – every day is different.* ◦ *He checks under the car for bombs as **a matter of** routine.* **2** [C] a regular series of movements, jokes or similar things used in a performance: *an **exercise/dance** routine* ◦ *He went into his usual 'I'm the head of the family' routine (= usual way of speaking).* **3** [C] specialized a part of a computer program that does a particular operation
▸**adj 1** done as part of what usually happens, and not for any special reason: *a routine **inspection**/medical **check-up*** **2** ordinary and not special or unusual: *a routine case of appendicitis* ◦ *He died during a routine **operation** which went wrong.* **3** (C2) disapproving ordinary and boring: *My job is so routine and boring – I hate it.*

routinely /ruːˈtiːn.li/ adv used for describing what often or usually happens: *Health and safety rules are routinely flouted/**ignored**.*

roux /ruː/ noun [C or U] (plural **roux**) a mixture made from equal amounts of fat and flour, used especially to make a sauce or soup thicker

rove /rəʊv/ (US) /roʊv/ verb [I + adv/prep, T] literary to move, travel, or look around an area, especially a large one: *His eye/gaze roved hungrily about the room.* ◦ *He spent most of his life roving the world in search of his fortune.*

roving /ˈrəʊ.vɪŋ/ (US) /ˈroʊ-/ adj [before noun] travelling from place to place: *And now a live report from our roving reporter, Martin Jackson.*

IDIOM **have a roving eye** old-fashioned humorous If you say that someone has a roving eye, you mean that they are always sexually interested in people other than their partner.

> **! Common mistake: row**
>
> **Warning:** choose the correct preposition!
>
> To talk about where someone or something is, don't say 'at/on the back/front/first row', say **in** the back/front/first row:
>
> ~~*We could only get seats on the back row.*~~
>
> *We could only get seats in the back row.*

row[1] /rəʊ/ (US) /roʊ/ noun; verb
▸noun **LINE** ▷ **1** (B1) [C] a line of things, people, animals, etc. arranged next to each other: *a row of houses/books/plants/people/horses* ◦ *We had seats **in** the front/back row **of** the theatre.* **2** [C] Row is also used in the names of some roads: *Prospect Row* **3 in a row** (B2) one after another without a break: *She's been voted Best Actress three years in a row.*
MOVING THROUGH WATER ▷ **4** [C usually singular] the activity of making a boat move through water using OARS (= poles with flat ends): *They've gone for a row to the island.*

IDIOM **a hard/tough row to hoe** US a difficult situation to deal with: *Teachers have a tough row to hoe in today's schools.*

▸verb [I or T] (B2) to cause a boat to move through water by pushing against the water with OARS (= poles with flat ends): *The wind dropped, so we had to row (the boat) back home.* • **rower** /ˈrəʊ.əʳ/ (US) /ˈroʊ.ɚ/ noun [C] • **rowing** /ˈrəʊ.ɪŋ/ (US) /ˈroʊ-/ noun [U] *I love rowing.*

row[2] /raʊ/ noun; verb
▸noun mainly UK **ARGUMENT** ▷ **1** [C] a noisy argument or fight: *My parents often **have** rows, but my dad does most of the shouting.* ◦ *What was a political row **over** government policy on Europe is fast becoming a diplomatic row **between** France and Britain.* **NOISE** ▷ **2** [S] loud noise: *I can't concentrate because of the row the builders are making.*
▸verb [I] mainly UK informal to argue, especially loudly: *My parents are always rowing (**about/over** money).*

rowan /ˈrəʊ.ən/, /ˈraʊ-/ (US) /ˈroʊ-/ noun [C] a small tree with small, bright red fruit

rowdy /ˈraʊ.di/ adj disapproving noisy and possibly violent: *a rowdy party* ◦ *rowdy behaviour* • **rowdily** /-dɪ.li/ adv • **rowdiness** /-nəs/ noun [U]

rowdy-sheeter /ˈraʊ.diˌʃiː.təʳ/ (US) /-t̬ɚ/ noun [C] Indian English a person who has a CRIMINAL RECORD (= an official record of the crimes that they have committed)

rowhouse /ˈrəʊˌhaʊs/ (US) /ˈroʊ-/ noun [C] US (UK ˈ**terraced** ˌ**house**) a house that is joined to the houses on either side of it by shared walls

ˈ**rowing** ˌ**boat** noun [C] UK (US **rowboat**) a small boat that is moved by pulling OARS (= poles with flat ends) through the water

rowlock /ˈrɒ.lək/, /ˈrəʊ.lɒk/ (US) /ˈrɑː.lək/, /ˈroʊ.lɑːk/ noun [C] (US **oarlock**) a U-shaped device or hole on each side of a rowing boat in which the OARS (= poles with flat ends used to move a boat) are held

royal /ˈrɔɪ.əl/ adj; noun
▸adj **1** (B2) (written abbreviation **R**) belonging or connected to a king or queen or a member of their family: *the royal **family*** ◦ *a royal visit* **2** good or excellent, as if intended for or typical of royalty: *The team was given a royal reception/welcome.* **3** mainly US big or great: *a royal pain/a royal mess*
▸noun [C usually plural] informal a member of the royal family: *The press follow the royals everywhere.*

ˌ**royal asˈsent** noun [U] UK specialized the official approval of a law by the British king or queen

ˌ**royal ˈblue** noun [U] a strong, bright blue colour • ˌ**royal-ˈblue adj**

ˌ**royal ˈflush** noun [C usually singular] in card games, a set of all the five highest cards in one suit

ˌ**Royal ˈHighness** noun **Her/His/Your Royal Highness** used when you are speaking about or to a royal person: *Thank you, Your Royal Highness.*

royalist /ˈrɔɪ.ə.lɪst/ noun [C] a person who supports a ruling king or queen or who believes that a king or queen should rule their country • **royalist adj** *royalist sympathies*

ˌ**royal ˈpardon** noun [C] an official order given by a king or queen to stop the punishment of a person accused of a crime → Compare **free pardon**

ˌ**royal preˈrogative** noun [U] the special rights of the ruling king or queen

royalty /ˈrɔɪ.əl.ti/ (US) /-t̬i/ noun **RULERS** ▷ **1** [U, + sing/pl verb] the people who belong to the family of a king and queen: *She believes she's related to royalty.* **PAYMENT** ▷ **2** [C usually plural] a payment made to writers, people who have invented things, owners of property, etc. every time their books, devices, land, etc. are bought or used by others

RP /ˌɑːˈpiː/ (US) /ˌɑːr-/ noun [U] abbreviation for **Received Pronunciation**

RPI /ˌɑː.piːˈaɪ/ (US) /ˌɑːr-/ noun [S] UK abbreviation for **retail price index**

rpm /ˌɑː.piːˈem/ (US) /ˌɑːr-/ abbreviation for revolutions per minute: used when stating the number of times something goes round during a minute

RR US **TRAIN** ▷ **1** written abbreviation for **railroad** **POST** ▷ **2** written abbreviation for rural route: used in addresses in some areas in the US

RRP written abbreviation for recommended retail price: the price that the company which makes a product says it should be sold for

RSI /ˌɑː.resˈaɪ/ (US) /ˌɑːr.es-/ noun [U] abbreviation for **repetitive strain injury**

RSS /ˌɑːr.esˈes/ noun [U] specialized abbreviation for really simple syndication: a way of publishing information on a website so that someone can take it and use it on another website

RSVP /ˌɑː.res.viːˈpiː/ (US) /ˌɑːr.es-/ used at the end of a written invitation to mean 'please answer': *RSVP by 9 October.*

RT /ˌɑːˈtiː/ (US) /ˌɑːr-/ noun; verb
▸noun [C] trademark abbreviation for **retweet**
▸verb [I or T] trademark abbreviation for **retweet**

Rt. Hon. /ˌraɪtˈɒn.ər.ə.bl/ (US) /ˌraɪtˈɑː.nɚ-/ abbreviation for Right Honourable: a title given to important British officials such as PRIVY COUNCILLORS and members of the government: *the Rt. Hon. Julian Smith MP*

rub /rʌb/ verb; noun
▸verb [I or T] (**-bb-**) (B2) to press or be pressed against something with a circular or up-and-down repeated movement: *She yawned and rubbed her eyes sleepily.* ◦ *He rubbed (**at**) the stain on his trousers and made it worse.* ◦ *We rubbed some polish **into** the surface of the wood.* ◦ *She gently rubbed the ointment **in**.* ◦ *First rub the baking tray well **with** butter.* ◦ [+ obj + adj] *Alice rubbed the blackboard **clean** for the teacher.* ◦ *Your cat*

R

*keeps on rubbing itself (**up**) **against** my leg.* ◦ *She was rubbing her hands (**together**) at the thought of winning.* ◦ *The branches rubbed **against** each other in the wind.* ◦ *The chair legs have rubbed holes in the carpet.* ◦ *My new shoes are rubbing (**against/on** my toe) and now I've got blisters.* ◦ *These marks will never rub **off** (= be cleaned off).*

IDIOMS **rub sb's nose in it** to say or do things which make someone remember that they failed or got something wrong: *Sue failed her exam, so just to rub her nose in it, I put my certificate up on the wall.* • **rub salt in/into the wound** to make a difficult situation even worse for someone: *Losing was bad enough, having to watch them receiving the trophy just rubbed salt into the wound.* • **rub shoulders (with)** (US also **rub elbows (with)**) to meet and spend time with someone: *She claims that she rubs shoulders with royalty all the time.* • **rub sb up the wrong way** UK (US **rub sb the wrong way**) to annoy someone without intending to: *As soon as they met they started to rub each other up the wrong way.*

PHRASAL VERBS **rub along** UK informal If two people rub along, they work or live together in a satisfactory way: *My flat-mate and I rub along okay **together**.* • **rub sth down** to rub something with a rough cloth, brush, or paper until its surface is smooth, or clean and shiny: *Rub the wood down **with** fine sandpaper till it is smooth.* ◦ *We rubbed the walls down **with** soap and hot water.* • **rub sth/sb down** to use a cloth to dry an animal or person: *I used a towel to rub the dog down after his bath.* • **rub sth in** C2 to talk to someone about something which you know they want to forget because they feel bad about it: *OK, I made a mistake, – you don't have to rub **it** in.* • **rub off** informal If a quality or characteristic that someone has rubs off, other people begin to have it because they have been with that person and learned it from them: *His enthusiasm is starting to rub off **on** the rest of us.* • **rub sth out** UK B2 to remove writing or a mark from something by rubbing it with a piece of rubber or a cloth: *It's in pencil, so you can rub it out if you need to.* • **rub sb out** US slang to murder someone: *He was rubbed out by the Mafia.*

▸**noun** [C] the act of rubbing something: *He **gave** her hair a good rub to dry it.*

IDIOM **the rub** formal the particular problem that makes a situation difficult or impossible: *You can't get a job unless you have experience, but **there's** the rub, you can't get experience unless you have a job.*

rubber /ˈrʌb.əʳ/ (US) /-ɚ/ noun **SUBSTANCE** ▷ **1** B2 [U] an ELASTIC substance (= that stretches) made either from the juice of particular tropical trees or artificially: *Tyres are almost always made of rubber.* **2** A2 [C] UK an **eraser** **3** [C] US slang for a **condom** **4** **rubbers** [plural] US old-fashioned for **overshoes** **GAME** ▷ **5** [C] a series of three or five games between two teams, especially in card games or cricket: *We played a rubber of bridge.*

IDIOM **a rubber check** US humorous a CHEQUE (= piece of paper from someone's bank that they sign and use for money) that is not worth anything because the person does not have enough money in the bank

ˌrubber ˈband noun [C] (also **eˌlastic ˈband**) a thin ring of rubber used for holding things together: *She put a rubber band around the box.*

ˌrubber ˈboot noun [C] US and Australian English a WATERPROOF boot that reaches almost to the knees → Compare **wellington**

ˌrubber ˈdinghy noun [C] a small rubber boat that has air in it to keep its shape

rubbernecker /ˈrʌb.ə.nek.əʳ/ (US) /-ɚ.nek.ɚ/ noun [C] (also **rubberneck**) a driver who drives more slowly to look at an accident, or a person who looks at something in a stupid way • **rubbernecking** /-ɪŋ/ noun [U]

ˈrubber ˌplant noun [C] a plant with dark green shiny leaves that comes originally from Asia

ˌrubber ˈstamp noun [C usually singular] a small device with raised letters made of rubber, used for printing the date, name of an organization, etc. on documents

ˌrubber-ˈstamp verb [T] disapproving to officially approve a decision or plan without thinking about it: *The boss makes the decisions and the committee just rubber-stamps them.*

ˈrubber ˌtree noun [C] a type of tropical tree from which LATEX (= the liquid used to make rubber) is obtained

rubbery /ˈrʌb.ᵊr.i/ (US) /-ɚ-/ adj feeling or bending like rubber: *My legs felt all rubbery (= weak) after the race.*

ˈrubbing ˌalcohol noun [U] US for **surgical spirit**

rubbish /ˈrʌb.ɪʃ/ noun; verb; adj

▸**noun** [U] **1** B1 mainly UK (US **garbage**, also **trash**) waste material or things that are no longer wanted or needed: *I forgot to put the rubbish out this morning.* ◦ *Put the empty box in the rubbish **bin**.* ◦ *Take the old furniture to the rubbish **dump**.* **2** B2 informal something that you think is very low quality or not true: *The film was rubbish.* ◦ *His ideas are **a load of** (**old**) rubbish.*

▸**verb** [T] UK informal to criticize something: *Why does everyone rubbish my ideas?*

▸**adj** UK informal completely without skill at a particular activity: *I'm rubbish at arithmetic.*

rubbishy /ˈrʌb.ɪ.ʃi/ adj mainly UK informal very low quality: *a rubbishy film*

rubble /ˈrʌb.l̩/ noun [U] **1** the piles of broken stone and bricks, etc. that are left when a building falls down or is destroyed: *The bomb **reduced** the house **to** rubble.* **2** small pieces of stone or rock used for building

rubdown /ˈrʌb.daʊn/ noun [C] an act of cleaning and smoothing something, or of drying a person or animal: *a cold shower and a rubdown with a towel*

rubella /ruːˈbel.ə/ noun [U] specialized → **German measles**

Rubicon /ˈruː.bɪ.kɒn/, /-kən/ (US) /-kɑːn/ noun **cross the Rubicon** to do something that you cannot later change and will strongly influence future events: *Most EU states have crossed the Rubicon and adopted the euro.*

rubicund /ˈruː.bɪ.kənd/ (US) /-bə.kʌnd/ adj literary having a red face

rubric /ˈruː.brɪk/ noun [C] formal a set of instructions, especially on an exam paper, usually printed in a different style or colour: *Read/Follow the rubric carefully.*

ruby /ˈruː.bi/ noun **1** [C or U] a transparent, dark red PRECIOUS STONE, often used in jewellery: *a ring with a large ruby* ◦ *a ruby necklace/ring* **2** [U] (also **ruby red**) a dark red colour • **ruby** adj (also **ruby red**) *ruby lips*

ˌruby ˈwedding (anniˌversary) noun [C] (also US **ˈruby anniˌversary**) the date exactly 40 years after someone's WEDDING

ruched /ruːʃt/ adj (of cloth) in tight ELASTIC folds: *elegant ruched curtains* ◦ *a ruched collar*

ruck /rʌk/ noun; verb

▸**noun** **CROWD** ▷ **1 the ruck** ordinary people or things,

R

that you consider boring: *Carter's brilliant second novel lifted her **out of** the ruck (of average writers).* **2** [C] specialized a group of players in RUGBY who are all together around the ball **FOLD** ▷ **3** [C] a fold
▸**verb**

PHRASAL VERB **ruck (sth) up** If material rucks up, it forms a LUMP (= mass) or folds, and if something rucks it up, it pushes the material into a lump or folds.

rucksack /ˈrʌk.sæk/ noun [C] A2 a **backpack**

ruckus /ˈrʌk.əs/ noun [C usually singular] mainly US informal a noisy situation or argument → Synonym **rumpus**

ructions /ˈrʌk.ʃənz/ noun [plural] mainly UK informal a noisy argument or angry complaint: *There'll be ructions if I'm not home by midnight.*

rudder /ˈrʌd.əʳ/ US /-ɚ/ noun [C] a flat piece of wood or metal at the back of a boat or aircraft, moved from side to side in order to control the direction of travel

rudderless /ˈrʌd.ə.ləs/ US /-ɚ-/ adj (of an organization) without anyone in control and therefore unable to take decisions

ruddy /ˈrʌd.i/ adj; adj, adv
▸**adj** red: *He was ruddy-cheeked from the walk in the cold.* ◦ *Her face was ruddy and healthy-looking.*
▸**adj** [before noun], **adv** UK old-fashioned informal used to avoid saying BLOODY to express anger: *Ruddy hell!*

rude /ruːd/ adj **NOT POLITE** ▷ **1** B1 not polite; offensive or embarrassing: *He's a very rude man.* ◦ ***It's** rude not **to** say 'Thank you' when you are given something.* ◦ *He's got no manners – he's rude **to** everyone.* **2** B2 relating to sex or going to the toilet: *He told a rude **joke**/story.* **SUDDEN** ▷ **3** [before noun] sudden and unpleasant: *We had a rude **awakening** (= unpleasant shock) when we saw our phone bill.* **SIMPLE** ▷ **4** old use or literary simply and roughly made: *We built a rude shelter from rocks on the beach.*
• **rudely** /ˈruːd.li/ adv C1 *She rudely interrupted my speech.* • **rudeness** /ˈruːd.nəs/ noun [U]

> **+ Other ways of saying rude**
>
> A more formal alternative to 'rude' is the word **impolite**:
>
> *She asks direct questions without being in any way **impolite**.*
>
> If someone is rude or does not show respect to a person who is older or has more authority, that person might be described as **impertinent** or **insolent**:
>
> *I found his questions **impertinent**.*
>
> The adjective **abrasive** describes someone's manner when being rude and unfriendly:
>
> *I thought he was kind of **abrasive**.*
>
> A person who is rude and unpleasant is sometimes described as **uncouth**:
>
> *She considers him loud-mouthed and **uncouth**.*
>
> Language which is rude, often because it refers to the body in an unpleasant way, can be described as **vulgar** or **crude**:
>
> *He told a pretty **vulgar** joke over dinner.*

rudimentary /ˌruː.dɪˈmen.tər.i/ US /-tɚ-/ adj formal **1** basic: *Her knowledge is still only rudimentary.* **2** describes methods, equipment, systems, etc. that are simple and not very well developed: specialized *Some unusual fish have rudimentary legs.*

the rudiments /ˈruː.dɪ.mənts/ noun [plural] the simplest and most basic facts about a subject or activity: *It only took me an hour to learn/pick up the rudiments **of** skiing.*

rue /ruː/ verb [T] (present tense **rueing** or **ruing**, past

tense and past participle **rued**) old-fashioned or literary to feel sorry about an event and wish it had not happened

IDIOM **rue the day** to feel very sorry about an event: *She'll rue the day (**that**) she bought that house.*

rueful /ˈruː.fəl/ adj literary feeling sorry and wishing that something had not happened: *He turned away with a rueful laugh.* • **ruefully** /-i/ adv

ruff /rʌf/ noun [C] a large, stiff collar with many folds, worn in Europe in the 16th and 17th centuries, or a circle of hair or feathers growing round the neck of a bird or animal

ruffian /ˈrʌf.i.ən/ noun [C] old-fashioned or humorous a violent, wild, and unpleasant person, usually a man

ruffle /ˈrʌf.l̩/ verb; noun
▸**verb 1** [T] to touch or move something smooth so that it is not even: *She affectionately ruffled his **hair** with her hand as she passed.* ◦ *The birds ruffled their **feathers** (**up**) in alarm.* **2** [T often passive] to annoy or upset someone, or to make them very nervous: *He's easily ruffled by criticism.*

IDIOM **ruffle sb's feathers** to upset or annoy someone: *She knows how to ruffle his feathers.*

▸**noun** [C] a series of small folds made in a piece of cloth or sewn onto it, as decoration

rug /rʌg/ noun [C] **1** B1 a piece of thick heavy cloth smaller than a carpet, used for covering the floor or for decoration: *My dog loves lying on the rug in front of the fire.* **2** a soft cover that keeps you warm or comfortable **3** slang for **toupée**

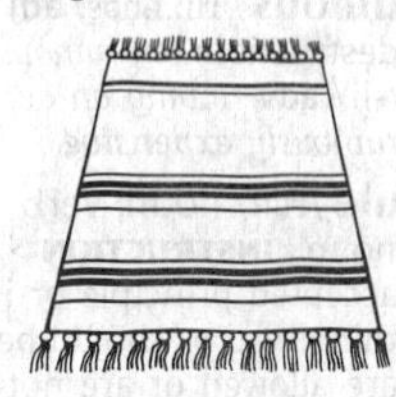
rug

rugby /ˈrʌg.bi/ noun [U] (formal ˌ**rugby** ˈ**football**) A2 a sport where two teams try to score points by carrying an oval ball across a particular line or kicking it over and between an H-shaped set of posts

ˌ**rugby** ˈ**league** noun [U] a form of rugby with 13 players in each team

ˌ**rugby** ˈ**union** noun [U] a form of rugby with 15 players in each team

rugged /ˈrʌg.ɪd/ adj **NOT EVEN** ▷ **1** (of land) wild and not even; not easy to travel over: *rugged landscape/terrain/hills/cliffs* **STRONG** ▷ **2** strong and simple; not delicate: *Jeeps are rugged vehicles, designed for rough conditions.* **3** describes a man's face that is strongly and attractively formed: *She fell for his rugged good looks.* • **ruggedly** /-li/ adv

rugger /ˈrʌg.əʳ/ US /-ɚ/ noun [U] UK informal for **rugby**

ruin /ˈruː.ɪn/ verb; noun
▸**verb** [T] **1** B2 to spoil or destroy something severely or completely: *Huge modern hotels have ruined this once unspoilt coastline.* ◦ *Her injury ruined her **chances** of winning the race.* **2** to cause a person or company to lose all their money or their reputation: *Cheap imported goods are ruining many businesses.* ◦ *If there's a scandal I'll be ruined!*
▸**noun 1** [U] the process or state of being spoiled or destroyed: *The car accident meant the ruin **of** all her hopes.* ◦ *They let the palace **fall into** ruin.* **2** C2 [U] a situation in which a person or company has lost all their money or their reputation: *Many companies are **on the edge/brink/verge of** ruin.* ◦ *Alcohol was my ruin (= the thing that spoiled my life)* **3** B1 [C] the broken parts that are left from an old building or

ruin

town: *We visited a Roman ruin.* ◦ *the ruins of the ancient city of Carthage* **4 be/lie in ruins a** (of a building or city) to be extremely badly damaged so that most of it has fallen down: *The town lay in ruins after years of bombing.* **b** C1 to be in an extremely bad state: *The economy was in ruins after the war.*

ruination /ˌruː.ɪˈneɪ.ʃᵊn/ noun [U] old-fashioned destruction: *Alcohol was the ruination* ***of*** *him.*

ruined /ˈruː.ɪnd/ adj destroyed or spoiled: *an ancient ruined* ***castle***

ruinous /ˈruː.ɪ.nəs/ adj formal causing great harm and destruction: *ten ruinous years of terrorism* • **ruinously** /-li/ adv *Having an accident without insurance can be ruinously* ***expensive****.*

rule /ruːl/ noun; verb

▸noun **INSTRUCTION** ▷ **1** B1 [C usually plural] an accepted principle or instruction that states the way things are or should be done, and tells you what you are allowed or are not allowed to do: *A referee must know all the rules of the game.* ◦ *The first/most important rule in life is always to appear confident.* ◦ *Before you start your own business you should be familiar with the government's rules* ***and regulations****.* ◦ *You must* ***follow/obey/observe*** *the rules.* ◦ *You must not* ***break*** *the rules.* ◦ *In special cases the manager will* ***bend/stretch*** *the rules (= allow the rules to be broken).* ◦ *You can trust Ruth because she always* ***plays (it) by/goes by/does things by*** *the rules (= follows instructions, standards, or rules).* ◦ [+ to infinitive] *It's* ***against*** *the rules (****of/in*** *boxing)* ***to*** *hit below the belt.* ◦ [+ that] *It's a club rule* ***that*** *new members must sing a song.* **CONTROL** ▷ **2** C2 [U] a period of time during which a particular person or group is in control of a country: *The period of Fascist rule is one people try to forget.* ◦ *We don't want one-party rule – we want rule* ***by*** *the people.* → See also **misrule**

> **Word partners for rule noun**
>
> *apply/enforce* a rule • *break/flout/violate* a rule • *bend/relax/stretch/waive* a rule • *follow/obey/observe* the rules • *establish/lay down/make* a rule • a rule *forbids/prevents/prohibits* sth • rules *governing* sth • a *strict/unwritten* rule • a rule *against* sth • be *against* the rules

IDIOMS **as a (general) rule** B2 usually: *As a general rule, I only read detective novels.* • **make it a rule** to act according to a principle: *I make it a rule not to eat fatty foods.* • **the rule** the usual situation: *In England, it often seems that rain is the rule all the year round.* • **rule of thumb** C1 a practical and approximate way of doing or measuring something: *A good rule of thumb is that a portion of rice is two handfuls.*

▸verb **CONTROL** ▷ **1** B2 [I or T] to control or be the person in charge of something such as a country: *Most modern kings and queens rule (their countries) only in a formal way, without real power.* ◦ *She rules her household* ***with an iron hand/fist*** *(= severely).* **2** B2 [I or T] to be the most important and controlling influence on someone: *Love ruled supreme in her heart.* ◦ *The desperate desire to go to Moscow ruled their lives.* **DECIDE** ▷ **3** [I or T] to decide officially: *Only the Appeal Court can rule* ***on*** *this point.* ◦ *The judge ruled* ***for/in favour of/against*** *the defendant.* ◦ [+ that] *The government has ruled* ***that*** *the refugees must be deported.* ◦ [+ obj + noun/adj] *The courts have ruled his brave action illegal.* → See also **overrule** **DRAW** ▷ **4** [T] to draw a straight line using something that has a straight edge: *She ruled two red lines under the title.*

IDIOMS **be ruled by sb** formal to take the advice of someone: *If you're wise you'll be ruled by your father.* • **rule OK** UK slang is the best: *The graffiti on the wall said 'Liverpool rules OK'.* • **rule the roost** to be the person who makes all the decisions in a group: *In that family it is the grandma who rules the roost.*

PHRASAL VERBS **rule sth or sb out** C2 to decide or say officially that something is impossible or will not happen, or that something or someone is not suitable: *The police haven't yet ruled out murder.* ◦ *I won't rule out a June election.* ◦ *The police have not ruled him out* ***as*** *a suspect.* • **rule sth out** to prevent something from happening: *This recent wave of terrorism has ruled out any chance of peace talks.*

rulebook /ˈruːl.bʊk/ noun [C usually singular] a book containing the official rules for an organization or activity

the ˌrule of ˈlaw noun [S] formal a set of laws that people in a society must obey: *Everyone is subject to the rule of law.*

ruler /ˈruː.ləʳ/ US /-lɚ/ noun [C] **LEADER** ▷ **1** C1 the leader of a country: *The country was without a ruler after the queen died.* **FOR DRAWING** ▷ **2** A2 (old-fashioned or formal **rule**) a long, narrow, flat piece of plastic, metal, or wood with straight edges where centimetres or INCHES, or both are printed. It is used for measuring things and for drawing straight lines.

ruling /ˈruː.lɪŋ/ noun; adj

▸noun [C] C2 a decision: [+ that] *The court has made a final ruling* ***on*** *the case* ***that*** *the companies acted illegally.*

▸adj [before noun] being in control and making all the decisions: *The Communists are the ruling party at the moment.*

IDIOM **ruling passion** most important interest: *His ruling passion is music.*

the ˌruling ˈclass noun [S] (also **ˌruling ˈclasses** [plural]) the most powerful people in a country

rum /rʌm/ noun; adj

▸noun [C or U] a strong alcoholic drink made from the juice of the SUGAR CANE plant: *I'll have a (glass of) rum.*

▸adj (**rummer**, **rummest**) UK old-fashioned unusual and strange: *She's a rum girl/lass/one.*

IDIOM **a rum do** UK old-fashioned a strange occasion

rumba (also **rhumba**) /ˈrʌm.bə/ noun [C] a type of dancing, originally from Cuba, or the music for this

rumble /ˈrʌm.bl̩/ verb **SOUND** ▷ **1** [I] to make a continuous low sound: *Please excuse my* ***stomach*** *rumbling – I haven't eaten all day.* ◦ *The tanks rumbled (= moved slowly, making a continuous noise) across the battlefield.* **DISCOVER** ▷ **2** [T usually passive] UK informal to discover the true facts about someone or something secret and often illegal: *I'm afraid our little tax*

R

dodge has been rumbled. **FIGHT** ▷ **3** [I] Australian English informal to take part in a physical fight • **rumble** noun [C] *We could hear the rumble **of** distant guns/thunder.*

rumbling /ˈrʌm.bl̩.ɪŋ/, /ˈ-blɪŋ/ noun **1** [C usually plural] a sign of anger or disagreement: *There are rumblings **of** annoyance throughout the workforce.* **2** [C usually singular] a continuous low sound: *the rumbling **of** distant guns/thunder*

ruminant /ˈruː.mɪ.nənt/ noun [C] specialized a type of animal that brings up food from its stomach and CHEWS it again, for example a cow, sheep, or DEER • **ruminant** adj *ruminant animals*

ruminate /ˈruː.mɪ.neɪt/ verb [I] **THINK** ▷ **1** formal to think carefully and for a long period about something: *She ruminated for weeks about whether to tell him or not.* **EAT** ▷ **2** specialized (of particular types of animal) to bring up food from the stomach and CHEW it again

ruminative /ˈruː.mɪ.nə.tɪv/ (US) /-neɪ.t̬ɪv/ adj formal thinking carefully and for a long period

rummage /ˈrʌm.ɪdʒ/ verb [I + adv/prep] to search for something by moving things around carelessly and looking into, under, and behind them: *She rummaged **in/through** all the drawers, looking for a pen.* • **rummage** noun [S] *I had a rummage **around/about** (the house), but I couldn't find my certificate anywhere.*

ˈrummage ˌsale noun [C] US for **jumble sale**

rummy /ˈrʌm.i/ noun [U] any of various card games in which two or more players try to collect cards that have the same value or whose numbers follow an ordered series

rumour UK (US **rumor**) /ˈruː.məʳ/ (US) /-mɚ/ noun [C or U] **1** (B2) an unofficial interesting story or piece of news that might be true or invented, which quickly spreads from person to person: *Rumours are **going round** (the school) **about** Mr Mason and his assistant.* ◦ [+ that] *She's **circulating/spreading** rumours **that** the manager is going to resign.* ◦ *I **heard a** rumour that she'd been seeing Luke Harrison.* **2 rumour has it** people are saying: *Rumour has it (**that**) you're going to be the next managing director. Is it true?*

rumoured UK (US **rumored**) /ˈruː.məd/ (US) /-mɚd/ adj describes a fact that people are talking about, which might be true or invented: *The rumoured stock market crash has yet to take place.* ◦ [+ to infinitive] *The president is rumoured **to** be seriously ill.*

ˈrumour ˌmill (US **ˈrumor ˌmill**) noun [S] used to refer to the situation when a number of people spread rumours about something: *Recently the rumour mill went into overdrive with suggestions that the couple might split.*

ˈrumour-ˌmonger noun [C] a person who spreads rumours

rump /rʌmp/ noun [C] **1** the back end of an animal **2** humorous a person's bottom **3** those few members of a group or organization who stay after the others have left or been forced out

rumple /ˈrʌm.pl̩/ verb [T] to make something become CREASED (= not smooth) or untidy: *You'll rumple your jacket if you don't hang it up properly.* • **rumpled** /-pl̩d/ adj *a rumpled suit/sheet/bed* ◦ *He hadn't brushed his hair and his clothes were rumpled.*

rumpus /ˈrʌm.pəs/ noun [S] informal a lot of noise, especially a loud and confused argument or complaint: *There was a real rumpus **going on** in the house next door last night.*

IDIOM **raise a rumpus** (UK also **kick up a rumpus**) to make a forceful complaint: *You should raise a rumpus about the lack of safety routines here.*

ˈrumpus ˌroom noun [C usually singular] US a room in a house intended for games and entertainment

run /rʌn/ verb; noun

▸verb (present participle **running**, past tense **ran**, past participle **run**) **GO QUICKLY** ▷ **1** (A1) [I or T] (of people and some animals) to move along, faster than walking, by taking quick steps in which each foot is lifted before the next foot touches the ground: [+ to infinitive] *The children had to run **to** keep up with their father.* ◦ *I can run a mile in five minutes.* ◦ *The sheep ran **away/off** in fright.* ◦ *A little girl ran **up to** (= came quickly beside) me, crying for her daddy.* ◦ *Are you running **against** each other or **against** the clock?* ◦ *The first two races will be run (**off**) (= will happen) in 20 minutes.* **2** [T] If you run an animal in a race, you cause it to take part: *Thompson Stables are running three horses **in** the next race.* **3** [I + adv/prep] to go quickly or in a hurry: *Would you run round to the post office and get me some stamps?* ◦ *You don't put on weight when you spend all day running round after small children.* **4 run for sth** to run fast in order to get or avoid something: *I ran for the bus but it drove off.* **5 run on the spot** to move your legs as if running, while you stay in one place: *I run on the spot to warm up before I play football.* **TRAVEL** ▷ **6** (B2) [I or T, usually + adv/prep] to (cause something to) travel, move, or continue in a particular way: *Trains are still running, despite the snow.* ◦ *A bus runs (= goes on a particular route at particular times) three times a day into town.* ◦ *Skis are waxed on the bottom so that they run smoothly over the snow.* ◦ *The route/railway/road runs (= goes) **across** the border/**into** Italy/**through** the mountains.* ◦ *A climbing rose bush runs (= grows) **around** the front door.* ◦ *There's a beautiful cornice running **around/round** all the ceilings.* ◦ *The film runs (= lasts) **for** two hours.* ◦ *The show/course/film runs (= continues) **for** another week.* ◦ *A magazine subscription usually only runs (= can be used) **for** one year.* ◦ *Buses are running an hour **late**, because of an earlier accident.* ◦ *The truck's brakes failed and it ran (= went) **off** the road.* ◦ *Trains run **on** rails (= move along on top of them).* ◦ *Electricity is running **through** (= moving along within) this cable.* ◦ *An angry muttering ran **through** (= went through) the crowd.* ◦ *A shiver of fear ran **through** his (body).* ◦ *She ran her finger **along/down** the page/list, looking for her name.* ◦ *Could you run the tape/film/video **back/forwards**, please?* ◦ *Could you possibly run me (= take me in your car) **home/to** the station?* ◦ *He ran (= pushed) his fingers **through** his hair and looked up at me.* **OPERATE** ▷ **7** (B2) [I or T] to (cause something to) operate: *Keep clear of the machines while they're running.* ◦ *The government took desperate measures to keep the economy running.* ◦ *Do you know how to run this sort of machinery?* ◦ *The mechanic asked me to run the engine (= switch it on and allow it to work) for a minute.* ◦ *They had the new computer system **up and** running (= working) within an hour.* ◦ *We've run the computer program, but nothing happens.* ◦ *We're running (= doing) an experiment.* **8** (B1) [T] to be in control of something: *He's been running a restaurant/his own company since he left school.* ◦ *The local college runs (= provides) a course in self-defence.* ◦ *a well-run/badly-run organization/business/course* **9 run a tight ship** to control a business or other organization firmly and effectively: *Ruth runs a tight ship and has no time for shirkers.* **10** [T] If you run a car, you own one, drive it, and pay for the costs: *I can't afford to run a car.* **11** [T] to organize the way you live or work: *Some people run their lives according to the movements of the stars.* **FLOW** ▷ **12** (B2) [I or T] to (cause something to) flow, produce liquid, or (especially of colours in

R

clothes) to come out or spread: *I can feel trickles of sweat running* ***down*** *my neck.* ◦ *Don't cry, or your make-up will run (= become liquid and move down your face).* ◦ *The walls were running* ***with*** *damp.* ◦ *The river runs (****down****)* ***to/into*** *the sea.* ◦ *The hot tap is running cold (= producing cold water)!* ◦ *I turned the tap on and ran some cold water* ***on*** *the burn.* ◦ [+ two objects] *I'll run you a hot bath (= fill a bath with water for you).* ◦ *My nose and eyes have been running all week because of hay fever.* ◦ *I must have washed my dress at too high a temperature, because the colour has run.* ◦ *If the first layer isn't dry before you add the next one, the colours will run* ***into*** *each other (= mix).* ◦ figurative *After twelve hours at her word processor, the words began to run* ***into*** *one another (= seem mixed together).* **BECOME** ▷ **13** [L only + adj] to be or become: *Differences between the two sides run* ***deep*** *(= are serious).* ◦ *The river/reservoir/well ran* ***dry*** *(= its supply of water finished).* ◦ *Supplies are running* ***low*** *(= there's not much left).* ◦ *We're beginning to run* ***short of*** *money/Money is beginning to run* ***short*** *(= there's not much left).* **HOLE** ▷ **14** [I] If TIGHTS (= thin clothing that covers the legs) run, a long, thin hole appears in them: *Oh no, my tights have run!* **SHOW** ▷ **15** C1 [T] to show something in a newspaper or magazine, on television, etc.: *All the newspapers ran (= printed) stories about the new peace talks.* ◦ *Channel 4 is running a series on the unfairness of the legal system.* **16** [I] Indian English If a film is running at a particular place, you can see it there: *What's running at the the Metro this week?* **POLITICS** ▷ **17** [I] to compete as a CANDIDATE in an election: *Mrs Thatcher wanted to run a fourth time.* ◦ *He's going to run* ***against*** *Smith/****for*** *president/****for*** *re-election.* **TAKE** ▷ **18** [T] to take guns or drugs illegally from one place to another: *He was arrested for running drugs* ***across*** *the border* ***into*** *America.*

Other ways of saying run

If someone runs very fast over a short distance, you can use the verb **sprint**:

I had to ***sprint*** *to catch the bus.*

Jog is used when someone runs at a slow, regular speed, especially as a form of exercise:

'What do you do to keep fit?' 'I ***jog*** *and go swimming.'*

If someone goes somewhere very quickly on foot, you can use the verbs **race**, **rush**, **dash**, or **hurry**:

He ***raced*** *up the stairs to answer the phone.*

Everyone ***rushed*** *to the door when the alarm went off.*

The verb **hurtle** can be used when someone is running so fast that it seems dangerous:

A little boy came ***hurtling*** *down the stairs.*

Bolt can be used when someone runs because he or she is frightened or is trying to escape:

He ***bolted*** *out of the door as soon as he saw her.*

If an animal runs somewhere with small, short steps, you can use the verbs **scamper** or **scurry**:

The dog ***scampered*** *off into another room.*

The mouse ***scurried*** *across the floor.*

IDIOMS **be running on empty** informal **1** to continue to work and be active when you have no energy left: *I get the impression he's been running on empty for months now. A holiday will do him good.* **2** mainly US and Australian English If a person or an organization is running on empty, they have no new ideas or are not as effective as they were before: *The fund-raising campaign was running on empty after ten years under the same leader.* • **run aground/ashore** (also **run onto the rocks**) If a ship or boat runs aground/ashore, it hits the coast, sometimes becoming stuck there. • **run a mile** UK informal to be extremely unwilling to be involved: *He'd run a mile if I asked him to marry me.* • **run and run** to be performed successfully for a long period of time: *This show will run and run.* • **run sb close** to be nearly as good, fast, etc. as someone else: *She got 90 percent, but Fred ran her close with 87 percent.* • **run errands** to go out to buy or do something: *After school he runs errands* ***for*** *his father.* • **run high** If feelings are running high, people are angry or excited. • **run in the family** If a quality, ability, disease, etc. runs in the family, many members of the family have it: *Intelligence seems to run in that family.* ◦ *We're all ambitious – it seems to run in the family.* • **run in/through sb's head/mind** If something is running in/through your head/mind, you cannot stop thinking about it or singing it silently: *I've had that tune running in my head all day.* • **run its course** to develop and finish naturally: *The doctor's advice is to let the fever run its course.* ◦ *I had to accept that the relationship had run its course.* • **run your eye over sth** to look quickly at the whole of something: *Can I have a copy of the article to run my eye over, before it's printed?* • **run yourself into the ground** informal to make yourself very tired by working too much: *We ran ourselves into the ground to meet the July deadline.* • **be running a fever** to be hotter than you should be because you are ill • **be running at sth** C2 to be at the rate of something: *Inflation is running at ten percent.* • **running with blood** describes a place where a lot of fighting is happening and many people are being hurt or killed: *During the revolution* ***the streets*** *were running with blood.* • **run sb ragged** informal If you run someone ragged, you make them very tired, usually by giving them too much work or work that is too demanding. • **run round in circles** UK informal to be very active but with few results: *Peter's been running round in circles since half his department resigned.* • **run the show** informal to be the leader, who is in control of a group of people doing something: *If you need help, ask Mark – he's running the show.* • **run through sb's mind/head** to suddenly think of something: *It ran through my mind that I was being tricked by Charlie.* • **run sb/sth to ground** (UK also **run sb/sth to earth**) to find someone or something after a lot of searching and problems: *Detectives finally ran the terrorists to ground in an apartment building in Chicago.* • **run wild** disapproving C2 If someone, especially a child runs wild, they behave as they want to and no one controls them.

PHRASAL VERBS **run across sb** informal to meet someone you know when you are not expecting to: *I ran across several old friends when I went back to my hometown.* • **run across sth** informal to experience a problem when you are not expecting to: *We've run across a slight problem with the instruction manual.* • **run after sb/sth** to chase someone or something that is moving away from you: *Why do dogs run after cats?* ◦ *She ran after me to hand me some papers I'd dropped.* • **run after sth** to try very hard to get or achieve something: *She has spent her life running after fame and fortune.* • **run after sb** informal disapproving to try to start a sexual relationship with someone: *He's always running after women.* • **run against sb/sth** to oppose or have an effect that is not helpful towards someone or something: *Luck is really running against you tonight!* ◦ *Public opinion is currently running against the banking industry.* • **run along!** old-fashioned said to children to tell them to go away: *Run along now, children!* • **run around** C2 to be very busy doing a lot of different things: *I'm exhausted – I've been running around all morning.* • **run around after sb** informal to do a lot of things for someone else, especially when they should be able to do more for themselves: *I seem to spend most of my time running around after those kids.* • **run around with sb** old-fashioned informal to spend a lot of time with someone: *She's running around with Micky and his friends these days.* • **run away LEAVE** ▷ **1** (B2) to leave a place or person secretly and suddenly: *He ran away* ***from*** *home when he was only twelve.* ◦ *Malcolm and my sister are planning to run away* ***together*** *to get married.* **AVOID** ▷ **2** to avoid dealing with a problem or difficult situation: *She accused him of running away* ***from*** *his responsibilities.* • **run away with sb RIDE** ▷ **1** If an animal or machine that someone is riding runs away with them, they lose control of it and it carries them away: *Her horse ran away with her.* **OF FEELING** ▷ **2** If a feeling or idea runs away with you, you cannot control it and it makes you behave stupidly: *Sometimes my imagination runs away with me and I convince myself that they are having an affair.* • **run away with sth** informal to win a competition or prize very easily: *She ran away with four first prizes.* • **run sth by sb** informal to tell someone about something so that they can give their opinion about it: *Would you run your idea by me one more time?* • **run sb/sth down CRITICIZE** ▷ **1** (C1) informal to criticize someone or something, often unfairly: *He's always running himself down.* **HIT** ▷ **2** to hit and injure a person or animal with a vehicle, especially intentionally: *Two masked men on motorbikes tried to run me down.* **FIND** ▷ **3** to find someone or something after following or searching for them for a long time: *I finally ran Mr Green down* ***in/to*** *a house in the country.* • **run (sth) down REDUCE** ▷ **1** UK to reduce a business or organization in size or importance, or to become reduced in this way: *The government is secretly running down the troop levels.* **LOSE POWER** ▷ **2** If a machine or device such as a clock or BATTERY runs down, it loses power, or if you run it down, you cause this to happen: *These batteries can be recharged when they run down.* ◦ *You'll run the battery down if you leave your car lights on.* • **run sth down** specialized If a large ship runs down a smaller one, it hits it. • **run sth in** UK (US **break sth in**) If you run in a vehicle, you use it carefully and slowly for a short time when it is new, so that you do not damage its engine. • **run sb in** old-fashioned If the police run someone in, they find them and take them to a police station. • **run (sth) into sth/sb** (B2) to drive a vehicle into an object or a person in another vehicle by accident: *I had to brake suddenly, and the car behind ran into me.* ◦ *He ran his motorbike into a tree.* • **run into sb** (B2) to meet someone you know when you are not expecting to: *Graham ran into someone he used to know at school the other day.* • **run into sth EXPERIENCE PROBLEMS** ▷ **1** If you run into problems, you begin to experience them: *We ran into bad weather/debt/trouble.* **REACH AN AMOUNT** ▷ **2** to reach a particular cost or amount, as a total: *The repairs will probably run into thousands of pounds.* • **run off** to leave somewhere or someone suddenly: *You can't run off (home) now, just when I need you!* ◦ *My wife has run off* ***with*** *another man.* • **run sth off 1** If you run off copies of something, you print them: [+ two objects] *Could you run me off five copies of this, please?* **2** to quickly and easily write something that is usually slow or difficult to write, such as a piece of poetry or music: *Kate can run off a sonnet in half an hour on any subject you like.* • **run off with sth** informal to leave a place or person suddenly after having stolen something from them: *He ran off with $10,000 of the company's money.* • **run on 1** If an event runs on, it continues for longer than expected: *The game/speech/discussion ran on* ***for*** *hours.* **2** If time runs on, it seems to pass quickly: ***Time's*** *running on – let's get this job finished soon!* • **run on sth** (C1) If a machine runs on a particular type or supply of power, it uses that power to work: *Some calculators run on solar power.* • **run out 1** (B1) to finish, use or sell all of something, so that there is none left: *I've run out* ***of*** *milk/money/ideas/patience.* ◦ *'Have you got any milk?' 'Sorry, I've run out.'* **2** (B2) If a supply of something runs out, all of it has been used or it is completely finished: *The milk has run out.* ◦ *My patience is beginning to run out.* **3** If a document or official agreement runs out, the period of time for which it lasts finishes. **4 time is running out** used to say that there is not much time left in which to achieve something: *Time is running out* ***for*** *the men trapped under the rubble.* • **run sb out** If you are run out in cricket, a player on the opposing team throws the ball at the WICKET you are running towards and hits it before you can reach it, and your turn as BATSMAN ends: *Their best batsman was run out* ***for*** *(= having scored) 99.* • **run out on sb/sth** to leave someone you are having a relationship with or something you are responsible for, without warning and usually causing problems: *She ran out on him two months ago, leaving him to look after their two children.* • **run sb/sth over** (B2) If a vehicle or its driver runs over someone or something, the vehicle hits and drives over them: *I'm afraid we've just run a rabbit over.* • **run over** If liquid runs over, it flows over the edges of something, because there is too much of it: *The water/The bath is running over – quick, turn the taps off.* • **run over (sth)** to continue after the expected finishing time: *I'm afraid we're starting to run over* ***time****, so could you make your speeches short please.* • **run over/through sth REPEAT** ▷ **1** (C2) to quickly say or practise something: *I'll just run over what's been said so far,* ***for*** *latecomers who missed the first speakers.* ◦ *She quickly ran over her speech before going on-stage.* ◦ *The director wants to run through the whole play this morning.* **EXPLAIN** ▷ **2** to examine a document or subject with someone in order to explain it or to get their help or their opinion on it: *I'd like to run over the main points of the article* ***with*** *you.* ◦ *I'm really struggling with this maths – could you run through it with me later?* • **run through sth EXAMINE** ▷ **1** to look at, examine, or deal with a set of things, especially quickly: *We ran through the list, but none of the machines seemed any good.* ◦ *I'd like to run through these points/questions* ***with*** *you, if that's okay, because you've made several mistakes.* **EXIST** ▷ **2** If a quality runs through something, it is in all parts of it: *Melancholy runs through all her stories.* **USE UP** ▷ **3** to use up an amount of something quickly: *It took him just a few months to run through all the money his father left him.* • **run sb/sth through** literary to push a SWORD or similar pointed weapon right into a person or animal: *He drew his sword and ran the villain through.* • **run to sth SIZE** ▷ **1** to reach a particular amount, level or size: *The new encyclopedia runs to several thousand pages.* **MONEY** ▷ **2** to have enough money to buy something or (of an income, etc.) to be enough to buy something: *I can lend you £1,000, but I can't run to more than that.* ◦ *My salary won't run to foreign holidays.* **ACTIVITY** ▷ **3** If your taste or skill runs to something, that is the type of thing that you enjoy or can manage to do: *I'm afraid my cooking skills don't run to fancy cakes and desserts.* • **run sth up DEBT** ▷ **1** If you run up a debt, you do things that cause you to owe a large amount of money: *She*

R

stayed two weeks at the hotel and ran up a ***bill*** *that she couldn't pay.* **MATERIAL** ▷ **2** to quickly make something such as a piece of clothing from material: [+ two objects] *I can run you up some curtains in a few hours, if you want.* **VALUE** ▷ **3** to make the price or value of something increase: *Heavy buying ran the price of stocks up higher than expected.* **FLAG** ▷ **4** UK to raise a flag into the air on a pole or MAST: *They've run up a British flag on the roof.* • **run up against sth** (C2) to experience an unexpected difficulty: *The community centre scheme has run up against strong local opposition.*

▸noun **GO QUICKLY** ▷ **1** (B1) [C] the action of running, especially for exercise: *We* ***go for/do*** *a three-mile run every evening after work.* ◦ *If you set off* ***at a*** *run (= running), you'll be exhausted later.* **TRAVEL** ▷ **2** [C] a journey: *The number of aircraft on the New York-Moscow run is being increased.* ◦ old-fashioned *Let's go for a run* (***out***) *in the car somewhere.* ◦ *The plane swooped in on its bombing run.* **3** [C] the period during which a play is performed: *The musical's London run was a disaster.* **BUY** ▷ **4** [C usually singular] a situation in which many people suddenly buy a particular product: *There's been a run* ***on*** *umbrellas because of all this rain.* **SELL** ▷ **5** [C usually singular] a situation in which many people suddenly sell a particular product: *A sudden run* ***on*** *the dollar has lowered its value.* **SERIES** ▷ **6 a run of sth** (C2) A run of something is a continuous period during which it lasts or is repeated: *a run of successes/defeats/bad luck* **ORDINARY** ▷ **7 the general/usual run of sth** the usual type of something: *Their food is the general run of hotel cooking.* **AREA** ▷ **8** [C] an area of ground of limited size for keeping animals: *a sheep/chicken/hen run* **POINT** ▷ **9** (B2) [C] in cricket and baseball, a single point, scored by running from one place to another: *England need 105 runs to win the game.* ◦ *a home run* **HOLE** ▷ **10** [C] a long, vertical hole in TIGHTS and STOCKINGS: *I've got a run in my tights from the nail on my chair.* **ILLNESS** ▷ **11 the runs** informal a condition of the bowels in which the contents are passed out of the body too often and in a form that is too liquid → Synonym **diarrhoea**

IDIOMS **give sb a run for their money** to not allow someone to win easily: *We're going to give the other candidate a run for her money.* • **have a good run for your money** to have a good enough time: *I've achieved a lot in my life and I feel I've had a good run for my money.* • **in the long run** (B2) at a time that is far away in the future: *It seems a lot of effort but I'm sure it's the best solution in the long run.* • **in the short run** at a time that is near in the future: *It's not a long term solution, but it will save money in the short run.* • **make a run for it** (C2) to suddenly start running in order to escape from somewhere: *One of the prisoners tried to make a run for it.* • **be on the run 1** to be trying to avoid being caught, especially by the police: *After a month on the run, the prisoners were finally recaptured by the police.* **2** to hurry from one activity to another: *She's always on the run and never has time for a chat.* • **on the run** while hurrying to go somewhere: *I eat breakfast on the run if I'm late for work.* • **the run of sth** the freedom to use something: *While she's away, I've got the run of her house.* ◦ *So do you have the run of the garden?*

runabout /ˈrʌn.ə.baʊt/ noun [C] (also **runaround**) a small car for short journeys

runaround /ˈrʌn.ə.raʊnd/ noun **give sb the runaround** to refuse to help someone, sending them to someone or somewhere else to get help: *I'm trying to get a new visa, but the embassy staff keep giving me the runaround.*

runaway /ˈrʌn.ə.weɪ/ **adj** out of control or escaped from somewhere: *A runaway bus/horse caused chaos on the streets.* ◦ *a runaway child sleeping on the streets* ◦ figurative *Her first novel's runaway* ***success*** *(= surprisingly big success) came as a great surprise.* • **runaway noun** [C] someone who has escaped from somewhere: *We're searching for a couple of runaways* ***from*** *the young offenders' institution.*

rundown /ˈrʌn.daʊn/ noun [usually S] **REPORT** ▷ **1** a detailed report: *Here's a rundown* ***on/of*** *the activities of our ten biggest competitors.* **REDUCTION** ▷ **2** a reduction in the size or quality of something: *the general run-down of the army*

ˌrun-ˈdown adj **1** describes buildings or areas that are in very bad condition: *a run-down building/cemetery* **2** [after verb] tired and not healthy, especially because of working too much: *My doctor said I was looking run-down.*

rune /ruːn/ **noun** [C] any of the letters of an ancient alphabet cut into stone or wood in the past by the people of northern Europe, or any similar mark with a secret or magic meaning • **runic** /ˈruː.nɪk/ **adj** *a runic letter/alphabet/message*

rung /rʌŋ/ **verb; noun**

▸verb past participle of **ring**

▸noun [C] any of the short bars that form the steps of a LADDER

IDIOM **be on the lowest/bottom rung of the ladder** to be at the lowest level of an organization: *I started my life on the bottom rung of the ladder in this company.*

ˈrun-in noun [C] informal If you have a run-in with someone, you have a serious argument with them or you get into trouble with them: *I* ***had*** *a run-in with the boss/the law/the police yesterday.*

runner /ˈrʌn.əʳ/ (US) /-ɚ/ **noun** [C] **GOING QUICKLY** ▷ **1** (A2) someone who runs, especially in competitions: *a long-distance runner* → See also **runner-up 2** a horse running in a race **3** a person who works for someone by taking messages, collecting money, etc. **4** a **running shoe BLADE** ▷ **5** one of two usually metal blades under a SLEDGE which allow it to move along easily **STEM** ▷ **6** a long stem of a plant that grows along the ground in order to put down roots in a new place **TAKING** ▷ **7** someone who takes illegal drugs or weapons from one place to another: *a gun-runner*

IDIOM **do a runner** UK informal to leave a place in order to avoid a difficult or unpleasant situation or to avoid paying for something

ˌrunner ˈbean noun [C usually plural] UK (US **ˌstring ˈbean**) a bean with long, green PODS that can be eaten, or the plant from which these beans grow

ˌrunner-ˈup noun [C] (plural **runners-up**) a person who comes second in a race or competition

running /ˈrʌn.ɪŋ/ **adj; noun**

▸adj [after noun] (C2) happening on a particular number of regular occasions: *You've been late three days running.* ◦ *They won the trophy* ***for the*** *third* ***year*** *running.*

IDIOMS **running battle** an argument that lasts over several different occasions: *I've had a running battle with the neighbours over whose responsibility that fence is.* • **(go and) take a running jump** UK informal said to someone when you want them to go away and stop annoying you

▸noun [U] **GOING QUICKLY** ▷ **1** (A2) the activity of going somewhere quickly on foot, as a sport or for pleasure: *running shoes/shorts* **OPERATION** ▷ **2** Ⓒ2 the activity of controlling or taking care of something: *She has control of the day-to-day running of the business.*

IDIOMS **in/out of the running** having/not having a reasonable chance of winning • **make (all) the running** UK to do the best and most work: *British companies have often made all the running in developing new ideas, but have then failed to market them.*

ˌrunning ˈcommentary noun [C] a description of an event, usually a sports event, given at the same time as it happens

ˈrunning ˌcosts noun [plural] **1** the money you need to spend regularly to keep a system or organization working **2** the money you need to spend in order to keep and use a vehicle

ˈrunning ˌmate noun [C] in the US, a political partner chosen for a politician who is trying to get elected: *If a candidate for president wins the election, his/her running mate becomes the vice president.*

ˈrunning ˌshoe noun [C] a type of light, comfortable shoe that is suitable for running

ˌrunning ˈsore noun [C] an injury that will not HEAL (= become well again) and keeps producing liquid

ˈrunning ˌstitch noun [U] a style of sewing that uses STITCHES that look like a series of short lines with small spaces in between

ˌrunning ˈwater noun [U] Ⓒ1 water supplied to a house by pipes: *Some of these older houses still don't have running water.*

runny /ˈrʌn.i/ adj **1** more liquid than usual: *The sauce looked runny so I added some more flour.* **2** If your nose is runny, it is producing more MUCUS than usual, usually because you are ill: *I've got a runny **nose**.*

ˈrun-off noun [C usually singular] an extra competition or election to decide the winner, because the leading competitors have finished equal: *In a run-off **for** the presidency of the assembly, Santos beat Gutiérrez.*

ˌrun-of-the-ˈmill adj ordinary and not special or exciting in any way: *He gave a fairly run-of-the-mill speech.*

runt /rʌnt/ noun [C] **1** the smallest and weakest animal of a group born at the same time to the same mother **2** informal a small or weak person who you dislike

ˈrun-through noun [C] the activity of performing or playing something from beginning to end in order to practise it: *We've got time for one more run-through before the concert.*

ˈrun-up noun **1** [C] In some sports, a run-up is a period or distance of running that you do in order to be going fast enough to perform a particular action: *The longer and faster your run-up is, the higher you can jump.* **2** [S] mainly UK the final period of time before an important event: *Everyone is very busy during the run-up **to** publication.*

runway /ˈrʌn.weɪ/ noun [C] **AIRCRAFT** ▷ **1** Ⓒ1 a long, level piece of ground with a specially prepared smooth, hard surface on which aircraft take off and land **FASHION** ▷ **2** mainly US the long, narrow stage that MODELS walk along in a FASHION SHOW → See also **catwalk**

rupee /ruːˈpiː/ ⓤⓢ /ˈruː.piː/ noun [C] the standard unit of money used in India, Pakistan, Mauritius, Nepal, Sri Lanka, and the Seychelles

rupiah /ruːˈpiː.ə/ noun [C] the standard unit of money used in Indonesia

rupture /ˈrʌp.tʃəʳ/ ⓤⓢ /-tʃɚ/ verb; noun

▸verb [I or T] **1** to (cause something to) explode, break or tear: *His appendix ruptured and he had to be rushed to hospital.* ◦ figurative *This news has ruptured (= violently ended) the delicate peace between the rival groups.* **2 rupture yourself** If you rupture yourself, you break apart the wall of muscle that keeps your stomach and your bowels in place, usually by lifting something too heavy.

▸noun [C] **1** an occasion when something explodes, breaks, or tears: *a rupture of the pipeline* ◦ figurative *a rupture (= an end to a friendly relationship) between the families* **2** a medical condition in which the wall of muscle holding the stomach and bowels in place inside the body is broken apart: *You're going to give yourself a rupture if you lift that.* → Synonym **hernia**

rural /ˈrʊə.rəl/ ⓤⓢ /ˈrʊr.əl/ adj Ⓑ2 in, of, or like the countryside: *The area is still very rural and undeveloped.* → Compare **urban**

ruse /ruːz/ noun [C] a trick intended to deceive someone

rush /rʌʃ/ verb; noun

▸verb **GO/DO QUICKLY** ▷ **1** Ⓑ2 [I or T, usually + adv/prep] to (cause to) go or do something very quickly: *Whenever I see him, he seems to be rushing (**about/around**).* ◦ *I rushed up the stairs/to the office/to find a phone.* ◦ *When she turned it upside down the water rushed out.* ◦ [+ to infinitive] *We shouldn't rush **to** blame them.* ◦ *You can't rush a job like this.* ◦ *The emergency legislation was rushed **through** Parliament in a morning.* ◦ *Don't rush me!* ◦ *The United Nations has rushed medical aid and food to the famine zone.* ◦ *He rushed the children off to school so they wouldn't be late.* **ATTACK** ▷ **2** [T] If a group of people rush an enemy or the place where an enemy is, they attack suddenly and all together: *We rushed the palace gates and killed the guards.* **AMERICAN FOOTBALL** ▷ **3** [I] In American football, to rush is to carry the football forward across the place on the field where play begins. Also, a member of the opposite team rushes when they force their way to the back of the field quickly to catch the player carrying the football.

PHRASAL VERBS **rush into sth** If you rush into something such as a job, you start doing it without having really decided if it is the right thing to do or having considered the best way to do it. • **rush sb into (doing) sth** to forcefully persuade someone to do something without giving them time to decide if they really want to do it • **rush sth out** to very quickly produce something and make it available to sell: *When the war started, several publishers rushed out books on the conflict.*

▸noun **HURRY** ▷ **1** Ⓑ2 [S] a situation in which you have to hurry or move somewhere quickly: *Slow down! What's the rush?* ◦ *Why is it always such a rush to get ready in the mornings?* ◦ *Everyone seemed to be **in a** rush.* ◦ *He was in a rush to get home.* ◦ *They were **in no** rush to sell the house.* **2** Ⓒ2 [S] a time when a lot of things are happening or a lot of people are trying to do or get something: *There's always a rush to get the best seats.* ◦ *I try to do my shopping before the Christmas rush.* ◦ *There's been a rush **for** (= sudden popular demand for) tickets.* **3** Ⓒ2 [S] the act of suddenly moving somewhere quickly: *There was a rush **of** air as she opened the door.* ◦ *They made a rush at him to get his gun.* **4** [S] a sudden movement of people to a certain area, usually because of some economic advantage: *the California gold rush* **5** [C] in American football, an attempt to run forwards carrying the ball, or an attempt to quickly reach and stop a player from the opposing team who is carrying the ball **SUDDEN FEELING** ▷ **6** [S] a sudden strong emotion or physical

R

feeling: *The memory of who he was came back to him with a rush.* ◦ *I had my first cigarette for a year and felt a sudden rush (of dizziness).* **PLANT** ▷ **7** [C usually plural] a plant like grass that grows in or near water and whose long, thin, hollow stems can be dried and made into floor coverings, containers, etc.: *a rush mat*

rushed /rʌʃt/ **adj** done in a hurry, or feeling that you must do something quickly: *Supper was rushed since the family had to go out that evening.* ◦ *I allowed plenty of time and didn't feel rushed.*

ˈrush ˌhour noun [C usually singular] **B2** the busy part of the day when towns and cities are crowded, either in the morning when people are travelling to work, or in the evening when people are travelling home: *rush hour traffic*

rushing /ˈrʌʃ.ɪŋ/ **adj** moving quickly

ˈrush ˌjob noun [C] a piece of work that is not as good as it could be, because you do it quickly: *The biography was a bit of a rush job.*

rusk /rʌsk/ **noun** [C] a type of very hard dry biscuit, eaten especially by babies

russet /ˈrʌs.ɪt/ **noun** [U] literary a reddish-brown colour • **russet adj** *russet leaves*

ˌRussian rouˈlette noun [U] a very dangerous game of chance where each player aims at their own head with a gun that has one bullet in it and five empty CHAMBERS (= spaces where bullets could go): figurative *Doctors' refusal to take the issue seriously is* ***playing*** *Russian roulette* ***with*** *(= taking unnecessary risks with) ordinary citizens' health.*

rust /rʌst/ **noun; verb**

▸**noun** [U] **1** a reddish-brown substance that forms on the surface of iron and STEEL as a result of reacting with air and water: *patches of rust* **2** a reddish-brown colour that looks like rust **3** any of various plant diseases that cause reddish-brown spots • **rust adj** having a reddish-brown colour

▸**verb** [I or T] to become or cause something to become covered with rust: *Older cars will begin to rust.* ◦ *Years of being left out in the rain had rusted the metal chairs.* ◦ *The floor of the car had rusted* ***away/through*** *(= been destroyed by rust), so I was careful where I put my feet.*

rustbelt /ˈrʌst.belt/ **noun** [C] an area where there was previously a lot of industry but where most factories are now closed: *a small town in the heart of the rustbelt*

rustic /ˈrʌs.tɪk/ **adj** simple and often rough in appearance; typical of the countryside: *a rustic bench/cabin* ◦ *The property has a certain rustic charm.*

rustle /rʌsl/ **verb; noun**

▸**verb MAKE NOISE** ▷ **1** [I or T] If things such as paper or leaves rustle, or if you rustle them, they move about and make a soft, dry sound: *The leaves rustled in the breeze.* ◦ *He rustled his papers (= noisily moved them about) to hide his embarrassment.* **STEAL** ▷ **2** [T] mainly US to steal farm animals

PHRASAL VERB **rustle sth up** informal to make something quickly, usually a meal from the food that is available: *Give me a minute and I'll rustle something up for supper.*

▸**noun** [S] the sound made by the movement of things such as leaves or paper

rustler /ˈrʌs.l̩.əʳ/, /-ləʳ/ US /-lɚ/ **noun** [C] a person who steals farm animals

rustling /ˈrʌs.l̩.ɪŋ/, /-lɪŋ/ **noun NOISE** ▷ **1** [C or U] the sound that paper or leaves make when they move: *I could hear (a) rustling in the bushes.* **STEALING** ▷ **2** [U] the crime of stealing farm animals

rustproof /ˈrʌst.pruːf/ **adj** protected against RUST (= metal decay) • **rustproof verb** [T] *Painting steel is a good way to rustproof it.*

rusty /ˈrʌs.ti/ **adj METAL** ▷ **1** **B2** covered with RUST (= metal decay): *a rusty car/nail* **NEEDING PRACTICE** ▷ **2** **B2** If a skill you had is rusty, it is not now good because you have forgotten it: *My Italian is a bit rusty these days.*

rut /rʌt/ **noun HOLE** ▷ **1** [C] a deep, narrow mark made in soft ground especially by a wheel **SEXUALLY ACTIVE PERIOD** ▷ **2** [S] the period of the year during which particular male animals, especially DEER and sheep, are sexually active: *During* ***the*** *rut, stags can be seen fighting for females.* **3 in rut** (of particular male animals) sexually excited

IDIOM **in a rut** **C2** If a person, organization, etc. is in a rut, they have become too fixed in one particular type of job, activity, method, etc.: *I've got to change jobs – after 15 years here I feel I'm (****stuck****) in a rut (= I'm bored).*

rutabaga /ˌruː.təˈbeɪ.gə/ US /-t̬ə-/ **noun** [C] US for **swede**

ruthless /ˈruːθ.ləs/ **adj** **C2** not thinking or worrying about any pain caused to others; cruel: *ruthless ambition* ◦ *a ruthless dictator* ◦ *Some people believe that to succeed in this world you have to be ruthless.* • **ruthlessly** /-li/ **adv** *She ruthlessly pursued her ambition, letting nothing get in her way.* • **ruthlessness** /-nəs/ **noun** [U]

rutted /ˈrʌt.ɪd/ US /ˈrʌt̬-/ **adj** If a surface is rutted, it has deep narrow marks in it made by wheels: *a deeply/badly rutted road*

rutting /ˈrʌt.ɪŋ/ US /ˈrʌt̬-/ **adj** relating to the period of the year during which particular male animals are sexually active: *the rutting season*

RV /ˌɑːˈviː/ US /ˌɑːr-/ **noun** [C] abbreviation for recreational vehicle: a **motor home**

Rx US written abbreviation for PRESCRIPTION (= a piece of paper on which a doctor writes the details of the medicine or drugs that someone needs)

rye /raɪ/ **noun** [U] **1** a type of grain, the seeds of which are used to make flour or WHISKY or to feed animals: *rye bread* **2** WHISKY made with rye: *a glass of rye*

ˈrye ˌbread noun [U] dark brown bread made with rye

S, s /es/ noun; adj
▸noun (plural **Ss, S's** or **s's**) **LETTER** ▷ **1** [C or U] the 19th letter of the English alphabet **SOUTH** ▷ **2** written abbreviation for **south** **SATISFACTORY** ▷ **3** US written abbreviation for **satisfactory**, when given as a mark for an exam or course
▸adj **SOUTH** ▷ **1** written abbreviation for **south** or **southern** **SMALL** ▷ **2** written abbreviation for small, used to show the size of a piece of clothing

s noun (also **sec**) written abbreviation for **second**

-s /-s, -z/ suffix (also **-es**) used to form the plural of nouns: *books* ◦ *sandwiches*

's /-s, -z/ short form of **1** is: *It's in the cupboard.* **2** has: *She's gone home.* **3** informal (only used in spoken questions) does: *How's this thing work?* **4** (only used after 'let') us: *Let's go swimming this afternoon.*

-s' /-s, -z/ suffix used to show that the following thing belongs to the people or things named: *the girls' books* ◦ *employees' rights*

-'s /-s, -z/ suffix **1** used to show that the following thing belongs to the person or thing named: *the cat's tail* ◦ *Patricia's dress* ◦ *today's paper* ◦ *the children's shoes* **2** the house belonging to the stated person: *The boys are at Alison's.* **3** UK the shop belonging to the stated person: *I got it at the greengrocer's.*

saag (also **sag**) /sɑːg/ noun [U] Indian English for **spinach**

the Sabbath /sæb.əθ/ noun [S] the day of the week kept by some religious groups for rest and worship. The Sabbath is Sunday for most Christians, Saturday for Jews, and Friday for Muslims: *to **keep/break** (= follow/not follow the religious rules for) the Sabbath*

sabbatical /səˈbæt.ɪ.kəl/ (US) /-ˈbæt̬-/ noun [C or U] a period of time when college or university teachers are allowed to stop their usual work in order to study or travel, usually while continuing to be paid: *to **take/have** a sabbatical* ◦ *She's **on** sabbatical for six months.*

sable /ˈseɪ.bl̩/ noun [C or U] **ANIMAL** ▷ **1** a small animal with thick, warm fur, or the fur of this animal used for making clothes and artists' brushes **COLOUR** ▷ **2** literary a very dark or black colour

sabotage /ˈsæb.ə.tɑːʒ/ verb [T] **1** to damage or destroy equipment, weapons, or buildings in order to prevent the success of an enemy or competitor: *The rebels had tried to sabotage the oil pipeline.* **2** to intentionally prevent the success of a plan or action: *This was a deliberate attempt to sabotage the ceasefire.*
• **sabotage** noun [U] *a campaign of **industrial** sabotage*

saboteur /ˌsæb.əˈtɜːr/ (US) /-ˈtɜː/ noun [C] a person who sabotages something

sabre mainly UK (US usually **saber**) /ˈseɪ.bər/ (US) /-bɚ/ noun [C] **1** a heavy SWORD with a wide, usually curved blade, used in the past by soldiers on horses **2** a light pointed SWORD with one sharp edge used in the sport of FENCING

ˈ**sabre-ˌrattling** UK disapproving (US ˈ**saber-ˌrattling**) noun [U] talking and behaving in a way that threatens military action

sac /sæk/ noun [C] specialized a part of a plant or animal that is like a bag and often contains liquid

saccharin /ˈsæk.ər.ɪn/ (US) /-ɚ-/ noun [U] a very sweet artificial substance that is used to replace sugar, especially by people who want to lose weight or who must not eat sugar: *saccharin tablets*

saccharine /ˈsæk.ər.iːn/ (US) /-ɚ-/ adj disapproving too sweet or too polite: *I don't trust her, with her saccharine smiles.* ◦ *saccharine love songs*

sachet /ˈsæʃ.eɪ/ (US) /sæʃˈeɪ/ noun [C] a small closed container made of paper or plastic, containing a small amount of something, usually enough for only one occasion: *a free sachet of shampoo*

sack /sæk/ noun; verb

sack

▸noun **BAG** ▷ **1** (C1) [C] a large bag made of strong cloth, paper, or plastic, used to store large amounts of something: *The corn was stored in large sacks.* ◦ *a sack **of** potatoes/coal/flour* → See also **haversack, knapsack, rucksack** **2** [C] US a paper or plastic bag used to carry things bought in a food shop: *a sack of groceries* **JOB** ▷ **3 the sack** (B2) a situation in which someone is removed from their job: *They **gave** him the sack **for** being late.* ◦ *Two workers **got** the sack **for** fighting in the warehouse.* **STEAL** ▷ **4** [S] the act of stealing all the valuable things from a town and sometimes destroying the town, during a war: ***The sack** (= destruction) **of** Rome by the Visigoths occurred in the fifth century.* **BED** ▷ **5 the sack** [S] US informal bed: *It's late – I'm going to **hit** the sack (= go to bed).* ◦ *He came home and found Judy and Brad **in** the sack (= in bed) together.* **6 in the sack** US informal If someone is good/bad in the sack, they are sexually skilled/not sexually skilled.
▸verb [T] **JOB** ▷ **1** (B2) to remove someone from a job, usually because they have done something wrong or badly, or sometimes as a way of saving the cost of employing them: *They sacked her **for** being late.* ◦ *He **got** sacked from his last job.* **STEAL** ▷ **2** to steal all the valuable things from a building, town, etc., and possibly destroy the building or town, usually during a war: *The invaders sacked every village they passed on their route.*

PHRASAL VERB **sack out** US informal to go to bed: *It's late – I'm going to sack out.*

sackcloth /ˈsæk.klɒθ/ (US) /-klɑːθ/ noun [U] (also **sacking**) the thick, rough material used to make sacks (= large strong bags)

IDIOM **wear sackcloth and ashes** to show by your behaviour that you are very sorry for something you did that was wrong

sackful /ˈsæk.fʊl/ noun [C] (also **sackload**) the amount contained in a sack: figurative *He got sackfuls **of** (= very many) letters from listeners following the show.*

sacking /ˈsæk.ɪŋ/ noun [C] an act of stopping employing someone: *Mr Ali said the sackings would save the company about $40 million a year.* → See also **sackcloth**

ˈ**sack ˌlunch** noun [C] US for **packed lunch**

ˈ**sack ˌrace** noun [C usually singular] a race in which people jump along with both legs in a cloth SACK that they hold up with their hands

sacrament /ˈsæk.rə.mənt/ noun **1** [C] an important religious ceremony in the Christian Church, such as

BAPTISM or COMMUNION **2** [C usually singular] the holy bread and wine eaten at HOLY COMMUNION (= a religious ceremony) • **sacramental** /ˌsæk.rəˈmen.təl/ (US) /-t̬əl/ adj

sacred /ˈseɪ.krɪd/ adj **1** C1 considered to be holy and deserving respect, especially because of a connection with a god: *sacred relics/temples* ◦ *This area is sacred* ***to*** *the Apaches.* **2** C1 connected with religion: *sacred music/writings* **3** C2 considered too important to be changed: *His daily routine is absolutely sacred* ***to*** *him.* ◦ humorous *The cricketers wore blue, not their usual white – is* ***nothing*** *sacred?* • **sacredness** /-nəs/ noun [U]

ˌsacred ˈcow noun [C] disapproving a belief, custom, etc. that people support and do not question or criticize: *They did not dare to challenge the sacred cow of parliamentary democracy.*

sacrifice /ˈsæk.rɪ.faɪs/ verb; noun

▸verb GIVE UP ▷ **1** C1 [T] to give up something that is valuable to you in order to help another person: *Many women sacrifice interesting careers* ***for*** *their family.* KILL ▷ **2** [I or T] to kill an animal or a person and offer them to a god or gods

IDIOM **be sacrificed on the altar of sth** literary to be destroyed by an activity, system, or belief that is bad but more important or more powerful: *Service and quality have been sacrificed on the altar of profit.*

▸noun [C or U] GIVING UP ▷ **1** C1 the act of giving up something that is valuable to you in order to help someone else: *We had to* ***make*** *sacrifices in order to pay for our children's education.* ◦ *They cared for their disabled son for 27 years,* ***at*** *great personal sacrifice.* KILLING ▷ **2** the act of killing an animal or person and offering them to a god or gods, or the animal, etc. that is offered: *The people offered a lamb on the altar as a sacrifice* ***for*** *their sins.*

IDIOM **make the ultimate/supreme sacrifice** formal to die while fighting for a principle

sacrificial /ˌsæk.rɪˈfɪʃ.əl/ adj offered as a sacrifice: *The priest held up the head of the sacrificial goat.* • **sacrificially** /-i/ adv

ˌsacrificial ˈlamb noun [C usually singular] someone or something that is given to people in authority and is expected to be harmed or destroyed, especially in order to prevent other people or things from being harmed or destroyed: *We knew the department would be a sacrificial lamb when the time came to cut staff.*

S

sacrilege /ˈsæk.rɪ.lɪdʒ/ noun [S or U] (an act of) treating something holy or important without respect: [+ to infinitive] *Muslims consider it sacrilege* ***to*** *wear shoes inside a mosque.* ◦ ***It*** *would be a sacrilege* ***to*** *put a neon sign on that beautiful old building.* • **sacrilegious** /ˌsæk.rɪˈlɪdʒ.əs/ adj • **sacrilegiously** /-li/ adv

sacristy /ˈsæk.rɪ.sti/ noun [C] a **vestry**

sacrosanct /ˈsæk.rə.sæŋkt/ adj thought to be too important or too special to be changed: *I'm willing to help on any weekday, but I'm afraid my weekends are sacrosanct.*

sad /sæd/ adj (**sadder**, **saddest**) NOT HAPPY ▷ **1** A1 unhappy or sorry: *I've just received some very sad news.* ◦ *She gave a rather sad smile.* ◦ [+ (that)] *It's sad* (***that***) *the trip had to be cancelled.* ◦ *I'm so sad* (***that***) *you can't come.* ◦ [+ to infinitive] ***It's*** *sad* ***to*** *see so many failures this year.* ◦ *I was sad* ***to*** *hear that they'd split up.* **2** informal If something looks sad, it looks worse than it should because it is not being cared for: *Give those flowers some water – they're looking a bit sad.* UNPLEASANT ▷ **3** [before noun] not satisfactory or pleasant: *The sad* ***fact/truth*** *is we can't afford to provide homes for all.* ◦ *a very sad state of affairs* **4 sad to say** C1 something you say when you are telling someone about something bad that happened: *Sad to say, the ring was never found.* BORING ▷ **5** UK slang showing that you are not fashionable or interesting or have no friends: *You enjoy reading timetables? You sad man!* • **sadness** /ˈsæd.nəs/ noun [U] B2 *Her sadness at her grandfather's death was obvious.*

Other ways of saying sad

Unhappy and **miserable** can mean the same as 'sad':

She'd had a very ***unhappy*** *childhood.*

I just woke up feeling ***miserable.***

Someone who is **upset** is unhappy because something bad has happened:

They'd had an argument and he was still ***upset*** *about it.*

Mike got very ***upset*** *when I told him the news.*

If you are **broken-hearted** or **heartbroken** you are very sad, often because someone you love has ended a relationship with you:

She was ***broken-hearted*** *when Richard left.*

If you are **devastated** or **distraught**, you are extremely upset:

He was ***devastated*** *when he lost his house.*

She was ***distraught*** *over the article and feared losing her job.*

The adjectives **depressed**, **down**, or **low** are often used when someone is very unhappy for a long time:

It makes her ***depressed*** *to think about the injury.*

I've been feeling a little ***down*** *recently.*

He was very ***low*** *for months after he lost his job.*

IDIOM **sadder but wiser** If someone is sadder but wiser after a bad experience, they have suffered but they have also learned something from it.

SAD /ˌes.eɪˈdiː/ noun [U] abbreviation for seasonal affective disorder: a medical condition in which a person does not have much energy and enthusiasm during the winter because of the reduced period of natural light

sadden /ˈsæd.ən/ verb [T] C2 to make someone sad: [+ to infinitive] ***It*** *saddens me* ***to*** *think that we'll never see her again.* ◦ *We are* ***deeply*** *saddened by this devastating tragedy.*

saddle /ˈsæd.l̩/ noun; verb

▸noun SEAT ▷ **1** C2 [C] a seat, often made of leather, used on a horse, bicycle, motorcycle, etc.: *He swung himself into the saddle and rode off.* → See also **sidesaddle 2 in the saddle a** riding a horse **b** in charge or in control: *The chairman is back in the saddle after his heart attack.* MEAT ▷ **3** [C or U] a large piece of meat taken from the middle of the back of an animal: *saddle of lamb*

▸verb [T] C2 to put a saddle on a horse: *She saddled (****up****) the horse for her friend.*

PHRASAL VERB **saddle sb with sth** informal C2 to give someone a responsibility or problem that they do not want and that will cause them a lot of work or difficulty: *The company is saddled with* ***debt.***

saddlebag /ˈsæd.l̩.bæg/ noun [C] a small bag that you fix to the back of your bicycle saddle, or one of a pair of bags that you put over the back of a horse or over the back wheel of a bicycle or motorcycle

saddler /ˈsæd.ləʳ/ (US) /-lə/ noun [C] a person who

makes, sells, and repairs saddles and other leather objects for horses

saddlery /ˈsæd.lə.ri/ (US) /-lɚ.i/ **noun** [U] leather objects, such as saddles and BRIDLES, for horses

ˈsaddle-sore adj having a sore bottom from sitting on a saddle for a long time

saddo /ˈsæd.əʊ/ (US) /-oʊ/ noun [C] UK slang someone, especially a man, who is not fashionable or interesting or has no friends: *So who says trainspotting is for saddos?*

sadhu /ˈsɑː.duː/ noun [C] a Hindu holy man, especially one who has chosen to live apart from society

sadism /ˈseɪ.dɪ.zəm/ (US) /ˈsæd.ɪ-/ noun [U] the activity of getting pleasure, sometimes sexual, from being cruel to or hurting another person

sadist /ˈseɪ.dɪst/ (US) /ˈsæd.ɪst/ noun [C] a person who gets pleasure, sometimes sexual, by being cruel to or hurting another person • **sadistic** /səˈdɪs.tɪk/ adj *sadistic behaviour/pleasure* • **sadistically** /səˈdɪs.tɪ.kəl.i/ adv

sadly /ˈsæd.li/ adv **NOT HAPPY** ▷ **1** (B2) in an unhappy way: *'He's gone away for six months,' she said sadly.* **UNPLEASANT** ▷ **2** (B2) in a way that is not satisfactory: *Sadly, the treatment doesn't work for all patients.* ◦ *If you think she'll let you do that, you're sadly (= completely)* ***mistaken***.

sadomasochism /ˌseɪ.dəʊˈmæs.ə.kɪ.zəm/ (US) /ˌsæd.oʊ-/ noun [U] (abbreviation **S & M, SM**) the activity of getting sexual pleasure from sadism and from MASOCHISM (= being hurt) • **sadomasochist** /-kɪst/ noun [C] • **sadomasochistic** /ˌseɪ.dəʊˌmæs.əˈkɪs.tɪk/ (US) /ˌsæd.oʊ-/ adj

ˈsad-sack adj informal boring and never likely to be successful: *He's just some sad-sack writer trying to get a book published.*

sae /ˌes.eɪˈiː/ noun [C] UK (US also **SASE**) abbreviation for stamped addressed envelope or self-addressed envelope: an envelope with a stamp and your name and address on it, which you send inside another ENVELOPE to an organization when you want a reply: *Write to the above address, enclosing an sae.*

safari /səˈfɑː.ri/ (US) /-ˈfɑːr.i/ noun [C or U] an organized journey to look at, or sometimes hunt, wild animals, especially in Africa: *to go/be* ***on*** *safari*

saˈfari ˌjacket noun [C] a jacket made of light cloth with short sleeves, pockets on the chest and a belt

saˈfari ˌpark noun [C] a large park where wild animals are kept and can move freely, and can be watched by visitors driving through in their cars

saˈfari ˌsuit noun [C] a safari jacket with matching trousers or a matching skirt

safe /seɪf/ adj; noun

▸adj **NOT IN DANGER** ▷ **1** (A1) not in danger or likely to be harmed: *In some cities you don't* ***feel*** *safe going out alone at night.* **2** (B1) not harmed or damaged: *She said that all the hostages were safe.* **3 safe and sound** (C2) completely safe and without injury or damage: *After three days lost in the mountains, all the climbers arrived home safe and sound.* **NOT CAUSING HARM** ▷ **4** (A2) not dangerous or likely to cause harm: *a safe play area for children* ◦ *a safe driver* ◦ *That ladder doesn't look safe.* ◦ *She wished us a safe journey.* ◦ *Is this medicine safe* ***for*** *children?* ◦ ***It's*** *safe* ***to*** *cross the road now.* **PLACE** ▷ **5** (C1) (of a place) where something is not likely to be lost or stolen: *Keep your passport in a safe place.* **NO RISK** ▷ **6** (C1) describes things that do not involve any risk: *I think we should go for the safest option (= the one that involves the least risks).* ◦ *He never usually remembers my birthday, so it's a safe* ***bet*** *(= I am*

certain) he'll forget again this time! **PARLIAMENT** ▷ **7** If an official position in parliament is safe, it is likely to be won by the political party that has won it at previous elections: *a safe Conservative* ***seat*** • **safeness** /ˈseɪf.nəs/ noun [U] *I'm a bit worried about the safeness of this machine for (= whether this machine will cause any danger to) children.*

> **! Common mistake: safe or save?**
>
> **Warning:** do not confuse the adjective **safe** with the verb **save**:
>
> ~~*You can safe a lot of time by booking your holiday online.*~~
>
> *You can save a lot of time by booking your holiday online.*

IDIOMS **as safe as houses** UK very safe • **in safe hands** (C1) being cared for or dealt with by someone skilled: *Dr Bailey is doing the operation, so your wife is in safe hands.* • **it's safe to say (that)** (C1) used to say that you are confident about what you are going to say: *I think it's safe to say that the crisis is now over.* • **(just) to be on the safe side** being especially careful in order to avoid something unpleasant: *I'm sure it won't rain, but I'll take an umbrella (just) to be on the safe side (= to be ready if it does rain).*

▸noun [C] a strong box or cupboard with special locks where valuable things, especially money or JEWELS (= precious stones), are kept: *Thieves* ***broke into/cracked*** *(= opened by force) the safe and stole everything in it.*

safebreaker /ˈseɪfˌbreɪ.kər/ (US) /-kɚ/ noun [C] UK (US **safecracker**) someone who opens safes using force and steals the valuable things from inside

ˌsafe ˈconduct noun [U] official protection from harm while travelling through an area, or a document that gives this: *In exchange for the hostages, the terrorists demanded safe conduct out of the country.*

ˈsafe deˌposit ˌbox noun [C] (also **ˈsafety deˌposit ˌbox**) a strong box in a bank where you can keep money or valuable things

safeguard /ˈseɪf.ɡɑːd/ (US) /-ɡɑːrd/ verb [T] to protect something from harm: *The union safeguards the* ***interests*** *of all its members.* • **safeguard** noun [C or U] *The disk has built-in safeguards to prevent certain errors.*

PHRASAL VERB **safeguard against sth** to do things that you hope will stop something unpleasant from happening: *A good diet will safeguard against disease.*

ˌsafe ˈhaven noun [C usually singular] a place where you are protected from harm or danger: *As long as the UN soldiers were present, the city was regarded as a safe haven for the refugees.*

ˈsafe ˌhouse noun [C] a house where someone can hide or shelter

safekeeping /ˌseɪfˈkiː.pɪŋ/ noun [U] protection from harm or loss: *I left my watch with Helen* ***for*** *safekeeping while I swam.*

safely /ˈseɪf.li/ adv (B1) in a safe way: *We all arrived safely.* ◦ *Drive safely! (= Do not take any risks!)* ◦ *Are the children safely fastened into their car seats?* ◦ *I think we can safely (= with no risk of being wrong) say they won't find us now.*

ˌsafe ˌperiod noun [S] the few days just before and during a woman's period when she is unlikely to become pregnant

ˌsafe ˈsex noun [U] the use of CONDOMS or other methods of avoiding catching a disease, especially

S

AIDS (= a serious disease that destroys the body's ability to fight infection), from sexual activity with someone else: *It's to be hoped that they're **practising** safe sex.*

safety /ˈseɪf.ti/ **noun** [U] (B2) a state in which or a place where you are safe and not in danger or at risk: ***For*** *your (comfort and) safety, we recommend you keep your seat belt loosely fastened during the flight.* ◦ *Journalists may enter the danger zone but unfortunately we cannot **guarantee/assure** their safety.* ◦ *The crew of the ship were winched to safety by a rescue helicopter.* ◦ *As the gunman opened fire, they all **ran/dived for** safety behind trees.* ◦ *Police are **concerned for** the safety **of** (= think that something bad might have happened to) the five-year-old.* ◦ *He was led to **a place of** safety (= somewhere he would not be in danger, especially of being found and harmed).*

> **!** Usage: **safety or security?**
>
> **Safety** is when you are safe or how safe something is:
>
> *Remember to wear your safety belt in the car.*
> *Children should have lessons in road safety.*
>
> **Security** means activities or people that protect you from harm, or that try to stop crime:
>
> *He works as a security guard.*
> *airport security*

> Word partners for **safety**
>
> *ensure/guarantee* sb's safety • *endanger/jeopardize/threaten* sb's safety • *improve/increase* safety • be *airlifted/hauled/winched to* safety • safety *checks/measures/precautions/standards* • a [good/poor] safety *record* • the safety *of* sb/sth • *in* safety

IDIOMS **safety first** said to mean that it is best to avoid any unnecessary risks and to act so that you stay safe • **there's safety in numbers** saying said to emphasize that being part of a group makes you less likely to be harmed

ˈ**safety** ˌ**belt** noun [C] a **seat belt**

ˈ**safety** ˌ**catch** noun [C] a small part on something dangerous, especially a machine or a gun, which prevents people from using it without intending to

ˈ**safety** ˌ**curtain** noun [C] in a theatre, a curtain made of material that will not burn that comes down between the stage and the part where people sit to prevent any possible fire from spreading

S

ˈ**safety de**ˌ**posit** ˌ**box** noun [C] a **safe deposit box**

ˈ**safety** ˌ**glass** noun [U] a type of glass, used especially for car windows, that either stays in one piece in an accident, or breaks into small pieces that are not sharp

ˈ**safety** ˌ**glasses** noun [plural] special pieces of strong glass or plastic in a frame which fits tightly to a person's face to protect their eyes from dangerous chemicals or machines

ˈ**safety** ˌ**match** noun [C] a match that will only start burning if you rub it along a special surface on its box

ˈ**safety** ˌ**net** noun [C] **NET** ▷ **1** a net put below people performing at a great height to catch them if they fall **HELP** ▷ **2** a system to help those who have serious problems and no other form of help: *The welfare state was set up to provide a safety net for the poor.*

ˈ**safety** ˌ**pin** noun [C] a pin used for fastening things, especially cloth, which has a round end into which the sharp point fits, so that it is covered and cannot stick into you

ˈ**safety** ˌ**razor** noun [C] a device for cutting hair on the face which has a blade that is partly covered, to prevent it from cutting the skin

ˈ**safety** ˌ**valve** noun [C] **MACHINE** ▷ **1** a small part on a machine, which allows steam or gas to escape if the pressure inside becomes too high **FEELINGS** ▷ **2** a way of getting rid of strong feelings without causing harm: *For many people who suffer from stress at work, sport is a vital safety valve.*

saffron /ˈsæf.rən/ **noun; adj**
▸**noun** [U] **SPICE** ▷ **1** a dark yellow substance obtained from a flower and used as a spice to give colour and flavour to food: *saffron rice* **COLOUR** ▷ **2** a dark yellow colour
▸**adj** having a dark yellow colour

sag /sæg/ **verb; noun**
▸**verb** [I] (**-gg-**) **1** to drop down to a lower level in the middle: *The shelf sagged **under** the weight of the heavy books.* ◦ *a sagging roof/floor/bed* **2** to become weaker: *The dollar held up well this morning but the pound sagged.*
▸**noun 1** [S or U] a movement or position in which something has dropped down to a lower level: *a sag in the roof* **2** [C usually singular] a reduction in something: *a sag in sales* **3** [U] **saag**

saga /ˈsɑː.gə/ **noun** [C] **1** a long story about past events over a long period of time, originally one told in the Middle Ages in Iceland or Norway: *a lengthy and compelling family saga* **2** a long complicated series of related usually negative events: *It was just another episode in an **ongoing** saga **of** marriage problems.*

sagacious /səˈgeɪ.ʃəs/ **adj** formal having or showing understanding and the ability to make good judgments: *a sagacious person/comment/choice* → Synonym **wise** • **sagaciously** /-li/ **adv** • **sagacity** /səˈgæs.ɪ.ti/ (US) /-ə.ti/ **noun** [U]

sage /seɪdʒ/ **adj; noun**
▸**adj** literary wise, especially as a result of great experience: *sage advice* • **sagely** /ˈseɪdʒ.li/ **adv** literary *He nodded his head sagely.*
▸**noun PLANT** ▷ **1** [U] a plant whose greyish-green leaves are used as a herb to give flavour to some foods **WISE** ▷ **2** [C] literary or humorous a person, especially an old man, who is wise

ˌ**sage** ˈ**green** adj, noun [U] greyish-green

Sagittarius /ˌsædʒ.ɪˈteə.ri.əs/ (US) /-ˈter.i-/ **noun** [C or U] the ninth sign of the ZODIAC, relating to the period 22 November to 22 December and represented by a CENTAUR (= half human, half horse) shooting an arrow, or a person born during this period • **Sagittarian** /-ən/ **noun** [C], **adj**

sago /ˈseɪ.gəʊ/ (US) /-goʊ/ **noun** [U] small white grains that are obtained from part of the TRUNK of a particular tree, used in cooking: *sago pudding*

said /sed/ **verb; adj**
▸**verb** past simple and past participle of **say**
▸**adj** [before noun] legal used before the name of a person or thing you have already mentioned: ***The*** *said Joseph Brown was seen outside the house on the night of 15 January.*

sail /seɪl/ **verb; noun**
▸**verb TRAVEL** ▷ **1** (B2) [I usually + adv/prep] When a boat or a ship sails, it travels on the water: *The boat sailed along/down the coast.* ◦ *As the battleship sailed by/past, everyone on deck waved.* ◦ *The ship was sailing **to** China.* **2** (B1) [I or T, usually + adv/prep] to control a boat that has no engine and is pushed by the wind: *He*

sailed the dinghy up the river. ◦ *She sailed around the world single-handed in her yacht.* **3** [I] When a ship sails, it starts its journey, and when people sail from a particular place or at a particular time, they start their journey in a ship: *Their ship sails* ***for*** *Bombay next Friday.* **MOVE QUICKLY** ▷ **4** [I + adv/prep] to move quickly, easily, and (of a person) confidently: *The ball went sailing* ***over*** *the garden fence.* ◦ *He wasn't looking where he was going, and just sailed* ***straight into*** *her.* ◦ *Manchester United sailed* ***on*** *(= continued easily)* ***to*** *victory in the final.*

IDIOMS **sail against the wind** to be trying to achieve something that is unlikely to succeed because most people would oppose it: *He's sailing against the wind in his attempt to stop women using the club.* • **sail close to the wind** to do something that is dangerous or only just legal or acceptable: *You were sailing a bit close to the wind there when you made those remarks about his wife.*

PHRASAL VERB **sail through (sth)** to succeed very easily in something, especially a test or exam

▸noun **MATERIAL** ▷ **1** C2 [C] a sheet of material fixed to a pole on a boat to catch the wind and make the boat move: *to hoist/lower the sails* **2** [C] On a WINDMILL, a sail is any of the wide blades that are turned by the wind in order to produce power. **TRAVEL** ▷ **3** [S] a journey in a boat or ship: *It's two days' sail/It's* ***a*** *two-day sail (= a journey of two days by sea) from here to the nearest island.* **4 set sail** C2 to begin a boat journey: *We set sail* ***from*** *Kuwait.* ◦ *They set sail* ***for*** *France.*

IDIOM **under sail** literary travelling in a boat or ship with sails: *After ten hours under sail, they reached dry land.*

sailboard /ˈseɪl.bɔːd/ US /-bɔːrd/ **noun** [C] a **windsurfer**

sailing /ˈseɪ.lɪŋ/ **noun** **1** A2 [U] the sport or activity of using boats with sails: *the sailing club* ◦ *She loves to* ***go*** *sailing.* **2** [C] an occasion when a ship leaves a port: *There are frequent sailings to Staten Island.*

ˈsailing ˌboat noun [C] UK (US **sailboat**) a small boat with sails

sailor /ˈseɪ.ləʳ/ US /-lɚ/ **noun** [C] **1** B1 a person who works on a ship, especially one who is not an officer **2** B1 a person who often takes part in the sport of using boats with sails **3 a good/bad sailor** someone who is not/often ill when they travel by boat

ˈsailor ˌsuit noun [C] a set of clothes, especially for a child, in the style of a sailor's uniform, usually blue and white with a large collar at the back

saint /seɪnt/, /sᵊnt/ **noun** **1** C1 [C] (written abbreviation **St**) (the title given to) a person who has received an official honour from the Christian, especially the Roman Catholic, Church for having lived in a good and holy way. The names of saints are sometimes used to name places and buildings: *Saint Peter* ◦ *St Andrew's school* ◦ *Saint Paul's Cathedral* **2** [C usually singular] a very good, kind person: *She must be a* ***real*** *saint to stay with him all these years.* ◦ *He has* ***the patience of a*** *saint with those kids.* • **sainthood** /ˈseɪnt.hʊd/ **noun** [U] • **saintliness** /ˈseɪnt.li.nəs/ **noun** [U] • **saintly** /ˈseɪnt.li/ **adj** *Her saintly manner concealed a devious mind.*

sainted /ˈseɪn.tɪd/ US /-t̬ɪd/ **adj** [usually before noun] given the title of saint by the Church, or considered to be like a saint: humorous *And where is my sainted (= extremely good) little sister?*

ˈsaint's ˌday noun [C] a day in the year when a particular saint is remembered and when people who have that saint's name often celebrate

sake[1] /seɪk/ **noun** **HELP** ▷ **1 for the sake of sb/for sb's sake** B2 in order to help or bring advantage to someone: *Please do it, for David's sake.* ◦ *Their parents only stayed together for the sake of the children.* ◦ *I hope for both our sakes that you're right!* **REASON** ▷ **2 for the sake of sth/for sth's sake** because of, or for the purpose of something: *Let's not disagree for the sake of (= because of) a few pounds.* ◦ *Let's say, just for the sake of argument/for argument's sake (= for the purpose of this discussion), that prices rise by three percent this year.* ◦ *You're only arguing for the sake of arguing (= because you like arguing).* **EMPHASIS** ▷ **3 for goodness', God's, Pete's, heaven's, etc. sake** used to emphasize requests or orders when you are angry or have lost patience: *For goodness' sake don't let her know I told you!*

sake[2] (also **saki**) /ˈsɑː.ki/ **noun** [C or U] a Japanese alcoholic drink made from rice and usually drunk warm

salaam /səˈlɑːm/ **verb** [I or T] (especially in Muslim countries) to greet someone by bending low from the waist with the front of the right hand against the top of the face • **salaam noun** [C], **exclamation**

salable /ˈseɪ.lə.bl/ **adj** mainly US for **saleable**

salacious /səˈleɪ.ʃəs/ **adj** disapproving causing or showing a strong interest in sexual matters: *a salacious film/book/joke/comment* • **salaciously** /-li/ **adv** • **salaciousness** /-nəs/ **noun** [U]

salad /ˈsæl.əd/ **noun** [C or U] **1** A2 a mixture of uncooked vegetables, usually including LETTUCE, eaten either as a separate dish or with other food: ***Toss*** *(= mix) the salad with a vinaigrette dressing.* ◦ *Serve the risotto with a* ***mixed*** *salad.* ◦ *a salad bowl* **2 cheese, egg, etc. salad** cheese, egg, etc. with salad **3** cooked or uncooked vegetables cut into very small pieces and often mixed with MAYONNAISE: *potato salad* ◦ *rice/pasta salad*

IDIOM **in your salad days** old-fashioned during the period of time when you were a young person and had little experience

ˈsalad ˌbar noun [C usually singular] a table where different salads are served in a restaurant or shop

ˈsalad ˌcream noun [U] UK a thick, cream-coloured liquid, similar to MAYONNAISE but sweeter, eaten with salad

ˈsalad ˌdressing noun [U] a cold sauce made from oil and VINEGAR, added to salads to give flavour

salamander /ˈsæl.ə.mæn.dəʳ/ US /-dɚ/ **noun** [C] a small animal which looks like a LIZARD but has soft skin and lives both on land and in water

salamander

salami /səˈlɑː.mi/ **noun** [U] a large sausage made from meat and spices that has a strong taste and is usually eaten cold in slices

salaried /ˈsæl.ᵊr.id/ US /-ɚ-/ **adj** being paid a salary: *salaried employees/workers/staff*

salary /ˈsæl.ᵊr.i/ US /-ɚ-/ **noun** [C or U] B1 a fixed amount of money agreed every year as pay for an employee, usually paid directly into his or her bank account every month: *an* ***annual*** *salary of £20,000* ◦ *His net* ***monthly*** *salary is £1,500.* ◦ *She's* ***on*** *quite a good/decent salary in her present job.* ◦ *He* ***took a drop in*** *(= accepted a lower) salary when he changed jobs.* ◦ *a ten percent salary* ***increase*** → Compare **wage**

Word partners for salary

draw/earn/get a salary • *pay* a salary • an *average/good/high/low* salary • an *annual/monthly* salary • a salary *cut/increase* • be *on* a salary *of* [£25,000, $50,000, etc.]

salaryman /ˈsæl.ər.i.mæn/ US /-ɚ-/ noun [C] (plural **-men** /-men/) a Japanese BUSINESSMAN who works very long hours every day

sale /seɪl/ noun **SELL** ▷ **1** B2 [C or U] an act of exchanging something for money: *The sale **of** cigarettes/alcohol is forbidden.* ◦ *The building company get commission on each house sale.* ◦ *I haven't **made** a sale all morning.* ◦ *They'll drop the price rather than **lose** the sale.* **2 for sale** A2 available to buy: *Is this painting for sale?* ◦ *Our neighbours **put** their house **up** for sale (= started to advertise that they want to sell it) last week.* **3 sales** [U, + sing/pl verb] the department of a company that organizes and does the selling of the company's products or services: *He works in Sales.* ◦ *the sales department/manager* **4 sales** [plural] B2 the number of products sold: *Sales this year exceeded the total for the two previous years.* → See also **telesales** **5** [C] an occasion when things are sold, especially by an organization such as a school or church, in order to make money for the organization: *a charity/Christmas/book sale* **6** [C] an AUCTION (= public sale): *a sale of antique furniture* ◦ *a cattle sale* **7 on sale** B1 UK available to buy in a shop: *On sale at record stores now.* **8 sale or return** a system by which goods are supplied to shops and can be returned if they are not sold within a particular period of time: *We can supply goods **on a** sale or return **basis**.*

Common mistake: sale or sell?

Warning: do not confuse the noun **sale** with the verb **sell**:

~~*The shop sales items made by local artists.*~~
The shop sells items made by local artists.

Common mistake: sale or sales?

Remember: to talk about the number of items sold, use the plural noun **sales**:

~~*The strike had a negative effect on this year's sale.*~~
The strike had a negative effect on this year's sales.

CHEAP PRICE ▷ **9** A2 [C] an occasion when goods are sold at a lower price than usual: *a mid-season/end-of-season sale* ◦ *a clearance/closing-down sale* ◦ *I bought this in the January sales.* ◦ *sale goods/prices* **10 on sale** A2 mainly US (UK usually **in the sale**) reduced in price: *Can you tell me if this dress is in the sale?*

saleable (mainly US **salable**) /ˈseɪ.lə.bl̩/ adj easy to sell or suitable for selling: *saleable commodities* ◦ *in saleable condition*

ˈsales asˌsistant noun [C] UK a **shop assistant**

salesclerk /ˈseɪlz.klɑːk/ US /-klɝːk/ noun [C] US for **shop assistant**

ˈsales ˌdrive noun [C] a special effort to sell more than usual

ˈsales ˌforce noun [C, + sing/pl verb] all the employees of a company whose job is persuading customers to buy their company's products or services

salesman /ˈseɪlz.mən/ noun [C] (plural **-men** /-mən/) B1 a man whose job is selling things in a shop or directly to customers: *a car salesman* ◦ *a travelling salesman* ◦ *a door-to-door salesman*

salesmanship /ˈseɪlz.mən.ʃɪp/ noun [U] skill in selling: *Clever salesmanship can persuade you to buy things you don't really want.*

salesperson /ˈseɪlzˌpɜː.sən/ US /-pɝː-/ noun [C] A2 a person whose job is selling things in a shop or directly to customers: *a car/computer salesperson*

ˈsales ˌpitch noun [S] a way of talking that is intended to persuade you to buy something: *He's got a good sales pitch.*

ˈsales ˌrep noun [C] (formal **ˈsales repreˌsentative**) someone who travels to different places trying to persuade people to buy their company's products or services

ˈsales ˌslip noun [C] US a **receipt**

ˈsales ˌtalk noun [U] a way of talking that is intended to persuade you to buy something

ˈsales ˌtax noun [C usually singular] US a tax paid by people when they buy goods or services → See also **VAT**

saleswoman /ˈseɪlzˌwʊm.ən/ noun [C] (plural **-women** /-wɪmɪn/) B1 a female SALESPERSON

salience /ˈseɪ.li.ənts/ noun [U] formal the fact of being important to or connected with what is happening or being discussed: *The salience of these facts was questioned by several speakers.*

salient /ˈseɪ.li.ənt/ adj formal The salient facts about something or qualities of something are the most important things about them: *She began to summarize the salient **features/points** of the proposal.* ◦ *The article presented the salient **facts** of the dispute clearly and concisely.*

saline /ˈseɪ.laɪn/ noun; adj

▸noun [U] specialized a liquid mixture of salt and pure water, which helps to kill bacteria or can be used to replace liquid lost from the body: *a saline drip*

▸adj specialized containing or consisting of salt: *saline deposits/springs* ◦ *saline solution* • **salinity** /səˈlɪn.ɪ.ti/ US /-ə.t̬i/ noun [U] *You should test the salinity of the water.*

saliva /səˈlaɪ.və/ noun [U] the liquid produced in your mouth to keep the mouth wet and to help to prepare food to be digested • **salivary** /-vər.i/ US /-vɚ.i/ adj [before noun] specialized

salivary gland /səˈlaɪ.vər.iˌglænd/ US /ˈsæl.ə.ver-/ noun [C] specialized one of the GLANDS that produce saliva and release it into the mouth

salivate /ˈsæl.ɪ.veɪt/ verb [I] specialized or humorous to produce saliva: *The thought of all that delicious food made me salivate.*

sallow /ˈsæl.əʊ/ US /-oʊ/ adj (of white-skinned people) yellowish and looking unhealthy: *a sallow complexion/face* • **sallowness** /-nəs/ US /-oʊ-/ noun [U]

sally /ˈsæl.i/ noun; verb

▸noun [C] a sudden attack on an enemy, especially when they are surrounding you

▸verb [I + adv/prep] to make a sally

IDIOM **sally forth** old-fashioned or humorous to leave a safe place in a brave or confident way in order to do something difficult: *The minister opened the door and sallied forth to face the angry crowd.*

the ˌSally ˈArmy noun UK informal for **the Salvation Army**

salmon /ˈsæm.ən/ noun [C or U] (plural **salmon**) B1 a medium-sized silver-coloured fish that lives in the sea and swims up rivers to produce its eggs. Its pink flesh is eaten as a food: *fresh/smoked/tinned salmon* ◦ *salmon mousse/fishcakes* ◦ *salmon fishing*

salmonella /ˌsæl.məˈnel.ə/ noun [U] **1** a type of bacteria that exists in several forms, some of which live in food and make the people who eat it ill:

S

salmonella poisoning **2** the illness caused by this bacteria: *an outbreak of salmonella*

ˌsalmon ˈpink noun [U] an orange-pink colour • **ˌsalmon-ˈpink** adj

salon /ˈsæl.ɒn/ (US) /səˈlɑːn/ noun [C] **SHOP** ▷ **1** (B1) a shop where you can get a particular service, especially connected with beauty or fashion: *a beauty salon* ◦ *a hairdressing/hair salon* **MEETING** ▷ **2** literary a meeting of writers, painters, etc., at the house of someone famous or important: *a **literary** salon*

saloon /səˈluːn/ noun [C] **CAR** ▷ **1** UK (US **sedan**) a car with seats for four or five people, two or four doors, and a separate area at the back for bags, boxes, and cases **BAR** ▷ **2** a public bar, especially in the past in the western US

saˈloon ˌbar noun [C] UK old-fashioned a bar in a pub or hotel that is more comfortable than the other bars, and in which you sometimes pay a little more money for your drink → Compare **public bar**

salsa /ˈsæl.sə/ (US) /ˈsɑːl-/ noun **SAUCE** ▷ **1** [C or U] a spicy sauce made from tomatoes, onions, and CHILLIES (= small, spicy, red or green seed cases) **MUSIC/DANCE** ▷ **2** [S or U] a type of South American music with a strong beat, or a dance done to this music

salt /sɒlt/ (US) /sɑːlt/ noun; adj; verb

▸noun **FOOD** ▷ **1** (A1) [U] a common white substance found in sea water and in the ground, used especially to add flavour to food or to preserve it: *salt and pepper* ◦ *Can you pass the salt please?* ◦ *Add **a pinch of** (= small amount of) salt to the sauce.* **CHEMICAL** ▷ **2** [C] specialized a chemical substance that is a combination of a metal or a BASE with an ACID: *Potassium nitrate and potassium chloride are potassium salts.*

IDIOMS **be the salt of the earth** If you say that someone is the salt of the earth, you mean that they are a very good and honest person. • **take sth with a pinch of salt** UK (US **take sth with a grain of salt**) to not completely believe something that you are told, because you think it is unlikely to be true: *You have to take everything she says with a pinch of salt, she does tend to exaggerate.*

▸adj [before noun] containing or preserved in salt: *salt water* ◦ *salt beef/pork*

▸verb [T] to add salt to or put salt on something: *Don't forget to salt the potatoes.* ◦ *When it's icy, the city salts the roads to thaw the ice.*

PHRASAL VERB **salt sth away** informal to save something, often money, secretly: *He salted away a fortune over the years and no one ever knew!*

SALT /sɒlt/ (US) /sɑːlt/ noun [U] abbreviation for Strategic Arms Limitation Talks: a series of discussions between the US and the USSR that took place from 1969 to 1979 and aimed to limit the number of nuclear weapons

ˌsalt-and-ˈpepper adj [before noun] US for **pepper-and-salt**

ˈsalt ˌcellar noun [C] (US **saltshaker**) a small container for salt, usually with one hole in the top

salted /ˈsɒl.tɪd/ (US) /ˈsɑːl.t̬ɪd/ adj containing or covered in salt: *salted peanuts* ◦ *lightly salted butter*

saltpetre UK (US **saltpeter**) /ˌsɒltˈpiː.tər/ (US) /ˈsɑːltˌpiː.t̬ɚ/ noun [U] a salty-tasting white powder used to preserve meat, and also used in producing explosives and FERTILIZERS (= substances that help plants grow)

ˈsalt ˌwater noun [U] sea water • **saltwater** /ˈsɒltˌwɔː.tər/ (US) /ˈsɑːltˌwɔː.t̬ɚ/ adj [before noun] *saltwater fish*

salty /ˈsɒl.ti/ (US) /ˈsɑːl.t̬i/ adj (B2) tasting of salt: *This bacon is too salty for me.* • **saltiness** /-nəs/ noun [U]

salubrious /səˈluː.bri.əs/ adj formal describes a place that is pleasant, clean, and healthy to live in: *He doesn't live in a very salubrious part of town.*

salutary /ˈsæl.jʊ.tᵊr.i/ (US) /-ter.i/ adj formal causing improvement of behaviour or character: *a salutary **experience*** ◦ *a salutary **reminder** of the dangers of mountain climbing*

salutation /ˌsæl.jʊˈteɪ.ʃᵊn/ noun [C or U] formal a greeting in words or actions, or the words used at the beginning of a letter or speech

salute /səˈluːt/ verb; noun

▸verb **SHOW RESPECT** ▷ **1** [I or T] (especially of people in the armed forces) to make a formal sign of respect to someone, especially by raising the right hand to the side of the head: *Whenever you see an officer, you must salute.* ◦ *The soldiers saluted the colonel.* **PRAISE** ▷ **2** [T] formal to honour or express admiration publicly for a person or an achievement: *On this memorable occasion we salute the wonderful work done by the association.* ◦ *We salute you **for** your courage and determination.*

▸noun [C] **SHOW OF RESPECT** ▷ **1** a sign of respect made to someone by raising the right hand to the side of the head: *The soldier **gave** a salute and the officer **returned** it.* **2** an action, such as FIRING a gun, done to show respect to someone: *Full military honours and a **21-gun** salute (= 21 guns fired at the same time) marked his funeral.* **PRAISE** ▷ **3** an action or sign to honour or show your admiration for a person or achievement

IDIOM **take the salute** When a person of high rank takes the salute, they stand and watch while soldiers march past saluting them.

salvage /ˈsæl.vɪdʒ/ verb [T] **1** to save goods from damage or destruction, especially from a ship that has sunk or been damaged or a building that has been damaged by fire or a flood: *gold coins salvaged from a shipwreck* ◦ *After the fire, there wasn't much furniture left worth salvaging.* **2** to try to make a bad situation better: *It was a desperate attempt to salvage the **situation**.* ◦ *After the fraud scandal he had to make great efforts to salvage his **reputation**.* • **salvage** noun [U] *They mounted a salvage **operation** after the fire.* • **salvageable** /-ə.bl̩/ adj

salvation /sælˈveɪ.ʃᵊn/ noun **1** [S or U] (a way of) being saved from danger, loss, or harm: *After the diagnosis, getting to know Mary was his salvation.* ◦ *a marriage beyond salvation* **2** [U] In the Christian religion, salvation of a person or their spirit is the state of being saved from evil and its effects by the death of Jesus on a cross: *The Gospel message is one of personal salvation.*

the Salˌvation ˈArmy noun (UK informal **the ˌSally ˈArmy**) an international Christian organization whose members have ranks and uniforms like an army, hold meetings with music, and work to help poor people: *a Salvation Army hostel for homeless men and women*

salve /sælv/ (US) /sæv/ noun; verb

▸noun old-fashioned **1** [C or U] a liquid or cream used to treat an injured, sore, or dry place on your body **2** [S] something that makes you feel better about a difficult situation

▸verb **salve your conscience** to do something so that you feel less guilty: *He salves his conscience by giving money to charity.*

salver /ˈsæl.vər/ (US) /-vɚ/ noun [C] a large metal plate used to bring food, drinks, or letters to people, especially in a formal situation: *a silver salver*

salvo /ˈsæl.vəʊ/ (US) /-voʊ/ noun [C] (plural **salvos** or

S

salvoes) **1** the action of FIRING several guns at the same time, either in a war or in a ceremony: *a salvo of guns/rockets* **2** a sudden loud sound made by many people at the same time: *Every joke the comedian made was greeted by a salvo of laughter from the audience.* **3** the first part of a speech or the first in a series of actions intended to get a particular result: *In his **opening** salvo the speaker fiercely attacked the government's record on healthcare.*

salwar /sʌlˈwɑːʳ/ US /-ˈwɑːr/ **noun** [C] (also **shalwar** /ʃʌlˈwɑːʳ/ US /-ˈwɑːr/) loose trousers often worn by women in South Asia with a KAMEEZ

salwar kaˈmeez noun [C] (also **shalwar kaˈmeez**) a type of suit, worn especially by Asian women, with loose trousers and a long shirt

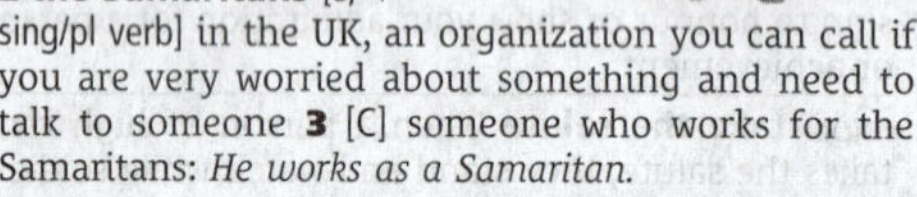
salwar kameez

SAM /sæm/ noun [C] abbreviation for **surface-to-air missile**

Samaritan /səˈmær.ɪ.tᵊn/ US /-ˈmer.ɪ.ţᵊn/ **noun** **1 a good Samaritan** someone who gives help to people who need it **2 the Samaritans** [S, + sing/pl verb] in the UK, an organization you can call if you are very worried about something and need to talk to someone **3** [C] someone who works for the Samaritans: *He works as a Samaritan.*

samba /ˈsæm.bə/ **noun** [C or U] an energetic dance originally from Brazil, or music for dancing this dance

same /seɪm/ **adj; pronoun; adv**

▸adj **EXACTLY LIKE** ▷ **1 the same** A1 exactly like another or each other: *My twin sister and I have got the same nose.* ◦ *She was wearing **exactly** the same dress **as** I was.* ◦ *Hilary's the same age **as** me.* ◦ *She brought up her children in **just** (= exactly) the same **way** her mother did.* → Compare **similar** **NOT ANOTHER** ▷ **2** A1 [before noun] not another different place, time, situation, person, or thing: *My brother and I sleep in **the** same room.* ◦ *Rachel's still going out with **the** same boyfriend.* ◦ ***That** (**very**) same day, he heard he'd passed his exam.* ◦ *I would do **the** same **thing** again if I had the chance.* ◦ *They eat at **the** same restaurant every week.* ◦ *Shall we meet up at **the** same time tomorrow?*

> **!** Common mistake: **same**
>
> **Remember: same** usually comes after **the**.
>
> Don't say 'same', say **the same**:
>
> ~~*My husband is same age as me.*~~
>
> *My husband is the same age as me.*

IDIOMS **at the same time** used to mention something that must be considered in addition to what you have just said: *No one likes conflict, but at the same time we have to deal with this problem.* • **be in the same boat** C2 to be in the same unpleasant situation as other people: *She's always complaining that she doesn't have enough money, but we're all in the same boat.* • **by the same token** C2 used to mean that something you are about to say is also true, for the same reasons as what has just been said: *I don't think that prices will go up but, by the same token, I don't see them going down either.* • **it all amounts/comes to the same thing** used to mean that any of several different possible actions will produce the same result: *It doesn't matter whether you do it first or last – it all amounts to the same thing.* • **it's the same old story** informal C1 said when talking about a bad situation that has happened many times before: *It's the same old story – the rich get richer and the poor get poorer.* • **not in the same league** not nearly as good as something or someone else: *Her golf is brilliant – I'm not in the same league.* • **one and the same** the same thing or person: *I was amazed to discover that Mary's husband and Jane's son are one and the same (person).* • **same difference** not standard said when you agree that what you said was not exactly correct, but you think the difference is not important: *'Did you see that bus?' 'Actually it was a coach.' 'Same difference.'* • **same old same old** informal used to say that a situation or someone's behaviour remains the same, especially when it is boring or annoying: *Most people just carry on doing the same old same old every day.*

▸pronoun **EXACTLY LIKE** ▷ **1 the same as** A2 exactly like: *People say I look **just** the same **as** my sister.* ◦ *John thinks the same as I do – it's just too expensive.* **2 the same** B2 not changed: *After all these years you look **exactly** the same – you haven't changed a bit.* ◦ *Charles is just the same **as** always.* **NOT ANOTHER** ▷ **3 the same a** B1 not another different thing or situation: *I'm hopeless at physics, and **it's** the same **with** chemistry – I get it all wrong.* **b** [before noun] humorous not another different person: *'Was that Marion on the phone?' 'The (very) same.'*

IDIOMS **all the same** C1 despite what has just been said: *It rained every day of our holiday – but we had a good time all the same.* • **be all the same to sb** to not be important to someone which of several things is chosen: *I don't mind whether we eat now or this evening, it's all the same to me.* ◦ *I'll have tea – **if** it's all the same to you.* • **not the same** not as good: *You can make shortbread with margarine instead of butter, but it isn't the same.* • **same again** informal said when you want another drink of the same type as you have just had: *'What are you having, David?' 'Same again, please.'* • **same here** informal said when you agree with what has been said or you have experienced the same thing as they have: *'I thought that film was awful!' 'Same here!'* • **same to you** informal used as an answer to someone who has greeted or insulted you in order to wish the same thing to them: *'Have a good holiday.' 'Same to you!' (= I hope you have a good holiday too.)*

▸adv **the same** B2 in the same way: *We treat all our children the same.* ◦ *I need some time to myself, the same **as** anybody else.*

sameness /ˈseɪm.nəs/ **noun** [U] the quality of being the same as or very similar to something else: *She was struck by the sameness of the houses.*

ˌsame-ˈsex adj A same-sex relationship, marriage, etc. is a romantic relationship between two men or between two women.

samey /ˈseɪ.mi/ **adj** UK informal disapproving not interesting because of being very similar: *His paintings all look a bit samey.*

samosa /səˈməʊ.sə/ US /-ˈmoʊ-/ **noun** [C] a South Asian food consisting of a small pastry case in the shape of a triangle, filled with vegetables or meat and spices and fried

samovar /ˈsæm.ə.vɑːʳ/ US /-vɑːr/ **noun** [C] a large metal container used, especially in Russia, to heat water for tea

sampan /ˈsæm.pæn/ **noun** [C] a small boat with a flat bottom, used along the coasts and rivers of China and Southeast Asia

sample /ˈsɑːm.pl/ (US) /ˈsæm-/ noun; verb
▸noun [C] **SMALL AMOUNT** ▷ **1** (B2) a small amount of something that shows you what the rest is or should be like: *a **free** sample **of** shampoo* ◦ *samples **of** carpet/curtain material* ◦ *Please bring some samples **of** your work to the interview.* **2** (C2) a small amount of a substance that a doctor or scientist collects in order to examine it: *a **blood**/urine sample* **3** (B2) a group of people or things that is chosen out of a larger number and is asked questions or tested in order to get information about the larger group: *a **random** sample **of** voters* ◦ *a nationally **representative** sample **of** 200 schools* **MUSIC** ▷ **4** a small part of a song that has been recorded and used to make a new piece of music
▸verb [T] **SMALL AMOUNT** ▷ **1** to taste a small amount of food or drink to decide if you like it: *As the food looked so good, he decided to sample a little from each dish.* **2** (C2) to experience a place or an activity, often for the first time: *So you're going to sample the **delights/pleasures** of the new restaurant?* **MUSIC** ▷ **3** specialized to record part of a song and use the recording to make a new piece of music: *This song has been heavily sampled.*

sampler /ˈsɑːm.pləʳ/ (US) /ˈsæm.plɚ/ noun [C] **CLOTH** ▷ **1** a decorative piece of cloth with letters, words, pictures, etc. sewed on it, made especially in the past and often hung on the wall like a picture **MUSIC** ▷ **2** specialized a device which allows you to record parts of other people's songs and then use these parts to create new pieces of music **PRODUCT** ▷ **3** a product, sometimes given free, that contains some examples or features of something, so that customers can get an idea of what it is like: *The Mozart Record Edition is on 45 compact disks by Philips, but Decca offers a more modest sampler of 12 compact disks.*

samurai /ˈsæm.ʊ.raɪ/ (US) /-ʊr.aɪ/ noun [C] (plural **samurai** or **samurais**) a member of a military class of high social rank from the 11th to the 19th century in Japan: *Samurai warriors*

sanatorium /ˌsæn.əˈtɔː.ri.əm/ (US) /-ˈtɔːr.i-/ noun [C] (plural **sanatoriums** or **sanatoria**) (US also **sanitarium**) a special type of hospital, usually in the countryside, where people can have treatment and rest, especially when getting better after a long illness

sanctify /ˈsæŋk.tɪ.faɪ/ verb [T] **1** formal to make an event or place holy **2** to make something socially or officially acceptable: *a practice sanctified **by** many years of tradition* • **sanctification** /ˌsæŋk.tɪ.fɪˈkeɪ.ʃən/ (US) /-t̬ɪ-/ noun [U] formal

sanctimonious /ˌsæŋk.tɪˈməʊ.ni.əs/ (US) /-ˈmoʊ-/ adj formal disapproving acting as if morally better than others • **sanctimoniously** /-li/ adv • **sanctimoniousness** /-nəs/ noun [U]

sanction /ˈsæŋk.ʃən/ noun; verb
▸noun **ORDER** ▷ **1** [C usually plural] an official order, such as the stopping of trade, that is taken against a country in order to make it obey international law: *Many nations have **imposed** sanctions **on** the country because of its attacks on its own people.* ◦ ***Trade/economic** sanctions will only be **lifted** (= stopped) when the aggressor nation withdraws its troops.* **2** (C2) [C] a strong action taken in order to make people obey a law or rule, or a punishment given when they do not obey: *Without realistic sanctions, some teachers have difficulty keeping order in the classroom.* **APPROVAL** ▷ **3** [U] approval or permission, especially formal or legal: *They tried to get **official** sanction **for** the scheme.*
▸verb [T] to formally give permission for something: *The government was reluctant to sanction intervention in the crisis.*

sanctity /ˈsæŋk.tɪ.ti/ (US) /-tə.t̬i/ noun **1 the sanctity of human life, marriage, etc.** the quality of being very important and deserving respect **2** [U] the quality of being holy: *the sanctity of a cemetery/tomb*

sanctuary /ˈsæŋk.tʃʊə.ri/ (US) /-tʃu.er.i/ noun **1** [C usually singular, U] protection or a safe place, especially for someone or something being chased or hunted: *Illegal immigrants **found/sought/took** sanctuary in a local church.* ◦ *The chapel became a sanctuary for the refugees.* ◦ figurative *If I want some peace and quiet, I **take** sanctuary in my study.* **2** [C] a place where birds or animals can live and be protected, especially from being hunted or dangerous conditions: *a wildlife/bird sanctuary* **3** [C] the most holy part of a religious building

sanctum /ˈsæŋk.təm/ noun formal **1 inner sanctum** a private place or room where someone is never interrupted **2** [C] a holy place

sand /sænd/ noun; verb
▸noun **1** (B1) [U] a substance that consists of very small grains of rock, found on beaches and in deserts: *a **grain of** sand* ◦ *The children played all day **in/on** the sand.* ◦ *coarse/fine sand* ◦ *Mix one part sand to three parts cement.* **2 sands** [plural] large flat areas of sand near the sea: *miles of **golden** sands*
▸verb [T] to make something smooth by rubbing it with something rough, especially SANDPAPER (= strong paper with sand fixed to it): *Sand the door (**down**) thoroughly before starting to paint.*

sandal /ˈsæn.dəl/ noun [C] (B1) a light shoe, especially worn in warm weather, consisting of a bottom part held onto the foot by straps: *a pair of sandals* ◦ *open-toed sandals*

sandalwood /ˈsæn.dəl.wʊd/ noun [U] the hard light-coloured wood of a tree that grows in Southeast Asia and Australia, or the pleasant-smelling oil from this tree

sandbag /ˈsænd.bæg/ noun; verb
▸noun [C] a bag filled with sand, used as a defence against floods, explosions, etc.
▸verb [T] (**-gg-**) to put sandbags in or around something: *They sandbagged the doors to stop the water coming in.*

sandbank /ˈsænd.bæŋk/ noun [C] a raised area of sand below the surface of the sea or a river, which you can only see when the water level is low

sandbar /ˈsænd.bɑːʳ/ (US) /-bɑːr/ noun [C] a long raised area of sand below the surface of the water, especially where a river enters the sea, usually formed by moving currents

sandblast /ˈsænd.blɑːst/ (US) /-blæst/ verb [T] to clean or decorate stone, metal, or glass with a machine that blows sand out at a high speed

sandcastle /ˈsændˌkɑː.sl/ (US) /-ˌkæs.l/ noun [C] a model castle of sand, usually made by children playing on the beach

ˈsand ˌdune noun [C] a hill of sand made by the wind on the coast or in a desert

sander /ˈsæn.dəʳ/ (US) /-dɚ/ noun [C] (also **ˈsanding maˌchine**) an electrical machine to which a sheet or disc of rough paper is fastened to rub other surfaces in order to make them smoother

S & M /ˌes.əndˈem/ noun [U], adj abbreviation for **sadomasochism**

the sandman /ˈsænd.mæn/ noun [S] child's word an imaginary man who spreads sand that makes children rub their eyes and go to sleep

sandpail /ˈsænd.peɪl/ noun [C] US for **bucket**

S

sandpaper /ˈsændˌpeɪ.pəʳ/ (US) /-pɚ/ **noun** [U] strong paper with sand or a similar rough substance stuck to one side, used for rubbing a surface in order to make it smoother: *coarse/fine sandpaper* • **sandpaper** verb [T]

sandpit /ˈsænd.pɪt/ **noun** [C] UK (US **sandbox** /-bɒks/ (US) /-bɑːks/) a hole in the ground, or a box, filled with sand in which children can play

sandstone /ˈsænd.stəʊn/ (US) /-stoʊn/ **noun** [U] a type of rock formed from sand

sandstorm /ˈsænd.stɔːm/ (US) /-stɔːrm/ **noun** [C] a strong wind in a desert carrying a large amount of sand

ˈsand ˌtrap noun [C] US a **bunker**

sandwich noun; verb

▸noun [C] /ˈsæn.wɪdʒ/ (US) /-wɪtʃ/ **1** A1 two pieces of bread, sometimes spread with butter or MARGARINE, and with some other usually cold food between them: *a tuna/ham sandwich* ◦ *a toasted sandwich* ◦ *a sandwich bar/box* ◦ *sandwich fillings* **2** (also **sandwich cake**) UK a cake consisting of two thin, round layers with a filling such as cream between them: *a jam and cream sandwich* ◦ *a Victoria sandwich*

▸verb

PHRASAL VERBS **sandwich sb/sth between sb/sth** [usually passive] informal If you are sandwiched between two people or things, you are in a small space between them: *On the train I was sandwiched between two very large men.* • **sandwich sth together** to put a layer of something between two things which sticks them together: *I sandwiched the cakes together* ***with*** *chocolate butter cream.*

ˈsandwich ˌbar noun [C] UK a small shop where you can buy sandwiches, especially to eat during the working day

ˈsandwich ˌboard noun [C] a pair of connected boards which a person hangs over their shoulders and walks around with in public places to advertise something

ˈsandwich ˌcourse noun [C] UK a college course consisting of periods of study with periods of work between them so that students get practical experience

ˈsandwich geneˌration noun [S] a way of referring to the group of people who have old parents as well as young children, so they have to take care both of their parents and of their children: *She has written a play about Alzheimer's that is aimed at the sandwich generation.*

sandy /ˈsæn.di/ adj **SAND** ▷ **1** B1 covered with sand or containing sand: *a lovely sandy* ***beach*** ◦ *sandy soil* **HAIR** ▷ **2** describes hair that is a pale brownish-orange colour

sane /seɪn/ adj C2 having a healthy mind and not mentally ill, or showing good judgment and understanding: *In the doctor's opinion he was sane at the time of the murder.* ◦ humorous *The only thing which* ***keeps*** *me sane after a hard day in the office is jogging!* ◦ *It was a sane (= sensible) decision and one we all respected.*

sang /sæŋ/ verb past simple of **sing**

sangfroid /ˌsɒ̃ˈfwɑː/ (US) /ˌsɑːŋ-/ **noun** [U] formal the ability to stay calm in a difficult or dangerous situation

sangria /sæŋˈgriː.ə/ (US) /sɑːn-/ **noun** [U] a cold Spanish drink made from red wine, fruit juice, FIZZY water (= water with bubbles), and sometimes BRANDY

sanguine /ˈsæŋ.gwɪn/ adj formal (of someone or their character) positive and hoping for good things: *They are less sanguine* ***about*** *the prospects for peace.* → See also **optimistic**

sanitarium /ˌsæn.ɪˈteə.ri.əm/ (US) /-ˈter.i-/ **noun** [C] (plural **sanitariums** or **sanitaria**) US for **sanatorium**

sanitary /ˈsæn.ɪ.tᵊr.i/ (US) /-ter.i/ adj **1** clean and not dangerous for the health, or protecting health by removing dirt and waste, especially human waste: *Cholera thrives in poor sanitary* ***conditions.*** ◦ *There were only very basic sanitary facilities on the site.* ◦ *His kitchen didn't look very sanitary (= clean).* **2** describes the things used by women during their PERIOD (= blood flow each month): *sanitary protection* ◦ *disposable sanitary products*

ˈsanitary ˌfittings noun [plural] UK (US **ˈbathroom ˌfittings**) the pieces of furniture that are in a bathroom, such as a toilet, bath, etc.

ˈsanitary ˌtowel noun [C] UK (US **ˈsanitary ˌnapkin**, Australian English **ˈsanitary ˌpad**) a piece of soft material worn by a woman to absorb blood during her PERIOD (= blood flow each month)

sanitation /ˌsæn.ɪˈteɪ.ʃᵊn/ **noun** [U] the systems for taking dirty water and other waste products away from buildings in order to protect people's health: *Many illnesses in these temporary refugee camps are the result of inadequate sanitation.*

saniˈtation ˌworker noun [C] US for **dustman**

sanitize (UK usually **sanitise**) /ˈsæn.ɪ.taɪz/ verb [T] **CLEAN** ▷ **1** mainly US to make something completely clean and free from bacteria **CHANGE** ▷ **2** disapproving to change something in order to make it less strongly expressed, less harmful, or less offensive: *The military wants to allow only a sanitized* ***report/version*** *of the incident to become public.* • **sanitization** mainly US (UK usually **sanitisation**) /ˌsæn.ɪ.taɪˈzeɪ.ʃᵊn/ **noun** [U]

sanity /ˈsæn.ɪ.ti/ (US) /-ə.ṭi/ **noun** [U] the state of having a healthy mind and not being mentally ill, or showing good judgment and understanding: *He'd been behaving so strangely that they began to* ***doubt/question*** *his sanity.* ◦ *Maybe Jenny can* ***bring some*** *sanity* ***into*** *(= think and act with good judgment in) this crazy situation.* ◦ *to keep/preserve/retain your sanity*

sank /sæŋk/ verb past simple of **sink**

sans /sænz/ **preposition** old use or humorous without: *It's great to have a grown-up meal out, sans kids!*

Santa Claus /ˈsæn.təˌklɔːz/ (US) /-ṭəˌklɑːz/ **noun** [S] (informal **Santa**) the imaginary old man with long, white hair and a BEARD and a red coat who is believed by children to bring them presents at CHRISTMAS, or a person who dresses as this character for children

ˌSanta's ˈgrotto noun [S] a place where children can receive presents from a person dressed as Santa Claus

sap /sæp/ verb; noun

▸verb [T] (**-pp-**) to make someone weaker or take away strength or an important quality from someone, especially over a long period of time: *Constant criticism saps you* ***of*** *your confidence.* ◦ *Looking after her dying mother had sapped all her energy.* • **sapping** /ˈsæp.ɪŋ/ adj *sapping heat/humidity*

▸noun **LIQUID** ▷ **1** [U] the liquid that carries food to all parts of a plant: *Maple syrup is obtained from the sap of the sugar maple tree.* **PERSON** ▷ **2** [C] mainly US informal a stupid person who can easily be tricked or persuaded to do something: *He's a sap* ***for*** *(= he can easily be persuaded to buy) any new machine.*

IDIOM **the sap is rising** humorous an expression used to mean that people start to have more energy and feel more interested in love and sex, for example in spring

sapling /ˈsæp.lɪŋ/ noun [C] a young tree

Sapphic /ˈsæf.ɪk/ adj SEXUALITY ▷ literary relating to LESBIANS (= women who are sexually attracted to other women): *Sapphic love/passion*

sapphire /ˈsæf.aɪəʳ/ (US) /-aɪr/ noun **1** [C or U] a PRECIOUS STONE, usually bright blue, that is often used in jewellery: *a ring with a large sapphire* ◦ *a sapphire ring/bracelet* **2** [U] (also **sapphire blue**) bright blue • **sapphire adj** (also **sapphire blue**) *a sapphire sea*

sappy /ˈsæp.i/ adj US informal describes something that is extremely emotional in an embarrassing way: *It's a sappy film – take some tissues when you see it.*

saprophyte /ˈsæp.rə.faɪt/ noun [C] specialized an organism, such as a FUNGUS or a BACTERIUM, that lives and feeds on dead and decaying plant and animal matter

sarcasm /ˈsɑː.kæz.ᵊm/ (US) /ˈsɑːr-/ noun [U] the use of remarks that clearly mean the opposite of what they say, made in order to hurt someone's feelings or to criticize something in a humorous way: *'You have been working hard,' he said with* ***heavy*** *sarcasm, as he looked at the empty page.* → Compare **irony**

sarcastic /sɑːˈkæs.tɪk/ (US) /sɑːr-/ adj (UK informal **sarky**) (C2) using sarcasm: *a sarcastic* ***comment/remark*** ◦ *Are you being sarcastic?* • **sarcastically** /-tɪ.kᵊl.i/ adv

sarcoma /sɑːˈkəʊ.mə/ (US) /sɑːrˈkoʊ-/ noun [C or U] (plural **sarcomas** or formal **sarcomata**) specialized a type of CANCEROUS LUMP in the bones, muscles, or JOINTS (= places where two bones are connected)

sarcophagus /sɑːˈkɒf.ə.gəs/ (US) /sɑːrˈkɑː.fə-/ noun [C] (plural **sarcophagi**) a stone COFFIN, which was used in ancient times and is often decorated

sardine /sɑːˈdiːn/ (US) /sɑːr-/ noun [C] a small sea fish that can be eaten: *a tin of sardines*

IDIOM **packed/squashed like sardines** If people are packed or squashed like sardines, they are positioned very close together so that they cannot move: *We were squashed like sardines in the rush-hour train.*

sardonic /sɑːˈdɒn.ɪk/ (US) /sɑːrˈdɑː.nɪk/ adj showing little respect in a humorous but unkind way, often because you think that you are too important to consider or discuss a matter: *a sardonic smile/look/comment* • **sardonically** /-ˈdɒn.ɪ.kᵊl.i/ (US) /-ˈdɑː.nɪ.kᵊl.i/ adv

sarge /sɑːdʒ/ (US) /sɑːrdʒ/ noun [S] informal for **sergeant**: [as form of address] *I'll be there straight away, sarge.*

sari (also **saree**) /ˈsɑː.ri/ (US) /ˈsɑːr.i/ noun [C] a dress, worn especially by South Asian women, consisting of a very long piece of thin cloth wrapped around the body

sarky /ˈsɑː.ki/ (US) /ˈsɑːr-/ adj UK informal for **sarcastic**

sarnie /ˈsɑː.ni/ (US) /ˈsɑːr-/ noun [C] UK informal for a **sandwich**

sarong /səˈrɒŋ/ (US) /-ˈrɑːŋ/ noun [C] a long piece of thin cloth that is worn wrapped around the waist

SARS /ˈsɑːz/ (US) /ˈsɑːrz/ noun [U] abbreviation for Severe Acute Respiratory Syndrome: a serious infectious illness which causes difficulty in breathing and sometimes death

sarsaparilla /ˌsɑː.spəˈrɪl.ə/, /ˌsæs.pə-/ noun [U] a plant with large roots and heart-shaped leaves which climbs up walls, or a drink whose flavour comes from the root of this plant

sartorial /sɑːˈtɔː.ri.əl/ (US) /sɑːrˈtɔːr.i-/ adj [before noun] formal relating to the making of clothes, usually men's clothes, or to a way of dressing: *sartorial elegance* • **sartorially** /-i/ adv

the SAS /ˌes.eɪˈes/ noun [+ sing/pl verb] abbreviation for the Special Air Service: a part of the British Army that has been specially trained for secret or very dangerous military activities

SASE /ˌes.eɪˌesˈiː/ noun [C] US (UK **sae**) abbreviation for self-addressed stamped envelope: an envelope with a stamp and your name and address on it, which you send inside another ENVELOPE to an organization when you want a reply: *Please enclose an SASE with your application.* → Compare **sae**

sash /sæʃ/ noun [C] CLOTHING ▷ **1** a long, narrow piece of cloth worn round the waist and fastened at the back, or a strip of cloth worn over the shoulder, often with a uniform at official ceremonies WINDOW ▷ **2** a frame with a piece of glass in it, used in windows and doors

sashay /ˈsæʃ.eɪ/ (US) /sæʃˈeɪ/ verb [I + adv/prep] to walk confidently while moving your hips from side to side in a way that attracts attention

sashimi /sæʃˈiː.mi/ noun [U] a Japanese dish consisting of small pieces of uncooked fish that are eaten with SOY SAUCE

sash ˈwindow noun [C] a window that has two frames fixed one above the other that open by being moved up and down

Sasquatch /ˈsæs.kwɒtʃ/ (US) /-kwɑːtʃ/ noun [C] a **Bigfoot**

sass /sæs/ noun; verb

▸noun [U] mainly US informal talk or behaviour that is rude and shows no respect: *I don't want to hear any more of your sass.*

▸verb [T] mainly US informal to talk to someone in a rude way: *Don't you sass your father like that!*

Sassenach /ˈsæs.ə.næk/ noun [C] (plural **Sassenachs**) Scottish English mainly disapproving an English person

sassy /ˈsæs.i/ adj mainly US informal **1** rude and showing no respect: *a sassy young girl* **2** fashionable, attractive, or confident: *a sassy little black dress*

sat /sæt/ verb past simple and past participle of **sit**

Sat. written abbreviation for **Saturday**

SAT /sæt/ noun [C] UK EDUCATION ▷ **1** abbreviation for Standard Assessment Task: a test taken by children in England and Wales at various ages to find out the level of the NATIONAL CURRICULUM that they have reached: *SATs* ***results*** US EDUCATION ▷ **2** trademark abbreviation for Scholastic Aptitude Test: a test taken in the US to measure students' abilities before they go to college

Satan /ˈseɪ.tᵊn/ noun formal the name used by Christians and Jews for the DEVIL (= a powerful evil force and the enemy of God)

satanic /səˈtæn.ɪk/ adj **1** connected with worshipping Satan: *a satanic cult/practice/rite* **2** very evil: *He gave a satanic smile.*

Satanism /ˈseɪ.tᵊn.ɪ.zᵊm/ noun [U] the worship of Satan

Satanist /ˈseɪ.tᵊn.ɪst/ noun [C] a person who worships Satan

satay /ˈsæt.eɪ/ (US) /sɑːˈteɪ/ noun [U] a Southeast Asian food consisting of small pieces of meat or fish cooked on a stick, and served with a spicy PEANUT sauce: *chicken satay*

satchel /ˈsætʃ.ᵊl/ noun [C] a rectangular leather bag with a long strap, used especially in the past by children for carrying books to school

sate /seɪt/ verb [T] formal or literary to satisfy someone by giving them something that is wanted or needed:

S

He searched for a book that would sate his ***desire*** *for all the details of Olympic history.*

sated /ˈseɪ.tɪd/ (US) /-t̬ɪd/ **adj** formal having had more of something than you can easily have at one time: *sated* ***with*** *drink/food*

satellite /ˈsæt.ᵊl.aɪt/ (US) /ˈsæt̬-/ **noun** [C] **IN SPACE** ▷ **1** (B2) a device sent up into space to travel round the Earth, used for collecting information or communicating by radio, television, etc.: *The World Cup was transmitted around the world* ***by*** *satellite.* ◦ *a spy/weather satellite* ◦ *satellite television/TV* **2** a natural object moving round a larger object in space: *The moon is the satellite of the Earth.* **COUNTRY** ▷ **3** (also **satellite state**) a country controlled by or depending on a more powerful country → Compare **client state**

ˈsatellite ˌdish **noun** [C] a round AERIAL for receiving television and radio signals broadcast from satellites

sati /sæ.tiː/ (US) /ˈsɑː.tiː/ **noun** [U] **suttee**

satiate /ˈseɪ.ʃi.eɪt/ **verb** [T often passive] formal to completely satisfy yourself or a need, especially with food or pleasure, so that you could not have any more: *He drank greedily until his thirst was satiated.*

satin /ˈsæt.ɪn/ (US) /ˈsæt̬.ᵊn/ **noun** **CLOTH** ▷ **1** [U] a type of cloth, sometimes made of SILK, that is smooth and shiny on one side but not on the other: *a cream satin dress* **PAINT** ▷ **2** [S or U] (also **satin finish**) a type of paint that is slightly shiny when it dries

satiny /ˈsæt.ɪ.ni/ (US) /ˈsæt̬.ᵊn.i/ **adj** smooth and soft

satire /ˈsæt.aɪəʳ/ (US) /-aɪr/ **noun** [C or U] a way of criticizing people or ideas in a humorous way, or a piece of writing or play which uses this style: *political satire* ◦ *Her play was a* ***biting/cruel*** *satire on life in the 80s.* • **satirical** /səˈtɪr.ɪ.kᵊl/ **adj** *satirical cartoons/magazines*

satirist /ˈsæt.ɪ.rɪst/ (US) /ˈsæt̬.ɚ.ɪst/ **noun** [C] a person who writes satire

satirize (UK usually **satirise**) /ˈsæt.ɪ.raɪz/ (US) /ˈsæt̬.ə.raɪz/ **verb** [T] to use satire to show that people or ideas have bad qualities or are wrong

satisfaction /ˌsæt.ɪsˈfæk.ʃᵊn/ (US) /ˌsæt̬-/ **noun** **1** (B2) [C or U] a pleasant feeling which you get when you receive something you wanted, or when you have done something you wanted to do: *She looked at the finished painting* ***with*** *satisfaction.* ◦ *She derived/obtained great satisfaction* ***from/out of*** *helping other people.* ◦ *For me,* ***job*** *satisfaction is more important than the money.* ◦ *She* ***had*** *the satisfaction* ***of*** *know****ing*** *that she'd done everything she could.* **2** [U] formal a way of dealing with a complaint or problem which makes the person who complained feel happy: *You've sold me a faulty product and I* ***demand*** *satisfaction (= you must return my money or give me a new product).* **3** [U] the act of FULFILLING (= achieving) a need or wish: *the satisfaction* ***of*** *one's sexual desires* **4 to sb's satisfaction a** (C2) in a way that a particular person can believe or accept: *The boy explained to the satisfaction of the court why he had lied.* **b** (C2) in a way that a particular person feels pleased or satisfied with: *He won't get paid until he completes the job to my satisfaction.*

satisfactory /ˌsæt.ɪsˈfæk.tᵊr.i/ (US) /ˌsæt̬.ɪˈsfæk.tɚ-/ **adj** (B2) good or good enough for a particular need or purpose: *The teachers seem to think his work is satisfactory.* ◦ *We hope very much to find a satisfactory solution to the problem.* ◦ *The result of the match was* ***highly*** *satisfactory (= very pleasing).* • **satisfactorily** /-ᵊl.i/ **adv** (C1) *I'm sure these problems can be satisfactorily resolved.*

satisfied /ˈsæt.ɪs.faɪd/ (US) /ˈsæt̬-/ **adj** **WANTING** ▷ **1** (B1) pleased because you have got what you wanted, or because something has happened in the way that you wanted: *Some people are never satisfied!* ◦ *a satisfied smile* ◦ *Are you satisfied* ***with*** *the new arrangement?* **BELIEVING** ▷ **2** (C1) [after verb, + (that)] If you are satisfied that something is true, you believe it: *The judge was satisfied* ***(that)*** *she was telling the truth.*

satisfy /ˈsæt.ɪs.faɪ/ (US) /ˈsæt̬-/ **verb** [T] **WANTING** ▷ **1** (B2) to please someone by giving them what they want or need: *They have 31 flavours of ice cream – enough to satisfy everyone!* ◦ *Come on, satisfy my* ***curiosity*** *(= tell me what I want to know), what happened last night?* **2 satisfy conditions/needs/requirements** (C1) to have or provide something that is needed or wanted: *She satisfies all the requirements for the job.* ◦ *There are three main conditions you must satisfy if you wish to be a member of the club.* **BELIEVING** ▷ **3** to make someone believe that something is true: *His explanation satisfied the court.* ◦ [+ (that)] *I satisfied myself* ***(that)*** *I had locked the door.* ◦ formal *The authorities were satisfied* ***of*** *(= they accepted) the seriousness of his situation.*

satisfying /ˈsæt.ɪs.faɪ.ɪŋ/ (US) /ˈsæt̬-/ **adj** making you feel pleased by providing what you need or want: *a satisfying meal/result* ◦ *It's an immensely satisfying job.* ◦ ***It is*** *very satisfying* ***to*** *know that the project was a success.*

satnav /ˈsæt.næv/ **noun** [U or C] abbreviation for satellite navigation: a system of computers and SATELLITES, used in cars and other places that tell you where something is, where you are, or how to get to a place: *Many cars are now fitted with satnav.*

satsuma /ˌsætˈsuː.mə/ **noun** [C] a fruit like a small orange with skin that can be removed easily

saturate **verb; noun**

►**verb** /ˈsæt.jʊ.reɪt/ (US) /-jʊr.eɪt/ **MAKE WET** ▷ **1** [T often passive] to make something or someone completely wet: *The grass had been saturated by overnight rain.* ◦ *He had cut his leg badly, and his trousers were saturated* ***with/in*** *blood.* **FILL** ▷ **2** [T] to fill a thing or place completely so that no more can be added: *The police saturated (= a large number of police officers were sent into) the area.* **3 saturate the market** to provide too much of a product so that there is more of this product available than there are people who want to buy it: *Since the US market has now been saturated, drug dealers are looking to Europe.* • **saturation** /ˌsæt.jʊˈreɪ.ʃᵊn/ (US) /-jʊr-/ **noun** [U] *market saturation*

►**noun** [C usually plural, U] /ˈsæt.jʊ.rət/ (US) /-jʊr-/ a **saturated fat** → Compare **polyunsaturate**

saturated /ˈsæt.jʊ.reɪ.tɪd/ (US) /-jʊr.eɪ.t̬ɪd/ **adj** completely wet: *It's pouring down outside – I'm absolutely saturated!*

ˌsaturated ˈfat **noun** [C or U] (also **saturate**) a type of fat found in meat, eggs, milk, cheese, etc. that is thought to be bad for your health: *Butter and cream contain a lot of saturated fats.* → See also **monounsaturated, polyunsaturated, unsaturated**

ˌsaturated soˈlution **noun** [C] specialized in chemistry, a SOLUTION (= a liquid containing a solid) in which as much solid as possible is dissolved

saturˈation ˌbombing **noun** [U] extremely heavy bombing

saturˈation ˌpoint **noun** **reach saturation point** to reach a stage where no more can be added, contained, or accepted: *Demand for cars in the developed world will have reached saturation point within 20 years.*

Saturday /ˈsæt.ə.deɪ/ (US) /ˈsæt̬.ɚ-/ **noun** [C or U] (written abbreviation **Sat.**) (A1) the day of the week after Friday and before Sunday: *He's leaving*

on *Saturday.* ◦ *Most football matches are played* **on** *Saturdays.* ◦ *The party is* **next** *Saturday.* ◦ *We went out for a lovely meal* **last** *Saturday.* ◦ *Joel was born on a Saturday.* ◦ *Saturday* ***morning/afternoon/evening/night***

ˌSaturday night ˈspecial noun [C] US informal any small gun that is cheap, often bought illegally and used by criminals

Saturn /ˈsæt.ən/ Ⓤⓢ /ˈsæţ.ɚn/ noun [S] the planet sixth in order of distance from the Sun, after Jupiter and before Uranus

Saturnalia /ˌsæt.əˈneɪ.li.ə/ Ⓤⓢ /ˌsæţ.ɚ-/ noun [C] (plural **Saturnalia** or **Saturnalias**) **1** an ancient Roman celebration which happened on 19 December **2** literary a party where people behave in an uncontrolled way

saturnine /ˈsæt.ə.naɪn/ Ⓤⓢ /ˈsæţ.ɚ-/ adj literary serious and unfriendly: *a saturnine character/look*

satyr /ˈsæt.əʳ/ Ⓤⓢ /ˈsæţ.ɚ/ noun [C] a god in Greek literature who is half man and half GOAT

sauce /sɔːs/ Ⓤⓢ /sɑːs/ noun **THICK LIQUID** ▷ **1** Ⓐ② [C or U] a thick liquid eaten with food to add flavour: *a savoury/sweet sauce* ◦ *tomato sauce* **2** [U] US slang alcohol: *Gran's been* ***on the*** *sauce again – she's passed out in the den.* **RUDENESS** ▷ **3** [U] old-fashioned remarks that are rude or which show no respect: *That's enough of your sauce, my girl!*

saucepan /ˈsɔː.spən/ Ⓤⓢ /ˈsɑː-/ noun [C] Ⓑ① a deep, round pan with straight sides, usually with a handle and a lid, used for cooking things over heat

saucepan

saucer /ˈsɔː.səʳ/ Ⓤⓢ /ˈsɑː.sɚ/ noun [C] Ⓑ① a small, curved plate which you put a cup on: *a* ***cup and*** *saucer* ◦ *She gave the cat a saucer* ***of*** *milk (= a small amount of milk on a saucer).*

saucy /ˈsɔː.si/ Ⓤⓢ /ˈsɑː-/ adj old-fashioned rude and showing no respect, or referring to sex, especially in a humorous way: *a saucy remark/manner/look* ◦ *a saucy postcard/magazine*

sauerkraut /ˈsaʊə.kraʊt/ Ⓤⓢ /ˈsaʊr-/ noun [U] CABBAGE that has been cut into small pieces and preserved in VINEGAR

sauna /ˈsɔː.nə/ Ⓤⓢ /ˈsaʊ-/ noun [C] (a period of time spent in) a room or small building, often with wood fixed to the walls, that is heated to a high temperature, usually with steam: *have/go for/take a sauna*

saunter /ˈsɔːn.təʳ/ Ⓤⓢ /ˈsɑːn.ţɚ/ verb [I usually + adv/prep] to walk in a slow and relaxed way, often in no particular direction: *He sauntered* ***by****, looking very pleased with himself.* • **saunter** noun [S]

sausage /ˈsɒs.ɪdʒ/ Ⓤⓢ /ˈsɑː.sɪdʒ/ noun [C or U] Ⓐ② a thin, tube-like case containing meat that has been cut into very small pieces and mixed with spices: *fried/grilled pork sausages* ◦ *half a pound of garlic sausage*

IDIOM **not a sausage** UK old-fashioned humorous nothing: *'Did you find anything out?' 'No, not a sausage.'*

ˈsausage ˌdog noun [C] UK informal a DACHSHUND (= a small dog with a long body and short legs)

ˈsausage maˌchine noun [C] UK disapproving a system that deals with things or people as if they are all the same

ˈsausage ˌmeat noun [U] the meat mixture used to make sausages

ˌsausage ˈroll noun [C] UK a tube of pastry filled with sausage meat

sauté /ˈsəʊ.teɪ/ Ⓤⓢ /sɔːˈteɪ/ verb [T] to cook food in oil or fat over heat, usually until it is brown • **sauté** /ˈsəʊ.teɪ/ Ⓤⓢ /sɔːˈteɪ/ adj [before noun] *sauté potatoes*

savage /ˈsæv.ɪdʒ/ adj; verb; noun

▸adj **1** extremely violent, wild or frightening: *a savage dog/beast* ◦ *a brutal and savage* ***attack*** **2** very serious or cruel: *savage* ***criticism*** **3** very large and severe: *savage* ***cuts*** *in education spending*

▸verb [T] If an animal savages someone, it attacks them violently and badly hurts them: *The child was savaged by a dog.*

▸noun [C] offensive a person whose way of life is at a very early stage of development: *Twelve thousand years ago, our ancestors were primitive savages living in caves.*

savagely /ˈsæv.ɪdʒ.li/ adv in a violent, cruel, or very severe way

savagery /ˈsæv.ɪdʒ.ri/ noun [C or U] (acts of) cruel and violent behaviour

savannah (also **savanna**) /səˈvæn.ə/ noun [C or U] a large, flat area of land covered with grass, usually with few trees, that is found in hot countries, especially in Africa

savant /ˈsæv.ənt/ Ⓤⓢ /sævˈɑːnt/ noun [C] formal a person with a high level of knowledge or skill, especially someone who is less able in other ways: *There are musical savants who are very awkward physically – until they sit at the piano.*

save /seɪv/ verb; noun; preposition

▸verb **MAKE SAFE** ▷ **1** Ⓑ① [T] to stop someone or something from being killed, injured, or destroyed: *Wearing seat belts has saved many lives.* ◦ *He fell in the river but his friend saved him* ***from*** *drown****ing****.* ◦ *He had to borrow money to save his business.* ◦ *He was desperately trying to save their failing marriage.* ◦ *We all need to do our bit to save* ***the planet****.* ◦ *The former tennis champion was now serving to save the* ***match*** *(= to win the next point so that the other player did not win this part of the competition).* **2 save sb's life a** Ⓑ① to stop someone from being killed **b** informal to help someone escape from a difficult or unpleasant situation: *Thanks for helping me with that report – you saved my life!* **KEEP** ▷ **3** Ⓐ② [I or T] to keep something, especially money, for use in the future: *Tom's been saving his pocket money every week.* ◦ *We're saving (up)* ***for*** *a new car.* ◦ *I save all my old letters in case I want to read them again.* ◦ *Save me a place at your table, will you?* **4** Ⓐ② [T] to put information on a computer onto a computer disk **NOT WASTE** ▷ **5** Ⓑ① [I or T] to prevent time, money or effort being wasted or spent: *You'll save time if you take the car.* ◦ [+ two objects] *Thanks for your help – it saved me a lot of work.* ◦ [+ -ing verb] *I'll lend you a bag for your trip – it'll save you buy****ing*** *one specially.* ◦ informal *Can you save* ***it for later*** *(= tell me your news later when I am less busy)?* **SPORT** ▷ **6** Ⓑ② [T] in football and similar games, to stop the ball from going into the goal when a player on the other team has kicked or hit it

IDIOMS **can't do sth to save your life** informal said to mean that you are extremely bad at doing something: *I can't draw to save my life.* • **save sb's bacon/neck** informal to help someone avoid getting into trouble • **save your breath** informal used to say that it is not worth talking to someone because they will not listen to you: *I don't know why I bother speaking to him – I might as well save my breath.* • **save your own skin/hide** informal to protect yourself from danger or difficulty, without trying to help other people • **save the day** to do something that prevents a likely defeat

S

or failure: *Newcastle seemed to be heading for disaster until a late goal saved the day.* • **saved by the bell** something that you say when a difficult situation is ended suddenly before you have to do or say something that you do not want to: *Luckily my bus arrived before I had time to reply. Saved by the bell.*

PHRASAL VERBS **save on sth** to avoid using something so that you do not have to pay for it: *It was a warm winter, so we saved on electricity.* • **save (sth) up** A2 to keep money so that you can buy something with it in the future: *It took me ages to save up enough money to go travelling.* ◦ *She's saving up* **for** *a new bike.*

▸**noun** [C] in football or similar games, when a player stops the ball from going into the goal when it is hit or kicked by a player from the other team: *The goalkeeper* **made** *a great save in the last minute of the match.*

▸**preposition** (also **save for**) formal or old-fashioned but or except for: *They found all the lost documents save one.*

saver /ˈseɪ.vəʳ/ US /-vɚ/ **noun** [C] a person who saves money regularly

-saver /-seɪ.vəʳ/ US /-vɚ/ **suffix** something that makes it possible for you to use less of the stated thing: *A washing machine is a great time-saver.*

saving /ˈseɪ.vɪŋ/ **noun 1 savings** [plural] B2 the money which you keep in an account in a bank or similar financial organization: *He spent all his savings on an expensive car.* **2** C1 [C] an amount of money that you do not need to spend: *You can* **make** *huge savings (= save a lot of money) by buying food in bulk.*

-saving /-seɪ.vɪŋ/ **suffix** making it possible to use less of the stated thing: *a time-saving recipe* ◦ *a money-saving offer* ◦ *a labour-saving device*

ˌsaving ˈgrace noun [S] a good quality that something or someone has which stops them from being completely bad: *The film's* **only/one** *saving grace is the excellent photography.*

ˈsavings acˌcount noun [C] an account in a bank or similar financial organization which earns interest → Compare **current account**

ˌsavings and ˈloan asˌsociation noun [C] US for **building society**

ˈsavings ˌbank noun [C] a bank which only offers accounts where your money earns interest

saviour (US **savior**) /ˈseɪ.vjəʳ/ US /-vjɚ/ **noun** [C] **1** UK a person who saves someone from danger or harm **2 the/our Saviour** in the Christian religion, a way of referring to Jesus

ˈsaviour ˌsibling noun [C] a child who is born with particular GENES that have been chosen in order to treat an older brother or sister who has a disease

savoir-faire /ˌsæv.wɑːˈfeəʳ/ US /-ˈfer/ **noun** [U] formal the ability to do and say the right thing in any social situation: *She possesses* **great** *savoir-faire.*

savour /ˈseɪ.vəʳ/ US /-vɚ/ **verb; noun**

▸**verb** [T] UK (US **savor**) to enjoy food or an experience slowly, in order to enjoy it as much as possible: *It was the first chocolate he'd tasted for over a year, so he savoured every mouthful.*

PHRASAL VERB **savour of sth** [never passive] formal to have particular characteristics or qualities that make people think of something, especially something unpleasant: *His behaviour does rather savour of hypocrisy.*

▸**noun** [S or U] UK literary (US **savor**) **1** pleasure and interest: *She felt that life had lost most of its savour.* **2** a smell or taste, especially a pleasant one

savoury UK (US **savory**) /ˈseɪ.vᵊr.i/ US /-vɚ-/ **adj 1** Savoury food is salty or spicy and not sweet in taste: *savoury dumplings/pancakes* **2** If you say that something is not savoury, you mean that it is not pleasant or socially acceptable: *That hotel doesn't have a very savoury* **reputation**.

savoy (cabbage) /səˌvɔɪˈkæb.ɪdʒ/ **noun** [C] a type of CABBAGE with curly leaves

savvy /ˈsæv.i/ **noun** [U] informal practical knowledge and ability: *She hasn't got much savvy.* ◦ *business savvy*

saw /sɔː/ US /sɑː/ **verb; noun**

▸**verb** past simple of **see**

▸**verb** (**sawed**, **sawn** or US **sawed**) **1** [I or T] to cut wood or other hard material using a saw: *They sawed the door in half.* ◦ *He sawed through the pipe.* **2** [I + adv/prep] to move something backwards and forwards as if using a saw: *He was sawing* **away** *at his violin, making a terrible noise!*

PHRASAL VERBS **saw sth down** to make something fall to the ground by cutting it with a saw • **saw sth off** to remove something by cutting it with a saw: *She sawed off the dead branches of the tree.* • **saw sth up** to cut something into smaller pieces using a saw: *I'll saw the logs up into smaller pieces.*

▸**noun** [C] a tool with a long or round blade and a row of sharp points along one edge, used for cutting hard materials such as wood or metal: *a hand/power/chain/circular saw* → See also **fretsaw, hacksaw, jigsaw**

sawdust /ˈsɔː.dʌst/ US /ˈsɑː-/ **noun** [U] the dust and small pieces of wood that are produced when you cut wood with a saw

sawmill /ˈsɔː.mɪl/ US /ˈsɑː-/ **noun** [C] a factory where trees are cut up into pieces with machines

ˌsawn-off ˈshotgun noun [C] UK (US **ˌsawed-off ˈshotgun**) a SHOTGUN (= gun) with most of the BARREL cut off

sax /sæks/ **noun** [C] informal for **saxophone**: *alto/tenor sax* ◦ *a sax player*

Saxon /ˈsæk.sᵊn/ **adj** relating to or belonging to a people who were originally from Germany and who came to live in Britain in the fifth and sixth centuries

saxophone /ˈsæk.sə.fəʊn/ US /-foʊn/ **noun** [C] (informal **sax**) a musical instrument, usually made of metal, that is played by blowing into it to make a REED VIBRATE. They are made in different sizes.

saxophonist /sækˈsɒf.ᵊn.ɪst/ US /-ˈsɑː.fᵊn-/ **noun** [C] (informal **ˈsax ˌplayer**) someone who plays the saxophone

say /seɪ/ **verb; exclamation; noun**

▸**verb** (**said**, **said**) **SPEAK** ▷ **1** A1 [T] to pronounce words or sounds, to express a thought, opinion, or suggestion, or to state a fact or instruction: *Small children find it difficult to say long words.* ◦ *She said* **goodbye** *to all her friends and left.* ◦ *Ben never forgets to say 'Please' and 'Thank you'.* ◦ *How do you say 'goodbye' in French?* ◦ *I'm sorry, what did you say?* ◦ *Do you know what she said* **to** *him?* ◦ *What did they say* **about** *the house?* ◦ [+ speech] *'I'm going out this evening,' she said.* ◦ *He said* **to himself** *(= thought), 'This will never work.'* ◦ [+ (that)] *The doctors say* **(that)** *it will take him a few weeks to recover.* ◦ [+ question word] *She didn't say* **wh***ether she was coming.* ◦ *Did she say (= tell you)* **why** *she wasn't coming?* ◦ [+ to infinitive] informal *He said (= told me)* **to** *meet him here.* ◦ *I've got* **something** *to* say to you. ◦ *The offer was so good that I* **couldn't** *say* **no** *(= couldn't refuse).*

! Common mistake: say or tell?

When talking about the truth, lies, jokes, news, stories, or secrets, don't use 'say', use **tell**:

~~*I knew that he was saying the truth.*~~

~~*Dave is always saying jokes and funny stories.*~~

~~*I have some fantastic news to say you.*~~

THINK ▷ **2** B1 [I or T] to think or believe: [+ (that)] *People/They say* **(that)** *he's over 100.* ◦ *'It's going to be a very hot summer.'* **'So** *they say (= that is what people believe).'* ◦ *She is a firm leader, too firm,* **some might** *say (= some people believe that she is too firm).* **3** B1 [I or T] to give (as) an opinion or suggestion about something: *'Who do you think will get the job?' 'I'd rather not say.'* ◦ *What are you saying, exactly? (= What do you mean?)* ◦ [+ (that)] *We've been driving all day – I say* **(that)** *we start looking for a hotel now.* ◦ informal *What do you say we sell the car? (= What do you think about selling it?)* **4** [T] to show what you think without using words: [+ (that)] *The look on his face said (= showed)* **(that)** *he knew what had happened.* **5** B2 [T always passive] When something or someone is said to be a particular thing, that is what people think or believe about them: [+ (that)] **It** *is said* **(that)** *Latin is a difficult language to learn.* ◦ [+ to be + noun/adj] *He's said* **to be** *over 100.* **GIVE INFORMATION** ▷ **6** B1 [T] to give information in writing, numbers, or signs: *My watch says three o'clock.* ◦ *Can you read what that notice says?* ◦ [+ (that)] *It says in the paper* **(that)** *they've found the man who did it.* ◦ [+ to infinitive] *It says on the bottle* **to** *take three tablets a day.*

+ Other ways of saying say

See also: **tell**

Utter is a slightly formal word which means 'say':

He sat through the meeting without **uttering** *a word.*

Remark or **comment** can be used instead of 'say' to talk about an opinion or thought, or in formal English you could use **observe**:

He **remarked/commented** *that she was looking thin.*

'I've always found German-made cars very reliable,' he **observed**.

If someone says something, especially clearly and carefully, you could use the verb **state**:

Union members **stated** *that they were unhappy with the proposal.*

Announce or **declare** are often used when someone says something publicly:

He suddenly **announced** *in the middle of dinner that they were getting married.*

She **declared** *that it was the best chocolate cake she had ever tasted.*

Claim can be used when someone says that something is true but they cannot prove it:

He **claimed** *that he was not responsible for the accident.*

If someone says something suddenly and unexpectedly, you could use the phrase **come out with**:

Young children **come out with** *very funny things sometimes.*

If you say something although it is difficult because other people are talking too, you could use the phrasal verb **get in**:

She couldn't **get** *a word* **in** *– he just loves to talk.*

IDIOMS **before you can say Jack Robinson** old-fashioned informal used to say that something happens very quickly: *Before you could say Jack Robinson, she'd jumped into the car and driven away.* • **does what it says on the tin** UK informal If something does what it says on the tin, it does exactly what it is intended to do: *The hotel does exactly what it says on the tin and offers customers a relaxing break.* • **have a lot to say for yourself** informal disapproving to talk too much and seem to have a high opinion of yourself • **have nothing to say for yourself** informal to not be willing to take part in conversations or express your opinions • **having said that** despite what has just been said: *He forgets most things, but having said that, he always remembers my birthday.* • **I wouldn't say no** informal used to say that you would like something that is offered to you: *'Would you like another drink?' 'I wouldn't say no.'* • **I'll say!** informal used to show that you agree very strongly with what has been said: *'Does he eat a lot?' 'I'll say!'* • **it goes without saying** B2 used to mean that something is obvious: *Of course, it goes without saying* **that** *you'll be paid for the extra hours you work.* • **not say boo 1** US informal to say nothing: *You didn't say boo to me about going to your mother's this weekend.* **2** US (UK **not say boo to a goose**) to be very nervous and easily frightened • **not to say** and possibly even: *It would be unwise, not to say stupid, to leave your first job after only six months.* • **(let's) say** used to introduce a suggestion or possible example of something: *Try and finish the work by, let's say, Friday.* ◦ *Say/Let's say (= if we accept)* **(that)** *the journey takes three hours, you'll arrive at two o'clock.* • **say goodbye to sth** to accept that you will not have something any more or that you will not get it: *If Europe fails to agree on this, we can say goodbye to any common foreign policy.* • **say no more** said to show that you understand exactly what the other person is suggesting: *'I saw him coming out of her flat.' 'Say no more!'* • **say the word** used to tell someone that you will do what they want at the time when they ask you: ***You only have to/Just*** *say the word,* ***and*** *I'll come and help.* • **say this/that much for sb/sth** to say something good about someone or something considered to be bad: *I'll say this much for Kay, she always agrees to help whenever we ask her.* • **say uncle** US informal to admit failure • **say when** said when you are pouring a drink for someone and you want them to tell you when to stop pouring • **that is to say ...** or more exactly: *Our friends, that is to say our son's friends, will meet us at the airport.* • **That's not saying much.** used to show that you do not think what someone has said is special • **there's little to be said for sth** said to mean that something has disadvantages: *Personally, I think there's little to be said for such a policy.* • **there's something to be said for** (also **there's a lot to be said for**) said to mean that something has advantages: *There's a lot to be said for living alone.* • **to say nothing of ...** C2 and in addition there is: *It would be an enormous amount of work, to say nothing of the cost.* • **to say the least** C1 used to show that what you are describing is in fact much more serious or important than you have suggested: *It's going to be awkward, to say the least.* • **what sb says, goes** informal said to mean that you must do whatever a particular person says: *Around here, mate, what I say, goes!* • **what have you got to say for yourself?** used to ask someone to explain why they have done something bad: *Well, you've ruined my car – what have you got to say for yourself?* • **when all is said and done** said when you

S

are about to tell someone the most important fact they should remember in a situation: *When all is said and done, you can only do your best.* • **who can say?** no one knows: *'Is it possible?' 'Who can say?'* • **you can say that again!** used to show that you completely agree with what someone has said • **you can't say fairer than that** UK informal used to say that you think an offer or arrangement is good • **you don't say!** informal used either to express surprise or lack of surprise in a humorous and slightly unkind way: *'He's lost his job.' 'You don't say!'* • **you said it!** informal used to say that you agree with what has just been said: *'How stupid of me to lend him that money!' 'You said it!'*

▸**exclamation** used to express surprise or pleasure, or to attract attention to what you are about to say: US *Say, that's really good of you!* ◦ US *Say, how about going out tonight?* ◦ UK old-fashioned or humorous ***I say**, what a splendid hat you're wearing!*

▸**noun** [S or U] (the right to give) an opinion about something: *Can't you keep quiet for a minute and let me **have** my say.* ◦ *The judge usually has the final say.*

IDIOM **have a, some, etc. say in sth** to be involved in making a decision about something: *When he's 18, he'll begin to have a/some say in the running of the family business.* ◦ *The staff had little/no say in the restructuring of the company.*

saying /ˈseɪ.ɪŋ/ **noun** [C] C1 a well-known and wise statement, which often has a meaning that is different from the simple meanings of the words it contains: *As the saying **goes**, 'Don't count your chickens before they're hatched'.*

ˈsay-so noun [S] informal **STATEMENT** ▷ **1** a statement made by someone without proof: *Don't just believe it **on** my say-so – find out for yourself.* **PERMISSION** ▷ **2** an instruction to do something, or permission given by someone to do something: *She's not allowed to do anything without her father's say-so.*

ˈS-bend noun [C usually singular] a bend in a road that is in the shape of the letter S

scab /skæb/ **noun SKIN COVERING** ▷ **1** [C] a rough surface made of dried blood that forms over a cut or broken skin while it is HEALING → Compare **scar 2** [U] a plant or animal disease which causes rough areas on the skin **WORKER** ▷ **3** [C] informal disapproving an insulting word for a person who continues working while other people in the organization are on STRIKE

S

scabbard /ˈskæb.əd/ US /-ɚd/ **noun** [C] a long, thin cover for the blade of a SWORD, usually fixed to a belt

scabby /ˈskæb.i/ **adj** covered in scabs or scab: *a scabby knee* ◦ *scabby potatoes*

scabies /ˈskeɪ.biːz/ **noun** [U] a skin disease which causes your skin to become rough and uncomfortable

scabrous /ˈskeɪ.brəs/ **adj** literary offensive or shocking, because describing or showing sex

scads /skædz/ **noun** [plural] US informal a large number or amount: *He earns scads **of** money.*

scaffold /ˈskæf.əʊld/ US /-foʊld/ **noun** [C] **1** a structure made of scaffolding for workers to stand on when they want to reach high parts of a building **2** a flat raised structure on which criminals are punished by having their heads cut off or by being hanged with a rope around the neck until they die

scaffolding /ˈskæf.əl.dɪŋ/ **noun** [U] a structure of metal poles and wooden boards put against a building for workers to stand on when they want to reach the higher parts of the building: *Scaffolding has been **erected** around the tower and repair work will start next week.*

scaffolding

scalability /ˌskeɪ.ləˈbɪl.ɪ.ti/ US /-ə.t̬i/ **noun** [U] specialized the ability of a business or system to grow larger: *There are doubts about the profitability and the scalability of the company's web business.*

scalable /ˈskeɪ.lə.bl/ **adj** specialized used to describe a business or system that is able to grow or to be made larger: *To receive this funding the schools will have to demonstrate that their idea is scalable from school level to state level.*

scalar /ˈskeɪ.ləʳ/ US /-lɚ/ **noun** [C] specialized something that has size but no direction, such as a quantity, distance, speed, or temperature → Compare **vector** • **scalar adj** *a scalar **quantity***

scalawag /ˈskæl.ɪ.wæg/ **noun** [C] US also for **scallywag**

scald /skɔːld/ US /skɑːld/ **verb; noun**

▸**verb** [T] **1** to burn the skin with boiling liquid or steam: *I dropped a pan of boiling water and scalded my leg.* **2** to put something in boiling water or steam in order to make it completely clean: *Scald the needles to sterilize them.* **3** specialized to heat a liquid until it almost boils: *Scald the milk and then add it to the egg and sugar mixture.*

▸**noun** [C] an injury to the skin caused by boiling liquid or steam

scalding /ˈskɔːl.dɪŋ/ US /ˈskɑːl-/ **adj LIQUID** ▷ **1** If a liquid is scalding, it is extremely hot: *scalding tea* ◦ *scalding hot water* **CRITICISM** ▷ **2** If criticism is scalding, it is very strong or violent.

scale /skeɪl/ **noun; verb**

▸**noun MEASURE** ▷ **1** B2 [C] a set of numbers, amounts, etc., used to measure or compare the level of something: *the Centigrade/Fahrenheit scale* ◦ *How would you rate his work **on a** scale **of** 1 to 5?* **2** B2 [C or U] the relation between the real size of something and its size on a map, model, or DIAGRAM: *a scale of 1:50,000* ◦ *This map is **large** scale (= things are shown in detail).* ◦ *Is the bridge drawn **to** scale (= so that it shows the exact shape of the bridge, but much smaller)?* ◦ *He was building a scale **model** of Concorde.* **SIZE** ▷ **3** B2 [S or U] the size or level of something, especially when this is large: *We don't yet know the scale **of the problem**.* ◦ *Nuclear weapons cause destruction **on** a massive scale (= cause a lot of destruction).* ◦ *My parents used to entertain friends **on a large/small** scale (= they had large/small parties).* **MACHINE** ▷ **4 scales** [plural] UK (US **scale**) B2 a device for weighing things or people: ***kitchen/bathroom** scales* **5 a pair of scales** UK a weighing device with two containers connected to a metal bar that is free to move up and down about its fixed central point. An object of known weight is put in one container and the thing to be weighed is put in the other. **MUSIC** ▷ **6** [C] a set of notes played or sung in order, going up or down: *the scale of G major* ◦ *You must practise your scales every day.* **SKIN** ▷ **7** [C usually plural] one of the many very small, flat pieces that cover the skin of fish, snakes, etc. **COVERING** ▷ **8** [U] (UK also **limescale**) a hard, white or grey layer of material that forms on the inside of pipes or containers that heat water

IDIOMS **large/small-scale** describes an event or activity that is large/small in size: *a large-scale investigation* • **the scales fall from sb's eyes** literary If the scales fall from your eyes, you suddenly know and understand the truth.

▸verb [T] CLIMB ▷ **1** to climb up a steep surface, such as a wall or the side of a mountain, often using special equipment: *The prisoner scaled the high prison wall and ran off.* CLEAN TEETH ▷ **2** specialized to remove TARTAR (= hard white substance) and PLAQUE (= soft substance in which bacteria breed) from teeth: *The dentist scaled and polished my teeth last week.*

IDIOM **scale the heights** If you scale the heights of a type of work, you are very successful in it: *At the age of 35, she had already scaled the heights* ***of*** *the acting profession.*

PHRASAL VERBS **scale sth down** (mainly US **scale sth back**) to make something smaller than it was or smaller than it was planned to be: *A shortage of money has forced them to scale down the project.* • **scale sth up** to increase the size, amount, or importance of something, usually an organization or process: *My company is scaling up its operations in the Middle East.*

ˌscaled-ˈdown adj [before noun] reduced in size or extent: *a scaled-down version/plan*

scalene triangle /ˌskeɪ.liːnˈtraɪ.æŋ.gl/ noun [C] specialized a triangle with three sides all of different lengths → Compare **equilateral, isosceles triangle**

scallion /ˈskæl.i.ən/ noun [C] US for **spring onion**

scallop /ˈskɒl.əp/ (US) /ˈskɑː.ləp/ noun [C] a sea creature that lives inside two joined flat, round shells and can be eaten

scallywag informal humorous (US usually **scalawag**) /ˈskæl.i.wæg/ noun [C] someone, especially a child, who has behaved badly but who is still liked

scalp /skælp/ noun; verb

▸noun [C] TOP OF HEAD ▷ **1** the skin on the top of a person's head where hair usually grows: *a dry/oily/itchy scalp* ◦ *Some tribes used to collect scalps to prove how many of the enemy they had killed in battle.* DEFEATED PERSON ▷ **2** someone you defeat in a competition or election: *Although they are expected to* ***take*** *some important scalps in the election, they are unlikely to form the next government.*

IDIOM **be out for/after sb's scalp** to want to defeat or punish someone in some way, especially to make them lose their job: *He's made one mistake too many, and now they're out for his scalp.*

▸verb [T] SELL ▷ **1** US informal to buy things, such as theatre tickets, at the usual prices and then sell them, when they are difficult to get, at much higher prices HEAD ▷ **2** to cut off the scalp of a dead enemy **3** humorous to cut someone's hair very short

scalpel /ˈskæl.pᵊl/ noun [C] a very sharp knife that is used for cutting through skin and flesh during an operation

scalper /ˈskæl.pər/ (US) /-pɚ/ noun [C] US informal someone who buys things, such as theatre tickets, at the usual prices and then sells them, when they are difficult to get, at much higher prices: *A scalper offered me a $10 ticket for the final match for $70.*

scaly /ˈskeɪ.li/ adj SKIN ▷ **1** If skin is scaly, it has small, hard, dry areas which fall off in small pieces: *I get scaly patches on my scalp.* COVERING ▷ **2** If the inside of a pipe or container that heats water is scaly, it is covered in a hard white or grey layer of material. • **scaliness** /-nəs/ noun [U]

scam /skæm/ noun [C] informal an illegal plan for making money: *an insurance scam*

scamp /skæmp/ noun [C] old-fashioned a child that behaves badly in a way that is funny rather than serious

scamper /ˈskæm.pər/ (US) /-pɚ/ verb [I + adv/prep] When small children and animals scamper, they run with small quick steps: *The children scampered* ***off*** *into the garden.*

scampi /ˈskæm.pi/ noun [U, + sing/pl verb] large PRAWNS (= small sea creatures that can be eaten) that are usually fried

scan /skæn/ verb; noun

▸verb (-nn-) LOOK ▷ **1** (C2) [T] to look at something carefully, with the eyes or with a machine, in order to get information: *She anxiously scanned the faces of the men leaving the train.* ◦ *Doug scanned* ***the horizon for*** *any sign of the boat.* **2** (C1) [I + adv/prep, T] to look through a text quickly in order to find a piece of information that you want or to get a general idea of what the text contains: *I scanned* ***through*** *the booklet but couldn't find the address.* ◦ *Scan the newspaper article quickly and make a note of the main points.* MAKE PICTURE ▷ **3** (C1) [I or T] to use a machine to put a picture of a document into a computer, or to take a picture of the inside of something: *I'll just scan the article into the computer.* ◦ *Volunteers' brains were scanned while they looked at the pictures.* ◦ *All hand luggage has to be scanned.* POEM ▷ **4** [I] specialized If a poem or part of a poem scans, it follows a pattern of regular beats: *This line doesn't scan – it's got too many syllables.*

▸noun **1** [S] a careful or quick look through something: *I gave the book a quick scan, and decided not to buy it.* **2** (C2) [C] a medical examination in which an image of the inside of the body is made using a special machine: *to do a brain scan* ◦ *to have an ultrasound scan*

scandal /ˈskæn.dᵊl/ noun **1** (B2) [C or U] (an action or event that causes) a public feeling of shock and strong moral disapproval: *a financial/political/****sex*** *scandal* ◦ *Their affair* ***caused/created*** *a scandal in the office.* ◦ *The scandal* ***broke*** *(= became public knowledge) right at the beginning of the Conservative Party Conference.* ◦ *If there is the slightest* ***suggestion/hint*** *of scandal, the public will no longer trust us.* **2** [U] reports about actions or events that cause shock and disapproval: *Some magazines contain nothing but scandal and gossip.* ◦ *to spread scandal* **3** [S] a situation that is extremely bad: [+ (that)] ***It's*** *a scandal* ***(that)*** *children could be treated in this way.*

scandalize (UK usually **scandalise**) /ˈskæn.dᵊl.aɪz/ verb [T often passive] If you are scandalized by someone's behaviour, you disapprove of it and are shocked by it because you think it is against moral laws.

scandalmonger /ˈskæn.dᵊlˌmʌŋ.gər/ (US) /-gɚ/ noun [C] disapproving a person who creates or spreads reports about actions and events that cause public shock and disapproval

scandalous /ˈskæn.dᵊl.əs/ adj making people shocked and upset: *scandalous stories* ◦ ***It's*** *scandalous* ***that*** *we do so little to prevent homelessness.* • **scandalously** /-li/ adv *scandalously expensive (= so expensive that it is annoying)*

Scandinavian /ˌskæn.dɪˈneɪ.vi.ən/ noun [C], adj (a person) coming from Sweden, Norway, or Denmark

scanner /ˈskæn.ər/ (US) /-ɚ/ noun [C] a device for making images of the inside of the body or for reading information into a computer system: *an ultrasound scanner* ◦ *bar code scanners*

scansion /ˈʃkæn.ʃᵊn/ noun [U] specialized the rhythm

S

of a line of poetry, or the process of examining the rhythm of a line of poetry

scant /skænt/ **adj** [before noun] very little and not enough: *He pays scant* ***attention*** *to the needs of his children.* ∘ *scant* ***regard*** *for the truth*

scantily /ˈskæn.tɪ.li/ (US) /-t̬ɪ-/ **adv** **scantily clad, dressed, etc.** wearing very little clothing: *scantily clad dancers*

scanty /ˈskæn.ti/ (US) /-t̬i/ **adj** smaller in size or amount than is considered necessary or is hoped for: *scanty evidence/information*

-scape /-skeɪp/ **suffix** used to form nouns referring to a wide view of a place, often one represented in a picture: *landscape* ∘ *seascape* ∘ *cityscape*

scapegoat /ˈskeɪp.ɡəʊt/ (US) /-ɡoʊt/ **noun** [C] a person who is blamed for something that someone else has done: *The captain was* ***made*** *a scapegoat* ***for*** *the team's failure.*

scapula /ˈskæp.jʊ.lə/ **noun** [C] (plural **scapulae** or **scapulas**) specialized for **shoulder blade**

scar /skɑːʳ/ (US) /skɑːr/ **noun; verb**

▸**noun** [C] **1** B2 a mark left on part of the body after an injury, such as a cut, has HEALED: *a prominent/noticeable/ugly scar* ∘ *That burn will* ***leave*** *a nasty scar.* ∘ *scar* ***tissue*** → Compare **scab 2** C1 a sign of damage to a person's mental state: *His early years in the refugee camp* ***left*** *a deep* ***psychological*** *scar.* **3** a sign of physical destruction in a place: *Every village* ***bears*** *the scars* ***of*** *war.*

▸**verb** [T often passive] (-rr-) C2 to leave a scar: *He was scarred as a result of the fire.* ∘ figurative *His experiences in the army left him scarred* ***for life*** *(= had a serious mental effect on him for the rest of his life).*

scarce /skeəs/ (US) /skers/ **adj** C1 not easy to find or get: *Food and clean water were becoming scarce.* ∘ *scarce resources*

IDIOM **make yourself scarce** informal to go away from a difficult situation in order to avoid trouble: *Dad's really angry with you, so you'd better make yourself scarce.*

scarcely /ˈskeəs.li/ (US) /ˈskers-/ **adv** **ONLY JUST** ▷ **1** C2 (literary **scarce**) only just or almost not: *I was scarcely able to move my arm after the accident.* ∘ *I* ***could*** *scarcely* ***believe*** *it when she said she wanted to marry me.* **2** used to say that something happened immediately after something else happened: *I had scarcely sat down/Scarcely had I sat down to eat* ***when*** *the phone rang.* **NOT** ▷ **3** certainly not: *I'd scarcely have done it if I didn't think it was absolutely necessary!* ∘ *He's only two – you can scarcely blame him for behaving badly.*

scarcity /ˈskeə.sɪ.ti/ (US) /ˈsker.sə.t̬i/ **noun** [U] C2 a situation in which something is not easy to find or get: *the scarcity* ***of*** *skilled workers*

scare /skeəʳ/ (US) /sker/ **verb; noun**

▸**verb** [I or T] C1 to (make a person or animal) feel frightened: *Sudden noises scare her.* ∘ *She's very brave – she doesn't scare easily.* ∘ *He scared me* ***out of*** *my* ***wits*** *(= made me extremely frightened) when he was driving so fast.* ∘ *Meeting new people scares me* ***stiff/to death*** *(= makes me extremely nervous and worried).* ∘ *She scared* ***the hell/life/living daylights out of*** *me (= frightened me very much) when she fell out of the tree.*

IDIOM **scare sb shitless** offensive to make someone extremely frightened

PHRASAL VERBS **scare sb/sth away/off** C1 to make a person or an animal so frightened that they go away: *Don't make too much noise or you'll scare away the birds.* ∘ *She scared off her attacker by screaming.* • **scare sb away/off** C1 to make someone so worried about doing something that they decide not to do it: *If you charge as much as that, you'll scare customers off.* • **scare sb into doing sth** to persuade someone to do something by frightening them: *The two boys scared the old man into handing over his wallet.* • **scare sth up** US informal to find or get something despite difficulties or limited supplies: *There's hardly any food in the house, but I'll scare something up* ***from*** *these leftovers.*

▸**noun 1** [S] a sudden feeling of fear or worry: *I* ***got/had*** *a scare (= I was very worried) when I looked at my bank statement this morning!* ∘ *You* ***gave*** *us a real scare (= frightened us) when you fainted, you know.* **2** [C] an occasion when a subject receives a lot of public attention and worries many people, often when there is no real danger: *a* ***bomb/health*** *scare* ∘ *The government are accused of employing scare* ***tactics*** *(= ways of frightening people in order to persuade them to do something).* ∘ *The press have been publishing scare* ***stories*** *(= newspaper reports which make people feel unnecessarily worried) about the mystery virus.*

scarecrow

scarecrow /ˈskeə.krəʊ/ (US) /ˈsker.kroʊ/ **noun** [C] a model of a person dressed in old clothes and put in a field of growing crops to frighten birds away

scared /skeəd/ (US) /skerd/ **adj** B1 frightened or worried: *He's scared* ***of*** *spiders.* ∘ *I'm scared* ***of*** *telling her what really happened.* ∘ *He's scared* ***to*** *tell her what really happened.* ∘ *I was scared (= very worried) (****that****) you might not be there.* ∘ *I was scared* ***stiff*** *(= extremely frightened).* ∘ *She had a scared look on her face.*

> ✚ Other ways of saying **scared**
>
> Other common ways of saying 'scared' are **afraid** and **frightened**.
>
> If someone is extremely scared, then you can use the adjectives **petrified, terrified, panic-stricken**, or the informal phrase **scared to death**:
>
> *I'm* ***petrified/terrified*** *of spiders.*
>
> *She was* ***panic-stricken*** *when her little boy disappeared.*
>
> *He's* ***scared to death*** *of having the operation.*
>
> If someone is scared because of worrying about something, then you can use adjectives like **afraid** or **worried**:
>
> *I'm* ***afraid/worried*** *that something will go wrong.*
>
> To talk about things that make you feel uncomfortable and scared, you could use the idiom **give me the creeps**:
>
> *Being alone in that big house* ***gives me the creeps.***

scaredy-cat /ˈskeə.di.kæt/ (US) /ˈsker-/ **noun** [C] child's expression someone, especially a child, who is easily frightened: *Come on, scaredy-cat – it won't bite you!*

scaremonger /ˈskeəˌmʌŋ.ɡəʳ/ (US) /ˈskerˌmʌŋ.ɡɚ/ **noun** [C] disapproving a person who spreads stories that cause public fear • **scaremongering** /-ɪŋ/ **noun** [U]

scarf /skɑːf/ (US) /skɑːrf/ **noun; verb**
▸**noun** [C] (plural **scarves** or **scarfs**) A2 a strip, square, or triangle of cloth, worn around the neck, head, or shoulders to keep you warm or to make you look attractive: *a knitted/woollen/silk scarf*
▸**verb** [T] US for **scoff**

scarlatina /ˌskɑː.ləˈtiː.nə/ (US) /ˌskɑːr-/ **noun** [U] specialized for **scarlet fever**

scarlet /ˈskɑː.lət/ (US) /ˈskɑːr-/ **noun** [U], **adj** bright red: *scarlet berries* ◦ *He **went** scarlet with shame.*

ˌscarlet ˈfever **noun** [U] (specialized **scarlatina**) an infectious illness of children which causes a sore throat, a high body temperature, and red spots on the skin

ˌscarlet ˈwoman **noun** [C] old-fashioned disapproving a woman who is considered to be IMMORAL because she has sex with a lot of men

scarper /ˈskɑː.pəʳ/ (US) /ˈskɑːr.pɚ/ **verb** [I] UK slang to leave very quickly, often to avoid getting into trouble: *The police are coming! We'd better scarper.*

SCART /skɑːt/ (US) /skɑːrt/ **noun** [U] trademark a system for connecting AUDIO-VISUAL equipment (= televisions, DVD players, etc.) that uses a CONNECTOR with 21 pins and a SOCKET with 21 holes: *a SCART **socket/connector***

scary informal (UK also **scarey**) /ˈskeə.ri/ (US) /ˈsker.i/ **adj** B1 frightening: *a scary movie/story*

scat /skæt/ **exclamation; noun**
▸**exclamation** informal said to an animal, especially a cat, or to a person to make them go away quickly
▸**noun** [U] a type of JAZZ singing that uses words with no meaning

scathing /ˈskeɪ.ðɪŋ/ **adj** criticizing someone or something in a severe and unkind way: *scathing **criticism*** ◦ *He was very scathing **about** the report, saying it was inaccurate.* • **scathingly** /-li/ **adv** *She spoke scathingly of the poor standard of work done by her predecessor.*

scatological /ˌskæt.əˈlɒdʒ.ɪ.kəl/ (US) /ˌskæţ.əˈlɑː.dʒɪ-/ **adj** solid human waste: *scatological humour*

scatter /ˈskæt.əʳ/ (US) /ˈskæţ.ɚ/ **verb** **MOVE** ▷ **1** [I or T] to (cause to) move far apart in different directions: *The protesters scattered at the sound of gunshots.* ◦ *The soldiers came in and scattered the crowd.* **COVER** ▷ **2** [T usually + adv/prep] to cover a surface with things that are far apart and in no particular arrangement: *Scatter the powder **around** the plants.* ◦ *I scattered grass seed all **over** the lawn.* ◦ *I scattered the whole lawn **with** grass seed.*

IDIOM **be scattered to the four winds** literary If a group of things or people are scattered to the four winds, they go or are sent to different places that are far away from each other.

scatterbrain /ˈskæt.ə.breɪn/ (US) /ˈskæţ.ɚ-/ **noun** [C] a person who forgets things easily or does not think seriously about things: *I'm such a scatterbrain – I'm always leaving my umbrella behind.* • **scatterbrained** /-breɪnd/ **adj**

ˈscatter ˌdiagram **noun** [C] specialized a GRAPH with points representing amounts or numbers on it, often with a line joining the points

scattered /ˈskæt.əd/ (US) /ˈskæţ.ɚd/ **adj** C2 covering a wide area: *Toys and books were scattered **about/around** the room.* ◦ *My family is scattered **all over** the world.* ◦ *The forecast is for scattered **showers** (= separate areas of rain) tomorrow.*

scattering /ˈskæt.ᵊr.ɪŋ/ (US) /ˈskæţ.ɚ-/ **noun** [C usually singular] a small number or amount of things in a particular area: *a scattering **of** houses*

scatty /ˈskæt.i/ (US) /ˈskæţ-/ **adj** UK informal silly and often forgetting things: *a scatty child* ◦ *scatty behaviour*

scavenge /ˈskæv.ɪndʒ/ **verb** [I or T] **1** to look for or get food or other objects in other people's rubbish: *The flood has left villagers and animals desperately scavenging **for** food.* ◦ *We managed to scavenge a lot of furniture **from** the local rubbish dump.* **2** If a wild animal scavenges, it feeds on the flesh of dead decaying animals.

scavenger /ˈskæv.ɪn.dʒəʳ/ (US) /-dʒɚ/ **noun** [C] a bird or animal which feeds on dead animals which it has not killed itself

scenario /sɪˈnɑː.ri.əʊ/ (US) /səˈner.i.oʊ/ **noun** [C] (plural **scenarios**) **POSSIBLE EVENT** ▷ **1** C2 a description of possible actions or events in the future: *There are several possible scenarios.* ◦ *a **horrific/nightmare** scenario such as a Third World War* → See also **worst-case scenario** **PLAN** ▷ **2** a written plan of the characters and events in a play or film

scene /siːn/ **noun** **THEATRE/FILM** ▷ **1** B1 [C] a part of a play or film in which the action stays in one place for a continuous period of time: *the funeral/wedding scene* ◦ *nude/sex scenes* ◦ *Juliet dies in Act IV, Scene iii.* **VIEW** ▷ **2** B2 [C] a view or picture of a place, event, or activity: *Lowry painted street scenes.* ◦ *scenes of everyday life* ◦ figurative *There were scenes **of** great joy as the hostages were re-united with their families.* **PLACE** ▷ **3** B2 [C usually singular] a place where an unpleasant event has happened: *The police arrived to find a scene **of** horrifying destruction.* ◦ *Evidence was found at the scene **of the crime**.* **AREA** ▷ **4** B2 [S] a particular area of activity and all the people or things connected with it: *the pop/political/drugs/gay scene* ◦ *Rap music **arrived/came/appeared on** the scene in the early 1980s.* ◦ informal *I'd rather go to a jazz concert – I'm afraid opera isn't really my scene (= is not the type of thing I like).* **ARGUMENT** ▷ **5** C2 [C] an expression of great anger or similar feelings, often between two people, or an occasion when this happens: *Please don't **make** a scene.* ◦ *There was a terrible scene and Jayne ended up in tears.*

IDIOMS **be on the scene** to arrive: *I phoned the police and they were on the scene within minutes.* • **behind the scenes** C2 If something happens behind the scenes, it happens without most people knowing about it, especially when something else is happening publicly: *A lot of hard work has been going on behind the scenes.* • **set the scene** **1** to describe a situation where something is about to happen: *First, let's set the scene – it was a dark, wet night with a strong wind blowing.* **2** to make something possible or likely to happen: *His resignation set the scene **for** a pre-election crisis.*

scenery /ˈsiː.nᵊr.i/ (US) /-nɚ-/ **noun** [U] **COUNTRYSIDE** ▷ **1** B1 the general appearance of the natural environment, especially when it is beautiful: *beautiful/breathtaking/spectacular scenery* ◦ *They stopped at the top of the hill to **admire** the scenery.* **THEATRE** ▷ **2** the large painted pictures used on a theatre stage to represent the place where the action is

IDIOM **blend into the scenery** to behave in the same way as people around you, so that you are not noticed

sceneshifter /ˈsiːnˌʃɪf.təʳ/ (US) /-tɚ/ **noun** [C] a person who changes the scenery in a theatre

scenic /ˈsiː.nɪk/ **adj** C1 having or allowing you to see beautiful natural features: *an area of outstanding*

S

scenic beauty ◦ *a scenic drive/railway* ◦ *We* ***took the*** *scenic* ***route*** *home.*

scent /sent/ **noun; verb**

▸**noun 1** B2 [C] a pleasant natural smell: *the scent of roses* **2** [C] a smell produced by an animal which acts as a signal to other animals: *The hounds had* ***lost*** *the scent of the fox near the river.* **3** [C or U] a pleasant-smelling liquid that people put on their skin: *a bottle of scent* → Synonym **perfume**

IDIOMS **on the scent** close to discovering: *'We're on the scent* ***of*** *something big,' said the police chief.* • **throw/put sb off the scent** to give someone false or confusing information to prevent them from discovering something that you do not want them to know about

▸**verb** [T] **1** If an animal scents something or someone, it knows they are there because it can smell them. **2** If a person scents something, they have a feeling that they are about to experience it: *Halfway through the match, the team could already scent* ***victory****.*

IDIOM **scent blood** to believe that someone you are competing against is having difficulties and to use this to get an advantage for yourself: *The manager has already made some serious errors of judgment and it is clear that other employees scent blood.*

scented /ˈsen.tɪd/ US /-t̬ɪd/ **adj** having a pleasant strong smell: *scented notepaper* ◦ *The air was scented* ***with*** *lavender.*

sceptic UK (US **skeptic**) /ˈskep.tɪk/ **noun** [C] a person who doubts the truth or value of an idea or belief: *People say it can cure colds, but I'm a bit of a sceptic.* ◦ *to convince the sceptics*

sceptical UK (US **skeptical**) /ˈskep.tɪ.kəl/ **adj** C2 doubting that something is true or useful: *Many experts* ***remain*** *sceptical* ***about/of*** *his claims.* • **sceptically** (US **skeptically**) /-kəl.i/ **adv** • **scepticism** (US **skepticism**) /-sɪ.zəm/ **noun** [U] *The company's environmental claims have been* ***greeted/regarded/treated with*** *scepticism by conservationists.*

sceptre UK (US **scepter**) /ˈsep.tər/ US /-tə/ **noun** [C] a decorated stick that is carried by a queen or king during some official ceremonies as a symbol of their authority

Schadenfreude /ˈʃɑː.dənˌfrɔɪ.də/ **noun** [U] a feeling of pleasure or satisfaction when something bad happens to someone else

S

schedule /ˈʃed.juːl/ US /ˈsked-/ **noun; verb**

▸**noun** [C] **1** B2 a list of planned activities or things to be done showing the times or dates when they are intended to happen or be done: *a production schedule* ◦ *a hectic/tight (= very busy) schedule* ◦ *Everything went* ***according to*** *schedule (= as had been planned).* **2** B1 US (UK **timetable**) a list of the times when events are planned to happen, especially the times when buses, trains, and planes leave and arrive **3** formal an official list of things: *a schedule* ***of*** *business expenses* **4 ahead of schedule** B2 early: *We expect the building work to be completed ahead of schedule.* **5 on schedule** B2 not early or late **6 fall behind schedule** to do less work than you planned to do by a particular point in time

▸**verb** [T often passive] B2 to arrange that an event or activity will happen at a particular time: *The* ***meeting*** *has been scheduled* ***for*** *tomorrow afternoon.* ◦ [+ to infinitive] *The train is scheduled* ***to*** *arrive at 8.45, but it's running 20 minutes late.* • **scheduled** /-juːld/ **adj** B2 *This program will be broadcast half an hour later than the scheduled time.*

ˈ**scheduled** ˌ**flight** **noun** [C] B2 a regular flight organized by the company which owns the aircraft

scheduler /ˈʃed.juː.lər/ US /ˈsked.juː.lə/ **noun** [C] a person who works for a broadcasting company putting the various programmes for the day, week, month, etc. into a particular order

schema /ˈskiː.mə/ **noun** [C] (plural **schemata** or **schemas**) specialized a drawing that represents an idea or theory and makes it easier to understand

schematic /skɪˈmæt.ɪk/ US /-ˈmæt̬-/ **adj** showing the main form and features of something, usually in the form of a drawing, which helps people to understand it: *a schematic diagram/outline* • **schematically** /-ɪ.kəl.i/ **adv**

scheme /skiːm/ **noun; verb**

▸**noun** [C] **1** B2 mainly UK an officially organized plan or system: *a training/housing/play scheme* ◦ *a pension/savings scheme* ◦ *There's a new scheme in our town* ***for*** *recycling plastic bottles.* ◦ *Class sizes will increase* ***under*** *the new scheme.* **2** a plan for getting an advantage for yourself, especially by deceiving others: *He's got a* ***hare-brained/crazy/daft*** *scheme* ***for*** *getting rich before he's 20.*

> Word partners for **scheme** noun
>
> *come up with/create/develop/devise/hatch* a scheme • *implement/introduce/launch/unveil* a scheme • a *crazy/harebrained/ill-conceived* scheme • a scheme *for* sth • *under* a scheme • a scheme *whereby*

IDIOM **the scheme of things** the way things are organized or happen in a particular situation, or the way someone wants them to be organized: *I was disappointed not to get the job, but it's not that important in the* ***great/grand*** *scheme of things (= when all things are considered).*

▸**verb** [I or T] disapproving to make clever secret plans which often deceive others: *All her ministers were scheming* ***against*** *her* ◦ [+ to infinitive] *For months he had been scheming* ***to*** *prevent her from getting the top job.* • **schemer** /ˈskiː.mər/ US /-mə/ **noun** [C] disapproving *He's a schemer who always finds a way of getting what he wants.* • **scheming** /ˈskiː.mɪŋ/ **adj** disapproving *a secretive and scheming politician*

scherzo /ˈskeət.səʊ/ US /ˈskert.soʊ/ **noun** [C] (plural **scherzos**) a fast and happy piece of music for instruments, often part of a longer piece

Schilling /ˈʃɪl.ɪŋ/ **noun** [C] the standard unit of money used in Austria before the euro

schism /ˈskɪz.əm/, /ˈsɪz-/ **noun** [C] a division into two groups caused by a disagreement about ideas, especially in a religious organization: *a schism* ***in/within*** *the Church*

schist /ʃɪst/ **noun** [U] specialized a type of rock that breaks easily into thin layers, formed of MICA or other minerals

schizo /ˈskɪt.səʊ/ US /-soʊ/ **noun** [C] (plural **schizos**) informal disapproving a person with very strange and usually violent or threatening behaviour

schizoid /ˈskɪt.sɔɪd/ **adj** specialized suffering from or behaving as if suffering from schizophrenia: *a schizoid personality*

schizophrenia /ˌskɪt.səˈfriː.ni.ə/ **noun** [U] **1** a serious mental illness in which someone cannot understand what is real and what is imaginary: *paranoid schizophrenia* **2** informal behaviour in which a person appears to have two different personalities

schizophrenic /ˌskɪt.səˈfren.ɪk/ **noun** [C] someone

who suffers from schizophrenia • **schizophrenic** adj • **schizophrenically** /-ɪ.kəl.i/ adv

schlep /ʃlep/ verb; noun
▸verb [I or T, + adv/prep] (-pp-) (also **schlepp**) mainly US informal to move yourself or an object with effort and difficulty: *Do I really have to schlep all that junk down to the cellar?*
▸noun [S] (also **schlepp**) mainly US informal something that takes a lot of effort to do: *It's a real schlep getting it all home.*

schlock /ʃlɒk/ US /ʃlɑːk/ noun [U] mainly US informal disapproving goods or artistic works that are cheap or low in quality: *markets selling schlock ◦ schlock TV shows* • **schlocky** /ˈʃlɒk.i/ US /ˈʃlɑː.ki/ adj

schlub /ʃlʌb/ noun [C] US informal someone who is stupid or not attractive

schmaltz (also **schmalz**) /ʃmɒlts/ US /ʃmɑːlts/ noun [U] informal disapproving artistic works, such as music or writing, that are intended to cause strong sad or romantic feelings but have no real artistic value: *Her second album was pure schmaltz.* • **schmaltzy** (also **schmalzy**) /ˈʃmɒlt.si/ US /ˈʃmɑːlt-/ adj

schmooze /ʃmuːz/ verb [I] informal to talk informally with someone, especially in a way that is not sincere or to win some advantage for yourself: *He spent the entire evening schmoozing **with** the senator.*

schmuck /ʃmʌk/ noun [C] mainly US informal a stupid or silly person: *Her husband is such a schmuck!*

schnapps /ʃnæps/ noun [C or U] a clear, strong alcoholic drink made in eastern and northern parts of Europe, usually from grain, potato, or fruit

schnitzel /ˈʃnɪt.səl/ noun [C or U] a thin slice of meat, usually VEAL (= young cow) that is covered in egg and very small pieces of bread before being fried

schnozzle (also **shnozzle**) /ˈʃnɒz.l/ US /ˈʃnɑː.zl/ noun (also **schnozz** /ʃnɒz/ US /ʃnɑːz/) **NOSE** ▷ **1** [C] informal humorous a person's nose **DRUG** ▷ **2** [U] slang **cocaine**

scholar /ˈskɒl.əʳ/ US /ˈskɑː.lɚ/ noun [C] **1** C1 a person who studies a subject in great detail, especially at a university: *a classics/history scholar ◦ Dr Miles was a **distinguished** scholar **of** Russian history.* **2** informal someone who is clever or good at learning by studying: *David's never been much of a scholar.*

scholarly /ˈskɒl.ə.li/ US /ˈskɑː.lɚ-/ adj **1** containing a serious, detailed study of a subject: *a scholarly article/book/work/journal* **2** describes someone who studies a lot and knows a lot about what they study: *a scholarly young woman*

scholarship /ˈskɒl.ə.ʃɪp/ US /ˈskɑː.lɚ-/ noun **1** [U] serious, detailed study: *a work of great scholarship* **2** C1 [C] an amount of money given by a school, college, university, or other organization to pay for the studies of a person with great ability but little money: *He **got/won** a scholarship **to** Eton. ◦ Paula went to the Royal College of Music **on** a scholarship.*

scholastic /skəˈlæs.tɪk/ adj relating to school and education: *scholastic achievements* • **scholastically** /-tɪ.kəl.i/ adv

school /skuːl/ noun; verb
▸noun **EDUCATION** ▷ **1** A1 [C or U] a place where children go to be educated: *a primary/secondary school ◦ Milton Road School ◦ They're building a new school in the village. ◦ She drives the kids to school every morning.* ◦ UK *I was **at** school **with** (= I went to the same school at the same time as) Luke's brother. ◦ Is Emily **in** school today or is she still ill? ◦ Which school do you **go to** (formal **attend**)? ◦ school meals/uniform ◦ school buildings/fees* **2** A1 [U] the period of your life during which you go to school, or the teaching and learning activities which happen at school: *British children **start/begin** school at the age of four or five. ◦ What do you want to do when you **leave** school (= finish studying at school)? ◦ I love/hate school.* ◦ US *My sister **teaches** school (= teaches children in a school) in New York City.* **3** A2 [U] the time during the day when children are studying in school: *before/after school ◦ School starts at 9 a.m. and finishes at 3.30 p.m.* **4** [C + sing/pl verb] all the children and teachers at a school: *The whole school is/are delighted about Joel's success in the championships.* **5** [C or U] a part of a college or university specializing in a particular subject or group of subjects: *the School of Oriental and African Studies ◦ She went to medical school in Edinburgh.* **6** A2 [C] a place where people, especially adults, can study a particular subject either some of the time or all of the time: *a driving/dancing school ◦ the London Business School* **7** B1 [U] US for **university**: *We first met at **graduate** school (= while doing a university course for a second or third degree).* **GROUP** ▷ **8** [C, + sing/pl verb] a group of painters, writers, poets, etc. whose work is similar, especially similar to that of a particular leader: *the Flemish School ◦ the Impressionist school **of** painting* **SEA CREATURES** ▷ **9** [C, + sing/pl verb] a large number of fish or other sea creatures swimming in a group: *a school of dolphins/whales*

> **Word partners for school**
> *attend/go to* school • *begin/leave/start* school • *expel* sb *from/play truant from/skip* school • *teach at* a school • a school *assembly/bus/dinner/report*

IDIOMS **school of hard knocks** If you learn something in the school of hard knocks, you learn it as a result of difficult or unpleasant experiences. • **school/university of life** humorous all the good and bad experiences that you have in your life and that you learn from

▸verb [T] formal **1** to train a person or animal to do something: *It takes a lot of patience to school a dog/horse.* ◦ [+ to infinitive] *You must school yourself **to** be tolerant.* **2** [T often passive] to teach a child: *Her children are **well** schooled **in** correct behaviour.*

schoolboy /ˈskuːl.bɔɪ/ noun; adj
▸noun [C] a boy who goes to school
▸adj [before noun] like a child's: *I must say I find his schoolboy **humour** rather tiresome.*

schoolchild /ˈskuːl.tʃaɪld/ noun [C] (plural **schoolchildren**) (informal **schoolkid**) A2 a child who goes to school: *We just sat there giggling like **naughty** schoolchildren.*

schooldays /ˈskuːl.deɪz/ noun [plural] the period of your life that you spend at school

schoolgirl /ˈskuːl.gɜːl/ US /-gɝːl/ noun [C] a girl who goes to school

schoolhouse /ˈskuːl.haʊs/ noun [C] mainly US a building used as a school, especially in a village

schooling /ˈskuː.lɪŋ/ noun [U] C2 education at school: *Jack didn't **receive** much **formal** schooling.*

ˌschool-ˈleaver noun [C] UK a young person who is about to leave or has just left SECONDARY school

ˈschool-ˌleaving ˌage noun [U] UK the lowest age at which a person can leave school

schoolmarm /ˈskuːl.mɑːm/ US /-mɑːrm/ noun [C] **1** disapproving a very formal and severe woman who likes to control other people and is easily shocked **2** mainly US old-fashioned a female school teacher

schoolmarmish /ˈskuːlˌmɑː.mɪʃ/ US /-ˌmɑːr-/ adj disapproving behaving like a schoolmarm

S

schoolmaster /ˈskuːlˌmɑː.stəʳ/ (US) /-ˌmæs.tɚ/ noun [C] old-fashioned a man who teaches children in a school

schoolmate /ˈskuːl.meɪt/ noun [C] a friend who is at the same school as you at the same time

schoolmistress /ˈskuːlˌmɪs.trəs/ noun [C] old-fashioned a woman who teaches children in a school

ˈschool ˌnight noun [C] an evening before a day when children have to go to school and adults have to go to work: humorous *I don't usually drink wine on a school night.*

ˌschool of ˈthought noun [C] a set of ideas or opinions which a group of people share about a matter: *There are several schools of thought about how the universe began.*

ˈschool ˌrun noun [C usually singular] UK the time when parents drive their children to or from school: *Next week it's my turn to* ***do*** *the school run.*

schoolteacher /ˈskuːlˌtiː.tʃəʳ/ (US) /-tʃɚ/ noun [C] someone who teaches children in a school

schoolwork /ˈskuːl.wɜːk/ (US) /-wɝːk/ noun [U] studying done by a child at school or at home

schoolyard /ˈskuːl.jɑːd/ (US) /-jɑːrd/ noun [C] mainly US an outside area next to a school where children can play games or sport when they are not studying

schooner /ˈskuː.nəʳ/ (US) /-nɚ/ noun [C] a sailing ship with two or more MASTS and with its SAILS parallel to the length of the ship, rather than across it

schwa (also **shwa**) /ʃwɑː/ noun [C] the weak vowel sound in some syllables that is not emphasized, such as the first syllable of 'about' and the second syllable of 'given', or the ə symbol that represents this sound

sciatica /saɪˈæt.ɪ.kə/ (US) /-ˈæt̬-/ noun [U] pain in the lower part of the back and the back of the legs

science /saɪəns/ noun **1** (A2) [U] (knowledge from) the careful study of the structure and behaviour of the physical world, especially by watching, measuring, and doing EXPERIMENTS, and the development of theories to describe the results of these activities: *pure/applied science ◦ recent developments in science and technology ◦ Space travel is one of the marvels/wonders of modern science.* **2** (B1) [C or U] a particular subject that is studied using scientific methods: *physical sciences ◦ Economics is not an* ***exact*** *science. ◦ advances in* ***medical*** *science* **3** (A2) [U] the study of science: *a science graduate/teacher ◦ a science course/lesson*

S

ˌscience ˈfiction noun [U] (informal ˈ**sci-fi**, also **SF**) (B1) books, films, or CARTOONS about an imagined future, especially about space travel or other planets

ˈscience ˌpark noun [C] mainly UK an area, often started or supported by a college or university, where companies involved in scientific work and new TECHNOLOGY are based

scientific /ˌsaɪənˈtɪf.ɪk/ adj **1** (B1) relating to science, or using the organized methods of science: *a scientific discovery/experiment/theory ◦ scientific data/evidence/research ◦ The project has attracted considerable criticism from* ***the*** *scientific* ***community*** *(= from scientists).* **2** careful and using a system or method: *We will have to adopt a more scientific* ***approach*** *in the future. ◦ I try to arrange things in some kind of a system, but I'm not very scientific* ***about*** *it.* • **scientifically** /-ɪ.kᵊl.i/ adv

scientist /ˈsaɪən.tɪst/ noun [C] (B1) an expert who studies or works in one of the sciences: *a research/nuclear scientist*

sci-fi /ˈsaɪ.faɪ/ noun [U] informal for **science fiction**

scimitar /ˈsɪm.ɪ.təʳ/ (US) /-t̬ɚ/ noun [C] a SWORD with a curved blade that is sharp only on its outer edge and gets wider towards its pointed end

scintilla /sɪnˈtɪl.ə/ noun formal **a scintilla of sth** a very small amount of something: *There's* ***not*** *a scintilla of truth in what he says.*

scintillating /ˈsɪn.tɪ.leɪ.tɪŋ/ (US) /-tᵊl.eɪ.t̬ɪŋ/ adj funny, exciting, and clever: *scintillating wit/repartee/conversation ◦ a scintillating personality/speech*

scion /ˈsaɪ.ən/ noun [C] literary a young member of a rich and famous family: *He's the scion* ***of*** *a very wealthy newspaper-publishing family.*

scirocco /sɪˈrɒk.əʊ/ (US) /ʃɪˈrɑː.koʊ/ noun [C] a **sirocco**

scissor /ˈsɪz.əʳ/ (US) /-ɚ/ adj [before noun] relating to or like scissors: *a scissor blade*

scissors /ˈsɪz.əz/ (US) /-ɚz/ noun [plural] (A2) a device used for cutting materials such as paper, cloth, and hair, consisting of two sharp blades that are joined in the middle, and two handles with holes to put your fingers through: *a pair of scissors ◦ Could you pass me the/those scissors, please.*

IDIOM **scissors and paste** mainly disapproving If something such as a piece of writing is a scissors and paste job, it is not original, but is made up from parts of other people's work.

sclera /ˈsklɪə.rə/ (US) /ˈsklɪr.ə/ noun [C usually sing] specialized the white layer that covers the outside of the eye

sclerosis /skləˈrəʊ.sɪs/ (US) /-ˈroʊ-/ noun [U] specialized a medical condition which causes body tissue or organs to become harder, especially the ARTERIES (= thick tubes carrying blood from the heart) • **sclerotic** /-ˈrɒt.ɪk/ (US) /-ˈrɑː.t̬ɪk/ adj specialized *sclerotic arteries* ◦ figurative disapproving *The tax cuts are designed to bring growth to a sclerotic (= very slowly developing and not easily changed) economy.*

scoff /skɒf/ (US) /skɑːf/ verb **LAUGH** ▷ **1** [I] to laugh and speak about a person or idea in a way which shows that you think they are stupid or silly: *The critics scoffed* ***at*** *his paintings. ◦ Years ago people would have scoffed* ***at*** *the idea that cars would be built by robots.* **EAT** ▷ **2** [T] (US also **scarf**) to eat something quickly and eagerly: *I baked a huge cake this morning, and the kids scoffed the lot.* • **scoff** noun [C usually plural] *Despite the scoffs of her colleagues, the experiment was completely successful.* • **scoffer** /ˈskɒf.əʳ/ (US) /ˈskɑː.fɚ/ noun [C usually plural] *I was able to prove the scoffers wrong.*

scold /skəʊld/ (US) /skoʊld/ verb [T] old-fashioned to tell off someone because you disapprove of their behaviour: *His mother scolded him* ***for*** *breaking her favourite vase.* • **scolding** /ˈskəʊl.dɪŋ/ (US) /ˈskoʊl-/ adj • **scolding** /ˈskəʊl.dɪŋ/ (US) /ˈskoʊl-/ noun [C] *He* ***gave*** *his son a scolding* ***for*** *coming home so late.*

sconce /skɒns/ (US) /skɑːns/ noun [C] specialized a device that is fixed to a wall to hold electric lights or candles

scone /skɒn/ (US) /skoʊn/ noun [C] a small, round cake like bread, made from flour, milk, and a little fat: *tea and buttered scones*

scoop /skuːp/ noun; verb

▸noun [C] **TOOL** ▷ **1** a tool with a deep bowl-shaped end that is used to dig out and move a soft substance or powder: *a measuring scoop ◦ an ice-cream scoop* **2** the amount held by a scoop: *Just one scoop of mashed potato for me, please.* **NEWS** ▷ **3** a story or piece of news discovered and published by one newspaper before all the others: *The paper managed to secure a major scoop and broke the scandal to the world.*

▸verb [T] **TOOL** ▷ **1** to move something with a scoop or with something used as a scoop: *He scooped the sand* *into a bucket with his hands.* **WIN** ▷ **2** to get a large number of votes or prizes: *The socialist party is expected to scoop* ***up*** *the majority of the working-class vote.* **NEWS** ▷ **3** to be the first newspaper to discover and print an important news story: *Just as we were about to publish the story, we were scooped by a rival paper.*

IDIOM **scoop the pool** UK informal to win all the prizes that are available: *Cuba scooped the pool in the boxing at this year's Olympics.*

PHRASAL VERBS **scoop sth out** to remove something that is inside something else with a spoon: *Cut the tomato in half and scoop out the seeds.* • **scoop sth/sb up** to lift something or someone with your hands or arms in a quick movement: *She scooped the children up and ran with them to safety.* ◦ *I scooped up my belongings into my handbag.*

ˌscoop-ˈneck adj describes a piece of women's clothing that is cut low around the neck in a U-shape

scoot /skuːt/ verb **1** [I usually + adv/prep] informal to go quickly: *I'm scooting* ***off*** *to St Andrews for a few days' golf.* ◦ *I'll have to scoot (= leave quickly) or I'll miss my train.* **2** [I + adv/prep] US informal to slide while sitting: *Scoot over and make room for your sister.*

scooter /ˈskuː.təʳ/ US /-t̬ɚ/ noun [C] **TOY** ▷ **1** A2 a child's vehicle with two or three small wheels joined to the bottom of a narrow board and a long vertical handle fixed to the front wheel. It is ridden by standing with one foot on the board and pushing against the ground with the other foot. **MOTORCYCLE** ▷ **2** a **motor scooter**

scope /skəʊp/ US /skoʊp/ noun; verb

▸noun [U] **RANGE** ▷ **1** C1 the range of a subject covered by a book, programme, discussion, class, etc.: *I'm afraid that problem is* ***beyond/outside the*** *scope* ***of*** *my lecture.* ◦ *Oil painting does not come* ***within the*** *scope* ***of*** *a course of this kind.* ◦ *We would now like to* ***broaden/widen the*** *scope* ***of*** *the enquiry and look at more general matters.* **OPPORTUNITY** ▷ **2** C2 the opportunity for doing something: *There is limited scope* ***for*** *further reductions in the workforce.*

▸verb

PHRASAL VERB **scope sth/sb out** US informal to look carefully to see if something or someone is interesting or attractive: *We scoped out the local shops and facilities to see if it would be a good place to rent a flat.*

-scope /-skəʊp/ US /-skoʊp/ suffix used to form nouns that refer to devices for looking at or discovering and measuring things: *a microscope* ◦ *a telescope* • **-scopic** /-skɒp.ɪk/ US /-skɑː.pɪk/ suffix used to form adjectives: *a telescopic lens*

scorch /skɔːtʃ/ US /skɔːrtʃ/ verb **BURN** ▷ **1** [I or T] to (cause to) change colour with dry heat, or to burn slightly: *The iron was too hot and he scorched the shirt.* ◦ *The surrounding buildings were scorched by the heat of the explosion.* **DRIVE FAST** ▷ **2** [I usually + adv/prep] old-fashioned informal (especially of motorcycles and cars) to travel or be driven very fast: *The sports car scorched* ***past*** *and disappeared into the distance.* • **scorch** noun [C] *The fire left scorch* ***marks*** *halfway up the wall.*

scorched /skɔːtʃt/ US /skɔːrtʃt/ adj slightly burned, or damaged by fire or heat: *The countryside was scorched after several weeks of hot sun.*

ˌscorched-ˈearth ˌpolicy noun [C usually singular] the act of an army destroying everything in an area such as food, buildings, or equipment that could be useful to an enemy

scorcher /ˈskɔː.tʃəʳ/ US /ˈskɔːr.tʃɚ/ noun [C] informal an extremely hot and SUNNY day: *Yesterday was a real scorcher.*

scorching /ˈskɔː.tʃɪŋ/ US /ˈskɔːr-/ adj, adv (also **ˌscorching ˈhot**) very hot: *a scorching summer day* ◦ *It was scorching* ***hot*** *inside the greenhouse.*

score /skɔːʳ/ US /skɔːr/ verb; noun

▸verb **WIN** ▷ **1** B1 [I or T] to win or get a point, goal, etc. in a competition, sport, game, or exam: *Tennant scored (a* ***goal****) in the last minute of the match.* ◦ *In American football, a touchdown scores (= is worth) six points.* ◦ *She scored 18 out of 20 in the spelling test.* **2** [I or T] to succeed in an activity or to achieve something: *She has certainly scored (****a success****) with her latest novel.* ◦ *Nearly every bomb scored* ***a hit****.* ◦ *You have a lot of patience – that's where you score* ***over*** *(= are better than) your opponents.* **3** [I] UK to record the number of points won by competitors: *We need someone to score for tomorrow's match.* **GET** ▷ **4** [T] US informal to get something: *I managed to score a couple of tickets to the World Cup final.* **5** [I or T] slang to get illegal drugs: *She tried to score some dope in a nightclub.* **6** [I] slang If someone scores, they have sex with someone that they have usually just met: *Did you score last night, then?* **MARK** ▷ **7** [T] to make a mark or cut on the surface of something hard with a pointed tool, or to draw a line through writing: *If you score the tile first, it will be easier to break.* → See also **underscore** **MUSICAL TEXT** ▷ **8** [T] to write or change a piece of music for particular instruments or voices: *This piece is scored* ***for*** *strings and woodwind.*

IDIOM **score points off/over sb** to make clever remarks in order to make someone look silly: *He's always trying to score points over people and it's really irritating.*

PHRASAL VERB **score sth out/through** to draw a line through a piece of writing: *He scored out two names on the list.*

▸noun **WIN** ▷ **1** B1 [C] (plural **scores**) the number of points, goals, etc. achieved in a game or competition: *a* ***high/low*** *score* ◦ *Have you heard the latest cricket score?* ◦ *At half time, the score* ***stood at*** *(= was) two all.* ◦ *The* ***final*** *score was 3–0.* ◦ *Could you* ***keep*** *(= record) the score at this afternoon's match?* **MUSIC** ▷ **2** [C] (plural **scores**) a piece of written music showing the parts for all the instruments and voices: *an orchestral score* **3** [C] (plural **scores**) the music written for a film, play, etc.: *a film score* ◦ *Rodgers wrote the score* ***for/of/to*** *'Oklahoma!'.* **ARGUMENT** ▷ **4** [C] (plural **scores**) an argument or disagreement that has existed for a long time: *It's time these* ***old*** *scores were forgotten.* **TWENTY** ▷ **5** [C usually singular] (plural **score**) formal 20 or approximately 20: *He lived to be three score years and ten (= until he was 70 years old).* **6 by the score** formal in large numbers: *People are leaving the Nationalist Party by the score.* **7 scores** [plural] a lot of things or people: *Benjamin received cards from scores* ***of*** *local well-wishers.* **SUBJECT JUST MENTIONED** ▷ **8 on this/that score** C2 about the thing or subject that has just been mentioned: *I'll let you have the money, so there's nothing to worry about on that score.*

> **Word partners for score noun**
>
> *keep* score • *even/level/tie* the score • the score *stands at* sth • a *good/high/impressive/top* score • an *average/low* score • the *final/latest* score • a score *of* sth

IDIOMS **settle a score** to punish someone for something wrong that they did to you in the past and that

S

you cannot forgive: *Police believe the killer was a gang member settling a score with a rival gang.* • **what's the score?** informal used to ask someone about what is going to happen, especially when arrangements have been confused: *What's the score, then – are they coming?*

scoreboard /ˈskɔː.bɔːd/ ⓤⓢ /ˈskɔːr.bɔːrd/ **noun** [C] a large board on which the score of a game is shown

scorecard /ˈskɔː.kɑːd/ ⓤⓢ /ˈskɔːr.kɑːrd/ **noun** [C] a small card for recording the score while watching or taking part in a game, race, or competition

scoreless /ˈskɔː.ləs/ ⓤⓢ /ˈskɔːr-/ **adj** In a scoreless game, no goals or points are scored: *After a scoreless first half, United went on to win 2–0.* ◦ *a scoreless* ***draw***

scoreline /ˈskɔː.laɪn/ ⓤⓢ /skɔːr-/ **noun** [C] the score achieved by the players in a game or competition: *The final scoreline was 5–3.*

scorer /ˈskɔː.rəʳ/ ⓤⓢ /ˈskɔːr.ɚ/ **noun** [C] **1** (US usually **scorekeeper**) the person who records the score in a game **2** someone who scores a point or goal in a game

scorn /skɔːn/ ⓤⓢ /skɔːrn/ **noun; verb**

▸**noun** [U] a very strong feeling of no respect for someone or something that you think is stupid or has no value: *She* ***has nothing but*** *scorn* ***for*** *the new generation of politicians.* ◦ *Why do you always* ***pour/heap*** *scorn* ***on*** *(= criticize severely and unfairly) my suggestions?*

▸**verb** [T] **1** to show scorn for someone or something: *So does he respect the press and media, or does he secretly scorn them?* ◦ *You scorned all my suggestions.* **2** to refuse advice or an offer because you are too proud: *She scorned all my offers of help.*

scornful /ˈskɔːn.fəl/ ⓤⓢ /ˈskɔːrn-/ **adj** showing or feeling scorn for someone or something: *a scornful look/remark/laugh/tone* ◦ *They are openly scornful* ***of*** *the new plans.* • **scornfully** /-i/ **adv**

Scorpio /ˈskɔː.pi.əʊ/ ⓤⓢ /ˈskɔːr.pi.oʊ/ **noun** [C or U] (plural **Scorpios**) the eighth sign of the ZODIAC, relating to the period 23 October to 21 November and represented by a scorpion, or a person born during this period

scorpion /ˈskɔː.pi.ən/ ⓤⓢ /ˈskɔːr-/ **noun** [C] a small creature similar to an insect that lives in hot, dry areas of the world and has a long body and a curved tail with a poisonous STING (= pointed part that can go through skin)

S

Scot /skɒt/ ⓤⓢ /skɑːt/ **noun** [C] **1** a person who comes from Scotland **2 the Scots** [plural] the people of Scotland

scotch /skɒtʃ/ ⓤⓢ /skɑːtʃ/ **verb** [T] formal to prevent something from being believed or being done: *Her remarks were intended to scotch rumours of an imminent election date.*

Scotch /skɒtʃ/ ⓤⓢ /skɑːtʃ/ **adj; noun**

▸**adj** (of products) of or from Scotland

▸**noun** [C or U] a type of WHISKY (= a strong alcoholic drink) made in Scotland: *a bottle of Scotch* ◦ *I'll have a Scotch (= a glass of Scotch).*

ˌScotch ˈbroth **noun** [U] a thick soup which usually contains BEEF, vegetables, and BARLEY

ˌScotch ˈegg **noun** [C] a boiled egg that has been covered with a mixture of crushed meat, spices, and bread, and then fried

ˌScotch ˈmist **noun** [U] a mixture of FOG and light rain

ˌScotch ˈtape **noun** [U] US trademark → **Sellotape**

scot-ˈfree **adv** without receiving the deserved or expected punishment or without being harmed: *The court* ***let*** *her* ***off*** *scot-free.*

Scotland Yard /ˌskɒt.lənd ˈjɑːd/ ⓤⓢ /ˌskɑːt.lənd ˈjɑːrd/ **noun** [+ sing/pl verb] the main office of the London police force, or the officers who work there, especially those involved in solving serious crimes: *Scotland Yard have/has been* ***called in*** *to investigate the murder.*

Scots /skɒts/ ⓤⓢ /skɑːts/ **adj; noun**

▸**adj** (also **Scottish**) of or from Scotland, used especially of people: *His wife is Scots* ◦ *a Scots accent* ◦ *Scots Gaelic*

▸**noun** [U] a language spoken in Scotland that is related to English, but has some important differences: *My grandparents still speak broad Scots at home.*

Scotsman /ˈskɒt.smən/ ⓤⓢ /ˈskɑːt-/ **noun** [C] (plural **-men** /-mən/) a man who comes from Scotland

Scotswoman /ˈskɒtˌswʊm.ən/ ⓤⓢ /ˈskɑːt-/ **noun** [C] (plural **-women**) a woman who comes from Scotland

Scottish /ˈskɒt.ɪʃ/ ⓤⓢ /ˈskɑː.t̬ɪʃ/ **adj** (also **Scots**) relating to Scotland: *Scottish dancing/music*

scoundrel /ˈskaʊn.drəl/ **noun** [C] old-fashioned or humorous a person, especially a man, who treats other people very badly and has no moral principles

scour /skaʊəʳ/ ⓤⓢ /skaʊ.ɚ/ **verb** [T] **CLEAN** ▷ **1** (also **scour out**) to remove dirt from something by rubbing it hard with something rough: *You'll have to scour out those old cooking pots before you use them.* **SEARCH** ▷ **2** to search a place or thing very carefully in order to try to find something: *The police are scouring the countryside* ***for*** *the missing child.* ◦ *I scoured the shops* ***for*** *a blue and white shirt, but I couldn't find one anywhere.* • **scour noun** [S]

PHRASAL VERB **scour sth out** to make a hole by a movement that is repeated continuously over a long period of time: *The fast-moving water had scoured out a channel in the rock.*

scourge /skɜːdʒ/ ⓤⓢ /skɝːdʒ/ **noun** [C usually singular] something or someone that causes great suffering or a lot of trouble: *the scourge* ***of*** *war* ◦ *AIDS has been described as the scourge* ***of*** *the modern world.*

ˈscouring ˌpad **noun** [C] (UK also **scourer** /ˈskaʊə.rəʳ/ ⓤⓢ /ˈskaʊ.ɚ.ɚ/) a small ball or rectangle of wire or stiff plastic NETTING (= material in the form of a net) that is used to clean dirt off surfaces

Scouse /skaʊs/ **noun; adj**

▸**noun** UK informal **PERSON** ▷ **1** [C] (also **Scouser**) a person who comes from the Liverpool area, in northwest England **LANGUAGE** ▷ **2** [U] the form of English spoken by a person from Liverpool

▸**adj** UK informal of the form of English spoken by a person from Liverpool

scout /skaʊt/ **noun; verb**

▸**noun** [C] **SOLDIER** ▷ **1** a person, especially a soldier, sent out to get information about where the enemy are and what they are doing **SEARCH** ▷ **2** a person employed to look for people with particular skills, especially in sport or entertainment: *a* ***talent*** *scout* ◦ *Manchester United's chief scout spotted him when he was playing for his school football team.* **3 a scout around/round** [S] informal a quick look around a place or area, especially in order to find something: *I had* ***a*** *quick scout around the house to check everything was okay.*

▸**verb** [I or T, usually + adv/prep] to go to look in various places for something you want: *He's scouting* ***about/around for*** *somewhere better to live.* ◦ *She's opened an office in Connecticut to scout* ***out*** *(= discover information about) the east coast housing market.*

Scout /skaʊt/ **noun** [C] **1** a boy or girl who is a member of the Scouts: *a group of Scouts* ◦ *a new Scout leader/troop* **2 the Scouts** [plural] UK (US **the Boy/Girl Scouts**) an international organization which encourages young people of all ages to take part in activities outside and to become responsible and independent → Compare **the Guides**

ˈScout ˌleader noun [C] (US also **Scoutmaster**, UK also **Scouter**) the adult leader of a group of Scouts

scowl /skaʊl/ verb [I] to look at someone or something with a very annoyed expression: *The boy scowled* ***at*** *her and reluctantly followed her back into school.* • **scowl** noun [C]

scrabble /ˈskræb.l̩/ verb [I + adv/prep] **1** to use your fingers to quickly find something that you cannot see: *He was scrabbling about* ***in*** *the sand searching for the ring.* **2** to try to get something quickly that is not easily available: *The government is scrabbling* ***around*** *for ways to raise revenue without putting up taxes.*

Scrabble /ˈskræb.l̩/ noun [U] trademark a game played on a board covered in squares in which players win points by creating words from letters with different values and connecting these words with ones already on the board

scraggly /ˈskræg.li/ adj mainly US informal growing in a way that is untidy and uneven: *long scraggly hair*

scraggy /ˈskræg.i/ adj disapproving very thin, especially so that the bones stick out: *He was wearing a high-necked pullover to hide his scraggy* ***neck***.

scram /skræm/ verb [I] (-mm-) informal to go away quickly: *Get out of here! Go on, scram!*

scramble /ˈskræm.bl̩/ verb; noun

▸verb **MOVE QUICKLY** ▷ **1** Ⓒ [I usually + adv/prep] to move or climb quickly but with difficulty, often using your hands to help you: *She scrambled* ***up*** *the steep hillside and* ***over*** *the rocks.* ◦ *He scrambled* ***into*** *his clothes (= put them on quickly) and raced to fetch a doctor.* ◦ *As the burning plane landed, the terrified passengers scrambled* ***for*** *the door (= tried to reach the door quickly).* **2** [I] to compete with other people for something there is very little of: [+ to infinitive] *People are scrambling* ***to*** *buy property before prices rise even further.* **CHANGE SIGNAL** ▷ **3** [T] to change a radio or phone signal so that it can only be understood using a special device **TAKE OFF** ▷ **4** [I or T] specialized to (cause a plane to) take off very quickly: *A helicopter was scrambled within minutes of the news.* **MIX** ▷ **5** [T] to mix eggs with a little milk and mix again as they are being fried

▸noun **CLIMBING** ▷ **1** [S] a climb that is difficult so that you have to use your hands to help you: *It was* ***a*** *real scramble to the top of the hillside.* **2** [S] an act of hurrying: [+ to infinitive] *As soon as the plane landed there was* ***a*** *mad/wild scramble* ***to*** *get out.* **QUICK MOVEMENT** ▷ **3** [S] a hurried attempt to get something: *After the death of the dictator there was* ***an*** *unseemly scramble* ***for*** *power among the generals.*

ˌscrambled ˈeggs noun [plural] eggs mixed with a little milk and mixed again as they are being fried: *scrambled eggs on toast*

scrambler /ˈskræm.bləʳ/ ⓤⓢ /-blɚ/ noun [C] an electronic device that scrambles radio or phone messages

scrambling /ˈskræm.blɪŋ/ noun [U] **motocross**

scrap /skræp/ verb; noun

▸verb (-pp-) **THROW AWAY** ▷ **1** Ⓒ [T] to not continue with a system or plan: *They're considering scrapping the tax and raising the money in other ways.* ◦ *We scrapped our* ***plans*** *for a trip to France.* **2** Ⓒ [T] to get rid of something that is no longer useful or wanted, often using its parts in new ways: *Hundreds of nuclear weapons have been scrapped.* **ARGUMENT** ▷ **3** [I] to have a fight or an argument

▸noun **METAL** ▷ **1** Ⓒ [U] old cars and machines or

pieces of metal, etc. that are not now needed but have parts that can be used to make other things: *scrap iron/****metal*** ◦ *We've sold our old car* ***for*** *scrap.* **SMALL PIECE** ▷ **2** Ⓒ [C] a small piece of something or a small amount of information: *Have you got a scrap* ***of*** *paper I could write on?* ◦ *I've read* ***every*** *scrap of information I can find on the subject.* ◦ *There's* ***not a*** *scrap* ***of*** *(= no) evidence to suggest that he committed the crime.* **3 scraps** [plural] small pieces of food that have not been eaten and are usually thrown away: *We give all our scraps to our cat.* **ARGUMENT** ▷ **4** [C] a fight or argument, especially a quick, noisy one about something not important: *A couple of kids were* ***having*** *a scrap in the street.*

scrapbook /ˈskræp.bʊk/ noun [C] a book with empty pages where you can stick newspaper articles, pictures, etc. which you have collected and want to keep

scrape /skreɪp/ verb; noun

▸verb **REMOVE** ▷ **1** [T] to remove an unwanted covering or a top layer from something, especially using a sharp edge or something rough: [+ obj + adj] *Scrape your boots clean before you come in.* ◦ *We'll have to scrape the snow* ***off*** *the car before we go out in it.* ◦ *Emily scraped* ***away*** *the dead leaves to reveal the tiny shoot of a new plant.* **RUB** ▷ **2** [I or T, usually + adv/prep] to (cause to) rub against a surface so that slight damage or an unpleasant noise is produced: *Jackie fell over and scraped her knee (****on*** *the pavement).* ◦ *I was woken up by the noise of branches scraping* ***against*** *my bedroom window.* **SUCCEED** ▷ **3** [I usually + adv/prep] to succeed in getting or achieving something, but only just or with great difficulty: *She scraped* ***into*** *university on very low grades.*

IDIOMS **scrape (the bottom of) the barrel** informal to use the worst people or things because that is all that is available: *Richard's in the team? – You really are scraping the barrel!* • **scrape a living** UK to only just earn enough money to provide yourself with food, clothing, and a place to live: *He settled in Paris, where he scraped a living writing short stories and magazine articles.* • **scrape home** UK to win by a very small amount in a competition: *The reigning champion scraped home just 2.9 seconds ahead of his nearest rival.*

PHRASAL VERBS **scrape by/along 1** to manage to live when you do not have enough money and other necessary things: *He lost his job, so the family had to scrape along* ***on*** *£95 a week.* **2** to manage with difficulty to get a successful result or to reach an acceptable standard: *I only learned Spanish for a year but I can just scrape by in most situations.* • **scrape through (sth)** to succeed in something but with a lot of difficulty: *He managed to scrape through his exam with 52 percent.* • **scrape sth/sb together/up** informal to manage with great difficulty to collect enough of something, especially money, or to find the things or people that you need: *I finally scraped together enough money for a flight home.* ◦ *Do you think we can scrape up a team for the match on Saturday?*

▸noun **SITUATION** ▷ **1** [C] informal a difficult or slightly dangerous situation which you cause by your own silly behaviour: *She's always* ***getting into*** *silly scrapes – I do wish she'd think before she does things.* ◦ *He had a couple of scrapes* ***with*** *the police and ended up in court.* **RUB** ▷ **2** [C or U] a slight injury or an unpleasant noise produced by rubbing against a surface: *'It's just a scrape,' said the boy looking down at his bleeding knee.* ◦ *I hate the scrape of chalk* ***on*** *a blackboard.*

scraper /ˈskreɪ.pəʳ/ ⓤⓢ /-pɚ/ noun [C] a tool for scraping

S

ˈscrap ˌheap noun **1** [C] a pile of old, unwanted things, especially pieces of metal **2** [S] If an idea or person is on the scrap heap, people are no longer interested in them: *Some people believe that Communism has been* ***relegated/consigned to the*** *scrap heap* ***of history.*** ◦ *Many top class players* ***end up on the*** *scrap heap after a short career.*

scrapie /ˈskreɪ.pi/ noun [U] a serious brain disease of sheep and goats which usually results in death

scrapings /ˈskreɪ.pɪŋz/ noun [plural] small pieces that are left on a surface or have been SCRAPED off

scrappage /ˈskræp.ɪdʒ/ noun [U] mainly UK the act of offering people money if they get rid of an old car or piece of equipment and buy a new one: *The government is offering scrappage grants to reduce the number of old vehicles on the road.*

ˈscrap ˌpaper noun [U] (US also **ˈscratch ˌpaper**) loose sheets of paper, often already partly used, for writing notes on

scrappy /ˈskræp.i/ adj **NOT ORGANIZED** ▷ **1** badly arranged or planned and consisting of parts which fit together badly: *I'm afraid your last essay was a very scrappy piece of work.* **ARGUMENT** ▷ **2** US describes a person who often wants to argue or fight • **scrappily** /-ɪ.li/ adv

scratch /skrætʃ/ verb; noun; adj

▸verb **CUT** ▷ **1** B2 [I or T] to cut or damage a surface or your skin slightly with or on something sharp or rough: *We scratched the paintwork trying to get the bed into Martha's room.* ◦ *Be careful not to scratch your****self on*** *the roses.* ◦ *A few chickens were scratching* ***about/around*** *(= searching with their beaks) in the yard* ***for*** *grain.* **2** B2 [T] If you scratch something on or off a surface, you add it or remove it by scratching: *People have been scratching their names* ***on*** *this rock for years.* ◦ *I'm afraid I scratched some paint* ***off*** *the door as I was getting out of the car.* **3** B2 [I] If an animal scratches, it rubs something with its CLAWS (= sharp nails): *The dog's scratching* ***at*** *the door – he wants to be let in.* **4** B2 [I or T] to rub your skin with your nails: *He was scratching (****at****) his mosquito bites.* ◦ *Hannah scratched her head thoughtfully.* **REMOVE** ▷ **5** [I or T] to remove yourself or another person or an animal from a competition before the start: *The world champion scratched* ***from*** *the 800 metres after falling ill three hours earlier.* ◦ *They scratched the horse* ***from*** *the race because she had become lame.*

IDIOMS **scratch your head** to think hard about something: *A lot of people must be scratching their heads about which way to vote.* • **scratch beneath the surface** to look further than what is obvious: *If you scratch beneath the surface you'll find she's really a very nice person.* • **you scratch my back and I'll scratch yours** informal used to tell someone that if they help you, you will help them

PHRASAL VERB **scratch around for sth** informal to look for something that is very difficult to find because it is rare: *The editor of the local paper says he's really scratching around for stories this week.*

▸noun **1** B2 [C] a mark made by scratching: *Her legs were covered in scratches and bruises after her walk through the forest.* ◦ *There was a scratch on the CD.* ◦ *Amazingly, he survived the accident* ***without a*** *scratch (= without suffering any injuries at all).* **2** [S] an act of scratching: *That dog is* ***having*** *a good scratch. It must have fleas.*

IDIOMS **from scratch** C1 from the beginning, without using anything that already exists: *Ben built the shed from scratch.* • **up to scratch** C2 reaching an acceptable standard: *Your last essay wasn't up to scratch/didn't* ***come*** *up to scratch.*

▸adj UK **scratch team/side/orchestra** a group of people brought together in a hurry in order to play together on a particular occasion

ˌscratch-and-ˈsniff adj [before noun] A scratch-and-sniff picture is one which releases a smell if you rub it.

ˈscratch ˌcard noun [C] UK a small card that you can buy to try to win a prize, with a thin layer that you rub off in order to see if you have winning numbers written on it: *a lottery scratch card*

scratchpad /ˈskrætʃ.pæd/ noun [C] US a set of sheets of paper, joined along one edge, used for writing notes on

ˈscratch ˌpaper noun [U] US for **scrap paper**

scratchy /ˈskrætʃ.i/ adj Scratchy clothes are rough and uncomfortable.

scrawl /skrɔːl/ (US) /skrɑːl/ verb; noun

▸verb [T] to write something quickly, without trying to make your writing tidy or easy to read: *I scrawled a quick note* ***to*** *Judith and put it under her door.* ◦ *Someone had scrawled graffiti* ***across*** *the wall.*

▸noun [S] untidy writing that is difficult to read: *I hope you can decipher my scrawl!*

scrawny /ˈskrɔː.ni/ (US) /ˈskrɑː-/ adj unpleasantly thin, often with bones showing: *He came home after three months at college looking terribly scrawny.*

scream /skriːm/ verb; noun

▸verb **MAKE NOISE** ▷ **1** B1 [I or T] to cry or say something loudly and usually on a high note, especially because of strong emotions such as fear, excitement, or anger: *A spider landed on her pillow and she screamed.* ◦ *Through the smoke, the rescuers could hear people screaming* ***for*** *help.* ◦ *He was screaming* ***in/with*** *pain and begging for anaesthetic.* ◦ *They screamed* ***with*** *laughter at her jokes.* ◦ *Ken screamed (****out****) a warning telling people to get out of the way.* ◦ *Mrs Brown screamed (= shouted angrily)* ***at*** *Joel* ***for*** *dropping the test-tube.* ◦ *I've never found screaming (****and shouting****) (= shouting angrily)* ***at*** *my staff to be very effective.* ◦ [+ speech] *'I wish you were dead!' she screamed (= shouted angrily).* ◦ *I tried to apologize, but he just screamed* ***abuse/obscenities*** *at me.* **2** [I + adv/prep] If a vehicle screams, it moves very quickly making a loud high sound: *The cars screamed* ***round*** *the bend/****past*** *the spectators.* **3** [I] to make a loud, high sound: *The ambulance raced round the corner with its tyres screaming.* **GET ATTENTION** ▷ **4** [I] (also **scream out**) If a word or image screams (out), it gets attention because it is very big or easy to notice: *'Royal Plane Disaster!' screamed the newspaper headlines the next day.*

IDIOMS **scream (out) for sth** to need something very much: *This matter is screaming out for attention.* • **scream yourself hoarse/silly** (also **scream the place down**, also **scream your head off**) to scream very loudly: *I screamed myself silly on the roller coaster.*

▸noun [C] **NOISE** ▷ **1** B1 a loud, high sound you make when very frightened, excited, or angry: *a scream* ***of*** *pain/rage/joy/laughter* ◦ *No one heard their screams.* ◦ *She* ***let out*** *a* ***piercing/shrill*** *scream.* **FUN** ▷ **2** informal a person, thing, or situation that is very funny: *Jane's such a scream – her jokes have me in stitches.*

screamingly /ˈskriː.mɪŋ.li/ adv informal extremely: *a screamingly* ***funny*** *story.* ◦ *The answer was suddenly screamingly* ***obvious*** *to me.*

scree /skriː/ noun [C or U] specialized (an area on the

S

side of a mountain covered with) large, loose broken stones

screech /skriːtʃ/ verb; noun

▸**verb** [I] to make an unpleasant loud, high, noise: *She was screeching at him at the top of her voice.* ◦ *He was screeching* ***with*** *pain/laughter.* ◦ [+ speech] *'Don't you dare touch me!' she screeched.* ◦ *The car screeched* ***to a halt/standstill*** *(= stopped very suddenly, making a loud high noise).* ◦ figurative *The economic recovery is likely to screech* ***to a halt/standstill*** *(= stop very suddenly) if taxes are increased.*

▸**noun** [C] a long, loud, high noise that is unpleasant to hear: *He* ***let out*** *a loud screech.* ◦ *The truck stopped with a screech* ***of*** *brakes.*

screeds /skriːdz/ noun [plural] a large amount of writing: *She's written screeds* ***(and screeds)*** *on the subject, but hardly any of it is worth reading.*

screen /skriːn/ noun; verb

▸**noun** [C] **PICTURE** ▷ **1** A2 a flat surface in a cinema, on a television, or as part of a computer, on which pictures or words are shown: *Our television has a 19-inch screen.* ◦ *Coming to your screens (= cinemas) shortly, the amazing adventures of 'Robin Hood'.* ◦ *Her ambition is to write for* ***the*** *screen (= for television and films).* ◦ *Write the letter on the computer, then you can make changes easily* ***on*** *screen.* **2 the small screen** television: *He's made several films for the small screen.* **3 the big screen** cinema: *So this is your first appearance on the big screen?* **SEPARATING** ▷ **4** a vertical structure that is used to separate one area from another, especially to hide something or to protect you from something unpleasant or dangerous: *The nurse pulled a screen around the bed so that the doctor could examine the patient in private.* ◦ *A screen* ***of*** *trees at the bottom of the garden hid the ugly factory walls.* **5** mainly US an activity that is not dangerous or illegal but is used to hide something that is: *That café's just a screen* ***for*** *their criminal activities.*

▸**verb** [T] **EXAMINE** ▷ **1** to test or examine someone or something to discover if there is anything wrong with them: *All women over 50 will be screened* ***for*** *breast cancer.* ◦ *Completely unsuitable candidates were screened* ***out*** *(= tested and refused) at the first interview.* **2 screen your calls** to delay your decision to speak to someone who is ringing you on the phone until you can discover who they are, either by listening to them leaving a message on your ANSWERING MACHINE or by seeing their phone number shown on your phone: *I always screen my calls while I'm eating dinner.* **PICTURE** ▷ **3** to show or broadcast a film or television programme: *The programme was not screened* ***on*** *British television.* **PROTECT** ▷ **4** to protect or hide: *She raised her hand to screen her eyes* ***from*** *the bright light.* **5** mainly US to protect someone by taking the blame yourself: *The husband says he's the murderer but we think it was his wife – he's just screening her.*

PHRASAL VERB **screen sth off** to separate one area from another using a wall or other vertical structure: *We can screen off part of the room and use it as a temporary office.*

ˈscreen ˌdoor noun [C] US a door consisting of a wire net with very small holes stretched over a frame, which allows air but not insects to move through it

screener /ˈskriː.nəʳ/ US /-nɚ/ noun [C] a person at an airport who checks with a special machine to see if passengers are carrying anything that could be dangerous: *airport screeners*

screening /ˈskriː.nɪŋ/ noun **CINEMA** ▷ **1** [C] a showing of a film: *There will be three screenings of the film – at 3 p.m., 5 p.m., and 7 p.m.* **EXAMINATION** ▷ **2** [C or U] a test or examination to discover if there is anything wrong with someone: *regular screening(s)* ***for*** *cervical cancer*

screenplay /ˈskriːn.pleɪ/ noun [C] the text for a film, including the words to be spoken by the actors and instructions for the cameras: *Who wrote/did the screenplay* ***for/of/to*** *the film 'Chariots of Fire'?*

ˈscreen-ˌprinting noun [U] a method of printing by forcing ink through a pattern cut into a piece of cloth stretched across a frame

screensaver /ˈskriːnˌseɪ.vəʳ/ US /-vɚ/ noun [C] on a computer, a program that protects the screen by automatically producing a moving image if the computer has not been used for a few minutes

screenwriter /ˈskriːnˌraɪ.təʳ/ US /-t̬ɚ/ noun [C] someone who writes the story for a film

screw /skruː/ noun; verb

▸**noun METAL OBJECT** ▷ **1** [C] a thin, pointed piece of metal with a raised edge twisting round along its length and a flat top with a cut in it, used to join things together, especially pieces of wood **PRISON GUARD** ▷ **2** [C] slang (a word used especially by prisoners) a prison guard **HAVE SEX** ▷ **3** [C] offensive the act of sex, or a sexual partner: *I never feel like a screw when I wake up in the morning.* ◦ *He's a really good screw.* **INSTRUMENT** ▷ **4 screws** [plural] **thumbscrew**

IDIOMS **have a screw loose** informal If you say that someone has a screw loose, you mean that they behave in a strange way and seem slightly mentally ill. • **put/tighten the screws on sb** informal to use force or threats to make someone do what you want: *They put the screws on him until he paid up.*

▸**verb TIGHT SHAPE** ▷ **1** [T + adv/prep] to tighten the muscles of your face or part of your face into a particular expression, especially one of disapproval or pain: *He screwed his eyes tight shut against the bright light.* ◦ *The woman at the breakfast table screwed her mouth* ***into*** *a grimace.* **2** [T + adv/prep] to twist and crush something, especially paper or cloth, roughly with your hands: *She screwed the bag* ***up*** *and threw it in the bin.* ◦ *He screwed the letter* ***into*** *a ball and flung it away.* **METAL OBJECT** ▷ **3** [T usually + adv/prep] to fasten something using a screw: *Screw this piece of wood* ***to*** *the wall.* ◦ *Screw these two pieces* ***together****.* **4** [T usually + adv/prep] to fasten something using an object similar to a screw: *We'll have to screw a hook* ***into*** *the wall.* **5 screw in/together** If something screws in/together, it fits or fastens together by being turned: *This light bulb screws in.* ◦ *The steel rods screw together.* **TURN** ▷ **6** [T usually + adv/prep] to fasten something by turning it or twisting it: *Screw the lid firmly* ***on*** *to the jar and shake well.* **CHEAT** ▷ **7** [T] slang to cheat or deceive someone: *It was only after we'd had the car for a few days that we realized we'd been screwed by the dealer.* **HAVE SEX** ▷ **8** [I or T] offensive to have sex with someone: *They say he's screwing the boss's wife.*

IDIOMS **screw it/you/them!** offensive used when expressing extreme anger: *'Screw it!' he said. 'If they won't give us the money, we'll just take it.'* ◦ *You don't like it? Well, screw you!* • **screw up your courage** to force yourself to be brave: *I screwed up my courage and went in to see the director.*

PHRASAL VERBS **screw around** offensive to have sex with a lot of people or with people other than your husband or wife • **screw sth out of sb** UK informal to get something from someone by using force or threats: *We'll screw every last penny out of him.* • **screw (sth) up** informal to make a mistake, or to

S

spoil something: *I reckon I screwed the chemistry exam up totally.* • **screw sb up** informal When bad experiences or people screw you up, they make you worried and unhappy or they damage your personality: *It really screwed him up when he saw his friend get killed.*

screwball /ˈskruː.bɔːl/ (US) /-bɑːl/ **noun; adj**
▸**noun** [C] **PERSON** ▷ **1** mainly US informal a person who behaves in a strange and funny way **BALL** ▷ **2** US a ball that is thrown during a baseball game so that it curves to one side
▸**adj** mainly US used to describe a type of film, etc. in which there are funny characters and silly situations: *a screwball comedy*

screwdriver

screwdriver /ˈskruːˌdraɪ.vəʳ/ (US) /-vɚ/ **noun** [C] a tool for turning screws, consisting of a handle joined to a metal rod shaped at one end to fit in the cut in the top of the screw

ˌscrewed ˈup **adj** informal unhappy and worried because of bad experiences: *He's been really screwed up since his wife died.*

ˌscrew ˈtop **noun** [C] a lid for a container which fastens by being turned • **ˈscrew-top adj** [before noun] (also **ˈscrew-topped**) *a screw-top jar*

screwy /ˈskruː.i/ **adj** old-fashioned informal very strange, silly, or unusual: *Pat's always coming up with screwy ideas.*

scribble /ˈskrɪb.l̩/ **verb; noun**
▸**verb** [I or T] to write or draw something quickly or carelessly: *The baby's just scribbled all over my new dictionary!* ◦ [+ two objects] *I'll just scribble Dad a note/scribble a note **to** Dad to say we're going out.*
▸**noun** [C or U] a careless piece of writing or drawing: *What are all these scribbles doing on the wallpaper?* ◦ *I hope you can read my scribble!*

scribbler /ˈskrɪb.ləʳ/ (US) /-lɚ/ **noun** [C] disapproving or humorous a writer of books or articles in newspapers or magazines, especially one who is not thought to be very good

scribe /skraɪb/ **noun** [C] **1** a person employed before printing was invented to make copies of documents **2** in BIBLICAL times, a teacher of religious law

scrimmage /ˈskrɪm.ɪdʒ/ **noun** [C] **1** a fight **2** US a practice game of American football

scrimp /skrɪmp/ **verb** [I] **1** to save money by spending less than is necessary to reach an acceptable standard: *There is a risk that the debt-ridden airline may be tempted to scrimp **on** maintenance or security.* **2 scrimp and save** If you scrimp and save, you manage to live on very little money in order to pay for something.

script /skrɪpt/ **noun** **TEXT** ▷ **1** (B2) [C] the words of a film, play, broadcast, or speech: *Bruce Robinson wrote the script **for** 'The Killing Fields'.* **2** [C] Australian English a piece of paper on which a doctor writes the details of the medicine or drugs that someone needs → Compare **prescription** **EXAM** ▷ **3** [C] UK an answer paper written by a student in an exam **WRITING** ▷ **4** (C2) [U] a set of letters used for writing a particular language: *Arabic/Cyrillic/Roman script* **5** [C or U] writing, especially when well-formed: *The invitation was written **in** beautiful italic script.* **COMPUTER** ▷ **6** [C or U] specialized a type of language for programming computers that is used for finding and showing websites on the internet

scripted /ˈskrɪp.tɪd/ **adj** A scripted speech or broadcast has been written before it is read or performed: *He read from a scripted speech and refused to answer any questions at all at the end of it.* → Opposite **unscripted**

scripture /ˈskrɪp.tʃəʳ/ (US) /-tʃɚ/ **noun** [C or U] the holy writings of a religion: *the Hindu/Buddhist/Muslim scriptures* ◦ *According to **Holy** Scripture (= the Bible), God created the world in six days.* • **scriptural** /-əl/ **adj** specialized *scriptural texts/passages*

scriptwriter /ˈskrɪptˌraɪ.təʳ/ (US) /-t̬ɚ/ **noun** [C] a person who writes the words for films or radio or television broadcasts

scroll /skrəʊl/ (US) /skroʊl/ **noun; verb**
▸**noun** [C] **1** a long roll of paper or similar material with usually official writing on it: *The ancient Egyptians stored information on scrolls.* **2** a decoration that looks like a roll of paper: *The tops of the marble pillars were decorated with scrolls.*
▸**verb** [I usually + adv/prep] (C2) to move text or other information on a computer screen in order to see a different part of it: *Scroll **to** the end of the document.*

ˈscroll ˌbar **noun** [C] specialized a long, thin strip at the side of a computer window, used for moving its contents up, down, or across

scrooge /skruːdʒ/ **noun** [C] disapproving someone who spends as little money as possible and is not generous: *He's a mean old scrooge!*

scrotum /ˈskrəʊ.təm/ (US) /ˈskroʊ.t̬əm/ **noun** [C] (plural **scrotums** or formal **scrota**) specialized in most male mammals, a bag of skin near the PENIS which contains the TESTICLES

scrounge /skraʊndʒ/ **verb; noun**
▸**verb** [I or T] informal to get things, especially money or food, by asking for them instead of buying them or working for them: *Peter never buys anything – he just scrounges (**off** his friends).* • **scrounger** /ˈskraʊn.dʒəʳ/ (US) /-dʒɚ/ **noun** [C] disapproving *He thinks that people who receive state benefits are scroungers.*

PHRASAL VERB **scrounge around** US informal to look in different places or in a particular place where you might find something that you need: *She scrounged around **in** the tool box **for** a tack or nail to hang the notice up with.*

▸**noun** disapproving or humorous **on the scrounge** Someone who is on the scrounge is asking people for things or for money.

scrub /skrʌb/ **verb; noun**
▸**verb** (-bb-) **CLEAN** ▷ **1** [I or T] to rub something hard in order to clean it, especially using a stiff brush, soap, and water: *She scrubbed (**at**) the mark on the wall for ages, but it wouldn't come off.* ◦ [+ obj + adj] *He scrubbed the old saucepan clean, and it looked as good as new.* **STOP** ▷ **2** [T] (US usually **scratch**) to decide not to do something you had planned to do: *We had to scrub our plans when I lost my job.* → Synonym **cancel**

PHRASAL VERB **scrub up** If a doctor scrubs up, they wash their hands and arms very carefully before performing a medical operation.

IDIOM **scrub up well** UK informal approving said about someone when they have made an effort to make their appearance as tidy and pleasant as possible and they look very attractive and stylish: *Mary scrubs up well.*

▸**noun** **PLANTS** ▷ **1** [U] (an area of land covered with) short trees and bushes, growing on dry ground of low quality **CLEAN** ▷ **2** [S] the act of rubbing something hard in order to clean it, especially using a stiff brush, soap, and water: *Kids, give your hands **a good** scrub and come and get your dinner!* • **scrubby** /ˈskrʌb.i/ **adj** covered with short trees and bushes: *scrubby vegetation*

scrubber /ˈskrʌb.əʳ/ ⓤⓢ /-ɚ/ **noun** [C] **CLEAN** ▷ **1** an object for scrubbing things to clean them: *a pan scrubber* **2** a system or piece of equipment for removing substances that are harmful to the environment from a gas: *Scrubbers in factory chimneys can extract harmful particles before they are vented into the atmosphere.* **WOMAN** ▷ **3** UK offensive disapproving an offensive word for a woman who has sex with a lot of men or who has an untidy, rough appearance

ˈ**scrubbing** ˌ**brush** **noun** [C] (US also ˈ**scrub** ˌ**brush**) a stiff brush used for cleaning floors

scruff /skrʌf/ **noun** **NECK** ▷ **1 by the scruff of the/your neck** by the skin at the back of the neck: *Cats carry their kittens by the scruff of the neck.* ◦ *I **took/grabbed** him by the scruff of his neck and threw him out of the hall.* **PERSON** ▷ **2** [C] UK informal a dirty and untidy person: *I feel a bit of a scruff in my jeans.*

scruffy /ˈskrʌf.i/ **adj** Ⓒ2 untidy and dirty: *They live in a rather scruffy part of town.* ◦ *a small, scruffy-**looking** man* • **scruffily** /-ɪ.li/ **adv**

scrum /skrʌm/ **noun** **1** [C] (also **scrummage**) in the sport of RUGBY, a group of attacking players from each team who come together with their heads down and arms joined, and push against each other, trying to take control of the ball **2** [S] a situation in which a group of people push each other to get to a place or obtain something • **scrummager** /ˈskrʌm.ɪ.dʒəʳ/ ⓤⓢ /-dʒɚ/ **noun** [C]

ˌ**scrum** ˈ**half** **noun** [C] (plural **scrum halves**) a RUGBY player who throws the ball into the scrum

scrump /skrʌmp/ **verb** [T] UK old-fashioned informal to steal fruit such as apples from trees

scrumptious /ˈskrʌmp.ʃəs/ **adj** (UK informal **scrummy**) tasting extremely good: *scrumptious cakes* → Synonym **delicious**

scrumpy /ˈskrʌm.pi/ **noun** [U] UK an alcoholic drink made from apples: *Scrumpy is a type of strong cider.*

scrunch /skrʌntʃ/ **verb** **MAKE A NOISE** ▷ **1** [I or T] to make the noise produced by hard things being pressed together, or to press hard things together so that they make a noise: *The pebbles scrunched beneath our feet.* ◦ *We scrunched snow under our feet.* **CRUSH** ▷ **2** [T] to crush material such as paper or cloth into a rough ball in the hand: *She scrunched the letter **up** and threw it in the bin.* **MAKE SMALL** ▷ **3** [I or T, + adv/prep] to make something or yourself smaller to fit into a small space: *The cat was hiding, scrunched **up** under the sofa.* **4** [I or T, usually + adv/prep] to make your face or part of your face into a tight shape in order to show an emotion, or to go into a tight shape which expresses an emotion: *He was red with anger and his face was all scrunched **up**.*

scrunchy (also **scrunchie**) /ˈskrʌn.tʃi/ **noun** [C] a piece of ELASTIC (= material that stretches) covered in often brightly coloured cloth that is used to hold long hair at the back of the head

scruple /ˈskruː.pl̩/ **noun**; **verb**

▸**noun** [C or U] a feeling that prevents you from doing something that you think is morally wrong or makes you uncertain about doing it: *Robin Hood **had** no scruples **about** robbing the rich to give to the poor.* ◦ *He is a man **without** scruple – he has no conscience.*

▸**verb** formal **not scruple to do sth** to not care that something you do is morally wrong or likely to have

bad results: *He wouldn't scruple to cheat his own mother if there was money in it for him.*

scrupulous /ˈskruː.pjʊ.ləs/ **adj** extremely honest, or doing everything correctly and exactly as it should be done: *A scrupulous politician would not lie about her business interests.* ◦ *The nurse told him to be scrupulous (= extremely careful) **about** keeping the wound clean.* • **scrupulously** /-li/ **adv** *She is always scrupulously honest/fair.* ◦ *A hospital must be kept scrupulously clean.*

scrutineer /ˌskruː.tɪˈnɪəʳ/ ⓤⓢ /-t̬ənˈɪr/ **noun** [C] UK a person who counts votes in an election or who makes certain that the counting has been done correctly

scrutinize (UK usually **scrutinise**) /ˈskruː.tɪ.naɪz/ ⓤⓢ /-t̬ən.aɪz/ **verb** [T] to examine something very carefully in order to discover information: *He scrutinized the men's faces carefully/closely, trying to work out who was lying.*

scrutiny /ˈskruː.tɪ.ni/ ⓤⓢ /-t̬ən.i/ **noun** [U] Ⓒ2 the careful and detailed examination of something in order to get information about it: *The government's record will **be subjected to/come under** (**close**) scrutiny in the weeks before the election.*

scuba diving /ˈskuː.bəˌdaɪ.vɪŋ/ **noun** [U] the sport of swimming underwater with special breathing equipment • ˈ**scuba** ˌ**diver** **noun** [C]

scud /skʌd/ **verb** [I usually + adv/prep] (**-dd-**) (especially of clouds and ships) to move quickly and without stopping in a straight line: *It was a windy day, and small white clouds were scudding **across** the blue sky.*

scuff /skʌf/ **verb** [T] to make a rough mark on a smooth surface, especially on a shoe or floor: *Please wear trainers in the gym, to avoid scuffing the floor.* ◦ *Have you got anything for getting rid of scuff **marks** on shoes?* ◦ *If you scuff your feet (= pull your shoes along the ground as you walk) like that, you'll ruin your shoes.* • **scuffed** /skʌft/ **adj** *The book's a bit scuffed along the spine, but it was the only copy left in the shop.*

scuffle /ˈskʌf.l̩/ **noun** [C] a short and sudden fight, especially one involving a small number of people: *Two police officers were injured in scuffles with fans at Sunday's National Football League contest.* • **scuffle** **verb** [I] *The youths scuffled **with** the policeman, then escaped down the lane.*

scullery /ˈskʌl.əʳ.i/ ⓤⓢ /ˈ-ɚ-/ **noun** [C] especially in a large old house, a room next to the kitchen where pans are washed and vegetables are prepared for cooking: *Our house has the original scullery.*

sculling /ˈskʌl.ɪŋ/ **noun** [U] the sport of ROWING in a small, narrow boat designed for one, two, or four people, who use two small OARS (= poles with flat ends) each, to move the boat

sculpt /skʌlpt/ **verb** **1** [I or T] to create solid objects that represent a thing, person, idea, etc. out of a material such as wood, clay, metal, or stone: *Johnny sculpted an old man's head **out of** wood.* **2** [T] to form into a particular shape: *The dripping water had sculpted strange shapes **out of** the rocks/sculpted the rocks **into** strange shapes.*

sculptor /ˈskʌlp.təʳ/ ⓤⓢ /-tɚ/ **noun** [C] someone who creates sculptures: *Henry Moore, who died in 1986, is one of Britain's best-known sculptors.*

sculpture /ˈskʌlp.tʃəʳ/ ⓤⓢ /-tʃɚ/ **noun** [C or U] Ⓑ1 the art of forming solid objects that represent a thing, person, idea, etc. out of a material such as wood, clay, metal, or stone, or an object made in this way: *Tom teaches sculpture at the local art school.* ◦ *The museum has several life-sized sculptures **of** people and animals.* • **sculptural** /ˈskʌlp.tʃə.rəl/ ⓤⓢ /-tʃɚ-/ **adj** specialized

S

*Her delicate sculptural **pieces** (= works of art) are now selling in the USA and Japan.*

sculptured /ˈskʌlp.tʃəd/ ⓤⓢ /-tʃɚd/ **adj 1** created as a sculpture: *a deer sculptured **in** wax* **2** describes a part of someone's body that has a strong, smooth shape: *his beautifully sculptured features*

scum /skʌm/ **noun** DIRT ▷ **1** [U] a layer of unpleasant or unwanted material that has formed on the top of a liquid: *The lake near the factory was covered with grey, foul-smelling scum.* IMMORAL PERSON ▷ **2** [C or U] (plural **scum**) informal a very bad or IMMORAL person or group of people: *People who organize dog fights are scum in my opinion!* ◦ *His boss treats him **like** scum (= very badly).* ◦ *racist scum* • **scummy** /ˈskʌm.i/ **adj**

IDIOM **the scum of the earth** informal the worst type of people that can be imagined: *These men are the scum of the earth.*

scumbag /ˈskʌm.bæg/ **noun** [C] offensive a very unpleasant person who has done something dishonest or unacceptable

scupper /ˈskʌp.əʳ/ ⓤⓢ /-ɚ/ **verb** [T] SINK ▷ **1** to sink your own ship on purpose SPOIL ▷ **2** to cause something such as a plan or an opportunity to fail: *Arriving late for the interview scuppered my **chances** of getting the job.*

scurf /skɜːf/ ⓤⓢ /skɝːf/ **noun** [U] very small pieces of dry dead skin → Compare **dandruff**

scurrilous /ˈskʌr.ɪ.ləs/ ⓤⓢ /ˈskɝː-/ **adj** formal expressing unfair or false criticism that is likely to damage someone's reputation: *a scurrilous remark/attack/article* • **scurrilously** /-li/ **adv**

scurry /ˈskʌr.i/ ⓤⓢ /ˈskɝː-/ **verb** [I usually + adv/prep] to move quickly, with small, short steps: *The mouse scurried **across** the floor.* ◦ *The noise of the explosion **sent** the villagers scurry**ing** back into their homes.* • **scurry noun** [S]

scurvy /ˈskɜː.vi/ ⓤⓢ /ˈskɝː-/ **noun** [U] an illness of the body tissues that is caused by not having enough VITAMIN C

scuttle /ˈskʌt.l̩/ ⓤⓢ /ˈskʌt̬-/ **verb; noun**

▸**verb** RUN ▷ **1** [I usually + adv/prep] to move quickly, with small, short steps, especially in order to escape: *A crab scuttled **away** under a rock as we passed.* ◦ *The children scuttled **off** as soon as the headmaster appeared.* SINK ▷ **2** [T] to intentionally sink a ship, especially your own, in order to prevent it from being taken by an enemy STOP ▷ **3** [T] to stop something happening, or to cause a plan to fail

▸**noun** [C] a **coal scuttle**

scuttlebutt /ˈskʌt.l̩.bʌt/ ⓤⓢ /ˈskʌt̬-/ **noun** [U] US informal news or information which may or may not be true: *Have you heard any scuttlebutt **about** the new boss?*

scuzzy /ˈskʌz.i/ **adj** informal (usually of people) unpleasant, dirty, and probably unable to be trusted

scythe /saɪð/ **noun; verb**

▸**noun** [C] a tool with a long, sharp, curved blade and a long handle held in two hands, used especially to cut long grass → Compare **sickle**

▸**verb 1** [T] to cut something using a scythe **2** [I + adv/prep] to move very quickly through a group of people or things: *The racing car left the track at 120 mph and scythed **through** the crowd of spectators, killing ten.*

the SDLP /ˌes.diːˌelˈpiː/ **noun** [+ sing/pl verb] abbreviation for the Social and Democratic Labour Party: a political party in Northern Ireland that supports UNION with the Republic of Ireland by peaceful methods

SE noun [U], **adj** written abbreviation for **southeast** or **southeastern**

sea /siː/ **noun 1** Ⓐ1 [C or U] the salty water that covers a large part of the surface of the Earth, or a large area of salty water, smaller than an ocean, that is partly or completely surrounded by land: *the Mediterranean Sea* ◦ *We went swimming **in the** sea.* ◦ *The sea was **calm/smooth/choppy/rough** when we crossed the Channel.* ◦ *The refugees were **at sea** (= in a boat on the sea a long way from land) for 40 days before reaching land.* ◦ *When we moved to the US, we sent our things **by** sea (= in a ship).* ◦ *We spent a lovely week **by the** sea (= on the coast) this year.* ◦ *Soon we had left the river estuary and were heading towards **the open** sea (= the part of the sea a long way from land).* **2 a sea of sth** a large amount or number of something: *The teacher looked down and saw a sea of smiling faces.* **3 put (out) to sea** (of a ship) to leave a port and start a journey: *The boats will put (out) to sea on this evening's high tide.* **4** [C] one of the large, flat areas on the moon which in the past were thought to be seas

IDIOM **at sea** confused: *I'm all/completely at sea **with** the new coins.*

ˈsea aˌnemone noun [C] a soft, brightly coloured sea creature which looks like a flower and often lives on rocks under the water

ˈsea ˌbass noun [C or U] a sea fish that you can eat

the seabed /ˈsiː.bed/ **noun** [S] the solid surface of the Earth which lies under the sea: *The ship has been lying on the seabed for more than 50 years.*

seabird /ˈsiː.bɜːd/ ⓤⓢ /-bɝːd/ **noun** [C] a bird that lives near the sea and gets its food from it

seaboard /ˈsiː.bɔːd/ ⓤⓢ /-bɔːrd/ **noun** [C usually singular] the long, thin area of a country that is next to the sea: *The company owns a chain of hotels **along/on** the Atlantic seaboard.* → Synonym **coast**

seaborne /ˈsiː.bɔːn/ ⓤⓢ /-bɔːrn/ **adj** carried in a ship: *seaborne trade/goods* ◦ *seaborne missiles/troops/reinforcements*

ˌsea ˈbreeze noun [C] a light, cool wind blowing from the sea onto the land

ˈsea ˌcaptain noun [C] a person in charge of a ship, especially one used for trading rather than for military purposes

ˈsea ˌchange noun [C] literary a complete change: *There will have to be a sea change in people's attitudes if public transport is ever to replace the private car.*

ˈsea ˌdog noun [C] literary or humorous an old sailor with many years of experience at sea: *With his white beard and blue cap he looked like an **old** sea dog.*

seafaring /ˈsiːˌfeə.rɪŋ/ ⓤⓢ /-ˌfer.ɪŋ/ **adj** [before noun] literary connected with travelling by sea: *a seafaring man (= a sailor)*

seafood /ˈsiː.fuːd/ **noun** [U] animals from the sea that can be eaten, especially fish or sea creatures with shells

seafront /ˈsiː.frʌnt/ **noun** [C usually singular] (also **front**) the part of a town on the coast next to the beach, often with a wide road or path and a row of houses and shops facing the sea: *We rented a house **on** the seafront for the summer.* ◦ *After dinner we went for a stroll **along** the seafront.*

seagoing /ˈsiːˌgəʊ.ɪŋ/ ⓤⓢ /-ˌgoʊ-/ **adj** [before noun] (of ships) built for use on journeys across the sea, not just for journeys near the coast and on rivers

seagull /ˈsiː.gʌl/ **noun** [C] (also **gull**) a bird which lives near the sea and has short legs, long wings, and white and grey feathers: *a flock of seagulls*

seahorse /ˈsiː.hɔːs/ ⓤⓢ /-hɔːrs/ **noun** [C] a small fish which swims in a vertical position and has a head like that of a horse

seagull

seal /siːl/ noun; verb

►noun [C] **ANIMAL** ▷ **1** B2 a large mammal that eats fish and lives partly in the sea and partly on land or ice **COVERING** ▷ **2** something fixed around the edge of an opening to prevent liquid or gas flowing through it: *Clean the seal* ***on/around*** *the fridge door regularly so that it remains airtight.* **3** a thin piece of material such as paper or plastic that covers the opening of a container and has to be broken in order to open the container and use the contents **MARK** ▷ **4** an official mark on a document, sometimes made with WAX, that shows that it is legal or has been officially approved: *The lawyer stamped the certificate with her seal.*

IDIOMS **seal of approval** a statement or sign that someone in an important position approves of something: *The government has* ***given*** *the proposal its seal of approval.* • **set/put the seal on sth** to make the result of something certain: *The meeting set the seal on the negotiations.*

►verb [T] **COVERING** ▷ **1** C2 to close an entrance or container so that nothing can enter or leave it **2** to cover a surface with a special liquid to protect it: *This floor has just been sealed (****with*** *varnish), so don't walk on it!* **3** C2 to close a letter or parcel by sticking the edges together: *Seal the package (****up****) with sticky tape.* ◦ *He sealed (****down****) the* ***envelope*** *and put a stamp on it.* **MARK** ▷ **4** to make an agreement more certain or to approve it formally: *The two leaders sealed their agreement* ***with*** *a handshake.*

IDIOM **seal sb's fate** If an action, event, or situation seals your fate, nothing can stop some unpleasant thing happening to you: *From the moment she stepped into the busy road her fate was sealed.*

PHRASAL VERBS **seal sth in** to prevent a substance or quality from being lost from something during a process such as cooking: *Fry the meat quickly in hot oil to seal in the flavour/juices.* • **seal sth off** C2 to prevent people from entering an area or building, often because it is dangerous

ˈsea ˌlane noun [C] a particular route across the sea regularly used by ships

sealant /ˈsiː.lənt/ noun [C or U] a substance such as paint or POLISH that is painted onto a surface to protect it from other liquids going into it, or is put in the space between two materials for the same reason

sealed /siːld/ adj closed: *The teacher opened the sealed envelope containing the exam papers.*

ˈsea ˌlegs noun [plural] a person's ability to keep their balance while walking on a moving ship and to not be ill

ˈsea ˌlevel noun [C] the average height of the sea where it meets the land: *The top of Mount Everest is 8,848 m* ***above*** *sea level.*

sealing /ˈsiː.lɪŋ/ noun [U] the hunting and killing of seals (= animals)

ˈsealing ˌwax noun [U] a type of WAX that is used for making seals because it melts easily and becomes hard quickly

ˈsea ˌlion noun [C] a large SEAL (= sea animal), found mainly in the Pacific, that has large ears and can move on land

sealskin /ˈsiːl.skɪn/ noun [U] the skin or fur of a SEAL (= sea animal), especially when it is used for making clothing

seam /siːm/ noun [C] **JOIN** ▷ **1** a line where two things join, especially a line of sewing joining two pieces of cloth or leather: *The bags we sell have very strong seams, so they will last for years.* ◦ *My old coat is* ***coming/falling apart at the*** *seams (= the stitches are coming out).* ◦ figurative *Their marriage is* ***coming/falling apart at the*** *seams (= likely to fail).* **LAYER** ▷ **2** a long, thin layer of a substance such as coal that has formed between layers of other rocks

IDIOMS **be a rich seam to mine** to be full of good material and ideas to use: *When she started writing novels, she found her time as a judge was a rich seam for her to mine.* • **bursting at the seams** informal If a place is bursting at the seams, it has a very large number of people or things in it: *Now that they've got six children, their little house is bursting at the seams.*

seaman /ˈsiː.mən/ noun [C] (plural **-men** /-mən/) a sailor, especially one who is not an officer

seamanship /ˈsiː.mən.ʃɪp/ noun [U] skill in managing a ship

seamed /siːmd/ adj literary covered in lines: *The old man's face was seamed and wrinkled.*

seamless /ˈsiːm.ləs/ adj **CLOTHES** ▷ **1** without any SEAMS (= lines of sewing joining different pieces of cloth) **WITHOUT STOPPING** ▷ **2** happening without any sudden changes, interruption, or difficulty: *The intention is to achieve a seamless* ***transition*** *with a continuity of management.* • **seamlessly** /-li/ adv *It's a kids' movie that seamlessly combines live action with computer-generated creatures.*

seamstress /ˈsiːm.strəs/, /ˈsem-/ noun [C] old-fashioned a woman whose job is sewing and making clothes

seamy /ˈsiː.mi/ adj (of a situation) unpleasant because of a connection with dishonest behaviour, violence, and illegal sex: *The film vividly portrays the seamy* ***side of life*** *in the London of the early 70s.*

séance /ˈseɪ.ɒns/ US /-ɑːns/ noun [C] a meeting where people try to talk with dead people: *They're* ***holding*** *a séance this evening.*

seaplane /ˈsiː.pleɪn/ noun [C] an aircraft that can take off from and land on water

seaport /ˈsiː.pɔːt/ US /-pɔːrt/ noun [C] (a city or town with) a port that can be used by ships

sear /sɪəʳ/ US /sɪr/ verb [T] **1** to burn the surface of something with sudden very strong heat: *The heat from the explosion seared their hands and faces.* **2** to fry a piece of meat quickly at a high temperature, in order to prevent liquid and flavour escaping from it **3** to have a strong unpleasant effect on someone's feelings or memories: *The disaster is indelibly seared* ***into*** *the villagers'* ***memory.***

search /sɜːtʃ/ US /sɝːtʃ/ verb; noun

►verb **1** B1 [I or T] to look somewhere carefully in order to find something: *The police searched the woods* ***for*** *the missing boy.* ◦ *She searched his face* ***for*** *some sign of forgiveness, but it remained expressionless.* ◦ *He searched (****in/through****) his pockets* ***for*** *some change.* ◦ *I've searched* ***high and low*** *(= everywhere), but I can't find my birth certificate.* ◦ *The detectives searched the house* ***from top to bottom*** *(= all over it), but they found no sign of the stolen goods.* ◦ figurative *She searched her* ***mind/memory for*** *the man's name, but she couldn't remember it.* ◦ figurative *People who are searching* ***after*** *inner peace sometimes turn to religion.* **2** C1 [I] to try to find the answer to a problem:

S

Philosophers have searched for millennia but they haven't found the meaning of life. **3** B2 [T] A police officer who searches you or your possessions looks for something you might be hiding: *The men were searched **for** drugs and then released.* **4** B1 [I or T] to look for information on a computer, the internet, etc.: *I searched the internet **for** the best deal.*

Other ways of saying search

Look and **hunt** are very common alternatives to 'search':

*She was **looking** in her handbag for a pen.*

*I'm **looking** for my keys. Have you seen them?*

*I've **hunted** all over the place but I can't find that book.*

Rummage can be used when someone searches in a drawer, bag, etc. for something:

*He **rummaged** through his pockets, looking for a pen.*

The phrasal verb **ferret out** can be used when someone searches for information, especially information that other people do not want known:

*The inspector general has broad powers to **ferret out** fraud on the state and local level.*

If someone searches a place very carefully in order to find something or someone, the words **comb** or **scour** are often used:

*Police **combed** the area for evidence.*

*Police **scoured** the countryside looking for the missing child.*

If someone searches a place in a violent and careless way, you could use the verb **ransack**:

*Burglars had **ransacked** the house and stolen three watches.*

If you are **on the lookout for** something, you are continuously searching for it:

*He is always **on the lookout for** a bargain.*

Common mistake: search

Remember: when **search** has an indirect preposition, use the preposition **for**.

To talk about the thing you are trying to find, don't say 'search something', say **search for something**:

~~He is still searching his lost dog.~~

S

IDIOM **search me!** informal something that you say when you do not know the answer to a question: *'Where's Jack?' 'Search me!'*

PHRASAL VERB **search sth/sb out** to find something or someone after searching: *Despite the warm weather, we searched out some snow and went skiing.*

Word partners for search noun

carry out/conduct/make/mount a search • *abandon/call off/give up* a search • *resume/step up* a search • a *careful/full-scale/painstaking/thorough* search • a *desperate/frantic* search • a search *for* sb/sth

▸**noun** **1** B1 [C] an attempt to find someone or something: *After a long search, they eventually found the missing papers.* ◦ *The police **carried out/conducted/made** a thorough/exhaustive search **of** the premises, but they failed to find any drugs.* **2** B2 [S] an attempt to find an answer to a problem: *the search **for** happiness* **3** B1 [C] an attempt to find information on a computer, on the internet, etc.: *I **did** a search **for** yoga clubs in my area.* **4 in search of sth** trying to find something: *She was shot by a sniper when she went out in search of firewood.*

searchable /ˈsɜːtʃ.ə.bl/ US /ˈsɝːtʃ-/ **adj** If computer files are searchable, it is possible to search for words, numbers, and other information in those files: *a fully searchable database*

ˈsearch ˌengine **noun** [C] a computer program which finds information on the internet by looking for words which you have typed in

searching /ˈsɜː.tʃɪŋ/ US /ˈsɝː-/ **adj** intended to find out the often hidden truth about something: *I think we need to ask some searching **questions** about how the money has been spent.* • **searchingly** /-li/ **adv**

searchlight /ˈsɜːtʃ.laɪt/ US /ˈsɝːtʃ-/ **noun** [C] a light with a very bright beam that can be turned in any direction, used especially to guard prisons or to see the movements of enemy aircraft in the sky

ˈsearch ˌparty **noun** [C] a group of people who look for someone who is lost: *A search party was **sent out** to look for the missing climbers.*

ˈsearch ˌwarrant **noun** [C] an official document which gives police officers the authority to search a building for stolen property, illegal goods, or information which might help to solve a crime

searing /ˈsɪə.rɪŋ/ US /ˈsɪr.ɪŋ/ **adj** **1** If something, such as a feeling or temperature, is described as searing, it is extreme: *A searing **pain** shot up her arm.* ◦ *The race took place in the searing **heat**.* **2** (especially of a criticism or story) very powerful and emotional or criticizing someone or something very strongly: *The article is a searing attack on government mismanagement.* ◦ *a searing tale of love and hate* • **searingly** /-li/ **adv**

seascape /ˈsiː.skeɪp/ **noun** [C] a painting of a view of the sea

seashell /ˈsiː.ʃel/ **noun** [C] the empty shell of a small sea creature, often one found lying on the beach

the seashore /ˈsiː.ʃɔːʳ/ US /-ʃɔːr/ **noun** [S] the land along the edge of the sea: *As we walked along the seashore we saw several different sorts of seaweed.*

seasick /ˈsiː.sɪk/ **adj** vomiting or having the feeling you will vomit because of the movement of the ship you are travelling in: *I **was/felt** seasick, so I went up on deck for some fresh air.* • **seasickness** /-ˌsɪk.nəs/ **noun** [U]

the seaside /ˈsiː.saɪd/ **noun** [S] B1 the area near the sea, especially where people spend their holidays and enjoy themselves: *Let's go to the seaside at the weekend!* ◦ *a seaside holiday/hotel/resort*

season /ˈsiː.zᵊn/ **noun; verb**

▸**noun** [C] **1** B1 one of the four periods of the year; spring, summer, autumn, or winter **2** B1 the period of the year when something that happens every year happens: *How long does the **dry/hurricane/monsoon** season last?* **3** B1 the period of the year during which a particular sport is played: *The British football season begins in August and ends in May.* **4 the holiday, summer, tourist, etc. season** the period when most people take their holidays, go to visit places, or take part in an activity outside work: *Air fares are more expensive during the holiday season.* **5** UK a period when a set of programmes, plays, or musical events are broadcast or performed: *There will be more documentaries and fewer quiz shows in the autumn season on TV.* ◦ *There's a season (US **festival**) **of** 1960s French films at the Arts Cinema next month.* **6 in season a** B2 If fruit and vegetables are in season, they are being produced in the area and are available and ready to eat: *Fruit is cheaper when it's in season.* **b** at the time of year when many people want to travel or have a holiday: *Hotel rooms are more expensive in season.* **c** A female animal that is in season is ready to have sex and able to become pregnant. **d** An animal that is in season can be hunted legally during a particular period of time. **7 out of season a** C1 If fruit and vegetables are out of season, they do not grow in the area during that time: *In Britain, tomatoes are out of season in winter.* **b** C2 during the period when fewer people want to travel or have a holiday **c** during the period when it is not legal to hunt animals

> Word partners for **season** noun
>
> the *monsoon/rainy/summer/winter* season • the *high/low/peak* season • the *festive/holiday* season • *be in/come into* season

IDIOM **the season of goodwill** the period around CHRISTMAS

▸verb [T] **FLAVOUR** ▷ **1** to improve the flavour of SAVOURY food by adding salt, herbs, or spices when cooking or preparing it: *Drain the rice, stir in the salmon and season **to taste** (= so that it has the taste you like).* **WOOD** ▷ **2** to make wood hard to make it ready for use, by drying it gradually

seasonable /ˈsiː.zᵊn.ə.bl̩/ adj expected at or suitable for a particular time of the year: *December brought some seasonable snow showers.*

seasonal /ˈsiː.zᵊn.ᵊl/ adj B2 relating to or happening during a particular period in the year: *seasonal vegetables*

ˌ**seasonal afˌfective disˈorder** noun [U] (abbreviation **SAD**) a medical condition in which a person does not have much energy and enthusiasm during the winter because of the reduced period of natural light

seasonally /ˈsiː.zᵊn.ᵊl.i/ adv relating to the particular season of the year: *Although total unemployment has decreased, the seasonally **adjusted** figure has risen slightly.*

seasoned /ˈsiː.zᵊnd/ adj having a lot of experience of doing something and therefore knowing how to do it well: *a seasoned **traveller*** ◦ *a seasoned **campaigner** for human rights*

seasoning /ˈsiː.zᵊn.ɪŋ/ noun [C or U] a substance that is added to SAVOURY food to improve its flavour: *Taste the soup and adjust the seasoning, adding more salt or pepper as desired.*

ˌ**season's ˈgreetings** exclamation, noun [plural] something written on a Christmas card as a way of expressing a Christmas greeting

ˈ**season ˌticket** noun [C] a ticket that can be used many times within a limited period and is cheaper than paying separately for each use: *I have a season ticket **for** all Manchester United's games.*

seat /siːt/ noun; verb

▸noun **FURNITURE** ▷ **1** A2 [C] a piece of furniture or part of a train, plane, etc. that has been designed for someone to sit on: *Chairs, stools and benches are different types of seat.* ◦ *Please **have/take** a seat (= sit down).* ◦ *A car usually has a **driver's** seat, a **front/passenger** seat and **back/rear** seats.* ◦ *My ticket says 22D but there's already someone **in** (= sitting on) that seat.* ◦ *Is this seat **free/taken** (= is anyone using it)?* ◦ *Would you **keep** (= stop anyone else from sitting in) my seat (**for** me) while I go to the buffet car?* ◦ formal *Please **keep** your seats (= stay sitting down) until asked to leave.* ◦ *Could I **book/reserve** two seats (= arrange for them to be officially kept for me) for tomorrow evening's performance?* **BOTTOM PART** ▷ **2** [C usually singular] the part of a piece of furniture or clothing on which a person sits: *I've spilled some coffee on the seat of the armchair.* ◦ *The seat of those trousers looks rather tight, Sir. Would you like to try a larger size?* **POSITION** ▷ **3** C2 [C] an official position as a politician or member of a group of people who control something: *She has a seat **on** the board of directors.* ◦ *He is expected to **lose** his seat **on** the council in next month's elections.* ◦ *She **won** her seat **in** Parliament in 1979.* ◦ *He has a very **safe** seat (= a position that is very unlikely to be lost in an election).* **4** [C] Indian English the place in an office where a particular person sits: *I'm sorry – he's not in his seat right now.* **5** [C] Indian English a place on a course to study something: *On receipt of the tuition fees, the college will issue a letter confirming your seat on the course.* **BASE** ▷ **6** [C] a place which acts as a base or centre for an important activity: *The seat **of government** in the US is in Washington, DC.* ◦ *St Petersburg was the seat **of** the Russian Revolution.*

IDIOMS **bums on seats** UK (US **fannies in the seats**) the number of people who have paid to watch a performance: *Lowering ticket prices should increase the number of bums on seats.* • **seat of learning** formal a place where people are educated: *The Sorbonne is a world-famous seat of learning.* • **by the seat of your pants** If you do something by the seat of your pants, you do it using only your own experience and trusting your own judgment.

▸verb **1** [T + adv/prep] to arrange for someone to have a particular seat: *The waiter greeted me with a big smile and seated us by the window.* **2 seat yourself** [usually + adv/prep] to sit somewhere: *'I'm so glad to see you!' she said, seating herself between Eleanor and Marianne.* **3** C2 [T not continuous] (of a building, room, table, or vehicle) to have enough seats for the stated number of people: *The new concert hall seats 1,500 people.*

-seat /-siːt/ suffix with enough seats for the particular number of people: *a 2,000-seat theatre*

ˈ**seat ˌbelt** noun [C] (also ˈ**safety ˌbelt**) a belt that fastens around someone travelling in a vehicle or aircraft and holds them in their seat, in order to reduce the risk of them being injured in an accident: *Do you know how to **fasten/do up** your seat belt?* ◦ *You must **wear** your seat belt.*

seated /ˈsiː.tɪd/ US /-t̬ɪd/ adj B2 sitting: *The woman seated opposite him refused to stop staring at him.* ◦ *You are requested to **remain** seated during take-off.* ◦ formal *Ladies and gentlemen, please **be** seated (= please sit down).*

-seater /-siː.təʳ/ US /-t̬ɚ/ suffix with enough seats for the particular number of people: *a 50,000-seater stadium*

seating /ˈsiː.tɪŋ/ US /-t̬ɪŋ/ noun [U] **1** the seats that are provided in a place: *The car has seating **for** six.* **2** how or where people will sit: *Have you worked out the seating **arrangements/plan** for the wedding reception?*

ˈ**sea ˌurchin** noun [C] a small sea creature that lives in water that is not very deep, has a round shell covered with sharp points like needles, and has flesh that can be eaten

ˌ**sea ˈwall** noun [C] a wall that protects land from being covered or damaged by the sea or protects a port from the action of powerful waves

seaweed /ˈsiː.wiːd/ noun [U] a green, brown, or dark red plant that grows in the sea or on land very close to the sea

seaworthy /ˈsiːˌwɜː.ði/ US /-ˌwɜː-/ adj (of a ship) in a condition that is good enough to travel safely on the sea • **seaworthiness** /-nəs/ noun [U]

sebaceous gland /sɪˈbeɪ.ʃəsˌglænd/ noun [C] spe-

S

cialized a very small organ in the skin which produces sebum

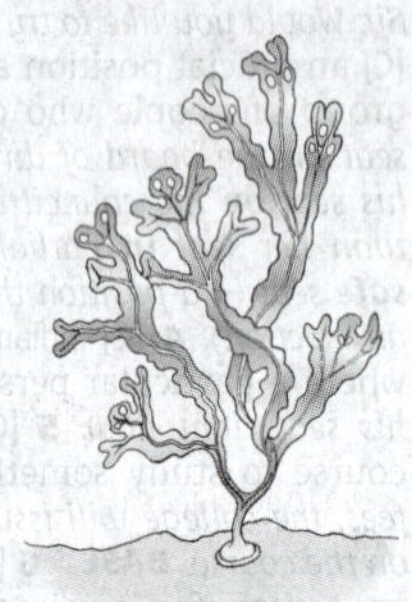

sebum /ˈsiː.bəm/ **noun** [U] specialized an oil-like substance produced by the sebaceous GLANDS in the skin that makes hair shiny and prevents skin from becoming dry

sec **noun** [C] /sek/ informal a very short period of time: *Would you mind waiting for me – I'll only be a couple of secs.*

sec. written abbreviation for **second**

secateurs /ˌsek.əˈtɜːz/ (US) /-ˈtɝz/ **noun** [plural] UK (US ˈ**pruning** ˌ**shears**) a garden tool that has two short sharp blades and is used for cutting plant stems

secede /sɪˈsiːd/ **verb** [I] formal to become independent of a country or area of government: *There is likely to be civil war if the region tries to secede* ***from*** *the south.* • **secession** /sesˈeʃ.ən/ **noun** [U] • **secessionist** /sesˈeʃ.ən.ɪst/ **noun** [C], **adj**

secluded /sɪˈkluː.dɪd/ **adj** C2 quiet, private, and not near people, roads, or buildings: *a secluded beach* ◦ *a secluded house in the forest*

seclusion /sɪˈkluː.ʒən/ **noun** [U] the state of being alone, away from other people: *He's been living* ***in*** *seclusion since he retired from acting.* ◦ *In some societies women are kept* ***in*** *seclusion, so that they are hardly ever seen in public.* ◦ *After being with a tour group all week I was glad to return to the seclusion* ***of*** *my own home.*

second[1] /ˈsek.ənd/ **ordinal number, determiner; adv; noun; verb**

▸**ordinal number**, **determiner** **1** A1 immediately after the first and before any others: *Is Brian her first or second child?* ◦ *This is the second time I've had flu this winter.* ◦ *Today is* ***the*** *second (****of*** *March).* **2** A1 the position in which a person finishes a race or competition if they finish immediately behind the winner: *First prize is a fortnight in Barbados and second* ***prize*** *is a weekend in Rome.* ◦ *Jones took second* ***place*** *in the long jump.* **3** B1 Second is used to show that only one thing is better, bigger, etc. than the thing mentioned: *St Petersburg is Russia's second (****biggest/largest****) city.* ◦ *Iraq's oil reserves are second* ***only to*** *Saudi Arabia's.* **4** B1 another: *She is often described as the second Marilyn Monroe.* ◦ *You really ought to make the most of the opportunity, because you won't get a second* ***chance****.* ◦ *Richard and Liz have a second* ***home*** *in France.* ◦ *Pay attention to what she's saying because she won't explain it a second* ***time****.* **5** happening only once out of every two possible times: *We've decided to hold the conference* ***every*** *second year.* → Compare **alternate**

IDIOMS **second best** not as good as the best and therefore not wanted so much: *She refuses to* ***settle for*** *second best – she strives for perfection.* • **second to none** as good as or better than all others: *The conditions that these prisoners are kept in are second to none.*

▸**adv** **1** B1 after the first and before any others: *Robertson won the race and Cameron* ***was/came/finished*** *second.* ◦ *In this business, money comes first and principles* ***come*** *a very* ***poor*** *second (= they are much less important).* **2** B2 (also **secondly**) used to introduce the second thing in a list of things you want to say or write: *There are two good reasons why we can't do it. First, we can't afford it, and second, we don't have time.*

▸**noun** **TIME** ▷ **1** A2 [C] (abbreviation **sec.**, **s**) a short unit of time that is equal to a 60th of a minute: *There are 60 seconds in a minute.* ◦ *These computers process millions of instructions* ***per*** *second.* ◦ *The new system can trace a phone call in a* ***fraction*** *of a second.* **2** B1 [C] a very short period of time: *'Come on, hurry up!' 'I'll* ***just/only*** *be a second – I've got to lock the back door.'* ◦ *Have you got a second, Paul? I'd like to have a word with you.* ◦ *It won't take a second (= it will be very quick).* ◦ *Wait* ***a couple of/a few*** *seconds before trying again.* **POSITION** ▷ **3** [S] the second person or thing to do or be something, or the second person or thing mentioned: *This is the second of the four tests.* **4 seconds** [plural] informal an extra amount of food that is given after the first amount has been eaten: *Would anyone like seconds* ***of*** *ice cream?* **MEASUREMENT** ▷ **5** [C] specialized the smallest unit used for measuring an angle: *There are 3,600 seconds in a degree.* **DAMAGED PRODUCT** ▷ **6** C2 [C] a product that is sold cheaply because it is damaged or not in perfect condition **HELPER** ▷ **7** [C] a person who takes care of someone who is fighting in a BOXING competition or, in the past, in a DUEL (= organized fight) **QUALIFICATION** ▷ **8** [C] (also ˌ**second-**ˌ**class de**ˈ**gree**) UK a degree qualification immediately below the highest level you can get from a British university **GEAR** ▷ **9** [U] (also **second gear**) in a vehicle, the GEAR that combines power with limited speed and is used when increasing or reducing speed: *You'll have to* ***change (down/up) into*** *second.*

▸**verb** [T] to make a formal statement of support for a suggestion made by someone else during a meeting so that there can be a discussion or vote: specialized *The* ***motion*** *was proposed by the club's chairwoman and seconded by the secretary.* ◦ *'I could do with a drink.' 'I'll second that (= I agree with you)!'* • **seconder** /ˈsek.ən.dəʳ/ (US) /-dɚ/ **noun** [C] *There was no seconder for (= person who was willing to support) the motion so it could not be debated.*

second[2] /sɪˈkɒnd/ (US) /-ˈkɑːnd/ **verb** [T] UK to send an employee to work somewhere else temporarily, either to increase the number of workers or to replace other workers, or to exchange experience or skills: *During the dispute, many police officers were seconded* ***from*** *traffic duty* ***to*** *the prison service.* • **secondment** /-mənt/ **noun** [C or U] UK *His involvement with the project began when he was on (a) secondment* ***from*** *NASA* ***to*** *the European Space Agency.*

secondary /ˈsek.ən.dri/ (US) /-der.i/ **adj** **EDUCATION** ▷ **1** B1 [before noun] relating to the education of children approximately between the ages of 11 and 18 years old: *secondary* ***education*** ◦ *Marcus has just started at secondary* ***school****.* **LESS IMPORTANT** ▷ **2** less important than related things: *Her health is what matters – the cost of the treatment is of secondary importance.* ◦ *The need for secrecy is secondary* ***to*** *the need to take immediate action.* **COMING AFTER** ▷ **3** developing from something similar that existed earlier: *The drug is not very effective against AIDS, though it may be used to treat secondary viral* ***infections****.* ◦ *You can't just rely on secondary* ***sources*** *for your research into her life history – you ought to look at primary sources such as her letters and diaries.* • **secondarily** /ˌsek.ənˈdeə.rɪ.li/ (US) /-ˈder.ɪ-/ **adv**

ˌ**second** ˈ**childhood** **noun** [S] a situation in which someone starts to behave like a child, especially because of mental weakness caused by old age: *Her grandfather's in his second childhood and talks nonsense most of the time.*

S

ˌsecond ˈclass adj; adv; noun
▸adj (also **ˌsecond-ˈclass**) NOT IMPORTANT ▷ **1** less important than other people: *Women are still treated as second class* ***citizens***. QUALIFICATION ▷ **2** a degree from a British university that is a good degree but not the best possible. LESS EXPENSIVE ▷ **3** relating to the less expensive way of travelling in a train, aircraft, etc., that most people use: *a second-class carriage/ticket* **4** UK Second-class post is less expensive and sent less quickly than FIRST-CLASS: *second-class mail/postage* ◦ *How much is a second-class stamp?*
▸adv **1** If you travel second class in a train, aircraft, etc., you use the less expensive type of ticket that most people use: *We always travel second class.* **2** UK If you send something second class, you send it using the less expensive type of post: *How much less would it cost to send it second class?*
▸noun [U] **1** the seats on a plane or in a train that are less good and less expensive than FIRST CLASS: *Second class is at the rear of the train.* **2** UK a less expensive and slower type of post than FIRST CLASS: *How much does it cost for second class?*

the ˌSecond ˈComing noun [S] the return of Jesus Christ to Earth from heaven that Christians expect will happen one day

ˌsecond ˈcousin noun [C] any person who is a child of a COUSIN of your mother or father

ˌsecond-deˈgree adj [before noun] US used to describe a crime that is not the most serious of its type, for example because it was not planned: *second-degree* ***murder/assault/felony*** → Compare **first-degree**

ˌsecond-ˌdegree ˈburn noun [C] a serious burn in which the skin develops BLISTERS → Compare **first-degree burn, third-degree burn**

the ˌsecond ˈfloor noun [S] in British English, the floor of a building that is two floors above ground level, or in American English, the floor that is directly above ground level: *I live* ***on*** *the second floor.* • **ˈsecond-ˌfloor** adj [before noun] *a second-floor apartment*

ˌsecond-ˈguess verb [T] GUESS ▷ **1** to guess what someone will do in the future: *She's always trying to second-guess the boss.* CRITICIZE ▷ **2** US to criticize someone's actions or an event after it has happened: *Of course it's easy to second-guess the management of the election campaign, but I do think serious mistakes were made.*

ˈsecond ˌhand noun [C usually singular] the long, thin piece on some clocks and watches that shows how many seconds have passed

ˌsecond-ˈhand adj, adv B1 not new; having been used in the past by someone else: *This bike is second-hand but it's still in good condition.* ◦ *She buys all her clothes second-hand.*

ˌsecond ˈhoneymoon noun [C usually singular] humorous a holiday taken by a couple who have been married for some time, especially in order to try to improve a relationship that is failing

ˌsecond-in-coˈmmand noun [S] someone who is almost as important as the person in charge: *Well, if the manager isn't available I'd like to speak to the second-in-command.*

ˌsecond ˈlanguage noun [C] a language that a person can speak that is not the first language they learned naturally as a child: *German is my second language.*

secondly /ˈsek.ənd.li/ adv (also **second**) B2 used when stating the second of two or more reasons or pieces of information: *I want two things from my boss – firstly, a pay rise, and secondly, a longer contract.*

ˈsecond ˌname noun [C] UK SURNAME (= the name that you share with other members of your family)

ˌsecond ˈnature noun [U] If something is second nature to you, you are so familiar with it that you can do it easily without needing to think very much about it: *I used to hate computers, but using them is second nature* ***to*** *me now.*

the ˌsecond ˈperson noun [S] B2 the form of a verb or PRONOUN that is used to a person that you are speaking to or writing to

ˌsecond-ˈrate adj not very good: *a second-rate film*

ˌsecond ˈsight noun [U] an unusual ability that some people are thought to have that allows them to know without being told what will happen in the future or what is happening in a different place

ˌsecond ˈthought noun [C] **1 without a second thought** If you do something without a second thought, you do it without first considering if you should do it or not: *She'll spend a hundred pounds on a dress without a second thought.* **2 have second thoughts** to change your opinion about something or start to doubt it: *You're not having second thoughts* ***about*** *getting married, are you?* **3 on second thoughts** UK (US **on second thought**) used when you want to change a decision you have made: *I'd like a cup of coffee, please – actually, on second thoughts, I'll have a beer.*

ˌsecond ˈwind noun [S] a return of strength or energy that makes it possible to continue in an activity that needs a lot of effort: *We started to feel we couldn't walk any further but when we saw the village in the distance we* ***got*** *a/our second wind.*

the ˌSecond ˌWorld ˈWar noun [S] the war from 1939 to 1945 in which many countries fought

secrecy /ˈsiː.krə.si/ noun [U] the state of being secret or of keeping something secret: *The content of her report is* ***shrouded in*** *secrecy (= being kept secret).* ◦ *I'd love to tell you about it, but Martin's* ***sworn*** *me* ***to*** *secrecy (= made me promise not to tell anyone).* ◦ *There has been strong criticism of the secrecy* ***surrounding*** *the negotiations.*

secret /ˈsiː.krət/ noun; adj
▸noun **1** B1 [C] a piece of information that is only known by one person or a few people and should not be told to others: *Why did you have to go and tell Bob about my illness? You just can't* ***keep*** *a secret, can you?* ◦ *A close couple should have no secrets* ***from*** *each other.* ◦ *Aren't you going to* ***let*** *me* ***in on*** *(= tell me) the secret?* ◦ *There's no secret (= everyone knows) about his homosexuality.* ◦ *She* ***makes no*** *secret* ***of*** *(= makes very clear) her dislike of her father.* ◦ *That restaurant is one of the* ***best-kept*** *secrets in London.* **2** [C] a fact about a subject that is not known: *the secrets of the universe* **3** B2 [S] the particular knowledge and skills needed to do something very well: *So what's the secret* ***of*** *being a good cook?*

> **Word partners for secret noun**
> ***harbour/have/keep*** a secret • ***let sb in on/reveal/tell sb*** a secret • a ***guilty/terrible/well-kept*** secret • a ***big*** secret • do sth ***in*** secret

IDIOMS **in secret 1** B2 in a private place with no one else present and without other people knowing: *The negotiators were meeting in secret for several months before the peace agreement was made public.* **2** only in someone's thoughts, without telling other people: *He says he loathes her, but I think in secret he really likes her.* • **your secret's safe with me** used to say that you will not tell anyone what you have just been told: *'I'd*

S

Other ways of saying secret

Covert is an alternative to 'secret', especially when talking about military or police actions:

*The government was accused of **covert** military operations.*

Clandestine is a formal word for 'secret', especially describing something that is not officially allowed:

*He arranged a **clandestine** meeting between his client and the candidate.*

If information is **confidential**, it is secret, especially in a formal or business situation, and should not be told to anyone else:

*All the information you give us will treated as strictly **confidential**.*

Official government information that is secret is described as **classified**:

*These documents contain **classified** information.*

Innermost or **private** can be used for thoughts or feelings which someone keeps secret:

*She never told anyone her **innermost** thoughts.*

*She kept her views on the subject **private**.*

If someone does something in a secret way because he or she does not want other people to see that action, you could use the adjectives **furtive** or **surreptitious**:

*He kept giving her **furtive** glances.*

*She took a **surreptitious** look at her watch.*

If something is **under wraps**, it is secret and you are deliberately not telling anyone about it yet:

*He is doing some research for a new book which is **under wraps** at the moment.*

appreciate it if you kept quiet about this.' 'Don't worry – your secret's safe with me.'

▸**adj 1** B1 If something is secret, other people are not allowed to know about it: *The president escaped through a secret passage underneath the parliament building.* ◦ *We ought to keep these proposals secret **from** the chairman for the time being.* ◦ *This is **top** (= extremely) secret information.* ◦ *Do you think we'll manage to **keep** the surprise party **secret** from Mum until her birthday?* **2** [before noun] describes someone who has a particular habit, hobby, or feeling but does not tell or show other people that they do: *a secret drinker* ◦ *a secret admirer* • **secretly** /-li/ **adv** B1 *She said she didn't care about it, but I believe she was secretly **delighted**.*

S

ˌsecret adˈmirer noun [C] humorous a person who likes another person but does not say so: *Who sent you those flowers – have you got a secret admirer?*

ˌsecret ˈagent noun [C] a government employee whose job involves getting secret information about the governments of unfriendly foreign countries → Synonym **spy**

secretarial /ˌsek.rəˈteə.ri.əl/ US /-ˈter.i-/ **adj** relating to the work of a secretary: *a secretarial college* ◦ *She's found some part-time secretarial work.*

secretariat /ˌsek.rəˈteə.ri.ət/ US /-ˈter.i-/ **noun** [C, + sing/pl verb] the office or people responsible for the management of an organization, especially an international or political one

secretary /ˈsek.rə.tᵊr.i/ US /-ter.i/ **noun** [C] **OFFICE** ▷ **1** A2 someone who works in an office, writing letters, making phone calls, and arranging meetings for a person or for an organization: *My secretary will phone you to arrange a meeting.* **COMMITTEE** ▷ **2** C1 the member of a COMMITTEE of an organization, club, etc. who keeps records of meetings, sends letters, emails, etc.: *The three elected members of the committee are the chair, secretary, and treasurer.* **OFFICIAL** ▷ **3** an official who has responsibility for the general management of an organization: *The **company** secretary has written to all the shareholders to apologize for the mistake.*

Secretary /ˈsek.rə.tᵊri/ US /-ter.i/ **noun** [C] **1** UK a **Secretary of State**: *the Foreign Secretary* ◦ *the Home Secretary* **2** US the head of a government department, chosen by the president and not a member of a law-making group: *the Secretary of Health and Human Services*

ˌsecretary ˈgeneral noun [C] (plural **secretaries general**) The secretary general of an organization is its most important official.

ˌSecretary of ˈState noun [C] **1** (also **Secretary**) in the UK, a Member of Parliament who is in charge of a government department: *She became Secretary of State **for** Education after spending three years as Environment Secretary.* ◦ *Was the conference a success, Foreign Secretary?* **2** in the US, an important government official who has responsibility for relationships with the governments of other countries

ˌsecret ˈballot noun [C or U] a method of voting in which each person writes their choice on a piece of paper so that no one else knows how they have voted: *The election of the government is carried out **by** secret ballot.*

secrete /sɪˈkriːt/ **verb** [T] **PRODUCE** ▷ **1** specialized (of animals or plants or their cells) to produce and release a liquid: *Saliva is a liquid secreted by glands in or near the mouth.* **HIDE** ▷ **2** formal to put something in a place where it is unlikely to be found: *He was arrested at the airport with a kilo of heroin secreted **in** his clothing.*

secretion /sɪˈkriː.ʃᵊn/ **noun** [C or U] specialized the process by which an animal or plant produces and releases a liquid, or the liquid produced: *The excessive secretion of gastric juices in the gut causes ulcers.* ◦ *toxic secretions*

secretive /ˈsiː.krə.tɪv/ US /-t̬ɪv/ **adj** mainly disapproving People who are secretive hide their feelings, thoughts, intentions, and actions from other people: *He's being very secretive **about** his new girlfriend.* • **secretively** /-li/ **adv** mainly disapproving • **secretiveness** /-nəs/ **noun** [U] mainly disapproving

ˌsecret poˈlice noun [U] a police force which secretly collects information about people who oppose the government and tries to make such opposition weaker, often using illegal and violent methods

ˌsecret ˈservice noun [S] a government organization that is responsible for things such as the safety of important politicians and for preventing secret information being discovered by possible enemy countries

ˌsecret ˈshopper noun [C] US (also **mystery shopper**) someone employed to test the service in shops and businesses by pretending to be a normal customer

ˌsecret soˈciety noun [C] an organization which does not allow people who are not members to find out about its activities and customs

ˌsecret ˈweapon noun [C] something or someone that no one knows about and that will give you an advantage over your competitors or enemies: *Johann was the bank robbers' secret weapon – he knew how the security system worked.*

sect /sekt/ **noun** [C] usually disapproving a religious group that has developed from a larger religion and is considered to have extreme or unusual beliefs or customs: *When he was 16 he ran away from home and joined a **religious** sect.*

sectarian /sekˈteə.ri.ən/ (US) /-ˈter.i-/ noun [C], adj mainly disapproving (a person) strongly supporting a particular religious group, especially in such a way as not to be willing to accept other beliefs: *a sectarian murder* ◦ *He called on terrorists on both sides of the sectarian divide to end the cycle of violence.* • **sectarianism** /-ə.nɪ.zᵊm/ noun [U] disapproving

section /ˈsek.ʃᵊn/ noun; verb
▸noun **PART** ▷ **1** (B1) [C] one of the parts that something is divided into: *the sports section **of** the newspaper* ◦ *the tail section **of** an aircraft* ◦ *Does the restaurant have a non-smoking section?* ◦ *The poorest sections **of** the community have much worse health.* ◦ *He was charged **under** section 17 of the Firearms Act (= according to that part of the law).* **CUT** ▷ **2** [C or U] specialized a cut made in part of the body in an operation **3** [C] specialized a **caesarean (section)** **4** [C] specialized a very thin slice of a part of an animal, plant, or other object made in order to see its structure: *Each section is mounted on a slide and examined under the microscope.* **5** [C] specialized a drawing or model which shows the structure of something by cutting part of it away: *This **vertical** section of the soil shows four basic soil layers.* **6** [C] the shape of a flat surface that is produced when an object is cut into separate pieces **7** **in section** showing what something would look like if the surface was cut away and you could see inside: *The first diagram is a view of the shop from the street, and the second shows it in section.*
▸verb [T] UK to officially force someone who has mental health problems to stay in a hospital and receive treatment because they might harm themselves or other people: *He was sectioned under section 4 of the Mental Health Act.*

sectional /ˈsek.ʃᵊn.ᵊl/ adj **1** US describes a piece of furniture that is made up of parts that can be arranged in various ways: *a sectional sofa* **2** Interests or aims that are sectional are limited to a particular group within an organization, society, or country and do not consider other groups: *The national interest is more important than any sectional or personal interests.*

sector /ˈsek.təʳ/ (US) /-tɚ/ noun [C] **ECONOMIC AREA** ▷ **1** (C1) one of the areas into which the economic activity of a country is divided: *In the **financial** sector, banks and insurance companies have both lost a lot of money.* ◦ *The new government's policy is to transfer state industries from the **public** sector to the **private** sector.* **CONTROLLED AREA** ▷ **2** an area of land or sea that has been divided from other areas and is controlled by a particular country: *What is the total oil output from the British sector of the North Sea?*

secular /ˈsek.jʊ.ləʳ/ (US) /-jə.lɚ/ adj not having any connection with religion: *We live in an increasingly secular society, in which religion has less and less influence on our daily lives.* ◦ *secular education* ◦ *a secular state*

ˌsecular ˈhumanism noun [U] a set of beliefs which emphasize the importance of reason and of people rather than religion • **ˌsecular ˈhumanist** noun [C]

secularism /ˈsek.jʊ.lᵊr.ɪ.zᵊm/ (US) /-jə.lɚ-/ noun [U] the belief that religion should not be involved with the ordinary social and political activities of a country • **secularist** /-ɪst/ noun [C], adj

secularize (UK usually **secularise**) /ˈsek.jʊ.lᵊr.aɪz/ (US) /-jə.lə.raɪz/ verb [T] When something is secularized, religious influence, power, or control is removed from it: *He claims that Western secularized society makes it difficult to live as a Christian.*

secure /sɪˈkjʊəʳ/ (US) /-ˈkjʊr/ adj; verb
▸adj **FIXED** ▷ **1** (B2) positioned or fixed firmly and correctly and therefore not likely to move, fall, or break: *That ladder doesn't look very secure to me.* ◦ *Check that all windows and doors are secure.* ◦ figurative *Her promotion has made her position in the company more secure.* ◦ figurative *The museum has been promised £22 million by the government, so its future is relatively secure.* **2** A secure place is one that it is difficult to get out of or escape from: *He killed the man just a month after his release from a secure mental hospital.* **PROTECTED** ▷ **3** (especially of objects, situations, etc.) able to avoid being harmed by any risk, danger, or threat: *Car manufacturers ought to produce vehicles which are more secure **against** theft.* ◦ *Endangered species need to be **kept** secure **from** poachers.* **CONFIDENT** ▷ **4** (B2) not doubting or being worried about yourself and your personal relationships: *Children need to feel secure in order to do well at school.*
▸verb **GET** ▷ **1** [T] formal to get something, sometimes with difficulty: *He was disappointed by his failure to secure the top job with the bank.* ◦ *The change in the law will make it harder for the police to secure **convictions**.* **PROTECT** ▷ **2** [I or T] to make certain something is protected from danger or risk: *The building has only one main entrance and would be easy to secure (**against/from** intruders).* ◦ *This form of investment is an excellent way of securing your children's financial future.* **FINANCE** ▷ **3** [T] to make certain that money which has been lent will be paid back, by giving the person who lends the money the right to own property belonging to the person who borrows it, if the money is not paid back: *a secured **loan*** ◦ *Her bank loan is secured **against/by/on** her house.* **FIX** ▷ **4** [T] to fasten one object firmly to another: *The gate won't stay open, so we'll have to secure it **to** that post.*

securely /sɪˈkjʊə.li/ (US) /-ˈkjʊr-/ adv **PROTECTED** ▷ **1** in a way that avoids someone or something being harmed by any risk, danger, or threat: *The door was securely fastened.* ◦ *The offices were securely guarded.* ◦ *This certificate is an important document, and should be kept securely (= in a place where it cannot be lost or stolen).* **FIXED** ▷ **2** positioned or fastened firmly and correctly and therefore not likely to move, fall, or break: *Please ensure that your seat belts are fastened securely.* ◦ figurative *He has given up political power, but he remains securely in control of the army.*

security /sɪˈkjʊə.rɪ.ti/ (US) /-ˈkjʊr.ə.t̬i/ noun **PROTECTION** ▷ **1** (B1) [U] protection of a person, building, organization, or country against threats such as crime or attacks by foreign countries: *The station was closed for two hours because of a security **alert**.* ◦ *30 demonstrators were killed in clashes with the security **forces** over the weekend.* ◦ *The tighter security **measures/precautions** include video cameras in the city centre.* ◦ *The students were deported because they posed a threat to **national** security.* ◦ *The proposed national identity card system would help to **tighten** security against fraud.* ◦ *The most dangerous criminals are held in **maximum**-security prisons (= prisons that are as difficult as possible to escape from).* **2** [U, + sing/pl verb] the group of people responsible for protecting a building **FIXED** ▷ **3** (C1) [U] the fact that something is not likely to fail or be lost: *If it's a choice between higher pay and **job** security, I'd prefer to keep my job.* ◦ *I'm on a temporary contract and have little financial security (= little certainty of having enough money to live on).* **FINANCE** ▷ **4** [U] property or goods that you promise to give to someone if you cannot pay them what you owe them: *She used her shares in the*

S

company **as** security **against** a £23 million bank loan. ◦ *The hotel held onto our baggage* ***as*** *security while we went to the bank to get money to pay the bill.* **5 securities** [plural] specialized INVESTMENT in a company or in government debt that can be traded on the financial markets and produces an income for the INVESTOR **CONFIDENCE** ▷ **6** C2 [U] the feeling of being confident in one's family and relationships: *Most children need the security of a stable family life.*

se'curity ˌblanket noun [C] **1** a soft object such as a small piece of cloth or a toy that is very familiar to a baby or young child and makes him or her feel safe **2** something that makes you feel safe or confident

se'curity ˌclearance noun [C or U] official permission given to someone to enter a building or area, after making certain that they are not a threat

the Se'curity ˌCouncil noun [+ sing/pl verb] a part of the United Nations whose purpose is to prevent war and keep peace

se'curity ˌguard noun [C] someone whose job involves preventing people going into places without permission, transporting large amounts of money, or protecting goods from being stolen

se'curity ˌrisk noun [C] something or someone likely to cause danger or difficulty: *The only reason she was considered a security risk was because her husband was a foreigner.*

sedan /sɪ'dæn/ noun [C] US for **saloon**

se'dan ˌchair noun [C] in the past, a seat for one person surrounded by walls and with horizontal poles at either side, designed to be lifted and carried by two people

sedate /sɪ'deɪt/ **adj; verb**

▸**adj** avoiding excitement or great activity and usually calm and relaxed: *The fight against a chemical storage site has transformed a normally sedate village into a battleground.* ◦ *The speed limit is a sedate 55 mph.* • **sedately** /-li/ adv

▸**verb** [T] to cause a person or animal to be very calm or go to sleep by giving them a drug: *When I saw him after the accident he was still in shock and was* ***heavily*** *sedated.* • **sedation** /sɪ'deɪ.ʃən/ noun [U] *She's* ***under*** *strong sedation and should not be disturbed.*

sedative /'sed.ə.tɪv/ US /-t̬ɪv/ noun [C] a drug used to calm a person or animal or to make them sleep

sedentary /'sed.ən.tər.i/ US /-ter.i/ **adj** C2 involving little exercise or physical activity: *a sedentary job/occupation* ◦ *My doctor says I should start playing sport because my* ***lifestyle*** *is too sedentary.*

S

sediment /'sed.ɪ.mənt/ **noun** **1** [C or U] a soft substance that is like a wet powder and consists of very small pieces of a solid material that have fallen to the bottom of a liquid: *There was a brown sediment in the bottom of the bottle.* **2 sediments** [plural] sand, stones, etc. that slowly form a layer of rock: *It is hoped that the oil slick will sink to the seabed where it would be covered within a few years by sediments and eventually decompose.* • **sedimentation** /ˌsed.ɪ.men'teɪ.ʃən/ noun [U]

sedimentary /ˌsed.ɪ'men.tər.i/ US /-t̬ɚ.i/ **adj** (of rock) made from sediment left by the action of water, ice, or wind: *sedimentary rock*

sedimen'tation ˌtank noun [C] specialized a large container in which dirty or waste water is stored until all the solid material in it falls to the bottom and the water can be released for further treatment

sedition /sɪ'dɪʃ.ən/ noun [U] formal language or behaviour that is intended to persuade other people to oppose their government • **seditious** /-əs/ **adj** *She was arrested after making a speech that the government considered to be seditious.*

seduce /sɪ'djuːs/ US /-'duːs/ **verb** **PERSUADE** ▷ **1** C2 [T] to persuade someone to have sex with you, often someone younger than you, who has little experience of sex: *Pete lost his virginity at 15 when he was seduced by his best friend's mother.* **ATTRACT** ▷ **2** C2 [T usually passive] to cause someone to do something that they would not usually consider doing by being very attractive and difficult to refuse: *I wouldn't normally have bought this, but I was seduced by the low price.* ◦ *They were seduced* ***into*** *buy****ing*** *the washing machine by the offer of a free flight to the United States.* **3** [T usually passive] If you are seduced by something, you like it because it seems attractive: *Almost every visitor to Edinburgh is seduced by its splendid architecture.*

seducer /sɪ'djuː.sər/ US /-'duː.sɚ/ **noun** [C] someone who seduces people: *The play tells the story of a wealthy woman who seeks revenge on her heartless seducer.*

seduction /sɪ'dʌk.ʃən/ **noun** **ATTRACTING** ▷ **1** [C usually plural] the attractive quality of something: *The seductions of life in a warm climate have led many Britons to live abroad, especially in Spain.* **PERSUADING** ▷ **2** [C or U] the act of seducing someone: *The film depicts Charlotte's seduction by her boss.*

seductive /sɪ'dʌk.tɪv/ **adj** **PERSUADING** ▷ **1** intended to seduce someone: *It was a seductive black evening dress.* ◦ *She gave him a seductive look.* **ATTRACTING** ▷ **2** making you want to do, have, or believe something, because of seeming attractive: *Television confronts the viewer with a succession of glittering and seductive* ***images.*** ◦ *The* ***argument*** *that sanctions should be given more time to work is seductive but fatally flawed.* • **seductively** /-li/ **adv** • **seductiveness** /-nəs/ **noun** [U]

seductress /sɪ'dʌk.trəs/ **noun** [C] a female seducer

sedulous /'sed.jʊ.ləs/ **adj** formal careful and using a lot of effort: *It was agreed that the few students sedulous enough to read the book deserved top marks for diligence.* • **sedulously adv** *Susan and Robert sedulously avoided all political discussion.*

see /siː/ **verb** (present participle **seeing**, past tense **saw**, past participle **seen**) **USE EYES** ▷ **1** A1 [I or T] to be conscious of what is around you by using your eyes: *Turn the light on so I can see.* ◦ *I* ***can*** *see you!* ◦ [+ (that)] *The teacher could see* (***that***) *the children had been fighting.* ◦ [+ infinitive without to] *Jacqui saw the car drive up outside the police station.* ◦ [+ -ing verb] *From the window we could see the children play****ing*** *in the yard.* ◦ [+ past participle] *His parents saw him award****ed*** *the winner's medal.* ◦ *See (= look at) p. 23 for prices and flight details.* ◦ *See* ***over*** *(= look at the next page) for further information.* **2** A2 [T] to watch a film, television programme, etc.: *Did you see that documentary on Channel 4 last night?* **3** C1 [T often passive] to be the time or place when something happens: *This summer has seen the end of water restrictions in the area thanks to a new reservoir.* **4 you ain't seen nothing yet** humorous said to mean that more surprising or exciting things are likely to happen **UNDERSTAND** ▷ **5** B1 [T] to understand, know, or realize: [+ (that)] *I see* (***that***) *the social club is organizing a theatre trip next month.* ◦ [+ question word] *He can't see* ***wh****at difference it makes to come (= he doesn't think it is important if he comes) on Thursday instead of Friday.* ◦ *They didn't see* ***the need/any need*** *(= understand that it was important) to notify their members of the changes in writing.* ◦ *They only refused to help because they're too busy, but he seems to see more* ***in*** *it than that.* ◦ *'I'm tired.'* ***'So*** *I see – you've been yawning all afternoon.'*

◦ *The chairwoman thought the new scheme was a great improvement, but I couldn't see* ***it*** *myself (= couldn't understand why it was thought to be good, or didn't agree).* ◦ *I was surprised that they couldn't see my point of view.* ◦ *The government didn't want to* **be** *seen* **to be** *making concessions to terrorists.* ◦ *After she read his book she started to see the issue* ***in another/a different/ a new light*** *(= differently).* **MEET** ▷ **6** Ⓐ1 [I or T] to meet or visit someone, or to visit a place: *We're seeing friends at the weekend.* ◦ *I haven't seen Jerry* ***around*** *(= in the places I usually meet him) in the last few weeks.* ◦ *No one has seen* ***much of*** *Daryl since he got married.* ◦ *They see* ***a lot of*** *each other (= are often together) at weekends.* ◦ *My mother is seeing the doctor again next week.* ◦ *The children wanted to see the circus.* ◦ *The agent said they could see the house* (UK also *see* ***round*** *the house) at 3 p.m.* **7** [T] to have a romantic relationship with someone: *How long has she been seeing him?* **CONSIDER** ▷ **8** Ⓑ2 [T] to consider or think about, especially to think about someone or something in a particular way, or to imagine someone doing a particular activity: *She didn't see herself* ***as*** *brave.* ◦ *It was easy to see the gift* ***as*** *a sort of bribe.* ◦ [+ obj + -ing verb] *I can't see her accept****ing*** *(= I don't think she will accept) the job in the present circumstances.* ◦ *As I see* ***it/things/the situation****, we'll have to get extra help.* ◦ *Try and see it my* ***way*** *– I'll be left without any help if you go to Edinburgh tomorrow.* **GO WITH** ▷ **9** [T usually + adv/prep] to take someone somewhere by going there with them: *He saw his visitors* ***to the door.*** ◦ *Her friends saw her* ***home.*** ◦ *The security guard saw the protesters* ***off*** *the premises.* **TRY TO DISCOVER** ▷ **10** Ⓑ2 [I + question word] to try to discover: *Will you see* ***if*** *you can get anyone to help?* ◦ *I'll see* ***wh****at I can do.* **MAKE CERTAIN** ▷ **11** Ⓒ2 [+ (that)] to make certain that something happens: *See* ***(that)*** *you're ready by five, or there'll be trouble.* ◦ *The receptionist said he'd see* ***(that)*** *she got the message.*

> **Other ways of saying see**
>
> See also: **look**
>
> If you see or become aware of something, the verbs **notice** or **perceive** are often used, or in formal English, **observe**:
>
> *I* ***noticed*** *a crack in the ceiling.*
>
> *Bill* ***perceived*** *a tiny figure in the distance.*
>
> *A teacher* ***observed*** *her climbing over the gate.*
>
> **Spot** is used when you see someone or something, especially when you are looking hard for that person or thing:
>
> *We* ***spotted*** *several dolphins swimming nearby.*
>
> The phrases **catch sight of** and **catch a glimpse of** are used when you suddenly see something for a moment:
>
> *He* ***caught sight of/caught a glimpse of*** *his reflection in the glass.*
>
> You use the verb **witness** when someone sees an event such as a crime or an accident:
>
> *Did anyone* ***witness*** *the attack?*
>
> The phrasal verb **make out** is used when you see something but with difficulty:
>
> *I could just* ***make out*** *a figure standing in the doorway.*

IDIOMS **can't see further than the end of your nose** If someone can't see further than the end of their nose, they do not notice what is happening around them. • **can't see the wood for the trees** UK (US **can't see the forest for the trees**) to be unable to understand a situation clearly because you are too involved in it • **have seen better days** to be old and in bad condition: *That jacket's seen better days. Why don't you get a new one?* • **have to be seen to be believed** to be so extreme that it is difficult to believe: *The mess the burglars left behind had to be seen to be believed.* • **I/ we'll (have to) see** Ⓒ1 used to say that you will make a decision about something later: *'Do you think there'll be time to stop for a meal?' 'We'll see.'* • **let me see/let's see** used when you want to think for a moment about something: *'Do you know a shop that sells sports clothes?' 'Let me see – I think there's one near the station.'* • **not see beyond sth** disapproving to have your attention fixed on something and therefore be unable to consider other things: *The government cannot see beyond next year's general election.* • **not see sb for dust** UK informal used to describe someone leaving quickly in order to avoid something: *If you let him know that Margaret's coming, you won't see him for dust.* • **not see hide nor hair of sb** informal to not see someone at all over a period of time: *I haven't seen hide nor hair of her since last Friday.* • **see sth coming** to expect something to happen: *No one else had expected the factory to close, but we saw it coming.* • **see sb in hell before ...** mainly UK informal If you would see someone in hell before you would do something they have suggested, you are very determined not to do it: *I'd see her in hell before I'd agree to an arrangement like that.* • **see sb right** UK informal to make certain that someone is helped or treated well: *Ask Mrs Martin at the desk over there about the invoices – she'll see you right.* • **see your way (clear) to doing sth** to agree to do or allow something: *Could you see your way to letting us borrow the machine on Wednesday?* • **see eye to eye** Ⓒ2 If two people see eye to eye, they agree with each other: *My sisters* ***don't*** *see eye to eye* ***with*** *me about the arrangements.* • **see fit** formal If you see fit to do something, you think it is good or necessary to do it: *She saw fit to take her son away from the school.* • **see in the New Year** to not go to bed on 31 December until after twelve o'clock at night in order to celebrate the start of a new year • **see life** to experience many different and often unexpected things: *As a volunteer on the childcare project, I really saw life.* • **see red** Ⓒ2 to become very angry: *People who don't finish a job really make me see red.* • **see sense/reason** Ⓒ2 to be reasonable and have good judgment: *We talked to her for an hour, but we couldn't make her see sense.* • **see stars** If you see stars, you are partly unconscious because you have been hit on the head. • **see the back of sb/sth** UK If you are pleased to see the back of something/someone, you are pleased that you no longer have to be involved with them: *The hotel staff were* ***glad*** *to see the back of such a difficult guest.* • **see the colour of sb's money** informal To see the colour of someone's money is to make certain that a person is going to pay for something: *'I'll have one of those.' 'Let's see the colour of your money first!'* • **see the joke** to understand something funny and find it funny yourself: *Everyone else laughed loudly but I didn't see the joke.* • **see the last of sth/sb** to not see something or someone again because they have gone away or are finished • **see the light** If you see the light, you suddenly understand something you didn't understand before. • **see the light of day** When something sees the light of day, it appears for the first time. • **see the point of sth** to understand the importance of or the reason for something: *They couldn't see the point of further training.* • **see you (later)** informal Ⓐ1 goodbye • **seeing is believing** saying said to mean that if you see something yourself, you will believe it to exist or be true, despite the fact that it is extremely

S

unusual or unexpected: *I never thought Simon would get out of bed before lunchtime on a Saturday, but seeing is believing!* • **seeing things** If you are seeing things, you are imagining that things are happening when they are not: *Didn't Marie come in just now? I must have been seeing things.* • **we'll (soon) see about that** used when you are angry about something that you feel is unfair and that you intend to stop happening: *He wants to park his car on my lawn? Well, we'll soon see about that!* • **what you see is what you get** saying said to show that there is nothing hidden → See also **WYSIWYG** • **wouldn't be seen dead** informal If someone wouldn't be seen dead in a particular place or doing a particular thing, they would never do it, usually because it would be too embarrassing: *I wouldn't be seen dead wearing a dress like that.* • **you see** C1 used when you hope someone else will understand what you are saying or asking: *Could you lend me £10? I need to do some shopping, you see.*

PHRASAL VERBS **see about sth** informal to prepare for or deal with an action or event, or to arrange for something to be done: *It's getting late – I'd better see about lunch.* ◦ [+ -ing verb] *You should see about getting your hair cut.* • **not see beyond sth** disapproving to have your attention fixed on something and therefore be unable to consider other things: *The government cannot see beyond next year's general election.* • **see sth in sb/sth** to believe that someone or something has a particular quality: *We don't travel on bank holiday weekends – I just can't see the pleasure in it. He's so boring – I don't know what she sees in him.* • **see sb off** SAY GOODBYE ▷ **1** B2 to go to the place that someone is leaving from in order to say goodbye to them: *My parents saw me off at the airport.* GET RID OF ▷ **2** to send away someone who is attacking you or who is not wanted, usually forcefully: *The caretaker ran out and saw off the boys who had been damaging the fence.* • **see sb/sth off** informal to defeat someone or something, or to deal with them effectively so that they can no longer cause harm: *England saw off Luxembourg 5–0.* • **see sth out** to wait or last until the end of a difficult event or situation: *The besieged town hasn't enough food to see the month out.* ◦ *They saw out the storm in the best shelter they could find.* • **see sb out** (also **see sb to the door**) to go to the door of a building or room with someone who does not live or work there, when they are leaving: *My secretary will see you out.* • **see yourself out** (also **see yourself to the door**) to leave a building or room by yourself after visiting someone there: *It's ok – I'll see myself out.* • **see sb through sth** to help or support someone during a difficult period in their life: *He was a prisoner of war for five years, but his courage saw him through.* ◦ *My brother's lent me £500 to see me through the next few weeks.* • **see sth through** to continue doing a job or activity until it is finished, especially when it is difficult: *The course would take me three years to complete, but I was determined to see it through.* • **see through sb/sth** B2 to realize that someone is trying to deceive you to get an advantage, or that someone's behaviour is intended to deceive you, and to understand the truth about the situation: *They were very friendly, but I quickly saw through them.* ◦ *She saw through his excuse at once.* • **see to sth/sb** B2 to deal with a person or task that needs to be dealt with or is waiting to be dealt with: *'These letters need posting.' 'I'll see to them later.'* ◦ *Mrs Chapman asked for some help with the orders – could you see to it?* ◦ [+ that] *Please see to it that no one comes in without identification.*

S

seed /siːd/ noun; verb
▸noun PLANT ▷ **1** B2 [C or U] a small, round or oval object produced by a plant and from which, when it is planted, a new plant can grow: ***Sow** the seeds (= put them in the ground) about three centimetres deep.* ◦ *The chemical will stop all seeds from **sprouting** (= starting to grow).* ◦ *The farmers grow these crops for seed (= for planting to grow more crops, rather than for eating).* **2** [U] literary **semen** **3 go/run to seed a** If a food plant goes or runs to seed, it produces flowers and seeds because it has not been picked early enough: *In hot weather lettuces can suddenly run to seed.* **b** If a person or place goes or runs to seed, their physical appearance becomes worse because no one cares for them: *After he retired, he really went to seed.* BEGINNING ▷ **4** C2 [C usually plural] the cause of a feeling or situation, or the early stages of it: *The seeds **of** friendship were sown early, and they remained lifelong companions.* ◦ *He may be **sowing** the seeds **of** his own destruction in the long term by using violence against his own people.* SPORT ▷ **5** [C] especially in tennis, a good player who is given a place on the list of those expected to win games in a particular competition because of the way they have played in the past: *Turner's opponent in the quarter-finals of the darts is the number one seed.*
▸verb PLANT ▷ **1** [I or T] to produce seeds: *The plants have seeded themselves (= their seeds have fallen) into the cracks between the paving stones.* **2** [T] (also **deseed**) to remove the seeds from a fruit or vegetable: *Wash, seed, and cut the pepper into small pieces.* SPORT ▷ **3** [T usually passive] to make a player a seed: [+ adj] *Jones, seeded second, has won her last ten matches.*

ˈseed ˌcorn noun [U] **1** grain that is kept for planting to produce new plants **2** something that is important because it is the starting point for future development: *Investment is the seed corn of economic progress.*

seeded /ˈsiː.dɪd/ adj PLANT ▷ **1** with the seeds removed: *Garnish with peeled, seeded, and diced tomatoes.* **2** containing seeds SPORT ▷ **3** especially of a tennis player, given a place on the list of those expected to win games in a particular competition because of the way they have played in the past: *seeded players*

-seeded /-siː.dɪd/ suffix PLANT ▷ **1** with the type of seed mentioned: *The walnut is a hard-seeded fruit.* SPORT ▷ **2** being seeded in the position mentioned: *The fifth-seeded Browne crushed the defending champion.*

seedless /ˈsiːd.ləs/ adj without seeds: *seedless grapes*

seedling /ˈsiːd.lɪŋ/ noun [C] a very young plant that has grown from a seed: ***Raise** the seedlings in the greenhouse.*

ˈseed ˌmoney noun [U] US money used to start a business or activity

ˈseed poˌtato noun [C] Seed potatoes are potatoes that are planted so that a plant will grow and more potatoes will be produced.

seedy /ˈsiː.di/ adj looking dirty or in bad condition and likely to be involved in dishonest or illegal activities: *a seedy hotel* • **seediness** /-nəs/ noun [U]

ˈseeing (that) conjunction (informal **seeing as**, not standard **seeing as how**) considering or accepting the fact that; as: *We may as well go to the concert, seeing as we've already paid for the tickets.*

Seeing ˈEye ˌdog noun [C] US trademark **guide dog**

seek /siːk/ verb (**sought**, **sought**) formal SEARCH ▷ **1** B2 [T] to try to find or get something, especially something that is not a physical object: *'Are you actively seeking jobs?' she asked.* ◦ *Hundreds of dissidents are seeking refuge/asylum in the US embassy.*

2 B2 [T] to ask for advice, help, approval, permission, etc.: *Legal advice should be sought before you take any further action.*

> **! Common mistake: seek**
>
> **Remember: seek** is not usually followed by a preposition.
>
> Don't say 'seek for something', say **seek something**:
>
> ~~*I went to the beach seeking for peace.*~~
>
> *I went to the beach seeking peace.*

TRY ▷ **3** C2 [I + to infinitive] to try or attempt: *They sought **to** reassure the public.* • **-seeking** /-ɪŋ/ **suffix** *A lot of bad behaviour is **attention**-seeking on the part of mixed-up kids.*

PHRASAL VERB **seek sb/sth out** to look for someone or something, especially for a long time until you find them: *While he was at the library, Steve decided to seek out some information on accommodation in the area.*

seeker /ˈsiː.kəʳ/ US /-kɚ/ **noun** [C] a person who is looking for the thing mentioned: *asylum seekers* ◦ *job-seekers*

seem /siːm/ **verb** [I + adv/prep, L] B1 to give the effect of being; to be judged to be: *He's 16, but he often seems (**to be**) younger.* ◦ *The children seemed (**as if/as though/like** they were) tired.* ◦ *I suspect his claims are **not all** they seem – he tends to exaggerate.* ◦ *Things are seldom **as/how/what** they seem.* ◦ [+ to infinitive] *I seem **to** know more about him than anyone else.* ◦ *They seem **to** be taking a long time to decide.* ◦ [+ (that)] ***It** seems (**that**) she can't come.* ◦ ***It** seems **to** me (**that**) (= I think that) he isn't the right person for the job.* ◦ formal ***It would** seem (**that**) we need to be at the airport two hours before take-off.* ◦ ***There** seems **to** have been a mistake – my name isn't on the list.* ◦ [after so] *'There's no reply – they've all gone home.' '**So** it seems.'* ◦ *'Was a decision made?' 'It seems **not/so**.'*

seeming /ˈsiː.mɪŋ/ **adj** [before noun] formal appearing to be something, especially when this is not true: *He said, with seeming embarrassment, that he would have to cancel the meeting.*

seemingly /ˈsiː.mɪŋ.li/ **adv** **1** C1 appearing to be something, especially when this is not true: *He remains confident and seemingly untroubled by his recent problems.* **2** according to the facts that you know: *The factory closure is seemingly inevitable.* ◦ *Seemingly, she's gone off to live with another man.*

seemly /ˈsiːm.li/ **adj** old-fashioned socially suitable and polite → Opposite **unseemly**

seen /siːn/ **verb** past participle of **see**

seep /siːp/ **verb** [I + adv/prep] to move or spread slowly out of a hole or through something: *Pesticides are seeping **out of** farmland and **into** the water supply.* ◦ figurative *Given the intense secrecy of the arms business, information only seeps **out** in company literature.* • **seepage** /ˈsiː.pɪdʒ/ **noun** [U or C] *Oil spills and seepage **from** refineries are common.*

seer /sɪəʳ/ US /sɪr/ **noun** [C] literary a person who says he or she can see what will happen in the future

seersucker /ˈsɪəˌsʌk.əʳ/ US /ˈsɪrˌsʌk.ɚ/ **noun** [U] a light cloth that has a pattern of raised and flat strips on it

seesaw

seesaw /ˈsiː.sɔː/ US /-sɑː/ **noun; verb**

▸**noun** [C] (US also ˌ**teeter-ˈtotter**) a long board that children play on. The board is balanced on a central point so that when a child sits on each end they can make the board go up and down by pushing off the ground with their feet.

▸**verb** [I] to change repeatedly from one emotion, situation, etc. to another and then back again: *His mind seesawed between hope and despair all through those weeks.* • **seesaw adj** [before noun] *The stock market's recent seesaw movements have made many investors nervous.*

seethe /siːð/ **verb** [I] FEEL ANGER ▷ **1** to feel very angry but to be unable or unwilling to express it clearly: *The class positively seethed **with** indignation when Julia won the award.* ◦ *By the end of the meeting he was seething.* MOVE ▷ **2** (of a large number or amount) to move about energetically in a small space: *The streets were seething (= busy and crowded) **with** tourists.* • **seething** /ˈsiː.ðɪŋ/ **adj** [before noun] *Their seething resentment led to angry jostling between team-mates.* ◦ *A seething **mass** of children crowded around the tables.*

ˈ**see-through adj** **1** describes a piece of clothing that is very thin and light, under which you can see other clothes or the body: *a see-through blouse* **2** transparent: *see-through partitions*

segment noun; verb

▸**noun** [C] /ˈseg.mənt/ any of the parts into which something (especially a circle or SPHERE) can be divided or into which it is naturally divided: *The salad was decorated with segments of orange.* ◦ *People over the age of 85 make up the fastest-growing population segment.*

▸**verb** [I or T] /segˈment/ US /ˈseg.ment/ specialized to divide something into different parts: *City Insurance segmented the market **into** three by issuing three types of policy.* • **segmentation** /ˌseg.menˈteɪ.ʃᵊn/ **noun** [U]

segregate /ˈseg.rɪ.geɪt/ **verb** [T] **1** to keep one group of people apart from another and treat them differently, especially because of race or sex: *a segregated school/society* ◦ *Blacks were segregated **from** whites in every area of life.* **2** to keep one thing separate from another: *The systems will have to be able to segregate clients' money **from** the firm's own cash.* • **segregated** /-geɪ.tɪd/ US /-geɪ.t̬ɪd/ **adj** *segregated schools* ◦ *The psychiatric section is segregated (= separated) **from** the rest of the prison.* • **segregation** /ˌseg.rɪˈgeɪ.ʃᵊn/ **noun** [U] *The system of **racial** segregation that used to exist in South Africa was called apartheid.*

segue /ˈseg.weɪ/ **verb** [I] to move easily and without interruption from one piece of music, part of a story, subject, or situation to another: *His performance of 'Alison' segued **into** a cover version of 'Tracks of My Tears'.* • **segue noun** [C usually singular]

seismic /ˈsaɪz.mɪk/ **adj** **1** [before noun] relating to or caused by an EARTHQUAKE: *seismic activity/waves* **2** having very great and damaging effects: *The news that the chairman would resign set off seismic waves in the business community.*

seismograph /ˈsaɪz.mə.grɑːf/ US /-græf/ **noun** [C] specialized a piece of equipment which measures and records the strength of an EARTHQUAKE

seismology /saɪzˈmɒl.ə.dʒi/ US /-ˈmɑː.lə-/ **noun** [U] the scientific study of the sudden, violent movements of the Earth connected with EARTHQUAKES • **seismologist** /-dʒɪst/ **noun** [C]

seize /siːz/ **verb** **1** B2 [T] to take something quickly and keep or hold it: *I seized his arm and made him turn to look at me.* ◦ *He seized the **chance/opportunity** of a free flight **with both hands** (= with eagerness or* *enthusiasm).* **2** C2 [T] to take using sudden force: *The rebels have seized ten soldiers to use as hostages.* ◦ *Political instability helped the army to seize* ***power.*** ◦ *Troops yesterday seized* ***control*** *of the broadcasting station.* **3** [T] If the police or other officials seize something, they take possession of it with legal authority: *Customs officers at Heathrow have seized 60 kilos of heroin.* **4** [usually passive] If a strong emotion or pain seizes you, you feel it suddenly: *I was suddenly seized* ***by/with*** *a feeling of great insecurity and loneliness.*

PHRASAL VERBS **seize on/upon sth** to use, accept, or take advantage of something quickly or enthusiastically: *The story was seized on by the tabloid press, who printed it under huge headlines.* • **seize up** informal to stop being able to move or work in the normal way: *The washing machine totally seized up on Thursday.* ◦ *The traffic had seized up for miles because of the roadworks.*

seizure /ˈsiː.ʒəʳ/ Ⓤⓢ /-ʒɚ/ noun **TAKING** ▷ **1** [C or U] the action of taking something by force or with legal authority: *seizure of power/property/control* ◦ *Seizures of illicit drugs have increased by 30 percent this year.* **MEDICAL** ▷ **2** [C] a very sudden attack of an illness in which someone becomes unconscious or develops violent movements: *an epileptic seizure* **3** [C] old use a sudden failure of the heart: *His aunt died of a seizure.* ◦ figurative humorous *When I told her how much it cost she nearly had a seizure* (= she was very shocked).

seldom /ˈsel.dəm/ adv B2 almost never: *Now that we have a baby, we seldom get the chance to go to the cinema.* ◦ formal *Seldom do we receive any apology when mistakes are made.*

select /sɪˈlekt/ verb; adj

▸verb [I or T] B1 to choose a small number of things, or to choose by making careful decisions: *There was a choice of four prizes, and the winner could select one of them.* ◦ *A mouse is a device which makes it easier to select different options* ***from*** *computer menus.* ◦ *How do you select people* ***for*** *promotion?* ◦ [+ obj + to infinitive] *He was selected* ***to*** *play for Australia at the age of only 18.* ◦ formal *The supermarket's policy is to select* ***out*** (= choose) *the best fruit and discard the rest.*

▸adj of only the best type or highest quality, and usually small in size or amount: *It's a very select club – I've been trying unsuccessfully to join it for years.* ◦ *These activities should be available to all pupils, not just a select* ***few.*** ◦ *Hamilton lives in a very select part of London.*

S

seˌlect comˈmittee noun [C] a group of politicians, from different political parties, chosen to report and advise on a particular subject: *She is a member of the Commons Select Committee* ***on*** *education.*

selection /sɪˈlek.ʃən/ noun **1** B2 [C or U] the act of choosing someone or something: *the selection* ***process*** ◦ *Success is achieved by the careful selection* ***of*** *projects.* ◦ *The coach* ***made*** *her selection* (= chose who she wanted) ***for*** *the team.* **2** B2 [C] a choice or range of different types of something: *Most schools would have* ***a*** *good selection* ***of*** *these books in their libraries.* ◦ *The larger shops are able to stock* ***a*** *wider selection* ***of*** *goods.* **3** [C] a person or thing that has been or will be chosen: *Their music was a mix of old stuff and selections* ***from*** *the new album.*

selective /sɪˈlek.tɪv/ adj C1 intentionally choosing some things and not others: *As a teacher she was very selective, accepting only a small number of exceptionally gifted pupils.* ◦ *He seemed to have a very selective recall of past events.* • **selectively** /-li/ adv • **selectivity** /ˌsɪl.ekˈtɪv.ɪ.ti/ Ⓤⓢ /səˌlekˈtɪv.ə.t̬i/ noun [U] (also **selectiveness** /-nəs/)

seˌlective ˈservice noun [U] US the system in the US in which men aged 18-26 must put their names on an official list so that they can be called to join the army if there is a war → Compare **national service**

selector /sɪˈlek.təʳ/ Ⓤⓢ /-tɚ/ noun [C] **1** a device that allows you to choose something: *a channel/gear/height selector* **2** UK a person who chooses a sports team: *His performance persuaded the selectors that he should be included in the team.*

selenium /səˈliː.ni.əm/ noun [U] (symbol **Se**) a chemical element used in PHOTOCELLS and photographic devices and also necessary in small amounts in the body

self /self/ noun **PERSONALITY** ▷ **1** C1 [C or U] (plural **selves**) the set of someone's characteristics, such as personality and ability, that are not physical and make that person different from other people: *The hero of the film finally* ***finds*** *his* ***true*** *self.* ◦ *When I saw them this afternoon they were more like their* ***old/normal*** *selves* (= as they were in the past). ◦ *a sense of self* **PERSONAL ADVANTAGE** ▷ **2** [U] formal disapproving interest only in your own advantage: *Her reply was typical of her constant regard for self.*

self- /self-/ prefix of or by yourself or itself: *self-educated* ◦ *a self-winding watch*

ˌself-abˈsorbed adj usually disapproving only interested in yourself and your own activities • **ˌself-abˈsorption** noun [U] *Her self-absorption is total – she talks you to death about her health problems.*

ˌself-ˈaccess noun [U] a method of learning in which students use books, videos, etc. to study on their own: *self-access material*

ˌself-adˈdressed adj (especially of an envelope) with the address of the person who has sent it: *Send a self-addressed* ***envelope*** *for our free catalogue.* → See also **sae, SASE**

ˌself-aˈppointed adj disapproving behaving as if you had responsibility or authority but without having been chosen by other people

ˌself-aˈssembly adj mainly UK designed to be made at home from a set of prepared parts by the person who buys it: *a self-assembly kitchen cabinet*

ˌself-aˈssertive adj giving your opinions in a powerful way so that other people will notice

ˌself-aˈssessment noun [C or U] **1** a judgment, sometimes for official purposes, which you make about your abilities, qualities, or actions **2** a system in which people calculate for themselves how much tax they must pay: *Make sure that you have* ***submitted*** *your self-assessment tax return and paid your tax for this year by 31 January .*

ˌself-aˈssured adj approving C2 having confidence in your own abilities: *The interview showed her as a self-assured and mature student.* • **ˌself-aˈssurance** noun [U]

ˌself-aˈwareness noun [U] C2 good knowledge and judgment about yourself • **ˌself-aˈware** adj

ˌself-beˈlief noun [U] trust in your own abilities

ˌself-ˈbuild noun **1** [U] a way of building your house yourself: *Self-build is becoming an increasingly popular choice.* **2** [C] a house that the owner has built • **ˌself-ˈbuild** adj [before noun] *self-build projects* • **ˌself-ˈbuild** verb [T] *We offer everything you need to self-build your dream home.*

ˌself-ˈcatering adj UK C1 (of a holiday) having a kitchen so that you can cook meals for yourself rather than having them provided for you: *self-catering apartments/accommodation* ◦ *a self-catering holiday* ◦

We decided to go for self-catering rather than stay in a hotel. • **ˌself-ˈcatering noun** [U] *This price is for self-catering.*

ˌself-ˈcensorship noun [U] control of what you say or do in order to avoid annoying or offending others, but without being told officially that such control is necessary: *These writers knew that unless they practised a form of self-censorship, the authorities would persecute them.*

ˌself-ˈcentred UK disapproving (US **ˌself-ˈcentered**) adj C1 only interested in yourself and your own activities: *Robert is a self-centred, ambitious, and bigoted man.*

ˌself-ˌcertifiˈcation noun [U] UK formal an official statement that you make about yourself, especially in connection with tax or illness: *You are able to notify up to eight days' illness by self-certification.*

ˌself-conˈfessed adj [before noun] admitting to having a characteristic that is considered to be bad or not acceptable: *New evidence from a self-confessed* ***liar*** *was not enough to justify a retrial.*

ˌself-ˈconfident adj approving B2 behaving calmly because you have no doubts about your ability or knowledge: *At school he was popular and self-confident, and we weren't surprised at his later success.* • **ˌself-ˈconfidence noun** [U] • **ˌself-ˈconfidently adv**

ˌself-conˌgratuˈlatory adj disapproving praising yourself or saying how well you have done something • **ˌself-conˈgratulation noun** [U]

ˌself-ˈconscious adj C1 nervous or uncomfortable because you know what people think about you or your actions: *He looked uncomfortable, like a self-conscious adolescent.* • **ˌself-ˈconsciously adv** • **ˌself-ˈconsciousness noun** [U]

ˌself-conˈtained adj **1** containing or having everything that is needed within itself: *The government wants to encourage viable self-contained rural communities.* **2** describes someone who does not have a large number of relationships with other people or does not depend on others for support: *She's very self-contained and isn't at all worried about moving to a big city where she won't know anybody.*

ˌself-ˌcontraˈdictory adj formal expressing one thing that is the opposite of another thing that was already said; saying two things which cannot both be correct: *He is a Texas oil millionaire and environmentalist, which might appear to be self-contradictory.*

ˌself-conˈtrolled adj usually approving having strong control over your emotions and actions: *He's always seemed very self-controlled, so I was amazed by his sudden outburst in the office.* • **ˌself-conˈtrol noun** [U] C2 *It took incredible self-control not to cry out with pain.*

ˌself-deˈception noun [U] the act of hiding the truth from yourself: *His claim to be an important and unjustly neglected painter is sheer self-deception – he's no good at all.*

ˌself-deˈclared adj [before noun] stated or announced by yourself: *The self-declared guardians of law and order held a press conference.* → See also **self-styled**

ˌself-deˈfeating adj describes something that causes or makes worse the problem it was designed to avoid or solve: *self-defeating regulations*

ˌself-deˈfence UK (US **ˌself-deˈfense**) noun [U] **1** protection of yourself, either by fighting or discussion: *He used the gun* ***in*** *self-defence.* ◦ ***In*** *self-defence, I have to say that I only did what you asked me to do.* **2** the skill of fighting without weapons to protect yourself: *She goes to self-defence classes for women.*

ˌself-deˈlusion noun [C or U] the act of allowing yourself to believe something that is not true: *It's self-delusion if he thinks he'll be offered a better contract.*

ˌself-deˈnial noun [U] the act of not taking or having something that you would like because you think it is good for you not to have it

ˌself-ˈdeprecating adj (also **ˌself-ˈdeprecatory**) trying to make yourself, your abilities, or your achievements seem less important: *a self-deprecating manner/remark* ◦ *self-deprecating humour/jokes* • **ˌself-ˈdeprecatingly adv** • **ˌself-ˌdepreˈcation noun** [U]

ˌself-deˈstruct verb [I] **1** If a machine or weapon self-destructs, it destroys itself, especially in a way that is planned: *An investigation is underway after a missile self-destructed shortly after it was launched.* **2 (the/sb's) self-destruct button** a characteristic in a person that makes them likely to fail because of their own actions: *At least he reached the semifinal before hitting the self-destruct button.* • **ˌself-deˈstruction noun** [U] • **ˌself-deˈstructive adj** *He is rebellious, aggressive and at times self-destructive.*

ˌself-deˌtermiˈnation noun [U] the ability or power to make decisions for yourself, especially the power of a nation to decide how it will be governed

ˌself-ˈdiscipline noun [U] approving C2 the ability to make yourself do things you know you should do even when you do not want to: *You need a lot of self-discipline when you're doing research work on your own.* • **ˌself-ˈdisciplined adj**

ˌself-diˈscovery noun [U] the process of learning about yourself and your beliefs: *Her own* ***journey/voyage*** *of self-discovery started as she was recovering from a severe illness.*

ˌself-ˈdoubt noun [U] a feeling of having no confidence in your abilities and decisions

ˌself-ˈdrive adj UK renting and driving a car yourself, rather than being driven by someone else: *a self-drive hire car*

ˌself-efˈfacing adj not making yourself noticeable, or not trying to get the attention of other people: *The captain was typically self-effacing when questioned about the team's successes, giving credit to the other players.* → Synonym **modest** • **self-effacement** /-mənt/ **noun** [U] • **self-effacingly** /-li/ **adv**

ˌself-emˈployed adj not working for an employer but finding work for yourself or having your own business: *a self-employed builder* ◦ *Do you pay less tax if you're self-employed?* • **ˌself-emˈployed noun** [plural] *They run an advice centre for* ***the*** *self-employed.* • **ˌself-emˈployment noun** [U]

ˌself-eˈsteem noun [U] C1 belief and confidence in your own ability and value: *The compliments she received after the presentation boosted her self-esteem.* ◦ *She suffers from* ***low*** *self-esteem and it prevents her from pursuing her goals.*

ˌself-ˈevident adj clear or obvious without needing any proof or explanation: *Solutions which seem self-evident* ***to*** *humans are often beyond the grasp of computers.* • **ˌself-ˈevidently adv** *Any growth in unemployment is self-evidently a matter of extreme seriousness.*

ˌself-exˈplanatory adj easily understood from the information already given and not needing further explanation: *a self-explanatory list of instructions*

ˌself-exˈpression noun [U] expression of your personality, emotions, or ideas, especially through art, music, or acting

ˌself-ˈfinancing adj paid for only by the money that an activity itself produces: *Fees will have to treble to make the courses self-financing.*

ˌself-fulˈfilling adj happening because it is expected

to happen: *Pessimism is self-fulfilling – expect the worst and it happens.*

ˌself-fulˌfilling ˈprophecy noun [C] something that you cause to happen by saying and expecting that it will happen

ˌself-fulˈfilment noun [U] a feeling of satisfaction that you have achieved what you wanted: *When the options are unemployment or a boring job, having babies can seem like the only means of self-fulfilment.* • **ˌself-fulˈfilled** adj

ˌself-ˈgovernment noun [U] the control of a country or an area by the people living there, or the control of an organization by a group of people independent of central or local government: *The poll showed that 80 percent of the population supported regional self-government.* • **ˌself-ˈgoverning** adj *self-governing trusts/schools*

ˌself-ˈharm verb [I] to deliberately hurt yourself, for example by cutting yourself, because you have emotional problems or are mentally ill • **ˌself-ˈharm** noun [U] the act of self-harming

ˌself-ˈhelp adj, noun [U] the activity of providing what you need for yourself and others with similar experiences or difficulties without going to an official organization: *It is a group providing self-help for single parents.* ◦ [before noun] *self-help groups*

ˌself-ˈimage noun [C usually singular] the way a person feels about his or her personality, achievements, and value to society: *Having a decent job contributes to a good self-image.*

ˌself-imˈportance noun [U] disapproving the belief that you are more important or have a higher value than other people: *He's a modest, mild-mannered man, without a trace of self-importance.* • **ˌself-imˈportant** adj • **ˌself-imˈportantly** adv

ˌself-imˈposed adj decided by yourself, without being influenced or ordered by other people: *The end of the year was their self-imposed deadline for finishing the building work.* ◦ *After the military coup, the family left for self-imposed* ***exile*** *in America.*

ˌself-incrimiˈnation noun [U] saying or doing something which shows that you are guilty of a crime: *A witness can legally refuse to give evidence to avoid self-incrimination.*

ˌself-inˈduced adj caused by yourself: *self-induced vomiting/hysteria*

S

ˌself-inˈdulgent adj allowing yourself to have or do anything that you enjoy: *I know it's self-indulgent of me, but I'll just have another chocolate.* • **ˌself-inˈdulgence** noun [S or U]

ˌself-inˈflicted adj If an injury or a problem is self-inflicted, you have caused it yourself: *self-inflicted pain/damage*

ˌself-ˈinterest noun [U] the act of considering the advantage to yourself when making decisions, and deciding to do what is best for you: *The company's donation was surely* ***motivated by*** *self-interest, as it attracted a lot of media attention.* • **ˌself-ˈinterested** adj *self-interested arguing*

selfish /ˈsel.fɪʃ/ adj disapproving B1 Someone who is selfish only thinks of their own advantage: *The judge told him: 'Your attitude shows a selfish disregard for others.'* • **selfishly** /-li/ adv disapproving • **selfishness** /-nəs/ noun [U] disapproving

ˌself-ˈknowledge noun [U] an understanding of yourself and your abilities

selfless /ˈself.ləs/ adj approving Someone who is selfless only thinks of other people's advantage: *selfless devotion to duty* • **selflessly** /-li/ adv approving • **selflessness** /-nəs/ noun [U] approving

ˌself-ˈmade adj C2 rich and successful as a result of your own work and not because of family money: *a self-made man/millionaire*

ˌself-ˈmedicate verb [I] to take medicine without asking a doctor: *90 percent of the people questioned self-medicated, usually for pain or colds.* • **ˌself-mediˈcation** noun [U] *The pain drove him to self-medication.*

ˌself-obˈsessed adj disapproving only interested in yourself and your own activities

ˌself-oˈpinionated adj disapproving having and expressing very strong feelings and beliefs, and believing that your own ideas are the only correct ones

ˌself-perˈpetuating adj disapproving having a system that prevents change and produces new things that are very similar to the old ones: *The fighting between the different groups has become a self-perpetuating spiral of death and hatred.*

ˌself-ˈpity noun [U] disapproving sadness for yourself because you think you have a lot of problems or have suffered a lot: *He faced his illness bravely and without any hint of self-pity.* • **ˌself-ˈpitying** adj

ˌself-ˈportrait noun [C] a picture, photograph, or piece of writing that you make of or about yourself

ˌself-poˈssession noun [U] the characteristic of being calm and in control of your emotions at all times: *He looked surprised but soon recovered his self-possession.* • **ˌself-poˈssessed** adj

self-ˌpreserˈvation noun [U] behaviour based on the characteristics or feelings which warn people or animals to protect themselves from difficulties or dangers: *It was his instinct for self-preservation that led him to abandon his former friends and transfer his allegiance to the new rulers.*

ˌself-proˈclaimed adj mainly disapproving said or announced about yourself: *He's a self-proclaimed expert on national defence.*

ˌself-proˈfessed adj said, announced, or admitted about yourself: *a self-professed gambler* ◦ *She's a self-professed supporter of prison reform.*

ˌself-proˈpelled adj able to move by its own power: *self-propelled artillery/guns*

ˌself-proˈtection noun [U] keeping yourself safe from injury or damage: *They claimed that they needed the weapons for self-protection.*

ˌself-raising ˈflour noun [U] UK (US **ˌself-rising ˈflour**) flour containing a substance that makes cakes swell when they are cooked

ˌself-refeˈrential adj A self-referential book, film, play, etc. refers to itself, its writer, or other work by that writer: *Modern television sitcoms are often ironic and self-referential.*

ˌself-reguˈlation noun [U] making certain yourself that you or your employees act according to the rules, rather than having this done by other people: *They favour the self-regulation of the industry, and strict codes of conduct have already been issued by the Advertising Association.* • **ˌself-ˈregulating** adj (also **ˌself-ˈregulatory**) *a self-regulating body/organization*

ˌself-reˈliant adj approving C2 not needing help or support from other people: *Lone parents have to be self-reliant and inventive.* • **ˌself-reˈliance** noun [U]

ˌself-reˈspect noun [U] C2 respect for yourself which shows that you value yourself: *He felt what he was being asked to do took away his dignity and self-respect.* • **ˌself-reˈspecting** adj [before noun] *No self-respecting*

government would allow such atrocities to be carried out in its name.

ˌself-reˈstraint noun [U] control of your own actions: *He was angry but managed, with great self-restraint, to reply calmly.*

ˌself-ˈrighteous adj disapproving believing that your ideas and behaviour are morally better than those of other people: *He's so self-righteous – you'd think he'd never done anything wrong in his life.* • **ˌself-ˈrighteously** adv • **ˌself-ˈrighteousness** noun [U]

ˌself-ˈrule noun [U] the act of a country, a part of a country, or a nation choosing its own government and controlling its own activities → See also **self-government**

ˌself-ˈsacrifice noun [U] approving giving up what you want so that other people can have what they want: *People say this is a selfish society, but frankly I've seen too much kindness, self-sacrifice and generosity to believe that.* ◦ *The job requires a lot of enthusiasm, dedication and self-sacrifice.* • **ˌself-ˈsacrificing** adj

selfsame /ˈself.seɪm/ adj [before noun] exactly the same: *The selfsame car has been parked outside three times this week.*

ˌself-ˈsatisfied adj disapproving very pleased with yourself and showing no criticism of yourself: *She was very smug and self-satisfied about getting the promotion.* • **ˌself-ˌsatisˈfaction** noun [U]

ˌself-ˈseeking adj formal disapproving interested in your own advantage in everything that you do: *The army felt that the politicians of the day were just self-seeking opportunists.*

ˌself-ˈservice adj B1 especially in a shop or restaurant, not being served by an employee but collecting goods or food yourself: *a self-service salad bar* ◦ *self-service petrol pumps* (US *gas pumps*) → Compare **full-service**

ˌself-ˈserving adj formal disapproving working or acting for your own advantage: *Politicians are seen as corrupt and self-serving.*

ˌself-ˈstarter noun [C] approving a person who is able to work effectively without regularly needing to be told what to do: *The successful applicant for the position will be a well-motivated self-starter who has excellent communication skills.*

ˌself-ˈstudy noun [U] a way of learning about a subject that involves studying alone at home, rather than in a classroom with a teacher: *The diploma is awarded following a course of self-study ending in a three-hour exam.* ◦ *self-study* ***materials/workbooks/programs***

ˌself-ˈstyled adj [before noun] usually disapproving given a name or title by yourself without any official reason for it: *The media appears to be full of self-styled 'experts' who are happy to give their views on subjects that they actually know very little about.*

ˌself-suˈfficient adj C2 able to provide everything you need, especially food, for yourself without the help of other people: *The programme aims to make the country self-sufficient* ***in*** *food production and to cut energy imports.* • **ˌself-suˈfficiency** noun [U]

ˌself-suˈpporting adj earning or having enough money to pay for your activities without receiving financial help from other people: *The vast majority of students here are self-supporting.* → See also **self-financing**

ˌself-ˈtan noun [U] a substance that you put on your skin to make it look darker as if you have been in the sun: *self-tan for your face* • **ˌself-ˈtan** adj *self-tan products* • **ˌself-ˈtanning** noun [U] rubbing a substance into your skin in order to make it look darker as if you have been in the sun

ˌself-ˈwilled adj disapproving determined to base your actions on your own decisions without listening to advice from other people

ˌself-ˈworth noun [U] the value you give to your life and achievements: *Many people derive their self-worth from their work.*

sell /sel/ verb (**sold**, **sold**) **MONEY** ▷ **1** A2 [I or T] to give something to someone else in return for money: [+ two objects] *I sold him my car/I sold my car to him* ***for*** *£600.* ◦ *We'll be selling the tickets* ***at/for*** *£50 each.* ◦ *The stall sells drinks and snacks.* ◦ *These baskets sell well* (= a lot of them are bought). **PERSUADE** ▷ **2** C2 [T] to persuade someone that an idea or plan is a good one and likely to be successful: *My boss is very old-fashioned and I'm having a lot of trouble selling the idea of working at home occasionally.* ◦ [+ two objects] *The chance of greater access to European markets would help sell the president the scheme/sell the scheme* ***to*** *the president.* ◦ *She's really sold* ***on*** *the idea of buying a new car.*

> **Other ways of saying sell**
>
> **Retail** is a word that means 'sell' when talking about companies selling things in stores or by mail:
> *The company makes and* ***retails*** *moderately priced sportswear.*
>
> The phrasal verb **deal in** can be used when someone sells and buys things as part of a business:
> *They mainly* ***deal in*** *rare books.*
>
> **Divest** or **sell off** means 'to sell something, especially a business or part of a business':
> *The company is* ***divesting/selling off*** *the less profitable parts of its business.*
>
> If a company or country sells goods to other countries, you could use the word **export**:
> *France* ***exports*** *a lot of cheese.*
>
> **Hawk** can be used when someone sells things informally in public places:
> *There were lots of street vendors* ***hawking*** *candy.*
>
> **Peddle** is a usually disapproving word when someone goes from place to place to sell things:
> *They were caught on the street* ***peddling*** *counterfeit CDs.*
>
> If you **auction** (**off**) something, you sell it at a public sale to the person who offers the most money:
> *The family is* ***auctioning off*** *its art collection.*
>
> **Sell out** (**of**) means to sell all of the supply that you have of something:
> *We* ***sold out of*** *the T-shirts within two hours.*

IDIOMS **sell sb a bill of goods** (UK also **sell sb a pup**) to deceive someone into buying something that has no value • **sell sb down the river** informal to put someone in a difficult or dangerous situation by not acting as you had promised to act, usually in order to win an advantage for yourself • **sell yourself/sth short** to not consider someone or something to be as valuable or good as they deserve: *Don't sell yourself short – you've got the skills and the experience.* • **sell your soul (to the devil)** to be persuaded to do something, especially something bad, because of the money or other reward you will receive for doing it

PHRASAL VERBS **sell sth off 1** to charge a low price for something to encourage people to buy it: *They're*

S

selling off last year's stock at half price. **2** to sell all or part of a business: *The company announced that it would be selling off its hotel business.* • **sell out** **SELL ALL** ▷ **1** to sell all of the supply that you have of something: *We sold out **of** the T-shirts in the first couple of hours.* **2** B2 If a supply of something sells out, there is no more of that thing to buy: *The first issue of the magazine sold out within two days.* **3** [passive] When a film, CONCERT, etc. is sold out, all of the tickets for it have been sold: *We couldn't get seats – the concert was sold out.* **SELL BUSINESS** ▷ **4** to sell your business or part of your business: *They decided to sell out **to** their competitors.* • **sell (sb) out** informal to not do what you have promised someone you will do or what you should do because you will get more advantages for yourself if you do something else: *French farmers feel they've been sold out by their government in the negotiations.* ◦ *They've sold out **to** the road transport lobby (= done what these people wanted).* • **sell up** UK to sell your house or company in order to go somewhere else or do something else: *They sold up and retired to the West Country.*

ˈsell-by ˌdate noun [C] UK (US **ˈpull ˌdate**) a date printed on a product such as food after which it should not be sold

seller /ˈsel.əʳ/ US /-ɚ/ noun [C] **1** B1 a person who is selling something: *flower/newspaper/souvenir sellers* ◦ *Do you think the seller will accept £300,000 for the house?* **2** a product which a lot of people buy: *This car is our **biggest** seller at the moment.*

ˈselling ˌpoint noun [C] a characteristic of a product which will persuade people to buy it: *Its best selling point is the price – it's the cheapest on the market.*

ˈsell-off noun [C] **1** a sale of an unwanted business at a low price to encourage someone to buy it **2** a sale of an INVESTMENT, such as SHARES in a company, that causes its value to fall **3** Australian English an occasion when the price of goods in a shop or factory is reduced so they can be sold quickly → Compare **closeout**

Sellotape /ˈsel.ə.teɪp/ noun [U] UK trademark (US trademark **ˌScotch ˈtape**) a long, thin strip of sticky and usually transparent material that is sold in a roll and is used for joining together things such as paper or card: *a roll of Sellotape* ◦ *I stuck the note to the door **with** Sellotape.* • **sellotape** verb [T] UK (US **ˈscotch-tape**) *When I got home, I found a mysterious message sellotaped **to** the front door.*

S

sellout /ˈsel.aʊt/ noun [C usually singular] **ALL SOLD** ▷ **1** a performance or sports event for which no more tickets are available, because it is so popular: *The concert was a sellout.* **BROKEN PROMISE** ▷ **2** disapproving a situation in which someone does not do what they have promised to do or what they should do: *Most of the workers see the union agreement as a sellout.*

seltzer /ˈselt.səʳ/ US /-sɚ/ noun [C or U] US for MINERAL WATER with bubbles

selves /selvz/ plural of **self**

semantic /sɪˈmæn.tɪk/ US /-t̬ɪk/ adj connected with the meanings of words • **semantically** /-tɪ.kəl.i/ adv

semantics /sɪˈmæn.tɪks/ US /-t̬ɪks/ noun [U] the study of meanings in a language

semaphore /ˈsem.ə.fɔːʳ/ US /-fɔːr/ noun [U] a system of communication using two flags held in your hands that are moved into different positions to represent different letters, numbers, or symbols

semaphore

semblance /ˈsem.bləns/ noun [U] formal a situation or condition that is similar to what is wanted or expected, but is not exactly as hoped for: *The city has now returned to **some** semblance **of** normality after last night's celebrations.* ◦ *He was executed without even **the** semblance **of** a fair trial.*

semen /ˈsiː.mən/ noun [U] a thick, whitish liquid containing SPERM that is produced by the sex organs of men and some male animals → See also **seminal**

semester /sɪˈmes.təʳ/ US /səˈmes.tɚ/ noun [C] A2 one of the periods into which a year is divided at a college or university, especially in the US and Australia: *the first/second semester* ◦ *the spring/fall semester* → Compare **term, trimester**

semi /ˈsem.i/ US /-aɪ/ noun [C] (plural **semis**) **HOUSE** ▷ **1** UK informal a house that is SEMI-DETACHED **VEHICLE** ▷ **2** US informal an ARTICULATED truck **COMPETITION** ▷ **3** informal for **semifinal**

semi- /sem.i-/, /-ɪ-/ US /-aɪ-/, /-i-/ prefix half or partly: *semi-literate* ◦ *semi-permanent* ◦ *semi-skilled workers* ◦ *a semi-autobiographical novel*

ˌsemi-ˈarid adj specialized a semi-arid area or CLIMATE (= general type of weather) has little rain but is not completely dry → Compare **arid**

ˌsemi-autoˈmatic adj partly automatic: *a semi-automatic gearbox/shotgun*

semibreve /ˈsem.i.briːv/ noun [C] mainly UK (US usually **ˈwhole note**) a musical note with a time value equal to two MINIMS or four CROTCHETS

semicircle /ˈsem.iˌsɜː.kl/ US /-ˌsɝː-/ noun [C usually singular] half a circle: *We arranged the chairs **in** a semicircle.* • **semicircular** /ˌsem.iˈsɜː.kjʊ.ləʳ/ US /-ˈsɝː.kjʊ.lɚ/ adj *The chairs were placed in a semicircular arrangement.*

semicircle

semicolon /ˌsem.iˈkəʊ.lɒn/ US /ˈsem.iˌkoʊ.lən/ noun [C] B2 the symbol ; used in writing between two parts of a sentence, usually when each of the two parts could form grammatical sentences on their own. A semicolon can also separate the things in a list.

semiconductor /ˌsem.i.kənˈdʌk.təʳ/ US /-tɚ/ noun [C] a material, such as SILICON, that allows electricity to move through it more easily when its temperature increases, or an electronic device made from this material: *Semiconductors are used for making integrated circuits and computers.* • **semiconducting** /-tɪŋ/ adj [before noun]

ˌsemi-deˈtached adj UK C1 A house that is semi-detached is one that is joined to another similar house on only one side: *They live in a semi-detached house.* → Compare **detached**

semifinal /ˌsem.iˈfaɪ.nəl/ noun [C usually plural] (informal **semi**) B2 one of the two games that are played to decide who will take part in the final game of a competition: *Who's in the semifinals?* ◦ *She's the youngest player ever to **get through to/advance to** a semifinal.*

seminal /ˈsem.ɪ.nəl/ adj **IMPORTANT** ▷ **1** formal containing important new ideas and having a great influence on later work: *She wrote a seminal article on the subject while she was still a student.* **LIQUID** ▷

2 [before noun] specialized connected with SEMEN: *seminal fluid*

seminar /ˈsem.ɪ.nɑːʳ/ (US) /-nɑːr/ noun [C] (B2) an occasion when a teacher or expert and a group of people meet to study and discuss something: *I **attended** practically every lecture and seminar when I was a student.* ◦ *I'm **giving** a seminar **on** the latest developments in genetic engineering next week.* ◦ *a seminar **room*** → Compare **lecture**

seminary /ˈsem.ɪ.nə.ri/ (US) /-ner.i/ noun [C] a college for training people to become priests

semiotics /ˌsem.iˈɒt.ɪks/ (US) /-ˈɑː.t̬ɪks/ noun [U] specialized the study of signs and symbols, what they mean, and how they are used • **semiotic** /-ɒt.ɪk/ (US) /-ˈɑː.t̬ɪk/ adj • **semiotician** /ˌsem.ɪ.əˈtɪʃ.ən/ noun [C]

semipermeable /ˌsem.iˈpɜː.mi.ə.bl/ (US) /ˈpɜːr-/ adj specialized describes something, for example a cell MEMBRANE, that allows some liquids and gases to pass through it, but not others

ˌsemi-ˈprecious adj [before noun] A semi-precious stone is one that is used for making jewellery but is not extremely valuable: *Jade and turquoise are semi-precious stones.*

ˌsemi-proˈfessional adj People who are semi-professional are paid for an activity that they take part in but do not do all the time: *semi-professional musicians/rugby players*

semiquaver /ˈsem.iˌkweɪ.vəʳ/ (US) /-vɚ/ noun [C] mainly UK (US usually **sixˈteenth ˌnote**) a musical note that has a time value of half a QUAVER or a 16th of a SEMIBREVE

ˌsemi-ˈskilled adj having or needing only a small amount of training: *semi-skilled jobs/workers/labour*

ˌsemi-ˈskimmed adj UK (US **ˌlow-ˈfat**) used to describe milk from which some of the cream has been removed → Compare **full-fat, skimmed milk**

semisweet chocolate /sem.iˌswiːtˈtʃɒk.lət/ (US) /-ˈtʃɑːk-/ noun [U] US for **dark chocolate**

Semitic /sɪˈmɪt.ɪk/ (US) /səˈmɪt̬-/ adj **1** relating to the race of people that includes Arabs and Jews, or to their languages: *Hebrew and Arabic are Semitic languages.* → See also **anti-Semitic 2** old use Jewish **3** describes races such as the Babylonians and Phoenicians that existed in ancient times

semitone /ˈsem.i.təʊn/ (US) /-toʊn/ noun [C or] (US usually **ˈhalf ˌstep**) the smallest difference in sound between two notes that are next to each other in the western musical SCALE

semolina /ˌsem.əlˈiː.nə/ noun [U] a powder made from WHEAT, used for making PASTA and sweet dishes

Semtex /ˈsem.teks/ noun [U] trademark a powerful explosive, used especially to make illegal bombs

Sen. noun [before noun] written abbreviation for **senator**

SEN /ˌes.iːˈen/ abbreviation for special educational needs: an expression used to refer to SPECIAL NEEDS (= the needs of people with particular disabilities or problems) relating to education

the Senate /ˈsen.ət/ noun POLITICS ▷ **1** the more important of the two groups of politicians who make laws in some countries such as the US, Australia, and France: *the French/Australian Senate* ◦ *The US Senate has 100 members.* ◦ *The law has no chance of being passed by the Senate.* EDUCATION ▷ **2** the group of people who control a college or university

senator /ˈsen.ə.təʳ/ (US) /-t̬ɚ/ noun [C] (written abbreviation **Sen.**) a politician who has been elected to a Senate: *Only two senators voted against the bill.* ◦ [as form of address] *It's a pleasure to meet you, Senator.*
• **senatorial** /ˌsen.əˈtɔː.ri.əl/ (US) /-ˈtɔːr.i-/ adj mainly US *a senatorial candidate/committee*

send /send/ verb [T] (**sent**, **sent**) POST/EMAIL ▷ **1** (A1) to cause something to go from one place to another, especially by post or email: [+ two objects] *I'll send her a letter/email/parcel/postcard next week.* ◦ *We'll send it **by post/airmail/sea**.* ◦ *Could you send a reply **to** them as quickly as possible?* ◦ *The news report was sent by satellite.* ◦ *She sent a message with John to say that she couldn't come.* ◦ *They sent her flowers for her birthday.* ◦ *Maggie sends her love and hopes you'll feel better soon.* CAUSE TO GO ▷ **2** (B2) to cause or order someone to go and do something: [+ to infinitive] *We're sending the children **to** stay with my parents for a couple of weeks.* ◦ *The commander has asked us to send reinforcements.* ◦ *They've sent their son (**away**) to school in Scotland.* ◦ *He was trying to explain but she became impatient and sent him away (= told him to leave).* CAUSE TO HAPPEN ▷ **3** (C2) to cause someone or something to do a particular thing, or to cause something to happen: *The explosion sent the crowd **into** a panic.* ◦ *Watching the television always sends me **to sleep**.* ◦ [+ adj] UK *His untidiness sends her crazy/mad/wild.* ◦ [+ -ing verb] *The announcement of the fall in profits sent the company's share price plummet**ing** (= caused it to go down a lot).* ◦ *The draught from the fan sent papers fly**ing** all over the room.*

IDIOMS **send sb packing** informal to ask someone to leave immediately: *There were some kids at the door asking for money but I sent them packing.* • **send sb to Coventry** UK old-fashioned If a group of people send someone to Coventry, they refuse to speak to that person, usually as a punishment for having done something to upset the group. • **send shivers down/up sb's spine** to make someone feel very frightened or excited: *The way he looked at me sent shivers down my spine.* • **send a signal to sb** to warn someone about something: *The rise in interest rates should send a signal to financial institutions that the government is serious about reducing inflation.* • **send word** to send a message: *She sent word with her secretary **that** she would be unable to attend the meeting.*

PHRASAL VERBS **send sth back** (B1) to return something to the person who sent it to you, especially because it is damaged or not suitable: *I had to send the shirt back because it didn't fit me.* • **send sb down** [M usually passive] PRISON ▷ **1** UK (US **send sb up**) to send someone to prison: *He was sent down **for** armed robbery.* ◦ *She was sent down for three years.* COLLEGE ▷ **2** UK old-fashioned to ask someone to leave a college or university without finishing their course because they have done something wrong: *She was sent down **from** Oxford for taking drugs.* • **send for sb** (C2) to send someone a message asking them to come to see you: *Do you think we should send for a doctor?* • **send (off/away) for/to sth** to write to an organization or place to ask them to send you something: *I've sent off for a catalogue.* ◦ *We had to send off to Ireland for a replacement part.* • **send sth in** to send something to an organization: *The magazine asked its readers to send in their comments about the new style of presentation.* • **send sb in** to send soldiers, police, etc. to a place in order to deal with a dangerous situation: *UN troops were sent in as the situation got worse.* • **send sth off** (B2) to send a letter, document, or parcel by post: *Have you sent off your application form yet?* • **send sb off** UK (US **eject**) to order a sports player to leave the playing area during a game because they have done something wrong: *He was sent off **for** swearing at the referee.* • **send sth on** to send

S

something from someone's old address to their new one: *Paul's moved back to New York and he's asked me to send on his letters.* • **send sth out** **PRODUCE** ▷ **1** C2 to produce something in a way that causes it to spread out from a central point: *The equipment sent out a regular high-pitched signal.* ◦ *The torch sends out a powerful beam of light.* ◦ *The bushes were sending out new shoots.* **POST/EMAIL** ▷ **2** to send something to a lot of different people, usually by post or email: *We sent out the wedding invitations about three weeks ago.* • **send out for sth** to ask for something to be brought to you from another place, by using the phone or sending a message: *There's not much to eat in the fridge. Should I send out for a pizza?* • **send sb/sth up** UK informal to make someone or something seem stupid by copying them in a funny way: *The show was very funny – they were sending up sports commentators.*

sender /ˈsen.dəʳ/ (US) /-dɚ/ **noun** [C] a person who sends something: *The letter came back with '**return to** sender – not known at this address' written on it.*

ˈsend-off noun [C usually singular] an occasion at which people can express good wishes and say goodbye to someone who is leaving a place: *We'll have to give her a good send-off when she leaves the office.*

ˈsend-up noun [C] UK informal an act of making someone or something seem stupid by copying them or it in a funny way: *He does a brilliant send-up of the president.*

senile /ˈsiː.naɪl/ (US) /ˈsen.aɪl/ **adj** showing poor mental ability because of old age, especially being unable to think clearly and make decisions: *He spent many years caring for his senile mother.* ◦ *I'm always losing my keys these days. I think I must be **going** senile.* • **senility** /sɪˈnɪl.ɪ.ti/ (US) /-ə.t̬i/ **noun** [U]

ˌsenile deˈmentia noun [U] specialized a medical condition that causes the memory and other mental abilities of old people to gradually become worse, leading them to behave in a confused manner

senior /ˈsiː.ni.əʳ/ (US) /-njɚ/ **adj; noun**

▸**adj** **OLDER** ▷ **1** B2 [before noun] older: *Senior pupils are expected to set an example to the younger children.* → Compare **junior** **2** (UK written abbreviation **Snr**, US written abbreviation **Sr.**) used after a man's name to refer to the older of two people in the same family who have the same name: *Hello, may I speak to Ken Griffey senior, please?* **HIGH RANK** ▷ **3** B2 high or higher in rank: *senior management* ◦ *a senior government minister* ◦ *She's senior **to** me, so I have to do what she tells me.* → Compare **junior**

IDIOM **have a senior moment** informal to forget something in a way that is thought to be typical of people who are old

▸**noun** **HIGH RANK** ▷ **1** [C] someone who is high or higher in rank: *It's important to impress your seniors if you want to be promoted.* **OLDER** ▷ **2** **20, 30, etc. years sb's senior** 20, 30, etc. years older than someone: *She married a man 20 years her senior.* ◦ *She's my senior by three years (= she is three years older than me).* **3** [C] US a student in their final year of high school or university

ˌsenior ˈcitizen noun [C] (US also **senior**) polite expression for an old person: *Discounts are available for senior citizens.*

seniority /ˌsiː.niˈɒr.ɪ.ti/ (US) /siːˈnjɔːr.ə.t̬i/ **noun** [U] **LONG TIME** ▷ **1** the advantage that you get by working for a company for a long time: *In future, promotion will be based on merit not seniority.* **HIGH RANK** ▷ **2** the state of being higher in rank than someone else: *I suppose I was impressed by his seniority.*

ˌsenior ˈnursing officer noun [C] UK (UK old-fashioned **matron**) the person in charge of all the nurses in a hospital

ˌsenior ˈstatesman noun [C] an experienced politician who is usually no longer working in government → See also **elder**

sensation /senˈseɪ.ʃᵊn/ **noun** **FEELING** ▷ **1** B2 [C or U] the ability to feel something physically, especially by touching, or a physical feeling that results from this ability: *a burning sensation* ◦ *I had no sensation **of** pain whatsoever.* ◦ *The disease causes a loss of sensation in the fingers.* **2** B2 [C usually singular] a general feeling caused by something that happens to you, especially a feeling which you cannot describe exactly: [+ (that)] *I had the odd sensation (**that**) someone was following me.* ◦ *I can remember the first time I went sailing – it was a wonderful sensation.* **EXCITEMENT** ▷ **3** B2 [S] something very exciting or interesting, or something which causes great excitement or interest: *Their affair **caused** a sensation.* ◦ *The books have been a publishing sensation on both sides of the Atlantic.* ◦ *The show was an overnight sensation (= was very successful immediately).*

sensational /senˈseɪ.ʃᵊn.ᵊl/ **adj** **1** C2 approving very good, exciting, or unusual: *a sensational sports car/dress* ◦ *She looks sensational (= extremely attractive) in her new dress.* **2** C1 disapproving describes news reports and articles that are intended to be shocking and exciting rather than serious: *Some of the more sensational newspapers have given a lot of coverage to the scandal.*

sensationalism /senˈseɪ.ʃᵊn.ᵊl.ɪ.zᵊm/ **noun** [U] disapproving the act by newspapers, television, etc. of presenting information in a way that is be shocking or exciting: *The newspaper has been accused of sensationalism in its coverage of the murders.* • **sensationalist** /-ɪst/ **adj** • **sensationalize** (UK usually **sensationalise**) /-aɪz/ **verb** [T]

sensationally /senˈseɪ.ʃᵊn.ᵊl.i/ **adv** **1** extremely; used to emphasize positive adjectives or adverbs: *sensationally popular/successful* ◦ *The book sold sensationally well.* **2** in an extremely interesting or exciting way: *The show ended sensationally with fireworks.*

sense /sens/ **noun; verb**

▸**noun** **ABILITY** ▷ **1** B2 [C] an ability to understand, recognize, value, or react to something, especially any of the five physical abilities to see, hear, smell, taste, and feel: *With her keen sense **of** smell, she could tell if you were a smoker from the other side of the room.* ◦ *My cold is so bad I've **lost** my sense **of** smell/taste (= I can't smell/taste anything).* **2** B1 [C or U] a general feeling or understanding: *Did you get any sense of how they might react?* ◦ *The helicopters hovering overhead added to the sense **of** urgency.* **3** **sense of fun** the ability to enjoy life and not be too serious: *Don't be angry – it was just a joke – where's your sense of fun?* **4** **sense of humour** B1 your ability to understand funny things: *She **has** a really good sense of humour.* ◦ *We **have** the same sense of humour.* ◦ *Come on, lighten up! Where's your sense of humour?* **5** **sense of occasion** UK the feeling people have when there is a very important event or celebration: *The decorations, flowers, and crowds gave the town a real sense of occasion.* **GOOD JUDGMENT** ▷ **6** B2 [U] the characteristic of having good judgment, especially when it is based on practical ideas or understanding: [+ to infinitive] *I hope they'll **have the** (**good**) sense/**have enough** sense **to** shut the windows before they leave.* ◦ ***It makes** (**good**) sense **to** buy a large packet because* it works out cheaper in the end. ◦ [+ -ing verb] ***There's no sense in*** *wait**ing*** (= it is not practical to wait) *– the next train isn't for two hours.* ◦ ***Where's/What's the*** *sense* (= what is the advantage) ***in*** *pay**ing*** *someone when you could get a volunteer?* ◦ *Planning so far ahead* ***makes no*** *sense – so many things will have changed by next year.* **7 senses** [plural] the ability to use good judgment: *Have you* ***taken leave of*** *your senses?* (= Have you lost your ability to make a good judgment?) ◦ *It's time you* ***came to*** *your senses* (= started to use your good judgment) *and realized that they are not going to help you.* ◦ *The accident* ***brought*** *him* ***to*** *his senses* (= caused him to use his good judgment again) *and made him stop drinking.* **MEANING** ▷ **8** (B2) [C] one of the possible meanings of a word or phrase: *They are not immigrants, at least not* ***in*** *any sense that I understand.* ◦ *The packaging is green – in both senses of the word* (= it is green in colour and it is good for the environment). ◦ *Security defined* ***in the broad/broadest*** *sense* ***of*** *the term means getting at the root causes of trouble and helping to reduce regional conflicts.* ◦ *This passage doesn't* ***make*** *(****any****) sense* (= the meaning is not clear). ◦ *I've read the letter twice, but I can't* ***make*** *(****any****) sense* ***of*** *it* (= I can't understand it). **9 in every sense** in every way or feature: *It's a book which is, in every sense, about different ways of seeing the world.* **10 in a sense** (C1) (also **in one sense**) thinking about something in one way, but not in every way: *She claims that the system is at fault and she's right, in a sense* (= she is partly right), *it could be improved.* **11 in no sense** not at all: *We are in no sense obliged to agree to this.*

> **Word partners for sense noun (ABILITY)**
>
> a *keen/powerful/strong* sense of sth • *convey/feel/get/have* a sense of sth • a sense of *achievement/decency/relief/purpose*

> **Word partners for sense noun (GOOD JUDGMENT)**
>
> *make* [little/perfect, etc.] sense • *talk* sense • *common* sense • *business/commercial/economic* sense • What's the sense *in* doing sth?

> **Word partners for sense noun (MEANING)**
>
> in a *broad/general/literal* sense • in the *true* sense *of the term/word* • in *every* sense

▸**verb** [T] (C2) to feel or experience something without being able to explain exactly how: *Although she said nothing, I could sense her anger* ◦ *He sensed something was about to happen.* ◦ [+ (that)] *He sensed* ***(that)*** *his guests were bored, although they were listening politely.* ◦ [+ question word] *Could you sense* ***wh****at was likely to happen?*

senseless /ˈsens.ləs/ adj **NO JUDGMENT** ▷ **1** (C2) not having good judgment or a good or useful purpose: *a senseless argument* ◦ *senseless killings/violence/deaths* **NOT CONSCIOUS** ▷ **2** unconscious: *Panos was* ***beaten*** *senseless by the burglars.* • **senselessly** /-li/ adv

ˈsense ˌorgan noun [C] a part of the body which makes it possible to experience the physical characteristics of a situation: *Your ears, eyes, tongue, nose, and skin are your sense organs.*

sensibility /ˌsen.sɪˈbɪl.ɪ.ti/ (US) /-səˈbɪl.ə.t̬i/ noun **1** (C2) [U] an understanding of or ability to decide about what is good or valuable, especially in connection with artistic or social activities: *literary/musical/artistic/theatrical/aesthetic sensibility* ◦ *The author has applied* ***a*** *modern sensibility* (= way of understanding things) *to the social ideals of an earlier age.* **2 sensibilities** [plural] feelings: *In a multicultural society we need to show respect for the sensibilities* ***of*** *others.*

sensible /ˈsen.sɪ.bl/ adj **GOOD JUDGMENT** ▷ **1** (B1) based on or acting on good judgment and practical ideas or understanding: *a sensible answer/approach/compromise/option* ◦ *a sensible person* ◦ *I think the sensible thing to do is phone before you go and ask for directions.* ◦ ***It*** *would be sensible* ***to*** *take an umbrella.* **2** Sensible clothes or shoes are practical and suitable for the purpose they are needed for, rather than being attractive or fashionable: *It could be cold and wet so pack some sensible clothes.* **AWARE** ▷ **3** formal having an understanding of a situation: *He did not appear to be sensible* ***of*** *the difficulties that lay ahead.*

sensibly /ˈsen.sɪ.bli/ adv (C1) in a sensible or practical way: *The police praised motorists for driving sensibly in the appalling conditions.*

sensitive /ˈsen.sɪ.tɪv/ (US) /-sə.t̬ɪv/ adj **UPSET** ▷ **1** (B2) easily upset by the things people say or do, or causing people to be upset, embarrassed, or angry: *Her reply showed that she was very sensitive* ***to*** *criticism.* ◦ *He was very sensitive* ***about*** *his scar and thought everyone was staring at him.* **2** (B2) A sensitive subject, situation, etc. needs to be dealt with carefully in order to avoid upsetting people: *Sex education and birth control are sensitive* ***issues****.* ◦ *The stolen car contained military documents described as very sensitive.* **KIND** ▷ **3** (B2) understanding what other people need, and being helpful and kind to them: *Representatives of the company claim their plan will be sensitive* ***to*** *local needs.* ◦ *In the movie, he plays a concerned and sensitive father trying to bring up two teenage children on his own.* **REACTING EASILY** ▷ **4** (B2) easily influenced, changed, or damaged, especially by a physical activity or effect: *Some people's teeth are highly sensitive* ***to*** *cold.* ◦ *sensitive* ***skin*** **5** (B2) Sensitive equipment is able to record small changes: *The patient's responses are recorded on a sensitive piece of equipment which gives extremely accurate readings.* • **-sensitive** /-sen.sɪ.tɪv/ (US) /-sə.t̬ɪv/ suffix *light-/heat-sensitive* • **sensitively** /-li/ adv *This is a very delicate situation and it needs to be handled sensitively.* • **sensitiveness** /-nəs/ noun [U]

sensitivity /ˌsen.sɪˈtɪv.ɪ.ti/ (US) /-səˈtɪv.ə.t̬i/ noun (also **sensitiveness**) **KINDNESS** ▷ **1** (C1) [C or U] an ability to understand what other people need, and be helpful and kind to them: *The police showed commendable sensitivity in their handling of the case.* **UPSETTING** ▷ **2** (C1) [U or C usually pl] the quality of being easily upset by the things people say or do, or causing people to be upset, embarrassed, or angry: *I should have warned you about her sensitivity to criticism.* **3** [U] the fact of a situation, subject, etc. needing to be dealt with carefully in order to avoid upsetting people: *Such is the sensitivity of the information that only two people are allowed to know it.* **REACTING EASILY** ▷ **4** [U or C] having a strong physical reaction to something: *One of the side effects of the drug is an increased sensitivity* ***to*** *sunlight.* **5** [U] the ability to record small changes in weight, temperature, etc.: *The sensitivity of the machine provides us with extremely accurate data.*

sensitize (UK usually **sensitise**) /ˈsen.sɪ.taɪz/ verb [T] **REACT EASILY** ▷ **1** to make someone sensitive to something: *It seems very likely that air pollutants are sensitizing people so that they become allergic to pollen.* **MAKE AWARE** ▷ **2** to make someone familiar with something such as a problem or bad situation: *The association aims to sensitize employers* ***to*** *the problems faced by left-handed people in the workplace.*

sensor /ˈsen.səʳ/ (US) /-sɚ/ noun [C] a device that is

S

used to record that something is present or that there are changes in something: *The security device has a heat sensor which detects the presence of people and animals.*

sensory /ˈsen.sᵊr.i/ (US) /-sɚ-/ **adj** [before noun] specialized connected with the physical senses of touch, smell, taste, hearing, and sight

sensual /ˈsen.sjuəl/ **adj** expressing or suggesting physical, especially sexual, pleasure or satisfaction: *sensual pleasure* ◦ *a sensual mouth/voice* ◦ *He is elegant, sensual, conscious of his body.* • **sensuality** /ˌsen.sjuˈæl.ɪ.ti/ (US) /-ə.t̬i/ **noun** [U] *She found his intense sensuality irresistible.*

sensuous /ˈsen.sjuəs/ **adj** **1** giving or expressing pleasure through the physical senses, rather than pleasing the mind or the intelligence: *She luxuriated in the sensuous feel of the silk sheets.* **2 sensual**: *He had a very sensuous mouth.* • **sensuously** /-li/ **adv** • **sensuousness** /-nəs/ **noun** [U]

sent /sent/ **verb** past simple and past participle of **send**

sentence /ˈsen.təns/ **noun; verb**

▸**noun** [C] **WORD GROUP** ▷ **1** (A1) a group of words, usually containing a verb, which expresses a thought in the form of a statement, question, instruction, or EXCLAMATION and starts with a capital letter when written: *He's very impatient and always interrupts me mid-sentence.* ◦ *Your conclusion is good, but the final sentence is too long and complicated.* **PUNISHMENT** ▷ **2** (B2) a punishment given by a judge in court to a person or organization after they have been found guilty of doing something wrong: *He got a* ***heavy/light*** *sentence (= he was severely/not severely punished).* ◦ *The offence* ***carries*** *a* ***jail/prison/life/five-year*** *sentence.* ◦ *He was given a* ***non-custodial/suspended*** *sentence.* **3 pronounce sentence** (of a judge) to say officially what a punishment will be: *The judge will pronounce sentence* ***on*** *the defendant this afternoon.*

▸**verb** [T] legal (B2) to decide and say officially what a punishment will be: *He was sentenced* ***to*** *life imprisonment.*

sententious /senˈten.ʃəs/ **adj** formal disapproving trying to appear wise, clever, and important: *The document was sententious and pompous.* • **sententiously** /-li/ **adv**

sentient /ˈsen.tɪ.ənt/, /ˈsen.ʃᵊnt/ **adj** formal able to experience physical and possibly emotional feelings

S

sentiment /ˈsen.tɪ.mənt/ (US) /-t̬ə-/ **noun** **IDEA** ▷ **1** (C2) [C or U] formal a thought, opinion, or idea based on a feeling about a situation, or a way of thinking about something: *Nationalist sentiment has increased in the area since the bombing.* ◦ *I don't think she* ***shares*** *my sentiments.* ◦ *His son was overwhelmed by the sentiments* ***of*** *love and support in the cards and letters he received.* ◦ formal *'It's a very bad situation.' 'My sentiments exactly (= I completely agree).'* **FEELINGS** ▷ **2** [U] often disapproving gentle feelings such as sympathy, love, etc., especially when considered to be silly or not suitable: *The film is flawed by slightly treacly sentiment.*

sentimental /ˌsen.tɪˈmen.tᵊl/ (US) /-t̬əˈmen.t̬ᵊl/ **adj** **1** (C2) describes someone who is strongly influenced by emotional feelings, especially about happy memories of past events or relationships with other people, rather than by careful thought and judgment based on facts: *Why be sentimental* ***about*** *that old coat? There's no point in keeping it just because you were wearing it when you first met me.* ◦ *It's a cheap ring but it has great sentimental* ***value*** *for me.* **2** disapproving too strongly influenced by emotional feelings: *silly sentimental songs/stories* • **sentimentally** /-i/ **adv**

sentimentalism /ˌsen.tɪˈmen.tᵊl.ɪ.zᵊm/ (US) /-t̬əˈmen.t̬ᵊl-/ **noun** [U] (also **sentimentality**) formal disapproving being sentimental: *Caring for animals is not sentimentality – it reinforces our respect for life.* • **sentimentalist** /-ɪst/ **noun** [C] • **sentimentalize** disapproving (UK usually **sentimentalise**) /-ˈmen.tᵊl.aɪz/ (US) /-ˈmen.t̬ə.laɪz/ **verb** [T] *Her book sentimentalizes parenthood and completely ignores the disadvantages of it.*

sentinel /ˈsen.tɪ.nᵊl/ (US) /-t̬ɪ-/ **noun** [C] **1** literary a person employed to guard something: *A policeman* ***stood*** *sentinel at the entrance.* → Synonym **sentry** **2** mainly US Sentinel is also used in the names of some newspapers: *the Fort Lauderdale Sun-Sentinel*

sentry /ˈsen.tri/ **noun** [C] a soldier who guards a place, usually by standing at its entrance: *My squad were on sentry* ***duty*** *last night.*

ˈsentry ˌbox **noun** [C] a small shelter in which a sentry stands while guarding a place

sepal /ˈsep.əl/ (US) /ˈsiː.pᵊl/ **noun** [C] specialized one of the parts forming the outer part of a flower that surround the petals and are usually small and green

separable /ˈsep.ᵊr.ə.bl/ (US) /-ɚ-/ **adj** formal able to be separated from each other → Compare **inseparable**

separate **adj; verb**

▸**adj** /ˈsep.ᵊr.ət/ (US) /-ɚ-/ (B1) existing or happening independently or in a different physical space: *The art department and the main college are in two separate buildings.* ◦ *I try to* ***keep*** *meat separate* ***from*** *other food in the fridge.* ◦ *I have my public life and my private life, and as far as possible I try to* ***keep*** *them separate.* ◦ *Three youths have been shot and killed in separate incidents this month.*

IDIOM **go your (own) separate ways** If two or more people go their separate ways, they stop being together: *In 1983 the group disbanded and went their separate ways.*

▸**verb** /ˈsep.ᵊr.eɪt/ (US) /-ə.reɪt/ **DIVIDE** ▷ **1** (B2) [I or T] to (cause to) divide into parts: *The north and south of the country are separated* ***by*** *a mountain range.* ◦ *You can get a special device for separating egg whites* ***from*** *yolks.* ◦ *The top and bottom sections are quite difficult to separate.* **MOVE APART** ▷ **2** (B2) [I or T] to make people move apart or into different places, or to move apart: *At school they always tried to separate Jane and me because we were troublemakers.* ◦ *Somehow, in the rush to get out of the building, I got separated* ***from*** *my mother.* ◦ *Perhaps we should separate now and meet up later.* **CONSIDER AS DIFFERENT** ▷ **3** [T] to consider two people or things as different or not related: *You can't separate morality* ***from*** *politics.* **LIQUID** ▷ **4** [I] If a liquid separates, it becomes two different liquids. **RELATIONSHIP** ▷ **5** (B2) [I] to start to live in a different place from your husband or wife because the relationship has ended: *My parents separated when I was six and divorced a couple of years later.*

separately /ˈsep.ᵊr.ət.li/ (US) /-ɚ-/ **adv** (B2) not together: *Detectives interviewed the men separately over several days.* ◦ *I tend to wear the jacket and skirt separately rather than as a suit.* ◦ *I think we'd better deal with these two points separately.*

separates /ˈsep.ᵊr.əts/ (US) /-ɚ-/ **noun** [plural] pieces of women's clothing that are bought separately and not as part of a suit: *Ladies' separates are on the next floor, madam.*

separation /ˌsep.ᵊrˈeɪ.ʃᵊn/ (US) /-əˈreɪ-/ **noun** **1** (B2) [U or S] a situation in which two or more people or things are separated: *During the war many couples had to endure long periods of separation (= not being together).*

∘ *After many years the government finally abandoned its apartheid system of racial separation.* **2** B2 [C or U] an arrangement, often legal, by which two married people stop living together as a couple: *Couples may agree to divorce each other after a separation.* ∘ *They're considering separation as an option.*

separatism /ˈsep.ᵊr.ə.tɪ.zᵊm/ US /-ɚ.ə.t̬ɪ-/ **noun** [U] the belief held by people of a particular race, religion, or other group within a country that they should be independent and have their own government or in some way live apart from other people: *Basque separatism*

separatist /ˈsep.ᵊr.ə.tɪst/ US /-ɚ.ə.t̬ɪst/ **noun** [C] someone who is a member of a particular race, religion, or other group within a country and who believes that this group should be independent and have their own government or in some way live apart from other people

sepia /ˈsiː.pi.ə/ **noun** [U] the reddish-brown colour of photographs in the past • **sepia adj**

sepoy /ˈsiː.pɔɪ/ **noun** [C] **1** in the past, an Indian soldier who got his orders from a European officer **2** Indian English a soldier or police officer of the lowest rank

sepsis /ˈsep.sɪs/ **noun** [U] specialized a severe medical condition in which bacteria enter the blood after an operation or accident

September /sepˈtem.bəʳ/ US /-bɚ/ **noun** [C or U] (written abbreviation **Sept.**) A1 the ninth month of the year, after August and before October: *My mother's birthday is* ***in*** *September.* ∘ *School starts* ***on*** *3 September.* ∘ *Claudia is starting school* ***next*** *September.*

septet /sepˈtet/ **noun** [C, + sing/pl verb] seven people who play musical instruments or sing as a group, or a piece of music written for seven people

septic /ˈsep.tɪk/ **adj** infected by bacteria which produce PUS: *I had my ears pierced and one of them* ***went*** *septic.*

septicaemia UK specialized (US **septicemia**) /ˌsep.tɪˈsiː.mi.ə/ **noun** [U] a serious illness in which an infection spreads through the blood

ˌseptic ˈtank noun [C] a large, usually underground container in which solid waste and urine are dissolved by the action of bacteria

septuagenarian /ˌsep.tjʊə.dʒɪˈneə.ri.ən/ US /-tu.ə.dʒəˈner.i-/ **noun** [C] a person who is between 70 and 79 years old

sepulchral /sɪˈpʌl.krᵊl/ **adj** literary suggesting death or places where the dead are buried: *The curtain rose to reveal a gloomy, sepulchral set for the play.*

sepulchre old use (US also **sepulcher**) /ˈsep.ᵊl.kəʳ/ US /-kɚ/ **noun** [C] a stone structure where someone is buried

sequel /ˈsiː.kwᵊl/ **noun** [C] **1** a book, film, or play that continues the story of a previous book, etc.: *I'm reading the sequel* ***to*** *'Gone with the Wind'.* → Compare **prequel 2** an event which happens after and is the result of an earlier event: *There was a dramatic sequel* ***to*** *last Thursday's scandalous revelations when the minister for trade suddenly announced his resignation.*

sequence /ˈsiː.kwəns/ **noun** **ORDERED SERIES** ▷ **1** C2 [C or U] a series of related things or events, or the order in which they follow each other: *The first chapter describes the strange sequence* ***of events*** *that led to his death.* ∘ *Is there a particular sequence in which you have to perform these tasks?* ∘ *For the sake of convenience the photographs are shown* ***in*** *chronological sequence* (= in the order in which they were taken). **FILM PART** ▷ **2** [C] a part of a film that shows a particular event or a related series of events: *The film's* ***opening*** *sequence is of a very unpleasant murder.*

sequencing /ˈsiː.kwən.sɪŋ/ **noun** [U] specialized the process of deciding the correct order of things: *A common sign of dyslexia is that the sequencing of letters when spelling words may be incorrect.*

sequential /sɪˈkwen.ʃᵊl/ **adj** formal following a particular order: *The publishers claim that the book constitutes 'the first sequential exposition of events and thus of the history of the revolution'.* • **sequentially** /-i/ **adv**

sequester /sɪˈkwes.təʳ/ US /-tɚ/ **verb** [T] **TAKE** ▷ **1** (also **sequestrate**) to take temporary possession of someone's property until they have paid back the money that they owe or until they have obeyed a court order **KEEP SEPARATE** ▷ **2** US legal to keep a JURY together in a place so that they cannot discuss the case with other people or read or hear news reports about it • **sequestration** /ˌsiː.kwesˈtreɪ.ʃᵊn/ **noun** [U] legal

sequestered /sɪˈkwes.təd/ US /-tɚd/ **adj** literary describes a place that is peaceful because it is far away from people: *I found a sequestered spot at the bottom of the garden and lay down with my book.*

sequin /ˈsiː.kwɪn/ **noun** [C] a small, shiny metal or plastic disc sewn onto clothes for decoration • **sequinned** (also **sequined**) /-kwɪnd/ **adj** *a shimmering, blue sequinned dress*

sequoia /sɪˈkwɔɪə/ **noun** [C] a large Californian EVERGREEN tree (= one that never loses its leaves) that can reach a height of more than 90 metres

sera /ˈsɪə.rə/ US /ˈsɪr.ə/ **noun** plural of **serum**

seraph /ˈser.əf/ **noun** [C] (plural **seraphim** or **seraphs**) an ANGEL of the highest rank

seraphic /səˈræf.ɪk/ **adj** literary approving beautiful in a way that suggests that someone is morally good and pure: *a seraphic smile* • **seraphically** /-ɪ.kᵊl.i/ **adv**

serenade /ˌser.əˈneɪd/ **verb; noun**

▸**verb** [T] to play a piece of music or sing for someone, especially for a woman while standing outside her house at night: *Romeo serenades Juliet in the moonlight.* ∘ *Shoppers are serenaded with live piano music.*

▸**noun** [C] **1** a song or piece of music sung or played for someone **2** a piece of CLASSICAL music in several parts: *'Moonlight Serenade'*

serendipity /ˌser.ᵊnˈdɪp.ɪ.ti/ US /-ə.t̬i/ **noun** [U] formal the fact of finding interesting or valuable things by chance • **serendipitous** /-təs/ US /-t̬əs/ **adj** *Reading should be an adventure, a personal experience full of serendipitous surprises.*

serene /səˈriːn/ **adj** C2 peaceful and calm; worried by nothing: *She has a lovely serene face.* • **serenely** /-li/ **adv** • **serenity** /səˈren.ɪ.ti/ US /-ə.t̬i/ **noun** [U] C2 *I admired her serenity in the midst of so much chaos.*

serf /sɜːf/ US /sɝːf/ **noun** [C] a member of a low social class in MEDIEVAL times who worked on the land and was the property of the person who owned that land

serfdom /ˈsɜː.dəm/ US /ˈsɝːf-/ **noun** [U] the state of being a serf or the system by which the serfs worked on the land

serge /sɜːdʒ/ US /sɝːdʒ/ **noun** [U] a strong cloth made from wool, used especially to make jackets and coats

sergeant /ˈsɑː.dʒᵊnt/ US /ˈsɑːr-/ **noun** [C] (also **Sergeant**, written abbreviation **Sgt**, informal **sarge**) **SOLDIER** ▷ **1** a soldier of middle rank: *Sergeant Lewis/Tom Lewis* ∘ [as form of address] *Dismiss the men, Sergeant.* **POLICE OFFICER** ▷ **2** in Britain, a police officer whose rank is above CONSTABLE and

S

below INSPECTOR, or, in the US, a police officer whose rank is below a CAPTAIN: *Sergeant Bates/Bill Bates* ◦ [as form of address] *Thank you, Sergeant.*

ˌsergeant ˈmajor noun [C] a soldier of middle rank

serial /ˈsɪə.ri.əl/ (US) /ˈsɪr.i-/ **adj; noun**

▸**adj** [before noun] **C1** describes a person who repeatedly commits the same serious crime, often using the same method, or a serious crime that is committed repeatedly by one person: *She wrote a thriller about a brutal serial* ***killer.*** ◦ *a serial rapist* ◦ *serial murders/killings*

▸**noun** [C] **C1** a story on television or radio or in a newspaper, etc. that is broadcast or printed in separate parts: *Most of her novels have been made into* ***television*** *serials at some time.*

serialize (UK usually **serialise**) /ˈsɪə.ri.əl.aɪz/ (US) /ˈsɪr.i.ə.laɪz/ **verb** [T] If a book is serialized, it is made into a number of television or radio programmes or published in a newspaper or a magazine in parts: *The novel was serialized* ***for*** *TV back in the 1990s.* • **serialization** (UK usually **serialisation**) /ˌsɪə.ri.əl.aɪˈzeɪ.ʃən/ (US) /ˌsɪr.i.əl-/ noun [C or U]

ˌserial moˈnogamy noun [U] humorous the fact or custom of having a number of sexual relationships one after another, but never more than one at a time

ˈserial ˌnumber noun [C] one of a set of numbers that is put on things produced in large quantities, such as computers, televisions, paper money, etc. so that each has a different number and can be recognized

ˈserial ˌport noun [C] specialized a part of a computer where wires from other pieces of equipment can be connected to it, sending through information one BIT (= unit of information) at a time → Compare **parallel port**

series /ˈsɪə.riːz/ (US) /ˈsɪr.iːz/ **noun** [C] (plural **series**) **SET OF EVENTS** ▷ **1** **B2** a number of similar or related events or things, one following another: *There has been a series* ***of*** *sexual attacks on women in the area.* ◦ *She gave a series* ***of*** *lectures at Warwick University last year on contemporary British writers.* **2** a number of games played by two teams: *The Yankees have a four-game series against the Orioles at home.* **3** **in series** Parts of an electrical system that are in series are arranged in a single line so that the current flows through each part, one after another. **SET OF BROADCASTS** ▷ **4** **B1** a set of television or radio broadcasts on the same subject or using the same characters but in different situations: *The footballer is to host a Channel 4* ***television*** *series on soccer skills* ◦ *a comedy series* ◦ *I missed the second episode of the series so I don't know what's going on now.* **SET OF BOOKS** ▷ **5** **B2** a set of books published by the same company which deal with the same subject: *They do a series* ***on*** *architecture throughout the ages.*

ˌseries ˈcircuit noun [C] specialized a CIRCUIT in which the electric current passes through each of the connected parts in turn → Compare **parallel circuit**

serious /ˈsɪə.ri.əs/ (US) /ˈsɪr.i-/ **adj** **BAD** ▷ **1** **B1** severe in effect; bad: *a serious illness* ◦ *There were no reports of serious injuries.* ◦ *The new tax regulations have landed some of the smaller companies in serious trouble.* ◦ *Drugs have become a serious problem in a lot of schools.* ◦ *This is a very serious offence.* ◦ *He's been taken to hospital where his condition is described as serious but stable.* **2** [after noun] mainly Indian English very ill **NOT JOKING** ▷ **3** **B1** not joking or intended to be funny: *Please don't laugh – I'm being serious.* ◦ *He was wearing a very serious expression and I knew something was wrong.* ◦ *On the surface it's a very funny novel but it does have a more serious underlying theme.* **4** **B1** A serious person is quiet, thinks carefully about things, and does not laugh a lot: *I remember her as a very serious child.* **DETERMINED** ▷ **5** [after verb] determined to follow a particular plan of action: *Is she serious* ***about*** *going to live abroad?* **6** [after verb] If two people who have a loving relationship are serious about each other, they intend to stay with each other for a long time and possibly marry: *She's had a lot of boyfriends but Simon's the only one she's been serious* ***about.*** **NEEDING ATTENTION** ▷ **7** **B2** [before noun] needing or deserving your complete attention: *That's an interesting job offer – I'd give it some serious consideration if I were you.* ◦ *We've got some serious talking to do, you and me.* **EXTREME** ▷ **8** informal extreme in degree or amount: *We did some fairly serious walking over the weekend.* ◦ *I mean we're talking serious (= a large amount of) money, right?* **9** informal very good of its type: *This is a serious wine, Belle, you've just got to try some.*

seriously /ˈsɪə.ri.əs.li/ (US) /ˈsɪr.i-/ **adv** **BADLY** ▷ **1** **B1** badly or severely: *He wasn't seriously injured – he just got a few cuts and bruises.* **NOT JOKING** ▷ **2** **B2** in a serious way, not joking: *Seriously now, did he really say that or are you just being silly?* ◦ *You're not seriously thinking of leaving, are you?* **NEEDING ATTENTION** ▷ **3** **take sb/sth seriously** **B2** to consider a person, subject, or situation to be important or dangerous and worth your attention or respect: *The police have to take any terrorist threat seriously.* ◦ *You don't take anything seriously, do you? It's all one big joke to you.* ◦ *She's sick of being seen as a sex symbol and wants to be taken seriously as an actress.* ◦ *These young actors take them****selves*** *so seriously!* **EXTREMELY** ▷ **4** informal very: *They do some seriously good desserts there.*

seriousness /ˈsɪə.ri.əs.nəs/ (US) /ˈsɪr.i-/ **noun** [U] **BAD** ▷ **1** the state of being very bad or severe: *I don't think he has any notion of the seriousness of the situation.* **NOT JOKING** ▷ **2** the state of being serious, rather than intending to be funny: ***In all*** *seriousness (= completely seriously) now – joking aside – I do think there's a problem here that we've got to get sorted.*

sermon /ˈsɜː.mən/ (US) /ˈsɝː-/ **noun** [C] **1** a part of a Christian church ceremony in which a priest gives a talk on a religious or moral subject, often based on something written in the BIBLE: *The Reverend William Cronshaw* ***delivered/preached*** *the sermon.* ◦ *Today's sermon was* ***on*** *the importance of compassion.* **2** disapproving a long talk in which someone advises other people how they should behave in order to be better people: *I really don't think it's a politician's job to go* ***delivering*** *sermons* ***on*** *public morality.*

sermonize (UK usually **sermonise**) /ˈsɜː.mə.naɪz/ (US) /ˈsɝː-/ **verb** [I] disapproving to give a long talk to people, telling them how they should behave in order to be better people: *My grandmother's all right until she starts sermonizing and then she's unbearable.*

serotonin /ˌse.rəˈtəʊ.nɪn/ (US) /-ˈtoʊ-/ **noun** [U] a NEUROTRANSMITTER (= a chemical in the body which carries messages from the brain) which helps you feel relaxed and happy

serpent /ˈsɜː.pənt/ (US) /ˈsɝː-/ **noun** [C] old use a snake

serpentine /ˈsɜː.pən.taɪn/ (US) /ˈsɝː-/ **adj** literary **1** curving and twisting like a snake: *We followed the serpentine course of the river.* **2** complicated and difficult to understand: *The film's serpentine plot was difficult to follow.*

serrated /səˈreɪ.tɪd/ (US) /-t̬ɪd/ **adj** having a row of sharp points along the edge: *You really need a knife*

S

with a serrated edge for cutting bread.

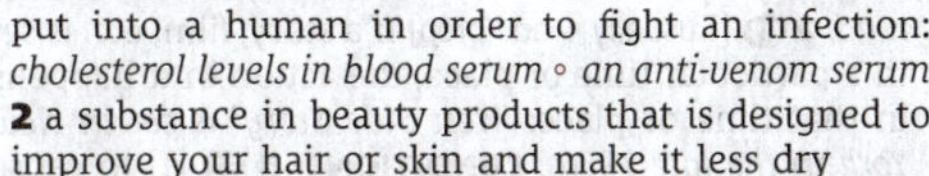

serried /ˈser.id/ **adj** literary pressed closely together, usually in lines: *We flew over the city with its serried* ***ranks*** *of identical grey houses.*

serum /ˈsɪə.rəm/ (US) /ˈsɪr.əm/ **noun** [C or U] (plural **sera** /ˈsɪə.rə/ (US) /ˈsɪr.ə/ or **serums**) **1** the part of the blood that has no colour, or this liquid taken from an animal and put into a human in order to fight an infection: *cholesterol levels in blood serum* ◦ *an anti-venom serum* **2** a substance in beauty products that is designed to improve your hair or skin and make it less dry

servant /ˈsɜː.vənt/ (US) /ˈsɝː-/ **noun 1** (B2) [C] a person who is employed in another person's house, doing jobs such as cooking and cleaning, especially in the past **2 public servant/servant of the state** a person who works for the government: *Public servants should be incorruptible.*

serve /sɜːv/ (US) /sɝːv/ **verb; noun**

▸verb **PROVIDE FOOD/DRINK** ▷ **1** (A2) [I or T] to provide food or drinks: *Do they serve meals in the bar?* ◦ *Breakfast is served in the restaurant between 7.00 and 9.00.* ◦ *We arrived at the hotel and were served* ***with*** *champagne and canapés.* ◦ *All recipes in this book, unless otherwise stated, will serve (= be enough for) four to five people.* ◦ [+ obj + adj] *Serve the tarts hot* ***with*** *custard or whipped cream.* **WORK** ▷ **2** (C1) [I or T] to work for; to do your duty to: *He served* ***in*** *the army in India for 22 years.* ◦ *She has served* ***on*** *the committee for the last 15 years.* ◦ *He served* ***under*** *Harold Wilson as Transport Minister.* **HELP ACHIEVE** ▷ **3** (C1) [I or T] to help achieve something or to be useful as something: *The minister said she did not consider that a public enquiry would serve any useful* ***purpose.*** ◦ *The judge said that the fine would serve* ***as*** *a warning to other motorists who drove without due care.* ◦ *In the absence of anything better the settee would serve (= could be used)* ***as*** *a bed for a couple of nights.* ◦ [+ to infinitive] *Nothing serves* ***to*** *explain the violent fighting we have seen recently.* ◦ old-fashioned *My umbrella will serve* ***for*** *a weapon.* **PROVIDE STH NECESSARY** ▷ **4** [T] to provide with something that is needed: *London's hospitals, so says the report, are out of touch with the communities that they serve.* **DEAL WITH CUSTOMER** ▷ **5** (B1) [T] in a shop, restaurant, or hotel, to deal with a customer by taking their order, showing or selling them goods, etc.: *Are you being served, madam?* ◦ *That's the restaurant where they refused to serve Giles because he was so rude.* **SPEND TIME** ▷ **6** (C2) [T] to spend a period of time doing something: *He served four years* ***in prison*** *for robbery.* ◦ *After he'd served his* ***apprenticeship*** *he found work overseas.* **7 serve time** to spend time in prison: *He's serving time for drugs offences.* **HIT BALL** ▷ **8** [I or T] in sports such as tennis, to hit the ball to the other player as a way of starting the game: *Whose turn is it to serve?* ◦ *That's the third ace you've served this game.* **GIVE DOCUMENT** ▷ **9** [T] legal to give a legal document to someone, demanding that they go to a law court or that they obey an order: *Less than two weeks ago Gough finally served* ***a writ on*** *Slater, claiming damages for alleged loss of royalties.* ◦ *Each person served* ***with*** *a summons will be given six weeks before they have to appear in the Magistrates' Court.*

IDIOMS **if my memory serves me right** if I remember correctly: *I think he was called Brian, if my memory serves me right.* • **serve sb right** informal If you say that something bad serves someone right, you mean that they deserve it: *'He hit me!' 'It serves you right. You shouldn't have been rude to him.'*

PHRASAL VERB **serve (sth) up/out** to put food on plates for people to eat: *Come on everyone, I'm ready to serve up.* ◦ *Jack, could you serve out the trifle?*

▸noun [C] (also **service**) in sports such as tennis, the act of hitting the ball to the other player to start play: *It's your serve.* ◦ *She's got a very fast service.*

server /ˈsɜː.vəʳ/ (US) /ˈsɝː.vɚ/ **noun** [C] **COMPUTING** ▷ **1** (B1) specialized a central computer from which other computers get information: *a client/network/file server* **PROVIDE FOOD/DRINK** ▷ **2** a large spoon, etc. that is used for serving food: ***salad*** *servers*

service /ˈsɜː.vɪs/ (US) /ˈsɝː-/ **noun; verb**

▸noun **PUBLIC NEED** ▷ **1** (B1) [C] a system or organization that provides for a basic public need: *the ambulance/health/postal/prison service* **2** (B1) [C or U] the operation of a system: *There isn't any railway service on Sundays.* ◦ *We hope to be* ***operating*** *a normal service as soon as possible.* **3 services** [plural] UK a place at the side of a large road at which fuel, food, drink, and other things that people want on their journey are sold: *We stopped at the services to get petrol.* **DEALING WITH CUSTOMER** ▷ **4** (B1) [U] the act of dealing with a customer in a shop, restaurant, or hotel by taking their order, showing or selling them goods, etc.: *The only trouble with this café is that the service is so slow.* **5** (B2) [U] an amount of money charged for serving a customer in a restaurant, often paid directly to the WAITER: *There is a ten percent service* ***charge*** *included in the bill.* **WORK** ▷ **6** (B2) [C] a government department that is responsible for a particular area of activity: *the diplomatic service* ◦ *the security services* **7** (C1) [C or U] the time you spend working for an organization: *She was given the award for a lifetime of* ***public*** *service.* **8 services** [plural] formal the particular skills that someone has and can offer to others: *I may be needing the services* ***of*** *a surveyor soon, as I'm buying a house.* **9 in service** in use: *The battleship has been in service since 1965.* **10 be in service** old-fashioned to be employed as a servant **ARMED FORCES** ▷ **11** (B2) [C or U] (work in) the armed forces: *He joined the air force in 1964 and spent ten years* ***in*** *the service.* ◦ *All men under 35 were told to report for* ***military*** *service.* ◦ *Service personnel are subject to the Official Secrets Act.* **12 the services** (B2) [plural] the army, navy, and/or air force: *a career in the services* **13 on active service** fighting in a war: *He was the first member of his regiment to die while on active service.* **RELIGIOUS CEREMONY** ▷ **14** [C] a formal religious ceremony: *A* ***memorial*** *service is being* ***held*** *on Sunday for victims of the bomb explosion.* **ON TABLE** ▷ **15** [C] a set of objects such as plates, cups, or other things that are used in providing and eating food: *a 24-piece dinner service* **REPAIR** ▷ **16** [C] mainly UK a check and repair of a vehicle or machine that is done after regular periods: *She took the car in for a service yesterday.*

IDIOMS **be of service (to sb)** to help someone: *'Thank you so much for that.' 'I'm glad to have been of service.'* • **do sb a service** formal to do something to help someone: *You've done me a great service – thank you.*

▸verb [T] **MACHINE** ▷ **1** to examine a machine and repair any damaged parts: *I'm taking the car in to have it serviced this afternoon.* **DEBT** ▷ **2** to make payments

S

to pay back a debt: *The country is still spending $3 million a week servicing debt.* • **servicing** /-ɪŋ/ **noun** [U] *Bryce has taken the car in for servicing.*

serviceable /ˈsɜː.vɪ.sə.bl̩/ (US) /ˈsɝː-/ **adj** suitable for use: *The shoes are slightly worn, but still serviceable.*

ˈservice ˌcharge noun [C] an amount of money added to the basic price of something to pay for the cost of dealing with the customer: *If you order the tickets by phone you have to pay a $2 service charge as well as $13.50 for each ticket.*

ˈservice ˌindustry noun [C] an industry that provides a service for people but does not result in the production of goods: *More than 70 percent of jobs in the area are in service industries, ranging from hotels to banking.*

serviceman /ˈsɜː.vɪs.mən/ (US) /ˈsɝː-/ **noun** [C] (plural **-men** /-mən/) a man who belongs to the armed forces

ˈservice ˌprovider noun [C] specialized an **ISP**

ˈservice ˌroad noun [C] a small road that is parallel to a bigger road and is used mainly by people travelling in the local area to homes or shops

ˈservice ˌstation noun [C] **1 petrol station 2** (also **services**) UK a place next to a MOTORWAY where you can buy petrol and food and go to the toilet

servicewoman /ˈsɜː.vɪsˌwʊm.ən/ (US) /ˈsɝː-/ **noun** [C] (plural **-women** /-ˈwɪmɪn/) a woman who belongs to the armed forces

serviette /ˌsɜː.viˈet/ (US) /ˌsɝː-/ **noun** [C] UK a square piece of cloth or paper used while you are eating for protecting your clothes or cleaning your mouth and fingers → Synonym **napkin**

servile /ˈsɜː.vaɪl/ (US) /ˈsɝː.vəl/ **adj** disapproving too eager to serve and please someone else in a way that shows you do not have much respect for yourself: *As a waiter you want to be pleasant to people without appearing totally servile.* • **servility** /sɜːˈvɪl.ɪ.ti/ (US) /sɝːˈvɪl.ə.t̬i/ **noun** [U] formal disapproving

serving /ˈsɜː.vɪŋ/ (US) /ˈsɝː-/ **adj; noun**

▸adj **WORKING** ▷ **1** [before noun] employed at the present time in a particular organization, especially the armed forces: *serving and retired military officers* **FOOD/DRINK** ▷ **2 serving dish, spoon, etc.** an object used for holding food before it is put onto plates, or for putting food onto plates

▸noun [C] an amount of one type of food that is given to one person: *The quantities given in the recipe should be enough for four servings.*

servitude /ˈsɜː.vɪ.tjuːd/ (US) /ˈsɝː.vɪ.tuːd/ **noun** [U] formal the state of being under the control of someone else and of having no freedom: *In the past, the majority of women were consigned to a lifetime of servitude and poverty.*

servomechanism /ˈsɜː.vəʊˌmek.ə.nɪ.zᵊm/ (US) /ˌsɝː.voʊˈmek-/ **noun** [C] (also **servo** /ˈsɜː.vəʊ/ (US) /ˈsɝː.voʊ/) a system that uses a small amount of power to control the power of a larger machine

servomotor /ˈsɜː.vəʊˌməʊ.təʳ/ (US) /ˈsɝː.voʊˌmoʊ.t̬ɚ/ **noun** [C] (also **servo**) a motor which provides the power for a servomechanism

sesame /ˈses.ə.mi/ **noun** [U] a herb grown for its small oval seeds and its oil: *sesame oil/seeds*

session /ˈseʃ.ᵊn/ **noun** **FORMAL MEETING** ▷ **1** [C or U] a formal meeting or series of meetings of an organization such as a parliament or a law court: *The **parliamentary** session is due to end on 27 May.* ◦ *The UN Security Council met **in** emergency session to discuss the crisis.* **ACTIVITY** ▷ **2** (B1) [C] a period of time or meeting arranged for a particular activity: *The 21-year-old runner twisted his ankle in a **training** session last Friday.* ◦ *As the European heads of state gathered, the press were allowed in for a **photo** session.* ◦ informal *Rob and I had a **heavy** session last night* (= we drank a lot of alcohol). **COLLEGE PERIOD** ▷ **3** [C or U] US or Scottish English at a college, any of the periods of time that a teaching year or day is divided into, or the teaching year itself: *The session begins on 1 October.* ◦ *Access is restricted when school is **in** session.*

set /set/ **verb; noun; adj**

▸verb (present tense **setting**, past tense and past participle **set**) **POSITION** ▷ **1** (B2) [T usually + adv/prep] to put something in a particular place or position: *He set a vase of flowers on the table.* ◦ *The campsite is set in the middle of a pine forest.* ◦ *Our house is set back from the road.* **2** (B1) [T usually + adv/prep] If a story, film, etc. is set in a particular time or place, the action in it happens in that time or place: *'West Side Story' is set **in** New York **in** the late 1950s.* **CONDITION** ▷ **3** (B2) [T] to cause something or someone to be in the stated condition or situation: *It is believed that the building was set **alight/ablaze/on fire** deliberately.* ◦ *The new director has set a lot of changes **in motion** in our department.* ◦ [+ adj] *After years in prison, the men who had wrongfully been found guilty of the bombing were finally set **free**.* ◦ *If I've made a mistake, then it's up to me to set it **right*** (= correct it). **4 set sb/sth doing sth** to cause someone or something to start doing something: *His remarks set me thinking.* ◦ *The thunderstorm set the radio crackling.* **5 set sb to work** to give someone work to do: *I was set to work tidying the bookshelves.* **ESTABLISH** ▷ **6** (B2) [T] to establish or decide something: *The school has been criticized for failing to set high **standards** for its students.* ◦ *The government has set new **limits** on spending.* ◦ *Lewis has set a new world **record**.* ◦ *The court's decision has set a legal **precedent**.* ◦ *Parents should set a good **example** to their children.* ◦ *He's set himself the **goal/target** of making his first million by the time he's 30.* **GET READY** ▷ **7** (B2) [T] to get something ready so that it comes into operation or can be used: [+ to infinitive] *The heating is set **to** come on at 5 p.m.* ◦ *Have you set **up** the DVD player?* ◦ *I usually set my watch **by** the time signal on the radio.* ◦ *He set the alarm **for** 7 a.m.* ◦ *Will you set the table* (= put plates, knives, forks, etc. on it ready for use), *please?* **8** [T] to put furniture and other things on a stage so that it represents the time and the place in which the action of a play, film, or television programme is going to happen: *During the interval the stage was set **for** the second act.* **FIX** ▷ **9** (B1) [T] to fix or make certain: *Has a **date/time** been set for the meeting yet?* ◦ *The **price** of the house has been set **at** £425,000.* **10 set into sth/be set with sth** If a PRECIOUS STONE is set in/into a piece of jewellery, or a piece of jewellery is set with a PRECIOUS STONE, the stone is fixed firmly to the piece of jewellery: *a gold tiepin with a diamond set into it* ◦ *a brooch set with rubies and pearls* **11** [T] When a doctor sets a broken bone, he or she puts it into a fixed position so that it will HEAL. **12** [I] When a broken bone sets, it HEALS in a fixed position. **13** [T] If you have your hair set, you have it arranged while it is wet so that it will be fixed in a particular style when it is dry. **14** [T] If you set a part of your body, you tighten the muscles around it in order to show that you are determined about something: *'I'm never going back to him,' she said, setting her **jaw** firmly.* ◦ *His face was set in determination.* **15** [I] If a liquid or soft material sets, it becomes firm or hard: *Leave the jelly in the fridge to set.* ◦ *Don't walk on the concrete until it has set.* **GIVE WORK** ▷ **16** (B2) [T] mainly UK (US usually **assign**) to give or provide a piece of work or task for someone to do: *My science teacher*

S

always sets a lot of homework. ◦ *What books have been set for this term?* ◦ [+ two objects] *We set the kids the task of clearing the snow from the front path.* **MUSIC** ▷ **17** [T] to write or provide music for a poem or other words so that they can be sung: *poems set* ***to music*** **SUN** ▷ **18** (B1) [I] (of the sun, moon, or planets) to go down below the HORIZON (= the line at which the Earth seems to join the sky): *We sat on the beach and watched the sun set.* ◦ *The setting sun cast long shadows across the lawn.* → See also **sunset**

IDIOMS **not set the world on fire** to not be very exciting or successful: *He has a nice enough voice but he's not going to set the world on fire.* • **set the scene/stage** (also **the scene/stage is set**) used to mean that conditions have been made right for something to happen, or that something is likely to happen: *This weekend's talks between the two leaders have set the scene* ***for*** *a peace agreement to be reached.* ◦ *The stage looks set* ***for*** *a repeat of last year's final.*

PHRASAL VERBS **set about sth** to start to do or deal with something: [+ -ing verb] *I've no idea how to set about chang****ing*** *a tyre on a car.* ◦ *I tried to apologize, but I think I set about* ***it*** *the wrong way.* • **set about sb** literary to attack someone: *Her attacker set about her* ***with*** *a knife.* • **set sb against sb** to cause one person to argue or fight with another person: *This war has set neighbour against neighbour.* • **set sth against sth** **COMPARE** ▷ **1** to consider something in relation to another thing and compare their different qualities or effects: *You have to set the advantages of the scheme against the disadvantages.* **FINANCE** ▷ **2** to use or record one thing, especially the cost of something, in order to reduce or remove the effect of another: *The cost of business travel and entertainment can be set against* ***tax***. • **set sth/sb apart** If a quality or characteristic sets someone/something apart, it shows them to be different from, and usually better than, others of the same type: *What set her apart* ***from*** *the other candidates for the job was that she had a lot of original ideas.* • **set sth aside** **PURPOSE** ▷ **1** to save something, usually money or time, for a special purpose: *He had some money in an account that he'd set aside* ***for*** *his kids.* ◦ [+ to infinitive] *I set aside half an hour every evening* ***to*** *hear Erik read.* **LEGAL DECISION** ▷ **2** If a judge or court sets aside a previous decision or judgment, they state that it does not now have any legal effect, usually because they consider it to have been wrong: *The Court of Appeal set aside his conviction.* **IGNORE** ▷ **3** to decide that you will not be influenced by your own feelings or opinions because they are not important at a particular time: *In times of war people tend to set aside political differences.* **4** to ignore or not think about a particular fact or situation while considering a matter: *Setting aside the question of cost, what do you think of the idea in principle?* • **set sb back (sth)** informal to cost someone a large amount of money: *Buying that suit must have set you back.* • **set sth/sb back** (C1) to delay an event, process, or person: *The opening of the new swimming pool has been set back by a few weeks.* ◦ *A war would inevitably set back the process of reform.* → See also **setback** • **set sth back** to reduce something to a weaker or less advanced state: *This result has set back their chances of winning the competition.* → See also **setback** • **set sth down** **WRITING** ▷ **1** [often passive] to write or print something, especially to record it in a formal document: *The rules of the club are set down in the members' handbook.* **AIRCRAFT** ▷ **2** to land an aircraft • **set sb down** If a vehicle sets down a passenger, it stops so that the passenger can get out: *The taxi set us down a long way from our hotel, and we had to walk.* • **set sth forth** formal for **set sth out** • **set in** When something unpleasant sets in, it begins and seems likely to continue in a serious way: *This rain looks as if it has set in* ***for*** *the rest of the day.* ◦ *If you get bitten by a dog, you have to make sure the wound is properly cleaned, or an infection could set in.* ◦ *Despair seems to have set in among the team.* • **set off/out** (B2) to start a journey: *What time will we have to set off* ***for*** *the station tomorrow?* ◦ *Jenny set off down the road on her new bike.* ◦ *They've just set off* ***on*** *a round-the-world cruise.* • **set sth off** **CAUSE** ▷ **1** (C2) to cause an activity or event, often a series of events, to begin or happen: *The court's initial verdict in the police officers' trial set off serious riots.* **2** to cause a loud noise or explosion, such as that made by a bomb or an ALARM (= a warning sound) to begin or happen: *Terrorists set off a bomb in the city centre.* ◦ *Somebody set the alarm off on my car.* **MAKE NOTICEABLE** ▷ **3** to make something look attractive by providing a CONTRAST (= attractive difference) to it: *The new yellow cushions nicely set off the pale green of the chair covers.* • **set sb off** informal to cause someone to start doing something: [+ -ing verb] *Every time I think about it, it sets me off laugh****ing***. ◦ *She's finally stopped crying – now don't set her off again.* • **set sb/sth on sb** to make an animal or person attack someone: *The security guards set their dogs on the intruders.* ◦ *If you do that again, I'll set my big brother on you!* • **set on/upon sb** **1** [often passive] to attack someone: *He was set upon by a vicious dog.* **2** to surround or catch someone and prevent them from escaping: *As he left the theatre, the singer was set upon by fans desperate for autographs.* • **set out** **1** (C2) to start an activity with a particular aim: *She set out* ***with*** *the aim of becoming the youngest ever winner of the championship.* ◦ [+ to infinitive] *They set out* ***to*** *discover a cure for cancer.* **2** to start a journey • **set sth out** **DETAILS** ▷ **1** (B2) (formal **set sth forth**) to give the details of something or to explain it, especially in writing, in a clear, organized way: *The management board has set out its goals/plans/proposals for the coming year.* ◦ *Your contract will set out the terms and conditions of your employment.* **ARRANGEMENT** ▷ **2** to arrange something, usually a number of things, in an attractive or organized way: *The market was full of brightly coloured vegetables set out on stalls.* • **set to** **WORK** ▷ **1** to start working or dealing with something in an energetic and determined way: *If we all set to, we should be able to finish the job in a week.* **FIGHT** ▷ **2** informal to begin to fight • **set sth up** **1** (B1) to formally establish a new company, organization, system, way of working, etc.: *A committee has been set up to organize social events in the college.* ◦ *She plans to set up her own business.* ◦ *They've set up a fund for victims of the earthquake.* **2** (B2) to arrange for an event or activity to happen: *We need to set up a meeting to discuss the proposals.* ◦ *The government has agreed to set up a public enquiry.* • **set sb up** **ESTABLISH** ▷ **1** to establish someone or yourself in a business or position: *After he left college, his father set him up* ***in*** *the family business.* ◦ *She set her****self*** *up* ***as*** *an interior designer.* **BENEFIT** ▷ **2** to provide the money that someone needs for an important task or activity that is expected to last a long time: *Winning the lottery has set them up* ***for life***. **3** to provide someone with the energy or health that you need for a particular period of time: *A good breakfast really sets you up* ***for*** *the day.* **DECEIVE** ▷ **4** [often passive] informal to trick someone in order to make them do something, or in order to make them seem guilty of something that they have not done: *They claimed that they weren't selling drugs, but that they'd been set up by the police.* • **set sth/sb up** to provide someone or something with all the

S

necessary things for a particular activity or period of time: *I think we're set up **with** everything we need **for** the journey.* ◦ *We went on a shopping trip and got him all set up for the new term.* • **set (sth) up** to prepare something for use, especially by putting the different parts of it together: *We only had a couple of hours to set up before the exhibition opened.* ◦ *I need one or two people to help me set up the equipment.* • **set yourself up as sth** often disapproving to say that you are a particular type of person: *He sets himself up as an expert on vegetable growing, but he doesn't seem to me to know much about it.*

▶noun **GROUP** ▷ **1** A2 [C] a group of similar things that belong together in some way: *We bought Charles and Mandy a set **of** cutlery as a wedding present.* ◦ *I always keep a tool set in the back of my car.* ◦ *The doctor said that he hadn't seen this particular set **of** symptoms before.* ◦ *We need to establish a new set **of** priorities.* **2** A2 [C] a number of objects or pieces of equipment needed for a particular activity, especially playing a game: *a chess/train/chemistry set* **3** [C] specialized In mathematics, a set is a group of objects with stated characteristics. **4** [C, + sing/pl verb] a group of people who have similar interests and ways of living: *the London set* ◦ *She's got in with a very arty set.* ◦ *The **smart** set is/are going to the Caprice restaurant this season.* **FILM/PLAY** ▷ **5** B2 [C] the place where a film or play is performed or recorded, and the pictures, furniture, etc. that are used: *a film set* ◦ *a stage set* ◦ *a set designer* ◦ *They first met **on** the set of 'Star Wars'.* **PART** ▷ **6** B2 [C] a part of a game of tennis: *They won in **straight** sets (= they won every set).* **7** C2 [C] a musical performance that forms part of a CONCERT, especially one of pop music or JAZZ: *The band's opening set lasted 45 minutes.* **POSITION** ▷ **8 the set of sth** the position in which you hold a part of your body: *I could tell from the set of his jaw that he was angry.* **9** [C] the act of having your hair set: *a **shampoo and** set* **TELEVISION** ▷ **10** [C] old-fashioned a television: *We need a new **television** set.*

▶adj **READY** ▷ **1** C1 [after verb] ready and prepared: *Shall we go now – is everyone set?* ◦ *Is everything **all** set for the party?* ◦ *At the start of the race, the starter said 'On your marks, **get** set, go'.* ◦ *We were just **getting** set **to** leave when Ben said he had something important to tell us.* **2** [after verb] likely or in a suitable condition: *He looks set **to** become world champion again this year.* **FIXED** ▷ **3** C2 fixed or never changing: *My parents say I have to be home by a set time.* ◦ *The restaurant does a set lunch (= a meal which is offered at a fixed price, but with little or no choice about what you have to eat) on Sundays.* ◦ *The receptionist had a bright set smile on his face, but I could tell that he was bored.* ◦ *My father has very set opinions/views on the matter.* **4 set expression/phrase** a phrase in which the words are always used in the same order **STUDY** ▷ **5** [before noun] a set book is one that must be studied for a particular course: *The students are reading 'Lord of the Flies' as one of their set **books/texts** this year.*

IDIOMS **be (dead) set against sth** to be determined not to do something: *Why are you so set against going to college?* ◦ *They are **dead** set against (= strongly opposed to) the plans to close the local hospital.* • **be set fair** UK old-fashioned (of the weather) to be clear and dry and not changing or expected to change • **be set in your ways** to do the same things every day and to not want to change those habits: *As people get older, they often become set in their ways.* • **be set on/upon sth** to be determined to do something: *She seems set on marrying him.*

ˈ**set-aside** noun [U] the act of paying farmers in order not to grow crops on areas of land, or land of this type

setback /ˈset.bæk/ noun [C] C1 something that happens which delays or prevents a process from developing: *Sally had been recovering well from her operation, but yesterday she **experienced/suffered** a setback.* ◦ *There has been a slight/temporary setback **in** our plans.* → See also **set sth/sb back, set sth back**

ˌ**set** ˈ**piece** noun [C usually singular] **1** part of a film, play, etc. that is exciting and attracts attention, but is often not a necessary part of the story **2** a move in a sports game that has been planned and practised

ˌ**set** ˈ**point** noun [C] If a tennis player has a set point, it means that if they win the next point, they will win the SET (= important part of a tennis competition).

ˈ**set** ˌ**square** noun [C] (also **triangle**) UK a flat piece of metal or plastic in the shape of a triangle with one angle of 90°, used for drawing angles → Compare **T-square**

settee /setˈiː/ noun [C] **1** a long, soft seat with a back and usually with arms → Synonym **sofa 2** US a long, wooden seat that has a back

setter /ˈset.əʳ/ US /ˈset̬.ɚ/ noun [C] a dog with long hair that can be trained to help HUNTERS find birds or animals to shoot. There are various types of setter: *an Irish setter* ◦ *a red setter*

setting /ˈset.ɪŋ/ US /ˈset̬-/ noun **POSITION** ▷ **1** B2 [C usually singular] the position of a house or other building: *Their cottage is in an idyllic rural setting.* **2** B2 [C usually singular] the time and the place in which the action of a book, film, play, etc. happens: *The play has its setting in a wartime prison camp.* **3** [C] a **place setting** **CONTROLS** ▷ **4** [C] a position on the controls of a piece of equipment: *My hairdryer has three settings – high, medium, and low.* ◦ *You don't need to **adjust** the setting every time you take a photo.* **JEWELLERY** ▷ **5** [C] the piece of metal in a ring, or other piece of jewellery, into which a PRECIOUS STONE is fixed: *a single diamond in a plain gold setting*

settle /ˈset.l/ US /ˈset̬-/ verb **AGREE** ▷ **1** B2 [T] to reach a decision or an agreement about something, or to end a disagreement: *Good, that's all settled – you send out the invitations for the party, and I'll organize the food.* ◦ [+ question word] *They haven't yet settled **when** the wedding is going to be.* ◦ *'The tickets are £40 each.' 'Well, **that** settles **that** then – I can't afford that much.'* ◦ *I'd like to get this matter settled **once and for all** (= reach a final decision on it).* **2** B2 [I or T] to arrange something: *The details of the contract have not yet been settled.* ◦ *Our lawyer advised us that it would be better to settle **out of court** (= reach an agreement in a legal case without it being decided in a court of law).* ◦ *It took months to settle (= bring to an end) the dispute/strike.* ◦ *My father and I have agreed finally to settle our **differences** (= stop arguing).* **MAKE COMFORTABLE** ▷ **3** [I or T, usually + adv/prep] to relax into a comfortable position: *After dinner we settled **in front of** the television for the evening.* ◦ *The dentist told her patient to settle **back** in the chair.* ◦ *He settled him**self** **down** with a newspaper, and waited for the train to arrive.* **LIVE** ▷ **4** B2 [I usually + adv/prep] to go and live somewhere, especially permanently: *After they got married, they settled **in** Brighton.* **5** [I or T, often passive] to arrive, especially from another country, in a new place and start to live there and use the land: *America was first settled by people who came across from Asia over 25,000 years ago.* **MOVE LOWER** ▷ **6** C1 [I] to move to a lower level and stay there; to drop: *The house had been empty for years, and dust had settled **on** all the surfaces.* ◦ *Do you think the snow will settle (= remain* *on the ground and other surfaces without melting)?* ◦ *The contents of this packet may settle (= fall towards the bottom of the container and so seem to be less).* **PAY** ▷ **7** Ⓒ2 [I or T] to pay, especially money that you owe: *Please settle your **account/bill** without further delay.* ◦ *It took the insurance company months to settle my **claim**.* ◦ formal *Payment of your account is now overdue, and we must ask you to settle (= pay the money you owe) immediately.* **QUIET** ▷ **8** [I or T] to become quiet and calm, or to make something or someone do this: *The weather is expected to settle towards the end of the week.* ◦ *I'll call you back as soon as I've settled the children for the night.* ◦ *Before a performance, she takes three deep breaths to settle her nerves.* ◦ *We're very busy this week, but things should settle (**down**) a bit after the weekend.* ◦ UK *Joe's parents are very worried about him because he doesn't seem to be able to settle **to** (= to give his whole attention to) anything.* **BE IN A CERTAIN STATE** ▷ **9** [I + adv/prep] to reach and remain at a certain level or in a certain state: *The pound rose slightly against the dollar today, then settled **at** $1.53.* ◦ *A peaceful expression settled **on** her face.* ◦ *After the recent riots, an uneasy calm has settled **on** the city.*

IDIOMS **settle an account** to harm someone because they have harmed you in the past • **settle your affairs** formal to decide what will happen to your possessions after your death, usually by making a legal document • **settle an (old) score** (also **settle (old) scores**) to harm someone because they have harmed you in the past: *The president used his speech to settle some old scores **with** his opponents.*

PHRASAL VERBS **settle down** **FEEL COMFORTABLE** ▷ **1** Ⓑ2 (also **settle into somewhere**) to become familiar with a place and to feel happy and confident in it: *She quickly settled down **in** her new house/job/school.* **MAKE HOME** ▷ **2** Ⓒ1 to start living in a place where you intend to stay for a long time, usually with your partner: *Eventually I'd like to settle down and have a family, but not yet.* • **settle (sb) down** Ⓒ2 to become quiet and calm, or to make someone become quiet and calm: *Come on children, stop chatting and settle down please!* ◦ *They settled down on the sofa to watch the film.* • **settle for sth** to accept or agree to something, or to decide to have something, although it is not exactly what you want or it is not the best: *They were hoping to sell their car for £2,000, but settled for £1,500.* ◦ *He wants a full refund and he won't settle for anything less.* ◦ *She never settles for second best.* • **settle in** Ⓒ1 to become familiar with somewhere new, such as a new house, job, or school, and to feel comfortable and happy there: *Once we've settled in, you must come round for dinner.* • **settle sb in** to help someone to become familiar with a new job or a new place where they will be living, working, or staying: *The nurse will be with you soon – she's settling a new patient in at the moment.* • **settle on sth** to agree on a decision: *Have you settled on a name for the baby?* • **settle sth on sb** legal to formally give money or property to someone: *When my uncle died, he settled £1,000 a year on me.* • **settle up** to pay someone the money that you owe them: *Would you like to settle up now, sir?* ◦ *You buy the tickets and I'll settle up **with** you later.*

settled /ˈset.ld/ (US) /ˈseṭ-/ **adj** **COMFORTABLE** ▷ **1** [after verb] If you feel settled in a job, school, etc., you have become familiar with it and are comfortable and happy there: *Now that the children are settled at school, we don't really want to move again.* ◦ *Although I worked there for over a year, I never really felt settled.* **HOME** ▷ **2** living somewhere, especially permanently: *After many years of travelling around, we're now enjoying a more settled life.* **QUIET** ▷ **3** Settled weather is calm and unlikely to change: *It looks as if we are in for a settled spell this week.*

settlement /ˈset.l̩.mənt/ (US) /ˈseṭ-/ **noun** **AGREE** ▷ **1** Ⓒ1 [C or U] an official agreement that finishes an argument: *It now seems unlikely that it will be possible to **negotiate/reach** a peaceful settlement **of** the conflict.* ◦ *As part of their divorce settlement, Geoff agreed to let Polly keep the house.* **2** Ⓒ2 [C] an arrangement to end a disagreement involving a law having been broken, without taking it to a law court, or an amount of money paid as part of such an arrangement: *They **reached** an **out-of-court** settlement.* **HOME** ▷ **3** Ⓒ2 [C or U] a place where people come to live or the process of settling in such a place: *A large Roman settlement has been discovered just outside the town.* ◦ *Many Native Americans were killed during the settlement **of** the American West by Europeans in the 19th century.* **PAYMENT** ▷ **4** [C or U] the action of paying money to someone: *The settlement **of** his debts took him several months.* ◦ *I enclose a cheque **in** settlement **of** your claim.* ◦ legal *Her mother **made** a settlement **on** her (= made a formal arrangement to give her money) when she started college.* **MOVEMENT LOWER** ▷ **5** [U] the process of the slow sinking of a building or the ground

settler /ˈset.ləʳ/ (US) /ˈseṭ-/ **noun** [C] a person who arrives, especially from another country, in a new place in order to live there and use the land

ˈset-to **noun** [C usually singular] informal a short argument or fight: *Dad **had** a bit of a set-to **with** the neighbours about their playing loud music all the time.*

ˌset-top ˈbox **noun** [C] an electronic device that makes it possible to watch DIGITAL broadcasts on ordinary televisions

ˈset-up **noun** **ARRANGE** ▷ **1** [S] the way in which things are organized or arranged: *When I started my new job, it took me a while to get used to the set-up.* ◦ *'Nice little set-up you've got here,' he said as we showed him round the house.* **TRICK** ▷ **2** [C usually singular] informal a situation in which someone is tricked into doing something or is made to seem guilty of something they have not done: *When drugs were found in her luggage, she claimed it was a set-up.*

seven /ˈsev.ən/ **number** Ⓐ1 the number 7: *The restaurant opens for dinner at seven (o'clock).* ◦ *We're open seven days a week (= every day).*

seventeen /ˌsev.ənˈtiːn/ **number** Ⓐ1 the number 17: *I'm nearly seventeen so I should be able to do what I want.* ◦ *They've been married for seventeen years.*

seventeenth /ˌsev.ənˈtiːnθ/ **ordinal number** 17th written as a word: *My mother's birthday is on **the** seventeenth (**of** June).*

seventh /ˈsev.ənθ/ **ordinal number; noun**

▸**ordinal number** Ⓐ2 7th written as a word: *It's **the** seventh (**of** May) today.* ◦ *Our team **was/came** seventh.*

IDIOM **be in seventh heaven** informal humorous to be extremely happy

▸**noun** [C] one of seven equal parts of something

ˌSeventh-Day ˈAdventist **noun** [C] a member of a Christian group that believes that Jesus Christ will return to the earth soon, and has Saturday as its day for worship

seventies /ˈsev.ən.tiz/ (US) /-ṭiz/ **noun** [plural] **1** A person's seventies are the period in which they are aged between 70 and 79: *He's very active considering he's **in** his seventies.* **2 the seventies** **a** the range of

S

temperature between 70° and 79°: *The temperature is expected to reach the seventies tomorrow.* **b** B2 the DECADE (= period of ten years) between 70 and 79 in any century, usually 1970–1979: *Flared trousers and platform shoes were fashionable* ***in*** *the seventies.*

seventieth /ˈsev.ən.ti.əθ/ US /-t̬i-/ **ordinal number** 70th written as a word

seventy /ˈsev.ən.ti/ US /-t̬i/ **number** [C] A2 the number 70: *sixty-nine, seventy, seventy-one* ◦ *This house was built seventy years ago.*

ˌseventy-ˈeight noun [C] (also **78**) an old-fashioned record that is played by being turned around 78 times every minute

ˌseven-year ˈitch noun [S] informal humorous If a married person has the seven-year itch, they are feeling unhappy with their marriage after seven years, and are considering having a sexual relationship with someone who is not their wife or husband.

sever /ˈsev.əʳ/ US /-ɚ/ **verb** [T] **1** to break or separate, especially by cutting: *The knife severed an artery and he bled to death.* ◦ *Her foot was severed* ***from*** *her leg in a car accident.* ◦ *Electricity cables have been severed by the storm.* **2** to end a connection with someone or something: *The US severed* ***diplomatic relations*** *with Cuba in 1961.* ◦ *The company has severed its connection/links/relationship/ties with its previous partners.*

several /ˈsev.ər.əl/ US /-ɚ-/ **determiner, pronoun; adj**
▸**determiner, pronoun** A2 some; an amount that is not exact but is fewer than many: *I've seen 'Gone with the Wind' several times.* ◦ *Several people have complained about the scheme.* ◦ *Several* ***of*** *my friends are learning English at language schools in Cambridge.*
▸**adj** [before noun] formal separate or different: *We are striving to reach an agreement which will satisfy the several interests of the parties concerned.* • **severally** /-i/ **adv**

severance /ˈsev.ər.əns/ US /-ɚ-/ **noun** [U] **1** money paid by an employer to an employee whose job the employer has had to bring to an end: *The management have offered employees one week's severance (****pay****) for each six months they have worked at the company.* ◦ *a severance agreement/deal/package* **2** formal the act of ending a connection, relationship, etc. or of being separated from a person, place, etc.: *The minister announced the severance* ***of*** *aid to the country.* ◦ *The hardest thing to cope with was the severance* ***from*** *his family.*

S

severe /sɪˈvɪəʳ/ US /-ˈvɪr/ **adj** VERY SERIOUS ▷ **1** B2 causing very great pain, difficulty, worry, damage, etc.; very serious: *a severe chest infection/leg injury/toothache* ◦ *This is a school for children with severe learning difficulties.* ◦ *In parts of Africa there is a severe food/water shortage.* ◦ *There is expected to be a severe frost tonight.* ◦ *Severe cutbacks in public spending have been announced.* **2** extreme or very difficult: *This will be a severe test of our strength.* NOT KIND ▷ **3** B2 not kind or showing sympathy; not willing to accept other people's mistakes or failures: *The headteacher spoke in a severe voice.* ◦ *The government is currently facing severe criticism.* ◦ *There are severe penalties for failing to declare all your income to the tax authorities.* PLAIN ▷ **4** often disapproving completely plain and without decoration: *She wore a severe black dress, and plain black shoes.* ◦ *I don't like these severe modern buildings.*

severely /sɪˈvɪə.li/ US /-ˈvɪr-/ **adv** VERY SERIOUSLY ▷ **1** B2 very seriously: *Their daughter was severely injured in a car accident.* ◦ *severely disabled/handicapped* ◦ *Job opportunities are severely limited/restricted at the moment.* NOT KINDLY ▷ **2** in a way that is not kind or does not show sympathy: *I was severely reprimanded by my boss.* ◦ *'I will not allow that kind of behaviour in my class,' the teacher said severely.* PLAINLY ▷ **3** completely plainly: *She dresses very severely.*

severity /sɪˈver.ɪ.ti/ US /-ə.t̬i/ **noun** [U] SERIOUS ▷ **1** C2 seriousness: *Even the doctors were shocked by the severity* ***of*** *his injuries.* NOT KIND ▷ **2** the quality of being very unkind or unpleasant: *He spoke with great severity.* ◦ *The severity* ***of*** *the punishment should match the seriousness of the crime.* PLAIN ▷ **3** plainness

sew /səʊ/ US /soʊ/ **verb** (**sewed, sewn** or **sewed**) **1** B1 [I or T] to join two pieces of cloth together by putting thread through them with a needle: *My grandmother taught me to sew.* ◦ *I made this skirt just by sewing two pieces of material* ***together***. ◦ *He sewed the badge neatly* ***onto*** *his uniform.* **2** B1 [T] to make a piece of clothing by joining pieces of cloth together by putting thread through them with a needle: *She sews all her children's clothes.* **3** [I or T] to use a needle and thread to join up the edges of a cut in the skin or other part of the body: *The muscle layer needs to be sewn first.* ◦ *His finger was cut off when he caught it in a machine, but the surgeon was able to sew it back* ***on***.

PHRASAL VERB **sew sth up** REPAIR ▷ **1** to close or repair something by sewing the edges together: *I've got to sew up that hole in your jeans.* ◦ *A nurse will come and sew up that wound for you soon.* BE SUCCESSFUL ▷ **2** [usually passive] informal If you have a competition or game sewn up, you are certain to win it or get control of it: *The Democrats appear to have the election sewn up.* **3** to complete all the arrangements for a successful business agreement: *It's going to take another week or two to sew up this deal.*

sewage /ˈsuː.ɪdʒ/ **noun** [U] **1** waste matter such as water or human urine or solid waste: *Some cities in the world do not have proper facilities for the disposal of sewage.* ◦ ***Raw/untreated*** *sewage is being pumped into the sea, from where it pollutes our beaches.* **2** the system of carrying away waste water and human waste from houses and other buildings through large underground pipes or passages

ˈsewage ˌworks noun [C] UK (UK also **ˈsewage ˌfarm**, US **ˌsewage ˈtreatment ˌplant**) a place where sewage is treated so that it can be safely got rid of or changed into FERTILIZER

sewer /sʊəʳ/ US /ˈsuː.ɚ/ **noun** [C] **1** a large pipe, usually underground, that is used for carrying waste water and human waste away from buildings to a place where they can be safely got rid of: *a sewer pipe* ◦ *A complicated system of sewers runs under the city.* **2 open sewer** a CHANNEL for carrying away waste water and waste from the human body that is above the ground and is not covered

sewerage /ˈsʊə.rɪdʒ/ US /ˈsuː.ɚ.ɪdʒ/ **noun** [U] **sewage**

sewing /ˈsəʊ.ɪŋ/ US /ˈsoʊ-/ **noun** [U] **1** a piece of cloth that is being or needs to be sewn: *She put her sewing down.* **2** C1 the skill or activity of making or repairing clothes or other things made from cloth: *I'm not very good at sewing.*

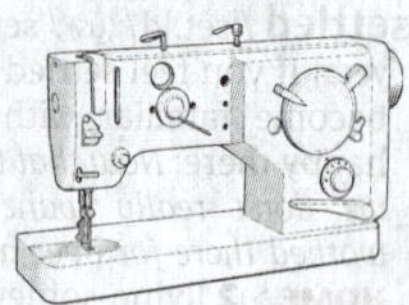
sewing machine

ˈsewing maˌchine noun [C] a machine that is used for joining together pieces of cloth, with a needle that is operated either by turning a handle or by electricity

sex /seks/ noun; verb

▸**noun** MALE/FEMALE ▷ **1** B1 [U] the state of being either male or female: *What sex is your cat?* ◦ *Some tests enable you to find out the sex **of** your baby before it's born.* ◦ *It's illegal to discriminate against people on the basis of (their) sex.* ◦ *She accused her employer of sex **discrimination** (= of treating her unfairly because she was a woman).* **2** C1 [C] all males considered as a group, or all females considered as a group: *She seems to regard all **members of** the male sex as inferior.* ◦ *Members of the **opposite** sex are not allowed in students' rooms overnight.* ACTIVITY ▷ **3** B1 [U] physical activity between people involving the sexual organs: *Sex before/outside marriage is strongly disapproved of in some cultures.* ◦ *She was complaining about all the sex and violence on television.* ◦ *She'd been **having** sex **with** a colleague at work for years.* ◦ *Most young people now receive sex **education** at school.* ◦ ***extramarital/premarital** sex* ◦ ***casual** sex (= sex with someone you do not know)* ◦ ***unprotected** sex (= sex without using something to prevent disease or becoming pregnant)*

▸**verb** [T] specialized to discover if an animal is male or female: *How do you sex fish?*

PHRASAL VERB **sex sth up** informal to make something seem more exciting or interesting: *How can we sex up science writing?*

sexagenarian /ˌsek.sə.dʒɪˈneə.ri.ən/ US /-ˈner.i-/ noun [C] a person who is between 60 and 69 years old

ˈsex apˌpeal noun [U] the quality of being sexually attractive

ˈsex ˌchange noun [C, usually singular] an operation which, together with HORMONE treatment, gives a man many of the characteristics of a woman, or a woman many of the characteristics of a man: [before noun] *a sex-change operation*

-sexed /sekst/ suffix relating to the amount of sexual DESIRE or interest that someone has: *highly-sexed*

sexism /ˈsek.sɪ.zəm/ noun [U] disapproving (actions based on) the belief that the members of one sex are less intelligent, able, skilful, etc. than the members of the other sex, especially that women are less able than men: *The university has been accused of sexism because it has so few women professors.*

sexist /ˈsek.sɪst/ adj disapproving Sexist jokes or remarks suggest that women are less able than men or refer to women's bodies, behaviour, or feelings in a negative way: *sexist comments/jokes* • **sexist** noun [C]

ˈsex ˌkitten noun [C] old-fashioned a sexually attractive young woman

sexless /ˈseks.ləs/ adj SEX ▷ **1** not being sexually attractive or not having an interest in sex: *I've always found her rather sexless.* MALE/FEMALE ▷ **2** without sexual characteristics → Compare **neuter**

ˈsex ˌlife noun [C] a person's sexual activities and relationships: *Many new parents find that having a baby seriously affects their sex life.*

ˈsex-ˌlinked adj If a characteristic of a living thing is sex-linked, it is found only among males or only among females.

ˌsex ˈmaniac noun [C] someone who always wants to have sex and thinks about it too much

ˈsex ˌobject noun [C] If you consider someone to be, or you treat someone like a sex object, you are only interested in them sexually, and not as a person: *She wanted to be regarded as more than just a sex object.*

ˈsex ofˌfender noun [C] a person who commits a crime involving a sexual attack: *Some parents are demanding access to the sex offenders' **register** (= a list, kept by the police, of all the people who have been found guilty in a court of a sexual offence).*

sexologist /sekˈsɒl.ə.dʒɪst/ US /-ˈsɑː.lə-ɪst/ noun [C] a person who studies human sexual behaviour

ˈsex ˌorgan noun [C] a part of the body involved in the production of babies, such as the VAGINA or PENIS

sexpot /ˈseks.pɒt/ US /-pɑːt/ noun [C] informal a woman who is sexually exciting or is very interested in sex. Some people, especially women, consider this offensive.

ˈsex ˌshop noun [C] a shop that sells products connected with sexual activity, including magazines, clothing, and equipment

ˈsex-starved adj having not had enough sex recently

ˈsex ˌsymbol noun [C] someone famous who is considered very sexually attractive by many people: *Marilyn Monroe is one of the cinema's most famous sex symbols.*

sextant /ˈsek.stənt/ noun [C] a device used on a ship or aircraft for measuring angles, such as those between stars or that between the sun and the Earth, in order to discover the exact position of the ship or aircraft

sextet /sekˈstet/ noun [C] a group of six musicians or singers who play or sing together, or a piece of music for six players or singers

ˈsex ˌtherapy noun [U] advice and/or training given by an expert to help people who have sexual problems • **ˈsex ˌtherapist** noun [C]

sexting /ˈsekst.ɪŋ/ noun [U] the activity of sending TEXT MESSAGES that are about sex or intended to sexually excite someone

sexton /ˈsek.stən/ noun [C] a person whose job is to take care of a church building and its GRAVEYARD, and sometimes to ring the church bells

ˈsex ˌtourism noun [U] the act of travelling to another country for the purpose of paying to have sex, especially with children

sextuplet /sekˈstjuː.plɪt/ US /-ˈstuː-/ noun [C] any of six children born to the same mother at the same time

sexual /ˈsek.sjuəl/ adj SEX ▷ **1** B2 relating to the activity of sex: *Most people remember their first sexual experience.* ◦ *a sexual relationship* ◦ *sexual **assault/harassment*** ◦ formal *sexual **intercourse** (= the act of having sex)* ◦ *sexual **orientation/preference** (= whether someone chooses to have sex with men, women, or both)* **2** relating to the production of young living things by the combining of a cell from a male with a cell from a female: *sexual reproduction* MALE/FEMALE ▷ **3** C1 relating to being male or female: *Sexual equality will not be achieved until there is more provision for childcare.* ◦ *Some steps have been taken towards ending sexual discrimination (= treating people unfairly because of which sex they are).*

ˌsexual aˈbuse noun [U] the activity of having sex with a child or old person or someone who is mentally ill, against their wishes or without their agreement

sexuality /ˌsek.sjuˈæl.ɪ.ti/ US /-ə.ţi/ noun [U] someone's ability to experience or express sexual feelings: *She was uncomfortably aware of her son's developing sexuality.*

sexually /ˈsek.sjuə.li/ adv SEX ▷ **1** to do with sexual activity: *She's fun to be with, but I don't find her sexually **attractive** (= do not want to have sex with her).* MALE/FEMALE ▷ **2** to do with being male or female: *sexually stereotyped behaviour (= behaviour which is considered to be typical of a male or a female)*

ˌsexually transˌmitted disˈease noun [C] (abbreviation **STD**) an illness that can be passed from one person to another by sexual activity

ˌsexually transˌmitted ˈillness noun [C] (abbreviation **STI**) UK an illness that can be passed from one person to another by sexual activity

ˌsexual orienˈtation noun [U] the fact of someone preferring to have sexual relationships either with men, or with women, or with both: *Everyone will be treated equally, regardless of sexual orientation.*

ˌsexual revoˈlution noun [S] the change in people's ideas about sex which happened in many countries in the 1960s

ˈsex ˌworker noun [C] polite word for **prostitute**

sexy /ˈsek.si/ adj **SEX** ▷ **1** B2 sexually attractive: *He's very sexy.* ◦ *a sexy smile* ◦ *sexy underwear* **INTERESTING** ▷ **2** informal describes something that attracts a lot of interest and excitement: *For most people, grammar isn't a very sexy subject.* • **sexily** /-sɪ.li/ adv

SF /ˌesˈef/ noun [U] abbreviation for **science fiction**

SGML /ˌes.dʒiː.emˈel/ noun [U] abbreviation for standard generalized markup language: a system for organizing and marking parts of a computer document

Sgt noun [before noun] written abbreviation for **sergeant**

sh (also **shh**, **ssh**) /ʃ:/ exclamation (also **shush**) used to tell someone to be quiet: *Sh, you'll wake the baby!*

Shabbat /ʃæbˈæt/ noun [U] the Jewish day of rest and religious worship, celebrated on Saturday

shabby /ˈʃæb.i/ adj **BAD CONDITION** ▷ **1** C1 looking old and in bad condition because of being used for a long time or not being cared for: *He wore a shabby old overcoat.* ◦ *Her home is a rented one-bedroom flat in a shabby part of town.* ◦ *The refugees were shabby (= wore old clothes in bad condition) and hungry.* **NOT FAIR** ▷ **2** C2 not HONOURABLE or fair; unacceptable: *She spoke out about the shabby way the case had been handled.* • **shabbily** /-ɪ.li/ adv *shabbily dressed* ◦ *The hostages were shabbily **treated** when they came home.* • **shabbiness** /-nəs/ noun [U]

IDIOM **not so shabby/not too shabby** slang used for saying that something is good: *It was a not so shabby week for the team who had three wins.*

shack /ʃæk/ noun; verb

▸noun [C] a very simple and small building made from pieces of wood, metal or other materials

▸verb

PHRASAL VERB **shack up** informal to start living in the same house as sexual partners, without being married: *I hear Tony and Helen have shacked up **together**.* ◦ *She's decided to shack up **with** her boyfriend.*

IDIOM **be shacked up** to be living with someone as a sexual partner when you are not married to them: *'Is Alan still living with Maria?' 'No, he's shacked up with someone else now.'*

shackle /ˈʃæk.l̩/ verb [T] If you are shackled by something, it prevents you from doing what you want to do: *The government is shackled by its own debts.*

shackles /ˈʃæk.l̩z/ noun [plural] **1** a pair of metal rings connected by a chain and fastened to a person's wrists or the bottom of their legs to prevent them from escaping: *The shackles had begun to cut into his ankles.* **2** something that prevents you from doing what you want to do: *The press, once heavily censored, has managed to shake off its shackles.*

shade /ʃeɪd/ noun; verb

▸noun **SLIGHT DARKNESS** ▷ **1** B1 [U] slight darkness caused by something blocking the direct light from the sun: *The sun was hot, and there were no trees to offer us shade.* ◦ *The children played **in/under the** shade **of** a large beach umbrella.* → See also **sunshade** **2** C2 [C] a covering that is put over an electric light in order to make it less bright: *The lamps all had matching purple shades.* **3** [U] (also **shading**) specialized the parts of a picture or painting that the artist has made slightly darker than the other parts: *A good artist can produce a very realistic effect using only **light and** shade.* **4 shades** [plural] informal dark glasses: *She was wearing a black leather jacket and shades.* **5** [C] US for **roller blind** **DEGREE** ▷ **6** B2 [C] a type or degree of a colour: *Their kitchen is painted an unusual shade **of** yellow/an unusual yellow shade.* ◦ *This hair colouring comes in several shades.* ◦ *The room has been decorated in **pastel** shades (= soft and light colours) throughout.* **7** [C] something that is slightly different from other, similar things: *They are hoping to satisfy all shades **of** public **opinion**.* ◦ *There are several shades **of meaning** in that sentence.* **8 a shade** C1 slightly: *Don't you think those trousers are a shade too tight?* ◦ *The journey took us a shade **over/under** three hours.* ◦ *Our new car cost us a shade **more/less** than we were expecting it to.* **9 shades of sth/sb** informal **a** similarities with something or someone: *I fancied there were shades of socialism in the way the school was run.* **b** said to mean that something or someone makes you remember something or someone similar in the past: *In his speech he said – shades of Martin Luther King Jr. – that he had a dream.*

IDIOMS **light and shade** different parts of the character of a person or the quality of a thing: *The orchestra's playing brought out the light and shade in the music.* • **put/leave sb in the shade** to be so good that another person or thing does not seem important or worth very much: *Although I thought I'd done well, my sister's exam results put mine in the shade.* • **shades of grey** the fact of it not being clear in a situation what is right and wrong: *The film presents a straightforward choice between good and evil, with no shades of grey.*

▸verb **STOP LIGHT** ▷ **1** [T] to prevent direct light from shining on something: *I shaded my **eyes** from the glare of the sun.* ◦ *The broad avenues are shaded by splendid trees.* **CHANGE** ▷ **2** [I usually + adv/prep] to gradually change or become: *At sunset, the sky shaded **from** pink **into** dark red.* ◦ *Their views shade **into** the policies of the extreme left of the party.* • **shaded** /ˈʃeɪ.dɪd/ adj *Nothing will grow in the shaded part of the garden.* ◦ *The shaded areas of the plans show where the houses will be built.*

PHRASAL VERB **shade sth in** to make part of a picture darker

ˈshade ˌtree noun [C] US a tree that is planted to provide shade

shadow /ˈʃæd.əʊ/ (US) /-oʊ/ noun; verb; adj

▸noun **DARKNESS** ▷ **1** B1 [C] an area of darkness, caused by light being blocked by something: *The children were playing, jumping on each other's shadows.* ◦ *Jamie followed his mother around all day like a shadow.* ◦ *The sun shone through the leaves, **casting/throwing***

shadows on the lawn. ◦ *This corner of the room is always* ***in*** *shadow (= slight darkness).* **2 the shadows** [plural] an area of darkness in which people and things cannot be seen: *Someone jumped out of the shadows and grabbed my handbag.* **3** [C] a small dark area of skin under your eye: *She put on some make-up to cover the dark shadows under her eyes.* **4 be in/under the shadow of sth a** to be very close to a larger building or place: *They live in a charming house in the shadow of the cathedral.* **b** to be in a situation in which something unpleasant either seems likely to happen and to have a bad effect on your life, or is already having a bad effect on your life: *We are all living under the shadow of* ***war.*** **SMALL AMOUNT** ▷ **5** [S] a small amount: *It is a tragic story, but there is a shadow of hope.* ◦ *There isn't a shadow* ***of doubt*** *that you've made the right decision.* **6 beyond/without a shadow of a doubt** Ⓒ If something is true beyond a shadow of a doubt, there is no doubt that it is true: *This is without a shadow of a doubt the best film I've seen all year.* **FOLLOW** ▷ **7** [C] someone who follows another person everywhere: *'I think we have a shadow on our tail,' muttered the detective.* ◦ *Ever since he was able to walk, Stephen has been his older brother's shadow (= has followed him and copied his actions).* **8** [C] a person, especially in industry, who follows someone else while they are at work in order to learn about that person's job

IDIOMS **be a shadow of your former self** to have less health or strength, or less influence, than you did before • **be in/under sb's shadow** to always receive less attention than someone else: *She's always been under her sister's shadow.* • **cast a shadow over/on sth** literary to spoil a good situation with something unpleasant: *Her father's illness had cast a shadow over the birth of her baby.*

▸verb [T] **FOLLOW** ▷ **1** to follow closely: *The police think that the robbers shadowed their victims for days before the crime.* ◦ *The euro has closely shadowed the dollar.* **2** to follow someone else while they are at work in order to learn about that person's job: *Your first week in the job will be spent shadowing one of our more experienced employees.* **DARKNESS** ▷ **3** to produce a shadow: *We came across a glade shadowed by large trees.*

▸adj [before noun] UK used in the title of important politicians in the main OPPOSITION party (= the party not in government): *the Shadow Foreign Secretary* ◦ *the Shadow Cabinet*

shadowbox /ˈʃæd.əʊ.bɒks/ ⓤⓢ /-oʊ.bɑːks/ verb [I] **1** to fight an imaginary enemy by hitting the air with your hands **2** to pretend to argue about or deal with a problem, often to avoid dealing with the most important problem

shadowy /ˈʃæd.əʊ.i/ ⓤⓢ /-oʊ-/ adj **1** dark and full of shadows: *She was startled by a sudden movement in the shadowy hallway.* **2** describes someone or something about which little is known: *The English king, Arthur, is a somewhat shadowy* ***figure*** *who may not have even existed.* ◦ *They are members of some shadowy extremist group.*

shady /ˈʃeɪ.di/ adj **SLIGHT DARKNESS** ▷ **1** sheltered from direct light from the sun: *We sat on the shady grass for our picnic.* **DISHONEST** ▷ **2** informal dishonest or illegal: *They know some very shady characters.* ◦ *He was involved in shady* ***deals*** *in the past.*

shaft /ʃɑːft/ ⓤⓢ /ʃæft/ noun; verb

▸noun [C] **POLE** ▷ **1** a pole or rod that forms the handle of a tool or weapon: *the shaft* ***of*** *a golf club* **2** a rod forming part of a machine such as an engine, that turns in order to pass power on to the machine: *the drive shaft of a car* ◦ *the propeller shaft of an aircraft* → See also **crankshaft 3 shaft of light** a beam of light: *A shaft of (sun)light came through the open door.* **PASSAGE** ▷ **4** a long, either vertical or sloping, passage through a building or through the ground: *a lift (US an elevator) shaft* ◦ *a ventilation/air shaft* ◦ *a well shaft* **REMARK** ▷ **5** literary a clever remark, especially one that is intended as an attack on someone or something: *John came out with an unexpected shaft* ***of*** *wit/wisdom.* **TREATMENT** ▷ **6 the shaft** US informal unfair treatment: *After years of loyal service, his boss* ***gave*** *him the shaft by firing him just before he would have qualified for a pension.*

▸verb [T] informal to cheat or trick someone, or to treat them unfairly: *She was shafted by her agent over the film rights to her book.*

shag /ʃæg/ verb; adj; noun

▸verb [I or T] (-gg-) UK offensive to have sex with someone

▸adj [before noun] (of a carpet) made of long thick threads: *shag* ***pile*** *(= the soft surface of a carpet formed by cut threads)*

▸noun **SEX** ▷ **1** [C] UK offensive an act of having sex, or a sexual partner **EFFORT** ▷ **2** [S] UK slang an activity that needs a lot of effort or causes small problems **BIRD** ▷ **3** [C] a large sea bird that has dark feathers, a long neck and body, and a curved beak

IDIOM **like a shag on a rock** Australian English slang completely alone

shagged /ʃægd/ adj [after verb] (also **shagged ˈout**) UK offensive extremely tired

IDIOM **can't be shagged** If you can't be shagged to do something, you do not have enough energy to do it.

shaggy /ˈʃæg.i/ adj having or covered with long, rough, and untidy hair, or (of hair) long, rough, and untidy: *a shaggy dog/pony* ◦ *the shaggy coat of a sheep* ◦ *a shaggy rug* • **shagginess** /-nəs/ noun [U]

ˌshaggy-ˈdog ˌstory noun [C] a long joke that has an intentionally silly or MEANINGLESS ending

Shah /ʃɑː/ noun [C] the title of a ruler of Iran in the past

shake /ʃeɪk/ verb; noun

▸verb (**shook, shaken**) **MOVE** ▷ **1** Ⓑ1 [I or T] to move backwards and forwards or up and down in quick, short movements, or to make something or someone do this: *A young boy climbed into the apple tree and shook the branches so that the fruit fell down.* ◦ *Babies like toys that make a noise when they're shaken.* ◦ *The explosion shook buildings for miles around.* ◦ [+ obj + adj] *People in southern California were shaken awake by an earthquake.* ◦ *She shook her hair* ***loose*** *from its ribbon.* ◦ *Anna shook some powdered chocolate* ***over*** *her coffee.* ◦ *Every time one of these big trucks goes through the village, all the houses shake.* ◦ *The child's body was shaking* ***with*** *sobs.* **2** Ⓑ2 [I] If you are shaking, your body makes quick short movements, or you feel as if it is doing so, because you are frightened or nervous: *She was shaking as she opened the letter.* ◦ *Her voice shook as she spoke about the person who attacked her.* ◦ *I was shaking* ***in*** *my* ***shoes/boots*** *(= very nervous) about having to tell Dad what I'd done.* ◦ *I was shaking* ***like a leaf*** *(= very nervous) before my exam.* **3 shake sb's hand/shake sb by the hand** Ⓑ1 to hold someone's hand and move it up and down, especially when you meet them for the first time or when you make an agreement with them: *'Pleased to meet you,' he said, shaking my hand.* ◦ *The Princess was photographed shaking hands* ***with*** *AIDS victims.* ◦ *It seems that we have a deal, so let's shake*

S

(hands) **on** it. ◦ *'Congratulations,' she said, shaking the winner by the hand.* **4 shake your head** B2 to move your head from side to side, in order to express disagreement, sadness, or that you do not want or believe something: *I asked Tim if he'd seen Jackie lately but he shook his head.* ◦ *'That's incredible!' he said, shaking his head in disbelief.* **5 shake your fist** to hold your hand up in the air with your fingers and thumb bent, and move it forcefully backwards and forwards, to show that you are angry: *He shook his fist at the driver who pulled out in front of him.* **UPSET** ▷ **6** [T] to cause to feel upset and worried: *The child seemed nervous and visibly shaken.* ◦ *The news has shaken the whole country.* **MAKE WEAKER** ▷ **7** [T] to make something less certain, firm, or strong: *What has happened has shaken the foundations of her belief.* ◦ *After six defeats in a row, the team's confidence has been badly shaken.* ◦ *This discovery may shake (**up**) traditional theories on how mountains are formed.* **GET RID OF** ▷ **8** C2 [T] to get rid of or escape from something: *It's very difficult to shake the habit of a lifetime.* ◦ *The company has so far been unable to shake (**off**) its reputation for being old-fashioned.*

IDIOMS **more (...) than you can shake a stick at** old-fashioned a lot of: *There are more whisky distilleries in this part of Scotland than you can shake a stick at.* • **shake a leg** old-fashioned informal used to tell someone to hurry or act more quickly: *Come on, Nick, shake a leg or we'll never be ready in time.*

PHRASAL VERBS **shake sb down** US informal to get money from someone by using threats or tricks • **shake sb/somewhere down** US informal to search a person or place carefully, usually in order to find things that are stolen or illegal • **shake down** informal to become organized or established after a period of change: *Give the new arrangements time to shake down – I'm sure they'll be OK.* • **shake sth off** informal C2 to get rid of an illness: *I hope I can shake off this cold before the weekend.* • **shake sb/sth off 1** to get away from someone or something that will not stop following you: *He drove through the red lights in an attempt to shake off the police car that was chasing him.* **2** informal to beat an opponent, or to free yourself from someone or something that is limiting you: *I have no doubt that we will be able to shake off the challenge from our rivals.* • **shake sth out** to hold something such as a piece of cloth at one end and shake it up and down to get rid of dirt or folds: *I was on the back doorstep shaking out a rug.* • **shake sb up** If an unpleasant experience shakes someone up, it makes them feel shocked and upset: *I think she was quite shaken up by the accident.* • **shake sth up** to cause large changes in something such as an organization, usually in order to make improvements: *Technological changes have shaken up many industries.* ◦ *The first thing the new chairman of the company did was to shake up the management.* ◦ *Several new players have been brought in to shake up the team.*

▸**noun 1** [C] an act of shaking something: *She **gave** the box a shake to see if there was anything inside it.* ◦ *'No, no, no,' he said with a shake **of** his head.* **2 the shakes** [plural] informal short, quick movements from side to side that your body makes because you are ill, are frightened, or have drunk too much alcohol: *I watched her hands as she prepared coffee and she definitely had the shakes.* **3** [C] informal a **milkshake**

IDIOM **in two shakes (of a lamb's tail)** (also **a couple of shakes**) old-fashioned informal very soon: *I'll be with you in two shakes.*

shakedown /ˈʃeɪk.daʊn/ **noun; adj**

▸**noun** US informal **THREAT** ▷ **1** [C] the activity of getting money from someone by threatening or tricking them **SEARCH** ▷ **2** [C usually singular] a careful search in order to find things that are stolen or illegal: *Two policemen gave his place a real shakedown.*

▸**adj** [before noun] US becoming organized after a period of change: *The new administration is still in the shakedown period.*

shakeout /ˈʃeɪk.aʊt/ **noun** [C usually singular] a situation in which people lose their jobs, or companies stop doing business, because of economic difficulties: *The shakeout in the labour market after Christmas usually makes January a bad month for unemployment.* ◦ *There has been a shakeout **of** inefficient corporations.*

shaker /ˈʃeɪ.kər/ US /-kɚ/ **noun** [C] **1** a container with a tightly fitting lid in which liquids can be mixed together by moving the container quickly from side to side: *a cocktail shaker* **2** a container with holes in its lid from which a powder can be put onto a surface, by holding the container upside down and shaking it: *a salt/pepper shaker* **3** a container into which DICE are put and moved quickly from side to side before being thrown onto a flat surface, usually during a game involving chance

ˈ**shake-up** **noun** [C usually singular] a large change in the way something is organized: *The company is undergoing a **radical** shake-up.* ◦ *The arrival of the new baby caused a thorough shake-up **of** their family life.*

shaky /ˈʃeɪ.ki/ **adj** **MOVEMENT** ▷ **1** moving with quick, short movements from side to side, not in a controlled way: *Soon after it was born, the calf got up and tried to stand on its shaky legs.* ◦ *The child wrote her name in large shaky letters.* ◦ *She's recovering well from her operation, but she's still a little shaky **on** her **feet**.* **UPSET** ▷ **2** upset: *The news left me feeling a little shaky.* **WEAK** ▷ **3** not firm or strong: *The building's foundations are rather shaky, and it could collapse at any time.* ◦ *The government is taking these steps to try to improve the country's shaky economy.* ◦ *Their marriage looks pretty shaky to me.* ◦ *I think you're on very shaky **ground** with that argument.* • **shakily** /-kɪ.li/ **adv** *The old man stood up and walked shakily across the room.* • **shakiness** /-nəs/ **noun** [U]

shale /ʃeɪl/ **noun** [U] a type of soft, grey rock, usually formed from clay that has become hard, that breaks easily into thin layers

shall strong /ʃæl/ weak /ʃəl/ **modal verb** **FUTURE** ▷ **1** B1 old-fashioned used instead of 'will' when the subject is 'I' or 'we': *If you do that one more time, I shall be very cross.* ◦ *I shall never forget you.* ◦ *Shall we be able to get this finished today, do you think?* ◦ *I'm afraid I shall not/shan't be able to come to your party.* ◦ formal *I shall look forward to meeting you next week.* ◦ *So we'll see you at the weekend, shall we (= is that right)?* ◦ *We shall (= intend to) let you know as soon as there's any news.* **SUGGEST** ▷ **2** A2 used, with 'I' or 'we', to make a suggestion: *'I'm cold.' 'Shall I close this window?'* ◦ *Shall we go out for dinner tonight?* ◦ *Shall I pick the children up from school today?* **CERTAINLY WILL** ▷ **3** used to say that something certainly will or must happen, or that you are determined that something will happen: *Don't worry, I shall be there to meet the train.* ◦ formai *The school rules state that no child shall be allowed out of the school during the day, unless accompanied by an adult.* ◦ *You shall go to the ball, Cinderella.*

shallot /ʃəˈlɒt/ US /-ˈlɑːt/ **noun** [C or U] a type of small onion

S

shallow /ˈʃæl.əʊ/ ⓤⓢ /-oʊ/ **adj; noun**
▸**adj** **NOT DEEP** ▷ **1** B2 having only a short distance from the top to the bottom: *The stream was quite shallow so we were able to walk across it.* ◦ *She told her children to stay in the shallow end (of the swimming pool).* ◦ *Fry the onions in a shallow pan.* ◦ *These beech trees have shallow roots (= roots which do not go very deep into the ground).* **2 shallow breathing** breathing in which you only take a small amount of air into your lungs with each breath **NOT SERIOUS** ▷ **3** C2 disapproving not showing serious or careful thought: *I found the film rather shallow.* ◦ *I think she found him physically quite attractive but a bit shallow.* • **shallowly** /-li/ ⓤⓢ /-oʊ-/ **adv** • **shallowness** /-nəs/ **noun** [U] *Because of the shallowness* ***of*** *the water, we could see the fish in it very clearly.* ◦ *The fine performances of the actors hide the shallowness* ***of*** *the play's script.*
▸**noun** **the shallows** [plural] the shallow part of an area of water: *Alligators live* ***in*** *the shallows.*

ˈshallow-fry **verb** [T] to cook food in a small amount of oil or fat

shalom /ʃəˈlɒm/ ⓤⓢ /-ˈlɑːm/ **exclamation** a form of greeting or a way of saying goodbye, used by Jewish people

shalt /ʃælt/ **modal verb** **thou shalt** old use you shall

sham /ʃæm/ **noun; verb; adj**
▸**noun** [C usually singular] disapproving something that is not what it seems to be and is intended to deceive people, or someone who pretends to be something they are not: *It turned out that he wasn't a real doctor at all – he was just a sham.* ◦ *They claimed that the election had been fair, but really it was a sham.*
▸**verb** [I or T] (**-mm-**) disapproving to pretend: *He isn't really upset – he's just shamming.*
▸**adj** disapproving only pretending to be real; false: *They made a fortune through some sham property deal.* ◦ *That jewellery looks sham to me.* ◦ *She's trapped in a sham (= not good or satisfying) marriage.*

shaman /ˈʃeɪ.mən/ **noun** [C] in particular religions, a person who has special powers to control or influence good and evil spirits which makes it possible for them to discover the cause of illness, bad luck, etc.

shamanism /ˈʃeɪ.mən.ɪ.zᵊm/ **noun** [U] a form of religion which includes a belief in the power of the shaman • **shamanistic** /ˌʃeɪ.məˈnɪs.tɪk/ **adj**

shamble /ˈʃæm.bl̩/ **verb** [I + adv/prep] to walk slowly and awkwardly, without lifting your feet correctly: *Sick patients shambled along the hospital corridors.* ◦ *He was a strange, shambling figure.*

shambles /ˈʃæm.bl̩z/ **noun** [S] informal a state of confusion, bad organization, or untidiness, or something that is in this state: *After the party, the house was* ***a total/complete*** *shambles.* ◦ *Our economy is* ***in a*** *shambles.* ◦ *The way these files are arranged is the biggest shambles I've ever seen.*

shambolic /ʃæmˈbɒl.ɪk/ ⓤⓢ /-ˈbɑː.lɪk/ **adj** UK informal confused and badly organized: *Things are often a bit shambolic at the beginning of the school year.* ◦ *Anna is far too shambolic to be able to run a business.* • **shambolically** /ʃæmˈbɒl.ɪ.kᵊl.i/ ⓤⓢ /-ˈbɑː.lɪ-/ **adv**

shame /ʃeɪm/ **noun; verb; exclamation**
▸**noun** **BAD LUCK** ▷ **1** A2 [S] If something is described as a shame, it is disappointing or not satisfactory: [+ that] ***It's a (great)*** *shame* ***that*** *the concert had to be cancelled.* ◦ [+ to infinitive] *Have some more vegetables –* ***it*** *would be* ***a*** *shame* ***to*** *waste them.* ◦ *'Douglas is having to miss the school concert because he's ill.' 'Oh,* ***what a*** *shame/****that's a*** *shame!'* **BAD FEELING** ▷ **2** C1 [U] an uncomfortable feeling of GUILT or of being ashamed because of your own or someone else's bad behaviour: *He said he felt no shame for what he had done.* ◦ *The children* ***hung/bowed*** *their* ***heads in*** *shame.* ◦ *The shame* ***of*** *the scandal was so great that he shot himself a few weeks later.* ◦ *You can't go out dressed like that –* ***have*** *you* ***no*** *shame (= don't you feel ashamed about being dressed like that)?* **3** [U] loss of honour and respect: *He thinks there's great shame in being out of work and unable to provide for his family.* ◦ *In some societies, if a woman leaves her husband, it* ***brings*** *shame* ***on*** *her and her family.* **4 put sb to shame** to make someone feel ashamed: *It puts me to shame that I still haven't replied to David's letter.* **5 to my shame** I feel ashamed because: *To my shame, I never wrote and thanked Mary for her present.* **6 shame on you** used to tell someone that they should feel sorry for something they did: *Shame on you* ***for*** *being so unkind.* ◦ humorous *You mean you were in town and you didn't come and see us – shame on you!* **COMPARE WELL** ▷ **7 put sb/sth to shame** to make someone or something seem not good by comparison: *Your cooking puts mine to shame.*

IDIOM **die of shame** informal to feel extremely ashamed: *If anyone found out that I took the money, I'd die of shame.*

▸**verb** [T] **BAD FEELING** ▷ **1** to make someone feel ashamed, or to make someone or something lose honour and respect: *It shames me that I treated her so badly.* ◦ *The behaviour of a few children has shamed the whole school.* **2 shame sb into/out of sth** to cause someone to do or not to do something by making them feel ashamed: [+ -ing verb] *The number of people out of work has shamed the government into tak****ing*** *action to prevent further job losses.* **COMPARE WELL** ▷ **3** to be so much better than something that is seems of a low standard by comparison: *The school's exam results shame those of the other schools in the area.*
▸**exclamation** used to express disapproval of something that a public speaker is saying: *To cries of 'Shame!', the minister announced that taxes were being increased.*

shamefaced /ˌʃeɪmˈfeɪst/ **adj** awkward and embarrassed or ashamed: *He looked somewhat shamefaced when he realized his mistake.* • **shamefacedly** /-li/, /-ˈfeɪ.sɪd.li/ **adv**

shameful /ˈʃeɪm.fᵊl/ **adj** disapproving C1 deserving blame, or being a reason for feeling ashamed: *I couldn't see anything shameful in what I had done.* ◦ *The crime figures are shameful.* • **shamefully** /-i/ **adv** disapproving *The children had been shamefully neglected.* • **shamefulness** /-nəs/ **noun** [U]

shameless /ˈʃeɪm.ləs/ **adj** disapproving **1** not ashamed, especially about something generally considered unacceptable: *She is quite shameless* ***about*** *her ambition.* ◦ *They seem to have a shameless disregard for truth.* **2** behaving in a way intended to attract sexual interest, without feeling ashamed about it: *She's a shameless* ***hussy****.* • **shamelessly** /-li/ **adv** disapproving *The government has shamelessly abandoned its principles.* ◦ *She's shamelessly having an affair with her friend's husband.* • **shamelessness** /-nəs/ **noun** [U]

shammy (leather) /ˈʃæm.iˌleð.əʳ/ ⓤⓢ /-ɚ/ **noun** [C or U] a **chamois**

shampoo /ʃæmˈpuː/ **noun; verb**
▸**noun** (plural **shampoos**) **1** A2 [C or U] a liquid used for washing hair, or for washing particular objects or materials: *an anti-dandruff shampoo* ◦ *a carpet shampoo* ◦ *Directions: wet hair, apply shampoo and massage into a rich lather.* **2** [C] an act of washing

S

something, especially your hair, with shampoo: *My hair/The rug/The dog needs a shampoo.* ◦ *She went to the hairdressers for a shampoo* ***and set.***
▸**verb** [T] to wash something with shampoo: *Duncan shampooed my hair and then Tracy cut it.*

shamrock /ˈʃæm.rɒk/ Ⓤⓢ /-rɑːk/ **noun** [C or U] a plant that has three round leaves on each stem

shandy /ˈʃæn.di/ **noun** [C or U] mainly UK a drink made by mixing together beer and LEMONADE or sometimes GINGER ALE: *Two shandies (= glasses of this drink), please.*

shank /ʃæŋk/ **noun** [C] **STRAIGHT PART** ▷ **1** a long, thin, straight part of particular objects, especially one which connects the end of a device or tool that you hold to the end of it which operates: *the shank* ***of*** *a screwdriver* ◦ *the shank* ***of*** *a key/nail* **LEG** ▷ **2** old-fashioned or humorous the leg of a person or animal, especially the part below the knee

shan't /ʃɑːnt/ Ⓤⓢ /ʃænt/ **short form of** shall not: *I shan't be able to come to your party.* ◦ *'Pick those books up immediately.' 'Shan't (= I refuse to)!'*

shanty /ˈʃæn.ti/ Ⓤⓢ /-t̬i/ **noun** [C] **HOUSE** ▷ **1** a small house, usually made from pieces of wood, metal, or cardboard, in which poor people live, especially on the edge of a city **SONG** ▷ **2** (also **chanty**, US also **chantey**) a song that sailors sang in the past while they were working on a ship

shantytown /ˈʃæn.ti.taʊn/ Ⓤⓢ /-t̬i-/ **noun** [C] an area in or on the edge of a city, in which poor people live in small, very cheaply built houses

shape /ʃeɪp/ **noun; verb**
▸**noun FORM** ▷ **1** Ⓑ1 [C or U] the particular physical form or appearance of something: *Clay can be moulded into almost any shape.* ◦ *These bricks are all different shapes.* ◦ *Kim's birthday cake was* ***in the*** *shape* ***of*** *a train.* ◦ *Our table is oval* ***in*** *shape.* ◦ *My bicycle wheel has got bent* ***out of*** *shape.* ◦ *This T-shirt has been washed so many times that it's* ***lost*** *its shape (= has become loose and lost its form).* **2** Ⓑ1 [C] an arrangement that is formed by joining lines together in a particular way or by the line or lines around its outer edge: *a round/square/circular/oblong shape* ◦ *A triangle is a shape with three sides.* ◦ *The children made patterns by sticking coloured shapes onto paper.* **3** [C] the physical form or appearance of a particular person or thing: *In the story, Faust is tempted by the Devil, who has* ***taken the*** *shape* ***of*** *a man.* ◦ *Life on Earth* ***takes*** *many shapes.* **4** [C] a person or object that you cannot see clearly because it is too dark, or because the person or object is too far away: *I could see a dark shape in the street outside.* **5 all shapes and sizes** Ⓒ2 many different types: *We sell all shapes and sizes* ***of*** *teddy bear.* ◦ *Cars* ***come in*** *all shapes and sizes.* **6 in any shape or form** of any type: *I'm opposed to war in any shape or form.* **CHARACTER** ▷ **7** [U] the way something is organized, or its general character or nature: *Technological developments have changed the shape* ***of*** *industry.* ◦ *We need to change the whole shape* ***of*** *our campaign.* **CONDITION** ▷ **8** Ⓑ2 [U] condition, or state of health: *He bought up businesses that were* ***in*** *bad/poor shape, and then sold them off bit by bit.* ◦ *'How are you?' 'Oh, I'm* ***in*** *great shape.'* ◦ *You're* ***in*** *no shape (= not in a good enough state of health) to go to work today.* **9** Ⓑ2 [U] good physical condition: *It's taken us five years to* ***get*** *our house* ***into*** *shape.* ◦ *She runs six miles every day to help keep herself* ***in*** *shape.* ◦ *I haven't had any exercise for weeks, and I'm really* ***out of*** *shape (= not in good physical condition).*

Word partners for shape (FORM)
change shape • sth *loses* its shape • sth *keeps/retains* its shape • *bend* sth *out of* shape • a *beautiful/regular/strange* shape • *in* the shape *of* sth • the shape *of* sth

Word partners for shape (CONDITION)
get in/get back in shape • *keep in/stay in* shape • *knock/lick/whip* sb/sth into shape • *bad/great/poor/tiptop* shape • *in* shape • *out of* shape

IDIOMS **in the shape of sth** in the form of something, or appearing as something: *Luckily, help arrived in the shape of a police officer.* • **knock/lick sth/sb into shape** (US usually **whip sth/sb into shape**) to take action to get something or someone into the good condition that you would like: *to knock the economy into shape* ◦ *A better teacher would have licked him into shape.* • **the shape of things to come** the form or style that is likely to develop or be popular in the future: *I hope the fashions pictured in this magazine are not the shape of things to come.* • **take shape** Ⓒ2 to start to develop a more clear or certain form: *We watched the vase begin to take shape in the potter's hands.* ◦ *Our ideas are beginning to take shape.*

▸**verb** [T] **CHARACTER** ▷ **1** Ⓒ2 to decide or influence the form of something, especially a belief or idea, or someone's character: *Many people are not able to shape their own destinies.* ◦ *My relationship with my father played a major part in shaping my attitude towards men.* ◦ *He was very influential in shaping the government's economic policy/strategy.* **FORM** ▷ **2** to make something become a particular shape: *The skirt has been shaped so that it hangs loosely.* ◦ *When you've made the dough, shape it* ***into*** *two loaves.* **3** formal to make an object from a physical substance: *Early humans shaped tools* ***out of*** *stone.*

PHRASAL VERB **shape up** informal **1** [usually continuous] to develop: ***How*** *are your plans shaping up?* ◦ *Things seem to be shaping up nicely.* ◦ *Colin is shaping up quite well in his new job.* **2** to improve your behaviour or performance: *I've been told that if I don't shape up, I'll lose my job.*

IDIOM **shape up or ship out!** informal said to tell someone that they must improve their performance or behaviour or they will have to leave

shaped /ʃeɪpt/ **adj** having a particular shape: *an unusually shaped carrot* ◦ *Jackie has a perfectly shaped figure.* ◦ *The lenses of her sunglasses were shaped* ***like*** *hearts.*

-shaped /-ʃeɪpt/ **suffix** having a particular shape: *sunglasses with heart-shaped lenses*

shapeless /ˈʃeɪp.ləs/ **adj** without a clear form or structure: *My clay pot ended up as just a shapeless lump.* ◦ *His ideas are interesting, but they're rather shapeless.* • **shapelessly** /-li/ **adv** *Her clothes hung shapelessly (= loosely and without fitting well) on her.* • **shapelessness** /-nəs/ **noun** [U]

shapely /ˈʃeɪ.pli/ **adj** approving used to describe something that has an attractive form, especially a woman's body or parts of a woman's body: *shapely legs* • **shapeliness** /ˈʃeɪ.pli.nəs/ **noun** [U]

shape-shifter /ˈʃeɪpˌʃɪf.təʳ/ Ⓤⓢ /-tɚ/ **noun** [C] an imaginary person or creature that can change into a different shape or form • ˈ**shape-ˌshifting noun** [U]

shard /ʃɑːd/ Ⓤⓢ /ʃɑːrd/ **noun** [C] a piece of a broken glass, cup, container, or similar object

share /ʃeəʳ/ Ⓤⓢ /ʃer/ **verb; noun**
▸**verb 1** Ⓐ2 [I or T] to have or use something at the same

time as someone else: *She's very possessive about her toys and finds it hard to share.* ◦ *Bill and I shared an office for years.* ◦ *I share a house **with** four other people.* **2** A2 [I or T] to divide food, money, goods, etc. and give part of it to someone else: *Will you share your sandwich **with** me?* ◦ *Let's share the sweets (**out**) **among/between** everyone.* ◦ *We should share (**in**) the reward.* **3** B2 [I or T] If two or more people share an activity, they each do some of it: *Shall we share the driving?* ◦ *We shared the preparation for the party **between** us, so it wasn't too much work.* **4** B1 [I or T] If two or more people or things share a feeling, quality, or experience, they both or all have the same feeling, quality, or experience: *We share an interest **in** sailing.* ◦ *All hospitals share some common characteristics.* ◦ *I don't share your views/beliefs.* ◦ *Management and the union both share **in** the responsibility for the crisis.* ◦ *She knew that he was the person she wanted to share her life **with**.* **5** C1 [T] to tell someone else about your thoughts, feelings, ideas, etc.: *He's not very good at sharing his worries.* ◦ *It's nice to have someone you can share your problems **with**.* ◦ *Come on, Bob, share the joke (**with** us).*

IDIOM **share and share alike** used to encourage everyone to have an equal amount of something: *Don't keep all those chocolates to yourself – share and share alike.*

▸noun **PART** ▷ **1** B2 [C or U] a part of something that has been divided between several people, which belongs to, is owed to, or has to be done by a particular person: *The total bill comes to £80, so our share is £20.* ◦ *We must make sure that everyone gets equal shares **of** the food.* ◦ *The party's share **of** the vote fell from 39 percent to 24 percent.* ◦ *She's not doing her share **of** the work.* ◦ *We must all accept some share **of** the responsibility.* **PART OF A BUSINESS** ▷ **2** C2 [C] one of the equal parts that the OWNERSHIP of a company is divided into, and that can be bought by members of the public: *The value of my shares has risen/fallen by eight percent.* ◦ *We've got some shares **in** Apple.* ◦ *He invests in **stocks and** shares.* ◦ *share **prices***

IDIOM **have your (fair) share of sth** C2 to have a lot or more than enough of something bad: *We've certainly got our share of problems at the moment.* ◦ *She's had her fair share of tragedies in her life.*

sharecropper /ˈʃeəˌkrɒp.əʳ/ US /ˈʃerˌkrɑː.pɚ/ **noun** [C] mainly US a farmer who rents land and who gives part of his or her crop as rent • **sharecropping** /-ˌkrɒp.ɪŋ/ US /-ˌkrɑː.pɪŋ/ **noun** [U] US

shared /ʃeəd/ US /ʃerd/ **adj** owned, divided, felt, or experienced by more than one person: *The company is in shared ownership.* ◦ *She and her husband have many shared interests.*

shareholder /ˈʃeəˌhəʊl.dəʳ/ US /ˈʃerˌhoʊl.dɚ/ **noun** [C] (mainly US **stockholder**) a person who owns shares in a company and therefore gets part of the company's profits and the right to vote on how the company is controlled: *Shareholders will be voting on the proposed merger of the companies next week.*

ˈshare-out **noun** [C usually singular] UK an act of dividing something between several people: *Everyone benefited from the share-out **of** the profits.*

shareware /ˈʃeə.weəʳ/ US /ˈʃer.wer/ **noun** [U] computer programs that you are allowed to use for a short period before you decide if you want to buy them: *I've found a really good shareware text editor.*

sharia /ʃəˈriː.ə/ **noun** [U] (also **shariah**) the holy laws of Islam, which cover all parts of a Muslim's life: *sharia law*

shark /ʃɑːk/ US /ʃɑːrk/ **noun** [C] (plural **shark** or **sharks**) **FISH** ▷ **1** B1 a large fish that has sharp teeth and a FIN on its back that can sometimes be seen above the water: *a great white shark* ◦ *a basking shark* ◦ *The movie 'Jaws' is about a man-eating shark.* **PERSON** ▷ **2** informal disapproving a dishonest person, especially one who persuades other people to pay too much money for something: *People who need a place to live can often find themselves at the mercy of local property sharks.*

sharp /ʃɑːp/ US /ʃɑːrp/ **adj**; **adv**; **adj, adv**; **noun**

▸adj **ABLE TO CUT** ▷ **1** B1 having a thin edge or point that can cut something or make a hole in something: *a knife with a sharp edge/blade.* ◦ *sharp teeth/claws/fingernails* ◦ *The point of this pencil isn't sharp enough.* **2** C2 producing or describing a quick, strong pain that makes you feel like you have been cut: *She nudged me with a sharp elbow, to tell me to be quiet.* ◦ *I have this sharp **pain** in my chest, doctor.* **3** describes a part of someone's face that is very pointed: *a thin face with a sharp nose* **4** If someone is sharp or makes a sharp statement, they speak or act in a severe and angry way that can hurt other people: *He was rather sharp **with** me when I asked him to help.* ◦ *The government's proposals came in for some sharp **criticism**.* **SUDDEN** ▷ **5** B2 happening suddenly, quickly, and strongly: *a sharp drop in temperature* ◦ *a sharp decline in the standard of living* ◦ *a sharp **rise/increase** in the number of cases of this illness* ◦ *a sharp **bend** in the road* ◦ *to suffer a sharp **blow** to the head* **TASTE** ▷ **6** sour in taste: *Lemons have a sharp **taste**.* ◦ *This cheese is rather sharp.* → Synonym **acid** **CLEAR** ▷ **7** C1 clear; easy to see or understand: *This TV gives a very sharp picture.* ◦ *The mountains stood **in** sharp **contrast** to the blue sky.* ◦ *There is a sharp **distinction** between crimes which involve injury to people and those that don't.* ◦ *It was a sharp **reminder** of how dangerous the world can be.* **CLEVER** ▷ **8** B2 mainly approving clever or quick to notice things: *Birdwatchers need to have sharp ears and eyes.* ◦ *She has a sharp eye for a bargain.* ◦ *Our new director is very sharp.* ◦ *She manages to combine a sharp **mind/intellect** with a sympathetic manner.* ◦ *He was a man of sharp **wit/sharp-witted** man who always spoke his mind.* ◦ *The play was full of sharp one-liners.* ◦ US *He may be old but he's still **as sharp as a tack**.* **FASHIONABLE** ▷ **9** informal fashionable: *Tony is a very sharp dresser.* ◦ *a sharp-**suited** business executive* • **sharpness** /ˈʃɑːp.nəs/ US /ˈʃɑːrp-/ **noun** [U] *She has a remarkable sharpness **of** mind.* ◦ *the sharpness **of** a photograph/image*

IDIOM **have a sharp tongue** (also **be ˌsharp-ˈtongued**) to be someone who often criticizes and speaks in a severe way: *Jane has rather a sharp tongue, I'm afraid.*

▸adv **SUDDENLY** ▷ **1** C1 suddenly or immediately: *After the church, turn sharp **left/right**.* **EXACTLY** ▷ **2** C1 exactly at the stated time: *The performance will start at 7.30 sharp.*

▸adj, adv higher than the correct or stated musical note: *The E string on my guitar is a bit sharp.* ◦ *This concerto is in the key of C sharp (= the set of musical notes a SEMITONE higher than the one based on the note C).* ◦ *to sing sharp* → Compare **flat, natural**

▸noun [C] (a symbol for) a note that is a SEMITONE higher than the stated note

sharpen /ˈʃɑː.pᵊn/ US /ˈʃɑːr-/ **verb** [T] **ABLE TO CUT** ▷

S

1 B2 to make something sharp or sharper: *My pencil is blunt – I'll have to sharpen it.* ◦ figurative *The company is cutting production costs in an attempt to sharpen its competitive edge (= in order to improve how competitive it is).* **MAKE STRONG** ▷ **2** to make something stronger: *Recent changes have sharpened competition between the airlines.* ◦ *The prison riots have sharpened the debate about how prisons should be run.* **3** to improve: *I hope this course will help me sharpen my computer skills.* ◦ *I went to university to sharpen my mind.* ◦ *We'll need to sharpen our **wits** if we're going to defeat Jack's team.* **CLEAR** ▷ **4** to make something clearer: *How do you sharpen the focus on this camera?* **MUSIC** ▷ **5** to make something play a higher musical note: *You need to sharpen the A string on your violin.*

PHRASAL VERB **sharpen (sth) up** to perform better, or to improve the performance of something: *If the company doesn't sharpen up soon, it will go out of business.*

IDIOM **sharpen up your act** to improve your behaviour or performance

the ˈsharp ˌend noun [S] UK informal the part of an activity, such as a job, where the most problems are likely to be found: *A job like hers would be much too demanding for me, but she enjoys being **at** the sharp end.*

sharpener /ˈʃɑː.pən.əʳ/ US /ˈʃɑːr.pən.ɚ/ noun [C] a machine or tool for making things such as pencils or knives sharper: *a pencil/knife sharpener*

ˌsharp-ˈeyed adj very good at noticing things: *A sharp-eyed secretary noticed the mistake just in time.*

sharpish /ˈʃɑː.pɪʃ/ US /ˈʃɑːr-/ adv UK informal quickly: *We'd better get out of here pretty sharpish.*

sharply /ˈʃɑː.p.li/ US /ˈʃɑːrp-/ adv **SUDDENLY** ▷ **1** B2 quickly and suddenly: *Inflation has **risen/fallen** sharply.* ◦ *His health **improved/deteriorated** sharply this week.* ◦ *The road bends sharply to the left.* **ABLE TO CUT** ▷ **2** in a way which will cut or make a hole: *a sharply pointed nail* **3** severely and angrily: *a sharply-worded letter of complaint* ◦ *He spoke sharply to his daughter.* ◦ *The police have been sharply criticized for their handling of the affair.* **CLEARLY** ▷ **4** clearly and obviously: *a sharply **focused** photograph* ◦ *We have sharply differing views.* **FASHIONABLE** ▷ **5** in a fashionable way: *to be sharply dressed* **CLEVER** ▷ **6** quickly noticing things: *Her ears are sharply attuned to her baby's cry.*

S

ˌsharp ˈpractice noun [U] a way of behaving, in business, that is dishonest but not illegal: *The building industry brought in rules to protect customers from sharp practice.*

sharpshooter /ˈʃɑːpˌʃuː.təʳ/ US /ˈʃɑːrpˌʃuː.t̬ɚ/ noun [C] a person who is skilled at FIRING a gun and accurately hitting what they are aiming at

shat /ʃæt/ verb past simple and past participle of **shit**

shatter /ˈʃæt.əʳ/ US /ˈʃæt̬.ɚ/ verb **1** [I or T] to (cause something to) break suddenly into very small pieces: *The glass shattered **into** a thousand tiny pieces.* ◦ *His leg was shattered in the accident.* **2** [T] to end or severely damage something: *The book shattered all her **illusions** about the Romans.* ◦ *Noisy motorbikes shattered **the peace**.* • **-shattering** /-ɪŋ/ suffix *a confidence-shattering defeat (= one which destroys confidence)* → See also **earth-shattering**

shattered /ˈʃæt.əd/ US /ˈʃæt̬.ɚd/ adj **BROKEN** ▷ **1** broken into very small pieces: *Shattered glass lay all over the road.* **UPSET** ▷ **2** C2 extremely upset: *The family were shattered at the news of Annabel's suicide.* **TIRED** ▷ **3** C2 UK informal extremely tired: *By the time I got home, I was shattered.*

shattering /ˈʃæt.ər.ɪŋ/ US /ˈʃæt̬.ɚ-/ adj making you feel extremely tired: *It was a shattering schedule – seven meetings in two days.*

shatterproof /ˈʃæt.ə-.pruːf/ US /ˈʃæt̬.ɚ-/ adj Shatterproof glass or plastic, etc. is made so that it will not break into small pieces: *a shatterproof windscreen*

shave /ʃeɪv/ verb; noun

shave

▸verb [I or T] B1 to remove hair from the body, especially a man's face, by cutting it close to the skin with a RAZOR, so that the skin feels smooth: *John has to shave twice a day.* ◦ *I always shave my legs in the bath.* ◦ *Do you shave under your arms?* ◦ *When my dad shaved his beard **(off)**, he looked ten years younger.*

PHRASAL VERBS **shave sth off/from sth** to cut a very thin piece from an object or surface: *She shaved a few millimetres off the bottom of the door, so that it would open more easily.* • **shave sth off sth** (also **shave sth by sth**) to reduce something by the stated amount: *The new high speed trains will shave 25 minutes off the journey time.* ◦ *Our prices have been shaved by five percent!*

▸noun [C] the act of shaving, especially a man's face: *I **need** a shave.* ◦ *He washed and **had** a shave.*

shaven /ˈʃeɪ.vən/ adj with the hair removed: *They all had shaven heads.*

shaver /ˈʃeɪ.vəʳ/ US /-vɚ/ noun [C] (also **electric razor**) an electric device for shaving hair from someone's face or body

shaving /ˈʃeɪ.vɪŋ/ adj [before noun] for using when you shave: *a shaving brush* ◦ *shaving cream/foam*

shavings /ˈʃeɪ.vɪŋz/ noun [plural] small, very thin pieces of a hard substance: *The floor was covered in **wood** shavings.*

shawl /ʃɔːl/ US /ʃɑːl/ noun [C] a large piece of cloth worn especially by women or girls over their shoulders and/or head

shawl

s/he pronoun written used in writing instead of 'she or he' to refer to a person whose sex is not known: *If any employee needs to take time off, s/he should contact the Personnel Department.* → See also **they**

she strong /ʃiː/ weak /ʃi/ pronoun; noun

▸pronoun **1** A1 used as the subject of a verb to refer to a woman, girl, or female animal that has already been mentioned: *I asked my mother if she'd lend me some money, but she said no.* **2** old-fashioned used instead of 'it' to refer to a country, ship, or vehicle: *After India became independent, she chose to be a member of the Commonwealth.* ◦ *Look at my new car – isn't she beautiful?*

▸noun [C] a female: *Is this kitten a she or a he?* • **she-** /ʃiː-/ prefix *a she-wolf (= a female wolf)*

shea butter /ˈʃeɪˌbʌt.əʳ/ US /-ˌbʌt̬.ɚ/ noun [U] a yellow fat from a type of nut, used in make-up and soap and as a food: *This product contains avocado oil and shea butter to leave your skin silky smooth.*

sheaf /ʃiːf/ noun [C] (plural **sheaves**) a number of things, especially pieces of paper or plant stems, that are held or tied together: *A lawyer walked in carrying a whole sheaf **of** papers.* ◦ *The corn was cut and tied in sheaves.*

shear /ʃɪəʳ/ (US) /ʃɪr/ verb (**sheared, sheared** or **shorn**) **CUT** ▷ **1** [T] to cut the wool off a sheep **2** [T] to cut the hair on a person's head close to the skin, especially without care: *He recalled the humiliation of having his hair shorn and exchanging his clothes for the prison uniform.* **3 be shorn of sth** to have something taken away from you: *The ex-president, although shorn of his official powers, still has influence.* **BREAK** ▷ **4** [I] specialized If part of something, especially something made of metal, shears, it breaks into two pieces, usually because of a sideways force: *The old screws holding the engine casing had sheared (**off**).* • **shearing** /ˈʃɪə.rɪŋ/ (US) /ˈʃɪr.ɪŋ/ noun [U] *sheep shearing*

shears /ʃɪəz/ (US) /ʃɪrz/ noun [plural] very large SCISSORS: *gardening/dressmaking shears* ◦ *a pair of shears*

sheath /ʃiːθ/ noun [C] **1** a close-fitting covering to protect something: *The cable has a copper wire surrounded by a plastic sheath.* ◦ *The nerves are protected by thin sheaths of fatty tissue.* **2** a cover into which a knife or SWORD fits so that the blade cannot cut someone when it is not being used: *He drew the knife from its jewelled leather sheath.* **3** UK a **condom** • **sheathing** /ˈʃiː.ðɪŋ/ noun [C or U] *The frame is covered by a glass and metal sheathing (= protective cover).*

sheathe /ʃiːð/ verb [T] **1** to put a knife back inside its sheath **2** literary to cover something in a thick or PROTECTIVE layer of a substance: *The landscape was sheathed **in** ice.*

ˈsheath ˌknife noun [C] a knife with a fixed blade

sheaves /ʃiːvz/ noun plural of **sheaf**

shebang /ʃɪˈbæŋ/ noun informal **the whole shebang** the whole of something, including everything that is connected with it: *The wedding's next week, but my parents are taking care of the whole shebang.*

she'd /ʃid/, /ʃiːd/ short form **1** she had: *She'd found the answer, at last.* **2** she would: *She'd be a great managing director, don't you think?*

shed /ʃed/ noun; verb

▸noun [C] **1** (B2) a small building, usually made of wood, used for storing things: *a garden shed* ◦ *a tool/bicycle shed* **2** a large, simple building used for a particular activity: *the lambing shed*

▸verb (present tense **shedding**, past tense and past participle **shed**) **GET RID OF** ▷ **1** [T] (often used in newspapers) to get rid of something you do not need or want: *900 jobs will be shed over the next few months.* ◦ *Psychotherapy helped him to shed some of his insecurity/inhibitions.* ◦ *I'm going on a diet to see if I can shed (= become thinner by losing) a few kilos.* **2** [T] to lose a covering, such as leaves, hair, or skin, because it falls off naturally, or to drop something in a natural way or by accident: *The trees shed their **leaves** in autumn.* ◦ *They ran down to the sea, shedding clothes as they went.* ◦ UK *A lorry had shed a load of gravel across the road.* **PRODUCE** ▷ **3 shed tears, blood, light, etc.** (C1) to produce tears, light, blood, etc.: *She shed a few tears at her daughter's wedding.* ◦ *So much blood has been shed (= so many people have been badly hurt or killed) in this war.*

shedload /ˈʃed.ləʊd/ (US) /-loʊd/ noun [C] UK informal a large amount: *The film has recently won **a** shedload **of** awards.* ◦ *Shedloads **of** cash are needed to improve the failing health service.*

sheen /ʃiːn/ noun [S] approving a bright, smooth surface: *The conditioner gives the hair a beautiful soft sheen.*

sheep /ʃiːp/ noun [C] (plural **sheep**) (A1) a farm animal with thick wool that eats grass and is kept for its wool, skin, and meat: *The farmer has several large **flocks** (= groups) of long-haired sheep.* ◦ *We heard sheep **bleating/baaing** in the field.* → See also **ewe, lamb, mutton, ram**

IDIOMS **be (like) sheep** disapproving If a group of people are (like) sheep, they all behave in the same way or all behave as they are told, and cannot or will not act independently. • **separate/sort out the sheep from the goats** UK to make clear which people in a particular group are of a higher ability than the others: *The uphill stages of the race will really sort the sheep from the goats.*

ˈsheep ˌdip noun [C or U] a liquid in which sheep are washed in order to kill harmful insects living in their wool, or the container in which the liquid is put

sheepdog /ˈʃiːp.dɒg/ (US) /-dɑːg/ noun [C] a dog trained to help people control sheep and move them in the direction wanted: *Two sheepdogs herded the sheep into pens.*

sheepish /ˈʃiː.pɪʃ/ adj embarrassed because you know that you have done something wrong or silly: *She gave me a sheepish smile and apologized.* • **sheepishly** /-li/ adv • **sheepishness** /-nəs/ noun [U]

sheepskin /ˈʃiːp.skɪn/ noun [C or U] the skin of a sheep with the wool still on it: *We've got a rug made from (a) sheepskin.* ◦ *a sheepskin coat*

sheer /ʃɪəʳ/ (US) /ʃɪr/ adj; verb

▸adj **COMPLETE** ▷ **1** (C1) [before noun] used to emphasize how very great, important, or powerful a quality or feeling is; nothing except: *The suggestion is sheer **nonsense**.* ◦ *His success was due to sheer willpower/determination.* ◦ *It was sheer coincidence that we met.* **STEEP** ▷ **2** (C2) extremely steep; almost vertical: *a sheer mountain side* ◦ *a sheer drop of 100 metres* **THIN** ▷ **3** describes clothing or material that is so thin, light, and delicate that you can see through it: *sheer nylon tights*

▸verb [I usually + adv/prep] to change direction suddenly: *I thought the boats were going to collide, but one sheered **off/away** at the last second.*

sheet /ʃiːt/ noun; verb

▸noun [C] **1** (A2) a large, thin, flat, usually rectangular piece of something, especially a piece of cloth used for sleeping on: *I've put clean sheets on the bed.* ◦ *a sheet **of** glass* ◦ *They fixed a **polythene/plastic** sheet over the broken window.* **2** (A2) a piece of paper: *some sheets **of** wrapping paper* ◦ *The application form was a single sheet **of paper**.* **3** a piece of paper with something printed on it: *The tourist office provides a weekly information sheet about things that are happening in the town.* **4 sheet of sth** a large, wide mass of something such as fire or ice: *A sheet of **flame** shot up into the air immediately after the explosion.* ◦ *A thick sheet of **ice** had formed over the water.* **5 sheets** [plural] a large quantity of rain: *The rain was coming down **in** sheets.*

▸verb informal **be sheeting** to be raining very hard: *We can't go out yet, it's sheeting **down** outside.* ◦ *The rain was sheeting **against** the windows.*

sheeting /ˈʃiː.tɪŋ/ (US) /-t̬ɪŋ/ noun [U] thin material, especially cloth, plastic, or metal

ˌsheet ˈlightning noun [U] LIGHTNING that lights up a large part of the sky

ˌsheet ˈmusic noun [U] music in its printed or

S

written form, especially single sheets of paper not formed into a book

sheikh (also **sheik**) /ʃeɪk/, /ʃiːk/ **noun** [C] an Arab ruler or head of a group of people

sheikhdom /ˈʃeɪk.dəm/, /ˈʃiːk-/ **noun** [C] an area of land or a country ruled by a sheikh

sheila /ˈʃiː.lə/ **noun** [C] Australian English slang a girl or a woman

shekel /ˈʃek.əl/ **noun** **1** [C] the standard unit of money used in Israel **2 shekels** [plural] slang humorous money

shelf /ʃelf/ **noun** [C] (plural **shelves**) **1** A2 a long, flat board fixed horizontally, usually against a wall or inside a cupboard so that objects can be stored on it: *a glass shelf* ◦ ***on** the top/bottom shelf* ◦ *One wall had shelves from floor to ceiling, crammed with books.* → See also **bookshelf** **2** specialized a flat area of rock underwater or on a CLIFF **3 off the shelf** If a product can be bought off the shelf, it does not need to be specially made or asked for: *It's often cheaper if you **buy** wallpaper off the shelf, rather than having to order it.* ◦ *off-the-shelf goods/clothes* **4 remove sth from your shelves** When a shop removes something from its shelves, that product stops being available for sale there.

IDIOM **on the shelf** **1** not noticed or not used: *It's important to apply research in a practical way and not **leave** it on the shelf.* **2** mainly UK informal describes someone, usually a woman, who is not married and is considered too old for anyone to want to marry them: *In those days, if you hadn't married by the time you were 30, you were definitely on the shelf.*

ˈshelf ˌlife **noun** [C usually singular] (plural **shelf lives**) **1** the length of time that a product, especially food, can be kept in a shop before it becomes too old to be sold or used: *Fresh fruit has a very short shelf life.* **2** the length of time that something remains useful, popular, or successful

shell /ʃel/ **noun; verb**

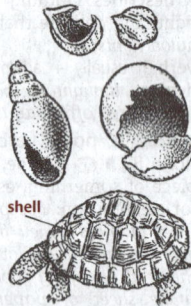

▸**noun** COVERING ▷ **1** B2 [C or U] the hard outer covering of something, especially nuts, eggs, and some animals: *Brazil nuts have very hard shells.* ◦ *A piece of shell fell into the cake mixture.* ◦ *the shell of a snail/crab/tortoise* ◦ *a shell necklace (= a piece of jewellery made out of the shells of small sea creatures)* → See also **eggshell, nutshell, seashell, shellfish** **2** [C] the basic outer structure of a building or vehicle, especially when the parts inside have been destroyed or taken or have not yet been made: *the shell **of** a burned-out farmhouse* EXPLOSIVE ▷ **3** [C] a container, usually with a pointed end, that is filled with explosives and shot from a large gun: ***Artillery** and **mortar** shells were landing in the outskirts of the city.* COMPANY ▷ **4** a company that is used to hide illegal activities: *The shell advertised bonds for sale to investors, but this offering was essentially a fraud because no bonds ever existed.*

shells

shell

IDIOMS **come out of your shell** (also **bring sb out of their shell**) If you come out of your shell, you become more interested in other people and more willing to talk and take part in social activities, and if someone brings you out of your shell, they cause you to do this: *Derek has really come out of his shell since he started working here.* • **crawl/go/retreat/retire into your shell** to become less interested in other people and less willing to talk and take part in social activities: *The more they tried to get her to talk about her experiences, the further she retreated **back** into her shell.*

▸**verb** [T] COVERING ▷ **1** to remove PEAS, nuts, etc. from their shells or their natural covering EXPLOSIVE ▷ **2** to fire shells at something: *They were under orders to shell the hospital and the town hall.* • **shelling** /ˈʃel.ɪŋ/ **noun** [U] *Shelling of enemy lines continued all day.*

PHRASAL VERB **shell (sth) out** informal to pay or give money for something, usually unwillingly: *Having shelled out £50 **for** the tickets, I wasn't going to miss the show.*

she'll /ʃil/, /ʃiːl/ **short form** she will: *She'll be here later.*

shellfish /ˈʃel.fɪʃ/ **noun** [C or U] (plural **shellfish**) sea creatures that live in shells and are eaten as food, or one of these creatures: *Lobsters, crabs, and oysters are all shellfish.*

ˈshell ˌshock **noun** [U] mental illness caused by experiences of war: *He said many of the men who were shot for cowardice were in fact suffering from shell shock.*

ˈshell-shocked **adj** **1** suffering from shell shock: *I was treating shell-shocked soldiers.* **2** extremely tired and nervous or frightened, especially after an unpleasant and unexpected event, or extremely surprised: *After the crash, the passengers were shell-shocked but there were no serious injuries.* ◦ *They were shell-shocked by the news.*

ˈshell ˌsuit **noun** [C] UK an informal loose top and trousers made of thin, light, smooth material with ELASTIC (= material that stretches) at the wrist and ANKLE

shelter /ˈʃel.təʳ/ US /-t̬ɚ/ **noun; verb**

▸**noun** [C or U] **1** B2 (a building designed to give) protection from bad weather, danger, or attack: *an air-raid shelter* ◦ *They opened a shelter to provide temporary housing for the city's homeless.* ◦ *The trees **gave/provided** some shelter **from** the rain.* **2 find/take shelter** B2 to protect yourself from bad weather, danger or attack: *We took shelter for the night **in** an abandoned house.*

▸**verb** PROTECT ▷ **1** C2 [I or T] to protect yourself, or another person or thing, from bad weather, danger, or attack: *We were caught in a thunderstorm, without anywhere to shelter.* ◦ *A group of us were sheltering **from** the rain under the trees.* **2** [T] to give someone a secret hiding place so that they will not be caught by the army, police, etc.: *Local people risked their own lives to shelter resistance fighters **from** the army.*

sheltered /ˈʃel.təd/ US /-t̬ɚd/ **adj** protected from wind, rain, or other bad weather: *We found a sheltered **spot** (= place) to have our picnic.*

IDIOM **have/lead a sheltered life** disapproving to have a life in which you are protected too much and experience very little danger, excitement, or change

ˌsheltered accommoˈdation **noun** [U] (also **ˌsheltered ˈhousing**) houses for old and ill people in a place where help can be given if it is needed: *She's just moved into sheltered accommodation.*

shelve /ʃelv/ **verb** DELAY ▷ **1** [T] to not take action on something until a later time: *I've had to shelve my **plans** to buy a new car, because I can't afford it at the moment.* SHELF ▷ **2** [T] to put something onto shelves, or to fix shelves somewhere SLOPE ▷ **3** [I] specialized When a surface such as the bottom of the sea shelves, it slopes down gradually.

S

shelves /ʃelvz/ noun plural of shelf

shelving /ˈʃel.vɪŋ/ noun [U] shelves: *The carpenter put up some shelving in the living room.*

shenanigans /ʃɪˈnæn.ɪ.gənz/ noun [plural] informal disapproving secret or dishonest activities, usually of a complicated and humorous or interesting type: *More business/political shenanigans were exposed in the newspapers today.*

shepherd /ˈʃep.əd/ US /-əd/ noun; verb
▸noun [C] a person whose job is to take care of sheep and move them from one place to another: *a shepherd boy*
▸verb [T usually + adv/prep] **PEOPLE** ▷ **1** to make a group of people move to where you want them to go, especially in a kind, helpful, and careful way: *He shepherded the old people towards the dining room.* **SHEEP** ▷ **2** to move sheep from one place to another: *The dogs shepherded the sheep into the pens.*

shepherdess /ˈʃep.ə.des/, /ˌʃep.əˈdes/ US /-ə-/ noun [C] a female shepherd

ˌshepherd's ˈpie noun [C or U] a dish consisting of a layer of small pieces of meat covered with a thick layer of MASHED POTATO

sherbet /ˈʃɜː.bət/ US /ˈʃɜː-/ noun [U] **1** UK an artificial powder with a fruit flavour eaten as a sweet or used to make a drink, especially for children **2** US **sorbet**

sheriff /ˈʃer.ɪf/ noun [C] **1** in the US, an official whose job is to be in charge of performing the orders of the law courts and making certain that the laws are obeyed within a particular COUNTY **2** in England and Wales, a person who represents the king or queen in a particular COUNTY, and whose duties are mainly in official ceremonies **3** the most important judge of a COUNTY in Scotland

Sherpa /ˈʃɜː.pə/ US /ˈʃɜː-/ noun [C] a member of a Himalayan people who are skilled mountain climbers and who are often employed to help visiting climbers

sherry /ˈʃer.i/ noun [C or U] a type of strong wine from southern Spain that is a pale yellow or brown colour, sometimes drunk before a meal: ***sweet/dry** sherry* ◦ *Would you like a glass of sherry/some sherry?* ◦ *Would you like a sherry (= a glass of sherry)?*

she's strong /ʃiːz/ weak /ʃiz/ **short form** **1** she is: *She's a writer.* **2** she has: *She's got the most elegant writing style.*

Shetland pony /ˌʃet.lənd'pəʊ.ni/ US /-'poʊ-/ noun [C] a very small horse with rough hair

Shia /ˈʃiː.ə/ noun [C] (also **Shiite**) a member of the second largest religious movement in Islam, based on the belief that Ali, a member of Mohammed's family, and the teachers who came after him were the true religious leaders • **Shia adj** (also **Shiite** /ˈʃiː.aɪt/) refers to Shias or their type of Islam

shiatsu /ʃiˈæt.su/ US /-ɑːt-/ noun [U] a treatment for pain or illness, originally from ancient Japan, in which particular places on the body are pressed

shibboleth /ˈʃɪb.əl.eθ/ noun [C] **1** formal a belief or custom that is not now considered as important and correct as it was in the past: *They still cling to many of the old shibboleths **of** education.* **2** a word, phrase, custom, etc. only known to a particular group of people, which you can use to prove to them that you are a real member of that group

shield /ʃiːld/ noun; verb
▸noun [C] **1** C2 in the past, a large, flat object made of metal or leather that soldiers held in front of their bodies to protect themselves **2** a large, flat object made of strong plastic that police officers hold in front of their bodies to protect themselves: *The police held up their **riot** shields against the flying rocks and bricks.* **3** something or someone used as protection or providing protection: *The anti-personnel mines were laid as a **protective** shield around the town.* ◦ *Anger can function as a shield **against** (= a way of avoiding) even more painful emotions of loss and hurt.* **4** a flat object with two straight sides, a rounded or pointed lower edge, and usually a straight top edge, on which there is a COAT OF ARMS **5** an object shaped like a shield that is given as a prize or used as a symbol or BADGE: *Our school won the county football shield this year.*
▸verb [T] C1 to protect someone or something: *She held her hand above her eyes to shield them **from** the sun.* ◦ *They are accused of trying to shield the General **from** US federal investigators.*

shift /ʃɪft/ verb; noun
▸verb **MOVE/CHANGE** ▷ **1** C1 [I or T] to (cause something or someone to) move or change from one position or direction to another, especially slightly: *She shifted (her weight) uneasily **from** one foot **to** the other.* ◦ *The wind is expected to shift (**to** the east) tomorrow.* **2** C1 [I] (of an idea, opinion, etc.) to change: *Society's attitudes towards women have shifted enormously over the last century.* ◦ *Media attention has shifted recently **onto** environmental issues.* **3** [T] mainly US to move the GEARS of a vehicle into different positions in order to make it go faster or slower: *In cars that are automatics, you don't have to bother with shifting **gears**.* **4** **shift house** Indian English to leave your home in order to live in a new one; MOVE HOUSE **GET RID OF** ▷ **5** [T] UK informal to get rid of something unwanted, or to sell something: *Modern detergents will shift most stains.* ◦ *The people at the toy shop expect to shift a lot of stock in the run-up to Christmas.*

IDIOMS **shift yourself** If you shift yourself when you have a job to do, you hurry to do the job as quickly as possible: *Come on, there's work to be done – shift yourself.* • **shift (your) ground** to change your opinion: *He's annoying to argue with because he keeps shifting his ground.*

PHRASAL VERB **shift for yourself** old-fashioned to earn your own income or buy and cook your own food, etc.: *He left home at 18 and had to shift for himself.*

▸noun **GROUP** ▷ **1** B2 [C, + sing/pl verb] a group of workers who do a job for a period of time during the day or night, or the period of time itself: *As the **night** shift leave/leaves, the **day** shift arrive/arrives.* ◦ *Are you on the **night** shift or the **day** shift? (= Do you work during the night period or the day period?)* **CHANGE** ▷ **2** C1 [C] a change in position or direction: *a shift **in** the wind/temperature* ◦ *The shift **in** the balance of power in the region has had far-reaching consequences.* ◦ *There has been a **dramatic** shift **in** public opinion **towards** peaceful negotiations.* **DRESS** ▷ **3** [C] a simple dress that hangs straight from the shoulders

shifting /ˈʃɪf.tɪŋ/ adj always changing or moving: *They lost their way in the shifting sands of the Sahara.*

ˈshift ˌkey noun [C] specialized a key on a keyboard that you press at the same time as you press a letter key in order to produce a capital letter

shiftless /ˈʃɪft.ləs/ adj disapproving lazy and not having much determination or a clear purpose: *He called the young people shiftless, lazy and good-for-nothing.*

shiftwork /ˈʃɪft.wɜːk/ US /-wɜːk/ noun [U] a system in which different groups of workers work somewhere at different times of the day and night: *The factory is run on shiftwork.*

shifty /ˈʃɪf.ti/ adj looking or seeming dishonest: *He's got shifty eyes.* ◦ *You're **looking** very shifty. What have*

S

you been up to? ◦ There's a couple of shifty-**looking** people standing on the street corner. • **shiftily** /-tɪ.li/ adv • **shiftiness** /-nəs/ noun [U]

shiitake (mushroom) (also **shitake**) /ʃɪˈtɑː.ki/ noun [C] a Japanese or Chinese MUSHROOM, used in cooking

Shiite (also **Shi'ite**) /ˈʃiː.aɪt/ noun [C] a **Shia**

shilling /ˈʃɪl.ɪŋ/ noun [C] **1** a unit of money used in Britain until 1971, equal to twelve old pence **2** the standard unit of money used in Kenya, Somalia, Tanzania, and Uganda

shilly-shally /ˈʃɪl.iˌʃæl.i/ verb [I] informal disapproving to spend too much time doing something or making a decision because you do not know what is the right thing to do: *Stop shilly-shallying and make a decision now!*

shimmer /ˈʃɪm.əʳ/ (US) /-ɚ/ verb; noun

▸verb [I] to shine in such a way that the light seems to shake slightly and quickly: *She could see her reflection in the water, shimmering in the moonlight.*

▸noun [S] the fact that something shimmers

shimmering /ˈʃɪm.ər.ɪŋ/ (US) /-ɚ-/ adj **1** reflecting a gentle light which seems to move slightly: *We drove across the desert, through the shimmering heat haze.* **2** literary attractive: *a shimmering new production of 'A Midsummer Night's Dream'*

shimmy /ˈʃɪm.i/ verb [I] to do a dance in which you shake your hips and shoulders: *She shimmied across the dance floor.*

shin /ʃɪn/ noun; verb

▸noun **1** [C] the front part of your leg between your knee and your foot: *She's got a nasty bruise on her shin.* **2** [C or U] a JOINT (= large piece) of meat from the lower leg of a cow: *a shin of beef*

▸verb [I usually + adv/prep] (**-nn-**) (US also **shinny**) to climb something such as a tree, using your hands and legs to move along quickly: *Several of us shinned **up** lampposts so that we could see over the crowd.*

shinbone /ˈʃɪn.bəʊn/ (US) /-boʊn/ noun [C] (specialized **tibia**) the bone at the front of your leg, between the knee and the foot

shindig /ˈʃɪn.dɪg/ noun [C] **1** informal a noisy event or situation, especially a large, energetic party, celebration, etc.: *Are you going to that shindig at the Town Hall tonight?* **2** mainly UK a noisy argument

S

shine /ʃaɪn/ verb; noun

▸verb (**shone** or **shined**) LIGHT ▷ **1** (B1) [I] to send out or reflect light: *Is that light shining **in** your eyes?* ◦ *The **sun** shone all afternoon.* ◦ *He polished the brass till it shone.* **2 shine with sth** (C1) If a person's eyes or face shine with a quality, you can see that quality in them very strongly: *Her eyes shone with delight.* **3** [T] to point a light in a particular direction: *The policeman walked along the street, shining a torch into every car.* **4** [T] to make something bright by rubbing it: *Guy ironed his shirt and shined his **shoes** for the interview.* ABILITY ▷ **5** (C2) [I] to be extremely good at an activity or skill, in an obvious way: *She's hopeless at languages, but she shines **at/in** science.* • **shining** /ˈʃaɪ.nɪŋ/ adj *a shining silver cup* ◦ *She looked at him with shining (= bright and happy) eyes.* ◦ *These pictures are shining (= excellent) **examples** of great photography.*

PHRASAL VERB **shine out 1** If people or things shine out, they are noticeable because they are very good: *The play has a very strong cast, but two actors in particular shine out.* **2** If a quality shines out of someone, it is strong and easy to see: *Her honesty and sincerity positively shine out.*

▸noun [S or U] the fact that something is bright from reflected light on its surface: *hair with body and shine* ◦ *Wax polish gives a lovely shine to wood furniture.*

IDIOM **take a shine to sb** informal to like someone immediately: *I think he's taken a bit of a shine to you.*

shiner /ˈʃaɪ.nəʳ/ (US) /-nɚ/ noun [C] informal a BLACK EYE (= an eye where the skin around it has gone dark because it has been hit): *I think you're going to have a real shiner there in the morning.*

shingle /ˈʃɪŋ.gl/ noun STONES ▷ **1** [U] small, round stones that cover a beach or the ground by the edge of a river: *a shingle beach* ◦ *I love the noise of the waves on the shingle.* PIECE ▷ **2** [C] a thin, flat TILE usually made of wood, that is fixed in rows to make a roof or wall covering DISEASE ▷ **3 shingles** [U] a disease caused by a virus that infects particular nerves and that produces a line or lines of painful red spots, especially around the waist

shinny /ˈʃɪn.i/ verb [I] US for **shin**

ˈshin ˌsplints noun [plural] severe pains in your SHIN (= front part of the lower leg), happening especially to runners and other people who do exercise involving a lot of running or jumping

Shinto /ˈʃɪn.təʊ/ (US) /-toʊ/ noun [U] (also **Shintoism**) a Japanese religion in which people worship past members of their family and various gods that represent nature

shiny /ˈʃaɪ.ni/ adj (B1) A shiny surface is bright because it reflects light: *beautiful shiny hair* ◦ *shiny black shoes* • **shininess** /-nəs/ noun [U]

ship /ʃɪp/ noun; verb

▸noun [C] (A2) a large boat for travelling on water, especially across the sea: *a sailing ship* ◦ *a merchant/naval ship* ◦ *They **boarded** (= went on to) a ship that was **sailing** (= leaving) the next day.*

IDIOM **like ships that pass in the night** If two people are like ships that pass in the night, they meet once or twice by chance for a short time then do not see each other again.

▸verb [T usually + adv/prep] (**-pp-**) to send something, usually a large object or a large quantity of objects or people, to a place far away: *We ship books **out** to New York every month.*

PHRASAL VERB **ship sb off** informal to send someone away somewhere: *The children were shipped off to their grandparents' house for the holidays.*

-ship /-ʃɪp/ suffix having the rank, position, skill, or relationship of the stated type: *lordship* ◦ *partnership* ◦ *craftsmanship* ◦ *friendship*

shipboard /ˈʃɪp.bɔːd/ (US) /-bɔːrd/ adj happening or used on a ship: *a shipboard romance* ◦ *a shipboard transmitter*

shipbuilder /ˈʃɪpˌbɪl.dəʳ/ (US) /-dɚ/ noun [C] a person or company that builds ships • **shipbuilding** /-dɪŋ/ noun [U] *industries such as shipbuilding, steel production, and coal mining*

shipmate /ˈʃɪp.meɪt/ noun [C] A sailor's shipmate is another sailor who works on the same ship as they do.

shipment /ˈʃɪp.mənt/ noun [C or U] a large amount of goods sent together to a place, or the act of sending them: *A shipment **of** urgent medical supplies is expected to arrive very soon.*

shipper /ˈʃɪp.əʳ/ (US) /-ɚ/ noun [C usually plural] a person or company whose job is to organize the sending of goods from one place to another: *wine shippers*

shipping /ˈʃɪp.ɪŋ/ noun [U] **1** ships considered as a

group: *This stretch of water is heavily used by shipping.* **2** the act of sending goods from one place to another, especially by ship: *The cost is $205 plus $3 for shipping.* ◦ *The fruit is picked and artificially ripened before shipping.*

ˌshipping and ˈhandling noun [U] US for **postage and packing**

shipshape /ˈʃɪp.ʃeɪp/ adj informal tidy and with everything in its correct place: *The builders have gone, but it'll take a while to **get** things shipshape again.*

shipwreck /ˈʃɪp.rek/ noun; verb

▸noun [C or U] (also **wreck**) an accident in which a ship is destroyed or sunk at sea, especially by hitting rocks, or a ship that has been destroyed or sunk in such an accident: *The danger of shipwreck is much greater in fog.* ◦ *There have been many shipwrecks along this dangerous stretch of coastline.*

▸verb [T] to make someone suffer a shipwreck: *They were shipwrecked **off** the coast of Newfoundland.* ◦ *a shipwrecked sailor*

shipyard /ˈʃɪp.jɑːd/ US /-jɑːrd/ noun [C] a place where ships are built or repaired

shire /ʃaɪəʳ/ US /ʃaɪr/ noun **1** [C] UK old use a COUNTY, now used in combination in the names of many British COUNTIES: *Yorkshire* ◦ *Oxfordshire* **2 the shires** [plural] UK the central RURAL COUNTIES of England, such as Leicestershire, Nottinghamshire, and Derbyshire

ˈshire ˌhorse noun [C] a large, strong English horse that has long hair covering its feet

shirk /ʃɜːk/ US /ʃɝːk/ verb [I or T] disapproving to avoid work, duties, or responsibilities, especially if they are difficult or unpleasant: *If you shirk your **responsibilities/duties** now, the situation will be much harder to deal with next month.*

shirker /ˈʃɜː.kəʳ/ US /ˈʃɝː.kɚ/ noun [C] someone who avoids something, especially work

shirt /ʃɜːt/ US /ʃɝːt/ noun [C] A1 a piece of clothing worn, especially by men, on the upper part of the body, made of light cloth like cotton and usually having a collar and buttons at the front: *a striped/white shirt* ◦ *a short-/long-sleeved shirt* ◦ *You've spilled something down your shirt front.* → See also **nightshirt, sweatshirt, T-shirt**

IDIOMS **keep your shirt on** (UK also **keep your hair on**) said to tell someone to stop being so angry or upset: *Keep your shirt on! Your car isn't badly damaged!* • **put your shirt on sth** UK informal to feel very certain that something will happen: *I'd put my shirt on the president being re-elected.* • **the shirt off sb's back** informal the last thing that someone has left: *He's the kind of man who'd **give** you the shirt off his back.*

shirtsleeve /ˈʃɜːt.sliːv/ US /ˈʃɝːt-/ noun [C] a sleeve of a shirt: *Susannah felt a hand tugging at her shirtsleeve.* ◦ *Jamie rolled up his shirtsleeves and set to work.*

IDIOM **in shirtsleeves** dressed informally, wearing a shirt with no jacket over it: *Because it was so hot, the men were all in their shirtsleeves.*

ˈshirt ˌtail noun the part at the back of a shirt which comes down below the waist of the person wearing it: *He tucked his shirt tail into his trousers.*

shirty /ˈʃɜː.ti/ US /ˈʃɝː.ţi/ adj UK informal annoyed or angry, especially in a rude way: *Don't get shirty **with** me – this is your fault, not mine.*

shish kebab /ˈʃiːʃ.kɪˌbæb/ US /ˈʃiːʃ.kɪˌbɑːb/ noun [C] (also **kebab**) a dish consisting of small pieces of meat and vegetables that have been put on a long, thin stick or metal rod and cooked together

shit /ʃɪt/ noun; verb; exclamation

▸noun **1** [U] offensive the solid waste that is released from the bowels of a person or animal: *There's so much dog shit on the pavement.* → Synonym **excrement** → See also **bullshit, shite** **2** [S] offensive the act of releasing solid waste from the bowels: *to **have** (US **take**) a shit.* **3 the shits** [plural] offensive DIARRHOEA (= a medical condition in which the contents of the bowels are passed out of the body too often): *Something I ate has given me the shits.* **4** [C or U] offensive someone or something you do not like, especially because they are unpleasant or of low quality: *She talks **a load of** shit.* ◦ *The man's a complete shit.* **5** [U] offensive insults, criticism, or unkind or unfair treatment: *Ben **gets** a lot of shit **from** his parents about the way he dresses.* ◦ *Jackie doesn't **take** (any) shit **from** anyone (= does not allow anyone to treat her badly).* **6** [U] US offensive used in negatives to mean 'anything': *He doesn't know shit about what's going on.*

IDIOMS **have/get your shit together** mainly US offensive to be or become effective, organized, and skilful: *One of these days I'll get my shit together.* • **no shit!** offensive an expression of surprise about information you have just heard: *'Richard's got the job in New York!' 'No shit!'* • **not give a shit** offensive to not be interested in or worried about something or someone: *I don't give a shit what Nigel thinks.* • **(the) shit hits the fan** (also **the shit flies**) When the shit hits the fan or when the shit flies, a situation suddenly causes a lot of trouble for someone: *I don't want to be here when the shit hits the fan.* • **the shit out of sb/sth** offensive used to emphasize the degree of force of an action which you are describing: *His dad would **beat/knock/kick** the shit out of him if he disobeyed.* ◦ *Don't creep up on me like that – you **scared** the shit out of me.*

▸verb (present tense **shitting**, past tense and past participle **shit**, **shat** or **shitted**) offensive **1** [I] to pass solid waste from the bowels: *That dog had better not shit in the house again!* ◦ mainly US *I need to shit real bad.* **2 shit yourself** to be extremely frightened: *She was shitting herself, especially when he pulled out a gun.*

PHRASAL VERB **shit on sb** to treat someone very badly and unkindly: *He was whinging that the boss had shat on him by not giving him a day off.*

▸exclamation offensive used to express anger or surprise: *Oh shit, we're going to be late!* ◦ *Shit – the damn thing's broken!*

shitake (mushroom) /ʃɪˈtɑː.ki/ noun [C] a **shiitake (mushroom)**

shite /ʃaɪt/ noun [C or U] UK offensive → **shit**

ˈshit-faced adj offensive extremely drunk

shithead /ˈʃɪt.hed/ noun [C] offensive a stupid, unpleasant, and unpopular person

ˌshit ˈhot adj UK offensive extremely good

shitload /ˈʃɪt.ləʊd/ US /-loʊd/ noun offensive **a shitload of sth** a lot of something: *He earns a shitload of money.*

ˈshit ˌstirrer noun [C] offensive someone who makes trouble for other people, especially by making known facts that they would prefer to keep secret

shitty /ˈʃɪt.i/ US /ˈʃɪţ.i/ adj offensive **1** unfair and unkind: *She's had really shitty treatment from the management.* **2** bad, difficult, or unpleasant: *Jamie's had a shitty week at work.* ◦ *Anna, if you're feeling shitty (= ill), just go home.*

shiver /ˈʃɪv.əʳ/ US /-ɚ/ verb; noun

▸verb [I] B2 When people or animals shiver, they shake

S

slightly because they feel cold, ill, or frightened: *The poor dog – it's shivering!* ◦ *He shivered* ***with*** *cold in his thin cotton shirt.*

▸**noun** [C] **1** the act of shaking slightly because you are frightened, cold, or ill: *I felt/gave a shiver as I looked out at the dark expanse of sea.* **2 the shivers** [plural] **a** a condition in which you shiver because you are ill: *She's aching and she's* ***got*** *the shivers, so I've sent her to bed.* **b** informal a feeling of being frightened of someone or something: *I don't like him – he* ***gives*** *me the shivers.*

IDIOM **shiver (up and) down your spine** informal a frightened or excited feeling: *At its most terrifying, his writing* ***sends*** *shivers up and down my spine.*

shivery /ˈʃɪv.ər.i/ (US) /-ɚ-/ **adj** informal shaking slightly because you feel cold, frightened, or ill: *She's very hot and shivery, so I think she must have flu.*

shoal /ʃəʊl/ (US) /ʃoʊl/ **noun** **FISH** ▷ **1** [C, + sing/pl verb] a large number of fish swimming as a group: *We could see shoals of tiny fish darting about.* ◦ *Piranhas often feed* ***in*** *shoals.* **2** [C usually plural] informal a large number of things or people: *In the summer, tourists visit the city* ***in*** *shoals.* **RAISED AREA** ▷ **3** [C] specialized a raised area of sand or rocks under the surface of the water

shock /ʃɒk/ (US) /ʃɑːk/ **noun; verb**

▸**noun** **SURPRISE** ▷ **1** (B1) [C or U] (the emotional or physical reaction to) a sudden, unexpected, and usually unpleasant event or experience: *Her mother's death* ***came as*** *a great shock – it was so unexpected.* ◦ *It was such a loud crash – it* ***gave*** *me/I* ***got*** *quite a shock.* ◦ ***It*** *was a shock* ***to*** *see her looking so ill.* ◦ *I was* ***in*** *(****a state of****) shock for about two weeks after the accident.* ◦ UK *The French suffered a shock* ***defeat*** *(= completely unexpected defeat) by the Italian side at the weekend.* **2 a shock to the system** an unpleasant feeling that you experience when something new or unusual happens: *It's really hard getting back to work after three months off – it's quite a shock to the system.* **ELECTRICITY** ▷ **3** (C2) [C] an **electric shock**: *Ow! – I got a shock from that lamp!* **ILLNESS** ▷ **4** [U] a medical condition caused by severe injury, pain, loss of blood, or fear which slows down the flow of blood around the body: *Several passengers from the wrecked vehicle were taken to hospital* ***suffering from*** *shock.* **DAMAGING EFFECT** ▷ **5** (C2) [U] the effect of one object violently hitting another, which might cause damage or a slight movement: *For running on hard roads, you need shoes with extra cushioning to* ***absorb*** *(= reduce) the shock.* **OFFENDED** ▷ **6** [U] a feeling of being offended or upset by something you consider wrong or unacceptable: *You should have seen the look of shock on her face when he started swearing!* **HAIR** ▷ **7** [S] a large and noticeable mass of hair: *She's got* ***a*** *shock* ***of*** *bright red hair.*

> Word partners for **shock noun**
>
> *come as* a shock • *get/have* a shock • *get over/recover from* a shock • a *big/great/nasty/real* shock • the *initial* shock • be *in for* a shock • a shock *to* sb • be *in a state of* shock

▸**verb** [I or T] **OFFEND** ▷ **1** (B2) to offend or upset someone by doing or saying something which they consider is IMMORAL or unacceptable: *The advertisements were designed to shock – that was the whole point of the campaign.* ◦ [+ obj + to infinitive] *I think it shocks him* ***to*** *hear women talking about sex.* **SURPRISE** ▷ **2** (B2) to make someone feel upset or surprised: *The photographs of starving children shocked people* ***into*** *giving money.* ◦ *The news of the accident shocked the family* ***deeply****.* • **shockable** /ˈʃɒk.ə.bl̩/ (US) /ˈʃɑːk.ə-/ **adj** *I have to be careful what I say to my mother – she's very shockable (= easily offended).* • **shocked** /ʃɒkt/ (US) /ʃɑːkt/ **adj** (B1) *After his announcement, there was a shocked silence.* ◦ [+ to infinitive] *We were shocked* ***to*** *see smoke pouring out of the roof.*

shock absorber /ˈʃɒk.əbˌzɔː.bər/ (US) /ˈʃɑːk.əbˌzɔːr.bɚ/ **noun** [C] a device on a vehicle, especially a car or an aircraft, which reduces the effects of travelling over rough ground or helps it to land more smoothly

shocker /ˈʃɒk.ər/ (US) /ˈʃɑː.kɚ/ **noun** [C] informal something that is likely to offend, especially something new or recently announced

shocking /ˈʃɒk.ɪŋ/ (US) /ˈʃɑː.kɪŋ/ **adj** **OFFENSIVE** ▷ **1** (B1) offensive, upsetting, or IMMORAL: *The sex scenes in the book were considered very shocking at the time when it was published.* ◦ *There are few crimes more truly shocking than the murder or abuse of children.* **VERY BAD** ▷ **2** mainly UK informal extremely bad or unpleasant, or of very low quality: *What shocking weather!* ◦ *My memory is shocking.* **SURPRISING** ▷ **3** extremely surprising: *The news came as a shocking blow.* • **shockingly** /-li/ **adv** mainly UK informal *The service was shockingly* ***bad****.* ◦ *The restaurant charges shockingly high prices for its food.* ◦ *Stories of abused and battered children are shockingly familiar.*

ˌshocking ˈpink **noun** [U] a very bright pink colour • **ˌshocking-ˈpink adj**

ˈshock ˌjock **noun** [C] mainly US a person who presents a radio programme and who often says things that are not considered acceptable by most people during the programme: *Howard Stern is one of America's best known shock jocks.*

shockproof /ˈʃɒk.pruːf/ (US) /ˈʃɑːk-/ **adj** describes a watch or other device that is not easily damaged if hit or dropped

ˈshock ˌtactics **noun** [plural] If you use shock tactics, you do something unexpected in order to shock someone or to get an advantage over them.

ˈshock ˌtherapy **noun** [U] (also **ˈshock ˌtreatment**) the treatment of particular mental illnesses by sending electric currents through the brain

ˈshock ˌtroops **noun** [plural] soldiers who are specially trained for making sudden attacks

ˈshock ˌwave **noun** [C] **1** a sudden wave of increased pressure or temperature, caused by an explosion, an EARTHQUAKE, or an object moving faster than the speed of sound **2** a very strong reaction that spreads through a group of people when something surprising or bad happens: *The assassination of the president* ***sent*** *shock waves across the world.*

shod /ʃɒd/ (US) /ʃɑːd/ **verb** past simple and past participle of **shoe**

shoddy /ˈʃɒd.i/ (US) /ˈʃɑː.di/ **adj** disapproving **BADLY MADE** ▷ **1** badly and carelessly made, using low quality materials: *shoddy goods* ◦ *shoddy workmanship* **NOT RESPECTFUL** ▷ **2** showing little respect, thought, or care: *They refused him sick pay when he was off ill, which is a shoddy way to treat an employee.* • **shoddily** /ˈʃɒd.ɪ.li/ (US) /ˈʃɑː.dɪ-/ **adv** *These clothes are very shoddily made.* ◦ *I've been treated very shoddily by the company.* • **shoddiness** /-nəs/ (US) /ˈʃɑː.di-/ **noun** [U]

shoe /ʃuː/ **noun; verb**

▸**noun** [C] **1** (A1) one of a pair of coverings for your feet, usually made of a strong material such as leather, with a thick leather or plastic SOLE (= base) and usually a HEEL: *flat/high-heeled shoes* ◦ *gym/tennis shoes* ◦ *He*

S

put on/took off his new *pair of* shoes. ◦ *Hurry and* ***do up/lace up*** *your shoes.* ◦ *a shoe shop* **2** a **horseshoe**

IDIOMS **be in sb's shoes** informal to be in the situation, usually a bad or difficult situation, that another person is in: *I wouldn't like to be in Mike's shoes when the boss hears what he's done!* • **if I were in your shoes** informal used when you want to tell someone what you would do in their situation: *If I were in your shoes, I think I'd write to her rather than try to explain over the phone.* • **step into sb's shoes** (also **fill sb's shoes**) to take someone's place, often by doing the job they have just left

▸verb [T] (present tense **shoeing**, past tense and past participle **shod** or US also **shoed**) If you shoe a horse, you nail a HORSESHOE (= a curved piece of metal) to one or each of its feet.

ˈshoe ˌbite noun [C] Indian English a painful place on the foot that contains liquid, caused by wearing new shoes that rub; a type of BLISTER

shoehorn /ˈʃuː.hɔːn/ (US) /-hɔːrn/ **noun; verb**

▸**noun** [C] a smooth, curved piece of plastic or metal which you hold in the back of your shoe when putting it on, to help your foot slide into it

▸**verb** [T often passive] informal to fit something tightly in a particular place, often between two other things: *This tiny restaurant is shoehorned* ***between*** *two major banks.*

shoelace /ˈʃuː.leɪs/ noun [C usually plural] (also **lace**, US also **shoestring**) a thin string or strip of leather used to fasten shoes: *My shoelaces came undone.* ◦ ***Do/Tie up*** *your shoelaces, Rosie.*

shoestring /ˈʃuː.strɪŋ/ noun [C usually plural] US for **shoelace**

IDIOM **on a shoestring** informal If you do something on a shoestring, you do it with a very small amount of money: *The film was made on a shoestring.*

shoetree /ˈʃuː.triː/ noun [C] a piece of wood or metal shaped like the inside of a shoe, for putting inside a shoe to keep its shape when it is not being worn

shone /ʃɒn/ (US) /ʃɑːn/ verb past simple and past participle of **shine**

shoo /ʃuː/ **exclamation; verb**

▸**exclamation** said to animals or children to make them go away: *'Shoo!' she shouted at the cat.*

▸**verb** [T usually + adv/prep] (present tense **shooing**, past tense and past participle **shooed**) informal to make sounds and movements in order to send animals or children away: *Go and shoo that cat* ***away*** *before it catches a bird.*

ˈshoo-in noun [C usually singular] someone who is certain to win an election or a competition: *He's a shoo-in* ***for*** *the White House.* ◦ *Manchester United's a shoo-in* ***to*** *win the title this season.*

shook /ʃʊk/ verb past simple of **shake**

shoot /ʃuːt/ **verb; noun**

▸**verb** (**shot, shot**) **WEAPON** ▷ **1** (B1) [I or T] to FIRE a bullet or an arrow, or to hit, injure, or kill a person or animal by FIRING a bullet or arrow at them: *If he's not armed, don't shoot.* ◦ *The kids were shooting arrows* ***at*** *a target.* ◦ *She was shot three times in the head.* ◦ *He has a licence to shoot pheasants on the farmer's land.* ◦ [+ obj + adj] *A policeman was shot* ***dead*** *in the city centre last night.* ◦ *The troops were told to shoot* ***to kill***. **SPORT** ▷ **2** (B1) [I] to try to score points for yourself or your team, in sports involving a ball, by kicking, hitting, or throwing the ball towards the goal: *He shot from the middle of the field and still managed to score.* **MOVE QUICKLY** ▷ **3** (C2) [I usually + adv/prep] to move in a particular direction very quickly and directly: *She shot* ***past*** *me several metres before the finishing line.* ◦ *He shot* ***out*** *of the office a minute ago – I think he was late for a meeting.* ◦ *They were just shooting* ***off*** *to town so we didn't stop to speak.* ◦ *Sylvester Stallone shot* ***to fame*** *(= became famous suddenly) with the film 'Rocky'.* **4** [T] to move through or past something quickly: informal *He shot three sets of* ***traffic lights*** *(= went past them when they gave the signal to stop) before the police caught him.* ◦ *It was so exhilarating shooting* ***the rapids*** *(= travelling through the part of a river where the water flows dangerously fast).* **FILM** ▷ **5** (C1) [I or T] to use a camera to record a film or take a photograph: *We shot four reels of film in Egypt.* ◦ *The film was shot* ***on location*** *in Southern India.* **PLAY** ▷ **6** [T] mainly US informal to play a game of POOL or CRAPS **DRUG** ▷ **7** [T] slang to take an illegal drug by INJECTING yourself with it: *By the time he was 16, he was shooting heroin twice a day.* • **shooter** /ˈʃuː.təʳ/ (US) /-t̬ɚ/ noun [C] *He's thought to be the best shooter in the league.*

IDIOMS **have shot your bolt** UK informal to have already achieved all that you have the power, ability, or strength to do and to be unable to do more: *He started off the game well but seemed to have shot his bolt by half-time.* • **shoot sth/sb down (in flames)** informal to refuse to accept someone's suggestion or idea and not consider it at all • **shoot yourself in the foot** to do something without intending to which spoils a situation for yourself • **shoot your mouth off** informal to talk too much in a loud and uncontrolled way: *It's just like Richard to go shooting his mouth off* ***about*** *other people's affairs.* • **shoot a glance at sb** to look at someone quickly: *She shot him a glance as he entered the room.* • **shoot for the moon** US to ask for the best or the most you could hope for: *You might as well shoot for the moon and ask for a promotion as well as a raise.* • **shoot questions at sb** to ask someone a lot of questions very quickly, one after the other: *He shot questions at me so quickly that I didn't even have time to answer.* • **shoot the breeze** US informal to spend time talking about things that are not important: *We sat out on the porch, just shooting the breeze.* • **sb should be shot** informal said when you think that someone's actions are extremely unreasonable: *They should be shot* ***for*** *selling drinks at that price!*

PHRASAL VERBS **shoot sth down** to destroy an aircraft or make an aircraft, bird, etc. fall to the ground by shooting at it: *He was killed during the war when his plane was shot down.* • **shoot sb down** to shoot and usually kill someone, showing no sympathy: *I saw Leonforte shoot him down like a dog in the street.* • **shoot for/at sth** US to try to do something: *It's worth taking chances when you're shooting at a chance of fame and wealth.* • **shoot it out** If opposing groups or people armed with guns shoot it out, they shoot at each other until one of the groups or people is dead or defeated. • **shoot through** Australian English informal to leave a place very quickly, especially in order to avoid having to do something • **shoot up INCREASE** ▷ **1** informal to grow in size, or increase in number or level, very quickly: *David has really shot up since I saw him last.* ◦ *Prices shot up by 25 percent.* **DRUGS** ▷ **2** slang to put illegal drugs into your blood using a special needle: *She saw a girl shooting up in the toilets.*

▸**noun PLANT** ▷ **1** [C] the first part of a plant to appear above the ground as it develops from a seed, or any new growth on an already existing plant: *Two weeks after we'd planted the seeds, little green shoots started to appear.* ◦ figurative *The first green shoots (= hopeful signs) of economic recovery have started to appear.* **FILM** ▷ **2** [C usually singular] an occasion when

S

photographers take a series of photographs, usually of the same person or people in the same place: *We **did** a **fashion** shoot on the beach, with the girls modelling swimwear.* **WEAPON** ▷ **3** [C] an occasion on which a group of people go to an area of the countryside to shoot animals

-shooter /-ʃuː.təʳ/ (US) /-t̬ɚ/ **suffix** a type of gun, etc. or a person that shoots: *a peashooter* ◦ *a sharpshooter* ◦ *a six-shooter*

shooting /ˈʃuː.tɪŋ/ (US) /-t̬ɪŋ/ **noun; adj**

▸**noun 1** B2 [U] the act of shooting bullets from guns or other weapons: *We heard some shooting in the night.* **2** B2 [C] an occasion when someone is injured or killed by a bullet shot from a gun: *There have been a number of shootings in the capital this week.* **3** [U] the sport of shooting animals or birds: *pheasant/grouse shooting* ◦ *He **goes** shooting most weekends.*

▸**adj** Indian English (of prices) rising very quickly to a high level

ˈshooting ˌgallery noun [C] **GUNS** ▷ **1** a closed area in which people shoot guns at targets, either for enjoyment or in order to improve their shooting skills **DRUGS** ▷ **2** US slang a place where people go to INJECT illegal drugs: *Police raided a well-known shooting gallery on Thursday night.*

ˈshooting ˌpains noun [plural] sudden severe pains which move through the body: *I get shooting pains up my spine whenever I try to move.*

ˌshooting ˈstar noun [C] informal for **meteor**

ˈshooting ˌstick noun [C] a walking stick that has a sharp point to push into the ground at one end and a folded part that opens out to use as a seat at the other

shootout /ˈʃuː.taʊt/ (US) /ˈʃuːt̬-/ **noun** [C] a fight in which two people or two groups of people shoot at each other with guns

shop /ʃɒp/ (US) /ʃɑːp/ **noun; verb**

▸**noun** [C] **PLACE TO BUY THINGS** ▷ **1** A1 (US usually **store**) a building, or a room in a building, where you can buy goods or get services: *a book/clothes/record/sweet shop* ◦ *a barber's/betting shop* ◦ *I need to go to the shops – I've got no food in the house.* **2** UK the act of shopping, especially of shopping for food and other things needed in the house: *I usually **do** the **weekly** shop on a Monday.* **3 be in the shops** to be available to buy: *His latest novel will be in the shops by Christmas.* **WORK AREA** ▷ **4** a place where a particular type of thing is made or repaired: *He runs an auto-tyre repair shop.* **BUSINESS** ▷ **5** informal a business

S

> Word partners for **shop noun**
>
> *have/open/run/work in* a shop • *go to* the shops • a *local* shop

IDIOM **set up shop** to start your own business

▸**verb** (-pp-) **BUY THINGS** ▷ **1** B1 [I] to buy things in shops: *I like to shop **at** Harrods for clothes.* ◦ *If I'm just shopping **for** food, I tend to go to the local supermarket.* **GIVE INFORMATION** ▷ **2** [T] UK slang to give the police information about a criminal: *His ex-wife shopped him **to** the police.*

PHRASAL VERB **shop around** to compare the price and quality of the same or a similar object in different shops before you decide which one to buy: *When you're buying a flight, you should always shop around for the best deal.*

shopaholic /ˌʃɒp.əˈhɒl.ɪk/ (US) /ˌʃɑː.pəˈhɑː.lɪk/ **noun** [C] informal a person who enjoys shopping very much and does it a lot: *A self-confessed shopaholic, Diane loved looking for new clothes with her two daughters.*

ˈshop asˌsistant noun [C] UK (US **salesclerk**) A2 someone who serves customers in a shop

the ˌshop ˈfloor noun [S] **1** the ordinary workers in a factory, or the place where they work **2 on the shop floor** among the ordinary workers at a factory: *There is concern on the shop floor over job security.*

shopfront /ˈʃɒpˈfrʌnt/ (US) /ˈʃɑːp.frʌnt/ **noun** [C] (US **storefront**) the outside part of a shop which faces the street

shopkeeper /ˈʃɒpˌkiː.pəʳ/ (US) /ˈʃɑːpˌkiː.pɚ/ **noun** [C] (US usually **storekeeper**) B2 a person who owns and manages a small shop

shoplifting /ˈʃɒpˌlɪf.tɪŋ/ (US) /ˈʃɑːp-/ **noun** [U] the illegal act of taking goods from a shop without paying for them: *He was charged with shoplifting.* • **shoplift** /-lɪft/ **verb** [I] *He was caught shoplifting by a store detective.* • **shoplifter** /-lɪf.təʳ/ (US) /-lɪf.tɚ/ **noun** [C] *Shoplifters will be prosecuted.*

shopper /ˈʃɒp.əʳ/ (US) /ˈʃɑː.pɚ/ **noun** [C] a person who is buying things from a shop or a number of shops: *crowds of **Christmas** shoppers*

shopping /ˈʃɒp.ɪŋ/ (US) /ˈʃɑː.pɪŋ/ **noun** [U] **1** A1 the activity of buying things from shops: *The store is open for late night shopping on Wednesdays.* ◦ *I'm **going** shopping this afternoon.* ◦ *My granddaughter **does** my weekly shopping for me.* ◦ ***Christmas** shopping* **2** A2 goods which you have bought from shops, especially food: *She had so many **bags of** shopping that she could hardly carry them.* ◦ *I forgot my shopping **list**.*

ˈshopping ˌbag noun [C] **1** UK (US **tote bag**) any bag intended to carry things bought in shops, especially one bought for this purpose and used many times **2** US for **carrier**

ˈshopping ˌbasket noun 1 [C] (often **basket**) UK a container with a handle that you use for carrying what you plan to buy in a shop **2** [S] a place on a shopping website where you collect things you plan to buy from the website

ˈshopping ˌcentre UK (US **ˈshopping ˌcenter**) **noun** [C] a group of shops with a common area for cars to park, which usually provides goods and services for local people

ˈshopping ˌchannel noun [C] a television CHANNEL which shows products that you can buy, and allows you to buy them by pushing a button on your television's REMOTE CONTROL

ˈshopping ˌmall noun [C] (also **mall**) mainly US a large usually covered shopping area where cars are not allowed

ˈshop-soiled adj UK (US **shopworn**) If goods sold in shops are shop-soiled, they are slightly dirty or damaged and therefore reduced in price.

ˌshop ˈsteward noun [C] a worker elected by workers in a factory or business to represent them in discussions with the management, usually a member of a TRADE UNION

shopworn /ˈʃɒp.wɔːn/ (US) /ˈʃɑːp.wɔːrn/ **adj 1** US for **shop-soiled 2** US If a story or joke is shopworn, it is boring or not interesting because it is so familiar to people.

shore /ʃɔːʳ/ (US) /ʃɔːr/ **noun; verb**

▸**noun 1** B1 [C or U] the land along the edge of a sea, lake or wide river: *You can walk for miles along the shore.* ◦ *The boat was about a mile **from/off** (the) shore when the engine suddenly died.* → See also **offshore, onshore 2 on shore** on the land and not in a ship: *We waited until we were on shore before repairing the sails.* **3 shores** [plural] literary a country or continent with a coast: *In 1992, Britain played host to the first multi-racial South African team to visit these shores.*

▸verb

PHRASAL VERB **shore sth up 1** to stop a wall or a building from falling down by supporting it with building materials such as wood or metal: *Boundary walls have had to be shored up.* **2** to support or improve an organization, agreement, or system that is not working effectively or that is likely to fail: *The new public relations manager has the difficult task of shoring up the company's troubled image.*

shoreline /ˈʃɔː.laɪn/ US /ˈʃɔːr-/ **noun** [C usually singular] the edge of a sea, lake, or wide river: *Oil from the wrecked tanker polluted more than 40 miles of the Normandy shoreline.*

shorn /ʃɔːn/ US /ʃɔːrn/ **verb** past participle of **shear**

short /ʃɔːt/ US /ʃɔːrt/ **adj; noun; verb; adv**

▸adj **DISTANCE** ▷ **1** A1 small in length, distance, or height: *a short skirt* ◦ *Her hair is much shorter than it used to be.* ◦ *It's only a short walk to the station.* ◦ *I'm quite short but my brother's very tall.* **2** B2 describes a name that is used as a shorter form of a name: *Her name's Jo – it's short* ***for*** *Josephine.* ◦ *Her name's Josephine, or Jo* ***for*** *short.* **TIME** ▷ **3** A1 being an amount of time that is less than average or usual: *a short film/visit* ◦ *He's grown so much in such a short time.* ◦ *I work much better if I take a short break every hour or so.* **4** A2 describes books, letters, and other examples of writing that do not contain many words and do not take much time to read: *It's a very short book – you'll read it in an hour.* **LACKING** ▷ **5 be short (of sth)** B1 to not have enough of something: *to be short* ***of*** *space/time* ◦ *We're a bit short* ***of*** *coffee – I must get some more.* ◦ *The bill comes to £85, but we're £15 short.* ◦ *I'm a little short (= I do not have much money) this week – could you lend me ten dollars?* **6 short of breath** unable to breathe very well, for example because you have been running or doing some type of energetic exercise **7 be in short supply** to be few or not enough in number: *Computers are in rather short supply in this office.* **8 go short** mainly UK to not have something, especially when it is something you need in order to live: *My parents didn't have much money, but they made sure we didn't go short (****of*** *anything).* **NOT PATIENT** ▷ **9** [after verb] saying little but showing slight IMPATIENCE or anger in the few words that you say: *I'm sorry if I was a bit short* ***with*** *you on the phone this morning.* • **shortness** /ˈʃɔːt.nəs/ US /ˈʃɔːrt-/ **noun** [U] *shortness of time* ◦ *The disease may cause sweating, nausea, vomiting, and shortness* ***of breath*** *(= difficulties in breathing).*

IDIOMS **be caught/taken short** UK informal to suddenly and unexpectedly need to go to the toilet, especially when it is not convenient for you to do so • **be short notice** to be very near the time when an event is expected to happen: *I will have to cancel this afternoon's class – I'm sorry it's such short notice.* • **draw/get the short straw** informal to have to do the least enjoyable of a range of duties, often because you have been chosen to do it: *Colin, I'm afraid you've drawn the short straw – you're cleaning out the toilets.* • **get the short end of the stick** US and Australian English to suffer the bad effects of a situation: *The people who get the short end of the stick are those whose income is just too high to qualify for help from the government.* • **have a short memory** to forget things quickly • **in short** C1 used before describing something or someone in as few words and as directly as possible: *He's disorganized, inefficient, never there when you want him – in short, the man's hopeless.* • **make short work of sth** informal to finish or deal with something quickly: *Well, you certainly made short work of the chocolate cake! There's none left for your dad.* • **not be short of a bob or two** UK informal to be rich: *Did you see his car? He's not short of a bob or two!* • **short and sweet** informal surprisingly short in a way that is pleasing: *This morning's lecture was short and sweet.* • **short sharp shock** (describing or relating to) punishment that is quick and effective: *He's in favour of the short sharp shock* ***treatment*** *for young offenders.*

▸noun [C] **DRINK** ▷ **1** UK informal a drink of SPIRITS (= type of strong alcohol) without water or any other liquid added: *She only drinks shorts, never wine or beer.* **FILM** ▷ **2** a short film, especially one made for showing before the main film at a cinema **ELECTRICITY** ▷ **3** informal for **short circuit**

▸verb [I or T] informal for ˌ**short-ˈcircuit** (**ˌshort ˈcircuit**): *The plumber's shorted the electric shower.*

▸adv before the arranged or expected time or place: *We wanted to explain the plans fully, but the chairman* ***stopped*** *us short, as there were other important matters to discuss.*

IDIOM **cut sth short** C2 to have to stop doing something before it is finished: *Their conversation was cut short by the arrival of more guests.* ◦ *We had to cut short our holiday because Richard was ill.*

short- /ʃɔːt-/ US /ʃɔːrt-/ **prefix** used with adjectives ending in -ed formed from nouns to describe something with a short part: *a short-haired dog (= a dog with short hair)* ◦ *a short-sleeved shirt (= a shirt with short sleeves)*

shortage /ˈʃɔː.tɪdʒ/ US /ˈʃɔːr.t̬ɪdʒ/ **noun** [C] B2 a situation in which there is not enough of something: *There's a shortage* ***of*** *food and shelter in the refugee camps.* ◦ *The long hot summer has led to serious water shortages.*

ˌ**short** ˌ**back and** ˈ**sides** **noun** [S] old-fashioned a hairstyle for men in which the hair is cut short at the back and sides, showing the ears

shortbread /ˈʃɔːt.bred/ US /ˈʃɔːrt-/ **noun** [U] (also **shortcake**) a type of sweet biscuit which contains a lot of butter: *traditional Scottish shortbread*

shortcake /ˈʃɔːt.keɪk/ US /ˈʃɔːrt-/ **noun 1** [U] **shortbread 2** [C or U] mainly US a type of cake that is often served in layers with fruit and cream: *Do you like* ***strawberry*** *shortcake?*

shortchange /ˌʃɔːtˈtʃeɪndʒ/ US /ˌʃɔːrt-/ **verb** [T] **1** to give someone back less money than they are owed when they are buying something from you: *I think I was shortchanged in the pub last night, because I've only got £5 in my purse when I should have £10.* **2** to treat someone unfairly, by giving them less than they deserve: *Children who leave school unable to read and write properly are being tragically shortchanged.*

ˌ**short** ˈ**circuit** **noun** [C] (informal **short**) a bad electrical connection which causes the current to flow in the wrong direction, often having the effect of stopping the power supply • ˌ**short-ˈcircuit** **verb** [I or T] (informal **short**) to cause a short circuit: *If those two wires touch, the appliance will short-circuit and probably go up in flames.*

shortcoming /ˈʃɔːtˌkʌm.ɪŋ/ US /ˈʃɔːrt-/ /ˌʃɔːtˈkʌm-/ **noun** [C usually plural] C1 a fault or a failure to reach a particular standard: *Whatever his shortcomings as a husband, he was a good father to his children.* ◦ *Like any political system, it has its shortcomings.*

shortcrust pastry /ˌʃɔːt.krʌstˈpeɪ.stri/ US /ˌʃɔːrt-/ **noun** [U] a type of soft pastry that breaks easily

shortcut /ˈʃɔːt.kʌt/ US /ˈʃɔːrt-/ **noun** [C] **1** a route that

S

leads from one place to another and is quicker and more direct than the usual route: *I know a shortcut **to** town.* **2** a quicker way of doing something in order to save time or effort **3** a quick way to start or use a computer program: *a shortcut key*

shorten /ˈʃɔː.tᵊn/ ⓤⓢ /ˈʃɔːr-/ **verb** [I or T] C1 to become shorter or to make something shorter: *As you grow older, your spine shortens by about an inch.* ◦ *I've asked him to shorten my grey trousers.* ◦ *The name 'William' is often shortened **to** 'Bill'.*

shortening /ˈʃɔː.tᵊn.ɪŋ/ ⓤⓢ /ˈʃɔːrt.nɪŋ/ **noun** [U] US butter or other fat that is used in cooking, especially to make pastry soft and CRUMBLY (= easily broken)

shortfall /ˈʃɔːt.fɔːl/ ⓤⓢ /ˈʃɔːrt.fɑːl/ **noun** [C] an amount that is less than the level that was expected or needed: *The drought caused serious shortfalls **in** the food supply.*

ˌshort-grain ˈrice **noun** [U] a type of rice with small, rounded seeds: *The Spanish dish paella is made with a type of short-grain rice.*

shorthand /ˈʃɔːt.hænd/ ⓤⓢ /ˈʃɔːrt-/ **noun** [U] (also **stenography**) a system of fast writing that uses lines and simple signs to represent words and phrases: *Their conversations were taken down **in** shorthand by a secretary.*

IDIOM **shorthand for sth** a short, simple phrase that is used instead of a longer and more complicated phrase

ˌshort-ˈhanded **adj** (UK also **ˌshort-ˈstaffed**) If a company or organization is short-handed, it does not have the usual or necessary number of workers.

ˌshorthand ˈtypist **noun** [C] UK someone who types and does shorthand as the main part of their job

ˈshort-haul **adj** [before noun] travelling a short distance: *short-haul flights*

shorthorn /ˈʃɔːt.hɔːn/ ⓤⓢ /ˈʃɔːrt.hɔːrn/ **noun** [C] a cow from a breed with short horns

shortish /ˈʃɔː.tɪʃ/ ⓤⓢ /ˈʃɔːr.t̬ɪʃ/ **adj** DISTANCE ▷ **1** quite short: *She's got shortish black hair* TIME ▷ **2** not long, but not very short: *'Is it a short film?' 'Well, shortish.'*

ˌshort-line ˈrailroad **noun** [C] (also **ˌshort-line ˈrailway**) US a railway company that operates over a fairly small area

shortlist UK (US **ˈshort list**) /ˈʃɔːt.lɪst/ ⓤⓢ /ˈʃɔːrt-/ **noun** [C, usually singular] a list of people who have been judged the most suitable for a job or prize, made from a longer list of people originally considered, and from which one person will be chosen: *We've **drawn up** (= decided) a shortlist for the job.* ◦ *She's **on** the shortlist for a teaching post.* • **shortlist** (US **ˈshort-list**) **verb** [T] *His latest novel has been shortlisted **for** the Booker prize.*

short-lived /ˌʃɔːtˈlɪvd/ ⓤⓢ /ˌʃɔːrtˈlaɪvd/ /-ˈlɪvd/ **adj** If a feeling or experience is short-lived, it only lasts for a short time.

shortly /ˈʃɔːt.li/ ⓤⓢ /ˈʃɔːrt-/ **adv** **1** B2 soon: *We will shortly be arriving in King's Cross Station.* **2** **shortly after/before sth** B1 a short time after or before something: *Shortly after you left, a man came into the office looking for you.*

ˌshort-order ˈcook **noun** [C] a person who works in a restaurant cooking food that can be prepared quickly

ˌshort-ˈrange **adj** **1** reaching a short distance: *short-range missiles/weapons* **2** relating to a short time: *a short-range weather forecast*

shorts /ʃɔːts/ ⓤⓢ /ʃɔːrts/ **noun** [plural] **1** A2 trousers that end above the knee or reach the knee, often worn in hot weather or when playing a sport: *tennis shorts* ◦ *She put on a **pair of** shorts and a T-shirt.* **2** US men's UNDERPANTS

short shrift /ˌʃɔːtˈʃrɪft/ ⓤⓢ /ˌʃɔːrt-/ **noun** [U] If you get or are given short shrift by someone, you are treated without sympathy and given little attention: *He'll **get** short shrift from me if he starts complaining about money again, now that I know how much he earns!*

IDIOM **make short shrift of sth** to deal with or get rid of something quickly: *Williams made short shrift of her opponent, letting her win only two games in the match.*

ˌshort-ˈsighted **adj** SIGHT ▷ **1** C2 (US also **near-sighted**) describes someone who can only clearly see objects that are close to them THOUGHT ▷ **2** C2 disapproving not thinking enough about how an action will affect the future: *It's very short-sighted of the government not to invest in technological research.* • **short-sightedness** /-nəs/ **noun** [U] (US also **nearsightedness**)

ˌshort-ˈstaffed **adj** UK for **short-handed**

ˌshort ˈstory **noun** [C] an invented story that is no more than about 10,000 words in length: *He published a book of short stories.*

ˌshort-ˈtempered **adj** If someone is short-tempered, they get angry easily, often for no good reason.

ˌshort-ˈterm **adj** **1** B2 lasting a short time: *short-term memory* **2** B2 relating to a short period of time: *a short-term weather forecast*

ˌshort ˈtime **noun** [U] (also **reˌduced ˈtime**) a situation in which the people who work at a factory or in an office work fewer days or hours than usual for less money because there is not much work to do: *He's been put **on** short time because business is so quiet.*

ˈshort ˌwave **noun** [U] (written abbreviation **SW**) a range of radio waves with a FREQUENCY between 3 and 30 MHz

shorty /ˈʃɔː.ti/ ⓤⓢ /ˈʃɔːr.t̬i/ **noun** [C] informal (UK offensive also **ˈshort-arse**) a short person: *That coat reaches your ankles, shorty!*

shot /ʃɒt/ ⓤⓢ /ʃɑːt/ **verb; noun; adj**

▸**verb** past simple and past participle of **shoot**

▸**noun** SPORT ▷ **1** B2 [C] a kick, hit, or throw of the ball that is intended to score points in cricket, football, tennis, or GOLF: *And that was a great shot by Márquez!* ◦ *Murray drove a forehand shot down the line to win the match.* WEAPON ▷ **2** B2 [C] the action of FIRING a gun or another weapon: *He **fired** four shots at the car as it drove off.* **3** **a good/poor shot** someone who is skilled/not skilled at aiming and FIRING a gun ATTEMPT ▷ **4** [C usually singular] informal an attempt to do or achieve something that you have not done before: *I thought I'd **have** a shot **at** making my own wine.* ◦ *I've never tried bowling before, but I thought I'd **give** it a shot.* FILM ▷ **5** B2 [C] a photograph: *I **got/took** some really good shots of the harbour at sunset.* **6** [C] a short piece in a film in which there is a single action or a short series of actions AMOUNT OF DRINK ▷ **7** [C] a small amount of an alcoholic drink: *a shot **of** whisky* DRUG ▷ **8** **a shot of sth** informal the amount of a drug that is put into the body by a single INJECTION: *The doctor **gave** him a shot of morphine.* METAL BALL ▷ **9** [C] a heavy metal ball thrown in a sports competition → See **shot put** **10** [U] a mass of small metal balls that are shot from a gun: *Shotgun cartridges contain **lead** shot.*

IDIOMS **a shot in the arm** something that has a sudden and positive effect on something, providing encouragement and new activity: *Fresh investment would provide the shot in the arm that this industry so* *badly needs.* • **a shot in the dark** informal an attempt to guess something when you have no information or knowledge about the subject and therefore cannot possibly know what the answer is • **give sth your best shot** informal to do something as well as you can • **like a shot** informal When someone does something like a shot, they do it extremely quickly and enthusiastically: *The moment I let go of the dog, she's off like a shot.*

▸adj **FREE** ▷ **1 get/be shot of sth** UK informal to get rid of or free of something, or to leave something: *I can't wait to get shot of this office for a week.* ◦ *I suspect he left home to get shot of that awful mother of his.* **CLOTH** ▷ **2** (of SILK) having small threads of a colour in it, so that the main colour appears to change depending on the angle at which the cloth is seen: *Her evening dress is made of green shot silk.* **DESTROYED** ▷ **3** informal no longer working or effective: *It's no good – these gears are shot.*

IDIOM **be shot through with sth** to show or contain a particular emotion or quality in a noticeable way all the way through: *Her novel is shot through with a haunting lyricism.* ◦ *The report was shot through with inaccuracies.* → See also **shoot through**

shotgun /ˈʃɒt.ɡʌn/ (US) /ˈʃɑːt-/ noun [C] a long gun that fires a large number of small metal bullets at one time, designed for shooting birds and animals: *The robbers used a **sawn-off** (US **sawed-off**) shotgun in the raid.*

ˌshotgun ˈwedding noun [C] old-fashioned informal (US also **shotgun ˈmarriage**) a marriage that is arranged very quickly and suddenly because the woman is pregnant

ˈshot put noun [S] a sports competition in which a heavy metal ball is thrown from the shoulder as far as possible: *He's practising for **the** shot put.* • **ˈshot-putter** noun [C] a person who competes in the shot put

should strong /ʃʊd/ weak /ʃəd/ **modal verb DUTY** ▷ **1** A2 used to say or ask what is the correct or best thing to do: *If you're annoyed with him, you should tell him.* ◦ *You should change trains at Peterborough if you're going to Newcastle.* ◦ *'Should I apologize to him?' 'Yes, I think you should.'* ◦ *You should be ashamed of yourselves.* ◦ *This computer isn't working as it should.* ◦ *There should be an investigation into the cause of the disaster.* ◦ *He said that I should see a doctor.* ◦ *I should **have** written to her but I haven't had time.* ◦ *It's very kind of you, but you really shouldn't **have** bothered.* ◦ *Where should (= do you suggest that) we meet tonight?* ◦ *It's rather cold in here. Should I (= do you want me to) turn the heating on?*

> **! Common mistake: should**
>
> **Should** is followed by an infinitive verb without 'to'.
>
> Don't say 'should to do something', say **should do something**:
>
> ~~*We should to spend the rest of our budget on books.*~~
>
> *We should spend the rest of our budget on books.*

PROBABLE ▷ **2** B1 used to show when something is likely or expected: *My dry cleaning should be ready this afternoon.* ◦ *You should find this guidebook helpful.* ◦ *I wonder what's happened to Annie. She should be (= it was expected that she would be) here by now.* ◦ *'Could you have the report ready by Friday?' 'Yes, I should think so (= it is likely that it will be ready).'* ◦ *This should be good (= this is likely to be interesting or amusing).* **POSSIBILITY** ▷ **3** formal used when referring to a possible event in the future: *If anyone should ask for me, I'll be in the manager's office.* ◦ *Should you (= if you) ever need anything, please don't hesitate to contact me.* **4** used after 'that' and adjectives or nouns that show an opinion or feeling: *It's odd **that** she should think I would want to see her again.* ◦ *It's so unfair **that** she should **have** died so young.* **5** used after 'that' to suggest that a situation possibly exists or might come into existence: *We agree **that** the money should be paid tomorrow.* **6** formal used after 'so that' and 'in order that' to show purpose: *He took his umbrella so that he shouldn't get wet.* **7** formal used after 'for fear that', 'in case' and 'lest': *He took his umbrella in case it should rain.* **REASON** ▷ **8** B2 used after 'why' when giving or asking the reason for something: *Why shouldn't she buy it if she can afford it?* **WOULD** ▷ **9** mainly UK formal used instead of 'would' when the subject is 'I' or 'we': *I should like a whisky before I go to bed.* ◦ *I shouldn't expect you to pay, of course.* **SURPRISE** ▷ **10** used to express surprise in sentences that are in the form of questions: *I was just getting off the bus when who should I see **but** my old school friend Pat!* **ADVISE** ▷ **11** UK used after 'I' when giving advice: *I shouldn't worry about it if I were you.* ◦ *I shouldn't (= I advise you not to) let it worry you.*

IDIOMS **how should I know?** I cannot be expected to know: *'Where's Mikey?' 'How should I know? He's hardly ever in the office these days.'* • **I should think not/so (too)!** said when you think what has been suggested is certainly not, or certainly is, the correct and expected thing: *'I bought her some flowers to say thank you.' 'I should think so **too**.'* ◦ *'I don't like to drink more than one bottle of wine in an evening.' 'I should think not.'* • **I should be so lucky!** informal said when what you want is extremely unlikely to happen: *'You might win first prize.' 'I should be so lucky.'* • **you should have seen/heard sth/sb** seeing or hearing something or someone would have interested or entertained you very much: *You should have seen her – she was furious!*

shoulder /ˈʃəʊl.dəʳ/ (US) /ˈʃoʊl.dɚ/ **noun; verb**

▸noun **BODY PART** ▷ **1** B1 [C] one of the two parts of the body at each side of the neck which join the arms to the rest of the body: *I rested my head on her shoulder.* ◦ *Then she put her arm round my shoulder and gave me a kiss.* ◦ *She **glanced** nervously **over** her shoulder to make sure no one else was listening.* **2 shoulders** [plural] **a** the top part of a person's back: *He was about six feet tall with **broad** shoulders.* ◦ *'I don't know what to do about it,' said Martha, **shrugging** her shoulders.* **b** the parts of a piece of clothing which cover the wearer's shoulders: *The shoulders look a bit tight. Do you want to try a larger size?* ◦ *a jacket with **padded** shoulders* **3** [C] the part of a bottle that curves out below its opening **4** [C] US for **hard shoulder** **RESPONSIBILITY** ▷ **5 sb's shoulders** used to refer to the responsibility that someone has or feels for something: *A huge **burden** was **lifted** from my shoulders (= I became much less worried) when I told my parents about my problem.* ◦ *Responsibility for the dispute **rests** squarely **on** the shoulders of the president.* **MEAT** ▷ **6** [C or U] a piece of meat which includes the upper part of an animal's front leg: *I've bought a shoulder of **lamb** for Sunday lunch.* • **-shouldered** /-dəʳd/ (US) /-dɚd/ suffix *to be **broad/narrow**-shouldered*

IDIOMS **a shoulder to cry on** C2 someone who is willing to listen to your problems and give you sympathy, emotional support, and encouragement: *I wish you'd been here when my mother died and I **needed** a shoulder to cry on.* • **shoulder to shoulder** If

S

people are shoulder to shoulder, they are close together and next to each other: *The refugees were packed shoulder to shoulder on the boat.* • **stand shoulder to shoulder with sb** to give someone or a group of people complete support during a difficult time

►verb **ACCEPT RESPONSIBILITY** ▷ **1 shoulder the blame, burden, responsibility, cost, etc.** to accept that you are responsible for something bad or difficult: *It is women who mainly shoulder responsibility for the care of elderly and disabled relatives.* ◦ *Teachers cannot be expected to shoulder all the blame for poor exam results.* **BODY PART** ▷ **2** [T] to put something on your shoulders to carry it: *Shouldering her pack, she strode off up the road.* **3** [T + adv/prep] to push something with one of your shoulders: *She was carrying two suitcases and had to shoulder the door open.* ◦ *He shouldered his **way** (= formed a way through by pushing with his shoulders) to the front of the crowd to get a better look.*

ˈshoulder ˌbag noun [C] a bag that hangs on a strap from the shoulder, especially one used for carrying small personal things

ˈshoulder ˌblade noun [C] (specialized **scapula**) a large, flat bone on each side of your back below your shoulder, that helps to increase the range of movement of your arm

ˈshoulder-ˌlength adj If your hair is shoulder-length, it goes down as far as your shoulders.

ˈshoulder ˌpad noun [C usually plural] a small piece of a soft material that is put into the shoulder of a piece of clothing to raise it or improve its shape

ˈshoulder ˌstrap noun [C] a narrow strip of material on a bag or a piece of clothing which hangs over the wearer's shoulder and holds the bag or clothing in position

shouldn't /ˈʃʊd.ənt/ short form of should not: *You shouldn't do things like that.*

should've /ˈʃʊd.əv/ short form of should have: *You should've come to the party last night, Manya.*

shout /ʃaʊt/ verb; noun

►verb **USE LOUD VOICE** ▷ **1** A2 [I] to speak with a very loud voice, often as loud as possible, usually when you want to make yourself heard in noisy situations, or when the person you are talking to is a long way away or cannot hear very well: *There's no need to shout, I can hear perfectly well.* ◦ [+ speech] *'I'll see you tomorrow,' shouted Eleni **above** the noise of the helicopter.* ◦ [+ that] *He shouted from the bottom of the garden **that** he'd be finished in about half an hour.* **2** A2 [I or T] to express strong emotions, such as anger, fear, or excitement, or to express strong opinions, in a loud voice: *Dad really shouted **at** me when I broke the window.* ◦ *He shouted **abuse** at the judge after being sentenced to five years' imprisonment.* ◦ *The fans were screaming and shouting **out** the names of the band members.* ◦ [+ to infinitive] *I shouted **at** him **to** put the gun down.* ◦ [+ speech] *'Stop this childish nonsense at once!' he shouted furiously.* **3** A2 [I] to try to attract attention in a loud voice: *I heard them shouting **for help**, but there was nothing I could do.* ◦ figurative *It's the charities that shout **loudest** (= attract the most public attention) that often get given the most money.*

IDIOMS **something/nothing to shout about** informal something that makes/does not make you feel excited or pleased: *At last, a 5–0 victory gives England's supporters something to shout about.* ◦ *The pay increase is nothing to shout about, but it's better than last year's.*

S

Other ways of saying shout

An alternative to 'shout' is **yell** or **bellow**:

*'What are you doing?' he **yelled**.*

*'Listen to me!' he **bellowed**.*

Holler (mainly US) is an informal word for shout:

*'Dinner's ready!' **hollered** Jackson from the kitchen.*

Call or **cry** is used when someone shouts something to attract attention:

*'I'm up here,' he **called**.*

*'Look out!' she **cried**.*

Scream is often used when someone shouts because of a strong emotion such as fear or anger:

*My sisters were always **screaming** at each other.*

*'Let go of me!' she **screamed**.*

When someone shouts to show approval or encouragement, you could use the verb **cheer**:

*The audience **cheered** as he came on stage.*

• **within shouting distance** very close: *We live within shouting distance **of** the station.*

PHRASAL VERB **shout sb down** to prevent someone who is speaking at a meeting from being heard, by shouting: *She was shouted down when she tried to speak on the issue of abortion.*

►noun [C] **LOUD VOICE** ▷ **1** B1 the act of saying something very loudly or making a very loud sound with your voice: *Her speech was interrupted by **angry** shouts from the audience.* **DRINKS** ▷ **2** UK informal a set of drinks for a group of people, or a particular person's turn to buy them: *Would you like another drink? It's my shout since you bought the last ones.*

IDIOM **give sb a shout** informal to tell someone: *Give me a shout **when** you've finished in the bathroom.*

shouting /ˈʃaʊ.tɪŋ/ US /-t̬ɪŋ/ noun [U] shouts: *We could hear shouting in the street outside.*

ˈshouting ˌmatch noun [C] informal disapproving an argument which involves people shouting at each other because they have very strong opinions: *The meeting soon degenerated into a shouting match.*

shouty /ˈʃaʊ.ti/ US /-t̬i/ adj informal **1** involving a lot of shouting: *shouty music* **2** Someone who is shouty shouts a lot because they get angry very easily.

shove /ʃʌv/ verb; noun

►verb **PUSH** ▷ **1** [I or T] to push someone or something forcefully: *She was jostled and shoved by an angry crowd as she left the court.* ◦ *Just wait your turn – there's no need to shove.* ◦ *Reporters **pushed and** shoved as they tried to get close to the princess.* **PUT** ▷ **2** [T + adv/prep] informal to put something somewhere in a hurried or careless way: *I'll just shove this laundry **in** the washer before we go out.* ◦ *'Where should I put this suitcase?' 'Shove it **down** there for the moment.'* ◦ *They can't just shove motorways anywhere they like, you know.* **MOVE BODY** ▷ **3** [I + adv/prep] informal to move your body to make space for someone else: *Shove **over/along**, Lena, and make some room for me.* ◦ UK *Why don't you shove **up** so that Brian can sit next to you?*

IDIOM **shove it** slang a rude expression showing you have no respect for someone or for something that they have said: *When I told him he'd have to work harder, he said I could take the job and shove it.*

PHRASAL VERBS **shove sb around/about 1** to push someone forcefully, in an unpleasant and threatening way: *The older boys at school are always shoving* *him around.* **2** informal to tell someone what to do, in a rude or threatening way: *Don't let them shove you around. You've got to stand up for your rights.* • **shove off!** informal used to tell someone angrily to go away: *Just shove off, will you?* • **shove off** to leave land in a boat, usually by pushing against the land with your foot or an OAR: *She jumped into the dinghy and shoved off.*

▸**noun** [C] the action of shoving someone or something: *Would you help me **give** the piano a shove?*

shovel /ˈʃʌv.əl/ **noun; verb**

shovel

▸**noun** [C] **1** C2 a tool consisting of a wide, square metal or plastic blade, usually with slightly raised sides, fixed to a handle, for moving loose material such as sand, coal, or snow **2** a similar part on a large machine, for picking up and holding loose material **3** (also **shovelful**) the amount of something that can fit on a shovel: *Should I put another shovelful **of** coal on the fire?*

▸**verb** [I or T] (**-ll-** or US usually **-l-**) to move with a shovel: *Would you give me a hand shovelling the snow away from the garage door?*

IDIOM **shovel sth into your mouth** (also **shovel sth down**) to put large quantities of food into your mouth very quickly: *He was sitting in front of the TV shovelling down a pizza.*

show /ʃəʊ/ US /ʃoʊ/ **verb; noun**

▸**verb** (**showed, shown**) **MAKE SEEN** ▷ **1** A1 [T] to make it possible for something to be seen: [+ two objects] *I must show you this new book I've just bought.* ◦ *On this map, urban areas are shown **in** grey.* ◦ *You ought to show that rash **to** your doctor.* ◦ [+ obj + question word] *Why won't you show me **wh**at you've got in your hand?* ◦ [+ obj + -ing verb] *The secretly filmed video shows the prince and princess kiss**ing**.* ◦ *These photographs show the **effects** of the chemical on the trees.* ◦ *He began to show **signs** of recovery.* ◦ *'I've got a Victorian gold coin here.' 'Have you? Show me (= allow me to see it).'* **RECORD** ▷ **2** B1 [T] to record or express a number or measurement: *The right-hand dial shows the temperature, and the left-hand one shows the air pressure.* ◦ *The company showed a loss of £2 million last year.* **EXPLAIN** ▷ **3** B1 [T] to explain something to someone, by doing it or by giving instructions or examples: [+ question word] *Can you show me **how** to set the DVD player?* ◦ *This dictionary contains many examples that show **how** words are actually used.* ◦ *Could you show me the **way** to the bus station?* **PROVE** ▷ **4** B2 [T] to prove something or make the truth or existence of something known: *She has shown her**self** (**to be**) a highly competent manager.* ◦ *His diaries show him **to have been** an extremely insecure person.* ◦ [+ (that)] *The diaries show (**that**) he was very insecure.* ◦ *Show me (**that**) I can trust you.* ◦ [+ question word] *Our research has shown (us) **how** little we know about this disease.* **EXPRESS** ▷ **5** B2 [T] to express ideas or feelings using actions or words: *He finds it difficult to show affection.* ◦ *She showed enormous courage when she rescued him from the fire.* ◦ [+ two objects] *You should show your parents more respect/show more respect **to** your parents.* **NOTICEABLE** ▷ **6** C1 [I] to be easy to see or notice: *'Oh no, I've spilled red wine on my jacket!' 'Don't worry, it doesn't show.'* ◦ *Whatever she's thinking, she never lets it show.* ◦ *I've painted over the graffiti twice, but it still shows **through**.* ◦ *The drug does not show **up** in blood tests because it is effective in very small quantities.* ◦ *When we moved in, the house hadn't been decorated for 20 years, and **it** showed.* → See also **show up 7 show your age** to look as old as you really are: *Recently, he's really **starting** to show his age.* **PUBLIC EVENT** ▷ **8** [T] to make an artist's work available for the public to see: *Our aim is to make it easier for young unknown artists to show their work.* **9** [I or T] If a cinema or a television station shows a film or programme, or if a film or programme is showing somewhere, you can see it there: *It's the first time this film has been shown on British television.* ◦ *Now showing at a cinema near you!* **ARRIVE** ▷ **10** [I] mainly US to **show up** **LEAD** ▷ **11** [T usually + adv/prep] to take someone somewhere by going there with them: *Could you show Dr Sanchez into the living room?* ◦ *The waiter showed us **to** our table.* **FAIL TO HIDE** ▷ **12** [T] to fail to hide something, or to make it possible to see or know something that is not intended to be seen or known: *Your shirt's so thin that it shows your bra.* ◦ *Light-coloured carpets show the dirt.* ◦ [+ question word] *His failure in the exams shows (**up**) just **how** bad his teachers are.* **MAKE UNDERSTAND** ▷ **13** [T + obj + question word] to make someone understand something by directing their attention to it: *Can you show me **wh**ere it hurts?* ◦ *Show me **wh**ich one you want.*

IDIOMS **have something/nothing to show for sth** If you have something/nothing to show for your work or effort, you have/have not won any advantage from it: *I worked for two weeks, and £50 was all I had to show for it.* • **show your face** to appear somewhere when you are not expected to because you have done something bad: *How **dare** you show your face in here after saying all those dreadful things!* • **show your hand** to allow people to know about intentions that you had previously kept secret: *Keep the names of the team secret – don't show your hand until the day of the match.* • **show sb the door** to make it obvious that you do not want someone to be present and that they should leave: *When I told my bank manager that I wanted to borrow £100,000, she showed me the door.* • **show (sb) the way** to do something original that others are likely to copy: *Sweden has shown the way **forward** on energy efficiency.* • **that will show sb** informal said of an action that you intend as a punishment for someone who has done something wrong: *The next time she's late home, I'll throw her dinner away. That'll show her!*

PHRASAL VERBS **show off** B2 to behave in a way that is intended to attract attention or admiration, and that other people often find annoying: *She only bought that sports car to show off and prove she could afford one.* ◦ *He's always showing off to his classmates.* • **show sth/sb off** to show something or someone you are proud of to other people, so that they will admire them: *She likes to wear short skirts to show off her legs.* • **show sb out** to go to the door of the building with someone who does not live or work there, when they are leaving: *If you'd like to come this way, I'll show you out.* • **show yourself out** to leave a building in which you do not live or work, without anyone going to the door with you: *Don't get up – I'll show myself out.* • **show sb over sth** UK to lead someone around a place that they are visiting in a formal or official way, while telling them about it: *After lunch the VIPs will be shown over the new Arts Centre.* • **show sb round/around (sth)** B1 to go with someone to all parts, or the main parts, of a place that they have not visited before, so that they can see what it is like or learn

S

about it: *Let me know when you're coming to Cambridge and I'll show you around.* ◦ *A guide showed us round the exhibition.* • **show up** (mainly US **show**) B1 to arrive somewhere in order to join a group of people, especially late or unexpectedly: *I invited him for eight o'clock, but he didn't show up until 9.30.* ◦ *We were expecting 30 people to come, but half of them never showed up.* • **show sb up** to behave in a way that makes someone you are with feel ashamed or embarrassed: *I wish you wouldn't show me up in front of my parents by getting so drunk.*

▸noun **ENTERTAINMENT** ▷ **1** A2 [C] a theatre performance or a television or radio programme that is entertaining rather than serious: *a* ***radio/television/stage*** *show* ◦ *a* ***quiz/game*** *show* ◦ *Why don't we go to London on Saturday and* ***see*** *a show?* ◦ *We had to raise £60,000 to* ***stage*** *the show.* ◦ *We had a* ***puppet*** *show for Jamie's birthday party.* → See also **roadshow** **PUBLIC EVENT** ▷ **2** B2 [C] an event at which a group of related things are available for the public to look at: *a* ***fashion/flower*** *show* ◦ *There were some amazing new cars at the* ***motor*** *show.* ◦ *They put on a* ***retrospective*** *show* ***of*** *his work at the National Museum of American Art.* → See also **airshow, peepshow, roadshow, showjumping, sideshow** **3 on show** C1 Something that is on show has been made available for the public to look at: *Her sculptures will be on show at the museum until the end of the month.* **EXPRESSION** ▷ **4** [C] an action that makes other people know what your feelings, beliefs, or qualities are: *In an unexpected show* ***of*** *solidarity, the management and workers have joined forces to campaign against the closure of the factory.* ◦ *Over 100 military vehicles paraded through the capital in a show of* ***strength.*** **5 a good, poor, etc. show** an activity or piece of work that appears to be done with great, little, etc. effort: *She may not have won, but she certainly* ***put up*** *a good show.* **FALSE APPEARANCE** ▷ **6** [C] an appearance of something that is not really sincere or real: *Despite its public show* ***of*** *unity, the royal family had its share of disagreements just like any other.* ◦ *They* ***put on*** *a show* ***of*** *being interested, but I don't think they really were.* **7 for show** Something that is for show has no practical value and is used only to improve the appearance of something else: *Do the lights on this phone have any useful function or are they* ***just/only*** *for show?* **ACTIVITY** ▷ **8** [U] informal an activity, business, or organization, considered in relation to who is managing it: *Who will* ***run*** *the show when Meg retires?* ◦ *The wedding is their show – let them do it their way.*

IDIOMS **get the/this show on the road** informal to begin an activity that has been planned: *Come on, let's get this show on the road or we'll be late.* • **the show must go on** saying said to encourage someone to continue with what they are doing, even if they are experiencing difficulties

S

ˌshow-and-ˈtell noun [U] a school activity for young children in which a child brings an object into the class and talks to the other children about it

ˈshow ˌbusiness noun [U] (informal **showbiz**) the entertainment business, especially the part that is considered to be popular but not very artistic or serious: *Stars of the entertainment world turned out to celebrate his 40th year* ***in*** *show business.*

showcase /ˈʃəʊ.keɪs/ US /ˈʃoʊ-/ noun; verb
▸noun [C] **CONTAINER** ▷ **1** a container with glass sides in which valuable or important objects are kept so that they can be looked at without being touched, damaged, or stolen **OPPORTUNITY** ▷ **2** a situation or event which makes it possible for the best features of something to be seen: *The Venice Film Festival has always been the showcase* ***of*** *Italian cinema.* ◦ *The exhibition is an annual showcase* ***for*** *British design and innovation.*
▸verb [T] to show the best qualities or parts of something: *The main aim of the exhibition is to showcase British design.*

showdown /ˈʃəʊ.daʊn/ US /ˈʃoʊ-/ noun [C] an important argument that is intended to end a disagreement that has existed for a long time: *The president is preparing for a showdown* ***with*** *his advisers* ***over*** *his plans to reform the economy.* ◦ *Millions of dollars were spent on lawyers in a courtroom showdown* ***between*** *the two companies.*

shower /ʃaʊəʳ/ US /ʃaʊr/ noun; verb
▸noun **WASHING DEVICE** ▷ **1** A1 [C] a device that releases drops of water through a lot of very small holes and that you stand under to wash your whole body: *The shower is broken – you'll have to have a bath.* ◦ *Many British homes have a shower* ***attachment*** *fixed to the bath taps.* ◦ *a shower* ***curtain/cap*** **2** A1 [C] a wash using such a device: *Have I got time to (UK)* ***have/(US) take*** *a shower before we go out?* **3** A1 [C] a place, usually in a bathroom, where a shower is situated: *He's* ***in*** *the shower at the moment. Would you like him to phone you back?* **RAIN** ▷ **4** B1 [C] a short period of rain or snow: *showers of rain, hail and sleet* ◦ *You're soaked! Did you get caught in the shower?* ◦ *There will be* ***thundery/wintry*** *showers over many parts of the country.* ◦ ***Snow*** *showers are expected at the end of the week.* **MASS** ▷ **5 a shower of sth** a lot of small objects or drops of liquid coming through the air: *There was a bang and a shower* ***of sparks.*** ◦ *The pipe burst, sending out a shower* ***of*** *water.* **PARTY** ▷ **6** [C] US a party held for a woman just before she gets married or gives birth to a child, when she is given presents for her future home or baby: *I bought the cutest baby clothes to take to Jacey's* ***baby*** *shower.* ◦ *We went to my cousin's* ***bridal*** *shower yesterday.*
▸verb **FALL** ▷ **1** [I or T, usually + adv/prep] to fall down or come out in a shower, or to make something do this: *I heard a massive explosion, and seconds later fragments of glass were showering (= falling) down on us.* ◦ *She shook the bottle violently and showered us* ***with*** *champagne.* **WASH** ▷ **2** B2 [I] to take a shower: *I shower every morning.*

PHRASAL VERB **shower sb with sth** (also **shower sth on sb**) C2 to give someone a lot of presents or praise: *She only sees her niece occasionally, so she showers her with* ***presents*** *when she does.* ◦ *His boss showered him with* ***praise.***

ˈshower ˌgel noun [U] a type of thick liquid soap used for washing your body in the shower

showerproof /ˈʃaʊə.pruːf/ US /ˈʃaʊr-/ adj UK (US **ˈwater-repellent**) Showerproof clothing or material does not absorb water when it is raining lightly: *This coat isn't waterproof, but it is showerproof.*

showery /ˈʃaʊə.ri/ US /ˈʃaʊr.i/ adj describes weather with light rain that is often not continuous: *showery weather*

showgirl /ˈʃəʊ.ɡɜːl/ US /ˈʃoʊ.ɡɝːl/ noun [C] a young woman who sings or dances in a musical theatre entertainment

ˈshow ˌhome noun [C] UK (UK also **ˈshow ˌhouse**, US **ˈmodel ˌhouse**) a new house or apartment that has been decorated and filled with furniture to show buyers what similar homes might be like when people are living in them

showing /ˈʃəʊ.ɪŋ/ US /ˈʃoʊ-/ noun **PERFORMANCE** ▷

1 [C usually singular] the quality of someone's performance in a competition: *She managed a **good/strong** showing in the world championship.* ◦ *She had a **dismal** showing in the opinion polls.* **PUBLIC EVENT** ▷ **2** [C] an opportunity for the public to see something: *This is the film's first showing on British television.*

showjumper /ˈʃəʊˌdʒʌm.pəʳ/ US /ˈʃoʊˌdʒʌm.pɚ/ **noun** [C] a rider or horse that takes part in showjumping

showjumping /ˈʃəʊˌdʒʌm.pɪŋ/ US /ˈʃoʊ-/ **noun** [U] a sport which involves riding horses in competitions which test their ability to jump quickly over large objects such as walls and fences

showjumping

showman /ˈʃəʊ.mən/ US /ˈʃoʊ-/ **noun** [C] (plural **-men** /-mən/) someone who is very good at entertaining people • **showmanship** /-ʃɪp/ **noun** [U] *His showmanship in the ring shouldn't detract from his considerable skill.*

shown /ʃəʊn/ US /ʃoʊn/ **verb** past participle of **show**

ˈshow-off **noun** [C] disapproving a person who SHOWS OFF (= behaves in a way intended to attract attention which other people often find annoying)

ˌshow of ˈhands **noun** [S] a vote in which people raise one of their hands to show that they support a suggestion: *Her re-election to the committee was defeated **on** a show of hands.*

showpiece /ˈʃəʊ.piːs/ US /ˈʃoʊ-/ **noun** [C] an extremely good example of something, which deserves to be admired

showroom /ˈʃəʊ.rʊm/, /-ruːm/ US /ˈʃoʊ-/ **noun** [C] a large shop in which people are encouraged to look at the goods that are on sale before buying them: *a car showroom*

showstopper /ˈʃəʊˌstɒp.əʳ/ US /ˈʃoʊˌstɑː.pɚ/ **noun** [C] approving a piece in a stage performance that the audience enjoy so much that their clapping and shouts of approval interrupt the performance • **showstopping** /-ˌstɒp.ɪŋ/ US /-ˌstɑː.pɪŋ/ **adj** [before noun] *a showstopping **performance***

ˈshow ˌtrial **noun** [C] a trial organized by a government in order to have an effect on public opinion and reduce political opposition, and not in order to find the truth

showy /ˈʃəʊ.i/ US /ˈʃoʊ-/ **adj** disapproving attracting a lot of attention by being very colourful or bright, but without any real beauty: *a showy production of a play* ◦ *Her dress was too showy for such a formal occasion.* • **showily** /-ɪ.li/ **adv** • **showiness** /-nəs/ **noun** [U]

shrank /ʃræŋk/ **verb** past simple of **shrink**

shrapnel /ˈʃræp.nəl/ **noun** [U] small pieces of metal that fly through the air when a bomb or similar weapon explodes and are intended to injure people: *Twelve people were **hit** by shrapnel in the attack.* ◦ *a shrapnel **wound***

shred /ʃred/ **noun; verb**

▸**noun** **SMALL AMOUNT** ▷ **1** [S] a very small amount of something: *There's still **a** shred **of** hope that a peace agreement can be reached.* ◦ *There isn't **a** shred **of evidence** to support her accusation.* **CUT** ▷ **2** [C usually plural] a very small, thin piece that has been torn from something: *Cut the radishes into shreds to garnish the plates* **3 in shreds a** very badly torn: *My shirt was in shreds when I took it out of the washer.* **b** badly damaged: *The report has left the prison governor's reputation in shreds.*

IDIOM **tear/rip sb/sth to shreds** **1** to strongly criticize a person or something they do, think, or say: *The critics tore his performance to shreds.* **2** to damage someone or something badly: *My trousers were torn to shreds when I fell off my bike.*

▸**verb** [T] (**-dd-**) **1** to cut or tear something roughly into thin strips: *Shred the lettuce and arrange it around the edge of the dish.* ◦ *shredded carrot/paper* **2** to destroy a document by tearing it into strips, especially in a machine: *He ordered his secretary to shred important documents when government inspectors started investigating his business affairs.*

shredder /ˈʃred.əʳ/ US /-ɚ/ **noun** [C] a tool or machine that is used for cutting things into very small pieces: *a paper/document/vegetable shredder* ◦ *Much of the documentary evidence against her had been put through the shredder before she was arrested.*

shrew /ʃruː/ **noun** [C] **ANIMAL** ▷ **1** an animal like a small mouse but with a longer pointed nose and small eyes **WOMAN** ▷ **2** old-fashioned disapproving an unpleasant woman who is easily annoyed and who argues a lot • **shrewish** /ˈʃruː.ɪʃ/ **adj** disapproving

shrewd /ʃruːd/ **adj** approving C2 having or based on a clear understanding and good judgment of a situation, resulting in an advantage: [+ to infinitive] *He was shrewd **enough** not **to** take the job when there was the possibility of getting a better one a few months later.* ◦ *She is a shrewd **politician** who wants to avoid offending the electorate unnecessarily.* ◦ *It was a shrewd **move** to buy your house just before property prices started to rise.* • **shrewdly** /ˈʃruːd.li/ **adv** *She shrewdly predicted the stock market crash.* • **shrewdness** /ˈʃruːd.nəs/ **noun** [U]

shriek /ʃriːk/ **noun; verb**

▸**noun** [C] a short, loud, high cry, especially one produced suddenly as an expression of a powerful emotion: *shrieks **of** delight* ◦ *He suddenly let out a **piercing** shriek.*

▸**verb** [I or T] to make such a cry: *We shrieked **with laughter** when we realized how stupid we'd been.* ◦ *I tried to apologize, but he just shrieked **abuse** at me.* ◦ [+ speech] *'Don't you dare do that ever again!' she shrieked.*

shrill /ʃrɪl/ **adj** **1** having a loud and high sound that is unpleasant or painful to listen to: *She had a shrill high-pitched voice.* **2** disapproving describes a way of arguing or criticizing that seems too forceful: *He launched a shrill attack on the prime minister.* • **shrillness** /ˈʃrɪl.nəs/ **noun** [U] • **shrilly** /ˈʃrɪl.li/ **adv**

S

shrimp /ʃrɪmp/ **noun** **ANIMAL** ▷ **1** B1 [C or U] (plural **shrimps** or **shrimp**) (UK also **prawn**) a small sea creature with a thin shell, ten legs, and a long tail, or its flesh eaten as food: *shrimp paste* **PERSON** ▷ **2** [C] (plural **shrimps**) informal disapproving an extremely short person

ˌshrimp ˈcocktail **noun** [C or U] US shrimp served cold in a glass with a spicy tomato sauce, usually eaten as a STARTER (= a small dish served before a main course) → Compare **prawn cocktail**

shrine /ʃraɪn/ **noun** [C] **1** a place for worship that is holy because of a connection with a holy person or object: *Islam's most sacred shrine is at Mecca.* **2** a special place in which you remember and praise someone who has died, especially someone famous: *She's turned her bedroom into a shrine **to** the dead pop star and covered the walls with pictures of him.*

shrink /ʃrɪŋk/ verb; noun

►verb (**shrank**, **shrunk**) **BECOME SMALLER** ▷ **1** B2 [I or T] to become smaller, or to make something smaller: *Your sweater will shrink if you wash it at too high a temperature.* ◦ *The company's profits have shrunk* ***from*** *£5.5 million* ***to*** *£1.25 million.* ◦ *The productivity improvements have shrunk our costs* ***by*** *25 percent.* → See also **shrunken** **BE FRIGHTENED** ▷ **2** [I usually + adv/prep] literary to move away from someone or something because you are frightened: *The child shrank behind the sofa as his father shouted at him.* ◦ *When she was younger she would shrink (****away****)* ***from*** *me whenever I spoke to her.* • **shrinkage** /ˈʃrɪŋ.kɪdʒ/ noun [U] *Synthetic fabrics are less susceptible to shrinkage than natural ones.*

PHRASAL VERB **shrink from sth** to avoid doing something that is unpleasant or difficult: *We must not shrink from our responsibilities.* ◦ [+ -ing verb] *We will not shrink from* ***using*** *force.*

►noun [C] informal a PSYCHIATRIST or PSYCHOANALYST: *I was so depressed that I ended up going to see a shrink.*

ˌshrinking ˈviolet noun [C] informal a person who is very shy or MODEST and does not like to attract attention: *She loves appearing on television and is* ***no*** *shrinking violet when it comes to expressing her views.*

ˈshrink-wrap noun [U] a thin, transparent plastic material which tightly covers the thing that it is wrapped around, used for protecting goods when they are being transported or sold • **ˈshrink-wrap** verb [T] *A lot of the fresh food sold in supermarkets is shrink-wrapped.*

shrivel /ˈʃrɪv.ᵊl/ verb (**-ll-** or US usually **-l-**) **1** [I or T] to become dry, smaller, and covered with lines as if by crushing or folding, or to make something do this: *The lack of rain has shrivelled the crops.* ◦ *You ought to pick those lettuces before they shrivel (****up****) and die.* **2** [I] to become much smaller than is needed or wanted: *Profits are shrivelling as the recession gets worse.* • **shrivelled** /-ᵊld/ adj

shroud /ʃraʊd/ noun; verb

►noun [C] **CLOTH** ▷ **1** a cloth or long, loose piece of clothing that is used to wrap a dead body before it is buried **HIDE** ▷ **2** a layer of something which covers or surrounds something: *Everything was covered in a thick shroud* ***of*** *dust.* **3** a situation which prevents something from being known or understood: *The truth about the accident remains hidden beneath a shroud* ***of*** *secrecy.*

►verb [T] to hide something by covering or surrounding it: *Visitors have complained about the scaffolding that shrouds half the castle.* ◦ *Suddenly all the lights went out and the house was shrouded* ***in*** *darkness.* ◦ *The* ***mist*** *shrouding the valley had lifted by eight o'clock.*

IDIOM **be shrouded in secrecy/mystery** to be a matter about which very little is known or understood: *Her whereabouts have been shrouded in secrecy since she received the death threat.*

Shrove Tuesday /ˌʃrəʊvˈtjuːz.deɪ/ US /ˌʃroʊvˈtuːz-/ noun [C or U] (UK also **ˈPancake ˌDay**) the day before the Christian period of LENT begins

shrub /ʃrʌb/ noun [C] a large plant with a rounded shape formed from many small branches growing either directly from the ground or from a hard stem, grown in gardens: *She planted some roses and other* ***flowering*** *shrubs.* → See also **bush**

shrubbery /ˈʃrʌb.ᵊr.i/ US /-ɚ-/ noun **1** [C] a part of a garden where a lot of shrubs have been planted **2** [U] a group of shrubs

shrug /ʃrʌg/ verb; noun

►verb [I or T] (**-gg-**) C2 to raise your shoulders and then lower them in order to say you do not know or are not interested: *'Where's Dad?' 'How should I know?' replied my brother, shrugging.* ◦ *He shrugged his* ***shoulders*** *as if to say that there was nothing he could do about it.* ◦ figurative *Thousands of people are starving to death while the world shrugs its shoulders (= shows no interest or care).*

PHRASAL VERB **shrug sth off** **NOT WORRY** ▷ **1** to treat something as if it is not important or not a problem: *The stock market shrugged off the economic gloom and rose by 1.5 percent.* ◦ *You're a father and you can't simply shrug off your* ***responsibility*** *for your children.* **NOT KEEP** ▷ **2** to get rid of something unpleasant that you do not want: *I hope I can shrug off this cold before I go on holiday.* ◦ *The city is trying to shrug off its industrial* ***image*** *and promote itself as a tourist centre.* → See also **shake sth off**

►noun [C] **SHOULDER MOVEMENT** ▷ **1** the action of raising and lowering your shoulders to express something: *'I'm afraid there's nothing I can do about your problem,' she said with a shrug.* ◦ *'Well, I suppose we'll just have to do what he says,' said Kim with a shrug* ***of*** *resignation.* **CLOTHES** ▷ **2** a short CARDIGAN for women

shrunk /ʃrʌŋk/ verb past participle of **shrink** → See also **preshrunk**

shrunken /ˈʃrʌŋ.kən/ adj smaller than before, and less important: *a shrunken old man* ◦ *The company faces shrunken profits for the third year in succession.*

shtick /ʃtɪk/ noun [C usually singular] mainly US **1** (also **schtick**) the type of humour typical of a COMEDIAN (= person whose job is to make people laugh): *Pratfalls and other physical gags are typical of Carey's shtick.* **2** a particular ability or behaviour that someone has and that they are well known for

shuck /ʃʌk/ verb [T] US to remove the shell or natural covering from something that is eaten: *to shuck corn/oysters*

PHRASAL VERB **shuck sth off** **1** to remove a piece of clothing, especially one that limits you: *The lifeguard shucked off his sweatshirt.* **2** to get rid of something that limits you or causes you problems: *They seem to be able to just shuck off guilt.*

shucks /ʃʌks/ exclamation US informal an expression of MODESTY, embarrassment, disappointment, or anger: *'You played brilliantly in the concert.' 'Shucks, do you honestly think so?'* ◦ *Shucks, I wish I could have gone to the party with Jessica.* → See also **aw-shucks**

shudder /ˈʃʌd.əʳ/ US /-ɚ/ verb; noun

►verb [I] **1** C2 to shake suddenly with very small movements because of a very unpleasant thought or feeling: *The sight of so much blood made him shudder.* ◦ *She shuddered* ***at the thought of*** *kissing him.* **2** When something shudders, it shakes violently and quickly: *I heard a massive explosion and the ground shuddered beneath me.* ◦ *There was a screech of brakes and the bus shuddered* ***to a halt*** *(= shook violently and stopped).*

IDIOMS **I shudder to think** said when you are worried about something unpleasant that might happen or might have happened: *I shudder to think what my parents will say when I tell them I've failed my exams.* • **shudder to a halt** If a system shudders to a halt, it suddenly stops working: *The economy has shuddered to a halt because of the civil war.*

►noun [C] the act of shuddering: *He* ***gave a*** *slight shudder as he considered how near he had come to* death. ◦ *She recalled **with a** shudder how her boss had once tried to kiss her.* ◦ figurative *America's second biggest supermarket chain has **sent a** shudder **through** (= has had a strong effect on) its rivals by slashing its prices.*

IDIOM **send shudders/a shudder down your spine** to cause you to feel extremely worried or frightened: *When I think of what might have happened in the accident, it sends shudders down my spine.*

shuffle /ˈʃʌf.l̩/ verb; noun

▸verb **WALK** ▷ **1** [I + adv/prep, T] to walk by pulling your feet slowly along the ground rather than lifting them: *I love shuffling **through** the fallen leaves.* ◦ *He shuffled **into** the kitchen, leaning on his walking stick.* ◦ *Don't shuffle your feet like that! Lift them properly.* **2** [I usually + adv/prep, T] to move your feet or bottom around, while staying in the same place, especially because you are uncomfortable, nervous, or embarrassed: *The woman in front of me kept shuffling around in her seat all the way through the performance.* ◦ *When I asked him where he'd been, he just looked at the ground and shuffled his feet.* **MOVE AROUND** ▷ **3** [T] to move similar things from one position or place to another, often to give an appearance of activity when nothing useful is being done: *She shuffled her **papers** nervously on her desk.* ◦ *Many prisoners have to be shuffled around police stations because of prison overcrowding.* **MIX CARDS** ▷ **4** [I or T] to mix a set of playing cards without seeing their values before beginning a game, so that their order is not known to any of the players: *It's your turn to shuffle the cards.*

▸noun **MOVE AROUND** ▷ **1** [C] the act of moving things around from one position to another: *She gave her papers a quick shuffle.* **2** [C] mainly US a **reshuffle** **MIX CARDS** ▷ **3** [C] the act of mixing a set of playing cards before giving them out: *Make sure you give the cards a good shuffle before you deal.* **WALK** ▷ **4** [S] a way of walking in which you pull your feet slowly along the ground rather than lifting them: *He's got arthritis and walks with a shuffle.*

shufti (also **shufty**) /ˈʃʊf.ti/ noun UK old-fashioned informal **have/take a shufti** to look at something quickly: *Can I have a shufti **at** your paper?*

shun /ʃʌn/ verb [T] (**-nn-**) **1** to avoid something: *She has shunned publicity since she retired from the theatre.* **2** to ignore someone and not speak to them because you cannot accept their behaviour, beliefs, etc.: *After the trial he was shunned by friends and family alike.*

shunt /ʃʌnt/ verb **TRAINS** ▷ **1** [T] to move a train or CARRIAGE onto a different track in or near a station using a special railway engine designed for this purpose **MOVE** ▷ **2** [T usually + adv/prep] to move someone or something from one place to another, usually because they are not wanted and without considering any unpleasant effects: *I spent most of my childhood being shunted (**about**) **between** my parents who had divorced when I was five.* ◦ *He shunts his kids **off** to a camp every summer.* ◦ *Viewers are fed up with their favourite sitcoms being shunted **to** later times to make way for live football coverage.* • **shunt** noun [C usually singular]

shunter /ˈʃʌn.təʳ/ (US) /-t̬ɚ/ noun [C] a small railway engine that is used for moving CARRIAGES around on the tracks rather than making journeys between stations

shush /ʃʊʃ/ exclamation; verb

▸exclamation informal used to tell someone to be quiet: *Shush! I want to listen to the news.*

▸verb [I or T] informal to (cause to) stop talking or making a noise: *I wish you children would shush and let me read the paper in peace.*

shut /ʃʌt/ verb; adj

▸verb [I or T] (present tense **shutting**, past tense and past participle **shut**) **CLOSE** ▷ **1** A2 to (cause to) close something: *Please shut the gate.* ◦ *I've got a surprise for you! Shut your eyes **tightly** and hold out your hand.* ◦ *Mary shut her book and put it down on the table.* ◦ *This window won't shut – it's jammed.* **STOP OPERATING** ▷ **2** A2 to (cause to) stop operating or being in service, either temporarily or permanently: *The shops shut at eight o'clock on Wednesday evenings.* ◦ *It's such a shame they shut that factory (**down**).*

IDIOMS **shut your eyes to sth** to ignore something: *Until now the president has shut his eyes to the homelessness problem.* • **shut your mouth/face** (UK also **shut your gob**) a rude and angry way of telling someone to stop talking: *He told me to shut my mouth or there'd be trouble.* ◦ *'You're a lazy slob!' 'You shut your mouth!' (= Don't talk to me like that!)* • **shut up shop** UK (mainly US **close up shop**) to end an activity, usually a business activity, either temporarily or permanently

PHRASAL VERBS **shut sb away** to put a person in a place which they are not allowed or able to leave: *He was ten years old when he was shut away in an asylum for stealing an apple.* • **shut sth away** to put something in a place where other people cannot see it or get it: *The diamonds are shut away in a bank vault somewhere.* • **shut yourself away** to go into a place that you are unwilling to leave and where you do not want to be interrupted by other people: *Andy shuts himself away in his studio for hours on end when he's recording a song.* • **shut (sth) down** B1 If a business or a large piece of equipment shuts down or someone shuts it down, it stops operating: *The company plans to shut down four factories and cut 10,000 jobs.* ◦ *The crew shut down the right-hand engine of the aircraft.* • **shut sb/sth in (sth)** to prevent someone or something from leaving a place, usually by closing or fastening a door or gate: *The cat was shut in the garage all night.* ◦ *He was so upset that he shut him**self** in his bedroom and refused to come out.* • **shut sth in sth** to catch part of your body or an object inside a device or container when it closes: *Steve was off work for a week after he shut his hand in the car door.* • **shut (sth) off** If a machine or system shuts off, it stops operating, and if someone or something shuts it off, they stop it from operating: *The engine shuts off automatically when the desired speed is reached.* • **shut sth off** **SUPPLY** ▷ **1** to stop the supply of something: *Did you remember to shut off the water and gas before you left the house?* ◦ *Oil supplies have been shut off.* **AREA** ▷ **2** to prevent something from being reached or seen: *The music room is shut off **from** the rest of the house by a soundproof partition.* ◦ *A row of tall fir trees shuts off the **view** of the street in front.* • **shut yourself off** to stop speaking to other people or stop being involved with them: *When her husband died she seemed to shut her**self** off **from** her friends and family.* • **shut sb/sth out** **PREVENT ENTRY** ▷ **1** to stop someone or something from entering or getting back inside a house or other building: *The wind blew the door closed behind me and now I'm shut out (**of** the house).* ◦ *Don't forget to shut the cat out when you leave for work.* **NOT INCLUDE** ▷ **2** to not include a person or organization in an activity: *Anna felt shut out **of** the conversation.* ◦ *What are the chances of peace if we shut the terrorists out **of** negotiations?* • **shut sth out** **1** to stop yourself thinking about something that upsets you or feeling something that hurts you: *She finds it impossible to shut out the memory of the accident.* **2** to prevent a

S

sound or light from being heard or seen: *The double glazing shuts out most of the traffic noise.* ◦ *She pulled the duvet over her head to try to shut out the light.* • **shut sb out** US to prevent your opponent in a sports competition from scoring any points: *She had shut out two of her first four opponents by identical scores.* • **shut (sb) up** informal **1** B2 to stop talking or making a noise, or to make someone do this: *I wish you'd shut up for a moment and listen to what the rest of us have to say.* ◦ *Just shut up and get on with your work!* ◦ *My dad never stops talking. It's impossible to shut him up!* ◦ figurative *If you breathe a single word to the police, we'll come round and shut you up* ***for good*** *(= kill you).* **2** to stop someone from talking about a particular subject or from complaining or asking for things: *The kids kept on about how hungry they were, so their father gave them some biscuits to shut them up.* • **shut sb/sth up** to keep a person or animal in a closed place: *She can't spend her whole life shut up* ***in*** *her office.* • **shut (sth) up** UK to close a shop or other business for a period of time, usually when business is finished for the day: *By the time we got there, all the market traders were shutting up.*

▸**adj** [after verb] B1 closed: *I suspected something was wrong when I noticed her curtains were still shut at lunchtime.* ◦ figurative *The government ought to have opened the door to Japanese investment instead of* ***slamming*** *it shut.* → See also **open-and-shut**

shutdown /ˈʃʌt.daʊn/ **noun** [C] an occasion when a business or large piece of equipment stops operating, usually for a temporary period: *It's just a regular maintenance shutdown.* ◦ *The emergency shutdown procedure was activated.*

shuteye /ˈʃʌt.aɪ/ US /ˈʃʌt̬-/ **noun** [U] old-fashioned informal sleep: *You look exhausted! Try to* ***get*** *some shuteye on the train.*

shutout /ˈʃʌt.aʊt/ US /ˈʃʌt̬-/ **noun** [C] US a situation in a sports competition in which a player or team wins without the other player or team scoring any points

shutter /ˈʃʌt.əʳ/ US /ˈʃʌt̬.ɚ/ **noun** [C] **PHOTOGRAPHY** ▷ **1** the part of a camera which opens temporarily to allow light to reach the film when a photograph is being taken **WINDOW COVER** ▷ **2** a wooden cover on the outside of a window which prevents light or heat from going into a room or heat from leaving it: *Shutters usually come in pairs and are hung like doors on hinges.* **3** a metal covering which protects the windows and entrance of a shop from thieves when it is closed • **shuttered** /-əd/ US /-ɚd/ **adj** *Shops are closed and shuttered on Sundays.*

S

shuttle /ˈʃʌt.l̩/ US /ˈʃʌt̬-/ **noun; verb**

▸**noun** [C] **VEHICLE** ▷ **1** C1 a vehicle or aircraft that travels regularly between two places: *To get across town, you can* ***take*** *the shuttle from Times Square to Grand Central.* ◦ *The American* ***(space)*** *shuttle was able to be used many times to put payloads in space.* **THREAD** ▷ **2** specialized in WEAVING, a device that is used to carry the thread that goes across the cloth between the threads that go down the cloth

▸**verb** [I or T, usually + adv/prep] to travel or take people regularly between the same two places: *A small train shuttles constantly* ***between*** *the concourse* ***and*** *the runways.*

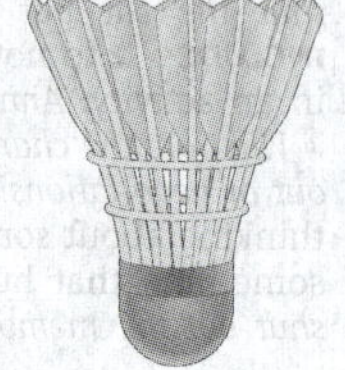
shuttlecock

shuttlecock /ˈʃʌt.l̩.kɒk/ US /ˈʃʌt̬.l̩.kɑːk/ **noun** [C] (informal **shuttle**, US **birdie**) a small, light object with a rounded end to which real or artificial feathers are fixed, that is hit over the net in the game of BADMINTON

ˈshuttle diˌplomacy noun [U] discussions between two or more countries, in which someone travels between the different countries, talking to the governments involved, carrying messages, and suggesting ways of dealing with problems

shy /ʃaɪ/ **adj; verb**

▸**adj NERVOUS** ▷ **1** B1 (**shyer**, **shyest**) nervous and uncomfortable with other people: *He was too shy to ask her to dance with him.* ◦ *She gave a shy smile.* ◦ *Children are often shy* ***of/with*** *people they don't know.* ◦ *The deer were shy (= unwilling to be near people) and hid behind some trees.* **LESS** ▷ **2** [after noun] less than: *We're only £100 shy* ***of*** *the total amount.*

▸**verb HORSES** ▷ **1** [I] (of a horse) to suddenly move sideways or backwards, especially because of fear: *The horse shied* ***at*** *the fence.* **THROW** ▷ **2** [T usually + adv/prep] old-fashioned informal to throw something suddenly, often in a sideways movement: *Two small boys were shying stones* ***at*** *a tree.*

PHRASAL VERB **shy away from sth** to avoid something that you dislike, fear, or do not feel confident about: *I've never shied away from hard work.*

-shy /-ʃaɪ/ **suffix** avoiding or not liking the thing mentioned: *camera-shy* ◦ *work-shy*

shyly /ˈʃaɪ.li/ **adv** in a shy way: *She smiled shyly at him.*

shyness /ˈʃaɪ.nəs/ **noun** [U] C1 the condition of being shy: *His face went red with shyness when he walked into the crowded room.*

shyster /ˈʃaɪ.stəʳ/ US /-stɚ/ **noun** [C] informal a dishonest person, especially a lawyer or politician: *He's a real shyster.* ◦ *What are those shyster politicians doing now?*

SI /es'aɪ/ **noun** [U] specialized abbreviation for Système International: the international system of units used for scientific measurements, with standard base units such as the metre and the kilogram: *The SI* ***unit*** *of electric current is the ampere.*

Siamese (cat) /ˌsaɪ.ə.miːzˈkæt/ **noun** [C] a cat that has short hair and pale fur, but darker ears, tail, and feet, and blue eyes

Siamese twins /ˌsaɪ.ə.miːzˈtwɪnz/ **noun** [plural] old-fashioned **conjoined twins** (= two people with the same mother who were born at the same time, with some part of their bodies joined together)

sibilant /ˈsɪb.ɪ.lənt/ **adj; noun**

▸**adj** literary making a 's' or 'sh' sound: *a sibilant whisper*

▸**noun** [C] formal a 's' or 'sh' sound

sibling /ˈsɪb.lɪŋ/ **noun** [C] formal C2 a brother or sister: *I have four siblings: three brothers and a sister.* ◦ *There was great sibling* ***rivalry*** *(= competition) between Peter and his brother.*

sibyl /ˈsɪb.əl/ **noun** [C] literary any of several women in the ancient world who were thought to be able to see into the future

sic /sɪk/ **adv** a word written in BRACKETS after a word that you have copied to show that you know it has been spelled or used wrongly: *The notice outside the cinema said 'Closed on Wedensday' (sic).*

sick /sɪk/ **adj; verb; noun**

▸**adj ILL** ▷ **1** A2 physically or mentally ill; not well or healthy: *a sick child* ◦ *a sick cow* ◦ *My father has been* ***off*** *sick (= not working because of illness) for a long time.* ◦ *Anyone who could hurt a child like that must be sick (= mentally ill).* ◦ *The old woman* ***fell/took/was taken*** *sick (= became ill) while she was away and had to come home.* ◦ *Sarah* ***called in/reported*** *sick (= told her employer that she was unable to go to work because* of illness). ◦ figurative *High rates of crime are considered by some people to be a sign of a sick society.* → See also **heartsick, homesick, lovesick**

> **Usage: sick, ill, and be sick**
>
> In British English **ill** is the word that is usually used to mean 'not well'. In American English the word for this is **sick**:
>
> *He went home early because he felt ill.* (British English)
>
> *He went home early because he felt sick.* (American English).
>
> In British English to **be sick** is to bring food up from the stomach. Another way of saying this is the word **vomit**, which is used both in British and American English:
>
> *The little boy in the back seat of the car was sick into a paper bag.* (British English)

VOMIT ▷ **2** A2 [after verb] feeling ill as if you are going to vomit: *Lucy **felt** sick the morning after the party.* ◦ *If you eat any more of that cake, you'll **make** yourself sick.* → See also **airsick, carsick, seasick 3 be sick** B1 to vomit: *She was sick after she ate too much chocolate.* **UNPLEASANT** ▷ **4** B2 [after verb] informal causing or expressing unpleasant emotions: *I'm sick **at** (US **over**) (= unhappy about) not getting that job.* ◦ *It **makes** me sick (= makes me very angry) to see people wearing fur coats.* ◦ UK informal *It's sick-**making** (= very annoying) that she's being paid so much for doing so little.* ◦ *I'm sick **(and tired/to death) of** (= very annoyed about) the way you're behaving.* ◦ *She was **worried** sick (= very worried) when her daughter didn't come home on time.* ◦ *Joan was not amused by the sick (= cruel or offensive) **joke** her brother told.* ◦ *I **felt** sick (= felt shocked and disgusted) when I heard about the prisoners being beaten.*

IDIOMS **sick as a dog** vomiting a lot: *I was sick as a dog after last night's meal.* • **sick as a parrot** UK humorous slang very disappointed: *He was sick as a parrot when his team lost the match.* • **sick at heart** literary very unhappy: *David was sick at heart about having to leave his family behind.* • **sick to your stomach 1** C2 likely to vomit: *I'm (feeling) sick to my stomach.* **2** feeling very upset, worried, or angry: *It **makes** me (feel) sick to my stomach when I remember my car accident.*

▸verb

PHRASAL VERB **sick sth up** UK informal to vomit something: *The baby sicked up some milk on his aunt's shoulder.*

▸noun **ILL** ▷ **1 the sick** [plural] people who are ill: *It's better for the sick to be cared for at home rather than in hospital.* **VOMIT** ▷ **2** [U] UK informal vomit: *a pool of sick on the floor*

sickbay /ˈsɪk.beɪ/ noun [C] a room with beds for people who are ill, especially on a ship

sickbed /ˈsɪk.bed/ noun [C] the bed of a person who is ill: *We visited my grandmother **on** her sickbed.*

ˌsick ˈbuilding ˌsyndrome noun [U] an illness that people who work in certain buildings can get, caused by poor air quality inside the building: *Air conditioning can contribute to sick building syndrome.*

ˈsick ˌday noun [C] a day for which an employee will receive pay while absent from work because of illness

sicken /ˈsɪk.ən/ verb **ILL** ▷ **1** [I] to become ill: literary *The child sickened and died.* ◦ UK *'You look feverish. Are you sickening **for** (= about to become ill with) something?'* **UNPLEASANT** ▷ **2** [T] to cause someone to feel unpleasant emotions, especially anger and shock: *The violence in the film sickened me.* ◦ *He was sickened **by/at** the number of people who were hurt in the crash.*

sickening /ˈsɪk.ən.ɪŋ/ adj **1** extremely unpleasant and causing you to feel shock and anger: *The slaves were treated with sickening cruelty.* ◦ *There was a sickening thud when the child fell from the tree and hit the ground.* **2** annoying: *It's sickening that I can't go to the party.* • **sickeningly** /-li/ adv

ˌsick ˈheadache noun [C] a severe pain in the head, especially a MIGRAINE

sickie /ˈsɪk.i/ noun UK informal **throw a sickie** to say to your employer that you are ill when you are not so that you do not have to go to your place of work for a day: *I just didn't feel like work so I threw a sickie.*

sickle /ˈsɪk.l̩/ noun [C] a tool with a short handle and a curved blade, used for cutting grass and grain crops → Compare **scythe**

sickle

ˈsick ˌleave noun [U] time away from work because of illness: *Mark is not in the office today. He broke his leg yesterday, so he's on/he's taken sick leave.*

ˌsickle cell aˈnaemia (mainly US **ˌsickle cell aˈnemia**) noun [U] a medical condition that causes pain and fever, passed from parent to child and found especially in black people

sickly /ˈsɪk.li/ adj **ILL** ▷ **1** weak, unhealthy, and often sick: *a sickly child/plant* **VOMIT** ▷ **2** disapproving causing a slight feeling of wanting to vomit: *A sickly smell of decaying fish came from the dirty river.* ◦ *The chocolate cake was sickly **sweet** (= too sweet).* **TOO EMOTIONAL** ▷ **3** disapproving emotional, in an unpleasant or embarrassing way: *His books are sometimes accused of sickly **sentimentality**.*

sickness /ˈsɪk.nəs/ noun [U] **ILL** ▷ **1** B2 the condition of being ill: *There's a lot of sickness around this winter.* **VOMIT** ▷ **2** vomiting: *Drinking unclean water can cause diarrhoea and sickness.*

ˈsickness ˌbenefit noun [U] UK money paid by the government to someone who cannot work because of illness

sicko /ˈsɪk.əʊ/ US /-oʊ/ noun [C] (plural **sickos**) slang someone, especially a man, who is mentally ill or who performs unpleasant, often sexual, acts: *She's afraid of being attacked in the park by a sicko.* • **sicko** adj

ˈsick ˌpay noun [U] money given by an employer to someone who cannot work because of illness

sickroom /ˈsɪk.rʊm/, /-ruːm/ noun [C] a room in which someone who is ill lies in bed

side /saɪd/ noun; verb; adj

▸noun **SURFACE** ▷ **1** A2 [C] a flat outer surface of an object, especially one that is not the top, the bottom, the front, or the back: *The names of ships are usually painted on their sides.* ◦ *My room is at the side of the house.* ◦ *Please write on one side of the paper only.* ◦ *I've already written four sides (= pages of writing) for my essay.* ◦ *Please use the side entrance.* **EDGE** ▷ **2** A2 [C] an edge or border of something: *A square has four sides.* ◦ *There are trees on both sides of the road.* ◦ *They were surrounded **on all** sides/**on every** side by curious children.* **NEXT TO** ▷ **3** B2 [U] a place next to something: *I have a small table **at/by** the side of (= next to) my bed.* ◦ *He stayed **at/by** her side (= with her) throughout her long illness.* → See also **alongside, aside, beside 4** [C] US informal **side dish 5 side by side** B2 next to each other: *The children sat side by side on the sofa watching television.* **PART** ▷ **6** A2 [C] a part

S

of something, especially in relation to a real or imagined central line: *He likes to sleep on the right side of the bed.* ◦ *In Britain, cars drive on the left side of the road.* ◦ *There is no money **on** my mother's side (**of the family**).* ◦ *I could just see Joan **on the far/other** side **of** the room.* ◦ *Children came running **from all** sides (= from all directions).* **7** C2 [C usually singular] the part of the body from under the arm to the top of the leg: *I have a pain in my side.* **8** [C] UK a television CHANNEL: *What side is 'Coronation Street' on?* **9 from side to side** B2 from left to right and from right to left: *The curtains were swinging from side to side in the breeze.* **10** [C usually singular] half of an animal's body, considered as meat: *She bought a side of lamb from the butcher's shop.* **OPPOSING GROUP** ▷ **11** B2 [C, + sing/pl verb] one of two or more opposing teams or groups: *This is a war which neither side can win.* ◦ *Our side (= team) lost again on Saturday.* ◦ *Whose/which side are you **on** (= which team are you playing for/supporting)?* ◦ *Don't be angry with me – I'm **on** your side (= I want to help you).* **12 take sides** to support one person or group rather than another, in an argument or war: *My mother never takes sides when my brother and I argue.* **13 take sb's side** B2 to support someone in an argument: *My mother always takes my father's side when I argue with him.* **OPINION** ▷ **14** B2 [C] an opinion held in an argument, or a way of considering something: *There are at least two sides **to** every question.* ◦ *I've listened to your side **of the story**, but I still think you were wrong to do what you did.* **PART OF SITUATION** ▷ **15** B2 [C] a part of a situation, system, etc. that can be considered or dealt with separately: *She looks after the financial side of things.* ◦ *Fortunately my boss did see the funny side of the situation.* **CHARACTER** ▷ **16** B2 [C] a part of someone's character: *She seems quite fierce, but actually she has a gentle side.* • **-sided** /-ɪd/ **suffix** *A square is a four-sided figure.* ◦ *a many-sided question* ◦ *a steep-sided hill*

IDIOMS **be two sides of the same coin** (also **be different/opposite sides of the same coin**) If two things are two sides of the same coin, they are very closely related although they seem different: *Violent behaviour and deep insecurity are often two sides of the same coin.* • **come down on one side of the fence or the other** to make a decision between two opposing points of view: *The election is next week, so you'll have to come down on one side of the fence or other by then.* • **get on the right/wrong side of sb** to make someone pleased/annoyed with you: *As a teenager, Clare was always getting on the wrong side of her mother.* • **have sth on your side** If you have something on your side, it gives you an advantage when you are trying to achieve something: *I thought I would get the job, but the other person who was being considered for it had experience on his side.* • **keep on the right side of sb** to try to make certain that someone is pleased with you: *Paul kept on the right side of his teachers by doing masses of work.* • **on the large, small, etc. side** too large, small, etc. for a particular purpose: *This dress is rather on the large side **for** me.* • **on the right/wrong side of 40, 50, etc.** looking younger/older than a particular age: *She looks to me as if she's on the wrong side of 50.* • **on the right/wrong side of the law** obeying/not obeying the law: *After coming out of prison, he tried to stay on the right side of the law.* • **on the side 1** C2 in addition to your main job: *He makes a little money on the side by cleaning windows in his spare time.* **2** secretly: *I think he has another woman on the side (= a relationship with a woman who is not his wife).* **3** mainly US (of food in a restaurant) served on another plate, or not on part of the meal: *I'd like a salad with the dressing on the side (= with the dressing served separately from the salad), please.* ◦ *I'll have a omelette with fries on the side, please.* • **the other side of the coin** a different way of considering a situation, making it seem either better or worse than it did originally: *I like having a white car, but the other side of the coin is that it soon gets dirty.* • **put/lay sth on/to one side** C2 to not use something, especially an amount of money, in order to keep it for later use: *We have put some money on one side for next year's summer holiday.* • **put/leave sth on/to one side** to stop talking about a particular subject: *Can we leave the issue of pay on one side for the moment?* • **take/lead sb on/to one side** to have a private talk with someone: *Bill's father took him to one side and told him to stop behaving so badly.* • **this side of sth** before reaching a particular age, date, place, etc.: *I can't believe she's this side of 50.* ◦ *We don't expect to see Gideon this side of Christmas.* ◦ *This is the best pizza I've eaten this side of (= anywhere other than) Rome.* ◦ *Parenting is the most rewarding thing I will do this side of **the grave** (= in life).* • **the wrong/other side of the tracks** a part of a town that is considered poor and dangerous: *Her boyfriend came from the wrong side of the tracks.*

▸verb

PHRASAL VERB **side with sb** to support one person or group in an argument: *If ever there was any sort of argument, she'd always side with my father **against** me.*

▸adj [before noun] not in or at the centre or main part of something: *We parked the car on a side **street/road** (= a small road, especially one that joins on to a main road).* ◦ *I think that's a side **issue** (= a subject which is separate from the main one) which we should talk about later.* ◦ *I'd like a side **dish** (US side **order**) of potatoes (= some potatoes on a separate plate).*

sidearm /ˈsaɪd.ɑːm/ (US) /-ɑːrm/ **noun** [C] a weapon worn on the side of the body, especially a small gun or SWORD

sidebar /ˈsaɪd.bɑːʳ/ (US) /-bɑːr/ **noun** [C] **1** a box or narrow area on a newspaper or magazine page that contains a short news story or extra information relating to a longer main story **2** a narrow area at the side of a page on a website, giving extra information or LINKS

sideboard /ˈsaɪd.bɔːd/ (US) /-bɔːrd/ **noun** [C] a piece of furniture with a flat top and cupboards at the bottom, usually used for holding glasses, plates, etc.

sideburns /ˈsaɪd.bɜːnz/ (US) /-bɝːnz/ **noun** [plural] (UK also **sideboards**) areas of hair grown down the sides of a man's face in front of the ears

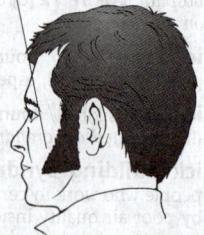

sidecar /ˈsaɪd.kɑːʳ/ (US) /-kɑːr/ **noun** [C] a small, one-wheeled vehicle fixed to the side of a motorcycle to hold a passenger

ˈside ˌdish **noun** [C] **1** (also **ˈside ˌorder**, US informal **side**) in a restaurant, an extra dish of food, for example vegetables or salad, that is served with the main dish, sometimes on a separate plate **2** a plate on which a side dish is served

ˈside ˌdrum **noun** [C] a small drum that is hit with hard sticks → Compare **snare drum**

ˈside efˌfect **noun** [C] **1** C1 an unpleasant effect of a drug that happens in addition to the main effect: *Does this drug **have** any side effects?* **2** an unexpected result of a situation: *A side effect of the new law is that fewer people will take out insurance.*

sidekick /ˈsaɪd.kɪk/ **noun** [C] informal a person who works with someone who is more important than they are

sidelight /ˈsaɪd.laɪt/ **noun** [C] **LIGHT** ▷ UK (US **parking light**) either of the two smaller lights fixed on the front of a car → Compare **headlight**

sideline /ˈsaɪd.laɪn/ **noun; verb**

▸**noun** [C] **JOB** ▷ **1** an activity that you do as well as your main job: *Jim works in a bank, but teaches French in the evenings **as** a sideline.* **SPORT** ▷ **2** mainly US a line that shows the position of the side areas of play, especially for football: *The ball fell just **inside/on/outside** the sideline.*

IDIOM **on/from the sidelines** If you are on the sidelines or do something from the sidelines, you are not actively involved in something: *Our party has been on the **political** sidelines for too long – we must now work towards getting into power.* ◦ *She could only **watch** from the sidelines as her brother's health deteriorated.*

▸**verb** [T] **1** If a sports player is sidelined they are prevented from playing or competing, and can only watch: *Johnson has been sidelined through injury.* **2** to stop someone taking an active and important part in something: *The minister was sidelined after he criticized party policy.*

sidelong /ˈsaɪd.lɒŋ/ (US) /-lɑːŋ/ **adj** [before noun], **adv** describes a short look at someone or something, moving your eyes to the side, and not looking directly: *He gave her a sidelong glance.* ◦ *He glanced at her sidelong and smiled.*

ˈ**side** ˌ**mirror** **noun** [C] US for **wing mirror**

ˌ**side-**ˈ**on** **adv, adj** from or on the side: *The bus hit the car side-on.* ◦ *a side-on collision*

ˈ**side** ˌ**order** **noun** [C] **side dish**

ˈ**side** ˌ**plate** **noun** [C] a small plate that you put your bread on when you are eating the main part of a meal

sidereal /saɪˈdɪə.ri.əl/ (US) /-ˈdɪr.i-/ **adj** [before noun] specialized of or calculated by the stars

siˈ**dereal** ˌ**time** **noun** [U] specialized time based on the movement of the Earth in relation to the stars

sidesaddle /ˈsaɪdˌsæd.l̩/ **noun** [C], **adv** (on) a SADDLE used especially in the past by women, on which the rider sits with both legs on the same side of the horse: *The Queen rode sidesaddle when she inspected the soldiers.*

sideshow /ˈsaɪd.ʃəʊ/ (US) /-ʃoʊ/ **noun** [C] **1** a small show or event in addition to the main entertainment: *Carol won a large soft toy at a sideshow at the fair.* **2** an event or subject that is connected to another event or subject but is considered to be much less important: *The media still regards women's sport as a sideshow to the main event.*

ˈ**side-**ˌ**splitting** **adj** extremely funny: *a side-splitting joke/story/film* • ˈ**side-**ˌ**splittingly** **adv** *side-splittingly funny*

sidestep /ˈsaɪd.step/ **verb** [I or T] (**-pp-**) **1** to step to the side in order to avoid something, especially being hit: *He sidestepped the blow/the tackle.* **2** to avoid talking about a subject, especially by starting to talk about something else: *The speaker sidestepped **the question** by saying that it would take him too long to answer it.*

sidestroke /ˈsaɪd.strəʊk/ (US) /-stroʊk/ **noun** [U] any of various ways of swimming lying on one side

sideswipe /ˈsaɪd.swaɪp/ **noun; verb**

▸**noun** [C] **REMARK** ▷ **1** a remark attacking something or someone made while talking about something else: *During her lecture on her discoveries, she **made/took** several sideswipes **at** the management.* **HIT** ▷ **2** a hit something on the side

▸**verb** [T] to hit on the side: *The motorcycle turned the corner too quickly, and sideswiped a car coming towards it.*

sidetrack /ˈsaɪd.træk/ **verb** [T usually passive] to direct a person's attention away from an activity or subject towards another one that is less important: *Ruth was looking for an envelope in a drawer when she was sidetracked by some old letters.* ◦ *The students side-tracked their teacher **into** talking about her hobby.* ◦ *I'm sorry I'm late – I **got** sidetracked.* • **sidetrack** **noun** [C]

sidewalk /ˈsaɪd.wɔːk/ (US) /-wɑːk/ **noun** [C] (B1) mainly US for **pavement**

sideways /ˈsaɪd.weɪz/ **adv, adj** in a direction to the left or right, not forwards or backwards: *The fence is leaning sideways.* ◦ *If you would move sideways to the left, I can get everyone in the picture.*

ˈ**side-wheeler** **noun** [C] US for **paddle steamer**

siding /ˈsaɪ.dɪŋ/ **noun** **RAILWAY** ▷ **1** [C] a short railway track connected to a main track, where CARRIAGES are kept when they are not being used **MATERIAL** ▷ **2** [U] US material which covers the surface of the outer walls of a building, usually in sloping layers: *vinyl/aluminum/wood siding*

sidle /ˈsaɪ.dl̩/ **verb** [I usually + adv/prep] to walk towards or away from someone, trying not to be noticed: *Tim sidled **up/over to** the girl sitting at the bar and asked if he could buy her a drink.* ◦ *She sidled **past** him, pretending that she had not seen him.*

SIDS /sɪds/ **noun** [U] (also ˈ**cot** ˌ**death**) abbreviation for sudden infant death syndrome: a medical condition in which a baby dies suddenly while it is sleeping for no obvious reason

siege /siːdʒ/ **noun** [C or U] the surrounding of a place by an armed force in order to defeat those defending it: *The siege **of** Mafeking lasted for eight months.* ◦ *The soldiers **laid** siege **to** (= started a siege of) the city.* ◦ *The castle was **under** siege for months.* ◦ figurative *That whole weekend at Cannes, Brigitte Bardot was **under** siege by photographers.* → See also **besiege**

ˈ**siege men**ˌ**tality** **noun** [S] disapproving a feeling that makes you frightened of people around you, and causes you not to trust them: *Years of international isolation has led the country to develop a siege mentality.*

sienna /siˈen.ə/ **noun** [U] a type of soil that is used to colour paint

sierra /siˈeə.rə/ (US) /-ˈer.ə/ **noun** [C] a range of steep mountains, especially in North and South America and Spain

siesta /siˈes.tə/ **noun** [C] a rest or sleep taken after LUNCH, especially in hot countries

sieve /sɪv/ **noun; verb**

▸**noun** [C] a tool consisting of a wood, plastic or metal frame with a wire or plastic net fixed to it. You use it either to separate solids from a liquid, or you rub larger solids through it to make them smaller: *Pass the sauce through a sieve to remove any lumps.*

IDIOM **memory/mind like a sieve** If you have a memory or mind like a sieve, you forget things very easily.

▸**verb** [T] to put a liquid or powder through a sieve: *To make the pastry, sieve the flour and salt into a bowl.*

sievert /ˈsiː.vət/ (US) /-vɚt/ noun [C] (plural **sievert** or **sieverts**) the standard unit for measuring the effect of RADIATION

sift /sɪft/ verb [T] **SEPARATE** ▷ **1** to put flour, sugar, etc. through a sieve (= wire net shaped like a bowl) to break up large pieces: *When the cake is cooked, sift some icing sugar over the top of it.* **EXAMINE** ▷ **2** to make a close examination of all the parts of something in order to find something or to separate what is useful from what is not: *The police are sifting the evidence very carefully to try and find the guilty person.* ◦ *After my father's death, I had to sift* ***through*** *all his papers.* ◦ *The police are trying to sift* ***out*** *the genuine warnings* ***from*** *all the hoax calls they have received.*

sifter /ˈsɪf.təʳ/ (US) /-tɚ/ noun [C] a container with many small holes in its lid for sifting substances, usually foods: *a flour sifter* ◦ *a sugar sifter*

sigh /saɪ/ verb; noun

▸verb [I] **1** (B2) to breathe out slowly and noisily, expressing tiredness, sadness, pleasure, etc.: *She sighed deeply and sat down.* ◦ [+ speech] *'I wish he was here,' she sighed (= she said with a sigh).* **2** If the wind sighs, it makes a long, soft sound as it moves through trees: *I lay on my back, listening to the sound of the wind sighing in the trees.*

▸noun [C] (B2) a slow, noisy breath: *He leaned back in his seat* ***with a*** *sigh.* ◦ *'Ah, you're here,' she said and* ***heaved/let out/gave*** *a sigh* ***of relief****.*

sight /saɪt/ noun; verb

▸noun **ABILITY TO SEE** ▷ **1** (B1) [U] the ability to see: *If your sight is poor, you should not drive a car.* ◦ *The old woman has* ***lost*** *her sight (= has become blind).* → See also **eyesight** **VIEW** ▷ **2** (B2) [C or S or U] something that is in someone's view: *The flowers at the annual flower show were a beautiful sight.* ◦ *You should always* ***keep*** *sight* ***of*** *your bags (= have them where you can see them) while you're at the airport.* ◦ informal *You can't go out in those clothes – you look* ***a real*** *sight (= look untidy or silly)!* ◦ *The child laughed* ***at the*** *sight* ***of*** *(= when she saw) the clockwork toy.* ◦ formal *The lawyer requested sight* ***of*** *(= to see) the papers.* ◦ *I dare not let the children* ***out of*** *my sight (= go where I cannot see them) in this park.* ◦ *The police officer was hidden* ***out of*** *sight (= where he could not be seen) behind a tree.* ◦ *The castle came* ***into*** *sight (= started to be able to be seen) as we went round a bend in the road.* ◦ *We're looking for a house which is* ***within*** *sight* ***of*** *(= from which it is possible to see) the mountains.* ◦ figurative *After three years of campaigning, the end is finally* ***in*** *sight (= will happen soon) for Jon.* ◦ *I* ***caught*** *sight* ***of*** *(= saw for a moment) my former teacher while I was out shopping today, but she turned a corner and I* ***lost*** *sight of (= could no longer see) her.* ◦ *'Do you know David Wilson?' 'I haven't met him, but I know him* ***by*** *sight (= I recognize him, but do not know him).'* ◦ informal *She hated/loathed* ***the*** *sight* ***of*** *(= hated) her former husband.* ◦ informal *They used to be very good friends, but now they* ***can't bear/stand the*** *sight* ***of*** *(= hate) each other.* ◦ *The question seemed easy* ***at first*** *sight (= when they first saw it), but when the students tried to answer it, they discovered how difficult it was.* **3 the sights** (B1) places of interest, especially to visitors: *We spent a fortnight in Rome looking at all the sights.* **4 sight unseen** without seeing something first: *I never buy anything sight unseen.* **MUCH** ▷ **5 a sight** informal a lot; much: *Food is* ***a*** *(darn/damn) sight* ***more*** *expensive than it used to be.* ◦ *He's a sight better than he was yesterday.* **GUN PART** ▷ **6** [C usually plural] a part of a gun or other device through which you look to help you aim at something: *Make sure you line up the sights before you fire the gun.*

> **Word partners for sight**
>
> *catch* sight of sb/sth • *disappear from/vanish from* sight • *lose* sight of sb/sth • *not let* sb/sth *out of* your sight • the sight *of* sb/sth • *in/within* sight • *out of* sight • an *amazing/common/depressing/ sorry* sight

IDIOMS **get out of my sight!** informal an angry way of telling someone to go away: *Get out of my sight, you idiot!* • **lose sight of sth** (C2) to forget about an important idea or fact because you are thinking too much about other things: *Some members of the peacekeeping force seem to have lost sight of the fact that they are there to help people.* • **lower your sights** to accept that you will only be able to get something less than you hoped for: *He had hoped to become a doctor, but he had to lower his sights after his disappointing exam results.* • **out of sight, out of mind** saying said to emphasize that when something or someone cannot be seen, it is easy to forget them • **set your sights on sth** (C2) to decide to achieve something: *Jenny has set her sights on winning the competition.* • **a sight for sore eyes** informal a way of saying that you are very pleased to see someone or that you think someone is very attractive: *You're a sight for sore eyes!*

▸verb [T] to suddenly see something or someone: *After days at sea, the sailors finally sighted land.*

sighted /ˈsaɪ.tɪd/ (US) /-t̬ɪd/ adj formal able to see

-sighted /-saɪ.tɪd/ (US) /-t̬ɪd/ suffix used when describing a particular way of seeing or thinking → See **clear-sighted, far-sighted, long-sighted, nearsighted, short-sighted**

sighting /ˈsaɪ.tɪŋ/ (US) /-t̬ɪŋ/ noun [C] an occasion when you see something or someone, especially that is rare or trying to hide: *This is the first sighting of this particularly rare bird in this country.*

sightless /ˈsaɪt.ləs/ adj literary unable to see

ˈsight-read verb [I or T] to play or sing written music the first time you see it • **ˈsight-ˌreader** noun [C] *She's an expert sight-reader.* • **ˈsight-ˌreading** noun [U]

sightseeing /ˈsaɪtˌsiː.ɪŋ/ noun [U] (A2) the activity of visiting interesting places, especially by people on holiday: *We* ***did*** *a bit of sightseeing in Paris.* ◦ *There was no time to* ***go*** *sightseeing in Rome.* • **sightseer** /-əʳ/ (US) /-ɚ/ noun [C]

sign /saɪn/ verb; noun

▸verb **WRITE** ▷ **1** (B1) [I or T] to write your name, usually on a written or printed document, to show that you agree with its contents or have written or created it yourself: *to sign a letter/cheque/contract/lease/agreement* ◦ *Sign here, please.* ◦ *He signed his name at the end of the letter.* ◦ [+ obj + noun] *He signed himself 'Mark Taylor'.* ◦ *She said the painting was by Picasso, but it wasn't signed.* **2** [T] in sport, to make a legal written agreement to employ a player: *The football club has just signed a new player.* **BODY MOVEMENT** ▷ **3** [T or I] to give an order or information, or make a request, using hand and body movements: [+ to infinitive] *He signed* ***for/to*** *the waiter* ***to*** *bring him another drink.* ◦ [+ that] *He signed* ***to*** *the waiter* ***that*** *he wanted another drink.* **4** [I or T] to use SIGN LANGUAGE (= language used by people who cannot hear or talk)

IDIOMS **sign your own death warrant** informal to do something that is harmful to your own position: *She signed her own death warrant by refusing to do what the boss demanded.* • **sign on the dotted line** informal to agree to do something, especially by signing an agreement: *If you want to join the club, all you have to do is sign on the dotted line.* • **signed and sealed** (also **signed, sealed, and delivered**) finished and official because all the necessary documents have been signed

PHRASAL VERBS **sign sth away** to give up your rights to something by signing a legal document: *Under the treaty, both sides will sign away a third of their nuclear weapons.* • **sign for sth** to sign a form to show that you have received something: *I had to sign for the parcel when I collected it from the post office.* • **sign for/with sb** (in sport) to sign a formal agreement saying that you will play for a particular team • **sign (sb) in** to sign your name or the name of someone who is visiting you in a book, in order to be allowed to enter a building such as an office or hotel: *New security measures require all visitors to sign in at reception and wear a visitor's badge.* • **sign (sth) off** to give a final message at the end of a letter or when communicating by radio, or at the end of a television or radio programme: *She signed off (her show) by wishing her listeners a Happy New Year.* • **sign off** STOP WORK ▷ **1** US informal to stop doing your work or a similar activity for a period of time: *As it's Friday, I think I'll sign off early today.* FINANCIAL SUPPORT ▷ **2** UK informal to report to a government EMPLOYMENT office that you now have a job and do not need to receive BENEFIT (= money paid by the government) • **sign on 1** UK informal to sign a form at a government office to say that you do not have a job and that you want to receive BENEFIT (= money paid by the government) **2** mainly US (UK **sign up**) to agree to become involved in an organized activity: [+ to infinitive] mainly US *I've signed on to help at the school fair.* **3** (also **sign up**) UK informal to sign a document saying that you will work for someone or do a particular job or activity: *She's signed on **with** a temp agency.* ◦ *Julie has signed up **for** courses on English and French this year.* • **sign (sb) out** to sign your name in a book when you leave a building such as an office or factory, or to write someone else's name in a book when they leave after visiting it: *Don't forget to sign out before you leave.* • **sign sth out** to record when you take something away, usually by signing your name in a book: *You have to sign books out when you borrow them from the library.* • **sign sth over** to give the legal rights to own or do something to someone else by formally signing a document: *Two years before her death she signed her property over **to** her children.* • **sign up** B1 to agree to become involved in an organized activity: [+ to infinitive] *I've signed up **to** do the sandwiches for the street party.* ◦ *She's signed up **for** evening classes at the community college.* → See also **sign on**

▸noun [C] NOTICE ▷ **1** A2 a notice giving information, directions, a warning, etc.: *a road sign* ◦ *a shop sign* BODY MOVEMENT ▷ **2** B1 a movement of the body that gives information or an instruction: *She pointed to her watch **as a** sign **that** it was getting late and she wanted to leave.* ◦ *She **made/gave** a sign to her husband **to** stop talking.* ◦ *The priest **made** the sign **of the cross** (= made the shape of a cross by moving his hand between four points on his chest) when he entered the church.* → See also **signal** SHOWING ▷ **3** B1 something showing that something else exists or might happen or exist in the future: *His inability to handle the situation is a sure sign **of** weakness.* ◦ [+ that] *The fact that he's eating more is a sign **that** he's feeling better.* ◦ *I've searched for my hat, but there's **no** sign **of** it anywhere (= I can't find it).* ◦ *There was no sign **of life** in the building (= there seemed to be no one in it).* ◦ *Billy's work at school has **shown** signs **of** improvement this year.* ◦ ***There is every** sign **that/All the** signs **are that** the worst is over.* → See also **signal** MARK ▷ **4** B2 a written or printed mark that has a standard

meaning: *+ and − are mathematical signs.* ◦ *£ is the sign for the British pound.*

IDIOM **sign of the times** usually disapproving something that is typical of the (bad) way things are now: *These riots in the north are a sign of the times.*

signage /ˈsaɪ.nɪdʒ/ noun [U] specialized **1** all the signs that advertise a product, etc.: *As part of its rebranding effort, the company will replace signage on 2,000 of its stores.* **2** signs that tell people what something is or where to go: *Lee suggested signage could make it clear that the area is open to the public.*

signal /ˈsɪg.nəl/ noun; verb; adj

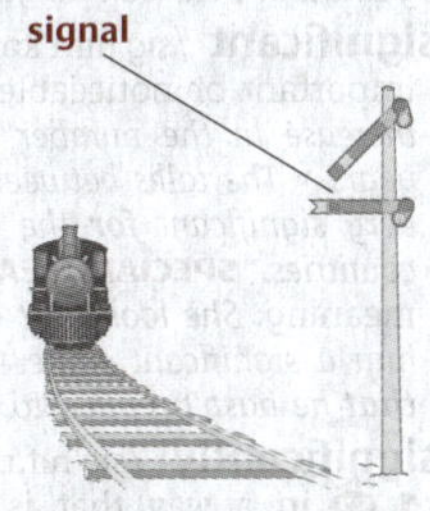

▸noun [C] ACTION ▷ **1** B2 an action, movement, or sound that gives information, a message, a warning, or an order: *When she **gave** (them) the signal, they all cheered.* ◦ [+ that] *The fire-work was a signal **that** the festival had started.* ◦ [+ to infinitive] *The police officer **gave** us a signal **to** stop.* ◦ *The signal **for** a race to start is often the firing of a gun.* **2** US for **indicator** WAVE ▷ **3** B2 a series of electrical or radio waves that are sent to a radio or television in order to produce a sound, picture, or message SHOWING ▷ **4** something that shows that something else exists or is likely to happen: *The poor result is a clear signal **of** his deteriorating confidence.* ◦ *The changing colour of the leaves on the trees is a signal **that** it will soon be autumn.* EQUIPMENT ▷ **5** equipment, especially on the side of a railway or road, often with lights, that tells drivers to stop, continue, or go more slowly: *a railway signal* ◦ *a traffic signal* ◦ *a road signal*

▸verb (-ll- or US usually -l-) ACTION ▷ **1** C2 [I or T] to make a movement, sound, flash, etc. that gives information or tells people what to do: *Flashing lights on a parked car usually signal a warning (**to** other motorists).* ◦ *He signalled left, and turned the lorry slowly.* ◦ *He was signalling (= giving a signal) with a red flag.* ◦ *She signalled **for** help.* ◦ [+ that] *She signalled **to** the cars behind **that** they were going the wrong way.* ◦ [+ obj + to infinitive] *The children's mother signalled them **to** be quiet.* ◦ [+ to infinitive] *The children's mother signalled **to/for** them **to** be quiet.* SHOW ▷ **2** [T] to show that you intend or are ready to do something: [+ that] *The union has signalled **that** the workers will strike.* ◦ *The union has signalled the workers' intention to strike.* ◦ *The death of Chairman Mao signalled (= marked) the end of an era in Chinese history.*

▸adj [before noun] formal noticeable and unusual: *a signal success/failure*

ˈsignal ˌbox noun [C] UK (US **ˈsignal ˌtower**) a building from which railway signals are operated

signally /ˈsɪg.nə.li/ adv formal obviously: *The council is signally failing to keep the streets clean.*

signalman /ˈsɪg.nəl.mən/, /-mæn/ noun [C] (plural **-men** /-mən/, /-men/) someone who operates a railway signal

signatory /ˈsɪg.nə.tᵊr.i/ (US) /-tɔːr.i/ noun [C] a person, organization, or country that has signed an agreement: *Most western European nations are signatories **to/of** the North Atlantic Treaty Organization.*

signature /ˈsɪg.nɪ.tʃəʳ/ (US) /-tʃɚ/ noun [C] B1 your name written by yourself, always in the same way, usually to show that something has been written or agreed by you → Compare **autograph**

S

ˈsignature ˌtune noun [C] a short tune used in broadcasting at the beginning and/or end of a particular programme or to mark the appearance of a particular performer

signet ring /ˈsɪg.nɪtˌrɪŋ/ noun [C] a finger ring with a flat piece at the front, which usually has a pattern cut into it

significance /sɪgˈnɪf.ɪ.kəns/ noun [U] **IMPORTANCE** ▷ **1** C1 importance: *The discovery of the new drug is* ***of*** *great significance* ***for/to*** *people suffering from heart problems.* **SPECIAL MEANING** ▷ **2** special meaning: *Do you think that look he gave you had any significance?*

significant /sɪgˈnɪf.ɪ.kənt/ adj **IMPORTANT** ▷ **1** B2 important or noticeable: *There has been a significant increase in the number of women students in recent years.* ◦ *The talks between the USA and the USSR were very significant* ***for*** *the relationship between the two countries.* **SPECIAL MEANING** ▷ **2** having a special meaning: *She looked at him across the table and gave him a significant smile.* ◦ *Do you think* ***it's*** *significant* ***that*** *he hasn't replied to my letter yet?*

significantly /sɪgˈnɪf.ɪ.kənt.li/ adv **IMPORTANT** ▷ **1** B2 in a way that is easy to see or by a large amount: *My piano playing has improved significantly since I've had a new teacher.* **SPECIAL MEANING** ▷ **2** in a way that suggests a special meaning

signification /ˌsɪg.nɪ.fɪˈkeɪ.ʃᵊn/ noun [C] specialized the meaning (of a word)

signify /ˈsɪg.nɪ.faɪ/ verb formal **MEAN** ▷ **1** [T] to be a sign of something; to mean: *Nobody really knows what the marks on the ancient stones signify.* ◦ [+ that] *The number 30 on a road sign signifies* ***that*** *the speed limit is 30 miles an hour.* **MAKE KNOWN** ▷ **2** [T] to make something known; to show: *She signified her agreement by nodding her head.* ◦ [+ (that)] *She signified (****that****) she was in agreement by nodding her head.* **BE IMPORTANT** ▷ **3** [I] to have importance or to MATTER: *Don't worry about being late – it doesn't signify.*

signing /ˈsaɪ.nɪŋ/ noun [C] in sport, a player who has been bought by one team from another

ˈsign ˌlanguage noun [U or C] **1** (also **sign** [U]) a system of hand and body movements representing words, used by and to people who cannot hear or talk **2** the movements that people sometimes make when talking to someone whose language they do not speak

ˌsign of the ˈzodiac noun [C] (plural **signs of the zodiac**) (also **ˈstar ˌsign, sign**) in ASTROLOGY, any of the twelve symbols that represent parts of the year: *the mosaic depicts the twelve signs of the zodiac* ◦ *'What sign are you?' 'Gemini.'*

signpost /ˈsaɪn.pəʊst/ US /-poʊst/ noun; verb

▸**noun** [C] **ROAD SIGN** ▷ **1** B1 a pole at the side of a road, especially at a point where two or more roads meet, which gives information about routes and distances: *The signpost said 'London 18 miles'.* **SHOW FUTURE** ▷ **2** something which shows what is going to happen, or what should happen, in the future: *This upturn in the country's economy is a splendid signpost* ***to*** *the future.*

signpost

▸**verb** **ROAD SIGN** ▷ [T usually passive] to show the direction of something on a signpost: *The road wasn't very well signposted (= provided with signposts).* ◦ *We found where we were going very easily, because it was signposted (= the direction was shown by signposts) all the way.*

Sikh /siːk/ noun [C] a member of the religion that developed in the 15th century, based on belief in a single god and on the teachings of Guru Nanak • **Sikh** adj *a Sikh temple* • **Sikhism** /ˈsiː.k.ɪ.zᵊm/ noun [U]

silage /ˈsaɪ.lɪdʒ/ noun [U] grass or other green plants that are cut and stored, without being dried first, to feed CATTLE in winter

silence /ˈsaɪ.ləns/ noun; verb

▸**noun** **QUIET** ▷ **1** B1 [U] a period without any sound; complete quiet: *A loud crash of thunder* ***broke*** *the silence of the night.* ◦ *Silence* ***reigned*** *(= there was complete silence) in the church.* **NO SPEAKING** ▷ **2** B1 [U] a state of not speaking or writing or making a noise: *The soldiers listened* ***in*** *silence as their captain gave the orders.* ◦ *'Silence! (= Stop talking!)' shouted the teacher.* ◦ *My request for help was* ***met with*** *silence (= I received no answer).* ◦ *Her silence* ***on/about*** *what had happened to her surprised everyone.* ◦ *Their mother's angry words* ***reduced*** *the children* ***to*** *silence.* ◦ *I don't expect to hear from her now, after three years' silence (= three years in which she has not spoken or written to me).* **3** B2 [C] a period of time in which there is complete quiet or no speaking: *Their conversation was punctuated by uncomfortable silences.*

> **Word partners for silence**
>
> *in* silence • *reduce* sb to silence • *break* the silence • *lapse into* silence • *meet with* silence • silence *descends/falls/follows* • a *shocked/stunned/stony* silence • *absolute/complete/total* silence • a *brief/long/short* silence • an *awkward/embarrassed/tense/uncomfortable* silence • a *deafening/eerie* silence

IDIOM **silence is golden** saying said to mean it is often better to say nothing

▸**verb** [T] to make someone or something be quiet: *The teacher raised his voice to silence the class (= to make them stop talking).* ◦ *Her remark about his appearance completely silenced him (= made him unable to answer).* ◦ figurative *Al Capone silenced his opponents (= prevented them from opposing him) by killing them.* ◦ figurative *The enemy's guns were silenced (= made to stop firing) in a surprise attack.*

silencer /ˈsaɪ.lən.səʳ/ US /-sɚ/ noun [C] **1** a piece of equipment that you use on a gun to reduce the noise made when it FIRES **2** UK (US and Australian English **muffler**) a part of a vehicle that reduces noise from the engine

silent /ˈsaɪ.lənt/ adj **QUIET** ▷ **1** B1 without any sound: *The empty house was completely silent.* ◦ literary *It was four o'clock in the morning and London was* ***as silent as the grave*** *(= completely silent).* **NO SPEAKING** ▷ **2** B2 without talking: *She whispered a silent prayer that her wounded brother would not die.* ◦ *The police officer told the criminal that he had* ***the right to remain*** *silent.* ◦ *The minister was silent* ***on/about*** *his plans for the future.* ◦ *Arthur has always been the* ***strong,*** *silent* ***type*** *(= a type of person, usually a man, who says very little).* • **silently** /-li/ adv

ˌsilent ˈfilm noun [C] (also **ˌsilent ˈmovie**) a film without any sound → Compare **talkie**

ˌsilent ˈletter noun [C] A silent letter in a word is one that is written but not pronounced, such as the 'b' in 'doubt'.

ˌsilent maˈjority noun [S] a large number of people

who have not expressed an opinion about something: *A few people have spoken in favour of the new car park, but I'm sure the silent majority are against it.*

ˌsilent ˈpartner noun [C usually singular] US for **sleeping partner**

silhouette /ˌsɪl.uˈet/ noun [C or U] a dark shape seen against a light surface: *The silhouette of the bare tree on the hill was clear **against** the winter sky.*

silhouetted /ˌsɪl.uˈet.ɪd/ (US) /-et̬-/ adj forming a silhouette: *The goats high up on the mountain were silhouetted **against** the snow.*

silica /ˈsɪl.ɪ.kə/ noun [U] a mineral that exists in various forms, including sand, QUARTZ, and FLINT, used to make glass and CEMENT

silicate /ˈsɪl.ɪ.kət/ noun [C or U] any of a large number of common minerals formed of silica, OXYGEN, and one or more other elements

silicon /ˈsɪl.ɪ.kən/ noun [U] (symbol **Si**) a grey chemical element that is found in rocks and sand and is used in making computers and other electronic machines

ˌsilicon ˈchip noun [C] a small piece of silicon that is used in computers, CALCULATORS, and other electronic machines

silicone /ˈsɪl.ɪ.kəʊn/ (US) /-koʊn/ noun [U] any of a number of COMPOUNDS of silicon that are used in making artificial rubber, paint, POLISH, VARNISH, etc.

ˈsilicone ˌimplant noun [C] something used to replace or increase the size of body parts that can be seen: *a silicone breast implant*

silicosis /ˌsɪl.ɪˈkəʊ.sɪs/ (US) /-ˈkoʊ-/ noun [U] a lung disease caused by breathing in SILICA dust, especially found among COAL MINERS and STONEMASONS

silk /sɪlk/ noun **CLOTH** ▷ **1** (B1) [U] a delicate, soft type of cloth made from a thread produced by SILKWORMS, or the thread itself: *a silk dress* ◦ *a silk shirt* **2 silks** [plural] the brightly coloured shirts worn by JOCKEYS (= people who ride horses in a race) **LAWYER** ▷ **3** [C] UK specialized a **QC**: a lawyer of high rank in some countries

IDIOM **take silk** UK specialized to become a QC

silken /ˈsɪl.kᵊn/ adj [usually before noun] literary soft, smooth, and shiny like silk: *The princess in the fairy story had long silken hair.*

silkscreen /ˈsɪlk.skriːn/ noun; verb

▸**noun** [U] a method of printing by forcing ink through a pattern cut into silk or other similar cloth, stretched across a frame: *silkscreen printing*

▸**verb** [I or T] to use the silkscreen method of printing

silkworm /ˈsɪlk.wɜːm/ (US) /-wɝːm/ noun [C] a type of CATERPILLAR (= a form of young insect that is small, long, and has many legs) that produces threads of silk from which it makes a COCOON (= a covering for its body)

silky /ˈsɪl.ki/ adj usually approving soft and smooth, like silk: *Persian cats have long, silky fur.* ◦ figurative *The villain leans over and speaks to her in a silky persuasive voice.* • **silkiness** /-nəs/ noun [U]

sill /sɪl/ noun [C] a flat piece of wood, stone, etc. which forms the base of a window or door → See also **windowsill**

silliness /ˈsɪl.i.nəs/ noun [U] silly behaviour

silly /ˈsɪl.i/ adj **1** (B1) showing little thought or judgment: *Don't do that, you silly boy!* ◦ *a silly mistake* ◦ *It was silly **of** you to go out in the sun without a hat.* ◦ *I feel silly (= embarrassed) in this dress.* → Synonym **foolish 2** (B1) not important, serious, or practical: *She gets upset over such silly things.* ◦ *We were served our drinks in these silly little glasses.*

IDIOMS **drink, laugh, etc. yourself silly** to drink, laugh, etc. so much that you are unable to think clearly or behave with good judgment: *I laughed myself silly at his jokes.* • **silly billy** informal a silly person, especially a child: *You're being a silly billy, now stop it.*

ˈsilly ˌseason noun [U] the time of year, usually in the summer, when newspapers are full of stories that are not important because there is no important, especially political, news

silo /ˈsaɪ.ləʊ/ (US) /-loʊ/ noun [C] (plural **silos**) **1** a large, round tower on a farm for storing grain or winter food for CATTLE **2** a large underground place for storing and FIRING MISSILES (= flying weapons)

silt /sɪlt/ noun; verb

▸**noun** [U] sand or soil that is carried along by flowing water and then dropped, especially at a bend in a river or at a river's opening

▸**verb**

PHRASAL VERB **silt (sth) up** to become blocked with silt, or to cause something to become blocked with silt: *The harbour silted up many years ago.*

silvan (also **sylvan**) /ˈsɪl.vən/ adj old use or literary of or having woods

silver /ˈsɪl.vəʳ/ (US) /-vɚ/ noun; adj; verb

▸**noun** [C or U] **1** (A2) (symbol **Ag**) a chemical element that is a valuable shiny white metal, used for making CUTLERY (= knives, spoons, etc.), jewellery, coins, and decorative objects: *We gave Alison and Tom a dish made of **solid** silver as a wedding present.* ◦ *Cleaning **the** silver (= silver objects) is a dirty job.* ◦ *Shall we use **the** silver (= knives, spoons, plates, etc. made of silver) for dinner tonight?* ◦ *I need some silver (= coins made of silver or a metal of similar appearance) for the ticket machine in the car park.* **2** (also **silver medal** [C]) a small disc of silver, or a metal that looks like silver, that is given to the person who comes second in a competition, especially in a sport: *Britain won (a) silver/a silver medal in the javelin.*

▸**adj** (A2) made of silver, or of the colour of silver: *a silver ring* ◦ *My grandmother has silver hair.*

▸**verb** [T often passive] to cover something, especially a window, with a thin layer of silver-coloured material in order to make a mirror

ˌsilver ˈbirch noun [C] a common type of BIRCH tree, which has a silver-coloured TRUNK and branches

silverfish /ˈsɪl.və.fɪʃ/ (US) /-vɚ-/ noun [C] (plural **silverfish** or **silverfishes**) a silver-white insect without wings which lives inside buildings

ˌsilver ˈjubilee noun [C usually singular] a date that is exactly 25 years after the date of an important event

ˌsilver ˈpaper noun [U] (also **ˌsilver ˈfoil**) UK shiny silver-coloured paper

ˌsilver ˈplate noun [U] objects made of metal with a thin covering of silver • **ˌsilver-ˈplated adj**

the ˌsilver ˈscreen noun [S] literary the film industry: *the stars of the silver screen*

silverside /ˈsɪl.və.saɪd/ (US) /-vɚ-/ noun [U] UK part of a leg of BEEF

silversmith /ˈsɪl.və.smɪθ/ (US) /-vɚ-/ noun [C] a person who makes or sells silver objects

ˌsilver-ˈtongued adj literary If you are silver-tongued, you are good at persuading people to do things.

silverware /ˈsɪl.və.weəʳ/ (US) /-vɚ.wer/ noun [U]

1 objects, especially knives, forks, spoons, etc., made of silver **2** C2 US knives, forks, spoons, etc. made of STEEL or other materials **3** UK silver cups, etc. that are won by sports teams in competitions

ˌsilver ˈwedding (anniversary) noun [C] the date exactly 25 years after the date of a marriage

silvery /ˈsɪl.vᵊr.i/ US /-vɚ-/ adj literary COLOUR ▷ **1** like silver: *The grass was silvery with frost.* SOUND ▷ **2** having a pleasant, clear musical sound: *We were woken early by the peal of silvery bells.*

SIM card /ˈsɪm.kɑːd/ US /-kɑːrd/ noun [C] a plastic card in a mobile phone that contains your personal information and that allows you to use the phone

simian /ˈsɪm.i.ən/ adj, noun [C] formal (of or like) a monkey

similar /ˈsɪm.ɪ.ləʳ/ US /-ə.lɚ/ adj B1 looking or being almost, but not exactly, the same: *My father and I have similar views on politics.* ◦ *I bought some new shoes which are very similar* ***to*** *a pair I had before.* ◦ *Paul is very similar* ***in*** *appearance* ***to*** *his brother.*

similarity /ˌsɪm.ɪˈlær.ɪ.ti/ US /-əˈler.ə.t̬i/ noun [C or U] B2 the fact that people or things look or are the same: *I can see the similarity* ***between*** *you and your mother.* ◦ *The book bears several striking similarities* ***to*** *last year's bestseller.*

similarly /ˈsɪm.ɪ.lə.li/ US /-ə.lɚ-/ adv C1 in a similar way: *The children were similarly dressed.* ◦ *Cars must stop at red traffic lights: similarly, bicycles should stop too.*

simile /ˈsɪm.ɪ.li/ noun [C or U] (the use of) an expression comparing one thing with another, always including the words 'as' or 'like': *The lines 'She walks in beauty, like the night...' from Byron's poem contain a simile.*

simmer /ˈsɪm.əʳ/ US /-ɚ/ verb **1** [I or T] to cook something liquid, or something with liquid in it, at a temperature slightly below boiling: *Leave the vegetables to simmer for a few minutes.* **2** [I] If a disagreement or negative emotion simmers, it grows slowly stronger over a period of time and could become more serious at any moment: *The strike has been simmering for weeks.* ◦ *She's been simmering* ***with*** *resentment ever since the meeting.* • **simmer** noun [S] *Bring the potatoes to a simmer.*

PHRASAL VERB **simmer down** informal to become less angry or excited about something: *Come on kids! Simmer down and get on with your work!*

S

simper /ˈsɪm.pəʳ/ US /-pɚ/ verb [I] to smile in a silly or annoying way: *She gave her teacher a simpering smile.* • **simper** noun [C]

simple /ˈsɪm.pl̩/ adj EASY ▷ **1** A2 easy to understand or do; not difficult: *The instructions were written in simple English.* ◦ ***It's*** *simple* ***to*** *find our house.* ◦ *I want an explanation, but* ***keep/make it*** *simple.* IMPORTANT ▷ **2** B2 [before noun] used to describe the one important fact, truth, etc.: *We didn't go swimming for the simple reason that the water was too cold.* PLAIN ▷ **3** B1 without decoration; plain: *I like simple food better than fancy dishes.* ONE PART ▷ **4** B1 [before noun] having or made of only one or a few parts: *A hammer is a simple tool.* ◦ *Simple forms of life have only one cell.* NATURAL ▷ **5** usually approving ordinary; traditional or natural rather than modern and complicated: *He was just a simple fisherman.* FOOLISH ▷ **6** describes a person who does not have a normal level of intelligence: *He's a bit simple, I'm afraid.*

ˌsimple ˈeye noun [C] specialized a basic type of eye consisting of a group of cells that are SENSITIVE to light, or having only one LENS, as found in some insects → Compare **compound eye**

ˌsimple ˈfracture noun [C] a broken bone that has not cut through the surrounding flesh or skin → Compare **compound fracture**

ˌsimple ˈinterest noun [U] money that is paid only on an original amount of money that has been borrowed or INVESTED, and not on the extra money that the original amount earns → Compare **compound**

ˌsimple ˈleaf noun [C] specialized a type of leaf that consists of one leaf on a leaf stem → Compare **compound leaf**

ˌsimple-ˈminded adj disapproving **1** describes a person who does not have the ability to use reason and understand **2** describes an action or opinion that is based on a limited understanding of a situation

ˈsimple ˌsugar noun [C] specialized a **monosaccharide**

simpleton /ˈsɪm.pl̩.tᵊn/ noun [C] old-fashioned a person without the usual ability to use reason and understand

simplicity /sɪmˈplɪs.ɪ.ti/ US /-ə.t̬i/ noun [U] EASY ▷ **1** C1 the fact that something is easy to understand or do: *The advantage of the plan is its simplicity.* ◦ *The exam was simplicity* ***itself*** *(= very easy).* NATURAL ▷ **2** the fact that something is ordinary, traditional, or natural, and not complicated: *The old people led a life of great simplicity (= with few possessions and little money).* PLAIN ▷ **3** the fact that something is plain and has no decoration

simplify /ˈsɪm.plɪ.faɪ/ US /-plə-/ verb [T] C1 to make something less complicated and therefore easier to do or understand: *the new simplified tax system* ◦ *He tried to simplify the story for the younger audience.* • **simplification** /ˌsɪm.plɪ.fɪˈkeɪ.ʃᵊn/ noun [C or U]

simplistic /sɪmˈplɪs.tɪk/ adj disapproving making something complicated seem simple by ignoring important parts of it

simply /ˈsɪm.pli/ adv IMPORTANT ▷ **1** B2 completely or as much as possible: *You look simply (= really) beautiful in that dress.* ◦ *The hunger in parts of Africa is terrible – there's* ***(quite)*** *simply (= without doubt) no other word for it.* **2** B2 only: *I don't like my job – I simply do it for the money.* EASY ▷ **3** B2 in an easy way: *He explained it as simply as he could, but the class still didn't understand.* PLAIN ▷ **4** in a plain way: *a simply decorated apartment*

simulacrum /ˌsɪm.jʊˈleɪ.krəm/ noun [C] (plural **simulacrums** or **simulacra**) formal something that looks like or represents something else

simulate /ˈsɪm.jʊ.leɪt/ verb [T] to do or make something which looks real but is not real: *In cheap furniture, plastic is often used to simulate wood.* ◦ formal *Ruth simulated pleasure at seeing Simon, but really she wished he hadn't come.* ◦ *Some driving teachers use computers to simulate (= represent) different road conditions for learners to practise on.* • **simulated** /-leɪ.tɪd/ US /-leɪ.t̬ɪd/ adj

simulation /ˌsɪm.jʊˈleɪ.ʃᵊn/ noun [C or U] C1 a model of a set of problems or events that can be used to teach someone how to do something, or the process of making such a model: *The manager prepared a computer simulation* ***of*** *likely sales performance for the rest of the year.*

simulator /ˈsɪm.jʊ.leɪ.təʳ/ US /-t̬ɚ/ noun [C] a piece of equipment that is designed to represent real conditions, for example in an aircraft or spacecraft: *People learning to fly often practise on a* ***flight*** *simulator.*

simulcast /ˈsɪm.ᵊl.kɑːst/ US /ˈsaɪ.mᵊl.kæst/ noun [C]

mainly US a broadcast on radio and television of the same programme at the same time

simultaneous /ˌsɪm.əlˈteɪ.ni.əs/ (US) /ˌsaɪ.məl-/ **adj** C1 happening or being done at exactly the same time: *There were several simultaneous explosions in different cities.* • **simultaneously** /-li/ **adv** B2 *Two children answered the teacher's question simultaneously.* • **simultaneousness** /-nəs/ **noun** [U] (also **simultaneity** /-təˈneɪ.ə.ti/ (US) /-təˈniː.ə.t̬i/)

sin /sɪn/ **noun; verb**

▸**noun** [C or U] C2 the offence of breaking, or the breaking of, a religious or moral law: *to **commit/confess** a sin* ◦ *He thinks a lot about sin.* ◦ [+ to infinitive] informal *I think **it's** a sin (= is morally wrong) **to** waste food, when so many people in the world are hungry.* ◦ humorous *For my sins (= as if it were a punishment), I'm organizing the office party this year.* • **sinless** /-ləs/ **adj**

IDIOM **as guilty/miserable/ugly as sin** informal very guilty, miserable or ugly

▸written abbreviation for **sine**

▸**verb** [I] (**-nn-**) to break a religious or moral law • **sinner** /ˈsɪn.əʳ/ (US) /-ɚ/ **noun** [C]

ˈsin bin **noun** [C] UK informal in some sports, an area off the field where a player who has done something that is against the rules can be sent • **ˈsin-bin verb** [T usually passive] (plural **-nn-**) to send a player to the sin bin: *Thomas was sin-binned for a professional foul.*

since /sɪns/ **adv; preposition; conjunction**

▸**adv** B2 from a particular time in the past until a later time, or until now: *Emma went to work in New York a year ago, and we haven't seen her since.* ◦ *He started working for the company when he left school, and has been there **ever** since (= and is still there).* ◦ *I've **long** since (= long ago) forgotten any Latin I ever learned.*

> **! Common mistake: since, from, or for?**
>
> **Remember:** To talk about when something began and ended, don't say 'since', say **from**:
>
> ~~*He worked for that company since 1998 to 2006.*~~
>
> *He worked for that company from 1998 to 2006.*
>
> To talk about something that has happened from a particular date, use **since**, but to talk about a general period of time use **for**:
>
> ~~*They have been in England since two years.*~~
>
> *They have been in England for two years.*
>
> *I have lived here since 1993.*

▸**preposition** A2 from a particular time in the past until a later time, or until now: *England have not won the World Cup in football since 1966.* ◦ *It was the hottest October since records began.*

▸**conjunction** **BECAUSE** ▷ **1** B1 because; as: *Since we've got a few minutes to wait for the train, let's have a cup of coffee.* **TIME** ▷ **2** B1 from a particular time in the past until a later time, or until now: *I've been very busy since I came back from holiday.*

sincere /sɪnˈsɪəʳ/ (US) /-ˈsɪr/ **adj** C1 (of a person, feelings, or behaviour) not pretending or lying; honest: *a sincere apology* ◦ *He seems so sincere.* → Opposite **insincere**

sincerely /sɪnˈsɪə.li/ (US) /-ˈsɪr-/ **adv** **1** honestly and without pretending or lying: *I'm sincerely grateful.* **2** **(yours) sincerely** B1 (US also **Sincerely yours**) used to end a formal letter that is sent to a particular person

sincerity /sɪnˈser.ɪ.ti/ (US) /-ə.t̬i/ **noun** [U] C2 honesty: *The priest was a man of deep sincerity.*

sine /saɪn/ **noun** [C] (written abbreviation **sin**) (in a triangle that has one angle of 90°) the RATIO of the length of the side opposite an angle less than 90° divided by the length of the HYPOTENUSE (= the side opposite the 90° angle) → Compare **cosine, tangent**

> **+ Other ways of saying sincere**
>
> See also: **honest**
>
> An alternative to 'sincere' is **genuine**:
>
> *His surprise was perfectly **genuine**.*
>
> *He's a very **genuine** person.*
>
> **True** or **real** can be used about feelings which are sincere:
>
> *He showed **true** concern for his students.*
>
> *She didn't show any **real** regret for what she had done.*
>
> If a feeling is strong and sincere, you could use the adjective **heartfelt**:
>
> *His **heartfelt** desire is to end world hunger.*

> **! Common mistake: sincerely**
>
> **Warning:** Check your spelling!
>
> **Sincerely** is one of the 50 words most often spelled wrongly by learners.

> **! Common mistake: sincerely**
>
> **Remember:** a formal letter should end with **Yours sincerely** or **Yours faithfully**.
>
> If the letter begins with 'Dear Sir' or 'Dear Madam', don't write 'Yours sincerely', write **Yours faithfully**.

sinecure /ˈsɪn.ɪ.kjʊəʳ/ (US) /ˈsaɪ.nə.kjʊr/ **noun** [C] disapproving a position which involves little work, but for which the person is paid

ˌsine qua ˈnon **noun** [S] formal a necessary condition without which something is not possible: *An interest in children is a sine qua non **of** teaching.*

sinew /ˈsɪn.juː/ **noun** **1** [C] a TENDON (= strong piece of tissue in the body connecting a muscle to a bone) **2** [C usually plural] a part of a structure or system that provides support and holds it together: *These steel posts form the sinews of the building.*

sinewy /ˈsɪn.juː.i/ **adj** with strong muscles and little fat: *The fighter had a strong, sinewy body.*

sinful /ˈsɪn.fəl/ **adj** **1** against the rules of a religion or morally wrong: *He confessed that he had sinful thoughts.* ◦ *Buying that sports car was a sinful waste of money.* **2** informal describes something that is very pleasant, but very bad for you: *This cream cake is sinful!* • **sinfully** /-i/ **adv** • **sinfulness** /-nəs/ **noun** [U]

sing /sɪŋ/ **verb; noun, adj**

▸**verb** (**sang, sung**) **MAKE MUSIC** ▷ **1** A1 [I or T] to make musical sounds with the voice, usually a tune with words: *The children sang two songs by Schubert at the school concert.* ◦ *We were woken early by the sound of the birds singing.* ◦ *Your grandmother would like you to sing **for/to** her.* ◦ [+ two objects] *Will you sing us a song/sing a song **to** us?* ◦ *She sang her baby **to sleep** every night.* ◦ *Pavarotti is singing Rodolfo (= singing the part of Rodolfo) in 'La Bohème' at La Scala this week.* ◦ *Please sing **up** (US **out**) (= sing louder).* **RING** ▷ **2** [I] to make or be filled with a (high) ringing sound: *A bullet sang **past** the top of the soldier's head.* • **singing** /ˈsɪŋ.ɪŋ/ **noun** [U]

IDIOMS **sing for your supper** old-fashioned to do something for someone else in order to receive something in return, especially food: *Dan's upstairs fixing my computer – I'm making him sing for his*

S

supper. • **sing the praises of sb/sth** to praise someone or something

PHRASAL VERB **sing along** to sing a piece of music while someone else is singing or playing it: *The radio station played a Billy Joel song, and I found myself singing along* ***to*** *it.*

▸noun, adj abbreviation for singular

singalong /ˈsɪŋ.ə.lɒŋ/ ⓊⓈ /-lɑːŋ/ **noun** [C usually singular] US for **singsong**

singe /sɪndʒ/ **verb; noun**

▸verb [I or T] (past tense and past participle **singeing**) to burn slightly on the surface, without producing flames: *My jumper started to singe when I leaned over a burning candle.*

▸noun [C] a slight burn mark: *The hot iron left a singe (**mark**) on my dress.*

singer /ˈsɪŋ.əʳ/ ⓊⓈ /-ɚ/ **noun** [C] A2 a person who sings: *Kiri Te Kanawa is a famous singer from New Zealand.*

single /ˈsɪŋ.ɡl̩/ **adj; verb; noun**

▸adj **ONE** ▷ **1** B2 [before noun] one only: *He knocked his opponent down with a single blow.* ◦ ***Not a*** *single person offered to help her.* ◦ *You haven't been listening to a single word I've been saying.* → Compare **double** **NOT MARRIED** ▷ **2** A2 not married, or not having a romantic relationship with someone: *a single woman/man/person* ◦ *He's been single for so long now, I don't think he'll ever marry.* ◦ *The number of single-parent* ***families*** *dependent on the state has risen enormously in recent years.* **SEPARATE** ▷ **3** B1 [before noun] considered on its own and separate from other things: *Patience is the single most important quality needed for this job.* ◦ *She lost every single thing when her house burned down.*

▸verb [I] A baseball player singles by hitting a ball that allows him to reach first base.

PHRASAL VERB **single sb/sth out** to choose one person or thing from a group for special attention, especially criticism or praise: *It's not fair the way my sister is always singled out* ***for*** *special treatment.*

▸noun [C] **1** a record or CD that has only one main song on it: *Have you heard Lady Gaga's new single?* **2** in cricket, one RUN (= point) **3** in baseball, a hit that allows the player to reach first base **4 singles** [U] a game, especially in tennis, played between one player on one side and one on the other → Compare **double** **5 singles** [plural] people who are not married and do not have a romantic relationship with someone **6 single (ticket)** B1 UK a ticket for a journey to a place, but not for the return: *May I have a single to London, please.* **7** a **single room**

S

ˌsingle ˈbed noun [C] A2 a bed for one person

ˌsingle-ˈbreasted adj [before noun] describes a jacket or coat that fastens in the centre, with only one row of buttons: *a single-breasted coat/jacket/suit*

ˌsingle ˈcombat noun [U] fighting between two people, usually with weapons: *The two soldiers met (= fought each other)* ***in*** *single combat.*

ˌsingle ˈcream noun [U] UK (US **ˈlight ˌcream**) a type of thin cream

single-decker /ˌsɪŋ.ɡl̩ˈdek.əʳ/ ⓊⓈ /-ɚ/ **noun** [C] a bus or other vehicle that has only one level

ˌsingle ˈfile noun [S] a way of walking with one person behind another: *The schoolchildren were told to walk* ***in*** *single file.*

ˌsingle-ˈhanded adj without any help from anyone else: *a single-handed voyage* • **single-handedly** /-li/ **adv**

ˌsingle-ˈminded adj very determined to achieve something: *She had a single-minded will to win.* • **single-mindedly** /-li/ **adv** • **single-mindedness** /-nəs/ **noun** [U]

singleness /ˈsɪŋ.ɡl̩.nəs/ **noun** **singleness of mind/purpose** attention to one thing: *He showed great singleness of mind in dealing with the problem.*

ˌsingle ˈparent noun [C] (also UK **ˌlone ˈparent**) B1 someone who has a child or children but no husband, wife, or partner who lives with them

ˌsingle ˈroom noun [C] (also **single**) A2 a room in a hotel for one person: *I'd like a single room, please.*

ˈsingles ˌbar noun [C] a bar where single people (= people with no partner) go to meet other single people

ˌsingle-ˈsex adj [before noun] describes a school that is for either girls or boys, but not both: *I went to a single-sex school.*

singlet /ˈsɪŋ.ɡlət/ **noun** [C] **1** mainly UK a piece of clothing without sleeves that is worn on the top part of the body under clothes, or for playing particular sports **2** Australian English a type of underwear, often with no sleeves, that covers the upper part of the body and is worn for extra warmth → Compare **vest**

singleton /ˈsɪŋ.ɡl̩.tən/ **noun** [C] humorous a man or woman who does not have a romantic or sexual partner

singly /ˈsɪŋ.ɡli/ **adv** one at a time: *Doctors usually see their patients singly.*

singsong /ˈsɪŋ.sɒŋ/ ⓊⓈ /-sɑːŋ/ **noun** **MUSICAL VOICE** ▷ **1** [S] a voice rising and falling in level: *She spoke in* ***a*** *singsong.* **SINGING** ▷ **2** [C] UK (US **singalong**) the informal singing of songs by a group of people: *It's nice to have a good old-fashioned singsong now and again.* • **singsong adj** [before noun] *a singsong voice*

singular /ˈsɪŋ.ɡjʊ.ləʳ/ ⓊⓈ /-lɚ/ **adj; noun**

▸adj **GRAMMAR** ▷ **1** A2 of or relating to the form of a word used when talking or writing about one thing: *a singular ending/form/noun/verb* ◦ *The word 'woman' is singular.* **NOTICEABLE** ▷ **2** [before noun] formal of an unusual quality or standard; noticeable: *It was a building of singular grace and beauty.* ◦ *He showed a singular lack of skill in painting.* **STRANGE** ▷ **3** formal unusual or strange; not ordinary

▸noun [S] A2 the form of a word used when talking or writing about one thing: *The singular* ***of*** *'children' is 'child'.* ◦ *The word 'teeth' is plural –* ***in*** *the singular it's 'tooth'.*

singularly /ˈsɪŋ.ɡjʊ.lə.li/ ⓊⓈ /-lɚ-/ **adv** **NOTICEABLE** ▷ **1** to an unusual degree: *singularly beautiful* ◦ *a singularly unattractive individual* **STRANGE** ▷ **2** formal strangely

sinister /ˈsɪn.ɪ.stəʳ/ ⓊⓈ /-stɚ/ **adj** making you feel that something bad or evil might happen: *The ruined house had a sinister appearance.* ◦ *A sinister-looking man sat in the corner of the room.*

sink /sɪŋk/ **verb; noun**

▸verb (**sank** or US also **sunk**, **sunk**) **GO DOWN BELOW** ▷ **1** B1 [I or T] to (cause something or someone to) go down below the surface or to the bottom of a liquid or soft substance: *The Titanic was a passenger ship which sank (**to the bottom of the ocean**) in 1912.* ◦ *The legs of the garden chair sank* ***into*** *the soft ground.* ◦ *Enemy aircraft sank two battleships.* ◦ *The dog sank her teeth* ***into*** *(= bit) the ball and ran off with it.* → See also **sunken** **FALL** ▷ **2** B2 [I] to (cause something or someone to) fall or move to a lower level: *The sun glowed red as it sank slowly below the horizon.* ◦ *Student numbers have sunk considerably this year.* ◦ informal *We sank (= drank) a bottle of wine each last* night. ◦ *The wounded soldier sank (= fell)* ***to*** *the ground.* ◦ *He sank* ***into*** *deep despair (= became very unhappy) when he lost his job.* **3** [T] to hit a ball into a hole or pocket, especially in GOLF or SNOOKER **DIG** ▷ **4** [T] to dig a hole in the ground, or to put something into a hole dug into the ground: *Sinking more wells is the best way of supplying the population with clean drinking water.* ◦ *The first stage of building the fence is sinking the posts* ***into*** *the ground.* → See also **sunken FAILURE** ▷ **5** [T] to cause something to fail or be in trouble: *This rain could sink our plans for the garden party.*

IDIOMS **sink your differences** UK to forget your disagreements: *Paul and Mark agreed to sink their differences and be friends.* • **sink like a stone** (also **sink like a lead balloon**) to attract no support, attention, or interest: *My suggestion that we all play tennis sank like a stone.* • **sink or swim** If someone leaves you to sink or swim, they give you no help so that you succeed or fail completely by your own efforts: *My employer gave me no help when I started my new job – I was just* ***left to*** *sink or swim.* • **sink to a whisper** to become very quiet: *The child's voice sank to a whisper as she admitted that she had broken the window.* • **sink to such a level/such depths** (also **sink so low**) to do something so bad: *I can't believe you would sink so low as to snitch on your best friends.* • **sink without (a) trace** informal to be forgotten about completely, or to not attract any attention or interest: *Since his last book five years ago, he seems to have sunk without trace.* ◦ *Her second symphony sank without a trace.* • **sinking fast** (of a person's health) getting much worse quickly so that death is likely: *Mrs Jones is sinking fast, and the doctor doesn't think she'll live much longer.* • **sinking feeling** a feeling that something bad is going to happen: *When I woke up this morning, I had a sinking feeling that it was going to be a difficult day.* • **sinking ship** a company or other organization that is failing: *He'd seen the accounts, realized he was on a sinking ship, and decided to get off.* • **sunk in thought** UK thinking deeply: *Rodin's sculpture 'The Thinker' is of a man sitting with his head in his hand, sunk in thought.*

PHRASAL VERBS **sink in** informal If an unpleasant or surprising fact or idea sinks in, you gradually start to believe it, understand it, or realize the effect it will have on you: *How many times do I have to tell you something before it sinks in?* ◦ *His voice trailed off as the seriousness of his position sank in.* • **sink in/sink into sth** If a liquid or soft substance sinks into something solid, it gradually passes into it through its surface: *You'd better wipe up that coffee you spilled on the carpet before it sinks in.* • **sink into sth** to slowly move your body into a sitting or lying position, in a relaxed or tired way: *I was so tired when I got home that all I wanted to do was sink into bed/an armchair/a hot bath.* • **sink sth into sth** to spend a large amount of money on a business or other piece of work: *We sank all our money into my brother's business.*

▸**noun** [C] A2 a bowl that is fixed to the wall in a kitchen or bathroom in which you wash dishes or your hands, etc.: *a bathroom/kitchen sink*

sinker /ˈsɪŋ.kəʳ/ US /-kɚ/ **noun** [C] a weight fixed to a fishing net or line to keep it under the water

ˈsinking ˌfund noun [C] specialized money saved by a company or government for the payment of future debts

ˈsink ˌunit noun [C] a piece of kitchen furniture into which a sink is fitted

Sinn Fein /ˌʃɪnˈfeɪn/ **noun** [+ sing/pl verb] an Irish political party that wants Northern Ireland to become part of the Republic of Ireland

Sino- /saɪ.nəʊ-/ US /-noʊ-/ **prefix** of or connected with China: *Sino-Cuban trade relations*

sinology /saɪˈnɒl.ə.dʒi/ US /-ˈnɑː.lə-/ **noun** [U] the study of Chinese language, literature, history, society, etc. • **sinologist** /-dʒɪst/ **noun** [C]

ˈsin ˌtax noun [C usually singular] US informal a tax on things such as cigarettes, alcohol, GAMBLING, and other things that are considered unnecessary in life

sinuous /ˈsɪn.ju.əs/ **adj** literary moving in a twisting, curving, or INDIRECT way, or having many curves: *He enjoyed watching the sinuous bodies of the dancers.* • **sinuously** /-li/ **adv**

sinus /ˈsaɪ.nəs/ **noun** [C] any of the spaces inside the head that are connected to the back of the nose

sip /sɪp/ **verb** [I or T] **(-pp-)** C1 to drink, taking only a very small amount at a time: *This tea is very hot, so sip it carefully.* ◦ *She slowly sipped* **(at)** *her wine.* • **sip noun** [C]

siphon /ˈsaɪ.fᵊn/ **noun; verb**

▸**noun** [C] (also **syphon**) **1** a tube that is bent in the shape of an 'n', with each end in a separate container at two different levels, so that liquid can be pulled up into it from the higher container and go down through it into the lower container **2** a **soda siphon**

▸**verb** [T usually + adv/prep] (also **syphon**) to remove liquid from a container using a siphon

PHRASAL VERB **siphon sth off** (also **syphon sth off**) to dishonestly take money from an organization or other supply, and use it for a purpose for which it was not intended: *He lost his job when it was discovered that he had been siphoning off money from the company for his own use.*

sir /sɜːʳ/ US /sɝː/ **noun** [as form of address] (also **Sir**) formal **1** B1 used as a formal and polite way of speaking to a man, especially one who you are providing a service to or who is in a position of authority: *Would you like to see the menu, sir?* ◦ *'Did you hear what I said?' 'Yes, Sir.'* → Compare **madam, Miss, Ms 2** mainly UK sometimes used by children to address or refer to teachers who are men: *Can I go to the toilet, sir?* **3** Indian English used after the name of a man, especially one who is in a position of authority, in order to be polite or show respect: *John Sir* **4 Dear Sir** B2 used to begin a formal letter to a man whose name you do not know. 'Dear Sirs' is an old fashioned way of beginning a letter to a company. **5 Dear Sir or Madam** used to begin a formal letter when you do not know if the person you are writing to is a man or a woman

IDIOM **no sir** US informal certainly not: *I'm not going to ride the subway, no sir!*

Sir strong /sɜːʳ/ US /sɝː/ weak /səʳ/ US /sɚ/ **noun** used as the title of a KNIGHT (= a man who has been given a rank of honour by a British king or queen), with a first name or with both first and family names, but never with just the family name: *Sir Walter (Scott)*

sire /saɪəʳ/ US /saɪr/ **noun; verb**

▸**noun** [C] **FATHER** ▷ **1** a male parent of an animal, especially a horse **KING** ▷ **2** old use used as a form of address to a king: *I will serve you always, sire.*

▸**verb** [T] to become the male parent of an animal or the father of a child: *The foal was sired by a cup-winning racehorse.* ◦ old use or humorous *At the age of 70, he married a much younger woman and went on to sire two more children.*

siren /ˈsaɪə.rən/ US /ˈsaɪr.ən/ **noun** [C] **DEVICE** ▷ **1** C2 a device for making a loud warning noise: *police sirens* ◦ *When the air raid siren went off people ran to*

S

their shelters. **WOMAN** ▷ **2** (in ancient Greek literature) one of the creatures who were half woman and half bird, whose beautiful singing encouraged sailors to sail into dangerous waters where they died **3** a woman who is considered to be very attractive, but also dangerous

sirloin (steak) /ˌsɜː.lɔɪnˈsteɪk/ (US) /ˌsɝː-/ **noun** [C or U] the best meat from the lower back of a cow

sirocco (plural **siroccos**) (also **scirocco**) /sɪˈrɒk.əʊ/ (US) /-ˈrɑː.koʊ/ **noun** [C] a hot wind which blows from the Sahara Desert to southern Europe

sis /sɪs/ **noun** [C] informal a sister

sisal /ˈsaɪ.səl/ (US) /ˈsɪs.əl/ /ˈsaɪ-/ **noun** [U] (a tropical plant whose leaves produce) strong threads that are used for making rope and floor coverings

sissy /ˈsɪs.i/ **noun** [C] (also **cissy**) informal disapproving a boy who other boys dislike and laugh at because they think he is weak or interested in activities girls usually like, or a person who is weak and COWARDLY (= not brave): *Kevin is such a sissy.* ◦ [as form of address] *Can't you climb that tree, you big sissy?* • **sissy adj**

sister /ˈsɪs.tər/ (US) /-tɚ/ **noun; adj**

▸**noun** [C] **1** (A1) a girl or woman who has the same parents as another person: *Sophie and Emily are sisters.* ◦ *Emily is Sophie's younger/little/older/big sister.* **2** a girl or woman who treats you in the kind way that a sister would: *Lynn's such a good friend – she's **like a** sister **to** me.* **3** a woman who shares an interest with you, especially that of improving women's rights: [as form of address] *'We must continue the fight, sisters!'* **4** US old-fashioned informal used to address a woman: [as form of address] *OK, sister, move it!* **5** UK a nurse who is in charge of a department of a hospital: *The sister told us that visiting hours were over.* ◦ [as form of address] *Excuse me, Sister, could I have some water?* **6** a female member of a religious group, especially a NUN: *Sister Bernadette* ◦ [as form of address] *God bless you, Sister.*

▸**adj** [before noun] belonging to a pair or group of similar and related things, such as businesses, usually owned or operated by the same person or organization: *our sister **company** in Australia* ◦ *the US battleship Missouri and her sister **ship**, the Wisconsin*

sisterhood /ˈsɪs.tə.hʊd/ (US) /-tɚ-/ **noun 1** [U] a strong feeling of friendship and support among women who are involved in action to improve women's rights **2** [C, + sing/pl verb] a society of women living a religious life **3 the sisterhood** [+ sing/pl verb] women involved in action to improve women's rights

S

ˈsister-in-law noun [C] (plural **sisters-in-law**) (B2) the wife of your brother or sister, or the sister of your husband or wife, or the wife of the brother or sister of your husband or wife

sisterly /ˈsɪs.təl.i/ (US) /-tɚ.li/ **adj** feeling or behaving like a sister: *I felt quite sisterly towards him, but I couldn't marry him.*

sit /sɪt/ **verb** (present tense **sitting**, past tense and past participle **sat**) **BE SEATED** ▷ **1** (A1) [I or T, usually + adv/prep] to (cause someone to) be in a position in which the lower part of the body is resting on a seat or other type of support, with the upper part of the body vertical: *to sit **at** a table/desk* ◦ *to sit **in** an armchair* ◦ *to sit **on** a chair/a horse/the ground* ◦ *He came and sat (**down**) next to me.* ◦ informal *Sit your**self down** and have a cup of tea.* ◦ *The child's father sat her (**down**) **on** a chair.* **2** [I usually + adv/prep] to be a model for a painter, photographer, etc.: *Monet's wife sat **for** him many times.* **3** [I] (of an animal such as a dog) to move into a position with its back legs bent and its tail end on the ground: *We're trying to train our dog to sit.* **4** [I usually + adv/prep] If a bird sits on its eggs, it covers them with its body to keep them warm before they HATCH. **POSITION** ▷ **5** [I usually + adv/prep] to stay in one place for a long time and not be used: *The encyclopedia sits **on** my shelf at home, gathering dust.* **6** [I usually + adv/prep] to be in a particular position: *The village sits **at/in** the bottom of a valley.* **7** [I usually + adv/prep] (of clothes) to fit someone in a particular way: *That coat sits very well **on** you.* **MEET** ▷ **8** [I] to hold an official meeting of a parliament, court, etc.: *The court will sit tomorrow morning.* ◦ *As an MP, I see much less of my family when Parliament is sitting.* **BE A MEMBER** ▷ **9** [I] to be a member of an official group: *I'm going to be sitting **on** the committee for one more year.* ◦ *Our member of Congress has sat **for** (= represented) this town for years.* ◦ US *All of the federal judges currently sitting (= in office) in Maryland hail from Baltimore.* **EXAM** ▷ **10** (B2) [T] mainly UK to take an exam: *After I've sat my exams, I'm going on holiday.* ◦ Australian English *I sat **for** my exams today.* **LOOK AFTER** ▷ **11** [I usually + adv/prep] to BABYSIT

IDIOMS **be sitting pretty** to be in a good situation, usually because you have a lot of money: *They bought their house while prices were low, so now they're sitting pretty.* • **sit at the feet of sb** to be a very admiring student of someone important • **sit in judgment on/over sb** mainly disapproving to make a judgment on someone especially when you have no right to do so: *I don't know why he thinks he can sit in judgment over us like that.* • **sit on your arse** UK (US **sit on your ass**) to do nothing, especially when you should be doing something • **sit on sb's stomach** informal Food that sits on your stomach makes you feel uncomfortably full. • **sit on the fence** to delay making a decision: *You can't sit on the fence any longer – you have decide whose side you're on.* • **sit right/well (with sb)** to be something that you agree or are pleased with: *Their decision/answer didn't sit well with the Board of Directors.* • **sit tight 1** to stay where you are: *You'd better sit tight and I'll call the doctor.* **2** mainly UK to refuse to change your mind: *My parents tried to persuade me not to go alone, but I sat tight.*

PHRASAL VERBS **sit around** (UK also **sit about**) to spend time sitting down and doing very little: *We sat around most of the evening, waiting for Jake and drinking beer.* • **sit back COMFORTABLE** ▷ **1** to sit comfortably with your back against the back of a chair **WAITING** ▷ **2** informal to wait for something to happen without making any effort to do anything yourself: *You can't just sit back **and** wait for job offers to come to you.* • **sit by** to fail to take action to stop something wrong from happening: *I can't just sit by **and watch** you waste all our money.* • **sit down** to move your body so that the lower part of it is resting on a seat or on the ground: *I sat down **on** the sofa next to Barbara.* • **sit down and do sth** to spend time discussing a problem in order to solve it or make a decision: *I think we should sit down and **talk** about this.* • **sit in COMPLAIN** ▷ **1** to go as a group into a public building and refuse to leave or to allow normal activities to continue there until a situation that you are complaining about is changed → See also **sit-in BE PRESENT** ▷ **2** to be present in a meeting or class, watching it but not taking part in it: *There will be a school inspector sitting in **on** your class this morning.* • **sit in for sb** to take the place of someone who would normally do a particular job or go to a particular meeting: *Mr Baker is ill today, so Miss Dixon is sitting in for him (**as** your teacher).* • **sit on sth** informal **DELAY** ▷ **1** to delay taking action about something: *The company has been sitting on my letter for weeks without dealing with my complaint.* **KEEP SECRET** ▷

2 mainly disapproving to prevent people from knowing a piece of information: *The government will presumably sit on the report until after the election.*

IDIOM **sit on your hands** to do nothing about a problem or a situation that needs dealing with: *Every day the crisis worsens and yet the government seems content to sit on its hands.*

• **sit on sb** informal to force someone to be silent or not to do something: *The boss is going to sit on him to make sure he says nothing.* • **sit sth out** ACTIVITY ▷ **1** to not take part in a physical activity such as a dance or a game, because you are tired or injured SITUATION ▷ **2** to wait for an unpleasant situation or event to finish, without leaving or taking some other action: *The government is prepared to sit out the strike rather than agree to union demands.* • **sit through sth** to stay until the end of an event such as a meeting or performance that is very long or boring: *We had to sit through two hours of speeches.* • **sit under sb** US to receive teaching from someone: *He sat under the most influential teacher in his field.* • **sit (sb) up** to move into a sitting position after you have been lying down, or to help someone else to do this: *Let me sit you up in the bed so you'll be more comfortable.* • **sit up** STRAIGHT ▷ **1** to sit with a straight back: *How many times do I have to tell you children to sit up* ***straight****?* STAY AWAKE ▷ **2** to stay awake and not go to bed although it is late: [+ -ing verb] *The book was so interesting that I sat up all night read****ing*** *it.* ◦ *I'll be late tonight, so don't sit up* ***for*** *(= wait for) me.* NOTICE ▷ **3** informal to show interest or surprise: *The news that he was getting married really made her sit up.*

IDIOM **sit up and take notice** informal to show interest or surprise: *She sat up and took notice when she heard he was getting married.*

sitar /ˈsɪt.ɑːʳ/ (US) /sɪˈtɑːr/ noun [C] a South Asian musical instrument with a round body, a long neck, and two sets of strings

sitcom /ˈsɪt.kɒm/ (US) /-kɑːm/ noun [C or U] a **situation comedy**

ˈsit-down adj; noun

▸adj [before noun] MEAL ▷ **1** describes a meal served to people who are sitting at a table: *We're having a sit-down meal at our wedding, rather than a buffet.* REFUSE TO WORK ▷ **2** describes a STRIKE in which workers refuse to leave their place of work until their employers have agreed to their demands: *The workers are holding a sit-down* ***strike****.*

▸noun [S] informal a short period of sitting in order to rest: *You look tired. Why don't you come and have a sit-down for a few minutes.*

site /saɪt/ noun; verb

▸noun [C] PLACE ▷ **1** B1 a place where something is, was, or will be built, or where something happened, is happening, or will happen: *a building site* ◦ *The council haven't yet chosen the site* ***for*** *the new hospital.* ◦ *This is the site* ***of*** *the accident.* **2 on site** C1 inside a factory, office building, etc.: *There are two restaurants on site.* ◦ *The office complex has an on-site nursery.* INTERNET ▷ **3** A2 a website

▸verb [T usually + adv/prep] formal to exist or be built in a particular place: *The company head office is sited in Rome.*

ˈsit-in noun [C] an occasion when a group of people go into a public building and refuse to leave or allow normal activities to continue there until a situation that they are complaining about is changed: *Students staged a sit-in in the university offices as part of their protest campaign.* → See also **sit in**

sitter /ˈsɪt.əʳ/ (US) /ˈsɪṭ.ɚ/ noun [C] **1** someone who is having their PORTRAIT (= picture of their face or body) painted **2** a **babysitter**

sitting /ˈsɪt.ɪŋ/ (US) /ˈsɪṭ-/ noun; adj

▸noun [C] BE SEATED ▷ **1** a period when a meal is served in a place like a hotel: *When the hotel is full, dinner is served in two sittings.* **2** a period spent by a model who is being painted, photographed, etc.: *The portrait was finished after only three sittings.* MEETING ▷ **3** a meeting of a parliament, court, etc.

IDIOM **at/in one sitting** during one limited period of time, without stopping: *I enjoyed the book so much that I read it all in one sitting.*

▸adj existing or continuing at the present time: *a sitting Member of Parliament.*

ˌsitting ˈduck someone or something that is very easy for an enemy to shoot or attack: *With their bullets all gone, the soldiers were sitting ducks for the enemy.*

ˌsitting ˈmember noun [C] UK formal the person who is the MEMBER OF PARLIAMENT for an area at the present time

ˈsitting ˌroom noun [C] A2 UK for **living room**

ˌsitting ˈtenant noun [C] a person with a legal right to stay in a property that they are renting: *We can't sell the house because we can't get rid of the sitting tenants.*

situate /ˈsɪt.ju.eɪt/ verb [T usually + adv/prep] formal to put something in a particular position: *They plan to situate the bus stop* ***at*** *the corner of the road.* ◦ *To understand this issue, it must first be situated* ***in*** *its context.*

situated /ˈsɪt.ju.eɪ.tɪd/ (US) /-ṭɪd/ adj [after verb] formal B1 in a particular position: *The school is situated near to the station.* ◦ [+ to infinitive] *With this new product, we are well situated* ***to*** *beat (= we have a good chance of beating) our competitors.*

situation /ˌsɪt.juˈeɪ.ʃən/ noun [C] **1** B1 the set of things that are happening and the conditions that exist at a particular time and place: *the economic/political situation* ◦ *Her news put me* ***in*** *a difficult situation.* ◦ *'Would you get involved in a fight?' 'It would* ***depend on the*** *situation.'* ◦ *I'll worry about it* ***if/when/as*** *the situation* ***arises*** *(= if/when/as it happens).* **2** old use a job: *My sister has a good situation* ***as*** *a teacher in the local school.* **3** formal the position of something, especially a town, building, etc.: *The house's situation in the river valley is perfect.*

> **Word partners for situation**
>
> a situation *arises* • *cope with/deal with/handle* a situation • *defuse/improve/remedy* a situation • *complicate/exacerbate* a situation • *create/lead to* a situation • *change* a situation • a situation *deteriorates/improves/worsens* • the *current/present* situation • a *difficult/dangerous/intolerable/stressful* situation • *in* a situation

situˌation ˈcomedy noun [C or U] (informal **sitcom**) a funny television or radio show in which the same characters appear in each programme in a different story

Situˌations ˈVacant noun [S or U] UK the part of a newspaper in which jobs are listed

ˈsit-up noun [C] a type of exercise in which someone sits up from a lying position, designed to make the ABDOMINAL muscles stronger

SI unit /ˌesˈaɪ.juː.nɪt/ noun [C] specialized a unit of measurement that is part of a system used for scientific and technical work all over the world: *The SI unit of length is the metre.*

S

six /sɪks/ **number; noun**
▸**number** A1 the number 6: *Look for a bus with a number six on the front of it.* ◦ *'How many grandchildren do you have now?' 'I've got six.'*

IDIOMS **at sixes and sevens** informal in a confused, badly organized, or difficult situation: *We've been at sixes and sevens in the office this week.* • **be six feet under** humorous to be dead and buried: *There's no point worrying about it – we'll both be six feet under by then.* • **six of one and half a dozen of the other** informal said when you think that neither of two choices is better than the other: *'Shall we go by car or train?' 'I don't know, it's six of one and half a dozen of the other.'* • **six of the best** UK old-fashioned a beating, usually of six hits with a stick

▸**noun** [C] in cricket, six RUNS (= points) scored when the player hits the ball to the edge of the playing area without it touching the ground first: *Richards hit a six.*

ˌsix-ˈfooter noun [C] informal a person who is at least six feet (1.83 metres) tall

ˈsix-pack noun [C] **1** informal six containers, usually bottles or CANS, of a particular type of beer or other drink that are sold together as one unit **2** humorous the well-developed muscles of a man's stomach

sixpence /ˈsɪks.pəns/ noun [C or U] a small silver-coloured coin used in Britain until 1971 which was worth six old PENNIES, or this amount of money

sixpenny /ˈsɪks.pən.i/ adj [before noun] worth or costing sixpence: *a sixpenny bit*

ˈsix-shooter noun [C] a small gun that holds six bullets

sixteen /ˌsɪkˈstiːn/ **number** A1 the number 16: *We've got sixteen (people) coming for lunch.* ◦ *He left school at sixteen (= when he was 16 years old).*

sixteenth /ˌsɪkˈstiːnθ/ **ordinal number** 16th written as a word: *Their anniversary is on **the** sixteenth (**of** June).*

sixˈteenth ˌnote noun [C] US for **semiquaver**

sixth /sɪksθ/ **ordinal number; noun**
▸**ordinal number** A2 6th written as a word: *I have to return my library books on **the** sixth (**of** July).* ◦ *England **were/came** sixth in the 100 metres.*
▸**noun** [C] one of six equal parts of something: *Cut the cake into sixths.*

ˈsixth ˌform noun [C] in Britain, the part of a school for students aged 16-18: *The sixth-form students are preparing to take their A levels.*

S

ˈsixth-ˌformer noun [C] a student in the sixth form

ˌsixth ˈsense noun [S] an ability that some people believe they have that seems to give them information without using the five senses of sight, hearing, touch, smell, or taste: *A sixth sense told me that the train was going to crash.*

sixties /ˈsɪk.stiz/ noun [plural] **1** A person's sixties are the period in which they are aged between 60 and 69: *Many people retire **in** their sixties.* **2 the sixties a** the range of temperature between 60° and 69° FAHRENHEIT: *The temperature is usually **in** the sixties at this time of year.* **b** B2 the DECADE (= period of ten years) between 60 and 69 in any century, usually 1960–1969: *The Beatles made their first hit records **in** the sixties.*

sixtieth /ˈsɪk.sti.əθ/ **ordinal number** 60th written as a word

sixty /ˈsɪk.sti/ **number** A2 the number 60: *fifty-nine, sixty, sixty-one* ◦ *She plans to retire at sixty (= when she is 60 years old).*

size /saɪz/ **noun; verb**
▸**noun** **AMOUNT** ▷ **1** A2 [C or U] how large or small something or someone is: *We are concerned about the size of our debt.* ◦ *Some kinds of trees grow to a huge size.* ◦ *What is the size of that window?* ◦ *The field was about ten acres **in** size.* ◦ *He had a lump on his head the size **of** (= the same size as) an egg.* ◦ *The baby is **a good** size (= quite large).* ◦ *I was amazed at the size of their garden (= it was very big).* **MEASURE** ▷ **2** A2 [C] one of the standard measures according to which goods are made or sold: *a size 14 dress* ◦ *Do these shoes come (= are they made) **in** children's sizes?* ◦ *What size are you?/What is your size?/What size do you **take**?* ◦ *Would you like to **try** the coat (**on**) **for** size (= see how well it fits you), sir?* ◦ *We'll need to get the carpet cut **to** size (= cut so that it fits).* **GLUE** ▷ **3** [U] specialized a substance like glue which gives stiffness and a hard, shiny surface to cloth, paper, etc.

> Word partners for **size** (**AMOUNT**)
>
> *vary in* size • *double/increase/reduce* the size of sth • a *good* size • the *sheer* size of sth • the size *of* sth

> Word partners for **size** (**MEASURE**)
>
> *take/wear* a size [10, 37, etc.] • *try* sth *on for* size • *cut* sth *to* size • *come in* [all/different/various] sizes • a *large/medium/small* size • *different/various/varying* sizes

IDIOM **that's about the size of it** informal used to show your agreement with someone who has said something correct: *'So you mean you won't come to the party with me?' 'Yes, that's about the size of it.'*

▸**verb** [T] to cover or treat cloth, paper, etc. with size

PHRASAL VERB **size sth/sb up** to examine something or someone carefully and decide what you think about them: *We must size up the situation before we decide what to do.* ◦ *The two cats walked in circles around each other, sizing each other up.*

sizeable mainly UK (mainly US **sizable**) /ˈsaɪ.zə.bl/ adj large: *a sizeable amount/area/house*

-sized /-saɪzd/ suffix of the size mentioned: *a good-sized (= large) garden* ◦ *a pocket-sized mobile phone (= one small enough to fit into a pocket)*

sizzle /ˈsɪz.əl/ verb [I] to make a sound like food cooking in hot fat: *The sausages are sizzling in the pan.*

sizzler /ˈsɪz.ləʳ/ US /-lɚ/ noun [C] informal a very hot day

sizzling /ˈsɪz.l.ɪŋ/, /-lɪŋ/ adv (also **ˌsizzling ˈhot**) very hot: *It's a sizzling hot day today!*

skank /skæŋk/ noun [C] US slang disapproving an unpleasant person, especially a woman who has sex with a lot of different people

skanky /ˈskæŋ.ki/ adj informal **1** extremely unpleasant, especially because of being dirty: *I found a pair of his skanky underpants on the floor.* **2** US of low quality or not stylish: *I wouldn't be caught dead in that skanky outfit!*

skate /skeɪt/ **noun; verb**
▸**noun** **BOOT** ▷ **1** A2 [C] (plural **skates**) a special boot with a thin metal bar fixed to the bottom that you wear to move quickly on ice, or a boot with four small wheels fixed to the bottom so that you can move over a hard surface: *a pair of **ice** skates* ◦ *a pair of **roller** skates* **FISH** ▷ **2** [C or U] (plural **skate** or **skates**) a large, flat sea fish, which can be eaten as food

IDIOM **get/put your skates on** UK informal used when you want to tell someone to hurry up: *Get your skates on, or we'll be late.*

▸**verb** [I + adv/prep, T] B1 to move, or make a particular movement on a surface, using skates: *The ice on the river is thick enough to skate **on/across/over**.* ◦ *Shall we **go** skating tomorrow?*

IDIOM **be skating on thin ice** to be doing something that is dangerous or involves risks: *He's skating on thin ice by lying to the police.*

PHRASAL VERB **skate over/round/around sth** to avoid dealing completely with something or to fail to pay enough attention to it: *Providing homeless people with somewhere to stay when the weather is cold only skates round the problem, it doesn't solve it.* ◦ *I didn't understand what the teacher said about prepositions, because she only skated over it.*

skateboard /ˈskeɪt.bɔːd/ (US) /-bɔːrd/ noun [C] (A2) a flat narrow board with two small wheels under each end, which a person stands on and moves forward by pushing one foot on the ground • **skateboarder** /-ˌbɔː.dəʳ/ (US) /-ˌbɔːr.dɚ/ noun [C]

skateboarding /ˈskeɪtˌbɔː.dɪŋ/ (US) /-ˌbɔːr-/ noun [U] (A2) the activity or sport of riding a skateboard

skatepark /ˈskeɪt.pɑːk/ (US) /-pɑːrk/ noun [C] a place where people do skateboarding, IN-LINE SKATING, etc.

skater /ˈskeɪ.təʳ/ (US) /-t̬ɚ/ noun [C] a person on skates

skating /ˈskeɪ.tɪŋ/ (US) /-t̬ɪŋ/ noun [U] (A2) the activity or sport of moving on skates: *ice/roller skating*

ˈskating ˌrink noun [C] a specially prepared area for skating

skedaddle /skɪˈdæd.l̩/ verb [I] informal to run away quickly: *OK, children, skedaddle!*

skein /skeɪn/ noun [C] **THREAD** ▷ **1** a length of wool or thread collected together into the shape of a loose ring **BIRDS** ▷ **2** a large group of wild birds such as GEESE or DUCKS in flight

skeletal /ˈskel.ɪ.təl/ (US) /-t̬əl/ adj **1** of or like a skeleton (= frame of bones): *Her body was skeletal (= very thin).* ◦ *He suffered serious skeletal injuries in the accident.* **2** describes something that exists in its most basic form: *The newspaper report gave only a skeletal account of the debate.*

skeleton /ˈskel.ɪ.tən/ (US) /-t̬ən/ noun [C] **1** (B2) the frame of bones supporting a human or animal body: *We found an old sheep skeleton up on the cliffs.* ◦ figurative *Her long illness reduced her to a skeleton (= made her very thin).* **2** the most basic form or structure of something: *The skeleton **of** my book is written/My book is **in** skeleton **form** – now I just have to add the details.*

IDIOM **skeleton in the/your cupboard/closet** an embarrassing secret: *Most families **have** one or two skeletons in the cupboard.*

ˈskeleton ˌkey noun [C] a key which will open several doors

ˈskeleton ˌservice noun [S] (C1) the operation of something such as a transport system in an extremely limited way at certain times: *The local bus company only runs a skeleton service on Sundays.*

ˈskeleton ˌstaff noun [S] (also **ˌskeleton ˈcrew**) (C1) the smallest number of people needed for a business or organization to operate: *The hospital has a skeleton staff at weekends.*

skeptic /ˈskep.tɪk/ noun [C] US for **sceptic**

sketch /sketʃ/ noun; verb

▸noun [C] **SIMPLE SHAPE/FORM** ▷ **1** (C1) a simple, quickly-made drawing which does not have many details: *My mother made a (pencil) sketch **of** my brother reading a book.* **2** (C2) a short written or spoken story which does not have many details **HUMOROUS PERFORMANCE** ▷ **3** (C1) a short, humorous part of a longer show on stage, television, or radio: *I thought the sketch about Queen Victoria was very funny.*

▸verb [I or T] to make a sketch of something: *The art students were told to sketch the landscape.* ◦ *The artist has sketched **out** a design for the new school.*

PHRASAL VERB **sketch sth out** (C2) to give a short description of something, containing few details: *She sketched out the plan in a few brief sentences.*

sketcher /ˈsketʃ.əʳ/ (US) /-ɚ/ noun [C] someone who makes sketches (= drawings)

sketchpad /ˈsketʃ.pæd/ noun [C] (also **sketchbook**) a number of sheets of plain paper fixed together for drawing on

sketchy /ˈsketʃ.i/ adj containing few details: *So far we only have sketchy information about what caused the explosion.* • **sketchily** /-ɪ.li/ adv

skew /skjuː/ verb; adj

▸verb [T] to cause something to be not straight or exact; to twist or DISTORT: *The company's results for this year are skewed because not all our customers have paid their bills.*

▸adj [after verb] not straight

skewer /skjʊəʳ/ (US) /ˈskjuː.ɚ/ noun; verb

▸noun [C] a long, thin metal pin used for holding together pieces of food, especially meat, during cooking

▸verb [T] to put pieces of food, especially meat, on a skewer

ˌskew-ˈwhiff adj [after verb] UK informal sloping instead of straight, or wrongly positioned: *You've got your hat on skew-whiff.*

ski /skiː/ noun; verb

▸noun [C] (plural **skis**) (B1) one of a pair of long, flat, narrow pieces of wood or plastic, which curve up at the front, and are fastened to boots so that the wearer can move quickly and easily over snow: *a pair of skis* ◦ *ski boots* ◦ *a ski club/resort*

▸verb [I or T] (B1) to move over snow on skis: *He skied **down** the hill.* ◦ *Shall we **go** skiing?*

skibob /ˈskiː.bɒb/ (US) /-bɑːb/ noun [C] a vehicle like a bicycle with skis instead of wheels, used for races

skid /skɪd/ verb; noun

▸verb [I] (**-dd-**) (especially of a vehicle) to slide along a surface so that you have no control: *Trevor's bus skidded **on** some ice and hit a tree.*

▸noun [C] **1** a sliding movement that cannot be controlled: *She was riding too fast on a wet road, and the motorbike **went into a** skid.* **2** one of two long flat pieces under some aircraft such as HELICOPTERS, which help the aircraft to land

IDIOMS **on skid row** mainly US informal poor, without a job or a place to live, and often drinking too much alcohol • **on the skids** informal experiencing difficulties and unlikely to continue successfully: *Their marriage seems to be on the skids.* • **put the skids under sth** UK informal to cause something such as a plan to fail: *Local residents have put the skids under plans to build a new shopping centre.*

ˈskid ˌmarks noun [plural] black marks made by the tyres of a car when it starts or stops moving very quickly: *There were skid marks on the road where a car had braked suddenly.*

skidpan /ˈskɪd.pæn/ noun [C] UK a specially prepared surface on which drivers can practise controlling skids

skier /ˈskiː.əʳ/ (US) /-ɚ/ noun [C] a person who skis

S

skiff /skɪf/ **noun** [C] a small, light boat for ROWING or sailing, usually used by only one person

skiffle /ˈskɪf.l̩/ **noun** [U] a type of music popular in the 1950s that is a mixture of JAZZ and FOLK music, in which players often perform on instruments they have made themselves

skiing /ˈskiː.ɪŋ/ **noun** [U] A2 the activity or sport of moving on skis: *a skiing trip/instructor*

ˈski ˌjump **noun** [S or U] a competition in which people on skis move very fast down a specially made steep slope which turns up at the end, and jump off from the bottom of it, landing on a lower level

skilful UK (US **skillful**) /ˈskɪl.fəl/ **adj 1** B2 good at doing something, especially because you have practised doing it: *Police officers have to be skilful drivers.* **2** C1 done or made very well: *a skilful piece of playing on the clarinet*

Other ways of saying skilful

A common phrase which means the same as 'skilful' is **good at**:

*She's very **good at** dealing with people.*

If someone is skilful and seems to have a special natural ability you could describe that person as **able**, **gifted**, or **talented**:

*She's a very **able** student.*

*She's a **gifted** musician.*

*He's a very **talented** actor.*

Adept and **deft** are used when someone is very skilful and clever at doing something:

*Her movements were **deft** and quick.*

*She's very **adept** at dealing with all management issues.*

Accomplished means skilful, especially when talking about someone who writes, plays music, etc.:

*He's an **accomplished** pianist.*

Someone who is skilful because he or she has practised something a lot can be described as **competent** or **proficient**:

*She's a very **competent** skier.*

*He's a **proficient** horseback rider.*

skilfully UK (US **skillfully**) /ˈskɪl.fəl.i/ **adv** with great skill

ˈski ˌlift **noun** [C usually singular] a machine consisting of seats hanging down from a continuously moving wire, which carries people on skis to the top of slopes which they can then ski down

S

skill /skɪl/ **noun** [C or U] B1 an ability to do an activity or job well, especially because you have practised it: *Ruth **had/possessed** great writing skills.* ◦ *I have no skill **at/in** sewing.*

Word partners for skill

have/possess a skill • *acquire/develop/learn/master* a skill • *need/require* a skill • *basic/necessary/useful* skills • *new/special* skills • *considerable/consummate/great* skill • *level* of skill • skill *at/in* sth

skilled /skɪld/ **adj; noun**

▸**adj 1** B2 having the abilities needed to do an activity or job well: *My mother is very skilled **at/in** dressmaking.* **2** Skilled work needs someone who has had special training to do it: *Nursing is a highly skilled job.*

▸**noun** [plural] **the skilled** people who have been trained for a job

skillet /ˈskɪl.ɪt/ **noun** [C] US for **frying pan**

skim /skɪm/ **verb** (-mm-) **MOVE ABOVE** ▷ **1** [I or T] to move quickly just above a surface without touching it: *The birds skimmed (**across/along/over**) the tops of the waves.* **2** [T] UK (US **skip**) to throw a flat stone horizontally over water so that it touches and rises off the surface several times: *We watched a child skimming stones across the lake.* **CONSIDER QUICKLY** ▷ **3** [I or T] to read or consider something quickly in order to understand the main points, without studying it in detail: *I've only skimmed (**through/over**) his letter; I haven't read it carefully yet.* ◦ *We've only skimmed **the surface of** (= considered a small part of) the problem.* **REMOVE** ▷ **4** [T] to remove something solid from the surface of a liquid: *Strain the cooking liquid and skim **off** the **fat**.* **STEAL** ▷ **5** [T] to secretly use a piece of equipment that records someone's CREDIT CARD details when they are paying for something, in order to use their CREDIT CARD account illegally

PHRASAL VERB **skim sb/sth off** to choose the best people or things from a group: *We've skimmed off the six people who seem to be the most suitable for the job.*

ˌskimmed ˈmilk **noun** [U] UK (US **ˌskim ˈmilk**) milk from which the cream has been removed

ˌskim ˈmilk **noun** [U] **skimmed milk**

skimp /skɪmp/ **verb** [I or T] to not spend enough time or money on something, or to not use enough of something in order to do a job or activity as it should be done: *Many old people skimp **on** food and heating in order to meet their bills.* ◦ *When choosing an overseas package tour, do not skimp.*

skimpy /ˈskɪm.pi/ **adj 1** disapproving not large enough: *a skimpy meal* **2** Skimpy clothing shows a lot of your body: *a skimpy dress*

skin /skɪn/ **noun; verb**

▸**noun NATURAL COVERING** ▷ **1** B1 [C or U] the natural outer layer that covers a person, animal, fruit, etc.: *dark/fair/pale/tanned skin* ◦ *skin cancer* ◦ *Babies have soft skins.* ◦ *Native Americans used to trade skins (= the skins of animals that have been removed from the body, with or without the hair).* ◦ *a banana/potato skin* **OUTER COVERING** ▷ **2** [C or U] any outer covering: *The bullet pierced the skin of the aircraft.* **LIQUID** ▷ **3** [S] a thin surface which forms on some liquids, such as paint, when they are left in the air, or others, such as heated milk, when they are left to cool **COMPUTER** ▷ **4** [C] specialized the part of a computer program that you can change in order to make pictures, designs, colours, etc. look different on a screen: *Many electronic devices let you create your own skins.* **5 drenched/soaked/wet to the skin** extremely wet: *We had no umbrellas so we got soaked to the skin in the pouring rain.* **6 thin/thick skin** easily/not easily upset by criticism: *I don't worry about what he says – I **have** a very thick skin.* → See also **thick-skinned, thin-skinned** • **-skin** /-skɪn/ **suffix** *I've got an old sheepskin coat.* • **-skinned** /-d/ **suffix** *pale-skinned*

IDIOMS **be no skin off sb's nose** (US also **be no skin off sb's back/teeth**) used when you want to say that it makes no difference to you what someone else does or thinks: *It's no skin off my nose if you don't take my advice.* • **be skin and bone(s)** to be extremely thin: *She was (just) skin and bone(s).* • **by the skin of your teeth** If you do something by the skin of your teeth, you only just succeed in doing it: *He escaped from the secret police by the skin of his teeth.* • **get under sb's skin** to annoy someone: *Jack really gets under my skin – he never buys anyone a drink.* • **jump/leap out of your skin** to be extremely surprised by something: *The loud noise made me jump out of my skin.* • **make sb's skin crawl** If someone or something makes your skin crawl, you think they are very unpleasant or frightening: *Just thinking about the way he had touched her made her skin crawl.*

▸**verb** [T] (-nn-) to remove the skin of something: *The hunters skinned the deer they had killed.* ◦ *I skinned my knee (= hurt my knee by rubbing skin off it) when I fell down the steps.*

IDIOM **skin sb alive** informal humorous to punish or tell someone off severely

ˌskin-ˈdeep adj not carefully considered or strongly felt: *After the first half-hour she realized that her new-found confidence was no more than skin-deep.*

ˈskin ˌdiving noun [U] the activity of swimming underwater with only simple breathing equipment and without a special suit • **ˈskin-ˌdiver** noun [C]

ˈskin ˌflick noun [C] US slang a film that shows sexual acts in a way that is intended to cause sexual excitement but that would be considered unpleasant and offensive by many people

skinflint /ˈskɪn.flɪnt/ noun [C] informal disapproving a person who is unwilling to spend money: *He's a real skinflint.*

skinful /ˈskɪn.fʊl/ noun [S] slang an amount of alcohol that is enough to make a person drunk: *By ten o'clock he'd **had** a skinful.*

ˈskin ˌgraft noun [C] a piece of skin taken from one part of the body and used to replace damaged skin in another part

skinhead /ˈskɪn.hed/ noun [C] a young person, especially a man, who has very short hair or no hair and is part of a group, often a violent group

skink /skɪŋk/ noun [C] a small LIZARD found in various hot parts of the world

skinless /ˈskɪn.ləs/ adj without a skin: *skinless, boneless fillets of fish*

skinny /ˈskɪn.i/ adj **THIN** ▷ **1** mainly disapproving very thin: *You should eat more, you're much too skinny.* **FOOD AND DRINK** ▷ **2** US informal low in fat: *a skinny latte* **CLOTHES** ▷ **3** narrow and fitting closely to the body: *skinny jeans*

ˈskinny-dip verb [I] informal to swim while naked • **ˈskinny-ˌdipping** noun [U]

skint /skɪnt/ adj [after verb] UK slang having no money: *I get paid each Friday, and by Tuesday I'm always skint.*

skintight /ˈskɪn.taɪt/ adj describes clothes that fit tightly around the body: *skintight jeans*

skip /skɪp/ verb; noun

▸**verb** (-pp-) **MOVE** ▷ **1** [I usually + adv/prep] to move lightly and quickly, making a small jump after each step: *She watched her little granddaughter skip **down** the path.* ◦ *The lambs were skipping **about** in the field.* **JUMP** ▷ **2** [I] (US **jump rope**, **skip rope**) to jump lightly over a rope that is held in both your hands, or by two other people, and turned repeatedly under your legs and over your head as exercise or a game: *Sports players often train by skipping.* **LEAVE** ▷ **3** (C1) [I or T] to leave one thing or place, especially quickly, in order to go to another: *This part of the book isn't very interesting, so I'm going to skip (**over**) it.* ◦ *The teacher kept skipping **from** one subject **to** another so it was difficult to follow what he was saying.* ◦ *We're skipping **over/across/off** (= making a quick journey) to France for the day.* ◦ *The police think that the bank robbers must have skipped (= left) **the country** by now.* ◦ *She skipped **off/out** (= left quickly and/or secretly) without saying goodbye.* **AVOID** ▷ **4** (B2) [T] informal to not do or not have something that you usually do or that you should do; to avoid: *I'm trying to lose weight, so I'm skipping (= not eating) **lunch** today.*

▸**noun** [C] **CONTAINER** ▷ **1** UK (US trademark **Dumpster**) a large metal container into which people put unwanted objects or building or garden waste, and brought to and taken away from a place by a special truck when people ask for it **MOVE** ▷ **2** a small, light, dancing or jumping step: *She gave a little skip of joy.*

ˈski ˌpants noun [plural] tight trousers, usually for women, that are made from a material that stretches easily and are held firmly in place by a strap worn under each foot

ˈski ˌpole noun [C] (UK also **ˈski ˌstick**) one of two short pointed poles that are held one in each hand by someone on skis to help them balance

skipper /ˈskɪp.əʳ/ (US) /-ɚ/ noun; verb

▸**noun** [C] the CAPTAIN of a ship or boat, a sports team, or an aircraft: *John is (the) skipper **of** the cricket team this year.* ◦ [as form of address] *Ready to go, skipper.*

▸**verb** [T] to be the CAPTAIN of a boat, team, aircraft, etc.

ˈskipping ˌrope noun [C] (US also **ˈjump ˌrope**) a rope that is used for skipping

skipping rope

skirmish /ˈskɜː.mɪʃ/ (US) /ˈskɝː-/ noun [C] **1** a fight between a small number of soldiers that is usually short and not planned, and happens away from the main area of fighting in a war **2** a short argument: *There was a **short** skirmish **between** the political party leaders when the government announced it was to raise taxes.* • **skirmish** verb [I] • **skirmisher** /-əʳ/ (US) /-ɚ/ noun [C]

skirt /skɜːt/ (US) /skɝːt/ noun; verb

▸**noun** [C] **1** (A1) a piece of clothing for women and girls that hangs from the waist and does not have legs: *a long/short skirt* **2** an outer covering or part to protect particular machines

▸**verb** [T, I + prep] (also **skirt around/round**) **1** to go around the edge of something: *Take the road which skirts (round) the village, not the one which goes through it.* **2** to avoid discussing a subject or problem, usually because there are difficulties that you do not want to deal with

ˈskirting ˌboard noun [C or U] UK (US **baseboard**) a piece of wood fixed along the bottom of a wall where it meets the floor

skit /skɪt/ noun [C] a short, funny play which makes a joke of something: *I thought the skit **on** politicians was really funny.*

skitter /ˈskɪt.əʳ/ (US) /ˈskɪt̬.ɚ/ verb [I usually + adv/prep] (especially of a small animal, bird, or insect) to move very quickly and lightly: *When I lifted the log, there were lots of beetles skittering **about/around** under it.*

skittish /ˈskɪt.ɪʃ/ (US) /ˈskɪt̬-/ adj (of people and animals) nervous or easily frightened, or (of a person) not serious and likely to change their beliefs or opinions often: *My horse is rather skittish, so I have to keep him away from traffic.* ◦ *Investors are skittish **about** the impact of an economic downturn.* ◦ *Marilyn was a complete child, playful and skittish one moment, sulky and withdrawn the next.* • **skittishly** /-li/ adv • **skittishness** /-nəs/ noun [U]

skittle /ˈskɪt.l̩/ (US) /ˈskɪt̬-/ noun **1 skittles** [U] a game played especially in Britain in which players roll a ball at objects shaped like bottles to try to knock them down and score points **2** [C] one of a set of objects

S

shaped like bottles that are knocked down with a ball as part of a game

skive /skaɪv/ **verb** [I or T] UK informal to be absent from work or school without permission: *Tom and Mike have skived (**off**) school today to watch the football match.*

skiver /ˈskaɪ.vəʳ/ ⓤⓢ /-vɚ/ **noun** [C] UK informal a person who is absent from work without permission

skivvy /ˈskɪv.i/ **noun; verb**

▸**noun** SERVANT ▷ **1** [C] UK informal a person, in the past a female servant, who does the dirty and unpleasant jobs in a house, such as cleaning: *He treats me like a skivvy.* CLOTHING ▷ **2** [C] Australian English a tight-fitting piece of clothing for the top part of the body, made of KNITTED cotton, with a high, round collar **3 skivvies** [plural] US informal men's underwear

▸**verb** [I] UK informal to do the dirty, unpleasant jobs in the house: *I'm not going to skivvy **for** you any more.*

skol /skɒl/ ⓤⓢ /skɑːl/ **verb** [T] (-ll-) Australian English informal to drink something, especially beer, all at once without a pause

skua /ˈskjuː.ə/ **noun** [C] UK a type of large bird which lives in the North Atlantic and steals food from other birds

skulduggery UK (US **skullduggery**) /ˌskʌlˈdʌg.ər.i/ ⓤⓢ /-ɚ-/ **noun** [U] secret and dishonest behaviour

skulk /skʌlk/ **verb** [I usually + adv/prep] to hide or move around as if trying not to be seen, usually with bad intentions: *I thought I saw someone skulking **in** the bushes – perhaps we should call the police.*

skull /skʌl/ **noun** [C] C2 the bones of the head, which surround the brain and give the head its shape: *The soldiers discovered a pile of human skulls and bones.*

IDIOM **get sth into your (thick) skull** informal to understand something with difficulty: *Has he got the truth into his thick skull yet?*

ˌskull and ˈcrossbones **noun** [S] a picture of a skull with two long bones crossing each other under it, which warns of death or danger, used in the past on PIRATE flags and now on containers or places containing dangerous substances or machinery

skullcap /ˈskʌl.kæp/ **noun** [C] a small, round hat that fits closely on the top of the head, worn especially by religious Jewish men or Roman Catholic priests of high rank

S

skunk /skʌŋk/ **noun** [C] ANIMAL ▷ **1** [C] a small, black and white North American animal that makes a strong, unpleasant smell as a defence when it is attacked PERSON ▷ **2** [C] US slang disapproving an unpleasant person: *He was an oily, opportunistic skunk.* DRUG ▷ **3** [U] **skunkweed**

skunkweed /ˈskʌŋk.wiːd/ **noun** [U] (also **skunk**) a type of strong CANNABIS

sky /skaɪ/ **noun** **1** A2 [S or U] the area above the earth, in which clouds, the sun, etc. can be seen: *a blue/cloudy/dark sky* ◦ *Can you see those birds high up **in** the sky?* ◦ *We **looked up at/into** the sky at the sound of the plane.* **2 skies** [plural] the sky in a particular state or place: *For weeks we had cloudless blue skies.* ◦ *We're off to the sunny skies **of** Spain.*

IDIOM **the sky's the limit** there is no limit: *The sky's the limit to what you can win in our competition.*

ˌsky ˈblue **noun** [U] a bright, light blue colour • **ˌsky-ˈblue** **adj**

skycap /ˈskaɪ.kæp/ **noun** [C] US a person who carries passengers' bags at an airport or receives them for putting onto an aircraft

skydiving /ˈskaɪˌdaɪ.vɪŋ/ **noun** [U] a sport in which a person jumps from an aircraft and falls for as long as possible before opening a PARACHUTE • **skydiver** /-vəʳ/ ⓤⓢ /-vɚ/ **noun** [C]

ˌsky-ˈhigh **adj, adv** describes a price or charge that is very high: *The price of oil **went** sky-high when war broke out.*

skylark /ˈskaɪ.lɑːk/ ⓤⓢ /-lɑːrk/ **noun** [C] a **lark**

skylight /ˈskaɪ.laɪt/ **noun** [C] a window built into a roof to allow light in: *Putting in a skylight made the attic seem big and bright.*

skyline /ˈskaɪ.laɪn/ **noun** [C usually singular] a shape or pattern made against the sky, especially by buildings: *You get a good view of the New York skyline from the Statue of Liberty.*

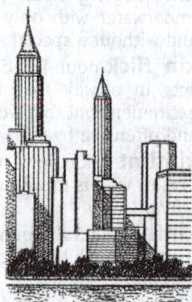

skyline

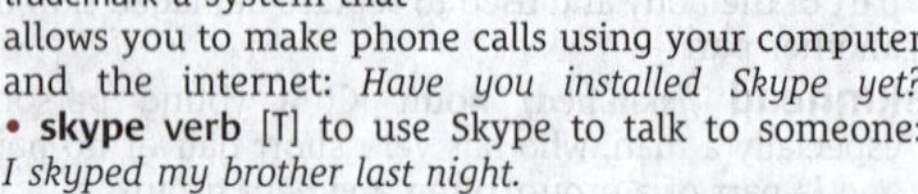

ˈsky ˌmarshal **noun** [C] an official person carrying a gun, dressed as a passenger, whose job is to protect other passengers on an aircraft

Skype /skaɪp/ **noun** [U] trademark a system that allows you to make phone calls using your computer and the internet: *Have you installed Skype yet?* • **skype** **verb** [T] to use Skype to talk to someone: *I skyped my brother last night.*

skyrocket /ˈskaɪˌrɒk.ɪt/ ⓤⓢ /-ˌrɑː.kɪt/ **verb** [I] to rise extremely quickly or make extremely quick progress towards success: *Housing prices have skyrocketed in recent months.* → Synonym **rocket**

skyscraper /ˈskaɪˌskreɪ.pəʳ/ ⓤⓢ /-pɚ/ **noun** [C] a very tall modern building, usually in a city

skyward /ˈskaɪ.wəd/ ⓤⓢ /-wɚd/ **adv, adj** (also **skywards**) in the direction of the sky: *He raised his eyes slowly skyward.* ◦ figurative *At the news, share prices **shot** skyward (= suddenly increased a lot).*

slab /slæb/ **noun** [C] a thick, flat piece of a solid substance, such as stone, wood, metal, food, etc., that is usually square or rectangular: *a concrete/marble slab*

slack /slæk/ **adj; noun; verb**

▸**adj** NOT TIGHT ▷ **1** not tight; loose: *These tent ropes are too slack – they need tightening.* NOT ACTIVE ▷ **2** showing little activity; not busy or happening in a positive way: ***Business** is always slack at this time of year.* ◦ disapproving *Discipline in Mr Brown's class has become very slack recently.* ◦ disapproving *The job is taking a long time because the workmen are so slack.* • **slackly** /ˈslæk.li/ **adv**

▸**noun** NOT TIGHT ▷ **1** [U] the fact that something is too loose: *There's too much slack in these ropes.* ◦ *The men pulled on the ropes to **take up** the slack (= to tighten them).* TROUSERS ▷ **2 slacks** [plural] old-fashioned a pair of trousers, usually of a type that fit loosely COAL ▷ **3** [U] very small pieces and dust from coal

IDIOM **pick up/take up the slack** to do the work that someone else has stopped doing but still needs to be done: *If Sue gets a job, Mick will have to take up the slack at home.*

▸**verb** [I] informal to work more slowly and with less effort than usual, or to go more slowly: *Everyone slacks **off/up** a bit at the end of the week.* ◦ disapproving *You'll be in trouble if you're caught slacking on the job like that.* ◦ *Slack **off** your **speed** as you approach the corner.*

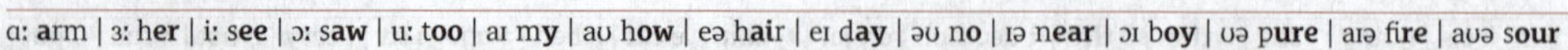

slacken /ˈslæk.ᵊn/ verb [I or T] LESS TIGHT ▷ **1** to (cause to) become loose: *Slacken the reins or you'll hurt the horse's mouth.* LESS ACTIVE ▷ **2** to (cause to) become slower or less active: *He stooped to pick it up, without slackening his **pace** (= without walking more slowly).* ◦ *The pace of trading slackened during the winter months.* ◦ *The management expects demand to slacken (**off**) in the New Year.* ◦ *The car's speed slackened (**off**) as it went up a steep hill.* ◦ *Most people slacken **off/up** at the end of a day's work.*

slacker /ˈslæk.əʳ/ (US) /-ɚ/ noun [C] informal disapproving a person who does not work hard enough: *Those slackers have gone home early again.*

ˌslack-ˈjawed adj with your mouth open in surprise

slackness /ˈslæk.nəs/ noun [U] NOT ACTIVE ▷ **1** the state of being slower and less active than usual: *Low sales figures were partly because of normal mid-summer slackness **in/of** demand.* **2** disapproving the fact that a person or organization is not working as well or as hard as they should: *The inspector criticized the slackness and incompetence of the staff.* NOT TIGHT ▷ **3** the state of not being tight

slag /slæg/ noun; verb

▸noun [U] WASTE ▷ **1** [U] waste material produced when coal is dug from the ground, or a substance produced by mixing chemicals with metal that has been heated until it is liquid in order to remove unwanted substances from it → See also **slag heap** WOMAN ▷ **2** [C] UK slang disapproving a woman who people disapprove of because she has had a lot of sexual partners LIQUID ▷ **3** [U] Australian English informal for **spit**

▸verb (-gg-)

PHRASAL VERB **slag sb off** UK informal to criticize someone: *I hate the way Ian is always slagging people off behind their backs.*

ˈslag heap noun [C] mainly UK a hill made from the waste material from a MINE

slain /sleɪn/ verb past participle of **slay**

slake /sleɪk/ verb [T] literary to satisfy a feeling of being thirsty or of wanting something: *After our long game of tennis, we slaked our **thirst** with a beer.* ◦ *I don't think Dick will ever manage to slake his lust for power.*

slalom /ˈslɑː.ləm/ noun [C] a race for people on skis or in CANOES (= long light narrow boats) in which they have to follow a route that bends in and out between poles

slam /slæm/ verb; noun

▸verb (-mm-) **1** (B2) [I or T] to (cause to) move against a hard surface with force and usually a loud noise: *The wind made the door/window slam (shut).* ◦ *Close the door carefully, don't slam it.* ◦ *He slammed the **brakes on** (= used them quickly and with force) when a child ran in front of his car.* ◦ *I had to stop suddenly, and the car behind slammed **into** the back of me.* **2** [T] informal to criticize: *Although the reviewers slammed the play, the audience loved it.*

▸noun [S] a sudden loud noise: *The door shut with a slam.*

ˈslam ˌdunk noun [C] a shot in BASKETBALL in which a player jumps up and pushes the ball down through the net • **ˈslam-dunk verb** [T] (also **dunk**) to jump up and force a BASKETBALL down through the net in order to score

IDIOM **be a slam dunk** mainly US to be a certain winner: *Although he's a strong candidate, he's not a slam dunk.*

the slammer /ˈslæm.əʳ/ (US) /-ɚ/ noun [S] slang prison

slander /ˈslɑːn.dəʳ/ (US) /ˈslæn.dɚ/ noun; verb

▸noun [C or U] a false spoken statement about someone which damages their reputation, or the making of such a statement: *The doctor is **suing** his partner **for** slander.* ◦ *She regarded his comment as a slander **on** her good reputation.* → Compare **libel**

▸verb [T] to damage someone's reputation by making a false spoken statement about them • **slanderer** /-əʳ/ (US) /-ɚ/ noun [C] • **slanderous** /-əs/ adj *a slanderous accusation/allegation/comment* • **slanderously** /-əs.li/ adv

slang /slæŋ/ noun; verb

▸noun [U] (C1) very informal language that is usually spoken rather than written, used especially by particular groups of people: *army slang* ◦ *a slang expression* ◦ *'Chicken' is slang **for** someone who isn't very brave.*

▸verb [T] UK to attack with angry, uncontrolled language: *The football players started slanging each other in the middle of the game.*

ˈslanging ˌmatch noun [C] UK informal an argument in which both people use angry uncontrolled language and insult each other

slangy /ˈslæŋ.i/ adj informal Slangy language contains a lot of slang expressions: *His language is very slangy.*

slant /slɑːnt/ (US) /slænt/ verb; noun

▸verb **1** [I or T] to (cause to) lean in a position that is not vertical; to (cause to) slope: *Italic writing slants **to** the right.* ◦ *The evening sun slanted (= shone with the light moving in a slope) **through** the narrow window.* **2** [T] often disapproving to present information in a particular way, especially showing one group of people, one side of an argument, etc. in such a positive or negative way that it is unfair: *The police claimed that reports in the media were slanted **against/towards** the defendant.*

▸noun **1** [S] a position that is sloping: *The house is built **on/at** a slant.* **2** [C usually singular] a particular way of showing or looking at something: *The book had a personal/political/sociological slant.* • **slantwise** /ˈslɑːnt.waɪz/ (US) /ˈslænt-/ adv (US also **slantways**)

slanted /ˈslɑːn.tɪd/ (US) /ˈslæn.t̬ɪd/ adj **1** sloping in one direction **2** disapproving showing information about one person, one side of an argument, etc. in such a positive or negative way that it is unfair: *Slanted media coverage is increasing public support for the war.*

slanting /ˈslɑːn.tɪŋ/ (US) /ˈslæn.t̬ɪŋ/ adj sloping in one direction: *Swiss chalets have steeply slanting roofs, so that snow does not settle on them.*

S

slap /slæp/ noun; adv; verb

▸noun HIT ▷ **1** (C2) [C] a quick hit with the flat part of the hand or other flat object: *She gave her son a slap for behaving badly.* **2 a slap in the face** (C2) informal an action that insults or upsets someone: *It was a real slap in the face for him when she refused to go out to dinner with him.* **3 a slap on the back** the action of hitting someone in a friendly way on the back in order to show praise for something they have done: *He's won – **give** him a slap on the back.* **4 a slap on the wrist** informal a gentle warning or punishment: *The judge **gave** Minna a slap on the wrist for not wearing her seat belt.* FOR FACE ▷ **5** [U] UK informal for **make-up**: *I'm just going to put a bit of slap on.*

IDIOM **slap and tickle** UK informal humorous sexual activity, especially when it involves playing or joking: *I think there's a bit of slap and tickle going on in the back of that car over there.*

▸adv (UK also ˌ**slap ˈbang**) directly or right: *The football* *player kicked the ball slap into the middle of the net.* → Synonym **smack**

▸verb [T] (-pp-) B2 to hit someone with the flat part of the hand or other flat object: *She slapped his face.* ◦ *She slapped him **across** the face.* ◦ *His friends slapped him **on the back** when he said he was getting married (= hit him lightly on the back in a friendly way to express pleasure at what he had done).* ◦ *When her ideas were rejected, she slapped her report (**down**) on the table and stormed out of the meeting.*

PHRASAL VERBS **slap sb around** [T] informal to hit someone repeatedly or often: *Her husband has been slapping her around, but she's afraid to go to the police.* • **slap sb down** usually disapproving to stop someone from talking or making suggestions, often in an unpleasant way: *I tried to suggest ways in which the plans could be improved, but he slapped me down.* • **slap sth on** to put or spread a substance over a surface very quickly or roughly: *We want to sell our house, so we've slapped some paint on the outside to make it look better.* • **slap sth on/onto (sth/sb)** informal disapproving When someone in authority slaps an unpleasant, difficult, or extra thing on someone or something, they suddenly make them or it provide or accept it: *The government has slapped more tax on cigarettes.* ◦ *The librarian slapped a fine on him for returning the books late.*

slapdash /ˈslæp.dæʃ/ **adj** informal disapproving done or made in a hurried and careless way: *He gets his work done quickly, but he's very slapdash.*

slaphappy /ˌslæpˈhæp.i/ **adj** informal happily careless and not thinking about the results of your actions: *He's slaphappy in his approach to rules and regulations.*

slaphead /ˈslæp.hed/ **noun** [C] UK very informal a person who is BALD (= has little or no hair on their head)

slapper /ˈslæp.əʳ/ US /-ɚ/ **noun** [C] UK offensive a woman who has sex with a lot of men: *She looked like a right **old** slapper.*

slapstick /ˈslæp.stɪk/ **noun** [U] a type of humorous acting in which the actors behave in a silly way, such as by throwing things, falling over, etc.

ˈslap-up **adj** [before noun] UK informal describes a meal that is especially large and good: *We went for a slap-up meal on our wedding anniversary.*

slash /slæʃ/ **verb; noun**

▸verb **1** [I or T] to cut with a sharp blade using a quick, strong movement: *The museum was broken into last night and several paintings were slashed.* ◦ *She tried to commit suicide by slashing her **wrists**.* ◦ *We had to slash (**our way**) **through** the long grass to clear a path.* **2** [T] informal to very much reduce something, such as money or jobs: *Prices have been slashed by 50 percent!*

▸noun **PUNCTUATION** ▷ **1** B2 [C] (UK also **oblique (stroke)**) the symbol / used in writing to separate letters, numbers, or words: *You often write a slash between alternatives, for example, 'and/or'.* → See also **backslash, forward slash** **CUT** ▷ **2** a long, deep cut **3** [C] a fast, long movement to hit something: *Ben took a wild slash **at** the ball and luckily managed to hit it.* **TOILET** ▷ **4** [S] UK slang the act of going to the toilet and urinating

ˌslash-and-ˈburn **adj** **1** relating to a type of farming that involves cutting and burning trees, crops, etc. before planting new ones **2** getting rid of a lot of people, systems, etc. in an organization: *The company rejected a slash-and-burn type restructuring program.*

slasher /ˈslæʃ.əʳ/ US /-ɚ/ **noun** [C] informal a person who kills or injures people using a knife

ˈslasher ˌmovie **noun** [C] mainly US informal a film in which people, especially young women, are killed very violently with knives

slat /slæt/ **noun** [C] a thin, narrow piece of wood, plastic, or metal used to make floors, furniture, window coverings, etc.: *The base of the bed was made of slats.*

slate /sleɪt/ **noun; verb; adj**

▸noun **ROCK** ▷ **1** [C or U] a dark grey rock that can be easily divided into thin pieces, or a small, thin piece of this used to cover a roof **COMPUTER** ▷ **2** [C] (also **slate PC**) a small computer with a screen that you can write on using a special pen **FOR WRITING** ▷ **3** [C] in the past, a small, thin, rectangular piece of slate (= rock), usually in a wooden frame, used for writing on, especially by children **CHOOSE** ▷ **4** [C] US the group of people who are chosen by a particular party to take part in an election: *The senator has not got a full slate **of** delegates in New York.*

IDIOMS **on the slate** UK informal (of the price of food or drink that a regular customer buys) recorded so that they can pay for it at another time: *Could you **put** these drinks on the slate?* • **with the slate wiped clean** with your past mistakes or crimes forgotten

▸verb [T] **CHOOSE** ▷ **1** **be slated** US to be expected to happen in the future or to be expected to be or do something in the future: [+ to infinitive] *Geoff is slated **to** be the next captain of the football team.* ◦ *The election is slated **for** (= the chosen day is) next Thursday.* **CRITICIZE** ▷ **2** UK informal to attack by criticizing; to write or say that something is very bad: *Her last book was slated by the critics.* **ROCK** ▷ **3** to cover a roof with slates

▸adj of a colour similar to slate: *slate **grey*** ◦ *slate **blue***

slather /ˈslæð.əʳ/ US /-ɚ/ **verb** [T] to spread something thickly on something else: *She slathered lotion **on/all over** her body.* ◦ *She slathered her toast **with** butter.*

slatted /ˈslæt.ɪd/ US /ˈslæt̬-/ **adj** made with slats: *slatted floors/doors/windows*

slattern /ˈslæt.ən/ US /ˈslæt̬.ɚn/ **noun** [C] **1** old use disapproving a dirty, untidy woman **2** US slang disapproving a woman who has many sexual partners, for pleasure or payment • **slatternly** /-li/ **adj**

slaughter /ˈslɔː.təʳ/ US /ˈslɑː.t̬ɚ/ **noun; verb**

▸noun **1** C2 [S or U] the killing of many people cruelly and unfairly, especially in a war: *Hardly anyone in the town escaped the slaughter when the rebels were defeated.* ◦ *We must find ways of reducing the slaughter which takes place on our roads (= death of many people in motor accidents) every year.* **2** [U] the killing of animals for meat: *The geese are being fattened for slaughter.* → See also **slaughterhouse** **3** [S] an occasion when one team is very easily defeated by the other: *Saturday's game was an absolute slaughter.*

▸verb [T] **1** to cruelly and unfairly kill a lot of people: *Thousands of people were slaughtered in the civil war.* **2** to kill an animal for meat: *The animals are slaughtered in abattoirs.* **3** to defeat someone very easily: *England slaughtered Germany 5–1 at football.*

slaughtered /ˈslɔː.təd/ US /ˈslɑː.t̬ɚd/ **adj** UK informal **get slaughtered** to get very drunk

slaughterhouse /ˈslɔː.tə.haʊs/ US /ˈslɑː.t̬ɚ-/ **noun** [C] mainly US for **abattoir**

Slav /slɑːv/ **noun** [C] a member of any of the Eastern European races of people who speak Slavic languages • **Slav adj** (also **Slavic**)

slave /sleɪv/ **noun; verb**

▸noun [C] B2 a person who is legally owned by someone else and has to work for them: *Black slaves used to work on the cotton plantations of the* southern United States. ◦ *I'm tired of being* ***treated like a slave****!*

IDIOM **be a slave to sth** disapproving to be influenced too much by something: *She's a slave to fashion.*

▸**verb** [I usually + adv/prep] informal to work very hard at something: *We slaved* ***away*** *all week* ***at*** *the report.* ◦ humorous *I've been slaving* ***over a hot stove*** *(= cooking) all morning.* → See also **enslave**

ˈslave ˌdriver noun [C] informal disapproving a person who makes other people work very hard: *My boss is a real slave driver.*

ˌslave ˈlabour noun [U] **1** work done by slaves **2** informal disapproving very hard work for which people are paid very little: *It's slave labour working in that office.*

slaver¹ /ˈslæv.əʳ/ US /-ɚ/ verb [I] **1** (especially of an animal) to allow liquid to come out of the mouth, especially because of excitement or hunger: *The dog slavered* ***with*** *excitement when told it was time for a walk.* **2** disapproving to show great interest or excitement in someone or something, in a way that is unpleasant to other people: *Stop slavering* ***over*** *that guitar, Stephen!*

slaver² /ˈsleɪ.vəʳ/ US /-vɚ/ noun [C] in the past, a ship used for carrying SLAVES, or a person who sold SLAVES

slavery /ˈsleɪ.vəʳr.i/ US /-ɚ-/ noun [U] C1 the activity of having SLAVES or the condition of being a SLAVE: *Millions of Africans were* ***sold into*** *slavery.*

ˈslave ˌtrade noun [U] the buying and selling of SLAVES, especially of African people who were taken to North America from the 16th to the 19th century

slavish /ˈsleɪ.vɪʃ/ adj disapproving obeying completely and having no original thoughts or ideas: *a slavish devotion* ***to*** *duty* ◦ *a slavish translation*

slavishly /ˈsleɪ.vɪʃ.li/ adv disapproving obeying completely; without any ideas of your own: *I followed the recipe slavishly.*

slaw /slɔː/ US /slɑː/ noun [U] US informal for **coleslaw**

slay /sleɪ/ verb [T] (**slew, slain**) **1** UK old use or literary to kill in a violent way: *St George slew the* ***dragon****.* **2** (used especially in newspapers) to murder someone: *He was found slain in an alley two blocks from his apartment.*

slaying /ˈsleɪ.ɪŋ/ noun [C] mainly US a murder

sleaze /sliːz/ noun **1** [U] activities, especially business or political, of a low moral standard: *The sleaze* ***factor*** *was the major reason for his electoral defeat.* **2** [C] US a **sleazebag**

sleazebag /ˈsliːz.bæg/ noun [C] (US also **sleazeball, sleaze**) a person who has low standards of honesty or morals

sleazy /ˈsliː.zi/ adj dirty, cheap, or not socially acceptable, especially relating to moral or sexual matters: *This part of town is full of sleazy bars and restaurants.*

sleb /sleb/ noun [C] slang often disapproving someone who is famous, especially in the entertainment business

sled /sled/ noun [C], verb [I or T] US for **sledge**

sledge /sledʒ/ noun; verb

▸**noun** [C] UK (US **sled**) an object used for travelling over snow and ice with long narrow strips of wood or metal under it instead of wheels. It can be either a low frame, or a vehicle like a CARRIAGE pulled by horses or dogs. → Compare **sleigh**

▸**verb** [I or T] UK (US **sled**) to ride or travel on snow using a sledge

sledgehammer /ˈsledʒˌhæm.əʳ/ US /-ɚ/ noun [C] **1** a large, heavy hammer with a long handle, used for breaking stones or other heavy material, or for hitting posts into the ground, etc. **2** describes a way of behaving that is too forceful: *They accused the prime minister of using sledgehammer tactics.*

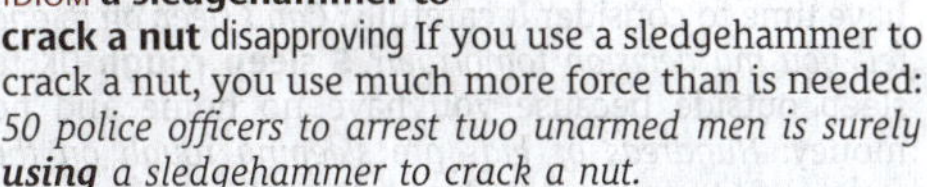
sledgehammer

IDIOM **a sledgehammer to crack a nut** disapproving If you use a sledgehammer to crack a nut, you use much more force than is needed: *50 police officers to arrest two unarmed men is surely* ***using*** *a sledgehammer to crack a nut.*

sledging /ˈsledʒ.ɪŋ/ noun [U] **1** the activity of travelling on the snow on a sledge **2** informal the act of one sports player insulting another during a game, in order to make them angry

sleek /sliːk/ adj; verb

▸**adj** (especially of hair, clothes, or shapes) smooth, shiny, and lying close to the body, and therefore looking well cared for; not untidy and with no parts sticking out: *The cat had sleek fur.* ◦ *Who owns that sleek black car parked outside your house?* ◦ disapproving *He's one of those sleek (= seeming rich and dishonest) businessman types.* • **sleekly** /ˈsliː.kli/ adv • **sleekness** /ˈsliːk.nəs/ noun [U]

▸**verb**

PHRASAL VERB **sleek back/down** to make something such as hair smooth, shiny, and flat: *Before going to the party, he sleeked back his hair with hair cream.*

sleep /sliːp/ noun; verb

▸**noun** NOT AWAKE ▷ **1** B1 [U] the resting state in which the body is not active and the mind is unconscious: *I must* ***get*** *some sleep – I'm exhausted.* → See also **sleepwalker** **2 get/go to sleep** B1 to succeed in sleeping: *I couldn't get to sleep at all last night for worrying.* ◦ *You'll find that your baby usually goes to sleep after a feed.* **3** B1 [C] a period of sleeping: *You must be tired after all that driving – why don't you* ***have*** *a little sleep?* ◦ *He* ***fell into a deep*** *sleep.* SUBSTANCE ▷ **4** [U] informal a yellowish substance sometimes found in the corners of the eyes after sleeping

> **Word partners for sleep**
>
> *drift into/go to* sleep • *get* [no/some] sleep • *have* a sleep • *lose* sleep (over sth) • be *deprived of* sleep • a *decent/deep/good/restful* sleep • a *disturbed/fitful/restless* sleep • a *good night's* sleep • a *lack of* sleep • *not get/have* a *wink of* sleep • *in* your sleep

IDIOMS **could do sth in their sleep** If someone could do something in their sleep, they can do it very easily, usually because they have done it so often: *I've done this recipe so many times I could do it in my sleep now.* • **go back to sleep!** informal used to tell someone off for not paying attention: *'Sorry, what did you say?' 'Oh, go back to sleep!'* • **go to sleep** informal If your arm or leg has gone to sleep, you cannot feel or control it, often because you have been sitting or lying for too long in a strange position. • **put sth to sleep** to kill an animal that is very ill or very old so that it does not suffer any more

▸**verb** (**slept, slept**) **1** A1 [I] to be in the state of rest when your eyes are closed, your body is not active, and your mind is unconscious: *I couldn't sleep because of all the noise next door.* ◦ *I slept* ***late*** *on Sunday morning.* ◦ *How can Jayne sleep* ***at night*** *with all those worries on her mind!* ◦ *We had dinner with Ann and*

S

*Charles and slept **the night** (with them)* (= *at their home*). → See also **oversleep, sleepout** **2** [T] If a vehicle, tent, etc. sleeps a particular number of people, it provides enough space or beds for that number of people to be able to sleep in it: *The caravan sleeps four comfortably.* **3 sleep like a log** informal to sleep very well: *I went to bed early and slept like a log.* **4 sleep on sth** C2 to delay making a decision about something important until the next day so that you have time to consider it carefully: *Can I sleep on it, and tell you my decision tomorrow?* **5 sleep rough** UK to sleep outside because you have no home and no money: *Hundreds of kids are sleeping rough on the streets of London.* • **sleeping** /ˈsliː.pɪŋ/ adj *She looked lovingly at the sleeping child.* → See also **asleep**

PHRASAL VERBS **sleep around** informal disapproving to have sex with a lot of different people without having a close or long relationship with any of them • **sleep in** informal to sleep until later in the morning than you usually do: *I usually sleep in at the weekends.* • **sleep sth off** If you sleep off something, especially a HANGOVER, you go to sleep so that you will feel better when you wake up. • **sleep over** informal to sleep in someone else's home for a night: *If you don't want to catch a train home at that time of night, you're welcome to sleep over.* • **sleep through sth** If you sleep through a lot of noise or an activity, it does not wake you or keep you awake: *I never heard the storm last night – I must have slept through it.* ◦ *I was so bored that I slept through the second half of the film.* • **sleep together** informal If two people sleep together, they have sex: *I don't think they sleep together any more.* • **sleep with sb** informal C2 to have sex with someone: *He found out that his wife had been sleeping with his best friend.*

sleepaway camp /ˈsliː.pə.weɪˌkæmp/ noun [C or U] US a place where children can go to stay without their parents and do activities

sleeper /ˈsliː.pəʳ/ US /-pɚ/ noun PERSON ▷ **1 a good/heavy/light sleeper** someone who sleeps in the stated way: *I'm a light sleeper – the slightest noise wakes me.* ◦ *You won't wake him – he's such a heavy sleeper.* ON TRAIN ▷ **2** a CARRIAGE in a train with beds for passengers to sleep in, or one of the beds in this CARRIAGE, or the type of train that has these carriages: *I'm travelling overnight so I've booked a sleeper.* ◦ *The 11.45 to Glasgow is a sleeper.* BLOCK ▷ **3** [C] UK (US **railroad tie**) one of the heavy horizontal blocks that supports a railway track RING ▷ **4** [C] UK a small gold or silver ring that is worn in an ear which is PIERCED (= has a hole in it) to stop the hole from closing while other EARRINGS are not being worn SUDDEN ACTIVITY ▷ **5** [C] a person or thing that is suddenly and surprisingly successful after a long period of not achieving anything **6** [C] a SPY who only becomes active a long time after being put in place by an organization or country

S

sleeping bag

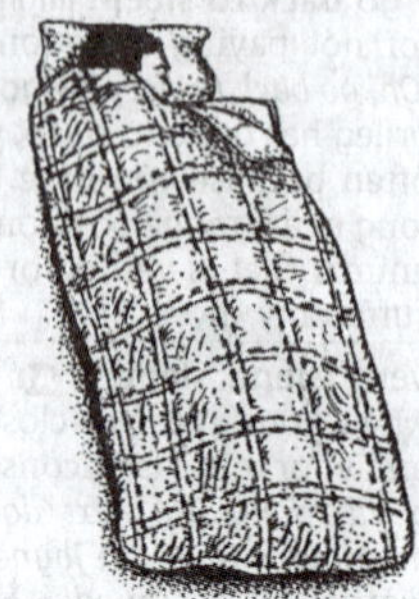

ˈ**sleeping ˌbag** noun [C] a large, thick bag for sleeping in, especially when you are sleeping outside, for example in a tent

ˈ**sleeping ˌcar** noun [C] (also **sleeper**) a railway CARRIAGE with beds for passengers to sleep in

ˌ**sleeping ˈpartner** noun [C] UK (US ˌ**silent ˈpartner**) a partner in a company who does not take an active part in its management, especially one who provides some of the money

ˈ**sleeping ˌpill** noun [C] (also ˈ**sleeping ˌtablet**) a pill which you take to help you to sleep better

ˌ**sleeping poˈliceman** noun [C] UK a **speed bump**

ˈ**sleeping ˌsickness** noun [U] an African disease which causes fever, severe loss of energy, weight loss, and sometimes death

sleepless /ˈsliː.p.ləs/ adj [before noun] **1** C1 without any sleep: *I've spent so many sleepless **nights** worrying about him.* **2** [after verb] not able to sleep: *Alone and sleepless, she stared miserably up at the ceiling.* • **sleeplessness** /-nəs/ noun [U]

sleepout /ˈsliː.p.aʊt/ noun [C] Australian English a small building in a garden or a covered outside part of a house that is used for sleeping in

sleepover /ˈsliː.p.əʊ.vəʳ/ US /-oʊ.vɚ/ noun [C] a type of party when a young person or a group of young people stay for the night at the house of a friend → See also **slumber party**

sleepwalker /ˈsliː.pˌwɔː.kəʳ/ US /-ˌwɑː.kɚ/ noun [C] a person who gets out of bed and walks around while they are sleeping • **sleepwalk** /-wɔːk/ US /-wɑːk/ verb [I] • **sleepwalking** /-ˌwɔː.kɪŋ/ US /-ˌwɑː.kɪŋ/ noun [U]

sleepy /ˈsliː.pi/ adj PERSON ▷ **1** B1 tired and wanting to sleep → See also **sleepyhead** PLACE ▷ **2** C1 A sleepy place is quiet and without much activity or excitement: *They retired to a sleepy little village in the west of Yorkshire.* • **sleepily** /-pɪ.li/ adv • **sleepiness** /-nəs/ noun [U]

sleepyhead /ˈsliː.pi.hed/ noun [C] informal a person, especially a child, who is tired and looks as if they want to sleep: [as form of address] *Come on, sleepyhead, let's get you to bed.*

sleet /sliːt/ noun [U] wet, partly melted falling snow: *Driving snow and sleet brought more problems to the county's roads last night.* • **sleet** verb [I] *It's sleeting.* • **sleety** /ˈsliː.ti/ US /-t̬i/ adj *sleety rain*

sleeve /sliːv/ noun [C] CLOTHING PART ▷ **1** B1 (also **arm**) the part of a piece of clothing that covers some or all of the arm: *short/long sleeves* ◦ *The sleeves are too long for me.* ◦ *You'd better **roll** your sleeves **up** or you'll get them dirty.* COVER ▷ **2** UK (US **jacket**) a cover to protect something **3** a tube-shaped covering to protect a part of a machine

IDIOM **have sth up your sleeve** informal C2 to have secret plans or ideas: *If I know Mark he'll have one or two tricks up his sleeve.*

-sleeved /-sliːvd/ suffix having the length of sleeves mentioned: *a short/long-sleeved blouse*

sleeveless /ˈsliːv.ləs/ adj A sleeveless piece of clothing has no sleeves: *a sleeveless blouse/dress/jacket*

ˈ**sleeve ˌnote** noun UK (mainly US ˈ**liner ˌnotes**) information about a performer or a performance that is supplied with a sound recording

sleigh /sleɪ/ noun [C] a type of SLEDGE pulled by animals, especially horses or dogs

sleight of hand /ˌslaɪt.əvˈhænd/ noun [U] **1** speed and skill of the hand when performing tricks: *Most of these conjuring tricks depend on sleight of hand.* **2** skilful hiding of the truth in order to win an advantage: *By some statistical sleight of hand the government have produced figures showing that unemployment has recently fallen.*

slender /ˈslen.dəʳ/ US /-dɚ/ adj **1** C2 thin and delicate, often in a way that is attractive: *He put his hands around her slender waist.* ◦ *The plant's leaves are long and slender.* **2** small in amount or degree: *a man of* *slender* ***means*** *(= without much money)* ◦ *The chances of settling this dispute through talks seem increasingly slender.* • **slenderness** /-nəs/ noun [U]

slenderize /ˈslen.dᵊr.aɪz/ (US) /-dɚ-/ verb [I or T] US to become thinner or to make something appear thinner: *We manufacture undergarments that tone and slenderize.* ◦ *Wearing dark clothes from the waist down will help to slenderize your figure.*

slept /slept/ verb past simple and past participle of **sleep**

sleuth /sluːθ/ noun [C] old-fashioned or humorous someone whose job is to discover information about crimes and find out who is responsible for them → Synonym **detective** • **sleuthing** /ˈsluː.θɪŋ/ noun [U] informal *A bit of sleuthing from our investigative reporter uncovered some interesting information on Mr Parkinson.*

slew[1] /sluː/ verb past simple of **slay**

slew[2] /sluː/ verb [I or T, + adv/prep] to turn or be turned round suddenly and awkwardly: *The car hit a patch of ice and slewed* ***around*** *violently.* ◦ *He slewed the van to the left to avoid the dog.*

slew[3] /sluː/ noun [C usually singular] US informal a large amount or number: *Mr Savino has been charged with three murders as well as a* ***whole*** *slew* ***of*** *other crimes.*

slice /slaɪs/ noun; verb

▸noun **PIECE** ▷ **1** (A2) [C] a flat, often thin, piece of food that has been cut from a larger piece: *a slice* ***of*** *bread/cake* ◦ *cucumber/lemon slices* ◦ *Would you like another slice of ham/beef?* **2** (C2) [S] a part of something, such as an amount of money: *We agreed before we did the deal that we'd both take an equal slice of the profit.* ◦ *The film presents us with a fascinating slice of history.* **3** [C] a kitchen UTENSIL with a wide blade, used for serving pieces of food: *a cake/fish slice* **HIT** ▷ **4** [C] in tennis, the action of hitting the bottom of the ball so that it does not BOUNCE very high when it hits the ground: *That wonderful backhand slice of Ben's sends the ball where his opponent just can't reach it.* **5** in the sports of GOLF and baseball, the action of hitting a ball so that it goes to one side rather than straight in front

IDIOMS **a slice of life** A film, piece of literature, or a play might be described as a slice of life if it describes or shows the ordinary details of real life. • **slice of the cake** Australian English informal If you want a slice of the cake, you want a share of any money that is being made from an activity.

▸verb **CUT** ▷ **1** (B2) [T] to cut something into thin, flat pieces: *Slice the mushrooms thinly and fry in butter.* ◦ [+ two objects] *Could you slice me a very thin piece of cake/slice a very thin piece of cake* ***for*** *me?* **2** [I + adv/prep] to easily cut into or through something with a sharp knife: *He screamed as the blade sliced* ***into*** *his leg.* ◦ figurative *She watched his slim strong body as it sliced effortlessly* ***through*** *the water.* **HIT** ▷ **3** [T] in the sports of golf and baseball, to hit a ball so that it goes to one side rather than straight in front: *Sara sliced the ball, sending it a hundred metres or so to the left.* **4** [T] If you slice the ball in a game of tennis, you hit the bottom of the ball so that it does not BOUNCE very high when it hits the ground.

IDIOM **any way you slice it** (also **no matter how you slice it**) mainly US informal in whatever way the situation is considered: *He shouldn't have hit her, any way you slice it.*

PHRASAL VERB **slice sth off** to remove an amount of something by cutting it: *She sliced off a piece of sausage.* ◦ *He accidentally sliced the top off his finger while he was cutting vegetables.* ◦ figurative *Amit won the race, slicing three seconds off his previous best time.*

sliced /slaɪst/ adj cut into thin, flat pieces: *sliced bread/ham/tomato*

slicer /ˈslaɪ.səʳ/ (US) /-sɚ/ noun [C] a machine or tool for slicing particular types of food: *an egg/bread/meat slicer*

slick /slɪk/ adj; noun; verb

▸adj **1** operating or performing skilfully and effectively, without problems and without seeming to need effort: *Manilow gave the slick, polished performance that we've come to expect.* **2** disapproving skilful and effective but not sincere or honest: *It's that sort of slick sales talk that I mistrust.*

▸noun [C] **OIL** ▷ **1** an **oil slick** **MAGAZINE** ▷ **2** US for **glossy magazine**

▸verb [T usually + adv/prep] to cause hair to be smooth and close to the head by brushing it flat, often using a substance to make it stick: *He'd slicked his hair* ***back*** *with gel.*

slicker /ˈslɪk.əʳ/ (US) /-ɚ/ noun [C] **city slicker**

slide /slaɪd/ verb; noun

▸verb (**slid, slid**) **MOVE** ▷ **1** (B2) [I or T] to (cause to) move easily and without interruption over a surface: *When I was little I used to like sliding on the polished floor in my socks.* ◦ *We've got one of those doors in the kitchen that slides open.* ◦ *He slid the letter into his pocket while no one was looking.* ◦ *sliding* ***doors*** **GET WORSE** ▷ **2** [I] to go into a worse state, often through lack of control or care: *The dollar slid against other major currencies.* ◦ *Car exports slid by 40 percent this year.* ◦ *He was improving for a while, but I fear he's sliding* ***back*** *into his old habits.* ◦ *I was doing really well with my diet, but I'm afraid I've* ***let it*** *slide* (= not tried as hard) *recently.* → See also **backslide**

▸noun **MOVEMENT** ▷ **1** [C] a sudden movement of a large mass of MUD (= wet earth) or rock down a hill: *a* ***mud/rock*** *slide* → See also **landslide** **2** [C] a structure for children to play on which has a slope for them to slide down and usually a set of steps leading up to the slope **3** a part that moves easily backwards and forwards on an instrument or machine: *the slide on a trombone* **WORSE STATE** ▷ **4** [C usually singular] the process of moving into a worse state, often through lack of control or care: *The government must take measures, he said, to* ***halt*** *the country's slide* ***into*** *recession.* **PHOTOGRAPHY** ▷ **5** [C] (specialized **transparency**) a small piece of photographic film in a frame that, when light is passed through it, shows a larger image on a screen or plain surface: *colour slides* **GLASS** ▷ **6** [C] a small piece of glass on which you put something in order to look at it through a MICROSCOPE **HAIR** ▷ **7** [C] UK short form of **hair slide**

ˈslide ˌrule noun [C] a long, narrow device for calculating numbers with a middle part which slides backwards and forwards

ˈslide ˌshow noun [C] **1** an occasion when you use a machine to show photographs on a wall **2** an occasion when a computer shows several different photographs one after another on a screen

ˌsliding ˈscale noun [C usually singular] a system in which the rate at which something is paid changes as a result of other conditions: *Charges are made on a sliding scale, which means that the amount you must pay increases with the level of your income.*

slight /slaɪt/ adj; verb; noun

▸adj **SMALL IN AMOUNT** ▷ **1** (B2) small in amount or degree: *a slight improvement* ◦ *a slight incline* ◦ *I've got a slight headache.* ◦ *I haven't the slightest* ***idea*** *what he's talking about.* **2** **not in the slightest** not at all: *'Does it worry you?' 'Not in the slightest.'* **THIN** ▷

S

3 (of people) thin and delicate: *Like most long-distance runners she is very slight.* • **slightness** /ˈslaɪt.nəs/ **noun** [U]

▸**verb** [T] to insult someone by not paying them any attention or treating them as if they are not important: *I felt slighted when my boss thanked everyone but me for their hard work.* • **slighted** /ˈslaɪ.tɪd/ Ⓤⓢ /-t̬ɪd/ **adj**

▸**noun** [C] an action that insults a person because someone fails to pay attention to them or to treat them with the respect that they deserve: *I regarded her failure to acknowledge my greeting as a slight.*

slightly /ˈslaɪt.li/ **adv** **SMALL IN AMOUNT** ▷ **1** B2 a little: *She's slightly taller than her sister.* ◦ *I'm slightly upset she forgot my birthday.* ◦ *I'm slightly worried that she'll get lost on the way.*

> **!** Common mistake: **slightly or slight?**
>
> **Warning:** do not confuse the adverb **slightly** with the adjective **slight**:
>
> ~~*There was a slightly decrease in sales in the summer.*~~
>
> *There was a slight decrease in sales in the summer.*

THIN ▷ **2** Someone who is slightly built is thin and delicate.

slim /slɪm/ **adj; verb; noun**

▸**adj** (**slimmer**, **slimmest**) approving A1 (especially of people) attractively thin: *slim hips/legs* ◦ *She's got a lovely slim figure.* ◦ figurative *They've only a slim **chance** of winning (= it's unlikely that they will win).* • **slimness** /ˈslɪm.nəs/ **noun** [U]

▸**verb** [I] (**-mm-**) UK to try to get thinner by eating less food and taking more exercise: *You haven't got much lunch – are you slimming?*

PHRASAL VERBS **slim down** to become thinner: *He's really slimmed down over the last few months.* • **slim sth down** to reduce the size of something: *It is not our intention to slim down the workforce.*

▸**noun** [U] East African for AIDS (= a serious disease that destroys the body's ability to fight infection)

slime /slaɪm/ **noun** [U] a sticky liquid substance that is unpleasant to touch, such as the liquid produced by fish and SNAILS and the greenish-brown substance found near water: *There was a revolting green slime in between the bathroom tiles.* ◦ *You could see trails of slime where the slugs had been.*

S

slimeball /ˈslaɪm.bɔːl/ Ⓤⓢ /-bɑːl/ **noun** [C usually singular] informal a very unpleasant person whose friendly manner is not sincere

ˈslim-ˌfit **adj** Slim-fit trousers, shirts, etc. fit your body quite closely.

slimline /ˈslɪm.laɪn/ **adj** UK **1** (of a drink) containing little or no sugar: *I'll have a gin and slimline **tonic**, please.* **2** designed to be less wide than the ordinary type: *a slimline dishwasher*

slimmer /ˈslɪm.əʳ/ Ⓤⓢ /-ɚ/ **noun** [C] UK a person who is trying to get thinner by eating less and doing more exercise

slimming /ˈslɪm.ɪŋ/ **noun; adj**

▸**noun** [U] UK the act of trying to become thinner by eating less food: *With all the diet-food and books on the market, slimming is big business these days.* ◦ *slimming aids/clubs/magazines*

▸**adj** **1** UK informal describes food that you can eat without getting fat: *Have a salad – that's slimming.* **2** US making you look thinner: *Black is very slimming.*

ˌslim ˈpickings **noun** [plural] informal little or no success in getting or achieving something: *Buyers who have waited for bargains at the end of the year will **find** slim pickings.*

slimy /ˈslaɪ.mi/ **adj** **1** covered in SLIME: *Although snakes look slimy their skin is actually dry to the touch.* **2** disapproving If you describe a person or their manner as slimy, you mean that they appear to be friendly but in a way that you find unpleasant: *He was the very worst sort of slimy salesman.* • **sliminess** /-nəs/ **noun** [U]

sling /slɪŋ/ **verb; noun**

▸**verb** [T usually + adv/prep] (**slung**, **slung**) **THROW** ▷ **1** informal to throw or drop something carelessly: *Don't just sling your bag on the floor!* ◦ *If any of the letters aren't interesting just sling them in the bin.* ◦ *I'll just sling **together** a few things (= put what I need to take with me in a bag) and I'll be ready to go.* **2** mainly UK informal to throw or give something to someone: [+ two objects] *Sling me a pen, will you?* **HANG** ▷ **3** to hang something over something, especially in a careless way: *I usually sling my jacket **over** the back of my chair.*

IDIOM **sling your hook** UK slang to leave: *She told him to sling his hook.*

PHRASAL VERBS **sling sb out** mainly UK informal to make someone leave a place because they have behaved badly: *She was slung out **of** college because she never did any work.* • **sling sth out** mainly UK informal to get rid of something unwanted: *What about these old magazines? Shall I just sling them out?*

▸**noun** [C] **1** a device that uses a strap, piece of cloth, or ropes for supporting, lifting, or carrying objects: *The cylinder was lifted from the seabed **in** a sling.* **2** a device for supporting a broken or damaged arm in which the arm is held in front of the body in a piece of cloth that is tied around the neck: *I had my arm **in** a sling for six weeks.* **3** a device like a bag for carrying a baby, tied to the front or the back of an adult's body **4** a simple weapon used mainly in the past in which a strap held at the ends was used for throwing stones

slingbacks /ˈslɪŋ.bæks/ **noun** [plural] women's shoes with a strap around the back of the HEEL instead of a full covering: *a pair of slingbacks* • **slingback** /-bæk/ **adj** [before noun] *slingback sandals/shoes*

slingshot /ˈslɪŋ.ʃɒt/ Ⓤⓢ /-ʃɑːt/ **noun** [C] US for **catapult**

slink /slɪŋk/ **verb** [I usually + adv/prep] (**slunk**, **slunk**) to walk away from somewhere quietly so that you are not noticed: *I tried to slink out of the room so that nobody would see me go.* ◦ disapproving *He usually slinks **off** (= leaves) at about 3.30.*

slinky /ˈslɪŋ.ki/ **adj** **1** (of women's clothes) made of delicate cloth and fitting the body closely in a way that is sexually attractive: *a slinky black dress* **2** UK (of music or dancing) slow and suggesting sex: *There's some very slinky dancing going on tonight!*

slip /slɪp/ **verb; noun**

▸**verb** (**-pp-**) **SLIDE** ▷ **1** B1 [I] to slide without intending to: *She slipped on the ice.* ◦ *Careful you don't slip – there's water on the floor.* ◦ *The razor slipped while he was shaving and he cut himself.* **2** C2 [I] to move out of the correct position: *Her hat had slipped over one eye.* ◦ *He could feel the rope slipping out of his grasp.* **DO QUICKLY** ▷ **3** C2 [I or T, usually + adv/prep] to go somewhere or put something somewhere quickly, often so that you are not noticed: *Just slip **out of** the room while nobody's looking.* ◦ *She slipped **between** the cool cotton sheets and was soon asleep.* ◦ *He slipped a piece of paper **into** my hand with his address on it.* ◦ [+ two objects] *If you slip the waiter some money/slip* *some money **to** the waiter he'll give you the best table.* **GET WORSE** ▷ **4** [I] to go into a worse state, often because of lack of control or care: *Productivity in the factory has slipped quite noticeably in the last year.* **ESCAPE** ▷ **5** [T] to get free from, leave, or escape something: *The ship slipped its moorings.* **VALUE** ▷ **6** [I] to go down in value: *The dollar slipped **against** the Japanese yen.*

IDIOMS **slip sb's memory/mind** C2 to be forgotten: *I forgot I'd arranged to meet Richard last night – it completely slipped my mind.* • **slip through sb's fingers** If you allow an opportunity or a person to slip through your fingers, you lose it or them through not taking care or making an effort: *You're surely not going to let a job/man like that slip through your fingers!* • **slip through the net** UK (US **slip through the cracks**) to escape a punishment or be missed by a system that should deal with or protect you: *Once again terrorists have slipped through the police net.* ◦ *There are laws there to protect the mentally ill, but now and then someone does slip through the net.*

PHRASAL VERBS **slip away 1** C2 to leave secretly: *He slipped away while we were all sleeping.* **2** C2 If a period of time slips away, it passes quickly: *Time was slipping away and she had to make a decision soon.* **3** C2 If someone's power or the possibility of someone winning or achieving something slips away, it disappears: *Political power was really in their hands and they let it slip away.* • **slip into sth** (also **slip sth on**) to quickly put on a piece of clothing: *If you could wait two minutes, I'm just going to slip into a smarter dress.* ◦ *You don't need to go into the changing rooms – just slip the jacket on over your sweater.* • **slip out** C2 If a remark slips out, you say it without intending to. • **slip out of sth** (also **slip sth off**) to quickly take off a piece of clothing: *Slip your shirt off and I'll listen to your heart.* • **slip up** C2 to make a mistake: *These figures don't make sense – have we slipped up somewhere?*

▸noun **PIECE OF PAPER** ▷ **1** [C] a small piece of paper: *a slip **of paper** ◦ If you want to order a book fill in the green slip.* **MISTAKE** ▷ **2** [C] a small mistake: *She's **made** one or two slips – mainly spelling errors – but it's basically well written.* **UNDERWEAR** ▷ **3** [C] a piece of underwear for a woman or girl that is like a dress or skirt **SMALL** ▷ **4 slip of a sth** old-fashioned small and thin, usually because of being young: *I knew her when she was a slip of a **girl**.* **ESCAPE** ▷ **5 give sb the slip** informal to escape from someone who is following or chasing you

IDIOM **slip of the tongue** something that you say by accident when you intended to say something else: *I called her new boyfriend by her previous boyfriend's name – it was just a slip of the tongue.*

slipcase /ˈslɪp.keɪs/ noun [C] a case to protect a book, usually made of cardboard, with one open end

slipcover /ˈslɪpˌkʌv.əʳ/ (US) /-ɚ/ noun [C] a cover for a chair or SOFA

slipknot /ˈslɪp.nɒt/ (US) /-nɑːt/ noun [C] a knot that can easily be made tighter or looser by pulling one of its ends

ˈslip-on noun [C usually plural] a shoe with no way of fastening it to the foot that can be quickly put on and taken off: *a pair of slip-ons ◦ slip-on shoes*

slippage /ˈslɪp.ɪdʒ/ noun [U] **1** a reduction in the rate, amount, or standard of something: *The party leader is said to be concerned at the slippage (= loss of popularity) in the recent opinion polls.* **2** a failure to happen or finish on time: *the slippage of the book's publication date*

ˌslipped ˈdisc UK (US **ˌslipped ˈdisk**) noun [C] a medical condition in which one of the DISCS (= flat pieces of tissue between the bones in the back) slides out of its usual place, causing pain

slipper /ˈslɪp.əʳ/ (US) /-ɚ/ noun [C] a type of soft, comfortable shoe for wearing inside the house: *a pair of slippers ◦ After a hard day's work, Flavio loved relaxing in his slippers.*

slippery /ˈslɪp.ᵊr.i/ (US) /-ɚ-/ adj **1** C1 If something is slippery, it is wet or smooth so that it slides easily or causes something to slide: *slippery soap ◦ a slippery floor ◦ The road was wet and slippery.* **2** informal disapproving Someone who is slippery cannot be trusted: *He's **as** slippery **as an eel** – you can never get a straight answer out of him. ◦ He's a slippery **customer** (= person), that Tim, I've never felt comfortable with him.*

ˌslippery ˈslope noun [S] a bad situation or habit which, after it has started, is likely to get very much worse: *You're **on** a slippery slope once you start lying about your age!*

slippy /ˈslɪp.i/ adj UK informal A slippy surface causes you to slip easily because it is wet or smooth: *Careful – I've just polished the floor and it's a bit slippy.* → See also **slippery**

ˈslip ˌroad noun [C] UK (US **ramp**) a short road on which vehicles join or leave a main road

slipshod /ˈslɪp.ʃɒd/ (US) /-ʃɑːd/ adj disapproving (especially of a piece of work) showing little care, effort, or attention

slipstream /ˈslɪp.striːm/ noun [C] a current of air behind a quickly moving object such as a car travelling extremely fast or an aircraft

ˈslip-up noun [C] a mistake or something which goes wrong

slipway /ˈslɪp.weɪ/ noun [C] a sloping track used to move boats into or out of the water

slit /slɪt/ verb; noun

▸verb [T] (present tense **slitting**, past tense and past participle **slit**) to make a long, straight, narrow cut in something: *He slit **open** the envelope with a knife. ◦ She killed herself by slitting her **wrists**. ◦ He was found the next day with his **throat** slit. ◦ She was wearing one of those skirts that's slit up the front.*

▸noun [C] a straight, narrow cut or opening in something: *Make a small slit in each chicken breast and push in a piece of garlic.*

slither /ˈslɪð.əʳ/ (US) /-ɚ/ verb [I usually + adv/prep] (of bodies) to move easily and quickly across a surface while twisting or curving: *She watched the snake slither away.*

sliver /ˈslɪv.əʳ/ (US) /-ɚ/ noun [C] formal a very small, thin piece of something, usually broken off something larger: *a sliver **of** glass ◦ Just a sliver **of** cake for me, please – I shouldn't really be having any.*

slob /slɒb/ (US) /slɑːb/ noun; verb

▸noun [C] informal disapproving a lazy, untidy, and often rude person: *He's a big **fat** slob of a man – I can't stand him.* • **slobbish** /ˈslɒb.ɪʃ/ (US) /ˈslɑː.bɪʃ/ adj

▸verb

PHRASAL VERB **slob around/about** informal disapproving to behave in a very lazy way, doing very little: *He won't get a job and just slobs around the house all day.*

slobber /ˈslɒb.əʳ/ (US) /ˈslɑː.bɚ/ verb; noun

▸verb [I] disapproving to allow SALIVA or food to run out of the mouth • **slobbery** /-i/ adj disapproving *a big, slobbery, (= wet) **kiss***

S

PHRASAL VERB **slobber over sb** informal disapproving to show how much you admire and like someone, in a way that shows little control: *Ted was slobbering over the pretty new assistant in marketing.*

▸noun [U] disapproving SALIVA or food that has run out of the mouth

sloe /sləʊ/ (US) /sloʊ/ noun [C] a small, bluish-black fruit which tastes sour

ˌsloe ˈgin noun [U] an alcoholic drink made from GIN with sloes in it

slog /slɒg/ (US) /slɑːg/ verb; noun

▸verb (-gg-) **WORK HARD** ▷ **1** [I usually + adv/prep] mainly UK informal to work hard over a long period, especially doing work that is difficult or boring: *I've been slogging* ***away*** *for days on this essay and I'm still not finished.* **2** [I + adv/prep] to travel or move with difficulty, for example through wet, sticky soil or snow, or when you are very tired: *Despite the rain, they slogged* ***on*** *for another six miles.* **HIT HARD** ▷ **3** [T] UK to hit a ball hard and often in an uncontrolled way

▸noun **HARD WORK** ▷ **1** [S] mainly UK informal a period of difficult or TIRING effort: *The exams were* ***a*** *real* ***hard*** *slog but I'm glad I did them.* ◦ *That last hill before the finishing-line was* ***a*** *long slog!* **HARD HIT** ▷ **2** [C] UK informal a very hard, and often uncontrolled hit: *And that was a real slog from Kumar.*

slogan /ˈsləʊ.gən/ (US) /ˈsloʊ-/ noun [C] (C1) a short easily remembered phrase, especially one used to advertise an idea or a product: *an advertising slogan* ◦ *a campaign slogan*

sloganeering /ˌsləʊ.gəˈnɪə.rɪŋ/ (US) /ˌsloʊ.gəˈnɪr.ɪŋ/ noun [U] mainly US disapproving *Without a coherent set of policies to persuade the electorate, the Republicans have resorted to sloganeering and empty rhetoric.*

sloop /sluːp/ noun [C] a small sailing boat with one MAST

slop /slɒp/ (US) /slɑːp/ verb; noun

▸verb [I or T, + adv/prep] (-pp-) to cause a liquid to flow over the edge of a container through not taking care or making a rough movement: *Careful, you've just slopped coffee all over the carpet!* ◦ *Water slopped out of the bucket as he carried it up the stairs.*

PHRASAL VERBS **slop about/around** informal to relax and do very little: *Jeans are all right just for slopping around the house, but I don't wear them for work.* • **slop out** UK When prisoners slop out, they empty the containers they use as toilets during the night in the rooms where they sleep.

▸noun **1** [U] informal disapproving food that is more liquid than it should be and is therefore unpleasant: *Have you tried the slop that they call curry in the canteen?* **2 slops** [plural] (also **slop**) liquid or wet food waste, especially when it is fed to animals: *We feed the slops to the pigs.* ◦ *There's a tray under each tap to catch the beer slops.*

slope /sləʊp/ (US) /sloʊp/ noun; verb

▸noun [C] **1** (B2) a surface which lies at an angle to the horizontal so that some points on it are higher than others: *The roof is at a slope (= at an angle to a horizontal surface) of 30°.* **2** (B2) (part of) the side of a hill or mountain: *a ski/mountain slope* ◦ *Snow had settled on some of the higher slopes.* ◦ *There's a very* ***steep*** *slope just before you reach the top of the mountain.* ◦ *There are some nice* ***gentle*** *(= not steep) slopes that we can ski down.*

▸verb [I] to be at an angle to the horizontal: *The path slopes* ***up/down*** *to the house.* ◦ *Our school football pitch sloped at the south end, so one half of the game always had to be played uphill.* • **sloping** /ˈsləʊ.pɪŋ/ (US) /ˈsloʊ-/ adj *sloping handwriting/shoulders* ◦ *The bedroom is in the roof so it's got a sloping ceiling.*

PHRASAL VERB **slope off** UK informal to leave somewhere quietly so that you are not noticed, usually to avoid work: *I saw you sloping off just after lunch yesterday!*

sloppy /ˈslɒp.i/ (US) /ˈslɑː.pi/ adj **TOO WET** ▷ **1** informal disapproving (of a substance) more liquid than it should be, often in a way that is unpleasant: *The batter was a bit sloppy so I added some more flour.* **LACKING CARE** ▷ **2** disapproving not taking care or making an effort: *Spelling mistakes always look sloppy in a formal letter.* ◦ *Another sloppy pass like that might lose them the whole match.* **3** describes clothes that are large, loose, and often untidy: *At home I tend to wear big sloppy jumpers and jeans.* **EMOTIONAL** ▷ **4** informal disapproving expressing feelings of love in a way that is silly or embarrassing: *a sloppy love song* • **sloppily** /ˈslɒp.ɪ.li/ (US) /ˈslɑː.pɪ-/ adv disapproving badly or carelessly: *a sloppily written letter* • **sloppiness** /-nəs/ noun [U]

slosh /slɒʃ/ (US) /slɑːʃ/ verb [I or T, usually + adv/prep] informal (of a liquid) to move around noisily in the bottom of a container, or to cause liquid to move around in this way by making rough movements: *I could hear you sloshing around in the bath.* ◦ *We sloshed through the puddles.* ◦ *She sloshed (= poured without care) some more brandy into her glass.*

sloshed /slɒʃt/ (US) /slɑːʃt/ adj [after verb] slang drunk: *He always* ***gets*** *sloshed at the annual office party.*

slot /slɒt/ (US) /slɑːt/ noun; verb

▸noun [C] **LONG HOLE** ▷ **1** (C1) a long, narrow hole, especially one for putting coins into or for fitting a separate piece into: *I put my money in the slot and pressed the button but nothing came out.* ◦ *The holder has slots for 100 CDs.* **AMOUNT OF TIME** ▷ **2** (C1) an amount of time that is officially allowed for a single event in a planned order of activities or events: *The programme will occupy that half-hour slot before the nine o'clock news.*

▸verb [I or T, + adv/prep] (-tt-) to put something into a slot or fit together using slots: *The legs of the chair are meant to slot* ***into*** *the holes at the back.* ◦ *Do these two pieces slot* ***together****?* ◦ *Slot piece A* ***into*** *piece B, taking care to keep the two pieces at right angles.*

PHRASAL VERB **slot sb/sth in** to find time to see someone or do something between various other arrangements that have already been made: *Doctor Meredith is busy this morning, but she might be able to slot you in around one o'clock.*

sloth /sləʊθ/ (US) /sloʊθ/ noun **NO EFFORT** ▷ **1** [U] literary unwillingness to work or make any effort: *The report criticizes the government's sloth in tackling environmental problems.* **ANIMAL** ▷ **2** [C] a mammal that moves slowly and lives in trees: *Sloths live in Central and South America.*

slothful /ˈsləʊθ.fəl/ (US) /ˈsloʊθ-/ adj literary lazy: *slothful adolescents*

ˈslot maˌchine noun [C] (UK also **ˈfruit maˌchine**) a machine that you try to win money from by putting coins into it and operating it, often by pressing a button or pulling a handle

slotted /ˈslɒt.ɪd/ (US) /ˈslɑː.t̬ɪd/ adj A slotted kitchen UTENSIL or tool has long narrow holes in it: *a slotted spoon/spatula/screw*

slouch /slaʊtʃ/ verb; noun

▸verb [I] to stand, sit or walk with the shoulders hanging forward and the head bent slightly over so that you look tired and bored: *Straighten your back – try not to slouch.* ◦ *A couple of boys were slouched over* the table reading magazines. ◦ A group of teenagers were slouching around outside the building.

▸**noun** [C usually singular] a way of standing, sitting, or walking with the shoulders hanging forward: *He's developed a slouch from leaning over his books all day.*

IDIOM **be no slouch** informal If you say that someone is no slouch at a particular activity, you mean that they work hard at it and produce good results: *She's no slouch when it comes to organizing parties.*

slough verb; noun

▸**verb** [T] /slʌf/ (of some animals) to have a layer of skin come off: *Snakes slough their skin regularly.*

PHRASAL VERB **slough sth off** **1** literary to get rid of something or someone unwanted: *He seemed to want to slough off all his old acquaintances.* **2** specialized When snakes and other reptiles slough off their skin, they get rid of an old, dead layer of skin.

▸**noun** /slaʊ/ (US) /sluː/ /slaʊ/ **SADNESS** ▷ **1** [S] literary a mental state of deep sadness and no hope: *She seems unable to pull herself out of this deep slough **of** self-pity.* **WET AREA** ▷ **2** [C] an area of soft, wet land

slovenly /ˈslʌv.ən.li/ adj untidy and dirty: *a slovenly appearance* ◦ *I'll have to improve my slovenly habits – my mother's coming to stay.* • **slovenliness** /-nəs/ noun [U]

slow /sləʊ/ (US) /sloʊ/ adj; verb; adv

▸**adj** **NOT FAST** ▷ **1** (A1) moving, happening, or doing something without much speed: *a slow runner/driver/reader* ◦ *She's a very slow eater.* ◦ *We're making slow but steady progress with the decorating.* ◦ *The government was very slow **to** react to the problem.* ◦ *Business is always slow during those months because everyone's on holiday.* → Opposite **fast**, or **quick** **NOT EXCITING** ▷ **2** (B2) describes a film, book, play, etc. that does not have much excitement and action: *His films are so slow they send me to sleep.* **NOT CLEVER** ▷ **3** A person might be described as slow if they are not very clever and do not understand or notice things quickly: *I feel so slow when I'm with Andrew – he's so much brighter than me.* ◦ *I was a bit slow **off the mark/on the uptake** there – I didn't follow his reasoning at all.* → See also **slow-witted** **TIME** ▷ **4** If a clock or watch is slow, it shows a time that is earlier than the real time: *That clock is ten minutes slow.*

▸**verb** [I or T] (C2) to reduce speed or activity, or to make something do this: *Business development has slowed in response to the recession.* ◦ *Traffic slows **to a crawl** (= goes so slowly it almost stops) during rush hour.* ◦ *The pilot was asked to slow his approach to the runway.*

PHRASAL VERBS **slow (sb/sth) down/up** (B2) to become slower, or to make someone or something become slower: *Slow down, you two, you're walking too fast!* ◦ *If I run with Christina she tends to slow me down.* ◦ *We slowed up when we saw the police.* • **slow down** (B2) to be less active and relax more: *The doctor has told him to slow down or he'll have a heart attack.*

▸**adv** at a slow speed: *I can't walk any slower.* ◦ *slow-moving traffic* ◦ *a slow-burning candle* ◦ mainly US *He drives too slow!*

ˌslow ˈburn noun [C usually singular] **ACTIVITY** ▷ **1** UK a period of not much activity: *Many workers have benefited from the new scheme, which allows careers to be put **on** a slow burn for months or years and then reactivated.* **ANGER** ▷ **2** US a slow, controlled show of anger: *When angered, Ellen was given to spontaneous outbursts, while her partner Terry would **do** a slow burn.*

ˈslow ˌcity noun [C] a town or city that tries to encourage a good environment, for example by providing a lot of parks and using food that is grown in the local area

slowcoach /ˈsləʊ.kəʊtʃ/ (US) /ˈsloʊ.koʊtʃ/ noun [C] UK (US **slowpoke**) someone, especially a child, who is walking or doing something too slowly: [as form of address] *Come on, slowcoach, we haven't got all day you know!*

slowdown /ˈsləʊ.daʊn/ (US) /ˈsloʊ-/ noun [C] **1** a reduction in speed, activity, or the rate that things are produced: *a worldwide economic slowdown* ◦ *a slowdown **in** production* **2** US for **go-slow**

ˈslow ˌfood noun [U] good food that is prepared and cooked carefully

ˌslow ˈhandclap noun [C usually singular] UK an occasion when a crowd watching a performance, sports event, etc. clap very slowly to show that they are annoyed

slowly /ˈsləʊ.li/ (US) /ˈsloʊ-/ adv **1** (A2) at a slow speed: *Could you please speak more slowly?* **2** **slowly but surely** carefully, in order to avoid problems: *Slowly but surely we made our way down the muddy hillside.*

ˌslow ˈmotion noun [U] a way of showing pictures from a film or television programme at a slower speed than normal: *They showed the goal **in** slow motion.*

slowpoke /ˈsləʊ.pəʊk/ (US) /ˈsloʊ.poʊk/ noun [C] US for **slowcoach**

ˌslow-ˈwitted adj not clever and therefore slow to notice or understand things

slowworm /ˈsləʊ.wɜːm/ (US) /ˈsloʊ.wɜːm/ noun [C] a small, brownish-grey LIZARD with no legs, found in Europe

SLR (camera) /ˌes.elˌɑːˈkæm.rə/ (US) /-ˌɑːr-/ noun [C] abbreviation for single-lens reflex (camera): a type of film camera in which the same LENS (= special piece of glass) is used for looking at and recording an image

sludge /slʌdʒ/ noun [U] soft, wet soil or a substance that looks like this: *We seemed to spend the last mile of the walk knee-deep in sludge.*

sludgy /ˈslʌdʒ.i/ adj disapproving soft, wet, and very thick: *a thick, sludgy pudding*

slug /slʌg/ noun; verb

▸**noun** [C] **CREATURE** ▷ **1** a small, usually black or brown creature with a long, soft body and no arms or legs, like a SNAIL but with no shell **2** mainly US informal a slow-moving, lazy person → See also **sluggish** **BULLET** ▷ **3** informal a bullet: *The poor guy wound up with a slug in his stomach.* **AMOUNT OF DRINK** ▷ **4** informal an amount of drink, especially strong alcoholic drink, that you can swallow at one time: *I had a slug **of** vodka to give me courage.* **COIN** ▷ **5** US a piece of metal used instead of a coin for putting in machines

▸**verb** [T] (-gg-) **1** informal to hit someone hard with the FIST (= closed hand): *She slugged him and he fell against the bar.* **2** US to hit a baseball hard

IDIOM **slug it out** If two people slug it out, they fight or argue violently until one of them wins.

slugger /ˈslʌg.əʳ/ (US) /-ɚ/ noun [C] US informal **1** a baseball player who hits the ball very hard **2** approving someone, especially a young boy, who tries very hard at something

sluggish /ˈslʌg.ɪʃ/ adj moving or operating more slowly than usual and with less energy or power: *A heavy lunch makes me sluggish in the afternoon.* ◦ *Something is wrong with the car – the engine feels a bit sluggish.* ◦ *The housing market has been very sluggish these past few years.* • **sluggishly** /-li/ adv • **sluggishness** /-nəs/ noun [U]

S

ˈslug ˌpellet noun [C usually plural] a small, hard piece of a substance that is poisonous to slugs (= small garden creatures harmful to plants)

sluice /sluːs/ noun; verb

▸noun [C] (also **sluiceway**) an artificial CHANNEL for carrying water, which has an opening at one end to control the flow of the water

▸verb [I usually + adv/prep] If water sluices out from somewhere, it flows in large amounts: *Water sluiced **out** from the pipes.*

PHRASAL VERB **sluice sth down/out** to wash something with a large amount of running water: *We had to sluice out the garage to get rid of the smell of petrol.*

slum /slʌm/ noun; verb

▸noun [C] **1** a very poor and crowded area, especially of a city: *an inner-city slum* ◦ *She was brought up in the slums of Lima.* **2** informal disapproving a very untidy or dirty place: *This flat would be an absolute slum if I wasn't here to clean it.*

▸verb informal **slum it** to spend time in conditions that are much less good than the standard that you are used to: *We ran out of money on holiday and had to slum it in cheap hostels.*

slumber /ˈslʌm.bəʳ/ (US) /-bɚ/ noun; verb

▸noun [C or U] literary sleep: *I fell into a gentle slumber.* ◦ *I didn't want to rouse you from your slumbers.* ◦ figurative *Sharp cuts in interest rates have failed to bring the economy out of its slumber.*

▸verb [I] literary to sleep

ˈslumber ˌparty noun [C] US a party when a group of children spend the night at one child's house → See also **sleepover**

slump /slʌmp/ verb; noun

▸verb REDUCE SUDDENLY ▷ **1** [I] (of prices, values, or sales) to fall suddenly: *The value of property has slumped.* ◦ *Car sales have slumped dramatically over the past year.* SIT/FALL ▷ **2** [I usually + adv/prep] to sit or fall heavily and suddenly: *She slumped into the chair, exhausted.*

▸noun [C] **1** a fall in the price, value, sales, etc. of something: *There's been a slump in the demand for new cars.* **2** a period when an industry or the economy is in a bad state and there is a lot of UNEMPLOYMENT: *an economic slump* ◦ *The airline industry is currently **in a** slump.*

slumped /slʌmpt/ adj having your head low and shoulders forward: *He sat slumped **over** his desk, the picture of misery.*

S

slung /slʌŋ/ verb past simple and past participle of **sling**

slunk /slʌŋk/ verb past simple and past participle of **slink**

slur /slɜːʳ/ (US) /slɝː/ verb; noun

▸verb [T] (-rr-) PRONOUNCE BADLY ▷ **1** to pronounce the sounds of a word in a way that is wrong or not clear: *Her **speech** was slurred but she still denied she was drunk.* MUSIC ▷ **2** to sing or play notes in a smooth and connected manner CRITICIZE ▷ **3** to harm someone's reputation by criticizing them: *The report slurs both the teachers and pupils.*

▸noun CRITICISM ▷ **1** [C] a remark that criticizes someone and is likely to have a harmful effect on their reputation: *Her letter contained several outrageous slurs **against/on** her former colleagues.* ◦ *His comments **cast** a slur **on** the integrity of his employees.* BAD PRONUNCIATION ▷ **2** [S] a way of pronouncing the sounds of a word that is unclear, uncontrolled, or wrong: *The drug affected her vision and made her speak with **a** slur.* MUSIC ▷ **3** [C] a curved line written over or under musical notes to show that they must be played in a smooth and connected manner

slurp /slɜːp/ (US) /slɝːp/ verb **1** [I or T] informal to drink a liquid noisily as a result of sucking air into the mouth at the same time as the liquid: *Do try not to slurp.* ◦ *I wish you wouldn't slurp your soup like that.* ◦ *He slurped **down** his coffee.* **2** [I] UK informal When a thick liquid slurps, it makes loud noises: *The lava slurped and bubbled down the mountainside.* • **slurp** noun [C] informal *She paused to take a slurp **of** tea.*

slurry /ˈslʌr.i/ (US) /ˈslɝː-/ noun [U] a mixture of water and small pieces of a solid, especially such a mixture used in an industrial or farming process

slush /slʌʃ/ noun SNOW ▷ **1** [U] snow that is lying on the ground and has started to melt **2** [C or U] mainly US a thick drink made from crushed ice and a sweet liquid: *a cherry/cola slush* ROMANTIC LANGUAGE ▷ **3** [U] language or writing that is too emotional and romantic and does not have any real importance or meaning

ˈslush ˌfund noun [C] an amount of money that is kept for dishonest or illegal activities in politics or business: *He used his party's slush fund to buy votes in the election.*

ˈslush ˌpile noun [C] a pile of MANUSCRIPTS (= early versions) of books that have been sent by writers to a publisher and that will probably not be published: *Her novel was rescued from the slush pile and made into a hit movie.*

slushy /ˈslʌʃ.i/ adj SNOW ▷ **1** Slushy snow is partly melted. ROMANTIC LANGUAGE ▷ **2** Slushy language is too emotional and romantic.

slut /slʌt/ noun [C] SEXUALLY ACTIVE WOMAN ▷ **1** slang disapproving a woman who has sexual relationships with a lot of men without any emotional involvement LAZY WOMAN ▷ **2** UK very informal disapproving a woman who is usually untidy and lazy • **sluttish** /ˈslʌt.ɪʃ/ (US) /ˈslʌt̬-/ adj (also **slutty**) slang disapproving

sly /slaɪ/ adj; noun

▸adj (**slyer**, **slyest**) **1** deceiving people in a clever way in order to get what you want: *He's a sly old devil – I wouldn't trust him with my money.* **2** [before noun] seeming to know secrets: *'You'll find out eventually,' said Mary with a sly **smile**.* • **slyly** /ˈslaɪ.li/ adv • **slyness** /ˈslaɪ.nəs/ noun [U]

▸noun **on the sly** If you do something on the sly, you do it secretly because you should not be doing it: *He drives his mother's car on the sly while she's at work.*

slyboots /ˈslaɪ.buːts/ noun [C] (plural **slyboots**) UK old-fashioned informal a person who avoids showing or telling other people what he or she is thinking or intending: [as form of address] ***You** old slyboots! Why didn't you tell us about your new girlfriend?*

ˈsly ˌgrog noun [U] Australian English informal illegally sold alcoholic drink

smack /smæk/ verb; noun; adv

▸verb **1** [T] to hit someone or something forcefully with the flat inside part of your hand, producing a short, loud noise, especially as a way of punishing a child: *I never smack my children.* ◦ *I'll smack your **bottom** if you don't behave yourself.* **2** [I or T, usually + adv/prep] to hit something hard against something else: *I smacked my head on the corner of the shelf.* ◦ *She smacked her books **down** on the table and stormed out of the room.*

IDIOM **smack your lips** to close and open your mouth loudly to express a strong wish to eat something you like a lot: *'I adore chocolate cake,' said Susannah, smacking her lips.*

PHRASAL VERB **smack of sth** If something smacks of an unpleasant quality, it seems to have that quality: *The whole affair smacks of mismanagement and incompetence.*

▸noun **HIT FORCEFULLY** ▷ **1** [C] a hit from someone's flat hand as a punishment: *You're going to get a smack **on** the bottom if you don't stop being such a naughty boy.* **2** [C] informal a hit given with the FIST (= closed hand): *I **gave** him a smack **on** the jaw.* **3** [C] a short, loud noise: *She slammed her case down on the desk with a smack.* **4** [C] informal a loud kiss: *a big smack **on** the lips* **DRUG** ▷ **5** [U] slang HEROIN (= a strong illegal drug): *How long has she been **on** smack?*

▸adv (UK also ˈ**smack bang**, US also ˈ**smack dab**) **EXACTLY** ▷ **1** exactly in a place: *She lives smack in the middle of London.* **DIRECTLY** ▷ **2** directly and forcefully, producing a short, loud noise: *I wasn't looking where I was going and walked smack into a lamppost.*

smacker /ˈsmæk.əʳ/ (US) /-ɚ/ noun **MOUTH** ▷ **1** [C] informal a loud or long kiss **2** [C] US the lips or the outer part of the mouth: *a kiss **on** the smacker* **MONEY** ▷ **3** [C usually plural] slang a pound or dollar: *It cost me 50 smackers to get that window fixed.*

smackhead /ˈsmæk.hed/ noun [C] UK informal a person who regularly takes HEROIN (= a strong illegal drug)

small /smɔːl/ (US) /smɑːl/ adj; adv; noun

▸adj **LITTLE** ▷ **1** (A1) little in size or amount when compared with what is typical or average: *a small dog/house/car/country* ◦ *I'd rather live in a small town than a big city.* ◦ *Would you like a large or small cola with your burger?* ◦ *Ella is the smallest girl in her class.* ◦ *That jacket's too small **for** you.* ◦ *He's small **for** his age.* ◦ *Only a small **number** of applicants are successful.* ◦ *The number of women in parliament is **pitifully** (= extremely) small.* ◦ *Liqueurs are usually drunk **in** small **quantities**.* **YOUNG** ▷ **2** (A1) describes a very young child that is older than a baby: *Looking after small children can be very tiring.* **LIMITED ACTIVITY** ▷ **3** [before noun] limited in the amount of an activity: *The government should give more help to small businessmen (= people whose businesses are of a limited size).* ◦ *Chris is quite a small **eater** so he won't want much.* ◦ *If you can help us in a small **way** (= to a limited degree) it would be greatly appreciated.* **NOT IMPORTANT** ▷ **4** (A2) not very important or not likely to cause problems: *She just made a couple of small mistakes in the test.* ◦ *I have a small problem I would like to discuss with you.* **ASHAMED** ▷ **5** ashamed or weak: *Talking to her makes me **feel** small.* ◦ *He's always trying to make me **look** small in front of my boss.* **LETTER SIZE** ▷ **6** [before noun] describes letters that are not capital letters: *The poet e. e. cummings wrote his name with small letters, not capital letters.* **7** UK A CONSERVATIVE with a small 'c' is someone who has traditional values, such as disliking change in society, rather than being a member or supporter of the CONSERVATIVE PARTY. We can use this structure with other words to say something is more general or less extreme than the usual meaning: *Management is all about politics with a small 'p'.* • **smallness** /ˈsmɔːl.nəs/ (US) /ˈsmɑːl-/ noun [U] *The smallness **of** the city often surprises first-time visitors.*

IDIOMS **grateful/thankful for small mercies** If someone should be grateful/thankful for small mercies, they should be grateful for something although it is not as good as they would like: *We've only raised a quarter of the money we needed, but I suppose we must be thankful for small mercies.* • **it's a small world** saying said to show your surprise that people or events in different places are connected: *So you know my old science teacher! Well, it's certainly a small world, isn't it?* • **a small fortune** informal a large amount of money: *You'll have to **spend** a small fortune in legal fees if you decide to sue for compensation.* • **small wonder** used to mean that something is not surprising: *After five years with the company she hadn't been promoted – small wonder then **that** she decided to quit her job.*

> **Other ways of saying small**
>
> **Little** is a very common alternative to 'small', and can describe things or people.
>
> If someone is extremely small, you can say that the person is **tiny**, and if something is extremely small, you can say that it is **minute**, **tiny**, or, in more formal contexts, **microscopic** or **minuscule**:
>
> *The Chihuahua is the **tiniest** breed of dog in the world.*
>
> *The phone he pulled out of his pocket was **minute**.*
>
> *The cost of vaccination is **minuscule** compared to the cost of treatment.*
>
> The adjectives **dwarf** and **miniature** are sometimes used to describe things that are smaller than the normal size:
>
> *There were **dwarf** fir trees in pots on the patio.*
>
> *It's a **miniature** bath for the doll's house.*
>
> If a person or thing is small in an attractive way, you can use the adjectives **dainty** or **petite**:
>
> *She had **dainty** feet.*
>
> *Emma was dark and **petite**.*
>
> The adjective **slight** is sometimes used with abstract nouns to describe things that are small and not important:
>
> *There was a **slight** difference in colour.*

▸adv in a small size: *The instructions are printed so small I can hardly read them.*

▸noun **UNDERWEAR** ▷ **1 smalls** [plural] UK old-fashioned informal underwear, especially when being washed or about to be washed **BODY** ▷ **2 the small of your back** the middle of the lower back: *I have a pain **in** the small of my back.*

ˈ**small** ˌ**ad** noun [C] UK **classified ad**

ˈ**small** ˌ**arms** noun [plural] small light guns that are held and FIRED in one or both hands

ˌ**small** ˈ**beer** noun [U] UK (US ˌ**small po**ˈ**tatoes**) something that does not seem important when compared to something else: *The insurance premium is small beer compared to what we'd have to pay if the house burned down.*

ˌ**small** ˈ**change** noun [U] **1** money that is in the form of coins of low value **2** something that is not considered to be expensive or important: *He spent $10 million on a race horse, but that's just small change to him.*

ˌ**small** ˈ**claims** ˌ**court** noun [C or U] a law court which deals with claims for small amounts of money, especially from people who believe that they have had money taken from them unfairly by a business

ˌ**smallest** ˈ**room** noun [S] UK informal old-fashioned for the TOILET (= room with a toilet)

ˈ**small** ˌ**fry** noun [U] informal people or things that are not considered to be important: *They may be key players in their own company, but they're small fry in the industry itself.*

S

smallholder /ˈsmɔːlˌhəʊl.dəʳ/ (US) /ˈsmɑːlˌhoʊl.dɚ/ noun [C] UK someone who owns a smallholding

smallholding /ˈsmɔːlˌhəʊl.dɪŋ/ (US) /ˈsmɑːlˌhoʊl-/ noun [C] UK an area of land that is used for farming but is much smaller than a typical farm

ˈsmall ˌhours noun [plural] the early hours of the morning, between twelve o'clock at night and the time when the sun rises: *She was up until* ***the*** *small hours of the morning trying to finish her essay.*

ˌsmall inˈtestine noun [C usually singular] the upper part of the bowels between the stomach and the LARGE INTESTINE

ˌsmall-ˈminded adj disapproving having fixed opinions and refusing to consider new or different ideas: *He has some very small-minded opinions about foreigners.* • **small-mindedness** /-nəs/ noun [U]

smallpox /ˈsmɔːl.pɒks/ (US) /ˈsmɑːl.pɑːks/ noun [U] an extremely infectious disease which causes a fever, spots on the skin, and often death

ˈsmall ˌprint noun [U] UK (US **ˈfine ˌprint**) text in a formal agreement that is printed smaller than the rest of the text, sometimes in the hope that it will not be noticed: *Don't sign anything until you've* ***read*** *the small print.*

the ˈsmall ˌscreen noun [S] television, especially when compared with cinema: *Her new detective series will be her debut on the small screen.*

ˈsmall ˌtalk noun [U] conversation about things that are not important, often between people who do not know each other well: *I don't enjoy parties where I have to* ***make*** *small talk with complete strangers.*

ˈsmall-time adj disapproving not very successful or important: *a small-time crook* ◦ *a small-time theatre* • **ˈsmall-timer** noun [C]

ˈsmall-town adj [before noun] describes small social groups where ordinary people live: *The film explores the life of small-town America in the 1930s.*

smarmy /ˈsmɑː.mi/ (US) /ˈsmɑːr-/ adj informal disapproving extremely polite or helpful or showing a lot of respect in a way that is annoying or does not seem sincere: *She was trying to be friendly, but she just seemed smarmy and insincere.* • **smarm** /smɑːm/ (US) /smɑːrm/ verb [I or T] *He's always trying to smarm his way into a promotion.*

smart /smɑːt/ (US) /smɑːrt/ adj; verb

▸adj **STYLISH** ▷ **1** (B1) mainly UK having a clean, tidy, and stylish appearance: *Guy* ***looks*** *very smart in his new suit, doesn't he?* ◦ *I need a smart jacket for my interview.* ◦ *She works in a very smart* ***new*** *office overlooking the river.* **2** (B1) mainly UK A place or event that is smart attracts fashionable, stylish, or rich people: *a smart restaurant* ◦ *We went to a very smart party on New Year's Eve.* **CLEVER** ▷ **3** (B1) mainly US intelligent, or able to think quickly or cleverly in difficult situations: *Gemma's teacher says she's one of the smartest kids in the class.* ◦ *Why don't you fix it if you're so smart?* ◦ *I'm not smart enough to understand computers.* ◦ *He's smart enough to know he can't run the business without her.* ◦ *Quitting that job was the smartest* ***move*** *I ever made.* **QUICK** ▷ **4** [before noun] done quickly with a lot of force or effort: *She gave him a smart smack on the bottom.* ◦ *We'll have to work at a smart pace if we're going to finish on time.* **WORKING BY COMPUTER** ▷ **5** (C1) A smart machine, weapon, etc. uses computers to make it work so that it is able to act in an independent way: *Until the advent of smart weapons, repeated attacks were needed to ensure the destruction of targets.* • **smartness** /ˈsmɑːt.nəs/ (US) /ˈsmɑːrt-/ noun [U] UK

▸verb [I] **1** to hurt with a sharp pain: *My eyes were smarting* ***from*** *the onions.* **2** to feel upset and angry because of failure or criticism: *The police are* ***still*** *smarting* ***from*** *their failure to prevent the robbery.*

smart alec (also **smart aleck**) /ˌsmɑːtˈæl.ɪk/ (US) /ˌsmɑːrt-/ noun [C] informal someone who tries to appear clever or who answers questions in a clever way that annoys other people

ˈsmart-ˌarse noun [C] UK (US **ˈsmart-ˌass**) someone who is always trying to seem more clever than other people in a way that is annoying: *I don't want some smart-arse from the city telling me how to manage my farm.*

ˈsmart ˌbomb noun [C] a bomb that is directed to the object it is intended to hit by a television signal or a LASER

ˈsmart ˌcard noun [C] a small plastic card that is used to make payments and to store personal information, and can be read when connected to a computer system

ˈsmart ˌdrug noun [C usually plural] a drug that is designed to make you more intelligent or help you think more clearly

smarten /ˈsmɑː.tᵊn/ (US) /ˈsmɑːr-/ verb

PHRASAL VERB **smarten (sb/sth) up** mainly UK to (cause to) become more clean, tidy, and stylish: *She's really smartened her****self*** *up since she left university.* ◦ *You'll have to smarten up if you want to work in television.*

IDIOM **smarten up your act** mainly UK to make more effort: *Why are you always so late? You'll have to smarten up your act if you want to keep your job.*

smartly /ˈsmɑːt.li/ (US) /ˈsmɑːrt-/ adv **STYLISH** ▷ **1** UK or US old-fashioned in a fashionable and slightly formal way: *Paul's always very smartly* ***dressed.*** **QUICK** ▷ **2** quickly or forcefully: *The good economic news caused share prices to rise smartly this afternoon.*

the ˈsmart ˌmoney noun [S] money that is INVESTED (= given to companies hoping to get more back) by experienced INVESTORS who know a lot about what they are doing: *The smart money is coming back into mortgages as the best investment now.*

IDIOM **the smart money is on/says...** If the smart money is on something or says something, that thing is considered to be likely to happen: *The smart money says she'll win the world championship.*

ˈsmart ˌmouth noun [C usually singular] US informal If someone has or is a smart mouth, they speak to other people in a way that shows little respect. • **ˌsmart-ˈmouthed** adj *a smart-mouthed little brat*

smartphone /ˈsmɑːt.fəʊn/ (US) /ˈsmɑːrt.foʊn/ noun [C] a mobile phone that can be used as a small computer and that connects to the internet

smarts /smɑːts/ (US) /smɑːrts/ noun [plural] US informal intelligence: *He's got* ***the*** *smarts to figure out what to do next.*

ˈsmart ˌset noun [U] UK people who are fashionable, rich, and often artistic or well educated: *The nightclub is popular with Berlin's smart set.*

smarty-pants /ˈsmɑː.ti.pænts/ (US) /ˈsmɑːr.t̬i-/ noun [C] (plural **smarty-pants**) informal someone who wants to appear to be clever: [as form of address] *Okay, smarty-pants, you tell me how to do it then.*

smash /smæʃ/ verb; noun

▸verb **BREAK NOISILY** ▷ **1** (B2) [I or T] to cause something to break noisily into a lot of small pieces: *Rioters ran through the city centre smashing* ***windows*** *and looting shops.* ◦ *She dropped her cup and watched it smash* ***to pieces/to smithereens*** *on the stone floor.* **MOVE**

FORCEFULLY ▷ **2** [I or T, + adv/prep] to cause something to move with great force against something hard, usually causing damage or injury: *Several boats were smashed against the rocks during the storm.* ◦ *He tried to smash the door* ***down*** *to get to me.* ◦ *The car was travelling very fast when it smashed* ***into*** *the tree.* ◦ *He threatened to smash* ***my face in*** *if I didn't give him the money.* **3** [I or T] in tennis, to hit the ball down towards the ground quickly and forcefully **DEFEAT** ▷ **4** [T] to defeat someone or to destroy something completely: *The government said it would do whatever was necessary to smash the rebellion.* **DO BETTER** ▷ **5** [T] to do much better than the best or fastest result recorded previously: *Petersen smashed the 400 metres record* ***by*** *over half a second.*

smash

PHRASAL VERB **smash sth up** to damage something in a violent way: *In the 60s he was famous for taking drugs and smashing up hotel rooms.*

▸noun **NOISE** ▷ **1** [S] the sound of something being smashed: *I was woken by the smash of glass.* **2** [C] the sound of something smashing against something: *The cars collided with a loud smash.* **ACCIDENT** ▷ **3** [C] a **smash-up** **TENNIS** ▷ **4** [C] in tennis, a powerful downward hit that sends the ball forcefully over the net **SUCCESSFUL FILM/SONG** ▷ **5** [C] an extremely popular and successful song, play, or film: *This CD contains all the latest smash* ***hits***. ◦ *Her first movie was an international* ***box-office*** *smash.*

ˌsmash-and-ˌgrab ˈraid noun [C] UK a crime in which thieves break the window of a shop and steal things before quickly escaping

smashed /smæʃt/ adj [after verb] slang extremely drunk, or powerfully affected by illegal drugs

smasher /ˈsmæʃ.əʳ/ ⓤⓢ /-ɚ/ noun [C] UK old-fashioned informal someone who is very attractive

smashing /ˈsmæʃ.ɪŋ/ adj UK old-fashioned extremely good, attractive, enjoyable, or pleasant: *There's a smashing view from her office.* ◦ *Jonathan would make a smashing dad.* ◦ *He* ***looks*** *smashing in his dinner suit.*

ˈsmash-up noun [C usually singular] (also **smash**) a road or train accident: *He hasn't driven since his smash-up two years ago.*

smattering /ˈsmæt.ər.ɪŋ/ ⓤⓢ /ˈsmæţ.ɚ-/ noun [C usually singular] a very small amount or number: *There's only a smattering* ***of*** *people who oppose the proposal.*

smear /smɪəʳ/ ⓤⓢ /smɪr/ verb; noun

▸verb **SPREAD** ▷ **1** [T usually + adv/prep] to spread a liquid or a thick substance over a surface: *The children had smeared peanut butter all* ***over*** *the sofa.* ◦ *Can you explain why the front of your car is smeared* ***with*** *blood?* **ACCUSE** ▷ **2** [T] to publicly accuse someone of something unpleasant, unreasonable, or unlikely to be true in order to harm their reputation: *She decided to sue for libel after the newspaper smeared her private life.*

▸noun [C] **SPREAD** ▷ **1** a dirty mark made by spreading a liquid or a thick substance over a surface **ACCUSING** ▷ **2** an attempt to harm someone's reputation by publicly accusing them of something that is unpleasant, unreasonable, or unlikely to be true: *The prime minister has dismissed the allegations as smears and innuendo.* ◦ *She claims she was the victim of a smear* ***campaign*** *(= repeated attempts to damage her reputation).* **MEDICAL TEST** ▷ **3** UK (also **smear test**, US **pap smear**) a medical test in which cells from a woman's CERVIX (= entrance to the WOMB) are removed and examined to discover if there is any disease

smell /smel/ verb; noun

▸verb (**smelled** or UK also **smelt**, **smelled** or UK also **smelt**) **CHARACTERISTIC** ▷ **1** Ⓑ① [I, L only + adj] to have a particular quality that others can notice with their noses: *My hands smell* ***of*** *(US* ***like****) onions.* ◦ *That cake smells good.* ◦ *There's something in the fridge that smells mouldy.* ◦ *Your feet smell (= have an unpleasant smell). Why don't you wash them?* **DISCOVER** ▷ **2** Ⓑ① [T] to notice or discover something using the nose: *Come and smell these flowers!* ◦ *Can you smell something* ***burning****?* ◦ [+ (that)] *Didn't you smell (****that****) the pie was burning?* ◦ *I can smell something nasty in the bottom of the fridge.* **3** [T] informal to know about or be aware of a situation without having to be told about it: *Brenda can smell* ***trouble*** *a mile off (= a long time in advance).* **ABILITY** ▷ **4** Ⓑ② [I] to have the ability to notice or discover that a substance is present by using your nose: *Humans can't smell as well as dogs.* ◦ *What I hate most about having a cold is not being able to smell.* • **-smelling** /-ɪŋ/ suffix ***sweet****-smelling flowers* ◦ ***foul****-smelling rubbish*

> **Other ways of saying smell**
>
> **Aroma** is often used when a smell is strong and pleasant, especially a smell from food or drink:
>
> *The delicious* ***aroma*** *of fresh bread wafted out of the bakery.*
>
> A sweet or pleasant natural smell is a **fragrance**, **perfume**, or **scent**:
>
> *the delicate* ***fragrance*** *of the roses*
> *The* ***perfume*** *of the flowers filled the room.*
> *She smelled the sweet* ***scent*** *of the lilies.*
>
> **Odour** is a slightly more formal word meaning 'smell' and is often used when the smell is unpleasant:
>
> *There was the unmistakable* ***odour*** *of sweaty feet.*
>
> The word **stench** and the informal words **reek** and **stink** can all be used when a smell is very unpleasant:
>
> *the* ***stench*** *of rotting fish*
> *The noisy engines filled the air with the* ***reek*** *of gasoline.*
> *There was a bad* ***stink*** *in the kitchen.*
>
> If a smell just lasts for a short time, carried on a current of air, you could use the word **whiff**:
>
> *He leaned towards me and I got a* ***whiff*** *of garlic.*

IDIOMS **come up/out smelling of roses** UK (US **come up/out smelling like roses**) to have people believe that you are good and honest after a difficult situation which could have made you seem bad or dishonest: *When the results of the fraud investigation were announced last week, the staff came up smelling of roses.* • **smell a rat** to recognize that something is not as it appears to be or that something dishonest is happening: *He's been working late with her every night this week – I smell a rat!* • **smell blood** to recognize an opportunity to take advantage of someone who is in a difficult situation: *When she smells blood, you don't get a second chance.*

PHRASAL VERBS **smell somewhere out** UK (US **smell somewhere up**) to fill a place with a smell, in an unpleasant way: *That aftershave of yours is smelling*

S

out the whole house. • **smell sth/sb out** mainly UK (US usually **sniff sth/sb out**) to discover where something or someone is by smelling: *At customs, dogs are used to smell out drugs in passengers' luggage.*

▸noun **CHARACTERISTIC** ▷ **1** (B1) [C] the characteristic of something that can be recognized or noticed using the nose: *What's your favourite smell?* ◦ *I love **the** smell **of** orange blossoms.* ◦ *The marketplace was filled with delightful smells.* ◦ *There's a **delicious** smell in here.* ◦ *I wish we could get rid of that smell (= bad smell) in the bathroom.* **2 the smell of sth** literary the particular character or feeling that someone or something has: *She's still enjoying the **sweet** smell (= pleasant experience) **of success** after her victory in the world championships.* **ABILITY** ▷ **3** (B2) [U] the ability to notice or discover that a substance is present by using your nose: *Smell is one of the five senses.* ◦ *Dogs have a very good **sense of** smell.* **DISCOVER** ▷ **4** [S] mainly UK the act of putting your nose near something and breathing in so that you can discover its characteristics with your nose: *Have **a** smell **of** this perfume.*

ˈsmelling ˌsalts noun [plural] a chemical with a strong smell that is put under the nose of people who have become unconscious in order to make them awake again

smelly /ˈsmel.i/ adj having an unpleasant smell: *smelly feet*

smelt¹ /smelt/ verb UK past simple and past participle of **smell**

smelt² /smelt/ verb [T] to get a metal from rock by heating it to a very high temperature, or to melt objects made from metal in order to use the metal to make something new • **smelting** /ˈsmel.tɪŋ/ (US) /-t̬ɪŋ/ noun [U]

smelter /ˈsmel.təʳ/ (US) /-t̬ɚ/ noun [C] a factory or machine in which metal is smelted

smidge /smɪdʒ/ noun [C usually singular] **smidgen**

smidgen (also **smidgin**, **smidgeon**) /ˈsmɪdʒ.ɪn/ noun [S] informal a very small amount: *Could I have **a** smidgen more wine?*

smile /smaɪl/ noun; verb

▸noun [C] (B1) a happy or friendly expression on the face in which the ends of the mouth curve up slightly, often with the lips moving apart so that the teeth can be seen: *Amy had a **big/broad** smile **on** her face.* ◦ *She has a nice smile.* ◦ *He winked and **gave** me a smile.* ◦ *It's nice to be able to **bring** a smile **to** people's faces (= make people smile).*

> **Word partners for smile noun**
>
> *break into/give/wear* a smile • *force/manage* a smile • *bring* a smile *to* sb/sb's face • a smile *crosses/plays across/spreads across* sb's face/lips • sb's smile *broadens* • sb's smile *disappears/fades/vanishes* • a *beaming/big/broad/wide* smile • a *faint/slight* smile • a *friendly/warm/wry* smile

IDIOM **be all smiles** to look happy and friendly, especially when other people are not expecting you to: *She's never been very friendly, but she was all smiles when she asked me to help her with her homework.*

▸verb **1** (B1) [I or T] to make a happy or friendly expression in which the corners of your mouth curve up: *He smiled and shook my hand.* ◦ *When he smiled **at** me I knew everything was all right.* ◦ *Esme's so cheerful – she's always smiling.* ◦ *I couldn't help smiling when I thought of how pleased she was going to be.* ◦ *He smiled **politely** as Mary apologized for her drunken friends.* ◦ *He smiled **to himself** as he thought about his new girlfriend.* ◦ *He smiled the **smile** of a man who knew victory was within reach.* **2** [T] to express or say something with a smile: *He smiled his congratulations and left without another word.* ◦ *'Don't you worry about a thing. Everything's going to be just fine,' smiled Robin reassuringly.*

PHRASAL VERB **smile on sth/sb** literary to feel positive about something or someone, or to treat them in a very positive way: figurative *The gods smiled on us and we had brilliant sunshine throughout the day.*

smiley /ˈsmaɪ.li/ noun; adj

▸noun [C] an EMOTICON (= a sideways image of a face, consisting of keyboard symbols, used in emails to express emotions)

▸adj (**smilier**, **smiliest**) informal A smiley person or someone who has a smiley face looks friendly and smiles a lot.

smiling /ˈsmaɪ.lɪŋ/ adj having a smile: *I really miss seeing their happy smiling **faces**.*

smilingly /ˈsmaɪ.lɪŋ.li/ adv If someone does something smilingly, they smile as they are doing it: *When I complained about how long we'd had to wait for our food, the bill was whisked away and smilingly returned without the service charge.*

smirk /smɜːk/ (US) /smɝːk/ noun; verb

▸noun [C] disapproving a smile that expresses satisfaction or pleasure about having done something or knowing something that is not known by someone else: *'Maybe your husband does things that you don't know about,' he said with a smirk.* ◦ *'I told you it would end in disaster,' said Polly with a self-satisfied smirk on her face.*

▸verb [I or T] disapproving to smile in this way: *I don't like the way he winks and smirks **at** me whenever he sees me.* ◦ *He smirked his way through the interview.*

smite /smaɪt/ verb [T] (**smote**, **smitten**) literary to hit someone forcefully or to have a sudden powerful or damaging effect on someone

smith /smɪθ/ noun [C], **suffix** someone who makes things out of metal, especially by heating it and hitting it with a hammer: *a goldsmith/silversmith* → See also **blacksmith**

smithereens /ˌsmɪð.əʳˈiːnz/ (US) /-əˈriːnz/ noun [plural] informal a lot of very small broken pieces: *Our city was bombed **to** smithereens during the war.* ◦ *So many films nowadays involve everyone and everything being **blown to** smithereens.*

smithy /ˈsmɪð.i/ noun [C] a place where things are made out of metal, especially iron or STEEL, by heating and using a hammer

smitten /ˈsmɪt.ən/ (US) /ˈsmɪt̬-/ adj [after verb] having suddenly started to like or love something or someone very much: *The story's about a man smitten **with** love for his wife's cousin.* ◦ *He was so smitten **by** her that he promised to move to Argentina to be near her.*

smock /smɒk/ (US) /smɑːk/ noun [C] a piece of clothing like a long shirt, worn loosely over other clothing to protect it when working, or a piece of women's clothing that is similar to this: *an artist's smock*

smocking /ˈsmɒk.ɪŋ/ (US) /ˈsmɑː.kɪŋ/ noun [U] decoration on a piece of clothing consisting of cloth pulled into tight folds that are held in position with decorative STITCHES

smog /smɒg/ (US) /smɑːg/ noun [S or U] (C1) a mixture of smoke, gases, and chemicals, especially in cities, that makes the atmosphere difficult to breathe and harmful for health: *Smog is a major problem in Athens.* ◦ *As we flew into the airport, we could see a* *murky yellow smog hovering over the city.* • **smoggy** /ˈsmɒg.i/ (US) /ˈsmɑː.gi/ **adj** *Mexico City is one of the world's smoggiest capitals.*

smoke /sməʊk/ (US) /smoʊk/ **noun; verb**

▸**noun** GREY GAS ▷ **1** (B1) [U] the grey, black, or white mixture of gas and very small pieces of carbon that is produced when something burns: ***cigarette** smoke* ◦ *a tiny smoke-**filled** pub* ◦ *The fire produced a **pall** (= large mass) **of** smoke visible 20 miles away.* ◦ ***Plumes of** smoke **billowed** from the chimney.* ◦ *She leaned back thoughtfully and blew **a puff of** (= a small amount of) smoke into the air.* **2 go up in smoke a** to be destroyed by burning: *Because of the fire, hundreds of houses went up in smoke.* **b** Something that goes up in smoke fails to produce the result that was wanted: *When the business went bankrupt, 20 years of hard work went up in smoke.* CIGARETTE ▷ **3** [S] the act of smoking a cigarette: *I really enjoy **a** smoke at the end of a meal.* **4** [C] informal a cigarette: *Would you buy me some smokes while you're out?* CITY ▷ **5 the (big) smoke** UK and Australian English informal any large city, especially London, Sydney, or Melbourne: *He was a young lad of 16 when he first came to the big smoke.*

IDIOM **there's no smoke without fire** UK saying (US **where there's smoke, there's fire**) If unpleasant things are said about someone or something, there is probably a good reason for it: *She says the accusations are not true, but there's no smoke without fire.*

▸**verb** BREATHE SMOKE ▷ **1** (A1) [I or T] to breathe smoke into the mouth and usually lungs from a cigarette, pipe, etc.: *Do you mind if I smoke?* ◦ *I used to smoke a packet (US pack) of cigarettes a day.* GREY GAS ▷ **2** [I] to produce smoke as a result of industrial activity or of something such as an electrical fault: *The skyline is dominated by smoking factory chimneys.* ◦ *Suddenly the TV went blank and started smoking.* PRESERVE ▷ **3** [T] to preserve meat, fish, or cheese using smoke from burning wood: *People in Egypt were salting, drying, and smoking fish and meat 6,000 years ago.* ◦ *She had champagne and smoked **salmon** sandwiches at her birthday party.*

PHRASAL VERB **smoke sb/sth out** If you smoke out an animal or person that is hiding, you force them to leave the place where they are by filling it with smoke: figurative *The finance minister has promised a tougher approach to smoking out (= finding) tax dodgers.*

ˌsmoke and ˈmirrors **noun** [plural] mainly US Something that is described as smoke and mirrors is intended to take attention away from an embarrassing or unpleasant situation

ˈsmoke ˌbomb **noun** [C] a device like a bomb which produces a lot of smoke instead of exploding

smoked /sməʊkt/ (US) /smoʊkt/ **adj** [before noun] describes glass or a window that has been made darker, as if by smoke: *She works in a modern office with smoked-glass windows.*

ˈsmoke deˌtector **noun** [C] a device that makes a loud noise when there is smoke present to tell people that there is a fire

ˌsmoke-filled ˈroom **noun** [C] a place where powerful people, such as politicians, meet to have discussions and make agreements in secret: *The whole business stinks of political corruption and decisions made in smoke-filled rooms.*

smokeless /ˈsməʊk.ləs/ (US) /ˈsmoʊk-/ **adj** **1** UK not causing or allowing smoke: *If you live in a smokeless **zone** you have to use smokeless **fuels** instead of coal.* **2 smokeless tobacco** US tobacco that is CHEWED or put in the mouth

smoker /ˈsməʊ.kəʳ/ (US) /ˈsmoʊ.kɚ/ **noun** [C] **1** (B2) someone who smokes tobacco regularly: *a **cigarette/pipe** smoker* ◦ *Chris is a **light/heavy** smoker (= smokes a little/a lot each day).* **2** UK old-fashioned a train CARRIAGE in which people are allowed to smoke tobacco

smokescreen /ˈsməʊk.skriːn/ (US) /ˈsmoʊk-/ **noun** [C] **1** something that hides the truth about someone's intentions: *Instead of doing something about the problem, the council is hiding **behind** a smokescreen of bureaucracy.* **2** an artificial cloud of smoke that is used to hide the movements or positions of soldiers from the enemy

ˈsmoke ˌsignal **noun** [C usually plural] **1** a message using smoke from a fire, which can be seen from a long distance **2** a statement that is a sign of what someone's intentions are: *The chancellor was **sending out** smoke signals about the new budget proposal.*

smokestack /ˈsməʊk.stæk/ (US) /ˈsmoʊk-/ **noun** [C] a tall, vertical pipe which takes smoke or steam into the air from an engine driven by steam or from a factory

ˈsmokestack ˌindustry **noun** [C] mainly US a traditional industry that produces large machines or materials used in other industries and creates POLLUTION in doing so: *There's been a steady decline in smokestack industries such as shipbuilding and steel.*

smoking /ˈsməʊ.kɪŋ/ (US) /ˈsmoʊ-/ **noun** [U] (A1) the action of smoking a cigarette, pipe, etc., or the activity of doing this regularly: *Smoking is not permitted anywhere in this theatre.* ◦ *The nicotine patches are designed to help people **give up/quit/stop** smoking.* ◦ ***Cigarette** smoking kills thousands of people every year.* ◦ ***No** smoking, please.*

ˌsmoking ˈgun **noun** [C usually singular] information which proves who committed a crime: *The tape recordings provided prosecutors with the smoking gun they needed to prove he'd been involved in the conspiracy.*

ˈsmoking ˌjacket **noun** [C] old-fashioned a comfortable coat for a man that is made from a soft material and is worn when relaxing at home, traditionally when smoking

smoky (**smokier, smokiest**) (also **smokey**) /ˈsməʊ.ki/ (US) /ˈsmoʊ-/ **adj** **1** (C2) If a place is smoky, there is a lot of smoke in it: *a smoky pub/restaurant* ◦ *a smoky fire* **2** describes something which appears to be similar to smoke: *a smoky blue colour* ◦ *This wine has a delicious smoky flavour.*

smolder /ˈsməʊl.dəʳ/ (US) /ˈsmoʊl.dɚ/ **verb** [I] US for **smoulder**

smooch /smuːtʃ/ **verb; noun**

▸**verb** [I] **1** informal to kiss, hold, and touch someone in a way that shows you love them: *Didn't I see you smooching **with** Mark at Kim's party?* **2** UK When two people are smooching, they are dancing slowly and very close together to slow, romantic music: *The dance floor was full of middle-aged couples smooching **to** slushy ballads.*

▸**noun** [C usually singular] **1** informal a kiss: *I was so embarrassed when I walked in on them **having a** smooch on the sofa.* **2** UK a slow, romantic dance: *Kate **had a** smooch with a very attractive young man at the Christmas party.*

smooth /smuːð/ **adj; verb**

▸**adj** REGULAR ▷ **1** (B1) having a surface or consisting of a substance that is perfectly regular and has no holes, LUMPS, or areas that rise or fall suddenly: *a smooth surface/texture/consistency* ◦ *This custard is deliciously smooth and creamy.* ◦ *Mix together the butter and sugar*

S

until smooth. ◦ *The road ahead was flat and smooth.* ◦ *This cream will help to keep your* ***skin*** *smooth.* **NOT INTERRUPTED** ▷ **2** C2 happening without any sudden changes, interruption, or difficulty: *We had a very smooth* ***flight*** *with no turbulence at all.* ◦ *The car's improved suspension gives a much smoother* ***ride*** *than earlier models.* ◦ *An efficient transport system is vital to the smooth* ***running*** *of a country's economy.* **TASTING PLEASANT** ▷ **3** having a pleasant flavour that is not sour or bitter: *This coffee is incredibly smooth and rich.* **NOT SINCERE** ▷ **4** very polite, confident, and able to persuade people, but in a way that is not sincere: *In job interviews, the successful candidates tend to be the smooth* ***talkers*** *who know exactly how to make the right impression.* • **smoothness** /ˈsmuːð.nəs/ **noun** [U] *The wine possesses a smoothness and balanced depth that is rare.* ◦ *I just love the smoothness of silk.*

IDIOM **as smooth as silk/a baby's bottom** extremely smooth: *Her skin was as smooth as silk.*

▸verb **MAKE FLAT** ▷ **1** [I or T] to move your hands across something in order to make it flat: *He straightened his tie nervously and smoothed (****down****) his hair.* **REMOVE PROBLEMS** ▷ **2** [T] to remove difficulties and make something easier to do or achieve: *We encourage parents to help smooth their children's* ***way*** *through school.* ◦ *We must do more to smooth the country's* ***path*** *to democratic reform.* **RUB** ▷ **3** [T + adv/prep] to cover the surface of something with a liquid or cream, using gentle rubbing movements: *Pour some oil into the palm of your hand and then smooth it over your arms and neck.*

PHRASAL VERBS **smooth sth away** to remove the difficulties from something: *My mother was always there to smooth away my fears.* • **smooth sth out** to reduce the difficulties or changes in a process or situation: *By investing small amounts regularly, you can smooth out the effects of sudden rises and falls in the stock market.* • **smooth sth over** to make problems, difficulties, or disagreements less serious or easier to solve, usually by talking to the people involved: *Would you like me to try to smooth* ***things*** *over between you and your parents?*

smoothie /ˈsmuː.ði/ noun [C] **DRINK** ▷ **1** a thick, cold drink made from fruit, ice, and often YOGURT or ice cream, mixed together until smooth **NOT SINCERE** ▷ **2** disapproving a man who is very polite, confident, and able to persuade people, but in a way that is not sincere: *He's such a smoothie – I just assumed he worked in sales.*

smoothly /ˈsmuːð.li/ adv **1** B2 easily and without interruption or difficulty: *The road was blocked for two hours after the accident, but traffic is now* ***flowing*** *smoothly again.* ◦ *Lead is added to fuel to make car engines* ***run*** *more smoothly.* ◦ *The pregnancy's* ***gone*** *very smoothly so far.* ◦ ***If all goes*** *smoothly, we should arrive by nine o'clock.* **2** C2 without any sudden movements or changes: *I drove through the gates, which closed smoothly behind me.*

smorgasbord /ˈsmɔː.gəs.bɔːd/ US /ˈsmɔːr.gəs.bɔːrd/ noun **1** [C] a mixture of many different hot and cold Scandinavian dishes which are arranged so that you can serve yourself **2** [C usually singular] many different types of something that are offered: *a smorgasbord* ***of*** *choices*

smote /sməʊt/ US /smoʊt/ verb past simple of **smite**

smother /ˈsmʌð.əʳ/ US /-ɚ/ verb [T] **COVER** ▷ **1** to kill someone by covering their face so that they cannot breathe: *They threatened to smother the animals with plastic bags.* **2** to kill something by covering it and preventing it from receiving the substances and conditions it needs for life: *Snow soon smothered the last of the blooms.* ◦ figurative *I tried desperately to smother a sneeze (= I tried not to sneeze) during his speech.* **3** to stop a fire from burning by covering it with something which prevents air from reaching it: *I threw a blanket over the cooker to smother the flames.* **NOT DEVELOP** ▷ **4** to prevent something from developing or growing freely: *The latest violence has smothered any remaining hopes for an early peace agreement.* **5** to give someone too much love and attention so that they do not feel independent or free: *I think she broke off their engagement because she felt smothered by him.*

PHRASAL VERB **smother sth in/with sth** to cover something completely with a substance or objects: *She took a slice of chocolate cake and smothered it in cream.*

smoulder UK (US **smolder**) /ˈsməʊl.dəʳ/ US /ˈsmoʊl.dɚ/ verb [I] **BURN** ▷ **1** to burn slowly with smoke but without flames: *a smouldering fire* ◦ *smouldering* ***embers*** ◦ *The fire was started by a smouldering cigarette.* **PROBLEM** ▷ **2** If a problem or unpleasant situation smoulders, it continues to exist and may become worse at any time: *The dispute is* ***still*** *smouldering, five years after the negotiations began.* **EMOTION** ▷ **3** If a strong emotion smoulders, it exists, but is prevented from being expressed: *She was smouldering* ***with*** *rage as she explained how her son had been killed.* **ROMANTIC FEELINGS** ▷ **4** A person who smoulders has strong sexual or romantic feelings but does not express them: *He gazed at her with smouldering* ***eyes****, wishing she wasn't married.*

SMS /ˌes.emˈes/ noun [U] abbreviation for short message service: a system for sending TEXT MESSAGES from one mobile phone to another

SMTP /esˌem.tiːˈpiː/ noun [U] specialized abbreviation for Simple Mail Transfer Protocol: a way of sending emails between computers

smudge /smʌdʒ/ noun; verb

▸noun [C] a mark with no particular shape that is caused, usually by accident, by rubbing something such as ink or a dirty finger across a surface: *Her hands were covered in dust and she had a black smudge on her nose.* ◦ figurative *She said we were nearly there, but the island was still no more than a distant smudge on the horizon.* • **smudgy** /ˈsmʌdʒ.i/ adj

▸verb [I or T] If ink, paint, etc. smudges or if someone smudges it, it becomes dirty or not clear because someone or something has touched it: *She was crying and her mascara had smudged.* • **smudging** /ˈsmʌdʒ.ɪŋ/ noun [U]

smudged /smʌdʒd/ adj dirty or not clear: *The signature was smudged and impossible to decipher.*

smug /smʌg/ adj (**smugger**, **smuggest**) disapproving too pleased or satisfied about something you have achieved or something you know: *a smug grin* ◦ *She deserved her promotion, but I wish she wasn't so damned smug* ***about*** *it.* ◦ *There was a hint of smug* ***self-satisfaction*** *in her voice.* ◦ *He's been* ***unbearably*** *smug since he gave up smoking.* • **smugness** /ˈsmʌg.nəs/ noun [U]

smuggle /ˈsmʌg.l/ verb [T usually + adv/prep] C2 to take things or people to or from a place secretly and often illegally: *She was caught trying to smuggle 26 kilos of heroin* ***out of/into*** *the country.* ◦ *They managed to smuggle a video of the captive journalists* ***out*** *of the prison.* • **smuggling** /-lɪŋ/ noun [U] *The murdered man is thought to have been involved in* ***drug*** *smuggling.*

smuggler /ˈsmʌg.ləʳ/ US /-lɚ/ noun [C] someone who smuggles

smugly /ˈsmʌg.li/ adv disapproving in a way that shows too much satisfaction or confidence: *'I own three cars and two boats,' he said smugly.*

smut /smʌt/ noun **SEXUAL MATERIAL** ▷ **1** [U] disapproving magazines, books, pictures, films, jokes, or conversations which offend some people because they relate to sex: *There's an awful lot of smut on television these days.* ◦ *Patrick's conversations are always full of smut.* **DIRT** ▷ **2** [C or U] dirt or ASH (= powder left when something has burned) that makes a mark on something

smutty /ˈsmʌt.i/ US /ˈsmʌt̬-/ adj disapproving related to or containing smut: *I was really embarrassed by his smutty **jokes**.* • **smuttiness** /-nəs/ noun [U]

snack /snæk/ noun; verb

▸noun [C] A2 a small amount of food that is eaten between meals, or a very small meal: *I had a huge lunch, so I'll only need a snack for dinner.* ◦ *Fresh or dried fruit makes an ideal snack.* ◦ *Many snack **foods** are high in salt, sugar, and fat.*

▸verb [I] to eat small amounts of food between meals: *I've been snacking all day.* ◦ *If you eat three good meals a day, you're less likely to snack **on** biscuits and crisps.*

ˈsnack ˌbar noun [C] a small, informal restaurant where small meals can be eaten or bought to take away

snaffle /ˈsnæf.l̩/ verb [I or T] UK informal to take something quickly for yourself, in a way that prevents someone else from having or using it: *Who's snaffled my pen?* ◦ *Martha snaffled (= ate) all the peanuts before the party had even begun!* ◦ *The company grew by snaffling **up** several smaller businesses.*

snafu /snæˈfuː/ noun [C] US informal a situation in which nothing has happened as planned

snag /snæg/ noun; verb

▸noun [C] **PROBLEM** ▷ **1** informal a problem, difficulty, or disadvantage: *We don't anticipate any snags **in/with** the negotiations.* ◦ *The drug is very effective – the **only** snag is that it cannot be produced in large quantities.* **DAMAGE** ▷ **2** a tear, hole, or loose thread in a piece of clothing or cloth caused by a sharp or rough object: *This sweater's full of snags.* **FOOD** ▷ **3** Australian English informal for **sausage**

▸verb (-gg-) **DAMAGE** ▷ **1** [T] If you snag something, it becomes caught on a sharp object and tears: *Be careful not to snag your coat **on** the barbed wire.* **PROBLEM** ▷ **2** [I or T] mainly US to cause problems or difficulties for someone or something: *Financial problems have snagged the project for the past six months.* ◦ *The negotiations have snagged **on** a dispute about who should chair them.* **GET** ▷ **3** [T] US informal to get or catch something by acting quickly: *They'd have gone bust if they hadn't snagged that contract **from** their rivals.* ◦ *The ball was hit well, but Silverman snagged it for the final out of the inning.*

snail /sneɪl/ noun [C] a small creature with a soft, wet body and a round shell, that moves very slowly and often eats garden plants

snail

IDIOM **at a snail's pace** extremely slowly: *The roads were full of traffic and we were travelling at a snail's pace for two hours.*

ˈsnail ˌmail noun [U] informal humorous letters or messages that are not sent by email, but by post: *We agreed the deal online, but we'll have to wait for snail mail to get the paperwork.*

snake /sneɪk/ noun; verb

▸noun [C] **1** A2 a reptile with a long body and no legs: *He's terrified of being **bitten** by a snake.* ◦ *a snake bite* ◦ *snake **venom*** **2 a snake (in the grass)** an unpleasant person who cannot be trusted

▸verb [I usually + adv/prep] to move along a route that includes a lot of twists or bends: *The river snakes through some of the most spectacular countryside in France.* ◦ *The queue for tickets snaked all the way around the block.*

IDIOM **snake its way** Something that snakes its way moves or is arranged in a twisting way: *A long queue had formed, snaking its way downstairs and out into the street.*

ˈsnake ˌcharmer noun [C] someone who seems to control the movements of snakes by playing music, in order to entertain people

ˌsnakes and ˈladders noun [U] UK (US trademark **ˌchutes and ˈladders**) a children's game played on a board that has pictures of snakes and LADDERS

snaky /ˈsneɪ.ki/ adj Australian English informal annoyed or angry

snap /snæp/ verb; noun; adj; exclamation

▸verb (-pp-) **BREAK** ▷ **1** C2 [I or T] to cause something that is thin to break suddenly and quickly with a CRACKING sound: *You'll snap that ruler if you bend it too far.* ◦ *Some vandal's gone and snapped **off** my car aerial again.* **2** C2 [I] to suddenly become unable to control a strong feeling, especially anger: *When she asked me to postpone my trip to help her move house, I just snapped (= got angry).* **MOVE QUICKLY** ▷ **3** [I or T, usually + adv/prep] to move into a position quickly, producing a short noise as if breaking: *Tendons store elastic energy by stretching and then snapping **back** into shape like rubber bands.* ◦ *Simply snap the pieces into place.* **4** [I + adv/prep] to quickly return to a previous place or condition: *After substantial losses last year, the company has snapped **back** to profitability (= started making profits again).* **5 snap shut** C2 If something snaps shut or is snapped shut, it closes quickly with a sudden sharp sound: *She snapped her book shut and got up to leave.* ◦ *Her mouth snapped shut when she realized he'd heard everything she'd said about him.* **ANIMAL** ▷ **6** [I] If an animal snaps, it tries to bite someone: *The guard dog was snarling and snapping behind the fence.* **SPEAK** ▷ **7** C2 [I or T] to say something suddenly in an angry way: *There's no need to snap **at** me – it's not my fault that you lost your wallet.* ◦ [+ speech] *'Well, I hate you too!' she snapped.* **PHOTOGRAPH** ▷ **8** [I or T] to take a lot of photographs quickly: *He was arrested for snapping photos of a military parade.* ◦ *She's very pleased with her new camera and was snapping **away** the whole time we were abroad.*

IDIOMS **snap your fingers** to a make a noise by pushing your second finger hard against your thumb and then releasing it suddenly so that it hits the base of your thumb: *He was snapping his fingers in time with the music.* • **snap sb's head off** to answer someone in an unreasonably angry way: *There's no point trying to discuss anything with him if all he's going to do is snap your head off.* • **snap at sb's heels** **1** If an animal is snapping at your heels, it is running behind you and trying to bite you. **2** to compete strongly with someone and have a chance of soon defeating or replacing them: *With so many younger women snapping at her heels, this year may be her last*

S

chance to win the championship. • **snap to it** UK (US **snap it up**) used to tell someone to do something more quickly: *We're leaving in five minutes so you'd better snap to it and finish your breakfast.*

PHRASAL VERBS **snap out of sth** informal to force yourself to stop feeling sad and upset: *He just can't snap out of the depression he's had since his wife died.* ◦ *Now come on, snap out of* ***it****. Losing that money isn't the end of the world.* • **snap sth up** informal to buy or get something quickly and enthusiastically because it is cheap or exactly what you want: *The tickets for the concert were snapped up within three hours of going on sale.* ◦ *The fall in property prices means that there are a lot of bargains waiting to be snapped up.* • **snap sb up** informal to immediately offer someone a job or position because you want them very much: *She was snapped up by a large law firm.*

▸noun **BREAKING NOISE** ▷ **1** [C usually singular] a sudden loud sound like something breaking or closing: *She broke the stick over her knee with a loud snap.* **2** [C] US for **press stud** **PHOTOGRAPH** ▷ **3** [C] UK informal an informal photograph that is not very skilful or artistic: ***holiday*** *snaps* ◦ *Did you* ***take*** *many snaps while you were away?* **GAME** ▷ **4** [U] a card game in which the players compete to call out the word 'snap' when they see two cards that have the same value: *a game of snap* **SOMETHING EASY** ▷ **5** [S] US informal something that can be done without any difficulty: *'Will you finish on time?' 'Sure thing. It's* ***a*** *snap.'* ◦ *Talking to girls is a snap* ***for*** *him.*

▸adj [before noun] done suddenly without allowing time for careful thought or preparation: *He always makes snap* ***decisions*** *and never thinks about their consequences.*

▸exclamation **1** 'Snap!' is what you say in the game of snap when two cards of the same value have been played. **2** UK informal something that you say when you notice that two things are the same: *Snap! We're wearing the same shirts!*

ˈsnap ˌbean noun [C] US for **sugar (snap) pea**

snapdragon /ˈsnæpˌdræg.ən/ noun [C] a garden plant with white, yellow, pink, or red flowers whose PETALS are shaped like a pair of lips that open when they are pressed

ˈsnap ˌfastener noun [C] UK a **press stud**

snapper /ˈsnæp.əʳ/ (US) /-ɚ/ noun [C] a fish that can be eaten which lives in warm seas

S

snappish /ˈsnæp.ɪʃ/ adj (also **snappy**) easily annoyed and often speaking in an angry way • **snappishly** /-li/ adv *'Of course I know what I'm doing!' she said, snappishly.*

snappy /ˈsnæp.i/ adj **STYLISH** ▷ **1** informal approving (especially of a man's clothes or of his appearance) modern and stylish: *He's a snappy* ***dresser****.* ◦ *That's a very snappy new suit you've got, Peter.* **EFFECTIVE** ▷ **2** approving immediately effective in getting people's attention or communicating an idea: *The magazine will be launched in September with a snappy new design.* ◦ *They're looking for a snappy slogan to communicate the campaign's message.* • **snappily** /-ɪ.li/ adv approving *The sales team are usually fairly snappily dressed.*

IDIOM **make it snappy** informal used to tell someone that you want them to do something immediately and to do it quickly: *I'd like my bill please, waiter, and make it snappy.*

snapshot /ˈsnæp.ʃɒt/ (US) /-ʃɑːt/ noun [C] informal **PHOTO** ▷ **1** a photograph **UNDERSTANDING** ▷ **2** a piece of information or short description that gives an understanding of a situation at a particular time: *Credit rating agencies provide a snapshot* ***of*** *the risks an investment poses at any one time.*

snare /sneəʳ/ (US) /sner/ noun; verb

▸noun [C] **1** a device for catching small animals and birds, usually with a rope or wire which tightens around the animal **2** a trick or situation which deceives you or involves you in some problem which you do not know about: *The legal system is full of snares for those who are not wary.*

▸verb [T] to catch an animal using a snare: *We used to snare small birds such as sparrows and robins.* ◦ figurative *She grew up in the days when a woman's main aim was to snare a rich husband.*

ˈsnare ˌdrum noun [C] a small drum with twisted wires stretched across the bottom that shake against it when it is hit → Compare **side drum**

snarf /snɑːf/ (US) /snɑːrf/ verb [T] informal **1** to take something without permission: *I snarfed the book off the table when he wasn't looking.* **2** to use a computer document or file without getting the writer's permission: *He hacked into the computer system and snarfed some images.* **3** (also **snarf down**) to eat something very quickly in a way that people think is GREEDY: *He snarfed down the whole cake.*

snarky /ˈsnɑː.ki/ (US) /ˈsnɑːr.ki/ adj informal criticizing someone in an annoyed way and trying to hurt their feelings: *There was some idiot at the back of the hall making snarky comments.*

snarl /snɑːl/ (US) /snɑːrl/ verb; noun

▸verb [I or T] (especially of dogs) to make a deep, rough sound while showing the teeth, usually in anger or (of people) to speak or say something angrily and forcefully: *The dogs started to snarl* ***at*** *each other so I had to separate them.* ◦ [+ speech] *'Go to hell!', he snarled.*

▸noun [C] a deep, rough sound, usually made in anger: *The dog gave a low snarl so I quickly drew my hand back.* ◦ *'Take your hands off me!' she said with a snarl.*

ˌsnarled ˈup adj UK (US usually **snarled**) describes a long line of traffic that is unable to travel forward because something is blocking the road: *The traffic was snarled up in both directions for two miles because of the accident.* • **ˈsnarl-up** noun [C] UK (US usually **snarl**)

snatch /snætʃ/ verb; noun

▸verb [T] **TAKE QUICKLY** ▷ **1** ⓒ to take hold of something suddenly and roughly: *He snatched the photos out of my hand before I had a chance to look at them.* ◦ figurative *Running the best race of his career, Fletcher snatched (= only just won) the gold medal from the Canadian champion.* **2** to take something or someone away by force: *The six-year-old girl was snatched from a playground and her body was found two days later.* ◦ *She had her purse snatched (= stolen) while she was in town.* **3** to do or get something quickly because you only have a short amount of time: *Perhaps you'll be able to snatch a couple of hours' sleep before dinner.*

IDIOM **snatch victory (from the jaws of defeat)** to win at the last moment possible, when it had previously seemed certain that you were going to lose

PHRASAL VERB **snatch at sth** **1** to try to take hold of something: *A man snatched at my bag, but he didn't get it.* **2** UK to try to use an opportunity quickly before it disappears: *I was desperate to find a way out of teaching so when this job came along I snatched at it.*

▸noun [C] **TAKE QUICKLY** ▷ **1** the action of trying to take something quickly and forcefully: *I felt someone* *behind me* ***make*** *a snatch at my bag.* **SHORT PART** ▷ **2** a short part of something: *I tried to hear what they were saying, but I only managed to catch a few snatches* ***of*** *conversation.* **SEX ORGAN** ▷ **3** offensive for the **vagina**

snatcher /ˈsnætʃ.əʳ/ (US) /-ɚ/ **noun** [C] someone who takes something or someone by force: *You have to watch out for bag/purse snatchers (= people who steal bags/*PURSES*).*

snazzy /ˈsnæz.i/ **adj** informal approving modern and stylish in a way that attracts attention: *Paula's wearing a very snazzy pair of shoes!* ◦ *He designs snazzy new graphics for software packages.* • **snazzily** /-ɪ.li/ **adv**

sneak /sniːk/ **verb; noun**

▸**verb** (**sneaked** or US also **snuck**, **sneaked** or US also **snuck**) **MOVE SECRETLY** ▷ **1** (C2) [I or T, usually + adv/prep] to go somewhere secretly, or to take someone or something somewhere secretly: *I managed to sneak* ***in*** *through the back door while she wasn't looking.* ◦ *Jan hasn't got a ticket but I thought we might sneak her* ***in****.* ◦ *I thought I'd sneak* ***up on*** *him (= move close to him without him seeing) and give him a surprise.* **TELL SECRETLY** ▷ **2** [I] UK slang disapproving to secretly tell someone in authority, especially a teacher, that someone else has done something bad, often in order to cause trouble: *She was always sneaking* ***on*** *other kids in the class.* **LOOK** ▷ **3 sneak a look/glance at sb/sth** (C2) to look at someone or something quickly and secretly: *I noticed him sneak a look at what I was writing.*

▸**noun** [C] UK slang disapproving (US **snitch**) a person who tells people in authority when someone else does something bad

sneaker /ˈsniː.kəʳ/ (US) /-kɚ/ **noun** [C] US (A2) a type of light, comfortable shoe that is suitable for playing sports

sneaking /ˈsniː.kɪŋ/ **adj** [before noun] If you have a sneaking feeling about someone or something, you have that feeling, although you are not certain it is correct: *I've got a sneaking* ***feeling/suspicion*** *that we're going the wrong way.*

ˌsneak ˈpeek **noun** [C] informal an opportunity to see something before it is officially available: *The company is offering a sneak peek at the new software.*

ˌsneak ˈpreview **noun** [C] an opportunity to see (a part of) something new before the rest of the public see it

sneaky /ˈsniː.ki/ **adj** doing things in a secret and unfair way: *a sneaky plan* • **sneakily** /-kɪ.li/ **adv**

sneer /snɪəʳ/ (US) /snɪr/ **verb; noun**

▸**verb** [I or T] to talk about or look at someone or something in an unkind way that shows you do not respect or approve of them: *You may sneer, but a lot of people like this kind of music.* ◦ *She'll probably sneer* ***at*** *my new shoes because they're not expensive.* ◦ [+ speech] *'Is that the best you can do?' he sneered.*

▸**noun** [C] disapproving an unkind expression on your face which shows you do not respect or approve of someone or something: *'How much did you say you earned last year?' she said with a sneer.*

sneering /ˈsnɪə.rɪŋ/ (US) /ˈsnɪr.ɪŋ/ **adj** disapproving rude and not showing respect: *I don't like that superior, sneering tone of his.* • **sneeringly** /-li/ **adv**

sneeze /sniːz/ **verb; noun**

▸**verb** [I] (B2) When you sneeze, air and often small drops of liquid suddenly come out of your nose and mouth in a way you cannot control: *Cats make him sneeze – I think he's allergic to them.*

IDIOM **not to be sneezed at** informal If you say that something, especially an amount of money, is not to be sneezed at, you mean that it is a large enough amount to be worth having: *Well, a five percent pay increase means an extra £700 a year, which is not to be sneezed at!*

▸**noun** [C] an act or sound of sneezing: *He's got all the classic symptoms of a cold – the coughs and sneezes and the sore throat.*

snick /snɪk/ **verb** [T] UK in sports, especially cricket, to hit the ball off the edge of the BAT: *Carlton snicked the ball low and fast to Lynch's right.* • **snick noun** [C]

snicker /ˈsnɪk.əʳ/ (US) /-ɚ/ **verb** [I], **noun** [C] US for **snigger**

snide /snaɪd/ **adj** (especially of remarks) containing unpleasant criticism that is not clearly stated: *She made one or two snide* ***remarks*** *about their house, which I thought was a bit unnecessary.* • **snideness** /ˈsnaɪd.nəs/ **noun** [U]

snidely /ˈsnaɪd.li/ **adv** rudely and CRITICALLY: *'Well, she's certainly better looking than her mother,' she said snidely.*

sniff /snɪf/ **verb; noun**

▸**verb 1** (C2) [I or T] to smell something by taking air in through your nose: *He sniffed his socks to see if they needed washing.* ◦ *Dogs love sniffing each other.* ◦ *She sniffed* ***at*** *her glass of wine before tasting it.* ◦ *Dogs are sometimes used at airports to sniff* ***out*** *(= find by smelling) drugs in people's luggage.* ◦ *He was expelled from school for sniffing* ***glue*** *(= taking in the gas from glue because of the feelings of pleasure that this gives).* **2** (C2) [I] to take air in quickly through your nose, usually to stop the liquid inside the nose from flowing out: *You were sniffing a lot – I presumed you had a cold.* **3** [T] to speak in an unpleasant way, showing that you have a low opinion of something: [+ speech] *'They didn't even serve wine at dinner!' she sniffed.*

PHRASAL VERBS **sniff at sth** **DISAPPROVE** ▷ **1** to show disapproval or a low opinion of something: *The men at City Hall, sniffing at anything too ideological, insist that big cuts are just not practical.* **SHOW INTEREST** ▷ **2** (also **sniff around (sth)**) to show that you are interested in something: *A few computer firms are sniffing at the project already.* ◦ *Chief executive David Prosser said the takeover speculation was wrong and no one was sniffing around.* • **sniff sth out** to search for and discover something: *Her job is to go round the big fashion shows sniffing out talent for a modelling agency.*

IDIOM **not to be sniffed at** informal valuable or worth having: *A £2 million profit is not to be sniffed at.*

▸**noun** [C] a quick breath in through the nose to smell something, or to stop liquid in the nose from coming out: *Have a sniff of this medicine – it smells revolting, doesn't it?* ◦ *'I don't think much of that idea,' she said with a sniff (= an expression of a low opinion).*

sniffer /ˈsnɪf.əʳ/ (US) /-ɚ/ **noun** [C] someone who sniffs chemicals for the feelings of pleasure it causes: *a* ***glue/paint*** *sniffer.*

ˈsniffer ˌdog **noun** [C] mainly UK informal a dog that is trained and used by the police or army to find hidden drugs or bombs by smelling them

sniffle /ˈsnɪf.l/ **verb; noun**

▸**verb** [I] (also **snuffle**) to breathe in quickly and repeatedly through the nose, usually because you are crying or because you have a cold: *You're sniffling a lot today – have you got a cold?*

▸**noun** (also **snuffle**) **1** [C] an act or sound of sniffling **2 a sniffle** (also **the sniffles**) a slight cold which

S

mainly affects your nose: *I had a cold a couple of weeks ago and it's left me with a bit of a sniffle.*

sniffy /ˈsnɪf.i/ **adj** informal showing disapproval and a low opinion: *She's a bit sniffy* ***about*** *my taste in music.*

snifter /ˈsnɪf.təʳ/ (US) /-tɚ/ **noun** [C] **DRINK** ▷ **1** old-fashioned informal a small drink of something alcoholic: *How about a snifter before dinner?* **GLASS** ▷ **2** US a bowl-shaped glass that is narrower at the top and has a short stem, used for drinking BRANDY

snigger /ˈsnɪg.əʳ/ (US) /-ɚ/ **verb** [I] (US also **snicker**) to laugh at someone or something in a silly and often unkind way: *They spent half the time sniggering* ***at*** *the clothes people were wearing.* ◦ *What are you two sniggering* ***at/about****?* • **snigger noun** [C] *We were* ***having*** *a snigger at the bride who was rather large and dressed in a tight, pale pink dress.*

snip /snɪp/ **verb; noun**

▸**verb** [I or T] (**-pp-**) to cut something with SCISSORS, usually with small, quick cuts: *Have you seen the scissors? I want to snip* ***off*** *this loose thread.* ◦ *I snipped* ***out*** *the article and gave it to her.*

▸**noun CUT** ▷ **1** [C] a quick, short cut with SCISSORS: *Give it a snip with the scissors.* **2 the snip** UK informal humorous a **vasectomy CHEAP PRODUCT** ▷ **3** [S] UK informal a product that is being sold cheaply, for less than you would expect: *The sunglasses are now available in major stores,* ***a*** *snip* ***at*** *£12 a pair.*

snipe /snaɪp/ **verb; noun**

▸**verb** [I] **1** to shoot at someone from a position where you cannot be seen: *The rebels have started sniping* ***at*** *civilians.* **2** to criticize someone unpleasantly: *The former minister has been making himself unpopular recently, sniping* ***at*** *his ex-colleagues.* • **sniping** /ˈsnaɪ.pɪŋ/ **noun** [U]

▸**noun** [C] (plural **snipe** or **snipes**) a bird with a long, straight beak which lives near rivers and MARSHES (= low land that is wet and sometimes covered with water)

sniper /ˈsnaɪ.pəʳ/ (US) /-pɚ/ **noun** [C] **SHOOT** ▷ **1** someone who shoots at people from a place where they cannot be seen: *He was shot and fatally injured by a sniper.* ◦ *Sniper fire has claimed countless lives these past few weeks.* **BUYER** ▷ **2** someone who waits until nearly the end of an AUCTION (= public competition to buy goods) on a website before saying how much money they will offer, in order to be more successful than other people trying to buy the same thing

snippet /ˈsnɪp.ɪt/ **noun** [C] informal a small and often interesting piece of news, information, or conversation: *I love listening to snippets* ***of*** *conversation in restaurants.*

snit /snɪt/ **noun** [C] US informal an angry mood: *He was* ***in*** *a snit this morning and I didn't dare approach him.*

snitch /snɪtʃ/ **verb TELL SECRETLY** ▷ **1** [I] informal disapproving to secretly tell someone in authority that someone else has done something bad, often in order to cause trouble: *He snitched* ***to*** *my boss that I'd been making long-distance calls at work!* ◦ *She's always snitching* ***on*** *someone.* **STEAL** ▷ **2** [T] informal to steal something: *'Where did you get that money?' 'I snitched it* ***from*** *my dad when he wasn't looking.'* • **snitch noun** [C] informal disapproving *You little snitch!*

snivel /ˈsnɪv.əl/ **verb** [I] (**-ll-** or US usually **-l-**) to cry slightly in a way that is weak and does not make other people feel sympathy for you

snivelling old-fashioned informal (US usually **sniveling**) /ˈsnɪv.əl.ɪŋ/ **adj** used to describe someone you do not like because they are weak and unpleasant: *That snivelling creep/coward!*

snob /snɒb/ (US) /snɑːb/ **noun** [C] disapproving (C2) a person who respects and likes only people who are of a high social class, and/or a person who has extremely high standards who is not satisfied by the things that ordinary people like: *He's a frightful snob – if you haven't been to the right school he probably won't even speak to you.* ◦ *I'm afraid I'm a bit of a wine snob/a snob where wine is concerned.*

snobbery /ˈsnɒb.ər.i/ (US) /ˈsnɑː.bɚ-/ **noun** [U] (also **snobbishness**) behaviour and opinions that are typical of a snob: *She accused me of snobbery because I sent my sons to a private school.*

snobbish /ˈsnɒb.ɪʃ/ (US) /ˈsnɑː.bɪʃ/ **adj** (informal **snobby**) (C2) like a snob: *My brother is very snobbish* ***about*** *cars.* • **snobbishly** /-li/ **adv** (also **snobbily**) in a snobbish way

snog /snɒg/ (US) /snɑːg/ **verb** [I or T] (**-gg-**) UK informal to kiss and hold a person in a sexual way: *I saw them snogging on the back seat of a bus.* ◦ *I've never snogged (****with****) a man with a beard.* • **snog noun** [C] *He caught us* ***having*** *a snog.*

snooker /ˈsnuː.kəʳ/ (US) /-kɚ/ **noun; verb**

▸**noun** [U] a game played by two people in which CUES (= long, thin poles) are used to hit 15 red balls and six balls of different colours into six holes around a table covered in soft cloth in a fixed order → Compare **pool**

▸**verb** [T] **1** UK informal to prevent someone from finishing an intended plan of action: *We had intended to go driving around Scotland, but unless I can get my licence we're snookered.* **2** US informal to deceive or trick someone

snoop /snuːp/ **verb; noun**

▸**verb** [I usually + adv/prep] informal disapproving **1** to look around a place secretly, in order to discover things or find out information about someone or something: *People were sent out to snoop* ***on*** *rival businesses.* ◦ *She's the sort of person you can imagine snooping* ***about/around*** *your room when you're not there.* **2** to try to find out about other people's private lives: *I don't mean to snoop, but is there something wrong?* ◦ *Clara's husband is snooping* ***on*** *her because he thinks she is seeing another man.*

▸**noun 1** [S] informal the act of snooping: *I think someone's been* ***having*** *a snoop around my office – I didn't leave that drawer open.* **2** [C] (also **snooper**) informal disapproving someone who snoops: *He's such a snoop – he's always going through my mail.*

snoot /snuːt/ **noun** [C] US slang a nose: *Keep your big snoot out of my business!*

IDIOM **stick your snoot in/into (sth)** US informal disapproving to try to discover things or influence events that are not really your affair: *Stop sticking your snoot into other people's business!*

snooty /ˈsnuː.ti/ (US) /-t̬i/ **adj** informal behaving in an unfriendly way because you believe you are better than other people: *She was one of those really snooty sales assistants that you often find in expensive shops.* • **snootily** /-tᵊ.li/ (US) /-t̬ᵊ.li/ **adv**

snooze /snuːz/ **verb** [I] informal to sleep lightly for a short while: *The dog's snoozing in front of the fire.* • **snooze noun** [C] *I* ***had*** *a nice little snooze in the back of the car.*

ˈsnooze ˌbutton noun [C] a button on an ALARM CLOCK (= a clock for waking you up) that you press after it has woken you up, so that you can sleep for a few minutes more before being woken up again by the clock

snore /snɔːʳ/ (US) /snɔːr/ **verb; noun**
▸**verb** [I] (B2) to breathe in a very noisy way while you are sleeping: *Sometimes my husband snores so loudly, it keeps me awake at night.* ◦ *Do you know any cures for snoring?* • **snorer** /ˈsnɔː.rəʳ/ (US) /ˈsnɔːr.ɚ/ **noun** [C] *He's a terrible snorer.*
▸**noun** [C] a very noisy breath while you are sleeping: *I could hear loud snores coming from Jim's bedroom.*

snorkel /ˈsnɔː.kəl/ (US) /ˈsnɔːr-/ **noun** [C] a tube that you hold in your mouth to help you breathe if you are swimming with your face underwater

snorkelling UK (US usually **snorkeling**) /ˈsnɔː.kəl.ɪŋ/ (US) /ˈsnɔːr-/ **noun** [U] the activity of swimming while using a snorkel: *We **went** snorkelling along the Great Barrier Reef.*

snort /snɔːt/ (US) /snɔːrt/ **verb; noun**
▸**verb 1** [I] to make an explosive sound by forcing air quickly up or down the nose: *He did an impression of a horse snorting.* ◦ *Camille snorts when she laughs.* ◦ informal *By this time I was snorting **with** laughter (= laughing a lot and loudly).* **2** [T] to take an illegal drug by breathing it in through the nose: *People were snorting **cocaine** in the toilets.* **3** [T] to suddenly express strong feelings of anger, disapproval, or disagreement, either by speaking or in a sound that you make: *'And you call that a first-class service?' snorted one indignant customer.*
▸**noun** [C] a loud sound made by forcing air through the nose: *The minister's speech drew loud snorts of derisive laughter.*

snot /snɒt/ (US) /snɑːt/ **noun** FROM NOSE ▷ **1** [U] informal MUCUS produced in the nose PERSON ▷ **2** [C] US informal disapproving a person who behaves badly and who you do not like: *Amber is such a snot!*

snotty /ˈsnɒt.i/ (US) /ˈsnɑː.t̬i/ **adj** FROM NOSE ▷ **1** informal covered with MUCUS from the nose: *You could have told me I had a snotty nose!* ◦ *I don't want to use your snotty handkerchief!* PERSON ▷ **2** UK informal disapproving behaving rudely to other people in a way that shows that you believe yourself to be better than them **3** US informal disapproving rude and behaving badly: *a snotty teenager* ◦ *She was so snotty to me!*

snout /snaʊt/ **noun** [C] **1** the nose and mouth which stick out from the face of some animals: *a pig's snout* **2** slang for a person's nose: *He has an enormous snout.*

snow /snəʊ/ (US) /snoʊ/ **noun; verb**
▸**noun** WEATHER ▷ **1** (A1) [U] the small, soft, white pieces of ice which sometimes fall from the sky when it is cold, or the white layer on the ground and other surfaces which it forms: *Outside the snow began to **fall**.* ◦ *Let's go and play in the snow!* ◦ ***A blanket of** snow lay on the ground.* ◦ *Her hair was jet-black, her lips ruby-red and her skin **as white as** snow.* **2** [C] a single fall of snow: *We haven't had many heavy snows this winter.* DRUG ▷ **3** [U] slang **cocaine**
▸**verb** WEATHER ▷ **1** (A2) [I] If it snows, snow falls from the sky: ***It's** snowing.* ◦ ***It's** starting to snow.* ◦ ***It** had snowed overnight and a thick white layer covered the ground.* **2 be snowed in** (C2) to be unable to travel away from a place because of very heavy snow: *We were snowed in for four days last winter.* TRICK ▷ **3** [T] US informal to deceive or trick someone by clever talk or by giving them a lot of information: *She always snowing the bosses **with** statistics.*

IDIOM **be snowed under (with sth)** (C2) to have so much work that you have problems dealing with it all: *I'm absolutely snowed under with work at the moment.*

snowball /ˈsnəʊ.bɔːl/ (US) /ˈsnoʊ.bɑːl/ **noun; verb**
▸**noun** [C] a ball of snow pressed together in the hands, especially for throwing

IDIOMS **not have a snowball's chance in hell** informal to have no chance of succeeding: *If he can't afford a good lawyer, he doesn't have a snowball's chance in hell **of** winning the case.* • **a snowball effect** a situation in which something increases in size or importance at a faster and faster rate: *The more successful you become, the more publicity you get and that publicity generates sales. It's a sort of snowball effect.*

▸**verb** [I] If a plan, problem, idea, etc. snowballs, it quickly grows bigger and more important: *I suggested a few drinks after work, and the whole thing snowballed **into** a company party.*

ˈ**snow** ˌ**bank** **noun** [C] mainly US a large pile of snow → Compare **snowdrift**

ˈ**snow** ˌ**blindness** **noun** [U] a temporary loss of sight that is caused by the brightness of light reflected by large areas of snow or ice • ˈ**snow-blind** **adj** *Halfway up the mountain I suddenly **went** snow-blind.*

snowboard /ˈsnəʊ.bɔːd/ (US) /ˈsnoʊ.bɔːrd/ **verb; noun**
▸**verb** [I] to slide on the snow by standing on a specially shaped board • **snowboarder** /-bɔː.dəʳ/ (US) /-bɔːr.dɚ/ **noun** [C] (informal **boarder**)
▸**noun** [C] (B1) a specially shaped board that you stand on to slide down a snow-covered slope

snowboarding /ˈsnəʊ.bɔː.dɪŋ/ (US) /ˈsnoʊ.bɔːr-/ **noun** [U] (A2) the activity or sport of moving over snow using a snowboard

snowboarding

snowbound /ˈsnəʊ.baʊnd/ (US) /ˈsnoʊ-/ **adj** (of vehicles or people) unable to travel because of heavy snow, or (of roads) not able to be travelled on or reached because of heavy snow: *Hundreds of vehicles have become snowbound.*

ˈ**snow-capped** **adj** Snow-capped mountains and hills have snow on the top of them.

snowdrift /ˈsnəʊ.drɪft/ (US) /ˈsnoʊ-/ **noun** [C] a large pile of snow formed by the wind

snowdrop /ˈsnəʊ.drɒp/ (US) /ˈsnoʊ.drɑːp/ **noun** [C] a plant which produces small, white, bell-shaped flowers in the early spring

snowfall /ˈsnəʊ.fɔːl/ (US) /ˈsnoʊ.fɑːl/ **noun** [C or U] the amount of snow that falls in a particular area during a particular period, or a fall of snow: *The annual snowfall for this region is 30 centimetres.* ◦ *Heavy snowfalls are predicted for tonight and tomorrow.*

snowflake /ˈsnəʊ.fleɪk/ (US) /ˈsnoʊ-/ **noun** [C] a small piece of snow

ˈ**snow** ˌ**job** **noun** [C] mainly US informal an attempt to persuade someone to do something, especially by praising them and using CHARM: *My boss **did** a snow job **on** me.*

ˈ**snow** ˌ**line** **noun** **the snow line** the level on a mountain above which snow is found for most or all of the year: ***above/below** the snow line*

snowman /ˈsnəʊ.mæn/ (US) /ˈsnoʊ-/ **noun** [C] (plural **-men** /-men/) a model of a person made of snow, especially by children

snowmobile /ˈsnəʊ.məˌbiːl/ (US) /ˈsnoʊ-/ **noun** [C] a small motor vehicle for travelling on snow and ice

ˈ**snow** ˌ**pea** **noun** [C] US for **mangetout**

S

snowplough UK (US **snowplow**) /ˈsnaʊ.plaʊ/ (US) /ˈsnoʊ-/ noun **VEHICLE** ▷ **1** [C] a vehicle or device for removing snow from roads or railways **SKIING** ▷ **2** [C usually singular] in skiing, a simple way of turning or stopping in which the points of the skis are turned towards each other

snowshoe /ˈsnaʊ.ʃuː/ (US) /ˈsnoʊ-/ **noun** [C] a flat frame with straps of material stretched across it that can be fixed to a boot to allow a person to walk on snow without sinking in

snowstorm /ˈsnaʊ.stɔːm/ (US) /ˈsnoʊ.stɔːrm/ **noun** [C] a heavy fall of snow that is blown by strong winds

snowsuit /ˈsnaʊ.suːt/ (US) /ˈsnoʊ-/ **noun** [C] a piece of winter clothing for a child that is warm and covers most of the body

ˈsnow ˌtyre UK (US **ˈsnow ˌtire**) **noun** [C] a tyre with a pattern of raised lines that are thicker than usual in order to stop a vehicle from sliding on ice or snow

ˌsnow ˈwhite noun [U] a pure white colour • **ˌsnow-ˈwhite adj**

snowy /ˈsnaʊ.i/ (US) /ˈsnoʊ-/ **adj** full of or like snow: *We've had a very snowy winter this year.* ◦ *I remember him as an old man with a snowy-**white** (= pure white) beard.*

Snr adj [after noun] UK (US **Sr**) written abbreviation for **senior**, used after a man's name to refer to the older of two people in the same family who have the same name

snub /snʌb/ **verb** [T] (**-bb-**) to insult someone by not giving them any attention or treating them as if they are not important: *I think she felt snubbed because Anthony hadn't bothered to introduce himself.* • **snub noun** [C] *I simply didn't recognize her and apparently she took it as a snub.*

ˈsnub ˌnose noun [C] a nose that is short and turns upwards at the end

ˌsnub-ˈnosed adj 1 describes a person with a nose that is short and turns up at the end **2** describes a gun that has a very short BARREL: *a snub-nosed revolver*

snuck /snʌk/ **verb** mainly US past simple and past participle of **sneak**

snuff /snʌf/ **noun; verb**

▸**noun** [U] tobacco in the form of a powder for breathing into the nose: *Very few people **take** snuff nowadays.*

▸**verb** [T] to put out a flame, especially from a candle, usually by covering it with something: *One by one she snuffed the candles.*

IDIOM **snuff it** mainly UK informal to die

PHRASAL VERBS **snuff sth out 1** informal to cause something to end suddenly: *The country has been able to celebrate the return of its independence so brutally snuffed out in 1940.* **2** to put out a flame, especially from a candle: *One by one she snuffed out the candles.* • **snuff sb out** US slang to kill someone

snuffle /ˈsnʌf.l̩/ **verb** [I], **noun** [C] **sniffle**

ˈsnuff ˌmovie noun [C] (UK also **ˈsnuff ˌfilm**) a violent film that shows a real murder, intended as entertainment

snug /snʌg/ **adj; noun**

▸**adj** (**snugger, snuggest**) **1** (of a person) feeling warm, comfortable, and protected, or (of a place, especially a small place) giving feelings of warmth, comfort, and protection: *We curled up in bed, all snug and warm, and listened to the storm outside.* ◦ *I bet your feet are nice and snug in your fur-lined boots!* **2** fitting closely: *These shoes are a bit too snug – do you have them in a larger size?* • **snugly** /ˈsnʌg.li/ **adv** *She's curled up snugly in the armchair, reading a book.* ◦ *If we put the washing machine over there the fridge will **fit** snugly (= closely) into this space.*

▸**noun** [C] (also **snuggery**) UK a small room or area in a pub where only a few people can sit

snuggle /ˈsnʌg.l̩/ **verb** [I usually + adv/prep] to move yourself into a warm and comfortable position, especially one in which your body is against another person or covered by something: *The children snuggled **up** to their mother to get warm.* ◦ *I was just snuggling **down** into my warm duvet when my phone rang.*

so adv; conjunction; adj; noun

▸**adv** /səʊ/ (US) /soʊ/ **VERY** ▷ **1** (A2) very, extremely, or to such a degree: *The house is so beautiful.* ◦ *Thank you for being so patient.* ◦ *Don't be so stupid!* ◦ *I didn't know she had so many children!* ◦ *You can only do so much to help (= there is a limit to how much you can help).* ◦ UK informal *She's **ever** so kind and nice.* ◦ *I'm so tired (**that**) I could sleep in this chair!* ◦ *I'm **not** so desperate **as to** agree to that.* ◦ *The word itself is so rare **as to be** almost obsolete.* **2** not standard used before a noun or before 'not' to emphasize what is being said: *Don't wear that – it's so last year (= it was fashionable last year but not now).* ◦ *I'm sorry, but she is so **not** a size 10 (= she is very much larger than a size 10).* **3** used at the end of a sentence to mean to a very great degree: *Is that why you hate him so?* ◦ *You worry so!* **SAME WAY** ▷ **4** (B1) used usually before the verbs 'have', 'be', or 'do', and other AUXILIARY VERBS to express the meaning 'in the same way' or 'in a similar way': *'I've got an enormous amount of work to do.' 'So have I.'* ◦ *'I'm allergic to nuts.' 'So is my brother.'* ◦ *Neil left just after midnight and so did Roz.* ◦ *Just **as** you like to have a night out with the lads, so I like to go out with the girls now and again.* **MENTIONED EARLIER** ▷ **5** (A2) used to avoid repeating a phrase mentioned earlier: *'I hope they stay together.' 'I hope so too.'* ◦ *'Do you think he's upset?' 'I don't think so.'* ◦ *James is coming tonight, or so he said.* **6** (B2) used to say that a situation mentioned earlier is correct or true: *'Is it true that we're not getting a pay increase this year?' 'I'm afraid so.'* ◦ *'Anthony and Mia don't get on very well.' 'Is that so?'* ◦ *'The forecast says it might rain.' 'If so, we'll have the party inside.'* **7** used to say that a fact that has just been stated is certainly true: *'My eyes are slightly different colours.' 'So they are.'* ◦ *'That's her brother – he looks like James Dean.' 'So he does.'* **8** used instead of repeating an adjective that has already been mentioned: *She's quite reasonable to work with – more so than I was led to believe.* ◦ *He's quite bright – well, certainly more so than his brother.* **9** US child's word used, especially by children, to argue against a negative statement: *'You didn't even see the movie.' 'I did so!'* **10 to do so** (C1) to act in the way mentioned: *Parents must take responsibility for their children. Failure to do so could mean a fine or a jail sentence.* **IN THIS WAY** ▷ **11** in this way, or like this: *The pillars, which are outside the building, are so placed in order to provide the maximum space inside.* ◦ *I've so arranged my trip that I'll be home on Friday evening.* **12** used when you are showing how something is done: *Just fold this piece of paper back, so, and make a crease here.* ◦ *Gently fold in the eggs **like** so.* **13** used when you are representing the size of something: *'How tall is he next to you?' 'Oh, about so big,' she said, indicating the level of her neck.* ◦ *'The table that I liked best was about so wide,' she said, holding her arms out a metre and a half.*

IDIOM **only so much/many** (C2) used to say that there are limits to something: *There are only so many hours* *in your working day – you cannot possibly do all the work.*

▸**conjunction** /səʊ/ (US) /soʊ/ **SENTENCE BEGINNING** ▷ **1** (A2) used at the beginning of a sentence to connect it with something that has been said or has happened previously: *So, there I was standing at the edge of the road with only my underwear on ... ◦ So, just to finish what I was saying earlier...* **2** (A2) used as a way of making certain that you or someone else understand something correctly, often when you are repeating the important points of a plan: *So we leave on the Thursday and get back the next Tuesday, is that right?* **3** (A2) used to refer to a discovery that you have just made: *So that's what he does when I'm not around!* **4** (A2) used as a short pause, sometimes to emphasize what you are saying: *So, here we are again – just you and me.* **5** (A2) used before you introduce a subject of conversation that is of present interest, especially when you are asking a question: *So, who do you think is going to win the election?* **6** informal used to show that you agree with something that someone has just said, but you do not think that it is important: *So the car's expensive – well, I can afford it.* **THEREFORE** ▷ **7** (A2) and for that reason; therefore: *My knee started hurting so I stopped running. ◦ I was lost so I bought a street map.*

IDIOMS **so there** informal humorous used for emphasis, or to show that something is being done against someone else's wishes: *Mine's bigger than yours, so there! ◦ No, I won't help you, so there!* • **so what?** informal used to mean 'it's not important' and 'I don't care': *So what **if** I'm 35 and I'm not married – I lead a perfectly fulfilling life! ◦ 'Andrew won't like it, you know.' 'So what? – I don't care what Andrew thinks!'*

▸**conjunction, adv** /səʊ/ (US) /soʊ/ **1** (B1) used before you give an explanation for the action that you have just mentioned: [+ (that)] *I deliberately didn't have lunch so (**that**) I would be hungry tonight. ◦ Leave the keys out so (**that**) I remember to take them with me.* **2 so as to** (B2) in order to: *I always keep fruit in the fridge so as to keep insects off it.* **3 so as not to** (C1) in order not to: *He did not switch on the light so as not to disturb her.*

▸**adj** /səʊ/ (US) /soʊ/ **just/exactly so** perfectly tidy and well arranged: *He's a perfectionist – everything has to be just so.*

▸**noun** [S] /səʊ/ (US) /soʊ/ the musical note **soh**

soak /səʊk/ (US) /soʊk/ **verb; noun**

▸**verb 1** (C1) [I + adv/prep, T] to make something very wet, or (of liquid) to be absorbed in large amounts: *The wind had blown the rain in and soaked the carpet. ◦ You'd better wipe up that red wine you've spilled before it soaks (= is absorbed) **into** the carpet. ◦ Blood had soaked **through** both bandages.* **2** (B2) [I or T] to leave something in liquid, especially in order to clean it, make it softer, or change its flavour: *You can usually soak **out** a stain. ◦ **Leave** the beans **to** soak overnight./**Let** the beans soak overnight. ◦ Soak the fruit **in** brandy for a few hours before you add it to the mixture.*

PHRASAL VERB **soak sth up LIQUID** ▷ **1** If a dry material or substance soaks up a liquid, it absorbs the liquid through its surface: *I tried to soak up most of the spilled milk with a cloth.* **EXPERIENCE** ▷ **2** (B2) to enjoy the effects or experience of something as much as possible: *I love to lie on the beach and soak up **the sun**. ◦ Just stroll around the bazaar and soak up **the atmosphere**.* **INFORMATION** ▷ **3** informal to understand and remember information well: *Given the right environment, children are like sponges and will soak up information.* **USE ALL** ▷ **4** to use up all or most of a supply of something, especially a supply of money: *The repairs on our house soaked up all our savings.*

▸**noun** [C] **MAKE WET** ▷ **1** a period of time during which something is in liquid: *Most dried beans need a soak before they're cooked. ◦ Showers are all right but there's nothing like a good long soak in the bath.* **PERSON** ▷ **2** old-fashioned informal a person who is often drunk

soaked /səʊkt/ (US) /soʊkt/ **adj** (B2) extremely wet: *I'm going to have to take these clothes off – I'm soaked **to the skin**! ◦ My shoes are soaked (**through**). ◦ His T-shirt was soaked **in** sweat.*

soaking /ˈsəʊ.kɪŋ/ (US) /ˈsoʊ-/ **adj** (B2) completely wet: *It's so hot outside – I've only been walking ten minutes and my shirt is soaking (**wet**)!*

ˈso-and-so noun informal **PERSON NOT NAMED** ▷ **1** [U] used instead of a particular name to refer to someone or something, especially when the real name is not important or you have forgotten it: *She always keeps me up to date with the latest gossip – you know, so-and-so from down the road is having a baby and so-and-so's just bought a car.* **UNPLEASANT PERSON** ▷ **2** [C] a polite way of referring to an unpleasant person: *Mr Baker was such a so-and-so – he didn't have a pleasant word to say about anyone!*

soap /səʊp/ (US) /soʊp/ **noun; verb**

▸**noun 1** (A2) [U or C] a substance used for washing the body that is usually hard, often has a pleasant smell, and produces a mass of bubbles when rubbed with water, or a piece of this: *a **bar** of soap ◦ liquid soap ◦ soap and water ◦ a soap dish/dispenser ◦ soap bubbles ◦ She bought me a box of prettily coloured soaps.* **2** (B1) [C] informal a **soap opera**

▸**verb** [T] to put soap on something: *Have you soaped yourself all over, Alice? ◦ Let me soap your back.*

soapbox /ˈsəʊp.bɒks/ (US) /ˈsoʊp.bɑːks/ **noun** [C] a rough wooden box or any raised, temporary surface for people to stand on while making informal public speeches

IDIOM **get on your soapbox** informal to express your opinions about a particular subject forcefully: *She never misses the chance to get on her soapbox **about** government reform.*

ˈsoap ˌflakes noun [plural] small, flat pieces of soap used for washing clothes, especially by hand: *a box of soap flakes*

ˈsoap ˌopera noun [C] (informal **soap**) (B1) a series of television or radio programmes about the lives and problems of a particular group of characters. The series continues over a long period and is broadcast (several times) every week.

soapstone /ˈsəʊp.stəʊn/ (US) /ˈsoʊp.stoʊn/ **noun** [U] a type of soft stone that feels like soap

soapsuds /ˈsəʊp.sʌdz/ (US) /ˈsoʊp-/ **noun** [plural] (also **suds**) the mass of small bubbles that form on the surface of water that has soap in it

soapy /ˈsəʊ.pi/ (US) /ˈsoʊ-/ **adj** containing or like soap: *I soaked it in some soapy water and the stains came out.*

soar /sɔːʳ/ (US) /sɔːr/ **verb RISE QUICKLY** ▷ **1** (C2) [I usually + adv/prep] to rise very quickly to a high level: *All night long fireworks soared into the sky. ◦ Temperatures will soar over the weekend, say the weather forecasters. ◦ House prices soared a further 20 percent.* **2** (C2) [T] to reach a great height: *The highest peak in the range soars 15,771 feet into the sky.* **FLY** ▷ **3** [I] (of a bird or aircraft) to rise high in the air while flying without moving the wings or using power: *She watched the gliders soaring effortlessly above her.* • **soaring** /ˈsɔː.rɪŋ/ (US) /ˈsɔːr.ɪŋ/ **adj** (C1) *soaring property prices*

sob /sɒb/ (US) /sɑːb/ **verb; noun**

▸**verb** [I] (**-bb-**) (B2) to cry noisily, taking in deep breaths:

I found her sobbing in the bedroom because she'd broken her favourite doll.

IDIOM **sob your heart out** to cry very much

▸noun [C] an act or sound of sobbing: *I could hear her sobs from the next room.*

S.O.B. /ˌes.əʊˈbiː/ (US) /-oʊ-/ noun [C usually singular] abbreviation for **son of a bitch**

sober /ˈsəʊ.bəʳ/ (US) /ˈsoʊ.bɚ/ adj; verb

▸adj **NOT DRUNK** ▷ **1** (C2) not drunk or affected by alcohol: *Are you sober enough to drive, Jim?* ◦ *I'd had no wine all evening so I was* ***stone cold*** *(= completely) sober.* **SERIOUS** ▷ **2** (C2) serious and calm: *In fact the whole wedding was a sober affair – no dancing, just people standing around in groups chatting politely.* ◦ *Anthony was in a very sober mood – I scarcely heard him laugh all night.* **NOT BRIGHT** ▷ **3** (C2) Clothes or colours that are sober are plain and not bright.

▸verb [I or T] to become more calm and serious, or to make someone do this: *News of the tragedy sobered us.*

PHRASAL VERB **sober (sb) up** to become less drunk, or to make someone become less drunk: *I went for a walk to try to sober up.* ◦ *Have a black coffee – that should sober you up!*

sobering /ˈsəʊ.bəʳr.ɪŋ/ (US) /ˈsoʊ.bɚ-/ adj making you feel serious or think about serious matters: *a sobering thought* ◦ *Surviving a car accident is a sobering experience.*

soberly /ˈsəʊ.bəl.i/ (US) /ˈsoʊ.bɚ.li/ adv seriously and reasonably: *She was dressed very soberly in a plain grey suit.*

sobriety /səˈbraɪ.ɪ.ti/ (US) /-ə.t̬i/ noun [U] formal **NOT DRUNK** ▷ **1** the state of being sober: US *The police said his car had been weaving all over the road, so they pulled him over and gave him a sobriety* ***test***. **SERIOUS** ▷ **2** seriousness: *We had the priest sitting at our table, which instilled a little sobriety into the occasion.*

sobriquet (also **soubriquet**) /ˈsəʊ.brɪ.keɪ/ (US) /ˈsoʊ-/ noun [C] formal a name given to someone or something that is not their real or official name: *These charms have earned the television programme's presenter the sobriquet 'the thinking woman's crumpet'.* → Synonym **nickname**

ˈsob ˌstory noun [C] informal disapproving a story or piece of information that someone tells you or writes about themselves that is intended to make you feel sympathy for them: *She came out with some sob story about not having enough money to go and see her father who was ill.*

S

ˌso-ˈcalled adj [before noun] **1** (B2) used to show that you think a word that is used to describe someone or something is not suitable or not correct: *It was one of his so-called friends who supplied him with the drugs that killed him.* **2** (B2) used to introduce a new word or phrase that is not yet known by many people: *It isn't yet clear how destructive this so-called 'super virus' is.*

soccer /ˈsɒk.əʳ/ (US) /ˈsɑː.kɚ/ noun [U] (UK also **football**) (A2) a game played between two teams of eleven people, where each team tries to win by kicking a ball into the other team's goal

ˈsoccer ˌmom noun [C] US informal a mother who spends a lot of time taking her children to activities such as music classes, sports, etc. It is often used to refer to a type of middle-class mother.

sociable /ˈsəʊ.ʃə.bl/ (US) /ˈsoʊ-/ adj approving (B1) describes someone who likes to meet and spend time with other people: *Rob's very sociable – he likes his parties.* ◦ *I had a headache and I wasn't feeling very sociable.* → Opposite **unsociable**

social /ˈsəʊ.ʃəl/ (US) /ˈsoʊ-/ adj; noun

▸adj **GOING OUT** ▷ **1** (B1) relating to activities in which you meet and spend time with other people and that happen during the time when you are not working: *I had an active social* ***life*** *when I was at college.* ◦ *I'm a social drinker – I only drink when I'm with other people.* ◦ *Most British schools organize social events for the students.* ◦ *I've just become a member of the company's sports and social club.* **SOCIETY** ▷ **2** (B2) [before noun] relating to society and living together in an organized way: *social classes/groups* ◦ *social disorder/trends/change/equality/justice/differences* ◦ *Monkeys are highly social* ***animals***.

▸noun [C] old-fashioned an occasion when the members of a group or organization meet informally to enjoy themselves: *a church social*

ˌsocial ˈclimber noun [C] disapproving someone who tries to improve their social position by being very friendly to people from a higher social class • **ˌsocial ˈclimbing** noun [U]

ˌsocial ˈconscience noun [S] If you have a social conscience, you worry about people who are poor, ill, old, etc. and try to help them.

ˌSocial ˈDemocrat noun [C] a member of the Social Democratic Party

ˌSocial Demoˈcratic ˌParty noun a political party which existed in the UK from 1981 to 1990

ˌsocial enginˈeering noun [U] the artificial controlling or changing of the groups within society

ˌsocial exˈclusion noun [U] a situation in which some people who are poor or who do not have a job do not feel part of the rest of society

ˌsocial inˈsurance noun [U] (in the US) money that employers and employees pay to the government so that people receive money when they are not able to work because of age, illness, etc.

socialism /ˈsəʊ.ʃəl.ɪ.zəm/ (US) /ˈsoʊ-/ noun [U] (C2) the set of beliefs which states that all people are equal and should share equally in a country's money, or the political systems based on these beliefs → Compare **capitalism, communism**

socialist /ˈsəʊ.ʃəl.ɪst/ (US) /ˈsoʊ-/ noun; adj

▸noun [C] a supporter of socialism or member of a socialist political party: *He was a socialist all his life.*

▸adj supporting or relating to socialism: *socialist policies*

socialite /ˈsəʊ.ʃəl.aɪt/ (US) /ˈsoʊ.ʃə.laɪt/ noun [C] someone, usually of high social class, who is famous because they go to a lot of parties and social events: *a wealthy socialite*

socialize (UK usually **socialise**) /ˈsəʊ.ʃəl.aɪz/ (US) /ˈsoʊ.ʃə.laɪz/ verb **GO OUT** ▷ **1** (B2) [I] to spend time when you are not working with friends or with other people in order to enjoy yourself: *I tend not to socialize* ***with*** *my colleagues.* ◦ *I hope Adrian's actually doing some work at college – he seems to spend all his time socializing!* **TRAIN** ▷ **2** [T] to train people or animals to behave in a way that others in the group think is suitable: *Here at the school we make every effort to socialize these young offenders.* • **socialization** (UK usually **socialisation**) /ˌsəʊ.ʃəl.aɪˈzeɪ.ʃən/ (US) /ˌsoʊ.ʃəl.ə-/ noun [U]

ˌsocialized ˈmedicine noun [U] US medical services provided or paid for by the government for anyone who needs them

socially /ˈsəʊ.ʃəl.i/ (US) /ˈsoʊ-/ adv **GOING OUT** ▷ **1** in or relating to a social situation: *I chat to him at work now and then but I've never seen him socially.* ◦ *Socially, she's a disaster – she's always offending someone or picking a fight.* **SOCIETY** ▷ **2** by or relating to society:

Drinking and driving is no longer socially acceptable. ◦ *Private education is often regarded as socially divisive.*

ˌsocial ˈmedia noun [U or plural] websites and computer programs that allow people to communicate and share information on the internet using a computer or mobile phone: *Companies are increasingly making use of social media in order to market their goods.*

ˌsocial ˈnetwork noun [C] **1** a website or computer program that allows people to communicate and share information on the internet using a computer or mobile phone: *We teach children how to deal with cyberbullying and the safe use of chat rooms and social networks.* **2** the different groups of people that you know: *Students graduating from high school have social networks they've been building for twelve years.*

ˌsocial ˈnetworking noun [U] B1 the use of websites and other internet services to communicate with other people and make friends: *social networking sites*

ˌsocial ˈscience noun [C or U] the study of society and the way people live

ˌsocial seˈcurity noun [U] **1** UK a system of payments made by the government to people who are ill, poor, or who have no job: *He's* ***on*** *social security.* **2 Social Security** US a system of payments made by the government to old people, people whose husbands or wives have died, and people who are unable to work because they are ill

ˌsocial ˈservices noun [plural] (also **ˌsocial ˈservice**) services provided by local or national government to help people who are old or ill or need support in their lives

ˈsocial ˌworker noun [U] a person who works for the social services or for a private organization providing help and support for people who need it • **ˈsocial ˌwork** noun [U]

societal /səˈsaɪ.ə.təl/ US /-t̬əl/ **adj** [before noun] formal relating to or involving society: *societal change/concerns/problems/values*

society /səˈsaɪ.ə.ti/ US /-t̬i/ **noun PEOPLE** ▷ **1** B1 [C or U] a large group of people who live together in an organized way, making decisions about how to do things and sharing the work that needs to be done. All the people in a country, or in several similar countries, can be referred to as a society: *a classless/multicultural/capitalist/civilized society* ◦ *These changes strike at the heart of British/American/modern society.* ◦ *There's a danger that we will end up blaming innocent children for society's problems.* ◦ *We must also consider the needs of the younger/older* ***members of*** *society.* **2** [U] (also **high society**) the part of society that consists of people who are rich, powerful, and fashionable: *a society hostess/ball/function* **3** [U] formal the state of being together with other people: *She prefers her own society (= likes to be alone).*

> **! Common mistake: society**
>
> **Remember:** it is not usual to use the definite article, 'the', when talking in a general way about all the people in a country or in several similar countries.
> Don't say 'the society', just say **society**:
> ~~*Homelessness is a serious problem for the society.*~~
> *Homelessness is a serious problem for society.*

ORGANIZATION ▷ **4** B2 [C] an organization to which people who share similar interests can belong: *an amateur dramatic society* ◦ *the Royal Society for the Protection of Birds*

> **Word partners for society**
>
> *build/create* a society • *live in* a society • a *member* of society • a *section/segment* of society • a *civilized/classless/democratic/multicultural* society • *modern* society • *in* society

socio- /səʊ.si.əʊ-/ US /soʊ.si.oʊ-/ **prefix** relating to society: *socioeconomic*

sociocultural /ˌsəʊ.si.əʊˈkʌl.tʃər.əl/ US /ˌsoʊ.si.oʊˈkʌl.tʃɚ.əl/ **adj** related to the different groups of people in society and their habits, traditions, and beliefs: *A good doctor has the ability to relate to the sociocultural background of his or her patients.*

socioeconomic /ˌsəʊ.si.əʊˌek.əˈnɒm.ɪk/ US /ˌsoʊ.si.oʊˌiː.kəˈnɑː.mɪk/ **adj** related to the differences between groups of people caused mainly by their financial situation: *socioeconomic groups/groupings* ◦ *socioeconomic factors* • **socioeconomically** /-nɒm.ɪ.kəl.i/ US /-ˈnɑː.mɪ.kəl.i/ **adv**

sociolect /ˈsəʊ.si.ə.lekt/ US /ˈsoʊ.si.oʊ-/ **noun** [C] specialized the form of a language that people in a particular social group speak

sociolinguistic /ˌsəʊ.si.əʊ.lɪŋˈgwɪs.tɪk/ US /ˌsoʊ.si.oʊ-/ **adj** connected with how language is used by different groups in society, or with the study of this: *a sociolinguistic analysis of how men and women talk to each other* ◦ *sociolinguistic research*

sociolinguistics /ˌsəʊ.si.əʊ.lɪŋˈgwɪs.tɪks/ US /ˌsoʊ.si.oʊ-/ **noun** [U] the study of how language is used by different groups in society

sociological /ˌsəʊ.si.əˈlɒdʒ.ɪ.kəl/ US /ˌsoʊ.si.əˈlɑː.dʒɪ-/ **adj** related to or involving sociology: *sociological theory/research* • **sociologically** /-kəl.i/ **adv**

sociologist /ˌsəʊ.siˈɒl.ə.dʒɪst/ US /ˌsoʊ.siˈɑː.lə-/ **noun** [C] someone who studies or is an expert in sociology

sociology /ˌsəʊ.siˈɒl.ə.dʒi/ US /ˌsoʊ.siˈɑː.lə-/ **noun** [U] the study of the relationships between people living in groups, especially in industrial societies: *She has a degree in sociology and politics.* ◦ *He specializes in the sociology* ***of*** *education/law/the family.*

sociopath /ˈsəʊ.si.ə.pæθ/ US /ˈsoʊ-/ **noun** [C] a person who is completely unable or unwilling to behave in a way that is acceptable to society: *I'm telling you he's a complete/total sociopath.*

sock /sɒk/ US /sɑːk/ **noun; verb**

▸**noun CLOTHES** ▷ **1** A2 [C] a piece of clothing made from soft material that covers your foot and the lower part of your leg: *a pair of socks* ◦ *nylon/woollen/cotton socks* ◦ *thermal socks* ◦ *ankle/knee socks* ◦ *Put on your* ***shoes and*** *socks.* ◦ *The little boy was wearing* ***odd*** (US usually ***mismatched***) *socks (= socks of different colours).* **HIT** ▷ **2** [C usually singular] old-fashioned slang a powerful hit: *a sock* ***on*** *the jaw*

IDIOMS **blow/knock your socks off** informal If something knocks your socks off, you find it extremely exciting or good: *I'm going to take you to a restaurant that'll knock your socks off.* • **put a sock in it!** informal humorous used to tell someone to be quiet or stop making so much noise

▸**verb** [T] **1** old-fashioned slang to hit someone with your FIST (= closed hand): *He socked the policeman* ***on*** *the jaw/****in*** *the eye.* **2** US in baseball, to hit a ball very powerfully

IDIOM **get socked with sth** mainly US to suddenly receive a lot of something which causes you problems: *If you don't pay your credit card bill on time, you'll get socked with a huge late fee.*

S

PHRASAL VERB **sock sth away** US informal to save money by putting it in a bank or by INVESTING it (= giving it to companies hoping to get more back): *He's socked away hundreds of dollars in a savings account.*

socket /ˈsɒk.ɪt/ (US) /ˈsɑː.kɪt/ noun [C] **ELECTRICAL** ▷ **1** the part of a piece of equipment, especially electrical equipment, into which another part fits: *an electrical socket* ◦ *a light socket* ◦ *He had forgotten to plug the television into the **mains** socket.* ◦ *The air freshener plugs into a car's **lighter** socket.* **BODY PART** ▷ **2** a part of the body into which another part fits: *a **tooth/eye** socket* ◦ *a **ball-and**-socket joint like the hip joint*

socket

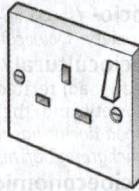

ˈsocket ˌset noun [C] a set of metal tools of different sizes, which fix onto one handle and are used to fasten and unfasten NUTS on pieces of equipment

sod /sɒd/ (US) /sɑːd/ **noun; verb; exclamation**

▸noun **PERSON** ▷ **1** [C] UK offensive something or someone considered unpleasant or difficult: *Apparently he's a sod to work for.* ◦ *What did you do that for, you stupid sod?* ◦ *It was a sod **of** a car to repair.* **2** [C] UK offensive a person: *He's won again – the lucky sod!* ◦ *The poor old sod – I don't suppose he's got a home.* **GRASS** ▷ **3** [S or C] specialized a rectangular piece that has been cut from an area of grass: *He worked fast, cutting and slicing the turf neatly, heaving the sod to one side.* **4** [S] literary soil or ground: *She sleeps beneath the sod (= she is dead and has been buried).*

IDIOM **not care/give a sod** UK offensive to not be worried about other people's opinions or actions: *I'm leaving and I don't give a sod **(about)** what Margaret thinks.* ◦ *She doesn't care a sod about her reputation.*

▸verb

PHRASAL VERB **sod off** [not continuous] UK offensive to go away: *Oh sod off, you stupid git!* ◦ *She told him to sod off.*

▸exclamation (also **sod it!**) UK offensive used to express anger: *Oh sod it – I've left my glasses behind!*

soda /ˈsəʊ.də/ (US) /ˈsoʊ-/ noun **1** [C] (also **ˈsoda ˌpop**) US any type of sweet FIZZY drink (= with bubbles) that is not alcoholic **2** [C or U] (also **ˈsoda ˌwater**, US also **ˌclub ˈsoda**) a type of FIZZY water (= with bubbles), often mixed with alcoholic drinks

ˌsod ˈall noun [S] UK offensive nothing: *Ann's just been chatting on the phone all morning – she's done sod all.*

ˈsoda ˌsiphon noun [C] a bottle for filling water with gas and forcing it out under pressure to use in drinks

sodden /ˈsɒd.ən/ (US) /ˈsɑː.dən/ adj (of something that can absorb water) extremely wet: *The football pitch was absolutely sodden.* ◦ *Her thin coat quickly became sodden.*

sodding /ˈsɒd.ɪŋ/ (US) /ˈsɑː.dɪŋ/ **adj** [before noun] UK offensive used to express anger: *Stupid sodding thing, why won't it move?*

sodium /ˈsəʊ.di.əm/ (US) /ˈsoʊ-/ **noun** [U] (symbol **Na**) a soft, silver-white chemical element that is found in salt

sodium bicarbonate /ˌsəʊ.di.əm.baɪˈkɑː.bən.ət/ (US) /ˌsoʊ.di.əm.baɪˈkɑːr-/ noun [U] specialized **bicarbonate of soda**

ˌsodium ˈcarbonate noun [U] specialized a chemical COMPOUND used as a WATER SOFTENER and in foods and industry, in the form of white powder or CRYSTALS

ˌsodium ˈchloride noun [U] specialized salt

sodium hydroxide /ˌsəʊ.di.əm.haɪˈdrɒk.saɪd/ (US) /ˌsoʊ.di.əm.haɪˈdrɑːk-/ noun [U] specialized a chemical COMPOUND used in soap and paper production and in powerful cleaning substances: **caustic soda**

ˌsodium ˈnitrate noun [U] specialized a chemical COMPOUND used to make explosives, FIREWORKS, and FERTILIZERS, and as a PRESERVATIVE for meat

sodomy /ˈsɒd.ə.mi/ (US) /ˈsɑː.də-/ **noun** [U] formal or legal the sexual act of putting the PENIS into another person's ANUS • **sodomite** /-maɪt/ **noun** [C] old use • **sodomize** (UK usually **sodomise**) /-maɪz/ verb [T]

Sod's ˈlaw noun [U] UK offensive → **Murphy's law**

sofa /ˈsəʊ.fə/ (US) /ˈsoʊ-/ noun [C] (UK also **settee**) (A2) a long, soft seat with a back and usually arms, on which more than one person can sit at the same time

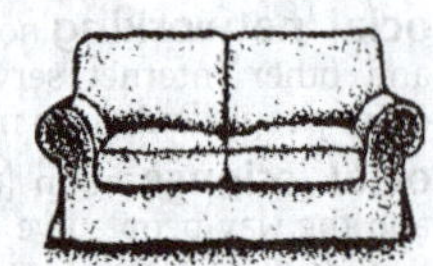
sofa

ˈsofa ˌbed noun [C] a sofa which opens to form a bed

soft /sɒft/ (US) /sɑːft/ adj **NOT HARD** ▷ **1** (A2) not hard or firm: *soft ground* ◦ *a soft pillow/mattress* ◦ *soft cheese* ◦ *I like chocolates with soft centres.* ◦ *Soft **tissue**, such as flesh, allows X-rays through.* **2** (A2) describes things, especially parts of the body, that are not hard or rough and feel pleasant and smooth when touched: *soft lips/cheeks/skin/hair* ◦ *soft leather* **3** informal disapproving Someone who is soft is not very healthy and strong: *Look at you! You need more exercise. You're **going/getting** soft.* **GENTLE** ▷ **4** (B1) not forceful, loud, or easily noticed: *a soft voice/sound* ◦ *soft music/lighting* ◦ *a soft glow* **5** disapproving not severe or forceful enough, especially in criticizing or punishing someone who has done something wrong: *She thinks I'm too soft **on** the kids when they misbehave.* ◦ *The government can't be seen to be **taking a** soft **line** (= not being severe enough) with criminals.* **EASY** ▷ **6** UK not difficult: *He's got a pretty soft job – he hardly seems to do anything all day.* **DRUGS** ▷ **7** [before noun] Soft drugs are illegal drugs that many people think are not dangerous. • **softness** /ˈsɒft.nəs/ (US) /ˈsɑːft-/ noun [U]

IDIOMS **be soft on sb** US to love someone or like them very much: *I think Matt must be soft on Tammy – he keeps sending her flowers and cards.* • **soft in the head** UK informal crazy or stupid: *Is the boss **going** soft in the head?*

softback /ˈsɒft.bæk/ (US) /ˈsɑːft-/ **adj, noun** [C] (US usually **softcover**) (a book) with a cover that can bend → Compare **hardback, paperback**

softball /ˈsɒft.bɔːl/ (US) /ˈsɑːft.bɑːl/ noun [U] a game similar to baseball but played with a larger, softer ball

ˌsoft ˈcorner noun **have a soft corner for sb** Indian English to feel that you like someone very much, often without knowing why → Compare **soft spot**

ˌsoft ˈdrink noun [C] (A2) a cold, usually sweet, drink which does not contain alcohol

soften /ˈsɒf.ən/ (US) /ˈsɑː.fən/ verb [I or T] **LESS HARD** ▷ **1** to become soft, or to make something soft: *You can soften the butter by warming it gently.* ◦ *These dried apples will soften **(up)** if you soak them in water.* **MORE GENTLE** ▷ **2** to become more gentle, or to make someone do this: *The news will upset him – we must think of a way to soften **the blow** (= make the news less*

S

unpleasant for him). ◦ *Would you say the government's stance on law and order has softened?*

PHRASAL VERB **soften sb up** to do things that will please someone so that they will do what you want: *You're trying to soften me up so I'll drive you to Jodie's house, aren't you?*

softener /ˈsɒf.ən.əʳ/ (US) /ˈsɑː.fən.ɚ/ **noun** [C or U] a substance used to make something soft: (a) *fabric softener*

ˌsoft ˈfruit noun [C or U] mainly UK a general name for small fruits such as STRAWBERRIES, RASPBERRIES, and BLACKCURRANTS which do not have a thick skin

ˌsoft ˈfurnishings noun [plural] UK (US **ˈsoft ˌgoods**) a general name for curtains, furniture coverings, and other things made of cloth which decorate a room

ˌsoft-ˈhearted adj kind and often feeling sympathy for other people → Compare **hard-hearted**

softie (also **softy**) /ˈsɒf.ti/ (US) /ˈsɑːf-/ **noun** [C] informal a kind, gentle person who is not forceful, looks for the pleasant things in life, and can be easily persuaded to do what you want them to

ˌsoft ˈlanding noun [C usually singular] an occasion when a person or vehicle comes down from the air to the ground without difficulty or damage

softly /ˈsɒft.li/ (US) /ˈsɑːft-/ **adv** (B1) gently: *She speaks softly but usually gets her own way.*

ˌsoftly-ˈsoftly adj UK **softly-softly approach** If you take a softly-softly approach, you try to solve a problem in a quiet and reasonable way.

ˌsoft ˈoption noun [C usually singular] UK the easiest of two or more possible choices: *The soft option is simply to say nothing for the moment.*

ˌsoft ˈpalate noun [C] specialized the soft piece of muscle and tissue that forms the top of the mouth at the back, separating the passages behind the nose from the throat → Compare **hard palate**

ˌsoft-ˈpedal verb [I or T] (**-ll-** or US usually **-l-**) to make something seem less important or less bad than it really is: *This is a rather sensitive issue – I think we'd better soft-pedal it for the moment.*

ˌsoft ˈporn noun [U] books and films showing sexual activity that is less extreme than other material of the same type

ˌsoft ˈsell noun [S] a way of trying to sell something to someone by persuading them gently: *The training brochure deliberately adopts a soft-sell approach.*

ˌsoft-ˈsoap verb [T] informal to try to persuade someone to do what you want by saying pleasant things to them

ˌsoft-ˈspoken adj having a quiet, pleasant voice

ˈsoft ˌspot noun **have a soft spot for sb** (C2) to feel that you like someone very much: *She'd always had a soft spot for her younger nephew.*

ˌsoft ˈtarget noun [C] something that is easy to attack or get an advantage from: *Major tourist attractions are a soft target **for** pickpockets.*

ˈsoft ˌtop noun [C] a CONVERTIBLE (= car with a soft roof that can be folded back)

ˌsoft ˈtouch noun [C usually singular] someone who you can easily persuade to do what you want

ˌsoft ˈtoy noun [C] UK (US **ˌstuffed ˈanimal**) a toy animal made from cloth and filled with a soft material so that it is pleasant to hold

software /ˈsɒft.weəʳ/ (US) /ˈsɑːft.wer/ **noun** [U] (A2) the instructions which control what a computer does; computer programs: *He's written a piece of software which calculates your tax returns for you.* → Compare **hardware**

! Common mistake: software

Software does not have a plural form and cannot be used with **a** or **an**.
To talk about an amount of **software**, do not say 'softwares', say **software**, **some software** or **a lot of software**:
~~*I recommend that we upgrade our softwares.*~~
I recommend that we upgrade our software.
To talk about **software** in the singular, do not say 'a software', say **a piece of software**:
~~*There was a demonstration of a software that I think we should buy.*~~
There was a demonstration of a piece of software that I think we should buy.

ˈsoftware ˌpackage noun [C] a computer program that is sold together with instructions on how to use it

ˌsoft ˈwater noun [U] water which does not contain a high level of minerals and allows soap to produce bubbles easily

softwood /ˈsɒft.wʊd/ (US) /ˈsɑːft-/ **noun** [U or C] wood from fast-growing EVERGREEN trees (= ones that never lose their leaves) like PINE, or a tree of this type: *window frames made from softwood* → Compare **hardwood**

soggy /ˈsɒg.i/ (US) /ˈsɑː.gi/ **adj** (of things that can absorb water, especially food) unpleasantly wet and soft: *soggy ground* ◦ *I hate it when cereal **goes** soggy.* • **soggily** /ˈsɒg.ɪ.li/ (US) /ˈsɑː.gɪ-/ **adv** • **sogginess** /-nəs/ **noun** [U]

soh (also **so**, **sol**) /səʊ/ (US) /soʊ/ **noun** [S] the fifth note in the SOL-FA musical SCALE

soil /sɔɪl/ **noun; verb**

▸**noun 1** (B2) [C or U] the material on the surface of the ground in which plants grow: *light/heavy/fertile soil* ◦ *sandy or chalky soils* **2** [U] literary a country: *It was the first time we had set foot on foreign/French/American soil* (= gone to a foreign country/France/America). **3 the soil** literary the activity of farming: *The government is trying to encourage a return to the soil.*

▸**verb** [T] formal to make something dirty, especially with solid waste: *soiled diapers/nappies/sheets*

IDIOM **not soil your hands** literary to not become involved in something unpleasant or bad: *These were top lawyers, the kind who wouldn't normally soil their hands with police work or criminal law.*

soiled /sɔɪld/ **adj** dirty: *soiled clothes*

ˈsoil ˌscience noun [U] the scientific study of soils

soirée /ˈswɑː.reɪ/ (US) /swɑːˈreɪ/ **noun** [C] formal an evening party, often with musical entertainment

sojourn /ˈsɒdʒ.ən/ (US) /ˈsoʊ.dʒɝːn/ **noun** [C] literary a short period when a person stays in a particular place: *My sojourn **in** the youth hostel was thankfully short.* • **sojourn** verb [I usually + adv/prep]

sol /sɒl/ (US) /sɑːl/ **noun** [S] (also **soh**, **so**) the fifth note in the SOL-FA musical SCALE

solace /ˈsɒl.ɪs/ (US) /ˈsɑː.lɪs/ **noun; verb**

▸**noun** [S or U] literary help and comfort when you are feeling sad or worried: *When his wife left him, he **found** solace **in** the bottle* (= drank alcohol). ◦ *Music was a great solace to me.*

▸**verb** [T] literary to give help and comfort to someone when they are feeling sad or worried

solar /ˈsəʊ.ləʳ/ (US) /ˈsoʊ.lɚ/ **adj** [before noun] (B2) of or from the sun, or using the energy from the sun to produce electric power: *solar radiation* ◦ *solar flares* ◦ *a solar cell/panel*

S

ˌsolar ˈenergy noun [U] (also **ˌsolar ˈpower**) energy that uses the power of the sun to produce electricity

solarium /səˈleə.ri.əm/ US /soʊˈler.i-/ noun [C] (plural **solariums** or **solaria**) **1** a room in which you can TAN (= make brown) your skin using either light from the sun or special equipment **2** US for **conservatory**.

ˌsolar ˈpanel noun [C] a device that changes energy from the sun into electricity: *Solar panels are used to power satellites.*

solar plexus /ˌsəʊ.ləˈplek.səs/ US /ˌsoʊ.lɚ-/ noun [S] the front part of the body below the chest: *a punch in the solar plexus*

ˌsolar ˈpower noun [U] **solar energy**

the ˈsolar ˌsystem noun [S] the sun and the group of planets which move around it

ˌsolar ˈyear noun [C] specialized the time it takes for the Earth to go round the sun, just over 365 days

sold /səʊld/ US /soʊld/ verb **1** past simple and past participle of **sell** **2** **sold out a** When a film, CONCERT, etc. is sold out, all of the tickets for it have been sold. **b** When a shop is sold out of something, there is no more of that thing left to buy in it.

solder /ˈsəʊl.dəʳ/ US /ˈsɑː.dɚ/ noun; verb

▸noun [U] a soft metal that is melted in order to join together pieces of metal so that they stick together when it cools and becomes hard again

▸verb [I or T] to join pieces of metal together using solder

ˈsoldering ˌiron noun [C] a tool which you use for heating solder

soldier /ˈsəʊl.dʒəʳ/ US /ˈsoʊl.dʒɚ/ noun; verb

▸noun [C] B1 a person who is in an army and wears its uniform, especially someone who fights when there is a war: *Soldiers were patrolling the streets.*

▸verb

PHRASAL VERB **soldier on** to continue doing something although it is difficult: *I admired the way she soldiered on when her business ran into trouble.*

soldiering /ˈsəʊl.dʒəʳ.rɪŋ/ US /ˈsoʊl.dʒɚ-/ noun [U] the job of being a soldier: *a life of soldiering*

ˌsoldier of ˈfortune noun [C] literary someone who fights for anyone who will pay, not only for their own country

sole /səʊl/ US /soʊl/ adj; noun; verb

▸adj [before noun] **1** C1 being one only; single: *My sole objective is to make the information more widely available.* ◦ *The sole **survivor** of the accident was found in the water after six hours.* **2** C1 not shared with anyone else: *She has sole **responsibility** for the project.* ◦ *I have sole charge of both children all day.*

▸noun [C] **FOOT** ▷ **1** (plural **soles**) the bottom part of the foot that touches the ground when you stand or walk, or the bottom part of a shoe that touches the ground, usually not including the HEEL: *a cut on the sole of her foot* ◦ *shoes with rubber soles* **FISH** ▷ **2** (plural **sole**) one of a number of flat, round fish that are eaten as food: *lemon sole* ◦ *Dover sole*

▸verb [T] to put a new sole on a shoe • **-soled** /-d/ suffix *leather-soled shoes*

solecism /ˈsɒl.ɪ.sɪ.zᵊm/ US /ˈsɑː.lə-/ noun [C] formal **1** behaviour that is a social mistake or is not polite: *to commit a social solecism* **2** a grammatical mistake: *a grammatical solecism*

solely /ˈsəʊl.li/ US /ˈsoʊl-/ adv C1 only and not involving anyone or anything else: *I bought it solely for that purpose.* ◦ *It seems he's not solely to blame for the accident.*

solemn /ˈsɒl.əm/ US /ˈsɑː.ləm/ adj **1** serious and without any humour: *a solemn face/voice* ◦ *solemn music* ◦ *Everyone looked very solemn.* **2** **solemn promise, commitment, undertaking, etc.** an agreement which you make in a serious way and expect to keep • **solemnly** /-li/ adv

solemnity /səˈlem.nɪ.ti/ US /-nə.t̬i/ noun **1** [U] (also **solemnness**) the quality of being serious: *the solemnity **of** a funeral service* **2** **solemnities** [plural] the ways of behaving or the activities that are considered suitable for a serious, formal, social ceremony, such as a funeral

solemnize (UK usually **solemnise**) /ˈsɒl.əm.naɪz/ US /ˈsɑː.ləm-/ verb specialized **solemnize a marriage** to perform the official marriage ceremony, especially as part of a religious ceremony in a church • **solemnization** (UK usually **solemnisation**) /ˌsɒl.əm.naɪˈzeɪ.ʃᵊn/ US /ˌsɑː.ləm.nəˈ-/ noun [U]

ˌsol-ˈfa noun [U] a type of musical SCALE in which the notes A to G have names, used especially in teaching music

solicit /səˈlɪs.ɪt/ verb **ASK FOR** ▷ **1** [T] formal to ask someone for money, information, or help: *to solicit donations for a charity* ◦ *It is illegal for public officials to solicit gifts or money in exchange for favours.* **OFFER** ▷ **2** [I] to offer sex for money, usually in a public place • **solicitation** /səˌlɪs.ɪˈteɪ.ʃᵊn/ noun [C or U] formal

soliciting /səˈlɪs.ɪ.tɪŋ/ US /-t̬ɪŋ/ noun [U] legal the act of offering to have sex for money

solicitor /səˈlɪs.ɪ.təʳ/ US /-t̬ɚ/ noun [C] C1 a type of lawyer in Britain and Australia who is trained to prepare cases and give advice on legal subjects and can represent people in lower courts: *a firm of solicitors*

solicitous /səˈlɪs.ɪ.təs/ US /-t̬əs/ adj formal showing care and helpful attention to someone: *He made a solicitous enquiry after her health.* • **solicitously** /-li/ adv • **solicitude** /-tjuːd/ US /-tuːd/ noun [U] (also **solicitousness** /-nəs/)

solid /ˈsɒl.ɪd/ US /ˈsɑː.lɪd/ adj; noun

▸adj **HARD** ▷ **1** B2 hard or firm, keeping a clear shape: *solid ground* ◦ *a solid object* ◦ *a solid structure* **2** B2 completely hard or firm all through an object, or without any spaces or holes: *solid rock* ◦ *a solid oak table* ◦ *solid doors/walls* ◦ *a solid line of traffic* ◦ *The lecture hall was **packed** solid (**with** students).* **3** C1 describes a metal or a colour that is pure and does not have anything else mixed together with it: *solid gold/silver candlesticks* ◦ *a white rose on a solid blue background* **NOT LIQUID/GAS** ▷ **4** C1 not liquid or gas: *Liquid and solid waste is collected in the tank.* ◦ *Freeze the mixture for about three hours or so until solid.* **5** describes food that is not in liquid form, especially when given to babies or people who are ill: *That rice pudding was the first solid **food** he's eaten since his operation.* **CERTAIN** ▷ **6** C2 certain or safe; of a good standard; giving confidence or support: *This provided solid evidence that he committed the crime.* ◦ *The drama course gives students a solid grounding in the basic techniques of acting.* **CONTINUOUS** ▷ **7** continuing for a period of time without stopping: *I slept for eleven solid hours.* ◦ *The hotel was booked solid all of December.*

▸noun **OBJECT** ▷ **1** [C] specialized an object that has a height, width, and length, and is not flat: *A cube and a pyramid are both solids.* **NOT LIQUID/GAS** ▷ **2** [C] a substance that is not liquid or gas **3** [C usually plural a food not in liquid form

solidarity /ˌsɒl.ɪˈdær.ɪ.ti/ US /ˌsɑː.lɪˈder.ə.t̬i/ noun [U] C1 agreement between and support for the members of a group, especially a political group: *The situation* raises important questions about solidarity among member states of the UN. ◦ The lecturers joined the protest march to show solidarity **with** their students.

ˌsolid ˈfuel noun [C or U] a solid substance used for fuel, such as coal or wood, rather than oil or gas

solidify /səˈlɪd.ɪ.faɪ/ verb [I or T] **NOT LIQUID/GAS** ▷ **1** to change from being a liquid or gas to a solid form, or to make something do this: *Molten volcanic lava solidifies as it cools.* ◦ *The chemical reaction solidifies the resin.* **CERTAIN** ▷ **2** to become or make something become certain: *Support for the policy is solidifying.* • **solidification** /səˌlɪd.ɪ.fɪˈkeɪ.ʃən/ noun [U]

solidity /səˈlɪd.ɪ.ti/ (US) /-ə.t̬i/ noun [U] (also **solidness**) **FIRM** ▷ **1** the quality of being hard or firm, not a liquid or gas **CERTAIN** ▷ **2** the quality of being certain or strong: *The agreement would give a new solidity to military cooperation between the two countries.*

solidly /ˈsɒl.ɪd.li/ (US) /ˈsɑː.lɪd-/ adv **HARD** ▷ **1** strongly and firmly: *The house seems very solidly built.* **CONTINUOUS** ▷ **2** in a regular or continuous way, without sudden changes: *The economy has been growing solidly for five years now.* **CERTAINLY** ▷ **3** agreeing with or supporting someone completely: *My colleagues are solidly* ***behind*** *me on this issue.*

ˌsolid-ˈstate adj [before noun] specialized describes an electronic device in which the flow of electrical current is through solid material and not through a VACUUM (= space without air)

soliloquy /səˈlɪl.ə.kwi/ noun [C] (plural **soliloquies**) specialized a speech in a play which the character speaks to him- or herself or to the people watching rather than to the other characters: *Hamlet's soliloquy 'To be or not to be'*

solipsism /ˈsɒl.ɪp.sɪ.zəm/ (US) /ˈsɑː.lɪp-/ noun [U] specialized the belief that only your own experiences and existence can be known • **solipsistic** /ˌsɒl.ɪpˈsɪs.tɪk/ (US) /ˌsɑː.lɪp-/ adj

solitaire /ˌsɒl.ɪˈteər/, /ˈsɒl.ɪ.teər/ (US) /ˈsɑː.lə.ter/ noun **JEWELLERY** ▷ **1** [C] a single JEWEL (= precious stone) that is part of a piece of jewellery, especially a ring, or the ring itself: *a solitaire diamond* **CARDS** ▷ **2** [U] US (UK **patience**) a game played with cards by one person

solitary /ˈsɒl.ɪ.tər.i/ (US) /ˈsɑː.lə.ter.i/ adj **1** (C2) A solitary person or thing is the only person or thing in a place: *On the hill, a solitary figure was busy chopping down trees.* ◦ *In the distance was a solitary building.* ◦ *He was a solitary child (= he enjoyed being alone).* **2** (C2) done alone: *solitary walks by the river* ◦ *fishing and other solitary pastimes*

ˌsolitary conˈfinement noun [U] a punishment in which someone is kept in a room alone, usually in a prison

solitude /ˈsɒl.ɪ.tjuːd/ (US) /ˈsɑː.lə.tuːd/ noun [U] (C1) the situation of being alone without other people: *a life of solitude* ◦ *After months of solitude at sea it felt strange to be in company.* ◦ *It provides one with a chance to reflect on spiritual matters* ***in*** *solitude.*

solo /ˈsəʊ.ləʊ/ (US) /ˈsoʊ.loʊ/ adj, adv; noun

▸adj [before noun], adv (B2) alone; without other people: *a solo performance/flight* ◦ *to sail/fly solo* ◦ *He used to play with a group but now he's* ***going*** *solo/pursuing a solo career.*

▸noun [C] (plural **solos**) (B2) a musical performance done by one person alone, or a musical performance in which one person is given special attention: *a trumpet solo* ◦ *Parker's solo on 'A Night in Tunisia' was so amazing that the pianist backing him simply stopped playing.*

soloist /ˈsəʊ.ləʊ.ɪst/ (US) /ˈsoʊ.loʊ-/ noun [C] a musician who performs a solo: *The soloist in the violin concerto was Yehudi Menuhin.*

solstice /ˈsɒl.stɪs/ (US) /ˈsɑːl-/ noun [C] either of the two occasions in the year when the sun is directly above either the furthest point north or the furthest point south of the EQUATOR that it ever reaches. These are the times in the year, in the middle of the summer or winter, when there are the longest hours of day or night: *the* ***summer/winter*** *solstice* → Compare **equinox**

soluble /ˈsɒl.jʊ.bl/ (US) /ˈsɑː.l-/ adj able to be dissolved to form a solution: *soluble aspirins* → Opposite **insoluble** • **solubility** /ˌsɒl.jʊˈbɪl.ɪ.ti/ (US) /ˌsɑː.l.jəˈbɪl.ə.t̬i/ noun [U]

solution /səˈluː.ʃən/ noun **ANSWER** ▷ **1** (B1) [C] the answer to a problem: *There's no easy solution* ***to*** *this problem.* ◦ *She just seems so unhappy and I don't know what the solution is.* ◦ *When you finish doing the crossword, the solution is on the back page.* ◦ *They help you talk through your problems but they don't give you any solutions.*

> **!** Common mistake: **solution**
>
> The correct preposition to use after **solution** is **to**.
>
> Don't say 'solution of/for something', say **solution to something**:
>
> ~~*We must find a solution for this problem.*~~
>
> *We must find a solution to this problem.*

LIQUID ▷ **2** [C or U] specialized a liquid into which a solid has been mixed and has dissolved: *an aqueous solution of salts* ◦ *copper sulphate* ***in*** *solution (= dissolved in water)*

> Word partners for **solution**
>
> *search for/seek* a solution • *find* a solution • *offer/provide* a solution • an *ideal/peaceful/perfect/satisfactory* solution • an *easy/obvious/possible/simple* solution • a *long-term/short-term* solution • a solution *to* sth

solvable /ˈsɒl.və.bl/ (US) /sɑːl-/ adj (also **soluble**) able to be solved

solve /sɒlv/ (US) /sɑːlv/ verb [T] (B1) to find an answer to a problem: *to solve a problem* ◦ *to solve a mystery/puzzle* ◦ *Just calm down – shouting won't solve anything!* ◦ *This strategy could cause more problems than it solves.* ◦ *Police are still no nearer to solving the crime.*

solvent /ˈsɒl.vənt/ (US) /ˈsɑːl-/ adj; noun

▸adj (especially of companies) having enough money to pay all the money that is owed to other people: *Many insurance companies are under pressure to increase premiums to* ***stay*** *solvent.* → Opposite **insolvent** • **solvency** /-vən.si/ noun [U]

▸noun [C] a liquid in which solids will dissolve → See also **dissolve**

ˈsolvent aˌbuse noun [U] formal the habit of breathing in the dangerous gases produced by some types of glue to achieve an excited mental condition

somatic /səˈmæt.ɪk/ (US) /soʊˈmæt̬-/ adj specialized relating to the body rather than the mind: *She may become angry and depressed, and show somatic symptoms such as headaches.*

sombre UK (US **somber**) /ˈsɒm.bər/ (US) /ˈsɑːm.bɚ/ adj **1** serious, sad, and without humour or entertainment: *a sombre atmosphere/voice/face* ◦ *The funeral was a sombre occasion.* ◦ *I left them in a sombre mood.* **2** dark

S

and plain: *He wore a sombre black suit.* • **sombrely** (US **somberly**) /-li/ adv • **sombreness** (US **somberness**) /-nəs/ noun [U]

sombrero /sɒmˈbreə.rəʊ/ (US) /sɑːmˈbrer.oʊ/ noun [C] (plural **sombreros**) a hat with a wide BRIM, worn especially by men in Mexico

some determiner; pronoun; adv

▸determiner **UNKNOWN AMOUNT** ▷ **1** A1 /sʌm, səm/ an amount or number of something that is not stated or not known; a part of something: *There's some cake in the kitchen if you'd like it.* ◦ *Here's some news you might be interested in.* ◦ *We've been having some problems with our TV over the last few weeks.* ◦ *Could you give me some idea of when the building work will finish?* ◦ *I've got to do some* ***more*** *work before I can go out.*

! Usage: **some or any?**

Some is used in positive sentences. **Any** is used in questions and negative sentences:

There are some flowers in the garden, but there aren't any trees.

Has he got any brothers or sisters?

Some is sometimes used in offers or requests, or other questions when we expect people to answer 'yes':

Would you like some more cake?

The same rules are true for **something** and **anything**, **someone** and **anyone**, and **somewhere** and **anywhere**.

LARGE AMOUNT ▷ **2** B2 /sʌm/ a large amount or number of something: *It'll be some time before we meet again.* ◦ *It was some years later when they next met.* ◦ *We discussed the problem at some length.* **PARTICULAR THING** ▷ **3** C1 /sʌm/ used to refer to a particular person or thing without stating exactly which one: *Some lucky person will win more than $1,000,000 in the competition.* ◦ *Some idiot's locked the door!* ◦ *There must be some way you can relieve the pain.* **ANGER** ▷ **4** /sʌm/ informal used before a noun, especially at the beginning of a sentence to show anger or disapproval, often by repeating a word that was not accurately used: *Some people just don't know when to shut up.* ◦ *Some help you were! You sat on your backside most of the afternoon!* ◦ *'A friend of mine sold me a radio that doesn't work.' 'Some friend!'* **EXCELLENT** ▷ **5** /sʌm/ informal used before a noun to show how good something or someone is: *Wow, that was some dinner!*

S

IDIOMS **and then some** informal and even more: *It looked like 20,000 people and then some at the demonstration.* • **some ... or other** refers to one of several possibilities when the exact one is not known or not stated: *They found the painting in some antique shop or other.*

▸**pronoun 1** A1 strong /sʌm/ weak /səm/ an amount or number of something that is not stated or not known; a part of something: *If you need more paper then just take some.* ◦ *'Would you like to have dinner with us?' 'No thanks, I've already had some.'* ◦ *Some* ***of*** *you here have already met Imran.* ◦ *Have some* ***of*** *this champagne – it's very good.* **2** /sʌm/ some people: *Some have compared his work to Picasso's.*

▸**adv** strong /sʌm/ weak /səm/ **APPROXIMATELY** ▷ **1** used before a number to mean approximately; about: *Some 50 tons of stone are taken from the quarry every day.* ◦ *The water is some 20 to 30 metres beneath the ground.* **SMALL AMOUNT** ▷ **2** US informal by a small amount or degree; a little: *She says she's feeling some better.* ◦ *We could turn down the heat some if that would make you more comfortable.*

somebody /ˈsʌm.bə.di/, /-ˌbɒd.i/ (US) /-ˌbɑː.di/ pronoun A2 someone

someday /ˈsʌm.deɪ/ adv at some time in the future that is not yet known or not stated: *Maybe someday you'll both meet again.* ◦ *Someday soon you're going to have to make a decision.*

somehow /ˈsʌm.haʊ/ adv **1** B1 (US informal also **someway**) in a way or by some means that is not known or not stated: *It won't be easy, but we'll get across the river somehow.* **2** B2 for a reason that is not clear: *I know what we're doing is legal, but somehow it doesn't feel right.*

someone /ˈsʌm.wʌn/ pronoun (also **somebody**) A2 used to refer to a single person when you do not know who they are or when it is not important who they are: *There's someone outside the house.* ◦ *Someone must have seen what happened.* ◦ *Eventually someone in the audience spoke.* ◦ *You'll have to ask someone* ***else***. ◦ *We'll need a software engineer* ***or*** *someone (= a person with skill of or like the stated type) on the project team.*

! Note:

Someone is not usually used in negatives and questions.

someplace /ˈsʌm.pleɪs/ adv B1 US for somewhere: *They live someplace in the South.* ◦ *If they don't like it here they can go someplace* ***else***.

somersault /ˈsʌm.ə.sɔːlt/ (US) /-ɚ.sɑːlt/ noun [C] a rolling movement or jump, either forwards or backwards, in which you turn over completely, with your body above your head, and finish with your head on top again: *She was so happy she* ***turned*** *three somersaults on the lawn.* • **somersault** verb [I] *The bus plunged down the embankment, somersaulted twice and finally landed on its side.*

something /ˈsʌm.θɪŋ/ pronoun **1** A1 an object, situation, quality, or action that is not exactly known or stated: *There's something sharp in my shoe.* ◦ *Something in the cupboard smells odd.* ◦ *We thought there must be something* ***wrong*** *because we hadn't heard from you.* ◦ *There's something wrong with the engine – it's making strange noises.* ◦ *Something's happened to upset him but we don't know what it is.* ◦ *I heard something rather worrying at work this morning.* ◦ *Is there something you'd like to say?* ◦ *Don't just stand there,* ***do*** *something.* ◦ ***There's*** *just something* ***odd*** *about him.*

! Note:

Something is not usually used in negatives and questions. See Note **some or any?** at **some**.

2 a thing for which you are grateful, especially because an unpleasant thing has also happened: *We were given five hundred pounds in compensation which isn't much but at least it's something.*

! Common mistake: **something or anything?**

Warning: choose the correct pronoun!

After a negative word like 'not' or 'nobody', don't say 'something', say **anything**:

~~*I have never seen something more amazing than the Grand Canyon.*~~

I have never seen anything more amazing than the Grand Canyon.

IDIOMS **be (really) something** informal C2 to be very special or admired: *Imagine England winning the World Cup – now that would be something.* • **be**

something of a sth informal C2 used to describe a person or thing in a way that is partly true but not completely or exactly: *It came as something of a surprise.* ◦ *He has a reputation as something of a troublemaker.* • **be/have something to do with sth** informal C1 to be related to something or a cause of something but not in a way that you know about or understand exactly: *I'm not sure what he does exactly – it's something to do with finance.* ◦ *It might have something to do with the way it's made.* • **have got something there** If you say that a person has got something there, you mean they have said or discovered an important or interesting thing. • **have something going with sb** informal If you have something going with someone, you are involved in a sexual relationship with them: *Didn't he have something going with one of his students?* • **or something (like that)** informal A2 used to show that what you have just said is only an example or you are not certain about it: *She works for a bank or something.* ◦ *Why don't you go to a movie or something?* • **something a little stronger** humorous a drink containing alcohol: *We have fruit juice but perhaps you'd like something a little stronger?* • **something for nothing** If someone gets something for nothing, they get something they want, such as money, without having to work or make any effort. • **something like** C2 similar to: *He cursed himself for not having foreseen that something like this might happen.* • **something like 96 percent, half, etc.** approximately, when talking about an amount or number: *Something like 60 percent of all married men will have an affair at some point in their marriage.* ◦ *He paid something like £90 for a T-shirt.* • **there's something in sth** used to admit that there is some value or truth in what someone does or says, although you do not completely approve of it: *I don't go along with all his theories but there's probably something in it.*

-something /-sʌm.θɪŋ/ **suffix** informal used after a number like 20, 30, etc. to refer to the age of a person who is between 20 and 29, 30 and 39 years old, etc., or to a person who is of this age: *I'd guess she's thirty-something.* ◦ *Most of these places are aimed at twenty-somethings.*

sometime /ˈsʌm.taɪm/ **adv; adj**

▸**adv** at a time in the future or the past that is not known or not stated: *sometime before June* ◦ *We really should meet sometime soon to discuss the details.* ◦ *sometime **in** the autumn*

> **! Common mistake: sometime or sometimes?**
>
> **Warning:** choose the correct adverb!
>
> To talk about something that happens on some occasions but not always or often, don't say 'sometime', say **sometimes**:
>
> ~~*Being visited can sometime be exhausting.*~~
>
> *Being visited can sometimes be exhausting.*

▸**adj** [before noun] formal (especially of a job or position) in the past but not any longer: *The enquiry will be headed by Lord Jones, sometime editor of the 'Daily News'.*

sometimes /ˈsʌm.taɪmz/ **adv** A1 on some occasions but not always or often: *Sometimes we take food with us and sometimes we buy food when we're there.* ◦ *Sometimes it's best not to say anything.*

someway /ˈsʌm.weɪ/ **adv** (also **someways**) US informal for **somehow**: *Don't worry – I'll get there someway.*

somewhat /ˈsʌm.wɒt/ US /-wɑːt/ **adv** formal **1** C1 to some degree; rather: *The resort has changed somewhat over the last few years.* ◦ *She's somewhat more confident than she used to be.* ◦ *We were somewhat tired after our long walk.* **2 somewhat of** to some degree: *She was known for being somewhat of a strange character.*

somewhere /ˈsʌm.weəʳ/ US /-wer/ **adv** **PLACE** ▷ **1** A2 (US also **someplace**) in or at a place having a position that is not stated or not known: *He was last heard of living somewhere on the south coast.* ◦ *You must have put their letter somewhere!* ◦ [+ to infinitive] *I'm looking for somewhere **to** eat/stay.* ◦ *Can we go somewhere **else** to talk – it's very noisy here.* ◦ *Wouldn't you like to go to Disneyland **or** somewhere (= or to a similar place)?*

> **! Note:**
>
> **Somewhere** is not usually used in negatives and questions. See Note **some or any?** at **some**.

APPROXIMATELY ▷ **2 somewhere around, between, etc.** B2 approximately; about: *Somewhere between 900 and 1,100 minor crimes are reported in this city every week.* ◦ *It will take us somewhere between three and four hours to get to Madrid.*

IDIOM **be getting somewhere** informal to be achieving something: *Right, that's the printer working. Now we're getting somewhere!*

somnambulism /sɒmˈnæm.bjʊ.lɪ.zᵊm/ US /sɑːm-/ **noun** [U] specialized the action, sometimes happening regularly, of a person walking around while they are sleeping → Compare **sleepwalker** • **somnambulist** /-lɪst/ **noun** [C]

somnolent /ˈsɒm.nəl.ənt/ US /ˈsɑːm-/ **adj** literary almost sleeping, or causing sleep: *a somnolent summer's afternoon* ◦ *the somnolent villages further north* • **somnolence** /-əns/ **noun** [U]

son /sʌn/ **noun** [C] **1** A1 your male child: *This is our son Raja.* ◦ *We have two sons and three daughters.* **2** used as an informal form of address by a man to a boy: *Come on, son, we haven't got all day.* **3 a son of somewhere** literary a man who was born in a particular place: *that notable son of Württemberg, Martin Brecht*

sonar /ˈsəʊ.nɑːʳ/ US /ˈsoʊ.nɑːr/ **noun** [U] equipment, especially on a ship, which uses sound waves to discover how deep the water is or the position of an object in the water, such as a group of fish

sonata /səˈnɑː.tə/ US /-t̬ə/ **noun** [C] a piece of music in three or four parts, either for a piano or for another instrument, such as a VIOLIN, sometimes also with a piano

son et lumière /ˌsɒn.eɪˌluː.miˈeəʳ/ US /ˌsɑːn.eɪˌluː.miˈer/ **noun** [U] an outside entertainment which uses sounds, lights, and often a spoken story to tell the history of a place

song /sɒŋ/ US /sɑːŋ/ **noun** **1** A2 [C] a usually short piece of music with words that are sung: *to sing a song* ◦ *a love/folk/pop song* → See also **swansong** **2** [U] the act of singing, or singing when considered generally: *He was so happy he wanted to **burst/break into** song (= start singing).* **3** [C or U] the musical sound that a bird makes: *bird song* ◦ *A thrush's song was the only sound to break the silence.*

IDIOMS **for a song** informal very cheaply: *She bought the bed for a song at an auction.* ◦ *Because the shop's closing down, most of the stock is **going** for a song (= being sold very cheaply).* • **make a song and dance about sth** UK informal to make something seem more important than it really is so that everyone notices it: *I only asked her to move her car but she made such a song and dance about it.* • **song and dance** mainly US

S

informal a long and complicated statement or story, especially one that is not true

songbird /ˈsɒŋ.bɜːd/ (US) /ˈsɑːŋ.bɝːd/ **noun** [C] any of many different types of bird that make musical sounds

songbook /ˈsɒŋ.bʊk/ (US) /ˈsɑːŋ-/ **noun** [C] a book containing a collection of songs showing both their words and their music

songfest /ˈsɒŋ.fest/ (US) /ˈsɑːŋ-/ **noun** [C] US for **singsong**

songster /ˈsɒŋ.stəʳ/ (US) /-stɚ/ **noun** [C] literary **1** a skilled singer **2** a bird with a musical song

songstress /ˈsɒŋ.strəs/ **noun** [C] literary a skilled female singer

ˈsong ˌthrush **noun** [C] a type of **thrush**

songwriter /ˈsɒŋˌraɪ.təʳ/ (US) /ˈsɑːŋˌraɪ.t̬ɚ/ **noun** [C] a person who writes the music and words of songs • **songwriting** /-tɪŋ/ (US) /-t̬ɪŋ/ **noun** [U]

sonic /ˈsɒn.ɪk/ (US) /ˈsɑː.nɪk/ **adj** specialized of sound or the speed at which sound travels in air → See also **supersonic**

ˌsonic ˈboom **noun** [C usually singular] an explosive sound made by an aircraft, bullet, etc. travelling faster than the speed at which sound travels

ˌsonic ˈbranding **noun** [U] using a sound in an advertisement for a product, so that when you hear the sound, you think of the product

ˈson-in-law **noun** [C] (plural **sons-in-law**) B2 the man who is married to your daughter or son

sonnet /ˈsɒn.ɪt/ (US) /ˈsɑː.nɪt/ **noun** [C] a poem that has 14 lines and a particular pattern of RHYME

sonny /ˈsʌn.i/ **noun** [S] old-fashioned a form of address used by an older person to a boy or a young man: *Look here, sonny, you've got a lot to learn!*

ˌson of a ˈbitch **noun** [C usually singular] (abbreviation **S.O.B.**) mainly US offensive an unpleasant man: *I'm going to beat that son of a bitch if it kills me!*

ˌson of a ˈgun **noun** [C] (plural **sons of guns**) US polite phrase for **son of a bitch**

sonogram /ˈsɒn.ə.græm/ (US) /ˈsɑː.nə-/ **noun** [C] specialized an image, especially of a baby that is still inside the WOMB, that is produced by ULTRASOUND (= sound waves)

sonorous /ˈsɒn.ᵊr.əs/ (US) /ˈsɑː.nɚ-/ **adj** formal having a deep pleasant sound: *a sonorous voice* • **sonorously** /-li/ **adv**

S

sook /sʊk/ **noun** [C] Australian English a shy or COWARDLY (= not brave) child or person

soon /suːn/ **adv** **1** A2 in or within a short time; before long; quickly: *She'll soon be here./She'll be here soon.* ◦ *It will soon be impossible for foreigners to enter the country.* ◦ *The sooner we leave, the sooner we'll get there.* ◦ *Soon* ***after*** *agreeing to go, she realized she'd made a mistake.* ◦ ***How*** *soon (= when) can we sign the contract?* ◦ *'When would you like to meet?'* ***'The*** *sooner* ***the*** *better.'* ◦ *I couldn't get out of that place soon enough.* **2 as soon as** B1 at the same time or a very short time after: *As soon as I saw her, I knew there was something wrong.* **3 as soon as possible** A2 If you do something as soon as possible, you do it as quickly as you can: *We need the repairs done as soon as possible.*

IDIOMS **no sooner ... than** C1 used to show that one thing happens immediately after another thing: *No sooner had I started mowing the lawn than it started raining.* • **no sooner said than done** used to say that you will do something immediately • **see you soon** A1 used for saying goodbye to someone you are going to meet again soon: *I'll see you soon!* • **sooner or later** B2 used to say that you do not know exactly when something will happen, but you are certain that it will happen: *Sooner or later she's going to realize what a mistake she's made.* • **would (just) as soon** (also **would sooner**) C2 If you would (just) as soon do something or would sooner do something, you would prefer to do it rather than something else that is possible: *'Would you like to go out for dinner?' 'I'd just as soon stay in – I'm not feeling very well.'*

soot /sʊt/ **noun** [U] a black powder composed mainly of carbon, produced when coal, wood, etc. is burned: *It can be dangerous to let too much soot accumulate inside a chimney.* • **sooty** /ˈsʊt.i/ (US) /ˈsʊt̬-/ **adj**

soothe /suːð/ **verb** [T] ANGER ▷ **1** to make someone feel calm or less worried: *to soothe a crying baby* PAIN ▷ **2** to make a part of the body less painful: *I had a long, hot bath to soothe my aching muscles.*

soothing /ˈsuː.ðɪŋ/ **adj** LESS ANGRY ▷ **1** C2 making you feel calm: *I put on some nice soothing music.* ◦ *Her words had a soothing effect.* LESS PAINFUL ▷ **2** making something less painful: *a soothing ointment* • **soothingly** /-li/ **adv**

soothsayer /ˈsuːθˌseɪ.əʳ/ (US) /-ɚ/ **noun** [C] old use a person who is believed to have the ability to know and tell what will happen in the future

sop /sɒp/ (US) /sɑːp/ **noun**; **verb**

▸**noun** [C usually singular] disapproving something of little importance or value that is offered to stop complaints or unhappiness: *Critics see the increase in defence spending as a sop* ***to*** *the armed forces rather than an improvement of national security.*

▸**verb** (-pp-)

PHRASAL VERB **sop sth up** to absorb liquid into a piece of something solid: *It's surprising how much milk the bread sops up.*

sophism /ˈsɒf.ɪ.zᵊm/ (US) /ˈsɑː.fɪ-/ **noun** [C] formal an argument which seems true but is really false and is used to deceive people

sophisticate /səˈfɪs.tɪ.kət/ **noun** [C] formal a person who is sophisticated

sophisticated /səˈfɪs.tɪ.keɪ.tɪd/ (US) /-t̬ɪd/ **adj** **1** B2 having a good understanding of the way people behave and/or a good knowledge of culture and fashion: *She was slim, svelte, and sophisticated.* ◦ *I don't suppose I have any books that would suit your sophisticated tastes.* **2** B2 clever in a complicated way and therefore able to do complicated tasks: *I think a more sophisticated approach is needed to solve this problem.* ◦ *These are among the most sophisticated weapons in the world.*

sophistication /səˌfɪs.tɪˈkeɪ.ʃᵊn/ **noun** [U] the quality of being sophisticated: *Her sophistication is evident from the way she dresses.* ◦ *The sophistication of computers is increasing.*

sophistry /ˈsɒf.ɪ.stri/ (US) /ˈsɑː.fɪ-/ **noun** [U] formal the clever use of arguments which seem true but are really false, in order to deceive people

sophomore /ˈsɒf.ə.mɔːʳ/ (US) /ˈsɑː.fə.mɔːr/ **noun** [C] US a student studying in the second year of a course at a US college or HIGH SCHOOL (= a school for students aged 15 to 18)

sophomoric /ˌsɒf.əˈmɒr.ɪk/ (US) /ˌsɑː.fəˈmɔːr-/ **adj** US silly and behaving like a child: *a sophomoric sense of humour*

soporific /ˌsɒp.ᵊrˈɪf.ɪk/ (US) /ˌsɑː.pəˈrɪf-/ **adj** causing sleep or making a person want to sleep: *the soporific effect of the heat* • **soporifically** /-ɪ.kᵊl.i/ **adv**

sopping /ˈsɒp.ɪŋ/ (US) /ˈsɑː.pɪŋ/ **adj** informal extremely wet: *The bottle had leaked in my bag and everything was sopping.* ◦ *You're sopping* ***wet*** *– go and get changed.*

soppy /ˈsɒp.i/ US /ˈsɑː.pi/ **adj** informal disapproving showing or feeling too much of emotions such as love or sympathy, rather than being reasonable or practical: *a film with a soppy ending* ◦ *That's one of the soppiest stories I've ever heard!* ◦ *Some people are really soppy* ***about*** *their pets.* • **soppily** /ˈsɒp.ɪ.li/ US /ˈsɑː.pɪ-/ **adv** informal • **soppiness** /-nəs/ **noun** [U] informal

soprano /səˈprɑː.nəʊ/ US /-ˈpræn.oʊ/ **noun** [C] (plural **sopranos**) a woman or girl with a voice that can sing the highest notes • **soprano adj, adv**

sorbet /ˈsɔː.beɪ/ US /sɔːrˈbeɪ/ **noun** [C or U] (US also **sherbet**) a frozen food made from fruit juice, water, and sugar: *lemon sorbet*

sorcerer /ˈsɔː.sᵊr.əʳ/ US /ˈsɔːr.sɚ.ɚ/ **noun** [C] in stories, a man who has magical powers and who uses them to harm other people

sorceress /ˈsɔː.sᵊr.əs/ US /ˈsɔːr.sɚ-/ **noun** [C] a female sorcerer

sorcery /ˈsɔː.sᵊr.i/ US /ˈsɔːr.sɚ-/ **noun** [U] a type of magic in which spirits, especially evil ones, are used to make things happen: *It seems that some people still believe in sorcery and black magic.*

sordid /ˈsɔː.dɪd/ US /ˈsɔːr-/ **adj** **DIRTY** ▷ **1** dirty and unpleasant: *There are lots of really sordid apartments in the city's poorer areas.* **IMMORAL** ▷ **2** morally wrong and shocking: *He told me he'd had an affair but he spared me the sordid* ***details****.* • **sordidly** /-li/ **adv** • **sordidness** /-nəs/ **noun** [U]

sore /sɔːʳ/ US /sɔːr/ **adj; noun**

▸**adj** **PAINFUL** ▷ **1** B1 painful and uncomfortable because of injury, infection, or too much use: *All the dust has made my eyes sore.* ◦ *I've got a sore* ***throat****.* ◦ *My feet were sore with all the walking.* **ANGRY** ▷ **2** US informal angry because you feel you have been unfairly treated: *He accused me of being a sore* ***loser*** *(= someone who does not accept defeat well).* • **soreness** /ˈsɔː.nəs/ US /ˈsɔːr-/ **noun** [U]

IDIOM **stand/stick out like a sore thumb** informal If someone or something stands/sticks out like a sore thumb, everyone notices them because they are very different from the people or things around them: *Everyone else was in jeans and casual gear and I had my office clothes on – I stuck out like a sore thumb.*

▸**noun** [C] a painful area on the surface of a body, especially an infected area: *The poor dog's back was covered with sores.* → See also **cold sore**

sorehead /ˈsɔː.hed/ US /ˈsɔːr-/ **noun** [C] US informal a person who is easily made angry: *Don't be such a sorehead – it was only meant to be a joke.*

sorely /ˈsɔː.li/ US /ˈsɔːr-/ **adv** formal extremely; very much: *I was sorely* ***tempted*** *to say exactly what I thought of his offer.* ◦ *You'll be sorely missed by everyone here, and we wish you success in your new job.*

ˌsore ˈpoint **noun** [C usually singular] C2 a subject that someone prefers not to talk about because it makes them angry or embarrassed: *'So how are your job applications going?' 'Oh, it's a bit of a sore point, I'm afraid.'*

sorghum /ˈsɔː.gəm/ US /ˈsɔːr-/ **noun** [U] a type of grain grown in hot countries

sorority /səˈrɒr.ɪ.ti/ US /-ˈrɔːr.ə.t̬i/ **noun** [C] a social organization for female students at some US colleges → Compare **fraternity**

sorrel /ˈsɒr.ᵊl/ US /ˈsɔːr-/ **noun** [U] a plant with sour leaves that are used in cooking and salads

sorrow /ˈsɒr.əʊ/ US /ˈsɔːr.oʊ/ **noun; verb**

▸**noun** [C or U] formal C2 (a cause of) a feeling of great sadness: *The sorrow she felt* ***over/at*** *the death of her husband was almost too much to bear.* ◦ *The sorrows of her earlier years gave way to joy in later life.*

▸**verb** [I usually + adv/prep] formal to feel great sadness: *For years she sorrowed* ***over*** *her missing son.*

sorrowful /ˈsɒr.əʊ.fᵊl/ US /ˈsɔːr.ə-/ **adj** literary very sad: *With a sorrowful sigh she folded the letter and put it away.* • **sorrowfully** /-i/ US /ˈsɔːr.ə-/ **adv**

sorry /ˈsɒr.i/ US /ˈsɔːr-/ **adj; exclamation**

▸**adj** **SAD** ▷ **1** A2 [after verb] feeling sadness, sympathy, or disappointment, especially because something unpleasant has happened or been done: *I'm just sorry* ***about*** *all the trouble I've caused her.* ◦ *He'd really upset her and he didn't seem at all sorry.* ◦ [+ (that)] *I'm sorry* ***(that)*** *you had such a difficult journey.* ◦ [+ to infinitive] *We were both sorry* ***to hear*** *you've been ill again.* ◦ *I* ***feel*** *so sorry* ***for*** *the children – it must be really hard for them.* **2 feel sorry for yourself** disapproving to feel sad because you have a problem and you feel that it is not fair that you are suffering so much: *He sounded very sorry for himself on the phone.* **3 I'm sorry to say** used to show that something which must be said causes sadness or disappointment: *I'm sorry to say* ***that*** *the project's funding has been cancelled.* ◦ *Most people who start the course do, I'm sorry to say, give up within the first two weeks.* **APOLOGY** ▷ **4** A1 [after verb] used to say that you wish you had not done what you have done, especially when you want to be polite to someone you have done something bad to: *Oh, I'm sorry – I didn't see you there.* ◦ *Tom, I'm so sorry* ***about*** *last night – it was all my fault.* ◦ *I've* ***said*** *I'm sorry.* **SAYING NO** ▷ **5 I'm sorry** B2 used to show politeness when refusing something or disagreeing: *I'm sorry but I think you've made a mistake.* ◦ *I'm sorry, I can't agree.* **BAD CONDITION** ▷ **6 sorry sight/state/tale** a bad condition or situation: *He was a sorry sight when he got home – soaking and covered in mud.* ◦ *It's a sorry state of affairs when there isn't any food in the house.*

▸**exclamation** **APOLOGY** ▷ **1** used when apologizing for something: *'That's my foot you're treading on.' 'Sorry!'* **POLITE NEGATIVE** ▷ **2** used to show politeness when refusing something or disagreeing: *Sorry, you can't go in there.* **3** mainly UK used when politely asking someone to repeat something or when politely interrupting someone: *'He's late.' 'Sorry?' 'I said he's late.'* ◦ *Sorry, could you just say that last sentence again please?*

sort /sɔːt/ US /sɔːrt/ **noun; verb**

▸**noun** **TYPE** ▷ **1** A2 [C] a group of things that are of the same type or which share similar qualities: *We both like the same sort* ***of*** *music.* ◦ *I'm going to have a salad* ***of some*** *sort.* ◦ *What sort* ***of*** *shoes will I need?* ◦ *We saw* ***all*** *sorts (= many types)* ***of*** *animals in the park.* ◦ *Many sorts* ***of*** *bacteria are resistant to penicillin.* ◦ *This sort* ***of*** *camera is very expensive.* ◦ *Plants* ***of*** *this sort need shady conditions.* **2 your sort** the type of thing or person that you like: *Hmm, this is my sort* ***of*** *wine!* ◦ *I'd have thought these black trousers were more your sort* ***of thing****.* ◦ *I wouldn't have thought he was your sort (= was the type of man you would be attracted to).* **3 (and) that sort of thing** B1 informal used to show that what you have just said is only an example from a much larger group of things: *They sell souvenirs, postcards, that sort of thing.* **PERSON** ▷ **4** [C usually singular] old-fashioned a person having the stated or suggested character: *He seemed like a decent sort to me.*

S

Other ways of saying sort

Kind, **type**, and **form** are alternative ways of saying 'sort':

*What **kind** of job are you looking for?*

*He's the **type** of man who never listens to what you're saying.*

*Swimming is the best **form** of exercise.*

If you are talking about the sort of design that something has, you could use the word **style**:

*The street is full of buildings in different **styles** of architecture.*

If you want to talk about the different sorts of something, you could use the word **variety**:

*The article was about the different **varieties** of Spanish spoken in South America.*

*This **variety** of rose is particularly hardy.*

If you are talking about a sort of animal, you could use the word **breed**:

*What **breed** of dog do you have?*

The words **brand** or **make** are used for talking about sorts of products:

*She always buys expensive **brands** of chocolate.*

*What is the **make** of your car?*

If things that are of the same sort are considered as a group, you could use the word **category**:

*There are three **categories** – standard, executive, and deluxe.*

IDIOMS **be out of sorts** old-fashioned to be slightly ill or slightly unhappy: *I've been feeling tired and headachy and generally out of sorts.* • **it takes all sorts (to make a world)** saying said to emphasize that people have different characters, opinions, and abilities, and that you should accept this • **of sorts** (also **of a sort**) used to describe something that is not a typical or good example of something: *He managed to make a curtain of sorts out of an old sheet.* • **(a) sort of** informal B1 used to describe something approximately: *It's a sort of pale orange colour.* • **sort of** informal B1 in some way or to some degree: *I was sort of hoping to leave early today.* ◦ *It's sort of silly, but I'd like a copy of the photograph.*

▸verb **ORDER** ▷ **1** B2 [I or T] to put a number of things in an order or to separate them into groups: *Paper, plastic, and cans are sorted for recycling.* ◦ *I'm going to sort these old books **into** those to be kept and those to be thrown away.* ◦ *You can use the computer to sort the newspaper articles alphabetically, **by** date, or **by** subject.* ◦ *She found the ring while sorting (**through**) some clothes.* **DEAL WITH** ▷ **2** [T] UK informal to deal with something by repairing or organizing it: *Can you sort the car by tomorrow?* ◦ *We must **get** the phone sorted soon.* ◦ *I must **get** this paperwork sorted before I go on holiday next week.*

PHRASAL VERBS **sort sth out** to separate one type of things from a group of things: *Sort out any clothes you want to throw away and give them to me.* → See also **sort-out** • **sort sth/sb out** B2 to deal successfully with a problem, a situation, or a person who is having difficulties: *We've sorted out the computer system's initial problems.* ◦ [+ question word] *It'll be difficult to sort out **how** much each person owes.* ◦ *Most of the job involves sorting out customers who have queries.* • **sort sb out** UK informal to punish or attack someone, usually to make them understand that they have behaved badly: *Has he been bothering you again – do you want me to sort him out?*

'sort ˌcode noun [C] (also **'sorting ˌcode**) an official number used to refer to a particular bank

sorted /ˈsɔː.tɪd/ US /ˈsɔːr.t̬ɪd/ **adj** [after verb], **exclamation** UK informal used to describe a situation in which everything is correctly organized or repaired, or when someone has the things they need: *Debbie's sorted for Tuesday night because she's found a babysitter.* ◦ *'Have you spoken to Grant about the party?' 'Sorted!'*

sortie /ˈsɔː.ti/ US /ˈsɔːr.t̬i/ **noun** [C] **1** a short, quick attack by a military force, such as a small group of soldiers or an aircraft, made against an enemy position: *A series of sorties was carried out at night by specially equipped aircraft.* **2** a short journey to somewhere you have not been before, often with a particular purpose: *It was our first sortie into the town centre.* **3** an attempt to do something: *This is the acclaimed historian John Taylor's first sortie into fiction.*

'sorting ˌoffice noun [C] a building where letters, parcels, etc. are taken after they have been posted and where they are then put into groups according to their addresses before being DELIVERED

'sort-out noun [C usually singular] UK informal an occasion when you put things in order or in their correct place: *I've **had** a sort-out in the bedroom – it's looking rather better.*

SOS /ˌes.əʊˈes/ US /-oʊˈ-/ **noun** [S] a request for help, especially because of danger: *Within an hour of the ship transmitting an SOS (**message/call**), six boats had arrived and started a rescue operation.* ◦ *The hospital sent out an SOS **for** extra blood supplies.*

ˌso-'so adj, adv informal between average quality and low quality; not good or well: *a so-so performance* ◦ *'How are you getting on with your new boss?' 'So-so.'*

sotto voce /ˌsɒt.əʊˈvəʊ.tʃeɪ/ US /ˌsɑː.t̬oʊˈvoʊ-/ **adv, adj** formal (said) in a quiet voice so that only people near can hear: *The remark was uttered sotto voce.*

sou /suː/ **noun** [S] UK old-fashioned a very small amount of money: *I don't have a sou.*

soubriquet /ˈsuː.brɪ.keɪ/ **noun** [C] formal a **sobriquet**

soufflé /ˈsuː.fleɪ/ US /suˈfleɪ/ **noun** [C or U] a light food that has a lot of air in it, is made mainly from eggs, and can be either sweet or SAVOURY: *a cheese soufflé* ◦ *a lemon soufflé*

sought /sɔːt/ US /sɑːt/ **verb** past simple and past participle of **seek**

'sought ˌafter adj wanted by many people and usually of high quality or rare: [before noun] *At the age of 17 she is already one of Hollywood's most sought-after actresses.*

souk /suːk/ **noun** [C] (also **suq**) a market in an Arab country

soul /səʊl/ US /soʊl/ **noun** **SPIRIT** ▷ **1** B2 [C] the spiritual part of a person that some people believe continues to exist in some form after their body has died, or the part of a person that is not physical and experiences deep feelings and emotions: *She suffered greatly while she was alive, so let us hope her soul is now at peace.* **DEEP FEELINGS** ▷ **2** [U] the quality of a person or work of art that shows or produces deep good feelings: *If you can't enjoy this music you've got **no** soul.* ◦ *For me her paintings somehow lack soul.* **3** A2 [U] **soul music** **PERSON** ▷ **4** B2 [C] a person of a stated type: *She's a happy little soul.* ◦ *Some poor soul had fallen 500 metres to their death.* **5 not a soul** B2 no one: *By the time I arrived there wasn't a soul there.* **BLACK CULTURE** ▷ **6** [U] US a deep understanding of and being proud of the culture of black people

'soul-deˌstroying adj mainly UK describes a job or

other activity that is so boring that it makes you very unhappy: *Repetitive work can become soul-destroying after a while.*

soulful /ˈsəʊl.fəl/ (US) /ˈsoʊl-/ adj DEEP FEELINGS ▷ **1** expressing deep feelings, often sadness: *a soulful performance/ballad* ◦ *The dog looked at me with its big, soulful, brown eyes.* BLACK CULTURE ▷ **2** US having a deep understanding of and proud of black culture • **soulfully** /-i/ adv • **soulfulness** /-nəs/ noun [U]

soulless /ˈsəʊl.ləs/ (US) /ˈsoʊl-/ adj disapproving showing no human influence or qualities: *a soulless building of grey concrete*

soulmate /ˈsəʊl.meɪt/ (US) /ˈsoʊl-/ noun [C] someone, usually your romantic or sexual partner, who you have a special relationship with, and who you know and love very much

ˈsoul ˌmusic noun [U] (also **soul**) A2 popular music which expresses deep feelings, originally performed by Black Americans: *Soul music is often an affirmation of, and a manifesto for, black dignity.*

ˈsoul-ˌsearching noun [U] deep and careful attention to private thoughts, especially about a moral problem: *After much soul-searching, he decided it was wrong to vote in the elections.*

sound /saʊnd/ noun; verb; adj; adv, adj

▸noun NOISE ▷ **1** A2 [C or U] something that you can hear or that can be heard: *They could **hear** the sound of a bell tolling in the distance.* ◦ *She stood completely still, not **making** a sound.* ◦ *Suddenly we heard a loud knocking sound from the engine.* ◦ *Sound can **travel** over very large distances in water.* **2** [U] the activity of recording and broadcasting sound such as from a performance of music or for a film: *a sound engineer/ recording* **3** [U] the volume or quality of the sound of a television or film: *Could you **turn** the sound **down/up** on the TV?* **4** [C] the particular quality of the music which a musician or a group of musicians produce: *The band's sound is a distinctive mixture of funk and rap.* SEEM ▷ **5 the sound of sth** C2 [S] how something seems to be, from what is said or written: *I like the sound of the beef in red wine sauce.* ◦ ***By/From** the sound of **it** I don't think it was her fault.* ◦ *So I'm going to be talking to over 90 people, am I? I don't like the sound of that!* WATER PASSAGE ▷ **6** [C] a passage of sea connecting two larger areas of sea, or an area of sea mostly surrounded by land: *the Kalmar Sound*

> **Word partners for sound**
>
> *emit/make/produce* a sound • *hear/listen to* a sound • a sound *carries/travels* • a sound *dies away/fades* • a *deafening/deep/loud* sound • a *distant/faint/muffled* sound • the sound *of* sth

▸verb SEEM ▷ **1 sound good, interesting, strange, etc.** A2 to seem good, interesting, strange, etc. from what is said or written: *Your job sounds really interesting.* ◦ *I know **it** sounds silly, but I'll miss him when he's gone.* **2 sound like/as if/as though** B1 to seem like something, from what is said or written: *That sounds like a good idea.* ◦ *It sounds like you've got a sore throat.* ◦ ***It** sounds as if they had a good holiday.* ◦ *You're going skiing with three friends? That sounds like fun.* **3 sound angry, happy, rude, etc.** B2 to seem angry, happy, rude, etc. when you speak: *He sounded very depressed when we spoke on the phone yesterday.* ◦ *At the press conference, he sounded at his most relaxed.* NOISE ▷ **4** [I or T] to make a noise: *If the alarm sounds, leave the building immediately.* ◦ *It sounds **like** a bird.* ◦ *He sounds (= speaks) just **like** someone I used to work with.* ◦ *Sounding the car's horn, she drove at high speed through the crowded streets.* **5 sound the alarm** to cause a noise to be made or say or shout a message to warn people about something: *Quick, sound the alarm – there's a fire in the machine room!* WATER DEPTH ▷ **6** [T] to measure the depth of a mass of water, such as the sea, usually by SONAR → See also **echo sounder**

PHRASAL VERBS **sound off** informal to express your opinions forcefully, especially without being asked for them: *He's always sounding off **about** how he thinks the country should be run.* • **sound sb out** to discover informally what someone thinks or intends to do about a particular thing, so that you can be prepared or take suitable action: *Perhaps you could sound the chairwoman out before the meeting, to see which way she's going to vote?*

▸adj GOOD CONDITION ▷ **1** not broken or damaged; healthy; in good condition: *It's an old building but it's still structurally sound.* ◦ *Considering his age, his body is quite sound.* ◦ *Was she **of** sound **mind** (= not mentally ill) at the time of the incident?* GOOD JUDGMENT ▷ **2** showing good judgment; able to be trusted: *She gave me some very sound **advice**.* ◦ *Are these pesticides environmentally sound (= will they not damage the environment)?* ◦ *Government bonds are a sound **investment**.* COMPLETE ▷ **3** complete: *How sound is her knowledge of the subject?*

IDIOM **be as sound as a bell** UK informal to be very healthy or in very good condition

▸adv, adj [before noun] (of sleep) deep and peaceful: *He was sound **asleep** within moments of getting into bed.*

the ˈsound ˌbarrier noun [S] a large increase in the force opposing a moving object as its speed reaches the speed at which sound travels: *There is usually a sonic boom when an aircraft **breaks** the sound barrier.*

soundbite /ˈsaʊnd.baɪt/ noun [C] a short sentence or phrase that is easy to remember, often included in a speech made by a politician and repeated in newspapers and on television and radio: *Most politicians want to master the art of the soundbite.*

soundboard /ˈsaʊnd.bɔːd/ (US) /-bɔːrd/ noun [C] a thin sheet of wood on a musical instrument, such as a guitar, that the strings go over and that helps to produce the sound

ˈsound ˌcard noun [C] a CIRCUIT BOARD (= small piece of electronic equipment) inside a computer that allows it to record and play sounds

ˈsound ˌcheck noun [C] a test of the musical instruments and recording equipment at a music show, especially before the players come on stage, to make certain that everything is working and that the sound quality is good

ˈsound efˌfect noun [C usually plural] in a radio or television programme or a film, one of the sounds other than speech or music that are added to make it seem more exciting or real

ˈsounding ˌboard noun [C usually singular] a person or group of people that you use to test something such as a new idea or suggestion to see if they will accept it or if they think it will work

soundings /ˈsaʊn.dɪŋz/ noun [plural] measurements that are taken of the depth of water: *They **took** soundings and found that the water was 120 feet deep.*

IDIOM **make/take soundings** to ask questions in order to collect information or opinions: *Can you take some discreet soundings to see what her future plans are?*

soundless /ˈsaʊnd.ləs/ adj formal without sound: *Above the mountain, eagles circled in soundless flight.* • **soundlessly** /-li/ adv

S

soundly /ˈsaʊnd.li/ adv **COMPLETELY** ▷ **1** completely: *The committee soundly rejected all of the proposed changes.* **SLEEP** ▷ **2** (of how someone sleeps) deeply: *I slept very soundly, thank you – the bed was really comfortable.*

soundness /ˈsaʊnd.nəs/ noun [U] **GOOD CONDITION** ▷ **1** the fact of being in good condition **GOOD JUDGMENT** ▷ **2** the quality of having good judgment

soundproof /ˈsaʊnd.pruːf/ adj (of a building or part of a building) not allowing sound to go through: *a soundproof room/wall/studio* • **soundproof** verb [T] *It was a well soundproofed building, so we didn't hear the traffic outside.* • **soundproofing** /-ˌpruː.fɪŋ/ noun [U]

ˈsound ˌsystem noun [C] a piece or several pieces of electronic equipment that can be used to play music from recordings, radio broadcasts, etc.

soundtrack /ˈsaʊnd.træk/ noun [C] B2 the sounds, especially the music, of a film, or a separate recording of this

ˈsound ˌwave noun [C] the form that sound takes when it passes through air, water, etc.

soup /suːp/ noun; verb

▸noun [C or U] A1 a usually hot, liquid food made from vegetables, meat, or fish: *chicken/oxtail/fish/tomato soup* ◦ *Would you like **a bowl of** soup?*

IDIOM **be in the soup** old-fashioned informal to be in an unpleasant or difficult situation

▸verb

PHRASAL VERB **soup sth up** informal to make something more powerful or more attractive by making changes to it, especially when it is old: *New circuit boards can be used to soup up existing machines.*

soupçon /ˈsuːp.sɔ̃/ US /-sɑ̃ː/ noun [S] mainly humorous a very small amount: *'Milk in your coffee?' 'Just a soupçon, please.'* ◦ *Do I detect a soupçon of sarcasm in what you just said?*

ˌsouped-ˈup adj [before noun] informal A souped-up vehicle or machine has been made more powerful or faster by having changes made to it: *a souped-up Mini*

ˈsoup ˌkitchen noun [C] a place where free soup or other food is given to people with no money or no home

ˈsoup ˌspoon noun [C] a rounded spoon used for eating soup

sour /saʊəʳ/ US /saʊr/ adj; verb; noun

▸adj **TASTE** ▷ **1** B1 having a sharp, sometimes unpleasant, taste or smell, like a lemon, and not sweet: *These plums are a bit sour.* **BAD FEELING** ▷ **2** unfriendly or easily annoyed: *Overnight, it seemed, their relationship had **turned** sour.* ◦ *She gave me a sour look.* • **sourly** /ˈsaʊə.li/ US /ˈsaʊr-/ adv • **sourness** /ˈsaʊə.nəs/ US /ˈsaʊr-/ noun [U]

IDIOM **sour grapes** If you describe someone's behaviour or opinion as sour grapes, you mean that they are angry because they have not got or achieved something that they wanted: *I don't think it's such a great job – and that's not just sour grapes because I didn't get it.*

▸verb [I or T] **TASTE** ▷ **1** to become sour or to make something become sour: *Hot weather sours milk.* ◦ *Milk sours in hot weather.* **BAD FEELING** ▷ **2** to (cause to) become unpleasant or unfriendly: *Her whole attitude to life soured as a result of that experience.* ◦ *This affair has soured relations between the two countries.*

▸noun [C] mainly US a drink made from strong alcohol, lemon or LIME juice, sugar, and ice: *a whisky sour*

source /sɔːs/ US /sɔːrs/ noun; verb

▸noun [C] **1** B2 the place something comes from or starts at, or the cause of something: *a source **of** heat/energy/light* ◦ *a heat/energy/light source* ◦ *Oranges are a good source **of** vitamin C.* ◦ *Experts are trying to track down the source of the contamination in the water supply.* ◦ *We walked up the river to its source in the hills.* ◦ *Money is often a source of tension and disagreements in young married couples.* **2** C1 someone or something that supplies information: *The journalist refused to reveal her sources (= say who had given the information to her).* ◦ *According to government sources (= people in the government) many MPs are worried about this issue.* ◦ *Always acknowledge your sources (= say which books you have used) at the end of an essay.* **3 at source** at the place where something comes from: *Tax is deducted from my income at source.*

▸verb [T often passive] to get something from a particular place: *Where possible the produce used in our restaurant is sourced locally.*

ˌsour ˈcream noun [U] (UK also **ˌsoured ˈcream**) cream made sour by adding special bacteria

sourdough /ˈsaʊə.dəʊ/ US /ˈsaʊr.doʊ/ noun [U] a mixture of flour and water that is left to FERMENT (= change in a chemical process) and then used to make bread: *sourdough bread*

sourpuss /ˈsaʊə.pʊs/ US /ˈsaʊr-/ noun [C] informal someone who always looks unhappy and annoyed

sousaphone /ˈsuː.zə.fəʊn/ US /-foʊn/ noun [C] a large TUBA (= metal musical instrument played by blowing) with tubes which go round the player's body, sometimes used in marching musical groups

souse /saʊs/ verb [T] to put something into a liquid, or to make something completely wet

soused /saʊst/ adj **1** (of fish) preserved in salty water or VINEGAR: *soused herring/mackerel* **2** old-fashioned informal drunk

south /saʊθ/ noun; adj; adv

▸noun [U] (also **South**) (written abbreviation **S**, UK also **Sth**, US also **So.**) **1** A2 the direction that goes towards the part of the Earth below the EQUATOR, opposite to the north, or the part of an area or country that is in this direction: *The points of the compass are north, south, east, and west.* ◦ *The best beaches are **in the** south (**of** the island).* ◦ *We usually spend our holidays **in the** south **of** France.* ◦ *Canberra **is/lies to the** south **of** Sydney.* **2 the South a** the southern states of the middle and eastern part of the US: *The American Civil War was fought between the North and the South partly over the issue of slavery.* **b** the developing countries of the world, most of which are below the EQUATOR → See also **the Third World**

▸adj (also **South**) (written abbreviation **S**, UK also **Sth**, US also **So**) **1** A2 in or forming the south part of something: *South Africa* ◦ *the South China Sea* ◦ *These plants grow well on a south-**facing** wall.* **2 south wind** a wind coming from the south

▸adv (also **South**) (written abbreviation **S**, UK also **Sth**, US also **So**) **1** A2 towards the south: *The Mississippi river flows south.* ◦ *They drove south towards the coast.* ◦ *He travelled **due** (= directly) south, towards the desert.* **2 down south** to or in the south of a country or region: *Alice got a job down south.*

ˌSouth Aˈmerica noun the continent that is to the south of North America, to the west of the Atlantic Ocean and to the east of the Pacific Ocean • **ˌSouth Aˈmerican** noun [C], adj

southbound /ˈsaʊθ.baʊnd/ adj, adv going or leading towards the south: *southbound passengers/traffic*

S

southeast /ˌsaʊθˈiːst/ noun; adj, adv
▸noun [U] (written abbreviation **SE**) **1** B1 the direction that is between south and east: *We live in **the** southeast **of** the city.* **2 the Southeast** an area of in the southeast of England, the US, or another country: *Most of the jobs and money are in the affluent counties of the Southeast.*
▸adj, adv (written abbreviation **SE**) **1** B1 in or towards the southeast: *Southeast Asia* ◦ *The mountains **are/lie** southeast **of** the city.* ◦ *They were moving southeast.* **2 southeast wind** a wind that comes from the southeast

southeasterly /ˌsaʊθˈiː.stə.li/ US /-stɚ-/ adj; noun
▸adj **1** towards the southeast: *The plane was flying in a southeasterly direction.* **2 southeasterly wind** a wind that comes from the southeast
▸noun [C] a wind that comes from the southeast

southeastern /ˌsaʊθˈiː.stᵊn/ US /-stɚn/ adj (written abbreviation **SE**) in or from the southeast: *The southeastern part of Britain is the most populated.*

southeastward adv; adj
▸adv /ˌsaʊθˈiːs.twəd/ US /-twɚd/ (also **southeastwards**) towards the southeast: *Looking southeastward, they could see the distant mountains.*
▸adj towards the southeast: *If we sail in a southeastward **direction** we'll reach land.*

southerly /ˈsʌð.ᵊl.i/ US /-ɚ.li/ adj; noun
▸adj **1** towards or in the south: *We walked in a southerly direction.* ◦ *Los Cristianos is the most southerly resort in Tenerife.* **2 southerly wind** a wind that comes from the south
▸noun [C] a wind that comes from the south

southern (also **Southern**) /ˈsʌð.ən/ US /-ɚn/ adj (written abbreviation **S**, US also **So**) B1 in or from the south part of an area: *a southern route* ◦ *the Southern Hemisphere*

the ˌSouthern ˈCross noun [S] the group of stars that points towards the South Pole and appears on the flags of Australia and New Zealand

southerner (also **Southerner**) /ˈsʌð.ə.nəʳ/ US /-ɚ.nɚ/ noun [C] a person who comes from the south of a country: *I could tell from his accent that he was a southerner.*

the ˌSouthern ˈLights noun [plural] **the aurora australis**

southernmost /ˈsʌð.ən.məʊst/ US /-ɚn.moʊst/ adj furthest towards the south of an area: *the southernmost tip of the island*

southpaw /ˈsaʊθ.pɔː/ US /-pɑː/ noun [C] **1** UK a **boxer** whose strongest hand is their left **2** US a person who uses their left hand to do most things, especially a PITCHER in the sport of baseball

the ˌSouth ˈPole noun the point on the earth's surface that is furthest south

southward /ˈsaʊθ.wəd/ US /-wɚd/ adv; adj
▸adv (also **southwards**) towards the south: *The rain moved slowly southward.* ◦ *They cycled southwards towards the sea.*
▸adj towards the south: *We walked in a southward **direction**.*

southwest /ˌsaʊθˈwest/ noun; adj, adv
▸noun [U] (written abbreviation **SW**) **1** B1 the direction that is between south and west: *We live in **the** southwest **of** Scotland.* **2 the Southwest** the area in the southwest of England, the US, or another country: *Have you been to Cornwall? It's **in** the Southwest.*
▸adj, adv (written abbreviation **SW**) **1** B1 in or towards the southwest: *I come from the southwest part of the island.* ◦ *They moved southwest in an attempt to find better land.* **2 southwest wind** a wind that comes from the southwest

southwester /ˌsaʊθˈwes.təʳ/ US /-tɚ/ noun [C] (also **sou'wester**) a strong wind coming from the southwest

southwesterly adj; noun
▸adj /ˌsaʊθˈwes.tə.li/ US /-tɚ-/ **1** towards the southwest: *They were travelling in a southwesterly direction.* **2 southwesterly wind** a wind that comes from the southwest
▸noun [C] a wind that comes from the southwest

southwestern /ˌsaʊθˈwes.tən/ US /-tɚn/ adj (written abbreviation **SW**) in or from the southwest: *The southwestern corner of Britain is the warmest.*

southwestward /ˌsaʊθˈwest.wəd/ US /-wɚd/ adj towards the southwest: *We sailed in a southwestward direction.* • **southwestwards** /-wədz/ US /-wɚdz/ adv (also **southwestward**) *They sailed southwestwards until they reached land.*

souvenir /ˌsuː.vᵊnˈɪəʳ/ US /-vəˈnɪr/ noun [C] B1 something you buy or keep to help you remember a holiday or special event: *He bought a model of a red London bus as a souvenir **of** his trip to London.* ◦ *We brought back a few souvenirs from our holiday in Greece.*

sou'wester /ˌsaʊˈwes.təʳ/ US /-tɚ/ noun [C] **1** a WATERPROOF hat with a wide piece at the back to protect the neck, worn especially by sailors **2** a **southwester**: a strong wind coming from the southwest

sovereign /ˈsɒv.ᵊr.ɪn/ US /ˈsɑːv.rən/ noun; adj
▸noun [C] **RULER** ▷ **1** a king or queen **COIN** ▷ **2** a British gold coin which was in use in Britain from 1817 to 1914 and was worth £1
▸adj **GOVERNMENT** ▷ **1** [before noun] having the highest power or being completely independent: *Sovereign power is said to lie with the people in some countries, and with a ruler in others.* ◦ *We must respect the rights of sovereign **states/nations** to conduct their own affairs.* **EXCELLENT** ▷ **2 sovereign remedy** old-fashioned or formal an extremely successful way of dealing with a problem: *Love is a sovereign remedy for unhappiness.*

sovereignty /ˈsɒv.rɪn.ti/ US /ˈsɑːv.rᵊn.i/ noun [U] the power of a country to control its own government: *Talks are being held about who should **have** sovereignty **over** the island.*

Soviet /ˈsəʊ.vi.ət/ US /ˈsoʊ-/ adj; noun
▸adj (in the past) of the USSR: *the Soviet people*
▸noun [plural] mainly US **the Soviets** the people of the USSR

soviet /ˈsəʊ.vi.ət/ US /ˈsoʊ-/ noun [C] an elected group at any of several levels in COMMUNIST countries, especially (in the past) the USSR

sow¹ /səʊ/ US /soʊ/ verb (**sowed**, **sown** or **sowed**)
PLANT ▷ **1** C1 [I or T] to put seeds in or on the ground so that plants will grow: *Sow the **seeds** in pots.* ◦ *We'll sow this field **with** barley.* **CAUSE** ▷ **2** [T] to cause a bad emotion or condition to begin somewhere, which will grow or continue: *Now that you've sown **doubts** in my mind, I'll never be sure I can trust him.*

IDIOMS **sow your wild oats** If a young man sows his wild oats, he has a period of his life when he does a lot of exciting things and has a lot of sexual relationships. • **sow the seeds of sth** to do something that will cause something to happen in the future: *He's sowing the seeds of his own downfall.*

sow² /saʊ/ noun [C] an adult female pig

soya /ˈsɔɪ.ə/ noun [U] (US **soy** /sɔɪ/) C1 soya beans as a crop

ˈsoya ˌbean noun [C usually plural] (mainly US **soybean**)

S

a small bean grown originally in Asia, used as a food for people and animals

ˈsoya ˌmilk noun [U] (US **ˈsoy ˌmilk**) a liquid from soya beans that people use instead of milk

ˌsoy ˈsauce noun [U] (UK also **ˌsoya ˈsauce**) a strong-tasting, dark brown liquid made from FERMENTED soya beans and used especially in Chinese and Japanese cooking

sozzled /ˈsɒz.l̩d/ (US) /ˈsɑː.zl̩d/ adj [after verb] UK informal very drunk

spa /spɑː/ noun [C] **1** a town where water comes out of the ground and people come to drink it or lie in it because they think it will improve their health: *Baden Baden in Germany and Bath in Britain are two of Europe's famous spa **towns**.* ◦ *spa water* **2** a place where people go in order to become more healthy, by doing exercises, eating special food, etc.

space /speɪs/ noun; verb

▸noun **EMPTY PLACE** ▷ **1** (A2) [C or U] an empty area that is available to be used: *Is there any space **for** my clothes in that cupboard?* ◦ *I've got to **make** (some) space for Mark's things.* ◦ *When the roads are wet, you've got to leave plenty of space **between** you and the car in front.* ◦ *The blank space at the end of the form is for your name.* ◦ *We found a **parking** space close to the museum.* → See also **airspace** **2** (B2) [U] the area around everything that exists, continuing in all directions: *He was absent-mindedly **staring/gazing into** space (= looking, but seeing nothing).* ◦ *Virtual reality gives us artificial worlds to explore, outside normal space and time.* **3 open space** land, especially in a town, that has no buildings on it: *What I like about Cambridge is that there's so much open space.* ◦ *I love the **wide** open spaces (= large areas of countryside) of central Australia.* **4 in/within a short space of time** very soon: *Within a short space of time you could be speaking perfect English!* **5 in/within the space of six weeks, three hours, etc.** during a period of six weeks, three hours, etc.: *It all happened in the space of ten minutes.* **BEYOND EARTH** ▷ **6** (B1) [U] the empty area outside the Earth's ATMOSPHERE, where the planets and the stars are: *space exploration/travel* ◦ *a space rocket* ◦ *Who was the first human being **in** space/the first to go **into** space?*

> **Word partners for space noun (EMPTY PLACE)**
>
> *create/make* space • *fill a/occupy a/take up* space • an *empty/vacant* space • a *confined/enclosed* space • be *short of* space • a *waste of* space • a *lack of/ plenty of* space • space *between* sth

> **Word partners for space noun (BEYOND EARTH)**
>
> *go into* space • *in* space • *deep/outer* space • a space *mission/programme* • space *exploration/ travel*

▸verb [T] to arrange things or people so that there is some distance or time between them: *That page looks badly spaced (= there is too much/too little distance between the lines or words).* ◦ *The flowers were spaced (**out**) evenly (= planted at equal distances) beside the path.* ◦ *If you're in financial difficulty, we're happy to let you space (**out**) your payments (= pay in smaller amounts over a longer period of time) **over** two years.*

ˈspace-age adj [before noun] very modern: *space-age technology*

ˈspace ˌbar noun [C usually singular] on a keyboard, the long bar below the letter keys that you press in order to make a space between words

ˈspace caˌdet noun [C] humorous someone who behaves strangely: *She's a bit of a space cadet but she's nice enough.*

spacecraft /ˈspeɪs.krɑːft/ (US) /-kræft/ noun [C] (plural **spacecraft**) a vehicle used for travel in space: *a manned/unmanned spacecraft (= with/without people inside)*

ˌspaced ˈout adj [after verb] (also **spacey**, **spacy**) describes someone who is not completely conscious of what is happening around them, often because of taking drugs or needing to sleep: *I hadn't slept for two days and was completely spaced out.*

spaceman /ˈspeɪs.mæn/ noun [C] (plural **-men** /-men/) **1** an **astronaut** (= person who travels into space) **2** in stories, a creature from another planet: *to be abducted by spacemen*

ˈspace ˌprobe noun [C] a small spacecraft, with no one travelling in it, sent into space to make measurements and send back information to scientists on Earth

ˈspace-ˌsaving adj [before noun] refers to a device, piece of furniture, etc. that takes up little room, for example a folding bed

spaceship /ˈspeɪs.ʃɪp/ noun [C] (especially in stories) a vehicle used for travel in space

ˈspace ˌshuttle noun [C usually singular] a vehicle in which people travel into space and back again, sometimes carrying a SATELLITE or other equipment into ORBIT (= a curved path through space)

ˈspace ˌstation noun [C] a vehicle in which people can travel round the Earth, outside its ATMOSPHERE, doing scientific tests

spacesuit /ˈspeɪs.suːt/ noun [C] a piece of clothing worn by a person who travels in space to protect the body when outside a spacecraft

spacesuit

ˌspace-ˈtime noun [U] specialized a part of Einstein's Theory of Relativity, which adds the idea of time to those of height, depth, and length

spacewalk /ˈspeɪs.wɔːk/ (US) /-wɑːk/ noun [C] an act of moving around in space outside a spacecraft but connected to it: *The crew are planning a four-hour spacewalk to carry out necessary repair work on the shuttle.*

spacey (also **spacy**) /ˈspeɪ.si/ adj → **spaced out**

spacing /ˈspeɪ.sɪŋ/ noun [U] the amount of distance between lines or words, especially on a printed page: *single/double/triple spacing*

spacious /ˈspeɪ.ʃəs/ adj approving (C1) large and with a lot of space: *a spacious house/living room* ◦ *spacious accommodation* • **spaciously** /-li/ adv approving • **spaciousness** /-nəs/ noun [U] approving

spade /speɪd/ noun

spade

TOOL ▷ **1** (C2) [C] a tool used for digging especially soil or sand, with a long handle and a flat blade: *a garden spade* ◦ *The kids took their **buckets and** spades to the beach.* **CARD** ▷ **2 spades** [plural or U] one of the four SUITS in playing cards, which has one or more black symbols like a pointed leaf with a short stem: *the Ace/*

S

Queen of spades **3** [C] a playing card from the SUIT of spades: *Don't you have any spades?* **PERSON** ▷ **4** [C] offensive old-fashioned an offensive word for a black person

IDIOM **in spades** informal in large amounts or to a very great degree: *My dog has personality in spades.*

spadework /ˈspeɪd.wɜːk/ ⓤⓢ /-wɝːk/ noun [U] UK hard, sometimes boring work done in preparation for something: *Now that the spadework's all been* ***done****, we can start to write the report itself.*

spaghetti /spəˈget.i/ ⓤⓢ /-ˈgeṭ-/ noun [U] PASTA made in the form of long, thin strings

spaˌghetti boloˈgnese noun [U] (UK informal **spag bol** /ˌspæg ˈbɒl/ ⓤⓢ /-ˈbɑːl/) a dish consisting of spaghetti with a tomato and meat sauce

spaˌghetti ˈwestern noun [C] a film about COWBOYS in the Wild West made cheaply in Europe, usually by an Italian DIRECTOR (= person in charge of making a film)

spake /speɪk/ verb old use or humorous past simple of **speak**: *Thus spake the expert.*

spam /spæm/ noun; verb

▸noun [U] **COMPUTING** ▷ **1** C1 informal disapproving unwanted email, usually advertisements: *I get so much spam at work.* **FOOD** ▷ **2** trademark a type of meat sold in metal containers, made mostly from PORK (= meat from a pig): *spam fritters*

▸verb [T] (-mm-) to send someone an advertisement by email that they do not want

spammer /ˈspæ.məʳ/ ⓤⓢ /ˈspæ.mɚ/ noun [C] a person or company that sends spam

span /spæn/ noun; verb

▸noun **TIME** ▷ **1** [C usually singular] the period of time that sometimes exists or happens: *He has a short* ***attention/concentration*** *span.* ◦ *an average* ***life*** *span of 70 years* ◦ ***Over a*** *span* ***of*** *just three years, the new government has transformed the country's economic prospects.* → See also **lifespan** **LENGTH** ▷ **2** [C] the length of something from one end to the other: *huge wings with a span of over a metre* → See also **wingspan** **3** [C] the area of a bridge, etc. between two supports: *The bridge crosses the river in a single span.*

▸verb **SPIN** ▷ **1** past simple of **spin** **TIME** ▷ **2** [T] (-nn-) to exist or continue for a particular length of time: *Tennis has a history spanning several centuries.* ◦ *Her acting career spanned almost six decades.* **BRIDGE** ▷ **3** [T] (-nn-) If a bridge spans a river, it goes from one side to the other: *An old bridge spans the river just outside the town.*

spandex /ˈspæn.deks/ noun [U] a type of material that stretches and is used especially for making clothes fit tightly: *spandex leggings*

spangle /ˈspæŋ.gl/ noun [C] a small piece of shiny metal or plastic, used especially in large amounts to decorate clothes → Synonym **sequin**

spangly /ˈspæŋ.gld/ adj (also **spangled**) covered with spangles: *a spangly top*

spaniel /ˈspæn.jəl/ noun [C] a type of dog with long hair and long ears that hang down

spank /spæŋk/ verb [T] **1** to hit a child with the hand, usually several times on the bottom as a punishment **2** to hit an adult on the bottom in order to get or give sexual pleasure

spanking /ˈspæŋ.kɪŋ/ adj; adv; noun

▸adj [before noun] informal approving very quick: *They raced by at a spanking* ***pace****.*

▸adv old-fashioned informal approving (used with some adjectives) very, completely: *a spanking* ***new*** *suit* ◦ *spanking white sheets*

▸noun [C or U] (also **spank**) the act of hitting someone with the hand, usually several times on the bottom as a punishment or for sexual pleasure: *He needs a* ***good*** *spanking.*

spanner /ˈspæn.əʳ/ ⓤⓢ /-ɚ/ noun [C] UK (US **wrench**) a metal tool with a shaped end, used to turn NUTS and BOLTS: *an open-ended/adjustable/ring spanner*

IDIOM **put/throw a spanner in the works** (US **throw a (monkey) wrench in the works**) to do something that prevents a plan or activity from succeeding: *The funding for the project was withdrawn so that really threw a spanner in the works.*

spar /spɑːʳ/ ⓤⓢ /spɑːr/ verb; noun

▸verb [I] (-rr-) **1** to practise BOXING, without hitting hard **2** to argue: *Frank and Jill always spar* ***with*** *each other at meetings, but they're good friends really.*

▸noun [C] specialized a strong pole, especially one used as a MAST to hold the sail on a ship

spare /speəʳ/ ⓤⓢ /sper/ adj; verb; noun

▸adj **EXTRA** ▷ **1** B1 If something is spare, it is available to use because it is extra: *a spare key/tyre* ◦ *spare sheets and blankets* ◦ *Have you got a spare pen?* ◦ *We've got a spare* ***room*** *if you want to stay overnight with us.* ◦ *Could I have a word with you when you've got a spare* ***moment/minute****?* ◦ UK informal *'Do you want this cake?' 'Yes, if it's* ***going*** *spare (= if no one else wants it).'* **2 spare time** A2 time when you are not working: *I like to do a bit of gardening* ***in*** *my spare time.* **THIN** ▷ **3** literary tall and thin: *He had the spare build of a runner.* **ANNOYED** ▷ **4 go spare** UK informal to get very upset or angry: *She goes spare if I'm so much as five minutes late.*

▸verb **SAVE** ▷ **1** [T] to not hurt or destroy something or someone: *They asked him to spare the women and children.* **AVOID** ▷ **2** [T + two objects] to prevent someone from having to experience something unpleasant: *Luckily, I was spared the embarrassment of having to sing in front of everyone.* ◦ *It was a nasty accident – but I'll spare you (= I won't tell you) the gruesome* ***details****.* **TRY HARD** ▷ **3 spare no effort/expense** C2 to use a lot of effort, EXPENSE, etc. to do something: [+ to infinitive] *We will spare no effort* ***to*** *find out who did this.* **4 not spare yourself** formal to try as hard as you can to achieve something: *She never spared herself in the pursuit of excellence.* **GIVE** ▷ **5** C1 [T] to give time, money, or space to someone especially when it is difficult for you: [+ two objects] *Could you spare me £10?* ◦ *I'd love to come, but I'm afraid I can't spare the time.* **6 spare a thought for sb** C2 to think about someone who is in a difficult or unpleasant situation: *Spare a thought for me tomorrow, when you're lying on a beach, because I'll still be here in the office!* **7 to spare** C1 left over or more than you need: *If you've got any wool to spare when you've finished the pullover, can you make me some gloves?* ◦ *I caught the plane with only two minutes to spare.*

IDIOM **spare sb's blushes** humorous to avoid making someone feel embarrassed

▸noun **1** [C] an extra thing that is not being used and can be used instead of a part that is broken, lost, etc. **2** [C usually plural] (also **spare part**) a piece that can be used to replace another similar piece in a car or other device

ˌspare-ˈpart ˌsurgery noun [U] UK (US **ˌorgan ˈtransplant ˌsurgery**) the process of taking a

S

healthy organ such as a heart or lung from a person who has just died and putting it into a living person to replace an organ that is not working properly

ˌspare ˈribs noun [plural] pig's RIBS (= curved bones) with most of the meat cut off them, cooked, and eaten: *barbecued spare ribs*

ˌspare ˈtyre UK (US **ˌspare ˈtire**) **noun** [C usually singular] unwanted fat around your waist

sparing /ˈspeə.rɪŋ/ US /ˈsper.ɪŋ/ **adj** using very little of something: *Be sparing **with** the butter as we don't have much left.* ◦ *He is sparing **with/in** his praise (= praises people very little).* • **sparingly** /-li/ **adv** *There wasn't enough coal during the war, so we had to use it sparingly.*

spark /spɑːk/ US /spɑːrk/ **noun; verb**

▸noun **CAUSE** ▷ **1** C2 [S] a first small event or problem that causes a much worse situation to develop: *That small incident was the spark that set off the street riots.* **FIRE/ELECTRICITY** ▷ **2** C2 [C] a very small piece of fire that flies out from something that is burning, or one that is made by rubbing two hard things together, or a flash of light made by electricity: *Sparks were flying out of the bonfire and blowing everywhere.* ◦ *You can start a fire by rubbing two dry pieces of wood together until you produce a spark.* **3 spark of anger, inspiration, life, etc.** a very small amount of a particular emotion or quality in a person

IDIOM **sparks fly** If sparks fly between two or more people, they argue angrily: *When they get together in a meeting **the** sparks really fly.*

▸verb [T] C2 to cause the start of something, especially an argument or fighting: *This proposal will almost certainly spark another countrywide debate about how to organize the school system.* ◦ *The visit of the G20 leaders sparked **off** (= caused the start of) mass demonstrations.*

sparkle /ˈspɑː.kl̩/ US /ˈspɑːr-/ **verb; noun**

▸verb [I] **1** to shine brightly with a lot of small points of light: *The snow/sea sparkled in the sunlight.* **2** If a person or performance sparkles, they are energetic, interesting, and exciting: *Alice is shy and quiet at parties, but her sister really sparkles!*

▸noun [U] **1** bright shine: *The radiant smile and the sparkle in her blue eyes were the clear signs of a woman still deeply in love.* **2** energy and interest: *Their latest performance of My Fair Lady really **lacked** sparkle.* ◦ *The sparkle **went out of/left** her (= she became unhappy) after her husband died.*

sparkler /ˈspɑː.kləʳ/ US /ˈspɑːr.klɚ/ **noun** [C] **1** a FIREWORK that children can hold in their hands and that produces a lot of sparks as it burns **2** slang a PRECIOUS STONE, especially a DIAMOND

sparkling /ˈspɑː.klɪŋ/ US /ˈspɑːr-/ **adj** **BRIGHT** ▷ **1** B2 shining brightly: *sparkling white teeth* **INTERESTING** ▷ **2** C1 energetic and interesting: *a sparkling performance* ◦ *sparkling conversation/wit* **BUBBLES** ▷ **3** B1 A sparkling drink is one that contains many small bubbles of gas: *Champagne is a sparkling wine.* → Compare **still**

ˈspark ˌplug noun [C] **ENGINE** ▷ **1** a device in an engine which produces an electrical SPARK which lights the fuel and makes the engine start **PERSON** ▷ **2** US a person who gives energy to an activity involving others: *She's the spark plug of the team.*

sparky /ˈspɑː.ki/ US /ˈspɑːr-/ **adj** informal energetic, clever, and enjoyable to be with

ˈsparring ˌpartner noun [C usually singular] **1** a person you practise BOXING with **2** someone you have friendly arguments with

sparrow /ˈspær.əʊ/ US /ˈsper.oʊ/ **noun** [C] a small, grey-brown bird that is especially common in towns

sparrowhawk /ˈspær.əʊ.hɔːk/ US /ˈsper.oʊ.hɑːk/ **noun** [C] a small HAWK (= a type of bird which catches and eats other birds or animals)

sparse /spɑːs/ US /spɑːrs/ **adj** small in numbers or amount, often spread over a large area: *a sparse population/audience* ◦ *sparse vegetation/woodland* ◦ *a sparse beard* ◦ *Information coming out of the disaster area is sparse.* • **sparsely** /ˈspɑːs.li/ US /ˈspɑːrs-/ **adv** *sparsely furnished/populated* • **sparseness** /ˈspɑːs.nəs/ US /ˈspɑːrs-/ **noun** [U] (also **sparsity** /ˈspɑː.sə.ti/ US /ˈspɑːr.sə.t̬i/)

spartan /ˈspɑː.tən/ US /ˈspɑːr-/ **adj** simple and severe with no comfort: *a spartan diet/meal* ◦ *spartan living conditions* ◦ *They lead a rather spartan life, with very few comforts and no luxuries.*

spasm /ˈspæz.ᵊm/ **noun** [C or U] **1** an occasion when a muscle suddenly becomes tighter in a way that cannot be controlled: *a muscle/muscular spasm* ◦ mainly UK *My leg suddenly **went into** spasm.* **2 spasm of sth** a short period of something, especially something that cannot be controlled: *a spasm of guilt/coughing/laughing*

spasmodic /spæzˈmɒd.ɪk/ US /-ˈmɑː.dɪk/ **adj** happening suddenly for short periods of time and not in a regular way: *He made spasmodic attempts to clean up the house.*

spastic /ˈspæs.tɪk/ **adj** **1** old-fashioned suffering from CEREBRAL PALSY (= a condition of the body which makes it difficult to control the muscles) **2** informal an offensive way of saying 'stupid', used especially by children • **spastic noun** [C]

spat /spæt/ **verb; noun**

▸verb past simple and past participle of **spit**

▸noun **ARGUMENT** ▷ **1** [C] informal a short argument, usually about something that is not important: *She was **having a** spat **with** her brother **about** who did the washing up.* **SHOE** ▷ **2** [C usually plural] a piece of cloth or leather covering the ANKLE and part of the shoe and fastening on the side, worn in the past by men

spate /speɪt/ **noun** [C usually singular] **1** a larger number of events than usual, especially unpleasant ones, happening at about the same time: *Police are investigating a spate **of** burglaries in the Kingsland Road area.* **2 in (full) spate** UK If a river is in (full) spate, it has more water in it and is flowing faster than it usually does.

spatial /ˈspeɪ.ʃᵊl/ **adj** relating to the position, area, and size of things: *This task is designed to test children's spatial **awareness** (= their understanding of where things are in relation to other things).* • **spatially** /-i/ **adv** *spatially aware*

spatter /ˈspæt.əʳ/ US /ˈspæt̬.ɚ/ **verb** [I or T] to drop small drops of liquid, etc. on a surface, or (of liquid) to fall, especially noisily, in small drops: *Two bikes raced by and spattered mud **over** our clothes.* ◦ *The bikes spattered them **with** mud.* ◦ *They could hear raindrops spattering **on** the roof of the caravan.* • **spatter noun** [C]

spattered /ˈspæt.əd/ US /ˈspæt̬.ɚd/ **adj** covered with small drops of a liquid: *a paint-spattered shirt* ◦ *His clothes were spattered **with** blood.*

spatula /ˈspæt.jʊ.lə/ **noun** [C] **1** a cooking UTENSIL with a wide, flat blade that is not sharp, used especially for lifting food out of pans **2** UK (US **tongue depressor**) a small piece of wood used by a doctor to hold someone's tongue down in order to examine their mouth or throat

spawn /spɔːn/ (US) /spɑːn/ **noun; verb**

▸**noun EGGS** ▷ [U] the eggs of fish, FROGS, etc. → See also **frogspawn**

▸**verb START** ▷ **1** [T] to cause something new, or many new things, to grow or start suddenly: *The new economic freedom has spawned hundreds of new small businesses.* ◦ *Her death spawned countless films and books.* **EGGS** ▷ **2** [I] to produce eggs: *The frogs haven't spawned yet.*

ˈspawning ˌground noun [C usually singular] a place where fish leave their eggs for FERTILIZATION

spay /speɪ/ verb [T] to remove the OVARIES of a female animal: *We're having the cat spayed.*

spaza /ˈspɑː.zə/ noun [C] South African English a small shop selling food, drinks, etc., especially one run from someone's home in a TOWNSHIP

speak /spiːk/ verb (**spoke, spoken**) **SAY WORDS** ▷ **1** (A1) [I or T] to say words, to use the voice, or to have a conversation with someone: *Would you mind speaking more slowly, please?* ◦ mainly UK *'Can I speak* ***to*** *Ian please?'* ◦ mainly US *'Can I speak* ***with*** *Ian please?'* ◦ *'Speaking.' (= This is Ian.)* ◦ *If he tells Julie what I said, I'll never speak* ***to*** *him again.* ◦ formal *She spoke* ***of*** *her sadness over her father's death.* ◦ *She speaks very* ***highly of*** *(= says good things about) the new director.* ◦ *I can certainly come but I can't speak* ***for*** *my wife (= I can't tell you whether she can or not).* ◦ formal *Who is going to speak* ***for*** *(= represent in a court of law) the accused?* ◦ *He's old enough to speak* ***for*** *him****self*** *(= to say what he thinks).* ◦ *I went with Ava – speaking* ***of*** *(= on the subject of) Ava, have you seen her new haircut?* ◦ *We've been invited to Rachel and Jamie's wedding – speaking* ***of which****, did you know that they're moving to Ealing?* ◦ *Speaking* ***as*** *(= with my experience as) a mother of four, I can tell you that children are exhausting.* ◦ *Sue speaks* ***with an*** *American* ***accent****.* ◦ *Why are you speaking* ***in a whisper*** *(= very quietly)?* ◦ *For five whole minutes, neither of them spoke* ***a word*** *(= they both said nothing).* **2 broadly, historically, strictly, etc. speaking** (B2) talking from a particular point of view: *Historically speaking, the island is of great interest.* ◦ *Generally speaking, it's quite a good school.* ◦ *Strictly speaking (= if I behave according to the rules), I should report it to the police.* **3 speak to sb** to tell someone that they have done something wrong: *The manager promised that she would speak to the person responsible.*

> **!** Common mistake: **speak or talk?**
>
> **Warning:** choose the correct verb!
>
> To talk about two people or a group of people having a conversation, the most usual verb is **talk**:
>
> ~~*They spoke all night about their memories.*~~
>
> *They talked all night about their memories.*

LANGUAGE ▷ **4** (A1) [T] to (be able to) talk in a language: *He speaks fluent French.* ◦ *How many foreign languages do you speak?* ◦ *I couldn't speak* ***a word of*** *(= I did not know any) Spanish when I got there.* ◦ *I couldn't work out what language they were speaking.* **FORMAL TALK** ▷ **5** (B2) [I] to give a formal talk to a group of people: *Who is speaking in the debate tonight?* ◦ *The Queen speaks* ***to*** *the nation on television every Christmas.* ◦ *Janet is speaking* ***for*** *the motion (= trying to persuade the people listening that the idea is good) and Peter is speaking* ***against*** *(it) (= trying to persuade them that it is bad).* **SUGGEST** ▷ **6** [I + adv/prep, T] literary to show or express something without using words: *She was silent, but her eyes spoke her real feelings for him.* ◦ *The whole robbery spoke* ***of*** *(= made it seem that there had been) inside knowledge on the part of the criminals.*

IDIOMS **be on speaking terms** (also **know sb to speak to**) to know someone well enough to talk to them • **none to speak of** (also **no sth to speak of**) very little of something: *'Did you get much rain while you were in Singapore?' 'None to speak of.'* • **not be on speaking terms** (C2) If you are not on speaking terms with someone, you refuse to speak to them because you are angry with them: *They had a quarrel last night and now they're not on speaking terms (****with*** *each other).* • **so to speak** (C2) used to explain that what you are saying is not to be understood exactly as stated: *In that relationship it's very much Lorna who wears the trousers, so to speak (= Lorna makes all the important decisions).* • **speak your mind** (C2) to say what you think about something very directly: *He's certainly not afraid to speak his mind.* • **speak for yourself** informal something you say to someone to tell them that the opinion that they have just expressed is not the same as your opinion: *'We had a really boring trip.' 'Speak for yourself! I had a wonderful time!'* • **speak too soon** to say something that is quickly shown not to be true: *He won't be home for ages yet ... Oh, I spoke too soon – here he is now!* • **speak to sb** If something speaks to you, it has a special meaning or importance for you: *That painting really speaks to me.* • **speak volumes** (C2) If something speaks volumes, it makes an opinion, characteristic, or situation very clear without the use of words: *She said very little but her face spoke volumes.* • **speaks for itself** (C2) If something speaks for itself, it is clear and needs no further explanation: *The school's excellent record speaks for itself.*

PHRASAL VERBS **speak out/up** to give your opinion about something in public, especially on a subject that you have strong feelings about: *If no one has the courage to speak out* ***against*** *the system, things will never improve.* • **speak up** (B2) to speak in a louder voice so that people can hear you: *Could you speak up? We can't hear at the back.* • **speak up for sb/sth** to support someone or something, especially by saying good things about them: *She has often spoken up for the rights of working mothers.*

-speak /-spiːk/ **suffix** informal mainly disapproving used to form nouns to mean the special language used in a particular subject area or business: *computer-speak* ◦ *marketing-speak*

speakeasy /ˈspiːkˌiː.zi/ noun [C] a place where alcohol was illegally sold and drunk in the US in the 1920s and 1930s

speaker /ˈspiː.kər/ (US) /-kɚ/ noun [C] **FORMAL TALK** ▷ **1** (B1) a person who gives a speech at a public event: *a good* ***public*** *speaker* ◦ *Please join with me in thanking our* ***guest*** *speaker tonight.* ◦ *The Democrats have chosen the Texas state treasurer as the* ***keynote*** *(= most important) speaker at their convention.* **LANGUAGE** ▷ **2** (B1) someone who speaks a particular language: *a French speaker* ◦ *a* ***fluent*** *Russian speaker* ◦ *non-English speakers* **ELECTRICAL** ▷ **3** (A2) the part of a radio, television, or computer, or of a piece of electrical equipment for playing recorded sound, through which the sound is played. A speaker can be part of the radio, etc. or be separate from it: *There's no sound coming out of the right-hand speaker.*

Speaker /ˈspiː.kər/ (US) /-kɚ/ noun [C] the person who controls the way in which business is done in an organization which makes laws, such as a parliament: *He served for eight years as Speaker of the House of*

Representatives. ◦ [as form of address] *Mr Speaker, my honourable friend has failed to consider the consequences of his proposal.*

speakerphone /ˈspiː.kə.fəʊn/ ⓤⓢ /-kɚ.foʊn/ **noun** [C] a phone which you can use without having to hold any part of it in your hand

-speaking /-spiː.kɪŋ/ **suffix** using the stated language: *a Spanish-speaking country*

spear /spɪəʳ/ ⓤⓢ /spɪr/ **noun; verb**

▸**noun** [C] **1** a weapon consisting of a pole with a sharp, usually metal, point at one end, that is either thrown or held in the hand **2** a thin pointed stem or leaf: *asparagus spears*

▸**verb** [T] **1** to push or throw a spear into an animal: *They catch the fish by spearing them.* **2** to catch something on the end of a pointed tool or object: *He speared a meatball with his fork.*

spearhead /ˈspɪə.hed/ ⓤⓢ /ˈspɪr-/ **verb; noun**

▸**verb** [T] to lead something such as an attack or a course of action: *British troops spearheaded the invasion.* ◦ *Joe Walker will be spearheading our new marketing initiative.*

▸**noun** [C usually singular] a person or group that leads something such as an attack or a course of action: *American troops formed the spearhead **of** the attack.*

spearmint /ˈspɪə.mɪnt/ ⓤⓢ /ˈspɪr-/ **noun** [U] a strong FLAVOURING with a fresh taste, or the plant from which this FLAVOURING comes: *spearmint chewing-gum/toothpaste*

spec /spek/ **noun** informal **1 on spec** taking a chance, without being sure that you will get what you want: *We just turned up at the airport on spec, hoping that we'd get tickets.* ◦ *You could always send your CV to a few companies on spec.* **2** [C] informal for **specification**: *We've had a spec **drawn up** for a new bathroom.*

ˈspec ˌbuilder **noun** [C] mainly Australian English a person or company that builds houses to sell to anyone who will buy them rather than for a particular customer

> **Other ways of saying special**
>
> See also: **unusual**
>
> If someone or something is special because of being better than usual, you can describe that person or thing as **exceptional** or **outstanding**:
>
> *Their standard of acting was very high but there was one **exceptional/outstanding** performance.*
>
> The adjective **extraordinary** is sometimes used to describe someone or something that is special in a surprising way:
>
> *Her capacity to remember things is **extraordinary**.*
>
> *She has an **extraordinary** talent.*
>
> The adjectives **deluxe** and **superior** are sometimes used to describe things you can buy that are special because they are particularly good quality:
>
> *The clerk tried to sell us the **deluxe** model.*
>
> The adjective **rare** is sometimes used instead of 'special' when it means 'unusual':
>
> *This is a **rare** opportunity to see the building.*

S

special /ˈspeʃ.əl/ **adj; noun**

▸**adj** NOT USUAL ▷ **1** A2 not ordinary or usual: *The car has a number of special safety features.* ◦ *Is there anything special that you'd like to do today?* ◦ *Passengers should tell the airline in advance if they have any special dietary needs.* ◦ *I don't expect special treatment – I just want to be treated fairly.* ◦ *Full details of the election results will be published in a special edition of tomorrow's newspaper.* ◦ *I have a suit for special **occasions**.* ◦ *There's a special **offer** on peaches* (UK also *peaches are **on** special **offer***) (= *they are being sold at a reduced price*) *this week.* **2** A2 especially great or important, or having a quality that most similar things or people do not have: *Could I ask you a special favour?* ◦ *I'm cooking something special for her birthday.* PARTICULAR ▷ **3** B1 [before noun] having a particular purpose: *Firefighters use special breathing equipment in smoky buildings.* ◦ *She works as a special adviser to the president.*

▸**noun** [C] **1** a television programme that is made for a particular reason or occasion and is not part of a series: *a three-hour election night special* **2** a dish that is available in a restaurant on a particular day that is not usually available: *Today's specials are written on the board.* **3** mainly US a product that is being sold at a reduced price for a short period: *Today's specials include T-shirts for only $2.99.*

ˈSpecial ˌBranch **noun** [+ sing/pl verb] the department of the UK police which deals with crimes such as TERRORISM that threaten the government of the UK

ˌspecial deˈlivery **noun** [U] the delivery of a letter or parcel that is much quicker, and more expensive, than normal delivery

ˌspecial eduˈcation **noun** [U] education for children with physical or mental problems, who need to be taught in a different way from other children

ˌspecial eduˈcational needs **noun** [plural] (abbreviation **SEN**) an expression used to refer to SPECIAL NEEDS relating to education in particular → Compare **learning difficulties**

ˌspecial efˈfect **noun** [C usually plural] B1 an unusual piece of action in a film, or an entertainment on a stage, created by using particular equipment: *The film's special effects are amazing.*

ˌspecial ˈinterest ˌgroup **noun** [C] (US also **ˌspecial ˈinterest**) a group of people who have particular demands and who try to influence political decisions involving them: *Much of the pressure for changing the law has come from special interest groups.*

specialism /ˈspeʃ.əl.ɪ.zəm/ **noun** **1** [C] UK (US **specialty**) a subject that someone knows a lot about: *His specialism is tax law.* **2** [U] limiting study or work to a few subjects: *I don't think too much specialism in schools is a good idea.*

specialist /ˈspeʃ.əl.ɪst/ **noun** [C] **1** B2 someone who has a lot of experience, knowledge, or skill in a particular subject: *a software specialist* ◦ *She's a specialist **in** modern French literature.* ◦ *specialist advice/help* **2** (UK also **consultant**) a doctor who has special training in and knowledge of a particular area of medicine: *She's a specialist **in** childhood illnesses.* ◦ *I've asked to be referred to a specialist about my back pain.* ◦ *a leading cancer/eye specialist*

speciality /ˌspeʃ.iˈæl.ɪ.ti/ ⓤⓢ /-ə.t̬i/ **noun** [C] PRODUCT ▷ **1** C1 UK (US **specialty**) a product that is extremely good in a particular place: *Oysters are a **local** speciality/a speciality **of** the area.* ◦ *Paella is a speciality **of the house*** (= *a food that is unusually good in a particular restaurant*). SUBJECT ▷ **2** C1 UK (US **specialty**) a subject that someone knows a lot about BEHAVIOUR ▷ **3** C1 humorous a particular thing that you regularly do or make: *Unkind remarks are one of his specialities.*

specialization (UK usually **specialisation**) /ˌspeʃ.əl.aɪˈzeɪ.ʃən/ **noun** [C or U] a particular area of knowledge or the process of becoming an expert in a particular area: *In the course I'm taking, there's no opportunity for specialization* (= *limiting my studying or work to one particular area*) *until the final year.* ◦ *The lawyer said* *that he was unable to help us because our case fell outside his specialization.*

specialize (UK usually **specialise**) /ˈspeʃ.əl.aɪz/ (US) /-ə.laɪz/ **verb** [I] B2 to spend most of your time studying one particular subject or doing one type of business: *She's hired a lawyer who specializes* ***in*** *divorce cases.* ◦ *a restaurant that specializes* ***in*** *seafood* ◦ *I enjoy working in general medicine, but I hope to be able to specialize in the future.*

specialized (UK usually **specialised**) /ˈspeʃ.əl.aɪzd/ (US) /-ə.laɪzd/ **adj** relating to one particular area or designed for a particular purpose: *Her job is very specialized (= involves only one limited area).* ◦ *The hospital is unable to provide the highly specialized care needed by very sick babies.* ◦ *specialized skills*

specially /ˈspeʃ.əl.i/ **adv** (also **especially**) **VERY** ▷ **1** extremely or in particular: *This is a specially good wine.* ◦ *'Is there anything you want to do this evening?' 'Not specially.'* ◦ *The children really liked the museum, specially the dinosaurs.* **FOR ONE PURPOSE** ▷ **2** B1 for a particular purpose: *I came here specially to see you.* ◦ *She has a wheelchair that was specially made for her.* ◦ *The opera 'Aida' was specially written for the opening of the Cairo opera house in 1871.*

ˌspecial ˈneeds **noun** [plural] specialized **1** the particular things needed by or provided to help people who have an illness or condition that makes it difficult for them to do the things that other people do: *carers for children with special needs* ◦ *a special needs teacher* **2** the people included in this group, for example within the educational system: *a special needs child*

the ˌSpecial Oˈlympics **noun** [plural] a set of international sports competitions for people who have lower than usual mental abilities

ˌspecial ˈpleading **noun** [U] the act of arguing from a particular case in order to get an unfair advantage in a more general situation

ˈspecial ˌschool **noun** [C] a school for children who have physical difficulties or problems with learning

specialty /ˈspeʃ.əl.ti/ **noun** [C] US for **speciality** or **specialism**

species /ˈspiː.ʃiːz/ **noun** [C] (plural **species**) B2 a set of animals or plants in which the members have similar characteristics to each other and can breed with each other: *Mountain gorillas are an* ***endangered*** *species.* ◦ *Over a hundred species* ***of*** *insect are found in this area.* ◦ figurative humorous *Women film directors in Hollywood are a rare species.* → See also **subspecies**

specific /spəˈsɪf.ɪk/ **adj** **PARTICULAR** ▷ **1** B2 relating to one thing and not others; particular: *The virus attacks specific cells in the brain.* ◦ *The money is intended to be used for specific purposes.* ◦ formal *The disease seems to be specific* ***to*** *(= only found in) certain types of plant.* ◦ *Is there anything specific you want from the shops?* **EXACT** ▷ **2** C1 clear and exact: *No specific allegations have yet been made about the prison officers' behaviour.* ◦ *Can you be more specific* ***about*** *where your back hurts?*

specifically /spəˈsɪf.ɪ.kəl.i/ **adv** **FOR ONE PURPOSE** ▷ **1** C1 for a particular reason, purpose, etc.: *These jeans are designed specifically* ***for*** *women.* ◦ [+ to infinitive] *I bought it specifically* ***to*** *wear at the wedding.* ◦ *We are aiming our campaign specifically at young people.* **EXACTLY** ▷ **2** C1 clearly, exactly, or in detail: *I specifically asked you not to be late.* ◦ *The law specifically prohibits acts of this kind.*

specification /ˌspes.ɪ.fɪˈkeɪ.ʃən/ **noun** [C or U] (informal **spec**) C1 a detailed description of how something should be done, made, etc.: *All products are made exactly* ***to*** *the customer's specifications.* ◦ *A specification has been* ***drawn up*** *for the new military aircraft.* ◦ *a job specification* ◦ *The cars have been built* ***to*** *a* ***high*** *specification (= a high standard).*

speˌcific ˈgravity **noun** [U] specialized the mass of a particular volume of a substance when compared with the mass of an equal volume of water at 4°C. A more modern name for this is RELATIVE DENSITY.

specificity /ˌspes.ɪˈfɪs.ɪ.ti/ (US) /-ə.t̬i/ **noun** [U] formal the quality of being SPECIFIC (= clear and exact)

specifics /spəˈsɪf.ɪks/ **noun** [plural] exact details: *I can't comment on the specifics* ***of*** *the case.* ◦ *The specifics of the plan still have to be worked out.*

specify /ˈspes.ɪ.faɪ/ **verb** [T] B2 to explain or describe something clearly and exactly: *He said we should meet but didn't specify a time.* ◦ *The peace treaty clearly specifies the terms for the withdrawal of troops.* ◦ [+ question word] *The newspaper report did not specify* ***how*** *the men were killed.* ◦ [+ (that)] *My contract specifies (****that****) I must give a month's notice if I leave my job.* ◦ *The loan must be repaid within a specified period/by a specified date.*

specimen /ˈspes.ə.mɪn/ **noun** [C] **1** C2 something shown or examined as an example; a typical example: *He has a collection of rare insect specimens.* ◦ *Museums will pay large amounts of money for good dinosaur fossil specimens.* ◦ *Astronauts brought back specimens* ***of*** *moon rock.* **2** a small amount of blood or urine used for testing: *They* ***took*** *blood and urine specimens for analysis.*

specious /ˈspiː.ʃəs/ **adj** formal disapproving seeming to be right or true, but really wrong or false: *a specious argument/claim* ◦ *specious allegations/promises* • **speciously** /-li/ **adv** • **speciousness** /-nəs/ **noun** [U]

speck /spek/ **noun** [C] a very small mark, piece, or amount: *He'd been painting the door and there were specks* ***of*** *paint all over the floor.* ◦ *There's not a speck* ***of*** *(= not any)* ***dust/dirt*** *in their house.* ◦ *We could see a speck (= a small amount)* ***of*** *light at the end of the tunnel.*

speckle /ˈspek.l̩/ **noun** [C usually plural] a very small mark of a different colour from the area around it, usually found with a large number of other marks of the same type: *A blackbird's egg is blue with brown speckles on it.*

speckled /ˈspek.l̩d/ **adj** covered with speckles: *a bird with a speckled breast*

spectacle /ˈspek.tɪ.kl̩/ **noun** **UNUSUAL EVENT** ▷ **1** [C] an unusual or unexpected event or situation that attracts attention, interest, or disapproval: *It was a strange spectacle to see the two former enemies shaking hands and slapping each other on the back.* ◦ *We witnessed the extraordinary spectacle* ***of*** *an old lady climbing a tree to rescue her cat.* **PUBLIC EVENT** ▷ **2** [C or U] a public event or show that is exciting to watch; an exciting appearance: *The carnival was a magnificent spectacle.* ◦ *The television show was mere spectacle (= had an exciting appearance, but little value).* **GLASSES** ▷ **3** **spectacles** [plural] (informal **specs**) old-fashioned glasses: *a pair of spectacles* ◦ *steel-rimmed spectacles* • **spectacle** /-kl/ **adj** [before noun] *a spectacle case*

IDIOM **make a spectacle of yourself** to do something that makes you look stupid and attracts other people's attention: *I wasn't going to make a spectacle of myself just to give you a laugh!*

spectacular /spekˈtæk.jʊ.ləʳ/ (US) /-lɚ/ **adj**; **noun**

▸**adj** **1** B1 very exciting to look at: *a spectacular*

S

view ◦ *He scored a spectacular goal in the second half.* ◦ *There was a spectacular sunset last night.* **2** B1 especially great: *We've had spectacular success with the product.*

▸**noun** [C] an event or performance that is very exciting to watch and involves a lot of people

spectacularly /spekˈtæk.jʊ.lə.li/ US /-lɚ-/ adv IMPRESSIVE ▷ **1** in a very beautiful way that people admire: *At night, the city is spectacularly lit.* EXTREMELY ▷ **2** extremely: *spectacularly beautiful countryside* ◦ *House prices have risen spectacularly.*

spectate /spekˈteɪt/ verb [I] to watch an activity, especially a sports event, without taking part

spectator /spekˈteɪ.tər/ US /-t̬ɚ/ noun [C] B2 a person who watches an activity, especially a sports event, without taking part: *They won 4–0 in front of over 40,000 cheering spectators.*

specˈtator ˌsport noun [C] a sport which people go to watch: *Football is certainly the biggest spectator sport in Britain.*

spectral /ˈspek.trəl/ adj GHOST ▷ **1** coming from or seeming to be the spirit of a dead person: *a spectral figure/presence* COLOURS ▷ **2** specialized of the set of colours into which a beam of light can be separated: *spectral light*

spectre UK UK (US **specter**) /ˈspek.tər/ US /-tɚ/ noun **1 the spectre of sth** the idea of something unpleasant that might happen in the future: *The awful spectre of civil war looms over the country.* ◦ *Drought and war have* ***raised*** *the spectre* ***of*** *food shortages for up to 24 million African people.* **2** [C] literary a **ghost**

spectrum /ˈspek.trəm/ noun [C] (plural **spectra** or **spectrums**) COLOURS ▷ **1** C2 the set of colours into which a beam of light can be separated, or a range of waves, such as light waves or radio waves: *The colours of the spectrum – red, orange, yellow, green, blue, indigo, and violet – can be seen in a rainbow.* RANGE ▷ **2** C1 a range of opinions, feelings, etc.: *He has support from across the whole* ***political*** *spectrum.* ◦ *The group includes students from both ends of the* ***social*** *spectrum (= range of social classes).* ◦ *A wide spectrum* ***of*** *opinion was represented at the meeting.*

speculate /ˈspek.jʊ.leɪt/ verb [I] GUESS ▷ **1** C2 to guess possible answers to a question when you do not have enough information to be certain: *I don't know why she did it – I'm just speculating.* ◦ *A spokesperson declined to speculate* ***on*** *the cause of the train crash.* ◦ *Journalists are speculating* ***about*** *whether interest rates will be cut.* ◦ [+ that] *The newspapers have speculated* ***that*** *they will get married next year.* TRADE ▷ **2** to buy and sell in the hope that the value of what you buy will increase and that it can then be sold at a higher price in order to make a profit: *He made his money speculating* ***on*** *the London gold and silver markets.* ◦ *The company has been speculating* ***in*** *property for years.*

speculation /ˌspek.jʊˈleɪ.ʃən/ noun [C or U] GUESS ▷ **1** C1 the activity of guessing possible answers to a question without having enough information to be certain: *Rumours that they are about to marry have been dismissed as* ***pure*** *speculation.* ◦ *Speculation* ***about*** *his future plans is rife.* ◦ [+ that] *News of the president's illness* ***fuelled/prompted*** *speculation* ***that*** *an election will be held later in the year.* TRADING ▷ **2** the act of speculating in order to make a profit

speculative /ˈspek.jʊ.lə.tɪv/ US /-t̬ɪv/ adj GUESS ▷ **1** based on a guess and not on information: *The article was dismissed as highly speculative.* TRADE ▷ **2** bought or done in order to make a profit in the future: *The office block was built as a speculative venture.* • **speculatively** /-li/ US /-t̬ɪv-/ adv

speculator /ˈspek.jʊ.leɪ.tər/ US /-t̬ɚ/ noun [C] a person who buys goods, property, money, etc. in the hope of selling them at a profit

speech /spiːtʃ/ noun SAY WORDS ▷ **1** B1 [U] the ability to talk, the activity of talking, or a piece of spoken language: *Children usually develop speech in the second year of life.* ◦ *People who suffer a stroke may experience a loss of speech.* **2** [U] the way a person talks: *His speech was slurred and I thought he was drunk.* **3** B1 [U] the language used when talking: *Some expressions are used more* ***in*** *speech than in writing.* **4** [C] a set of words spoken in a play: *Do you know the words to Hamlet's famous speech at the beginning of Act III?* FORMAL TALK ▷ **5** B2 [C] a formal talk given usually to a large number of people on a special occasion: *I had to* ***give/make*** *a speech at my brother's wedding.* ◦ *The Governor of New York* ***delivered*** *a rousing speech to the national convention.* ◦ *He gave the* ***after-dinner*** *speech (= a talk given after a formal evening meal at which a large number of people are present).* ◦ *Did you hear her* ***acceptance*** *speech at the Oscars ceremony?* → See also **speak**

> Word partners for **speech** (SAY WORDS)
>
> *careful/fluent* speech • *colloquial/normal/ordinary* speech • *slur* your speech • speech *patterns*

> Word partners for **speech** (FORMAL TALK)
>
> *deliver/give/make* a speech • *write* a speech • an *impassioned/rousing* speech • *in* a speech • a speech *about/on* sth

ˈspeech ˌbubble noun [C] a round shape next to the head of a character in a CARTOON inside which the character's words or thoughts are written

ˈspeech ˌday noun [C] a day each year in some British schools when prizes and formal talks are given

speechify /ˈspiː.tʃɪ.faɪ/ verb [I] informal disapproving to give a speech, especially in a boring way or in a way that shows you think you are important

ˈspeech imˌpediment noun [C] a difficulty in speaking clearly, such as a LISP or STAMMER

speechless /ˈspiːtʃ.ləs/ adj C1 unable to speak because you are so angry, shocked, surprised, etc.: *The news* ***left*** *us speechless.* ◦ *She was speechless* ***with*** *indignation.* • **speechlessly** /-li/ adv • **speechlessness** /-nəs/ noun [U]

ˌspeech recogˈnition ˌsoftware noun [U] computer SOFTWARE that allows a computer to understand spoken words

ˌspeech ˈtherapy noun [U] the treatment of people who have difficulty speaking: *She needed speech therapy after she suffered severe head injuries in a car accident.* • **ˌspeech ˈtherapist** noun [C] *A speech therapist helped him overcome his stammer.*

speechwriter /ˈspiːtʃˌraɪ.tər/ US /-t̬ɚ/ noun [C] a person whose job is to write formal speeches for someone else, usually for politicians

speed /spiːd/ noun; verb

▸**noun** RATE OF MOVEMENT ▷ **1** B1 [C or U] how fast something moves: *He was travelling* ***at a*** *speed* ***of*** *90 mph.* ◦ *The car has a* ***top*** *speed* ***of*** *155 miles per hour.* ◦ *You should* ***lower/reduce*** *your speed as you approach a junction.* ◦ *On a clear, straight road you can* ***gather/pick up*** *speed.* ◦ *He came off the road while driving his car round a bend at* ***high/breakneck*** *speed (= very fast).* ◦ *There are speed* ***restrictions*** *(= controls on how fast traffic is allowed to move) on this part of the road.*

∘ *an electric drill with two speeds (= rates at which it turns)* **2** B2 [U] very fast movement: *I get a real thrill from speed.* ∘ *He put on a sudden burst of speed.* ∘ *Both cars were travelling* ***at*** *speed (= very fast) when the accident happened.* **3** [U] how fast something happens: *We were surprised at the speed* ***of*** *the response to our enquiry.* ∘ *It was the speed at which it all happened that shocked me.* ∘ *She got through her work* ***with*** *speed (= quickly) and efficiency.* **4 the speed of light/sound** the rate at which light or sound travels: *The speed of light is 300 million metres per second.* ∘ *These planes travel at twice the speed of sound.* **5** [C] a **gear**: *a bicycle with ten speeds* ∘ *a ten-speed bicycle* **6** [C] the rate at which a photographic film absorbs or reacts to light: *What speed film do I need for taking photographs indoors?* **7 shutter speed** the length of time for which part of a camera is open to allow light to reach the film when a photograph is being taken: *a high/low shutter speed* **DRUG** ▷ **8** [U] slang for **amphetamine** (= a drug that makes the mind or body more active): *She was* ***on*** *speed at the time.*

> Word partners for **speed noun**
>
> *gain/gather/increase/pick up* speed • *lower/reduce* speed • *reach* a speed • *full/high/maximum/top* speed • *blinding/breakneck/dizzying/lightning* speed • a *burst* of speed • an *average/constant/steady* speed • *at* a speed *of* [100 kph/70 mph]

IDIOM **up to speed** C1 If you are up to speed with a subject or activity, you have all the latest information about it and are able to do it well: *We arranged for some home tutoring to* ***get*** *him up to speed with the other children in his class.* ∘ *Before we start the meeting I'm going to* ***bring*** *you up to speed with the latest developments.*

▸verb [I or T, usually + adv/prep] (**sped** or **speeded**, **sped** or **speeded**) **1** to (cause to) move, go or happen fast: *The train sped* ***along*** *at over 120 miles per hour.* ∘ *The actress then sped* ***away/off*** *in a waiting car.* ∘ *We sped* ***down*** *the ski slopes.* ∘ *This year is speeding* ***by/past***. ∘ *Ambulances sped the injured people (= moved them quickly) away from the scene.* ∘ *The best thing you can do to speed your recovery (= make it quicker) is to rest.* **2 be speeding** to be driving faster than you are legally allowed to do: *He was* ***caught*** *speeding.*

PHRASAL VERB **speed (sth) up** to happen or move faster, or to make something happen or move faster: *This drug may have the effect of speeding up your heart rate.* ∘ *Can the job be speeded up in some way?* ∘ *The tape speeded up towards the end.* ∘ *I think you need to speed up a bit (= drive faster) – we're going to be late.* ∘ *The economy shows signs of speeding up (= increasing activity).*

speedboat /ˈspiːd.bəʊt/ US /-boʊt/ noun [C] a small boat with a powerful engine that travels very fast

speedboat

ˈ**speed** ˌ**bump** noun [C or] (UK also ˈ**speed** ˌ**hump**, **sleeping policeman**) a small raised area built across a road to force people to drive more slowly

ˈ**speed** ˌ**camera** noun [C] a camera at the side of the road which takes pictures of cars that are going faster than is legally allowed

ˈ**speed** ˌ**dating** noun [U] a way of meeting people for possible romantic relationships which involves talking with a lot of people for a short time to see if you like them

ˈ**speed** ˌ**dial** noun [U] mainly US a feature on a phone that makes it possible for you to call a number by pressing only one button • ˈ**speed-**ˌ**dial** verb [I or T]

speeding /ˈspiː.dɪŋ/ noun [U] driving faster than is allowed in a particular area: *She was* ***fined for*** *speeding last month.*

ˈ**speed** ˌ**limit** noun [C] the fastest rate at which you are allowed to drive in a particular area: *a 50 mph speed limit* ∘ *Slow down – you're* ***breaking*** *the speed limit.* ∘ *Try not to go* ***over*** *the speed limit, Daniel.*

speedometer /spiːˈdɒm.ɪ.təʳ/ US /spɪˈdɑː.mə.t̬ɚ/ noun [C] (UK informal **speedo**) a device in a vehicle which shows how fast the vehicle is moving

Speedos /ˈspiː.dəʊz/ US /-doʊz/ noun [plural] trademark a style of tight SWIMWEAR (= clothing worn for swimming) for men

ˈ**speed** ˌ**skating** noun [U] the sport of racing on ice, usually around an oval track

ˈ**speed** ˌ**trap** noun [C] a place on a road where the police use special hidden equipment to see if drivers are going faster than is allowed in a particular area

ˈ**speed-up** noun [S] an increase in the rate of change or growth: *Measures should be taken to halt the speed-up* ***in*** *population growth.*

speedway /ˈspiːd.weɪ/ noun [C or U] (a special racing track used for) the sport of racing special cars, or light motorcycles without BRAKES

speedy /ˈspiː.di/ adj quick: *He's a very speedy worker.* ∘ *We need to take speedy action/make a speedy decision.* ∘ *Everyone is hoping for a speedy* ***end*** *to the conflict (= hoping that an end to it will happen quickly).* ∘ *We wished her a speedy* ***recovery*** *from her illness (= that she would get better quickly).* • **speedily** /-dɪ.li/ adv *The problem was speedily solved.* • **speediness** /-nəs/ noun [U]

speleologist /ˌspiː.liˈɒl.ə.dʒɪst/ US /-ˈɑː.lə-/ noun [C] specialized someone who studies caves, or who climbs in them for sport

speleology /ˌspiː.liˈɒl.ə.dʒi/ US /-ˈɑː.lə-/ noun [U] specialized **1** the scientific study of caves **2** the sport of walking and climbing in caves

spell /spel/ verb; noun

▸verb **FORM WORDS** ▷ **1** A2 [I or T] (**spelled** or UK also **spelt**) to form a word or words with the letters in the correct order: *How do you spell 'receive'?* ∘ *Shakespeare did not always spell his own name the same way.* ∘ *Our address is 1520 Main Street, Albuquerque – shall I spell that* ***(out)*** *(= say in the correct order the letters that form the word) for you?* ∘ *I think it's important that children should be taught to spell.* **RESULT** ▷ **2 spell disaster, trouble, etc.** to cause something bad to happen in the future: *This cold weather could spell trouble for gardeners.* **DO INSTEAD** ▷ **3** [T] (**spelled, spelled**) mainly US to do something that someone else would usually be doing, especially in order to allow them to rest: *You've been driving for a while – do you want me to spell you?*

PHRASAL VERB **spell sth out** to explain something in a very clear way with details: *The government has so far refused to spell out its plans/policies.* ∘ informal *What do you mean you don't understand – do I have to spell* ***it*** *out for you?*

▸noun [C] **PERIOD** ▷ **1** a period of time for which an activity or condition lasts continuously: *I lived in London* ***for*** *a spell.* ∘ *She* ***had*** *a brief spell* ***as*** *captain of the team.* ∘ *I keep having/getting* ***dizzy*** *spells (= periods of feeling as if I'm turning around).* **2** a short period of a particular type of weather: *a spell of dry weather* **DO**

S

INSTEAD ▷ **3** US a period when you do something that someone else would usually be doing, especially in order to allow them to rest: *If we take spells (**with**) doing the painting, it won't seem like such hard work.* **MAGIC** ▷ **4** spoken words that are thought to have magical power, or (the condition of being under) the influence or control of such words: *The witch **cast/put** a spell **on** the prince and he turned into a frog.* ◦ *A beautiful girl would have to kiss him to **break** (= stop) the spell.* ◦ *Sleeping Beauty lay **under** the wicked fairy's spell until the prince woke her with a kiss.*

IDIOM **be under sb's spell** to be strongly attracted to someone and influenced by them

spellbinding /ˈspelˌbaɪn.dɪŋ/ **adj** holding your attention completely: *He gave a spellbinding performance.*

spellbound /ˈspel.baʊnd/ **adj** having your attention completely held by something, so that you cannot think about anything else: *The children **listened** to the story spellbound.* ◦ *He **held** his audience spellbound.*

spellcheck /ˈspelˌtʃek/ **verb** [T] to use a computer program that makes certain that the words in a document have the correct letters in the correct order • **spellcheck noun** [C] *It's always a good idea to **run** a spellcheck once you've finished writing.*

spellchecker /ˈspelˌtʃek.əʳ/ ⓤⓢ /-ɚ/ **noun** [C] a computer program that makes certain that the words in a document have the correct letters in the correct order: *After you've finished each chapter, **run** the spellchecker.*

speller /ˈspel.əʳ/ ⓤⓢ /-ɚ/ **noun** **good/bad speller** someone who is good/bad at spelling

spelling /ˈspel.ɪŋ/ **noun** **1** A2 [U] forming words with the correct letters in the correct order, or the ability to do this: *He's hopeless at spelling.* ◦ *My computer has a program which corrects my spelling.* ◦ *Your essay is full of spelling **mistakes/errors**.* **2** [C] the way a particular word is spelled: *This dictionary includes both British and American spellings **of** words.*

ˈspelling ˌbee **noun** [C] US a competition in which the winner is the person or group who is able to form correctly the highest number of the words they are asked to form

spelunking /spəˈlʌŋ.kɪŋ/ **noun** [U] US (UK **potholing**) the sport of walking and climbing in caves: *Shall we **go** spelunking at the weekend?* • **spelunker** /-kəʳ/ ⓤⓢ /-kɚ/ **noun** [C] US (UK **potholer**)

S

spend /spend/ **verb; noun**

▸**verb** (**spent, spent**) **MONEY** ▷ **1** A2 [I or T] to give money as a payment for something: *How much did you spend?* ◦ *I don't know how I managed to spend so much in the pub last night.* ◦ *We spent **a fortune** when we were in New York.* ◦ *She spends a lot of **money on** clothes.* ◦ *We've just spent £1.9 million **on** improving our computer network.* ◦ *We went on a spending **spree** (= we bought a lot of things) on Saturday.*

> **!** **Common mistake: spend**
>
> When **spend** is followed by an indirect object, the correct preposition is **on**.
>
> Don't say 'spend money for/in something', say **spend money on something**:
>
> ~~*I spend £150 per week for rent.*~~
>
> *I spend £150 per week on rent.*

TIME ▷ **2** A2 [T] to use time doing something or being somewhere: *I think we need to spend more **time** together.* ◦ *I spent a lot of time clean**ing** that room.* ◦ *I've spent years build**ing** up my collection.* ◦ *I spent an hour at the station wait**ing** for the train.* ◦ *How long do you spend **on** your homework?* ◦ *My sister always spends ages in the bathroom.* ◦ *We spent the weekend in London.* ◦ *You can spend the night here if you like.* **FORCE** ▷ **3** [T] to use energy, effort, force, etc., especially until there is no more left: *For the past month he's been spending all his energy trying to find a job.* ◦ *They continued firing until all their ammunition was spent (= there was none of it left).* ◦ *The hurricane will probably have spent most of its force (= most of its force will have gone) by the time it reaches the northern parts of the country.* ◦ *Her anger soon spent **itself*** (= stopped).

> **!** **Common mistake: spend**
>
> In the past tense, don't say 'spend', say **spent**:
>
> ~~*I spend two weeks in London, and I enjoyed it.*~~
>
> *I spent two weeks in London, and I enjoyed it.*

> **+** **Other ways of saying spend**
>
> The most common alternative is the verb **pay**:
>
> *When you bought the tickets, how much did you **pay**?*
>
> *I **paid** an extra £30 to get a double room.*
>
> The verb **invest** is used when someone spends money on something and hopes to get a profit:
>
> *She's **invested** all her savings in the business.*
>
> If someone spends a lot of money on something, the phrasal verb **pay out** is sometimes used:
>
> *I've just **paid out** $700 to get the car fixed.*
>
> If someone spends a lot of money on something that he or she wants but does not need, you can use the verb **splurge**:
>
> *We've just **splurged** on new kitchen appliances.*
>
> If someone spends a lot of money on something that seems like a waste of money, in informal English you can use the verb **blow**:
>
> *We won a £15 million settlement in court and we **blew** it all in six years.*
>
> The phrasal verb **dip into** is sometimes used when someone spends part of a supply of money that has been kept or saved:
>
> *We had to **dip into** our savings to pay for the repairs.*
>
> If someone spends money on something but does not want to, the phrasal verbs **fork out** and **shell out** are often used:
>
> *We had to **shell out** £2,000 to get the roof fixed.*
>
> *I'm not going to **fork out** another £20 for their tickets.*

IDIOMS **spend a penny** UK old-fashioned polite phrase for to urinate: *If you'll excuse me, I need to spend a penny.* • **spend the night together** (also **spend the night with sb**) polite phrase for to have sex with someone: *Did you spend the night together?*

▸**noun** [S] UK informal the amount of money that is spent on something: *The total spend **on** the project was almost a million pounds.*

spender /ˈspen.dəʳ/ ⓤⓢ /-dɚ/ **noun** [C] someone who spends money: *Tourists are often **big** spenders (= they buy a lot of things).*

spending /ˈspen.dɪŋ/ **noun** [U] C2 the money that is used for a particular purpose, especially by a government or organization: *government spending **on** health* ◦ *spending cuts* ◦ *Consumer spending has more than doubled in the last ten years.*

ˈspending ˌmoney **noun** [U] money that you can spend on activities you enjoy, entertainment, personal things, etc.: *How much spending money are you taking on holiday?*

spendthrift /ˈspend.θrɪft/ **noun** [C] someone who spends a lot of money in a way that wastes it • **spendthrift adj** [before noun]

spent /spent/ **verb; adj**

▸**verb** past simple and past participle of **spend**

▸**adj 1** Something that is spent has been used so that it no longer has any power or effectiveness: *spent bullets/matches* ◦ *After several defeats in a row, people are starting to say that the team is a spent **force**.* **2** literary tired: *We arrived home spent after our long journey.*

sperm /spɜːm/ (US) /spɝːm/ **noun** (plural **sperm** or **sperms**) **1** [C] a sex cell produced by a man or male animal: *In human reproduction, one female egg is usually fertilized by one sperm.* **2** [U] informal for **semen** (= the liquid produced by the male sex organs that contains sperm)

spermatozoon /ˌspɜː.mə.təˈzəʊ.ɒn/ (US) /ˌspɝː.mə.t̬ə-ˈzoʊ.ɑːn/ **noun** [C] (plural **spermatozoa** /-ə/) specialized for **sperm**

ˈ**sperm** ˌ**bank noun** [C] a place in which human sperm is stored in order to be used by doctors to try to help women become pregnant

ˈ**sperm** ˌ**count noun** [C] the number of live male sperm cells in a particular amount of the liquid in which they are contained: *He has a **low/high** sperm count.*

spermicidal /ˌspɜː.mɪˈsaɪ.dəl/ (US) /ˌspɝː-/ **adj** containing a substance that kills sperm: *spermicidal jelly* ◦ *spermicidal cream*

spermicide /ˈspɜː.mɪ.saɪd/ (US) /ˈspɝː-/ **noun** [C or U] a substance that kills sperm, used especially on CONDOMS or by a woman before she has sex in order to stop herself becoming pregnant

ˈ**sperm** ˌ**whale noun** [C] a large WHALE with a very large, long head

spew /spjuː/ **verb** [I or T, + adv/prep] If something spews liquid or gas, or liquid or gas spews from something, it flows out in large amounts: *The volcano spewed a giant cloud of ash, dust, and gases **into** the air.* ◦ *The drains spew (**out**) millions of gallons of raw sewage **into** the river.* ◦ *Paper came spewing from the computer printer.*

PHRASAL VERB **spew (sth) up** slang to vomit: *I was spewing up all night after those mussels.*

SPF /ˌes.piːˈef/ **noun** [C] abbreviation for sun protection factor: the letters on a bottle of SUNSCREEN (= substance which prevents the skin from burning in the sun) which show how effective the SUNSCREEN is

sphere /sfɪəʳ/ (US) /sfɪr/ **noun** [C] **ROUND OBJECT** ▷ **1** an object shaped like a round ball: *Doctors have replaced the top of his hip bone with a metal sphere.* **AREA** ▷ **2** (C1) a subject or area of knowledge, work, etc.: *the political sphere* ◦ *exchanges with other countries, particularly **in** cultural, scientific, and economic spheres*

spherical /ˈsfer.ɪ.kəl/ **adj** round, like a ball: *The Earth is not perfectly spherical.*

spheroid /ˈsfɪə.rɔɪd/ (US) /ˈsfɪr.ɔɪd/ **noun** [C] specialized a solid object that is almost spherical: *The Earth is a spheroid.*

sphincter /ˈsfɪŋk.təʳ/ (US) /-tɚ/ **noun** [C] specialized a muscle that surrounds an opening in the body and can tighten to close it: *the anal sphincter* ◦ *a sphincter muscle*

sphinx /sfɪŋks/ **noun** [C] (plural **sphinx** or **sphinxes**) **1** an ancient imaginary creature with a lion's body and a woman's head **2 the Sphinx** a large stone STATUE with a lion's body and a person's head, that stands in the desert near Cairo in Egypt

ˈ**sphinx-like adj** mysterious and not allowing people to know what you are thinking: *He sat silently with a sphinx-like smile on his face.*

spic (also **spick**, **spik**) /spɪk/ **noun** [C] US offensive a person from a Spanish-speaking country

spice /spaɪs/ **noun; verb**

▸**noun FOOD** ▷ **1** (B1) [C or U] a substance made from a plant, used to give a special flavour to food: *Cinnamon, ginger, and cloves are all spices.* ◦ *Spices are widely used in South Asian cooking.* **INTEREST** ▷ **2** (C2) [S or U] something that makes something else more exciting and interesting: *A scandal or two **adds** a little spice to office life.*

▸**verb** [T] to use spice to add flavour to food or drink: *coffee spiced **with** cinnamon* ◦ *a **highly** spiced curry*

PHRASAL VERB **spice sth up** to add excitement or interest to a speech, story, or performance: *He'd spiced up his speech **with** a few rude jokes.* ◦ *It was one of those articles on how to spice up your sex life.*

spick /spɪk/ **adj; noun**

▸**adj** informal **spick and span** (especially of a place) very clean and tidy: *Their house is always spick and span.*

▸**noun** [C] offensive a **spic**

spicy /ˈspaɪ.si/ **adj FOOD** ▷ **1** (B1) containing strong flavours from spices: *Do you like spicy food?* **EXCITING** ▷ **2** exciting and interesting, especially because of being shocking or dealing with sexual matters: *a spicy novel* ◦ *spicy details* • **spiciness** /-nəs/ **noun** [U]

spider /ˈspaɪ.dəʳ/ (US) /-dɚ/ **noun** [C] (B1) a small creature with eight thin legs which catches insects in a WEB (= a net made from sticky threads): *a spider's web*

ˈ**spider** ˌ**monkey noun** [C] a small, thin South American monkey which uses its long tail to help it to move around in the branches of trees

ˈ**spider** ˌ**plant noun** [C] a plant commonly found in houses and offices, with long, flat, thin green leaves with white lines

ˈ**spider's web noun** [C] UK (US **spiderweb** /ˈspaɪ.də.web/ (US) /-dɚ-/) a structure like a net of sticky SILK threads made by a SPIDER for catching insects

spidery /ˈspaɪ.dər.i/ (US) /-dɚ-/ **adj** consisting of thin, dark, bending lines, like a SPIDER'S legs: *spidery handwriting* ◦ *a spidery pattern*

spiel /ʃpiːl/ **noun** [C] informal disapproving a speech, especially one that is long and spoken quickly and is intended to persuade the person listening about something: *a sales spiel* ◦ *They gave us a long spiel **about** why we needed to install double glazing in our house.*

spiff /spɪf/ **verb**

PHRASAL VERB **spiff sb/sth up** US informal to make someone or something look more stylish, or cleaner and tidier: *He's really spiffed up his wardrobe since he started his new job.*

spiffy /ˈspɪf.i/ **adj** US informal stylish, attractive, or pleasing: *a spiffy haircut/dresser*

spigot /ˈspɪɡ.ət/ **noun** [C] **1** a device used to control the flow of liquid from something such as a BARREL **2** US a **tap**, especially on the outside of a building

spik /spɪk/ **noun** [C] offensive a **spic**

spike /spaɪk/ **noun; verb**

▸**noun** [C] **SHAPE** ▷ **1** a narrow, thin shape with a sharp point at one end, or something, especially a piece of metal, with this shape: *There were large spikes on top of the railings to stop people climbing over them.*

S

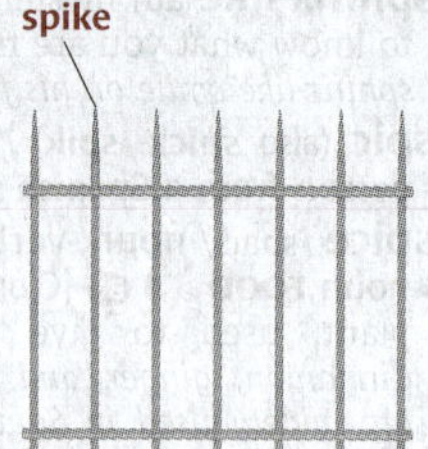

◦ Some types of dinosaur had sharp spikes on their tails. **2 spikes** a set of short, pointed pieces of metal or plastic fixed to the bottom of shoes worn for particular sports, which stop the person wearing the shoes from sliding on the ground, or shoes with these pointed pieces **LEVEL** ▷ **3** a very high amount, price, or level, usually before a fall: *If* ***price*** *spikes continue, people will not be able to afford the new houses they want.*

▸verb [T] **STOP** ▷ **1** informal to decide not to publish an article in a newspaper: *The story was deemed too controversial and so they spiked it.* **MAKE STRONGER** ▷ **2** to make a drink stronger by adding alcohol, or to add flavour or interest to something: *She claimed that someone had spiked her* ***drink*** *with whisky.* ◦ *The pasta was served in a cream sauce spiked* ***with*** *black pepper.* ◦ *His writing is spiked* ***with*** *humour.* **HIT** ▷ **3** in the sport of VOLLEYBALL, to hit the ball so that it goes almost straight down on the other side of the net **POINT** ▷ **4** to push a sharp point into something or someone: *She got badly spiked when one of the runners trod on her heel.* **LEVEL** ▷ **5** [I] to rise to a higher amount, price, or level, usually before going down again: *The jobless rate in October spiked* ***to*** *a five-year high.*

IDIOM **spike sb's guns** to spoil someone's plans: *We wanted to build an extra room onto the side of our house, but our neighbours spiked our guns.*

spiked /spaɪkt/ **adj** with a sharp point or points: *spiked helmets*

ˌspike ˈheels **noun** [plural] mainly US STILETTO HEELS (= very narrow, high heels on a woman's shoes)

spiky /ˈspaɪ.ki/ **adj** **POINTED** ▷ **1** covered with spikes or having that appearance: *a spiky cactus* ◦ *spiky leaves* ◦ *spiky hair* **BAD MOOD** ▷ **2** informal easily annoyed and not polite: *a spiky teenager*

spill /spɪl/ **verb; noun**

▸verb [I or T, usually + adv/prep] (**spilled** or UK also **spilt**, **spilled** or UK also **spilt**) B1 to (cause to) flow, move, fall or spread over the edge or outside the limits of something: *I spilled coffee* ***on*** *my silk shirt.* ◦ *You've spilled something* ***down*** *your tie.* ◦ *Let's see if I can pour the juice into the glass without spilling it.* ◦ *He dropped a bag of sugar and it spilled all* ***over*** *the floor.* ◦ *Crowds of football fans spilled* ***onto*** *the field at the end of the game.*

IDIOMS **spill blood** literary to kill or hurt people • **spill the beans** to tell people secret information: *So who spilled the beans about her affair with David?* • **spill your guts** US and Australian English informal to tell someone all about yourself, especially your problems: *Why do people take part in these shows and spill their guts on camera in front of a studio audience?*

PHRASAL VERBS **spill out 1** to flow or fall out of a container: *All the shopping had spilled out* ***of*** *my bag.* ◦ *The contents of the truck spilled out across the road.* **2** If people spill out of a place, large numbers of them come out of it: *People were spilling out* ***of*** *the wine bar* ***onto*** *the street.* • **spill (sth) out** to talk about or express an emotion freely: *All his resentment spilled out.* ◦ *I listened quietly as she spilled out all her anger and despair.* • **spill over 1** If an activity or situation spills over, it begins to affect another situation or group of people, especially in an unpleasant or unwanted way: *I try not to let my work spill over* ***into*** *my life outside the office.* ◦ *The conflict threatens to spill over* ***into*** *neighbouring regions.* **2** to continue for a longer time than expected: *The talks between the two leaders look likely to spill over* ***into*** *the weekend.*

▸noun [C] an amount of something that has come out of a container: *a fuel spill on the road* ◦ *Could you wipe up that spill, please?*

IDIOM **take a spill** informal to fall off something, usually a bicycle or a horse

spillage /ˈspɪl.ɪdʒ/ **noun** [C or U] formal a spill: *oil spillages*

spillover /ˈspɪl.əʊ.vəʳ/ US /-ˌoʊ.vɚ/ **noun** [C] mainly US **LIQUID** ▷ **1** an amount of liquid that has become too much for the object that contains it and flows or spreads out: *The spillover from the adjacent river flooded the lower fields.* **EFFECTS** ▷ **2** the effects of an activity that have spread further than was originally intended: *We are now witnessing a spillover of the war into neighbouring regions.*

spin /spɪn/ **verb; noun**

▸verb (present participle **spinning**, past tense **spun**, past participle UK also **span**) **TURN** ▷ **1** C1 [I or T] to (cause to) turn around and around, especially fast: *The Earth spins on its axis.* ◦ *The roulette players silently watched the wheel spin* ***around/round.*** ◦ *He was killed when his car hit a tree and spun off the road.* ◦ *Spin the ball (= make it turn around and around as you throw it) and it will change direction when it hits the ground.* **2 head/room spins** If your head or the room spins, you feel as if it is turning around and around, and you cannot balance: *The room started spinning and I felt faint.* **MAKE THREAD** ▷ **3** [I or T] to make thread by twisting FIBRES, or to produce something using thread: *The final stage of the production of cotton is when it is spun* ***into*** *thread.* ◦ *Spiders spin webs.* **4 spin (sb) a story/tale/yarn** to tell a story, either to deceive someone or for entertainment: *He spun some tale about needing to take time off work because his mother was ill.* ◦ [+ two objects] *They spun us a story about being in desperate need of money.* **DRIVE** ▷ **5** [I + adv/prep] informal (of a vehicle) to move quickly, or to move quickly in a vehicle: *We were spinning* ***along,*** *when suddenly one of our tyres burst.* ◦ *Chris spun* ***past*** *in a flashy new car.*

IDIOMS **spin a coin** to make a coin turn around and around on its edge so that someone can guess which side will land facing upwards: *Let's spin a coin to decide who'll have the first turn.* → Compare **toss** • **spin out of control** If activities or events spin out of control, they change very quickly and in an uncontrolled way: *The country's economy seemed to be spinning out of control.* • **spin your wheels** US informal to waste time doing things that achieve nothing: *If we're just spinning our wheels, let us know and we'll quit.*

PHRASAL VERBS **spin sth off PRODUCT** ▷ **1** to produce a useful and unexpected result in addition to the intended result: *The American space program has spun off new commercial technologies.* ◦ *Every new job that is created spins off three or four more in related fields.* **COMPANY** ▷ **2** mainly US to form a separate company from part of an existing company: *The company is trying to spin off part of its business.* • **spin sth out** to make something such as an activity or story last longer than usual or necessary, or as long as possible: *Can we spin our holiday out for a few more days?* ◦ *Somehow, she managed to spin her story out so that it took her the whole train journey to tell it.* • **spin (sb) round** UK (US **spin (sb) around**) C2 to quickly turn your own or someone else's body to face the

S

opposite direction: *She spun round to see what had happened.*

▸noun **TURN** ▷ **1** [C or U] the movement of something turning round very quickly: *I hit something on the road, which sent the car* ***into*** *a spin.* ◦ *Suddenly, the plane went* ***into*** *a spin.* ◦ *These clothes need another spin (= to be turned round very fast in a machine to get water out of them) – they're still very wet.* ◦ *She* ***put*** *a lot of spin on the ball (= threw or hit it in a way that made it spin).* **CHANGE IDEAS** ▷ **2** [S or U] informal a way of describing an idea or situation that makes it seem better than it really is, especially in politics: *They have tried to* ***put*** *a positive spin* ***on*** *the situation.* ◦ *This report* ***puts*** *a different spin* ***on*** *the issue.* **DRIVE** ▷ **3** [C usually singular] old-fashioned informal a short journey in a car for pleasure: *Rupert took me* ***for a*** *spin in his new car.*

IDIOM **in a spin** informal worried and confused: *She's in a spin over the arrangements for the party.* ◦ *News of the director's resignation* ***sent/threw*** *the management into a spin.*

spina bifida /ˌspaɪ.nəˈbɪf.ɪ.də/ noun [U] a serious condition in which part of the SPINE is not correctly developed at birth, leaving the nerves in the back without any protection

spinach /ˈspɪn.ɪtʃ/ noun [U] B1 a vegetable with wide dark green leaves that are eaten cooked or uncooked: *spinach lasagne/salad*

spinal /ˈspaɪ.nəl/ adj of the SPINE: *a spinal injury*

ˌspinal ˈcolumn noun [C] the **spine**

ˌspinal ˈcord noun [C] the set of nerves inside the SPINE that connect the brain to other nerves in the body

ˈspin ˌbowler noun [C] a cricket player who BOWLS (= throws) the ball in such a way that it turns around and around and changes direction when it hits the ground • **ˈspin ˌbowling** noun [U]

spindle /ˈspɪn.dl/ noun [C] a part of a machine around which something turns, or a rod onto which thread is twisted when it is SPUN (= made by twisting)

spindly /ˈspɪnd.li/ adj long or tall and thin, and looking weak: *spindly legs* ◦ *a plant with a spindly stem*

ˈspin ˌdoctor noun [C] mainly disapproving someone whose job is to make ideas, events, etc. seem better than they really are, especially in politics

ˌspin-ˈdryer (also **ˌspin-ˈdrier**) noun [C] UK a machine into which you put wet clothes, which turns them around and around very fast in order to get most of the water out of them → Compare **tumble dryer** • **ˌspin-ˈdry** verb [T] *The label says 'Do not spin-dry'.*

spine /spaɪn/ noun [C] **BONE** ▷ **1** C1 the line of bones down the centre of the back that provides support for the body and protects the SPINAL CORD: *She injured her spine in a riding accident.* ◦ figurative *The Apennine mountains form the spine (= central row of mountains) of Italy.* **POINT** ▷ **2** a long, sharp point like a needle growing out of an animal such as a HEDGEHOG or a plant such as a CACTUS **BOOK PART** ▷ **3** the narrow strip where the cover of a book is joined to the pages, usually with the title and writer's name printed on it

ˈspine-ˌchilling adj (also **ˈspine-ˌtingling**) very frightening: *He told them a spine-chilling ghost story.*

spineless /ˈspaɪn.ləs/ adj disapproving describes someone who does not have much determination and is not willing to take risks: *He was, she concluded, a spineless individual.* • **spinelessly** /-li/ adv • **spinelessness** /-nəs/ noun [U]

ˈspine-ˌtingling adj very special and exciting: *Watching Bolt win the Olympic hundred metres was one of those spine-tingling moments.*

spinifex /ˈspɪn.ɪ.feks/ noun [U] a grass with sharp SPINES which grows especially on sand hills in Australia

spinner /ˈspɪn.əʳ/ US /-ɚ/ noun [C] **SPORT** ▷ **1** in cricket, a BOWLER who makes the ball turn around and around as he or she throws it, or a ball that is BOWLED in that way **MAKING THREAD** ▷ **2** a person who makes thread by twisting FIBRES

spinneret /spɪn.əˈret/ noun [C] specialized an organ that produces the sticky SILK thread that SPIDERS and CATERPILLARS use to make WEBS and COCOONS with

spinney /ˈspɪn.i/ noun [C] mainly UK a small wood → Synonym **copse**

Spinning /ˈspɪn.ɪŋ/ noun [U] trademark a form of exercise that is done inside a building on a machine like a bicycle, that you ride very fast without moving forward

ˈspinning ˌtop noun [C] a toy with rounded sides, a flat top, a vertical handle, and a point at the bottom, which turns round and round on the point when the handle is pushed and pulled up and down or twisted

ˈspinning ˌwheel noun [C] a small machine used, especially in the past, at home for producing thread from FIBRES by turning them on a wheel operated by foot

ˈspin-off UK (US **spinoff**) noun [C] **1** a product that develops from another more important product: *The research has had spin-offs in the development of medical equipment.* **2** a programme or other show involving characters from a previous programme or film: *The stage show is a spin-off* ***from*** *a television programme.*

spinster /ˈspɪn.stəʳ/ US /-stɚ/ noun [C] old-fashioned a woman who is not married, especially a woman who is no longer young and seems unlikely ever to marry

spiny /ˈspaɪ.ni/ adj covered with SPINES (= long, sharp points like needles)

spiracle /ˈspaɪ.rə.kəl/ noun [C] specialized **1** in an insect or SPIDER, one of the small holes that allow air in and out through the surface of the body **2** in some fish such as SHARKS, a small hole behind each eye used for breathing, by allowing water through to the GILLS

spiral /ˈspaɪə.rəl/ US /ˈspaɪr.əl/ noun; verb; adj

▸noun [C] **1** a shape made up of curves, each one above or wider than the one before: *A corkscrew is spiral-****shaped****.* **2 downward spiral** C2 a situation in which a price, etc. becomes lower, or a situation gets worse and is difficult to control because one bad event causes another: *This year's downward spiral of house prices has depressed the market.* ◦ *We must avoid the downward spiral in which unemployment leads to homelessness and then to crime.*

▸verb [I usually + adv/prep] (**-ll-** or US usually **-l-**) **1** to move in a spiral: *With one wing damaged, the model airplane spiralled downwards.* **2** If costs, prices, etc. spiral, they increase faster and faster: *Spiralling costs have squeezed profits.* **3 spiral downwards** (of prices, etc.) to get less, at a faster and faster rate

▸adj [before noun] shaped in a series of curves, each one above or wider than the one before: *a spiral staircase* ◦ *a spiral galaxy*

ˌspiral-ˈbound adj (of a book) having a spiral-shaped piece of metal or plastic holding its pages together

spire /spaɪəʳ/ US /spaɪr/ noun [C] a tall, pointed structure on top of a building, especially on top of a church tower

S

spirit /ˈspɪr.ɪt/ noun; verb

▸noun **WAY OF FEELING** ▷ **1** B2 [S or U] a particular way of thinking, feeling, or behaving, especially a way that is typical of a particular group of people, an activity, a time, or a place: *The players have a very strong* ***team*** *spirit (= loyalty to each other).* ◦ *As rock musicians in the 1960s, they were very much part of the spirit* ***of the age/times****.* ◦ *We acted* ***in*** *a spirit* ***of*** *cooperation.* **2 spirits** B2 [plural] the way a person is feeling: *I've been* ***in high/low*** *spirits (= feeling happy/ sad) lately.* ◦ *Her spirits* ***lifted/rose*** *(= she felt happier) as she read the letter.* ◦ *The negative reply* ***dashed*** *his spirits (= made him unhappy).* **3 the spirit of a law, rule, etc.** the principle which a law, rule, etc. was created to make stronger, rather than the particular things it says you must or must not do: *They followed neither the spirit nor the letter of the law.* **4 enter/get into the spirit** to show enthusiasm and enjoyment **5 that's the spirit** used to approve or encourage someone's positive ATTITUDE (= way of thinking) or action: *'Come on, we can win this game.' 'That's the spirit.'* **NOT BODY** ▷ **6** C1 [U] the characteristics of a person that are considered as being separate from the body, and that many religions believe continue to exist after the body dies: *Although he's now living in America, I feel he's with me* ***in*** *spirit (= I feel he is present and is influencing me, in a way that is not physical).* **7** B2 [C] the form of a dead person, similar to a GHOST, or the feeling that a dead person is present although you cannot see them: *an evil spirit* ◦ *The spirits of long-dead warriors seemed to haunt the area.* **ENTHUSIASM** ▷ **8** [U] approving enthusiasm, energy, or courage: *The orchestra performed The Rite of Spring* ***with*** *great spirit.* ◦ *The torture failed to* ***break*** *the prisoner's spirit.* **ALCOHOL** ▷ **9** C1 [C or U] a strong alcoholic drink: *Vodka is a type of spirit.* **10** [U] Some types of spirit are alcoholic liquids used especially for cleaning, mixing with paint, etc.: *Thin the paint with* ***white*** *spirit.*

IDIOM **as, if, when, etc. the spirit moves sb** taking action only when you feel is the right time, not following a plan: *It's impossible to predict what he'll do – he just acts when the spirit moves him.*

▸verb **spirit sb/sth away, off, out, etc.** to move someone or something out of or away from a place secretly: *Somehow the prisoners managed to spirit news out to the world outside.*

S

spirited /ˈspɪr.ɪ.tɪd/ US /-t̬ɪd/ adj approving enthusiastic and determined: *The home team's spirited playing ensured them a comfortable victory.*

-spirited /-spɪr.ɪ.tɪd/ US /-t̬ɪd/ suffix in the mood mentioned: ***low****-spirited (= sad)* ◦ *The children are rather* ***high****-spirited (= excited and happy).*

spiritless /ˈspɪr.ɪt.ləs/ adj disapproving having no energy and enthusiasm: *It was a spiritless performance.*

ˈspirit ˌlevel noun [C] UK (US **level**) a tool that contains a tube of liquid with an air bubble in it, used to show if a surface is level

spiritual /ˈspɪr.ɪ.tju.əl/ adj; noun

▸adj B2 relating to deep feelings and beliefs, especially religious beliefs • **spiritually** /-ə.li/ adv

▸noun [C] (also **ˌnegro ˈspiritual**) a type of religious song, originally developed by African Americans in the US

ˌspiritual ˈhome noun [C usually singular] a place where you feel you belong, although you were not born there, because you have a lot in common with the people, the culture, and the way of life

spiritualism /ˈspɪr.ɪ.tju.əl.ɪ.zᵊm/ noun [U] the belief that living people can communicate with people who have died • **spiritualist** /-ɪst/ noun [C] *A spiritualist had told her he could give her a message from her dead husband.*

spirituality /ˌspɪr.ɪ.tjuˈæl.ɪ.ti/ US /-ə.t̬i/ noun [U] approving the quality that involves deep feelings and beliefs of a religious nature, rather than the physical parts of life

spirogyra /ˌspaɪə.rəˈdʒaɪə.rə/ US /ˌspaɪ.roʊˈdʒaɪ-/ noun [U] specialized a type of FRESHWATER ALGAE (= very simple plants) formed of cells that contain a green SPIRAL of CHLOROPLAST

spit /spɪt/ verb; noun

▸verb (present tense **spitting**, past tense and past participle **spat**) **FORCE OUT** ▷ **1** C2 [I or T] to force out the contents of the mouth, especially SALIVA: *Bob Ewell spat contemptuously right in the lawyer's face.* ◦ *He spat the meat* ***out*** *in disgust.* ◦ *They bought watermelons and ate them as they walked, spitting* ***out*** *the seeds.* **2** [I] If something hot, such as a fire, spits, it produces short, sharp noises and throws out little pieces. **RAIN** ▷ **3** [I] informal to rain very slightly: *If* ***it's*** *only spitting* ***(with rain)****, perhaps we don't need waterproofs.*

IDIOMS **be the spitting image of sb** (also **be the spit (and image) of sb**) to look extremely similar to someone: *Josie is the spitting image of her granny at the same age.* ◦ *The old man was the* ***(dead)*** *spit of Winston Churchill.* • **in/within spitting distance** informal If something is in or within spitting distance, it is very close: *The house is within spitting distance* ***of*** *the sea.* • **spit blood/venom** (US also **spit nails**, Australian English also **spit tacks**) to speak in an angry way, or to show anger: *I thought he was going to spit blood when he saw what had happened.* • **spit it out!** informal used to tell someone to start speaking or to speak more quickly, when they are unwilling to speak or are speaking slowly: *Come on, spit it out, who told you about this?*

PHRASAL VERB **spit sth out** to say something quickly and angrily: *He spat out an insult and marched out of the room.*

▸noun **STICK** ▷ **1** [C] a long, thin, metal stick put through a piece of food, especially meat, so that it can be cooked above a fire: *Roast the lamb* ***on*** *a spit.* **LAND** ▷ **2** [C] a long, thin, flat beach which goes out into the sea **FROM MOUTH** ▷ **3** [U] (formal **spittle**, Australian informal **slag**) SALIVA, especially when it is outside the mouth: *She used a little spit on a tissue to wipe the mirror clean.*

IDIOM **spit and polish** informal careful cleaning and shining: *The car needs some spit and polish.*

spitball /ˈspɪt.bɔːl/ US /-bɑːl/ noun [C] US a piece of paper that has been CHEWED and then rolled into a ball to be thrown or shot at someone

spite /spaɪt/ noun; verb

▸noun **DESPITE** ▷ **1 in spite of sth** B1 (used before one fact that makes another fact surprising) despite: *In spite of his injury, Ricardo will play in Saturday's match.* **2 in spite of yourself** used when you do something that you do not intend to do and are trying not to do: *She started to laugh, in spite of herself.* **HURT** ▷ **3** C2 [U] a feeling of anger towards someone that makes a person want to annoy, upset, or hurt them, especially in a small way: *He's the sort of man who would let down the tyres on your car just* ***out of/ from*** *spite.* • **spiteful** /-fᵊl/ adj disapproving • **spitefully** /-fᵊl.i/ adv disapproving • **spitefulness** /-fᵊl.nəs/ noun [U] disapproving

▸verb [T] to intentionally annoy, upset, or hurt

someone: *I almost think he died without making a will just to spite his family.*

spittoon /spɪˈtuːn/ noun [C] (US also **cuspidor**) especially in the past, a metal container on the floor in a public place for spitting into

spiv /spɪv/ noun [C] UK old-fashioned informal disapproving a man, especially one who is well-dressed in a way that attracts attention, who makes money dishonestly

splash /splæʃ/ verb; noun

▸verb **LIQUID** ▷ **1** B2 [I or T, usually + adv/prep] (UK informal also **splosh**) If a liquid splashes or if you splash a liquid, it falls on or hits something or someone: *Water was splashing from a hole in the roof.* ◦ *Unfortunately some paint splashed **onto** the rug.* ◦ *She splashed her face with cold water.* ◦ *She poured a large gin and splashed soda **into** it from a siphon.* **2** B2 [I usually + adv/prep] (UK informal also **splosh**) to move in water so that drops of it go in all directions: *The kids were splashing (**about/around**) in the shallow end of the swimming pool.* **SHOW** ▷ **3** [T + adv/prep] to print or show something in a very noticeable way: *Several newspapers splashed colour pictures of the Prince **across** their front pages.*

PHRASAL VERB **splash out (sth)** UK C2 to spend a lot of money on buying things, especially things that are pleasant to have but that you do not need: *They splashed out £3,000 **on** a holiday.* → See also **splurge**

▸noun [C] **LIQUID** ▷ **1** C2 a small amount of a liquid that has fallen or been dropped: *There were several splashes of white paint on the carpet.* **2** B2 the noise of something hitting or moving in water: *We heard a splash and then saw that Toni had fallen in the river.* **SHOW** ▷ **3** something or someone bright or very noticeable: *The little girl in her flowery dress provides the only splash **of colour** in the picture.* • **splash** adv *The ball fell splash into the river.*

IDIOM **make a splash** C2 to become suddenly very successful or very well known: *Jodie Foster made quite a splash in the film 'Taxi Driver'.*

splashdown /ˈsplæʃ.daʊn/ noun [C usually singular, U] a landing by a spacecraft in the sea

ˈsplash ˌguard noun [C] mainly US for **mudflap**

splashy /ˈsplæʃ.i/ adj US more expensive, exciting, etc. than necessary: *Hollywood tends to make splashy films with lots of star actors.*

splat /splæt/ noun [U] informal the sound of something wet hitting a surface or of something hitting the surface of a liquid • **splat** adv *She fell splat into the water.*

splatter /ˈsplæt.əʳ/ (US) /ˈsplæṭ.ɚ/ verb [I or T] (especially of a thick liquid) to hit and cover a surface with small drops, or to cause this to happen: *The bike was splattered **with** mud.*

splay /spleɪ/ verb [I or T] to spread wide apart: *At one point the dancers flipped onto their backs and splayed their legs.* ◦ *The petals splay **out** from the middle of the flower.*

spleen /spliːn/ noun **ORGAN** ▷ **1** [C] an organ near the stomach which produces and cleans the body's blood **ANGER** ▷ **2** [U] formal a feeling of anger and disagreement: mainly UK *She threatened, in a **fit/burst of** spleen, to resign.* ◦ *Shareholders used the conference as an opportunity to **vent** their spleen **on** (= get angry with) the Board of Directors.*

splendid /ˈsplen.dɪd/ adj formal C1 excellent, or beautiful and impressive: *We had splendid food/a splendid holiday/splendid weather.* ◦ *You look splendid in that outfit.* → See also **resplendent** • **splendidly** /-li/ adv

splendiferous /splenˈdɪf.ər.əs/ (US) /-ɚ-/ adj humorous excellent, or very beautiful and special

splendour UK (US **splendor**) /ˈsplen.dəʳ/ (US) /-dɚ/ noun **1** C2 [U] great beauty which attracts admiration and attention: *They bought a decaying 16th-century manor house and restored it to its original splendour.* **2 splendours** (mainly US **splendors**) [plural] the beautiful features or qualities of a place, etc.: *the splendours **of** Venice*

splice /splaɪs/ verb; noun

▸verb [T] to join two pieces of rope, film, etc. together at their ends in order to form one long piece

IDIOM **get spliced** old-fashioned informal to get married

▸noun [C] a join between two pieces of something so that they form one long piece

spliff /splɪf/ noun; verb

▸noun [C] slang a cigarette containing the drug CANNABIS

▸verb slang

PHRASAL VERB **spliff up** to make and light a CANNABIS cigarette

splint /splɪnt/ noun [C] a long, flat object used as a support for a broken bone so that the bone stays in a particular position while it HEALS: *The doctor put a splint **on** the arm and bandaged it up.*

splinter noun; verb

▸noun [C] /ˈsplɪn.təʳ/ (US) /-tɚ/ a small, sharp, broken piece of wood, glass, plastic, or similar material: *The girl had a splinter (**of** wood) in her toe.*

▸verb [I] /ˈsplɪn.təʳ/ (US) /-ṭɚ/ to break into small, sharp pieces: *The edges of the plastic cover had cracked and splintered.* ◦ figurative *The danger is that the Conservative Party may splinter **into** several smaller political parties.*

ˈsplinter ˌgroup noun [C] a group of people who have left a political party or other organization and formed a new separate organization: *The Socialist Workers' Party seemed to split into several splinter groups.*

split /splɪt/ verb; noun

▸verb (present participle **splitting**, past tense and past participle **split**) **DIVIDE** ▷ **1** B2 [I or T] to (cause to) divide into two or more parts, especially along a particular line: *The prize was split **between** Susan and Kate.* ◦ *Split the aubergines **in** half and cover with breadcrumbs.* ◦ *The teacher split the children (**up**) **into** three groups.* ◦ informal *I'll split (= share) this croissant **with** you.* ◦ *His trousers split when he tried to jump the fence.* ◦ [+ obj + adj] *The woman had split her head **open** (= got a long, deep wound in her head) when she was thrown off the horse.* **2** C2 [I or T] If the people in an organization or group split, or if something splits them, they disagree and form smaller groups: *The childcare issue has split the employers' group.* ◦ *The union executive has split **down the middle** (= divided into two equal-sized groups who disagree with each other) on what to do next.* ◦ *A group of extremists split (**off**) **from** the Labour Party to form a new 'Workers' Party'.* **3 split the difference** If you split the difference, you agree on a number or amount that is exactly in the middle of the difference between two other numbers or amounts. **TELL** ▷ **4** [I] UK old-fashioned informal to tell other people secret and damaging information about someone: *They knew Josie wouldn't split **on** them **to** the teacher.* **LEAVE** ▷ **5** [I] old-fashioned informal to leave a place

IDIOMS **split your sides** to laugh a lot at something: *We nearly split our sides **laughing/with laughter***

S

watching Paul trying to get the dog into the bicycle basket. • **split hairs** disapproving to argue about small details of something

PHRASAL VERB **split up** informal B1 If two people split up, they end their relationship or marriage: *She split up* ***with*** *her boyfriend last week.* → See also **split-up**

▸noun [C] **1** a long, thin hole in something where it has broken apart: *Rain was getting in through a split* ***in*** *the plastic sheeting.* **2** a situation in which a group of people is divided into smaller groups because they disagree about something: *There is a widening split* ***between*** *senior managers and the rest of the workforce.* ◦ *The tax issue has caused a split* ***in/within*** *the government.* ◦ *There was a 75/25 split in the voting.* **3 the splits** [plural] UK (US **split**) the action of sitting on the floor with your legs straight out and flat along the floor in opposite directions: *Can you* ***do*** *the splits?* ◦ *Carly* ***did*** *a split.*

ˌsplit ˈend noun [C usually plural] a hair that has divided into several parts at its end

ˌsplit inˈfinitive noun [C] specialized a phrase in which an adverb or other word is put between 'to' and an INFINITIVE. Some people consider split infinitives to be bad grammar, but they are becoming more acceptable: *'To quickly decide' is an example of a split infinitive.*

ˌsplit-ˈlevel adj A split-level building or room has floors at slightly different heights.

ˌsplit ˈpea noun [C usually plural] a dried PEA that has been separated into its two halves, used especially in soups

ˌsplit personˈality noun [C usually singular] Someone with a split personality behaves so differently at different times that they seem to have more than one character.

ˌsplit ˈpin noun [C] a thin metal rod divided into two parts which open out in order to fasten parts of a machine

ˌsplit ˈsecond noun [S] a very short moment of time: *They brought out guns and for a split second nobody moved.* ◦ *We had to make a split-second (= very quick) decision.*

splitting /ˈsplɪt.ɪŋ/ US /ˈsplɪţ-/ adj **splitting headache** a very severe pain that you feel in your head

ˈsplit-up noun [C usually singular] informal an occasion when two people end their relationship → See also **split**

S

splodge /splɒdʒ/ US /splɑːdʒ/ noun [C] mainly UK (US usually **splotch**) a mark or spot that does not have a regular shape: *He put his hand on the bed, and left a splodge of blood on the bedspread.*

splosh /splɒʃ/ US /splɑːʃ/ verb [I], noun [C] mainly UK informal for **splash**.

splurge /splɜːdʒ/ US /splɝːdʒ/ verb [I or T] informal to spend a lot of money on buying goods, especially expensive goods: *I feel like splurging* ***(out) on*** *a new dress.* → Synonym **splash out (sth)** • **splurge** noun [C]

splutter /ˈsplʌt.əʳ/ US /ˈsplʌţ.ɚ/ verb [I] (of a person) to speak in a quick and confused way, producing short, unclear noises because of surprise, anger, etc., or (of a person or thing) to make a series of noises similar to this: *The old gentleman was spluttering* ***with*** *indignation.* ◦ [+ speech] *'But, er ... when, um, ... how?' he spluttered.* ◦ *She took too big a gulp of whisky and started to cough and splutter.* • **splutter** noun [C]

spod /spɒd/ US /spɑːd/ noun [C] UK informal a person who is boring, not fashionable, and studies very hard

spoil /spɔɪl/ verb; noun

▸verb (**spoiled** or **spoilt**, **spoiled** or **spoilt**) DESTROY ▷ **1** B1 [T] to destroy or reduce the pleasure, interest, or beauty of something: *He tried not to let the bad news spoil his evening.* ◦ *The oil spill has spoiled the whole beautiful coastline.* ◦ *I haven't seen the film, so don't spoil it* ***for*** *me by telling me what happens.* ◦ *You'll spoil your* ***appetite*** *for dinner if you have a cake now.* **2** [I or T] When food spoils or is spoiled, it is no longer good enough to eat: *The dessert will spoil if you don't keep it in the fridge.* **3** [T] UK specialized to mark a BALLOT PAPER so that it cannot be officially counted as a vote: *Since she supported none of the candidates, she spoiled her ballot paper.* TREAT WELL ▷ **4** [T] to treat someone very or too well, especially by being extremely generous: *When I'm feeling miserable I go shopping and spoil myself – a couple of new dresses always make me feel better.* CHILD ▷ **5** C1 [T] disapproving to allow a child to do or have everything that it wants to, usually so that it expects to get everything it wants and does not show respect to other people: *Mr Harvey, unable for once to do exactly as he wanted, sulked just like a spoilt* ***child***.

> **Other ways of saying spoil**
>
> **Ruin** is a very common alternative to 'spoil':
>
> *I put too much salt in the sauce and* ***ruined*** *it.*
>
> The verb **deface** is sometimes used when someone spoils the appearance of something by writing or drawing on it:
>
> *Many of the library books had been* ***defaced***.
>
> The verb **disfigure** is sometimes used when a person's physical appearance has been spoiled:
>
> *Her face was* ***disfigured*** *by the scar.*
>
> If something spoils a friendship or other relationship, you can use the verbs **sour** or **poison**:
>
> *The long dispute has* ***poisoned/soured*** *relations between the two countries.*
>
> In informal situations you can use the phrasal verbs **mess up** and **screw up** to say that something has been spoiled:
>
> *Laurie's illness has completely* ***messed up*** *all our holiday plans.*
>
> *That new software has really* ***screwed up*** *my computer.*

IDIOMS **be spoiling for a fight** to be very eager to fight or argue: *Local councillors are spoiling for a fight over plans to close two village schools.* • **be spoilt for choice** to be unable to choose because there are so many possible good choices: *There's so much good theatre and cinema in London, really one is spoilt for choice.* • **spoil sb's party** (also **spoil the party for sb**) to cause trouble for someone at a moment when they are enjoying a success • **spoil sb rotten** to do whatever someone wants you to do or to give them anything they want: *The children are spoiled rotten by their grandparents.*

▸noun EARTH ▷ **1** [U] earth, stones, etc. dug out from a hole in the ground: *a spoil heap* PROFITS ▷ **2 spoils** [plural] formal goods, advantages, profits, etc. that you get by your actions or because of your position or situation: *The spoils* ***of victory/war*** *included mounds of treasure and armour.*

spoiler /ˈspɔɪ.ləʳ/ US /-lɚ/ noun [C] CAR PART ▷ **1** a device on a car or aircraft that is positioned so that it stops the air from flowing around the vehicle in a smooth way and so helps to control it TAKING ATTENTION ▷ **2** a newspaper article, television programme, etc. that is produced just before or at the same time as another similar one in order to take attention away from it

spoilsport /ˈspɔɪl.spɔːt/ US /-spɔːrt/ noun [C] informal disapproving a person who stops other people from enjoying themselves: *She did ask her dad if she could have a big party, but the old spoilsport refused.*

spoke /spəʊk/ (US) /spoʊk/ **verb; noun**
▸**verb** past simple of **speak**
▸**noun** [C] any of the rods that join the edge of a wheel to its centre, so giving the wheel its strength: *a bicycle spoke*

IDIOM **put a spoke in sb's wheel** informal to make it difficult for someone to achieve something they had planned to do

spoken /ˈspəʊ.kᵊn/ (US) /ˈspoʊ-/ **verb 1** past participle of **speak 2 the spoken word** language that is spoken, not written or sung: *The library holds recordings of the spoken word as opposed to music.*

-spoken /-spəʊ.kᵊn/ (US) /-spoʊ-/ **suffix** speaking in a particular way: *a softly-spoken young man ∘ a well-spoken lady*

ˈspoken ˌfor adj [after verb] **1** describes something that is not available because someone has already bought or asked for it: *Most of the best paintings in the exhibition were already spoken for.* **2** old-fashioned describes someone who is not available for a romantic relationship because they are already having one with someone else: *Both girls were spoken for.*

spokesman /ˈspəʊks.mən/ (US) /ˈspoʊks-/ **noun** [C] (plural **-men** /-mən/) (also **spokesperson**) (C1) someone who is chosen by a group or organization to speak officially to the public for them: *a government spokesperson*

spokesperson /ˈspəʊksˌpɜː.sᵊn/ (US) /ˈspoʊksˌpɝː-/ **noun** [C] (C1) a person who is chosen to speak officially for a group or organization: *A spokesperson for the airline said that flights would run as scheduled.*

spokeswoman /ˈspəʊksˌwʊm.ən/ (US) /ˈspoʊks-/ **noun** [C] a female spokesperson: *a spokeswoman **for** the environmental group Greenpeace*

spondulicks (also **spondulix**) /spɒnˈduː.lɪks/ (US) /spɑːn-/ **noun** [plural] old-fashioned informal humorous for money

sponge /spʌndʒ/ **noun; verb**
▸**noun SUBSTANCE** ▷ **1** [C] a soft substance that is full of small holes and can absorb a lot of liquid, and is used for washing and cleaning **2** [S] the action of rubbing something or someone with a wet sponge or cloth in order to clean them: *Give it **a** sponge **with** a damp cloth – that will remove the blood stains.* **CAKE** ▷ **3** [C or U] (also **sponge cake**) a soft cake made with eggs, sugar, and flour but usually no fat
▸**verb GET MONEY** ▷ **1** [I or T] disapproving to get money, food, etc. from other people, especially in order to live without working: *sponging **off** the state* **CLEAN** ▷ **2** [T] (also **sponge down**) to rub something or someone with a wet sponge or cloth, especially to clean them: *Most food stains will come off if you sponge the material with a little detergent. ∘ The doctor told me to sponge Erik down with cold water in order to lower his temperature.*

ˈsponge ˌbag noun [C] UK a small WATERPROOF bag used for carrying your TOOTHBRUSH, FACECLOTH, soap, etc. when you are travelling

sponger /ˈspʌn.dʒəʳ/ (US) /-dʒɚ/ **noun** [C] disapproving a person who gets money, food, etc. from other people, especially in order to live without working

ˌsponge ˈrubber noun [U] US for **foam rubber**

spongy /ˈspʌn.dʒi/ **adj** soft and able to absorb or having already absorbed a lot of liquid, like a sponge

sponsor /ˈspɒn.səʳ/ (US) /ˈspɑːn.sɚ/ **verb** [T] (B2) to support a person, organization, or activity by giving money, encouragement, or other help: *The team is sponsored by JVC, so the players wear the letters JVC on their shirts. ∘ Eva said she was doing a ten-mile walk for charity and asked if I'd sponsor her **for** £1 a mile.* • **sponsor noun** [C] (B2) *All the major theatres now have sponsors, especially **for** high-cost productions.* • **sponsorship** /-ʃɪp/ **noun** [U] (C1) *The orchestra receives £2 million a year **in** sponsorship from companies.*

spontaneous /spɒnˈteɪ.ni.əs/ (US) /spɑːn-/ **adj** happening or done in a natural, often sudden way, without any planning or without being forced: *His jokes seemed spontaneous, but were in fact carefully prepared beforehand. ∘* approving *She's such a spontaneous, lively woman.* • **spontaneity** /ˌspɒn.təˈneɪ.ɪ.ti/ (US) /ˌspɑːn.təˈneɪ.ə.ţi/ **noun** [U] approving *The script has a refreshing spontaneity and sparkle.* • **spontaneously** /-li/ **adv** *The liquid spontaneously ignited.*

sponˌtaneous comˈbustion noun [U] a situation in which something suddenly starts to burn without any obvious cause

spoof /spuːf/ **noun; verb**
▸**noun** [C] a funny and silly piece of writing, music, theatre, etc. that copies the style of an original work: *They did a spoof **on/of** the Nine O'Clock News. ∘ It was a spoof cowboy film.*
▸**verb** [I or T] US informal to try to make someone believe in something that is not true, as a joke

spook /spuːk/ **noun; verb**
▸**noun** [C] **SPIRIT** ▷ **1** informal for **ghost PERSON** ▷ **2** US for **spy**
▸**verb** [T] to frighten a person or animal: *Seeing the police car outside the house really spooked them.*

spooky /ˈspuː.ki/ **adj** informal strange and frightening: *It was a spooky coincidence.*

spool /spuːl/ **noun** [C] a tube-shaped object with top and bottom edges that stick out and around which a length of thread, wire, film, etc. is wrapped in order to store it: *a spool **of** cotton/film*

spoon /spuːn/ **noun; verb**
▸**noun** [C] **1** (A2) an object consisting of a round, hollow part and a handle, used for mixing, serving, and eating food **2** (used as a combining form): *a soup spoon ∘ a teaspoon* **3** (also **spoonful**) an amount held in a particular spoon: *a couple of spoons **of** sauce*
▸**verb** [T + adv/prep] to move something, especially food, using a spoon: *He spooned the mush **into** the baby's open mouth. ∘ Spoon a little sauce **over** the fish.*

spoonerism /ˈspuː.nᵊr.ɪ.zᵊm/ (US) /-nɚ-/ **noun** [C] a mistake made when speaking in which the first sounds of two words are exchanged with each other to produce a not intended and usually funny meaning: *The Reverend William Spooner used to produce spoonerisms such as 'a scoop of boy trouts', instead of what he had meant to say – 'a troop of boy scouts'.*

ˈspoon-feed verb [T] **FEED** ▷ **1** to feed a baby or other person using a spoon **PROVIDE INFORMATION** ▷ **2** disapproving to give someone so much help or information that they do not need to try themselves: *By giving out printed sheets of facts and theories, the teachers spoon-fed us **with** what we needed for the exam.*

spoonful /ˈspuːn.fʊl/ **noun** [C] (plural **spoonfuls** or **spoonsful**) an amount held in a particular spoon: *a spoonful of mustard*

spoor /spɔːʳ/ (US) /spʊr/ **noun** [S] specialized the marks left by a wild animal as it travels

sporadic /spəˈræd.ɪk/ adj happening sometimes; not regular or continuous: *sporadic gunfire* ◦ *a sporadic electricity supply* ◦ *More than 100 people have been killed this year in sporadic outbursts of ethnic violence.* → Synonym **occasional** • **sporadically** /-ɪ.kəl.i/ adv

spore /spɔːr/ (US) /spɔːr/ noun [C] a REPRODUCTIVE cell produced by some plants and simple organisms such as FERNS and MUSHROOMS

sporran /ˈspɒr.ən/ (US) /ˈspɔːr.ən/ noun [C] a small bag, usually made of fur, worn in front of the KILT (= a type of skirt) by a person wearing traditional Scottish clothes

sport /spɔːt/ (US) /spɔːrt/ noun; verb

▸noun **GAME** ▷ **1** A1 [C] a game, competition, or activity needing physical effort and skill that is played or done according to rules, for enjoyment and/or as a job: *Football, cricket, and hockey are all team sports.* ◦ *I enjoy winter sports like skiing and skating.* **2** A1 [U] UK all types of physical activity which people do to keep healthy or for enjoyment: *She used to **do/play** a lot of sport when she was younger.* **3** [U] old-fashioned enjoyment in doing things

> **!** Common mistake: **sport or sports**
>
> The correct word to use before a noun to refer to something relating to sport is **sports**.
>
> Before another noun, don't say 'sport', say **sports**:
>
> *A new sports centre is being built near our office.*

PERSON ▷ **4** [C] old-fashioned informal a pleasant, positive, generous person who does not complain about things they are asked to do or about games that they lose: *Oh, Douglas – be a (**good**) sport and give me a lift to the station.* → See also **spoilsport** **5** [C] Australian English a friendly way of talking to a man or boy: [as form of address] *Hello sport – how are you?*

> Word partners for **sport**
>
> *do/play* a sport • a *spectator/team* sport • *winter* sports

▸verb [T] to wear or be decorated with something: *Back in the 1960s he sported platform heels and hair down past his shoulders.* ◦ *The front of the car sported a German flag.*

sporting /ˈspɔː.tɪŋ/ (US) /ˈspɔːr.t̬ɪŋ/ adj **1** relating to sports: *The Olympics is the biggest sporting **event** in the world.* **2** old-fashioned showing fairness and respect towards an opposing team or player

S

ˌsporting ˈchance noun [S] If there is a sporting chance that something good will happen, it is possible that it will happen: *It's not definite that they'll accept our offer, but there's a sporting chance.*

sports /spɔːts/ (US) /spɔːrts/ adj [before noun] B1 relating to sport: *sports equipment.* ◦ *It's the school sports day on Monday.*

ˈsports ˌcar noun [C] a fast, low car, often for two people only

sportscaster /ˈspɔːtsˌkɑː.stər/ (US) /ˈspɔːrtsˌkæs.t̬ɚ/ noun [C] mainly US someone who appears on television or radio, giving information and news about sports events

ˈsports ˌcentre noun [C] UK (US **ˈsports ˌcenter**) A2 a building where you can play different sports

ˈsports ˌjacket noun [C] a man's jacket made of TWEED (= thick cloth made from wool)

sportsman /ˈspɔːts.mən/ (US) /ˈspɔːrts-/ noun [C] (plural **-men** /-mən/) **1** a man who plays sport, especially one who plays it well **2** someone who plays sport in a way that shows respect and fairness towards the opposing player or team: *He'll be remembered both as a brilliant footballer and as a true sportsman.*

sportsmanlike /ˈspɔːts.mən.laɪk/ (US) /ˈspɔːrts-/ adj behaving in a way that is fair and shows respect towards the other players when playing sport

sportsmanship /ˈspɔːts.mən.ʃɪp/ (US) /ˈspɔːrts-/ noun [U] behaviour in sport that is fair and shows respect to the other players

sportsperson /ˈspɔːtsˌpɜː.sən/ (US) /ˈspɔːrtsˌpɝː-/ noun [C] someone who plays sport, especially one who plays it well: *He was voted Sportsperson of the Year.*

sportswear /ˈspɔːts.weər/ (US) /ˈspɔːrts.wer/ noun [U] (used especially in shops) clothes that are worn for sports or other physical activities

sportswoman /ˈspɔːtsˌwʊm.ən/ (US) /ˈspɔːrts-/ noun [C] a woman who plays sport, especially one who plays it well: *a famous/keen/talented sportswoman*

sporty /ˈspɔː.ti/ (US) /ˈspɔːr.t̬i/ adj **FOR SPORT** ▷ **1** C1 describes someone who enjoys sport and is good at it: *Guy wasn't really the sporty type.* **2** describes clothes that are bright and informal, often looking like the type of clothes that you could wear for sports **FAST** ▷ **3** A sporty car is a fast, low car, often for two people only.

spot /spɒt/ (US) /spɑːt/ noun; verb

▸noun [C] **CIRCLE** ▷ **1** B1 a small, usually round area of colour that is differently coloured or lighter or darker than the surface around it: *He had a spot of grease on his tie.* **2** B1 one of many spots, that form a pattern: *I wore that skirt with the green spots.* **3** B2 UK a raised, pale red circle on the skin that is temporary: *Teenagers often suffer a lot from spots.* **4** mainly UK a small amount: *I felt a few spots of rain.* ◦ *Shall we stop for a spot of lunch?* ◦ *I'm having a spot of **bother** (= some trouble) with one of my back teeth.* **PLACE** ▷ **5** B2 a particular place: *This looks like a nice spot for a picnic.* **6 on the spot a** at the place where an event is happening or has recently happened: *The police were called and they were on the spot within three minutes.* **b** C2 immediately: *You can be sacked on the spot for stealing.* **PART OF A SHOW** ▷ **7** a short length of time in a show that is given to a particular performer: *She's doing a regular five-minute spot on his show.*

IDIOM **put sb on the spot** C2 If you put someone on the spot, you cause them embarrassment or difficulty by forcing them at that moment to answer a difficult question or make an important decision.

▸verb (-tt-) **SEE** ▷ **1** B2 [T] to see or notice someone or something, usually because you are looking hard: *I've just spotted Malcolm – he's over there, near the entrance.* ◦ *If you spot any mistakes in the article just mark them with a pencil.* ◦ [+ -ing verb] *The police spotted him driv**ing** a stolen car.* ◦ [+ question word] *I soon spotted **wh**at was wrong with the printer.* ◦ [+ that] *The policewoman spotted **that** I hadn't got my seat belt on and signalled me to stop.* **2 well spotted** UK used to praise someone who has noticed something: *'I've just seen your glasses – they're under the table.' 'Ah, well spotted!'* **RAIN** ▷ **3** [I] UK If someone says it's spotting (with rain), they mean that a few drops of rain are falling.

ˌspot ˈcheck noun [C] a quick examination of a few members of a group instead of the whole group: *The police are doing spot checks **on** motorists to test alcohol levels.*

ˈspot ˌfine noun [C] a FINE (= money you have to pay as a punishment) that is given to you at the time of breaking the law

spotless /ˈspɒt.ləs/ (US) /ˈspɑːt-/ adj **CLEAN** ▷ **1** C2 extremely clean: *Her home is spotless.* **GOOD** ▷ **2** spot-

less character, record, reputation, etc. a very good and honest character, etc.: *She was young and pretty, with a spotless reputation.* • **spotlessly** /-li/ **adv** *The kitchen is spotlessly* ***clean***.

spotlight /ˈspɒt.laɪt/ Ⓤⓢ /ˈspɑːt-/ **noun; verb**

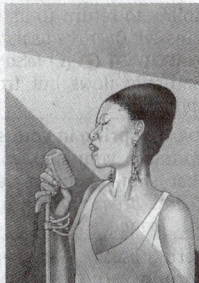

spotlight

▸**noun** [C] **1** C2 (UK informal **spot**) a LAMP whose beam can be directed, or a circle of light produced by such a lamp **2 in the spotlight** C2 (of a person) receiving a lot of public attention

▸**verb** [T] (**spotlighted** or **spotlit**, **spotlighted** or **spotlit**) **1** to light something or someone with a spotlight: *The paintings in the alcove were spotlit from below.* **2** If something spotlights a particular situation, it directs public attention to it.

ˌspot ˈon **adj** [after verb] UK informal exactly right: *'How old do I reckon she is? I'd say 38.' 'Spot on.'*

spotted /ˈspɒt.ɪd/ Ⓤⓢ /ˈspɑː.t̬ɪd/ **adj** covered in small, usually round areas of colour: *a spotted toad* ◦ *She was wearing a black and white spotted dress.*

ˌspotted ˈdick **noun** [C or U] UK a hot, sweet dish, consisting of cake and dried fruit

-spotter /-spɒt.əʳ/ Ⓤⓢ /-spɑː.t̬ɚ/ **suffix** describes a person whose job or interest is to notice people or things of the type mentioned: *a talent-spotter* ◦ UK *a train-spotter* • **-spotting** /-spɒt.ɪŋ/ Ⓤⓢ /-spɑː.t̬ɪŋ/ **suffix** *talent-spotting*

spotty /ˈspɒt.i/ Ⓤⓢ /ˈspɑː.t̬i/ **adj** **SKIN** ▷ **1** UK describes a person with spots on their skin: *I knew him when he was just a spotty youth.* **NOT ALWAYS GOOD** ▷ **2** US (UK **patchy**) bad in some parts: *She has a fairly spotty work record.* ◦ *Sales have picked up a little but they're still spotty.*

ˈspot-ˌwelding **noun** [U] a way of joining together two pieces of wire or two flat pieces of metal by sending an electric current through small areas of them

spousal /ˈspaʊ.zəl/ **adj** [before noun] formal done by a person's husband or wife, or relating to husbands and wives: *spousal abuse* ◦ *a spousal relationship*

spouse /spaʊs/ **noun** [C] formal or legal C2 a person's husband or wife: *In 60 percent of the households surveyed both spouses went out to work.*

spout /spaʊt/ **verb; noun**

▸**verb** **SPEAK** ▷ **1** [T, I + adv/prep] disapproving to speak a lot, in a way that is boring or annoying for other people: *He spouts a load of pretentious nonsense and people are stupid enough to believe him!* ◦ *I really don't want to listen to Mike spouting* ***on/off*** *all afternoon.* **FLOW** ▷ **2** [I + adv/prep, T] to flow or send out liquid or flames quickly and with force, in a straight line: *Flames spouted* (***out***) *from the oil wells.* ◦ *The gash was spouting blood.*

▸**noun** [C] **OPENING** ▷ **1** a tube-shaped opening which allows liquids to be poured out of a container **FLOW** ▷ **2** a stream of liquid coming out of something with some force: *A spout of water shot out of the geyser.*

IDIOMS **be up the spout** UK slang to be pregnant • **up the spout** UK slang wasted or spoiled: *Peter lost his job so that was our holiday plans up the spout.*

sprain /spreɪn/ **verb** [T] to cause an injury to a JOINT (= a place where two bones are connected) by a sudden movement: *She sprained her ankle playing squash.* • **sprain noun** [C] *He hasn't broken anything – it's just a bad sprain.*

sprang /spræŋ/ **verb** past simple of **spring**

sprat /spræt/ **noun** [C] a small sea fish that can be eaten

sprawl /sprɔːl/ Ⓤⓢ /sprɑːl/ **verb; noun**

▸**verb** disapproving **BODY** ▷ **1** [I] to spread the arms and legs out carelessly and untidily while sitting or lying down: *I knocked into her in the corridor and* ***sent*** *her sprawling (= knocked her over).* **CITY** ▷ **2** [I usually + adv/prep] (especially of a city) to cover a large area of land with buildings that have been added at different times so that it looks untidy: *The refugee camps sprawl across the landscape.* • **sprawled** /sprɔːld/ Ⓤⓢ /sprɑːld/ **adj** [after verb] *He was sprawled* (***out***) ***on*** *the floor.* • **sprawling** /ˈsprɔː.lɪŋ/ Ⓤⓢ /ˈsprɑː-/ **adj** *sprawling suburbs*

▸**noun** disapproving **BODY** ▷ **1** [U] a position with the arms and legs spread out carelessly and untidily while sitting or lying down **CITY** ▷ **2** [C usually singular] a large area of land covered with buildings that have been added at different times so that it looks untidy: *the* ***urban*** *sprawl of South Florida*

spray /spreɪ/ **noun; verb**

▸**noun** **LIQUID** ▷ **1** [U] a mass of very small drops of liquid carried in the air: *Can you feel the spray from the sea/waterfall?* **2** B2 [C] a liquid that is forced out of a special container under pressure so that it becomes a mass of small liquid drops like a cloud: *a quick spray of perfume/polish* **3** B2 [C] a mass of small drops of liquid spread onto plants and crops, etc. from a special piece of equipment, or the piece of equipment itself: *Farmers use a lot of* ***chemical*** *sprays on crops.* **FLOWERS** ▷ **4** [C] a single small branch or stem with leaves and flowers on it: *All the wedding guests wore sprays of carnations.*

▸**verb** [I or T, usually + adv/prep] B2 to spread liquid in small drops over an area: *She sprayed her****self with*** *perfume.* ◦ *Vandals had sprayed graffiti on the wall.* ◦ *The pipe burst and water was spraying everywhere.* ◦ figurative *Rush hour commuters were sprayed* ***with bullets*** *by a gunman in a car.*

sprayer /ˈspreɪ.əʳ/ Ⓤⓢ /-ɚ/ **noun** [C] a device for spraying liquid, especially chemicals used in the garden

ˈspray ˌgun **noun** [C] a device that is held in the hand and used for spraying liquid such as paint in very small drops

ˈspray ˌtan **noun** [C or U] a type of FAKE TAN (= substance to make skin look darker) that is sprayed onto someone's skin, usually using a special machine: *She's gone to the salon for a spray tan.*

spread /spred/ **verb; noun**

▸**verb** [I or T] (**spread**) B2 to (cause to) cover, reach, or have an effect on a wider or increasing area: *The fire spread very rapidly because of the strong wind.* ◦ *It started off as cancer of the liver but it spread* ***to*** *other areas of the body.* ◦ *The redundancies are spread* ***across*** *the banking and building industries.* ◦ *We spread the picnic rug* ***out*** *on the ground and sat down to eat.* ◦ *The virus is spread (= given to other people) through contact with blood and other body fluids.* ◦ *Are you spreading (= telling a lot of people)* ***gossip/rumours*** *again?* ◦ *If we spread (= divide) the work between us, it won't seem so bad.* ◦ *She spread her toast* ***with*** *a thick layer of butter./She spread a thick layer of butter* ***on*** *her toast.* ◦ *It's a special sort of butter that spreads easily even when cold.* ◦ *The suburbs spread* (***out***) *for miles to either side of the city.* ◦ *Slowly a smile spread across her face.*

S

IDIOMS **spread your wings** to use your abilities for the first time in your life to do new and exciting things: *She'd been working for the same company for 15 years and it was time to leave and spread her wings.* • **spread the word** to communicate a message to a lot of people: *We've arranged a meeting for next Thursday so if you see anyone do spread the word.* • **spread yourself too thin** to try to do too many things at the same time, so that you cannot give enough time or attention to any of them: *I realized I'd been spreading myself too thin so I resigned as secretary of the golf club.*

PHRASAL VERBS **spread out** B2 If people spread out, they move from being close together in a group to being in different places across a larger area: *They spread out to search the whole area.* • **spread sth over sth** C2 to arrange for something to happen in stages during a period of time: *The course is spread over two years.* ◦ *The repayments on the loan can be spread **out** over three years.*

▸noun **AREA COVERED** ▷ **1** B2 [S] the development or growth of something so that it covers a larger area or affects a larger number of people: *The spread of the disease in the last few years has been alarming.* **2** [S] the area or range covered by something: *The survey found **a** wide spread of opinion over the proposed new building.* **3** [C] a large article or advertisement covering one or more pages in a newspaper or magazine: *There's a double-page spread on the latest fashions.* **SOFT FOOD** ▷ **4** [C or U] a soft food for putting on bread and biscuits: *cheese/chocolate/fish spread* **LAND** ▷ **5** [C] US for **ranch** **MEAL** ▷ **6** [C] UK old-fashioned or US a meal, especially one for a special occasion with a lot of different dishes arranged on a table: *Sheila **laid on** (= made) a lovely spread for us.* **DIFFERENCE** ▷ **7** [C] the difference between two amounts, such as two prices or interest rates: *The issue was priced at a spread of 115 basis points above Treasury bonds.*

ˌspread ˈbetting noun [U] **1** a form of GAMBLING in which you try to win money by saying what the result of events such as sports games will be **2** specialized the activity of risking money on changes in the price of company SHARES, without buying the shares themselves

spreadeagled /ˌspredˈiː.ɡl̩d/ adj [usually after verb] describes someone who is lying with their arms and legs stretched out: *William was lying spreadeagled on the grass, blind drunk.*

S

spreadsheet /ˈspred.ʃiːt/ noun [C] B2 a computer program, used especially in business, which allows you to do financial calculations and plans

spree /spriː/ noun [C] a short period of doing a particular, usually enjoyable, activity much more than is usual: *I **went on** a drinking/shopping/spending spree on Saturday.* ◦ *20 people were shot dead in the city, making it the worst killing spree since the riots.*

sprig /sprɪɡ/ noun [C] a single small plant stem with leaves on it: *Garnish the dish with sprigs of parsley.*

sprightly /ˈspraɪt.li/ adj (especially of old people) energetic and in good health: *He's a sprightly old man of 75.* • **sprightliness** /-nəs/ noun [U]

spring /sprɪŋ/ noun; verb

▸noun **SEASON** ▷ **1** A2 [C or U] the season of the year between winter and summer, lasting from March to June north of the EQUATOR, and from September to December south of the equator, when the weather becomes warmer, leaves and plants start to grow again and flowers appear: *Many bulbs bloom **in** (**the**) spring.* ◦ *Janet's coming over for a couple of weeks **next** spring.* ◦ *It's been a very wet spring.* ◦ *a spring day/morning* ◦ *spring flowers/weather* **CURVED METAL** ▷ **2** [C] a piece of curved or bent metal that can be pressed into a smaller space but then returns to its usual shape: *The children have jumped on the couch so much that they've ruined the springs.* **3** [U] something's ability to return to its usual shape after it has been pressed: *Over the years the mattress has lost its spring.* **WATER** ▷ **4** C1 [C] (also **springs**) a place where water naturally flows out from the ground: *bubbling/hot springs*

IDIOM **a spring in your step** If you walk with or have a spring in your step, you walk energetically in a way that shows you are feeling happy and confident: *There's been a definite spring in his step ever since he met Joanna.*

▸verb [I usually + adv/prep] (**sprang** or US also **sprung**, **sprung**) **MOVE QUICKLY** ▷ **1** C2 to move quickly and suddenly towards a particular place: *I sprang out of bed to answer the door.* ◦ *The organization is ready to spring **into action** (= start taking action) the moment it receives its funding.* ◦ *He always springs **to** his **feet** when she walks in the room.* ◦ figurative *I noticed the way you sprang **to** his **defence** when Caroline started joking about his clothes.* ◦ *The lid of the box sprang shut.* **APPEAR SUDDENLY** ▷ **2** C2 to appear or start to exist suddenly: *Thousands of new businesses have sprung **up** in the past couple of years.* ◦ informal *'Where did you spring **from**? – I didn't see you come in!'*

IDIOMS **spring to life** to suddenly become very active or busy: *After about eight o'clock the city springs to life.* • **spring to mind** C2 to come quickly into your mind: *Say the word 'Australia' and a vision of beaches and blue seas immediately springs to mind.*

PHRASAL VERBS **spring from sth** C2 to come from or be a result of something: *His need to be liked obviously springs from a deep-rooted insecurity.* • **spring sth on sb** to suddenly tell or ask someone something when they do not expect it: *I hope he's not going to spring any nasty surprises on us at the meeting this morning.*

springboard /ˈsprɪŋ.bɔːd/ US /-bɔːrd/ noun [C] **SPORT** ▷ **1** a board that can bend which helps you to jump higher when jumping or DIVING into a swimming pool or when doing GYMNASTICS **GOOD START** ▷ **2** something which provides you either with the opportunity to follow a particular plan of action, or the encouragement that is needed to make it successful: *The firm's director is confident that the new project will act as a springboard **for/to** further contracts.*

springbok /ˈsprɪŋ.bɒk/ US /-bɑːk/ noun [C] (plural **springboks** or **springbok**) an animal that lives in southern Africa that is reddish-brown with a white back end, has HOOFS, and can jump very high

ˌspring ˈchicken noun humorous **be no spring chicken** to be no longer young

ˌspring-ˈclean verb [T] to clean all of a place, especially your house, very well, including parts you do not often clean • **ˌspring-ˈclean** noun [S] UK *I gave the kitchen a spring-clean at the weekend.* • **ˌspring-ˈcleaning** noun [U] *to do some spring-cleaning*

springform tin /ˌsprɪŋ.fɔːmˈtɪn/ US /-fɔːrmˈ-/ noun [C] UK (US **ˌspringform ˈpan**) a type of TIN for baking cakes that has sides that can be removed from the base

ˌspring ˈgreens noun [plural] UK the leaves of young CABBAGE plants, eaten as vegetables

ˌspring ˈonion noun [C] UK (US **ˌgreen ˈonion**) a long, thin, green and white onion that is often eaten uncooked

spring 'roll noun [C] (UK also **pancake 'roll**, US also **egg 'roll**) a SAVOURY Chinese PANCAKE that is rolled up, filled with small pieces of vegetables and sometimes meat, and fried

springtime /'sprɪŋ.taɪm/ **noun** [U] the season of spring: ***In (the)*** *springtime the woods are full of bluebells.*

springy /'sprɪŋ.i/ **adj** returning quickly to the usual shape, after being pulled, pushed, crushed, etc.: *The turf feels very springy underfoot.*

sprinkle /'sprɪŋ.kl̩/ verb; **sprinkle** noun

▸verb [T] ⓑ to drop a few pieces or drops of something over a surface: *Sprinkle a few herbs* ***on*** *the pizza./Sprinkle the pizza* ***with*** *a few herbs.* ◦ figurative *The speech was liberally sprinkled with (= contained many) jokes about the incident.*

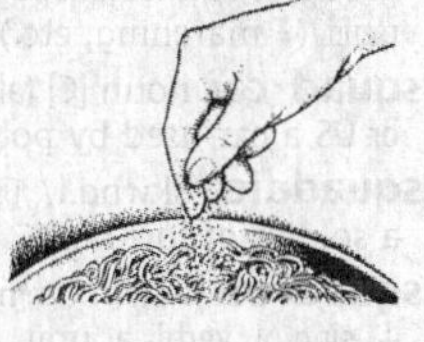

▸noun [C usually singular] (US also **sprinkling**) a very light fall of rain or snow which lasts only a short time

sprinkler /'sprɪŋ.kl̩.əʳ/ ⓤⓢ /-ɚ/ noun [C] **1** a piece of equipment for putting water onto fires in a lot of small drops to put them out **2** a device with a lot of small holes which you put on the end of a HOSE in order to water plants, grass, etc.

sprinkling /'sprɪŋ.kl̩.ɪŋ/ noun [C usually singular] small pieces or drops of something that are dropped over a surface: *Top each bowl with* ***a*** *generous sprinkling* ***of*** *fresh mint.* ◦ figurative *The audience were mainly women with* ***a*** *sprinkling (= a small number)* ***of*** *earnest-looking men.* ◦ figurative *Looking young for his 40 years, he has just* ***a*** *sprinkling (= a small number)* ***of*** *grey hairs at the temples.*

sprint /sprɪnt/ verb; noun

▸verb [I] to run as fast as you can over a short distance, either in a race or because you are in a great hurry to get somewhere: *We had to sprint to catch the bus.* • **sprinter** /'sprɪn.təʳ/ ⓤⓢ /-t̬ɚ/ **noun** [C] *a world-class sprinter*

▸noun **1** [C] a short and very fast race, such as the 100 metres, or the last part of a longer race that is run as fast as possible: *the 100-metre sprint* **2** [S] a very fast run that someone makes when they are in a great hurry to get somewhere: *He suddenly* ***broke into*** *(= started) a sprint.*

sprite /spraɪt/ noun [C] literary a FAIRY (= a small imaginary person with wings) especially one connected with water: *a sea/water sprite*

spritz /sprɪts/ verb [I] US to SPRAY a mass of very small drops of liquid out of a container, usually by pressing a part of the container: *After you've applied your powder, spritz with a little mineral water.* • **spritz noun** [C] *A quick spritz of scent and I'm ready.*

spritzer /'sprɪt.səʳ/ ⓤⓢ /-sɚ/ **noun** [C] a drink made with white wine and usually SODA WATER (= water with bubbles)

spritzig /'sprɪt.sɪg/ **adj** mainly Australian English describes wine that is slightly FIZZY (= with bubbles)

sprocket (wheel) /'sprɒk.ɪt.wiːl/ ⓤⓢ /'sprɑː.kɪt-/ noun [C] specialized a device like a wheel with one or more rows of tooth-like parts sticking out which keeps a chain moving on a bicycle or pulls film, paper, etc. through a machine

sprog /sprɒg/ ⓤⓢ /sprɑːg/ **noun; verb**

▸noun [C] UK slang a baby or young child: *She's got a couple of sprogs now.*

▸verb [I] (-gg-) UK slang to have a baby: *Has she sprogged yet?*

sprout /spraʊt/ verb; noun

▸verb **1** [I or T] to produce leaves, hair, or other new developing parts, or (of leaves, hair, and other developing parts) to begin to grow: *It takes about three days for the seeds to sprout.* ◦ *Your hair is sticking up – it looks like you're sprouting horns!* **2** [I] (also **sprout up**) If a large number of things sprout (up), they suddenly appear or begin to exist: *New factories have sprouted up everywhere.*

▸noun [C] **1** a part of a plant that is just beginning to grow **2** mainly UK a **Brussels sprout**

spruce /spruːs/ noun; adj; verb

▸noun [C or U] an EVERGREEN tree (= one that never loses its leaves) with leaves like needles, or the pale-coloured wood from this tree

▸adj approving (of a person) tidy and clean in appearance: *He looked spruce and handsome in a clean white shirt.*

▸verb

PHRASAL VERB **spruce sb/sth up** informal to make someone or something cleaner and tidier or to improve the way they appear generally: *I thought I'd have a shave and generally spruce my****self*** *up for the interview.* ◦ *They've employed an advertising agency to spruce up the company image.*

sprung /sprʌŋ/ verb; adj

▸verb past participle of **spring**

▸adj UK (US **spring**) (of furniture) using SPRINGS (= curved pieces of metal) to give support

spry /spraɪ/ **adj** (especially of older people) active and able to move quickly and energetically: *He was amazingly spry for a man of almost 80.*

spud /spʌd/ noun [C] informal a potato

spun /spʌn/ **verb** past simple and past participle of **spin**

spunk /spʌŋk/ noun **COURAGE** ▷ **1** [U] old-fashioned informal courage and determination **SEXUAL LIQUID** ▷ **2** [U] offensive SEMEN (= liquid sent out through the PENIS during sexual activity) **ATTRACTIVE MAN** ▷ **3** [C] mainly Australian English informal a sexually attractive man

spunky /'spʌŋ.ki/ **adj BRAVE** ▷ **1** old-fashioned informal brave and determined **ATTRACTIVE** ▷ **2** Australian English informal describes a man who is sexually attractive

spur /spɜːʳ/ ⓤⓢ /spɝː/ verb; noun

▸verb [T] (-rr-) **ENCOURAGE** ▷ **1** ⓒ to encourage an activity or development or make it happen faster: *Rising consumer sales have the effect of spurring the economy* ***to*** *faster growth.* ◦ *Spurred* ***(on)*** *by her early success, she went on to write four more novels in rapid succession.* **SHARP OBJECT** ▷ **2** to push spurs into the side of a horse to make it go faster: *He spurred his horse* ***on*** *and shouted 'Faster! Faster!'*

▸noun [C] **SHARP OBJECT** ▷ **1** a sharp, wheel-shaped metal object that is fixed to the HEEL of boots worn by people riding horses and is used to encourage the horse to go faster **MOUNTAIN** ▷ **2** a high piece of land that sticks out from a mountain or a group of mountains **ENCOURAGEMENT** ▷ **3** something that acts as an encouragement for an activity or development: *The manager said that the team's win on Saturday would be a spur* ***to*** *even greater effort this season.*

IDIOMS **on the spur of the moment** informal ⓒ describes a decision, action, etc. that is sudden and done without any planning: *We just jumped in a car on the spur of the moment and drove to the seaside.* • **win/**

S

gain your spurs to achieve something that proves that you are skilled in a particular type of activity and to therefore win the respect of other people: *He won his political spurs fighting hospital closures during his time as a local councillor in Bristol.*

spurious /ˈspjʊə.ri.əs/ (US) /ˈspjʊr.i-/ **adj** false and not what it appears to be, or (of reasons and judgments) based on something that has not been correctly understood and therefore false

spurn /spɜːn/ (US) /spɝːn/ **verb** [T] formal to refuse to accept something or someone because you feel that they are not worth having: *She spurned my offers of help.* ◦ *Ellis plays the part of the young lover spurned by his mistress.*

spurt /spɜːt/ (US) /spɝːt/ **verb; noun**

▸**verb** [I or T] **LIQUID** ▷ **1** to (cause to) flow out suddenly and with force, in a fast stream: *Blood was spurting out all over the place.* ◦ *His arm was spurting blood where the vein had been severed.* **INCREASE** ▷ **2** mainly US to increase or grow very quickly, or to suddenly increase by a particular amount: *Shares of the jewellery store chain spurted $6.*

▸**noun** [C] **INCREASE** ▷ **1** a sudden and short period of increased activity, effort, or speed: *There was a sudden spurt **of** activity in the housing market.* ◦ *He tends to work **in** spurts.* **LIQUID** ▷ **2** a sudden fast stream of liquid: *The water came out **in** spurts.*

sputter /ˈspʌt.əʳ/ (US) /ˈspʌt̬.ɚ/ **verb** **SOUND** ▷ **1** [I or T] to make several quick explosive sounds: *The car sputtered once or twice and then stopped.* **ACTIVITY** ▷ **2** [I] literary If an activity sputters, it is weak and varied, and does not make people feel confident about it: *Russia's presidential campaign sputtered to an uneasy close on Monday.* • **sputter** noun [C] *The engine wouldn't start – it **gave** one or two sputters but that was all.*

sputum /ˈspjuː.təm/ (US) /-t̬əm/ **noun** [U] specialized liquid from the passages in your body which go to the lungs → Compare **phlegm**

spy /spaɪ/ **noun; verb**

▸**noun** [C] (B1) a person who secretly collects and reports information about the activities of another country or organization

▸**verb** **FIND SECRETS** ▷ **1** (C1) [I] to secretly collect and report information about the activities of another country or organization: *He was arrested for spying **on** missile sites.* **2 spy out** informal to get knowledge secretly, especially of a place: *I generally like to spy out restaurants before I go to eat in them.* **SEE** ▷ **3** [T] old-fashioned or humorous to see or notice someone or something usually when it involves looking hard: *I think I've just spied Andrew in the crowd.*

IDIOM **spy out the land** If you spy out the land, you try to get knowledge of something before you do something: *We drove around the area where our new house is to spy out the land.*

PHRASAL VERB **spy on sb/sth** (C2) to watch someone or something secretly, often in order to discover information about them: *He was spying on her through the keyhole.*

spyhole /ˈspaɪ.həʊl/ (US) /-hoʊl/ **noun** [C] UK a **peephole**

spyware /ˈspaɪ.weəʳ/ (US) /-wer/ **noun** [U] software that collects information about how someone uses the internet, or personal information such as PASSWORDS, without the user knowing about it

sq. adj [before noun] written abbreviation for **square**, in measurements of length

S

squabble /ˈskwɒb.l̩/ (US) /ˈskwɑː.bl̩/ **noun** [C] an argument over something that is not important: *Polly and Susie were **having** a squabble about who was going to hold the dog's lead.* • **squabble** verb [I]

squad /skwɒd/ (US) /skwɑːd/ **noun** [C, + sing/pl verb] **1** (C2) a small group of people trained to work together as a unit: *An army **bomb** squad arrived and defused the bomb.* ◦ *the seizure of a large amount of heroin by the **drug** squad* ◦ *The company was under investigation by the **fraud** squad.* **2** (C2) a team in sports from which the players for a match are chosen: *Eight of their 24-man squad are injured.* **3** In the army, a squad is a small group of soldiers, especially one brought together for DRILL (= marching, etc.).

ˈsquad ˌcar noun [C] (also paˈtrol ˌcar) UK old-fashioned or US a car used by police officers

squaddie /ˈskwɒd.i/ (US) /ˈskwɑː.di/ **noun** [C] UK slang a soldier of low rank

squadron /ˈskwɒd.rᵊn/ (US) /ˈskwɑː.drən/ **noun** [C, + sing/pl verb] a unit of one of the armed forces, especially (in Britain) the air force or the navy

ˈsquadron ˌleader noun [C] an officer in the air force of the UK and some other countries

squalid /ˈskwɒl.ɪd/ (US) /ˈskwɑː.lɪd/ **adj** **DIRTY** ▷ **1** disapproving (of places) extremely dirty and unpleasant, often because of lack of money: *Many prisons, even today, are overcrowded and squalid places.* **IMMORAL** ▷ **2** (of situations and activities) not moral; involving sex and drugs, etc. in an unpleasant way: *It's the usual squalid rock star tale of drugs, sex, and overdoses.* • **squalor** /ˈskwɒl.əʳ/ (US) /ˈskwɑː.lɚ/ noun [U] *It was a dirty, damp, smelly flat – the usual student squalor.*

squall /skwɔːl/ (US) /skwɑːl/ **noun; verb**

▸**noun** [C] **STRONG WIND** ▷ **1** a sudden strong wind or short storm: *Violent squalls signalled the approach of the hurricane.* **SHOUT** ▷ **2** a loud, sharp noise • **squally** /ˈskwɔː.li/ (US) /ˈskwɑː-/ adj

▸**verb** [I] (especially of a baby) to make a loud, sharp noise

squander /ˈskwɒn.dəʳ/ (US) /ˈskwɑːn.dɚ/ **verb** [T] (C2) to waste money or supplies, or to waste opportunities by not using them to your advantage: *They'll quite happily squander a whole year's savings on two weeks in the sun.* ◦ *Ireland squandered several chances, including a penalty that cost them the game.*

square /skweəʳ/ (US) /skwer/ **noun; adj; verb**

▸**noun** [C] **SHAPE** ▷ **1** (A2) a flat shape with four sides of equal length and four angles of 90°: *First draw a square.* ◦ *It's a square-shaped room.* **2** (A2) any square-shaped object: *When cooled, cut the chocolate brownies into squares.* **3** (A2) an area of approximately square-shaped land in a city or a town, often including the buildings that surround it: *Are they still living at 6 Eaton Square?* ◦ *A band were playing **in** the town square.* **4** a particular space on a board used for playing games: *She moved her castle forward three squares.* **5** US a tool for drawing or testing a RIGHT ANGLE **BORING PERSON** ▷ **6** old-fashioned informal a boring person who does not like new and exciting ideas: *He's a bit of a square.* **MULTIPLY** ▷ **7** the result of multiplying a number by itself: *The square of 7 is 49.*

IDIOM **go/be back to square one** informal to be forced to think of a new course of action because your first course of action failed: *The deal with the house fell through so I'm afraid we're back to square one.*

▸**adj** **SHAPE** ▷ **1** (A2) having the shape of a square: *The recipe recommends that you use a square cake tin.* ◦ *He's got that square-jawed masculinity that a lot of women seem to find attractive.* **2** (written abbreviation

sq., specialized **2)** used with units of measurement of length to express the total size of an area: *The floor is 3 m wide by 5 m long, so its total area is 15 sq m.* ◦ *The city itself covers 13 square miles.* ◦ specialized *Ensure that the exposed area is less than 2 cm^2.* **3** Square is used immediately after measurements of length when expressing the length of the four sides of a square-shaped area: *So you want carpet for a room that's eight metres square (= eight metres long and eight metres wide).* **EQUAL** ▷ **4** informal equal or level: *Could you stand back from these shelves and tell me if they're square (= level)?* **5 (all) square** informal If two people are all square, one of them has paid off a debt to the other and neither now owes or is owed any money. **STRAIGHT** ▷ **6** in a straight line **BORING PERSON** ▷ **7** old-fashioned informal describes a person who is boring and does not like new and exciting things: *Do you think my new haircut makes me look a bit square?*

IDIOM **square peg (in a round hole)** informal a person whose character makes them unsuitable for the job or other position they are in: *He never quite fitted in when he was working here – he was always a bit of a square peg.*

▸verb **MULTIPLY** ▷ **1** [T] to multiply a number by itself: *10 squared equals a hundred.* ◦ *4^2 means four squared, and equals 16.* **SHAPE** ▷ **2 square your shoulders** to pull your shoulders up and back because you feel determined to do something: *He squared his shoulders and took a deep breath before diving into the pool.*

IDIOMS **square the accounts/books** to make certain that you have paid and received all the money that you owed or that others owed you • **square the circle** If you try to square the circle, you try to do something that is very difficult or impossible.

PHRASAL VERBS **square off** US to prepare to fight, compete, or argue with someone: *The two giants in the fast-food industry are squaring off this month with the most aggressive advertising campaigns yet.* • **square up FIGHT** ▷ **1** UK to prepare to fight, compete, or argue with someone: *The players squared up to each other and started shouting.* **PAY** ▷ **2** informal to pay someone the money that you owe them: *If you pay for both tickets now, I'll square up **with** you later.* • **square up to sb/sth** UK (US **face up to sb/sth**) to deal with a problem or difficult person bravely and with determination • **square (sth) with sth** to match or agree with something, or to think that one thing is acceptable together with another thing: *Her story doesn't quite square with the evidence.* ◦ *I don't think I could spend that much money on a jacket – I couldn't square it with my conscience (= I would feel too guilty).*

ˌsquare ˈbrackets noun [plural] the [ ] BRACKETS that are shaped like two halves of a square

squared /skweəd/ (US) /skwerd/ adj covered with squares: *Squared paper (= paper with squares printed on it) is better for drawing graphs on.*

ˈsquare ˌdance noun [C] in the US, a traditional dance in which four pairs of dancers dance together

ˌsquare ˈdeal noun [C] informal a fair agreement: *I reckon we got a square deal on that car.*

ˌsquare-ˈeyed adj UK informal If you say someone is or will go square-eyed, you mean they are watching too much television: *You'll **go** square-eyed if you sit in front of that TV any more!*

ˈsquare ˌknot noun [C] US for **reef knot**

squarely /ˈskweə.li/ (US) /ˈskwer/ adv **DIRECTLY** ▷ **1** (also **square**) directly and firmly: *She refused to come down squarely on either side of the argument.* ◦ *She punched him square on the jaw.* **STRAIGHT** ▷ **2** with weight equally balanced on each side, not to one side: *She stood squarely, with her feet apart.*

ˌsquare ˈmeal noun [C] a satisfying meal that fills you and provides you with all the different types of food that your body needs in order to stay healthy

the ˌSquare ˈMile noun UK used to refer to the City of London, the business and financial district of London: *The retail sector was the talk of the Square Mile yesterday.*

ˌsquare ˈroot noun [C] The square root of a particular number is the number that was multiplied by itself to reach that number: *The square root of 49 is 7.*

squash /skwɒʃ/ (US) /skwɑːʃ/ **verb; noun**

▸verb **MAKE FLAT** ▷ **1** (B2) [T] to crush something into a flat shape: *He accidentally sat on her hat and squashed it.* **PUSH** ▷ **2** (B2) [I or T, usually + adv/prep] to push yourself, a person, or thing into a small space: *The room was so full you couldn't squash another person **in**.* ◦ *If you all squashed **up** (= moved closer together), we could fit an extra person in the car.* ◦ *He tried to squash his ripped jeans **into** the suitcase while his mother wasn't looking.* **END** ▷ **3** [T] to stop something from continuing to exist or happen, by forceful action: ***Rumours** of a possible takeover of the company were soon squashed by the management.*

▸noun **PUSH** ▷ **1** [S] a situation when there is not much room: *There are over two hundred people coming to the party so it might be a bit of **a** squash.* **SPORT** ▷ **2** (B1) [U] a game played between two or four people on a special closed playing area that involves hitting a small rubber ball against a wall **DRINK** ▷ **3** [U] UK a drink made from fruit juice, water, and sugar or SWEETENER **VEGETABLE** ▷ **4** [C or U] mainly US a type of large vegetable with a hard skin and a lot of seeds at its centre that is very common in America

squashy /ˈskwɒʃ.i/ (US) /ˈskwɑː.ʃi/ adj soft and easy to crush: *I've bought some squashy pillows for the couch.*

squat /skwɒt/ (US) /skwɑːt/ **verb; adj; noun**

▸verb (-tt-) **SIT** ▷ **1** [I] to position yourself close to the ground balancing on the front part of your feet with your legs bent under your body: *She squatted on the ground and warmed her hands by the fire.* ◦ *He squatted **down** and examined the front wheel of his bike.* **LIVE** ▷ **2** [I or T] to live in an empty building or area of land without the permission of the owner: *They squatted (**in**) an old house in King's Cross when their money ran out.*

▸adj (**squatter**, **squattest**) short and wide, usually in a way that is not attractive: *a row of ugly, squat houses* ◦ *a heavily built, squat man*

▸noun **SITTING** ▷ **1** [C] a squatting position or exercise **PLACE TO LIVE** ▷ **2** [C] the place that you live in when you are squatting: *They're living in a damp squat with no electricity.* **ANYTHING** ▷ **3** [U] US slang anything: *She shouldn't talk – she doesn't know squat about it.* ◦ *His opinion isn't worth squat.*

squatter /ˈskwɒt.əʳ/ (US) /ˈskwɑː.t̬ɚ/ noun [C] **1** a person who lives in an empty building without permission **2** Australian English someone in the past who took land that did not officially belong to them in order to use it for farming

ˈsquat ˌthrust noun [C] a type of physical exercise in which your hands are kept on the floor while your legs move from a position in which they are bent under the body to one in which they are straight out behind you

squattocracy /ˌskwɒtˈɒk.rə.si/ (US) /ˌskwɑːˈt̬ɑː.krə-/ noun [C or U] Australian English the group of rich families who own large amounts of land

S

squaw /skwɔː/ (US) /skwɑː/ noun [C] old-fashioned a Native American woman, especially a wife. This word is now considered offensive by many people.

squawk /skwɔːk/ (US) /skwɑːk/ verb [I] **1** to make an unpleasantly loud, sharp cry: *As the fox came into the yard, the chickens began squawking in alarm.* **2** informal disapproving to complain about something noisily: *Environmental groups have been squawking **about** the decision to build the motorway through a forest.* • **squawk** noun [C]

squeak /skwiːk/ verb; noun
▸verb **SOUND** ▷ **1** (C2) [I] to make a short, very high cry or sound: *The mice in the cupboard squeaked.* ◦ *The door squeaked as it swung back and forth on its rusty hinges.* **SUCCEED** ▷ **2** [I + adv/prep] US to only just succeed in something such as a test or competition: *He squeaked **through** the exam.*
▸noun [C] a short, very high cry or sound: *She let out a squeak of fright at the sight of the spider.* ◦ *If I hear one more squeak out of you (= if you say anything else), there'll be trouble!*

squeaker /ˈskwiː.kəʳ/ (US) /-kɚ/ noun [C] US a competition or race which you only just win or lose: *The Buffalo Bills lost a squeaker to the Dallas Cowboys.*

squeaky /ˈskwiː.ki/ adj **SOUND** ▷ **1** (C2) making a very high sound **SUCCESS** ▷ **2** US only just succeeding in a game, competition, etc.: *The president had a squeaky six-vote win (= he won by only six votes) in Congress.*

ˌsqueaky-ˈclean adj informal **1** completely clean: *I love the squeaky-clean feel of my hair after I've washed it.* **2** Someone who is squeaky-clean is completely good and honest and never does anything bad: *Journalists have been trying to discover if the senator really is as squeaky-clean as he claims to be.*

squeal /skwiːl/ verb; noun
▸verb [I] **1** to make a long, very high sound or cry: *We could hear the piglets squealing as we entered the farmyard.* ◦ *The brakes squealed as the van rounded the corner.* ◦ *The two children squealed **with** joy.* **2** informal to complain about something loudly: *The threat of further changes in the education system is making teachers squeal.* **3** slang disapproving to give information to the police about people you know who have committed a crime: *When he finds out who squealed **on** him, he's going to make them very sorry.*
▸noun [C] a long, very high sound or cry: *Erik collapsed into giggles and squeals as Penny began tickling him.* ◦ *The train ground to a halt with a squeal **of brakes**.*

S

squeamish /ˈskwiː.mɪʃ/ adj easily upset or shocked by things which you find unpleasant or which you do not approve of: *She's really squeamish and can't stand the sight of blood.* ◦ *Many cooks are squeamish about putting live shellfish into boiling water.* • **squeamishness** /-nəs/ noun [U]

IDIOM **not for the squeamish** describes something that is unpleasant, and will upset people who are squeamish: *'The Silence of the Lambs' is an entertaining but violent movie and is not for the squeamish.*

squeamishly /ˈskwiː.mɪʃ.li/ adv in a way that shows how easily upset or shocked you are by something

squeegee /ˈskwiː.dʒiː/ noun [C] a tool with a rubber blade and a short handle that is used for removing water from a surface such as a window or mirror after it has been washed • **squeegee** verb [T]

squeeze /skwiːz/ verb; noun
▸verb **PRESS TOGETHER** ▷ **1** (B2) [T] to press something firmly, especially from all sides in order to change its shape, reduce its size, or remove liquid from it: *Cut the lemon in half and squeeze the juice into the bowl.* ◦ *As she waited to go into the exam, he squeezed her hand (= pressed it affectionately with his hand) and wished her good luck.* ◦ *Once he had finished cleaning the floor, he squeezed the cloth **out**.* ◦ *He reloaded the gun, took aim, and then squeezed (= pulled back) the **trigger**.* ◦ figurative *The studio is using all sorts of marketing tricks to squeeze as much profit **from** the movie as they can.* **2** [T] If you are squeezed by financial demands, they cause you financial problems: *Small businesses are being squeezed by heavy taxation.* **MOVE** ▷ **3** (C1) [I + adv/prep] to get in, through, under, etc. with difficulty: *She squeezed **through** the crowd and found a seat at the front.* ◦ *They managed to squeeze **under** the fence and get into the festival without paying.*

IDIOM **squeeze sb dry** If you squeeze someone dry, you get as much from them as possible: *When they got divorced, his wife squeezed him dry and took everything.*

PHRASAL VERBS **squeeze (sb/sth) in/squeeze (sb/sth) into sth** (B2) to succeed in getting someone or something into a small space or object, often by pushing or forcing: *The car's quite full, but we could manage to squeeze another couple of people in.* ◦ *I must have put on a lot of weight over Christmas because I can only just squeeze **into** my jeans.* • **squeeze sb/sth in** (C2) to manage to do something or see someone in a short period of time or when you are very busy: *While we're in Australia, we're hoping to squeeze in a trip to the Barrier Reef.* ◦ *I'm very busy this week but I could squeeze you in at 2.30 on Tuesday.* • **squeeze sth out of sb** (also **squeeze sth from sb**) to persuade or force someone to give you money or information: *During the negotiations, the union managed to squeeze several concessions from the management.*

▸noun **PRESS** ▷ **1** [C] the act of pressing something firmly: *She gave the present a quick squeeze and tried to guess what was inside.* ◦ *Garnish the fish with some fresh parsley and a squeeze of lemon.* **LIMIT** ▷ **2** [C usually singular] a reduction or limit: *The squeeze **on** profits in the oil industry has led to thousands of redundancies.* ◦ *The squeeze **on** local spending means that many services will have to be cut.* **3** [C usually singular] a period in which the supply of money is limited by the government because of economic difficulties: *The government has imposed a sharp **credit** squeeze in an attempt to hold down inflation.* **SPACE** ▷ **4** [S] a situation in which people or things are pushed or forced into a small space: *I can give you a lift, but it'll be a **tight** squeeze as I'm taking four other people as well.*

ˈsqueeze ˌbottle noun [C] US a plastic container whose contents can be forced out through a narrow hole at the top by pressing the sides of the bottle together

squeezebox /ˈskwiːz.bɒks/ (US) /-bɑːks/ noun [C] old-fashioned informal an **accordion**

squeezer /ˈskwiː.zəʳ/ (US) /-zɚ/ noun [C] a device which removes the juice from fruit by pressing it: *Have you got a **lemon** squeezer?*

squelch /skweltʃ/ verb; noun
▸verb **SOUND** ▷ **1** [I usually + adv/prep] to make a sucking sound like the one produced when you are walking on soft, wet ground: *He got out of the car and squelched through the mud to open the gate.* **STOP** ▷ **2** [T] US to quickly end something that is causing you problems: *A spokeswoman at the White House has squelched **rumors** about the president's ill health.* **3** [T] US to silence someone by criticizing them: *The senator*

thoroughly squelched the journalist who tried to interrupt him during his speech.

▸**noun** [C usually singular] a sucking sound like the one produced when you are walking on soft, wet ground: *As the hikers walked down the path by the house, she could hear the squelch of their boots in the mud.* • **squelchy** /ˈskwel.tʃi/ **adj**

squib /skwɪb/ **noun** [C] a small FIREWORK consisting of a tube filled with powder which makes a HISSING noise when it is lit

squid /skwɪd/ **noun** [C or U] (plural **squid**) a sea creature with a long body and ten arms situated around the mouth, or this animal eaten as food

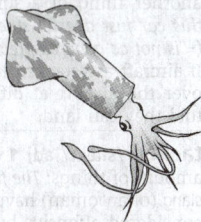

squidgy /ˈskwɪdʒ.i/ **adj** UK informal soft and wet and changing shape easily when pressed: *Bread which has just come out of the oven is often still squidgy in the middle.*

squiffy /ˈskwɪf.i/ **adj** informal old-fashioned (US also **squiffed**) slightly drunk: *'I've only had one glass of sherry and I feel squiffy already,' she said.*

squiggle /ˈskwɪg.l̩/ **noun** [C] a short line that has been written or drawn and that curves and twists in a way that is not regular: *His signature was an illegible squiggle at the bottom of the page.* • **squiggly** /-l̩.i/ **adj**

squillion /ˈskwɪl.i.ən/ US /-jən/ **noun** [C] informal humorous a very large number or amount, especially a large amount of money: *He made squillions from selling his business.* ◦ *I get squillions **of** emails every day.*

squillionaire /ˌskwɪl.i.əˈneəʳ/ US /-jəˈner/ **noun** [C] humorous someone who has a lot of money

squinch /skwɪntʃ/ **verb** [T] US to press together the features of the face or the muscles of the body: *He squinched **up** his face in a look that left no doubt about his displeasure.*

squint /skwɪnt/ **verb; noun**

▸**verb** [I] to partly close your eyes in order to see more clearly: *The sun was shining straight in her eyes which made her squint.*

▸**noun** [C] **EYE CONDITION** ▷ **1** a condition caused by a weakness of the eye muscles which makes the eyes look in different directions from each other: *As a child she wore thick glasses and **had** a bad squint.* **LOOK** ▷ **2** informal old-fashioned a quick look: *'The back wheel of my bike doesn't seem straight.' 'I'll **have/take** a squint at it if you like.'*

squire /skwaɪəʳ/ US /skwaɪr/ **noun** [C] **1** in the past in England, a man who owned most of the land around a village **2** UK old-fashioned informal used as a friendly form of address by one man to another who might be of a higher social class: *'I don't know if all my luggage is going to fit in the back of the taxi.' 'Don't worry, squire, I'll get it in.'*

squirm /skwɜːm/ US /skwɜːm/ **verb** [I] to move from side to side in an awkward way because of nervousness, embarrassment, or pain: *Nobody spoke for at least five minutes and Rachel squirmed in her chair **with** embarrassment.* ◦ *The fish squirmed on the ground for a few moments and then lay still.* • **squirm noun** [C]

squirrel /ˈskwɪr.əl/ US /ˈskwɜː-/ **noun; verb**

▸**noun** [C] a small animal covered in fur with a long tail, which climbs trees and feeds on nuts and seeds

▸**verb**

PHRASAL VERB **squirrel sth away** informal to hide or store something, especially money, in order to use it in the future: *As soon as I get paid, I squirrel some money away so I won't be tempted to spend it.*

squirt /skwɜːt/ US /skwɜːt/ **verb; noun**

▸**verb** **1** [I or T, usually + adv/prep] (to force a liquid) to flow out through a narrow opening in a fast stream: *He squirted some tomato sauce **on** his burger.* ◦ *There was a leak in one of the pipes and water was squirting **out** all over the kitchen floor.* **2** [T] to hit someone or something with a liquid or gas: *She was squirting the neighbours with a water pistol.*

▸**noun** [C] **LIQUID** ▷ **1** an amount of liquid or gas that is squirted out: *The door should stop squeaking once I've given it a few squirts of oil.* **PERSON** ▷ **2** old-fashioned a young or small person who you do not consider to be important and who has behaved rudely towards you

ˈsquirt ˌgun **noun** [C] US for a **water pistol**

squish /skwɪʃ/ **verb** [T] informal to crush something that is soft: *Don't sit on that bag – you'll squish the sandwiches.* • **squish noun** [C] *He could hear the squish of the damp ground beneath his boots.* • **squishy** /ˈskwɪʃ.i/ **adj** *a squishy banana*

Sr **adj** [after noun] US (UK **Snr**) written abbreviation for **senior**, used after a man's name to refer to the older of two people in the same family who have the same name

SS /ˌesˈes/ **noun** abbreviation for **steamship**

ssh /ʃː/ **exclamation sh**

st written abbreviation for **stone**: *He weighs 12 st 3 lb.*

St **noun** written abbreviation for **saint**: used only before personal names: *St Andrew*

St. **noun** (also **St**) written abbreviation for Street, used in writing in the name of a street: *My address is 27 Lind St.*

stab /stæb/ **verb; noun**

▸**verb** (-bb-) **1** B2 [T] to injure someone with a sharp pointed object such as a knife: *She was stabbed several times **in** the chest.* ◦ *He was jailed for 15 years for stabbing his wife **to death**.* **2** [I or T] to make a short, forceful pushing movement with a finger or a long, thin object: *As she spoke she stabbed the air with her finger.* ◦ *He stabbed **at** the meat with his fork.*

IDIOM **stab sb in the back** to do something harmful to someone who trusted you: *He had been lied to and stabbed in the back by people that he thought were his friends.* → See also **backstabber**

▸**noun** [C] **1** the act of pushing a knife into someone, or an injury caused by stabbing: *He was admitted to hospital with stab **wounds**.* **2** a sudden feeling, especially an unpleasant one such as pain: *She felt a stab **of** envy when she saw all the expensive presents Zoe had been given for Christmas.* **3** an action or remark that attacks someone's reputation: *Her criticism of the company's plans was a stab **at** the chairman himself.*

IDIOM **have/make a stab at sth** informal to attempt to do something although you are not likely to be very successful

stabbing /ˈstæb.ɪŋ/ **noun; adj**

▸**noun** [C] an occasion when someone stabs someone:

S

There have been several stabbings in our neighbourhood recently.
▸**adj stabbing pain** a sudden pain: *She was awoken by a **sharp** stabbing pain in her chest.*

stability /stəˈbɪl.ɪ.ti/ (US) /-ə.t̬i/ **noun** [U] (C1) a situation in which something is not likely to move or change: *a period of political stability*

stabilize (UK usually **stabilise**) /ˈsteɪ.bɪ.laɪz/ **verb 1** [I] If something stabilizes, it becomes fixed or stops changing: *He suffered a second heart attack two days ago but his condition has now stabilized.* **2** [T] If you stabilize something, you cause it to become fixed or to stop changing: *In China, the policy of one child per family was introduced to stabilize the country's population **at** 1.6 billion.* • **stabilization** (UK usually **stabilisation**) /ˌsteɪ.bɪ.laɪˈzeɪ.ʃən/ (US) /-əˈ-/ **noun** [U]

stabilizer (UK usually **stabiliser**) /ˈsteɪ.bɪ.laɪ.zəʳ/ (US) /-zɚ/ **noun** [C] **CONTROL** ▷ **1** UK a method used to limit sudden changes in prices or to limit the level of production **CHEMICAL** ▷ **2** specialized a chemical that is added to something so that it stays in the same state **FOR BALANCE** ▷ **3** a device that helps an aircraft, ship, or vehicle to balance **4 stabilizers** [plural] (US **training wheels**) small wheels fixed to each side of the back wheel of a bicycle to prevent it falling over when a child is learning to ride it

stable /ˈsteɪ.bl̩/ **adj; noun; verb**
▸**adj 1** (C1) firmly fixed or not likely to move or change: *If the foundations of the house aren't stable, collapse is possible.* ◦ *After several part-time jobs, he's now got a stable job in a bank.* ◦ *The hospital said she was in a stable condition (= not likely to get worse) following the operation.* **2** (C1) describes someone who is mentally healthy: *She seems more stable these days.* **3** specialized describes a substance that keeps the same chemical or ATOMIC state
▸**noun** [C] **1** (C2) a building in which horses are kept **2** a group of RACEHORSES that are owned or trained by one person **3** a group of people who perform a similar activity and who are trained by the same person or employed by the same organization: *During the 1950s, Sun Records' stable **of** singers included Johnny Cash and Jerry Lee Lewis.*
▸**verb** [T] to keep a horse in a stable

ˈstable ˌboy noun [C] (UK also **ˈstable ˌlad**) a young man who works in a stable and takes care of the horses

S

stablemate /ˈsteɪ.bl̩.meɪt/ **noun** [C] something that is similar to something else or is part of the same organization as something else: *the Daily News and its stablemate the Weekly News*

stabling /ˈsteɪ.bl̩.ɪŋ/, /ˈ-blɪŋ/ **noun** [U] a stable (= building for horses)

staccato /stəˈkɑː.təʊ/ (US) /-t̬oʊ/ **adj, adv 1** describes musical notes that are short and separate when played, or this way of playing music: *The music suddenly changed from a smooth melody to a staccato rhythm.* ◦ *She played the whole piece staccato to improve her technique.* **2** describes a noise or way of speaking that consists of a series of short and separate sounds: *She gave staccato replies to every question.*

stack /stæk/ **noun; verb**
▸**noun** [C] **PILE** ▷ **1** a pile of things arranged one on top of another: *He chose a cartoon from the stack of DVDs on the shelf.* **2** informal a large amount: *Don't worry, we've got stacks of time.* **3 the stacks** a set of shelves in a library that are positioned close together so that a lot of books can be stored on them **ACCIDENT** ▷ **4** Australian English informal a car accident, especially one that causes damage
▸**verb** [T] to arrange things in an ordered pile: *Once the last few people had left the hall, the caretaker began stacking (**up**) the chairs.*

IDIOMS **have the odds/cards stacked against you** to be very unlikely to succeed because you are not in an good position • **stack the cards** UK (US **stack the deck**) to arrange something in a dishonest way in order to achieve the result you want

PHRASAL VERBS **stack up** informal to compare with another thing of a similar type: *The new model of this car just doesn't stack up **against** previous models (= is not as good as previous models).* • **be stacked up** If aircraft are stacked up over an airport, they circle over the airport at different heights, waiting to be told they can land.

stacked /stækt/ **adj 1** covered or filled with a large amount of things: *The fridge is stacked with food.* **2** US slang (of a woman) having large breasts. This sense is considered offensive by many women.

ˈstack-up noun [C] informal a road accident involving a row of cars

stadium /ˈsteɪ.di.əm/ **noun** [C] (plural **stadiums** or **stadia**) (B2) a large closed area of land with rows of seats around the sides and often with no roof, used for sports events and musical performances: *Thousands of football fans packed into the stadium to watch the match.*

staff /stɑːf/ (US) /stæf/ **noun; verb**
▸**noun PEOPLE** ▷ **1** (A2) [S, + sing/pl verb] the group of people who work for an organization: *There is a good relationship between staff and pupils at the school.* ◦ *The staff are not very happy about the latest pay increase.* ◦ *There are over a hundred staff in the company.* ◦ *He is **on** (= a member of) the editorial staff of the magazine.* **2** [C usually singular] Indian English a person who works for an organization

> **! Common mistake: staff**
> **Warning:** Group noun!
> **Staff** always refers to a group of people. It does not have a plural form with 's'. Don't write 'staffs', write **staff**:
> ~~*The company employs around 150 staffs.*~~
> *The company employs around 150 staff.*
> If you want to refer to a single person who is part of the group, don't write 'staff', write **a member of staff**:
> ~~*Is there a staff who can speak Spanish?*~~
> *Is there a member of staff who can speak Spanish?*

STICK ▷ **3** [C] formal a long, strong stick held in the hand that is used as a support when walking, as a weapon, or as a symbol of authority **4** [C] (also **flagstaff**) formal a **flagpole MUSIC** ▷ **5** [C] US for **stave**

> **Word partners for staff**
> *appoint/employ/recruit/take on* staff • *cut/lay off* staff • *employ/have* a staff *of* [500/750, etc.] • *join* the staff • *train* staff • a *member* of staff • *experienced/junior/professional/senior* staff • *full-time/part-time/permanent/temporary* staff • *on* the staff

IDIOM **the staff of life** literary bread, considered as one of the most important foods we eat

▸**verb** [T] to be or provide the people who work for an organization: *Many charity shops in Britain are staffed **by/with** volunteers.*

staffer /ˈstɑː.f.əʳ/ (US) /ˈstæf.ɚ/ **noun** [C] mainly US an employee, often of a political organization: *White House staffers briefed reporters before the president arrived.*

ˈstaff ˌnurse noun [C] UK a person who works in a hospital taking care of the ill and injured and whose rank is below that of a SISTER

ˈstaff ˌofficer noun [C] an army officer who helps the officer in charge to plan military activities

staffroom /ˈstɑːf.rʊm/, /-ruːm/ (US) /ˈstæf-/ noun [C] a room in a school that is for the use of the teachers when they are not teaching: figurative *The government proposal to test 14-year-olds has been causing controversy in the staffroom (= among teachers).*

stag /stæɡ/ noun; verb

▸noun [C] **ANIMAL** ▷ **1** (plural **stags** or **stag**) an adult male DEER **PERSON** ▷ **2** (plural **stags**) UK a person who buys SHARES in a company that is being sold to the public with the intention of selling them immediately for profit

IDIOM **go stag** mainly US If a man goes stag to an event, he goes without a partner.

▸verb [I or T] (**-gg-**) UK to buy SHARES in a company that is being sold to the public with the intention of selling them immediately for profit

stage /steɪdʒ/ noun; verb

▸noun [C] **PART** ▷ **1** (B2) a part of an activity or a period of development: *The project is* ***in*** *its final stages and should be completed by August.* ◦ *They did the last stage of their journey on foot.* ◦ *Our marriage is going through a difficult stage at the moment.* ◦ *Their youngest child is* ***at*** *the stage* ***where*** *she can say individual words but not full sentences.* ◦ *I'm not tired at the moment but I will need a rest* ***at some*** *stage (= at some time) during the walk.* ◦ *Andrew spends all his spare time playing with his computer but it's probably* ***just*** *a stage he's* ***going through*** *(= a period of development that will end soon).* **2 in stages** If you do something in stages, you divide the activity into parts and complete each part separately: *We're decorating the house in stages so it won't be ready for another couple of months.* **3** specialized one of the separate parts of a ROCKET, each part having its own engine: *Once its fuel supply runs out, each stage separates from the main part of the rocket and falls back to Earth.* **THEATRE** ▷ **4** (A2) the area in a theatre that is often raised above ground level and on which actors or ENTERTAINERS perform: *Hamlet is* ***on*** *stage for most of the act.* ◦ *The orchestra* ***went on/off*** *stage to great applause.* ◦ *The play is a stage adaptation of William Golding's novel.* ◦ *The opera singer returns to the London stage (= will perform again in London) this summer.* **5** a particular area of public life: *The president was extremely popular on the* ***world*** *stage but was disliked in his own country.* **6 take the stage** to go onto the stage and start to perform

IDIOMS **be on the stage** to be an actor: *Her daughter is an artist and her son is on the stage.* • **go on the stage** to become an actor: *At the age of ten, he decided that he wanted to go on the stage.* • **take centre stage** to be at the centre of attention: *She always likes to take centre stage in whatever she does.*

▸verb [T] **1** (C2) to arrange and perform a play or show: *The local drama group is staging a production of the musical 'Grease'.* **2** to organize an event: *London staged the Olympic Games in 2012.*

stagecoach /ˈsteɪdʒ.kəʊtʃ/ (US) /-koʊtʃ/ noun [C] (in the past) a covered vehicle pulled by horses that carried passengers and goods on regular routes

ˈstage diˌrection noun [C] a description or instruction in the text of a play which explains how the play should be performed

ˌstage ˈdoor noun [C] the door that is used by the actors and theatre workers when entering and leaving the theatre

ˈstage ˌfright noun [U] Actors or performers who have stage fright are nervous because they are about to perform.

stagehand /ˈsteɪdʒ.hænd/ noun [C] a person who is employed in a theatre to move the equipment on the stage

ˌstage ˈleft noun [U], adv the part of the stage to the left of the actors when they are facing the people watching the performance

ˈstage-ˌmanage verb [T] to arrange and control an event carefully in order to achieve the result you want: *Many people have become cynical about the stage-managed debates between politicians which regularly appear on television.*

ˈstage ˌmanager noun [C] the person who is responsible for the equipment and the use of the stage during a play or performance

ˈstage ˌname noun [C] the name, different from his or her real name, that an actor or performer is publicly known by: *David Bowie is the stage name of the singer David Jones.*

ˌstage ˈright noun [U], adv the part of the stage to the right of the actors when they are facing the people watching the performance

ˈstage-struck adj If you are stage-struck, you are extremely interested in the theatre and want to become an actor.

ˈstage ˌwhisper noun [C] **1** If an actor says something in a stage whisper, it is intended to be heard by the people watching the play, and the other actors on the stage pretend not to hear it. **2** If you say something in a stage whisper, you intend it to be heard by people other than the ones you are talking to.

stagflation /stæɡˈfleɪ.ʃᵊn/ noun [U] specialized an economic situation in which prices keep rising but economic activity does not increase

stagger /ˈstæɡ.əʳ/ (US) /-ɚ/ verb; noun

▸verb **MOVE** ▷ **1** (C2) [I usually + adv/prep] to walk or move with difficulty as if you are going to fall: *After he was attacked, he managed to stagger* ***to*** *the phone and call for help.* ◦ figurative *The company is staggering* ***under*** *a $15 million debt and will almost certainly collapse by the end of the year.* **SHOCK** ▷ **2** [T] to cause someone to feel shocked or surprised because of something unexpected or very unusual happening: *He staggered all his colleagues by suddenly announcing that he was leaving the company at the end of the month.* **ARRANGE** ▷ **3** [T] to arrange things, especially hours of work, holidays or events, so that they begin at different times from those of other people: *Some countries have staggered school holidays so that holiday resorts do not become overcrowded.* **4** [T] If the start of a race is staggered, the competitors start at different times or in different positions.

▸noun [C usually singular] a way of walking or moving in which you almost fall: *He left the bar with a drunken stagger.*

staggered /ˈstæɡ.əd/ (US) /-ɚd/ adj [after noun] very shocked or surprised: *I was staggered* ***at*** *the prices.*

ˌstaggered ˈjunction noun [C] UK a place where several roads meet a main road at a slight distance apart so that they do not all come together at the same point

staggering /ˈstæɡ.ᵊr.ɪŋ/ (US) /-ɚ-/ adj (C1) very shock-

S

ing and surprising: *It costs a staggering $50,000 per week to keep the museum open to the public.* • **staggeringly** /-li/ adv *staggeringly expensive*

staging /ˈsteɪ.dʒɪŋ/ noun [C] the performance of a play or show: *The production is a modern staging of the fairy tale 'Cinderella'.*

ˈstaging ˌarea noun [C] a place where soldiers and equipment are brought together and prepared before military activity

ˈstaging ˌpost noun [C] UK a place where stops are regularly made on long journeys: *Hong Kong is often used as a staging post on flights from Melbourne to London.* ◦ figurative *For people who have spent a long time in a mental hospital, a hostel acts as an important staging post (= a place to stay temporarily) between the hospital and a home of their own.*

stagnant /ˈstæg.nənt/ adj **NOT FLOWING** ▷ **1** (of water or air) not flowing or moving, and smelling unpleasant: *a stagnant pond* **NOT BUSY** ▷ **2** not growing or developing: *a stagnant economy*

stagnate /stægˈneɪt/ (US) /ˈstæg.neɪt/ verb [I] to stay the same and not grow or develop: *The electronics industry is showing signs of stagnating after 15 years of growth.* • **stagnation** /stægˈneɪ.ʃən/ noun [U]

ˈstag ˌnight/ˌparty noun [C] (US also **ˈbachelor ˌparty**) a party for a man who is going to get married, to which only his male friends are invited → Compare **hen night**

stagy (also **stagey**) /ˈsteɪ.dʒi/ adj disapproving like in a theatre and not very natural

staid /steɪd/ adj serious, boring, and slightly old-fashioned: *In an attempt to change its staid image, the newspaper has created a new section aimed at younger readers.*

stain /steɪn/ verb; noun

▸verb **MARK** ▷ **1** (C2) [I or T] to leave a mark on something that is difficult to remove: *Tomato sauce stains terribly – it's really difficult to get it out of clothes.* ◦ *While she was changing the wheel on her car, her coat had become stained **with** oil.* **2** [I] If a material stains, it absorbs substances easily, causing it to become covered with marks, or coloured by a chemical: *This carpet is ideal for the kitchen because it doesn't stain easily.* **3** [T] to change the colour of something using a chemical: *She stripped the floorboards and stained them dark brown.* **SPOIL** ▷ **4** (C2) [T] literary to permanently spoil something such as someone's reputation: *Several important politicians have had their reputations stained **by** this scandal.* ◦ *The country's history is stained **with** the blood of (= the country is guilty of killing) millions of innocent men and women.*

▸noun **MARK** ▷ **1** (B1) [C] a dirty mark on something that is difficult to remove: *a blood/grass stain* ◦ *You can remove a red wine stain from a carpet by sprinkling salt over it.* **2** [C] a chemical for changing the colour of something **DAMAGE** ▷ **3** [S] literary permanent damage to someone's reputation or character: *His solicitor said, 'He leaves this court without a stain **on** his character.'*

-stained /-steɪnd/ suffix marked with the thing mentioned: ***tear**-stained faces* ◦ *a **blood**-stained blanket*

ˌstained ˈglass noun [U] glass that has been coloured and cut into various shapes to form pictures or patterns, used especially in church windows: *a stained glass window*

stainless steel /ˌsteɪn.ləsˈstiːl/ noun [U] a type of STEEL containing CHROMIUM that is not damaged by air or water and does not change its colour

stair /steər/ (US) /ster/ noun **1 stairs** [plural] (A2) a set of steps which lead from one level of a building to another: *Go up the stairs and her office is on the right.* ◦ *I had to climb a steep **flight** (= set) of stairs to her front door.* ◦ *He stood at the **foot** (= bottom) of the stairs and called out, 'Breakfast's ready!'* **2** [C] one of the steps in a set of steps which lead from one level of a building to another: *The top stair creaked as she went upstairs and the noise woke up her mother.* **3** [S] old use or literary a set of stairs: *He climbed the wooden stair and knocked on his grandfather's door.*

IDIOM **below/above stairs** UK old use In a large house, below stairs was the part of the house in which the servants worked and lived, and above stairs was the part in which the family of the owner of the house lived.

staircase /ˈsteə.keɪs/ (US) /ˈster-/ noun [C] (C1) a set of stairs inside a building, usually with a bar fixed on the wall or onto vertical poles at the side for you to hold on to: *She descended the **sweeping** (= long and wide) staircase into the crowd of photographers and journalists.*

stairway /ˈsteə.weɪ/ (US) /ˈster-/ noun [C] a passage in a public place with a set of steps that leads from one level to another

stairwell /ˈsteə.wel/ (US) /ˈster-/ noun [C] a long, vertical passage through a building around which a set of stairs is built

stake /steɪk/ noun; verb

▸noun [C] **SHARE** ▷ **1** a SHARE or a financial involvement in something such as a business: *He **holds** (= owns) a 40 percent stake **in/of** the company.* **2 have a stake in sth** If you have a stake in something, it is important to you because you have a personal interest or involvement in it: *Employers have a stake in the training of their staff.* **RISK** ▷ **3** the amount of money which you risk on the result of something such as a game or competition: *She spent two weeks in Las Vegas playing **high**-stakes blackjack at the casinos.* **4 the stakes** [plural] In an activity or competition, the stakes are the reward for the person who wins or succeeds in it: *The team is playing for enormous stakes – the chance to play in the final.* **5 the Stakes** used in the names of horse races in which the prize money is provided by all the owners of the horses that are competing in the race **6 the beauty, popularity, etc. stakes** a situation where someone is judged on how much of a particular quality they have: *The prime minister is not very high **in** the popularity stakes (= he is not very popular) at the moment.* **7 raise/up the stakes a** to increase the prize or reward in a competition or any activity in which you are competing **b** to make a situation more urgent or more difficult to ignore: *The stowaways are trying to raise the stakes by refusing to eat until they are given money and aid.* **STICK** ▷ **8** a strong stick or metal bar with a pointed end: *The stakes are pushed or hammered into the ground and can be used for supporting a plant or forming part of a fence.* **9 the stake** in the past, a wooden post to which people were tied before being burned to death as a punishment: *In medieval Europe, many women were accused of being witches and were **burned at** the stake.*

IDIOMS **at stake** (C2) If something that is valuable is at stake, it is in a situation where it might be lost: *Thousands of lives will be at stake if emergency aid does not arrive in the city soon.*

▸verb [T] **RISK** ▷ **1** to risk an amount of money: *At the roulette table, he staked $10,000 **on** number 21.* **USE STICK** ▷ **2** to hold up and support something by fastening it to stakes: *Tomato plants should be staked.*

IDIOM **stake a claim** If you stake a claim to something, you say or show that you have a right to it and that it should belong to you: *He marked the spot on his map where he had seen the gold and returned later that month to stake his claim.*

PHRASAL VERBS **stake sth on sth** to risk harming or losing something important if an action, decision, or situation does not have the result you want or expect: *I think she'll be head of this company in five year's time – I'd stake my reputation on it.* • **stake sth out** **WATCH** ▷ **1** to watch a place continuously in order to catch criminals or to see a famous person: *The police staked out the hotel where the two terrorists were reported to be staying.* **MAKE CLEAR** ▷ **2** to establish or make clear your opinion or position on something: *Two of the president's chief advisers have staked out opposite positions on this issue.* ◦ *New software companies are going to find it hard staking out a position in an already crowded market.* • **stake somewhere/sth out** **1** to mark the limits of an area or a piece of land with wooden sticks in order to claim that you own it **2** to show clearly that you claim the right to own, control, or use a particular area, for example by putting personal things there: *Each gang in the city has staked out its territory and defends it from other gangs.* ◦ *They arrived early for the concert and staked out a place at the front of the queue.* • **stake sb to sth** US to provide someone with a particular thing or with what they need to get it: *The governor has promised to stake the city's homeless to what they need for a fresh start.*

stakeholder /ˈsteɪkˌhəʊl.dəʳ/ (US) /-ˌhoʊl.dɚ/ noun [C] **SHARE** ▷ **1** a person or group of people who own a share in a business **2** a person such as an employee, customer, or CITIZEN who is involved with an organization, society, etc. and therefore has responsibilities towards it and an interest in its success **RISK** ▷ **3** a person who is in charge of the prize money given by people BETTING on the result of a game or competition and who gives it to the winner

stakeout /ˈsteɪk.aʊt/ noun [C] the continuous watching of a building or area, especially by the police

stalactite /ˈstæl.ək.taɪt/ noun [C] a column of rock that hangs from the roof of a cave and is formed over a very long period of time by drops of water containing LIME falling from the roof

stalagmite /ˈstæl.əg.maɪt/ noun [C] a column of rock that rises from the floor of a cave, formed over a very long period of time by drops of water containing LIME falling from the roof of the cave

stale /steɪl/ adj **1** (C1) no longer new or fresh, usually as a result of being kept for too long: *The bread/biscuits/cake had* ***gone*** *stale.* ◦ *The morning after the party, their apartment smelled of stale cigarette smoke.* **2** not fresh and new; boring because too familiar: *stale jokes/news* **3** describes someone who has lost interest in what they are doing because they are bored or are working too hard: *They had been working together for over five years and they had both become a little stale.* • **staleness** /ˈsteɪl.nəs/ noun [U]

stalemate /ˈsteɪl.meɪt/ noun [C or U] **1** a situation in which neither group involved in an argument can win or get an advantage and no action can be taken: *Tomorrow's meeting between the two leaders is expected to* ***break*** *a diplomatic stalemate that has lasted for ten years.* ◦ *Despite long discussions, the workers and the management remain* ***locked in*** *stalemate.* **2** in CHESS, a position in which one player is unable to move, but their king is not being attacked, which means that neither of the two players wins → Compare **checkmate**

stalk /stɔːk/ (US) /stɑːk/ noun; verb
▸noun [C] **1** the main stem of a plant, or the narrow stem that joins leaves, flowers, or fruit to the main stem of a plant: *She trimmed the stalks of the tulips before putting them in a vase.* **2** a narrow structure that supports a part of the body in some animals: *The eyes of shrimps are on movable stalks.*

IDIOM **eyes out on stalks** UK humorous If your eyes are out on stalks, they are wide open with surprise: *His eyes were out on stalks as he watched his neighbour drive past in a brand new Porsche.*

▸verb **FOLLOW** ▷ **1** [T] to follow an animal or person as closely as possible without being seen or heard, usually in order to catch or kill them: *The police had been stalking the woman for a week before they arrested her.* **2** [I or T] to illegally follow and watch someone, usually a woman, over a period of time: *He was arrested for stalking.* **3** [T] literary If something unpleasant stalks a place, it appears there in a threatening way: *When night falls, danger stalks the streets of the city.* **WALK** ▷ **4** [I + adv/prep] to walk in an angry or proud way: *She refused to accept that she was wrong and stalked furiously* ***out of*** *the room.*

stalker /ˈstɔː.kəʳ/ (US) /ˈstɑː.kɚ/ noun [C] a person who illegally follows and watches someone, especially a woman, over a period of time

ˈstalking ˌhorse noun [C] If someone is a stalking horse, they compete for a position that they have no chance of winning, in order to divide the opposition to a particular group or to take attention away from another person who that group really wants to win.

stall /stɔːl/ (US) /stɑːl/ noun; verb
▸noun **SHOP** ▷ **1** (B1) [C] a large table or a small shop with an open front from which goods are sold in a public place: *In the village market, the stalls are piled high with local vegetables.* **SMALL AREA** ▷ **2** [C] a small closed area within a farm building in which there is space for one animal to be kept **3** [C] a small area of a room that is separated from the main part of the room by walls or curtains: *There was one bathroom with a* ***shower*** *stall in the corner.* **SEATS** ▷ **4 the stalls** [plural] **a** rows of fixed seats in a church, often with the sides and backs connected **b** UK (US **the orchestra**) the seats on the main floor of a theatre or cinema, not at a higher level → Compare **circle, gallery**
▸verb **ENGINE** ▷ **1** [I or T] If an engine stalls, or if you stall it, it stops working suddenly and without you intending it to happen: *A car may stall due to the driver braking too suddenly.* **DELAY** ▷ **2** [I] to delay taking action or avoid giving an answer in order to have more time to make a decision or get an advantage: *She says she'll give me the money next week but I think she's just stalling* (***for time***). **3** [T] If you stall a person, you delay them or prevent them from doing something for a period of time: *I managed to stall him for a few days until I'd got enough money to pay back the loan.* ◦ mainly US *The thief broke into the office while his accomplice stalled* ***off*** *the security guard.* **4** [I] to stop making progress: *Japan's economic growth has stalled, with industrial production contracting in June for the fourth straight month.* **5** [T] If you stall an event, you delay it or prevent it from making progress: *Commandos stalled the enemy attack by destroying three bridges.* ◦ *Fears are growing that a tax increase may stall economic recovery.*

stallholder /ˈstɔːlˌhəʊl.dəʳ/ (US) /ˈstɑːlˌhoʊl.dɚ/ noun [C] mainly UK a person who rents or owns a stall in a market

S

stallion /ˈstæl.jən/ noun [C] an adult male horse that is used for breeding → Compare **mare**

stalwart /ˈstɔːl.wət/ (US) /ˈstɑːl.wɚt/ **adj; noun**
▸adj **LOYAL** ▷ **1** loyal, especially for a long time; able to be trusted: *She has been a stalwart supporter of the party for many years.* **STRONG** ▷ **2** formal (especially of a person) physically strong • **stalwartly** /-li/ adv
▸noun [C] a person who has been loyal for a long time: *Let me introduce Bob, one of the club's stalwarts.*

stamen /ˈsteɪ.mən/ noun [C] specialized the male part of a flower, consisting of a thin stem which holds an ANTHER

stamina /ˈstæm.ɪ.nə/ noun [U] (C1) the physical and/or mental strength to do something that might be difficult and will take a long time: *The triathlon is a great test of stamina.*

stammer /ˈstæm.əʳ/ (US) /-ɚ/ verb [I or T] to speak or say something with unusual pauses or repeated sounds, either because of speech problems or because of fear and ANXIETY: [+ speech] *'Wh-when can we g-go?' she stammered.* ◦ *He dialled 999 and stammered (**out**) his name and address.* → Compare **stutter** • **stammer** noun [C usually singular] *Robert **has** a bit of a stammer.* • **stammeringly** /-ɪŋ.li/ adv

stammerer /ˈstæm.ᵊr.əʳ/ (US) /-ɚ.ɚ/ noun [C] a person who stammers

stamp /stæmp/ **noun; verb**
▸noun **LETTER** ▷ **1** (A2) [C] (formal **postage stamp**) a small piece of paper with a picture or pattern on it that is stuck onto a letter or package before it is posted, to show that the cost of sending it has been paid: *I stuck a 50p stamp on the envelope.* **MARK** ▷ **2** [C] a tool for putting a mark on an object either by printing on it or pushing into it, or the mark made in this way: *A date stamp inside the front cover of a library book shows when it should be returned.* **QUALITY** ▷ **3** [U] a particular quality in something or someone, or a quality in something that shows it was done by a particular person or group of people: *Although this painting clearly bears the stamp **of** genius, we don't know who painted it.* ◦ *Each manager has left his or her own stamp **on** the way the company has evolved.* **FOOT** ▷ **4** [C] an act of putting the foot down on the ground hard, or the noise made in doing so: *With a stamp of her foot she stormed out.*
▸verb **MARK** ▷ **1** (B2) [T] to put a mark on an object either by printing on it or pushing into it with a small tool: *It is necessary to stamp your passport.* ◦ *Every carton of yogurt is stamped **with** a sell-by date.* **MOVE FOOT** ▷ **2** (C2) [I or T] (US also **stomp**) to put a foot down on the ground hard and quickly, making a loud noise, often to show anger: *The little boy was stamping his foot and refusing to take his medicine.* ◦ *She stood by the road, stamping her feet to stay warm.* ◦ *I wish those people upstairs would stop stamping (**about/around**).* ◦ *Why did you stamp **on** that insect?* → Compare **stomp** **SHOW QUALITY** ▷ **3** [T] to mark with a particular quality or show that someone has a particular quality: *Our new administrator seems to be trying to stamp her authority **on** every aspect of the department.*

IDIOM **stamped on sb's memory** If a particular event, etc. is stamped on someone's memory, the person will always remember it: *The awful sound of the crash will be stamped on her memory forever.*

PHRASAL VERBS **stamp on sth** to use force to stop or prevent something that you consider to be wrong or harmful: *Any opposition to the new government was immediately stamped on by the army.* • **stamp sth out** to get rid of something that is wrong or harmful: *The new legislation is intended to stamp out child prostitution.*

ˌstamped adˌdressed ˈenvelope noun [C] (also **sae**) an envelope with a stamp and your name and address on it, which you send inside another envelope to an organization when you want a reply

stampede /stæmˈpiːd/ **noun; verb**
▸noun [C] an occasion when many large animals or many people suddenly all move quickly and in an uncontrolled way, usually in the same direction at the same time, especially because of fear: *Two shoppers were injured in the stampede as shop doors opened on the first day of the sale.*
▸verb [I or T] When animals or people stampede, they all move quickly in the same direction, often because they are frightened: *A loud clap of thunder made the herd stampede.* ◦ figurative *No amount of pressure will stampede (= force) this committee **into** making hasty decisions.*

ˈstamping ˌground noun [C] informal a place or area which someone is very familiar with and where they like to spend time: *Do you ever go back to any of our old stamping grounds?*

stance /stɑːns/ (US) /stæns/ noun [C] **OPINION** ▷ **1** (C2) a way of thinking about something, especially expressed in a publicly stated opinion: *The doctor's stance **on** the issue of abortion is well known.* **POSITION** ▷ **2** a particular way of standing: *Jenny took up a stance with her feet slightly apart, ready to catch the ball.*

stanch /stɑːntʃ/ verb [T] US for **staunch**.

stanchion /ˈstɑːn.tʃᵊn/ (US) /ˈstæn-/ noun [C] a fixed vertical bar or pole used as a support for something

stand /stænd/ **verb; noun**
▸verb (**stood, stood**) **VERTICAL** ▷ **1** (A2) [I or T] to be in a vertical state or to put into a vertical state, especially (of a person or animal) by making the legs straight: *Granny says if she stands (**up**) for a long time her ankles hurt.* ◦ *As a sign of politeness you should stand (**up**) when she comes in.* ◦ *Stand **still** and be quiet!* ◦ *After the earthquake not a single building was left standing in the village.* ◦ *Stand the bottles **on** the table over there.* **STATE** ▷ **2** (C1) [I, L only + adj] to be in, cause to be in, or get into a particular state or situation: *How do you think your chances stand (= are) of being offered the job?* ◦ *The national debt stands **at** 55 billion dollars.* ◦ *The house stood **empty** for years.* ◦ *Martina is currently standing second in the world listings.* ◦ [+ to infinitive] *Our firm stands **to** lose (= will lose) a lot of money if the deal is unsuccessful.* ◦ *We really can't allow the current situation to stand (= to exist in its current form).* ◦ *Newton's laws of mechanics stood (= were thought to be completely true) for over two hundred years.* ◦ *Leave the mixture to stand (= do not touch it) for 15 minutes before use.* ◦ *It would be difficult for her to stand much lower/higher **in** my **opinion** (= for me to have a worse/better opinion of her) after the way she behaved at the party.* ◦ *She's very blunt, but at least you know where you stand with her (= you know what she thinks and how she is likely to behave).* ◦ formal *You stand **accused of** murder, how do you plead?* **3 stand trial** (C2) to be put on trial in a law court: *Two other men are to stand trial next month **for** their part in the bombing.* **PLACE** ▷ **4** (B2) [I or T, usually + adv/prep] to be in, cause to be in, or put into a particular place: *The room was empty except for a wardrobe standing in one corner.* ◦ *Stand the paintings against the wall while we decide where to hang them.* ◦ *The photograph shows the happy couple standing beside a banana tree.* **5** [I usually + adv/prep] Vehicles that are standing are waiting: *The train now standing **at** platform 8 is the 15.17 for Cardiff.*

ACCEPT ▷ **6** B1 [T usually in negatives] to successfully accept or bear something that is unpleasant or difficult: *I can't stand her voice.* ◦ *Our tent won't stand another storm like the last one.* ◦ [+ -ing verb] *I can't stand hearing her cry.* **POLITICS** ▷ **7** C2 [I] UK (mainly US **run**) to compete, especially in an election, for an official position: *The president has announced she does not intend to stand **for** re-election.* **8 stand a chance** C2 to have a chance of success: *She stands a good chance **of** passing her exam if she works hard.* **HEIGHT** ▷ **9** [L only + noun] to be a stated height: *Even without his shoes he stood over two metres tall.* **BUY** ▷ **10** [T + two objects] to buy something, especially a meal or a drink, for someone: *I couldn't get to the bank, so could you stand me lunch?* **OPINION** ▷ **11** C2 [I usually + adv/prep] to have as an opinion: *How/Where does he stand **on** foreign policy issues?*

IDIOMS **can't stand the sight of sb/sth** to hate someone or something: *Aunt Gloria can't stand the sight of cats.* • **from where sb stands** being in a particular position and having your particular experience, beliefs, and responsibilities: *You can see why they refused her demand for a pay rise, but from where she stands it probably seemed perfectly reasonable to ask.* • **I stand corrected** formal used to admit that something you have said or done was wrong: *I stand corrected – the date of foundation was 1411, and not 1412 as I had written.* • **it stands to reason** C2 said when something is obvious or clear from the facts: *If 20 percent of the Earth's population has 80 percent of its resources, then it stands to reason **that** 80 percent of the population has only 20 percent of the resources.* • **know where you stand** C2 to know what your opinion or situation is: *I know where I stand **on** this issue – I'm against the war.* ◦ *When we've paid all our debts we'll know where we stand.* • **stand (up) and be counted** to make your opinions known even if doing so might cause you harm or difficulty: *Those who did have the courage to stand up and be counted were arrested and imprisoned.* • **stand your ground** C2 to refuse to be pushed backwards, or to continue in your beliefs in an argument: *The battalion stood its ground in the face of repeated attacks.* ◦ *Clare stood her ground in the meeting and refused to be intimidated even when Michael got angry.* • **stand sb in good stead** If an experience stands a person in good stead, it is or will be of great use to them: *Getting some work experience now will stand you in good stead (**for**) when you apply for a permanent job.* • **stand sth on its head** to cause something such as an established belief to be doubted, especially because of new information or discoveries: *New data has stood the traditional explanation of the island's origin on its head.* • **stand and deliver!** said in the past by HIGHWAYMEN when they stopped a CARRIAGE (= vehicle pulled by horses) on a road to demand objects of value from the travellers • **stand bail** to pay money temporarily to a court so that someone can be released from prison until the date of their trial: *She can't be released from police custody until someone stands bail **for** her.* • **stand fast/firm** to be determined: *Stand firm **on** your decision and you're more likely to get the result you want.* • **stand in the way of sth/sb** (also **stand in sb's way**) to try to stop or prevent something or someone: *You know I won't stand in your way if you want to apply for a job abroad.* • **stand on your hands/head** to support yourself only on your hands, or only on your head and hands, with your feet up as high as possible • **stand on your own (two) feet** informal to be able to provide all of the things you need for living without help from anyone else: *She'll have to get a job and **learn to** stand on her own two feet sooner or later.* • **stand on ceremony** to behave in a formal way: *Please sit down and make yourself comfortable, we don't stand on ceremony here.* • **stand or fall by sth** to depend completely on something for success • **stand the test of time** If something stands the test of time, it is still popular, strong, etc. after a long time: *Which songs from the last year will stand the test of time?* • **standing on your head** informal If someone can do something standing on their head, they can do it very easily: *It's the sort of program Andrew could write standing on his head.*

PHRASAL VERBS **stand about/around** to spend time standing somewhere and doing very little: *We stood around in the cold for about an hour, waiting for the demo to start.* • **stand aside 1** to leave a job or position so that someone else can have it instead: *It's time he stood aside and let a more qualified person do the job.* **2** to step sideways to make a space for someone else: *Stand aside, please, so the doctor can get through.* • **stand back** B2 to move a short distance away from something or someone: *Please stand back – then all of you will be able to see what I'm doing.* • **stand by sb** B2 to continue to support or help someone who is in a difficult situation: *She has vowed to stand by her husband during his trial.* • **stand by BE READY** ▷ **1** to be waiting and ready to do something or to help: *Cabin crew, please stand by **for** take-off.* → See also **standby** **DO NOTHING** ▷ **2** to allow something unpleasant to happen without doing anything to stop it: *We can't stand by while millions of people starve.* → See also **bystander** • **stand by sth 1** to continue doing what you said you would when you made a decision, agreement, or promise: *Despite its financial problems, the company is standing by the no-redundancy agreement.* **2** to continue to believe that something you have said before is still true: *I stand by the statement I made earlier – there is no reason for the minister to resign.* • **stand clear** to move a short distance away from something so that you are safe: *'Stand clear!' shouted the policewoman, 'It might fall any minute.'* • **stand down** UK to give up your official job or position: *He's decided to stand down after 15 years as managing director.* • **stand for sth ACCEPT** ▷ **1** If you will not stand for something, you will not accept a situation or a particular type of behaviour: *I wouldn't stand for that sort of behaviour from him, if I were you.* **REPRESENT** ▷ **2** B2 to support or represent a particular idea or set of ideas: *This party stands for low taxes and individual freedom.* **3** B2 If one or more letters stand for a word or name, they are the first letter or letters of that word or name and they represent it: *'GMT' stands for Greenwich Mean Time.* • **stand in** (US usually **fill in**) C2 to do the job that another person was going to do or usually does, or to take their place at an event, because they cannot be there: *Paula stood in **for** Jane, while Jane was on holiday.* • **stand out 1** B2 to be very noticeable: *The black lettering really stands out on that orange background.* **2** B2 to be much better than other similar things or people: *We had lots of good applicants for the job, but one stood out **from** the rest.* • **stand out against sth/sb** to publicly oppose something or someone: *More and more people are standing out against what is a very unpopular piece of legislation.* • **stand over sb** to stand close to someone and watch what they are doing: *Don't stand over me all the time – it makes me nervous.* • **stand together** If a group of people stand together on a particular matter, they agree strongly about it and take action together about it. • **stand up** If an idea or some information

S

stands up, it is proved to be true or correct: *Their evidence will never stand up in court.* ◦ *Their argument won't stand up* ***to*** *detailed criticism (= when it is studied critically).* • **stand sb up** [usually passive] informal B2 to intentionally fail to meet someone when you said you would, especially someone you were starting to have a romantic relationship with: *I don't know if I've been stood up or if she's just late – I'll wait another half hour.* • **stand up for sth/sb** (also **stick up for sth/sb**) B2 to defend or support a particular idea or a person who is being criticized or attacked: *It's high time we all stood up for our rights around here.* ◦ *Don't be bullied, learn to stand up for your****self*** *and what you believe in.* • **stand up to sb/sth** C1 to defend yourself against a powerful person or organization when they treat you unfairly: *He wasn't afraid to stand up to bullies.* • **stand up to sth** to not be changed or damaged by something: *Will the lorries stand up to the journey over rough roads?*

▸noun **SPORT** ▷ **1** [C] UK a large structure at a sports ground, usually with a sloping floor and sometimes a roof, where people either stand or sit to watch a sports event → Compare **grandstand** **2** **stands** [plural] a stand: *Fighting broke out in the stands five minutes before the end of the match.* **OPINION** ▷ **3** [C] an opinion, especially one that is public: *What's her stand* ***on*** *sexual equality?* **COURT** ▷ **4** [C] US for **witness box**: *The witness* ***took*** *the stand (= went to the place in a court where you stand and answer questions).* **SHOP** ▷ **5** C1 [C] a small shop or STALL or an area where products can be shown, usually outside or in a large public building, at which people can buy things or get information: *a hotdog stand* ◦ *Over three thousand companies will have stands at this year's microelectronics exhibition.* → See also **newsstand** **FRAME** ▷ **6** C2 [C] a frame or piece of furniture for supporting or putting things on: *a music stand* ◦ *a hatstand* **OPPOSITION** ▷ **7** C2 [C usually singular] an act of opposition, especially in order to defend someone or something: *Environmental groups are* ***making a*** *stand* ***against*** *the new road through the valley.* → See also **stand out against sth/sb** **PERFORMANCES** ▷ **8** [C usually singular] US a particular number or period of performances: *The Orioles will be in town for a three-game stand.*

ˈstand-aˌlone adj [before noun] A stand-alone computer or business can operate on its own without needing help from another similar thing.

standard /ˈstæn.dəd/ US /-dɚd/ noun; adj

▸noun **QUALITY** ▷ **1** B2 [C or U] a level of quality: *This essay is not* ***of*** *an acceptable standard – do it again.* ◦ *This piece of work is* ***below*** *standard/is not* ***up to*** *standard.* ◦ *We have very high safety standards in this laboratory.* ◦ *Not everyone judges success by the same standards – some people think happiness is more important than money.* ◦ *Her technique became a standard against which all future methods were compared.* **2** C2 [C usually plural] a moral rule that should be obeyed: *Most people agree that there are standards (****of behaviour****) that need to be upheld.* **USUAL** ▷ **3** [C usually singular] a pattern or model that is generally accepted: *This program is an industry standard for computers.* **4** [C] a song or other piece of music that has been popular and often played over a long period of time **CAR** ▷ **5** [C] US a car with GEARS that are changed by hand **FLAG** ▷ **6** [C] a flag, especially a long, narrow one ending with two long points: *the royal standard*

▸adj **1** B2 usual rather than special, especially when thought of as being correct or acceptable: *White is the standard colour for this model of refrigerator.* ◦ *These are*

> **Word partners for standard noun**
>
> *come up to* standard • *improve/maintain/raise* standards • *implement/set* standards • *adhere to/comply with/conform to/meet* standards • a *good/high/low/poor* standard • *exacting/rigorous/strict/stringent* standards • standards *of* sth • *above/below/(not) up to* standard

standard ***procedures*** *for handling radioactive waste.* ◦ *The metre is the standard unit for measuring length in the SI system.* ◦ mainly UK *Your new TV comes with a two year guarantee* ***as*** *standard.* → See also **substandard** **2** Language described as standard is the form of that language that is considered acceptable and correct by most educated users of it: *Most announcers on the BBC speak standard* ***English****.* ◦ *In Standard* ***American****, 'gotten' is used as a past participle of 'get'.* **3** [before noun] A standard book or writer is the one that is most commonly read for information on a particular subject: *Her book is still a standard text in archaeology, even though it was written more than 20 years ago.*

ˈstandard-ˌbearer noun [C] the person or thing that seems to lead a group of people having similar ideas or moral opinions: *Mr Everhart wants Caltech to be the standard-bearer for excellence in scientific research of all kinds.*

standardize (UK usually **standardise**) /ˈstæn.də.daɪz/ US /-dɚ-/ verb [T] to make things of the same type all have the same basic features: *We standardize parts such as rear-view mirrors, so that one type will fit any model of car we make.* • **standardization** (UK usually **standardisation**) /ˌstæn.də.daɪˈzeɪ.ʃən/ US /-dɚ.də-/ noun [U]

ˈstandard ˌlamp noun [C] UK (US **ˈfloor ˌlamp**) an electric light supported by a tall pole that is fixed to a base that rests on the floor of a room

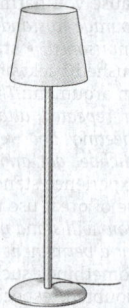

standard lamp

ˌstandard of ˈliving noun [C usually singular] (also **ˈliving ˌstandard**) B2 the amount of money and comfort people have in a particular society: *The standard of living in many developing countries is low.* → Compare **cost of living**

ˌstandard ˈoperating ˌprocedure noun [U] (abbreviation **SOP**) US the usual way of doing something: *Checking references before we lend money is standard operating procedure.*

ˈstandard ˌtime noun [U] In a country or a part of a country, standard time is the time that is officially used. → Compare **Greenwich Mean Time**

standby /ˈstænd.baɪ/ noun [C] (plural **standbys**) **READY** ▷ **1** something that is always ready for use, especially if a regular one fails: *Board games are a good standby to keep the children amused if the weather is bad.* ◦ *There are standby generators but these usually only have to work for a few hours a year during power cuts.* **2** **on standby** When a person or a thing is on standby, they are ready to be used if necessary: *Hospitals are on standby ready to deal with casualties from the crash.* **TICKET** ▷ **3** (also **standby ticket**) a cheap ticket sold just before a flight or a performance if there is a seat available

ˈstand-in noun [C] a person who takes the place or does the job of another person for a short time, for example because the other person is ill or on holiday: *The lecturer didn't turn up, so we had to find a stand-in.*

standing /ˈstæn.dɪŋ/ **noun; adj**

▸**noun** [U] **REPUTATION** ▷ **1** reputation, rank, or position in an area of activity, system, or organization: *As a pathologist of considerable standing, his opinion will have a lot of influence.* ◦ *A financial scandal would shake the Institute's standing* ***in*** *the international academic community.* **TIME** ▷ **2** formal the time for which something has existed: *One member,* ***of*** *twelve years' standing on the committee, resigned in protest at the changes.* → See also **long-standing**

▸**adj** [before noun] permanent, rather than formed or created when necessary: *a standing committee* ◦ *You know you have a standing* ***invitation*** *to come and stay anytime you're in town.*

IDIOM **from a standing start** from not moving: *This car can reach 60 mph from a standing start in six seconds.*

ˌstanding ˈjoke noun [C usually singular] something which a particular group of people are familiar with and laugh about often, especially in an unkind way: *The fact that Debbie is always late has become a standing joke among her friends.*

ˌstanding ˈorder noun [C] UK an instruction to a bank to pay a particular amount of money at regular times from a person's bank account to another bank account → Compare **direct debit**

ˌstanding oˈvation noun [C] an occasion when the people in an audience stand up to clap at the end of a performance or speech because they liked it very much: *She* ***received*** *a standing ovation at the end of her speech.*

ˈstanding ˌroom noun [U] space in a sports ground, theatre, bus, etc. where people can stand, especially if all of the seats have people sitting in them: *All the seats were gone, so there was standing room* ***only***.

standoff /ˈstænd.ɒf/ (US) /-ɑːf/ noun [C] a situation in which agreement in an argument does not seem possible → Synonym **stalemate**

standoffish /ˌstændˈɒf.ɪʃ/ (US) /-ˈɑː.fɪʃ/ adj informal disapproving behaving in a slightly unfriendly and too formal way • **standoffishly** /-li/ adv • **standoffishness** /-nəs/ noun [U]

standout /ˈstænd.aʊt/ noun [C] US an excellent or the best example of something: *While all the desserts are pretty good, the clear standout is the lemon pie.*

standpipe /ˈstænd.paɪp/ noun [C] a vertical pipe that is connected to a water supply and provides water to a public place such as a road

standpoint /ˈstænd.pɔɪnt/ noun [C] **C2** a set of beliefs and ideas from which opinions and decisions are formed: *'I have to put aside my emotions,' he says, 'and consider it from a professional standpoint.'*

standstill /ˈstænd.stɪl/ noun [S] a condition in which all movement or activity has stopped: *The runaway bus eventually* ***came to a*** *standstill when it rolled into a muddy field.* ◦ *Fighting and shortages have* ***brought*** *normal life* ***to a*** *virtual standstill in the city.*

ˈstand-up adj; noun

▸**adj** [before noun] describes COMEDY performed by a single person telling jokes: *stand-up comedy* ◦ *a stand-up comedian*

▸**noun** [C] a person who performs stand-up COMEDY; a stand-up COMEDIAN

stank /stæŋk/ verb past simple of **stink**

Stanley knife /ˈstæn.li.naɪf/ noun [C] trademark a sharp knife with a short blade that can be replaced or put inside the handle if not being used

stanza /ˈstæn.zə/ noun [C] a group of lines of poetry forming a unit → Compare **verse**

stapes /ˈsteɪ.piːz/ noun [C usually sing] (plural **stapes**) specialized one of three very small bones that carry sound from the EARDRUM to the INNER ear → See also **incus, malleus**

staple /ˈsteɪ.pl̩/ **noun; adj; verb**

▸**noun** [C] **WIRE** ▷ **1** a short, thin piece of wire used to fasten sheets of paper together. It has sharp ends that are pushed through the paper and then bent flat by a special device. **2** a U-shaped piece of metal with sharp ends that is fixed into a surface to hold something, such as a wire fence, in a particular position **BASIC** ▷ **3** a main product or part of something: *Shortages mean that even staples (= basic foods) like bread are difficult to find.* ◦ *Phosphate has been a staple* ***of*** *this area for many years.* ◦ *Romantic fiction and reference books are a staple* ***of*** *many public libraries.*

▸**adj** [before noun] basic or main; standard or regular: *The staple* ***diet*** *here is fish and boiled potatoes.* ◦ *Prices of staple* ***foods*** *such as wheat and vegetables have also been increasing.* ◦ *Her latest film is the staple offering of action and comedy that we have come to expect.*

▸**verb** [T] to fasten something using staples: *Would you mind stapling the reports* ***together***?

ˈstaple-gun noun [C] a tool which you hold in your hand and use to push staples into a surface

stapler /ˈsteɪ.pləʳ/ (US) /-plɚ/ noun [C] a small device which you can hold in your hand or use on a table to push staples through pieces of paper

star /stɑːʳ/ (US) /stɑːr/ **noun; verb; adj**

▸**noun OBJECT IN SPACE** ▷ **1** **A2** [C] a very large ball of burning gas in space that is usually seen from Earth as a point of light in the sky at night: *Stars* ***twinkled*** *above them as they lay on the hill.* **PERFORMER** ▷ **2** **A2** [C] a very famous, successful, and important person, especially a performer such as a musician, actor, or sports player: *a rock/movie/football star* ◦ *Kids wanting to be stars come to Hollywood from all over America.* → See also **co-star, superstar** **SYMBOL** ▷ **3** **A2** [C] a symbol with four or more points: *star-shaped* ◦ *How many stars (= symbols showing quality) has this restaurant got?* ◦ *The teacher gave Tom a gold star (= a paper symbol rewarding good work) for his drawing.* **4** **two-star, three-star, etc.** **C1** used to show how good a restaurant, hotel, etc. is: *The cheaper two-star hotels are also within the range of the budget traveller.* **5** a symbol made of metal or cloth worn by particular officials to show their rank: *a sheriff's star* ◦ *a four-star general* **6** [C] an ASTERISK (= a symbol *) **LUCK** ▷ **7** [C] informal any planet or other object in the sky thought of in ASTROLOGY as influencing a person's luck: *She was* ***born under*** *a lucky/an unlucky star.* → See also **star sign** **8** **stars** [plural] informal **horoscope**: *I always like to see what* ***the*** *stars say in the newspaper.*

IDIOM **you're a star!** informal something you say to someone when they have been kind and helpful to you

▸**verb** [I + prep, T] (**-rr-**) **B1** If a film, play, etc. stars someone, or if someone stars in a film, play, etc., they are the main actor in it: *Ben Kingsley starred* ***in*** *the film 'Gandhi'.*

▸**adj** [before noun] informal **C1** best or most important: *Natalie is, without a doubt, the star student in this year's ballet class.* ◦ *This afternoon the prosecution will call its star witness.*

starboard /ˈstɑː.bəd/ (US) /ˈstɑːr.bɚd/ noun [U] special-

S

ized the right side of a ship or aircraft as you are facing forward → Opposite **port**

starch /stɑːtʃ/ US /stɑːrtʃ/ noun; verb

▸noun [U] FOOD ▷ **1** a white substance that exists in large amounts in potatoes and particular grains such as rice: *Corn starch is used as a thickener in stews.* → Compare **carbohydrate** CLOTH ▷ **2** a white substance from potatoes and particular grains, used to make cloth stiff

▸verb [T] to make clothes stiff by washing them with starch: *She wore a starched white apron over her black dress.*

starchily /ˈstɑː.tʃɪ.li/ US /ˈstɑːr-/ adv informal disapproving in a formal way and without humour

starchy /ˈstɑː.tʃi/ US /ˈstɑːr-/ adj FORMAL ▷ **1** informal disapproving behaving in a formal way and without humour: *Museums are trying to shake off their starchy image.* FOOD ▷ **2** containing a lot of starch: *starchy foods*

ˌstar-ˈcrossed adj literary unlucky: *star-crossed lovers*

stardom /ˈstɑː.dəm/ US /ˈstɑːr-/ noun [U] C2 the quality of being famous, especially for being a singer, actor, etc.: *From childhood, Britney Spears seemed destined for stardom.*

stardust /ˈstɑː.dʌst/ US /ˈstɑːr-/ noun [U] literary (something which causes) a pleasant dream-like or romantic feeling

stare /steəʳ/ US /ster/ verb; noun

▸verb [I or T] B2 to look for a long time with the eyes wide open, especially when surprised, frightened, or thinking: *Don't stare **at** people like that, it's rude.* ◦ *Chuck sat quietly for hours staring into the distance, thinking of what might have been.* ◦ *During the press conference, each boxer tried to stare the other **down** (= force the other to look away by continual staring).* • **staring** /ˈsteə.rɪŋ/ US /ˈster.ɪŋ/ adj *In the darkness we could just make out the blank, staring eyes of a child.*

IDIOMS **be staring at sth** If you are staring at a bad situation or problem, you know you must experience it or deal with it very soon: *By late in the first half United were staring at a seven-goal deficit and almost certain defeat.* • **stare sb in the face** informal If something stares someone in the face, it is very easy to see or obvious: *The answer has been staring us in the face all along!*

▸noun [C] a long look at something or someone with your eyes wide open: *She gave him a long stare but didn't answer his question.*

S

starfish /ˈstɑː.fɪʃ/ US /ˈstɑːr-/ noun [C] (plural **starfish** or **starfishes**) a flat animal that lives in the sea and has five arms which grow from its body in the shape of a star

starfruit /ˈstɑː.fruːt/ US /ˈstɑːr-/ noun [C] (also **carambola**) a yellow tropical fruit with smooth skin and five pointed, curved parts, making a star shape when you cut through it

stargazer /ˈstɑːˌgeɪ.zəʳ/ US /ˈstɑːrˌgeɪ.zɚ/ noun [C] informal a person who is involved in ASTRONOMY or ASTROLOGY • **stargazing** /-zɪŋ/ noun [U]

stark /stɑːk/ US /stɑːrk/ adj; adv

▸adj empty, simple, or obvious, especially without decoration or anything that is not necessary: *It was a stark room with a bed and chair as the only furniture.* ◦ *The stark **reality** is that we are operating at a huge loss.* ◦ *In the suburbs the spacious houses stand in stark (= extreme) **contrast** to the slums of the city's poor.* → Synonym **severe** • **starkness** /ˈstɑːk.nəs/ US /ˈstɑːrk-/ noun [U]

▸adv completely or extremely: *The children were splashing in the river, stark **naked**.* ◦ *I think he's stark **raving mad** (UK also stark **staring mad**) to spend his time watching trains!*

starkers /ˈstɑː.kəz/ US /ˈstɑːr.kɚz/ adj [after verb] UK informal often humorous naked

starkly /ˈstɑː.kli/ US /ˈstɑːr-/ adv very obviously and clearly: *Her later sensual works contrast starkly with the harsh earlier paintings.*

starlet /ˈstɑː.lət/ US /ˈstɑːr-/ noun [C] often disapproving a young female actor who hopes to be or is thought likely to be famous in the future

starlight /ˈstɑː.laɪt/ US /ˈstɑːr-/ noun [U] the light produced by stars • **starlit** /-lɪt/ adj *a starlit night*

starling /ˈstɑː.lɪŋ/ US /ˈstɑːr-/ noun [C] a common bird with black or dark brown feathers which lives in large groups in many parts of the world

Star of David /ˌstɑː.rəvˈdeɪ.vɪd/ US /ˌstɑːr.əv-/ noun [C] a star with six points which represents Judaism

ˈstar ˌquality noun [C or U] a special ability that makes someone seem very successful or better than other people: *He is a player who has the star quality to delight his fans.*

starred /stɑːd/ US /stɑːrd/ adj SYMBOL ▷ **1** marked with an ASTERISK (= the symbol *): *The starred items on the agenda are the most important.* RANK ▷ **2** A starred hotel or restaurant is one that has been given one or more stars for quality.

starry /ˈstɑː.ri/ US /ˈstɑːr.i/ adj lit by stars or shining like a star: *a starry night/sky*

ˌstarry-ˈeyed adj If a person is starry-eyed, they have a lot of thoughts and opinions that are unreasonably positive, so they do not understand things as they really are.

ˌStars and ˈStripes noun the US flag

ˈstar ˌsign noun [C] in ASTROLOGY, any of the twelve symbols that represent parts of the ZODIAC: *'What's your star sign?' 'I'm a Leo.'*

ˌStar-Spangled ˈBanner noun the NATIONAL ANTHEM (= song) of the US

ˈstar-struck adj often disapproving feeling great or too much respect for famous or important people, especially famous actors or performers: *It's the story of a star-struck young girl who goes to Hollywood to make her fortune.*

ˈstar-ˌstudded adj informal If a group of people, a film, or a show is star-studded, there are a lot of famous people in it.

start /stɑːt/ US /stɑːrt/ verb; noun

▸verb BEGIN ▷ **1** A1 [I or T] to begin doing something: *When do you start your course/your new job?* ◦ *We'll be starting (the session) at six o'clock.* ◦ *Can you start (= begin a new job) on Monday?* ◦ [+ -ing verb] *They started build**ing** the house in January.* ◦ [+ to infinitive] *I'd just started **to** write a letter when the phone rang.* **2** B2 [I or T] (also **start up**) If a business or other organization starts, or if someone starts one, it is created and starts to operate: *She started her own software company.* ◦ *A lot of new restaurants have started up in the region.* **3** B1 [I or T] to begin to happen or to make something begin to happen: *A new series of wildlife programmes has started on Monday evenings.* ◦ *Police believe the fire was started by arsonists.* **4** A1 [I or T] to begin a set of activities with the thing or person mentioned: *The speaker started **with** a description of her journey to China.* ◦ *Give me your answers one by one, starting **with** Lucy.* ◦ *You could start **by** weed**ing** the flowerbeds.* ◦ *He started his working life **as** an engineer but later became a teacher.* **5** [I] informal to begin to complain or be annoying in some way: *Don't start – we're not going and that's that!* ◦ informal *'It would help if Richard did some work.' 'Oh, **don't get** me started on Richard!'* **6 get started** to begin: *When can we get started?* **7 start a family** to have your first child **8 start work** to begin being employed: *He started work at 16 in a local bakers.* **9 to start with** B2 at the beginning, or as the first of several things: *We only knew two people in London to start with, but we soon made friends.* ◦ *To start with, we need better computers – then we need more training.* **FIRST POINT** ▷ **10** [I usually + adv/prep] to begin at one point and then move to another, in distance or range: *The bus starts **at/from** the main depot.* ◦ *We'll need to start **(off/out)** early because the journey takes six hours.* ◦ *Tell me what happened – start **at the beginning**.* ◦ *Ticket prices start **at/from** £20 and go up to £100.* **MOVE SUDDENLY** ▷ **11** [I] to move your body suddenly because something has surprised or frightened you: *He started **at** the sound of the phone.* **WORK** ▷ **12** B2 [I or T] (also **start up**) to (cause to) begin to work or operate: *I'm having trouble starting the car.* ◦ *The engine won't start.*

PHRASAL VERBS **start (sth) off** B1 to begin by doing something, or to make something begin by doing something: *She started off the meeting with the monthly sales report.* ◦ *I'd like to start off by thanking you all for coming today.* • **start sb off 1** to help someone to start an activity, especially a piece of work: *I'll start her off on some fairly basic stuff and see how she gets on.* **2** to make someone start to laugh, cry, or talk about something that they often talk about: *I could see Emma trying not to laugh and of course that started me off.* • **start on sth** to start to deal with something, or to start to use something: *I'm just about to start on the cleaning.* ◦ *Shall we start on the wine or wait till Colin gets here?* • **start on at sb** to start complaining angrily to someone about something they have done: *She started on at him about the way he's always looking at other women.* • **start out** C1 to begin your life, or the part of your life when you work, in a particular way: *My dad started out **as** a sales assistant in a shop.* • **start over** US (UK **start afresh**) to begin to do something again, sometimes in a different way: *We decided to abandon the first draft of the report and start over.* ◦ *The agreement allows old expectations to be forgotten and everyone can start afresh.* • **start (sth) up BUSINESS** ▷ **1** If a business or other organization starts up, or if someone starts one up, it is created and starts to operate: *Many small businesses started up in the 1980s to cater to this growing market.* ◦ *We ought to start up a drama group.* **ENGINE** ▷ **2** If a vehicle or engine starts up, or someone starts it up, it starts to work: *The car wouldn't start up this morning.*

▸noun **BEGINNING** ▷ **1** B1 [S] the beginning of something: *We were doubtful about the product's usefulness **from** the start.* ◦ *They announced the start **of** a new commercial venture.* ◦ *The weather was good **at** the start (= in the first part) of the week.* ◦ *The event **got off to** a shaky/poor start with the stage lights failing in the first few minutes.* **2** C2 [C] the act of beginning to do something: *We need to **make** a start **on** (preparing) the brochure next week.* **3 from start to finish** C1 including all of something, from the beginning to the end: *The whole course was a disaster from start to finish.* **4 for a start** C1 UK first, or as the first in a set of things: *We'll take names and phone numbers for a start, then later on we can get more details.* **ADVANTAGE** ▷ **5** C2 [S] an advantage that you have over someone else when you begin something: *We gave the youngest children a five-second start (= in a race).* **SUDDEN MOVEMENT** ▷ **6** [S] a sudden movement of the body that you make when something has surprised or frightened you: *He woke **with a** start.* ◦ *She **gave a** start as I entered.*

starter /ˈstɑː.təʳ/ US /ˈstɑːr.t̬ɚ/ **noun** [C] **1** a person, animal, or organization that is involved at the beginning of an activity, especially a race: *Of the ten starters (= horses which started in the race), two fell at the first fence.* **2** [C] mainly UK a small dish served as the first part of a meal: *We had soup/pâté/pasta as a starter.*

IDIOMS **for starters** informal used to say that something is the first in a list of things: *Try this exercise for starters.* ◦ *'Why did you decide not to go to the concert?' 'Well, for starters, the tickets were ridiculously expensive.'* • **under starter's orders** ready for the signal to start a race

ˈstarter ˌmotor noun [C] an electrical device which causes an engine to begin to operate

ˈstarting ˌdate noun [C] (also **ˈstart ˌdate**) the planned day for the start of an important activity: *The starting date for the construction work is 23 June.*

ˈstarting ˌline noun [C] a line drawn on the ground behind which competitors wait for a signal to begin a race

ˈstarting ˌpistol noun [C] a small gun that makes a loud noise instead of FIRING bullets and is used for starting races

ˈstarting ˌpoint noun [C usually singular] (UK also **ˈstart ˌpoint**) a place or position where something begins: *The starting point for the guided tour of the town is in the market square.* ◦ *The committee emphasized that its report was only meant as a starting point **for** discussion.*

ˈstarting ˌprice noun [C] (abbreviation **SP**) UK the amount of money offered just at the start of a race by a BOOKMAKER for a winning BET (= money risked)

ˈstarting ˌsalary noun [C] the amount of money received when starting a particular type of job for the first time

ˈstarting ˌtime noun [C] (also **ˈstart ˌtime**) the planned time for starting an official activity: *The starting time for our monthly meetings will be 6.30.*

startle /ˈstɑː.tl/ US /ˈstɑːr.t̬l/ **verb** [T] to do something unexpected which surprises and sometimes worries a person or animal: *She was concentrating on her book and his voice startled her.* ◦ *The noise of the car startled the birds and the whole flock flew up into the air.* ◦ *Her article on diet startled many people **into** changing their eating habits.* • **startled** /-tld/ US /-t̬ld/ **adj** *a startled expression*

startling /ˈstɑː.tlɪŋ/ US /ˈstɑːr.t̬lɪŋ/ **adj** surprising and sometimes worrying: *startling results* ◦ *He made some startling admissions about his past.* • **startlingly** /-li/ **adv** *startlingly poor results*

ˈstart-up noun [C] a small business that has just been started: *Start-ups are very vulnerable in the business world.*

ˌstar ˈturn noun [C usually singular] the main performer in a film, play, or other show, or an extremely good performance by someone

starvation /stɑːˈveɪ.ʃᵊn/ US /stɑːr-/ **noun** [U] C2 the state of having no food for a long period, often causing death: *20 million people **face** starvation unless a vast emergency aid programme is launched.* ◦ *The animals had **died of** starvation.* ◦ figurative *They pay starvation **wages** (= not enough money to live on).*

starˈvation ˌdiet noun [C] the act of eating only a very small amount of food in order to lose weight

S

quickly: *She **went on** a starvation diet and ended up in hospital.*

starve /stɑːv/ (US) /stɑːrv/ verb **1** C1 [I or T] to (cause someone to) become very weak or die because there is not enough food to eat: *Whole communities starved **to death** during the long drought.* ◦ *From talking to former prisoners in the camps, an obvious conclusion is that they have been starved.* **2** [T often passive] If you are starved of something necessary or good, you do not receive enough of it: *People starved **of** sleep start to lose their concentration and may hallucinate.*

starved /stɑːvd/ (US) /stɑːrvd/ adj **1** mainly US informal very hungry **2 half-starved** dangerously thin: *A lot of these fashion models look half-starved to me.*

starving /ˈstɑː.vɪŋ/ (US) /ˈstɑːr-/ adj **NO FOOD** ▷ **1** B2 dying because of not having enough food: *The cats were neglected and starving.* **2** B2 informal very hungry: *Isn't lunch ready yet? I'm starving.*

stash /stæʃ/ verb [T] informal to store or hide something, especially a large amount: *The stolen pictures were stashed **(away)** in a London warehouse.* • **stash** noun [C] *They discovered a stash **of** money hidden at the back of a drawer.*

stasis /ˈsteɪ.sɪs/ noun [U] formal a state which does not change: *She was bored – her life was **in** stasis.*

state /steɪt/ noun; verb; adj

▸noun **CONDITION** ▷ **1** B2 [C] a condition or way of being that exists at a particular time: *The building was in **a** state **of** disrepair.* ◦ *She was found wandering in a confused state **(of mind)**.* ◦ *Give me the keys – you're in no fit state to drive.* ◦ *After the accident I was in a state **of shock**.* ◦ *I came home to an unhappy state **of affairs** (= situation).* ◦ *The kitchen was in its original state, with a 1920s sink and stove.* **2 the state of play** UK the present situation: *The article provides a useful summary of the current state of play **in** the negotiations.* **COUNTRY** ▷ **3** C1 [C or U] a country or its government: *The drought is worst in the central African states.* ◦ *Britain is one of the **member** states of the European Union.* ◦ *The government was determined to reduce the number of state-owned industries.* ◦ *Some theatres receive a small amount of funding from the state.* ◦ formal *His diary included comments on **affairs/matters of** state (= information about government activities).* **4** B1 [C] a part of a large country with its own government, such as in Germany, Australia, or the US: *Alaska is the largest state in the US.* ◦ *Representatives are elected from each state.* **5 the States** informal used to refer to the US **6 in state** If a king, queen, or government leader does something in state, they do it in a formal way as part of an official ceremony: *The Queen rode in state to the opening of Parliament.*

IDIOM **be in/get into a state** mainly UK to become nervous and upset: *She got into a real state before her driving test.*

▸verb [T] formal B2 to say or write something, especially clearly and carefully: *Our warranty clearly states the limits of our liability.* ◦ [+ (that)] *Union members stated **(that)** they were unhappy with the proposal.* ◦ [+ question word] *Please state **why** you wish to apply for this grant.* ◦ *Children in the stated (= named) areas were at risk from a lack of food, the report said.*

▸adj [before noun] **1** B2 provided, created, or done by the state (= government of a country): *state education/industries* ◦ *state legislature/law* ◦ *state control* ◦ *state funding/pensions/subsidies* **2** State events are formal official ceremonies that involve a leader of a country or someone who represents the government: *the state opening of Parliament*

statecraft /ˈsteɪt.krɑːft/ (US) /-kræft/ **noun** [U] the skill of governing a country

ˈState Deˌpartment noun the part of the US government which deals with foreign matters

statehood /ˈsteɪt.hʊd/ noun [U] the condition of being a country or a part of a large country that has its own government: *The US-Mexican War of 1846–48 was sparked by a dispute over Texas statehood.*

stateless /ˈsteɪt.ləs/ adj A stateless person has no country that they officially belong to.

ˌstate ˈline noun [C usually singular] US a border between two US states

stately /ˈsteɪt.li/ adj formal formal, slow, and having a style and appearance that causes admiration: *The procession moved through the mountain village at a stately **pace**.* ◦ *He always walked with a stately **bearing**.* • **stateliness** /-nəs/ noun [U]

ˌstately ˈhome noun [C] UK a large, old house that usually has beautiful furniture, decorations, and gardens

statement /ˈsteɪt.mənt/ noun [C] **1** B2 something that someone says or writes officially, or an action done to express an opinion: *The government is expected to issue a statement about the investigation **to** the press.* ◦ *He produced a signed statement from the prisoner.* ◦ *He threw paint over the fur coats because he wanted to **make** a statement about cruelty to animals.* ◦ [+ that] *We were not surprised by their statement **that** the train services would be reduced.* **2** C2 (also **bank statement**) a record of the amounts of money paid into and taken out of your bank account during a particular period of time

> Word partners for **statement**
>
> *issue/make/prepare/release* a statement • *retract/withdraw* a statement • a *false/joint/public/sworn* statement • a *general* statement • a statement *about/on* sth • a statement *of* sth

ˌstate ocˈcasion noun [C] an official formal occasion, which has traditional ceremonies connected with it, and at which important members of the government, royal family, etc. are present

ˌstate of eˈmergency noun [C] a temporary system of rules to deal with an extremely dangerous or difficult situation: *After the floods the government **declared** a state of emergency.*

ˌstate-of-the-ˈart adj C1 very modern and using the most recent ideas and methods: *a state-of-the-art computer*

ˌstate ˈpremier noun [C] the leader of an Australian state government

stateroom /ˈsteɪt.rʊm/, /-ruːm/ noun [C] a large room, especially in a castle or PALACE, used for formal or important occasions: *the staterooms at Windsor Castle*

ˈstate ˌschool noun [C] UK (US **ˌpublic ˈschool**) a school that is free to go to because the government provides the money for it

ˌstate's ˈevidence noun [U] US for **Queen's evidence** or **King's evidence**

stateside /ˈsteɪt.saɪd/ adj, adv US related to the US; in or towards the US: *a stateside job* ◦ *Some girls dream of finding an American husband to transport them stateside (= to the US).*

statesman /ˈsteɪt.smən/ noun [C] (plural **-men** /-mən/) approving an experienced politician, especially one who is respected for making good judgments • **statesmanship** /-ʃɪp/ noun [U]

statesmanlike /ˈsteɪts.mən.laɪk/ adj approving having or showing the qualities of a statesman: *a statesmanlike speech*

ˌstate ˈvisit noun [C] an official formal visit by the leader of one country to another

statewide /ˈsteɪt.waɪd/ adj in every part of a state: *statewide elections*

static /ˈstæt.ɪk/ (US) /ˈstæt̬-/ adj; noun

▸adj staying in one place without moving, or not changing for a long time: *Oil prices have **remained** static for the last few months.*

▸noun [U] **1** noise on a radio or television caused by electricity in the air: *There's so much static on this radio I can't hear what they're saying.* **2** (also **static electricity**) an electrical charge which collects on the surface of objects made from some types of material when they are rubbed

statin /ˈstæt.ɪn/ (US) /ˈstæt̬-/ noun [C] a drug that reduces the level of CHOLESTEROL (= substance containing a lot of fat in your blood that can cause heart disease)

station /ˈsteɪ.ʃən/ noun; verb

▸noun [C] **BUSES/TRAINS** ▷ **1** A1 a building and the surrounding area where buses or trains stop for people to get on or off: *a train/rail station* ◦ *a bus/coach station* ◦ UK *a railway station* ◦ *Our office is near the station.* ◦ *We looked on our map to find the nearest **underground/tube*** (US ***subway/metro***) *station.* **BROADCASTING** ▷ **2** B1 a company that broadcasts radio or television programmes: *a radio/television station* ◦ *a commercial/foreign station* ◦ *a pirate (= illegal) station* ◦ *The reception is not very good – try to **tune in to** another station.* **SERVICE** ▷ **3** a building or place used for a particular service or type of work: *a petrol* (US *gas*) *station* ◦ *a police/fire station* ◦ *a biological research station* **4** mainly Australian English a large farm with animals in Australia and New Zealand: *a sheep station* **POSITION** ▷ **5** a particular position that someone has been ordered to move into or to stay in: *The police **took up** their stations at the edge of the road, holding back the crowd.*

> **!** Usage: **station or stop?**
>
> **Station** is used for trains:
>
> *I'll meet you at the station in an hour.*
> *a railway station*
> *an underground station*
>
> **Stop** or **bus stop** is used for buses:
>
> *I stood at the bus stop for over half an hour.*
> *Get off at the third stop.*
>
> A **bus station** is a place where many buses start or end their journeys.

IDIOM **out of station** Indian English away; not present in a place: *I am at present out of station and will reply on my return.*

▸verb [T + adv/prep] to cause especially soldiers to be in a particular place to do a job: *I hear your son's in the army – where's he stationed?* ◦ *The regiment was stationed **in** Singapore for several years.* ◦ *Armed guards were stationed around the airport.*

stationary /ˈsteɪ.ʃən.ər.i/ (US) /-ʃə.ner-/ adj not moving, or not changing: *a stationary car/train* ◦ *The traffic got slower and slower until it was stationary.* ◦ *The rate of inflation has been stationary for several months.*

ˈstation ˌbreak noun [C] US a pause in a television or radio broadcast for the broadcasting station to give its name

stationer /ˈsteɪ.ʃən.ər/ (US) /-ɚ/ noun [C] **1** a person or business that sells stationery **2 stationer's** (plural **stationers**) a shop that sells stationery

stationery /ˈsteɪ.ʃən.ər.i/ (US) /-ʃə.ner-/ noun [U] **1** the things needed for writing, such as paper, pens, pencils, and envelopes **2** good quality paper for writing letters on and matching envelopes

ˈstation ˌhouse noun [C] US informal for **police station** or **fire station**

stationmaster /ˈsteɪ.ʃənˌmɑː.stər/ (US) /-ˌmæs.tɚ/ noun [C] the person who is in charge of a railway station

ˈstation ˌwagon noun [C] US for **estate**

statistic /stəˈtɪs.tɪk/ noun **1 statistics a** B2 [plural] (informal **stats**) information based on a study of the number of times something happens or is present, or other NUMERICAL facts: *Statistics **show/suggest** that women live longer than men.* ◦ *According to **official** statistics, the Japanese work longer hours than workers in most other industrialized countries.* **b** [U] the science of using information discovered from studying numbers **2** C1 [C] a fact in the form of a number that shows information about something: *The city's most shocking statistic is its high infant mortality rate.*

statistical /stəˈtɪs.tɪ.kəl/ adj C1 relating to statistics: *statistical errors/evidence* • **statistically** /-kəl.i/ adv *Statistically speaking, you're more likely to die from a bee sting than win the lottery.*

statistician /ˌstæt.ɪˈstɪʃ.ən/ noun [C] someone who studies or is an expert in statistics

stative verb /ˌsteɪ.tɪvˈvɜːb/ (US) /-t̬ɪvˈvɝːb/ noun [C] specialized a verb that describes a state and not an action: *'Be', 'seem', and 'understand' are stative verbs.*

statuary /ˈstætʃ.u.ər.i/ (US) /-er-/ noun [U] formal statues: *a display of garden statuary*

statue /ˈstætʃ.uː/ noun [C] B1 an object made from a hard material, especially stone or metal, to look like a person or animal: *a statue **of** a boy* ◦ *They planned to **put up/erect** a statue **to** the president.*

statue

statuesque /ˌstætʃ.uˈesk/ adj A statuesque woman is attractively tall and large.

statuette /ˌstætʃ.uˈet/ noun [C] a statue that is small enough to stand on a table or shelf

stature /ˈstætʃ.ər/ (US) /-ɚ/ noun **REPUTATION** ▷ **1** [U] the good reputation a person or organization has, based on their behaviour and ability: *an artist **of** great stature* ◦ *His stature **as** an art critic was tremendous.* ◦ *If the school continues to **gain in** stature, it will attract the necessary financial support.* **HEIGHT** ▷ **2** [C usually singular] formal (especially of people) height: *His red hair and short stature made him easy to recognize.*

status /ˈsteɪ.təs/ (US) /-t̬əs/ noun [U] **OFFICIAL POSITION** ▷ **1** C1 an accepted or official position, especially in a social group: *The association works to promote the status of retired people as useful members of the community.* ◦ *There has been an increase in applications for refugee status.* ◦ *The success of her book has given her unexpected celebrity status.* ◦ *Applicants* *should have a degree or a qualification of equal status.* **RESPECT** ▷ **2** the amount of respect, admiration, or importance given to a person, organization, or object: *high/low status* ◦ *As the daughter of the president, she enjoys high status among her peers.* ◦ *The leaders were often more concerned with status and privilege than with the problems of the people.* **SOCIAL MEDIA** ▷ **3** on a SOCIAL MEDIA website, especially FACEBOOK™, a piece of information that you publish about yourself telling people what you are doing, thinking, etc. at a particular time

the status quo /ˌsteɪ.təsˈkwəʊ/ (US) /-t̬əsˈkwoʊ/ **noun** [S] the present situation: *Certain people always want to **maintain** the status quo.*

ˈstatus ˌsymbol noun [C] a thing which people want to have because they think other people will admire them if they have it: *Among young people, this brand of designer clothing is the **ultimate** status symbol.*

statute /ˈstætʃ.uːt/ **noun** [C or U] **1** a law that has been formally approved and written down **2 statute book** UK When a law is on or reaches the statute book, it has been formally approved and written down and can be used in a law court.

statutory /ˈstæt.jʊ.tᵊr.i/ (US) /-tɔːr-/ **adj** decided or controlled by law: *statutory obligations*

staunch /stɔːntʃ/ (US) /stɑːntʃ/ **adj; verb**

▸**adj** always loyal in supporting a person, organization, or set of beliefs or opinions: *a staunch friend and ally* ◦ *He gained a reputation as being a staunch **defender/supporter** of civil rights.* • **staunchness** /ˈstɔːntʃ.nəs/ (US) /ˈstɑːntʃ-/ **noun** [U]

▸**verb** [T] (US also **stanch**) to stop something happening, or to stop liquid, especially blood, from flowing out: *The country's asylum laws were amended to staunch the **flow/flood** of economic migrants.* ◦ *Mike pressed hard on the wound and staunched the **flow** of blood.*

staunchly /ˈstɔːntʃ.li/ (US) /stɑːntʃ-/ **adv** strongly: *staunchly loyal/independent*

stave /steɪv/ **noun; verb**

▸**noun** [C] UK (US **staff**) the five lines and four spaces between them on which musical notes are written

▸**verb** (**staved** or **stove**)

PHRASAL VERBS **stave sth in** mainly UK to push or hit something such as a door or other surface so that it breaks and falls towards the inside: *The front of the ship was stove in where it had hit the rock.* • **stave sth/sb off** to stop something bad from happening, or to keep an unwanted situation or person away, usually temporarily: *We were hoping to stave off these difficult decisions until September.*

staves /steɪvz/ **noun** plural of **staff** and **stave**

stay /steɪ/ **verb; noun**

▸**verb NOT LEAVE** ▷ **1** (A1) [I] to not move away from or leave a place or situation: *They need an assistant who is willing to stay **for** six months.* ◦ *Stay **until** the rain has stopped.* ◦ *Can you stay after work to play tennis?* ◦ *Because of the snow, children were told to stay **at home*** (US usually *stay **home***). **CONTINUE** ▷ **2** (B1) [I usually + adv/prep, L] to continue doing something, or to continue to be in a particular state: *Stay away from the edge of the cliff.* ◦ *He's decided not to stay **in** teaching/medicine/the army.* ◦ *The final figures showed that most departments had stayed within budget.* ◦ *It was so warm we stayed (**out**) in the garden until ten that night.* ◦ *Put a lid on the pan so the food will stay hot.* ◦ *The shops stay open until nine o' clock.* ◦ *They stayed friends after their divorce.* **LIVE** ▷ **3** (A2) [I] to live or be in a place for a short time as a visitor: *I stayed **in** Montreal for two weeks then flew home.* ◦ *They said they'd stay **at/in** a hotel.* ◦ *The children usually stay **with** their grandparents for a week in the summer.* **4 stay overnight** (also **stay the night**) to sleep somewhere for one night: *We've arranged to stay overnight at my sister's house.* **5** [I] Indian English or Scottish English to live somewhere permanently: *I still stay with my parents.*

> **!** Common mistake: **stay**
>
> **Warning:** choose the correct preposition!
>
> To talk about the town/country/region you are visiting, don't say 'stay at/to/on', say **stay in**:
>
> *We stayed in Rome for three nights.*
>
> To talk about the building where you stay during your visit, remember to use the preposition **in** or **at**:
>
> *We stayed in a nice hotel in the city centre.*
>
> *I stayed at my brother's house.*
>
> To talk about the person or people you are visiting, don't say 'stay at/in', say **stay with**:
>
> *We stayed with a very nice host family.*

IDIOMS **here to stay** If something is here to stay, it has stopped being unusual and has become generally used or accepted: *Blogging is here to stay.* • **stay on the sidelines** If you stay on the sidelines, you are not an important part of what is happening. • **stay put** (C2) to remain in the same place or position: *Just stay put with the cases, while I go and find a taxi.* • **stay the course** to continue doing something until it is finished or until you achieve something you have planned to do: *She interviewed slimmers who had failed to stay the course to find out why they had given up.*

PHRASAL VERBS **stay away from sb/sth** (C1) to not go near or become involved with someone; to avoid something that will have a bad effect on you: *My parents told me to stay away from her.* ◦ *I drink a lot of water and I stay away from greasy, heavy foods.* • **stay behind** (B1) to not leave a place when other people leave: *I stayed behind after class.* • **stay in** (B1) to stay in your home: *Let's stay in tonight and watch a movie.* • **stay on** (C1) to continue to be in a place, job, or school after the other people who were with you have left: *Gill decided to stay on at university to do further research.* ◦ *We asked him to stay on **as** youth leader for another year.* • **stay out** [usually + adv/prep] (B2) to not come home at night, or to go home late: *Our cat usually stays out at night.* ◦ *My mum won't let me stay out **late**.* • **stay out of sth** (C2) to not become involved in an argument or discussion: *It's better to stay out of their arguments.* ◦ *You don't know anything about this, so just stay out of **it**!* • **stay over** (B2) to sleep at someone's house for one night: *Why don't you stay over and drive back in the morning?* • **stay up** (B2) to go to bed later than usual: *We stayed up (**late**) to watch a film.*

▸**noun VISIT** ▷ **1** (B1) [C] a period of time that you spend in a place: *She planned a short stay **at/in** a hotel to celebrate their anniversary.* **2 stay of execution, deportation, etc.** legal an order by a judge which stops a judgment being performed until new information can be considered

ˈstay-at-ˌhome noun [C] informal disapproving someone who does not like to go to parties or events outside the home and is considered boring

staycation /steɪˈkeɪ.ʃᵊn/ **noun** [C] informal a holiday that you take in your own country or at home rather than travelling to another country: *It's easy to have a staycation in a place like NYC.*

stayer /ˈsteɪ.əʳ/ (US) /-ɚ/ noun [C] CONTINUING ▷ **1** a person or animal that continues to try hard rather than giving up: *The horse isn't very fast but it's a stayer and always finishes even the longest races.* IN A PLACE ▷ **2** someone who stays in a place: *The longest stayers are the British, who visit Australia to see friends and relatives.*

ˈstaying ˌpower noun [U] If someone has staying power, they always manage to continue doing what they have to do until it is finished.

St Bernard /ˌseɪntˈbɜː.nəd/, /ˌsənt-/ (US) /ˌseɪnt.bɚˈnɑːrd/ noun [C] a very large, strong dog used especially in Switzerland in the past to find people lost in the mountains

std adj written abbreviation for **standard**.

STD /ˌes.tiːˈdiː/ noun DISEASE ▷ **1** [C] abbreviation for **sexually transmitted disease** PHONE ▷ **2** [U] abbreviation for subscriber trunk dialling: a system in the UK and Australia by which people make phone calls over long distances

stead /sted/ noun **1 in sb's stead** formal in place of someone: *The marketing manager was ill and her deputy ran the meeting in her stead.* **2 stand sb in good stead** → See at **stand**

steadfast /ˈsted.fɑːst/, /-fəst/ (US) /-fæst/ adj approving staying the same for a long time and not changing quickly or unexpectedly: *a steadfast friend/ally* ◦ *steadfast loyalty* ◦ *The group **remained** steadfast **in** its support for the new system, even when it was criticized in the newspapers.* • **steadfastness** /-nəs/ noun [U]

steadfastly /ˈsted.fɑːst.li/, /-fəst-/ (US) /-fæst-/ adv strongly and without stopping: *She was steadfastly in support of women's rights.*

steadily /ˈsted.ɪ.li/ adv GRADUALLY ▷ **1** (B2) gradually: *Prices have risen steadily.* CONTROLLED ▷ **2** calmly and in a controlled way: *She returned his gaze steadily.*

steady /ˈsted.i/ adj; verb; adv

▸adj GRADUAL ▷ **1** (B2) happening in a smooth, gradual, and regular way, not suddenly or unexpectedly: *The procession moved through the streets at a steady pace.* ◦ *Orders for new ships are rising, after several years of steady decline.* ◦ *Over the last ten years he has produced a steady **flow/stream/trickle** of articles and papers.* ◦ *Progress has been **slow but** steady.* FIRM ▷ **2** (B2) fixed and not moving or changing suddenly: *I'll **hold** the boat steady while you climb in.* ◦ *Most rental prices have **held** steady this year.* ◦ *Young people assume that if you are in a steady **relationship**, you don't have to worry about HIV.* **3 steady job/work** (C2) work that is likely to continue for a long time and for which you will be paid regularly: *Owning your own home and having a steady job will help when applying for a loan.* CONTROLLED ▷ **4** (B2) under control: *a steady voice/look/gaze* ◦ *You need steady **nerves** to drive in city traffic.* ◦ *Painting these small details needs a steady **hand**.* **5** describes someone who can be trusted to show good judgment and act in a reasonable way: *a steady friend* • **steadiness** /-nəs/ noun [U]

IDIOMS **go steady on sth** UK (US **go easy on sth**) to not use too much of something: *Go steady on the milk, Dan – that's our last bottle.* • **steady on!** UK informal used to tell someone that what they are saying is too extreme: *Steady on, Chris – she's nice but she's not that nice!*

▸verb [T] STOP MOVING ▷ **1** to make something stop shaking or moving: *He wobbled about on the bike and then steadied himself.* CONTROL ▷ **2** to become calm and controlled, or to make someone do this: *Some people say that a drink will steady your nerves.*

▸adv old-fashioned **go steady (with sb)** to have a romantic relationship with one person for a long period: *She's been going steady with Mike for six months.*

steak /steɪk/ noun [C or U] (A2) a thick, flat piece of meat or fish, especially meat from a cow: ***T-bone/sirloin** steaks* ◦ *salmon/turkey steaks* ◦ *Shall we have steak for dinner?*

steakhouse /ˈsteɪk.haʊs/ noun [C] a restaurant that specializes in serving steak

ˈsteak ˌknife noun [C] a sharp knife with small teeth-like parts along one edge which cuts meat easily

ˌsteak tarˈtare noun [U] steak (= meat from a cow) cut into very small pieces and eaten without being cooked

steal /stiːl/ verb; noun

▸verb [I or T] (**stole**, **stolen**) TAKE ▷ **1** (A2) to take something without the permission or knowledge of the owner and keep it: *She admitted stealing the money **from** her employers.* ◦ *The number of cars which are stolen every year has risen.* ◦ *They were so poor they had to steal in order to eat.* DO QUICKLY ▷ **2** to do something quickly or without being noticed: *She stole **a glance** at her watch.* ◦ *He stole **out** of the room while no one was looking.*

> **Other ways of saying steal**
>
> **Take** is often used instead of 'steal':
>
> *Someone **took** their car from outside the house.*
>
> If someone steals something from a shop, you could use the verb **shoplift**:
>
> *He was caught **shoplifting** by a store detective.*
>
> If someone steals something from a place or person, often in a violent way, you could use the verb **rob**:
>
> *He **robbed** a bank of about $5,000.*
>
> **Burgle** is used when someone illegally enters a building and steals things:
>
> *When she got home from work, she discovered that her house had been **burgled**.*
>
> **Pilfer** is used when people steal things that are not very valuable:
>
> *Employees **pilfering** paper, pens, etc. can cost employers a lot.*
>
> If large numbers of people steal things from shops and houses during a violent event, you could use the word **loot**:
>
> *During the riots, stores were **looted** and cars set on fire.*
>
> **Embezzle** can be used when someone steals money that belongs to the company or organization that person works for:
>
> *She **embezzled** thousands of dollars from the charity.*

IDIOMS **steal sb's thunder** to do what someone else was going to do before they do it, especially if this takes success or praise away from them: *Sandy stole my thunder when she announced that she was pregnant two days before I'd planned to tell people about my pregnancy.* • **steal a march on sb** If you steal a march on someone, you get an advantage over them by acting before they do: *Our rival company managed to steal a march on us by bringing out their software ahead of ours.* • **steal the limelight** to get more attention than anyone or anything else in a situation: *The experimental car certainly stole the limelight at the motor show.* • **steal the show/scene** to be the most

S

popular or the best part of an event or situation: *The child with the dog stole the show.*

▸noun [S] mainly US informal a product that has a very low price, or a price that is much lower than the original cost: *I picked up a new iron at the sale – it was a steal.*

stealth /stelθ/ **noun** [U] movement that is quiet and careful in order not to be seen or heard, or secret action: *These thieves operate* ***with*** *terrifying stealth – they can easily steal from the pockets of unsuspecting travellers.* ◦ *The weapons had been acquired* ***by*** *stealth.* • **stealthy** /ˈstel.θi/ **adj** *stealthy footsteps* • **stealthily** /ˈstel.θɪ.li/ **adv**

ˈstealth ˌbomber noun [C] (also **ˈstealth ˌfighter**) an aircraft that cannot be seen on RADAR

ˈstealth ˌtax noun [C] a new tax that is collected in a way that is not very obvious, so people may not realize that they are paying it

steam /stiːm/ **noun; verb**

▸noun [U] (B2) the hot gas that is produced when water boils: *Steam rose from the simmering stew.* ◦ *steam turbines* ◦ *a steam engine/locomotive* ◦ *the age of steam (= the period when steam provided power for railways and factories)* ◦ *The pump is driven* ***by*** *steam.*

IDIOMS **run out of steam** to suddenly lose the energy or interest to continue doing what you are doing: *The peace talks seem to have run out of steam.* • **get/pick up steam** to start working much more effectively: *After the first three months, the fundraising project really started to pick up steam.* • **let/blow off steam** (C2) to do or say something that helps you to get rid of strong feelings or energy: *He lifts weights after work to let off steam.* • **under your own steam** If you do something under your own steam, you do it without help: *Do you want a lift or will you get there under your own steam?*

▸verb **1** [I] to move by steam power: *The train/ship steamed* ***out*** *of the station/harbour.* **2** [T] to cook food using steam: *steamed vegetables* **3** [T usually + adv/prep] to use steam to make something softer, especially glue so that something can be removed: *Ross steamed* ***open*** *the envelope to see if it was a love letter.*

PHRASAL VERB **steam (sth) up** If glass or something with a glass or similar surface steams up, it becomes covered with a thin layer of water caused by steam touching it, and if you steam it up, you cause this to happen: *The bathroom mirror steamed up during my shower.*

IDIOM **steamed up** angry, especially about something that other people do not think is important: *She* ***got*** *all steamed up* ***about*** *the books being left on the tables.*

steamboat /ˈstiːm.bəʊt/ (US) /-boʊt/ **noun** [C] a boat which moves by steam power

steamer /ˈstiː.məʳ/ (US) /-mɚ/ **noun** [C] **BOAT** ▷ **1** a boat or ship that moves by steam power **CONTAINER** ▷ **2** a container with holes in the bottom that is put over boiling water in order to cook food in steam, or a machine which cooks food with steam: *a rice steamer* ◦ *a vegetable steamer*

steaming /ˈstiː.mɪŋ/ **adj** producing steam: *a steaming bowl of soup*

ˈsteam ˌiron noun [C] an electrical IRON that has water inside and produces steam to help make clothes smooth

steampunk /ˈstiːm.pʌŋk/ **noun** [U] books or movies about an imagined time when machines use steam for power rather than modern engines and methods, or a style of fashion based on this

steamroller /ˈstiːmˌrəʊ.ləʳ/ (US) /-ˌroʊ.lɚ/ **noun; verb**

▸noun [C] **VEHICLE** ▷ **1** a vehicle that moves forward on a large, heavy wheel in order to make a road surface flat **FORCE** ▷ **2** informal a person who forces other people to agree with them and prevents any opposition

▸verb [T] informal to use great force either to make someone do something or on something to make it happen or be successful: *He steamrollered the plan through the committee.* ◦ *I hate being steamrollered* ***into doing*** *something I don't want to.*

steamship /ˈstiːm.ʃɪp/ **noun** [C] a ship which moves by steam power

ˈsteam ˌshovel noun [C] US for **excavator**

steamy /ˈstiː.mi/ **adj** **1** filled with steam, or hot and wet like steam: *steamy summer weather* ◦ *a steamy kitchen/bathroom* **2** informal sexually exciting or including a lot of sexual activity: *a steamy love scene* ◦ *His new novel is advertised as his steamiest yet.*

steed /stiːd/ **noun** [C] literary a horse that is ridden: *a fine, white steed*

steel /stiːl/ **noun; verb**

▸noun [U] (B2) a strong metal that is a mixture of iron and carbon, used for making things that need a strong structure, especially vehicles and buildings: *steel girders/rods/struts* ◦ *a steel helmet* ◦ *a steel-plated army truck*

▸verb **steel yourself** to force yourself to get ready to do something unpleasant or difficult: [+ to infinitive] *She steeled herself* ***to*** *jump out of the plane.*

ˌsteel ˈband noun [C] a group of musicians who play steel drums

ˌsteel-ˈcapped adj → **steel-toecapped**

ˌsteel ˈdrum noun [C usually plural] a large oil container that has been made into a musical instrument and is played like a drum

ˈsteel ˌmill noun [C] a factory where steel is made

steel-toecapped /ˌstiːlˈtəʊ.kæpt/ (US) /-ˈtoʊ-/ **adj** (also **ˌsteel-ˈcapped**, US **ˌsteel-ˈtoed**) used for describing a shoe or boot with a metal part in the end to protect your toes, worn especially by people in the building industry

ˌsteel-ˈtoed adj → **steel-toecapped**

ˌsteel ˈwool noun [U] (UK also **ˌwire ˈwool**) a thick layer of thin steel threads twisted together, small pieces of which can be used to rub a surface smooth

steelworker /ˈstiːlˌwɜː.kəʳ/ (US) /-ˌwɝː.kɚ/ **noun** [C] a person who works in a factory making steel

steelworks /ˈstiːl.wɜːks/ (US) /-wɝːks/ **noun** [C, + sing/pl verb] (plural **steelworks**) a factory where steel is made

steely /ˈstiː.li/ **adj** **COLOUR** ▷ **1** like steel in colour: *steely grey* **STRONG** ▷ **2** very strong and determined: *steely eyes/nerves* ◦ *steely determination* ◦ *a steely look/stare*

steep /stiːp/ **adj; verb**

▸adj **NOT GRADUAL** ▷ **1** (B1) (of a slope) rising or falling at a sharp angle: *a steep slope* ◦ *It's a steep* ***climb*** *to the top of the mountain, but the view is worth it.* ◦ *The castle is set on a steep* ***hill/hillside.*** **2** (C1) A steep rise or fall is one which goes very quickly from low to high or from high to low: *There has been a steep* ***increase/rise*** *in prices.* **TOO MUCH** ▷ **3** informal (especially of prices) too much, or more than is reasonable: *They are having to face very steep taxes.* ◦ *We enjoyed our meal at the restaurant, but the bill was* ***a bit*** *steep.* ◦ *The*

S

membership fees at the golf club are **pretty** steep.
• **steepness** /ˈstiːp.nəs/ **noun** [U]

▸**verb** [I or T] to cause to stay in a liquid, especially in order to become soft or clean, or to improve flavour: *Leave the cloth to steep in the dye overnight.* ◦ *We had pears steeped in red wine for dessert.*

IDIOM **steeped in blood** literary describes a place where many people have died in a violent way, or a person responsible for the deaths of many people: *The castle's history is steeped in blood.*

PHRASAL VERB **steep sth/sb in sth** [usually passive] If something or someone is steeped in something, they are completely surrounded by or involved in it, or they know a lot about it: *The college is steeped in* ***history/tradition***. ◦ *These ancient scholars were steeped in poetry and painting, as well as maths and astronomy.*

steepen /ˈstiː.pᵊn/ **verb 1** [I or T] to become steeper, or to make something do this: *The trail began to steepen near the top of the hill.* **2** [I] If something such as a cost steepens, it increases: *Our costs have steepened since we began this project.*

steeple /ˈstiː.pl̩/ **noun** [C] a pointed structure on the top of a church tower, or the tower and the pointed structure considered as one unit: *a church steeple*

steeplechase /ˈstiː.pl̩.tʃeɪs/ **noun** [C] a long race in which horses or people have to jump over fences, bushes, etc., either across the countryside or, more usually, on a track

steeplejack /ˈstiː.pl̩.dʒæk/ **noun** [C] a person whose job is to climb high buildings in order to repair, paint, clean them, etc.

steeply /ˈstiːp.li/ **adv** suddenly or by a large amount: *The beach* ***slopes*** *steeply down to the sea.* ◦ *The value of the land has* ***risen*** *steeply.*

steer /stɪəʳ/ (US) /stɪr/ **verb; noun**

▸**verb 1** (B2) [I or T] to control the direction of a vehicle: *She carefully steered the car around the potholes.* ◦ *This car is very easy to steer.* **2** [I or T] If a vehicle steers, it follows a particular route or direction: *The ship passed Land's End, then steered towards southern Ireland.* **3** [T usually + adv/prep] to take someone or something, or cause them to go, in the direction in which you want them to go: *She steered her guests into the dining room.* ◦ *I'd like to steer our discussion* ***back to*** *our original topic.* ◦ *The main task of the new government will be to steer the country* ***towards*** *democracy.*

IDIOMS **steer a course/path** to take a series of actions, usually of a particular type, carefully and intentionally: *It will be difficult to steer a* ***middle*** *course* ***between*** *the competing claims of the two sides in the conflict.* • **steer clear of sb/sth** (C2) to avoid someone or something that seems unpleasant, dangerous, or likely to cause problems: *Her speech steered clear of controversial issues.* ◦ *They warned their children to steer clear of drugs.*

▸**noun** [C] a young male of the CATTLE family that has had its sex organs removed, usually kept for meat

ˈsteering ˌcolumn **noun** [C] the part of a vehicle that the steering wheel is connected to: *My car has an adjustable steering column.*

ˈsteering comˌmittee **noun** [C, + sing/pl verb] a group of people who are chosen to direct the way something is dealt with

ˈsteering ˌwheel **noun** [C] (B2) a wheel in a vehicle which the driver turns in order to make the vehicle go in a particular direction

stegosaurus /ˌsteg.əˈsɔː.rəs/ **noun** [C] specialized a large, plant-eating DINOSAUR with four legs that has pointed PLATES (= flat pieces) all along its back

stein /staɪn/ **noun** [C] **1** a very large cup, usually made of clay and often decorated, which has a handle and a lid, and is used for drinking beer **2** US for **tankard**

stellar /ˈstel.əʳ/ (US) /-ɚ/ **adj 1** of a star or stars: *a stellar explosion* ◦ *stellar light* **2** informal describes people or their activities that are of an extremely high standard: *a stellar performance/player/team*

stem /stem/ **noun; verb**

▸**noun** [C] **CENTRAL PART** ▷ **1** a central part of something from which other parts can develop or grow, or which forms a support **2** the stick-like central part of a plant that grows above the ground and from which leaves and flowers grow, or a smaller thin part that grows from the central part and supports the leaves and flowers: *flower stems* **3** the vertical part of a glass or similar container which supports the part into which you put liquid: *Champagne glasses usually have long stems.* **WORD** ▷ **4** the part of a word that is left after you take off the ending: *From the stem 'sav-' you get 'saves', 'saved', 'saving' and 'saver'.* **WATCH** ▷ **5** US the small part on the side of a watch that you turn to move the HANDS (= parts that point to the numbers), or to make the watch operate **SHIP** ▷ **6** the main supporting structure at the front of a ship

IDIOM **from stem to stern** US from one end of something to the other: *We overhauled the car from stem to stern.*

▸**verb** [T] (**-mm-**) **1** to stop something unwanted from spreading or increasing: *These measures are designed to stem the rise of violent crime.* ◦ *We must take action to stem the* ***tide*** *of resignations.* **2** to stop the flow of a liquid such as blood: *She tied a handkerchief around the wound to stem the* ***flow*** *of blood.*

PHRASAL VERB **stem from sth** (C1) to start or develop as the result of something: *Her problems stem from her difficult childhood.* ◦ *Their disagreement stemmed from a misunderstanding.*

ˈstem ˌcell **noun** [C] a cell, especially one taken from a person or animal in a very early stage of development, that can develop into any other type of cell

-stemmed /-stemd/ **suffix** having the stated type of stem: *a thick-stemmed plant* ◦ *a long-stemmed wine glass*

stench /stentʃ/ **noun 1** [C usually singular] a strong, unpleasant smell: *the stench* ***of*** *rotting fish/burning rubber/cigarette smoke* ◦ *an* ***overpowering*** *stench* **2** [S] literary a bad effect that follows an unpleasant event or situation and is noticeable for a long time: *For some time after the minister's resignation, the stench* ***of*** *scandal hung over the government.*

stencil /ˈsten.sᵊl/ **noun; verb**

▸**noun** [C] **1** a piece of card, plastic, metal, etc. into which shapes have been cut, used to draw or paint patterns onto a surface **2** a picture made by drawing or painting through the holes in such a piece of card, etc. onto a surface: *She did a stencil* ***of*** *a rainbow on her daughter's bedroom wall.*

▸**verb** [T] (**-ll-** or US usually **-l-**) to draw or paint something using a stencil

stenographer /stəˈnɒg.rə.fəʳ/ (US) /-ˈnɑː.grə.fɚ/ **noun** [C] (US informal also **steno**) a **shorthand typist**

stenography /steˈnɒg.rə.fi/ (US) /stəˈnɑː.grə-/ **noun** [U] **shorthand** (= system of fast writing)

stentorian /stenˈtɔː.ri.ən/ (US) /-ˈtɔːr.i-/ **adj** formal using a very loud voice, or (of a voice) very loud

S

step /step/ verb; noun

▸verb [I + adv/prep] (-pp-) B1 to move by lifting your foot and putting it down in a different place, or to put your foot on or in something: *She stepped* ***backwards*** *and fell over a chair.* ◦ *They stepped* ***out*** *onto the balcony.* ◦ *Be careful not to step* ***in*** *the mud.* ◦ *Ow, you stepped* ***on*** *my foot!* ◦ mainly US *I'm afraid Mr Taylor has just stepped (= gone)* ***out*** *for a few minutes, but I'll tell him you called.* ◦ formal *Would you care to step this way please, sir?*

IDIOMS **step back (in time)** to go back into the past: *Visiting her house was like stepping back in time/stepping back 50 years.* • **step into the breach** If you step into the breach, you do someone else's work when they are unable to do it: *Gill's sudden illness meant that Kathy had to step into the breach.* • **step on it** informal used to tell someone to drive faster or to hurry: *Could you step on it? I'm late.* • **step out of line** to behave in a way that is unacceptable or not expected: *Step out of line one more time Peters, and you're fired!*

PHRASAL VERBS **step aside** formal to step sideways to make a space for someone else: *Step aside, please – this lady needs a doctor.* • **step aside/down** C2 to leave an important job or position, especially to allow someone else to take your place: *He has decided to step down* ***as*** *captain of the team.* ◦ *He is unwilling to step aside* ***in favour of*** *a younger person.* • **step back** mainly UK to temporarily stop being involved in an activity or situation in order to think about it in a new way: *Let's just step back* ***from*** *the problem and think about what we could do.* • **step sth down** to reduce the amount, supply, or rate of something: *The doctor has said that I can start stepping down my medication in a few days' time.* ◦ *This device is used for stepping down the* ***voltage***. • **step forward** to offer to provide or do something, or to help with something: *No one has yet stepped forward* ***to*** *claim responsibility for the attack.* ◦ *At the last minute another company stepped forward* ***with*** *a bid.* • **step in** to become involved in a difficult situation or argument in order to help find a solution: [+ to infinitive] *An outside buyer has stepped in* ***to*** *save the company from going out of business.* ◦ *When the leading actress broke her leg, Isobel stepped in and took over.* • **step into sth** UK informal If you step into a job, you get it very easily: *He just stepped* ***straight*** *into a job as soon as he left college.* • **step on sb** informal to treat someone unfairly or unkindly • **step out on sb** US informal If you step out on your husband, wife, or usual sexual partner, you have sexual relationships with people other than them. • **step sth up** to increase the size, amount, or speed of a process that is intended to achieve something: *The police are stepping up their efforts to fight crime.* ◦ *Security has been stepped up at the airport.*

S

▸noun STAGE ▷ **1** B2 [C] a stage in a process: *What's the next step in the programme?* ◦ *We must stay one step* ***ahead*** *of our competitors.* ◦ *Most people believe that the decision to cut interest rates was a step* ***in the right direction***. ◦ *Let's take things* ***a*** *step/****one*** *step* ***at a time*** *(= slowly).* ◦ *Following the success of our products in Europe, our logical* ***next*** *step is to move into the American market.* **2** B2 [C] an action in a series of actions taken for a particular purpose: *The country is* ***taking*** *its first tentative steps towards democracy.* ◦ *We need to* ***take*** *drastic steps* ***to*** *reduce pollution.* ◦ *The president* ***took*** *the unusual step* ***of*** *altering his prepared speech in order to condemn the terrorist attack.* **3 step by step** C1 dealing with one thing and then another thing in a fixed order: *step-by-step instructions* ◦ *Don't worry – I'll go through the procedure with you step by step.*

> **! Common mistake: step**
>
> **Warning:** Choose the right verb!
>
> Don't say 'make a step', say **take a step**:
>
> ~~*He made an important step towards achieving his dream.*~~
>
> *He took an important step towards achieving his dream.*

STAIR ▷ **4** B1 [C] one of the surfaces that you walk on when you go up or down stairs: *a flight of steps* ◦ *We had to* ***climb*** *some steps to reach the front door.* ◦ *I asked them to leave the parcel on the (****front****) step (= outside the door to the house).* ◦ ***Mind the*** *step as you leave the train.* ◦ *It's difficult for people in wheelchairs to* ***negotiate*** *(= move up and down) steps.* ◦ *One of the steps* ***on*** *the ladder is broken.* **5 steps** [plural] another word for **stepladder**: *kitchen steps* ◦ *library steps* FOOT MOVEMENT ▷ **6** B1 [C] the act of lifting one foot and putting it down on a different part of the ground, such as when you walk or run: *Sophie* ***took*** *her first steps when she was eleven months old.* ◦ *He rose to his feet and* ***took*** *a couple of steps* ***towards*** *her.* ◦ ***With*** *every step, her feet hurt her more and more.* ◦ *I* ***retraced*** *my steps, looking for my lost keys.* → See also **footstep** **7** [C] the distance you cover when you take a step: *I'd only gone a few steps down the road when I realized I'd forgotten to lock the door.* **8** [U] the way you move your feet when you are walking or running, which can sometimes show how you are feeling: *She walked out of the office with* ***a spring in*** *her step (= in a way that showed she was happy).* ◦ *The driver told us to* ***mind/watch*** *our step (= walk carefully) as we got off the bus.* **9** [C] a particular movement that you make with your feet when you dance: *She's teaching me some basic* ***dance*** *steps.* **10 in step a** When people walk in step, they lift their feet off the ground and put them down again at the same time: *The soldiers marched in step.* **b** describes opinions, ideas, or ways of living that are the same as those of other people: *Television companies need to* ***keep*** *in step* ***with*** *public opinion.* **11 out of step a** When someone is out of step, they do not lift the same foot and put it down again at the same time as other people: *I'm no good at dancing – I always get hopelessly out of step.* **b** describes opinions, ideas, or ways of living that are different from those of other people: *The Republicans are out of step* ***with*** *the country, Williams said.* ◦ *He thinks that everyone is out of step except him.* MUSIC ▷ **12** [C] US (UK **tone**) the largest difference in sound between two notes that are next to each other in the western musical SCALE

IDIOMS **a few/couple of steps** informal a short distance: *The museum is just a few steps from the hotel.* • **mind/watch your step** be careful about how you behave, or you will get into trouble: *You need to watch your step, young lady!* • **one step forward, two steps back** If you take one step forward, two steps back, you make progress but then experience events that cause you to be further behind than you were when you made the progress. • **a step backwards** (also **a backward step**) going back to a worse or less developed state: *The changes that have been introduced are being seen as a step backwards.* • **a step forward** an improvement or development: *No one is sure whether this plan will work, but it's a step forward.*

step- /step-/ prefix being of the stated relationship to someone through the previous marriage of their husband or wife, or through their mother or father marrying again: *stepfather* ◦ *stepmother* ◦ *stepchildren*

ˈstep aeˌrobics noun [U] (also **step**) a type of exercise usually done to music in which you quickly step on and off a slightly raised surface

stepbrother /ˈstepˌbrʌ.ðəʳ/ ⓤⓢ /-ðɚ/ noun [C] not your parents' son, but the son of a person that one of your parents has married → Compare **half-brother**

ˈstep ˌchange noun [C] a change in a situation that is much bigger than usual: *There is a step change taking place in communications technology.*

stepchild /ˈstep.tʃaɪld/ noun [C] (plural **stepchildren**) the child of your husband or wife from a previous marriage

stepdad /ˈstep.dæd/ noun [C] US informal for **stepfather**

stepdaughter /ˈstepˌdɔː.təʳ/ ⓤⓢ /-ˌdɑː.t̬ɚ/ noun [C] the daughter of your husband or wife from a previous marriage

stepfather /ˈstepˌfɑː.ðəʳ/ ⓤⓢ /-ðɚ/ noun [C] B2 the man who is married to someone's mother but who is not their real father

stepladder /ˈstepˌlæd.əʳ/ ⓤⓢ /-ɚ/ noun [C] (UK also **steps**) a piece of equipment with steps for climbing up and down that can stand on its own or be folded for carrying: *I can't reach the top shelf unless I use a stepladder.*

stepmother /ˈstepˌmʌð.əʳ/ ⓤⓢ /-ɚ/ noun [C] B2 the woman who is married to someone's father but who is not their real mother

stepmum /ˈstep.mʌm/ noun [C] UK (US **stepmom**) informal for **stepmother**

stepney /ˈstep.ni/ noun [C] Indian English an extra wheel for a car that is available to use when you need it

stepparent /ˈstepˌpeə.rᵊnt/ ⓤⓢ /-ˌper.ᵊnt/ noun [C] the man or woman who is married to someone's mother or father but who is not their real father or mother

steppe /step/ noun [C usually plural, U] a large area of land with grass but no trees, especially in south-eastern Europe, Russia, and northern Asia: *These people have lived for centuries on **the** Russian steppes.*

ˈstepping ˌstone noun **STONE** ▷ **1** [C] one of a row of large, flat stones on which you can walk in order to cross a stream or river that is not deep **STAGE** ▷ **2** [S] an event or experience that helps you achieve something else: *I see this job just as a stepping stone **to** better things.*

stepsister /ˈstepˌsɪs.təʳ/ ⓤⓢ /-tɚ/ noun [C] not your parents' daughter, but the daughter of a person one of your parents has married → Compare **half-sister**

stepson /ˈstep.sʌn/ noun [C] the son of your husband or wife from a previous marriage

-ster /-stəʳ/ ⓤⓢ /-stɚ/ suffix a person who is associated with something: *gangster*

stereo /ˈster.i.əʊ/ ⓤⓢ /-oʊ/ noun **1** [U] a way of recording or playing sound so that it is separated into two signals and produces more natural sound: *The concert will be broadcast **in** stereo.* **2** [C] a piece of electrical equipment for playing music, listening to the radio, etc. that sounds very natural because the sounds come out of two SPEAKERS (= parts for playing sound) • **stereo** adj (formal **stereophonic**) *a stereo system* → Compare **mono, quadraphonic**

stereotype /ˈster.i.ə.taɪp/ noun; verb

▸noun [C] disapproving C1 a fixed idea that people have about what someone or something is like, especially an idea that is wrong: *racial/sexual stereotypes* ◦ *He doesn't **conform to/fit/fill** the national stereotype **of** a Frenchman.* ◦ *The characters in the book are just stereotypes.*

▸verb [T] disapproving to have a fixed idea about what a particular type of person is like, especially an idea that is wrong: *The study claims that British advertising stereotypes women.*

stereotypical /ˌster.i.əˈtɪp.ɪ.kᵊl/ adj disapproving C2 having the qualities that you expect a particular type of person to have • **stereotypically** /-i/ adv

sterile /ˈster.aɪl/ ⓤⓢ /-ᵊl/ adj **UNABLE TO PRODUCE** ▷ **1** (of a living being) unable to produce young, or (of land) unable to produce plants or crops: *Mules are usually sterile.* ◦ *One of the side effects of the drug could be to make men sterile.* **2** having no imagination, new ideas or energy: *a sterile argument* **CLEAN** ▷ **3** completely clean and free from dirt and bacteria: *The operation must be carried out under sterile conditions.*

sterility /stəˈrɪl.ɪ.ti/ ⓤⓢ /-ə.t̬i/ noun [U] **1** (in animals and people) the condition of being unable to produce young, or (in plants) the condition of being unable to produce plants or crops **2** the state of having no imagination, new ideas, or energy: *Over a bottle of wine, we shared our despair over the emotional sterility **of** our marriages.*

sterilization (UK usually **sterilisation**) /ˌster.ɪ.laɪˈzeɪ.ʃᵊn/ ⓤⓢ /ˌster.ɪ.ləˈ-/ noun [U] **STOP CHILDREN** ▷ **1** the process of having a medical operation to make it impossible to have children: *My wife and I have discussed sterilization, but we haven't made a decision about it yet.* **CLEANING** ▷ **2** the process of making something completely clean and free from bacteria

sterilize (UK usually **sterilise**) /ˈster.ɪ.laɪz/ verb [T] **STOP CHILDREN** ▷ **1** to perform a medical operation on someone in order to make them unable to have children: *After having five children, she decided to be sterilized.* **CLEAN** ▷ **2** to make something completely clean and free from bacteria: *All equipment must be sterilized before use.*

sterilizer (UK usually **steriliser**) /ˈster.ɪ.laɪ.zəʳ/ ⓤⓢ /-zɚ/ noun [C] a machine for making things completely clean and free from bacteria

sterilizing (UK usually **sterilizing**) /ˈster.ɪ.laɪ.zɪŋ/ adj making something completely clean and free from bacteria: *I put my contact lenses in sterilizing **solution** every night.*

sterling /ˈstɜː.lɪŋ/ ⓤⓢ /ˈstɝː-/ noun; adj

▸noun [U] British money: *The value of sterling increased against several other currencies yesterday.* ◦ *If you buy things on the plane, you can either pay for them in **pounds** sterling (= British pounds) or in US dollars.*

▸adj **METAL** ▷ **1** (of precious metal, especially silver) of a fixed standard of PURITY: *a sterling silver candlestick* **VERY GOOD** ▷ **2** approving of a very high standard: *You've done a sterling job.* ◦ *Everyone has made a sterling effort.*

stern /stɜːn/ ⓤⓢ /stɝːn/ adj; noun

▸adj **1** C2 severe, or showing disapproval: *a stern look/warning/voice* ◦ *She is her own sternest critic.* ◦ *Journalists received a stern warning not to go anywhere near the battleship.* **2** If something, such as a job, is stern, it is difficult: *The president is facing the sternest test of his authority since he came to power five years ago.* • **sternness** /ˈstɜːn.nəs/ ⓤⓢ /ˈstɝːn-/ noun [U]

IDIOM **made of sterner stuff** If someone is described as being made of sterner stuff, they are very strong and determined: *I was ready to give up the fight, but Nicky was made of sterner stuff and wanted us to carry on.*

▸noun [C] the back part of a ship or boat → Compare **bow**

S

sternly /ˈstɜːn.li/ Ⓤⓢ /ˈstɝːn-/ **adv** in a way that shows disapproval

sternum /ˈstɜː.nəm/ Ⓤⓢ /ˈstɝː-/ **noun** [C] (plural **sternums** or **sterna**) specialized the **breastbone**

steroid /ˈste.rɔɪd/, /ˈstɪər.ɔɪd/ Ⓤⓢ /ˈster.ɔɪd/, /ˈstɪr.ɔɪd/ **noun** [C] **1** one of the different types of chemical substances that are produced in the body **2** an artificial form of a natural chemical substance that is used for treating particular medical conditions: *I'm taking steroids/I'm* ***on*** *steroids for my asthma.* **3** a drug that increases the development of your muscles, sometimes taken illegally by people taking part in sports competitions

stethoscope /ˈsteθ.ə.skəʊp/ Ⓤⓢ /-skoʊp/ **noun** [C] a piece of medical equipment which doctors use to listen to your heart and lungs

Stetson /ˈstet.sᵊn/ **noun** [C] trademark a hat with a wide, curving lower edge, especially worn by COWBOYS

stevedore /ˈstiː.və.dɔːʳ/ Ⓤⓢ /-dɔːr/ **noun** [C] a **docker**

stew /stjuː/ Ⓤⓢ /stuː/ **noun; verb**

▸**noun** [C or U] a type of food consisting usually of meat or fish and vegetables cooked slowly in a small amount of liquid: *lamb/bean/fish stew* ◦ *She prepared a* ***hearty*** *stew for dinner.*

IDIOM **in a stew** informal If someone is in a stew, they are in a difficult situation that causes them to feel worried or upset: *William is in a stew* ***about/over*** *the demand he received from the tax office.*

▸**verb** **1** [T] to cook meat, fish, vegetables, or fruit slowly and gently in a little liquid **2** [I] informal to be angry: *You're not still stewing about what happened yesterday, are you?* **3** [I] UK to do nothing useful: *With jobs so scarce, many young people spend long hours with little to do but drink and stew.*

IDIOM **stew (in your own juice)** informal to think about or suffer the results of your own silly actions, without anyone giving you any help

steward /ˈstjuː.əd/ Ⓤⓢ /ˈstuː.ɚd/ **noun** [C] **1** a person whose job it is to organize a particular event, or to provide services to particular people, or to take care of a particular place: *Stewards will be inspecting the race track at 9.00.* ◦ *If you need help at any time during the conference, one of the stewards will be pleased to help you.* **2** (female **stewardess**) a person who serves passengers on a ship or aircraft **3** UK a person who organizes the supply and serving of food at a CLUB: *He's the steward* ***of*** *the City of Wakefield's Working Men's Club.*

S

stewardship /ˈstjuː.əd.ʃɪp/ Ⓤⓢ /ˈstuː.ɚd-/ **noun** [U] Someone's stewardship of something is the way in which that person controls or organizes it: *The company has been very successful while it has been* ***under*** *the stewardship* ***of*** *Mr White.*

stewed /stjuːd/ Ⓤⓢ /stuːd/ **adj** **1** UK describes tea that has been kept too long before it is poured, and is therefore strong and bitter **2** mainly US informal drunk

ˈ**stewing** ˌ**steak** **noun** [U] UK meat from CATTLE that is usually cut into small pieces and cooked slowly in liquid

STI /ˌes.tiːˈaɪ/ **noun** [C] UK abbreviation for **sexually transmitted illness**

stick /stɪk/ **noun; verb**

▸**noun** THIN PIECE ▷ **1** Ⓑ1 [C] a thin piece of wood or other matierial: *The old man was carrying a load of sticks.* ◦ *Police said that the child had been beaten with a stick.* ◦ *Find some dry sticks and we'll make a campfire.* ◦ *A lollipop is a sweet on a stick .* **2** Ⓑ1 [C] mainly UK a long, thin wooden pole that especially old or injured people use to help them walk: *a* ***walking*** *stick* ◦ *At 84 he's still quite active, although he walks with the aid of a stick.* **3** Ⓑ1 [C] a long, thin piece of wood used in playing various sports: *a hockey/lacrosse/polo stick* **4** [C] a long, thin piece of something: *carrot/bread sticks* ◦ *a stick of* ***celery/rhubarb/chewing gum/chalk/dynamite*** **5** [C] informal a piece of furniture: *When they got married, they didn't have a stick* ***of furniture.*** CRITICISM ▷ **6** [U] UK informal severe criticism: *I really* ***got/took*** *stick from my boss about being late for work again.* ◦ *We* ***gave*** *him some stick for wearing that silly hat.* COUNTRYSIDE ▷ **7 the sticks** [plural] informal disapproving an area in the countryside that is far from a town or city: *I'm fed up with living* ***in*** *the sticks.* ◦ *They live* ***out in*** *the sticks somewhere.*

IDIOMS **a stick to beat sb with** UK something that you can use to criticize, influence, or cause difficulty for someone or something you dislike or disapprove of: *The party has a number of sticks with which to beat the prime minister into submission.* • **sticks and stones may break my bones, (but words can never hurt me)** child's expression said in order to show that people cannot be hurt by unpleasant things that are said to them • **up sticks** UK (US **pull up stakes**) to take all the things that you own and go and live in a different place

▸**verb** (**stuck, stuck**) FIX ▷ **1** Ⓑ1 [I or T] to cause something to become fixed, for example with glue or another similar substance: *I tried to stick the pieces together with some glue/tape.* ◦ *He stuck* ***up*** *a notice on the board* ***with*** *pins.* ◦ *This glue won't stick.* ◦ *My car's stuck* ***in*** *the mud.* ◦ *Stir the sauce so that it doesn't stick* ***to*** *the pan.* ◦ *My book got wet and all the pages have stuck* ***together.*** → Compare **non-stick, stuck** **2** [I] If a name sticks, it continues to be used: *Although her name is Clare, her little sister called her Lali, and somehow the name stuck.* PUT ▷ **3** informal to put something somewhere, especially in a not very careful way: *'Where shall I put these books?' 'Oh, just stick them on the table for now.'* ◦ *She stuck her fingers in her ears so that she couldn't hear the noise.* ◦ *I'll pay for lunch – I can stick it on my expenses.* **4** [T usually + adv/prep] offensive If you tell someone to stick something or where they can stick something, it means that you do not want to keep that thing: *'I've had enough of working here,' she said, 'You can stick your job!'* PUSH INTO ▷ **5** Ⓑ2 [I or T, usually + adv/prep] to push a pointed object into or through something, or (of a pointed object) to be pushed into or through something and stay there: *She stuck the needle* ***into*** *my arm.* ◦ *We decided where to go for our holiday by closing our eyes and sticking a pin* ***in*** *the map.* ◦ *A thorn stuck* ***in*** *her finger.* ◦ *The metal springs were sticking* ***through*** *the mattress.* NOT CONTINUE ▷ **6** [I] In some card games, if you stick, you say that you do not want to be given any more cards. ACCEPT ▷ **7** [T] UK informal to bear or accept something or someone unpleasant: *I don't think I can stick this job a day longer.* ◦ [+ -ing verb] *I don't know how you can stick* ***living*** *in this place.*

IDIOMS **make sth stick** informal to show something bad that has been said about someone is true: *They've arrested him for fraud but they'll never make the* ***charges*** *stick.* • **stick in sb's mind/head/memory** informal to remember something • **stick in sb's throat/craw** to make you angry: *It really sticks in my throat* ***that*** *I did all the work, and she's getting all the credit.* • **stick to sb's ribs** If you describe food as sticking to your ribs, you mean that it makes you feel like you have eaten a lot.

PHRASAL VERBS **stick around** informal to stay somewhere for a period of time: *You go – I'll stick around here a bit longer.* • **stick at sth** (also **stick to/with sth**) UK to continue trying hard to do something difficult: *You'll never learn to play the piano if you're not prepared to stick at it.* • **stick by sth/sb** C1 to continue to support something or someone, especially in a difficult situation: *We must stick by our decision.* • **stick out 1** B2 to go past the surface or edge of something: *Paul's ears stick out a bit, don't they.* ◦ *There was a handkerchief sticking out of his jacket pocket.* **2** informal to be very easy to notice: *She certainly sticks out in a crowd.* • **stick (sth) out** to come forward from the rest of your body, or to make part of your body do this: *Mum, Lewis stuck out his tongue at me!* ◦ *He stuck his arm out of the window and waved at us.* ◦ *I wish my stomach didn't stick out so much.*

IDIOM **stick your neck out** to take a risk

• **stick it out** informal to continue to the end of a difficult or unpleasant situation: *I know things are difficult at the moment, but if we just stick it out, I'm sure everything will be OK in the end.* • **stick out for sth** UK to continue to demand or try to get something: *The unions have said that they are going to stick out for a ten percent rise.* • **stick to sth 1** B2 to limit yourself to doing or using one particular thing and not change to anything else: *Could you stick to the point, please?* ◦ *We'd better stick to the main road, because the other roads are blocked with snow.* **2** If you stick to a law, rule, or promise, you obey it or do what it states: *If you make a promise, you should stick to it.* **3** US for **stick at sth**

IDIOM **stick to your guns** to continue to have your beliefs or continue with a plan of action, even if other people disagree with you: *Despite harsh criticism, she's sticking to her guns* ***on*** *this issue.*

• **stick together 1** B2 informal If people stick together, they support and help each other: *The country's foreign minister said that it was important for small nations to stick together.* **2** If people stick together, they stay close to each other: *The two brothers always stick together at school.* • **stick up** to point up above the surface of something and not lie flat: *When I get up in the morning, my hair is always sticking up.* ◦ *There were some large rocks sticking up* ***out of*** *the water.* • **stick sth/sb up** mainly US informal to steal from a place or person, using a gun as a threat: *Did you hear that someone stuck up the post office last night?* → See also **stick-up** • **stick up for sth/sb** informal C1 to support or defend someone or something, especially when they are being criticized: *I can stick up for myself.* ◦ *It's sweet the way he sticks up for his little brother.* • **stick with sth/sb** informal B2 to continue doing something or using someone to do work for you, and not stop or change to something or someone else: *He said that he was going to stick with the traditions established by his grandfather.* ◦ *He's a good car mechanic – I think we should stick with him.*

IDIOM **stick with it** to continue doing something although it is difficult: *Things are hard at the moment, but if we stick with it, they are bound to get better.*

sticker /ˈstɪk.əʳ/ US /-ɚ/ **noun** [C] a small piece of paper or plastic with a picture or writing on one side and glue or another similar substance on the other side, so that it will fasten to a surface: *a bumper/window sticker* ◦ *Sophie's notebook is covered with stickers.* ◦ *There were two different* ***price*** *stickers on the shoes I wanted to buy.*

ˈsticker ˌprice **noun** [C] US the official price of something such as a car, given by the company that made it: *I got my truck for $2,000 less than the sticker price.*

ˈstick ˌfigure **noun** [C] (also **ˈmatchstick ˌfigure**) a simple picture of a person in which the head is drawn as a circle and the body, arms, and legs are drawn as lines

stickiness /ˈstɪk.i.nəs/ **noun** [U] SUBSTANCE ▷ **1** the quality of being STICKY (= staying fixed to any surface that is touched) BUSINESS ▷ **2** qualities that encourage people to spend a long time in a shop, on a website, etc.: *The company is using multimedia to increase the stickiness of visits to its Oxford Street store.*

ˈsticking ˌplaster **noun** [C or U] UK (US trademark **ˈBand-Aid**) a piece of material that you can put over a small cut in the skin in order to protect it and keep it clean: *Timmy had sticking plasters on both knees.*

ˈsticking-ˌplaster **adj** [before noun] UK disapproving dealing with a problem in a temporary and unsatisfactory way: *a sticking-plaster approach/solution/measure*

ˈsticking ˌpoint **noun** [C] A sticking point in a discussion is a point on which it is not possible to reach an agreement: *Exactly how the land is to be divided up is the main sticking point of the peace talks.*

ˈstick ˌinsect **noun** [C] a large insect with a long, thin body and legs: *She's as thin as a stick insect.*

stick insect

ˈstick-in-the-ˌmud **noun** [C] informal disapproving someone who is old-fashioned and too serious and avoids enjoying themselves: *My dad's a real stick-in-the-mud.*

stickleback /ˈstɪk.l̩.bæk/ **noun** [C] a small fish that has sharp points along its back

stickler /ˈstɪk.ləʳ/ US /-lɚ/ **noun** [C] informal a person who thinks that a particular type of behaviour is very important, and always follows it or tries to make other people follow it: *He's a stickler* ***for*** *detail/accuracy/efficiency.*

ˌstick of ˈrock **noun** [C] UK a long, hard, stick-shaped sweet

ˈstick-on **adj** [before noun] describes something that has glue on one side of it, so that it can fix to a surface: *a stick-on label*

ˈstick ˌshift **noun** [C] US for **gear lever**

stick-to-it-iveness /stɪkˈtuː.ɪt.ɪv.nəs/ **noun** [U] US informal the ability and determination to continue doing something despite difficulties

ˈstick-up **noun** [C] old-fashioned informal the act of threatening someone with a gun in order to steal from them: *Two men ran into the bank, shouting 'This is a stick-up!'*

sticky /ˈstɪk.i/ **adj** NOT DRY/SMOOTH ▷ **1** B1 made of or covered with a substance that stays fixed to any surface it touches: *sticky tape* ◦ *sticky fingers* ◦ *The floor's still sticky where I spilled the juice.* ◦ *The children's faces were sticky* ***with*** *chocolate.* → Compare **non-stick, stuck 2** If the weather is sticky, it is very hot and the air feels wet. DIFFICULT ▷ **3** informal difficult: *There were a few sticky moments during the meeting, but everything turned out all right in the end.* NOT WILLING ▷ **4** UK informal unwilling to agree: *Their bank manager was sticky* ***about*** *lending them the money they wanted to borrow.* BUSINESS ▷ **5** used to describe a website or shop where people like to spend

S

a long time: *Big media groups are drawn to social networking sites because of their 'sticky' nature.*

IDIOMS **come to/meet a sticky end** UK humorous to die in an unpleasant way: *He comes to a sticky end halfway through the movie.* • **have sticky fingers** informal to be likely to steal: *The last person we hired in the shop turned out to have sticky fingers.*

ˈsticky ˌtape noun [U] UK informal for **Sellotape**

ˌsticky ˈwicket noun [C usually singular] UK a difficult situation: *This is something of a sticky wicket you've got us into.*

stiff /stɪf/ adj; adv; noun

▸adj FIRM ▷ **1** B2 firm or hard: *stiff cardboard* ◦ *a stiff collar* ◦ *His clothes were stiff with dried mud.* ◦ *This hair spray has made my hair stiff.* ◦ *Mix the powder and water into a stiff paste.* **2** B2 not easily bent or moved: *The handle on this door is rather stiff.* ◦ *The man's body was (**as**) stiff **as a board** when it was found in the snow.* **3** B2 If you are stiff or part of your body is stiff, your muscles hurt when they are moved: *Sitting still at a computer terminal all day can give you a stiff neck.* NOT RELAXED ▷ **4** C2 behaving in a way that is formal and not relaxed: *The general is a tall man with steel spectacles and a stiff, rather pompous **manner**.* SEVERE ▷ **5** C2 severe and difficult: *The athlete was given a stiff punishment for using drugs.* ◦ *They are campaigning for stiffer penalties for people who drink and drive.* ◦ *There has been stiff **opposition/resistance** to the proposed tax increases.* ◦ *It's a stiff climb to the top of the hill.* ◦ *Some college courses have stiffer entry requirements than others.* ◦ *Both companies are worried about losing business in the face of stiff **competition**.* **6 a stiff breeze/wind** a strong wind **7 a stiff drink, brandy, gin, etc.** C2 an alcoholic drink that is very strong: *A stiff whisky – that's what I need.* **8** A stiff price is very expensive: *We had to pay a stiff membership fee to join the health club.*

▸adv B2 very much, or to a great degree: *I got **frozen** stiff (= very cold) waiting at the bus stop.* ◦ *I was **scared** stiff when I heard someone moving around upstairs.*

▸noun [C] PERSON ▷ **1** US informal a person of the type described: *a working stiff* ◦ *you lucky stiff* BODY ▷ **2** slang a dead body: *They found a stiff in the river.*

stiffen /ˈstɪf.ən/ verb FIRM ▷ **1** [I] to become firm or more difficult to bend: *Beat the cream until it begins to stiffen (= become firm).* ◦ *His body stiffened in fear.* LESS RELAXED ▷ **2** [I] to become less relaxed and more formal: *She stiffened when her former husband walked into the room.* MORE SEVERE ▷ **3** [I or T] to become or make something stronger or more difficult: *These events have stiffened our resolve to succeed.* ◦ *Penalties for selling illegal drugs have been stiffened.* ◦ *Stiffening competition in the market has led to a reduction in the company's profits this year.*

stiffly /ˈstɪf.li/ adv FIRM ▷ **1** straight and not bending: *The soldiers stood stiffly to attention.* NOT RELAXED ▷ **2** in a way that is too formal: *'I don't think that it's anything to do with you,' he said stiffly.* SEVERE ▷ **3** severely: *I wrote a stiffly worded letter of complaint to the council.*

stiffness /ˈstɪf.nəs/ noun [U] NOT RELAXED ▷ **1** the quality of being very formal and not relaxed: *Her initial stiffness began to wear off as we got to know her.* FIRM ▷ **2** C2 the quality of being firm, hard, or unable to bend: *the stiffness of her muscles* SEVERE ▷ **3** the quality of being very severe, strong, or difficult: *Everyone was surprised at the stiffness **of** the sentence/punishment/penalty/sanctions.*

ˌstiff ˌupper ˈlip noun [C usually singular] Someone who has a stiff upper lip does not show their feelings when they are upset: *He was taught at school to **keep** a stiff upper lip, whatever happens.*

stiffy /ˈstɪf.i/ noun [C] UK offensive an ERECTION (= when a man's PENIS is harder and bigger than usual and points up): *to **get/have** a stiffy*

stifle /ˈstaɪ.fl̩/ verb NO AIR ▷ **1** [I or T] to (cause to) be unable to breathe because you have no air: *He is said to have stifled his victim with a pillow.* ◦ *We almost stifled in the heat of the city.* PREVENT HAPPENING ▷ **2** [T] to prevent something from happening, being expressed, or continuing: *She stifled a cough/yawn/scream/sneeze.* ◦ *I don't know how I managed to stifle my anger.* ◦ *We should be encouraging new ideas, not stifling them.*

stifling /ˈstaɪ.fl̩.ɪŋ/ adj NO AIR ▷ **1** extremely hot and unpleasant: *I can't bear this stifling humidity.* ◦ *Several hundred people were crammed into the stifling room.* PREVENT HAPPENING ▷ **2** preventing something from happening: *stifling bureaucracy* • **stiflingly** /-li/ adv *It's stiflingly hot in here.*

stigma /ˈstɪg.mə/ noun FEELING ▷ **1** [C usually singular, U] a strong feeling of disapproval that most people in a society have about something, especially when this is unfair: *There is no longer any stigma **to** being divorced.* ◦ *Being an unmarried mother no longer **carries** the **social** stigma that it used to.* FLOWER PART ▷ **2** [C] the top of the central female part of a flower, where POLLEN is received

stigmata /ˈstɪg.mə.tə/, /stɪgˈmɑː-/ US /stɪgˈmɑː.t̬ə/ noun [plural] marks that appear on a person's body in the same places as those made on Jesus' body when he was fastened to a cross with nails

stigmatize (UK usually **stigmatise**) /ˈstɪg.mə.taɪz/ verb [T often passive] to treat someone or something unfairly by disapproving of them: *People should not be stigmatized on the basis of race.*

stile /staɪl/ noun [C] a set of usually two steps which you climb over in order to cross a fence or a wall, especially between fields

stile

stiletto /stɪˈlet.əʊ/ US /-ˈlet̬.oʊ/ noun [C] (plural **stilettos**) a woman's shoe with a narrow, high HEEL: *She was wearing a short skirt and stilettos.* ◦ *stiletto **heels***

still /stɪl/ adv; adj; verb; noun

▸adv CONTINUING ▷ **1** A2 continuing to happen or continuing to be done: *I'm still hungry.* ◦ *I still haven't finished my essay.* ◦ *There is still no news about the hostages.* ◦ *Do you still work for the government?* ◦ *Hope is fading that the missing child is still alive.* ◦ *There's still time for us to get to the cinema before the film starts.* DESPITE ▷ **2** B1 despite that: *You may not approve of what he did, but he's still your brother.* ◦ *I know you don't like her, but you still don't have to be so rude to her.* ◦ *Even though she hasn't really got the time, she still offered to help.* GREATER DEGREE ▷ **3** B2 to an even greater degree or in an even greater amount: *The number of people killed in the explosion is likely to rise still higher.* ◦ *The company is hoping to extend its market still further.* ◦ *Still more snow fell overnight.* ◦ *I'll meet you at the theatre. No, **better** still, let's meet in a pub and have a drink first.* ◦ *I'm worried that his car has broken down, or **worse** still, that he's had an*

> **! Common mistake: still**
>
> **Warning:** check your word order!
>
> **Still** usually goes directly before the main verb in a sentence.
>
> Don't say 'do still something', say **still do something**:
>
> ~~I still can remember the day we met.~~
>
> *I can still remember the day we met.*
>
> But if the main verb is **am/is/are/was/were, still** usually goes directly after it:
>
> ~~She still is my best friend.~~
>
> *She is still my best friend.*

accident. ◦ *Why do you have to tell me still (= even) more lies?*

▸**adj 1** B2 staying in the same position; not moving: *Children find it difficult to **sit/stand/stay** still for very long.* ◦ *I can't brush your hair if you don't **keep/hold** still.* ◦ *She sat perfectly still while I took her photograph.* ◦ *The **air** was so still (= there was so little wind) that not even the leaves were moving.* ◦ *She dived into the still (= calm and not flowing) **water** of the lake.* **2** B1 mainly UK A still drink is one that is not FIZZY (= with bubbles): *Would you like still or sparkling water?* • **stillness** /ˈstɪl.nəs/ **noun** [U]

> **+ Other ways of saying still**
>
> **Motionless** means the same as 'still':
>
> *He stood **motionless** when he saw the snake.*
>
> The expression **not move a muscle** can also be used when someone is completely still:
>
> *He sat there the whole time and did**n't move a muscle**.*
>
> **Immobile** or **inert** can be used when someone is still or unable to move:
>
> *She sat **immobile**, wondering what to do next.*
>
> *The **inert** figure of a man could be seen lying in front of the car.*
>
> If something is still and firm, you could use the adjective **steady**:
>
> *I'll hold the boat **steady** while you climb in.*
>
> **Stationary** is usually used for vehicles which are not moving:
>
> *We sat **stationary** in heavy traffic for close to an hour.*
>
> If someone becomes completely still because of being frightened, you can say that the person **freezes**:
>
> *She saw someone outside the window and **froze**.*

▸**verb** [T] to make something stop moving or become more calm: *He tried to still the swaying of the hammock.* ◦ literary *She cuddled her baby to still its cries.*

▸**noun NOT MOVING** ▷ **1** [C] specialized a photograph of a piece of action in a film **2** [U] literary a time when it is quiet and calm: *In the still **of the night**, nothing moved.* **EQUIPMENT** ▷ **3** [C] a piece of equipment used for making alcohol

stillbirth /ˈstɪl.bɜːθ/ (US) /-bɝːθ/ **noun** [C] the birth of a dead baby → Compare **abortion, miscarriage**

stillborn /ˌstɪlˈbɔːn/ (US) /-ˈbɔːrn/ /ˈstɪl.bɔːn/ **adj 1** born dead: *a stillborn baby* ◦ *The child was stillborn.* **2** If an idea or event is stillborn, it is unsuccessful or does not happen.

ˌstill ˈlife noun [C or U] (plural **still lifes**) a type of painting or drawing of an arrangement of objects that do not move, such as flowers, fruit, bowls, etc.

stilt /stɪlts/ **noun** [C usually plural] **1** one of a set of long pieces of wood or metal used to support a building so that it is above the ground or above water: *The houses are built **on** stilts to protect them from the annual floods.* **2** one of two long pieces of wood with supports for the feet which allow you to stand and walk high above the ground: *to walk **on** stilts*

stilted /ˈstɪl.tɪd/ (US) /-t̬ɪd/ **adj** disapproving (of a person's behaviour or way of speaking or writing) too formal and not smooth or natural: *He writes in a formal and rather stilted style.* ◦ *The dialogue sounded stilted and unnatural, perhaps because of the translation from the original Russian.* • **stiltedly** /-li/ **adv**

Stilton /ˈstɪl.tᵊn/ **noun** [U] a white and blue English cheese with a strong flavour

stimulant /ˈstɪm.jʊ.lənt/ **noun** [C] **1** something which makes or causes something else to grow or develop: *Tourism has acted as a stimulant **to** the country's economy.* **2** a substance, such as a drug, which makes the mind or body more active: *Caffeine, which is found in coffee and tea, is a mild stimulant.*

stimulate /ˈstɪm.jʊ.leɪt/ **verb 1** B2 [T] to encourage something to grow, develop, or become active: *The government plans to cut taxes in order to stimulate the economy.* **2** B2 [I or T] to make someone excited and interested about something: *The film was intended to stimulate and amuse.* ◦ [+ obj + to infinitive] *Good teachers should ask questions that stimulate students **to** think.* ◦ *Erotic images are often more sexually stimulating to men than to women.* **3** [T] specialized to cause part of the body to operate: *The drugs stimulate the damaged tissue **into** repairing itself.* ◦ *Standing on your head is supposed to stimulate hair growth.*

stimulating /ˈstɪm.jʊ.leɪ.tɪŋ/ (US) /-t̬ɪŋ/ **adj 1** If something is stimulating, it encourages new ideas: *a stimulating discussion* ◦ *Universities have been asked to make their courses more attractive and stimulating.* **2** describes someone who makes you feel enthusiastic and full of ideas: *a really stimulating teacher* **3** If an activity is stimulating, it causes your body to be active: *Aerobics is one of the most stimulating forms of exercise.*

stimulation /ˌstɪm.jʊˈleɪ.ʃᵊn/ **noun** [U] an action or thing which causes someone or something to become more active or enthusiastic, or to develop or operate: *While she was at home looking after her children, she felt deprived of **intellectual** stimulation.* ◦ specialized *Electric stimulation can help to heal fractured bones.*

stimulus /ˈstɪm.jʊ.ləs/ **noun** [C] (plural **stimuli**) **1** C2 something that causes growth or activity: *Foreign investment has been a stimulus **to** the industry.* ◦ *The book will provide a stimulus **to** research in this very important area.* **2** specialized something which causes part of the body to react: *The tip of the tongue is sensitive to salt and sweet stimuli and the back of the tongue is sensitive to bitter stimuli.*

sting /stɪŋ/ **verb; noun**

▸**verb** (**stung, stung**) **HURT** ▷ **1** [I or T] If an insect, plant, or animal stings, it produces a small but painful injury, usually with a poison, by brushing against the skin or making a very small hole under the skin: *Do all types of bee sting?* ◦ *I got stung by a wasp yesterday.* ◦ *I didn't see the nettles until I was stung by them.* **2** [I or T] to cause sharp but usually temporary pain: *The soap/smoke/sweat stung my eyes.* ◦ *This type of disinfectant doesn't sting, even if you put it on a fresh cut.* **3** [I or T] If someone's unkind remarks sting, they make you feel upset and annoyed: *She knew he was right, but his words still stung.* ◦ *He was stung by her criticisms.* ◦ *She managed to give a*

S

stinging reply (= an angry answer intended to upset), *before slamming down the phone.* **CHARGE** ▷ **4** [T] informal to charge someone a surprisingly large amount of money for something: *The bank stung me* ***for*** *£50 in charges when I went overdrawn.*

▸noun **HURT** ▷ **1** [C or S] a sudden burning pain in your eyes, on your skin, etc., or the ability to cause such pain: *She had several bee stings.* ◦ *the sting of salt in a wound* ◦ *Some types of jellyfish have a powerful sting.* **2** [S] the feeling of being upset by something: *the sting of defeat* **3** [C] UK (US **stinger**) a pointed part of an insect, plant, or animal that goes through a person's or animal's skin and leaves behind poison **GETTING STH** ▷ **4** [C] US a clever and complicated act of stealing **5** [C] mainly US a police action to catch criminals in which the police pretend to be criminals: *a sting operation*

IDIOMS **have a sting in the/its tail** UK If something, such as a story or joke, has a sting in the/its tail, it has a surprising or unpleasant part which only becomes clear at the end. • **take the sting out of sth** If something takes the sting out of an unpleasant situation, it makes it less unpleasant: *The new policy of shorter working hours will serve to take the sting out of the pay cut.*

ˈstinging ˌnettle noun [C] a wild plant that has leaves with very short hairs that sting

stingray /ˈstɪŋ.reɪ/ noun [C] a large, flat, round fish with a long tail that has poisonous points on it

stingy /ˈstɪn.dʒi/ adj informal disapproving unwilling to spend money: *He's really stingy and never buys the drinks when we go out.* ◦ *The owners are so stingy – they've refused to pay for new carpets.* • **stinginess** /-nəs/ noun [U]

stink /stɪŋk/ verb; noun

▸verb [I] (**stank** or US and Australian English also **stunk**, **stunk**) informal **SMELL** ▷ **1** to smell very unpleasant: *Your feet stink!* ◦ *The morning after the party, the whole house stank* ***of*** *beer and cigarettes.* ◦ *He hadn't washed for over a week and stank* ***to high heaven*** *(= greatly).* ◦ *The woman next to me sprayed on some perfume and stank* ***out*** *(US stank* ***up****) the whole place (= filled it with an unpleasant smell).* **BE BAD** ▷ **2** to be extremely bad or unpleasant: *I think her whole attitude stinks.* ◦ *His acting stinks but he looks good, so he's offered lots of movie roles.*

▸noun [C usually singular] informal a strong unpleasant smell: *The stink* ***of*** *rotting seaweed was strong along the seashore.*

IDIOMS **cause a stink** informal to cause trouble and make people angry: *The article about political corruption caused a real stink.* • **create/kick up/raise a stink** informal to make a strong public complaint: *She created a stink* ***about*** *the lack of recycling facilities in the town.* • **like stink** UK informal If someone works like stink, they work extremely hard.

ˈstink ˌbomb noun [C] a small device that gives off an extremely bad smell: *The two boys were caught letting off stink bombs in the school toilets.*

stinker /ˈstɪŋ.kəʳ/ (US) /-kɚ/ noun [C] old-fashioned informal someone or something that is very unpleasant: *What a stinker that man is!* ◦ *She'd had a real stinker* ***of a*** *day at work.*

stinking /ˈstɪŋ.kɪŋ/ adj informal **SMELL** ▷ **1** having a very unpleasant smell: *a pile of stinking rotten food* **BAD** ▷ **2** describes something that is very unpleasant or bad: *I hate this stinking job!* ◦ *She had a stinking* ***cold*** *and felt very sorry for herself.*

IDIOM **be stinking rich** to be extremely rich

stinky /ˈstɪŋ.ki/ adj informal having or producing an unpleasant smell: *stinky cheese* ◦ *The job is dirty, a little stinky, and far from glamorous.*

stint /stɪnt/ noun; verb

▸noun [C] a fixed or limited period of time spent doing a particular job or activity: *He has just finished a stint of compulsory military service.* ◦ *Perhaps her most productive period was her five-year stint as a foreign correspondent in New York.*

▸verb [I or T, usually in negatives] to provide, take, or use only a small amount of something: *The bride's parents did not stint* ***on*** *the champagne – there was plenty for everyone.* ◦ *Don't stint yourself – take another slice of cake.* → See also **unstinting**

stipend /ˈstaɪ.pend/ noun [C] **1** a fixed regular income: *an annual stipend* **2** the income paid to a priest in the UK

stipendiary /staɪˈpen.di.ᵊr.i/ (US) /-er-/ adj UK A stipendiary CLERGYMAN or MAGISTRATE receives a fixed income: *He was appointed as a stipendiary* ***priest*** *in the diocese of York.*

stipple /ˈstɪ.pᵊl/ verb [T] specialized to draw or paint something using small spots or marks: *She tried to create the impression of strong sunlight by stippling the canvas in yellow and white.* • **stippling** /-ɪŋ/ noun [U] specialized the activity of drawing or painting using small spots or marks

stippled /ˈstɪp.ld/ adj specialized drawn, painted, or coloured using small spots or marks: *The divers saw tropical fish stippled in gold and black.*

stipulate /ˈstɪp.jʊ.leɪt/ verb [T] formal to say exactly how something must be or must be done: *She agreed to buy the car, but stipulated racing tyres and a turbo-powered engine.* ◦ [+ that] *The law stipulates* ***that*** *new cars must have seat belts for the driver and every passenger.* ◦ [+ question word] *We have signed a contract which stipulates* ***wh****en the project must be completed.*

stipulation /ˌstɪp.jʊˈleɪ.ʃᵊn/ noun [C or U] formal a rule that must be followed or something that must be done: *Is there any stipulation as regards qualifications?* ◦ [+ that] *The only stipulation is* ***that*** *candidates must be over the age of 35.*

stir /stɜːʳ/ (US) /stɝː/ verb; noun

▸verb (-rr-) **MIX** ▷ **1** (B1) [I or T] to mix a liquid or other substance by moving an object such as a spoon in a circular pattern: *Stir the sauce gently until it begins to boil.* ◦ *Stir the egg yolks* ***into*** *the mixture.* ◦ *She paused to stir some milk* ***into*** *her coffee.* ◦ *Slowly add the flour, stirring until completely blended.* **MOVE** ▷ **2** (C2) [I or T] to move or to cause something to move slightly: *A light breeze stirred the leaves lying on the path.* ◦ *He stirred in his sleep as I kissed him.* **3 stir (yourself)** to wake up or begin to move or take action: *Come on, stir yourselves, or you'll be late!* ◦ *The alarm clock went off, but she didn't stir.* **CAUSE EMOTION** ▷ **4** (C2) [T] If something stirs you, it makes you feel a strong emotion: *I was deeply stirred by her performance.* ◦ [+ obj + to infinitive] *The speech stirred the crowd* ***to*** *take action.* **5** [I] literary If an emotion stirs within you, you begin to feel it: *Hope stirred within her heart.* **6** [I] UK informal disapproving to cause trouble intentionally between other people, especially by telling false or secret information: *There's a lot of gossip about me going around. Have you been stirring?* → See also **stir sth up**

IDIOM **stir the blood** (also **stir your blood**) If something stirs the blood, it makes you feel excited: *tales to stir the blood*

PHRASAL VERB **stir sth up** EMOTION ▷ **1** B2 to cause an unpleasant emotion or problem to begin or grow: *The teacher told him to stop stirring up* ***trouble.*** ◦ *The photographs stirred up some painful memories.* SUBSTANCE ▷ **2** to cause a substance such as soil or dust to move and rise up: *The helicopter stirred up clouds of dust.*

▸noun MIX ▷ **1** [C usually singular] the act of stirring a liquid or other substance in order to mix it: *Could you* ***give*** *the soup a quick stir?* EXCITEMENT ▷ **2** [U] informal a lot of interest or excitement: *The scandal* ***caused/created*** *quite a stir at the time.* MARCH ▷ **3** [C usually singular] Indian English an occasion when a group of people march or stand together to show that they disagree with or support something or someone; a DEMONSTRATION

ˈstir-ˌcrazy adj informal upset or angry because you have been prevented from going somewhere or doing something for a long time: *I've been laid up for two weeks with this broken leg and I'm beginning to* ***go*** *stir-crazy.*

ˈstir-fry verb; noun

▸verb [I or T] to fry small pieces of meat, vegetables, etc. quickly while mixing them around: *Stir-fry the chicken for one minute, then add the vegetables.*

▸noun [C or U] a method of frying food while mixing it quickly, or food cooked this way: *We're having a vegetable stir-fry for supper tonight.*

stirrer /ˈstɜː.rəʳ/ US /ˈstɝː.ɚ/ noun [C] mainly UK informal disapproving a person who intentionally causes trouble between other people: *He's such a stirrer!*

stirring /ˈstɜː.rɪŋ/ US /ˈstɝː.ɪŋ/ adj; noun

▸adj approving A stirring speech or song is one which produces strong positive emotions. • **stirringly** /-li/ adv

▸noun [C] the beginning of something, such as an emotion or thought: *She felt a faint stirring* ***of*** *envy when she heard that one of her colleagues had been promoted.*

stirrup /ˈstɪr.əp/ noun [C] one of a pair of pieces of metal shaped like the letter D that hang from the side of a horse's SADDLE, used for resting your foot when you are riding

stitch /stɪtʃ/ noun; verb

▸noun THREAD ▷ **1** C2 [C] a piece of thread sewn in cloth, or the single movement of a needle and thread into and out of the cloth which produces this: *Secure the two pieces together with a couple of stitches.* **2** [C] one of the small circles of wool that you make when you are KNITTING: *He* ***cast on/off*** *a stitch (= added/removed a length of thread from the needle).* ◦ *I've* ***dropped*** *a stitch (= lost a length of thread from the needle).* **3** [C] a particular type of stitch made in sewing or KNITTING, or the pattern which this produces: *a pearl/satin stitch* ◦ *The bedspread was embroidered with cross-stitch.* **4** C2 [C] a length of special thread used to join the edges of a deep cut in the flesh: *Her head wounds needed 50 stitches.* ◦ *He got hit with a broken bottle and needed five stitches* ***in*** *his cheek.* **5 not a stitch** informal without any clothes: *I haven't got a stitch to wear (= I have not got anything to wear) for this party tonight.* ◦ *She ran down the corridor to the bathroom without a stitch on (= naked).* PAIN ▷ **6** [C usually singular] a sharp pain in the side of your stomach or chest, often caused by not breathing enough when running or laughing: *I* ***got*** *a stitch after running for the bus.*

IDIOM **in stitches** informal If a joke or funny story has you in stitches, it makes you laugh a lot.

▸verb **1** [I or T] to sew two things together, or to repair something by sewing: *This button needs to be stitched back* ***onto*** *my shirt.* ◦ *Stitch the pieces* ***together*** *along the fold.* **2** [T] Indian English to make a piece of clothing • **stitching** /ˈstɪtʃ.ɪŋ/ noun [U] *The stitching along my coat hem is coming undone.*

PHRASAL VERBS **stitch sth together** informal disapproving to create or form something quickly or roughly: *Britain is likely to stitch together some sort of political deal to avoid a confrontation.* • **stitch sth/sb up** to join the two sides of something with stitches, for example torn clothing or a deep cut, or to treat someone who has a deep cut by doing this: *I've ripped my trousers – can you stitch them up for me?* ◦ *After giving birth, she was stitched up by a junior doctor.* • **stitch sb up** UK slang to deliberately make someone look guilty of doing something which they did not do: *He claims he was stitched up by the police.*

ˈstitch-up noun [C usually singular] UK slang a situation in which someone is deliberately made to look guilty of doing something that they did not do: *a police stitch-up*

stoat /stəʊt/ US /stoʊt/ noun [C] a small, thin animal that has brown fur in summer and white fur in winter

stock /stɒk/ US /stɑːk/ noun; verb; adj

▸noun SUPPLY ▷ **1** C1 [C or U] a supply of something for use or sale: *It is now halfway through winter and food stocks are already low.* ◦ *The local shop has a good stock* ***of*** *postcards and guidebooks.* ◦ *Much of the city's housing stock (= the number of houses in the city) is over 100 years old.* **2** B2 [U] the total amount of goods or the amount of a particular type of goods available in a shop: *This shop sells its old stock at very low prices.* ◦ *We'll be getting our new stock* ***in*** *on Friday.* ◦ *The new edition is* ***in/out of*** *stock (= available/not available) in major bookshops.* MONEY ▷ **3** [U] the amount of money that a company has through selling SHARES to people: *They own 20 percent of the company's stock.* **4** [C or U] part of the OWNERSHIP of a company that can be bought by members of the public: *Stock* ***prices*** *fell yesterday in heavy trading.* ◦ *She buys and sells stocks* ***and shares.*** **5** [C or U] UK money that people INVEST in the government, producing a fixed rate of interest: *government stock(s)* LIQUID ▷ **6** [U] a liquid used to add flavour to food, made by boiling meat or fish bones or vegetables in water: *vegetable/beef/chicken stock* ANIMALS ▷ **7** [U] animals, such as cows or sheep, kept on a farm OPINION ▷ **8** [U] formal the degree to which a person or organization is popular and respected: *At present, the prime minister's stock is* ***high/low.*** ORIGIN ▷ **9** [U] formal the family or group that a person or animal comes from: *He's an American* ***of*** *Irish stock.* ◦ *She's* ***of*** *peasant/noble stock.* ◦ *Some of the animals will be kept as breeding stock.* HANDLE ▷ **10** [C] the support or handle of a tool, especially the part of a gun that rests against your shoulder FRAME ▷ **11 the stocks** [plural] (in Europe in the Middle Ages) a wooden frame that was fixed around someone's feet, hands, and sometimes head, so that they were forced to sit or stand for a long time in public as a punishment PLANT ▷ **12** [C] a garden plant with small pleasant-smelling, brightly coloured flowers

IDIOMS **put stock in sth** If you put stock in something that someone says or does, you have a high opinion of it: *He's been wrong before, so I don't put much stock in what he says any more.* • **take stock** C2 To take

S

stock (of something) is to think carefully about a situation or event and form an opinion about it, so that you can decide what to do: *After two years spent teaching abroad, she returned home for a month to take stock **of** her life.*

▸**verb** [T] **1** C1 If a shop or factory stocks something, it keeps a supply of it: *Most supermarkets stock a wide range of wines.* **2** to fill something such as a cupboard or shelves with food or goods: *He has a Saturday job stocking shelves in the local supermarket.* ◦ *I always stock **up** the fridge before my sister comes to stay.*

PHRASAL VERB **stock up** to buy a large quantity of something: *During the emergency, people stocked up **on** essential items.*

▸**adj** (of an idea, expression, or action) usual or typical, and used or done so many times that it is no longer original: *a stock phrase/response* ◦ *'Don't worry – worse things happen at sea' is her stock expression for whenever anything goes wrong.*

stockade /stɒkˈeɪd/ US /stɑːˈkeɪd/ **noun** [C] a strong wooden fence built around an area to defend it against attack

stockbroker /ˈstɒkˌbrəʊ.kəʳ/ US /ˈstɑːkˌbroʊ.kɚ/ **noun** [C] a person or company that buys and sells stocks and SHARES for other people • **stockbroking** /-kɪŋ/ **noun** [U]

ˈstockbroker ˌbelt noun [C] UK the area near London where many rich people live in large houses and from where they travel to work in the City (= the financial area of London)

ˈstock ˌcar noun [C] an ordinary car that has been made stronger and faster so that it can be driven in special races

ˈstock conˌtrol noun [U] In a company or shop, stock control is the system of making certain that new supplies are ordered and that goods have not been stolen.

ˈstock ˌcube noun [C] (US usually **ˈbouillon ˌcube**) a small block of dried FLAVOURING that you dissolve in hot water before using it in some dishes such as soups

ˈstock exˌchange noun [C usually singular] (also **ˈstock ˌmarket**) a place where SHARES in companies are bought and sold, or the organization of people whose job is to do this buying or selling: *They bought some shares **on** the London stock exchange.* ◦ *Stock markets around the world are reacting to news of the US president's announcement.*

stockholder /ˈstɒkˌhəʊl.dəʳ/ US /ˈstɑːkˌhoʊl.dɚ/ **noun** [C] US for **shareholder**

Stockholm syndrome /ˈstɒk.həʊmˌsɪn.drəʊm/ US /ˈstɑːk.hoʊmˌsɪn.droʊm/ **noun** [U] the situation when a person who has been taken prisoner starts to like or trust the person or people who have taken them: *In hostage-taking situations, it is not uncommon for Stockholm syndrome to develop.*

stocking /ˈstɒk.ɪŋ/ US /ˈstɑː.kɪŋ/ **noun** [C] C1 one of a pair of tight-fitting coverings for the feet and legs made of light material and worn by women: ***nylon/silk** stockings.* → Compare **nylons**, **tights**

IDIOM **in your stocking(ed) feet** wearing only socks or stockings and not shoes: *Jerome stands 1 m 75 in his stocking feet.*

ˈstocking ˌcap noun [C] US a close-fitting KNITTED hat with a long tail

ˈstocking ˌfiller noun [C] UK (US **ˈstocking ˌstuffer**) a small, usually cheap Christmas present

ˈstocking ˌmask noun [C] a stocking which thieves pull over their heads to hide their faces

ˌstock-in-ˈtrade noun [U] **1** the typical characteristics or behaviour of someone or something: *The song was perfect for the soft vocals that are her stock-in-trade.* **2** old-fashioned the tools and other objects that you need for your job

stockist /ˈstɒk.ɪst/ US /ˈstɑː.kɪst/ **noun** [C] UK a shop that sells a particular type of goods: *a health food stockist*

ˈstock ˌmarket noun [C] C1 a **stock exchange**

stockpile /ˈstɒk.paɪl/ US /ˈstɑːk-/ **noun; verb**

▸**noun** [C] a large amount of food, goods, or weapons that are kept ready for future use: *They have a stockpile of weapons and ammunition that will last several months.*

▸**verb** [T] to store a large supply of something for future use: *The rebels have been stockpiling weapons.*

stockroom /ˈstɒk.rʊm/, /-ruːm/ US /ˈstɑːk-/ **noun** [C] a room in a shop, factory, or office that is used for storing a supply of goods or materials

ˈstock ˌroute noun [C] Australian English a road on which traffic must stop so that CATTLE and sheep that are being moved from one place to another can go past

ˌstock-ˈstill adv without moving; completely still: *On seeing us, the deer **stood** stock-still for a moment, then turned and retreated into the forest.*

stocktaking /ˈstɒkˌteɪ.kɪŋ/ US /ˈstɑːk-/ **noun** [U] UK the counting of all the goods, materials, etc. kept in a place such as a shop

stocky /ˈstɒk.i/ US /ˈstɑː.ki/ **adj** describes a person, especially a man, whose body is wide across the shoulders and chest and who is short: *The man was described as short and stocky and very strong.* → Synonym **thickset** • **stockily** /ˈstɒk.ɪ.li/ US /ˈstɑː.kɪ-/ **adv** *a stockily-built man* • **stockiness** /-nəs/ **noun** [U]

stockyard /ˈstɒk.jɑːd/ US /ˈstɑːk.jɑːrd/ **noun** [C] a set of areas surrounded by fences where farm animals are kept before being sold or killed

stodge /stɒdʒ/ US /stɑːdʒ/ **noun** [U] UK informal disapproving heavy food, such as potatoes, bread, and rice, which contains too much STARCH and makes you feel very full

stodgy /ˈstɒdʒ.i/ US /ˈstɑː.dʒi/ **adj** UK informal disapproving **FOOD** ▷ **1** describes food that is heavy and unhealthy, sometimes in an unpleasant way: *I've been eating too many stodgy puddings.* **BORING** ▷ **2** boring, serious, and formal: *Neither company has succeeded in shedding its stodgy image.* ◦ *Younger consumers, it is said, regard their products as stodgy and unfashionable.* • **stodginess** /-nəs/ **noun** [U]

stoep /stuːp/ **noun** [C] South African English a small VERANDA (= raised area) or set of steps outside a house, where people can sit

stoic /ˈstəʊ.ɪk/ US /ˈstoʊ-/ **adj; noun**

▸**adj** (also **stoical**) determined not to complain or show your feelings, especially when something bad happens to you: *We knew she must be in pain, despite her stoic attitude.* ◦ *He showed a stoic resignation towards his fate.* ◦ *Local people were stoical **about** the damage caused by the hurricane.* • **stoically** /-ɪ.kəl.i/ **adv** *Stoically, and with great determination, the people set about rebuilding the village.*

▸**noun** [C] formal someone who does not complain or show their emotions: *My father is a stoic by nature and found it hard to express his grief when my mother died.*

stoicism /ˈstəʊ.ɪ.sɪ.zəm/ US /ˈstoʊ-/ **noun** [U] formal the quality of experiencing pain or trouble without

S

complaining or showing your emotions: *He endured the pain of his wounds with great stoicism.*

stoke /stəʊk/ (US) /stoʊk/ **verb** [I or T] (also **stoke up**) **1** to add fuel to a large fire and move the fuel around with a stick so that it burns well and produces a lot of heat: *Once the fire had been stoked up, the room began to get warm.* **2** to encourage bad ideas or feelings in a lot of people: *He's been accused of stoking up racial hatred in the region.* ◦ *Rumours of an emergency meeting of the finance ministers stoked the atmosphere of crisis.*

PHRASAL VERB **stoke up on/with sth** informal to eat a lot of a particular food in order to avoid feeling hungry or weak later: *As it was a cold morning, she stoked up on bacon, eggs, and beans on toast.*

stoker /ˈstəʊ.kər/ (US) /ˈstoʊ.kɚ/ **noun** [C] a person whose job is adding fuel to a large closed fire

stole /stəʊl/ (US) /stoʊl/ **verb; noun**

▸verb past simple of **steal**

▸noun [C] **1** formal a long, narrow piece of cloth or fur that is worn around the shoulders by women, usually on special occasions: *a **mink** stole* **2** specialized a long, narrow piece of cloth, especially SILK, worn over the shoulders by some priests in the Christian Church during religious ceremonies

stolen /ˈstəʊ.lən/ (US) /ˈstoʊ-/ **verb** past participle of **steal**

stolid /ˈstɒl.ɪd/ (US) /ˈstɑː.lɪd/ **adj** disapproving (of a person) calm and not showing emotion or excitement, or (of a thing) not interesting or attractive: *He's a very stolid, serious man.* ◦ *The college is a stolid-looking building with no lawn.* • **stolidly** /-li/ **adv**

stollen /ˈstɒl.ən/, /ˈstəʊ.lən/ **noun** [C or U] a German cake containing dried fruit and MARZIPAN (= a food made from nuts), usually eaten at Christmas

stoma /ˈstəʊ.mə/ (US) /ˈstoʊ-/ **noun** [C] (plural **stomata**) specialized one of the many PORES (= very small holes in the surface) on a leaf or stem of a plant through which gases are able to pass in and out

stomach /ˈstʌm.ək/ **noun; verb**

▸noun [C] (plural **stomachs**) (A2) an organ in the body where food is digested, or the soft front part of your body just below the chest: *He was punched in the stomach.* ◦ *The doctor asked him to lie down **on** his stomach.* ◦ *The sight of blood always **churns/turns** my stomach (= makes me feel as if I am going to vomit).* ◦ *She's got a very **delicate** stomach and doesn't eat spicy food.* ◦ *I was hungry and my stomach had started **growling/rumbling** (= making noises).* ◦ *He felt a knot of nervousness in the **pit** (= bottom) of his stomach.* ◦ *I suggested that a cup of tea might **settle** (= calm) her stomach.*

IDIOMS **have a strong stomach** to be able to smell, taste, or see unpleasant things without feeling ill or upset: *You need to have a very strong stomach to watch some of the surgery scenes.* • **not have the stomach for sth** (also **have no stomach for sth**) to not feel brave or determined enough to do something unpleasant: *I didn't have the stomach for another fight.*

▸verb [T usually in negatives] to be able to accept an unpleasant idea or watch something unpleasant: *He can't stomach the idea that Peter might be the next chairman.* ◦ *She found the violence in the film **hard to** stomach.*

ˈstomach ˌache **noun** [C or U] (A2) pain in your stomach: *I ate too much and got a terrible stomach ache.*

ˈstomach ˌpump **noun** [C] a medical device with a long tube that is pushed down the throat to remove the contents of the stomach when someone has swallowed poison

stomp /stɒmp/ (US) /stɑːmp/ **verb** **1** [I usually + adv/prep] to walk with intentionally heavy steps, especially as a way of showing that you are annoyed: *She stomped up the stairs and slammed her bedroom door.* ◦ *He woke up in a bad mood and stomped off to the bathroom.* **2** [I or T] US for **stamp**.

PHRASAL VERB **stomp on sb/sth** mainly US **1** to step down hard on someone or something: *I stomped on his toes and ran away.* **2** to treat someone or something badly, or to defeat them

stone /stəʊn/ (US) /stoʊn/ **noun; verb**

▸noun ROCK ▷ **1** (B1) [C or U] the hard, solid substance found in the ground that is often used for building, or a piece of this: *a stone wall/floor* ◦ *a flight of stone steps* ◦ *a primitive stone axe* ◦ *They cut enormous blocks of stone out of the hillside.* ◦ *Some demonstrators were arrested for **throwing** stones at the police.* **2** [C] a piece of hard material that can form in some organs in the body and cause severe pain: ***kidney/gall** stones* WEIGHT ▷ **3** [C] (plural **stone** or **stones**) (written abbreviation **st**) UK a unit of weight equal to 14 pounds or 6.35 kilograms, used especially when talking about a person's weight: *I weigh ten and a half stone.* ◦ *She has **put on/lost** a stone (= is a stone heavier/lighter).* JEWEL ▷ **4** (B1) [C] a small piece of a hard, valuable substance, such as a DIAMOND, that is found in the ground and used in jewellery: *a **precious/semi-precious** stone* ◦ *The large central diamond is surrounded by eight smaller stones.* SEED ▷ **5** (C2) [C] (plural **stones**) (US also **pit**) a large, hard seed inside some types of fruit: *Peaches, plums, and olives all contain stones.* → Compare **pip**

IDIOMS **not be set/carved in stone** UK (US **not be carved/etched in stone**) to not be fixed and able to be changed: *These are just a few ideas – nothing is set in stone yet.* • **a stone's throw** (C2) a very short distance: *The cottage is just a stone's throw **from** the sea.* ◦ *'Is your house far from here?' 'No, it's only a stone's throw **away**.'*

▸verb [T] THROW ROCKS ▷ **1** to throw stones at something or someone: *Rioters set up barricades and stoned police cars.* **2** **stone sb to death** to kill someone as a punishment by throwing stones at them REMOVE SEED ▷ **3** (US usually **pit**) to remove the stone from a fruit: *Could you stone the cherries for me?*

IDIOM **stone the crows!** (also **stone me!**) UK old-fashioned used as an expression of surprise: *Well, stone the crows – it's five o'clock already!*

ˈstone-ˌage **adj** informal disapproving describes something that is very basic, simple, and not well developed: *The organization is criticized for its surly service and stone-age software.*

the ˈStone ˌAge **noun** [S] the early period in human history when people made tools and weapons only out of stone: *a Stone Age settlement/site* ◦ figurative *My gran's TV looks **like something out of** the Stone Age (= is very old-fashioned)!* → Compare **the Bronze Age, the Iron Age**

stoneclad /ˈstəʊn.klæd/ (US) /ˈstoʊn-/ **adj** Stoneclad buildings, walls, etc. are covered with a layer of stone.

ˌstone-ˈcold **adj** very or completely cold: *Your dinner's been on the table for over an hour and it's stone-cold.*

ˌstone-cold ˈsober **adj** [after verb] not having drunk any alcohol

stoned /stəʊnd/ (US) /stoʊnd/ **adj** DRUGS ▷ **1** slang

S

experiencing the effects of a drug, such as CANNABIS: *They spent the evening **getting** stoned.* **SEED** ▷ **2** (US usually **pitted**) with the stone (= seed) removed: *stoned olives*

ˌstone-ˈdead **adj** [after verb] dead: *By the time the paramedics got to him, he was stone-dead.*

IDIOM **kill sth stone-dead** to cause something to be completely unsuccessful or to stop completely: *One bad review can kill a film stone-dead.*

ˌstone-ˈdeaf **adj** completely unable to hear anything: *She has been stone-deaf since birth.*

stonefish /ˈstəʊn.fɪʃ/ (US) /ˈstoʊn-/ **noun** [C] (plural **stonefish** or **stonefishes**) a tropical fish with sharp, poisonous SPINES

stoneground /ˈstəʊn.graʊnd/ (US) /ˈstoʊn-/ **adj** Flour that is stoneground has been made by crushing grain between two large stones.

stonemason /ˈstəʊnˌmeɪ.sən/ (US) /ˈstoʊn-/ **noun** [C] (also **mason**) a person whose job it is to cut, prepare, and use stone for building

stoner /ˈstəʊ.nər/ (US) /ˈstoʊ.nɚ/ **noun** [C] slang someone who smokes or takes a lot of the drug CANNABIS

stonewall /ˈstəʊn.wɔːl/ (US) /ˈstoʊn.wɑːl/ **verb** [I or T] to stop a discussion from developing by refusing to answer questions or by talking in such a way that you prevent other people from giving their opinions: *The interviewer accused the minister of stonewalling on the issue of tax increases.*

stoneware /ˈstəʊn.weər/ (US) /ˈstoʊn.wer/ **noun** [U] plates, dishes, cups, etc. that are made from a special clay baked at a very high temperature

stonewashed /ˈstəʊn.wɒʃt/ (US) /ˈstoʊn.wɑːʃt/ **adj** (of a new piece of clothing, especially one made of DENIM) washed together with small pieces of stone in order to make it lose some of its colour and look older: *stonewashed **jeans***

stonework /ˈstəʊn.wɜːk/ (US) /ˈstoʊn.wɝːk/ **noun** [U] the parts of a building that are made of stone

stonkered /ˈstɒŋ.kəd/ (US) /ˈstɑːŋ.kɚd/ **adj** UK slang very tired: *I was completely stonkered after that game of squash.*

stonking /ˈstɒŋ.kɪŋ/ (US) /ˈstɑːŋ-/ **adj** UK slang used to emphasize how good something is: *We had a stonking good time at the party last night.* • **stonker** **noun** [C usually singular] UK slang something very good: *Christmas this year will be a stonker – we're going skiing.*

stony /ˈstəʊ.ni/ (US) /ˈstoʊ-/ **adj** **GROUND** ▷ **1** describes ground that contains a lot of stones: *The island has several stony beaches which are usually deserted.* **PERSON** ▷ **2** A stony expression or way of behaving is one that shows no sympathy or kindness: *She gave me a stony glare as I walked into the room.* ◦ *Most of her comments were met with a stony **silence**.*

IDIOM **fall on stony ground** If a request or a piece of advice falls on stony ground, it is ignored or unpopular.

ˌstony ˈbroke **adj** [after verb] UK (US **ˌstone ˈbroke**) describes someone who has no money

stood /stʊd/ **verb** past simple and past participle of **stand**

stooge /stuːdʒ/ **noun** [C] disapproving **1** a person who is forced or paid by someone in authority to do an unpleasant or secret job for them: *The newly appointed mayor is widely regarded as a government stooge.* **2** an actor in a funny show in the theatre or on television whose job is to allow the main actor to make him or her look silly

stool /stuːl/ **noun** [C] **SEAT** ▷ **1** (B2) a seat without any support for the back or arms: *a bar/kitchen/piano stool* ◦ *a three-legged stool* → See also **footstool** **EXCRETION** ▷ **2** specialized a piece of solid waste from the body: *He told the doctor he had been **passing** bloody stools.*

ˈstool ˌpigeon **noun** [C] slang disapproving a person, often a criminal, who gives information in secret to the police so that they can catch other criminals

stoop /stuːp/ **verb; noun**

▸**verb** [I] **1** to bend the top half of the body forward and down: *The doorway was so low that we had to stoop to go through it.* ◦ *Something fell out of her coat pocket and she stooped **down** and picked it up.* **2** If someone stoops, their head and shoulders are always bent forwards and down: *He's over six feet tall, but the way he stoops makes him look shorter.* • **stooped** /stuːpt/ **adj** *She is small and slightly stooped.*

PHRASAL VERB **stoop to sth** disapproving to lower your moral standards by doing something that is unpleasant, dishonest, or unfair: *I don't believe she would ever stoop to bribery or blackmail.* ◦ [+ -ing verb] *He was amazed that a reputable firm would stoop to sell**ing** the names of their clients to other companies.*

▸**noun** **STEPS** ▷ **1** [C] US a raised flat area in front of the door of a house, with steps leading up to it: *She got home to find the kids sitting on the stoop waiting for her.* **BEND** ▷ **2** [S] a way of standing or walking with the head and shoulders bent slightly forwards and down: *He is a tall man with **a** slight stoop.*

stop /stɒp/ (US) /stɑːp/ **verb; noun**

▸**verb** (-pp-) **FINISH** ▷ **1** (A1) [I or T] to finish doing something that you were doing: *Once I start eating chocolate, I can't stop.* ◦ [+ -ing verb] *Stop shout**ing** – you're giving me a headache!* ◦ *I couldn't stop laugh**ing**.* ◦ *Stop it!/Stop that!* **2** (B1) [I or T] to not continue to operate: *My watch must have stopped.* ◦ *The air conditioner has stopped working.* **3** (B1) [I or T] to not move any more or to make someone or something not move any more: *Stop the car, I want to get out!* ◦ *I heard him shout 'Stop, or I'll shoot!'* **4** (A1) [I + -ing verb] to finish doing something that you do regularly or as a habit: *Apparently she's stopped drink**ing**.* ◦ *I stopped see**ing** him last year.* **5** (A2) [I] to pause in a journey or an activity for a short time: *Does this train stop **at** Finsbury Park?* ◦ *Why don't you just stop somewhere and ask for directions?* ◦ [+ to infinitive] *I stopped **to** pick up a letter that I'd dropped.* **PREVENT** ▷ **6** (B1) [T] to prevent someone from doing something: *If she really wants to leave, I don't understand what's stopping her.* ◦ [+ -ing verb] *They've put barriers up to stop people (**from**) gett**ing** through.* ◦ *Something must be done to stop the fighting.* **7** **stop a cheque** UK (US **stop payment on a check**) to tell your bank not to deal with a CHEQUE which you have written, so that the money is not paid from your bank account **STAY** ▷ **8** [I] to stay in a place: *Are you coming with me or are you stopping here?* ◦ *I can't stop – Malcolm's waiting for me outside.* ◦ UK *Now that you're here, why don't you stop for some tea?* ◦ UK *I've been out every night this week, so I thought I'd stop **in** (= stay at home) tonight.* ◦ UK *We stopped **up** (= did not go to bed) until two o'clock last night watching the late film.* **BLOCK** ▷ **9** [T] to block a hole: *We stopped (**up**) the gap with some rags.*

IDIOMS **stop at nothing** (C1) If you stop at nothing to achieve something, you are willing to do anything in order to achieve it, even if it involves danger, great effort, or harming other people: *She'll stop at nothing* to get her revenge. • **stop short of sth** Ⓒ2 If you stop short of doing or saying something, you decide not to do or say it although you almost do: *I stopped short of telling him the brutal truth, but only just.*

PHRASAL VERBS **stop by (somewhere)** to visit someone for a short time, usually on the way to another place: *I was passing your house, so I thought I'd stop by for a chat.* • **stop in 1** informal to visit a person or place for a short time, usually when you are going somewhere else: *I stopped in* ***at*** *work on the way home to check my mail.* **2** UK informal to stay at home, especially in the evening • **stop off somewhere** to visit or stay at a place for a short time when you are going somewhere else: *I'll stop off* ***at*** *the shops on my way home and get some wine.* ◦ *We're going to stop off* ***in*** *Paris for a couple of days before heading south.* • **stop over** Ⓑ2 to stay at a place for one night or a few nights on the way to somewhere else or before returning home: *They're stopping over in Malaysia for a couple of nights on the way to Australia.* ◦ UK *Come round for dinner one night and you can stop over.* → See also **stopover**

▸**noun** [C] **1** Ⓑ1 the act of stopping an activity or journey, or a period of time when you stop: *Please remain in your seat until the plane* ***comes to a*** *complete stop.* ◦ *We'd have been here sooner, but we made several stops along the way.* ◦ *At the beginning of the project there were a lot of stops* ***and starts****.* → See also **doorstop 2** Ⓐ1 a place where vehicles, especially buses, stop in order to allow passengers to get off and on: *a* ***bus*** *stop* ◦ *I'm getting off at the next stop.* ◦ *Is this our stop (= where we must get off)?* **3** UK short form of **full stop 4** specialized a consonant that is made by completely stopping the flow of air **5 put a stop to sth** Ⓒ1 to stop an unpleasant, unwanted activity or habit from continuing: *He used to smoke in bed when I first got to know him, but I soon put a stop to that!*

ˌstop-and-ˈgo adj US A stop-and-go activity is one in which there are short periods of movement with regular interruptions: *stop-and-go traffic on city streets*

stopcock /ˈstɒp.kɒk/ Ⓤⓢ /ˈstɑːp.kɑːk/ **noun** [C] a VALVE in a pipe which controls the flow of liquid through it

stopgap /ˈstɒp.gæp/ Ⓤⓢ /ˈstɑːp-/ **noun** [C] something intended for temporary use until something better or more suitable can be found: *Hostels are usually provided* ***as a*** *stopgap until the families can be housed in permanent accommodation.* ◦ *We might have to employ someone temporarily as a stopgap* ***measure*** *until we can fill the post.*

ˌstop-ˈgo adj [before noun] UK describes a situation in which there are periods of development and activity quickly followed by periods without activity, especially in a country's economy

stoplight /ˈstɒp.laɪt/ Ⓤⓢ /ˈstɑːp-/ **noun** [C] US for **traffic light**

stopover /ˈstɒpˌəʊ.vəʳ/ Ⓤⓢ /ˈstɑːpˌoʊ.vɚ/ **noun** [C] UK (US **layover**) Ⓑ2 a short stay in a place that you make while you are on a longer journey to somewhere else: *Our tickets to Australia include a stopover for two nights in Singapore.*

stoppage /ˈstɒp.ɪdʒ/ Ⓤⓢ /ˈstɑː.pɪdʒ/ **noun** [C] **NOT WORKING** ▷ **1** a time when work is stopped because of a disagreement between workers and employers **MONEY** ▷ **2** UK (US and Australian English **deduction**) an amount that is taken away from the money that you are paid before you officially receive it: *Stoppages include things like pension contributions and national insurance.* **BUS** ▷ **3** Indian English an occasion when a bus stops to allow passengers to get on and off

ˈstoppage ˌtime noun [U] UK → **injury time**

stopper /ˈstɒp.əʳ/ Ⓤⓢ /ˈstɑː.pɚ/ **noun** [C] an object which fits into the top of a bottle or other container

-stopper /-stɒp.əʳ/ Ⓤⓢ /-stɑː.pɚ/ **suffix** something that stops the thing mentioned: *a conversation stopper* ◦ *a crowd-stopper* ◦ *a heart-stopper* → See also **show-stopper**

ˈstopping ˌdistance noun [C] the distance travelled between the time when someone decides to stop a vehicle moving, and the time when the vehicle completely stops: *The stopping distance depends on several factors, including the road surface and the driver's reflexes.*

ˈstopping ˌtrain noun [C] UK a train that stops at a lot of stations on a route and is therefore slower than a direct train

ˌstop ˈpress noun [U] UK Stop press refers to a particular space on the front or back page of a newspaper which contains very recent news which was added to the newspaper after the printing process had started.

ˈstop ˌsign noun [C] a sign on the road which tells drivers of vehicles to stop and not to continue until all other vehicles have gone past

stopwatch /ˈstɒp.wɒtʃ/ Ⓤⓢ /ˈstɑːp.wɑːtʃ/ **noun** [C] a watch that can be started and stopped in order to measure the exact time of an event, especially a sports event

stopwatch

storage /ˈstɔː.rɪdʒ/ Ⓤⓢ /ˈstɔːr.ɪdʒ/ **noun** [U] **1** Ⓑ2 the putting and keeping of things in a special place for use in the future: *We've had to build some cupboards to give us more storage* ***space****.* **2 in storage** If things such as furniture are in storage, they are being kept safe in a special building while they are not needed.

ˈstorage ˌbattery noun [C] US for **accumulator**

ˈstorage deˌvice noun [C] a piece of computer equipment in which information and instructions can be kept

ˈstorage ˌheater noun [C] UK an electric device for heating rooms which uses electricity during the hours when it is cheapest in order to store warmth for later use

S

store /stɔːʳ/ Ⓤⓢ /stɔːr/ **noun; verb**

▸**noun** [C] **SHOP** ▷ **1** Ⓑ1 UK a large shop where you can buy many different types of goods: *a department store* ◦ *a DIY/furniture store* **2** Ⓐ1 US any type of shop: *a clothing/liquor store* ◦ *a convenience store* **STH KEPT** ▷ **3** an amount of something that is being kept for future use: *He's got an impressively large store* ***of*** *wine in his cellar.* ◦ *Food stores are reported to be running dangerously low in the capital.* ◦ figurative *I'm afraid my great store of wit is rather depleted (= I'm not able to be very amusing) this evening.* **4** a building in which things are kept until they are needed: *a grain/weapons store*

IDIOMS **in store** Ⓒ1 going to happen soon: *You never know what's in store* ***for*** *you.* ◦ *There's a bit of a shock in store* ***for*** *him when he gets home tonight!* • **set great, little, etc. store by sth** to consider something to be of great, little, etc. importance or value: *She's setting a lot of store by this job interview – I only hope she gets it.*

▸**verb** [T usually + adv/prep] Ⓑ2 to put or keep things in a special place for use in the future: *The data is stored* ***on*** *a hard disk and backed up on a CD.* ◦ *I stored my possessions* ***in*** *my mother's house while I was living in Spain.* ◦ *I've stored my thick sweaters and jackets* ***(away)*** *until next winter.* ◦ *Squirrels store* ***(up)*** *nuts for the winter.*

PHRASAL VERB **store sth up 1** (C2) to keep a lot of something in one place, to be used in the future: *We believe that he has been training an army and storing up arms.* **2** (C1) to remember things, usually so that you can tell people about them later: *I listen in to their conversations and store it all up to tell you later.*

IDIOM **store up trouble/problems** to act in a way that will make your problems much worse in the future: *If you don't deal with the problem now, you'll be storing up trouble* ***for yourself*** *in the future.*

ˈstore-bought adj US (UK **ˈshop-bought**) describes food bought in a shop and not made at home: *Why use store-bought pastry when it's so easy to make your own?*

ˈstore ˌbrand noun [U] US for **own brand**

ˈstore ˌcard noun [C] a small plastic card that can be used as a method of payment at a particular shop, with the money being taken from you at a later date

ˌstored ˈenergy noun [U] specialized in physics, the energy stored by something → Synonym **potential energy**

ˈstore deˌtective noun [C] a person who works in a large shop, especially a DEPARTMENT STORE, watching the customers so that they do not steal goods

storefront /ˈstɔː.frʌnt/ (US) /ˈstɔːr-/ noun [C] US (UK **shopfront**) the part of a shop that faces the road: *A number of storefronts were damaged in the riots.*

storehouse /ˈstɔː.haʊs/ (US) /ˈstɔːr-/ noun [C] US for **warehouse**

storekeeper /ˈstɔːˌkiː.pəʳ/ (US) /ˈstɔːrˌkiː.pɚ/ noun [C] US for **shopkeeper**

storeroom /ˈstɔː.rʊm/, /-ruːm/ (US) /ˈstɔːr-/ noun [C] a room for keeping things in while they are not being used

storey UK (US **story**) /ˈstɔː.ri/ (US) /ˈstɔːr.i/ noun [C] (B2) a level of a building: *a three-storey house* ◦ *Their new house has four storeys including the attic.* • **storeyed** (US **storied**) /ˈstɔː.rid/ (US) /ˈstɔːr.id/ adj *It's a normal two-storeyed house.*

storied /ˈstɔː.rid/ (US) /ˈstɔːr.id/ adj [before noun] mainly US **1** often spoken of or written about: *Theirs was the most storied romance in Hollywood.* ◦ *Charlton Heston's storied film career* **2** US for **storeyed**

stork /stɔːk/ (US) /stɔːrk/ noun [C] a large, white bird with very long legs which walks around in water to find its food

storm /stɔːm/ (US) /stɔːrm/ noun; verb

▸noun **VIOLENT WEATHER** ▷ **1** (A2) [C] an extreme weather condition with very strong wind, heavy rain, and often thunder and LIGHTNING: *A lot of trees were blown down in the recent storms.* ◦ *They're still clearing up the storm damage.* **EMOTIONAL REACTION** ▷ **2** [C usually singular] a very angry reaction from a lot of people: *There was a storm* ***of*** *protest when the new tax was announced.* **ATTACK** ▷ **3 take sb/sth by storm** to be suddenly extremely successful in a place or with a group of people: *Her performance has taken the London critics by storm.*

> **Word partners for storm noun**
>
> an *approaching/gathering* storm • a *big/fierce/severe/violent* storm • a storm *blows in/brews/rolls in* • a storm *breaks/hits/strikes/wreaks havoc* • a storm *abates/passes* • the *centre/eye* of a storm • storm *clouds/damage*

IDIOMS **cook up, dance up, talk up, etc. a storm** informal to do something with a lot of energy and often skill: *Rob was in the kitchen cooking up a storm.* • **storm in a teacup** UK (US **tempest in a teapot**) a lot of unnecessary anger and worry about a matter that is not important

▸verb **ATTACK** ▷ **1** [T] to attack a place or building by entering suddenly in great numbers: *The fortress was stormed by hundreds of soldiers.* **EMOTIONAL REACTION** ▷ **2** [I or T] literary to express anger in a loud and often uncontrolled way: [+ speech] *'Get out and never come back!' he stormed.* **3 storm in/into/out** to enter or leave a place in a way that shows that you are angry: *He stormed out of the house, slamming the door as he went.*

-storm /-stɔːm/ (US) /-stɔːrm/ suffix used to form words for particular types of violent weather: *a rainstorm* ◦ *a sandstorm* ◦ *a snowstorm* ◦ *a thunderstorm* ◦ *a windstorm*

ˈstorm ˌcloud noun **1** [C usually singular] a large, dark cloud which brings rain or comes before a storm **2 storm clouds** [plural] literary trouble, especially trouble that is going to happen soon: *Economic storm clouds are* ***gathering*** *over India.* ◦ *The storm clouds* ***of war*** *seem to be looming over the east.*

ˈstorm ˌdoor/ˌwindow noun [C] US an extra door or window that is fitted to the usual door or window for protection in bad weather

stormily /ˈstɔː.mɪ.li/ (US) /ˈstɔːr-/ adv angrily

ˈstorm ˌsurge noun [C] an occasion when a lot of water is pushed from the sea onto the land, usually caused by a HURRICANE (= a violent storm with very high winds)

ˈstorm ˌtrooper noun [C] a soldier in the private army of the Nazi party in Germany before and during the Second World War

stormy /ˈstɔː.mi/ (US) /ˈstɔːr-/ adj **VIOLENT WEATHER** ▷ **1** (B2) with strong wind, heavy rain, and often thunder and LIGHTNING: *stormy* ***weather*** ◦ *The sky was dark and stormy.* **EMOTIONAL REACTION** ▷ **2** (C1) involving a lot of strong argument and shouting: *a stormy debate* ◦ *They had a passionate and often stormy relationship.*

story /ˈstɔː.ri/ (US) /ˈstɔːr.i/ noun [C] **DESCRIPTION** ▷ **1** (A2) a description, either true or imagined, of a connected series of events: *Will you* ***read/tell*** *me a story, daddy?* ◦ *Martha chose her favourite book of* ***bedtime*** *stories.* ◦ *He writes* ***children's*** *stories.* ◦ *I don't know if it's true but it's a good story (= entertaining to listen to although probably not true).* ◦ *She gave me her version of what had happened, but it would be interesting to hear his* ***half/side of the*** *story (= the events as described by him).* ◦ *Apparently his first words to her were 'Will you marry me?'* ***or so*** *the story* ***goes*** (= that is what people say happened). **2** (B2) a report in a newspaper or on a news broadcast of something that has happened: *The main story in the papers today is the president's speech.* **3** (C2) a lie: *He* ***made up*** *some story about having to be at his aunt's wedding anniversary.* **LEVEL** ▷ **4** US for **storey**

Other ways of saying story

Tale is an alternative to 'story', especially when it might be invented or difficult to believe:

*The book is a well-told **tale** about life during the Civil War.*

Narrative is a formal word for a story:

*It's a moving **narrative** of wartime adventure.*

If a story is someone's description of an event, you could use the word **account**:

*She gave a thrilling **account** of her life in the jungle.*

A short, amusing story, especially about something that someone has done, is an **anecdote**:

*He told one or two amusing **anecdotes** about his years as a police officer.*

The story of a book, film, etc. is its **plot**:

*The movie has a very simple **plot**.*

If a story is ancient and about famous people or events, the word **legend** is often used:

*The dance was based on several Hindu **legends**.*

Myths are ancient stories that explain the history of a group of people or are about natural events:

*Greek **myths***

A **fable** is a story that tells a general truth or is only partly based on facts:

*the **fable** of the hare and the tortoise*

Stories for children which involve magic and imaginary creatures are often called **fairy tales**.

IDIOM **it's/that's the story of my life** humorous said when something bad happens to you that has happened to you many times before: *Honestly, it's the story of my life – I meet a totally gorgeous bloke and he's leaving for Australia the next day!*

storyboard /ˈstɔː.ri.bɔːd/ (US) /ˈstɔːr.i.bɔːrd/ **noun** [C] (in films and television) a series of drawings or images showing the order of images planned for a film

storybook /ˈstɔː.ri.bʊk/ (US) /ˈstɔːr.i-/ **adj** [before noun] (of real life situations) happy and pleasant in the way that situations in children's stories usually are: *If you're looking for a storybook romance, you're always going to be disappointed.*

storyline /ˈstɔː.ri.laɪn/ (US) /ˈstɔːr.i-/ **noun** [C] (in a book, film, play, etc.) the PLOT (= the series of events which happen in it)

storyteller /ˈstɔː.riˌtel.əʳ/ (US) /ˈstɔːr.iˌtel.ɚ/ **noun** [C] a person who writes, tells, or reads stories

stout /staʊt/ **adj; noun**

▸**adj** **PERSON** ▷ **1** (especially of older people) quite fat and solid-looking, especially around the waist: *Mrs Blower was the rather stout lady with the glasses.* **OBJECT** ▷ **2** approving describes objects that are strongly made from thick, strong materials: *I've bought myself a pair of good stout boots for hiking.* **CHARACTER** ▷ **3** [before noun] literary strong and determined: *He needed a stout **heart** and nerves of steel.*

▸**noun** [U] a dark, bitter type of beer

stouthearted /ˌstaʊtˈhɑː.tɪd/ (US) /-ˈhɑːr.t̬ɪd/ **adj** old-fashioned literary brave and determined

stoutly /ˈstaʊt.li/ **adv** **CHARACTER** ▷ **1** in a firm and determined way: *They have stoutly denied the recent rumours that there are problems with their marriage.* **OBJECT** ▷ **2** in a strong way: *stoutly-made boots*

stove /stəʊv/ (US) /stoʊv/ **noun** [C] **1** a piece of equipment which burns fuel or uses electricity in order to heat a place **2** (A2) mainly US a cooker

stovetop /ˈstəʊv.tɒp/ (US) /ˈstoʊv.tɑːp/ **noun** [C] US for **hob**

stow /stəʊ/ (US) /stoʊ/ **verb** [T] to store something: *There's a big cupboard under the stairs for stowing toys.*

PHRASAL VERBS **stow away** to hide on a ship, aircraft, or other vehicle in order to escape from a place or to travel without paying • **stow (sth) away** to put something in a safe place so that it can be used in the future: *I think I'll stow the camping equipment away in the loft until next summer.*

stowage /ˈstəʊ.ɪdʒ/ (US) /ˈstoʊ-/ **noun** [U] space for storing things on a boat or plane

stowaway /ˈstəʊ.əˌweɪ/ (US) /ˈstoʊ-/ **noun** [C] a person who hides on a ship, aircraft, or other vehicle

straddle /ˈstræd.l̩/ **verb** [T] **1** to sit or stand with your legs on either side of something: *He pulled on his helmet and straddled the motorbike.* **2** Something that straddles a line, such as a border or river, exists on each side of it or goes across it: *Our farm straddles the railway line.* **3** to combine different styles or subjects: *It's described as a new kind of dance music which straddles jazz and soul.* **4** mainly US disapproving to be unable to decide which of two opinions about a subject is better and so partly support both opinions: *It's not the first time this year that the president has been accused of straddling an **issue**.*

strafe /streɪf/ **verb** [T] to attack an enemy by shooting from aircraft that are flying low in the sky

straggle /ˈstræg.l̩/ **verb** [I usually + adv/prep] to move or spread untidily and in small numbers or amounts: *I tie my hair up because I don't like it straggling down my back.* ◦ *A year after the hurricane, tourists are beginning to straggle (= come in small numbers) back to the region.*

straggler /ˈstræg.ləʳ/ (US) /-lɚ/ **noun** [C] a person or animal that is last in a group to do something or the last to get to or leave a place: *We watched the last of the stragglers come in, three hours after the first runner.*

straggly /ˈstræg.li/ **adj** growing or spreading out in an untidy way: *He has a long, straggly grey beard.*

straight /streɪt/ **adj; adv; adj; noun**

▸**adj, adv** **NOT CURVING** ▷ **1** (A2) continuing in one direction without bending or curving: *a straight line* ◦ *She's got straight blonde hair.* ◦ *Skirts this summer are long and straight.* ◦ *Can't you see it? – it's straight **ahead** (of you)!* ◦ *The dog seemed to be coming straight **at/for** me.* ◦ *Go straight along this road and turn left at the traffic lights.* **HONEST** ▷ **2** (B2) honest: *Just be straight with her and tell her how you feel.* ◦ informal ***Tell** me straight, would you rather we didn't go tonight?* → Compare **bent 3** **straight out** If you tell someone something straight out, you tell them directly and honestly, without trying to make what you are saying more pleasant: *I told her straight out that I didn't love her any more.*

IDIOMS **straight arrow** US someone who is very honest and careful to behave in a socially acceptable way: *Friends described Menendez as a straight arrow who rarely drank and was close to his family.* • **(as) straight as a die 1** extremely straight: *The road runs (as) straight as a die for 50 or so miles.* **2** completely honest: *She's as straight as a die, I can trust her to tell me what she's really thinking.* • **straight up** slang used to show that you are telling the truth: *You're a really attractive woman, straight up!* ◦ *'You're not telling me she's 16! Straight up?' (= Are you telling the truth?)*

▸**adv** **IMMEDIATELY** ▷ **1** (B1) immediately: *I got home and went straight to bed.* ◦ *Shall we go straight to the party*

S

or stop off at a pub first? ◦ Time is short so I'll get straight **to the point** (= explain the matter immediately). → See also **straightaway 2 straight away/off** B1 mainly UK immediately: *I knew straight away what you were thinking. ◦ We don't need to go straight off – we can stay for a little while.* **CLEAR** ▷ **3** C1 clearly: *You know you've had too much to drink when you can't **see** straight. ◦ I'm so tired I can't **think** straight any more.*

▸adj **CLEAR** ▷ **1** C1 [before noun] clear or not complicated: *It's a straight choice – either you leave him or you stay. ◦ Let's **get this** straight – you're travelling to Frankfurt on Monday and Brussels on Tuesday, is that correct?* → See also **straightforward LEVEL** ▷ **2** B2 level and not sloping to either side: *This picture's not straight. ◦ The shelf isn't straight – it sags in the middle.* **TIDY** ▷ **3** [after verb] mainly UK tidy, or arranged in order: *It only took an hour to get the flat straight after the party. ◦ Have you got a mirror? – I'll just put my **hair** straight.* **PLAIN** ▷ **4** plain and basic, or without anything added: *No tonic for me, please, I like my vodka straight. ◦ Straight pasta is very bland – you need some kind of sauce to make it interesting.* **FOLLOWING EACH OTHER** ▷ **5** [before noun] following one after another without an interruption: *They're the only team to have won ten straight games this season.* **TRADITIONAL** ▷ **6** informal traditional or serious: disapproving *He was a nice enough bloke, but he was so straight – I always felt I had to be on my best behaviour with him. ◦ There's a lot of straight theatre at the festival as well as the newer, more experimental stuff.* **SEXUAL PREFERENCE** ▷ **7** informal not gay **NO DRUGS** ▷ **8** informal not using illegal drugs or alcohol: *He's been straight for five months.* **NOT OWING MONEY** ▷ **9** [after verb] informal neither owing nor owed any money: *You bought the tickets, so if I pay for the taxi, we'll be straight.*

IDIOM **put/set someone straight** to make certain that someone knows the real facts about a situation: *Don't worry, I set him straight (**on** this matter).*

▸noun [C] **SPORTS TRACK** ▷ **1** (US usually **straightaway**) the straight part of a RACETRACK (= the track on which competitors race): *And the runners are just coming up to the **finishing** straight.* **SEXUAL PREFERENCE** ▷ **2** informal a person who is not gay

IDIOM **the straight and narrow** humorous If you keep on the straight and narrow, you behave in a way that is honest and moral: *The threat of a good beating should **keep** him **on** the straight and narrow.*

S

ˌstraight-ˈA adj [before noun] getting the best results in all examinations: *She had always been a straight-A student until she met him.*

ˈstraight ˌangle noun [C] specialized an angle of 180°: *Two right angles make a straight angle, which is a straight line.*

straightaway /ˌstreɪt.əˈweɪ/ (US) /ˌstreɪt̬-/ adv; noun

▸adv B1 immediately: *We don't have to go straightaway, do we?*

▸noun [C] US for a **straight**.

ˌstraight-edge ˈrazor noun [C] US for **cutthroat razor**

straighten /ˈstreɪ.tᵊn/ (US) /-ᵊn/ verb **NOT CURVING** ▷ **1** [I or T] to become straight or to make something become straight: *He straightened his tie. ◦ Her hair is naturally curly but she always straightens it. ◦ The road straightens **out** after a few miles.* **LEVEL** ▷ **2** [T] to make something level: *The picture fell while I was trying to straighten it.* **TIDY** ▷ **3** [T] to make something tidy: *She stood up and straightened her clothes. ◦ Pepe was careful to straighten his room before leaving.*

PHRASAL VERBS **straighten sb out** informal to improve someone's behaviour: *I thought that once he got a girlfriend that would straighten him out.* • **straighten sth out SITUATION** ▷ **1** to solve a problem or to deal successfully with a confusing situation: *Once we get these problems straightened out, we should be all right.* **PLACE** ▷ **2** to make something tidy or organized: *Could you straighten out these cupboards, please?* • **straighten up POSITION** ▷ **1** to stand straight after bending at the waist **BEHAVIOUR** ▷ **2** US to behave well after behaving badly: *You'd better straighten up or else!* • **straighten sth up** to make a place tidy: *Mark and I managed to straighten up the house before our parents got home.*

straighteners /ˈstreɪ.tᵊn.əz/ (US) /-ɚz/ noun [plural] (also **ˈhair ˌstraighteners**, US **straightener**) a piece of electrical equipment that you heat up and move through SECTIONS of your hair to make it straight

ˌstraight ˈface noun [C usually singular] a serious expression on your face that you use when you do not want someone to know that you think something is funny: *Brian looked ridiculous in leather trousers, and I was desperately trying to **keep** a straight face.*

ˌstraight-ˈfaced adj without laughing or smiling: *We laughed, but Chris was straight-faced and seemed a little offended by the joke.*

straightforward /ˌstreɪtˈfɔː.wəd/ (US) /-ˈfɔːr.wɚd/ adj **SIMPLE** ▷ **1** B2 easy to understand or simple: *Just follow the signs to Bradford – it's very straightforward.* **HONEST** ▷ **2** (of a person) honest and not likely to hide their opinions: *Roz is straightforward and lets you know what she's thinking.* • **straightforwardly** /-li/ adv

straightjacket /ˈstreɪt.dʒæk.ɪt/ noun [C] a **strait-jacket**

ˈstraight ˌman noun [C usually singular] In a COMEDY act between two men, the straight man is the more serious of the two who is often made to look stupid by his partner.

ˌstraight ˈrazor noun [C] US for **cutthroat razor**

strain /streɪn/ noun; verb

▸noun **PRESSURE** ▷ **1** B2 [C usually singular or U] a force or influence that stretches, pulls, or puts pressure on something, sometimes causing damage: *The hurricane **put** such a strain **on** the bridge that it collapsed. ◦ As you get older, excess weight **puts** a lot of strain **on** the heart. ◦ Their constant arguments were **putting** a strain **on** their marriage. ◦ The recent decline in the dollar has **put a** bigger strain **on** the economic system. ◦ Migration into the cities is **putting** a strain **on** already stretched resources.* **2** C2 [C] an injury to a muscle or similar soft part of the body caused by using that part too much: *a groin/hamstring strain* → See also **eyestrain 3** B2 [C or U] something that makes you feel nervous and worried: *She's a lot better than she was but she's still not ready to face the **stresses and** strains of a job. ◦ He's been **under** a lot of strain recently.* **TYPE** ▷ **4** [C] a particular type or quality: *A strain **of** puritanism runs through all her work.* **5** [C] an animal or plant from a particular group whose characteristics are different in some way from others of the same group: *Scientists have discovered a new strain **of** the virus which is much more dangerous.* **MUSIC** ▷ **6 strains** [plural] the sound of music being played or performed: *I could hear the strains **of** Mozart in the background.*

▸verb **SEPARATE** ▷ **1** [T] to separate liquid food from solid food, especially by pouring it through a UTENSIL with small holes in it: *Could you strain the vegetables,* please. ◦ *I usually strain the juice **off** the pineapple and use it in another recipe.* **PRESSURE** ▷ **2** B2 [I or T] to become stretched or to experience pressure, or to make something do or experience this: *I've put on such a lot of weight recently – this dress is straining at the seams.* ◦ *I strained a muscle in my back playing squash.* ◦ *Don't watch TV in the dark – you'll strain your **eyes**!* ◦ [+ to infinitive] figurative *I really had to strain (= try very hard) **to** reach those top notes.* ◦ figurative *I was straining (**my ears**) (= listening hard) to hear what they were saying.* → Compare **restrain** **MONEY** ▷ **3** C2 [T] to cause too much of something to be used, especially money: *Increases in wholesale oil prices have strained the company's finances.*

IDIOMS **be straining at the leash** to be very eager to do something that you are being prevented from doing at the present time: *Meanwhile we hear that our soldiers have reached a peak of fitness and are straining at the leash.* • **strain every nerve** to make the greatest possible effort: *She's straining every nerve to get the work finished on time.*

strained /streɪnd/ **adj** **1** If a relationship is strained, problems are spoiling that relationship: *Relations between the two countries have become strained (= difficult) recently.* **2** showing that someone is nervous or worried: *Jean felt uncomfortable but managed to force a strained smile.*

strainer /ˈstreɪ.nəʳ/ US /-nɚ/ **noun** [C] a kitchen UTENSIL with a lot of holes in it for separating liquid from solid: *a **tea** strainer*

strait /streɪt/ **noun** **WATER** ▷ **1** [C usually plural] a narrow area of sea which connects two larger areas of sea: *the Straits of Gibraltar* **DIFFICULTY** ▷ **2** **straits** [plural] a difficult situation, especially because of financial problems: *So many companies are **in** such **dire/difficult** straits that their prices have come right down.*

straitened /ˈstreɪ.tᵊnd/ **adj** [before noun] formal describes a situation that is difficult because there is much less money available to you than there was in the past: *A lot of people are finding themselves in very straitened **circumstances** these days.*

straitjacket (also **straightjacket**) /ˈstreɪtˌdʒæk.ɪt/ **noun** [C usually singular] **1** a strong piece of special clothing which ties the arms to the body and is used for limiting the movements of dangerous prisoners and mentally ill patients whose behaviour is violent: *Brody was locked in a padded cell and forced to wear a straitjacket.* **2** disapproving something that severely limits development or activity in a way that is damaging: *He refused to be fitted into any ideological straitjacket.*

strait-laced /ˌstreɪtˈleɪst/ US /ˈstreɪt.leɪst/ **adj** disapproving having old-fashioned and fixed morals, especially relating to sexual matters

strand /strænd/ **noun** [C] **THREAD** ▷ **1** C2 a thin thread of something, often one of a few, twisted around each other to make a string or rope: *a strand of cotton* ◦ *She tucked a loose strand of hair behind her ears.* **PART** ▷ **2** C2 a part which combines with other parts to form a whole story, subject, or situation: *There are so many different strands to the plot that it's quite hard to follow.* **COAST** ▷ **3** literary a **shore**

stranded /ˈstræn.dɪd/ **adj** C2 unable to leave somewhere because of a problem such as not having any transport or money: *He **left** me stranded in town with no car and no money for a bus.* ◦ *If the tide comes in, we'll be stranded on these rocks.*

strange /streɪndʒ/ **adj** **UNUSUAL** ▷ **1** A2 unusual and unexpected, or difficult to understand: *He's got some very strange ideas about women!* ◦ *You say the strangest things sometimes.* ◦ *I had a strange feeling that we'd met before.* ◦ ***It's** strange **that** tourists almost never visit this village.* ◦ ***That's** strange – I'm sure I put my glasses in my bag and yet they're not there.* **2** **feel strange** to feel uncomfortable and not normal or correct: *I hope that fish was all right – my stomach feels a bit strange.* **NOT FAMILIAR** ▷ **3** B1 not known or familiar: *I don't usually accept lifts from strange men.* ◦ *With so many strange faces around her, the baby started to cry.* ◦ *I've never been here before either, so it's all strange **to** me too.*

> **Other ways of saying strange**
>
> See also: **unusual**
>
> Other ways of saying 'strange' are **odd**, **bizarre**, and **weird**:
>
> *I always thought there was something a bit **odd** about her.*
>
> *I had a really **bizarre/weird** dream last night.*
>
> If something is strange because it is not what you usually expect, you can use the adjectives **curious**, **funny**, or **peculiar**:
>
> *This lemonade tastes **funny**.*
>
> *The chicken had a **peculiar** smell.*
>
> *A **curious** thing happened to me yesterday.*
>
> If someone always behaves strangely, you might describe that person as **eccentric**:
>
> *The whole family is **eccentric**.*

strangely /ˈstreɪndʒ.li/ **adv** B2 in a way that is unusual, unexpected, or difficult to understand: *She was strangely calm – I found it quite disturbing.*

IDIOM **strangely enough** B2 used to remark that something is surprising but true: *Strangely enough, when it came to the exam I actually felt quite relaxed.*

strangeness /ˈstreɪndʒ.nəs/ **noun** [U] **UNUSUAL** ▷ **1** the quality of being unusual, unexpected, or difficult to understand **NOT FAMILIAR** ▷ **2** the quality of not being familiar: *She was struck by the strangeness of her surroundings.*

stranger /ˈstreɪn.dʒəʳ/ US /-dʒɚ/ **noun** [C] **1** B1 someone you do not know: *My mother always warned me not to talk to strangers.* ◦ *I'd never met anyone at the party before – they were **complete** strangers.*

> **Note:**
>
> Do not confuse with **foreigner** (= a person from another country).

2 A stranger in a particular place is someone who has never been there before: *Do you know the way to St Peter's church or are you a stranger here too?*

IDIOMS **be no stranger to sth** formal to be familiar with a particular experience or activity: *He is no stranger to hard work.* • **hello stranger** humorous said to a person that you know but have not seen for a long time: *Hello stranger, I haven't seen you for weeks!*

strangle /ˈstræŋ.gl̩/ **verb** [T] **1** to kill someone by pressing their throat so that they cannot breathe: *She had been strangled with her own scarf and her body dumped in the woods.* **2** to stop something from developing: *For years, the organization was strangled by excessive bureaucracy.* ◦ *There is a great deal of fear that the new restrictions might strangle the country's economy.*

strangled /ˈstræŋ.gl̩d/ **adj** [usually before noun] describes a weak, high, interrupted sound made by

S

an extremely frightened or worried and nervous person: *It came again, a strangled **cry** from the room next door.*

stranglehold /ˈstræŋ.gl̩.həʊld/ (US) /-hoʊld/ **noun** [C usually singular] disapproving a position of complete control that prevents something from developing: *The two major companies have been **tightening** their stranglehold **on** the beer market.*

strangler /ˈstræŋ.gləʳ/ (US) /-glɚ/ **noun** [C] a person who kills people by pressing their throats so that they cannot breathe: *The newspapers dubbed him 'the Boston Strangler'.*

strangulate /ˈstræŋ.gjʊ.leɪt/ **verb** [T] Indian English to kill someone by pressing their throat so that they cannot breathe; STRANGLE

strangulated /ˈstræŋ.gjʊ.leɪ.tɪd/ (US) /-t̬ɪd/ **adj** **BODY PART** ▷ **1** specialized describes an organ or other part inside the body that has become tightly pressed, blocking the flow of blood or air through it: *a strangulated hernia* **SOUND** ▷ **2** (US also **strangled**) describes a sound that is not full or relaxed, but made when your throat is tight, for example because of fear or anger: *He let out a strangulated squeak of outrage.*

strangulation /ˌstræŋ.gjʊˈleɪ.ʃən/ **noun** [U] the action of killing someone by pressing their throat so that they cannot breathe, or the act of dying in this way: *The post-mortem showed that the boy had died from strangulation.*

strap /stræp/ **noun; verb**

▸**noun** [C] **1** (C2) a narrow piece of leather or other strong material used for fastening something or giving support: *Could you help me fasten this strap around my suitcase?* **2** with this meaning as a combining form: *a **watch** strap* ◦ *shoes with **ankle** straps*

▸**verb** [T usually + adv/prep] (**-pp-**) to fasten something in position by fixing a narrow piece of leather or other strong material around it: *Are the kids strapped into their car seats?* ◦ *We strapped the surfboard **to** the car roof.*

PHRASAL VERBS **strap sb in** to fasten a SEAT BELT around someone in a car, aircraft, or other vehicle, for safety purposes: *Are you kids strapped in back there?* • **strap sth up** [often passive] UK (US **tape sth up**) to wrap a leg, arm, or other part of the body in a BANDAGE (= strip of material for wrapping around injuries): *He injured himself playing football and his arm was strapped up.*

S

strapless /ˈstræp.ləs/ **adj** describes a piece of women's clothing, such as a dress or BRA (= piece of underwear) which does not have pieces of material going over the shoulders: *a strapless taffeta evening gown*

strapped /stræpt/ **adj** informal not having enough money: *I'd love to come to Malaysia with you, but I'm afraid I'm a bit strapped (**for cash**) at the moment.*

strapping /ˈstræp.ɪŋ/ **adj** [before noun] informal mainly humorous describes someone who is tall and strong-looking: *A big strapping **lad** like you shouldn't have much difficulty lifting that!*

strappy /ˈstræp.i/ **adj** informal having straps: *a pair of strappy **sandals***

stratagem /ˈstræt.ə.dʒəm/ (US) /ˈstræt̬-/ **noun** [C or U] a carefully planned way of achieving or dealing with something, often involving a trick: *Her stratagem **for** dealing with her husband's infidelities was to ignore them.* ◦ *He was a master of stratagem.*

strategic /strəˈtiː.dʒɪk/ **adj** **1** (C1) helping to achieve a plan, for example in business or politics: *strategic planning* ◦ *a strategic withdrawal/advance* ◦ *Their bombs are always placed **in** strategic **positions** to cause as much chaos as possible.* **2** Strategic weapons, war, or places provide military forces with an advantage: *There are plans to modernize the US strategic **forces**.* ◦ *strategic arms reduction talks* • **strategically** /-dʒɪ.kəl.i/ **adv** *Her scarf was strategically **placed** to hide a tear in her shirt.* ◦ *Central Asia is a fragile region, politically weak but strategically **important**.*

strategist /ˈstræt.ə.dʒɪst/ (US) /ˈstræt̬-/ **noun** [C] someone with a lot of skill and experience in planning, especially in military, political, or business matters: *He's the president's chief **political** strategist.*

strategy /ˈstræt.ə.dʒi/ (US) /ˈstræt̬-/ **noun** [C or U] (B2) a detailed plan for achieving success in situations such as war, politics, business, industry, or sport, or the skill of planning for such situations: *The president held an emergency meeting to discuss military strategy with his defence commanders yesterday.* ◦ *Their marketing strategy **for** the product involves obtaining as much free publicity as possible.* ◦ [+ to infinitive] *We're working on new strategies **to** improve our share of the market.*

stratify /ˈstræt.ɪ.faɪ/ (US) /ˈstræt̬-/ **verb** [T] to arrange the different parts of something in separate layers or groups: *The sample of people questioned was drawn from the university's student register and stratified **by** age and gender.* • **stratification** /ˌstræt.ɪ.fɪˈkeɪ.ʃən/ (US) /ˌstræt̬-/ **noun** [U] formal *The prime minister wants to reduce **social** stratification and make the country a classless society.*

stratocumulus /ˈstræ.təʊˌkjuː.mjə.ləs/ (US) /ˈstræ.t̬oʊ-/ **noun** [U] specialized a type of CUMULUS (= tall, rounded, white cloud with a flat base) formed in a thick layer and found at low height → Compare **altocumulus, cirrocumulus**

the stratosphere /ˈstræt.ə.sfɪəʳ/ (US) /ˈstræ.t̬ə.sfɪr/ **noun** [S] the layer of gases surrounding the Earth at a height of between 15 and 50 kilometres that is not affected by the weather and in which the temperature increases with height: *During the 1980s, the amount of ozone in the stratosphere above Europe decreased by about eight percent.* → Compare **the ionosphere**

IDIOM **go into the stratosphere** informal to go up to an extremely high level: *Property prices have gone into the stratosphere.*

stratum /ˈstrɑː.təm/ (US) /ˈstræ.t̬əm/ **noun** [C] (plural **strata**) **1** one of the parts or layers into which something is separated: *The report shows that drugs have penetrated every stratum **of** American society.* **2** specialized a layer of rock, soil, or similar material: *The cliffs are characterized by remarkable zigzagging strata of shale and sandstone.*

stratus /ˈstreɪ.təs/ (US) /ˈstreɪ.t̬əs/ **noun** [U] specialized a type of flat, grey cloud found at the lowest level, below all other cloud types, and causing DULL weather or light rain → Compare **cirrus, cumulus, nimbus**

straw /strɔː/ (US) /strɑː/ **noun** **DRIED STEMS** ▷ **1** (C1) [U] the dried, yellow stems of crops such as WHEAT, used as food for animals or as a layer on the ground for animals to lie on, and for making traditional objects: *a **bale** of straw* ◦ *a straw basket/hat* ◦ *straw-**coloured** hair* **TUBE** ▷ **2** (C2) [C] a thin tube made of plastic or WATERPROOF paper that is used to suck liquid into the mouth: *Why don't you drink your milkshake **through** a straw?*

IDIOMS **clutch/grasp at straws** to be willing to try anything to improve a difficult or unsatisfactory situation, even if it has little chance of success: *She offered to take a pay cut to keep her job, but she was just* *clutching at straws.* • **the final/last straw** (also **the straw that breaks the camel's back**) C1 the last in a series of unpleasant events which finally makes you feel that you cannot continue to accept a bad situation: *Losing my job was bad enough, but being evicted was the final straw.* ◦ *She's always been rude to me, but it was the last straw when she started insulting my mother.* • **straw in the wind** UK something that suggests what might happen

strawberry /ˈstrɔː.bᵊr.i/ US /ˈstrɑːˌber.i/ **noun** [C] B1 a small JUICY red fruit that has small brown seeds on its surface, or the plant with white flowers on which this fruit grows: *I thought we'd have strawberries **and cream** for dessert.* ◦ *strawberry **jam***

ˌstrawberry ˈblonde adj describes hair that is a pale reddish-yellow colour • **ˌstrawberry ˈblonde noun** [C] *Who was that strawberry blonde in the red dress?*

ˈstrawberry ˌmark noun [C] a permanent dark red mark on a person's skin which has existed since birth

ˌstraw ˈboater noun [C] a stiff hat with a flat top and wide, straight BRIM, traditionally worn in a boat on a river to protect the wearer from the sun

ˌstraw ˈman noun [C] (also **ˌman of ˈstraw**) mainly UK an argument, claim, or opponent that is invented in order to win or create an argument

ˌstraw ˈpoll noun [C] an unofficial vote that is taken to discover what people think about an idea or problem or how they intend to vote in an election: *A straw poll **of** local inhabitants concluded that British tourists were the most stylish.*

stray /streɪ/ **verb; noun; adj**

▸**verb** [I] **1** to travel along a route that was not originally intended, or to move outside a limited area: *A herd of cattle had strayed into the road.* ◦ *They got lost when they strayed **too far from** the footpath.* ◦ *The ship strayed off course during the storm.* **2** to start thinking or talking about a different subject from the one you should be giving attention to: *I think we've strayed **too far from** our original plan.* ◦ *Sorry – I've strayed **from the subject**.*

▸**noun** [C] a pet that no longer has a home or cannot find its home: *a stray dog* ◦ *'Who owns that cat?' 'I don't know. I think it must be a stray.'*

▸**adj** [before noun] Stray things have moved apart from similar things and are not in their expected or intended place: *There are still a few stray spots of paint on the window pane.* ◦ *Several journalists have been killed or injured by stray **bullets** while reporting on the civil war.*

streak /striːk/ **noun; verb**

▸**noun** [C] **MARK** ▷ **1** a long, thin mark that is easily noticed because it is very different from the area surrounding it: *The window cleaner has left dirty streaks on the windows.* ◦ *I dye my hair to hide my grey streaks.* ◦ *Meteors produce streaks **of** light as they burn up in the Earth's atmosphere.* **CHARACTERISTIC** ▷ **2** an often unpleasant characteristic that is very different from other characteristics: *Her **stubborn** streak makes her very difficult to work with sometimes.* ◦ *You need to have a **competitive** streak when you're working in marketing.* **SHORT PERIOD** ▷ **3** a short period of good or bad luck: *I just hope my **lucky** streak continues until the world championships.* ◦ *Their longest **losing** streak has been three games.* ◦ *After winning a couple of bets, he thought he was **on** a winning streak.*

IDIOM **like a streak of lightning** informal extremely quickly: *She grabbed the money and ran out of the shop like a streak of lightning.*

▸**verb MOVE FAST** ▷ **1** [I usually + adv/prep] to move somewhere extremely quickly, usually in a straight line: *The motorbike streaked off **down** the street.* ◦ *Did you see that bird streak **past** the window?* **RUN NAKED** ▷ **2** [I] to run naked through a public place in order to attract attention or to express strong disapproval of something **MARK** ▷ **3 be streaked** to have long, thin noticeable lines of a different colour: *Doesn't Chris look good with her hair streaked?* ◦ *Her clothes were streaked **with** mud.* ◦ *White marble is frequently streaked **with** grey, black, or green.*

PHRASAL VERB **streak ahead** to be much more successful than your competitors: *The study revealed that Asian youngsters are streaking ahead in the race to get into university.*

streaker /ˈstriː.kəʳ/ US /-kɚ/ **noun** [C] a person who runs naked through a public place in order to attract attention or to express strong disapproval of something: *The match was interrupted when two streakers ran onto the field with a banner.*

streaky /ˈstriː.ki/ **adj** covered with long, thin lines: *This door needs another coat of paint – it's looking rather streaky.* ◦ UK *Streaky **bacon** contains strips of fat.*

stream /striːm/ **noun; verb**

▸**noun** [C] **SMALL RIVER** ▷ **1** B1 water that flows naturally along a fixed route formed by a CHANNEL cut into rock or ground, usually at ground level: *a **mountain** stream* ◦ *underground streams* ◦ *There's a lovely stream that **flows** through their garden.* **CONTINUOUS FLOW** ▷ **2** any current of water or liquid: *the level of cholesterol in your **blood** stream* **3** the direction in which water is moving: *She stopped rowing and let the boat float with the stream.* **4** B2 a continuous flow of things or people: *There has been a **steady** stream of phone calls from worried customers.* ◦ *I had a **constant** stream of visitors while I was ill.* **STUDENTS** ▷ **5** UK (US **track**) a group of school students with similar ability who are approximately the same age and are taught together: *I'm in the A stream for maths, and the B stream for English.* ◦ *the top/bottom stream*

IDIOM **on stream** UK Something in industry or business that is on stream is being produced or is available for use: *The company's increased sales were primarily a result of new stores **coming** on stream.*

▸**verb FLOW** ▷ **1** [I usually + adv/prep] to flow somewhere or produce liquid, quickly and in large amounts without stopping: *There were **tears** streaming **down** his **face**.* ◦ *One woman was carried from the scene of the accident with **blood** streaming **from** her head.* ◦ UK *I've got a terrible cold and my nose has been streaming all week.* **2 stream in, out, through, etc.** to move continuously in one direction: *We were all very excited as we streamed **out of** our final exam.* ◦ *Officials estimate that 20,000 refugees streamed **into** the city last week.* ◦ *His hair streamed **out** behind him as he rode off.* **INTERNET** ▷ **3** [T] to listen to or watch sound or video on a computer directly from the internet rather than DOWNLOADING it and saving it first **STUDENTS** ▷ **4** [T] UK (US **track**) to group and teach together school students with similar abilities who are approximately the same age: *We start to stream the children in the third form.*

streamer /ˈstriː.məʳ/ US /-mɚ/ **noun** [C] a long, narrow strip of brightly coloured paper that is used as a decoration for special occasions such as parties

streaming /ˈstriː.mɪŋ/ **noun** [U] **INTERNET** ▷ **1** the activity of listening to or watching sound or video directly from the internet **STUDENTS** ▷ **2** UK (US **tracking**) the act of putting school students with similar abilities in a group and teaching them

S

together: *Some people object to streaming because it gives an unfair advantage to intelligent children.*

streamline /ˈstriːm.laɪn/ verb [T] **SHAPE** ▷ **1** to shape something so that it can move as effectively and quickly as possible through a liquid or gas: *Streamlining cars increases their fuel efficiency.* ◦ *The bodies of dolphins are more streamlined than those of porpoises.* **IMPROVE** ▷ **2** to improve the effectiveness of an organization such as a business or government, often by making the way activities are performed simpler: *The cost-cutting measures include streamlining administrative* ***procedures*** *in the company.* ◦ *The government recently announced details of its plan to streamline the taxation system.* ◦ *Streamlining management could save at least 15 percent in costs.*

ˌstream of ˈconsciousness noun [U] specialized a style in literature that is used to represent a character's feelings and thoughts as they experience them, using long, continuous pieces of text without obvious organization or structure: *a stream-of-consciousness novel/style*

street /striːt/ noun [C] **1** A1 a road in a city, town, or village that has buildings that are usually close together along one or both sides: *The streets were strewn with rubbish after the carnival.* ◦ *a street map* ◦ *Our daughter lives just* ***across*** *the street from us.* ◦ *Diane's house is* ***in*** (US ***on***) *Cherry Street.* ◦ *Builders jeer at us even when we're just* ***walking down the*** *street.* ◦ *Be sure to look both ways when you* ***cross*** *the street.* ◦ *The town's streets were* ***deserted*** *by dusk.* ◦ *At five in the morning, there were still crowds of people* ***roaming*** *the streets.* ◦ *I bought these sunglasses from a street* ***vendor*** *in Florence.* **2 take to the streets** When people take to the streets, they express their opposition to something in public and often violently: *Thousands of people have taken to the streets to protest against the military coup.*

IDIOMS **be streets ahead** UK informal C2 to be much better or much more advanced than another thing or person: *The latest sales figures show that we're streets ahead* ***of*** *the competition.* • **be up your street** UK (US **be up your alley**) to be the type of thing that you are interested in or that you enjoy doing: *Carpentry isn't really up my street. I'd rather pay someone else to do it.* ◦ *I've got a little job for you which is* ***right*** (= exactly) *up your street.* • **the man/woman/person in/on the street** an ordinary, average person whose opinions are considered to represent most people: *To win the election he needs to appeal to the typical man in the street.* • **on the streets** (US also **on the street**) without a home: *Some of these people have been* ***living*** *on the streets for years.* • **the streets are paved with gold** literary said about a place where it is easy to get rich, or where people imagine that it is: *Many asylum seekers appear to be economic migrants, convinced that the streets of Europe are paved with gold.* • **the whole street** informal everyone living along a particular road: *Keep your voice down, we don't want the whole street to hear us!*

streetcar /ˈstriːt.kɑːʳ/ US /-kɑːr/ noun [C] US for **tram**: *The cheapest way of seeing the city is to* ***take*** *a streetcar.*

ˈstreet cred noun [U] (also **ˈstreet crediˌbility**) UK a quality that makes you likely to be accepted by ordinary young people who live in towns and cities because you have the same fashions, styles, interests, culture, or opinions: *Many celebrities develop a working class accent to increase their street credibility.* ◦ *That jacket won't do much for your street cred. It looks awful!* • **ˈstreet-ˌcredible adj**

ˈstreet ˌfurniture noun [U] UK specialized equipment such as lights and road signs, positioned at the side of a road for use by the public

streetlight /ˈstriːt.laɪt/ noun [C] (also **streetlamp**) a light in or at the side of a road or public area that is usually supported on a tall post

ˈstreet ˌpeople noun [plural] US people who do not have a home and who often sleep outside in cities

ˈstreet-smart adj US for **streetwise**

ˈstreet ˌsmarts noun [plural] US the ability to manage or succeed in difficult or dangerous situations, especially in big towns or cities: *You haven't got the street smarts to last ten minutes in New York without getting ripped off.*

ˈstreet ˌvalue noun [C usually singular, U] the price that is paid for something illegal, especially a drug, by the person who uses it: *Customs officers at Felixstowe discovered heroin with a street value* ***of*** *£6 million.*

streetwalker /ˈstriːtˌwɔː.kəʳ/ US /-ˌwɑː.kɚ/ noun [C] old-fashioned a PROSTITUTE who looks for customers outside in public places

streetwise /ˈstriːt.waɪz/ adj (US also **ˈstreet-smart**) able to deal successfully with dangerous or difficult situations in big towns or cities where there is a lot of crime: *McDonald was as streetwise as any of the criminals he had investigated.*

strength /streŋθ/ noun **POWER** ▷ **1** B2 [U] the ability to do things that need a lot of physical or mental effort: *She had the strength and stamina to take the lead and win the gold medal.* ◦ *Admitting you've made a mistake is a sign of strength, not weakness.* ◦ *He showed great strength* ***of character*** *when he refused to accept the bribes.* ◦ *We shall struggle on,* ***drawing*** *our strength from the courage of others.* ◦ *Much of the country's military strength lies in its missile force.* **2** C2 [C usually singular] the degree to which something is strong or powerful: *Opinion polls put the* ***combined*** *strength of the two parties at 15 percent nationwide.* ◦ *You can* ***gauge*** (= measure) *the strength of a democracy by the way it treats its minorities.* **GOOD FEATURE** ▷ **3** C1 [C] a good characteristic: *She's well aware of her strengths and weaknesses as an artist.* ◦ *His greatest strengths are his determination and resilience.* **NUMBER** ▷ **4** [U] the number of people in a group: *What's the current strength* ***of*** *the Cambridgeshire police force?* **5 in strength** in large numbers: *Demonstrators arrived in strength to protest against the closure of the factory.* **6 below strength** UK If a group is below strength, it consists of fewer people or members than usual: *The office will be below strength in August when a lot of people will be away.* **7 at full strength** with the complete number of people who are usually in a group: *Staff cuts have meant that we haven't been* ***working*** *at full strength for a year.*

> Word partners for **strength**
>
> *have* the strength (to do sth) • *find/muster/summon (up)* strength • *build up* sb's strength • *draw* strength *from* sb/sth • *conserve* strength • *gauge* the strength of sth • a *show/test* of strength • sb/sth's strength *lies in* sth • *considerable/full/great/superhuman* strength

IDIOMS **give me strength!** mainly UK something that you say when you find someone else's stupid behaviour or their being unable to do something annoying but quite funny: *Oh, give me strength! Do you want me to do it for you?* • **go from strength to strength** mainly UK C1 to gradually become more successful: *The firm's gone from strength to strength since the new factory was built.* • **on the strength of**

S

sth If you do something on the strength of something such as advice, you do it because you have been influenced by it or believe it: *I invested in the company on the strength of my brother's advice.*

strengthen /ˈstreŋ.θən/ verb [I or T] B2 to make something stronger or more effective, or to become stronger or more effective: *They have been strengthening their border defences in preparation for war.* ◦ *His battle against cancer has strengthened his* ***belief*** *in God.* ◦ *The accident strengthens the* ***case*** *for better safety measures at fairgrounds.* ◦ *The bank loan has greatly strengthened our financial position.* ◦ *The organization's aim is to strengthen the cultural ties between Britain and Germany.* ◦ *The rise in US interest rates caused the dollar to strengthen (= increase in value)* ***against*** *all the Asian currencies.*

IDIOM **strengthen sb's hand** to give someone more power: *The police want tougher laws to strengthen their hand* ***against*** *drug traffickers.*

strenuous /ˈstren.ju.əs/ adj C2 needing or using a lot of physical or mental effort or energy: *He rarely does anything more strenuous than changing the channels on the television.* ◦ *His doctor advised him not to take any strenuous* ***exercise.*** ◦ *Strenuous* ***efforts*** *were made throughout the war to disguise the scale of civilian casualties.* • **strenuously** /-li/ adv *He strenuously* ***denies*** *all the allegations against him.* ◦ *Most local residents strenuously* ***object*** *to the building proposals.*

ˌstrep ˈthroat noun [C or U] mainly US a severe infection of the throat

streptococcus /ˌstrep.təˈkɒk.əs/ US /-ˈkɑː.kəs/ noun [C] (plural **streptococci**) (mainly US informal **strep** /strep/) a BACTERIUM, many types of which cause disease: *Tonsillitis is normally caused by infection with streptococci.* • **streptococcal** /-ˈkɒk.l̩/ US /-ˈkɑː.kl̩/ adj *Pneumonia tends to be caused by streptococcal or viral infection.*

stress /stres/ noun; verb

▸noun **WORRY** ▷ **1** B1 [C or U] great worry caused by a difficult situation, or something which causes this condition: *People* ***under*** *a lot of stress may experience headaches, minor pains, and sleeping difficulties.* ◦ *Yoga is a very effective technique for* ***combating*** *stress.* ◦ *the stresses* ***and strains*** *of the job* ◦ *stress-****related*** *illness* **PRONUNCIATION** ▷ **2** B2 [C or U] the way that a word or syllable is pronounced with greater force than other words in the same sentence or other syllables in the same word: *The meaning of a sentence often depends on stress and intonation.* ◦ *When 'insert' is a verb, the stress is* ***on*** *the second syllable, but when it is a noun, the stress is* ***on*** *the first syllable.* **FORCE** ▷ **3** [C or U] specialized a force that acts in a way which often changes the shape of an object: *Computers work out the stresses that such a craft will encounter in flight.* ◦ *Jogging* ***puts*** *a lot of stress* ***on*** *your knee joints.* ◦ *He needs to have an operation for a stress* ***fracture*** *in his foot.* **EMPHASIS** ▷ **4** C1 [U] emphasis: *During his speech, he* ***laid*** *particular stress on the freedom of the press.*

> **Word partners for stress noun**
>
> *suffer from* stress • *cope with/deal with/handle* stress • *alleviate/combat/reduce/relieve* stress • be *under* stress • *great/severe/undue* stress • *signs/symptoms* of stress • stress *levels* • the stresses *and strains* of sth

▸verb **EMPHASIZE** ▷ **1** B2 [T] to give emphasis or special importance to something: [+ (that)] *He is careful to stress* ***(that)*** *the laboratory's safety standards are the best in the country.* ◦ *I'd just like to stress* ***the importance of*** *neatness and politeness in this job.* **PRONOUNCE** ▷ **2** B2 [T] to pronounce a word or syllable with greater force than other words in the same sentence or other syllables in the same word, or to play a musical note with greater force than others in a group: *In the word 'engine', you should stress the first syllable.* **WORRY** ▷ **3** [I] to feel worried and nervous: *Don't stress over it – we'll soon sort it out.*

PHRASAL VERB **stress sb out** to make someone feel very nervous and worried: *Interviews always stress me out.*

ˌstressed (ˈout) adj [after verb] B1 worried and nervous: *She's been* ***feeling*** *very stressed since she started her new job.* ◦ *I was really stressed out before the exam.*

stressful /ˈstres.fəl/ adj B1 making you feel worried and nervous: *a stressful day/job* ◦ *Police work is physically demanding and stressful.* ◦ *She's very good at coping in stressful* ***situations.***

ˈstress-reˌlated adj caused by stress: *stress-related illness/disease*

stressy /ˈstres.i/ adj informal **1** worried and nervous: *He's been stressy all day.* **2** making you feel worried and nervous: *I've had a very stressy week.*

stretch /stretʃ/ verb; noun

▸verb **REACH** ▷ **1** B2 [T usually + adv/prep] to cause something to reach, often as far as possible, in a particular direction: *I tripped on a piece of wire that someone had stretched across the path.* ◦ *She stretched out her* ***hand*** *and helped him from his chair.* **2** B2 [I] to make your body or your arms and legs straight so that they are as long as possible, in order to exercise the JOINTS (= place where two bones are connected) after you have been in the same place or position for a long time: *'I'm so tired,' she said, yawning and stretching.* ◦ *It's a good idea to stretch before you take vigorous exercise.* **SPREAD** ▷ **3** C2 [I usually + adv/prep] to spread over a large area or distance: *A huge cloud of dense smoke stretched* ***across*** *the horizon.* ◦ *The Andes stretch* ***for*** *7,250 km along the west coast of South America.* ◦ *Unsettled weather will stretch* ***from*** *the middle Mississippi Valley* ***to*** *the southern Middle Atlantic States.* ◦ *The refugee camps stretch* ***as far as the eye can see.*** **GO PAST** ▷ **4** [T] to go as far as or past the usual limit of something: *Many families' budgets are already stretched* ***to breaking point.*** ◦ *We can't work any harder, Paul. We're already* ***fully*** *stretched.* ◦ *This movie really stretches the patience of the audience* ***to the limit.*** ◦ *We don't normally allow in people under 18, but I suppose we could stretch the* ***rules*** *for you as it's your birthday tomorrow.* **MAKE LONGER** ▷ **5** B2 [I or T] to (cause a material to) become longer or wider than usual as a result of pulling at the edges: *an exercise to stretch the leg muscles* ◦ *That elastic band will snap if you stretch it too far.* ◦ *This substance stretches* ***to*** *any shape you want.* **6** B2 [I] If a material stretches, it can become longer or wider when pulled and then return to its original size: *to stretch* ***fabrics*** **LONG TIME** ▷ **7** [I usually + adv/prep] to spread over a long period of time: *The dispute stretches* ***back*** *over many years.* ◦ *Although we were supposed to finish this month, it looks like the work will stretch well* ***into*** *next year.* **8** [T] (also **stretch out**) to make a process or task continue for a longer period of time than was originally planned: *I'd like to stretch my mortgage payments* ***out*** *over a longer period if possible.* **DO MORE** ▷ **9** [T] If jobs or tasks stretch you, they make you learn new things that use your skill and experience more than you have done before: *My*

S

present job doesn't stretch me, so I'm looking for something more demanding.

IDIOMS **be stretching it** to be going further than the truth: *She's very clever, but it's stretching it a bit **to** call her a genius.* • **stretch your legs** to go for a walk, especially after sitting in the same position for a long time: *The car journey took three hours, including a couple of stops to stretch our legs.* • **stretch a point** to make a claim that is not completely true, or to do something that goes further than what is considered to be reasonable: *They claim to be the biggest company in the world, which is stretching a point.* • **stretch the truth** to say something that is not completely honest in order to make someone or something seem better than it really is

PHRASAL VERBS **stretch (yourself) out** to lie with your legs and arms spread out in a relaxed way: *I just want to get home and stretch out on the sofa.* • **stretch to sth** UK informal to manage to give or pay a particular amount, often a larger amount than you might expect: *'How much money do you want to borrow?' 'Could you stretch to £50?'*

▸**noun** **PART** ▷ **1** C1 [C usually singular] a continuous area of land or water: *This particular stretch **of** coast is especially popular with walkers.* ◦ *Traffic is at a standstill **along** a five-**mile** stretch of the M11 just south of Cambridge.* ◦ *Some very rare birds inhabit our stretch **of** the river.* **2** [C usually singular] a stage in a race, or a part of a RACETRACK: *She looked certain to win as she entered the **final** stretch.* ◦ *He fell as he galloped down the **home** stretch (= towards the finish).* **REACH** ▷ **3** [C usually singular] an act of stretching: *I always **have** a good stretch when I get up in the morning.* **GO PAST** ▷ **4** [C usually singular] the fact that something has gone past its usual limits: *His thesis may be a stretch, but it's not outside the realm of possibility.* **MAKE LONGER** ▷ **5** [U] the degree to which a material can be made longer or wider by pulling: *This fabric doesn't have much stretch in it, does it?* **TIME** ▷ **6** [C usually singular] a continuous period of time: *The elderly generally need far less rest than the young, and tend to sleep in several short stretches.* **7** [C usually singular] informal a period of time that a criminal spends in prison: *Her brother's doing a ten-year stretch for armed robbery.* **8 at a stretch** mainly UK continuously or without any interruptions: *There's no way I could work **for** ten **hours** at a stretch.* **ACTOR** ▷ **9** [C usually singular] the fact that an actor finds it difficult to play a character who is very different from their own personality: *Playing a budding opera star was not much of a stretch for this classically trained singer.*

S

IDIOM **by no stretch of the imagination** (also **not by any stretch of the imagination**) used to describe things that are impossible to believe, even with a lot of effort: *By no stretch of the imagination could he be seriously described as an artist.*

stretcher /ˈstretʃ.əʳ/ US /-ɚ/ **noun** [C] a light frame made from two long poles with a cover of soft material stretched between them, used for carrying people who are ill, injured, or dead: *She was carried off the track on a stretcher.* • **stretcher verb** [T]

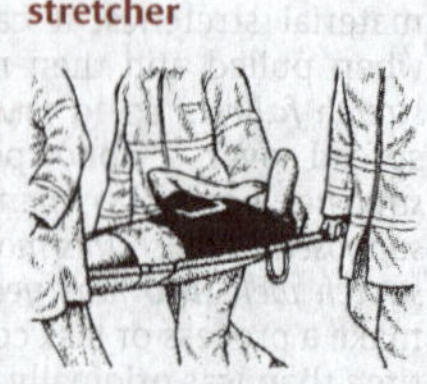
stretcher

ˈ**stretcher-ˌbearer** **noun** [C] someone who carries a stretcher, with another person at its other end, especially in a war or emergency

ˌ**stretch limouˈsine** **noun** [C] (informal ˌ**stretch** ˈ**limo**) a large, expensive car that has been specially made longer to provide extra space or seats, often used by rich, famous people

stretchmarks /ˈstretʃ.mɑːks/ US /-mɑːrks/ **noun** [plural] thin lines or marks on the front or sides of the body of a woman who has given birth: *She's worried about having children because she doesn't want to get stretchmarks or lose her figure.*

stretchy /ˈstretʃ.i/ **adj** Stretchy material stretches or can be stretched: *stretchy leggings* ◦ *stretchy material*

strew /struː/ **verb** [T] (**strewed**, **strewn** or **strewed**) to spread things untidily over a surface, or to be spread untidily over a surface: *They marked the end of the war by strewing flowers over the graves of 18,000 soldiers.* ◦ *Wine bottles and dirty dishes were strewn **across** the lawn.* ◦ *Her clothes lay strewn **on** the floor.* ◦ *The park was strewn **with** litter after the concert.*

strewth /struːθ/ **exclamation** UK old-fashioned or Australian informal used to express surprise or disappointment: *Strewth, look at the size of that steak!*

striated /straɪˈeɪ.tɪd/ US /-t̬ɪd/ **adj** specialized having long, thin lines, marks, or strips of colour: *The canyon walls were striated **with** colour.*

striation /straɪˈeɪ.ʃᵊn/ **noun** [C usually plural] specialized a long, thin line, mark, or strip of colour: *What has caused the striations in this rock?*

stricken /ˈstrɪk.ᵊn/ **adj** literary suffering severely from the effects of something unpleasant: *All the oil from the stricken tanker has now leaked into the sea.* ◦ *My country has been stricken **by** war for the past five years.* ◦ *He has been stricken with **grief** since the death of his wife.* ◦ *emergency aid for **famine**-stricken countries* ◦ *a **poverty**-stricken area*

Other ways of saying strict

If someone is very strict in the way he or she deals with others, you can describe that person as **firm**:

*I was always very **firm** with my children.*

If someone is very strict in the way he or she deals with a particular thing, you could say that person **takes a hard line on** something:

*The school **takes a hard line on** bullying.*

A person, government, system, etc. that is strict in a way you disapprove of can be described as **authoritarian**:

*His manner is extremely **authoritarian**.*

Rules, laws, etc. that are strict can be described as **stringent**, **tough**, or **tight**:

***Stringent** safety regulations were introduced after the accident.*

*We need **tough** new measures to combat crime.*

***Tighter** security has resulted in longer waits at airports.*

If you think rules are unreasonably strict, you can use the adjective **draconian**:

*He criticized the **draconian** measures used by the police in controlling the demonstrators.*

strict /strɪkt/ **adj** **1** B1 strongly limiting someone's freedom to behave as they wish, and likely to severely punish them if they do not obey: *My parents were very strict **with** me when I was young.* ◦ *Stricter **controls** on air pollution would help to reduce acid rain.* ◦ *A strict **curfew** has been imposed from dusk till dawn.* ◦ *We follow very strict **guidelines** on the use and storage of personal details on computers.* ◦ *Do you think stricter gun **laws** would reduce the murder rate in the United States?* ◦ *The drug should only be administered under* strict medical **supervision**. ◦ *The negotiations took place in strict (= total)* **secrecy**. → See also **restrict** **2** C2 exactly correct: *a strict translation of the text* ◦ *He would be found guilty under a strict* **interpretation** *of the law.* **3** B2 describes someone who follows the rules and principles of a belief or way of living very carefully and exactly, or a belief or principle that is followed very carefully and exactly: *His parents were strict Catholics.* ◦ *She's a strict* **vegetarian** *and refuses to eat any poultry or fish.* **4 in a strict sense** in the most limited meaning of a word, phrase, etc.: *In a strict sense, frost refers simply to a temperature of zero degrees Celsius or less.*

IDIOM **in the strictest confidence** If you tell someone something in the strictest confidence, you expect them not to tell it to anyone else.

strictly /ˈstrɪkt.li/ adv **1** B2 in a way that would bring severe punishment if not obeyed: *The speed limit is strictly* **enforced** *on urban roads.* ◦ *The use of cameras in this museum is strictly* **forbidden.** **2** in a very limited or limiting way: *Should I mark this letter to your accountant 'strictly* **confidential**'? ◦ *The proposed change in the law would make abortion illegal except for strictly* **defined** *medical reasons.* ◦ *This unrepeatable offer is only available for a strictly* **limited** *period.* **3** B2 exactly or correctly: *I have acted strictly* **in accordance with** *the regulations at all times.* ◦ *It is essential that the safety procedures are strictly* **adhered to**. ◦ *Their salaries are not strictly* **comparable** *(= cannot be directly compared) because of the differences in UK and US tax rates.* ◦ *Are all these questions strictly (= really)* **necessary**?

IDIOM **strictly speaking** B2 being completely accurate: *Strictly speaking, Great Britain consists of Scotland, Wales, and England.*

strictness /ˈstrɪkt.nəs/ noun [U] the ability of something to limit someone's freedom very much: *the increased strictness of the immigration rules*

stricture /ˈstrɪk.tʃəʳ/ (US) /-tʃɚ/ noun [C] formal CRITICISM ▷ **1** a statement of severe criticism or disapproval: *The strictures of the United Nations have failed to have any effect on the warring factions.* LIMIT ▷ **2** a severe moral or physical limit: *religious/financial strictures* ◦ *the Taliban's strictures* **on** *women's rights and education*

stride /straɪd/ noun; verb

▸noun DEVELOPMENT ▷ **1** [C] an important positive development: *The West* **made** *impressive strides* **in** *improving energy efficiency after the huge rises in oil prices during the 70s.* ◦ *The group has made strides* **to** *expand internationally.* STEP ▷ **2** [C] a long step when walking or running: *She attributes her record-breaking speed to the length of her stride.* CLOTHES ▷ **3 strides** [plural] Australian English informal trousers: *a new* **pair of** *strides*

IDIOMS **get into your stride** mainly UK (US usually **hit your stride**) to become familiar with and confident at something you have recently started doing: *Let's wait until she's got into her stride before we ask her to negotiate that contract.* • **not break your stride** to not stop walking or running at the same speed: *Without pausing for breath or breaking her stride, she pushed open the door of his private office.* • **put sb off their stride/stroke** mainly UK to take someone's attention away from something they are doing for a short time, making it more difficult to do: *The slightest noise puts him off his stride when he's performing.* • **take sth in your stride** UK (US **take sth in stride**) to deal with a problem or difficulty calmly and not to allow it to influence what you are doing: *When you become a politician, you soon learn to take criticism in your stride.*

▸verb [I usually + adv/prep] (**strode**, **stridden**) to walk somewhere quickly with long steps: *She strode* **purposefully** *up to the desk and demanded to speak to the manager.* ◦ *He strode* **across/into/out of** *the room.*

strident /ˈstraɪ.dᵊnt/ adj LOUD ▷ **1** describes a sound that is loud, unpleasant, and rough: *People are put off by his strident voice.* FORCEFUL ▷ **2** expressing or expressed in forceful language that does not try to avoid upsetting other people: *a strident newspaper article* ◦ *They are becoming increasingly strident in their criticism of government economic policy.* • **stridency** /-dᵊn.si/ noun [U] • **stridently** /-li/ adv *She has always stridently denied the accusations against her.* ◦ *He is stridently opposed to abortion.*

strife /straɪf/ noun [U] formal violent or angry disagreement: *What are the prospects for overcoming the strife* **between** *the Christian minority and Muslim majority?* ◦ *20 years of* **civil** *strife have left the country's economy in ruins.*

strike /straɪk/ verb; noun

▸verb (**struck**, **struck**) STOP WORK ▷ **1** B2 [I] to refuse to continue working because of an argument with an employer about working conditions, pay levels, or job losses: *Democratization has brought workers* **the right to** *strike and join a trade union.* ◦ *We're striking* **for** *a reduction in the working week and improved safety standards.* CAUSE SUFFERING ▷ **2** C2 [I or T] to cause a person or place to suffer severely from the effects of something very unpleasant that happens suddenly: *I've got a life insurance policy that will look after my family if* **disaster** *strikes.* ◦ *The disease has struck the whole community, sometimes wiping out whole families.* ◦ *They predict that a large* **earthquake** *will strike the east coast before the end of the decade.* HIT ▷ **3** B1 [I or T] to hit or attack someone or something forcefully or violently: *Her car went out of control and struck an oncoming vehicle.* ◦ *The police have warned the public that the killer could strike again.* ◦ *The autopsy revealed that his murderer had struck him* **on** *the head with an iron bar.* ◦ *Have you ever been struck* **by** *lightning?* **4** [I or T] When a clock strikes, its bells ring to show what the time is: *The clock was striking ten as we went into the church.* **5** [I] When a particular time strikes, a clock's bells ring to tell people what time it is: *Midnight had just struck when I went upstairs to bed.* **6** C2 [T] If you strike a match, you cause it to burn by rubbing it against a hard rough surface: *She struck a match and lit another cigarette.* ◦ *He lent down and struck a match* **on** *the sole of his boot.* REMOVE ▷ **7** [T usually + adv/prep] formal to remove something officially from a document: *Please strike my name* **from** *your mailing list immediately.* ◦ *Several unreliable dealers have been struck* **off** *our list of authorized suppliers.* **8 strike camp** to take down your tents in preparation for leaving the place where you have been CAMPING: *We woke up late and it was ten o'clock before we struck camp.* DISCOVER ▷ **9** C2 [T] to discover a supply of oil, gas, or gold underground: *The first person to strike* **oil** *in the US was Edwin Laurentine Drake.* AGREE ▷ **10** [T] to reach or make an agreement: *Do you think the government should try to strike a* **deal** *with the terrorists?* FEEL/THINK ▷ **11** B2 [T] to cause someone to have a feeling or idea about something: *Doesn't it strike you* **as** *rather* **odd** *that he never talks about his family?* ◦ *I was immediately struck* **by** *the similarities between the two murders.* ◦ *So how does my proposition strike you? (= What do you think of it?)* ◦ [+ (that)] ***It*** *strikes me* (**that**) *you'd be better off working*

S

for someone else. **12** (B2) [T] If a thought or idea strikes you, you suddenly think of it: [+ that] ***It's** just struck me **that** I still owe you for the concert tickets.* ◦ *Sitting at her desk, she was struck by the thought that there must be something more to life.* **MOVE BODY** ▷ **13 strike a pose/attitude** formal to move your body into a particular position: *Bainbridge struck the pose **of** a fearless sea captain.* **MAKE COINS** ▷ **14** [T] to make a metal disc-shaped object such as a coin with a machine that quickly presses a picture into a piece of metal: *When was the first pound **coin** struck?* ◦ *A special medal has been struck to celebrate the end of the war.*

IDIOMS **be struck dumb** to be so surprised by something that you cannot say anything: *We were struck dumb when she announced she was pregnant.* • **strike a balance** (C1) If you strike a balance between two things, you accept parts of both things in order to satisfy some of the demands of both sides in an argument, rather than all the demands of just one side: *It's a question of striking the right balance **between** quality and productivity.* • **strike a blow against/at sth** to do something which harms something severely: *Her resignation has struck a blow against the company's plans for expansion.* • **strike a blow for sth** to do something which supports or defends something: *The judge's ruling has struck a blow for racial equality.* • **strike a chord 1** If something strikes a chord, it causes people to approve of it or agree with it: *The party's policy on childcare facilities has struck a **responsive** chord **with** women voters.* ◦ *Her speech struck a **sympathetic** chord **among** business leaders.* **2** If something strikes a chord, it causes people to remember something else because it is similar to it. • **strike a note** to express and communicate a particular opinion or feeling about something: *I find it really difficult to strike **the right** note when I'm writing job applications.* ◦ *At the end of her speech, she struck a note **of** warning about the risks involved in the project.* • **strike at the heart of sth** to damage something severely by attacking the most important part of it: *By its nature, terrorism is designed to strike at the heart of our democratic values.* • **strike fear/terror into sb** to make someone extremely frightened: *The brutal military regime has struck terror into the whole population.* • **strike gold** literary **1** to win a gold MEDAL in a sports competition: *She is the favourite to strike gold in the 400 metres hurdles.* **2** to make large profits or to become rich: *A few lucky people have struck gold by investing in this company.* • **strike home** to hit the intended place or have the intended effect: *The laser guidance system dramatically increases the likelihood that the missile will strike home.* ◦ *The government's message about the dangers of smoking seems to have struck home.* • **strike it lucky** (UK also **strike lucky**) to suddenly have a lot of unexpected luck: *What would you do if you struck it lucky in the national lottery?* • **strike it rich** to become rich suddenly and unexpectedly: *His father struck it rich in the diamond business.* • **strike while the iron is hot** to take advantage of an opportunity as soon as it exists, in case the opportunity goes away and does not return: *He doesn't often make such offers – I'd strike while the iron is hot if I were you.* • **within striking distance 1** near: *We live within striking distance **of** both Baltimore and Washington.* **2** very near to getting or achieving something: *His victory in the Brazilian Grand Prix puts him within striking distance **of** the world championship.*

S

PHRASAL VERBS **strike back** to attack someone who has attacked you • **strike sb down** [M often passive] If someone is struck down, they die suddenly or start to suffer from a serious illness: *It's a tragedy that these young people were struck down in their prime.* ◦ *He was struck down **by** polio when he was a teenager.* • **strike sb off (sth)** UK If someone with a responsible job such as a doctor or lawyer is struck off, they are officially not allowed to continue in that work because they have done something seriously wrong: *A solicitor who insulted two officials from the Law Society was struck off **for** abusive behaviour.* • **strike on/upon sth** to discover or think of something: *She struck on the idea for her novel while she was travelling in Russia.* • **strike out (somewhere)** to start on a long or difficult journey in a determined way: *In heavy rain, we struck out across the field.* ◦ *She struck out **for** the opposite bank.* • **strike out START** ▷ **1** to start doing something new, independently of other people: *After working for her father for ten years, she felt it was time to strike out **on** her **own**.* **FAIL** ▷ **2** US informal to be unsuccessful: *I really struck out **with** her – she wouldn't even kiss me good night.* • **strike (sb) out** to fail three times to hit the ball successfully in baseball and therefore to lose one of your team's chances to score, or to cause someone to do this: *The pitcher struck out both batters in the ninth inning and saved the game.* • **strike sth out/through** to draw a line through text in a document to show that it does not relate to you or is not correct: *Please strike out whichever option does not apply to you.* • **strike up (sth)** to start to play or sing something: *When the applause had died down, a regimental band struck up the national anthem.* • **strike up sth** to start a relationship or conversation with someone: *He gets really jealous if his girlfriend strikes up a **friendship** with another man.* ◦ *It can be difficult to strike up a **conversation** with a complete stranger.*

▸**noun** [C] **STOP WORK** ▷ **1** (B2) a period of time when workers refuse to work because of an argument with an employer about working conditions, pay levels, or job losses: *After last year's long and bitter strike, few people want further industrial action.* ◦ *Most of the workers have ignored their union's **call** for strike **action**.* ◦ *Some miners were **calling for** a nationwide strike in support of 20 colleagues who'd been fired.* ◦ *They have voted to stage **lightning** (= sudden and short) strikes in pursuit of their demands.* ◦ *We've voted to **stage** a series of **one-day** strikes.* ◦ *A **wave of** strikes swept the country.* ◦ *The result of the strike **ballot** will be known tomorrow morning.* **2 on strike** (UK also **out on strike**) taking part in a strike: *The city's bus drivers have been on strike for three weeks.* **3 go on strike** to start to strike: *All 2,500 employees went on strike in protest at the decision to close the factory.* **HIT** ▷ **4** a sudden and powerful hit or attack: *Lightning conductors protect buildings and tall structures from **lightning** strikes.* → See also **strike force** **5** a sudden, short military attack, especially one by aircraft or MISSILES: *The United Nations has authorized the use of **air** strikes.* ◦ *The violence is unlikely to stop without **military** strikes **against** terrorist bases.* ◦ *Would you support a **nuclear** strike to bring an end to a war?* ◦ *We have no intention of **launching** a **pre-emptive** strike, but we will retaliate if provoked.* **DISCOVERY** ▷ **6** the discovery underground of a valuable substance: *The population and settlement of Colorado expanded after the **gold** strike of 1858.* **FAILURE** ▷ **7** (in baseball) a ball that has been thrown by the PITCHER and not been hit successfully when it should have been: *A batter is out after three strikes.* **8** US a failure, mistake, or disadvantage: *California's 'three strikes and you're out' bill means that from now on criminals found guilty of three crimes* are jailed for life. ◦ One strike **against** him as a candidate is his perceived lack of charisma.

strikebound /ˈstraɪk.baʊnd/ **adj** describes a place that is closed or unable to operate because the people employed there are refusing to work: *The factory has been strikebound for two months because of a pay dispute.*

strikebreaker /ˈstraɪkˌbreɪ.kəʳ/ US /-kɚ/ **noun** [C] someone who continues working during a strike or who takes the job of a worker who is involved in a strike • **strikebreaking** /-kɪŋ/ **noun** [U]

ˈstrike ˌforce noun [C] a group of people, especially soldiers or police officers, who are organized and trained to take strong, sudden action to stop something harmful or unpleasant from continuing

strikeout /ˈstraɪk.aʊt/ **noun** [C] (in baseball) the act of failing three times to hit the ball, or of making a BATTER (= person trying to hit the ball) do this: *He averaged 14 strikeouts per game last season.*

ˈstrike ˌpay noun [U] money that is paid to people involved in a strike by their UNION from an amount of money saved specially for this purpose

striker /ˈstraɪ.kəʳ/ US /-kɚ/ **noun** [C] **STOP WORK** ▷ **1** C1 someone who is involved in a strike: *Many people sympathize with the strikers.* **SPORT** ▷ **2** C2 a player in a game such as football whose main purpose is to try to score goals rather than to prevent the opposing team from scoring: *The club's new manager is a former England striker.* ◦ *The 24-year-old striker scored 35 goals for Newcastle United last season.*

striking /ˈstraɪ.kɪŋ/ **adj** **1** B2 very unusual or easily noticed, and therefore attracting a lot of attention: *She **bears** a striking **resemblance** to her mother.* ◦ *There's a striking **contrast** between what he does and what he says he does.* ◦ *St Peter's Church is a striking **example** of modern architecture.* ◦ *There are striking **similarities** between the two cases.* ◦ *Their production of Macbeth was the most **visually** striking performance I've ever seen.* **2** more attractive than usual: *He's quite good-looking, but he's not as striking as his brother.* • **strikingly** /-li/ **adv** *Her latest novel is strikingly **different** from her earlier work.* ◦ *They gave a strikingly **original** performance of the play.* ◦ *Her husband is strikingly **handsome**.*

Strimmer /ˈstrɪm.əʳ/ US /-ɚ/ **noun** [C] UK trademark (US trademark **ˈWeed ˌwhacker**) an electric or MECHANICAL tool that is held in the hand and is used for cutting grass in places that are difficult to reach with a larger machine

string /strɪŋ/ **noun; adj; verb**

▸**noun** **ROPE** ▷ **1** B2 [C or U] (a piece of) strong, thin rope made by twisting very thin threads together, used for fastening and tying things: *a parcel tied with string* ◦ *a **ball/piece of** string* ◦ *When you **pull** the strings, the puppet's arms and legs move.* **2** [C] a set of objects joined together in a row on a single rope or thread: *a string of **beads/pearls*** ◦ *A string **of** onions hung from a beam in the kitchen.* **SERIES** ▷ **3** C2 [C] a series of related things or events: *What do you think of the recent string **of** political scandals?* ◦ *He had a string of top-20 **hits** during the 80s.* **MUSIC** ▷ **4** B2 [C] a thin wire that is stretched across a musical instrument and is used to produce a range of notes depending on its thickness, length, and tightness: *A violin has four strings.* ◦ ***Guitar** strings nowadays are made from steel or nylon.* ◦ *You can **pluck** the strings on a guitar with your fingers or a plectrum.* ◦ *a twelve-string guitar* **5 strings** [plural] the group of instruments that have strings and are played with a BOW or with the fingers, or the players in a musical group who play these instruments **SPORT** ▷ **6** [C] one of the thin plastic strings that are stretched between the sides of the frame of a RACKET used in sport **COMPUTING** ▷ **7** [C] specialized a usually short piece of text consisting of letters, numbers, or symbols that is used in computer processes such as searching through large amounts of information: *If you type in the **search** string 'ing', the computer will find all the words containing 'ing'.*

IDIOMS **have another/more than one string to your bow** to have another interest or skill which you can use if your main one cannot be used: *I enjoy my work, but I'd like to have another string to my bow in case I lose my job.* • **strings attached** C2 If something such as an agreement has strings attached, it involves special demands or limits: *Most of these so-called special offers come **with** strings attached.* ◦ *The bank's agreed to lend me £1,000, **no** strings attached.*

▸**adj** consisting of or relating to STRING INSTRUMENTS: *the string section* ◦ *a string quartet* → See also **string instrument**

▸**verb** [T] (**strung, strung**) **MUSIC** ▷ **1** to put strings on a musical instrument: *First you need to learn how to string and tune your guitar.* **SPORT** ▷ **2** to put new strings onto a RACKET used in sport: *You ought to have your racket re-strung before the competition.* **BEADS, ETC.** ▷ **3** to put a string through a number of objects: *Would you help me string these beads?*

PHRASAL VERBS **string sb along** to deceive someone for a long time about what you are really intending to do: *She's been promising to pay back the money for six months, but I reckon she's just stringing me along.* ◦ *He strung her along for years, saying he'd marry her and divorce his wife.* • **string sth out** **GROUP** ▷ **1** If a group of similar things or people are strung out, they are in a long line with spaces between each of them: *Most of Canada's population is strung out along its 5,525-mile border with the US.* ◦ *The geese were strung out along the river bank.* **ACTIVITY** ▷ **2** to make an activity last longer than necessary: *I think the lawyer's just stringing out the case so that he'll earn more money.* • **string sth together** If you string words or sentences together, you manage to say something that other people can understand: *People tend to be very impressed if you can string together a couple of sentences in Japanese.* • **string sb up** informal **1** to kill someone by hanging them by the neck from a rope, usually as a punishment for a crime: *He reckons they're too soft on mass murderers and says they ought to be strung up.* **2** to punish someone severely: *He ought to be strung up for what he said about his mother.* • **string sth up** to tie or fix the ends of a long, thin object to two points that are high up, allowing the rest of it to hang freely: *Let's string up a banner in the garden to welcome him home.*

ˌstring ˈbean noun [C] US for **runner bean**

ˈstringed ˌinstrument noun [C] a **string instrument**

stringent /ˈstrɪn.dʒənt/ **adj** **SEVERE** ▷ **1** having a very severe effect, or being extremely limiting: *The most stringent **laws** in the world are useless unless there is the will to enforce them.* ◦ *We need to introduce more stringent security **measures** such as identity cards.* ◦ *Stringent safety **regulations** were introduced after the accident.* **LIMITING MONEY** ▷ **2** specialized involving not enough money being available for borrowing as a result of firm controls on the amount of money in an economy: *Already low living standards have been worsened by stringent economic reforms.* • **stringency** /ˈstrɪn.dʒᵊn.si/ **noun** [U] *The stringency of the safety regulations threatens to put many manufac-*

S

turers out of business. ◦ Greater **financial** stringency is needed to eradicate inflation from the economy. • **stringently** /-li/ adv *Fire regulations are stringently enforced in all our factories.*

ˈstring ˌinstrument noun [C] (also **ˈstringed ˌinstrument**) a musical instrument with a set of strings that VIBRATE to produce sound when they are pulled, hit, or rubbed with a BOW: *Guitars, pianos, and cellos are different types of string instrument.*

ˌstring quarˈtet noun [C] **1** a group of four instruments with strings that play together: *A string quartet consists of two violins, a viola, and a cello.* **2** a piece of music written for such a group: *Haydn's works include 84 string quartets.*

ˌstring ˈvest noun [C] a piece of underwear for the top part of a man's body that is made from material with a pattern of large holes, like a net

stringy /ˈstrɪŋ.i/ adj similar to string: *These beans are rather stringy (= hard and difficult to chew).*

strip /strɪp/ verb; noun

▸verb (-pp-) **REMOVE COVER** ▷ **1** [T] to remove, pull, or tear the covering or outer layer from something: *Because of the pollution, the trees are almost completely stripped **of** bark.* ◦ *The paintwork was so bad that we decided to strip **off** all the paint and start again.* ◦ [+ adj] *During the summer months, the sheep strip the mountains **bare**.* **REMOVE CLOTHING** ▷ **2** [I or T] (UK also **strip off**) to remove your clothing, or to remove all the clothing of someone else: UK *Suddenly he stripped off and ran into the sea.* ◦ *It was so hot that we stripped **off** our shirts.* ◦ [+ adj] *He was interrogated, stripped **naked** and then beaten.* **REMOVE PARTS** ▷ **3** [T] to remove parts of a machine, vehicle, or engine in order to clean or repair it: *I've decided to strip **down** my motorbike and rebuild it.* **4** [T] mainly US to remove the parts of a car, etc. in order to sell them

PHRASAL VERBS **strip sth away** to gradually reduce something important or something that has existed for a long time: *Stripping away all the waffle, he said that no Conservative government would let Britain be drawn into a European superstate.* • **strip (down) to sth** to remove everything except for a particular piece of clothing or above a particular part of the body: *I had to strip down to my underwear for my medical examination.* ◦ *He was stripped to the waist.* • **strip sb of sth** to take something important, such as a title, away from someone as a punishment: *He was stripped of his knighthood after he was convicted of stealing from the company.* • **strip sth out** to ignore particular numbers or facts in a situation in order to understand what is really important: *After stripping out property sales, the firm's operating profits rose ten percent.*

▸noun **PIECE** ▷ **1** C1 [C] a long, flat, narrow piece: *a **narrow** strip **of** land* ◦ *He didn't have a bandage, so he ripped up his shirt into **thin** strips.* ◦ *Protect the **magnetic** strip on your credit card from scratches, heat, or other damage.* **CLOTHING** ▷ **2** [C usually singular] UK the clothing worn by a football team which has the team's colours on it: *The team will be wearing its new strip at next Saturday's match.* **REMOVE CLOTHING** ▷ **3** [S] an entertainment in which the performer removes all his or her clothing: *He jumped up on the table and started to **do** a strip.*

ˌstrip carˈtoon noun [C] UK **comic strip**

ˈstrip ˌclub noun [C] (informal **ˈstrip ˌjoint**) a bar where the main entertainment is performers removing their clothes while dancing to music: *The city is notorious for its red-light district and strip clubs.* ◦ *She worked in a strip joint before she became a model.*

stripe /straɪp/ noun [C] **COLOURED STRIP** ▷ **1** B1 a strip on the surface of something that is a different colour from the surrounding surface: *The zebra is a wild African horse with black and white stripes.* **ON UNIFORM** ▷ **2** (US also **bar**) a strip of material that is sewn onto the arm of a military uniform to show the rank of the person wearing it: *By the age of 25 he'd already earned his third stripe and become a sergeant.*

IDIOM **of every stripe/of all stripes** of all types: *Governments of every stripe (= of all political opinions) have a bad habit of interfering in state broadcasting.*

striped /straɪpt/ adj Something that is striped has stripes on it: *green and white striped **pyjamas*** ◦ *Do you prefer plain or striped **shirts**?*

striped

ˈstrip ˌlight noun [C] UK (US **ˌfluorescent ˈlight**) a FLUORESCENT electric light in the form of a thin glass tube, often with a plastic cover

ˈstrip ˌlighting noun [U] UK (US **fluorescent ˈlighting**) one or more strip lights

ˈstrip ˌmining noun [U] US a method of removing substances such as coal from the ground, which involves removing the top layer of soil instead of digging deep holes underground

stripper /ˈstrɪp.ər/ US /-ɚ/ noun **REMOVER** ▷ **1** [C or U] a liquid chemical or an electric tool that is used for removing things such as paint: *a can of **paint** stripper* **PERFORMER** ▷ **2** [C] someone whose job is removing all their clothing to entertain other people: *We organized a male stripper for her 50th birthday party.*

strippergram (also **strippagram**) /ˈstrɪp.ə.græm/ US /-ɚ-/ noun [C] UK a surprise visit on a special occasion from a person who is paid to remove most or all of their clothes before giving someone a message from their friends or relations: *They'd arranged a strippergram for Nigel's leaving party.*

ˌstrip ˈpoker noun [U] a card game in which players remove a piece of clothing each time they lose

ˈstrip search noun [C] the process of removing the clothes of a prisoner, or someone thought to have committed a crime, by a police officer or government official in order to find any illegal things, such as drugs, hidden in their clothing or on their body • **ˈstrip-search** verb [T] *We were stopped by customs officers at the airport and strip-searched for no apparent reason.*

ˈstrip ˌsteak noun [C or U] US a thick, flat piece of meat cut from the side of a cow

striptease /ˈstrɪp.tiːz/, /ˌstrɪpˈtiːz/ noun [C or U] a form of entertainment in which a performer takes off his or her clothes in a way that is sexually exciting to the people who are watching: *I'm not the sort of person who'd **do** a striptease.* ◦ *a striptease **club/artist***

stripy (**stripier**, **stripiest**) (also **stripey**) /ˈstraɪ.pi/ adj with stripes or a pattern of stripes: *stripy shirts*

strive /straɪv/ verb [I] (**strove** or **strived**, **striven** or **strived**) C2 to try very hard to do something or to make something happen, especially for a long time or against difficulties: [+ to infinitive] *Mr Roe has kindled expectations that he must now strive **to** live up to.* ◦ *In her writing she strove **for** a balance between innovation and familiar prose forms.*

strobe (light) /ˈstrəʊb̩laɪt/ (US) /ˈstroʊb-/ noun [C] a light which quickly flashes on and off: *The strobes and loud music in the club made her want to dance.*

strode /strəʊd/ (US) /stroʊd/ verb past simple of **stride**.

stroganoff /ˈstrɒg.ə.nɒf/ (US) /ˈstrɔː.gə.nɔːf/ noun [C or U] a type of food consisting of meat or MUSHROOMS in a sauce that contains SOUR CREAM

stroke /strəʊk/ (US) /stroʊk/ noun; verb

▸noun **ILLNESS** ▷ **1** B2 [C] a sudden change in the blood supply to a part of the brain, sometimes causing a loss of the ability to move particular parts of the body: *She **suffered/had** a stroke which left her unable to speak.* **MARK** ▷ **2** C2 [C] (a line or mark made by) a movement of a pen or pencil when writing or a brush when painting: *a brush stroke* ◦ *With a few **bold** strokes, she signed her name.* **3** [C] UK used in spoken English to mean an OBLIQUE or SLASH symbol **HIT** ▷ **4** [C] an act of hitting a ball when playing a sport: *She returned the volley with a powerful stroke to win the game.* **5** [C] old-fashioned an act of hitting someone with a weapon: *The punishment was 20 strokes of the lash.* **SWIMMING** ▷ **6** C1 [C] (a particular movement which is usually repeated in) a method of swimming: *What's your best stroke when you're swimming?* → See also **backstroke, breaststroke, sidestroke** **EVENT** ▷ **7 a stroke of luck, genius, etc.** C2 something that happens or succeeds suddenly because of luck, intelligence, etc.: *By a stroke of luck, someone else was walking along the path and heard my shouts for help.* **WORK** ▷ **8** [S] informal a small amount of work: *She's been gossiping and hasn't **done a** stroke (**of work**) all morning.* **ACTION** ▷ **9** [C] a quick, forceful action: *Ending negotiations was seen as a **bold** stroke by many commentators.* ◦ *By computerizing we could, **at a (single)/in one** stroke, improve efficiency and reduce costs.* **CLOCK SOUND** ▷ **10** [C] one of the sounds which some clocks make at particular times, especially by ringing a bell once for each number of the hour: *How many strokes did you count?* **TOUCH** ▷ **11** [C] an act of moving your hand, another part of the body, or an object gently over something or someone, usually repeatedly and for pleasure: *Don't be frightened, just give the horse a stroke.*

IDIOM **at/on the stroke of sth** exactly at a particular time: *Fireworks started at the stroke of ten.*

▸verb [T] **TOUCH** ▷ **1** B2 to move a hand, another part of the body, or an object gently over something or someone, usually repeatedly and for pleasure: *Stroke the dog if you like, it won't bite.* ◦ *She lovingly stroked Chris's face with the tips of her fingers.* **HIT** ▷ **2** to hit a ball: *The batsman stroked the ball effortlessly to the boundary.*

stroll /strəʊl/ (US) /stroʊl/ verb [I] C1 to walk in a slow, relaxed manner, especially for pleasure: *We could stroll into town if you like.* • **stroll** noun [C] *The whole family was enjoying a **leisurely** stroll in the sunshine.*

stroller /ˈstrəʊ.ləʳ/ (US) /ˈstroʊ.lɚ/ noun [C] **1** someone who strolls **2** mainly US for **pushchair**

strong /strɒŋ/ (US) /strɑːŋ/ adj; adv

▸adj **NOT WEAK** ▷ **1** A2 powerful; having or using great force or control: *She must be very strong to carry such a weight on her back.* ◦ *It is surely the duty of the stronger members in a society to help those who are weak.* ◦ *My grandmother had a strong **influence/effect** on my early childhood.* ◦ *Strong winds are forecast in the area for the next few days.* ◦ *It's surprising what strong memories a photograph can produce.* ◦ *Get Carl to lift it – he's **as strong as an ox** (= very strong).* **2** B2 effective; of a good quality or level and likely to be successful: *We will need strong policies if our economic problems are to be solved.* ◦ *I can give you stronger pain-killing drugs if these aren't strong enough.* ◦ *Strong trading links exist between us and many South American countries.* **3** B2 clever or good at doing things: *Without a doubt, she's the strongest candidate we've interviewed for the post.* ◦ *As a guitarist, he's strong **on** (= good at) technique but perhaps lacks feeling in some pieces.* **DETERMINED** ▷ **4** B2 difficult to argue with; firm and determined: *She has strong **opinions** about religion.* ◦ *He has a strong **personality**, but don't let him bully you.* ◦ *Most of the group have strong **views** on the subject of divorce.* **NOTICEABLE** ▷ **5** B1 If a taste, smell, etc. is strong, it is very noticeable or powerful: *A strong light was shining straight in my eyes.* ◦ *There's a really strong smell of bleach in the corridor.* ◦ *I don't like coffee/tea if it's too strong.* ◦ *The room was decorated in very strong colours.* ◦ *What a strong likeness there is between the brothers.* **DIFFICULT TO BREAK** ▷ **6** B1 difficult to break, destroy, or make ill, or able to support a heavy weight or force: *a strong box/chair* ◦ *The window is made from very strong glass – it won't shatter.* ◦ *He's never been very strong, and I'm afraid all the excitement was too much for him.* ◦ *He had such a strong will to live – he simply refused to die.* → See also **strength** **LIKELY** ▷ **7** very likely to happen: *There's a strong **possibility/likelihood** of finding the child within the next few hours.* ◦ *The treatment's **chances** of success are stronger if it is started as soon as the disease is diagnosed.* **IN NUMBER** ▷ **8** [after noun] having the stated number of people, members, etc.: *Our social club is currently about 80 strong.* → See also **strength** **CHEMISTRY** ▷ **9** specialized describes an ACID, ALKALI, or chemical BASE that produces many IONS (= atoms with an electrical charge) when it is dissolved in water

IDIOMS **be going strong** C2 to continue to exist and be successful or work well, after a long period: *After two hundred years, the town's theatre is still going strong.* ◦ *His father is still going strong (= is alive and well) at 94.* • **strong nerves** (also **a strong stomach**) an ability to not be upset by unpleasant things: *You need a strong stomach to work in the accident department.*

▸adv informal **come on strong** to behave in a way which makes it clear that you are sexually interested in a particular person, or to behave towards another person in a way which many people think is too severe: *He's always coming on strong to me – I wish he'd stop.* ◦ *You came on too strong then – she didn't do it deliberately.*

ˈstrong-arm adj disapproving **a strong-arm tactic/method** a method or a type of behaviour that involves using force and threats to make people do what you demand: *Police resorted to strong-arm tactics to break up the protest.*

strongbox /ˈstrɒŋ.bɒks/ (US) /ˈstrɑːŋ.bɑːks/ noun [C] mainly US a specially made box that is fastened with a lock and is very difficult to break, used to keep valuable objects safe

stronghold /ˈstrɒŋ.həʊld/ (US) /ˈstrɑːŋ.hoʊld/ noun [C] **1** a building or position that is strongly defended: *a rebel stronghold* ◦ *They captured the last stronghold **of** the presidential guard.* **2** a place or area where a particular belief or activity is common: *Rural areas have been traditionally thought of as a stronghold **of** old-fashioned attitudes.*

ˌstrong ˈlanguage noun [U] C1 speech that states ideas forcefully, sometimes using words that may be considered offensive

strongly /ˈstrɒŋ.li/ (US) /ˈstrɑːŋ-/ adv **NOT WEAK** ▷ **1** B2 very much or in a very serious way: *Many locals are strongly **opposed** to the development.* **DIFFICULT TO**

S

BREAK ▷ **2** in a way or form that is difficult to break: *Equipment will have to be strongly made to endure the weather conditions on the ice cap.*

strongman /ˈstrɒŋ.mæn/ (US) /ˈstrɑːŋ-/ **noun** [C] (plural **-men** /-men/) **1** a man who is employed or famous for his great physical strength: *If she talks to the police, Joey's strongmen will be paying her a visit.* **2** literary a person who is very powerful and able to cause change, especially of a political type

ˌstrong-ˈminded adj If someone is strong-minded, they are determined and unwilling to change their opinions and beliefs: *You'll have to be strong-minded if you're going to push the changes through.*

ˈstrong ˌpoint noun [C] mainly UK (mainly US **ˈstrong ˌsuit**) (C1) a particular skill or ability that a person has: *Tact is **not** her strong point, judging by the way she behaved.*

strongroom /ˈstrɒŋ.rʊm/, /-ruːm/ (US) /ˈstrɑːŋ-/ **noun** [C] a special room with strong walls and a strong door where valuable things can be kept safe: *the bank's strongroom*

ˌstrong-ˈwilled adj If you are strong-willed, you are determined to behave in a particular way although there might be good reasons for not doing so: *She's very strong-willed and if she's decided to leave school, nothing will stop her.*

strontium /ˈstrɒn.ti.əm/ (US) /ˈstrɑːn.ʃi.əm/ **noun** [U] (symbol **Sr**) a chemical element that is a soft, silver-white metal that burns easily with a bright red flame, used in FIREWORKS and some televisions

strop /strɒp/ (US) /strɑːp/ **noun** [C] UK informal a bad mood, especially one in which a person will not do what they are asked and is unpleasant to other people: *Don't go in unless you have to – she's **in a (real)** strop.*

IDIOM **have a strop on** informal to be in a bad mood: *Why have you got such a strop on – what's happened?*

stroppy /ˈstrɒp.i/ (US) /ˈstrɑː.pi/ **adj** UK informal angry and unpleasant or rude to other people: *a stroppy **teenager** ◦ It's no use **getting** stroppy – I said no and I meant it!* • **stroppily** /ˈstrɒp.ɪ.li/ (US) /ˈstrɑː.pɪ-/ **adv** • **stroppiness** /-nəs/ **noun** [U]

strove /strəʊv/ (US) /stroʊv/ **verb** past simple of **strive**

struck /strʌk/ **verb** past simple and past participle of **strike**

S

structural /ˈstrʌk.tʃər.əl/ (US) /-tʃɚ-/ **adj** **ARRANGEMENT** ▷ **1** (C2) relating to the way in which parts of a system or object are arranged: *The political reforms have led to major structural changes in the economy.* **BUILDING** ▷ **2** relating to the structure of a building or similar object: *Hundreds of houses in the typhoon's path suffered structural **damage**.* • **structurally** /-i/ **adv** *Few buildings were left structurally safe after the earthquake.*

structuralism /ˈstrʌk.tʃər.əl.ɪ.zəm/ (US) /-tʃɚ-/ **noun** [U] specialized a system of ideas used in the study of language, literature, art, ANTHROPOLOGY, and SOCIOLOGY, which emphasizes the importance of the basic structures and relationships of that particular subject • **structuralist** /-ɪst/ **adj, noun** [C]

structure /ˈstrʌk.tʃər/ (US) /-tʃɚ/ **noun; verb**

▸**noun** **ARRANGEMENT** ▷ **1** (B2) [C or U] the way in which the parts of a system or object are arranged or organized, or a system arranged in this way: *the grammatical structure of a sentence ◦ The structure **of** this protein is particularly complex. ◦ They have a very old-fashioned management structure. ◦ Some people like the sense of structure that a military lifestyle imposes.* **BUILDING** ▷ **2** (C2) [C] something that has been made or built from parts, especially a large building: *The proposed new office tower is a steel and glass structure 43 storeys high.*

▸**verb** [T] (C2) to plan, organize, or arrange the parts of something: *We must carefully structure and rehearse each scene. ◦ a well-structured argument*

structured /ˈstrʌk.tʃəd/ (US) /-tʃɚd/ **adj** (C2) organized so that the parts relate well to each other: *In today's competitive climate, success is most likely to come to those who understand the need for a structured approach to job hunting. ◦ The course provides hands-on experience within a structured programme of study.*

strudel /ˈstruː.dəl/ **noun** [C or U] a type of cake made from fruit, wrapped in a thin layer of pastry and then baked: *(an) apple strudel*

struggle /ˈstrʌɡ.l̩/ **verb; noun**

▸**verb** **EFFORT** ▷ **1** (B2) [I] to experience difficulty and make a very great effort in order to do something: [+ to infinitive] *The dog had been struggling **to** get free of the wire noose. ◦ I've been struggling **to** understand this article all afternoon. ◦ Fish struggle **for** survival when the water level drops in the lake.* **2 struggle along, through, out, etc.** to move somewhere with great effort: *He struggled along the rough road holding his son. ◦ By this time he'd managed to struggle out of bed.* **3** [I] informal to be in danger of failing or being defeated: *After the first half, United were really struggling at 1–3 down.* **FIGHT** ▷ **4** (B2) [I] to fight, especially with your hands: *He struggled **with** his attacker who then ran off.* **5** (C2) [I usually + adv/prep] to use a lot of effort to defeat someone, prevent something, or achieve something: *For years she struggled **with/against** the establishment **to** get her theories accepted.*

PHRASAL VERB **struggle on** to continue dealing with a difficult situation or to continue doing something difficult: *When Bobbie leaves, we'll have to struggle on until we find a replacement.*

▸**noun** [C] **EFFORT** ▷ **1** (B2) a very difficult task that you can do only by making a great effort: *It was a terrible struggle for him to accept her death. ◦ The people of this country will continue in their struggle **for** independence. ◦* [+ to infinitive] *She never **gave up** the struggle **to** have her son freed from prison. ◦ It's going to be an **uphill** struggle (= very difficult) to get your ideas accepted.* **FIGHT** ▷ **2** (B2) a physical or mental fight: *a struggle **with** an armed robber ◦ the struggle **between** good and evil ◦ Clearly there will be a **power** struggle within the party.*

> **Word partners for struggle noun (EFFORT)**
>
> a *constant/hard/ongoing/uphill* struggle • a struggle *for* [justice/survival, etc.] • *continue with/give up* a struggle

> **Word partners for struggle noun (FIGHT)**
>
> a *bitter/heroic* struggle • be *engaged in/locked in* a struggle • *without* a struggle • a struggle *over* sth • a struggle *against/between* sth

struggling /ˈstrʌɡ.lɪŋ/ **adj** unsuccessful but trying hard to succeed: *It's the story of a struggling artist who marries a rich woman.*

strum /strʌm/ **verb** [I or T] (**-mm-**) to move your fingers across the strings of a guitar or similar instrument

strumpet /ˈstrʌm.pɪt/ **noun** [C] old use a female PROSTITUTE

strung /strʌŋ/ **verb** past simple and past participle of **string**

ˌ**strung ˈout** adj [after verb] slang experiencing the strong effects of drugs such as HEROIN or COCAINE: *For most of her teenage years, she was strung out **on** crack.* → See also **string sth out**

ˌ**strung ˈup** adj [after verb] UK informal nervous or worried: *She always gets strung up before a performance.*

strut /strʌt/ verb; noun

▸**verb** [I] (-tt-) to walk in a proud way trying to look important: *The boys strutted **around** trying to get the attention of a group of girls who were nearby.*

IDIOM **strut your stuff 1** informal mainly humorous to dance in a confident and usually sexually exciting way, especially trying to be noticed by other people: *Hey baby, why don't you get out on the floor and strut your stuff?* **2** informal to show your abilities: *Wimbledon is the opportunity for all the world's best tennis players to strut their stuff.*

▸**noun** [C] a strong rod, usually made from metal or wood, which helps to hold something such as a vehicle or building together

strychnine /ˈstrɪk.niːn/ noun [U] specialized a poisonous substance with a bitter taste that comes from the seeds of a tropical tree and is used as a RAT poison

stub /stʌb/ noun; verb

▸**noun** [C] the short part of something that is left after the main part has been used, especially a cigarette after it has been smoked or one of the small pieces of paper left in a book from which CHEQUES or tickets have been torn

▸**verb stub your toe** to hurt your toe by hitting it against a hard object by accident

PHRASAL VERB **stub sth out** to stop a cigarette from burning by pressing the burning end against a hard surface

stubble /ˈstʌb.əl/ noun [U] **1** the short hair which grows on a man's face if he has not cut the hair for a few days: *With the back of his hand, he rubbed the stubble on his chin.* **2** the short stems left after a crop such as WHEAT has been cut: *In the distance, a wisp of smoke rose from **burning** stubble.* • **stubbly** /-i/ adj

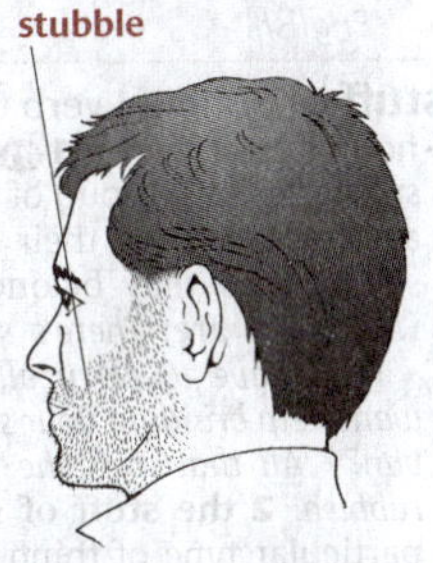

stubborn /ˈstʌb.ən/ (US) /-ən/ adj **1** (B2) disapproving describes someone who is determined to do what they want and refuses to do anything else: *They have massive rows because they're both so stubborn.* **2** Things that are stubborn are difficult to move, change, or deal with: *He was famed for his stubborn **resistance** and his refusal to accept defeat.* ◦ *Stubborn **stains** can be removed using a small amount of detergent.* • **stubbornly** /-li/ adv *She stubbornly **refused** to sign the document.* • **stubbornness** /ˈstʌb.ən.nəs/ (US) /-ən-/ noun [U]

IDIOM **be as stubborn as a mule** to be very stubborn

stubby /ˈstʌb.i/ adj short and thick: *He had rather unattractive, stubby fingers.*

stucco /ˈstʌk.əʊ/ (US) /-oʊ/ noun [U] a type of PLASTER used for covering walls and ceilings, especially one that can be formed into decorative patterns • **stuccoed** /-əʊd/ (US) /-oʊd/ adj

stuck /stʌk/ verb; adj

▸**verb** past simple and past participle of **stick**

▸**adj 1** (B2) unable to move, or fixed in a particular position, place, or way of thinking: *This door seems to be stuck – can you help me push it open?* ◦ *Seven of us were stuck **in** the lift for over an hour.* ◦ *I hate being stuck (= having to be) behind a desk – I'd rather work outside.* **2** in a difficult situation, or unable to change or get away from a situation: *We'd be stuck if your sister hadn't offered to come round and look after the children tonight.* **3** (C1) not able to continue reading, answering questions, etc. because something is too difficult: *I'm really stuck – have you got any ideas how to answer these questions?* **4 be stuck with sb/sth** (C2) to have to deal with someone or something unpleasant because you have no choice or because no one else wants to: *We were stuck with him for the entire train journey!*

IDIOMS **be stuck on sb/sth** old-fashioned informal to like a person or an idea very much: *Nick's really stuck on Maria – he doesn't talk about anything else.* • **get stuck in** (also **get stuck into sth**) UK informal to start doing something enthusiastically: *We showed them where the crates had to be moved to, and they got stuck in straightaway.* ◦ *You really got stuck into your food (= ate your food quickly) – you must have been hungry.* ◦ *Mum brought in the sandwiches and told us to get stuck in.*

ˌ**stuck ˈup** adj informal disapproving too proud and considering yourself to be very important: [before noun] *a bunch of stuck-up mummy's boys*

stud /stʌd/ noun **HORSE** ▷ **1** [C] a group of animals, especially high-quality horses, kept for breeding: *David Grenfell runs a 170-acre stud farm in Co. Wexford, Ireland.* **2 put (out) to stud** specialized kept for breeding **MAN** ▷ **3** [C] slang a man who is thought to have sex a lot and be good at it: *He thinks he's a real stud.* **DECORATION** ▷ **4** [C usually plural] a small nail or piece of metal, with a large, rounded top, that is fixed to the surface of something, usually for decoration **JEWELLERY** ▷ **5** [C] a small piece of metal jewellery that is put through a part of your body such as your ear or nose: *gold studs* ◦ *a nose stud* **BOOT** ▷ **6** [C] UK (US **cleat**) any of the small, pointed objects that stick out from the bottom of some boots and shoes used in particular sports, especially football **FASTENER** ▷ **7** [C] a FASTENER made from two small flat parts joined together by a short bar, used for clothing, especially in the past to fix collars onto shirts

studded /ˈstʌd.ɪd/ adj **1** made with metal studs fixed into the surface in a pattern: *a studded dog collar/leather jacket* **2 studded with sth** literary If something is studded with many objects of the same type, those objects are arranged regularly across it, or across the surface of it: *a baked ham studded with cloves* ◦ *Elaine looked up at the black, velvety sky studded with tiny, twinkling stars.*

student /ˈstjuː.dənt/ (US) /ˈstuː-/ noun [C] **1** (A1) a person who is learning at a college or university, or sometimes at a school: *a law student (= someone learning about law)* ◦ *a postgraduate student* ◦ *a student teacher (= a person training to become a teacher)* ◦ *He was a student **at** the University of Chicago.* **2** If someone is a student of a stated subject, they know about it and are interested in it, but need not have studied it formally: *When you're a nurse, you get to be a bit of a student of (= to know about) human nature.*

ˌ**student ˈloan** noun [C] an agreement by which a student at a college or university borrows money from a bank to pay for their education and then pays the money back after they finish studying and start a job

S

ˌstudent ˈunion noun [C usually singular] (also **ˌstudents' ˈunion**) **1** an organization of students in a college or university that arranges social events and sometimes helps to provide health services and places to live **2** the building or part of a building specially used by students to meet socially

studied /ˈstʌd.id/ **adj** very carefully and intentionally done, made, or considered, rather than in a completely honest or sincere way: *After a pause, he gave a studied answer.* ◦ *She listened to his remarks with studied indifference.*

studio /ˈstjuː.di.əʊ/ (US) /ˈstuː.di.oʊ/ **noun** [C] (plural **studios**) RECORDING ROOM ▷ **1** (B1) a room with special equipment where television or radio programmes or music recordings are made: *She spent three months in the studio working on her latest album.* ◦ *a studio **audience** (= people who watch a programme while it is being made in the studio)* **2** (B1) a building or place where films are made for the cinema, or a company which makes them: *Ealing Studios made some famous British comedies in the 40s and 50s.* **3** a room or building where dancing is taught or practised: *a dance studio* ARTIST'S ROOM ▷ **4** (B2) a room in which an artist works, especially a painter or photographer **5** a company making artistic or photographic products HOME ▷ **6** (UK also **studio flat**, US **studio apartment**) a small apartment designed to be lived in by one or two people, usually with one large room for sleeping and living in, a bathroom and sometimes a separate kitchen

studious /ˈstjuː.di.əs/ (US) /ˈstuː-/ **adj** LEARNING ▷ **1** describes someone who enjoys studying or spends a lot of time studying: *She was a studious child, happiest when reading.* CAREFUL ▷ **2** [before noun] very careful or paying attention to all the small details: *The report was obviously prepared with studious **care** and **attention**.* • **studiously** /-li/ **adv** *They studiously **avoided/ignored** each other.* • **studiousness** /-nəs/ **noun** [U]

study /ˈstʌd.i/ verb; noun

▸verb LEARN ▷ **1** (A1) [I or T] to learn about a subject, especially in an educational course or by reading books: *to study biology/chemistry* ◦ *Next term we shall study plants and how they grow.* ◦ *She's been studying **for** her doctorate for three years already.* EXAMINE ▷ **2** (B2) [T] to examine something very carefully: *I want time to study this contract thoroughly before signing it.* ◦ [+ question word] *Researchers have been studying **how** people under stress make decisions.*

> **! Common mistake: study**
>
> **Warning:** Check your verb endings!
>
> Many learners make mistakes when using **study** in the past tense. The past simple and past participle are **studied**. The **-ing** form is stud**ying**.

PHRASAL VERB **study under sb** to be taught by someone: *As a young painter, he studied under Picasso.*

▸noun EXAMINING ▷ **1** (B2) [C] the activity of examining a subject in detail in order to discover new information: *a five-year study of the relationship between wildlife and farming* ◦ *Some studies have suggested a link between certain types of artificial sweetener and cancer.* **2** [C] a drawing which an artist makes in order to test ideas before starting a painting of the same subject LEARNING ▷ **3** (B2) [U] the act of learning about a subject, usually at school or university: *the study of English literature* **4 studies** (A2) [plural] **a** studying or work involving studying: *Adam doesn't spend enough time on his studies.* **b** used in the names of some

> **Other ways of saying study**
>
> If someone is studying something as his or her main subject at a college or university, you can use the verb **major in** (US):
>
> *She **majored in** philosophy at Harvard.*
>
> **Cram**, **revise** (UK), or **review** (US) can be used when someone is studying very hard just before an exam:
>
> *She's **cramming** for her history exam.*
>
> *I'm **revising** for the test tomorrow.*
>
> If someone is studying a subject in order to discover new facts, the verb **research** is often used:
>
> *Scientists are **researching** possible new treatments for cancer.*

> **Word partners for study noun**
>
> *carry out/conduct/undertake* a study • *commission* a study • be *based on* a study • a study *concludes/finds/shows/suggests* • a study *examines/focuses on* sth • a *careful/comprehensive/detailed/exhaustive* study • a study *into* sth

educational subjects and courses: *the department of **business/media** studies* **5** (B1) [C] a room, especially in a house, used for quiet work such as reading or writing

ˈstudy ˌholiday noun [C usually plural] Indian English one of a number of days that students spend preparing for an exam when there are no classes at school, college, or university

> **! Common mistake: stuff or staff?**
>
> **Warning:** choose the correct word!
>
> To talk about the group of people who work for an organization, don't say 'stuff', say **staff**:
>
> *The staff do not have an adequate command of English.*

stuff /stʌf/ noun; verb

▸noun SUBSTANCE ▷ **1** (B1) [U] informal used to refer to a substance or a group of things, ideas, etc., often with a description of their general type or quality or saying who they belong to, without saying exactly what they are: *There's sticky stuff all over the chair.* ◦ *We'll have to carry all our camping stuff.* ◦ *Do you want help bringing your stuff (= possessions) in from the van?* ◦ *All that stuff she has been saying about Lee is rubbish.* **2 the stuff of sth** literary something that a particular type of thing is made of or based on: *Her appetite for shopping became the stuff of **legend**.* QUALITY ▷ **3 the stuff of sth** literary the most necessary, important, or typical part of something: *A thwarted love affair is the **(very)** stuff of fiction.*

IDIOMS **do your stuff** informal to do what you should do or what is expected of you: *If all the members of the team do their stuff, we should win easily.* • **good/great stuff!** something you say to encourage or praise someone: *'The sales figures are up this week.' 'Great stuff!'* • **stuff and nonsense** old-fashioned an expression used to show that you think something is not true and/or is silly

▸verb FILL ▷ **1** [T] to completely fill a container with something: *Stuff the cushion and then sew up the final seam.* ◦ *Under her bed, they found a bag stuffed **with** money.* **2** (C2) [T] informal to push something into a small space, often quickly or in a careless way: *This case is absolutely full – I can't stuff another thing **into** it.* **3** [T] to fill the body of a dead animal with special material so that it looks as if it is still alive FOOD ▷ **4** [T] to fill food with STUFFING: *Stuff the turkey, then put it into a pre-heated oven.* EAT ▷ **5 stuff yourself**

S

informal to eat a lot: *They'd been stuffing themselves* ***with*** *snacks all afternoon, so they didn't want any dinner.*

IDIOMS **get stuffed!** mainly UK very informal used to show anger or disagreement: *'I'll give you ten quid for the car.' 'Get stuffed!'* • **stuff it, them, you, etc.** mainly UK slang used to show anger or disapproval about a situation or person, or that you refuse to obey someone: *He's expecting us to work late, well stuff that/him!* ◦ *'Shall we tidy up now?' 'No, stuff it!'* • **stuff your face** informal to eat a lot: *I've been stuffing my face all morning.*

stuffed /stʌft/ adj **FULL** ▷ **1** A stuffed animal or bird is filled with special material so that it keeps the shape it had when it was alive: *a collection of stuffed birds* **2** [after verb] informal (of a person) having eaten enough or too much: *'No more for me thanks – I'm stuffed.'* **COOKING** ▷ **3** filled with a STUFFING: *stuffed peppers*

ˌstuffed ˈanimal noun [C] US for **soft toy**: *Her bed is covered with stuffed animals.*

ˌstuffed ˈshirt noun [C] informal disapproving someone who behaves in a very formal and old-fashioned way and thinks that they are very important

ˌstuffed ˈup adj If you are stuffed up, your nose is blocked with MUCUS, usually because you have a cold: *He sounds all stuffed up – is he all right?* ◦ [before noun] *a stuffed-up nose*

stuffing /ˈstʌf.ɪŋ/ noun [U] **MATERIAL** ▷ **1** material that is pushed inside something to make it firm: *This cushion is losing its stuffing.* **FOOD** ▷ **2** a mixture of food, such as bread, onions, and herbs, that is used to fill something that is going to be eaten, such as a chicken or a vegetable, before being cooked: *a stuffing for the turkey* ◦ *sage and onion stuffing*

IDIOMS **beat/kick/knock the stuffing out of sb** informal to hit or kick someone very severely • **knock/take the stuffing out of sb/sth** informal to make someone or something become very weak: *Her illness has really knocked the stuffing out of her.*

stuffy /ˈstʌf.i/ adj disapproving **WITHOUT AIR** ▷ **1** A stuffy room or building is unpleasant because it has no fresh air: *a stuffy office* ◦ *It's really hot and stuffy in here – let's open the window.* ◦ *The bedroom gets a bit stuffy in the summer.* **FORMAL** ▷ **2** old-fashioned, formal, and boring: *Sir William had the ability to conduct proceedings in a dignified manner without ever becoming stuffy.* ◦ *He is trying to promote a less stuffy image of the Conservatives.* • **stuffily** /-ɪ.li/ adv • **stuffiness** /-nəs/ noun [U]

stultifying /ˈstʌl.tɪ.faɪ.ɪŋ/ (US) /-t̬ə-/ adj formal disapproving preventing new ideas from developing: *These countries are trying to shake off the stultifying effects of several decades of state control.* • **stultify** /ˈstʌl.tɪ.faɪ/ (US) /-t̬ə-/ verb [T] *She felt the repetitive exercises stultified her musical technique so she stopped doing them.* • **stultifyingly** /-li/ adv *stultifyingly* ***dull/boring***

stumble /ˈstʌm.bl̩/ verb **WALK** ▷ **1** (C2) [I] to step awkwardly while walking or running and fall or begin to fall: *Running along the beach, she stumbled* ***on*** *a log and fell on the sand.* ◦ *In the final straight Meyers stumbled, and although he didn't fall it was enough to lose him first place.* **2** [I usually + adv/prep] to walk in a way which does not seem controlled: *We could hear her stumbling* ***about/around*** *the bedroom in the dark.* ◦ *He pulled on his clothes and stumbled* ***into*** *the kitchen.* **PAUSE** ▷ **3** (C2) [I] to make a mistake, such as repeating something or pausing for too long, while speaking or playing a piece of music: *When the poet stumbled* ***over*** *a line in the middle of a poem, someone in the audience corrected him.*

PHRASAL VERB **stumble across/on/upon sth/sb** (C2) to discover something by chance, or to meet someone by chance: *Workmen stumbled upon the mosaic while digging foundations for a new building.*

ˈstumbling ˌblock noun [C] something which prevents action or agreement: *Lack of willingness to compromise on both sides is the* ***main/major*** *stumbling block* ***to*** *reaching a settlement.*

stump /stʌmp/ noun; verb

▸noun **PART LEFT** ▷ **1** [C] the part of something such as a tree, tooth, arm, or leg that is left after most of it has been removed: *the stump* ***of*** *a tree* ◦ *Her smile broadened to reveal two rows of brown stumps.* **CRICKET** ▷ **2 stumps** [plural] the three vertical wooden poles at which the ball is thrown in cricket

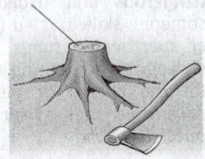

▸verb **NO ANSWER** ▷ **1 be stumped** informal to be unable to answer a question or solve a problem because it is too difficult: *I'm* ***completely*** *stumped – how did she manage to escape?* ◦ *Scientists are stumped* ***by*** *this mystery virus.* **WALK** ▷ **2** [I usually + adv/prep] to **stomp** **POLITICS** ▷ **3** [T] US to travel around an area giving speeches and trying to get political support: *She remembers when her dad ran for governor and stumped the north of the state.* **CRICKET** ▷ **4** [T usually passive] If the person hitting the ball in cricket is stumped, their turn to try scoring points is ended by a member of the other team knocking the BAILS off the stumps with the ball while they are outside a safe area.

PHRASAL VERB **stump up (sth)** UK informal to pay an amount or type of money for something, especially unwillingly: *It can be cheaper to stump up* ***for*** *a new washing machine than to get your old one repaired.* ◦ *Chissano said Western governments should stump up* ***the cash*** *to fund land redistribution.*

stumpy /ˈstʌm.pi/ adj informal mainly disapproving short and thick: *There was a large ring on each of her stumpy fingers.*

stun /stʌn/ verb [T] (-nn-) **SHOCK** ▷ **1** to shock or surprise someone very much: *News of the disaster stunned people throughout the world.* ◦ *She was stunned by the amount of support she received from well-wishers.* **MAKE UNCONSCIOUS** ▷ **2** to make a person or animal unconscious, or to cause them to lose the usual control of their mind, especially by hitting their head hard: *Stunned by the impact, he lay on the ground wondering what had happened.* ◦ *This injection stuns the rhinoceros, so we can examine it.*

stung /stʌŋ/ verb past simple and past participle of **sting**

ˈstun ˌgun noun [C] a device which produces a small electric shock in order to stop an animal or human from moving temporarily without harming them permanently

stunk /stʌŋk/ verb past simple and past participle of **stink**

stunned /stʌnd/ adj (C2) very shocked or surprised: *They stood in stunned* ***silence*** *beside the bodies.* ◦ *I am stunned and saddened by this news.*

stunner /ˈstʌn.əʳ/ (US) /-ɚ/ noun [C] old-fashioned informal a person or thing that is very beautiful, especially a woman: *The new administrator in accounts is a **real** stunner.*

stunning /ˈstʌn.ɪŋ/ adj BEAUTIFUL ▷ **1** B2 extremely beautiful or attractive: *a stunning dress* ◦ *a stunning view over the bay of Saint Tropez* SHOCKING ▷ **2** shocking or very impressive: *All the ideas have a stunning simplicity.* • **stunningly** /-li/ adv *a stunningly beautiful/attractive woman* ◦ *He's stunningly naive for a person of his age.*

stunt /stʌnt/ noun; verb

▸noun [C] EXCITING ACTION ▷ **1** an exciting action, usually in a film, that is dangerous or appears dangerous and usually needs to be done by someone skilled: *It's a typical action film with plenty of **spectacular** stunts.* GET ATTENTION ▷ **2** mainly disapproving something that is done to get attention for the person or people responsible for it: *an advertising stunt* ◦ *Their marriage was just a cheap **publicity** stunt.*

IDIOM **pull a stunt** informal to do something silly and dangerous: *What did you want to pull a stupid stunt like that for?*

▸verb [T] to prevent the growth or development of something from reaching its limit: *Drought has stunted (the **growth** of) this year's cereal crop.*

stunted /ˈstʌn.tɪd/ US /-ɪd/ adj prevented from growing or developing to the usual size: *A few stunted trees were the only vegetation visible.* ◦ *children with stunted growth*

stuntman /ˈstʌnt.mæn/ noun [C] (plural **-men** /-men/) a man who performs stunts, especially instead of an actor in a film or television programme

stuntwoman /ˈstʌntˌwʊm.ən/ noun [C] (plural **-women** /-wɪmɪn/) a woman who performs stunts, especially instead of an actor in a film or television programme

stupa /ˈstuː.pə/ noun [C] a building with a DOME (= rounded roof), that is a holy place for Buddhists

stupefy /ˈstjuː.pɪ.faɪ/ US /ˈstuː-/ verb [T] TIRE ▷ **1** to make someone tired and unable to think clearly SURPRISE ▷ **2** to surprise or shock someone very much • **stupefaction** /ˌstjuː.pɪˈfæk.ʃᵊn/ US /ˌstuː-/ noun [U] formal *Because of the drugs, he was in **a state of** stupefaction by the time we found him.* • **stupefied** /ˈstjuː.pɪ.faɪd/ US /ˈstuː-/ adj *Stupefied by tiredness, she just sat in front of the fire.* ◦ *We were so stupefied by the news that we all sat in silence for a long time.* • **stupefying** /-ɪŋ/ adj *stupefying **heat/noise*** ◦ *stupefying arrogance* • **stupefyingly** /-ɪŋ.li/ adv *stupefyingly **dull/boring*** ◦ *stupefyingly rich*

S

stupendous /stjuːˈpen.dəs/ US /stuː-/ adj very surprising, usually in a pleasing way, especially by being large in amount or size: *He ran up stupendous debts through his extravagant lifestyle.* ◦ *Stupendous news! We've won £500,000!* • **stupendously** /-li/ adv *Our charity appeal has been stupendously successful.*

stupid /ˈstjuː.pɪd/ US /ˈstuː-/ adj **1** B1 silly or unwise; showing poor judgment or little intelligence: *She was really stupid to quit her job like that.* ◦ *Whose stupid idea was it to travel at night?* ◦ *He now thinks that retiring early was a stupid **thing** to do.* ◦ *How could you be so stupid?* **2** informal annoying, or causing a problem: *Have your stupid book back if it's so important to you.* ◦ *I hate doing this stupid exercise, I just can't get it right.* • **stupid** noun [as form of address] informal *Don't lock it, stupid!* • **stupidly** /-li/ adv *Sorry, I stupidly forgot to bring my copy of the report – could I look at yours?*

> **Other ways of saying stupid**
>
> Some common alternatives to 'stupid' are **foolish** and **silly**:
>
> *She was really **foolish** to quit her job like that.*
>
> *It was **silly** of you to go out in the sun without a hat.*
>
> If something or someone is stupid enough to be funny or strange, you can use the words **absurd**, **ridiculous**, or **ludicrous**:
>
> *What an **absurd** thing to say!*
>
> *Do I look **ridiculous** in this hat?*
>
> *I think giving young children such expensive jewellery is a **ludicrous** idea.*
>
> You can describe a stupid person as a **fool** or an **idiot**:
>
> *You were a **fool** not to take that job.*
>
> *Some **idiot** dropped a lighted match in the waste-paper basket.*
>
> In informal situations, if you think people have been stupid, you can say that they are **out of** their **mind**:
>
> *You must be **out of your mind** spending so much money on a car.*

stupidity /stjuːˈpɪd.ɪ.ti/ US /stuːˈpɪd.ə.t̬i/ noun [U] C2 the state of being silly or unwise: *a moment/act of stupidity* ◦ *Her stupidity is beyond belief sometimes.* ◦ *It was **sheer** stupidity to refuse at the price they were offering.*

stupor /ˈstjuː.pəʳ/ US /ˈstuː.pɚ/ noun [C usually singular] a state in which a person is almost unconscious and their thoughts are not clear: *He was lying under the table **in a drunken** stupor.*

sturdy /ˈstɜː.di/ US /ˈstɝː-/ adj **1** physically strong and solid or thick, and therefore unlikely to break or be hurt: *sturdy walking boots* ◦ *a sturdy table* ◦ *sturdy little legs* **2** [before noun] literary strong and determined: *They put up a sturdy defence of their proposal.* • **sturdily** /-dɪ.li/ adv *We could see the boat was sturdily built/constructed.* • **sturdiness** /-nəs/ noun [U]

sturgeon /ˈstɜː.dʒᵊn/ US /ˈstɝː-/ noun [C] a type of fish that lives in northern parts of the world and is usually caught for its eggs, which are eaten as CAVIAR

stutter /ˈstʌt.əʳ/ US /ˈstʌt̬.ɚ/ verb [I] SPEAK ▷ **1** to speak or say something, especially the first part of a word, with difficulty, for example pausing before it or repeating it several times: *She stutters a bit, so let her finish what she's saying.* ◦ [+ speech] *'C-c-can we g-go now?' stuttered Jenkins.* → Compare **stammer** NOT SMOOTH ▷ **2** to work or happen in a way that is not smooth or regular: *Suddenly the engine stuttered and then it stopped completely.* • **stutter** noun [C] *Toni's developed a slight stutter over the last few months.* • **stuttering** /-ɪŋ/ US /ˈstʌt̬.ɚ-/ adj *Stuttering (= sometimes good and sometimes bad) productivity figures over the last two years have made the industry unattractive to investors.*

sty /staɪ/ noun [C] STRUCTURE ▷ **1** a **pigsty** SWELLING ▷ **2** (also **stye**) a small, sore swelling on the edge of an EYELID

Stygian /ˈstɪdʒ.i.ən/ adj literary extremely and unpleasantly dark: *Stygian **gloom***

style /staɪl/ noun; verb

▸noun WAY ▷ **1** B1 [C or U] a way of doing something, especially one that is typical of a person, group of people, place, or period: *Jones favours a dynamic, hands-on style **of** management.* ◦ *His office is very utilitarian **in** style, with no decoration.* **2 be your style** informal to be the type of thing that you would

do: *He wouldn't try to mislead you – it's not his style.* **FASHION** ▷ **3** B1 [C or U] fashion, especially in clothing: *a style consultant* ◦ *I read the fashion pages in the newspapers to keep up with the latest styles.* ◦ *The classic black dress is always* ***in*** *style.* **DESIGN** ▷ **4** B1 [C] a particular shape or design, especially of a person's hair, clothes, or a piece of furniture: *a formal style* ***of*** *hat* ◦ *Her hair was cut in a really nice style.* → See also **hairstyle** **HIGH QUALITY** ▷ **5** B2 [U] approving high quality in appearance, design, or behaviour: *That car's* ***got real*** *style, which is no surprise considering how much it cost.* ◦ *When she decides to do something, she always does it* ***in/with*** *great style.* **FLOWER PART** ▷ **6** [C] specialized the middle part of the CARPEL (= female part) of a flower, connecting the OVARY to the STIGMA
▸verb [T] **DESIGN** ▷ **1** to shape or design something such as a person's hair or an object like a piece of clothing or furniture, especially so that it looks attractive: *You've had your hair styled – it really suits you.* ◦ *This range of jackets is styled to look good whatever the occasion.* **TITLE** ▷ **2** to give a title to a person or group: [+ noun] *She styles herself 'Doctor' but she doesn't have a degree.* → See also **self-styled**

-style /-staɪl/ suffix in the style mentioned: *Japanese-style management* ◦ *antique-style furniture*

styling /staɪl/ noun [U] used in the name of products or devices that are used for giving a particular shape or style to a person's hair: *styling mousse/gel* ◦ *a styling comb*

stylish /ˈstaɪ.lɪʃ/ adj approving B1 of a high quality in appearance, design, or behaviour: *The film's direction is subtle and stylish.* • **stylishly** /-li/ adv approving *stylishly dressed* • **stylishness** /-nəs/ noun [U] approving

stylist /ˈstaɪ.lɪst/ noun [C] **1** a person whose job is to shape or design something: *the latest exciting new car designed by our team of stylists* ◦ *I've been going to the same* (***hair***) *stylist for years.* **2** a writer who is very careful in the way they style their work: *She's no stylist, but she writes very exciting stories.*

stylistic /staɪˈlɪs.tɪk/ adj relating to a particular style of doing something: *In their second album, the band tried to expand their stylistic range.* ◦ *Notice the stylistic similarities in the work of these three sculptors.* • **stylistically** /-tɪ.kəl.i/ adv *stylistically similar*

stylistics /staɪˈlɪs.tɪks/ noun [U] the study of style used in language

stylized (UK usually **stylised**) /ˈstaɪə.laɪzd/ adj If something is stylized, it is represented with an emphasis on a particular style, especially a style in which there are only a few simple details: *The rock drawings depict a variety of stylized mythological figures and patterns.*

stylus /ˈstaɪ.ləs/ noun [C] **1** a small, pointed device on a RECORD PLAYER which picks up the sound signals stored on a record **2** a small, pointed metal or plastic stick that you use to make some computer devices work

stymie /ˈstaɪ.mi/ verb [T often passive] (present participle **stymieing**) informal to prevent something from happening or someone from achieving a purpose: *In our search for evidence, we were stymied by the absence of any recent documents.*

Styrofoam /ˈstaɪ.rə.fəʊm/ US /-foʊm/ noun [U] US trademark **polystyrene**

suave /swɑːv/ adj describes a man who is very polite, pleasant, and usually attractive, often in a way that is slightly false: *He's very suave and sophisticated.* • **suavely** /ˈswɑːv.li/ adv • **suavity** /ˈswɑː.vɪ.ti/ US /-və.t̬i/ noun [U]

sub /sʌb/ noun; verb
▸noun [C] **MONEY** ▷ **1** UK informal for **subscription**: *Have you paid your tennis club sub yet?* **CHANGE** ▷ **2** UK and US informal for **substitute**: *One of the players was injured during the match, so a sub was brought on.* **SHIP** ▷ **3** informal for **submarine**: *a nuclear sub* **BREAD** ▷ **4** US informal for **submarine sandwich**
▸verb [I] (**-bb-**) to replace someone, especially in a game of football: *Travis subbed* ***for*** *the injured defender.*

sub- /sʌb-/ prefix **BELOW** ▷ **1** under or below: *Winter weather brought sub-zero (= less than 0 degrees) temperatures to much of the country.* **NOT QUITE** ▷ **2** almost or nearly: *subhuman* ◦ *subtropical* **SMALLER** ▷ **3** being a smaller part of a larger whole: *a subcontinent* ◦ *to subdivide*

subaltern /ˈsʌb.əl.tən/ US /səbˈɔːl.tən/ noun [C] UK an army officer whose rank is lower than CAPTAIN

ˌsub-ˈaqua adj [before noun] UK relating to sports that involve swimming underwater: *a sub-aqua club*

subarctic /sʌbˈɑːk.tɪk/ US /-ˈɑːrk-/ adj belonging or relating to the cold regions of the world immediately south of the ARCTIC CIRCLE, such as northern Scandinavia, Alaska, and Siberia: *the subarctic climate* ◦ *subarctic peoples/cultures*

subatomic /ˌsʌb.əˈtɒm.ɪk/ US /-ˈtɑː.mɪk/ adj specialized smaller than or within an atom

subaˌtomic ˈparticle noun [C] specialized an extremely small piece of matter that is smaller than an atom or found inside an atom, such as a PROTON, NEUTRON, or ELECTRON

subcommittee /ˈsʌb.kəˌmɪt.i/ US /-ˌmɪ-/ noun [C] a number of people chosen from a COMMITTEE (= a small group of people who represent a larger organization and make decisions for it) to study and report on a particular subject: *Several subcommittees will be* ***set up*** *to deal with specific environmental issues.*

subcompact /ˈsəb.kəm.pækt/ noun [C] US a very small car

subconscious /ˌsʌbˈkɒn.ʃəs/ US /-ˈkɑːn-/ noun; adj
▸noun [S] the part of your mind that notices and remembers information when you are not actively trying to do so, and influences your behaviour even though you do not realize it: *The memory was buried deep within my subconscious.*
▸adj [before noun] relating to this part of your mind: *subconscious thoughts/fears* ◦ *Such memories exist only* ***on/at*** *the subconscious level.* ◦ *Our subconscious* ***mind*** *registers things which our conscious mind is not aware of.* → Compare **conscious** • **subconsciously** /-li/ adv C2 *I think I must have known subconsciously that something was going on between them.*

subcontinent /ˌsʌbˈkɒn.tɪ.nənt/ US /ˈsʌbˌkɑːn.ən.ənt/ noun [C] a large area of land that is part of a continent, often referring to South Asia: *the* ***Indian*** *subcontinent* ◦ *He has written a book about the history of railways in* ***the*** *subcontinent.*

subcontract /ˌsʌb.kənˈtrækt/ US /sʌbˈkɑːn.trækt/ verb [T] to pay someone else to do part of a job that you have agreed to do: *Most of the bricklaying has been subcontracted* (***out***) ***to*** *a local builder.*

subcontractor /ˌsʌb.kənˈtræk.tər/ US /-kɑːn.træk.tɚ/ noun [C] a person or company that does part of a job which another person or company is responsible for

subculture /ˈsʌbˌkʌl.tʃər/ US /-tʃɚ/ noun [C] the way of life, customs, and ideas of a particular group of people within a society that are different from the rest of that society: *youth subcultures* ◦ *the gay subculture*

S

subcutaneous /ˌsʌb.kjuˈteɪ.ni.əs/ **adj** specialized existing under the skin: *subcutaneous fat/muscle*

subdivide /ˌsʌb.dɪˈvaɪd/ **verb** [T] to divide something into smaller parts: *Each chapter is subdivided* ***into*** *smaller sections.*

subdivision /ˈsʌb.dɪˌvɪʒ.ən/, /ˌsʌb.dɪˈvɪʒ-/ **noun 1** [C or U] any of the parts into which something is divided, or the act of creating these: *Each category has several subdivisions.* ◦ *They agreed that subdivision of the house* ***into*** *apartments would be a good idea.* **2** [C] US for **housing estate**

subdue /səbˈdjuː/ (US) /-ˈduː/ **verb** [T] to reduce the force of something, or to prevent something from existing or developing: *The fire burned for eight hours before the fire crews could subdue it.* ◦ *He criticized the school for trying to subdue individual expression.*

subdued /səbˈdjuːd/ (US) /-ˈduːd/ **adj** **NOT STRONG** ▷ **1** If a colour or light is subdued, it is not very bright: *subdued lighting* **2** If a noise is subdued, it is not loud: *subdued laughter/cheers* **MOOD** ▷ **3** If a person is subdued, they are not as happy as usual or they are quieter than usual: *He seemed a bit subdued at lunch – is he all right?*

subheading /ˈsʌbˌhed.ɪŋ/ **noun** [C] a word, phrase, or sentence that is used to introduce part of a text: *The subheadings are numbered within each chapter.*

subhuman /ˌsʌbˈhjuː.mən/ **adj** disapproving having or showing behaviour or characteristics that are much worse than those expected of ordinary people: *Their treatment of prisoners is subhuman.*

subject **noun; verb; adj**

▸**noun** [C] /ˈsʌb.dʒekt/ **AREA OF DISCUSSION** ▷ **1** (B1) the thing which is being discussed, considered, or studied: *Our subject for discussion is homelessness.* ◦ *She has made a series of documentaries* ***on the*** *subject* ***of*** *family relationships.* ◦ *The guest lecturer* ***took as*** *her subject (= decided to speak about) 'punishment and imprisonment in modern society'.* ◦ *The number of planes flying over the town has been* ***the*** *subject* ***of*** *(= has caused) concern since last summer.* **AREA OF STUDY** ▷ **2** (A1) an area of knowledge that is studied in school, college, or university: *My favourite subjects at school were history and geography.* ◦ mainly UK *Her subject (= special area of study) is low-temperature physics.* **3** **change the subject** (B2) to start talking about a different subject: *I'd tried to explain the situation, but he just changed the subject.* **STORY/PAINTING** ▷ **4** (C2) a person, thing, or situation that is written about in a book, article, etc. or shown in a picture, etc.: *The mill by the bridge was the subject of an unfinished painting by J. M. W. Turner.* **GRAMMAR** ▷ **5** (B1) specialized the person or thing that performs the action of a verb, or is joined to a description by a verb: *'Bob' is the subject of the sentence 'Bob threw the ball'.* → Compare **object** **PERSON** ▷ **6** a person who lives in or who has the right to live in a particular country, especially a country with a king or queen: *He is a British subject.* → Compare **citizen**

> Word partners for **subject noun**
>
> *bring up/broach/discuss/raise* a subject • *get onto* a subject • *change/drop/get off* a subject • *keep off/stay off* a subject • a subject *for discussion/debate* • a *controversial/emotive/sensitive/touchy* subject • *on* the subject (of sth) • a subject *area*

▸**verb** [T] /səbˈdʒekt/ to defeat people or a country and then control them against their wishes and limit their freedom: *The invaders quickly subjected the local tribes.*

PHRASAL VERB **subject sb/sth to sth** [often passive] (C2) to make someone or something experience an unpleasant or worrying thing: *The inquiry found that they had been subjected to unfair treatment.* ◦ *'I didn't want to subject him to such a long journey,' she said.*

▸**adj** /ˈsʌb.dʒekt/ **HAVING** ▷ **1 be subject to sth** (C1) to have or experience a particular thing, especially something unpleasant: *Cars are subject to a high domestic tax.* ◦ *In recent years, she has been subject to attacks of depression.* **DEPEND** ▷ **2 subject to sth** (C2) only able to happen if something else happens: *We plan to go on Wednesday, subject to your approval.* ◦ *Moving all the books should not take long, subject to there being (= if there are) enough helpers.* **GOVERN** ▷ **3** [before noun] under the political control of another country or state: *subject peoples/states*

subjection /səbˈdʒek.ʃən/ **noun** [U] the state of being under the political control of another country or state: *The book discusses the political subjection of the island by its larger neighbour.*

subjective /səbˈdʒek.tɪv/ **adj** (C1) influenced by or based on personal beliefs or feelings, rather than based on facts: *I think my husband is the most handsome man in the world, but I realize my judgment is rather subjective.* ◦ *More specific and less subjective criteria should be used in selecting people for promotion within the company.* → Compare **objective** • **subjectively** /-li/ **adv** • **subjectivity** /ˌsʌb.dʒekˈtɪv.ɪ.ti/ (US) /-ə.t̬i/ **noun** [U] *There's always an element of subjectivity in decision-making.*

ˈsubject ˌmatter **noun** [C] the things that are being talked or written about, or used as the subject of a piece of art, etc.: *The programme's subject matter was quite unsuitable for children.*

sub judice /ˌsʌbˈdʒuː.dɪ.si/ **adj** [after verb] legal being studied or decided in a law court at the present time: *In Britain, cases which are sub judice cannot be publicly discussed in the media.*

subjugate /ˈsʌb.dʒʊ.geɪt/ **verb** [T] formal **DEFEAT** ▷ **1** to defeat people or a country and rule them in a way which allows them no freedom **CONTROL** ▷ **2** to treat yourself, your wishes, or your beliefs as being less important than other people or their wishes or beliefs: *She subjugated her**self to** her mother's needs.* ◦ *Journalists must subjugate personal political convictions* ***to*** *their professional commitment to balance.* • **subjugation** /ˌsʌb.dʒʊˈgeɪ.ʃən/ **noun** [U] *They are bravely resisting subjugation by their more powerful neighbours.*

subjunctive /səbˈdʒʌŋk.tɪv/ **noun** [S] specialized in some languages, a verb form that refers to actions that are possibilities rather than facts: *In the sentence 'I wish I were rich', the verb 'were' is* ***in the*** *subjunctive.*

sublet /ˌsʌbˈlet/ (US) /ˈsʌb.let/ **verb** [T] (present tense **subletting**, past tense and past participle **sublet**) to allow someone to rent all or part of a house or other building which you are renting from someone else: *Our rental contract states that we are not allowed to sublet the house.*

ˌsub lieuˈtenant **noun** [C] an officer of low rank in the British navy

sublimate /ˈsʌb.lɪ.meɪt/ **verb** [T] specialized to express strong emotions or use energy by doing an activity, especially an activity that is considered socially acceptable: *Hostile feelings and violent responses often seem to be sublimated* ***into*** *sporting activities.* • **sublimation** /ˌsʌb.lɪˈmeɪ.ʃən/ **noun** [U]

S

sublime /sə'blaɪm/ **adj; noun**
▸**adj 1** extremely good, beautiful, or enjoyable: *sublime beauty ◦ The book has sublime descriptive passages.* **2** very great: *He possesses sublime self-confidence.* • **sublimity** /sə'blɪm.ɪ.ti/ ⓤⓢ /-ə.t̬i/ **noun** [U]
▸**noun the sublime** something that is sublime: *A great deal of literature is only the obvious transformed into the sublime.*

IDIOM **from the sublime to the ridiculous** from something that is very good or very serious to something very bad or silly: *The dresses in the fashion show **went/ranged** from the sublime to the ridiculous.*

sublimely /sə'blaɪm.li/ **adv** extremely: *At times the writing is sublimely funny.*

subliminal /ˌsʌb'lɪm.ɪ.nəl/ **adj 1** not recognized or understood by the conscious mind, but still having an influence on it: *The prime minister was interviewed in front of a factory to give the subliminal **message** that he was a man of the people.* **2** describes advertising that uses INDIRECT ways of influencing people to be attracted to a product, such as using a picture of a farm to advertise food to suggest that it is fresh

submachine gun /ˌsʌb.mə'ʃiːŋ.gʌn/ **noun** [C] a type of automatic gun that is light enough to be carried easily

submarine /ˌsʌb.mə'riːn/, /'sʌb.mə.riːn/ **noun; adj**
▸**noun** [C] (informal **sub**) a ship that can travel underwater: *a nuclear submarine ◦ a submarine base/commander*
▸**adj** specialized existing below the surface of the sea

ˈ**submarine ˌsandwich noun** [C] (informal **sub**) US a long, thin LOAF of bread filled with salad and cold meat or cheese

submerge /səb'mɜːdʒ/ ⓤⓢ /-'mɝːdʒ/ **verb 1** [I or T] to go below or make something go below the surface of the sea or a river or lake: *The submarine submerged when enemy planes were sighted. ◦ She was taken to hospital after being submerged **in** an icy river for 45 minutes.* **2** [T] literary to cover or hide something completely: *She has submerged her identity in the role of photographer's wife and muse.* • **submersion** /-'mɜː.ʃən/ ⓤⓢ /-'mɝː.ʒən/ **noun** [U] *The fruit was preserved by submersion **in** alcohol.*

PHRASAL VERB **submerge yourself in sth** to put all your effort into doing a particular activity: *She is an actress who always tries to submerge herself completely in a role.*

submersible /səb'mɜː.sɪ.bl/ ⓤⓢ /-'mɝː-/ **noun** [C] specialized a type of ship that can travel underwater, especially one that operates without people being in it

submission /səb'mɪʃ.ən/ **noun GIVING** ▷ **1** [C or U] the act of giving something for a decision to be made by others, or a document formally given in this way: *No date has yet been set for the submission of applications. ◦ The final deadline for submissions is 21 February.* ◦ [+ that] formal *The judge will hear the defence's submission (= suggestion) **that** the case be dismissed.* **ACCEPTING** ▷ **2** [U] the act of allowing someone or something to have power over you: *They thought the country could be bombed **into** submission. ◦ The teachers agreed to a special meeting, **in** submission **to** parents' demands.*

submissive /səb'mɪs.ɪv/ **adj** describes someone who allows themselves to be controlled by other people: *He was looking for a quiet, submissive wife who would obey his every word.* • **submissively** /-li/ **adv** • **submissiveness** /-nəs/ **noun** [U]

submit /səb'mɪt/ **verb** (**-tt-**) **GIVE** ▷ **1** B2 [T] to give or offer something for a decision to be made by others: *You must submit your application before 1 January. ◦ The developers submitted building plans **to** the council for approval.* **2** [T + that] formal to suggest: *In conclusion, I submit **that** the proposal will not work without some major changes.* **ALLOW** ▷ **3** C2 [I or T] to allow another person or group to have power or authority over you, or to accept something unwillingly: *We protested about the changes for a long time, but in the end we had to submit. ◦ She decided to resign from the party rather than submit her**self to** the new rules.*

submultiple /ˌsʌb'mʌl.tɪ.pəl/ ⓤⓢ /-t̬ə-/ **noun** [C] specialized a number that divides into another number an exact number of times: *4 is a submultiple of 12.*

subnormal /ˌsʌb'nɔː.məl/ ⓤⓢ /-'nɔːr-/ **adj** below an average or expected standard, especially of intelligence: *mentally subnormal ◦ subnormal temperatures*

subordinate adj; noun; verb
▸**adj** /sə'bɔː.dɪ.nət/ ⓤⓢ /-'bɔːr-/ having a lower or less important position: *a subordinate role ◦ subordinate status ◦ The individual's needs are subordinate **to** those of the group.*
▸**noun** [C] /sə'bɔː.dɪ.nət/ ⓤⓢ /-'bɔːr-/ a person who has a less important position than you in an organization: *He left the routine checks to one of his subordinates.*
▸**verb** [T] /sə'bɔː.dɪ.neɪt/ ⓤⓢ /-'bɔːr-/ to put someone or something into a less important position

suˌbordinate ˈclause noun [C] specialized in grammar, a CLAUSE that cannot form a sentence on its own but can be joined to a main clause to form a sentence

subordination /səˌbɔː.dɪ'neɪ.ʃən/ ⓤⓢ /-ˌbɔːr-/ **noun** [U] the act of giving someone or something less importance or power: *She claims that society is still characterized by male domination and female subordination. ◦ subordination of high standards **to** quick results*

subplot /'sʌb.plɒt/ ⓤⓢ /-plɑːt/ **noun** [C] a part of the story of a book or play which develops separately from the main story

subpoena /sə'piː.nə/ **verb; noun**
▸**verb** [T] legal **1** to order someone to go to a law court to answer questions: *A friend of the victim was subpoenaed **as** a witness by lawyers representing the accused.* ◦ [+ to infinitive] *They were subpoenaed **to** testify before the judge.* **2** to order that documents must be produced in a law court
▸**noun** [C] legal a legal document ordering someone to appear in a law court: *Subpoenas were issued to several government employees.*

subprime (also ˌ**sub-ˈprime**) /ˌsʌb'praɪm/ **adj** specialized used to describe the practice of lending money, especially to buy a house, to people who may not be able to pay it back: *subprime mortgages/loans/lending*

subrogation /ˌsʌb.rə'geɪ.ʃən/ **noun** [U] specialized the ability that an INSURANCE company has to get the money it has paid to a customer back from the person who caused the accident, damage, etc.

subscribe /səb'skraɪb/ **verb** [I or T] **1** to pay money to an organization in order to receive a product, use a service regularly, or support the organization: *She subscribes **to** several women's magazines. ◦ I subscribe £10 a month **to** the charity.* **2** specialized to offer to buy something or pay an amount for something as part of your business activities: *Existing shareholders subscribed **to** only 49 percent of the new share issue.*

S

PHRASAL VERB **subscribe to sth** to agree with or support an opinion, belief, or theory: *Frank subscribed firmly to the belief that human kindness would overcome evil.*

subscriber /səbˈskraɪ.bəʳ/ (US) /-bɚ/ **noun** [C] someone who subscribes to a product, service, or organization

subscription /səbˈskrɪp.ʃᵊn/ **noun** **REGULAR PAYMENT** ▷ **1** [C] (informal **sub**) an amount of money that you pay regularly to receive a product or service or to be a member of an organization: UK *We bought our niece an **annual** subscription **to** the tennis club.* ◦ *I decided to **take out** (= pay for) a subscription **to** a gardening magazine.* **2** [C] (also **subscription ticket**) a **season ticket** for cultural events **SHARES** ▷ **3** [C or U] an opportunity to buy SHARES in a company: *You will soon have the opportunity to purchase stock through a subscription **offering**.*

subsection /ˈsʌbˌsek.ʃᵊn/ **noun** [C] one of the smaller parts into which the main parts of a document or organization are divided: *Further details can be found in section 7 subsection 4 of the report.*

subsequent /ˈsʌb.sɪ.kwənt/ **adj** C1 happening after something else: *The book discusses his illness and subsequent resignation from the government.* ◦ *Those explosions must have been subsequent **to** our departure, because we didn't hear anything.* • **subsequently** /-li/ **adv** C1 *In 1982 he was arrested and subsequently convicted on drug trafficking charges.*

subservient /səbˈsɜː.vi.ənt/ (US) /-ˈsɝː-/ **adj** disapproving willing to do what other people want, or considering your wishes as less important than those of other people: *to adopt a subservient **role/position*** ◦ *The government was accused of being subservient **to** the interests of the pro-Europe campaigners.* • **subservience** /-əns/ **noun** [U] • **subserviently** /-li/ **adv**

subset /ˈsʌb.set/ **noun** [C] specialized a SET (= a group of similar numbers, objects, or people) that is part of another, larger set

subside /səbˈsaɪd/ **verb** [I] **LESS STRONG** ▷ **1** If a condition subsides, it becomes less strong or extreme: *The police are hoping that the violence will soon subside.* ◦ *As the pain in my foot subsided, I was able to walk the short distance to the car.* **LOWER LEVEL** ▷ **2** If a building, land, or water subsides, it goes down to a lower level: *There is a danger that many homes will subside because of the drought.* ◦ *Eventually the flood waters began to subside.*

subsidence /səbˈsaɪ.dᵊns/, /ˈsʌb.sɪ-/ **noun** [U] the process by which land or buildings sink to a lower level: *The building had to be demolished because of subsidence.*

subsidiarity /ˌsʌb.sɪd.iˈær.ɪ.ti/ (US) /-er.ə.t̬i/ **noun** [U] specialized the principle that decisions should always be taken at the lowest possible level or closest to where they will have their effect, for example in a local area rather than for a whole country

subsidiary /səbˈsɪd.i.ᵊr.i/ (US) /-er-/ **adj; noun**
▸**adj** describes something less important than something else with which it is connected: *a subsidiary role/factor*
▸**noun** [C] a company that is owned by a larger company

subsidize (UK usually **subsidise**) /ˈsʌb.sɪ.daɪz/ **verb** [T] to pay part of the cost of something: *£50 would help to subsidize the training of an unemployed teenager.* ◦ *The refugees live in subsidized housing provided by the authorities.* • **subsidization** (UK usually **subsidisation**) /ˌsʌb.sɪ.daɪˈzeɪ.ʃᵊn/ (US) /-dəˈ-/ **noun** [U]

subsidy /ˈsʌb.sɪ.di/ **noun** [C] C1 money given as part of the cost of something, to help or encourage it to happen: *The company received a substantial government subsidy.* ◦ *The government is planning to abolish subsidies **to** farmers.*

subsist /səbˈsɪst/ **verb** [I] formal to get enough food or money to stay alive, but no more: *The prisoners were subsisting **on** a diet of bread and water.*

subsistence /səbˈsɪs.tᵊns/ **noun** [U] formal the state of having what you need in order to stay alive, but no more: *The money is intended to provide basic subsistence and should not be paid to someone who receives other income.* ◦ *The family were living **at** subsistence **level**.*

subˈsistence ˌcrop **noun** [C] specialized a crop that people grow to use or eat themselves, rather than to sell → Compare **cash crop**

subˈsistence ˌfarming **noun** [U] specialized farming that provides enough food for the farmer and their family to live on, but not enough for them to sell

subsoil /ˈsʌb.sɔɪl/ **noun** [U] the layer of soil that is under the surface level → Compare **topsoil**

subsonic /sʌbˈsɒn.ɪk/ (US) /-ˈsɑː.nɪk/ **adj** slower than the speed of sound

subspecies /ˈsʌbˌspiː.ʃiːz/ **noun** [C] (plural **subspecies**) specialized a particular type within a SPECIES, the members of which are different in some clear ways from those of other types of the SPECIES

substance /ˈsʌb.stᵊns/ **noun** **MATERIAL** ▷ **1** B2 [C or U] material with particular physical characteristics: *an organic/chemical substance* ◦ *What sort of substance could withstand those temperatures?* **2** **illegal substance** formal an illegal drug **IMPORTANCE** ▷ **3** C2 [U] the most important part of what someone has said or written: *Later that year, the substance of their secret conversation appeared in a newspaper article.* **4** [U] importance, seriousness, or relationship to real facts: *There is no substance **in/to** the allegation.* ◦ *This new information **gives** substance **to** the stories we have heard.*

> **Word partners for substance**
>
> a *carcinogenic/dangerous/hazardous/toxic* substance • an *oily/powdery/sticky* substance • a *banned/controlled/illegal/illicit* substance • a *hallucinogenic/mood-altering/performance-enhancing* substance • an *addictive* substance • substance *abuse/misuse*

ˈsubstance aˌbuse **noun** [U] formal the use of a drug to get pleasure, or to improve a person's performance of an activity, or because a person cannot stop using it

substandard /sʌbˈstæn.dəd/ (US) /-dɚd/ **adj** below a satisfactory standard: *substandard housing/accommodation* ◦ *substandard work/goods*

substantial /səbˈstæn.ʃᵊl/ **adj** **LARGE** ▷ **1** B2 large in size, value, or importance: *The findings show a substantial difference between the opinions of men and women.* ◦ *She inherited a substantial fortune from her grandmother.* ◦ *The first draft of his novel needed a substantial amount of rewriting.* **GENERAL** ▷ **2** [before noun] formal relating to the main or most important things being considered: *The committee were in substantial agreement (= agreed about most of the things discussed).*

substantially /səbˈstæn.ʃᵊl.i/ **adv** **LARGE** ▷ **1** C1 to a large degree: *The new rules will substantially change how we do things.* **GENERAL** ▷ **2** generally: *This model has a few extra fittings, but the two cars are substantially the same.*

S

substantiate /səbˈstæn.ʃi.eɪt/ verb [T] formal to show something to be true, or to support a claim with facts: *We have evidence to substantiate the* ***allegations*** *against him.* ◦ *Reports that children had been hurt have not been substantiated.* • **substantiation** /səbˌstæn.ʃiˈeɪ.ʃən/ noun [U] formal *The company produced receipts* ***in*** *substantiation* ***of*** *(= to support) its claim.*

substantive /səbˈstæn.tɪv/ ⓤⓢ /-t̬ɪv/ adj formal important, serious, or related to real facts: *Substantive research on the subject needs to be carried out.* ◦ *The documents are the first substantive information obtained by the investigators.*

substation /ˌsʌbˈsteɪ.ʃən/ noun ELECTRICITY ▷ **electricity substation** a place which allows electricity to go from one part of the electricity production system to another

substitute /ˈsʌb.stɪ.tjuːt/ ⓤⓢ /-tuːt/ verb; noun
▸verb **1** [T] B2 to use something or someone instead of another thing or person: *You can substitute oil* ***for*** *butter in this recipe.* ◦ *Dayton was substituted* ***for*** *Williams in the second half of the match.* **2 substitute for sth** to perform the same job as another thing or to take its place
▸noun [C] **1** B2 a thing or person that is used instead of another thing or person: *Tofu can be used as a meat substitute in vegetarian recipes.* ◦ *Vitamins should not be used as a substitute* ***for*** *a healthy diet.* **2** (informal **sub**) in sports, a player who is used for part of a game instead of another player: *Johnson* ***came on*** *as a substitute towards the end of the match.* ◦ *The manager* ***brought on*** (US also ***sent in***) *another substitute in the final minutes of the game.* **3 there is no substitute for sth** nothing is as good as the stated thing: *You can work from plans of a garden, but there's no substitute for visiting the site yourself.* **4** (also **substitute teacher**, informal **sub**) US for **supply teacher**

substitution /ˌsʌb.stɪˈtjuː.ʃən/ ⓤⓢ /-ˈtuː-/ noun [C or U] C1 the use of one person or thing instead of another: *It looks as though the coach is going to* ***make a*** *substitution (= change one player for another in the game).*

substrate /ˈsʌb.streɪt/ noun [C] specialized **1** a substance or surface which an organism grows and lives on and is supported by **2** a substance which an ENZYME (= chemical made by living cells) acts on to produce a chemical reaction

substructure /ˈsʌbˌstrʌk.tʃər/ ⓤⓢ /-tʃɚ/ noun [C] a firm structure which supports something built on top of it: *The explosion damaged the bridge, but the substructure remained intact.*

subsume /səbˈsjuːm/ ⓤⓢ /-ˈsuːm/ verb [T] formal to include something or someone as part of a larger group: *Soldiers from many different countries have been subsumed* ***into*** *the United Nations peace-keeping force.* ◦ *All the statistics have been subsumed* ***under*** *the general heading 'Facts and Figures'.*

subtenant /ˌsʌbˈten.ənt/ noun [C] a person who rents a building or part of a building from someone who is renting it from the owner

subterfuge /ˈsʌb.tə.fjuːdʒ/ ⓤⓢ /-tɚ-/ noun [C or U] a trick or a dishonest way of achieving something: *It was clear that they must have obtained the information by subterfuge.*

subterranean /ˌsʌb.tərˈeɪ.ni.ən/ ⓤⓢ /-təˈreɪ-/ adj under the ground: *subterranean passages* ◦ *a subterranean river*

subtext /ˈsʌb.tekst/ noun [C] a hidden or less obvious meaning: *The political subtext of her novel is a criticism of government interference in individual lives.*

subtitle /ˈsʌbˌtaɪ.tl/ ⓤⓢ /-t̬l/ noun **1** [C] a word, phrase, or sentence that is used as the second part of a book title and is printed under the main title at the front of the book **2 subtitles** C1 [plural] words shown at the bottom of a film or television picture to explain what is being said: *The Chinese film was shown with English subtitles.* ◦ *The evening news has subtitles for the deaf.* • **subtitled** /-tld/ ⓤⓢ /-t̬ld/ adj *a subtitled film/programme*

subtle /ˈsʌt.əl/ ⓤⓢ /ˈsʌt̬-/ adj approving **1** C2 not loud, bright, noticeable, or obvious in any way: *The room was painted a subtle shade of pink.* ◦ *The play's message is perhaps too subtle to be understood by young children.* **2** small but important: *There is a subtle difference between these two plans.* **3** C2 achieved in a quiet way that does not attract attention to itself and is therefore good or clever: *a subtle plan/suggestion* ◦ *subtle questions* • **subtly** /-li/ adv *This discovery had subtly* ***changed/altered*** *the way I thought about myself.*

subtlety /ˈsʌt.l̩.ti/ ⓤⓢ /ˈsʌt̬.l̩.t̬i/ noun approving **1** [U] the quality of being subtle: *Listening to the interview, I was impressed by the subtlety of the questions.* **2** [C] a small but important detail: *All the subtleties of the music are conveyed in this new recording.*

subtotal /ˈsʌbˌtəʊ.təl/ ⓤⓢ /-ˌtoʊ.t̬əl/ noun [C] the total of one set of numbers to which other numbers will be added: *You have to add the cost of postage to the subtotal.*

subtract /səbˈtrækt/ verb [T] to remove a number from another number: *Four subtracted* ***from*** *ten equals six.* → Compare **add, divide, multiply**

subtraction /səbˈtræk.ʃən/ noun [U] the process of removing one number from another: *The test involves simple calculations, such as addition and subtraction.*

subtropical /ˌsʌbˈtrɒp.ɪ.kəl/ ⓤⓢ /-ˈtrɑː.pɪ-/ adj belonging to or relating to parts of the world that are immediately south or north of the TROPICS (= the hottest areas) and have very hot weather at some times of the year: *a subtropical climate* ◦ *Subtropical regions are cooler than equatorial regions.*

the subtropics /sʌbˈtrɒp.ɪks/ ⓤⓢ /-ˈtrɑː.pɪks/ noun [plural] specialized the parts of the world that are immediately south or north of the TROPICS and have very hot weather at some times of year

suburb /ˈsʌb.ɜːb/ ⓤⓢ /-ɝːb/ noun **1** B2 [C] an area on the edge of a large town or city where people who work in the town or city often live: *Box Hill is a suburb of Melbourne.* ◦ *We drove from middle-class suburbs to a very poor inner-city area.* **2 the suburbs** [plural] the outer area of a town, rather than the shopping and business centre in the middle: *The company decided to relocate to the suburbs because the rent was much cheaper.*

suburban /səˈbɜː.bən/ ⓤⓢ /-ˈbɝː-/ adj **1** relating to a suburb: *suburban schools/housing* ◦ *They live in suburban Washington.* **2** disapproving used to suggest that something is boring and has no excitement: *suburban life*

suburbanite /səˈbɜː.bə.naɪt/ ⓤⓢ /-ˈbɝː-/ noun [C] US a person who lives in the suburbs of a large town or city

suburbia /səˈbɜː.bi.ə/ ⓤⓢ /-ˈbɝː-/ noun [U] mainly disapproving **1** the outer parts of a town, where there are houses, but no large shops, places of work, or places of entertainment: *They live in a two-bedroomed house in the heart of suburbia.* **2** the way of life of people who live in the outer parts of a town: *He has written a book about middle-class suburbia.*

subversion /səbˈvɜː.ʃən/ ⓤⓢ /-ˈvɝː-/ noun [U] formal the act of trying to destroy or damage an established

S

system or government: *He was found guilty of subversion and imprisoned.*

subversive /səbˈvɜː.sɪv/ (US) /-ˈvɝː-/ adj formal trying to destroy or damage something, especially an established political system: *subversive elements/groups in society* ◦ *subversive ideas/influences* • **subversively** /-li/ adv • **subversiveness** /-nəs/ noun [U]

subvert /səbˈvɜːt/ (US) /-ˈvɝːt/ verb [T] formal to try to destroy or damage something, especially an established political system: *The rebel army is attempting to subvert the government.* ◦ *Our best intentions are sometimes subverted by our natural tendency to selfishness.*

subway /ˈsʌb.weɪ/ noun [C] **PASSAGE** ▷ **1** B2 UK an underground passage which allows people on foot to cross a busy road **RAILWAY** ▷ **2** A1 mainly US a railway system in which electric trains travel along passages below ground: *We took the subway uptown to Yankee Stadium.*

sub-ˈzero adj Sub-zero temperatures are temperatures below zero degrees.

succeed /səkˈsiːd/ verb **ACHIEVE SOMETHING** ▷ **1** B1 [I] If you succeed, you achieve something that you have been aiming for, and if a plan or piece of work succeeds, it has the results that you wanted: *She's been trying to pass her driving test for six years and she's finally succeeded.* ◦ *You need to be pretty tough to succeed **in** the property world.* ◦ *The campaign has certainly succeeded **in** raising public awareness of the issue.* ◦ humorous *Richard succeeded **in** offending (= managed unintentionally to offend) just about everybody in the room!*

> **!** Common mistake: **succeed**
>
> **Remember: succeed** is usually followed by the preposition **in**.
>
> Don't say 'succeed something', say **succeed in something**:
>
> ~~*I hope you will succeed your new job.*~~
>
> *I hope you will succeed in your new job.*
>
> When **succeed in** is followed by a verb, that verb is usually in the **-ing** form:
>
> Don't say 'succeed to do something' or 'succeed doing something', say **succeed in doing something**:
>
> *They finally succeeded in catching the killer.*

FOLLOW ▷ **2** [I or T] to take an official job or position after someone else: *He succeeded his father **as** editor of the paper.* ◦ *When the Queen dies, her eldest son will succeed **to** the throne.* **3** to come after another person or thing in time: *In the weeks that succeeded, five more patients showed similar symptoms.* ◦ *Almost from its beginnings, New York has produced succeeding generations of intellectuals.*

S

success /səkˈses/ noun **1** B1 [U] the achieving of the results wanted or hoped for: *The success of almost any project depends largely on its manager.* ◦ *I've been trying to persuade her to take on more staff, but so far **without** success.* ◦ *I'm not **having** much success **in** communicating with him at the moment.* ◦ *The success **rate** for this operation is very low.* **2** B1 [C] something that achieves positive results: *Both films have been a big box-office success in this country.* ◦ *She's determined to make a success of this project.* ◦ *That salmon dish was a success, wasn't it?*

successful /səkˈses.fəl/ adj **1** B1 achieving the results wanted or hoped for: *a successful operation* ◦ *My second attempt at making flaky pastry was a bit more successful.* ◦ *This year's harvest was one of the most successful since the record crop of 1985.* → Opposite **unsuccessful** **2** B2 having achieved a lot, become popular, and/or made a lot of money: *a successful career* ◦ *She runs a very successful computer business.* ◦ *He's the author of several **hugely** successful children's books (= books which have been bought by a lot of people).* ◦ *The Birmingham Royal Ballet has had a highly successful season.* → Opposite **unsuccessful** • **successfully** /-i/ adv B2 *A number of patients have been successfully treated with the new drug.*

> **!** Common mistake: **successful**
>
> **Warning:** Check your spelling!
>
> **Successful** is one of the 50 words most often spelled wrongly by learners. Remember: the correct spelling has 'cc' and 'ss', but only one 'l'.

> **!** Common mistake: **successful**
>
> **Warning:** Common word-building error!
>
> Adjectives which end in the suffix **-ful** have only one 'l'. Don't write 'successfull', write **successful**.

succession /səkˈseʃ.ən/ noun **1** [S] a number of similar events or people that happen, exist, etc. after each other: *A succession **of** scandals and revelations has undermined the government over the past year.* ◦ *Life was just an endless succession **of** parties and dinners.* **2 in succession** happening one after another: *She had her first three children in **rapid** succession.* ◦ *This is the seventh year in succession that they've won the cup.* **3** [U] a process in which someone automatically takes an official position or job after someone else: *Divorce would not prevent the Prince of Wales's succession **to** the throne.* ◦ *Who comes after the vice-president in the presidential **line of** succession?*

successive /səkˈses.ɪv/ adj [before noun] C2 happening one after the other without any break: *It was the team's fourth successive defeat.* ◦ *He won the World Championship for the third successive year.* • **successively** /-li/ adv *Since the championship began, they have finished successively ninth, seventh, and fifth.*

successor /səkˈses.əʳ/ (US) /-ɚ/ noun [C] C1 someone or something that comes after another person or thing: *The university is seeking a successor **to** its vice chancellor, who retires this Easter.* ◦ *This range of computers is very fast, but their successors will be even faster.*

sucˈcess ˌstory noun [C] something or someone that achieves great success, often by making a lot of money: *Angela Black's biscuit company is a rare success story in these times of recession.*

succinct /səkˈsɪŋkt/ adj approving said in a clear and short way; expressing what needs to be said without unnecessary words: *Keep your letter succinct and to the point.* • **succinctly** /-li/ adv *I thought she expressed her feelings most succinctly in the meeting.* • **succinctness** /-nəs/ noun [U]

succour /ˈsʌk.əʳ/ (US) /-ɚ/ noun; verb

▸**noun** [U] UK literary (US **succor**) help given to someone, especially someone who is suffering or in need: *Her organization **gave** succour and strength **to** those who had been emotionally damaged.*

▸**verb** [T] UK literary (US **succor**) to help someone, especially someone who is suffering or in need: *to succour the poor, help the helpless, support the weak*

succulent /ˈsʌk.jʊ.lənt/ adj; noun

▸**adj** approving Succulent food is pleasantly JUICY: *a succulent peach.* ◦ *a big piece of succulent steak* • **succulence** /-ləns/ noun [U]

▸**noun** [C] specialized a plant such as a CACTUS in which the leaves and stem are thick and can store a lot of water: *Succulents often have thick waxy cuticles to minimize water loss.*

succumb /səˈkʌm/ verb [I] formal **1** C2 to lose the determination to oppose something; to accept defeat: *The town finally succumbed last week after being pounded with heavy artillery for more than two months.* ◦ *I'm afraid I succumbed **to** temptation and had a piece of cheesecake.* ◦ *I felt sure it would only be a matter of time before he succumbed **to** my charms.* **2** C2 to die or suffer badly from an illness: *Thousands of cows have succumbed **to** the disease in the past few months.*

such /sʌtʃ/ **predeterminer, determiner, pronoun 1** A2 used before a noun or noun phrase to add emphasis: *That's such a good film.* ◦ *It seems like such a long way to drive for just one day.* ◦ *Oh Richard, you're such an idiot!* ◦ *Such cruelty really is beyond my comprehension.* ◦ *I'd put on such a lot of weight **that** I couldn't get into my trousers.*

> **!** Common mistake: **such**
>
> **Remember:** when it refers to a singular countable noun, **such** is followed by **a** or **an**.
>
> Don't say 'such person/event/situation', say **such a person, event, situation:**
>
> ~~*We had such good holiday in Greece last year.*~~
>
> *We had such a good holiday in Greece last year.*

2 B2 of a particular or similar type: *Small companies such **as** ours are very vulnerable in a recession.* ◦ *I'm looking for a cloth for cleaning silver. Do you have such **a thing**?* ◦ *Present on this grand occasion were Andrew Davies, Melissa Peters, and other such stars.* ◦ *I tried to tell her in such **a way that** she wouldn't be offended.* ◦ *He said it was an Edwardian washstand or **some** such thing – I can't remember exactly.* ◦ old-fashioned informal *I just bought one or two things – bread and milk **and** such* (also ***suchlike***). ◦ formal *Our lunch was such (= of a type) that we don't really need an evening meal.* **3 such as** A2 for example: *That sum of money is to cover costs such as travel and accommodation.* **4 as such** in the true or exact meaning of the word or phrase: *There wasn't much vegetarian food as such, although there were several different types of cheese.* ◦ *We don't have a secretary as such, but we do have a student who comes in to do a bit of filing.*

IDIOMS **such as it is** used to suggest that something you have referred to is of low quality or not enough: *You're welcome to borrow my tennis racket, such as it is.* • **such is life** used to refer to an event that has happened and that you must accept, because you know that this is the way life is: *So here I am, without a girlfriend again. Oh well, such is life.* • **there's no such thing/person (as)** B2 used to say that something or someone does not exist: *There's no such thing as ghosts!*

ˈsuch and ˌsuch adj informal used to refer to something which you do not want to name or say exactly: *If they tell you to arrive at such and such a time, just get there a couple of minutes early.*

suchlike /ˈsʌtʃ.laɪk/ **determiner, pronoun** things of that type: *There's a shop in the hospital where they sell flowers and chocolates and suchlike.*

suck /sʌk/ verb; noun

▸verb **PULL IN** ▷ **1** C2 [I or T] to pull in liquid or air through your mouth without using your teeth, or to move the tongue and muscles of the mouth around something inside your mouth, often in order to dissolve it: *She was sitting on the grass sucking lemonade through a straw.* ◦ *I sucked my **thumb** until I was seven.* ◦ *I tried sucking (**on**) a mint to stop myself coughing.* **2** [T + adv/prep] Something that sucks a liquid or an object in a particular direction pulls it with great force: *The waves came crashing over my head and I could feel myself being sucked under by the currents.* ◦ figurative *Continued rapid growth in consumer spending will suck **in** (= encourage) more imports.* **BE BAD** ▷ **3** [I] slang If someone or something sucks, they are bad or unpleasant: *Man, this job sucks!* ◦ *While my brother was sick, I had to do all of his chores and it sucked.*

IDIOMS **suck it and see** UK informal to try something to find out if it will be successful: *I'm not sure whether this paint is the right colour for the bedroom – we'll just have to suck it and see.*

PHRASAL VERBS **suck sb/sth in/suck sb/sth into sth** [M often passive] to cause someone or something to gradually become involved in an unpleasant situation or harmful activity: *I really don't want any part in this whole argument, but I can feel myself being sucked into it.* • **suck sb off** offensive to use the tongue, lips, and mouth on someone's sexual organs to give them pleasure • **suck up to sb** informal disapproving to try to make someone who is in authority approve of you by doing and saying things that will please them: *'Why do you think he offered to take all that work home?' 'Ah, he's just sucking up to the boss.'*

▸noun [C usually singular] the action of sucking something: *Can I have a suck of your lollipop, please?*

sucker /ˈsʌk.əʳ/ US /-ɚ/ **noun; verb**

▸noun **STICKING DEVICE** ▷ **1** [C] something that helps an animal or object to stick to a surface: *The leech has a sucker at each end of its body.* **2** informal for **suction cup PLANT PART** ▷ **3** [C] specialized a new growth on an existing plant that develops under the ground from the root or the main stem, or from the stem below a GRAFT (= part where a new plant has been joined on) **FOOLISH PERSON** ▷ **4** [C] informal disapproving a person who believes everything they are told and is therefore easy to deceive: *You didn't actually believe him when he said he had a yacht, did you? Oh, Annie, you sucker!* **5 be a sucker for sth** informal to like something so much that you cannot refuse it or judge its real value: *I have to confess I'm a bit of a sucker **for** musicals.* **THING/PERSON** ▷ **6** [C] US informal used to refer to a thing or person that is unpleasant or difficult: *I've been working on that paper for weeks and almost have the sucker finished.* ◦ *He's a nasty little sucker, isn't he?* **SWEET** ▷ **7** [C] US informal for **lollipop**

▸verb

PHRASAL VERB **sucker sb into sth** US informal to persuade someone to do something by deceiving them: [+ -ing verb] *We were suckered into doing the job for free.*

suckle /ˈsʌk.l̩/ verb [I or T] to feed a baby, especially a baby animal, with milk from the organ in the mother that produces milk, or (of a baby, especially a baby animal) to drink milk from the mother: *We watched the cow suckling her calves.* ◦ *The puppies went back to their mother to suckle.*

suckling /ˈsʌk.lɪŋ/, /ˈ-l̩.ɪŋ/ **noun** [C], **adj** [before noun] old-fashioned (an animal that is) still young enough to be drinking milk from its mother: *The main course of the feast was roast suckling pig.*

sucrose /ˈsuː.krəʊz/ US /-kroʊs/ **noun** [U] specialized the type of sugar that exists naturally in most plants that grow on land

suction /ˈsʌk.ʃᵊn/ **noun** [U] the act of removing air from a space resulting in a lower pressure in that space, either causing liquid, gases, or other substances to enter, or causing two surfaces to stick together: *a suction pump*

ˈsuction ˌcup noun [C] (UK also **sucker**) a circular piece of rubber which sticks to surfaces when pressed against them

sudden /ˈsʌd.ən/ adj B2 happening or done quickly and without warning: *Drop the gun, put your hands in the air, and don't make any sudden movements.* ◦ *He had a sudden heart attack while he was on holiday.* ◦ *First they announce their engagement and then they tell me Angie's pregnant – it's all a bit sudden really.* • **suddenness** /-nəs/ noun [U] *It was the suddenness of his illness that came as such a shock.*

IDIOM **all of a sudden** informal B2 very quickly: *It seemed to happen all of a sudden – I felt dizzy and I just collapsed.*

ˌsudden ˈdeath noun [U] (in some sports) a rule that the first person or team to score after a particular time will win the game: *With the score tied after extra time, the game went to sudden death.*

ˌsudden infant ˈdeath ˌsyndrome noun [U] (abbreviation **SIDS**) a medical condition in which a baby who is sleeping dies suddenly for no obvious reason

suddenly /ˈsʌd.ən.li/ adv B1 quickly and unexpectedly: *'Do you remember much about the accident?' 'No, it all happened so suddenly.'* ◦ *I was just dozing off to sleep when suddenly I heard a scream from outside.* ◦ *I suddenly realized what I'd said, but it was too late.*

sudoku /suˈdɒk.uː/, /suˈdəʊ.kuː/ US /-ˈdɑː.kuː/, /-ˈdoʊ.kuː/ noun [U or C] a number game in which you have to write a number between 1 and 9 in each small box of a 9x9 square

suds /sʌdz/ noun [plural] **1** (also **soapsuds**) the mass of small bubbles that forms on the surface of water that has soap in it **2** US a mass of small bubbles that forms on the surface of any liquid **3** US old-fashioned informal for beer

sudsy /ˈsʌd.zi/ adj US covered in soap bubbles

sue /suː/ verb [I or T] C2 to take legal action against a person or organization, especially by making a legal claim for money because of some harm that they have caused you: *He was so furious about the accusations in the letter that he threatened to sue.* ◦ *She sued the paper **for** (= in order to get) damages after they wrongly described her as a prostitute.* ◦ *She is suing her husband **for** (= in order to get a) divorce.*

S

suede /sweɪd/ noun [U] leather that is slightly rough to touch and is not shiny: *suede shoes*

suet /ˈsuː.ɪt/ noun [U] a type of hard fat used in cooking, taken from around the KIDNEYS of animals such as sheep and cows: *suet **pudding***

suffer /ˈsʌf.əʳ/ US /-ɚ/ verb **FEEL PAIN** ▷ **1** B1 [I] to experience physical or mental pain: *I think he suffered quite a lot when his wife left him.* ◦ *She suffers terribly in the winter when it's cold and her joints get stiff.* ◦ *She's been suffering **from** (= been ill with) cancer for two years.* ◦ *Johnny suffers **from** (= is often ill with) asthma.* ◦ *If you're not happy with it, you should complain. Don't just suffer **in silence** (= without saying anything).* **EXPERIENCE** ▷ **2** B2 [I or T] to experience or show the effects of something bad: *The Democrats suffered a crushing defeat in the last election.* ◦ *25 policemen suffered minor injuries during the protest.* ◦ *The city suffered another **blow** last month with the closure of the local car factory.* ◦ *If you will insist on eating three helpings of dessert, I'm afraid you'll have to suffer **the consequences**!* ◦ [+ obj + -ing verb] *I had to suffer her father moaning for half an hour on the phone last night!* ◦ *When you're working such long hours, it's inevitable that your marriage will start to suffer.* ◦ *Like a lot of his films, it suffers **from** being a bit too long.*

IDIOM **not suffer fools gladly** to have very little patience with people who you think are silly or have stupid ideas

sufferance /ˈsʌf.ər.əns/ US /-ɚ-/ noun **on sufferance** formal with unwilling permission: *He gave me a bed for a couple of nights but I felt I was there on sufferance.*

sufferer /ˈsʌf.ər.əʳ/ US /-ɚ.ɚ/ noun [C] C2 a person who has or often gets a particular illness: *Almost 50 percent of cancer sufferers are treated successfully.* ◦ *A new drug may give new hope to thousands of hay-fever sufferers.*

suffering /ˈsʌf.ər.ɪŋ/ US /-ɚ-/ noun [C or U] B2 physical or mental pain that a person or animal is feeling: *The war will cause widespread human suffering.*

suffice /səˈfaɪs/ verb [I] formal to be enough: *I'm taking £400 – I think that should suffice.*

IDIOM **suffice (it) to say** it is enough to say: *Suffice (it) to say, Mike won't be going to Tina's birthday party after what he said about her to her boss.*

sufficiency /səˈfɪʃ.ən.si/ noun [S] formal an amount of something that is enough for a particular purpose: *'More ham, Mr Fletcher?' 'No thank you – it was delicious, but I've had **a** sufficiency (= I have eaten enough).'*

sufficient /səˈfɪʃ.ənt/ adj B2 enough for a particular purpose: *This recipe should be sufficient **for** five people.* ◦ *It was thought that he'd committed the crime but there wasn't sufficient evidence **to** convict him.* → Opposite **insufficient** • **sufficiently** /-li/ adv C1 *McGeechan has not recovered sufficiently to play in the semifinal tomorrow.* ◦ *The case was sufficiently serious to warrant investigation by the police.*

suffix /ˈsʌf.ɪks/ noun [C] B2 a letter or group of letters added at the end of a word to make a new word: *The suffix '-ness' added to the end of the word 'sweet' forms the word 'sweetness', changing an adjective into a noun.*

suffocate /ˈsʌf.ə.keɪt/ verb [I or T] **DIE** ▷ **1** to (cause someone to) die because they do not have enough OXYGEN: *The report said that the victims had suffocated in the fumes.* ◦ *She suffocated him by holding a pillow over his head.* **PREVENT** ▷ **2** to prevent something or someone from improving or developing in a positive way • **suffocation** /ˌsʌf.əˈkeɪ.ʃən/ noun [U]

suffocating /ˈsʌf.ə.keɪ.tɪŋ/ US /-t̬ɪŋ/ adj **NO AIR** ▷ **1** informal Something that is suffocating makes you feel uncomfortably hot or unable to breathe: *I've got to open the window – it's suffocating in here!* ◦ *suffocating smoke/fumes* **PREVENTING** ▷ **2** preventing something or someone from improving or developing in a positive way: *The book tells the story of a woman escaping from a suffocating marriage.*

suffrage /ˈsʌf.rɪdʒ/ noun [U] the right to vote in an election, especially for REPRESENTATIVES in a parliament or similar organization: *universal suffrage (= the right of all adults to vote)*

suffragette /ˌsʌf.rəˈdʒet/ noun [C] a woman in Britain, Australia, or the US in the early 20th century who was a member of a group that demanded the right of women to vote and that increased knowledge of the subject with a series of public protests

suffragist /ˈsʌf.rə.dʒɪst/ noun [C] someone who

supports suffrage, especially a supporter of the right of women to vote in the early 20th century

suffuse /sə'fju:z/ verb [T often passive] literary to spread through or over something completely: *His voice was low and suffused **with** passion.*

Sufi /'su:.fi/ noun [C] a member of an Islamic religious group that tries to become united with God by living a simple life and by praying and MEDITATING • **Sufic** /-fɪk/ adj (also **Sufi**) *He's a member of a Sufic order.* • **Sufism** /-fi.zᵊm/ noun [U]

sugar /'ʃʊg.əʳ/ (US) /-ɚ/ **noun; exclamation; verb**

▸**noun 1** (A1) [C or U] a sweet substance especially from the plants sugar cane and sugar beet, used to make food and drinks sweet: *I don't take sugar in my coffee, thanks.* ◦ *How many sugars (= spoonfuls or lumps of sugar) do you take in your tea?* **2** [C] specialized any of several types of simple CARBOHYDRATE that dissolves in water: *Glucose and lactose are sugars.* **3** [as form of address] mainly US a friendly way of talking to someone that you know: *Hi, sugar, did you have a good day at school?*

IDIOM **sugar and spice** If you describe someone, especially a woman or a girl, as being sugar and spice, you mean that they are behaving in a kind and friendly way: *She could be **all** sugar and spice when she wanted to be.*

▸**exclamation** polite word for **shit**, used when something annoying happens: *Oh sugar, I've just spilled coffee all down my jacket!*

▸**verb** [T] to put sugar in something: *Oh, I forgot to sugar your coffee.*

'sugar ˌbeet noun [C or U] a plant from whose white root sugar can be produced

'sugar ˌcane noun [U] a tropical plant from whose tall thick stems sugar can be produced

ˌsugar-'coated adj **SWEET** ▷ **1** (of foods or pills) covered with a thin layer of sugar **DECEIVING** ▷ **2** disapproving An announcement or promise that is sugar-coated is intended to seem positive or pleasant, although in fact it will result in something unpleasant or unacceptable. • **'sugar-ˌcoat** verb [T]

'sugar ˌdaddy noun [C] informal a rich and usually older man who buys presents for or gives money to a young person, especially a woman, usually in order to spend time with them or have a sexual relationship with them

ˌsugar-'free adj Sugar-free foods do not contain sugar and usually contain an artificial SWEETENER instead: *sugar-free chewing gum*

ˌsugar (ˌsnap) 'pea noun [C usually plural] UK (US **'snap ˌbean**) a long, thin, green POD, eaten as a vegetable

sugary /'ʃʊg.ᵊr.i/ (US) /-ɚ-/ adj **1** containing sugar: *all those sugary snacks that kids eat* **2** disapproving too good or kind or expressing feelings of love in a way that is not sincere: *It's that sugary smile of his that I can't bear – it makes me want to puke!*

suggest /sə'dʒest/ verb [T] **MENTION** ▷ **1** (B1) to mention an idea, possible plan, or action for other people to consider: *They were wondering where to hold the office party and I suggested the Italian restaurant near the station.* ◦ formal *Might I suggest a white wine with your salmon, sir?* ◦ [+ (that)] *I suggest (**that**) we wait a while before we make any firm decisions.* ◦ *Liz suggested (**that**) I try the shop on Mill Road.* ◦ [+ -ing verb] *I suggested putt**ing** the matter to the committee.* ◦ [+ question word] *Can you suggest **wh**ere I might find a chemist's?* **SHOW/EXPRESS** ▷ **2** (B2) to communicate or show an idea or feeling without stating it directly or giving proof: [+ (that)] *There's no absolute proof, but all the evidence suggests (**that**) he's guilty.* ◦ *Are you suggesting (**that**) I look fat in these trousers?* ◦ *Something about his manner suggested a lack of interest in what we were doing.* **PRODUCE AN IDEA** ▷ **3** formal to produce an idea in the mind: *Does anything suggest **itself**? (= Have you got any ideas about what we should do?)*

> **! Common mistake: suggest**
>
> When **suggest** is followed directly by another verb, that verb cannot be in the infinitive with 'to'.
>
> Do not say 'suggest to do something', say **suggest doing something**:
>
> ~~*I suggest to plan an indoor activity in case it rains.*~~
>
> *I suggest planning an indoor activity in case it rains.*
>
> You can also say **suggest someone does something**:
>
> *I suggest you plan an indoor activity in case it rains.*

suggestible /sə'dʒes.tɪ.bl/ (US) /-tə-/ adj formal disapproving describes someone who is easily influenced by other people's opinions: *The success of advertising proves that we are all **highly** suggestible.*

suggestion /sə'dʒes.tʃᵊn/ noun [C or U] **1** (B1) an idea, plan, or action that is suggested or the act of suggesting it: *I don't know what to wear tonight – do you **have** any suggestions?* ◦ *She **made** some very helpful suggestions but her boss **rejected** them all.* ◦ [+ that] *They didn't like my suggestion **that** we should all share the cost.* ◦ *I have a few favourite restaurants that I tend to go back to, but I'm always **open to** new suggestions (= willing to try new ones that people suggest).* ◦ *I went to the Park Street dentist's **at** Ann's suggestion (= as a result of Ann suggesting it) and I was really impressed.* **2** communication of an idea without stating it directly: *the suggestion of his guilt* **3** a very small amount of something: *a suggestion of an Irish accent*

> **! Common mistake: suggestion**
>
> **Warning:** Choose the right verb!
>
> Don't say 'do a suggestion' or 'give a suggestion', say **make/put forward/offer a suggestion**:
>
> ~~*He did some suggestions about how to improve our service.*~~
>
> *He made some suggestions about how to improve our service.*

> **Word partners for suggestion**
>
> *have* a suggestion • *make/offer/put forward* a suggestion • *accept/act on/welcome* a suggestion • *deny/dismiss/refute/reject* a suggestion • a *constructive/helpful/practical/sensible* suggestion • an *outrageous/ridiculous* suggestion • an *alternative* suggestion • a suggestion *about* sth • *at* sb's suggestion

suggestive /sə'dʒes.tɪv/ adj **SEXUAL** ▷ **1** often used to describe something that makes people think about sex: *Some of his lyrics are rather suggestive.* **GIVE IDEA** ▷ **2** formal If something is suggestive of something else, it makes you think about it: *The amplified sounds are suggestive of dolphins chatting to each other under the sea.* • **suggestively** /-li/ adv

suicidal /ˌsu:.ɪ'saɪ.dᵊl/ adj **DEATH** ▷ **1** People who are suicidal want to kill themselves or are in a mental

S

Other ways of saying suggestion

If someone suggests a plan or action, especially in business, you can use nouns such as **proposal** or **proposition**:

*The **proposal** for a new stadium has been rejected.*

*He wrote to me with a very interesting business **proposition**.*

A suggestion about what to do is sometimes described as a **thought** or **idea**:

*Rebecca has a few **ideas** about how we could improve things.*

*I've had a **thought** about what we might do this summer.*

state in which it is likely that they will try to do so: *Pete was so depressed after his girlfriend left him that I actually thought he was suicidal.* **2** describes behaviour that is likely to result in death: *He took some suicidal risks.* **DEFEAT** ▷ **3** A suicidal act causes the defeat of the person who does it: *It would be suicidal for the prime minister to call an election at a time when he's so unpopular.* • **suicidally** /-i/ **adv**

suicide /ˈsuː.ɪ.saɪd/ **noun DEATH** ▷ **1** B2 [C or U] the act of killing yourself intentionally, or a person who has done this: *to **attempt/commit** suicide* ◦ *The suicide rate among men between the ages of 16 and 25 has risen alarmingly.* ◦ *Many suicides occur in prisons.* → Compare **manslaughter, murder DEFEAT** ▷ **2** [U] any act that has the effect of causing your own defeat: [+ to infinitive] *As a leader he knows that it is political suicide **to** appear indecisive.*

ˈsuicide ˌbomber noun [C] a person who has a bomb hidden on their body and who kills themselves in the attempt to kill others

ˈsuicide ˌpact noun [C] an agreement between two or more people to kill themselves together at the same time

suit /suːt/, /sjuːt/ US /suːt/ **noun; verb**

►**noun SET OF CLOTHES** ▷ **1** A2 [C] a jacket and trousers or a jacket and skirt that are made from the same material: *All the businessmen were wearing pinstripe suits.* ◦ *She wore a dark blue suit.* **2** [C] a set of clothes or a piece of clothing to be worn in a particular situation or while doing a particular activity: *a diving/protective/ski, etc. suit* ◦ *a swimsuit* ◦ *a spacesuit* ◦ *a suit **of** armour* **LEGAL PROBLEM** ▷ **3** [C] (also **lawsuit**) a problem taken to a law court by an ordinary person or an organization rather than the police in order to obtain a legal decision: *He **brought** (US usually **filed**) a $12 million libel suit against the newspaper, claiming his reputation had been damaged.* ◦ *a malpractice/negligence/paternity suit* **PLAYING CARDS** ▷ **4** [C] any of the four types of card in a set of playing cards, each having a different shape printed on it: *The four suits in a pack of cards are hearts, spades, clubs, and diamonds.* **PERSON** ▷ **5** [C often plural] informal disapproving a man who works in an office and wears a suit, especially a man with a high position in a company who is considered not to have human feelings and good ideas

►**verb** [T] **BE RIGHT** ▷ **1** B2 to be right for a particular person, situation, or occasion: *Corn is grown a lot in this area – the soil seems to suit it very well.* ◦ *The city lifestyle seems to suit her – she's certainly looking very well.* **2** B2 (usually of a colour or style of clothes) to make someone look more attractive: *You should wear more red – it suits you.* ◦ *Short skirts don't really suit me – I haven't got the legs for them.* **BE CONVENIENT** ▷ **3** B2 to be convenient and cause the least difficulty for someone: *We could go now or this afternoon – whatever time suits you best.* ◦ *'How about eight o'clock outside the cinema?' 'That suits me **fine**.'*

Common mistake: suit

Remember that **suit** is not followed by a preposition.

Don't say 'suit to/for someone' or 'suit to/for something', say **suit someone/something**:

~~*We need to find a solution that suits to everyone.*~~

We need to find a solution that suits everyone.

IDIOMS **suit yourself!** informal an expression used either humorously or angrily to mean 'do what you want to do': *'I don't think I'll come to the party tonight.' 'All right, suit yourself!'* • **suit sb (right) down to the ground** If something suits someone down to the ground, it suits them perfectly, usually because it is convenient for them: *Part-time work would suit me **right** down to the ground.*

suitable /ˈsuː.tə.bl̩/, /ˈsjuː-/ US /ˈsuː.t̬ə-/ **adj** B1 acceptable or right for someone or something: *The film is suitable **for** children.* ◦ *My mother doesn't like me wearing short skirts to church – she doesn't think they're suitable.* → Opposite **unsuitable** • **suitability** /ˌsuː.təˈbɪl.ɪ.ti/, /ˌsjuː-/ US /ˌsuː.t̬əˈbɪl.ə.t̬i/ **noun** [U] • **suitably** /-bli/ **adv** B2 *a suitably qualified person*

Other ways of saying suitable

A common alternative to 'suitable' is the adjective **appropriate**:

*Is this film **appropriate** for young children?*

*You should bring **appropriate** footwear.*

If an action is suitable for a particular situation, you can use the adjectives **apt** or **fitting**:

*'Unusual', yes, that's a very **apt** description.*

*The promotion was a **fitting** reward for all his hard work.*

The adjective **right** can also be used to show that someone or something is suitable for a particular situation:

*I'm not sure that she's the **right** person for the job.*

*Is this the **right** way to do it?*

If someone or something is very suitable, you can use the adjective **perfect**:

*It's a **perfect** day for a picnic.*

*She'd be **perfect** for the job.*

The expression **in keeping with** is sometimes used when something is suitable for a particular style or tradition:

*The antique desk was very much **in keeping with** the rest of the furniture in the room.*

suitcase /ˈsuːt.keɪs/, /ˈsjuːt-/ US /ˈsuːt-/ **noun** [C] (UK also **case**) A2 a large, rectangular case with a handle for carrying clothes and possessions while travelling: *Have you packed/unpacked your suitcase yet?*

suite /swiːt/ **noun** [C] **SET OF ROOMS** ▷ **1** a set of connected rooms, especially in a hotel: *The singer was interviewed in his **hotel** suite.* ◦ *They've got a whole suite **of** offices on the 34th floor.* **SET OF FURNITURE** ▷ **2** a set of furniture for one room, of matching design and colour: *We're having a new bathroom/bedroom suite fitted at the weekend.* ◦ *I've ordered a new three-piece suite for the living-room.* **MUSIC** ▷ **3** a piece of music with several parts, usually all in the same KEY **COMPUTER** ▷ **4** a set of related SOFTWARE (= computer program) products

suited /ˈsuː.tɪd/, /ˈsjuː-/ US /ˈsuː.t̬ɪd/ **adj 1** C1 right for

S

someone or something: *With her qualifications and experience, she would seem to be ideally suited **to/for** the job.* **2** If two people who have a relationship are suited, they have a good relationship that will probably last, often because they share a lot of interests: *They were never suited (**to each other**) from the start – they've got nothing in common.*

suiting /ˈsuː.tɪŋ/, /ˈsjuːt-/ (US) /ˈsuː.t̬ɪŋ/ noun [U] cloth that is used for making SUITS

suitor /ˈsuː.tər/, /ˈsjuː-/ (US) /ˈsuː.t̬ɚ/ noun [C] **1** literary a man who wants to marry a particular woman: *It's the story of a young woman who can't make up her mind which of her many suitors she should marry.* **2** specialized a person or company who wants to take control of another company: *PJH Corporation said it had been approached by two possible suitors who had submitted bids to buy the company.*

sulfur /ˈsʌl.fər/ (US) /-fɚ/ noun [U] US for **sulphur**

sulk /sʌlk/ verb; noun

▸verb [I] disapproving to be silent and refuse to smile or be pleasant to people because you are angry about something that they have done: *He's sulking in a corner somewhere because I wouldn't let him have a second bar of chocolate.*

▸noun [C] disapproving a period of time when someone refuses to smile or be pleasant because they are angry about something: *If she doesn't get what she wants she **goes into a** sulk just like a child.* ◦ *Jim's in one of his sulks again – just ignore him.* • **sulkiness** /ˈsʌlk.i.nəs/ noun [U] • **sulky** /ˈsʌlk.i/ adj *She brought along a couple of sulky kids who didn't say a word all evening.*

sullen /ˈsʌl.ən/ adj angry and unwilling to smile or be pleasant to people: *His daughters stared back at him with an expression of sullen resentment.* ◦ literary *She looked up at the sullen (= dark and unpleasant) sky and shuddered.* • **sullenly** /-li/ adv *She turned her back to him and stared sullenly out of the window.* • **sullenness** /-nəs/ noun [U]

sully /ˈsʌl.i/ verb [T] formal **1** to spoil something that is pure or someone's perfect reputation: *His reputation, he said, had been unfairly sullied half-truths and innuendos.* **2** to make something dirty: *No speck of dirt had ever sullied his hands.*

sulphate (mainly US **sulfate**) /ˈsʌl.feɪt/ noun [C or U] a chemical formed from sulphur, OXYGEN, and another element

sulphide (mainly US **sulfide**) /ˈsʌl.faɪd/ noun [C or U] a chemical formed from sulphur and another element

sulphur UK (US **sulfur**) /ˈsʌl.fər/ (US) /-fɚ/ noun [U] (symbol **S**) a pale yellow chemical element that exists in various physical forms. It burns with a blue flame and a strong smell and is used in medicine and industry. • **sulphurous** (mainly US **sulfurous**) /-əs/ adj

ˌsulphur diˈoxide noun [U] a gas that has a strong, unpleasant smell and dissolves in water. It is used in various industrial processes, and can cause air POLLUTION.

sulphuric acid (mainly US **sulfuric acid**) /sʌlˌfjʊə.rɪk ˈæs.ɪd/ (US) /-ˌfjʊr.ɪk/ noun [U] a strong ACID with no colour

sultan /ˈsʌl.tən/ noun [C] a ruler, especially in the past, of some Muslim countries: *the Sultan **of** Brunei*

sultana /sʌlˈtɑː.nə/ noun [C] mainly UK (US usually **ˌgolden ˈraisin**) a dried white GRAPE

sultanate /ˈsʌl.tə.nət/ noun [C] a country ruled by a sultan

sultry /ˈsʌl.tri/ adj **WARM** ▷ **1** (of weather) uncomfortably warm and with air that is slightly wet **SEXY** ▷ **2** (especially of a woman's face or voice) sexually attractive in a way that suggests sexual DESIRE: *She's the sultry blonde in that new chocolate commercial.* • **sultriness** /-nəs/ noun [U]

sum /sʌm/ noun; verb

▸noun **AMOUNT OF MONEY** ▷ **1** (B1) [C] an amount of money: *Huge sums **of** money are spent on national defence.* ◦ *He'll get £50,000 from the company when he retires, which is a **tidy** (= large) sum.* ◦ humorous *I worked for three whole weeks for which I received the **princely** (= very low) sum of $100.* **CALCULATION** ▷ **2** [C] a calculation, especially a simple one, using such processes as adding, taking away, multiplying, or dividing: *I remember how much I hated **doing** sums when I was at school.* **TOTAL** ▷ **3** [S] the whole number or amount when two or more numbers or amounts have been added together: *The sum of 13 and 8 is 21.* **4 in sum** formal considered as a whole: *The meeting was, in sum, a disaster.* **5 the sum of sth** all of something: *I'm afraid that's the pitiful sum of my knowledge on the subject!*

IDIOM **get/have your sums right/wrong** mainly UK to calculate the cost of something correctly/wrongly

▸verb (-mm-)

PHRASAL VERBS **sum (sth/sb) up** (B2) to describe or express the important facts or characteristics about something or someone: *The best way of summing up the situation in our office is to say that it is 'absolute chaos'.* ◦ *I'd just like to sum up **by saying** that it's been a tremendous pleasure to work with you.* ◦ *He's a small man with a big ego – that about sums him up, doesn't it?* • **sum sth/sb up 1** An action or object that sums something or someone up represents the most typical qualities of that person or thing: *For me, her paintings sum up the restless spirit of America.* **2** to quickly form an opinion about someone or something: *She summed up the situation quickly and took charge.* • **sum up** When a JUDGE sums up towards the end of a trial, he or she makes a speech to the JURY telling them again of the main matters they should consider in the case.

summarize (UK usually **summarise**) /ˈsʌm.ər.aɪz/ (US) /-ə.raɪz/ verb [I or T] (C1) to express the most important facts or ideas about something or someone in a short and clear form: *I'll just summarize the main points of the argument in a few words if I may.*

summary /ˈsʌm.ər.i/ (US) /-ɚ-/ noun; adj

▸noun [C] (formal **summation**) (B2) a short, clear description that gives the main facts or ideas about something: *At the end of the news, they often give you a summary of the main stories.*

▸adj [before noun] done suddenly, without discussion or legal arrangements: *summary arrest/dismissal/execution* • **summarily** /ˌsʌmˈer.ɪ.li/ adv

summer /ˈsʌm.ər/ (US) /-ɚ/ noun [C or U] (A1) the season of the year between spring and autumn when the weather is warmest, lasting from June to September north of the EQUATOR and from December to March south of the equator: *We have breakfast on the balcony **in** (**the**) summer.* ◦ ***Last** summer they went to Australia, and two summers ago they went to Brazil.* ◦ *That year it was a hot, dry summer.* ◦ *summer weather/sun* ◦ *a summer/summer's day* → See also **Indian summer**

ˈsummer ˌcamp noun [C or U] in the US, a place where children can go, usually to stay, and do activities: *Her children were away at summer camp.*

summerhouse /ˈsʌm.ə.haʊs/ (US) /-ɚ-/ noun [C] **1** a small building in a garden used for sitting in during the summer **2** US a house at the beach or in the mountains that you live in for part or all of the summer

ˈsummer ˌschool noun [C] **1** an educational course that happens during the summer when other courses have finished **2** US one or more educational courses taken during the summer which replace courses that were missed or failed, or which make it possible for students to move more quickly towards a degree or GRADUATION

summertime /ˈsʌm.ə.taɪm/ ⓤⓢ /-ɚ-/ noun [U] the season of summer: *You should see the garden* ***in*** *(****the****) summertime – it's beautiful.*

summery /ˈsʌm.ər.i/ ⓤⓢ /-ɚ-/ adj typical of or suitable for summer: *Clare walked by looking very summery in a pale blue sundress.*

ˌsumming-ˈup noun [C usually singular] a speech made by a JUDGE or lawyer to the JURY towards the end of a trial, telling them again about the main matters they should consider in the case: *The judge referred to this point several times in his summing-up.*

summit /ˈsʌm.ɪt/ noun [C] **MEETING ▷ 1** ⓒ2 an important formal meeting between leaders of governments from two or more countries: *a summit* ***meeting*** ◦ *World leaders will meet next week for their annual economic summit.* **HIGHEST POINT ▷ 2** ⓒ1 the highest point of a mountain: *On this day in 1784, Dr Michel Paccard and Jacques Balmat* ***reached*** *the summit of Mont Blanc.* **3 the summit** the highest, most successful, or most important point in something: *I certainly haven't reached the summit of my career.*

summon /ˈsʌm.ən/ verb [T] **ORDER ▷ 1** ⓒ2 to order someone to come to or be present at a particular place, or to officially arrange a meeting of people: *General Rattigan summoned reinforcements to help resist the attack.* ◦ humorous *I'm afraid I'll have to go – I'm being summoned by my wife.* ◦ *On 20 July, the council was summoned* ***to*** *hear an emergency report on its finances.* **PRODUCE STRENGTH ▷ 2** ⓒ2 to increase your courage or strength, especially with an effort: *It took me six months to summon* ***(up)*** *the* ***courage*** *to ask him out for a drink.*

summons /ˈsʌm.ənz/ noun [C] **1** an order to come and see someone: *I sat outside the boss's office awaiting my summons.* **2** legal an official demand to appear in a law court: *Mr Clarke's insurance company had* ***issued*** *a summons for unpaid mortgage repayments.*

S

sumo wrestling /ˌsuː.məʊˈres.lɪŋ/ ⓤⓢ /-moʊ-/ noun [U] a style of WRESTLING (= a fighting sport) originally from Japan, in which each man tries to defeat the other either by pushing him outside of a special ring or by forcing him to touch the ground with a part of his body other than the bottom part of the foot • **ˈsumo ˌwrestler** noun [C]

sump /sʌmp/ noun [C] a hole or container, especially in the lower part of an engine, into which a liquid that is not needed can flow

sumptuous /ˈsʌmp.tju.əs/ adj LUXURIOUS and showing that you are rich: *The celebrity guests turned up dressed in sumptuous evening gowns.* • **sumptuously** /-li/ adv

ˌsum ˈtotal noun [U] The sum total of something is the whole of it, or everything: *It's the sum total of what you eat over a long period that matters and not what you consume in a day.*

sun /sʌn/ noun; verb

▸noun [S or U] ⓐ1 the star that the Earth moves around, which provides light and heat for the Earth, or the light or heat that the Earth receives from this star: *The sun* ***rises*** *in the east and* ***sets*** *in the west.* ◦ *The sun's rays are at their most powerful at midday.* ◦ *I think I've had a bit too much sun today – I've got a headache.* ◦ *Shall we go and sit out* ***in*** *the sun?* ◦ *We thought we'd go out for a walk while the sun was* ***shining****.*

IDIOMS **everything under the sun** everything that exists or is possible: *I've tried everything under the sun on this stain, but I just can't get rid of it.* • **the sun sets on sth** literary If the sun sets on something, it ends: *It used to be said that Britain ruled an empire on which the sun would never set.* • **think the sun shines out (of) sb's arse/backside** UK offensive to love and admire someone so much that you do not think they have any bad qualities

▸verb **sun yourself** to lie or sit somewhere where there is a lot of sun, especially in order to make your skin darker: *I sat on the balcony sunning myself.*

Sun. written abbreviation for Sunday

ˈsun-baked adj [before noun] An area of land or a place that is sun-baked is very dry and obviously receives a lot of sun: *We strolled along the sun-baked streets of Naples.*

sunbathe /ˈsʌn.beɪð/ verb [I] ⓑ1 to sit or lie in the sun in order to make your skin darker: *I like to sunbathe in the morning when the sun is not so hot.* • **sunbathing** /-ˌbeɪ.ðɪŋ/ noun [U] *the risks associated with sunbathing*

sunbeam /ˈsʌn.biːm/ noun [C] UK (US **sunray**) a beam of light from the sun that you can see

sunbed /ˈsʌn.bed/ noun [C] UK (US **ˈtanning ˌbed**) a structure like a bed containing a device for producing light, which you lie on in order to make the skin go darker

the Sunbelt /ˈsʌn.belt/ noun [S] the southern part of the US: *The Sunbelt stretches from Florida to southern California.*

sunblind /ˈsʌn.blaɪnd/ noun [C] Australian English a cloth or plastic cover fastened to a building or structure and supported by a frame, used to protect someone or something from the sun or rain → Compare **awning**

sunblock /ˈsʌn.blɒk/ ⓤⓢ /-blɑːk/ noun [U] **sunscreen**

sunburn /ˈsʌn.bɜːn/ ⓤⓢ /-bɝːn/ noun [U] a condition in which your skin is sore and red because you have spent too long in the strong heat of the sun → Compare **suntan**

sunburned (also **sunburnt**) /ˈsʌn.bɜːnd/ ⓤⓢ /-bɝːnd/ adj describes the condition of skin that has become red and sore by being in the strong heat of the sun for too long, or that is very SUNTANNED: *When you go out in the hot sun, you should always put cream on your skin to avoid getting sunburned.* ◦ *Fishermen with sunburned faces sat on the beach mending their nets.*

sundae /ˈsʌn.deɪ/ noun [C] a food made from ice cream, with pieces of fruit, nuts, cream, sweet sauce, etc. on top of it

Sunday /ˈsʌn.deɪ/ noun [C or U] (written abbreviation **Sun.**) ⓐ1 the day of the week after Saturday and before Monday, when most people in Western countries do not go to work: *We're going to visit my aunt and uncle* ***on*** *Sunday.* ◦ *They go to church* ***on*** *Sundays.* ◦ *The choir is giving a concert* ***next*** *Sunday.* ◦ *I haven't done any exercise since* ***last*** *Sunday.* ◦ *New Year's Day this year is a Sunday.* ◦ *Sunday* ***morning/afternoon/evening/night*** ◦ *In Britain the traditional Sunday* ***lunch*** *consists of roast meat.*

ˌSunday ˈbest noun **your Sunday best** old-fashioned your best clothes which you wear on special occasions

ˌSunday ˈdriver noun [C] disapproving someone who drives too slowly, often annoying other drivers

ˌSunday ˈpaper noun [C] (UK also **Sunday**) a newspaper that is sold on Sundays and is usually bigger than newspapers sold on other days, often having several parts

ˈSunday ˌschool noun [C usually singular] a class held on Sundays in which especially Christian children are given religious teaching

ˈsun deck noun [C] a part of a ship or a flat area next to or on the roof of a house where you can sit and enjoy the sun

sundial /ˈsʌn.daɪl/ noun [C] a device used outside, especially in the past, which consists of a thin piece of metal fixed to a flat surface printed with numbers. It shows the time by the metal making a dark line on the surface as the sun moves across the sky.

sundown /ˈsʌn.daʊn/ noun [U] the time in the evening when you last see the sun in the sky: *We left early, anxious to make it back to Florence **before/by** sundown.*

ˈsun-drenched adj [before noun] A place that is sun-drenched receives a lot of sun: *sun-drenched beaches*

sundress /ˈsʌn.dres/ noun [C] an informal dress without sleeves that is worn in hot weather

ˈsun-dried adj [before noun] describes vegetables that have been dried by leaving them in the sun so that their flavour becomes much stronger: *sun-dried tomatoes*

sundries /ˈsʌn.driz/ noun [plural] various different small things that are considered together, usually because they are not important enough to be considered separately: *There's an item on the hotel bill for sundries.*

sundry /ˈsʌn.dri/ adj [before noun] formal several different; various: *Sundry distant relatives, most of whom I hardly recognized, turned up for my brother's wedding.*

IDIOMS **all and sundry** mainly UK informal everyone: *I don't want all and sundry knowing about our problems.* • **various and sundry** mainly US informal many different: *He spent an hour telling me about various and sundry ideas he has for making money.*

sunflower /ˈsʌnˌflaʊəʳ/ (US) /-ˌflaʊr/ noun [C] a plant, usually having a very tall stem and a single large, round, flat, yellow flower, with many long, thin, narrow PETALS close together

sung /sʌŋ/ verb past participle of **sing**

sunglasses /ˈsʌŋˌglɑː.sɪz/ (US) /ˈsʌnˌglæs.ɪz/ noun [plural] (also ˌ**dark** ˈ**glasses**, informal **shades**) A2 dark glasses which you wear to protect your eyes from bright light from the sun: *a **pair of** sunglasses*

ˈsun god noun [C] a god who represented the sun in some ancient religions

ˈsun ˌhat noun [C] a hat to protect your head from the sun

sunk /sʌŋk/ verb past simple and past participle of **sink**

sunken /ˈsʌŋ.kən/ adj **1** having fallen to the bottom of the sea: *They're diving for sunken **treasure**.* **2** at a lower level than the surrounding area: *It was a luxurious bathroom, with a sunken bath.* **3** (of eyes or cheeks) seeming to have fallen further into the face, especially because of tiredness, illness, or old age: *She looked old and thin with sunken cheeks and hollow eyes.*

ˈsun-kissed adj [before noun] describes a place that receives a lot of sun, or a person whose appearance is attractive because they have recently been in the sun

sunlamp /ˈsʌn.læmp/ noun [C] a device that produces ULTRAVIOLET light, used for getting a SUNTAN: *She spends several hours a week **under** a sunlamp to keep her skin looking tanned.*

sunless /ˈsʌn.ləs/ adj literary without any sun: *It was a grey and sunless day and our spirits were low.*

sunlight /ˈsʌn.laɪt/ noun [U] B2 the light that comes from the sun: *a ray/beam/shaft/pool of sunlight* ◦ *The morning/afternoon/evening sunlight shone through the curtains.* ◦ *The lake sparkled **in** the bright sunlight.*

sunlit /ˈsʌn.lɪt/ adj (of a room, etc.) receiving a lot of light from the sun: *a sunlit room/courtyard/patio*

ˈsun ˌlotion noun [C or U] **sunscreen**

Sunni /ˈsʊn.i/ adj, noun [C] (a member) of the largest Islamic religious group, which follows the teachings only of Mohammed, not those of any of the religious leaders who came after him: *a Sunni Muslim*

sunnies /ˈsʌn.iz/ noun [plural] informal **sunglasses**

sunny /ˈsʌn.i/ adj **BRIGHT** ▷ **1** A2 bright because of light from the sun: *We're having the party in the garden, so I'm praying it'll be sunny.* **HAPPY** ▷ **2** describes someone who is usually happy and relaxed and does not usually get worried or angry: *She has a very sunny disposition.*

sunray /ˈsʌn.reɪ/ noun [C] US for **sunbeam**

sunrise /ˈsʌn.raɪz/ noun **1** B1 [U] (US informal also ˈ**sun-up**) the time in the morning when the sun starts to rise in the sky: *They went out **at** sunrise to go bird-watching.* ◦ *We have to leave before sun-up tomorrow.* **2** B1 [C] the appearance of the sky when the sun starts to rise: *There was a beautiful sunrise this morning.*

sunroof /ˈsʌn.ruːf/ noun [C] part of a roof of a car that can be opened to allow air and light from the sun to come in

sunroom /ˈsʌn.rʊm/ noun [C] a room with a lot of windows that is designed so that a lot of sun comes in

sunscreen /ˈsʌn.skriːn/ noun [C or U] (also **sunblock**) a substance that you put on your skin to prevent it from being burned by the sun

sunset /ˈsʌn.set/ noun **1** B1 [U] the time in the evening when you last see the sun in the sky: *The fishermen set out **at sunset** for a night's fishing.* **2** B1 [C] the appearance of the sky in the evening before the sun goes down: *We sat on the beach watching a spectacular sunset.*

IDIOM **ride, drive, walk, etc. (off) into the sunset** to begin a new, happy life at the end of a story: *At the end of the film, the pair of them ride off into the sunset.*

sunshade /ˈsʌn.ʃeɪd/ noun [C] **1** an object similar to an UMBRELLA that you carry to protect yourself from light from the sun **2** (US also **umbrella**) a larger folding frame of this type that you put into the ground to form an area that is sheltered from the light of the sun **3** US for **awning**

sunshine /ˈsʌn.ʃaɪn/ noun [U] **LIGHT** ▷ **1** B1 the light and heat that come from the sun: *The children were out playing **in** the sunshine.* **PLEASURE** ▷ **2** informal happiness or pleasure: *Their grandchildren have **brought** sunshine into their lives.* **3** mainly UK informal used as a form of address, either in a friendly way, or to express unwillingness to accept another person's delays, bad behaviour, etc.: *Hello, sunshine!* ◦ *Come on, sunshine, get a move on.*

sunspot /ˈsʌn.spɒt/ (US) /-spɑːt/ noun [C] a dark spot on the surface of the sun which appears for a few days or weeks and then disappears

sunstroke /ˈsʌn.strəʊk/ (US) /-stroʊk/ noun [U] an illness caused by spending too much time in strong

S

heat and light from the sun: *Someone who is suffering from sunstroke feels dizzy and has a high temperature, but does not sweat.*

suntan /ˈsʌn.tæn/ noun [C] (also **tan**) pleasantly brown skin caused by being in hot sun: *She's on the beach all day, trying to get a really deep suntan.* → Compare **sunburn** • **suntanned** /-tænd/ adj (also **tanned**) *suntanned arms*

suntrap /ˈsʌn.træp/ noun [C] UK a room or place that receives a lot of light and heat from the sun

sunup /ˈsʌn.ʌp/ noun [U] US for **sunrise**

ˈsun ˌvisor noun [C] (also **visor**) a flat piece at the top of the front window of a vehicle which protects the driver's eyes from strong sun

ˈsun-ˌworshipper noun [C] someone who enjoys lying in the sun

sup /sʌp/ verb [I usually + adv/prep, T] (**-pp-**) mainly UK to drink or to eat: Northern English *He spends most of his evenings in the pub, supping beer.* ◦ old-fashioned *They supped **on/off** cold meat.*

super /ˈsuː.pəʳ/ (US) /-pɚ/ **adj; noun**

▸adj old-fashioned informal excellent: *The Natural History Museum is a super place for kids.* ◦ *'Did you enjoy the film?' 'Yes, I thought it was super.'*

▸noun **1** [C] UK informal for **superintendent** **2** [U] (also **super petrol**) Australian English the highest quality LEADED fuel that can be used in cars → Compare **four-star** **3** [U] Australian English informal for **superannuation**

super- /suː.pəʳ-/ (US) /-pɚ-/ prefix **MORE THAN USUAL** ▷ **1** larger, more effective, more powerful, or more successful than usual; very or more than usually: *a supercomputer* ◦ *a supermodel* ◦ *the super-rich* ◦ *superfine stockings* **OVER** ▷ **2** over; above: *a superstructure*

superabundant /ˌsuː.pəʳ.əˈbʌn.dənt/ (US) /-pɚ-/ adj existing in very large amounts: *Grapes and olives are superabundant in this part of France.* • **superabundance** /-dəns/ noun [S]

superannuated /ˌsuː.pəʳˈæn.ju.eɪ.tɪd/ (US) /-pɚˈæn.ju.eɪ.t̬ɪd/ adj formal old, and almost no longer suitable for work or use

superannuation /ˌsuː.pəʳˌæn.juˈeɪ.ʃən/ (US) /-pɚ-/ noun [U] mainly UK money which people pay while they are working, so that they will receive payment when they stop working when they are old, or the payment they receive when they stop working

S

superb /suːˈpɜːb/ (US) /-ˈpɝːb/ adj (B2) of excellent quality; very great: *He is a superb dancer.* ◦ *Taylor scored a superb goal at the end of the first half.* • **superbly** /-li/ adv *The orchestra played superbly.*

ˈSuper ˌBowl noun [C usually singular] in the US, a game of American football played each year between the winners of the two football LEAGUES (= groups) in order to decide which is the best team in the country

superbug /ˈsuː.pə.bʌɡ/ (US) /-pɚ-/ noun [C] a type of bacteria that causes an illness that cannot be cured by ANTIBIOTICS

supercharge /ˈsuː.pə.tʃɑːdʒ/ (US) /-pɚ.tʃɑːrdʒ/ verb [T] to make an engine more powerful by forcing in more air and fuel than usual

supercharged /ˈsuː.pə.tʃɑːdʒd/ (US) /-pɚ.tʃɑːrdʒd/ adj informal **FAST** ▷ **1** very fast or energetic: *The economy has expanded at a supercharged pace.* **EMOTIONAL** ▷ **2** containing or expressing very strong emotions: *There was a supercharged **atmosphere** during the debate in the House of Commons last night.*

supercharger /ˈsuː.pəˌtʃɑː.dʒəʳ/ (US) /-pɚˌtʃɑːr.dʒɚ/ noun [C] a device which produces more power in an engine by forcing more air into the part of it in which fuel burns

supercilious /ˌsuː.pəˈsɪl.i.əs/ (US) /-pɚ-/ adj disapproving behaving as if you are better than other people, and that their opinions, beliefs, or ideas are not important • **superciliously** /-li/ adv • **superciliousness** /-nəs/ noun [U]

superconductor /ˈsuː.pə.kənˌdʌk.təʳ/ (US) /-pɚ.kənˌdʌk.tɚ/ noun [C] a substance, especially a metal, that allows an electrical current to move freely through it at a very low temperature • **superconductivity** /ˌsuː.pə.kɒn.dʌkˈtɪv.ɪ.ti/ (US) /-pɚ.kɑːn.dʌkˈtɪv.ə.t̬i/ noun [U]

superdelegate /ˈsuː.pə.del.ɪ.ɡət/ (US) /ˈsuː.pɚ-/ noun [C] US a DELEGATE to the Democratic National Convention or the Republican National Convention who has not been elected, usually one who has been given the position because they are a party leader or an official

superego /ˌsuː.pəˈriː.ɡəʊ/ (US) /-pɚˈiː.ɡoʊ/ noun [C] (plural **superegos**) specialized in PSYCHOANALYSIS, the part of your mind that knows what is right and what is wrong, and causes you to feel guilty when you do something wrong → Compare **ego, id**

superficial /ˌsuː.pəˈfɪʃ.əl/ (US) /-pɚ-/ adj **NOT SERIOUS** ▷ **1** (C2) disapproving (of a person) never thinking about things that are serious or important: *He's fun to be with, but he's very superficial.* **NOT COMPLETE** ▷ **2** (C2) usually disapproving not complete and involving only the most obvious things: *I thought that article was written at a very superficial level.* ◦ *The documentary's treatment/analysis of the issues was very superficial.* ◦ *I only have a superficial (= slight) knowledge of French.* **FALSE APPEARANCE** ▷ **3** appearing to be real or important when this is not true or correct: *There are superficial similarities between the two cars, but actually they're quite different in terms of performance.* **ONLY ON SURFACE** ▷ **4** only on the surface of something: *superficial damage* ◦ *The driver only received superficial injuries/cuts/wounds.* • **superficiality** /-ˌfɪʃ.iˈæl.ɪ.ti/ (US) /-ˌfɪʃ.iˈæl.ə.t̬i/ noun [U] • **superficially** /-i/ adv (C2) *The job I've been offered is superficially (= seems to be) attractive/appealing, but I think I might find it boring after a while.* ◦ *Religious education is poorly and superficially taught in most schools.*

superfluous /suːˈpɜː.flu.əs/ (US) /-ˈpɝː-/ adj (C2) more than is needed or wanted: *The report was marred by a mass of superfluous detail.* • **superfluity** /ˌsuː.pəˈfluː.ɪ.ti/ (US) /-pɚˈfluː.ə.t̬i/ noun [C] formal • **superfluously** /-li/ adv • **superfluousness** /-nəs/ noun [U]

superfood /ˈsuː.pə.fuːd/ (US) /ˈsuː.pɚ-/ noun [C] a food that is considered to be very good for your health

superglue /ˈsuː.pə.ɡluː/ (US) /-pɚ-/ noun [U] a very strong, quick-drying glue

supergrass /ˈsuː.pə.ɡrɑːs/ (US) /-pɚ.ɡræs/ noun [C] UK a person, especially a criminal, who gives the police a lot of information about the activities of criminals, especially serious ones

superhero /ˈsuː.pəˌhɪə.rəʊ/ (US) /ˈsuː.pɚ-/ noun [C] (plural **superheroes**) **1** a character in a film or story who has special strength and uses it to do good things and help other people **2** someone who has done something very brave to help someone else

superhighway /ˈsuː.pəˌhaɪ.weɪ/ (US) /-pɚ-/ noun [C] US a large, wide road on which traffic travels at high speed

superhuman /ˌsuː.pəˈhjuː.mən/ (US) /-pɚ-/ adj having more powers than, or seeming outside the powers of, a human: *I'll never get all this work done in a week – I'm not superhuman!* ◦ *Thanks to the superhuman* *efforts of local volunteers, aid is now getting through to the disaster areas.*

superimpose /ˌsuː.pə.rɪmˈpəʊz/ US /-pɚ.ɪmˈpoʊz/ **verb** [T] to put especially a picture, words, etc. on top of something else, especially another picture, words, etc., so that what is in the lower position can still be seen, heard, etc.: *The book cover had a picture of a dove superimposed* ***on*** *a battle scene.*

superintend /ˌsuː.pə.rɪnˈtend/ US /-pɚ.ɪn-/ **verb** [T] formal to be in charge of something: *Her job is to superintend the production process.*

superintendent /ˌsuː.pə.rɪnˈten.dənt/ US /-pɚ.ɪn-/ **noun** [C] **1** a person who is in charge of work done in a particular department, office, etc., or who is responsible for keeping a building or place in good condition: *In the US, a school superintendent is in charge of the schools in a particular area.* ◦ *We asked the superintendent* (also US informal ***super***) *to fix the broken window in our apartment.* **2** a British police officer of high rank

superior /suːˈpɪə.ri.əʳ/ US /-ˈpɪr.i.ɚ/ **adj; noun**
▸**adj** **BETTER** ▷ **1** C1 better than average or better than other people or things of the same type: *This is clearly the work of a superior artist.* ◦ *She was chosen for the job because she was the superior candidate.* ◦ *For babies, breastfeeding is superior* ***to*** *bottle-feeding.* ◦ *The government troops were superior* ***in*** *numbers* (= *there were more of them*). → Compare **inferior** **2** C2 disapproving describes someone who believes that they are better than other people and acts in such a way: *a superior manner/smile* ◦ *I can't bear Amanda – she's so superior.* **HIGHER** ▷ **3** higher in rank or social position than others: *The soldier was reported to his superior officer for failing in his duties.*
▸**noun** [C] C1 a person or group of people who are higher in rank or social position than others: *I will pass your complaint on to my superiors.*

superiority /suːˌpɪə.riˈɒr.ɪ.ti/ US /-ˌpɪr.iˈɔːr.ə.t̬i/ **noun** [U] **BETTER** ▷ **1** C2 the fact that one person or thing is better, stronger, etc. than another: *The Australian team soon demonstrated their superiority* ***over*** *the opposition.* → Compare **inferiority** **2** C2 an unpleasant way of behaving that a person has when they think they are better than other people: *Her sense of superiority makes her very unpopular.* **HIGHER** ▷ **3** the state of being of a higher rank or social position than others

superlative /suːˈpɜː.lə.tɪv/ US /-ˈpɝː.lə.t̬ɪv/ **noun; adj**
▸**noun** [C] A2 the form of an adjective or adverb which expresses that the thing or person being described has more of the particular quality than anything or anyone else of the same type: *'Richest' is* ***the*** *superlative* ***of*** *'rich'.* ◦ *The magazine article contained so many superlatives that I found it hard to believe that what it was saying was true.*
▸**adj** **BEST** ▷ **1** of the highest quality; the best: *We went to a superlative restaurant.* **GRAMMAR** ▷ **2** relating to the superlative of an adjective or adverb

superlatively /suːˈpɜː.lə.tɪv.li/ US /-ˈpɝː.lə.t̬ɪv-/ **adv** extremely: *The company has been superlatively successful this year.*

superman /ˈsuː.pə.mæn/ US /-pɚ-/ **noun** [C] (plural **-men** /-men/) a man who has greater strength, ability, intelligence, etc. than other men: *The film portrays Gandhi as a kind of superman.*

supermarket /ˈsuː.pəˌmɑː.kɪt/ US /-pɚˌmɑːr-/ **noun** [C] A1 a large shop which sells most types of food and other goods needed in the home, in which people take from shelves the things they want to buy and pay for them as they leave

ˌsupermarket ˈtabloid **noun** [C] US a newspaper sold in supermarkets that contains reports about famous people's private lives, or other things that have happened that are often hard to believe

supermodel /ˈsuː.pəˌmɒd.əl/ US /-pɚˌmɑː.dəl/ **noun** [C] a very famous MODEL (= person, especially a woman, whose job is to wear clothes to show them to possible buyers)

supernatural /ˌsuː.pəˈnætʃ.ər.əl/ US /-pɚˈnætʃ.ɚ-/ **adj** **1** B2 caused by forces that cannot be explained by science: *Ghosts and evil spirits are supernatural.* ◦ *She is said to have supernatural* ***powers*** *and to be able to communicate with the dead.* **2** **the supernatural** B2 things that cannot be explained by science: *I don't believe in* ***the*** *supernatural.* • **supernaturally** /-i/ US /-pɚˈnætʃ.ɚ-/ **adv**

supernova /ˌsuː.pəˈnəʊ.və/ US /-pɚˈnoʊ-/ **noun** [C] (plural **supernovae** /-viː/ or **supernovas**) a star that has exploded, strongly increasing its brightness for a few months

superpower /ˈsuː.pəˌpaʊəʳ/ US /-pɚˌpaʊr/ **noun** [C] a country that has very great political and military power: *Since the disintegration of the USSR, there has been only one superpower – the US.*

superscript /ˈsuː.pə.skrɪpt/ US /-pɚ-/ **noun** [U], **adj** (a word, letter, number, or symbol) written or printed just above a word, letter, number, or symbol, usually in a smaller size: *References to the notes are given* ***in*** *superscript.*

supersede /ˌsuː.pəˈsiːd/ US /-pɚ-/ **verb** [T] to replace something, especially something older or more old-fashioned: *Most of the old road has been superseded by the great interstate highways.*

supersize /ˈsuː.pə.saɪz/ US /-pɚ-/ **adj; verb**
▸**adj** [before noun] US **1** describes the largest size of meal or drink available in a FAST FOOD RESTAURANT **2** (also **supersized**) very large: *Unhealthy food is producing supersized kids.*
▸**verb** US **1** [I or T] to give a customer in a FAST FOOD RESTAURANT the largest size of meal or drink: *'A burger and a Coke please.' 'Can I supersize it for you?'* **2** [T] to increase a lot in size, or to make something increase a lot in size: *We offer tips on how to supersize your business.* • **supersizing** **noun** [U] informal

supersonic /ˌsuː.pəˈsɒn.ɪk/ US /-pɚˈsɑː.nɪk/ **adj** faster than the speed of sound: *a supersonic fighter plane*

superstar /ˈsuː.pə.stɑːʳ/ US /-pɚ.stɑːr/ **noun** [C] an extremely famous actor, singer, musician, sports player, etc.: *a rock superstar* • **superstardom** /-stɑː.dəm/ US /-.stɑːr.dəm/ **noun** [U]

superstate /ˈsuː.pə.steɪt/ US /-pɚ-/ **noun** [C] a large and powerful state formed when several smaller countries unite: *a European/Federal superstate*

superstition /ˌsuː.pəˈstɪʃ.ən/ US /-pɚ-/ **noun** [C or U] belief that is not based on human reason or scientific knowledge, but is connected with old ideas about magic, etc.: *According to superstition, if you walk under a ladder it brings you bad luck.* ◦ *I don't believe in the old superstition* ***that*** *the number 13 is unlucky.*

superstitious /ˌsuː.pəˈstɪʃ.əs/ US /-pɚ-/ **adj** based on or believing in superstitions: *superstitious nonsense* ◦ *Some people are superstitious* ***about*** *spilling salt on the table.* • **superstitiously** /-li/ **adv**

superstore /ˈsuː.pə.stɔːʳ/ US /-pɚ.stɔːr/ **noun** [C] an extremely large shop which sells food and/or other goods usually for use in the home: *a DIY superstore* ◦ *an out-of-town superstore*

superstructure /ˈsuː.pəˌstrʌk.tʃəʳ/ US /-pɚˌstrʌk.tʃɚ/ **noun** [C] **1** (of a building) the part above the ground:

S

The foundations are finished and work has now begun on building the superstructure of the new library. **2** (of a ship) the part above the main DECK **3** the ideas and systems of a society or organization which develop from more basic ideas and systems

supertanker /ˈsuː.pəˌtæŋ.kəʳ/ (US) /-pɚˌtæŋ.kɚ/ **noun** [C] a very large ship that transports especially oil

supertitle /ˈsuː.pəˌtaɪ.tl̩/ (US) /-pɚˌtaɪ.t̬l̩/ **noun** [C] US for **surtitle**

superuser /ˈsuː.pə.juː.zəʳ/ (US) /-pɚ.juː.zɚ/ **noun** [C] someone who knows a lot about a computer program and can help other people to use it

supervise /ˈsuː.pə.vaɪz/ (US) /-pɚ-/ **verb** [I or T] (B2) to watch a person or activity to make certain that everything is done correctly, safely, etc.: *The UN is supervising the distribution of aid by local agencies in the disaster area.* ◦ *The children play while two teachers supervise (= make certain that they behave correctly and are safe).*

supervision /ˌsuː.pəˈvɪʒ.ən/ (US) /-pɚ-/ **noun** [U] (C1) the act of watching a person or activity and making certain that everything is done correctly, safely, etc.: *Students are not allowed to handle these chemicals unless they are* ***under*** *the supervision* ***of*** *a teacher.*

supervisor /ˈsuː.pə.vaɪ.zəʳ/ (US) /-pɚ.vaɪ.zɚ/ **noun** [C] **1** (C1) a person whose job is to supervise someone or something **2** in some colleges, a teacher with responsibility for a particular student **3** US A town or COUNTY supervisor is an elected official who manages local government services. • **supervisory** /ˌsuː.pəˈvaɪ.zər.i/ (US) /-pɚˈvaɪ.zɚ-/ **adj** *We need to employ more supervisory staff.*

superwoman /ˈsuː.pəˌwʊm.ən/ (US) /-pɚ-/ **noun** [C] (plural **-women** /-wɪmɪn/) a woman who has greater strength, ability, intelligence, etc. than other women: *She said that she was tired of being expected to be a superwoman.*

supine /ˈsuː.paɪn/, /ˈsjuː-/ **adj** BODY ▷ **1** formal (lying) flat on your back, looking up: *We walked along the beach, past the rows of supine bodies soaking up the sun.* → Compare **prone** CHARACTER ▷ **2** disapproving If you are supine, you are weak and willing to accept the control of others: *The new director has introduced a series of changes against little opposition from the supine staff.* • **supinely** /-li/ **adv** formal

supper /ˈsʌp.əʳ/ (US) /-ɚ/ **noun** [C or U] (A2) a main meal eaten in the evening, or a small meal eaten in the late evening: *We usually have tea at about 5.30 p.m., then supper before we go to bed.* ◦ *Would you like to come to supper tonight?* ◦ *They had an early supper before going to the theatre.*

S

supplant /səˈplɑːnt/ (US) /-ˈplænt/ **verb** [T] formal to replace: *Printed books will soon be supplanted by e-books.* ◦ *Small children can often feel supplanted in their parents' affections (= that their parents no longer like them as much) when a new brother or sister is born.*

supple /ˈsʌp.l̩/ **adj** BENDING ▷ **1** bending or able to be bent easily; not stiff: *I'm not supple enough (= my body doesn't bend easily enough) to touch the floor.* ◦ *The gloves were made of very supple leather.* ABLE TO CHANGE ▷ **2** literary able to change quickly and successfully to suit different conditions: *She has shown that she has a supple mind.* ◦ *We need a more supple monetary policy.* • **suppleness** /-nəs/ **noun** [U]

supplement noun; verb

▸**noun** [C] /ˈsʌp.lɪ.mənt/ **1** (C2) something that is added to something else in order to improve it or complete it; something extra: *The doctor said she should be taking vitamin supplements.* ◦ *The money I get from teaching evening classes provides a supplement* ***to*** *my main income.* ◦ *We paid a supplement (= an extra amount of money) so that we could have a cabin on board the ship.* **2** a part of a magazine or newspaper, either produced separately or as part of the magazine or newspaper: *The newspaper publishes a sports supplement every Monday.* **3** an extra part of a book, either produced separately or included at the end of the book, containing information that was not available when the book was first published: *There is a supplement* ***to*** *the dictionary containing new words.*

▸**verb** [T] /ˈsʌp.lɪ.ment/ (C2) to add something to something to make it larger or better: *He supplements (= adds to) his income by working in a bar in the evening.* ◦ *Some vegetarians like to supplement their diets* ***with*** *iron tablets.*

supplementary /ˌsʌp.lɪˈmen.tər.i/ (US) /-t̬ɚ-/ **adj** EXTRA ▷ **1** (C2) (US also **supplemental**) extra: *a supplementary income* ANGLE ▷ **2** specialized If an angle is supplementary to another angle, it forms 180° when combined with it.

supplicant /ˈsʌp.lɪ.kənt/ **noun** [C] formal a person who asks a god or someone who is in a position of power for something in a nervous way that shows that they do not think of themselves as very important • **supplication** /ˌsʌp.lɪˈkeɪ.ʃən/ **noun** [U] *Inside the temple, worshippers were kneeling* ***in*** *supplication.*

supplier /səˈplaɪ.əʳ/ (US) /-ɚ/ **noun 1** (B2) [C] a company, person, etc. that provides things that people want or need, especially over a long period of time: *They used to be a leading supplier* ***of*** *military equipment.* ◦ *He said that he had got the drugs from his usual supplier (= person who sells drugs illegally).* **2 suppliers** [plural] a company which sells something: *I'll contact* ***the*** *suppliers and see if I can get the paint you want by Friday.*

supply /səˈplaɪ/ **verb; noun**

▸**verb** [T] (B2) to provide something that is wanted or needed, often in large quantities and over a long period of time: *Electrical power is supplied by underground cables.* ◦ *Three people have been arrested for supplying arms* ***to*** *the terrorists.* ◦ *The company has supplied the royal family (= provided them with something they need) for years.* ◦ *At the beginning of term, students are supplied* ***with*** *a list of books that they are expected to read.*

▸**noun 1** [C or U] an amount of something that is available for use: *Whenever she goes out with her baby, she always takes a large supply* ***of*** *baby food with her.* ◦ *In London, demand for cheap housing far outstrips supply (= what is provided).* **2 supplies** (B2) [plural] food or other things necessary for living: *The refugees are urgently in need of food and medical supplies.* **3 the gas, electricity, etc. supply** the system used for supplying gas, electricity, etc. to people: *Someone has turned off the electricity supply.* **4 in short supply** describes a situation in which there is little of something available: *Strawberries are in short supply at the moment.*

IDIOM **supply and demand** the idea that the price of goods and services depends on how much of something is being sold and how many people want to buy it

suˈpply ˌchain **noun** [C] (also **suˌpply ˈnetwork, loˈgistics ˌnetwork**) the system of people and things that are involved in getting a product from the place where it is made to the person who buys it

suˈpply ˌside **noun** [S] the part of a country's economy that involves producing goods and supplying services • **sup'ply-ˌside** adj [before noun] *supply-side economics/policies*

sup'ply ˌteacher noun [C] UK (US **'substitute ˌteacher**) a teacher who replaces teachers who are absent from work

support /sə'pɔːt/ (US) /-'pɔːrt/ verb; noun

▸verb [T] **ENCOURAGE** ▷ **1** (B2) to agree with and give encouragement to someone or something because you want them to succeed: *My father supported the Labour Party all his life.* ◦ *The majority of people in the town strongly support the plans to build a by-pass.* ◦ *I think it's important to support local businesses by buying locally.* **2** (B1) mainly UK (US usually **root for**) If you support a sports team or a sports player, you want them to win, and might show it by going to watch them play: *Which team do you support?* **HELP** ▷ **3** (B1) to help someone emotionally or in a practical way: *Alcoholics Anonymous is a group which supports people who are trying to stop drinking too much alcohol.* ◦ *My family has always supported me* ***in*** *whatever I've wanted to do.* **PROVIDE** ▷ **4** (B1) to give a person the money they need in order to buy food and clothes and pay for somewhere to live: *He has a wife and four children to support.* **5** (B2) If you support an activity or a habit, you provide the money needed to pay for it: *The drug company is supporting cancer research.* ◦ *I don't know how they manage to support their expensive lifestyle.* ◦ *Some drug addicts turn to crime in order to support their habit.* **6** to provide the right conditions, such as enough food and water, for life: *The land is so poor here that it cannot support any crops.* **STOP FROM FALLING** ▷ **7** (C2) to hold something firmly or carry its weight, especially from below to stop it from falling: *The church dome is supported* ***by/on*** *marble pillars.* ◦ *When babies first learn to stand, they hold on to something to support themselves (= to stop themselves from falling).* ◦ *My ankle is rather weak, so I always put a bandage on it to support it when I play tennis.* ◦ figurative *The Bank of England has taken measures to support the pound (= to stop it from being reduced in value).* **PROVE** ▷ **8** (C1) to help to show something to be true: *These figures support my argument.* ◦ *You can't make a statement like that without any supporting documentation.* **ACCEPT** ▷ **9** formal to accept something and allow it to happen: *The headteacher told the boys that he would not support that kind of behaviour.*

▸noun **ENCOURAGEMENT** ▷ **1** (B2) [U] agreement with and encouragement for an idea, group, or person: *Environmental groups are fast gaining support among young people.* ◦ *We've succeeded in* ***drumming up*** *a lot of local support* ***for*** *our attempt to stop the hospital being closed.* ◦ *I signed a petition* ***in*** *support* ***of*** *the campaign to end the marketing of baby milk in developing countries.* **HELP** ▷ **2** (B1) [C or U] emotional or practical help: *Liz gave me a lot of support when I lost my job.* ◦ *You've been a great support* ***to*** *my mum in this difficult time.* **MONEY** ▷ **3** (B2) [U] the money someone needs in order to buy food and clothes and pay for somewhere to live: *He is dependent on his father for support.* **HOLDING** ▷ **4** [C or U] something that holds something firmly or carries its weight, especially from below to stop it from falling: *The floor is held up by wooden supports.* ◦ *I've hurt my wrist, so I've got it bandaged to give it some support.* **5** [C] a device worn to hold part of the body, especially a weak part, firmly in position: *Jim always wears a knee support when he goes running.* **PROOF** ▷ **6** [U] something that shows that a fact is true: *This new evidence lends support to the theory that she was murdered.* ◦ *We had to send a doctor's report* ***in*** *support* ***of*** *our claim to the insurance company.*

> **Word partners for support noun**
>
> *attract/get/have/win* support • *express/give/lend/offer* support • *drum up/enlist/rally* support • *lose* support • *full/overwhelming/strong/wholehearted* support • *popular/public/widespread* support • support *for* sth • *in* support *of* sb/sth

supportable /sə'pɔː.tə.bl̩/ (US) /-'pɔːr.t̬ə-/ adj formal **TRUE** ▷ **1** A supportable argument, statement, etc. can be shown to be true using EVIDENCE. **ABLE TO CONTINUE** ▷ **2** If something bad is supportable, you are able to accept it or continue despite it: *He looked for something to make his wait more supportable.* **3** used to describe an activity that can continue without problems: *Their economy has shrunk by a barely supportable 15–20 percent.*

supporter /sə'pɔː.tər/ (US) /-'pɔːr.t̬ɚ/ noun [C] **1** (B2) someone who supports a particular idea, group, or person: *He is one of the prime minister's strongest supporters within industry.* **2** (B1) UK (US **fan**) someone who wants a particular team to win and might show it by going to watch them play: *Thousands of supporters have travelled to London for the cup final.*

sup'port ˌgroup noun [C] a group of people who have had similar experiences, especially difficult ones, and who provide help to each other: *After their baby died, they joined a local support group.*

supporting /sə'pɔː.tɪŋ/ (US) /-'pɔːr.t̬ɪŋ/ adj **supporting actor/part/role** not the most important actor or part in a film or play: *She had a small supporting part in the play.*

supportive /sə'pɔː.tɪv/ (US) /-'pɔːr.t̬ɪv/ adj **1** (C1) showing agreement and giving encouragement: *Doubts about the government's policies are being expressed even by people who have been supportive* ***of*** *the government in the past.* **2** approving giving help and encouragement: *Children with supportive parents often do better at school than those without.* • **supportively** /-li/ adv • **supportiveness** /-nəs/ noun [U]

sup'port ˌnetwork noun [C] a group of people who provide emotional and practical help to someone in serious difficulty: *It's very hard for battered women to rebuild their lives without a good support network.*

suppose /sə'pəʊz/ (US) /-'poʊz/ verb; conjunction

▸verb **THINK LIKELY** ▷ **1** (A2) [T] to think that something is likely to be true: [+ (that)] *I couldn't get any reply when I called Dan, so I suppose (****that****) he's gone out.* ◦ *He found it a lot more difficult to get a job than he supposed it would be.* ◦ [+ (that)] *Do you suppose (****that****) Gillian will marry him?* ◦ ***It*** *is widely supposed (****that****) the minister will be forced to resign.* ◦ [+ to infinitive] *We all supposed him* ***to*** *be German, but in fact he was Swiss.* ◦ *Her new book is supposed* ***to*** *be (= generally people think it is) very good.* **2** [+ (that)] used in making polite requests: *I don't suppose (****that****) you could/I suppose you couldn't lend me £5 till tomorrow, could you?* **3** [+ (that)] used to show that you think something is so, although you wish that it were not: *I suppose (****that****) all the tickets will be sold by now.* **4** [+ (that)] used when you are annoyed: *I suppose (****that****) you're going to be late again.* ◦ *I suppose (****that****) you think that's funny. Well, I certainly don't.* **5** (B1) used to show unwillingness to agree: *'Can I go out tonight?' 'Oh, I suppose* ***so****.'* ◦ [+ (that)] *I don't agree with it, but I suppose (****that****) it's for the best.* **NEED** ▷ **6** [T] formal to expect and need: *Investment of this kind supposes (= would not be possible without) an increase in the company's profits this year.* → See also **presuppose**

▸conjunction (also **supposing**) (C1) used at the begin-

S

ning of a sentence or CLAUSE to mean 'what would happen if': *Suppose we miss the train – what will we do then?* ◦ *We'd love to come and see you on Saturday, supposing (= if) I don't have to work that day.*

supposed /sə'pəʊzd/ (US) /-'poʊzd/ **adj** DUTY ▷ **1 be supposed to** (B2) to have to; to have a duty or a responsibility to: *The children are supposed to be at school by 8.45 a.m.* ◦ *You're not supposed (= allowed) to park here.* INTENDED ▷ **2 be supposed to** (B1) to be intended to: *These batteries are supposed to last for a year.* ◦ *We were supposed to have gone away this week, but Debbie's ill so we couldn't go.* ◦ *How am I supposed to (= how can I) find that much money by the end of the week?* OTHERS' OPINION ▷ **3** [before noun] used to show that you do not believe that something or someone really is what many other people consider them to be: *a supposed genius* ◦ *The costs of the scheme outweigh its supposed benefits.*

supposedly /sə'pəʊ.zɪd.li/ (US) /-'poʊ-/ **adv** (C1) used to show that you do not believe that something you have been told is true: *Well, the tickets are supposedly in the mail.*

supposition /ˌsʌp.ə'zɪʃ.ən/ **noun** [C or U] the fact of believing something is true without any proof or something that you believe to be true without any proof: *That article was based on pure supposition.*

suppository /sə'pɒz.ɪ.tər.i/ (US) /-'pɑː.zə.tɔːr.i/ **noun** [C] a small, solid pill containing a drug that is put inside the ANUS, where it dissolves easily

suppress /sə'pres/ **verb** [T] END BY FORCE ▷ **1** (C2) to end something by force: *The Hungarian uprising in 1956 was suppressed by the Soviet Union.* PREVENT ▷ **2** (C2) to prevent something from being seen or expressed or from operating: *She couldn't suppress her anger/annoyance/delight.* ◦ *His feelings of resentment have been suppressed for years.* ◦ *The government tried to suppress the book because of the information it contained about the security services.* ◦ *The virus suppresses the body's immune system.* • **suppression** /-'preʃ.ən/ **noun** [U] *brutal police suppression **of** the riots* ◦ *suppression **of** evidence/emotions/free speech, etc.*

suppressor /sə'pres.ər/ (US) /-ɚ/ **noun** [C] a thing or person that prevents something bad from happening: *Plastic is a good weed suppressor (= a substance which stops them from growing).*

suppurate /'sʌp.jʊ.reɪt/ **verb** [I] specialized (of an injury, etc.) to form or give out a thick, yellow liquid because of infection: *a suppurating sore/wound*

supranational /ˌsuː.prə'næʃ.ən.əl/ **adj** involving more than one country, or having power or authority that is greater than that of single countries

supremacist /suː'prem.ə.sɪst/ **noun** [C] disapproving someone who believes that a particular type or group of people should lead or have control over other types or groups of people because they believe they are better: *a white supremacist*

supremacy /suː'prem.ə.si/ **noun** [U] HIGHEST ▷ **1** the leading or controlling position: *The company has begun to challenge the supremacy **of** the current leading manufacturers in the textiles industry.* ◦ *The allies have established **air** supremacy (= military control of the sky).* GREATEST ▷ **2** the position of being the best: *a struggle for supremacy* ◦ *This victory clearly proves the supremacy **of** the Brazilians in football.*

supreme /suː'priːm/ **adj, adv; adj**

▸**adj, adv** (C1) having the highest rank, level, or importance: *the supreme commander of the armed forces* ◦ *the Supreme Court* ◦ *The present constitution gives supreme authority to the presidency.* ◦ *Beethoven **reigns** supreme among classical composers.*

▸**adj** very great, or the best: *She was awarded a medal for showing supreme bravery.* ◦ *For me, dieting requires a supreme effort of will.*

the ˌSupreme 'Being **noun** [S] literary a name for God

the Suˌpreme 'Court **noun** the most important law court in the US

supremely /suː'priːm.li/ **adv** extremely: *Wales are supremely confident of winning the match.*

supremo /suː'priː.məʊ/ (US) /-moʊ/ **noun** [C] (plural **supremos**) UK informal the person in charge of an organization or who is considered to have most skill and authority in a particular type of activity: *the entertainment supremo, Simon Cowell*

Supt **noun** [before noun] written abbreviation for **superintendent**

surcharge /'sɜː.tʃɑːdʒ/ (US) /'sɝː.tʃɑːrdʒ/ **noun; verb**

▸**noun** [C] a charge in addition to the usual amount paid for something, or the amount already paid: *A surcharge may be made **for** deliveries outside normal hours.*

▸**verb** [I or T] to charge an extra amount

sure /ʃɔːr/ (US) /ʃʊr/ **adj; adv**

▸**adj 1** (A2) certain; without any doubt: *'What's wrong with him?' 'I'm not really sure.'* ◦ *I'm sure **(that)** I left my keys on the table.* ◦ *I **feel** absolutely sure **(that)** you've made the right decision.* ◦ *It now **seems** sure **(that)** the election will result in another victory for the government.* ◦ *Simon isn't sure **whether/if** he'll be able to come to the party or not.* ◦ *Is there anything you're not sure **of/about**?* ◦ *There is only one sure way (= one way that can be trusted) of finding out the truth.* → See also **cocksure** **2 be sure of/about sb** to have confidence in and trust someone: *Henry has only been working for us for a short while, and we're not really sure about him yet.* ◦ *You can always be sure of Kay.* **3 for sure** (B1) certain or certainly: *I know for sure that I won't be able to go to the party.* ◦ *One thing's for sure – once the baby's born, your lives will never be the same again.* **4 be sure of yourself** (B2) to be very or too confident: *She's become much more sure of herself since she got a job.* **5 be sure of sth** (B2) be confident that something is true: *He said that he wasn't completely sure of his facts.* **6 be sure of getting/winning sth** to be certain to get or win something: *We arrived early, to be sure of getting a good seat.* ◦ *A majority of Congress members wanted to put off an election until they could be sure of winning it.* **7 be sure to** (C1) to be certain to: *She's sure to win.* ◦ *I want to go somewhere where we're sure to have good weather.* **8 make sure (that)** (A2) to look and/or take action to be certain that something happens, is true, etc.: *Make sure you lock the door behind you when you go out.* **9** If you have a sure knowledge or understanding of something, you know or understand it very well: *I don't think he has a very sure understanding of the situation.*

IDIOMS **(as) sure as eggs is eggs** UK old-fashioned for certain: *One day he'll realize that I was right, as sure as eggs is eggs.* • **(as) sure as hell** slang used for emphasis: *There better be another way in – I'm sure as hell not climbing up all those steps.* • **a sure thing** (C1) something that is certain to happen: *The president's re-election is now far from a sure thing.* • **sure enough** (C2) as expected: *He said he'd left the book on the desk, and sure enough, here it was.* • **sure thing** mainly US informal used to show agreement: *'Could you give me a lift home tonight?' 'Sure thing!'* • **to be sure** formal certainly: *This is not his best book, to be sure, but it is still worth reading.*

▸adv informal A2 certainly: *'Do you want to come swimming with us?' 'Sure.'* ◦ mainly US *'Will you help me with this?' 'Sure I will.'* ◦ US *I sure am hungry.*

surefire /ˈʃɔː.faɪəʳ/ US /ˈʃʊr.faɪr/ adj [before noun] informal certain or likely, especially to succeed: *The film looks a surefire Oscar winner.* ◦ *Running into the road like that is a surefire way to get hurt.*

surefooted /ˈʃɔːˌfʊt.ɪd/ US /ˈʃʊrˌfʊt̬-/ adj NOT FALLING ▷ **1** able easily to walk on rough ground, without falling: *a surefooted goat/llama/mule* CONFIDENT ▷ **2** showing confidence and the ability to make good judgments in a difficult situation • **surefootedly** /-li/ adv • **surefootedness** /-nəs/ US /ˌʃʊrˈfʊt̬-/ noun [U]

surely /ˈʃɔː.li/ US /ˈʃʊr-/ adv **1** B2 used to express that you are certain or almost certain about something: *The fault surely lies in the design of the equipment.* ◦ US *'May I sit here?' 'Surely.'* (= *Yes, certainly.*) ◦ *Without more food and medical supplies, these people will surely not survive.* **2** B2 used to express surprise that something has happened or is going to happen: *Surely you don't expect me to believe that?* ◦ *Surely you're not going out on a night like this?*

sureness /ˈʃɔː.nəs/ US /ˈʃʊr-/ noun [U] confidence and control: *We admired the sureness* ***of*** *the orchestra's playing.* ◦ *She has an enviable sureness* ***of touch*** (= *she deals with things confidently and well*).

surety /ˈʃɔː.rə.ti/ US /ˈʃʊr.ə.t̬i/ noun [C or U] legal a person who accepts legal responsibility for another person's debt or behaviour, or money given as a promise that someone will do something that they have said they will do, such as pay a debt or appear in court: *Her brothers are acting as sureties* ***for*** *her.* ◦ *No one has yet been found who is willing to* ***stand*** (= *act as a*) *surety* ***for*** *Mr Naylor.* ◦ *What are you able to provide as a surety that you will repay the loan?*

surf /sɜːf/ US /sɝːf/ verb; noun

▸verb [I or T] INTERNET ▷ **1** A2 to spend time visiting a lot of websites: *Many towns and cities have cybercafés where you can surf the internet/Net/Web.* WAVES ▷ **2** B1 to ride on a wave as it comes towards land, while standing or lying on a special board: *They* ***go*** *surfing every weekend.* → See also **bodysurf, windsurfing**

▸noun [U] the tops of the waves on the sea when they are near to the coast or hit against rocks: *We were almost deafened by the crash/roar of the surf.*

surface /ˈsɜː.fɪs/ US /ˈsɝː-/ noun; verb; adj

▸noun TOP ▷ **1** B2 [C] the outer or top part or layer of something: *Tropical rain forests used to cover ten percent of the Earth's surface.* ◦ *The marble has a smooth, shiny surface.* ◦ *Neil Armstrong was the first person to set foot* ***on*** *the surface* ***of*** *the moon.* **2** [C] the top layer of a field or track on which sports are played: *The match will be played on an artificial/all-weather surface.* **3** [C] the flat top part of a table, cupboard, etc.: *a work surface* ◦ *Don't put anything wet* ***on*** *a polished surface, or it will leave a mark.* APPEARANCE ▷ **4** B2 [S] The surface of a situation or person is what they appear to be, or the features they have that are not hidden or difficult to see: ***On*** *the surface, this seems like a difficult problem, but in fact there's an easy solution to it.* ◦ ***Beneath/Below/Under*** *the surface of contemporary West Indian life lurk memories of slavery.* ◦ *Suddenly, all her anger* ***came/rose to*** *the surface* (= *became obvious*).

> Word partners for **surface noun**
> *above/below/beneath/on* the surface

IDIOM **scratch/scrape the surface** to deal with only a very small part of a subject or a problem: *There's far more to be said – I've only had time to scratch the surface in this talk.* ◦ *The amount of aid which has been offered is hardly going to scratch the surface of the problem.*

▸verb TOP ▷ **1** [I] to rise to the surface of water: *The submarine surfaced a few miles off the coast.* **2** [T] to cover a road or other area with a hard surface KNOWN ▷ **3** [I] If a feeling or information surfaces, it becomes known: *Doubts are beginning to surface* ***about*** *whether the right decision has been made.* ◦ *A rumour has surfaced that the company is about to go out of business.* OUT OF BED ▷ **4** [I] informal to get out of bed: *He never surfaces until at least 11.00 a.m. on a Sunday.*

▸adj TOP ▷ **1** working or operating on the top of the land or sea, rather than under the land or sea, or by air APPEARANCE ▷ **2** [before noun] appearing in a particular way but not always showing the truth: *his surface appearance of calm confidence*

ˈsurface ˌarea noun [C usually sing] specialized the area of a surface or of all of the outer surfaces of something: *the surface area of a cube*

ˈsurface ˌmail noun [U] a way of sending letters, parcels, etc. by road, sea, or train and not by aircraft, or things sent in this way: *I sent the parcel by surface mail.*

ˌsurface ˈtension noun [C] the natural force existing in a liquid which holds its surface together

ˌsurface-to-ˌair ˈmissile noun [C] (abbreviation **SAM**) a MISSILE (= flying weapon) that is FIRED from land or the sea towards aircraft or other MISSILES

ˌsurface-to-ˌsurface ˈmissile noun [C] a MISSILE (= flying weapon) that is FIRED from land or the sea towards a place on land or a ship

surfboard /ˈsɜːf.bɔːd/ US /ˈsɝːf.bɔːrd/ noun [C] a long, narrow board made of wood or plastic, used for riding on waves as they come in towards the beach

surfeit /ˈsɜː.fɪt/ US /ˈsɝː-/ noun [C usually singular] formal an amount that is too large, or is more than is needed: *The country has* ***a*** *surfeit* ***of*** *cheap labour.*

surfer /ˈsɜː.fəʳ/ US /ˈsɝː.fɚ/ noun [C] **1** a person who rides on a wave on a special board → See also **windsurfer** **2** a person who spends a lot of time looking at websites on the internet

surfing /ˈsɜː.fɪŋ/ US /ˈsɝː.fɪŋ/ noun [U] WAVES ▷ **1** A2 the sport of riding on a wave on a special board → See also **windsurfing** INTERNET ▷ **2** the activity of spending time visiting different websites on the internet: *internet surfing*

surge /sɜːdʒ/ US /sɝːdʒ/ noun; verb

▸noun [C] **1** C1 a sudden and great increase: *An unexpected surge* ***in*** *electrical power caused the computer to crash.* ◦ *There has been a surge* ***in*** *house prices recently.* → See also **resurgence** **2** a sudden and great movement forward: *At the end of the game, there was a surge* ***of*** *fans onto the field.* ◦ *A* ***tidal*** *surge* (= *sudden and great rise in the level of the sea*) *caused severe flooding in coastal areas.* **3** a sudden increase of an emotion: *She was overwhelmed by a surge* ***of*** *remorse.*

▸verb [I] **1** C1 to increase suddenly and strongly: *The company's profits have surged.* **2** to move quickly and powerfully: *An angry crowd surged through the gates of the president's palace.* ◦ *A few metres before the end of the race, Jenkins surged* ***into the lead.*** **3** (of an emotion) to develop strongly and quickly: *She felt a wave of resentment surging* (***up***) *inside her.*

surgeon /ˈsɜː.dʒᵊn/ US /ˈsɝː-/ noun [C] C1 a doctor who is specially trained to perform medical operations

S

ˌSurgeon ˈGeneral noun [C usually singular] In the US, the Surgeon General is the person who is in charge of the public health service.

surgery /ˈsɜː.dʒᵊr.i/ (US) /ˈsɝː.dʒɚ-/ noun **MEDICAL OPERATION** ▷ **1** (B2) [U] the treatment of injuries or diseases in people or animals by cutting open the body and removing or repairing the damaged part: *The patient* ***had/underwent*** *surgery* ***on*** *his heart.* ◦ *He made a good recovery after surgery* ***to*** *remove a brain tumour.* **ADVICE** ▷ **2** (B2) [C or U] UK (US **office**) a place where you can go to ask advice from or receive treatment from a doctor or dentist: *If you come to the surgery at 10.30, the doctor will see you then.* ◦ *On Saturday mornings, surgery (= the fixed period of opening of the place where you can go to see your doctor) is from 9.00 to 12.00.* **3** [C] the regular period of time when a person can visit their MEMBER OF PARLIAMENT to ask advice: *Our MP* ***holds*** *a weekly surgery on Friday mornings.*

surgical /ˈsɜː.dʒɪ.kᵊl/ (US) /ˈsɝː-/ adj **1** used for medical operations: *surgical supplies/instruments/gloves, etc.* **2** involved in performing medical operations: *surgical procedures/techniques/intervention* ◦ *surgical staff* **3** (of clothing) worn in order to treat a particular medical condition: *a surgical shoe/collar/corset* • **surgically** /-i/ adv

ˌsurgical ˈspirit noun [U] UK (US **ˈrubbing ˌalcohol**) a liquid for cleaning medical equipment or a person's skin so that it is free from bacteria

ˌsurgical ˈstrike noun [C] a type of military attack that is made in an exact way on a particular place

surly /ˈsɜː.li/ (US) /ˈsɝː-/ adj often in a bad mood, unfriendly, and not polite: *We were served by a very surly waiter.* ◦ *He gave me a surly look.* • **surliness** /-nəs/ noun [U]

surmise /sə.maɪz/ (US) /sɚ-/ verb; noun

▸verb [T] formal to guess something, without having much or any proof: [+ (that)] *The police surmise* ***(that)*** *the robbers have fled the country.*

▸noun [C or U] formal a guess: *My surmise turned out to be right.* ◦ *The article is* ***pure*** *surmise and innuendo.*

surmount /səˈmaʊnt/ (US) /sɚ-/ verb [T] formal **DEAL WITH** ▷ **1** to deal successfully with a difficulty or problem: *They managed to surmount all opposition/objections to their plans.* ◦ *There are still a few technical problems/obstacles/hurdles to be surmounted before the product can be put on sale to the public.* **BE ON TOP** ▷ **2** to be on top of something tall: *The central twelve-foot column is surmounted by a bronze angel with outspread wings.* • **surmountable** /-ˈmaʊn.tə.bᵊl/ (US) /-ˈmaʊn.t̬ə.bᵊl/ adj

surname /ˈsɜː.neɪm/ (US) /ˈsɝː-/ noun [C] (US usually **ˈlast ˌname**, UK also **ˈsecond ˌname**) (A2) the name that you share with other members of your family; last name: *Her first name is Sarah but I don't know her surname.*

surpass /səˈpɑːs/ (US) /sɚˈpæs/ verb [T] formal (C2) to do or be better than: *His time for the 100 metres surpassed the previous world record* ***by*** *one hundredth of a second.* ◦ *The book's success has surpassed everyone's expectations.* ◦ *The director has really surpassed* ***himself*** *(= done better than he has done before) with this new film.*

surpassing /səˈpɑː.sɪŋ/ (US) /sɚˈpæs.ɪŋ/ adj [before noun] literary extremely great: *a face of surpassing loveliness*

surplice /ˈsɜː.plɪs/ (US) /ˈsɝː-/ noun [C] specialized a white, loose piece of clothing, worn over other clothing during religious ceremonies by some Christian priests and members of groups who sing in churches

surplus /ˈsɜː.pləs/ (US) /ˈsɝː-/ noun [C or U], adj **1** (C2) (an amount that is) more than is needed: *The world is now producing large food surpluses.* ◦ *We are unlikely to produce any surplus this year.* ◦ *The government has authorized the army to sell its surplus weapons.* ◦ UK *The store is selling off stock that is surplus* ***to requirements*** *(= more than they need to have).* **2** the amount of money you have left when you sell more than you buy, or spend less than you own: *a budget/trade surplus* ◦ *Fortunately the school's bank account is currently* ***in*** *surplus.*

> **Other ways of saying surprise**
>
> A strong way of saying 'surprise' is **amaze**:
>
> *It would* ***amaze*** *me if they win the competition.*
>
> Things that are very surprising can be described as **incredible** or **amazing**:
>
> *After missing so much school, it was* ***incredible*** *that she passed her exams.*
>
> *The team has made an* ***amazing*** *comeback after last season's poor showing.*
>
> Something that is so surprising that it is almost difficult to believe is sometimes described as a **miracle**:
>
> *It's a* ***miracle*** *that she survived the accident.*
>
> An unpleasant surprise is often described as a **shock**:
>
> *It will be a terrible* ***shock*** *if their income is cut.*
>
> The expression **a rude awakening** is sometimes used if someone has an unpleasant surprise when he or she discovers the truth about a situation:
>
> *She'll be in for* ***a rude awakening*** *when she has to pay her own bills.*
>
> If you want to say informally that an event is a surprise to you, you can use the expression **be news to**:
>
> *Sarah is leaving? Well that****'s news to*** *me.*
>
> You can use the idiom **a bolt from the blue** for something that is a surprise because you were not expecting it at all:
>
> *The news of his marriage was* ***a bolt from the blue.***

surprise /səˈpraɪz/ (US) /sɚ-/ noun; verb

▸noun **EVENT** ▷ **1** (A2) [C] an unexpected event: *Don't tell Anne we've arranged a party for her – I want it to be a surprise.* ◦ *It was a lovely/nasty, etc. surprise to get home and find the letter.* ◦ *Last night's heavy snow* ***came as*** *a complete surprise.* ◦ *You're always* ***full of*** *surprises (= doing unexpected things).* ◦ *I wish you wouldn't keep* ***springing*** *surprises* ***on*** *me (= telling me unexpected things or causing unexpected things to happen).* ◦ *They mounted a surprise attack at dawn.* ◦ *My uncle paid us a surprise visit yesterday.* → Compare **shock** **FEELING** ▷ **2** (B2) [U] the feeling caused by something unexpected happening: *He looked at her* ***in/with*** *surprise.* ◦ ***To*** *my great surprise, they agreed to all our demands.*

> **Word partners for surprise noun**
>
> *come as* a surprise • *express* surprise • *catch/take* sb *by* surprise • *have* a surprise *for* sb • *spring* a surprise *on* sb • a *big/complete/nice/unpleasant* surprise • a surprise *to* sb • *to* sb's surprise

IDIOM **surprise, surprise 1** said when someone has done something or when something has happened in a way that you expected and that you do not approve of: *'I've forgotten my keys again.' 'Surprise, surprise!'*

2 said when you are telling someone about a situation in which something unexpected and pleasant has happened: *I asked him if he wanted to come to dinner, and surprise, surprise, he said yes!*

▸verb [T] **1** B1 to make someone feel surprise: *The news surprised everyone.* ◦ [+ that] *It doesn't surprise me* ***that*** *their parents don't want them to get married.* ◦ [+ to infinitive] *It will not surprise anyone* ***to*** *learn that the offer has been rejected.* ◦ [+ question word] *Janet was surprised* ***how*** *quickly the time passed.* **2** to find, catch, or attack someone when they are not expecting it: *The robbers had just opened the safe when they were surprised by the police.* ◦ [+ -ing verb] *His mother surprised him help****ing*** *himself to her gin.*

surprised /səˈpraɪzd/ US /sɚ-/ adj A2 feeling or showing surprise because something has happened that you did not expect: *We were very surprised* ***at*** *the result.* ◦ *It's not like you to behave like this, Alice – I'm surprised* ***at*** *you (= I feel disappointed with you)!* ◦ *I'm not surprised* ***(that)*** *he didn't keep his promise.* ◦ *I'm surprised* ***to*** *see you here.* ◦ *I've managed to fix your car for now, but* ***don't be*** *surprised* ***if*** *it breaks down again (= it probably will stop working again).* ◦ *She looked at him with a surprised expression on her face.*

surprising /səˈpraɪ.zɪŋ/ US /sɚ-/ adj B1 unexpected: *He gave a rather surprising answer.* ◦ ***It's hardly/ scarcely/not*** *surprising* ***(that)*** *you're putting on weight, considering how much you're eating.* ◦ *I must say that* ***it's*** *surprising* ***to*** *find you agreeing with me for once.*

surprisingly /səˈpraɪ.zɪŋ.li/ US /sɚ-/ adv B1 unexpectedly or in a way that is unusual: *The restaurant turned out to be surprisingly cheap.* ◦ *Not surprisingly, the jury found them guilty.*

surreal /səˈrɪəl/ adj strange; not seeming real; like a dream: *Driving through the total darkness was a slightly surreal experience.*

surrealism /səˈrɪə.lɪ.zᵊm/ noun [U] specialized a type of 20th-century art and literature in which unusual or impossible things are shown happening • **surrealist** /-lɪst/ noun [C], adj

surrealistic /səˌrɪəˈlɪs.tɪk/ adj not seeming real; very unusual or impossible

surrender /sᵊrˈen.dəʳ/ US /səˈren.dɚ/ verb; noun

▸verb ACCEPT DEFEAT ▷ **1** C2 [I] to stop fighting and admit defeat: *They would rather die than surrender* ***(to*** *the invaders).* **2** [I] If you surrender to an experience or emotion, you stop trying to prevent or control it: *I finally surrendered* ***to*** *temptation, and ate the last remaining chocolate.* GIVE ▷ **3** [T] to give something that is yours to someone else because you have been forced to do so or because it is necessary to do so: *The police demanded that the gang surrender their weapons.* ◦ *Neither side is willing to surrender any territory/any of their claims.*

▸noun [C or U] the act of stopping fighting and officially admitting defeat: *The rebels are on the point of surrender.*

surreptitious /ˌsʌr.əpˈtɪʃ.əs/ US /ˌsɝː-/ adj done secretly, without anyone seeing or knowing: *She seemed to be listening to what I was saying, but I couldn't help noticing her surreptitious glances at the clock.* • **surreptitiously** /-li/ adv • **surreptitiousness** /-nəs/ noun [U]

surrogacy /ˈsʌr.ə.gə.si/ US /ˈsɝː-/ noun [U] the action of a woman having a baby for another woman who is unable to do so herself

surrogate /ˈsʌr.ə.gət/ US /ˈsɝː-/ adj; noun

▸adj [before noun] replacing someone else or used instead of something else: *Because she had no children of her own, her friend's son became a kind of surrogate child to her.*

▸noun **1** [C] something that replaces or is used instead of something else: *For some people, reading travel books is a surrogate* ***for*** *actual travel.* **2** (also **surrogate mother**) a woman who has a baby for another person who is unable to have a baby: *She has agreed to act as a surrogate* ***mother*** *for her sister.*

surround /səˈraʊnd/ verb; noun

▸verb [T] B1 to be everywhere around something: *Snow-capped mountains surround the city.* ◦ *Gwen sat at her desk, surrounded by books and papers.* ◦ *Mystery still surrounds the exact circumstances of Stalin's death.* ◦ *She said that she wanted to die surrounded by the people she loves (= with them all present).* ◦ *Early this morning, armed police surrounded (= moved into a position so that they were everywhere around) a house which they thought contained an escaped prisoner.* • **surrounding** /-ˈraʊn.dɪŋ/ adj [before noun] B2 *A lot of the children at the school do not live in the town, but come in from the surrounding countryside.*

▸noun **1** [C] the area or border around something: *Our bath has a tiled surround.* **2** **surrounds** [plural] US the area that is near: *I don't think there are any bookstores in the immediate surrounds.*

surroundings /səˈraʊn.dɪŋz/ noun [plural] **1** B2 the place where someone or something is and the things that are in it: *Some butterflies* ***blend in with*** *their surroundings so that it's difficult to see them.* **2** B2 the place where someone lives and the conditions they live in: *They live in very comfortable/pleasant/drab/ bleak surroundings.*

> **! Common mistake: surroundings**
>
> **Warning:** Plural noun!
>
> **Surroundings** does not have a singular form.
>
> Don't write 'surrounding', write **surroundings**:
>
> ~~*The campsite is in a very beautiful surrounding.*~~
>
> *The campsite is in very beautiful surroundings.*

surˈround ˌsound noun [U] a system for playing sounds, especially in cinemas, that uses three or more LOUDSPEAKERS so that the person listening seems to be surrounded by the sound

surtax /ˈsɜː.tæks/ US /ˈsɝː-/ noun [U] an extra tax that is paid by people who earn more than a particular large amount, or an extra tax that is added to something that is already taxed: *a surtax on company profits*

surtitle /ˈsɜːˌtaɪ.tl̩/ US /ˈsɝːˌtaɪ.t̬l̩/ noun [C] (US usually **supertitle**) a written form in the listener's own language of the words that are being sung in an OPERA, shown above the stage during a performance

surveillance /səˈveɪ.ləns/ US /sɚ-/ noun [U] the careful watching of a person or place, especially by the police or army, because of a crime that has happened or is expected: *The police have* ***kept*** *the nightclub* ***under*** *surveillance because of suspected illegal drug activity.* ◦ *More banks are now installing surveillance* ***cameras.***

survey noun; verb

▸noun [C] /ˈsɜː.veɪ/ US /ˈsɝː-/ QUESTIONS ▷ **1** B2 an examination of opinions, behaviour, etc., made by asking people questions: *A recent survey* ***found/ revealed/showed*** *that 58 percent of people did not know where their heart is.* ◦ *to* ***conduct/carry out/do*** *a survey* EXAMINING ▷ **2** the measuring and recording of the details of an area of land: *a* ***geological*** *survey* **3** a description of the whole of a subject: *His new book*

S

! Common mistake: survey

Warning: Choose the right verb!

Don't say 'make a survey', say **do/carry out/ conduct a survey**:

~~*We should make a survey to find out what our customers want.*~~

We should conduct a survey to find out what our customers want.

*is a survey **of** European theatre in the 19th century.* **4** UK (US and Australian English **inspection**) an examination of the structure of a building by a specially trained person

▸verb LOOK AT ▷ **1** C1 /sə'veɪ/ US /'sɜː.veɪ/ [T] formal to look at or examine all of something, especially carefully: *He got out of the car to survey the damage.* ◦ *She has written a book which surveys (= describes in detail) the history of feminism.* **2** /sə'veɪ/ US /'sɜː.veɪ/ [T] to measure an area of land, and to record the details of it, especially on a map: *Before the new railway was built, its route was carefully surveyed.* **3** /sə'veɪ/ US /'sɜː.veɪ/ [T often passive] UK (US and Australian English **inspect**) If a building is surveyed, it is examined carefully by a specially trained person, in order to discover if there is anything wrong with its structure. QUESTIONS ▷ **4** C1 /'sɜː.veɪ/ US /'sɝː-/ [T] to ask people questions in order to find out about their opinions or behaviour: *The researchers surveyed the attitudes of 2,500 college students.* ◦ *Many of the listeners surveyed said that they were not satisfied with the station's programmes.*

IDIOM **lord/master/mistress/king/queen of all you survey** humorous If you are lord, master, mistress, king, or queen of all you survey, you own or control the place in which you live or work.

surveyor /sə'veɪ.əʳ/ US /sɚ'veɪ.ɚ/ noun [C] **1** a person whose job is to measure and record the details of areas of land **2** UK (US **structural engineer**) a person who is specially trained to examine buildings and discover if there are any problems with their structure

survivable /sə'vaɪ.və.bl̩/ US /sɚ-/ adj formal (of an accident or injury) very serious but not causing death

survival /sə'vaɪ.vəl/ US /sɚ-/ noun; adj

▸noun **1** B2 [U] the fact of a person, organization, etc. continuing to live or exist: *The doctors told my wife I had a 50/50 chance of survival.* ◦ *His main concern is to ensure his own political survival.* ◦ *England are fighting for survival (= trying not to be defeated) in the match.* **2** [C] something that has continued to exist from a previous time: *Most of these traditions are survivals from earlier times.*

▸adj continuing to exist or wanting to continue to exist: *We all have a strong survival **instinct**.* ◦ *The survival **rate** for people who have this form of cancer is now more than 90 percent.*

sur'vival ˌkit noun [C] a small box containing things that you need in order to stay alive if you are in a difficult or dangerous situation in which you are unable to get help

surˌvival of the 'fittest noun [U] the principle that animals and plants suited to the conditions they live in are more likely to stay alive and produce other animals and plants than those that are not suited

survive /sə'vaɪv/ US /sɚ-/ verb **1** B2 [I or T] to continue to live or exist, especially after coming close to dying or being destroyed or after being in a difficult or threatening situation: *The baby was born with a heart problem and only survived for a few hours.* ◦ *These plants cannot survive in very cold conditions.* ◦ *None of Shakespeare's plays survives in its original manuscript form.* ◦ *The family are struggling to survive **on** very little money.* ◦ *The front passengers were lucky to survive the accident.* ◦ *The prime minister succeeded in surviving the challenge to his authority.* ◦ *'How are you?' 'Oh, (I'm) surviving (= life is satisfactory, but not very good).'* **2** [T] to continue to live after someone, especially a member of your family, has died: *He is survived by his wife and four children.*

surviving /sə'vaɪ.vɪŋ/ US /sɚ-/ adj [before noun] continuing to live or exist: *The rhinoceros is one of the world's oldest surviving species.* ◦ *Her estate was divided between her three surviving children (= those who continued to live after her death).*

survivor /sə'vaɪ.vəʳ/ US /sɚ'vaɪ.vɚ/ noun [C] **1** B2 a person who continues to live, despite nearly dying: *He was the **sole** (= only) survivor **of** the plane crash.* ◦ *She's a cancer survivor/a survivor **of** cancer.* **2** a person who is able to continue living their life successfully despite experiencing difficulties: *He's one of life's survivors.* **3** US A person's survivors are the members of his or her family who continue to live after he or she has died.

susceptibility /səˌsep.tɪ'bɪl.ɪ.ti/ US /-ə.t̬i/ noun **1** [U] the fact that someone or something can easily be influenced, harmed, or infected **2 susceptibilities** [plural] the feelings someone has that are likely to be hurt: *I didn't mean to offend/upset/hurt your susceptibilities.*

susceptible /sə'sep.tɪ.bl̩/ adj INFLUENCED ▷ **1** easily influenced or harmed by something: *She isn't very susceptible **to** flattery.* ◦ *These plants are particularly susceptible **to** frost.* ◦ *Among particularly susceptible children, the disease can develop very fast.* **2** describes someone who is easily emotionally influenced: *They persuade susceptible teenagers to part with their money.* POSSIBLE ▷ **3** [after verb] formal (especially of an idea or statement) able to be understood, proved, explained, etc. in a particular way: *Shakespeare's plays are susceptible **to** various interpretations.* ◦ UK *The facts are susceptible **of** other explanations.*

sushi /'suː.ʃi/ noun [U] a type of Japanese food consisting of squares or balls of cold boiled rice, with small pieces of other food, especially RAW fish on top

suspect verb; noun; adj

▸verb [T] /sə'spekt/ THINK LIKELY ▷ **1** B2 to think or believe something to be true or probable: *So far, the police do not suspect foul play.* ◦ [+ (that)] *We had no reason to suspect **(that)** he might try to kill himself.* ◦ *'Do you think she'll have told them?' 'I suspect **not/so**.'* THINK GUILTY ▷ **2** B2 to think that someone has committed a crime or done something wrong: *No one knows who killed her, but the police suspect her husband.* ◦ *The police suspect him **of** carrying out two bomb attacks.* ◦ *Three suspected terrorists have been arrested.* DOUBT ▷ **3** C2 to not trust; to doubt: *I have no reason to suspect her honesty/loyalty.* ◦ *We suspected his motives in making his offer.* • **suspected** /-'spek.tɪd/ adj *He has a suspected broken leg.*

▸noun [C] /'sʌs.pekt/ B2 a person believed to have committed a crime or done something wrong, or something believed to have caused something bad: *Police have issued a photograph of the suspect.* ◦ *The **prime** suspect **in** the case committed suicide.* ◦ *No one knows what caused the outbreak of food poisoning, but shellfish is the main suspect (= is thought to have caused it).*

IDIOM **the usual suspects** the people you would expect to be present somewhere or doing a particular thing: *'Who was at Adrian's party?' 'Oh, Paula, Roz, Lucy – the usual suspects.'*

▸adj /ˈsʌs.pekt/ possibly false or dangerous: *The study was carried out with such a small sample that its results are suspect.* ◦ *A suspect parcel was found at the station.*

suspend /səˈspend/ verb **STOP** ▷ **1** C1 [T] to stop something from being active, either temporarily or permanently: *The ferry service has been suspended for the day because of bad weather.* ◦ *The president has suspended the constitution and assumed total power.* ◦ *When you go to the theatre, you have to be willing to suspend* ***disbelief*** *(= to act as if you believe that what you are seeing is real or true, although you know that it is not).* ◦ *I'm suspending* ***judgment*** *(= not forming an opinion) on the book I'm reading until I've finished it.* ◦ legal *Mr Young was given a six-month jail* ***sentence*** *suspended for two years (= if he commits another crime within two years, he will have to go to prison for six months for his original crime).* **2** B2 [T] If someone is suspended from work, school, etc., they are temporarily not allowed to work, go to school, or take part in an activity because they have done something wrong: *She was suspended* ***from*** *school for fighting.* ◦ *He was suspended for four matches after arguing with the referee.* **HANG** ▷ **3** [T usually + adv/prep] to hang: *The builders worked on wooden platforms, suspended by ropes* ***from*** *the roof of the building.* ◦ *It was very uncomfortable lying on the hospital bed with my legs suspended* ***in the air.*** **4** [T usually + adv/prep] If small pieces of solid material are suspended in a gas or a liquid, they hang or float in the gas or liquid: *The drug is suspended* ***in*** *a saline solution.* ◦ *A cloud of smoke was suspended* ***in*** *the air.*

su,spended aniˈmation noun [U] a state in which life in a body is temporarily slowed down or stopped: *Some animals, such as hedgehogs, exist in a state of suspended animation during the winter.*

suspender /səˈspen.dəʳ/ US /-dɚ/ noun **1** [C] UK (US **garter**) a type of button that fastens onto a woman's STOCKINGS to hold them up **2 suspenders** [plural] US for **brace**

suˈspender ˌbelt noun [C] UK (US ˈ**garter ˌbelt**) a piece of women's underwear worn round the waist, with suspenders fixed to it for holding up STOCKINGS

suspense /səˈspens/ noun [U] C2 the feeling of excitement or nervousness which you have when you are waiting for something to happen and are uncertain about what it is going to be: *She* ***kept*** *him* ***in*** *suspense for several days before she said that she would marry him.* ◦ *The suspense* ***is killing*** *me (= I am extremely eager to know what is going to happen).* ◦ *There is a gradual build-up of suspense throughout the film, until it comes to an unexpected ending.*

suspension /səˈspen.ʃən/ noun **STOP** ▷ **1** [U] the act of stopping something happening, operating, etc. for a period of time: *The suspension* ***of*** *fighting is to take effect at 6 a.m. on Monday.* ◦ *There have been calls for the drug's immediate suspension, following reports that it has dangerous side effects.* **2** [C or U] a punishment in which a person is temporarily not allowed to work, go to school, or take part in an activity: *The union is protesting about the suspension* ***of*** *a restaurant worker.* ◦ *The player is likely to receive a three-match suspension following an incident in yesterday's game.* **VEHICLE** ▷ **3** [U] equipment fixed to the wheels of a vehicle which reduces the uncomfortable effects of going over road surfaces that are not even **LIQUID** ▷ **4** [C] a liquid in which small pieces of solid are contained, but not dissolved: *a suspension of fine cornflour* ***in*** *corn oil*

suˈspension ˌbridge noun [C] a bridge that is

suspension bridge

supported by strong STEEL ropes hung from a tower at each end of the bridge

suspicion /səˈspɪʃ.ən/ noun **THINK LIKELY** ▷ **1** B2 [C] a belief or idea that something may be true: [+ that] *I* ***have*** *a suspicion* ***that*** *he only asked me out because my brother persuaded him to.* ◦ *She* ***had*** *a* ***nagging/sneaking*** *suspicion* ***that*** *she might have sent the letter to the wrong address.* **2** [S] a small amount: *He gave just* ***a*** *suspicion* ***of*** *a smile.* ◦ *I have* ***a*** *suspicion* ***of*** *doubt about whether I should accept his invitation or not.* **THINK GUILTY** ▷ **3** C1 [C or U] a feeling or belief that someone has committed a crime or done something wrong: *'I'm arresting you* ***on*** *suspicion* ***of*** *illegally possessing drugs,' said the police officer.* ◦ mainly UK *She is* ***under*** *suspicion* ***of*** *murder.* ◦ *In this particular case, they are* ***above/beyond*** *suspicion (= cannot be thought to be guilty).* ◦ *His strange behaviour aroused/raised his neighbours' suspicions.* **DOUBT** ▷ **4** [C or U] doubt or lack of trust: *Since they discovered the truth about his background, his colleagues have regarded him with suspicion.* ◦ *They feel that she* ***harbours*** *(= has) suspicions* ***of*** *their politics.*

suspicious /səˈspɪʃ.əs/ adj **SEEM GUILTY** ▷ **1** B2 making you feel that something illegal is happening or that something is wrong: *Her behaviour was very suspicious.* ◦ *The fire at the bank is being treated as suspicious.* ◦ ***It's*** *a bit suspicious* ***that*** *no one knows where he was at the time of the murder.* ◦ *There were some suspicious characters hanging around outside.* ◦ *There's a suspicious-****looking*** *van parked at the end of the road.* ◦ *His new book bears a suspicious resemblance to a book written by someone else. (= His book is so similar to the other book that it seems as if he has copied it.)* **DOUBT** ▷ **2** B2 feeling doubt or no trust in someone or something: *His colleagues became suspicious (= thought that there was something wrong) when he did not appear at work, since he was always punctual.* ◦ *They are* ***deeply/highly*** *(= very) suspicious* ***of*** *one another/****of*** *each other's motives.* ◦ *My mother has a very suspicious nature (= does not trust people).*

S

suspiciously /səˈspɪʃ.əs.li/ adv **DOUBT** ▷ **1** B2 in a way that makes you think that something is wrong: *He looked at her suspiciously.* ◦ *The children are suspiciously quiet (= are so quiet that they are probably doing something wrong).* **SEEM GUILTY** ▷ **2** in a way that makes you think someone is guilty of something wrong or illegal: *The officers noticed two men acting suspiciously (= as if they were doing something wrong).* **SEEM LIKELY** ▷ **3** in a way that makes you think something may be true: *She brushed away what looked suspiciously like (= looked as if it probably was) a tear.*

suss /sʌs/ verb; adj

▸verb [T] UK informal to realize, understand, or discover: [+ that] *He never sussed* ***(out) that*** *they'd tricked him.* ◦ *She thinks she's got me sussed* ***(out)*** *(= she thinks she understands me), but she's wrong.* ◦ *I'll visit the college and suss it* ***out*** *before I decide whether to apply or not.*

▸adj Australian English informal for **suspicious**

sustain /sə'steɪn/ verb [T] **CONTINUE** ▷ **1** Ⓑ2 to cause or allow something to continue for a period of time: *The economy looks set to sustain its growth into next year.* ◦ *He seems to find it difficult to sustain relationships with women.* ◦ US *The judge sustained (= accepted) the lawyer's objection.* **2** Ⓒ2 to keep alive: *The soil in this part of the world is not rich enough to sustain a large population.* **SUFFER** ▷ **3** formal to suffer or experience, especially damage or loss: *She sustained multiple injuries in the accident.* ◦ *The company has sustained heavy losses this year.* **SUPPORT** ▷ **4** to support emotionally: *She was sustained by the strength of her religious faith.*

sustainable /sə'steɪ.nə.bḷ/ adj **1** Ⓒ1 able to continue over a period of time: *That sort of extreme diet is not sustainable over a long period.* **2** Ⓒ1 causing little or no damage to the environment and therefore able to continue for a long time: *A large international meeting was held with the aim of promoting sustainable* ***development*** *in all countries.* • **sustainability** /-nə'bɪl.ɪ.ti/ Ⓤⓢ /-nə'bɪl.ə.ṭi/ noun [U]

sustained /sə'steɪnd/ adj **1** continuing for a long time: *The president's speech was greeted by sustained applause.* **2** determined: *We must make a sustained effort to get this task finished this week.*

sustenance /'sʌs.tɪ.nəns/ noun [U] formal **FOOD** ▷ **1** food: *During this freezing weather, the food put out by householders is the only form of sustenance that the birds have.* **2** the ability of food to provide people and animals with what they need to make them strong and healthy: *A stick of celery does not provide much sustenance.* **SUPPORT** ▷ **3** emotional or mental support: *When her husband died, she* ***drew*** *sustenance* ***from****/she* ***found*** *sustenance* ***in*** *her religious beliefs.*

suttee /'sʌt.iː/ noun [U] (also **sati**) the Hindu custom, no longer legal, of a woman being burned alive in the same fire as that in which her dead husband's body is burned

suture /'suː.tʃəʳ/ Ⓤⓢ /-tʃɚ/ noun; verb

▸**noun** [C] specialized a STITCH used to sew up a cut in a person's body

▸**verb** [T] specialized to sew together a cut in a person's body

SUV /ˌes.juː'viː/ noun [C] mainly US sport utility vehicle: a large car with an engine that supplies power to all four wheels that is usually used for ordinary driving

svelte /svelt/ adj attractively thin, GRACEFUL, and stylish

SW adj; noun

▸**adj** written abbreviation for **southwest** or **southwestern**

▸**noun** [U] **SOUTHWEST** ▷ **1** written abbreviation for **southwest** **RADIO** ▷ **2** written abbreviation for **short wave**

swab /swɒb/ Ⓤⓢ /swɑːb/ noun; verb

▸**noun** [C] a small piece of soft material used for cleaning a cut or for taking a small amount of substance from a body, or the substance itself which can then be tested: *The nurse cleaned the cut on my leg with a swab.* ◦ *'I'm just going to take a swab* ***of*** *your ear,' said the doctor.*

▸**verb** [T] (**-bb-**) **WASH** ▷ **1** to wash a surface, especially the open, flat areas of a ship, with a wet cloth or MOP **MEDICINE** ▷ **2** to clean a cut or take a small amount of substance from a body using a small piece of soft material

swaddle /'swɒd.ḷ/ Ⓤⓢ /'swɑː.dḷ/ verb [T] old-fashioned to wrap a baby tightly in cloth: *Swaddling a baby tightly* ***in*** *a blanket can be a good way to stop it crying.*

swadeshi /swæ'deʃ.i/ adj Indian English made and sold or used in India

swag /swæg/ noun [U] **STOLEN** ▷ **1** old-fashioned slang stolen goods: *The cartoon showed a picture of a robber carrying a bag with 'swag' written on it.* **POSSESSIONS** ▷ **2** Australian English old-fashioned possessions wrapped in a cloth and carried by a person who does not have a home or a job, but walks around from place to place

swagger /'swæg.əʳ/ Ⓤⓢ /-ɚ/ verb; noun

▸**verb** [I] to walk or act in a way that shows that you are very confident and think that you are important: *They swaggered into the room.* • **swaggerer** /-əʳ/ Ⓤⓢ /-ɚ/ noun [C] • **swaggeringly** /-ɪŋ.li/ adv

▸**noun** [S or U] a way of walking or acting that shows you are confident: *He walked out of the room with* ***a*** *self-confident swagger.* ◦ *Underneath all his swagger he's actually quite nervous.*

swallow /'swɒl.əʊ/ Ⓤⓢ /'swɑː.loʊ/ verb; noun

▸**verb** **THROAT** ▷ **1** Ⓑ2 [I or T] to cause food, drink, pills, etc. to move from your mouth into your stomach by using the muscles of your throat: *My throat is so sore that it really hurts when I swallow.* ◦ *He put a grape into his mouth and swallowed it* ***whole****.* **2** [I] to use the muscles of your throat, as if moving something from your mouth into your stomach, because you are nervous or frightened, or are about to say something: *He swallowed* ***hard*** *and said, 'Dad, I've got something to tell you.'* **TAKE AWAY** ▷ **3** [T] If something large swallows (up) another thing, it makes it disappear or stop existing separately by making it part of itself: *An increasing amount of the countryside is being swallowed* ***(up)*** *by the town.* ◦ *Many small businesses have been swallowed* ***(up)*** *by large companies.* **4** [T] to use or take away a large part of something valuable: *Taxes have swallowed up nearly half of my pay increase.* **ACCEPT** ▷ **5** Ⓒ2 [T] informal to accept something without question or without expressing disagreement: *Not surprisingly, this excuse was too much for them to swallow.* ◦ *He swallowed her story* ***whole****.* ◦ *She swallowed his sales pitch* ***hook, line, and sinker*** *(= believed it completely).* **NOT EXPRESS** ▷ **6** Ⓒ2 [T] to not express or show something: *She swallowed her disappointment, saying, 'That's OK, it doesn't matter.'*

IDIOMS **swallow your words** to be forced to admit that something you have said has been shown to be wrong: *I had to swallow my words when the scheme turned out to be a great success.* • **swallow the bait** If you swallow the bait, you completely accept something, especially an offer that is a trick or way of getting something from you.

▸**noun** [C] **THROAT** ▷ **1** an act of using the muscles of your throat, or the amount of something you move into your stomach from your mouth by using the muscles of your throat: *He gave a swallow, then began speaking.* **BIRD** ▷ **2** a small bird with pointed wings and a tail with two points, which flies quickly and catches insects to eat as it flies

swallow ˌdive noun [C] UK (US **'swan ˌdive**) a **dive** in which you hold your arms out from your sides until you are close to the water

swam /swæm/ verb past simple of **swim**

swami /'swɑː.mi/ noun [C] (the title of) a Hindu religious teacher

swamp /swɒmp/ Ⓤⓢ /swɑːmp/ noun; verb

▸**noun** [C or U] (an area of) very wet, soft land: *an alligator-infested swamp* ◦ *The Everglades are an area of swamp in southern Florida.*

▸**verb** **COVER** ▷ **1** [T] to cover a place or thing with a large amount of water: *High tides have swamped the*

S

coast. ◦ *The boat was swamped **by** an enormous wave.* TOO MUCH/BIG ▷ **2** [T often passive] If something swamps a person, system, or place, they receive more of it than they can easily deal with: *Foreign cars have swamped the UK market.* ◦ *I'm swamped **with** work at the moment.* ◦ *Don't let feelings of depression swamp you.* **3** [T] informal If clothes swamp you, they are much too big for you.

ˈswamp ˌgas noun [C usually singular] a gas produced in a swamp by decaying plants that are covered by water: *You could smell the swamp gas a mile off.*

swampland /ˈswɒmp.lænd/ (US) /ˈswɑːmp-/ noun [C or U] specialized an area of swamp

swampy /ˈswɒm.pi/ (US) /ˈswɑːm-/ adj describes land that is soft and very wet

swan /swɒn/ (US) /swɑːn/ noun; verb

swan

▸noun [C] (B2) a large, usually white bird with a long neck that lives on rivers and lakes: *We watched the swans glide by.*

▸verb [I usually + adv/prep] (**-nn-**) UK informal disapproving to travel, move, or behave in a relaxed way for pleasure and without worrying that others may feel annoyed: *She swanned into the room, carrying a glass of wine, taking no notice of the fact that she'd kept us all waiting for hours.* ◦ *He's been swanning **around** the States (= travelling and not doing any work) all summer.*

ˈswan ˌdive noun [C] US for **swallow dive**

swank /swæŋk/ verb; noun

▸verb [I] informal disapproving to behave or speak too confidently because you think that you are very important, in order to attract other people's attention and admiration: *Just because you won, there's no need to swank.* ◦ *People around here don't swank **about** their money.*

▸noun [U] informal disapproving behaviour that is too confident: *In spite of all his swank, he's never really achieved very much.*

swanky /ˈswæŋ.ki/ adj **1** informal very expensive and fashionable, in a way that is intended to attract people's attention and admiration: *We stayed in a swanky hotel.* **2** disapproving behaving too confidently: *I'm sick of his swanky talk.*

swansong /ˈswɒn.sɒŋ/ (US) /ˈswɑːn.sɑːŋ/ noun [S] a person's last piece of work, achievement, or performance: *This weekend's match was his swansong as the team's captain.*

swap /swɒp/ (US) /swɑːp/ verb; noun

▸verb [I or T] (**-pp-**) (UK also **swop** (**-pp-**)) (C1) to give something and be given something else instead: *When you've finished reading your book, and I've finished mine, shall we swap?* ◦ *We swapped addresses **with** the people we met on holiday.* ◦ *When he got a job in a bank, he had to swap his jeans and T-shirt **for** a suit (= he had to wear formal clothes instead of informal ones).* ◦ [+ two objects] *I'll swap you my chocolate bar **for** your peanuts.* ◦ *We spent the evening in the pub, swapping (= telling each other) stories/jokes.* → Synonym **exchange**

▸noun [C] (UK also **swop**) an exchange, or something that is going to be or has been exchanged: *I thought Simon's food looked nicer than mine, so we **did a** swap.* ◦ *This comic is a swap (= something that was exchanged) that I got from Nick.*

ˈswap ˌmeet noun [C] US for **car boot sale**

swarm /swɔːm/ (US) /swɔːrm/ noun; verb

▸noun **1** [C] a large group of insects all moving together: *a swarm **of** bees/wasps/ants/locusts* ◦ *The dead sheep was covered with swarms **of** flies.* **2** [C, + sing/pl verb] a large group of people all moving together: *A swarm **of**/Swarms **of** journalists followed the film star's car.*

▸verb [I] **1** When insects swarm, they come together in a large group. **2** When people swarm somewhere, they move there in a large group or in large numbers: *After the game, thousands of football fans swarmed onto the pitch.*

PHRASAL VERB **swarm with sth** If a place is swarming with people or things, there are large numbers of them moving around it: *The garden is swarming with wasps.* ◦ *Something must be going on – the town is swarming with police.*

swarthy /ˈswɔː.ði/ (US) /ˈswɔːr-/ adj (of a person or their skin) dark: *a swarthy face/complexion* ◦ *a swarthy fisherman*

swashbuckling /ˈswɒʃˌbʌk.lɪŋ/ (US) /ˈswɑːʃ-/ adj [before noun] behaving in a brave and exciting way, especially like a fighter in the past: *a swashbuckling hero/pirate*

swastika /ˈswɒs.tɪ.kə/ (US) /ˈswɑː.stɪ-/ noun [C] a symbol in the form of a cross with each of its arms bent at a 90° (degree) angle half way along, used in the 20th century as the symbol of the NAZI party

swat /swɒt/ (US) /swɑːt/ verb [T] (**-tt-**) to hit something, especially an insect, with a flat object or your hand: *I swatted the fly with a rolled-up newspaper.* ◦ *He tried to swat the ball too hard, and missed it entirely.* ◦ figurative *These missiles are capable of swatting enemy planes with deadly accuracy.* • **swat** noun [C] *He gave the mosquito a swat.*

swatch /swɒtʃ/ (US) /swɑːtʃ/ noun [C] a small piece of cloth used as an example of the colour and type of the cloth

swathe /sweɪð/ noun; verb

▸noun (also **swath**) AREA ▷ **1** [C] a long strip or large area especially of land: *Huge swathes **of** rainforest are being cleared for farming and mining.* **2** [S] literary a large part of something that includes several different things: *These people represent a **broad/wide** swathe **of** public opinion.* CLOTH ▷ **3** [C] a long strip of cloth: *His head was wrapped in swathes **of** bandages.*

▸verb [T] to wrap round or cover with cloth: *He came out of the hospital swathed **in** bandages.* ◦ *I love to swathe (= dress) my**self in** silk.*

SWAT team /ˈswɒt.tiːm/ (US) /swɑːt-/ noun [C] mainly US abbreviation for Special Weapons and Tactics team: a group of police officers who are specially trained to deal with dangerous situations

sway /sweɪ/ verb; noun

▸verb MOVE ▷ **1** [I] to move slowly from side to side: *The trees were swaying in the wind.* ◦ *The movement of the ship caused the mast to sway **from side to side/backwards and forwards**.* ◦ *A drunk was standing in the middle of the street, swaying uncertainly and trying hard to stay upright.* **2** [T] to cause something to move or change: *Recent developments have swayed the balance of power in the region.* PERSUADE ▷ **3** [T] to persuade someone to believe or do one thing rather than another: *Her speech failed to sway her colleagues **into** supporting the plan.*

▸noun [U] formal control or influence: *In the 1980s, the organization came **under the** sway **of** (= became strongly influenced by) Christian fundamentalism.*

S

◦ *Her parents no longer seem to have much sway* ***over*** *her.* ◦ *The party could* ***hold sway*** *(= have an important influence) on some crucial votes.*

swear /sweəʳ/ (US) /swer/ verb (**swore**, **sworn**) **USE RUDE WORDS** ▷ **1** B2 [I] to use words that are rude or offensive as a way of emphasizing what you mean or as a way of insulting someone or something: *It was a real shock, the first time I heard my mother swear.* ◦ *When the taxi driver started to swear* ***at*** *him, he walked off.* **PROMISE** ▷ **2** B2 [I or T] to promise or say firmly that you are telling the truth or that you will do something or behave in a particular way: *I don't know anything about what happened, I swear (****it****).* ◦ [+ (that)] *You might find it difficult to believe, but I swear (****that****) the guy just came up to me and gave me the money.* ◦ informal *She swore* ***blind*** *(= promised definitely) (****that****) she didn't know what had happened to the money.* ◦ [+ to infinitive] *New gang members must swear* ***to*** *obey the gang leaders at all times.* ◦ *In some countries, witnesses in court have to swear* ***on*** *the Bible.* ◦ *I swore an* ***oath*** *to tell the truth, the whole truth, and nothing but the truth.* ◦ *A few of us knew what was going to happen, but we were sworn* ***to*** *secrecy (= we were made to promise to keep it a secret).* ◦ *I think his birthday is on the 5th, but I wouldn't/couldn't swear* ***to*** *it (= I am not completely certain about it).*

PHRASAL VERBS **swear by sth** [not continuous] informal to believe strongly that something is effective or useful: *My dad swears by these vitamin pills.* • **swear sb in** legal When someone is sworn in, they make a formal promise to be honest or loyal, either because they are in a law court or because they are starting a new official job: *The next witness was sworn in.* ◦ *Obama was sworn in* ***as*** *president.* • **swear off sth** to make a decision to stop doing, using, or being involved with something harmful, such as drugs or alcohol, or something that is not good or helpful: *After years of addiction, he swore off drugs completely.*

swearing /ˈsweə.rɪŋ/ (US) /ˈswer.ɪŋ/ noun [U] rude or offensive language that someone uses, especially when they are angry

ˌswearing-ˈin noun [S] an official ceremony in which someone starting a new official job formally promises to be loyal and honest and to perform their duties well: *She had a good seat at the president's swearing-in ceremony.*

ˈswear ˌword noun [C] a rude or offensive word: *All swear words, even mild ones such as 'damn', were deleted from the text.*

sweat /swet/ noun; verb

▸noun **LIQUID** ▷ **1** B2 [U] the clear, salty liquid that you pass through your skin: *The dancers were* ***dripping with/pouring with*** *sweat after a morning's rehearsal.* ◦ *By the time we'd climbed to the top of the hill, we were* ***covered in*** *sweat.* ◦ *She wiped the* ***beads*** *(= drops)* ***of*** *sweat from her forehead.* ◦ figurative *The cathedral was built by human toil and sweat (= effort).* **CLOTHES** ▷ **2 sweats** [plural] US (UK **tracksuit**) a loose top and trousers, worn either by people who are training for a sport or exercising, or as informal clothing

IDIOMS **get in a sweat** informal to worry: *He tends to get in a sweat* ***about*** *flying.* • **no sweat** informal If you say that something is no sweat, you mean that it will not be difficult or cause problems: *'Can you fix my car for me?' 'No sweat!'*

▸verb [I] **1** B2 to pass sweat through the skin because you are hot, ill, or frightened: *It was so hot when we arrived in Tripoli that we started to sweat as soon as we got off the plane.* ◦ *The prisoners were sweating* ***with*** *fear.* ◦ informal *I was so afraid, I was sweating* ***like a pig*** *(= sweating a lot).* **2** If something sweats, it produces drops of liquid on the outside: *The walls in older houses sometimes sweat* ***with*** *damp.*

IDIOMS **make sb sweat** informal to make someone wait nervously: *It seemed that the authorities had delayed the news just to make us sweat.* • **sweat blood** (also **sweat your guts out**) to make a great effort: *We sweated blood to get the work finished on time.* ◦ *I've been sweating blood over this report.* • **sweat bullets** US informal to be extremely nervous and worried about something: *I was sweating bullets* ***over*** *this interview.* • **sweat it out** informal **1** to wait nervously for an unpleasant situation to end or improve: *My exams finish next week, and then I'll be sweating it out for a month waiting for the results.* **2** to do hard physical exercise: *I like to sweat it out in the gym for a couple of hours every day.*

PHRASAL VERB **sweat over sth** to work very hard using or doing something: *She's been sweating over that essay all afternoon.* ◦ *I've been sweating over* ***a hot stove*** *(= cooking) all morning.*

sweatband /ˈswet.bænd/ noun [C] a thin strip of material that someone doing sport or exercise wears round their head to stop sweat going into their eyes, or wears around their wrists to stop sweat going onto their hands

sweated /ˈswet.ɪd/ (US) /ˈswet̬-/ adj [before noun] disapproving involving workers who are paid very little and who work many hours in very bad conditions: *The textile industry still relies to some extent on sweated* ***labour****.*

sweater /ˈswet.əʳ/ (US) /ˈswet̬.ɚ/ noun [C] (UK also **jumper**) A2 a piece of clothing with long sleeves that is usually made from wool, worn on the upper part of the body: *Put a sweater on if you're cold.* ◦ *a V-necked sweater* → Compare **cardigan**

ˈsweat ˌgland noun [C usually plural] one of the small organs under the skin which produce SWEAT

sweatpants /ˈswet.pænts/ noun [plural] **tracksuit bottoms**

sweatshirt /ˈswet.ʃɜːt/ (US) /-ʃɝːt/ noun [C] B1 a piece of informal clothing with long sleeves, usually made of thick cotton, worn on the upper part of the body: *She was dressed casually in jeans and a sweatshirt.*

sweatshop /ˈswet.ʃɒp/ (US) /-ʃɑːp/ noun [C] disapproving a small factory where workers are paid very little and work many hours in very bad conditions

sweatsuit /ˈswet.suːt/ noun [C] a **tracksuit**

sweaty /ˈswet.i/ (US) /ˈswet̬-/ adj covered in SWEAT or smelling of SWEAT: *a sweaty face* ◦ *sweaty clothes* ◦ *We spent the evening in a sweaty pub (= one that causes you to sweat).*

swede /swiːd/ noun [C or U] mainly UK (US usually **rutabaga**) a round vegetable with dark yellow flesh and a brown or purple skin

sweep /swiːp/ verb; noun

▸verb (**swept**, **swept**) **CLEAN** ▷ **1** B2 [T] to clean especially a floor by using a brush to collect the dirt into one place from which it can be removed: *sweep the floor* **MOVE** ▷ **2** C2 [I + adv/prep] to move, especially quickly and powerfully: *Everyone looked up as she swept* ***into*** *the room.* ◦ *The fire swept (= spread quickly)* ***through*** *the house.* ◦ *The National Party swept* ***into power*** *(= easily won the election) with a majority of almost 200.* **3** [T] to quickly spread through and influence an area: *A 1970s fashion revival is sweeping Europe.* **4** [T] to travel across all of an area, especially when looking for something: *American minesweepers are sweeping the Arabian Sea.* **5** [I usually + adv/prep] If a road, river, range of mountains, set of steps, etc. sweeps in a particular direction, they follow a particular curved path: *The road sweeps down to the coast.* **REMOVE** ▷ **6** (B2) [T usually + adv/prep] to remove and/or take in a particular direction, especially in a fast and powerful way: *A large wave swept* ***away*** *half the sandcastle.* ◦ *She swept the pile of papers and books* ***into*** *her bag.* ◦ *The boat was swept* ***out to sea*** *(= away from land) by the tide.* ◦ *Government troops swept* ***aside*** *the rebel forces (= caused them to move away from the area in which they were).* **WIN** ▷ **7** [T] US informal to win all the parts of a competition, or to win very easily: *The Yankees swept a four-game series* ***from*** *the Blue Jays.*

IDIOMS **sweep sb off their feet** to make someone become suddenly and completely in love with you: *The first time he met her, he was completely swept off his feet.* • **sweep sth under the carpet** UK (US **sweep sth under the rug**) to hide a problem or try to keep it secret instead of dealing with it: *The committee is being accused of sweeping financial problems under the carpet to avoid embarrassment.* • **sweep the board** to win everything that is available: *Australia swept the board in the swimming, with gold medals in every race.*

PHRASAL VERBS **sweep sb along** [M often passive] If a feeling or someone's behaviour sweeps you along, it makes you feel very enthusiastic about an activity and very involved in it: *We were swept along by her eloquence.* • **sweep sth aside** to refuse to consider something or to treat it as important: *They swept his doubts and objections aside.*

▸**noun CLEAN** ▷ **1** [C usually singular] the act of sweeping something to clean it: *I've given the kitchen floor* ***a*** *sweep (= I have swept it).* **2** [C] old-fashioned for **chimney sweep MOVEMENT** ▷ **3** [C] a movement, especially a quick, powerful one or one to search an area: *With a sweep (= horizontal movement)* ***of*** *its tail, the alligator knocked her under the water.* **4** [C] a long, often curved, area of land, sea, river, etc.: *A broad sweep* ***of*** *flat countryside stretched to the horizon in all directions.* **5 sweeps** [plural] US a period of time when measurements of the number of people watching different television stations are made so that the cost of advertising on each station can be set **WIN** ▷ **6 a clean sweep** a situation in which one player, team, etc. wins everything that is available: *Romania* ***made*** *a clean sweep of the medals.*

sweeper /ˈswiː.pəʳ/ (US) /-pɚ/ noun [C] **CLEANING** ▷ **1** someone or something that sweeps something clean: *a carpet sweeper (= a machine for cleaning carpets)* ◦ *a road sweeper (= a person whose job is cleaning the roads)* **FOOTBALL** ▷ **2** In football, a sweeper is a player whose position is behind the other DEFENDERS (= players whose main aim is to stop points from being scored).

sweeping /ˈswiː.pɪŋ/ adj [before noun] **GENERAL** ▷ **1** affecting many things or people; large: *It is obvious that sweeping* ***changes*** *are needed in the legal system.* ◦ *We need to make sweeping* ***cuts*** *to our budget.* **2 sweeping statement/generalization** disapproving something that you say or write that is too general and that has not been carefully thought about: *Sweeping generalizations about this complex and difficult situation are not helpful.* **WIN** ▷ **3** A sweeping win or VICTORY is an easy or complete win: *The party have failed to win the sweeping victory they expected.*

sweepstake /ˈswiːp.steɪk/ noun [C] (informal **sweep**) a type of GAMBLING, often on a horse race, in which people pay a small amount of money and choose a particular horse, team, etc. The person who chooses the winning horse, team, etc. receives all the money paid by everyone else.

sweet /swiːt/ adj; noun

▸**adj TASTE** ▷ **1** (A1) (especially of food or drink) having a taste similar to that of sugar; not bitter or salty: *The pineapple was sweet and juicy.* ◦ *Do you want your pancakes sweet or savoury?* **PLEASANT** ▷ **2** If an emotion or event is sweet, it is very pleasant and satisfying: *She was enjoying the sweet* ***smell of success.*** **3** If a sound is sweet, it is pleasant and easy to like: *She has a sweet singing voice.* **4** (A2) (especially of something or someone small) pleasant and attractive: *They live in a sweet little house.* ◦ *What a sweet baby!* **5** (B1) kind and pleasant: *I think Alex is really sweet.* ◦ ***It*** *was sweet* ***of*** *you to help me.*

IDIOMS **be sweet on sb** old-fashioned informal to like someone very much in a romantic way: *She's still sweet on him after all this time!* • **keep sb sweet** to try to keep someone satisfied and pleased with you: *We're allowing the French engineers to use our computers, to keep them sweet in case we need their help later on.* • **sweet Fanny Adams** (abbreviation **sweet FA**) old-fashioned slang nothing: *And what does she know about it? Sweet Fanny Adams!*

▸**noun 1** (A2) [C] UK (US **candy**) a small piece of sweet food, made of sugar: *She bought a packet of sweets to suck on the journey.* **2** [C] US any food with a lot of sugar in it **3** [C or U] UK sweet food eaten at the end of a meal: *There was only one sweet on the menu – chocolate cake with cream.*

IDIOM **my sweet** old-fashioned a way of talking to someone you love

ˌsweet-and-ˈsour adj [before noun] describes food with a flavour that is both sweet and sour: *sweet-and-sour pork*

sweetbread /ˈswiːt.bred/ noun [C usually plural] the PANCREAS (= organ near the stomach) of a young sheep or cow, used as food

ˌsweet ˈchestnut noun [C] UK (US **chestnut**) a large tree with leaves divided into five parts and large round nuts that are cooked and eaten hot

ˌsweet ˈcider noun [C] Australian English juice from crushed apples, used as a drink or to make VINEGAR → Compare **cider, rough cider**

sweetcorn /ˈswiːt.kɔːn/ (US) /-kɔːrn/ noun [U] (US usually **corn**) the yellow seeds of a particular type of the MAIZE plant, eaten as a vegetable

sweeten /ˈswiː.tᵊn/ verb [T] **TASTE** ▷ **1** to make something taste sweet: *The apple mixture can be sweetened* ***with*** *honey.* **MORE PLEASANT** ▷ **2** to make something more attractive: *The management sweetened the deal by offering an extra two percent to staff on the lowest end of the pay scale.* **3** to make a person or a mood happier or friendlier: *I think you should try to sweeten him* ***up*** *before you ask him for the loan.*

sweetener /ˈswiːt.nəʳ/ (US) /-nɚ/ noun **TASTE** ▷ **1** [C or U] an artificial substance that has a similar taste to sugar, or a small pill made of this **MONEY** ▷ **2** [C] mainly UK a present or money given to persuade someone to do something, especially in a way that is secret and often dishonest: *a financial sweetener*

sweetheart /ˈswiːt.hɑːt/ (US) /-hɑːrt/ noun [C] **1** a person you love, especially a person you have a romantic relationship with: *She eventually married her* ***childhood*** *sweetheart.* ◦ [as form of address] *'Happy birthday, sweetheart,' he said.* **2** a kind and generous person: *'Oh, you're a sweetheart,' she said, when I placed the breakfast tray on her lap.*

S

ˌ**sweetheart ˌdeal** noun [C] an agreement that you make in which you get something that is to your advantage, especially by agreeing to give up something else

sweetie /ˈswiː.ti/ (US) /-t̬i/ noun FOOD ▷ **1** [C] UK child's word a sweet PERSON ▷ **2** [C] informal a very pleasant or kind person: *He's a real sweetie.* **3** [S] informal a friendly way of talking to someone

sweetly /ˈswiːt.li/ adv in a kind way: *He smiled sweetly at her.*

sweetmeat /ˈswiːt.miːt/ noun [C] old-fashioned a small piece of sweet food, made of or covered in sugar

sweetness /ˈswiːt.nəs/ noun [U] the quality of being sweet

IDIOM **be (all) sweetness and light** to be very peaceful and friendly: *They'd had a big argument yesterday, but by this morning it was all sweetness and light again.*

ˌ**sweet ˈnothings** noun [plural] humorous romantic and loving talk: *They're the couple in the corner,* ***whispering/murmuring*** *sweet nothings to each other.*

ˌ**sweet ˈpea** noun [C] a climbing plant with sweet-smelling flowers that are often a pale colour

ˌ**sweet ˈpepper** noun [C] a **pepper**

ˌ**sweet poˈtato** noun [C] (also **yam**) a pink vegetable which looks like a potato and has yellow or white flesh and a sweet taste

ˈ**sweet ˌspot** noun [C] the part of a surface that is the best or most effective possible place to hit something: *The new tennis rackets are lighter, stronger, and have a bigger sweet spot.*

ˈ**sweet talk** noun [U] informal a way of talking to someone in a pleasing or clever way in order to persuade them to do or believe something • ˈ**sweet-talk** verb [T] *The salesman tried to sweet-talk me* ***into*** *buying a bigger car.*

ˌ**sweet ˈtooth** noun [S] If you have a sweet tooth, you like eating sweet foods, especially sweets and chocolate.

swell /swel/ verb; noun; adj; adv

▸verb (**swelled**, **swollen** or **swelled**) **1** C2 [I or T] to become larger and rounder than usual; to (cause to) increase in size or amount: *It was obvious she had broken her toe, because it immediately started to swell* (***up***). ◦ *25 employees have joined the union in this month alone, swelling its* ***ranks*** *(= increasing its size) to 110.* ◦ literary *His heart/breast swelled* ***with pride*** *(= he felt very proud) as he stood watching his son graduate.* **2** [I] If music swells, it becomes louder.

▸noun [S] WAVES ▷ **1** the slow up and down movement of the sea with large but smooth waves → See also **groundswell** SOUND ▷ **2** an increase in sound produced by a musical instrument or instruments

▸adj US old-fashioned informal very good or pleasant: *That's a swell idea!*

▸adv US old-fashioned informal very well: *Everything's going real swell.*

swelling /ˈswel.ɪŋ/ noun [C or U] a part of your body that has become bigger because of illness or injury

swelter /ˈswel.təʳ/ (US) /-tɚ/ verb [I] (of a person) to feel very hot: *The soldiers were sweltering in their uniforms.*

sweltering /ˈswel.tᵊr.ɪŋ/ (US) /-tɚ-/ adj extremely and uncomfortably hot: *In the summer,* ***it's*** *sweltering in the smaller classrooms.*

swept /swept/ verb past simple and past participle of **sweep**

ˌ**swept-ˈback** adj [before noun] having a front edge which faces backwards at an angle: *a swept-back hairstyle* ◦ *an aircraft with swept-back wings*

swerve /swɜːv/ (US) /swɝːv/ verb [I] **1** to change direction, especially suddenly: *The bus driver swerved to avoid hitting the cyclists.* **2** If you do not swerve from a principle or certain actions, you continue to think or act as you did in the beginning: *She is one of those rare politicians whom one can trust not to swerve* ***from*** *policy and principle.* → Compare **unswerving** • **swerve** noun [C]

swift /swɪft/ adj; noun

▸adj C2 happening or moving quickly or within a short time, especially in a smooth and easy way: *The local police took swift action against the squatters.* ◦ *Thank you for your swift reply.* ◦ *The gazelle is one of the swiftest and most graceful of animals.* • **swiftly** /ˈswɪft.li/ adv C2 *Walking swiftly, he was at the station within minutes.* • **swiftness** /ˈswɪft.nəs/ noun [U]

▸noun [C] a small bird with curved, pointed wings that can fly very fast

swig /swɪɡ/ verb [T] (**-gg-**) informal to drink, especially by swallowing large amounts in a series of single actions • **swig** noun [C] *She* ***took*** *a swig of whisky, straight from the bottle.*

swill /swɪl/ verb; noun

▸verb MOVE LIQUID ▷ **1** [T usually + adv/prep] to cause a liquid to flow around or over something, often in order to clean it: *The dentist handed me a glass of water to swill my mouth* ***out*** *with.* DRINK ▷ **2** [T] informal often disapproving to drink, especially alcohol, quickly and in large amounts

▸noun LIQUID ▷ **1** [S] the movement of liquid over or around something, often in order to clean it: *Give the sink* ***a*** *quick swill to get it clean.* FOOD ▷ **2** [U] US for **pigswill**

swim /swɪm/ verb; noun

▸verb (present participle **swimming**, past tense **swam**, past participle **swum**) MOVE IN WATER ▷ **1** A1 [I or T] to move through water by moving the body or parts of the body: *We spent the day on the beach but it was too cold to* ***go*** *swimming.* ◦ *Her ambition is to swim* (***across***) *the English Channel.* ◦ *I swam two miles this morning.* **2 be swimming in/with sth** disapproving If food is swimming in/with a liquid, it has too much of that liquid in it or on it: *The salad was swimming in oil.* SEEM TO MOVE ▷ **3** [I] (of an object) to seem to move about: *Getting up too suddenly made the room swim before her eyes.* **4** [I] If your head swims, you feel confused and are unable to think or see clearly: *After the second or third drink, my* ***head*** *began to swim.*

▸noun [S] A2 a time when you swim: *Shall we* ***go for/have*** *a swim this afternoon?* • **swimmer** /ˈswɪm.əʳ/ (US) /-ɚ/ noun [C] B1 *Oliver is a very* ***strong*** *swimmer.* • **swimming** /ˈswɪm.ɪŋ/ noun [U] A2 *The doctor recommended swimming as the best all-round exercise.*

ˈ**swim ˌbladder** noun [C] specialized an organ like a bag inside a fish that holds air so that it does not sink and stays in the correct position

swimmers /ˈswɪm.əz/ (US) /-ɚz/ noun [plural] Australian English informal for **swimming costume** or **swimming trunks**

ˈ**swimming ˌbaths** noun [C, + sing/pl verb] UK old-fashioned a public swimming pool

ˈ**swimming ˌcostume** noun [C] UK A2 a piece of clothing that women wear for swimming

swimmingly /ˈswɪm.ɪŋ.li/ adv old-fashioned informal successfully and without any problems: *Everything* ***went*** *swimmingly until Peter started talking about money.*

ˈ**swimming ˌpool** noun [C] A1 an artificial area of

water for swimming, or a building containing this: *an **indoor/outdoor** swimming pool*

ˈswimming ˌtrunks noun [plural] mainly UK a piece of men's clothing that is worn when swimming

swimsuit /ˈswɪm.suːt/, /-sjuːt/ ⓤⓢ /-suːt/ noun [C] A2 a piece of clothing that you wear for swimming

swimwear /ˈswɪm.weəʳ/ ⓤⓢ /-wer/ noun [U] clothes that you wear for swimming

swindle /ˈswɪn.dəl/ verb [T] to get money dishonestly from someone by deceiving or cheating them: *They swindled local businesses **out of** thousands of pounds.* • **swindle** noun [C] *Fraud squad officers are investigating a £5.6 million swindle.* • **swindler** /-əʳ/ ⓤⓢ /-ɚ/ noun [C]

swine /swaɪn/ noun [C] **PERSON** ▷ **1** (plural **swine** or **swines**) old-fashioned a person who you consider to be extremely unpleasant and unkind: *You **filthy** swine!* ◦ *Her ex-husband sounds like an absolute swine.* **ANIMAL** ▷ **2** (plural **swine**) old use or specialized a pig

ˈswine ˌfever noun [U] a serious disease of pigs

swing /swɪŋ/ verb; noun

▸verb (**swung, swung**) **MOVE SIDEWAYS** ▷ **1** B2 [I or T] to move easily and without interruption backwards and forwards or from one side to the other, especially from a fixed point, or to cause something or someone to do this: *He walked briskly along the path swinging his rolled-up umbrella.* ◦ *The door swung open.* **2** [I] to change: *His **mood** swings **between** elation and despair.* **BE EXCITING** ▷ **3** [I] informal to be exciting and enjoyable: *You need music to make a **party** swing.* **MUSIC** ▷ **4** [I or T] to play music in a strong, exciting style like JAZZ, or (of music) to be played in this way **ARRANGE** ▷ **5** [T] informal to arrange for something to happen, by persuading people and often by acting slightly dishonestly: *If you want an interview with Pedro, I could probably swing **it** (**for** you).*

IDIOMS **swing both ways** informal to be sexually attracted to both men and women • **swing for it** UK informal to be punished severely for something that has happened: *If there's an error in the calculations, you know who'll swing for it!* • **swing into action** to quickly start working: *The emergency services swung into action as soon as the news of the bomb explosion reached them.* • **swing the balance** If something swings the balance, it is the thing that causes a particular situation to happen or a particular decision to be made instead of other situations or decisions that are possible: *This latest election promise might just swing the balance in the government's favour.*

PHRASAL VERBS **swing at sb** to try to hit someone • **swing for sb** UK old-fashioned informal to hit someone • **swing (sth/sb) round** UK (US **swing (sth/sb) around**) to turn round quickly, or to turn something or someone round quickly

▸noun **SIDEWAYS MOVEMENT** ▷ **1** [C] a swinging movement **2** [C] an attempt to hit someone: *The drunk **took** a wild swing **at** Harry.* **3** [C] a change: *He experiences severe **mood** swings (= sudden changes from one extreme mood to another).* ◦ *The Democrats only need a five percent swing (= need five percent of voters to change to supporting them) to win this election.* **SEAT** ▷ **4** B2 [C] a seat joined by two ropes or chains to a metal bar or a tree, on which you can sit and move backwards and forwards **BE EXCITING** ▷ **5 go with a swing** UK informal If an event, especially a party, goes with a swing, it is very exciting and successful. **MUSIC** ▷ **6** [U] a type of dance music that was popular in the 1930s and 40s

IDIOM **get into the swing of it/things** informal to start to understand, enjoy, and be active in something: *I hadn't worked in an office for several years, so it took me a while to get back into the swing of it.*

ˈswing ˌbridge noun [C usually singular] a bridge that can be turned to a position that is at 90° to its usual position, so that ships can go through

ˌswing ˈdoor noun [C] UK (US **ˈswinging ˌdoor**) a door that can swing open in both directions

swingeing /ˈswɪn.dʒɪŋ/ adj UK formal extreme and having a serious and unpleasant effect: *We are going to have to make swingeing **cuts** in the budget.*

swinger /ˈswɪŋ.əʳ/ ⓤⓢ /-ɚ/ noun [C] old-fashioned slang a person who dresses in a fashionable way and who goes to a lot of parties and NIGHTCLUBS, or someone who is willing to have sex often with many different people

swinging /ˈswɪŋ.ɪŋ/ adj old-fashioned informal exciting and fashionable: *It's a nostalgia trip back into the youth culture of the swinging 60s.*

ˈswing ˌvoter noun [C] someone who has not yet decided who they will vote for in an election

swipe /swaɪp/ verb; noun

▸verb **HIT** ▷ **1** [I or T, usually + adv/prep] to hit or try to hit something, especially with a sideways movement: *She opened the window and swiped **at** the flies with a rolled-up newspaper to make them go out.* ◦ *She swiped him **round** the head.* ◦ mainly US *The car swiped the garage door as he pulled out.* → See also **sideswipe** **STEAL** ▷ **2** [T] informal to steal: *Okay, who's swiped my keys?* **MOVE** ▷ **3** [T] to move a card containing information stored on a MAGNETIC strip through a device that reads this information

▸noun **CRITICISM** ▷ **1** [C usually singular] a criticism of someone or something, or an attempt to damage or annoy them: *In a recent interview, she **takes** a swipe **at** the theatre management.* **HIT** ▷ **2** [C] an act of hitting or trying to hit someone or something: *Edwin **took** a swipe **at** the ball and missed.*

ˈswipe ˌcard noun [C] a plastic card that you slide through a machine in order to be allowed into a building, pay for something, etc.

swirl /swɜːl/ ⓤⓢ /swɝːl/ verb [I or T, usually + adv/prep] to (cause to) move quickly with a twisting, circular movement: *Swirl a little oil **around** the frying pan.* ◦ *The fog swirled thickly **around** us.* • **swirl** noun [C] *The truck went by in a swirl of dust.*

swish /swɪʃ/ verb; adj; noun

▸verb [I or T] to (cause to) move quickly through the air making a soft sound: *I heard the rope swish through the air.* ◦ *The horses swished their tails to get rid of the flies hovering around them.*

▸adj informal fashionable or expensive: *a swish hotel*

▸noun [C] **MOVEMENT** ▷ **1** a quick movement through the air, making a soft sound: *With a swish of the curtains, the stage was revealed.* **LIKE A WOMAN** ▷ **2** US slang disapproving a man who behaves or appears in a way that is generally considered more suited to a woman, and who does not have traditional male qualities

ˌSwiss ˈchard noun [U] (also **chard**) a vegetable with large, dark green leaves and white stems, which can be cooked and eaten

ˌSwiss ˈroll noun [C] UK (US **ˌjelly ˈroll**) a cake that has been spread with cream, jam, or chocolate and then rolled into a cylinder shape

switch /swɪtʃ/ noun; verb

▸noun **DEVICE** ▷ **1** B1 [C] a small device, usually pushed up or down with your finger, that controls and turns on or off an electric current: *a light switch* ◦ *Can you*

S

flip the switch? **2 switches** [plural] US for **points** CHANGE ▷ **3** [C] a sudden or complete change, especially of one person or thing for another
▸verb [T, I usually + adv/prep] DEVICE ▷ **1** B1 to use a switch to change a device from one state or type of operation to another: *switch the TV* ***off/on*** CHANGE ▷ **2** B2 to change suddenly or completely, especially from one thing to another, or to exchange by replacing one person or thing with another: *She started studying English at college, but switched* ***to*** *Business Studies in her second year.* ◦ *In 1971, Britain switched* ***over*** *(= changed completely)* ***to*** *a decimal currency.* ◦ *After the bank robbery, the gang switched cars (= left one car and got into another).*

PHRASAL VERBS **switch off** informal to stop giving your attention to someone or something • **switch sth on** usually disapproving If someone switches on a particular emotion or behaviour, they suddenly start to feel or behave in that way, but usually not sincerely: *When a customer walks in, she switches on the charm.*

switchback /ˈswɪtʃ.bæk/ noun [C] a path, road, or railway that forms very sharp bends from one direction to almost the opposite direction as it goes up and down steep slopes

switchblade /ˈswɪtʃ.bleɪd/ noun US for **flick knife**

switchboard /ˈswɪtʃ.bɔːd/ US /-bɔːrd/ noun [C] a piece of equipment that is used to direct all the phone calls made to and from a particular building or area: *Tearful fans* ***jammed*** *the radio station's switchboard after the singer's death (= so many people rang that all the phones were busy).*

ˈswitchboard ˌoperator noun [C] a person whose job is to receive phone calls and connect them to other numbers

ˌswitched ˈon adj old-fashioned informal quick to know about or be involved with the most recent fashions and ideas

swivel /ˈswɪv.əl/ verb; adj
▸verb [I or T] (-ll- or US usually -l-) to (cause to) turn round a central point in order to face in another direction: *She swivelled* ***round*** *to look out of the window.* ◦ *The ostrich swivelled its head in our direction.*
▸adj [before noun] turning around a central point to face in another direction: *a swivel chair* ◦ *a swivel lamp*

S

swizz (also **swiz**) /swɪz/ noun [S] UK old-fashioned informal something that is disappointing or unfair: *'There's only half as much in the new packets.* ***'What a*** *swizz!'*

swizzle stick /ˈswɪz.əlˌstɪk/ noun [C] a small glass or plastic rod for mixing drinks

swollen /ˈswəʊ.lən/ US /ˈswoʊ-/ verb; adj
▸verb past participle of **swell**
▸adj B2 larger than usual: *a bruised, swollen face* ◦ *The stream is swollen because of the heavy rain.*

ˌswollen ˈhead noun [C usually singular] (US usually also **ˌswelled ˈhead**) If someone has a swollen head, they think they are more intelligent and more important than they really are: *Don't compliment him any more, or he'll* ***get*** *a swollen head.* → Compare **bighead** • **ˌswollen-ˈheaded** adj informal disapproving

swoon /swuːn/ verb; noun
▸verb [I] **1** to feel a lot of pleasure, love, etc. because of something or someone: *The audience swooned* ***with*** *delight.* **2** old-fashioned literary to **faint**
▸noun [C] old-fashioned literary a **faint** (= state of suddenly becoming unconscious)

swoop /swuːp/ verb [I] **1** to move very quickly and easily through the air, especially down from a height in order to attack: *The eagle swooped* ***down*** *to snatch a young rabbit.* **2** informal to make a sudden attack on a place or group of people in order to surround and catch them: *Undercover police swooped* ***on*** *three houses in Bristol at 5.00 this morning.* • **swoop** noun [C]

swoosh /swuːʃ/ verb; noun
▸verb [I] informal to make the sound of air or water that is moving quickly
▸noun [C] informal SOUND ▷ **1** the sound of air or water that is moving quickly: *The geese took off with a swoosh of their wings.* SHAPE ▷ **2** a curved shape that is used as a symbol representing the name of a company or product. The word was originally used for the symbol of the Nike company.

swop /swɒp/ US /swɑːp/ verb [I or T] (-pp-) mainly UK for **swap**

sword /sɔːd/ US /sɔːrd/ noun [C] B2 a weapon with a long, sharp metal blade and a handle, used especially in the past

sword

IDIOMS **beat/turn swords into ploughshares** literary to change to a peaceful way of life and spend money on peaceful things rather than weapons • **put sb to the sword** literary to kill someone: *Thousands of innocents were put to the sword.* • **sword of Damocles** If you have a sword of Damocles hanging over you/your head, something bad seems very likely to happen to you: *Government threats to cut the budget by 50 percent are hanging over the Opera House* ***like a*** *sword of Damocles.*

swordfish /ˈsɔː.d.fɪʃ/ US /ˈsɔːrd-/ noun [C or U] (plural **swordfish** or **swordfishes**) a large, long fish with a very long pointed part like a beak at the front of its head, often eaten as food

swordsman /ˈsɔːdz.mən/ US /ˈsɔːrdz-/ noun [C] (plural **-men** /-mən/) a person skilled in fighting with a sword

swordsmanship /ˈsɔːdz.mən.ʃɪp/ US /ˈsɔːrdz-/ noun [U] the skill of fighting with a sword

swore /swɔːr/ US /swɔːr/ verb past simple of **swear**

sworn /swɔːn/ US /swɔːrn/ verb; adj
▸verb past participle of **swear**
▸adj [before noun] formally and officially stated as being true: *a sworn testimony*

ˌsworn ˈenemy noun [C] Sworn enemies are people who will always hate each other.

swot /swɒt/ US /swɑːt/ verb; noun
▸verb [I] (-tt-) UK informal or child's word to study hard, usually by reading about or learning something, especially before taking an exam

PHRASAL VERB **swot up (sth)** to learn as much as you can about a subject, especially before an exam: *She's at home, swotting up* ***on*** *her maths.*

▸noun [C] (plural -tt-) UK informal or child's word someone, usually a child, who studies very hard

SWOT /swɒt/ US /swɑːt/ noun [U] abbreviation for strengths, weaknesses, opportunities, threats: a way of considering all the good and bad features of a business situation or a company: *a SWOT analysis*

swum /swʌm/ verb past participle of **swim**

swung /swʌŋ/ verb past simple and past participle of **swing**

sybarite /ˈsɪb.ᵊr.aɪt/ (US) /-ə.raɪt/ noun [C] formal a person who loves expensive things and pleasure → Compare **hedonist (hedonism)** • **sybaritic** /ˌsɪb.ᵊrˈɪt.ɪk/ (US) /-əˈrɪt̬-/ adj

sycamore /ˈsɪk.ə.mɔːʳ/ (US) /-mɔːr/ noun [C] a tree with leaves divided into five parts and seeds that turn around slowly to the ground when they fall

sycophantic /ˌsɪk.əˈfæn.tɪk/ adj formal disapproving (of a person or of behaviour) praising people in authority in a way that is not sincere, usually in order to get some advantage from them: *There was sycophantic laughter from the audience at every one of his terrible jokes.* • **sycophancy** /ˈsɪk.ə.fən.si/ noun [U] • **sycophant** /ˈsɪk.ə.fænt/ noun [C] *The prime minister is surrounded by sycophants.*

sylˌlabic ˈconsonant noun [C] specialized a consonant that is a whole syllable: *The /l/ at the end of 'bottle' is a syllabic consonant.*

syllable /ˈsɪl.ə.bl̩/ noun [C] (B2) a single unit of speech, either a whole word or one of the parts into which a word can be separated, usually containing a vowel • **syllabic** /sɪˈlæb.ɪk/ adj specialized

syllabub /ˈsɪl.ə.bʌb/ noun [U] a sweet, cold dish consisting of cream mixed with sugar, white wine, and sometimes the WHITE of an egg

syllabus /ˈsɪl.ə.bəs/ noun [C] (plural **syllabuses** or **syllabi**) (C2) (a plan showing) the subjects or books to be studied in a particular course, especially a course which leads to an exam: *Which novels are **on** the syllabus this year?* → Compare **curriculum**

syllogism /ˈsɪl.ə.dʒɪ.zᵊm/ noun [C] specialized (in PHILOSOPHY) a process of LOGIC in which two general statements lead to a more particular statement • **syllogistic** /ˌsɪl.əˈdʒɪs.tɪk/ adj

sylphlike /ˈsɪlf.laɪk/ adj usually humorous (of a woman or girl) attractively thin and delicate

symbiosis /ˌsɪm.baɪˈəʊ.sɪs/ (US) /-ˈoʊ-/ noun [U] **1** specialized a relationship between two types of animal or plant in which each provides for the other the conditions necessary for its continued existence **2** a relationship between people or organizations that depend on each other equally • **symbiotic** /-ˈɒt.ɪk/ (US) /-ˈɑː.t̬ɪk/ adj specialized *a symbiotic relationship* • **symbiotically** /-ˈɒt.ɪ.kᵊl.i/ (US) /-ɑː.t̬ɪ.kᵊl.i/ adv specialized

symbol /ˈsɪm.bᵊl/ noun [C] **1** (B2) a sign, shape, or object that is used to represent something else: *A heart shape is the symbol of love.* ◦ *The wheel in the Indian flag is a symbol **of** peace.* → Compare **emblem** **2** something that is used to represent a quality or idea: *Water, a symbol **of** life, recurs as an image throughout her poems.* **3** a number, letter, or sign used in mathematics, music, science, etc.: *The symbol **for** oxygen is O.* **4** An object can be described as a symbol of something else if it seems to represent it because it is connected with it in a lot of people's minds: *The private jet is a symbol **of** wealth.*

symbolic /sɪmˈbɒl.ɪk/ (US) /-ˈbɑː.lɪk/ adj (also **symbolical**) **1** (C2) representing something else: *The skull at the bottom of the picture is symbolic **of** death.* **2** refers to an action that expresses or seems to express an intention or feeling, but has little practical influence on a situation: *Five hundred troops were sent in, more as a symbolic **gesture** than as a real threat.* • **symbolically** /-ɪ.kᵊl.i/ adv

symbolism /ˈsɪm.bᵊl.ɪ.zᵊm/ noun [U] **1** the use of symbols in art, literature, films, etc. to represent ideas: *Religious symbolism is very characteristic of the paintings of this period.* **2** specialized a type of art and literature developed in the late 19th century that tries to express ideas or states of mind rather than represent the real world, using the power of words and images → Compare **naturalism, realism, expressionism**

symbolist /ˈsɪm.bᵊl.ɪst/ noun [C] specialized a writer or an artist connected with symbolism • **symbolist** adj specialized *symbolist poets*

symbolize (UK usually **symbolise**) /ˈsɪm.bᵊl.aɪz/ (US) /-bə.laɪz/ verb [T] to represent something: *The lighting of the Olympic torch symbolizes peace and friendship among the nations of the world.*

symmetry /ˈsɪm.ə.tri/ noun [U] **1** the quality of having parts that match each other, especially in a way that is attractive, or similarity of shape or contents: *The design of the house had a **pleasing** symmetry, its oblong shape being picked up in its elongated windows.* → Compare **asymmetry (asymmetric)** **2** specialized in mathematics, the quality of having two parts that match exactly, either when one half is like an image of the other half in a mirror, or when one part can take the place of another if it is turned 90° or 180° • **symmetrical** /sɪˈmet.rɪ.kᵊl/ adj (also **symmetric**) • **symmetrically** /sɪˈmet.rɪ.kᵊl.i/ adv

sympathetic /ˌsɪm.pəˈθet.ɪk/ (US) /-ˈθet̬-/ adj UNDERSTANDING ▷ **1** (B2) describes someone who shows, especially by what they say, that they understand and care about someone's suffering: *He suffers from back trouble too, so he was very sympathetic **about** my problem.* ◦ *She just needed someone who would **lend a** sympathetic **ear** to her (= listen to her in a kind and understanding way) once in a while.* → Opposite **unsympathetic** **2** If a character in a book or film is sympathetic, they are described or shown in such a way that you are able to understand their feelings and the reasons for their actions, and so you like them: *She comes across as a more sympathetic character in the film.* SUPPORT ▷ **3** (C2) agreeing with or supporting: *The Labour party are supposed to be sympathetic **to/towards** the unions.* ◦ *Did he give your proposal/complaints a sympathetic **hearing**?* • **sympathetically** /-ɪ.kᵊl.i/ adv

sympathize (UK usually **sympathise**) /ˈsɪm.pə.θaɪz/ verb [I] UNDERSTAND ▷ **1** (C2) to understand and care about someone's problems: *I know what it's like to have migraines, so I do sympathize (**with** you).* SUPPORT ▷ **2** to support and agree with someone or something: *I sympathize **with** the general aims of the party, but on this particular issue I'm afraid I disagree.*

sympathizer (UK usually **sympathiser**) /ˈsɪm.pə.θaɪ.zəʳ/ (US) /-zɚ/ noun [C] a person who supports a political organization or believes in a set of ideas

sympathy /ˈsɪm.pə.θi/ noun UNDERSTANDING ▷ **1** (B2) [U] (an expression of) understanding and care for someone else's suffering: *The president has sent a message of sympathy to the relatives of the dead soldiers.* ◦ *I don't have much sympathy **for** her – I think she's brought her troubles on herself.* → Compare **empathy** **2 offer/send your sympathies** formal to express your sadness to someone because a relation or friend of theirs has recently died: *I went along to the funeral in order to offer my sympathies.* SUPPORT ▷ **3** (C2) [U] support and agreement: *I must confess I have some sympathy **with** his views.* **4 sympathies** [plural] support: *Of those people questioned, 93 percent said their sympathies were **with** the teachers.* ◦ *He is known to have right-wing sympathies.* **5 come out in sympathy with sb** to stop working in order to show

S

your support for other workers who are ON STRIKE: *The railway workers came out in sympathy with the miners.*

ˌsympathy ˌvote noun [S] UK informal an occasion when a lot of people vote for or support a particular person because he or she has suffered recently: *He won the award, but some suspected it was a sympathy vote following his struggle with cancer.*

symphony /ˈsɪm.fə.ni/ noun [C] a long piece of music for an ORCHESTRA, usually with four MOVEMENTS (= parts): *Mahler's ninth symphony* • **symphonic** /sɪmˈfɒn.ɪk/ (US) /-ˈfɑː.nɪk/ adj

symposium /sɪmˈpəʊ.zi.əm/ (US) /-ˈpoʊ-/ noun [C] (plural **symposia** or **symposiums**) formal an occasion at which people who have great knowledge of a particular subject meet in order to discuss a matter of interest: *a symposium* ***on*** *European cinema*

symptom /ˈsɪmp.təm/ noun [C] **1** B2 any feeling of illness or physical or mental change that is caused by a particular disease: *He's complaining of all the usual flu symptoms – a high temperature, headache, and so on.* ◦ *He's been HIV-positive for six years, but just recently he's started to* ***develop*** *the symptoms of AIDS.* **2** C2 any single problem that is caused by and shows a more serious and general problem: *It's her feeling that the recent outbreaks of violence are a symptom of the dissatisfaction that is currently affecting our society.*

symptomatic /ˌsɪmp.təˈmæt.ɪk/ (US) /-ˈmæt̬-/ adj If something bad is symptomatic of something else, it is caused by the other thing and is proof that it exists: *Jealousy within a relationship is usually symptomatic* ***of*** *low self-esteem in one of the partners.*

synagogue /ˈsɪn.ə.gɒg/ (US) /-gɑːg/ noun [C] a building in which Jewish people worship and study their religion

synapse /ˈsaɪ.næps/ noun [C] specialized the point at which electrical signals move from one nerve cell to another • **synaptic** /sɪˈnæp.tɪk/ adj

sync /sɪŋk/ noun; verb

▸noun [U] (also **synch**) **1** informal for **synchronization (synchronize)**: *He's putting himself forward as a president whose ideas are* ***in sync with*** *(= are suited to and show an understanding of) a nation demanding change.* **2 in/out of sync** If two things are in/out of sync, they reach the same or related stage at the same time/at different times.

▸verb [I or T] (also **synch**) **1** informal for **synchronize**: *The action on the screen syncs perfectly with the music.* **2** to connect two electronic devices so that they both have the latest information or files: *How do I sync my iPhone to my computer?*

synchronicity /ˌsɪŋ.krəˈnɪs.ɪ.ti/ (US) /-ə.t̬i/ noun [U] specialized the happening by chance of two or more related or similar events at the same time

synchronize (UK usually **synchronise**) /ˈsɪŋ.krə.naɪz/ verb **1** [I or T] to (cause to) happen at the same time: *The show was designed so that the lights synchronized* ***with*** *the music.* **2** [T] When people synchronize their watches, they make sure that all their watches show the same time: *We'd better synchronize our watches if we all want to be there at the same time.* • **synchronization** (UK usually **synchronisation**) /ˌsɪŋ.krə.naɪˈzeɪ.ʃən/ (US) /-əˈ-/ noun [U]

ˌsynchronized ˈswimming noun [U] a sport in which a group of people make smooth, attractive movements like dancing in the water at the same time

synchronous /ˈsɪŋ.krə.nəs/ adj formal happening or done at the same time or speed: *The dancers perform a sequence of wonderfully synchronous movements.* → Opposite **asynchronous**

syncline /ˈsɪŋ.klaɪn/ noun [C] specialized a downward, U-shaped fold in the layers of rock in the Earth's surface → Compare **anticline**

syncopated /ˈsɪŋ.kə.peɪ.tɪd/ (US) /-t̬ɪd/ adj (of a tune) having a rhythm in which strong notes are not on the beat: *syncopated jazz rhythms* • **syncopation** /ˌsɪŋ.kəˈpeɪ.ʃən/ noun [U]

syndicate /ˈsɪn.dɪ.kət/ noun **GROUP** ▷ **1** [C, + sing/pl verb] a group of people or companies who join together in order to share the cost of a particular business operation for which a large amount of money is needed: *A syndicate* ***of*** *banks is/are financing the deal.* **NEWSPAPERS** ▷ **2** [C] an organization that supplies articles and photographs to different newspapers and magazines for publishing • **syndicate** /ˈsɪn.dɪ.keɪt/ verb [T] • **syndication** /ˌsɪn.dɪˈkeɪ.ʃən/ noun [U]

syndicated /ˈsɪn.dɪ.keɪ.tɪd/ (US) /-t̬ɪd/ adj **1** (of articles and photographs) sold to several different newspapers and magazines for publishing **2** mainly US (of television or radio programmes) sold to several different broadcasting organizations

syndrome /ˈsɪn.drəʊm/ (US) /-droʊm/ noun **1** [C] a combination of medical problems that commonly go together, which might show the existence of a particular disease or mental condition → See also **Down's syndrome** **2** [U] used in the names of various illnesses: *irritable bowel syndrome* **3** [C] a type of negative behaviour or mental state that is typical of a person in a particular situation: *It's a classic case of the bored-housewife syndrome – she's got nothing to do all day except drink and go shopping.*

synergy /ˈsɪn.ə.dʒi/ (US) /-ɚ-/ noun [U] (also **synergism**) the combined power of a group of things when they are working together that is greater than the total power achieved by each working separately • **synergistic** /sɪn.əˈdʒɪs.tɪk/ (US) /sɪn.ɚ-/ adj *the synergistic effect of two drugs given at the same time*

synod /ˈsɪn.əd/, /-ɒd/ noun [C] specialized a regular meeting of Church members for the discussion of religious matters

synonym /ˈsɪn.ə.nɪm/ noun [C] C2 a word or phrase that has the same or nearly the same meaning as another word or phrase in the same language: *The words 'small' and 'little' are synonyms.* → Compare **antonym**

synonymous /sɪˈnɒn.ɪ.məs/ (US) /-ˈnɑː.nə-/ adj **1** C2 having the same meaning: *The words 'annoyed' and 'irritated' are more or less synonymous.* **2** C2 If you say that one thing is synonymous with another, you mean that the two things are so closely connected in most people's minds that one suggests the other: *Oscar Wilde's name is synonymous* ***with*** *wit.*

synopsis /sɪˈnɒp.sɪs/ (US) /-ˈnɑːp-/ noun [C] (plural **synopses**) a short description of the contents of something such as a film or book

synovial fluid /saɪˌnəʊ.vi.əlˈfluː.ɪd/ (US) /-ˌnoʊ-/ noun [U] specialized a transparent, sticky liquid produced in our JOINTS (= places where two bones are connected) that allows the bones and TENDONS to move smoothly

syntax /ˈsɪn.tæks/ noun [U] specialized the grammatical arrangement of words in a sentence • **syntactic** /sɪnˈtæk.tɪk/ adj • **syntactically** /sɪnˈtæk.tɪ.kəl.i/ adv

synthesis /ˈsɪn.θə.sɪs/ noun **CHEMICAL PRODUCTION** ▷ **1** [U] specialized the production of a substance from simpler materials after a chemical reaction → See also **photosynthesis** **MIX** ▷ **2** [C] (plural **syntheses**) formal the mixing of different ideas, influences, or things to make a whole that is different or new: *He describes his latest record as 'a synthesis of African and Latin rhythms'.*

synthesize specialized (UK usually **synthesise**) /ˈsɪn.θə.saɪz/ **verb** [T] to produce a substance by a chemical reaction in plants or animals: *There are many vitamins that the body cannot synthesize itself.*

synthesizer (UK usually **synthesiser**) /ˈsɪn.θə.saɪ.zəʳ/ ⓤⓢ /-zɚ/ **noun** [C] an electronic keyboard instrument that can produce and combine a large range of recorded sounds, often in order to copy other musical instruments or voices

synthetic /sɪnˈθet.ɪk/ ⓤⓢ /-ˈθeṭ-/ **adj** **1** describes products that are made from artificial substances, often copying a natural product: *synthetic fibres* **2** disapproving false or artificial: *She criticized the synthetic charm of television presenters.* • **synthetically** /-ɪ.kəl.i/ **adv**

syphilis /ˈsɪf.ɪ.lɪs/ **noun** [U] a disease caught during sexual activity with an infected person which spreads slowly from the sex organs to all parts of the body

syphon /ˈsaɪ.fən/ **noun** [C] a **siphon**

syringe /sɪˈrɪndʒ/ **noun; verb**

▸**noun** [C] a hollow, cylinder-shaped piece of equipment used for sucking liquid out of something or pushing liquid into something, especially one with a needle that can be put under the skin and used to INJECT drugs, remove small amounts of blood, etc.

▸**verb** [T] to clean the inside of the ears by pushing water into them and then sucking it out of them using a syringe

syrup /ˈsɪr.əp/ **noun** [U] **1** a very sweet, thick, light-coloured liquid made by dissolving sugar in water **2** a type of sweet liquid medicine: *cough syrup*

syrupy /ˈsɪr.əp.i/ **adj** **1** thick and sweet **2** disapproving too good or kind or expressing feelings of love in a way which is not sincere: *syrupy love songs*

system /ˈsɪs.təm/ **noun** **SET** ▷ **1** B1 [C] a set of connected things or devices that operate together: *a central-heating system* **2** B1 [C] a set of computer equipment and programs used together for a particular purpose: *The system keeps crashing and no one is able to figure out why.* **3** C2 [C] a set of organs or structures in the body that have a particular purpose: *the immune system* ◦ *the nervous system* **4** [C] the way that the body works, especially the way that it digests food and passes out waste products: *A run in the morning is good for the system – it wakes the body up and gets everything going.* **METHOD** ▷ **5** B2 [C] a way of doing things: *We'll have to work out a proper filing system.* ◦ ***Under** our education system, you're supposed to be able to choose the type of schooling that your child receives.* ◦ *The legal system **operates** very differently in the US and Britain.* **6** B2 [C] a particular method of counting, measuring, or weighing things: *the metric system of measuring and weighing* **7** [U] approving the intentional and organized use of a system: *There doesn't seem to be any system to the books on these shelves – they're certainly not in alphabetical order.* **8 the system** disapproving unfair laws and rules that prevent people from being able to improve their situation: *He has his own ways of **beating** the system, making sure that he has good relationships with influential people.*

IDIOM **get sth out of your system** informal If you get something out of your system, you get rid of a wish or emotion, especially a negative one, by allowing yourself to express it: *I had a really good shout at him this morning and got it out of my system.*

systematic /ˌsɪs.təˈmæt.ɪk/ ⓤⓢ /-ˈmæṭ-/ **adj** C2 using a fixed and organized plan: approving *We've got to be a bit more systematic in the way that we approach this task.* ◦ disapproving *We're hearing reports of the systematic rape and torture of prisoners.* • **systematically** /-ɪ.kəl.i/ **adv**

systematize specialized (UK usually **systematise**) /ˈsɪs.tə.mə.taɪz/ **verb** [T] to plan a system for something • **systematization** (UK usually **systematisation**) /ˌsɪs.tə.mə.taɪˈzeɪ.ʃən/ ⓤⓢ /-tə.mə.ṭəˈ-/ **noun** [U]

systemic /sɪˈstem.ɪk/ **adj** **1** specialized A systemic drug, disease, or poison reaches and has an effect on the whole of a body or a plant and not just one part of it. **2** formal A systemic problem or change is a basic one, experienced by the whole of an organization or a country and not just particular parts of it: *The current recession is the result of a systemic change within the structure of the country's economy.*

ˈsystems ˌanalyst **noun** [C] a person who examines complicated industrial and business operations in order to find ways of improving them, especially by the introduction of computer programs and equipment • **ˈsystems aˌnalysis** **noun** [U]

T

T, t /tiː/ **noun** [C or U] (plural **Ts, T's** or **t's**) the 20th letter of the English alphabet

ta /tɑː/ **exclamation** UK informal thank you

tab /tæb/ **noun** [C] **SMALL OBJECT** ▷ **1** a small piece of paper, metal, etc. that is fixed to something larger and is used for giving information, fastening, opening, etc.: *Make a file for these documents and write 'finance' on the tab.* ◦ *Insert Tab A into Slot A and glue, before standing the model upright.* **2** US (UK **ringpull**) the small piece of metal, often joined to a ring, that is pulled off or pushed into the top of a CAN (= metal drink container) to open it **3** Northern English a cigarette **4** (also **tab of acid**) a small piece of paper containing the drug LSD **COMPUTER** ▷ **5** a small symbol on a computer screen or website that allows you to open different documents or pages: *Move between pages by clicking on the tabs at the top of the screen.* **6** a fixed position on a line of text that can be reached by pressing the TAB KEY on a keyboard **BILL** ▷ **7 the tab** informal the total money charged in a restaurant or hotel for food, drinks, etc.: *He kindly offered to* ***pick up*** *the tab (= pay).*

IDIOM **keep tabs on sth/sb** to watch something or someone carefully: *I like to keep tabs on my bank account so that I don't overdraw.*

tabard /ˈtæb.ɑːd/ (US) /-ɚd/ **noun** [C] a piece of clothing consisting of a back and a front part without sleeves and a hole for the head, sometimes worn to protect the clothes underneath when working

Tabasco /təˈbæs.kəʊ/ (US) /-koʊ/ **noun** [U] trademark a red sauce with a hot taste, used on food to add flavour

tabbouleh (also **tabouli**) /təˈbuː.leɪ/ **noun** [U] a Middle Eastern dish, eaten cold, that is made with WHEAT grains, herbs, and vegetables

tabby /ˈtæb.i/ **adj, noun** [C] (a cat) having dark-coloured marks on grey or brown fur

tabernacle /ˈtæb.əˌnæk.l̩/ (US) /-ɚ-/ **noun** [C] **1** a place of worship for some groups of Christians **2** in a Roman Catholic church, the box in which holy bread and wine are kept

ˈtab ˌkey noun [C] the key on a computer keyboard that allows you to move the CURSOR (= a symbol that shows where you are working) forward a few spaces

tabla /ˈtæb.lə/ (US) /ˈtɑː.blə/ **noun** [C] an Indian musical instrument consisting of a pair of small drums that you play with your PALMS and fingers

table /ˈteɪ.bl̩/ **noun; verb**

▸**noun FURNITURE** ▷ **1** (A1) [C] a flat surface, usually supported by four legs, used for putting things on **2** [+ sing/pl verb] the people sitting at a table: *There was a really noisy table behind us celebrating someone's birthday.* **3** [C] Indian English a table that you work at in an office → See also **desk 4 lay/set the table** (B1) to put a cloth, knives, and forks, etc. on the table in preparation for a meal: *Could you lay the table* ***for*** *lunch, please?* **INFORMATION** ▷ **5** (B1) [C] an arrangement of facts and numbers in rows or blocks, especially in printed material **6** [C] a **multiplication table 7 table of contents** a list of the information that is contained in a book

IDIOMS **on the table** If a plan or suggestion has been put/laid on the table, it has been made available for people to hear, read, or discuss. • **under the table** If something is done under the table, it is a secret, hidden action: *They offered him money under the table to change his mind.*

▸**verb** [T] **1** UK to suggest something for discussion: *An amendment to the proposal was tabled by Mrs James.* **2** US to delay discussion of a subject: *The suggestion was tabled for discussion at a later date.*

tableau /ˈtæb.ləʊ/ (US) /-loʊ/ **noun** [C] (plural **tableaux**) an arrangement of people who do not move or speak, especially on a stage, who represent a view of life, an event, etc.

tablecloth /ˈteɪ.bl̩.klɒθ/ (US) /-klɑːθ/ **noun** [C] (B2) a large piece of cloth that covers a table during a meal and protects or decorates it

tablecloth

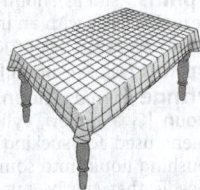

table d'hôte /ˌtɑː.bləˈdəʊt/ (US) /-bl̩ˈdoʊt/ **noun** [U] food that is served in a restaurant as a complete meal at a fixed price but with little choice of dishes → Compare **à la carte**

ˌtable ˈfootball noun [C] (US also **foosball**) a game played on a table using a small ball and model players fixed to poles, based on football

ˈtable ˌlamp noun [C] a small electric light that is used on a table

ˈtable ˌlinen noun [U] the TABLECLOTHS and NAPKINS that are put on a table for a meal

ˈtable ˌmanners noun [plural] the way you eat your food, or the socially acceptable way to eat your food, especially when eating a meal with others: *Your table manners are appalling – don't you know how to use a knife and fork?*

ˈtable ˌmat noun [C] a small cover that protects a table against heat damage from food containers or plates

tablespoon /ˈteɪ.bl̩.spuːn/ **noun** [C] (written abbreviation **tbsp**) (the amount held by) a large spoon used for measuring or serving food: *three tablespoons of sugar* → Compare **dessertspoon, teaspoon**

tablespoonful /ˈteɪ.bl̩ˌspuːn.fʊl/ **noun** [C] (plural **tablespoonsful** or **tablespoonfuls**) (written abbreviation **tbsp.**) the amount a tablespoon can hold: *Sprinkle a tablespoonful of grated cheese over the pasta.*

tablet /ˈtæb.lət/ **noun** [C] **MEDICINE** ▷ **1** (B1) a small, solid piece of medicine: *a sleeping tablet* ◦ *a vitamin tablet* **BLOCK** ▷ **2** a thin, flat, often square piece of hard material such as wood, stone, or metal: *The poem was engraved on a tablet of stone.* ◦ UK *a tablet* ***of soap*** **COMPUTER** ▷ **3** (also **ˌtablet comˈputer**) trademark a small, flat computer that is controlled by touching the screen or by using a special pen

ˈtable ˌtennis noun [U] (A2) a game that is played on a large table where two or four players hit a ball over a low net using small, round BATS

tabletop sale /ˌteɪ.bl̩.tɒpˈseɪl/ (US) /-tɑːp-/ **noun** [C] a sale of a mixed collection of things that people no longer want, especially in order to make money for an organization. The items for sale are arranged on tables.

tableware /ˈteɪ.bl̩.weəʳ/ (US) /-wer/ **noun** [U] formal the

T

knives, forks, spoons, plates, glasses, etc. used for meals

ˈtable ˌwine noun [C or U] a wine that is not very expensive and is of average quality

tabloid /ˈtæb.lɔɪd/ adj, noun [C] B2 (of or relating to) a type of popular newspaper with small pages that has many pictures and short, simple reports: *the tabloid press* ◦ *a tabloid newspaper*

taboo /təˈbuː/ noun [C] (plural **taboos**) (an action or word) avoided for religious or social reasons: *In this society there is a taboo* ***on/against*** *any sort of public display of affection.* ◦ *For some people, death is a taboo* ***subject***.

tabouli /təˈbuːli/ noun [U] **tabbouleh**

tabular /ˈtæb.jʊ.ləʳ/ US /-lɚ/ adj [before noun] formal (of information, especially in printed material) in the form of a TABLE (= an arrangement of facts and numbers in rows or blocks)

tabulate /ˈtæb.jʊ.leɪt/ verb [T] formal to show information in the form of a TABLE (= an arrangement of facts and numbers in rows or blocks)

tachograph /ˈtæk.ə.græf/, /-grɑːf/ US /-græf/ noun [C] a machine inside a vehicle such as a truck that records speed, distance travelled, and stopping periods, used to control the driver's legal hours of work

tachometer /tækˈɒm.ɪ.təʳ/ US /-ˈɑː.mɪ.t̬ɚ/ noun [C] (informal ˈ**rev** ˌ**counter**) a device for measuring the rate at which something turns

tacit /ˈtæs.ɪt/ adj understood without being expressed directly: *tacit agreement/approval/support* • **tacitly** /-li/ adv

taciturn /ˈtæs.ɪ.tɜːn/ US /-ə.tɝːn/ adj tending not to speak much: *He's a reserved, taciturn person.*

tack /tæk/ noun; verb

▸noun **NAIL** ▷ **1** [C] a small, sharp nail with a flat end **SEWING** ▷ **2** [C] a long, loose STITCH **RIDING EQUIPMENT** ▷ **3** [U] all the objects that the rider of a horse needs, including SADDLES and BRIDLES **BOAT'S DIRECTION** ▷ **4** [C] the direction or distance that a boat moves at an angle to the direction of the wind, so that the boat receives the wind on its sails: *The ship was* ***on*** *the starboard tack.*

▸verb **FASTEN** ▷ **1** [T] to fasten something to a place with tacks **SEW** ▷ **2** [I or T] (US also **baste**) to sew with a long, loose STITCH that holds two pieces of material together temporarily, before they are sewn together in a more tidy or permanent way **BOAT** ▷ **3** [I usually + adv/prep] (of a boat) to turn so that it is at an angle to the direction of the wind and receives the wind on its sails • **tacking** /ˈtæk.ɪŋ/ noun [U]

PHRASAL VERB **tack sth on** informal to add something that you had not planned to add, often without much preparation or thought: *At the last minute they tacked on a couple of extra visits* ***to*** *my schedule.*

tackie noun [C usually plural] South African English a **takkie**

tackle /ˈtæk.l̩/ verb; noun

▸verb **DEAL WITH** ▷ **1** B2 [T] to try to deal with something or someone: *There are many ways of tackling this problem.* ◦ *I tackled him* ***about*** *his careless work.* **SPORT** ▷ **2** B2 [I or T] (especially in football or HOCKEY) to try to take the ball from a player in the other team, or (in RUGBY or American football) to do this by taking hold of the player and making them fall

▸noun **SPORT** ▷ **1** [C] (especially in football or HOCKEY) an act of tackling someone **EQUIPMENT** ▷ **2** [U] all the objects needed for a particular activity: *fishing tackle* **SEXUAL ORGANS** ▷ **3** [U] (also **wedding tackle**) UK slang humorous the male sexual organs

tacky /ˈtæk.i/ adj **LOW QUALITY** ▷ **1** informal disapproving of cheap quality or in bad style: *The shop sold tacky souvenirs and ornaments.* **STICKY** ▷ **2** sticky; (especially of paint or glue) not completely dry • **tackiness** /-nəs/ noun [U]

taco /ˈtæk.əʊ/ US /ˈtɑː.koʊ/ noun [C] (plural **tacos**) a hard, folded TORTILLA (= thin flat bread) filled with meat, cheese, etc. and hot, spicy sauce

tact /tækt/ noun [U] C2 the ability to say or do the right thing without making anyone unhappy or angry: *He's never had much tact and people don't like his blunt manner.*

tactful /ˈtækt.fəl/ adj C2 careful not to say or do anything that could upset someone: *Mentioning his baldness wasn't very tactful.* • **tactfully** /-i/ adv

tactic /ˈtæk.tɪk/ noun **1** C1 [C usually plural] a planned way of doing something: *These bomb attacks represent a change of tactics by the terrorists.* **2 tactics** [plural] the organization and use of soldiers and equipment in war

tactical /ˈtæk.tɪ.kəl/ adj **1** relating to tactics or done in order to achieve something: *It was a tactical vote.* **2** describes weapons that are for use over short distances and, especially in the case of nuclear weapons, have a local effect only • **tactically** /-i/ adv

ˌtactical ˈvest noun [C] a piece of BULLETPROOF clothing (= designed to prevent bullets going through it) worn on the top half of a soldier's or police officer's body to protect his or her chest and back

ˌtactical ˈvoting noun [U] the act of voting for a political party that you do not usually support in order to prevent another party from winning • **ˌtactical ˈvote** noun [C]

tactician /tækˈtɪʃ.ən/ noun [C] someone who is skilled in using tactics

tactile /ˈtæk.taɪl/ US /-təl/ adj **1** related to the sense of touch **2** If something is tactile, it has a surface that is pleasant or attractive to touch: *Her paintings have a very tactile quality.* **3** describes someone who touches other people a lot

tactless /ˈtækt.ləs/ adj not careful about saying or doing something that could upset someone: *It was rather tactless of you to invite his ex-girlfriend.* • **tactlessly** /-li/ adv • **tactlessness** /-nəs/ noun

tad /tæd/ noun [S] informal **a tad** a little, slightly: *The fish was OK, but the chips were a tad greasy.*

tadpole /ˈtæd.pəʊl/ US /-poʊl/ noun [C] a small, black creature with a large head and long tail that lives in water and develops into a FROG or TOAD

T

tae kwon do /ˌtaɪˈkwɒn.dəʊ/ US /ˌtaɪ.kwɑːnˈdoʊ/ noun [U] a sport originally from Korea, in which people fight with arms, legs, and feet. It is similar to KARATE.

taffeta /ˈtæf.ə.tə/ US /-ɪ.t̬ə/ noun [U] a stiff, shiny cloth made from SILK or artificial material, used especially for dresses to be worn at special events: *a taffeta ball gown*

Taffy /ˈtæf.i/ noun [C] (also **Taff** /tæf/) UK offensive a Welshman

tafn written abbreviation for that's all for now: used at the end of an email or when you finish taking part in a discussion in an internet CHAT ROOM

tag /tæg/ noun; verb

▸noun **SMALL PART** ▷ **1** [C] a small piece of paper, cloth, or metal, on which there is information, fixed onto something larger: *a **price** tag* **GAME** ▷ **2** [U] a game played by two or more children in which one child chases the others and tries to touch one of them. This child then becomes the one who does the chasing. **GRAMMAR** ▷ **3** [C] a phrase such as 'he is' or 'isn't it?', added on to a sentence for emphasis, or to turn it into a question, usually to get agreement or to check information

▸verb [T] (-gg-) **SMALL PART** ▷ **1** to put a tag on something **COMPUTING** ▷ **2** specialized to mark computer information so that you can process it later

PHRASAL VERBS **tag along** informal to go somewhere with a person or group, usually when they have not asked you to go with them: *I don't know her, she just tagged along **with** us.* • **tag sth on** (also **tag sth onto sth**) to add something to what you have said or written at a later time: *Tag on a couple of paragraphs about recent events.*

tagger /ˈtæg.əʳ/ noun [C] slang someone who paints their name or a special mark on buildings • **tagging** /-ɪŋ/ noun [U] slang

tagine /tæˈʒiːn/ noun [C or U] another spelling of **tajine**

tagliatelle /ˌtæl.jəˈtel.i/ (US) /ˌtɑːl-/ noun [U] a type of PASTA shaped into long, thin, flat strips

tahini /tɑːˈhiː.ni/ noun [U] a soft substance that is made from crushed SESAME SEEDS, and used in cooking

t'ai chi /ˌtaɪˈtʃiː/ noun [U] a form of exercise involving slow movements of muscles, originally done in China

tail /teɪl/ noun; verb

▸noun [C] **ANIMAL** ▷ **1** (B2) a part of an animal's body, sticking out from the base of the back, or something similar in shape or position: *The dog **wagged** its tail excitedly.* **PERSON FOLLOWING** ▷ **2** informal someone who follows another person to discover where the other person goes to, who they speak to, what they do, etc. **COIN SIDE** ▷ **3 tails** [U] the side of a coin that does not have a picture of someone's head on it → Compare **head JACKET** ▷ **4 tails** [plural] a **tailcoat**

IDIOMS **be on sb's tail** to follow someone closely: *That driver's been on my tail for miles.* • **get off your tail** US slang to stop being lazy and start doing something: *You've just got to get off your tail and start looking for a job.* • **leave, go off, etc. with your tail between your legs** to leave, feeling ashamed and embarrassed because you have failed or made a mistake: *The losing team went off with their tails between their legs.* • **the tail wagging the dog** a situation in which a large group has to do something to satisfy a small group

▸verb [T] to follow and watch someone very closely, especially in order to get information secretly: *That car has been tailing me for the last ten minutes.*

PHRASAL VERBS **tail back** UK If traffic tails back, it forms a long line and moves very slowly or stops: *There is traffic tailing back along the motorway for ten miles.* • **tail off** to reduce in amount or become lower in level: *His voice tailed off as he drifted into sleep.* ◦ *The profits tailed off after a few years.*

tailback /ˈteɪl.bæk/ noun [C] mainly UK a line of vehicles that have stopped or are moving only very slowly, because of an accident or other problem on the road in front of them: *Yesterday there was a four-mile tailback on the main road into the city after a crash.*

tailboard /ˈteɪl.bɔːd/ (US) /-bɔːrd/ noun [C] (US **tailgate**) the door or board at the back of a vehicle that can be brought down to put in goods

tailcoat /ˈteɪl.kəʊt/ (US) /-koʊt/ noun [C] (also **tails**) an old-fashioned type of man's coat, waist-length at the front and with the lower half of the back divided into two pieces, now only worn on very formal occasions

-tailed /-teɪld/ suffix having a tail of the type mentioned: *a furry-tailed animal*

the ˌtail ˈend noun [S] (C2) the final part: *I only saw the tail end **of** the TV news.* ◦ *She was at the head of the queue but I was at the tail end.*

tailgate /ˈteɪl.geɪt/ verb [I or T] mainly US disapproving to drive too closely behind the vehicle in front • **tailgating** /-geɪ.tɪŋ/ (US) /-geɪ.t̬ɪŋ/ noun [U]

ˈtail ˌlight noun [C] US a **rear light**

tailor /ˈteɪ.ləʳ/ (US) /-lɚ/ noun; verb

▸noun [C] someone whose job is to repair, make, and ADJUST (= make changes to) clothes, especially someone who makes jackets, trousers, coats, etc. for men

▸verb [T] to make or prepare something following particular instructions

tailored /ˈteɪ.ləd/ (US) /-lɚd/ adj **CLOTHES** ▷ **1** describes a piece of clothing that is shaped to fit a person's body closely: *a tailored suit* **2** describes clothing that is made for a particular person by a tailor **FOR PURPOSE** ▷ **3** made or changed especially to be suitable for a particular situation or purpose: *The project clearly requires a tailored computer system.*

tailor-ˈmade adj **1** specially made for a particular purpose: *a tailor-made course* **2 be tailor-made for sth** to have all the right skills and abilities for a particular task: *It sounds as though you're tailor-made for the job.*

tailpipe /ˈteɪl.paɪp/ noun [C] (C1) US for **exhaust pipe**

tailspin /ˈteɪl.spɪn/ noun **1** [C usually singular] a situation in which a plane turns round and round as it falls quickly towards the ground **2** [S] a situation in which something starts to fail or lose value and gets more and more out of control: *Share prices **went into a** tailspin when the president resigned.*

tailwind /ˈteɪl.wɪnd/ noun [C] a wind blowing from behind a vehicle

taint /teɪnt/ verb [T] to spoil something, especially food or blood, by adding a harmful substance, or to spoil people's opinion of someone: *His reputation was permanently tainted by the financial scandal.* • **taint** noun [C usually singular, U] *The enquiry cleared him of any taint **of** suspicion/dishonesty.*

tajine (also **tagine**) /tæˈʒiːn/ noun **1** [C or U] a Moroccan dish consisting of meat, fruit, vegetables, and spices that are cooked together very slowly **2** [C] a clay dish used for cooking a tajine

take /teɪk/ verb; noun

▸verb (**took**, **taken**) **REMOVE** ▷ **1** (B1) [T] to remove something, especially without permission: *Has anything been taken (= stolen)?* ◦ *Here's your pen, I took it by mistake.* ◦ *All her possessions had been taken **from** her.* **2** (B2) [T] to SUBTRACT a number (= remove it from another number): *If you take 4 **from** 12 you get 8.* → See also **take sth away** **MOVE** ▷ **3** (A1) [T] to move something or someone from one place to another: *The weather forecast said rain, so take your umbrella (**with** you) when you go out.* ◦ *The suitcases were taken **to** Madrid by mistake.* ◦ *Take the book up/down to the third floor of the library.* ◦ [+ two objects] *I suggested that he should take her some chocolates/take some chocolates **to** her (= bring them to her as a present).* **ACCEPT** ▷ **4** (B1) [T] to accept or have: *Do they take credit cards here?* ◦ *Do you take milk in your tea?* ◦ *This*

T

container will take (= has room for) six litres. ◦ *Which newspaper do you take (= regularly buy)?* ◦ *He continually abuses her, and she just sits there and takes it.* ◦ *If you think I'm going to take that* ***lying down*** *(= accept it without complaining), you're very much mistaken.* ◦ *I take* ***the****/your* ***point*** *(= accept the argument), but I still don't think you should have gone.* **5 take part** B1 to be involved in an activity with other people: *She doesn't usually take part* ***in*** *any of the class activities.* **6** [T] used when you want to mention something as a particular example of what you are talking about: *I've been very busy recently. Take last week, I had meetings on four evenings.* **7 take to be/take for sth** If you take someone or something to be something, or if you take them for something, you accept or believe that they are that thing: [+ to infinitive] *These creatures are generally taken to be descended from primitive fishes.* ◦ *I could have taken him for (= believed that he was) your brother.* ◦ *I'm not going to forge his signature for you! What do* ***you*** *take* ***me*** *for? (= You should not believe I could do a thing like that.)* **8 can't take sth** B2 to not be able to deal with an unpleasant situation: *I can't take it* ***any more****. I'm leaving.* **9 take it or leave it** accept or refuse the offer completely: *That's my final offer – you can take it or leave it.*

> **! Common mistake: take part**
>
> The correct preposition to use after **take part** is **in**.
>
> Don't say 'take part at/of something', say **take part in something**:
>
> *My team would like to take part in the competition.*

> **! Common mistake: take part or take place?**
>
> **Warning:** choose the correct verb!
>
> To talk about something happening, don't say something 'takes part', say something **takes place**:
>
> ~~*The concert will take part at the Albert Hall, in London.*~~
>
> *The concert will take place at the Albert Hall, in London.*

HOLD ▷ **10** B1 [T] to move in order to hold something in the hand(s): *Can you take this bag while I open the door?* ◦ *He took my arm and led me outside.* ◦ *Take an egg and break it into the bowl.* ◦ *He took* ***hold of*** *the plant's root and pulled.* **GO WITH** ▷ **11** A1 [T] to go somewhere with someone, often paying for them or being responsible for them: *We're taking the children* ***to*** *the zoo on Saturday.* ◦ [+ to infinitive] *I took my elderly parents* ***to*** *look at some new houses.* ◦ [+ -ing verb] *Will you take me swimm****ing*** *tomorrow?* **12** [T] to show someone how to get to somewhere by going there with them: *Let me take you* ***to*** *your room.* **13** [T] to go to a social event with someone: *Who's taking you* ***to*** *the dance?* **TRANSPORT** ▷ **14** A2 [T] to travel somewhere by using a particular form of transport or a particular vehicle, route, etc.: *I always take the train – it's less hassle than a car.* ◦ *She took the 10.30 flight to Edinburgh.* ◦ *If you take the road on the left, you'll come to the post office.* **NEED** ▷ **15** B2 [T] to need: *Parachuting takes a lot of nerve.* ◦ *Transitive verbs take a direct object.* ◦ [+ -ing verb] *His story took* ***some*** *believ****ing*** *(= was difficult to believe).* **16** B1 to wear a particular size of clothes or shoes: *What size shoes do you take?* **17** A2 [L only + noun] If something takes a particular time, that period is needed in order to complete it: *The cooking process only takes ten minutes.* ◦ [+ to infinitive] *How long does this paint take* ***to*** *dry?* ◦ [+ obj + noun] ***It*** *took us all day* ***to*** *drive home.* **18 not take long** A2 to act or happen over a short period of time: *I'm just going to the shops – I won't take long.* **19 take time** to need a long time: *Broken bones always take time to mend.* **MEASURE** ▷ **20** C2 to measure something: *Nurses took my temperature and blood pressure.* **DRUG/MEDICINE** ▷ **21** A2 to swallow or use a medicine or drug, especially in a regular way: *Take this medicine three times a day.* ◦ *Do you think she takes drugs?* **ACT** ▷ **22** B1 [T] to do or perform: *The Archbishop took our service of thanksgiving.* ◦ *Shelley is taking (= studying) economics at university.* ◦ UK *Mr Marshall takes us* ***for*** *(= teaches us) physics.* **23** B1 [T] used with many nouns to make a verb phrase that is equal in meaning to the related verb: *I think we'll take a break (= we'll stop for a break) there.* ◦ *If you're tired you should take a rest (= you should rest).* ◦ *I always like to take a walk (= to walk) after lunch.* **THINK ABOUT** ▷ **24** B2 [T] to think about something or someone in a particular way: *We're taking the bomb threats very* ***seriously****.* **UNDERSTAND** ▷ **25** C2 to understand something in a particular way: *We were only teasing, but he took it the wrong way.* ◦ *I'm not sure whether to take that* ***as*** *a compliment or an insult.* ◦ *She gave a nod, which we took to mean that she was in agreement.* **REACTION** ▷ **26** B2 [T] to have or come to have a particular feeling or opinion: *He doesn't take any* ***interest in*** *his children.* ◦ *Don't take any* ***notice of*** *the cameras.* ◦ *She takes* ***offence*** *too easily.* ◦ *They took* ***pity on*** *the stray cat and fed it.* ◦ *I take* ***the view that*** *fuel should be heavily taxed to reduce road use.* **27 take sb unawares** (also **take sb by surprise**) to surprise someone: *The sudden noise took her unawares.* **MONEY** ▷ **28** [T] to receive money from sales or as payment for entrance to an event: *The show took an astonishing $100,000 in its first week.* → See also **takings** **CATCH** ▷ **29** B2 [T] to get possession of something or someone: *Rebels ambushed the train and took several prisoners.* ◦ *The Liberals need just 200 more votes to take the seat* ***from*** *Labour.* ◦ *Centre-left parties look set to take* ***power****.* ◦ *Adam, I'd like you to take* ***control*** *of the aircraft now.* **WRITE** ▷ **30** B1 [T] to write: *I hope you're all taking notes.* **PERFORM WELL** ▷ **31** [I] to work or perform as expected: *These new plants haven't taken – they don't like this dry soil.*

IDIOMS **be like taking candy from a baby** (also **be as easy as taking candy from a baby**) US informal to be very easy: *Beating them was the easiest thing in the world – it was like taking candy from a baby.* • **can take it or leave it** said about something that you quite like, but that you do not love or need strongly: *My sister's absolutely crazy about chocolate whereas I can take it or leave it.* • **I take it** (also **can take it**) C2 said if you think that what you say is likely to be true, although it is not proved: *You'll be staying the night, I take it?* ◦ *So we can take it you've resigned?* • **if you take my meaning** UK used to say that you have left out information or your opinion from what you have just said, but that you expect the person listening still to understand it: *Let's just say we had 'problems', if you take my meaning.* • **point taken** used to say you accept what someone has said • **take your time 1** C1 said to mean that you can spend as much time as you need in doing something, or that you should slow down **2** C1 disapproving to do something too slowly: *The builders are really taking their time.* • **take one (thing) at a time** to do or deal with one thing before starting to do or deal with another • **take sth as it comes** C2 to deal with something as it happens, without planning for it: *Just take each day as it comes*

T

and do what you feel is right. • **take that!** informal said as someone hits someone else, especially in humorous films or CARTOONS • **take the time** to make the effort to do something: *She didn't even take the time* ***to*** *wish me good morning.* • **take a walk!** US informal a rude way of telling someone to go away: *The guy kept pestering her, and finally she told him to take a walk.* • **will not take no for an answer** to not allow someone to refuse what you have offered: *I've told Steve I'm not interested, but he keeps asking me out – he won't take no for an answer.*

PHRASAL VERBS **take sb aback** to surprise or shock someone so much that they do not know how to behave for a short time: *I was a little taken aback at the directness of the question.* ◦ *The news really took us aback.* • **take after sb** B2 to be similar to an older member of your family in appearance or character: *He takes after his mother/his mother's side of the family.* • **take against sb** UK to begin to dislike someone: *I think she took against me when I got the promotion she wanted.* • **take sth apart** to separate something into its different parts: *We took the engine apart to see what the problem was.* • **take sb apart** informal to defeat someone very easily in a sport: *He took their defence apart, scoring three goals in the first 20 minutes.* • **take sth away** **REMOVE** ▷ **1** B2 to remove something: *Take these chairs away – we don't need them.* ◦ *Supermarkets are taking business away* ***from*** *small local shops.* **CALCULATE** ▷ **2** B1 to SUBTRACT a number (= remove it from another number): *Four take away two is two.* ◦ *If you take 4 away* ***from*** *12 you get 8.* **FOOD** ▷ **3** B1 UK to buy food in a restaurant and eat it somewhere else: *Is that to eat in or take away?* • **take sth back** **SOMETHING BOUGHT** ▷ **1** B1 to return something you have bought to a shop: *Is it too small? Take it back and get a refund.* **STATEMENT** ▷ **2** to admit that something you said was wrong: *All right, I take* ***it all*** *back. It wasn't your fault.* • **take sb back** **PARTNER** ▷ **1** to allow a partner who previously left your home because of a disagreement or another relationship to come back to live with you: *His wife said she would never take him back.* **MEMORY** ▷ **2** If something takes you back, it makes you remember a period or an event: *That piece of music really took me back (***to*** *my schooldays).* • **take sth down** **REMOVE** ▷ **1** B2 to remove something that is on a wall or something that is temporary, or to remove a structure by separating its different parts: *I've taken the pictures down.* **WRITE** ▷ **2** to write something that another person has just said: *He took down my address and phone number and said he'd phone back.* • **take sth from sb** [often passive] If you take words, information, or ideas from another person or piece of work, you use or develop them in some way: *The plot is taken from Shakespeare.*

IDIOM **take it from me** (also **take my word for it**) C1 accept that what I say is true, because I know or have experienced it: *It won't work – take it from me.*

• **take sth in** **UNDERSTAND** ▷ **1** C2 to understand completely the meaning or importance of something: *I had to read the letter twice before I could take it all in.* **INCLUDE** ▷ **2** to include something: *The new town takes in three former villages.* **WATCH** ▷ **3** mainly US to go to watch a film or performance, or to visit a place such as a museum: *I thought we might get something to eat and then take in a movie.* **CLOTHES** ▷ **4** to make a piece of clothing narrower, by changing the position of some of the STITCHES joining it together: *I'll have to take this dress in* ***at*** *the waist – it's too big.* **WORK** ▷ **5** to do paid work for other people, such as washing or sewing, in your home: *She supported her family by taking in laundry.* • **take sb in** **CARE FOR** ▷ **1** to take care of someone and provide a place in your home for them: *Several families take in foreign students.* **DECEIVE** ▷ **2** B2 [often passive] to cause someone to believe something that is not true, or to trick or deceive someone: *I can't believe she was taken in by him.* **POLICE** ▷ **3** If the police take you in, they take you to the police station: *Detectives on the murder inquiry have taken in a new suspect for questioning.* • **take sth off** **REMOVE** ▷ **1** A2 to remove something, especially clothes: *He took off his clothes and got into the bath.* ◦ *After the poisoning scare, the product was taken off the shelves/the market (= removed from sale).* **NOT WORK** ▷ **2** B2 to spend time away from your work: *He took off two weeks in September.* • **take off** **FLY** ▷ **1** A2 If an aircraft, bird, or insect takes off, it leaves the ground and begins to fly: *The plane took off at 8.30 a.m.* → See also **take-off** **SUCCEED** ▷ **2** B2 to suddenly start to be successful or popular: *Her singing career had just begun to take off.* **LEAVE** ▷ **3** informal to suddenly leave somewhere, usually without telling anyone that you are going: *When he saw me, he took off in the other direction.* • **take sb off** UK informal to copy the way a particular person speaks or behaves, or the way something is done, usually in order to entertain other people → See also **take-off** → Compare **impersonate** • **take sth on** C1 to accept a particular job or responsibility: *She took too much on and made herself ill.* • **take on sth** to begin to have a particular quality: *Her voice took on a troubled tone.* • **take sb on** **EMPLOY** ▷ **1** B2 to employ someone: *She was taken on* ***as a*** *laboratory assistant.* **FIGHT** ▷ **2** to compete against or fight someone: *The government took on the unions and won.* • **take sth out** **REMOVE** ▷ **1** B1 to remove something from somewhere: *I've had a tooth taken out.* **MONEY** ▷ **2** B2 to get money from a bank account: *I took out some money for the weekend.* • **take sb out** B1 to go somewhere and do something with someone, usually something you plan and pay for: *Dad's taking the whole family out* ***to*** *the cinema.* ◦ *Our boss took us out* ***for*** *a meal.* • **take sb/sth out** slang to kill someone or destroy something: *The soldiers said that they were trying to take out the snipers.* • **take it out of sb** (also **take a lot out of sb**) to make someone very tired: *Digging in the garden certainly takes it out of me these days.* • **take sb out of themselves** UK to change someone's mood and stop them from thinking about what was making them unhappy • **take sth out on sb** to treat someone badly because you are upset or angry, even if they have done nothing wrong: *I know you've had a bad day, but there's no need to take it out on me!* • **take (sth) over** **START DOING** ▷ **1** B2 to start doing a job or being responsible for something that another person did or had responsibility for before: *He took over* ***from*** *the previous headmaster in February.* ◦ *She took over* ***as*** *manager two weeks ago.* ◦ *Colin Lamb has taken over responsibility for this project.* **GET CONTROL** ▷ **2** to get control of a company by buying enough of the SHARES in it: *The company he works for has recently been taken over.* → See also **takeover** **BECOME MORE POWERFUL** ▷ **3** C2 to become more successful or powerful than something or someone else that is involved in the same type of activity: *It's only a matter of time before they take over completely.* • **take sb round (sth/somewhere)** B2 to walk through a building or visit a place with someone, showing them the most interesting or important parts: *You will be taken round the museum by one of the guides.* • **take sb through sth** to explain something to someone: *I'll take you through it one more time, then you can try it yourself.* • **take to sb/sth** C1 to start to like someone or something: *His wife* took to her new neighbours at once. ◦ *She's taken to tennis* ***like a duck to water*** *(= she likes it and is good at it).* • **take to sth** to start doing something often: *She was so depressed she took to drink.* ◦ [+ -ing verb] *He's taken to staying out very late.* • **take to somewhere** to go somewhere, usually because you are in a difficult or dangerous situation: *The refugees took to the hills for safety.* • **take sth up** FILL ▷ **1** B2 to fill an amount of space or time: *This desk takes up too much room.* ◦ *Too much of this report is taken up* ***with*** *out-of-date figures.* START ▷ **2** B1 to start doing a particular job or activity: *He's taken up the post of supervisor.* ◦ [+ -ing verb] *Have you ever thought of taking up acting?* ◦ *Ian took up (= continued) the story where Sue had left off.* **3 take up office** to start an official job: *The minister took up office in December.* DISCUSS ▷ **4** to discuss something or deal with something: *The school took the matter up* ***with*** *the police.* ◦ UK *I'd like to take you up* ***on*** *your sales figures for June.* ◦ *A leading law firm took up his case.* CLOTHING ▷ **5** to make a piece of clothing, such as a skirt or trousers, shorter • **take sb up on sth** to accept an offer that someone has made: *Could I take you up on that offer of a lift, Rob?* • **take up with sb** to become friendly or start a relationship with someone, especially someone who might have a bad influence on you: *She's taken up with a strange crowd of people.*

▸**noun** MONEY ▷ **1** [U] money that is received from sales or as payment for entrance to an event: *The box office take was huge for the new show.* FILM ▷ **2** [C] the filming of a SCENE (= small part of a film): *This scene of the film needed ten takes before we felt it was right.*

IDIOM **on the take** US trying to profit in a personal and usually financial way from a situation: *I honestly don't trust him – he always seems to be on the take.* → Compare **be on the make**

takeaway /ˈteɪk.ə.weɪ/ noun [C] UK (US **takeout**) B1 a meal cooked and bought at a shop or restaurant but taken somewhere else, often home, to be eaten, or the shop or restaurant itself: *a Chinese takeaway*

ˈtake-home ˌpay noun [U] the amount of earnings that you have left after tax, etc.

ˈtake-home ˌtest noun [C] US a test that students complete at home, especially because there would not be enough time to do it in class

taken /ˈteɪ.kᵊn/ verb; adj

▸**verb** past participle of **take**

▸**adj taken with/by sth** believing something to be deserving of respect or admiration: *The committee was very taken with your proposals.*

ˈtake-off noun AIRCRAFT ▷ **1** [C or U] the moment when an aircraft leaves the ground and begins to fly: *Night take-offs and landings are banned at this airport.* COPY ▷ **2** [C] a piece of acting or writing, etc. that copies the way a particular person speaks or behaves, or the way something is done, usually to entertain other people: *It was the best take-off* ***of*** *the prime minister that I have ever seen.*

takeout /ˈteɪk.aʊt/ noun [C] US B1 **takeaway**

takeover /ˈteɪkˌəʊ.vəʳ/ US /-ˌoʊ.vɚ/ noun [C] **1** C1 a situation in which a company gets control of another company by buying enough of its SHARES: *They were involved in a takeover last year.* **2 make a takeover bid for sth** to try to get control of something: *The company made a takeover bid for a rival firm.*

taker /ˈteɪ.kəʳ/ US /-kɚ/ noun ACCEPT ▷ **1** someone who accepts or wants what someone is offering **2 few/no/not many takers** few, no, or not many people interested in what has been offered: *I put an advert in the paper to sell my bike but I haven't had any takers.* DRUG USER ▷ **3** someone who uses a drug or medicine: *a drug taker* HOLD ▷ **4** someone who takes or holds someone or something: *a hostage taker*

ˈtake-up noun [S] how much people start to use or accept a service, or sometimes a product, that has become available to them: *We are calling for government action to improve the take-up of state benefits.*

takings /ˈteɪ.kɪŋz/ noun [plural] all the money that a business gets from selling things: *Our takings were down this week because the weather was so bad.*

takkie (also **tackie**) /ˈtæk.i/ noun [C usually plural] South African English a light, comfortable shoe suitable for playing sports → See also **trainer, sneaker**

talcum powder /ˈtæl.kəmˌpaʊ.dəʳ/ US /-dɚ/ noun [C or U] (also **talc**) a powder, usually having a pleasant smell, put on the skin to make it feel smooth or to help it stay dry

tale /teɪl/ noun [C] B2 a story, especially one which might be invented or difficult to believe: *He* ***told*** *some fascinating tales about his life in India.* ◦ *She told me/invented/concocted a tale about missing the bus to explain her lateness.*

IDIOM **tale of woe** a report of the bad things that have happened: *I asked how he was and he gave me a real tale of woe.*

talent /ˈtæl.ᵊnt/ noun NATURAL ABILITY ▷ **1** B1 [C or U] (someone who has) a natural ability to be good at something, especially without being taught: *Her talent* ***for*** *music showed at an early age.* ◦ *His artistic talents were wasted in his boring job.* ATTRACTIVE PEOPLE ▷ **2** [U] UK slang mainly humorous people who are sexually attractive: *There was plenty of talent at the party last night.* • **talentless** /-ləs/ adj

ˈtalent ˌcontest noun [C] an event in which people compete to show who is the most skilled, especially at being entertaining

talented /ˈtæl.ᵊn.tɪd/ US /-ɪd/ adj B1 with talent; able or skilful: *a talented footballer/pianist*

ˈtalent ˌscout noun [C] someone who looks for people who have the skills they want, especially in entertainment or sport

talisman /ˈtæl.ɪz.mən/ noun [C] (plural **talismans**) an object believed to bring good luck or to keep its owner safe from harm

talk /tɔːk/ US /tɑːk/ verb; noun

▸**verb** [I] SAY WORDS ▷ **1** A1 to say words aloud; to speak to someone: *We were just talking* ***about*** *Simon's new girlfriend.* ◦ *My little girl has just started to talk.* ◦ *She talks* ***to*** *her mother on the phone every week.* DISCUSS ▷ **2** B2 to discuss something with someone, often to try to find a solution to a disagreement: *The two sides have agreed to talk.* **3 talk business, politics, etc.** C1 to discuss a particular subject: *Whenever they're together, they talk politics.* LECTURE ▷ **4** B2 to give a lecture on a subject: *The next speaker will be talking about endangered insects.*

IDIOMS **be like talking to a brick wall** If talking to someone is like talking to a brick wall, the person you are speaking to does not listen: *I've tried to discuss my feelings with her, but it's like talking to a brick wall.* • **give sb something to talk about** to provide someone with an interesting subject to discuss: *Our new car will give the neighbours something to talk about.* • **look who's talking!** (also **you're a fine one to talk!**, also **you can/can't talk!**, US also **you should talk!**) something you say when someone criticizes you for something that they do themselves: *I'm lazy? You're a fine one to talk!* • **talk sb's head off** informal to

T

Other ways of saying talk

The most common alternatives are **speak** and **say**:

*Could you **speak** more quietly, please?*

*I couldn't hear what they were **saying**.*

The verb **chat** or the expression **have a chat** are often used if a person is talking with someone in a friendly, informal way:

*We were just **chatting** about the party.*

*Give me a call and we'll **have a chat**.*

If people talk for a long time about things that are not important, the verb **chatter** is sometimes used:

*They spent the morning **chattering** away.*

If people talk for a long time about things that are important, the verb **discuss** can be used:

*We need to **discuss** arrangements for next week.*

If someone talks about something too much in an annoying way, you can use the expression **go on (and on)**:

*He's always **going on and on** about how much he hates his work.*

If someone talks quietly so that the voice is difficult to hear, often because the person is complaining about something, then the verbs **mumble** and **mutter** are used:

*She walked past me, **muttering** to herself.*

*He **mumbled** something about it being a waste of time.*

The verb **whisper** is used when someone talks extremely quietly so that other people cannot hear:

*What are you two girls **whispering** about?*

talk to someone for a long time, usually loudly: *She talked my head off.* • **talk a blue streak** US informal to talk quickly and without stopping: *He talked a blue streak all through breakfast.* • **talk about ...** informal used to emphasize that something is very noticeable in the stated way: *What a film – talk about boring!* • **talk dirty** informal to describe sexual acts to another person using rude words • **talk nonsense** (UK also **talk rubbish**) to say things that are not reasonable or have no meaning: *Is it just me or was she talking nonsense in the meeting?* • **talk sense** to speak in a reasonable way: *Why don't you talk sense!* • **talk shop** to talk about your job with those you work with when not at work: *Even at a party they have to talk shop!* • **talk the hind leg(s) off a donkey** UK informal to talk without stopping for a long time • **talk the talk ... walk the walk** If you say that someone talks the talk but does not walk the walk, you mean that they do not act in a way that agrees with the things they say: *When it comes to recycling he talks the talk but he doesn't walk the walk.* • **talk through your hat** informal to talk about something without understanding what you are talking about • **talk turkey** US informal to discuss something honestly and directly • **talking of sb/sth** (also **speaking of sb/sth**) while we are talking about a particular person or thing: *Talking of John, I saw a friend of his last week.*

PHRASAL VERBS **talk about sth/doing sth** C2 to think about or make plans to do something in the future: *They're always talking about selling the house and moving away.* • **talk at sb** to speak to someone without listening to them or allowing them to speak: *What discussion? You weren't talking to me, you were talking at me!* • **talk back** If a child talks back, they reply rudely to someone they should be polite to: *Children who talk back are regarded as cheeky and disrespectful.* • **talk sth down** to talk about something in a way that makes it seem less important or less serious than it really is: *He began his lecture by talking down the initiatives of a rival company.* • **talk sb down** PREVENT ▷ **1** to speak loudly or without stopping to prevent someone else from speaking: *I tried to explain, but he just talked me down.* PERSUADE ▷ **2** to persuade someone who is threatening to kill themselves not to jump from a high place: *The policeman talked the girl down after she had been on the roof for two hours.* • **talk down to sb** to talk to someone as if they were less intelligent than you or not important: *I wish politicians wouldn't talk down to us as if we were idiots.* • **talk sb into sth** B2 to persuade someone to do something: *He's against the idea, but I think I can talk him into **it**.* • **talk sth out** to discuss something such as a problem or plan completely in order to find a solution or an agreement: *If you two don't talk out the differences between you, it'll be very difficult for you to continue working together.* • **talk sb out of sth** C2 to persuade someone not to do something: [+ -ing verb] *Her parents tried to talk her out of getting engaged.* • **talk sth over** B2 to discuss a problem or situation with someone, often to find out their opinion or to get advice before making a decision about it: *I'd like to talk it over **with** my wife first.* • **talk sb round** UK to persuade someone to agree with you or to do what you want them to do: *She's not keen on the idea but we think we can talk her round.* • **talk round/around sth** to avoid speaking directly about something: *I felt that he just talked round the subject and didn't tackle the main issues.* • **talk sth through** C2 to discuss all the details of something, often before making a decision: *It is very important to try and talk all the issues through so that they can be dealt with in an appropriate manner.* • **talk sth up** to speak with enthusiasm about something: *If we talk up the event, people will surely come.*

►**noun 1** B1 [C] a conversation between two people, often about a particular subject: *I asked him to **have** a talk **with** his mother **about** his plan.* **2** B2 [C] a speech given to a group of people to teach or tell them about a particular subject: *He **gave** a talk **about/on** his visit to America.* **3 talks** C2 [plural] serious and formal discussions on an important subject, usually intended to produce decisions or agreements: *Talks were **held** in Madrid **about** the fuel crisis.* **4** C2 [U] the action of talking about what might happen or be true, or the subject people are talking about: *Talk won't get us anywhere.* ◦ ***The** talk/Her talk was all about the wedding.*

Word partners for talk noun

have a talk (*with* sb) • a talk *about* sth • a *long/serious/short* talk

Word partners for talks

begin/enter into/have/hold talks • *resume/revive/reopen* talks • talks *take place* • talks *break down/collapse/fail/stall* • talks *aimed at* doing sth • *direct/face-to-face/secret/urgent* talks • talks *about/on* sth • *in* talks (*with* sb)

IDIOMS **be all talk (and no action)** (also **be just talk**) used to describe someone who talks about doing something but never does it: *She's all talk when it comes to doing something about the problem.* • **be the talk of somewhere** to be what people are discussing in a particular place: *Her behaviour is the talk of the neighbourhood/office.* • **be the talk of the town** to be

T

what everyone is talking about: *The new statue in the park is the talk of the town.*

talkative /ˈtɔː.kə.tɪv/ ⓤⓢ /ˈtɑː.kə.t̬ɪv/ adj C1 talking a lot: *She's a lively, talkative person.*

talkback /ˈtɔːk.bæk/ ⓤⓢ /ˈtɑːk-/ noun [C] Australian English a radio programme in which people listening take part by phone → Compare **call-in, phone-in**

talker /ˈtɔː.kəʳ/ ⓤⓢ /ˈtɑː.kɚ/ noun [C] a person who talks a lot, too much or in a particular way: *I'm afraid he's more of a talker than a doer, which is why he never finishes anything.* ◦ *What a talker your mum is – I couldn't get off the phone!*

talkie /ˈtɔː.ki/ ⓤⓢ /ˈtɑː-/ noun [C] old-fashioned a cinema film with speech and sound made during the period when most films were silent → Compare **silent film**

ˌtalking ˈbook noun [C] a spoken recording of a book, used especially by blind people

ˈtalking ˌpoint noun [C] something which encourages discussion

ˈtalking-to noun [C usually singular] informal a severe talk with someone who has done something wrong: *I **gave** her a good talking-to **about** doing her homework on time.*

ˈtalk ˌshow noun [C] B1 a radio or television programme on which famous guests are asked questions about themselves, or members of the public discuss a particular subject

tall /tɔːl/ ⓤⓢ /tɑːl/ adj A1 of more than average height, or of a particular height: *a tall girl* ◦ *a tall building* ◦ *He's six feet tall.* ◦ *She's much taller **than** me.* • **tallness** /ˈtɔːl.nəs/ ⓤⓢ /ˈtɑːl-/ noun [U]

IDIOMS **be a tall order** to be something that is difficult to do: *Getting the essay done on time will be a tall order.* • **stand/walk tall** to act in a proud and confident way: *You'd have more chance of success if you'd stand tall.* • **a tall tale** a story or statement that is difficult to believe because it is too exciting or interesting: *He told me a tall tale about having met some top models in a night club.*

ˌtall ˈclaim noun [C] Indian English for **tall story**

ˌtall-grass ˈprairie noun [C or U] US a wide area of flat land in the central part of the US where various types of tall grass grow

tallish /ˈtɔː.lɪʃ/ ⓤⓢ /ˈtɑː-/ adj quite tall: *He's tallish, with fair hair and glasses.*

tallow /ˈtæl.əʊ/ ⓤⓢ /-oʊ/ noun [U] fat from animals, used for making soap and, especially in the past, candles

ˌtall ˈpoppy ˌsyndrome noun [U] informal UK the fact that people do not like and often criticize other people who are successful

ˌtall ˈstory noun [C usually singular] a story or fact that is difficult to believe: *After dinner she told me a tall story about her pet.*

tally /ˈtæl.i/ verb; noun

▸verb [I] to match or agree with something else: *Our figures don't tally – you've made it £20 more than me.* ◦ *Your plans don't tally **with** mine.*

PHRASAL VERB **tally (sth) up** informal to calculate the total of something

▸noun [C usually singular] a record or count of a number of things: *Will you **keep a tally of** the number of customers going in and out?*

tally-ho /ˌtæl.iˈhəʊ/ ⓤⓢ /-ˈhoʊ/ **exclamation** a shout made by someone hunting who sees a FOX

ˈtally-ˌroom noun [C usually singular] Australian English a room in which votes are collected after an election

the Talmud /ˈtæl.mʊd/ ⓤⓢ /ˈtɑːl-/ noun [S] the collection of ancient Jewish laws and traditions for religious and social matters • **Talmudic** /tælˈmʊd.ɪk/ ⓤⓢ /tɑːl-/ adj

talon /ˈtæl.ən/ noun [C] a sharp nail on the foot of a bird which it uses when hunting animals

tamarind /ˈtæm.ᵊr.ɪnd/ ⓤⓢ /-ɚ.ɪnd/ noun [C or U] (fruit of) a type of tropical tree

tambourine /ˌtæm.bəˈriːn/ noun [C] a small musical instrument consisting of a circular wooden frame with metal discs loosely fixed to it, shaken or hit with the hand to make the discs ring

tame /teɪm/ adj; verb

▸adj **NOT WILD** ▷ **1** (especially of animals) not wild or dangerous, either naturally or because of training or long involvement with humans: *After a few months' contact the monkeys become very tame.* **NOT EXCITING** ▷ **2** disapproving not interesting or exciting: *It was a tame film in comparison to some that she's made.*

▸verb [T] **1** to make a wild animal tame **2** to control something dangerous or powerful: *He'll need to tame his temper if he wants to succeed.* • **tameable** /ˈteɪ.mə.bl̩/ adj • **tamer** /ˈteɪ.məʳ/ ⓤⓢ /-mɚ/ noun [C] someone who tames something that is wild, especially an animal: *a lion-tamer*

tamp /tæmp/ verb [T] to press something such as soil or tobacco down firmly

Tampax /ˈtæmpæks/ noun [C] trademark a type of tampon

tamper /ˈtæm.pəʳ/ ⓤⓢ /-pɚ/ verb

PHRASAL VERB **tamper with sth** to touch or make changes to something which you should not, usually without enough knowledge of how it works or when you are trying to damage it: *I could see at once that the lock had been tampered with.*

tampon /ˈtæm.pɒn/ ⓤⓢ /-pɑːn/ noun [C] a small cylinder of cotton or other material which a woman puts in her VAGINA to absorb blood during her PERIOD

tan /tæn/ noun; adj; verb; abbreviation

▸noun [C] (also **suntan**) B2 pleasantly brown skin caused by being in the hot sun: *a deep tan*

▸adj pale yellowish-brown in colour • **tan noun** [U]

▸verb (-nn-) **COLOUR** ▷ **1** [I or T] to become brown, or to make someone's body or skin, etc. brown, from being in the sun: *Her skin tans very quickly in the summer.* ◦ *I need to tan my legs before the holiday.* ◦ *Tanned workmen were sitting around the dock.* **LEATHER** ▷ **2** [T] to change animal skin into leather using special chemicals such as TANNIN

IDIOM **tan sb's hide** old-fashioned (UK also **tan the hide off sb**) to beat someone: *I'll tan his hide if I catch him.*

▸abbreviation written abbreviation for **tangent**

tandem /ˈtæn.dəm/ noun [C] a bicycle made for two people who sit one behind the other • **tandem adv** *riding tandem*

IDIOM **in tandem 1** at the same time: *The heart and lungs will be transplanted in tandem.* **2** If two pieces of equipment, people, etc. are working in tandem, they are working together, especially well or closely: *I want these two groups to work/operate in tandem on this project.*

tandoori /tænˈdʊə.ri/ ⓤⓢ /tɑːnˈdʊr.i/ noun [U] a particular South Asian method of cooking food in a clay cooker: *tandoori chicken*

tang /tæŋ/ noun [S] a strong, sharp taste or smell: *the tang of the sea air*

tangent /ˈtæn.dʒᵊnt/ noun [C] **CIRCLE** ▷ **1** a straight line which touches but does not cut into a curve **TRIANGLE** ▷ **2** (written abbreviation **tan**) (in a triangle that has one angle of 90°) the RATIO of the length of the side opposite an angle less than 90° divided by the length of the shorter of the two sides that are next to the angle → Compare **cosine, sine** • **tangential** /tænˈdʒen.ʃəl/ adj

IDIOM **go/fly off at a tangent** UK (US **go off on a tangent**) to suddenly start talking or thinking about a completely new subject: *It's hard to get a firm decision out of him – he's always going off at a tangent.*

tangerine /ˌtæn.dʒəˈriːn/ US /ˈtæn.dʒə.riːn/ noun; adj
▸noun **FRUIT** ▷ **1** [C] a fruit like a small orange with a loose skin **COLOUR** ▷ **2** [U] a dark orange colour
▸adj of a dark orange colour

tangible /ˈtæn.dʒə.bl̩/ adj C2 real and not imaginary; able to be shown, touched, or experienced: *We need tangible* ***evidence*** *if we're going to take legal action.* ◦ *Other tangible* ***benefits*** *include an increase in salary and shorter working hours.* • **tangibly** /-bli/ adv

tangle /ˈtæŋ.gl/ noun; verb
▸noun [C] an untidy mass of things that are not in a state of order, or a state of confusion or difficulty: *a tangle* ***of*** *wires*
▸verb [I or T] informal to become or form, or to make something into, an untidy mass → See also **entangle** • **tangled** /-gl̩d/ adj *tangled string*

PHRASAL VERB **tangle with sb** to become involved with someone, usually by arguing or fighting with them: *He was a self-opinionated, overbearing tyrant, and he was the last man she should want to tangle with.*

tango /ˈtæŋ.gəʊ/ US /-goʊ/ noun [C] (plural **tangos**) an energetic dance from South America for two people, or the music for this dance • **tango** verb [I] (**tangoed**, **tangoed**)

tangy /ˈtæŋ.i/ adj A tangy flavour is pleasantly strong and sharp: *a deliciously tangy lemon tart*

tank /tæŋk/ noun; verb
▸noun [C] **CONTAINER** ▷ **1** C2 a container which holds liquid or gas: *a water tank* ◦ *a fuel/petrol tank* **VEHICLE** ▷ **2** C1 a large military fighting vehicle designed to protect those inside it from attack, driven by wheels that turn inside moving metal belts **POOL** ▷ **3** Indian English an artificial pool or lake, especially a lake for supplying water to an area
▸verb [I] informal to go down in price, value, etc., or to become less successful: *The state was expecting an increase in tax revenues, but that was before the economy tanked.* ◦ *Car exports in the year to April tanked 23 percent.*

T

tankard /ˈtæŋ.kəd/ US /-kəd/ noun [C] a large usually metal drinking cup with sloping sides and a handle and sometimes a lid, mainly used for drinking beer

ˌtanked ˈup adj informal drunk

tanker /ˈtæŋ.kəʳ/ US /-kɚ/ noun [C] a ship or vehicle that is built to carry liquid or gas: *an* ***oil*** *tanker*

tankful /ˈtæŋk.fʊl/ noun [C] the amount that can be held by a tank (= container)

tankini /tæŋˈkiː.ni/ noun [C] a two-piece SWIMMING COSTUME for women in which the top part covers the whole of the chest and a large part of the back

ˈtank ˌtop noun [C] a piece of clothing that covers the upper part of the body but not the arms, and usually has a U-shaped opening at the neck

tanner /ˈtæn.əʳ/ US /-ɚ/ noun [C] **JOB** ▷ **1** a person who TANS leather **COIN** ▷ **2** old use informal a **sixpence**

tannery /ˈtæn.ər.i/ US /-ɚ-/ noun [C] the place where leather is made

tannin /ˈtæn.ɪn/ noun [C or U] (also **tannic acid** /ˌtæn.ɪkˈæs.ɪd/) (one of) a group of chemicals that are found in plant cells, especially in leaves, BARK (= a tree's outer covering), and fruit that is not yet ready to eat

ˈtanning ˌbooth noun [C] a small room where a person can go to have their skin turned brown by ULTRAVIOLET RAYS

Tannoy /ˈtæn.ɔɪ/ noun [C usually singular] UK trademark a system of equipment that is used for making speech loud enough for a large number of people to hear, especially in order to give information

tantalize (UK usually **tantalise**) /ˈtæn.təl.aɪz/ US /-ə.laɪz/ verb [T] to make someone feel excited or attracted by an offer or a suggestion of something that is, in fact, unlikely to happen

tantalizing (UK usually **tantalising**) /ˈtæn.tə.laɪ.zɪŋ/ US /-t̬ə-/ adj describes something that causes DESIRE and excitement in you, but is unlikely to provide a way of satisfying that desire: *I caught a tantalizing glimpse of the sparkling blue sea through the trees.* • **tantalizingly** (UK usually **tantalisingly**) /-li/ adv

tantamount /ˈtæn.tə.maʊnt/ US /-t̬ə-/ adj formal **tantamount to sth** being almost the same or having the same effect as something, usually something bad: *Her refusal to answer was tantamount to an admission of guilt.*

tantrum /ˈtæn.trəm/ noun [C] a sudden period of uncontrolled anger like a young child's: *Johnny* ***had/threw*** *a tantrum in the shop because I wouldn't buy him any sweets.* ◦ *If she doesn't get her own way she has* ***temper*** *tantrums.*

Taoiseach /ˈtiː.ʃək/ noun [C] the leader of the government of the Republic of Ireland

Taoism (also **Daoism**) /ˈtaʊ.ɪ.zəm/ US /ˈdaʊ.ɪ-/ noun [U] a religion developed originally in ancient China which emphasizes a simple and natural life • **Taoist** /-ɪst/ adj, noun [C] *a Taoist temple* ◦ *Taoist philosophy*

tap /tæp/ verb; noun
▸verb (-pp-) **HIT** ▷ **1** B2 [I or T] to hit something gently, and often repeatedly, especially making short, sharp noises: *The branches tapped* ***against*** *the window.* ◦ *I could hear him tapping his fingers on the desk.* ◦ *I was tapping my feet (= hitting the floor gently with my feet) to the music.* ◦ *Someone tapped me* ***on the shoulder.*** **GET** ▷ **2** [T] to get or make use of something: *For more than a century, Eastern cities have expanded their water supplies by tapping ever more remote sources.* ◦ *There is a rich vein of literary talent here just waiting to be tapped by publishers.* **PHONE** ▷ **3** [T] to use a small device fixed to a phone in order to listen secretly to what people are saying: *He suspected that his* ***phone*** *had been tapped.*

PHRASAL VERBS **tap sb for sth** old-fashioned informal to get money from someone • **tap into sth** to manage to use something in a way that brings good results: *If only we could tap into all that energy and creativity.*

▸noun **DEVICE** ▷ **1** B1 [C] UK (US **faucet**) a device that controls the flow of liquid, especially water, from a pipe: *the hot/cold tap* ◦ ***Turn the*** *tap* ***on/off.*** **2** [C] UK a device that controls the flow of gas from a pipe **3 on tap a** used to describe beer that is served from a BARREL through a tap **b** available for use at any time: *Working in a library as I do, I have all this information on tap.* **HIT** ▷ **4** B2 [C] a gentle knock or touch, or the noise made by knocking something gently: *I gave her a tap on the shoulder and she turned around.* ◦ *There was a tap on the window – Dad was outside!* **DANCE** ▷ **5** [U] **tap dancing**: *He teaches tap and ballroom.* **PHONE** ▷ **6** [C] a small piece of equipment that can be fixed to a phone in order to listen secretly to someone's phone calls: *He claims that he knew nothing of government* ***phone*** *taps on journalists during those years.* **SPEECH SOUND** ▷ **7** [C] specialized a sound made by the tongue moving upwards and downwards very quickly and hitting the alveolar area

tapas /ˈtæp.əs/ **noun** [plural] small amounts of Spanish food that are served, especially with alcoholic drinks, in Spanish bars and restaurants: *a tapas* ***bar***

ˈtap ˌdancing noun [U] (also **tap**) a type of dance in which the rhythm is kept by the noise of the dancer's shoes on the floor: *I did tap classes as well as ballet.* • **ˈtap ˌdance** noun [C or U] • **ˈtap-ˌdancer** noun [C]

tape /teɪp/ **noun; verb**

▸**noun** [C or U] **RECORDING** ▷ **1** thin plastic in a long narrow strip with a magnetic covering that allows sounds or sounds and pictures to be recorded and played again, especially one on which sound is (to be) recorded: *magnetic tape* ◦ *I've got that film* ***on*** *tape (= recorded) if you want to borrow it.* ◦ *If you give me a* ***blank*** *tape (= one with nothing on it) I'll record it for you.* **STRIP** ▷ **2** a long, narrow strip of material that is sometimes sticky on one side: UK *sticky tape* **3 the (finishing) tape** a tape stretched across the finishing line of a race that the winner breaks as they finish

▸**verb** [T] **RECORD** ▷ **1** to record something on tape **USE STICKY STRIPS** ▷ **2** to use strips of sticky material, especially to fix two things together or to fasten a parcel: *She taped a note to the door.*

IDIOM **have sb taped** (also **have sb on tape**) UK informal to know about and be able to deal with a person or situation

ˈtape ˌmeasure noun [C] a strip of plastic or metal used for measuring that can be rolled up when not being used → Compare **ruler**

tape measure

taper /ˈteɪ.pəʳ/ (US) /-pɚ/ **verb; noun**

▸**verb** [I or T] to become gradually narrower at one end, or to make something do this: *Turn left where the road tapers* ***(off)*** *into a track.* • **tapering** /ˈteɪ.pə.rɪŋ/ (US) /-pɚ.ɪŋ/ **adj**

PHRASAL VERB **taper off** to become gradually smaller or weaker, or happen less often: *Sales have gradually tapered off.*

▸**noun** [C] a very thin candle or a very thin strip of wood, used especially in the past for lighting candles, fires, etc.

ˈtape reˌcorder noun [C] a machine that is used for playing and recording sound onto tape, usually one that is light and small enough to be carried

tapestry /ˈtæp.ɪ.stri/ **noun** [C] a piece of cloth with a pattern or picture that is created by sewing or weaving different coloured threads onto a special type of strong cloth

tapeworm /ˈteɪp.wɜːm/ (US) /-wɝːm/ **noun** [C] a long, flat parasite (= organism which lives in another from which it gets its food) which lives inside the bowels of humans and other animals

tapioca /ˌtæp.iˈəʊ.kə/ (US) /-ˈoʊ-/ **noun** [U] small, hard pieces of the dried and crushed root of the cassava plant, usually cooked with milk and sugar to make a sweet food: *tapioca pudding*

tapir /ˈteɪ.pəʳ/, /-pɚ/ **noun** [C] an animal with hoofs, a long nose that bends, and a smooth coat, which lives in the forests of Southeast Asia and Central and South America

tappet /ˈtæp.ɪt/ **noun** [C] a part of a machine which causes another part to move by hitting it

taproot /ˈtæp.ruːt/ **noun** [C] specialized a main thick root found in some plants, such as the carrot, which stores food and grows straight down vertically

ˈtap ˌwater noun [U] the water that comes out of the taps in a building that are connected to the main supply of the local water system

tar /tɑːʳ/ (US) /tɑːr/ **noun; verb**

▸**noun** [U] **1** a black substance, sticky when hot, used especially for making roads **2** one of the poisonous substances found in tobacco: *a low tar cigarette*

IDIOM **beat/knock/whale the tar out of sb** US informal to hit someone forcefully and repeatedly: *The boxer knocked the tar out of his opponent.*

▸**verb** [T] (-rr-) to put tar on a surface

IDIOMS **tar sb with the same brush** to think that someone has the same bad qualities as another person: *Because they worked so closely in the same department, John was tarred with the same brush as Tim.* • **tar and feather sb** to cover someone in tar and feathers as a punishment

taramasalata /ˌtær.ə.mə.səˈlɑː.tə/ (US) /ˌtɑːr.ə.mə.sə-ˈlɑː.t̬ə/ **noun** [U] a pale pink food, originally from southeastern Europe, that is made from a mixture of fish eggs, bread, and oil

tarantula /təˈræn.tjʊ.lə/ **noun** [C] any of various large spiders covered in hair, some of which have a poisonous bite

tarantula

tardy /ˈtɑː.di/ (US) /ˈtɑːr-/ **adj** formal slow or late in happening or arriving • **tardiness** /-nəs/ **noun** [U]

tare /teəʳ/ (US) /ter/ **noun** [U or S] (also **tare weight**) the weight of a vehicle or container when empty

target /ˈtɑː.ɡɪt/ (US) /ˈtɑːr-/ **noun; verb**

▸**noun** **OBJECT SHOT AT** ▷ **1** (B2) [C] an object shot at during shooting practice, often a circle with a pattern of rings, or any object or place at which bullets, bombs, etc. are aimed: *I had four shots but I didn't even* ***hit*** *the target.* ◦ *Any major airport or station is potentially a* ***terrorist*** *target.* **PERSON/GROUP** ▷ **2** (C2) [C usually singular] a person or a particular group of people that something is directed at, or that something is intended for: *The target audience* ***for*** *the TV series are young people aged 13 to 18.* **3** (C1) [C usually singular] one or more people who are criticized or laughed at, or who experience unpleasant treatment from others: *Recently she has been the target* ***of*** *a series of obscene phone calls.* **AIM** ▷ **4** (B2) [C] a level or situation which you intend to achieve: *The government's target of 3.5 percent annual growth seems easily attainable.*

> Word partners for **target** (**OBJECT SHOT AT**)
>
> *attack/hit/miss/strike* a target • *identify* a target • a *likely/possible/potential* target • an *obvious/prime* target • an *easy/soft* target • the *intended* target • a target *for* sth

IDIOM **on target** If you are on target with a piece of work, you are making good progress and likely to achieve what you planned.

▸**verb** [T] **DIRECT** ▷ **1** (C2) to direct advertising, criticism, or a product at someone: *The paper is targeted specifically* ***at*** *young people.* **ATTACK** ▷ **2** to aim an

T

Word partners for target (PERSON/GROUP)

become a target • the *main/prime* target • a target *for* sth • the target *audience/group/market*

Word partners for target (AIM)

set a target • *achieve/meet/reach* a target • a target *date/figure/price/weight* • an *achievable/realistic/reasonable* target • a target *of* sth • a target *for* sth

attack, or a bullet, bomb, etc., at a particular object, place, or person: *It is hoped that civilians will not be targeted during the war.*

ˈtarget ˌlanguage noun [C usually singular] specialized a language that you are changing spoken or written words into

tariff /ˈtær.ɪf/ noun [C] a charge or list of charges either for services or on goods entering a country

tarmac /ˈtɑː.mæk/ (US) /ˈtɑːr-/ noun [U] (also **tarmacadam**) **1** (an area of) black material used for building roads, etc., which consists of TAR mixed with small stones **2 the tarmac** an area covered in tarmac, especially the area in an airport where aircraft land and take off • **tarmac** verb [T] (**tarmacking**, **tarmacked**, **tarmacked**) UK

tarn /tɑːn/ (US) /tɑːrn/ noun [C] a small mountain lake

tarnish /ˈtɑː.nɪʃ/ (US) /ˈtɑːr-/ verb **METAL** ▷ **1** [I or T] to make or (especially of metal) become less bright or a different colour **GOOD OPINION** ▷ **2** [T] to make people think that someone or something is less good: *By this time a series of scandals had severely tarnished the leader's* ***image/reputation***. • **tarnished** /-nɪʃt/ adj

taro /ˈtær.əʊ/ (US) /-oʊ/ noun [C] (plural **taros**) a tropical plant which has a root that is cooked and eaten

tarot /ˈtær.əʊ/ (US) /-oʊ/ noun [S or U] a set of 78 cards with pictures on, used for trying to find out what will happen to someone in the future

tarpaulin /tɑːˈpɔː.lɪn/ (US) /tɑːrˈpɑː-/ noun [C or U] (US usually **tarp**) (a large piece of) heavy WATERPROOF cloth used as a covering

tarragon /ˈtær.ə.gən/ (US) /-gɑːn/ noun [U] a plant with whitish flowers whose narrow leaves taste similar to LIQUORICE and are used in cooking as a herb

tarry /ˈtær.i/ verb [I] old use to stay somewhere for longer than expected and delay leaving

tart /tɑːt/ (US) /tɑːrt/ noun; adj; verb

▸noun **FOOD** ▷ **1** [C or U] an open pastry case with a filling, usually of something sweet such as fruit: *apple/strawberry/custard tart* **WOMAN** ▷ **2** [C] very informal disapproving a woman who intentionally wears the type of clothes and make-up that attract sexual attention in a way that is too obvious **3** [C] old-fashioned slang a female PROSTITUTE

▸adj **SOUR** ▷ **1** (especially of fruit) tasting sour or ACIDIC: *You might need some sugar on the rhubarb – it's a bit tart.* **BEHAVIOUR** ▷ **2** (especially of a way of speaking) quick or sharp and unpleasant: *a tart remark/comment/reply* • **tartly** /ˈtɑːt.li/ (US) /ˈtɑːrt-/ adv • **tartness** /ˈtɑːt.nəs/ (US) /ˈtɑːrt-/ noun [U]

▸verb

PHRASAL VERBS **tart yourself up** UK informal disapproving or humorous to try to make yourself look more attractive by putting on make-up, jewellery, and fashionable clothes: *She's still in the bathroom, tarting herself up.* • **tart sth up** UK informal often disapproving to make something look more attractive or decorative, usually by making very quick or very obvious changes: *He made his money by tarting up slum houses and selling them at a huge profit.*

tartan /ˈtɑː.tᵊn/ (US) /ˈtɑːr.ᵊn/ noun [C or U] a pattern of different coloured straight lines crossing each other at 90 degree angles, or a cloth with this pattern: *a tartan kilt*

tartar /ˈtɑː.təʳ/ (US) /ˈtɑːr.t̬ɚ/ noun **SUBSTANCE** ▷ **1** [U] a hard substance that forms on the teeth **PERSON** ▷ **2** [C] old-fashioned disapproving a person who is often angry and unkind

tartaric acid /tɑːˌtær.ɪkˈæs.ɪd/ (US) /tɑːr-/ noun [U] an ACIDIC substance, found in many plants and fruits, that is used to make CREAM OF TARTAR

ˈtartar ˌsauce (also **ˈtartare ˌsauce**) noun [U] a cold, white sauce containing small pieces of herbs and vegetables, usually eaten with fish

tarty /ˈtɑː.ti/ (US) /ˈtɑːr.t̬i/ adj informal disapproving intentionally attracting sexual attention in a way that is too obvious: *I always think short skirts and high heels look a bit tarty.*

taser /ˈteɪ.zəʳ/ (US) /-zɚ/ noun [C] trademark a gun that fires small objects which give someone a small ELECTRIC SHOCK and make them unable to move for a short time

task /tɑːsk/ (US) /tæsk/ noun; verb

▸noun **WORK** ▷ **1** (B2) [C] a piece of work to be done, especially one done regularly, unwillingly or with difficulty: *We usually ask interviewees to* ***perform*** *a few simple tasks on the computer just to test their aptitude.* ◦ *The government now faces the* ***daunting*** *task of restructuring the entire health service.* **SPEAK ANGRILY** ▷ **2 take sb to task** to criticize or speak angrily to someone for something that they have done wrong: *She took her assistant to task* ***for/over*** *her carelessness.*

▸verb [T usually passive] to give someone a task: *We have been tasked* ***with*** *setting up camps for refugees.*

taskbar /ˈtɑːsk.bɑːʳ/ (US) /ˈtæsk.bɑːr/ noun [C] a set of symbols on a computer screen that shows the programs you are using and allows you to change them

ˈtask ˌforce noun [C usually singular] a group of people who are brought together to do a particular job, or a large military group who have a military aim to achieve

tassel /ˈtæs.ᵊl/ noun [C] a group of short threads or ropes held together at one end, used as a hanging decoration on hats, curtains, furniture, etc. • **tasselled** (US usually **tasseled**) /-ᵊld/ adj

taste /teɪst/ noun; verb

▸noun **FLAVOUR** ▷ **1** (B1) [C or U] the flavour of something, or the ability of a person or animal to recognize different flavours: *I love the taste* ***of*** *garlic.* ◦ *Olives are perhaps an* ***acquired*** *taste (= you only like them after you have become familiar with their taste).* ◦ *When you've got a cold you often lose your* ***sense of*** *taste.* → See also **aftertaste** **2 a taste for sth** (C2) the fact of liking or enjoying something: *I acquired a taste for classical music when I was living in Vienna.* **3** [S] a small amount of food: *Have a taste of the sauce and tell me if it needs salt.* **JUDGMENT** ▷ **4** [C or U] a person's approval of and liking for particular things: *I've never really cared much for flash new cars – old vintage cars are more* ***to*** *my taste (= what I like).* **5** (B2) [U] approving a person's ability to judge and recognize what is good or suitable, especially relating to such matters as art, style, beauty, and behaviour: *He* ***has*** *the most awful taste so you can probably imagine what his house looks like.* ◦ *His taste* ***in*** *clothes leaves a little to be desired.*

6 tastes (B2) [plural] the things a person likes: *I'm afraid I **have** expensive tastes (= I like expensive things).* **EXPERIENCE** ▷ **7** (B2) [S] a short experience of something: *I **had** a taste **of** office work during the summer and that was quite enough.*

> **Word partners for taste noun (FLAVOUR)**
> *improve/spoil* the taste • *disguise/take away* the taste • *like/love* the taste of sth • *savour* the taste • sb's *sense* of taste • a *bitter/bland/pleasant/ strong* taste • a *distinctive/unusual* taste

> **Word partners for taste noun (JUDGMENT)**
> *acquire/develop/get/have* a taste *for* sth • *give* sb a taste *for* sth • *different/expensive* tastes • *for* [my, your, etc.] taste • taste *in* sth • *to* sb's taste

IDIOMS **be in good, the best possible, etc. taste** (C2) to be acceptable in a way that will not upset or anger people: *The film must be in good taste for public viewing.* • **be in bad, poor, the worst possible, etc. taste** (C2) to be unacceptable in a way that will upset or anger people: *He told a joke about death that I thought was in rather poor taste considering that Steve's father had just died.*

▸verb [T] **FOOD/DRINK** ▷ **1** (B1) to put food or drink in your mouth to find out what flavour it has: *Taste this sauce and tell me if it needs seasoning.* ◦ *Whatever's this? I've never tasted anything like it.* **2 taste good, bad, sweet, etc.** (B1) to have a particular flavour: *This sauce tastes strange.* ◦ *The bread tastes **of** onions.* ◦ *This coffee tastes **like** dishwater!* **EXPERIENCE** ▷ **3** to experience something for a short time: *Once you've tasted luxury it's very hard to settle for anything else.*

ˈtaste ˌbuds noun [plural] a group of cells, found especially on the tongue, which allow different tastes to be recognized

tasteful /ˈteɪst.fəl/ adj (C2) attractive and chosen for style and quality: *It's very tasteful, their house, but I can't help thinking it lacks a little character.* • **tastefully** /-i/ adv *tastefully decorated*

tasteless /ˈteɪst.ləs/ adj **LIKELY TO UPSET** ▷ **1** (C2) likely to upset someone: *tasteless jokes* **NO FLAVOUR** ▷ **2** (C1) having no flavour: *The meat was dry and tasteless.* **NOT STYLISH** ▷ **3** (C2) not stylish: *the tasteless decor in the house* • **tastelessly** /-li/ adv

taster /ˈteɪ.stəʳ/ (US) /-stɚ/ noun [C] **JOB** ▷ **1** a person who tastes food or drink as a job: *a **wine**-taster* **SMALL AMOUNT** ▷ **2** a small amount or short experience of something that is intended either to make you understand what it is like or to make you want more of it

-tasting /-teɪ.stɪŋ/ suffix having a particular flavour: *sweet-tasting* ◦ *foul-tasting*

tasty /ˈteɪ.sti/ adj **FOOD** ▷ **1** (B1) describes food that has a strong and very pleasant flavour: *This soup is very tasty.* **PERSON** ▷ **2** informal describes someone who is very sexually attractive

tat /tæt/ noun **LOW QUALITY** ▷ **1** [U] informal anything that looks cheap, is of low quality or in bad condition: *Like most souvenir shops, it sells a lot of old tat.* **DECORATION** ▷ **2** [C] informal for **tattoo**

ta-ta /təˈtɑː/, /tætˈɑː/ (US) /tɑːˈtɑː/ exclamation UK informal goodbye

tattered /ˈtæt.əd/ (US) /ˈtæţ.ɚd/ adj (especially of cloth or paper) badly torn: *The flag was tattered and threadbare.* ◦ *a tattered old letter*

tatters /ˈtæt.əz/ (US) /ˈtæţ.ɚz/ noun [plural] **in tatters** **a** (especially of cloth) badly torn: *Her clothes were old and in tatters.* **b** badly damaged or completely spoiled: *After the newspaper story appeared his reputation was in tatters.*

tattletale /ˈtæt.l̩.teɪl/ (US) /ˈtæţ-/ noun [C] US for **telltale**

tattoo /təˈtuː/, /tætˈuː/ noun; verb

tattoo

▸noun [C] (plural **tattoos**) **DECORA·TION** ▷ **1** (informal **tat**) a permanent image, pattern, or word on the skin that is created by using needles to put colours under the skin **MILITARY SHOW** ▷ **2** an outside show, with several military performances especially of marching and music

▸verb [T] (**tattooed**) to put a tattoo or tattoos on someone or something: *He had her name tattooed on his arm.* • **tattooed** /təˈtuːd/, /tætˈuːd/ adj

tattooist /təˈtuː.ɪst/, /tætˈuː.ɪst/ noun [C] (also **tatˈtoo ˌartist**) someone whose job is putting tattoos on people

tatty /ˈtæt.i/ (US) /ˈtæţ-/ adj old and in bad condition: *tatty **old** jeans*

taught /tɔːt/ (US) /tɑːt/ verb past simple and past participle of **teach**

taunt /tɔːnt/ (US) /tɑːnt/ verb [T] to intentionally annoy and upset someone by making unkind remarks to them, laughing at them, etc.: *The other children used to taunt him in the playground because he was fat and wore glasses.* • **taunt** noun [C] *The protesters shouted taunts at the police.*

Taurus /ˈtɔː.rəs/ (US) /ˈtɔːr.əs/ noun [C or U] the second sign of the ZODIAC, relating to the period 21 April to 22 May, represented by a BULL, or a person born during this period

taut /tɔːt/ (US) /tɑːt/ adj **TIGHT** ▷ **1** tight or completely stretched: *a taut rope* ◦ *He kept his eyes on the road ahead, his face taut **with** concentration.* → Compare **slack** **EXCITED/NERVOUS** ▷ **2** literary excited or nervous: *His latest film was described in today's paper as a taut thriller.* ◦ *There was a taut edge to Niall's voice.* **WRITING/SPEECH** ▷ **3** literary describes writing or speech that is controlled, clear, and short: *taut prose* • **tautly** /ˈtɔːt.li/ (US) /ˈtɑːt-/ adv • **tautness** /ˈtɔːt.nəs/ (US) /ˈtɑːt-/ noun [U]

tauten /ˈtɔː.tən/ (US) /ˈtɑː.ţ-/ verb [I or T] to become taut (= tight): *The muscles in his face suddenly tautened.*

tautology /tɔːˈtɒl.ə.dʒi/ (US) /tɑːˈtɑː.lə-/ noun [C or U] the unnecessary and usually unintentional use of two words to express one meaning • **tautological** /ˌtɔː.təˈlɒdʒ.ɪ.kəl/ (US) /ˌtɑː.ţəˈlɑː.dʒɪ-/ adj • **tautologically** /ˌtɔː.təˈlɒdʒ.ɪ.kəl.i/ (US) /ˌtɑː.ţəˈlɑː.dʒɪ-/ adv

tavern /ˈtæv.ən/ (US) /-ɚn/ noun [C] old use a place where alcohol is sold and drunk

tawdry /ˈtɔː.dri/ (US) /ˈtɑː-/ adj looking bright and attractive but in fact cheap and of low quality • **tawdriness** /-nəs/ noun [U]

tawny /ˈtɔː.ni/ (US) /ˈtɑː-/ adj of a light yellowish-brown colour, like that of a lion

tax /tæks/ noun; verb

▸noun [C or U] (B1) (an amount of) money paid to the government that is based on your income or the cost of goods or services you have bought: *They're putting up the tax **on** cigarettes.* ◦ *Tax **cuts** (= reductions in taxes) are always popular.* ◦ *What do you earn **before/***

T

Word partners for tax noun

impose/introduce/levy/raise a tax • *cut/increase/reduce/raise* tax • *deduct/pay* tax • *high/low* taxes • a tax *on* sth • [pay £100/25%] *in* tax • a *tax cut/increase*

after *tax (= before/after you have paid tax on the money you earn)?*

▸**verb** [T] **MONEY** ▷ **1** C1 to make someone pay a tax: *Husbands and wives may be taxed independently/together.* **NEED EFFORT** ▷ **2** to need someone to make a lot of effort, either physical or mental: *He only has to read a short report – it shouldn't tax him unduly.*

taxable /ˈtæk.sə.bl/ **adj** If something is taxable, you must pay tax on it: *taxable* ***income***

ˈtax alˌlowance noun [C usually singular] the amount of income on which you do not have to pay tax

taxation /tækˈseɪ.ʃən/ noun [U] the system of taxing people

ˈtax aˌvoidance noun [U] the reduction, by legal methods, of the amount of tax that a person or company pays

ˈtax ˌcredit noun [C] an amount of money that is taken off the amount of tax you must pay

ˌtax-deˈductible adj If an amount of money that you spend is tax-deductible, it can be taken away from the total amount of income you must pay tax on.

ˈtax ˌdisc noun [C] UK a small, round sign that you put in the corner of the front window of your car or other vehicle to show that you have paid the tax to use it

ˈtax eˌvasion noun [U] ways of illegally paying less tax than you should

ˌtax-eˈxempt adj **1** used to describe a product, service, or financial arrangement on which no taxes have to be paid: *The poorest families pay no grocery tax because their food stamp purchases are tax-exempt.* **2** used to describe a person or an organization that does not have to pay tax: *the tax-exempt* ***status*** *of college athletic departments*

ˈtax ˌexile noun [C] a rich person who has moved to another place where taxes are lower than in their own country: *The island is a haven for tax exiles.*

ˌtax-ˈfree adj If something is tax-free, you do not pay tax on it.

ˈtax ˌhaven noun [C] a place where people pay less tax than they would pay if they lived in their own country

T

taxi /ˈtæk.si/ noun; verb

▸**noun** [C] (also **taxicab**, also **cab**) A1 a car with a driver who you pay to take you somewhere: *I* ***took*** *a taxi from the station to the hotel.* ◦ *a taxi* ***driver***

▸**verb** [I] (present tense **taxiing**, past tense and past participle **taxied**) (of an aircraft) to move slowly on the ground

taxicab /ˈtæk.si.kæb/ noun [C] a taxi

taxidermist /ˈtæk.sɪ.dɜː.mɪst/ US /-dɝː-/ noun [C] a person whose job is taxidermy

taxidermy /ˈtæk.sɪ.dɜː.mi/ US /-dɝː-/ noun [U] the activity of cleaning, preserving, and filling the skins of dead animals with special material to make them look as if they are still alive

taxing /ˈtæk.sɪŋ/ adj difficult or needing a lot of thought or effort: *I like a bit of light reading when I'm on holiday – nothing too taxing.*

ˈtaxi ˌrank noun [C] UK (US **cabstand**) a place where taxis wait for customers

taxiway /ˈtæk.si.weɪ/ noun [C] a long path which aircraft travel along in order to get to or return from a RUNWAY (= place where aircraft take off and land)

the taxman /ˈtæks.mæn/ noun [S] the government department that is responsible for collecting taxes

taxonomy /tækˈsɒn.ə.mi/ US /-ˈsɑː.nə-/ noun [C or U] specialized a system for naming and organizing things, especially plants and animals, into groups which share similar qualities • **taxonomic** /ˌtæk.səˈnɒm.ɪk/ US /-ˈnɑː.mɪk/ adj *a taxonomic group/system*

taxpayer /ˈtæksˌpeɪ.əʳ/ US /-ɚ/ noun **1** C2 [C] a person who pays tax **2 the taxpayer** all the people who pay tax to the government

ˈtax preˌparer noun [C] US a person whose job is to prepare tax returns (= forms that give information about how much money has been earned in a year) for people or businesses

ˈtax reˌlief noun [U] the system of allowing someone not to pay tax on a part of their income

ˈtax reˌturn noun [C] a form that a some people must fill in to give information about how much they have earned in a year

ˈtax ˌshelter noun [C] a financial arrangement by which INVESTMENTS can be made without paying tax

ˈtax ˌyear noun [C] **financial year**

TB /ˌtiːˈbiː/ noun [U] abbreviation for **tuberculosis**

ˌT-bone ˈsteak noun [C] (also **ˈT-bone**) a piece of thickly cut BEEF that has a T-shaped bone in it

tbsp. written abbreviation for **tablespoonful** or **tablespoon**

ˈT-cell noun [C] a type of white blood cell that helps protect the body against diseases such as viruses, infections, or CANCER

te /tiː/ noun [S] the musical note **ti**

tea /tiː/ noun **DRINK** ▷ **1** A1 [C or U] (a drink made by pouring hot water onto) dried and cut leaves and sometimes flowers, especially the leaves of the tea plant: *China/Indian tea* ◦ *iced/lemon tea* ◦ *a selection of herbal teas* ◦ *I'd love a* ***cup of*** *tea, please.* ◦ *'Shall I pour the tea?' 'No, let it* ***brew*** *(= get stronger) a while.'* ◦ *Tea* ***and biscuits*** *will be provided at eleven o'clock.* ◦ *How do you like your tea –* ***strong*** *or* ***weak****?* ◦ *We sat in the shade of a tree,* ***sipping*** *tea and eating scones.* ◦ *I'm not much of a tea* ***drinker****.* ◦ UK informal *How about* ***a nice cup of*** *tea? That'll make you feel better.* **2** [C] a cup of tea: *Two teas, please.* **MEAL** ▷ **3** [U or C] a meal that is eaten in the early evening and is usually cooked **4** B1 [U or C] a small meal eaten in the late afternoon, usually including cake and a cup of tea

IDIOMS **tea and sympathy** old-fashioned kindness and sympathy that you show to someone who is upset • **would not do sth for all the tea in China** old-fashioned used to say that nothing could persuade you to do something: *I wouldn't take that job for all the tea in China.*

teabag /ˈtiː.bæg/ noun [C] a small paper bag filled with enough tea leaves to make tea for one person

teabag

ˈtea ˌball noun [C] mainly US a small wire ball that is filled with tea leaves and put into hot water to make tea

ˈtea ˌbreak noun [C usually singular] UK a short rest from working, usually spent drinking tea or something similar: *We had a chat in our tea break.*

ˈtea ˌcaddy noun [C] a container to keep tea leaves in

teacake /ˈtiː.keɪk/ noun [C] UK a small, round, sweet cake containing dried fruit, often cut open, heated, and eaten with butter: *toasted teacakes*

teach /tiːtʃ/ verb [I or T] (**taught**, **taught**) **1** A1 to give someone knowledge or to train someone; to INSTRUCT: *She taught English **to** foreign students.* ◦ [+ to infinitive] *Who taught you **to** cook?* **2 teach school** US to be a teacher in a school: *Ever since she was a child her dream has been to teach school.*

> **! Common mistake: teach**
>
> **Warning:** Check your verb endings!
>
> Many learners make mistakes when using **teach** in the past tense. The past simple and past participle are **taught**. Don't write 'teached', write **taught**.

> **+ Other ways of saying teach**
>
> **Instruct** can sometimes be used instead of 'teach':
>
> *His job is to **instruct** people in the use of the gym equipment.*
>
> **Train** can be used when you are teaching people how to do a job or activity:
>
> *She **trains** new hairdressers.*
>
> If someone teaches special classes in sports or a school subject, especially to one person or a small group, you could use the verb **coach**:
>
> *She **coaches** students in French.*
>
> *He **coaches** young football players.*
>
> **Tutor** could also be used when talking about teaching a school subject to one person or a small group:
>
> *She **tutors** students in French.*
>
> **Educate** means 'to teach someone, especially using the formal system of school or college':
>
> *How much does it cost to **educate** a child privately?*

IDIOMS **teach sb a lesson** C2 A person or experience that teaches you a lesson improves your future behaviour by making you experience the bad effects of your actions: *Having my car stolen really taught me a lesson – I'll never leave it unlocked again.* ◦ *She decided to teach the boy a lesson.* • **that'll teach sb** If someone says that they or an unpleasant experience will teach someone (not) to do something, they mean that they will stop that person from doing it in future by making them experience the bad effects of their action: *So Roger spent the night in a freezing garage, did he? That'll teach him **to** (= show him that he should not) go out without his house keys!*

teacher /ˈtiː.tʃəʳ/ US /-tʃɚ/ noun [C] A1 someone whose job is to teach in a school or college

ˌ**teacher's** ˈ**pet** noun [C] disapproving a student in a class who is liked best by the teacher and therefore treated better than the other students

ˌ**teacher-ˈtraining** ˌ**college** noun [C] UK (US ˈteacher's ˌcollege, Australian English ˈteachers ˌcollege) a college where teachers are trained

ˈ**tea** ˌ**chest** noun [C] a large wooden box used first for storing tea and after that for other things, especially when someone is moving from one house to another

ˈ**teach-in** noun [C] old-fashioned a meeting for discussion on a subject of public interest, often held among college students

teaching /ˈtiː.tʃɪŋ/ noun **JOB** ▷ **1** B1 [U] the job of being a teacher: *He's always wanted to go into teaching.* ◦ *modern teaching methods* **OPINIONS** ▷ **2 teachings** [plural] moral, religious, or political opinions, especially of a famous leader: *Christ's teachings*

ˈ**tea** ˌ**cloth** noun [C] UK **tea towel**

ˈ**tea** ˌ**cosy** noun [C] a thick covering, like a hat, that is put on a TEAPOT to keep the tea warm

teacup /ˈtiː.kʌp/ noun [C] a cup with a handle from which tea is drunk

ˈ**tea** ˌ**garden** noun [C] UK **RESTAURANT** ▷ **1** an outside restaurant where drinks and small meals are served **AREA OF LAND** ▷ **2** a tea PLANTATION (= large area of land where tea plants are grown)

teahouse /ˈtiː.haʊs/ noun [C] in China and Japan, a small building in which tea is served

teak /tiːk/ noun [U] (the wood of) a type of large tropical tree: *a teak forest* ◦ *teak furniture*

teakettle /ˈtiːˌket.l/ US /-ˌket-/ noun US a **kettle**

teal /tiːl/ noun **BIRD** ▷ **1** [C] a small wild DUCK **COLOUR** ▷ **2** [U] a dark greenish-blue colour • **teal** adj having a dark greenish-blue colour

team /tiːm/ noun; verb

▸noun [C, + sing/pl verb] **1** A2 a number of people or animals who do something together as a group: *a basketball/hockey/netball team* ◦ *a team **of** investigators* **2** used in a number of phrases which refer to people working together as a group in order to achieve something: *It was a real team **effort** – everyone contributed something to the success of the project.*

> **Word partners for team**
>
> be *in/on* a team • *join/play for* a team • *choose/pick* (sb for) a team • a team *captain/coach/member* • a team *effort* • a team *game/sport* • the *home/opposing* team • [operate/work] *as* a team

▸verb

PHRASAL VERB **team up** to join another person, or form a group with other people, in order to do something together: *They teamed up for a charity performance.*

ˈ**team** ˌ**building** noun [U] the process of encouraging members of a group to work well together, for example by having them take part in activities or games: *The company puts a lot of emphasis on cooperation and team building.* ◦ *a team-building exercise/course*

teammate /ˈtiːm.meɪt/ noun [C] a player on the same team

ˈ**team** ˌ**player** noun [C] someone who is good at working closely with other people

teamster /ˈtiːm.stəʳ/ US /-stɚ/ noun [C] US someone who drives a truck as a job

teamwork /ˈtiːm.wɜːk/ US /-wɝːk/ noun [U] C1 the ability of a group of people to work well together: *Brilliant teamwork and old fashioned grit got the team a last minute point.* ◦ *Her determination, teamwork skills and leadership capabilities convinced us that she was perfect for the job.*

ˈ**tea** ˌ**party** noun [C] an occasion when people meet in the afternoon to drink tea and eat a small amount of food

the ˈ**Tea** ˌ**Party** noun a RIGHT-WING political movement in the US that wants to reduce government spending and cut taxes

teapot /ˈtiː.pɒt/ US /-pɑːt/ noun [C] a container for making and serving tea with a handle and a shaped opening for pouring

tear[1] /teəʳ/ US /ter/ verb; noun

▸verb (**tore**, **torn**) **PULL APART** ▷ **1** B1 [I or T] to pull or

T

be pulled apart, or to pull pieces off: *You have to be very careful with books this old because the paper tends to tear very easily.* ◦ *I tore my skirt on the chair as I stood up.* ◦ *A couple of pages had been torn* ***out of/from*** *the book.* **HURRY** ▷ **2** [I + adv/prep] informal to move very quickly: *He went tearing along the road after the bus.*

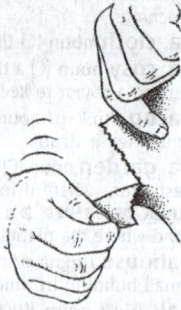

IDIOMS **be in a tearing hurry** UK old-fashioned to be going somewhere very quickly, usually because you are late • **tear your hair out** If you tear your hair out over a problem, you are worrying a lot about it: *She's been tearing her hair out* ***over*** *the final chapter of her novel for the last month.* • **tear sb's heart out** to make someone very sad: *The thought of those poor, hungry children is tearing my heart out.* • **tear a strip off sb** (also **tear sb off a strip**) UK informal to criticize someone in a forceful way

PHRASAL VERBS **tear sth apart** **PULL VIOLENTLY** ▷ **1** to pull something so violently that it breaks into two or more pieces: *A dog can tear a rabbit apart in seconds.* **DIVIDE PEOPLE** ▷ **2** (C2) to make a group of people that was united, such as a country, family, or political party, argue or fight with each other by dividing it into two or more parts: *Ethnic rivalries threaten to tear this country apart.* ◦ *He resigned, depressed at the way that the party was tearing it****self*** *apart.* **DESTROY** ▷ **3** to destroy a building or room: *The blast had torn the building apart.* • **tear sb/sth apart** (C2) to criticize something or someone severely: *The speaker was applauded as he tore apart the prime minister's policies.* • **tear sb apart** informal to make someone very unhappy: *Seeing the children suffer really tears me apart.* • **tear sb away** to make someone stop doing something that they enjoy, usually because they have to go somewhere or do something else: *I'll bring Tim, if I can tear him away* ***from*** *the football.* ◦ *You could come to the party with us. That's if you can tear your****self*** *away* ***from*** *that new boyfriend of yours!* • **tear sth down** (C2) to intentionally destroy a building or other structure because it is not being used or it is not wanted any more: *They're going to tear down the old hospital and build a new one.* • **tear into sb** informal to criticize someone or something very strongly: *Unfortunately, if he doesn't agree with you, he tends to tear into you.* • **tear sth off** to remove your clothes quickly and carelessly: *I tore my sweaty clothes off and jumped into the shower.* • **tear off** informal to leave very quickly: *He got in his car and tore off down the road.* • **tear sth up** **PAPER** ▷ **1** (C1) to tear paper into a lot of small pieces: *He tore the letter up and threw it away.* **AGREEMENT** ▷ **2** If you tear up an agreement, you refuse to accept it or be controlled by it any more: *She tore up the contract and walked out.*

▸**noun** [C] a hole in a piece of paper, cloth, or other material, where it has been torn

tear² /tɪəʳ/ (US) /tɪr/ **noun** **1** (B1) [C usually plural] a drop of salty liquid which flows from the eye, as a result of strong emotion, especially unhappiness, or pain: *tears* ***of*** *remorse/regret/happiness/joy/laughter* ◦ *Did you notice the tears* ***in*** *his* ***eyes*** *when he talked about Diane?* ◦ *Why do arguments with you always* ***reduce*** *me* ***to*** *tears (= make me cry)?* ◦ *I won't* ***shed*** *(****any****) tears (= I will not be unhappy) when he goes, I can tell you!* **2** **burst into tears** (B1) to suddenly start to cry **3** **in tears** (B1) crying: *I found him in tears in his bedroom.*

tearaway /ˈteə.rə.weɪ/ (US) /ˈter.ə-/ **noun** [C] UK informal a young person, usually male, who behaves in an uncontrolled way and is often causing trouble: *He was a real tearaway at school – he was always in trouble with teachers or with the police.*

teardrop /ˈtɪə.drɒp/ (US) /ˈtɪr.drɑːp/ **noun** [C] a single TEAR (= drop from the eye)

tearful /ˈtɪə.fəl/ (US) /ˈtɪr-/ **adj** crying or likely to cry: *After a tearful farewell at the station, we went our separate ways.* ◦ *Katy's always a bit tearful when it's time to go back to school.* • **tearfully** /-i/ **adv** • **tearfulness** /-nəs/ **noun** [U]

ˈtear ˌgas **noun** [U] a gas used by some police and armed forces to control crowds of people. It hurts the eyes and makes them produce TEARS.

tearjerker /ˈtɪəˌdʒɜː.kəʳ/ (US) /ˈtɪrˌdʒɜː.kɚ/ **noun** [C] informal a book, film, play, etc. that has a sad story intended to make people cry or be sad: *I'd recommend that you take a pile of tissues with you when you see that film – it's a* ***real*** *tearjerker!*

ˈtea ˌroom **noun** [C] (also **ˈtea ˌshop**) UK a small restaurant where drinks and small meals, such as tea and cakes, are served

tease /tiːz/ **verb**; **noun**

▸**verb** [I or T] (B2) to laugh at someone or say unkind things about them, either because you are joking or because you want to upset them: *I used to hate being teased* ***about*** *my red hair when I was at school.* ◦ *I was only teasing, I didn't mean to upset you.*

> **Other ways of saying tease**
>
> If someone is teasing a person as a joke by telling that person something that is not true, you could use the verbs **joke** or, in informal English, **kid**:
>
> *I've lost your passport. Only* ***joking****!*
>
> *I'm sorry I forgot to get you a birthday present. Only* ***kidding****!*
>
> You can also use the informal phrase **pull someone's leg**:
>
> *Is that really your car or are you* ***pulling my leg****?*
>
> If someone is teasing a person in a friendly way, you can use the verb **rib**:
>
> *His brothers were* ***ribbing*** *him about his new girlfriend.*
>
> If someone is teasing a person in order to upset him or her, the phrase **make fun of** is often used:
>
> *The other children* ***made fun of*** *him because he wore glasses.*
>
> If someone is teasing a person in order to upset him or her, you could in more formal situations use **mock** or **ridicule**:
>
> *It was not unusual for our greatest inventors to be* ***mocked*** *and thought crazy.*
>
> *She didn't say what she thought for fear of being* ***ridiculed****.*

PHRASAL VERB **tease sth out** **GET INFORMATION** ▷ **1** to try to get information or understand a meaning that is hidden or not clear: *It took me a while to tease the truth out* ***of*** *him.* **SEPARATE** ▷ **2** to use your fingers to gradually separate hairs or threads that are stuck or twisted together: *While it was still wet, I gently teased out the tangled knots in Rosie's hair.*

▸**noun** [C] **1** someone who is always teasing people: *Johnny, don't be such a tease – leave your sister alone!* **2** slang disapproving someone who enjoys causing sexual excitement and interest in people she or he does not intend to have sex with

T

teaser /ˈtiː.zəʳ/ US /-zɚ/ noun [C] a **brainteaser**

ˈ**tea** ˌ**set** noun [C] (also ˈ**tea** ˌ**service**) a set of small plates, cups, etc., with a matching design, for serving tea and small amounts of food such as cakes and sandwiches

teaspoon /ˈtiː.spuːn/ noun [C] B2 a small spoon used to STIR (= mix) tea or coffee in a cup → Compare **dessertspoon, tablespoon**

teaspoonful /ˈtiː.spuːn.fʊl/ noun [C] (plural **teaspoonsful** or **teaspoonfuls**) (written abbreviation **tsp.**) the amount a teaspoon can hold

ˈ**tea** ˌ**strainer** noun [C] an object that is used to collect the tea leaves when tea is poured through it into a cup

teat /tiːt/ noun [C] **ANIMAL** ▷ **1** a part of a female mammal's body through which milk passes to her babies **BOTTLE** ▷ **2** UK (US **nipple**) a piece of rubber or SILICONE for feeding a baby from a bottle

teatime /ˈtiː.taɪm/ noun [U] the time in the afternoon when some people eat a small meal

ˈ**tea** ˌ**towel** noun [C] (UK also ˈ**tea** ˌ**cloth**, US **dishtowel**) a cloth used for drying plates, knives and forks, etc., after you have washed them

ˈ**tea** ˌ**tray** noun [C] a small TRAY (= flat surface for carrying especially food and drink)

ˈ**tea tree** ˌ**oil** noun [U] a pale oil taken from the leaves of an Australian plant called the tea tree, used for its strong, pleasant smell or as a medicine

ˈ**tea** ˌ**trolley** noun [C] UK (mainly US ˈ**tea** ˌ**wagon/cart**) a small table on wheels, sometimes with an upper and a lower shelf, for serving drinks and food

tech /tek/ adj, noun [U] abbreviation for **technical** or **technology**

techie (also **techy**) /ˈtek.i/ noun [C] informal someone who knows a lot about computers or other electronic equipment

technical /ˈtek.nɪ.kəl/ adj **1** B2 relating to the knowledge, machines, or methods used in science and industry: *a few technical* ***problems*** **2** relating to the knowledge and methods of a particular subject or job: *Personally, I found some parts of the book a little too technical to follow.* **3** B2 relating to practical skills and methods that are used in a particular activity: *In her performance as the Snow Queen she showed great technical brilliance.*

technicality /ˌtek.nɪˈkæl.ə.ti/ US /-nəˈkæl.ə.t̬i/ noun [C] a detail or small matter: *He was disqualified from the competition* ***on a*** *technicality.*

technically /ˈtek.nɪ.kəl.i/ adv **1** C2 according to an exact understanding of rules, facts, etc.: *Technically, the country's economic problems are over but recovery will be slow.* ◦ *young people who are technically still children* **2** C1 in a way that relates to the knowledge, machines, or methods used in science and industry: *technically advanced weapons* **3** in a way that relates to practical skills and methods that are used in a particular activity: *It was a technically brilliant performance.*

ˈ**technical** ˌ**school** noun [C] Australian English a school where students learn skills which involve working with their hands → Compare **trade school**

ˌ**technical sup**ˈ**port** noun [U] an advice service provided, usually over the phone, to help people who have problems using a computer: *We had to make five calls to technical support to get the computer working.*

technician /tekˈnɪʃ.ən/ noun [C] **1** C1 a worker trained with special skills, especially in science or ENGINEERING: *a laboratory technician* **2** a person whose technique is very good

technicolor /ˈtek.nɪˌkʌl.əʳ/ US /-ɚ/ adj; noun
▸adj (UK also **technicolour**) having a lot of bright colours
▸noun (UK also **technicolour**)

IDIOM **in glorious technicolor** US (UK also **in glorious technicolour**) very colourful or too brightly coloured: *Her room was painted in glorious technicolor.*

Technicolor /ˈtek.nɪˌkʌl.əʳ/ US /-ɚ/ noun [U] trademark a special process for making cinema films in colour

technique /tekˈniːk/ noun [C or U] B1 a way of doing an activity which needs skill: *We have developed a new technique* ***for*** *detecting errors in the manufacturing process.* ◦ *She's a wonderfully creative dancer but she doesn't have the technique of a truly great performer.*

techno /ˈtek.nəʊ/ US /-noʊ/ noun [U] C1 fast electronic dance music with a regular beat: *Thousands of ravers came to Berlin yesterday for the world's largest techno* ***music*** *party.*

techno- /tek.nə-/ /tek.nəʊ-/ US /tek.noʊ-/ prefix relating to or involving TECHNOLOGY: *a technophile (= a person who loves technology)*

technobabble /ˈtek.nəʊˌbæb.əl/ US /-noʊˌ-/ noun [U] informal disapproving technical language that is difficult for ordinary people to understand

technological /ˌtek.nəˈlɒdʒ.ɪ.kəl/ US /-ˈlɑː.dʒɪ-/ adj B2 relating to, or involving, technology: *Technological* ***advances*** *in computing and telecommunications have reduced the need for many people to travel to work.* • **technologically** /-kəl.i/ adv

technologist /tekˈnɒl.ə.dʒɪst/ US /-ˈnɑː.lə-/ noun [C] someone who works with a particular technology: *an architectural technologist* ◦ *a food technologist*

technology /tekˈnɒl.ə.dʒi/ US /-ˈnɑː.lə-/ noun [C or U] B1 (the study and knowledge of) the practical, especially industrial, use of scientific discoveries: *computer technology* ◦ ***Modern*** *technology is amazing, isn't it?* ◦ *What this country needs is a long-term policy for investment in* ***science and*** *technology.* → See also **biotechnology**

> **!** Common mistake: **technology**
>
> To talk in general about the practical use of scientific discoveries, don't say 'the technology', just say **technology**:
>
> ~~*Advances in the technology have made our lives easier.*~~
>
> *Advances in technology have made our lives easier.*

> Word partners for **technology**
>
> *develop/harness* technology • *have* the technology to do sth • *advanced/cutting-edge/modern/new* technology • the *latest* technology

technophobe /ˈtek.nə.fəʊb/ US /-foʊb/ noun [C] someone who dislikes new technology, especially computers, and is not able to use it with confidence

tectonic /tekˈtɒn.ɪk/ US /-ˈtɑː.nɪk/ adj specialized relating to the structure of the surface of the Earth and the way it is formed, changed, and moved by forces inside it: *the motion of Earth's tectonic* ***plates*** *(= sections of the planet's surface)* • **tectonics** /-ˈtɒn.ɪks/ US /-ˈtɑː.nɪks/ noun [U] ***plate*** *tectonics*

teddy /ˈted.i/ noun [C] **TOY** ▷ **1** (also **teddy bear**) a soft toy BEAR **CLOTHES** ▷ **2** a piece of women's underwear for the upper body

ˈ**Teddy** ˌ**boy** noun [C] (informal **ted**) a young man, especially in the 1950s in the UK, who typically dressed in narrow trousers, a long, loose jacket, and shoes with thick SOLES

T

tedious /ˈtiː.di.əs/ adj C1 boring: *a tedious job* • **tediously** /-li/ adv • **tediousness** /-nəs/ noun [U]

tedium /ˈtiː.di.əm/ noun [U] the quality of being boring for a long time: *Soldiers often say that the worst thing about fighting is not the moments of terror, but all the hours of tedium in between.*

tee /tiː/ noun; verb

▸noun [C] a short plastic stick with a cup-shaped top on which a GOLF BALL is put to be hit, or the area where this is used to start the play for each hole

IDIOM **to a tee** old-fashioned perfectly or completely: *That job would suit you to a tee.*

▸verb

PHRASAL VERBS **tee sb off** US informal to make someone angry: *It really tees me off when she doesn't listen to me.* • **tee off** to hit a golf ball off the tee, or to begin a game of golf by doing this: *We'll tee off at ten o'clock.* • **tee (sth) up** to put a golf ball on the tee in preparation for playing

teem /tiːm/ verb [I] (also **teem down**) UK to rain heavily: ***It's** been teeming down all day.* ◦ ***It's teeming with** rain.*

PHRASAL VERB **teem with sth** to contain large numbers of animals or people: *The mall was teeming with shoppers that Saturday.*

teeming /ˈtiː.mɪŋ/ adj If a place is teeming, it is full of people: *the teeming metropolis*

teen /tiːn/ adj; noun

▸adj **teenage (teenager)**

▸noun [C] **teenager**

teenager /ˈtiːnˌeɪ.dʒəʳ/ US /-dʒɚ/ noun [C] (informal **teen**) A2 a young person between 13 and 19 years old: *The magazine is aimed at teenagers and young adults.* • **teenage** /-eɪdʒ/ adj [before noun] (also **teenaged** /-eɪdʒd/, informal **teen**) B1 *a teenage nephew*

teens /tiːnz/ noun [plural] **1** A person's teens are the period in which they are aged between 13 and 19: *Both my daughters are **in** their teens.* ◦ *He's in his **early/mid/late** teens.* **2 the teens a** the range of temperature between 13° and 19°: *The temperature is expected to be **in** the teens tomorrow.* **b** the period of years between 11 and 19 in any century, usually 1911–1919 or 2011–2019: *This type of building was built **in** the teens and twenties.*

teeny /ˈtiː.ni/ adj (also **ˌteeny-ˈweeny**) informal very small: *Just a teeny slice of cake for me, please.*

teenybopper /ˈtiː.niˌbɒp.əʳ/ US /-ˌbɑː.pɚ/ noun [C] informal a teenager, especially a girl, who eagerly follows the most recent fashion, music, and other interests of her age group

teepee /ˈtiː.piː/ noun [C] another spelling of **tepee**

ˈtee shirt noun [C] a **T-shirt**

teeter /ˈtiː.təʳ/ US /-t̬ɚ/ verb [I usually + adv/prep] to appear to be about to fall while moving or standing: *Delia was teetering around in five-inch heels.*

IDIOM **teeter on the brink/edge of sth** If something is teetering on the brink/edge of a bad situation, it is likely that the situation will happen soon: *What we are seeing now is a country teetering on the brink of civil war.*

ˌteeter-ˈtotter noun [C] US for **seesaw**

teeth /tiːθ/ noun plural of tooth

teethe /tiːð/ verb [I] If a baby or small child is teething, its first teeth are growing, usually causing it pain.

ˈteething ˌtroubles noun [plural] (also **ˈteething ˌproblems**) UK problems which happen in the early stages of doing something new: *There were the usual teething troubles at the start of the project, but that's to be expected.*

teetotal /ˌtiːˈtəʊ.tᵊl/ US /-ˈtoʊ.t̬ᵊl/ adj never drinking alcohol or opposed to the drinking of alcohol • **teetotaller** UK (US usually **teetotaler**) /-əʳ/ US /-ɚ/ noun [C]

TEFL /ˈtef.l/ noun [U] abbreviation for Teaching English as a Foreign Language

Teflon /ˈtef.lɒn/ US /-lɑːn/ noun [U] trademark a plastic that is very smooth and does not have chemical reactions with other substances. It is used in industry and as a surface for cooking pans so that food does not stick to the pan.

tel. noun (also **tel. no.**) written abbreviation for telephone number

tele- /tel.ɪ-/ US /tel.ə-/ prefix over a long distance, done by phone, or on or for television

telecommunications /ˌtel.ɪ.kəˌmjuː.nɪˈkeɪ.ʃᵊnz/ US /-ə-/ noun [plural] (informal **telecoms**) B2 the sending and receiving of messages over distance, especially by phone, radio, and television: *the telecommunications industry*

telecommuting /ˌtel.ɪ.kəˈmjuː.tɪŋ/ US /-t̬ɪŋ/ noun [U] **teleworking** • **telecommute** /-ˈmjuːt/ verb [I] to **telework** • **telecommuter** /-ˈmjuː.təʳ/ US /-t̬ɚ/ noun [C]

telecoms /ˈtel.ɪ.kɒmz/ US /-kɑːmz/ noun [U, + sing/pl verb] short for telecommunications

teleconference /ˌtel.ɪˈkɒn.fᵊr.ᵊns/ US /-ˈkɑːn.fɚ-/ noun [C] a meeting involving people who are in different places, but who are connected by video and computers • **teleconferencing** /-ᵊn.sɪŋ/ noun [U] *Medical researchers in many countries exchange information through email and video teleconferencing.*

telecottage /ˈtel.ɪˌkɒt.ɪdʒ/ US /-ˌkɑː.t̬ɪ-/ noun [C] an office, usually in a village, provided with computers and electronic communications equipment for use by people and businesses in the area • **telecottaging** /-ɪ.dʒɪŋ/ noun [U] the activity of working from a telecottage

telegenic /ˌtel.ɪˈdʒen.ɪk/ US /-ə-/ adj approving (especially of a person) appearing attractive on television: *With their new youthful and telegenic leader, the party looks set to woo the voters.*

telegram /ˈtel.ɪ.græm/ noun [C] (US also **wire**) (especially in the past) a piece of paper with a message sent by telegraph • **telegrammatic** /ˌtel.ɪ.grəˈmæt.ɪk/ US /-ə.grəˈmæt̬-/ adj

telegramese /ˌtel.ɪ.græmˈiːz/ US /-ə-/ noun [U] (also **telegraphese**) a style of writing which leaves out words that are not important

telegraph /ˈtel.ɪ.grɑːf/, /-græf/ US /-ə-/ noun [U] (especially in the past) a method of sending and receiving messages by electrical or radio signals, or the special equipment used for this purpose: *The news came **by** telegraph.* • **telegraph** verb [T]

ˈtelegraph ˌpole noun [C] UK (US **ˈtelephone ˌpole**) a tall wooden pole to which phone wires are fixed

telemarketing /ˈtel.ɪˌmɑː.kɪ.tɪŋ/ US /-əˌmɑːr.kə.t̬ɪŋ/ noun [U] mainly US for **telesales**

telemedicine /ˈtel.ɪˌmed.ɪ.sən/ noun [U] the treatment of people who are ill, by sending information from one place to another by computer, video, etc.

telemetry /təˈlem.ə.tri/ noun [U] specialized the science or process of collecting information about objects that are far away and sending the information somewhere electronically

teleology /ˌtiː.liˈɒl.ə.dʒi/ (US) /-ˈɑː.lə-/ **noun** [U] specialized (in PHILOSOPHY) the belief that everything has a special purpose or use • **teleological** /-əˈlɒdʒ.ɪ.kəl/ (US) /-ˈlɑː.dʒɪ.kəl/ **adj** *a teleological argument*

telepathy /təˈlep.ə.θi/ **noun** [U] the ability to know what is in someone else's mind or communicate with them mentally, without using words or other physical signals • **telepathic** /ˌtel.ɪˈpæθ.ɪk/ (US) /-ə-/ **adj**

telephone /ˈtel.ɪ.fəʊn/ (US) /-ə.foʊn/ **noun; verb**
▸**noun** [C or U] (A2) a **phone**
▸**verb** [I or T] (A2) to use a phone

ˈtelephone ˌbooth noun [C] US a **phone box**

ˈtelephone ˌbox noun [C] a **phone box**

ˈtelephone diˌrectory noun [C] (informal **ˈphone book**) a large book containing all the phone numbers for a particular area, organization, etc.

ˈtelephone exˌchange noun [C] the building that contains the equipment for connecting phone calls

ˈtelephone ˌkiosk noun [C] UK a **phone box**

ˈtelephone ˌnumber noun [C] a **phone number**

telephonist /təˈlef.ən.ɪst/ **noun** [C] UK a **switchboard operator**

telephony /təˈlef.ə.ni/ **noun** [U] the activity or process of communicating by phone: *We provide support for users of mobile and fixed-line telephony.*

telephoto lens /ˌtel.ɪˌfəʊ.təʊˈlenz/ (US) /-əˌfoʊ.t̬oʊ-/ **noun** [C] a camera LENS that makes objects far away look nearer and larger when they are photographed

teleport /ˈtel.ɪ.pɔːt/ (US) /-ə.pɔːrt/ **verb** [I or T] to (cause to) travel by an imaginary very fast form of transport that uses special TECHNOLOGY or special mental powers

teleprinter /ˈtel.ɪˌprɪn.təʳ/ (US) /-t̬ɚ/ **noun** [C] (mainly US **teletypewriter**) a type of electric printer for sending and receiving messages down a phone line → See also **telex**

teleprompter /ˈtel.ɪˌprɒmp.təʳ/ (US) /-ˌprɑːmp.tɚ/ **noun** [C] US (US trademark **Autocue**) an electronic device that makes it possible for people speaking on a television programme to read text while looking directly at the television camera

telesales /ˈtel.ɪ.seɪlz/ **noun** [U] (US **telemarketing**) the advertising or selling of goods or services by phone

telescope /ˈtel.ɪ.skəʊp/ (US) /-ə.skoʊp/ **noun; verb**

telescope

▸**noun** [C] (B2) a cylinder-shaped device for making objects that are far away look nearer and larger, using a combination of LENSES, or LENSES and curved mirrors • **telescopic** /ˌtel.ɪˈskɒp.ɪk/ (US) /-əˈskɑː.pɪk/ **adj** *a telescopic lens*
▸**verb** [I or T] to make or become shorter by reducing the length of the parts: *We had to telescope five visits into two days.*

Teletext /ˈtel.ɪ.tekst/ (US) /-ə-/ **noun** [U] trademark a system for giving written information on many subjects (such as news and sports results) by television

telethon /ˈtel.ɪ.θɒn/ (US) /-ə.θɑːn/ **noun** [C usually singular] a television show, usually several hours long, whose purpose is to make money for CHARITY

televangelism /ˌtel.ɪˈvæn.dʒə.lɪ.zəm/ **noun** [U] (especially in the US) the activity of PREACHING (= giving religious speeches) on television in order to persuade people to become Christians and give their money to religious organizations • **televangelist** /-lɪst/ **noun** [C]

televise /ˈtel.ɪ.vaɪz/ (US) /-ə-/ **verb** [T] to show or broadcast on television: *The match will be televised* ***live*** *(= shown as it is being played) on BBC Scotland.* • **televised** /-vaɪzd/ (US) /-ə-/ **adj**

television /ˈtel.ɪ.vɪʒ.ən/, /ˌtel.ɪˈvɪʒ-/ (US) /-ə-/ **noun** [C or U] (also **TV**, UK informal **telly**) (A1) a device shaped like a box with a screen which receives electrical signals and changes them into moving images and sound, or the method or business of sending images and sound by electrical signals: *a 3D/an HD television* ◦ *Could you turn the television down?* ◦ *It's one of the few television* ***programmes*** *that I always make a point of watching.* ◦ *Is there anything interesting* ***on*** *television tonight?* ◦ *Clare has worked* ***in*** *television since she left college.* ◦ *Your problem is that you* ***watch*** *too much television.*

> **! Common mistake: television**
>
> **Remember:** the most usual preposition to use with **television** is **on**:
>
> Don't say 'in/at television', say **on television**:
> *What's on television tonight?*

> **Word partners for television**
>
> *watch* television • *see/watch* sth on television • *appear* on television • be *aired/broadcast/shown* on television • be *glued to* the television • *on* (the) television • a television *channel/presenter/programme/series* • *children's/daytime/prime-time* television

televisual /ˌtel.ɪˈvɪʒ.u.əl/ (US) /-ə-/ **adj** mainly UK relating to television: *the televisual age*

teleworking /ˈtel.ɪˌwɜː.kɪŋ/ (US) /-əˌwɝː-/ **noun** [U] (also **telecommuting**) the activity of working at home, while communicating with your office by phone or email • **telework** /-wɜːk/ (US) /-wɝːk/ **verb** [I] (also **telecommute**) • **teleworker** /-kəʳ/ (US) /-kɚ/ **noun** [C] (also **telecommuter**)

telex /ˈtel.eks/ **noun** [C or U] a method of sending written messages down a phone line from one TELEPRINTER to another, the machine that does this, or the message itself: *The details were sent* ***by*** *telex.* • **telex verb** [I or T] [+ two objects] *We telexed him the news at once.*

tell /tel/ **verb** (**told, told**) **SPEAK** ▷ **1** (A1) [T] to say something to someone, often giving them information or instructions: *Tell me* ***about*** *your holiday then.* ◦ [+ two objects] *Can you tell me the way to the station?* ◦ [+ obj + (that)] *Did you tell anyone (****that****) you were coming to see me?* ◦ [+ obj + speech] *'I'm leaving you,' she told him.* ◦ [+ obj + to infinitive] *I told her* ***to*** *go home.* ◦ formal *He told us* ***of*** *his extraordinary childhood.* ◦ *I can't tell you how grateful I am for your help.* **2 tell a lie/lies** to say something/things that are not true: *She's always telling lies.* **3 tell it like it is** informal to tell the facts without hiding anything **4 tell tales** disapproving If someone, usually a child, tells tales, they tell someone such as a teacher about something bad that someone else has done: *Your classmates won't trust you if you're always telling tales, Alvin.* → See also **telltale 5 tell the truth** to speak honestly: *How do you know she's telling the truth?* **6 to tell (you) the truth** to be honest: *To tell (you) the truth, I didn't understand a word of what he was saying.* **KNOW** ▷ **7** (B2) [I or T] to know, recognize, or be certain: *'He's Dutch.' 'How can you tell?'* ◦ [+ (that)] *I could tell (****that****) you were unhappy.* **8** (B2) [T] If something tells you something, it gives you information: *What does*

! Common mistake: tell or say?

Remember: when **tell** is followed by a 'that' clause, it must have an indirect object.

Don't say 'tell that...', say **tell someone that...**:

~~Rory told that he was leaving.~~

Rory told Julie that he was leaving.

To make a sentence without an indirect object, don't use 'tell', use **say**:

Rory said that he was leaving.

the survey tell us ***about*** *the lives of teenagers?* **9 tell the difference** C1 to notice a difference in quality between two things: *This coffee is about half the price of that one and yet you really can't tell the difference.* **10 tell sb's fortune** (also **tell fortunes**) to say what will happen in someone's future: *At the fair, there was a lady who told your fortune.* **11 tell the time** to be able to understand a clock: *My daughter has just learned to tell the time.* **12 there is no telling** there is no way of knowing: *There is no telling* ***wh****at the future will hold for them.* **13 you never can tell** B2 (also **you can never tell**) said to mean that you can never know or be certain: *Who knows what will happen to Peter and me in the future – you can never tell.* **HAVE AN EFFECT** ▷ **14** [I] to have an effect: *She's been under a lot of stress recently and it's starting to tell.*

+ Other ways of saying tell

See also: **say**

Let someone know is a common phrase that means the same as 'tell':

Let me know *if you'd like to come.*

The verb **give** can be used when you tell someone some information:

Can you ***give*** *the message to Jo?*

He ***gave*** *me a few details of what had happened to him.*

Inform or **notify** can be used when someone tells a person some facts, especially in an official situation:

The names of the injured will not be released until their relatives have been ***informed*** *of the accident.*

The school is required to ***notify*** *parents if their children fail to arrive at school.*

If someone tells a person official information, you could, in formal English, use the verb **advise**:

They were ***advised*** *of their rights.*

The verbs **relate** and **recount** are used in formal English when someone tells a story or talks about a series of events that have happened:

She ***related*** *the events of the previous week to the police.*

He ***recounted*** *his adventures since he had left.*

The phrasal verb **pass something on** can be used when you tell someone something that another person has told you:

John told me they were getting engaged but please don't ***pass it on*** *to anyone else.*

If someone tells something to a lot of people, the phrase **spread the word** is sometimes used:

I've arranged the meeting for next Tuesday so if you see anyone, ***spread the word.***

If you tell someone some bad news which will affect that person, you could use the phrase **break the news**:

I didn't want to be the one to ***break the news*** *to him.*

T

IDIOMS **I told you so!** informal C2 said when something bad happens after you warned someone that it would happen • **(I'll) tell you what** C2 used to suggest a plan: *I'll tell you what – we'll split the money between us.* • **tell me another!** UK informal (US informal **tell me another one!**) used to say that you do not believe what someone has told you: *'I worked all day yesterday.' 'Oh yeah, tell me another!'* • **you're telling me!** informal used to say that you strongly agree with what someone has just said: *'Stephen's in such a bad mood today.' 'You're telling me!'*

PHRASAL VERBS **tell against sb/sth** UK formal to make someone or something more likely to fail: *His reputation as a troublemaker told against him when he tried to change his job.* • **tell sth/sb apart** to be able to see the difference between two very similar things or people: *As babies, the twins were so alike that I just couldn't tell them apart.* • **tell sb off** B2 to speak angrily to someone because they have done something wrong: *The teacher told me off* ***for*** *swearing.* • **tell on sb INFORM** ▷ **1** informal to give information about someone, usually something bad that they have said or done, especially to a person in authority **AFFECT BADLY** ▷ **2** to have a bad effect on someone's health or behaviour: *A succession of late nights had begun to tell on him and his work was suffering.*

teller /ˈtel.əʳ/ (US) /-ɚ/ noun [C] **1** a person who counts votes at an election **2** US and Australian English a person employed in a bank to receive and pay out money

telling /ˈtel.ɪŋ/ adj showing the truth about a situation or showing what someone really thinks: *a telling comment*

ˌtelling-ˈoff noun [C usually singular] (plural **tellings-off**) informal the act of speaking angrily to someone because they have done something wrong: *He* ***gave*** *me a* ***good*** *telling-off* ***for*** *forgetting the meeting.*

telltale /ˈtel.teɪl/ adj; noun

▸adj [before noun] allowing a secret to become known: *She found lipstick on his shirts – the telltale* ***sign*** *that he was having an affair.*

▸noun [C] (US **tattletale**) a person, especially a child, who secretly tells someone in authority, especially a teacher, that someone else has done something bad, often in order to cause trouble

telly /ˈtel.i/ noun [C or U] UK C1 informal for television: *What's* ***on*** *telly tonight?*

temerity /təˈmer.ɪ.ti/ (US) /-ə.t̬i/ noun [U] formal disapproving a willingness to do or say something that shocks or upsets other people: [+ to infinitive] *She* ***had the*** *temerity* ***to*** *call me a liar.*

temp /temp/ noun [C] informal a person employed to work for a short period, especially in an office while another person is absent or when there is extra work • **temp** verb [I] *I decided to temp for a while so that I could try different kinds of jobs.*

temper /ˈtem.pəʳ/ (US) /-pɚ/ noun; verb

▸noun **1** B2 [C often singular] the ability to become angry very quickly: *She* ***has*** *a real temper.* ◦ *He's got a really bad temper.* **2 lose your temper** B2 to suddenly become angry: *The children behaved so badly that I lost my temper.* **3 keep your temper** C2 to succeed in staying calm and not becoming angry: *I found it hard to keep my temper with so many things going wrong.* **4 be in a bad, foul, etc. temper** to be feeling angry: *I'd avoid her if I were you – she's in a foul temper.* **5** [S or U] formal or literary mood or emotional state: *He appears to be a man of calm and even temper.*

IDIOM **tempers get frayed** If you say that tempers are getting (rather) frayed, you mean that people are getting angry with each other.

▸verb [T] **REDUCE** ▷ **1** formal to make something less strong, extreme, etc.: *My enthusiasm for the venture was somewhat tempered by my knowledge of the work that would be involved.* ◦ *I learned to temper my criticism.* **METAL** ▷ **2** to heat and then cool a metal in order to make it hard: *tempered steel*

tempera /ˈtem.pᵊr.ə/ ⓊⓈ /-pɚ.ə/ **noun** [U] specialized a method of painting with colours that are mixed with egg and water

temperament /ˈtem.pᵊr.ə.mənt/, /-prə.mənt/ ⓊⓈ /-pɚ.ə-/ **noun** [C or U] the part of your character that affects your moods and the way you behave: *a fiery temperament*

temperamental /ˌtem.pᵊr.əˈmen.tᵊl/, /-prə-/ ⓊⓈ /-pɚ.əˈmen.tᵊl/ **adj** **PERSON** ▷ **1** describes someone whose mood often changes very suddenly: *Be careful how you approach her – she's very temperamental.* **2** caused by your own character and feelings: *There are temperamental similarities between the brothers.* **MACHINE** ▷ **3** informal describes a machine that sometimes works and sometimes does not: *You have to treat our DVD player very carefully – it's rather temperamental.* • **temperamentally** /-i/ **adv**

temperance /ˈtem.pᵊr.ᵊns/, /-prəns/ ⓊⓈ /-pɚ.ᵊns/ **noun** [U] formal **1** control of your own behaviour, such as not drinking or eating too much **2** the habit of not drinking alcohol because you believe it is dangerous or wrong

temperate /ˈtem.pᵊr.ət/, /-prət/ ⓊⓈ /-pɚ.ət/ **adj** **WEATHER** ▷ **1** (of weather conditions) neither very hot nor very cold: *a temperate **climate*** **2** describes plants that grow naturally in places where the weather is neither very hot nor very cold **BEHAVIOUR** ▷ **3** formal If someone's behaviour is temperate, it is calm and controlled. → Opposite **intemperate**

temperature /ˈtem.prə.tʃəʳ/ ⓊⓈ /-pɚ.ə.tʃɚ/ **noun** **HEAT LEVEL** ▷ **1** Ⓐ② [C or U] the measured amount of heat in a place or in the body: *Preheat the oven to a temperature of 200 degrees Celsius.* ◦ *There has been a rise in temperature over the past few days (= the weather has become warmer).* ◦ *The doctor examined him and **took** his temperature (= measured it).* **2 run/have a temperature** Ⓐ② to have a higher body temperature than normal and to be ill **OF A SITUATION** ▷ **3** [U] If you say that the temperature in a particular situation is rising, you mean that it is likely to become violent because people have become angry: *The temperature of the discussion started to rise as each side added its own arguments.*

> **Word partners for temperature**
>
> temperatures *drop/fall/plummet/plunge* • temperatures *rise/soar* • temperatures *hover around* [30 degrees/10 degrees] • *take* sb's temperature • *average/extreme/high/low* temperatures • *at* a temperature of sth

-tempered /-tem.pəd/ ⓊⓈ /-pɚd/ **suffix** having or showing the stated type of TEMPER: *even-tempered* ◦ *bad-tempered*

tempest /ˈtem.pɪst/ **noun** [C] literary a violent storm

tempestuous /temˈpes.tju.əs/ **adj** **EMOTIONS** ▷ **1** If something such as a relationship or time is tempestuous, it is full of strong emotions: *They got divorced in 2010 after a tempestuous marriage.* **STORM** ▷ **2** literary of or relating to a tempest • **tempestuously** /-li/ **adv**

template /ˈtem.pleɪt/ **noun** [C] **1** a pattern made of metal, plastic, or paper, used for making many copies of a shape or to help cut material accurately **2** something that is used as a pattern for producing other similar things: *We used the structure of his report as the template for ours.* **3** a system that helps you arrange information on a computer screen: *a letter template*

temple /ˈtem.pl/ **noun** **BUILDING** ▷ **1** Ⓑ① [C] a building used for the worship of a god or gods in some religions **BODY PART** ▷ **2** [C often plural] the flat area on each side of your head in front of the top of your ear

tempo /ˈtem.pəʊ/ ⓊⓈ /-poʊ/ **noun** (plural **tempos** or specialized **tempi**) **1** [C] the speed at which an event happens: *We're going to have to **up** the tempo (= work faster) if we're to finish on time.* **2** [C or U] specialized the speed at which a piece of music is played: *a change **in** tempo*

temporal /ˈtem.pᵊr.ᵊl/ ⓊⓈ /-pɚ.əl/ **adj** formal relating to practical matters or physical things, rather than spiritual ones

temporary /ˈtem.pᵊr.ᵊr.i/, /-prᵊr-/ ⓊⓈ /-pə.rer.i/ **adj** Ⓑ① not lasting or needed for very long: *The ceasefire will only provide a temporary solution to the crisis.* ◦ *temporary staff* → Compare **permanent** • **temporarily** /-pᵊr.er.ɪ.li/ ⓊⓈ /-pə.rer.ɪ.li/ **adv** Ⓑ② *This office is closed temporarily for redecoration.*

> **Other ways of saying temporary**
>
> The phrase **for now** can be used to say that something should happen or be done now but can be changed later:
>
> *Just put everything on the table **for now** – I'll sort it all out later.*
>
> The adjective **disposable** can be used to describe objects which are intended to be used temporarily and then thrown away:
>
> *I bought a **disposable** camera at the airport.*
>
> If something is temporary and low quality, you can say that it is **makeshift**:
>
> *We built a **makeshift** shelter under the trees.*
>
> The adjective **short-lived** can be used instead of temporary when it means 'lasting for a short time':
>
> *I had a few relationships in college, most of which were fairly **short-lived**.*
>
> The adjectives **provisional** or **interim** can be used when something is temporary because it is likely to change soon:
>
> *After the war, a **provisional** government was set up.*
>
> *This is only an **interim** solution.*
>
> The adjective **acting** is often used to describe someone who does a job temporarily while the person who usually does it is not there:
>
> *He'll be the **acting** director until they appoint a permanent one.*

temporize formal (UK usually **temporise**) /ˈtem.pᵊr.aɪz/ ⓊⓈ /-pə.raɪz/ **verb** [I] to delay making a decision or stating your opinion in order to get an advantage

tempt /tempt/ **verb** [T] **1** to make someone want to have or do something, especially something that is unnecessary or wrong: *The offer of free credit tempted her **into** buying a new car.* ◦ [+ to infinitive] *They tempted him **to** join the company **by** offering him a large salary and a company car.* **2 be tempted** Ⓑ② to want something or to want to do something: *'Did you apply for that job?' 'Well, I was very tempted but in the end I decided not to.'* ◦ *I was **sorely** (= very) tempted **to** resign after my boss was so rude to me.*

IDIOM **tempt fate/providence** If you tempt fate or providence by doing something, you take a silly risk by doing it and depend too much on your good luck:

T

You're tempting fate by riding your bike without wearing a cycle helmet.

temptation /temp'teɪ.ʃᵊn/ **noun 1** B2 [C or U] the wish to do or have something which you know you should not do or have: [+ to infinitive] *As a young actress, she managed to* ***resist*** *the temptation* ***to*** *move to Hollywood.* **2** [C] something that makes you want to do or have something that you know you should not: *He knew it was wrong to steal, but the money just lying there was too great a temptation.*

tempting /'temp.tɪŋ/ **adj** If something is tempting, you want to do or have it: *a tempting offer* ◦ *That pie looks very tempting.* ◦ [+ to infinitive] *It's tempting* ***to*** *blame television for the increase in crime.* • **temptingly** /-li/ **adv**

temptress /'temp.trɪs/ **noun** [C] literary or humorous a woman who tries to sexually attract men

tempura /tem'pʊə.rə/ US /'tem.pʊ.rɑː/ **noun** [U] a type of Japanese food, made by covering small pieces of fish or vegetables in BATTER and frying them

ten /ten/ **number** A1 the number 10: *Her father died ten years ago.* ◦ *We can take ten (people) in the minibus.*

IDIOM **ten to one** If you say ten to one something will or will not happen, you mean it is very likely that it will or will not happen: *Ten to one he won't be there tonight.*

tenable /'ten.ə.bl/ **adj** formal (of an opinion or position) able to be defended successfully or held for a particular period of time: *His theory is no longer tenable in the light of the recent discoveries.* ◦ *The university fellowship is tenable* ***for*** *(= lasts for) three years.*

tenacious /tə'neɪ.ʃəs/ **adj** holding tightly onto something, or keeping an opinion in a determined way: *The baby took my finger in its tenacious little fist.* ◦ *There has been tenacious local opposition to the new airport.* • **tenaciously** /-li/ **adv**

tenacity /tə'næs.ə.ti/ US /-t̬i/ **noun** [U] the determination to continue what you are doing

tenancy /'ten.ᵊn.si/ **noun 1** [C or U] the right to use land or live in a building in exchange for rent **2** [C] the period of time for which you have the right to use a building or piece of land: *a two-year tenancy*

tenant /'ten.ənt/ **noun** [C] C2 a person who pays rent for the use of land or a building

the ˌTen Comˈmandments **noun** [plural] in the Bible, the rules of behaviour which God gave to Israel through Moses

T

tend /tend/ **verb** BE LIKELY ▷ **1** B2 [I] to be likely to behave in a particular way or have a particular characteristic: [+ to infinitive] *We tend* ***to*** *get cold winters and warm, dry summers in this part of the country.* CARE ▷ **2** [T] formal to care for something or someone: *He carefully tended his sunflower plants.* ◦ *The nurse gently tended the patient's cuts and bruises.*

PHRASAL VERB **tend to sb/sth** to deal with the problems or needs of a person or thing: *Would you mind waiting? I'm tending to another customer at the moment.* ◦ *Nurses tended to the injured.*

tendency /'ten.dən.si/ **noun** [C] **1** C1 If someone has a tendency to do or like something, they will probably do it or like it: [+ to infinitive] *His tendency* ***to*** *exaggerate is well known.* **2** If there is a tendency for something to happen, it is likely to happen or it often happens: *There is a tendency* ***for*** *unemployment to rise in the summer.* **3** If there is a tendency to do something, it starts to happen more often or starts to increase: [+ to infinitive] *There is a growing tendency* ***to*** *regard money more highly than quality of life.*

tendentious /ten'den.ʃəs/ **adj** formal (of speech or writing) expressing or supporting a particular opinion which many other people disagree with • **tendentiously** /-li/ **adv** • **tendentiousness** /-nəs/ **noun** [U]

tender /'ten.dəʳ/ US /-dɚ/ **adj; verb; noun**

▸**adj** GENTLE ▷ **1** C2 gentle, loving, or kind: *a tender look/smile* ◦ *What you need is some tender* ***loving care.*** PAINFUL ▷ **2** (of part of the body) painful, sore, or uncomfortable when touched: *My arm was very tender after the injection.* SOFT ▷ **3** C2 (of meat or vegetables) easy to cut or CHEW (= crush with the teeth): *My steak was beautifully tender.* **4** describes plants that are easily damaged by cold weather YOUNG ▷ **5** C2 literary young: *He was sent off to boarding school* ***at*** *the tender* ***age of*** *seven.* • **tenderly** /-li/ **adv** • **tenderness** /-nəs/ **noun** [U]

▸**verb 1** [I] If you tender for a job, you make a formal offer to do it for a stated price: *Five companies have tendered* ***for*** *the hospital contract.* **2** [I] specialized If you tender for something such as SHARES, you make a formal offer to buy them for a stated price. **3** [T] formal to give or offer something: *Please tender the exact fare.* ◦ *The health minister has tendered her* ***resignation*** *(= has offered to leave her job).*

▸**noun** [C] OFFER ▷ **1** a written or formal offer to supply goods or do a job for an agreed price: *The council has* ***invited*** *tenders for the building contract.* **2** specialized a written offer to buy or sell SHARES in a company **3 put sth out to tender** UK If you put work out to tender, you ask people to make offers to do it: *Education departments in all the prisons are being put out to tender.* CONTAINER ▷ **4** specialized a vehicle used for transporting water, wood, or coal, especially one that is pulled behind a railway engine or used by the fire service, or a small boat used for transporting people or goods between a larger boat and the coast

ˌtender-ˈhearted **adj** very kind and showing a lot of sympathy

tenderize (UK usually **tenderise**) /'ten.dᵊr.aɪz/ US /-də.raɪz/ **verb** [T] to make meat easy to cut or CHEW (= crush with the teeth) by beating it or preparing it in a particular way

tenderloin /'ten.dᵊ.lɔɪn/ US /-dɚ-/ **noun** [U] a strip of meat taken from the lower back of cows or pigs, which does not contain a lot of fat and is easy to cut or CHEW (= crush with the teeth)

tendon /'ten.dən/ **noun** [C] a strong piece of tissue in the body connecting a muscle to a bone

tendril /'ten.drᵊl/ **noun** [C] a thin, stem-like part of a climbing plant which holds on to walls or other plants for support

tenement /'ten.ə.mənt/ **noun** [C] a large building divided into apartments, usually in a poor area of a city

tenet /'ten.ɪt/ **noun** [C] formal one of the principles on which a belief or theory is based: *It is a tenet of contemporary psychology that an individual's mental health is supported by having good social networks.*

ˌten-ˈfour **exclamation** (also **10-4**) mainly US said to mean that a message has been received

tenner /'ten.əʳ/ US /-ɚ/ **noun** [C] UK informal ten pounds, or a note worth ten pounds → See also **fiver**

tennis /'ten.ɪs/ **noun** [U] A1 a game played between two or four people on a special playing area which involves hitting a small ball across a central net using a RACKET

ˌtennis ˈelbow **noun** [U] a painful swelling near the

ELBOW that is caused by repeatedly twisting the hand and arm

ˈtennis ˌshoe noun [C] a sports shoe with a rubber bottom and a top made of leather or strong cotton

tenon /ˈten.ən/ noun [C] specialized the end of a piece of wood that is shaped to fit into a MORTISE (= an opening) in another piece of wood to form a JOINT

ˈtenon ˌsaw noun [C] UK (US **ˈback saw**) a small tool with a sharp, thin blade and a strong metal back

tenor /ˈten.əʳ/ (US) /-ɚ/ noun **MUSIC** ▷ **1** [C] a male singer with a high voice, or (especially in combinations) a musical instrument that has the same range of notes as the tenor singing voice: *a tenor saxophone* **CHARACTER** ▷ **2** [U] formal the general meaning, character, or pattern of something: *What was the general tenor **of** his speech?*

ˌtenpin ˈbowling noun [U] (US **tenpins**) → **bowling**

tense /tens/ noun; adj; verb

▸noun [C] B1 any of the forms of a verb which show the time at which an action happened: *'I sing' is in the **present** tense and 'I will sing' is in the **future** tense.*

▸adj **NERVOUS** ▷ **1** B2 nervous and worried and unable to relax: *She was very tense as she waited for the interview.* **2** B2 If a situation is tense, it causes feelings of worry or nervousness: *There were some tense moments in the second half of the game.* **STRETCHED** ▷ **3** (of your body or part of the body) stretched tight and stiff ▷**4** specialized (of a speech sound) made with more force than other speech sounds → Compare **lax** • **tensely** /ˈtens.li/ adv • **tenseness** /ˈtens.nəs/ noun [U]

▸verb [I or T] (also **tense up**) **1** If you or your muscles tense, your muscles become stiff and tight because you are frightened or nervous, or are preparing yourself to do something: *Don't tense your shoulders, just relax.* ◦ *I could feel myself tense up as he touched my neck.* **2 tensed up** very nervous and worried and unable to relax because of something that is going to happen: *You seem very tensed up. Are you still waiting for that call?*

tensile /ˈten.saɪl/ (US) /-sɪl/ adj specialized If a material is tensile, it can be stretched.

ˈtensile ˌstrength noun [U] specialized the ability of a material or object to be stretched or pulled without breaking

tension /ˈten.ʃᵊn/ noun **FEELING** ▷ **1** B2 [U] a feeling of nervousness before an important or difficult event: *You could feel the tension in the room as we waited for our exam results.* **2** B2 [C usually plural or U] a feeling of fear or anger between two groups of people who do not trust each other: *ethnic/racial tension* **STRETCH** ▷ **3** [U] The tension of a wire or rope is the degree to which it is stretched.

tent /tent/ noun [C] B1 a shelter made of CANVAS or a similar material and supported by poles and ropes, that you can fold up and carry with you

tentacle /ˈten.tə.kl̩/ (US) /-t̬ə-/ noun [C] one of the long, thin parts like arms of some sea creatures, used for feeling and holding things, catching food, or moving

tentative /ˈten.tə.tɪv/ (US) /-t̬ə.ɪv/ adj (of a plan or idea) not certain or agreed, or (of a suggestion or action) said or done in a careful but uncertain way because you do not know if you are right: *I have made tentative plans to take a trip to Seattle in July.* • **tentatively** /-li/ adv If you do or say something tentatively, you do or say it in an uncertain way. • **tentativeness** /-nəs/ noun [U]

ˌtent ˈcity noun [C] a large group of tents that provide a temporary place for people to live, especially people who do not have a home

tenterhooks /ˈten.tə.hʊks/ (US) /-t̬ɚ-/ noun [plural] **on tenterhooks** worried or nervous about something that is going to happen: *We were on tenterhooks all morning waiting for the phone to ring.*

tenth /tenθ/ ordinal number; noun

▸ordinal number 10th written as a word: *This is his tenth year of working for the company.* ◦ *Our next meeting is on **the** tenth (**of** April).* ◦ *The team **was/came** tenth in the league.*

▸noun [C] one of ten equal parts of something: *He receives a tenth of the profits.*

tenuous /ˈten.ju.əs/ adj A tenuous connection, idea, or situation is weak and possibly does not exist: *We were only able to make a tenuous connection between the two robberies.* • **tenuously** /-li/ adv

tenure /ˈten.jəʳ/, /-jʊəʳ/ (US) /-jɚ/ /-jʊr/ noun [U] formal **1** being the legal owner of land, a job, or an official public position, or the period of time during which you own it: *During his tenure as dean, he had a real influence on the students.* **2** the right to remain permanently in a job: *She is one of the few lecturers in this department who **has** tenure.* ◦ ***Tenure-track** professors (= those likely to get tenure) who don't publish enough work may not be offered tenure.*

tepee (also **teepee**, **tipi**) /ˈtiː.piː/ noun [C] a type of tent in the shape of a cone made from animal skins that is the typical shelter of some Native Americans

tepid /ˈtep.ɪd/ adj **NOT WARM** ▷ **1** (of liquid) not very warm **NOT ENTHUSIASTIC** ▷ **2** describes a reaction that is not enthusiastic: *I got a tepid response to my suggestion.*

tequila /təˈkiː.lə/ noun [C or U] a strong alcoholic drink originally from Mexico

teˌquila ˈslammer noun [C] a drink consisting of tequila mixed with a sweet FIZZY drink (= one with bubbles) that is shaken and then drunk very quickly

terabyte /ˈter.ə.baɪt/ noun [C] (written abbreviation **TB**) specialized a unit of computer information, consisting of approximately 100 GIGABYTES

terawatt /ˈter.ə.wɒt/ (US) /-wɑːt/ noun [C] a unit for measuring electrical power that is equal to one million MEGAWATTS

tercentenary /ˌtɜː.senˈtiː.nᵊr.i/, /-ˈten.ᵊr-/ (US) /tɚˈsen.tᵊn.er-/ noun [C] mainly UK (mainly US **tercentennial**) the day or year that is 300 years after an important event

term /tɜːm/ (US) /tɝːm/ noun; verb

▸noun **TIME** ▷ **1** [C] the fixed period of time which something lasts for: *He received a prison term **for** drunk driving.* ◦ *The government's term **of office** (= the period in which they have power) expires at the end of the year.* **2** A2 [C] mainly UK one of the periods into which a year is divided at school, college, or university: *In Britain, the spring term starts in January and ends just before Easter.* ◦ *We're very busy in term-**time** (= during the term).* → Compare **quarter, semester, trimester** **3** [C] formal the period of time which a legal agreement lasts for: *The lease on our house is near the end of its term.* **4** [U] specialized the end of a pregnancy when a baby is expected to be born: *Her last pregnancy went **to** term (= the baby was born after the expected number of weeks).* ◦ *a full-term pregnancy* **5 in the long/medium/short term** B2 for a long, medium or short period of time in the future: *Taking this decision will cost us more in the short term, but will be beneficial in the long term.* **DESCRIPTION** ▷ **6** B2 [C] a word or expression used in relation to a particular subject, often to describe something official or technical: *'Without let or hindrance' is a*

T

legal term which means 'freely'. **7 term of abuse** an unkind or unpleasant name to call someone **8 term of endearment** a kind or friendly name to call someone **9 in terms of/in ... terms** (B2) used to describe which particular area of a subject you are discussing: *In financial terms, the project was not a success.* ◦ *In terms of money, I was better off in my last job.* **10 in no uncertain terms** (C2) in a very clear way: *She told him what she thought of his behaviour in no uncertain terms (= she made her disapproval very clear).* **11 in strong, etc. terms** using language which clearly shows your feelings: *He complained in the strongest terms.* ◦ *She spoke of his achievements in* ***glowing*** *terms (= in a very approving way).* **RULES** ▷ **12 terms** (B2) [plural] the conditions which control an agreement, arrangement, or activity: *terms* ***of*** *employment* ◦ ***Under the*** *terms* ***of*** *their contract, employees must give three months' notice if they leave.* **13 on easy terms** If you buy something on easy terms, you pay for it over a period of time. **14 on equal terms** (also **on the same terms**) having the same rights, treatment, etc.: *British and overseas companies will compete for the government contract on equal terms.* **15 terms of reference** formal the matters to which a study or report is limited

IDIOMS **come to terms with sth** (C2) to gradually accept a sad situation, often the death of someone you love: *I think he's still coming to terms with the death of his wife.* • **be on good, friendly, etc. terms (with sb)** (C2) to have a good, friendly, etc. relationship with someone: *My ex-wife and I are still on friendly terms.* ◦ *Are you on good terms with your boss?*

▸verb [T] to give something a name or to describe it with a particular expression: *Technically, a horse which is smaller than 1.5 metres at the shoulder is termed a pony.*

-term /-tɜːm/ (US) /-tɝːm/ suffix **long/medium/short-term** lasting a long/medium/short time: *The project will have long-term benefits.*

termagant /ˈtɜː.mə.gᵊnt/ (US) /ˈtɝː-/ noun [C] disapproving a woman who argues noisily to get or achieve what she wants

terminal /ˈtɜː.mɪ.nəl/ (US) /ˈtɝː-/ adj; noun

▸adj **ILLNESS** ▷ **1** (of a disease or illness) leading gradually to death: *She has terminal cancer.* **2** A terminal patient is one who is seriously ill and will die soon. **EXTREME** ▷ **3** extreme, when referring to something unpleasant or negative: *He has nothing to do all day and is suffering from terminal* ***boredom***. ◦ *She claims that the shipbuilding industry is in terminal* ***decline***. • **terminally** /-nə.li/ adv *a terminally ill child*

▸noun [C] **BUILDING** ▷ **1** (B2) the area or building at a station, airport, or port that is used by passengers leaving or arriving by train, aircraft, or ship: *Your flight to Perth will leave from Terminal 4.* **COMPUTER** ▷ **2** a piece of equipment consisting of a keyboard and screen, used for communicating with the part of a computer system that deals with information **ELECTRICITY** ▷ **3** specialized the point at which a connection can be made in an electric CIRCUIT

terminate /ˈtɜː.mɪ.neɪt/ (US) /ˈtɝː-/ verb [I or T] formal **1** to (cause something to) end or stop: *They terminated my contract in October.* ◦ *This train will terminate at the next stop – passengers who wish to continue should change trains.* **2** specialized to end a pregnancy intentionally, usually by a medical operation

termination /ˌtɜː.mɪˈneɪ.ʃᵊn/ (US) /ˌtɝː-/ noun **1** [C or U] specialized the intentional ending of a pregnancy, usually by a medical operation **2** [U] formal the act of ending something or the end of something: *The termination of the bus service was a severe blow to many villagers.*

ˈterminator ˌgene noun [C] a GENE (= part of a cell which controls development) that has been designed to make a plant unable to produce new young plants

terminology /ˌtɜː.mɪˈnɒl.ə.dʒi/ (US) /ˌtɝː.mɪˈnɑː.lə-/ noun [C or U] special words or expressions used in relation to a particular subject or activity: *scientific terminology* → Compare **jargon** • **terminological** /-nəˈlɒdʒ.ɪ.kᵊl/ (US) /-nəˈlɑː.dʒɪ.kᵊl/ adj • **terminologically** /-nəˈlɒdʒ.ɪ.kᵊl.i/ (US) /-nəˈlɑː.dʒɪ.kᵊl.i/ adv

ˈterm inˌsurance noun [U] a type of INSURANCE which lasts for a limited time period → Compare **life insurance**

terminus /ˈtɜː.mɪ.nəs/ (US) /ˈtɝː-/ noun [C] (plural **terminuses** or **termini** /ˈtɜː.mɪ.naɪ/ (US) /ˈtɝː-/) the last stop or the station at the end of a bus or railway route

termite /ˈtɜː.maɪt/ (US) /ˈtɝː-/ noun [C] (also **ˌwhite ˈant**) a small, white tropical insect that eats wood

ˈterm ˌpaper noun [C] US the main report written by a student for a particular class or subject in the middle of each school TERM

tern /tɜːn/ (US) /tɝːn/ noun [C] a small black and white sea bird with long, pointed wings and a divided tail

terrace /ˈter.əs/ noun; verb

▸noun **GROUND** ▷ **1** [C] a flat raised area **2** (B2) a flat area of stone or grass outside a house, where people sit and sometimes eat **3** one of several narrow strips of land that are built like steps on the slope of a hill, used for growing crops on **4 the terraces** [plural] UK specialized wide steps on which people stand to watch a football match **HOUSE** ▷ **5** [C] UK (US **row**) a row of often small houses joined together along their side walls

▸verb [T] to build narrow strips of land on a slope so that people can plant crops there

terraced /ˈter.ɪst/ adj **HOUSE** ▷ **1** (also **terrace**) UK built as or belonging to a row of often small houses joined together along their side walls: *a terraced street* ◦ *We rented a little terraced* ***house*** *in South London.* **GROUND** ▷ **2** (of land, fields, etc.) built in step-like terraces on a slope

terracotta /ˌter.əˈkɒt.ə/ (US) /-ˈkɑː.t̬ə/ noun [U] **1** hard, baked, reddish-brown clay: *Our kitchen tiles are made from terracotta.* ◦ *The courtyard was full of exotic plants in terracotta pots.* **2** a reddish-brown colour • **terracotta adj** having a reddish-brown colour

terra firma /ˌter.əˈfɜː.mə/ (US) /-ˈfɝː-/ noun [U] usually humorous dry land, when compared with the sea or air: *It was good to get back on terra firma again after that awful sea crossing.*

terrain /təˈreɪn/ noun [U] an area of land, when considering its natural features: *The car handles particularly well on rough terrain.*

terra incognita /ˌter.ə.ɪŋˈkɒg.nɪ.tə/ (US) /-ɪnˈkɑːg.niː.t̬ə/ noun [U] often humorous a place, subject, or situation that you are not familiar with: *Dealing with children is terra incognita to me.*

terrapin /ˈter.ə.pɪn/ noun [C] (plural **terrapin** or **terrapins**) a type of small North American TURTLE which lives in warm rivers and lakes

terrestrial /təˈres.tri.əl/ adj **EARTH** ▷ **1** formal relating to the planet Earth → Compare **extraterrestrial** **ANIMALS** ▷ **2** specialized (of animals) living on the land rather than in the sea or air **TELEVISION** ▷ **3** formal describes television CHANNELS that are broadcast from stations on the ground and do not use SATELLITES

terrible /ˈter.ə.bl̩/ adj **UNPLEASANT** ▷ **1** A2 very unpleasant or serious or of low quality: *The weather was terrible.* ◦ *We have just received some terrible news.* **VERY GREAT** ▷ **2** informal used to emphasize the great degree of something: *This project is a terrible waste of money.* ◦ *She's a terrible nuisance.*

ˌterrible ˈtwins noun [plural] UK informal two people who behave in a way which attracts attention

terribly /ˈter.ə.bli/ adv **VERY BADLY** ▷ **1** B2 very badly: *I slept terribly last night.* **VERY MUCH** ▷ **2** B1 informal very: *I'm terribly pleased to hear that you've got a job.* ◦ *She was terribly sorry not to have seen you last Saturday.*

terrier /ˈter.i.əʳ/ US /-ɚ/ noun [C] a breed of small, active dog, originally used for hunting and chasing animals into or out of their underground holes

terrific /təˈrɪf.ɪk/ adj informal **VERY GOOD** ▷ **1** B1 very good: *a terrific opportunity* ◦ *You look terrific!* **VERY GREAT** ▷ **2** C1 used to emphasize the great amount or degree of something: *The police car drove past at a terrific speed.* • **terrifically** /-ɪ.kəl.i/ adv

terrified /ˈter.ə.faɪd/ adj B1 very frightened: *He huddled in the corner like a terrified child.* ◦ *I'm terrified **of** the dark.* ◦ *She's terrified **(that)** her mother might find out her secret.*

terrify /ˈter.ə.faɪ/ verb [T] B2 to frighten someone very much: *The idea of parachuting out of a plane terrifies me.*

terrifying /ˈter.ə.faɪ.ɪŋ/ adj B2 very frightening: *a terrifying experience/ordeal* • **terrifyingly** /-li/ adv

terrine /təˈriːn/ noun **1** [C or U] a dish made of small pieces of cooked meat, fish, or vegetables pressed into a rectangular shape **2** [C] the type of cooking dish in which a terrine is made

territorial /ˌter.ɪˈtɔː.ri.əl/ US /-ˈtɔːr.i-/ adj C2 relating to TERRITORY: *a territorial dispute* ◦ *Some animals and birds are territorial (= they mark out areas which they defend against others).*

Territorial /ˌter.ɪˈtɔː.ri.əl/ US /-ˈtɔːr.i-/ noun [C] a member of the Territorial Army

the ˌTerritorial ˈArmy noun UK a group of men and women who, without payment and during the time when they are not working, are trained as soldiers

ˌterritorial ˈsea noun specialized **1** [C usually plural] → **territorial waters** **2** [U] the area of sea that lies over the CONTINENTAL SHELF at the edge of a continent

ˌterritorial ˈwaters noun [plural] the area of sea that is around the coast of a country and is thought to belong to it, often going out to twelve NAUTICAL MILES

territory /ˈter.ɪ.tər.i/ US /-tɔːr.i/ noun [C or U] **AREA** ▷ **1** B2 (an area of) land, or sometimes sea, that is considered as belonging to or connected with a particular country or person: *He was shot down in enemy territory.* ◦ *The UN is sending aid to the **occupied** territories.* **2** B2 an area that an animal or person tries to control or thinks belongs to them: *The robin keeps other birds off that part of the garden – that's his territory.* **SUBJECT** ▷ **3** C2 a subject that you know about or have experience in: *The director is back **on familiar** territory with his latest film.*

IDIOM **go/come with the territory** to be an expected fact or result of a particular situation or position: *The public attention that famous people get just goes with the territory.*

terror /ˈter.əʳ/ US /-ɚ/ noun **1** B2 [C or U] (violent action which causes) extreme fear: *They fled from the city **in** terror.* ◦ *There was **sheer/abject** terror in her eyes when he came back into the room.* ◦ *Lots of people have **a** terror **of** spiders.* ◦ *What he said **struck** terror in my heart (= made me very frightened).* ◦ *The separatists started a **campaign of** terror (= violent action causing fear) to get independence.* ◦ *Heights **have/hold** no terrors for me (= do not frighten me).* **2** [C] informal someone, especially a child, who behaves badly and is difficult to control: *My brother is a little terror.*

IDIOM **in terror of your life** frightened that you will be killed

terrorism /ˈter.ə.rɪ.zəm/ US /-ɚ.ɪ-/ noun [U] B2 (threats of) violent action for political purposes: *Governments must cooperate if they are to fight/combat international terrorism.* ◦ *The bomb explosion was one of the worst **acts of** terrorism that the country had experienced in recent years.*

terrorist /ˈter.ə.rɪst/ US /-ɚ.ɪst/ noun [C] B2 someone who uses violent action, or threats of violent action, for political purposes: *Several terrorists have been killed by their own bombs.* ◦ *There has been an increase in terrorist **attacks**.* ◦ *The government has said that it will not be intimidated by terrorist threats.*

terrorize (UK usually **terrorise**) /ˈter.ə.raɪz/ verb [T] to make someone feel very frightened by threatening to kill or hurt them: *Street gangs have been terrorizing the neighbourhood.*

ˈterror-ˌstricken adj extremely frightened

terry /ˈter.i/ noun [U] (UK also **ˌterry ˈtowelling**, US also **ˈterry ˌcloth**) a type of thick cotton cloth with short threads on each side, used especially for making TOWELS (= thick cloths used for drying)

terse /tɜːs/ US /tɝːs/ adj using few words, sometimes in a way that seems rude or unfriendly: *'Are you feeling any better?' 'No!' was the terse **reply**.* • **tersely** /ˈtɜːs.li/ US /ˈtɝː-/ adv • **terseness** /ˈtɜːs.nəs/ US /ˈtɝː-/ noun [U]

tertiary /ˈtɜː.ʃər.i/ US /ˈtɝː.ʃi.er-/ adj **THIRD** ▷ **1** formal relating to a third level or stage **EDUCATION** ▷ **2** C1 [before noun] UK relating to education in colleges and universities: *tertiary education* **SERVICE** ▷ **3** [before noun] specialized describes an industry that provides a service and is not involved with getting the materials with which products are made, or with making products

Terylene /ˈter.ə.liːn/ noun [U] UK trademark (cloth made from) an artificial material

TESL /ˈtes.l̩/ noun [U] abbreviation for Teaching English as a Second Language

TESOL /ˈtiː.sɒl/ US /-sɑːl/ noun [U] abbreviation for Teaching English to Speakers of Other Languages

tessellate (US also **tesselate**) /ˈtes.əl.eɪt/ verb [I] specialized (of shapes) to fit together in a pattern with no spaces in between • **tessellation** (US also **tesselation**) /ˌtes.əlˈeɪ.ʃən/ noun [C or U]

tessellated (US also **tesselated**) /ˈtes.əl.eɪ.tɪd/ US /-t̬ɪd/ adj specialized A tessellated floor is one made from small pieces of coloured stone fitted together to make a pattern or picture.

test /test/ noun; verb

▸noun [C] **1** A1 a way of discovering, by questions or practical activities, what someone knows, or what someone or something can do or is like: *The class are **doing/having** a spelling test today.* ◦ *She had to **take/do/sit** an aptitude test before she got the job.* **2** B1 a medical examination of part of your body in order to find out how healthy it is or what is wrong with it: *a blood/urine test* ◦ *an eye test* ◦ *a pregnancy test* ◦ *The*

T

doctors have ***done*** *some tests to try and find out what's wrong with her.* **3** an act of using something to find out if it is working correctly or how effective it is: *The new missiles are currently* ***undergoing*** *tests.* **4** B2 a situation which shows how good something is: *Driving on that icy road was a real test* ***of*** *my skill.* **5** a **test match**: *Australia won the test by 197 runs.*

> Word partners for **test noun**
>
> *do/have/sit/take* a test • *fail/flunk /pass* a test • a test *on* sth • *in* a test • a test *paper/result/score*

IDIOM **put sth to the test** to find out how good something is: *Her constant questions really put my patience to the test!*

▸verb [T] **1** B2 to do something in order to discover if something is safe, works correctly, etc., or if something is present: *The manufacturers are currently testing the new engine.* ◦ *They tested her blood* ***for*** *signs of the infection.* **2** B1 to give someone a set of questions, in order to measure their knowledge or ability: *Will you test me* ***on*** *the chemical formulae I've been learning?* **3** B2 If a situation tests someone, it proves how good, strong, etc. they are: *That lecture really tested my powers of endurance, it was so boring.* **4** to do a medical examination of part of someone's body or of a particular physical ability

IDIOM **test the water(s)** to find out what people's opinions of something are before you ask them to do something

PHRASAL VERB **test sth out** to test something, especially a theory or an idea, to find out how it works in a practical situation or how people react to it: *The students tested out their cost-cutting ideas in several companies.*

testa /ˈtes.tə/ noun [C] (plural **testae**) specialized in plants with flowers, a hard layer that covers and protects the surface of a seed

testament /ˈtes.tə.mənt/ noun [C or U] formal proof: *The detail of her wildlife paintings is (a) testament* ***to*** *(= proof of) her powers of observation.*

testate /ˈtes.teɪt/ adj formal (of a person) having left a WILL (= document saying who should get their possessions) → Opposite **intestate**

ˈ**test ˌban** noun [C] an agreement between countries to stop the practice of exploding nuclear weapons in order to examine their effectiveness: *a test ban treaty*

ˈ**test ˌcard** noun [C] UK (US ˈ**test ˌpattern**) a picture or pattern that is broadcast so that the quality of the television picture received can be examined and improved if necessary by using the controls on the equipment

ˈ**test ˌcase** noun [C] a case in a law court that establishes principles in relation to which other similar cases are considered in the future

ˈ**test ˌdrive** noun [C] an act of driving a car that you are considering buying, in order to see if you like it

tester /ˈtes.təʳ/ US /-tɚ/ noun [C] **1** a person or a machine which tests something **2** a small container of a product which you can try in order to see if you like it

ˈ**test-fire** verb [T] to explode a nuclear weapon in order to see how effective it is: *The country has test-fired a missile capable of hitting the US.*

testicle /ˈtes.tɪ.kl/ noun [C] (specialized **testis**) either of the two round male sex organs that produce SPERM and are contained in the SCROTUM (= bag of skin) below and behind the PENIS

testicular /tesˈtɪk.jə.ləʳ/ /-lɚ/ adj relating to the testicles: *testicular cancer.*

testify /ˈtes.tɪ.faɪ/ verb [I or T] C2 to speak seriously about something, especially in a law court, or to give or provide proof: [+ that] *He testified* ***that*** *he had seen the man leaving the building around the time of the murder.*

testimonial /ˌtes.tɪˈməʊ.ni.əl/ US /-ˈmoʊ-/ noun [C] **1** a statement about the character or qualities of someone or something **2** formal or old-fashioned a formal written description of someone's character and qualities given by a previous employer

testiˈ**monial ˌmatch** noun [C] (in sport) a match played to honour and make money for a famous player

testimony /ˈtes.tɪ.mᵊn.i/ US /-moʊ.ni/ noun [C or U] formal **1** (an example of) spoken or written statements that something is true, especially those given in a law court: *Some doubts have been expressed about his testimony.* **2 be (a) testimony to sth** to be clear proof of something: *The reports are testimony to the many hours of research completed by this committee.*

testing /ˈtes.tɪŋ/ adj mainly UK difficult: *These are very testing* ***times*** *for our family.* ◦ *This testing circuit is a challenge for any racing driver.*

testis /ˈtes.tɪs/ noun [C] (plural **testes** /ˈtes.tiːz/) specialized a **testicle**

ˈ**test ˌmatch** noun [C] (also **test**) a game of cricket or RUGBY played by the national teams of two countries

testosterone /ˌtesˈtɒs.tᵊr.əʊn/ US /-ˈtɑː.stɚ.oʊn/ noun [U] a male HORMONE that causes a stage of growth in older boys and development of their sexual organs

ˈ**test ˌpilot** noun [C] someone whose job is to fly new aircraft in order to make certain that they are effective

ˈ**test ˌtube** noun [C] a small glass tube with one closed and rounded end, used in scientific EXPERIMENTS

ˌ**test-tube** ˈ**baby** noun [C] a baby that developed from sex cells that were joined outside the body and then put in the mother to grow

testy /ˈtes.ti/ adj easily annoyed and not patient: *a testy old man* ◦ *testy comments* • **testily** /-tɪ.li/ adv • **testiness** /-nəs/ noun [U]

tetanus /ˈtet.ᵊn.əs/ noun [U] (old-fashioned informal **lockjaw**) a serious disease caused by bacteria entering the human body through small cuts, causing the muscles, especially around the mouth, to become tight and stop working

tetchy /ˈtetʃ.i/ adj easily made angry, unhappy, or upset: *Be careful what you say to Anna – she's in a rather tetchy mood.* • **tetchily** /-ɪ.li/ adv • **tetchiness** /-nəs/ noun [U]

tête-à-tête /ˌteɪt.əˈteɪt/ noun; adv

▸noun [C] an informal private conversation between two people, especially friends: *We must* ***have*** *a tête-à-tête sometime.*

▸adv in private with only two people together: *We dined tête-à-tête.*

tether /ˈteð.əʳ/ US /-ɚ/ noun [C] a rope or chain used to tie especially an animal to a post or other fixed place, usually so that it can move freely within a small area • **tether** verb [T] • **tethered** /-əd/ US /-ɚd/ adj

IDIOM **at the end of your tether** C2 having no strength or patience left: *By six o'clock after a busy day I'm at the end of my tether.*

tetrahedron /ˌtet.rəˈhiː.drᵊn/ noun [C] (plural **tetrahedrons** or **tetrahedra** /-drə/) specialized a solid shape whose four surfaces are triangles

Teutonic /tjuːˈtɒn.ɪk/ US /tuːˈtɑː.nɪk/ **adj** of, or thought to be typical of, the groups of people in northwestern Europe of German origin: *a Teutonic language*

Tex-Mex /ˌteksˈmeks/ **adj** referring to the Mexican-American culture existing in the southern US

text /tekst/ **noun; verb**

▸**noun 1** B1 [U] the written words in a book, magazine, etc., not the pictures: *The book has 100 pages of closely printed text.* **2** A2 [C] a **text message**: *I'll send you a text as soon as I have any news.* **3 the text of sth** the exact words of a speech, etc.: *Can we see the full text of your speech before Tuesday?* **4** B1 [C] a book or piece of writing that you study as part of a course: *'Ulysses' is a* ***set*** *text for the exam.* **5** [C usually singular] a sentence or piece of writing from the Bible which a priest reads aloud in church and talks about

▸**verb** [T] A2 to send someone a text message by phone: *I texted her to arrange a time to meet.* • **texting** /ˈtekst.ɪŋ/ **noun** [U]

textbook /ˈtekst.bʊk/ **noun; adj**

▸**noun** [C] A2 a book that contains detailed information about a subject for people who are studying that subject: *a science textbook*

▸**adj** [before noun] (of an example of something) extremely good, or thought to be usual or typical: *That was a textbook goal from Taylor.* ◦ *It was a textbook* ***example*** *of how to deal with the problem.*

textile /ˈtek.staɪl/ **noun** [C] a cloth made by hand or machine: *the textile* ***industry***

ˈtext ˌmessage **noun** [C] (also **text**) A2 a written message, often containing short forms of words, sent from one mobile phone or PAGER to another: *He sent me a text message to say he would be late.* • **ˈtext-ˌmessaging noun** [U] (also **texting**)

textual /ˈteks.tju.əl/ US /-tʃu-/ **adj 1** relating to written or printed material **2** related to the way in which something has been written: *textual analysis*

texture /ˈteks.tʃəʳ/ US /-tʃɚ/ **noun 1** C1 [C or U] the quality of something that can be decided by touch; the degree to which something is rough or smooth, or soft or hard: *a smooth/rough/coarse texture* ◦ *This artificial fabric has the texture of silk.* **2** [U] the character of a piece of writing or music: *The writing has a rich texture.*

textured /ˈteks.tʃəd/ US /-tʃɚd/ **adj** describes something that has a surface that is not smooth but has a raised pattern on it: *textured wallpaper*

-textured /-teks.tʃəd/ US /-tʃɚd/ **suffix** having a texture of the stated type: *coarse-textured*

thalamus /ˈθæl.ə.məs/ **noun** [C] one of the two oval-shaped parts of the brain that control feeling and all the senses apart from the sense of smell

thalidomide /θəˈlɪd.ə.maɪd/ **noun** [U] a drug that was once used to help people relax or sleep. It was found to cause damage to babies inside the WOMB, especially by stopping the development of their arms and legs, when it was taken by their mothers.

thallium /ˈθæl.i.əm/ **noun** [U] a very poisonous chemical element used in PHOTOCELLS, and used as poison in the past

than strong /ðæn/ weak /ðən/ **preposition, conjunction 1** A1 used to join two parts of a comparison: *My son is a lot taller than my daughter.* ◦ *You always walk faster than I do!* ◦ *You're earlier than usual.* **2** A2 used with 'more' or 'less' to compare numbers or amounts: *I spent more than I intended to.* ◦ *It cost less than I expected.*

Common mistake: than or then?

Warning: Choose the right word!

These two words look similar, but they are spelled differently and have completely different meanings.

thank /θæŋk/ **verb** [T] A2 to express to someone that you are pleased about or are grateful for something that they have done: *He thanked me* ***for*** *taking him home.*

IDIOMS **have sb to thank** If you have someone to thank for something, they are responsible or to blame for it: *You have John to thank for this problem.* • **I'll thank you to do sth** formal used to ask someone, in an annoyed way, to do something: *I'll thank you to leave my private papers alone.* • **thank sb for sth** If you thank someone for something, you mean that they are responsible or to blame for it: *You can thank John for the mess we're in.* • **thank your lucky stars** to be very grateful for something: *She thanked her lucky stars that she had taken out insurance, when she was in an accident on holiday.* • **thank God, goodness, heaven(s), etc.** B1 said to express happiness that something bad has been avoided or has finished: *Thank God you found the key.* • **won't thank you for doing sth** If someone won't thank you for doing something, they will not be pleased if you do it: *She won't thank you for telling everyone how old she is.*

thankful /ˈθæŋk.fəl/ **adj** C1 pleased or grateful for something: [+ that] *I was thankful* ***that*** *the meeting didn't last long, because I had a train to catch.* • **thankfulness** /-nəs/ **noun** [U]

thankfully /ˈθæŋk.fəl.i/ **adv** C1 used, usually at the beginning of a sentence, to show you are pleased or grateful about something: *Thankfully, nobody was hurt.*

thankless /ˈθæŋk.ləs/ **adj** describes a piece of work that is difficult or unpleasant, and for which people do not thank you: *Keeping the children's rooms tidy is a thankless* ***task/job.***

thanks /θæŋks/ **exclamation; noun**

▸**exclamation** informal A1 **thank you**: *'Shall I do that for you?' 'No, thanks.'*

IDIOM **thanks for nothing** (also **thanks a bunch**, also **thanks a lot**) used to show you are annoyed when someone has done something you are unhappy about or has failed to help you in some way: *'I told Dad you'd love to wash his car.' 'Thanks a lot.'* ◦ *Thanks a lot for supporting me.* (= *You did not support me.*)

▸**noun** [plural] B2 words or actions that show you are grateful or pleased about something: *They expressed their thanks to the organizers.* ◦ *He wrote a* ***letter of*** *thanks to the hospital.* ◦ *Let us* ***give*** *thanks to God.*

IDIOMS **no thanks to sb** despite: *It's no thanks to you that I arrived on time.* • **thanks to sb/sth** B2 because of someone or something: *It's thanks to Sandy that I heard about the job.* ◦ disapproving *The baby is awake thanks to your shouting.*

thanksgiving /ˌθæŋksˈɡɪv.ɪŋ/ **noun** [U] the act of saying or showing that you are grateful, especially to God

ˌThanksˈgiving (ˌDay) **noun** [C or U] a public holiday and celebration, held on the fourth Thursday of November in the US and on the second Monday of October in Canada, to remember the thanks that the people who first came from Europe gave to God when they collected crops for the first time in their new country

T

ˈthank ˌyou exclamation; noun

▸**exclamation** (informal **thanks**) **1** A1 used to tell someone that you are grateful because they have given you something or done something for you: *That was a delicious lunch, thank you.* ◦ *'Here's your coffee.' 'Thank you* ***very much*** *(****indeed****).'* ◦ *Thank you* ***for*** *my birthday present.* **2** said when you are answering a polite question or remark: *'How are you?' 'I'm fine, thank you.'* ◦ *'You look very nice in that dress.' 'Thank you* ***very much****.'* **3** A2 said to politely accept or refuse something that has been offered to you: *'Would you like some more cake?' 'Yes, I will have a small piece, thank you.'* ◦ *'Do you need any help?' 'No, thank you.'* **4** said to show your disapproval of something: *I don't want to hear that kind of language, thank you (****very much****).*

▸**noun** [C usually singular] B1 something that you say or do in order to show that you are grateful for something: *I'd like to say a* ***big*** *thank you* ***to*** *everyone for all their help.* ◦ *He wrote a thank-you* ***note/letter*** *to his granny to thank her for the birthday present she sent him.*

that determiner; conjunction; pronoun; adv

▸**determiner** /ðæt/ (plural **those**) **1** A1 used to refer to a person, object, idea, etc. that is separated from the speaker by space or time: *I've never liked that cousin of hers.* ◦ *Who's that? Is that the girl you told me about?* ◦ *How much are those shoes?* ◦ formal *His handwriting is like that (= the writing)* ***of*** *a much younger child.* **2** A1 used to refer to something that has been mentioned or was involved earlier, or to something that is already known about: *Where's that pen (= the one I was using earlier) gone?* ◦ *She lives in that house by the bus station (= you know which one I mean).*

> **!** Common mistake: **that or than?**
>
> **Warning:** Choose the right word!
>
> These two words look similar, but they are spelled differently and have completely different meanings.

> **!** Usage: **this/these or that/those?**
>
> Use **this** or **these** to talk about people and things that are close to the speaker in space or time:
>
> *This is Sarah, who will be working with us for a few months.*
>
> *Do you like these earrings I'm wearing?*
>
> Use **that** or **those** to talk about people and things which are further away from the speaker in space or time:
>
> *That girl over there is called Sarah.*
>
> *I liked those earrings you wore last night.*

IDIOMS **... at that** informal in addition to that: *It's too expensive, and probably out-of-date at that.* • **that is (to say)** C1 said when you want to give further details or be more exact about something: *I'll meet you in the city, that is, I will if the trains are running.* • **that will do** said to mean that you do not want any more of something: *'More peas?' 'No, that'll do, thank you.'* ◦ *That will do, Charles. I don't want to see any more of that kind of behaviour.* • **that's it 1** B1 used to say that something has ended: *Well, that's it, we've finished – we can go home now.* ◦ *That's it! I'm not putting up with any more of her rudeness.* **2** B2 used to say that something is correct: *You switch the computer on at the back. That's it.* • **that's life!** saying said when something bad has happened that you cannot change • **that's that** (also **that was that**) C1 an expression that shows that something has ended: *I won't agree to it and that's that (= I won't discuss it any longer).*

▸**conjunction** strong /ðæt/ weak /ðət/ A2 used to introduce a CLAUSE that reports something or gives further information, although it can often be left out: *She said (that) she'd collect it for me after work.* ◦ *Is it true (that) she's gone back to teaching?* ◦ *We'll be there at about 7.30,* ***provided/providing*** *(that) there's a suitable train.* ◦ *It was* ***so*** *dark (that) I couldn't see anything.*

▸**pronoun** strong /ðæt/ weak /ðət/ (plural **those**) **1** B1 used as the subject or object of a verb to show which person or thing you are referring to, or to add information about a person or thing just mentioned. It is used for both people and things. It can often be left out: *I can't find the books (that) I got from the library.* ◦ *Is this the train that stops at Cambridge?* ◦ *Have you been to the restaurant that's just opened in town?* **2** A2 used to make a connection with an earlier statement: *My usual train was cancelled. That's why I'm so late.* ◦ *Lucy has just ruined her new dress. That's children* ***for you*** *(= such behaviour is typical of children).* **3** B2 used to express a reaction to something: *I didn't know she'd been so ill. That's terrible.* ◦ *Turn the engine on, then put the car in gear. That's* ***right*** *(= you are doing it correctly).* ◦ *Smile for the camera. That's* ***more like it*** *(= that smile is better than before).*

▸**adv** /ðæt/ B2 as much as suggested: *She's too young to walk that far.* ◦ *It wasn't (****all****) that (= very) good.*

thatch /θætʃ/ verb; noun

▸**verb** [T] to make a roof for a building with STRAW or REEDS • **thatched** /θætʃt/ **adj** *They live in a thatched* ***cottage****/a cottage with a thatched* ***roof****.*

▸**noun 1** [U] STRAW or REEDS used to make roofs **2 thatch of hair** a mass of thick or untidy hair

thatcher /ˈθætʃ.əʳ/ US /-ɚ/ noun [C] a person whose job is thatching roofs

thaw /θɔː/ US /θɑː/ verb; noun

▸**verb** BECOME NOT FROZEN ▷ **1** [I or T] to (cause to) change from a solid, frozen state to a liquid or soft one, because of an increase in temperature: *Allow the meat to thaw properly before cooking it.* ◦ *The sun came out and thawed the ice.* ◦ ***It's*** *beginning to thaw (= the weather is warm enough for snow and ice to melt).* → Compare **freeze** BECOME FRIENDLY ▷ **2** [I] to become friendlier or more relaxed: *The report shows that* ***relations*** *between the two enemies may be thawing.*

PHRASAL VERB **thaw out** If you thaw out, you gradually get warm again after being very cold.

▸**noun** [S] FRIENDLY ▷ **1** an increase in friendliness: *There are signs of* ***a*** *thaw in relations between the two countries.* WEATHER ▷ **2 the thaw** a period of warmer weather when snow and ice begin to melt: *The thaw has* ***set in*** *early this year.*

the strong /ðiː/ weak /ðə/ determiner PARTICULAR ▷ **1** A1 used before nouns to refer to particular things or people that have already been talked about or are already known or that are in a situation where it is clear what is happening: *I just bought a new shirt and some new shoes. The shirt was quite expensive, but the shoes weren't.* ◦ *Please would you pass the salt.* ◦ *I'll pick you up at the station.* **2** A1 used before some nouns that refer to place when you want to mention that type of place, without showing exactly which example of the place you mean: *We spent all day at the beach.* ◦ *Shall we go to the movies this evening?* ◦ *I must go to the bank and change some money.* **3** A1 used before noun phrases in which the range of meaning of the noun is limited in some way: *I really enjoyed the book I've just finished reading.* ◦ *Do you like the other students in your class?* **4** A1 used to refer to things or people when only one exists at any one time: *What will happen in the future?* ◦ *After I leave college, I want to travel round the world.* ◦ *They live in the north of Spain.* ◦ *Ed Koch was for many years the mayor of New York.* ◦ *When we went to Paris, we went up the Eiffel Tower.* **5** A2 used before SUPERLATIVES and other words, such as 'first' or 'only' or numbers showing something's position in a list, to refer to only one thing or person: *That was one of the best films I've ever seen.* ◦ *What's the highest mountain in Europe?* ◦ *I shall never forget the first time we met.* ◦ *You're the fifth person to ask me that question.* **6** used to say that the particular person or thing being mentioned is the best, most famous, etc. In this use, 'the' is usually given strong pronunciation: *Harry's Bar is the place to go.* ◦ *You don't mean you met the Richard Gere, do you?* **7** used before some adjectives to turn the adjectives into nouns which refer to one particular person or thing described by the adjective: *It seems that the deceased (= this particular dead person) had no living relatives.* ◦ *I suppose we'll just have to wait for the inevitable (= the particular thing that is certain to happen).* **8** used before some adjectives to turn the adjectives into nouns which refer to people or things in general that can be described by the adjective: *She lives in a special home for the elderly.* ◦ *The French were defeated at Waterloo in 1815.* **9** used before a singular noun to refer to all the things or people represented by that noun: *The panda is becoming an increasingly rare animal.* ◦ *The car is responsible for causing a lot of damage to our environment.* **10** used before a family name to refer to two people who are married or to a whole family: *The Jacksons are coming to lunch on Saturday.* **11** used before some nouns referring to musical instruments or dances to mean the type of instrument or dance in general: *Nico is learning to play the piano.* ◦ *Can you do the waltz?* **12** used before a noun to represent the activity connected with that noun: *I've got to go under the surgeon's knife (= have a medical operation) next week.* ◦ *It's not a good idea to spend more than three hours at the wheel (= driving a vehicle) without a break.* **13** B2 used before numbers that refer to periods of ten years: *the 60s* **14** B2 used before each of two COMPARATIVE adjectives or adverbs when you want to show how one amount gets bigger or smaller in relation to the other: *The sooner I get this piece of work finished, the sooner I can go home.* **15** used before COMPARATIVE adjectives or adverbs when you want to show that someone or something has become more or less of a particular state: *She doesn't seem to be any the worse **for** her bad experience.* **16** used for emphasis when you are expressing a strong opinion about someone or something: *André's got a new job, the lucky devil.* **YOUR** ▷ **17** B1 used instead of a possessive adjective such as your, her or my: *He held his daughter by the arm.* ◦ *I can't remember where I parked the (= my) car.* **ENOUGH** ▷ **18** enough: *I'd like to go out this evening, but I don't think I've got the energy.* ◦ [+ to infinitive] *I haven't got the time **to** talk to you now.* **EACH** ▷ **19** each; every: *It does 30 miles to the gallon.*

theater /ˈθɪə.təʳ/ US /ˈθiː.ə.t̬ɚ/ noun [C] **1** A2 US for theatre **2** (also **movie theater**) US a cinema

theatre UK (US **theater**) /ˈθɪə.təʳ/ US /ˈθiː.ə.t̬ɚ/ noun **BUILDING/ROOM** ▷ **1** A2 [C] a building, room, or outside structure with rows of seats, each row usually higher than the one in front, from which people can watch a performance or other activity: *the Lyceum Theatre* ◦ *a lecture theatre* **2** [C] UK **operating theatre** **PERFORMING ARTS** ▷ **3** [S or U] (the writing or performance of) plays, OPERA, etc., written to be performed in public: *His latest play has delighted theatre **audiences** and theatre **critics** alike.* ◦ *She made her career **in the** theatre.* **BEHAVIOUR** ▷ **4** [U] behaviour that is not sincere and is intended just to produce a particular effect or to attract attention: *Her tears were **pure** theatre.* **MILITARY** ▷ **5** [C] an area or place in which important military events happen: *a theatre of war*

theatregoer (US usually **theatergoer**) /ˈθɪə.təˌgəʊ.əʳ/ US /ˈθiː.ə.t̬ɚˌgoʊ.ɚ/ noun [C] someone who regularly goes to the theatre

ˌtheatre in the ˈround noun [C or U] a theatre where people sit on all sides of the performers, not just in front of them, or a type of performance which tries to involve the people watching.

theatrical /θiˈæt.rɪ.kəl/ adj **PERFORMING ARTS** ▷ **1** belonging or relating to the theatre, or to the performance or writing of plays, OPERA, etc.: *theatrical make-up* **BEHAVIOUR** ▷ **2** describes behaviour that is not sincere and too extreme and that is intended to attract attention: *a theatrical gesture* • **theatricality** /θiˌæt.rɪˈkæl.ɪ.ti/ US /-ə.t̬i/ noun [U] • **theatrically** /-i/ adv

theatricals /θiˈæt.rɪ.kəlz/ noun [plural] stage performances by people who are not trained or paid to act, but who practise and perform in the time when they are not working: *amateur theatricals*

thee /ðiː/ pronoun old use you; object form of THOU; used when speaking to one person: *With this ring, I thee wed.*

theft /θeft/ noun [C or U] B2 (the act of) dishonestly taking something which belongs to someone else and keeping it: *Unfortunately, we have had several thefts in the building recently.* ◦ *Shoplifting is theft.* → See also **thief**

their /ðeəʳ/ US /ðer/ determiner **1** A1 of or belonging to them: *He gave them their coats.* **2** B1 used to refer to one person in order to avoid saying 'his or her': *One of the students has left their book behind.*

> **! Common mistake: their or there?**
>
> **Warning:** Choose the right word!
>
> These two words look similar, but they are spelled differently and have completely different meanings.

theirs /ðeəz/ US /ðerz/ pronoun A2 the one(s) belonging to or connected with them: *Which children are theirs?* ◦ *I think she's a relation **of** theirs.* ◦ *Theirs is that little house with the big tree outside.*

theism /ˈθiː.ɪ.zəm/ noun [U] belief in the existence of a god or gods → Compare **atheism**, **deism**

T

them pronoun; determiner

▸**pronoun** strong /ðem/ weak /ðəm/ **1** A1 used, usually as the object of a verb or preposition, to refer to people, things, animals, situations, or ideas that have already been mentioned: *I've lost my keys. I can't find them anywhere.* ◦ *It's them. They've arrived early.* **2** B1 used to refer to one person whose sex is not known instead of saying 'him' or 'her': *When each passenger arrives, we ask them to fill in a form.*

> **! Note:**
>
> Some people do not like this use, and prefer to use **him or her**:
>
> *When each passenger arrives, we ask him or her to fill in a form.*

IDIOM **them and us** informal used when describing disagreements or differences, especially between different social groups: *The senior staff have their own restaurant. – It's definitely a case of them and us.*

▸**determiner** /ðem/ not standard for **those**: *Who gave you them sweets?*

thematic /θɪˈmæt.ɪk/ US /θiːˈmæţ-/ **adj** relating to or based on subjects or a theme: *In her study, the author has adopted a thematic rather than a chronological approach.*

theme /θiːm/ **noun** [C] MAIN SUBJECT ▷ **1** B2 the main subject of a talk, book, film, etc.: *The theme of loss runs through most of his novels.* TUNE ▷ **2** a song or tune that is played several times in a film, etc. and represents a character, situation, etc.: *a theme song/tune* **3** a short, simple tune on which a piece of music is based

ˈ**theme** ˌ**park** **noun** [C] (US also **aˈmusement ˌpark**) a large permanent area for public entertainment, with entertaining activities and big machines to ride on or play games on, restaurants, etc., all connected with a single subject

themselves /ðəmˈselvz/ **pronoun** **1** A2 used when the subject of the verb is 'they' or a group of people, and the object is the same group of people: *They asked themselves where they had gone wrong.* ◦ *Did the children enjoy themselves at the party?* **2** used for emphasis when the subject is 'they': *They themselves had no knowledge of what was happening.* **3 (all) by themselves** alone or without help from anyone else: *Small children should not be left by themselves.* ◦ *They collected the evidence all by themselves.* **4 (all) to themselves** for their use only: *They had the whole campsite to themselves.*

> ! Common mistake: **themselves**
>
> **Remember:** plural reflexive pronouns end in **-selves.**
>
> Don't write 'themselfs' or 'theirselfs', write **themselves**:
>
> ~~The children really enjoyed themself at the zoo.~~

IDIOM **keep (themselves) to themselves** to spend time alone, not talking to other people very much: *We don't see much of our neighbours – they keep themselves to themselves.*

then /ðen/ **adv, adj; adv**

▸**adv, adj** [before noun] A1 (at) that time (in the past or in the future): *I was working in the city then.* ◦ formal *I wanted to live in the city, but my then husband (= the man who was my husband at that time) preferred the country.* ◦ *Give it to me next week – I won't have time to read it before/until then.* ◦ *I'll phone you tomorrow – I should have the details by then.*

> ! Common mistake: **then or than?**
>
> **Warning:** Choose the right word!
>
> These two words look similar, but they are spelled differently and have completely different meanings.

IDIOMS **from then on** from that time: *She had a car accident a year ago and suffered from back pain from then on.* • **then and there** (also **there and then**) immediately: *I suggested he phone his mother and he did it there and then.*

▸**adv** NEXT ▷ **1** A1 next or after that: *Let me finish this job, then we'll go.* ◦ *Give her the letter to read, then she'll understand.* IN ADDITION ▷ **2** B2 in addition: *This is the standard model, then there's the deluxe version which costs more.* RESULT ▷ **3** A2 as a result; in that case; also used as a way of joining a statement to an earlier piece of conversation: *Have a rest now, then you won't be so tired this evening.* ◦ *You'll be selling your house, then?*

IDIOM **but then (again)** but when you think about the matter more or in another way: *I agree she types accurately, but then again, she's very slow.*

thence /ðens/ **adv** old-fashioned or formal from there: *We travelled to my parents' home and thence to my sister's.*

thenceforth /ˌðensˈfɔːθ/ US /-ˈfɔːrθ/ **adv** (also **thenceforward**) old-fashioned or formal after that; from that time forward: *The property was known thenceforth as The Manor.*

theocracy /θiˈɒk.rə.si/ US /-ˈɑː.krə-/ **noun** **1** [C] a country that is ruled by religious leaders **2** [U] government by religious leaders • **theocratic** /ˌθiː.əˈkræt.ɪk/ US /-ˈkræţ-/ **adj**

theodolite /θiˈɒd.əl.aɪt/ US /-ˈɑː.də.laɪt/ **noun** [C] specialized a piece of equipment like a small TELESCOPE, used for measuring horizontal and vertical angles: *The surveyor set up his theodolite and took some measurements.*

theologian /ˌθiː.əˈləʊ.dʒən/ US /-ˈloʊ-/ **noun** [C] a student of theology

theological /ˌθiː.əˈlɒdʒ.ɪ.kəl/ US /-ˈlɑː.dʒɪ-/ **adj** relating to the study of religion and religious belief: *They met at theological college.* • **theologically** /-i/ **adv**

theology /θiˈɒl.ə.dʒi/ US /-ˈɑː.lə-/ **noun** **1** [U] the study of religion and religious belief **2** [C or U] a set of beliefs about a particular religion

theorem /ˈθɪə.rəm/ US /ˈθiː.ɚ.əm/ **noun** [C] specialized (especially in mathematics) a formal statement that can be shown to be true by LOGIC: *a mathematical theorem*

theoretical /θɪəˈret.ɪ.kəl/ US /ˌθiː.əˈreţ-/ **adj** **1** C2 based on the ideas that relate to a subject, not the practical uses of that subject: *theoretical physics* **2** C2 related to an explanation that has not been proved

theoretically /θɪəˈret.ɪ.kəl.i/ US /ˌθiː.əˈreţ-/ **adv** C2 in a way that obeys some rules but is not likely: *It is theoretically possible.*

theorist /ˈθɪə.rɪst/ US /ˈθiː.ɚ.ɪst/ **noun** [C] someone who develops ideas about the explanation for events: *a political theorist*

theorize (UK usually **theorise**) /ˈθɪə.raɪz/ US /ˈθɪr.aɪz/ **verb** [I] to develop a set of ideas about something: *It's easy to theorize* ***about*** *what might have happened.*

> Word partners for **theory**
>
> *develop/formulate/test* a theory • *have/propound* a theory • *challenge/prove/reject* a theory • *subscribe to/support* a theory • a *new/plausible/popular* theory • the theory *of* sth • a theory *about* sth

theory /ˈθɪə.ri/ US /ˈθɪr.i/ **noun** [C or U] **1** B2 a formal statement of the rules on which a subject of study is based or of ideas that are suggested to explain a fact or event or, more generally, an opinion or explanation: *economic theory* ◦ *scientific theory* ◦ *Darwin's theory* ***of*** *evolution* ◦ *He* ***has*** *a theory* ***that*** *the hole was caused by a meteorite.* **2 in theory** B2 If something is possible in theory, it should be possible, but often it does not happen in that way: *In theory, the journey ought to take three hours, but in practice it usually takes four because of roadworks.*

therapeutic /ˌθer.əˈpjuː.tɪk/ US /-ţɪk/ **adj** C1 causing someone to feel happier and more relaxed or to be more healthy: *I find gardening very therapeutic.*

therapist /ˈθer.ə.pɪst/ **noun** [C] C1 someone whose job is to treat a particular type of mental or physical

T

illness or DISABILITY, usually with a particular type of therapy: *a speech therapist* ◦ *a music/an art therapist* ◦ *I'm seeing my therapist on Friday morning.*

therapy /ˈθer.ə.pi/ **noun** [C or U] B2 a treatment which helps someone feel better, grow stronger, etc., especially after an illness: *occupational therapy* ◦ *speech therapy* ◦ *group therapy* ◦ *Joining a club can be **a** therapy **for** loneliness.*

there /ðeəʳ/ US /ðer/ **adv; exclamation**

▸**adv PLACE** ▷ **1** A1 (to, at or in) that place: *Put the chair there.* ◦ *The museum is closed today. We'll go there tomorrow.* ◦ *There's that book you were looking for.* ◦ *I'll have to stop you there, we've run out of time.* ◦ *I've left the boxes over/out/under there.* **2 get there a** A1 to arrive somewhere: *We'll never get there in time.* **b** B2 informal to succeed: *Try again, you'll get there in the end.* **INTRODUCING SUBJECT** ▷ **3** A1 used to introduce the subject of a sentence, especially before the verbs be, seem, and appear: *There's someone on the phone for you.* ◦ *There's no doubt who is the best candidate.* ◦ *I took out my wallet but there was no money in it.* ◦ *By the time I got back, there was no food left.* ◦ *There appeared/seemed to be some difficulty in fixing a date for the meeting.* ◦ not standard *There's (= there are) lives at stake and we can't afford to take any risks.* **4** literary used to begin some children's stories written in a traditional style: *There once was/lived a poor widow who had a beautiful daughter.*

> **!** Common mistake: **there or their?**
> **Warning:** Choose the right word!
> These two words look similar, but they are spelled differently and have completely different meanings.

IDIOMS **be there for sb** to be available to provide help and support for someone: *We haven't always been close, but she was there for me when I needed her.* ◦ *Best friends are always there for each other in times of trouble.* • **there you go again** a way of emphasizing that an action is often repeated: *There they go again, making trouble.* • **there and back** adding together the distance or time to and from a particular place: *It was 20 miles there and back.* • **there you are 1** A2 (informal **there you go**) used when giving something to someone, usually after a request for the thing, such as giving someone goods that they have bought **2** used to mean 'I told you so': *There you are, I knew you'd forget if you didn't write it down.* • **there you go** used to express the fact that you cannot change a situation so you must accept it: *We didn't win the competition, but there you go – we can always try again next year.* • **there's a good boy/girl/dog!** used to show approval or encouragement: *Tie your shoelaces, there's a good girl!*

▸**exclamation** used to express sympathy or satisfaction: *There, I've made it work at last.*

IDIOM **there, there** (also **there now**) something you say to comfort someone, especially a child: *There, there, don't cry.*

thereabouts /ˈðeə.rə.baʊts/, /ˌðeə.rəˈbaʊts/ US /ˈðer.ə.baʊts/ **adv** approximately: *He's lived in Norwich for 40 years, or thereabouts.*

thereafter /ˌðeəˈrɑːf.təʳ/ US /ˌðerˈæf.tɚ/ **adv** formal C2 continuing on from a particular point in time, especially after something else has stopped happening: *He left the priesthood in 1970 and settled in the Washington area **shortly** thereafter (= soon after that).*

thereby /ˌðeəˈbaɪ/ US /ˌðer-/ **adv** formal or old-fashioned C1 as a result of this action: *Diets that are high in saturated fat clog up our arteries, thereby reducing the blood flow to our hearts and brains.*

therefore /ˈðeə.fɔːʳ/ US /ˈðer.fɔːr/ **adv** B1 for that reason: *We were unable to get funding and therefore had to abandon the project.*

therein /ˌðeəˈrɪn/ US /ˌðerˈɪn/ **adv** old-fashioned formal in or into a particular place, thing, etc.

IDIOM **therein lies** in what has just been mentioned we see the reason or explanation for (a particular situation, quality, or problem): *Her book is simply a collection of memories, told without conceit or self-absorption – and therein lies its power.*

thereof /ˌðeəˈrɒv/ US /ˌðerˈɑːv/ **adv** formal of or about the thing just mentioned: *Please refer to the Regulations and in particular Articles 99 and 100 thereof.*

thereto /ˌðeəˈtuː/ US /ˌðer-/ **adv** formal or literary to the thing just mentioned: *The government has the right to inspect any such establishment or any papers or records relating thereto.*

thermal /ˈθɜː.məl/ US /ˈθɝː-/ **adj; noun**

▸**adj** [before noun] specialized connected with heat: *thermal **conductivity** (= ability of a substance to carry heat)* ◦ *It was the Romans who first recognized the medicinal benefits of Hungary's thermal **springs** (= ones which produce hot water).* • **thermally** /-mə.li/ **adv**

▸**noun HOT AIR** ▷ **1** [C] specialized a large column of hot air rising from the ground **CLOTHES** ▷ **2 thermals** [plural] informal for **thermal underwear**

ˌthermal ˈimaging **noun** [U] the use of special electronic equipment, in conditions in which it is difficult to see, to create a picture based on the heat produced by a person or object

ˌthermal ˈunderwear **noun** [U] (informal **thermals**) underwear that has been specially designed to keep you warm

thermo- /θɜː.məʊ-/ US /θɝː.moʊ-/ **prefix** connected with heat or temperature: *a thermonuclear device*

thermodynamics /ˌθɜː.məʊ.daɪˈnæm.ɪks/ US /ˌθɝː.moʊ-/ **noun** [U] specialized the area of physics connected with the action of heat and other types of energy, and the relationship between them • **thermodynamic** /-ɪk/ **adj** [before noun]

thermometer /θəˈmɒm.ɪ.təʳ/ US /θɚˈmɑː.mə.t̬ɚ/ **noun** [C] B2 a device used for measuring temperature, especially of the air or in a person's body

Thermos /ˈθɜː.məs/ US /ˈθɝː-/ **noun** [C] (UK also **ˈThermos ˌflask**, US also **ˈThermos ˌbottle**) a **vacuum flask**

thermostat /ˈθɜː.mə.stæt/ US /ˈθɝː-/ **noun** [C] a device which keeps a building, engine, etc. within a usually limited temperature range by automatically switching the supply of heat on and off

thesaurus /θɪˈsɔː.rəs/ US /-ˈsɔːr.əs/ **noun** [C] (plural **thesauruses** or formal **thesauri** /θɪˈsɔː.raɪ/ US /-ˈsɔːr.aɪ/) a type of dictionary in which words with similar meanings are arranged in groups

these /ðiːz/ **determiner, pronoun plural of** A1 **this**

thesis /ˈθiː.sɪs/ **noun** [C] (plural **theses** /ˈθiː.siːz/) **1** B2 a long piece of writing on a particular subject, especially one that is done for a higher college or university degree: *a doctoral thesis (= for a PhD)* **2** C2 formal the main idea, opinion, or theory of a person, group, piece of writing, or speech: *Their main thesis was that war was inevitable.*

thespian /ˈθes.pi.ən/ **adj; noun**

▸**adj** formal connected with acting and the theatre

▸**noun** [C] formal an actor

they /ðeɪ/ **pronoun 1** A1 used as the subject of a verb to refer to people, animals, or things already mentioned or, more generally, to a group of people not clearly described: *I've known the Browns for a long time. They're very pleasant people.* ◦ *Where are my glasses? They were on the table just now.* ◦ *They (= people who know) say things will be better in the new year.* **2** B1 used to avoid saying 'he or she': *'There's someone on the phone for you.' 'What do they want?'*

they'd /ðeɪd/ **short form 1** they had: *They'd had three bottles of wine and were very drunk.* **2** they would: *They'd love to see the film.*

they'll /ðeɪl/ **short form** they will: *They'll be here any minute, if their train's on time.*

they're /ðeəʳ/ US /ðer/ **short form** they are: *They're so in love.*

they've /ðeɪv/ **short form** they have: *They've really made a mess of things now.*

thiamine /ˈθaɪ.ə.miːn/, /-mɪn/ **noun** [U] specialized **vitamin** B_1

thick /θɪk/ **adj NOT THIN** ▷ **1** B1 having a large distance between two sides: *a thick rope* ◦ *a thick layer of dust* ◦ *She picked up a thick volume and began to read out loud.* ◦ *The walls are two metres thick.* ◦ *a thick (= made of thick material) sweater/coat* **CLOSE TOGETHER** ▷ **2** B1 growing close together and in large amounts: *thick forest* ◦ *thick, dark hair* **3** B2 difficult to see through: *Thick, black smoke was pouring out of the chimney.* **NOT FLOWING** ▷ **4** (of a liquid) not flowing easily: *thick soup* ◦ *a thick sauce* ◦ *thick paint* → Opposite **thin,** or **runny STUPID** ▷ **5** informal stupid: *I told you not to touch that – are you deaf or just thick?* • **thickly** /ˈθɪk.li/ **adv**

IDIOMS **be (as) thick as thieves** informal to be very close friends and share secrets, etc.: *I'm sure she tells Ruth everything we say – they're as thick as thieves, those two.* • **(as) thick as two short planks** slang very stupid: *He's a very skilled footballer but he's as thick as two short planks.* • **thick and fast** C2 quickly and in large numbers: *Distress calls were pouring in, thick and fast, from all over the area.* • **thick on the ground** mainly UK informal existing in large numbers: *Female engineers are not too thick on the ground.* • **through thick and thin** C2 If you support or stay with someone through thick and thin, you always support or stay with them, even if there are problems or difficulties: *She has stuck with me through thick and thin.*

T

thicken /ˈθɪk.ən/ **verb** [I or T] to (cause to) become thicker: *Thicken the sauce with a little flour.* ◦ *The smoke thickened rapidly.*

thickener /ˈθɪk.ən.əʳ/ US /-ɚ/ **noun** [C or U] (also **thickening**) a substance that is used to make a liquid thicker: *Cornflour can be used as a thickener in sauces.*

thicket /ˈθɪk.ɪt/ **noun** [C] an area of trees and bushes growing closely together

thickness /ˈθɪk.nəs/ **noun 1** [U] the quality of being thick: *The thickness of the mulch will prevent weeds growing around the shrubs.* ◦ *Just feel the thickness of this carpet!* **2** [C or U] the distance between the opposite sides of something: *How do you measure the thickness of paper?* ◦ *Look at the thickness of that tree trunk.* **3** [C] a layer of something: *Put several thicknesses **of** newspaper on the table before you start painting.*

thicko /ˈθɪk.əʊ/ US /-oʊ/ **noun** [C] (plural **thickos**) informal a stupid person

thickset /ˌθɪkˈset/ **adj** describes a person, especially a man, whose body is wide across the shoulders and chest and who is short: *A thickset young man appeared in the doorway.* → Synonym **stocky**

ˌthick-ˈskinned adj Someone who is thick-skinned does not appear to be easily hurt by criticism: *You do need to be thick-skinned to survive as a politician here.* → Opposite **thin-skinned**

thief /θiːf/ **noun** [C] (plural **thieves**) B1 a person who steals: *A post office was broken into last night, and the thieves got away with £120,000.* → See also **theft**

IDIOM **like a thief in the night** secretly or unexpectedly and without being seen

thieving /ˈθiː.vɪŋ/ **adj; noun**

▸**adj** [before noun] informal used to describe people who steal things: *Those thieving kids tried to steal my car.*

▸**noun** [U] formal the activity of stealing: *His was a life of thieving and cheating.*

thigh /θaɪ/ **noun** [C] B2 the part of a person's leg above the knee

thimble /ˈθɪm.bl̩/ **noun** [C] a small cover, usually made of metal or plastic, worn to protect the finger which pushes the needle when sewing

thimbleful /ˈθɪm.bl̩.fʊl/ **noun** [C] informal a very small amount of liquid: *He poured **a** thimbleful **of** whisky into the glass.*

thin /θɪn/ **adj; verb**

▸**adj** (**thinner, thinnest**) **NOT THICK** ▷ **1** A2 having a small distance between two opposite sides: *a thin book* ◦ *thin black lines* ◦ *a thin jacket (= made from thin material)* **NOT FAT** ▷ **2** A2 (of the body) with little flesh on the bones: *Did you notice how thin her wrists were?* ◦ *Thin, hungry dogs roamed the streets.* → Opposite **fat 3 be as thin as a rake** (also US **be as thin as a rail**) to be very thin: *He eats like a horse and yet he's as thin as a rake.* **TRANSPARENT** ▷ **4** not difficult to see through: *thin mist/cloud* → Opposite **thick FEW** ▷ **5** having only a small number of people or a small amount of something: *Attendance at the meeting was rather thin.* **FLOWING EASILY** ▷ **6** (of a liquid) flowing easily: *a thin soup* → Opposite **thick WEAK** ▷ **7** weak or of poor quality: *a thin excuse* ◦ *a thin disguise* ◦ *a thin smile* • **thinness** /ˈθɪn.nəs/ **noun** [U] *the thinness of his hair* ◦ *The author discusses why female beauty has become linked to thinness.*

Other ways of saying thin

Skinny or **scrawny** are words that mean 'very thin' and are usually used when you disapprove:

*You should eat more. You're much too **skinny**.*

*He hated his **scrawny** legs.*

Slim or **slender** can be used when someone is thin in an attractive way:

*He was tall, very **slim**, with pale, deep-set eyes.*

*He put his arms around her **slender** waist.*

If a woman is short and thin in an attractive way, you could describe her as **petite**:

*She was a **petite** woman with long, blonde hair.*

Emaciated is a formal word that you could use to describe someone who is thin and weak, especially because of illness or extreme hunger:

***Emaciated** refugees streamed into the city.*

Gaunt can be used when someone looks thin and ill:

*He looked at her tired and **gaunt** face.*

Bony can be used about parts of someone's body when they are very thin:

*long, **bony** fingers*

IDIOMS **be thin on the ground** UK to exist only in small numbers or amounts: *Traditional bookshops are thin on the ground these days.* • **be thin on top** informal to have lost some of the hair on your head: *He's a bit thin on top nowadays, isn't he?* • **disappear/vanish into thin air** C2 to disappear suddenly and completely • **have a thin time (of it)** to have bad or unhappy experiences: *He's been having a thin time (of it) since his accident.* • **out of thin air** from nothing: *I can't come up with £10,000 out of thin air.* • **the thin end of the wedge** UK the start of a harmful development: *Identity cards for football supporters could be the thin end of the wedge – soon everyone might have to carry identification.*

▸verb (-nn-) LESS THICK ▷ **1** [T] to make a substance less thick, often by adding a liquid to it: *Thin the sauce **down** with a little stock.* FEWER ▷ **2** [I or T] (also **thin out**) When a crowd or a group thins (out), it becomes fewer in number, and when you thin (out) a group of plants or other things, you remove some to make them fewer: *The traffic will thin out after the rush hour.*

PHRASAL VERB **thin down** informal If you thin down, you become less fat.

thine /ðaɪn/ **pronoun** old use yours: the POSSESSIVE PRONOUN form of THOU, used when speaking to one person

thing /θɪŋ/ noun OBJECT ▷ **1** A1 [C] used to refer in an approximate way to an object or to avoid naming it: *What's that thing over there?* ◦ *There are some nice things in the shops this summer.* ◦ *I don't eat sweet things (= sweet food).* ◦ *How does this damn thing work?* **2 things** [plural] **a** A1 your possessions or a particular set of your possessions: *All their things were destroyed in the fire.* ◦ *Bring your swimming things if the weather's nice.* **b** a particular set of objects: *Let me help you clear away the tea things (= cups, plates, etc. that are used for having tea).* IDEA/EVENT ▷ **3** A2 [C] used to refer in an approximate way to an idea, subject, event, action, etc.: *That was an unkind thing to say.* ◦ *I've got so many things to do I don't know where to start.* ◦ *Your information is correct but you left out one thing.* ◦ *'What's the matter?' 'It's this insurance thing. I'm really worried about it.'* **4 the thing** [C] the exact fact, object, idea, event, etc.: *Your letter has told me precisely the thing I needed to know.* **5 the real thing** something that is not false or a copy: *The fire alarm goes off accidentally so often that when it's the real thing (= when it really does happen) nobody will take any notice.* **6 the same thing** B1 the same: *Training isn't the same thing **as** education.* **7 the whole thing** B2 everything that has been planned or discussed: *Let's call the whole thing off.* ◦ *I want to forget the whole thing.* **8 above all things** more than everything else: *I value my freedom above all things.* **9 in all things** in every situation or subject; in everything: *Be true to yourself in all things.* **10 if there's one thing I want to know, find out, etc.** said before describing what it is that you especially want to know: *If there's one thing I want to know, it's where he goes on Thursday afternoons.* SITUATION ▷ **11 things** B1 [plural] used to refer to the general situation: *Things have been going very well recently.* **12 it's a good thing** B2 If it's a good thing that something happened, it is lucky that it happened: *It's a good thing (**that**) we booked our tickets early.* **13 the way things are** (also **as things stand**) in the present situation: *The way things are, I'll never have this ready by June.* ANYTHING/EVERYTHING ▷ **14 a thing** B1 [S] used instead of 'anything' or 'everything' to emphasize what you are saying: *Don't worry about a thing (= anything). I'll take care of it.* **15 not a (single) thing** B2 not anything: *After the guests had gone, there wasn't a thing left to eat.* **16 not have a thing to wear** B1 (also **have nothing to wear**) to have no clothes that are suitable for an occasion: *I'm going to a wedding on Saturday and I don't have a thing to wear.* **17 there isn't a thing you can do** you cannot do anything: *He broke his promise and there wasn't a thing we could do **about** it.* ACTION ▷ **18 a/one thing** [S] used to talk about a particular action, agreement, etc.: *I went by plane, a thing I hardly ever do.* ◦ *One thing you'll have to agree to is working in the evenings.* **19 the … thing** [S] used to make noun phrases with particular adjectives and adverbs: *The **first** thing (to do) is to write your name at the top of the page.* REASON ▷ **20 for one thing** C2 used to introduce a reason for something: *'Why won't you come to New York with me?' 'For one thing, I don't like flying, and for another, I can't afford it.'* PERSON/ANIMAL ▷ **21** B2 [C] used after an adjective to refer to a person or animal with love or sympathy: *The poor things were kept in small cages without room to move.* ◦ [as form of address] *You lucky thing, winning a car!*

> **!** Common mistake: **thing or think?**
>
> **Warning:** Choose the right word!
>
> These two words look similar, but they are spelled differently and have completely different meanings.

IDIOMS **a close/near thing** UK (mainly US **a close call**) something bad that almost happened: *The car just missed the child but it was a very close thing.* • **all things being equal** if everything happens as expected: *All things being equal, I'll be at home on Tuesday.* • **all things considered** C1 Someone might say that something is good all things considered to mean it was generally good although the situation was not perfect: *I think the party was great, all things considered – I mean we didn't have much time to prepare and no help, but it still went well.* • **all things to all men/people** If you try to be all things to all men/people, you try to do things that will please everyone. • **and another thing** used to introduce one more in a series of arguments or complaints: *And another thing, why didn't you tell me you were going out?* • **a thing of the past** something that no longer happens: *Giving up your seat to an older person seems to be a thing of the past.* • **a thing or two** some matters, facts, or information: *I'm having trouble paying attention – I have a thing or two on my mind.* ◦ *Why don't you ask Andrew about it? He **knows** a thing or two **about** (= has some knowledge of) computers.* ◦ *She thinks she knows everything about raising children, but I **could tell** her a thing or two (= some information she does not know).* • **be hearing/imagining/seeing things** informal to think you are experiencing something that is not really happening: *I'm sure I saw my glasses on this table, but they're not here now. I must have been seeing things.* • **be one thing after another** (also **be one thing after the other**) You say that it is one thing after another/the other when many things are happening in a short time: *I've been so busy today. It's been one thing after another.* • **be on to a good thing** informal to have an easy and pleasant life or job in which it is not necessary to work hard: *He's on to a good thing, he has free accommodation in return for answering the phone when the family are out.* • **do your own thing** informal C2 to do what you want without worrying about what anyone else thinks of you • **does things to you** informal Something or someone that does things to

T

you has a strong, usually enjoyable, effect on you: *That music really does things to me.* • **have a thing about sth/sb** informal to like or dislike something or someone very much: *Ben's got a thing about Triumph motorbikes – he's got three of them.* ◦ *She's got a thing about spiders – she won't touch them.* • **how are things (with you)?** B1 informal for 'how are you?' • **if it's not one thing, it's another** saying used when bad things keep happening to you • **just the thing** (also **the very thing**) exactly what is needed: *A week's rest would be just the thing **for** her.* • **make a big thing (out) of sth** informal to give something too much importance: *I want a party, but I don't want to make a big thing of it.* • **not the done thing** mainly UK (US usually **not the thing to do**) not socially acceptable: *Smoking during a meal is not the done thing.* • **(just) one of those things** informal said to mean that there was no way of planning to avoid something: *The road was blocked, so we missed the meeting – it was just one of those things.* • **one thing leads to another** If one thing leads to another, there is a series of events in which each event was caused by the previous one: *At first, we were just dancing together, but one thing led to another, and I ended up in bed with him.* • **take things easy** to relax and not work too hard: *My doctor's told me to take things easy for a while.* • **the done thing** mainly UK (US usually **the thing to do**) what you are expected to do in a social situation: *Don't forget to shake hands – it's the done thing, you know.* • **the last thing you want, need, etc.** something that you certainly do not want, need, etc.: *Go home? That's the last thing I want to do!* • **the (latest) thing** something that is very new and fashionable: *Biodegradable plastic is the latest thing.* • **the thing is 1** B2 informal used to introduce an explanation or an excuse: *The thing is, my parents like me to be home by ten o'clock.* ◦ *The thing is, the shops close early on Sundays.* **2** used to emphasize the importance of what you are saying: *The thing is to be watchful even when you think your child is safe.* • **things that go bump in the night** humorous used to describe anything unknown that might be frightening, especially a noise • **what with one thing and another** informal You say what with one thing and another when you want to explain that the reason you have failed to do something is because you have been very busy: *What with one thing and another, I forgot to phone you yesterday.*

thingamabob /ˈθɪŋ.ə.mə.bɒb/ US /-bɑːb/ noun [C] (also **thingamajig**, UK also **thingummy**) a word used, especially in spoken English, when the name of an object has been forgotten: *I need one of those red thingamabobs for this – have you got one?* → See also **thingy**

thingy /ˈθɪŋ.i/ noun [S] informal sometimes used if you can't remember someone's or something's name: *Ask thingy over there, he'll know.*

think /θɪŋk/ verb; noun

▸verb (**thought**, **thought**) CONSIDER ▷ **1** A1 [I or T] to believe something or have an opinion or idea: [+ (that)] *I think **(that)** I've met you before.* ◦ *I don't think Emma will get the job.* ◦ *'Do you think **(that)** you could get me some stamps while you're in town?'* ◦ [+ noun/adj] *Salmon used to be thought expensive/thought a luxury.* ◦ [+ to infinitive] *He was thought **to** have boarded the plane in New York.* ◦ *What did you think **of** the film?* ◦ *What do you think **about** this latest government scheme?* ◦ *I think it is important to learn English.* **2** B2 [I] to consider a person's needs or wishes: *She's always thinking **of** others.*

> **! Common mistake: think**
>
> If you use the verb 'to be' after **think** to talk about an opinion or idea that you have, remember to use the subject pronoun **it**.
>
> Don't say 'think is important/difficult/necessary', say **think it is important/difficult/necessary**:
>
> ~~*I think is very important to learn English.*~~
>
> *I think it is very important to learn English.*

DECIDE ▷ **3** A2 to use the brain to decide to do something: [+ of+ -ing verb] *I'm thinking of taking up running.* ◦ [+ (that)] *I think **(that)** I'll go swimming after lunch.* ◦ *I'm thinking **about** buying a new car.*

> **! Common mistake: think**
>
> **Remember:** when talking about deciding to do something, **think** is usually followed by **of/about** and the **-ing** form.
>
> Don't say 'think to do something', say **think about/of doing something**:
>
> ~~*I'm thinking to have my hair cut short.*~~
>
> *I'm thinking about having my hair cut short.*

REASON ▷ **4** B1 [I] to use the brain to plan something, solve a problem, understand a situation, etc.: *What are you thinking, Peter?* ◦ *He just does these things without thinking and he gets himself into such a mess.* ◦ *You think too much – that's your problem.* ◦ *I'm sorry I forgot to mention your name. I just **wasn't thinking**.* **5 think long and hard** (also **think twice**) C1 to think very carefully about something: *I should think long and hard before you make any important decisions.* ◦ *If burglars could realize how deeply they hurt people by invading their homes and stealing their treasured belongings, they might think twice before doing it.* **6 think aloud** UK (US **think out loud**) to automatically say what you are thinking: *'What did you say?' 'Oh, nothing, I was just thinking aloud.'* REMEMBER ▷ **7** B1 [I usually + adv/prep] to remember or imagine: *I was just thinking **about** you when you phoned.* ◦ *She was so busy she didn't think to tell me about it.*

IDIOMS **couldn't think** did not know: *She couldn't think **what** to do next.* • **I can't think** I do not know: *I can't think **why** she hasn't phoned.* • **I think not** a formal way of disagreeing or saying no: *'Will you be going tonight, James?' 'I think not.'* • **I thought as much** used to say that you are not surprised by what someone has said or done: *'I came to ask you a favour.' 'I thought as much.'* • **not be thinking straight** to not be thinking clearly or using good judgment: *I'm sorry, that was a stupid thing to do – I wasn't thinking straight.* • **not think twice** C1 to do something immediately, without considering if it is a good idea: *They didn't think twice about making hundreds of workers redundant.* • **think again** to form a new opinion about something or decide to change your decision on it, often after learning more about it: *When the children are misbehaving, it makes me think again **about** having a large family.* • **think better of sth** to decide that something is not a good idea: *Originally we were going to buy John's old car, but we thought better of it.* • **think big** to have plans to be very successful or powerful: *You need to think big if you want to succeed.* • **think nothing of sth** to consider that an activity is easy and not unusual: *When I was younger, I thought nothing of cycling 50 miles in a day.* • **think on your feet** to make a quick decision or give an answer quickly: *I'd never heard about the firm before, so I had to think on my feet.* • **think outside the box** to think IMAGINATIVELY using new ideas instead of traditional or expected ideas • **to sb's way of thinking** in a particular person's opinion:

Other ways of saying think

See also: **believe**

If you are thinking about a possibility or about making a decision, the verb **consider** is often used:

Don't make any decisions before you've ***considered*** *the matter.*

If someone spends a lot of time thinking about something in a serious way, you can use the verbs **contemplate**, **ponder**, or **mull over**:

He lay in a hospital bed ***contemplating*** *his future.*

She sat back for a minute to ***ponder*** *her next move in the game.*

I need a few days to ***mull*** *things* ***over*** *before I decide.*

Reflect is a formal word that means 'to think carefully, especially about possibilities and opinions':

I spent a lot of time ***reflecting*** *on what he'd said.*

If you think about something anxiously for a long time, you could use the verb **agonize**:

She ***agonized*** *for days about whether she should take the job.*

Brood or **dwell on** are used when someone thinks about something for a long time in a way that makes the person unhappy:

She sat ***brooding*** *in her room for days after she and Gary split up.*

There's no point in ***dwelling on*** *the past.*

If you suddenly think about something, you can say that something **crosses your mind** or that something **strikes you**:

The thought suddenly ***crossed my mind*** *that I might not see him again.*

It's just ***struck me*** *that I haven't paid you yet for the tickets.*

If you are thinking very hard to remember something or to find a way to do something, you can use the phrase **rack your brain**:

I've been ***racking my brain*** *all day but I can't remember where I put my keys.*

If you think again about something in order to change or improve it, you can use the verbs **rethink** or **reconsider**:

Her family's disapproval made her ***rethink*** *her plans.*

He was ***reconsidering*** *whether to accept or not.*

To my way of thinking, the plan should never have been approved. • **who would have thought it?** (C2) used to say that you are very surprised something has happened: *So, Adrian is going out with Emma, is he? Who would have thought it?*

PHRASAL VERBS **think ahead** (C2) to think carefully about what might happen in the future, or to make plans for things you want to do in the future: *The new year is a natural time to think ahead and make plans for the future.* • **think back** (C2) to remember something that happened in the past: *It might help you to understand Elaine if you think back* ***to*** *when you were her age.* • **think for yourself** to make your own decisions and form your own opinions, without depending on other people: *It's no good asking me all the time, Anna – you're going to have to learn to think for yourself.* • **think of sth** (B1) to produce a new idea or plan: *We'll have to think of a pretty good excuse for being late.* • **think of sth/sb 1** (A1) If you think of something or someone in a particular way, you have that opinion about them: *I think of him* ***as*** *someone who will always help me.* ◦ *What do you think of (= do you like) my new dress?* **2 think highly, well, a lot, etc. of sb** (C2) (also **think the world of sb**) to have a good opinion of someone or something: *She thinks very highly of her boss.* **3 not think much of sb/sth** (C2) to have a low opinion of someone or something: *I don't think much of having to work on Saturdays.* • **think of/about sb/sth** (B1) to remember or imagine someone or something: *I thought of you immediately when they said they wanted someone who could speak English.* ◦ *He was thinking about the time he spent in the army.* • **think sth out** to consider all the possible details of something: *The scheme was well thought out.* • **think sth over** (B2) to consider an idea or plan carefully before making a decision: *I'll think it over and give you an answer next week.* • **think sth through** (B2) to carefully consider the possible results of doing something: *I need some time to think it through – I don't want to make any sudden decisions.* • **think sth up** to produce a new idea or plan: *I don't want to go tonight but I can't think up a good excuse.*

▸**noun** **have a think** UK to consider something for some time: *Let me have a think* ***about*** *it before I decide.* ◦ *Have a think over the weekend and tell me what you've decided.*

thinker /ˈθɪŋ.kər/ (US) /-kɚ/ **noun** [C] (C2) someone who considers important subjects or produces new ideas: *a political/religious thinker* ◦ *He was known for being an original thinker.*

thinking /ˈθɪŋ.kɪŋ/ **noun; adj**

▸**noun** [U] **1** the activity of using your mind to consider something: *I'll have to* ***do*** *some thinking about how best to arrange the books.* **2** someone's ideas or opinions: *What's the thinking* ***behind*** *the decision to combine the two departments?*

IDIOM **put your thinking cap on** to think seriously about something: *I'm in need of some interesting suggestions so if you can put your thinking cap on I'd be grateful.*

▸**adj** [before noun] describes people who use their minds to consider things carefully: *All thinking people realize that we must stop wasting our natural resources.*

IDIOM **the thinking woman's/man's crumpet** UK humorous a way of describing a man or a woman who is popular with the opposite sex because they are intelligent as well as being physically attractive: *Paxman is surely the ultimate thinking woman's crumpet.*

ˈ**think** ˌ**tank** **noun** [C usually singular, + sing/pl verb] a group of experts brought together, usually by a government, to develop ideas on a particular subject and to make suggestions for action

thinly /ˈθɪn.li/ **adv** NOT THICK ▷ **1** made or done so that something is not thick: ***thinly-sliced*** *ham* FEW ▷ **2** with only a small number of people or things, or without the people or things being close to each other: *a thinly populated area* ◦ *thinly planted seedlings* TRANSPARENT ▷ **3** in a way that is not difficult to see through or to recognize: *A light mist thinly covered the summit.* ◦ *a thinly disguised lie*

thinner /ˈθɪn.ər/ (US) /-ɚ/ **noun** [U] a substance added especially to paint to make it flow more easily: *paint thinner*

ˌ**thin-**ˈ**skinned** **adj** easily hurt by criticism or easily made unhappy → Opposite **thick-skinned**

third /θɜːd/ (US) /θɝːd/ **ordinal number; noun**

▸**ordinal number** [S] (A2) 3rd written as a word: *the third road on the right* ◦ *the third time* ◦ *'What's the date*

T

today?' 'It's ***the*** *third (****of*** *July).'* ◦ *She* ***was/came*** *third in the competition.*

IDIOM **the third degree** informal asking serious questions and/or giving someone rough treatment to get information: *I* ***got*** *the third degree when I got home last night.*

▸noun [C] **PART** ▷ **1** B2 one of three equal parts of something: *He cut the cake into thirds* (= three equal parts). **QUALIFICATION** ▷ **2** [C] (also ˌ**third-class deˈgree**) a degree qualification from a British university that is below a 2:2

ˌ**third-ˌdegree ˈburn** noun [C] a very serious burn in which the flesh is destroyed → Compare **first-degree burn, second-degree burn**

ˌ**third-geneˈration** adj [before noun] (abbreviation **3G**) describes TECHNOLOGY that is new and improved, especially MOBILE PHONES on which you can use the internet, watch television, etc.

thirdly /ˈθɜːd.li/ US /ˈθɝːd-/ adv used in order to introduce the third thing in a list: *There are three factors to take into account: firstly cost, secondly time, and thirdly staff.*

ˌ**third ˈparty** noun [C usually singular] legal a third person or organization less directly involved in a matter than the main people or organizations that are involved

ˌ**third-ˌparty inˈsurance** noun [U] INSURANCE that will pay money to a person or group damaged in some way by the person or group who has this INSURANCE

the ˌthird ˈperson noun [S] B2 the form of a verb or PRONOUN that is used about another person you are speaking about or writing about

ˌ**third-ˈrate** adj of low quality: *I don't want to work for some third-rate company.*

the ˌThird ˈWorld noun the countries of Africa, South America, and Asia which have less developed industries: *She does a lot of work in the Third World.* ◦ *a Third-World country/economy*

thirst /θɜːst/ US /θɝːst/ noun; verb

▸noun **NEED FOR DRINK** ▷ **1** B2 [S or U] a need for something to drink: *Hundreds of refugees collapsed from hunger and thirst.* ◦ *I've got a terrible thirst after all that running.* ◦ *I woke up with a thumping headache and a* ***raging*** (= extreme) *thirst.* **WISH** ▷ **2** C2 [S] literary a strong wish: *He's always had* ***a thirst for*** *adventure.*

▸verb

PHRASAL VERB **thirst after/for sth** literary to feel very strongly that you want and need a particular thing: *to be thirsting for justice/truth/adventure*

ˈ**thirst-ˌquenching** adj describes a drink that stops you feeling thirsty: *I'd like something thirst-quenching – an orange juice, I think.*

thirsty /ˈθɜː.sti/ US /ˈθɝː-/ adj **NEED FOR DRINK** ▷ **1** A2 needing to drink: *I felt/was hot and thirsty after my game of squash.* **WISH** ▷ **2** literary Someone who is thirsty for power, knowledge, etc. wants to have it very much. • **thirstily** /-stɪ.li/ adv

ˌ**thirsty ˈwork** noun [U] informal hard physical work that makes you thirsty: *Sawing wood is thirsty work.*

thirteen /θɜːˈtiːn/ US /θɝː-/ number A1 the number 13: *Some people think that thirteen is an unlucky number.* ◦ *There were twelve or thirteen people waiting at the bus stop.*

thirteenth /θɜːˈtiːnθ/ US /θɝː-/ ordinal number 13th written as a word: *My birthday is on* ***the*** *thirteenth (****of*** *October).*

thirties /ˈθɜː.tiz/ US /ˈθɝː.t̬iz/ noun [plural] **1** B2 A person's thirties are the period in which they are aged between 30 and 39: *My brother is* ***in*** *his thirties.* **2 the thirties a** the range of temperature between 30° and 39°: *The temperature is expected to be* ***in*** *the thirties tomorrow.* **b** B2 the DECADE (= period of ten years) between 30 and 39 in any century, usually 1930–1939: *My family fled Germany* ***in*** *the thirties.*

thirtieth /ˈθɜː.ti.əθ/ US /ˈθɝː.t̬i-/ ordinal number 30th written as a word

thirty /ˈθɜː.ti/ US /ˈθɝː.t̬i/ number A2 the number 30: *twenty-nine, thirty, thirty-one* ◦ *She got married when she was thirty (years old).*

this /ðɪs/ determiner; adv

▸determiner (plural **these**) **1** A1 used for a person, object, idea, etc. to show which one is referred to: *Can you sign this form here for me?* ◦ *These books are too heavy for me to carry.* ◦ informal *We met this girl* (= the girl I am going to tell you about) *in the hotel.* ◦ *This is the one I want.* ◦ *What's this? Is this what you're looking for?* ◦ *What's this I hear about your moving to Scotland?* **2 by this time** (also **before this**) already: *I thought you'd have finished by this time.*

IDIOM **this and that** (also **this, that, and the other**) C2 various things: *'What were you talking about?' 'Oh, this and that.'*

▸adv C1 as much as shown or to a particular degree: *It was only about this high off the ground.* ◦ *She has never been this late for school before.*

thistle /ˈθɪs.l̩/ noun [C] a wild plant with sharp points on the leaves and, typically, purple flowers

thistledown /ˈθɪs.l̩.daʊn/ noun [U] the mass of thin, soft, white threads that are joined to thistle seeds and help them to be blown through the air

thither /ˈðɪð.əʳ/ US /-ɚ/ adv old use to that place, in that direction

thnq written abbreviation for thank you: used in emails and text messages

thong /θɒŋ/ US /θɑːŋ/ noun [C] **NARROW PIECE** ▷ **1** a narrow piece of especially leather used to fasten something or as part of a WHIP **UNDERWEAR** ▷ **2** a piece of underwear or the bottom part of a BIKINI with a very narrow part at the back which does not cover the bottom **SHOE** ▷ **3** US and Australian English a **flip-flop**

thorax /ˈθɔː.ræks/ US /ˈθɔːr.æks/ noun [C] (plural **thoraces** /ˈθɔː.rə.siːz/ or **thoraxes**) specialized **1** in humans and animals, the middle part of the body below the neck and above the waist **2** in insects, the middle part of the body, between the head and the ABDOMEN (= end part) • **thoracic** /θɔːˈræs.ɪk/ adj

thorn /θɔːn/ US /θɔːrn/ noun [C] a small, sharp pointed growth on the stem of a plant

IDIOM **thorn in your flesh/side** a person or thing that repeatedly annoys you or causes you pain: *A relentless campaigner, he was a thorn in the government's side for a number of years.*

thorny /ˈθɔː.ni/ US /ˈθɔːr-/ adj **PROBLEM/SUBJECT** ▷ **1** [before noun] describes a problem or subject that is difficult to deal with: *the thorny* ***issue of*** *taxation* **PLANT** ▷ **2** having thorns: *a thorny rose bush*

thorough /ˈθʌr.ə/ US /ˈθɝː-/ /-oʊ/ adj **CAREFUL** ▷ **1** B2 detailed and careful: *a thorough revision of the manuscript* ◦ *They did a thorough search of the area but found nothing.* **COMPLETE** ▷ **2** complete, very great, or very much: *It was a thorough waste of time.* • **thoroughness** /-nəs/ noun [U]

thoroughbred /ˈθʌr.ə.bred/ US /ˈθɝː-/ /-oʊ-/ adj, noun [C] (a horse) with parents that are of the same breed and have good qualities: *a thoroughbred racehorse*

thoroughfare /ˈθʌr.ə.feəʳ/ (US) /ˈθɝː.ə.fer/ /-oʊ-/ noun [C] formal **1** a main road for public use or a passage through somewhere **2 no thoroughfare** On road signs, no thoroughfare means no ENTRY or do not go in.

thoroughgoing /ˌθʌr.əˈɡəʊ.ɪŋ/, /ˈθʌr.əˌɡəʊ-/ (US) /ˌθɝː.əˈɡoʊ-/ adj formal complete, detailed, careful: *a thoroughgoing reform of the economy*

thoroughly /ˈθʌr.ə.li/ (US) /ˈθɝː-/ /-oʊ-/ adv **VERY MUCH** ▷ **1** B2 completely, very much: *I thoroughly enjoyed the performance.* **CAREFULLY** ▷ **2** B2 in a detailed and careful way: *We went through the report thoroughly but the information we wanted wasn't given anywhere.*

those /ðəʊz/ (US) /ðoʊz/ determiner, pronoun A1 plural of **that**

thou pronoun; noun
▸pronoun /ðaʊ/ old use you, used when speaking to one person
▸noun [C] /θaʊ/ (plural **thou**) informal for **thousand**, especially when referring to an amount of money: *'How much do you reckon it cost him?' 'About thirty thou.'*

though /ðəʊ/ (US) /ðoʊ/ conjunction; adv
▸conjunction **1** B1 despite the fact that: *She hasn't phoned, **even** though she said she would.* **2** B2 but: *They're coming next week, though I don't know which day.* **3 as though** B2 as if: *You look as though you've had a bad time!*
▸adv B2 despite this: *We were at school together. I haven't seen her for years, though.*

thought /θɔːt/ (US) /θɑːt/ verb; noun
▸verb past simple and past participle of **think**
▸noun [C or U] B1 the act of thinking about or considering something, an idea or opinion, or a set of ideas about a particular subject: *Ask me again tomorrow. I'll have to **give** it some thought.* ◦ *She doesn't **give** any thought **to** her appearance.* ◦ *Let me have your thoughts **on** that report by Friday.* ◦ ***Spare a** thought **for** (= think about) all those without shelter on a cold night like this.* ◦ *He's the author of a book on the history of European thought.* ◦ *You sent her a card? That was a kind thought.*

> **Word partners for thought**
> *have* a thought • a thought *occurs to/strikes* sb • *give* sth *some* thought • *spare* a thought *for* sb • your thoughts *turn to* sth • *can't bear* the thought *of* sth/doing sth • an *interesting/secret/scary/sobering* thought • thoughts *about/on* sth

IDIOMS **that's a thought** that's a good idea: *'Shall we go on Thursday instead of Friday?' 'That's a thought.'* • **the thought crosses sb's mind** If the thought of (doing) something crosses someone's mind, they think about it for a short time: *The thought had crossed my mind **that** I might need some help with the project.* • **with no thought for sth** not thinking about a particular thing: *With no thought for his own safety, he rushed towards the burning car.*

thoughtful /ˈθɔːt.fəl/ (US) /ˈθɑːt-/ adj **1** B2 carefully considering things: *He has a thoughtful approach to his work.* **2** C2 quiet because you are thinking about something: *You look thoughtful.* **3** kind and always thinking about how you can help other people: *Thank you for phoning when I was ill – it was very thoughtful of you.* ◦ *She's a very thoughtful person.* → Opposite **thoughtless** • **thoughtfully** /-i/ adv *He gazed thoughtfully into the distance.* ◦ *There were sandwiches, thoughtfully provided by his wife.* • **thoughtfulness** /-nəs/ noun [U]

thoughtless /ˈθɔːt.ləs/ (US) /ˈθɑːt-/ adj C2 not considering how your actions or words may upset someone: *It was thoughtless not to phone and say you'd be late.* ◦ *She's not intentionally unkind – she's just a little thoughtless sometimes.* • **thoughtlessly** /ˈθɔːt.ləs.li/ (US) /ˈθɑːt-/ adv • **thoughtlessness** /ˈθɔːt.ləs.nəs/ (US) /ˈθɑːt-/ noun [U]

ˌthought ˈout adj If something is carefully/well/badly thought out, it is carefully/well/badly planned: *To me the whole scheme seems to be badly thought out.* ◦ [before noun] *a well-thought-out plan*

ˈthought-proˌvoking adj making you think a lot about a subject: *a thought-provoking book/film*

thousand /ˈθaʊ.zənd/ number (plural **thousand** or **thousands**) **1** A2 the number 1,000: *They had driven over a/one thousand miles.* ◦ *The population of the village is about three thousand.* ◦ *The damage will cost thousands **of** dollars to repair.* **2 a thousand/thousands of sth** B2 informal a large number: *I've got a thousand things to do before we go on holiday.* **3 the thousands** numbers between 1,000 and 1,000,000: *His latest work is expected to sell in the thousands.*

> **! Common mistake: thousands or thousand?**
> When **thousand** is used after a particular number, it is used in the singular form and without 'of'.
> Don't say 'five/ten/fifteen thousands of sth', say five/ten/fifteen **thousand** sth:
> ~~*The stadium can hold fifty thousands of fans.*~~
> *The stadium can hold fifty thousand fans.*
> When **thousand** is used without a particular number, it is used in the plural form and is sometimes followed by 'of':
> *The stadium can hold thousands (of fans).*

thousandth /ˈθaʊ.zənθ/ ordinal number 1,000th written as a word: *Sir Alex Ferguson celebrated his thousandth match as manager of Manchester United.*

thrall /θrɔːl/ (US) /θrɑːl/ noun [U] **in thrall** literary If you are in thrall to someone or something or in their or its thrall, they or it have or has a lot of power to control you: *Her love for him was like a madness, and she was completely in its thrall.*

thrash /θræʃ/ verb **HIT** ▷ **1** [T] to hit a person or animal hard many times as a punishment: *His father used to thrash him when he was a boy.* **MOVE** ▷ **2** [I] to move from side to side in a violent or uncontrolled way: *He was screaming and thrashing **around** on the floor.* **DEFEAT** ▷ **3** [T] informal to defeat someone very easily in a game or sports competition: *We thrashed the visiting team 6–0.* **REMOVE SEEDS** ▷ **4** [I or T] to **thresh**

PHRASAL VERB **thrash sth out** informal to discuss a problem in detail until you reach an agreement or find a solution: *If we've got an important decision to make, we sometimes spend a whole day thrashing it out in a meeting.*

ˌthrash ˈmetal noun [U] a very fast type of HEAVY METAL music, that also has some features of PUNK ROCK

thread /θred/ noun; verb
▸noun **FIBRE** ▷ **1** C2 [C or U] (a length of) a very thin FIBRE: ***needle and** thread* ◦ *loose threads* **2** [C] a long, thin line of something such as light or smoke: *A thin thread **of** light made its way through the curtains.* **CONNECTION** ▷ **3** C2 [C] The thread of a book, discussion, speech, etc. is its story or the way that it develops, one part connecting with another: *One of*

the main threads of the film is the development of the relationship between the boy and his uncle. ◦ *Unfortunately my attention wandered for a moment and I* **lost** *the thread of (= forgot) what I was saying.* **4** C2 [C] a connected group of pieces of writing on the internet, where people are talking about a particular subject: *I was so pleased to find this thread, and to know that lots of people have the same problem as me!* **SCREW** ▷ **5** [C] a continuous raised line, such as the one which goes around the outside of a SCREW or BOLT or the inside of a hole
▸verb [T] C2 to put something long and thin such as string or thread through a narrow hole or into a small space: *to thread a* **needle** ◦ *The sari had gold strands threaded through the material.*

IDIOM **thread your way through, between, etc. sth** C2 to move carefully through a crowded space, changing direction in order to avoid people or things: *She threaded her way through the crowded market place.*

threadbare /ˈθred.beəʳ/ US /-ber/ **adj THIN** ▷ **1** describes material or clothes that have become thin or damaged because they have been used a lot: *a threadbare coat* **WEAK** ▷ **2** A threadbare excuse, argument, or idea is not strong and no longer persuades people because it is old or has been used too much: *a threadbare excuse*

threat /θret/ **noun** [C] **1** B2 a suggestion that something unpleasant or violent will happen, especially if a particular action or order is not followed: [+ to infinitive] *She* **carried out** *her threat* **to** *throw away any clothes that were left on the floor.* ◦ *The threat* **of** *jail failed to deter him from petty crime.* ◦ *Drunken drivers* **pose** *a serious threat (= cause a lot of harm)* **to** *other road users.* ◦ *He says he'll tell the authorities but it's just an* **empty** *threat (= it will not happen).* **2 be under threat of sth** to be in a situation where people are threatening you with something bad or unpleasant: *She left the country under threat of arrest if she returned.*

> **Word partners for threat**
> *be/pose* a threat • *issue/make* a threat • *receive* a threat • *carry out* a threat • a threat *hangs over* sb • a *growing/major/real/serious* threat • an *idle/immediate/potential/renewed* threat • a threat *to* sth/sb • the threat *of* sth

threaten /ˈθret.ən/ **verb 1** B2 [T] to tell someone that you will kill or hurt them, or cause problems for them if they do not do what you want: *They threatened the shopkeeper* **with** *a gun.* ◦ [+ to infinitive] *They threatened* **to** *kill him unless he did as they asked.* **2** C1 [T] to be likely to cause harm or damage to something or someone: *Changing patterns of agriculture are threatening the countryside.* **3** C2 [I] If something bad threatens to happen, it is likely to happen: *Look at those clouds! There's a storm threatening.*

threatening /ˈθret.ən.ɪŋ/, /-nɪŋ-/ **adj** expressing a threat of something unpleasant or violent: *threatening behaviour* • **threateningly** /-li/ **adv**

three /θriː/ **number** A1 the number 3: *I've got three sisters.* ◦ *School finishes at three (o'clock).*

IDIOM **the three Rs** informal used to refer to the basic areas of education: reading, writing, and mathematics

ˌthree-diˈmensional adj (abbreviation **3-D**) having or appearing to have three DIMENSIONS (= length, width, and height) and therefore looking real: *The picture had a three-dimensional* **effect**.

ˌthree-ˈlegged ˌrace noun [C] a race in which the right leg of one person is tied to the left leg of another person, and the two people run together as if they had three legs

ˌthree-line ˈwhip noun [C usually singular] In the UK a three-line whip is an instruction given to Members of Parliament by the leaders of their party telling them they must vote in the way that the party wants them to on a particular subject.

threepence /ˈθrʌp.əns/ **noun** [U] old use a small BRASS coin used in Britain until 1971, or an earlier silver-coloured coin, which was worth three old PENNIES, or this amount of money

threepenny /ˈθrepən.i/ **adj** [before noun] old use worth or costing three old PENNIES: *a threepenny* **bit**

ˌthree-piece ˈsuit noun [C] a matching jacket, trousers, and WAISTCOAT (= a top without sleeves that is worn over a shirt) especially for men

ˌthree-piece ˈsuite noun [C] UK (US **ˈliving room ˌsuite**) a SOFA with two matching chairs

ˈthree-ply adj, noun [U] **PAPER/WOOD** ▷ **1** (wood, TISSUES, TOILET PAPER, etc.) made of three layers joined together **WOOL** ▷ **2** (wool) consisting of three threads

ˌthree-point ˈturn noun [C] a method of turning a car round to face the other direction by moving forwards across the road, then backwards in the opposite direction across the road and then forwards again

ˌthree-quarter ˈlength adj A three-quarter length coat is between the length of a jacket and a coat.

ˌthree ˈquarters determiner three fourths of something

threesome /ˈθriː.səm/ **noun** [C] informal three people as a group

ˌthree-ˈstar adj Something such as a service or a hotel that is three-star is of good quality.

ˌthree-ˈwheeler noun [C] a vehicle with three wheels

thresh /θreʃ/ **verb** [I or T] (also **thrash**) to remove the seeds of crop plants by hitting them, using either a machine or a hand tool

threshold /ˈθreʃ.həʊld/ US /-hoʊld/ **noun ENTRANCE** ▷ **1** [C] the floor of an entrance to a building or room **LEVEL** ▷ **2** C2 [C usually singular] the level or point at which you start to experience something, or at which something starts to happen: *I have a* **low/high** *boredom threshold (= I do/don't feel bored easily).* ◦ *His secretary earns £268 a month, well below the threshold for paying tax.*

IDIOM **on the threshold of sth** C2 at the start of a new and important time or development: *We are on the threshold of a new era in European relations.*

threw /θruː/ **verb** past participle of **throw**

thrice /θraɪs/ **adv** old use or Indian English three times

thrift /θrɪft/ **noun** [U] **AVOIDING WASTE** ▷ **1** the careful use of money, especially by avoiding waste **PLANT** ▷ **2** a small plant with, typically, pink flowers on long stems which often grows wild on CLIFFS by the sea **BANK** ▷ **3** [C] a type of bank in the US that allows you to save money or borrow money to buy a house: *These days, thrifts place most of their money into boring but safe mortgages.*

ˈthrift ˌshop noun [C] US (UK **ˈcharity ˌshop**) a shop that sells clothes and other goods that people no longer want, in order to raise money for people who are ill or have no food, homes, etc.

thrifty /ˈθrɪf.ti/ **adj** showing a careful use of money, especially by avoiding waste: *They have plenty of money now, but they still tend to be thrifty.* • **thriftily** /-tɪ.li/ **adv** • **thriftiness** /-nəs/ **noun** [U]

thrill /θrɪl/ noun; verb
▸noun [C] C1 a feeling of extreme excitement, usually caused by something pleasant: *the thrill of winning a competition ◦ So why do people still go hunting – is it the thrill of the chase? ◦ It **gave** me a real thrill to see her again after so many years. ◦ The video shows the thrills **and spills** (= excitement and accidents) of motor racing.*
▸verb [I or T] C2 to make someone feel very excited and pleased: *McIlroy thrilled the golf world with his performance.*

thrilled /θrɪld/ adj B2 extremely pleased: [+ that] *I was thrilled **that** so many people turned up to the party.*

IDIOM **thrilled to bits** informal extremely pleased: *She was thrilled to bits with her present.*

thriller /ˈθrɪl.əʳ/ US /-ɚ/ noun [C] B1 a book, play, or film that has an exciting story, often about solving a crime: *It's described here as a taut psychological thriller.*

thrilling /ˈθrɪl.ɪŋ/ adj B2 extremely exciting: *The book is a thrilling adventure story.*

thrive /θraɪv/ verb [I] (**thrived** or US also **throve**, **thrived** or US also **thriven**) C1 to grow, develop, or be successful: *His business thrived in the years before the war. ◦ She seems to thrive **on** stress.* • **thriving** /ˈθraɪ.vɪŋ/ adj

throat /θrəʊt/ US /θroʊt/ noun [C] B1 the front of the neck, or the space inside the neck down which food and air can go: *A fish bone got **stuck in** my throat. ◦ a **sore** throat ◦ He **cleared** his throat (= coughed so he could speak more clearly) and started speaking.*

IDIOMS **at each other's throats** If two people are at each other's throats, they are arguing angrily: *Those two are always at each other's throats.* • **force/ram sth down sb's throat** to force someone to listen to opinions and ideas and to try to get them to accept them: *I can't bear it when someone starts ramming their views down your throat.*

-throated /-θrəʊ.tɪd/ US /-θroʊ.t̬ɪd/ suffix of or with a particular kind of throat: *a red-throated bird ◦ a **full-throated** (= loud) roar*

throaty /ˈθrəʊ.ti/ US /ˈθroʊ.t̬i/ adj describes a sound that is low and rough: *a throaty voice/laugh/cough* • **throatily** /-tɪ.li/ US /-t̬ɪ.li/ adv • **throatiness** /-nəs/ noun [U]

throb /θrɒb/ US /θrɑːb/ verb [I] (**-bb-**) **1** to produce a strong, regular beat: *Both records have a good throbbing bass which is great to dance to.* **2** If a part of your body throbs, you feel pain in it in a series of regular beats: *His **head** throbbed, and his body ached. ◦ The throbbing pain in his leg was becoming unbearable.* • **throb** noun [S] *the throb of the engine* → See also **heartthrob**

throes /θrəʊz/ US /θroʊz/ noun [plural] **in the throes of sth** experiencing or doing something that is difficult, unpleasant, or painful: *The country is presently in the throes of the worst recession since the Second World War. ◦ He's in the throes of a mid-life crisis that makes him rather difficult to live with.* → See also **death throes**

thrombosis /θrɒmˈbəʊ.sɪs/ US /θrɑːmˈboʊ-/ noun [C] (plural **thromboses**) a medical condition in which the flow of blood in the body is blocked by a CLOT (= half solid mass) of blood

throne /θrəʊn/ US /θroʊn/ noun [C] **1** C2 the special chair used by a ruler, especially a king or queen **2 the throne** C2 the state of being a ruler: *Elizabeth II **ascended/came to** the throne (= became queen of Britain) when her father died. ◦ Queen Victoria was **on** the throne (= was queen) at that time. ◦ Charles is **next in line to** the throne (= will become king next).*

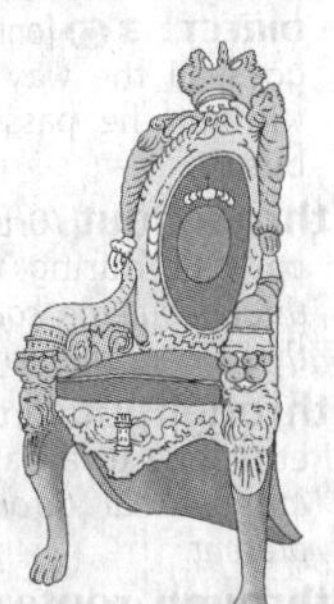
throne

throng /θrɒŋ/ US /θrɑːŋ/ noun; verb
▸noun [C, + sing/pl verb] a crowd or large group of people: *A huge throng had gathered round the speaker.*
▸verb [I + adv/prep, T] to be or go somewhere in very large numbers: *Crowds thronged the market place. ◦ The narrow streets were thronged **with** summer visitors.* ◦ [+ to infinitive] *Thousands of people thronged **to** see the exhibition while it was in London.*

throttle /ˈθrɒt.l̩/ US /ˈθrɑː.t̬l̩/ noun; verb
▸noun [C] a VALVE which allows more or less fuel to go into an engine and so changes the power with which the engine operates

IDIOM **at full/half throttle** at full/half speed or power: *He's working at full throttle (= as hard as he can) to get the job finished. ◦ The captain of the boat had his engines at full throttle.*

▸verb [T] **PRESS THROAT** ▷ **1** to press someone's throat very tightly so that they cannot breathe: informal *Sometimes he annoys me so much that I could throttle him.* **PREVENT** ▷ **2** to prevent something from succeeding: *The reduction in funds is throttling the development of new programmes.*

PHRASAL VERB **throttle (sth) back/down** to reduce speed, or to reduce the power and speed being produced by an engine: *The pilot throttled back (the engines) as he came in to land.*

through /θruː/ preposition, adv; preposition; adj
▸preposition, adv **PLACE** ▷ **1** A2 (also US not standard **thru**) from one end or side of something to the other: *They walked slowly through the woods. ◦ The boy waded through the water to reach his boat. ◦ He struggled through the crowd till he reached the front. ◦ How long the journey takes will depend on how long it takes to **get** through the traffic. ◦ Her words kept running through my mind/head (= I kept hearing her words in my imagination). ◦ We drove through the tunnel. ◦ I saw him drive through **a red light** (= he did not stop at the red traffic light). ◦ I'll put you through (= connect you by phone) (**to** the sales department).* **TIME** ▷ **2** B1 from the beginning to the end of a period of time: *It rained **all/right** through June and into the first half of July. ◦ We sat through two lectures and then left. ◦ She had just enough energy to **get** through the day.* ◦ US *She works Monday through Thursday (= from Monday to Thursday).*

IDIOM **through and through** completely: *My mother is Irish through and through.*

▸preposition **RESULT** ▷ **1** B1 as a result of: *The company lost the order through production delays.* **USING** ▷ **2** B1 by; using: *I got my car through my brother who works in a garage. ◦ We sold the bike through advertising in the local paper.*
▸adj **FINISHED** ▷ **1** having finished using or doing something: *I've got some work to do but I should be through in an hour if you can wait. ◦ Are you through **with** that atlas?* **SUCCESSFUL** ▷ **2 be through (to sth)** to achieve success in an exam, competition, etc. and progress to the next stage or a higher level: *'Has she heard about her entrance exams yet?' 'Yes, she's*

T

through.' ◦ *She's through to the next round of interviews.* **DIRECT** ▷ **3** C1 [only before noun] A through train or bus goes all the way from one place to another place without the passenger having to change trains or buses.

throughout /θruːˈaʊt/ **preposition, adv** B2 in every part, or during the whole period of time: *People throughout the country are out of work.* ◦ *He yawned throughout the performance.*

throughput /ˈθruː.pʊt/ **noun** [U] an amount of work, etc. done in a particular period of time: *We need to improve our throughput because demand is high at present.*

ˈthrough ˌroute noun [C] a road which avoids a town centre

ˈthrough ˌtraffic noun [U] traffic which does not want to stop in a town

throve /θrəʊv/ US /θroʊv/ US past simple and past participle of **thrive**

throw /θrəʊ/ US /θroʊ/ **verb; noun**

▸**verb** (**threw**, **thrown**) **SEND THROUGH AIR** ▷ **1** A2 [I or T] to send something through the air with force, especially by a sudden movement of the arm: *My friend threw the **ball** back over the fence.* ◦ *The coat was thrown over the back of the chair.* ◦ *She threw her**self** into a chair, exhausted.* ◦ *The rider was thrown as the horse jumped the fence.* ◦ *He threw **a punch** at* (= hit) *his attacker.* **2 throw a glance/look** to look quickly or suddenly: *The boy threw a frightened look in the direction of the house.* **MOVE QUICKLY** ▷ **3** C2 [T] to cause to move or act quickly or carelessly: *She threw **back** her hair.* ◦ *David threw **open** the window to get some air.* **CONFUSE** ▷ **4** [T] to confuse or shock someone or cause difficulty for them: *I wasn't expecting a visitor. I was really thrown.* ◦ *The news of the coup threw them into a state of panic.* **PARTY** ▷ **5 throw a party** to have a party: *Flavio threw a party for Colin's 50th birthday.* **ANGER** ▷ **6 throw a fit/tantrum** to experience and show a strong feeling of anger, especially suddenly: *My mother threw a fit when she saw what a mess we'd made of her kitchen.* **SHAPE** ▷ **7** [T] specialized to shape clay on a special round table that spins

> **Other ways of saying throw**
>
> **Toss** and, in informal English, **chuck**, can be used when someone throws something in a careless way:
>
> *She **tossed** the keys into her bag and went out.*
>
> *He read the letter and **chucked** it into the trash can.*
>
> If someone throws something somewhere with a lot of force, you could use the verbs **fling** or **hurl**:
>
> *He crumpled up the letter and **flung** it into the fire.*
>
> *In a fit of temper he **hurled** the book across the room.*
>
> **Lob** is used when someone throws something in a high curve:
>
> *The boys spent an hour **lobbing** stones into the lake.*
>
> If someone **pelts** a person or thing, they throw a lot of things at that person or thing very quickly:
>
> *They **pelted** each other with snowballs on the way home from school.*

IDIOMS **throw the baby out with the bathwater** to lose valuable ideas or things in your attempt to get rid of what is not wanted • **throw sth back in sb's face** to say unkind things about someone's behaviour in the past during an argument: *She threw all his failures back in his face.* • **throw the book at sb** to severely punish someone: *After the accident, the safety inspector threw the book at the company directors.* • **throw caution to the wind/winds** C2 to do something without worrying about the risk or negative results: *I threw caution to the wind and bought the most expensive one.* • **throw cold water on sth** to be negative about someone's ideas or plans: *You're always throwing cold water on my suggestions.* • **throw (sb) a curve (ball)** mainly US and Australian English informal to surprise someone with something that is difficult or unpleasant to deal with: *The weather threw a curve at their barbecue and they had to eat indoors.* • **throw good money after bad** to waste money by spending more money on something you have already spent money on that is no good: *Trying to fix that old car would just be throwing good money after bad.* • **throw in the towel/sponge** to admit defeat • **throw (your) money/cash around** informal disapproving to spend money, especially in an obvious and careless way, on things that are not necessary: *He lost his job, but still seems to have plenty of money to throw around.* • **throw money at sth** to spend a lot of money on trying to solve a problem: *We won't solve this problem by throwing money at it.* • **throw sb off balance** to confuse or upset someone for a short time by saying or doing something that they are not expecting: *The question threw him off balance for a moment.* • **throw sb to the dogs** to allow someone to be criticized or attacked, often in order to protect yourself from being criticized or attacked: *I really felt as if I'd been thrown to the dogs just to save other people's reputations.* • **throw up your hands in horror/despair** to show that you are shocked or that you disagree strongly with something: *They threw up their hands in horror at his suggestion.* • **throw your voice** to make something that is not real, such as a toy, seem to be speaking • **throw your weight around/about** disapproving to act as if you have a lot of power or authority

PHRASAL VERBS **throw yourself at sb** informal disapproving to make it very obvious to someone that you want a sexual relationship with them: *I don't know what it is about John, but women just seem to throw themselves at him.* • **throw sth away/out** B1 to get rid of something that you do not want any more: *So when are you going to throw away those old magazines?* • **throw sth away** to waste a skill or opportunity: *You've spent three years studying – don't throw it all away.* • **throw sth in** If a person or business selling goods throws something in, they provide it for free when you buy something else from them: *When I bought my new glasses, they threw in a free pair of prescription sunglasses.* • **throw yourself into sth** C1 to do something actively and enthusiastically: *She's thrown herself into this new job.* • **throw sth off CLOTHES** ▷ **1** If you throw off your clothes, you take them off quickly and carelessly: *They threw off their clothes and jumped in the sea.* **ILLNESS** ▷ **2** to stop suffering from a cold or other illness that is not serious: *I can't seem to throw off this cold.* • **throw sth/sb off** to escape from something or someone following you: *They threw the police off the scent by travelling on false passports.* • **throw sth open OBJECT** ▷ **1** to open something that was closed, usually suddenly and completely: *She drew back the curtains and threw open all the windows.* **EVENT** ▷ **2** to allow people to enter or become involved in an event: *The competition has been thrown open to the public.* • **throw sth out GET RID OF** ▷ **1** B1 see **throw sth away/out** **NOT ACCEPT** ▷ **2** If people in authority throw out a plan, idea, case, etc. they refuse to accept or use it: *The case was thrown out by the courts due to lack of evidence.* • **throw sb out** B2 to force someone to leave a college, school, house or organization: *She was thrown out **of** college for not attending lectures.* ◦ *They had a big row and she threw him out (= made him leave the house).* • **throw sb over** old-fashioned informal to finish a relationship with someone and start one with another person: *She threw him over **for** a richer man.* • **throw sth together** informal to make something quickly without special care or preparation: *I had to throw a meal together at the last minute.* • **throw sb together** [usually passive] If two people are thrown together, they meet each other in a way that was not planned, or events cause them to meet unexpectedly: *We were thrown together by chance at a conference.* • **throw (sth) up** informal B2 to vomit: *I spent the night throwing up.* ◦ *He threw up his breakfast all over the back seat of the car.* • **throw sth up** JOB ▷ **1** UK informal If you throw up your job, you choose to leave it or stop doing it: *He's thrown up his job and gone off to Africa to work for a children's charity.* IDEA ▷ **2** to produce new problems or ideas: *The meeting threw up some interesting ideas.*

▸noun THROWING ▷ **1** [C] an act of throwing something: *a throw of the dice* EACH ▷ **2 a throw** [S] informal used to mean each thing or for each time: *We could get a coffee in there but they charge two quid a throw.*

throwaway /ˈθrəʊ.ə.weɪ/ US /ˈθroʊ-/ adj [before noun] **1** made to be destroyed after use: *throwaway cups and plates* ◦ *We live in a throwaway society.* **2 throwaway comment/line/remark** something that someone says without thinking carefully and is not intended to be serious

throwback /ˈθrəʊ.bæk/ US /ˈθroʊ-/ noun [C usually singular] a person or thing that is similar to an earlier type: *He's an unappealing throwback **to** the days of 80s City slickers.*

thru /θruː/ preposition US not standard through

thrush /θrʌʃ/ noun BIRD ▷ **1** [C] (also **song thrush**) a brown bird with a pale breast with spots on it that is known for its singing INFECTION ▷ **2** [U] an infection of the VAGINA or mouth

thrust /θrʌst/ verb; noun

▸verb [I or T, usually + adv/prep] (**thrust, thrust**) to push suddenly and strongly: *She thrust the money **into** his hand.* ◦ *They thrust a microphone in front of me and fired questions at me.* ◦ *She thrust the papers **at** me (= towards me).* ◦ *The bodyguards thrust past the crowd to get at the cameraman.*

PHRASAL VERB **thrust sth on/upon sb** [often passive] to force someone to accept or deal with something: *Fatherhood had been thrust on him.*

▸noun IDEA ▷ **1** [S] the main idea, subject or opinion that is discussed or written about: *The **main** thrust **of** her argument was that women are compromised by the demands of childcare.* PUSH ▷ **2** [C] a strong push **3** [U] specialized the driving force produced by, for example, an aircraft engine

thud /θʌd/ noun [C] the sound that is made when something heavy falls or hits something else: *The boy fell to the ground **with a** thud.* ◦ *I could hear the thud **of** horses' hoofs down the track.* • **thud** verb [I] (plural **-dd-**)

thug /θʌɡ/ noun [C] a man who acts violently, especially to commit a crime: *Some thugs smashed his windows.* • **thuggish** /ˈθʌɡ.ɪʃ/ adj informal *a thuggish-looking youth with a shaven head and tattoos on his arms*

thumb /θʌm/ noun; verb

▸noun [C] B1 the short, thick finger on the side of your hand which makes it possible to hold and pick things up easily

IDIOMS **all (fingers and) thumbs** informal very awkward with your hands: *Can you untangle this thread for me? I'm all thumbs today.* • **thumbs down** informal used to show disapproval of something: *They've **given** our plan the thumbs down (= they have disagreed with our plan).* • **thumbs up** informal used to show approval of something • **under sb's thumb** under someone's control: *He's got the committee firmly under his thumb – they agree to whatever he asks.*

▸verb **1 thumb a lift** informal to stand near the edge of a road and hold out your hand with the thumb raised as a signal for a vehicle to stop and take you somewhere: *We thumbed a lift **to** London.* **2 thumb your nose at sb/sth** to show no respect, or to raise the end of your thumb to the end of your nose to show that you do not respect someone: *He has thumbed his nose at authority all his life.*

PHRASAL VERB **thumb through sth** to turn the pages of a book, magazine, or a document quickly and only read small parts of it: *'Have you read the report?' 'Well, I thumbed through it quickly on the train.'*

thumbnail /ˈθʌm.neɪl/ noun [C] FINGER ▷ **1** the nail on the thumb PICTURE ▷ **2** a small picture of an image or page on a computer screen

ˌthumbnail ˈsketch noun [C] a short description mentioning only the most important features

thumbscrew /ˈθʌm.skruː/ noun [C] (also **screws**) a device used especially in the past to TORTURE people (= cause them great pain) by crushing their thumbs

thumbtack /ˈθʌm.tæk/ noun [C] US for **drawing pin**

thump /θʌmp/ verb; noun

▸verb [I or T] **1** to hit someone with your FIST (= closed hand) or to hit something and cause a noise: *He thumped him in the face.* ◦ *He thumped **on** the door but nobody came.* **2 sb's head thumps** If your head thumps, you can feel pain in strong beats in your head: *When I woke up my mouth was dry and my head was thumping.* **3 sb's heart thumps** If your heart thumps, it beats more strongly and quickly than usual, because of exercise, fear, or excitement: *She stood outside his room, her heart thumping.*

▸noun [C usually singular] **1** an act of thumping someone or something: *If he does that again I'm going to **give** him a thump (= hit him with my closed hand).* **2** the sound of something heavy hitting something: *She fell to the floor with a thump.*

thumping /ˈθʌm.pɪŋ/ adj; adv

▸adj [before noun] informal **1** very big or important: *a thumping defeat/victory* ◦ *They won by a thumping majority.* **2 thumping headache** a bad headache that is felt in strong, painful beats

▸adv informal extremely or importantly: *I'm not carrying that thumping **great** thing around with me!*

thunder /ˈθʌn.dəʳ/ US /-dɚ/ noun; verb

▸noun **1** B1 [U] the sudden loud noise which comes from the sky especially during a storm: *a **clap** of thunder* ◦ *thunder **and lightning*** **2** [S] a continuous loud noise: *I couldn't hear what he was saying over the thunder **of** the waterfall.*

▸verb **1** [I] When it thunders, a loud noise comes from the sky: *The sky grew dark and it started to thunder.* **2** [I + adv/prep] to move, making a lot of noise: *The train thundered past, shaking the whole house.* **3** [I] to shout angrily: [+ speech] *'I never want to see you here again!' he thundered.* • **thundering** /-ɪŋ/ noun [U] *We could*

T

hear the thundering (= continuous loud noise) of the guns all night.

thunderbolt /'θʌn.də.bəʊlt/ (US) /-dɚ.boʊlt/ **noun** **THUNDER** ▷ **1** [C] a flash of LIGHTNING and the sound of thunder together **SURPRISE/SHOCK** ▷ **2** [S] an announcement, event, or idea that is completely unexpected or shocking: *He dropped a thunderbolt on us this morning, when he told us that we were closing down.*

thunderclap /'θʌn.də.klæp/ (US) /-dɚ-/ **noun** [C] a single loud sound of thunder

thundercloud /'θʌn.də.klaʊd/ (US) /-dɚ-/ **noun** [C usually plural] a large, dark cloud which produces thunder and LIGHTNING

thunderous /'θʌn.dᵊr.əs/ (US) /-dɚ.əs/ **adj** [before noun] extremely loud: *thunderous applause*

thunderstorm /'θʌn.də.stɔːm/ (US) /-dɚ.stɔːrm/ **noun** [C] (A2) a storm with thunder and LIGHTNING and usually heavy rain

thunderstruck /'θʌn.də.strʌk/ (US) /-dɚ-/ **adj** [after verb] very surprised: *Ruth was thunderstruck when he presented her with an engagement ring.*

thundery /'θʌn.dᵊr.i/ (US) /-dɚ.i/ **adj** describes weather or a storm, etc. in which there is thunder

Thur. (also **Thurs.**) written abbreviation for Thursday

Thursday /'θɜːz.deɪ/ (US) /'θɝːz-/ **noun** [C or U] (written abbreviation **Thur.**, **Thurs.**) (A1) the day of the week after Wednesday and before Friday: *I'm having my hair cut after work* ***on*** *Thursday.* ◦ *The shops stay open late* ***on*** *Thursdays.* ◦ *Bye! See you* ***next*** *Thursday!* ◦ *Do you remember that book we were talking about* ***last*** *Thursday?* ◦ *This year my birthday is on a Thursday.* ◦ *Thursday* ***morning/afternoon/evening/night***

thus /ðʌs/ **adv** formal **1** in this way: *Bend from the waist, thus.* **2** (B2) with this result: *They planned to reduce staff and thus to cut costs.* **3 thus far** as far as this or until now: *We haven't had any problems thus far.*

thwack /θwæk/ **noun; verb**

▸**noun** [C] the short, loud sound of something like a stick hitting a surface: *I heard the thwack of the whip against the horse's side.*

▸**verb** [T] to hit something, making a short, loud sound

thwart /θwɔːt/ (US) /θwɔːrt/ **verb** [T] to stop something from happening or someone from doing something: *My holiday plans have been thwarted by the strike.*

thx written abbreviation for thanks

thy /ðaɪ/ **determiner** old use your: the possessive form of THOU, used when speaking to one person

T

thyme /taɪm/ **noun** [U] a herb used in cooking

thyroid (gland) /'θaɪ.rɔɪd,glænd/ (US) /'θaɪ-/ **noun** [C] a GLAND (= an organ) in the front of the neck that is involved in controlling the way the body develops and works

thyroxine (also **thyroxin**) /θaɪ'rɒk.sɪn/ (US) /-'rɑːk-/ **noun** [U] specialized a HORMONE produced by the thyroid GLAND that controls METABOLISM (= chemical processes in the body) and is important for normal development in children

thyself /ðaɪ'self/ **pronoun** old use yourself: the REFLEXIVE form or strong form of THOU, used when speaking to one person

ti (also **te**) /tiː/ **noun** [S] the seventh note in the SOL-FA musical SCALE

tia written abbreviation for thanks in advance: used in an email when you ask someone for information or want them to do something for you

tiara /ti'ɑː.rə/ (US) /-'er.ə/ **noun** [C] a piece of metal in the shape of half a circle decorated with JEWELS (= precious stones) that is worn on the head by a woman, especially a queen, etc., at very formal social occasions

tiara

tibia /'tɪb.i.ə/ **noun** [C] (plural **tibiae** /'tɪb.i.iː/ or **tibias**) specialized the large bone at the front of the lower leg)

tic /tɪk/ **noun** [C] a sudden and uncontrolled small movement, especially of the face, especially because of a nervous illness

tick /tɪk/ **noun; verb**

▸**noun** **MARK** ▷ **1** (A2) [C] mainly UK (US usually **check**) a mark (✓) that shows that something is correct or has been done: ***Put*** *a tick* ***by/against*** *the names of the people who have accepted the invitation.* **SHORT TIME** ▷ **2** [C] UK informal a very short time: ***Hold on/Hang on a*** *tick – I'm not quite ready.* ◦ *I'll* ***be with you in a tick/in two*** *ticks.* **SOUND** ▷ **3** [C usually singular] the sound clocks and watches make every second **PAYING LATER** ▷ **4 on tick** UK old-fashioned informal If you buy something on tick, you pay for it later. **ANIMAL** ▷ **5** [C] a very small creature like an insect which lives on and sucks the blood of other animals

▸**verb** **SOUND** ▷ **1** (C2) [I] When a clock or watch ticks, it makes a sound every second. **MARK** ▷ **2** (A1) [T] mainly UK (US usually **check**) to mark something with a tick: *Tick* ***(off)*** *each item on the list as you complete it.*

IDIOM **what makes sb tick** If you know what makes someone tick, you understand why they behave the way they do.

PHRASAL VERBS **tick away/by** If time ticks away/by, it goes past: *With the final seconds ticking away, Milan scored a goal.* • **tick sb off** **SPEAK SEVERELY** ▷ **1** UK informal to speak severely to and criticize someone who has done something wrong: *I had to tick him off for being late again.* **ANNOY** ▷ **2** US informal to annoy someone: *It really ticks me off when she doesn't keep her promises.* • **tick over** **ACTIVITY** ▷ **1** If a business, job, or system is ticking over, it continues to work but makes little progress: *I'll be able to* ***keep*** *things ticking over in the office until you get back.* **ENGINE** ▷ **2** If the engine of a vehicle is ticking over, the engine is operating slowly although the vehicle is not moving: *I've left the car with the engine ticking over.*

ticker /'tɪk.əʳ/ (US) /-ɚ/ **noun** [C] **HEART** ▷ **1** informal a heart **SCREEN** ▷ **2** a moving area on a screen that shows changing information such as news or SHARE prices: *A* ***stock*** *ticker runs along the screen, so that you can check your portfolio.*

'ticker ˌtape **noun** [U] **1** a long, thin strip of paper, used in the past for printing changing information on, for example SHARE prices **2** a moving area on a screen that shows changing information such as SHARE prices

'ticker-tape paˌrade **noun** [C] US a special celebration in which someone who is being shown respect for achieving something very important walks or drives along streets in a city and small pieces of paper are thrown over them from the windows of tall buildings

ticket /'tɪk.ɪt/ **noun** [C] **PROOF OF PAYMENT** ▷ **1** (A1) a small piece of paper or card given to someone, usually to show that they have paid for an event, journey, or activity: *a concert ticket* ◦ *a train/bus/plane ticket* ◦ *a lottery/raffle ticket* ◦ *a ticket office* ◦ *a ticket collector* **PRICE CARD** ▷ **2** a piece of card or paper that is put on an object to show its size or price: ***a price***

ticket **3** a note telling you that you must pay some money as a punishment for not obeying a rule or law: *a parking ticket* **POLITICS** ▷ **4** mainly US the range of ideas and plans that someone supports when they are in an election: *She's standing on an education ticket.* **5** US the group of people representing a particular political party in an election: *the Republican/Democratic ticket*

Word partners for ticket

book/buy/get/purchase a ticket • a *one-way/return/single* ticket • a *valid* ticket • an *adult/family/student* ticket • a ticket *for/to* sth • a ticket *collector/machine/office*

IDIOM **just the ticket** old-fashioned informal very suitable and exactly what is needed

ticketing /ˈtɪk.ɪ.tɪŋ/ (US) /-t̬ɪŋ/ **noun** [U] the production or selling of tickets: *Electronic ticketing now allows customers to buy airline seats over the phone.*

ticketless /ˈtɪk.ɪt.ləs/ **adj, adv** **1** without a ticket: *Ticketless fans were told to stay away from the match.* ◦ *Over 17,000 people were fined for travelling ticketless in March.* **2** without using a printed ticket: *Travel is ticketless and bookings are confirmed by email.* ◦ *By the end of the year, 30 percent of passengers will be flying ticketless.*

ˌticking ˈoff noun [S] mainly UK informal severe criticism because you have done something wrong: *I **gave** her a real ticking off yesterday.*

tickle /ˈtɪk.l̩/ **verb; noun**

▸verb **RUB SKIN** ▷ **1** [T] to touch someone lightly with your fingers, making them slightly uncomfortable and often making them laugh: *Stop! You're tickling me!* ◦ *I tickled her feet and she laughed.* **2** [I or T] If a part of the body tickles, or if something tickles it, it feels slightly uncomfortable and you want to rub it: *My nose is tickling, I think I'm going to sneeze.* **PLEASE** ▷ **3** [T often passive] informal If something tickles you, you find it funny or it pleases you: old-fashioned *I was tickled **pink** (= very pleased) to hear the news.*

IDIOM **tickle sb's fancy** informal If something tickles your fancy, you like it and want to have it: *Does anything on the menu tickle your fancy?*

▸noun [S] **TOUCH** ▷ **1 give sb a tickle** to tickle someone **COUGH** ▷ **2** an unpleasant feeling in your throat which makes you want to cough

ticklish /ˈtɪk.l̩.ɪʃ/, /-lɪʃ/ **adj** **SKIN** ▷ **1** If someone is ticklish, they quickly feel uncomfortable when someone lightly touches their skin to make them laugh. **DIFFICULT** ▷ **2** A ticklish situation is one that needs to be dealt with carefully: *This leaves me with the ticklish job of explaining to Debbie that she is not invited.*

tic-tac-toe (also **tick-tack-toe**) /ˌtɪk.tækˈtəʊ/ (US) /-ˈtoʊ/ **noun** [U] US for **noughts and crosses**

tidal /ˈtaɪ.dəl/ **adj** relating to the TIDE: *a tidal river*

ˈtidal ˌwave noun [C] **SEA** ▷ **1** an extremely large wave caused by movement of the earth under the sea, often caused by an EARTHQUAKE (= a shaking of the earth) → Compare **tsunami** **LARGE NUMBER** ▷ **2** a sudden large number of things: *a tidal wave **of** complaints*

tidbit /ˈtɪd.bɪt/ **noun** [C] US for **titbit**

tiddler /ˈtɪd.l.əʳ/, /-ləʳ/ (US) /-l̩.ɚ/, /-lɚ/ **noun** [C] informal **1** something very small, especially a fish **2** a child

tiddly /ˈtɪd.l̩.i/, /-li/ **adj** informal **SMALL** ▷ **1** extremely small: *All you ate was a tiddly little piece of cake.* **DRUNK** ▷ **2** UK old-fashioned slightly drunk

tiddlywinks /ˈtɪd.l̩.i.wɪŋks/, /-li-/ **noun** [U] a game in which players try to get small plastic discs into a cup by pressing one piece against another to make it fly through the air • **tiddlywink** /-wɪŋk/ **noun** [C] one of the pieces used in the game of tiddlywinks

tide /taɪd/ **noun; verb**

▸noun **SEA** ▷ **1** (B2) [C] the rise and fall of the sea that happens twice every day: *high/low tide* ◦ *The tide is **out/in**.* **CHANGE** ▷ **2** [S] literary a noticeable change in a situation or increase in a particular type of behaviour: *We must look for ways of **stemming** (= stopping) the rising tide **of** protest.*

IDIOMS **go/swim against the tide** to not follow what everyone else is doing • **go/swim with the tide** to follow what everyone else is doing: *I thought I'd just swim with the tide and leave when everyone else does.*

▸verb

PHRASAL VERB **tide sb over (sth)** to help someone to work or operate normally through a difficult period, usually by lending them money: *Can you lend me some money to tide me over till the weekend?*

-tide /-taɪd/ **suffix** old use a period of time: *Yuletide*

tidemark /ˈtaɪd.mɑːk/ (US) /-mɑːrk/ **noun** [C] **1** (also **high water mark**) a line of waste left on a beach which marks the highest point the sea reaches **2** UK a dirty mark around a bath or SINK, left by the water

ˈtide ˌtable noun [C] a list of the times at which the tide in a particular place is high each day

tidings /ˈtaɪ.dɪŋz/ **noun** [plural] old use news: *tidings of great joy*

tidy /ˈtaɪ.di/ **adj; noun; verb**

▸adj **ORDERED** ▷ **1** (A2) having everything ordered and arranged in the right place, or liking to keep things like this: *The house was clean and tidy.* ◦ *My flatmate isn't very tidy.* ◦ ***neat and** tidy* ◦ *a tidy solution* **LARGE** ▷ **2** [before noun] informal (of amounts of money) large: *His business deals make him a tidy sum.* • **tidily** /-dɪ.li/ **adv** *Put your clothes away tidily.* • **tidiness** /-nəs/ **noun** [U]

▸noun **a desk, car, sink, etc. tidy** a small container for a few objects, that makes it easier for you to keep your desk, car, etc. tidy

▸verb [I or T] (A2) to make a place or a collection of things tidy: *Tidy (**up**) these papers before you leave, please.* ◦ *I'm tired of asking you to tidy your room (**up**).* ◦ *Have you tidied **up** yet, kids?* • **ˌtidy-ˈup** **noun** [S] *Let's have/do a quick tidy-up before mum gets home.*

PHRASAL VERB **tidy sth away** to put things back in drawers, cupboards, and other places where they are kept, after you have used them: *The children were expected to tidy away their toys before bedtime.*

tie /taɪ/ **verb; noun**

▸verb (present tense **tying**, past tense and past participle **tied**) **FASTEN** ▷ **1** (B1) [I or T] to fasten together two ends of a piece of string or other long, thin material, or to (cause to) hold together with a long, thin piece of string, material, etc.: *Could you tie this piece of string for me?* ◦ *This skirt ties at the waist.* ◦ *She tied the ribbon tightly **in** a bow/knot.* ◦ *I tie my hair **back** when it's hot.* ◦ *Tie (**up**) your shoelaces, or you'll trip over.* **2 be tied to sth/sb** If you are tied to a job, place, or person, you are forced to stay with them: *I felt tied to the job while I had a mortgage to pay.* **RELATE** ▷ **3** [T] to relate to or connect to: *Is the allergy tied **to** dairy products, for example?* ◦ *Can you tie his behaviour **up with** anything that's happened recently?* **FINISH EQUAL** ▷ **4** [I] to finish at the same time or score the same number of points, etc. in a competition as

T

someone or something else: *Jane and I tied (**for** first place) in the spelling test.* ◦ *We tied **with** a team from the south in the championships.*

IDIOMS **tie sb (up) in knots** informal to confuse someone: *The Director of Studies tied me up in knots by asking tricky questions.* • **tie the knot** informal C2 to get married: *So when are you two going to tie the knot?* • **tied to your mother's/wife's apron strings** disapproving If you say that someone, especially a man, is tied to his mother's/wife's apron strings, it means that he is strongly influenced and controlled by that person: *George never comes out with the rest of us – he's tied to his wife's apron strings.*

PHRASAL VERBS **tie sb down** informal **LIMIT** ▷ **1** [M often passive] to limit someone's freedom: *He's tied down **by** having to work every Saturday.* ◦ *We'd like to travel more, but having children at school really ties us down.* **GET DECISION** ▷ **2** to make someone give you a clear decision: *I'll try to tie her down **on** her plans.* • **tie (sth) in** When ideas or statements tie in, they agree or are closely connected, and if you tie them in, you make them agree or connect closely: *I can't tie in what he said today **with** what he told me last week.* • **tie (sth) in with sth** to plan an event or activity so that it combines with or happens at the same time as another, or to be planned in this way: *We're trying to tie our holiday in with Simon's lecture tour.* • **tie sb up** **FASTENED** ▷ **1** B2 to make a person unable to move by tying a rope or something similar around their body or part of their body: *The burglars had tied him up (**to** the bed).* **NOT AVAILABLE** ▷ **2** When someone is tied up, they are busy or are prevented from doing something, such as speaking to someone or going somewhere, because they are involved in another event or activity: *Mrs Moran is tied up **in** a meeting at the moment, but I'll ask her to call you later.* • **tie sth up** **FASTENED** ▷ **1** to fasten something together using string, rope or something similar: *Could you tie up the parcel for me?* **NOT AVAILABLE** ▷ **2** to cause something, often money or possessions, not to be available for use: *All my money is tied up **in** property.* ◦ *He tied up the printer all morning, printing out his reports.*

▸**noun** [C] **FASTENING** ▷ **1** A2 (US also **necktie**) a long, thin piece of material that is worn under a shirt collar, especially by men, and tied in a knot at the front: *He always wears a jacket and tie to work.* **2** any piece of string, plastic, metal, etc. that is used to fasten or hold together something: *Can you see the ties for the rubbish bags in the cupboard?* **CONNECTION** ▷ **3 ties** C2 [plural] the friendly feelings that people have for other people, or special connections with places: *Family ties are weaker if you move a long way away.* ◦ *I no longer feel any ties **with** my home town.* ◦ *He urged governments worldwide to break **diplomatic** ties with the new regime.* **EQUAL FINISH** ▷ **4** C2 a situation in which two or more people finish at the same time or score the same number of points: *It's a tie **for** first place.* ◦ *They have changed the scoring system because there have been too many ties.*

ˈtie-ˌbreaker noun [C] (UK also **ˈtie-ˌbreak**) extra play at the end of a game when both teams have the same points, to decide who is the winner

ˌtied ˈcottage noun [C] (also **ˌtied ˈhouse**) UK a house owned by your employer that you can live in for as long as you are employed in a particular job

ˌtied ˈhouse noun [C] UK a pub that is owned by a particular beer company and only sells that company's products → Compare **free house**

ˈtie-dye verb [T] (present tense **tie-dyeing**, past tense and past participle **tie-dyed**) to colour cloth by tying it in knots so that when it is put in a DYE (= substance for changing the colour of cloth) the tied areas absorb less colour and produce circular patterns when unfastened: *There are pictures of us in the 60s wearing flares and tie-dyed T-shirts.*

ˈtie-in noun [C] a product such as a toy or book that is related to a film, television programme, etc. • **ˈtie-in** adj [before noun] *The movie has a tie-in book.*

tiepin /ˈtaɪ.pɪn/ noun [C] a small, thin, often decorative piece of metal used to hold the two parts of a TIE together

tier /tɪəʳ/ US /tɪr/ **noun; verb**

▸**noun** [C] one of several layers or levels: *We sat in one of the upper tiers of the football stands.* ◦ *My wedding cake had four tiers, each supported by small pillars.* ◦ *I don't understand why you think we need yet another tier of management.*

▸**verb** [T often passive] to arrange or organize something in tiers: *The seats in the theatre were steeply tiered.* • **-tiered** /tɪəd/ US /tɪrd/ **suffix** *a two-tiered structure* ◦ *a three-tiered cake*

ˈtie-up noun [C] **CONNECTION** ▷ **1** mainly UK a connection or agreement that joins two things or organizations: *Cambridge University Press arranged a tie-up **with** the German publisher Klett.* **DELAY** ▷ **2** US a temporary problem that delays progress, such as too much traffic on the road: *I missed my flight because of a tie-up on the interstate.*

tiff /tɪf/ noun [C] informal a slight argument: *Have you two **had** a **lovers'** tiff?*

tiffin /ˈtɪf.ɪn/ noun [U] old use or Indian English a small meal, especially one that you eat in the middle of the day

ˈtiffin-ˌcarrier noun [C] Indian English a container in which your lunch can be carried to work, school, etc.

tiger /ˈtaɪ.gəʳ/ US /-gɚ/ noun [C] (female also **tigress**) B1 a large wild animal of the cat family with yellowish-orange fur with black lines that lives in parts of Asia

tight /taɪt/ **adj, adv; adj**

▸**adj, adv** B2 (held or kept together) firmly or closely: *I can't untie the knot – it's too tight.* ◦ *This lid is on very tight.* ◦ *The people stood talking in tight groups.* ◦ *Hold on tight when we go round this corner.* ◦ *Check that windows and doors are shut tight (= completely closed) before you leave.* ◦ *The plastic cover was stretched tight (= stretched as much as it could be) across the tank.* → See also **airtight, watertight**

▸**adj** **UNCOMFORTABLE** ▷ **1** B1 Clothes or shoes that are tight fit the body too closely and are uncomfortable: *That jacket's too tight – you want a bigger size.* **2** If you have a tight feeling in your chest you have an uncomfortable feeling of pressure, caused by illness, fear, etc. **LIMITING** ▷ **3** B2 Controls or rules that are tight are ones that severely limit what can happen: *tight security* **NOT MUCH** ▷ **4** B2 If time or money is tight, there is only just enough of it: *I'm sorry I can't stop, time's really tight.* ◦ *They're raising three kids on one small salary so money is very tight.* **NOT GENEROUS** ▷ **5** informal disapproving **tight-fisted** **DRUNK** ▷ **6** old-fashioned informal having drunk too much alcohol: *Jim, you're tight!* → Synonym **drunk** **RELATIONSHIP** ▷ **7** informal If you are tight with someone, you know them very well and like them a lot: *We're tight – we've been best friends since we were at school.* • **tightness** /ˈtaɪt.nəs/ noun [U]

IDIOM **be in a tight corner/spot** C2 to be in a difficult situation

tighten /ˈtaɪ.tᵊn/ verb [I or T] B2 to become tighter or to make something become tighter, firmer, or less easy to move: *Tighten the straps so they don't rub.* ◦ *As he struggled, the ropes tightened even more.*

IDIOMS **tighten your belt** C2 to spend less money than you did before because you have less money: *I've had to tighten my belt since I stopped working full-time.* • **tighten the net** (especially of the police) to become closer to catching someone, especially a criminal: *The police are tightening the net **around** the smugglers.*

PHRASAL VERBS **tighten sth up** to make something become tighter, firmer, or less easy to move: *Now tighten up the screws.* • **tighten (sth) up** to make a rule, system, or law stronger and more difficult to avoid or ignore: *Are there any plans to tighten up **on** advertising controls?*

ˌtight-ˈfisted adj (also **tight**) informal disapproving unwilling to spend money: *Don't imagine Gillian will buy you a drink – she's too tight-fisted.*

ˌtight-ˈlipped adj If someone is tight-lipped, they are pressing their lips together to avoid showing anger or they are refusing to speak about something: *He's been very tight-lipped about what happened at the meeting.*

tightly /ˈtaɪt.li/ adv B2 firmly or closely: *The baby was clutching his dummy tightly in his grubby fist.* ◦ *Many commuters are forced to stand, tightly packed in, like sardines.*

tightrope /ˈtaɪt.rəʊp/ US /-roʊp/ noun [C] a tightly stretched wire or rope fixed high above the ground, which skilled people walk across, especially in order to entertain others: *One of the acrobats who **walked** the tightrope at the circus did it blindfolded.*

IDIOM **walk/tread a tightrope** If you walk/tread a tightrope, you have to deal with a difficult situation, especially one involving making a decision between two opposing plans of action: *Many manufacturers have to walk a tightrope **between** pricing their goods too high and not selling them, and pricing them low and losing money.*

tights /taɪts/ noun [plural] **1** A2 UK (US **pantyhose**) a piece of clothing made of thin material that covers the legs and lower part of the body below the waist, worn by women and girls: *She bought a new **pair of** tights.* ◦ *Oh no, I've got a ladder/run/hole in my tights.* **2** the same type of clothing made from thicker material and worn by dancers and people doing exercise

ˌtight ˈturn noun [C] (also **ˌtight ˈbend**) a sudden, sharp turn

tightwad /ˈtaɪt.wɒd/ US /-wɑːd/ noun [C] US slang disapproving a person who is not willing to spend money: *There's no point in asking Joe to pay for it – he's a real tightwad.*

tigress /ˈtaɪ.grəs/ noun [C] **ANIMAL** ▷ **1** a female TIGER **WOMAN** ▷ **2** a woman who is behaving very violently: *Jean can be a real tigress if she feels criticized.*

tike /taɪk/ noun [C] **tyke**

tikka /ˈtɪk.ə/, /ˈtiːk.ə/ noun [C or U] Indian English **1** in South Asian cooking, a mixture of spices and YOGURT (= slightly sour, thick milk) used in preparing meat, cheese, etc. for some dishes and in the names of these dishes: *chicken tikka* **2** in South Asian cooking, meat in small pieces

tilde /ˈtɪl.də/ noun [C] (used when writing some languages) a ~ mark made above a letter, especially n, to show that the letter has a special sound

tile /taɪl/ noun; verb

▸noun [C] a thin, usually square or rectangular piece of baked clay, plastic, etc. used for covering roofs, floors, walls, etc.: *roof tiles* ◦ *floor tiles* ◦ *ceramic tiles*

IDIOM **be/go out on the tiles** UK informal to enjoy yourself at night by going out to NIGHTCLUBS, parties, or bars: *I was out on the tiles last night and I've got such a headache this morning.*

▸verb [T] to cover a wall or floor with tiles: *We're going to tile the bathroom.*

tiled /taɪld/ adj (of a surface) covered with tiles: *The kitchen has a tiled floor.*

tiler /ˈtaɪ.ləʳ/ US /-lɚ/ noun [C] a person who fixes tiles to a surface: *Can you recommend a good tiler?*

till /tɪl/ preposition, conjunction; noun; verb

▸preposition, conjunction A2 up to (the time that); until: *We waited till half past six for you.* ◦ ***Up** till 1918, women in Britain were not allowed to vote.* ◦ *How long is it till your baby is due?*

▸noun [C] mainly UK (US usually **register**) the drawer in a CASH REGISTER (= a machine which records sales in a shop, and in which money is kept) or the CASH REGISTER itself: *Next time you have the till open, could you give me some change?* ◦ *I think these items have been **rung up** wrongly **on** the till.*

▸verb [T] to prepare and use land for growing crops: *This piece of land has been tilled for hundreds of years.*

tiller /ˈtɪl.əʳ/ US /-ɚ/ noun [C] a long handle fixed to and used to turn a RUDDER (= blade at the back of a boat used to control the boat's direction)

tilt /tɪlt/ verb; noun

▸verb [I or T] to (cause to) move into a sloping position: *He tilted his chair backwards and put his feet up on his desk.* ◦ *Anna looked up at him with her head tilted to one side.* ◦ *The front seats of the car tilt.*

IDIOMS **tilt at windmills** literary to fight enemies who do not really exist • **tilt the balance/scales** (also **tip the balance/scales**) If something tilts the balance, it is the thing that causes a particular situation to happen or a particular decision to be made when other situations or decisions are possible: *This might just tilt the balance in the government's favour.*

▸noun [C usually singular] a sloping position or a move in a particular direction, especially up or down: *She wore her hat **at** a tilt.* ◦ figurative *There has been a tilt **to/towards/away from** the socialists among some groups of young people.*

IDIOM **at full tilt** as fast as possible: *The plant is operating at full tilt to cope with demand.*

timber /ˈtɪm.bəʳ/ US /-bɚ/ noun; exclamation

▸noun **1** C2 [U] trees that are grown so that the wood from them can be used for building: *a timber forest* ◦ *These trees are being grown for timber.* **2** C2 [U] UK (US **lumber**) wood used for building: *a timber merchant* **3** C2 [C] a long piece of wood used for building, especially houses and ships: *roof timbers* ◦ *a timber-framed building*

▸exclamation shouted when a tree that has been cut is about to fall

the timberline /ˈtɪm.bə.laɪn/ US /-bɚ-/ noun [U] US for **the treeline**

timbre /ˈtæm.bəʳ/ US /-bɚ/ noun [U] specialized a quality of sound which makes voices or musical instruments different from each other: *He has a wonderful singing voice, with a rich timbre and resonant tone.*

time noun; verb

▸noun **MINUTES/DAYS/YEARS** ▷ **1** A2 [U] that part of existence that is measured in seconds, minutes,

T

hours, days, weeks, months, years, etc., or this process considered as a whole: *He wants to* ***spend*** *more time with his family.* ◦ *Time* ***passes*** *so quickly when you're enjoying yourself.* ◦ *She grew more and more fascinated by the subject as time* ***went on/by***. ◦ *The curtains have faded* ***over/with*** *time (= as years have gone past).* ◦ *You'll forget her* ***in*** *time (= in the future).* ◦ *Over the course of time (= as years have gone past), holes have formed in the rock.* ◦ *I only worked there for a short* ***period of*** *time.* ◦ *I'd like to visit them all but time* ***is short*** *(= there is little time left).* **2 all the time** A2 continuously: *I wish you'd stop criticizing me all the time.* **3 at the same time** B1 If two things happen at the same time, they happen together: *We arrived at the same time.* **4 for some time** B2 for a fairly long period of time: *I've been doing yoga for some time.* **5 waste time** A2 to not make good use of the hours, etc. that you have available: *If you'd got on with your work instead of wasting time chatting, you'd be finished by now.* **6 in no time** C1 (also **in next to no time**) very quickly or very soon: *The children ate their dinner in no time.* **7 no time to lose** If you say there is or that you have no time to lose, it means that you must do quickly whatever it is that you want to do: *Come on, there's no time to lose, we must get home before John finds out.* **8 for all time** literary always: *I will love you for all time.* **9 of all time** that has ever lived or existed: *She's been called the greatest opera singer of all time.* **ABLE TO DO STH** ▷ **10 have time** B1 If you have got time, you have enough time to do something: *We haven't got much time before the train leaves.* ◦ *Have you got time* ***for*** *a quick drink after work?* ◦ *I'd like to learn to sail, but I haven't* ***the*** *time (= I am too busy).* ◦ [+ to infinitive] *I haven't got time* ***to*** *go to the shops today.* **11 run out of time** B1 to not have enough hours, etc. available to finish something you are trying to do: *She ran out of time and didn't finish the last question.* **12 be (all) out of time** to not have enough minutes, etc. available: *I'd like to continue this discussion but we're all out of time.* **13 time's up** informal there are no more minutes, hours, etc. available: *OK everyone, time's up for this week – see you all again at next week's class.* **PARTICULAR POINT** ▷ **14** A1 [C or S or U] a particular point in the day, as expressed in hours and minutes or shown on a clock, or a particular point in the day, week, month, or year, etc.: *'What's* ***the*** *time?' 'It's ten o'clock.'* ◦ *What time is it?* ◦ *What time do you finish work?* ◦ *Have you got* ***the*** *time? (= Do you know what time it is?)* ◦ *He's teaching his daughter to* ***tell*** *the time (= to recognize what time it is by looking at a clock).* ◦ *Did you find out the times* ***of*** *the trains to London (= the particular points in the day at which they leave)?* ◦ *The estimated time* ***of*** *arrival/departure of this flight is 11.15.* ◦ *Oh dear, is that the* ***(right)*** *time (= is it really so late)?* ◦ *The kitchen clock is* ***gaining/losing*** *time (= is showing a particular point in the day that is increasingly later or earlier than the real one).* ◦ *My watch has never* ***kept*** *very good time (= been correct in showing what particular point in the day it is).* ◦ *We always have dinner* ***at the same*** *time every day.* ◦ *I was exhausted* ***by the*** *time (= when) I got home.* ◦ *'What would be the best time* ***of day*** *for us to deliver the table?' 'Oh, any time will be OK.'* ◦ *Today's temperatures will be normal* ***for the*** *time* ***of*** *year (= will be as they are expected to be at this particular point in the year).* ◦ *Just think,* ***this*** *time (= at the same particular point during) next week we'll be in Mauritius.* ◦ *We regret that* ***at the present*** *time* (US also ***at this time***) *(= for now, although it is hoped not in the future) we are unable to supply the goods you ordered.* ◦ *The time is fast* ***drawing near/approaching*** *when (= it will soon be the particular point at which) we'll have to make a decision one way or the other.* **15** C1 [U] the system of recording hours used in different parts of the world: *Greenwich Mean Time* ◦ *daylight saving time* **SUITABLE POINT** ▷ **16** B1 [S or U] a particular point of the day, week, month, year, etc. that is suitable for a particular activity, or at which something is expected to happen: *holiday time* ◦ *party time* ◦ *Put your toys away now, it's time* ***for*** *bed.* ◦ *It's time* ***(that)*** *I was leaving.* ◦ [+ to infinitive] *Is it time* ***to*** *go home yet?* ◦ *When would be* ***a*** *good time for me to call you?* ◦ *This is not the time (= not a suitable moment) to be thinking about buying a house.* ◦ *This is no time (= not a suitable moment) to change your mind.* ◦ *I feel that the time has* ***come*** *(= now is a suitable moment) for me to move on.* ◦ *The repairs to the road were finished two weeks* ***ahead of*** *time (= sooner than was expected).* ◦ *Why is it that the trains never run* ***on*** *time (= make their journeys in the expected number of hours, etc.)?* ◦ *She's grown old* ***before*** *her time (= sooner than she might have been expected to have done).* **17 in time** B1 early enough: *I got home just in time – it's starting to rain.* ◦ *If we don't hurry up, we won't be in time* ***to*** *catch the train.* ◦ *We arrived in* ***good*** *time (= we arrived early)* ***for*** *the start of the match.* **18 (bang/dead/right) on time** informal happening or done at the particular moment that it was expected to happen or be done: *The bus arrived dead on time.* **19 ahead of time** mainly US earlier than a particular moment: *Let's meet for lunch. I'll call you ahead of time to fix up exactly when and where.* **20 about time** C1 (also **high time**) If it is about time/high time that someone did something, it should have been done sooner or a long time ago: *It's about time* ***(that)*** *the school improved its meals service.* ◦ *It is high time* ***for*** *Europe to take responsibility for its own defence.* **21 about time (too)** (also **not before time**) said when someone does something or something happens that you think should have been done or have happened much sooner: *'So Ben's finally found a job.' 'Yes, and about time too.'* **OCCASION** ▷ **22** A2 [C] an occasion or period, or the experience connected with it: *The last time we went to Paris, it rained every day.* ◦ ***Every*** *time/****Each*** *time I ask you to do something, you always say you're too busy.* ◦ *They go swimming three or four times a week.* ◦ *There are times* ***when*** *I wish I didn't live where I do.* ◦ *The four-times* (US *four-time*) *champion (= the person who had been the winner on four occasions in the past) was defeated in the second round.* ◦ *If I'd known* ***at*** *the time (= then) that she was his former wife, I'd never have said what I did.* ◦ *Sometimes I enjoy my English lessons, but* ***at*** *other times (= on other occasions) I find them really boring.* ◦ ***For*** *the* ***umpteenth/hundredth/thousandth*** *time, (= I've told you on many occasions to) stop hitting your sister.* ◦ *Did you* ***have*** *a* ***bad/good*** *time (= an unenjoyable/enjoyable experience) at the conference?* ◦ *She had an* ***easy/hard*** *time* ***of it*** *(= a comfortable/uncomfortable experience) with the birth of her second baby.* **23 at all times** continuously: *When you're at the airport, you should make sure you have your luggage with you at all times.* **24 at (any) one time** (also **at a time**, also **at any given time**) at or during any particular point or moment in the day: *Only a certain number of people are allowed in the building at any one time.* ◦ *I'm sorry, but I'm too busy to help you now – I can only do one thing at a time.* **25 at times** C1 sometimes: *You can be really annoying at times, you know.* **26 the times** UK on many occasions: *The times I've told you, ask before you borrow my clothes.* **HISTORICAL PERIOD** ▷ **27** B2 [C] (also **times**) a period in history: *Charles Dickens' novel 'A Tale of Two Cities' is set at the time* ***of*** *the French Revolution.* ◦ ***In/***

T

During medieval times, women thought to be witches were burned at the stake. ◦ ***In*** *times gone by, all crops were harvested by hand.* ◦ *Times* ***were hard*** *(= the conditions of life were uncomfortable) when I was a boy.* ◦ *He is widely regarded as one of the best writers of* ***modern/our*** *times (= the present or very recent past).* ◦ *I never thought it would happen* ***in*** *my time (= before I died).* ◦ *We sat and talked about* ***old*** *times (= things that had happened to us in the past.)* **28 at one time** Ⓒ2 in the past: *At one time, George Eliot lived here.* **29 ahead of your time** (UK also **before your time**) having new ideas, opinions, or ways of living long before most other people do **30 before your time** If something or someone is before your time, they happened or existed before you were born or were old enough to remember them: *I don't remember The Beatles – they were before my time.* → See also **ahead of your time** **31 time was** said to mean that there was a period in the past when something used to happen or be true: *Time was (****when****) you could buy a loaf of bread for sixpence.* **RACE** ▷ **32** [C or U] Your time in a race is the number of minutes, hours, etc. you take to complete it: *Her time* ***for*** *the marathon was just under three hours.* ◦ *He won the 100 metres in* ***record*** *time.* **MUSIC** ▷ **33** [U] the number of beats in a BAR of music, or the speed at which a piece of music is intended to be played: *This piece is written* ***in*** *4/4 time.* ◦ *Small children often have difficulty singing* ***in*** *time* ***with*** *the music (= at the same speed at which the music is being played).* ◦ *It seemed to me as if the violins were playing* ***out of*** *time (= at a different speed from the other instruments playing the same piece of music).* ◦ *To* ***beat*** *time is to make a regular series of sounds at the same speed as a piece of music is intended to be played.* ◦ *Watching the conductor will help you to* ***keep*** *time (= to play the music at the speed at which it is intended to be played).* **PRISON** ▷ **34 do time** informal to spend a period of weeks, months, years, etc. in prison: *It's not always easy to find a job after you've done time.* **DRINKING** ▷ **35** [U] the particular point in the day at which people who are drinking in a bar in Britain have to finish their drinks and leave: *'Time, please,' called the landlord.* ◦ *Is it time already?*

IDIOMS **all the time in the world** a large number of minutes, hours, etc. available: *The doctor made me feel as if she had all the time in the world to listen to my problems.* • **behind the times** Ⓒ1 If someone or something is behind the times, they are old-fashioned. • **be pressed for time** to be in a hurry: *I'd love to stop and chat but I'm rather pressed for time.* • **change with/keep up with/move with the times** to change your ideas, opinions, or way of living or working to make them modern: *I don't really like working on a computer, but you have to move with the times, I suppose.* • **give sb a hard time** informal Ⓒ2 to make things difficult or unpleasant for someone: *Her kids always give her a hard time when she takes them shopping.* ◦ *My mother gave me a really hard time (= was angry with me) about staying out late.* • **give sb the time of day** If someone will not give you the time of day, they are unfriendly and refuse to speak to you: *We had an argument with our neighbours, and now they won't even give us the time of day.* • **have a lot of time for sb** informal to like someone and be interested in them: *She's really nice – I have a lot of time for Helen.* • **have no time for sb** Ⓒ2 to disapprove of someone and not want to be involved with them: *I've got no time for people who are always complaining.* • **have time to kill** to have nothing to do for a particular period: *We've got some time to kill before our train arrives – shall we have a drink?* • **a matter/question of time** used when you think that something will happen at some point in the near future: *If you carry on driving like that, it'll only be a matter of time before you have an accident.* • **there's no time like the present** saying said to encourage someone to take action immediately instead of waiting • **time flies** saying Ⓒ2 used to mean that time passes very and surprisingly quickly: *Time flies when you're having fun.* • **time is money** saying said to emphasize that you should not waste time, because you could be using it to earn money • **time is of the essence** formal said to encourage someone to hurry • **time is on sb's side** (also **have time on your side**) If you say that time is on your side, or that you have time on your side, you mean that you do not have to do quickly whatever it is that you want or have to do: *We don't have to make a final decision till next week, so time is on our side.* • **the time is ripe** If you say that the time is ripe, you mean that it is a suitable point for a particular activity: *I'm waiting till the time is ripe before I tell my parents that I failed my exams.* • **the time of your life** an extremely enjoyable experience: *We had the time of our lives at Ali's party.* • **have time on your hands** to have nothing to do: *Now that her children are all at school, Mary has found that she has time on her hands, so she is taking a college course.* • **time stands still** When time stands still, everything around you seems to stop: *I saw the car coming straight towards me, and for a moment time stood still.* • **(only) time will/can tell** used to say that the truth or a result will only be known in the future after events have happened: *Only time will tell whether we made the right decision.*

▸**verb** [T] /taɪm/ **1** to decide that something will happen at a particular time: [+ to infinitive] *We timed our trip* ***to*** *coincide with my cousin's wedding.* **2** Ⓑ2 to measure how long it takes for something to happen or for someone to do something: *Will you time me to see how long it takes me to swim a length?* **3** to arrange something so that it happens at an exactly suitable time: *If you time your departure carefully, you should be able to miss the worst of the traffic.* ◦ *She won the game with a brilliantly timed shot (= one played at exactly the right moment).*

-time /-taɪm/ **suffix** the stated period of time during the year, day, etc.: *springtime* ◦ *Christmas-time* ◦ *daytime* ◦ *night-time*

ˌtime and a ˈhalf noun [U] the usual pay for a job with half the usual pay added on to it

ˌtime-and-ˈmotion ˌstudy noun [C usually singular] a study of work methods, especially in industry or business, in order to find the most effective way of operating

ˈtime ˌbomb noun [C usually singular] **BOMB** ▷ **1** a bomb containing a device that makes it explode at a particular time **DIFFICULT SITUATION** ▷ **2** a situation that is likely to become difficult to deal with or control: *By ignoring the wishes of their employees, the managers are* ***setting/creating*** *a time bomb for themselves.* ◦ *The prison governors are* ***sitting on*** *a time bomb (= are having to deal with a bad situation that is likely to become difficult to deal with or control).*

ˈtime ˌcapsule noun [C] a container that is filled with objects considered to be typical of the present period in history and then buried, so that it can be dug up and studied much later

ˈtime ˌclock noun [C] a clock which employees use to record the particular point in the day at which they arrive at and leave work

ˈtime-conˌsuming adj Ⓒ1 describes a task that takes

a lot of time to do: *Producing a dictionary is a very time-consuming job.*

ˌtimed ˈticket noun [C] a ticket which allows you to go into a place, such as a famous building which the public is able to visit, at a particular time

ˈtime ˌframe noun [C] a period of days, weeks, months, etc. within which an activity is intended to happen: *Have you* ***set*** *a time frame* ***for*** *completing the job?* ◦ *The government plans to introduce these changes* ***in/within*** *a fairly long/short time frame.*

ˈtime-ˌhonoured adj [before noun] A time-honoured tradition, practice, or method is respected because it has been done or used in the same way for many years: humorous *The developers dealt with the problem* ***in*** *the time-honoured* ***fashion/way****, burying the industrial waste in landfill sites.*

timekeeper /ˈtaɪmˌkiː.pəʳ/ ⓤⓢ /-pɚ/ noun [C] **1** an object or person that records (an amount of) time: *There's no point in having a clock which looks attractive if it isn't a good timekeeper (= if it doesn't show the correct time).* **2** a person who records the amount of time that people taking part in a race or competition take to finish the race or competition, or the amount of time that people at work spend working on their jobs **3 a good/bad timekeeper** a person who usually arrives on time/late for something, especially work

timekeeping /ˈtaɪmˌkiː.pɪŋ/ noun [U] the ability to arrive at a place at the time expected

ˈtime ˌlag noun [C usually singular] a period between two related events: *There's a time lag of about a week* ***between*** *having the blood test and getting the results.*

ˈtime-lapse adj [before noun] describes a method of filming very slow actions by taking a series of single pictures over a period of time and then putting them together to show the action happening very quickly: *time-lapse photography* ◦ *a time-lapse camera/sequence*

timeless /ˈtaɪm.ləs/ adj **NOT CHANGING** ▷ **1** describes something that does not change as the years go past: *The city has a timeless quality as if it had existed forever.* **NOT LIMITED** ▷ **2** having a value that is not limited to a particular period but will last for ever: *a timeless book/play/film/classic* ◦ *timeless values/questions* ◦ *Rothko's paintings have a timeless quality.* • **timelessly** /-li/ **adv** • **timelessness** /-nəs/ **noun** [U]

ˈtime ˌlimit noun [C usually singular] the greatest length of time someone is allowed to spend doing something: *We've set a time limit* ***of*** *ten minutes* ***for*** *each child's turn on the trampoline.* ◦ *There's a 30-minute time limit* ***on*** *internet use in the library.*

T

timeline /ˈtaɪm.laɪn/ noun [C] **1** a line that shows the time and the order in which events have happened **2** a plan which shows how long something will take or when things will happen

timely /ˈtaɪm.li/ adj happening at a suitable moment: *a timely reminder* ◦ *The change in the exchange rate provided a timely boost to the company's falling profits.* • **timeliness** /-nəs/ **noun** [U]

ˈtime maˌchine noun [C usually singular] (especially in stories and films) a machine in which people can travel into the past or the future

timeout /ˌtaɪmˈaʊt/ noun; exclamation, noun

▸**noun** [C usually singular] a short period during a game in some sports when the players stop playing in order to rest, plan what they are going to do next, etc.: *The coach* ***called*** *a timeout to discuss strategy.*

▸**exclamation, noun** US used to tell people to stop what they are doing, especially when they are having a disagreement: *OK, timeout, everyone, let's all quiet down and talk about this calmly.*

timepiece /ˈtaɪm.piːs/ noun [C] old-fashioned or formal a clock or watch

timer /ˈtaɪ.məʳ/ ⓤⓢ /-mɚ/ noun [C] **1** a device which records when a particular number of minutes, hours, etc. have gone past: *He* ***set*** *the timer on the oven to/for 20 minutes (= to record when 20 minutes had gone past).* **2** (UK also **time switch**) a device on a machine which causes the machine to start or stop working at a particular point in the day

ˈtime-reˌlease adj (also **ˈtimed-reˌlease**) (of a pill) releasing its contents gradually during the day

times /taɪmz/ preposition, predeterminer, adv; predeterminer, adv

▸**preposition, predeterminer, adv** B2 multiplied by: *Two times two equals four (2 x 2 = 4).* ◦ *The area of a rectangle is its height times its width.*

▸**predeterminer, adv 1** B1 used to show the difference in amount of two things, by multiplying one of them by the stated number: *She earns five times* ***as much as*** *I do./She earns five times* ***more than*** *I do.* ◦ *My foot swelled up to three times the normal size when it was stung by a wasp.* **2 ten, a hundred, etc. times better, longer, etc.** informal much better, longer, etc.: *This work is ten times better than the last piece you did.*

timesaving /ˈtaɪmˌseɪ.vɪŋ/ adj reducing the amount of time needed for doing something: *Washing machines and vacuum cleaners are timesaving devices.*

timescale /ˈtaɪm.skeɪl/ noun [C] the period of time over which something happens: *Police officers are trying to construct the timescale* ***of*** *events leading up to the murder.* ◦ *What's the timescale* ***for*** *this? (= How long will it take?)*

ˈtime-scale proˌmotion noun [C or U] Indian English the act of giving someone a higher or more important position or rank at work because they have been doing their job for a certain length of time

ˈtime-ˌserver noun [C] disapproving **1** a person who does not work very hard at their job, and who is just waiting until they reach the age at which they can stop work **2** someone who changes their ideas and opinions in order to make them more like those that are held by people in power, especially because they believe it will be to their advantage • **ˈtime-ˌserving** adj *time-serving politicians*

timeshare /ˈtaɪm.ʃeəʳ/ ⓤⓢ /-ʃer/ noun **1** [C] a holiday house or apartment that is owned by several different people who each use it for a particular period of the year: *We've bought a timeshare in Spain.* ◦ *timeshare holiday/property/developments* **2** [U] (also **timesharing**) the activity of owning and using a timeshare

timesharing /ˈtaɪmˌʃeə.rɪŋ/ ⓤⓢ /-ˌʃer-/ noun [U] **COMPUTER** ▷ **1** the use of a central computer by several other smaller computers connected to it **HOLIDAY** ▷ **2** → **timeshare**

timesheet /ˈtaɪm.ʃiːt/ noun [C] (US also **ˈtime card**) a piece of paper on which an employee records the number of hours they have worked

ˈtime ˌsignal noun [C usually singular] a signal that is broadcast on the radio at an exact time, for example one o'clock, to show accurately what the time is

ˈtime ˌsignature noun [C] a symbol, usually in the form of two numbers, one above the other, written at the beginning of a piece of music to show how many beats there are in each BAR

ˈtime ˌswitch noun [C] UK a **timer**

timetable /ˈtaɪmˌteɪ.bl̩/ noun; verb

▸**noun** [C] UK (US **schedule**) **1** B1 a list of the times when events are planned to happen, especially the times when buses, trains, and planes leave and arrive: *Do you have a Birmingham to London train timetable* that I could borrow? ◦ The timetable **for** our trip to Paris includes visits to Notre-Dame and the Louvre. ◦ Here is the timetable **of** events **for** the day. ◦ I've got a very busy timetable next week (= I have a lot of activities planned). **2** A2 a list of the times when classes in school happen: *The first lesson **on** the timetable **for** Monday morning is history.*

▸**verb** [T usually passive] UK (US **schedule**) to plan when something is going to happen: [+ to infinitive] *We are timetabled **to** go to the British Museum on Thursday and the Tower of London on Friday.* ◦ *The lecture is timetabled **for** 5.00 p.m.*

ˈtime-ˌtested adj mainly US describes something, for example a method, that has been used for a long period and has been proved to work well

ˈtime ˌtravel noun [U] the idea of travelling into the past or the future

ˈtime ˌwarp noun [C usually singular] **1** the idea of a change in the measurement of time, in which people and events from one part of history are imagined as existing in another part **2 be/live in a time warp** figurative to be old-fashioned in your behaviour or opinions: *He's living in a time warp – he even wears a suit to work!*

timeworn /ˈtaɪm.wɔːn/ US /-wɔːrn/ adj (no longer of interest or value because of) having been used a lot over a long period of time: *a timeworn expression/excuse* ◦ *a timeworn path*

ˈtime ˌzone noun [C] one of many equal parts into which the world is divided. In any place within each part, the particular point in the day is the same, and is an hour in front of or behind that in the parts on either side: *If you go from New York to London, you **cross** five time zones.*

timid /ˈtɪm.ɪd/ adj C2 shy and nervous; without much confidence; easily frightened: *Lucy is a rather timid child.* ◦ *My horse is a bit timid and is easily frightened by traffic.* • **timidity** /tɪˈmɪd.ɪ.ti/ US /-ə.t̬i/ noun [U] • **timidly** /-li/ adv *'Um, excuse me,' he said timidly.*

timing /ˈtaɪ.mɪŋ/ noun **1** B2 [U or C] the time when something happens: *'Have we arrived too early?' 'No, your timing is perfect – dinner is almost ready.'* ◦ *The bomb contained a timing **device** set to make it go off at rush hour.* **2 timings** [plural] Indian English the hours when someone is usually at work, or when an office or business is open **3** [U] the ability to do something at exactly the right time: *To be a good tennis player, you have to have **good** timing.* **4** [U] the ability to play or sing all the notes in a piece of music at the correct speed: *My singing teacher says I must try and improve my timing.*

timorous /ˈtɪm.ər.əs/ US /-ɚ.əs/ adj literary nervous and without much confidence → Synonym **timid** • **timorously** /-li/ adv • **timorousness** /-nəs/ noun [U]

timpani /ˈtɪm.pə.ni/ noun [plural] a set of KETTLEDRUMS (= large metal drums with round bottoms) played in an ORCHESTRA

timpanist /ˈtɪm.pə.nɪst/ noun [C] a person who plays the timpani

tin /tɪn/ noun **METAL** ▷ **1** C2 [U] (symbol **Sn**) a chemical element that is a silver-coloured metal, often combined with other metals or used to cover and protect other metals **CONTAINER** ▷ **2** B1 [C] UK (UK and US also **can**) a closed metal container in which food is sold: *a tin **of** beans* ◦ *piles of soup tins* **3** B1 [C] UK (US **can**) the contents of a tin, or the amount of something a tin contains: *The children ate two tins **of** beans.* ◦ *We used four tins **of** paint when we painted the ceiling.* **4** B2 [C] UK (US **cookie jar**) a metal container with a lid used for keeping cakes or biscuits: *a biscuit tin* **5** B2 [C] UK (US **can**) a cylindrical metal container with a lid used for keeping liquid substances such as paint: *a tin **of** paint* **6** [C] UK (US **pan**) a metal container without a lid used for cooking food in the oven: *Put both cake tins in the oven for half an hour.* **7** [C] Australian English a closed metal container in which beer is sold: *a tin of beer* → Compare **can**

tincture /ˈtɪŋk.tʃər/ US /-tʃɚ/ noun [C or U] a medicine which consists of a mixture of alcohol and a small amount of a drug: *a/some tincture **of** iodine/myrrh*

tinder /ˈtɪn.dər/ US /-dɚ/ noun [U] small pieces of something dry that burns easily, used for lighting fires: *We used some dry grass as tinder to light the campfire.* ◦ *The grass is tinder-**dry** (= so dry that it will burn easily), so there's a risk of fire.*

tinderbox /ˈtɪn.də.bɒks/ US /-dɚ.bɑːks/ noun [C] a dangerous and uncontrolled situation in which violence is likely to happen: *The racial tension in the area makes it a tinderbox ready to ignite.*

tinfoil /ˈtɪn.fɔɪl/ noun [U] shiny, metal material, as thin as paper, that is used especially for wrapping food in order to store it or cook it

ting /tɪŋ/ adv, noun [C] (with) a clear, high ringing sound: *The bell on the hotel receptionist's desk **went** ting when I pressed it.*

ting-a-ling /ˌtɪŋ.əˈlɪŋ/ exclamation (mainly US **ding-a-ling** /ˌdɪŋ.əˈlɪŋ/) said, especially by children, to represent the sound of a bell

tinge /tɪndʒ/ noun; verb

▸**noun** [C] a very slight amount of a colour or of a feeling: *His hair is starting to show tinges **of** grey.* ◦ *I have a tinge **of** regret that I didn't accept her offer.*

▸**verb** [T usually passive] to contain a slight amount of: *Her joy at the birth of her son was tinged **with** sadness that her father had not lived to see him.* • **tinged** /tɪndʒd/ adj *Her dark hair is now tinged **with** grey.*

tingle /ˈtɪŋ.gəl/ verb; noun

▸**verb** [I] **1** to have a feeling as if a lot of sharp points are being put quickly and lightly into your body: *My toes and fingers are tingling **with** the cold.* ◦ *There's a line in that poem that makes my **spine** tingle every time I read it.* **2** When you tingle with an emotion, such as excitement or fear, you feel it very strongly: *She tingled **with** fear as she entered the dark alleyway.*

▸**noun** [C] a feeling as if a lot of sharp points are being put quickly and lightly into your body: *There's a slight tingle in my wrists.* ◦ *She stroked his head, sending tingles down his spine.* • **tingly** /-i/ adj causing a tingle: *My massage had left me with a pleasant tingly sensation.*

ˌtin ˈgod noun [C] (also **ˌlittle tin ˈgod**) literary disapproving someone who behaves as if they are more important or powerful than they really are

ˌtin ˈhat noun [C] informal a metal hat worn by soldiers to protect their heads

tinker /ˈtɪŋ.kər/ US /-kɚ/ verb; noun

▸**verb** [I usually + adv/prep] to make small changes to something, especially in an attempt to repair or improve it: *He spends every weekend tinkering (**about**) **with** his car.* ◦ *I wish the government would stop tinkering **with** the health service.* → Compare **fiddle**

▸**noun** **TRAVELLER** ▷ **1** [C] especially in the past, a person who travelled from place to place, repairing pans or other metal containers **CHILD** ▷ **2** [C] UK old-fashioned informal a child who behaves badly: *Don't be such a tinker.* **CHANGES** ▷ **3** [S] UK the activity of making small changes to something: *I'll just have **a** tinker **with** the TV and see if I can get it to work.*

tinkle /ˈtɪŋ.kl̩/ noun; verb

▸**noun** **SOUND** ▷ **1** [S] a light ringing sound: *In the*

T

distance we heard the **silvery** tinkle of a stream. PHONE CALL ▷ **2 give sb a tinkle** old-fashioned informal to make a phone call to someone: *I'll give you a tinkle some time next week.* TOILET ▷ **3** [C] informal or child's word an act of URINATION

▸verb [I] SOUND ▷ **1** to make a light ringing sound: *Some small old-fashioned shops still have a bell which tinkles when you push the door open.* TOILET ▷ **2** informal or child's word to urinate

tinned /tɪnd/ adj UK (US **canned**) Something, especially food, that is tinned is put in a tin in order to preserve it: *I don't like tinned tomatoes/spaghetti/milk.*

tinnie /ˈtɪn.i/ noun [C] **tinny**

tinnitus /ˈtɪn.ɪ.təs/ ⓤⓢ /-t̬əs/ noun [U] specialized a condition of the ear in which the person suffering from it hears noises such as ringing

tinny /ˈtɪn.i/ adj; noun

▸adj SOUND ▷ **1** describes a sound that is of low quality or like metal being hit: *a tinny piano* ◦ *a tinny recording* POOR QUALITY ▷ **2** informal disapproving If something made of metal is tinny, it is not strong and not of good quality: *a cheap, tinny toy car*

▸noun [C] (also **tinnie**) Australian English informal a CAN of beer

ˈtin ˌopener noun [C] UK (mainly US ˈ**can ˌopener**) a device for opening TINS of food

ˌTin ˌPan ˈAlley noun [S] informal the people who write, perform, and produce popular music, especially those who were active in the first half of the 20th century

tinplate /ˈtɪn.pleɪt/ noun [U] thin sheets of iron or STEEL covered with a thin layer of TIN • **tinplated** /ˌtɪnˈpleɪ.tɪd/ ⓤⓢ /-t̬ɪd/ adj

tinpot /ˈtɪn.pɒt/ ⓤⓢ /-pɑːt/ adj [before noun] informal disapproving not important, or having little value: *a tinpot dictator*

tinsel /ˈtɪn.səl/ noun [U] **1** long pieces of thin, shiny material used as decoration, especially at Christmas: *a Christmas tree decorated with tinsel* **2** disapproving something, especially the entertainment business or someone's way of living, that seems exciting and attractive, but is really of low quality or value: *The show was all tinsel and glitter.* • **tinselly** /-i/ adj

tint /tɪnt/ noun; verb

▸noun [C] **1** a small amount of a colour: *The paint we're using for the bathroom is white with a yellow tint.* ◦ *The evening sky was deep pink, with tints* ***of*** *purple and red in it.* **2** a small amount of DYE, especially used on the hair, or the act of using such a substance: *She's had blonde tints put in her hair.* ◦ *I'm going to the hairdresser's for a tint.*

▸verb [T] to slightly change the colour of something

tinted /ˈtɪn.tɪd/ ⓤⓢ /-t̬ɪd/ adj [before noun] (of glass) with colour added: *Tinted* ***glasses*** *(= glasses with slightly darkened lenses) are good for driving in bright sunlight.* ◦ *The president arrived at the airport in a car with tinted* ***windows*** *(= windows with darkened glass so that people cannot see into the car).*

ˌtin ˈwhistle noun [C] a small musical instrument consisting of a thin metal tube that the player blows into.

tiny /ˈtaɪ.ni/ adj B1 extremely small: *a tiny flower* ◦ *a tiny helping of food* ◦ *a tiny baby* ◦ *a tiny* ***bit*** *late*

tip /tɪp/ verb; noun

▸verb (-pp-) ONE SIDE HIGHER ▷ **1** C2 [I or T] to (cause to) move so that one side is higher than another side: *The table tipped and all our drinks fell on the floor.* ◦ *If you put too many books on one end of the shelf, it'll tip* ***up.*** ◦ *Don't tip your chair* ***back*** *like that, you'll fall.* **2 tip the scales at** to weigh: *The baby tipped the scales at 3.75 kg.* POUR ▷ **3** C2 [T usually + adv/prep] UK to pour a substance from one container into another or onto a surface: *She tipped the contents of her purse out onto the table.* ◦ *He tipped his breakfast cereal into a bowl.* ◦ *The child picked up the box and tipped the toys* ***out*** *all over the floor.* **4 be tipping (it) down** UK informal When it is tipping it down, a lot of rain is falling: *We won't be able to go to the beach today –* ***it's*** *tipping it down.* END ▷ **5** [T usually passive] to cover the end of something pointed with a liquid, a colour, etc.: *The giraffe was killed with a spear that had been tipped* ***with*** *poison.* PAYMENT ▷ **6** [I or T] to give someone who has provided you with a service an extra amount of money to thank them: *The taxi driver was so rude to her that she didn't tip him.* ◦ [+ two objects] *They tipped the waiter £5.* INFORMATION ▷ **7** [T often passive] mainly UK to say that someone is likely to be successful or achieve something: *He is being tipped* ***as*** *the next prime minister.* ◦ [+ to infinitive] *Davis is being tipped* ***to*** *win the championship.* RUBBISH ▷ **8** [I or T, usually + adv/prep] UK (US also **dump**) to get rid of rubbish by putting it in a place where it should not be: *A lot of waste is being tipped into the sea.* ◦ *The sign by the side of the road said 'No tipping'.*

IDIOMS **tip your hand** US If you tip your hand, you say what you are going to do or what you believe: *Despite weeks of media speculation, the president refused to tip his hand about his plans for re-election.* • **tip the scales** (also **tip the balance**) If something tips the scales, it is the thing that causes a particular situation to happen or a particular decision to be made, when other situations or decisions are possible: *The teams were evenly matched until two quick goals from Robson tipped the balance* ***in favour of*** *England.* ◦ *She was a good candidate, but her lack of computer skills tipped the scales* ***against*** *her.* • **tip sb the wink** (also **tip the wink to sb**) UK informal to give someone a piece of secret or private information that might bring an advantage to them: *Thanks for tipping me the wink* ***about*** *those cheap tickets, Bill.*

PHRASAL VERBS **tip sb off** C2 to warn someone secretly about something that will happen, so that they can take action or prevent it from happening: [+ that] *Somebody must have tipped the burglars off* ***that*** *the house would be empty.* ◦ *The robber was caught when someone tipped off the police.* • **tip (sth/sb) over** to (cause to) fall over onto one side: *Be careful not to tip that cup of coffee over.* • **tip over into sth** If something tips over from something into something else, it stops being the first thing, and becomes the second: *At various points in the play, the action tips over from comedy into farce (= stops being amusing and becomes ridiculous).*

▸noun [C] INFORMATION ▷ **1** B1 a useful piece of information, especially about how to do something or about the likely winner of a race or competition: *gardening/cooking/sewing tips* ◦ *She* ***gave*** *me a useful/helpful/valuable/practical tip* ***about/for*** *growing tomatoes.* ◦ *Our racing correspondent has the following tips* ***for*** *the 3.15 and the 3.45 at Newmarket (= thinks that particular horses will be the winners in those races).* ◦ *I've got a* ***hot*** *tip* ***for*** *you (= I can tell you about a particular likely winner of a race or competition, or give you a valuable piece of information).* PAYMENT ▷ **2** B1 a small amount of money given to someone who has provided you with a service, in addition to the official payment and for their personal use: *a 15 percent tip* ◦ *He* ***gave*** *the porter a tip.* ◦ *We don't need to* ***leave*** *a tip* ***for*** *the waiter, because there's a service charge* *included in the bill.* **END** ▷ **3** C1 the usually pointed end of something, especially something that is long and thin: *We had asparagus tips for dinner.* ◦ *If I stand* ***on*** *the tips* ***of*** *my toes, I can just reach the top shelf.* ◦ *The Keys are coral islands off the southern tip* ***of*** *Florida.* ◦ *There's paint* ***on*** *the tip* ***of*** *your nose.* **4** a small part fitted to the end of something, especially something that is long and thin: *a walking cane with a metal tip* ◦ *the filter tip* ***of*** *a cigarette* **RUBBISH** ▷ **5** C2 UK (mainly US **dump**) a place where especially large pieces of rubbish can be taken and left: *a rubbish/waste tip* ◦ *We need to take this old carpet to the tip.* ◦ UK informal *This room is a complete/absolute/real tip* (= *is very untidy*) *– tidy it up at once.*

IDIOMS **be on the tip of your tongue** If something that you want to say is on the tip of your tongue, you think you know it and that you will be able to remember it very soon: *Her name is on the tip of my tongue.* • **tip of the iceberg** C2 a small, noticeable part of a problem, the total size of which is really much greater: *These small local protests are just the tip of the iceberg.*

ˈtip-off noun [C usually singular] informal a secret warning or piece of secret information: *Acting on a tip-off, the police arrested the drug dealers.*

ˈtipper ˌtruck/ˌlorry noun [C] UK a **dumper truck**

Tipp-Ex /ˈtɪp.eks/ noun [U] UK trademark (US trademark **Wite-Out**) a white liquid used for painting over mistakes in a piece of writing

ˈtipping ˌpoint noun [S or U] the time at which a change or an effect cannot be stopped: *The Earth has already passed the tipping point in terms of global warming.*

tipple /ˈtɪp.l/ noun [C] informal an alcoholic drink: *What's your tipple?* (= *What alcoholic drink do you usually drink?*)

tippler /ˈtɪp.l̩.əʳ/, /-ləʳ/ US /-l̩.ɚ/ /-lɚ/ noun [C] informal someone who often drinks alcohol

tipster /ˈtɪp.stəʳ/ US /-stɚ/ noun [C] a person who gives information to people, usually in exchange for money, especially about the likely winner of a race or competition, or who gives information to an official organization, especially about someone who has done something wrong: *All the tipsters were wrong about the gold medal winner.* ◦ *An anonymous tipster has leaked confidential government information to the press.*

tipsy /ˈtɪp.si/ adj informal slightly drunk: *Auntie Pat is getting a little tipsy again.* • **tipsily** /-sɪ.li/ adv • **tipsiness** /-nəs/ noun [U]

tiptoe /ˈtɪp.təʊ/ US /-toʊ/ noun; verb

▸noun **on tiptoe(s)** on your toes with the HEEL of your foot lifted off the ground: *The children stood on tiptoe in order to pick the apples from the tree.* ◦ *They walked across the room on tiptoe so as not to waken the baby.*

▸verb [I usually + adv/prep] to walk on your toes with the HEEL of your foot lifted off the ground, especially in order not to make a noise: *He waited until his daughter was asleep, then tiptoed quietly out of the room.*

PHRASAL VERB **tiptoe round/around sth/sb** informal to avoid dealing with a difficult subject, problem, or person: *Guy keeps tiptoeing round the problem, instead of confronting it.*

ˈtip-top adj informal excellent; perfect: *I try and keep in tip-top* ***shape*** *by exercising every day.* ◦ *Even though our house is in tip-top* ***condition****, we're having problems selling it.* ◦ *The hotel we stayed in was absolutely tip-top.*

ˈtip ˌtruck noun [C] Australian English a large truck for transporting heavy LOADS, with a back part that can be raised at one end so that its contents fall out → Compare **dumper truck**

tirade /taɪˈreɪd/, /tɪ-/ US /ˈtaɪ.reɪd/ noun [C] a long, angry speech expressing strong disapproval: *She launched into an* ***angry/furious*** *tirade* ***about*** *how she had been unfairly treated.* ◦ *In a furious tirade* ***of*** *abuse, the opposition spokesperson demanded the minister's resignation.*

tiramisù /ˌtɪr.ə.mɪˈsuː/ US /-ˈmiː.suː/ noun [C or U] a sweet, cold Italian dish, consisting of soft cheese, cake, alcohol, and coffee

tire verb; noun

▸verb [I or T] /taɪəʳ/ US /taɪr/ C2 to begin to feel as if you have no energy and want to rest or go to sleep, or to make someone feel this way: *She's been leading throughout the race, but it now looks as if she's tiring.* ◦ *Even doing the garden tires me these days.*

PHRASAL VERBS **tire of sth/sb** C2 to become bored with someone or something, or to stop enjoying an activity: *This is the kind of toy that children will soon tire of.* ◦ *He* ***never*** *tires* ***of*** (= *he enjoys*) *playing games on his computer.* • **tire of sth** to be annoyed by something • **tire sb out** to make someone very tired: *Let the kids run around in the garden and that'll soon tire them out.*

▸noun [C] /taɪəʳ/ US /taɪɚ/ US for **tyre**

tired /taɪəd/ US /taɪrd/ adj **NEEDING REST** ▷ **1** A1 in need of rest or sleep: *I was so tired when I got home from work last night that I had a quick nap.* ◦ *My legs are tired.* ◦ *She spoke in a tired voice.* **NOT INTERESTING** ▷ **2** disapproving describes people, ideas, or subjects that are not interesting because they are very familiar: *It's always the same tired* ***old*** *faces at these meetings.* **3 be tired of sth/sb** B1 to be bored with an activity or person: *I'm so tired of doing the same job, day after day.* ◦ *Don't you* ***get*** *tired of quarrelling all the time?* ◦ *I'm* ***sick and*** *tired of you telling me what to do all the time.* • **tiredly** /ˈtaɪəd.li/ US /ˈtaɪrd-/ adv feeling or showing a need to rest or sleep • **tiredness** /ˈtaɪəd.nəs/ US /taɪrd-/ noun [U] B2 *He said that it was tiredness that led him to make the mistake.* ◦ *I was overtaken by a sudden wave of tiredness.*

Other ways of saying tired

If someone is extremely tired, you can say that the person is **exhausted** or **worn out**:

I'm too ***exhausted*** *to take the dog for a walk.*

I was completely ***worn out****.*

You can describe someone who is tired because he or she has been working very hard as **burned out** or **drained**:

He was completely ***burned out*** *after a full week of performances.*

I'd worked a twelve-hour day and was absolutely ***drained****.*

If someone is tired and wants to go to sleep, you can describe that person as **drowsy** or **sleepy**:

The heat had made me ***drowsy/sleepy****.*

IDIOM **tired and emotional** UK humorous or polite phrase for **drunk**

ˌtired ˈout adj [after verb] very much in need of rest or sleep: *We were all really tired out after our long journey.*

tireless /ˈtaɪə.ləs/ US /ˈtaɪr-/ adj working energetically and continuously: *Tony is a tireless worker.* ◦ *The prisoner's family is conducting a tireless campaign for his release.* ◦ *The police have been tireless* ***in*** *their search for the child's killer.* • **tirelessly** /-li/ adv

T

tiresome /ˈtaɪə.səm/ (US) /ˈtaɪr-/ **adj** (C2) annoying and making you lose patience: *I find it very tiresome doing the same job day after day.* ◦ *He has the tiresome habit of finishing your sentences for you.* • **tiresomely** /-li/ **adv** *a tiresomely repetitive speech* ◦ *a tiresomely long wait*

tiring /ˈtaɪə.rɪŋ/ (US) /ˈtaɪ-/ **adj** (B1) making you feel tired: *I've had a very tiring day.* ◦ *Looking after the kids is extremely tiring.*

'tis /tɪz/ old use short form of it is: *'Tis the season to be jolly!*

tisane /tɪˈzæn/ **noun** [C or U] (also ˌ**herbal** ˈ**tea**) a drink made by pouring boiling water onto particular types of dried or fresh flowers or leaves

tissue /ˈtɪʃ.uː/, /ˈtɪs.juː/ **noun** **CELLS** ▷ **1** [U] a group of connected cells in an animal or plant that are similar to each other, have the same purpose, and form the stated part of the animal or plant: *human tissue* ◦ *plant tissue* ◦ *brain/lung/muscle/fat tissue* ◦ *His face is covered with scar tissue where he was badly burned.* **PAPER** ▷ **2** (B1) [C or U] soft paper that is used for cleaning, especially your nose, and is thrown away after use, or a small rectangular piece of this: *She handed me a tissue just as I sneezed.* ◦ *I always keep a box of tissues in the car.* ◦ *He used a piece of tissue to clean his sunglasses.* → Compare **handkerchief** **3** [U] (also **tissue paper**) thin, light paper used especially for wrapping delicate things: *The shop assistant wrapped the vase carefully in tissue paper.*

ˈ**tissue** ˌ**culture** **noun** specialized **1** [U] the scientific process of growing tissue (= cells) outside an organism, in a substance containing the necessary NUTRIENTS **2** [C] a particular quantity of tissue grown in this way

tit /tɪt/ **noun** [C] **BIRD** ▷ **1** a common small bird found in the northern half of the world **BREAST** ▷ **2** offensive a woman's breast: *He says he likes women with big tits.* **PERSON** ▷ **3** UK slang a stupid person. This word is considered offensive by some people: *Why did you do that, you stupid great tit?*

IDIOM **get on sb's tits** UK offensive to annoy someone: *Stop it, Joe, you're really getting on my tits.*

titan /ˈtaɪ.tᵊn/ **noun** [C] literary a person who is very important, powerful, strong, big, clever, etc.: *an intellectual titan* ◦ *The final will be a* ***clash of the*** *(= a hard struggle and competition between) titans.* ◦ *The soft drink titans (= big companies who produce these drinks) are struggling for control of the market.*

T

titanic /taɪˈtæn.ɪk/ **adj** extremely powerful, strong, important, or large: *titanic mountains* ◦ *a titanic battle/performance/struggle*

titanium /tɪˈteɪ.ni.əm/, /taɪ-/ **noun** [U] (symbol **Ti**) a chemical element that is a light, strong, white metal

titbit /ˈtɪt.bɪt/ (US usually **tidbit**) **noun** [C] a small piece of interesting information, or a small dish of pleasant-tasting food: *Our guide gave us some interesting titbits* ***about*** *the history of the castle.* ◦ *This magazine is full of* ***juicy*** *titbits (= small pieces of interesting information, especially about other people's private lives).* ◦ *Grandma always has a few titbits for the children if they're visiting at lunchtime.*

titch /tɪtʃ/ **noun** [C] UK child's word a small person, especially a child: *I don't need to take any notice of a titch like you.* ◦ [as form of address] *Come on, titch.*

titchy /ˈtɪtʃ.i/ **adj** UK child's word extremely small: *We've got a great big car, and you've only got a titchy little one.*

ˌ**tit for** ˈ**tat** **noun** [U] disapproving actions done intentionally to punish other people because they have done something unpleasant to you: *I noticed she didn't send me a card – I think it was tit for tat because I forgot her birthday last year.* • ˌ**tit-for-**ˈ**tat** **adj** [before noun] *Recent months have seen a pattern of tit-for-tat killings between the two sides.*

tithe /taɪð/ **noun** [C] a tenth part of someone's produce or income that they give or pay as a tax to the Church

titillate /ˈtɪt.ɪ.leɪt/ **verb** [I or T] to make someone excited intentionally but only a little, usually with sexual images or descriptions: *So many adverts nowadays are designed to titillate.* ◦ humorous *Carter's biography is only spoiled by the fact that he refuses to titillate (= interest) his readers with any gossip.* • **titillation** /ˌtɪt.ɪˈleɪ.ʃᵊn/ **noun** [U]

titillating /ˈtɪt.ɪ.leɪ.tɪŋ/ (US) /-t̬ɪŋ/ **adj** **1** describes sexual images or descriptions, etc. that intentionally cause excitement, but not in a serious way: *The photos, which include some mildly titillating semi-nude shots of the actress, will be on display for a week.* **2** humorous interesting and shocking: *It seems that people can't resist titillating headlines, especially if they concern the Royal Family.*

titivate /ˈtɪt.ɪ.veɪt/ (US) /ˈtɪt̬.ə-/ **verb** [I or T] informal to improve the small details of someone's appearance by arranging their hair, putting on make-up, etc.

title /ˈtaɪ.tl̩/ (US) /-t̬l̩/ **noun** **NAME** ▷ **1** (B1) [C] the name of a film, book, painting, piece of music, etc.: *The title* ***of*** *Evelyn Waugh's first novel was 'Decline and Fall'.* ◦ *And this next record is the title* ***track*** *on the album 'The Red Shoes' (= the piece of music and the record are both called 'The Red Shoes').* → See also **subtitle, surtitle** **2** **titles** [plural] (also **credits**) the information given at the end or beginning of a film or television programme, stating the names of the people who acted in it or were involved in its production **3** [C] specialized a book: *Last year we published over a hundred new titles.* **PERSON** ▷ **4** [C] a word that is used before someone's name, stating their social rank, qualifications, position in an organization, sex, etc.: *What's her title – is she Professor or just Doctor?* ◦ *He will retain the honorary title* ***of*** *non-executive chairman.* ◦ *What's your* ***job*** *title now – are you managing director?* **SPORTS PRIZE** ▷ **5** (C2) [C] the position you get by beating all other competitors in a sports competition: *Hendry won the world snooker title after a tense 35-frame final.* **LEGAL RIGHT** ▷ **6** [U] the legal right to own a piece of land or a building: *If you wish to sell the property, you will first have to prove your title to it.*

ˈ**title** ˌ**bar** **noun** [C] specialized the long, narrow coloured part along the top of your computer screen that shows the title of the document or program that is open

titled /ˈtaɪ.tl̩d/ (US) /-t̬l̩d/ **adj** **PERSON** ▷ **1** A person who is titled has a special word, such as SIR or LADY, before their own name, showing that they have a high social rank: *one of his titled friends* **BOOK/FILM/PAINTING, ETC.** ▷ **2** [after verb] with the title of: *Reed wrote a novel about de Sade titled 'When the Whip Comes Down'.*

ˈ**title** ˌ**deed** **noun** [C usually plural] a document which states and proves a person's legal right to own a piece of land or a building

titleholder /ˈtaɪ.tl̩ˌhəʊl.dəʳ/ (US) /-t̬l̩ˌhoʊl.dɚ/ **noun** [C] a person who is in the position of having beaten all other competitors in a sports competition: *The field includes Rosa Mota, the Olympic, world and European titleholder.*

ˈ**title** ˌ**page** **noun** [C usually singular] a page at the front of a book on which you find the name of the book, the writer, and the publisher

ˈtitle ˌrole noun [C usually singular] A title role in a play or film is the character referred to in its name, usually the main part: *She is currently to be seen at the National Theatre playing the title role in Pam Gems' play 'Queen Christina'.*

titration /taɪˈtreɪ.ʃən/ noun [U] specialized a method of finding exactly how much of a substance there is in a solution by gradually adding measured amounts of another substance which reacts to it in a known way, for example by causing a colour change

titter /ˈtɪt.əʳ/ US /ˈtɪt̬.ɚ/ verb [I] to laugh nervously, often at something that you feel you should not be laughing at: *A couple of the younger teachers tittered at his smutty jokes.* • **titter** noun [C] *The love scene raised a few titters from a party of schoolboys.*

tittle-tattle /ˈtɪt.l̩ˌtæt.l̩/ US /ˈtɪt̬.l̩ˌtæt̬-/ noun [U] old-fashioned informal talk about other people's lives that is usually unkind, disapproving or not true → Synonym **gossip**

titty /ˈtɪt.i/ US /ˈtɪt̬-/ noun [C] informal a **tit**

titular /ˈtɪt.jʊ.ləʳ/ US /ˈtɪtʃ.ə.lɚ/ adj [before noun] having the title of a position but not the responsibilities, duties, or power; in name only: *It is already agreed that Mr Alfonso Escamez will be the titular head of the new bank.*

tizzy /ˈtɪz.i/ noun [S] (UK also **tizz**) a temporary state of worry and confusion: *She got herself* ***in a*** *real tizzy because she couldn't find her car keys.*

ˈT-ˌjunction noun [C] UK a place where one road meets another without crossing it, forming the shape of a letter T

TLA /ˌtiː.elˈeɪ/ abbreviation for three-letter abbreviation: three letters that are a short form of a phrase: *FAQ and PFI are TLAs.*

TNT /ˌtiː.enˈtiː/ noun [U] a powerful, yellow explosive substance

to preposition; adv

▸**preposition** strong /tuː/ weak /tʊ, tu, tə/ US /tə/ **INFINITIVE** ▷ **1** A1 used before a verb to show that it is in the INFINITIVE **2** A1 used after some verbs, especially when the action described in the INFINITIVE will happen later: *She agreed to help.* ◦ *I'll have to tell him.* ◦ *Sadly, she didn't live to see her grandchildren.* **3** A1 used after many verbs of agreeing, needing, and wanting: *I need to eat something first.* ◦ *I'd love to live in New York.* ◦ *That child ought to be in bed.* **4** A2 used instead of repeating a verb CLAUSE: *'Are you going tonight?' 'I'm certainly hoping to.'* **5** A1 used in phrases where there are reported orders and requests: *He told me to wait.* ◦ *Did anyone ask Daniel to book the room?* **6** A1 used after some adjectives: *It's not likely to happen.* ◦ *Three months is* ***too*** *long to wait.* ◦ *She's not strong* ***enough*** *to go walking up mountains.* **7** used after some nouns: *He has this enviable ability to ignore everything that's unpleasant in life.* ◦ *This will be my second attempt to make flaky pastry.* **8** A CLAUSE containing to + INFINITIVE can be used as the subject of a sentence: *To go overseas on your own is very brave.* ◦ *My plan was to get it all arranged before I told anyone.* **9** A1 used after question words: *I don't know what to do.* ◦ *Can you tell me how to get there?* **10** A2 used with an INFINITIVE to express use or purpose: *I'm going there to see my sister.* ◦ *This tool is used to make holes in leather.* ◦ *To make this cake, you'll need two eggs, 175 grams of sugar, and 175 grams of flour.* ◦ *He works to get paid, not because he enjoys it.* **11** You can introduce a CLAUSE with a phrase containing to + INFINITIVE: *To be honest (= speaking honestly), Elaine, I prefer you in the grey shirt.* ◦ *To be quite truthful with you, Betty, I never really liked the man.* **12** A1 used with an INFINITIVE after 'there is' or 'there are' and a noun: *There's an awful lot of work to be done.* **13 to be going on with** UK To be going on with means in order to continue with the present activity or situation: *Do we have enough paint to be going on with, or should I get some more while I'm out?* **SHOWING DIRECTION** ▷ **14** A1 in the direction of: *We're going to town on the bus, okay?* ◦ *We went to Prague last year.* ◦ *I asked someone the way to the town centre.* ◦ *You can walk* ***from*** *here to the station in under ten minutes.* ◦ *I've asked Helen and Ben to dinner (= invited them to come and eat dinner with me) next week.* ◦ *We received another invitation to a wedding this morning.* ◦ *I had my back to them, so I couldn't see what they were doing.* ◦ *She walked* ***over*** *to the window.* ◦ *He went* ***up*** *to a complete stranger and started talking.* ◦ *You've got your sweater on* ***back*** *to* ***front*** *(= with the back of the sweater on the chest).* **RECEIVING** ▷ **15** A2 used for showing who receives something or who experiences an action: *I lent my bike to my brother.* ◦ *I told that to Glyn and he was horrified.* ◦ *Who's the letter addressed to?* **16** A2 With many verbs that have two objects, 'to' can be used before the INDIRECT OBJECT: *Give me that gun./Give that gun to me.* **UNTIL** ▷ **17** B1 until a particular time, state, or level is reached: *It's only two weeks to Christmas.* ◦ *Unemployment has risen to almost eight million.* ◦ *He drank himself to death.* ◦ *She nursed me back to health.* **18** A1 used when saying the time, to mean before the stated hour: *It's twenty to six.* **EXTREME** ▷ **19** used to suggest an extreme state: *Look at your shirt – it's torn to shreds!* ◦ *She was thrilled to bits.* ◦ *I was bored to tears.* **CONNECTION** ▷ **20** B1 in connection with: *What was their response to your query?* ◦ *She was so rude to me.* ◦ *There's a funny side to everything.* **21** B1 used to say where something is fastened or connected: *The paper was fastened to the wall with tape.* ◦ *A fast rail service connects us to the city.* **FUTURE** ▷ **22** used before an INFINITIVE, usually with 'be', to indicate a future action: *The government announced today that it is to cut funding for the arts for next year.* → See also **to-be** **23** used in this pattern to say what someone should do or to give an order: *You're not to (= you must not) bite your nails like that.* **24** Newspapers often use to + infinitive without 'be' in their HEADLINES (= titles of articles) when reporting planned future events: *France to send troops in.* **CAUSING** ▷ **25** C2 causing a particular feeling in a particular person: *That's when I learned, to my horror, that she was coming here.* **CONSIDERED BY** ▷ **26** considered by: *I realize it may sound strange to you.* ◦ *I mean, £50 is nothing to him (= he would not consider it a large amount).* ◦ informal *'I hear you've been going out with Sally.' 'Well,* ***what's it*** *to you?' (= It should not interest you, and you have no right to ask about it.)* **SERVING** ▷ **27** B1 serving: *As a personal trainer to the rich and famous, he earns over a million dollars a year.* **AGAINST** ▷ **28** against or very near: *Stand back to back.* ◦ *They were dancing cheek to cheek.* **BELONGING** ▷ **29** matching or belonging to: *He's given me the keys to his car – the fool!* ◦ *I've lost the trousers to this jacket.* **30** having as a characteristic feature: *She has a mean side to her.* ◦ *There is a very moral tone to this book.* **COMPARED WITH** ▷ **31** B1 compared with: *She's earning a reasonable wage, but* ***nothing*** *to what she could if she was in the private sector.* ◦ *Paul beat me by three games to two (= he won three and I won two).* ◦ *He was old enough to be her father – she looked about 30 to his 60.* **32** B1 used to show the position of something or someone in comparison with something or someone else: *John's*

T

standing to the left of Adrian in the photo. ◦ *The Yorkshire Dales are twenty miles to the north of the city.* **IN HONOUR OF** ▷ **33** in honour or memory of: *I proposed a toast to the bride and the groom.* ◦ *The record is dedicated to her mother, who died recently.* **FOR EACH** ▷ **34** for each: *How many francs are there to the pound?* ◦ *This car does about 50 miles to the gallon.* ◦ *If we go swimming together I do six lengths to her twelve.* → Compare **per** **BETWEEN** ▷ **35** B2 used in phrases which show a range: *There must have been 30 to 35 (= a number between 30 and 35) people there.* **AT THE SAME TIME AS** ▷ **36** at the same time as music or other sound: *I like exercising to music.* ◦ *He left the stage to the sound of booing.* **POSITIVE** ▷ **37** relating to a positive reaction or result: *Is the room to your* ***liking****, madam?* ◦ *I think being present at the meeting would be to your* ***advantage****.*

> **!** Common mistake: **to or too?**
>
> **Warning:** Choose the right word!
>
> These two words look similar, but they are spelled differently and have completely different meanings.

▸adv /tuː/ into a closed position: *I'll just push the door to.*

toad /təʊd/ US /toʊd/ **noun** [C] **ANIMAL** ▷ **1** a small, brownish-green animal, similar to a FROG, that has big eyes and long back legs for swimming and jumping: *Toads have dryer, lumpier skins than frogs and spend less time in the water.* **MAN** ▷ **2** informal an extremely unpleasant man, especially one who is not very physically attractive: [as form of address] *You lying toad!*

ˌtoad-in-the-ˈhole **noun** [U] UK a dish made with sausages cooked in a mixture of eggs, milk, and flour

toadstool /ˈtəʊd.stuːl/ US /ˈtoʊd-/ **noun** [C] a poisonous FUNGUS with a round top and a narrow stem → Compare **mushroom**

toady /ˈtəʊ.di/ US /ˈtoʊ-/ **noun** [C] disapproving a person who praises and is artificially pleasant to people in authority, usually in order to get some advantage from them • **toady verb** [I] *She was always toadying* ***to*** *the boss.*

ˌto and ˈfro **adv** [before noun], **adj** in one direction and then in the opposite direction, a number of times: *I was disturbed by all the people walking to and fro outside the office.* ◦ *She was gazing out of the window, rocking rhythmically to and fro.*

toast /təʊst/ US /toʊst/ **noun; verb**

▸**noun** **BREAD** ▷ **1** A2 [U] sliced bread made warm, CRISP (= hard enough to break), and brown by being put near a high heat: *a* ***slice of*** *toast* ◦ *I have toast* ***and*** *marmalade for breakfast.* ◦ *I'm having beans* ***on*** *toast for supper.* **DRINK** ▷ **2** C1 [C] an expression of good wishes or respect for someone which involves holding up and then drinking from a glass of alcohol, especially wine, after a short speech: *Now, if you'd all please raise your glasses, I'd like to* ***propose*** *a toast* ***to*** *the bride and groom.* ◦ *Champagne corks popped and the guests* ***drank*** *a toast* ***to*** *the happy couple.*

IDIOM **the toast of sth** old-fashioned The toast of a particular place is a person who is very much admired there for something they have recently done: *Not so long ago Viviana was a little-known actress playing in a provincial theatre – these days she's the toast of New York/****the town****.*

▸**verb** [T] **HEAT** ▷ **1** to make bread or other food warm, CRISP (= hard enough to break), and brown by putting it near a high heat: *Do you want this bread toasted?* ◦ *Can I have a toasted* ***sandwich****, please?* **2** informal to warm yourself or part of your body: *He's just toasting his feet by the fire.* **DRINK** ▷ **3** to hold up your glass and then drink as an expression of good wishes or respect: *We toasted the happy couple.*

toaster /ˈtəʊ.stəʳ/ US /ˈtoʊ.stɚ/ **noun** [C] an electric device for making toast

ˈtoasting ˌfork **noun** [C] a fork with a long handle used for holding slices of bread near a fire to make toast

ˈtoast ˌrack **noun** [C] a device for holding pieces of toast which supports them vertically

toasty /ˈtəʊ.sti/ US /ˈtoʊ-/ **adj; noun**

▸**adj** **WARM** ▷ comfortably and pleasantly warm: *My feet feel so warm and toasty in the new slippers.*

▸**noun** [C] (also **toastie**) UK a sandwich that has been toasted: *a cheese/ham/tuna toasty*

tobacco /təˈbæk.əʊ/ US /-oʊ/ **noun** [U] C1 a substance smoked in cigarettes, pipes, etc. that is prepared from the dried leaves of a particular plant: *28 percent of people asked thought that the advertising of tobacco (= tobacco and products made from it, such as cigarettes) and alcohol should be banned.*

tobacconist /təˈbæk.ən.ɪst/ **noun** [C] a person who is in charge of a shop where tobacco, cigarettes, etc. are sold

to-ˈbe **suffix** in the near future: *a bride-to-be*

toboggan /təˈbɒg.ən/ US /-ˈbɑː.gən/ **noun** [C] an object used for sliding over snow and ice which consists of a low frame on which a person or people sit • **toboggan verb** [I] *We could* ***go*** *tobogganing on Primrose Hill.*

toboggan

tocopherol /tɒˈkɒ.fə.rɒl/ US /-ˈkɑː.fə.ɑːl/ **noun** [U] specialized **vitamin E**

tod /tɒd/ US /tɑːd/ **noun** UK old-fashioned informal **on your tod** alone: *Are you on your tod tonight – where's your missus?*

today /təˈdeɪ/ **adv, noun** **1** A1 (on) the present day: *What's the date today?* ◦ *He's going to ring you at some point today.* ◦ *Today is even hotter than yesterday!* ◦ *Is that today's paper?* ◦ *He should be back today* ***week****/****a week*** *today (= one week from today).* **2** B2 used more generally to mean the present time: *Today, people are much more concerned about their health than they were in the past.* ◦ *With today's technology almost anything seems possible.* ◦ *The youth* ***of*** *today don't know how lucky they are.*

toddle /ˈtɒd.l̩/ US /ˈtɑː.dl̩/ **verb** [I] **1** (especially of a young child) to walk with short steps, trying to keep the body balanced: *I watched my two-year-old nephew toddling around after his puppy.* **2** informal to walk somewhere: *I'm just toddling* ***off/round*** *to the shops.*

toddler /ˈtɒd.ləʳ/ US /ˈtɑː.d.lɚ/ **noun** [C] C2 a young child, especially one who is learning or has recently learned to walk

to-ˈdie-for **adj** [before noun] informal extremely good or beautiful: *They sell beautiful shoes and to-die-for handbags.*

to-ˈdo **noun** [S] informal a show of anger, worry, or excitement that is unnecessary or greater than the situation deserves: *What a to-do that was, getting my passport renewed!*

toe /təʊ/ US /toʊ/ **noun; verb**

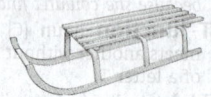

▸**noun** [C] **1** A2 any of the five separate parts at the end of the foot: *your big toe (= your largest toe)* ◦ *your little toe (= your smallest toe)* ◦ *I* ***stubbed*** *(= knocked) my toe*

on the edge of the bed. **2** the part of a sock, shoe, or other foot covering that goes over the toes

IDIOMS **on your toes** C2 Someone or something that keeps you on your toes forces you to continue directing all your attention and energy to what you are doing: *I work with people who are half my age so that **keeps** me on my toes.* • **tread/step on sb's toes** If you tread/step on someone's toes, you say or do something that upsets or annoys them, especially by involving yourself in matters that are their responsibility.

▸verb **toe the line** C2 to do what you are ordered or expected to do: *Ministers who wouldn't toe the **party** line were swiftly got rid of.*

ˈtoe ˌcap noun [C] a hard covering to protect the toes in a shoe or boot: *metal toe caps*

ˈtoe-ˌcurling adj UK informal making you feel extremely embarrassed and ashamed for someone else: *I saw the worst comedy act I've ever seen last night – it was absolutely toe-curling!*

-toed /-təʊd/ US /-toʊd/ suffix having toes as described: *open-toed sandals* ◦ *the two-toed sloth*

TOEFL /ˈtəʊ.fl̩/ US /ˈtoʊ-/ noun [U] trademark abbreviation for Test of English as a Foreign Language: a test of English for speakers of other languages

toehold /ˈtəʊ.həʊld/ US /ˈtoʊ.hoʊld/ noun [C] **IN ROCK** ▷ **1** a small hole or surface on a rock that is just big enough for a climber to put the end of his or her foot in or on: *I searched desperately for a toehold in the rock face.* **STRONG FIRST POSITION** ▷ **2** a strong first position from which further progress can be made: *Insurance is a very difficult market to **get** a toehold **in**.*

toenail /ˈtəʊ.neɪl/ US /ˈtoʊ-/ noun [C] B2 the hard, slightly curved part that covers and protects the end of a toe: *She was cutting/painting her toenails.*

toerag /ˈtəʊ.ræg/ US /ˈtoʊ-/ noun [C] UK informal an extremely unpleasant person

toff /tɒf/ US /tɑːf/ noun [C] UK old-fashioned a rich person from a high social class: *Gone are the days when champagne-drinking was just for toffs.*

toffee /ˈtɒf.i/ US /ˈtɑː.fi/ noun [C or U] a hard, CHEWY, often brown sweet that is made from sugar boiled with butter

IDIOM **for toffee** UK informal If you say that someone cannot do something for toffee, you mean that they are extremely bad at it: *He can't paint for toffee!*

ˈtoffee ˌapple noun [C] an apple covered with a sticky layer of toffee and held on a stick

ˈtoffee-nosed adj UK informal disapproving People who are toffee-nosed consider themselves to be better than other people, especially than people of a lower social class: *He's a toffee-nosed git – take no notice of him!*

tofu /ˈtəʊ.fuː/ US /ˈtoʊ-/ noun [U] (also **ˈbean ˌcurd**) a soft, pale food that has very little flavour but is high in PROTEIN, made from the seed of the SOYA plant

tog /tɒg/ US /tɑːg/ noun; verb

▸noun **UNIT** ▷ **1** [C] UK a unit of measurement showing the degree of warmth of a bed cover, especially a DUVET **CLOTHES** ▷ **2 togs** [plural] **a** informal clothes: *Get your togs on, love, then we can go.* **b** Australian English informal for **swimming costume** or **swimming trunks**

▸verb informal **be/get yourself togged up/out** to dress yourself in clothes that are specially for a particular occasion or activity: *We got (ourselves) togged up in walking gear for the hike.* ◦ *They were **all** togged out **in** dinner jackets and ballgowns.*

toga /ˈtəʊ.gə/ US /ˈtoʊ-/ noun [C] a piece of clothing worn by people in ancient Rome, consisting of a long piece of cloth wrapped around the body and hanging loosely from the shoulders

together /təˈgeð.əʳ/ US /-ɚ/ adv; adj

▸adv **WITH EACH OTHER** ▷ **1** A1 with each other: *We used to go to aerobics together.* ◦ *We worked together on a project a couple of years back.* ◦ *Could you add these figures together for me?* ◦ *You mix all the dry ingredients together before you add the milk.* ◦ *I like both flavours separately but I don't like them together.* ◦ *You could stick that back together (= join the separate parts to each other) with a bit of glue.* ◦ *She said, 'Never trust a man whose eyes are so **close** together!'* ◦ *The waiter asked if we were **all** together so I explained that we were two separate parties.* ◦ *We should **get** together (= meet each other socially) some time and have a drink.* → See also **altogether 2** If two people are described as together, they have a close romantic and often sexual relationship with each other: *Mira and Ellis have been together now for almost five years.* **3 get (it) together** informal If two people get together or get it together, they start a sexual relationship with each other. **AT THE SAME TIME** ▷ **4** B1 at the same time: *Everyone seemed to arrive together.* ◦ *We can deal with the next two items on the list together.* **COMBINED** ▷ **5** B2 combined: *Together they must earn over $80,000 a year.* ◦ *She's got more sense than the rest of you **put** together.* **IN ONE PLACE** ▷ **6** B2 in one place: *I'll just gather my things together and then we can go.* **AND ALSO** ▷ **7 together with** B2 in addition to; and also: *The money that I owe you for the phone together with the rent equals £300.* ◦ *That bottle of champagne together with those chocolates will make a nice present.*

▸adj informal approving **1** organized, confident of your abilities, and able to use them to achieve what you want: *He's strikes me as a fairly together sort of a guy.* **2 get it together** to get something organized: *We were going to do something more ambitious over Christmas this year but we never got it together.*

togetherness /təˈgeð.ə.nəs/ US /-ɚ-/ noun [U] the pleasant feeling of being united with other people in friendship and understanding: *War had given to the community a greater sense of togetherness.*

toggle /ˈtɒg.l̩/ US /ˈtɑː.gl̩/ noun; verb

▸noun [C] **FASTENER** ▷ **1** a small bar of wood or plastic that is used to fasten something by being put through a hole or LOOP **COMPUTER SWITCH** ▷ **2** a key or button on a computer that is pressed to turn a feature on and then off: *Select the function you require by pointing to the toggle (= image of a button on the screen) with the mouse and then clicking.*

▸verb [I or T] to switch a feature on a computer on and off by pressing the same button or key: *Use this key to toggle **between** the two typefaces.* ◦ *By toggling this key, you can switch the italics on and off.*

toil /tɔɪl/ noun; verb

▸noun [U] hard work, especially work which makes you feel physically tired: *Lindi has achieved her comfortable life only after years of **hard** toil.* ◦ humorous *Well, after a day's toil in the office I like to relax a little.*

▸verb [I] **WORK HARD** ▷ **1** to work hard: *England's cricketers have been toiling in the 100-degree heat over the past week.* ◦ *I was relaxing in the bath, having toiled **away** in the garden all afternoon.* **MOVE** ▷ **2** to move in a particular direction, slowly and with great effort: *I was toiling up the hill with four heavy bags when he took pity on me.*

toilet /ˈtɔɪ.lət/ noun **CONTAINER** ▷ **1** A1 [C] a bowl-shaped device with a seat which you sit on or stand

T

near when emptying the body of urine or solid waste, or another device used for this purpose: *I was **on** (= using) the toilet when the phone rang.* ◦ *Don't forget to **flush** the toilet.* ◦ *Excuse me, Miss Lewis, I **need/want** (to go to) the toilet.* ◦ *The toilet **seat** was cracked and there was no paper.* **2** [C] UK (US **bathroom**) a room with a toilet in it: *Someone's in the toilet.* **3 go to the toilet** A2 to empty the body of urine or solid waste, usually using a toilet to do so: *It's going to be a long journey, kids, so if you want to go to the toilet do so now.* **4 toilets** A2 [plural] UK (US **restroom**, US also **ladies'/men's room**) a room or small building in a public place in which there are several toilets: *Do you know where the ladies' toilets are?*

> **!** Usage: **toilet**
>
> **Toilet** is the most general word. In British English the informal word **loo** is often used. In American English **bathroom** is often used to mean toilet, especially in the home. In public places toilets are usually called **the ladies** or **the gents** in British English and the **men's room**, **ladies' room**, or **restroom** in American English. The **lavatory** is a slightly formal word for toilet, and **WC** is only used in British English. **WC** is usually only used in advertisments describing houses, hotels, etc.

WASHING ▷ **5** [U] old-fashioned formal the process of washing and dressing yourself: *Virginia had spent longer than usual **over** her toilet that evening, with pleasing results.*

ˈtoilet ˌbag noun [C] a bag in which you put things for keeping yourself clean and tidy, especially when you are travelling

ˈtoilet ˌbrush noun [C] a brush with a long handle that is used to clean the inside of a toilet

ˈtoilet ˌpaper noun [U] soft paper, usually in a long roll, used to clean yourself when you have been to the toilet

toiletries /ˈtɔɪ.lə.triz/ noun [plural] objects and substances that you use in washing yourself and preventing the body from smelling unpleasant: *Women's toiletries are at the other end of the shop, madam.*

ˈtoilet ˌroll noun [C] UK a long, narrow length of toilet paper, rolled around a cardboard cylinder

ˈtoilet ˌsoap noun [C or U] sweet-smelling soap that is intended for washing the body

ˈtoilet ˌtissue noun [U] **toilet paper**

ˈtoilet-trained adj **potty-trained**

ˈtoilet ˌwater noun [C or U] a weak PERFUME (= liquid with a pleasant smell, used on the skin)

to-ing and fro-ing /ˌtuː.ɪŋ.əndˈfrəʊ.ɪŋ/ US /-ˈfroʊ-/ noun [U] **1** repeated movement from one place to another: *Inevitably, when both parents have custody of the child, there's a lot of to-ing and fro-ing between them for the child concerned.* **2** (also **to-ings and fro-ings**) many different and repeated discussions and activities: *The legal to-ings and fro-ings could delay the start of the trial.*

token /ˈtəʊ.kᵊn/ US /ˈtoʊ-/ noun; adj

▸noun [C] **SYMBOL** ▷ **1** C1 something that you do, or a thing that you give someone, that expresses your feelings or intentions, although it might have little practical effect: ***As a** token **of** our gratitude for all that you have done, we would like you to accept this small gift.* ◦ *It doesn't have to be a big present – it's just a token.* **PAPER WORTH MONEY** ▷ **2** UK (US **gift certificate**) a piece of paper with a particular amount of money printed on it that can be exchanged in a shop for goods of that value: *a £20 **book/gift/record** token* **DISC** ▷ **3** C1 a round metal or plastic disc that is used instead of money in some machines

▸adj [before noun] **1** used to describe actions that are done to show that you are doing something, even if the results are limited in their effect: *The troops in front of us either surrendered or offered only token (= not much) resistance.* ◦ *They were the only country to argue for even token recognition of the Baltic states' independence.* **2** disapproving describes something that is done to prevent other people complaining, although it is not sincerely meant and has no real effect: *The truth is that they appoint no more than a token number of women to managerial jobs.*

tokenism /ˈtəʊ.kᵊn.ɪ.zᵊm/ US /ˈtoʊ-/ noun [U] disapproving actions that are the result of pretending to give advantage to those groups in society who are often treated unfairly, in order to give the appearance of fairness

told /təʊld/ US /toʊld/ past simple and past participle of **tell**

IDIOM **all told** as a complete total: *There were 550 people at the festival all told.*

tolerable /ˈtɒl.ᵊr.ə.bl/ US /ˈtɑː.lɚ-/ adj of a quality that is acceptable, although certainly not good: *At their best the conditions in these prisons are scarcely tolerable.* ◦ *For me it's friendships that make life tolerable.*

tolerably /ˈtɒl.ᵊr.ə.bli/ US /ˈtɑː.lɚ-/ adv formal to a limited degree or quite: *I play the piano tolerably **well**, though I have no particular talent for it.*

tolerance /ˈtɒl.ᵊr.ᵊns/ US /ˈtɑː.lɚ-/ noun **ACCEPTANCE** ▷ **1** C2 [U] (formal **toleration**) willingness to accept behaviour and beliefs that are different from your own, although you might not agree with or approve of them: *This period in history is not noted for its **religious** tolerance.* ◦ *Some members of the party would like to see it develop a greater tolerance **of/towards** contrary points of view.* **ABILITY TO DEAL WITH** ▷ **2** [U] the ability to deal with something unpleasant or annoying, or to continue existing despite bad or difficult conditions: *My tolerance **of** heat is considerably greater after having lived in the Far East for a couple of years.* **3** [U] specialized an animal's or plant's ability not to be harmed by a drug or poison over a long period of time: *a greater tolerance **of/to** the drug* **VARIATION** ▷ **4** [C or U] specialized the amount by which a measurement or calculation might change and still be acceptable: *parts that are made to tolerances of a thousandth of an inch*

tolerant /ˈtɒl.ᵊr.ᵊnt/ US /ˈtɑː.lɚ-/ adj **ACCEPTING** ▷ **1** C1 willing to accept behaviour and beliefs that are different from your own, although you might not agree with or approve of them: *The present government is even less tolerant **of** dissent.* ◦ *On the continent people are more tolerant **of** children in public places.* **ABLE TO DEAL WITH** ▷ **2** able to deal with something unpleasant or annoying, or to continue existing despite bad or difficult conditions: *I think men are less tolerant **of** stress than women.* ◦ *Compared to other plants, rye is more tolerant **of** drought.* • **tolerantly** /-li/ adv *I would tell my grandmother about all the crazy things I'd been doing and she would just smile tolerantly.*

tolerate /ˈtɒl.ᵊr.eɪt/ US /ˈtɑː.lə.reɪt/ verb [T] **ACCEPT** ▷ **1** B2 to accept behaviour and beliefs that are different from your own, although you might not agree with or approve of them: *I will not tolerate that sort of behaviour in my class.* ◦ [+ -ing verb] *I won't tolerate lying.* **DEAL WITH** ▷ **2** C2 to deal with something unpleasant or annoying, or to continue existing despite bad or difficult conditions: *These ants can tolerate temperatures that would kill other species.*

toll /təʊl/ (US) /toʊl/ **noun; verb**

▸**noun** **CHARGE** ▷ **1** (C1) [C] a small amount of money that you have to pay to use a road, cross a bridge, etc.: *He's just got a job collecting tolls at the start of the motorway.* **2** [C] US the money a LONG-DISTANCE phone call costs: *Is Bayonne a toll **call** (= a more expensive phone call) from New York?* **SUFFERING** ▷ **3** (C2) [U] suffering, deaths, or damage: *Independent sources say that the **death** toll from the earthquake runs into thousands.*

IDIOM **take its/a toll** (C2) If something takes its/a toll, it causes suffering, deaths, or damage: *The problems of the past few months have taken their toll **on** her health and there are shadows beneath her eyes.* ◦ *The deepening recession has also taken its toll in the south of the country, where unemployment is rife.*

▸**verb** [I or T] to (cause a large bell to) ring slowly and repeatedly: *In the distance, a church bell tolled the hour (= showed the time by ringing).*

tollbooth /ˈtɒl.buːθ/ (US) /ˈtoʊl-/ **noun** [C] US a **tollgate**

ˌtoll-ˈfree **adj** US A toll-free phone call is free for the person making the call.

tollgate /ˈtəʊl.geɪt/ (US) /ˈtoʊl-/ **noun** [C] (US usually **tollbooth**) a gate at the start of a road or bridge at which you pay an amount of money in order to be allowed to use the road or bridge

tollhouse /ˈtəʊl.haʊs/ (US) /ˈtoʊl-/ **noun** [C] especially in the past, a small house at a tollgate, in which the person who collects the money lives

ˈtoll ˌplaza **noun** [C] US a place on a road where there is a line of TOLLBOOTHS

tom /tɒm/ (US) /tɑːm/ **noun** [C] a **tomcat**

tomahawk /ˈtɒm.ə.hɔːk/ (US) /ˈtɑː.mə.hɑːk/ **noun** [C] a small fighting AXE used by Native Americans

tomato /təˈmɑː.təʊ/ (US) /-ˈmeɪ.t̬oʊ/ **noun** [C or U] (plural **tomatoes**) (A1) a round, red, sharp-tasting fruit with a lot of seeds, eaten cooked or uncooked as a vegetable, for example in salads or sauces

toˌmato ˈketchup **noun** [U] a sweet, red tomato sauce, eaten cold and usually poured from a bottle

tomb /tuːm/ **noun** [C] (B2) a large stone structure or underground room where someone, especially an important person, is buried

tombola /tɒmˈbəʊ.lə/ (US) /tɑːmˈboʊ-/ **noun** [C] UK a game in which tickets with different numbers are bought from a spinning container and small prizes are won when the numbers on the tickets are the same as the numbers on the prizes: *I won a bottle of port **on** the tombola at the fair.*

tomboy /ˈtɒm.bɔɪ/ (US) /ˈtɑːm-/ **noun** [C] a girl who acts and dresses like a boy, liking noisy, physical activities

tombstone /ˈtuːm.stəʊn/ (US) /-stoʊn/ **noun** [C] a **gravestone**

tombstoning /ˈtuːm.stəʊ.nɪŋ/ (US) /-stoʊ-/ **noun** [U] mainly UK the dangerous activity of jumping from very high rocks or structures into water while keeping the body straight

tomcat /ˈtɒm.kæt/ (US) /ˈtɑːm-/ **noun** [C] (also **tom**) a male cat

Tom, Dick, and/or Harry /ˌtɒmˌdɪk.ənˈhær.i/ (US) /ˌtɑːmˌdɪk.ənˈher.i/ **noun** [S] disapproving an ordinary person/all ordinary people: *You'd better get a qualified electrician to sort this out – you don't want **any** Tom, Dick or Harry messing around with your electrics.*

tome /təʊm/ (US) /toʊm/ **noun** [C] usually humorous a large, heavy book: *She's written several **weighty** tomes on the subject.*

tomfoolery /ˌtɒmˈfuː.lər.i/ (US) /ˌtɑːmˈfuː.lə-/ **noun** [U] old-fashioned silly behaviour, especially done as a joke

tommy gun /ˈtɒm.i.gʌn/ (US) /ˈtɑː.mi-/ **noun** [C] a light MACHINE GUN (= a gun that fires many bullets quickly) that is held in the hand

tomorrow /təˈmɒr.əʊ/ (US) /-ˈmɔːr.oʊ/ **adv, noun** [U] **1** (A1) (on) the day after today: *I've arranged to see Rachel tomorrow night.* ◦ *Oh, leave it till tomorrow.* ◦ *Is John coming to tomorrow's meeting?* ◦ *He'll be back tomorrow **week/a week** tomorrow (= a week from tomorrow).* **2** (C2) used more generally to mean the future: *Today's problem child may be tomorrow's criminal.* ◦ *We make sacrifices now to give our children a better tomorrow.*

IDIOM **like there is/was no tomorrow** informal If someone does something like there is/was no tomorrow, they do it very fast, in large amounts and without thinking carefully: *After his win on the football pools, he began spending money like there was no tomorrow.*

ˈtom-tom **noun** [C] a drum that is usually beaten with the hands

ton /tʌn/ **noun** [C] (plural **tons** or **ton**) **WEIGHT** ▷ **1** (B2) (specialized **metric ton**, specialized **tonne**) a unit of weight equal to 1,000 kilograms **2** (B2) (specialized **long ton**) a unit of weight equal to 1,016 kilograms **3** (B2) (specialized **short ton**) a unit of weight equal to 907 kilograms **4 tons** (B2) [plural] informal an extremely large amount: *We've got tons **of** food left over from the party.* **MONEY** ▷ **5** [singular] UK informal £100: *It'll cost you a ton or more.* **SPEED** ▷ **6 do a ton** UK old-fashioned informal to drive at 100 miles an hour

IDIOM **like a ton of bricks** very strongly or forcefully: *If father finds out what you've been doing, he'll **come down on** (= punish) you like a ton of bricks!*

tonal /ˈtəʊ.nəl/ (US) /ˈtoʊ-/ **adj** specialized **MUSICAL QUALITY** ▷ **1** relating to the quality of sound of a musical instrument or singing voice **MUSICAL NOTES** ▷ **2** Tonal music is music that is based on MAJOR and MINOR KEYS (= sets of notes). → Compare **atonal**

tone /təʊn/ (US) /toʊn/ **noun; verb**

▸**noun** **VOICE EXPRESSION** ▷ **1** (B2) [U] a quality in the voice that expresses the speaker's feelings or thoughts, often towards the person being spoken to: *I tried to use a sympathetic tone **of voice**.* ◦ *Don't speak to me in that tone **of voice** (= angrily), young lady!* ◦ *It wasn't so much what she said that annoyed me – it was her tone.* **2 tones** [plural] literary the quality of someone's voice: *She recounted the story to me **in** shocked tones (= in a shocked voice).* **3** [U] specialized a change in how high or low the voice is that can change the meaning of a word or sentence **GENERAL MOOD** ▷ **4** (C2) [S] the general mood or main qualities of something: *I didn't like the jokey tone of the article – I thought it inappropriate.* ◦ *Trust you to **lower** the tone of the evening by telling vulgar jokes, Martin!* ◦ *Well, I thought it might **raise** the moral tone of the evening if I invited a vicar to the party.* ◦ *He was in a very bad mood when he arrived, and that **set** the tone **for** the whole meeting.* **COLOUR** ▷ **5** [C] a form or degree of a colour: *warm tones of brown and yellow* **TIGHTNESS** ▷ **6** [U] the healthy tightness of the body, especially the muscles: *After you've had a baby you lose the **muscle** tone in your stomach.* **DIFFERENCE IN SOUND** ▷ **7** [C] (US also **step**) the largest difference in sound between

T

two notes which are next to each other in the Western musical SCALE: *The interval from G to A is a **whole** tone.* **MUSICAL QUALITY** ▷ **8** [C or U] the quality of sound of a musical instrument or singing voice: *the beautiful rich tones of his tenor voice* **PHONE NOISE** ▷ **9** B2 [C] one of the continuous sounds that you hear on a phone that tell you if the other phone is ringing, if it is ENGAGED, etc.: *I've called him several times but I keep getting the engaged tone.* ◦ *Please wait until you hear the **dialling** tone* (US ***dial*** *tone*) (= *the sound that a phone makes when it is ready to be used*).

▸verb [T] (also **tone up**) If you tone a part of the body, you make it firmer and stronger, usually by taking physical exercise: *This is a good exercise for toning up the thighs.*

PHRASAL VERBS **tone sth down** to make something less forceful or offensive, usually a piece of writing or a speech: *Some of the **language** in the original play has been toned down for the television version.* • **tone in** When colours tone in, they match and look pleasant together: *The green of your scarf tones in **with** your shoes.*

toned /təʊnd/ US /toʊnd/ **adj** (of a body) firm and strong

-toned /-təʊnd/ US /-toʊnd/ **suffix** having the tone or tones described: *Low-toned mutterings could be heard in the next room.*

ˌtone-ˈdeaf adj Someone who is tone-deaf is not able to recognize different notes or sing tunes accurately.

ˈtone ˌlanguage noun [C] specialized a language in which the same series of sounds can represent different meanings, depending on how high or low they are spoken: *Chinese is a tone language.*

toneless /ˈtəʊn.ləs/ US /ˈtoʊn-/ **adj** literary (of a voice) not expressing any emotion • **tonelessly** /-li/ **adv**

toner /ˈtəʊ.nəʳ/ US /ˈtoʊ.nɚ/ **noun INK** ▷ **1** [U] ink for a printer or PHOTOCOPIER: *The copier is out of toner.* **FOR SKIN** ▷ **2** [C or U] a substance that you put on your face after you have cleaned it to make the skin feel firm

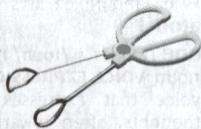

tongs /tɒŋz/ US /tɑːŋz/ **noun** [plural] a device used for picking up objects, consisting of two long pieces joined at one end and pressed together at the other end in order to hold an object between them: *coal tongs* ◦ *a pair of tongs*

tongs

tongue /tʌŋ/ **noun MOUTH PART** ▷ **1** B1 [C] the large, soft piece of flesh in the mouth that you can move, and is used for tasting, speaking, etc.: *I burned my tongue on some soup last night.* **2** [U] the tongue of an animal, used as food **SHOE** ▷ **3** [C] a part of an object that is tongue-shaped, especially the piece of material that is under the LACES in a shoe **LANGUAGE** ▷ **4** [C] literary a language: *immigrants struggling to learn a foreign tongue* ◦ *an ancient tongue* **STYLE OF EXPRESSION** ▷ **5** [S] a person's way of expressing their ideas and feelings: *She is a prolific writer with critical views and a **sharp*** (= *severe and critical*) *tongue.*

IDIOMS **get your tongue round/around sth** to pronounce a difficult word or phrase: *It's one language that I have real difficulty getting my tongue round.* • **loosen sb's tongue** to make someone speak very honestly: *A few whiskies should loosen his tongue.* • **stick/put your tongue out** to make a rude sign by putting the tongue outside the mouth: *An old man was staring at her so she stuck her tongue out **at** him.* • **tongue in cheek** (also **with your tongue in your cheek**) If you say something tongue in cheek, you intend it to be understood as a joke, although you might appear to be serious: *He said that he was America's greatest lover, although I suspect it was tongue in cheek.* • **tongues wagging** informal If what someone says or does starts tongues wagging, it causes other people to start talking and guessing things about their private lives: *Do you think if we leave the party together it will **set/start** tongues wagging?* ◦ *They tried to keep their affair secret, but it wasn't long before tongues began to wag.*

-tongued /-tʌŋd/ **suffix** used to form adjectives that describe the way someone uses words to express their ideas and feelings: *Coleman plays the part of the **sharp**-tongued* (= *severe and critical*) *lawyer.* ◦ *He was younger than her, in his forties, and had a **silver**-tongued charm* (= *said charming things*).

ˌtongue-in-ˈcheek adj [before noun] describes something that is meant to be understood as a joke, although it might appear to be serious: *Her latest play is a firmly tongue-in-cheek look at the world of advertising.*

ˈtongue-ˌlashing noun [C] informal If you give someone a tongue-lashing, you speak angrily to them about something that they have done wrong.

ˈtongue-tied adj If you get tongue-tied, you find it difficult to express yourself, usually because you are nervous.

ˈtongue-ˌtwister noun [C] a sentence or phrase that is intended to be difficult to say, especially when repeated quickly and often: *'She sells seashells on the seashore' is a well-known tongue-twister.*

tonic /ˈtɒn.ɪk/ US /ˈtɑː.nɪk/ **noun MEDICINE** ▷ **1** [C] a liquid medicine that has the general effect of making you feel better rather than treating a particular health problem that you might have **2** [S] informal something that makes you feel stronger or happier: *The magazine is lively and interesting – the pictures alone are a tonic.* **DRINK** ▷ **3** [C or U] (also **tonic water**) FIZZY (= with bubbles) water with a bitter taste which can be drunk on its own or added to alcoholic drinks: *Two gin and tonics, please.*

tonight /təˈnaɪt/ **adv, noun** [U] A1 (during) the night of the present day: *Tonight will be my first opportunity to meet her.* ◦ *Tonight's meeting will take place in the main school hall.*

tonnage /ˈtʌn.ɪdʒ/ **noun** [U] the size of a ship or the weight of goods that a ship is able to carry

tonne /tʌn/ **noun** [C] (plural **tonnes** or **tonne**) (also **ˌmetric ˈton**) 1,000 kilograms: *Oil deliveries will fall 2.5 million tonnes short this year.* ◦ *a 7,554-tonne ocean liner*

tonsil /ˈtɒn.səl/ US /ˈtɑːn-/ **noun** [C usually plural] one of two small, soft organs at the back of the mouth

tonsillitis /ˌtɒn.sɪˈlaɪ.təs/ US /ˌtɑːn.sɪˈlaɪ.t̬əs/ **noun** [U] a painful infection of the tonsils

tonsure /ˈtɒn.ʃəʳ/ US /ˈtɑːn.ʃɚ/ **noun** [C] the top back part of a MONK's head from which a circle of hair has been removed

too /tuː/ **adv MORE** ▷ **1** A1 more than is needed or wanted; more than is suitable or enough: *I'm too fat.* ◦ *I can't reach the shelf – it's **(a bit)** too high.* ◦ *There were **(far)** too many people for such a small room.* ◦ *It's too difficult **(for** me**) to** explain.* ◦ formal *It was too expensive **a** desk **for** a child's room.* ◦ *It's **(all)** too much* (= *more than I can deal with*) *– I can't bear it.* **2 all too** used before an adjective or adverb to emphasize a negative meaning: *The holidays flew by all too quickly.*

T

3 only too used before an adjective to emphasize a positive meaning: *'Would you like to make a donation?' 'I'd be only too pleased.'* **ALSO** ▷ **4** A1 (especially at the end of a sentence) in addition, also: *I'd like to come too.* ◦ informal *'I love chocolate.' 'Me too.'* **5** used to show surprise: *It's a wonderful picture of light shining through trees – and by a child too!* → Compare **well, moreover, what's more** **VERY** ▷ **6** A2 very, or completely: *He wasn't too **pleased/happy** when I told him about the mistake.* ◦ *My mother hasn't been too **well** recently.* ◦ formal *Thank you, you're too **kind**.* **CERTAINLY** ▷ **7** US informal used to emphasize a positive answer to a negative statement: *'I'm not going to school today.' 'You are too!'*

IDIOMS **in too deep** too involved in a difficult situation • **too bad** informal B1 If you say something is too bad, you can mean either that you feel sympathy about a problem, or that you do not. The difference is in what is being talked about and the way that you say it: *It's too bad that you can't come to see Mark in his school play.* ◦ *'I can't come on Friday.' 'That's too bad – I've already bought the tickets so you'll still have to pay.'* • **too good to be true** so good that it is hard to believe, or seeming very good but not real: *Her new job sounds too good to be true.* ◦ *I'm not surprised the offer wasn't genuine, it **sounded** too good to be true.* • **too good to miss** If you say that something is too good to miss, you mean that it is a very good opportunity and that people should see it, do it, etc.: *Henri's latest show is simply too good to miss.* • **too much like hard work** describes an activity that you do not want to do because it needs a lot of effort: *I don't like gardening – it's too much like hard work.* • **too much of a good thing** the fact that something pleasant becomes unpleasant because you have or do too much of it: *You can **have** too much of a good thing.*

took /tʊk/ past simple of **take**

tool /tuːl/ noun [C] **EQUIPMENT** ▷ **1** a piece of equipment which you use with your hands to make or repair something: *power tools* ◦ *machine tools* **2** something that helps you to do a particular activity: *A free low-interest credit card can be a **useful** budgeting tool.* **3 tool of the trade** A tool of the trade is something you need to use to do your job: *For the modern sales executive, a Blackberry is one of the tools of the trade.* **PERSON** ▷ **4** disapproving someone whose decisions and actions are unfairly controlled by others: *The president was widely regarded as the tool **of** the military.* **PENIS** ▷ **5** offensive a PENIS

> **Word partners for tool**
> *use* a tool • an *effective/essential/useful/valuable* tool • a tool *for* sth/doing sth

toolbar /ˈtuːl.bɑːʳ/ noun [C] on a computer screen, a row of ICONS (= small pictures that you choose in order to make the computer do something)

toolbox /ˈtuːl.bɒks/ US /-bɑːks/ noun [C usually singular] a container in which you keep and carry small tools, especially those used in the house or for repairing a car

tooled /tuːld/ adj Something, especially a piece of leather, that is tooled is covered with decorative patterns using a special tool: *a tooled leather belt*

ˌtooled ˈup adj [after verb] slang carrying a weapon, especially a gun

toolkit /ˈtuːlˌkɪt/ noun [C] a set of tools

toolshed /ˈtuːlˌʃed/ noun [C] a small building in which tools and garden equipment are kept

tooltip /ˈtuːl.tɪp/ noun [C] a message with information that appears when you hold a CURSOR over a piece of text or an ICON on a website or in a software program

toot /tuːt/ verb [I or T] to make a short sound or series of short sounds, especially with the HORN of a car as a warning: *The driver tooted (her horn).* • **toot** noun [C] *The waiting taxi **gave** a toot **on** its horn.*

tooth /tuːθ/ noun (plural **teeth**) **MOUTH** ▷ **1** A1 [C] one of the hard, white objects in the mouth that are used for biting and CHEWING (= crushing food): *a broken/missing tooth* ◦ *front/back teeth* ◦ ***false** teeth* ◦ ***Brush/Clean** your teeth thoroughly morning and night.* ◦ *I had to have a tooth **out** (US **pulled**) (= removed).* → See also **eyetooth** **POINT** ▷ **2** [C usually plural] any of the row of points which stick out from the edge of a tool or piece of equipment, such as a COMB, SAW, or ZIP → See also **fine-tooth comb** **POWER** ▷ **3 teeth** [plural] effective force or power: *This committee can make recommendations but it has no real teeth.*

IDIOMS **fight tooth and nail** to try very hard to get something you want: *We fought tooth and nail to get the route of the new road changed.* • **get your teeth into sth** to deal with something or become involved in something with great energy and enthusiasm: *I'm so bored at work, I wish they'd give me something I could really get my teeth into.* • **in the teeth of sth** If something happens or is done in the teeth of difficulties, the difficulties cause problems but do not stop it: *The road was built in the teeth of fierce opposition from the public.* • **set sb's teeth on edge** If something, especially a noise, sets your teeth on edge, it annoys you very much: *That DJ's voice really sets my teeth on edge.*

toothache /ˈtuːθ.eɪk/ noun [C or U] A2 pain caused by something being wrong with one of your teeth: *I've got terrible toothache.*

toothbrush /ˈtuːθ.brʌʃ/ noun [C] A2 a small brush with a long handle which you use to clean your teeth

-toothed /-tuːθt/ suffix with the teeth described: *gap-toothed (= with a space between the top two front teeth)*

ˈtooth ˌfairy noun [C] an imaginary being who children believe takes away a BABY TOOTH that has come out and leaves them money instead

toothless /ˈtuːθ.ləs/ adj **NO TEETH** ▷ **1** having no teeth: *an ugly toothless old hag* **NO POWER** ▷ **2** describes an organization or a rule that has no power: *This well-intentioned but toothless law will do nothing to improve the situation.*

toothpaste /ˈtuːθ.peɪst/ noun [U] B1 a substance which you put onto a toothbrush to clean your teeth: *a tube of toothpaste*

toothpick /ˈtuːθ.pɪk/ noun [C] a small, thin, pointed stick of wood, plastic, or metal that can be used for removing pieces of food from between the teeth, especially after a meal

toothpick

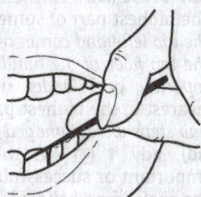

toothsome /ˈtuːθ.səm/ adj (especially of food) attractive or pleasant

toothy /ˈtuː.θi/ adj showing a lot of teeth when you smile: *He gave me a toothy **grin**.*

tootle /ˈtuː.tl/ US /-t̬l/ verb [I usually + adv/prep] informal to go, especially to drive, slowly: *The car in front was just tootling along through the beautiful scenery.*

tootsie /ˈtʊt.si/ noun [C] **FOOT** ▷ **1** (also **tootsy**) a toe or a foot: *Don't get your tootsies cold.* **WOMAN** ▷ **2** (also

T

toots) mainly US informal a woman: [as form of address] *See you later, toots. I'll be home around eight.*

top /tɒp/ (US) /tɑːp/ **noun; adj, adv; adj, exclamation; verb**

▸**noun HIGHEST PART** ▷ **1** (A2) [C] the highest place or part: *She waited for me **at** the top **of** the stairs.* ◦ *There were flags **on** the tops of many of the buildings.* ◦ *There was a pile of books **on** top **of** (= on) the table.* → See also **clifftop, hilltop, mountaintop, rooftop, the treetops** → Compare **bottom, summit 2** [C] the flat upper surface of something: *The top of the table/desk was badly scratched.* **CLOTHES** ▷ **3** (B1) [C] any piece of light clothing worn on the part of the body above the waist: *a skimpy top* ◦ *a pyjama top* ◦ *I need a top to go with these trousers.* **LID** ▷ **4** (C1) [C] the cover or lid used to close a container or pen: *a screw-on top* ◦ *a bottle top* **MOST IMPORTANT** ▷ **5 the top** (C2) [S] the most important position in a group or organization: *At 40, he was **at** the top **of** his profession.* ◦ *Life **at** the top is stressful.* **TOY** ▷ **6** [C] a **spinning top** **EARRING** ▷ **7** [C usually plural] Indian English a piece of jewellery, usually one of a pair, worn in a hole in the ear or fixed to the ear by a CLIP; an EARRING **EXCELLENT** ▷ **8 the tops** [S] old-fashioned the best: *You're the tops, Linda!*

IDIOMS **at the top of your voice** extremely loudly: *She shouted his name at the top of her voice.* • **be on top of sth** informal to be able to control a situation or deal with it • **from top to bottom** (C2) If you search, paint, etc. a building from top to bottom, you search, paint, etc. all parts of it: *They cleaned the house from top to bottom.* • **from top to toe** (also **from head to foot**) (of the clothes a person is wearing, etc.) all in the same style, colour, etc.: *A woman came into the room dressed in red from top to toe.* • **get on top of you** If a difficult situation gets on top of you, it makes you feel so upset that you cannot deal with it: *She's had a few financial problems and I think things have just been getting on top of her.* • **off the top of your head** from the knowledge you have in your memory: *'What's the capital of Mauritania?' 'I couldn't tell you off the top of my head, but I could go and look it up.'* • **on top of sth** (B2) in addition to something, especially something unpleasant: *We missed the train, and on top of that we had to wait for two hours for the next one.* • **on top of the world** (C2) extremely happy: *She was feeling on top of the world.* • **over the top** (abbreviation **OTT**) UK informal (C2) too extreme and not suitable, or demanding too much attention or effort, especially in an uncontrolled way: *I thought the decorations were **way** (= very) over the top.* ◦ *The speech was a bit OTT.* ◦ *He realized he'd gone over the top with the seating arrangements.*

T

▸**adj** [before noun] **HIGHEST PART** ▷ **1** (B1) [before noun] at the highest part of something: *There's a dirty mark on the top left-hand corner of the photo.* ◦ *The offices are on the top floor of the building.* ◦ *He was standing on the top rung of a ladder.* **UPPER PART** ▷ **2** in the part nearest to the highest part; in the upper part: *The top few steps were damaged and broken.*

▸**adj, adv 1** (B1) (in the position of being) most important or successful; best: *So what would be your top choice for a holiday?* ◦ *As a chess player he's among the top ten percent in the country.* **2** (B1) Top people, organizations, or activities are the most important or successful ones: *top athletes/executives* ◦ *top jobs* ◦ *top universities* **3 at top speed** as fast as possible: *The train thundered through the station at top speed.* **4 be/come top** (B2) to be the student with the best results: *She came top **of the class** in English.* ◦ *Sam was top **at/in** Science.* **5 on top form** UK (US **in top form**) feeling or doing things as well as possible: *Paul's back on top form after his illness.*

▸**adj, exclamation** UK informal excellent: *'How was your party?' 'Top, mate.'* ◦ *'You coming, then?' 'Yeah, top!'*

▸**verb (-pp-) HIGHEST PART** ▷ **1** (C2) [T] (also **top off**) to be on the upper surface of something, especially as a decoration: *The dessert was topped off **with** cream and pieces of fruit.* **MOST IMPORTANT** ▷ **2** (C2) [T] to be the most important, most successful, etc.: *The song topped **the charts** (= sold the largest number of recordings) for five weeks.* ◦ *She topped **the bill** (= was the most important act in the show).* **BEST** ▷ **3** [T] to do, pay, etc. more or better than anyone else: *'They've offered me £1,000.' 'I'm afraid we can't top that.'* ◦ *She topped my suggestion **with** an even better one of her own.* **KILL** ▷ **4 top yourself** UK slang to kill yourself

IDIOMS **top and tail** to cut off the hard parts at each end of a fruit or vegetable when you prepare it for cooking: *Top and tail the beans.* • **to top it all** (US and Australian English **to top it all off**) (C2) If you have been describing bad things that happened, and then say that to top it all something else happened, you mean that the final thing was even worse: *The washing machine flooded, my car broke down, then to top it all I locked myself out of the house.*

PHRASAL VERBS **top sth off** (C2) to finish something in an enjoyable or successful way: *She topped off her performance **with** a dazzling encore.* • **top sth up LIQUID** ▷ **1** UK (US **top sth off**) to add liquid in order to fill to the top a container that is already partly full: *Shall I top up your drink?* ◦ *Mix together some lemon juice and sugar, then top it up **with** water.* **MONEY** ▷ **2** to add more of something, especially money, to an existing amount to create the total you need: *This is the easiest way to top up your mobile phone card.* ◦ *top-up fees/payments* • **top sb up** informal to put more drink into someone's glass or cup: *Your glass is nearly empty. Let me top you up.*

top- /tɒp-/ (US) /tɑːp-/ **prefix** used with many different words to mean 'best': *a top-class athlete* ◦ *top-ranking officers*

topaz /ˈtəʊ.pæz/ (US) /ˈtoʊ-/ **noun** [C or U] a transparent, yellow stone used in jewellery

ˌtop ˈbrass noun [U, + sing/pl verb] the people with the highest positions of authority, especially in the armed forces

topcoat /ˈtɒp.kəʊt/ (US) /ˈtɑːp.koʊt/ **noun** [C or U] a final layer of paint put onto a surface over another layer, or the type of paint used to do this → Compare **undercoat**

ˌtop ˈdog noun [C usually singular] informal a person who has achieved a position of authority

ˌtop-ˈdown adj [before noun] describes a situation in which decisions are made by a few people in authority rather than by the people who are affected by the decisions: *a top-down approach/strategy*

topee /ˈtəʊ.piː/ (US) /ˈtoʊ-/ **noun** [C] (also **topi**) a **pith helmet**

ˌtop-ˈflight adj [before noun] highest in standard or quality: *He's one of our top-flight engineers.*

ˌtop ˈhat noun [C] (informal **topper**) a tall, black or grey hat worn by men on some formal occasions

ˌtop-ˈheavy adj [after verb] If something is top-heavy, it has more weight in the higher part than in the lower part and will not balance correctly: *The main reason the ship capsized was that it was top-heavy.* ◦ figurative *If they sacked a hundred senior managers, they would be less top-heavy.*

topiary /ˈtəʊ.pjər.i/ (US) /ˈtoʊ.pi.er-/ noun [U] specialized the art of cutting bushes into attractive shapes, especially of animals and birds

topic /ˈtɒp.ɪk/ (US) /ˈtɑː.pɪk/ noun [C] (B1) a subject that is discussed, written about, or studied: *Our discussion ranged over various topics, such as acid rain and the hole in the ozone layer.*

topical /ˈtɒp.ɪ.kəl/ (US) /ˈtɑː.pɪ-/ adj HAPPENING NOW ▷ **1** of interest at the present time; relating to things that are happening at present: *a topical joke* ◦ *The discussion focused on topical issues in medicine.* MEDICINE ▷ **2** specialized describes a medical product that is used on the outside of the body: *This lotion is for topical application only.* • **topicality** /ˌtɒp.ɪˈkæl.ə.ti/ (US) /ˌtɑː.pɪˈkæl.ə.t̬i/ noun [U] • **topically** /-kəl.i/ adv

topknot /ˈtɒp.nɒt/ (US) /ˈtɑːp.nɑːt/ noun [C] long hair tied up onto the top part of the back of the head

topless /ˈtɒp.ləs/ (US) /ˈtɑːp-/ adj, adv describes someone, usually a woman, wearing nothing on the upper part of their body, or something connected with this way of dressing: *topless dancers/bars/sunbathing* ◦ *Many women now **go** topless on European beaches.*

ˌtop-ˈlevel adj [before noun] describes an activity in which the most important people in an organization or country take part: *top-level talks/negotiations/discussions*

topmost /ˈtɒp.məʊst/ (US) /ˈtɑːp.moʊst/ adj [before noun] highest: *We couldn't reach the apples on the topmost branches.*

ˌtop-ˈnotch adj informal excellent: *That restaurant's really top-notch.*

ˌtop-of-the-ˈrange adj UK (US **ˌtop-of-the-ˈline**) used for describing something that is the most expensive in a group of similar products: *a top-of-the-range Mercedes*

topography /təˈpɒg.rə.fi/ (US) /təˈpɑː.grə-/ noun [U] specialized the physical appearance of the natural features of an area of land, especially the shape of its surface • **topographer** /-fər/ (US) /-fɚ/ noun [C] • **topographical** /ˌtɒp.əˈgræf.ɪ.kəl/ (US) /ˌtɑː.pə-/ adj • **topographically** /ˌtɒp.əˈgræf.ɪ.kəl.i/ (US) /ˌtɑː.pə-/ adv

topology /tɒpˈɒl.ə.dʒi/ (US) /təˈpɑː.lə-/ noun [C or U] specialized the way the parts of something are organized or connected: *Globalization and the rise of information technology have changed the topology of the corporation.*

topper /ˈtɒp.ər/ (US) /ˈtɑː.pɚ/ noun [C] HAT ▷ **1** informal for **top hat** STUDENT ▷ **2** Indian English the best student in a class or school

topping /ˈtɒp.ɪŋ/ (US) /ˈtɑː.pɪŋ/ noun [C or U] a substance, especially a sauce, cream, or pieces of food, that is put on top of other food to give extra flavour and to make it look attractive: *pizza topping* ◦ *a topping of toasted almonds*

topple /ˈtɒp.l̩/ (US) /ˈtɑː.pl̩/ verb FALL ▷ **1** [I or T] to (cause to) lose balance and fall down: *The statue of the dictator was toppled (**over**) by the crowds.* ◦ *The tree toppled and fell.* GOVERNMENT ▷ **2** [T] to force a leader or government out of power: *The church was prominently involved in the struggle that toppled the dictatorship.*

ˌtop ˈsecret adj (of information) extremely secret and not to be told to anyone outside a particular group of people: *These papers are top secret.* ◦ *a top secret military research project*

ˌtop-seˈcurity adj [before noun] a top-security prison or hospital is very strongly protected because it contains dangerous people

topsoil /ˈtɒp.sɔɪl/ (US) /ˈtɑːp-/ noun [U] (the soil which forms) the top layer of ground in which plants grow → Compare **subsoil**

topspin /ˈtɒp.spɪn/ (US) /ˈtɑːp-/ noun [U] a forward turning movement of a ball as it travels through the air

topsy-turvy /ˌtɒp.siˈtɜː.vi/ (US) /ˌtɑː.p.siˈtɝː-/ adj, adv informal (in a state of being) confused, not well organized, or giving importance to unexpected things: *The government's topsy-turvy priorities mean that spending on education remains low.* → Synonym **upside down**

ˈtop-up noun [C usually singular] LIQUID ▷ **1** the act of putting more drink into someone's glass or cup: *Your glass is nearly empty. Would you like a top-up?* **2** the act of adding liquid in order to fill to the top a container that is already partly full MONEY ▷ **3** an extra amount of something, especially money, that is added to an existing amount to create the total you need: *The bank agreed to lend me a top-up of £500.*

ˈtop-up ˌcard noun [C] a card you can buy which gives you a special number so that you can use your mobile phone for longer

the Torah /ˈtɔː.rə/ (US) /ˈtɔːr.ə/ noun [S] the first five books of the Jewish BIBLE that deal with the law of God

torch /tɔːtʃ/ (US) /tɔːrtʃ/ noun; verb

▸noun **1** (B2) [C] UK (US **flashlight**) a small light that is held in the hand and usually gets its power from BATTERIES: *She **flashed/shone** the torch into the dark room.* **2** [C] a thick stick with material that burns tied to the top of it, used to give light: *a flaming/blazing torch* ◦ literary *Many buildings were **put to the** torch (= burned intentionally) during the riots.* **3** [S] approving used as a symbol of a political movement or idea that has an important positive influence: ***the** torch **of** socialism.*

▸verb [T] to burn a building or other large thing, intentionally and usually illegally

torchlight /ˈtɔːtʃ.laɪt/ (US) /ˈtɔːrtʃ-/ noun; adj

▸noun LIGHT ▷ **1** [U] the light from a torch: *I saw the blade of an open knife shine in his hand **in** the torchlight.* TORCH ▷ **2** [C] Indian English a **torch**

▸adj [before noun] (also **torchlit**) describes an event that is lit by burning torches: *a torchlight/torchlit procession*

tore /tɔːr/ (US) /tɔːr/ past simple of **tear**

toreador /ˈtɒr.i.ə.dɔːr/ (US) /ˈtɔːr.i.ə.dɔːr/ noun [C] a person, usually a man, who takes part in a BULLFIGHT riding a horse → Compare **matador, picador**

torment noun; verb

▸noun /ˈtɔː.ment/ (US) /ˈtɔːr-/ **1** [U] great mental suffering and unhappiness, or great physical pain: *The family said they had **endured** years of torment and abuse at the hands of the neighbours.* ◦ *Waiting for the result of the medical tests was sheer torment.* ◦ *He spent the night **in** torment, trying to decide what was the best thing to do.* **2** **torments** [plural] great mental suffering and unhappiness: *Nothing can describe the torments we **went through** while we were waiting for news.* **3** [C] something or someone that causes great suffering or anger: *The tax forms were an annual torment **to** him.*

▸verb [T] /tɔːˈment/ (US) /tɔːr-/ to cause a person or animal to suffer or worry: *The animals are tormented mercilessly by flies and mosquitoes.* ◦ *The camera focused on a group of women whose faces were tormented **by/with** (= showed that they were suffering)* *grief.* ◦ *It tormented me all day – did I remember to lock the door when I left the house?* • **tormentor** /-ˈmen.təʳ/ ⓤⓢ /-ˈmen.tɚ/ noun [C]

torn /tɔːn/ ⓤⓢ /tɔːrn/ past participle of **tear**

IDIOM **torn between** C2 If you are torn between two possibilities, you find it very difficult to choose between them.

tornado /tɔːˈneɪ.dəʊ/ ⓤⓢ /tɔːrˈneɪ.doʊ/ noun [C] (plural **tornadoes** or **tornados**) (US informal also **twister**) B2 a strong, dangerous wind that forms itself into an upside-down spinning cone and is able to destroy buildings as it moves across the ground

torpedo /tɔːˈpiː.dəʊ/ ⓤⓢ /tɔːrˈpiː.doʊ/ noun; verb

▸**noun** [C or U] (plural **torpedoes**) a long, thin bomb that travels underwater in order to destroy the ship at which it is aimed

▸**verb** [T] **1** to use a torpedo to destroy something **2** informal to destroy: *He accused them of trying to torpedo the peace process.*

torpid /ˈtɔː.pɪd/ ⓤⓢ /ˈtɔːr-/ adj formal not active; moving or thinking slowly, especially as a result of being lazy or feeling that you want to sleep: *If you have a sudden loss of cabin pressure at 20,000 feet, passengers will become torpid and then lose consciousness.* • **torpidly** /-li/ adv

torpor /ˈtɔː.pəʳ/ ⓤⓢ /ˈtɔːr.pɚ/ noun [U] (also **torpidity** /tɔːˈpɪd.ə.ti/ ⓤⓢ /tɔːrˈpɪd.ə.t̬i/) **1** formal the state of not being active and having no energy or enthusiasm **2** specialized the state of reduced activity that some animals experience during the winter

torque /tɔːk/ ⓤⓢ /tɔːrk/ noun [U] specialized a force which causes something to ROTATE (= turn in a circle)

torrent /ˈtɒr.ᵊnt/ ⓤⓢ /ˈtɔːr-/ noun **1** [S] a sudden large or too large amount, especially one which seems to be uncontrolled: *He let out* ***a*** *torrent* ***of*** *abuse/angry words.* ◦ *They are worried that the flow/trickle/stream of tourists could swell into* ***an*** *unmanageable torrent if there are no controls.* **2** [C] a large amount of water that is moving quickly: *Heavy rainfall turned the river into a rushing/raging torrent.* **3 torrents** [plural] large amounts: *torrents of rain* ◦ *The rain came down/fell* ***in*** *torrents.* ◦ *We have received torrents of letters/requests/criticism.*

torrential /təˈren.ʃᵊl/ ⓤⓢ /tɔːˈren.ʃᵊl/ adj C2 used to refer to very heavy rain: *torrential rain* ◦ *a torrential downpour/storm*

torrid /ˈtɒr.ɪd/ ⓤⓢ /ˈtɔːr.ɪd/ adj EMOTIONS ▷ **1** involving strong emotions, especially those of sexual love: *a torrid romance* WEATHER ▷ **2** formal extremely hot: *the torrid heat of August*

IDIOM **a torrid time** UK a period when you experience a lot of problems

torsion /ˈtɔː.ʃᵊn/ ⓤⓢ /ˈtɔːr-/ noun [U] specialized the act of twisting, the force which causes twisting, or the state of being twisted

torso /ˈtɔː.səʊ/ ⓤⓢ /ˈtɔːr.soʊ/ noun [C] (plural **torsos**) the human body considered without head, arms, or legs, or a STATUE (= artistic model) representing this: *The airbag will protect the head and torso.* ◦ *a famous marble torso*

tort /tɔːt/ ⓤⓢ /tɔːrt/ noun [C] legal an action that is wrong but can be dealt with in a CIVIL court rather than a criminal court

torte /tɔːt/ ⓤⓢ /tɔːrt/ noun [C or U] a round, flat, sweet cake, often with cream and fruit: *chocolate/almond/blackcurrant torte*

tortellini /ˌtɔː.tᵊlˈiː.ni/ ⓤⓢ /ˌtɔːr.t̬əˈliː-/ noun [U] a type of PASTA in folded shapes that are filled with meat, cheese, or vegetables

tortilla /tɔːˈtiː.ə/ ⓤⓢ /tɔːrˈtiː.jə/ noun **1** [C] a type of thin, round Mexican bread made from MAIZE flour **2** [C or U] a thick Spanish OMELETTE (= a flat, round food made by frying eggs that have been mixed together) with potato and sometimes onion in it

torˈtilla ˌchip noun [C usually plural] a small, fried piece of tortilla, often eaten with a spicy sauce

tortoise /ˈtɔː.təs/ ⓤⓢ /ˈtɔːr.t̬əs/ noun [C] an animal with a thick, hard shell that it can move its head and legs into for protection. It eats plants, moves very slowly, and sleeps during the winter.

tortoiseshell /ˈtɔː.təʃ.ʃel/ ⓤⓢ /ˈtɔːr.t̬əs-/ noun [U] the hard shell of a TURTLE that is yellow, orange, and brown and that is used to make decorative objects, or an artificial substance made to look like this: *glasses with tortoiseshell frames*

ˌtortoiseshell ˈbutterfly noun [C] a type of BUTTERFLY with yellow, orange, and brown marks on its wings

tortuous /ˈtɔː.tʃu.əs/ ⓤⓢ /ˈtɔːr-/ adj with many turns and changes of direction; not direct or simple: *He took a tortuous* ***route*** *through back streets.* ◦ *The path to peace seems at last to be clear, although it may be a long and tortuous one.* • **tortuously** /-li/ adv • **tortuousness** /-nəs/ noun [U]

torture /ˈtɔː.tʃəʳ/ ⓤⓢ /ˈtɔːr.tʃɚ/ noun; verb

▸**noun 1** C2 [U] the act of causing great physical or mental pain in order to persuade someone to do something or to give information, or to be cruel to a person or animal: *Half of the prisoners died after torture and starvation.* ◦ *He revealed the secret* ***under*** *torture.* **2** C1 [C or U] informal a very unpleasant experience: *The rush-hour traffic was* ***sheer*** *torture as usual.*

▸**verb** [T] **1** C2 to cause great physical or mental pain to someone intentionally: *It is claimed that the officers tortured a man* ***to death*** *in a city police station.* **2** to cause mental pain: *He tortured him****self*** *for years* ***with*** *the thought that he could have stopped the boy from running into the road.* • **torturer** /-əʳ/ ⓤⓢ /-ɚ/ noun [C]

tortured /ˈtɔː.tʃəd/ ⓤⓢ /ˈtɔːr.tʃɚd/ adj involving suffering and difficulty: *the country's tortured past*

Tory /ˈtɔː.ri/ ⓤⓢ /ˈtɔːr.i/ adj, noun [C] (a member) of the British Conservative Party: ***The*** *Tories (= the Tory party) have dropped in the opinion poll ratings.* ◦ *Tory voters.* • **Toryism** /-ɪ.zᵊm/ noun [U]

tosh /tɒʃ/ ⓤⓢ /tɑːʃ/ noun [U] old-fashioned informal nonsense: *It's just a lot of tosh.*

toss /tɒs/ ⓤⓢ /tɑːs/ verb; noun

▸**verb** THROW ▷ **1** C2 [T usually + adv/prep] to throw something carelessly: *He glanced at the letter and then tossed it into the bin.* ◦ *The bull tossed him up into the air.* ◦ [+ two objects] *Andrew tossed him the ball.* FOOD ▷ **2** [T] When you toss food you shake or mix small pieces of it together with a sauce or DRESSING: *a tossed salad* ◦ *carrots tossed* ***in*** *butter* **3 toss a pancake** UK to quickly and suddenly lift the pan in which a PANCAKE (= a thin, flat, round cake) is cooking so that the pancake goes up into the air and turns over before falling back into the pan MOVE ▷ **4** [T] If you toss your hair or a part of your body you move it up and back suddenly: *She tossed her head in annoyance.* ◦ *She tossed back her hair.* **5 toss and turn** C2 [I] to move about from side to side or turn a lot in bed, especially because you cannot sleep: *I was tossing and turning all night.* COIN ▷ **6** C1 [I or T] (also **toss sb for sth**, also **toss up**) to throw a coin up into the air and guess which side will land facing up, as a way of making a decision: *Let's toss **a coin**/Let's toss up to see who'll go first.* ◦ *'I'll toss you for it – heads or tails?'*

PHRASAL VERBS **toss sth about/around** informal If you toss ideas, suggestions, or phrases about, you mention them and discuss them with other people. • **toss sth aside** literary to throw away or get rid of something • **toss sth away** informal to spend or lose something carelessly: *That much money is not to be tossed away lightly.* • **toss sth off** informal to do something quickly, especially in a careless way or with little effort: *She tossed off a reply to the letter before she left for the meeting.* • **toss (sb) off** UK offensive to give someone sexual pleasure by rubbing their sex organs, or to do this to yourself

▸noun **MOVEMENT** ▷ **1** [C usually singular] a sudden quick movement: *'I don't care,' she replied with a toss **of her head**.* **THROW** ▷ **2 a toss of a coin** an act of throwing a coin in the air and guessing which side will land facing upward as a way of deciding something **3 win/lose the toss** to guess correctly/wrongly which side of a coin will be facing up when it lands on the ground after being thrown **4** [C] an act of throwing something in a careless or relaxed way

IDIOM **not give/care a toss** UK very informal to not be worried at all by something: *I don't give a toss what he thinks.*

tosser /ˈtɒs.əʳ/ (US) /ˈtɑː.sɚ/ noun [C] UK offensive a stupid or unpleasant person: *Barry's such a tosser.*

ˈtoss-up noun [C] informal If you describe a situation as a toss-up, you mean that either of two possibilities is equally likely: *It's **a** toss-up **between** Angela and Moira for the editor's job.*

tot /tɒt/ (US) /tɑːt/ noun; verb

▸noun [C] **CHILD** ▷ **1** informal a young child: *These are good, strong toys for **tiny** tots.* **DRINK** ▷ **2** a small drink of alcohol: *He poured them each a generous tot **of** whisky/rum.*

▸verb (-tt-)

PHRASAL VERB **tot sth up** informal to add up numbers or amounts of something, or to have a particular number or amount as a total when added up: *She quickly totted up our bill and added an amount for the waiter.* ◦ *That tots up **to** £20.*

total /ˈtəʊ.təl/ (US) /ˈtoʊ.t̬əl/ noun; adj; verb

▸noun [C] (B1) the amount you get when several smaller amounts are added together: *At that time of day, cars with only one occupant accounted for almost 80 percent of the total.* ◦ ***A** total **of** 21 horses were entered for the race.* ◦ *We made £700 **in** total, over three days of trading.*

> **Word partners for total noun**
>
> sth *brings/takes* the total *to* [500/1,000] • *reach* a total of [700/200] • the *final/net/overall/sum* total • the *annual/monthly* total • a total *of* [500/3,000] • [600/30] *in* total • [50/30] *out of* a total of [90/100]

▸adj **AMOUNT** ▷ **1** (B1) [before noun] including everything: *the total cost* ◦ *Total losses were $800.* **VERY GREAT** ▷ **2** (B2) very great or of the largest degree possible: *total secrecy* ◦ *a total disregard for their feelings* ◦ *total silence* ◦ *The organization of the event was a total shambles (= very bad).* ◦ *The collapse, when it came, was total.*

▸verb [L only + noun, T] (-ll- or US usually -l-) (C1) to have as a complete amount, or to calculate this: *This is the eighth volume in the series, which totals 21 volumes in all.* ◦ *We totalled (**up**) the money we had each earned, and then shared it equally among the three of us.*

totalitarian /təʊˌtæl.ɪˈteə.ri.ən/ (US) /toʊˌtæl.əˈter.i-/

adj disapproving (C2) of or being a political system in which those in power have complete control and do not allow people freedom to oppose them: *a totalitarian regime/state* • **totalitarianism** /-ə.nɪ.zəm/ noun [U]

totality /təʊˈtæl.ə.ti/ (US) /toʊˈtæl.ə.t̬i/ noun [U] formal the whole of something: *We need to consider this very serious issue **in its** totality.*

totally /ˈtəʊ.təl.i/ (US) /ˈtoʊ.t̬əl-/ adv (B1) completely: *Her second husband is totally different from Mark.* ◦ *I totally agree with you.*

> **Common mistake: totally**
>
> **Warning:** Common word-building error! If an adjective ends with 'l', add '-ly' to make an adverb. Don't write 'totaly', write **totally.**

tote /təʊt/ (US) /toʊt/ verb; noun

▸verb [T] informal to carry something, especially something heavy or awkward: *She usually toted the baby **around** in a backpack.* ◦ *The building was surrounded with bodyguards toting sub-machine **guns**.* ◦ ***Gun**-toting security men were posted at all the entrances.*

▸noun **RACING** ▷ **1 the Tote** [S] trademark a system of putting BETS on horses or dogs in a race **BAG** ▷ **2** [C] a **tote bag**

ˈtote ˌbag noun [C] (also **tote**) a large, strong bag

totem /ˈtəʊ.təm/ (US) /ˈtoʊ.t̬əm/ noun [C] an object that is respected by a group of people, especially for religious reasons: *Television could be seen as a totem of modern society.* • **totemic** /təʊˈtem.ɪk/ (US) /toʊ-/ adj

ˈtotem ˌpole noun [C] a tall wooden pole with symbols cut or painted on it that is part of the tradition of the Native Americans of the west coast of Canada and the northern US

totter /ˈtɒt.əʳ/ (US) /ˈtɑː.t̬ɚ/ verb [I] **1** to walk with difficulty in a way that looks as if you are about to fall: *She tottered unsteadily down the stairs in her high-heeled shoes.* → Compare **stagger, teeter 2** to shake and move from side to side: *Several tall piles of books tottered and fell.* **3** (of a company, government, etc.) to become weaker and less likely to carry on existing: *The industry has tottered from crisis to crisis now for two years.* • **tottering** /-ɪŋ/ adj *She walked slowly with tottering steps.* ◦ *It was the last decision of a tottering government.* • **tottery** /-i/ adj *a tottery old man*

totty /ˈtɒt.i/ (US) /ˈtɑː.t̬i/ noun [U] UK slang sexually attractive people: *Any totty around last night?*

toucan /ˈtuː.kən/ (US) /-kæn/ noun [C] a South American bird that has a brightly coloured beak

toucan

touch /tʌtʃ/ verb; noun

▸verb **PUT HAND ON** ▷ **1** (B1) [I or T] to put your hand or another part of your body lightly onto and off something or someone: *That paint is wet – don't touch (it).* ◦ *He touched the girl **on** the arm to get her attention.* ◦ *The child touched the worm **with** (= using, in his hand) a twig.* ◦ figurative *The setting sun touched the trees **with** red (= made them appear red for a short time).* **BE CLOSE TOGETHER** ▷ **2** (B2) [I or T] (of two or more things) to be so close together that there is no space between; to be in CONTACT: *He fell asleep as soon as his head touched the pillow.* ◦ *She pushed the two bookcases together until they touched/were touching.* **HARM/DAMAGE** ▷ **3** (C2) to

T

harm someone, or use or damage something: *Please don't touch any of my things while I'm away.* **EAT/DRINK** ▷ **4** [T] informal (usually used in negative sentences) to eat or drink something: *They hadn't touched any of the food we had left for them.* ◦ *Honestly, I haven't touched **a drop** (= drunk any alcohol) all night.* **INFLUENCE** ▷ **5** [T] to influence someone or something emotionally, or cause feelings of sympathy in someone: *Tragedy touched their lives when their son was 16.* ◦ *The TV report about the children's work for charity touched thousands of people's hearts.* **BE AS GOOD** ▷ **6** [T] (usually used in negative sentences) to have or reach the same STANDARD (= level of quality) as someone or something: *Her novels **can't** touch (= are not as good as) those of her sister.* ◦ ***There's no one to** touch him **as** an illustrator of children's books.*

IDIOMS **touch base** to talk to someone for a short time to find out how they are or what they think about something: *I just wanted to quickly touch base **with** you: did you get an email from my secretary about the meeting?* • **touch wood** UK (US **knock on wood**) said in order to avoid bad luck, either when you mention good luck that you have had in the past or when you mention hopes you have for the future: *The deal will be agreed on Wednesday, touch wood.* • **touch/strike/hit a (raw) nerve** to upset someone: *The newspaper article touched a raw nerve – people still resent the closure of the local school.* • **wouldn't touch sth with a barge pole** UK (US also **wouldn't touch sth with a ten-foot pole**) used to mean that you certainly do not want to buy something or be involved with something

PHRASAL VERBS **touch down** When an aircraft touches down, it lands. → See also **touchdown** • **touch sth off** to cause a violent or difficult series of events to suddenly begin: *The plans for a new airport have touched off a storm of protest.* • **touch on/upon sth** to mention a subject quickly when speaking or writing about another subject: *The talk was about educational opportunities for adults, and the speaker also touched upon sources of finance.* • **touch sth up** to improve something by making small changes or additions: *She touched up her lipstick and brushed her hair.* ◦ *We thought the photo had probably been touched up, because he looked so much younger in it.* • **touch sb up** UK (US **feel sb up**) informal to touch someone's body in a sexual way without their permission: *She claimed that he had tried to touch her up.*

▸noun **SMALL AMOUNT** ▷ **1** C2 [S] a small amount: *'Would you like milk?' 'Just **a** touch.'* ◦ *There was a touch **of** irony/humour in her voice.* **2** [S] informal To show that an illness is not too serious, you can say you have had a touch of it: *I've had a touch of flu/hay fever.* **3** C2 [C] a small addition or detail which makes something better: *The speech had several comic touches.* ◦ *Using a sailing ship as the company badge was a touch **of genius** (= a good/clever idea or action).* ◦ *The flowers on the table provided the **finishing** touch.* **4 a touch** slightly: *The weather has turned a touch too cold for my liking.* **FEELING** ▷ **5** B2 [U] the ability to know what something is like by feeling it with the fingers: *the sense of touch* ◦ *I found the right coin in the dark **by** touch.* **6 to the touch** B2 (also **to your touch**) used after an adjective to express how something feels when you put your hand on it: *The material was soft to the touch.* **MOVEMENT ONTO/OFF** ▷ **7** B2 [C usually singular] a quick, light movement of one thing, especially a hand, onto and off another thing: *I felt a cold touch on my arm.* ◦ *At a/the touch **of** a button, the door opened.* **COMMUNICATION** ▷ **8 be, get, keep, etc. in touch** B1 to communicate or continue to communicate with someone by using a phone or writing to them: *Are you still in touch with any of your old school friends?* ◦ *No, Jane and I never kept in touch after college.* ◦ *We're in **close** touch with our office in Spain.* **9 lose touch** B2 to stop communicating with someone, usually because they do not live near you now: *We lost touch over the years.* **ABILITY** ▷ **10** [S or U] an ability to do things in the stated, especially positive, way: *He has a deft touch with tricky painting jobs.* ◦ *She gave the job her own special/magic/professional/personal touch.* ◦ *I admire her lightness/sureness of touch as a cook.* ◦ *He used to be a good writer but I think he's **losing** his touch.* **SPORT** ▷ **11** [U] the area outside either of the long edges of the space on which football and similar games are played: *Playing for safety, he kicked the ball **into** touch.* → See also **touchline** **KNOWLEDGE** ▷ **12 be in/out of touch** C2 If you are in touch/out of touch with a subject, activity, or situation, your knowledge about it is recent/not recent: *He's not really in touch with what young people are interested in.* ◦ *I didn't look at a newspaper all the time I was on holiday, so I'm completely out of touch.*

ˌtouch-and-ˈgo adj informal C2 describes a situation that is uncertain: *The doctor says that it's touch-and-go **whether** Mary will be okay.*

touchdown /ˈtʌtʃ.daʊn/ noun [C] **LANDING** ▷ **1** the landing of an aircraft or of some types of spacecraft: *One of the plane's tyres burst on touchdown.* → See also **touch down** **FOOTBALL** ▷ **2** (in RUGBY) the act of scoring points by putting the ball down on the ground behind the other team's goal **3** (in American football) the act of scoring points by carrying the ball across the other team's goal line or throwing the ball so that it is caught by a member of your team who is across the other team's goal line

touché /tuːˈʃeɪ/ **exclamation** used to admit that someone has made a good point against you in an argument or discussion: *'You say we should support British industries, but you always drink French wines.' 'Touché.'*

touched /tʌtʃt/ adj [after verb] **GRATEFUL** ▷ **1** B2 grateful for something kind that someone has done: *I was very touched by all the cards my friends sent me when I was in hospital.* ◦ [+ that] *He was touched **that** you remembered his birthday.* **STRANGE** ▷ **2** old-fashioned informal behaving in an unusual and strange way: *You must think I'm a bit touched, hanging around in graveyards.*

ˌtouch ˈfootball noun [U] US an informal type of football in which play stops if a player puts their hand onto the person who has the ball

touching /ˈtʌtʃ.ɪŋ/ **adj** making you feel sadness, sympathy, etc.: *a touching story* • **touchingly** /-li/ **adv**

touchline /ˈtʌtʃ.laɪn/ **noun** [C] UK (US **sideline**) one of the two lines that show the position of the long edges of the area in which particular games, such as football, are played: *She spends her Saturday afternoons standing on the touchline, watching her boyfriend play rugby.*

touchpad /ˈtʌtʃ.pæd/ **noun** [C] **1** a special area on a LAPTOP or other computer that you touch in order to move the CURSOR or give an instruction **2** a small area that you touch to choose something or give an instruction on a device such as a MICROWAVE

touchpaper /ˈtʌtʃˌpeɪ.pər/ (US) /-pɚ/ **noun** [C] a small piece of paper on one end of a FIREWORK, which you light in order to start the firework burning: *The instructions on the fireworks said 'Light the blue touchpaper, and stand well clear.'*

touchscreen /ˈtʌtʃ.skriːn/ **noun** [C] a computer screen that you touch to get information, buy something, etc.: *Customers use a touchscreen to buy tickets.* ◦ *Voters in Georgia will use a touchscreen voting system.* ◦ *touchscreen technology*

touchstone /ˈtʌtʃ.stəʊn/ US /-stoʊn/ **noun** [C] an established standard or principle by which something is judged: *Until relatively recently, the Japanese car industry was the touchstone **of** international success.*

ˈTouch-Tone **adj** trademark describes a phone that produces different sounds when the different buttons with numbers on them are pressed: *You can call your bank and perform a transaction using a Touch-Tone phone.*

ˈtouch-type **verb** [I] to use a keyboard without looking at the keys

touchy /ˈtʌtʃ.i/ **adj** **1** easily offended or upset: *You have to be careful what you say to Kevin – he's rather touchy.* ◦ *She's very touchy **about** the fact that her husband has been married before.* **2** needing to be dealt with carefully: *This is a touchy **subject/issue/point**, so we'd better avoid it.* • **touchily** /-ɪ.li/ **adv** • **touchiness** /-nəs/ **noun** [U] *Everyone is aware of the touchiness **of** the situation (= that it needs to be dealt with carefully).*

touchy-feely /ˌtʌtʃ.iˈfiː.li/ **adj** informal kind and loving, especially by touching and holding people more than is usual, often in a way that makes other people uncomfortable: *a touchy-feely approach*

tough /tʌf/ **adj; verb; noun**

▸**adj** **STRONG** ▷ **1** B2 strong; not easily broken or made weaker or defeated: *These toys are made from tough plastic.* ◦ *Children's shoes need to be tough.* ◦ *You have to be tough to be successful in politics.* ◦ informal *Their lawyer is a real tough **customer/nut** (= person).* **2** C2 strong and determined: *Tough new safety standards have been introduced for cars.* ◦ *There have been calls for tougher controls/restrictions on what newspapers are allowed to print.* ◦ *After some tough bargaining, we finally agreed on a deal.* ◦ *I think it's time the police **got** tougher **on/with** (= treated more severely) people who drink and drive.* ◦ *The government is continuing to take a tough **line** on terrorism.* **DIFFICULT** ▷ **3** B2 difficult to do or to deal with: *They've had an exceptionally tough life.* ◦ *They will be a tough team **to** beat.* ◦ *The company is going through a tough **time** at the moment.* ◦ *We've had to make some very tough **decisions**.* ◦ *My boss has given me a tough **job/assignment**.* ◦ *Many homeless people are facing a tough **winter**.* **FOOD** ▷ **4** B2 describes food that is difficult to cut or eat: *This steak is very tough.* **VIOLENT** ▷ **5** likely to be violent or to contain violence; not kind or pleasant: *a tough neighbourhood* ◦ *Many of the country's toughest criminals are held in this prison.* **UNLUCKY** ▷ **6** C2 informal unlucky: *'I've been told I've got to work late today because I'm very behind on my work.' 'Oh, tough **luck**!'* ◦ *It's tough **on** Geoff that he's going to miss the party.* **7** informal sometimes used to show that you have no sympathy for someone's problems or difficulties: *'I haven't got any money left.' 'Well, (**that's** just) tough – you shouldn't have spent it all on cigarettes.'* • **toughly** /ˈtʌf.li/ **adv** *These boots are very toughly (= strongly) made.* ◦ *The newspaper published a toughly worded article about racist behaviour.* ◦ *We live in a toughly **competitive** world.* • **toughness** /ˈtʌf.nəs/ C2 *She has a reputation for toughness (= being strong and determined).* ◦ *They can't face the toughness **of** the **competition**.*

IDIOMS **it's tough at the top** humorous saying used to mean that people in important positions have a lot of advantages and get a lot of good things: *'The managing director always flies first class.' 'It's tough at the top, isn't it?'* • **(as) tough as old boots** **1** very strong, and not easily made weaker: *He might be in his eighties but he's tough as old boots, that man.* **2** (US also **(as) tough as shoe leather**) describes food that is very difficult to cut or eat • **tough luck** (offensive **tough shit**) said to show that you have no sympathy for someone's problems or difficulties: *'They lost a lot of money on their investment.' 'Tough luck – they should have been more careful.'*

▸**verb**

PHRASAL VERB **tough sth out** informal to deal with a difficult period or situation without becoming any less certain or determined in your plans or opinions: *It's a difficult situation, but if we can just tough **it** out, things are bound to get better soon.*

▸**noun** [C] (also **toughie**) mainly US or old-fashioned informal a violent person: *Bands of armed toughs roamed the city.*

toughen /ˈtʌf.ən/ **verb** **MAKE STRONG** ▷ [T] to make something or someone tough, strong, or stronger: *The UN announced its intentions to toughen sanctions still further.* ◦ *The government wants to toughen (**up**) the existing drug laws/controls.* ◦ *His time in the army certainly toughened him **up**.* ◦ *Car windows are usually made from toughened glass.*

toughie /ˈtʌf.i/ **noun** [C] informal **DIFFICULT THING** ▷ **1** a difficult question or problem: *That last question was a real toughie.* **PERSON** ▷ **2** mainly US or old-fashioned informal a violent person **3** a strong person who is not easily made weaker or defeated

ˌtough ˈlove **noun** [U] the fact of deliberately not showing too much kindness to a person who has a problem so that the person will start to solve their own problem

toupée /ˈtuː.peɪ/ US /tuːˈpeɪ/ **noun** [C] a piece of artificial hair worn by a man to cover part of his head where there is no hair

tour /tʊəʳ/, /tɔːʳ/ US /tʊr/ **noun; verb**

▸**noun** **1** A2 [C] a visit to a place or area, especially one during which you look round the place or area and learn about it: *We **went on** a **guided** tour **of** the cathedral/museum/factory.* ◦ *A bus took us **on** a **sightseeing** tour **of** the city.* ◦ *a tour **guide*** **2** A2 [C] a journey made for pleasure, especially as a holiday, visiting several different places in an area: *a **cycling** tour **of** Provence* ◦ *They've just come back from a tour **of*** (UK also ***round***) *Cornwall.* ◦ *Tour **operators** (= companies which arrange holidays for people) have reported a drop in bookings.* **3** A2 [C or U] a planned visit to several places in a country or area made for a special purpose, such as one made by a politician, sports team, or group of performers: *a lecture/concert tour* ◦ *The Queen is **making** a two-week tour **of** Australia.* ◦ *She is performing in Birmingham tonight, on the third **leg of** (= stage of) her **nationwide** tour.* ◦ *The England cricket team is **on** tour in Pakistan.* **4** [C] a **tour of duty**

▸**verb** **1** B1 [I or T] to go on a tour somewhere: [+ prep] *We spent a month touring (**around/round/in**) Kenya.* ◦ *The New Zealand team will be touring (**in**) Europe this winter.* ◦ *The president toured US military bases yesterday.* ◦ *The band are currently touring to promote their new album.* **2** [T] If a play tours a particular area, it is performed in several places there: *The play will be performed first in London, and will then tour the rest of the country.* • **touring** /ˈtʊə.rɪŋ/, /ˈtɔː.rɪŋ/ US /ˈtʊr.ɪŋ/ **adj** [before noun] *a touring opera **company***

ˌtour de ˈforce **noun** [S] an achievement or performance which shows great skill and attracts ad-

T

miration: *a technical/musical/political tour de force* ◦ *The painting/book/film is a tour de force.*

Tourette's syndrome /tʊəˈretsˌsɪn.drəʊm/ (US) /tʊˈretsˌsɪn.droʊm/ **noun** [U] a rare illness of the brain in which a person makes noises and movements that he or she cannot control, often saying offensive words without meaning to

tourism /ˈtʊə.rɪ.zəm/, /ˈtɔː-/ (US) /ˈtʊr.ɪ-/ **noun** [U] B1 the business of providing services such as transport, places to stay, or entertainment for people who are on holiday: *Tourism is Venice's main industry.* ◦ *These beautiful old towns have remained relatively untouched by tourism.*

tourist /ˈtʊə.rɪst/, /ˈtɔː-/ (US) /ˈtʊr.ɪst/ **noun** [C] **1** A2 someone who visits a place for pleasure and interest, usually while they are on holiday: *Millions of tourists visit Rome every year.* ◦ *Hordes (= very large groups) of tourists flock to the Mediterranean each year.* ◦ *Disneyworld is one of Florida's major tourist* ***attractions***. ◦ *The island is very busy during the tourist* ***season***. **2** UK a member of a sports team who is travelling from place to place in a foreign country, playing games: *The West Indies easily defeated the tourists.*

ˈtourist ˌclass **noun** [U] the ordinary travelling conditions passengers on a plane or ship get when they buy the cheapest tickets

ˈtourist ˌoffice **noun** [C] an office that supplies information to people who are visiting an area for pleasure or interest: *The local tourist* ***information*** *office provides a free map of the region.*

ˈtourist ˌtrap **noun** [C] disapproving a crowded place which provides entertainment and things to buy for tourists, often at high prices

touristy /ˈtʊə.rɪ.sti/, /ˈtɔː-/ (US) /ˈtʊr.ɪ-/ **adj** disapproving describes a place that is not attractive because a lot of tourists visit it and it is full of things for them to buy and do: *This used to be an attractive seaside town, but now it's become very touristy.*

tournament /ˈtʊə.nə.mənt/, /ˈtɔː-/ (US) /ˈtɜː-/ **noun** [C] (US also **tourney**) B1 a competition for teams or single players in which a series of games is played, and the winners of each game play against each other until only one winner is left: *a tennis/chess/golf tournament* ◦ *They were defeated in the first* ***round of*** *the tournament.*

tourniquet /ˈtʊə.nɪ.keɪ/, /ˈtɔː-/ (US) /ˈtɜː.nɪ.kɪt/ **noun** [C] a strip of cloth that is tied tightly around an injured arm or leg to stop it BLEEDING: *If it continues to bleed, you may have to* ***apply*** *a tourniquet* ***to*** *the limb.*

T

ˌtour of ˈduty **noun** [C] (also **tour**) a period of time which someone, especially a soldier or an official, spends working in a foreign country: *The soldiers have just completed a six-month tour* ***in*** *the Philippines.*

tousled /ˈtaʊ.zl̩d/ **adj** having hair that looks untidy, as if it has been rubbed: *Naomi stood in front of them, her face flushed, her* ***hair*** *tousled.* ◦ *He came to breakfast, all tousled, in last night's clothes.*

tout /taʊt/ **verb; noun**

▸**verb** **MAKE KNOWN** ▷ **1** [T] to advertise, talk about, or praise something or someone repeatedly, especially as a way of encouraging people to like, accept, or buy something: *The minister has been touting these ideas for some time.* ◦ *He is being widely touted* ***as*** *the next leader of the Social Democratic party.* ◦ *Several insurance companies are now touting their* ***services/wares*** *on local radio.* **2** [I] to repeatedly try to persuade people to buy your goods or services: *There were hundreds of taxis at the airport, all touting* ***for*** *business/custom.* **SELL UNOFFICIALLY** ▷ **3** [T] UK (US **scalp**) to sell tickets for something such as a sports game or theatre performance unofficially, usually at a much higher price than the official price: *£30 seats for the match were being touted* ***for*** *£500.*

▸**noun** [C] UK (US **scalper**) a person who touts tickets: *Britain's best-known* ***ticket*** *tout once boasted that he could get you tickets for anything.*

tow /təʊ/ (US) /toʊ/ **verb; noun**

▸**verb** [T] to pull a car, boat, etc. along, using a rope or a chain tied to another vehicle or boat: *You shouldn't drive fast when your car is towing a caravan.* ◦ *The road was closed while the vehicles that had been involved in the accident were towed* ***away/off***. ◦ *The damaged boat was towed to safety.*

PHRASAL VERB **tow sth away** [often passive] to lift a vehicle that has been parked illegally onto an official truck and take it to a place from which you have to pay to collect it: *You're not allowed to park here – your car will be towed* ***away***.

▸**noun** **1** **give sb/sth a tow** to pull someone's vehicle using a rope or chain tied to your vehicle: *When my car broke down, a police car gave me a tow to the nearest garage.* **2** **on tow** UK (US **in tow**, Australian English also **under tow**) being pulled along: *The car in front of us is on tow – that's why we're going so slowly.* ◦ *The damaged boat drifted for days before it was finally* ***taken*** *in tow.*

IDIOM **in tow** informal If you go somewhere with a particular person in tow, they are with you: *She arrived at the party, with a tall, silver-haired man in tow.*

towards /təˈwɔːdz/ (US) /tʊˈwɔːrdz/ **preposition** mainly UK (mainly US **toward**) **MOVEMENT** ▷ **1** B1 in the direction of, or closer to someone or something: *She stood up and walked towards him.* ◦ *He leaned towards his wife and whispered, 'Can we go home soon?'* ◦ *She kept glancing towards the phone.* ◦ *The country seems to be drifting towards war.* ◦ *There is a trend towards healthier eating among all sectors of the population.* **RELATION** ▷ **2** B2 in relation to something or someone: *They've always been very friendly towards me.* ◦ *There has been a change in government policy towards energy efficiency.* ◦ *He feels a lot of anger/hostility/antagonism/animosity towards his father.* ◦ *A lot of people think that most newspapers are biased towards one particular political party.* **POSITION** ▷ **3** C1 near to, just before, or around a time or place: *Our seats were towards the back of the theatre.* ◦ *I often get hungry towards the middle of the morning.* ◦ *We're getting towards winter and it's getting dark earlier.* **PURPOSE** ▷ **4** C1 for the purpose of buying or achieving something: *I'm saving up to buy a car, and Dad has given me some money towards it.* ◦ *Would you like to make a contribution (= give some money) towards a present for Linda?* ◦ *The work that students do during the term counts towards their final grade.*

ˈtow-away **noun** [C usually singular] an act of a car being officially removed from a place where it has been illegally left: *I couldn't find a parking meter, so I decided to park illegally and risk a tow-away.* ◦ *This part of town is a tow-away* ***area/zone*** *(= one in which cars left illegally will be removed).*

ˈtow ˌbar **noun** [C] a bar fixed to the back of a car that is used for pulling a CARAVAN or TRAILER

towel /taʊəl/ **noun; verb**

▸**noun** [C] A2 a piece of cloth or paper used for drying someone or something that is wet: *She came downstairs after her shower, wrapped in a towel.* ◦ *The school* provides **paper** towels for the children to dry their hands on.

IDIOM **throw/chuck in the towel** C2 to stop trying to do something because you have realized that you cannot succeed: *Three of the original five candidates for the Democratic presidential nomination have now thrown in the towel.*

▸verb [T] (-ll- or US usually -l-) to rub something with a towel to dry it: [+ adj] *She towelled her hair dry.* ◦ *After our swim, we quickly towelled our**selves down**.*

towelette /ˌtaʊəˈlet/ **noun** [C] a small square of wet paper, used especially for cleaning your face and hands with when there is no water available: *On the plane, the flight attendant brings you a towelette after your meal.*

towelling (US usually **toweling**) /ˈtaʊə.lɪŋ/ **noun** [U] a soft, thick cloth used especially for making towels or clothing: *a towelling bathrobe*

ˈtowel ˌrail **noun** [C] UK (US **ˈtowel ˌrack**) a horizontal bar on the wall, or a frame with a horizontal bar, used to hang towels on: *We have a heated towel rail in our bathroom.*

tower /taʊəʳ/ (US) /taʊɚ/ **noun; verb**

▸noun [C] **1** B1 a tall, narrow structure, often square or circular, which either forms part of a building or stands alone: *the Eiffel tower* ◦ *There's a clock on the **church** tower.* ◦ *He works in an **office** tower in downtown San Francisco.* **2** a tall, usually metal structure used for broadcasting: *a radio/transmission tower*

IDIOM **a tower of strength** a person who gives you help and support when you are in a difficult situation: *Polly was a tower of strength **to** me when I was ill.*

▸verb [I usually + adv/prep] to be very tall or large, usually in a way that makes people feel respect: *We turned the corner and there was the cathedral, towering in front of us.*

PHRASAL VERBS **tower above/over sb/sth** to be very tall in comparison with someone or something else: *Canary Wharf towers above the Dockland area of London.* ◦ *Although he's only twelve, David towers over his mother.* • **tower above/over sth** to be much bigger and more successful than another thing of the same type: *One computer manufacturer towers above all the rest.*

ˈtower ˌblock **noun** [C] UK (US **ˈhigh-rise**) a tall building divided into apartments or offices

towering /ˈtaʊə.rɪŋ/ (US) /ˈtaʊɚ.ɪŋ/ **adj** **1** literary very high and making people feel respect: *the towering walls of the Acropolis* **2** very great: *a towering figure in the British art world* ◦ *Laurence Olivier's Othello was a towering performance.*

town /taʊn/ **noun** **1** A1 [C or U] a place where people live and work, containing many houses, shops, places of work, places of entertainment, etc., and usually larger than a village but smaller than a city: *a seaside/industrial town* ◦ *a fishing/mining town* ◦ *He was born in the small town **of** Castleford, in Yorkshire.* ◦ *We stayed in the best hotel **in** town.* ◦ *the main road **into/out of** town* → See also **downtown, hometown, uptown** **2** A2 [S or U] the part of a town where the main shops are: *I'm going **into/to** town at lunchtime to do some shopping.* ◦ *I met Charles while I was **in** town.* **3** [U] the most important city or town in a country or area: *We went **up to** town to see a play.* ◦ *Many people go **into** town (= New York) from New Jersey on weekends.* **4** B1 [U] mainly US the place where you live or work: *I'm leaving town for a few days.* ◦ *Barbara is **out of** town on business this week.* **5 the town** [S] **a** a town or city, rather than the countryside: *I've always lived in the town.* **b** [+ sing/pl verb] the people who live in the town: *The **whole** town is/are hoping that their football team will win the final tomorrow.*

IDIOMS **go to town** to do something in a detailed and enthusiastic way, especially by spending a lot of money: *They've really gone to town **on** their wedding.* • **on the town** enjoying yourself by going to places of entertainment in a town or city: *I was **out** on the town/I had **a night** on the town last night, and I'm exhausted!*

ˌtown ˈcouncil **noun** [C] the local government of a town: *Mr Dunn has been a **member of** the town council for many years.* • **ˌtown ˈcouncillor** **noun** [C]

ˌtown ˈhall **noun** [C] a building in which local government officials and employees work and have meetings

townhouse /ˈtaʊn.haʊs/ **noun** [C] US a house that is joined to another house

ˈtown ˌhouse **noun** [C] UK a house in a town or city, usually a comfortable, expensive one in a fashionable area: *a beautiful four-storey town house*

townie /ˈtaʊ.ni/ **noun** [C] **1** informal disapproving a person who lives in a town where there is a college but who is not involved with the college **2** UK (US and Australian English **city slicker**) a person who lives in a town, and has no experience of or knowledge about living in the countryside: *A couple of townies walked into the village pub, looking very out of place in their smart suits.*

ˌtown ˈmeeting **noun** [C] US a meeting of the people who live or pay taxes in a town, for the purpose of governing the town

ˌtown ˈplanning **noun** [U] the planning of the way in which towns and cities are built in order to make them pleasant to live in: *He studied town planning at college.* • **ˌtown ˈplanner** **noun** [C]

township /ˈtaʊn.ʃɪp/ **noun** [C] **1** a South African town where only black people lived during APARTHEID: *a black township* ◦ *the township **of** Soweto* ◦ *township music* **2** in the US and Canada, a unit of local government consisting of a town and the area surrounding it: *the township **of** Dulce, New Mexico* ◦ *Princeton Township*

townspeople /ˈtaʊnzˌpiː.pl/ **noun** [plural] (also **townsfolk**) **1** people who live in a particular town, considered as a group: *The townspeople have raised $9 million for a new museum.* **2** people who live in towns rather than in the countryside

towpath /ˈtəʊ.pɑːθ/ (US) /ˈtoʊ.pæθ/ **noun** [C] a path that goes along the side of a river or CANAL, used in the past by horses pulling boats: *We walked **along** the towpath.*

ˈtow rope **noun** [C] a rope or chain that a vehicle uses to pull another vehicle

ˈtow ˌtruck **noun** [C] (UK also **ˈbreakdown ˌtruck**) a truck with special equipment for pulling a vehicle that is not working to a place where it can be repaired

toxaemia specialized (mainly US **toxemia**) /tɒkˈsiː.mi.ə/ (US) /tɑːk-/ **noun** [U] the condition of having a poisonous substance or substances in your blood

toxic /ˈtɒk.sɪk/ (US) /ˈtɑːk-/ **adj** **POISONOUS** ▷ **1** B2 poisonous: *toxic waste/chemicals/effluent* **UNPLEASANT** ▷ **2** informal very unpleasant or unacceptable **3** informal causing you a lot of harm and unhappiness over a long period of time: *toxic parents* ◦ *a toxic relationship* • **toxicity** /tɒkˈsɪs.ɪ.ti/ (US) /tɑːkˈsɪs.ə.t̬i/ **noun** [U] *Tests of the chemical have shown that it has a*

T

high level of toxicity. ◦ The toxicity **of** the drug severely limits its use.

ˌtoxic ˈasset noun [C] a financial ASSET (= something a person or company owns) whose price has fallen by a large amount and that cannot be easily sold

ˌtoxic ˈdebt noun [C or U] a debt or debts that have little chance of being paid back or of being paid back with interest

toxicology /ˌtɒk.sɪˈkɒl.ə.dʒi/ (US) /ˌtɑːk.sɪˈkɑː.lə-/ noun [U] the scientific study of the characteristics and effects of poisons • **toxicologist** /-dʒɪst/ noun [C] a person who studies or knows a lot about poisons

toxin /ˈtɒk.sɪn/ (US) /ˈtɑːk-/ noun [C] a poisonous substance, especially one produced by bacteria, that causes disease

toy /tɔɪ/ noun; adj; verb

▸noun [C] **1** (A2) an object for children to play with: *a cuddly/soft/stuffed toy* ◦ *a clockwork/wind-up toy* ◦ *a toy train/farm/soldier* ◦ UK *toy bricks* (US *toy blocks*) ◦ *Put your toys away now – it's time for bed.* ◦ *Leave daddy's camera alone – it isn't a toy!* **2** an object that is used by an adult for pleasure rather than for serious use: *His latest toy is an underwater camera.* ◦ *She has several* ***executive*** *toys on her desk.*

▸adj [before noun] belonging or relating to a very small breed of dog that is kept as a pet: *a toy poodle/spaniel*

▸verb

PHRASAL VERBS **toy with sth** CONSIDER ▷ **1** to consider something or doing something, but not in a very serious way, and without making a decision: *We're toying with* ***the idea*** *of going to Peru next year.* TOUCH ▷ **2** to touch an object or move it around with your hand, without any purpose but while thinking about something else: *She just toyed with her salad.* ◦ *He toyed nervously with a button on his jacket as he was speaking.* • **toy with sb/sth** old-fashioned to not care seriously about someone or about their feelings, especially during a romantic friendship

ˈtoy ˌboy noun [C] informal a young man who has a sexual or romantic relationship with an older woman

tptb written abbreviation for the powers that be: used, in emails for example, when you are referring to people who have authority and control: *If it were up to me, I'd say yes, but I'll have to check with tptb.*

trace /treɪs/ verb; noun

▸verb [T] FIND ▷ **1** (C1) to find someone or something that was lost: *The police are trying to trace the mother of a newborn baby found abandoned outside a hospital.* ◦ *Attempts to trace* ***the whereabouts of*** *a man seen leaving the scene of the crime have so far been unsuccessful.* ◦ *Their missing daughter was finally traced* ***to*** *(= found in) Manchester.* **2** (C1) to find the origin of something: *The phone company were unable to trace the call.* ◦ *No one has yet been able to trace the source of the rumour.* **3** to discover the cause or origin of something by examining the way in which it has developed: *The outbreak of food poisoning was traced* ***to*** *some contaminated shellfish.* ◦ *The practice of giving eggs at Easter can be traced* ***back to*** *festivals in ancient China.* ◦ *Rivalries between the gangs can be traced* ***back to*** *(= first happened in) the 1950s in some black and Hispanic neighbourhoods.* **4** to describe the way in which something has developed: *The film traces the events leading up to the Russian Revolution in 1917.* DRAW ▷ **5** to copy a drawing or pattern, etc. by drawing over its lines through a thin piece of transparent paper: *Did you draw this picture yourself, or did you trace it?* ◦ *She learned to write her name by tracing* ***out*** *the letters.* **6** to draw a shape by showing the main or outer lines: *The child was tracing patterns* ***in/on*** *the sand with a stick.*

▸noun SIGN/RECORD ▷ **1** (B2) [C or U] a sign that something has happened or existed: *He attempted to cover up all the traces* ***of*** *his crime.* ◦ *When she moved out, she* ***left*** *no trace* ***of*** *having been there.* ◦ *My wallet has been missing for several days and I can't find any trace* ***of*** *it.* ◦ *He seems to have vanished* ***without*** *(a) trace (= no one knows where he is).* **2** [C] an act of finding information about something electronically, or the record of the information found in this way: *The phone company* ***put*** *a trace on the call.* SLIGHT AMOUNT ▷ **3** [C] a very slight amount: *Traces* ***of*** *drugs were found in his blood.* ◦ *There is just a trace* ***of*** *grey in his hair.* ◦ *She speaks English without the slightest trace* ***of*** *an accent.* ◦ *There was the faintest trace* ***of*** *a smile on her lips.* ◦ *'How wonderful!' she said, without any trace* ***of*** *sarcasm.*

traceable /ˈtreɪ.sə.bl̩/ adj possible to trace: *In theory, most phone calls should be traceable.* ◦ *His medical problems were shown to be traceable* ***to*** *(= to have been caused by) his having been exposed to dangerous chemicals.*

ˈtrace ˌelement noun [C] one of several types of simple chemical substance that is necessary for healthy growth and development, and exists in animals and plants in very small amounts

tracer /ˈtreɪ.səʳ/ (US) /-sɚ/ noun [C] a bullet which leaves a line of flame or smoke behind it when it is fired, so that you can see the direction it has taken: *Tracer* ***bullets*** *streaked through the sky.* ◦ *The sky was bright with tracer* ***fire****.*

trachea /trəˈkiː.ə/ (US) /ˈtreɪ.kiə/ noun [C] (plural **tracheae** or **tracheas**) specialized **windpipe**

tracheotomy /ˌtræk.iˈɒt.ə.mi/ (US) /ˌtreɪ.kiˈɑː.t̬ə-/ noun [C or U] (also **tracheostomy** /-ˈɒst.ə.mi/ (US) /-ˈɑːs.t̬ə.mi/) a medical operation in which an opening is made in a person's neck and trachea, usually in order to help them to breathe

tracing /ˈtreɪ.sɪŋ/ noun [C] a copy of a drawing or pattern made by drawing over it through a piece of thin, transparent paper: *He made a tracing* ***of*** *the picture.*

ˈtracing ˌpaper noun [U] thin, transparent paper which you use for copying a picture by putting it on top of the picture and drawing over its lines

track /træk/ noun; verb

▸noun PATH ▷ **1** (B1) [C] a path or rough road that is made of soil rather than having a surface covered with stone or other material: *The house is at the end of a dirt/an unmade track.* **2** (C1) [C or U] the pair of long metal bars fixed on the ground at an equal distance from each other, along which trains travel: *a ten-mile stretch of track* ◦ *Passengers are requested not to walk across the tracks.* SPORT ▷ **3** (B1) [C] a type of path or road, often in the shape of a ring, which has been specially designed and built for sports events, especially racing: *an all-weather track* ◦ *a dog/horse track* ◦ *The runners are now on their final lap of the track.* → See also **racetrack** **4** (B2) [U] US a sport in which people compete with each other by running a race on a specially prepared circular path: *a track event* **5** [U] (also **track and field**) US for **athletics** MARKS ▷ **6** (B2) [C usually plural] a mark or line of marks left on the ground or on another surface by an animal, person, or vehicle that has moved over it, showing the direction they moved in: *Police found tyre tracks in the mud.* ◦ *The hunters followed the tracks* ***of*** *the deer for hours.* ◦ *The burglars were careful not to* ***leave*** *any tracks behind them.* **7 be on the track of sb/sth** to be examining marks or pieces of information that show where a person or animal has gone, in order to catch them: *The police are on the track of the killer.* **DIRECTION** ▷ **8** [C] the direction that something has taken or will take through the air: *People living in the track **of** the hurricane have been advised to leave their homes until it has passed.* **DEVELOPMENT** ▷ **9** C2 [C or U] the direction in which someone's job or education develops: *She was a lawyer, but then she changed track completely and became a doctor.* **10** [C usually singular] the way in which a thought or idea has developed or might develop: *I found it difficult to follow the track **of** his argument.* **11 get off the track** to start talking about something that is not part of what you should be talking about: *I think we're getting off the track here – we're supposed to be discussing our advertising campaign.* **MUSIC** ▷ **12** B2 [C] one of several songs or pieces of music on a CD or other musical recording: *The album includes four previously unreleased tracks.* → See also **soundtrack** **13** [C] a part of a MAGNETIC strip onto which sound can be recorded, with several tracks on one magnetic strip

IDIOMS **in your tracks** in the exact place where you are standing: *He fell dead in his tracks.* ◦ *A sudden loud scream **stopped** me (**dead**) in my tracks (= caused me suddenly to stop what I was doing).* • **keep track** C1 to make certain that you know what is happening or has happened to someone or something: *My sister has had so many different jobs, I find it hard to keep track (**of** what she's doing).* • **lose track** B2 to no longer know what is happening, or not to remember something: *What he was saying was so complicated that I lost track after the first couple of sentences.* ◦ *I've lost track **of** the number of times he's asked me to lend him money.* • **make tracks** informal to leave somewhere to go home: *It's getting late, Jim – I think we should make tracks.* • **on track** C1 making progress and likely to succeed: *They're on track **to** make record profits.*

▸verb **FOLLOW** ▷ **1** C2 [T] to follow a person or animal by looking for proof that they have been somewhere, or by using electronic equipment: *It's difficult to track an animal over stony ground.* ◦ *The military use radar satellites to track targets through clouds and at night.* ◦ *The terrorists were tracked **to** (= found in) Amsterdam.* → See also **backtrack, sidetrack** **2** C2 [T] to record the progress or development of something over a period: *The study tracked the careers of 1,226 doctors who trained at the Medical School.* **MOVE** ▷ **3** [I] If a television or film camera tracks in a particular direction, it moves along while it is filming: *The film ends with a long tracking **shot** around the deserted house.* **FINANCE** ▷ **4** [T] to follow the level of an interest rate, SHARE price, etc.: *The mortgage deal will track the Bank of England base rate plus 0.75 percent.*

PHRASAL VERB **track sth/sb down** C2 to find something or someone after looking for them in a lot of different places: *He finally managed to track down the book he wanted.*

ˌtrack and ˈfield noun [U] (also **track**) US for **athletics**: *The team had no chance of striking gold in track and field.*

trackball /ˈtræk.bɔːl/ noun [C] a ball on the keyboard of a LAPTOP or other computer that you roll with your finger in order to move the CURSOR on the screen

tracker /ˈtræk.əʳ/ US /-ɚ/ noun [C] a person who is able to find animals or people by following the marks they leave on the ground as they move over it

ˈtracker ˌdog noun [C] a dog specially trained to help the police find people they are looking for, using their sense of smell: *The body was found after an extensive search by police with tracker dogs.*

ˈtrack eˌvent noun [C] a sports event in which people compete with each other by running a race on a specially prepared circular path → See also **field event**

ˈtracking ˌstation noun [C] a place where electrical waves are used to follow the direction of objects, such as spacecraft, in space

ˈtrack ˌmeet noun [C] US a sports competition between two or more teams, involving various different running races and jumping and throwing events

ˈtrack ˌrecord noun [C usually singular] all the achievements or failures that someone or something has had in the past: *The school has an impressive/strong track record in getting its students through exams.*

tracksuit /ˈtræk.suːt/ US /-suːt/ noun [C] UK (US **sweats**) B1 a loose top and trousers, worn either by people who are training for a sport or exercising, or as informal clothing • **tracksuited** /-suː.tɪd/ US /-suː.t̬ɪd/ adj UK wearing a tracksuit: *a tracksuited runner*

ˈtracksuit ˌbottoms noun [plural] (informal also **ˈtrackie ˌbottoms, sweatpants**) soft, loose trousers that you wear for doing sport or exercise, or as informal clothing

tract /trækt/ noun [C] **WRITING** ▷ **1** a short piece of writing, especially on a religious or political subject, that is intended to influence other people's opinions: *a moral/religious/socialist tract* **LAND** ▷ **2** a large area of land: *The house is surrounded by **vast** tracts **of** woodland.* **3** US a measured area of land that is used for a particular purpose, such as building houses or digging for oil: *a 132-acre tract in Irving* **TUBE** ▷ **4** a system of connected tubes and organs in the body of a person or an animal, which has a particular purpose: *the **urinary/respiratory/digestive** tract*

tractable /ˈtræk.tə.bl̩/ adj formal easily dealt with, controlled or persuaded: *The problem turned out to be rather less tractable than I had expected.* • **tractability** /ˌtræk.təˈbɪl.ɪ.ti/ US /-ə.t̬i/ noun [U]

ˈtract ˌhouse noun [C] US one of a large number of very similar-looking houses built on a single area of land

traction /ˈtræk.ʃən/ noun [U] **WHEEL/TYRE** ▷ **1** the ability of a wheel or tyre to hold the ground without sliding: *In deep snow, people should use snow tyres on their vehicles to give them better traction.* **PULLING** ▷ **2** specialized the pulling of a heavy LOAD over a surface, or the power used in this: *steam traction* **3** specialized a form of medical treatment that involves using special equipment to pull gently an injured part of the body, especially an arm or leg, for a long period of time: *After her hip operation poor Mira was **in/on** traction for six weeks.*

ˈtraction ˌengine noun [C] a large, heavy vehicle, operated by steam power, used especially in the past for pulling heavy LOADS along roads

tractor /ˈtræk.təʳ/ US /-tɚ/ noun [C] C2 a motor vehicle with large back wheels and thick tyres, used on farms for pulling machinery

ˌtractor-ˈtrailer noun [C] US for **juggernaut**

trad /træd/ noun [U] UK **trad jazz**

trade /treɪd/ noun; adj; verb

▸noun **BUYING AND SELLING** ▷ **1** B1 [U] the activity of buying and selling, or exchanging, goods and/or services between people or countries: *The country's trade **in** manufactured goods has expanded in the last ten years.* ◦ *70 percent of the country's trade is **with***

T

Europe. ◦ *The two countries have signed a trade* ***agreement*** *for one year only.* **2** [U] business activity: *Since the supermarket opened, many small local shops have lost up to 50 percent of their trade.* ◦ *In hot weather, shops do a* ***roaring/brisk*** *trade* ***in*** *(= sell a lot of) cold drinks and ice creams.* ◦ *This level of confidence in the economy is good for trade generally.* **BUSINESS ▷ 3** Ⓒ1 [C] a particular business or industry: ***the*** *building/catering/tourist trade* ◦ ***the*** *book/car/fur trade* ◦ *He worked* ***in*** *the same trade all his life.* **4** Ⓑ2 [C or U] a job, especially one that needs special skill, that involves working with your hands: *After she left school, she went to college to learn a trade.* ◦ *He's a carpenter* ***by*** *trade.* **5 the trade** [S] the people who work in a particular business or industry or in the same one: *People who work* ***in*** *the trade can buy their books at a discount.* ◦ *The company only supplies its goods to the (building/catering) trade, not direct to the public.*

> Word partners for **trade noun**
>
> *foreign/global/international/local* trade • a trade *agreement/deal/policy* • trade *negotiations/relations/talks* • trade *barriers/restrictions/sanctions* • trade *between* [two countries/regions] • trade *with* [a country] • trade *in* sth • the trade *of* sth

▸adj **trade publication/journal/magazine/paper** a newspaper, etc. produced for people working in a particular business or industry: *a steel industry trade journal*

▸verb **BUY AND SELL ▷ 1** Ⓑ2 [I or T, usually + adv/prep] to buy and sell goods or services, especially between countries: *For centuries, Native Americans traded* ***with*** *European settlers.* ◦ *The company has been trading* ***in*** *oil for many years.* ◦ *The two countries have become close trading* ***partners.*** ◦ *Our books are traded right across Asia.* → See also **ˈhorse-ˌtrade 2** [I or T] to be bought and sold, or to buy and sell SHARES, on the STOCK EXCHANGE: *On London's Stock Exchange, 18.5 million* ***shares*** *were traded yesterday.* ◦ *Shares in the company traded* ***actively.*** **EXCHANGE ▷ 3** [T] to exchange something, or to stop using or doing something and start using or doing something else instead: *The children traded comics.* ◦ [+ two objects] *I'll trade you some of my chocolate* ***for*** *some of your ice cream.* ◦ *I wouldn't trade you* ***for*** *the world (= I do not want a different partner).* → See also **trade sth in 4** [T] If people trade statements of a particular type, they say or tell them to each other: *We sat around the dinner table, trading stories.* ◦ *The two politicians didn't really discuss the issues, they just traded* ***insults.***

T

PHRASAL VERBS **trade sth in** to give something you own as part of your payment for something you buy, especially a new type of the same thing: *He recently traded in his Jeep* ***for*** *a red Mercedes.* • **trade sth off** to accept a disadvantage or bad feature in order to have something good: *It may be possible to trade off manpower costs* ***against*** *computer costs.* • **trade on sth** to use something, especially a characteristic, for your own advantage and usually in an unfair way: *People are always trading on his generosity.* ◦ *This kind of advertising trades on people's fears.* ◦ *He trades on his good looks.* • **trade up/down** to buy something, usually a house or car, that is of higher or lower value than the one you already have: *My car is costing me too much to run, so I'm going to trade down* ***to*** *a cheaper model.*

ˈtrade ˌbalance noun [C usually singular] a country's BALANCE OF TRADE → See **balance of payments**

ˈtrade ˌdeficit noun [C] (also **ˈtrade ˌgap**) a situation in which the value of goods a country IMPORTS (= buys from other countries) is greater than the value of goods it EXPORTS (= sells to other countries), or the size of this difference

ˈtrade ˌfair noun [C] (US also **ˈtrade ˌshow**) a large event at which companies show and sell their products and try to increase their business

ˈtrade ˌfigures noun [plural] A country's trade figures are a record of how much the country has paid for goods which it has bought from other countries, compared with how much it has been paid for goods which it has sold to other countries: *The last set of trade figures showed exceptionally strong export growth.*

ˈtrade-in noun [C] a method of buying something new by giving something you own as part of the payment for it: *We got a good trade-in* ***price*** *for our old car.*

trademark /ˈtreɪd.mɑːk/ Ⓤⓢ /-mɑːrk/ noun [C] **PRODUCT ▷ 1** a name or symbol on a product that shows it was made by a particular company, and that it cannot be used by other companies without permission: *Velcro is a* ***registered*** *trademark.* **TYPICAL ▷ 2** something very noticeable that a person typically has or does: *He was wearing one of the brightly coloured ties that are his trademark.* ◦ *She gave one of her trademark smiles.*

ˈtrade ˌname noun [C] a **brand name**

ˈtrade-off noun **1** [C] a situation in which you balance two opposing situations or qualities: *There is a trade-off* ***between*** *doing the job accurately and doing it quickly.* ◦ *She said that she'd had to make a trade-off* ***between*** *her job and her family.* **2** [C usually singular] a situation in which you accept something bad in order to have something good: *For some car buyers, lack of space is an acceptable trade-off* ***for*** *a sporty design.*

ˈtrade ˌprice noun [C] UK (US **wholesale**) the price at which goods are sold to shops by the people who produce them, rather than the price which the customer usually pays in the shop: *I bought my coat direct from the factory* ***at*** *trade price.*

trader /ˈtreɪ.dəʳ/ Ⓤⓢ /-dɚ/ noun [C] **1** Ⓒ2 a person who buys and sells things: *a wool/sugar trader* ◦ *His father is a* ***market*** *trader, selling fruit and vegetables.* **2** a person who buys and sells company SHARES or money: *a stock/currency/futures trader* ◦ *He is a well-known trader on the floor of the New York Stock Exchange.*

ˈtrade ˌroute noun [C] a route, often covering a long distance, that people buying and selling goods often used in the past

ˈtrade ˌschool noun [C] US a school where students learn skills which involve working with their hands: *At trade school, he learned to be an auto mechanic.*

ˌtrade ˈsecret noun [C] **1** a piece of information about a product that is known only to the particular company that makes it: *The exact ingredients of Coca-Cola are a trade secret.* **2** informal a piece of information that you are not willing to tell anyone: *My aunt won't tell anyone her age – she says that it's a trade secret.*

tradesman /ˈtreɪdz.mən/ noun [C] (plural **-men** /-mən/) **1** mainly UK someone who buys and sells goods, especially someone who owns a shop: *Local tradesmen are objecting to plans for a big new out-of-town shopping centre.* **2** someone who works in a trade which needs skill at using your hands, usually in the building industry

tradespeople /ˈtreɪdzˌpiː.pl̩/ noun [plural] people who buy and sell goods, especially people who own a shop

ˈtrade ˌsurplus noun [C] specialized a situation in which the value of goods a country EXPORTS (= sells to other countries) is greater than the value of goods it IMPORTS (= buys from other countries), or the size of this difference

ˌtrade ˈunion noun [C] UK (UK also **ˌtrades ˈunion**, US **ˈlabor ˌunion**) an organization that represents the people who work in a particular industry, protects their rights, and discusses their pay and working conditions with employers: *The rally was organized by local trade union officials.* → See also **the TUC** • **ˌtrade ˈunionism** noun [U] • **ˌtrade ˈunionist** noun [C]

trading /ˈtreɪ.dɪŋ/ noun [U] **1** the activity of buying and selling goods and/or services: *She doesn't approve of **Sunday** trading (= shops being open on Sunday).* **2** the buying and selling of SHARES and money: *The stock market moved ahead slightly in active trading today.* → See also **insider dealing**

ˈtrading esˌtate noun [C] UK an **industrial estate**

ˈtrading ˌpost noun [C] a small place, especially in the past, far from other places in which people live, where goods can be bought and sold or exchanged: *New York was originally a Dutch trading post.*

tradition /trəˈdɪʃ.ən/ noun [C or U] B2 a belief, principle, or way of acting which people in a particular society or group have continued to follow for a long time, or all of these beliefs, etc. in a particular society or group: *Fireworks have long been an American tradition on the Fourth of July.* ◦ *Switzerland has a **long** tradition **of** neutrality.* ◦ [+ that] *There's a tradition **in** our office **that** when it's somebody's birthday, they bring in a cake for us all to share.* ◦ *We decided to **break with** tradition (= not behave as usual) this year and go away for Christmas.* ◦ ***According to** tradition, a headless ghost walks through the corridors of the house at night.*

> Word partners for **tradition**
>
> *follow* tradition • *break with/buck* tradition • *preserve/revive/uphold* a tradition • a tradition *dates back to* [1925, the 19th century, etc.] • an *ancient/long/old* tradition • a *great/proud/rich/strong* tradition • a *local/national* tradition • the tradition *of* sth/doing sth

IDIOM **in the tradition of sb/sth** having characteristics similar to a particular person or thing: *His paintings are in the tradition of those of Bacon and Spencer.*

traditional /trəˈdɪʃ.ən.əl/, /-ˈdɪʃ.nəl/ adj B1 following or belonging to the customs or ways of behaving that have continued in a group of people or society for a long time without changing: *The villagers retain a strong attachment to their traditional values/customs/beliefs.* ◦ *The school uses a combination of modern and traditional methods for teaching reading.* ◦ *The dancers were wearing traditional Hungarian dress/costume.* ◦ *She's very traditional (in her ideas and opinions).*

traditionalism /trəˈdɪʃ.ən.əl.ɪ.zəm/, /-nəl-/ noun [U] the belief in, or act of following, traditional ideas and ways of doing things: *The building's design is an interesting blend of traditionalism and modernism.*

traditionalist /trəˈdɪʃ.ən.əl.ɪst/, /-nəl-/ noun [C] someone who believes in and follows traditional ideas: *Religious traditionalists objected to theories of evolution being taught in schools.* • **traditionalist** adj *She holds traditionalist Muslim views.* ◦ *This production of 'Swan Lake' is in traditionalist style.*

traditionally /trəˈdɪʃ.ən.əl.i/, /-ˈdɪʃ.nəl-/ adv B2 according to tradition; in a traditional way: *Quaker meetings are traditionally held in silence.* ◦ *Traditionally, the company's main markets have been Britain and the US.*

ˌtrad ˈjazz noun [U] UK (also **trad**, US **dixieland**) a type of JAZZ, which was first played in the 1920s, in which the players invent the music as they play it

traduce /trəˈdjuːs/, /-ˈdʒuːs/ (US) /-ˈduːs/ verb [T] formal to strongly criticize someone, especially in a way that harms their reputation

traffic /ˈtræf.ɪk/ noun; verb

▸noun [U] VEHICLES ▷ **1** A2 the number of vehicles moving along roads, or the number of aircraft, trains, or ships moving along a route: *There was **heavy/a lot of** traffic on the roads this morning.* ◦ *We got **stuck in** traffic for several hours.* ◦ *New measures have been introduced to try and ease traffic **congestion** in the city.* ◦ *Five people were injured in a traffic **accident** (= one involving vehicles).* ◦ ***Air** traffic has increased 30 percent in the last decade.* **2** people or goods transported by road, air, train, or ship, as a business: *The airline halved its overseas service because of a sharp reduction in traffic.* ◦ *Environmental groups want more **passenger** and **freight** traffic moved off the roads and onto trains.* TRADE ▷ **3** illegal trade: *to cut down the traffic **in drugs**/the **drug** traffic* ◦ *Police are looking for ways of curbing the traffic **in** guns.*

> Word partners for **traffic**
>
> *ease/reduce* traffic • *increase* traffic • *block (off)/disrupt/halt/slow (down)* traffic • *divert/reroute* traffic • traffic *builds up* • *bad/heavy/slow-moving* traffic • be *stuck in* traffic • the *volume* of traffic

▸verb [I] (present tense **trafficking**, past tense and past participle **trafficked**) to buy and sell goods illegally: *They were arrested for trafficking **in** the eggs of protected species of birds.* • **trafficking** /-ɪ.kɪŋ/ noun [U] *arms/drugs trafficking*

ˈtraffic ˌcalming noun [U] UK the act of building raised areas, small ROUNDABOUTS, or other similar structures on roads, usually roads where there are houses, so that vehicles are forced to move more slowly along them: *Local residents are demanding that traffic-calming **measures** are introduced to reduce the number of accidents on the road.*

ˈtraffic ˌcircle noun [C] US for **roundabout**

ˈtraffic ˌcone noun [C] a cone-shaped, usually red and white or yellow object used to keep vehicles away from an area of road temporarily, usually because repairs are being done to it: *One lane of the road was closed off by traffic cones.*

ˈtraffic ˌisland noun [C] **1** (also **island**) a raised area in the middle of a road where people who are crossing the road can wait safely for traffic to go past **2** US for **central reservation**

ˈtraffic ˌjam noun [C] B1 a large number of vehicles close together and unable to move or moving very slowly: *Roadworks have caused traffic jams throughout the city centre.* ◦ *I was **stuck in** a traffic jam for an hour yesterday.*

trafficker /ˈtræf.ɪ.kər/ (US) /-kɚ/ noun a person who trades in illegal goods, especially drugs: ***drug** traffickers*

ˈtraffic ˌlight noun [C usually plural] A2 one of a set of red, yellow, and green lights that control the movement of vehicles, usually at a point where two or more roads join: *The police pulled him over for failing to stop at a red traffic light.* ◦ *Turn left **at the** traffic lights.* ◦ *The traffic lights turned green as we approached the junction.*

ˈtraffic ˌwarden noun [C] UK someone whose job is

T

to make certain that people do not leave their cars in illegal places: *A traffic warden gave me a ticket for parking on a double yellow line.*

tragedy /ˈtrædʒ.ə.di/ noun [C or U] **1** B2 a very sad event or situation, especially one involving death or suffering: *The pilot averted a tragedy when he succeeded in preventing the plane from crashing.* ◦ *Hitler's invasion of Poland led to the tragedy **of** the Second World War.* ◦ *His life was touched by hardship and **personal** tragedy.* ◦ *They had only recently arrived in London when tragedy **struck** – their son was killed in a traffic accident.* ◦ [+ (that)] *It's a tragedy (**that**) so many young people are unable to find jobs.* **2** a play about death or suffering with a sad end, or this type of play generally: *Shakespeare's tragedies include 'Hamlet', 'King Lear' and 'Othello'.* ◦ *In Greek tragedy, the role of the chorus is to express the audience's reactions to what is happening in the play.*

tragic /ˈtrædʒ.ɪk/ adj **1** B2 very sad, often involving death and suffering: *His friends were deeply shocked and saddened by the tragic **news** of his death.* ◦ *The bomb explosion resulted in a tragic loss of life.* ◦ *Hospital authorities admitted that a tragic mistake/error had taken place.* ◦ ***It** is tragic **that** the theatre has had to close.* **2** belonging or relating to literature about death or suffering: *During his acting career, he has played all Shakespeare's great tragic heroes.* • **tragically** /-ɪ.kəl.i/ adv C2 *She died tragically young.* ◦ *Tragically, the side-effects of the drug were not discovered until many people had been seriously damaged by it.*

tragicomedy /ˌtrædʒ.ɪˈkɒm.ə.di/ US /-ˈkɑː.mə-/ noun [C or U] a (type of) play or story that is both sad and funny • **tragicomic** /-ˈkɒm.ɪk/ US /-ˈkɑː.mɪk/ adj

trail /treɪl/ noun; verb

▸noun **PATH** ▷ **1** B2 [C] a path through the countryside, often made or used for a particular purpose: *a forest/mountain trail* **SIGNS** ▷ **2** C2 [C] the smell or series of marks left by a person, animal, or thing as it moves along: *The dogs are specially trained to **follow** the trail left by the fox.* ◦ *He **left a** trail **of** muddy footprints behind him.* **S** ▷ **3** [S] various pieces of information which together show where someone you are searching for has gone: *The police admit that the thieves have **left** no trail for them to follow up.* **4 be on the trail of sb/sth** to be searching for someone or something by examining information you find about where they went: *The three men went to the Bahamas, on the trail of a sunken 17th-century galleon full of treasure.*

▸verb **MOVE SLOWLY** ▷ **1** [I or T, usually + adv/prep] to (allow something to) move slowly along the ground or through the air or water, after someone or something: *Katherine, your skirt's trailing **in** the mud!* ◦ *As the boat moved along, he trailed his hand **in** the water.* **2** C2 [I usually + adv/prep] to move slowly and without energy or enthusiasm: *The delegates trailed **back** into the conference room for the afternoon session.* ◦ *After a mile or two the youngest children were trailing **behind**.* **IN A COMPETITION/GAME** ▷ **3 be trailing** C2 to be losing to your competitor in a competition: *The Swiss team are trailing **by** six points.* ◦ *The Nationalist Party is trailing (**behind**) the Liberals in the opinion polls.* **FOLLOW** ▷ **4** [T] to follow the trail of someone or something

PHRASAL VERB **trail away/off** When a person's voice or a similar sound trails away/off, it becomes quieter and less confident and then stops completely: *His voice trailed off as he saw the look on her face.*

trailblazer /ˈtreɪlˌbleɪzər/ US /-zɚ/ noun [C] the first person to do something or go somewhere, who shows that it is also possible for other people: *Orville and Wilbur Wright were aviation trailblazers.*

trailer /ˈtreɪ.lər/ US /-lɚ/ noun [C] **VEHICLE** ▷ **1** a box on wheels that is pulled by a car and is used for taking things from one place to another: *The car was **pulling** a trailer with a motorcycle on it.* **2** the separate back part of a large truck **3** US for a **caravan** **ADVERTISEMENT** ▷ **4** an advertisement for a film or a television or radio programme, consisting of short parts taken from it: *I saw a trailer **for** the latest Spielberg film.*

ˈtrailer ˌpark noun [C] US for **caravan site**

trailing /ˈtreɪ.lɪŋ/ adj [before noun] describes plants that grow along the ground or over the surface of something: *a trailing rose*

train /treɪn/ noun; verb

▸noun **VEHICLE** ▷ **1** A1 [C] a railway engine connected to CARRIAGES for carrying people or to wheeled containers for carrying goods: *a goods/freight/passenger train* ◦ *the train to/from Bristol* ◦ *a train journey/station* ◦ *Did you come **by** train?* ◦ *She **caught/took** the train to Edinburgh.* ◦ *Hurry up, or we'll **miss** (= arrive too late for) the train.*

> **!** Common mistake: **train**
>
> **Remember:** choose the correct preposition!
>
> Don't say 'get in/into the train', say **get on the train**:
>
> *I got on the train and sat down.*
>
> To talk about leaving a train, don't say 'get out of', say **get off**:
>
> *You need to get off the train at the last stop.*
>
> During the journey, you are **on the train**, not 'in the train'.

SERIES ▷ **2 train of thought/events** C2 a series of connected thoughts or events: *What amazing train of thought led you from Napoleon to global warming?* ◦ *The book describes the train of events that led up to the assassination.* **3** [C] a line of animals, people, or things moving along together: *a wagon train* ◦ *a mule/camel train* **PART OF DRESS** ▷ **4** [C] the part of a long dress that spreads out onto the floor behind the person wearing it: *an elaborate wedding dress with a long train*

IDIOM **put/set sth in train** formal to start a process: *The reform process was put in train in 1985.*

▸verb **PREPARE** ▷ **1** B1 [I or T] to prepare someone or yourself for a job, activity or sport, by learning skills and/or by mental or physical exercise: *She trained **as** a pilot.* ◦ [+ to infinitive] *Isn't Michael training **to** be a lawyer?* ◦ [+ to infinitive] *I've had to train my**self to** be more assertive at work.* ◦ *She trained hard **for** the race, sometimes running as much as 60 miles a week.* ◦ humorous *I'm trying to train my boyfriend **to** do the occasional bit of housework.* **AIM** ▷ **2** [T usually + adv/prep] formal to aim or point a gun, camera, light, etc. at someone or something: *With five guns suddenly trained **on** him, he was understandably nervous.* **DIRECT GROWTH** ▷ **3** [T] to direct the growth of a plant in a particular direction by cutting it and tying it: *The vines were trained **over** an arch, providing shade as well as fruit.*

trained /treɪnd/ adj having been prepared for a particular job or activity, by learning skills, getting qualifications, etc.: *I didn't realize Philippa was a trained nurse.* ◦ *Are you trained **in** the use of this equipment?* ◦ humorous *'Did I hear you say your children cleared up after the party?' 'Oh yes, I've got them **well**-trained!'*

T

trainee /ˌtreɪˈniː/ noun [C] C1 a person who is learning and practising the skills of a particular job: *a trainee dentist/electrician*

trainer /ˈtreɪ.nəʳ/ US /-nɚ/ noun **PERSON** ▷ **1** B1 [C] a person who teaches skills to people or animals and prepares them for a job, activity, or sport: *They showed pictures of the horse and its trainer (= the person who prepared it for its races).* ◦ *A lot of wealthy people have their own* ***personal*** *trainer (= a person they employ to help them exercise).* **SHOE** ▷ **2** A2 [C usually plural] UK (UK also **training shoe**, US **sneaker**) a type of light, comfortable shoe that is suitable for playing sport

training /ˈtreɪ.nɪŋ/ noun [U] **1** B1 the process of learning the skills you need to do a particular job or activity: *a training course* ◦ *a teacher-training college* ◦ *New staff* ***have/receive*** *a week's training* ***in*** *how to use the system.* **2 be in training for sth** to exercise a lot and eat particular food in order to prepare yourself for a competition **3 be good training for sth** to be a useful experience that will be helpful when doing a particular thing in the future: *His experience as a teacher was good training for parenthood.*

> **!** Common mistake: **training**
>
> **Training** does not have a plural form.
>
> Do not say 'trainings'. Only say **training**:
>
> ~~*Our staff need trainings in how to operate the system.*~~
>
> *Our staff need training in how to operate the system.*
>
> To talk about **training** in the singular, don't say 'a training', say **a training session** or **a training course**.

> Word partners for **training**
>
> *have/receive/undergo* training • *give* sb training • *provide* training • training *in/on* sth • *advanced/basic/formal/intensive* training • *in-house/in-service/on-the-job* training • a training *course/day/programme/session* • training *facilities/materials*

ˈtrain ˌset noun [C] a toy train, together with the equipment, toy houses, etc. that go with it

trainspotting /ˈtreɪnˌspɒt.ɪŋ/ US /-ˌspɑː.t̬ɪŋ/ noun [U] UK the activity of watching trains and writing down the numbers that each railway engine has • **trainspotter** /-ˌspɒt.əʳ/ US /-ˌspɑː.t̬ɚ/ noun [C]

traipse /treɪps/ verb [I usually + adv/prep] informal to walk from one place to another, often feeling tired or bored: *I spent the day traipsing* ***round*** *the shops, but found nothing suitable for her.* ◦ *It was awful having the builders traipsing* ***through*** *our home every day.*

trait /treɪt/ noun [C] C2 a particular characteristic that can produce a particular type of behaviour: *His sense of humour is one of his better traits.* ◦ *Arrogance is a very unattractive* ***personality/character*** *trait.*

traitor /ˈtreɪ.təʳ/ US /-t̬ɚ/ noun [C] disapproving a person who is not loyal or stops being loyal to their own country, social class, beliefs, etc.: *The leaders of the rebellion were hanged as traitors.* ◦ *The Chinese Communist Party* ***branded*** *(= called) Mr Gorbachev 'a traitor* ***to*** *socialism'.* • **traitorous** /-əs/ adj formal disapproving

trajectory /trəˈdʒek.tᵊr.i/ US /-tɚ.i/ noun [C] specialized the curved path that an object follows after it has been thrown or shot into the air: *the trajectory of a bullet/missile*

IDIOM **be on an upward/downward trajectory** to be getting higher or lower: *The government is now claiming that inflation is on a downward trajectory.*

tram /træm/ noun [C] UK (US usually **streetcar**, US also **trolley**) A2 an electric vehicle that transports people, usually in cities, and goes along metal tracks in the road

tramlines /ˈtræm.laɪnz/ noun [plural] **TRACK** ▷ **1** two metal tracks set in the road, along which a tram goes **SPORT** ▷ **2** UK two parallel painted lines along the edge of the playing area used in tennis and BADMINTON: *In doubles, the ball is not out if it lands between the tramlines.*

tramp /træmp/ noun; verb

▸noun **POOR PERSON** ▷ **1** [C] a person with no home, job, or money who travels around and asks for money from other people **WOMAN** ▷ **2** [C] US slang disapproving a woman who has sex often, with a lot of different partners **WALK** ▷ **3** [S] the sound of people all walking together with heavy steps: *The streets echoed with the tramp* ***of*** *soldiers' feet.* **4** [C] a long walk: *The girls* ***went for*** *a tramp* ***through*** *the countryside.*

▸verb [I usually + adv/prep, T] to walk, especially long distances or with heavy steps: *to tramp* ***through*** *the forest/undergrowth* ◦ *We spent a week tramping the streets of Rome, looking for movie locations.*

trample /ˈtræm.pl̩/ verb [I or T, usually + prep] **STEP HEAVILY ON** ▷ **1** to step heavily on something or someone, causing damage or injury: *Somebody trampled* ***all over*** *my flowerbeds in the night!* ◦ *Eight people were trampled* ***to death*** *(= killed) when the stadium collapsed and the crowd rushed out onto the football pitch.* **TREAT WITHOUT RESPECT** ▷ **2** to act without any respect for someone or something: *She accused the government of trampling* ***on*** *the needs and rights of the ordinary citizen.* ◦ *He argues that Congress trampled the constitutional rights of legal immigrants in the new welfare reform law.*

trampoline /ˈtræm.pᵊl.iːn/ US /ˌtræm.pəˈliːn/ noun [C] a piece of sports equipment that you jump up and down on, consisting of a piece of strong material joined by SPRINGS to a frame • **trampolining** /-ɪŋ/ noun [U] *Rebecca's main hobby is trampolining.*

trance /trɑːns/ US /træns/ noun **MENTAL CONDITION** ▷ **1** [C] a temporary mental condition in which someone is not completely conscious of and/or not in control of themselves and of what is happening to them: *First she* ***goes/falls into*** *a deep trance and then the spirit voices start to speak through her.* ◦ *When a hypnotist* ***puts*** *you* ***in(to)*** *a trance, you no longer have conscious control of yourself.* ◦ *He sat staring out of the window as if* ***in*** *a trance.* **MUSIC** ▷ **2** [U] fast, electronic dance music with a regular beat, keyboards, but usually no singing

tranche /trɑːntʃ/ noun [C] specialized one of several parts of a financial arrangement, payment, amount, etc.: *Next month, they will sell a further tranche of shares worth up to €500 million.*

tranquil /ˈtræŋ.kwɪl/ US /ˈtræn-/ adj C1 calm and peaceful and without noise, violence, worry, etc.: *She stared at the tranquil surface of the water.* ◦ *The hotel is in a tranquil rural setting.* ◦ *A spasm of pain crossed his normally tranquil features.* • **tranquilly** /-kwɪ.li/ adv

tranquillity (US usually **tranquility**) /træŋˈkwɪl.ɪ.ti/ US /trænˈkwɪl.ə.t̬i/ noun [U] C2 a peaceful, calm state, without noise, violence, worry, etc.: *living in* ***peace and*** *tranquillity* ◦ *I love the tranquillity of the countryside.*

T

tranquillize (US usually **tranquilize**, UK usually **tranquillise**) /ˈtræŋ.kwɪ.laɪz/ (US) /ˈtræn-/ **verb** [T] to make an animal or person become unconscious or calm, especially with a drug: *a tranquillizing drug* ◦ *The dogs were tranquillized with a dart gun and taken to a shelter.*

tranquillizer (US usually **tranquilizer**, UK usually **tranquilliser**) /ˈtræŋ.kwɪ.laɪ.zəʳ/ (US) /ˈtræn.kwɪ.laɪ.zɚ/ **noun** [C] a drug used to make a person or animal calmer: *She was* ***on*** *tranquillizers for a long time after her son died.*

trans- /træns-/, /trænz-/ **prefix** ACROSS ▷ **1** across: *a transatlantic flight* ◦ *the trans-Alaskan pipeline* CHANGED ▷ **2** having changed from one thing to another: *Kate has transformed (= completely changed the appearance of) that house since she moved in.* ◦ *She is a transsexual (= she has changed from being a man to a woman).*

transact /trænˈzækt/ **verb** [T] formal to do and complete a business activity: *The sale was transacted in conditions of the greatest secrecy.*

transaction /trænˈzæk.ʃən/ **noun** [C or U] C1 an occasion when someone buys or sells something, or when money is exchanged or the activity of buying or selling something: *a business transaction* ◦ *Each transaction at the foreign exchange counter seems to take forever.* ◦ *We need to monitor the transaction of smaller deals.*

transatlantic /ˌtræn.zətˈlæn.tɪk/ (US) /-zætˈlæn.t̬ɪk/ **adj** crossing the Atlantic ocean, or relating to countries on both sides of the Atlantic Ocean: *transatlantic flights*

transcend /trænˈsend/ **verb** [T] formal to go further, rise above, or be more important or better than something, especially a limit: *The best films are those which transcend national or cultural barriers.* ◦ *The underlying message of the film is that love transcends everything else.*

transcendent /trænˈsen.dənt/ **adj** formal greater, better, more important, or going past or above all others: *transcendent power/beauty/love* ◦ *He describes seeing Pelé play football as one of the transcendent* ***moments*** *of his life.* • **transcendence** /-dəns/ **noun** [U]

transcendental /ˌtræn.senˈden.təl/ (US) /-t̬əl/ **adj** formal describes an experience, event, object or idea that is extremely special and unusual and cannot be understood in ordinary ways: *a transcendental vision of the nature of God*

ˌTranscendental Meditˈation **noun** [U] trademark a method of making the mind calm and becoming relaxed by silently repeating a special word or series of words many times

transcontinental /ˌtrænz.kɒn.tɪˈnen.təl/, /ˌtræns-/ (US) /-kɑːn-/ **adj** crossing a continent: *The transcontinental railway goes from New York to San Francisco.*

transcribe /trænˈskraɪb/ **verb** [T] RECORD ▷ **1** to record something written, spoken, or played by writing it down: *Recordings of conversations are transcribed and entered into the database.* CHANGE ▷ **2** to change a piece of writing or music into another form, for example into a different writing system or into music for different instruments: *Transcribing the Ethiopian text* ***into*** *the English alphabet was their first task.* ◦ *The quintet had been transcribed* ***for*** *clarinet and piano.*

transcript /ˈtræn.skrɪpt/ **noun** [C] an exact written copy of something: *Mysteriously, the transcript* ***of*** *what was said at the trial went missing.*

transcription /trænˈskrɪp.ʃən/ **noun** **1** [C] a written record of words or music: *This is a* ***phonetic*** *transcription* ***of*** *the conversations that were recorded on tape.* **2** [U] the process of transcribing something

transducer /trænzˈdjuː.səʳ/ (US) /trɑːnsˈduː.sɚ/ **noun** [C] specialized any electronic device that changes one form of energy into another, such as a MICROPHONE, which changes sound waves into electrical signals

transept /ˈtræn.sept/ **noun** [C] either of the two side parts of a cross-shaped church that are at an angle of 90 degrees to the main part

trans fat /ˈtrænz.fæt/ **noun** [C or U] (also **ˌtrans-fatty ˈacid**) a type of fat that is produced by HYDROGENATION (= when vegetable oil is made into solid fat) and is used in MARGARINE, fried foods, etc.: *An excess of trans fats in the diet can cause high cholesterol levels.*

transfer **verb**; **noun**

▸**verb** /trænsˈfɜːʳ/ (US) /ˈtræns.fɝː/ (**-rr-**) **1** B1 [T] to move someone or something from one place, vehicle, person, or group to another: *He has been transferred* ***to*** *a psychiatric hospital.* ◦ *She transferred her gun* ***from*** *its shoulder holster* ***to*** *her handbag.* ◦ *We were transferred* ***from*** *one bus* ***into*** *another.* ◦ *Police are investigating how £20 million was illegally transferred* ***from/out of*** *the Trust's bank account.* ◦ *The aim is to transfer* ***power/control/responsibility to*** *self-governing regional councils.* ◦ *I'll be upstairs, so could you transfer my phone calls (= arrange that I can receive them)* ***up*** *there, please?* **2** B2 [I or T, usually + adv/prep] to change to a different job, team, place of work, etc., or to make someone do this: *After a year he transferred* ***to*** *University College, Dublin.* ◦ *Some very high-profile British players have transferred* ***to*** *clubs abroad.* ◦ *He threatened to give up football if his club didn't transfer him (= sell him to another team).* **3** [T] to make something the legal property of another person: *She transferred the house* ***to*** *her daughter before she died.* • **transferable** /trænsˈfɜː.rə.bl̩/ (US) /-ˈfɝː.ə-/ **adj** *The tickets were marked 'Not Transferable'.*

> **!** Common mistake: **transfer**
>
> **Warning:** Check your verb endings!
>
> Many learners make mistakes when using **transfer** in the past tense. The past simple and past participle have 'rr'. Don't write 'transfered', write **transferred**. The **-ing** form is **transferring**.

▸**noun** /ˈtræns.fɜːʳ/ (US) /-fɝː/ MOVE/CHANGE ▷ **1** B2 the movement of something or someone from one place, position, etc. to another: *the transfer of information* ◦ *Black's transfer* ***to*** *the LA office came as a shock his colleagues.* ◦ *The official transfer* ***of*** *ownership will take a few days to complete.* SPORTS ▷ **2** [C] a player who has moved from one sports team to another: *They've a new transfer* ***from*** *Tottenham playing for them.* TRAVEL TICKET ▷ **3** [C] US a ticket that allows a passenger to change routes or to change from one bus or train to another PATTERN ▷ **4** [C] a picture or pattern that can be fixed to a surface by pressing it against the surface and then rubbing or heating it: *The kids bought transfers and ironed them onto their T-shirts.* → Compare **decal**

transference /trænsˈfɜː.rəns/ (US) /ˈtræns.fɚ.əns/ **noun** [U] formal the process of moving something or someone from one place, position, etc. to another: *UN observers were there to ensure the smooth transference of power.*

ˈtransfer ˌfee **noun** [C] UK the amount of money which a sports team pays in order to buy a new player from another team

ˈtransfer ˌlist **noun** [C usually singular] UK a football or RUGBY team's list of players that are available to be sold: *The club's top goalkeeper is* ***on*** *the transfer list.*

transfigure /træns'fɪg.əʳ/ (US) /-jɚ/ **verb** [T] formal to change the appearance of a person or thing very much, usually in a very positive and often spiritual way: *As she gazed down at the baby, her face was transfigured* ***with*** *tenderness.* ◦ *The assassination somehow transfigured Kennedy* ***into*** *a modern American saint.* • **transfiguration** /ˌtræns.fɪ.gəʳ'eɪ.ʃən/ (US) /-fɪg.jə'reɪ-/ **noun** [U]

transfix /træns'fɪks/ **verb** [T] literary **UNABLE TO MOVE** ▷ to make a person or animal unable to move or stop looking at something because they are so interested, surprised, or frightened, usually because their interest in or fear of something is so strong: *The conference delegates were transfixed by her speech.* • **transfixed** /-'fɪkst/ **adj** *Rabbits transfixed in the glare of car headlights are common victims on the roads.*

transform /træns'fɔːm/ (US) /-'fɔːrm/ **verb** [T] (B2) to change completely the appearance or character of something or someone, especially so that they are improved: *The reorganization will transform the British entertainment industry.* ◦ *Whenever a camera was pointed at her, Marilyn would instantly transform her****self into*** *a radiant star.*

transformation /ˌtræns.fə'meɪ.ʃən/ (US) /-fɚ-/ **noun** [C or U] (C1) a complete change in the appearance or character of something or someone, especially so that they are improved: *Local people have mixed feelings about the planned transformation of their town* ***into*** *a regional capital.* ◦ *I'd never seen Carlo in smart evening clothes before – it was quite a transformation.*

transformer /træns'fɔː.məʳ/ (US) /-'fɔːr.mɚ/ **noun** [C] specialized a device which changes the VOLTAGE or other characteristic of electrical energy as it moves from one CIRCUIT to another: *You may need a transformer if you want to run a personal stereo off mains electricity.*

transfusion /træns'fjuː.ʒən/ **noun** [C or U] **1** the process of adding an amount of blood to the body of a person or animal, or the amount of blood itself: *She suffered kidney failure and needed a* ***blood*** *transfusion.* **2 transfusion of sth** the act of putting a new quantity of something powerful, effective, or important into an organization, group, or place: *a transfusion of talent/energy/money*

transgender /trænz'dʒen.dəʳ/ (US) /-dɚ/ **adj** (informal **trans** /trænz/) used to describe someone who feels that they are not the same GENDER (= sex) as their physical body, or who does not fit easily into being either a male or a female

transgenic /trænz'dʒen.ɪk/ **adj** specialized describes an animal or plant that contains one or more GENES that have been added from another type of plant or animal

transgress /trænz'gres/ **verb** [I or T] formal to break a law or moral rule: *Those are the rules, and anyone who transgresses will be severely punished.* • **transgression** /-'greʃ.ən/ **noun** [C or U] *Who is supposed to have* ***committed*** *these transgressions?* • **transgressor** /-əʳ/ (US) /-ɚ/ **noun** [C] *The system seems to be designed to punish the transgressor (= the person breaking the rules) rather than help his victim.*

transient /'træn.zi.ənt/ (US) /-ʃənt/ **adj; noun**

▸**adj** formal lasting for only a short time; temporary: *A glass of whisky has only a transient warming effect.* ◦ *The city has a large transient population (= many people who are living in it only temporarily).*

▸**noun** [C] mainly US formal someone who lives only temporarily in a place: *It's an organization set up to provide money and help for transients.* • **transience** /-əns/ **noun** [U] formal *the transience of human existence/fame*

transistor /træn'zɪs.təʳ/ (US) /-'zɪs.tɚ/ **noun** [C] **1** a small electrical device containing a SEMICONDUCTOR, used in televisions, radios, etc. to control or increase an electric current **2** (also **transistor radio**, informal **trannie**) a small radio containing transistors, used especially in the past

transistorized (UK usually **transistorised**) /træn'zɪs.tər.aɪzd/ (US) /-tə.raɪzd/ **adj** describes a device that uses transistors rather than VALVES: *transistorized amplifiers*

transit /'træn.zɪt/ **noun** [U] the movement of goods or people from one place to another: *It is possible to make an insurance claim for any goods lost or damaged* ***in*** *transit.* ◦ *The question is whether road transit is cheaper than rail.* ◦ *a* ***rapid****-transit train*

Transit /'træn.zɪt/ **noun** [C] trademark a type of road vehicle used especially for carrying goods: *He was seen driving a white Transit* ***van*** *near Leeds.*

'transit ˌcamp **noun** [C] a place where REFUGEES stay in tents or other temporary structures when they have nowhere to live permanently

transition /træn'zɪʃ.ən/ **noun** [C or U] (C2) a change from one form or type to another, or the process by which this happens: *The health-care system is* ***in*** *transition at the moment.* ◦ *There will be an interim government to oversee the transition* ***to*** *democracy.*

transitional /træn'zɪʃ.ən.əl/ **adj** belonging or relating to a change, or the process of change, from one form or type to another: *a transitional government*

tran'sition ˌmetal **noun** [C] (also **tran'sition ˌelement**) any of a group of metal chemical elements including COPPER and gold that show more than one VALENCY (= the number of HYDROGEN atoms that can combine with one of its atoms to form a COMPOUND)

transitive /'træn.sə.tɪv/, /'trɑːn-/, /-zə-/ (US) /'træn.sə.t̬ɪv/ /-zə-/ **adj; noun**

▸**adj** specialized (B2) (of a verb) having or needing an object: *In this dictionary, transitive verbs, such as 'put', are marked [T].* → Compare **ditransitive, intransitive** • **transitively** /-li/ **adv** *Can 'cry' be used transitively?* • **transitivity** /ˌtræn.sə'tɪv.ɪ.ti/, /'trɑːn-/, /-zə-/ (US) /ˌtræn.sə.t̬ɪv-/ /-zə-/ **noun** [U]

▸**noun** [C] specialized a transitive verb

transitory /'træn.zɪ.tər.i/ (US) /-tɔː.ri/ **adj** formal lasting for only a short time: *the transitory nature of life*

translate /træns'leɪt/, /trænz-/ **verb** [I or T] **1** (B1) to change words into a different language: *We were asked to translate a list of sentences.* ◦ *She works for the EU, translating* ***from*** *English* ***into*** *French.* → Compare **interpret 2** (C2) to change something into a new form, especially to turn a plan into something real: *So how does this theory translate* ***into*** *practical policy?* ◦ *The ways of working that he had learned at college did not translate* ***well*** *(= were not suitable)* ***to*** *the world of business.* **3 translate sth as sth** to decide that words, behaviour, or actions mean a particular thing: *He mumbled something which I translated as agreement.*

translation /træns'leɪ.ʃən/, /trænz-/ **noun** [C or U] **1** (B1) something that is translated, or the process of translating something, from one language to another: *The children do one French translation a week.* ◦ *A* ***literal*** *translation* ***of*** *'euthanasia' would be 'good death'.* ◦ *The English version is boring – perhaps it has* ***lost*** *something* ***in*** *translation (= is not as good as the original).* **2 in translation** changed into someone's own language, not in the original language: *She reads Proust in translation.*

translator /træns'leɪ.təʳ/, /trænz-/ (US) /-t̬ɚ/ **noun** [C] a person whose job is changing words, especially

T

written words, into a different language → Compare **interpreter**

transliterate /trænzˈlɪt.ᵊr.eɪt/ (US) /trænsˈlɪt̬.ə.reɪt/ verb [T] specialized to write words using a different alphabet: *On the road signs, the Greek place names have been transliterated **into** the Roman alphabet.* • **transliteration** /ˌtrænz.lɪ.tᵊrˈeɪ.ʃᵊn/ (US) /trænsˌlɪt̬.əˈreɪ-/ noun [C or U]

translucent /trænzˈluː.sᵊnt/ (US) /træns-/ adj often approving If an object or a substance is translucent, it is almost transparent, allowing some light through it in an attractive way: *This china is so fine and delicate that it's translucent.* ◦ *Delia's skin has a translucent **quality**.* → Compare **opaque, transparent** • **translucence** /-sᵊns/ noun [U]

transmission /trænzˈmɪʃ.ᵊn/ (US) /træns-/ noun RADIO/TELEVISION ▷ **1** (C2) [C or U] the process of broadcasting something by radio, television, etc., or something that is broadcast: *We apologize for the interruption to our transmissions this afternoon.* PASSING ▷ **2** (C2) [U] the process of passing something from one person or place to another: *the transmission **of** disease* VEHICLE ▷ **3** [C or U] the machinery that brings the power produced by the engine to the wheels of a vehicle: *automatic transmission* ◦ *The car had a faulty transmission.*

transmit /trænzˈmɪt/ (US) /træns-/ verb (-tt-) RADIO/TELEVISION ▷ **1** (C1) [I or T] to broadcast something, or to send out or carry signals using radio, television, etc.: *Radio Seven transmits **on** 201 medium wave (= uses those particular radio waves to broadcast on).* ◦ *The information is transmitted electronically to the central computer.* PASS ▷ **2** (C2) [T] to pass something from one person or place to another: *a sexually transmitted disease* ◦ *Cholera is transmitted **through** contaminated water.* ◦ *Some diseases are transmitted **from** one generation **to** the next.* ◦ *Somehow your panic and fear transmits it**self to** the horse that you're riding.*

transmitter /trænzˈmɪt.əʳ/ (US) /trænsˈmɪt̬.ɚ/ noun [C] a piece of equipment for broadcasting radio or television signals: *a TV/radio transmitter*

transmogrify /trænzˈmɒg.rɪ.faɪ/ (US) /trænsˈmɑː.grə-/ verb [I or T] humorous to change or be changed completely: *Almost overnight, that sweet, little child had transmogrified into an antisocial monster.* • **transmogrification** /ˌtrænz.mɒg.rɪ.fɪˈkeɪ.ʃᵊn/ (US) /trænsˌmɑː.grə-/ noun [C or U]

transmute /trænzˈmjuːt/ (US) /træns-/ verb [I or T, usually + adv/prep] formal to change something completely, especially into something different and better: *A few centuries ago alchemists thought they could transmute lead **into** gold.* ◦ specialized *Plutonium transmutes **into/to** uranium when it is processed in a nuclear reactor.* • **transmutation** /ˌtrænz.mjuːˈteɪ.ʃᵊn/ (US) /ˌtræns-/ noun [C or U]

transnational /ˌtrænzˈnæʃ.ᵊn.ᵊl/ adj involving several nations: *transnational crime/issues*

transom /ˈtræn.səm/ noun [C] **1** specialized a horizontal bar of stone or wood across a window, or separating the top of a window or door from a small window above **2** (also **transom window**) US for **fanlight**

transparency /trænˈspær.ᵊn.si/ (US) /-ˈsper-/ noun SEE THROUGH ▷ **1** [U] the characteristic of being easy to see through: *The old-fashioned type of plastic lacked transparency.* **2** [C] specialized a photograph or picture printed on plastic which you can see on a screen by shining a light through it OPEN ▷ **3** [U] the quality of being done in an open way without secrets: *We want more transparency **in** government.*

transparent /trænˈspær.ᵊnt/ (US) /trænˈsper-/ adj SEE THROUGH ▷ **1** (B2) If a substance or object is transparent, you can see through it very clearly: *Grow the bulbs in a transparent plastic box, so the children can see the roots growing.* ◦ *Her blouse was practically transparent!* → Compare **opaque, translucent** OBVIOUS ▷ **2** clear and easy to understand or recognize: *I think we should try to make the instructions more transparent.* WITHOUT SECRETS ▷ **3** open and honest, without secrets: *We are committed to being totally transparent about our charges.*

transpire /trænˈspaɪəʳ/ (US) /-ˈspaɪɚ/ verb BECOME KNOWN ▷ **1** [I] formal If it transpires that something has happened, a previously secret or unknown fact becomes known: [+ that] *It may yet transpire **that** ministers knew more than they are admitting at the moment.* ◦ *As it later transpired, she had known him at school.* HAPPEN ▷ **2** [I] formal to happen: *No one is willing to predict what may transpire at the peace conference.* LOSE WATER ▷ **3** [I or T] specialized If a body or plant transpires, it loses water through its surface or skin. • **transpiration** /ˌtræn.spɪˈreɪ.ʃᵊn/ noun [U] specialized

transplant /trænˈsplɑːnt/ (US) /-ˈsplænt/ verb; noun

▸verb [I or T, usually + adv/prep] to move something, or to be moved, from one place or person to another: *The plants should be grown indoors until spring, when they can be transplanted outside.* → Compare **implant**
• **transplantation** /ˌtræn.splɑːnˈteɪ.ʃᵊn/ (US) /-splæn-/ noun [U] *Transplantation of organs from living donors raises ethical issues.*

▸noun **1** (C2) [C or U] a medical operation in which a new organ is put into someone's body: *a liver/kidney transplant* ◦ *transplant surgery* ◦ *He **had** a heart transplant (= doctors gave him a different, healthier heart instead of his old one).* **2** [C] something, especially a new organ, that has been transplanted: *His body accepted/rejected the transplant.*

transponder /trænˈspɒn.dəʳ/ (US) /-ˈspɑːn.dɚ/ noun [C] specialized an electronic device that gives out a radio signal when it receives a similar signal telling it to: *Aircraft are required by law to carry transponders, so that they can be identified.*

> **! Common mistake: transport**
>
> **Transport** does not have a plural form and cannot be used with **a** or **an**.
>
> To talk about **transport** in general, do not say 'transports', say **transport**:
>
> ~~*Public transports were not frequent in the evenings.*~~
> *Public transport was not frequent in the evenings.*
>
> To talk about **transport** in the singular, do not say 'a transport', say **a form/means/mode of transport**:
>
> ~~*The bicycle is a convenient transport.*~~
> *The bicycle is a convenient means of transport.*

transport noun; verb

▸noun /ˈtræn.spɔːt/ (US) /-spɔːrt/ GOODS/PEOPLE ▷ **1** (B2) [U] the movement of people or goods from one place to another: *the transport of live animals* ◦ *The company will arrange transport from the airport.* **2** (B1) [U] UK (US **transportation**) a system of vehicles, such as buses, trains, aircraft, etc. for getting from one place to another: *the Department of Transport* ◦ *investment in **public** transport (= buses, trains, etc. available for everyone to use)* ◦ *Do you have your own transport (= vehicle)?* ◦ *Bicycles are a cheap and efficient **form of*** *transport.* **FEELING** ▷ **3 in transports (of delight)** literary extremely pleased or happy

> **Word partners for transport**
>
> *arrange/provide* transport • *improve* transport • *cheap/free* transport • a *form/means/mode* of transport • transport *links/network/services/system*

▸**verb** [T] /træn'spɔːt/ (US) /-'spɔːrt/ **GOODS/PEOPLE** ▷ **1** (B2) to take goods or people from one place to another: *The pipeline was constructed to transport oil* ***across*** *Alaska* ***to*** *ports on the coast.* ◦ *Such heavy items are expensive to transport (****by*** *plane).* **2** (in the past) to send a criminal to a country far away, to live, as a punishment: *162,000 convicts were transported* ***to*** *Australia from 1788 to 1868.* **FEELING** ▷ **3** literary If something transports you to a different time or place, it makes you feel as if you are in it: *The film transported us* ***back to*** *the New York of the 1950s.*

transportation /ˌtræn.spɔː'teɪ.ʃən/ (US) /-spɚ-/ **noun** [U] **1** (B2) the movement of people or goods from one place to another: *In the past, British convicts could be sentenced to transportation (****to*** *Australia).* **2** (B1) US (UK **transport**) a vehicle or system of vehicles, such as buses, trains, etc. for getting from one place to another: *In Los Angeles many companies encourage their employees to use alternative* ***means of*** *transportation, rather than the car.*

ˈtransport ˌcafé noun [C] UK (US **ˈtruck ˌstop**) a cheap restaurant next to a main road, used mainly by truck drivers

transporter /træn'spɔː.tər/ (US) /-'spɔːr.t̬ɚ/ **noun** [C] a long vehicle used for moving several large objects such as cars from one place to another: *a car transporter*

ˈtransport ˌplane noun [C] an aircraft used especially for taking soldiers or military supplies from one place to another

ˈtransport ˌship noun [C] a ship used especially for taking soldiers or military supplies from one place to another

transpose /træn'spəʊz/ (US) /-'spoʊz/ **verb** [T] **1** formal to change something from one position to another, or to exchange the positions of two things: *In their latest production they have reworked 'King Lear', transposing it* ***to*** *pre-colonial Africa.* ◦ *The confusion was caused when two numbers were accidentally transposed by a Social Security clerk.* **2** specialized to play or write a piece of music in a different KEY (= set of musical notes based on a particular note) from the one used originally: *The pianist transposed the song* ***into*** *C.* • **transposition** /ˌtræn.spə'zɪʃ.ən/ **noun** [C or U]

transsexual /trænz'sek.sjuəl/, /-sju.əl/ (US) /-ʃu.əl/ **noun** [C] **1** a person, especially a man, who feels that they should have been the opposite sex, and therefore behaves and dresses like a member of that sex **2** a person who has had a medical operation to change their sex

transubstantiation /ˌtræn.səbˌstæn.ʃi'eɪ.ʃən/ **noun** [U] specialized the belief, especially by Roman Catholics, that during MASS (= a religious ceremony) bread and wine are changed into the body and blood of Jesus Christ

transverse /trænz'vɜːs/ (US) /træns'vɜːrs/ **adj** specialized in a position or direction that is at an angle of 90° to something else: *The main roof beams are given extra support by the smaller transverse beams.*

ˈtransverse ˌwave noun [C] specialized in physics, a wave moving through a substance in which the PARTICLES are VIBRATING (= moving quickly backwards and forwards) at a 90 degree angle to the direction of the wave → Compare **longitudinal wave**

transvestite /trænz'ves.taɪt/ (US) /træns-/ **noun** [C] a person, especially a man, who wears the clothes of the opposite sex, often for sexual pleasure → Compare **transsexual** • **transvestism** /-tɪ.zəm/ **noun** [U] formal

trap /træp/ **noun; verb**

▸**noun STH THAT PREVENTS ESCAPE** ▷ **1** (B2) [C] a device or hole for catching animals or people and preventing their escape: *The fox got its foot* ***caught in*** *a trap.* **2** (B2) [S] a dangerous or unpleasant situation which you have got into and from which it is difficult or impossible to escape: *The undercover agents went to the rendezvous knowing that it might be a trap.* ◦ *She's too clever to* ***fall into*** *the trap of doing any unpaid work.* **MOUTH** ▷ **3** [C] slang a mouth: *Oh,* ***shut*** *your trap (= stop talking) – I'm bored of listening to you!* ◦ *I've told him it's a secret and he's to* ***keep*** *his trap* ***shut*** *(= not say anything about it).* **VEHICLE** ▷ **4** [C] a light CARRIAGE with two wheels pulled by a horse, used especially in the past

▸**verb** [T] **(-pp-) 1** to catch an animal in a trap: *She survived in the forest by eating berries and trapping small animals and birds.* **2** to keep something such as heat or water in one place, especially because it is useful: *A greenhouse stays warm because the glass traps the heat of the sun.* **3 be trapped** (B2) If someone or something is trapped, they are unable to move or escape from a place or situation: *The two men died when they were trapped* ***in*** *a burning building.* ◦ *Fire officers used cutting equipment to free his legs, which were trapped under a steel beam.* ◦ figurative *Jack left the job after ten years because he was beginning to* ***feel*** *trapped.* **4 be trapped into (doing) sth** to be forced or tricked into doing something that you do not want to do: *In his book, Holden speculates that Shakespeare was an unfaithful husband who was trapped into marriage.* ◦ *She had been trapped into saying something she did not mean.*

trapdoor /'træp.dɔːr/ (US) /-dɔːr/ **noun** [C] a small door in a ceiling or floor: *There's a trapdoor* ***into*** *the attic.*

trapeze /trə'piːz/ **noun** [C] a short bar hanging high up in the air from two ropes, which ACROBATS use to perform special movements: *A glamorous couple performed* ***on*** *the* ***flying*** *trapeze.* ◦ *trapeze* ***artists***

trapezium /trə'piː.zi.əm/ **noun** [C] (plural **trapezia** /trə'piː.zi.ə/ or **trapeziums**) UK specialized (US **trapezoid**) a flat shape with four sides, where two of the sides are parallel

trapezoid /'træp.ɪ.zɔɪd/ **noun** [C] UK (US **trapezium**) a shape with four sides of different lengths, none of which are parallel

trapper /'træp.ər/ (US) /-ɚ/ **noun** [C] a person who catches wild animals, usually to sell their fur: *a fur trapper*

trappings /'træp.ɪŋz/ **noun** [plural] all the things that are part of or typical of a particular job, situation, or event: *He enjoyed the trappings* ***of power****, such as a chauffeur-driven car and bodyguards.* ◦ *The demonstration had* ***all the*** *trappings* ***of*** *a typical 1960s peace demo.*

Trappist monk /ˌtræp.ɪst'mʌŋk/ **noun** [C] (also **Trappist**) a member of a Roman Catholic organization with very extreme rules, such as no talking

trapshooting /'træpˌʃuː.tɪŋ/ (US) /-t̬ɪŋ/ **noun** [U] the sport of shooting at CLAY PIGEONS (= round, flat clay objects that are thrown into the air)

trash /træʃ/ **noun; verb**

▸**noun** [U] **THINGS** ▷ **1** (C2) informal something that is of

T

low quality: *I can't believe that someone of his intelligence can read such trash!* **2** B1 US for rubbish: *The trash really stinks – why don't you take it out?* **PEOPLE** ▷ **3** [+ sing/pl verb] US informal an insulting way of referring to a group of people that you have no respect for: *We don't have anything to do with the people in the apartment below us – they're trash.*

IDIOM **talk trash 1** informal to say things that do not have a lot of meaning: *There are too many radio shows featuring idiots who call in and talk trash all day.* **2** US informal to criticize other people, especially unfairly or cruelly

▸verb [T] informal **THROW AWAY** ▷ **1** to throw something away: *I simply trash that sort of mail.* **DAMAGE** ▷ **2** to destroy or severely damage something: *The guys got angry and trashed the bar.* **CRITICIZE** ▷ **3** to criticize something or someone severely: *The boss completely trashed her work, in front of everyone.*

ˈtrash ˌbag noun [C] US for **bin bag**

ˈtrash ˌcan noun [C] US for **dustbin** or **bin**

ˈtrash can ˌliner noun [C] US for **bin bag**

trashy /ˈtræʃ.i/ adj informal of low quality; with little or no value: *trashy programmes*

trauma /ˈtrɔː.mə/, /ˈtraʊ-/ US /ˈtrɑː-/ noun [C or U] **SHOCK** ▷ **1** C2 (a) severe emotional shock and pain caused by an extremely upsetting experience: *the trauma **of** marriage breakdown* ◦ *He had psychotherapy to help him deal with his childhood traumas.* **INJURY** ▷ **2** specialized (a) severe injury, usually caused by a violent attack or an accident

traumatic /trɔːˈmæt.ɪk/, /traʊ-/ US /trɑːˈmæt̬-/ adj **1** C2 If an experience is traumatic, it causes you severe emotional shock and upset: *Some of the most disturbed children had witnessed really traumatic things, such as rape and murder.* **2** informal frightening and causing worry: *Don't you find exams traumatic?*
• **traumatically** /-ɪ.kəl.i/ adv

traumatize (UK usually **traumatise**) /ˈtrɔː.mə.taɪz/, /ˈtraʊ-/ US /ˈtrɑː-/ verb [T usually passive] to shock and upset someone severely and for a long time: *She was completely traumatized by the death of her mother.*
• **traumatized** (UK usually **traumatised**) /-taɪzd/ adj *The whole experience left him traumatized.*

travails /ˈtræv.eɪlz/, /trəˈveɪlz/ noun [plural] old-fashioned or literary the difficulties that are experienced as part of a particular situation: *The travails of the British car industry are seldom out of the news.*

> **! Common mistake: travel**
>
> **Warning:** Check your verb endings!
>
> Many learners make mistakes when using **travel** in the past tense. The past simple and past participle are trave**ll**ed in UK English, and, usually, trave**l**ed in US English. The **-ing** form is trave**ll**ing in UK English, and, usually, trave**l**ing in US English.

travel /ˈtræv.əl/ verb; noun

▸verb (-ll- or US usually -l-) **1** A1 [I or T] to make a journey, usually over a long distance: *After leaving school, she spent a year travelling, mostly in Africa and Asia.* ◦ *I travel **to** work **by** train.* ◦ *He travelled over 100 miles to be at the wedding.* ◦ *As a young man he had travelled (= been to many parts of) **the world**.* **2** B1 [I] to move or go from one place to another: *Supersonic planes can travel faster than the speed of sound.* **3** [I] If something such as food travels well/badly, it does/does not stay in good condition if it is moved long distances: *They say that real Yorkshire beers don't travel well.* **4 really travel** informal to move very fast: *We were doing 90 mph, so the car that passed us must have been really travelling!* ◦ *That bike can really travel!* **5 travel light** to make a journey without taking a lot of heavy things with you: *I always try to travel light.*

▸noun **1** B1 [U] the activity of travelling: *air/space travel* ◦ *business travel* ◦ *We share a love of food and travel.* ◦ *I heard on the travel **news** that there'd been an accident.* **2 travels** C1 [plural] journeys: *a record of her travels **in/around** the Far East*

> **! Common mistake: travel, trip, or journey?**
>
> **Warning:** Choose the right word!
>
> **Travel** is an uncountable noun and refers to the activity of travelling:
>
> *Air travel has become much cheaper.*
>
> To talk about a particular occasion where you go somewhere and come back again, don't say 'travel', say **trip**:
>
> ~~*I met him on a recent travel to London.*~~
>
> *I met him on a recent trip to London.*
>
> To talk about the part of a 'trip' you spend in a vehicle, don't say 'travel', say **journey**:
>
> ~~*The travel from the airport takes about 20 minutes.*~~
>
> *The journey from the airport takes about 20 minutes.*

ˈtravel ˌagency noun [C] a company or shop that makes travel arrangements for people

ˈtravel ˌagent noun [C] B1 a person or company that arranges tickets, hotel rooms, etc. for people going on holiday or making a journey

travelled (US usually **traveled**) /ˈtræv.əld/ adj **1 well/much/little travelled** describes a journey or route that many/few people travel on **2 well/widely travelled** describes people who have visited many countries: *They're a well-travelled couple.*

traveller (US usually **traveler**) /ˈtræv.əl.əʳ/, /-ləʳ/ US /-əl.ɚ/ noun [C] **1** B1 someone who travels: *This hotel is for serious travellers, rather than tourists on two-week package holidays.* **2** UK a **gypsy**

ˈtraveller's ˌcheque UK (US **ˈtraveler's ˌcheck**) noun [C] a piece of paper that you buy from a bank or a travel company and that you can use as money or exchange for the local money of the country you visit

travelling /ˈtræv.əl.ɪŋ/, /-lɪŋ/ noun; adj

▸noun [U] (US usually **traveling**) the activity of making journeys; travel: *I love the work but I hate the travelling that's involved.*

▸adj [before noun] (US usually **traveling**) **1** moving from one place to another, especially to perform or while working, etc.: *a travelling opera company/circus* **2** relating to or used for travel

ˌtravelling ˈsalesman old-fashioned (US usually **ˌtraveling ˈsalesman**) noun [C] a **sales rep**

travelogue /ˈtræv.əl.ɒg/ US /-ə.lɑːg/ noun [C] a film or book about travelling to or in a particular place: *Peter Jackson's latest book 'Africa' is part travelogue, part memoir.*

ˈtravel ˌsickness noun [U] (also **ˈmotion ˌsickness**) a feeling of illness, especially of needing to vomit, that some people get in a moving vehicle

traverse /trəˈvɜːs/ US /-ˈvɜːs/ verb [T] formal to move or travel through an area: *Stanley traversed the continent from west to east.*

travesty /ˈtræv.ə.sti/ noun [C] formal something which fails to represent the values and qualities that it is intended to represent, in a way that is shocking or offensive: *Their production of 'Macbeth' was quite* the worst I've ever seen – it was a travesty. ◦ Langdale described the court ruling as a travesty **of justice**. → Compare **parody**

trawl /trɔːl/ (US) /trɑːl/ verb; noun
▸verb **FISH** ▷ **1** [T] to pull a large, cone-shaped net through the sea at a deep level behind a special boat in order to catch fish: *They trawl these waters **for** cod.* **SEARCH** ▷ **2** [I or T, usually + adv/prep] to search among a large number or many different places in order to find people or information you want: *The newspaper had trawled its files **for** photos of the new minister.* ◦ *You need to trawl **through** a lot of data to get results that are valid.*
▸noun [C] **SEARCH** ▷ **1** a search among a large number or many different places in order to find people or information you want: *We **did** a wide trawl to find the right person to play the part.* **NET** ▷ **2** (also **trawl net**) a large, cone-shaped net used for trawling the water for fish

trawler /ˈtrɔː.ləʳ/ (US) /ˈtrɑː.lɚ/ noun [C] a large boat that uses a wide, cone-shaped net to catch fish

tray /treɪ/ noun [C] **1** (B2) a flat object, usually with raised edges, used for carrying food and drinks: *She was carrying a tray **of** drinks.* **2** mainly UK a flat, open container with raised edges which you put on your desk for keeping papers in: *She put the letter in your **in** tray.* ◦ *I don't know where I put that article – it must be in the bottom of my tray.* → See also **ashtray**

treacherous /ˈtretʃ.ər.əs/ (US) /-ɚ-/ adj **DANGEROUS** ▷ **1** If the ground or sea is treacherous, it is extremely dangerous, especially because of bad weather conditions: *Snow and ice have left many roads treacherous, and motorists are warned to drive slowly.* **NOT LOYAL** ▷ **2** A person who is treacherous deceives someone who trusts them, or has no loyalty: *Vargas plays the part of a treacherous aristocrat who betrays his king and country.* ◦ *I feel a bit treacherous **to** my own sex if I ever make general criticisms of women.*

treachery /ˈtretʃ.ər.i/ (US) /-ɚ-/ noun [U] formal behaviour which deceives, or is not loyal to, someone who trusts you: *Corley said she was standing down as leader because of the treachery of her own colleagues.*

treacle /ˈtriː.kl̩/ noun [U] UK **1** (also **black treacle**) a sweet, dark, thick liquid that is used in cooking sweet dishes and sweets: *treacle toffee* → Compare **syrup 2 golden syrup**: *treacle tart*

treacly /ˈtriː.kəl.i/, /-kli/ adj **STICKY** ▷ **1** dark and sticky, like treacle: *He'd coated the shelves with a thick treacly varnish.* **FEELINGS** ▷ **2** disapproving too pleasant or kind, or expressing feelings of love in a false way: *The film is spoilt by a slightly treacly sentimentality.*

tread /tred/ verb; noun
▸verb [I or T, usually + adv/prep] (**trod** or US also **treaded**, **trodden** or US and Australian English also **trod**) **1** (C2) mainly UK to put your foot on something or to press something down with your foot: *I kept treading **on** his toes when we were dancing.* ◦ *Yuck! Look what I've just trodden **in**!* ◦ *A load of food had been trodden **into** the carpet.* ◦ *Before the days of automation, they used to tread **grapes** to make wine.* **2** literary to walk: *He trod heavily and reluctantly up the stairs.* ◦ *I sometimes see him flash past in his sports car as I tread **my weary way** (= walk in a tired way) to work.* **3 tread water** to float vertically in the water by moving the legs and the arms up and down

IDIOMS **be treading water** to not be advancing in any way: *I think she feels that she's just treading water in that job.* • **tread carefully/gently/lightly** to speak or behave carefully to avoid upsetting or causing offence to anyone: *The government know they have to tread carefully on this issue.* • **tread the boards** old-fashioned or humorous to act in plays: *It's three years now since you've trodden the boards, Ken – how does it feel to be back?*

▸noun **PATTERN ON TYRE** ▷ **1** [C or U] the pattern of raised lines on a tyre which prevents a vehicle from sliding on the road: *The tread on your tyres is very worn.* **STEP** ▷ **2** [S] the sound that your feet make on the ground as you walk: *Then I heard someone's tread on the stairs.* **3** [S] the horizontal part of a step on which you put your foot

treadle /ˈtred.l̩/ noun [C] a part of a machine which, when operated by the foot, gives the power to turn a wheel in the machine: *My grandmother still uses her old treadle sewing machine.*

treadmill /ˈtred.mɪl/ noun **REPEATED WORK** ▷ **1** [S] any type of repeated work that is boring and makes you feel tired and seems to have no positive effect and no end: *There were days when child-rearing seemed like an endless treadmill of feeding, washing, and nappy-changing.* **EXERCISE MACHINE** ▷ **2** [C] an exercise machine that consists of a moving strip or two step-like parts on which you walk without moving forward **WHEEL** ▷ **3** [C] a wide wheel turned by the weight of people climbing on steps around its edge, used in the past to provide power for machines or, more usually, as a punishment for prisoners

treason /ˈtriː.zən/ noun [U] (the crime of) showing no loyalty to your country, especially by helping its enemies or trying to defeat its government: *Guy Fawkes was executed for treason.*

treasonable /ˈtriː.zən.ə.bl̩/ adj (also **treasonous**) A treasonable act, crime, etc. is, or is considered to be, treason: *a treasonable offence* ◦ *treasonable activities*

treasure /ˈtreʒ.əʳ/ (US) /-ɚ/ noun; verb
▸noun **VALUABLE THINGS** ▷ **1** (B2) [U] very valuable things, usually in the form of a store of precious metals, PRECIOUS STONES, or money: *Stories about pirates often include a search for **buried** treasure.* ◦ *When they opened up the tomb they found treasure beyond their wildest dreams.* **2 treasures** [plural] very valuable things, especially pieces of art: *stolen **art** treasures* ◦ *The museum houses many priceless treasures.* **PERSON** ▷ **3** [C] informal someone who is very helpful and valuable to you: *I don't know what I'd have done without Lizzie when I was ill – she was an absolute treasure.* **4** [C] mainly UK old-fashioned informal a friendly way of talking to someone, especially a child: *Come on, treasure, let's go and see Granny.*
▸verb [T] (C2) to take great care of something because you love it or consider it very valuable: *I shall always treasure those **memories** of her.* ◦ *This pen that my grandfather gave me is one of my most treasured **possessions**.*

ˈtreasure ˌhunt noun [C] a game in which the players are given a series of CLUES (= pieces of information) to direct them to a hidden prize

treasurer /ˈtreʒ.ər.əʳ/ (US) /-ɚ.ɚ/ noun [C] a person who is responsible for an organization's money

treasure trove /ˈtreʒ.əˌtrəʊv/ (US) /-ɚˌtroʊv/ noun [C or U] **1** a large number of valuable objects found hidden somewhere and seeming to belong to no one: *A Roman soldier's pay, found by a metal detector enthusiast in Norfolk, has been **declared** treasure trove.* **2 a treasure trove of sth** a place that is full of something good: *a treasure trove of information*

the Treasury /ˈtreʒ.ər.i/ (US) /-ɚ-/ noun the government department, in the UK and some other countries, that is responsible for financial matters such as spending and tax → Compare **the Exchequer**

T

treat /triːt/ verb; noun

▸verb DEAL WITH ▷ **1** B2 [T usually + adv/prep] to behave towards someone or deal with something in a particular way: *My parents treated us all the same when we were kids.* ◦ *He treated his wife very badly.* ◦ *It's wrong to treat animals **as if** they had no feelings.* ◦ *I treat remarks like that **with** the contempt that they deserve.* GIVE MEDICAL CARE ▷ **2** B2 [T] to use drugs, exercises, etc. to cure a person of a disease or HEAL an injury: *He is being treated **for** a rare skin disease.* ◦ *Western medicine tends to treat **the symptoms** and not the cause.* PAY FOR ▷ **3** B2 [T] to buy or pay for something for another person: *Put your money away – I'm going to treat you (**to** this).* ◦ *I'm going to treat my**self to** (= buy for myself) a new pair of sandals.* PUT ON ▷ **4** [T] to put a special substance on material such as wood, cloth, metal, etc. or put it through a special process, in order to protect it from damage or decay: *The material has been treated **with** resin to make it waterproof.*

IDIOMS **treat sb like dirt** to treat someone extremely badly: *For years I allowed him to treat me like dirt.* • **treat sb like royalty** to treat someone extremely well: *The staff in the hotel treated us like royalty.*

▸noun SPECIAL EXPERIENCE ▷ **1** C2 [C] a special and enjoyable occasion or experience: *We're going to Italy for the weekend – it's my **birthday** treat.* ◦ *As a **special** treat, I'll take you to my favourite restaurant.* PAY FOR ▷ **2 my, your, etc. treat** [S] an occasion when I, you, etc. buy or pay for something for another person: *No, you paid for dinner last time – this is my treat.*

IDIOM **a treat** UK informal very well; with good results: *To prevent red wine from staining, put some salt on it – it **works** a treat.* ◦ *That soup **went down** a treat (= tasted very good)!* ◦ *I polished that old desk of grandma's and it **came up** a treat (= its appearance improved).*

treatise /ˈtriː.tɪs/ US /-t̬ɪs/ noun [C] a formal piece of writing that considers and examines a particular subject: *a six-volume treatise **on** trademark law*

treatment /ˈtriːt.mənt/ noun DEALING WITH ▷ **1** B2 [U] the way you deal with or behave towards someone or something: *Peter gets **special** treatment because he knows the boss.* **2** [C or U] the way something is considered and examined: *The same subject matter gets a very different treatment by Chris Wilson in his latest novel.*

> Word partners for **treatment** (DEALING WITH)
>
> *put up with/receive/suffer* (bad, cruel, etc.) treatment • treatment *meted out to* sb • *cruel/harsh/rough* treatment • *preferential/special* treatment • *equal/fair/the same* treatment • treatment *of* sb/sth

MEDICAL CARE ▷ **3** B2 [C or U] the use of drugs, exercises, etc. to cure a person of an illness or injury: *free **dental** treatment* ◦ *Perhaps it's time to try a new **course of** treatment.* ◦ *This disease doesn't generally **respond to** (= improve as a result of) treatment.* ◦ *There are various treatments **for** this complaint.*

> Word partners for **treatment** (MEDICAL CARE)
>
> *get/have/receive/undergo* treatment • *give/provide* treatment • *need/require* treatment • *respond to* treatment • *appropriate/early/effective/emergency* treatment • treatment is *available* • treatment *for* sth • a *course of* treatment

treaty /ˈtriː.ti/ US /-t̬i/ noun [C] C2 a written agreement between two or more countries, formally approved and signed by their leaders: *a **peace** treaty* ◦ *the treaty **on** European union* ◦ [+ to infinitive] *We've **signed/concluded** a treaty **with** neighbouring states **to** limit emissions of harmful gases.*

treble /ˈtreb.l̩/ predeterminer; verb; adv, adj; noun

▸predeterminer three times greater in amount, number or size: *He earns almost treble the amount that I do.*

▸verb [I or T] to increase three times in size or amount, or to make something do this: *The price of property has almost trebled in the last ten years.*

▸adv, adj [before noun] being or relating to a boy's voice which sings the highest notes, or an instrument that plays the highest notes: *He sings treble.* ◦ *a treble voice*

▸noun [C] someone with a treble voice: *This part is for a **boy** treble.* → Compare **soprano**

ˌtreble ˈclef noun [C usually singular] (also **ˈG clef**) a sign on a STAVE (= the five lines on which music is written) which shows that the notes are above MIDDLE C (= the C near the middle of a piano keyboard)

tree /triː/ noun [C] **1** A1 a tall plant that has a wooden TRUNK and branches that grow from its upper part: *a plum/apple/chestnut tree* ◦ *We sat under a tree for shade.* **2** another type of tall plant, without a wooden TRUNK: *palm trees*

ˈtree ˌfern noun [C] a large tropical FERN (= plant with leaves like feathers) with a thick stem

ˈtree ˌhouse noun [C] a small building, structure, or shelter built among the branches of a tree: *I spent hours in our tree house when I was a kid.*

ˈtree ˌhugger noun [C] informal humorous often disapproving someone who is very interested in protecting the environment

the treeline /ˈtriː.laɪn/ noun [S] (also **the timberline**) the height above sea level or the distance south or north of the EQUATOR after which trees do not grow

ˈtree-lined adj A tree-lined road has trees on both sides of it.

the treetops /ˈtriː.tɒpz/ US /-tɑːpz/ noun [plural] the upper branches of a group of trees: *Monkeys were playing **in** the treetops.*

trek /trek/ verb; noun

▸verb [I usually + adv/prep] (**-kk-**) to walk a long distance, usually over land such as hills, mountains, or forests: *We spent the day trekking through forests and over mountains.* ◦ informal *I trekked (= walked a long and tiring distance) all the way into town to meet him and he didn't even turn up.*

▸noun [C] **1** C1 a long walk over land such as hills, mountains, or forests: *We did an eight-hour trek yesterday.* **2** informal a walk that is long and difficult or makes you feel very tired: *You can walk to town from here, but it's a bit of a trek.*

trekking /ˈtrek.ɪŋ/ noun [U] B2 the activity of walking long distances on foot for pleasure: *We want to **go** trekking in the Himalayas.*

trellis /ˈtrel.ɪs/ noun [C] a light frame made of bars of wood or metal crossed over each other, fixed to a wall for plants to grow up

tremble /ˈtrem.bl̩/ verb; noun

▸verb [I] B2 to shake slightly, usually because you are cold, frightened, or very emotional: *When he came out of the water, he was trembling **with** cold.* ◦ *Her **bottom lip** trembled and tears welled up in her eyes.* ◦ *His **voice** started to tremble and I thought he was going to cry.*

IDIOM **tremble to think** If you say that you tremble to think about a possible future event, you are worried or frightened about it: *I tremble to think what will happen when he finds out.*

T

▸**noun** [C or S] a slight shake: *There was a slight tremble in her voice as she recalled her husband.*

tremendous /trɪˈmen.dəs/ **adj** B2 very great in amount or level, or extremely good: *They were making the most tremendous amount of noise last night.* ◦ *She's been a tremendous (= very great) help to me over the last few months.* ◦ *You won? That's tremendous!* • **tremendously** /-li/ **adv** B2 *We all enjoyed ourselves tremendously.*

tremolo /ˈtrem.əl.əʊ/ US /-ə.loʊ/ **noun** [C] (plural **tremolos**) specialized when singing or playing an instrument, a shaking sound that is achieved by repeating the same note extremely quickly or by playing two notes very quickly, one after the other → Compare **vibrato**

tremor /ˈtrem.əʳ/ US /-ɚ/ **noun** [C] **1** a slight shaking movement in a person's body, especially because of nervousness or excitement: *The disease mostly affects people over 50, causing paralysis and uncontrollable tremors.* ◦ *There was a slight tremor in her voice.* ◦ figurative *A tremor* ***of*** *excitement went through the audience as he came on stage.* **2** a slight EARTHQUAKE: *The tremor was felt as far as 200 miles away.*

tremulous /ˈtrem.jʊ.ləs/ **adj** literary If a person's voice or a part of their body is tremulous, it is shaking slightly: *He watched her tremulous hand reach for the teacup.* ◦ *In a tremulous* ***voice*** *she whispered: 'Who are you people?'* • **tremulously** /-li/ **adv**

trench /trentʃ/ **noun** **1** [C] a narrow hole that is dug into the ground: *A workman was killed when the sides of the trench he was working in collapsed.* **2** [C usually plural] a deep hole dug by soldiers and used as a place from which they can attack the enemy while being hidden: ***the*** *trenches of the First World War* ◦ *trench* ***warfare*** → Compare **foxhole**

trenchant /ˈtren.tʃənt/ **adj** formal severe, expressing strong criticism or forceful opinions: *His most trenchant* ***criticism*** *is reserved for the party leader, whom he describes as 'the most incompetent and ineffectual the party has known'.* ◦ *Dorothy Parker's writing is characterized by a trenchant wit and sophistication.* • **trenchancy** /-tʃən.si/ **noun** [U] • **trenchantly** /-li/ **adv**

ˈtrench ˌcoat **noun** [C] a long, loose coat with a belt, usually made from WATERPROOF material (= not allowing water through) and similar in style to a military coat

trencher /ˈtren.tʃəʳ/ US /-tʃɚ/ **noun** [C] **1** Australian English a black hat with a square, flat top, worn on formal occasions by some teachers and students at college or university, and in the past by some school teachers → Compare **mortarboard** **2** in the past, a flat, wooden dish used to serve food

trend /trend/ **noun; verb**

▸**noun** [C] **1** B1 a general development or change in a situation or in the way that people are behaving: *Surveys show a trend* ***away from*** *home-ownership and toward rented accommodation.* ◦ *There's been a* ***downward/upward*** *trend in sales in the last few years.* **2** a new development in clothing, make-up, etc.: *Whatever the latest* ***fashion*** *trend, you can be sure Nicki will be wearing it.* ◦ *The trend at the moment is for a more natural and less made-up look.* **3 on trend** fashionable: *Her long skirt is right on trend this winter.*

▸**verb** [I] to be one of the words, subjects, or names that is being mentioned most often on TWITTER™ at a particular time: *Within minutes of the incident her name was trending on Twitter.*

trendsetter /ˈtrendˌset.əʳ/ US /-ˌset̬.ɚ/ **noun** [C] a person, organization, etc. that starts new fashions, especially in clothes: *They are not only the biggest fast food chain, but also the industry's trendsetter.*

trendspotter /ˈtrendˌspɒt.əʳ/ US /-ˌspɑː.t̬ɚ/ **noun** [C] a person who notices and reports on new fashions, ideas, or activities that are becoming popular: *Trendspotter Faith Starr believes a revolution is going on in the world of conferencing.*

trendy /ˈtren.di/ **adj; noun**

▸**adj** informal C1 modern and influenced by the most recent fashions or ideas: *trendy clothes* ◦ *a trendy nightclub* ◦ *He writes for some trendy magazine for the under-30s.*

▸**noun** [C] informal mainly disapproving a person who is very influenced by the most recent ideas and fashions: *This is where all the North London trendies go for a night out.*

trepidation /ˌtrep.ɪˈdeɪ.ʃən/ **noun** [U] formal fear or worry about what is going to happen: *We view future developments* ***with*** *some trepidation.*

trespass /ˈtres.pəs/ US /-pæs/ **verb; noun**

▸**verb** [I] **BREAK LAW** ▷ **1** to go onto someone's land or enter their building without permission: *I hope this is a public footpath and we're not trespassing* ***on*** *someone's land.* **NOT MORAL** ▷ **2** old use to do something or act in a way that is not morally acceptable • **trespasser** /-pə.səʳ/ US /-pæs.ɚ/ **noun** [C] *Can't you read the sign? It says 'Trespassers will be prosecuted!'*

PHRASAL VERB **trespass on/upon sth** formal to take unfair advantage of a good quality in someone's character: *They said we should stay another night, but I didn't want to trespass on their hospitality.*

▸**noun** **BREAK LAW** ▷ **1** [C or U] the crime of going onto someone's land or entering their building without permission: *the law of trespass* **NOT MORAL** ▷ **2** [C] old use an offence in which you break a moral or religious law: *Forgive us our trespasses.*

tresses /ˈtres.ɪz/ **noun** [plural] literary a woman's hair, especially long hair: *Her black tresses lay around her on the pillow.*

trestle /ˈtres.l̩/ **noun** [C] **1** a supporting structure for a table, consisting of a flat piece of wood supported at each end by two pairs of sloping legs **2** specialized a set of sloping supports holding a horizontal structure, used especially for railway bridges

ˈtrestle ˌtable **noun** [C] a table which consists of a board supported by a trestle

trews /truːz/ **noun** [plural] trousers: *a pair of* ***tartan*** *trews*

tri- /traɪ-/ **prefix** three: *a triangle* ◦ *a tripod*

triad /ˈtraɪ.æd/ **noun** **CHINESE ORGANIZATION** ▷ **1** [C] a secret Chinese organization involved in illegal activities such as selling drugs **THREE THINGS** ▷ **2** [S] literary three related things that form a group

triage /ˈtriː.ɑːʒ/ **noun** [U] **1** the process of quickly examining patients who are taken to a hospital in order to decide which ones are the most seriously ill and must be treated first: *The triage* ***nurse*** *told him he would have to wait.* **2** the process of examining problems in order to decide which ones are the most serious and must be dealt with first • **triage** **verb** [T] *The casualties were triaged.*

trial /traɪəl/ **noun; verb**

▸**noun** **LEGAL PROCESS** ▷ **1** B2 [C or U] the hearing of statements and showing of objects, etc. in a law court to judge if a person is guilty of a crime or to decide a case or a legal matter: *trial proceedings* ◦ *Trial* ***by jury*** *is a fundamental right.* ◦ *It was a very complicated trial that went on for months.* ◦ *She's* ***going on/standing***

T

trial ***for*** *fraud.* → See also **try** **TEST** ▷ **2** Ⓒ1 [C or U] a test, usually over a limited period of time, to discover how effective or suitable something or someone is: *They're doing* ***clinical*** *trials on a new drug.* ◦ *They've employed her for a six-month trial* (***period***)*.* ◦ *You can buy the equipment* ***on*** *trial* (US usually ***on a*** *trial*) ***basis****, and if you don't like it you can give it back.* **PROBLEM** ▷ **3** [C] a person or thing that is annoying and causes a lot of problems: *She was a real trial* ***to*** *her parents when she was younger.* ◦ *The book is all about the trials of growing up.*

> **Word partners for trial noun**
>
> *face/go on/stand* trial • *come to/go to* trial • *bring* sb *to/put* sb *on* trial • *await/face* trial • a trial *begins/continues/opens/resumes* • sth *comes to/goes to* trial • *adjourn* a trial • a *fair* trial • *on* trial (*for* sth) • a trial *court/date/judge*

IDIOM **trials and tribulations** literary or humorous troubles and events that cause suffering: *the trials and tribulations of marriage*

▸verb [T] (**-ll-** or **-l-**) to test something in a formal way to discover how effective or suitable it is: *We will trial the new drug in several hospitals.*

ˌtrial and ˈerror noun [U] Ⓒ2 a way of achieving an aim or solving a problem by trying a number of different methods and learning from the mistakes that you make: *There's no instant way of finding a cure – it's just a* ***process of*** *trial and error.*

ˌtrial ˈrun noun [C] a practical test of something new or unknown to discover its effectiveness: *We're holding a tournament in the new ice-hockey stadium, as a trial run for next year's Winter Olympics.*

triangle /ˈtraɪ.æŋ.gl/ noun [C] **1** Ⓑ2 a flat shape with three straight sides: *an equilateral/isosceles triangle* **2** anything that has three straight sides: *Which earrings did you buy in the end – the triangles or the circles?* **3** a musical instrument consisting of a thin metal bar bent into a triangle shape that is hit with a metal bar to make a sound **4** US for **set square**

triangular /traɪˈæŋ.gjʊ.ləʳ/ Ⓤ /-lɚ/ adj shaped like a triangle: *a triangular plot of land* ◦ *The play is performed on a triangular stage.*

triangulation /traɪˌæŋ.gjʊˈleɪ.ʃᵊn/ noun [U] specialized the division of a map or plan into triangles for measurement purposes, or the calculation of positions and distances using this method

Triassic /traɪˈæs.ɪk/ adj specialized from or referring to the period of GEOLOGICAL time between around 245 and 208 million years ago, in which DINOSAURS first appeared: *the Triassic period* ◦ *Triassic plants* • **the Triassic** noun the Triassic period

triathlon /traɪˈæθ.lɒn/ Ⓤ /-lɑːn/ noun [C] a competition in which the people competing must swim, ride a bicycle, and run particular distances without stopping between events • **triathlete** noun [C] someone who competes in a triathlon

tribal /ˈtraɪ.bᵊl/ adj Ⓒ2 relating to a tribe: *tribal dress/leaders* ◦ informal figurative *The fierce tribal* ***loyalty*** *among soccer supporters leads to violence between opposing fans.*

tribalism /ˈtraɪ.bᵊl.ɪ.zᵊm/ noun [U] the state of existing as a tribe, or a very strong feeling of loyalty to your tribe

tribe /traɪb/ noun [C, + sing/pl verb] **1** Ⓑ2 a group of people, often of related families, who live together, sharing the same language, culture, and history, especially those who do not live in towns or cities: *a tribe of Amazonian Indians* ◦ *the Masai tribe* **2** informal a large family or other group that someone belongs to: *We've invited Carol's sisters and brothers and their spouses and children – the whole Cassidy tribe.*

tribesman /ˈtraɪbz.mən/ noun [C] (plural **-men** /-mən/) a man who belongs to a tribe

tribespeople /ˈtraɪbzˌpiː.pl/ noun [plural] people who belong to a tribe

tribeswoman /ˈtraɪbzˌwʊm.ən/ noun [C] (plural **-women** /-wɪmɪn/) a woman who belongs to a tribe

tribulation /ˌtrɪb.jʊˈleɪ.ʃᵊn/ noun [C or U] formal a problem or difficulty → See **trials and tribulations**

tribunal /traɪˈbjuː.nəl/ noun [C] a special court or group of people who are officially chosen, especially by the government, to examine (legal) problems of a particular type: *a war crimes tribunal*

tribune /ˈtrɪb.juːn/ noun [C] **1** used in the titles of some newspapers: *The New York Tribune* **2** in ancient Rome, an elected official whose job was to protect people's rights

tributary /ˈtrɪb.jʊ.tᵊr.i/ Ⓤ /-ter.i/ noun [C] a river or stream that flows into a larger river or a lake: *the Indre, a lesser tributary* ***of*** *the Loire*

tribute /ˈtrɪb.juːt/ noun **RESPECTFUL ACTION** ▷ **1** Ⓒ2 [C or U] something that you say, write, or give which shows your respect and admiration for someone, especially on a formal occasion: *Tributes have been pouring in from all over the world for the famous actor who died yesterday.* ◦ ***floral*** *tributes* (*= flowers sent to someone's funeral*) **2** **pay tribute to sb/sth** Ⓒ2 to praise someone or something: *The minister paid tribute to the men who had fought the blaze.* **BENEFICIAL EFFECT** ▷ **3** **be a tribute to sth/sb** to show clearly how good, strong, or effective something or someone is: *I've never known a five-year-old as well behaved as your son – he's a tribute* ***to*** *you!* ◦ *It is a tribute to his determination over his 22 years that he has achieved so much.*

ˈtribute ˌband noun [C] a group of musicians who play the music of a famous pop group and pretend to be that group: *a Beatles tribute band*

trice /traɪs/ noun [S] informal **in a trice** in a very short time: *Jim had the wheel mended in a trice.*

triceps /ˈtraɪ.seps/ noun [C] (plural **triceps**) the large muscle at the back of the upper arm → Compare **biceps**

trick /trɪk/ noun; verb; adj

▸noun [C] **ACT OF DECEIVING** ▷ **1** Ⓑ1 an action that is intended to deceive, either as a way of cheating someone, or as a joke or form of entertainment: *She* ***played*** *a really nasty trick* ***on*** *me – she put syrup in my shampoo bottle!* ◦ *My niece was showing me all the tricks that she's learned to* ***do*** *with her new magic set.* ◦ *It's a bit of trick* ***photography*** *– she's meant to look like she's walking on water.* **2** **be a trick of the light** to be an effect caused by light, making something appear different: *For a moment I thought you had a patch of grey hairs, but it's just a trick of the light.* **METHOD** ▷ **3** Ⓑ2 an effective or quick way of doing something: *What's the trick* ***of*** *getting this chair to fold up?* ◦ *On page 21, some tricks to speed up your beauty routine.*

> **Word partners for trick noun**
>
> *play* a trick (*on* sb) • *do/perform* a trick • a *cheap/cruel/dirty/sneaky* trick • a *clever/cunning* trick

IDIOMS **do the trick** informal Ⓒ2 If something does the trick, it has the necessary or wanted effect: *This sauce needs a bit of flavour – I know, some lemon juice* ***should/ought to*** *do the trick.* • **every trick in the book** every possible way: *I've tried every trick in the book to seduce him and still no luck!* • **how's tricks?** informal how are you?: *'Hi, how's tricks?' 'Oh, fine, how are you doing?'* • **trick of the trade** a clever method used by people who are experienced in a particular type of work or activity: *Newspapers often improve photographs before they print them – it's one of the tricks of the trade.*

▸verb [T] B2 to deceive someone, often as a part of a plan: *Dean tricked the old lady **into** giving him eight hundred pounds.*

▸adj [before noun] **DECEIVING** ▷ **1** used to deceive someone, either as a joke or form of entertainment or so that they make a mistake: *a trick question* **WEAK** ▷ **2** US describes a part of the body, especially a JOINT (= place where two bones are connected), that sometimes feels weak suddenly and unexpectedly: *I've got a trick ankle that gives me problems if I do much running.*

trickery /ˈtrɪk.ər.i/ (US) /-ɚ-/ noun [U] disapproving the activity of using tricks to deceive or cheat people: *The government, he said, had resorted to political trickery in its attempts to retain power.*

trickle /ˈtrɪk.l̩/ verb; noun

▸verb [I] **LIQUID** ▷ **1 trickle down, from, out of, etc. sth** If liquid trickles somewhere, it flows slowly and without force in a thin line: *Blood trickled out of the corner of his mouth.* ◦ *Oil was trickling from a tiny hole in the tank.* **SMALL NUMBER** ▷ **2 trickle in, out, back, etc.** to arrive or move somewhere slowly and gradually, in small numbers: *Gradually people trickled back into the theatre for the second half.*

▸noun **SMALL NUMBER** ▷ **1** [S] a very small number of people or things arriving or leaving somewhere: *We usually only get a trickle of customers in the shop in the mornings.* **LIQUID** ▷ **2** [C] a small amount of liquid that is flowing slowly in a thin line: *A trickle of melted butter made its way down his chin.*

ˌtrickle-ˈdown adj [before noun] describes a situation in which something that starts in the high parts of a system spreads to the whole of the system: *The supposed trickle-down **effect** of lower taxes for the rich has not yet resulted in greater prosperity for society as a whole.*

ˈtrickle ˌfeed noun [T] the process of supplying continuous small amounts of something: *Trickle-feed techniques allow continuous update of the data.* • **ˈtrickle-ˌfeed** verb [T] *The media were trickle-fed information about the department's problems.*

ˌtrick-or-ˈtreating noun [U] **1** an activity in which children dress up in frightening or strange clothes on HALLOWEEN (= 31 October) and visit people's homes to demand sweets or a small amount of money **2 go trick or treating** If children go trick or treating, they visit people's houses on HALLOWEEN to ask for sweets.

ˌtrick ˈquestion noun [C] a question which makes you believe you should answer it in one way, when the question you are really meant to answer is hidden within it

trickster /ˈtrɪk.stər/ (US) /-stɚ/ noun [C] disapproving a person who deceives people: *a confidence trickster*

tricky /ˈtrɪk.i/ adj **DIFFICULT** ▷ **1** B2 If a piece of work or problem is tricky, it is difficult to deal with and needs careful attention or skill: *Those bird models are quite tricky **to** make, aren't they?* ◦ *I'm in a bit of a tricky situation really – whatever I do I'll offend someone.* **DISHONEST** ▷ **2** likely to deceive people: *He's a tricky character, that one.*

tricolour UK (US **tricolor**) /ˈtrɪk.əl.ər/ (US) /ˈtraɪˌkʌl.ɚ/ noun [C] a flag that is divided into three equal parts of different colour: *the French tricolour*

tricycle /ˈtraɪ.sɪ.kl̩/ noun [C] (also **trike**) a CYCLE with two wheels at the back and one at the front, used especially by young children

trident /ˈtraɪ.dənt/ noun [C] a weapon used in the past consisting of a pole with three sharp metal points on the end: *Neptune's trident*

Trident /ˈtraɪ.dənt/ noun [C or U] a type of BALLISTIC MISSILE (= explosive weapon) that is sent from under the sea: *a Trident missile/submarine*

tried /traɪd/ verb; adj

▸verb past simple and past participle of **try**

▸adj **tried and tested/trusted** used many times before and proved to be successful: *I'll give you my mother's tried and tested recipe for wholemeal bread.*

triennial /traɪˈen.i.əl/ adj happening every three years: *the party's triennial congress*

trier /ˈtraɪ.ər/ (US) /-ɚ/ noun [C] approving someone who tries hard to succeed in what they do, even if they fail: *She's a real trier, I'll give her that.*

trifle /ˈtraɪ.fl/ noun; verb

▸noun **SWEET DISH** ▷ **1** [C or U] a sweet cold dish consisting of a layer of fruit and SPONGE (= cake), a layer of CUSTARD (= thick, sweet, yellow sauce) and a top layer of cream: *a sherry trifle* **UNIMPORTANT THING** ▷ **2** [C] formal a matter or object of little value or importance: *I brought a few trifles back from India – bits of jewellery and material mainly.* **3 a trifle** slightly: *I'm a trifle confused about the arrangements for tonight.*

▸verb

PHRASAL VERB **trifle with sb/sth** formal or old-fashioned to treat someone or something carelessly or without respect: *He trifled with her **affections** (= feelings).* ◦ *As you know, Caroline O'Neill is not a woman to be trifled with.*

trifling /ˈtraɪ.fl.ɪŋ/, /-flɪŋ/ adj formal A trifling matter or amount of money is small or not important.

trig /trɪg/ noun [U] informal **trigonometry**

trigger /ˈtrɪg.ər/ (US) /-ɚ/ noun; verb

▸noun **GUN PART** ▷ **1** [C] a part of a gun which causes the gun to fire when pressed: *It's not clear who actually **pulled** the trigger.* **START** ▷ **2** [C usually singular] an event or situation, etc. that causes something bad to start: *There are fears that the incident may be a trigger **for** further violence in the capital.*

▸verb [T] C1 to cause something bad to start: *Some people find that certain foods trigger their headaches.* ◦ *The racial killings at the weekend have triggered **off** a wave of protests.*

ˈtrigger ˌfood noun [C] a food that causes someone to have an ALLERGIC reaction

ˈtrigger-ˌhappy adj **1** informal describes someone who often uses his or her gun, shooting with very little reason: *Their police are worryingly trigger-happy.* **2** disapproving ready to use violence or force immediately, without careful thought

trigonometry /ˌtrɪg.əˈnɒm.ə.tri/ (US) /-ˈnɑː.mə-/ noun [U] (informal **trig**) a type of mathematics that deals with the relationship between the angles and sides of triangles, used in measuring the height of buildings, mountains, etc.: *Trigonometry concerns the functions of angles, such as sine, cosine, and tangent.*

trike /traɪk/ noun [C] informal a **tricycle**

trilby /ˈtrɪl.bi/ noun [C] mainly UK a man's hat made of FELT (= thick firm cloth) with a deep fold along its top

trilingual /ˌtraɪˈlɪŋ.gwəl/ adj able to speak three languages → Compare **bilingual**

T

trill /trɪl/ verb; noun
▸verb [I] **1** When birds trill, they sing a series of quickly repeated high notes. **2** literary to speak in a very high voice: [+ speech] *'Tea is ready,' trilled Daphne.*
▸noun [C] **MUSIC** ▷ **1** specialized (the effect achieved by) the fast playing of a note and the note above or below it, one after the other **BIRD** ▷ **2** a series of quickly repeated high notes sung by a bird: *We heard the familiar trill of the lark.* **SPEECH** ▷ **3** specialized a sound that is made by very small, quick movements of one of the organs used in speech

trillion /ˈtrɪl.jən/ number (plural **trillion** or **trillions**) the number 1,000,000,000,000: *a/one trillion* ◦ *Four light years is 25 trillion miles.* ◦ *trillions* ***of*** *dollars* • **trillionth** /-jənθ/ **ordinal number, noun** [C]

trilobite /ˈtraɪ.lə.baɪt/ (US) /-loʊ-/ noun [C] specialized a simple, flat sea creature that lived in the earliest period of life on Earth, with a hard outer layer and a body in three parts

trilogy /ˈtrɪl.ə.dʒi/ noun [C] (C2) a series of three books, plays, etc. written about the same situation or characters, forming a continuous story

trim /trɪm/ verb; adj; noun
▸verb [T] (**-mm-**) **CUT** ▷ **1** to make something tidier or more level by cutting a small amount off it: *to trim the hedge* ◦ *My hair needs trimming.* ◦ *Trim* ***off*** *the leafy ends of the vegetable before cooking.* **REDUCE** ▷ **2** to reduce the amount or size of something: *They're trying to trim their costs, so staff who leave are not being replaced.*
▸adj (**trimmer**, **trimmest**) **THIN** ▷ **1** approving thin in an attractive and healthy way: *You're looking very trim – have you lost weight?* **TIDY** ▷ **2** tidy and well ordered: *trim lawns and neat flower beds*
▸noun **CUT** ▷ **1** [S] an act of making something, especially someone's hair, tidier or more level by cutting a small amount off it: *I asked the hairdresser for* ***a*** *trim.* ◦ *Just* ***give*** *the ends* ***a*** *trim, please.* **MATERIAL** ▷ **2** [C or U] **trimming** **PREPARED** ▷ **3** **in trim** informal physically prepared and ready, or in good condition: *Are you in trim* ***for*** *the run on Sunday?*

trimaran /ˈtraɪ.mə.ræn/ noun [C] a small, fast sailing boat that has a central HULL (= floating part) that is joined to two other smaller HULLS, one at each side

trimester /trɪˈmes.təʳ/, /traɪ-/ (US) /traɪˈmes.tɚ/ noun [C] **1** a three-month period **2** any of the three three-month periods that a human pregnancy is divided into: *The second trimester is generally the easiest part of a pregnancy.* **3** US any of the three-month periods into which the school or college year is sometimes divided: *Many students arrange internships or work-study placements during the second trimester.*
→ Compare **semester**

trimmed /trɪmd/ adj [after verb] If clothes and other things made of cloth are trimmed, they are decorated, especially around the edges: *She was wearing a black suit trimmed* ***with*** *white.*

trimmer /ˈtrɪm.əʳ/ (US) /-ɚ/ noun [C] a device used for making something tidier or more level by cutting a small amount off it: *a hedge trimmer*

trimming /ˈtrɪm.ɪŋ/ noun (also **trim**) **1** [C or U] (a piece of) decorative material added around the edge of something: *I want a plain black jumper with no fancy trimmings.* ◦ *I wore my red jacket with the black trim.* **2** **trimmings** [plural] extra things which complete or improve the appearance of something: *a big wedding celebration* ***with all the*** *trimmings* ◦ *the traditional trimmings* ***of*** *fame/success*

trinity /ˈtrɪn.ɪ.ti/ noun [C usually singular] literary a group of three things or people: *British culture now appears to revolve around the* ***unholy*** *trinity of sport, shopping, and sex.* ◦ *Above all Amenabar worships the trinity* ***of*** *Hitchcock, Kubrick, and Spielberg.*

the ˈTrinity noun [S] (also **the ˌHoly ˈTrinity**) in Christianity, the existence of one God in three forms, the Father, the Son, and the Holy Spirit

trinket /ˈtrɪŋ.kɪt/ noun [C] a small decorative object, or a piece of jewellery that is cheap or of low quality: *She always returns from vacation with a few souvenirs, even if they're only* ***cheap*** *trinkets.*

trio /ˈtriː.əʊ/ (US) /-oʊ/ noun (plural **trios**) **1** (C2) [C, + sing/pl verb] a group of three people or things: *There was disappointment for our trio* ***of*** *200 metre runners, all of whom failed to reach the final.* **2** [C, + sing/pl verb] a group of three musicians or singers who perform together: *Many* ***jazz*** *trios consist of piano, guitar, and double bass.* **3** [C] a piece of music that has been written to be performed by three people: *The final item in today's programme is Beethoven's Trio in B flat.*

trip /trɪp/ noun; verb
▸noun **JOURNEY** ▷ **1** (A2) [C] a journey in which you go somewhere, usually for a short time, and come back again: *The trip* ***from*** *York* ***to*** *Newcastle takes about an hour by train.* ◦ *Do you want to go* ***on*** *the school trip to France this year?* ◦ *I thought we might hire a motorboat and* ***take*** *a trip* ***round/around*** *the bay.* ◦ mainly UK *We can't afford another trip* ***abroad*** *this year.* ◦ *It's a ten-mile trip from the airport to the city centre.* ◦ *She's away on a* ***business*** *trip and won't be back until next week.* ◦ *I was thinking we might go on a* ***shopping*** *trip to Paris on Saturday.* **FALL** ▷ **2** [C usually singular] an occasion when you knock your foot against something and fall or lose your balance, or someone causes you to do this, when you are walking or running: *She broke her ankle when she had a nasty trip on the stairs.* **EXPERIENCE** ▷ **3** [C] slang an experience in which someone sees, hears or feels things that do not exist as a result of taking an illegal drug: *If you take this stuff when you're depressed, you'll* ***have*** *a really* ***bad*** *trip.* **4** **guilt/power/ego trip** disapproving a period of time when you experience a particular feeling strongly: *She's been* ***on*** *a real* ***power*** *trip since she became the office manager.* ◦ *I suffer from the classic working mother's* ***guilt*** *trip.*

> **Word partners for trip noun**
>
> *go on/take* a trip • *arrange/book/organize/plan* a trip • *cancel/postpone* a trip • a *day/short/two-day/weekend* trip • *on* a trip • a trip *across/around/from/through/to* sth

▸verb (**-pp-**) **LOSE BALANCE** ▷ **1** (B2) [I or T] to lose your balance after knocking your foot against something when you are walking or running, or to cause someone to do this: *He tripped and fell over, grazing his knee.* ◦ *That cable is dangerous. Someone might trip* ***over*** *it.* ◦ *He was sent off for deliberately tripping Robson when he was about to score a goal.* **MOVE** ▷ **2** [I usually + adv/prep] to move with quick, gentle steps: *She looked stunning as she tripped* ***down*** *the stairs in her ball gown.* **SWITCH** ▷ **3** [T] to move a switch that operates an electrical system, or to cause such a system to start or stop working by moving a switch: *A special system prevents the circuitry being tripped accidentally by a power surge or lightning strike.* **EXPERIENCE** ▷ **4** [I] slang to experience the effects of taking an illegal drug which causes the user to see, hear, or feel things that do not exist: *When I was a student I spent a lot of time tripping* ***out on*** *LSD.*

IDIOM **trip off the tongue** Something that trips off the tongue is easy to say or pronounce: *The new company* *will need to have a name that trips off the tongue and is easy to remember.*

PHRASAL VERB **trip (sb) up** **FALL** ▷ **1** to fall because you hit your foot on something, or to make someone fall by putting your foot in front of their foot: *I'm terribly sorry. I didn't mean to trip you up.* ◦ *She tripped up **on** the rug.* **FAIL** ▷ **2** informal to make a mistake, or to cause someone to make a mistake: *The exam went quite well, except at the end when I tripped up **on** the final question.* ◦ *At the interview, they were trying to trip me up all the way through.*

tripartite /ˌtraɪˈpɑː.taɪt/ US /-pɑːr.t̬aɪt/ **adj** formal involving three people or organizations, or existing in three parts: *A tripartite agreement brought together government, industry, and trade unions in an effort to reduce unemployment.*

tripe /traɪp/ **noun** [U] **FOOD** ▷ **1** the covering of the inside of the stomach of an animal, such as a cow or sheep, used for food: *stewed tripe* **STUPID IDEAS** ▷ **2** informal ideas, suggestions, or writing that are stupid, silly, or have little value: *She said my last essay was complete tripe.* ◦ *People **talk a lot of** tripe about fashion.*

ˈtrip-ˌhop **noun** [U] a type of popular dance music that has a slow beat, and is intended to create a relaxed mood. It is a mixture of HIP-HOP and REGGAE.

triphthong /ˈtrɪf.θɒŋ/, /ˈtrɪp-/ US /-θɑːŋ/ **noun** [C] specialized a vowel sound in which the tongue changes position to produce the sound of three vowels → Compare **diphthong, monophthong**

triple /ˈtrɪp.l̩/ **adj; verb**

▸**adj** **1** having three parts of the same type, or happening three times: *Her trainer is a triple Olympic **champion**.* ◦ *There's a triple **bill** of Hitchcock films (= three films) on at the cinema next Sunday.* **2 triple sth** three times as large as something: *The number of one-parent households reached 10.1 million in 1991, **nearly** triple that of 1971.*

▸**verb** [I or T] to increase three times in size or amount, or to make something do this: *We have tripled our output over the past two years.* ◦ *The workforce has tripled **in size** since the new factory opened.*

the ˈtriple ˌjump **noun** [S] a sports event in which the competitor jumps from one foot and lands on it, then jumps from one foot and lands on the other, and finally jumps with both feet: *She's the European triple jump champion.* • **ˈtriple jumper noun** [C]

triplet /ˈtrɪp.lət/ **noun** [C] one of three children born to the same mother at the same time: *I was amazed when my doctor told me I was going to have triplets.*

triplicate /ˈtrɪp.lɪ.kət/ **adj** [before noun] formal existing in three parts that are exactly the same

IDIOM **in triplicate** When a document is prepared or written in triplicate, two exact copies of it are made also: *The application has to be completed in triplicate, with the original being kept by the bank and the copies going to the customer and the tax office.*

tripod

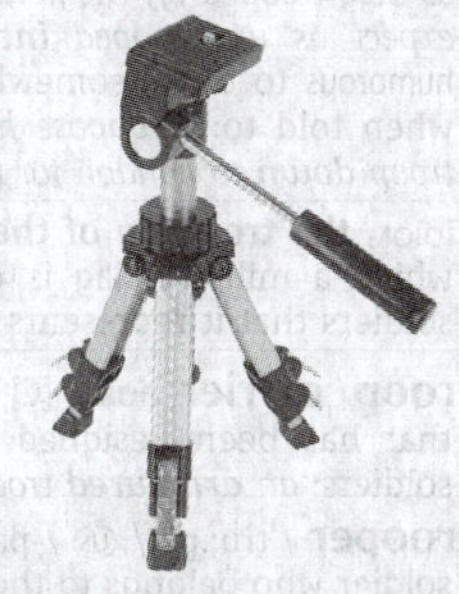

tripod /ˈtraɪ.pɒd/ US /-pɑːd/ **noun** [C] a support with three legs for a piece of equipment such as a camera: *For photographs requiring long exposure times, your camera should be **mounted on** a tripod.*

tripper /ˈtrɪp.əʳ/ US /-ɚ/ **noun** [C] mainly UK someone who visits a place for a short time, often with a large group of people: *Thousands of **day** trippers flock to resorts on the south coast.* ◦ *The café was full of **coach** trippers.*

trippy /ˈtrɪp.i/ **adj** slang relating to the effect produced by taking a PSYCHEDELIC drug (= one that affects the mind and the way that someone sees things): *Staring at this visual creates a trippy and powerful optical illusion.*

triptych /ˈtrɪp.tɪk/ **noun** [C] specialized a piece of art made of three paintings connected to each other in a way that allows the two outer ones to fold in towards the larger central one: *A medieval triptych hung above the altar.*

tripwire /ˈtrɪp.waɪəʳ/ US /-waɪr/ **noun** [C] a wire stretched low above the ground which operates an explosive device, a gun, or a device for catching animals when it is touched by the foot of a person or animal

trite /traɪt/ **adj** disapproving expressed too often to be interesting or seem sincere: *His lyrics about love and peace are too trite for me to take them seriously.* ◦ *I know it will **sound** trite, but I've loved being part of this club.* • **tritely** /ˈtraɪt.li/ **adv** • **triteness** /ˈtraɪt.nəs/ **noun** [U]

triumph /ˈtraɪ.əmf/ **noun; verb**

▸**noun** [C or U] C1 a very great success, achievement, or VICTORY (= when you win a war, fight, or competition), or a feeling of great satisfaction or pleasure caused by this: *The book celebrates the hostages' remarkable triumph **over** appalling adversity.* ◦ *The signing of the agreement was a **personal** triumph **for** the prime minister.* ◦ *It was the Republican Party's third **election** triumph in a row.* ◦ *The eradication of smallpox by vaccination was one of medicine's greatest triumphs.* ◦ *The constitutional changes have been **hailed as** a triumph **for** democracy.* ◦ *The match ended **in** triumph for the French team.* ◦ *He **returned in** triumph from the sales with a half-price stereo system.*

▸**verb** [I] to have a very great success or VICTORY: *I believe that sooner or later good must triumph **over** evil.* ◦ *The Democrats once again triumphed in recent elections.*

triumphal /traɪˈʌm.fəl/ **adj** describes something that celebrates a great VICTORY (= winning a war or competition)or success: *Shortly after his triumphal **entry** into Havana in January 1959, Castro spoke on television for seven hours without a break.* ◦ *Her popularity has declined since her triumphal **return** from exile two years ago.*

triumphalism /traɪˈʌm.fəl.ɪ.zəm/ **noun** [U] disapproving an unpleasant show of pleasure and satisfaction because you have won or done better than someone: *There wasn't a hint of triumphalism in her acceptance speech at the awards ceremony.* • **triumphalist** /-ɪst/ **adj, noun** [C] *a triumphalist victory parade*

triumphant /traɪˈʌm.fənt/ **adj** having achieved a great VICTORY (= winning a war or competition) or success, or feeling very happy and proud because of such an achievement: *It seemed as though the whole city had turned out for their team's triumphant homecoming.* ◦ *She **emerged** triumphant from the court after all the charges against her were dropped because of a lack of evidence.* ◦ *She made a triumphant **return** to the stage after several years working in television.* • **triumphantly** /-li/ **adv** *Bob triumphantly announced his promotion.*

triumvirate /traɪˈʌm.vɪ.rət/ **noun** [C] formal a group of three people who are in control of an activity or

T

organization: *The shape of post-war Europe was decided in Potsdam in 1945 by the Allied triumvirate of Churchill, Truman, and Stalin.*

trivet /ˈtrɪv.ɪt/ **noun** [C] specialized a metal stand which you put on a table to protect its surface from hot dishes or pans

trivia /ˈtrɪv.i.ə/ **noun** [plural] details or information that are not important: *She has an encyclopedic knowledge of pop trivia.* ◦ *I'm fascinated by the trivia of everyday life.*

trivial /ˈtrɪv.i.əl/ **adj 1** B2 having little value or importance: *I don't know why he gets so upset about something that is **utterly** trivial.* ◦ *Sexual harassment in the workplace is not a trivial **matter**.* **2** describes a problem that is easy to solve: *Getting computers to understand human language is not a trivial problem.*

triviality /ˌtrɪv.iˈæl.ə.ti/ US /-t̬i/ **noun 1** [C usually plural] something that is not important: *I'm a busy man – don't bother me with trivialities.* **2** [U] the state of not being important: *The prison sentence seemed rather harsh, considering the triviality of the offence.*

trivialize disapproving (UK usually **trivialise**) /ˈtrɪv.i.ə.laɪz/ **verb** [T] to make something seem less important than it really is: *I don't want to trivialize the problem, but I do think there are more important matters to discuss.*

trod /trɒd/ US /trɑːd/ past simple and past participle of **tread**: *It really hurt when Mark trod **on** my foot.*

trodden /ˈtrɒd.ən/ US /ˈtrɑː.dən/ past participle of **tread**

troglodyte /ˈtrɒg.lə.daɪt/ US /ˈtrɑː.glə-/ **noun** [C] specialized a person who lives in a cave: *Most people associate troglodytes with prehistoric times, but troglodyte communities still exist in Tunisia and China.*

troika /ˈtrɔɪ.kə/ **noun** [C] formal a group of three people, especially government officials: *She is a member of the president's troika of close advisers.*

Trojan horse /ˌtrəʊ.dʒənˈhɔːs/ US /ˌtroʊ.dʒənˈhɔːrs/ **noun** [S] **1** literary a person or thing that joins and deceives a group or organization in order to attack it from the inside **2** (also **Trojan**) a computer program that has been deliberately designed to destroy information, or allow someone to steal it

troll /trəʊl/, /trɒl/ US /troʊl/ **noun; verb**

▸**noun** [C] **CREATURE** ▷ **1** an imaginary, either very large or very small creature in traditional Scandinavian stories, that has magical powers and lives in mountains or caves **COMPUTING** ▷ **2** someone who leaves an intentionally annoying message on the internet, in order to get attention or cause trouble **3** a message that someone leaves on the internet that is intended to annoy people: *A well-constructed troll will provoke irate or confused responses from flamers and newbies.*

▸**verb** [I or T] **SEARCH** ▷ **1** mainly US to search among a large number or many different places in order to find people or information you want: *They are trolling the internet **for** new customers.* **COMPUTING** ▷ **2** to leave an insulting message on the internet in order to annoy someone: *Getting trolled is one of the most annoying things about buying stuff on the internet.*

trolley /ˈtrɒl.i/ US /ˈtrɑː.li/ **noun** [C] (plural **trolleys** or **trollies**) **FOR CARRYING** ▷ **1** B2 UK (US **cart**) a small vehicle with two or four wheels that you push or pull to transport large or heavy objects: *a shopping trolley* ◦ *The hospital is so overcrowded that some patients are being treated on trolleys in the corridors.* ◦ *Why will **supermarket** trolleys never move in the direction that you push them in?* **2** UK (US **cart**) a table on four small wheels with one or more shelves under it, used for serving food or drinks: *Betty almost ran me over with her **tea** trolley as I was walking into the office!* ◦ *Every 30 minutes or so the flight attendant would **wheel** the **drinks** trolley down the aisle.* **VEHICLE** ▷ **3** (also **trolleycar**) US for **tram**: *You can catch the number 47 trolley from the train station.*

trolley

IDIOM **off your trolley** UK informal behaving in an extremely unusual way or doing something very silly: *Anyone who saw us doing this would think we were off our trolleys.* ◦ *Have you **gone** completely off your trolley? You'll never get away with it!*

trolleybus /ˈtrɒl.i.bʌs/ US /ˈtrɑː.li-/ **noun** [C] a public transport vehicle with rubber tyres which travels along ordinary roads in towns and is driven by electricity supplied from a wire above the road: *The trolleybus does not run on tracks.*

trolleyed /ˈtrɒl.id/ US /ˈtrɑː.lid/ **adj** [after verb] UK informal extremely drunk

trollop /ˈtrɒl.əp/ US /ˈtrɑː.ləp/ **noun** [C] old-fashioned or humorous disapproving a woman who has had a lot of sexual relationships without any emotional involvement: *That woman's a real trollop. Every time I see her she's with a different man.*

trombone /trɒmˈbəʊn/ US /trɑːmˈboʊn/ **noun** [C] a large, BRASS musical instrument that you play by blowing into it and sliding a U-shaped tube in and out to change the length and produce different notes: *The main orchestral brass instruments are the horn, trumpet, trombone, and tuba.* • **trombonist** /-ˈbəʊ.nɪst/ US /-ˈboʊ.nɪst/ **noun** [C] someone who plays a trombone: *My cousin is a **jazz** trombonist.*

troop /truːp/ **noun; adj; verb**

▸**noun 1 troops** C2 [plural] soldiers on duty in a large group: *Traditionally, United Nations troops have been **deployed** only in a peacekeeping role.* ◦ *The major powers have said they will not send in **ground** troops (= soldiers who fight on land).* ◦ *In 1988, about 220,000 American troops were **stationed** in Western Europe.* ◦ *All troops will be **withdrawn** by the end of the year.* **2** [C] a group of soldiers, especially ones who fight in strong military vehicles or on horses: *the King's Troop of the Royal Horse Artillery* **3** [C] an organized group of young people who are Scouts: *We've got a troop of Scouts camping in one of our fields this weekend.*

▸**adj** [before noun] for, relating to, or involving troops: *Satellite photographs provide us with a lot of information about their troop **movements**.*

▸**verb 1** [I usually + adv/prep] to walk somewhere in a large group, usually with one person behind another: *The little boys trooped **after** him across the playing fields.* ◦ *The Norwich fans gave their team a loud cheer as they trooped **off** the field.* ◦ *None of us knew what to expect as we trooped **into** her office.* **2** [I] informal humorous to travel somewhere as a group, especially when told to: *I suppose head office expects us all to troop **down** to London for this meeting.*

IDIOM **the trooping of the colour** UK a ceremony in which a military flag is carried in public with the soldiers that it represents marching behind it

ˈ**troop** ˌ**carrier** **noun** [C] a vehicle, ship, or aircraft that has been designed for transporting a lot of soldiers: *an **armoured** troop carrier*

trooper /ˈtruː.pər/ US /-pɚ/ **noun** [C] **SOLDIER** ▷ **1** a soldier who belongs to the lowest rank in the part of

T

an army that fights in strong military vehicles or on horses **POLICE OFFICER** ▷ **2** US a police officer in one of the forces of the 50 states of the US: ***state** troopers* ◦ *Troopers are called out in emergencies or dangerous situations.*

IDIOM **swear like a trooper** to use a lot of offensive language: *He was extremely drunk and swearing like a trooper.*

troopship /ˈtruːp.ʃɪp/ noun [C] a ship that is used for transporting large numbers of soldiers, especially one that was previously used for carrying goods

trope /trəʊp/ (US) /troʊp/ noun [C] specialized something such as an idea, phrase, or image that is often used in a particular artist's work, in a particular type of art, etc.: *Human-like robots are a classic trope of science fiction.*

trophy /ˈtrəʊ.fi/ (US) /troʊ-/ noun [C] **1** (B2) a prize, such as a gold or silver cup, that is given to the winner of a competition or race, and often returned after a year to be given to the winner of the competition in the following year: *He's an excellent snooker player, but he's never **won** a major trophy.* ◦ *The Duchess of Cambridge will be **presenting** the trophies.* **2** something used as a symbol of success from hunting or war: *That stuffed pike is Pat's trophy from a fishing holiday.*

ˌtrophy ˈwife/ˈgirlfriend noun [C] disapproving a young, attractive woman who is the partner of a rich and successful older man and acts as a symbol of his social position

tropic /ˈtrɒp.ɪk/ (US) /ˈtrɑː.pɪk/ noun **1** [C] one of the two imaginary lines around the Earth at approximately 23.5 degrees north and 23.5 degrees south of the EQUATOR **2 the tropics** [plural] the hottest area of the Earth, between the Tropic of Cancer and the Tropic of Capricorn: *She's a botanist and spent several years researching in the tropics.*

tropical /ˈtrɒp.ɪ.kəl/ (US) /ˈtrɑː.pɪ-/ adj **1** (B2) from or relating to the area between the two tropics: *tropical fish* ◦ *a tropical island/region/climate* ◦ *Leprosy is one of the few tropical **diseases** which could be eradicated early in the 21st century.* ◦ *She specializes in tropical **medicine** (= the treatment of diseases from the tropical areas of the world).* ◦ *The Amazon river basin contains the world's largest tropical **rainforest**.* ◦ *The hurricane was downgraded to a tropical **storm** when its speed dropped to 70mph.* → See also **subtropical 2** informal extremely hot and feeling wet: *The weather was positively tropical last summer.*

the ˌTropic of ˈCancer noun [S] the northern tropic

the ˌTropic of ˈCapricorn noun [S] the southern tropic

the troposphere /ˈtrɒp.əs.fɪəʳ/ (US) /ˈtrɑː.pəs.fɪr/ noun [S] specialized the layer of gases surrounding the Earth from the surface up to a height of about ten kilometres → Compare **the mesosphere, the stratosphere**

trot /trɒt/ (US) /trɑːt/ verb; noun

▸verb (-tt-) **RUN** ▷ **1** [I usually + adv/prep] If a horse or similar animal with four legs trots, it runs at its slowest speed, using short steps in which a front leg and the back leg on the opposite side move together: *We were trotting **along** the lane when a car suddenly appeared from nowhere and almost made me fall off my pony.* ◦ *The dog trotted **down** the path to greet me.* → Compare **canter, gallop HURRY** ▷ **2** [I usually + adv/prep] informal When people trot somewhere, they go there in a quick or busy way: *She left her purse on the counter, so I had to trot **down** the street after her.* ◦ *'I'm in a bit of a rush. I'll give you a ring,' said James, and **off** he trotted.* ◦ *Although she retired from politics five years ago, she still trots around the globe, giving speeches and meeting world leaders.* → See also **globetrotter 3** [I + adv/prep] to speak or do something too quickly: *She was rather nervous and trotted **through** her speech a bit too quickly.*

PHRASAL VERBS **trot sth out** disapproving to provide an excuse, idea, opinion, or fact, especially one that has been used often before or one that is silly: *You trot out that argument whenever I try to discuss this matter with you.* ◦ *Whenever I ask him why his essay's late, he just trots out the same **old** excuses.* • **trot sb out** [M often passive] disapproving to send someone to represent or defend your idea or opinion in public, in a boring and familiar way: *Whenever the president is in difficulties, her spokesman is trotted out to face the press.*

▸noun **RUN** ▷ **1** [S] the speed or movement of a horse or similar animal when it trots: *He climbed onto his horse and set off **at a** relaxed trot down the lane.* **2** [S] a slow run by a human: *The team warmed up for the match with a trot around the pitch.* **ILLNESS** ▷ **3 the trots** [plural] informal DIARRHOEA (= a condition in which the contents of the bowels are emptied too often): *to get/have the trots* ◦ *That prawn curry gave me the trots.*

IDIOMS **on the trot** UK informal If you do things on the trot, you do them directly after each other without pausing: *They won three games on the trot.* ◦ *She worked 30 hours on the trot to get the job finished on time.* • **a (quick/brisk) trot through sth** informal an occasion when you examine or explain the whole of a subject, method or piece of work quickly without stopping or getting slower: *In this book, John Pemble takes a **brisk** trot through the history and mysteries of Venice.*

trotter /ˈtrɒt.əʳ/ (US) /ˈtrɑː.t̬ɚ/ noun [C usually plural] a pig's foot used for food: *a dish of pigs' trotters*

troubadour /ˈtruː.bə.dɔːʳ/ (US) /-dɔːr/ noun [C] a male poet and singer who travelled around southern France and northern Italy between the 11th and 13th centuries entertaining rich people

trouble /ˈtrʌb.l̩/ noun; verb

▸noun **DIFFICULTIES** ▷ **1** (B1) [C or U] problems or difficulties: *The form was terribly complicated and I **had** a lot of trouble **with** it.* ◦ *Their problems seem to be over for the moment, but there could be more trouble **ahead**.* ◦ *The trouble **started/began when** my father came to live with us.* ◦ [+ -ing verb] *Parents often **have** trouble **finding** restaurants that welcome young children.* ◦ *You'll only be **storing up** trouble **for** the future if you don't go to the dentist now.* ◦ *I should get it finished over the weekend without **too much** trouble.* ◦ *She thought her troubles would be over once she'd got divorced.* ◦ *My Christmas shopping is **the least of** my troubles at the moment – I haven't even got enough money to pay the rent.* ◦ *Most of the current troubles stem from (= are caused by) our new computer system.* **2** (B2) [U] a characteristic of someone or something that is considered a disadvantage or problem: ***The** trouble **with** this carpet is that it gets dirty very easily.* ◦ *It's a brilliant idea. **The only** trouble **is that** we don't know how much it will cost.* ◦ *Ron**'s** trouble is that he's too impatient.* **3** (B1) [U] a situation in which you experience problems, usually because of something you have done wrong or badly: *He's never **been in** trouble **with** his teachers before.* ◦ *She'll be in **big** trouble if she crashes Sam's car.* ◦ *He got into **financial** trouble after his divorce.* ◦ *I hope you won't **get into** trouble because of what I said to your dad.* ◦ *The camp is a great way of getting kids off the street and **keeping***

T

them ***out of*** *trouble.* ◦ *I hope I haven't* ***landed*** *you* ***in*** *trouble with your boss.* ◦ *The marriage* ***ran into*** *trouble because of her husband's heavy drinking.* ◦ *The company will be in* ***serious/real*** *trouble if we lose this contract.* ◦ *He's* ***stayed out of*** *trouble since he was released from jail last year.* **4** Ⓒ [U] problems or difficulties caused by something failing to operate as it should: *The plane developed* ***engine*** *trouble shortly after take-off.* ◦ *They have a good reputation for building reliable trouble-****free*** *cars.* ◦ *Her* ***knee*** *trouble is expected to keep her out of the game for the rest of the season.* **5** Ⓑ2 [U] problems in the form of arguments, fighting, or violence: *Listen, I don't want any trouble in here, so please just finish your drink and leave.* ◦ *You can only go to the match if you promise to leave* ***at the first sign of*** *trouble.* ◦ *My little brother's always trying to* ***stir up*** (= create) *trouble* ***between*** *me and my boyfriend.*

! Usage: **trouble or problem?**

Problem means 'a situation that causes difficulties and that needs to be dealt with'. You can talk about **a problem** or **problems**:

Tell me what the problem is.

There's a problem with the engine.

He's having a few problems at work.

Trouble means 'problems, difficulties, or worries' and is used to talk about problems in a more general way. **Trouble** is almost always uncountable so do not use the determiner 'a' before it:

We had some trouble while we were on holiday.

He helped me when I was in trouble.

I had trouble with the car last night.

~~*I had a trouble with the car last night.*~~

Troubles is used in a small number of particular phrases to talk about all of the problems that someone has or that a country/organization has. You should not use **troubles** unless you are sure that it is correct:

~~*The report outlines the troubles caused by unemployment.*~~

The report outlines the problems caused by unemployment.

INCONVENIENCE ▷ **6** Ⓑ2 [U] slight problems or effort: *I didn't mean to* ***cause*** *you any trouble.* ◦ *'I'd love some more tea, if it isn't too much trouble.' 'Oh, it's* ***no*** *trouble* ***at all.****'* ◦ *I don't want to* ***put*** *you* ***to*** *any trouble* (= create any work for you). ◦ [+ to infinitive] *If you* ***took the*** *trouble* ***to*** *listen to what I was saying, you'd know what I was talking about.* ◦ *They* ***went to a lot of*** *trouble* (= made a lot of effort) ***for*** *their dinner party, but half the guests didn't bother to turn up.* ◦ *It's annoying, but I don't think I'll* ***go to the*** *trouble* ***of*** *making an official complaint.*

IDIOMS **be asking for trouble** to be likely to cause problems or difficulties for yourself: *Giving him such a powerful car when he's only just learned to drive is asking for trouble.* • **get sb into trouble** old-fashioned If a man gets a woman or girl who is not married into trouble, he makes her pregnant: *When he got his girlfriend into trouble, they had to choose between marriage and an abortion.* • **more trouble than it's worth** (also **not worth the trouble**) If something is more trouble than it's worth or is not worth the trouble, it is not important or useful enough to make an effort doing it: ***It's*** *more trouble than it's worth* ***to*** *take it back to the shop and ask for a replacement.* ◦ *It's not* ***worth the*** *trouble (****of****) applying for that job. You've no chance of getting it.* • **spell trouble** to suggest that there may be problems in the future: *The latest opinion polls spell trouble* ***for*** *the government.*

Word partners for **trouble** noun (**DIFFICULTIES**)

have trouble (*with* sth) • *get into/run into* trouble • *avoid* trouble • *forget* your troubles • be *beset by* troubles • *teething* troubles • *without* any trouble

Word partners for **trouble** noun (**INCONVENIENCE**)

cause sb [a lot of/some/any] trouble • *go to/take* a lot of trouble • *put sb to* [a lot of/any] trouble • *save* trouble

▸verb **WORRY** ▷ **1** [T] to cause someone to be worried or nervous: *What's troubling you, dear? You look ever so worried.* ◦ formal *Many of us are deeply troubled* ***by*** *the chairman's decision.* ◦ [+ (that)] ***It*** *troubles me (****that****) you didn't discuss your problems with me earlier.* **CAUSE DIFFICULTIES** ▷ **2** [T often passive] to cause someone to have a problem or difficulties: *He has been troubled by a knee injury for most of the season.* **CAUSE EFFORT** ▷ **3** [T] formal to cause someone a small amount of effort: *May I trouble you* ***for*** (= please give me) *some more wine, please?* ◦ [+ obj + to infinitive] *Could I trouble you* ***to*** *open that window? I'm afraid I can't reach it.* ◦ *Let's not trouble our****selves*** (= make the effort to think) ***about*** *the details at the moment.*

troubled /ˈtrʌb.ḷd/ adj **HAVING DIFFICULTIES** ▷ **1** Ⓒ1 having problems or difficulties: *The survival package involves selling off the unprofitable parts of the troubled* ***company.*** ◦ *This troubled* ***region*** *has had more than its fair share of wars over the centuries.* ◦ *In these troubled* ***times****, it makes a change to hear some good news.* **WORRIED** ▷ **2** worried or nervous: *He is clearly a very troubled man.*

troublemaker /ˈtrʌb.ḷˌmeɪ.kəʳ/ ⓊⓈ /-kɚ/ noun [C] someone who intentionally causes problems for other people, especially people who are in a position of power or authority: *I was worried that I would be regarded as a troublemaker if I complained about the safety standards.*

troubleshooting /ˈtrʌb.ḷˌʃuː.tɪŋ/ ⓊⓈ /-t̬ɪŋ/ noun [U] discovering why something does not work effectively and offering suggestions about how to improve it • **troubleshoot** /ˈtrʌb.ḷ.ʃuːt/ verb [I or T] (**troubleshot, troubleshot**) *I've been brought in to troubleshoot – to go in, sort out the problem, and get out again.* ◦ *A top German engineer has been appointed to troubleshoot the cause of the accident.* • **troubleshooter** /-ˌʃuː.təʳ/ ⓊⓈ /-ˌʃuː.t̬ɚ/ noun [C] *A troubleshooter is being appointed to make the prison service more efficient.*

troublesome /ˈtrʌb.ḷ.səm/ adj Ⓒ causing a lot of problems for someone: *Her hip has been troublesome for quite a while, and she'll probably need surgery on it.* ◦ *The negotiations have* ***proven*** *more troublesome than any of us expected.*

ˈtrouble ˌspot noun [C] a place where trouble, especially political violence, happens regularly: *There is increasing demand for the United Nations to intervene in trouble spots throughout the world.*

troubling /ˈtrʌb.lɪŋ/ adj Something that is troubling makes you worried or nervous: *Some troubling* ***questions*** *remain about the legal status of frozen embryos.* • **troublingly** /-li/ adv

trough /trɒf/ ⓊⓈ /trɑːf/ noun; verb

▸noun [C] **CONTAINER** ▷ **1** a long, narrow container without a lid that usually holds water or food for farm animals: *cows at the feeding trough* **LOW POINT** ▷ **2** a low point in a regular series of high and low points: *Investing small amounts regularly is a good way of smoothing out the **peaks and** troughs of the stock market.* **3** specialized (in the study of weather patterns) a long area of low air pressure between two areas of high air pressure: *A trough **of low pressure** over hilly areas will bring heavy thunderstorms overnight.*

IDIOM **have/get your snout in the trough** informal to have or get a share of a supply of money or some other advantage which people eagerly and sometimes dishonestly take: *The council had been handing out grants indiscriminately, and people were hurrying to get their snouts in the trough.*

▸verb informal **EAT** ▷ **1** [T] to eat something quickly and eagerly, especially in large amounts: *She was sitting there troughing chocolate.* **LOW LEVEL** ▷ **2** [I] to reach a low level, price, etc. before going up again: *The economy troughed six months ago and is now growing again.* • **trougher** noun [C] informal someone who eats a lot of food very quickly

trounce /traʊns/ verb [T] informal to defeat a competitor by a large amount: *France trounced Germany **by** five goals to one in the qualifying match.* ◦ *She trounced her rivals in the election.*

trouncing /ˈtraʊn.sɪŋ/ noun [C usually singular] informal a serious defeat: *the party's trouncing in the local elections* ◦ *Major changes are expected in the team following their 3–0 trouncing.*

troupe /truːp/ noun [C, + sing/pl verb] a group of performers such as singers or dancers who work and travel together: *She joined a **dance** troupe and travelled all over Europe.* ◦ *A troupe **of dancers** from Beijing is one of the leading attractions in the festival.*

trouper /ˈtruː.pəʳ/ (US) /-pɚ/ noun [C] **1** a successful ENTERTAINER who has had a lot of experience **2** approving anyone with a lot of experience who can be depended on and does not complain: *Good old Edna – she's a **real** trouper to do the washing-up without even being asked!* ◦ *He took his disappointment **like a** trouper.*

trouser /ˈtraʊ.zəʳ/ (US) /ˈtraʊ.zɚ/ adj [before noun] (US usually **pants**) belonging or relating to trousers: *'Just look at this scar,' said Brian proudly, rolling up his trouser **leg**.*

ˈtrouser ˌpress noun [C] a device for making or keeping trousers smooth by pressing them between two boards

trousers /ˈtraʊ.zəz/ (US) /-zɚz/ noun [plural] (US Usually **pants**) (A1) a piece of clothing that covers the lower part of the body from the waist to the feet, consisting of two cylinder-shaped parts, one for each leg, that are joined at the top: *I need a new **pair of** trousers to go with this jacket.* ◦ *Why aren't you **wearing** any trousers, David?*

ˈtrouser ˌsuit noun [C] UK (US **pantsuit**) a matching jacket and pair of trousers that is worn by women on formal occasions: *She's bought a very smart trouser suit for her job interviews.*

trousseau /ˈtruː.səʊ/ (US) /-soʊ/ noun [C] old-fashioned a collection of personal possessions, such as clothes, that a woman takes to her new home when she gets married

trout /traʊt/ noun **FISH** ▷ **1** [C or U] (plural **trout** or **trouts**) a fish that is a popular food, especially a brown type that lives in rivers and lakes or a silver type that lives in the sea but returns to rivers to produce its eggs: *Thousands of young salmon and trout have been killed by the pollution.* ◦ *Loch Leven is famous for its trout **fishing**.* **2** [U] the flesh of this fish eaten as food: *I love smoked trout, don't you?* **PERSON** ▷ **3** [C] (plural **trouts**) UK informal an old person, especially a woman, who is unpleasant or not attractive: *She's a miserable **old** trout who complains about everything.*

ˈtrout ˌpout noun [C] informal very big lips that women get if they have too much COLLAGEN put in their lips in an operation to make them look bigger

trowel

trowel /traʊəl/ noun [C] **1** a small tool consisting of a flat metal blade joined to a handle, used for spreading building materials such as CEMENT **2** a small tool with a curved pointed metal blade, used in the garden for digging small holes and removing small plants from the ground

truancy /ˈtruː.ən.si/ noun [U] (UK also **truanting**) the problem or situation of children being absent from school regularly without permission: *My daughter's school has very good exam results and hardly any truancy.* ◦ *Truanting was a serious problem in a fifth of the schools surveyed.*

truant /ˈtruː.ənt/ noun; verb

▸noun **1** [C] a child who is regularly absent from school without permission: *Police reports showed that the vast majority of crime committed by children was carried out by truants.* **2 play truant** (US usually **play hooky**) to be regularly absent from school without permission: *Most parents are horrified when they discover their children have been playing truant **from school**.*

▸verb [I] mainly UK Children who truant are regularly absent from school, usually while pretending to their parents that they have gone to school: *You'll fail all your exams if you carry on truanting.*

truce /truːs/ noun [C] a short interruption in a war or argument, or an agreement to stop fighting or arguing for a period of time: *After years of rivalry the two companies have **agreed** (US **agreed to**) a truce.* ◦ *We've got to spend the weekend together, so we might as well **call** (= have) a truce.* ◦ *Following last month's riots, the two big gangs in Los Angeles have finally **declared** a truce, ending years of bloodshed.* ◦ *The fragile truce **between** the two sides is not expected to last long.*

truck /trʌk/ noun; verb

▸noun **VEHICLE** ▷ **1** (B1) [C] (UK also **lorry**) a large road vehicle that is used for transporting large amounts of goods: *The road was completely blocked by an overturned truck.* ◦ *a truck driver* → See also **dumper truck** **2** [C] UK (US **car**) a part of a train that is used for carrying goods or animals: *Hundreds of refugees were herded into **cattle** trucks for the gruelling ten-hour journey.* **INVOLVEMENT** ▷ **3 have no truck with sth/sb** informal to refuse to become involved with something or someone because you do not approve of them

▸verb [T usually + adv/prep] mainly US to transport something somewhere in a truck: *Most of the aid is being trucked into the city, although some is arriving by boat.* • **trucking** /ˈtrʌk.ɪŋ/ noun [U] US (UK **road haulage**) *The railroads have lost a lot of business to trucking **companies**.*

IDIOM **keep on trucking** informal to continue to do something that is ordinary and boring: *'How's work going?' 'Oh, okay. I just keep on trucking.'*

trucker /ˈtrʌk.əʳ/ (US) /-ɚ/ noun [C] someone whose job is driving trucks

T

ˈtruck ˌfarm noun [C] US a small farm where fruit and vegetables are grown for selling to the public: *We buy all our produce from the local truck farm.* • **ˈtruck ˌfarmer** noun [C] *The floods have had a severe effect on the livelihoods of truck farmers in the area.*

truckie /ˈtrʌk.i/ noun [C] Australian English someone whose job is driving trucks → Compare **trucker**

truckle bed /ˈtrʌk.lˌbed/ noun [C] UK (US **ˈtrundle ˌbed**) a low bed on wheels that is stored under an ordinary bed ready for use by visitors

truckload /ˈtrʌk.ləʊd/ (US) /-loʊd/ noun [C] the amount of something that can be carried by a truck: *Truckloads* ***of*** *rice have been brought in to the areas affected by drought.* ◦ *Donations of food and medicines have been arriving* ***by*** *the truckload all week.*

ˈtruck ˌstop noun [C] US an area next to an important road with a restaurant, fuel, and repair services, where the main customers are truck drivers wanting to eat and drink cheaply

truculent /ˈtrʌk.jʊ.lənt/ adj unpleasant and likely to argue a lot: *a truculent teenager* ◦ *I found him truculent and most unpleasant.* • **truculence** /-ləns/ noun [U] • **truculently** /-li/ adv

trudge /trʌdʒ/ verb; noun

▸verb [I usually + adv/prep] C2 to walk slowly with a lot of effort, especially over a difficult surface or while carrying something heavy: *We trudged back up the hill.* ◦ *I'd had to trudge* ***through*** *the snow.*

PHRASAL VERB **trudge through sth** humorous to do work or a particular task slowly and with effort or difficulty: *I spent the whole weekend trudging through this report, and I still haven't finished reading it.*

▸noun [S] a long walk which makes you feel very tired: *We came back from our trudge across the moor wet and tired.*

true /truː/ adj; noun; adv

▸adj **NOT FALSE** ▷ **1** A2 (especially of facts or statements) right and not wrong; correct: [+ that] *Is* ***it*** *true* ***that*** *Lucy and Mark are getting married?* ◦ *The allegations,* ***if*** *true, could lead to her resignation.* ◦ *Her story is only* ***partly*** *true.* ◦ *Would* ***it*** *be true* ***to say*** *that you've never liked Jim?* ◦ *I suspect she gave a true* ***picture*** *(= accurate description) of what had happened.* ◦ *I don't believe these exam results are a true* ***reflection*** *of your abilities.* ◦ *The movie is based on the true* ***story*** *of a London gangster.* ◦ *She has since admitted that her earlier statement was not* ***strictly*** *(= completely) true.* ◦ *It used to be very cheap but that's no longer true (= that situation does not now exist).* ◦ *Alcohol should be consumed in moderation, and this is particularly true* ***for*** *pregnant women.* ◦ *Parents of young children often become depressed, and* ***this is*** *especially true* ***of*** *single parents.* → See also **truth** **REAL** ▷ **2** B1 [before noun] being what exists, rather than what was thought, intended, or stated: *true love* ◦ *a true friend* ◦ *There cannot be true democracy without reform of the electoral system.* ◦ *The true* ***horror*** *of the accident did not become clear until the morning.* **3 come true** B1 If a hope, wish, or dream comes true, it happens although it was unlikely that it would: *I'd always dreamed of owning my own house, but I never thought it would come true.* ◦ *After all the problems I'd had getting pregnant, Oliver's birth was a* ***dream*** *come true.* **SINCERE** ▷ **4** C2 sincere or loyal, and likely to continue to be so in difficult situations: *There are few true believers in communism left in the party.* ◦ *She has vowed to remain true* ***to*** *the president whatever happens.* ◦ *He said he'd repay the money the next day, and true* ***to*** *his* ***word*** *(= as he had promised), he gave it all back to me the following morning.* **5 be true to yourself** to behave according to your beliefs and do what you think is right **6 true to form/type** Someone who does something true to form or type behaves as other people would have expected from previous experience: *True to form, when it came to his turn to buy the drinks, he said he'd left his wallet at home.* **HAVING NECESSARY QUALITIES** ▷ **7** [before noun] having all the characteristics necessary to be accurately described as something: *Only true deer have antlers.* ◦ formal *It was said that the portrait was a very true* ***likeness*** *of her (= looked very much like her).* ◦ *In true Hollywood* ***style*** *(= in a way that is typical of Hollywood), she's had four marriages and three facelifts.* **ACCURATE** ▷ **8** [after verb] fitted or positioned accurately: *None of the drawers were true.*

IDIOMS **ring true** If something someone says or writes rings true, it seems to be true: *Something about his explanation didn't quite ring true.* • **so ... it's not true** mainly UK used to emphasize an adjective: *Julie's brother's so handsome it's not true.*

▸noun [U] **be out of true** to not be in the correct position or to be slightly bent out of the correct shape: *This door won't shut properly. I think the frame must be out of true.*

▸adv straight and without moving to either side: *Make sure you hit the nails in true.*

ˌtrue-ˈblue adj completely loyal to a person or belief: *They want control of the company to remain in true-blue hands.*

ˌtrue-life ˈstory noun [C] a story that is based on real rather than imaginary events

ˌtrue ˈnorth noun [U] the direction towards the top of the Earth along an imaginary line at an angle of 90° to the EQUATOR: *True north runs parallel to the Earth's axis.*

ˌtrue to ˈlife adj showing things and people as they really are, or seeming to be real: *She was saying how true to life the characters in the film were.* ◦ *a true-to-life story.*

truffle /ˈtrʌf.l/ noun [C] **RARE FOOD** ▷ **1** a type of FUNGUS that grows underground and can be eaten. Truffles are expensive because they are very rare: *The Dordogne region's gastronomic specialities include truffles and foie gras.* ◦ *Use truffle* ***oil*** *to add flavour to the dish.* **CHOCOLATE** ▷ **2** a small, round, very soft chocolate: *rum truffles*

trug /trʌg/ noun [C] a wooden container with a handle that you use for carrying garden tools, flowers, etc.

truism /ˈtruː.ɪ.zəm/ noun [C] a statement that is so obviously true that it is almost not worth saying: *As far as health is concerned, it's a truism that prevention is better than cure.*

truly /ˈtruː.li/ adv **EMPHASIZING TRUTH** ▷ **1** B2 used to emphasize that what you are saying is true: *At this time of year the river is a truly beautiful sight.* ◦ *She was a truly great actress.* ◦ *This is a truly remarkable achievement.* ◦ *It was a truly terrifying experience.* **REALLY** ▷ **2** really existing; in fact: *These will be the first truly democratic elections in the country's history.* ◦ *This is a desperate situation which requires a truly radical solution.* **SINCERELY** ▷ **3** C1 formal sincerely: *Truly, I could not have done this without you.* ◦ *He truly* ***believes*** *he can cure himself by willpower alone.* **4 yours truly** formal mainly US used to end a letter: *I look forward to hearing from you. Yours truly, Taylor Champinski.* **EXACTLY** ▷ **5** in an exact way: *Mushrooms aren't truly vegetables, but many people think they are.*

T

! Common mistake: truly

Warning: Common word-building error!
To make the adjective **true** into an adverb, first remove the 'e' and then add '-ly'. Don't write 'truely' or 'truelly', write **truly.**

trump /trʌmp/ noun; verb
▸noun **1** [C] a card that belongs to the group of cards that has been chosen to have the highest value in a particular game: *I played a trump.* ◦ *Luckily, I* ***drew*** *a trump.* **2 trumps** [plural] one of the four groups in a set of playing cards that has been chosen to have the highest value during a particular game or part of a game: *Diamonds are trumps.* **3 no trump(s)** a situation in which all four groups of cards have equal value in a game of BRIDGE

IDIOM **turn/come up trumps** UK to complete an activity successfully or to produce a good result, especially when you were not expected to: *John's uncle came up trumps, finding us a place to stay at the last minute.*

▸verb [T] **1** If you trump another player's card, you beat it with a card that belongs to the group of cards that has been chosen to have the highest value in the game you are playing. **2** to beat someone or something by doing or producing something better: *Their million-pound bid for the company was trumped at the last moment by an offer for almost twice as much from their main competitor.*

PHRASAL VERB **trump sth up** to accuse someone of something they have not done in order to have an excuse for punishing them

ˈtrump ˌcard noun [C usually singular] an advantage that makes you more likely to succeed than other people, especially something that other people do not know about: *Anthea was about to* ***play*** *her trump card – without her signature none of the money could be released.*

ˌtrumped-ˈup adj [before noun] deliberately based on false information so that someone will be accused of doing something wrong and punished: *She was imprisoned on trumped-up corruption* ***charges****.*

trumpet /ˈtrʌm.pɪt/ noun; verb
▸noun [C] B1 a BRASS musical instrument consisting of a metal tube with one narrow end, into which the player blows, and one wide end. Three buttons are pressed in order to change notes.
▸verb **ANIMAL CALL** ▷ **1** [I] (of a large animal, especially an ELEPHANT) to produce a loud call: *We could hear the elephants trumpeting in the distance.* **ANNOUNCE** ▷ **2** [T] mainly disapproving to announce or talk about something proudly to a lot of people: *The museum has been* ***loudly*** *trumpeting its reputation as one of the finest.* ◦ *Their* ***much-****trumpeted price cuts affect only five percent of the goods that they sell.*

trumpeter /ˈtrʌm.pɪ.təʳ/ noun [C] a musician who plays a trumpet: *a jazz trumpeter*

truncate /trʌŋˈkeɪt/ verb [T] to make something shorter or quicker, especially by removing the end of it: *Television coverage of the match was truncated by a technical fault.* • **truncated** /-ˈkeɪ.tɪd/ US /-ˈkeɪ.t̬ɪd/ adj • **truncation** /trʌŋˈkeɪ.ʃən/ noun [U]

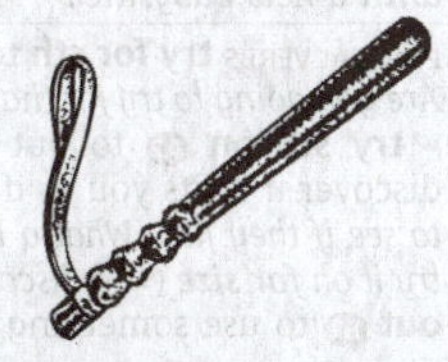
truncheon

truncheon /ˈtrʌn.tʃən/ noun [C] UK (US **nightstick**) a thick, heavy stick used as a weapon by police officers

trundle /ˈtrʌn.dl̩/ verb **1** [I or T, usually + adv/prep] (to cause something) to move slowly on wheels: *She trundled the wheelbarrow down the garden.* ◦ *Hundreds of trucks full of fruit and vegetables trundle across the border each day.* **2** [I + adv/prep] informal disapproving to develop or operate slowly: *The negotiations have been trundling* ***on*** *for months and there's still no end in sight.*

PHRASAL VERB **trundle sth out** informal to produce in a boring way something that has often been seen or used before: *They seem to trundle out the same old films every Christmas.*

ˈtrundle ˌbed noun [C] US (UK **ˈtruckle ˌbed**) a low bed on wheels that is stored under an ordinary bed ready for use by visitors

trunk /trʌŋk/ noun **MAIN PART** ▷ **1** B2 [C] the thick main stem of a tree, from which its branches grow **2** [C] the main part of a person's body, not including the head, legs, or arms **NOSE** ▷ **3** [C] the long, tube-shaped nose of an ELEPHANT **CASE** ▷ **4** [C] a large, strong case that is used for storing clothes and personal possessions, often when travelling or going to live in a new place **CLOTHES** ▷ **5 trunks** [plural] (UK also **swimming trunks**) a piece of men's clothing that covers the hips and bottom and the top part of the legs and is worn when swimming **CAR** ▷ **6** B1 [C] US (UK **boot**) a covered space at the back of a car, for storing things in: *I always keep a blanket and a toolkit in the trunk for emergencies.* ◦ *Her husband's dismembered body was later discovered in the trunk of her car.*

ˈtrunk ˌroad noun [C] UK an important road for travelling long distances at high speed

truss /trʌs/ verb; noun
▸verb [T] **1** (also **truss up**) to tie the arms and legs of someone together tightly and roughly with rope to prevent them from moving or escaping: *Police said the couple had been trussed up and robbed before being shot.* **2** to prepare a bird for cooking by tying its wings and legs to its body
▸noun [C] **FOR A BODY PART** ▷ **1** a device for holding an organ of the body, especially part of the INTESTINE, in its correct position after it has moved because of an injury **FOR A ROOF/BRIDGE** ▷ **2** specialized a support for a roof or bridge that is usually made of stone or brick

trust /trʌst/ verb; noun
▸verb **BELIEVE** ▷ **1** B1 [I or T] to believe that someone is good and honest and will not harm you, or that something is safe and reliable: *My sister warned me not to trust him.* ◦ *Trust me – I know about these things.* ◦ *Trust your instincts and do what you think is right.* ◦ *I don't trust air travel – it's unnatural.* ◦ [+ obj + to infinitive] *I trust him* ***to*** *make the right decision.* ◦ *That man is* ***not to be*** *trusted.* ◦ *I wouldn't trust him* ***with*** *my car.* ◦ *Sometimes you simply have to trust* ***in*** *the goodness of human nature.* ◦ *However much you plan an expedition like this, you still have to trust* ***to luck*** *to a certain extent.* **HOPE** ▷ **2** C1 [I] formal to hope and expect that something is true: [+ (that)] *I trust* ***(that)*** *you slept well?* ◦ *The meeting went well, I trust.*

IDIOMS **I wouldn't trust sb as far as I could throw them** informal something that you say which means you do not trust someone at all: *He's very charming but I wouldn't trust him as far as I could throw him.*
• **trust sb (to do sth)!** mainly UK informal used to say that it is typical of someone to do something stupid: *Trust Chris to leave the tickets at home!*

▸noun **BELIEF** ▷ **1** B2 [U] the belief that you can trust someone or something: *a relationship based on trust and understanding* ◦ *We were obviously wrong to* ***put***

T

our trust ***in*** *her.* ◦ *He's in* ***a position of*** *trust (= a position with responsibilities, especially to the public).* **2 take sth on trust** to believe that something is true although you have no proof **LEGAL ARRANGEMENT** ▷ **3** [C] a legal arrangement in which a person or organization controls property and/or money for another person or organization: *Under the terms of the trust he receives interest on the money, but he cannot get at the money itself.* ◦ *The money that her father left her is being* ***held/kept in*** *trust (= being controlled) for her until she's 30.* **ORGANIZATION** ▷ **4** [C] an organization that controls property and/or money for another person: *He works for a charitable trust.* ◦ *Housing trusts help to provide houses for people who are not well off.* **5** [C] US used in the name of some banks: *Morgan Guaranty Trust*

> **Word partners for trust noun**
>
> *have* trust (*in* sb/sth) • *place/put* your trust in sb/sth • *earn/gain/get/win* sb's trust • *betray/undermine* sb's trust • *build* (*up*) trust • *lose* trust *in* sb/sth • a *betrayal/breach* of trust • trust *between* [two people]

trustee /ˌtrʌsˈtiː/ **noun** [C] a person, often one of a group, who controls property and/or money for another person or an organization: *the museum's* ***board of*** *trustees*

trusteeship /ˌtrʌsˈtiː.ʃɪp/ **noun** [C or U] the position or responsibility of a trustee

ˈtrust ˌfund noun [C] an amount of money that is being controlled for a person or organization by another person or organization: *There are some tax advantages in setting up a trust fund for each of your children.*

trusting /ˈtrʌs.tɪŋ/ **adj** (also **trustful**) always believing that other people are good or honest and will not harm or deceive you: *The child gave a lovely, trusting smile.* ◦ *You shouldn't be so trusting – people take advantage of you.*

trustworthy /ˈtrʌstˌwɜː.ði/ (US) /-ˌwɝː-/ **adj** (C1) able to be trusted • **trustworthiness** /-nəs/ **noun** [U]

trusty /ˈtrʌs.ti/ **adj** [before noun] mainly humorous able to be trusted, especially because of having been owned and used for a long time: *I did the entire three hundred miles on my own – just me and my trusty bike.*

truth /truːθ/ **noun 1** (B2) [U] the quality of being true: *There would seem to be some truth* ***in*** *what she says.* ◦ *There is no truth* ***in*** *the reports of his resignation.* ◦ *You cannot question the truth* ***of*** *his alibi.* ◦ *And yet what he says contains at least* ***a grain of*** *(= a small amount of) truth.* **2 the truth** (B1) [S] the real facts about a situation, event or person: *But was he* ***telling*** *the truth?* ◦ *I don't suppose we'll ever know the truth* ***about*** *what happened that day.* ◦ ***To tell*** *(****you****) the truth (= speaking honestly) I'm quite pleased he's not coming.* **3 in truth** formal used to show or emphasize that something is true: *In truth we feared for her safety although we didn't let it be known.* **4** (C2) [C] formal a fact or principle that is thought to be true by most people: *It would seem to be a general truth that nothing is as straightforward as it at first seems.* ◦ *The entire system of belief is based on a few simple truths.*

> **Common mistake: truth or true?**
>
> **Warning:** do not confuse the noun **truth** with the adjective **true**:
>
> ~~*Nothing that she wrote in her letter was truth.*~~
> *Nothing that she wrote in her letter was true.*

> **Word partners for truth**
>
> *tell* the truth • *discover/find out/learn/uncover* the truth • *confess/reveal* the truth • *conceal/hide/withhold* the truth • the truth *comes out/emerges* • the truth *dawns on* sb • the *awful/honest/simple/whole* truth • an *element/grain* of truth • the *ring* of truth • the truth *about* sb/sth

truthful /ˈtruːθ.fəl/ **adj** honest and not containing or telling any lies: *The public has a right to expect truthful answers from politicians.* ◦ *Are you being quite truthful* ***with*** *me?* • **truthfully** /-i/ **adv** • **truthfulness** /-nəs/ **noun** [U]

try /traɪ/ **verb; noun**

▸**verb ATTEMPT** ▷ **1** (A2) [I or T] to attempt to do something: *Keep trying and you'll find a job eventually.* ◦ *If I don't get into the academy this year, I'll try* ***again*** *next year.* ◦ *I've tried really* ***hard*** *but I can't persuade him to come.* ◦ *I'm trying my* ***best/hardest****, but I just can't do it.* ◦ [+ to infinitive] *I tried* ***to*** *open the window.* ◦ [+ -ing verb] *Perhaps you should try gett****ing*** *up (= you should get up) earlier.* **TEST** ▷ **2** (B1) [T] to test something to see if it is suitable or useful or if it works: *I tried that recipe you gave me last night.* ◦ *I'm afraid we don't sell newspapers – have you tried the shop on the corner?* ◦ [+ -ing verb] *Try us****ing*** *a different shampoo.* ◦ *I thought I might try parachut****ing****.* ◦ *I've forgotten my door-keys – we'd better try the window (= test it to see if it is open).* **3 tried and tested/trusted** (US **tried and true**) used by many people and proved to be effective: *Most people would prefer to stick to tried and true methods of birth control.* **LAW** ▷ **4** (C2) [T] to examine a person accused of committing a crime in a law court by asking them questions and considering known facts, and then decide if they are guilty: *Because of security implications the officers were tried in secret.* ◦ *They are being tried* ***for*** *murder.* → See also **trial WORRY** ▷ **5** [T] to worry or annoy someone or upset a person's patience with many, often slight, difficulties: *The demands of the job have tried him* ***sorely****.* ◦ *He's been trying my* ***patience*** *all morning with his constant questions.* ◦ *Her endless demands would try* ***the patience of a saint*** *(= are very annoying).*

> **Common mistake: try**
>
> **Warning:** Check your verb endings!
> Many learners make mistakes when using **try** in the past tense. In the past simple and past participle, don't write 'tryed', write **tried**. The **-ing** form is **trying**.

IDIOMS **try sth for size** UK (US **try sth on for size**) to test something or to think about an idea in order to decide if it works or if you can use it • **try your hand at sth** to try doing something for the first time: *I might try my hand at a bit of Chinese cookery.* • **try your luck** to try to achieve something although you know you might not succeed: *He'd always wanted to act and in 1959 came to London to try his luck on the stage.* • **try it on** UK informal to deceive someone or behave badly, especially in order to discover how much of your bad behaviour will be allowed: *He's not really ill – he's just trying it on.* ◦ *The kids often try it on* ***with*** *a new babysitter.*

PHRASAL VERBS **try for sth** to attempt to get something: *Are you going to try for that job in the sales department?* • **try sth on** (A2) to put on a piece of clothing to discover if it fits you or if you like it: *Try on the shoes to see if they fit.* ◦ *What a lovely dress – why don't you try it on* ***for size*** *(= to discover whether it fits)?* • **try sth out** (B2) to use something to discover if it works or if

Other ways of saying try

Attempt is a common alternative to 'try':

*I have never **attempted** to run a marathon.*

Endeavour means the same as 'try' but is slightly more formal:

*Engineers are **endeavouring** to locate the source of the problem.*

Seek is a formal word that means 'try':

*They **sought** to reassure the public.*

The verbs **battle**, **strive**, and **struggle** can be used when someone is trying to do something in a difficult situation:

*He was **battling** to fix the roof in the rain.*

*With limited resources, they are **striving** to make the school a better one.*

*I've been **struggling** to understand this article all afternoon.*

If someone tries very hard to do something, you can say that the person **goes to great lengths**:

*She knew that her parents would **go to great lengths** to see that she got a good education.*

you like it: *Don't forget to try out the equipment before setting up the experiment.* • **try out for sth** US to compete for a position in a sports team or a part in a play: *Luke's trying out for the college football team.*

▸**noun** ATTEMPT ▷ **1** B2 [C usually singular] an attempt to do something: *They might just have a place left on the course – why don't you **give it/have** a try?* ◦ *This will be her third try **at** jumping the bar.* ◦ *You could ask him if he's willing – it's **worth a** try.* SPORT ▷ **2** [C] (in the game of RUGBY) the act of a player putting the ball on the ground behind the opposing team's goal line, which scores points for the player's team

trying /ˈtraɪ.ɪŋ/ **adj** annoying and difficult: *I've had a very trying day at work.* ◦ *He can be rather trying at times.*

ˈtry-out **noun** [C] informal a test to see how useful or effective something or someone is: *After a try-out in Bath, the play is due to open in Edinburgh next month.* ◦ *The try-outs **for** the team will be next weekend.*

tryst /trɪst/ **noun** [C] old use or humorous a meeting between two people who are having a romantic relationship, especially a secret one

tsar (also **tzar**, US usually **czar**) /zɑːʳ/ (US) /zɑːr/ **noun** [C] RULER ▷ **1** (until 1917) the male Russian ruler: *Tsar Nicholas I* OFFICIAL ▷ **2** a person who has been given special powers by the government to deal with a particular matter: *The government has appointed a drugs tsar to coordinate the fight against drug abuse.* LEADER ▷ **3** a powerful person in business or politics • **tsarist** (also **tzarist**, US usually **czarist**) /ˈzɑː.rɪst/ (US) /ˈzɑːr.ɪst/ **adj, noun** [C] *the tsarist empire* ◦ *Tsarist Russia*

tsarina (also **tzarina**, US usually **czarina**) /zɑːˈriː.nə/ (US) /zɑːrˈiː-/ **noun** [C] (until 1917) the wife of a tsar or the female Russian ruler

tsetse fly /ˈtet.si ˌflaɪ/ **noun** [C] one of various types of African fly which feed on blood and can cause serious diseases to the person or animal they bite

ˈT-shirt **noun** [C] (also **tee shirt**) A1 a simple piece of clothing, usually with short sleeves and no collar, that covers the top part of the body: *She was wearing jeans and a T-shirt.*

tsk /tɪsk/ **exclamation** (also **ˌtsk ˈtsk**) **tut**

tsp. written abbreviation for **teaspoonful**: *Add one tsp. of ground coriander.*

ˈT-square **noun** [C] a long, flat, T-shaped piece of wood, metal, or plastic, used to draw parallel lines → Compare **set square**

tsunami /tsuːˈnɑː.mi/ **noun** [C] an extremely large wave caused by a violent movement of the earth under the sea

ttfn written abbreviation for ta-ta for now: a way of saying goodbye at the end of an email

tub /tʌb/ **noun** [C] CONTAINER ▷ **1** a large, round container with a flat base and an open top: *Outside was a stone patio with tubs of flowering plants.* ◦ *We've got a tub for compost at the bottom of our garden.* **2** a small plastic container with a lid, used for storing food: *a tub of ice cream/margarine* BATH ▷ **3** US for **bath**: *It's good to sink into a hot tub at the end of a hard day's work.*

tuba /ˈtjuː.bə/ (US) /ˈtuː-/ **noun** [C] a BRASS musical instrument consisting of a long, bent metal tube which the player blows into, producing low notes

tubby /ˈtʌb.i/ **adj** informal (of a person) fat: *Our chef was a genial, slightly tubby man.*

tube /tjuːb/ (US) /tuːb/ **noun** PIPE ▷ **1** B2 [C] a long cylinder made from plastic, metal, rubber, or glass, especially used for moving or containing liquids or gases: *Gases produced in the reaction pass through this tube and can then be collected.* **2** [C] in biology, any hollow, cylinder-shaped structure in the body that carries air or liquid: *the bronchial tubes* CONTAINER ▷ **3** B1 [C] a long, thin container made of soft metal or plastic that is closed at one end and has a small hole at the other, usually with a cover, used for storing thick liquids: *a tube of toothpaste* **4** [C] Australian English informal for a CAN or bottle of beer: *a tube of lager* TRAIN ▷ **5 the tube** B1 [S] (often **the Tube**) UK informal London's underground train system: *I got the Tube to Camden Town.* ◦ *I go to work **on** the tube.* ◦ *a Tube station* TELEVISION ▷ **6 the tube** [S] mainly US the television: *What's on the tube this weekend?*

IDIOM **go down the tubes** informal to fail completely: *If business doesn't pick up soon, the company will go down the tubes.*

tuber /ˈtjuː.bəʳ/ (US) /ˈtuː.bɚ/ **noun** [C] a swollen underground stem or root of a plant from which new plants can grow, as in the potato • **tuberous** /ˈtjuː.bə.rəs/ (US) /ˈtuː.bɚ.əs/ **adj**

tuberculosis /tjuːˌbɜː.kjuˈləʊ.sɪs/ (US) /tuːˌbɝː.kjəˈloʊ-/ **noun** [U] (abbreviation **TB**) a serious disease that is infectious and can attack many parts of a person's body, especially their lungs • **tubercular** /-ˈbɜː.kju.ləʳ/ (US) /-ˈbɝː.kjə.lɚ/ **adj**

tubing /ˈtjuː.bɪŋ/ (US) /ˈtuː-/ **noun** [U] material in the form of a tube or tubes: *Rubber tubing can perish after a few years.*

ˈtub-ˌthumping **adj** [before noun] informal disapproving describes a style of speaking that is forceful or violent: *a tub-thumping speech/campaigner*

tubular /ˈtjuː.bjʊ.ləʳ/ (US) /ˈtuː.bjə.lɚ/ **adj** made in or having the shape of a tube: *tubular steel*

the TUC /ˌtiː.juːˈsiː/ **noun** abbreviation for the Trades Union Congress: an organization for British TRADE UNIONS that has a large meeting every year

tuck /tʌk/ **verb; noun**

▸**verb** [T usually + adv/prep] TIDY ▷ **1** to push a loose end of a piece of clothing or material into a particular place or position, especially to make it tidy or comfortable: *Should I tuck my shirt **into** my trousers?* ◦ *He tucked the bottom of the sheet **under** the mattress.* STORE SAFELY ▷ **2** to put something into a safe or convenient place: *Tuck your gloves **in** your pocket so*

T

that you don't lose them. ◦ She had a doll tucked **under** her arm. ◦ Eventually I found the certificate tucked **under** a pile of old letters. ◦ Tuck your chair **in** (= put it so that the seat of it is under the table) so that no one trips over it. **BODY** ▷ **3** to hold part of your body in a particular position: *Stand up straight, tuck your tummy* ***in*** *and tuck your bottom* ***under.*** ◦ *She sat with her legs tucked* ***under*** *her.* **HIDDEN** ▷ **4 be tucked (away)** to be in a place that is hidden or where few people go: *Tucked along/down this alley are some beautiful old houses.* ◦ *A group of tiny brick houses is tucked away behind the factory.*

PHRASAL VERBS **tuck sth away** to put something in a private, safe place: *Grandma always kept a bit of money tucked away in case there was an emergency.* • **tuck sb in** (UK also **tuck sb up**) to make someone comfortable in their bed, especially a child, by arranging the covers round them: *Daddy, if I go to bed now will you tuck me in?* ◦ *The children are safely tucked up in bed.* • **tuck in/tuck into sth** UK informal to start eating something eagerly: *There's plenty of food, so please tuck in.*

▸noun **FOLD** ▷ **1** [C] a narrow fold sewn into something, especially a piece of material, either for decoration or to change its shape **MEDICAL OPERATION** ▷ **2** [C] an operation to remove unwanted fat from a part of the body: *a tummy tuck* **FOOD** ▷ **3** [U] UK old-fashioned child's word food, especially sweets and cakes: *a tuck shop* → See also **tucker**

tucker /ˈtʌk.əʳ/ US /-ɚ/ noun [U] Australian English informal food: *a tucker bag*

'tude /tjuːd/ US /tuːd/ noun [U] slang an unpleasant way of behaving towards someone. 'Tude is short for 'attitude': *Don't give me that 'tude, girl!*

Tue. (also **Tues.**) written abbreviation for Tuesday

Tuesday /ˈtjuːz.deɪ/ US /ˈtuːz-/ noun [C or U] (written abbreviation **Tue.**, **Tues.**) A1 the day of the week after Monday and before Wednesday: *We'll meet at eight* ***on*** *Tuesday.* ◦ *We always meet* ***on*** *Tuesdays.* ◦ *The work has to be finished by* ***next*** *Tuesday.* ◦ *Where were you* ***last*** *Tuesday?* ◦ *The 29th is a Tuesday, isn't it?* ◦ *Tuesday* ***morning/afternoon/evening/night***

tuft /tʌft/ noun [C] a number of short pieces of hair, grass, etc. which closely grow together or are held together near the base: *He had a few tufts* ***of*** *hair on his chin, but you could hardly call it a beard.*

tufted /ˈtʌf.tɪd/ adj with, or made of, a tuft or tufts: *the tufted duck* ◦ *tufted carpet*

tug /tʌg/ verb; noun

▸verb [I or T] (-gg-) to pull something quickly and usually with a lot of force: *Tom tugged* ***at*** *his mother's arm.*

▸noun [C] **BOAT** ▷ **1** (also **tugboat**) a boat with a powerful engine that can change direction easily and is used to pull large ships into and out of port **PULL** ▷ **2** a sudden strong pull on something: *Feeling a tug at his sleeve, he turned to see Joe beside him.*

ˌtug of ˈlove noun [S] UK informal used, especially in newspapers, to refer to a situation in which one of the separated parents of a child takes care of the child but the other parent claims that right, or a situation in which a child is being taken care of by people other than the child's parents but the parents claim that right: [before noun] *a tug-of-love battle*

ˌtug of ˈwar noun [C usually singular] a type of sport in which two teams show their strength by pulling against each other at the opposite ends of a rope, and each team tries to pull the other over a line on the ground

tuition /tjuːˈɪʃ.ən/ US /tuː-/ noun [U] **1** C1 mainly UK teaching, especially when given to a small group or one person, such as in a college or university: *All students receive tuition* ***in*** *logic and metaphysics.* ◦ *tuition* ***fees*** **2** mainly US the money paid for this type of teaching: *Few can afford the tuition of $12,000 a term.*

tulip /ˈtjuː.lɪp/ US /ˈtuː-/ noun [C] a plant with a large, brightly coloured, bell-shaped flower on a stem that grows from a BULB, or the flower itself

tulle /tjuːl/ US /tuːl/ noun [U] a light cloth like a net of SILK or similar material, used on dresses, to decorate hats, or for particular types of VEIL

tumble /ˈtʌm.bl̩/ verb; noun

▸verb [I] **1** to fall quickly and without control: *I lost my footing and tumbled* ***down*** *the stairs.* ◦ *At any moment the whole building could tumble* ***down.*** ◦ *He lost his balance and tumbled* ***over.*** **2** to fall a lot in value in a short time: *Share prices tumbled yesterday.* **3** to move in an uncontrolled way, as if falling or likely to fall: *An excited group of children tumbled* ***out*** *of school/the bus.*

PHRASAL VERB **tumble to sth** UK old-fashioned informal to suddenly understand something: *I think he's tumbled to our plan.*

▸noun [C] a sudden fall: *She* ***had*** *a nasty tumble on her way to work and grazed her arm.*

IDIOM **take a tumble** to fall suddenly to a lower level: *Company profits took a tumble last year.*

tumbledown /ˈtʊm.bl̩.daʊn/ adj [before noun] (of a building) in a very bad condition, especially in a state of decay: *a tumbledown cottage*

ˈtumble ˌdryer UK (US **ˈtumble ˌdrier**) noun [C] (also **dryer**) a machine that dries wet clothes by turning them in hot air → Compare **spin-dryer**

tumbler /ˈtʌm.bləʳ/ US /-blɚ/ noun [C] a glass drinking container which does not have a handle or a stem

tumbleweed /ˈtʌm.bl̩.wiːd/ noun [U] a plant of North America and Australia which breaks near the ground when it dies and is then rolled about in large balls by the wind

tumescent /tjuːˈmes.ənt/ US /tuː-/ adj specialized (especially of parts of the body) swollen or becoming swollen: *a tumescent penis* • **tumescence** /-ənts/ noun [U]

tummy /ˈtʌm.i/ noun [C] informal or child's word the stomach, or the lower front part of the body: *a tummy ache*

ˈtummy ˌbutton noun [C] UK informal or child's word for **navel**

tumour UK (US **tumor**) /ˈtjuː.məʳ/ US /ˈtuː.mɚ/ noun [C] a mass of DISEASED cells which might become a LUMP or cause illness: *They found a* ***malignant*** *tumour in her breast.* ◦ *a benign tumour* ◦ *a brain tumour*

tumult /ˈtjuː.mʌlt/ US /ˈtuː-/ noun [C or U] formal a loud noise, especially that produced by an excited crowd, or a state of confusion, change, or UNCERTAINTY: *You couldn't hear her speak over the tumult from the screaming fans.* ◦ *From every direction, people were running and shouting and falling over each other in a tumult* ***of*** *confusion.* ◦ *The financial markets are* ***in*** *tumult.*

tumultuous /tjuːˈmʌl.tjuəs/ US /tuː-/ adj formal very loud, or full of confusion, change, or UNCERTAINTY: *Dame Joan appeared to tumultuous* ***applause*** *and a standing ovation.* ◦ *After the tumultuous events of 1990, Eastern Europe was completely transformed.* • **tumultuously** /-li/ adv

tuna /ˈtjuː.nə/ US /ˈtuː-/ noun **1** B1 [C] (plural **tuna** or

tunas) a large fish which lives in warm seas: *shoals of tuna* **2** B1 [U] the flesh of this fish eaten as food: *a can of tuna (fish)*

tundra /ˈtʌn.drə/ noun [U] (part of) the very large area of land in Northern Asia, North America, and Northern Europe where, because it is cold, trees do not grow and ground below the surface is permanently frozen: *Reindeer roam the tundra in large herds.* ◦ *Few plants grow in tundra regions.*

tune /tjuːn/ US /tuːn/ noun; verb

▸noun **MUSICAL NOTES** ▷ **1** A2 [C] a series of musical notes, especially one that is pleasant and easy to remember: *He was humming a tune as he dried the dishes.* ◦ *a theme tune* ◦ *That's a very (= easy to remember and pleasant)* ***catchy*** *tune.* → Synonym **melody 2 in tune** C1 singing or playing notes that are at the right PITCH (= level) or that agree with others being sung or played **3 out of tune** C1 singing or playing notes that are at the wrong PITCH (= level) or that do not agree with others being sung or played: *I'm afraid the piano is out of tune.* **UNDERSTANDING** ▷ **4 be in/out of tune with sb/sth** C2 If you are in tune with people or ideas, you understand or agree with them, and if you are out of tune with them, you do not: *Much of his success comes from being in tune with what his customers want.* ◦ *Her theories were out of tune with the scientific thinking of the time.* **AMOUNT** ▷ **5 to the tune of** to the stated amount: *The City Council had financed the new building to the tune of over four million pounds.* **ENGINE** ▷ **6** [C usually singular] UK a **tune-up**

▸verb [T] **INSTRUMENT** ▷ **1** to change a part of a musical instrument so that the instrument produces the correct sounds when played: *Get into the habit of tuning your guitar every day before you practise.* ◦ *She tuned (****up****) her violin before the concert.* **RADIO** ▷ **2** to move the controls on a radio, television, etc. so that it receives programmes broadcast from a particular station: *His radio is constantly tuned* ***to*** *KROQ-FM, the local rock station.* **ENGINE** ▷ **3** to make slight changes to an engine so that it works as well as possible: *The* ***engine*** *certainly needs tuning but there's nothing wrong with the car.* ◦ *Could you tune (****up****) the* ***engine*** *for me, please?*

PHRASAL VERBS **tune in TV/RADIO** ▷ **1** to watch or listen to a particular television or radio programme or station: *Be sure to tune in* ***to*** *next week's show.* ◦ *Millions of viewers tune in every weekday for 'News at Night'.* **UNDERSTANDING** ▷ **2 be tuned in** to have a good understanding of what is happening in a situation or what other people are thinking: *She just doesn't seem to be tuned in* ***to*** *her students' needs.* • **tune (sb/sth) out** US informal to ignore someone or not give your attention to something or to what is happening around you: *He talks such garbage that I just tune him out.* • **tune (sth) up INSTRUMENT** ▷ **1** If musicians who are preparing to play tune up their instruments, they make small changes to them so that they produce the correct notes: *After the orchestra had tuned up, the conductor walked on to the stage.* ◦ *He began to tune up his violin.* **ENGINE** ▷ **2** to tune an engine

tuneful /ˈtjuːn.fəl/ US /ˈtuːn-/ adj with a pleasant tune: *The first track on the album is surprisingly tuneful.* • **tunefully** /-i/ adv • **tunefulness** /-nəs/ noun [U]

tuneless /ˈtjuːn.ləs/ US /ˈtuːn-/ adj having no tune and unpleasant: *tuneless whistling* • **tunelessly** /-li/ adv *She sang rather tunelessly.*

tuner /ˈtjuː.nər/ US /ˈtuː.nɚ/ noun [C] **1** the part of a radio or television that allows you to choose the broadcasting station you want to listen to or watch **2** a radio that is part of a MUSIC SYSTEM

ˈtune-up noun [C usually singular] (UK also **tune**) the act of making small changes to an engine so that it works as well as possible

tungsten /ˈtʌŋ.stən/ noun [U] (symbol **W**) a chemical element that is a hard metal used in making light BULBS and strong types of STEEL: *tungsten steel*

tunic /ˈtjuː.nɪk/ noun [C] a piece of clothing which fits loosely over a person's body, reaches to the waist or knees, and often has no sleeves: *a soldier's tunic*

tuning /ˈtjuː.nɪŋ/ US /ˈtuː-/ noun [U] the way an instrument is TUNED: *The tuning on this piano is awful.*

ˈtuning ˌfork noun [C] a metal object with two long, thin parts joined to a short handle, which, when hit gently, produces a particular note. It is used when TUNING musical instruments.

ˈtuning ˌpeg noun [C] (also **ˈtuning ˌpin**) a short wooden or metal stick with a flat, rounded end that is turned to make the strings on a musical instrument tighter or looser

tunnel /ˈtʌn.əl/ noun; verb

▸noun [C] B1 a long passage under or through the ground, especially one made by people: *The train went into the tunnel.*

▸verb [I or T] (**-ll-** or US usually **-l-**) to dig a tunnel: *The decision has not yet been made whether to tunnel* ***under*** *the river or build a bridge over it.* ◦ *The alternative is to tunnel a route through the mountain.* ◦ *He was trapped in a collapsed building but managed to tunnel his* ***way*** *out.* • **tunneller** UK (US **tunneler**) /-ər/ US /-ɚ/ noun [C]

ˌtunnel ˈvision noun [U] **SEEING** ▷ **1** a medical condition that makes someone see only things that are directly in front of them **THINKING** ▷ **2** disapproving the fact that someone considers only one part of a problem or situation, or holds a single opinion rather than having a more general understanding

tuppence /ˈtʌp.əns/ noun [U] (also **twopence**) two old or new British pence

IDIOM **not care/give tuppence** UK old-fashioned to not care about something or someone in any way

tuppenny /ˈtʌp.ən.i/, /-ni/ adj [before noun] (also **twopenny**) old-fashioned informal costing two pence

Tupperware /ˈtʌp.ə.weər/ US /-ɚ.wer/ noun [U] trademark plastic containers, usually for storing food, and usually having lids which fit tightly

tuque /tuːk/ noun [C] Canadian for **bobble hat**

turban /ˈtɜː.bən/ US /ˈtɝː-/ noun [C] **1** a head covering for a man, worn especially by Sikhs, Muslims, and Hindus, made from a long piece of cloth that is wrapped around the top of the head many times **2** a hat for women in this style • **turbaned** /-bənd/ adj *a turbaned man*

turbid /ˈtɜː.bɪd/ US /ˈtɝː-/ adj formal (of a liquid) not transparent because a lot of small pieces of matter are held in it: *Several different species of fish inhabit these turbid shallow waters.* • **turbidity** /tɜːˈbɪd.ɪ.ti/ US /tɝːˈbɪd.ə.t̬i/ noun [U]

turbine /ˈtɜː.baɪn/ US /ˈtɝː-/ noun [C] a type of machine through which liquid or gas flows and turns a special wheel with blades in order to produce power: *a steam turbine* ◦ *a turbine engine*

turbocharger /ˈtɜː.bəʊˌtʃɑː.dʒər/ US /ˈtɝː.boʊˌtʃɑːr.dʒɚ/ noun [C] a small turbine turned by the waste gases from an engine which pushes the fuel and air mixture into the engine at a higher pressure, so increasing the power produced by the engine • **turbocharged** /-tʃɑːdʒd/ (US) /-tʃɑːrdʒd/ **adj** *a turbocharged engine*

turbofan /ˈtɜː.bəʊ.fæn/ (US) /ˈtɝː.boʊ-/ **noun** [C] a turbine used as an engine, especially for an aircraft, which provides some force for movement from the gas that it pushes out, and some by turning a large special wheel with blades which also pushes air out, or an aircraft driven by this type of engine

turbojet /ˈtɜː.bəʊ.dʒet/ (US) /ˈtɝː.boʊ-/ **noun** [C] a TURBINE used as an engine, especially for an aircraft, which provides a forward force for movement from the gas it pushes out, or an aircraft driven by this type of engine

turboprop /ˈtɜː.bəʊ.prɒp/ (US) /ˈtɝː.boʊ.prɑːp/ **noun** [C] a **turbine** used as an aircraft engine which provides most force for movement by turning a PROPELLER, or an aircraft driven by this type of engine

turbot /ˈtɜː.bət/ (US) /ˈtɝː-/ **noun** **1** [C] (plural **turbot** or **turbots**) a fish with a flat body which lives near to the coast in European seas **2** [U] the flesh of this fish eaten as food

turbulence /ˈtɜː.bjʊ.ləns/ (US) /ˈtɝː.bjə-/ **noun** [U] **CONFUSION** ▷ **1** a state of confusion without any order: *The era was characterized by political and cultural turbulence.* ◦ *There are signs of turbulence ahead for the economy.* **AIR/WATER MOVEMENT** ▷ **2** strong sudden movements within air or water: *We might be experiencing some turbulence on this flight due to an approaching electrical storm.*

turbulent /ˈtɜː.bjʊ.lənt/ (US) /ˈtɝː.bjə-/ **adj** **SITUATION/TIME** ▷ **1** (C2) involving a lot of sudden changes, arguments, or violence: *a turbulent marriage* ◦ *This has been a turbulent week for the government.* **AIR/WATER** ▷ **2** Turbulent air or water moves very strongly and suddenly: *The sea was too turbulent for us to be able to take the boat out.*

turd /tɜːd/ (US) /tɝːd/ **noun** [C] offensive **1** a piece of solid waste: *dog turds on the pavement* **2** a rude word for someone who you think is unpleasant: *I'm not doing business with that little turd.*

tureen /tjʊˈriːn/ (US) /tə-/ **noun** [C] a large bowl, usually with a lid, from which soup or vegetables are served

turf /tɜːf/ (US) /tɝːf/ **noun; verb**

▸**noun** **GRASS** ▷ **1** [C or U] (plural **turfs** or UK **turves**) the surface layer of land on which grass is growing, consisting of the grass and the soil in which its roots grow, or a piece of this that is cut from the ground and is usually rectangular **HORSE RACING** ▷ **2** **the turf** [S] the sport of horse racing **AREA** ▷ **3** [U] informal a subject in which a person or group has a lot of knowledge or influence: *Antiques are very much her turf.* **4** [U] mainly US informal the area that a group considers its own: *Judges feel that the courtroom is their private turf.* ◦ *The gymnastics team won the championship on home turf.*

▸**verb** [T] to cover a piece of land with turf

PHRASAL VERBS **turf sth out** UK informal to get rid of a number of things or something large that you do not want: *I turfed out a load of old shoes last week.* • **turf sb out** mainly UK informal to force someone to leave a place or an organization: *She'll be turfed out **of** the study group if she carries on being disruptive.*

ˈturf acˌcountant **noun** [C] UK formal a **bookmaker**

ˈturf ˌwar **noun** [C] a fight or an argument to decide who controls an area or an activity

turgid /ˈtɜː.dʒɪd/ (US) /ˈtɝː-/ **adj** **TOO SERIOUS** ▷ **1** formal (of speech, writing, style, etc.) too serious about its subject matter; boring: *a couple of pages of turgid prose* **NOT FLOWING** ▷ **2** formal (of water) not flowing easily **SWOLLEN** ▷ **3** specialized (of an organ or living tissue) swollen • **turgidity** /tɜːˈdʒɪd.ɪ.ti/ (US) /tɝːˈdʒɪd.ə.t̬i/ **noun** [U] formal or specialized • **turgidly** /-li/ **adv** formal

turkey /ˈtɜː.ki/ (US) /ˈtɝː-/ **noun** **BIRD** ▷ **1** (B1) [C] a large bird grown for its meat on farms: *a wild turkey* **2** (B1) [U] the flesh of this bird used as food: *roast turkey* **FAILURE** ▷ **3** [C] informal something that fails badly: *His last film was a complete turkey.* **4** [C] US informal a stupid or silly person: *What did you do that for, you turkey?*

Turkish bath /ˌtɜː.kɪʃˈbɑːθ/ (US) /ˌtɝː.kɪʃˈbæθ/ **noun** [C] a health treatment in which you sit in a room full of steam and are then MASSAGED (= rubbed) and washed, or a building in which this treatment is available → Compare **sauna**

Turkish delight /ˌtɜː.kɪʃ.dɪˈlaɪt/ (US) /ˌtɝː-/ **noun** [U] a soft type of sweet, usually in the form of square pink pieces covered with powdered sugar

turmeric /ˈtɜː.mᵊr.ɪk/ (US) /ˈtɝː.mɚ-/ **noun** [U] a yellow powder, used as a spice to flavour particular foods, especially CURRY, and give them a yellow colour. It is made from the root of an Asian plant.

turmoil /ˈtɜː.mɔɪl/ (US) /ˈtɝː-/ **noun** [S or U] (C2) a state of confusion, UNCERTAINTY, or DISORDER: *The whole region is **in** turmoil.* ◦ *The country is in a state of political turmoil.* ◦ *The Stock Exchange is **in** turmoil following a huge wave of selling.*

turn /tɜːn/ (US) /tɝːn/ **verb; noun**

▸**verb** **GO ROUND** ▷ **1** (B2) [I or T] to (cause to) move in a circle round a fixed point or line: *The Earth turns **on** its axis once every 24 hours.* ◦ *She turned **on** her toes, holding out her skirt.* ◦ *The wheels started to turn (**round**).* ◦ *Turn the steering wheel as quickly as you can.* ◦ *She turned the doorknob and quietly opened the door.* ◦ *Slowly, I turned the door handle.* **CHANGE DIRECTION** ▷ **2** (A2) [I or T] to (cause to) change the direction in which you are facing or moving: *Turn right at the traffic lights.* ◦ *The path **twists and** turns for the next half mile.* ◦ *We have to turn down/into/up the next road on the right.* ◦ *Plants tend to turn towards the source of light.* ◦ *She turned to face him.* ◦ *He turned **round** and waved to us.* ◦ *He turned **on his heel** (= turned quickly to face the opposite direction) and left the room.* ◦ *The person on my left turned **to** me and whispered 'Not another speech!'* ◦ *His wife tried to speak to him, but he turned his back (**on** her)/turned away (from her) (= moved himself round and away from her to show his anger).* ◦ *At about three o'clock, **the tide** started to turn (= the sea started to come closer to or move away from the beach).* ◦ *He turned his head to me to listen.* ◦ *I'll just turn the car **round** and go back the way we've come.* ◦ *We watched until the car had turned (= gone round) the corner.* ◦ *The army turned their guns **on** (= pointed them at and started to shoot at) the protesters.* ◦ *She can turn (= perform) a **somersault**.* **CHANGE POSITION** ▷ **3** (B1) [I or T] to move, or to move an object or page, so that a different side or surface is on the top: *Now turn the page, please, and start work on Exercise 2.* ◦ *She turned the vase **over** to look for the price.* ◦ *He turned **over** two or three pages.* ◦ *She put out the light, turned **over** (= rolled in order to face in another direction) and went to sleep.* ◦ *Now turn **to** (= open the book at) page 23 and look at the first paragraph.* **BECOME** ▷ **4** (B2) [L, I or T usually + adv/prep] to (cause to) become, change into, or come to be something: *The weather has suddenly turned cold.* ◦ *When I refused to pay, he turned nasty.* ◦ *She turned pale and started to shiver.* ◦ *The mood of the meeting*

T

turned solemn when the extent of the problem became known. ◦ *The companies worked well together for a time, but eventually the relationship turned sour (= became bad).* ◦ *Keele, pop star turned business tycoon, has launched a new range of cosmetics.* ◦ *The dry weather turned the soil* ***into/to*** *concrete.* ◦ *By the end of September, the leaves have started to turn (= become brown).* ◦ *Her attitude turned* ***from*** *politely interested* ***to*** *enthusiastic during the course of our conversation.* **5 turn 16, nine o'clock, etc.** C1 to become a particular age or time: *She turned 18 last year.* ◦ *It's just turned ten o'clock.* **SWITCH** ▷ **6** A2 [I or T, usually + adv/prep] to use a control to switch a piece of equipment or a power or water supply on or off, or to increase or reduce what it is producing: *Turn* ***off/out*** *the light.* ◦ *Who turned the telly* ***on****?* ◦ *I asked him to turn* ***down*** *the heating.* ◦ *Turn the sound* ***up*** *– I can't hear what they're saying.* ◦ *This sort of heater turns* ***off*** *(= can be switched off) at the mains.* **WOOD** ▷ **7** [T] specialized to shape a piece of wood while it is fixed to a machine that SPINS it: *a turned bowl*

IDIOMS **not turn a hair** to not show any emotion when you are told something bad or when something bad happens: *I was expecting him to be horrified when he heard the cost but he didn't turn a hair.* • **turn a blind eye** C1 to ignore something that you know is wrong: *Management often turn a blind eye* ***to*** *bullying in the workplace.* • **turn a deaf ear** to ignore someone when they complain or ask for something: *In the past they've tended to turn a deaf ear* ***to*** *such requests.* • **turn your back on sth** (also **turn away from sth**) C2 to stop being involved in something: *Spain cannot afford to turn its back on tourism.* • **turn your back on sb** C2 to refuse to help someone: *Surely you won't turn your back on them?* • **turn your hand to sth** If you say that someone could turn their hand to an activity or skill, you mean they could do it well although they have no experience of it: *Stella's very talented – she could turn her hand to anything.* • **turn your nose up** C2 to not accept something because you do not think it is good enough for you: *They turned their noses up* ***at*** *the only hotel that was available.* • **turn sth on its head** to cause something to be the opposite of what it was before: *These new findings turn the accepted theories on their head.* • **turn over a new leaf** C2 to start behaving in a better way • **turn sb's stomach** to make someone feel sick, often because they are angry or upset about something: *The sight of Joe eating raw fish is enough to turn your stomach.* ◦ *Just the smell makes my stomach turn.* • **turn sth upside down** to search everywhere for something, sometimes leaving a place very untidy: *I turned the apartment upside down but I couldn't find those photos.* • **turn tail** to turn around and run away, usually because you are frightened • **turn the clock back** If you try to turn the clock back, you want things to be the way they were in the past. • **turn the corner** If something or someone turns the corner, their situation starts to improve after a difficult period: *After nine months of poor sales we've finally turned the corner.* • **turn the other cheek** to not do anything to hurt someone who has hurt you: *Neither nation is renowned for turning the other cheek.* • **turn the tables on sb** to change a situation so that you now have an advantage over someone who previously had an advantage over you: *She turned the tables on her rival with allegations of corruption.*

PHRASAL VERBS **turn (sb) against sb/sth** to start not to like or agree with someone or something, or to make someone do this: *After six years of fighting public opinion has turned against the war.* ◦ *The girl's natural father claimed that her stepfather was turning her against him.* • **turn sth around/round** to change an unsuccessful business, plan, or system so that it becomes successful: *The new management team turned the ailing company around in under six months.* • **turn away** to move your face so you are not looking at something: *When they show an operation on TV, I have to turn away.* • **turn sb away** to not allow someone to enter a place: *They turned us away at the entrance because we hadn't got tickets.* • **turn (sb) back** B2 to return in the direction you have come from, or to make someone do this: *We're lost – we'll have to turn back.* • **turn sth/sb down** B2 to refuse an offer or request: *He offered her a trip to Australia but she turned it/him down.* ◦ *He turned down the job because it involved too much travelling.* • **turn in** informal to go to bed: *I usually turn in at about midnight.* • **turn sb in** to take a criminal to the police, or to go to them yourself to admit a crime: *The hit-and-run driver turned him****self*** *in* ***to*** *the police the day after the accident.* • **turn sth in RETURN** ▷ **1** to return something to an organization or a person in authority: *Please turn your old parking permits in at the end of the week.* **PRODUCE** ▷ **2** to produce results, usually good results: *Both companies turn in pretax profits of over 5.5 million annually.* • **turn (sb/sth) into sb/sth** B1 to change and become someone or something different, or to make someone or something do this: *The council was hoping to turn a children's home into a residence for adolescent girls.* ◦ *The town turned* ***from*** *a small seaside resort into a major commercial centre when oil was discovered.* • **turn off (sth)** to leave the road you are travelling on and travel along another one: *Turn off the motorway at the next exit.* • **turn sb off** informal to stop someone feeling interested or excited, especially sexually: *I should think the smell of her breath would turn any man off.* • **turn sth on** to start to show a particular quality: *He can really turn on* ***the charm*** *when he wants to.* • **turn on sb** to attack or criticize someone suddenly and unexpectedly: *Suddenly she just turned on me and accused me of undermining her.* • **turn on sth** If something turns on something else, it depends on it or is decided by it: *The success of the talks turns on* ***wh****ether both sides are willing to make some concessions.* • **turn sb on** informal to make someone feel interested or excited, especially sexually: *Short men really turn me on.* ◦ *'In my spare time I make models out of matchsticks.' 'Oh well,* ***whatever*** *turns you on, I suppose (= that would not interest me).'* • **turn out HAPPEN** ▷ **1** B2 to happen in a particular way or to have a particular result, especially an unexpected one: *As events turned out, we were right to have decided to leave early.* ◦ *How did the recipe turn out?* **2** B2 to be known or discovered finally and surprisingly: [+ to infinitive] *The truth turned out* ***to*** *be stranger than we had expected.* ◦ [+ that] ***It*** *turns* ***out that*** *she had known him when they were children.* **GO** ▷ **3** B2 If people turn out for an event, they go to be there or to watch: *Thousands of people turned out to welcome the England team home.* → Compare **turn up (somewhere)** • **turn sth out PRODUCE** ▷ **1** to produce or make something, often quickly or in large amounts: *They turn out thousands of these games every week.* **EMPTY** ▷ **2** If you turn out a container or the things in it, you empty it completely: *We turned out all the cupboards and drawers and found things we hadn't seen for years.* • **turn sb out REMOVE** ▷ **1** to force someone to leave: *He was turned out* ***of*** *his flat because he couldn't pay the rent.* **DRESS** ▷ **2 be beautifully, well, etc. turned out** to be beautifully, well, etc. dressed: *She's always beautifully turned out.* • **turn (sth) over** UK to change to a different television station: *This programme's*

T

boring – shall I turn over to BBC? • **turn over sth** If a business turns over a particular amount of money, it does that amount of business during a stated period: *The profits are not high, but the company turns over a large sum every year.* • **turn sth over** USE ▷ **1** to use or allow something to be used for a different purpose: *Grants are being offered to farmers who agree to turn over their land* ***to*** *woodland and forests.* THINK ▷ **2** to think about something for a period of time: *His father had been turning the idea over* ***in his mind*** *for some time.* • **turn somewhere/sth over** informal to steal something from a place or to search it, making it very untidy or causing damage: *Did you hear Paul's flat got turned over last week?* • **turn sth over to sb** to give something to someone in authority or someone who has a legal right to it, or to give someone legal responsibility for something: *They turned the videos over to the police.* ◦ *All documents are to be turned over to the court.* → See also **turn sth in** • **turn sb over to sb** to take a criminal to the police or other authority: *He was working here illegally and was terrified that his boss would turn him over to the police.* • **turn to sb/sth** B2 to ask a person or organization for help or support: *Without someone to turn to* ***for*** *advice, making the most appropriate choice can be difficult.* ◦ *Her family lived a long way away, and she had* ***no one to*** *turn to.* • **turn to sth** to start to do or use something bad, especially because you are unhappy: *She turned to drugs after the break-up of her marriage.* • **turn (sth) to sth** If someone turns to a particular subject or they turn their thoughts or attention to it, they begin to speak, think, or write about it: *I'd like us now to turn our* ***attention*** *to next year's budget.* ◦ *We're now going to turn to an issue that concerns us all – racism.* • **turn up (somewhere)** informal B2 to arrive or appear somewhere, usually unexpectedly or in a way that was not planned: *Do you think many people will turn up?* ◦ *She turned up at my house late one night.* • **turn up** HAPPEN ▷ **1** informal If a better situation or an opportunity to do something turns up, it happens or becomes available unexpectedly or in a way that was not planned: *Don't worry about it – something will turn up, you'll see.* ◦ *This job turned up just when I needed it.* FIND ▷ **2** If something that you have been looking for turns up, you find it unexpectedly: *The missing letter eventually turned up inside a book.* • **turn sth up** FOLD ▷ **1** to make a piece of clothing or part of a piece of clothing shorter, by folding the material and sewing it into position: *You could always turn the sleeves up.* DISCOVER ▷ **2** informal to discover something, especially information, after a lot of searching: *See what you can turn up about the family in the files.*

▸noun TIME TO DO STH ▷ **1** B1 [C] an opportunity or a duty to do something at a particular time or in a particular order, before or after other people: *Is it my turn yet?* ◦ [+ to infinitive] *I waited so long for my turn* ***to*** *see the careers adviser that I missed my train.* ◦ *It's your turn* ***to*** *do the washing up!* ◦ *In this game if you give the wrong answer you have to* ***miss*** *a turn.* → Compare **go** **2** **take turns** B2 (mainly UK **take it in turn(s)**) When a number of people take turns, they do the same thing one after the other: *We take turns* ***to*** *answer the phone.* **3** **in turn** C1 (also **by turns**) one after the other in an agreed order: *Each of us collects the mail in turn.* GO ROUND ▷ **4** [C] an action that causes something to move in a circle round a fixed point: *Give the screw a couple of turns to make sure it's tight.* CHANGE IN DIRECTION ▷ **5** B2 [C] a change in the direction in which you are moving or facing: *We got as far as the school, and there we had to* ***make*** *a right turn.* ◦ *The path was full of* ***twists and*** *turns.* **6** **on the turn** Something that is on the turn is about to change direction: *The tide is on the turn.* **7** **the turn of sth** C2 the point at which something changes or moves in a different direction: *the turn of the tide* ◦ *She was born around the turn of the century (= around 1900, 2000, etc.).* DEVELOPMENT ▷ **8** **take a … turn** to develop in a particular way: *The situation took a nasty turn and the police were called.* ◦ *Events took an unexpected turn when her mother suddenly arrived.* **9** **take a turn for the better/worse** C2 to suddenly become better or worse: *Their relationship took a turn for the worse when he lost his job.* PERFORMANCE ▷ **10** [C] a stage act or performance: *The first couple of turns were children singing and dancing.* ILLNESS ▷ **11** [C] old-fashioned informal a slight illness, a strange feeling, or a nervous shock: *After the accident I started having funny turns.* ◦ *It* ***gave*** *me quite* ***a*** *turn to see him after all these years.*

IDIOMS **a good/bad turn** [C usually singular] an action that helps/harms someone: *That's my good turn for the day!* ◦ *You* ***did*** *me a good turn warning me that Abigail was going to be there.* • **at every turn** If something unpleasant happens at every turn, it happens every time you try to do something: *They do their best to frustrate my efforts at every turn.* • **a turn of the screw** an action which makes a bad situation worse, especially one that forces someone to do something: *Each letter from my bank manager is another turn of the screw.* • **cooked/done to a turn** old-fashioned cooked for exactly the right amount of time: *The beef was done to a turn.* • **one good turn deserves another** saying said when you do a helpful or kind act for someone who has done something good for you • **speak/talk out of turn** to say something which you should not have said: *I'm sorry if I've spoken out of turn, but I thought everyone had already been told.*

turnabout /ˈtɜːn.ə.baʊt/ US /ˈtɝːn-/ noun [C] a complete change from one situation or condition to its opposite: *What accounts for the dramatic turnabout* ***in*** *Britain's international trading performance?*

turnaround /ˈtɜːn.ə.raʊnd/ US /ˈtɝːn-/ noun TIME TAKEN ▷ **1** [U] (UK usually **turnround**) the amount of time taken for something to happen after a vehicle, an instruction, or an order for goods arrives at a place: *We'll have to improve the turnaround – three days is too long.* ◦ *Turnaround* ***time*** *for the information is some four days and the average cost £12.* → See also **turn sth around/round** BIG CHANGE ▷ **2** [S] (UK also **turnround**) an occasion when a business, plan, or system suddenly becomes successful: *The chairman was responsible for the turnaround in the company's fortunes.* **3** [S] (UK also **turnround**) any change from one thing to its opposite: *What a turnaround – they were losing 3–0, but in the end they won 4–3.*

turncoat /ˈtɜːŋ.kəʊt/ US /ˈtɝːn-/ noun [C] disapproving a person who changes from one opinion to an opposite one in a way which shows they are not loyal to people who share the original opinion

turning /ˈtɜː.nɪŋ/ US /ˈtɝː-/ noun [C] B1 a place, especially a road, track or path, where you can leave the road you are on: ***Take*** *the third turning on the left after the traffic lights.*

ˈturning ˌcircle noun [C usually singular] (US usually **ˈturning ˌradius**) the amount of space a vehicle needs in order to go round in a complete circle

ˈturning ˌpoint noun [C usually singular] the time at which a situation starts to change in an important way: *ASH, the anti-smoking group, called the new regulations a turning point* ***in*** *the campaign against*

smoking. ◦ *The turning point in her political career came when she was chosen to fight a crucial by-election.*

turnip /ˈtɜː.nɪp/ (US) /ˈtɝː-/ noun [C] a rounded, white root that is eaten cooked as a vegetable, or the plant which produces it

turnkey /ˈtɜːŋ.kiː/ (US) /ˈtɝːn-/ adj [before noun] (of a piece of equipment) ready to be used immediately by the person who is buying or renting it: *More and more manufacturers are offering to tailor-make a turnkey system from their own components.*

ˌturn of eˈvents noun [C usually singular] (C2) a change in a situation: *an unexpected/strange/dramatic turn of events*

ˈturn-off noun **ROAD** ▷ **1** [C] a road which leaves another road to go in a different direction: *It's four kilometres to the turn-off **for** Norwich/the Norwich turn-off.* → See also **turn off (sth)** **DISLIKE** ▷ **2** [C usually singular] informal something which you dislike or which you do not find interesting or sexually exciting: *This system may provide a powerful tool for adults who find computers a turn-off yet need to learn to use them.* ◦ *Hairy backs are for me the ultimate turn-off.* → See also **turn sb off,** at **turn**

ˌturn of ˈmind noun [S] a characteristic way of thinking: *His natural supporters are the urban poor, and educated people of a liberal turn of mind.*

ˌturn of ˈphrase noun [C usually singular] **1** a way of saying something: *'Significant other' meaning 'partner' – now that's an interesting turn of phrase.* **2** the ability to express yourself well: *She has a nice turn of phrase, which should serve her well in journalism.*

ˈturn-on noun [C] informal something which you find exciting, especially sexually: *The smell of leather on a man is a real turn-on.* → See also **turn sb on**

turnout /ˈtɜː.naʊt/ (US) /ˈtɝːn-/ noun [C] the number of people who are present at an event, especially the number who go to vote at an election: *Good weather on polling day should ensure a good turnout.*

turnover /ˈtɜːnˌəʊ.vəʳ/ (US) /ˈtɝːnˌoʊ.vɚ/ noun **BUSINESS** ▷ **1** (C1) [C or U] the amount of business that a company does in a period of time: *Large supermarkets have **high** turnovers (= their goods sell very quickly).* ◦ *The business has an **annual** turnover of £50,000.* **EMPLOYEES** ▷ **2** (C2) [S or U] the rate at which employees leave a company and are replaced by new people: *The large number of temporary contracts resulted in a high turnover of staff.* ◦ US *They've had a lot of turnover at the factory recently.* **CAKE** ▷ **3** [C] a small cake made from a folded piece of pastry with fruit inside: *an apple turnover*

turnpike /ˈtɜː.n.paɪk/ (US) /ˈtɝːn-/ noun [C] (informal **pike**) US a main road that you usually have to pay to use

ˈturn ˌsignal noun [C] US for **indicator**

turnstile /ˈtɜːn.staɪl/ (US) /ˈtɝːn-/ noun [C] a device that controls the way into or out of a building, room, or area of land, especially one that you have to pay to enter. It is a post with a number of short poles sticking out from it that have to be pushed round as each person walks through the entrance: *The number of spectators going through the turnstiles is up on last season.*

turntable /ˈtɜːnˌteɪ.bl̩/ (US) /ˈtɝːn-/ noun [C] **1** a circular surface on a RECORD PLAYER on which the record is played **2** a circular surface on which a railway engine is turned around

ˈturn-up noun **FOLD** ▷ **1** [C] mainly UK (US usually **cuff**) a piece of material at the bottom of a trouser leg that is folded back: *trouser turn-ups* **EVENT** ▷ **2** [S] UK informal something that happens in an unexpected way or in a way that was not planned

IDIOM **turn-up for the book(s)** UK (US **one for the books**) a surprising or unexpected event: *Well, that's a turn-up for the books – I never thought he'd get the job.*

turpentine /ˈtɜː.pᵊn.taɪn/ (US) /ˈtɝː-/ noun [U] (informal **turps**) a clear liquid with a strong smell that burns easily. It is sometimes used in products for removing paint from brushes.

turpitude /ˈtɜː.pɪ.tjuːd/ (US) /ˈtɝː.pɪ.tuːd/ noun [U] formal evil: *acts/crimes of **moral** turpitude*

turquoise /ˈtɜː.kwɔɪz/ (US) /ˈtɝː.kɔɪz/ noun; adj
▸noun **1** [C or U] a bluish-green SEMI-PRECIOUS STONE that is often used in jewellery **2** [U] a bluish-green colour
▸adj bluish-green in colour: *the clear turquoise water of the bay*

turret /ˈtʌr.ət/ noun [C] **TOWER** ▷ **1** a small, circular tower that is part of a castle or a large building **GUN PART** ▷ **2** a part of a military vehicle that contains a large gun or guns and can be moved to face any direction • **turreted** /-ɪ.tɪd/ (US) /-ə.t̬ɪd/ adj with turrets

turtle /ˈtɜː.tl/ (US) /ˈtɝː.t̬l/ noun [C] (plural **turtles** or **turtle**) an animal which lives in or near water and has a thick shell covering its body into which it can move its head and legs for protection

ˈturtle dove noun [C] a small, pale brown bird that makes a soft pleasant sound

turtleneck /ˈtɜː.tl.nek/ (US) /ˈtɝː.t̬l-/ noun [C] **1** US for **polo neck** **2** UK (US **mock turtleneck**) a high, round collar that does not fold over on itself, or a JUMPER with this type of collar: *a turtleneck sweater*

turves /tɜːvz/ (US) /tɝːvz/ UK plural of **turf**

tush exclamation; noun
▸exclamation /tʌʃ/ old use used to say that something is stupid or not true
▸noun [C] /tʊʃ/ US slang the part of your body that you sit on; bottom: *I slipped on the ice and landed right on my tush!*

tusk /tʌsk/ noun [C] either of the two long, pointed teeth of some animals such as ELEPHANTS

tussle /ˈtʌs.l̩/ verb; noun
▸verb [I] **DISAGREE** ▷ **1** to have difficult disagreements or strong arguments: *During his twelve years in Congress he has tussled **with** the power companies on behalf of the ordinary person.* ◦ *The residents are still tussling **over** the ever-scarcer street parking.* **FIGHT** ▷ **2** to fight with another person using your arms and body: *The boys started to tussle in the corridor.*

PHRASAL VERB **tussle with sth** informal to try hard to understand or deal with a difficult idea or problem: *It's an idea that I've been tussling with for quite a while.*

▸noun **DISAGREEMENT** ▷ **1** [C] a difficult disagreement or violent argument: *a boardroom/bureaucratic/legal tussle* **FIGHT** ▷ **2** [C usually singular] a fight with another person using your arms and body: *From the state of his clothes and hair, he had been **in a** tussle.*

tut /tʌt/ exclamation; verb
▸exclamation (also **ˌtut-ˈtut**) used in writing to represent the sound made to show you disapprove of something, or a word said twice in a humorous way to suggest disapproval: *Tut, it's raining – I'm going to get soaked.* ◦ *You're late again – tut tut!*
▸verb [I] (**-tt-**) to make a disapproving sound or speak in a disapproving way: *He walked off, tutting to himself.* ◦ [+ speech] *'Still not out of bed?' she tutted (= said in a disapproving way).*

tutelage /ˈtjuː.tɪ.lɪdʒ/ (US) /ˈtuː.t̬ᵊl.ɪdʒ/ noun [U] formal help, advice, or teaching about how to do something: ***Under the** tutelage **of** Professor Roberts, the 900 delegates assessed and discussed the social market economy.*

tutor /ˈtjuː.təʳ/ ⓊⓈ /ˈtuː.t̬ɚ/ **noun** [C] **B2** a teacher who works with one student or a small group, either at a British college or university or in the home of a child: *His tutor encouraged him to read widely in philosophy.* ◦ *During my illness I was taught by a series of **home** tutors.* • **tutor verb** [T] *Children are routinely tutored for hours after school.*

tutorial /tjuːˈtɔː.ri.əl/ ⓊⓈ /tuːˈtɔːr.i-/ **noun** [C] a period of study with a tutor involving one student or a small group

tutu /ˈtuː.tuː/ **noun** [C] a very short skirt made of many layers of very thin, stiff material, worn by female BALLET dancers

tu-whit tu-whoo /tʊˌwɪt.tʊˈwuː/ **exclamation** used in writing to represent the sound made by an OWL

tuxedo /tʌkˈsiː.dəʊ/ ⓊⓈ /-doʊ/ **noun** [C] (plural **tuxedos**) (informal **tux**) mainly US for **dinner jacket**

TV /ˌtiːˈviː/ **noun** [C or U] **A1** abbreviation for television: *We ate **in front of** (= while watching) the TV.* ◦ *What's **on** TV tonight?* ◦ *You **watch** too much TV!* ◦ *TV personalities*

> **! Common mistake: TV**
>
> Remember that **TV** is written with capital 'T' and capital 'V' and without full stops.
>
> Don't write 'tv' or 't.v.', write **TV**:
>
> ~~*What's on t.v. tonight?*~~
>
> *What's on TV tonight?*

ˌTV ˈdinner noun [C] a meal that can be bought already prepared from a shop and only needs to be heated before being eaten, especially while watching television

twaddle /ˈtwɒd.l̩/ ⓊⓈ /ˈtwɑː.dl̩/ **noun** [U] informal speech or writing that is silly or not true: *She dismissed the findings as **utter** twaddle/**a load of old** twaddle.* → Synonym **nonsense**

twain /tweɪn/ **number** old use two

twang /twæŋ/ **verb; noun**

▸**verb** [I or T] to make a noise like that of a tight string being quickly pulled and released: *He twanged the guitar string/his braces.* ◦ *The springs twanged.*

▸**noun** [C usually singular] **SOUND** ▷ **1** a noise like that of a tight string being quickly pulled and released: *We heard a twang as the cable broke.* **VOICE** ▷ **2** a quality of the human voice, produced by air passing out through the nose as you speak: *a nasal/southern twang*

'twas /twɒz/ ⓊⓈ /twɑːz/ old use short form of it was: *'Twas the night before Christmas.*

twat /twæt/ **noun** [C] **SEX ORGAN** ▷ **1** offensive offensive for the **vagina PERSON** ▷ **2** UK offensive a stupid or unpleasant person

tweak /twiːk/ **verb** [T] **PULL** ▷ **1** to pull and twist something with a small sudden movement: *Standing in front of the mirror she tweaked a strand of hair into place.* **CHANGE SLIGHTLY** ▷ **2** to change something slightly, especially in order to make it more correct, effective, or suitable: *The software is pretty much there – it just needs a little tweaking.* ◦ *You just need to tweak the last paragraph and then it's done.* • **tweak noun** [C] *He gave the boy's nose a tweak.*

twee /twiː/ **adj** mainly UK informal disapproving artificially attractive or too perfect: *The village has escaped all modern developments, yet without becoming twee or 'preserved'.*

tweed /twiːd/ **noun 1** [C or U] a thick material made from wool of several different colours: *a tweed jacket* **2 tweeds** [plural] clothes made from tweed, especially a jacket and matching trousers/skirt: *He wore tweeds and smoked a pipe.*

tweedy /ˈtwiː.di/ **adj 1** of or like tweed: *a tweedy sports jacket* **2** describes the life of rich people with homes in the countryside and an interest in sports like hunting: *We met a tweedy man walking a couple of dogs.*

tween /twiːn/ **noun** [C] US a child between the ages of approximately eight and twelve: *Here are some of the best gifts for tweens.* ◦ *tween clothing*

tweenager /ˈtwiːn.eɪ.dʒəʳ/ ⓊⓈ /-dʒɚ/ **noun** [C] a young person between the ages of approximately eight and twelve

tweet /twiːt/ **noun; verb**

▸**noun** [C] informal **BIRD** ▷ **1** a short, high sound made by a bird **SOCIAL MEDIA** ▷ **2** trademark a short remark or piece of information published on TWITTER™

▸**verb BIRD** ▷ **1** [I] When a bird tweets, it makes a short, high sound: *We could hear the baby birds tweeting.* **SOCIAL MEDIA** ▷ **2** [I or T] trademark to publish a short remark or piece of information on TWITTER™: *He tweeted **that** he was just about to meet the president.*

tweeter /ˈtwiː.təʳ/ ⓊⓈ /ˈtwiː.t̬ɚ/ **noun** [C] **SOUND SYSTEM** ▷ **1** a LOUDSPEAKER designed to produce the high notes in a SOUND SYSTEM → Compare **woofer SOCIAL MEDIA** ▷ **2** a person who uses the SOCIAL NETWORKING service TWITTER™

tweezers /ˈtwiː.zəz/ ⓊⓈ /-zɚz/ **noun** [plural] (US also **tweezer**) a small piece of equipment made of two narrow strips of metal joined at one end. It is used to pull out hairs or to pick up small objects by pressing the two strips of metal together with the fingers: *a pair of tweezers* ◦ *eyebrow tweezers*

twelfth /twelfθ/ **ordinal number** 12th written as a word: *Our next meeting is on **the** twelfth (**of** May).*

ˌtwelfth ˈman noun [C] (plural **twelfth men**) UK in a cricket team, a RESERVE (= extra player)

ˌTwelfth ˈNight noun [C or U] 6 January, twelve days after Christmas, or the evening before

twelve /twelv/ **number A1** the number 12: *The cafeteria opens for lunch at twelve (o'clock).* ◦ *a twelve-seater minibus* → See also **dozen**

twenties /ˈtwen.tiz/ ⓊⓈ /-t̬iz/ **noun** [plural] **1 B2** A person's twenties are the period in which they are aged between 20 and 29: *I'd guess she's **in** her twenties.* **2 the twenties a** the range of temperature between 20° and 29°: *The temperature is expected to be **in** the twenties tomorrow.* **b B2** the DECADE (= period of ten years) between 20 and 29 in any century, usually 1920–1929 or 2020–2029: *She was born **in** the twenties.*

twentieth /ˈtwen.ti.əθ/ ⓊⓈ /-t̬i-/ **ordinal number** 20th written as a word

twenty /ˈtwen.ti/ ⓊⓈ /-t̬i/ **number A1** the number 20: *nineteen, twenty, twenty-one* ◦ *space for twenty people* → See also **score**

ˌtwenty-ˈfirst ordinal number; noun

▸**ordinal number** 21st written as a word: *the twenty-first century*

▸**noun** [C] (also **ˌtwenty-first ˈbirthday**) the day on

which a person reaches the age of 21 and is traditionally said, in Western societies, to become an adult: *It's Jamie's twenty-first next Friday.* ◦ *Her dad gave her a car for her twenty-first.*

ˌtwenty-four-ˌhour ˈclock noun [S] the **24-hour clock**

ˌtwenty-four ˈseven adv, adj (also **24/7**) 24 hours a day, 7 days a week; all the time: *a football website updated 24/7* ◦ *Having a kid is a 24/7 job.*

ˌtwenty-ˌtwenty ˈvision noun [U] (also **20/20 vision**) perfect sight, especially as measured by a standard test: *The optician told me I had twenty-twenty vision.*

'twere /twɜːʳ/ US /twɝː/ old use short form of it were: *We hold, as 'twere, the mirror up to nature to find out who we are.*

twerp (also **twirp**) /twɜːp/ US /twɝːp/ noun [C] old-fashioned informal a stupid person

twice /twaɪs/ predeterminer, adv A2 two times: *I've already asked him twice.* ◦ *The post comes twice daily (= two times every day).* ◦ *There are twice as many houses in this area as there used to be.* ◦ *The state is at least twice as big as England.* ◦ *He's twice her size (= much bigger than she is).*

twiddle /ˈtwɪd.l̩/ verb; noun

▸verb [I or T] to move something repeatedly between your fingers, especially without any purpose: *She was twiddling (**with**) a pencil/her hair.* ◦ *Twiddle **a dial/knob** on a radio in Britain and you may hear voices speaking French or German.*

IDIOM **twiddle your thumbs** to do nothing for a period of time, usually while you are waiting for something to happen: *I arrived early for the meeting so I was twiddling my thumbs for half an hour.*

▸noun [C] an act of turning something with the fingers: *At the twiddle of a knob the operators can focus on a tiny amount of airspace or scan the whole area.*

twiddly /ˈtwɪd.l̩.i/, /-li/ adj informal curly or decorative, especially in an unnecessary way: *The frame has twiddly **bits** at the corners which get very dusty.*

twig /twɪɡ/ noun; verb

▸noun [C] a small, thin branch of a tree or bush, especially one removed from the tree or bush and without any leaves: *We collected dry twigs to start the fire.*

▸verb [I or T] (**-gg-**) informal to suddenly realize something: [+ question word] *Then he twigged **what** I meant.* ◦ *She's six months pregnant and he still hasn't twigged.*

twilight /ˈtwaɪ.laɪt/ noun; adj

▸noun EVENING ▷ **1** [U] the period just before it becomes completely dark in the evening: *I could make out a dark figure in **the** twilight.* FINAL PART ▷ **2 the twilight of sth** literary the final part of a period: *I knew him when he was **in** the twilight of his career.*

IDIOM **twilight years** the last years of someone's life: *Old people often rely on pets for comfort and companionship in their twilight years.*

▸adj literary used to describe a way of life that involves illegal or immoral activities, and is on the edge of normal society: *The remaining inhabitants of this once-prosperous market town have got used to a twilight **existence**.* ◦ *Leaving a secure job for the twilight **world** of pop music was perhaps a mistake.*

IDIOM **twilight zone** an area where two different ways of life or states of existence meet: *the twilight zone **between** life and death*

twilit /ˈtwaɪ.lɪt/ adj literary in the twilight; becoming dark but not yet completely dark: *a twilit street/room*

twill /twɪl/ noun [U] a strong cotton cloth that has raised DIAGONAL (= sloping) lines on the surface

twin /twɪn/ noun; adj; verb

▸noun [C] **1** B1 either of two children born to the same mother on the same occasion: *My sister has twin sons.* ◦ *a twin sister* **2** one of two very similar things: *The two countries are often regarded as economic twins.*

▸adj [before noun] **1** used to describe two similar things that are a pair: *twin towers* ◦ *a car with twin exhausts* **2** existing at the same time: *his twin obsessions – women and cars*

▸verb UK **be twinned with** If a town in one country is twinned with a town in another country, the two towns have a special relationship: *Cambridge is twinned with Heidelberg.*

ˌtwin ˈbed noun [C] one of a pair of two beds that are each big enough for one person • **twin-ˈbedded** adj *I'd like to book one twin-bedded room and one double room.*

twine /twaɪn/ verb; noun

▸verb [I or T, usually + adv/prep] to (cause to) wrap round an object several times: *The vine twines **round/up** the pole.* ◦ *Twine the different coloured threads **together**.* → See also **entwine, intertwine** • **twining** /ˈtwaɪ.nɪŋ/ adj *a twining plant*

▸noun [U] strong string made of two or more pieces of string twisted together: *a ball of twine* ◦ *garden twine*

twinge /twɪndʒ/ noun [C] a sudden short feeling of physical or mental pain: *I **felt a** twinge in my knee.* ◦ *He was feeling twinges from a calf injury after 20 minutes of the game.* ◦ *I admit I felt a twinge **of** guilt as we left.*

twinkle /ˈtwɪŋ.kl̩/ verb; noun

▸verb [I] (of light or a shiny surface) to shine repeatedly strongly then weakly, as if flashing on and off very quickly: *The lights of the town twinkled in the distance.* ◦ *The stars twinkled in the clear sky.* ◦ *His brown eyes twinkled behind the gold-rimmed glasses.*

▸noun [S] an act of twinkling: *the twinkle of the stars/lights/diamonds* ◦ *He was holding the phone with a mischievous twinkle **in** his **eye** (= expression of amusement).*

IDIOM **when sb was a (mere) twinkle in their father's eye** humorous at a time before someone was born

twinkling /ˈtwɪŋ.kl̩.ɪŋ/, /-klɪŋ/ noun [S] old-fashioned a very short time: *I shall be there **in a** twinkling.*

IDIOM **in the twinkling of an eye** If something happens in the twinkling of an eye, it happens very quickly: *Microprocessors do the calculations in the twinkling of an eye.*

twinset /ˈtwɪn.set/ noun [C] a woman's JUMPER and CARDIGAN that have the same colour or pattern and are worn together: *She always wore a twinset **and pearls**.*

ˌtwin ˈtown noun [C] UK (US **ˈsister ˌcity**) a town or city which shares planned activities and visits with a similar town in another country: *Cambridge and Heidelberg are twin towns.*

twirl /twɜːl/ US /twɝːl/ verb [I or T, usually + adv/prep] to (cause to) give a sudden quick turn or set of turns in a circle: *She danced and twirled across the room.* ◦ *He twirled the ribbon round the stick.* ◦ *He twirled his **umbrella** as he walked.* ◦ *She twirled her baton high in the air as she led the parade.* • **twirl** noun [C] *She **did a** twirl (= turned quickly round) in her new skirt.*

twirler /ˈtwɜː.ləʳ/ US /ˈtwɝː.lɚ/ noun [C] (also **majorette**) US a girl who marches as part of a group while

T

turning a BATON (= short metal stick) or throwing it in the air and then catching it

twirling /ˈtwɜː.lɪŋ/ (US) /ˈtwɝː-/ noun [U] US the action or skill of spinning a BATON

twirly /ˈtwɜː.li/ (US) /ˈtwɝː-/ adj informal with turns or curls: *a twirly moustache* ◦ *twirly writing*

twirp /twɜːp/ (US) /twɝːp/ noun [C] a **twerp**

twist /twɪst/ verb; noun

▸verb **TURN** ▷ **1** (C2) [I or T] to turn something, especially repeatedly, or to turn or wrap one thing around another: *The path twists* ***and turns*** *for over a mile.* ◦ *She sat there nervously twisting the ring around on her finger.* ◦ *She twisted her head (round) so she could see what was happening.* ◦ *Twist the rope tightly round that post over there.* **2** (C1) [T] If you twist a part of your body, such as your ANKLE, you injure it by suddenly turning it: *She slipped on the ice and twisted her knee.* **CHANGE** ▷ **3** (C2) [T] disapproving to change information so that it gives the message you want it to give, especially in a way that is dishonest: *This report shows how she twisted the truth to claim successes where none, in fact, existed.* ◦ *You're twisting my words – that's not what I said at all.*

IDIOMS **twist sb's arm** to persuade someone to do something they do not want to do: *I didn't want to go but Linda twisted my arm.* • **twist sb around/round your little finger** to be able to persuade someone to do anything you want, usually because they like you so much

▸noun **TURN** ▷ **1** [C] an act of twisting something: *She gave the cap another twist to make sure it was tight.* **2** [C] the shape of or a piece of something that has been twisted: *a twist* ***of*** *hair* ◦ *a twist* ***of*** *lemon* **3** [C] a tight bend: *a path with many twists* ***and turns*** **CHANGE** ▷ **4** [C] a change in the way in which something happens: *The story* ***took*** *a surprise twist today with media reports that the doctor had resigned.* ◦ *The incident was the* ***latest*** *twist in the continuing saga of fraud and high scandal in banks and stockbroking firms.* ◦ *But for a cruel twist* ***of fate/fortune***, *he could now be running his own business.* ◦ *There's an unexpected twist* ***in/to*** *the plot towards the end of the film.* **5** [C] a complicated situation or plan of action: *the twists* ***and turns*** *of fate* ◦ *It has proved very difficult to unravel the twists* ***and turns*** *and contradictions of the evidence.* **DANCE** ▷ **6 the twist** [S] a dance in which people stay in one place and twist their bodies from side to side to music

IDIOM **be/go round the twist** (also **send sb round the twist**) to be, become, or make someone else become angry or unable to behave in a reasonable way: *If I'd stayed there any longer, I'd have gone round the twist.*

twisted /ˈtwɪs.tɪd/ adj **BENT** ▷ **1** (B2) bent so that the original shape is changed or destroyed: *a twisted tree trunk* ◦ *a twisted ankle* ◦ *twisted metal* **STRANGE** ▷ **2** (C2) strange and slightly unpleasant or cruel: *The letter was clearly the product of a twisted* ***mind***. ◦ *The experience had left her* ***bitter and*** *twisted.*

twister /ˈtwɪs.təʳ/ (US) /-tɚ/ noun [C] US informal a **tornado** or a **whirlwind**

ˈ**twist tie** noun [C] mainly US a short piece of wire covered in plastic or paper that is used to fasten a plastic bag

twisty /ˈtwɪs.ti/ adj informal describes a road with many turns

twit /twɪt/ noun [C] informal a stupid person: *He's such a twit!* ◦ *You stupid twit!*

twitch /twɪtʃ/ verb; noun

▸verb **MOVE SLIGHTLY** ▷ **1** [I or T] (to cause) to make a sudden small movement with a part of the body, usually without intending to: *He tried to suppress a smile but felt the corner of his mouth twitch.* ◦ *She twitched her nose like a rabbit.* **PULL** ▷ **2** [T] to give something a sudden light pull: *You'll feel something twitch the line when you get a fish.*

▸noun [C] **UNCONTROLLED MOVEMENT** ▷ **1** a sudden small, usually unintentional, movement of a part of the body: *I've got a twitch at the corner of my eye.* **PULL** ▷ **2** a sudden light pull or movement

twitcher /ˈtwɪtʃ.əʳ/ (US) /-ɚ/ noun [C] UK informal a BIRDWATCHER (= someone whose hobby is studying wild birds in their natural environment)

twitchy /ˈtwɪtʃ.i/ adj nervous and worried, sometimes showing this through sudden movements or movements which do not appear smooth or relaxed: *On camera he appears twitchy and ill at ease.* ◦ *The president is getting twitchy about the fall in his popularity.*

twitter /ˈtwɪt.əʳ/ (US) /ˈtwɪt̬.ɚ/ verb [I] **BIRD** ▷ **1** (of a bird) to make a series of short, high sounds: *I was woken up by a bird twittering just outside my window.* **PERSON** ▷ **2** to talk quickly and nervously in a high voice, saying very little of importance or interest: *She comes in here when I'm trying to work and just twitters* ***on*** *about nothing.* • **twitter** noun [C]

Twitter /ˈtwɪt.əʳ/ (US) /ˈtwɪt̬.ɚ/ noun [U] trademark a website where people or organizations can publish short remarks or pieces of information, and where you can see information published by people or organizations that you choose: *I always read her column, and I follow her* ***on*** *Twitter.*

ˈ**twixt** /twɪkst/ preposition old use or literary between

two /tuː/ number (A1) the number 2: *They've got two houses.* ◦ *He'll be two (years old) in February.*

IDIOMS **be in two minds** UK (US **be of two minds**) (C1) to be unable to decide about something: *I was in two minds whether or not to come this morning.* • **be two of a kind** If two people are two of a kind, they are very similar: *'Patrick and Glyn got on really well, didn't they?' 'Yes, well they're two of a kind.'* • **have two left feet** humorous to move in a very awkward way when dancing: *When we danced together, I discovered he had two left feet.* • **it takes two to tango** saying said when you want to emphasize that both people involved in a difficult situation must accept the blame, or that an activity needs two people who are willing to take part for it to happen • **(there's) no two ways about it.** something that you say in order to emphasize that something is true: *She was the meanest person I've ever met – no two ways about it.* • **or two** (B1) used to talk about a small number or amount of something: *It will only take a minute or two.* • **put two and two together** informal to guess the truth about a situation from what you have seen or heard: *'How did you know they were having an affair?' 'I'd seen them out together a couple of times so I just put two and two together.'* • **put two and two together and make five** informal humorous to understand a particular situation wrongly, often in a way that is more shocking or exciting than the truth: *'Why ever did she think you were pregnant?' 'I was sick once or twice and I suppose she just put two and two together and made five.'* • **that makes two of us** something that you say to tell someone that you are in the same unpleasant situation, or have the same negative feelings as them: *'I have no idea what's going on.' 'That makes two of us!'* • **two can play at that game** informal something that you say when you intend to harm someone in the same way as they have harmed you:

Well, when I found out that my husband had been having an affair I thought two can play at that game! • **your two cents' worth** US informal your spoken opinion on a particular matter: *I thought I'd just* ***throw in*** *(= add) my two cents' worth.* • **two's company, three's a crowd** saying said when two people are relaxed and enjoying each other's company but another person would make them feel less comfortable

ˈtwo-bit adj [before noun] US informal disapproving worth very little, or not very important: *He plays a two-bit Chicago gangster in the play.*

ˌtwo ˈbits noun [plural] US informal 25 CENTS

ˌtwo-diˈmensional adj **SHAPE** ▷ **1** flat, having width and length but not depth **TOO SIMPLE** ▷ **2** disapproving A person or story that is two-dimensional is too simple, showing little deep, serious thought, or understanding: *I didn't believe in any of the characters in the book – they were somehow two-dimensional.*

ˌtwo-ˈedged adj **BLADE** ▷ **1** having two sharp edges for cutting: *a two-edged sword* **TWO MEANINGS** ▷ **2** A two-edged remark can be understood in two very different ways, one of them positive and one of them negative: *'That was amazingly generous of you!' 'Well, that was a two-edged comment – are you saying I'm usually mean?'*

ˌtwo-ˈfaced adj disapproving describes someone who is not sincere, saying unpleasant things about you to other people while seeming to be pleasant when they are with you

ˌtwo ˈfingers noun [plural] UK in Britain, a sign that is considered rude, made by holding your hand up with your PALM facing towards you and your first and second fingers held in a V shape: *She drove past and* ***stuck*** *two fingers* ***up at*** *him.*

ˌtwo-ˈhanded adj Something that is two-handed needs or involves the use of both hands at the same time: *a two-handed saw* ◦ *My tennis is really improving – I've got a formidable two-handed backhand.*

two-hander /ˌtuːˈhæn.dəʳ/ (US) /-dɚ/ noun [C] UK a play written for two actors

twopence /ˈtʌp.ᵊns/ noun [C or U] **tuppence**

twopenny /ˈtʌp.ᵊn.i/, /-ni/ adj [before noun] (also **tuppenny**) costing or worth two pence: *a twopenny chew (= type of sweet)*

ˈtwo-ˌpiece noun [C usually singular] a set of clothes which consists of two separate matching parts, especially a woman's clothes for swimming, or a man's matching jacket and trousers

ˈtwo-ˌply adj, noun [U] Two-ply material, wood, or wool consists of two layers or two sets of thread for added thickness or strength.

ˌtwo-ˈseater noun [C] a car that has seats for only two people

twosome /ˈtuː.səm/ noun [C] two people considered together: *Zoe and I were inseparable as kids – my mother used to call us the terrible twosome.*

ˈtwo-time verb [T] informal A person who two-times someone they are having a relationship with deceives them by having a secret sexual relationship with someone else at the same time: *I finished with him when I found out he was two-timing me.*

ˈtwo-ˌtimer noun [C] informal a person who deceives their partner by having a secret sexual relationship with someone else

ˈtwo-tone adj Clothes or shoes that are two-tone are two different colours or are a lighter and a darker type of the same colour.

'twould /twʊd/ old use short form of it would: *'Twould do me good to hear of such a thing.*

two-ˌup two-ˈdown noun [C] UK informal a small house on two levels that has just two main rooms on the ground floor and two bedrooms on the top floor: *a modest two-up two-down*

ˈtwo-way adj **DIRECTION** ▷ **1** [before noun] moving or allowing movement in both directions: *a two-way street* **RADIO** ▷ **2** [before noun] describes radios that can both send out and receive signals **RELATIONSHIP** ▷ **3** describes a situation that involves two people or two groups of people working together to achieve a shared aim: *Negotiations are a two-way thing – both sides have to come to a compromise.* ◦ *Remember, friendships are a* ***two-way street*** *(= both people have to make an effort).*

ˌtwo-way ˈmirror noun [C] a mirror that can be used in the usual way from one side but is transparent from the other side and can therefore be used to watch people without them knowing

ˌtwo-ˈwheeler noun [C] a vehicle with two wheels such as a motorcycle or MOTOR SCOOTER

tycoon /taɪˈkuːn/ noun [C] a person who has succeeded in business or industry and has become very rich and powerful: *a business/property/shipping tycoon*

tyke (also **tike**) /taɪk/ noun [C] **1** UK informal a child who behaves badly in a way that is funny rather than serious: *Come here, you cheeky little tyke!* **2** informal a young child

Tylenol /ˈtaɪ.lə.nɒl/ (US) /-nɑːl/ noun [C or U] US trademark a common drug in the US which reduces pain: *I was taking Tylenol for my arthritis.*

type /taɪp/ noun; verb

▸**noun GROUP** ▷ **1** (A2) [C] a particular group of people or things which share similar characteristics and form a smaller division of a larger set: *There were so many different types* ***of*** *bread that I didn't know which to buy.* ◦ *What type* ***of*** *clothes does she wear?* ◦ *It was dark so I didn't notice what type* ***of*** *car it was.* ◦ *He's the type* ***of*** *man you could take home to your mother.* ◦ *He's very attractive, if you like the blond, athletic type.* ◦ *They sell dried flowers and baskets and that type* ***of thing***. ◦ *We have a range of moisturizers for all different skin types.* ◦ *She was young and she was wearing student-type clothes so I assumed she was studying here.* ◦ *He took me to a pub in Soho full of actor types speaking at the tops of their voices.* **2** (C1) [C] specialized a person who seems to represent a particular group of people, having all the qualities that you usually connect with that group: *He doesn't use fully rounded characters in his plays – he uses types.* **3 be sb's type** (C2) to be the type of person that someone thinks is attractive: *He's a nice enough guy – he's just not my type.* ◦ *I'd have thought Ben was more your type.* **PRINTED LETTERS** ▷ **4** [C or U] (specialized **typeface**) the style and size of printed letters used in a piece of printed writing such as in a newspaper, book, or article: *Use bold type for your headings.* ◦ *The software allows you to choose from over 20 sorts of typeface.*

▸**verb** [I or T] **WRITE** ▷ (B1) to write using a machine, either a computer keyboard or a TYPEWRITER: *She asked me to type a couple of letters.* ◦ *He can type very quickly.* ◦ *I was typing* ***away*** *into the early hours of the morning just to get the thing finished.*

PHRASAL VERBS **type sth in** If you type an instruction or piece of information in, you press the necessary letters, numbers, or other keys on your computer keyboard: *Type in your password.* • **type sth up** to

T

make a typed copy of a piece of text that is written by hand: *Could you type up the minutes from the meeting, please?*

typecast /ˈtaɪp.kɑːst/ ⓤⓢ /-kæst/ verb [T] (**typecast, typecast**) to always give an actor the same type of character to play, usually because he or she is physically suited to that type of part: *She soon found herself typecast **as** a dizzy blonde.*

typeface /ˈtaɪp.feɪs/ noun [C] letters and numbers in a particular design, used in printing or on a computer screen

typescript /ˈtaɪp.skrɪpt/ noun [C] a typed copy of a piece of writing such as a book

typewriter /ˈtaɪpˌraɪ.təʳ/ ⓤⓢ /-t̬ɚ/ noun [C] a machine with keys that you press to produce letters and numbers on paper: *He still uses an old typewriter.*

typewritten /ˈtaɪpˌrɪt.ən/ ⓤⓢ /-ˌrɪt̬-/ adj printed using a typewriter or computer: *a typewritten memo*

typhoid (fever) /ˌtaɪ.fɔɪdˈfiː.vəʳ/ ⓤⓢ /-vɚ/ noun [U] an infectious disease spread by dirty water and food, causing a high body temperature, red spots on the upper body, severe pains in the bowels, and sometimes death

typhoon /taɪˈfuːn/ noun [C] a violent wind that has a circular movement, found in the West Pacific Ocean: *The 169,000-ton vessel went down during a typhoon in the South China Sea.*

typhus /ˈtaɪ.fəs/ noun [U] an infectious disease spread by LICE (= small insects which live on the body) causing a high body temperature, severe pains in the head, and purple spots on the body

typical /ˈtɪp.ɪ.kəl/ adj **1** Ⓑ1 showing all the characteristics that you would usually expect from a particular group of things: *I must look like the typical tourist with my shorts and my camera.* ◦ *This sort of hot and spicy food is very typical **of** the food in the south of the country.* ◦ *Typical symptoms would include severe headaches, vomiting and dizziness.* **2** disapproving showing all the bad characteristics that you expect from someone or something, often in a way that is annoying: *It's just typical **of** Ian to spend all that money on the equipment and then lose interest half way through the course.* ◦ *'He phoned in at the last minute to say he wasn't coming.' 'Typical!'*

typically /ˈtɪp.ɪ.kəl.i/ adv **1** Ⓑ2 in a way that shows all the characteristics that you would expect from the stated person, thing, or group: *She has that reserve and slight coldness of manner which is typically English.* ◦ *Paul, in typically rude fashion, told him he was talking rubbish.* **2** Ⓑ1 used when you are giving an average or usual example of a particular thing: *Typically, a doctor will see about 30 patients a day.* ◦ *Tickets for such events will typically cost around thirty dollars.*

typify /ˈtɪp.ɪ.faɪ/ verb [T, not continuous] **1** Something which typifies a particular group of things shows all the characteristics that you would usually expect from it: *With her cropped hair and her mannish clothes, she typifies the sort of feminist often feared by men.* **2** to be characteristic of something

typing /ˈtaɪ.pɪŋ/ noun [U] using a computer keyboard or a TYPEWRITER to produce documents or text: *It's the usual boring secretarial job – a bit of typing and some filing.* ◦ *a typing error*

typist /ˈtaɪ.pɪst/ noun [C] **1** used to say how good someone is at typing: *I'm a poor typist.* **2** old-fashioned a person whose job is to TYPE letters, reports, and other documents

typo /ˈtaɪ.pəʊ/ ⓤⓢ /-poʊ/ noun [C] informal a small mistake in a text made when it was TYPED or printed

typography /taɪˈpɒg.rə.fi/ ⓤⓢ /-ˈpɑː.grə-/ noun [U] the design of the writing in a piece of printing or on a computer screen • **typographical** /ˌtaɪ.pəˈgræf.ɪ.kəl/ ⓤⓢ /-poʊ-/ adj (also **typographic**) *a typographical error*

typology /taɪˈpɒl.ə.dʒi/ ⓤⓢ /-ˈpɑː.lə-/ noun [C or U] the study of types, or a system of dividing things into types

tyrannical /tɪˈræn.ɪ.kəl/ adj using, showing, or relating to the unfair and cruel use of power over other people in a country, group, etc.: *a tyrannical leader/regime/political system* • **tyrannically** /-i/ adv

tyrannize (UK usually **tyrannise**) /ˈtɪr.ən.aɪz/ verb [T] to treat someone cruelly, controlling everything that they do: *He was one of those school bullies who tyrannized the whole playground.*

tyrannosaurus /tɪˌræn.əˈsɔː.rəs/, /taɪ-/ ⓤⓢ /-ˈsɔːr.əs/ noun [C] (also **tyrannosaur**) a very large DINOSAUR with large, powerful back legs, small front legs and a long tail

tyranny /ˈtɪr.ən.i/ noun [U] **1** government by a ruler or small group of people who have unlimited power over the people in their country or state and use it unfairly and cruelly: *This, the president promised us, was a war against tyranny.* **2** a situation in which someone or something controls how you are able to live, in an unfair way: *Women, the play seems to suggest, must resist **the** tyranny **of** domesticity.*

tyrant /ˈtaɪə.rənt/ ⓤⓢ /ˈtaɪ-/ noun [C] a ruler who has unlimited power over other people, and uses it unfairly and cruelly: *Tamir, one of several sons of the exiled ruler, vowed he would liberate his country from the tyrant.* ◦ figurative humorous *Overnight my boss seems to have turned into a tyrant.*

tyre UK (US **tire**) /taɪəʳ/ ⓤⓢ /taɪr/ noun [C] Ⓐ2 a thick rubber ring, often filled with air, that is fitted around the outer edge of the wheel of a vehicle, allowing the vehicle to stick to the road surface and to travel over the ground more easily: *I've got a **flat** tyre (= the air has gone out of it).* ◦ *He was driving along the motorway when his tyre burst.* ◦ *I keep a **spare** tyre in the back of the car.*

tyro /ˈtaɪ.rəʊ/ ⓤⓢ /-roʊ/ noun [C] (plural **tyros**) a person who is new to an activity: *I look forward to seeing this young tyro's next ballet.*

tzar /zɑːʳ/ ⓤⓢ /zɑːr/ noun [C] a **tsar**

tzetze fly /ˈtet.siˌflaɪ/ noun [C or U] a **tsetse fly**

T

U, u /juː/ noun; adj

▸**noun** (plural **Us**, **U's** or **u's**) **LETTER** ▷ **1** [C or U] the 21st letter of the English alphabet **COLLEGE** ▷ **2** [U] US written abbreviation for **university**: *She goes to Kansas U/Sydney U.* **FILM** ▷ **3** [C or U] abbreviation for **universal**: a film or a symbol for a film that is considered suitable for children of any age

▸**adj** **FILM** ▷ abbreviation for **universal**: used to refer to a film that is considered suitable for children of any age

the UAE /juː.eɪˈiː/ noun abbreviation for the United Arab Emirates

ˈ**U-bend** noun [C] a U-shaped piece of pipe, especially one fixed under a toilet or sink, which holds water in its lower part and prevents unpleasant gases from getting out

über- (also **uber-**) /ˈuː.bəʳ/ (US) /-bɚ/ **prefix** humorous used before nouns to mean 'extreme' or 'extremely good/successful': *über-model, Giselle* ◦ *über-billionaire*

ubiquitous /juːˈbɪk.wɪ.təs/ (US) /-wə.t̬əs/ **adj** formal or humorous seeming to be in all places: *Leather is very much in fashion this season, as of course is* ***the*** *ubiquitous denim.* ◦ *The Swedes are not alone in finding their language under pressure from* ***the*** *ubiquitous spread of English.* ◦ *The radio, that most ubiquitous of consumer-electronic appliances, is about to enter a new age.* • **ubiquitously** /-li/ **adv**

ubiquity /juːˈbɪk.wɪ.ti/ (US) /-wə.t̬i/ **noun** [U] formal the fact that something or someone seems to be everywhere: *the ubiquity of fast-food outlets*

ˈ**U-boat** noun [C] a German SUBMARINE, used especially in World Wars I and II

udder /ˈʌd.əʳ/ (US) /-ɚ/ **noun** [C] the organ of a cow, sheep, or other animal, that produces milk and hangs like a bag between the legs

udon /ˈuː.dɒn/ (US) /-dɑːn/ **noun** [plural] thick NOODLES (= long strips made from flour or rice) used in Japanese cooking

UFO /juː.efˈəʊ/ (US) /-ˈoʊ/ **noun** [C] abbreviation for unidentified flying object: an object seen in the sky that is thought to be a spacecraft from another planet: *Several UFO sightings have been reported.*

ugh /ʊx/, /ɜː/ **exclamation** used to express a strong feeling of DISGUST (= disapproval and dislike) at something very unpleasant: *Ugh, I've got something horrible on the bottom of my shoe!*

ugly /ˈʌg.li/ **adj** **NOT ATTRACTIVE** ▷ **1** B1 unpleasant to look at; not attractive: *I find a lot of modern architecture very ugly.* ◦ *Yesterday in town I saw the ugliest baby I've ever seen in my life.* ◦ *I feel really fat and ugly today.* ◦ *He was a really unpleasant man and* ***as*** *ugly* ***as sin*** *(= very ugly).* **THREATENING** ▷ **2** C2 unpleasant and threatening or violent: *There were ugly scenes outside the stadium.* ◦ *The demonstration turned ugly when a group of protesters started to throw bottles at the police.* • **ugliness** /-nəs/ **noun** [U] *the ugliness of the buildings*

ˌ**ugly** ˈ**duckling** noun [C] someone or something that is ugly and not successful when young or new but will later become beautiful or successful

uh /ɜː/, /ʌ/ **exclamation** used in writing to represent the sound that people sometimes make when they are thinking what to say next: *It's not too far – it's about, uh, five miles from here.*

UHF /juː.eɪtʃˈef/ **noun** [U] abbreviation for ultra-high frequency: radio waves between 300 MHz and 3,000 MHz → Compare **VHF**

uh-ˈhuh **exclamation** informal used in writing to represent the sound that people sometimes make in order to agree with or show understanding of something that has just been said: *'Did you hear what I just said?' 'Uh-huh.'* ◦ *'You know that strange guy we saw yesterday?' 'Uh-huh.'* ◦ *'I'll be back a little late because I'm going via town.' 'Uh-huh.'*

ˌ**uh-ˈoh** **exclamation** informal used in writing to represent the sound that people make when they discover that they have made a mistake or done something wrong: *Uh-oh, I think I just locked my keys in the car.*

UHT /juː.eɪtʃˈtiː/ **adj** [before noun] UK abbreviation for ultra heat treated: describes milk that has been heated to a very high temperature so that it will last for a long time if it is kept in a container that has not been opened, or a product made from this: *UHT milk/cream* • **UHT noun** [U] *a pint of UHT*

ˈ**uh-ˌuh** **exclamation** informal used in writing to represent the sound that people sometimes make to give a negative answer: *'You didn't have time to go to the store?' 'Uh-uh, no chance.'*

the UK /juːˈkeɪ/ **noun** abbreviation for the United Kingdom: the country of Great Britain and Northern Ireland: *When were you last in the UK then?* • **UK adj** [before noun] *the UK ambassador to Sweden*

> **! Common mistake: UK**
>
> **Remember:** you usually use **the** before any country that has 'State', 'Republic', 'Kingdom', or 'Isles' in its name.
>
> Don't say 'UK' or 'United Kingdom', say **the UK** or **the United Kingdom**:
>
> ~~*I first visited UK in 2001.*~~

ukulele (also **ukelele**) /juː.kəˈleɪ.li/ **noun** [C] a small guitar or BANJO with four strings

ulcer /ˈʌl.səʳ/ (US) /-sɚ/ **noun** [C] a break in the skin or on the surface of an organ inside the body, which does not HEAL naturally: *a mouth/stomach ulcer* • **ulcerous** /-əs/ **adj**

ulcerated /ˈʌl.sᵊr.eɪ.tɪd/ (US) /-sɚ.eɪ.t̬ɪd/ **adj** describes skin that is covered in ulcers: *She had lain in bed for so long that her shoulder blades had become ulcerated.* • **ulceration** /ˌʌl.sᵊrˈeɪ.ʃᵊn/ (US) /-səˈreɪ-/ **noun** [U]

ulna /ˈʌl.nə/ **noun** [C] specialized a long, thin bone in the lower part of your arm → Compare **radius**

ulterior /ʌlˈtɪə.ri.əʳ/ (US) /-ˈtɪr.i-/ **adj** **ulterior motive, reason, purpose, etc.** a secret purpose or reason for doing something: *He claims he just wants to help Lisa but I suspect he has an ulterior motive.*

ultimate /ˈʌl.tɪ.mət/ (US) /-t̬ə-/ **adj; noun**

▸**adj** [before noun] B2 most extreme or important because either the original or final, or the best or worst: *Of course the ultimate responsibility for the present conflict without doubt lies with the aggressor.* ◦ *The ultimate decision about who to employ lies with Andrew.* ◦ *Infidelity is the ultimate betrayal.* ◦ *the ultimate luxury cruiser*

▸**noun** **the ultimate in sth** the best or most extreme example of something: *It describes the hotel as 'the* *ultimate in luxury'.* ◦ *I mean, tackling six men single-handedly – that really is the ultimate in stupidity!*

ultimately /ˈʌl.tɪ.mət.li/ ⓤⓢ /-t̬ə-/ **adv 1** C1 finally, after a series of things have happened: *Everything will ultimately depend on what is said at the meeting with the directors next week.* ◦ *Ultimately, of course, he'd like to have his own business but that won't be for some time.* **2** C2 used to emphasize the most important fact in a situation: *Ultimately, he'll have to decide.*

ultimatum /ˌʌl.tɪˈmeɪ.təm/ ⓤⓢ /-t̬əˈmeɪ.t̬əm/ **noun** [C] (plural **ultimatums** or **ultimata**) a threat in which a person or group of people are warned that if they do not do a particular thing, something unpleasant will happen to them. It is usually the last and most extreme in a series of actions taken to bring about a particular result: *He* ***gave*** *her an ultimatum – she could either stop seeing Peter and come back to him or it was divorce.* ◦ *On Wednesday night the UN* ***issued*** *its toughest ultimatum to date, demanding that all troops withdraw from the city.*

ultra- /ʌl.trə-/ **prefix** extreme or extremely: *ultra-expensive* ◦ *ultra-modern architecture* ◦ *ultra-sensitive* ◦ *an ultra-short haircut*

ultralight /ˈʌl.trəˌlaɪt/ **noun** [C] US for **microlight**

ultramarine /ˌʌl.trə.məˈriːn/ **noun** [U] a bright blue colour • **ultramarine adj** of a bright blue colour

ultrasonic /ˌʌl.trəˈsɒn.ɪk/ ⓤⓢ /-ˈsɑː.nɪk/ **adj** describes sound that is too high for people to hear

ultrasound /ˈʌl.trə.saʊnd/ **noun 1** [U] special sound waves used in such processes as examining organs inside the body and directing the route of SUBMARINES: *They'll use ultrasound to monitor her ovaries.* ◦ *ultrasound scanning/imaging* **2** [C] an ultrasound SCAN

ultraviolet /ˌʌl.trəˈvaɪə.lət/ **adj** (abbreviation **UV**) describes light with a WAVELENGTH that is after the VIOLET (= light purple) end of the range of colours that can be seen by humans. Light of this type causes the skin to become darker in the sun.

um /əm/ **exclamation** used in writing to represent the sound that people make when they are pausing or deciding what to say next: *'What do you think of this jacket?' 'Um, I don't know if I like the colour.'* ◦ *'So what did you talk about?' 'Um, I don't remember.'*

umami /uːˈmɑː.mi/ **noun** [U] a strong, salty taste that is found in foods such as cheese, fish, or MUSHROOMS: *Vegetables develop umami as they ripen.*

umbilical cord /ʌmˈbɪl.ɪ.kəlˌkɔːd/ ⓤⓢ /-ˌkɔːrd/ **noun** [C usually singular] the long, tube-like structure that connects a baby that has not yet been born to its mother's PLACENTA (= the organ that provides it with food and OXYGEN)

U

umbrage /ˈʌm.brɪdʒ/ **noun** [U] formal **take umbrage** to feel upset or annoyed, usually because you feel that someone has been rude or shown no respect to you: *You don't think she'll take umbrage if she isn't invited to the wedding, do you?*

umbrella /ʌmˈbrel.ə/ **noun** [C] **DEVICE** ▷ **1** A2 a device for protection against the rain which consists of a stick with a folding frame covered in material at one end and usually a handle at the other, or a similar, often larger, device used for protection against the sun: *I felt a few spots of rain so I put my umbrella up.* ◦ *I left another umbrella on the bus yesterday.* ◦ *a folding umbrella* **GROUP** ▷ **2** something which includes or represents a group or range of similar things: *There are 980 community agencies* ***under the*** *umbrella* ***of*** *the National Community Action Foundation.* ◦ *Donations should be sent to the Disaster Emergency Committee, an umbrella* ***organization*** *for UK-based aid agencies.* ◦ *Existentialism was really an umbrella* ***term*** *to lump together the works of several philosophers and writers.*

umlaut /ˈʊm.laʊt/ **noun** [C] a mark put over a vowel in some languages, such as German, to show that the pronunciation of the vowel is changed: *The German word 'Gebäude', which means 'building', has an umlaut over the 'a'.*

umpire /ˈʌm.paɪəʳ/ ⓤⓢ /-paɪr/ **noun** [C] a person who is present at a sports competition in order to make certain that the rules of that particular game are obeyed and to judge if particular actions are acceptable: *a cricket/tennis umpire* • **umpire verb** [I or T] *Starmers has been chosen to umpire the next cricket test match.*

umpteen /ʌmpˈtiːn/, /ˈʌmp.tiːn/ **determiner, pronoun** informal very many; a lot (of): *We've been there umpteen times and she still can't remember the way.* • **umpteenth** /ʌmpˈtiːnθ/, /ˈʌmp.tiːnθ/ **determiner** informal *I drank my umpteenth cup of coffee.* ◦ *For the umpteenth time, Anthony, knives and forks go in the middle drawer!*

'un /ən/ **noun** [C] not standard one: *Mira'll fit in the back of the car – she's only a little 'un!*

un- /ʌn-/ **prefix** used to add the meaning 'not', 'lacking', or 'the opposite of' before adjectives, adverbs, verbs, and nouns: *unrealistic* ◦ *unhappily* ◦ *unscrew* ◦ *unfairness*

the UN /juːˈen/ **noun** [+ sing/pl verb] abbreviation for the United Nations: an international organization that was established in 1945 and aims to solve world problems in a peaceful way: *The UN has decided to impose sanctions.* • **UN adj** [before noun] *the UN Security Council* ◦ *UN troops*

unabashed /ˌʌn.əˈbæʃt/ **adj** without any worry about possible criticism or embarrassment: *She is to this day unabashed in her patriotism.* ◦ *He is an unabashed capitalist.* → Compare **abashed**

unabated /ˌʌn.əˈbeɪ.tɪd/ ⓤⓢ /-t̬ɪd/ **adj** [usually after verb] formal without becoming weaker in strength or force: *The fighting* ***continued*** *unabated throughout the night.* → Compare **abate**

unable /ʌnˈeɪ.bl̩/ **adj be unable to do sth** B1 to not be able to do something: *We were unable to contact him at the time.*

unabridged /ˌʌn.əˈbrɪdʒd/ **adj** An unabridged book, speech, or article is in its original form and has not been made shorter.

unacceptable /ˌʌn.əkˈsep.tə.bl̩/ ⓤⓢ /-t̬ə-/ **adj** B2 too bad to be accepted, approved of, or allowed to continue: *The unions have described the latest pay offer as unacceptable.* ◦ *The taking of hostages, said the minister, was totally unacceptable under any circumstances.* ◦ *The report found what it described as 'unacceptable levels of air pollution' in several major cities.*

IDIOM **the unacceptable face of sth** UK the bad side to a particular system or set of beliefs: *The paper showed a picture of homeless people sleeping on the streets with the caption underneath 'the unacceptable face of capitalism'.*

unacceptably /ˌʌn.əkˈsep.tə.bli/ **adv** in a way that cannot be accepted, approved of, or allowed to continue: *unacceptably high risks*

unaccompanied /ˌʌn.əˈkʌm.pən.id/ **adj 1** not having anyone with you when you go somewhere: *To everyone's great surprise, the princess arrived at the ball unaccompanied.* **2** describes music produced by a singer or by someone playing a musical instrument without anyone else singing or playing at the same time: *She sang the first three verses with a piano and the last verse unaccompanied.*

unaccountable /ˌʌn.əˈkaʊn.tə.bl̩/ (US) /-t̬ə-/ adj **NOT RESPONSIBLE** ▷ **1 be unaccountable to sb/sth** to not be expected to explain or provide a reason to a particular person or organization for your actions: *When Knight became leader, the council was run by a clique of officers largely unaccountable to the elected members.* **SURPRISING** ▷ **2** not able to be explained or understood: *For some unaccountable **reason**, he keeps his wallet in his underwear drawer.* • **unaccountably** /-li/ adv *I felt unaccountably happy this morning.*

unaccustomed /ˌʌn.əˈkʌs.təmd/ adj **1** [after verb] not familiar with something, or not used to something: *The weather presented a particular challenge, especially for American servicemen unaccustomed **to** subarctic conditions.* **2** [before noun] not usual: *The Olympic and world champion finished in the unaccustomed position of fourth.* → Opposite **accustomed**

unadulterated /ˌʌn.əˈdʌl.tᵊr.eɪ.tɪd/ (US) /-ə.reɪ.t̬ɪd/ adj **1** not spoiled or made weaker by the addition of other substances; pure: *People injecting drugs can never be sure that they're using unadulterated substances.* **2** [before noun] complete: *I've never heard such unadulterated nonsense in my life!*

unaffected /ˌʌn.əˈfek.tɪd/ adj **NOT CHANGED** ▷ **1** (C2) not influenced, harmed, or interrupted in any way: *The west of the city was largely unaffected **by** the bombing.* ◦ *It is hoped that train services on the main lines will be unaffected **by** today's industrial action.* **SINCERE** ▷ **2** approving natural and sincere in your behaviour: *For someone who has spent 40 years in show business she remains remarkably unaffected by it all.* • **unaffectedly** /-li/ adv

unaffordable /ˌʌn.əˈfɔː.də.bl̩/ (US) /-ˈfɔːr-/ adj (C1) too expensive for people to be able to buy or pay for: *For many people, this type of treatment remains unaffordable.*

unaided /ʌnˈeɪ.dɪd/ adj, adv without any help from anyone else; independently: *Since his accident, he hasn't been able to walk unaided.*

unalienable /ʌnˈeɪ.li.ə.nə.bl̩/ adj **inalienable**

unalloyed /ˌʌn.əˈlɔɪd/ adj literary (especially of a positive feeling) not spoiled by any amount of negative feeling; pure: *Spending time with one's family is never an unalloyed pleasure (= there are bad things about it too).* ◦ *We had the perfect holiday – two weeks of unalloyed bliss.*

unambiguous /ˌʌn.æmˈbɪg.ju.əs/ adj expressed in a way which makes it completely clear what is meant: *The minister said she would give a clear and unambiguous **statement** on the future of the coal industry at the earliest possible opportunity.* • **unambiguously** /-li/ adv

ˌun-Aˈmerican adj US disapproving guilty of activities, behaviour, or beliefs that show opposition or no loyalty to the US and its political system: *From 1940 to 1943, he was general counsel of the House committee investigating un-American **activities**.*

unanimity /ˌjuː.nəˈnɪm.ɪ.ti/ (US) /-ə.t̬i/ noun [U] formal the state of being unanimous

unanimous /juːˈnæn.ɪ.məs/ adj (C2) If a group of people are unanimous, they all agree about one particular matter or vote the same way, and if a decision or judgment is unanimous, it is formed or supported by everyone in a group: *The jury returned a unanimous **verdict** of guilty after a short deliberation.* ◦ *After a lengthy discussion we reached a unanimous **decision** on the proposal.* ◦ *The new format has unanimous support.* • **unanimously** /-li/ adv (C2) *All four proposals to the committee were unanimously approved.*

unannounced /ˌʌn.əˈnaʊnst/ adj, adv; adj

▸**adj, adv** If someone arrives unannounced, they arrive suddenly and unexpectedly: *She appeared unannounced and took control of the meeting.*

▸**adj** not made publicly known: *The Texan singer will be supported by two other bands, as yet unannounced.*

unanswerable /ʌnˈɑːn.sᵊr.ə.bl̩/ (US) /-ˈæn.sɚ-/ adj **CLEARLY TRUE** ▷ **1** formal If an argument or claim is unanswerable, people cannot disagree with it because it is so clearly true: *In economic terms the need to reduce inflation is unanswerable.* **WITHOUT AN ANSWER** ▷ **2** (of a question) without an answer: *As to how long this war will last, it's an unanswerable question.*

unanswered /ʌnˈɑːn.səd/ (US) /-ˈæn.sɚd/ adj not answered or explained: *Questions from local residents remained unanswered.*

unappealing /ˌʌn.əˈpiː.lɪŋ/ adj not attractive or interesting

unappreciative /ˌʌn.əˈpriː.ʃi.ə.tɪv/ (US) /-t̬ɪv/ adj not showing that you understand how good something is, or not grateful for something

unapproachable /ˌʌn.əˈprəʊ.tʃə.bl̩/ (US) /-ˈproʊ-/ adj Someone who is unapproachable has an unfriendly and slightly frightening manner which often makes other people less likely to speak to them: *As a boss I found him rather unapproachable.*

unarguable /ʌnˈɑː.g.ju.ə.bl̩/ (US) /-ˈɑːrg-/ adj not able to be argued

unarmed /ʌnˈɑːmd/ (US) /-ˈɑːrmd/ adj not armed

unashamed /ˌʌn.əˈʃeɪmd/ adj not ashamed; without hiding behaviour or opinions that other people might consider unacceptable: *Afterwards he spent five minutes with the president, of whom he is an unashamed admirer.* ◦ *We then checked into the hotel for a weekend of unashamed luxury.* • **unashamedly** /-ˈʃeɪ.mɪd.li/ adv *The school's headmistress is unashamedly traditional and refuses to allow the girls to wear trousers.*

unassailable /ˌʌn.əˈseɪ.lə.bᵊl/ adj **1** in such a strong position that you cannot be defeated: *The result has given the team an unassailable lead.* ◦ *The president looked unassailable with over 60 percent of the vote.* **2** impossible to doubt or argue with: *unassailable logic* ◦ *The conclusions were unassailable.* **3** impossible to attack: *an unassailable fortress*

unassuming /ˌʌn.əˈsjuː.mɪŋ/ (US) /-ˈsuː-/ adj approving Someone who is unassuming is quiet and shows no wish for attention or admiration: *He was shy and unassuming and not at all how you expect an actor to be.*

unattached /ˌʌn.əˈtætʃt/ adj **NOT MARRIED** ▷ **1** not married or not having a relationship with anyone; single: *He's gorgeous, he's got his own house and, what's more, he's unattached.* **NOT CONNECTED** ▷ **2** not connected: *Please enclose your signed cheque and payment slip unattached and unfolded.*

unattainable /ˌʌn.əˈteɪ.nə.bl̩/ adj (C2) not able to be achieved: *an unattainable ideal* ◦ *Some economists think that full employment in Europe is an unattainable **goal**.*

unattended /ˌʌn.əˈten.dɪd/ adj not being watched or taken care of: *Please do not leave your luggage unattended.* ◦ *According to the report, most accidents occur when young children are left unattended in the home.*

U

unattractive /ˌʌn.əˈtræk.tɪv/ **adj 1** B2 unpleasant to look at: *This is modern architecture at its most unattractive.* ◦ *He was short and overweight and generally fairly unattractive.* **2** C1 having no good or positive features: *The options were decidedly unattractive.* • **unattractively** /-li/ **adv**

unauthorized (UK usually **unauthorised**) /ʌnˈɔː.θə.raɪzd/ US /-ˈɑː-/ **adj** without someone's official permission to do something or be in a particular place: *No admittance to unauthorized personnel.* ◦ *This unauthorized biography of the star has sold over 10,000 copies in its first week in print.*

unavailable /ˌʌn.əˈveɪ.lə.bl̩/ **adj 1** C1 [after verb] If someone is unavailable, they are not able to talk to people or meet people, usually because they are doing other things: *The Minister accused of misleading parliament was unavailable* ***for comment*** *last night.* **2** B2 If something is unavailable, you cannot get it or use it: *This information was previously unavailable to the public.*

unavailing /ˌʌn.əˈveɪ.lɪŋ/ **adj** formal or literary When an attempt to do something is unavailing, it is unsuccessful or has no positive effect: *Diplomatic efforts at peace-making have so far proved unavailing.*

unavoidable /ˌʌn.əˈvɔɪ.də.bl̩/ **adj** C1 impossible to avoid • **unavoidably** /-bli/ **adv**

unaware /ˌʌn.əˈweər/ US /-ˈwer/ **adj** [after verb] B2 not understanding or realizing something: [+ that] *He was unaware* ***that*** *the police were watching him.* ◦ *I was quite unaware* ***of*** *the problem.*

unawares /ˌʌn.əˈweəz/ US /-ˈwerz/ **adv** suddenly and unexpectedly without any warning: *The overnight invasion* ***took*** *the military experts unawares.* ◦ *The prime minister seemed to have been* ***caught*** *unawares by (= was not expecting) this sudden attack of criticism.*

unbalance /ʌnˈbæl.əns/ **verb** [T] **NOT FIRM** ▷ **1** to cause something or someone to be unbalanced: *The result was to further unbalance the monetary-fiscal policy mix.* **MENTALLY ILL** ▷ **2** to make someone mentally ill, especially temporarily **NOT FAIR** ▷ **3** to make something unfair or not equal

unbalanced /ʌnˈbæl.ənst/ **adj NOT FIRM** ▷ **1** not firm but likely to fall or change position suddenly **MENTALLY ILL** ▷ **2** C2 mentally ill: *His relatives have said he became unbalanced after the death of his father.* **NOT FAIR** ▷ **3** C2 not fair or equal; false: *unbalanced reporting* ◦ *He gave an unbalanced* ***view*** *of the situation.* **FOOD** ▷ **4** not consisting of a combination of the correct types and amounts of food: *an unbalanced diet* ◦ *an unbalanced meal*

unbearable /ʌnˈbeə.rə.bl̩/ US /-ˈber.ə-/ **adj** B2 too painful or unpleasant for you to continue to experience: *All I remember of childbirth was the unbearable pain and the relief when it was all over.* ◦ *The atmosphere at work at the moment is quite unbearable.* ◦ *The heat was unbearable.* • **unbearably** /-bli/ **adv** *The sun was almost unbearably hot today.*

unbeatable /ʌnˈbiː.tə.bl̩/ US /-t̬ə-/ **adj** approving unable to be defeated or improved because of excellent quality: *The 23-year-old US tennis star looks unbeatable this season.* ◦ *For good pizzas at a reasonable price they're unbeatable.*

unbeaten /ʌnˈbiː.tən/ **adj** in sports, having won every game: *Manchester United remain unbeaten this season so far.*

unbecoming /ˌʌn.bɪˈkʌm.ɪŋ/ **adj 1** formal describes clothes that do not look attractive on a particular person **2** describes behaviour that is not correct or not acceptable: *Any officer who is convicted of conduct unbecoming (****to****) an officer shall be court-martialled.*

unbeknown /ˌʌn.bɪˈnəʊn/ US /-ˈnoʊn/ **adv** (also **unbeknownst**) **unbeknown/unbeknownst to sb** without a particular person knowing: *Unbeknown to me, he'd gone and rented out the apartment in my absence.*

unbelievable /ˌʌn.bɪˈliː.və.bl̩/ **adj SURPRISING** ▷ **1** B1 extremely surprising: *She eats an unbelievable amount of food.* ◦ *You've had such bad luck it's unbelievable.* **UNLIKELY** ▷ **2** B2 unable to be believed because unlikely: *I found most of the characters in the play totally unbelievable.*

unbelievably /ˌʌn.bɪˈliː.və.bli/ **adv** in a way that is very surprising or difficult to believe: *He works unbelievably hard.* ◦ *It was still an unbelievably stupid thing to do.*

unbeliever /ˌʌn.bɪˈliː.vər/ US /-vɚ/ **noun** [C] a person who does not have any religious beliefs: *Most church schools are open to unbelievers.*

unbend /ʌnˈbend/ **verb** [I] (**unbent**, **unbent**) to relax and become less formal and serious in your manner: *I'd hoped that after a glass or two of wine she might unbend a little.*

unbending /ʌnˈben.dɪŋ/ **adj** formal describes someone who often makes fixed judgments and decisions which they are unwilling to change

unbiased /ʌnˈbaɪəst/ **adj** C2 able to judge fairly because you are not influenced by your own opinions: *unbiased advice* ◦ *an unbiased opinion*

unbidden /ʌnˈbɪd.ən/ **adj** [usually after verb] literary not invited or wanted: *At night, images would come unbidden into her mind.*

unbleached /ʌnˈbliːtʃt/ **adj** describes flour or material that is not made white artificially by the use of chemicals: *unbleached cotton* ◦ *unbleached flour*

unblemished /ʌnˈblem.ɪʃt/ **adj** describes a reputation, character, etc. that has no faults and is not spoiled in any way: *For six years his championship record was unblemished.*

unborn /ʌnˈbɔːn/ US /-ˈbɔːrn/ **adj** not yet born; in the mother's WOMB: *the protection of the unborn child*

unbounded /ʌnˈbaʊn.dɪd/ **adj** describes a positive feeling that is very great and seems to have no limits: *her unbounded enthusiasm for her subject*

unbreakable /ʌnˈbreɪ.kə.bl̩/ **adj** impossible to break: *unbreakable glass/plastic*

unbridgeable /ʌnˈbrɪdʒ.ə.bl̩/ **adj** used for describing differences or divisions between people that are so big they will never be made smaller: *There is an unbridgeable divide between the country's two main political camps.*

unbridled /ʌnˈbraɪ.dl̩d/ **adj** [usually before noun] not controlled or limited: *unbridled ambition/enthusiasm/lust*

unbroken /ʌnˈbrəʊ.kən/ US /-ˈbroʊ-/ **adj** continuous and with no pauses: *The Giants' winning streak remained unbroken for an impressive 19 games.*

unbuckle /ʌnˈbʌk.l̩/ **verb** [T] to release the BUCKLE (= metal fastener) of a shoe, belt, etc. so that you can remove it

unburden /ʌnˈbɜː.dən/ US /-ˈbɝː-/ **verb unburden yourself** to free yourself of something that is worrying you, by talking about it to someone: *He'll unburden himself to anyone who'll listen.*

uncalled-for /ʌnˈkɔːld.fɔː/ US /-kɑːld.fɔːr/ **adj** disapproving describes a criticism, insult, remark, or action that is unfair, rude, or unkind and therefore considered to be unnecessary: *an uncalled-for re-*

mark ◦ *There's no need to make personal remarks – that was quite uncalled-for.*

uncanny /ʌnˈkæn.i/ **adj** strange or mysterious; difficult or impossible to explain: *an uncanny resemblance* • **uncannily** /-ɪ.li/ **adv** *Her predictions turned out to be uncannily accurate.*

uncared for /ʌŋˈkeəd.fɔː/ (US) /-ˈkerd.fɔːr/ **adj** not taken care of well enough: *He looked unwashed and uncared for.*

uncaring /ʌnˈkeə.rɪŋ/ (US) /-ˈker.ɪŋ/ **adj** disapproving not worrying about other people's troubles or doing anything to help them: *The bishop criticized the government for its 'callous, uncaring attitude' to the homeless and the unemployed.*

unceasing /ʌnˈsiː.sɪŋ/ **adj** formal continuing and unlikely to stop or become less: *The authors are grateful for the unceasing support of the editors in London and New York.* • **unceasingly** /-li/ **adv**

unceremonious /ʌnˌser.ɪˈməʊ.ni.əs/ (US) /-ˈmoʊ-/ **adj** formal done in a rude, sudden, or informal way: *an unceremonious refusal* • **unceremoniously** /-li/ **adv** *He was unceremoniously removed from the list of members, for gross misconduct.*

uncertain /ʌnˈsɜː.tᵊn/ (US) /-ˈsɝː-/ **adj** **1** (B2) not knowing what to do or believe, or not able to decide about something: [+ question word] *She's uncertain **whether** to go to New Zealand or not.* ◦ *Bridie was uncertain **about** meeting him.* **2** (B2) not known or fixed, or not completely certain: *New arrivals face an uncertain **future**.* ◦ *The political outlook is **still** uncertain.* • **uncertainly** /-li/ **adv**

uncertainty /ʌnˈsɜː.tᵊn.ti/ (US) /-ˈsɝː.tᵊn.t̬i/ **noun** [C or U] (C1) a situation in which something is not known, or something that is not known or certain: *Nothing is ever decided, and all the uncertainty is very bad for staff morale.* ◦ *Life is full of uncertainties.*

unchallenged /ʌnˈtʃæl.ɪndʒd/ **adj** accepted without asking questions or criticizing: *We can't allow her comments to **go** unchallenged.*

unchanged /ʌnˈtʃeɪndʒd/ **adj** [usually after verb] (B2) staying the same: *The area has remained virtually unchanged in 50 years.*

uncharacteristic /ʌnˌkær.ɪk.təˈrɪs.tɪk/ (US) /-ˌker-/ **adj** not typical • **uncharacteristically** /-tɪ.kᵊl.i/ **adv**

uncharitable /ʌnˈtʃær.ɪ.tə.bl̩/ (US) /-ˈtʃer.ə.t̬ə-/ **adj** unkind and unfair: *The uncharitable explanation is that she's too afraid to ask.* • **uncharitably** /-bli/ **adv**

uncharted /ʌnˈtʃɑː.tɪd/ (US) /-ˈtʃɑːr.t̬ɪd/ **adj** literary An uncharted place or situation is completely new and therefore has never been described before: *Nuclear fusion has taken physicists into uncharted **seas/territory/waters*** (= a new and unknown area).

unchecked /ʌnˈtʃekt/ **adj** describes something harmful that is continuing or increasing without or despite any limits or attempts to prevent it: *If present trends **go/continue** unchecked there will be a major epidemic of heart disease in the next five years.* ◦ *The war raged on, unchecked **by** the UN's efforts to stop it.*

uncivil /ʌnˈsɪv.ᵊl/ **adj** formal not polite: *He was most uncivil **to** your father – called him an old fool.* → See also **incivility** • **uncivilly** /-i/ **adv**

uncivilized (UK usually **uncivilised**) /ʌnˈsɪv.ɪ.laɪzd/ **adj** not CIVILIZED, especially below the usual standards of Western society: *Conditions in these inner-city housing estates can be pretty uncivilized.*

IDIOM **uncivilized hour** UK informal a very early or very late time in the day: *Sorry to phone you at such an uncivilized hour.*

unclaimed /ʌnˈkleɪmd/ **adj** If something is unclaimed, no one has said that it belongs to them or that they should have it: *unclaimed prizes* ◦ *More than £2.5 million lies unclaimed in bank accounts.*

uncle /ˈʌŋ.kl̩/ **noun** [C] **1** (A2) the brother of someone's mother or father, or the husband of someone's aunt or uncle: *I've got several uncles and aunts.* ◦ *We invited my Uncle Steve round.* ◦ [as form of address] *Did you bring me a present, Uncle Jack?* **2** Indian English any male adult that you know who is older than you: *John Uncle*

unclean /ʌnˈkliːn/ **adj** **1** not clean and therefore likely to cause disease: *The health risk from drinking unclean water is considerable.* **2** formal not clean or pure, or morally bad, as described by the rules of a religion: *Jews and Muslims consider pigs unclean.*

unclear /ʌnˈklɪəʳ/ (US) /-ˈklɪr/ **adj** **1** (B2) not obvious or easy to see or know: *The ownership of the painting remains unclear.* ◦ [+ question word] *It's unclear **what** actually happened that night.* ◦ *It's unclear **whether** he arrived before or after the shot was fired.* **2** (B2) If you are unclear about something, you are not certain about it: *I'm unclear about a couple of points in your proposal – could you go over them again?* ◦ *I'm unclear (**as to**) **whether** we're meant to stay here or not.* • **unclearly** /-li/ **adv**

Uncle Sam /ˌʌŋ.kl̩ˈsæm/ **noun** [S not after the] informal the US, or its government, sometimes represented by an image of a tall, thin man with a white BEARD and a tall hat

Uncle Tom /ˌʌŋ.kl̩ˈtɒm/ (US) /-ˈtɑːm/ **noun** [C usually singular] offensive disapproving a black person who is considered to be too eager to agree with white people or too willing to be treated in a way that is not equal to white people

uncomfortable /ʌnˈkʌmf.tə.bl̩/ (US) /-ˈkʌm.fɚ.t̬ə-/ **adj** **1** (B1) not feeling comfortable and pleasant, or not making you feel comfortable and pleasant: *I've eaten so much, I'm really quite uncomfortable.* ◦ *These shoes are really uncomfortable.* **2** (C1) slightly embarrassed, or making you feel slightly embarrassed: *an uncomfortable silence* • **uncomfortably** /-bli/ **adv** (C1) *I was warm but not uncomfortably so.*

uncommitted /ˌʌn.kəˈmɪt.ɪd/ (US) /-ˈmɪt̬-/ **adj** having made no promise to support any particular group, plan, belief, or action: *25 senators have admitted they are still uncommitted **on** the taxation question.*

uncommon /ʌnˈkɒm.ən/ (US) /-ˈkɑː.mən/ **adj** **NOT FREQUENT** ▷ **1** (C1) not seen, happening, or experienced often: *Accidents due to failure of safety equipment are uncommon nowadays.* ◦ *It's not uncommon for people to become ill when they travel.* **EXTREME** ▷ **2** old-fashioned formal describes a quality, especially a human quality, that is larger in amount or degree than usual: *a woman of uncommon beauty*

uncommonly /ʌnˈkɒm.ən.li/ (US) /-ˈkɑː.mən-/ **adv** old-fashioned formal extremely

uncommunicative /ˌʌn.kəˈmjuː.nɪ.kə.tɪv/ **adj** not willing to talk: *He had a headache and was rather uncommunicative.*

uncomplaining /ˌʌn.kəmˈpleɪ.nɪŋ/ **adj** approving willing to do boring or difficult work without complaining or becoming angry: *The work is boring, but he's always cheerful and uncomplaining.* • **uncomplainingly** /-li/ **adv**

uncomplimentary /ʌnˌkɒm.plɪˈmen.tᵊr.i/ (US) /-ˌkɑːm.pləˈmen.ɚ-/ **adj** rudely criticizing: *She had some very uncomplimentary things to say about Stephen.*

uncompromising /ʌnˈkɒm.prə.maɪ.zɪŋ/ (US)

U

/-ˈkɑːm-/ **adj** If people or their beliefs are uncompromising, they are fixed and do not change, especially when faced with opposition: *The city council has taken an uncompromising stand against the proposals for the new building.* • **uncompromisingly** /-li/ **adv**

unconcerned /ˌʌn.kənˈsɜːnd/ (US) /-ˈsɝːnd/ **adj** not worried or not interested, especially when you should be worried or interested: *The baby seemed quite unconcerned **by** the noise.* ◦ *Are you as unconcerned **about** the situation as you appear?* • **unconcernedly** /-ˈsɜː.nɪd.li/ (US) /-ˈsɝː.nɪd.li/ **adv**

unconditional /ˌʌn.kənˈdɪʃ.ən.əl/ **adj** C2 complete and not limited in any way: *the unconditional love that one has for one's child* ◦ *unconditional surrender* ◦ *We demand the immediate and unconditional release of all political prisoners.* • **unconditionally** /-i/ **adv**

unconfirmed /ˌʌn.kənˈfɜːmd/ (US) /-fɝːmd/ **adj** If facts are unconfirmed, it is not certain if they are true: *According to unconfirmed **reports**, two people were killed in the riots last night.*

unconnected /ˌʌn.kəˈnek.tɪd/ (US) /-t̬ɪd/ **adj** not connected; not related: *It's no longer possible to argue that crime is unconnected **with** unemployment.* ◦ *A series of apparently unconnected events led to his resignation.*

unconscionable /ʌnˈkɒn.ʃən.ə.bl̩/ (US) /-ˈkɑːn-/ **adj** formal disapproving An unconscionable size, amount, or length of time is too great and is unacceptable: *They had both drunk an unconscionable quantity of red wine the previous night.* • **unconscionably** /-bli/ **adv**

unconscious /ʌnˈkɒn.ʃəs/ (US) /-ˈkɑːn-/ **adj; noun**

▸**adj** **1** B2 in the state of not being awake, especially as the result of a head injury: *She was hit on the head by a stone and **knocked** unconscious.* **2** C2 An unconscious thought or feeling is one that you do not know you have: *my unconscious desire to impress him* • **unconsciously** /-li/ **adv** • **unconsciousness** /-nəs/ **noun** [U]

▸**noun** **the unconscious** the part of your mind that contains feelings and thoughts that you do not know about, and that influences the way you behave

unconsidered /ˌʌn.kənˈsɪd.əd/ (US) /-ɚd/ **adj** formal (of an action or remark) not carefully thought about

unconstitutional /ʌnˌkɒn.stɪˈtjuː.ʃən.əl/ (US) /-ˌkɑːn.stɪˈtuː-/ **adj** not allowed by the CONSTITUTION (= set of rules for government) of a country or organization: *Such a change in the law would be unconstitutional.* • **unconstitutionally** /-i/ **adv**

uncontrollable /ˌʌn.kənˈtrəʊ.lə.bl̩/ (US) /-ˈtroʊ-/ **adj** too strong or violent to be controlled: *I was suddenly overcome with an uncontrollable desire to hit him.* • **uncontrollably** /-bli/ **adv** *I arrived home to find him **sobbing** uncontrollably on the doorstep.* • **uncontrolled** /-ˈtrəʊld/ (US) /-ˈtroʊld/ **adj** *uncontrolled aggression*

unconventional /ˌʌn.kənˈven.ʃən.əl/ **adj** C1 different from what is usual or from the way most people do things: *an unconventional childhood/lifestyle/marriage* • **unconventionally** /-i/ **adv**

unconvincing /ˌʌn.kənˈvɪn.sɪŋ/ **adj** If an explanation or story is unconvincing, it does not sound or seem true or real: *They produced some rather unconvincing explanations for the system failure.* ◦ *The dialogue was unconvincing, partly because it was American actors trying to speak London English.* • **unconvincingly** /-li/ **adv**

uncooked /ʌnˈkʊkt/ **adj** not having been cooked: *Do not store cooked and uncooked meat together.*

uncool /ʌnˈkuːl/ **adj** informal embarrassing and not fashionable: *My dad's so uncool.* ◦ *Wearing homemade clothes was seen as very uncool.*

uncooperative /ˌʌn.kəʊˈɒp.ər.ə.tɪv/ (US) /-koʊˈɑː.pɚ.ə.t̬ɪv/ **adj** not willing to work with or be helpful to other people: *I found him rude and uncooperative.* • **uncooperatively** /-li/ **adv** • **uncooperativeness** /-nəs/ **noun** [U]

uncoordinated /ˌʌn.kəʊˈɔː.dɪn.eɪ.tɪd/ (US) /-koʊˈɔːr.dɪ.neɪ.t̬ɪd/ **adj** with different parts failing to work or move well together: *The marketing campaign was an uncoordinated effort by several different departments.* ◦ *She was clumsy and uncoordinated as a girl.*

uncork /ʌnˈkɔːk/ (US) /-ˈkɔːrk/ **verb** [T] to open a bottle by pulling out its CORK (= a cylinder-shaped piece of soft wood used to close it): *'Who's for some more wine?' asked Polly, uncorking another bottle.*

uncountable /ʌnˈkaʊn.tə.bl̩/ (US) /-t̬ə-/ **adj** specialized B1 An uncountable noun is not used with 'a' or 'an' and cannot be made plural: *Words like 'electricity', 'blood' and 'happiness' are uncountable.* → Compare **countable**

uncouple /ʌnˈkʌp.l̩/ **verb** [T] to separate two things that are joined together: *The engine had been uncoupled **from** the rest of the train.*

uncouth /ʌnˈkuːθ/ **adj** disapproving behaving in a rude, unpleasant way

uncover /ʌnˈkʌv.ər/ (US) /-ɚ/ **verb** [T] **1** C1 to discover something secret or hidden or remove something covering something else: *The investigation uncovered evidence of a large-scale illegal trade in wild birds.* ◦ *The biography is an attempt to uncover the inner man.* **2** to find something buried under the ground by removing the earth on top of it: *Digging in her garden, she uncovered a hoard of gold dating back to the ninth century.*

uncritical /ʌnˈkrɪt.ɪ.kəl/ (US) /-ˈkrɪt̬-/ **adj** often disapproving accepting something too easily, because of being unwilling or unable to criticize: *an adoring, uncritical audience* • **uncritically** /-i/ **adv**

uncrowned /ˌʌnˈkraʊnd/ **adj** **uncrowned king/queen** a man or woman who is considered to be the best, the most famous, or the most powerful in a particular area of life, especially when they do not have an official rank or title: *Django Reinhardt, **the** uncrowned king **of** jazz guitarists*

uncrushable /ˌʌnˈkrʌʃ.ə.bl̩/ **adj** describes cloth or clothing made of an artificial material and designed to stay free of unwanted folds: *an uncrushable hat*

unctuous /ˈʌŋk.tju.əs/ **adj** formal disapproving describes people or behaviour expressing too much praise, interest, friendliness, etc., in a way that is false and unpleasant: *his unctuous manner/voice/smile*

uncut /ʌŋˈkʌt/ **adj** complete and in its original form: *the original, uncut version of a film* ◦ *Uncut diamonds are worth less than those that have been cut and shaped.*

undated /ʌnˈdeɪ.tɪd/ (US) /-t̬ɪd/ **adj** An undated document has no date on it: *The cheque/letter was undated.*

undaunted /ʌnˈdɔːn.tɪd/ (US) /-ˈdɑːn.t̬ɪd/ **adj** [after verb] still determined and enthusiastic, despite problems or no success: *Undaunted **by** the cold and the rain, people danced until 2 a.m.* ◦ *The team **remain** undaunted, despite three defeats in a row.*

undecided /ˌʌn.dɪˈsaɪ.dɪd/ **adj** **1** If you are undecided, you have not yet made a decision or judgment about something: *Are you still undecided **about** the job in Brussels?* ◦ *54 percent of voters were in favour, 30 percent against, and the rest were undecided.* **2** not decided or finished: *The whole question is still undecided.*

undefeated /ˌʌn.dɪˈfiː.tɪd/ (US) /-t̬ɪd/ **adj** in sports, having won every game: *The team managed to remain undefeated in the final weeks of the season.*

undefinable /ˌʌn.dɪˈfaɪ.nə.bl̩/ **adj** US for **indefinable**

undelete /ʌn.dɪˈliːt/ **verb** [T] to make something that has been DELETED (= removed from a computer) able to be seen again

undeniable /ˌʌn.dɪˈnaɪ.ə.bl̩/ **adj** (C1) certainly true: *an undeniable fact* ◦ *a woman of undeniable brilliance* • **undeniably** /-bli/ **adv** (C2) *She is undeniably good at her job.*

under /ˈʌn.dəʳ/ (US) /-dɚ/ **preposition; adv**

▸**preposition** LOWER POSITION ▷ **1** (A1) in or to a position below or lower than something else, often so that one thing covers the other: *He hid under the bed.* ◦ *In AD 79 the city of Pompei was buried under a layer of ash seven metres deep.* ◦ *She put the thermometer under my tongue.* ◦ *She was holding a file under her arm (= between her upper arm and the side of her chest).* ◦ *They stood under a tree (= below its branches) to avoid getting wet.* **2** If a book, article, or piece of information is under a particular title, you can find it below or following that title in a list, book, library, etc.: *Books on Cecil Beaton will probably be under Art or Photography rather than Drama.* ◦ *Trifle? That **comes** under Puddings and Desserts.* LESS THAN ▷ **3** (A2) less than: *All items cost/are under a pound.* ◦ *The discount applies only to children under (**the age of**) ten (= younger than ten).* ◦ *If you get under 50 percent, you've failed the exam.* → Opposite **over** EXPERIENCING ▷ **4** (B2) happening during, as a result of, or according to a particular situation, event, rule, etc.: *The work was completed under very difficult conditions.* ◦ *Now that the deadline is approaching we all feel under pressure.* ◦ *The chair broke under his weight (= because he was too heavy for it).* ◦ *Under the present rules, you can buy ten litres of wine.* **5 under attack, consideration, discussion, etc.** (B2) in the process of being attacked, considered, discussed, etc.: *The town is under **fire** (= is being attacked) from the air.* ◦ *The proposals are now under **consideration** by the Board of Governors.* ◦ *The situation is still not under **control**.* **6 under sedation, anaesthetic, etc.** UK treated in the way mentioned: *The patient is being kept under heavy sedation.* ◦ *She'll have to go under anaesthetic for the operation.* **7 be under an impression/belief** (B2) to believe something, often wrongly: *He was under the mistaken belief that I was in charge.* CONTROL ▷ **8** controlled or governed by a particular person, organization, or force: *He's a Colonel, with hundreds of soldiers under him (= obeying his orders).* ◦ *I wonder what Britain was like under the Romans (= during the time when the Romans controlled Britain).* ◦ *People born under (= during the period of) the star sign Pisces are supposed to be dreamy and artistic.* **9 be under orders** to have been ordered to do something: *They're under strict orders not to discuss the situation.* ◦ *He's under **doctor's** orders (= has been told by a doctor) to cut down on fatty food and to drink no alcohol for at least six months.* NAME ▷ **10** using a particular name, especially one that is not your real name: *He writes under **the name** (**of**) John le Carré.* ◦ *For his own safety, he has to operate under a false name/an alias.*

IDIOM **be/fall under sb's influence/spell** to be affected by someone in a strong and often negative way: *She fell under his spell when he was her tutor at university.*

▸**adv** below the surface of something: *Because I'm a bad swimmer, I often go under and swallow a lot of water.*

IDIOM **go under** informal If a company goes under, it is unsuccessful and has to stop doing business: *Thousands of companies went under during the recession.*

under- /ʌn.dəʳ-/ (US) /-dɚ-/ **prefix 1** not enough or not done as well or as much as is necessary: *undercooked potatoes* ◦ *underprivileged children* ◦ *We're all overworked and underpaid.* ◦ *His boss says he's underperforming (= not doing as well as he should) at work.* → Compare **over- 2** below: *underwear* ◦ *an underpass*

underachieve /ˌʌn.də.rəˈtʃiːv/ (US) /-dɚ.ə-/ **verb** [I] to do less well than you could or should: *Like a lot of boys his age, he's underachieving.*

underachiever /ˌʌn.də.rəˈtʃiː.vəʳ/ (US) /-dɚ.əˈtʃiː.vɚ/ **noun** [C] someone who is less successful than they should be at school or at work

underage /ˌʌn.dəˈreɪdʒ/ (US) /-dɚˈeɪdʒ/ **adj** younger than the lowest age at which a particular activity is legally or usually allowed: *There are laws against underage sex and underage drinking.* ◦ *He was prosecuted for having sex with a girl who was underage.*

underarm /ˈʌn.də.rɑːm/ (US) /-dɚ.ɑːrm/ **adj; adj, adv**

▸**adj** [before noun] of or for use in the ARMPIT (= hollow place under the arm where the arm joins the body): *underarm deodorants/hair*

▸**adj, adv** (US also **underhand**) (done by) moving the arm below shoulder level: *underarm bowling* ◦ *He bowled underarm for the younger children.* → Opposite **overarm**

underbelly /ˈʌn.dəˌbel.i/ (US) /-dɚ-/ **noun** [S] literary the weakest or most unpleasant part of something that is most likely to fail or be easily defeated: *a film **exposing** the sordid underbelly of modern urban society* ◦ *Small businesses are the **soft** underbelly (= weakest parts) of the British economy, and they need as much government support as possible.*

underbrush /ˈʌn.dəˌbrʌʃ/ (US) /-dɚ-/ **noun** [U] US **undergrowth**

undercarriage /ˈʌn.dəˌkær.ɪdʒ/ (US) /-dɚˌker-/ **noun** [C] UK the set of wheels and other parts which support a plane when it is on the ground and make it possible to take off and land

undercharge /ˌʌn.dəˈtʃɑːdʒ/ (US) /-dɚˈtʃɑːrdʒ/ **verb** [I or T] to charge someone less than the correct price for something: *The sales assistant made a mistake and undercharged me **by** £2.* → Opposite **overcharge**

underclass /ˈʌn.də.klɑːs/ (US) /-dɚ.klæs/ **noun** [C usually singular] a group of people with a lower social and economic position than any of the other classes of society: *The long-term unemployed now constitute a sort of underclass.*

underclothes /ˈʌn.də.kləʊðz/ (US) /-dɚ.kloʊðz/ **noun** [plural] (also **underclothing**) formal for **underwear**

undercoat /ˈʌn.də.kəʊt/ (US) /-dɚ.koʊt/ **noun** [C or U] a first layer of paint that is put on a surface in order to improve the appearance of the final one, or the paint used for this → Compare **topcoat**

undercook /ˌʌn.dəˈkʊk/ (US) /-dɚ-/ **verb** [T often passive] to not cook something enough • **undercooked** /-ˈkʊkt/ **adj** *People can become infected after eating raw or undercooked **meat**.*

undercover /ˌʌn.dəˈkʌv.əʳ/ (US) /-dɚˈkʌv.ɚ/ **adj** [before noun] working secretly using a false appearance in order to get information for the police or government: *an undercover police operation* ◦ *an undercover detective* • **undercover adv** *He was working undercover at the time, almost certainly for the British Secret Service.*

undercurrent /ˈʌn.dəˌkʌr.ənt/ (US) /-dɚˌkɝː-/ **noun** [C] an emotion, belief, or characteristic of a situation that is hidden and usually negative or dangerous but that has some effect: *undercurrents of racism/anxiety/violence* ◦ *Beneath the smooth surface of political life, one senses powerful and dangerous undercurrents.*

undercut /ˌʌn.dəˈkʌt/ ⓤⓢ /-dɚ-/ verb [T] (present tense **undercutting**, past tense and past participle **undercut**) **CHARGE LESS THAN** ▷ **1** to charge less than a competitor: *Big supermarkets can undercut all rivals, especially small high-street shops.* ◦ *They claim to undercut their competitors* ***by*** *at least five percent.* **DAMAGE** ▷ **2** to damage something or to make it fail: *He suspected it was an attempt to undercut his authority.* → Synonym **undermine**

underdeveloped /ˌʌn.də.dɪˈvel.əpt/ ⓤⓢ /-dɚ-/ adj C2 (especially of a country) without modern industry or modern services that provide transport, hospitals, etc.: *an underdeveloped country* ◦ *It's in the poorer, underdeveloped eastern region of the country that the biggest problems exist.*

underdog /ˈʌn.də.dɒg/ ⓤⓢ /-dɚ.dɑːg/ noun **1 the underdog** [S] a person or group of people with less power, money, etc. than the rest of society: *As a politician, her sympathy was always for the underdog in society.* **2** [C usually singular] in a competition, the person or team considered to be the weakest and the least likely to win

underdone /ˌʌn.dəˈdʌn/ ⓤⓢ /-dɚ-/ adj describes food, especially meat, that is cooked for only a short time, or for less time than is necessary: *I like my steak underdone.* ◦ *These potatoes are underdone – I'll put them back in the oven.*

underdressed /ˌʌn.dəˈdrest/ ⓤⓢ /-dɚ-/ adj wearing clothes that are not attractive enough or formal enough for a particular occasion: *Everyone else was in smart suits and I felt a bit underdressed.*

underemployed /ˌʌn.dərɪmˈplɔɪd/ ⓤⓢ /-dɚ-/ adj not having enough work to do, or having a job that does not use all your skills

underestimate /ˌʌn.dəˈres.tɪ.meɪt/ ⓤⓢ /-dɚˈes-/ verb **AMOUNT** ▷ **1** B2 [I or T] to fail to guess or understand the real cost, size, difficulty, etc. of something: *Originally the builders gave me a price of £2,000, but now they say they underestimated and it's going to be at least £3,000.* ◦ *One shouldn't underestimate the difficulties of getting all the political parties to the conference table.* → Opposite **overestimate PERSON** ▷ **2** C1 [T] to fail to understand how strong, skilful, intelligent, or determined someone, especially a competitor, is: *Never underestimate your opponent!* • **underestimate** /-mət/ noun [C] *Clearly £25 was a serious underestimate.*

U

underexpose /ˌʌn.də.rɪkˈspəʊz/ ⓤⓢ /-dɚ.ɪkˈspoʊz/ verb [T] to give too little light to a piece of photographic film when taking a photograph

underfloor /ˌʌn.dəˈflɔːr/ ⓤⓢ /-dɚˈflɔːr/ adj [before noun] mainly UK under the surface of a floor: *an underfloor heating system*

underfoot /ˌʌn.dəˈfʊt/ ⓤⓢ /-dɚ-/ adv under your feet as you walk; on the ground: *The grass was cool and pleasant underfoot.* ◦ *Many people were* ***trampled/crushed*** *underfoot when the police tried to break up the demonstration.*

underfunded /ˌʌn.dəˈfʌn.dɪd/ ⓤⓢ /-dɚ-/ adj If an organization is underfunded, it does not receive a large enough income: *The government does not admit that the Hospital Service is underfunded.*

undergarment /ˈʌn.dəˌgɑː.mənt/ ⓤⓢ /-dɚˌgɑːr-/ noun [C] formal a piece of underwear

undergo /ˌʌn.dəˈgəʊ/ ⓤⓢ /-dɚˈgoʊ/ verb [T] (present participle **undergoing**, past tense **underwent**, past participle **undergone**) C1 to experience something that is unpleasant or something that involves a change: *She underwent an operation on a tumour in her left lung last year.* ◦ *Cinema in Britain is undergoing a revival of popularity.*

undergrad /ˈʌn.də.græd/ ⓤⓢ /-dɚ-/ noun [C] informal an undergraduate

undergraduate /ˌʌn.dəˈgræd.ju.ət/ ⓤⓢ /-dɚ-/ noun [C] a student who is studying for their first degree at college or university → Compare **graduate, postgraduate**

underground adj, adv; noun

▸adj, adv /ˌʌn.dəˈgraʊnd/ ⓤⓢ /-dɚ-/ **BELOW EARTH** ▷ **1** B2 below the surface of the Earth; below ground: *an underground cave/passage/cable* ◦ *Moles live underground.* **SECRET** ▷ **2** describes an activity that is secret and usually illegal: *an underground newspaper/movement* ◦ *The Communist Party was forced (to* ***go****) underground, and its leaders went into hiding.*

▸noun /ˈʌn.də.graʊnd/ ⓤⓢ /-dɚ-/ **TRANSPORT** ▷ **1 the underground** A2 [S] (also **the tube**) UK a railway system in which electric trains travel along passages below ground: ***the*** *London Underground* ◦ *They went* ***on the*** *underground.* **PEOPLE** ▷ **2** [U] people in a society who are trying new and often shocking or illegal ways of living or forms of art: *In Britain and the USA in the 1970s,* ***the*** *underground was a powerful subversive force.* **3 the underground** a group of people who secretly fight against the government: *He was a member of* ***the*** *underground, harassing the invading army.*

undergrowth /ˈʌn.də.grəʊθ/ ⓤⓢ /-dɚ.groʊθ/ noun [U] a mass of bushes, small trees, and plants growing under the trees of a wood or forest: *Police discovered the body hidden in thick undergrowth.*

underhand /ˌʌn.dəˈhænd/ ⓤⓢ /-dɚ-/ adj; adj, adv

▸adj (US usually **underhanded**) done secretly, and sometimes dishonestly, in order to achieve an advantage: *What really angered her was the dirty, underhand way they had tricked her.*

▸adj, adv US for **underarm**

underlay /ˈʌn.də.leɪ/ ⓤⓢ /-dɚ.leɪ/ noun [U] UK thick material put between a carpet and the floor for extra comfort and to protect the carpet

underlie /ˌʌn.dəˈlaɪ/ ⓤⓢ /-dɚ-/ verb [T] (present participle **underlying**, past tense **underlay**, past participle **underlain**) to be a hidden cause of or strong influence on something: *Psychological problems very often underlie apparently physical disorders.*

underline /ˌʌn.dəˈlaɪn/ ⓤⓢ /-dɚ-/ verb [T] (also **underscore**) **1** B1 to draw a line under a word, especially in order to show its importance: *All the technical words have been underlined* ***in*** *red.* **2** B2 to emphasize: *She put the figures up on the board to underline the seriousness of the situation.* ◦ *To underline their disgust, the crowd started throwing bottles at the stage.*

underling /ˈʌn.dəl.ɪŋ/ ⓤⓢ /-dɚ.lɪŋ/ noun [C] disapproving a person of low rank and little authority who works for someone more important: *She surrounded herself with underlings who were too afraid of her to answer back.*

underlying /ˌʌn.dəˈlaɪ.ɪŋ/ ⓤⓢ /-dɚ-/ adj [before noun] **NOT OBVIOUS** ▷ **1** C2 real but not immediately obvious: *And what might be the underlying significance of these supposedly random acts?* **BASED ON** ▷ **2** used to describe something on which something else is based: *The price of the investment fell below the value of the underlying* ***assets***. **UNDER** ▷ **3** positioned under the surface of something: *The currents are affected by the shape of the underlying rocks.*

undermanned /ˌʌn.dəˈmænd/ (US) /-dɚ-/ **adj under-staffed**

undermentioned /ˌʌn.dəˈmen.ʃᵊnd/ (US) /-dɚ-/ **adj** [before noun] formal used to refer to information that can be found in a later part of the same text: *The undermentioned staff all wish to join the union.* → Compare **above-mentioned**

undermine /ˌʌn.dəˈmaɪn/ (US) /-dɚ-/ **verb** [T] (C2) to make someone less confident, less powerful, or less likely to succeed, or to make something weaker, often gradually: *The president has accused two cabinet ministers of working secretly to undermine his position/him.* ◦ *Criticism just undermines their confidence.*

underneath /ˌʌn.dəˈniːθ/ (US) /-dɚ-/ **preposition, adv; noun**

▸**preposition, adv** (B1) under or below: *The tunnel goes right underneath the city.* ◦ *They found a bomb underneath the car.* ◦ *Underneath that shy exterior, she's actually a very warm person.* ◦ *He was wearing a garish T-shirt underneath his shirt.*

▸**noun** **the underneath** [S] the lower part or the bottom surface of something: *Bake for half an hour – the top should be crisp, and the underneath moist and succulent.* ◦ *She found the key taped to the underneath of the table, as always.*

undernourished /ˌʌn.dəˈnʌr.ɪʃt/ (US) /-dɚˈnɝː-/ **adj** not eating enough food to continue to be in good health: *Many of the children are undernourished and suffering from serious diseases.*

underpants /ˈʌn.də.pænts/ (US) /-dɚ-/ **noun** [plural] (UK also **pants**) (B1) a piece of underwear covering the area between the waist and the tops of the legs: *a pair of underpants*

underpass /ˈʌn.də.pɑːs/ (US) /-dɚ.pæs/ **noun** [C] (UK also **subway**) a road or path that goes under something such as a busy road, allowing vehicles or people to go from one side to the other

underpay /ˌʌn.dəˈpeɪ/ (US) /-dɚ-/ **verb** [T] (**underpaid, underpaid**) to pay someone too little for the work they do • **underpaid** /-ˈpeɪd/ **adj** (C1) *They're ridiculously underpaid, especially as the work is so dangerous.*

underpin /ˌʌn.dəˈpɪn/ (US) /-dɚ-/ **verb** [T] (**-nn-**) to give support, strength, or a basic structure to something: *He presented the figures to underpin his argument.* ◦ *Gradually the laws that underpinned (= formed part of the basic structure of) apartheid were abolished.* ◦ specialized *When restoring the building, the first priority was to underpin the exterior walls by adding wooden supports along the foundations.* • **underpinning** /ˈʌn.dəˌpɪn.ɪŋ/ (US) /-dɚ-/ **noun** [C or U] *After a while, we found ourselves questioning the spiritual and philosophical underpinning of the American way of life.*

underplay /ˌʌn.dəˈpleɪ/ (US) /-dɚ-/ **verb** [T] to make something such as a dangerous situation seem less important or dangerous than it really is: *While not wanting to underplay the seriousness of the situation, I have to say that it is not as bad as people seem to think.*

underprivileged /ˌʌn.dəˈprɪv.ɪ.lɪdʒd/ (US) /-dɚ-/ **adj; noun**

▸**adj** without the money, possessions, education, opportunities, etc. that the average person has: *Children from an underprivileged family background are statistically more likely to become involved in crime.*

▸**noun** [plural] **the underprivileged** polite phrase for poor people: *The charity raises money for holidays for the underprivileged.*

underrate /ˌʌn.dəˈreɪt/, /ˌʌn.dɚ-/ **verb** [T] to fail to understand how skilful, important, etc. someone or something is: *The company has consistently underrated the importance of a well-trained workforce.* • **underrated** /-ˈreɪ.tɪd/ (US) /-ˈreɪ.t̬ɪd/ **adj** *In my opinion, fennel is an underrated vegetable.*

ˌunder-repreˈsented **adj** If a type of person or thing is under-represented in a group or organization, there are not enough of them in it: *Hispanics are under-represented in US political institutions.*

underscore **verb; noun**

▸**verb** [T] /ˌʌn.dəˈskɔːʳ/ (US) /-dɚˈskɔːr/ to **underline**

▸**noun** [C or U] /ˈʌn.də.skɔːʳ/ (US) /-dɚ.skɔːr/ the character _ on a computer keyboard, used to draw a line under a letter or word, and also used in file names where a space is not allowed

undersea /ˌʌn.dəˈsiː/ (US) /-dɚ-/ **adj** [before noun] below the surface of the sea: *undersea exploration*

undersecretary /ˌʌn.dəˈsek.rə.tᵊr.i/ (US) /-dɚˈsek.rə.ter.i/ **noun** [C] a person who works for and has a slightly lower rank than the SECRETARY (= person in charge) of a government department: *She's Undersecretary of State for Foreign Affairs.*

undersell /ˌʌn.dəˈsel/ (US) /-dɚ-/ **verb** [T] (**undersold, undersold**) **SELL CHEAPLY** ▷ **1** to sell goods at a price lower than a competitor: *A big supermarket can usually undersell a small local store.* **BE MODEST** ▷ **2** to not give something or someone, especially yourself, the praise they deserve: *Don't undersell yourself – you've got a lot to offer a company.*

undershirt /ˈʌn.də.ʃɜːt/ (US) /-dɚ.ʃɝːt/ **noun** [C] US for **vest**

underside /ˈʌn.də.saɪd/ (US) /-dɚ-/ **noun** [C usually singular] the side of something that is usually nearest the ground

the undersigned /ˌʌn.dəˈsaɪnd/ (US) /-dɚ-/ **noun** [plural] formal the people whose SIGNATURES appear below in the text, usually at the end of a formal letter: *We, the undersigned, strongly object to the closure of St. Mary's Hospital: Jack James (Dr), Philippa Curry (Dr), Hugh Edwards.*

undersized /ˌʌn.dəˈsaɪzd/ (US) /ˈʌn.dɚ-/ **adj** (also **undersize**) smaller than average, or smaller than the correct size: *an undersized, malnourished boy*

understaffed /ˌʌn.dəˈstɑːft/ (US) /-dɚˈstæft/ **adj** (also **undermanned**) If a shop, business, or organization is understaffed, it does not have enough employees. → Opposite **overstaffed**

understand /ˌʌn.dəˈstænd/ (US) /-dɚ-/ **verb** (**understood, understood**) **KNOW** ▷ **1** (A1) [I or T] to know the meaning of something that someone says: *She explained the whole idea again, but I still didn't understand.* ◦ *Is there anyone here who understands Arabic?* ◦ *I think he was phoning from a pub – it was so noisy I couldn't understand (= recognize) a word he said.* **2** (A2) [I or T] to know why or how something happens or works: [+ question word] *We still don't fully understand how the brain works.* **3** (B1) [I or T] to know how someone feels or why they behave in a particular way: *My wife doesn't understand me.* ◦ *Sometimes I don't understand James.* ◦ [+ question word] *You don't understand **what** it's like/**how** it feels to have to beg on the streets.* **4** **understand sb to mean sth** to think, especially wrongly, that someone means a particular thing: *When he said three o'clock, I understood him to mean in the afternoon.* **5** **understand one another/each other** When two people understand one another, they both know what the other means and wants and they have an agreement: *Both sides must try to understand one another, to recognize each other's rights and beliefs.* **REALIZE** ▷ **6** (C1) [T] formal to know or

U

realize something because you have been told it: [+ (that)] *I understand (**that**) you are interested in borrowing some money from us.* ◦ [+ that] *The Director had **given** her **to** understand (= told her) **that** she would be promoted.* ◦ [+ obj + to infinitive] *A secret buyer is understood **to** have paid £1 million for the three pictures (= there is unofficial news that this has happened).* **7** [I or T] formal used when making certain that someone knows what you mean and that they will do as you want: *I don't want you to see that boy again. Understand?/Do you understand?/Is that understood?* **8 it is understood** formal used to refer to something such as a rule that everyone knows and accepts: *In the library it is understood **that** loud talking is not permissible.*

> **+ Other ways of saying understand**
>
> See also: **realize**
>
> **Comprehend** is a slightly more formal way of saying 'understand':
>
> *He doesn't seem to **comprehend** the scale of the problem.*
>
> The phrase **get the picture** can be used in more informal situations to mean 'understand':
>
> *OK. Don't say any more. I **get the picture**.*
>
> **Follow** can be used when someone understands something as it is being said:
>
> *It was so complicated I couldn't **follow** what he was saying.*
>
> If you understand something that is difficult, the verb **grasp** can be used:
>
> *I think I **grasped** the main points of the lecture.*
>
> If you understand something that you read or hear after taking time, you could use the verb **digest**:
>
> *This chapter is so difficult to **digest**. I'll have to read it again later.*
>
> **Fathom** can be used when someone understands something that is mysterious:
>
> *For years, people have been trying to **fathom** the mysteries of the whale's song.*
>
> If you understand a joke, the verb **get** is sometimes used:
>
> *I told him a joke, but he didn't **get** it.*

IDIOM **make yourself understood** C2 to communicate effectively: *Since they spoke only Swahili, we used signs and gestures to make ourselves understood.*

understandable /ˌʌn.dəˈstæn.də.bl/ US /-dɚ-/ **adj** **1** easy to understand: *You've got to put the facts into a form that's understandable **to** everyone.* **2** B2 You say that something, for example someone's behaviour, is understandable, if you feel that it is usual and not strange or difficult to understand: *Their refusal to cooperate is perfectly/completely understandable, considering the circumstances.* • **understandably** /ˌʌn.dəˈstæn.də.bli/ US /-dɚ-/ **adv**

understanding /ˌʌn.dəˈstæn.dɪŋ/ US /-dɚ-/ **noun; adj**

▸**noun** KNOWLEDGE ▷ **1** B2 [U] knowledge about a subject, situation, etc. or about how something works: *She doesn't have any understanding **of** politics/human nature/what it takes to be a good manager.* ◦ *My understanding **of** the agreement (= what I think it means) is that they will pay £50,000 over two years.* SYMPATHY ▷ **2** B2 [S or U] a positive relationship between two people or groups in which they feel sympathy for each other: *For peace to exist in the region there needs to be a much improved understanding **between** all the parties concerned.* AGREEMENT ▷ **3** C1 [C] an informal agreement between people: *It took several hours of discussion before they could **come to/reach** an understanding.* **4 on the understanding (that)** If you do something on the understanding that something else can or will happen, you do it because someone else has promised that it can or will: *We bought the cupboard on the understanding that we could return it if it wasn't suitable.*

▸**adj** approving B2 describes someone who has the ability to know how someone else is feeling or what their situation is, and can forgive them if they do something wrong: *He had expected her to be horrified, but she was actually very understanding.*

understate /ˌʌn.dəˈsteɪt/ US /-dɚ-/ **verb** [T] to describe something in a way that makes it seem less important, serious, bad, etc. than it really is: *She believes the research understates the amount of discrimination women suffer.*

understated /ˌʌn.dəˈsteɪ.tɪd/ US /-dɚˈsteɪ.t̬ɪd/ **adj** not trying to attract attention or IMPRESS people: approving *He's very elegant, in an understated way.*

understatement /ˌʌn.dəˈsteɪt.mənt/ US /-dɚ-/ **noun** [S or U] a statement that describes something in a way that makes it seem less important, serious, bad, etc. than it really is, or the act of making such statements: *To say that her resignation was a shock would be an understatement – it caused panic.* ◦ *That New York City is not a peaceful place to live is **the** understatement **of the** year/month/century.*

understudy /ˈʌn.dəˌstʌd.i/ US /-dɚ-/ **noun** [C] an actor who learns the parts of other actors in a play, so that he or she can replace them if necessary, for example if they are ill • **understudy verb** [T]

undertake /ˌʌn.dəˈteɪk/ US /-dɚ-/ **verb** [T] (**undertook, undertaken**) DO ▷ **1** C1 formal to do or begin to do something, especially something that will take a long time or be difficult: *Students are required to undertake simple experiments.* PROMISE ▷ **2** C2 formal to promise that you will do something: [+ to infinitive] *She undertook not **to** publish the names of the people involved.* ◦ [+ that] *The government undertook **that** the buildings would not be redeveloped.*

undertaker /ˈʌn.dəˌteɪ.kər/ US /-dɚˌteɪ.kɚ/ **noun** [C] (US also **mortician**) a person whose job is to prepare dead bodies that are going to be buried or CREMATED (= burned) and to organize funerals

undertaking /ˌʌn.dəˈteɪ.kɪŋ/ US /ˈʌn.dɚˌteɪ.kɪŋ/ **noun** [C] JOB ▷ **1** C2 a job, business, or piece of work: *The construction of the tunnel is a large and complex undertaking.* PROMISE ▷ **2** formal a formal promise: [+ that] formal *The manager **gave** a written undertaking **that** no one would lose their job.*

undertone /ˈʌn.də.təʊn/ US /-dɚ.toʊn/ **noun** CHARACTERISTIC ▷ **1** [C] a particular but not obvious characteristic that a piece of writing or speech, an event, or a situation has: *I thought her speech had slightly sinister undertones.* ◦ *It was a comedy act with an undertone **of** cruelty.* QUIET VOICE ▷ **2 in an undertone** in a very quiet voice: *Freddie muttered something to me in an undertone.*

undertow /ˈʌn.də.təʊ/ US /-dɚ.toʊ/ **noun** [C usually singular] a strong current flowing underwater in a different direction to the way the water on the surface is moving, especially one that flows away from the beach at the same time as a wave hits the beach

undertrial /ʌn.dəˈtraɪəl/ US /-dɚ-/ **noun** [C] Indian English a person who is appearing in a law court because they have been accused of committing a crime

underused /ˌʌn.dəˈjuːzd/ US /-dɚ-/ **adj** not used as

U

much as it could or should be: *Since the main hospital was built, the local clinics have been rather underused.*

undervalue /ˌʌn.dəˈvæl.juː/ (US) /-dɚ-/ **verb** [T] to consider someone or something as less valuable or important than they really are: *The company had undervalued the building* ***by*** *£20,000.* ◦ *He felt undervalued and underpaid.*

underwater /ˌʌn.dəˈwɔː.təʳ/ (US) /-dɚˈwɑː.t̬ɚ/ **adj, adv** B2 under the surface of the water, especially under the surface of the sea: *an underwater camera* (= a camera that you can use underwater) ◦ *Some species of turtle can remain underwater for 24 hours.*

underway (also ˌ**under** ˈ**way**) /ˌʌn.dəˈweɪ/ (US) /-dɚ-/ **adj** [after verb] **1** C2 If something is underway, it is happening now: *Economic recovery is* ***already*** *underway.* **2 get underway** C2 to begin: *The film festival gets underway on 11 July .*

underwear /ˈʌn.də.weəʳ/ (US) /-dɚ.wer/ **noun** [U] B1 clothes worn next to the skin, under other clothes

underweight /ˌʌn.dəˈweɪt/ (US) /-dɚ-/ **adj** Underweight people weigh too little and are too thin: *According to the hospital chart he's four kilos underweight.* → Opposite **overweight**

underwent /ˌʌn.dəˈwent/ (US) /-dɚ-/ **verb** past simple of **undergo**

underwhelmed /ˌʌn.dəˈwelmd/ (US) /-dɚ-/ **adj** humorous feeling no excitement about or admiration for something or someone: *I get the feeling that the staff are distinctly underwhelmed by John's latest proposal.*

underwired /ˌʌn.dəˈwaɪəd/ (US) /-dɚˈwaɪrd/ **adj** (US **underwire**) used to describe women's clothing made with a piece of wire under the breasts for extra support: *an underwired bra*

underworld /ˈʌn.də.wɜːld/ (US) /-dɚ.wɝːld/ **noun** [S] **CRIME** ▷ **1** the part of society consisting of criminal organizations and activities **IN STORIES** ▷ **2 the underworld** in MYTHOLOGY, a place under the earth where the spirits of the dead go → Compare **Hades**

underwrite /ˌʌn.dəˈraɪt/ (US) /ˈʌn.dɚ.raɪt/ **verb** [T] (**underwrote, underwritten**) **1** If a bank or other organization underwrites an activity, it gives it financial support and takes responsibility for paying any costs if it fails. **2** specialized If a company underwrites an INSURANCE POLICY, someone's property, etc., they have an agreement to pay out money in cases of damage or loss. • **underwriter** /-ˌraɪ.təʳ/ (US) /-ˌraɪ.t̬ɚ/ **noun** [C]

undesirable /ˌʌn.dɪˈzaɪə.rə.bl̩/ (US) /-ˈzaɪr.ə-/ **adj** disapproving C2 not wanted, approved of, or popular: *Houses near industrial sites often do not sell so quickly because they are regarded as undesirable.*

undesirables /ˌʌn.dɪˈzaɪə.rə.bl̩z/ (US) /-ˈzaɪr.ə-/ **noun** [plural] often humorous people whose behaviour or appearance makes them unacceptable in society or at a particular occasion: *There are guards on the door to keep out (the) undesirables.*

undeveloped /ˌʌn.dɪˈvel.əpt/ **adj** C2 An undeveloped place or piece of land has not been built on or used for farming.

undid /ʌnˈdɪd/ **verb** past simple of **undo**

undies /ˈʌn.diz/ **noun** [plural] informal → **underwear**

undiluted /ˌʌn.daɪˈluː.tɪd/ (US) /-ˈluː.t̬ɪd/ **adj** **1** If a liquid is undiluted it has not been mixed with water to make it less strong. **2** If the truth or a fact, etc. is undiluted it is stated in a simple, clear way, without trying to disguise it or make it easier to accept.

undisclosed /ˌʌn.dɪsˈkləʊzd/ (US) /-ˈkloʊzd/ **adj** If official information is undisclosed, it is secret: *The meeting is taking place at an undisclosed location.*

undisguised /ˌʌn.dɪsˈgaɪzd/ **adj** describes a feeling that is clearly shown or expressed, when it is usually kept hidden: *She looked at him with undisguised contempt.*

undisputed /ˌʌn.dɪˈspjuː.tɪd/ (US) /-t̬ɪd/ **adj** If something is undisputed, everyone agrees about it: *an undisputed fact* ◦ *the undisputed champion/winner*

undisturbed /ˌʌn.dɪˈstɜːbd/ (US) /-ˈstɝːbd/ **adj** not interrupted or changed in any way: *eight hours of undisturbed sleep*

undivided /ˌʌn.dɪˈvaɪ.dɪd/ **adj** **1** existing as a whole, not in separate parts **2 undivided attention** complete attention: *If you just wait till I've finished this bit of work you will* ***have****/I will* ***give*** *you my undivided attention.*

undo /ʌnˈduː/ **verb** [T] (present participle **undoing**, past tense **undid**, past participle **undone**) **UNFASTEN** ▷ **1** B2 to unfasten something that is fastened or tied: *Can someone help me to undo my seat belt?* **REMOVE EFFECTS** ▷ **2** B2 to remove the good or bad effects of an action or several actions: *I did a really tough aerobics class and then went out for a meal and undid* ***(all) the good work!*** ◦ *It's very difficult to undo* ***the damage*** *that's caused by inadequate parenting in a child's early years.*

undocumented /ʌnˈdɒk.jə.men.tɪd/ (US) /-ˈdɑː.kjə.men.t̬ɪd/ **adj** **1** not having any documents to prove that you are living or working in a country legally: *undocumented immigrants/aliens/workers* **2** not supported by written proof: *People should not stop eating fish because of some undocumented risk of cancer.*

undoing /ʌnˈduː.ɪŋ/ **noun** [S] formal the cause of someone's failure, or of their loss of power or money: *Greed has been* ***the*** *undoing* ***of*** *many a businessman.*

undone /ʌnˈdʌn/ **adj** **NOT FASTENED** ▷ **1** unfastened: *Why didn't you tell me my zip was undone!* ◦ *Damn, my shoe-laces have* ***come*** *undone again.* **DISAPPOINTED** ▷ **2 be undone** old use to be without hope for the future, having experienced great disappointment, loss of money, etc.

undoubted /ʌnˈdaʊ.tɪd/ (US) /-t̬ɪd/ **adj** [usually before noun] C2 used to emphasize that something is true: *She is the undoubted star of British ballet.* • **undoubtedly** /-li/ **adv** B2 *She was undoubtedly the best candidate.*

undreamed of /ʌnˈdriːmd.əv/ **adj** (also **undreamt of** /ʌnˈdremt.əv/) describes WEALTH, success, or progress that is better or greater than anyone would think possible: *We in the West enjoy a standard of living undreamed of by the majority of people in the world.* ◦ [before noun] *These two lads have enjoyed undreamed-of success with their first album.*

undress /ʌnˈdres/ **verb; noun**

▸**verb** [I or T] B1 to remove your clothes or remove the clothes from someone else: *Could you undress the kids for bed, Steve?* ◦ *He undressed and got into the bath.* • **undressed** /-ˈdrest/ **adj** [usually after verb] B2 *You two kids* ***get*** *undressed, and I'll run the bath.*

IDIOM **undress sb with your eyes** informal to look at someone's body with strong, and often unpleasant, sexual DESIRE

▸**noun** formal or humorous **in a state of undress** not wearing many or any clothes: *He came to the door in a state of undress.*

undue /ʌnˈdjuː/ (US) /-ˈduː/ **adj** [before noun] formal C2 to a level that is more than is necessary, acceptable, or reasonable: *Such a high increase will impose an undue*

U

burden on the local tax payer. • **unduly** /-li/ adv *There's no need to be unduly* ***pessimistic*** *about the situation.*

undulating /ˈʌn.djʊ.leɪ.tɪŋ/ (US) /-t̬ɪŋ/ adj formal **1** describing or having small hills and slopes that look like waves: *undulating roads* ◦ *I love the gently undulating hills of the Dales.* **2** moving gently up and down: *undulating waves* • **undulate** /-leɪt/ verb [I]

undying /ʌnˈdaɪ.ɪŋ/ adj [before noun] literary Undying feelings or beliefs are permanent and never end: *He pledged undying love/loyalty.*

unˌearned ˈincome noun [U] money that you get from INVESTMENTS and property that you own, instead of earning by working

unearth /ʌnˈɜːθ/ (US) /-ˈɝːθ/ verb [T] **1** to discover something in the ground: *Building at the site was halted after human remains were unearthed earlier this month.* **2** to discover proof or some other information, especially after careful searching: *A private detective has apparently unearthed some fresh evidence.*

unearthly /ʌnˈɜːθ.li/ (US) /-ˈɝːθ-/ adj **NOT CONVENIENT** ▷ **1** informal describes a time that is not at all convenient because it is too early in the morning or too late at night: *I was woken up* ***at some*** *unearthly* ***hour*** *of the morning by someone knocking on my door.* **STRANGE** ▷ **2** strange in a mysterious and sometimes frightening way: *Cats' cries have an unearthly quality.*

uneasiness /ʌnˈiː.zi.nəs/ noun [U] (also **unease**) worry or ANXIETY: ***Growing*** *unease* ***at*** *the prospect of an election is causing fierce arguments within the party.*

uneasy /ʌnˈiː.zi/ adj **1** (B2) If you are uneasy, you are slightly worried or uncomfortable about a particular situation: *I feel a bit uneasy* ***about*** *asking her to do me such a big favour.* **2** describes a situation or condition that makes people slightly worried, often because it may not continue successfully: *Who can predict how long this uneasy peace between the two countries will last?* ◦ *She has a rather uneasy relationship with her mother-in-law.* • **uneasily** /-zɪ.li/ adv

uneconomic /ʌnˌiː.kəˈnɒm.ɪk/, /-ˌek.ə-/ (US) /-ˈnɑː.mɪk/ adj (also **uneconomical**) **1** describes businesses and industries that are not making enough profit or are losing money: *The minister maintained that the coal mines were uneconomic and would have to be closed.* **2** Uneconomic processes or activities waste money, time, or materials, and are likely to result in a loss of money.

unedifying /ʌnˈed.ɪ.faɪ.ɪŋ/ adj formal unpleasant and causing people to feel no respect: *We were treated to the unedifying* ***spectacle*** *of two cabinet ministers fighting over a seat.*

uneducated /ʌnˈed.jʊ.keɪ.tɪd/ (US) /-t̬ɪd/ adj having received little or no education

U

unemployed /ˌʌn.ɪmˈplɔɪd/ adj; noun

▸adj (B1) not having a job that provides money: *He's been unemployed for over a year.*

▸noun [plural] (C1) people who do not have a job that provides money: *There are now over four million unemployed in this country.* ◦ *Tickets are £10 or £5 for* ***the*** *unemployed.*

unemployment /ˌʌn.ɪmˈplɔɪ.mənt/ noun [U] **1** (B1) the number of people who do not have a job which provides money: *Unemployment has* ***fallen/risen*** *again for the third consecutive month.* **2** the state of being unemployed **3** (also **unemployment compensation**, also **unemployment insurance**) US for **jobseeker's allowance**

unemˈployment ˌbenefit noun [U] UK (US **unemˈployment ˌbenefits**) money that the government pays to unemployed people who are looking for a job → Compare **jobseeker's allowance**

> **Word partners for unemployment**
>
> unemployment *drops/falls/increases/rises* • *combat/tackle* unemployment • *high/low/rising/soaring* unemployment • unemployment *figures/levels/numbers/statistics* • the unemployment *rate* • a *growth/increase/rise* in unemployment • a *decrease/drop/fall* in unemployment

unending /ʌnˈen.dɪŋ/ adj formal describes activities or events, especially unpleasant ones, when they seem to continue for ever: *Motherhood seemed to her an unending cycle of cooking, washing, and cleaning.*

unendurable /ˌʌn.ɪnˈdjʊə.rə.bl̩/ (US) /-ˈdʊr.ə-/ adj formal If a situation or experience is unendurable, it is so unpleasant or painful that it is almost impossible to bear: *unendurable pain/suspense*

unenforceable /ˌʌn.ɪnˈfɔː.sə.bl̩/ (US) /-ˈfɔːr-/ adj If a rule or law is unenforceable, it is impossible to force people to obey it.

unenviable /ʌnˈen.vi.ə.bl̩/ adj describes a duty or necessary action that is unpleasant or difficult: *I had the unenviable* ***task*** *of cleaning up after the party.*

unequal /ʌnˈiː.kwəl/ adj **NOT THE SAME** ▷ **1** formal different in size, level, amount, etc.: *She cut two slices of noticeably unequal size.* **NOT FAIR** ▷ **2** not treating everyone the same; unfair: *Until women are paid as much as men, they will be competing on unequal terms.* ◦ *They have a rather unequal relationship.* **NOT ABLE** ▷ **3 be unequal to sth** formal to not have the necessary ability, power, or qualities to achieve something: *He tried to cheer her up but found himself unequal to* ***the task***. • **unequally** /-i/ adv

unequalled formal (US usually **unequaled**) /ʌnˈiː.kwəld/ adj better or more extreme than any other: *Though small, this restaurant offers a range of fish dishes unequalled anywhere else in London.*

unequivocal /ˌʌn.ɪˈkwɪv.ə.kəl/ adj total, or expressed in a clear and certain way: *The prime minister, he said, had the party's unequivocal support.* ◦ *The church has been unequivocal in its condemnation of the violence.* • **unequivocally** /-i/ adv

unerring /ʌnˈɜː.rɪŋ/ (US) /-ˈer.ɪŋ/ adj **1** never failing to hit a target **2** always accurate in your judgment or ability: *He has an unerring talent for writing catchy melodies.* • **unerringly** /-li/ adv

UNESCO (also **Unesco**) /juːˈnes.kəʊ/ (US) /-koʊ/ noun [+ sing/pl verb] abbreviation for United Nations Educational, Scientific, and Cultural Organization: a department of the United Nations which aims to encourage peace between countries through education, science, and culture

unethical /ʌnˈeθ.ɪ.kəl/ adj (C2) not ETHICAL (= based on moral beliefs)

uneven /ʌnˈiː.vən/ adj **NOT EVEN** ▷ **1** (C2) not level, equal, flat, or continuous: *Take care when you walk on that path – the paving stones are rather uneven.* ◦ *There is an uneven distribution of wealth across the country from the north to the south.* ◦ *The contest was very uneven – the other team was far stronger than us.* **NOT GOOD** ▷ **2** different in quality; often used to avoid saying bad: *Your work has been rather uneven this term, Matthew.* • **unevenly** /-li/ adv • **unevenness** /-nəs/ noun [U]

unˌeven ˈbars noun [plural] US for **asymmetric bars**

uneventful /ˌʌn.ɪˈvent.fəl/ adj (C2) describes a time or situation in which nothing interesting or surprising happens: *It was an uneventful journey.* • **uneventfully** /-i/ adv

unexceptionable /ˌʌn.ɪk'sep.ʃᵊn.ə.bl̩/ adj formal not bad; having nothing that anyone could criticize or disapprove of: *an unexceptionable speech*

unexceptional /ˌʌn.ɪk'sep.ʃᵊn.ᵊl/ adj ordinary, not EXCEPTIONAL

unexpected /ˌʌn.ɪk'spek.tɪd/ adj B1 not expected: *Well, fancy seeing you here! This really is an unexpected* ***pleasure!*** • **unexpectedly** /-li/ adv

unexplained /ʌn.ɪk'spleɪnd/ adj describes events, behaviour, etc. for which people do not know or understand the reason: *an unexplained death/noise* ◦ *He was shot dead earlier this year in unexplained* ***circumstances.***

unexplored /ʌn.ɪk'splɔːd/ US /-'splɔːrd/ adj **PLACE** ▷ **1** describes a place where people have not been to find out what is there: *unexplored territory* **PLAN** ▷ **2** describes a plan, idea, or subject that has not been examined to find out what it involves: *The subject of alternative medical care for older people has been entirely unexplored.*

unexpurgated /ʌn'ek.spə.geɪ.tɪd/ US /-spɚ.geɪ.t̬ɪd/ adj describes a book, article, film, etc. that is complete and contains everything, including parts considered likely to cause offence

unfailing /ʌn'feɪ.lɪŋ/ adj describes a positive quality of someone's character when it shows itself at all times: *unfailing enthusiasm* • **unfailingly** /-li/ adv *She's unfailingly cheerful no matter what the circumstances.*

unfair /ʌn'feəʳ/ US /-'fer/ adj B1 not treating people in a equal way, or not morally right: *an unfair system* ◦ [+ to infinitive] *It's unfair to blame Roger.* • **unfairly** /-li/ adv • **unfairness** /-nəs/ noun [U]

> **Other ways of saying unfair**
>
> **Unjust** is an alternative to 'unfair':
>
> *It seems* ***unjust*** *that people should be expected to pay twice.*
>
> If something is unfair because it shows an unreasonable like or dislike for someone that is based on personal opinions, you could use the words **biased** or **slanted**:
>
> *The newspaper gave a very* ***biased*** *report of the meeting.*
>
> *The report was* ***slanted*** *in favour of the developers.*
>
> **Discriminatory** is often used when something is unfair because it treats people differently because of their sex, skin colour, religion, etc.:
>
> *The company has a zero-tolerance policy toward* ***discriminatory*** *practices.*
>
> In formal English, the word **inequitable** is often used when something is unfair because it is good for some people and bad for other people:
>
> *The current health care system is* ***inequitable.***

unfaithful /ʌn'feɪθ.fᵊl/ adj having a sexual relationship or experience with a person who is not your husband, wife, or usual sexual partner: *If a man was unfaithful* ***to*** *me I'd leave him no matter what the circumstances.* • **unfaithfulness** /-nəs/ noun [U]

unfaltering /ʌn'fɒl.tᵊr.ɪŋ/ US /-'fɑːl.t̬ɚ-/ adj never stopping or losing strength; not FALTERING: *unfaltering commitment/support/belief*

unfamiliar /ʌn.fə'mɪl.i.əʳ/ US /-jɚ/ adj **1** B2 not known to you: *I noticed several unfamiliar faces in the meeting room.* ◦ *His name was unfamiliar* ***to*** *me.* **2 be unfamiliar with sth** B2 to not have any knowledge or

experience of something: *Many older people are unfamiliar with computers.*

unfashionable /ʌn'fæʃ.ᵊn.ə.bl̩/ adj B2 not modern or popular: *They paid less for the house because it was in an unfashionable part of town.*

unfasten /ʌn'fɑː.sᵊn/ US /-'fæs-/ verb [I or T] to release or open something that is fixed or closed: *I can't unfasten this button/belt.* ◦ *This blouse unfastens (= can be unfastened) at the back.*

unfathomable /ʌn'fæð.ə.mə.bl̩/ adj formal impossible to understand: *For some unfathomable reason they built the toilet next to the kitchen.* • **unfathomably** /-bli/ adv formal

unfavourable UK (US **unfavorable**) /ʌn'feɪ.vᵊr.ə.bl̩/ US /-vɚ-/ adj **1** C2 not giving you an advantage or a good chance of success **2** C2 negative and showing that you do not like something: *He always talks about her in an unfavourable way.* ◦ *Of those surveyed, 62 percent said they had an unfavourable opinion of the president.* → Opposite **favourable** • **unfavourably** /-bli/ adv

unfazed /ʌn'feɪzd/ adj informal not surprised or worried: *She seems unfazed by her sudden success and fame.*

unfeasible /ʌn'fiː.zɪ.bl̩/ adj not FEASIBLE (= able to be done or achieved) • **unfeasibly** /-bli/ adv

unfeeling /ʌn'fiː.lɪŋ/ adj disapproving not feeling sympathy for other people's suffering

unfettered /ʌn'fet.əd/ US /-'fet̬.ɚd/ adj formal not limited by rules or any other controlling influence: *In writing poetry, one is unfettered* ***by*** *the normal rules of sentence structure.*

unfiltered /ʌn'fɪl.təd/ US /-t̬ɚd/ adj **1** not having had solids removed with a FILTER: *unfiltered apple juice* **2** with no information removed: *The radio station provides millions of people with unfiltered news and political debate.* **3** used for referring to cigarettes or CIGARS without FILTERS in one end to remove harmful substances

unfinished /ʌn'fɪn.ɪʃt/ adj **1** not ended or completed **2 unfinished business** a matter, especially a disagreement, that is not yet decided or agreed: *I still have some unfinished business* ***with*** *you.*

unfit /ʌn'fɪt/ adj **NOT HEALTHY** ▷ **1** B1 not healthy because you do too little exercise: *I used to take plenty of exercise, but now I'm terribly unfit.* **NOT GOOD ENOUGH** ▷ **2** B2 not suitable or good enough for a particular purpose or activity: *The building was declared unfit* ***for*** *human habitation.*

unflagging /ʌn'flæg.ɪŋ/ adj If a quality, such as energy, interest, or enthusiasm, is unflagging, it never becomes weaker: *He thanked Tony for his unflagging energy and support.*

unflappable /ʌn'flæp.ə.bl̩/ adj not likely to get worried, nervous, or angry even in difficult situations: *She's totally unflappable – you have to be when working in such a highly-pressured environment.*

unflattering /ʌn'flæt.ᵊr.ɪŋ/ US /-'flæt̬.ɚ-/ adj making someone look less attractive or seem worse than they usually do: *an unflattering photo/dress/colour* ◦ *The book portrays her in a most unflattering* ***light.***

unflinching /ʌn'flɪn.tʃɪŋ/ adj not frightened of or trying to avoid a dangerous or unpleasant situation: *It is a brave and unflinching account of prison life.*

unfold /ʌn'fəʊld/ US /-'foʊld/ verb **OPEN** ▷ **1** C1 [T] to open or spread out something that has been folded: *If we unfold the table we can fit eight people around it.* ◦ *He watched her expression as she unfolded the letter.*

U

DEVELOP ▷ **2** C2 [I] If a situation or story unfolds, it develops or becomes clear to other people: *Like a lot of people, I've watched the **events** of the last few days unfold on TV.* ◦ *As the plot unfolds, you gradually realize that all your initial assumptions were wrong.* **3** [T] formal to tell someone about something, especially a plan, and explain it in detail: *I've arranged a lunch with him next Thursday at which I intend to unfold my proposal.*

unfollow /ʌnˈfɒl.əʊ/ US /-ˈfɑː.loʊ/ verb [T] to stop FOLLOWING someone on Twitter (= stop reading the messages that they have published)

unforeseen /ˌʌn.fəˈsiːn/ US /-fɚ-/ adj C1 not expected: *Due to unforeseen **circumstances** the cost of the improvements has risen by 20 percent.* ◦ *Unless there are any unforeseen problems the whole project should be finished by the spring.*

unforgettable /ˌʌn.fəˈget.ə.bl̩/ US /-fɚˈt̬ge-/ adj B1 An unforgettable experience has such a strong effect or influence on you that you cannot forget it. • **unforgettably** /-bli/ adv

unfortunate /ʌnˈfɔː.tʃən.ət/ US /-ˈfɔːr-/ adj; noun

▸adj UNLUCKY ▷ **1** B2 unlucky or having bad effects: *She has inherited her father's large nose, which is very unfortunate.* ◦ [+ (that)] ***It** was just unfortunate (that) he phoned exactly as our guests were arriving.* NOT SUITABLE ▷ **2** formal (of remarks or behaviour) unsuitable in a way which could cause embarrassment or offence: *The housing director's remark that 'the homeless could do more to help themselves' was unfortunate to say the least.*

▸noun [C] formal or humorous an unlucky person who is in a bad situation: *He was one of the **poor** unfortunates who invested in the company and now finds himself a few thousand pounds poorer.*

unfortunately /ʌnˈfɔː.tʃən.ət.li/ US /-ˈfɔːr-/ adv A2 used to say that something is sad, disappointing, or has a bad effect: *Unfortunately, I didn't have my credit card with me or I'd certainly have bought it.*

> **!** Common mistake: **unfortunately**
>
> **Warning:** Common word-building error!
>
> If an adjective ends with 'te', just add 'ly' to make an adverb. Don't write 'unfortunatly' or 'unfortunatelly', write **unfortunately.**

unfounded /ʌnˈfaʊn.dɪd/ adj describes a claim or piece of news that is not based on fact: *I'm pleased to see that our fears about the weather **proved** totally unfounded.*

unfriend /ʌnˈfrend/ verb [T] → **defriend**

unfriendly /ʌnˈfrend.li/ adj B1 showing dislike and no sympathy → Opposite **friendly** • **unfriendliness** /-nəs/ noun [U]

unfulfilled /ˌʌn.fʊlˈfɪld/ adj **1** If a wish, hope, promise, etc. is unfulfilled, it has not happened or been achieved: *an unfulfilled ambition/dream* **2** unhappy because you think you should be achieving more in your life

unfurl /ʌnˈfɜːl/ US /-ˈfɝːl/ verb [I or T] If a flag, sail, or BANNER unfurls, it becomes open from a rolled position, and if you unfurl a flag, etc., you make it do this: *The demonstrators unfurled a large banner.*

unfurnished /ʌnˈfɜː.nɪʃt/ US /-ˈfɝː-/ adj describes a room, house, or other building without furniture in it: *unfurnished accommodation*

ungainly /ʌnˈgeɪn.li/ adj awkward and without GRACE (= moving smoothly and attractively) in movement: *Ducks are ungainly on land.*

unglamorous /ʌnˈglæm.ər.əs/ US /-ɚ-/ adj not GLAMOROUS (= especially attractive and exciting): *unglamorous work/surroundings*

unglued /ʌnˈgluːd/ adj US informal **come unglued** to experience difficulties and fail: *When the secret arrangements came unglued, the president was revealed to have ordered the burglary.*

ungodly /ʌnˈgɒd.li/ US /-ˈgɑːd-/ adj [before noun] informal extreme or unacceptable: *I had to get up at some ungodly **hour** in the morning to take her to the airport.*

ungovernable /ʌnˈgʌv.ən.ə.bl̩/ US /-ɚ.nə-/ adj unable to be governed or controlled

ungrammatical /ˌʌn.grəˈmæt.ɪ.kəl/ US /-ˈmæt̬-/ adj not GRAMMATICAL

ungrateful /ʌnˈgreɪt.fəl/ adj not showing or expressing any thanks → Opposite **grateful**

unguarded /ʌnˈgɑː.dɪd/ US /-ˈgɑːr-/ adj **1** not guarded or protected: *You shouldn't leave your bag unguarded in a pub like that.* **2** If you make an unguarded remark or say something in an unguarded moment, you tell someone something that you would usually keep secret, sometimes in a way that shows bad judgment: *In an unguarded moment, I said that I didn't trust Carlo.*

unhappy /ʌnˈhæp.i/ adj A2 sad or not satisfied: *That's enough to make anyone unhappy.* ◦ *an unhappy marriage* ◦ *I was very unhappy **with** the service.* • **unhappily** /-ɪ.li/ adv • **unhappiness** /-nəs/ noun [U]

> **+** Other ways of saying **unhappy**
>
> **Sad** and **miserable** mean the same as 'unhappy':
>
> *I felt so **sad** after he left.*
>
> *I just woke up feeling **miserable**.*
>
> If someone is **upset**, that person is unhappy because something bad has happened:
>
> *They'd had an argument and she was still **upset** about it.*
>
> *Mike got very **upset** when I told him the news.*
>
> If someone is **broken-hearted** or **heartbroken** that person is very sad because someone he or she loves has ended their relationship:
>
> *She was **broken-hearted** when Richard left.*
>
> Someone who is **devastated** or **distraught** is extremely upset:
>
> *She was **devastated** when he died.*
>
> ***Distraught** relatives waited for word of loved ones missing after the earthquake.*
>
> The adjectives **depressed**, **down**, or **low** are often used when someone is unhappy for a long time:
>
> *She became deeply **depressed** after her cat died.*
>
> *I've been feeling a bit **down** recently.*
>
> *He was very **low** for months after he lost his job.*

unharmed /ʌnˈhɑːmd/ US /-ˈhɑːrmd/ adj [after verb] not hurt or damaged: *Both children escaped unharmed from the burning building.*

unhealthy /ʌnˈhel.θi/ adj B1 not good for your health, or not strong and well: *an unhealthy diet* • **unhealthily** /-θɪ.li/ adv

unheard /ʌnˈhɜːd/ US /-ˈhɝːd/ adj **go unheard** to not be listened to or considered: *We complained but as usual our voices went unheard.*

unˈheard-of adj surprising or shocking because not known about or previously experienced: *It was unheard-of for an unmarried couple to live together.*

unhelpful /ʌnˈhelp.fəl/ adj **1** C1 not improving a difficult situation: *The instructions were badly written and unhelpful.* **2** B2 not wanting to help someone, in a way that seems unfriendly: *The shop assistant was rude and unhelpful.*

unhinged /ʌnˈhɪndʒd/ **adj** mentally ill: *I sometimes think that your mother is a little unhinged.* • **unhinge** /-ˈhɪndʒ/ **verb** [T]

unholy /ʌnˈhəʊ.li/ Ⓤⓢ /-ˈhoʊ-/ **adj** CAUSING HARM ▷ **1** describes a combination of things when it is very bad, harmful, or unpleasant: *Religious fanatics have formed an unholy **alliance** with right wing groups.* ◦ *There was a smell emanating from the fridge – an unholy **combination of** over-ripe cheese and unwrapped fish.* EXTREME ▷ **2** [before noun] informal extreme and unacceptable: *an unholy mess/row/noise*

unhurt /ʌnˈhɜːt/ Ⓤⓢ /-ˈhɝːt/ **adj** not harmed

uni /ˈjuː.ni/ **noun** [C] UK informal for **university**: *Which uni was she at?*

uni- /juː.nɪ-/ **prefix** having or consisting of only one: *unilateral* ◦ *unisex*

UNICEF /ˈjuː.nɪ.sef/ **noun** [+ sing/pl verb] abbreviation for United Nations Children's Fund: a department of the United Nations whose aim is improving children's health and education, especially in poor countries

unicellular /ˌjuː.nɪˈsel.jə.ləʳ/ Ⓤⓢ /-lɚ/ **adj** specialized A unicellular organism is made of only one cell: *Most algae are unicellular.* → Compare **multicellular**

unicorn /ˈjuː.nɪ.kɔːn/ Ⓤⓢ /-kɔːrn/ **noun** [C] an imaginary white creature like a horse with a single horn growing from the front of its head

unicycle /ˈjuː.nɪˌsaɪ.kl̩/ **noun** [C] a vehicle like a bicycle with only one wheel

unicycle

unidentified /ˌʌn.aɪˈden.tɪ.faɪd/ Ⓤⓢ /-t̬ə-/ **adj** whose name is not known or is being kept secret: *Police are investigating the death of an unidentified man whose body was found in Crackley Woods yesterday.* ◦ *The airline is currently having merger talks with an unidentified rival.* → See also **UFO**

uniform /ˈjuː.nɪ.fɔːm/ Ⓤⓢ /-fɔːrm/ **noun; adj**

▸**noun** [C or U] **1** Ⓐ2 a particular set of clothes that has to be worn by the members of the same organization or group of people: *military/school uniform* ◦ *a nurse's uniform* ◦ *I love a man **in** uniform!* → Compare **mufti** **2** [C] a type of clothes that is connected with a particular group of people: *Photographs show him wearing the scruffy T-shirt and jeans that were the student's uniform of the time.* • **uniformed** /-fɔːmd/ Ⓤⓢ /-fɔːrmd/ **adj** *uniformed officers/police/soldiers*

▸**adj** the same; not changing or different in any way: *As in so many offices that you see, the walls and furniture are a uniform grey.* ◦ *Small businesses are demanding that they receive uniform treatment from the banks.* • **uniformity** /ˌjuː.nɪˈfɔː.mɪ.ti/ Ⓤⓢ /-ˈfɔːr.mə.t̬i/ **noun** [U] • **uniformly** /-li/ **adv** *Critics were uniformly enthusiastic about the production.*

unify /ˈjuː.nɪ.faɪ/ **verb** [T] to bring together; combine: *If the new leader does manage to unify his warring party it will be quite an achievement.* • **unification** /ˌjuː.nɪ.fɪˈkeɪ.ʃən/ **noun** [U] *the unification of East and West Germany* • **unified** /-faɪd/ **adj**

unilateral /ˌjuː.nɪˈlæt.ər.əl/ Ⓤⓢ /-ˈlæt̬.ɚ-/ **adj** involving only one group or country: *The party leader has actually declared her support for unilateral nuclear **disarmament** (= giving up her country's nuclear weapons without first waiting for other countries to do the same).* → Compare **bilateral, multilateral** • **unilateralism** /-ɪ.zəm/ **noun** [U] • **unilateralist** /-ɪst/ **noun** [C] • **unilaterally** /-i/ **adv**

unimaginable /ˌʌn.ɪˈmædʒ.ɪ.nə.bl̩/ **adj** Ⓒ2 describes something that is difficult to imagine because it is so bad, good, big, etc.: *unimaginable pain/wealth* • **unimaginably** /-bli/ **adv**

unimaginative /ˌʌn.ɪˈmædʒ.ɪ.nə.tɪv/ Ⓤⓢ /-t̬ɪv/ **adj** not new, original, or clever; not showing any imagination

unimpeachable /ˌʌn.ɪmˈpiː.tʃə.bl̩/ **adj** formal approving of such a high standard of honesty and moral goodness that it cannot be doubted or criticized: *Lord Fletcher, said the Bishop, was a man of unimpeachable integrity and character.*

unimportant /ˌʌn.ɪmˈpɔː.tənt/ Ⓤⓢ /-ˈpɔːr-/ **adj** Ⓑ1 not important: *Staffing is still a **relatively** unimportant issue compared to the other problems that we're encountering.*

unimpressed /ˌʌn.ɪmˈprest/ **adj** [after verb] not IMPRESSED (= made to feel admiration or respect): *They looked the house over, but they seemed unimpressed (**by** it).* • **unimpressive** /-ˈpres.ɪv/ **adj**

uninformed /ˌʌn.ɪnˈfɔːmd/ Ⓤⓢ /-ˈfɔːrmd/ **adj; noun**

▸**adj** not having much information about something; not INFORMED: *Individuals and businesses appear woefully uninformed about this aspect of the information age.*

▸**noun** [plural] **the uninformed** people who do not have much information or knowledge about something: *Individuals with knowledge must attempt to educate the uninformed.*

uninhabitable /ˌʌn.ɪnˈhæb.ɪ.tə.bl̩/ Ⓤⓢ /-t̬ə-/ **adj** not HABITABLE (= suitable to live in): *If there's no roof then the house is uninhabitable.*

uninhabited /ˌʌn.ɪnˈhæb.ɪ.tɪd/ Ⓤⓢ /-t̬ɪd/ **adj** Ⓒ2 describes a place with no people living in it: *an uninhabited island*

uninhibited /ˌʌn.ɪnˈhɪb.ɪ.tɪd/ Ⓤⓢ /-t̬ɪd/ **adj** approving free and natural, without embarrassment or too much control: *The students we spoke to were surprisingly uninhibited in talking about sex.* ◦ *We watched two hours of glorious, uninhibited football.* ◦ *She gave a loud, uninhibited laugh.*

the uninitiated /ˌʌn.ɪˈnɪʃ.i.eɪ.tɪd/ Ⓤⓢ /-t̬ɪd/ **noun** [plural] mainly humorous people who are without knowledge or experience of a particular subject or activity: *Michelle, for the uninitiated, is the central female character in ITV's latest comedy series.* • **uninitiated adj**

uninjured /ʌnˈɪn.dʒəd/ Ⓤⓢ /-dʒɚd/ **adj** not injured: *The driver of the car was shocked but uninjured.*

uninspired /ˌʌn.ɪnˈspaɪəd/ Ⓤⓢ /-ˈspaɪrd/ **adj** not exciting or interesting: *an uninspired performance*

uninspiring /ˌʌn.ɪnˈspaɪə.rɪŋ/ Ⓤⓢ /-ˈspaɪr.ɪŋ/ **adj** not making you feel excited or interested: *The menu looked fairly uninspiring.*

uninstall /ˌʌn.ɪnˈstɔːl/ Ⓤⓢ /-ˈstɑːl/ **verb; adj**

▸**verb** [T] to remove a computer program from a computer: *The program ran so slowly, I had to uninstall it.*

▸**adj** [before noun] describes a computer program which removes other programs from a computer: *There is still a lot of software that comes without an uninstall **program**.*

unintelligible /ˌʌn.ɪnˈtel.ɪ.dʒə.bl̩/ **adj** not able to be understood: *He muttered something unintelligible.*

unintended /ˌʌn.ɪnˈten.dɪd/ **adj** not intended: *The*

group argues that many of the proposed reforms will have unintended **consequences**.

unintentional /ˌʌn.ɪnˈten.ʃən.əl/ **adj** not intentional • **unintentionally** /-i/ **adv**

uninterested /ʌnˈɪn.tər.es.tɪd/ (US) /-tɚ-/ **adj** B1 not interested

uninteresting /ʌnˈɪn.tər.es.tɪŋ/ (US) /-tɚ-/ **adj** B1 not interesting

uninterrupted /ʌnˌɪn.tərˈʌp.tɪd/ (US) /-t̬əˈrʌp-/ **adj** (especially of a period of time) continuous: *The present government has had eight uninterrupted years in office.* • **uninterruptedly** /-li/ **adv**

uninviting /ˌʌn.ɪnˈvaɪ.tɪŋ/ (US) /-t̬ɪŋ/ **adj** (especially of a place) not attractive

union /ˈjuː.ni.ən/ **noun** JOINING ▷ **1** B2 [S or U] the act or the state of being joined together: *Meanwhile the debate on European political and monetary union continues.* ◦ formal *She believes that the union (= marriage) of man and woman in holy matrimony is for ever.* WORKERS ▷ **2** B1 [C, + sing/pl verb] a **trade union**: *the electricians' union*

ˈ**union-ˌbasher** **noun** [C] informal someone who strongly criticizes TRADE UNIONS and tries to limit their power • ˈ**union-ˌbashing** **noun** [U] strong criticism of TRADE UNIONS

unionize (UK usually **unionise**) /ˈjuː.ni.ən.aɪz/ **verb** [T] to organize workers to become members of a TRADE UNION: *They're about to launch a campaign to unionize workers at all major supermarkets in the area.* ◦ *unionized employees/labour/workers* • **unionization** (UK usually **unionisation**) /ˌjuː.ni.ən.aɪˈzeɪ.ʃən/ **noun** [U]

ˌ**Union** ˈ**Jack** **noun** [C usually singular] (also ˌ**Union** ˈ**flag**) the red, white, and blue flag of the UK

unique /jʊˈniːk/ **adj** B2 being the only existing one of its type or, more generally, unusual or special in some way: *Each person's genetic code is unique except in the case of identical twins.* ◦ *Do not miss this unique opportunity to buy all six pans at half the recommended price.* ◦ *As many as 100 species of fish, some unique **to** (= only found in) these waters, may have been affected by the pollution.* • **uniquely** /-li/ **adv** • **uniqueness** /-nəs/ **noun** [U]

unisex /ˈjuː.nɪ.seks/ **adj** intended for use by both males and females: *unisex clothes* ◦ *a unisex hairdresser's*

unison /ˈjuː.nɪ.sən/ **noun** SINGING TOGETHER ▷ **1** [U or C] the playing or singing of notes at the same PITCH by different instruments or voices: *unison singing* ◦ *Here the tenors are **in unison with** the basses.* ACTING TOGETHER ▷ **2 in unison** acting or speaking together, or at the same time: *'We want ice cream!' the children chanted in unison.*

U

unit /ˈjuː.nɪt/ **noun** SEPARATE PART ▷ **1** B1 [C] a single thing or a separate part of something larger: *The first year of the course is divided into four units.* ◦ *Each unit of the course book focuses on a different grammar point.* **2** [C] a piece of furniture or equipment that is intended to be fitted as a part of a set of similar or matching pieces: *kitchen/shelf/sink units* **3** [C] a small machine or part of a machine that has a particular purpose: *the central processing unit of a computer* ◦ *a waste-disposal unit* **4** [C] specialized a single complete product of the type that a business sells **5** [C] US a single apartment in a bigger building: *a multiple-unit dwelling* ◦ *a public housing unit* PEOPLE ▷ **6** C1 [C, + sing/pl verb] a group of people living or working together, especially for a particular purpose: *the traditional family unit* ◦ *Dr Nussbaum is director of the Civil Liberties Research Unit at King's College, London.* ◦ *Both soldiers spent two weeks in training before being allowed to rejoin their unit (= the particular part of the army to which they belonged).* MEASUREMENT ▷ **7** [C] a standard measure that is used to express amounts: *A centimetre is a unit of length.* ◦ *The standard unit of currency in the US is the dollar.* **8** [C] UK a standard measure of alcohol: *Experts say that women should not drink more than 14 units of alcohol a week.* HOSPITAL DEPARTMENT ▷ **9** [C] a department in a hospital for the treatment of people with similar illnesses or conditions: *She's in the burns/paediatric/psychiatric unit.* SINGLE NUMBER ▷ **10** [C] any whole number less than ten: *Tens go in the left-hand column and units in the right.* **11** [C] specialized the number 1

Unitarian /ˌjuː.nɪˈteə.ri.ən/ (US) /-ˈter.i-/ **noun** (a member of) a Christian Church that does not believe in the TRINITY • **Unitarian** **adj** *a Unitarian church/minister*

unitary /ˈjuː.nɪ.tər.i/ (US) /-ter.i/ **adj** UK of a system of local government in the UK in which official power is given to one organization that deals with all matters in a local area instead of to several organizations that each deal with only a few matters

unite /jʊˈnaɪt/, /juː-/ **verb** [I or T] C1 to join together as a group, or to make people join together as a group; to combine: *If the opposition groups manage to unite, they may command over 55 percent of the vote.* ◦ *If ever a dance company could unite the differing worlds of rock and ballet, the Joffrey Ballet is it.* → See also **reunite**

united /jʊˈnaɪ.tɪd/, /juː-/ (US) /-t̬ɪd/ **adj** **1** B2 joined together as a group: *Factions previously at war with one another are now united **against** the common enemy.* ◦ *The whole village was united **in** their grief.* ◦ *It was the first film festival to take place in a united Germany.* → See also **the UK** **2** B2 If people are united, they all agree about something: *On that issue, we're united.* **3 a united front** an appearance of agreement: *The party's main failing has been their inability to **present** a united front to the people.*

the Uˌnited ˈKingdom **noun** (abbreviation **the UK**) the country that consists of England, Scotland, Wales, and Northern Ireland; → See also **British, Briton**

the Uˌnited ˈNations **noun** [+ sing/pl verb] (abbreviation **the UN**) an international organization that was established in 1945 and aims to solve world problems in a peaceful way

ˌ**unit** ˈ**trust** **noun** [C] UK (US ˈ**mutual** ˌ**fund**) a service where financial experts INVEST the money of many people in many different companies

unity /ˈjuː.nɪ.ti/, /juː-/ (US) /-nə.t̬i/ **noun** [U] C1 the state of being joined together or in agreement: *European political and economic unity* ◦ *a call for national unity*

universal /ˌjuː.nɪˈvɜː.səl/ (US) /-ˈvɝː-/ **adj** B2 existing everywhere or involving everyone: *a universal truth* ◦ *Food, like sex, is a subject of almost universal interest.* ◦ *The new reforms have not met with universal approval within the government.* • **universality** /-vɜː-ˈsæl.ɪ.ti/ (US) /-vɝːˈsæl.ə.t̬i/ **noun** [U] formal • **universally** /-i/ **adv**

ˌ**universal** ˈ**indicator** **noun** [C] specialized a chemical solution made from a mixture of substances which produce many different colour changes according to different PH levels, used to discover how ACID or ALKALINE something is

ˌ**universal** ˈ**joint** **noun** [C] a JOINT in a machine or engine which connects two parts and allows movement in all directions

universe /ˈjuː.nɪ.vɜːs/ (US) /-vɝːs/ **noun** **1** B1 [S] everything that exists, especially all physical matter, including all the stars, planets, GALAXIES, etc. in space: *Is there intelligent life elsewhere in **the** universe?* **2** [S] the world, or the world that you are familiar with: *The characters in his novels inhabit a bleak and hopeless universe.* ◦ *His family is his whole universe (= everything that is important to him).*

university /juː.nɪˈvɜː.sɪ.ti/ (US) /-ˈvɝː.sə.t̬i/ **noun** [C] A1 a college or collection of colleges at which people study for a degree: *Which university did you **go to**/were you **at** (= did you study at)?* ◦ *She teaches at the University of Connecticut.* ◦ *a university campus/course/lecturer*

> **Word partners for university**
>
> *go to* university • *read/study* sth at university • *graduate from/leave* university • *at* university • a university *graduate/student/lecturer/professor* • a university *course/degree/education*

unjust /ʌnˈdʒʌst/ **adj** disapproving not fair • **unjustly** /-li/ **adv**

unjustifiable /ʌnˌdʒʌs.tɪˈfaɪ.ə.bl̩/ **adj** unacceptable and wrong because without any good or fair reason: *His behaviour was unjustifiable.* ◦ *unjustifiable expense* • **unjustifiably** /-bli/ **adv** disapproving

unjustified /ʌnˈdʒʌs.tɪ.faɪd/ **adj** disapproving C1 wrong and/or not deserved: *The defendant had supreme and, as it turned out, unjustified confidence in his own judgment.*

unkempt /ʌnˈkempt/ **adj** disapproving untidy; not cared for: *an unkempt lawn*

unkind /ʌnˈkaɪnd/ **adj** B1 slightly cruel: *an unkind remark* ◦ ***It** was unkind **of** you **to** take his rattle away.* • **unkindly** /-li/ **adv** • **unkindness** /-nəs/ **noun** [U]

unknowing /ʌnˈnəʊ.ɪŋ/ (US) /-ˈnoʊ-/ **adj** literary not conscious of a particular situation or problem: *He took secret pictures of his unknowing victims.* • **unknowingly** /-li/ **adv**

unknown /ʌnˈnəʊn/ (US) /-ˈnoʊn/ **adj; noun**

▸**adj** B1 not known or familiar: *The exact number of people carrying the virus is unknown.* ◦ *As recently as six months ago her name was almost unknown in Britain.* ◦ *Unknown **to** me, she'd organized a party for my birthday.*

▸**noun** **1** C1 [S] what is not familiar or known: *Racism is in some ways just a fear of **the** unknown.* **2** [C] a person, especially a performer or sports player, who is not famous: *For her latest film she deliberately chose a cast of unknowns.* **3** [C] mainly US something that cannot be guessed at or calculated because so little is known about it: *It's the big unknowns that make insurance companies uneasy.*

ˌunknown ˈquantity **noun** [C usually singular] C2 a person or a thing whose abilities, powers, or effects are not yet known: *The third candidate for the party leadership is a relatively unknown quantity.*

unlawful /ʌnˈlɔː.fəl/ (US) /-ˈlɑː-/ **adj** not allowed by law: *unlawful possession of guns* • **unlawfully** /-i/ **adv**

unleaded /ʌnˈled.ɪd/ **adj; noun**

▸**adj** describes a type of petrol or other substance that does not contain lead: *Does your car use unleaded petrol?*

▸**noun** [U] unleaded petrol: *They cut 2p per litre off the price of unleaded.*

unlearn /ʌnˈlɜːn/ (US) /-ˈlɝːn/ **verb** [T] to make an effort to forget your usual way of doing something so that you can learn a new and sometimes better way

unleash /ʌnˈliːʃ/ **verb** [T] to suddenly release a violent force that cannot be controlled: *At worst, nuclear war could be unleashed.* ◦ *Rachel's arrival on the scene had*

unleashed passions in him that he could scarcely control.

unleavened /ʌnˈlev.ənd/ **adj** describes bread or similar food that is made without YEAST and is therefore flat

unless /ənˈles/ **conjunction** B1 except if: *You can't get a job unless you've got experience (= you can only get a job if you have experience).* ◦ *Unless you call me to say you're not coming, I'll see you at the theatre (= I will see you there if you do not call to say you are not coming).*

unlicensed /ʌnˈlaɪ.sənst/ **adj** not having a LICENCE (= a document giving legal permission) to do something, for example to sell alcohol, or use or own something, for example a gun: *an unlicensed restaurant*

unlike /ʌnˈlaɪk/ **preposition** **DIFFERENT FROM** ▷ **1** B2 different from: *Dan's actually quite nice, unlike his father.* ◦ *Unlike you, I'm not a great dancer.* **NOT TYPICAL** ▷ **2** C2 not typical or characteristic of: *It's unlike you to be quiet – is something wrong?*

unlikely /ʌnˈlaɪ.kli/ **adj** **NOT PROBABLE** ▷ **1** B1 not probable or LIKELY to happen: [+ (that)] ***It's** pretty unlikely (that) they'll turn up now – it's nearly ten o'clock.* **NOT EXPECTED** ▷ **2** [only before noun] not the same as you would normally expect: *He seems an unlikely-looking doctor (= he is not what I expect a doctor to look like).* **PROBABLY NOT TRUE** ▷ **3** C2 [only before noun] probably not true: *When I asked what he was doing there, he came up with some unlikely explanation.*

unlimited /ʌnˈlɪm.ɪ.tɪd/ (US) /-t̬ɪd/ **adj** B2 not limited; having the greatest possible amount, number, or level: *Passes are available for one month's unlimited travel within Europe.* ◦ *Demand for healthcare appears virtually unlimited.*

unlisted /ʌnˈlɪs.tɪd/ (US) /-t̬ɪd/ **adj** **1** not included in a list of STOCK EXCHANGE company prices: *unlisted securities/shares* **2** US not included in the public list of phone numbers belonging to the customers of a telephone company: *Doctors most often have unlisted home phone numbers to protect their privacy.*

unload /ʌnˈləʊd/ (US) /-ˈloʊd/ **verb** **REMOVE** ▷ **1** C1 [I or T] to remove the contents of something, especially a LOAD of goods from a vehicle, the bullets from a gun or the film from a camera: *We watched a ship unloading (sacks of flour).* **TELL** ▷ **2** [I or T] informal to tell someone about your problems, the things that worry you, etc.: *I'm afraid I've been unloading my worries **on** poor Ann here.* **3** [I] US informal to express strong emotions such as anger freely to another person

unlock /ʌnˈlɒk/ (US) /-ˈlɑːk/ **verb** [T] **1** B2 to open something, especially a door that is LOCKED (= fastened with a lock) using a key or an electronic device: *I keep worrying that I've left the garage door unlocked.* **2** **unlock the mystery/secret of sth** to discover important new facts about something: *A chemical has been discovered that may be the key to unlocking the mysteries of Parkinson's disease.* **3** **unlock the imagination** to make the imagination more active, producing interesting ideas and images: *One of poetry's functions is to somehow unlock the imagination.*

unlooked-for /ʌnˈlʊkt.fɔːr/ (US) /-fɔːr/ **adj** [before noun] not expected: *unlooked-for joy*

unlovable /ʌnˈlʌv.ə.bl̩/ **adj** not easy to love

unloved /ʌnˈlʌvd/ **adj** formal not loved: *He found himself alone and unloved.*

unlucky /ʌnˈlʌk.i/ **adj** [often + to infinitive] B1 not lucky: *The couple were unlucky **enough to** be in the*

U

hotel when the terrorist group struck. • **unluckily** /-ɪ.li/ adv

unmade /ʌnˈmeɪd/ adj If a bed is unmade, its sheets and covers are still untidy from having been slept in.

unmanageable /ʌnˈmæn.ɪ.dʒə.bl̩/ adj impossible to deal with or manage: *74 percent of teachers found the paperwork was unmanageable.* ◦ *Within weeks, a difficult boy had become unmanageable.*

unmanned /ʌnˈmænd/ adj describes a spacecraft, or a place where military guards work, that has no people present to operate or be in charge of it: *an unmanned mission to the planet Mars*

unmarked /ʌnˈmɑːkt/ (US) /-ˈmɑːrkt/ adj having no signs or marks showing what something is: *an unmarked police car* ◦ *She died penniless and was buried in an unmarked grave.*

unmarried /ʌnˈmær.ɪd/ (US) /-ˈmer-/ adj C1 not married: *an unmarried mother* ◦ *Their youngest son is still unmarried.*

unmask /ʌnˈmɑːsk/ (US) /-ˈmæsk/ verb [T] to show the bad, and previously hidden, truth about someone or something: *The conspirators were unmasked and summarily shot.*

unmatched /ʌnˈmætʃt/ adj formal having no equal; better than any other of the same type: *For years they have enjoyed a standard of living unmatched **by** any other country in Europe.*

unmentionable /ʌnˈmen.ʃən.ə.bl̩/ adj shocking and embarrassing and therefore not allowed or disapproved of as a subject of conversation: *What's the matter with him – or is it some unmentionable disease that he doesn't like people to know about?*

unmentionables /ʌnˈmen.ʃən.ə.bl̩z/ noun [plural] old-fashioned or humorous underwear

unmindful /ʌnˈmaɪnd.fəl/ adj formal **unmindful of sth** not remembering, noticing, or being careful about something

unmissable /ʌnˈmɪs.ə.bl̩/ adj informal An unmissable film or play, etc. is so good that it must be seen: *It's fairly entertaining as films go, but I wouldn't describe it as unmissable.*

unmistakable /ˌʌn.mɪˈsteɪ.kə.bl̩/ adj not likely to be confused with something else: *There was an unmistakable smell of incense in the air.* • **unmistakably** /-bli/ adv

unmitigated /ʌnˈmɪt.ɪ.geɪ.tɪd/ (US) /-ˈmɪ.ə.geɪ.t̬ɪd/ adj [usually before noun] complete, often describing something bad or unsuccessful that has no good or positive points: *The whole venture has been an unmitigated **disaster**.*

U

unmoved /ʌnˈmuːvd/ adj [after verb] not feeling any emotion: *Both men appeared unmoved as the judge read out their sentence.*

unnamed /ʌnˈneɪmd/ adj An unnamed person or thing is talked about, but their name is not known or mentioned: *The article quoted an unnamed source from the White House.*

unnatural /ʌnˈnætʃ.ər.əl/ (US) /-ɚ-/ adj B2 not natural • **unnaturally** /-i/ adv

unnecessary /ʌnˈnes.ə.ser.i/ adj **1** B1 not needed or wanted, or more than is needed or wanted: *I found a lot of the violence in the film totally unnecessary.* ◦ *The idea is to kill the animal as quickly as possible without causing unnecessary suffering.* **2** describes an offensive remark or action that could have been avoided: *He just humiliated her in front of everyone – it was so unnecessary.* • **unnecessarily** /-ɪ.li/ adv C1 *Of course we don't want to alarm people unnecessarily, but they should be alerted to potential dangers.*

unnerve /ʌnˈnɜːv/ (US) /-ˈnɝːv/ verb [T] to make someone feel less confident and slightly frightened: *I think it unnerved me to be interviewed by so many people.* • **unnerving** /-ˈnɜː.vɪŋ/ (US) /-ˈnɝː.vɪŋ/ adj *Meeting a twin brother I didn't know I had was an unnerving experience.* • **unnervingly** /ʌnˈnɜː.vɪŋ.li/ (US) /-ˈnɝː-/ adv

unnoticed /ʌnˈnəʊ.tɪst/ (US) /-ˈnoʊ.t̬ɪst/ adj, adv C1 without being seen or noticed: *We managed to slip away unnoticed.* ◦ *His rude comments are not likely to **go** unnoticed.*

unobtainable /ˌʌnəbˈteɪ.nə.bl̩/ adj not able to be obtained → Opposite **obtainable**

unobtrusive /ˌʌn.əbˈtruː.sɪv/ adj approving not noticeable; seeming to fit in well with the things around it or them: *Make-up this season is unobtrusive and natural-looking.* • **unobtrusively** /-li/ adv • **unobtrusiveness** /-nəs/ noun [U]

unofficial /ˌʌn.əˈfɪʃ.əl/ adj not official; not from a person in authority, the government, etc.: *unofficial estimates/figures/reports* • **unofficially** /-i/ adv

unoriginal /ˌʌn.əˈrɪdʒ.ɪ.nəl/ adj the same as a lot of other things and therefore not interesting or special

unorthodox /ʌnˈɔː.θə.dɒks/ (US) /-ˈɔːr.θə.dɑːks/ adj different from what is usual or expected in behaviour, ideas, methods, etc.: *Steiner was recognized as an original if unorthodox thinker.*

unpack /ʌnˈpæk/ verb REMOVE ▷ **1** B1 [I or T] to remove things from a SUITCASE, bag, or box: *I haven't even had time to unpack (my bag/clothes).* EXPLAIN ▷ **2** [T] to explain or to make a meaning clearer: *He read the agreed statement to the group and then began to unpack it for them.*

unpaid /ʌnˈpeɪd/ adj **1** C1 describes a debt, tax, etc. that has not been paid: *$50,000 in unpaid taxes* **2** C1 describes work that you do without getting any money for it: *unpaid work/employment*

unpalatable /ʌnˈpæl.ə.tə.bl̩/ (US) /-t̬ə-/ adj formal **1** describes a fact or idea that is unpleasant or shocking and therefore difficult to accept: *the unpalatable truth/facts about the war* **2** describes food that is unpleasant to taste or eat

unparalleled /ʌnˈpær.əl.eld/ (US) /-ˈper-/ adj formal having no equal; better or greater than any other: *They enjoyed success on a scale unparalleled by any previous pop group.*

unpick /ʌnˈpɪk/ verb [T] SEWING ▷ **1** to cut or remove the STITCHES from a line of sewing IDEAS ▷ **2** If you unpick a difficult subject, you separate and examine its different parts carefully: *As long as two years ago, Mandelson tried to unpick the reasons for the disaster.* DESTROY ▷ **3** to gradually destroy or remove the good effects of what someone has done or created: *The former leader now has to watch his successor unpicking what he strived so hard to achieve.*

unpitched /ʌnˈpɪtʃt/ adj (also **untuned**) refers to PERCUSSION instruments that do not produce sounds of a definite PITCH → Compare **pitched**

unplaced /ʌnˈpleɪst/ adj in horse racing, not one of the first three horses to finish a race: *The sole British runner, White Knight, was unplaced.*

unplanned /ʌnˈplænd/ adj not planned or expected: *an unplanned pregnancy*

unplayable /ʌnˈpleɪ.ə.bl̩/ adj SPORT ▷ **1** describes a ball that is hit or thrown so hard or skilfully that it is impossible to hit **2** describes an area of ground usually used for sports, that cannot be played on, especially because of bad weather conditions

MUSIC ▷ **3** describes a piece of music that is too difficult to perform

unpleasant /ʌnˈplez.ᵊnt/ **adj 1** B1 not enjoyable or pleasant: *an unpleasant surprise* ◦ *the unpleasant truth* **2** C1 [after verb] rude and angry: *The waiter got quite unpleasant with us.* • **unpleasantly** /-li/ **adv** • **unpleasantness** /-nəs/ **noun** [C or U]

unplug /ʌnˈplʌg/ **verb** [T] **1** to take the PLUG of a piece of electrical equipment out of the place where it is connected to the electricity supply: *Have you unplugged the iron?* **2** US to remove what is blocking something: *The video shows you how to unplug a bath drain full of hair.*

unplugged /ʌnˈplʌgd/ **adj, adv** describes musicians performing without electric instruments and without AMPLIFICATION (= electronic equipment that makes sound louder)

unpopular /ʌnˈpɒp.jʊ.ləʳ/ US /-ˈpɑː.pjə.lɚ/ **adj** B2 not liked by many people: *Night flights from the airport are deeply unpopular.* ◦ *The government is becoming increasingly unpopular.* • **unpopularity** /ˌʌn.pɒp.jʊˈlær.ɪ.ti/ US /-pɑː.pjʊˈler.ə.t̬i/ **noun** [U]

unprecedented /ʌnˈpres.ɪ.den.tɪd/ US /-t̬ɪd/ **adj** C2 never having happened or existed in the past: *This century has witnessed environmental destruction* ***on an*** *unprecedented* ***scale***.

unpredictable /ˌʌn.prɪˈdɪk.tə.bl̩/ **adj** B2 likely to change suddenly and without reason and therefore not able to be PREDICTED (= expected before it happens) or depended on: *The weather there can be a bit unpredictable – one minute it's blue skies and the next minute it's pouring down.* ◦ *The hours in this job are very unpredictable – you sometimes have to work late at very short notice.* • **unpredictability** /ˌʌn.prɪ.dɪk.təˈbɪl.ɪ.ti/ US /-ə.t̬i/ **noun** [U] • **unpredictably** /-bli/ **adv**

unpremeditated /ˌʌn.priːˈmed.ɪ.teɪ.tɪd/ US /-t̬ɪd/ **adj** (especially of a crime or something unpleasant) done without being planned → Opposite **premeditated**

unprepared /ˌʌn.prɪˈpeəd/ US /-ˈperd/ **adj** not prepared; not ready: *He was completely/totally/wholly unprepared* ***for*** *what he saw.* ◦ *The extreme cold weather* ***caught*** *them unprepared.*

unpretentious /ˌʌn.prɪˈten.ʃəs/ **adj** approving simple and/or sincere; not PRETENTIOUS: *The food is delicious and unpretentious.* → Opposite **pretentious**

unprincipled /ʌnˈprɪn.sɪ.pld/ **adj** having or showing no moral rules or standards of good behaviour

unprintable /ʌnˈprɪn.tə.bl̩/ US /-t̬ə-/ **adj** containing offensive language and therefore not acceptable in printed form, for example in a newspaper: *The taxi driver entertained us with unprintable observations/remarks/views about government ministers all the way to the airport.*

unproductive /ˌʌn.prəˈdʌk.tɪv/ **adj 1** C1 not producing very much → Opposite **productive 2** C1 not having positive results: *It was such an unproductive meeting – we achieved hardly anything.*

unprofessional /ˌʌn.prəˈfeʃ.ᵊn.ᵊl/ **adj** C1 not showing the standard of behaviour or skill that is expected of a person in a skilled job: *Doctor Rivers was charged with unprofessional conduct and improper use of dangerous drugs.* • **unprofessionally** /-i/ **adv**

unprofitable /ʌnˈprɒf.ɪ.tə.bl̩/ US /-ˈprɑː.fɪ.t̬ə-/ **adj** not making a profit: *Rural railway lines risk being axed because they are unprofitable.*

unpromising /ʌnˈprɒm.ɪ.sɪŋ/ US /-ˈprɑː.mɪ-/ **adj** Something that is unpromising does not show any signs that it will be enjoyable or successful: *It was a rather unpromising start to the holiday.*

unprompted /ʌnˈprɒmp.tɪd/ US /-ˈprɑːmp-/ **adj** without being told to say or do something: *Jim was remarkably charming this evening – he even said, unprompted, how nice Margot looked in her dress.*

unpronounceable /ˌʌn.prəˈnaʊn.sə.bl̩/ **adj** difficult to say or (of something written) difficult to know how to say: *She's got some unpronounceable name which seems to be all consonants.*

unprotected /ˌʌn.prəˈtek.tɪd/ **adj 1** not protected and therefore able to be harmed or damaged: *Water and other liquids can stain unprotected wood surfaces.* ◦ *Although some marine mammals are protected by environmental laws, many remain unprotected.* ◦ *The lack of a shell leaves the larvae unprotected against predators.* **2 unprotected sex** sexual activity without a CONDOM

unprovoked /ˌʌn.prəˈvəʊkt/ US /-ˈvoʊkt/ **adj** describes an unpleasant action or remark when it has not been caused by anything and is therefore unfair: *an unprovoked* ***attack*** *on her character*

unpublished /ʌnˈpʌb.lɪʃt/ **adj** written but not yet published: *After his death, his daughter found an unpublished manuscript among his papers.*

unpunished /ʌnˈpʌn.ɪʃt/ **adj** [after verb] not punished: *If a referee allows a foul like that to* ***go*** *unpunished he's asking for trouble.*

unputdownable /ˌʌn.pʊtˈdaʊ.nə.bl̩/ **adj** informal describes a book that is so exciting that you do not want to stop reading it: *'Was it a good read?' 'Oh, totally unputdownable – I finished it in two days.'*

unqualified /ʌnˈkwɒl.ɪ.faɪd/ US /-ˈkwɑː.lɪ-/ **adj** **PERSON** ▷ **1** C1 An unqualified person does not have the qualifications needed for a particular job. **COMPLETE** ▷ **2** not limited in any way; to the largest degree possible: *We achieved a lot but I wouldn't say that the project has been an unqualified* ***success***. ◦ *The proposal has the unqualified* ***support*** *of the entire committee.*

unquestionable /ʌnˈkwes.tʃə.nə.bl̩/ **adj** obvious and impossible to doubt → Compare **questionable** • **unquestionably** /-bli/ **adv**

unquestioned /ʌnˈkwes.tʃənd/ **adj** accepted as true or right by everyone, or trusted and respected by everyone: *He's the unquestioned leader in his field (= no one would say that he is not the leader).*

unquestioning /ʌnˈkwes.tʃə.nɪŋ/ **adj** mainly disapproving Unquestioning OBEDIENCE is total, and given without thinking, asking questions, or doubting: *Like all tyrannical leaders, he demanded unquestioning obedience from his followers.* • **unquestioningly** /-li/ **adv**

unquiet /ʌnˈkwaɪət/ **adj** literary troubled and worried; not peaceful or calm: *One can only hope that his unquiet spirit found some peace in the grave.*

unravel /ʌnˈræv.ᵊl/ **verb** (**-ll-** or US usually **-l-**) **CLOTH** ▷ **1** [I or T] If a piece of WOOLLEN or WOVEN cloth, a knot, or a mass of thread unravels, it separates into a single thread, and if you unravel it, you separate it into a single thread: *You'd better mend that hole before the whole sweater starts to unravel.* ◦ *I had to unravel one of the sleeves because I realized I'd knitted it too small.* **SUBJECT** ▷ **2** [I or T] If you unravel a mysterious, unknown, or complicated subject, you make it known or understood, and if it unravels, it becomes known or understood: *We've got a long way to go before we unravel the secrets of genetics.* **PROCESS** ▷ **3** [I, T usually passive] If a process or achievement that was slow and complicated unravels or is unravelled, it is destroyed:

U

As talks between the leaders broke down, several months of careful diplomacy were unravelled.

unreadable /ʌnˈriː.də.bl̩/ adj **1** too boring, complicated, or badly written to be worth reading: *I found James Joyce's 'Ulysses' totally unreadable.* **2** ILLEGIBLE (= impossible to read because not clear or untidy): *completely unreadable handwriting*

unreal /ʌnˈrɪəl/ US /-ˈriːl/ adj **IMAGINARY** ▷ **1** as if imagined; strange and dream-like: *The whole bizarre evening had an unreal quality to it.* **SURPRISING** ▷ **2** C1 slang extremely or surprisingly good: *He gave you £5,000? Man, that's unreal!* • **unreality** /ˌʌn.riˈæl.ɪ.ti/ US /-ə.t̬i/ noun [U] *There was an air of unreality about the visit, as if I'd stepped into another world for two weeks.*

unrealistic /ˌʌn.rɪəˈlɪs.tɪk/ US /-riː.ə-/ adj B2 having a wrong idea of what is likely to happen or of what you can really do; not based on facts: *I think these sales forecasts are unrealistic, considering how slow sales are at present.* ◦ [+ to infinitive] ***It's** unrealistic **to** expect an answer before next week.* • **unrealistically** /-tɪ.kəl.i/ adv

unreasonable /ʌnˈriː.zən.ə.bl̩/ adj B2 not fair or acceptable: *unreasonable demands* ◦ [+ to infinitive] *It seems unreasonable **to** expect one person to do both jobs.* • **unreasonably** /-bli/ adv

unreasoning /ʌnˈriː.zən.ɪŋ/ adj formal describes feelings or beliefs that are not based on reason or judgment: *unreasoning hatred*

unreconstructed /ˌʌn.riː.kənˈstrʌk.tɪd/ adj often humorous having opinions or behaving in a way not considered to be modern or politically acceptable in modern times: *She describes herself as an unreconstructed feminist.*

unrefined /ˌʌn.rɪˈfaɪnd/ adj in a natural state, without having been through a chemical or industrial process to remove unwanted parts; not REFINED: *unrefined sugar*

unregulated /ʌnˈreg.jʊ.leɪ.tɪd/ US /-t̬ɪd/ adj describes a type of business or activity that is not controlled and directed by fixed rules or laws: *Parents have the right to expect information to guide them through a growing, yet unregulated **market** (**place**).*

unrelated /ˌʌn.rɪˈleɪ.tɪd/ US /-t̬ɪd/ adj C1 having no connection: *Police said his death was unrelated **to** the attack.*

unrelenting /ˌʌn.rɪˈlen.tɪŋ/ US /-t̬ɪŋ/ adj formal extremely determined; never becoming weaker or admitting defeat: *She will be remembered as an unrelenting opponent of racial discrimination.* • **unrelentingly** /-li/ adv

unreliable /ˌʌn.rɪˈlaɪə.bl̩/ adj B2 not able to be trusted or believed: *The bus service is unreliable.* ◦ *unreliable evidence* → Opposite **reliable**

U

unrelieved /ˌʌn.rɪˈliːvd/ adj [usually before noun] formal When a bad situation or emotion is unrelieved, it is continuous and never improves, not even for a short period: *She held the family together through years of unrelieved poverty.* • **unrelievedly** /-ˈliː.vɪd.li/ adv

unremarkable /ˌʌn.rɪˈmɑː.kə.bl̩/ US /-ˈmɑːr-/ adj ordinary and not interesting: *an unremarkable town*

unremitting /ˌʌn.rɪˈmɪt.ɪŋ/ US /-ˈmɪt̬-/ adj formal never stopping, becoming weaker, or failing: *Our thanks are due to Bob Lawrence whose unremitting labours have ensured the success of the whole scheme.* • **unremittingly** /-li/ adv

unrepeatable /ˌʌn.rɪˈpiː.tə.bl̩/ US /-t̬ə-/ adj **EVENTS** ▷ **1** [usually before noun] describes an event, price, etc. that cannot happen again: *an unrepeatable offer/opportunity* **WORDS** ▷ **2** describes a word or remark used by another person which was too rude or too difficult for you to repeat: *an unrepeatable joke/name*

unrepentant /ˌʌn.rɪˈpen.tənt/ adj not REPENTANT (= feeling sorry for something that you have done)

unrepresentative /ˌʌn.rep.rɪˈzen.tə.tɪv/ US /-ə.t̬ɪv/ adj not typical of a larger group of people or things; not REPRESENTATIVE

unrequited /ˌʌn.rɪˈkwaɪ.tɪd/ US /-t̬ɪd/ adj formal or humorous If love that you feel for someone is unrequited, it is not felt in the same way by the other person: *It's just another poem on the pain of unrequited **love**.*

unreserved /ˌʌn.rɪˈzɜːvd/ US /-ˈzɝːvd/ adj formal without any doubts or feeling uncertain; total: *He was a good strong leader, she said, who deserved his party's unreserved support.* • **unreservedly** /-ˈzɜː.vɪd.li/ US /-ˈzɝː.vɪd.li/ adv *The paper's editor has **apologized** unreservedly to the senator.*

unresolved /ˌʌn.rɪˈzɒlvd/ US /-ˈzɑːlvd/ adj formal If a problem or difficulty is unresolved, it is not solved or ended: *The question of contracts **remains** unresolved.*

unresponsive /ˌʌn.rɪˈspɒn.sɪv/ US /-ˈspɑːn-/ adj not RESPONSIVE (= reacting in a quick or positive way to something)

unrest /ʌnˈrest/ noun [U] C2 disagreements or fighting between different groups of people: *It is feared that the civil unrest we are now witnessing in this country could lead to full-scale civil war.*

unrestrained /ˌʌn.rɪˈstreɪnd/ adj not limited or controlled: *unrestrained joy/anger/criticism*

unrivalled (US usually **unrivaled**) /ʌnˈraɪ.vəld/ adj having no equal; better than any other of the same type: *The museum boasts an unrivalled collection of French porcelain.*

unroll /ʌnˈrəʊl/ US /-ˈroʊl/ verb [I or T] to open and become flat from a rolled position, or to cause something to do this: *She unrolled the most beautiful carpet.*

unruffled /ʌnˈrʌf.l̩d/ adj calm; not nervous or worried, usually despite a difficult situation: *For a man in danger of losing his job, he appeared quite unruffled.*

unruly /ʌnˈruː.li/ adj **1** Unruly people are difficult to control and often do not obey rules: *an unruly class of adolescents* **2** Unruly hair is difficult to keep tidy, often sticking up or out: *an unruly mop of black hair* • **unruliness** /-nəs/ noun [U]

unsaddle /ʌnˈsæd.l̩/ verb [T] to take the SADDLE off a horse or to cause someone riding a horse to fall off

unsafe /ʌnˈseɪf/ adj **IN DANGER** ▷ **1** C1 not safe **LAW** ▷ **2** UK legal describes a decision that someone is guilty which can be APPEALED against (= considered again) in court: *an unsafe conviction/verdict*

unsaid /ʌnˈsed/ adj [after verb] not said, although thought of or felt: *I know she's put on weight, Michael, but some things are **better left** unsaid!* → See also **unspoken**

unsanitary /ʌnˈsæn.ɪ.tər.i/ US /-ter.i/ adj (UK also **insanitary**) dirty or unhealthy and therefore likely to cause disease: *unsanitary toilets* ◦ *unsanitary living conditions*

unsatisfactory /ʌnˌsæt.ɪsˈfæk.tər.i/ US /-ˌsæt̬.ɪsˈfæk.tɚ-/ adj B2 not satisfactory

unsatisfied /ʌnˈsæt.ɪs.faɪd/ US /-ˈsæt̬-/ adj **1** feeling that something is not enough or not good enough: *After the meal he still felt unsatisfied.* **2** If you have an unsatisfied wish, you have not got what you wanted:

There is unsatisfied demand for the product. ◦ *unsatisfied curiosity/desire*

unsatisfying /ʌnˈsæt.ɪs.faɪ.ɪŋ/ (US) /-ˈsæt̬-/ **adj** not satisfying

unsaturated /ʌnˈsætʃ.ᵊr.eɪ.tɪd/ (US) /-t̬ɪd/ **adj** specialized describes a fat or oil that is either MONOUNSATURATED or POLYUNSATURATED, found in plants, vegetable oil, and fish and thought to be better for your health than SATURATED FAT

unsavoury UK (US **unsavory**) /ʌnˈseɪ.vᵊr.i/ (US) /-vɚ-/ **adj** unpleasant, or morally offensive: *unsavoury sexual practices* ◦ *an unsavoury reputation*

unscathed /ʌnˈskeɪðd/ **adj** [after verb] without injuries or damage being caused: *Her husband died in the accident but she, amazingly, escaped unscathed.*

unscientific /ˌʌn.saɪənˈtɪf.ɪk/ **adj** disapproving not obeying scientific methods or principles: *an unscientific account/claim/method*

unscramble /ʌnˈskræm.bl̩/ **verb** [T] to discover the meaning of information given in a secret or complicated way: *You need a decoding device to unscramble some of the signals sent out by satellite and cable TV.* → Synonym **decode**

unscrew /ʌnˈskruː/ **verb** [T] **LID** ▷ **1** to take the lid or top off something by twisting it round: *I can't unscrew the top of this jar – it's really tight.* **SCREWS** ▷ **2** to remove something by taking the SCREWS out of it

unscripted /ʌnˈskrɪp.tɪd/ **adj** describes a speech or broadcast that has not been written before it is made

unscrupulous /ʌnˈskruː.pjʊ.ləs/ **adj** disapproving (C2) behaving in a way that is dishonest or unfair in order to get what you want: *an unscrupulous financial adviser*

unseasonable /ʌnˈsiː.zᵊn.ə.bl̩/ **adj** (also **unseasonal**) describes weather that is not usual or suitable for the time of year: *When you're used to snow in January, warm sunny weather feels unseasonable.* • **unseasonably** /-bli/ **adv** (also **unseasonally**) *unseasonably warm weather*

unseat /ʌnˈsiːt/ **verb** [T] **POLITICIAN** ▷ **1** to remove someone from power, especially as a result of an election **RIDER** ▷ **2** If a horse unseats its rider, it throws them from its back.

unseeded /ʌnˈsiː.dɪd/ **adj** not SEEDED in a tennis competition

unseemly /ʌnˈsiːm.li/ **adj** formal not SEEMLY (= socially suitable and polite) • **unseemliness** /-nəs/ **noun** [U]

unseen /ʌnˈsiːn/ **adj** not seen or not able to be seen: *She found the side-door open and slipped into the house unseen.* ◦ *Unseen birds sang in the trees above us.*

unselfish /ʌnˈsel.fɪʃ/ **adj** Someone who is unselfish thinks about what is good for other people, not just about their own advantage. • **unselfishly** /-li/ **adv** • **unselfishness** /-nəs/ **noun** [U]

unsettled /ʌnˈset.l̩d/ (US) /-ˈset̬-/ **adj** **CHANGING** ▷ **1** likely to change suddenly; not calm or having a regular pattern: *a period of unsettled weather* ◦ *an unsettled political climate* **WORRIED** ▷ **2** nervous and worried; unable to relax: *Children tend to get unsettled if you keep on changing their routine.*

unsettling /ʌnˈset.ᵊl.ɪŋ/ (US) /-ˈset̬-/ **adj** **CHANGING** ▷ **1** causing change **WORRYING** ▷ **2** causing worry or ANXIETY: *One of the film's many unsettling images is of a child playing with her father's gun.* • **unsettle** /-ᵊl/ **verb** [T] *The airline's decision to cut air fares is likely to unsettle the market.* ◦ *Even the most experienced of West Indian batsmen was unsettled by the sheer speed of this bowler.*

unshakeable (also **unshakable**) /ʌnˈʃeɪ.kə.bl̩/ **adj** If someone's trust or belief is unshakeable, it is firm and cannot be made weaker or destroyed: *She was blessed with an unshakeable belief in her own abilities.*

unshaven /ʌnˈʃeɪ.vᵊn/ **adj** not having had the hair removed: *an unshaven chin/man*

unsightly /ʌnˈsaɪt.li/ **adj** formal not attractive; ugly: *He had undone the buttons of his shirt, exposing an unsightly expanse of white flesh.*

unskilled /ʌnˈskɪld/ **adj** Unskilled people have no particular work skills, and unskilled work does not need any particular skills: *unskilled workers* ◦ *unskilled labour/work/jobs*

unsliced /ʌnˈslaɪst/ **adj** not sliced: *unsliced bread*

unsmiling /ʌnˈsmaɪ.lɪŋ/ **adj** not smiling: *Cabinet members were tight-lipped and unsmiling as they emerged from Downing Street.*

unsociable /ʌnˈsəʊ.ʃə.bl̩/ (US) /-ˈsoʊ-/ **adj** not liking to meet people or to spend time with them

unsocial /ʌnˈsəʊ.ʃᵊl/ (US) /-ˈsoʊ-/ **adj** UK happening during the days of the week or hours of the day when most people do not have to work: *I don't want to work unsocial **hours**.*

unsold /ʌnˈsəʊld/ (US) /-ˈsoʊld/ **adj** not sold: *stocks of unsold goods*

unsolicited /ˌʌn.səˈlɪs.ɪ.tɪd/ (US) /-t̬ɪd/ **adj** not asked for: *unsolicited advice*

unsolved /ˌʌnˈsɒlvd/ (US) /-ˈsɑːlvd/ **adj** (C1) that has not been solved: *an unsolved mystery*

unsophisticated /ˌʌn.səˈfɪs.tɪ.keɪ.tɪd/ (US) /-t̬ɪd/ **adj** not complicated, or not showing a good understanding of culture and fashion; not SOPHISTICATED

unsound /ʌnˈsaʊnd/ **adj** **NOT ACCEPTABLE** ▷ **1** If a person's activities or judgment are unsound, they are not good enough, acceptable, or able to be trusted: *unsound accounting practices* ◦ *unsound police evidence* **WEAK** ▷ **2** If a building or other structure is unsound, it is in bad condition and likely to fall down or fail: *The bridge is one of several said to be structurally unsound.*

unsparing /ʌnˈspeə.rɪŋ/ (US) /-ˈsper.ɪŋ/ **adj** **HIDING NOTHING** ▷ **1** showing no kindness and no wish to hide the unpleasant truth: *The documentary went through all the graphic details of the operation in unsparing detail.* **GENEROUS** ▷ **2** formal extremely generous with money, time, help, etc.: *Last of all, our thanks go to the caterers who have been unsparing **in** their efforts to make this afternoon such a success.*

unspeakable /ʌnˈspiː.kə.bl̩/ **adj** too bad or shocking to be expressed in words: *unspeakable crimes* ◦ *No report can convey the unspeakable suffering that this war has caused.* ◦ *The stench coming from the toilets was quite unspeakable.* • **unspeakably** /-bli/ **adv**

unspecified /ʌnˈspes.ɪ.faɪd/ **adj** If something is unspecified, you are not told what it is: *The court awarded her an unspecified amount of money.*

unspoiled /ʌnˈspɔɪld/, /-ˈspɔɪlt/ **adj** (UK also **unspoilt**) (C1) An unspoiled place is beautiful because it has not been changed or damaged by people: *an island with clean, unspoiled beaches*

unspoken /ʌnˈspəʊ.kᵊn/ (US) /-ˈspoʊ-/ **adj** not spoken, although thought of or felt: *unspoken doubts/fears* ◦ *There's an unspoken assumption in the department that Sue will take over the post when Ian leaves.*

unsporting /ʌnˈspɔː.tɪŋ/ (US) /-ˈspɔːr.t̬ɪŋ/ **adj** not SPORTING (= showing fairness and respect, especially to opposing teams or players)

unsportsmanlike /ʌnˈspɔːts.mən.laɪk/ (US) /-ˈspɔːrts-/ **adj** not showing fairness or respect to other people,

U

especially towards the opposing team or player when playing sport

unstable /ʌnˈsteɪ.bl̩/ adj **1** not solid and firm and therefore not strong, safe, or likely to last: *That chair looks a bit unstable to me.* ◦ *It is a poor and politically unstable society.* **2** describes someone who suffers from sudden and extreme changes in their mental and emotional state: *emotionally unstable*

unsteady /ʌnˈsted.i/ adj moving slightly from side to side, as if you might fall: *She's been in bed with the flu and she's still a bit unsteady* ***on her feet.*** • **unsteadily** /-ɪ.li/ adv

unstinting /ʌnˈstɪn.tɪŋ/ (US) /-t̬ɪŋ/ adj formal extremely generous with time, money, praise, help, etc.: *unstinting support/generosity* ◦ *She was quite unstinting* ***in*** *her praise.*

unstoppable /ʌnˈstɒp.ə.bl̩/ (US) /-ˈstɑː.pə-/ adj unable to be stopped or prevented from developing: *The band has enjoyed a seemingly unstoppable rise in popularity.*

unstuck /ʌnˈstʌk/ adj **NOT FIXED** ▷ **1** [after verb] no longer stuck: *The sticky tape on the parcel* ***came*** *unstuck and the whole thing came undone.* **NOT SUCCESSFUL** ▷ **2 come unstuck** informal to experience difficulties and fail: *It was in the third round of the championships that they came unstuck.*

unsubscribe /ˌʌn.səbˈskraɪb/ verb [I or T] to get an organization or business to remove your name from its MAILING LIST so that you no longer receive email or post from them, or to remove someone's name from such a list

unsuccessful /ˌʌn.səkˈses.fəl/ adj (B2) not achieving the hoped for result: *They made several unsuccessful* ***attempts*** *to reach the men.* ◦ *His application was unsuccessful.* • **unsuccessfully** /-i/ adv

unsuitable /ʌnˈsuː.tə.bl̩/, /-ˈsjuː-/ (US) /-ˈsuː.t̬ə-/ adj (B2) not acceptable or right for someone or something; not suitable: *The software blocks material that is unsuitable* ***for*** *children.* • **unsuitably** /-bli/ adv

unsuited /ʌnˈsuː.tɪd/, /-ˈsjuː-/ (US) /-ˈsuː.t̬ɪd/ adj not right for someone or something, usually in character: *Liberman realized Kurt was unsuited* ***to*** *office life, but offered him a contract anyway.*

unsullied /ʌnˈsʌl.id/ adj formal not damaged or made dirty by anything: *his unsullied reputation*

unsung /ˌʌnˈsʌŋ/ adj not noticed or praised for hard work, courage, or great achievements: *an unsung hero/heroine* ◦ *Many of her achievements* ***went unsung*** *until after her death.*

U

unsupported /ˌʌn.səˈpɔː.tɪd/ (US) /-ˈpɔːr.t̬ɪd/ adj **OPINION** ▷ **1** If someone's opinions or statements are unsupported, they do not have any proof or EVIDENCE to show that they are true: *unsupported allegations* **PERSON** ▷ **2** not receiving any help or encouragement from other people: *He made several attempts to reach the North Pole unsupported.* **STRUCTURE** ▷ **3** describes a structure or object that does not use any other object or person to support its weight, especially from below to stop it from falling: *to stand unsupported* ◦ *the largest unsupported marble dome in the world*

unsure /ʌnˈʃɔːr/ (US) /-ˈʃʊr/ adj **1** (B2) not certain or having doubts: *I'm a bit unsure* ***about*** *what to do next – can you help me?* **2 unsure of yourself** (C2) without confidence in yourself: *As a new teacher I was very unsure of myself when I was in front of a class.*

unsurpassed /ˌʌn.səˈpɑːst/ (US) /-səˈpæst/ adj better than anyone or anything else: *His knowledge of the subject is unsurpassed.*

unsurprising /ˌʌn.səˈpraɪ.zɪŋ/, /-sə-/ adj not making you feel surprised: ***It is*** *unsurprising* ***that*** *many people do not support the government.* • **unsurprisingly** /-li/ adv *Perhaps unsurprisingly, the film was not a success.*

unsuspected /ˌʌn.səˈspek.tɪd/ adj not known or thought to exist: *an unsuspected talent/complication/problem/illness*

unsuspecting /ˌʌn.səˈspek.tɪŋ/ adj trusting; not realizing there is any danger or harm: *The killer lured his unsuspecting victims back to his apartment.*

unsustainable /ˌʌn.səˈsteɪ.nə.bəl/ adj **1** (C2) Something that is unsustainable cannot continue at the same rate: *This level of spending on pensions is unsustainable.* **2** (C2) causing damage to the environment by using more of something than can be replaced naturally: *unsustainable fishing methods*

unswerving /ʌnˈswɜː.vɪŋ/ (US) /-ˈswɝː-/ adj If someone's trust or belief is unswerving, it is always strong and never becomes weaker: *unswerving loyalty/devotion/support/faith*

unsympathetic /ˌʌn.sɪm.pəˈθet.ɪk/ (US) /-ˈθet̬-/ adj not SYMPATHETIC (= showing that you understand or care about someone's suffering)

untangle /ʌnˈtæŋ.gl̩/ verb [T] **KNOTS** ▷ **1** to remove the knots from an untidy mass of string, wire, etc. and separate the different threads **PROBLEM** ▷ **2** to make a complicated subject or problem, or its different parts, clear and able to be understood: *It took years to untangle the legal complexities of the case.*

untapped /ʌnˈtæpt/ adj If a supply of something valuable is untapped, it is not yet used or taken advantage of: *untapped assets/resources/markets/talent*

untenable /ʌnˈten.ə.bl̩/ adj formal **1** describes a theory or argument that cannot be supported or defended against criticism **2** describes a situation that cannot continue as it is: *If three people in four no longer support the government, isn't this an untenable situation?*

unthinkable /ʌnˈθɪŋ.kə.bl̩/ adj; noun

▸adj (C1) so shocking that it cannot be imagined: *You can't imagine what it would be like to have your child die – it's quite unthinkable.*

▸noun [S]

IDIOM **the unthinkable** an unthinkable event or situation: *The unthinkable had happened – his secret activities had been discovered by the press.*

unthinking /ʌnˈθɪŋ.kɪŋ/ adj formal mainly disapproving not based on serious thought or an examination of the information: *What annoys me about these people is their unthinking hostility to anything foreign or unfamiliar.* • **unthinkingly** /-li/ adv *I really didn't mean to offend her – I just said it unthinkingly.*

untidy /ʌnˈtaɪ.di/ adj (B1) not tidy: *an untidy room* ◦ *She's really untidy at home.* • **untidily** /-dɪ.li/ adv • **untidiness** /-nəs/ noun [U]

untie /ʌnˈtaɪ/ verb [T] (present tense **untying**, past tense and past participle **untied**) (B2) to unfasten a knot or something tied

until /ənˈtɪl/, /ˈʌn-/ preposition, conjunction (also **till**) **TIME** ▷ **1** (A1) up to (the time that): *I was up until three o'clock trying to get it finished!* ◦ *Hadn't we better wait until Antony's here?* **2 not until** (B1) not before a particular time or event: *We didn't eat till past midnight.* ◦ *Once he starts a decorating job he won't stop until it's finished.* **DISTANCE** ▷ **3** (A2) as far as: *You should stay on the train until Manchester and then change.*

> **! Common mistake: until now or so far?**
>
> **Warning:** choose the correct adverb!
>
> Use 'until now' to talk about a situation that existed, but has just ended:
>
> *The weather was lovely until now. I hope the rain stops soon.*
>
> To talk about a situation that still exists and may continue to exist, don't say 'until now', say **so far**:
>
> ~~*The weather has been lovely until now. I hope it will continue.*~~
>
> *The weather has been lovely so far. I hope it will continue.*

> **! Common mistake: until**
>
> **Warning:** Check your spelling!
>
> **Until** is one of the 50 words most often spelled wrongly by learners. Remember: the correct spelling has only one 'l'. You can also use **till** with the same meaning, but remember that it has two 'l's.

untimely /ʌnˈtaɪm.li/ **adj** formal describes something bad that happens unexpectedly early or at a time that is not suitable: *It was this passion for fast cars that led to his untimely **death** at the age of 43.*

untiring /ʌnˈtaɪə.rɪŋ/ Ⓤⓢ /-ˈtaɪr.ɪŋ/ **adj** If someone has untiring energy, interest, or enthusiasm, their energy, interest, or enthusiasm never becomes weaker: *We'd like to thank George for his untiring efforts on our behalf.*

unto /ˈʌn.tuː/, /-tu/, /-tə/ **preposition** old use to: *And the Lord spake unto (= spoke to) him.*

untold /ʌnˈtəʊld/ Ⓤⓢ /-ˈtoʊld/ /ˈʌn.təʊld/ **adj** so great in amount or level that it can not be measured or expressed in words: *untold riches* ◦ *Words alone cannot convey the untold **misery** endured by people in these refugee camps.*

untouchable /ʌnˈtʌtʃ.ə.bl̩/ **adj; noun**
▸**adj** **PROTECTED** ▷ **1** not able to be punished, criticized, or changed in any way: *We've got to change the present system in which high court judges are regarded as somehow untouchable.* **NOT DEFEATED** ▷ **2** not able to be defeated or to be as good as: *Coventry City have proved untouchable this season – they've just won their sixth consecutive game.*
▸**noun** [C] a member of the lowest social group in Indian society

untouched /ʌnˈtʌtʃt/ **adj** **1** Ⓒ1 not changed or spoiled in any way: *Most of the east coast remains mercifully untouched by tourism.* **2** If food is untouched, it has not been eaten: *She took a few spoonfuls of soup but left her main course untouched.*

untoward /ˌʌn.tuˈwɔːd/ Ⓤⓢ /-ˈtə.wɔːrd/ **adj** unexpected and not convenient or unpleasant: *Unless anything untoward happens we should arrive just before midday.*

untrained /ʌnˈtreɪnd/ **adj** **1** never having been taught the skills for a particular job: *untrained staff* **2 to the untrained eye** to someone without the skill or knowledge to judge what they see: *To the untrained eye, most fake diamonds look real.*

untrammelled formal (US usually **untrammeled**) /ʌnˈtræm.əld/ **adj** not limited by rules or any other controlling influence: *Self-governing schools are untrammelled by education authority rules.*

untreated /ʌnˈtriː.tɪd/ Ⓤⓢ /-t̬ɪd/ **adj** **1** describes a substance that is not cleaned and has not had special substances added to protect it or make it safe to use: *untreated water/sewage/waste* ◦ *untreated timber* **2** describes illnesses, injuries, people, or animals that do not receive medical treatment: *untreated illness/disease/depression* ◦ *It is a form of anaemia which is nearly always fatal if left untreated.*

untrue /ʌnˈtruː/ **adj** Ⓒ1 not true; false

untruth /ʌnˈtruːθ/ **noun** **1** [C] a statement that is not true: *It's not the first time that the paper has been in trouble for printing untruths about people's private lives.* **2** [U] the fact that something is not true: *The untruth of this statement was immediately clear to me.*

untuned /ʌnˈtjuːnd/ Ⓤⓢ /-tuːnd/ **adj** **unpitched**

untutored /ʌnˈtjuː.təd/ Ⓤⓢ /-ˈtuː.t̬əd/ **adj** formal **1** having no knowledge of or education in a particular subject **2 to the, my, etc. untutored eye** if or because you are, I am, etc. an untutored person: *You see, to my untutored eye that just looks like a load of random brush strokes and yet it's a very valuable painting.*

untypical /ʌnˈtɪp.ɪ.kəl/ **adj** not typical: *Her angry outburst was untypical; she's usually a very quiet woman.* ◦ *It is **not** untypical **of** girls of her age to be concerned about their appearance.*

unusable /ʌnˈjuː.zə.bl̩/ **adj** describes something that cannot be used, especially because it is broken or not safe: *The normal supply of water has turned brown and unusable.* ◦ *The virus deletes files and corrupts essential core microchips, leaving computers unusable.*

unused **adj** **NOT USED** ▷ **1** /ʌnˈjuːzd/ not being used at present, or never having been used: *You might as well take your father's car – there's no point in having it sit there unused in the garage.* **NOT FAMILIAR** ▷ **2 be unused to sth** /ʌnˈjuːst/ to not be familiar with a particular habit or experience: *If you're unused to exercise your joints may ache the next day.* ◦ *I'm unused to getting up so early.*

> **✚ Other ways of saying unusual**
>
> See also: **different**, **special**, **strange**
>
> **Uncommon** or **rare** can be used instead of 'unusual' when saying that something is unusual because it does not happen or exist very often:
>
> *It's not **uncommon** for people to become ill when they travel.*
>
> *This is a **rare** opportunity to visit the building.*
>
> If something is unusual because it is different from the way most people do things, the adjective **unconventional** can be used:
>
> *I had a very **unconventional** childhood.*
>
> **Unique** is used when something only happens once or only one of a particular thing exists:
>
> *This is your chance to own a **unique** piece of jewellery.*
>
> **Exotic** can be used for describing things which are unusual and exciting, especially because they relate to a foreign country:
>
> *The room was decorated with **exotic** flowers.*
>
> If something is unusual in an interesting and slightly odd way, you can use the words **quirky** or **offbeat**:
>
> *He has a very **quirky** sense of humour.*
>
> *The movie is an **offbeat** romantic comedy.*
>
> If a person is very unusual in a nice way, you can say that he or she is **one of a kind**:
>
> *He was truly **one of a kind**, and will be missed.*

unusual /ʌnˈjuː.ʒu.əl/ **adj** Ⓐ2 different from others of the same type in a way that is surprising, interesting, or attractive: *'Do you like the new settee?' 'Very much, it's most unusual.'* ◦ [+ to infinitive] ***It's** unusual **to** have adult conversation like that with such a young child.* ◦ *I was actually on time, which is unusual for me.*

unusually /ʌnˈjuː.ʒu.ə.li/ **adv** **1** B2 more than is usual or expected, or in a way that is not usual: *He was unusually polite.* **2 unusually for sb** C2 in a way that is not usual for someone: *Unusually for me, I felt deeply embarrassed.*

unutterable /ʌnˈʌt.ər.ə.bl/ US /-ˈʌţ.ɚ-/ **adj** formal too bad to be expressed in words; extreme: *unutterable boredom*

unutterably /ʌnˈʌt.ər.ə.bli/ US /-ˈʌţ.ɚ-/ **adv** formal extremely: *She came home exhausted and unutterably sad.*

unvarnished /ʌnˈvɑː.nɪʃt/ US /-ˈvɑːr-/ **adj** [before noun] describes a statement that is expressed in a plain and honest way: *It's a bit optimistic to expect a politician to tell you the unvarnished* ***truth***.

unveil /ʌnˈveɪl/ **verb** [T] **1** to remove a covering like a curtain from a new structure at a formal ceremony in order to show the opening or finishing of a new building or work of art: *The memorial to those who had died in the war was unveiled by the Queen.* **2** If you unveil something new, you show it or make it known for the first time: *A new government policy on forests is due to be unveiled in April.*

the unwaged /ˌʌnˈweɪdʒd/ **noun** [plural] UK unemployed people: *The entrance fee is six pounds, two pounds for the unwaged.* • **unwaged adj**

unwanted /ʌnˈwɒn.tɪd/ US /-ˈwɑːn.ţɪd/ **adj** C1 not wanted: *How can I stop unwanted emails?*

unwarranted /ʌnˈwɒr.ən.tɪd/ US /-ˈwɔːr.ən.ţɪd/ **adj** formal not having a good reason and therefore annoying or unfair: *People need to be protected against such unwarranted intrusions into their private lives by journalists.*

unwary /ʌnˈweə.ri/ US /-ˈwer.i/ **adj** not conscious of or careful about possible risks and dangers: *Meanwhile, the cowboy trader is free to carry on ripping off unwary customers.* ◦ *A range of tax and technical issues can trip up* ***the*** *unwary (= unwary people).*

unwashed /ʌnˈwɒʃt/ US /-ˈwɑːʃt/ **adj** not washed

unwavering /ʌnˈweɪ.vər.ɪŋ/ **adj** NOT MOVING ▷ **1** never moving or looking away from something: *She met his unwavering stare.* NOT CHANGING ▷ **2** never changing or becoming weaker: *Her belief in the project has been unwavering.*

unwelcome /ʌnˈwel.kəm/ **adj** not wanted: *unwelcome news* ◦ *an unwelcome visitor*

unwelcoming /ʌnˈwel.kəm.ɪŋ/ **adj** not making a guest or visitor feel happy, comfortable, or wanted: *The house was damp and unwelcoming.*

unwell /ʌnˈwel/ **adj** [after verb] B1 not well; ill: *I hear you've been unwell recently.*

unwieldy /ʌnˈwiːl.di/ **adj** DIFFICULT TO MOVE ▷ **1** An unwieldy object is difficult to move or handle because it is heavy, large, or a strange shape: *A piano is a very unwieldy item to get down a flight of stairs.* NOT EFFECTIVE ▷ **2** An unwieldy system is slow and not effective, usually because it is too big, badly organized, or involves too many different organizations or people: *One disadvantage for the bank is that its huge size – over 15,000 staff – makes it unwieldy and slow-moving.*

unwilling /ʌnˈwɪl.ɪŋ/ **adj** B2 not willing: *an unwilling helper* • **unwillingly** /-li/ **adv** • **unwillingness** /-nəs/ **noun** [U] C1 *her unwillingness to help*

unwind /ʌnˈwaɪnd/ **verb** (**unwound**, **unwound**) UNFASTEN ▷ **1** C2 [I or T] If you unwind something that is wrapped around an object, you unfasten it, and if it unwinds, it becomes unfastened: *In a nearby*

> **Other ways of saying unwilling**
>
> If someone is unwilling to do something, you can say formally that the person is **loath to** do it:
>
> *I was* ***loath to*** *spend all the money at once.*
>
> The verb **balk** can be used when someone is unwilling to do something or unwilling for something to happen:
>
> *The governor* ***balked*** *at a proposal to raise the state sales tax.*
>
> **Reluctant** can be used when someone is unwilling to do something and therefore is slow to do it:
>
> *I was* ***reluctant*** *to leave because I was having such a good time.*
>
> If someone is unwilling to do something but does it anyway, you can say that the person does it **grudgingly** or **under protest**:
>
> *He* ***grudgingly*** *agreed to a meeting.*
>
> *He did pay, but* ***under protest***.

medical tent, a US Army doctor gently unwinds Metruk's bandage. RELAX ▷ **2** C1 [I] (also **wind down**) to relax and allow your mind to be free from worry after a period of work or some other activity that has made you worried: *A glass of wine in the evening helps me to unwind after work.*

unwise /ʌnˈwaɪz/ **adj** C2 stupid and likely to cause problems • **unwisely** /-li/ **adv**

unwitting /ʌnˈwɪt.ɪŋ/ US /-ˈwɪţ-/ **adj** [before noun] formal without knowing or planning: *The two women claimed they were the unwitting victims of a drugs dealer who planted a large quantity of heroin in their luggage.* • **unwittingly** /-li/ **adv** *I regret any anxiety which I may, unwittingly, have caused.*

unwonted /ʌnˈwəʊn.tɪd/ US /-ˈwɑːn.ţɪd/ **adj** [before noun] formal unusual; not often experienced or shown: *He sprang to the phone with unwonted eagerness.*

unworkable /ʌnˈwɜː.kə.bl/ US /-ˈwɝː-/ **adj** describes a plan that is not practical or that you cannot really do successfully: *To be honest, I think the scheme is completely unworkable.*

unwrap /ʌnˈræp/ **verb** [T] (**-pp-**) to remove the paper or other covering from something: *Aren't you going to unwrap your presents?*

unwritten /ʌnˈrɪt.ən/ US /-ˈrɪţ-/ **adj** **1** describes something that does not exist in a written or printed form: *an unwritten constitution* **2** describes a rule or law that does not exist officially but that people generally accept and obey: *There's an unwritten* ***rule*** *that you don't wear jeans to work.*

unyielding /ʌnˈjiːl.dɪŋ/ **adj** NOT CHANGING ▷ **1** completely unwilling to change a decision, opinion, demand, etc.: *Korea is unyielding in its demands for a new treaty.* NOT BENDING ▷ **2** RIGID (= not able to be bent or moved)

unzip /ʌnˈzɪp/ **verb** [T] (**-pp-**) **1** to open something by using a ZIP: *He unzipped his suitcase.* **2** to return a computer file to its original size after it has been ZIPPED (= reduced in size so that it can be easily sent or stored)

up /ʌp/ **adv; preposition; adj; noun; verb**

▸**adv** HIGHER ▷ **1** A2 towards a higher position; towards a higher value, number, or level: *Put those books up on the top shelf.* ◦ *A gravel road leads through the jungle and up into the Andes.* ◦ *Pushing the number of unit sales up every quarter can't be continued indefinitely.* ◦ *The water was up* ***to****/had come up* ***to*** *the level of the windows.* **2** out of the ground: *He spent the afternoon digging carrots up.* **3 up and down** B2 from a higher to a lower position repeatedly: *My little daughter started **jumping** up and down with rage when she heard she couldn't go.* **VERTICAL** ▷ **4** A1 in or into a vertical position: *Would you stand up for a moment, I want to see how tall you are.* → Compare **down** **TOP** ▷ **5** A2 in a high position; at the top: *Our boardroom is up on the 23rd floor.* ◦ *You can tell which **way** up the crates have to be because they all say 'TOP'.* → Compare **down** **NEAR** ▷ **6** B1 very near: *Carrying a gun, he walked up **to** the cashier and demanded money.* ◦ *A limousine **drew** up (= parked) outside the hotel.* **INCREASE** ▷ **7** B2 to a greater degree; in order to increase: *The fire **heats** the room up (= makes it warmer) within minutes.* ◦ *Grandma always **turns** the TV up really loud because she can't hear very well.* ◦ *Try not to get **worked** up (= increasingly excited or angry), I'm sure we can sort the problem out.* **8** B2 If a level or amount is up, it has increased: *The cost of car insurance is up, but not very much.* ◦ *Last year the company's turnover was $240 billion, up three percent **on** (= compared with) the previous year.* **NOT IN BED** ▷ **9** B1 not in bed: *It's time to **get** up now!* ◦ *Oh, I've been up all night, finishing my essay.* **10 up and about/around** to be able to get out of bed and move around again after a period of illness, because your health has improved enough **EXIST** ▷ **11** into existence, view, or attention: *Originally the charity was **set** up to help orphans in urban areas.* ◦ *Sorry darling, something unexpected has **come** up (= has happened) at the office, and I'll be home late.* ◦ ***Coming** up (= happening next) after the break, we have a man who claims he can communicate with fish.* ◦ *Would this be a good time to **bring** up the issue of salary?* **EQUAL** ▷ **12** so as to be equal in quality, knowledge, or achievement: *She couldn't go to school for a few weeks because of illness, but she'll be able to **catch** up (**with** her lessons) quickly.* ◦ *So much scientific research is being performed that it's virtually impossible to **keep** up (**with** all the new developments).* ◦ US informal *Kate and I were both playing well, and after ten minutes the score was 6 up (= 6 points each).* **TOGETHER** ▷ **13** in a state of being together with other similar things: *You've got half an hour to gather up anything you'll need for the journey.* ◦ ***Add** up the column of figures in your head and then tell me what the sum is.* **TIGHTLY** ▷ **14** tightly or firmly in order to keep something safe or in position: *Can you **do** my shoelaces up for me?* ◦ ***Tie** up the top of the bag so the rubbish doesn't fall out.* ◦ *You'd better **wrap** up (= wear warm clothes) – it's cold outside.* **SMALLER** ▷ **15** broken or cut into smaller pieces; made smaller in area: *He **cut** the letter up into a hundred pieces.* ◦ *She **folded** the newspaper up and put it in her bag.* ◦ *The car **blew** up (= exploded) when flames reached its fuel tank.* **AGE** ▷ **16** to a greater age: *No one said that **growing** up would be easy or painless.* ◦ *Many single parents struggle to **bring** their children up on a low income.* **PROBLEM** ▷ **17** B1 [after verb] used when talking or asking about what is happening: *Everyone was talking in whispers, and I could tell something was up (= something unusual was happening).* ◦ ***What's** up? (= What is happening or what is wrong?)* **FINISHED** ▷ **18** [after verb] When a period of time is up, it is finished: *When the two hours were up nobody had answered all of the questions.* ◦ *Your **time** is up – it's someone else's turn on the training equipment now.* **IMPROVE** ▷ **19** into an improved position or state: *By lap 26, Hamilton had **moved** up into second position.* ◦ *Stein had a bad start to the race, but by the ninth lap she was up **with** the leaders.* → Compare **down** **END** ▷ **20** B2 to an end, finish, or state of being complete: ***Finish** up the old packet of biscuits before you open a new one.* ◦ *Crime won't help – you'll **end** up in prison.* ◦ *I'd like to **round** up the meeting by thanking all those who were able to attend at such short notice.* **DIRECTION** ▷ **21** towards the north or towards a more important place, especially a city: *On Tuesday she'll be travelling up **to** Newcastle from Birmingham.* ◦ *She comes up **from** her village about once a month on the train.* **INTENDED** ▷ **22 up for sth** intended, suggested, or being considered for something: *That house at the end of our road is up for sale again.* ◦ *Are you really up for promotion?* **EAGER** ▷ **23 up for (doing) sth** informal willing and able to do or take part in an activity: *After a long day at work I wasn't really up for a party.* ◦ *We're going swimming. Are you up for it?* ◦ *I'm up for organizing the meeting if nobody else wants to do it.* **TRIAL** ▷ **24** [after verb] on trial in a court: *If he doesn't pay the fine soon, he'll be up **before** the magistrate.* ◦ *Max is up **for** armed robbery.* **ROAD** ▷ **25** [after verb] UK When a road is up, it is being repaired and so is unsuitable for use: *The council has got the road up because of a broken sewer.* **HAIR** ▷ **26** If someone's long hair is up, it is arranged on the top or back of their head: *You look lovely with your **hair** up.*

IDIOMS **be up there with sb** informal to be equal to someone else in ability or in a particular skill: *As a composer, he was up there with the best.* • **up and down** sometimes happy and sometimes sad: *She's been very up and down since her husband went into hospital.* • **up and down somewhere** everywhere in a particular area: *Cinemas up and down **the country** are reporting huge audiences for the film.* • **up to (doing) sth 1** good enough for a particular activity: *He wants to compete at international level, but frankly I don't think he's up to it.* **2** strong enough for a particular activity: *It was a serious fall – it'll be a while before you feel up to walking again.* • **be up to sth** B1 to be doing something: *What are you up to at the moment?* • **up with** old-fashioned informal shouted or written on notices to show support: *Up with freedom, down with repression!*

▸**preposition HIGHER** ▷ **1** A2 to or in a higher level or position: *We followed her up the stairs to a large meeting room.* **TOP** ▷ **2** at the top of: *You'll find a dusty attic up these stairs.* ◦ *If you want Fred, he's up that ladder.* **ALONG** ▷ **3** A2 (further) along: *The car shot off up the road at high speed.* ◦ *They live just up the road.* **4 up and down** B2 along the surface of something first in one direction and then in the opposite direction, usually repeatedly: *He was running up and down the path, shouting.* **ORIGIN** ▷ **5** towards the starting point of something, especially a river or stream: *Rowing up (the) river against the current was very hard work.* → See also **upriver, upstream** **TO** ▷ **6** UK not standard to or at: *Are you **going** up the club tonight?* → Compare **down**

IDIOMS **be up yourself** UK slang to think that you are better and more important than other people: *She's so up herself since she landed this new job, it's unbearable.* • **up yours!** offensive used to show that you very much dislike someone or the things that someone has just said or done

▸**adj RISING** ▷ **1** moving up: *an up escalator* → See also **upper** **IN OPERATION** ▷ **2** [after verb] When a system, computer, or similar machine is up, it is operating, especially in its usual way: *Andy, do you know when the network will be up again?* → Opposite **down** **HAPPY** ▷ **3** informal feeling happy: *She's been really up since she started her new job.*

IDIOM **up and running** If something, especially a system or a machine, is up and running it is

U

operating: *The engineer soon got the air-conditioning up and running again.*

▸noun

IDIOM **on the up (and up) 1** mainly US informal describes someone who is honest and can be trusted **2** UK improving all the time: *Her career has been on the up and up since she moved into sales.*

▸verb informal **INCREASE** ▷ **1** [T] (-pp-) to increase something such as a price: *We won't be able to make a profit on the deal without upping the sale price.* ◦ *It looks like tax rates are going to be upped again.* **GO AWAY** ▷ **2 up and ...** used with another verb to emphasize that someone left a place or did something in a sudden and possibly unexpected way: *After dinner they just upped and* ***left/went*** *without saying goodbye.*

up- /ʌp-/ prefix higher or improved: *uphill* ◦ *uplift*

ˌup-and-ˈcoming adj [usually before noun] likely to achieve success soon or in the near future: *up-and-coming young actresses*

ˌup-and-ˈdown adj sometimes successful and sometimes not successful

upbeat /ʌpˈbiːt/, /ˈʌp.biːt/ adj informal full of hope, happiness, and good feelings: *Live music and a parade set an upbeat mood for the official opening.* → Opposite **downbeat**

upbraid /ʌpˈbreɪd/ verb [T] formal to forcefully or angrily tell someone they should not have done a particular thing and criticize them for having done it: *In newspaper articles she consistently upbraided those in authority who overstepped their limits.*

upbringing /ˈʌpˌbrɪŋ.ɪŋ/ noun [C usually singular] B2 the way in which someone is treated and educated when they are young, especially by their parents, especially in relation to the effect which this has on how they behave and make moral decisions: *Is it right to say all the crimes he committed were simply the result of his upbringing?* → See also **bring sb up**

upcoming /ˈʌpˌkʌm.ɪŋ/ adj [before noun] mainly US (UK usually **forthcoming**) C1 happening soon: *Tickets are selling well for the group's upcoming concert tour.*

upcycling /ˈʌpˌsaɪ.klɪŋ/ noun [U] using waste materials or old products to make new materials or products of better quality

update verb; noun

▸verb [T] /ʌpˈdeɪt/ **1** B2 to make something more modern or suitable for use now by adding new information or changing its design: *an updated version of the software* **2** B1 to give someone the most recent information: *We'll update you* ***on*** *this news story throughout the day.*

▸noun [C] /ˈʌp.deɪt/ **1** B2 an act of updating something or someone with new information: *Jo's just doing an update* ***on*** *the mailing list.* ◦ *I'll need regular updates* ***on*** *your progress.* **2** B2 a new form of something which existed at an earlier time: *It's an update* ***of*** *an old 60s movie.*

upend /ʌpˈend/ verb [T] to push or move something so that the part which usually touches the ground does so no longer: *She upended the chessboard halfway through the game because she was losing.*

upfront /ʌpˈfrʌnt/ adj [after verb] speaking or behaving in a way which makes intentions and beliefs clear: *She's very upfront* ***about*** *why she wants the job – she'd earn a lot more money.* → See also **up front** at **front**

upgradation /ˌʌp.ɡrəˈdeɪ.ʃən/, /ˌʌp.ɡreɪ-/ noun [U] Indian English the process of improving the quality or usefulness of something, or of giving a person a more important job: *The Centre has approved projects worth about Rs 40 crore for the upgradation of industrial estates in the city.*

upgrade verb; noun

▸verb [T] /ʌpˈɡreɪd/ B2 to improve the quality or usefulness of something, such as a machine or a computer program, or give a person a more important job or state that their job is more important than it was in the past: *It's quite simple to upgrade the indexing software.* ◦ *Congratulations, I hear you've been upgraded* ***to*** *divisional manager.* → Opposite **downgrade**

▸noun [C] /ˈʌp.ɡreɪd/ B2 a piece of software or equipment that improves the quality or usefulness of a computer or machine: *a hardware upgrade* ◦ *The upgrade to version 5.0 costs $395.*

upheaval /ʌpˈhiː.vəl/ noun [C or U] (a) great change, especially causing or involving much difficulty, activity, or trouble: *Yesterday's coup brought further upheaval to a country already struggling with famine.* ◦ *It would cause a tremendous upheaval to install a different computer system.*

uphill /ˌʌpˈhɪl/ adj, adv **1** C2 leading to a higher place on a slope: *an uphill climb* ◦ *running uphill* → Compare **downhill 2** C2 needing a large amount of effort: *It'll be an uphill* ***struggle/battle/fight*** *to get the new proposals accepted.* → Compare **downhill**

uphold /ʌpˈhəʊld/ US /-ˈhoʊld/ verb [T] (**upheld, upheld**) C2 to defend or keep a principle or law, or to say that a decision that has already been made, especially a legal one, is correct: *As a police officer you are expected to uphold the law whether you agree with it or not.* ◦ *Judge Davis upheld the county court's decision.* • **upholder** /-ˈhəʊl.dər/ US /-ˈhoʊl.dɚ/ noun [C]

upholster /ʌpˈhəʊl.stər/ US /-ˈhoʊl.stɚ/ verb [T] to cover a chair or other type of seat with suitable cloth and fill it with a suitable substance • **upholstered** /-stəd/ US /-stɚd/ adj *a nicely upholstered sofa* • **upholsterer** /-ər/ US /-ɚ/ noun [C]

upholstery /ʌpˈhəʊl.stər.i/ US /-ˈhoʊl.stɚ-/ noun [U] **1** the cloth used for covering a seat and/or the substance used for filling it: *an old sofa with faded green upholstery* **2** the activity of upholstering objects

upkeep /ˈʌp.kiːp/ noun [U] C2 the cost or process of keeping something, such as a building, in good condition: *The upkeep* ***of*** *larger old properties is very expensive.* ◦ *Council employees are responsible for the upkeep* ***of*** *the gardens.*

upland /ˈʌp.lənd/ adj; noun

▸adj describes an area of land that is high up, such as on a hill or mountain: *The whole plateau comprises one vast upland plain.*

▸noun **uplands** [plural] high areas of land

uplift noun; verb

▸noun /ˈʌp.lɪft/ **IMPROVEMENT** ▷ **1** [U] formal improvement of a person's moral or spiritual condition: *We are counting on your speech, bishop, to give some moral uplift to the delegates.* **SUPPORT** ▷ **2** [U] support or forces that raise an object or hold it up: *The wings are designed to provide uplift when the plane is flying horizontally.* ◦ *an uplift* ***bra*** **INCREASE** ▷ **3** [C or U] an increase in value: *Shares have now recovered to 481p – this represents a huge uplift* ***of*** *almost 50 percent in their value.*

▸verb [T] /ʌpˈlɪft/ **IMPROVE** ▷ **1** to improve a person's moral or spiritual condition **RAISE** ▷ **2** specialized to raise something to a higher position **COLLECT** ▷ **3** Scottish English to collect goods or people from one place, in order to take them to another: *Coaches will* *set down and uplift passengers only as directed by the police in the streets mentioned.*

uplifted /ʌpˈlɪf.tɪd/ adj formal raised: *With uplifted arms, he ran towards them.*

uplifting /ʌpˈlɪf.tɪŋ/ adj making someone feel better: *For me it was a marvellously uplifting performance.*

upliftment /ʌpˈlɪft.mənt/ noun [U] Indian English improvement of a person's moral or spiritual condition

uplighter /ˈʌp.laɪ.təʳ/ (US) /-t̬ɚ/ noun [C] (also **uplight**) a light that sends light up towards the ceiling

upload verb; noun

▸verb [T] /ʌpˈləʊd/ (US) /-ˈloʊd/ B1 to copy or move programs or information to a larger computer system or to the internet → Compare **download**

▸noun [C] /ˈʌp.ləʊd/ (US) /-loʊd/ a computer program or information that can be uploaded

upmarket /ˌʌpˈmɑː.kɪt/ (US) /ˈʌp.mɑːr-/ adj, adv mainly UK (mainly US **upscale**) describes goods and products that are of very high quality and intended to be bought by people who are quite rich: *an upmarket brand name* ◦ *Many garment exporters want to move upmarket.* → Compare **downmarket**

upon /əˈpɒn/ (US) /-ˈpɑːn/ preposition **1** B2 formal on: *Upon her head she wore a black velvet hat.* ◦ *You can never place enough emphasis upon the importance of safety.* ◦ *Upon your arrival (= as soon as you arrive), please report to the reception desk.* **2 be upon sb** formal to be something that someone will experience or have to deal with soon: *Another couple of weeks and the holidays will be upon us.*

upper /ˈʌp.əʳ/ (US) /-ɚ/ adj; noun

▸adj [before noun] B1 at a higher position or level than something else, or being the top part of something: *The office block's upper floors were being repainted.* ◦ *If the infection is not checked it will probably spread to the upper body.* → Opposite **lower**

▸noun [C] SHOE PART ▷ **1** the top part of a shoe which covers a person's foot and to which the HEEL and the SOLE are fixed: *These shoes have leather uppers and synthetic soles.* DRUG ▷ **2** informal a drug which causes a person taking it to feel very active and excited → Opposite **downer**

IDIOM **be on your uppers** old-fashioned informal to be very poor

ˌupper ˈcase noun [U] specialized If letters are in upper case, they are written as capitals. → Compare **lower case** • **ˌupper-ˈcase** adj *upper-case letters*

ˌupper ˈclass noun [S, + sing/pl verb] (also **the ˌupper ˈclasses** [plural]) C1 a social group consisting of the people who have the highest social rank and who are usually rich: *The upper classes usually send their children to expensive private schools.* → Compare **lower class, middle class, working class** • **ˌupper-ˈclass** adj C1 *She comes from a very upper-class family.*

the ˌupper ˈcrust noun [S, + sing/pl verb] informal people who have the highest social position and are usually rich: *Many treasures were brought back to Britain because its upper crust was wealthy and liked travelling abroad.*

the ˌupper ˈhand noun [S] C If you have the upper hand, you have more power than anyone else and so have control: *After hours of fierce negotiations, the president **gained/got/had** the upper hand.*

ˌupper ˈhouse noun [C usually singular] (also **ˌupper ˈchamber**) one of the two parts that some parliaments are divided into, usually the one with less political power: *In the UK, the upper house is the House of Lords.* → Compare **lower house**

uppermost /ˈʌp.ə.məʊst/ (US) /-ɚ.moʊst/ adj, adv in the highest position or having the most importance: *The office block's uppermost floors were engulfed with flames.* ◦ *Store the canisters with their lids uppermost.* ◦ *What's uppermost **in** your **mind** just before a race?*

uppity /ˈʌp.ɪ.ti/ (US) /-ə.t̬i/ adj informal disapproving describes a person who behaves in an unpleasant way because they think that they are more important than they really are: *He **got/became** very uppity when his fashion designs were criticized.*

upright /ˈʌp.raɪt/ adj; adv; noun

▸adj STRAIGHT ▷ **1** B2 straight up or vertical: *Please return your seat to an upright position and fasten your belt.* **2** describes something that is taller than it is wide: *an upright freezer/vacuum cleaner* MORAL ▷ **3** approving honest, responsible, and moral: *She behaved as any upright **citizen** would have under the circumstances.*

▸adv B2 vertical and as straight as possible: *to sit/stand upright* ◦ *The sound of breaking glass made her sit **bolt** upright (= sit with her back straight).*

▸noun [C] **1** a vertical part of something that supports other parts: *Firmly secure the two uprights to opposite walls in the alcove and then slot the shelves in between them.* **2** UK informal for **goalpost 3** (also **upright piano**) a piano in which the strings are vertical → Compare **grand piano**

uprightly /ˈʌp.raɪt.li/ adv approving in an honest, responsible, and moral way

uprightness /ˈʌp.raɪt.nəs/ noun [U] approving the quality of being honest, responsible, and moral

uprising /ˈʌpˌraɪ.zɪŋ/ noun [C] (also **rising**) an act of opposition, sometimes using violence, by many people in one area of a country against those who are in power: *Following a determined resistance in the east, there was eventually a **popular** uprising in the capital.*

upriver /ˌʌpˈrɪv.əʳ/ (US) /-ɚ/ adv, adj [before noun] towards the place where a river starts: *We paddled upriver for a couple of hours.*

uproar /ˈʌp.rɔːʳ/ (US) /-rɔːr/ noun [S or U] a situation in which a lot of people complain about something angrily or make a lot of noise: *The book **caused** an uproar in France.* ◦ *The whole hall was **in** uproar after the announcement.*

uproarious /ʌpˈrɔː.ri.əs/ (US) /-ˈrɔːr.i-/ adj **1** extremely noisy and confused: *an uproarious debate* **2** extremely funny: *It's a very amusing play with an uproarious final act.* • **uproariously** /-li/ adv *They laughed uproariously.*

uproot /ʌpˈruːt/ verb [T] PLANT ▷ **1** to pull a plant including its roots out of the ground: *Hundreds of mature trees were uprooted in the storm.* PERSON ▷ **2** to remove a person from their home or usual environment: *The war has uprooted nearly two thirds of the country's population.*

U

ˌups and ˈdowns noun [plural] If someone or something experiences ups and downs, a mixture of good and bad things happens to them: *Like most married couples we've had our ups and downs, but life's like that.*

upscale /ˈʌp.skeɪl/ adj US for **upmarket**

upselling /ʌpˈsel.ɪŋ/ noun [U] specialized the act of trying to persuade a customer who is already buying something to buy more, or to buy something more expensive: *The salesmen always look for opportunities for upselling.*

upset verb; adj; noun

▸verb [T] /ʌpˈset/ (present tense **upsetting**, past tense and past participle **upset**) **WORRY** ▷ **1** B2 to make someone worried, unhappy, or angry: *It still upsets him when he thinks about the accident.* ◦ *Don't upset your**self** by thinking about what might have been.* **CHANGE** ▷ **2** to change the usual or expected state or order of something, especially in a way which stops it from happening or working: *Any mechanical problems would upset our plans of driving across the desert.* **KNOCK** ▷ **3** to push or knock something out of its usual position, usually by accident, especially causing it to fall: *Our dog upset the picnic table, spilling food everywhere.* **MAKE SICK** ▷ **4** to make someone feel slightly sick: *He can't eat grapes – they upset him/his stomach.*

IDIOM **upset the apple cart** to cause trouble, especially by spoiling someone's plans

▸adj /ʌpˈset/ **WORRIED** ▷ **1** A2 [after verb] worried, unhappy, or angry: *Don't get upset **about** the dress – there's only a little stain on it.* ◦ [+ to infinitive] *She was very upset **to** hear that the holiday had been cancelled.* ◦ [+ that] *He was very upset **that** you didn't reply to his letters.* **ILL** ▷ **2** B2 informal If you have an upset stomach you feel slightly ill, especially because of something you have eaten or drunk: *I've got an upset **stomach/tummy** – serves me right for eating so much.*

▸noun /ˈʌp.set/ **CHANGE** ▷ **1** [U] confusion and problems: *How much upset will the new monitoring procedures cause?* **2** [C] an occasion when someone beats the team or player that was expected to win: *It would be quite an upset if the favourite didn't win.* **ILLNESS** ▷ **3** [C] informal a slight illness of the stomach: *Melanie's got a **stomach/tummy** upset so she won't be going to school today.*

upsetting /ʌpˈset.ɪŋ/ US /-ˈset̬-/ **adj** making someone feel worried, unhappy, or angry: *Seeing her again would be an upsetting experience after so many years.*

the upshot /ˈʌp.ʃɒt/ US /-ʃɑːt/ **noun** [S] something which happens as a result of other actions, events, or decisions: *The upshot **of** the discussions is that there will be no redundancies.*

upside /ˈʌp.saɪd/ **noun** [S] the advantage of a situation: *It's annoying that we can't travel until Thursday, but the upside is that the fare's cheaper then.* → Compare **downside**

ˌupside ˈdown adv, adj B2 having the part that is usually at the top turned to be at the bottom: ***Turn** the jar upside down and shake it.* ◦ *The plane was flying upside down at high speed.*

upside down

IDIOM **turn (sth) upside down** to (cause something to) change completely and in a bad way: *Their lives were turned upside down when their son was arrested.*

upskill /ʌpˈskɪl/ **verb** [I or T] to learn new skills or to teach workers new skills: *The program is aimed at people working in IT who want to upskill.* ◦ *We are upskilling the team.*

upskilling /ʌpˈskɪl.ɪŋ/ **noun** [U] the process of learning new skills or of teaching workers new skills

upstage verb; adv, adj

▸verb [T] /ʌpˈsteɪdʒ/ to take people's attention away from someone and make them listen to or look at you instead

▸adv, adj [before noun] /ʌpˈsteɪdʒ/ US /ˈʌp.steɪdʒ/ towards or at the part of a theatre stage that is furthest from the people watching the performance: *He looks upstage to where the body is lying.* → Opposite **downstage**

upstairs /ʌpˈsteəz/ US /-ˈsterz/ **adv** [before noun], **adj** A2 towards or on the highest floor or floors of a building: *an upstairs landing/window* ◦ *He heard glass breaking and ran upstairs to see what had caused it.* → Opposite **downstairs** • **upstairs** noun [S] *Sadly, **the** upstairs of the house was gutted by fire.*

upstanding /ʌpˈstæn.dɪŋ/ **adj** formal behaving in a good and moral way: *She is regarded as an upstanding **citizen** in the local community.*

upstart /ˈʌp.stɑːt/ US /-stɑːrt/ **noun** [C] **PERSON** ▷ **1** disapproving a person, especially a young one, who has suddenly got power or an important position and takes advantage of this in an unpleasant way **BUSINESS** ▷ **2** a new competitor: *Larger drug companies are buying up many of the upstart **firms**.*

upstate /ˈʌp.steɪt/ **adj** [before noun], **adv** US towards or of the northern parts of a state in the US, especially those that are far from cities where a lot of people live: *upstate New York* ◦ *We're going upstate for our vacation.*

upstream /ˌʌpˈstriːm/ **adv, adj** [before noun] **1** (moving) on a river or stream towards its origin: *Salmon swim upstream against very strong currents to reach their breeding areas.* **2** relating to an earlier stage in a process or series of events: *The company's upstream **business** includes oil exploration and production.* → Opposite **downstream**

upsurge /ˈʌp.sɜːdʒ/ US /-sɝːdʒ/ **noun** [C] a sudden and usually large increase in something: *An upsurge **of/in** violence in the district has been linked to increased unemployment.*

upswing /ˈʌp.swɪŋ/ **noun** [C] an increase or improvement: *Many analysts are predicting an upswing **in** the economy.*

uptake /ˈʌp.teɪk/ **noun** [S or U] **1** specialized the rate or act of taking something in: *Plants in their growth stage exhibit an increased uptake **of** nutrients.* **2** UK the rate or act of accepting something: *There is a 90 percent uptake **of** vaccination in this country.* ◦ *Uptake **of** places on the training course has been disappointing.*

IDIOM **be quick/slow on the uptake** informal If someone is quick/slow on the uptake they understand things easily/with difficulty: *He's a bit slow on the uptake, so you may have to repeat the instructions a few times.*

ˌup-ˈtempo **adj, adv** describes music that is played at a fast beat

uptight /ˌʌpˈtaɪt/ **adj** informal worried or nervous and not able to relax: *Don't get uptight **about** the exam – just do your best.*

ˈup ˌto adv; preposition

▸adv B1 used to say that something is less than or equal to but not more than a stated value, number, or level: *Up to two hundred people were on board the ship.* ◦ *We can teach dancers up to intermediate level here.*

▸preposition **UNTIL** ▷ **1** B1 (also **up until**) until: *Up to yesterday, we had no idea where the child was.* **RESPONSIBILITY** ▷ **2 be up to sb** B1 to be the responsibility of someone: *It's up to the manager to make the final decision.* **DOING** ▷ **3 be up to sth** B1 informal to be doing something, often something bad or illegal, usually secretly: *She's up to **no good** (= doing something bad or forbidden) – you can always tell* because she stays in her room. ◦ He looks very suspicious hanging around by the bins – I'm sure he's up to **something**.

ˌup to ˈdate adj B1 modern, recent, or containing the latest information: *Great trouble is taken to keep our database up to date.* ◦ [before noun] *up-to-date information* → See also **update**

ˌup-to-the-ˈminute adj most recent; containing the most recent information: *Now we're going live to our reporter in Washington for up-to-the-minute news on the crisis.*

uptown /ˌʌpˈtaʊn/ adv, adj [before noun] US in or towards the northern part of a city or town, especially if there is not much business or industry there: *We could walk uptown or we could take the train.* ◦ *I can get lunch in Chinatown for half of what it costs uptown.* → Compare **downtown**

upturn /ˈʌp.tɜːn/ US /-tɝːn/ noun [C] (especially in economics) an improvement or a change to a higher level or value: *a sharp upturn* ***in*** *the economy* → Opposite **downturn**

upturned /ˌʌpˈtɜːnd/ US /-ˈtɝːnd/ adj pointing or looking up, or having the part that is usually at the bottom turned to be at the top: *An upturned boat on the beach provided shelter.*

upward /ˈʌp.wəd/ US /-wɚd/ adj C1 moving towards a higher position, level, or value: *With an upward trend in inflation, you expect prices to rise.* → Opposite **downward**

upwardly mobile /ˌʌp.wəd.liˈməʊ.baɪl/ US /-wɚd.li-ˈmoʊ.bəl/ adj moving or able to move to a higher social class, for example by becoming richer: *The meeting attracted upwardly mobile professional and political women.* • **ˌupward moˈbility** noun [U]

ˈupward(s) ˌof preposition C2 If you say something is upward(s) of a number or value, you mean it is at least the stated amount and probably more: *Upwards of 50,000 people assembled in the main square.*

upwards /ˈʌp.wədz/ US /-wɚdz/ adv (US usually **upward**) C1 towards a higher position, level, or value: *She turned her face upwards to the midday sun.* ◦ *The cost of completion has been revised upwards again due to inflation.* → Opposite **downwards**

upwind /ˌʌpˈwɪnd/ adv [before noun], adj in the direction from which the wind is blowing: *Stay upwind* ***of*** *the fumes if you can.* → Opposite **downwind**

ur- /ɔːr/ prefix original or earliest: *He is not an actual historical person but represents the ur-man.*

uranium /jʊˈreɪ.ni.əm/ noun [U] (symbol **U**) a chemical element that is a heavy, RADIOACTIVE metal, used in the production of nuclear power and in some types of nuclear weapon

Uranus /ˈjʊə.rən.əs/, /jʊˈreɪ.nəs/ US /ˈjʊr-/ /jʊˈreɪ-/ noun [S] the planet seventh in order of distance from the Sun, after Saturn and before Neptune

urban /ˈɜː.bən/ US /ˈɝː-/ adj [before noun] B2 of or in a city or town: *urban development* → Compare **rural**

urbane /ɜːˈbeɪn/ US /ɝː-/ adj approving (especially of a man) confident, comfortable, and polite in social situations: *Herschel was an urbane, kindly, and generous man.* • **urbanely** /-li/ adv • **urbanity** /-ˈbæn.ɪ.ti/ US /-ˈbæn.ə.t̬i/ noun [U]

urbanite /ˈɜː.bən.aɪt/ US /ˈɝː-/ noun [C] someone who lives in a city or enjoys the type of life in a city: *More than half of UK urbanites have an iPod.*

urbanization (UK usually **urbanisation**) /ˌɜː.bən.aɪ-ˈzeɪ.ʃən/ US /ˌɝː-/ noun [U] the process by which more and more people leave the countryside to live in cities

urbanize (UK usually **urbanise**) /ˈɜː.bən.aɪz/ US /ˈɝː-/ verb [T] to build houses, offices, etc. in an area of countryside so that it becomes a town • **urbanized** (UK usually **urbanised**) /-aɪzd/ adj *The UK is a highly urbanized country.*

ˌurban ˈjungle noun [C usually singular] disapproving city life, especially the unpleasant parts of it: *Traffic noise, pollution, huge concrete buildings – how can people survive in the urban jungle?*

ˌurban ˈmyth noun [C] (also **ˌurban ˈlegend**) a story or statement that is not true but is often repeated, and believed by many to be true

urchin /ˈɜː.tʃɪn/ US /ˈɝː-/ noun [C] old-fashioned or humorous a small child, especially one who behaves badly and is dirty or untidily dressed: *a street urchin*

Urdu /ˈʊə.duː/, /ˈʊr-/, /ˈɜː.duː/ US /ˈɝː-/ noun [U] the official language of Pakistan, also spoken by many people in India

urea /jʊəˈriː.ə/ US /jʊ-/ noun [U] specialized a substance found in urine and also made from AMMONIA, used in FERTILIZERS, animal feed, and in the plastics industry

ureter /jʊəˈriː.tər/ US /jʊˈriː.t̬ɚ/ noun [C] specialized a tube on each side of the body that takes urine from the KIDNEY to the BLADDER

urethra /jʊəˈriː.θrə/ US /juː-/ noun [C] (plural **urethras** or specialized **urethrae**) specialized the tube in most mammals that carries urine from the BLADDER out of the body. In males it also carries SEMEN.

urge /ɜːdʒ/ US /ɝːdʒ/ noun; verb

▸**noun** [C] C2 a strong wish, especially one that is difficult or impossible to control: *The two of them seem unable to control their sexual urges.* ◦ [+ to infinitive] *The urge* ***to*** *steal is very strong in many of the young men we look after here.*

▸**verb** [I or T] C1 to strongly advise or try to persuade someone to do a particular thing: [+ to infinitive] *Lawyers will urge the parents* ***to*** *take further legal action.* ◦ [+ that] *Investigators urged* ***that*** *safety procedures at the site should be improved.* ◦ *Police urged continued vigilance in the fight against crime.* ◦ *The dogs are urged* ***into*** *fighting more fiercely by loud shouts from the crowd.* ◦ *We shall continue to urge* ***for*** *leniency to be shown to these prisoners.* • **urging** /ˈɜː.dʒɪŋ/ US /ˈɝː-/ noun [C or U] *He was happy to comply without any further urging from me.* ◦ *It was only because of Alison's urgings that he sold the house.*

PHRASAL VERB **urge sb on** C2 to encourage someone to do or achieve something: *The crowd was cheering and urging her on all through the race.*

urgent /ˈɜː.dʒənt/ US /ˈɝː-/ adj **IMPORTANT** ▷ **1** B1 needing attention very soon, especially before anything else, because important: *He's got to sign that paper – will you tell him it's urgent?* ◦ *The most urgent thing in a fire is to make sure everyone is out of the building.* ◦ *Many people are* ***in*** *urgent* ***need of*** *food and water.* **REPEATED** ▷ **2** formal (especially of a person's actions) repeated and determined in trying to get or do something: *His urgent pleas of innocence made no difference to the judge's decision.* • **urgency** /-dʒən.si/ noun [U] *It now is a matter of urgency that aid reaches the famine area.* • **urgently** /-li/ adv B1 *Help is urgently needed.*

uric /ˈjʊə.rɪk/ US /ˈjʊr.ɪk/ adj [before noun] specialized of urine: *uric acid*

urinal /jʊˈraɪ.nəl/ US /ˈjʊr.ən.əl/ noun [C] a device, usually fitted to a wall, into which men or boys can urinate, or a building which contains one or more of these devices

U

urinary /ˈjʊə.rɪ.nər.i/ (US) /ˈjʊr.ɪ.ner-/ **adj** relating to urine or to the parts of the body which produce and carry urine: *urinary tract infections*

urinate /ˈjʊə.rɪ.neɪt/ (US) /ˈjʊr.ɪ-/ **verb** [I] to pass urine from the body • **urination** /ˌjʊə.rɪˈneɪ.ʃən/ (US) /ˌjʊr.ɪ-/ **noun** [U]

urine /ˈjʊə.rɪn/ (US) /ˈjʊr.ɪn/ **noun** [U] the yellowish liquid waste that is released from the body when you urinate

URL /ˌjuː.ɑːrˈel/ **noun** [C] abbreviation for uniform resource locator: a website address

urn /ɜːn/ (US) /ɝːn/ **noun** [C] **1** a container, especially a large, round one on a stem, that is used for decorative purposes in a garden, or one that has a lid and is used for holding a dead person's ASHES (= the powder that is left after a dead body has been burned) **2** a large, cylinder-shaped metal container with a lid, used for holding a large amount of a drink such as tea or coffee and keeping it hot: *a tea urn*

urogenital /ˌjʊə.rəʊˈdʒen.ɪ.təl/ (US) /ˌjʊr.oʊˈdʒen.ə.t̬əl/ **adj** (also **urinogenital**) relating to the parts of the body which produce and carry urine, and also the GENITALS (= outer sexual organs)

us strong /ʌs/ weak /əs/ **pronoun** **GROUP** ▷ **1** (A1) used as the object of a verb or a preposition to refer to a group that includes the speaker and at least one other person: *Thank you for driving us to the station.* ◦ *Many of us in the editorial department disagree with the changes that are happening.* **ME** ▷ **2** UK not standard (especially used in spoken English) me: *Give us a light, mate.* ◦ *Give us it here and I'll see if I can mend it.*

the US /ˌjuːˈes/ **noun** [+ sing/pl verb] abbreviation for the United States: *A new study of education in the US has just been published.* ◦ *When did you become a US citizen?*

the USA /ˌjuː.esˈeɪ/ **noun** [+ sing/pl verb] abbreviation for the United States of America

> **!** Common mistake: **USA**
>
> **Remember:** you usually use **the** before any country that has 'State', 'Republic', 'Kingdom', or 'Isles' in its name.
>
> Don't say 'US/USA' or 'United States (of America)', say **the US/USA** or **the United States (of America)**.

usable /ˈjuː.zə.bl̩/ **adj** that can be used: *The specific software is also usable in other areas of research.*

the USAF /ˌjuː.es.eɪˈef/ **noun** [+ sing/plural verb] abbreviation for the United States Air Force

usage /ˈjuː.sɪdʒ/ **noun** **WORD** ▷ **1** (C1) [C or U] the way a particular word in a language, or a language in general, is used: *a guide to common English usage* ◦ *The earliest recorded usage of the word is in the twelfth century.* **2** (C1) [U] the way something is treated or used: *Sports equipment is designed to withstand hard usage.* **PERSON** ▷ **3** [U] formal the bad and unfair way someone treats you: *Many had complained about the usage they'd received at his hands.*

USB /ˌjuː.esˈbiː/ **noun** [C] abbreviation for Universal Serial Bus: a part of a computer to which extra devices such as printers, scanners, and digital cameras can be connected easily: *a USB **port***

use verb; noun

▸**verb** **PURPOSE** ▷ **1** (A1) /juːz/ [T] (**used, used**) to put something such as a tool, skill, or building to a particular purpose: *This glass has been used – please fetch me a clean one.* ◦ [+ to infinitive] *Use scissors **to** cut the shapes out.* ◦ *Going on the expedition gives me a chance to use all the training I've had.* ◦ *The old hospital isn't used any more.* ◦ *These lights are used **for** illuminating the playing area.* ◦ *To use military force **against** the protesters would be unacceptable.* ◦ informal *I could use (= I would like) some help putting these decorations up if you're not too busy.* **REDUCE** ▷ **2** (B1) /juːz/ [T] (**used, used**) to reduce the amount of or finish something, by eating it, burning it, writing on it, or by a chemical reaction: *We've used (**up**) nearly all of the bread – will you buy some more?* ◦ *Does she still use drugs?* ◦ *Don't worry if you use the polish **up** (= finish it) – I'm going shopping tomorrow.* → Compare **consume** **WORD** ▷ **3** (B2) /juːz/ [T] (**used, used**) to say or write a particular word or phrase: *'Autumn' is used in British English and 'fall' in American English.* ◦ *That's an expression she often uses to describe how she feels.* **TAKE ADVANTAGE** ▷ **4** (C2) /juːz/ [T] (**used, used**) usually disapproving to take advantage of a person or situation; to EXPLOIT: *He's just using you – he'll steal your ideas and then take the credit for them himself.* ◦ *It might be possible to use their mistake to help us get what we want.* ◦ *Within the relationship he feels **ill** (= badly) used most of the time.* **IN THE PAST** ▷ **5 use to** /ˈjuːs.tə/ In negative sentences and questions, 'use to' replaces 'used to' when it follows 'did' or 'didn't': *Did he use to be the doctor in 'Star Trek'?* ◦ *We didn't use to go out much in the winter months.*

IDIOM **use your head** (UK old-fashioned informal **use your loaf**) used to tell someone in a slightly angry way that they should think more carefully about what they are doing: *Why didn't you use your head and cover the furniture before you started painting?*

PHRASAL VERB **use sth up** (B2) to finish a supply of something: *Don't use up all the milk, we need some for breakfast.* ◦ *The Earth's resources are being used up at an alarming rate.*

▸**noun** /juːs/ **PURPOSE** ▷ **1** (B1) [C or U] a purpose for which something is used: *A food processor has a variety of uses in the kitchen.* ◦ *Don't throw that cloth away, you'll find a use **for** it one day.* ◦ *No, I don't want to buy a boat – I have no use **for** one!* **2** (A2) [U] the act of using something, or a period of time when something is being used or can be used: *You should be able to **put** your experience in electronics **to** (**good**) use in your new job.* ◦ *Don't touch the machine when it's **in** use.* ◦ *Sorry but the escalator is **out of** (US usually **not in**) use (= not operating).* ◦ *There has been some increase in **the** use **of** casual labour over recent years.* ◦ *Traditional farming methods are **going out of/coming into** use (= used less and less/more and more) in many areas.* **3 make use of sth** (B2) to use something that is available: *We might as well make use of the hotel's facilities.* **4 the use of sth** (C2) permission to use something, or the ability to use something: *They said we could **have** the use of their flat at the coast whenever they weren't there.* ◦ *She hurt her arm in the fall and **lost** the use of her fingers temporarily.* **REDUCTION** ▷ **5** [C or U] an action that reduces or finishes the amount of something available, by eating it, burning it, writing on it, or by a chemical reaction: *Building a dam would be a use **of** financial resources which this country cannot afford.* **WORD** ▷ **6** [C] one of the meanings of a word, or the way that a particular word is used: *Can you list all the uses of the word 'point'?*

IDIOMS **be (of) (any/some) use** (B2) to be useful: *Perhaps his advice will be of use to you when you're older.* • **be (of) no use** (B2) to not be useful, helpful, or possible: *His advice turned out to be no use at all.* ◦ ***There** is no use (**in**) argu**ing** any more.* ◦ ***It** is no use try**ing** (= there is no purpose in trying) to escape – no* *one ever gets out of here.* ◦ *It's no use (= I cannot succeed) – I just can't get this lid off.* • **what's the use of...?** (also **what use is...?**) used to tell someone to stop worrying because worrying will not help: *Try not to get depressed – after all, what's the use of worrying?*

used verb; adj

▸verb /ju:st/ **used to** B1 used to show that a particular thing always happened or was true in the past, especially if it no longer happens or is no longer true: *She used to live in Glasgow.* ◦ *She used to love cats but she doesn't like them any more.* ◦ *You don't come and see me like you used to.* ◦ *When we were younger, we used not to be allowed to drink coffee.* ◦ not standard *He did used to work there, didn't he?*

> **! Common mistake: used to**
>
> **Used to** meaning 'in the past' is followed by a verb in the infinitive without 'to'.
>
> Do not say 'used to doing something', say **used to do something**:
>
> ~~*My parents used to living in a house by the beach.*~~
>
> *My parents used to live in a house by the beach.*

▸adj FAMILIAR ▷ **1 be used to sth/sb** /ju:st/ B1 to be familiar with something or someone: *We're used to tourists here – we get thousands every year.* ◦ [+ -ing verb] *She was not used to speak**ing** Cantonese.* **2 get used to sth/sb** B1 to become familiar with something or someone: *Eventually you'll get used to the smells of the laboratory.* ◦ [+ -ing verb] *I just can't get used to getting up early.*

> **! Common mistake: be used to sth**
>
> When **be used to** is followed by a verb, that verb cannot be in the infinitive without 'to'.
>
> Do not say 'be used to do something', say **be used to doing something**:
>
> ~~*I am used to work flexible hours.*~~
>
> *I am used to working flexible hours.*

NOT NEW ▷ **3** /ju:zd/ that has already been put to the purpose it was intended for; not new: *a used airline ticket* ◦ *The blackmailers demanded to be paid in used £20 notes.* ◦ *I could only afford a used car (= one that has already been owned by others).*

useful /ˈju:s.fᵊl/ adj A2 effective; helping you to do or achieve something: *A good knife is probably one of the most useful things you can have in a kitchen.*

> **! Common mistake: useful**
>
> **Warning:** Common word-building error!
>
> Adjectives which end in the suffix **-ful** have only one 'l'. Don't write 'usefull', write **useful**.

IDIOMS **come in useful** UK C2 to be useful and help someone to do or achieve something: *You should keep that paint – it might come in useful one day.* • **make yourself useful** a way of telling someone to start being helpful: *Now you're here, you might as well make yourself useful – there's a lot of clearing up to do.*

usefully /ˈju:s.fᵊl.i/ adv in an effective or helpful way: *We could usefully spend the free time sightseeing.*

usefulness /ˈju:s.fᵊl.nəs/ noun [U] C1 the quality or state of being useful: *Some people think this system of education has **outlived** its usefulness (= is no longer useful).*

useless /ˈju:s.ləs/ adj B1 of no use; not working or not achieving what is needed: *Without fuel, the vehicles will become useless **for** moving supplies.* ◦ [+ to infinitive] ***It's** useless **to** speculate without more information.* ◦ *She's very good at methodical work, but useless when there's a lot of pressure.* ◦ informal *You're absolutely useless (= not able to act effectively) – can't you even go to the shops without getting lost!* • **uselessly** /-li/ adv • **uselessness** /-nəs/ noun [U]

> **+ Other ways of saying useful**
>
> See also: **valuable**
>
> If something is useful because it helps you do or achieve something, you can describe it as **helpful** or **valuable:**
>
> *They gave us some really **helpful** advice.*
>
> *He was able to provide the police with some **valuable** information.*
>
> The adjective **invaluable** means 'extremely useful':
>
> *The internet is an **invaluable** resource for teachers.*
>
> An activity which is useful but requires a lot of effort is sometimes described as **worthwhile:**
>
> *It's a difficult course but it's very **worthwhile**.*
>
> Something which is useful because it is simple to use is often described as **handy**:
>
> *That's a **handy** little gadget.*
>
> If speech or writing contains a lot of useful information, you can describe it as **informative** or **instructive**:
>
> *It's an interesting and highly **informative** book.*

user /ˈju:.zəʳ/ US /-zɚ/ noun [C] B1 someone who uses a product, machine, or service: *Unemployed people are the main users of this advice centre.* ◦ *drug users*

ˌuser-ˈfriendly adj If something, especially something related to a computer, is user-friendly, it is simple for people to use: *a user-friendly interface/printer* • **ˌuser-ˈfriendliness** noun [U]

ˈuser ˌgroup noun [C] specialized a group of people who are interested in a particular area of computer science or use the same product and who use the internet to share information about it

username /ˈju:.zə.neɪm/ US /-zɚ-/ noun [C] (also **ˌuser IˈD**) a name or other word that you sometimes need to type in together with a PASSWORD before you are allowed to use a computer or the internet: *Please enter your username and password.*

usher /ˈʌʃ.əʳ/ US /-ɚ/ verb; noun

▸verb [T usually + adv/prep] to show someone where they should go, or to make someone go where you want them to go: *She ushered us **into** her office and offered us a coffee.* ◦ *Officials quickly ushered the protesters **out** of the hall.*

PHRASAL VERB **usher sth in** to be at the start of a new period, especially when important changes or new things happen, or to cause important changes to start happening: *Yesterday's match between Arsenal and Spurs ushered in the start of the new football season.* ◦ *Banksie threw a huge party to usher in (= celebrate) the New Year.*

▸noun [C] a man who shows people where they should sit, especially at a formal event such as a WEDDING or at a theatre or cinema

usherette /ˌʌʃ.əˈret/ noun [C] a woman who works in a theatre or cinema, whose job is to show people to their seats and to sell sweets and drinks

the USN /ˌju:.esˈen/ noun [+ sing/pl verb] abbreviation for the United States Navy

USP /ˌju:.esˈpi:/ noun [C] abbreviation for unique selling proposition: a feature of a product that makes it different from and better than other similar products and that can be emphasized in advertisements for the product

USS /ˌjuː.esˈes/ abbreviation for United States Ship: used before the names of ships in the US navy

the USSR /ˌjuː.es.esˈɑːʳ/ (US) /-ˈɑːr/ **noun** abbreviation for the Union of Soviet Socialist Republics

usu. written abbreviation for usually

usual /ˈjuː.ʒu.əl/ **adj; noun**

▸**adj** A2 normal; happening, done, or used most often: *I went to bed at my usual time.* ◦ *There was more rainfall **than** usual this summer in the mountain areas.* ◦ *You'll find the cutlery in its usual place.* ◦ *Terry was, **as** usual, slow to respond.* ◦ *This shop is open for business **as** usual despite the shortages.*

▸**noun** [S] informal Someone's usual is the drink, especially an alcoholic one, which they most often have, for example when they are in a bar: *A gin and tonic for my dad, and I'll have **the/my** usual.*

usually /ˈjuː.ʒu.ə.li/ **adv** A2 in the way that most often happens: *He usually gets home about six o'clock.* ◦ *I usually just have a sandwich for lunch.* ◦ *Is your friend usually so rude?* ◦ *Usually we go to France in August.* ◦ *'Does this shop open on Sundays?' 'Usually.'*

usurp /juːˈzɜːp/, /-ˈsɜːp/ (US) /-ˈzɝːp/ /-ˈsɝːp/ **verb** [T] formal to take control of a position of power, especially without having the right to: *The powers of local councils are being usurped by central government.* • **usurper** /juːˈzɜː.pəʳ/, /-ˈsɜː-/ (US) /-ˈzɝː.pɚ/ /-ˈsɝː-/ **noun** [C]

usury /ˈjuː.zjʊ.ri/ (US) /-ʒɚ.i/ **noun** [U] formal disapproving the activity of lending someone money with the agreement that they will pay back a very much larger amount of money later

ute /juːt/ **noun** [C] Australian English a PICK-UP TRUCK (= a small vehicle with an open part at the back in which goods can be carried)

utensil /juːˈten.sɪl/ **noun** [C] a tool with a particular use, especially in a kitchen or house: *In the drawer was a selection of **kitchen** utensils – spoons, spatulas, knives, and whisks.*

uterus /ˈjuː.tᵊr.əs/ (US) /-t̬ɚ-/ **noun** [C] (plural **uteri** or **uteruses**) specialized a **womb** • **uterine** /-tᵊr.aɪn/ (US) /-t̬ə.rɪn/ **adj**

utilitarian /ˌjuː.tɪ.lɪˈteə.ri.ən/ (US) /-ˈter.i-/ **adj** designed to be useful rather than decorative: *Like many factories, it's a very ugly utilitarian building.*

utilitarianism /ˌjuː.tɪ.lɪˈteə.ri.ə.nɪ.zᵊm/ (US) /-ter.i-/ **noun** [U] the system of thought which states that the best action or decision in a particular situation is the one which brings most advantages to the most people

utility /juːˈtɪl.ɪ.ti/ (US) /-ə.t̬i/ **noun** SERVICE ▷ **1** [C] formal a service that is used by the public, such as an electricity or gas supply or a train service: *utility bills* USE ▷ **2** [U] formal the usefulness of something, especially in a practical way

uˈtility ˌroom **noun** [C] a room, especially in a house, where large pieces of useful equipment such as a washing machine can be kept and where things can be stored

utilize formal (UK usually **utilise**) /ˈjuː.tɪ.laɪz/ (US) /-t̬ᵊl.aɪz/ **verb** [T] to use something in an effective way: *The vitamins come in a form that is easily utilized by the body.* • **utilizable** (UK usually **utilisable**) /ˈjuː.tɪ.laɪ.zə.bl̩/ (US) /-t̬ᵊl.aɪ-/ **adj** • **utilization** (UK usually **utilisation**) /ˌjuː.tɪ.laɪˈzeɪ.ʃᵊn/ (US) /-t̬ᵊl.ɪ-/ **noun** [U] *Sensible utilization of the world's resources is a priority.*

utmost /ˈʌt.məʊst/ (US) /-moʊst/ **adj; noun**

▸**adj** [before noun] (formal **uttermost** /ˈʌt.ə-/ (US) /ˈʌ.t̬ɚ-/) C1 used to emphasize how important or serious something is: *a matter of the utmost importance* ◦ *The situation needs to be handled **with the** utmost care.*

▸**noun** [S] (formal **uttermost** /ˈʌt.əˌməʊst/ (US) /ˈʌ.t̬ɚmoʊst/ the greatest amount or degree possible: *The new model of the car offers **the** utmost **in** power and performance.*

IDIOM **do/try your utmost** C1 to do something as well as you can by making a great effort: *She did her utmost **to** finish on time.*

utopia /juːˈtəʊ.pi.ə/ (US) /-ˈtoʊ-/ **noun** [C or U] (the idea of) a perfect society in which everyone works well with each other and is happy

utopian /juːˈtəʊ.pi.ən/ (US) /-ˈtoʊ-/ **adj** relating to or aiming for a perfect society in which everyone works well with each other and is happy: *a utopian vision* ◦ *utopian aims*

utter /ˈʌt.əʳ/ (US) /ˈʌ.t̬ɚ/ **verb; adj**

▸**verb** [T] formal C2 to say something or to make a sound with your voice: *She sat through the whole meeting without uttering a word.*

▸**adj** [before noun] C2 complete or extreme: *utter confusion/misery/chaos* ◦ *utter nonsense/rubbish/drivel* ◦ *The meeting was a **complete and** utter waste of time.* ◦ *Lying back in the hot bath was utter bliss.* • **utterly** /ˈʌt.ᵊl.i/ (US) /ˈʌ.t̬ɚ.li/ **adv** C1 *What an utterly stupid thing to do!*

utterance /ˈʌt.ᵊr.ᵊns/ (US) /ˈʌ.t̬ɚ-/ **noun** [C] **1** formal something that someone says: *The senator's recent utterances were promptly rebutted by three of his colleagues on Monday.* **2 give utterance to sth** literary to express your ideas or feelings in spoken words

ˈU-turn **noun** [C] (informal **U-ie** /ˈjuːi/) **1** a turn made by a car in order to go back in the direction from which it has come: *It is illegal to **do/make** a U-turn on a motorway.* **2** mainly disapproving a complete change from one opinion or plan of action to an opposite one: *The prime minister **did/made** a quick U-turn in response to all the adverse publicity.*

UV /juːˈviː/ **adj** abbreviation for **ultraviolet**: *UV light*

UVA /ˌjuːviːˈeɪ/ **noun** [U] RADIATION from the sun with fairly long WAVELENGTHS. UVA is short for 'ultraviolet A'.

UVB /ˌjuːviːˈbiː/ **noun** [U] RADIATION from the sun with fairly short WAVELENGTHS. UVB is short for 'ultraviolet B'.

uvula /ˈjuː.vjə.lə/ **noun** [C] (plural **uvulae** or **uvulas**) specialized the soft piece of flesh that hangs down at the back of the mouth

uvular /ˈjuː.vjə.ləʳ/ (US) /-lɚ/ **noun** [C] specialized a consonant sound that is made by the back of the tongue touching the uvula

V

V, v /viː/ noun [C or U] (plural **Vs**, **V's** or **v's**) **LETTER ▷ 1** the 22nd letter of the English alphabet **NUMBER ▷ 2** (also **v**) the sign used in the Roman system for the number 5

V /viː/ **preposition; noun**
▸**preposition** (also **v.**, **vs**) **1** abbreviation for **versus**: *I need to consider the advantages v the disadvantages.* **2** used to show who is competing in a game: *Newcastle United v Wigan* **3** used to show the two sides involved in a court case: *the 1973 Supreme Court decision, Roe v Wade*
▸**noun** (also **v.**) written abbreviation for verb

V. adv **1** written abbreviation for very: *The teacher wrote 'v. good' on my essay.* **2** written abbreviation for **vide**

vac /væk/ noun **PERIOD ▷ 1** [C] UK informal for **vacation**: *Have you managed to get a job for the **long** (= summer) vac?* **EQUIPMENT ▷ 2** [C] informal for **vacuum 3** [S] UK informal for an act of cleaning something with a VACUUM CLEANER: *Could you give the bedrooms a vac?*

vacancy /ˈveɪ.kᵊn.si/ noun [C] **1** C1 a space or place that is available to be used: *We wanted to book a hotel room in July but there were no vacancies.* ◦ *The dentist can't see you today but she has a vacancy tomorrow morning.* ◦ *There are still some vacancies **for** students in science and engineering courses, but the vacancies in humanities have been **filled**.* **2** C1 a job that no one is doing and is therefore available for someone new to do: *There is a vacancy for a shop assistant on Saturdays.*

vacant /ˈveɪ.kᵊnt/ adj **EMPTY ▷ 1** B2 not filled or OCCUPIED; available to be used: *The hospital has no vacant beds.* → Compare **engaged 2** B2 A vacant job is one that no one is doing and is therefore available for someone new to do: *When the post **fell** (= became) vacant, Dennis Bass was appointed to fill it.* **NOT INTERESTED ▷ 3** showing no interest or activity: *She had a vacant **look/expression** on her face.*

vacantly /ˈveɪ.kᵊnt.li/ adv showing no interest or activity: *She **gazed/stared** vacantly into space/ahead.*

ˌvacant posˈsession noun [U] UK specialized the fact that no one is living in or using a house or property at the moment when someone buys it

vacate /vəˈkeɪt/, /veɪ-/ verb [T] formal to leave a room, building, chair, etc. so that it is available for other people: *Hotel guests are requested to vacate their rooms by noon.* ◦ *Denis vacates his job at the end of the week.*

vacation /veɪˈkeɪ.ʃᵊn/ noun **1** A1 [C or U] US a holiday, especially when you are travelling away from home for pleasure: *We're **taking** a vacation in June.* ◦ *They went to Europe **on** vacation.* ◦ *I've still got some vacation left before the end of the year.* **2** [C] mainly US (UK informal **vac**) a period of the year when schools or colleges are closed, or when law courts do not operate: *the Christmas/Easter/summer/long vacation* • **vacation** verb [I] US *Remember that time we were vacationing **in** Vermont?*

vacationer /veɪˈkeɪ.ʃᵊn.əʳ/ US /-ɚ/ noun [C] US for **holidaymaker**

vaccinate /ˈvæk.sɪ.neɪt/ verb [T] C2 to give someone a vaccine, usually by INJECTION, to prevent them from getting a disease: *The children were vaccinated **against** the major childhood diseases.* → See also **inoculate, immunize** • **vaccination** /ˌvæk.sɪˈneɪ.ʃᵊn/ noun [C or U] C2 *All the children have received two vaccinations **against** measles.*

vaccine /ˈvæk.siːn/ noun [C or U] C2 a substance that contains a form that is not harmful of a virus or bacterium and is given to a person or animal to prevent them from getting the disease which the virus or bacterium causes: *This vaccine protects against some kinds of the bacteria.*

vacillate /ˈvæs.ɪ.leɪt/ verb [I] disapproving to be uncertain what to do, or to change often between two opinions: *Her mood vacillated **between** hope and despair.* • **vacillation** /ˌvæs.ɪˈleɪ.ʃᵊn/ noun [C or U]

vacuole /ˈvæk.ju.əʊl/ US /-oʊl/ noun [C] specialized a space that contains air or liquid inside a living cell, often storing an important chemical or food substance

vacuous /ˈvæk.ju.əs/ adj formal not expressing or showing intelligent thought or purpose: *a vacuous remark/question/expression/smile* • **vacuously** /-li/ adv • **vacuousness** /-nəs/ noun [U] (also **vacuity** /vəˈkjuː.ə.ti/ US /-ə.t̬i/)

vacuum /ˈvæk.juːm/ **noun; verb**
▸**noun EMPTY SPACE ▷ 1** [C or U] a space from which most or all of the air, gas, or other material has been removed or is not present **2** [S] a lack of something: *The withdrawal of troops from the area has created a security vacuum which will need to be **filled**.* **3 in a vacuum** kept separate from other people and activities: *No artist works in a vacuum – we are all of us influenced by others.* **CLEANER ▷ 4** [C] a **vacuum cleaner**
▸**verb** [I or T] (UK also **hoover**) to use a VACUUM CLEANER to collect dust, dirt, etc.: *Vacuum **(up)** the cake crumbs, would you?*

ˈvacuum ˌcleaner noun [C] (also **vacuum**, informal **vac**, UK also trademark **Hoover**) a machine that cleans floors and other surfaces by sucking up dust and dirt

vacuum cleaner

ˈvacuum ˌflask noun [C] UK (US **ˈvacuum ˌbottle**) a container that keeps hot liquids hot or cold liquids cold → See also **flask**

ˈvacuum-ˌpacked adj Something, especially food, that is vacuum-packed is in a soft container from which the air has been removed so that the contents can be stored longer.

ˈvacuum ˌpump noun [C] a piece of equipment for removing air or gas from a container, creating a vacuum inside

vagabond /ˈvæg.ə.bɒnd/ US /-bɑːnd/ noun [C] old use or literary a person who has no home and usually no job, and who travels from place to place: *They live a vagabond life/existence, travelling around in a caravan.* → Compare **vagrant**

vagaries /ˈveɪ.gᵊr.iz/ US /-gɚ-/ noun [plural] formal unexpected events or changes that cannot be controlled and can influence a situation: *The success of the event will be determined by **the** vagaries **of** the **weather**.* ◦ *She had her own style and was not influenced by **the** vagaries **of fashion**.*

vagina /vəˈdʒaɪ.nə/ noun [C] the part of a woman or other female mammal's body which connects her outer sex organs to her WOMB • **vaginal** /-nəl/ adj *vaginal intercourse* • **vaginally** /-nəl.i/ adv

vagrant /ˈveɪ.grənt/ noun [C] formal or legal a person who is poor and does not have a home or job: *The town has shelters and food handouts for vagrants.* → Synonym **tramp** • **vagrancy** /-grən.si/ noun [U] *Most European countries have abandoned laws that make vagrancy a crime.*

vague /veɪg/ adj **1** C1 not clearly expressed, known, described, or decided: *I do have a vague memory of meeting her many years ago.* ◦ *The patient had complained of vague pains and backache.* **2** C1 not clear in shape, or not clearly seen: *Through the mist I could just make out a vague figure.* **3** C2 describes someone who is not able to think clearly, or who, sometimes as a way of hiding what they really think, does not express their opinions clearly: *My aunt is incredibly vague – she can never remember where she's left things.* ◦ *Their report is **studiously** vague (= intentionally not exact) on future economic prospects.* • **vaguely** /-li/ adv *I vaguely remembered having met her before.* • **vagueness** /-nəs/ noun [U]

vain /veɪn/ adj **NOT SUCCESSFUL** ▷ **1** C2 unsuccessful; of no value: *The doctors gave him more powerful drugs in the vain **hope** that he might recover.* ◦ formal ***It** was vain **to** pretend to himself that he was not disappointed.* **2 in vain** C1 unsuccessfully: *I tried in vain to start a conversation.* ◦ *All the police's efforts to find him were in vain.* **SELFISH** ▷ **3** C2 too interested in your own appearance or achievements: *He was very vain **about** his hair and his clothes.*

vainly /ˈveɪn.li/ adv unsuccessfully: *He tried vainly to make them listen.*

valance /ˈvæl.əns/ noun [C] **1** a short piece of material which hangs down especially around the base of a bed **2** US a **pelmet**

vale /veɪl/ noun [C] **1** used in the name of some valleys: *the Vale of Evesham* **2** old-fashioned or literary a valley: *a cloud that floats on high o'er hills and vales*

IDIOM **this vale of tears** literary This vale of tears is the world we live in, seen as sad and difficult.

valediction /ˌvæl.əˈdɪk.ʃən/ noun [C or U] formal the act of saying goodbye, especially formally, or a formal speech in which someone says goodbye

valedictorian /ˌvæl.ə.dɪkˈtɔː.ri.ən/ US /-ˈtɔːr.i-/ noun [C] US a student, usually one who has been the most successful in a particular class, who makes a speech at a special ceremony at the end of a school year

valedictory /ˌvæl.əˈdɪk.tər.i/ US /-tə-/ adj formal relating to saying goodbye, especially formally: *a valedictory speech*

V

valency /ˈveɪ.lən.si/ noun [C] (also **valence**) a measurement which shows the number of HYDROGEN atoms that can combine with one atom of a particular chemical element to make a COMPOUND, used to describe how easily an element can connect in a chemical way with others: *Zinc has a valency of 2.*

valentine /ˈvæl.ən.taɪn/ noun [C] **1** someone you love or would like to have a romantic relationship with: *The message on the card said 'Be my Valentine'.* **2** (also **valentine card**) a decorative card that you send, usually without your name on it, on 14 February (Valentine's Day) to someone you love: *Did you get any valentines?*

ˈValentine's ˌDay noun [C or U] 14 February, a day when you give a valentine card to someone you have, or would like to have, a romantic relationship with

valerian /vəˈlɪə.ri.ən/ noun [U] specialized a plant with small white or pink flowers and a root that is used in medicines, especially as a SEDATIVE (= drug to calm you or make you sleep)

valet noun; verb

▸**noun** [C] /ˈvæl.eɪ/ US /vəˈleɪ/ **1** someone in a hotel who cleans clothes **2** US someone at a hotel or restaurant who puts your car in a parking space for you **3** the personal male servant of a rich man, especially in the past

▸**verb** [T] /ˈvæl.eɪ/, /-ɪt/ US /vəˈleɪ/ UK to clean, especially the inside of, something: *There's a service which will valet your **car** for you while it is parked.*

ˈvalet ˌparking noun [U] the service offered by a restaurant, hotel, etc. of putting your car in a parking space

ˈvalet ˌservice noun [U] the service of cleaning clothes offered by a hotel to people staying there

valiant /ˈvæl.i.ənt/ adj very brave or bravely determined, especially when things are difficult or the situation gives no cause for hope: *The company has made a valiant **effort/attempt** in the last two years to make itself more efficient.* • **valiantly** /-li/ adv

valid /ˈvæl.ɪd/ adj **1** B2 based on truth or reason; able to be accepted: *a valid argument/criticism/reason* ◦ *My way of thinking might be different from yours, but it's equally valid.* → Compare **invalid** **2** B2 A ticket or other document is valid if it is based on or used according to a set of official conditions which often include a time limit: *My passport is valid for another two years.* **3** having legal force: *Is this contract/ticket/agreement still valid?* • **validity** /vəˈlɪd.ɪ.ti/ US /vəˈlɪd.ə.t̬i/ noun [U] C2 *This research seems to **give/lend** some validity to the theory that the drug might cause cancer.* • **validly** /-li/ adv

validate /ˈvæl.ɪ.deɪt/ verb [T] to make something officially acceptable or approved, especially after examining it: *It is a one-year course validated by London's City University.* ◦ *The data is validated automatically by the computer after it has been entered.* • **validation** /ˌvæl.ɪˈdeɪ.ʃən/ noun [U] *External validation of the teachers' assessments is recommended.*

Valium /ˈvæl.i.əm/ noun [C or U] trademark a drug which makes you calm and helps you to stop worrying, or a pill containing this: *She was **on** (= using) Valium for a few months after the accident.* ◦ *to take a couple of Valium*

valley /ˈvæl.i/ noun [C] B1 an area of low land between hills or mountains, often with a river running through it: *the Nile Valley* ◦ *the Thames valley* ◦ *There was snow on the hill tops but not in the valley.*

valour UK formal (US **valor**) /ˈvæl.ər/ US /-ɚ/ noun [U] great courage: *He was promoted to the rank of major in recognition of his valour during the battle.*

valuable /ˈvæl.jʊ.bl̩/ adj **MONEY** ▷ **1** B1 worth a lot of money: *These antiques are extremely valuable.* ◦ *This is losing valuable business for the company.* → Opposite **worthless**

> **! Note:**
> Invaluable means 'extremely useful'.

IMPORTANT ▷ **2** B2 Valuable information, advice, etc. is very helpful or important: *He was able to provide the police with some valuable information.* ◦ *Parents gave the school valuable support in its case for getting its facilities improved.*

valuables /ˈvæl.jʊ.bl̩z/ noun [plural] small objects,

Other ways of saying valuable

See also: **useful**

If something is valuable because it helps you do or achieve something, you can describe it as **helpful** or **useful**:

*They gave us some really **helpful** advice.*

*She made a really **useful** contribution to the project.*

Something which is valuable because it produces useful results may be described as **constructive**, **productive**, or **fruitful**:

*It was a very **constructive** discussion.*

*We had a very **productive** meeting and dealt with a lot of problems.*

*It was a **fruitful** partnership for both organizations.*

An activity which is valuable but requires a lot of effort is sometimes described as **worthwhile**:

*It's a difficult course but it's very **worthwhile**.*

If speech or writing contains a lot of valuable information, you can describe it as **informative** or **instructive**:

*It's an interesting and highly **informative** book.*

especially jewellery, which might be sold for a lot of money

valuation /ˌvæl.juˈeɪ.ʃən/ **noun** [C or U] the act of deciding how much money something might be sold for or the amount of money decided on: *You can receive a home loan of up to 95 percent of the official valuation of the property.*

value /ˈvæl.juː/ **noun; verb**

▸**noun MONEY** ▷ **1** B1 [C or U] the amount of money that can be received for something: *She had already sold everything **of** value that she possessed.* ◦ *What is the value **of** the prize?* ◦ *The value **of** the pound **fell** against other European currencies yesterday.* ◦ *Property values have fallen since the plans for the airport were published.* ◦ *I thought the offer was **good** value (**for money**)* (US also ***a good** value*) (= *a lot was offered for the amount of money paid*). **IMPORTANCE** ▷ **2** [S or U] the importance or worth of something for someone: *For them, the house's main value lay in its quiet country location.* ◦ *They are known to **place/put/set a** high value **on** good presentation.* **3** B1 [U] how useful or important something is: *The photos are **of** immense historical value.* ◦ *His contribution was of little or no **practical** value.* ◦ *The necklace had great **sentimental** value.* ◦ *It has **novelty** value because I've never done anything like it before.* **4 values** [plural] B2 the beliefs people have about what is right and wrong and what is most important in life, which control their behaviour: *family/moral/traditional values*

Word partners for value noun (MONEY)

the value *of* sth • *of* (any/great/real) value • *calculate/estimate/work out* the value of sth • values *go up/increase/rise/soar* • values *decrease/fall/go down/plummet* • a *drop/increase/reduction/rise* in value

Word partners for value noun (IMPORTANCE)

place/put/set [a high/great] value *on* sth • value *lies in* sth • *great/doubtful/dubious/immense* value • *of* [great/little/no/some] value

▸**verb** [T] **MONEY** ▷ **1** C2 UK (US **appraise**) to give a judgment about how much money something might be sold for: *He valued the painting **at** $2,000.* ◦ *The insurance company said I should have my jewellery valued.* **IMPORTANCE** ▷ **2** B2 to consider something important: *I've always valued her advice.*

ˌvalue-ˈadded adj Value-added products or services are worth more because they have been improved or had something added to them.

valued /ˈvæl.juːd/ **adj** formal useful and important: *a valued member of staff*

ˈvalue ˌjudgment noun [C] a statement of how good or bad you think an idea or action is: *People often **make** value judgments about things without considering them carefully.*

valueless /ˈvæl.jʊ.ləs/ **adj MONEY** ▷ **1** not worth any money: *We thought the chair was an antique worth a lot of money, but it turned out to be a valueless replica.* **IMPORTANCE** ▷ **2** not important or helpful: *His comments were so general as to be nearly valueless.*

valuer /ˈvæl.juː.ər/ US /-ɚ/ **noun** [C] UK (US **appraiser**) a person whose job is to say how much something is worth

valve /vælv/ **noun** [C] **1** a device which opens and closes to control the flow of liquids or gases, or a similar structure in the heart and the VEINS, which controls the flow of blood: *The valve failed to **open/close**.* ◦ *It was a weak **heart** valve that caused her death.* **2** part of a musical instrument such as a TRUMPET which changes the sound by controlling the flow of air

vamp /væmp/ **noun; verb**

▸**noun** [C] a woman who is conscious of and makes use of being attractive to men in order to get what she wants • **vampish** /ˈvæm.pɪʃ/ **adj** *vampish behaviour*

▸**verb**

PHRASAL VERB **vamp sth up** to make something more exciting: *The dress is simple and elegant, but you could vamp it up for evening wear with some stunning jewellery.*

vampire /ˈvæm.paɪər/ US /-paɪr/ **noun** [C] (in stories) a dead person who comes back to life and sucks blood from other people at night: *The most famous vampire is Count Dracula of Transylvania.*

ˈvampire ˌbat noun [C] a small Central and South American flying animal which sucks blood from other animals

van /væn/ **noun VEHICLE** ▷ **1** B1 [C] a medium-sized road vehicle used especially for carrying goods, which often has no windows in the sides at the back: *a delivery van* ◦ *a Transit van* ◦ *a van driver* **2** [C] US a medium-sized vehicle with windows all round, used for carrying more people than an ordinary car **FRONT** ▷ **3 in the van of sth** UK formal at the front, or in the most advanced position, of something: *The US is in the van of the quest to establish contact with other planets.* → See also **the vanguard**

vanadium /vəˈneɪ.di.əm/ **noun** [U] (symbol **V**) a chemical element that is a silver-grey metal, used to make STEEL ALLOYS (= mixtures of metals) and in CERAMICS (= making objects out of baked clay)

vandal /ˈvæn.dəl/ **noun** [C] a person who intentionally damages property belonging to other people: *Vandals smashed windows and overturned cars in the downtown shopping district.*

vandalism /ˈvæn.dəl.ɪ.zəm/ **noun** [U] **1** C2 the crime of intentionally damaging property belonging to other people: *Beset by violence and vandalism, this is one of the most unpleasant areas in the city.* ◦ *These schools are known to be vulnerable to vandalism.* **2** any activity that is considered to be damaging or destroying something that was good: *Cutting down the old* *forest was* ***an act of*** *vandalism.* ◦ *The advertising industry's use of classic songs is vandalism of popular culture, he said.*

vandalize (UK usually **vandalise**) /ˈvæn.dəl.aɪz/ **verb** [T] to intentionally damage property belonging to other people: *When I got back, my car had been vandalized.* ◦ *They are the type of teenagers likely to vandalize phone boxes.*

vane /veɪn/ **noun** [C] a flat, narrow part of a FAN, PROPELLER, etc. which turns because of the pressure of air or liquid against it

the vanguard /ˈvæŋ.gɑːd/ (US) /-gɑːrd/ **noun** [S] **1** the part of an army or navy that leads an attack on an enemy → Compare **rearguard 2** a group of people who lead the development of new ideas, or a leading position in the development of something: *He is* ***in*** *the vanguard* ***of*** *economic reform.* → See also **the forefront**

vanilla /vəˈnɪl.ə/ **noun; adj**

▸**noun** [U] a substance made from the seeds of a tropical plant, used to give flavour to sweet foods: *vanilla essence/extract* ◦ *vanilla ice cream/yogurt* ◦ *a vanilla milkshake* ◦ *Add two teaspoons of vanilla and stir.* ◦ *a vanilla* ***pod*** (US ***bean***) (= *seed container*)

▸**adj** used to describe a product or service that is basic and has no special features: *I just want a vanilla bank account with low charges.*

vanish /ˈvæn.ɪʃ/ **verb** [I] (B2) to disappear or stop being present or existing, especially in a sudden, surprising way: *The child vanished while on her way home from school.* ◦ *We rushed out of the shop in hot pursuit, but the thief had vanished* ***into thin air*** (= *had completely disappeared*). ◦ *Cheap rural housing is vanishing in the south of the country.*

vanished /ˈvæn.ɪʃt/ **adj** not now present or existing: *The temple ruins are a distant reminder of a vanished empire.*

vanity /ˈvæn.ɪ.ti/ (US) /-ə.t̬i/ **noun** **SELFISH** ▷ **1** (C2) [U] disapproving the fact that you are too interested in your appearance or achievements: *He wants the job purely for reasons of vanity and ambition.* **FURNITURE** ▷ **2** [C] US for **dressing table 3** [C] US for a **vanity unit**

ˈ**vanity ˌplates** **noun** [plural] US NUMBER PLATES on a vehicle that have particular numbers or letters on them that the vehicle's owner has specially chosen and paid to have

ˈ**vanity ˌpress** **noun** [C] a publishing company where writers pay to have their books produced

ˈ**vanity ˌunit** **noun** [C] UK a small cupboard which stands on the floor in a bathroom and has a WASHBASIN (= a fixed bowl-shaped container for water) in the top

vanquish /ˈvæŋ.kwɪʃ/ **verb** [T] literary to defeat an enemy or opponent, especially in war: *Napoleon was vanquished at the battle of Waterloo in 1815.* ◦ *The vanquished army surrendered their weapons.*

Vantage /ˈvɑːn.tɪdʒ/ (US) /ˈvæn.t̬ɪdʒ/ **noun** [U] a fairly high level of ability in a foreign language according to the Common European Framework (= a description of language ability levels created by the Council of Europe)

vantage point /ˈvɑːn.tɪdʒˌpɔɪnt/ (US) /ˈvæn.t̬ɪdʒ-/ **noun** **PLACE** ▷ **1** [C] a place, especially a high place, which provides a good, clear view of an area: ***From*** *our lofty vantage point, we could see the city spread out below us.* **OPINION** ▷ **2** [C usually singular] formal a particular personal way of thinking or set of opinions: *The documentary contains a first-hand description of political life in Havana* ***from*** *the vantage point* ***of*** *a senior bureaucrat.*

vapid /ˈvæp.ɪd/ **adj** formal showing no intelligence or imagination: *a vapid television programme* • **vapidity** /væpˈɪd.ɪ.ti/ (US) /-ə.t̬i/ **noun** [U] *the spiritual vapidity of Western materialism*

vaporize (UK usually **vaporise**) /ˈveɪ.pər.aɪz/ (US) /-pɚ.aɪz/ **verb** [I or T] to turn, or cause something to turn, from a solid or liquid state into gas: *During surgery, doctors sometimes use a laser beam to vaporize tiny blood vessels.* ◦ *Most meteorites striking the Earth vaporize instantly.*

vapour UK (US **vapor**) /ˈveɪ.pər/ (US) /-pɚ/ **noun** **GAS** ▷ **1** [C or U] gas or extremely small drops of liquid which result from the heating of a liquid or solid: *The hollow glass tank contains hot mercury vapour.* ◦ *Poisonous vapours burst out of the factory during the accident.* **ILLNESS** ▷ **2 the vapours** old use UK (US **the vapors**) [plural] a condition in which someone suddenly feels ill and weak, usually because of a shock

ˈ**vapour ˌtrail** UK (US ˈ**vapor ˌtrail**) **noun** [C] water vapour that looks like a line of white smoke behind an aircraft as it flies

vapourware humorous (US **vaporware**) /ˈveɪ.pə.weər/ (US) /-pɚ.wer/ **noun** [U] a computer program that is advertised but is not yet or is never made available

variable /ˈveə.ri.ə.bl̩/ (US) /ˈver.i-/ **adj; noun**

▸**adj** (C1) likely to change often: *a variable interest rate* ◦ *British weather is perhaps at its most variable in the spring.* • **variability** /ˌveə.ri.əˈbɪl.ɪ.ti/ (US) /ˌver.i.əˈbɪl.ə.t̬i/ **noun** [U]

▸**noun** [C] specialized (C1) a number, amount, or situation that can change: *The variables in the equation are X, Y, and Z.* ◦ *The data was analysed according to neighbourhoods, but other key variables like credit rating and marital status were ignored altogether.*

variance /ˈveə.ri.əns/ (US) /ˈver.i-/ **noun** **1** [C or U] formal the fact that two or more things are different, or the amount or number by which they are different: *There has been some unusual variance in temperature this month.* ◦ *I could detect subtle variances in fragrance as we strolled through the garden.* **2** [C] US legal official permission to do something that is not normally allowed: *We had to get* ***a*** *(****zoning****) variance before we could build the extension on our house.* **3 be at variance with sb/sth** to be in disagreement with someone or something, or to be different from them: *Young people's reactions to world events are often at variance with those of their parents.* ◦ *Most heavy metal fans are under 20 – this is at variance with the age of the bands themselves, who are often over 40.*

variant /ˈveə.ri.ənt/ (US) /ˈver.i-/ **noun; adj**

▸**noun** [C] something that is slightly different from other similar things: *There are many colas on the market now, all variants* ***on*** *the original drink.* ◦ *There are four variants* ***of*** *malaria, all transmitted to humans by a particular family of mosquitoes.*

▸**adj** different: *a variant form* ◦ *Words spelled with 'ae', such as 'encyclopaedia', have a variant* ***spelling*** *with 'e', as in 'encyclopedia'.*

variation /ˌveə.riˈeɪ.ʃən/ (US) /ˌver.i-/ **noun** **CHANGE** ▷ **1** (B2) [C or U] a change in amount or level: *Unemployment rates among white-collar workers show much less regional variation than corresponding rates among blue-collar workers.* ◦ *The medical tests showed some variation* ***in*** *the baby's heart rate.* ◦ *global temperature variations over the last 140 years* **DIFFERENCE** ▷ **2** (C2) [C] something that is slightly different from the usual form or arrangement: *There are* ***wide*** *variations in the way pensioners have benefited from the system.* ◦ *The films she makes are all variations* ***on*** *the* *same* **theme.** **3** [C] specialized one of several short tunes that are based on the same simple tune, but are different from it and from the others: *symphonic variations*

varicose vein /ˌvær.ɪ.kəʊs'veɪn/ US /ˌver.ɪ.koʊs-/ noun [C usually plural] a swollen and often painful VEIN, especially in the legs: *Pregnant women often get varicose veins.*

varied /'veə.rɪd/ US /'ver.ɪd/ adj B2 containing or changing between several different things or types: *a varied group of people* ◦ *a lengthy and varied career* ◦ *With its varied climate, the country attracts both winter and summer sports enthusiasts.*

variegated /'veə.rɪ.geɪ.tɪd/ US /'ver.i.ə.geɪ.t̬ɪd/ adj having a pattern of different colours or marks: *variegated leaves* ◦ *a variegated plant* • **variegation** /ˌveə.rɪ'geɪ.ʃən/ US /ˌver.i.ə-/ noun [U]

variety /və'raɪə.ti/ US /-t̬i/ noun **CHANGE** ▷ **1** B1 [U] the characteristic of often changing and being different: *When preparing meals, you need to think about variety and taste as well as nutritional value.* ◦ *Sexual reproduction serves to create genetic variety.* ◦ *Work on the production line is monotonous and lacks variety.* **TYPE** ▷ **2** [C] a different type of something: *The article was about the different varieties* ***of*** *Spanish spoken in South America.* ◦ *This variety* ***of*** *rose is especially hardy and drought-resistant.* ◦ *Our supermarket stocks apples in several different varieties.* **3** A2 [S] many different types of things or people: *She does a variety* ***of*** *fitness activities.* ◦ *Manufacturers need large sales to justify offering a big variety in export markets.* **ENTERTAINMENT** ▷ **4** [U] a type of entertainment which includes several separate short performances, such as singing, dancing, magic tricks, and telling jokes: *a variety show*

> **Word partners for variety**
>
> a *bewildering/infinite/large/wide* variety • a *whole* variety of sth • *offer/provide* a variety of sth

IDIOM **variety is the spice of life** saying said to emphasize that doing many different things, or often changing what you do, makes life interesting

var'iety ˌstore noun [C] US a shop which sells many different things, usually at low prices

various /'veə.ri.əs/ US /'ver.i-/ adj A2 many different: *We had various problems on our journey, including a puncture.* ◦ *The author gave various reasons for having written the book.* ◦ *Various people whom we weren't expecting turned up at the meeting.*

> **! Common mistake: various or varied?**
>
> **Warning:** choose the correct adjective!
>
> To describe something that changes between or contains several different things or types, don't say 'various', say **varied**:
>
> ~~*The school organizes a rich and various social programme.*~~
>
> *The school organizes a rich and varied social programme.*

variously /'veə.ri.əs.li/ US /'ver.i-/ adv in several different ways, at several different times, or by several different people: *It is one of a class of electronic products variously called 'personal communicators' or 'personal digital assistants'.* ◦ *The number of cases this year of salmonella poisoning has been variously put at 46, 49, or 51.*

varnish /'vɑː.nɪʃ/ US /'vɑːr-/ noun; verb

▸noun [C or U] a liquid that is painted onto wood or paintings to protect the surface, or the hard shiny surface it produces when it dries: *Polyurethane varnish provides a tough, scratch-resistant finish.* ◦ *a final* ***coat of*** *(clear) varnish*

▸verb [T] **1** to put varnish on a surface: *They decided to spend the weekend varnishing their boat.* **2** UK to use NAIL VARNISH

varnished /'vɑː.nɪʃt/ US /'vɑːr-/ adj covered with varnish: *a varnished surface* ◦ *varnished wood*

varsity adj; noun

▸adj [before noun] /'vɑː.sə.ti/ US /'vɑːr.sə.t̬i/ US used to describe sports teams at schools or colleges that are at the most skilled level of play: *He was a member of the varsity baseball team.*

▸noun [C] /'vɑː.sɪ.ti/ US /'vɑːr.sə.t̬i/ old-fashioned or Indian English or South African English a university

vary /'veə.ri/ US /'ver.i/ verb [I or T] **BE DIFFERENT** ▷ **1** B2 If things of the same type vary, they are different from each other, and if you vary them, you cause them to be different from each other: *Salary scales vary* ***between*** *states/****from*** *state* ***to*** *state/****according to*** *state/****with*** *each state.* ◦ *The samples varied* ***in*** *quality but were generally acceptable.* **CHANGE** ▷ **2** B2 to change or cause something to change in amount or level, especially from one occasion to another: *My taste in classical music varies* ***greatly/widely****, but I usually prefer Mozart or Brahms.* ◦ *Some people give a regular monthly donation while others vary the amount they give.*

vascular /'væs.kjʊ.lər/ US /-lɚ/ adj specialized relating to the tubes which carry blood or liquids in animals and plants: *the vascular* ***system*** ◦ *vascular disease* ◦ *a vascular surgeon*

vase /vɑːz/ US /veɪs/ noun [C] B1 a container for holding flowers or for decoration: *a vase of flowers*

vase

vasectomy /və'sek.tə.mi/ noun [C or U] the medical operation of cutting the tubes through which a man's SPERM move, in order to stop his partner getting pregnant

Vaseline /'væs.ə.liːn/ noun [U] trademark a soft, yellow or white substance made from oil, used especially on the skin to protect it or on surfaces to stop them sticking or rubbing together

vassal /'væs.əl/ noun [C] **1** in MEDIEVAL Europe, a man who agreed to fight for a king or LORD (= rich and powerful land owner) when needed, in exchange for land to live on **2** (also **vassal state**) a country that is controlled by a more powerful country, and has to provide military support or pay money to it when needed

vast /vɑːst/ US /væst/ adj B2 extremely big: *A vast audience watched the broadcast.* ◦ *The amount of detail the book contains is vast.* ◦ *The people who have taken our advice have saved themselves vast* ***amounts/sums*** *of money.* ◦ *The vast* ***majority*** *of pupils attend state-funded schools.*

vastly /'vɑːst.li/ US /'væst.li/ adv very much: *vastly different* ◦ *vastly superior* ◦ *vastly improved*

vat /væt/ noun [C] a large container used for mixing or storing liquid substances, especially in a factory: *a vat* ***of*** *wine/oil*

VAT (also **Vat**) /ˌviː.eɪ'tiː/, /væt/ noun [U] value added tax (= a type of tax in European countries that is paid by the person who buys goods and services)

VATable /'væt.ə.bl/ US /'væt̬-/ adj UK describes goods

on which VAT has to be paid: *The rich spend more than the poor on VATable goods.*

the Vatican /ˈvæt.ɪ.kən/ US /-ˈvæţ-/ **noun** [S] **1** the POPE (= the leader of the Catholic Church) or the officials who represent the Pope: *The Vatican released a statement condemning the recent terrorist attacks.* ◦ *The information was given by a Vatican official.* **2** the main offices of the Catholic Church in Rome, which include the building where the Pope lives: *No tour of Rome is complete without a visit to the Vatican/the Vatican **City**.*

vaudeville /ˈvɔː.də.vɪl/ US /ˈvoud.vɪl/ **noun** [U] US (UK ˈ**music ˌhall**) a type of theatre entertainment in the 1800s and early 1900s that included music, dancing, and jokes

vault /vɒlt/ US /vɑːlt/ **noun; verb**

▸**noun** [C] **ARCH** ▷ **1** a type of ARCH that supports a roof or ceiling, especially in a church or public building, or a ceiling or roof supported by several of these arches **ROOM** ▷ **2** (UK also **vaults**) a room, especially in a bank, with thick walls and a strong door, used to store money or valuable things in safe conditions: *a **bank** vault* ◦ *She entered the vault with an armed guard.* **3** a room under a church or a small building in a CEMETERY where dead bodies are buried: *She was buried in the **family** vault.*

▸**verb** **1** [I usually + adv/prep, T] to jump over something by first putting your hands on it or by using a pole: *He vaulted **over** the gate.* ◦ *She vaulted the wall and kept running.* ◦ specialized *He has vaulted 6.02 m in indoor competitions this year.* → See also **pole vault** **2** [T] formal to move someone or something suddenly to a much more important position: *Last week's changes vaulted the general **to** the top, over the heads of several of his seniors.*

vaulted /ˈvɒl.tɪd/ US /ˈvɑːl.ţɪd/ **adj** related to or having a vault: *a vaulted ceiling* ◦ *a vaulted room*

vaulting noun [U] /ˈvɒl.tɪŋ/ US /ˈvɑːl.ţɪŋ/ ARCHES which support a ceiling or room: *After the explosion nothing of the walls or vaulting remained intact.*

vaunted /ˈvɔː.n.tɪd/ US /ˈvɑːn.ţɪd/ **adj** formal praised often in a way that is considered to be more than acceptable or reasonable: *His (**much**) vaunted new scheme has been shown to have serious weaknesses.*

VC /ˌviːˈsiː/ **noun** [C usually singular] UK abbreviation for Victoria Cross: a MEDAL that is the highest honour for courage that can be given to a British soldier, or a soldier who has received this medal: *My grandfather was awarded **the** VC.*

VCR /ˌviː.siːˈɑːʳ/ US /-ˈɑːr/ **noun** [C] abbreviation for videocassette recorder: a machine used to record and play television programmes or films on VIDEOCASSETTES

VD /ˌviːˈdiː/ **noun** [U] abbreviation for venereal disease: a disease that is spread through sexual activity with an infected person

VDT /ˌviː.diːˈtiː/ **noun** [C] US abbreviation for video display terminal: a piece of equipment with a screen on which information from a computer can be shown

VDU /ˌviː.diːˈjuː/ **noun** [C] UK abbreviation for visual display unit: a piece of equipment with a screen on which information from a computer can be shown

've /-v/, /-əv/ **short form of** have: *I've been waiting for ages.*

veal /viːl/ **noun** [U] meat from a very young cow

vector /ˈvek.təʳ/ US /-tɚ/ **noun** [C] specialized **CALCULATION** ▷ **1** something physical such as a force that has size and direction → Compare **scalar** **ANIMAL** ▷ **2** an insect or animal that carries a disease from one animal or plant to another: *Mosquitoes are the vectors of malaria.*

Veda /ˈveɪ.də/ **noun** [C] one or all of the holy books of writings of Hinduism • **Vedic** /-dɪk/ **adj**

Vedanta /vɪˈdæn.tə/ **noun** [U] one of the main systems of Hindu thought

veep /viːp/ **noun** [C] US informal a **vice president**

veer /vɪəʳ/ US /vɪr/ **verb** [I + adv/prep] to change direction: *All of a sudden, the car veered **off** the road.* ◦ *Moments before crashing, the jet was seen veering sharply **to** the right.* ◦ *Three men were feared dead last night after a helicopter veered **off course** into an oil platform.* ◦ *Our talk soon veered **onto** the subject of football.*

veg /vedʒ/ **noun; verb**

▸**noun** [U or plural] UK informal vegetables: *a fruit and veg stall* ◦ *He still prefers the old-fashioned British meal of meat and two veg.*

▸**verb** (**-gg-**)

PHRASAL VERB **veg out** informal to relax and spend time doing very little: *I'm exhausted – I think I'll just go home and veg out in front of the TV tonight.*

vegan /ˈviː.gən/ **noun; adj**

▸**noun** [C] a person who does not eat or use any animal products, such as meat, fish, eggs, cheese, or leather: *Vegans get all the protein they need from nuts, seeds, and cereals.* → Compare **vegetarian**

▸**adj** not eating, using, or including any animal products: *a vegan diet* ◦ *She decided to **turn** vegan after watching a documentary about how poultry is raised.*

vegeburger /ˈvedʒ.ɪˌbɜː.gəʳ/ US /-ˌbɝː.gɚ/ **noun** [C] UK for **veggie burger**

vegetable /ˈvedʒ.tə.bl̩/ **noun; adj**

▸**noun** **FOOD** ▷ **1** A1 [C] (US informal **veggie**) a plant, root, seed, or POD that is used as food, especially in dishes that are not sweet: *fresh/frozen vegetables* ◦ *vegetable soup/stew/curry* ◦ *fruit and vegetables* ◦ *The potato is the most popular vegetable in Britain.* ◦ *In the winter we tend to eat more **root** vegetables, such as carrots and parsnips.* ◦ ***Raw** vegetables contain more potassium than **cooked** ones.* ◦ *a vegetable knife* → Compare **fruit** **PERSON** ▷ **2** [C] informal a person who does not do anything or has no interest in doing anything: *Sitting at home all day in front of the TV slowly turned her into a vegetable.* **3** [C] offensive a person who is unable to think or move correctly because of severe brain damage

▸**adj** made or obtained from a plant, or growing in the form of a plant: *vegetable matter/dye*

ˌ**vegetable** ˈ**oil** **noun** [C or U] cooking oil made from plants

vegetarian /ˌvedʒ.ɪˈteə.ri.ən/ US /-ˈter.i-/ **noun; adj**

▸**noun** [C] (UK informal **veggie**) B1 a person who does not eat meat for health or religious reasons or because they want to avoid being cruel to animals: *Of the four million people who have become vegetarians in Britain, nearly two thirds are women.* → Compare **vegan** • **vegetarianism** /-ə.nɪ.zᵊm/ **noun** [U] *Vegetarianism is very popular among young people in Britain, especially among teenage girls.*

▸**adj** (informal **veggie**) B1 not eating or including meat: *vegetarian cooking/food* ◦ *a vegetarian dish/meal* ◦ *a vegetarian restaurant* ◦ *She's recently gone/become vegetarian.*

vegetate /ˈvedʒ.ɪ.teɪt/ **verb** [I] to live in a way that has no physical and mental activity: *A report has shown that children spend too much time vegetating in front of the TV.*

vegetation /ˌvedʒ.ɪˈteɪ.ʃᵊn/ **noun** [U] C1 plants in

V

general, or plants that are found in a particular area: *The railway track will have to be cleared of vegetation if it is to be used again.* ◦ *Much of the region's native vegetation has been damaged by developers who are building hotels along the coast.*

vegetative /ˈvedʒ.ɪ.te.tɪv/ (US) /-ə.teɪ.t̬ɪv/ **adj** specialized alive but showing no brain activity

veggie /ˈvedʒ.i/ **adj; noun**
▸**adj** (also **veggy**) UK informal **vegetarian**
▸**noun** [C] (also **veggy**) **1** UK informal a **vegetarian** **2** US and Australian English informal a vegetable

ˈveggie ˌburger noun [C] a type of food similar to a HAMBURGER but made without meat, by pressing together small pieces of vegetables, seeds, etc. into a flat, round shape

vehement /ˈviː.ə.mənt/ **adj** expressing strong feelings, or shown by strong feelings or great energy or force: *Despite vehement opposition from his family, he quit school and became an actor.* ◦ *Both men were vehement **in** their denial of the charges against them.* ◦ *They launched a vehement attack on the government's handling of environmental issues.* • **vehemence** /-məns/ **noun** [U] *She argued **with** such vehemence against the proposal that they decided to abandon it.*

vehemently /ˈviː.ə.mənt.li/ **adv** in a strong and emotional way: *The president has vehemently **denied** having an extra-marital affair.*

vehicle /ˈviː.ɪ.kl/ **noun** **MACHINE** ▷ **1** (B1) [C] formal a machine, usually with wheels and an engine, used for transporting people or goods on land, especially on roads: *A truck driver died last night when his vehicle overturned.* ◦ ***Road** vehicles include cars, buses, and trucks.* ◦ *Tractors are **farm** vehicles.* ◦ *The number of thefts of **motor** vehicles rose by a third last year.* **METHOD** ▷ **2** (C2) [C usually singular] a way of achieving, producing, or expressing something: *The conference was seen as an ideal vehicle **for** increased cooperation between the member states.* **3** [C usually singular] a show, film, EXHIBITION, etc. that is used to show the special skills or qualities of one particular performer or artist: *The play seems to be little more than a vehicle for its director and star.* • **vehicular** /vɪˈhɪk.jʊ.ləʳ/ (US) /viːˈhɪk.jʊ.lɚ/ **adj** formal *The cottage has no vehicular access but can be reached by a short walk across the moor.*

veil /veɪl/ **noun; verb**
▸**noun** **MATERIAL** ▷ **1** (C1) [C] a piece of thin material worn by women to cover the face or head: *After the ceremony, the bride **lifted** up her veil to kiss her husband.* ◦ *The women wore black veils which covered all but their eyes.* **2 take the veil** A Christian woman who takes the veil becomes a NUN. **3 take/adopt the veil** A Muslim woman who takes or adopts the veil decides to wear traditional Muslim clothing. **UNCLEAR** ▷ **4** [S] literary a thin covering of something, which you can see through, but not very clearly: *The view over the lake was obscured by a veil **of** mist that hung in the air.* **5** (C2) [S] literary something that prevents you from knowing what is happening: *The government has been urged to **lift** the veil **of secrecy** surrounding the minister's unexpected resignation.* **6 draw a veil over sth** literary to not talk any more about a subject because it could cause trouble or embarrassment: *I think we should draw a veil over everything that happened at the party, don't you?*

veil

▸**verb** **MATERIAL** ▷ **1** [T often passive] to cover something, especially the face or body, with a veil: *In some societies, women are expected to be veiled when they go out in public.* **HIDE** ▷ **2** [T] to hide or cover something so that you cannot see it clearly: *Thick fog veiled the city.*

veiled /veɪld/ **adj** describes words or ways of behaving that are not direct or expressed clearly: *a veiled reference/threat/warning* ◦ *a **thinly** veiled **attack** on his abilities as a leader*

vein /veɪn/ **noun** **TUBE** ▷ **1** (C1) [C] a tube that carries blood to the heart from the other parts of the body **2** [C] the frame of a leaf or an insect's wing **LAYER** ▷ **3** [C] a narrow layer of a substance which forms in or fills a CRACK in rock: *A **rich** vein **of** iron ore was found in the hillside.* **4** [S] a particular quality or characteristic: *A vein **of** satirical anger runs through all his work.* ◦ *In its bid to be elected, the party is attempting to **tap** (= use) an underlying vein **of** nationalism in the country.* **MOOD** ▷ **5** [S or U] a style or a temporary mood: *The opening scene is very violent, and the rest of the film continues **in** (**a**) similar vein.* ◦ *After laughing over the photo, they began to talk **in** (**a**) more serious vein about the damaging effect it could have on his career.*

veined /veɪnd/ **adj** with many veins, or covered with lines that look like veins: *A thin, veined hand lay on the coverlet.* ◦ *veined cheese/marble* • **-veined suffix**

velar /ˈviː.ləʳ/ (US) /-lɚ/ **adj** specialized (of a consonant sound) made by the tongue touching the VELUM: *In English, /k/ and /g/ are examples of velar sounds.*

Velcro /ˈvel.krəʊ/ (US) /-kroʊ/ **noun** [U] trademark material that consists of two pieces of cloth that stick together, used to fasten clothes

veld (also **veldt**) /velt/ **noun** [S] flat, open country with few trees that is characteristic of parts of southern Africa

vellum /ˈvel.əm/ **noun** [U] **1** a thick, cream-coloured, very high-quality writing paper **2** a material used in the past for writing on or for covering a book, made from the skins of young animals, especially cows or sheep

velocity /vəˈlɒs.ɪ.ti/ (US) /-ˈlɑː.sə.t̬i/ **noun** [C or U] formal the speed at which an object is travelling: *Light travels at the highest achievable velocity in the universe.* ◦ *He always used **high** velocity lead bullets in his rifle.*

velour (also **velours**) /vəˈlʊəʳ/ (US) /-ˈlʊr/ **noun** [U] a material similar to velvet that has a soft surface, used for clothes and for covering furniture

velum /ˈviː.ləm/ **noun** [C] specialized the soft area at the top in the mouth

velvet /ˈvel.vɪt/ **noun; adj**
▸**noun** [U] (C2) a cloth usually made from SILK or cotton with a thick, soft surface: *Her skin was **as soft as** velvet.*
▸**adj** **CLOTH** ▷ **1** made of velvet: *a velvet dress* ◦ *velvet curtains/cushions* **QUALITY** ▷ **2** (also **velvety**) describes something that has a beautiful soft, smooth quality or appearance, usually something dark or deep: *under a wonderful velvet **sky*** ◦ *His velvety **brown** eyes had been his passport to fame.*

vena cava /ˌviː.nəˈkeɪ.və/ **noun** [C] (plural **venae cavae**) specialized one of the two very large VEINS through which blood returns to the heart, one from the upper body and head and one from all of the body below the chest: *The **superior** (= upper) and **inferior** (= lower) venae cavae collect blood that has circulated around the body.*

venal /ˈviː.nəl/ **adj** formal **1** A venal person is willing to behave in a way that is not honest or moral in exchange for money: *a venal ruler* **2** A venal activity is done in order to get money: *a venal regime* • **venality** /viːˈnæl.ɪ.ti/ (US) /vɪˈnæl.ə.t̬i/ **noun** [U]

vendetta /venˈdet.ə/ (US) /-ˈdet̬-/ **noun** [C] a long and violent argument between people or families, in which one group tries to harm the other in order to punish them for things that happened in the past: *He saw himself as the victim of a personal vendetta being* ***waged*** *by his political enemies.*

vending /ˈven.dɪŋ/ **noun** [U] formal the selling of goods: *He had his street vending licence taken away.*

ˈvending maˌchine **noun** [C] (UK also **ˈslot maˌchine**) a machine from which you can buy small things such as cigarettes, drinks, and sweets by putting coins into it: *The vending machine in the office* ***dispenses*** *really tasteless coffee.*

vendor /ˈven.dər/ (US) /-dɚ/ **noun** [C] someone who is selling something: *For the past few months she's been working as a* ***street*** *vendor, selling fruit and veg.* ◦ legal *The vendor of the house wants to exchange contracts this week.*

veneer /vəˈnɪər/ (US) /-ˈnɪr/ **noun** **1** [C or U] a thin layer of decorative wood or plastic used to cover a cheaper material: *The wardrobe is made of chipboard with a pine veneer.* **2** [S] something which hides something unpleasant or unwanted: *She managed to hide her corrupt dealings under a veneer* ***of respectability***. • **veneered** /-ˈnɪəd/ (US) /-ˈnɪrd/ **adj** *a veneered bookcase/surface/table*

venerable /ˈven.ər.ə.bl̩/ **adj** **1** formal deserving respect because of age, high position, or religious or historical importance: *a venerable tradition/company/family* **2** informal mainly humorous describes something that has been in use, or someone who has been involved in something, for a long time: *In recent years there has been a noticeable decline in such venerable British* ***institutions*** *as afternoon tea and the Sunday roast.*

Venerable /ˈven.ər.ə.bl̩/ **adj** **1 the Venerable** used as a title for an ARCHDEACON in the Church of England **2** used as a title for a person who is considered holy by the Roman Catholic Church but who has not yet been made a SAINT **3** used as a title for a MONK in Buddhism

venerate /ˈven.ər.eɪt/ (US) /-ɚ.eɪt/ **verb** [T] formal to honour or very much respect a person or thing: *Robert Burns is Scotland's most venerated poet.* • **veneration** /ˌven.ərˈeɪ.ʃən/ (US) /-ɚˈeɪ-/ **noun** [U] *Gandhi became an object of widespread veneration because of his unceasing struggle for freedom and equality.*

venereal /vəˈnɪə.ri.əl/ (US) /-ˈnɪr.i-/ **adj** caused or spread by sexual activity with another person: *a venereal infection*

V

veˌnereal disˈease **noun** [C or U] (abbreviation **VD**) a disease that is spread through sexual activity with an infected person → Compare **sexually transmitted disease, sexually transmitted illness**

venetian blind /vəˌniː.ʃənˈblaɪnd/ **noun** [C] a cover for a window made of thin, horizontal pieces of wood, plastic, or metal, which can be moved in order to change the amount of light that is allowed in

vengeance /ˈven.dʒəns/ **noun** [U] the punishing of someone for harming you or your friends or family, or the wish for such punishment to happen: *On the day after the terrorist attack, the overall mood in the town was one of vengeance.* ◦ *As he cradled his daughter's lifeless body in his arms, he* ***swore*** *(****to take****) vengeance* ***on*** *her killers.*

IDIOM **with a vengeance** with great force or extreme energy: *He's been working with a vengeance over the past few weeks to make up for lost time.* ◦ *Flared trousers are* ***back*** *with a vengeance (= very popular again) this summer.*

vengeful /ˈvendʒ.fəl/ **adj** formal expressing a strong wish to punish someone who has harmed you or your family or friends: *She sprayed red paint all over his car in one last vengeful act before leaving him for good.* • **vengefully** /-i/ **adv** • **vengefulness** /-nəs/ **noun** [U]

venial /ˈviː.ni.əl/ **adj** formal describes a wrong action that is not serious and therefore easy to forgive: *a venial sin/error*

> **Note:**
> Do not confuse with **venal**.

venison /ˈven.ɪ.sən/ **noun** [U] meat that comes from a DEER

Venn diagram /ˌvenˈdaɪ.ə.græm/ **noun** [C] specialized a mathematical plan consisting of OVERLAPPING circles which show how things that belong to mathematical sets relate to each other

venom /ˈvenəm/ **noun** [U] **POISON** ▷ **1** a poisonous liquid which some snakes, insects, etc. produce and can put into another animal's body by biting or STINGING **HATE** ▷ **2** literary the expression of feelings of hate or extreme anger: *He was shocked at the* ***sheer*** *venom of her reply.*

venomous /ˈven.ə.məs/ **adj** **POISON** ▷ **1** poisonous: *a venomous snake* **HATE** ▷ **2** full of anger or hate: *Ms Brown has launched a venomous* ***attack*** *against the newspaper.* • **venomously** /-li/ **adv**

venous /ˈviː.nəs/ **adj** specialized of or relating to the VEINS: *venous blood* ◦ *the venous system* → See also **intravenous**

vent /vent/ **noun; verb**

►**noun** **OPENING** ▷ **1** [C] a small opening that allows air, smoke, or gas to enter or leave a closed space: *If you have a gas fire in a room, you should have some kind of outside vent.* **2** [C] a cut in the bottom of a piece of clothing to allow the person wearing it to move more easily: *The skirt is long and straight with two side vents.* **EXPRESS FEELINGS** ▷ **3 give vent to sth** (C2) to express a negative emotion in a forceful and often unfair way: *The meeting will be an opportunity for everyone to give vent to their feelings.*

►**verb** [T] (C2) to express a negative emotion in a forceful and often unfair way: *Please don't shout – there's no need to vent your* ***frustration/anger/rage/spleen on*** *me.*

ventilate /ˈven.tɪ.leɪt/ (US) /-t̬əl.eɪt/ **verb** [T] **PROVIDE AIR** ▷ **1** to cause fresh air to enter and move around a closed space: *I work in a very well-/poorly-ventilated building.* **MAKE KNOWN** ▷ **2** formal to express an opinion or mention a subject so that it can be discussed by others: *She used the meeting to ventilate all her* ***grievances***.

ventilation /ˌven.tɪˈleɪ.ʃən/ (US) /-t̬əlˈeɪ-/ **noun** [U] the movement of fresh air around a closed space, or the system that does this: *Her room had* ***poor*** *ventilation and in summer it became unbearably stuffy.* ◦ *a ventilation* ***system***

ventilator /ˈven.tɪ.leɪ.tər/ (US) /-t̬əl.eɪ.tɚ/ **noun** [C] **1** an opening or a device that allows fresh air to come into a closed space **2** a machine that helps people breathe correctly by allowing air to flow in and out of their lungs: *He was brought into intensive care shortly after the crash and immediately* ***put on*** *a ventilator.*

ventral /ˈven.trəl/ adj [before noun] specialized of, on, or near the UNDERSIDE of an animal → Compare **dorsal**

ventricle /ˈven.trɪ.kl̩/ noun [C] specialized either of two small, hollow spaces, one in each side of the heart, which force blood into the tubes leading from the heart to the other parts of the body

ventriloquism /venˈtrɪl.ə.kwɪ.zəm/ noun [U] the ability to speak without moving your lips so that your voice seems to be coming from someone or something else, usually as a way of entertaining people • **ventriloquist** /-kwɪst/ noun [C]

venˌtriloquist's ˈdummy noun [C] a toy in the shape of a small person that ventriloquists operate, so that it seems to be alive

venture /ˈven.tʃər/ (US) /-tʃɚ/ noun; verb

▸noun [C] C2 a new activity, usually in business, which involves risk or UNCERTAINTY: *She advised us to look abroad for more lucrative* ***business*** *ventures.* ◦ *There are many* ***joint*** *ventures between American and Japanese companies.*

▸verb [I usually + adv/prep, T] formal C2 to risk going somewhere or doing something that might be dangerous or unpleasant, or to risk saying something that might be criticized: *She rarely ventured* ***outside****, except when she went to stock up on groceries at the corner shop.* ◦ *As we set off into the forest, we felt as though we were venturing* ***(forth) into*** *the unknown.* ◦ *She tentatively ventured* ***the opinion*** *that the project would be too expensive to complete, but the boss ignored her.*

IDIOM **nothing ventured, nothing gained** saying C2 You have to take a risk in order to get something good.

PHRASAL VERB **venture on/upon sth** to try to do something difficult or dangerous: *The wind was so strong that when we did finally venture on a walk, we were nearly swept away.*

ˈventure ˌcapital noun [U] money that is INVESTED or is available for INVESTMENT in a new company, especially one that involves risk: *They'll need to raise £1 million in venture capital if they're to get the business off the ground.* • **ˈventure ˌcapitalist** noun [C]

venturesome /ˈven.tʃə.səm/ (US) /-tʃɚ-/ adj formal describes a person who is willing to take risks, or an action or behaviour that involves risks

venue /ˈven.juː/ noun [C] **1** B2 the place where a public event or meeting happens: *The hotel is an ideal venue* ***for*** *conferences and business meetings.* ◦ *The stadium has been specifically designed as a venue* ***for*** *European Cup matches.* **2** US specialized the city or COUNTY in which a trial happens

Venus /ˈviː.nəs/ noun [S] the planet second in order of distance from the Sun, after Mercury and before the Earth. It is the nearest planet to the Earth.

Venus flytrap /ˌviː.nəsˈflaɪ.træp/ noun [C] a plant which feeds on insects and catches them by quickly closing its leaves when their surface is touched so that the insects cannot escape

veracity /vəˈræs.ɪ.ti/ (US) /vəˈæs.ə.t̬i/ noun [U] formal the quality of being true, honest, or accurate: *Doubts were cast on the veracity of her alibi after three people claimed to have seen her at the scene of the robbery.*

veranda (US also **verandah**) /vəˈræn.də/ noun [C] (also **porch**) a raised, covered, sometimes partly closed area, often made of wood, on the front or side of a building: *Every evening we sat* ***on*** *the veranda watching the sun go down.*

verb /vɜːb/ (US) /vɝːb/ noun [C] A2 a word or phrase that describes an action, condition, or experience: *The words 'run', 'keep', and 'feel' are all verbs.*

verbal /ˈvɜː.bəl/ (US) /ˈvɝː-/ adj SPOKEN ▷ **1** C2 spoken rather than written: *a verbal agreement/description/explanation* ◦ *Airport officials received a stream of verbal* ***abuse*** *from angry passengers whose flights had been delayed.* IN WORDS ▷ **2** C1 relating to words: *It can sometimes be difficult to give a verbal description of things like colours and sounds.* • **verbally** /-i/ adv

ˌverbal diarˈrhoea noun [U] informal humorous **have verbal diarrhoea** to talk continuously or too much

verbalize formal (UK usually **verbalise**) /ˈvɜː.bəl.aɪz/ (US) /ˈvɝː.bə.laɪz/ verb [I or T] to express ideas, opinions, or emotions in words: *He found it hard to verbalize his* ***feelings*** *towards his son.*

verbatim /vɜːˈbeɪ.tɪm/ (US) /vɝːˈbeɪ.t̬əm/ adv using exactly the same words as were originally used: *She had an amazing memory and could recall verbatim quite complex conversations.* • **verbatim** adj [before noun] *a verbatim account*

verbiage /ˈvɜː.bi.ɪdʒ/ (US) /ˈvɝː-/ noun [U] formal disapproving language that is very complicated and contains a lot of unnecessary words: *His explanation was wrapped up in so much technical verbiage that I simply couldn't understand it.*

verbose /vɜːˈbəʊs/ (US) /vɚˈboʊs/ adj formal disapproving using or containing more words than are necessary: *a verbose explanation/report/speech/style* ◦ *He was a notoriously verbose after-dinner speaker.* • **verbosely** /-li/ adv • **verbosity** /-ˈbɒs.ɪ.ti/ (US) /-ˈbɑː.sə.t̬i/ noun [U]

verdant /ˈvɜː.dənt/ (US) /ˈvɝː-/ adj literary covered with healthy green plants or grass: *Much of the region's verdant* ***countryside*** *has been destroyed in the hurricane.*

verdict /ˈvɜː.dɪkt/ (US) /ˈvɝː-/ noun [C] C1 an opinion or decision made after judging the facts that are given, especially one made at the end of a trial: *The jury* ***reached/returned*** *a* ***unanimous*** *verdict of* ***(not) guilty****.* ◦ *Voters* ***gave*** *their verdict* ***on*** *the government's economic record last night by voting overwhelmingly for the opposition.* → See also **open verdict**

verdigris /ˈvɜː.dɪ.grɪs/ (US) /ˈvɝː-/ noun [U] a blue-green layer that forms on COPPER, BRASS, or BRONZE

verdure /ˈvɜː.djər/ (US) /ˈvɝː.dʒɚ/ noun [U] literary (the green colour of) fresh, healthy plants

verge /vɜːdʒ/ (US) /vɝːdʒ/ noun; verb

▸noun [C] **1** the edge or border of something: *They set up camp on the verge of the desert.* **2** UK (US **shoulder**) the strip of land which borders a road or path: *She left her car by the side of the road and walked along the* ***grass*** *verge to the emergency phone.*

IDIOM **on the verge (of)** (also **to the verge of**) C2 If you are on the verge of something or come to the verge of something, you are very near to experiencing it: *on the verge of collapse/success/tears/death/disaster/war* ◦ *Her husband's violent and abusive behaviour* ***drove*** *her to the verge of despair.*

▸verb

PHRASAL VERB **verge on sth** to be almost a particular state, quality, or feeling, especially one that is very bad or very good: *At times, his performance verged on brilliance, but at others it was only ordinary.*

verger /ˈvɜː.dʒər/ (US) /ˈvɝː.dʒɚ/ noun [C] an official in some Churches who takes care of the inside of a church building and performs some simple duties during services

verifiable /ˈver.ɪ.faɪ.ə.bl̩/ adj able to be proved:

V

Throughout the trial, he didn't produce a single verifiable fact.

verify /ˈver.ɪ.faɪ/ **verb** [T] C1 to prove that something exists or is true, or to make certain that something is correct: *Are you able to verify your account/allegation/report/theory?* ◦ *These figures are surprisingly high and they'll have to be verified.* ◦ [+ (that)] *Under interrogation, she verified (**that**) the tapes were authentic.* • **verification** /ˌver.ɪ.fɪˈkeɪ.ʃən/ **noun** [U]

verily /ˈver.ɪ.li/ **adv** old use in a completely honest way

verisimilitude /ˌver.ɪ.sɪˈmɪl.ɪ.tjuːd/ US /-tuːd/ **noun** [U] formal the quality of seeming true or of having the appearance of being real: *She has included photographs in the book to lend verisimilitude to the story.*

veritable /ˈver.ɪ.tə.bl/ US /-ə.t̬ə-/ **adj** [before noun] used to describe something as another, more exciting, interesting, or unusual thing, as a way of emphasizing its character: *My garden had become **a** veritable jungle by the time I came back from holiday.* • **veritably** /-bli/ **adv**

verity /ˈver.ɪ.ti/ US /-ə.t̬i/ **noun** formal **1** [U] the quality of being true: *In the film, he plays a spy whose mission is to confirm the verity of a secret military document.* **2** [C] a belief, idea, or principle that is generally accepted as being true: *She has spent her life in a search for eternal/scientific/universal verities.*

vermicelli /ˌvɜː.mɪˈtʃel.i/ US /ˌvɝː-/ **noun** [U] **1** a type of PASTA made in long, thin threads **2** UK extremely small pieces of chocolate used for decorating cakes

vermilion (also **vermillion**) /vəˈmɪl.i.ən/ US /vɚˈmɪl.jən/ **noun** [C or U] a bright red colour: *She was wearing a jacket of bright vermilion.* • **vermilion adj** having a bright red colour

vermin /ˈvɜː.mɪn/ US /ˈvɝː-/ **noun** [plural] **1** small animals and insects that can be harmful and are difficult to control when they appear in large numbers: *Flies, lice, and cockroaches can all be described as vermin.* **2** offensive disapproving people who are unpleasant and harmful to society: *He thought all terrorists were vermin.*

verminous /ˈvɜː.mɪ.nəs/ US /ˈvɝː-/ **adj** formal covered with insects: *an old verminous blanket*

vermouth /vəˈmuːθ/, /ˈvɜː.məθ/ US /vɚ-/ **noun** [U] a strongly alcoholic red or white wine FLAVOURED with herbs and spices

vernacular /vəˈnæk.jʊ.ləʳ/ US /vɚˈnæk.jə.lɚ/ **noun** [C usually singular] **1** the form of a language that a particular group of speakers use naturally, especially in informal situations: *The French I learned at school is very different from the local vernacular of the village where I'm now living.* ◦ *Many Roman Catholics regret the replacing of the Latin mass by **the** vernacular.* **2** specialized in ARCHITECTURE, a local style in which ordinary houses are built **3** specialized dance, music, art, etc. that is in a style liked or performed by ordinary people • **vernacular adj** *His lively vernacular style goes down well with younger viewers.* ◦ *old stone vernacular buildings*

V

vernal /ˈvɜː.nəl/ US /ˈvɝː-/ **adj** [before noun] literary relating to or happening in the spring

ˌvernal ˈequinox noun [C usually singular] the time in the spring when the sun crosses the EQUATOR, and when night and day are of equal length

verruca /vəˈruː.kə/ **noun** [C] (plural **verrucas** or **verrucae**) a small, hard infectious growth on the skin, usually on the bottom of the foot

versatile /ˈvɜː.sə.taɪl/ US /ˈvɝː.sə.t̬əl/ **adj** approving C2 able to change easily from one activity to another or able to be used for many different purposes: *He's a very versatile young actor who's as happy in horror films as he is in TV comedies.* ◦ *A leather jacket is a timeless and versatile garment that can be worn in all seasons.* • **versatility** /ˌvɜː.səˈtɪl.ɪ.ti/ US /ˌvɝː.səˈtɪl.ə.t̬i/ **noun** [U]

verse /vɜːs/ US /vɝːs/ **noun** **1** [U] writing that is arranged in short lines with a regular rhythm; poetry: *comic/light/satirical verse* ◦ *Shakespeare wrote mostly **in** verse.* **2** B2 [C] one of the parts that a poem or song is divided into: *Each verse was sung as a solo and then everyone joined in on the chorus.* **3** [C] one of the series of short parts that the writing of a holy book is divided into: *She **recited** a verse from the Bible/the Koran.*

versed /vɜːst/ US /vɝːst/ **adj** formal **be versed in sth** to know a lot about a particular subject or be experienced in a particular skill: *I'm not sufficiently versed in computers to understand what you're saying.*

version /ˈvɜː.ʃən/, /-ʒən/ US /ˈvɝː-/ **noun** [C] B2 a particular form of something that is slightly different from other forms of the same thing: *The **official** version **of** events is that the police were attacked and were just trying to defend themselves.* ◦ *You can make a reduced fat version **of** the cheesecake by using cottage cheese instead of cream cheese.* ◦ *An English-language version **of** the book is planned for the autumn.*

versus /ˈvɜː.səs/ US /ˈvɝː-/ **preposition** **1** C1 (written abbreviation **v** or **vs**) used to say that one team or person is competing against another: *Tomorrow's game is Newcastle versus Arsenal.* **2** (written abbreviation **v** or **vs**) used in legal cases to show who a person is fighting against: *Abortion was legalized nationally in the United States following the Roe versus Wade case.* **3** C1 used to compare two things or ideas, especially when you have to choose between them: *private education versus state education*

vertebra /ˈvɜː.tɪ.brə/ US /ˈvɝː.t̬ə-/ **noun** [C] (plural **vertebrae**) specialized one of the small bones that form the SPINE (= back bone) • **vertebral** /-brəl/ **adj** *The vertebral **column** surrounds and protects the spinal cord.*

vertebrate /ˈvɜː.tɪ.brət/ US /ˈvɝː.t̬ə-/ **adj**; **noun**
▸**adj** specialized having a SPINE (= back bone)
▸**noun** [C] specialized an animal that has a SPINE: *Birds, fish, and reptiles are all vertebrates.* → Compare **invertebrate**

vertex /ˈvɜː.teks/ US /ˈvɝː.teks/ **noun** [C] (plural **vertices** or **vertexes**) specialized **1** (in mathematics) the point where two lines meet to form an angle, or the point that is opposite the base of a shape: *the vertex of a triangle/cone/pyramid* **2** the highest point of something

vertical /ˈvɜː.tɪ.kəl/ US /ˈvɝː.t̬ə-/ **adj**; **noun**
▸**adj** standing or pointing straight up or at an angle of 90° to a horizontal surface or line: *vertical lines/stripes* ◦ *She looked over the cliff and found she was standing at the edge of a vertical **drop**.* → Compare **horizontal** • **vertically** /-i/ **adv** *A wall of rock towered vertically up on one side of the narrow mountain path.*
▸**noun** [C usually singular] a vertical line, surface, or position: *In a two-stage operation, the steel structure will be raised to **the** vertical.*

ˈvertical ˌaxis noun [S] specialized → the **y-axis**

ˌvertical ˈblind noun [C] a cover for a window made of vertical strips of stiff cloth which can be moved in order to change the amount of light that is allowed in

ˌvertical ˈfarm noun [C] a place where plants or LIVESTOCK (= animals for food) are grown or kept in tall buildings with many floors • **ˌvertical ˈfarming noun**

[U] *Vertical farming promises to increase food supplies without using more land.*

ˌvertical ˈgardening noun [U] the activity of making plants grow up a wall or out of a wall, often because there is not much space available on the ground

ˌvertical inteˈgration noun [U] specialized a process in business where a company buys another company that supplies it with goods or that buys goods from it in order to control all the processes of production

ˌvertical ˈtake-off noun [C] a way of leaving the ground in which an aircraft rises straight up

vertiginous /vɜːˈtɪdʒ.ɪ.nəs/ US /vɚ-/ adj formal causing or experiencing the feeling that everything is spinning around: *The two skyscrapers were connected by a vertiginous walkway.*

vertigo /ˈvɜː.tɪ.ɡəʊ/ US /ˈvɝː.t̬ə.ɡoʊ/ noun [U] a feeling of spinning around and being unable to balance, caused by looking down from a height: *She can't stand heights and has always* ***suffered from*** *vertigo.*

verve /vɜːv/ US /vɝːv/ noun [U] great energy and enthusiasm: *She delivered her speech* ***with*** *tremendous wit and verve.*

very /ˈver.i/ adv; adj

▸adv **1** A1 (used to add emphasis to an adjective or adverb) to a great degree or extremely: *The situation is very serious.* ◦ *We're very, very sorry about what's happened.* ◦ *Think about it very carefully before deciding.* ◦ *'Are you tired?' 'No, not very.'* ◦ *Thank you very* ***much****.* ◦ *'Did you enjoy the play?' 'Very* ***much so****.'* (= Yes.) ◦ *I* ***can't*** *very* ***well*** (= *it would not be right for me to*) *say sorry when I didn't do anything wrong.* **2** used to add force to a SUPERLATIVE adjective or to the adjectives 'own' or 'same': *This is* ***the*** *very* ***best*** *chocolate cake I've ever tasted.* ◦ *She always leaves her homework to* ***the*** *very* ***last*** *moment.* ◦ *We now have our very* ***own*** *post office in the village.* ◦ *This is* ***the*** *very* ***same*** (= *exactly the same*) *place we sat in the last time we came.*

> **! Common mistake: very**
>
> Use **very** to emphasize adjectives that do not have a strong meaning.
>
> If an adjective already has a strong meaning, don't say 'very', say **really/absolutely**:
>
> *Their house is very big.*
>
> *Their house is really huge.*

IDIOMS **all very well/fine/good** You say that something is all very well/fine/good if it seems good by itself but you think that there are problems connected with it: *It's all very well to want to get rich quickly,* ***but*** *don't expect any sympathy from me if things go wrong.* • **very good** UK old-fashioned a way of saying yes to someone who is in a higher position or rank than you: *'Higgins, you may go now.' 'Very good, sir.'* • **very well** formal a way of saying yes to someone or of agreeing to do what they ask: *'Can't I stay for five minutes longer?' 'Oh, very well.'*

▸adj [before noun] EXACT ▷ **1** C2 (used to add emphasis to a noun) exact or particular: *This is the very book I've been looking for all month.* ◦ *You're the very person we need for the job.* ◦ *The letter was sent on Monday from Manchester and arrived in London the very* ***same/next*** *day.* ◦ *The very* ***idea/thought*** *of having her friends to stay fills me with dread.* FURTHEST POINT ▷ **2** used to describe or emphasize the furthest point of something: *He found the piece of paper he had lost at* ***the*** *very* ***bottom*** *of the pile.* ◦ *We were at* ***the*** *very* ***end*** *of the queue and so didn't manage to get any tickets.*

IDIOM **be the very thing** to be exactly what is needed: *Why not take garlic? It's the very thing* ***for*** *preventing colds.*

the ˌVery ˈReverend adj [before noun] used as a title of respect for particular important Church officials

vespers /ˈves.pəz/ US /-pɚz/ noun [U] the evening ceremony in some Churches

vessel /ˈves. əl/ noun [C] SHIP ▷ **1** formal a large boat or a ship: *a cargo/fishing/naval/patrol/sailing/supply vessel* CONTAINER ▷ **2** formal a curved container that is used to hold liquid: *The remains of some Roman earthenware vessels were found during the dig.* PERSON ▷ **3** literary a person who has a particular quality or who is used for a particular purpose: *As a young and spirited politician, he seems a worthy vessel for the nation's hopes.* TUBE ▷ **4** a tube that carries liquids such as blood through the body: *A heart attack is caused by the* ***blood*** *vessels that supply the blood to the heart muscle getting blocked.*

vest /vest/ noun; verb

▸noun [C] **1** C1 UK (US **undershirt**) a type of underwear, often with no sleeves, that covers the upper part of the body, worn for extra warmth: *a cotton/woollen/string vest* ◦ *She always wore a long-sleeved* ***thermal*** *vest in winter.* **2** (also **vest top**) UK a shirt without sleeves, usually made out of cotton, that is worn in the summer or for sport: *The cyclists were all dressed in tight lycra shorts and* ***the*** *official team vest.* ◦ *He wore a vest top and a pair of luminous shorts to the beach party.* **3** C2 US for **waistcoat**

▸verb

PHRASAL VERB **be vested in sb/sth** (also **be vested with sth**) If power or authority is vested in someone or something, or if they are vested with power or authority, it is officially given to them: ***Control*** *has been vested in local authorities.* ◦ *He has been vested with the* ***power/authority*** *to implement whatever changes he sees fit.*

vested interest /ˌves.tɪdˈɪn.tər.est/ US /-t̬ɚ-/ noun **1** [C] a strong personal interest in something because you could get an advantage from it: *As both a teacher and parent, she* ***had*** *a vested interest* ***in*** *seeing the school remain open.* **2 vested interests** [plural] often disapproving people or organizations who have a financial or personal interest in a business, company, or existing system: *A compromise has to be reached between all the powerful vested interests before any restoration work in the city can take place.*

vestibule /ˈves.tɪ.bjuːl/ noun [C] **1** formal a small room just inside the outer door of a public building where you can leave your coat, etc.: *I'll wait for you in the vestibule.* **2** US a small closed area on the front of a house → Synonym **porch**

vestige /ˈves.tɪdʒ/ noun [C] formal a still existing small part or amount of something larger, stronger, or more important that existed in the past but does not exist now: *These old buildings are the* ***last*** *vestiges* ***of*** *a colonial past.* ◦ *There is now no vestige* ***of*** *hope that the missing children will be found alive.*

vestigial /vesˈtɪdʒ.i.əl/ adj **1** [before noun] being a small remaining part or amount **2** specialized describes something, especially a part of the body, that has not developed completely, or has stopped being used and has almost disappeared: *a vestigial organ/limb/tail* • **vestigially** /-i/ adv

V

vestments /ˈvest.mənts/ **noun** [plural] the special clothes worn by priests during church ceremonies

vestry /ˈves.tri/ **noun** [C] (also **sacristy**) a room in a church, especially one in which priests and the group of people who sing in church put on the special clothes they wear for church ceremonies, and in which things used in church ceremonies are sometimes kept

vet /vet/ **noun; verb**

▸**noun** [C] **ANIMAL DOCTOR** ▷ **1** B1 (UK formal **veterinary surgeon**, US formal **veterinarian**) a person with a medical degree trained to take care of the health of animals: *The farmer called the vet out to treat a sick cow.* **2** (UK also **vet's**) the office where a vet works: *We took our cat to the vet's for its annual cat flu injection.* **ARMED FORCES** ▷ **3** US informal for **veteran** (= a person who has served in the armed forces)

▸**verb** [T] (**-tt-**) to examine something or someone carefully to make certain that they are acceptable or suitable: *During the war, the government vetted all news reports before they were published.* ◦ *The bank carefully vets everyone who applies for an account.*

veteran /ˈvet.ər.ən/ US /ˈve.t̬ɚ-/ **noun; adj**

▸**noun** [C] **1** C2 a person who has had a lot of experience of a particular activity: *a 20-year veteran **of** the New York Police Department* **2** C2 (US informal **vet**) someone who has been in the armed forces during a war: *a Vietnam veteran* ◦ *the surviving veterans **of** World War II*

▸**adj** [before noun] having been involved in a particular activity for a long time: *She's also a veteran campaigner for human rights.*

ˌ**veteran ˈcar** **noun** [C] UK a car made before 1919 or (sometimes) 1905 → Compare **classic car, vintage car**

ˈ**Veterans ˌDay** **noun** [C or U] a legal holiday on 11 November in the US and Canada, when people honour members of their countries' armed forces who have fought in wars

veterinarian /ˌvet.ər.ɪˈneə.ri.ən/ US /-ˈner.i-/ **noun** [C] US formal for **vet**

veterinary /ˈvet.ər.ɪ.nər.i/ US /-ner-/ **adj** [before noun] connected with taking care of the health of animals: *veterinary medicine*

ˌ**veterinary ˈsurgeon** **noun** [C] UK formal for **vet**

veto /ˈviː.təʊ/ US /-t̬oʊ/ **noun; verb**

▸**noun** [C or U] (plural **vetoes**) an official power or right to refuse to accept or allow something: *The Ministry of Defence has the power of veto **over** all British arms exports.* ◦ *The Senate voted to override the president's veto **of** the proposed measures.* ◦ mainly UK *Mum has **put** a veto **on** our watching television for more than two hours an evening.*

▸**verb** [T] to refuse to allow something: *In 1961, President De Gaulle vetoed Britain's entry into the Common Market.* ◦ [+ -ing verb] *My boss vetoed my tak**ing** any more time off this year.*

V

vex /veks/ **verb** [T] old-fashioned to cause difficulty to someone, or to cause someone to feel angry, annoyed, or upset: *This issue looks likely to continue to vex the government.*

vexation /vekˈseɪ.ʃən/ **noun** old-fashioned **1** [U] worry or anger: *After several unsuccessful attempts to start his car, he swore in vexation.* **2** [C] something that is worrying or annoying

vexatious /vekˈseɪ.ʃəs/ **adj** old-fashioned difficult to deal with and causing a lot of anger, worry, or argument: *This settlement will resolve one of the most vexatious (= difficult) problems in the field of industrial relations.* • **vexatiously** /-li/ **adv**

vexed /vekst/ **adj** [before noun] difficult to deal with and causing a lot of disagreement and argument: *The government has to deal with the vexed **question** of how to reduce spending.*

VHF /ˌviː.eɪtʃˈef/ **noun** [U] abbreviation for very high frequency: radio waves between 30 to 300 MHz: *a VHF radio/transmitter/frequency* → Compare **UHF**

via /ˈvaɪə/, /ˈviː.ə/ **preposition** **JOURNEY** ▷ **1** B1 going through or stopping at a place on the way to another place: *The London-Addis flight goes via Rome.* **USING** ▷ **2** B1 using a particular machine, system, or person to send or receive something: *Reports are coming in via satellite.* ◦ *I only found out about it via my sister.*

viability /ˌvaɪ.əˈbɪl.ɪ.ti/ US /-ə.t̬i/ **noun** [U] **1** ability to work as intended or to succeed: *Rising costs are threatening the viability **of** many businesses.* **2** specialized ability to continue to exist or develop as a living being: *As the world population of Hawaiian geese has shrunk to very small numbers, the bird's continuing viability is in doubt.*

viable /ˈvaɪ.ə.bl̩/ **adj** **1** C2 able to work as intended or able to succeed: *In order to make the company viable, it will unfortunately be necessary to reduce staffing levels.* ◦ *I am afraid your plan is not commercially/economically/financially/politically viable.* **2** specialized able to continue to exist as or develop into a living being: *There is a continuing debate about the age at which a human foetus can be considered viable.* • **viably** /-bli/ **adv**

viaduct

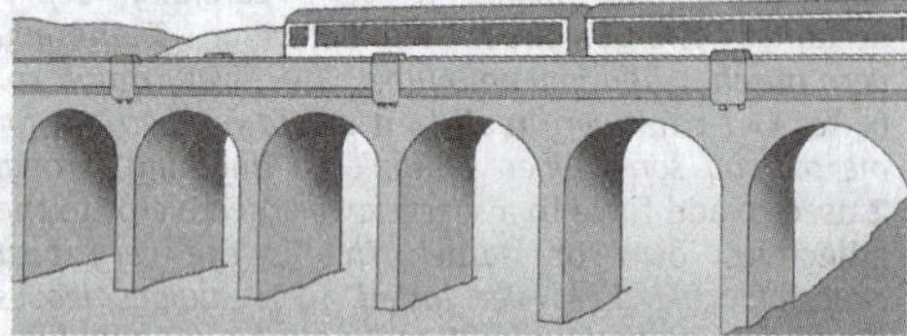

viaduct /ˈvaɪə.dʌkt/ **noun** [C] a long, high bridge, usually held up by many ARCHES, which carries a railway or a road over a valley: *a railway viaduct*

Viagra /vaɪˈæg.rə/ **noun** [U] trademark a drug for treating men who are IMPOTENT (= who cannot have sex because their PENIS cannot become or stay hard)

vial /vaɪl/ **noun** [C] a **phial**

vibe /vaɪb/ **noun** **1** [S] the mood or character of a place, situation, or piece of music: *The music has a soothing vibe.* **2** **vibes** [plural] **a** informal the general mood a person or place seems to have and the way they make you feel: *I didn't like the place – it had bad vibes.* **b** informal for **vibraphone**

vibrant /ˈvaɪ.brənt/ **adj** **1** energetic, exciting, and full of enthusiasm: *a vibrant young performer* ◦ *a vibrant personality* ◦ *a vibrant city* ◦ *The hope is that this area will develop into a vibrant commercial centre.* **2** describes colour or light that is bright and strong: *He always uses vibrant colours in his paintings.* • **vibrancy** /-si/ **noun** [U] *No one can fail to be struck by the vibrancy **of** New York.* • **vibrantly** /-li/ **adv**

vibraphone /ˈvaɪ.brə.fəʊn/ US /-foʊn/ **noun** [C] (informal **vibes**) a musical instrument consisting of a set of metal bars in a frame that have electrical devices fixed to them so that when they are hit they produce notes which shake slightly

vibrate /vaɪˈbreɪt/ US /ˈvaɪ.breɪt/ **verb** [I or T] to shake slightly and quickly, or to cause something to do this, in a way that is felt rather than seen or heard: *The whole station seemed to vibrate as the express train rushed through.* ◦ *His voice vibrated **with** anger.*

vibration /vaɪˈbreɪ.ʃᵊn/ **noun** [C or U] continuous quick, slight shaking movement: *Vibrations were felt hundreds of miles from the centre of the earthquake.* ◦ *Aircraft manufacturers want to reduce vibration for the sake of safety.*

vibrato /vɪˈbrɑː.təʊ/ (US) /-t̬oʊ/ **noun** [C or U] (plural **vibratos**) specialized a repeated slight shaking in a musical note, either when played on an instrument or sung, which gives a fuller sound to the note: *He sang the aria with a rich vibrato.* → Compare **tremolo**

vibrator /vaɪˈbreɪ.təʳ/ (US) /-t̬ɚ/ **noun** [C] a device that shakes slightly and quickly, held against the body to give sexual pleasure

vicar /ˈvɪk.əʳ/ (US) /-ɚ/ **noun** [C] a priest in the Church of England who is in charge of a church and the religious needs of people in a particular area: *We were married by our local vicar.* ◦ [as form of address] *Good evening, Vicar!*

vicarage /ˈvɪk.ᵊr.ɪdʒ/ (US) /-ɚ-/ **noun** [C] the house in which a vicar lives

vicarious /vɪˈkeə.ri.əs/ (US) /-ˈker.i-/ **adj** [before noun] experienced as a result of watching, listening to, or reading about the activities of other people, rather than by doing the activities yourself: *They get a vicarious thrill from watching motor racing.* • **vicariously** /-li/ **adv** *Through her letters we were able vicariously to experience her excitement.* • **vicariousness** /-nəs/ **noun** [U]

ˌVicar of ˈChrist **noun** [S] a title sometimes given to the POPE (= the leader of the Catholic Church)

vice /vaɪs/ **prefix; noun**

▸**prefix** (also **vice-**) used as part of the title of particular positions. The person who holds one of these positions is next below in authority to the person who holds the full position and can act for them: *the vice captain of the team* ◦ *a vice admiral*

▸**noun** FAULT ▷ **1** (C2) [C or U] a moral fault or weakness in someone's character: *Greed, pride, envy, and lust are considered to be vices.* ◦ mainly humorous *My one real vice (= bad habit) is chocolate.* **2** [U] illegal and IMMORAL activities, especially involving illegal sex, drugs, etc.: *The chief of police said that he was committed to wiping out vice in the city.* TOOL ▷ **3** mainly UK (US usually **vise**) [C] a tool with two parts that can be moved together by tightening a SCREW so that an object can be held firmly between them while it is being worked on: *Vices are often used to hold pieces of wood that are being cut or smoothed.* ◦ *Her hand tightened like a vice around his arm.*

ˌvice ˈchancellor **noun** [C] **1** UK the person in charge of a British college or university **2** US the person in charge of some parts of a college or university in the US

ˈvice-like **adj** (US usually **viselike**) very tight: *He holds his tennis racket **in/with** a vice-like **grip**.*

ˌvice ˈpresident **noun** [C] **1** (US abbreviation **VP**, US informal **veep**) the person who has the position immediately below the president in some countries, and who is responsible for the president's duties if he or she is unable to do them: *Vice President Cheney* **2** US the person who is responsible for a large, important part of a company or organization: *She's vice president of sales and marketing.*

ˈvice ˌring **noun** [C, + sing/pl verb] a group of people involved in IMMORAL illegal activities, especially illegal sex or drugs

viceroy /ˈvaɪs.rɔɪ/ **noun** [C] someone who represents a king or queen and rules for him or her in another country: *the viceroy of India*

ˈvice ˌsquad **noun** [C, + sing/pl verb] a special group of police officers whose job is to stop crimes that involve sex and drugs

vice versa /ˌvaɪsˈvɜː.sə/ (US) /ˌvaɪ.səˈvɝː-/ **adv** (C1) used to say that what you have just said is also true in the opposite order: *He doesn't trust her, and vice versa (= she also doesn't trust him).*

vichyssoise /ˌviː.ʃiˈswɑːz/ **noun** [C or U] a soup made with potatoes, LEEKS, and cream, often eaten cold

vicinity /vɪˈsɪn.ɪ.ti/ (US) /vəˈsɪn.ə.t̬i/ **noun** [S] (C2) the immediately surrounding area: *There are several hotels **in the immediate** vicinity **of** the station.*

IDIOM **in the vicinity of** approximately: *The team is believed to have paid in the vicinity of £3 million for Domingo.*

vicious /ˈvɪʃ.əs/ **adj** **1** (C2) describes people or actions that show an intention or wish to hurt someone or something very badly: *a vicious thug* ◦ *a vicious dog* ◦ *The police said that this was one of the most vicious attacks they'd ever seen.* ◦ *He gave her a vicious look.* **2** (C2) describes an object, condition, or remark that causes great physical or emotional pain: *a large collection of vicious medieval torture instruments* ◦ *I've got a vicious headache.* ◦ *Make sure you wrap up warmly – there's a vicious (= extremely strong and unpleasant) wind out there.* ◦ *a vicious lie/accusation/rumour* • **viciously** /-li/ **adv** • **viciousness** /-nəs/ **noun** [U]

ˌvicious ˈcircle **noun** [S] a continuing unpleasant situation, created when one problem causes another problem which then makes the first problem worse: *Many people get **caught/trapped in** a vicious circle of dieting and weight gain.*

vicissitudes /vɪˈsɪs.ɪ.tjuːdz/ (US) /-tuːdz/ **noun** [plural] formal changes which happen at different times during the life or development of someone or something, especially those which result in conditions being worse: *Losing your job is just one of the vicissitudes **of** life.*

victim /ˈvɪk.tɪm/ **noun** [C] **1** (B2) someone or something that has been hurt, damaged, or killed or has suffered, either because of the actions of someone or something else, or because of illness or chance: *to provide financial aid to hurricane/flood, etc. victims* ◦ *victims of crime* ◦ *The children are the innocent/helpless victims **of** the fighting.* ◦ *The new drug might help save the lives of cancer victims.* ◦ *We appear to have been the victims **of** a cruel practical joke.* ◦ *Our local hospital has become the latest victim **of** the cuts in government spending.* **2** **fall victim to sth** to be hurt, damaged, or killed because of something or someone: *In 1948, Gandhi fell victim to a member of a Hindu gang.* ◦ *The company has fallen victim to increased competition.*

IDIOM **be a victim of your own success** to have problems because of your success: *The school has become a victim of its own success as parents with children who have special needs now actively seek it out.*

victimize (UK usually **victimise**) /ˈvɪk.tɪ.maɪz/ **verb** [T] to treat someone in an intentionally unfair way, especially because of their race, sex, or beliefs: *He claimed he'd been victimized by the police.* ◦ *Nixon felt that he was being victimized by the media.* • **victimization** (UK usually **victimisation**) /ˌvɪk.tɪ.maɪˈzeɪ.ʃᵊn/ **noun** [U]

victimless /ˈvɪk.tɪm.ləs/ **adj** In a victimless crime no one suffers directly, sometimes because the people affected by the crime have agreed to take part in it:

Stock market fraud is sometimes regarded as a victimless crime.

ˌvictim supˈport noun [U] UK the act of providing emotional and practical help for people who suffer because of a crime, or an organization that provides this: *a victim support group/scheme* ◦ *The police put me in touch with Victim Support.*

victor /ˈvɪk.təʳ/ (US) /-tɚ/ noun [C] the winner of a game, competition, election, war, etc.: *The victor* ***in/of*** *the 1960 US presidential election was John F. Kennedy.*

Victorian /vɪkˈtɔː.ri.ən/ (US) /-ˈtɔːr.i-/ adj; noun

▸adj **HISTORY** ▷ **1** belonging to, made in, or living in the time when Queen Victoria was queen of the UK (1837–1901): *a Victorian terraced house* ◦ *Charles Dickens is one of the best-known Victorian novelists.* **2** Victorian ideas, beliefs, etc. are ones considered to be typical of the time when Queen Victoria was queen, such as a belief in strict moral and religious rules and in the importance of family life: *Victorian values*

▸noun [C] a person who was alive while Queen Victoria was queen

victorious /vɪkˈtɔː.ri.əs/ (US) /-ˈtɔːr.i-/ adj having won a game, competition, election, war, etc.: *The victorious team were loudly cheered by their fans.* ◦ *The German player* ***emerged*** *victorious after a long five-hour match.* • **victoriously** /-li/ adv

victory /ˈvɪk.tᵊr.i/ (US) /-tɚ-/ noun [C or U] (B2) an occasion when you win a game, competition, election, war, etc. or the fact that you have won: *The Redskins opened the season by* ***scoring*** *a resounding/stunning/impressive 25–3 victory* ***against/over*** *Detroit.* ◦ *Grant* ***won/achieved/gained*** *a comfortable/easy victory* ***against/over*** *Cooper in yesterday's match.* ◦ *This result is a triumphant victory* ***for*** *democracy.* → See also **Pyrrhic victory** → Opposite **defeat**

IDIOM **be a victory for common sense** to be a very reasonable result in a particular situation: *There is no doubt that the court's decision is a victory for common sense.*

victuals /ˈvɪt.ᵊlz/ (US) /ˈvɪt̬-/ noun [plural] old-fashioned or humorous food and drink: *'I can't bear to see good victuals wasted,' said Martha.*

vide /ˈvaɪ.di/ verb [T] (abbreviation **v.**) see; used as a written instruction to tell a reader to look at a particular book, page, etc. for more information

video /ˈvɪd.i.əʊ/ (US) /-oʊ/ noun; adj; verb

▸noun (plural **videos**) **FILM** ▷ **1** (A2) [U or C] a recording of moving pictures and sound, especially as a DIGITAL file, DVD, etc.: *My new laptop handles video really well.* ◦ *People can upload videos of their pets to this website.* ◦ *'Avatar' is now available* ***on*** *video.* → See also **tape** **2** (A2) [C] (also **music video**) a short film made to advertise a popular song **MACHINE** ▷ **3** [C] UK for **videocassette recorder**

▸adj **1** using video: *a video recording* **2** specialized connected with or used in the showing of moving pictures by television: *video frequencies*

▸verb [T] (also **tape**) to record a programme from the television, or to use a video camera to film an event: *There's a play on TV tonight that I'd like to video.* ◦ *We videoed the school concert.*

ˈvideo ˌcamera noun [C] a camera that records moving pictures and sound either as a DIGITAL file or, especially in the past, onto special TAPE: *Many shops have video cameras fixed to their walls or ceilings for security reasons.* → Compare **camcorder**

ˈvideo ˌcard noun [C] a CIRCUIT BOARD (= small piece of electronic equipment) inside a computer that allows it to receive and show moving images

videocassette /ˌvɪd.i.əʊ.kəˈset/ (US) /-oʊ.kəˈset/ noun [C] a recording of moving pictures and sound on a long, narrow strip of MAGNETIC material inside a plastic box, that can be played on a special machine

ˌvideocasˈsette reˌcorder noun [C] (also **VCR**) a machine used to record and play television programmes or films on videocassettes

ˈvideo ˌclip noun [C] (B1) a short video: *Video clips from a security camera showed the men breaking into the store.*

ˈvideo ˌconferencing noun [U] a system which allows two or more people who are in different parts of the world to talk to each other and see each other on television screens

ˈvideo ˌgame noun [C] (A2) a game in which the player controls moving pictures on a screen by pressing buttons

ˈvideo ˌmonitor noun [C] US a device with a screen on which moving pictures can be shown

videophone /ˈvɪd.i.əʊ.fəʊn/ (US) /-oʊ.foʊn/ noun [C] a mobile phone that can record moving pictures

ˈvideo reˌcorder noun [C] a **videocassette recorder**

videotape /ˈvɪd.i.əʊ.teɪp/ (US) /-oʊ-/ noun; verb

▸noun **1** [U] special MAGNETIC TAPE used for recording moving pictures and sounds: *They had captured the whole thing* ***on*** *videotape.* **2** [C] a **videocassette**

▸verb [T] to record a film, television programme, or event on videotape

vie /vaɪ/ verb [I] (present tense **vying**, past tense and past participle **vied**) to compete with other people to achieve or get something: *Six candidates are currently vying* ***for*** *the Democratic presidential nomination.* ◦ *The two older children tend to vie* ***with*** *the younger one* ***for*** *their mother's attention.* ◦ [+ to infinitive] *The two groups of scientists are vying* ***to*** *get funding for their research projects.*

view /vjuː/ noun; verb

▸noun **OPINION** ▷ **1** (B1) [C] an opinion, belief or idea, or a way of thinking about something: *Do you have any views* ***about/on*** *what we should do now?* ◦ ***In*** *my view, her criticisms were completely justified.* ◦ [+ that] *It's my view* ***that*** *the price is much too high.* ◦ *Many people* ***have/hold/share/take*** *the view* ***that*** *children should not be smacked.* ◦ *Everyone will have a chance to* ***make*** *their views* ***known*** *at the meeting.* ◦ *We had a friendly* ***exchange of*** *views (= discussion).* ◦ *I* ***take*** *a very* ***dim/poor*** *view* ***of*** *this kind of behaviour (= think that this type of behaviour is unacceptable).* **2 world view** a way of thinking about the world: *Our world view is quite different from that of writers in the fourth century BC.* **SIGHT** ▷ **3** (A2) [C or U] what you can see from a particular place, or the ability to see from a particular place: *The view* ***from*** *the top of the mountain is breathtaking/magnificent/spectacular.* ◦ *The rooftop restaurant* ***affords*** *a panoramic view (= allows you to see a wide area) across the bay.* ◦ *Don't stand in front of me – you're* ***blocking/obstructing*** *my view* ***of*** *the stage.* ◦ *The cloud lifted, and the tops of the mountains suddenly* ***came into*** *view (= could be seen).* ◦ *She turned a corner, and disappeared* ***from*** *view/****out of*** *view.* **4** [C] a picture of a particular place: *He paints rural views (= pictures of the countryside).* **5 in view** UK close enough to be seen: *I always make sure I keep the children in view whenever we're in a public place.* **6 on view** If something is on view, it is arranged so that it can be seen by the public: *The plans for the new road will soon be on view* ***to*** *the public in the library.*

IDIOMS **in view of sth** B2 because of a particular thing, or considering a particular fact: *In view of what you've said, I think we should reconsider our proposed course of action.* • **with a view to doing sth** C1 with the aim of doing something: *These measures have been taken with a view to increasing the company's profits.*

▸verb HAVE OPINION ▷ **1** C2 [T] to have a particular opinion or way of thinking about someone or something: *The journalist asked the minister how he viewed recent events.* ◦ *She is viewed **as** a strong candidate for the job.* ◦ *We view these latest developments **with** concern/suspicion/satisfaction.* ◦ *If we view the problem **from** a different **angle**, a solution may become more obvious.* ◦ *How do you view your prospects/chances (= what do you consider your chances to be) in tomorrow's race?* SEE ▷ **2** C2 [I or T] to watch something: *There's a special area at the airport where you can view aircraft taking off and landing.* ◦ *Viewing **figures** (= the number of people watching programmes) for the show were very low.* **3** [I or T] to look at something in a complete or careful way: *I haven't had a chance to actually view the house yet.* ◦ *The extent of the flooding can only be fully appreciated when viewed from the air.*

viewer /ˈvjuː.əʳ/ US /-ɚ/ noun [C] **1** B2 a person who watches something, especially television: *Millions of viewers will be glued to their sets for this match.* **2** a device for looking at SLIDES (= photographs on small pieces of film)

viewfinder /ˈvjuːˌfaɪn.dəʳ/ US /-dɚ/ noun [C] the part of a camera that you look through to see what it is that you are taking a photograph of

viewing /ˈvjuː.ɪŋ/ noun [C] (UK also **view**) an occasion for a special look at an EXHIBITION, film, etc.: *We've been invited to a **private** viewing, before the exhibition opens.*

viewpoint /ˈvjuː.pɔɪnt/ noun [C] SIGHT ▷ **1** UK (US **overlook**) a place from where a person can look at something, especially at an area of natural beauty: *The viewpoint by the side of the road gave us a stunning panorama of the whole valley.* OPINION ▷ **2** C1 a **point of view**

vigil /ˈvɪdʒ.ɪl/ noun [C or U] (an act of) staying awake, especially at night, in order to be with an ill person, or to express especially political disagreement, or to pray: *His parents **kept** vigil beside his bed for weeks before he died.* ◦ *Supporters of the peace movement **held** an all-night candlelit vigil outside the cathedral.*

vigilance /ˈvɪdʒ.ɪ.ləns/ noun [U] more careful attention, especially in order to notice possible danger: *The police said that it was thanks to the vigilance **of** a neighbour that the fire was discovered before it could spread.*

vigilant /ˈvɪdʒ.ɪ.lənt/ adj always being careful to notice things, especially possible danger: *Following the bomb scare at the airport, the staff have been warned to be extra vigilant.* • **vigilantly** /-li/ adv

vigilante /ˌvɪdʒ.ɪˈlæn.ti/ US /-ˈlæn.t̬i/ noun [C] a person who tries in an unofficial way to prevent crime, or to catch and punish someone who has committed a crime, especially because they do not think that official organizations, such as the police, are controlling crime effectively. Vigilantes usually join together to form groups. • **vigilantism** /-tɪ.zᵊm/ US /-t̬ɪ.zᵊm/ noun [U]

vignette /vɪˈnjet/ noun [C] a short piece of writing, music, acting, etc. which clearly expresses the typical characteristics of something or someone: *She wrote several vignettes **of** small-town life.*

vigorous /ˈvɪg.ᵊr.əs/ US /-ɚ-/ adj **1** very forceful or energetic: *a vigorous debate* ◦ *There has been vigorous opposition to the proposals for a new road.* ◦ *He takes plenty of vigorous exercise.* **2** healthy and strong: *Cutting the bush back in the autumn will help promote vigorous growth in the spring.* • **vigorously** /-li/ adv

vigour UK (US **vigor**) /ˈvɪg.əʳ/ US /-ɚ/ noun [U] **1** strength, energy, or enthusiasm: *They set about their work **with** youthful vigour and enthusiasm.* **2** strength of thought, opinion, expression, etc.: *His book is written **with** considerable vigour.*

Viking /ˈvaɪ.kɪŋ/ noun [C] a person belonging to a race of Scandinavian people who travelled by sea and attacked parts of northern and southern Europe between the 8th and the 11th centuries, often staying to live in places they travelled to

vile /vaɪl/ adj **1** unpleasant, IMMORAL, and unacceptable: *This vile policy of ethnic cleansing must be stopped.* **2** informal extremely unpleasant: *This cheese smells vile.* ◦ *He's in a vile mood/temper today.* • **vilely** /ˈvaɪl.li/ adv • **vileness** /ˈvaɪl.nəs/ noun [U]

vilify /ˈvɪl.ɪ.faɪ/ verb [T] formal to say or write unpleasant things about someone or something, in order to cause other people to have a bad opinion of them: *He was vilified by the press **as** a monster of perversity.* • **vilification** /ˌvɪl.ɪ.fɪˈkeɪ.ʃᵊn/ noun [U]

villa /ˈvɪl.ə/ noun [C] a house, usually in the countryside or near the sea, especially in southern Europe, and often one which people can rent for a holiday

village /ˈvɪl.ɪdʒ/ noun **1** A1 [C] a group of houses and other buildings that is smaller than a town, usually in the countryside: *a fishing village* ◦ *a mountain village* ◦ *a village shop* ◦ *a village green (= an area of grass in the middle of a village)* ◦ *Many people come from the outlying/surrounding villages to work in the town.* **2** [C usually singular, + sing/pl verb] all the people who live in a village: *The village is/are campaigning for a by-pass to be built.*

villager /ˈvɪl.ɪ.dʒəʳ/ US /-dʒɚ/ noun [C] C2 a person who lives in a village

villain /ˈvɪl.ən/ noun **1** [C] a bad person who harms other people or breaks the law: *Some people believe that Richard III was not the villain he is generally thought to have been.* ◦ *He's either a hero or a villain, depending on your point of view.* **2** [C] UK informal a criminal: *Bert's just a small-time villain.* **3** [C] a character in a book, play, film, etc. who harms other people: *He made his reputation as an actor playing villains.* **4** [C usually singular] informal something or someone considered harmful or dangerous: *We've always been told that cholesterol was a major cause of heart disease but, actually, saturated fat is the worst villain.*

IDIOM **villain of the piece** informal The villain of the piece is someone or something that is seen as being the cause of trouble on a particular occasion.

villainous /ˈvɪl.ə.nəs/ adj [before noun] describes a person or an action that is evil: *a villainous dictator* • **villainy** /-ni/ noun [U]

villus /ˈvɪl.əs/ noun [C usually plural] (plural **villi** /ˈvɪl.aɪ/) specialized one of many very small finger-like parts on the inside surface of the SMALL INTESTINE (= part of body where food goes after the stomach), which help food to be absorbed

vim /vɪm/ noun [U] old-fashioned energy and enthusiasm: *At 87, Minna's still full of vim **and vigour**.*

vinaigrette /ˌvɪn.ɪˈgret/ noun [U] (UK also ˌ**French**

'**dressing**) a cold sauce made from oil and VINEGAR, used especially on salad

vindicate /ˈvɪn.dɪ.keɪt/ **verb** [T] **1** to prove that what someone said or did was right or true, after other people thought it was wrong: *The decision to include Morris in the team was completely vindicated when he scored three goals.* ◦ *The investigation vindicated her complaint about the newspaper.* **2** to prove that someone is not guilty or is free from blame, after other people blamed them: *They said they welcomed the trial as a chance to vindicate themselves.* • **vindication** /ˌvɪn.dɪˈkeɪ.ʃən/ **noun** [S or U] *The army's victory is being seen as (a) vindication* ***of*** *their tactics.*

vindictive /vɪnˈdɪk.tɪv/ **adj** disapproving having or showing a wish to harm someone because you think that they have harmed you; unwilling to forgive: *In the film 'Cape Fear', a lawyer's family is threatened by a vindictive former prisoner.* • **vindictively** /-li/ **adv** • **vindictiveness** /-nəs/ **noun** [U]

vine /vaɪn/ **noun** [C] **1** C1 (also **grapevine**) the climbing plant that produces GRAPES as its fruit → See also **vineyard** **2** any type of plant that climbs or grows along the ground and has twisting stems: *Ivy is a type of vine.*

vine

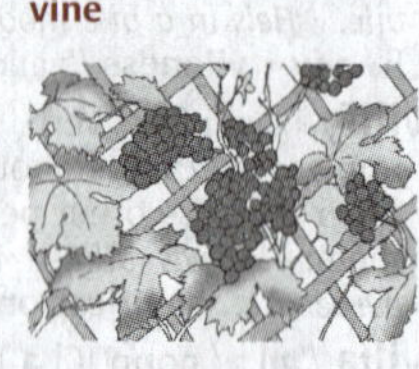

vinegar /ˈvɪn.ɪ.ɡəʳ/ (US) /-ɡɚ/ **noun** [U] B2 a sharp-tasting liquid, made especially from sour wine, MALT, or CIDER, that is used to add flavour to or to preserve food: *wine vinegar* ◦ *Would you like* ***oil and*** *vinegar on your salad?*

vinegary /ˈvɪn.ɪ.ɡər.i/ (US) /-ɡɚ-/ **adj** **1** tasting of vinegar **2** angry and unpleasant, or giving a lot of criticism

vineyard /ˈvɪn.jɑːd/ (US) /-jɚd/ **noun** [C] a piece of land on which vines are grown

vino /ˈviː.nəʊ/ (US) /-noʊ/ **noun** [U] informal for **wine**: *Would you like a drop more vino?*

vintage /ˈvɪn.tɪdʒ/ (US) /-t̬ɪdʒ/ **adj**; **noun**

▸**adj** HIGH QUALITY ▷ **1** of high quality and lasting value, or showing the best and most typical characteristics of a particular type of thing, especially from the past: *a vintage aircraft* ◦ *a vintage comic book* ◦ *This film is vintage (= has the best characteristics typical of films made by) Disney.* ◦ *She loves buying vintage clothing.* WINE ▷ **2** [before noun] describes wine of high quality that was made in a particular year and can be kept for several years in order to improve it: *vintage champagne/port/claret*

▸**noun** **1** [C] the wine made in a particular year, or a particular year in which wine has been made: *The 1983 vintage was one of the best.* ◦ *What vintage is this wine? (= In what year was it made?)* **2** [U] literary a group of things which were produced, or a group of people who were active, during the same particular period: *He is undoubtedly England's best captain* ***of recent*** *vintage.*

ˌvintage ˈcar **noun** [C] UK a car made between 1919 and 1930 → Compare **classic car, veteran car**

vintner /ˈvɪnt.nəʳ/ (US) /-nɚ/ **noun** [C] a person whose job it is to buy and sell wine

vinyl /ˈvaɪ.nəl/ **noun** [U] strong plastic that can be bent, used for making floor coverings, furniture, clothing, etc., or (in the past) records

viol /ˈvaɪəl/ **noun** [C] a wooden musical instrument with strings and FRETS, popular from the 15th to the 17th century. Viols are held vertically and played with a BOW, like a CELLO.

viola /viˈəʊ.lə/ (US) /viˈoʊ.lə/ **noun** [C] a wooden musical instrument with four strings, held against the shoulder and played by moving a BOW across the strings. It is slightly larger than the VIOLIN.

violate /ˈvaɪə.leɪt/ **verb** [T] **1** to break or act against something, especially a law, agreement, principle, or something that should be treated with respect: *They were charged with violating federal law.* ◦ *It seems that the planes deliberately violated the ceasefire agreement.* ◦ *The doctor has been accused of violating professional ethics.* **2** to go, especially forcefully, into a place or situation which should be treated with respect and in which you are not wanted or not expected to be: *The fishermen claimed that ships from another country had violated their territorial waters.* ◦ *Questions of this kind violate my privacy and I am not willing to answer them.* **3** formal to RAPE someone: *She said that she had been treated so roughly by the hospital staff that she felt violated.* • **violator** /-leɪ.təʳ/ (US) /-leɪ.t̬ɚ/ **noun** [C]

violation /ˌvaɪəˈleɪ.ʃən/ **noun** [C or U] an action that breaks or acts against something, especially a law, agreement, principle, or something that should be treated with respect: *He claimed that the way he'd been treated was a gross violation* ***of*** *his civil/constitutional/human rights.* ◦ *The takeover of the embassy constitutes a flagrant/blatant violation* ***of*** *international law.* ◦ *It was clear that they had not acted* ***in*** *violation* ***of*** *the rules.*

violence /ˈvaɪə.ləns/ **noun** [U] **1** B2 actions or words that are intended to hurt people: *It seems that the attack was a gratuitous/random/mindless* ***act of*** *violence.* ◦ *The recent* ***outbreak/eruption*** *of racial violence in the area is very troubling.* ◦ *The report documents the staggering amount of domestic violence* ***against*** *women.* **2** C2 extreme force: *We were all surprised at the violence* ***of*** *his anger/rage.* ◦ *The storm turned out to be one of unexpected violence.*

> **Word partners for violence**
>
> *erupt into/lead to/resort to/use* violence • *advocate/promote* violence • *condemn/renounce* violence • violence *breaks out/erupts/flares* • be *marred by* violence • the *amount/degree/level* of violence • *escalating/extreme/gratuitous/mindless* violence • violence *against/towards* sb

violent /ˈvaɪə.lənt/ **adj** CAUSING HURT ▷ **1** B2 using force to hurt or attack: *He shouts a lot but I don't think he's ever been physically violent towards her.* **2** B2 describes a situation or event in which people are hurt or killed: *a violent crime* ◦ *There was a violent clash/confrontation between rival supporters after the match.* ◦ *The more violent scenes in the film were cut when it was shown on television.* ◦ *Her family are still trying to come to terms with her violent* ***death*** *(= death caused suddenly and unexpectedly by the use of physical force, especially murder).* STRONG ▷ **3** C2 sudden and powerful: *He has a violent temper.* ◦ *violent thunderstorms* ◦ *The speaker launched into a violent attack on (= spoke forcefully against) the government's policies.* **4** [before noun] describes a colour that is extremely or unpleasantly bright: *She was wearing a violent pink sweater and orange trousers.*

violently /ˈvaɪə.lənt.li/ **adv** **1** B2 in a forceful way that causes people to be hurt: *He claimed to have been violently assaulted while in detention.* **2** strongly or extremely: *She violently disagreed with what we said.* ◦ *He was violently sick.*

Other ways of saying violent

If someone is angry and violent, you could describe that person as **aggressive**:

*She was very **aggressive** toward the TV reporters.*

Ferocious and **savage** both mean 'fierce and violent':

*a **ferocious/savage** dog*

Brutal can be used when someone is violent, cruel, and does not seem to have any feelings for people:

*He was jailed for the **brutal** crime.*

You could use **vicious** if someone is violent and seems to want to hurt someone very badly:

*It was a **vicious** crime.*

Bloody or **gory** can be used about things which are violent and involve a lot of blood:

*She refuses to watch **gory** horror movies.*

violet /ˈvaɪə.lət/ adj; noun
▸adj having a bluish-purple colour
▸noun [C] **PLANT** ▷ **1** [C] a small plant with pleasant-smelling purple, blue, or white flowers **COLOUR** ▷ **2** [U] a bluish-purple colour

violin /ˌvaɪəˈlɪn/ noun [C] A2 a wooden musical instrument with four strings that is held against the neck and played by moving a BOW across the strings

violinist /ˌvaɪəˈlɪn.ɪst/ noun [C] a person who plays a violin

violoncello /ˌvaɪə.lənˈtʃel.əʊ/ US /ˌviː.ə.lɑːnˈtʃe.loʊ/ noun [C] (plural **violoncellos**) formal a **cello**

VIP /ˌviː.aɪˈpiː/ noun [C] a very important person; a person who is treated better than ordinary people because they are famous or INFLUENTIAL (= having a lot of influence) in some way: *They were in the VIP **lounge** at the airport.* ◦ *We were given the full VIP **treatment**.*

viper /ˈvaɪ.pər/ US /-pɚ/ noun [C] **1** a small poisonous snake **2** literary a very unpleasant person who you cannot trust: *When I started my new job, I didn't realize that I was walking into **a nest of** vipers.*

virago /vɪˈrɑː.gəʊ/ US /-ˈgoʊ/ noun [C] (plural **viragos** or **viragoes**) old-fashioned a violent, unpleasant woman who shouts a lot

viral /ˈvaɪə.rəl/ US /ˈvaɪ-/ adj **DISEASE** ▷ **1** caused by a virus: *viral **infections*** **INTERNET** ▷ **2** used to describe something that quickly becomes very popular or well known by being published on the internet or sent from person to person by email, phone, etc.: *Here's a list of the top ten viral videos this week.* ◦ *Within days the film clip **went** viral.*

virgin /ˈvɜː.dʒɪn/ US /ˈvɝː-/ noun; adj
▸noun [C] **1** C2 someone who has never had sex: *She remained a virgin till she was over thirty.* ◦ *D'you think he's still a virgin?* **2** humorous a person with no experience of a particular activity
▸adj **NATURAL** ▷ **1** C2 describes a forest or an area of land that has not yet been CULTIVATED (= used to grow crops) or used by people: *The railway is being extended into areas of virgin **forest**.* **2** describes oil, especially OLIVE OIL, that is made directly from pressing the fruit, rather than by using heat: ***extra** virgin olive oil* **3** [before noun] literary pure and not spoiled, especially when describing something white: *a virgin sheet of paper (= one not written on)* **PERSON** ▷ **4** [before noun] never having had sex: *a virgin bride* • **virginal** /-dʒɪ.nəl/ adj *virginal innocence/modesty/purity* • **virginity** /vəˈdʒɪn.ɪ.ti/ US /vɚˈdʒɪn.ə.t̬i/ noun [U] *She **lost** her virginity at the age of 16 **to** the boy next door.*

IDIOM **virgin territory** a completely new area of activity: *The BBC is moving into virgin territory by producing comic programmes of this type.*

Virginia creeper /vəˌdʒɪn.jəˈkriː.pə/ US /vɚˌdʒɪn.jəˈkriː.pɚ/ noun [C or U] (US also **woodbine**) a VINE (= climbing plant) often grown on walls, the leaves of which become dark red in autumn

Virgo /ˈvɜː.gəʊ/ US /ˈvɝː.goʊ/ noun [C or U] (plural **Virgos**) the sixth sign of the ZODIAC, relating to the period 23 August to 22 September , represented by a young woman, or a person born during this period

Virgoan /vɜːˈgəʊ.ən/ US /vɝːˈgoʊ-/ noun [C], adj relating to, or (a person) born in, the period between 23 August and 22 September: *Perfectionism is a Virgoan trait.*

virile /ˈvɪr.aɪl/ US /-əl/ adj **MAN** ▷ **1** approving describes a man, especially a young man, full of sexual strength and energy in a way that is considered attractive: *She likes her men young and virile.* **POWER** ▷ **2** literary approving powerful, strong, and energetic: *In this role, Durante is able to give full expression to that wonderfully virile **voice**.*

virility /vɪˈrɪl.ɪ.ti/ US /vəˈrɪl.ə.t̬i/ noun [U] approving **MAN** ▷ **1** male sexual strength or qualities: *There was no doubting his virility.* **POWER** ▷ **2** strength or power: *a country's economic virility*

virology /vaɪəˈrɒl.ə.dʒi/ US /vaɪˈrɑː.lə-/ noun [U] the scientific study of viruses and the diseases that they cause

virtual /ˈvɜː.tju.əl/ US /ˈvɝː-/ adj **ALMOST** ▷ **1** C1 [before noun] almost a particular thing or quality: *Ten years of incompetent government had brought about the virtual collapse of the country's economy.* **COMPUTER** ▷ **2** B2 describes something that can be done or seen using a computer and therefore without going anywhere or talking to anyone: *virtual shopping*

virtually /ˈvɜː.tju.ə.li/ US /ˈvɝː-/ adv **ALMOST** ▷ **1** B2 almost: *Their twins are virtually identical.* ◦ *That wine stain on my shirt has virtually disappeared.* **BY COMPUTER** ▷ **2** B2 in a way that uses a computer to do or see something instead of someone going to a place or talking to a person: *Nowadays all these things can be experienced virtually.*

ˌvirtual ˈmemory noun [U] space that can be used on the HARD DRIVE of a computer to store information temporarily so that there is more memory available when it is needed by software such as a computer game → Compare **RAM, ROM**

ˌvirtual reˈality noun [U] B2 a set of images and sounds produced by a computer, which seem to represent a place or a situation that a person can take part in

virtue /ˈvɜː.tjuː/ US /ˈvɝː-/ noun **GOOD MORALS** ▷ **1** C2 [C or U] a good moral quality in a person, or the general quality of being morally good: *Patience is a virtue.* → Compare **vice** **ADVANTAGE** ▷ **2** C2 [C or U] an advantage or good thing: *It always looks odd to see an actress on TV **extolling** (= praising) the virtues **of** washing-up liquid.* ◦ *Would there be any virtue **in** taking an earlier train?* **BECAUSE OF** ▷ **3** **by virtue of** C2 formal because of; as a result of: *She succeeded by virtue of her tenacity rather than her talent.*

IDIOM **make a virtue (out) of sth** to use something, especially a bad situation, to your advantage: *I had a couple of months to spare between jobs so I thought I'd make a virtue of **necessity** by acquiring a few new skills.*

virtuoso /ˌvɜː.tjuˈəʊ.səʊ/ (US) /ˌvɝː.tʃuˈoʊ.soʊ/ **noun; adj**

▸**noun** [C] (plural **virtuosos** or **virtuosi**) a person who is extremely skilled at something, especially at playing an instrument or performing: *Famous mainly for his wonderful voice, Cole was also a virtuoso* ***on*** *the piano.*

▸**adj** [before noun] extremely skilled: *The Times critic described her dancing as 'a virtuoso* ***performance*** *of quite dazzling accomplishment'.* • **virtuosity** /ˌ-ˈɒs.ɪ.ti/ (US) /-ˈɑː.sə.t̬i/ **noun** [U] formal

virtuous /ˈvɜː.tju.əs/ (US) /ˈvɝː-/ **adj 1** having good moral qualities and behaviour: *He described them as a virtuous and hard-working people.* **2** disapproving describes a person who thinks himself or herself morally better than other people: *I'm convinced he only does that charity work so he can feel virtuous.* • **virtuously** /-li/ (US) /ˈvɝː-/ **adv**

virulence /ˈvɪr.ʊ.lᵊns/ **noun** [U] **1** the danger and speed of spreading of a disease: *The virulence of the disease is causing great concern in medical circles.* **2** formal very strong feelings of hating or opposing something or someone: *We are witnessing racism of a virulence that we haven't seen in Europe since the 1940s.*

virulent /ˈvɪr.ʊ.lᵊnt/ **adj 1** A virulent disease or poison is dangerous and spreads or affects people very quickly: *A particularly virulent* ***strain*** *of flu has recently claimed a number of lives in the US.* **2** formal full of hate and violent opposition: *She is a virulent* ***critic*** *of US foreign policy.*

virus /ˈvaɪə.rəs/ (US) /ˈvaɪ-/ **noun** [C] **DISEASE** ▷ **1** (B2) an extremely small piece of ORGANIC material which causes disease in humans, animals, and plants: *a chicken pox/flu/herpes/mumps virus* ◦ *Evidence suggested that the AIDS virus was* ***spreading*** *very quickly among the heterosexual community.* **2** (B2) a disease caused by a virus: *I don't know exactly what's wrong with her – I think it's some sort of virus.* **COMPUTER PROBLEM** ▷ **3** (B1) a computer program or part of a computer program that can make copies of itself and is intended to prevent the computer from working normally

> **Word partners for virus**
>
> a *deadly/killer/rare* virus • *contract/have/be infected with* a virus • *carry/transmit* a virus • a virus *attacks/causes* sth • the *spread/transmission* of a virus • a *strain* of a virus

visa /ˈviː.zə/ **noun** [C] (B1) an official mark made in a PASSPORT which allows you to enter or leave a particular country: *We travelled to Argentina* ***on*** *a tourist visa.*

visage /ˈvɪz.ɪdʒ/ **noun** [C] literary the face

vis-à-vis /ˌviːz.əˈviː/ **preposition** formal **1** in relation to: *I've got to speak to James Lewis vis-à-vis the arrangements for Thursday.* **2** in comparison with: *The decline in the power of local authorities vis-à-vis central government is worrying.*

viscera /ˈvɪs.ᵊr.ə/ (US) /-ɚ-/ **noun** [plural] specialized the large organs inside the body, including the heart, stomach, lungs, and INTESTINES

visceral /ˈvɪs.ᵊr.ᵊl/ (US) /-ɚ-/ **adj EMOTIONAL** ▷ **1** literary based on deep feeling and emotional reactions rather than on reason or thought: *visceral hatred/excitement* ◦ *His approach to acting is visceral rather than intellectual.* **BODY PARTS** ▷ **2** specialized relating to the large organs inside the body, including the heart, stomach, lungs, and INTESTINES

viscose /ˈvɪs.kəʊs/ (US) /-koʊs/ **noun** [U] a smooth material similar to SILK but made from CELLULOSE

viscount /ˈvaɪ.kaʊnt/ **noun** [C] (the title of) a British man of high social rank, between an EARL and a BARON

viscountess /ˌvaɪ.kaʊnˈtes/ **noun** [C] a woman who has the rank of viscount, or a woman who is married to a viscount

viscous /ˈvɪs.kəs/ **adj** specialized describes a liquid that is thick and sticky and does not flow easily • **viscosity** /vɪˈskɒs.ɪ.ti/ (US) /-ˈskɑː.sə.t̬i/ **noun** [U]

vise /vaɪs/ **noun** [C] US for **vice**

visibility /ˌvɪz.ɪˈbɪl.ɪ.ti/ (US) /-ə.t̬i/ **noun** [U] **1** how clearly objects can be seen, or how far you can see clearly, usually because of the weather conditions: *Mist is still causing* ***poor*** *visibility – down to five metres in parts of the southeast.* **2** the degree to which something is seen by the public: *The increasing visibility of the nation's poor and homeless has forced the government into taking action.*

visible /ˈvɪz.ɪ.bl̩/ **adj 1** (B2) able to be seen: *You should wear something light-coloured when you're cycling at night so that you're more visible.* ◦ *The writing on the tombstone was* ***barely*** *visible.* ◦ *There are few visible* ***signs*** *of the illness that kept her in hospital for so long.* ◦ *The comet should be visible* ***to the naked eye.*** **2** (C1) able or likely to attract public attention and be noticed: *In a very short period of time, she has become a* ***highly*** *visible national leader.*

visibly /ˈvɪz.ɪ.bli/ **adv** in a way that can be noticed; obviously: *The Princess, visibly moved, kept her head bowed during the ceremony.*

vision /ˈvɪʒ.ᵊn/ **noun MENTAL IMAGE** ▷ **1** (B2) [C] an idea or mental image of something: *We see in his novels his sinister, almost apocalyptic, vision* ***of*** *the future.* ◦ *Johnny was late home and, as usual, I* ***had*** *visions* ***of*** *him lying dead in some alley.* **2** [C] an experience in which you see things which do not exist physically, when your mind is affected powerfully by something such as deep religious thought or drugs or mental illness: *She* ***had*** *visions in which the angel Gabriel appeared to her.* **VIEW OF THE FUTURE** ▷ **3** (C1) [U] the ability to imagine how a country, society, industry, etc. could develop in the future and to plan in a suitable way: *He didn't have the mental agility or vision required for a senior politician.* ◦ *a person of great artistic vision* **ABILITY** ▷ **4** (B2) [U] the ability to see: *She has very little vision in her left eye.* **BEAUTIFUL SIGHT** ▷ **5** [S] literary or humorous (used when referring to a person) a beautiful and impressive sight: *And that vision* ***of loveliness*** *over there is my wife, Sandra.* ◦ *She emerged from the bedroom, a vision* ***in*** *cream silk.*

visionary /ˈvɪʒ.ᵊn.ri/ (US) /-er.i/ **noun; adj**

▸**noun** [C] **RELIGIOUS EXPERIENCE** ▷ **1** a person who has a religious or spiritual experience in which they see a holy person who is not living or they see a holy event that cannot be explained scientifically **VIEW OF THE FUTURE** ▷ **2** a person who has the ability to imagine how a country, society, industry, etc. will develop in the future and to plan in a suitable way

▸**adj VIEW OF THE FUTURE** ▷ **1** with the ability to imagine how a country, society, industry, etc. will develop in the future: *a visionary author* ◦ *visionary thinking* **RELIGIOUS EXPERIENCE** ▷ **2** relating to a religious vision

visit /ˈvɪz.ɪt/ **verb; noun**

▸**verb 1** (A1) [I or T] to go to a place in order to look at it, or to a person in order to spend time with them: *We visited a few galleries while we were in Prague.* ◦ *Will you visit me when I'm in hospital?* ◦ *When did you last visit the dentist/doctor?* **2** (A2) [T] to go to a website on the internet

PHRASAL VERBS **visit sth on/upon sb** old use or formal to cause damage to a place or to harm a person: *He left*

V

Common mistake: visit

Remember that when **visit** is a verb it is never followed by 'to'.
Don't say 'visit to someone/somewhere', say **visit someone/somewhere**:
~~I am pleased you decided to visit to my country.~~
I am pleased you decided to visit my country.

in 1983, horrified by the devastation that warfare and famine had visited on his homeland. • **visit with sb** US to spend time talking with or staying with someone you know: *I was hoping to visit with Katie while I was in town.*

▸**noun** [C] **1** (B1) an occasion when you visit a place or person: *We had a visit from the school inspector last week.* ◦ *I can't stop for a cup of tea – this is just a* ***flying*** (= *very short*) *visit.* **2 pay a visit** (B2) to visit a person or place, usually for a short time: *I think I'll pay a visit* ***to*** *the library while I'm in town.*

Word partners for visit noun

pay sb a visit • *have* a visit *from* sb • a *brief/fleeting/flying/whirlwind* visit • *frequent/occasional/rare/regular* visits • a visit *to* sth • *on* a visit

visitation /ˌvɪz.ɪˈteɪ.ʃᵊn/ **noun 1** [C] an official visit from someone important: humorous *We're awaiting a visitation from the inspector.* ◦ *In 1917 three shepherd children reported a visitation* ***from*** *the Virgin Mary.* **2** [U] US an arrangement in which a DIVORCED parent may spend time with the children he or she no longer lives with, at agreed times and under agreed conditions: *The mother agreed to visitation* ***rights*** *for the boys' father.* **3** [C] formal an event that is considered to be a message or a punishment from God

ˈvisiting ˌhours noun [plural] the times when you are allowed to go and spend time with someone who is in a hospital, prison, etc.: *Visiting hours are between 6 and 9 p.m.*

visitor /ˈvɪz.ɪ.təʳ/ (US) /-t̬ɚ/ **noun** [C] **1** (A2) someone who visits a person or place: *Ben, you've got some visitors to see you.* **2** someone who goes to a website on the internet

ˈvisitors' ˌbook noun [C] a book sometimes found in a hotel or a place of interest in which people who are visiting are asked to write their name, address, and anything they would like to say about their visit

visor /ˈvaɪ.zəʳ/ (US) /-zɚ/ **noun** [C] a part of a HELMET that can be pulled down to cover the face, or a curved piece of stiff material that is worn above the eyes to give protection from strong light from the sun

vista /ˈvɪs.tə/ **noun** [C] **1** literary a view, especially a beautiful view from a high position: *After a hard climb, we were rewarded by a picture-postcard vista* ***of*** *rolling hills under a deep blue summer sky.* **2** a possible future action or event that you can imagine: *As leader, he* ***opened up*** *exciting vistas of global cooperation.*

visual /ˈvɪʒ.u.əl/ **adj** (B2) relating to seeing: *visual stimulus/impact/abilities* → See also **VDU**

ˌvisual ˈaid noun [C] something that you are shown, such as a picture, film, or map, in order to help you understand or remember information

the ˌvisual ˈarts noun [plural] the arts of painting and SCULPTURE, rather than literature and music

visualize (UK usually **visualise**) /ˈvɪʒ.u.ᵊl.aɪz/ **verb** [T] to form a picture of someone or something in your mind, in order to imagine or remember them: *I was so surprised when he turned up – I'd visualized someone much older.* • **visualization** formal (UK usually **visualisation**) /ˌvɪʒ.u.ᵊl.aɪˈzeɪ.ʃᵊn/ **noun** [U]

visually /ˈvɪʒ.u.ə.li/ **adv** relating to seeing or appearance: *Guide dogs open up the lives of the blind or visually* ***impaired.*** ◦ *Books for children have to be visually very exciting.*

vital /ˈvaɪ.tᵊl/ (US) /-t̬ᵊl/ **adj** IMPORTANT ▷ **1** (B2) necessary for the success or continued existence of something; extremely important: *A strong opposition is vital* ***to*** *a healthy democracy.* ◦ *She had found out some information of vital* ***importance.*** ◦ *The kidney plays a vital* ***role/part*** *in the removal of waste products from the blood.* ◦ [+ that] ***It's*** *absolutely vital* ***that*** *you do exactly as I say.* ◦ [+ to infinitive] ***It*** *is vital* ***to*** *get medical supplies to the area as soon as possible.* LIVELY ▷ **2** formal approving energetic: *He had never felt so vital and full of life.* **3** formal relating to life • **vitally** /-i/ **adv** (C2) *It's not vitally* ***important*** *that we get extra funding for the project but it would help.*

vitality /vaɪˈtæl.ɪ.ti/ (US) /-ə.t̬i/ **noun** [U] approving (C2) energy and strength: *According to the packet, these vitamin pills will restore lost vitality.*

ˌvital ˈorgans noun [plural] the main organs inside the body, such as the heart, lungs, and brain, that are necessary for life

ˌvital staˈtistics noun [plural] OFFICIAL FACTS ▷ **1** a group of official facts which show such things as the number of births, deaths, and marriages in a particular country, area, etc. WOMAN'S BODY ▷ **2** UK old-fashioned humorous the measurements of a woman's breasts, waist, and hips

vitamin /ˈvɪt.ə.mɪn/ (US) /ˈvaɪ.t̬ə-/ **noun** [C] (B2) any of a group of natural substances that are necessary in small amounts for the growth and good health of the body: *a vitamin pill* ◦ *Oranges are full of vitamin C.*

ˌvitamin ˈA noun [U] (specialized **retinol**) a vitamin found in foods such as butter, egg YOLK, milk, and fish oils, or produced in the body from the CAROTENE in green vegetables with a lot of leaves or orange vegetables, important for normal growth, healthy skin, and the ability to see well, especially at night

ˌvitamin ˈB ˌcomplex noun [S, + sing/pl verb] a group of vitamins that dissolve in water and are found in food

ˌvitamin ˈC noun [U] (specialized **asˌcorbic ˈacid**) a vitamin found in foods such as CITRUS fruit, green vegetables with a lot of leaves, tomatoes, and potatoes, important for healthy bones, JOINTS, teeth, and GUMS (= the part of the mouth from which the teeth grow), and for fighting infection

ˌvitamin ˈD noun [U] any of a group of vitamins found in foods such as LIVER, some fish, and egg YOLK, important for healthy bones and teeth

ˌvitamin ˈE noun [U] (specialized **tocopherol**) a vitamin found in foods such as vegetable oils, whole grains, green vegetables with a lot of leaves, and fish, important for healthy blood and cells

ˌvitamin ˈK noun [U] a vitamin found in foods such as green vegetables with a lot of leaves, LIVER, vegetable oils, and egg YOLK, important for healthy blood

vitiate /ˈvɪʃ.i.eɪt/ **verb** [T] formal to destroy or damage something: *He said that American military power should never again be vitiated by political concerns.*

viticulture /ˈvɪt.ɪˌkʌl.tʃəʳ/ (US) /-t̬ɪˌkʌl.tʃɚ/ **noun** [U] specialized the growing of GRAPES, or the science or study of this

vitreous /ˈvɪt.ri.əs/ **adj** made of or similar to glass: *vitreous china/enamel*

ˈvitreous ˌhumour noun [U] specialized the thick,

V

clear liquid substance inside the eye between the LENS at the front and the RETINA at the back

vitriol /ˈvɪt.ri.əl/ noun [U] violent hate and anger expressed through severe criticism: *He is a writer who has often been criticized by the press but never before **with** such vitriol.* • **vitriolic** /ˌvɪt.riˈɒl.ɪk/ (US) /-ˈɑː.lɪk/ adj *He launched a vitriolic **attack** on the prime minister, accusing him of shielding corrupt friends.* • **vitriolically** /ˌvɪt.riˈɒl.ɪ.kəl.i/ (US) /-ˈɑː.lɪ-/ adv

vituperative /vaɪˈtjuː.pər.ə.tɪv/ (US) /-ˈtuː.pə.reɪ.t̬ɪv/ adj formal A vituperative spoken or written attack is full of angry criticism: *Miss Snowden yesterday launched a vituperative attack on her ex-boss and former lover.* • **vituperation** /vaɪˌtjuː.pərˈeɪ.ʃən/ (US) /-ˌtuː.pəˈreɪ-/ noun [U]

viva¹ /ˈvaɪ.və/ noun [C] (also **viva voce** /ˌvaɪ.vəˈvəʊ.si/ (US) /-ˈvoʊ-/) a spoken exam for a college qualification

viva² /ˈviː.və/ exclamation mainly US used to express approval or good wishes: *Throngs of his supporters were shouting 'Viva, Ollie, viva!'*

vivacious /vɪˈveɪ.ʃəs/ adj approving C2 A vivacious person, especially a woman or girl, is attractively energetic and enthusiastic: *He brought along his wife, a vivacious blonde, some 20 years his junior.* • **vivaciously** /-li/ adv • **vivacity** /vɪˈvæs.ɪ.ti/ (US) /-ə.t̬i/ noun [U]

vivid /ˈvɪv.ɪd/ adj **1** B2 Vivid descriptions, memories, etc. produce very clear, powerful, and detailed images in the mind: *He gave a very vivid and often shocking account/description of his time in prison.* ◦ *He's one of those people with a very vivid **imagination** – every time he hears a noise he's convinced it's someone breaking in.* **2** B2 very brightly coloured: *She was wearing a vivid pink shirt.* • **vividly** /-li/ adv B2 *I vividly remember my first day at school.* • **vividness** /-nəs/ noun [U]

viviparous /vɪˈvɪp.ər.əs/ (US) /-ɚ-/ adj specialized giving birth to young that have already developed inside the mother's body rather than producing eggs

vivisection /ˌvɪv.ɪˈsek.ʃən/ noun [U] the use of living animals in tests that are intended to increase human knowledge of human diseases and the effects of using particular drugs

vivisectionist /ˌvɪv.ɪˈsek.ʃən.ɪst/ noun [C] a person who is involved in or believes in the use of vivisection

vixen /ˈvɪk.sən/ noun [C] **1** a female FOX **2** old-fashioned an unpleasant woman

viz. /vɪz/ adv old-fashioned used, especially in written English, when you want to give more detail or be more exact about something you have just written: *We both shared the same ambition, viz., to make a lot of money and to retire at 40.*

vlog /vlɒg/ (US) /vlɑːg/ noun [C] a video BLOG: a record of your thoughts, opinions, or experiences that you film and publish on the internet → Compare **blog**

ˈV-neck noun [C] a V-shaped opening for your neck on a piece of clothing, or a piece of clothing with this opening: *I'm going to wear my black dress with the V-neck.* ◦ *a V-neck jumper* • **ˈV-necked** adj *a V-necked dress*

vocab /ˈvəʊ.kæb/ (US) /ˈvoʊ-/ noun [U] informal for **vocabulary**

vocabulary /vəˈkæb.jʊ.lər.i/ (US) /voʊˈkæb.jə.ler-/ noun **1** A2 [C] all the words known and used by a particular person: *a **wide/limited** vocabulary* ◦ *By the age of two a child will have a vocabulary of about two hundred words.* **2** C1 [C or U] all the words which exist in a particular language or subject: *Every week our French teacher gives us a list of vocabulary (= words) to learn.* ◦ *Computing, like any subject, has its own vocabulary.*

IDIOM **not be in sb's vocabulary** humorous You say that a particular quality is not in your vocabulary if you never show it or experience it: *Did you say 'tact'? The word isn't in his vocabulary!*

vocal /ˈvəʊ.kəl/ (US) /ˈvoʊ-/ adj; noun

▸adj **OF THE VOICE** ▷ **1** relating to or produced by the voice, either in singing or speaking: *a piece of vocal music* **OFTEN HEARD** ▷ **2** often expressing opinions and complaints in speech: *He had always been a very vocal **critic** of the president.* ◦ *During these years, suffrage demands by women became increasingly vocal.* • **vocally** /-i/ adv

▸noun [C usually plural] the singing in a piece of popular music: *The vocals are shared by two members of the band.* ◦ *Is that Tamsin Palmer **on** vocals (= singing)?*

ˈvocal ˌcords noun [plural] (also **ˈvocal ˌfolds**) a pair of folds at the upper end of the throat whose edges move quickly backwards and forwards and produce sound when air from the lungs moves over them

vocalist /ˈvəʊ.kəl.ɪst/ (US) /ˈvoʊ-/ noun [C] a person who sings, especially with a group who play popular music: *She won the Grammy Award for Best Female Vocalist.*

vocalize /ˈvəʊ.kə.laɪz/ (US) /ˈvoʊ-/ verb [T] to express feelings or ideas in words: *Most patients find it very difficult to vocalize feelings of shame.*

vocation /vəʊˈkeɪ.ʃən/ (US) /voʊ-/ noun [C or U] C2 a type of work that you feel you are suited to doing and to which you should give all your time and energy, or the feeling that a type of work suits you in this way: *I feel I've **found/missed** my true vocation.* ◦ *'We need teachers who regard their profession as a vocation, not just a job,' said the Minister.* ◦ *To work in medicine, you should **have** a vocation **for** it.*

vocational /vəʊˈkeɪ.ʃən.əl/ (US) /voʊ-/ adj C1 providing skills and education that prepare you for a job: *The Swedes regard vocational **training** as a part of a youngster's education.* • **vocationally** /-i/ adv

vociferous /vəˈsɪf.ər.əs/ (US) /-ɚ-/ adj Vociferous people express their opinions and complaints loudly and repeatedly in speech, and vociferous demands, etc. are made repeatedly and loudly: *Local activist groups have become increasingly vociferous as the volume of traffic passing through the village has grown.* ◦ *A vociferous **opponent** of gay rights, he is well-known for his right-wing views.* • **vociferously** /-li/ adv

VOD /ˌviː.əʊˈdiː/ (US) /-oʊ-/ noun [U] abbreviation for video on demand: a system for watching films or recorded programmes on the internet or television at any time

vodcast /ˈvɒd.kɑːst/ (US) /ˈvɑːd.kæst/ noun [C] a VIDEO stored in a DIGITAL form (= one that uses signals in the form of numbers) that you can DOWNLOAD from the internet and play on a computer or on an MP3 PLAYER → Compare **podcast**

vodka /ˈvɒd.kə/ (US) /ˈvɑːd-/ noun [C or U] a clear, strong alcoholic drink made especially from grain or potatoes: *'What would you like to drink?' 'Vodka and tonic please.'* ◦ *This is my third vodka (= glass of vodka).*

vogue /vəʊg/ (US) /voʊg/ noun [S or U] a fashion or general liking, especially one that is temporary: *In the 1920s, short hair for women became **the** vogue.* ◦ *The postwar vogue **for** tearing down buildings virtually destroyed the city's architecture.* ◦ *The short hemline is very much **in** vogue (= fashionable) this spring.* ◦ *'Community' is one of the vogue words of the new government.*

voice /vɔɪs/ noun; verb

▸noun **SOUNDS** ▷ **1** B1 [C] the sounds that are made when people speak or sing: *She **has** a loud/quiet/soft voice.* ◦ *a low-pitched/high-pitched voice* ◦ *a booming/breathy/clear/deep/fruity/gravelly/husky/squeaky voice* ◦ *a baritone/soprano singing voice* ◦ *You could tell from her voice that she wasn't pleased.* ◦ *'I don't know what you mean,' said Fran **in** a quavering voice.* ◦ *She **lowered** her voice to a whisper.* ◦ *You'll have to **raise** your voice (= speak louder) if you want to be heard in here.* ◦ *I've got a cold and I think I'm **losing** my voice (= becoming unable to speak).* ◦ *He's at that age when his voice is **breaking** (= changing from a boy's to a man's).* ◦ *She's done a lot of work with voice-**activated** computers.* **OPINION** ▷ **2** C2 [C often singular, U] (the right to) an expression of opinion: *There was only one dissenting voice during the discussion.* ◦ *Unfortunately a strike was the only way to **make** our voices **heard**.* ◦ *The committee represents **the** voice **of** the students.* ◦ *Developing countries are demanding a stronger voice (= right to express opinions) in the debate.* **3** C2 [S] an important quality or opinion which someone expresses, or the person who is able to express it: *She just won't listen to the voice **of reason**.* ◦ *I wouldn't work for Peter if I were you – this is the voice **of experience** talking!*

> **Word partners for voice noun**
>
> a *deep/gravelly/husky/low* voice • a *high-pitched/nasal/shrill/squeaky* voice • a *booming/loud* voice • *in* a [bored/stern/tender] voice • *drop/lower/raise* your voice • *lose* your voice • sb's voice *breaks/cracks/falters/quivers* • sb's *tone* of voice

IDIOMS **give voice to sth** to express your thoughts or feelings in words: *I always had doubts about the scheme but I never gave voice to them.* • **voice within you** your CONSCIENCE (= the part of you which tells you when you are doing something wrong): *Suddenly this voice within her told her to stop being so stupid.* • **with one voice** formal If a group of people express an opinion or decide something with one voice, they all agree: *The committee decided with one voice to accept the proposal.*

▸verb [T] **1** C2 to say what you think about a particular subject, especially to express a doubt, complaint, etc. that you have about it: *I have voiced my objections to the plan to management.* **2** specialized to produce a sound by making the VOCAL CORDS move very quickly several times

ˈvoice-ˌactivated adj Voice-activated machines, systems, etc. work when you speak instructions to them: *The phone has voice-activated dialling.*

ˈvoice ˌbox noun [C usually singular] a **larynx**

voiced /vɔɪst/ adj specialized (of a speech sound) produced by making the VOCAL CORDS move very quickly several times: *Most vowels in most languages are voiced.*

-voiced /-vɔɪst/ suffix having the type of voice mentioned: *my loud-voiced friend, Roz*

voiceless /ˈvɔɪs.ləs/ adj **1** literary describes a group of people who do not have the power or the legal right to express their opinions: *A committed socialist, he upheld the rights of the voiceless and the under-privileged.* **2** specialized (of a speech sound) produced without making the VOCAL CORDS move

voicemail /ˈvɔɪ.s.meɪl/ noun [C or U] a phone message recorded by someone when you do not answer their call, or a number of these messages

ˈvoice-over noun [C] on a television programme or film, the spoken words of a person that you cannot see: *Famous actors often provide voice-overs for adverts.*

ˌvoice recogˈnition noun [U] the ability of a computer or other machine to understand spoken instructions or to recognize who a human voice belongs to: *voice-recognition software/technology*

void /vɔɪd/ noun; adj; verb

▸noun **1** [C usually singular] a large hole or empty space: *She stood at the edge of the chasm and stared into the void.* ◦ *Before Einstein, space was regarded as a formless void.* **2** [S] a feeling of unhappiness because someone or something is missing: *They tried to describe their attempts to **fill** the void **left** by their son's death.*

▸adj **NOT ACCEPTABLE** ▷ **1** having no legal authority and therefore unacceptable: *The lawyers **declared** the contract (**null and**) void.* → See also **null and void** **WITHOUT** ▷ **2** **void of** literary without; lacking in: *He's completely void of charm so far as I can see.*

▸verb [T] to remove the legal force from something such as a legal agreement

voilà /ˌvwɑːˈlɑː/ exclamation used when showing to other people something that you have just made or got and are pleased with: *Corn tortillas can be cut into strips, fried until golden, and sprinkled with salt – voilà! tortilla chips.*

VoIP /vɔɪp/ noun [U] specialized abbreviation for Voice over Internet Protocol: TECHNOLOGY that allows people to make phone calls over the internet

vol. written abbreviation for **volume**

volatile /ˈvɒl.ə.taɪl/ US /ˈvɑː.lə.t̬əl/ adj **1** likely to change suddenly and unexpectedly or suddenly become violent or angry: *Food and fuel prices are very volatile in a war situation.* ◦ *The situation was made more volatile by the fact that people had been drinking a lot of alcohol.* ◦ *He had a rather volatile temper and can't have been easy to live with.* **2** A volatile liquid or solid substance will change easily into a gas. • **volatility** /ˌvɒl.əˈtɪl.ɪ.ti/ US /ˌvɑː.ləˈtɪl.ə.t̬i/ noun [U]

vol-au-vent /ˈvɒl.ə.vɒ̃/ US /ˌvɔː.loʊˈvɑ̃ː/ noun [C] a small, light, cup-shaped pastry case filled with meat, fish, or vegetables in a sauce: *chicken/mushroom/prawn vol-au-vents*

volcano /vɒlˈkeɪ.nəʊ/ US /vɑːlˈkeɪ.noʊ/ noun [C] (plural **volcanoes** or **volcanos**) B2 a mountain with a large, circular hole at the top through which LAVA (= hot liquid rock) gases, steam, and dust are or have been forced out: *an extinct/dormant volcano* ◦ *an active volcano* ◦ ***Erupting** volcanoes discharge massive quantities of dust into the stratosphere.* • **volcanic** /-ˈkæn.ɪk/ adj *volcanic ash/activity/rock*

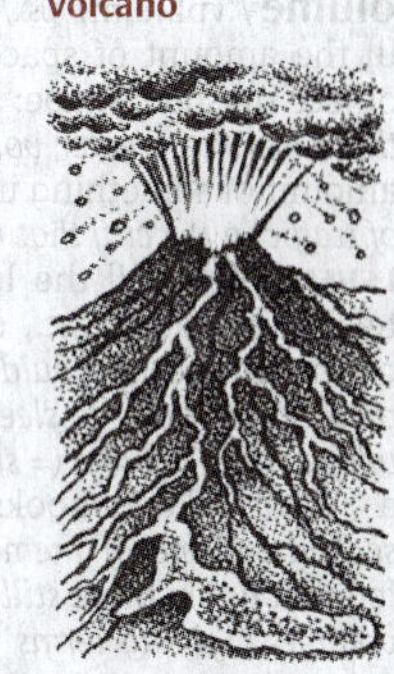
volcano

vole /vəʊl/ US /voʊl/ noun [C] a small animal similar to a mouse with a thick body, short tail, and small ears

volition /vəˈlɪʃ.ən/ noun [U] formal the power to make your own decisions: *The Minister wished it to be known that he had left the cabinet (**out**) **of** his **own** volition (= it was his decision).*

V

volley /ˈvɒl.i/ Ⓤⓢ /ˈvɑː.li/ **noun; verb**

▸**noun BULLETS** ▷ **1** [C] a large number of bullets (seeming to be) FIRED at the same time: *Even as the funeral took place, guerrillas hidden nearby* ***fired/let off*** *a fresh volley* ***of*** *machine-gun fire.* **A LOT** ▷ **2** [C usually singular] a lot of similar things that are said or produced, or that happen, quickly one after the other: *I'm afraid my proposal was met with a volley* ***of*** *criticisms.* **SPORTS** ▷ **3** [C] (in sports) a kick or hit in which a player returns a moving ball before it touches the ground: *That was a marvellous backhand volley.*

▸**verb** [I or T] (in sports) to hit or kick a moving ball before it touches the ground

volleyball /ˈvɒl.i.bɔːl/ Ⓤⓢ /ˈvɑː.li.bɑːl/ **noun** [U] Ⓐ② a game in which two teams use their hands to hit a large ball backwards and forwards over a high net without allowing the ball to touch the ground

volt /vɒlt/ Ⓤⓢ /voʊlt/ **noun** [C] the standard unit used to measure how strongly an electrical current is sent around an electrical system: *Electricity in Britain is 240 volts, AC.*

voltage /ˈvɒl.tɪdʒ/ Ⓤⓢ /ˈvoʊl.t̬ɪdʒ/ **noun** [C or U] the force of an electric current, measured in volts: ***high/low*** *voltages*

volte-face /ˌvɒltˈfæs/ Ⓤⓢ /ˌvoʊlt-/ **noun** [C usually singular] (plural **volte-face**) literary a sudden change from one set of beliefs or plan of action to the opposite: *In 1986 he* ***made*** *a very public and dramatic political volte-face from Left to Right.*

voltmeter /ˈvəʊltˌmiː.təʳ/ Ⓤⓢ /ˈvoʊltˌmiː.t̬ɚ/ **noun** [C] specialized any of various devices used for measuring the voltage between two points on an electric CIRCUIT

voluble /ˈvɒl.jʊ.bl̩/ Ⓤⓢ /ˈvɑːl-/ **adj** formal **1** speaking a lot, with confidence and enthusiasm: *Many see Parker as the obvious leader, whose voluble style works well on TV.* **2** expressed in many words: *It's not often that one hears such voluble praise for this government.* • **volubly** /-bli/ **adv**

volume /ˈvɒl.juːm/ Ⓤⓢ /ˈvɑːl-/ **noun AMOUNT** ▷ **1** [C or U] the amount of space that is contained within an object or solid shape: *Which of these bottles do you think has the greater volume?* **2** Ⓑ② [U] the number or amount of something in general: *It's the* ***sheer*** *volume of traffic in the city that is causing the problems.* **SOUND LEVEL** ▷ **3** Ⓑ① [U] the level of sound produced by a television, radio, etc., or the switch or other device controlling this: *Could you turn the volume down, please, I'm trying to sleep.* ◦ *I'll turn it up if you tell me which is the volume (= switch).* **BOOK** ▷ **4** Ⓒ② [C] one in a set of related books: *Now 'Realms Of Strife', his second volume* ***of*** *memoirs, is available too.* **5** Ⓒ② [C] formal a book: *While still an undergraduate, his first slim volume 'Fighting Terms' enjoyed a considerable success.*

voluminous /vəˈluː.mɪ.nəs/ **adj** formal **1** A voluminous piece of clothing is large and consists of a lot of cloth: *Her voluminous silk dress billowed out behind her.* **2** A voluminous piece of writing is long and detailed: *Have you read McClelland's voluminous account of his life?*

voluntary /ˈvɒl.ən.tᵊr.i/ Ⓤⓢ /ˈvɑː.lᵊn.ter.i/ **adj 1** Ⓒ① done, made, or given willingly, without being forced or paid to do it: *They chose to take voluntary redundancy.* ◦ *She does voluntary work for the Red Cross two days a week.* **2** describes an organization that is controlled and supported by people who give their time and money to it without being paid, and that exists to help other people: *The hospital has asked various voluntary organizations to help raise money for the new operating theatre.* • **voluntarily** /-trᵊl.i/ Ⓤⓢ /-ter.ᵊl.i/ **adv**

volunteer /ˌvɒl.ənˈtɪəʳ/ Ⓤⓢ /ˌvɑː.lənˈtɪr/ **noun; verb**

▸**noun** [C] Ⓑ② a person who does something, especially helping other people, willingly and without being forced or paid to do it: *The Health clinic is relying on volunteers to run the office and answer the phones.* ◦ *Since it would be a highly dangerous mission, the Lieutenant asked for volunteers.* ◦ *It's a volunteer army with no paid professionals.* → Compare **conscript**

▸**verb 1** Ⓒ① [I or T] to offer to do something that you do not have to do, often without having been asked to do it and/or without expecting payment: [+ to infinitive] *During the emergency many staff volunteered* ***to*** *work through the weekend.* ◦ *I volunteered myself* ***for*** *the post of Health and Safety Representative.* ◦ *My mates volunteered me* ***to*** *do the talking.* ◦ *He volunteered* ***for*** *the army (= he joined even though he did not have to).* **2** [T] to give information without being asked: *If I were you, I wouldn't volunteer any details of what happened.* ◦ [+ speech] *'I saw her going out of the main entrance at about half past two,' he volunteered.*

voluptuous /vəˈlʌp.tju.əs/ **adj 1** describes a woman who has a soft, curved, sexually attractive body: *a voluptuous body/mouth/figure* **2** literary describes an experience or object that gives you a lot of pleasure because it feels extremely soft and comfortable or it sounds or looks extremely beautiful: *such voluptuous pleasure* ◦ *I sank into the bed's voluptuous warmth.* • **voluptuously** /-li/ **adv** literary • **voluptuousness** /-nəs/ **noun** [U]

vomit /ˈvɒm.ɪt/ Ⓤⓢ /ˈvɑː.mɪt/ **verb** [I or T] Ⓒ② to empty the contents of the stomach through the mouth: *He came home drunk and vomited all over the kitchen floor.* ◦ *She was vomiting (**up**) blood.* • **vomit noun** [U]

voodoo /ˈvuː.duː/ **noun** [U] **1** a type of religion involving magic and the worship of SPIRITS (= people who cannot be seen), especially common in Haiti **2** informal bad luck: *They felt as if there was some sort of voodoo* ***on*** *the band, because everything just went wrong.*

voracious /vəˈreɪ.ʃəs/ **adj** very eager for something, especially a lot of food: *He has a voracious* ***appetite*** *(= he eats a lot).* ◦ *He's a voracious reader of historical novels (= he reads a lot of them eagerly and quickly).* • **voraciously** /-li/ **adv** • **voraciousness** /-nəs/ **noun** [U]

vortex /ˈvɔː.teks/ Ⓤⓢ /ˈvɔːr.t̬eks/ **noun** (plural **vortexes** or **vortices** /-tɪ.siːz/ Ⓤⓢ /-t̬ə-/) **1** [C] specialized a mass of air or water that SPINS around very fast and pulls objects into its empty centre **2** [C usually singular] literary a dangerous or bad situation in which you become more and more involved and from which you cannot escape: *I was* ***sucked into*** *a vortex* ***of*** *despair.*

vote /vəʊt/ Ⓤⓢ /voʊt/ **verb; noun**

▸**verb** [I or T] Ⓑ① to express your choice or opinion, especially by officially writing a mark on a paper or by raising your hand or speaking in a meeting: *She was too young to vote* ***in*** *the national election.* ◦ *The committee voted* ***on*** *the proposal, and accepted it unanimously.* ◦ *Did you vote* ***for*** *or* ***against*** *the motion?* ◦ *Over 55 percent voted Liberal.* ◦ [+ to infinitive] *Staff voted* ***to*** *accept the offer of an eight percent pay rise.* ◦ [+ (that)] *I vote (**that**) we (= it is my opinion that we should) go to the cinema first and eat afterwards.* ◦ [+ obj + noun] *The evening was voted a* *tremendous success (= this was most people's opinion).* ◦ *It was the younger members who voted Smith* ***onto*** *the committee.* ◦ *The Republican Party was voted* ***into/out of office*** *(= was chosen in an election to become/stop being the government).*

IDIOM **vote with your feet** If you vote with your feet, you leave an organization or stop supporting, using, or buying something, and change to a new organization, service, or product: *When the price of skiing doubled, tourists voted with their feet and just stopped going.*

PHRASAL VERBS **vote sth down** to defeat something such as a law or plan by voting against it: *The proposal to build a new road through the forest was voted down by the local council.* • **vote sth through** to accept and make possible something such as a law or plan by voting for it: *The committee voted through a proposal to cut the defence budget.*

▸**noun 1** B1 [C] the act of showing your choice or opinion in an election or meeting by writing a cross on an official piece of paper or putting your hand up: *The suggestion was approved, with 25 votes in favour, and seven against.* ◦ *She* ***cast*** *her vote (= voted) for the Communist Party.* **2** B2 [C usually singular] a way of making a decision by asking a group of people to vote: *We called a meeting in order to* ***take/hold*** *a vote* ***on*** *the issue.* **3 the vote** [S] **a** the total number of votes given or received in an election: *The party* ***got/took*** *25 percent of the vote.* ◦ *They are trying to capture the working-class vote (= to persuade those people to vote for them).* **b** C1 the fact of being officially allowed to vote: *In some countries women still don't* ***have*** *the vote.* **4 put sth to the/a vote** to vote on something: *The proposal was read out and then put to the vote.*

vote-getter /ˈvəʊtˌget.əʳ/ US /ˈvoʊtˌget̬.ɚ/ **noun** [C usually singular] US something that will win votes because it is popular with the voters: *Her stance on taxation could be a big vote-getter in this election.*

ˌvote of ˈconfidence noun [C usually singular] **1** formal an occasion when the members of a parliament or other organization are asked to say that they support the people in authority and agree with their actions: *The government* ***held*** *a vote of confidence and lost/won it.* **2** a sign that you are pleased with the quality of something or what someone has done or produced: *I think the fact that so many of you are here tonight is a vote of confidence* ***in*** *the quality of our local performers.*

ˌvote of ˌno ˈconfidence noun [C usually singular] an occasion when most of the members of a parliament or other organization say that they do not support the people in authority and that they disagree with their actions

ˌvote of ˈthanks noun [C usually singular] an act of formally and publicly thanking a person or organization for something they have done: *The new Chairperson stood up and* ***proposed*** *(= said) a vote of thanks* ***to*** *the retiring Chair* ***for*** *all her hard work.*

voter /ˈvəʊ.təʳ/ US /ˈvoʊ.t̬ɚ/ **noun** [C] C2 a person who votes or who has a legal right to vote, especially in an election: *Of course, tax cuts are usually popular with (the) voters.* ◦ *Are you a Labour voter?*

voting /ˈvəʊ.tɪŋ/ US /-t̬ɪŋ/ **noun** [U] the activity of choosing someone or something in an election: *Voting was brisk in spite of the bad weather.* ◦ *Pollsters asked people their voting intentions.*

ˈvoting maˌchine noun [C] mainly US a machine used to automatically record and count votes in an election

votive /ˈvəʊ.tɪv/ US /ˈvoʊ.t̬ɪv/ **adj** specialized given or done to honour and thank a god: *votive offerings*

vouch /vaʊtʃ/ **verb** [+ that] to be able from your knowledge or experience to say that something is true: *As a medical examiner I* ***can*** *vouch from experience* ***that*** *his death was accidental.*

PHRASAL VERB **vouch for sth/sb** to say that you know from experience that something is true or good, or that someone is honest and has a good character: *Patricia has checked the reports and can vouch for the accuracy of the information.*

voucher /ˈvaʊ.tʃəʳ/ US /-tʃɚ/ **noun** [C] UK a piece of paper that can be used to pay for particular goods or services or that allows you to pay less than the usual price for them: *The voucher is valid between July and December and entitles you to ten percent off all overseas flights.*

vouchsafe /ˌvaʊtʃˈseɪf/ **verb** [T] formal to tell or give something to someone: *He vouchsafed the information that the meeting had been postponed.*

vow /vaʊ/ **verb; noun**

▸**verb** [T] C2 to make a determined decision or promise to do something: [+ (that)] *The guerrillas vowed (****that****) they would overthrow the government.* ◦ [+ to infinitive] *After the awful meals we had last Christmas, I vowed* ***to*** *do more of the cooking myself.*

▸**noun** [C] C2 a serious promise or decision: [+ to infinitive] *She* ***took/made*** *a vow never to lend money to anyone again.*

vowel /vaʊəl/ **noun** [C] **1** B1 a speech sound produced by humans when the breath flows out through the mouth without being blocked by the teeth, tongue, or lips: *A* ***short*** *vowel is a short sound as in the word 'cup'.* ◦ *A* ***long*** *vowel is a long sound as in the word 'shoe'.* → Compare **consonant 2** B1 a letter that represents a sound produced in this way: *The vowels in English are a, e, i, o, and u.*

vox pop /ˌvɒksˈpɒp/ US /ˌvɑːksˈpɑːp/ **noun** UK informal **1** [U] the opinions of people recorded talking informally in public places **2** [C] a broadcast for radio or television in which people going past in a public place are asked their opinion on a particular subject

voyage /ˈvɔɪ.ɪdʒ/ **noun; verb**

▸**noun** [C] B2 a long journey, especially by ship: *He was a young sailor* ***on*** *his first sea voyage.* ◦ figurative *The first year of a loving relationship is a voyage (= period)* ***of*** *discovery.*

▸**verb** [I] literary to travel: *In their little boat they planned to voyage* ***to*** *distant lands.*

voyager /ˈvɔɪ.ɪ.dʒəʳ/ US /-dʒɚ/ **noun** [C] a person who goes on a long and sometimes dangerous journey

voyeur /vwɑːˈjɜːʳ/ US /-ˈjɝː/ **noun** [C] disapproving a person who gets sexual pleasure from secretly watching other people in sexual situations, or (more generally) a person who watches other people's private lives: *I felt like a voyeur visiting the war zone and seeing badly injured people being dragged from their bomb-shattered homes.* • **voyeurism** /ˈvwɑː.jɜː.rɪ.zᵊm/ US /-jɝː-/ **noun** [U] • **voyeuristic** /ˌvwɑː.jɜːˈrɪ.stɪk/ US /-jəˈrɪs.tɪk/ **adj**

VP /ˌviːˈpiː/ US abbreviation for **vice president**

vroom /vruːm/, /vrʊm/ **exclamation** informal used in writing to represent the sound of a car engine at high speed

vs preposition written abbreviation for **versus**

ˈV-shaped adj shaped like a V

ˈV-sign noun [C] **1** UK a sign meaning VICTORY or peace that is made by holding up the first two fingers of one hand in the shape of a V, while the thumb and other

V

fingers are folded down and face out → Compare **peace sign 2** (also **two fingers**) UK offensive a similar sign, made with the back of the hand facing out, used for expressing extreme dislike or anger towards someone: *The driver shouted rudely at the cyclist and* ***gave*** *her a/the V-sign.*

vulcanized (UK usually **vulcanised**) /ˈvʌl.kə.naɪzd/ **adj** Vulcanized rubber has been made stronger by a chemical process.

vulgar /ˈvʌl.gəʳ/ (US) /-gɚ/ **adj** disapproving **NOT SUITABLE** ▷ **1** not suitable, simple, DIGNIFIED or beautiful; common or not in the style preferred by the upper classes of society: *a vulgar patterned shirt* ◦ *I've no idea how much the clothes cost because there was nothing so vulgar as a price tag in evidence.* ◦ *Isn't it rather vulgar to talk about how much money you earn?* **RUDE** ▷ **2** rude and likely to upset or anger people, especially by referring to sex and the body in an unpleasant way: *It was an extremely vulgar joke.* • **vulgarity** /vʌlˈgær.ɪ.ti/ (US) /-ə.t̬i/ **noun** [U] • **vulgarly** /-li/ **adv**

ˌvulgar ˈfraction **noun** [C] (also **ˌcommon ˈfraction**) a FRACTION in which there is a horizontal line with one number above it and one number below it → Compare **improper fraction, proper fraction**

vulnerable /ˈvʌl.nᵊr.ə.bl̩/, /ˈvʌn.rə-/ (US) /ˈvʌl.nɚ.ə-/ **adj** (C2) able to be easily physically, emotionally, or mentally hurt, influenced, or attacked: *I felt very vulnerable, standing there without any clothes on.* ◦ *It is on economic policy that the government is most vulnerable.* ◦ *Tourists are more vulnerable* ***to*** *attack, because they do not know which areas of the city to avoid.* • **vulnerability** /ˌvʌl.nᵊr.əˈbɪl.ɪ.ti/, /ˌvʌn.rə-/ (US) /ˌvʌl.nɚ.əˈbɪl.ə.t̬i/ **noun** [U]

vulture /ˈvʌl.tʃəʳ/ (US) /-tʃɚ/ **noun** [C] **1** a large bird with almost no feathers on its head or neck, that eats the flesh of dead animals **2** disapproving a person or organization that is eager to win an advantage from other people's difficulties or problems: *When a company is in crisis like this, the vultures are always hovering.*

vulva /ˈvʌl.və/ **noun** [C] (plural **vulvas**) the parts of the female sex organs that are outside the body

vying /ˈvaɪ.ɪŋ/ present participle of **vie**

W

W, w noun; adj
▸noun /ˈdʌb.l̩.juː/ (plural **Ws, W's** or **w's**) **LETTER** ▷ **1** [C or U] the 23rd letter of the English alphabet **WEST** ▷ **2** written abbreviation for **west**: *W Africa* **ELECTRICITY** ▷ **3** written abbreviation for **watt**
▸adj written abbreviation for **west** or **western**

wack /wæk/ adj US slang **1** not good **2** strange

wacko /ˈwæk.əʊ/ (US) /-oʊ/ noun [C] (plural **wackos**) mainly US informal a person whose behaviour is strange and different from that of most people

wacky /ˈwæk.i/ adj informal unusual in a pleasing and exciting or silly way: *He decided to become a clown to join the wacky world of the circus.* • **wackiness** /-nəs/ noun [U]

wad /wɒd/ (US) /wɑːd/ noun [C] a number of especially flat and/or small objects pressed tightly together: *a wad of banknotes* ◦ *a wad of gum* ◦ *She used a wad (= a mass) of tissues to wipe away the blood.*

wadding /ˈwɒd.ɪŋ/ (US) /ˈwɑː.dɪŋ/ noun [U] any soft material used for filling a space, especially in order to protect something or to give something shape

waddle /ˈwɒd.l̩/ (US) /ˈwɑː.dl̩/ verb [I usually + adv/prep] (usually of a person or animal with short legs and a fat body) to walk with short steps, moving the body from one side to the other • **waddle** noun [C]

waddy /ˈwɒd.i/ (US) /ˈwɑː.di/ noun [C] Australian English a heavy stick

wade /weɪd/ verb **1** [I usually + adv/prep, T] to walk through water with difficulty because of the pressure of the water against your legs: *The river was full but we managed to wade* ***across***. ◦ *We waded a shallow river.* **2** [I] US for **paddle**

PHRASAL VERBS **wade in** to start to do or say something in a forceful way, often without thinking about it carefully: *Even when she knows nothing about it, she wades in* ***with*** *her opinion.* ◦ *When the crowd started throwing stones, the police waded in* ***with*** *tear gas.* • **wade into sth** to become involved in a difficult situation, often without thinking about it carefully • **wade through sth** informal to spend a lot of time and effort doing something boring or difficult, especially reading a lot of information: *We had to wade through pages of legal jargon before we could sign the contract.*

wader /ˈweɪ.dəʳ/ (US) /-dɚ/ noun **BIRD** ▷ **1** [C] a bird with long legs and a long neck, that lives near water and eats fish **BOOTS** ▷ **2 waders** [plural] rubber boots that cover the whole leg to keep a person dry in water: *The fishermen put on their waders.*

wadge /wɒdʒ/ (US) /wɑːdʒ/ noun [C] UK informal a **wodge**

wadi /ˈwɒd.i/ (US) /ˈwɑː.di/ noun [C] specialized a valley that has a river that is usually dry except when it has rained, common in desert areas of North Africa and Southwest Asia

ˈwading ˌpool noun [C] US for **paddling pool**

wafer /ˈweɪ.fəʳ/ (US) /-fɚ/ noun [C] **1** a very thin, dry biscuit that is often sweet **2** specialized a very thin, round piece of dry bread that the priest gives to people to eat during HOLY COMMUNION **3** Indian English a very thin, often round piece of fried potato or other vegetable, sometimes with a flavour added → See also **crisp**

ˌwafer-ˈthin adj extremely thin: *The rooms were divided only by a wafer-thin partition.*

waffle /ˈwɒf.l̩/ (US) /ˈwɑː.fl̩/ verb; noun
▸verb [I] disapproving to talk or write a lot without giving any useful information or any clear answers: *If you don't know the answer, it's no good just waffling* ***(on)*** *for pages and pages.*
▸noun **CAKE** ▷ **1** [C] a thin, light cake, the surface of which is formed into a pattern of raised squares, eaten especially in the US and Canada **TALK** ▷ **2** [U] disapproving talk or writing that uses a lot of words but does not give any useful information: *'What did he say?' 'Oh, it was a load of waffle – nothing important at all.'*

waft /wɒft/ (US) /wɑːft/ verb; noun
▸verb [I or T, usually + adv/prep] literary to (cause to) move gently through the air: *A gentle breeze wafted the scent of roses in through the open window.* ◦ *The sound of a flute wafted down the stairs.*
▸noun [C] literary a smell or smoke which moves through the air: *Caroline caught the heady waft of the other woman's perfume.* ◦ *A waft of smoke engulfed her.*

wag /wæg/ verb; noun
▸verb [I or T] **(-gg-)** (especially of a tail or finger) to move from side to side or up and down, especially quickly and repeatedly, or to cause this to happen: *The little dog's tail wagged in delight.* ◦ *He wagged his finger sternly at the two boys.*
▸noun **MOVE** ▷ **1** [C usually singular] (especially of a tail or finger) a movement from side to side or up and down: *With a single wag of her finger she managed to convey her total disapproval.* **PERSON** ▷ **2** [C] old-fashioned informal a humorous person who likes to make jokes **3** a **WAG** • **waggish** /ˈwæg.ɪʃ/ adj old-fashioned informal saying humorous things

WAG (also **wag**) /wæg/ noun [C usually plural] informal abbreviation for wife and girlfriend: a woman who is a wife or girlfriend, especially of a football player

wage /weɪdʒ/ noun; verb
▸noun [S] (also **wages** [plural]) (B1) a fixed amount of money that is paid, usually every week, to an employee, especially one who does work that needs physical skills or strength, rather than a job needing a college education: *a very low/high wage* ◦ *an hourly/daily/weekly/annual wage* ◦ *He gets/earns/is paid a good wage, because he works for a fair employer.* ◦ *The smaller shops pay very low wages.* → Compare **income, salary**
▸verb [T] formal to fight a war or organize a series of activities in order to achieve something: *Surely the president needs Congress' permission to wage war* ***on*** *another country?* ◦ *They've been waging a long campaign to change the law.*

ˈwage ˌearner noun [C] a person who works at a job for money

ˈwage ˌfreeze noun [C usually singular] an occasion when a company or government fixes the amount paid to workers and will not allow any increases

ˈwage ˌpacket noun [C usually singular] UK (US **paycheck**) the money that you earn, especially when it is given to you in notes and coins in an envelope: *cash a monthly/weekly wage packet* ◦ *She got £25 in cash* ***in*** *her first wage packet.*

wager /ˈweɪ.dʒəʳ/ (US) /-dʒɚ/ noun; verb
▸noun [C] an amount of money that you risk in the

W

hope of winning more, by trying to guess something uncertain, or the agreement that you make to take this risk: *She put a **cash** wager of £50 **on** the biggest horse race of the year.* ◦ *He tried to eat 50 hard-boiled eggs, **for** a wager.* → Synonym **bet**

▸**verb 1** [I or T] to risk money by guessing the result of something: [+ two objects, + that] *I'll wager you £5 **that** they'll get there first.* **2** [I] old-fashioned used to say that you are certain that something is true or will happen in the future: [+ (that)] *I'd wager (**that**) she's interested in you.*

waggle /ˈwæg.l/ **verb** [I or T] to (cause to) move quickly up and down or from side to side: *One of his party tricks is to waggle his **ears**.*

wagon (UK also **waggon**) /ˈwæg.ən/ **noun** [C] **1** a vehicle with four wheels, usually pulled by horses or OXEN, used for transporting heavy goods, especially in the past: *The first white settlers journeyed across America in **covered** wagons.* → See also **bandwagon, station wagon, Welcome Wagon 2** UK (US **freight car**) a large wheeled container for transporting goods, that is pulled by a train: *a **goods** wagon*

IDIOMS **fall off the wagon** informal to start drinking alcohol, after a period when you have drunk none: *When her husband died, she fell off the wagon.* • **on the wagon** informal If you are on the wagon, you have decided not to drink any alcohol for a period of time: *He was on the wagon for ten years, when he was living in Connecticut.*

wagon-lit /ˌvæg.ɒnˈliː/ **noun** [C] UK a **sleeping car**

ˈ**wagon** ˌ**train** **noun** [C] a long line of wagons pulled by horses or OXEN, used by people in the 19th century who were travelling to the western US with their possessions in order to live there

waif /weɪf/ **noun** [C] literary a child or animal without a home or enough food and care, usually thin and dirty in appearance

IDIOM **waifs and strays** UK people with no homes: *Her house is always full of waifs and strays.*

ˈ**waif-like** **adj** very thin and delicate in appearance: *waif-like supermodels*

wail /weɪl/ **verb; noun**

▸**verb 1** [I or T] to make a long, high cry, usually because of pain or sadness: *The women gathered around the coffin and began to wail, as was the custom in the region.* ◦ [+ speech] *'My finger hurts,' wailed the child.* **2** [I] informal to complain loudly or strongly: [+ that] *Business people wailed **that** their trade would be ruined.*

▸**noun** [C] a long, high, loud cry, especially because of something unpleasant: *a wail of anguish* ◦ *the wail of the police sirens*

waist /weɪst/ **noun** [C] **1** B2 the part of the body above and slightly narrower than the hips: *a small/narrow/tiny/large/thick waist* ◦ *These trousers are a bit tight around my waist.* **2** the part of a piece of clothing that goes around or covers the area between the hips and the RIBS: *The skirt had an elasticated waist.*

W

waistband /ˈweɪst.bænd/ **noun** [C] a strip of material that forms the waist of a pair of trousers or a skirt: *He had a gun tucked into the waistband of his trousers.*

waistcoat /ˈweɪs.kəʊt/ (US) /-koʊt/, /ˈwes.kət/ **noun** [C] UK (US **vest**) a piece of clothing that covers the upper body but not the arms and usually has buttons down the front, worn over a shirt

waisted /ˈweɪs.tɪd/ **adj** (of a piece of clothing) narrow at the waist: *This particular jacket is rather waisted.*

-waisted /-weɪs.tɪd/ **suffix** used with adjectives to describe the type of waist that a person or piece of clothing has: *a slim-waisted boy* ◦ *a **high**-waisted pair of trousers*

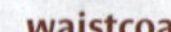
waistcoat

waistline /ˈweɪst.laɪn/ **noun** [C] an imaginary line going round the narrowest part of your waist: *a bulging/expanding waistline* ◦ *She started jogging twice a week to try to reduce her waistline.*

ˈ**waist** ˌ**pack** **noun** [C] US for **bumbag**

wait /weɪt/ **verb; noun**

▸**verb** [I] **1** A1 to allow time to go by, especially while staying in one place without doing very much, until someone comes, until something that you are expecting happens or until you can do something: *I waited **for** her in the corridor, while she went in to see the doctor.* ◦ *The dentist kept me waiting **for** ages.* ◦ [+ to infinitive] *There were a lot of people waiting **to** use the phone.* **2** to be done or to happen at a later time: *The meeting will **have to** wait until tomorrow, because I'm too busy now.* ◦ *The paperwork **can't** wait until tomorrow* (= is urgent and must be done now). **3 no waiting** UK (US **no standing**) used on signs to mean vehicles are not allowed to park, even for short periods of time

> **! Common mistake: wait**
>
> **Remember:** when **wait** is followed by an indirect object, remember to use the preposition **for.**
>
> Don't say 'wait something', say **wait for something**:
>
> ~~*I waited the bus but it never came.*~~
>
> *I waited for the bus but it never came.*

> **+ Other ways of saying wait**
>
> In formal English **await** means the same as 'wait for':
>
> *We are **awaiting** the committee's decision.*
>
> If people are waiting in a place, usually for no obvious reason, you can use the phrasal verb **hang around** or the verb **loiter**:
>
> *There were a lot of teenagers **hanging around/loitering** outside the store.*
>
> If people are waiting in a line to buy something, the verb **line up** is used:
>
> *People were **lining up** for tickets.*
>
> **Stay** and **remain** (*slightly formal*) are used when someone waits in a place until something else happens:
>
> ***Stay** there until I get back.*
>
> *Please **remain** in your seats until the plane has come to a complete stop.*
>
> If you want to tell someone to wait, you can use the phrase **hang on**:
>
> ***Hang on**, I'll be ready in a minute.*

IDIOMS **can't wait** (also **can hardly wait**) A2 to be very excited about something and eager to do or experience it: *I can't wait **to** see you.* • **wait your turn** to wait until it is really your turn to do or get something: *If people were more polite, they would wait their turn.* • **wait a minute/moment/second** B1 said in order to interrupt someone, or to get their attention or when you have suddenly thought of something important: *Now, wait a moment – I don't agree with that.* ◦ *Wait a minute – I've just had an idea.* • **wait and see** C1 to wait to discover what will happen: *No decision will be made until next year, so you'll just have to wait and see.* • **wait at table(s)** UK (US **wait on table(s)**) to serve meals to people in a restaurant, as your job • **wait for it** UK informal **1** to not start until the correct moment: *Wait for it! I haven't said 'go' yet.* **2** You say 'wait for it' to show that you are about to say something surprising, funny, or difficult to believe: *The new soap opera will be screened, wait for it, five times each day.* • **wait in the wings** If someone or something is waiting in the wings, they are not yet active or important, but are ready or likely to be so soon: *The team has several talented young players waiting in the wings.* • **wait till/until ...** said when you are excited about seeing another person's reaction to something special or unusual: *Wait till you see what Rachel's wearing!* • **(just) you wait** used as a way of threatening someone: *Just you wait, Maria, till I get my hands on you!*

PHRASAL VERBS **wait around** (UK also **wait about**) to stay in a place and do nothing while you wait for someone to arrive or something to happen: *We spent the whole day waiting around **for** something exciting to happen, but nothing did.* • **wait behind** to stay in a place after all the other people have left: *The teacher made us wait behind after class.* • **wait for sb/sth** If someone is waiting for someone or something, they are expecting them and prepared to deal with them: *When the thieves left the building, the police were waiting for them.* • **wait for sb** If something is waiting for you, it has been left or prepared for you to collect, use, enjoy, or deal with when you arrive: *An envelope was waiting for me when I got home.* ◦ *Uma had a cup of tea waiting for me, along with a plate of biscuits.* • **wait sth for sb** US to delay serving a meal until someone arrives: *Don't wait dinner for me – I'll be home late.* • **wait in** UK to stay at home because you are expecting someone or something to arrive, or someone to phone you: *I waited in **for** the plumber all morning, but he didn't turn up.* • **wait on sb/sth** mainly US to serve food and drink, especially to customers in a restaurant: *The staff who waited on us at dinner were excellent.* ◦ *She waited on **tables** (= served meals as a job) to earn some extra money.* • **wait on sb** to do everything for someone so that they do not have to do anything for themselves: *While she was pregnant, her husband waited on her **hand and foot** (= did everything for her).* • **wait on sth** formal to wait until you know the result of an activity before doing or deciding something: *The lawyers are waiting on the jury's verdict.* • **wait sth out** US to wait until something unpleasant has ended: *I'd rather wait out the storm than drive home immediately.* • **wait up** to not go to bed at night because you are expecting someone to arrive: *I'll be home after midnight, so don't wait up **for** me.*

▸**noun** [S] B2 a period of time when you stay in one place until someone comes, or something happens, or until you can do something: *We **had** a three-hour wait before we could see the doctor.* ◦ *The long wait **for** the doctor/**to** see the doctor really made me anxious.*

IDIOM **lie in wait** to hide, ready to attack: *The gunmen were lying in wait when Mr Predit came out of the hotel.*

waiter /ˈweɪ.təʳ/ (US) /-t̬ɚ/ **noun** [C] A1 a man whose job is to bring the food to customers at their tables in a restaurant

ˈwaiting ˌgame **noun** [S] a situation in which you delay taking any action, so that you can watch how a situation develops and see what it is best for you to do: *In a contest like this, the stronger side can afford to **play a** waiting game.*

ˈwaiting ˌlist **noun** [C usually singular] a list of people who have asked for something that is not immediately available but will be in the future: *The hospital has a two-year waiting list **for** minor operations.* ◦ *I'm afraid the course is full, but I can put you **on** the waiting list, in case someone else cancels.*

ˈwaiting ˌroom **noun** [C] a room in a place where people can sit and rest while waiting, as in a railway station or a doctor's office

waitress /ˈweɪ.trəs/ **noun** [C] A1 a woman whose job is to bring the food to customers at their tables in a restaurant

waive /weɪv/ **verb** [T] formal to not demand something you have a right to, or not cause a rule to be obeyed: *The bank manager waived the charge (= said we didn't have to pay), as we were old and valued customers.* ◦ *If the government waives (= removes) the time limit, many more applications will come in.* ◦ *He persuaded the delegates to waive (= give up) their objections.*

waiver /ˈweɪ.vəʳ/ (US) /-vɚ/ **noun** [C] an agreement that you do not have to pay or obey something: *We had to sign a waiver, giving up any rights to the land in the future.*

wake /weɪk/ **verb; noun**

▸**verb** [I or T] (past tense **woke** or **waked**, past participle **woken** or **waked**) (also **wake up**) A1 to (cause someone to) become awake and conscious after sleeping: *Did you wake at all during the night?* ◦ *Please wake me early tomorrow.* ◦ *I woke **up** with a headache.* ◦ *Jane's hand on my shoulder woke me **out of/from** a bad dream.*

IDIOMS **wake up!** something you say to tell someone to listen or to become involved when they have not been listening or paying attention: *Wake up, Daniel! It's your turn.* • **wake up and smell the coffee** informal used to tell someone that they are wrong about a particular situation and that they must realize what is really happening

PHRASAL VERBS **wake (sb) up** STOP SLEEPING ▷ **1** A1 to (cause to) become conscious after sleeping: *Come on, wake up – breakfast is ready.* ◦ *He woke himself up with his own snoring!* REACT ▷ **2** to start to react to a situation after a period in which you have done very little, or to make someone start to react to a situation: *Companies need to wake up and take notice of the public's increasing concern with the environment.* • **wake up to sth** to start to understand that a situation or problem exists: *Governments are finally waking up to the fact that the environment should be cleaned up.*

▸**noun** [C] WATER ▷ **1** the waves that a moving ship or object leaves behind: *The wake spread out in a v-shape behind the ship.* FUNERAL ▷ **2** an occasion when the family and friends of a dead person meet in order to look at the dead body the night before it is buried, or when they meet after a dead person has been buried to drink and talk about the person's life

IDIOMS **in the wake of sth** If something happens in the wake of something else, it happens after and often because of it: *Airport security was extra tight in the wake of yesterday's bomb attacks.* • **leave sth in your wake** to go somewhere new, leaving problems, confusion, etc. behind you, that you have caused: *The*

soldiers rampaged through the town centre, leaving chaos in their wake.

wakeful /ˈweɪk.fəl/ **adj** formal not able to sleep, or used to describe a period of time when you are not able to sleep: *We spent a wakeful night worrying about where he was.* ◦ *She lay there wakeful the whole night.* • **wakefulness** /-nəs/ **noun** [U]

waken /ˈweɪ.kən/ **verb** [I or T] formal to (cause to) wake from sleep: *I shook him but he didn't waken.* ◦ *Waken me at 7.00, would you?*

ˈwake-up ˌcall **noun** [C] **1** If something that happens is a wake-up call, it should make you realize that you need to take action to change a situation. **2** a phone call that you arrange to be made, for example in a hotel, to wake you up at a certain time

wakey-wakey /ˌweɪ.kiˈweɪ.ki/ **exclamation** humorous said to someone in order to wake them up from sleep: *Gloria knocked on the door and shouted 'Wakey-wakey!'*

waking /ˈweɪ.kɪŋ/ **noun; adj**

▸**noun** [U] the moment when you wake: *For a moment, between waking and sleeping, he couldn't understand where he was.*

▸**adj** [before noun] describes a period of time or an experience during which you are awake: *Children are in school for 15 percent of their waking **hours/life** between birth and the age of 16.* ◦ *She seems to spend **every** waking **moment/minute/hour*** (= all her available time) *at the piano.*

walk /wɔːk/ (US) /wɑːk/ **verb; noun**

▸**verb** **MOVE ON FOOT** ▷ **1** (A1) [I or T] to move along by putting one foot in front of the other, allowing each foot to touch the ground before lifting the next: *I walked home.* ◦ *A cat was walking along the top of the fence.* ◦ *He walks two miles to work every morning.* → See also **jaywalk, sleepwalk (sleepwalker)** **2** (B1) [T] to go with someone to a particular place, for example because you want to protect them from danger, or show them the way: *He offered to walk her home/**to** the station.* **3** (B1) [T] to take an animal, especially a dog, for a walk: *She walks the dog for an hour every afternoon.* **4** **a walking disaster, encyclopedia, etc.** someone who seems to be a human form of disaster, encyclopedia, etc.: *You've broken another pair of glasses? – Oh, you're a walking disaster!* **DO EASILY** ▷ **5** [T] UK informal to pass or win something, such as an exam or game, easily: *She'll walk the interview – the job is practically hers already.*

IDIOMS **walk all over sb** to treat someone very badly or defeat them very easily: *If you don't want to work at the weekend, say so – don't let the boss walk all over you.* • **walk it** UK informal to win or succeed easily: *The team should walk it on Saturday.* • **walk on air** to feel extremely excited or happy: *After the delivery of her baby, she was walking on air.* • **walk on eggs/eggshells** If you are walking on eggs/eggshells, you are being very careful not to offend someone or do anything wrong: *When my mother is staying at our house, I feel like I'm walking on eggshells.* • **walk right into sth** If you walk right into something, you are caught or tricked by it because you did not know what was happening: *We set a trap and they walked right into it.*

PHRASAL VERBS **walk away** **DIFFICULT SITUATION** ▷ **1** disapproving to stop being involved in a situation because it is difficult to deal with or does not give you any advantages: *You can't just walk away **from** a marriage at the first sign of a problem.* **ACCIDENT** ▷ **2** to escape an accident without being badly hurt: *She overturned the car, but walked away **from** it **without a** scratch.* • **walk away with sth** to win a prize or competition very easily: *He walked away with all three gold medals.* • **walk in on sb** to go into a room and see what someone is doing, when they did not want to be seen: *She walked in on me when I was getting undressed.* • **walk into sth** to get a job very easily: *She walked **straight** into a well-paid job after leaving university.* • **walk off (somewhere)** to leave a place because you are angry or unhappy about something: *She threatened to walk off the film set because of the conditions.* ◦ *He refused to discuss it and just walked off in a huff.* • **walk sth off** to go for a walk in order to get rid of an illness, often a HEADACHE, or the feeling of having eaten too much: *I'm going out to walk off this headache.* ◦ *Let's go to the park and walk off all that lunch.* • **walk off with sth** **WIN** ▷ **1** to win something easily: *She walked off with the top prize.* **STEAL** ▷ **2** to steal something or take something without asking permission: *Who's walked off with my cup?* • **walk out** **LEAVE** ▷ **1** to leave an event such as a meeting or performance because you are angry or disapprove of something: *All the parents walked out (**of** the meeting) in protest.* **2** to suddenly leave your husband, wife, or partner and end your relationship with them: *He walked out **on** his wife and two kids.* **STOP WORK** ▷ **3** to stop working or leave your job because of a disagreement with your employer: *Workers are threatening to walk out.* → See also **walkout** • **walk sb through sth** to slowly and carefully explain something to someone or show someone how to do something: *She walked me through the six-page document.* ◦ *He'll walk you through the procedure.*

Other ways of saying walk

If someone walks somewhere very quickly in a determined way, you could use the verbs **stride** or **march**:

*She **strode/marched** purposefully up to the desk and demanded to speak to the manager.*

Stroll, **wander**, and **amble** can be used when someone walks in a slow and relaxed way:

*We **strolled/wandered** along the beach.*

*She **ambled** down the street, looking in shop windows.*

If someone is walking slowly because he or she is tired or bored, you could use the verb **plod**:

*We **plodded** on until we reached the cottage.*

Pace is used when someone walks in one direction and back in the other direction several times because the person is anxious:

*He **paced** up and down the hospital corridor waiting for news.*

If someone is walking in a very confident way, especially when you find it annoying, you could use the verb **swagger**:

*He was **swaggering** around like he owned the place.*

Stagger can be used when someone walks in a very unsteady way:

*He **staggered** under the weight of all our luggage.*

To say that someone walks somewhere very quietly, you could use the verbs **creep** or **tiptoe**:

*Someone was **creeping** around outside.*

*He waited until the baby was asleep and **tiptoed** out of the room.*

Hike and **trek** can be used when someone walks a long way in the countryside:

*They **hiked** through Mount Rainier National Park.*

*They spent the day **trekking** through forests.*

▸noun **1** A2 [C] a journey that you make by walking, often for enjoyment: *He **went for/took** a walk around the block, to get some air.* ◦ *They went on a ten-mile walk to raise money for charity.* ◦ *Every afternoon she takes her grandad out for a walk.* → See also **jaywalk, sleepwalk (sleepwalker)**, **boardwalk, catwalk, crosswalk, sidewalk, spacewalk** **2** C1 [C] a path or route where people can walk for enjoyment: *Do you know any nice walks around here?* **3** [S] a way of walking: *He's got a strange waddling sort of walk.* **4** [S] walking speed: *She slowed the horses to a walk.* **5 a short, five-minute, ten-minute, etc. walk** a journey that takes a short time, five minutes, ten minutes, etc. when you walk: *The station is only a five-minute walk **away**.*

IDIOMS **a walk in the park** something that is very easy to do, and usually pleasant: *He's used to hard physical work – this is a walk in the park to him.* • **walk of life** When people talk about walk(s) of life, they are referring to different types of jobs and different levels of society: *We've got lawyers in this club, and builders and hairdressers – people from all (**different**) walks of life.*

walkabout /ˈwɔː.kə.baʊt/ US /ˈwɑː-/ noun [C] mainly UK informal an occasion when an important person walks around a public place, meeting and talking to members of the public: *The princess **went on** a walkabout in the town centre.*

IDIOM **go walkabout** informal humorous If you say that an object has gone walkabout you mean that it is missing, often because someone has taken it: *My pen was here this morning but it seems to have gone walkabout.*

walkaway /ˈwɔː.k.ə.weɪ/ noun [C] US for **walkover**

walker /ˈwɔː.kəʳ/ US /ˈwɑː.kɚ/ noun [C] **1** C1 a person who walks, especially for exercise or enjoyment: *She's a very fast/slow walker.* ◦ *They've been keen walkers ever since they read about the benefits of exercise.* **2** US for **Zimmer frame**

walkies /ˈwɔː.kiz/ US /ˈwɑː-/ exclamation, noun [plural] UK informal said to a dog to tell it that it is time for a walk: *Walkies, Shem, come on, walkies!*

walkie-talkie /ˌwɔː.kiˈtɔː.ki/ US /ˌwɑː.kiˈtɑː-/ noun [C] a small radio held in the hand, used for both sending and receiving messages: *The policeman was speaking to HQ **on** his walkie-talkie.*

ˈwalk-in adj [before noun] STORAGE ▷ **1** describes a space used for storing things that is large enough for a person to enter and walk around in: UK *a walk-in wardrobe* ◦ US *a walk-in closet* NOT ARRANGED ▷ **2** mainly US describes a place that you can go to without having already made an arrangement: *It's a walk-in dental clinic.*

walking /ˈwɔː.kɪŋ/ US /ˈwɑː-/ noun [U] **1** A2 the activity of going for a walk, especially for pleasure in the countryside: *We're **going** walking in Wales for a week.* ◦ *a pair of walking/hiking boots* ◦ *a walking stick* **2** the sport of walking fast over long distances

ˈwalking ˌframe noun [C] UK → **Zimmer frame**

ˈwalking ˌpapers noun [plural] US for **marching orders**

ˈwalk-on (ˌpart) noun [C] A walk-on (part) in a play is a very small part in which the actor is on the stage for a short time and speaks very few or no words.

walkout /ˈwɔːk.aʊt/ US /ˈwɑːk-/ noun [C] the act of leaving an official meeting as a group in order to show disapproval, or of leaving a place of work to start a STRIKE: *Senior union workers **staged** (= had) a walkout this afternoon at the annual conference over the proposed changes in funding.* → See also **walk out**

walkover /ˈwɔːkˌəʊ.vəʳ/ US /ˈwɑːkˌoʊ.vɚ/ noun [C] **1** (US also **walkaway**) a game or sports event that is won very easily by one side or one person: *The semifinal should be a walkover for France.* **2** the act of winning one stage of a competition without having to compete in it because the person that you should be playing against is no longer taking part

ˈwalk-up noun [C] US a building with several floors and no LIFT (= a device for going from one floor to another) or an apartment or office in such a building

ˈwalk-up ˌprice noun [C] the price you pay for something such as a ticket if you buy it just before using it, rather than buying it some time earlier: *Tickets booked online for the same day will be charged at the full walk-up price.*

walkway /ˈwɔː.kweɪ/ US /ˈwɑː-/ noun [C] a passage or path, especially one that is covered or raised above the ground

wall /wɔːl/ US /wɑːl/ noun; verb

▸noun **1** A1 [C] a vertical structure, often made of stone or brick, that divides or surrounds something: *The walls in this apartment are so thin you can hear just about every word the neighbours say.* ◦ *The walls look a bit bare – can't we put some pictures up?* ◦ *We had to climb over a ten-foot wall to get into the garden.* ◦ *The Berlin Wall came down in 1989.* **2** [C] any outer part of a hollow structure in the body: *the wall of the womb/stomach* ◦ *an artery wall* **3** [C] a mass of people or things formed in such a way that you cannot get through or past them: *The demonstrators formed a solid wall to stop the police from getting past them.* **4** [S] literary a large, powerful, usually fast moving mass of something: *After the rains, the houses were washed away by a wall **of** mud/water.* **5** [S] a way of feeling or behaving that completely prevents two groups of people from communicating with or understanding each other: *There is a wall **of** mistrust between the two groups.*

IDIOMS **drive sb up the wall** to make someone extremely angry: *My flat-mate is driving me up the wall at the moment.* • **go to the wall** If a company goes to the wall it is destroyed financially: *After nine months of massive losses the company finally went to the wall.* • **off the wall** surprising and unusual: *an off-the-wall joke* ◦ *off-the-wall leisure pursuits* • **walls have ears** saying something you say to warn someone that it is not safe to speak at that particular time because other people might be listening • **wall-to-wall** **1** (especially of carpets) covering the whole floor: *a wall-to-wall carpet* **2** continuous or happening very often or everywhere around you: *I went away to college thinking it would be wall-to-wall parties and all the freedom I wanted.*

▸verb

PHRASAL VERBS **wall sth off** to build a wall around a place: *They've walled off the electric sub-station for safety reasons.* • **wall sth up** to fill a space in a wall with brick or stone: *We had to wall up an old window.*

wallaby /ˈwɒl.ə.bi/ US /ˈwɑː.lə-/ noun [C] an animal found in Australia and New Guinea that is a small KANGAROO

wallah /ˈwɒl.ə/ US /ˈwɑː.lə/ noun [C] UK informal or Indian English (in compounds) a person who has a particular duty: *I made the tea yesterday so it's Mira's turn to be tea-wallah this afternoon.*

-wallah /-wɒl.ə/ US /-wɑː.lɑː/ suffix Indian English

W

added to nouns to describe a person who has a particular duty or job, or with a particular appearance: *a rickshawallah*

walled /wɔːld/ (US) /wɑːld/ **adj** surrounded by a wall: *Why not visit the beautiful walled city of York?*

wallet /ˈwɒl.ɪt/ (US) /ˈwɑː.lɪt/ **noun** [C] **1** A2 (US also **billfold**) a small folding case for carrying paper money, CREDIT CARDS and other flat objects, used especially by men: *He pulled out a big, fat wallet stuffed with bank notes.*

wallet

→ Compare **purse 2** (also **document wallet**) a large, flat case that is made of card and used for holding documents

wallflower /ˈwɔːlˌflaʊəʳ/ (US) /ˈwɑːlˌflaʊr/ **noun** [C] **PLANT** ▷ **1** a pleasant smelling garden plant that has yellow, orange, or brown flowers that grow in groups **SHY PERSON** ▷ **2** informal a shy person, especially a girl or woman, who is frightened to involve herself in social activities and does not attract much interest or attention: *Sooner or later someone would take pity on the poor wallflower and ask her to dance.*

ˈwall ˌhanging **noun** [C] a large piece of material or sewing that is hung on a wall as a decoration

wallop /ˈwɒl.əp/ (US) /ˈwɑː.ləp/ **verb** [T] informal to hit someone hard, especially with the flat part of the hand or with something held in the hand, or to defeat someone easily, especially in sports: *She walloped him across the back of the head.* ◦ *'How did your tennis match go last night?' 'Oh, I was walloped again.'* • **wallop noun** [C] *My mother **gave** me such a wallop when she eventually found me.*

walloping /ˈwɒl.ə.pɪŋ/ (US) /ˈwɑː.lə-/ **adj; noun**

▸**adj** [before noun] informal humorous very big or great: *He cut me a walloping (**great**) slice of cake.*

▸**noun** [S] informal an act of punishing someone by hitting them hard: *I **got** such a walloping from my father when he came home.*

wallow /ˈwɒl.əʊ/ (US) /ˈwɑː.loʊ/ **verb** [I] (especially of particular animals) to lie or roll about slowly in deep, wet earth, sand, or water: *a hippopotamus wallowing **in** mud* • **wallow noun** [C usually singular] informal *He likes a good wallow in the bath.*

PHRASAL VERB **wallow in sth** **ENJOY** ▷ **1** to allow yourself to enjoy something completely: *My idea of a holiday is to book myself into a five-star hotel and just wallow in the luxury for a week.* **REMAIN UNHAPPY** ▷ **2** to remain in an unhappy emotional state without trying to get out of it, as if you are enjoying it or trying to get sympathy from other people: *I wish she'd do something to help herself instead of just wallowing in self-pity!*

wallpaper /ˈwɔːlˌpeɪ.pəʳ/ (US) /ˈwɑːlˌpeɪ.pɚ/ **noun; verb**

▸**noun** **WALL** ▷ **1** [C or U] a thick, often decorative, paper used for covering the walls and sometimes ceilings of a room: *a **roll** of wallpaper* ◦ *We thought we'd **put up/hang** some wallpaper in the children's bedroom to make it brighter.* ◦ *I saw a wallpaper today that would be just right for the bathroom.* ◦ *We'll need some wallpaper **paste** and a big brush.* **COMPUTER** ▷ **2** [U] specialized a design or image that you choose to appear on the DESKTOP (= main) screen of your computer

▸**verb** [T] to put wallpaper on the walls of a room: *We've wallpapered the bedrooms.*

W

ˈWall ˌStreet **noun** [U] a street in New York which represents the financial centre of the US: *On Wall Street today, the Dow Jones rose 55 points following good economic figures.*

wally /ˈwɒl.i/ (US) /ˈwɑː.li/ **noun** [C] UK informal a stupid person: *I'll look a right wally in these shorts!*

walnut /ˈwɔːl.nʌt/ (US) /ˈwɑːl-/ **noun** [C or U] a nut with a slightly bitter taste and a series of folds in it and a hard shell, or (the expensive, light brown wood from) the tree that produces these nuts

walrus /ˈwɔːl.rəs/ (US) /ˈwɑːl-/ **noun** [C] (plural **walruses** or **walrus**) a mammal which lives in the sea and on beaches in the Arctic. It is similar to a SEAL but larger, with two TUSKS and long hairs growing near its mouth.

ˌwalrus mousˈtache **noun** [C] a MOUSTACHE that is long and hangs down at both sides of the mouth

waltz /wɒls/ (US) /wɑːls/ **noun; verb**

▸**noun** [C] a formal dance in which two people holding each other move around a large room, turning as they go, or a piece of music with three beats in a BAR written for this style of dancing

▸**verb** **WALK** ▷ **1** [I usually + adv/prep] informal to walk somewhere quickly and confidently, often in a way that annoys other people: *You can't just waltz **into** my bedroom without knocking – it's private!* ◦ *My idiot wife has gone and waltzed **off with** my car keys and left me without any means of transport!* **DANCE** ▷ **2** [I] to dance a waltz

PHRASAL VERB **waltz through sth** informal to complete something such as a test easily and successfully: *He waltzed through the first two rounds of the competition.*

wan /wɒn/ (US) /wɑːn/ **adj** (**wanner**, **wannest**) literary (of a person's face) more pale than usual and tired-looking • **wanly** /ˈwɒn.li/ (US) /ˈwɑːn-/ **adv** *She smiled wanly (= showing no energy or enthusiasm).*

WAN /wæn/ **noun** [C] specialized abbreviation for Wide Area Network: a computer network that connects separate machines over a wide area, for example in different countries, using telecommunication systems → Compare **LAN**

wand /wɒnd/ (US) /wɑːnd/ **noun** [C] a special thin stick waved by a person who is performing magic tricks: *The fairy godmother **waved** her magic wand over the cabbages and they turned into horses.*

wander /ˈwɒn.dəʳ/ (US) /ˈwɑːn.dɚ/ **verb** **WALK** ▷ **1** B2 [I or T] to walk around slowly in a relaxed way or without any clear purpose or direction: *We spent the morning wandering **around** the old part of the city.* ◦ *She was found several hours later, wandering **the streets**, lost.* ◦ *He was here a moment ago but he's wandered **off** somewhere.* **SUBJECT** ▷ **2** [I] to start talking about a different subject from the one you were originally discussing: *We've wandered **off/from the point** somewhat.* **3** C2 [I] If your mind or your thoughts wander, you stop thinking about the subject that you should be giving your attention to and start thinking about other matters: *Halfway through the meeting my **mind** started to wander.* **4** [I] If you say that an old person's mind is beginning to wander, you mean that they are starting to get very confused because of their age: *Her **mind** is beginning to wander and she doesn't always know who I am.* • **wander noun** [C usually singular] informal *While you're in your meeting I can **go for/have/take** a wander around the city.*

wanderings /ˈwɒn.dᵊr.ɪŋz/ (US) /ˈwɑːn.dɚ-/ **noun** [plural] time spent travelling around or going from one place or country to another: *After all her wanderings she had come back home to stay.* ◦ humorous *If you see Alan **in/on your** wanderings, will you tell him he's wanted in the office?*

wanderlust /ˈwɒn.də.lʌst/ US /ˈwɑːn.dɚ-/ noun [U] the wish to travel far away and to many different places: *In July wanderlust takes over the whole nation.*

wane /weɪn/ verb; noun
▸verb [I] **1** to become weaker in strength or influence: *By the late 70s the band's popularity was beginning to wane.* **2** formal The moon wanes when it gradually appears less and less round, after the FULL MOON. → Compare **wax**
▸noun **on the wane** becoming less strong, powerful, popular, etc.: *There are signs that support for the party is on the wane.*

wangle /ˈwæŋ.gl/ verb [T] informal to succeed in getting or doing something by persuading someone or by being clever in some way: *I'll be so jealous if you manage to wangle an invitation to his house.* ◦ *He's only been here two months and already he's managed to wangle **his way into** the biggest property company in London.* ◦ *If I can think of some excuse to wangle **my way out of** going tonight I will do!*

wank /wæŋk/ verb [I] UK offensive to MASTURBATE • **wank** noun [C usually singular] *to **have** a wank*

wanker /ˈwæŋ.kəʳ/ US /-kɚ/ noun [C] UK offensive **1** a very stupid or unpleasant person, usually a man: *They're all a bunch of wankers!* **2** less commonly, a person who MASTURBATES

wanna /ˈwɒn.ə/ US /ˈwɑː.nə/ short form not standard 'want to' or 'want a': [+ infinitive without to] *D'you wanna go now?* ◦ *I wanna hamburger, Mom.*

wannabe /ˈwɒn.ə.bi/ US /ˈwɑː.nə-/ noun [C], adj informal disapproving a person who is trying to become famous, usually unsuccessfully: *The bar is frequented by wannabe actresses and film directors.*

want /wɒnt/ US /wɑːnt/ verb; noun
▸verb [T] **WISH** ▷ **1** A1 to wish for a particular thing or plan of action. 'Want' is not used in polite requests in British English: *I want some chocolate.* ◦ *She wants a word with you.* ◦ *He's everything you'd ever want in a man – funny and attractive.* ◦ [+ to infinitive] *What do you want **to** eat?* ◦ [+ obj + to infinitive] *Do you want me **to** take you to the station?* ◦ [+ obj + past participle] *This letter – do you want it sent first class?* ◦ [+ obj + adj] *Do you want this pie hot?* ◦ [+ obj + -ing verb] *I don't want a load of traffic go**ing** past my house all night, waking me up.* ◦ *You wait – by next year she'll be wanting a bigger house!* → Compare **like 2** to wish or need someone to be present: *Am I wanted at the meeting tomorrow?* ◦ *He is wanted by the police (= they are searching for him).* **3 want in/out of** informal to want to start or stop being involved in something: *I want out of the whole venture before it's too late.*

> **!** Common mistake: **want**
>
> When **want** is followed by a verb, that verb cannot be in the infinitive without 'to'.
>
> Do not say 'want do something', say **want to do something**:
>
> ~~*Some women do not want stay at home and look after children.*~~
>
> *Some women do not want to stay at home and look after children.*

NEED ▷ **4** to need something: *Do you think this soup wants a bit of salt?* ◦ [+ -ing verb] *The wine is in the fridge – it just wants cool**ing** for a couple of minutes.* ◦ *If you ask me that child wants a good slap!* **5 want to** used in giving advice to mean that someone should do something: *You want to tell him now, before it's too late.*

IDIOMS **not/never want for anything** formal to have all the basic things you need to lead a satisfactory life: *As children we never wanted for anything.* • **tried and found wanting** tried and discovered to be not effective: *This government's policies, said the speaker, have been tried and found wanting.*

▸noun **LACK** ▷ **1** [U] a lack of something: ***For** want **of** anything better to do I watched television for a while.* ◦ *If we fail it won't be **for** want **of** trying (= we have tried even if we fail).* **NEED** ▷ **2 in want of** needing: *He appeared tired and in want of a shave.* **3 wants** [plural] formal needs: *Our wants are few.*

want ˌad noun [C] US for **classified ad**

wanted /ˈwɒn.tɪd/ US /ˈwɑːn.t̬ɪd/ adj **1** wished for and loved by other people: *She was a much wanted baby.* **2** being searched for by the police because of a crime: *He's a wanted man.*

wanting /ˈwɒn.tɪŋ/ US /ˈwɑːn.t̬ɪŋ/ adj formal not having something; lacking: *I think she's perhaps a little wanting **in** charm.*

wanton /ˈwɒn.tən/ US /ˈwɑːn.tᵊn/ adj **WITHOUT CARE** ▷ **1** formal (of something bad, such as damage, CRUELTY, waste) extreme and showing no care at all: *wanton destruction of human life* ◦ *wanton extravagance* **SEXUAL** ▷ **2** old use or humorous (of a woman) behaving or appearing in a very sexual way • **wantonly** /-li/ adv • **wantonness** /-nəs/ noun [U] old use or humorous

WAP /wæp/ noun [U] abbreviation for Wireless Application Protocol: a system which allows you to use the internet using a type of mobile phone

wapiti /ˈwɒp.ɪ.ti/ US /ˈwɑː.pə.t̬i/ noun [C] (plural **wapitis** or **wapiti**) (US also **elk**) a large DEER with brownish-red fur and large ANTLERS (= horns like branches) that lives in the forests of North America

war /wɔːʳ/ US /wɔːr/ noun [C or U] **1** A2 armed fighting between two or more countries or groups, or a particular example of this: *nuclear war* ◦ *a war film/grave/hero/poet* ◦ *If this country **goes to** (= starts to fight in a) war we will have to face the fact that many people will die.* ◦ *Britain and France **declared** war **on** Germany in 1939 as a result of the invasion of Poland.* ◦ *War **broke out** between the two countries after a border dispute.* ◦ *They've been **at** war for the last five years.* ◦ *He died in the First World War/the Vietnam war.* **2 war of attrition** a war that is fought over a long period and only ends when one side has neither the soldiers and equipment nor the determination left to continue fighting **3 war of nerves** a situation, often before a competition or BATTLE, in which two opposing sides attempt to frighten or DISCOURAGE each other by making threats or by showing how strong or clever they are **4** C2 any situation in which there is strong competition between opposing sides or a great fight against something harmful: *The past few months have witnessed a **price** war between leading supermarkets.* ◦ *The government are to step up their attempt to **wage** war **against/on** drugs.*

> Word partners for **war**
>
> war ***breaks out*** • ***go to*** war • ***wage/fight*** a war • ***declare*** war (**on** sb) • an ***all-out/full-scale*** war • a war ***against/with*** sb • a war ***between*** sb and sb • be ***at*** war

IDIOMS **be in the wars** UK informal to have injuries to many different parts of the body: *You've got a cut on your arm as well, you poor thing. You really have been in the wars!* • **war clouds are gathering** (also **clouds of war are gathering**) If someone says that war clouds are gathering over a particular country, they mean that a war seems increasingly likely there: *It*

was the 1930s and war clouds were gathering on the horizon in Europe.

warble /ˈwɔː.bl/ (US) /ˈwɔːr-/ **verb** [I] **1** (of a bird) to sing pleasantly **2** humorous to sing, especially in a high voice: *Was that you I heard warbling in the bathroom this morning?*

warbler /ˈwɔː.bləʳ/ (US) /ˈwɔːr.blə/ **noun** [C] a small bird that lives in trees and sings

ˈwar ˌbride **noun** [C] a girl or woman who, during a war, marries a member of the armed forces from a different country

ˈwar ˌcrime **noun** [C] a crime committed during a war which breaks the accepted international rules of war: *Genocide is a war crime.*

ˈwar ˌcriminal **noun** [C] someone who commits war crimes: *He was a Nazi war criminal.*

ˈwar ˌcry **noun** [C usually singular] (also **ˈbattle ˌcry**) a phrase or word shouted by people as they start to fight, intended to give them the strength and wish to fight harder: figurative *The phrase 'burn your bra!' was the feminists' war cry of the 1970s.*

ward /wɔːd/ (US) /wɔːrd/ **noun; verb**

▸noun [C] **HOSPITAL/PRISON** ▷ **1** B2 one of the parts or large rooms into which a hospital is divided, usually with beds for patients: *a geriatric/maternity/psychiatric ward* **2** US one of the parts into which a prison is divided **CITY AREA** ▷ **3** (in many countries) one of the areas into which a city or town is divided, having its own elected political REPRESENTATIVE or its own organizations for managing services **CHILD** ▷ **4** legal a person, especially a child, who is legally put under the protection of a law court or a GUARDIAN: *The girl was made a ward **of court** to stop her father taking her out of the country.*

▸verb

PHRASAL VERB **ward sth off** to prevent something unpleasant from harming or coming close to you: *In the winter I take vitamin C to ward off colds.* ◦ *She was given a magic charm to ward off evil spirits.*

-ward /-wəd/ (US) /-wəd/ **suffix** towards the stated place or direction: *At least we're homeward bound.* • **-wards** /-wədz/ (US) /-wədz/ **suffix** *Take a couple of steps backwards/forwards.*

> **!** Usage: **ward or wards?**
>
> Generally, adjectives are formed using **-ward** and adverbs are formed using **-wards**:
>
> *an eastward journey*
> *moving slowly backwards*
>
> The **-ward** form of the adverb is also possible, especially in American and Australian English.

ˈwar ˌdance **noun** [C] a formal dance, performed by some TRIBAL people, either before they fight or after they have won a fight

warden /ˈwɔː.dᵊn/ (US) /ˈwɔːr-/ **noun** [C] **MANAGER** ▷ **1** a person who is in charge of (the people in) a particular building: *She's the warden of a home for mentally handicapped people.* **2** UK the head of a college: *He's the warden of Robinson College, Cambridge.* **3** US the person in charge of a prison: *a prison warden* **OFFICIAL** ▷ **4** a person whose job is to make certain that members of the public obey particular rules: *a dog warden* ◦ *a park warden* ◦ *a traffic warden*

warder /ˈwɔː.dəʳ/ (US) /ˈwɔːr.də/ **noun** [C] (female old-fashioned also **wardress**) UK a person who is in charge of people in prison

wardrobe /ˈwɔː.drəʊb/ (US) /ˈwɔːr.droʊb/ **noun** **1** B1 [C or U] a tall cupboard in which you hang your clothes, or all of the clothes that a person owns: *She was showing me her new **built-in** (UK also **fitted**) wardrobes.* ◦ *I sometimes feel that my summer wardrobe is rather lacking (= I don't have many clothes for summer).* **2** [U] a department in a theatre, film company, etc. that is in charge of the clothes that the actors wear on stage, making certain that they are clean, repairing them and sometimes making them

-ware /-weəʳ/ (US) /-wer/ **suffix** used, often in shops, to refer to objects of the same material or type, especially things used in cooking and serving food: *tableware* ◦ *the kitchenware department*

warehouse /ˈweə.haʊs/ (US) /ˈwer-/ **noun; verb**

▸noun [C] UK (US **storehouse**) C2 a large building for storing things before they are sold, used, or sent out to shops, or a large shop selling a large number of a particular product at a cheap rate: *The goods have been sitting in a warehouse for months because a strike has prevented distribution.* ◦ *We bought both sofas from a big furniture warehouse that's just off the motorway.*

▸verb [T] UK to store something in a warehouse: *The division was only able to sell 40 systems, leaving 80 units warehoused and unsold.* • **warehousing** **noun** [U] *The company has sold its warehousing and distribution operation.*

wares /weəz/ (US) /werz/ **noun** [plural] **1** small products for selling, in a market or on the street but not usually in a shop: *Some displayed their wares on stalls, while others had just spread them out on the pavement.* **2** informal a company's products: *The company must do more to promote their wares overseas.*

warfare /ˈwɔː.feəʳ/ (US) /ˈwɔːr.fer/ **noun** [U] the activity of fighting a war, often including the weapons and methods that are used: *guerrilla/naval/nuclear/trench warfare*

warfarin /ˈwɔː.fᵊr.ɪn/ (US) /ˈwɔːr.fə-/ **noun** [U] trademark a substance that is used to kill RATS and is also used in a slightly different form as a medical treatment in order to prevent blood from CLOTTING (= becoming solid)

ˈwar ˌgame **noun** [C] a pretend military BATTLE that is performed only for the purpose of training

warhead /ˈwɔː.hed/ (US) /ˈwɔːr-/ **noun** [C] the front part of a bomb or MISSILE that contains explosives: *a conventional/nuclear warhead*

warhorse /ˈwɔː.hɔːs/ (US) /ˈwɔːr.hɔːrs/ **noun** **PERSON** ▷ **1** [C] informal an old and experienced politician, soldier, or ATHLETE, especially one who is still active **SHOW** ▷ **2** [C usually singular] often disapproving a piece of music, television show, play, or other performed piece of work that has often been performed or shown and is very famous: *I don't understand why a ballet company can't perform fresh new material instead of just bringing out the same **old** warhorses year after year.*

warlike /ˈwɔː.laɪk/ (US) /ˈwɔːr-/ **adj** formal often involved in and eager to start wars: *It has often been said, perhaps unfairly, that they are a warlike **nation/people**.*

warlord /ˈwɔː.lɔːd/ (US) /ˈwɔːr.lɔːrd/ **noun** [C] mainly disapproving a military leader who controls a country or, more often, an area within a country

warm /wɔːm/ (US) /wɔːrm/ **adj; verb**

▸adj **TEMPERATURE** ▷ **1** A1 having or producing a comfortably high temperature, although not hot: *Are you warm enough or do you want the fire on?* ◦ *I've got my hands in my pockets to keep them warm.* **2** A2 describes clothes and covers made of a material that keeps you warm: *I don't have a warm winter coat.* ◦ *Those gloves look nice and warm.* **3** A warm colour is one that is based on or contains a colour such as red, yellow, or orange that suggests warmth. **4 the warm** UK a warm place: *It's cold standing out there – come into the warm.* **FRIENDLY** ▷ **5** B1 friendly and loving: *They're a very warm family.* ◦ *He has a lovely warm smile.* ◦ *I'd like to give a warm **welcome** to our guests this evening.* **NEAR** ▷ **6** [after verb] informal (especially in children's games) near to guessing a correct answer or to discovering a hidden object: *You're **getting** warmer!* • **warmly** /ˈwɔːm.li/ US /ˈwɔːrm-/ **adv** B2 *He shook my hand warmly.* ◦ *You're not dressed warmly enough – put a sweater on.* • **warmth** /wɔːmθ/ US /wɔːrmθ/ **noun** [U] B2 *I've put a T-shirt on under my sweater for extra warmth.*

▸**verb** [I or T] B2 to (cause to) become warm (= less cold): *You're so cold – come and warm your hands by the fire.* ◦ *Your supper's just warming **through** in the oven.* ◦ *We can warm (**up**) the room quite quickly with this electric fire.*

PHRASAL VERBS **warm sth over** US disapproving to use an idea that has been used before or to discuss a subject that has already been discussed before: *Voters are bored with politicians warming over old policies.* • **warm to sb** to start to like someone: *I wasn't sure about Sarah at first, but I warmed to her after we'd been out together a few times.* • **warm to sth** If you warm to an idea, you start to become interested in or enthusiastic about it: *Unfortunately, I had to leave just as the speaker was warming to his theme.* • **warm (sb/sth) up** to become warmer or to make someone or something warmer: *The house soon warms up with the heating on.* ◦ *I'll just warm up the engine while you're getting your coats on.* • **warm (sb) up** to entertain people while they are waiting for a performance to start, for example by telling jokes: *He's got a job warming up for TV studio audiences.* ◦ *He was warming the audience up with his world-famous jokes.* • **warm sth up** to heat food that has already been cooked: *I might just warm up the leftovers from yesterday's meal in the microwave.* • **warm up** **EVENT** ▷ **1** informal If an event warms up, it starts to become more interesting, enjoyable, or exciting: *The party was only just starting to warm up as I left.* **EXERCISE** ▷ **2** to prepare yourself for a physical activity by doing some gentle exercises and stretches: *If you don't warm up before taking exercise, you risk injuring yourself.*

ˌwarm-ˈblooded adj having a body temperature which stays the same and does not change with the temperature of the environment: *Birds and mammals are warm-blooded.* → Compare **cold-blooded**

ˌwarmed-ˈover adj [before noun] mainly US disapproving using an idea that has been used before and is not new or interesting: *These commercials are just warmed-over imitations of earlier TV ads.*

ˈwar meˌmorial noun [C] a large structure, made especially of stone, that is built in honour of those people who died in a particular war

ˌwarm-ˈhearted adj kind and loving: *She's a good, warm-hearted woman.*

warming /ˈwɔː.mɪŋ/ US /ˈwɔːr-/ **adj** approving describes a type of food or drink that makes you feel warm: *Have a nice warming bowl of soup.*

warmonger /ˈwɔːˌmʌŋ.gəʳ/ US /ˈwɔːrˌmʌŋ.gɚ/ **noun** [C] disapproving a politician or other leader who is often encouraging a country to go to war • **warmongering** /-ɪŋ/ **noun** [U]

warmth /wɔːmθ/, /wɔːmθ/ **noun** [U] **HEAT** ▷ **1** B2 *I've put a T-shirt on under my sweater for extra warmth.* **FEELING** ▷ **2** B2 a friendly and enthusiastic quality in someone or something: *I still remember the warmth of their welcome.*

ˈwarm-up noun [C] something that you do to prepare yourself for an activity, especially gentle exercises before a physical activity: *A warm-up is important before a run so as not to strain any muscles.* ◦ *Let's do a few warm-up exercises.*

warn /wɔːn/ US /wɔːrn/ **verb** [I or T] B1 to make someone realize a possible danger or problem, especially one in the future: [+ obj + to infinitive] *We were warned not **to** eat the fish which might give us a slight stomach upset.* ◦ [+ obj + (that)] *Have you warned them (**that**) there will be an extra person for dinner?* ◦ *I was warned **against/off** going to the east coast because it was so full of tourists.* ◦ *There were signs warning **of** fog as soon as we got onto the motorway.* ◦ *This particular curry is extremely hot – **be** warned!* ◦ *Put that ball down and come over here, Laura – I'm warning you (= I will punish you if you do not)!*

warning /ˈwɔː.nɪŋ/ US /ˈwɔːr-/ **noun** [C or U] **1** B1 something that makes you understand there is a possible danger or problem, especially one in the future: *Completely without warning he turned up on my doorstep with all four children!* ◦ *There's a warning on the cigarette packet that says 'Tobacco seriously damages health'.* ◦ *I'm not surprised you feel ill – **let it be a** warning to you!* ◦ *Just a **word of** warning – restaurants in this area can be very expensive.* ◦ formal *The government have today **issued** a warning about the dangers of sunbathing.* ◦ *They can't dismiss you just like that – they have to **give** you a **written** warning first.* ◦ *The police fired warning **shots** but the protesters took no notice.* **2 warning sign** a physical condition that shows someone has a disease: *The warning signs **of** the illness are respiratory problems and dizziness.*

> **Word partners for warning**
>
> ***deliver/give/issue/sound*** a warning • ***heed*** a warning • ***ignore*** a warning • a ***blunt/clear/dire/final*** warning • ***without*** warning • a warning ***about*** sth

IDIOM **hear warning bells** (also **warning bells start to ring/sound**) used to describe a situation when people see signs that something bad has started or is going to happen: *For me, the warning bells started to ring when she stopped eating properly and lost all that weight.*

warp /wɔːp/ US /wɔːrp/ **verb; noun**

▸**verb** **BEND** ▷ **1** [I or T] If wood warps, or if water or heat warps it, it becomes damaged by bending or twisting: *If I put the shelves near the radiator, the heat might warp them.* **STRANGE** ▷ **2** [T] to make a person or their behaviour strange, in an unpleasant or harmful way: *Prison warps people. Had it warped Kelley enough that he would kill a stranger?*

▸**noun** **the warp** [S] specialized the threads that go along the length of a piece of cloth or a LOOM (= a special frame for making cloth) → Compare **the weft**

warpaint /ˈwɔː.peɪnt/ US /ˈwɔːr-/ **noun** [U] **1** a paint used by some TRIBAL people to decorate the face and body before fighting **2** humorous make-up

warpath /ˈwɔː.pɑːθ/ US /ˈwɔːr.pæθ/ **noun** informal mainly humorous **on the warpath** angry and likely to argue or punish: *If there was one thing she couldn't face in the morning it was her mother on the warpath.*

warped /wɔːpt/ US /wɔːrpt/ **adj** **STRANGE** ▷ **1** disapproving or humorous strange and unpleasant: *I suppose I shouldn't be laughing about death – perhaps I've got a warped **mind/sense of humour**!* **BENT** ▷ **2** bent

W

because of damage by heat or water: *Have you noticed how warped these shelves are?*

warrant /ˈwɒr.ənt/ (US) /ˈwɔːr-/ **verb; noun**
▸verb **MAKE NECESSARY** ▷ **1** [T] to make a particular activity necessary: *Obviously what she did was wrong, but I don't think it warranted quite such severe punishment.* ◦ *It's a relatively simple task that really doesn't warrant a great deal of time be**ing** spent on it.* → See also **unwarranted** **PROMISE** ▷ **2** [I or T] old-fashioned to say that you are certain about something
▸noun **DOCUMENT** ▷ [C] an official document, signed by a judge or other person in authority, which gives the police permission to search someone's home, arrest a person, or take some other action: *a search warrant* ◦ *Judge La Riva had issued an arrest warrant/a warrant **for** his arrest.*

ˈ**warrant** ˌ**officer** noun [C] a rank in the armed forces, between a COMMISSIONED OFFICER and an NCO: *Warrant Officer First Class*

warranty /ˈwɒr.ən.ti/ (US) /ˈwɔːr.ən.t̬i/ **noun** [C] a written promise from a company to repair or replace a product that develops a fault within a fixed period of time, or to do a piece of work again if it is not satisfactory: *The warranty **covers** the car mechanically for a year, with unlimited mileage.* → Synonym **guarantee**

ˈ**war-**ˌ**ravaged** adj **war-torn**

warren /ˈwɒr.ən/ (US) /ˈwɔːr-/ **noun** [C] **1** (also **rabbit warren**) a series of connecting underground passages and holes in which RABBITS live **2** mainly disapproving a very crowded and confusing building or part of a city in which it is easy to get lost: *They live on a great concrete warren of a housing estate.*

warring /ˈwɔː.rɪŋ/ (US) /ˈwɔːr.ɪŋ/ **adj** [before noun] describes countries or groups of people that are at war with each other or who are arguing violently with each other: *The Labour Party, he said, had disintegrated into warring **factions**.*

warrior /ˈwɒr.i.əʳ/ (US) /ˈwɔːr.i.ɚ/ **noun** [C] (C1) a soldier, usually one who has both experience and skill in fighting, especially in the past: *a Samurai warrior* ◦ *a warrior king/nation*

warship /ˈwɔː.ʃɪp/ (US) /ˈwɔːr-/ **noun** [C] a ship supplied with guns, for use in war

wart /wɔːt/ (US) /wɔːrt/ **noun** [C] a small, hard LUMP (= raised area) which grows on the skin, often on the face and hands

IDIOM **warts and all** informal describing or including all the bad qualities in a person's character, with no attempt to hide them: *He tried to paint the president as he really was, warts and all.*

warthog /ˈwɔːt.hɒg/ (US) /ˈwɔːrt.hɑːg/ **noun** [C] an African wild pig with a large head, TUSKS, and little raised areas on the male's face that look like warts

wartime /ˈwɔː.taɪm/ (US) /ˈwɔːr-/ **noun** [U] a period of time during which a war is being fought: ***In** wartime, food is often scarce.* ◦ *The film is set in wartime England.* → Opposite **peacetime**

ˈ**war-torn** adj (also ˈ**war-**ˌ**ravaged**) severely damaged by a long war, especially between different groups from the same country: *It is a long-term task to rebuild the infrastructure of a war-torn country such as Angola.*

warty /ˈwɔː.ti/ (US) /ˈwɔːr.t̬i/ **adj** having warts

wary /ˈweə.ri/ (US) /ˈwer.i/ **adj** (C2) not completely trusting or certain about something or someone: *I'm a bit wary **of/about** giving people my address when I don't know them very well.* • **warily** /ˈweə.rɪ.li/ (US) /ˈwer.ɪ-/ **adv** • **wariness** /-nəs/ **noun** [U]

ˈ**war** ˌ**zone** noun [C] a place where people are fighting in a war: *Some people mistakenly believe that Croatia is still a war zone.*

was strong /wɒz/ (US) /wɑːz/ weak /wəz/ **verb** past simple of **be**

wasabi /wəˈsɑː.bi/ **noun** [U] a strong-tasting green root used in Japanese cooking

wash /wɒʃ/ (US) /wɑːʃ/ **verb; noun**
▸verb **CLEAN** ▷ **1** (A1) [T] to clean something using water: *wash your hair/hands* ◦ *wash the car/clothes/floor* ◦ *These sheets need washing.* ◦ *I'll wash the bottle **out** (= clean its inside) and use it again.* **2** (A1) [I] (US also **wash up**) to clean yourself, or a part of yourself, with water and usually soap: *I'd like to wash before dinner.* **3 wash well** If a particular material or piece of clothing washes well, it is not damaged or spoiled by repeated washing. **FLOW** ▷ **4** [I usually + adv/prep] literary If water washes somewhere, it flows there, usually repeatedly: *She stood on the shore and let the water wash **over** her tired feet.* **5 wash sb/sth up/ashore/overboard** (of the sea) to carry something or someone to or away from a place: *Overnight the sea had washed up a lot of rubbish.* ◦ *More than 400 dead dolphins had been washed ashore.* ◦ *A Spanish crew member had been washed overboard (= carried off a ship into the sea by the force of the water) in the storm.*

> **Other ways of saying wash**
>
> **Rinse** is used when you wash something in water to remove the soap or dirt from it:
>
> *She **rinsed** the cloth in the sink.*
>
> If you wash something using soap, water, and a stiff brush, you could use the verb **scrub**:
>
> *He tried to **scrub** the pen marks off the wall.*
>
> **Soak** is used when you wash something by leaving it in some water for a long time:
>
> *She **soaked** the T-shirt overnight to get rid of the stains.*
>
> When you wash yourself, you can say that you **have a wash**:
>
> *I'll just **have a wash** and then I'll be ready.*

IDIOMS **wash (with sb)** informal If an excuse or argument won't wash (with someone), they are unlikely to believe or accept it. • **wash your dirty linen in public** disapproving People who wash their dirty linen in public discuss, or allow to be discussed in public, matters which should be kept private. • **wash your hands of sth** If you wash your hands of something that you were previously responsible for, you intentionally stop being involved in it or connected with it in any way: *She couldn't wait to wash her hands of the whole project.* • **wash your mouth out (with soap/soapy water)** humorous an expression used humorously when someone has used a rude or offensive word

PHRASAL VERBS **wash sth away** If water or rain washes something away, it removes it or carries it away: *The blood on the pavement had been washed away by the rain overnight.* • **wash sth down** **CLEAN** ▷ **1** to clean a large object or surface with a liquid: *He washed the car down with soapy water.* **EAT** ▷ **2** informal to eat food or swallow medicine with a drink that helps or improves it: *Supper was fresh salmon and vegetables, washed down **with** a bottle of white wine.* • **wash (sth) out** If a colour or dirty mark washes out, or if you wash it out, it disappears when you wash it: *Do you think these stains will wash out?* • **wash sth out** [usually passive] If an event or sports competition is washed out, it is prevented from happening or stopped early because of heavy rain: *The men's semifinals in the tennis were* washed out this morning. → See also **washout** • **wash (sth) up** A2 to clean the plates, pans, and other things that you have used for cooking and eating: *He washed up his mug and put it back on the shelf.* • **wash up** US to wash your hands, especially before a meal: *Go and wash up – your dinner's ready.*

▸**noun** CLEANING ▷ **1** A2 [C usually singular] the action of washing something or a part of your body: *Those curtains need a **good** (= careful) wash.* ◦ *Erik needed a **good** wash after playing in the garden.* **2 the wash** [S] **a** all the clothes, sheets, etc. that are washed together, especially in a washing machine: *Can I **put** this shirt **in** (**with**) the white wash?* ◦ *'Where's my pink shirt?' 'It's **in** the wash'* (= being washed or in a pile of clothes that is going to be washed). **b** US for **washing 3 have a wash** to wash your body or a part of it: *I need to have a wash before dinner* **4 do a wash** to clean clothes, sheets, etc., usually in a washing machine: *Are you doing a wash tonight?* THIN LAYER ▷ **5** [C] a thin layer of water or paint mixed with water, especially one that is brushed lightly over a painting to make the lines softer: *a blue wash/ a wash **of** blue* EVEN SITUATION ▷ **6** [C usually singular] US an event or situation in which positive and negative things balance each other: *If pollution controls are enforced here, the factories will move to where they're allowed to pollute, so it'll be a wash as far as clear air goes.* FLOW ▷ **7** [S] literary (the sound made) when the sea moves against land, etc.: *Outside the flat, she could hear the gentle wash of the waves on the beach.*

washable /ˈwɒʃ.ə.bl̩/ US /ˈwɑː.ʃə-/ **adj** able to be washed in a washing machine without being damaged: *I never buy clothes that aren't **machine-washable**.*

washbasin /ˈwɒʃˌbeɪ.sən/ US /ˈwɑːʃ-/ **noun** [C] UK (US **sink**) a bowl that is fixed to the wall in a bathroom or near a toilet and has pipes to supply and carry away water, in which you wash your hands, face, etc.

washcloth /ˈwɒʃ.klɒθ/ US /ˈwɑːʃ.klɑːθ/ **noun** [C] US for **facecloth**

ˌwashed ˈout adj NOT BRIGHT ▷ **1** describes cloth that has become less bright as a result of being washed a lot: *She was wearing an old washed-out T-shirt and jeans.* TIRED ▷ **2** feeling or looking very tired: [before noun] *I have to wear a bit of make-up in the winter or I look completely washed out.*

ˌwashed ˈup adj If you are washed up, the job for which you are trained is finished and you have no further chances of success in the future: *The tragedy of being a dancer is that you're **all** washed up by the time you're 35.* ◦ [before noun] *a bunch of washed-up celebrities*

washer /ˈwɒʃ.ər/ US /ˈwɑː.ʃɚ/ **noun** [C] RING ▷ **1** a flat ring of metal, rubber, or plastic that is put somewhere, especially between a SCREW or BOLT and a surface, or between joined pipes, in order to make a better connection between them MACHINE ▷ **2** informal a **washing machine**

ˌwasher-ˈdryer noun [C] a large electric machine for washing and drying clothes

washing /ˈwɒʃ.ɪŋ/ US /ˈwɑː.ʃɪŋ/ **noun** [U] (US also **the wash**) **1** the act of washing clothes: ***Doing** the washing is such a bore!* **2** clothes, sheets, etc. that need to be or have just been washed: *I **do** the washing and then I **hang/peg** it **out** in the garden.*

ˈwashing maˌchine noun [C] A2 a machine for washing clothes, sheets, and other things made of cloth: *a front/top-loading washing machine* ◦ *Could you empty/load the washing machine, please?*

ˈwashing ˌpowder/ˌliquid noun [C or U] UK (US **ˈlaundry deˌtergent**) a DETERGENT in the form of a powder or liquid that is used for washing clothes and other things made of cloth

Washington's Birthday /ˌwɒʃ.ɪŋ.tənz.ˈbɜː.θ.deɪ/ US /ˌwɑː.ʃɪŋ.tənz.ˈbɝːθ-/ **noun** (also **ˈPresident's ˌDay**) a US holiday on the third Monday in February when people remember George Washington and other former presidents

ˌwashing-ˈup noun [U] UK (US **dishes**) A2 the act of cleaning plates, pans, glasses, knives, forks, etc. after a meal, or the objects needing to be washed: *You **do** the washing-up and I'll do the drying.* ◦ *There's an enormous pile of washing-up in the sink.*

ˌwashing-ˈup ˌliquid noun [U] UK (US **ˈdish ˌliquid**) a thick liquid DETERGENT, added to hot water when washing pans, knives and forks, etc.

washout /ˈwɒʃ.aʊt/ US /ˈwɑː.ʃaʊt/ **noun** FAILURE ▷ **1** [C usually singular] informal a complete failure: *The last party was a bit of a washout – hardly anyone turned up.* CANCELLED EVENT ▷ **2** [C] an event or sports competition that is prevented from happening or stopped early because of heavy rain → See also **wash sth out**

washroom /ˈwɒʃ.rʊm/, /-ruːm/ US /ˈwɑːʃ-/ **noun** [C] US old-fashioned for TOILET (= a room with a toilet in it)

washstand /ˈwɒʃ.stænd/ US /ˈwɑːʃ-/ **noun** [C] a small table for holding a container of water for washing, used especially in the past

wasn't /ˈwɒz.ənt/ US /ˈwɑː.zənt/ **short form of** was not: *It was you who told me that, wasn't it?*

wasp /wɒsp/ US /wɑːsp/ **noun** [C] B2 a black and yellow flying insect that can STING (= produce a small, painful skin injury): *There's a wasps' **nest** in that old tree.* ◦ *a wasp **sting***

WASP (also **Wasp**) /wɒsp/ US /wɑːsp/ **noun** [C] mainly US disapproving White Anglo-Saxon Protestant (= a white American whose family originally came from northern Europe, and is therefore part of a group often considered as having the most influence and the most money in American society): *My mother comes from an old WASP family which has been in this country for 350 years.* • **Waspy** /ˈwɒs.pi/ US /ˈwɑː.spi/ **adj** (also **Waspish**)

waspish /ˈwɒs.pɪʃ/ US /ˈwɑː.spɪʃ/ **adj** disapproving likely to make sharp, slightly cruel remarks; having a slightly angry and unpleasant manner: *She had a waspish tongue which could hurt.*

wastage /ˈweɪ.stɪdʒ/ **noun** [U] **1** the amount that is wasted: *Water companies have got to cut down on wastage.* **2** UK for **natural wastage 3** UK (US **attrition**) the people who leave an educational or training course before it has finished: *The wastage rates on the degree courses are a cause for concern.*

waste /weɪst/ **noun; verb**

▸**noun** BAD USE ▷ **1** B1 [S or U] an unnecessary or wrong use of money, substances, time, energy, abilities, etc.: *That meeting achieved absolutely nothing – it was **a** complete waste **of time**.* ◦ *She's been unemployed for two years and it's such **a** waste **of** her talents.* ◦ *My mother couldn't bear waste – she always made us eat everything on our plates.* **2 go to waste** to not be used, eaten, etc.: *'Go on, finish off this tart, Paul.' 'Well, it seems a shame to let it go to waste.'* UNWANTED MATTER ▷ **3** B1 [C or U] unwanted matter or material of any type, especially what is left after useful substances or parts have been removed: *Britain produces 20 million tonnes of household waste each year.* ◦ *He opposes any kind of nuclear waste being dumped at sea.* ◦ *Millions of gallons of untreated human*

waste (= excrement) flow into the river every day. ◦ *Oil spills are common, as is the dumping of toxic industrial wastes.* ◦ *The Japanese recycle more than half of their waste* ***paper.*** **EMPTY GROUND** ▷ **4 waste ground** an area of ground in or near a city that is not built on, used to grow crops, or used in any way: *His body had been dumped in an area of waste ground just outside the city.* → See also **wasteland 5 wastes** [plural] large areas of land that are not used to grow crops and have few living animals or plants: *the Arctic wastes of northern Siberia*

> Word partners for **waste** (**BAD USE**)
>
> a waste *of* sth • a *complete/terrible/total/tragic* waste

> Word partners for **waste** (**MATTER**)
>
> *create/produce* waste • *cut down on/minimize/ reduce* waste • *dispose of/dump/get rid of* waste • *recycle/reprocess/reuse* waste • *hazardous/toxic* waste • *household/industrial* waste • *waste* disposal

IDIOM **waste of space** informal a person or thing that is not useful or helpful: *He's a total waste of space, that man.*

▸**verb** [T] **USE BADLY** ▷ **1** (B1) to use too much of something or use something badly when there is a limited amount of it: *You waste a lot of water by having a bath instead of a shower.* ◦ *Come on, let's get started – we've wasted enough* ***time*** *already.* ◦ *Don't waste your* ***money*** *on me, love, keep it for yourself.* **KILL** ▷ **2** US slang to kill someone

IDIOMS **not waste words** If someone does not waste words, they talk only about what is important using as few words as possible: *He explained the whole system in about 30 seconds – he doesn't waste words, does he?* • **waste your breath** If you waste your breath, you spend time and energy trying to give advice that is ignored: *Honestly, you're wasting your breath – he doesn't want to hear what anyone else has got to say.* • **waste not, want not** saying said to advise someone not to waste anything, because they might need it in the future • **wasted on sb** (C2) If you say that something is wasted on someone, you mean that it is too clever or its quality is too high for them and they will not understand its true value: *I'm not going to serve that good coffee to Chris and Melanie – it would be wasted on them.*

PHRASAL VERB **waste away** to gradually get thinner and weaker, in a way that is unhealthy: *You get thinner every time I see you, Sara – you're wasting away!*

wastebasket /ˈweɪstˌbɑː.skɪt/ (US) /-ˌbæs.kɪt/ **noun** [C] US (UK ˈ**wastepaper** ˌ**basket**) (A2) an open container that stands on the floor inside buildings and is used for putting rubbish in, especially paper

wasted /ˈweɪs.tɪd/ **adj BADLY USED** ▷ **1** wasted time, money, etc. is time, money, etc. that is not used effectively because it does not produce the result you wanted: *He wasn't in when I got there, so it was a completely wasted journey.* **THIN** ▷ **2** very thin and weak as a result of being ill or having no food: *Underneath the hospital blankets I could see the outline of her poor wasted* ***body.*** **DRUNK** ▷ **3** slang very drunk or ill from drugs: *He was too wasted to drive.* ◦ *Paula was completely wasted after only one drink.*

ˈ**waste disˌposal** noun [C] UK (US ˈ**garbage disˌposal**) an electrical machine connected to a kitchen sink which cuts up food waste so that it will flow easily through the pipes

wasteful /ˈweɪst.fᵊl/ **adj** disapproving using something in a careless way and causing some of it to be wasted: *It's wasteful the way you throw so much food away!* • **wastefully** /-i/ **adv** disapproving

wasteland /ˈweɪst.lænd/ **noun 1** [C or U] an empty area of land, especially in or near a city, that is not used to grow crops or built on, or used in any way: *The car was dumped in a stretch of wasteland in the south of the city.* **2** [S] literary disapproving a place, time, or situation that does not contain or produce anything positive, or that is completely without a particular quality or activity: *the* ***spiritual*** *wasteland of the 1980s*

wastepaper basket /ˈweɪst.peɪ.pəˌbɑː.skɪt/ (US) /-pəˌbæs.kɪt/ **noun** [C] UK (US **wastebasket**) an open container that stands on the floor inside buildings and is used for putting rubbish in, especially paper: *Most of the letters they receive end up in the wastepaper basket.*

ˈ**waste ˌproduct** noun [C] a substance of no value or use that is made during a process in which something useful is produced: *Cadmium is a toxic waste product of the electronics industry.*

waster /ˈweɪ.stəʳ/ (US) /-stɚ/ **noun** [C] **1** informal disapproving a person or thing who wastes something: *He's a time waster.* ◦ *This project is nothing but a money waster.* **2** UK informal disapproving a person who does nothing positive with their life, making no use of their abilities or the opportunities that are offered them

ˈ**wasting diˌsease** noun [C usually singular] a disease that causes a person to gradually become very thin and weak: *She suffers from a little-known* ***muscle-wasting*** *disease.*

wastrel /ˈweɪ.strᵊl/ **noun** [C] literary a person who does nothing positive with their life, making no use of their abilities or the opportunities that are offered them

watch /wɒtʃ/ (US) /wɑːtʃ/ **verb; noun**

▸**verb LOOK AT** ▷ **1** (A1) [I or T] to look at something for a period of time, especially something that is changing or moving: *I had dinner and watched TV for a couple of hours.* ◦ *He spent the entire afternoon watching a cricket match.* ◦ [+ obj + infinitive without to] *I watched him get into a taxi.* ◦ *I got the feeling I was being watched.* ◦ [+ obj + -ing verb] *I sit by the window and watch people walk****ing*** *past.* ◦ [+ question word] *Just watch* ***how*** *he slides that ball in past the goalkeeper.* ◦ *Bonner watched helplessly as the ball sneaked in at the near post.* ◦ *She'll pretend that she hasn't seen us – you watch.* **2** [T] to stay with something or someone such as a child for a short time to make certain that they are safe: *If you want me to watch the kids for a couple of hours while you go out, just let me know.* ◦ *Could you watch my bags for me, while I go to the toilet?* **BE CAREFUL** ▷ **3** (B2) [T] to be careful of something: *I have to watch my* ***weight*** *(= be careful not to become too heavy) now I'm not doing so much sport.* ◦ *Watch your language (= do not use rude words) in front of ladies, young man!* ◦ [+ (that)] *Watch (****that****) you don't get glue on your fingers, won't you?* ◦ [+ question word] *Watch* ***wh****at you're doing with that knife, Jim, it's sharp.* ◦ *You want to (= you should) watch him – he's a bit of a strange character.*

IDIOMS **watch your back** to be careful of the people around you, making certain that they do nothing to harm you: *I have to watch my back at work – there are a lot of people who would like my job.* • **watch your step** to be very careful about how you behave: *He'll have to watch his step if he wants to keep that job of* *his!* • **watch it** informal used to tell someone to be careful: *Watch it, you nearly knocked my head off with that plank!* • **watch paint dry** informal humorous used to refer to an activity that you consider extremely boring: *'So you don't want to watch the football?' 'To be honest I would rather watch paint dry'.* • **watch the clock** disapproving to often notice the time and wish that it was later, especially when you are doing work that you do not like • **watch the world go by** to look at people as they go past: *I love sitting in outdoor cafes watching the world go by.* • **watch this space** If someone says watch this space, they mean that there will very soon be an exciting change in their situation.

PHRASAL VERBS **watch out** B2 used to warn someone of danger or an accident that seems likely to happen: *'Watch out!' he shouted, but it was too late – she had knocked the whole tray of drinks on the floor.* • **watch out for sb/sth** to be careful to notice someone or something interesting: *Watch out for his latest movie, out next month.* • **watch over sb** to protect someone and make certain that they are safe: *The prince has two bodyguards watching over him every hour of the day.*

▸**noun** SMALL CLOCK ▷ **1** A1 [C] a small clock that is worn on a strap around the wrist or, sometimes, connected to a piece of clothing by a chain: *My watch seems to have stopped (= stopped working).* ◦ *He glanced nervously* ***at*** *his watch.* LOOKING ▷ **2** [S or U] the activity of watching or giving attention to something or someone, especially to make certain nothing bad happens: *Once your name has been linked with a drug offence, the police* ***keep*** *a close watch* ***on*** *you.* ◦ *The soldiers slept at night, except for one who stayed awake* ***on*** *watch/to* ***keep*** *watch.* **3** [S] a person or group of soldiers or guards whose duty is to protect a person, place, or thing from danger or attack **4** [C] a fixed period of time during which a person or a group of soldiers or guards has the duty of protecting and warning of danger

IDIOM **a watch out** the activity of watching carefully and looking for someone or something: ***Keep*** *a watch out* ***for*** *Nicki and Steve – they should be here somewhere.*

watchable /ˈwɒtʃ.ə.bl̩/ US /ˈwɑː.tʃə-/ adj informal approving describes a television programme or film that is entertaining: *It's not the most profound series I've ever seen but it's very watchable.*

watchdog /ˈwɒtʃ.dɒɡ/ US /ˈwɑːtʃ.dɑːɡ/ noun [C] ORGANIZATION ▷ **1** a person or organization responsible for making certain that companies obey particular standards and do not act illegally: *The Countryside Commission was set up as the government's official watchdog* ***on*** *conservation.* DOG ▷ **2** US for **guard dog**

watcher /ˈwɒtʃ.əʳ/ US /ˈwɑː.tʃɚ/ noun [C] a person who watches television or films: *The new channel is certainly good news for the movie watcher.* → See also **viewer**

-watcher /-wɒtʃ.əʳ/ US /-wɑː.tʃɚ/ suffix used with nouns to describe a person who is interested in and enjoys watching a particular thing: *Royal-watchers have once again been speculating on the health of the princess.*

watchful /ˈwɒtʃ.fəl/ US /ˈwɑːtʃ-/ adj paying careful attention and ready to deal with problems: ***Under the*** *watchful* ***eye of*** *their mother, the two boys played on the shore.* ◦ *She* ***keeps a*** *watchful* ***eye on*** *her husband to see that he behaves himself.* • **watchfully** /-i/ adv • **watchfulness** /-nəs/ noun [U]

watchman /ˈwɒtʃ.mən/ US /ˈwɑːtʃ-/ noun [C] (plural **-men** /-mən/) a person who is employed to guard a building or several buildings

watchstrap /ˈwɒtʃ.stræp/ US /ˈwɑːtʃ-/ noun [C] mainly UK (US **watchband**) a strip of leather or other material or a metal chain which fastens a watch onto your wrist

watchtower /ˈwɒtʃˌtaʊəʳ/ US /ˈwɑːtʃˌtaʊr/ noun [C] a tower built especially around the edges of prisons and army CAMPS, the top of which provides a good position from which to see anyone who is coming close

watchword /ˈwɒtʃ.wɜːd/ US /ˈwɑːtʃ.wɝːd/ noun [C usually singular] (a word or phrase which represents) the main ideas or principles directing the way that someone behaves or the way that something is done: *And remember, let caution be your watchword.*

water /ˈwɔː.təʳ/ US /ˈwɑː.t̬ɚ/ noun; verb

▸**noun** **1** A1 [U] a clear liquid, without colour or taste, that falls from the sky as rain and is necessary for animal and plant life: *a bottle/drink/glass of water* ◦ *bottled/mineral/tap water* ◦ *hot/cold water* ◦ *Can I have a* ***drop*** *of water in my whisky, please?* ◦ *Is the water hot enough for a bath?* ◦ *The human body is about 50 percent water.* **2** A2 [U] an area of water, such as the sea, a lake, or a swimming pool: *The water's warm – are you coming for a swim?* ◦ *I don't like getting my head* ***under*** *(= in) water.* ◦ *Dad, I swam a whole length of the pool* ***under*** *water (= with the whole head and body below the surface of the water)!* **3** [U] the level of an area of water: *High water this morning at Portsmouth is at 11.17.* **4 waters** [plural] **a** the area of sea near to and belonging to a particular country: *St Lucia depends on its clean coastal waters for its income.* **b** the water contained in a particular lake, river, or part of the sea: *In the shallow waters of the Gulf of Mexico, oil rigs attract fish.* **c** UK (US **water**) the liquid that surrounds a baby inside a pregnant woman's WOMB: *At 3 a.m. her waters broke, and the baby was born soon after.* **5 the waters** [plural] water from a spring, especially when used in the past for drinking or swimming in, in order to improve the health: *People used to come to this city to* ***take*** *(= drink or swim in) the waters.*

IDIOMS **water off a duck's back** C2 criticisms of or warnings to a particular person that have no effect on that person: *I've told him that he's heading for trouble, but he doesn't listen – it's just water off a duck's back.* • **water under the bridge** problems that someone has had in the past that they do not worry about because they happened a long time ago and cannot now be changed: *Yes, we did have our disagreements but that's water under the bridge now.* • **murky/uncharted waters** a situation that is not familiar and may be dangerous: *In the last two chapters of the book, she* ***enters*** *the murky waters of male sexuality.* ◦ *After the Wall Street crash, the American economy* ***moved into*** *uncharted waters.*

▸**verb** GIVE WATER ▷ **1** B2 [T] to pour water on to plants or the soil that they are growing in: *I've asked my neighbour to water the plants while I'm away.* **2** [T] to give an animal water to drink: *The horses had been fed and watered.* PRODUCE LIQUID ▷ **3** C2 [I] If your mouth waters, it produces a lot of saliva, usually because you can see or smell some food that you would like to eat: *The smell of that bread is making my mouth water!* **4** [I] When your eyes water, they produce tears but not because you are unhappy: *How do you stop your eyes from watering when you're cutting up onions?*

PHRASAL VERB **water sth down** DRINK ▷ **1** to add water to a drink, usually an alcoholic drink, in order to make it less strong IDEA ▷ **2** to deliberately make an idea or opinion less extreme, usually so that other people will accept it: *The party has watered down its ideals in order to appeal to the centre ground.*

-water /-wɔː.təʳ/ (US) /-wɑː.t̬ɚ/ **suffix** used to form adjectives: *freshwater fish* ◦ *a saltwater lagoon*

waterbed /ˈwɔː.təˌbed/ (US) /ˈwɑː.t̬ɚˌbed/ **noun** [C] a bed that is filled with water

ˈwater ˌbill noun [C] a regular charge that is made to people for the use of their local water supply

ˈwater ˌbird noun [C] any bird that lives near or on water

ˈwater ˌbiscuit noun [C] a thin, hard biscuit, often eaten with cheese

waterborne /ˈwɔː.tə.bɔːn/ (US) /ˈwɑː.ɚ.bɔːrn/ **adj** carried by or through water: *The disease, causing extreme stomach upsets, is caused by a waterborne parasite.*

ˈwater ˌbottle noun [C] **1** a container for carrying drinking water on a journey **2** Indian English a bottle of water

ˈwater ˌbuffalo noun [C or U] a large Asian animal like a cow with horns that curve backwards, often used for pulling farming tools

ˈwater ˌbutt noun [C] UK (US **ˈrain ˌbarrel**) a large container for collecting rain that can then be used to water plants

ˈwater ˌcannon noun [U] a device which sends out a powerful stream of water and is used in order to make large groups of people move away: *Police used water cannon to break up the demonstration.*

ˈwater ˌcloset noun [C usually singular] UK old-fashioned for a **WC**

watercolour UK (US **watercolor**) /ˈwɔː.təˌkʌl.əʳ/ (US) /ˈwɑː.t̬ɚˌkʌl.ɚ/ **noun** [C or U] a paint that is mixed with water and used to create pictures, or a picture that has been done with this type of paint: *I prefer painting with watercolours.* ◦ *some lovely watercolours*

ˌwater-ˈcooled adj If something such as an engine is water-cooled, it is surrounded by water to keep it at the correct operating temperature.

ˈwater ˌcooler noun [C] a machine for cooling and providing drinking water, usually in an office or other public place

watercourse /ˈwɔː.tə.kɔːs/ (US) /ˈwɑː.t̬ɚ.kɔːrs/ **noun** [C] a stream of water such as a river or CANAL, or the CHANNEL along which it flows

watercress /ˈwɔː.tə.kres/ (US) /ˈwɑː.t̬ɚ-/ **noun** [U] a plant which grows in water, whose green leaves taste hot and are used as food, often eaten uncooked in salads

ˌwatered-ˈdown adj [before noun] A watered-down idea or opinion has been made less extreme than it originally was, usually so that people are more likely to accept it: *They have returned with a watered-down version of the proposal.*

waterfall /ˈwɔː.tə.fɔːl/ (US) /ˈwɑː.t̬ɚ.fɑːl/ **noun** [C] (B1) water, especially from a river or stream, dropping from a higher to a lower point, sometimes from a great height

ˈwater ˌfeature noun [C] a small area of water or a FOUNTAIN that someone has in their garden

ˈwater ˌfilter noun [C] a device for removing unwanted substances such as bacteria or harmful chemicals from drinking water

ˈwater ˌfountain noun [C] a device, usually in a public place, which supplies water for drinking

waterfowl /ˈwɔː.tə.faʊl/ (US) /ˈwɑː.t̬ɚ-/ **noun** [C or U] (plural **waterfowl**) any bird that spends much of its life on or around a river or lake, especially one that is shot for food or sport

waterfront /ˈwɔː.tə.frʌnt/ (US) /ˈwɑː.t̬ɚ-/ **noun** [C usually singular] a part of a town that is next to an area of water such as a river or the sea: *She owns a popular tourist restaurant **on** the town's waterfront.*

waterhole /ˈwɔː.tə.həʊl/ (US) /ˈwɑː.t̬ə.hoʊl/ **noun** [C] a small pool of water in a dry area where animals go to drink

ˈwater ˌice noun [C] UK old-fashioned for **sorbet**

ˈwatering ˌcan noun [C] a container for water with a handle and a long tube used for pouring water onto garden plants

watering can

ˈwatering ˌhole noun [C] humorous a pub or bar where people go to drink alcohol

ˈwater ˌjump noun [C] an area of water with a fence before it, which people or horses jump over in a competition

ˈwater ˌlily noun [C] a plant whose large, flat leaves and cup-shaped PETALS float on the surface of lakes and pools

the waterline /ˈwɔː.tə.laɪn/ (US) /ˈwɑː.t̬ɚ-/ **noun** [S] specialized the level that the water reaches on the side of a ship

waterlogged /ˈwɔː.tə.lɒgd/ (US) /ˈwɑː.t̬ɚ.lɑːgd/ **adj** (of land) full of water and almost covered by a layer of it, or (of a boat) full of water and therefore unable to keep moving or floating: *Unfortunately the game was cancelled because of a waterlogged **pitch** (US **field**).*

ˈwater ˌmain noun [C usually plural] the main underground pipe in a system of pipes supplying water to an area

watermark /ˈwɔː.tə.mɑːk/ (US) /ˈwɑː.t̬ɚ.mɑːrk/ **noun** [C] PAPER ▷ **1** a mark made in some types of paper during its production that can only be seen if it is held against the light RIVER/SEA ▷ **2** a mark showing the highest or lowest level that a river or the sea reaches

ˈwater ˌmeadow noun [C] a field which floods with water from a river when there is a lot of rain

watermelon /ˈwɔː.təˌmel.ən/ (US) /ˈwɑː.t̬ɚ-/ **noun** [C or U] a large, round or oval-shaped fruit with dark green skin, sweet pink flesh, and a lot of black seeds

watermill /ˈwɔː.tə.mɪl/ (US) /ˈwɑː.t̬ɚ-/ **noun** [C] a MILL (= a machine that produces flour) whose power is provided by a large wheel that is turned by moving water, especially a river

ˈwater ˌpark noun [C] mainly US a large area containing several different pools with equipment and activities for swimmers, which visitors pay to use

ˈwater ˌpistol noun [C] (US also **ˈsquirt ˌgun**) a toy gun with which you can send out a stream of water to hit people or things

ˈwater ˌpolo noun [U] a game played in water in which two teams of swimmers try to get the ball into the other team's goal

waterproof /ˈwɔː.tə.pruːf/ (US) /ˈwɑː.t̬ɚ-/ **adj; verb; noun**

▸**adj** (B2) not allowing water to go through: *Canvas boots are all right but they're not as waterproof as leather.*

▸**verb** [T] to put a special substance on the surface of

something which will prevent water from going through it
▸noun [C] mainly UK a coat or other piece of clothing which keeps you dry because it does not allow water in

ˈwater-reˌpellent adj **showerproof**

watershed /ˈwɔː.tə.ʃed/ (US) /ˈwɑː.t̬ɚ-/ **noun** BIG CHANGE ▷ **1** [S] an event or period that is important because it represents a big change in how people do or think about something: *The year 1969 was **a** watershed **in** her life – she changed her career and changed her partner.* HIGH GROUND ▷ **2** [C] specialized an area of high ground from which water flows down to a river TELEVISION ▷ **3 the watershed** [S] UK in Britain, the time in the evening, usually 9 p.m., when television programmes that are not suitable for children may start to be shown

the waterside /ˈwɔː.tə.saɪd/ (US) /ˈwɑː.t̬ɚ-/ **noun** [S] an area of land near a river, lake, or sea: *They're building a new sports complex on the waterside.* ◦ *a waterside café*

waterskiing /ˈwɔː.təˌskiː.ɪŋ/ (US) /ˈwɑː.t̬ɚ-/ **noun** [U] a sport in which you are pulled along the surface of the water by a boat, while balancing on a pair of skis

ˈwater ˌsoftener noun [C] a substance or device that removes chemicals such as CALCIUM from water

ˈwater-ˌsoluble adj A water-soluble substance can dissolve in water: *Are these tablets water-soluble?*

ˈwater ˌsports noun [plural] sports which take place on or in water: *Popular water sports include surfing and waterskiing.*

waterspout /ˈwɔː.tə.spaʊt/ (US) /ˈwɑː.t̬ɚ-/ **noun** [C] mainly US a TORNADO (= violently spinning column of air) filled with water that forms over the sea

ˈwater supˌply noun [C usually singular] the water that is provided and treated for a particular area

ˈwater ˌtable noun [C usually singular] the level below the surface of the ground at which you start to find water

ˈwater ˌtank noun [C] Australian English a large container for collecting rain that can then be used to water plants → Compare **water butt**

ˈwater ˌtaxi noun [C] a small boat on a river or other area of water, operated by a person who you pay to take you where you want to go

watertight /ˈwɔː.tə.taɪt/ (US) /ˈwɑː.t̬ɚ-/ **adj** NO WATER ▷ **1** having no openings to allow water to get in: *They're doing some repairs to make the roof more watertight.* NO DOUBTS ▷ **2** (of a theory, plan, or agreement) formed very carefully in every detail so that nothing is uncertain or in doubt: *This book is designed to be provocative rather than a watertight piece of economic analysis.*

ˈwater ˌtower noun [C] a device to provide water pressure by positioning a large container for water on top of a tower-like structure

ˈwater ˌvapour noun [U] water in the form of a gas resulting from heating water or ice

waterway /ˈwɔː.tə.weɪ/ (US) /ˈwɑː.t̬ɚ-/ **noun** [C] a narrow area of water, such as a river or CANAL, which ships or boats can sail along

waterwheel /ˈwɔː.tə.wiːl/ (US) /ˈwɑː.t̬ɚ-/ **noun** [C] a large wheel that is turned by flowing water and used to provide the power for machinery

waterwings /ˈwɔː.tə.wɪŋz/ (US) /ˈwɑː.t̬ɚ-/ **noun** [plural] US (UK **armband**) hollow, ring-shaped pieces of plastic filled with air, which children who cannot swim wear on their arms in water to help them float

waterworks /ˈwɔː.tə.wɜːks/ (US) /ˈwɑː.t̬ɚ.wɝːks/ **noun**

[plural] **1** a system of buildings and pipes in which a public supply of water is stored and treated and from which it is sent out **2** UK polite word the parts of the body that deal with removing urine: *The doctor asked if I'd had any problems with my waterworks.*

IDIOM **turn on the waterworks** old-fashioned disapproving to start crying, especially too much or in a way that does not seem necessary or real: *You can turn on the waterworks all you like – I'm not going to change my mind!*

watery /ˈwɔː.tᵊr.i/ (US) /ˈwɑː.t̬ɚ.i/ **adj** **1** containing or filled with water: *watery eyes* ◦ *a thin, watery fluid* **2** disapproving (of food or drink) containing too much water and therefore weak in taste: *watery soup/coffee* **3** pale or weak in colour or strength: *The sun shed its thin watery **light** over the sea.*

IDIOM **watery grave** literary death by DROWNING (= dying because you cannot breathe underwater): *It was off the coast of Italy that Shelley **went to** his watery grave.*

watt /wɒt/ (US) /wɑːt/ **noun** [C] (written abbreviation **W**) the standard measure of electrical power: *Do you want 60-watt light bulbs for this room?* • **wattage** /ˈwɒt.ɪdʒ/ (US) /ˈwɑː.t̬ɪdʒ/ **noun** [U] *For lower wattage ovens, heating time must be increased.*

wattle and daub /ˌwɒt.l̩.ᵊndˈdɔːb/ (US) /ˌwɑː.t̬l̩.ᵊndˈdɑːb/ **noun** [U] a mixture of sticks, earth, and clay, used in some parts of the world as a building material: [before noun] *a wattle-and-daub hut*

wave /weɪv/ **verb; noun**

▸verb [I or T] MOVE HAND ▷ **1** (B1) to raise your hand and move it from side to side as a way of greeting someone, telling them to do something or adding emphasis to an expression: *I waved **to/at** him from the window but he didn't see me.* ◦ *I was waving my hand madly but he never once looked in my direction.* ◦ *She was so annoyed she wouldn't even wave us **goodbye**/wave goodbye **to** us.* ◦ *She waves her hands **about/around** a lot when she's talking.* **2 wave sb away, on, etc.** to make a movement with your hand that tells someone to move in a particular direction: *You'll have to wait till the policeman waves this line of traffic on.* ◦ *You can't just wave me away as if I were a child!* MOVE REPEATEDLY ▷ **3** (C1) to move from side to side, or to make something move like this while holding it in the hand: *The corn waved gently in the summer breeze.* ◦ *A crowd of football fans ran down the street waving banners.* ◦ *He seems to think I can wave a magic wand and everything will be all right.* CURL HAIR ▷ **4** If hair waves, it curls slightly: *If she leaves her hair to dry on its own, it just waves naturally.*

IDIOM **wave/say goodbye to sth** informal humorous to accept that you will no longer have something you value or that you will not get something you hoped to receive: *Well, if you've argued with senior management you can wave goodbye to any chances of promotion!*

PHRASAL VERBS **wave sth aside** to refuse to consider what someone says: *She waved aside all my objections.* • **wave sb/sth down** to make a driver stop their vehicle by waving your arms up and down: *If a car comes along, wave it down.* • **wave sb off** to wave to someone as they leave a place in order to say goodbye: *We went to the station to wave her off.*

▸noun [C] WATER ▷ **1** (B1) a raised line of water that moves across the surface of an area of water, especially the sea: *At night, I listened to the sound of the waves **breaking/crashing** against the shore.* HAND MOVEMENT ▷ **2** (C2) the action of raising your hand and moving it from side to side as a way of greeting someone, etc.: *Give Grandpa a wave.* **ENERGY** ▷ **3** B2 the pattern in which some types of energy, such as sound, light, and heat, are spread or carried: *radio waves* **LARGE NUMBER** ▷ **4** C2 a larger than usual number of events of a similar, often bad, type, happening within the same period: *a crime wave* ◦ *The country was swept by a wave **of** strikes.* **5 a new, second, etc. wave of sth** an activity that is happening again or is being repeated after a pause: *A new wave of job losses is expected this year.* **STRONG FEELING** ▷ **6** C2 A wave of an emotion or feeling is a sudden strong feeling that gets stronger as it spreads: *A wave **of** panic swept through the crowd.* → See also **brainwave** **HAIR CURVES** ▷ **7** a series of slight curves in a person's hair: *Your hair has a natural wave whereas mine's just straight.* → See also **wavy**

IDIOMS **make waves** informal C2 to be very active so that other people notice you, often in a way that intentionally causes trouble: *If a member of the Cabinet started making waves, the prime minister simply got rid of them.* • **wave after/upon wave** literary large quantities or groups of something, one after another: *Allied planes launched wave after wave of air attacks on the city.*

ˌwave and ˈpay noun [U] a way of paying for goods using a CREDIT CARD and a machine that can read the information on the card when you place the card on it

waveband /ˈweɪv.bænd/ noun [C] a set of radio waves of similar length that are used for broadcasting radio programmes

wavelength /ˈweɪv.leŋθ/ noun [C] the distance between two waves of energy, or the length of the radio wave used by a particular radio station for broadcasting programmes: *I don't know which wavelength the station is **on** – is it on long wave?*

IDIOM **be on the same wavelength** C2 (of two or more people) to think in a similar way and to understand each other well: *I can't seem to get on with him – we're just not on the same wavelength.*

waver /ˈweɪ.vəʳ/ US /-vɚ/ verb [I] **1** to lose strength, determination, or purpose, especially temporarily: *I'm afraid my concentration began to waver as lunch approached.* ◦ *He has never wavered **in** his support for the leader.* **2** If you waver between two possibilities, you cannot decide which of them to choose or you keep choosing one way and then the other: *'What are you having?' 'Er, I'm wavering **between** the fish soup and the mushroom tart.'* • **wavering** /-ɪŋ/ adj *It's the party's last attempt to persuade some of the nation's wavering voters to support them.*

wavy /ˈweɪ.vi/ adj having a series of curves: *Sarah's got lovely wavy blond hair.*

wax /wæks/ noun; verb

▸noun **1** [U] a solid substance containing a lot of fat that becomes soft and melts when warm: *She watched the wax as it dripped down the side of the candle.* → See also **beeswax** **2** [U] the soft, yellowish substance inside your ears

▸verb **USE WAX** ▷ **1** [T] to put a thin layer of wax on the surface of something, either to make it WATERPROOF or to improve its appearance: *I've waxed the floor so I'm afraid it's a bit slippery.* **2** [T] to remove hair from someone's body by covering it in a thin layer of warm wax that is then pulled off: *She **had** her legs waxed.* **MOON** ▷ **3** [I] formal When the moon waxes, it gradually appears larger and rounder each day. **SPEAK** ▷ **4 wax lyrical, eloquent, etc.** old use or formal to speak or write in the stated way: *My mother always used to wax lyrical about the lemon trees in the family garden.* • **waxed** /wækst/ adj *a waxed jacket*

IDIOM **wax and wane** to grow stronger and then weaker again: *His commitment to democracy and free markets has waxed and waned with his political fortunes.*

ˌwaxed ˈpaper noun [U] a type of paper that has a thin layer of wax on it and is used for wrapping food

waxen /ˈwæk.sᵊn/ adj literary describes a face that has pale, shiny skin and does not look healthy: *a waxen complexion*

waxhead /ˈwæks.hed/ noun [C] Australian English informal someone who SURFS on waves

waxing /ˈwæk.sɪŋ/ noun [U] a beauty treatment in which hair is removed from someone's body by covering it in a thin layer of warm WAX that is then pulled off: *We offer manicures, facials, and waxing.*

waxwork /ˈwæks.wɜːk/ US /-wɝːk/ noun **1** [C] a WAX model of a person **2 waxworks** [plural] a place where there are a lot of WAX models of famous people for the public to look at

waxy /ˈwæk.si/ adj slightly shiny; looking like WAX

way /weɪ/ noun; adv

▸noun **ROUTE** ▷ **1** A2 [C] a route, direction, or path: *Do you know the way **to** the train station?* ◦ *I've only been living in Madrid for a couple of weeks so I don't really know my way **around** it yet.* ◦ *We'll have to stop for fuel **on the** way to the airport.* ◦ *Can you **find** your own way **out of** the building?* ◦ *It's getting late – we should **make** our way (= go) home soon.* ◦ *He **elbowed/pushed** his way (= hit/pushed people so that he could go past them) to the front of the crowd.* ◦ *The coach stopped for us to eat lunch but within half an hour we were **on** our way/**under** way (= travelling) again.* ◦ *There's no way **through** the centre of town in a vehicle – it's for pedestrians only.* ◦ *You'll have to go **by** way **of** (= travel through) Copenhagen if you want to go to Southern Sweden from here.* ◦ *Many people have **lost** their way (= become lost) in the forest.* ◦ *Only a local person could **find** their way **through** the maze of narrow streets.* **2 make your way** B2 to travel or move to a place: *We slowly made our way down the river.* ◦ *It's getting late – we should make our way home soon.* **3** B1 [C] used to talk about the direction in which something is facing: *'Which way does the room face?' 'North.'* ◦ *Which way **up** should this box be? (= Which side should be on top?)* ◦ *The numbers are the wrong way **round** – it should be 71, not 17.* **4 the other way round/around** B2 happening in the opposite way: *I thought the older people would be more offended than the young people, but it was the other way round.* **5 Way** used in the names of some roads: *Our offices are at 17 King's Way.* **DISTANCE** ▷ **6** B1 [S] (US **ways**) distance or a period of time: *We walked **a long** way yesterday.* ◦ *The holidays seem like they're **a long** way **off**.* ◦ figurative *There were people of every political belief at university, ranging **all the** way from communists to fascists.* ◦ US *They still have a ways to go.* **POSSIBILITY** ▷ **7** B1 [C or U] a particular choice, opinion, belief, or action, especially from among several possibilities: *I like the way you've had your hair done.* ◦ ***In some/many** ways it would be better if we met on Monday rather than Wednesday.* ◦ ***In a** way (= partly), I would prefer it if they didn't come because it would mean extra work.* ◦ *He might have to resign or he might be demoted, but **either** way, his career is effectively over.* ◦ *They don't write songs **the** way (= as) they used to.* **MANNER** ▷ **8** C1 [S] the manner in which someone behaves or thinks, or in which something happens: *Don't be alarmed – it's just his way.* ◦ *He looked at me **in** a sinister way.* ◦ *It's* *amazing* **the** *way she manages to stay so calm.* ◦ *The way he was shouting, you'd have thought he was badly hurt.* ◦ ***To*** *my way of thinking, they shouldn't be building so many roads.* ◦ *It's* ***always the*** *way at work – either I've got nothing to do or I'm rushed off my feet!* **9 ways** [plural] types of behaviour: *Over the years we've got used to his funny little ways.* **METHOD** ▷ **10** A2 [C] an action that can produce the result you want; a method: *There are many ways* ***of*** *solv****ing*** *the problem.* ◦ [+ to infinitive] *That's not the way* ***to*** *do it – let me show you.* ◦ *That method hasn't worked, so let's try your way.* **FREE SPACE** ▷ **11** C2 [S] the space needed for a particular movement or action: *'Sorry, am I* ***in*** *your way? I'll move.'* ◦ *I couldn't see the stage because there was a pillar* ***in the*** *way (= between me and the stage).* ◦ *Please* ***make*** *way so the ambulance can get by.* ◦ *The best thing you can do if you're near to a tornado is get* ***out of*** *its way.* ◦ figurative *She's determined to succeed and she won't let anything* ***get/stand in*** *her way (= prevent her).* **WANT** ▷ **12** C1 [S] informal If someone gets or has their way, what they want happens: *If she doesn't* ***get/have*** *her* **(*own*)** *way, she sulks like a four-year-old.* **CONDITION** ▷ **13** [S] the bad condition or state of someone or something, especially the state of a person's health: *He's been in* ***a bad*** *way (= very ill) ever since the operation.*

> **! Common mistake: way**
>
> **Remember:** to talk about an action that produces the result you want, use **way to do sth** or **way of doing sth**:
>
> *What is the best way to send a parcel?*
> *What is the best way of sending a parcel?*
>
> After a possessive, don't say 'way to do sth', say **way of doing sth**:
>
> *It was his way of telling me he was proud of me.*
>
> If you are using a noun to talk about how something is achieved, don't say 'way of', say **means/method of**:
>
> ~~*way of communication/transport.*~~
> *means of communication/transport.*

> **! Common mistake: way**
>
> To talk about a method for doing something, don't say 'way how', just say **way**:
>
> ~~*We must find a way how to reduce queues.*~~
> *We must find a way to reduce queues.*

IDIOMS **all the way** as much as possible or completely: *If you want to take it up with the boss, I'll support you all the way.* • **all the way to** as far as someone or something at a high level in a process or structure: *I'll take my complaint all the way to the managing director.* • **(in) any way, shape, or form** in any way at all: *I have never been involved in any way, shape, or form with criminal activities.* • **be on the way to sth** to be close to doing something: *I'm* ***well*** *on the way to complet****ing*** *the report.* • **be out of the way** If a place or a building is out of the way, it is a long distance from where most people live: *It's a very beautiful village but it's a bit out of the way.* • **by the way** A2 used to introduce a new subject to be considered or to give further information: *I think we've discussed everything we need to – by the way, what time is it?* ◦ *Oh, by the way, my name's Julie.* • **by way of** C1 as a type of: *He sent me some flowers by way of an apology.* • **the easy way out** C1 what is easiest in a difficult situation: *As soon as things got difficult he* ***took*** *the easy way out.* • **find a way** to discover how to achieve or deal with something: *Finding a way* ***through*** *the legislation is impossible without expert advice.* • **get sth out of the way** C2 to finish something: *I like to get my homework out of the way on a Friday night so that I can enjoy the weekend.* • **give way to sth** (also **make way for sth**) UK C2 to be replaced by something, especially because it is better, cheaper, easier, etc.: *In some areas, modern intensive farming is giving way to the re-introduction of traditional methods.* • **go your own (sweet) way** to do what you want without considering other people: *It doesn't matter how much advice I give Cathy, she always goes her own sweet way.* • **go your own way** When people or groups of people choose to go their own way, they decide to live or work without continuing their previous personal or business relationship: *After a couple of years together, we realized we weren't suited to one another and decided to go our own ways.* • **go all the way** informal to have sex, especially after a period of kissing and touching: *Did you go all the way last night?* • **go out of your way** C2 to try very hard to do something, especially for someone else: *They really went out of their way* ***to*** *make us feel welcome by giving us the best room in the house.* • **have it both ways** to get advantages from two opposing things: *You* ***can't*** *have it both ways – you either work longer and get paid more or have more leisure time and get paid less.* • **in no way** C1 not at all: *She added that she had in no way intended to offend anybody.* • **make your way** C2 to be successful and make progress in your life and work: *He will teach you how to build a career and make your way in the world.* • **no way** informal **1** B1 used to tell someone that something is impossible: *I'm sorry but* ***there's*** *no way we can help you.* ◦ *No way will she agree to you leaving early.* **2 no way!** used to say 'no' in a forceful way: *'Go on, lend me your bike.' 'No way!'* • **point the way** to show how something can be done better in the future: *Recent medical discoveries are already pointing the way* ***to*** *more efficient vaccines.* • **talk your way into/out of sth** informal to persuade people that you should do something/not do something by the reasons you give: *He talked his way into the job.* ◦ *You might be able to talk your way out of most things but you still have to clean the dishes!* • **way of life** B1 the manner in which a person lives: *Sleeping in doorways, begging for food and money – it's not a very enviable way of life.* • **way/direction the wind blows** If a person tries to discover which way the wind blows/is blowing, they try to discover information about a situation, especially other people's opinions, before they take action: *I think I'll* ***see*** *which way the wind is blowing before I vote at the board meeting.* • **ways and means** The ways and means of achieving something are the methods and other things needed to make it happen: *With computer technology, even people working on their own have the ways and means to produce professional-looking documents.* • **work your way up/to the top** to make progress in a process or structure: *He started as an office junior and worked his way up through the company to become a director.* • **wouldn't have it any other way** If a person says they wouldn't have something any other way, they mean they would not change any of it, especially despite connected difficulties: *It's never going to be easy having kids but I wouldn't have it any other way.*

▸**adv** /weɪ/ **EMPHASIS** ▷ **1** informal used to emphasize degree or separation, especially in space or time: *After the third lap, she was way behind the other runners.* ◦ *She spends way too much money on clothes.* **PLACE** ▷ **2** old-fashioned in the direction of: *I think they live Birmingham way.*

waylay /ˌweɪˈleɪ/ verb [T] (**waylaid**, **waylaid**) to wait for and then stop someone, especially either to attack them or talk to them: *A man on his way to deposit $12,000 in a bank was waylaid by two men who snatched his bag.* ◦ *I meant to leave earlier but I was waylaid on the way out of a meeting by my manager.*

ˌ**way-ˈout** adj old-fashioned informal unusual, especially because very modern in style: *A lot of experimental theatre is too way-out for me.*

-ways /-weɪz/ suffix (used in adverbs) in the stated direction or manner: *edgeways* ◦ *lengthways*

wayside /ˈweɪ.saɪd/ noun **fall by the wayside** If someone falls by the wayside, they fail to finish an activity, and if something falls by the wayside, people stop doing it, making it, or using it: *So why does one company survive a recession while its competitors fall by the wayside?*

Waystage /ˈweɪ.steɪdʒ/ noun [U] a low to middle level of ability in a foreign language according to the Common European Framework (= a description of language ability levels created by the Council of Europe)

ˈ**way** ˌ**station** noun [C] US a place where people can stop when travelling from one place to another

wayward /ˈweɪ.wəd/ (US) /-wɚd/ adj old-fashioned doing only what you want and often changing your behaviour in a way that is difficult to control • **waywardness** /-nəs/ noun [U]

wazz /wæz/ noun [S] slang an act of URINATING (= passing urine from the body)

WC /ˌdʌb.l̩.juˈsiː/ noun [C] UK abbreviation for water closet: a toilet, or a room containing a toilet: *The wooden staircase leads to three bedrooms, the bathroom, and a separate WC.*

we strong /wiː/ weak /wi/ pronoun **GROUP** ▷ **1** (A1) used as the subject of a verb to refer to a group including the speaker and at least one other person: *Can we all go to the swimming pool this afternoon?* ◦ *If you don't hurry up we'll be late.* **2** used by a speaker or a writer to refer to themselves and the people listening or reading: *In today's lecture, we will be exploring the world economic situation.* **ALL PEOPLE** ▷ **3** (B1) used as the subject of a verb to refer to all people, especially when considered as a group: *This planet on which we **all** live should be cherished and not exploited.* **YOU** ▷ **4** informal used as the subject of a verb to mean 'you', especially when talking to a child or someone who is ill: *Now we don't want to be late for school, do we?* ◦ *'How are we this morning, Mrs Flanagan?' said the doctor.* **I** ▷ **5** formal used by a queen or king when speaking officially to mean 'I'

weak /wiːk/ adj **NOT STRONG** ▷ **1** (B1) not strong, or not strong enough to work, last, succeed, persuade, or be effective: *It's not surprising you feel weak if you haven't eaten properly for days.* ◦ *The electromagnetic field strength becomes weaker as you move further away from high voltage cables.* ◦ *He was a weak king surrounded by corrupt advisers.* ◦ *Any evidence that exists to support the hypothesis is fairly weak.* ◦ *He gave the weakest of excuses when asked why he was late.* **2** (B2) describes a drink that contains a lot of water compared to its other contents, so that it does not have a strong flavour: *I can't stand weak coffee/tea.* **3** specialized describes an ACID, ALKALI, or chemical BASE that does not produce many IONS (= atoms with an electrical charge) when it is dissolved in water **NOT GOOD** ▷ **4** (B1) not good enough, especially in ability, skill, or quality: *He was always weak **at/in** languages but strong at/in science.* ◦ *Our quiz team is a bit weak **on** sport.* ◦ *In the end I think the film was spoilt by a weak story line.* • **weakly** /-li/ adv

> **Other ways of saying weak**
>
> If someone is physically weak because of being small, you could describe that person as **puny** or a **weakling**:
>
> *He was **puny** as a child.*
>
> *It would take more than a few exercises to turn a ninety-pound **weakling** into a heavyweight boxer.*
>
> If someone is physically weak because of being old or ill, you could use the adjective **frail**:
>
> *a **frail**, grey-haired lady*
>
> If someone is weak and could easily be hurt, you can describe that person as **defenceless** or **vulnerable**:
>
> *a small, **defenceless** child*
>
> *The disease most often affects **vulnerable** people such as children and the elderly.*

IDIOM **weak at the knees** If you go weak at the knees, you lose your strength and feel you are going to fall over, usually because of seeing or talking about either someone you are very attracted to or because of something unpleasant or frightening: *The thought of kissing him made me **go** weak at the knees.*

weaken /ˈwiː.kᵊn/ verb [I or T] (C1) to (cause to) become less strong, powerful, or determined: *You could see the poor dog weakening daily as the disease spread through its body.* ◦ *Another defeat in parliament would seriously weaken the president's ability to govern.* ◦ *We know that prolonged exposure to vibration can weaken aircraft components.* ◦ *She's weakening – ask her some more questions and see if she confesses.*

the ˈ**weaker** ˌ**sex** noun [S, + sing/pl verb] used to refer to women in general: considered offensive by many people

ˈ**weak** ˌ**form** noun [C] specialized the way that word is pronounced when there is no STRESS on it

ˌ**weak-ˈkneed** adj [after verb] **1** informal disapproving not brave or determined enough to defend your beliefs against others: *Instead of defending traditional values, the church frequently seems weak-kneed and irresolute.* **2** made to feel weak and likely to fall by emotion: *She stood dazed and weak-kneed beside the coffin.*

weakling /ˈwiː.klɪŋ/ noun [C] disapproving someone who is weak, either physically or in character: *It would need more than a few exercises to turn a seven-stone weakling into a heavyweight boxer.*

ˌ**weak** ˈ**link** noun [C usually singular] a weak part, especially the weakest part of something: *They're a fairly good team – their only weak link is a relatively inexperienced goalkeeper.* ◦ *A chain can only be as strong as its weakest link, so we must look at the least committed country to see if the alliance will hold.*

ˌ**weak-ˈminded** adj showing no determination, or stupid

weakness /ˈwiːk.nəs/ noun **1** (B2) [U] the fact or state of not being strong or powerful: *Any change of policy will be interpreted as a sign of weakness.* **2** (B2) [C] a particular part or quality of someone or something that is not good or effective: *There are definite weaknesses in their security arrangements.* ◦ *His main weakness as a manager is his inability to delegate.* ◦ *The later novels show none of the weaknesses of his earlier work.* **3 weakness for** (C2) a strong liking, usually for something which might have unpleasant or unwanted effects: *My diet would be fine if only I didn't have this weakness for sweet things.*

W

ˈweak ˌspot noun [C] a weak part in something: *Targeting the opponent's weak spots is a typical technique in politics.*

ˌweak-ˈwilled adj not having the determination that is needed to continue with a difficult course of action: *My diets are never successful – I'm just too weak-willed.*

weal /wiːl/ noun [C] a raised mark on the skin caused by being hit or injured in some other way: *His back was covered with weals where he had been repeatedly beaten.*

wealth /welθ/ noun **MONEY** ▷ **1** B2 [U] a large amount of money or valuable possessions that someone has: *During a successful business career, she accumulated a great amount of wealth.* **LARGE AMOUNT** ▷ **2** C2 [S] a large amount of something good: *Jim has **a** wealth **of** teaching experience.* ◦ *Russia has **a** wealth **of** coal and timber.*

wealthy /ˈwel.θi/ adj; noun

▸adj B2 rich: *He's a very wealthy man.* ◦ *With their natural resources they are potentially a very wealthy country.*

▸noun [plural] **the wealthy** rich people

wean /wiːn/ verb [T] to cause a baby or young animal to stop feeding on its mother's milk and to start eating other food, especially solid food, instead: *The studies were carried out on calves that had been weaned at five weeks of age.* • **weaning** /ˈwiː.nɪŋ/ noun [U]

PHRASAL VERBS **wean sb off sth** (US also **wean sb from sth**) to make someone gradually stop using something that is bad for them: *It's difficult to wean an addict off cocaine once they're hooked.* ◦ *The whole scheme is intended to wean people off welfare dependency.* • **wean sb on sth/sb** [usually passive] If someone is weaned on something or someone, they have learned about and been influenced by them when they were young: *This generation has been weaned on computer games.*

weapon /ˈwep.ən/ noun [C] B2 any object used in fighting or war, such as a gun, bomb, knife, etc.: *a lethal weapon* ◦ *chemical/nuclear/biological weapons* ◦ *The youths were dragged from their car and searched for weapons.*

> **Word partners for weapon**
>
> *deploy/possess/stockpile* weapons • *biological/chemical/nuclear* weapons • *carry* a weapon • a weapons *programme*

weaponize (UK usually **weaponise**) /ˈwep.ən.aɪz/ verb [T] to turn bacteria, poisonous chemicals, etc. into weapons that could kill or injure many people

weaponry /ˈwep.ən.ri/ noun [U] weapons in general: *nuclear/conventional weaponry* ◦ *All hi-tech weaponry demands frequent servicing to ensure accuracy.*

ˈweapons-ˌgrade adj of the quality or type that can be used to make nuclear weapons

ˌweapons of ˌmass deˈstruction noun [plural] weapons, like nuclear bombs, which cause a lot of damage and kill many people

wear /weəʳ/ US /wer/ verb; noun

▸verb (**wore**, **worn**) **ON BODY** ▷ **1** A1 [T] to have clothing, jewellery, etc. on your body: *Tracey is wearing a simple black dress.* ◦ *What are you wearing **to** Caroline's wedding?* ◦ *Some musicians don't like to wear rings when they're playing.* ◦ *He wears glasses for reading.* ◦ *She wears very little makeup.* **2** C2 [T] to show a particular emotion on your face: *The minister wore a confident smile throughout the interview.* **3** B2 [T] to arrange your hair in a particular way: *When she's working she wears her hair **in** a ponytail.* ◦ *You should wear your hair **up** (= so that it does not hang down) more often – it suits you.* **WEAKEN** ▷ **4** [I] to become weaker, damaged, or thinner because of continuous use: *I'm very fond of this shirt but it's starting to wear at the collar.* ◦ *The wheel bearings have worn over the years, which is what's causing the noise.* **5** [T usually + adv/prep] to produce something such as a hole or loss of material by continuous use, rubbing, or movement: *I always seem to wear **a hole** in the left elbow of my sweaters.* ◦ *Over many years, flowing water wore deep grooves **into** the rock.* ◦ *Wind and water slowly wore **down** the mountain's jagged edges.* **ALLOW** ▷ **6** [T] UK old-fashioned informal to allow or accept something: *I'd ask my boss for some time off but I don't think she'd wear **it**.*

IDIOMS **wear your heart on your sleeve** to make your feelings and emotions obvious rather than hiding them • **wear the trousers** UK (US **wear the pants**) (especially of a woman) to be the person in a relationship who is in control and who makes decisions for both people: *Brian may seem bossy, but I'll tell you it's Lisa that really wears the trousers in that relationship.* • **wear thin** informal **1** C2 If your patience wears thin, you become less and less patient: *I've warned you several times about being late and my patience **is wearing** thin.* **2** C2 If something such as a joke wears thin, it becomes boring or annoying or stops being funny or effective, because it has been seen, heard, or used too much: *Tony, the joke is beginning to wear thin now and a lot of us have had enough.* ◦ *Her standard excuse for being late was beginning to wear thin.*

PHRASAL VERBS **wear (sth) away** to become thin and disappear after repeated use or rubbing, or to cause something to become thin and disappear in this way: *In some diseases, the protective layer in a joint wears away.* • **wear sb down** to make someone feel tired and less able to deal successfully with a situation: *Both sides are trying to wear the other down by being obstinate in the negotiations.* ◦ *All the stress and extra travel is beginning to wear him down.* • **wear off** B2 If a feeling or the effect of something wears off, it gradually disappears: *Most patients find that the numbness from the injection wears off after about an hour.* • **wear on** If a period of time wears on, it seems to pass very slowly: *She felt less confident about completing the course as the week wore on.* • **wear sb out** B2 to make someone extremely tired: *Walking around a museum all day really wears you out.* • **wear (sth) out** B1 to use something so much that it is damaged and cannot be used any more, or to become damaged in this way: *Moving parts in engines wear out much more quickly than stationary parts.*

▸noun [U] **CLOTHES** ▷ **1** (also **wear**) clothes suitable for a particular use or clothes of a particular type: *casual wear* ◦ *leisure wear* ◦ *knitwear* **USE** ▷ **2** the amount or type of use an object has had or can be expected to have, especially before showing damage: *I've had a lot of wear **out of** these boots – I've had them for five years.* ◦ *I've only worn the shirt a couple of times and it's already showing **signs of** wear (= damage).*

wearable /ˈweə.rə.bl/ US /ˈwer.ə-/ adj Clothes that are wearable are easy to wear because they are comfortable, acceptable in most social situations, and look attractive in combination with other clothes.

ˌwear and ˈtear noun [U] the damage which happens to an object in ordinary use during a period: *Seat covers on trains **take** a lot of wear and tear.*

wearer /ˈweə.rəʳ/ US /ˈwer.ɚ/ noun [C] the person wearing something: *In medieval times the sapphire* was believed to offer protection to its wearer. ◦ *Clothes, of course, say a lot about the wearer.*

wearing /ˈweə.rɪŋ/ (US) /ˈwer.ɪŋ/ **adj** making you feel tired: *Looking after three children all day is very wearing.*

wearisome /ˈwɪə.rɪ.səm/ (US) /ˈwɪr.ɪ-/ **adj** formal causing a person to be tired and/or bored: *Simple repetitive tasks can be very wearisome.*

weary /ˈwɪə.ri/ (US) /ˈwɪr.i/ **adj; verb**

▸**adj 1** (C2) very tired, especially after working hard for a long time: *I think he's a little weary after his long journey.* ◦ *Here, sit down and rest your weary legs.* **2 weary of** (C2) bored with something because you have experienced too much of it: *I've been going out with the same people to the same clubs for years and I've just* ***grown*** *weary of it.*

▸**verb** formal **1** [T] to make someone feel tired: *Children weary me all day with their constant inquiries and demands.* **2** [I] to start to feel that something or someone is boring: *Some people never seem to weary* ***of*** *eating the same type of food every day.* • **wearily** /ˈwɪə.rɪ.li/ (US) /ˈwɪr.ɪ-/ **adv** *I dragged myself wearily out of bed at five o'clock this morning.* • **weariness** /-nəs/ **noun** [U]

wearying /ˈwɪə.ri.ɪŋ/ (US) /ˈwɪr.i-/ **adj** making you feel tired: *a long wearying journey*

weasel /ˈwiː.zəl/ **noun; verb**

▸**noun** [C] a small mammal with reddish-brown fur and a long body that can kill other small animals such as mice and birds for food

▸**verb**

PHRASAL VERB **weasel out of sth** mainly US informal to avoid doing something that you have agreed to do, especially by being dishonest: *Although they had signed the contract they tried to weasel out of the deal later.*

ˈweasel ˌwords **noun** [plural] informal something that someone says either to avoid answering a question clearly or to make someone believe something that is not true

weather /ˈweð.əʳ/ (US) /-ɚ/ **noun; verb**

▸**noun** [U] (A1) the conditions in the air above the earth such as wind, rain, or temperature, especially at a particular time over a particular area: *bad/good/cold/dry/hot/stormy/warm/wet/etc. weather* ◦ *The weather in the hills can change very quickly, so take suitable clothing.* ◦ *We're going to have a picnic, weather* ***permitting*** *(= if the weather is good enough).*

> **Word partners for weather**
>
> weather ***brightens up/clears (up)/improves*** • weather ***closes in/deteriorates/worsens*** • weather ***conditions/patterns*** • ***adverse/bad/poor/severe*** weather • ***dry/fine/good/mild*** weather • ***cold/stormy/wet/windy*** weather • ***hot/sunny/warm*** weather

IDIOMS **be/feel under the weather** informal (C2) to be or feel ill: *I'm feeling a bit under the weather – I think I've caught a cold.* • **in all weathers** If something is done in all weathers, it is done in every type of weather: *He's a real enthusiast – he goes fishing in all weathers.*

▸**verb** **DEAL WITH** ▷ **1** [T] to deal successfully with a difficult situation or a problem: *As a small new company they did well to weather the recession.* **AIR CONDITIONS** ▷ **2** [I or T] to change in colour or form over a period of time because of the effects of sun, wind, or other weather conditions: *Rock is weathered by the action of ice and changes in temperature.* ◦ *The paint on the outside walls has weathered* ***badly*** *(= has changed and been damaged by the weather).* • **weathered** /-əd/ (US) /-ɚd/ **adj** *weathered stone/tiles*

IDIOM **weather the storm** If someone or something weathers the storm, they successfully deal with a very difficult problem: *In the next few days we shall see if the ambassador can weather the political storm caused by his ill-advised remarks.*

ˈweather-ˌbeaten **adj** describes something, such as skin or a building material that has been changed or damaged by the weather: *a weather-beaten face (= a face which is brown and has many deep lines)* ◦ *ancient, weather-beaten columns*

weatherboarding /ˈweð.əˌbɔː.dɪŋ/ (US) /-ɚˌbɔːr-/ **noun** [U] a set of boards fixed across the bottom of a door to stop water from entering a building

weathercock /ˈweð.ə.kɒk/ (US) /-ɚ.kɑːk/ **noun** [C] a type of WEATHER VANE (= a device for showing which way the wind is blowing) in the shape of a chicken

ˈweather ˌforecast **noun** [C] (B1) a statement of what the weather is likely to be for the next day or few days, usually broadcast on television or radio or printed in a newspaper

ˈweather ˌforecaster **noun** [C] **1** someone who scientifically studies weather conditions and says what the weather is likely to be in the future **2** a **weatherman** or **weathergirl**

weathergirl /ˈweð.ə.gɜːl/ (US) /-ɚ.gɜːl/ **noun** [C] informal a female weather forecaster on television or radio

weatherman /ˈweð.ə.mæn/ (US) /-ɚ-/ **noun** [C] (plural **-men** /-men/) a male weather forecaster on television or radio

weatherproof /ˈweð.ə.pruːf/ (US) /-ɚ-/ **adj** not allowing wind or rain to go through: *a weatherproof tent/coat* → Compare **waterproof**

ˈweather ˌstation **noun** [C] a building or place where information is collected about local weather conditions

weathervane /ˈweð.ə.veɪn/ (US) /-ɚ-/ **noun** [C] a metal object, usually with a part shaped like an arrow, that is put on top of a high building and turns to show which way the wind is blowing from

weathervane

weave /wiːv/ **verb; noun**

▸**verb** **MAKE** ▷ **1** [I or T] (**wove** or US also **weaved**, **woven** or US also **weaved**) to make cloth by repeatedly crossing a single thread through two sets of long threads on a LOOM (= special frame): *This type of wool is woven* ***into*** *fabric which will make jackets.* **2** [T] (**wove** or US also **weaved**, **woven** or US also **weaved**) to twist long objects together, or to make something by doing this: *We were shown how to roughly weave ferns and grass* ***together*** *to make a temporary shelter.* ◦ *It takes great skill to weave a basket* ***from/out of*** *rushes.* **3** [T] (**wove** or US also **weaved**, **woven** or US also **weaved**) literary to form something from several different things or to combine several different things, in a complicated or skilled way: *The biography is woven* ***from*** *the many accounts which exist of things she did.* **MOVE QUICKLY** ▷ **4** [I usually + adv/prep] (**weaved**, **weaved**) to go or make a path by moving quickly and changing direction often, especially to avoid hitting things: *To escape from police officers the thief weaved* ***through/between/in and out*** *of stationary traffic on a bicycle.* • **weaver** /ˈwiː.vəʳ/ (US) /-vɚ/ **noun** [C] a person whose job is weaving cloth and other materials: *basket weavers* • **weaving** /ˈwiː.vɪŋ/ **noun** [U]

IDIOM **get weaving** UK old-fashioned informal If you tell someone to get weaving, you either want them to start something or to hurry what they are doing: *We'd better get weaving – we've got a lot to do today.*

▸**noun** [C usually singular] the way in which cloth has been woven, for example with the threads pulled firmly together, or the pattern produced by this process: *a tight weave* ◦ *a striped/traditional weave*

web /web/ **noun** [C] **NET** ▷ **1** B1 a fixed net used to catch insects, made by a SPIDER from the sticky thread that its body produces: *a spider's web* ◦ *We watched a spider* ***spin*** *a web between three tall grass stems.* ◦ figurative *Those involved in the fraud created an* ***intricate*** *web of trading companies to hide their activities.* → See also **cobweb** **SKIN** ▷ **2** the skin connecting the toes of some birds and other animals living by or on water which helps them when swimming

the Web /web/ **noun** [S] A2 the system of connected documents on the internet: *Jane's been* ***surfing*** *the Web all morning.*

Web 2.0 **noun** a name for all the internet features and websites that allow users to create, change, and share internet CONTENT (= information, pictures, etc.)

ˈ**web aˌddress** **noun** [C] (US ˌ**web** ˈ**address**) an email or website address

webbed /webd/ **adj** describes the toes of some birds and animals that are connected by skin to help them when swimming: *webbed toes/feet*

webbing /ˈweb.ɪŋ/ **noun** [U] threads of strong material twisted into strong strips, used to make belts and straps and to support springs in furniture

ˈ**web ˌbrowser** (also **browser**) **noun** [C] a computer program that makes it possible for you to read information on the internet

webcam /ˈweb.kæm/ **noun** [C] B1 a camera that records moving pictures and sound and allows these to be broadcast on the internet as they happen

webcast /ˈweb.kɑːst/ (US) /-kæst/ **noun** [C] a broadcast made on the internet: *Click here to join our live webcast, Current Consumer Issues.*

ˈ**web deˌsigner** **noun** [C] a person who designs websites

ˈ**web-eˌnabled** **adj** able to connect to the internet or be used on the internet: *web-enabled TV/content*

ˌ**web-ˈfooted** **adj** (also ˌ**web-ˈtoed**) (of an animal) having feet with skin between the toes

ˈ**web ˌhosting** **noun** [U] the service of keeping and managing websites on a SERVER (= large central computer)

webinar /ˈweb.ɪ.nɑːʳ/ (US) /-ə.nɑːr/ **noun** [C] an occasion when a group of people go on the internet at the same time to study and discuss something

weblog /ˈweb.lɒg/ (US) /-lɑːg/ **noun** [C] (also **blog**) a regular record of your thoughts, opinions, and experiences, put on the internet for others to read, that often contains LINKS (= words or pictures that connect to other places on the internet)

ˈ**web ˌpage** **noun** [C] (also **page**) A2 a page of information on the internet about a particular subject, that forms (a part of) a website: *A website may have many different web pages for you to click on and explore.*

ˈ**web ˌserver** **noun** [C] specialized a computer system or program that sends websites and information to internet users

website /ˈweb.saɪt/ **noun** [C] (also **site**) A1 a set of pages of information on the internet about a particular subject, published by a single person or organization: *For more information about other Cambridge publications and courses,* ***visit*** *our website* ***at*** *www.cambridge.org.*

webzine /ˈweb.ziːn/ **noun** [C] a magazine that is published on the internet and not on paper

we'd strong /wiːd/ weak /wid/ **short form of 1** we had: *We'd better be more careful in the future.* **2** we would: *We'd be grateful for an answer.*

wed /wed/ **verb** [I or T] (present tense **wedding**, past tense and past participle **wedded** or **wed**) literary (used especially in newspapers) to marry someone: *The couple eventually wed after an 18-year engagement.* → See also **newlywed**

Wed. written abbreviation for **Wednesday**

wedded /ˈwed.ɪd/ **adj** **BELIEF** ▷ **1 wedded to** believing firmly in an idea or theory and unwilling to change that belief: *The Social Democrats are still wedded to the concepts of high taxation and regulation.* **MARRIED** ▷ **2** [before noun] literary married: *your lawful wedded husband/wife* ◦ *Elaine and Ian have been living in wedded* ***bliss*** *for almost half a year now.*

wedding /ˈwed.ɪŋ/ **noun** [C] B1 a marriage ceremony and any celebrations such as a meal or a party which follow it: *a wedding cake/dress/invitation/present/reception* ◦ *Do you know the date of Caroline and Matthew's wedding?*

ˈ**wedding ˌband** **noun** [C] US for a **wedding ring**

ˈ**wedding ˌlist** **noun** [C usually singular] a list of all the things that two people who are soon to be married would like to receive as presents, often kept at a particular shop

ˈ**wedding ˌplanner** **noun** [C] a person or company whose job is to organize weddings for other people

ˈ**wedding reˌception** **noun** [C] (also **reception**) a party to celebrate the marriage ceremony of two people: *The wedding will be held at St Martin's Church and the wedding reception at Crathorne Hotel.*

ˈ**wedding ˌring** **noun** [C] (US also ˈ**wedding ˌband**) a ring, usually made of gold, worn to show that you are married

wedge /wedʒ/ **noun; verb**

▸**noun** **SHAPE** ▷ **1** [C] a piece of metal, wood, rubber, etc. with a pointed edge at one end and a wide edge at the other, either pushed between two objects to keep them still or forced into something to break pieces off it: *Push a wedge under the door to keep it open while we're carrying the boxes in.* ◦ *Pieces of stone can be split off by forcing wedges* ***between*** *the layers.* **2** [C] a piece of something, especially food, in the shape of a triangle: *Auntie Ann put a huge wedge of fruit cake on my plate.* ◦ *a wedge of cheese* **SHOES** ▷ **3 wedges** [plural] women's shoes with a HEEL all the way under the shoe

▸**verb** [T] **1** to make something stay in a particular position by using a wedge: [+ adj] *Find something to wedge the window* ***open/closed*** *with.* **2** to put something into a very small or narrow space, so that it cannot move easily: *Her shoe came off and got wedged between the bars.* ◦ *I was standing waiting for a bus, wedged* ***between*** *(= fixed between and unable to move away from) two old ladies and their bags of shopping.*

wedlock /ˈwed.lɒk/ (US) /-lɑːk/ **noun** [U] old-fashioned or humorous the state of being married

Wednesday /ˈwenz.deɪ/ **noun** [C or U] (written abbreviation **Wed.**) A1 the day of the week after Tuesday and before Thursday: *Did you say the meeting is* ***on*** *Wednesday?* ◦ *The restaurant is always closed* ***on*** *Wednesdays.* ◦ ***Next*** *Wednesday is my birthday.* ◦ *I didn't go to school* ***last*** *Wednesday.* ◦ *29 April is a Wednesday.* ◦ *Wednesday* ***morning/afternoon/evening/night***

wee /wiː/ **adj; verb; noun**
▸**adj** [before noun] Scottish English or informal small; little: *There's a wee cottage inside the grounds.* ◦ *Would you care for a wee* ***bit*** *more to eat?*
▸**verb** [I] (also ˈ**wee-wee**) informal or child's word to URINATE: *Daddy, I want to wee!*
▸**noun 1** [C usually singular] (also child's word ˈ**wee-wee**) informal an act of URINATING: *'I really need a wee!' she said.* ◦ child's word *Do you* ***need/want*** *(****to do****)* ***a*** *wee-wee before we go out?* **2** [U] urine

weed /wiːd/ **noun; verb**
▸**noun PLANT** ▷ **1** C [C] any wild plant which grows in an unwanted place, especially in a garden or field where it prevents the CULTIVATED plants from growing freely **2** [U] slang **cannabis 3** [U] UK old-fashioned informal **tobacco PERSON** ▷ **4** [C] UK informal disapproving someone who is thin and physically weak or who is weak in character: *He looks like a real weed in those shorts.*
▸**verb** [I or T] to remove wild plants from a place where they are not wanted: *I've been weeding (the vegetable garden).* • **weeding** /ˈwiː.dɪŋ/ **noun** [U] *There's plenty of weeding to* ***do*** *now that the growing season's started.*

PHRASAL VERB **weed sth/sb out** to get rid of unwanted things or people from a group: *The first round of interviews only really serves to weed out the very weakest of applicants.*

weedkiller /ˈwiːdˌkɪl.əʳ/ US /-ɚ/ **noun** [C or U] a chemical used for killing weeds

ˈ**Weed** ˌ**Whacker noun** [C] US trademark (UK trademark **Strimmer**) an electric tool that is held in the hand and is used for cutting grass and weeds in places that are difficult to reach

weedy /ˈwiː.di/ **adj WEAK** ▷ **1** UK informal disapproving describes a person who is thin and physically weak: *a weedy child* **PLANT** ▷ **2** containing a lot of weeds: *a weedy pavement*

week /wiːk/ **noun** [C] **1** A1 a period of seven days, especially either from Monday to Sunday or from Sunday to Saturday: *last/this/next week* ◦ *We go to the cinema about once a week.* ◦ *Will you be going to next week's class?* ◦ *It usually takes about four weeks to get the forms processed.* ◦ *Don't do anything strenuous for a week* ***or two.*** ◦ *It'll be weeks (= several weeks) before the flood damage is cleared up.* **2** A1 the five days from Monday to Friday, the usual working period for many people: *We're usually too tired to do much socializing during the week.* **3** one week after the day mentioned: *The first performance of the play is a week* ***today/tomorrow.*** ◦ *Our holiday starts a week* ***on*** *Saturday.* ◦ *She has to go back to see the doctor Friday week.* **4** one week before the day mentioned: *The problems with the TV started a week* ***last*** *Monday.* ◦ *It was his birthday a week* ***ago this*** *Friday.* **5** the amount of hours spent working during a week or the number of days on which a person works: *A lot of farm labourers* ***work*** *a six-day week.* **6 week by week** each week during a period of time: *We could see his health deteriorate week by week.* **7 week after week** (also **week in, week out**) regularly or continuously for many weeks: *I go to aerobics three times a week, week in, week out.*

IDIOM **of the week** A thing or person of the week is one that has been chosen as the best in a particular week: *Book of the Week: Dog Breeds by A J Barker and H A Barker.*

weekday /ˈwiːk.deɪ/ **noun** [C] A2 any day of the week except Sunday and usually Saturday: *On weekdays I'm usually in bed by ten o'clock.*

weekend /ˌwiːkˈend/ /ˈwiːk.end/ **noun** [C] **1** A1 Saturday and Sunday, or Friday evening until Sunday night; the part of the week in which many people living in the West do not go to work: *Have you got anything planned for* ***the*** *weekend?* ◦ *This/Next weekend we're going to see some friends.* **2** a holiday or a visit taken at a weekend: *How much would a weekend for two in Amsterdam cost?* ◦ *They've got a weekend cottage in Sussex.* **3 at the weekend** UK (US **on the weekend**) on Saturday or Sunday, or on both Saturday and Sunday: *What did you do at the weekend?* ◦ *We go out once in a while after work and on the weekend.* **4 at weekends** UK (US **on (the) weekends**) between Friday evening and Sunday night, or on Saturdays and Sundays: *They usually go windsurfing at weekends.*

> **! Common mistake: weekend**
> Remember that **weekend** should be written as one word.
> Don't write 'week end' or 'week-end', write **weekend**.

weekly /ˈwiː.kli/ **adj, adv; noun**
▸**adj, adv** A2 happening once a week or every week: *a weekly magazine/report* ◦ *a twice-weekly meeting* ◦ *The fire alarm has a weekly test/is tested weekly.*
▸**noun** [C] a newspaper or magazine that is published once every week

weeknight /ˈwiːk.naɪt/ **noun** [C] the evening or night of any day of the week except Sunday and usually Saturday

weeny /ˈwiː.ni/ **adj** informal extremely small: *All right, I'll have a slice of cake then – but just a weeny bit.*

weep /wiːp/ **verb** (**wept, wept**) **CRY** ▷ **1** C [I or T] literary to cry tears: *People in the street wept* ***with*** *joy when peace was announced.* ◦ *She wept* ***buckets*** *(= cried a lot) when Paul left.* **INJURY** ▷ **2** [I] (of an injury) to produce liquid such as PUS: *The sore is still weeping a lot so you'll have to change the dressing once a day.* • **weep noun** [S] literary *It might help you to* ***have a*** *good weep.*

ˌ**weeping** ˈ**willow noun** [C] a type of WILLOW tree that has long, thin branches which hang down

weepy /ˈwiː.pi/ **adj; noun**
▸**adj** sad and likely to cry: *I'd just waved Peter off at the airport and was feeling a bit weepy.*
▸**noun** [C] (also **weepie**) a film or a book which makes people want to cry because it is sad: *If I were you I'd take some tissues to the cinema – it's a real weepy.*

weevil /ˈwiː.vəl/ **noun** [C] any of various BEETLES which destroy crops such as grains and cotton

the weft /weft/ **noun** [S] specialized the threads that go across the length of a piece of cloth or a LOOM (= a special frame for making cloth) → Compare **warp**

weigh /weɪ/ **verb HEAVINESS** ▷ **1** B1 [L only + noun, T] to have a heaviness of a stated amount, or to measure the heaviness of an object: *Yesterday a satellite weighing 15 tonnes was successfully placed in orbit.* ◦ *She weighs her****self*** *every week on the scales in the bathroom.* ◦ *Your luggage must be weighed before it is* *put on the aircraft.* **INFLUENCE** ▷ **2** [I usually + adv/prep] (of something such as a fact or an event) to have an influence or be important: *Easy access to a railway network weighed heavily **with** us when we chose a site for the new factory.* **CONSIDER** ▷ **3** (B2) [T] to carefully consider, especially by comparing facts or possibilities, in order to make a decision: *Only when we have weighed all the factors involved can we decide when would be the best time to start.* ◦ *Economic benefits must be carefully weighed **against** the possible dangers of handling radioactive waste.* → Compare **outweigh** **SHIP** ▷ **4 weigh anchor** to lift the ANCHOR (= a heavy metal object) of a ship from under the water so that it can move freely

IDIOMS **weigh your words** (also **weigh each word**) to carefully think about everything you are going to say before you say it: *He gave evidence to the court, weighing each word as he spoke.* • **weigh a ton** informal to be very heavy: *What on earth have you got in this bag, Elaine? It weighs a ton!*

PHRASAL VERBS **weigh sb/sth down** [M usually passive] If someone or something is weighed down with something, they are carrying a lot of or too much of it: *Weighed down **with** supplies, they found the steep path difficult to climb.* • **weigh sb down** [M usually passive] to make a person feel worried and unhappy because of problems, responsibilities, and duties: *I thought she looked somehow older, weighed down **by** all her new responsibilities.* ◦ *Too much responsibility when too young can weigh down **on** a child.* • **weigh in** **SPORT** ▷ **1** to be officially weighed before competing in a sport, especially BOXING or horse racing: *Tyson weighed in **at** 245 lb for the fight.* **DISCUSSION** ▷ **2** informal to become involved in an argument or discussion in a forceful way: *Several leading architects weighed in **with** criticisms regarding the design of the new museum.* • **weigh on sb/sth** If a problem or responsibility weighs on you, it makes you worried or unhappy: *He's under huge pressure at work and it's really weighing on him.* ◦ *She knew she had treated him badly and it weighed **heavily** on her mind for a long time.* • **weigh sth out** to measure an amount of something: *Will you weigh out two kilograms of flour for me please?* • **weigh sth up** (B2) to think carefully about the advantages or disadvantages of a situation before making a decision: *I'm weighing up my options before I decide to apply for the job.* • **weigh sb up** to form an opinion about a situation or someone's abilities and character by thinking about them carefully: *I weighed up my chances of escape, and decided to wait for a better moment.* ◦ *When you're a detective you learn to weigh people up quickly.*

weighbridge /ˈweɪ.brɪdʒ/ **noun** [C] a machine for weighing vehicles and their LOADS, that you drive onto

> **Word partners for weight**
>
> *gain/lose/put on* weight • *bear/carry/support* a weight • *buckle under/collapse under* the weight (of sth) • weight *increase/loss* • [a kilo/pound] *in* weight • the weight *of* sth

weight /weɪt/ **noun; verb**

▸**noun** **HEAVINESS** ▷ **1** (B1) [C or U] the amount that something or someone weighs: *What weight can this lorry safely carry?* ◦ *There was a slight decrease **in** his weight after a week of dieting.* **2** [C] a piece of metal of known heaviness that can be used to measure the heaviness of other objects **3** (B2) [C] any object that is heavy: *Try not to lift heavy weights.* ◦ *I lift weights twice a week at the gym.* **INFLUENCE** ▷ **4** (C2) [U] respect, influence, trust, or importance: *Her experience does give her opinions quite a bit of weight.* ◦ *After he was voted out of power, few people **attached** much weight **to** what he said.* ◦ *Radical views don't **carry** much weight any more.*

IDIOMS **be/take a weight off your mind** to allow you to stop worrying about a particular thing: *It's a great weight off my mind **to** know that the building is finally finished.* ◦ *It was a weight off my mind know**ing** that our finances were taken care of.* • **take the weight off your feet/legs** If you take the weight off your feet/legs, you sit down, especially after standing or walking for a long time: *You must be exhausted after all that shopping – why don't you take the weight off your feet!*

▸**verb** [T] to fasten something heavy to something: *Paper tablecloths need to be weighted **down** or they blow away in the wind.*

weightage /ˈweɪ.tɪdʒ/ (US) /-t̬ɪdʒ/ **noun** [U] Indian English the value or importance of something when compared with another thing: *The entrance test carries 40 percent weightage in the final result.*

ˈweight-ˌbearing **adj** supporting the weight of your body or a building: *weight-bearing joints such as the knees* ◦ *Weight-bearing exercise is very good for the bones.* ◦ *a weight-bearing wall*

weighted /ˈweɪ.tɪd/ (US) /-t̬ɪd/ prepared and arranged in a way that is likely to produce a particular effect, usually an advantage, rather than any other: *The system of benefits is weighted **in favour of** those who have children.*

weighting /ˈweɪ.tɪŋ/ (US) /-t̬ɪŋ/ **noun** UK **1** [U] an increase in an amount, especially extra money paid to someone because they work in an area where it is expensive to live: *Do they pay London weighting?* **2** [C or U] a value that is given to a number or a group of numbers to show how important they are when compared with each other: *When the final marks are calculated greater weighting is given to the practical tests than to the written work.*

weightless /ˈweɪt.ləs/ **adj** having or appearing to have no weight: *There is a lot of interest in carrying out experiments in the weightless conditions which are experienced aboard space stations.* • **weightlessly** /-li/ **adv** • **weightlessness** /-nəs/ **noun** [U]

weightlifting /ˈweɪtˌlɪf.tɪŋ/ **noun** [U] the activity of lifting heavy objects either as a sport or for exercise • **weightlifter** /-tər/ (US) /-tɚ/ **noun** [C]

ˈweight ˌtraining **noun** [U] the activity of lifting heavy objects for exercise, especially to improve the strength of muscles and the appearance of the body: *I do/go weight training in a gym during the week.* → Compare **bodybuilding, weightlifting**

weighty /ˈweɪ.ti/ (US) /-t̬i/ **adj** **HEAVY** ▷ **1** heavy **SERIOUS** ▷ **2** describes a subject, book, or piece of work that is important or serious: *weighty matters/issues*

weir /wɪər/ (US) /wɪr/ **noun** [C] a wall built under the water across a river, over which the water flows from one level to another in a controlled way

weird /wɪəd/ (US) /wɪrd/ **adj** (B2) very strange and unusual, unexpected, or not natural: *He was sitting alone by a window with a weird contraption on the bench in front of him.* ◦ *Her boyfriend's a bit weird but she's all right.* ◦ *That's weird – I thought I'd left my keys on the table but they're not there.* ◦ *There is nothing to rival the weird **and wonderful** things that come out on the streets at carnival time.* • **weirdly** /ˈwɪəd.li/ (US) /ˈwɪrd-/ **adv** • **weirdness** /ˈwɪəd.nəs/ (US) /ˈwɪrd-/ **noun** [U]

weirdo /ˈwɪə.dəʊ/ (US) /ˈwɪr.doʊ/ **noun** [C] (plural **weirdos**) informal disapproving a person who behaves strangely: *What did he mean by that? Weirdo!*

welch /weltʃ/, /welʃ/ **verb** [I] (also **welsh**) informal disapproving to avoid doing something you have promised to do, especially not to pay a debt: *Their competitors' behaviour gave them a great opportunity to welch **on** their promises.*

welcome /ˈwel.kəm/ **verb; adj; noun; exclamation**
▸**verb** [T] **ENCOURAGE** ▷ **1** B2 to be pleased about and encourage or support something: *The new appointment has been widely welcomed.* **MEET** ▷ **2** B1 to meet and speak to someone in a friendly way when they come to the place where you are: *The visitors to the College were **warmly** welcomed by the Warden.* ◦ *Browning stood at the door, welcoming newcomers with a large smile and a pat on the arm.* ◦ *Please welcome (= please clap for) our guest of honour, George Taylor.*
▸**adj** **MEETING** ▷ **1** B1 If someone is welcome, you are pleased when they visit you: *Come and see us whenever you're in town – you're always welcome/you'll always be welcome.* ◦ *Out in the desert the traveller is a welcome **guest**.* **2 make sb welcome** B1 to show someone that you are pleased that they are with you: *The restaurant made the children very welcome.* **PLEASED** ▷ **3** B2 If something is welcome, you are pleased to have or do it: *The holiday was a welcome **change/break/relief**.* ◦ *She offered him the welcome **chance/opportunity** to do something different.* ◦ *A nice cup of tea would be very welcome.* **4 be welcome to do sth** B1 used to tell someone that they can certainly do something: *Anyone who is interested is welcome to come along.*

IDIOMS **be welcome to** informal If someone is welcome to someone or something, they can have it or do it, especially because it is not wanted by anyone else: *You're welcome to it – I can never get it to work right.* ◦ *If they want to change the rules, they are welcome to try.* • **you're welcome** A2 said as a polite answer when someone thanks you for doing something: *'It was very kind of you to help.' 'You're welcome.'*

▸**noun** **MEETING** ▷ **1** B1 [C or U] the way in which someone is met and spoken to when they arrive in a place: *They were **given** a **warm** (= very friendly) welcome.* ◦ *The opposition leader returned to a **hero's/heroine's** welcome after seven years in exile.* ◦ *She referred to his previous visit in her **speech of** welcome/welcome **speech**.* **2 outstay/overstay your welcome** C2 to stay too long: *I left after two days – I didn't want to overstay my welcome.* **REACTION** ▷ **3** [S] a reaction to a decision or suggestion: *Their supporters **gave** the decision a guarded/cautious welcome.*
▸**exclamation** A2 said as a greeting to someone arriving at a place: *Welcome – please come in.* ◦ *Welcome **home/back** – we've missed you!* ◦ *Welcome **to** Cambridge.*

W

ˈwelcome ˌmat **noun** [C] a small piece of strong material with 'Welcome' written on it that is put on the floor by the door to greet people as they come in: figurative *A new immigration law means the US will be **dusting off the** welcome mat for (= will be ready to welcome) famous people who want to live in the country.* ◦ figurative *We had better **put the** welcome mat **out** (= be ready to welcome), if your mother is coming to visit.*

welcoming /ˈwel.kəm.ɪŋ/ **adj** friendly or making you feel welcome: *She gave everyone a welcoming smile.*

weld /weld/ **verb; noun**
▸**verb** [T] **JOIN METAL** ▷ **1** to join two pieces of metal together permanently by melting the parts that touch: *Iron spikes have been welded **(on) to** the railings around the embassy.* **JOIN PEOPLE** ▷ **2** to make separate people into a group who can work together successfully: *He is a born leader, who welded a collection of gifted individualists **into** a real team.*
▸**noun** [C] a JOINT made by welding

welder /ˈwel.dəʳ/ (US) /-dɚ/ **noun** [C] a person whose job is welding

welding /ˈwel.dɪŋ/ **noun** [U] the activity of joining metal parts together

welfare /ˈwel.feəʳ/ (US) /-fer/ **noun** [U] **HELP** ▷ **1** C2 help given, especially by the state or an organization, to people who need it, especially because they do not have enough money: *This national fund pays for welfare **benefits** such as unemployment and sickness pay.* ◦ UK *After her month's sick leave, she was summoned to see the company's welfare **officer**.* **2 on welfare** US receiving financial help from the state because you are poor or have not been employed for a long time **HEALTH AND HAPPINESS** ▷ **3** B2 physical and mental health and happiness, especially of a person: *The police are very concerned for the welfare **of** the missing child.* ◦ *These organizations have fought very hard for the rights and welfare **of** immigrants.* ◦ *animal welfare*

ˌwelfare ˈstate **noun** [C usually singular] a system that allows the government of a country to provide social services such as HEALTHCARE, UNEMPLOYMENT BENEFIT, etc. to people who need them, paid for by taxes

we'll strong /wiːl/ weak /wil/ **short form of** we will: *We'll do better next time, I'm sure.*

well /wel/ **adv; adj; exclamation; noun; verb**
▸**adv** (**better**, **best**) **IN A GOOD WAY** ▷ **1** A1 in a good way, to a high or satisfactory standard: *The documentary presented both sides of the problem very well.* ◦ *The concert was well enough advertised but ticket sales were poor.* ◦ *a well-cut suit* ◦ *a well-paid job* ◦ *Her points were well **put** (= expressed in a good or clever way).* ◦ *His point about the need to reduce waste was well **taken** (= it was accepted as a good criticism).* ◦ *They took two hours to discuss the plans and considered it time well **spent** (= it had been a useful discussion).* ◦ *I can't do it **as** well **as** Marie can.* **TO A GREAT DEGREE** ▷ **2** A2 very much, to a great degree, or completely: *Knead the dough well, then divide it into four pieces.* ◦ *He could well imagine how much his promise was going to cost him.* ◦ *I can't catch the bus – there are no buses after midnight, as you well know.* ◦ *He's plays the piano well **enough** (= to a satisfactory standard).* **3** C1 used to emphasize some prepositions: *The results are well **above/below** what we expected.* ◦ *Keep well **away from** the edge of the cliff.* ◦ *It cost well **over** £100.* ◦ *Stand well clear of the doors!* **4** B2 used to emphasize some adjectives: *The police are well **aware** of the situation.* ◦ *The museum is well **worth** a visit.* ◦ *Some machines look more like cheap, plastic toys – **leave** these well **alone**.* **5** UK slang very: *The film was well **good**.* ◦ *Watch out for those two – they're well **hard** (= strong and willing to use violence).* **REASONABLY** ▷ **6** B2 with good reason: *She might well be the best person to ask.* ◦ *I **can't very** well (= it would not be acceptable to) refuse their kind offer.* **IN ADDITION** ▷ **7 as well (as)** A1 in addition (to): *Invite Emlyn – and Simon as well.* ◦ *I want to visit Andrew as well **as** Martin.*

IDIOMS **all is well** B1 everything is in a good or acceptable state: *I hope all is well with Jack.* • **all very well** (also **all well and good**) If something is all very

! Common mistake: as well

Warning: as well usually goes at the end of a clause:

~~*As well, the hotel offers a discount for students.*~~

The hotel offers a discount for students as well.

At the beginning of a sentence, use **also** or **in addition**:

Also, the hotel offers a discount for students.

well, it is quite useful or good in some situations but not excellent and not useful or good in every situation: *Electric heating is all very well until there's a power cut.* • **be all very well** C1 used to show that you do not agree with something or that you are annoyed about something: *Patience is all very well as long as you don't have to be patient for too long.* • **be just as well** (mainly UK **be as well**) B2 to be a good thing to do, or to be a lucky thing to happen or be done: *It's just as well you're not here – you wouldn't like the noise.* ◦ *He left at three, which was just as well or he'd have missed the train.* ◦ *It **would** be as well to check the small print.* • **may/might as well** B2 used to suggest doing something, often when there is nothing better to do: *We might as well walk there.* ◦ *We may as well start the meeting – the others will be here soon.* • **well and truly** completely: *The party was well and truly over when he arrived.* • **well away** UK informal **1** completely involved in what you are doing: *He was soon well away on (= talking a lot about) his favourite subject of steam train conservation.* **2** very drunk: *After five pints of lager and a couple of whiskies I was well away (= drunk).* • **well done** A1 used as a way of praising someone and saying that you are pleased about and approve of something they have done: *'I passed my exam.' 'Well done!'* → See also **well done** • **well in (with)** UK informal (US **in well with**) to have a good relationship with someone in which they like you and from which you get an advantage: *He's well in with the boss, these days.* • **well out of sth** UK informal lucky not to be involved: *'Did I tell you the company went bust the month after I left?' 'Really? Oh, you're well out of **that**!'*

▸**adj** [usually after verb] (**better**, **best**) A1 healthy; not ill: *He hasn't been too well lately.* ◦ *When she came home from school she really didn't **look** well.* ◦ *I'm sorry you're ill – I hope you **get** well soon.* ◦ *They sent a get well card.*

▸**exclamation** A1 used to introduce something you are going to say, often to show surprise, doubt, slight disagreement, or anger, or to continue a story: *Well, what shall we do now?* ◦ *Well now/then, how are we going to arrange things?* ◦ *'Who was that?' 'Well, I'm afraid I can't remember her name.'* ◦ *'He's decided to give up his job and move to the north with her.' 'Well, well – that's what love does for you.'* ◦ *Well, really, how thoughtless of him!* ◦ *Well? What did you do next?* ◦ *Well, after that we went camping in the mountains.* ◦ *Well/**Oh** well, it doesn't matter – I can always buy another one.* ◦ ***Very** well, if you insist I'll meet him next week.*

▸**noun** [C] a deep hole in the ground from which you can get water, oil, or gas → See also **stairwell**

well

▸**verb** [I usually + adv/prep] (of liquid) to appear on the surface of something or come slowly out from somewhere: *Dirty water welled (**up**) **out of** the damaged pipe.* ◦ *As she read the letter tears welled **up** in her eyes.* ◦ figurative *Conflicting emotions welled **up** in his heart.*

ˌwell adˈjusted adj describes a person who is reasonable and has good judgment and whose behaviour is not difficult or strange: [before noun] *a quiet, well-adjusted man*

ˌwell adˈvised adj [after verb] formal showing good judgment: [+ to infinitive] *You would be well advised **to** book in advance.*

ˌwell apˈpointed adj formal having a good supply of comfortable or necessary furniture and attractive decorations: [before noun] *The hotel has spacious, well-appointed public rooms and bedrooms.*

ˌwell ˈargued adj described or asked for in an effective and clever way: [before noun] *She presented a well-argued case for banning smoking in public places.*

ˌwell atˈtended adj describes an event where many people are present: [before noun] *The information was given at an unusually well-attended press conference yesterday.*

ˌwell ˈbalanced adj **1** containing a mixture of ideas, people, etc. with each one being represented equally or fairly: *The team is unusually well balanced.* ◦ [before noun] *a well-balanced article* **2** B2 describes a group of foods which together provide a good range of the things you need to stay healthy: [before noun] *a well-balanced meal/diet* **3** C1 describes someone who is calm and reasonable and who shows good judgment: [before noun] *happy, well-balanced children*

ˌwell beˈhaved adj approving behaving in a way that is accepted as correct: [before noun] *a well-behaved child*

ˌwell-ˈbeing noun [U] C1 the state of feeling healthy and happy: *People doing yoga benefit from an increased feeling of well-being.*

ˌwell ˈbred adj **1** speaking or behaving in a way that is generally considered correct and polite: [before noun] *A television announcer with a well-bred voice was reading the news.* **2** old-fashioned coming from a family that has a high social position: [before noun] *a well-bred young English woman*

ˌwell brought ˈup adj approving describes people, especially children, who are polite and who act in a quiet and pleasant way, because they have been taught this behaviour at home: [before noun] *He was a very well-brought-up young man.*

ˌwell ˈbuilt adj **1** B2 describes a person who is large and strong **2** UK polite word for **fat** **3** US having a strong, attractive body: [before noun] *I was always a trim, well-built guy until I turned 40.*

ˌwell ˈchosen adj carefully chosen: [before noun] *These debates have made a successful series, mostly because of well-chosen speakers and lively topics.*

IDIOM **a few well-chosen words** a short speech: *He introduced the visitors with a few well-chosen words.*

ˌwell conˈnected adj having friends or family members who are important or powerful people: [before noun] *She was born in 1940 into a very well-connected family.*

ˌwell deˈfined adj clearly expressed, explained, or described: [before noun] *Scientists follow several well-defined steps in investigating unexpected outbreaks of disease.*

ˌwell deˈveloped adj having grown or increased in a positive way: *These areas are less well developed and so less attractive as investment prospects.* ◦ [before noun] *She is a physically well-developed teenager with the mental level of a four-year-old.*

ˌwell disˈposed adj friendly and helpful: *If you've got a good feeling about yourself, you are more likely to feel well disposed* ***to/towards*** *other people.*

ˌwell ˈdocumented adj having been often recorded: *The medicinal value of garlic is well documented.*

ˌwell ˈdone adj (of meat) cooked so that it is firm and has a grey-brown colour all the way through: *'How would you like your steak?' 'Well done.'* → See also **well done** at **well**

ˌwell ˈdressed adj B1 wearing attractive and stylish clothes

ˌwell ˈearned adj UK deserved because of what you have done or experienced: [before noun] *Liz won't be at work next week – she's having a well-earned rest.*

ˌwell ˈeducated adj C1 having had a good education: [before noun] *well-educated and highly motivated workers*

ˌwell enˈdowed adj **1** having a lot of something, especially money or possessions: *The city is well endowed* ***with*** *modern medical facilities.* ◦ [before noun] *It is a very well-endowed college.* **2** humorous approving (of a man) having large sexual organs, or (of a woman) having large breasts: *He's very well endowed!*

ˌwell eˈstablished adj having a recognized position, or being generally known about: *The rules, though not written down, are fairly well established.* ◦ *World Music is now well established and popular with mass audiences.*

ˌwell-ˈfed adj having a lot to eat: *It should be possible to be warm and well-fed, and to enjoy all the good things of life, while respecting the needs of the planet.*

ˌwell ˈfounded adj based on facts: [before noun] *He had to show that he had a well-founded fear of persecution on religious or political grounds to qualify as a refugee.*

ˌwell ˈgroomed adj having a tidy and pleasant appearance that is produced with care: [before noun] *He is the sort of well-groomed man you expect to inhabit an executive-size corporate office.*

ˌwell ˈgrounded adj being based on or having a good knowledge of facts: *The young players all seemed very well grounded* ***in*** *the rich history of the music they were performing.* ◦ *The claim must be well grounded* ***in*** *fact.* ◦ [before noun] *a well-grounded criticism*

ˌwell ˈheeled adj informal rich: *His family was very well heeled.*

wellie (also **welly**) /ˈwel.i/ noun [C] UK informal for **wellington**

ˌwell inˈformed adj C1 having a lot of knowledge or information about a particular subject or things in general: *He was well informed and shrewd, with good, calm judgment.*

wellington /ˈwel.ɪŋ.tən/ noun [C usually plural] UK (UK also **ˌwellington ˈboot**, UK informal **wellie**, US or Australian English **ˌrubber ˈboot**) a WATERPROOF boot that reaches almost to the knees: *He left his muddy wellingtons outside the back door.*

ˌwell inˈtentioned adj wanting to have good effects, but sometimes having bad effects which were not expected: [before noun] *Well-intentioned development projects can have unintended negative effects on population control.* → See also **well meaning**

ˌwell ˈkept adj TIDY ▷ **1** clean, tidy, and cared for: [before noun] *He was astonished to find nice streets and well-kept houses.* HIDDEN ▷ **2** [mainly before noun] A well-kept secret has not been told or shown to anyone: *The details of the new car were a well-kept* ***secret.***

ˌwell ˈknown adj A2 known or recognized by many people: *Her views on the subject are already well known.* ◦ [+ that] *It is well known* ***that*** *he never gives interviews.* ◦ *The restaurant is well known* ***for*** *its friendly atmosphere and excellent service.* ◦ *a well-known local artist* ◦ [before noun] *a well-known face/voice*

> **!** Common mistake: **well known or well-known?**
>
> Remember that when we use **well known** directly before a noun, we add a hyphen between 'well' and 'known':
>
> *It is well known that people live longer these days.*
>
> *It is a well-known fact that people live longer these days.*

ˌwell ˈliked adj liked by many people: *A colleague described him as well liked and respected by all.*

ˌwell ˈmannered adj behaving in a pleasant and polite way: *The other visitors were too well mannered to complain.*

ˌwell ˈmatched adj similar or equal (to something): *At the start of the competition the three teams looked extremely well matched.* ◦ *Her skills are well matched* ***to*** *the job.*

ˌwell ˈmeaning adj wanting to have a good effect, but not always achieving one: *I know he's well meaning, but I wish he'd leave us alone.*

ˌwell ˈmeant adj said or done in order to be helpful, but not always achieving this: [before noun] *a well-meant suggestion*

wellness /ˈwel.nəs/ noun [U] mainly US the state of being healthy

ˌwell-ˈnigh adv almost or very nearly: *With no help, finishing the job in a day was well-nigh* ***impossible.***

ˌwell ˈoff adj; noun
▸adj RICH ▷ **1** C1 rich: *Her family was very well off.* ◦ [before noun] *a well-off neighbourhood* HAVING A LOT ▷ **2** [after verb] having a lot of or a number of: *The city is well off* ***for*** *parks and gardens.*
▸noun [plural] **the well-off** rich people: *It is a resort that clearly caters for the well-off.*

ˌwell ˈoiled adj DRUNK ▷ **1** slang drunk EFFECTIVE ▷ **2** working easily and effectively: [before noun] *a well-oiled political machine*

ˌwell ˈpreserved adj **1** (especially of something old) kept in good condition: [before noun] *It was a pretty town with a picturesque harbour and well-preserved buildings.* **2** often humorous (of an older person) not looking as old as they really are: [before noun] *A well-preserved male model can go on working into his forties.*

ˌwell ˈqualified adj [+ to infinitive] C1 having suitable experience or formal qualifications: *Ken has more than ten years of experience in photography behind him, so he is well qualified* ***to*** *offer advice.* ◦ *He seems well qualified* ***for*** *the job.*

ˌwell ˈread adj describes someone who has learned a lot of information on different subjects by reading

ˌwell ˈrounded adj involving or having experience in a wide range of ideas or activities: *The article is well rounded and is fair to both sides of the dispute.* ◦ [before noun] *She describes herself as a 'well-rounded individual' who works hard but has a varied social life.*

ˌwell ˈspoken adj approving having a pleasant and polite way of speaking that is considered socially acceptable

wellspring /ˈwel.sprɪŋ/ noun [S] literary the place something comes from or starts at, or the cause of something: *the wellspring of the creative spirit* → Synonym **source**

ˌ**well** ˈ**thought of** adj considered by other people as good; admired, and approved of: *He was efficient at his job and well thought of by everyone.* ◦ [before noun] *It's a well-thought-of school.*

ˌ**well thought** ˈ**out** adj planned in an effective way: *The training schedule wasn't very well thought out.* ◦ [before noun] *a well-thought-out scheme for traffic control*

ˌ**well** ˈ**thumbed** adj describes a book, magazine, etc. whose slightly damaged appearance shows that it has been used many times.

ˌ**well** ˈ**timed** adj happening or caused to happen at a suitable or effective time: [before noun] *A well-timed joke stopped the disagreement developing into something more serious.*

ˌ**well-to-**ˈ**do** adj rich: *well-to-do families*

ˌ**well** ˈ**tried** adj used many times before and known to be effective: [before noun] *a well-tried recipe*

ˌ**well** ˈ**trodden** adj **1** much used or visited: [before noun] *We followed the well-trodden tourist* ***route*** *from Paris to Chartres.* **2** describes a set of actions that many people have done or a subject that many people have dealt with previously: [before noun] *The survey showed that people become managers by well-trodden* ***paths***.

ˌ**well** ˈ**turned** adj cleverly expressed: [before noun] *a well-turned phrase*

ˌ**well** ˈ**versed** adj knowing a lot about something: *He was well versed* ***in*** *modern history.*

ˈ**well-**ˌ**wisher** noun [C] a person who encourages or supports you: *He was clutching the award he had just won for Best Newcomer, surrounded by fans and well-wishers.*

ˌ**well** ˈ**woman/man** ˌ**clinic** noun [C] a place that provides tests and advice relating especially to the health of women/men, or a fixed period when it is open: *There's a well woman clinic at the health centre on Wednesday afternoons.*

ˌ**well** ˈ**worn** adj **1** describes clothes that have been worn often and are becoming old: [before noun] *a well-worn sports jacket* **2** used very often or too often: [before noun] *Ecology can be written about without relying on well-worn examples such as tropical rain forests.*

welly /ˈwel.i/ noun [C] mainly UK informal for **wellington**

welsh /welʃ/ verb [I] to **welch**

Welsh rarebit /ˌwelʃˈreə.bɪt/ (US) /-ˈrer-/ noun [U] (also ˌ**Welsh** ˈ**rabbit**) a piece of TOAST with cheese on it that is heated until the cheese melts

welt /welt/ noun [C] a raised, red area of skin caused by being hit or by cuts HEALING

welter /ˈwel.təʳ/ (US) /-t̬ɚ/ noun [S] a large and especially badly organized number of things: *We are reducing the company's welter* ***of*** *development projects and will streamline sales and marketing.*

welterweight /ˈwel.tə.weɪt/ (US) /-t̬ɚ-/ noun [C] a BOXER whose body weight is between LIGHTWEIGHT and MIDDLEWEIGHT

wench /wentʃ/ noun [C] old use or humorous a young woman

wend /wend/ verb **wend your way** to move slowly and not directly: *The thieves then wended their way through the dark back streets to the docks.*

ˈ**Wendy** ˌ**house** noun [C] UK a toy house or PLAYHOUSE

went /went/ verb past simple of **go**

wept /wept/ verb past simple and past participle of **weep**

we're /wɪəʳ/ (US) /wɪr/ short form we are: *We're here, Diane.*

were strong /wɜːʳ/ (US) /wɜː/ weak /wəʳ/ (US) /wɚ/ verb past simple of **be**

> **! Common mistake: were or where?**
>
> **Warning:** Choose the right word!
>
> These two words look similar, but they are spelled differently and have completely different meanings.

weren't /wɜːnt/ (US) /wɝːnt/ short form of were not: *Weren't we lucky with the weather?*

werewolf /ˈwɪə.wʊlf/, /ˈweə-/ (US) /ˈwɪr-/ /ˈwer-/ noun [C] (plural **werewolves**) someone who, in stories, changes into a WOLF at the time of the FULL MOON (= when the moon is a complete circle)

west /west/ noun; adj; adv

▸noun [U] (also **West**) (written abbreviation **W**) **1** (A2) the direction in which the sun goes down in the evening, opposite to the east, or the part of an area or country which is in this direction: *The points of the compass are north, south, east, and west.* ◦ *The sun rises* ***in the*** *east and sets* ***in the*** *west.* ◦ *Most of the country will be dry tomorrow, but* ***the*** *west will have some rain.* ◦ *The Black Country* ***is/lies to the*** *west of Birmingham.* **2 (the) West a** (B2) North America and western Europe: *There has been concern* ***in/throughout*** *the West about the effects of this measure.* ◦ *East-West relations* **b** In the US, the West is the part of the country west of the Mississippi river which only became developed in the late 1800s: *the Wild West* **3 out west** US to or in the west of the US: *Travis moved out west after college.*

IDIOM **go west** UK informal If something goes west, it is lost, damaged, or spoiled in some way: *I couldn't get a ticket – that's my last chance to see the show gone west.*

▸adj (also **West**) (written abbreviation **W**) **1** (A2) in or forming the west part of something: *West Africa* ◦ *the west coast of Ireland* ◦ *Ireland is west* ***of*** *Britain.* **2 west wind** a wind coming from the west

▸adv (also **West**) (written abbreviation **W**) (A2) towards the west: *Go* ***due*** *(= directly) west until you see a lake.* ◦ *The balcony* ***faces*** *west.*

westbound /ˈwest.baʊnd/ adj, adv going or leading towards the west: *The accident occurred on the westbound carriageway of the motorway.* ◦ *We crossed six time zones westbound on our flight.*

the ˌ**West** ˈ**Coast** noun the area of the Pacific coast in the US which includes California: *They're moving to the West Coast.* ◦ *West Coast companies*

the ˈ**West** ˌ**Country** noun the area in the southwest of Britain: *We spent our holiday in the West Country.* ◦ *a West Country accent*

the ˌ**West** ˈ**End** noun the part of central London where there are many theatres and many large, expensive shops and hotels: *We went to a restaurant in the West End.* ◦ *a West End theatre*

westerly /ˈwes.tᵊl.i/ (US) /-tɚ.li/ adj; noun

▸adj **1** in or towards the west: *So far, only the westerly part of the site has been developed.* ◦ *We travelled in a westerly direction.* **2 westerly wind** a wind that comes from the west

▸noun [C] a wind that comes from the west

western /ˈwes.tən/ (US) /-tɚn/ adj; noun

▸adj (also **Western**) DIRECTION ▷ **1** (B1) (written abbreviation **W**) in or from the west of a place: *western Europe* ◦ *California and other western states* COUNTRIES ▷ **2** (B1) relating to countries in the west part

of the world, especially North America and countries in the west of Europe: *western opinion/culture* ◦ *a Western-educated engineer* ◦ *western medicine*
▸noun [C] (also **Western**) (UK also **cowboy film**, US also **cowboy movie**) a film based on stories about life in the west of the US in the past

westerner (also **Westerner**) /ˈwes.tə.nəʳ/ (US) /-tɚ.nɚ/ **noun** [C] **1** a person who comes from a country in North America or western Europe: *Some of the Buddhists came from Sri Lanka and Southeast Asia, while others were Westerners by birth.* **2** a person who comes from the west of a country, especially the US: *Easterners and westerners were equally affected by these changes in American life.*

westernize (UK usually **westernise**) /ˈwes.tən.aɪz/ (US) /-tɚ.naɪz/ **verb** [T] to cause the ideas and ways of doing things that are common in North America and most of Europe to be used and accepted by someone or something in or from another part of the world • **westernization** (UK usually **westernisation**) /ˌwes.tᵊn.aɪˈzeɪ.ʃᵊn/ (US) /-tɚ.nə-/ **noun** [U]

westernized (UK usually **westernised**) /ˈwes.tən.aɪzd/ (US) /-tɚ.naɪzd/ **adj** having a culture like North America and western Europe: *As the political emphasis shifts, Bulgaria will inevitably become more westernized.*

westernmost /ˈwes.tən.məʊst/ (US) /-tɚn.moʊst/ **adj** furthest towards the west of an area: *Ouessant is the westernmost point of France.*

ˌ**West ˈIndian** **noun** [C], **adj** (a person) of or from the West Indies: *a West Indian poet* ◦ *a family of West Indians*

Westminster /ˌwestˈmɪn.stəʳ/ (US) /-stɚ/ **noun** [S] the UK parliament, or the part of London where the parliament buildings are

westward /ˈwest.wəd/ (US) /-wɚd/ **adv; adj**
▸**adv** (also **westwards**) towards the west: *We followed a road leading westward.* ◦ *The boat drifted westwards.*
▸**adj** towards the west: *He set off in a westward* ***direction***.

wet /wet/ **adj; verb; noun**
▸**adj** (**wetter**, **wettest**) **NOT DRY** ▷ **1** (A2) covered in water or another liquid: *a wet floor* ◦ *a wet umbrella* ◦ *wet hair* ◦ *My bike* ***got*** *wet in the rain.* ◦ *I had to cycle in the rain and got* ***soaking*** *(= very) wet.* ◦ informal *You poor thing – you're* ***all*** *(= very) wet.* **2** (B1) describes paint, ink, or a similar substance when it has not had time to dry and become hard: *The paint's still wet.* ◦ *a notice saying 'Wet paint!'* **3** (A2) describes weather or periods of time when rain falls: *We've had wet weather all week.* ◦ *This is the first wet day for two months.* ◦ *The presentation will take place indoors if* ***it's*** *wet.* **4 be wet through** to be completely wet: *Come in quickly – you're wet through.* **WEAK** ▷ **5** describes someone who has a weak character and does not express any forceful opinions: *Don't be so wet.* • **wetly** /ˈwet.li/ **adv** • **wetness** /ˈwet.nəs/ **noun** [U]

IDIOMS **a wet weekend** a very boring and disappointing experience or person: *He sounds about* ***as much fun as*** *a wet weekend in Carmarthenshire.* • **be wet behind the ears** to be young and without experience

▸**verb** [T] **1** to make something wet: *Wet the powder thoroughly and mix to remove lumps.* ◦ *He wetted a cloth and tried to rub the mark away.* **2 wet yourself** to urinate in your clothes by accident **3 wet the/your bed** to urinate in your bed by accident: *She still sometimes wets the bed at night.*

IDIOM **wet your whistle** old-fashioned informal to have an alcoholic drink

▸**noun** **WATER** ▷ **1** [U] liquid, especially water: *Don't put your newspaper down in the wet.* **2 the wet** mainly UK wet weather: *Don't leave it out there in the wet.* **PERSON** ▷ **3** [C] UK disapproving someone who has a weak character and does not express any forceful opinions: *Come on Tom, don't be such a wet!*

ˌ**wet ˈblanket** **noun** [C usually singular] disapproving a person who says or does something that stops other people enjoying themselves

ˌ**wet ˈdream** **noun** [C] a sexually exciting dream in a man that causes an EJACULATION (= release of SEMEN)

wetland /ˈwet.lənd/, /-lænd/ **noun** [C or U] a large area of land covered with SWAMP or MARSH

ˈ**wet-look** **adj** [before noun] shiny: *wet-look hair gel*

ˈ**wet ˌnurse** **noun** [C] in the past, a woman employed to give her breast milk to another woman's baby

wetsuit /ˈwet.suːt/ **noun** [C] a piece of clothing, made from rubber, which covers the whole body closely and is designed to keep you warm when you are swimming in especially the sea for long periods: *divers* ***in*** *wetsuits*

we've /ˈwiːv/, /wiv/ **short form of** we have: *We've been married eight years.*

whack /wæk/ **verb; noun**
▸**verb** **1** [T] to hit someone or something noisily: *He whacked the tree trunk with his stick.* ◦ *She whacked him in the mouth.* **2** [T + adv/prep] informal to quickly put something somewhere: *'Where shall I put my bag?' 'Just whack it in the corner there.'*
▸**noun** **SHARE** ▷ **1** [S or U] informal a share or part: *Low earners will pay only half the charge but high earners will have to* ***pay full*** *whack (= pay the whole amount).* ◦ *That's not a* ***fair*** *whack.* **2 top whack** UK informal the highest possible price or payment: *They're prepared to pay top whack for goods like this.* **NOT RIGHT** ▷ **3 out of whack** US informal not operating correctly or looking right: *You can use Carol's old bike – the gears are out of whack, but it still goes.* **HIT** ▷ **4** [C] the action of hitting someone or something noisily: *He* ***gave*** *the ball a whack with his stick.*

whacked /wækt/ **adj** (also ˌ**whacked ˈout**) **1** informal very tired: *Go and pour yourself a drink, love – you look whacked.* **2** US informal suffering the effects of drugs or alcohol: *He was whacked-out on speed, jabbering a mile a minute and making no sense at all.*

whacking /ˈwæk.ɪŋ/ **adj, adv** informal very big: *a whacking (great) boulder* ◦ *a whacking fine*

whacky informal (US usually **wacky**) /ˈwæk.i/ **adj** strange or unusual: *The place is stuffed with whacky memorabilia like a sculpture of the Seven Dwarfs that Walt Disney gave to Debbie Reynolds.*

whale /weɪl/ **noun** [C] (B1) a very large sea mammal that breathes air through a hole at the top of its head

IDIOMS **have a whale of a time** informal to enjoy yourself very much: *We had a whale of a time on holiday.* • **a whale of a** US informal describes a very great amount of something or a very good thing: *That's a whale of a story.* ◦ *Another thousand dollars would make a whale of a difference.*

whaler /ˈweɪ.ləʳ/ (US) /-lɚ/ **noun** [C] a boat that is designed for hunting whales, or a person who works on such a boat

whaling /ˈweɪ.lɪŋ/ **noun** [U] the activity of hunting whales

wham /wæm/ **exclamation** informal **SOUND** ▷ **1** used to suggest the sound of a sudden hit: *The boys in the cartoon were punching each other – wham, zap!* **SUDDENLY** ▷ **2** used to show that something you are describing happened suddenly: *Everything was fine until, wham, the wire snapped.*

wharf /wɔːf/ (US) /wɔːrf/ **noun** [C] (plural **wharves**) an area like a wide wall built near the edge of the sea or a river where ships can be tied and goods can be taken off them

what /wɒt/ (US) /wɑːt/ **determiner, pronoun, exclamation; pronoun; predeterminer, determiner; pronoun, exclamation**

▸**determiner, pronoun, exclamation** QUESTION ▷ **1** A1 used to ask for information about people or things: *What time is it?* ◦ *What books did you buy?* ◦ *What did you wear?* ◦ *What size shoes do you take?* ◦ *What happened after I left?* ◦ *What caused the accident?* **2** used in questions which show you are surprised or do not believe something: *'I've just told Peter.' 'What?/You did what?'* ◦ *What's this I hear? You're leaving?* **3 what... for?** B2 used to ask about the reason for something: *What are these tools for?* ◦ *What are you doing that for?* ◦ *'We need a bigger car.' 'What for?'*

> **!** Common mistake: **what**
>
> **Warning:** check your word order!
>
> When **what** is used in a main clause to ask a question, remember to put the verb before the subject:
>
> ~~*What you are doing this summer?*~~
>
> *What are you doing this summer?*
>
> When **what** is used in a subordinate clause, do not put the verb before the subject:
>
> ~~*I'm writing to ask you what are you doing this summer.*~~
>
> *I'm writing to ask you what you are doing this summer.*

IDIOMS **what about?** A2 used to suggest something: *What about Lola – shall we invite her?* ◦ *What about taking a few days off?* • **what if?** B1 used to ask about something that could happen in the future, especially something bad: *What if the train's late?* ◦ *What if you don't pass your exams?* • **what is he, are they, etc. like?** said to ask someone to describe someone or something to you: *What was her boyfriend like?* ◦ *You've seen their new house, haven't you? What's it like?* • **what of it?** informal used to rudely say that you do not think something is important: *'That's the third time you've done that!' 'Yeah, what of it?'* • **what's on** used to mean 'what is happening'. This phrase is often used as the title of the part of a newspaper which tells you about events and entertainment happening in the next week or month. • **what's that (all) about (then)?** UK informal used when you do not understand why something or someone is so popular or fashionable: *Pierced tongues – what's that about, then?* • **what's up?** informal used to ask someone what the problem is: *What's up – why does everyone look so serious?* ◦ *What's up **with** Terry?*

▸**pronoun** THAT WHICH ▷ **1** B1 the thing(s) which; that which: *What I wanted to find out first was how long it was going to take.* ◦ *What really concerned her was how unhappy the child was.* ◦ *She wouldn't tell me what he said.* ◦ *I hadn't got much money on me but I gave them what I had.* ◦ *The letter showed clearly what they were planning.* ◦ *I can't decide what **to** do next.* ◦ *Have you thought about what **to** send as a present?* **2** used to introduce something you are going to say: *You'll never **guess** what – Laurie won first prize!* ◦ *I'll **tell you** what – we'll collect the parcel on our way to the station.*

IDIOMS **and what have you** informal and other similar things: *There were a couple of bags full of old records, magazines, and what have you.* • **what with** informal C2 used to talk about the reasons for a particular situation, especially a bad or difficult situation: *I'm very tired, what with travelling all day yesterday and having a disturbed night.* • **what/whatever sb says goes** What/whatever someone says goes means you have to do what they say: *It was Helen's idea and what Helen says goes.* • **what's more** B2 used to add something surprising or interesting to what you have just said: *The decorations were absolutely beautiful **and** what's more, the children had made them themselves.*

> **!** Common mistake: **what or which?**
>
> **Warning:** choose the correct pronoun!
>
> To add extra information to a previous clause, don't say 'what', say **which**:
>
> ~~*I also speak English, what might be useful in this job.*~~
>
> *I also speak English, which might be useful in this job.*

▸**predeterminer, determiner** OPINION ▷ B1 used to introduce your opinion: *'She can't come.' 'What a shame/pity.'* ◦ *What a lovely view!* ◦ *What nonsense/rubbish!* ◦ *What strange clothes he was wearing.*

▸**pronoun, exclamation** informal QUESTION ▷ used to ask someone to say something again: *'I think we should leave at twelve.' 'What?' 'I said I think we should leave at twelve.'*

whatchamacallit /ˈwɒtʃ.ə.məˌkɔː.lɪt/ (US) /ˈwɑː.tʃə.məˌkɑː.lɪt/ **noun** [C] informal used when you are speaking about something or someone whose name you can not remember: *I need a – a whatchamacallit – one of those things that you can caramelize sugar with.*

whatever /wɒtˈev.əʳ/ (US) /wɑːˈt̬ev.ɚ/ **pronoun, determiner; pronoun; adv**

▸**pronoun, determiner** NOT IMPORTANT WHAT ▷ **1** B2 it is not important what is; it makes no difference what (is): *We'll go whatever the weather.* ◦ *Whatever happens, you know that I'll stand by you.* ◦ *Whatever else may be said of him, Mr Meese is not scared of a fight.* ◦ *Whatever the outcome of the war, there will be no winners.* ◦ *Whatever the reason, more Britons are emigrating to Australia today than at any time since the 1950s.* ANYTHING ▷ **2** B1 anything or everything: *I eat whatever I want and I still don't seem to put on weight.* ◦ *'What shall we do tonight then?' 'It's up to you – whatever you want.'* ◦ *Whatever I say I always seem to get it wrong.* ◦ *Don't, whatever **you do**, tell Patrick (= you certainly should not tell him).* ◦ *Do whatever you want – it won't affect me.* ◦ *'So I'll bring red wine then.' 'Sure, whatever (= bring that or anything else).'* ◦ *Apparently he 'discovered himself' in India, whatever **that means** (= although I do not know what that means).*

▸**pronoun** SURPRISE ▷ used instead of 'what' to add emphasis to a phrase, usually expressing surprise: *Whatever is he doing with that rod?* ◦ *Whatever's that yellow thing on your plate?* ◦ *Whatever did you say that for?* ◦ *Whatever does she see in him – he's revolting!* ◦ *Whatever made him buy that jacket?*

▸**adv** EMPHASIS ▷ **1 whatsoever**: *There is no evidence whatever to show that this is in fact the case.* DISRESPECT ▷ **2** informal something that is said to show no respect to someone who is asking you to agree with them or agree to do something: *'Bryce, could you do what I ask you to once in a while?' 'Whatever.'*

whatnot /ˈwɒt.nɒt/ (US) /ˈwɑːt.nɑːt/ **noun** informal **and**

W

whatnot/and what have you and other similar things: *You can buy crisps and whatnot at the bar.* ◦ *That'll leave you a bit of time so that you can get the table set and whatnot.*

ˈwhat's-her-name noun [S] (also **whatsername**) informal used for referring to a woman or girl when you cannot remember or do not know her name: *I gave the report to what's-her-name – the new marketing assistant.*

ˈwhat's-his-name (also **whatsisname**) noun [S] informal used for referring to a man or boy when you cannot remember or do not know his name: *Have you invited Mike Whatsisname to the party?*

whatsit /ˈwɒt.sɪt/ (US) /ˈwɑːt-/ noun [C] informal any object or person whose name you have temporarily forgotten or do not know: *Where's the whatsit that you change channels with?* ◦ *You'd better tell whatsit – what's his name – the guy in charge of stationery.*

whatsoever /ˌwɒt.səʊˈev.əʳ/ (US) /ˌwɑːt.soʊˈev.ɚ/ adv (also **whatever**) C1 used after a negative phrase to add emphasis to the idea that is being expressed: *He has no respect for authority whatsoever.* ◦ *I can honestly say that I have no interest whatsoever in the royal family.* ◦ *There is no evidence whatever to show that this is in fact the case.* ◦ *'Had you any idea what was happening at the time?' 'None whatsoever.'*

wheat /wiːt/ noun [U] B2 a plant whose yellowish-brown grain is used for making flour, or the grain itself: *wheat fields* ◦ *Wheat is a staple crop for millions of people across the world.* → See also **wholewheat**

IDIOM **separate the wheat from the chaff** to separate things or people that are of high quality or ability from those that are not: *The first round of interviews really separates the wheat from the chaff.*

ˌwheat comˈplexion noun [C] Indian English If a person has a wheat complexion, the skin on their face is light brown in colour.

wheatgerm UK (US **wheat germ**) /ˈwiːt.dʒɜːm/ (US) /-dʒɝːm/ noun [U] the central part of a grain of wheat, sometimes added to food, especially bread, because it contains substances that are good for health

wheatmeal /ˈwiːt.miːl/ noun [U] UK brown flour which contains some but not all of the outer covering and central part of the wheat grain

wheedle /ˈwiː.dəl/ verb [I, T + adv/prep] disapproving to try to persuade someone to do something or give you something by praising them or being intentionally CHARMING: *She's one of those children who can wheedle you **into** giving her anything she wants.* ◦ *She wasn't invited, but somehow she managed to wheedle her **way in**.* ◦ *I tried all manner of different approaches – I wheedled, threatened, demanded, cajoled.* • **wheedling** /-ɪŋ/ adj *I knew by your wheedling tone that you wanted something from me.*

wheel /wiːl/ noun; verb

▸noun **1** A2 [C] a circular object connected at the centre to a bar, used for making vehicles or parts of machines move: *I got my bag caught in the wheel of my bicycle.* ◦ *He lost control of his car when a front/rear wheel hit a stone as he approached the first bend.* → See also **Ferris wheel, flywheel, waterwheel** **2 on wheels** Something that is on wheels has wheels under it so that it can be pulled or pushed along: *My suitcase is on wheels so that makes life a little easier.* ◦ *I bought my niece one of those toy dogs on wheels.* **3 the wheel** B2 a STEERING WHEEL (= a wheel inside a vehicle that the driver turns to make the vehicle go in a particular direction): *Keep your hands on the wheel!* ◦ *I never feel safe with Richard **at/behind** the wheel (= driving).* ◦ *Do you think you could **take** the wheel (= drive) for a couple of hours?* **4** [C] a wooden or metal wheel that is turned to make a ship go in a particular direction **5 wheels** [plural] old-fashioned informal a car: *I've got to get some wheels – this public transport system's a joke!*

IDIOMS **a fifth/third wheel** US someone who is in a situation where they are not needed or are ignored by most people • **set the wheels in motion** to do something that will cause a series of actions to start: *I thought a phone call to the right person might set the wheels in motion.* • **wheels within wheels** hidden or unknown things that influence a particular situation, making it more complicated than it at first seems

▸verb PUSH ▷ **1** [T usually + adv/prep] to push an object that has wheels so that it moves in a particular direction: *I saw her last night wheeling a buggy along Green Lane.* ◦ *Halfway through the talk someone wheeled in a trolley laden with drinks.* ◦ *Doctors put her on a respirator and wheeled her downstairs to intensive care.* FLY IN CIRCLES ▷ **2** [I] to fly repeatedly in a circular pattern: *She watched a flock of seagulls wheeling high above her.*

PHRASAL VERBS **wheel sth out** disapproving to use something or someone that you have used many times before in a way that is boring for other people: *Every time we have this argument you wheel out the same old statistics, and I'm still not convinced!* ◦ *Year after year they wheel out the same third-rate celebrities to entertain us.* • **wheel round** UK (US **wheel around**) to turn round quickly: *She wheeled round to face him and saw him take out a gun.*

ˌwheel and ˈdeal verb [I] informal to try to make a profit or get an advantage using clever or complicated methods and often deceiving people or breaking the usual rules: *He spends his time wheeling and dealing on the stock exchange.* • **ˌwheeling and ˈdealing** noun [U] *It's an article about all the wheeling and dealing that goes on in financial markets.*

wheelbarrow /ˈwiːlˌbær.əʊ/ (US) /-ˌber.oʊ/ noun [C] (also **barrow**) a large, open container for moving things in, which has a wheel at the front and two handles at the back, used especially in the garden

wheelbarrow

wheelbase /ˈwiːl.beɪs/ noun [C usually singular] the distance between the front and the back wheels of a motor vehicle

wheelchair /ˈwiːl.tʃeəʳ/ (US) /-tʃer/ noun [C] B1 a chair on wheels which people who are unable to walk use for moving around: *He spent the last ten years of his life **in a** wheelchair after a fall which left him paralysed from the waist down.* ◦ *The building isn't designed very well from the point of view of wheelchair access.*

ˈwheel ˌclamp noun [C] UK (US **boot**, **Denver ˈboot**) a metal device fixed to the wheel of an illegally parked car which will only be removed when the owner pays an amount of money: *I hope we're not going to find a wheel clamp on my car when we get back.* • **ˈwheel-clamp** verb [T]

-wheeled /-wiːld/ suffix with the stated number of wheels: *It looks like a motorized version of a child's two-wheeled scooter.*

-wheeler /-wiː.ləʳ/ (US) /-lɚ/ suffix used with numbers to form a noun which describes a vehicle with the

W

stated number of wheels: *He drives a three-wheeler (= a car with three wheels).*

ˌwheeler-ˈdealer noun [C] informal someone who WHEELS AND DEALS: *He worked in the property business for a number of years, acquiring a reputation as a formidable wheeler-dealer.*

wheelie /ˈwiː.li/ noun [C] informal an act of raising the front wheel of a bicycle off the ground and keeping it in the air while riding the bicycle: *I can* ***do*** *great wheelies on this bike.*

ˈwheelie ˌbin noun [C] a container for rubbish that has wheels so that it can be moved easily: *We put our wheelie bin out to be emptied every Thursday morning.*

wheelie bin

wheeze /wiːz/ verb; noun

▸verb [I] to make a high, rough noise while breathing because of some breathing difficulty: *I could hear the old man behind me wheezing.* ◦ *I know when I've been smoking too much because I start to wheeze when I run for a train.* • **wheezy** /ˈwiː.zi/ adj *He's got a very wheezy chest that hasn't been helped by a recent cold.*

▸noun [C] **PLAN** ▷ **1** UK old-fashioned informal a clever and often unusual idea or plan, especially one that is intended to achieve a profit or some other advantage: *As a part of their latest marketing wheeze they've planted £50 notes in a number of the crisp packets.* ◦ *So the public actually pay to feed the animals in the zoo? That seems like a* ***good*** *wheeze.* ◦ *I've* ***had*** *a wheeze – why don't we put both kids in the small room and that will leave the back room free.* **BREATH** ▷ **2** a high, rough noise made when someone cannot breathe easily: *The cough, wheeze, and shortness of breath are things that go with smoking, not with age.*

whelk /welk/ noun [C] a soft sea creature, similar to a SNAIL, that lives in a hard shell

when /wen/ adv, conjunction; pronoun; conjunction

▸adv, conjunction (A1) at what time; at the time at which: *'I did tell you about it.' 'When? I don't remember.'* ◦ *When are you going?* ◦ *When's the baby due?* ◦ *We'll go when you're ready.* ◦ *Tell me when* ***to*** *start.* ◦ *Ask him when he's next coming home.* ◦ *When do you expect to have the project completed (****by****)?* ◦ *She was only 20 when she had her first baby.* ◦ *He was quite shocked when I told him.* ◦ *I hate it when there's no one in the office.* ◦ *I went there when I was a child.* ◦ *I was just getting into the bath when the phone rang.*

> **!** Common mistake: **when**
>
> **Remember:** if you are using **when** to talk about something happening in the future, use the present simple tense.
>
> Don't say 'when sth will happen', say **when something happens**:
>
> ~~*Say 'hello' to Sarah for me when you will see her.*~~
>
> *Say 'hello' to Sarah for me when you see her.*
>
> However, if a clause beginning with **when** is the object of the sentence, it is possible to use 'will':
>
> *I don't know when I will see Sarah again.*

▸pronoun what/which time: *'Did you know Lucy was back in England?' 'Is she –* ***since*** *when?'*

IDIOM **since when** used angrily in speech to ask someone why they believe a situation to be different from how it really is: *Since when did you have the right to tell me what to do?*

> **!** Common mistake: **when or if?**
>
> **Warning:** choose the correct conjunction!
>
> To talk about a situation that is not certain but may be true, or may be possible in the future, don't say 'when', say **if**:
>
> ~~*It would be better for the environment when everyone cycled to work.*~~
>
> *It would be better for the environment if everyone cycled to work.*

▸conjunction **CONSIDERING THAT** ▷ **1** (B2) considering the fact that: *How can you say you don't like something when you've never even tried it!* ◦ *You can't complain of being lonely when you don't make any effort to meet people.* ◦ *Why is she training to be a teacher when she doesn't even like children?* ◦ *I don't suppose I can really call myself a vegetarian when I eat fish.* **ALTHOUGH** ▷ **2** (B2) despite the fact that: *He says he hasn't got any money when in fact he's got thousands of dollars in his account.* ◦ *I don't understand how he can say that everything's fine when it's so obvious that it's not.*

whence /wens/ adv, conjunction formal (from) where: *It has been returned to the shop* ***from*** *whence it came.*

whenever /wenˈev.əʳ/ (US) /-ɚ/ adv, conjunction; adv

▸adv, conjunction (B1) every or any time: *I blush whenever I think about it.* ◦ *Whenever I go there they seem to be in bed.* ◦ *I try to use olive oil whenever possible.* ◦ *'Will it be okay if I do it tomorrow?' 'Sure, whenever (= then or at any other time).'* ◦ *Do it in a spare moment at the weekend or whenever – it really doesn't matter.* ◦ *I'm talking about last July or whenever it was you got back from India.*

▸adv used instead of 'when' to add emphasis to a phrase, usually expressing surprise: *Whenever do you get the time to do these things?* ◦ *Whenever did Jane see a fortune teller?*

where /weəʳ/ (US) /wer/ adv, conjunction **1** (A1) to, at, or in what place: *Where does he live?* ◦ *'I put it on your desk.' 'Where? I can't see it?'* ◦ *Where are we going?* ◦ *Now where did I put my glasses?* ◦ *Where's the party being held?* ◦ *Could you tell me where Barker Drive is please?* ◦ *Where did you put my umbrella?* ◦ *I've left my keys somewhere and I don't know where.* ◦ *You've found my diary – where* ***on Earth*** *was it?* ◦ *I've been meaning to ask you where you get your hair cut.* ◦ *Bradford, where Bren comes from, has a lot of good curry restaurants.* ◦ *She lived in Rome for a couple of years, where she taught English.* ◦ *You see where Mira is standing? Well, he's behind her.* ◦ *I like to have him next to me where I can keep an eye on him.* ◦ *I read it somewhere – I don't know where (= in which book, newspaper, etc.).* **2** (B2) used when referring to a particular stage in a process or activity: *You reach a point in any project where you just want to get the thing finished.* ◦ *I've reached the stage where I just don't care any more.* **3** in what situation: *You're not available on the 12th and Andrew can't make the 20th – so where does that leave us?* ◦ *Where do you see yourself five years from now?*

IDIOMS **be where it's at** to be very fashionable and popular: *In the classical music world these days, authentic instruments are where it's at.* • **know/see where sb is coming from** If you say to someone you know or see where they are coming from, you mean you understand why they have a particular opinion, often although you do not have that opinion: *I could*

> **! Common mistake: where or were?**
>
> **Warning:** Choose the right word!
>
> These two words look similar, but they are spelled differently and have completely different meanings.

> **! Common mistake: where or when?**
>
> **Warning:** choose the correct conjunction!
>
> When using a relative clause to talk about what happened at a particular time, don't say 'where', say **when**:
>
> ~~*I worked there until 2001, where the company went bankrupt.*~~
>
> *I worked there until 2001, when the company went bankrupt.*

> **! Common mistake: where**
>
> **Warning:** check your word order!
>
> When **where** is used in a main clause to ask a question, the verb comes before the subject:
>
> *Where is the nearest hospital?*
>
> When **where** is used in a subordinate clause to talk about what place something is at/in, or moving towards, do not put the verb before the subject:
>
> ~~*I don't know where is the nearest hospital.*~~
>
> *I don't know where the nearest hospital is.*

see where they were coming from when they started quoting the Bible at me.

whereabouts noun; adv
▸**noun** [U, + sing/pl verb] /ˈweə.rə.baʊts/ ⓤⓢ /ˈwer.ə-/ C2 the place where a person or thing is: *Trupin is thought to be in the Caribbean, although his exact whereabouts are/is a mystery.*
▸**adv** /ˌweə.rəˈbaʊts/ ⓤⓢ /ˌwer.ə-/ C2 in what part or area: *Whereabouts in Madrid do you live?* ◦ *Whereabouts is your office, then?*

whereas /weərˈæz/ ⓤⓢ /werˈæz/ **conjunction** B2 compared with the fact that; but: *He must be about 60, whereas his wife looks about 30.* ◦ *You eat a massive plate of food for lunch, whereas I have just a sandwich.*

whereby /weəˈbaɪ/ ⓤⓢ /wer-/ **adv, conjunction 1** C2 by which way or method: *They've set up a plan whereby you can spread the cost over a period.* ◦ *We need to devise some sort of system whereby people can liaise with each other.* **2** not standard in which, or with which: *It's put me in a position whereby I can't afford to take a job.*

wherefores /ˈweə.fɔːz/ ⓤⓢ /ˈwer.fɔːrz/ **noun** [plural] → See at **why**

wherein /weəˈrɪn/ ⓤⓢ /werˈɪn/ **adv, conjunction** old use or formal in which, or in which part: *He gazed once more around the room, wherein were assembled his entire family.*

wheresoever /ˌweə.səʊˈev.əʳ/ ⓤⓢ /ˌwer.soʊˈev.ɚ/ **adv, conjunction** formal for **wherever**

whereupon /ˌweə.rəˈpɒn/ ⓤⓢ /ˌwer.əˈpɑːn/ **conjunction** immediately after which: *I told her she looked fat, whereupon she threw the entire contents of a saucepan at me and burst into tears.*

wherever /weəˈrev.əʳ/ ⓤⓢ /werˈev.ɚ/ **adv, conjunction; adv**
▸**adv, conjunction 1** B1 to or in any or every place: *We can go wherever you like.* ◦ *Wherever I go I always seem to bump into him.* ◦ *All across Europe, wherever you look, marriage is in decline and divorce rates are soaring.* ◦ *Wherever you choose to live there are always going to be disadvantages.* ◦ *He lives, apparently, in Little Overington, wherever that is.* **2** B2 in every case: *Wherever possible I use honey instead of sugar.*
▸**adv** used instead of 'where' to add emphasis to a phrase, usually expressing surprise: *Wherever did you find that hat!* ◦ *Wherever did you get that idea!* ◦ *Wherever does he get the money from to go on all these exotic journeys?*

the wherewithal /ˈweə.wɪ.ðɔːl/ ⓤⓢ /ˈwer.wɪ.ðɑːl/ **noun** [S] the money necessary for a particular purpose: *I'd like to buy a bigger house, but I don't have the wherewithal.* ◦ [+ to infinitive] *Poor families* ***lack*** *the wherewithal* ***to*** *hire good lawyers.*

whet /wet/ **verb** (**-tt-**) **INTEREST** ▷ **1 whet sb's appetite** to increase someone's interest in and wish for something, usually by giving them a small experience of it: *I've read an excerpt of the book on the Web and it's whetted my appetite.* ◦ *That one kiss had whetted his appetite.* **SHARPEN** ▷ **2** [T] old use to SHARPEN the blade of a knife or similar tool: *He whetted his knife against the stone.*

whether /ˈweð.əʳ/ ⓤⓢ /-ɚ/ **conjunction 1** B1 (used especially in reporting questions and expressing doubts) if, or not: *I wasn't sure whether you'd like it.* ◦ *She asked me whether I was interested in working for her.* ◦ *I'm wondering whether to have the fish or the beef.* ◦ *I doubt whether it'll work.* ◦ *I was merely questioning whether we have the money to fund such a project.* ◦ *It all depends on whether* ***or not*** *she's got the time.* ◦ *Anyway, it's a good story, whether* ***or not*** *it's true.* **2 whether...or** B1 (used to introduce two or more possibilities) it is not important if: *I'm going, whether she likes it or* ***not***. ◦ *Someone's got to tell her, whether it's you or me.* ◦ *Let's face it – you're going to be late whether you go by bus or train.*

> **! Common mistake: whether**
>
> **Warning:** Check your spelling!
>
> **Whether** is one of the 50 words most often spelled wrongly by learners. Remember: the correct spelling has 'h' after the 'w'.

whetstone /ˈwet.stəʊn/ ⓤⓢ /-stoʊn/ **noun** [C] a stone used for SHARPENING the blades of knives or other cutting tools

whew! /fhjuː/ **exclamation** informal **phew!**

whey /weɪ/ **noun** [U] the liquid part of milk that is separated from the solid CURDS during the process of making cheese

which /wɪtʃ/ **determiner, pronoun; pronoun**
▸**determiner, pronoun QUESTION** ▷ **1** A1 (used in questions and structures in which there is a fixed or limited set of answers or possibilities) what one or ones: *Which party would you prefer to go to – Anna's or Ian's?* ◦ *Which doctor did you see – Sewards?* ◦ *Which time suits you better – 12.30 or one o'clock?* ◦ *'Jacinta was there with her boyfriend.' 'Which one? She's got several.'* ◦ *Which is mine? The smaller one?* ◦ *See if you can guess which one is me in my old school photo.* ◦ *It's either Spanish or Portuguese that she speaks, but I've forgotten which.* ◦ *Which* ***of*** *the desserts did you have?* ◦ *Which of your parents do you feel closer to?* **ADDS INFORMATION** ▷ **2** B1 used to add extra information to a previous CLAUSE, in writing usually after a COMMA: *That bar on Milton Street, which by the way is very nice, is owned by Trevor's brother.* ◦ *She says it's Charlotte's fault, which is rubbish, and that she blames her.* ◦ *Anyway, that evening, which I'll tell you more about later, I ended up staying at Rachel's place.* ◦ *It's the third in a sequence of three books, the first of*

! Common mistake: which or what?

Warning: choose the correct pronoun!
'Which' is used when the question is about a choice between a limited number of things:
Which is your favourite subject – maths or geography?
If the question is about a choice between a number of things that is not known or mentioned, don't say 'which', say **what**:
~~*Which is your favourite subject?*~~
What is your favourite subject?

! Common mistake: which

Warning: Check your spelling!
Which is one of the 50 words most often spelled wrongly by learners. Remember: the correct spelling has 'h' after 'w'.

which I really enjoyed. ◦ *He showed me round the town, which was very kind of him.* ◦ *The picking of the fruit, for which work they receive no money, takes about a week.*

▸pronoun **USED TO REFER** ▷ A2 used as the subject or object of a verb to show what thing or things you are referring to, or to add information about the thing just mentioned. It is usually used for things, not people: *These are principles which we all believe in.* ◦ *You know that little Italian restaurant – the one which I mentioned in my letter?* ◦ *Is that the film in which he kills his mother?* ◦ *The death of his son was an experience from which he never fully recovered.* ◦ *It isn't a subject to which I devote a great deal of thought.*

! Common mistake: which or who?

Warning: choose the correct pronoun!
'Which' is usually used for things, not people.
To add information about the person or people just mentioned, don't say 'which', say **who**:
I met a girl called Marcia who had just finished college.

IDIOM **which is which** used in expressions that relate to being able to see the difference between two very similar things or people: *For the first few months the babies looked so alike I couldn't* ***tell*** *which was which.*

whichever /wɪˈtʃev.əʳ/ (US) /-ɚ/ **determiner, pronoun; determiner**

▸**determiner, pronoun** B2 any one from a limited set: *We can go to the seven o'clock performance or the eight – whichever suits you best.* ◦ *Either Thursday or Friday – choose whichever day is best for you.*

▸**determiner** B2 it is not important which: *It's going to be expensive whichever way you do it.* ◦ *Whichever option we choose there'll be disadvantages.*

whiff /wɪf/ **noun** [C usually singular] **1** a slight smell, carried on a current of air: *He leaned towards me and I* ***caught/got a*** *whiff* ***of*** *garlic.* ◦ *During the first few months of pregnancy the slightest whiff* ***of*** *food cooking made my stomach turn.* **2 a whiff of sth** a slight sign of something: *They regularly hold elections without a whiff of corruption or violence.*

whiffy /ˈwɪf.i/ **adj** UK informal smelling unpleasant: *He hadn't showered for a couple of days and was starting to get whiffy.*

Whig /wɪg/ **noun** [C] a member of a British political party in the 17th, 18th, and 19th centuries that supported political and social change

while /waɪl/ **conjunction; noun; verb**

▸**conjunction DURING** ▷ **1** A2 (mainly UK formal **whilst**) during the time that, or at the same time as: *I read it while you were drying your hair.* ◦ *While I was in Italy I went to see Alessandro.* ◦ *I thought I heard him come in while we were having dinner.* ◦ *'I'm going to the post office.' 'While you're there can you get me some stamps?'* **ALTHOUGH** ▷ **2** B2 (mainly UK formal **whilst**) despite the fact that; although: *While I accept that he's not perfect in many respects, I do actually quite like the man.* ◦ *While I fully understand your point of view, I do also have some sympathy with Michael's.* **BUT** ▷ **3** B1 compared with the fact that; but: *He gets £50,000 a year while I get a meagre £20,000!* ◦ *Tom is very extrovert and confident while Katy's shy and quiet.* ◦ *I do every single bit of housework while he just does the dishes now and again.*

▸**noun a while** B1 a length of time: *I only stayed for a short while.* ◦ *You were there* ***quite*** *a while (= a long time), weren't you?* ◦ *'When did that happen?' 'Oh, it was a while* ***ago*** *(= a long time ago).* ◦ *I haven't seen him* ***for*** *a while (= for a long time).* ◦ *I'll be fine* ***in*** *a while (= soon).* → See also **worthwhile**

IDIOM **all the while** for all of a period of time: *There I was thinking you were hard at work and you were upstairs in bed all the while!*

▸**verb**

PHRASAL VERB **while sth away** to spend time in a relaxed way because you have nothing to do or you are waiting for something else to happen: *We whiled away the afternoon playing cards in front of the fire.* ◦ *That's the bar where Sara and I used to while away the hours between lectures.*

whim /wɪm/ **noun** [C] C2 a sudden wish or idea, especially one that cannot be reasonably explained: *We booked the holiday* ***on a*** *whim.* ◦ *You can add what you like to this mixture – brandy, whisky, or nothing at all – as the whim takes you.* ◦ *Oh for a husband who would indulge my* ***every*** *whim!*

whimper /ˈwɪm.pəʳ/ (US) /-pɚ/ **verb** [I] (especially of an animal) to make a series of small, weak sounds, expressing pain or unhappiness: *A half-starved dog lay in the corner, whimpering pathetically.* ◦ *I said she couldn't have an ice cream and she started to whimper.* • **whimper noun** [C] *She* ***gave*** *a little whimper as the vet inspected her paw.*

whimsical /ˈwɪm.zɪ.kəl/ **adj** unusual and strange in a way that might be funny or annoying: *a whimsical tale* ◦ *Despite his kindly, sometimes whimsical air, he was a shrewd observer of people.* • **whimsically** /-i/ **adv** • **whimsicality** /ˌwɪm.zɪˈkæl.ɪ.ti/ (US) /-ə.t̬i/ **noun** [U] formal

whimsy /ˈwɪm.zi/ **noun** [C or U] disapproving something that is intended to be strange and humorous but in fact has little real meaning or value: *Personally I've always considered mime to be a lot of whimsy.*

whine /waɪn/ **verb; noun**

▸**verb** [I] **1** to make a long, high, sad sound: *Leon's dog was sitting by the door whining, so I thought I'd better take it for a walk.* **2** disapproving If you whine, especially as a child, you complain or express disappointment or unhappiness repeatedly: *Alice, if you carry on whining like that I won't take you – do you understand!*

▸**noun** [C usually singular] an unpleasant high sound or voice: *the whine of a circular saw* ◦ *She delivered the speech in a high-pitched nasal whine.*

whiner /ˈwaɪ.nəʳ/ (US) /-nɚ/ **noun** [C] disapproving a

W

person, especially a child, who complains or expresses disappointment or unhappiness repeatedly

whinge /wɪndʒ/ **verb** [I] (past tense and past participle **whingeing** or **whinging**) UK informal disapproving to complain, especially about something which does not seem important: *Oh stop whinging, for heaven's sake!* ◦ *She's always whingeing* **(on)** ***about*** *something.* • **whinge noun** [C usually singular] *We were just* ***having a*** *whinge about our boss – nothing new.*

whinger /ˈwɪn.dʒəʳ/ Ⓤⓢ /-dʒɚ/ **noun** [C] UK informal disapproving a person who complains repeatedly: *His friend Jon is such a whinger.*

whinny /ˈwɪn.i/ **verb** [I] (of a horse) to make a soft, high sound: *A horse whinnied into the cold morning.*

whiny /ˈwaɪn.i/ **adj** disapproving complaining a lot in an annoying way, especially in a high, sad voice: *The children were tired and whiny.* ◦ *a whiny voice*

whip /wɪp/ **noun; verb**

▸**noun DEVICE FOR HITTING** ▷ **1** [C] a piece of leather or rope that is fastened to a stick, used for hitting animals or people: *She lashed the horses mercilessly with her long whip.* ◦ *The lion-tamer* ***cracked*** *his whip.* **POLITICS** ▷ **2** [C] (in many elected political systems) a member of a political party in parliament or in the LEGISLATURE whose job is to make certain that other party members are present at voting time and also to make certain that they vote in a particular way: *Hargreaves is the MP who got into trouble with his party's* ***chief*** *whip for opposing the tax reform.* **3** [C] in British politics, a written order ordering that party members be present in parliament when there is to be an important vote, or that they vote in a particular way: *In 1970 he defied the* ***three-line*** *(= most urgent) whip against EC membership.* **SWEET FOOD** ▷ **4** [C or U] a sweet food made from cream or beaten egg mixed together with fruit

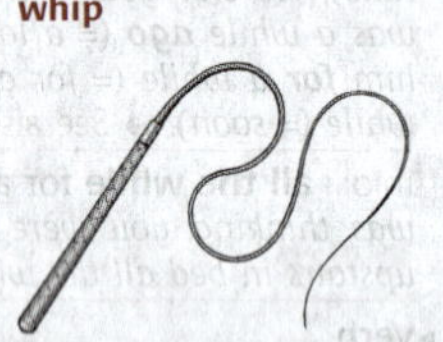

IDIOM **have/hold the whip hand** to be the person or group that has the most power in a situation: *During the last decade the right wing of the party has held the whip hand.*

▸**verb** (-pp-) **DO QUICKLY** ▷ **1** [T usually + adv/prep] to bring or take something quickly: *She whipped a handkerchief* ***out of*** *her pocket and wiped his face.* ◦ *He whipped the covers* ***off*** *the bed.* ◦ *I was going to pay but before I knew it he'd whipped* ***out*** *his credit card.* ◦ *They whipped my plate* ***away*** *before I'd even finished.* **2** [I or T, + adv/prep] literary to (cause something to) move quickly and forcefully: *The wind whipped across the half-frozen lake.* **BEAT FOOD** ▷ **3** [T] to beat food, especially cream with a special piece of equipment in order to make it thick and firm: *Could you whip the cream for me?* ◦ *Try whipping a little brandy or other liqueur* ***into*** *the cream.* ◦ *Top with whipped* ***cream*** *and a sprinkle of sugar.* **HIT** ▷ **4** [T] to hit a person or animal with a whip: *I don't like the way the drivers whip their horses.* **STEAL** ▷ **5** [T] UK old-fashioned informal to steal something

PHRASAL VERBS **whip sb into sth** If you whip someone into a particular state, you quickly and effectively cause them to be in that state: *Karl Smith, the 19-year-old singer, had whipped the crowd of teenage girls into* ***a frenzy*** *merely by removing his shirt.* ◦ *The prime minister's final speech had the desired effect, whipping his party into a patriotic fervour.* • **whip sth up EMOTION** ▷ **1** to encourage or cause people to have strong feelings about something: *She criticized the government for trying to whip up anti-German prejudice.* ◦ *He was trying to whip up some enthusiasm for the project.* **FOOD** ▷ **2** informal to make food or a meal very quickly and easily: *I think I've just about got enough time to whip up an omelette.*

whiplash /ˈwɪp.læʃ/ **noun** [C or U] a neck injury caused by a sudden forward movement of the upper body, especially in a car accident: *a whiplash injury*

whippersnapper /ˈwɪp.əˌsnæp.əʳ/ Ⓤⓢ /-ɚˌsnæp.ɚ/ **noun** [C] old-fashioned or humorous a young person who is too confident and shows no respect towards other, especially older, people: *I'm not going to have some* ***young*** *whippersnapper tell me what to do!*

whippet /ˈwɪp.ɪt/ **noun** [C] a thin dog, like a small GREYHOUND, often used for racing

whipping /ˈwɪp.ɪŋ/ **noun** [C usually singular] the punishment of being hit by a WHIP

ˈ**whipping** ˌ**boy noun** [C usually singular] someone or something that is blamed or punished for problems that are caused by someone or something else

ˈ**whipping** ˌ**cream noun** [U] cream that gets thicker when it is WHIPPED

ˈ**whip-round noun** [C usually singular] UK informal a collection of money made by a group of people that is then given to a particular person or used to buy a present for them: *We usually* ***have*** *a whip-round at work* ***for*** *people who are leaving.*

whirl /wɜːl/ Ⓤⓢ /wɝːl/ **verb; noun**

▸**verb** [I or T] to (cause something to) turn around in circles: *She saw a mass of bodies whirling round on the dance floor.* ◦ *He stepped out into the night and the whirling snow.* ◦ *He whirled her* ***round*** *until she felt quite sick.*

IDIOM **head/mind is whirling** If your head/mind is whirling, your mind is full of thoughts and images and you are so excited that you cannot relax.

▸**noun ACTIVITY** ▷ **1** [S] a continuous and exciting period of activity: *The next two days passed in a whirl* ***of*** *activity.* ◦ *I found myself swept up in the* ***social*** *whirl of college life and scarcely had time for work.* **TURN** ▷ **2** [C usually singular] the action of turning around in circles or something that turns around in circles: *a whirl of snow*

IDIOMS **be in a whirl** to be excited and confused and unable to think clearly • **give it a whirl** informal to attempt to do something, often for the first time: *I've never danced salsa before but I'll give it a whirl.*

whirligig /ˈwɜː.lɪ.gɪg/ Ⓤⓢ /ˈwɝː-/ **noun** [C] something that is full of fast activity and always changing: *By June of this year the whirligig* ***of*** *politics had kicked the Conservatives out and put the Liberal Democrats in.*

whirlpool /ˈwɜːl.puːl/ Ⓤⓢ /ˈwɝːl-/ **noun** [C] a small area of the sea or other water in which there is a powerful, circular current of water that can pull objects down into its centre

whirlwind /ˈwɜːl.wɪnd/ Ⓤⓢ /ˈwɝːl-/ **noun; adj**

▸**noun** [C] (US also **twister**) a tall, spinning column of air that moves across the surface of the land or sea

▸**adj** [before noun] describes an event that happens very fast, and often unexpectedly: *They married three months after they met – it was a real whirlwind* ***romance.*** ◦ *a whirlwind tour/visit*

whirlybird /ˈwɜː.lɪ.bɜːd/ Ⓤⓢ /ˈwɝː.lɪ.bɝːd/ **noun** [C] US old-fashioned **helicopter**

whirr (mainly US **whir** (-rr-)) /wɜːʳ/ Ⓤⓢ /wɝː/ **verb** [I] (especially of machines) to make a low, soft, continuous sound: *I could hear the washing machine* *whirring in the kitchen.* • **whirr** (mainly US **whir**) noun [C usually singular] *the whirr of machinery*

whisk /wɪsk/ verb; noun

whisk

▸verb **REMOVE** ▷ **1** [T usually + adv/prep] to take something or someone somewhere else suddenly and quickly: *Our coffees were whisked* ***away*** *before we'd even finished them.* ◦ *We only had half an hour to see her before she was whisked* ***off to*** *some exotic location.* ◦ *Her husband whisked her* ***off to*** *Egypt for her birthday.* **BEAT FOOD** ▷ **2** [T] to beat eggs, cream, etc. with a special tool in order to add air and make the food light: *Whisk the egg whites until stiff.* ◦ *Remove mixture from heat and whisk in the brandy and vanilla essence.*

▸**noun** [C] a kitchen tool which you use for beating food such as eggs and cream in order to add air and make it light: *an electric whisk* ◦ *a hand-held whisk*

whisker /ˈwɪs.kəʳ/ ⓤⓢ /-kɚ/ noun **1** [C] any of the long, stiff hairs growing on the face of a cat, mouse, or other mammal: *He watched the cat cleaning the milk off her whiskers.* **2 whiskers** [plural] old-fashioned or humorous the hair growing on a man's face, especially the sides and/or the lower part

IDIOMS **by a whisker** by a very small amount: *Last time she raced against the Brazilian, she won by a whisker.* • **come within a whisker of (doing) sth** If you come within a whisker of doing something, you almost do it or it almost happens to you: *Twice now she had come within a whisker of death.*

whiskered /ˈwɪs.kəd/ ⓤⓢ /-kɚd/ **adj** old-fashioned having whiskers

whisky mainly UK (mainly US and Irish English **whiskey**) /ˈwɪs.ki/ **noun** [C or U] **B2** a strong, pale brown alcoholic drink, originally from Scotland and Ireland, made from grain such as BARLEY, MAIZE, or RYE

whisper /ˈwɪs.pəʳ/ ⓤⓢ /-pɚ/ verb; noun

▸verb **SPEAK** ▷ **1 B2** [I or T] to speak very quietly, using the breath but not the voice, so that only the person close to you can hear you: *She leaned over and whispered something in his ear.* ◦ *What are you two girls whispering about?* ◦ [+ speech] *'Where are the toilets?' she whispered.* ◦ *It's rude to whisper!* **SUGGEST** ▷ **2** [+ that] to suggest privately that something might be true: *People are whispering* ***that*** *she's going to retire next year.*

▸**noun SPEECH** ▷ **1** [C] a way of speaking very quietly, using the breath but not the voice, so that only the person close to you can hear you: *I heard whispers outside my room.* ◦ *She said it* ***in a*** *whisper so I presumed it wasn't common knowledge. 'You see,' she said, lowering her voice to a whisper, 'he hasn't been well recently.'* **2** [S] literary a soft, low noise: *The silence was broken only by the whisper* ***of*** *the leaves in the gentle breeze.* **SUGGESTION** ▷ **3** [C] a suggestion or piece of information that you hear privately from someone: *I've heard a whisper* ***that*** *they're heading for divorce.*

ˈwhispering camˌpaign noun [C usually singular] disapproving the intentional damaging of an important person's reputation by saying unpleasant things about them that may not be true

whist /wɪst/ **noun** [U] a card game played between two pairs of players in which each side tries to win more cards than the other

ˈwhist ˌdrive noun [C] UK a social occasion at which people play whist

whistle /ˈwɪs.l̩/ verb; noun

whistle

▸verb **1 B2** [I or T] to make a high sound by forcing air through a small hole or passage, especially through the lips, or through a special device held to the lips: *He whistled as he worked.* ◦ *On the days when she wore a skirt the men on the building site would whistle* ***at*** *her.* ◦ *Someone was whistling Beatles tunes outside my window.* ◦ *The referee whistled and the game was over.* **2** [I + adv/prep] to make a long, high sound while moving quickly through or past something: *She heard the wind whistling* ***through*** *the trees and the howl of a distant wolf.* ◦ *I stepped out of the building and immediately a bullet whistled* ***past*** *my head.* **3** [I] When birds whistle, they sing in high musical notes: *The birds were whistling in the early morning quiet.*

▸**noun** [C] **1 B2** the sound made by someone or something whistling: *From the bottom of the garden I recognized my father's tuneless whistle.* ◦ *It sounded like the whistle of an old-fashioned steam train.* ◦ *She listened to the whistle of the wind through the trees.* **2** an object which you hold to your lips and blow through in order to make a loud, high sound: *The referee* ***blew*** *his whistle for half-time.*

ˈwhistle-ˌblower noun [C] a person who tells someone in authority about something illegal that is happening, especially in a government department or a company

ˌwhistle-stop ˈtour noun [C] a series of short visits to different places, made usually by a politician

whit /wɪt/ **noun** formal **not a whit** not any amount: *There's not a whit* ***of*** *sense in that head of his!*

white /waɪt/ **adj; noun**

▸**adj COLOUR** ▷ **1 A1** of a colour like that of snow, milk, or bone: *a white T-shirt* ◦ *white walls* ◦ *a black and white dog* ◦ *He's white-haired now.* ◦ *'How do you like your coffee?' 'White (= with milk or cream) and no sugar, please.'* **2 C2** having a pale face because you are not well, or you are feeling shocked: *She was white, and her lips were pale.* **3 A2** used in the names of various food and drink products, many of which are not pure white but slightly cream, yellow, grey, or transparent: *white bread* ◦ *white chocolate* ◦ *white flour* ◦ *white sugar* **PEOPLE** ▷ **4 B1** of a person who has skin that is pale in colour: *He had a black mother and a white father.* ◦ *a predominantly white neighbourhood* • **whiteness** /ˈwaɪt.nəs/ **noun** [U] the quality of being white

IDIOMS **(as) white as a sheet** If someone is (as) white as a sheet, their face is very pale, usually because of illness, shock, or fear. • **whiter than white** never doing anything wrong: *I was never convinced by the image of the whiter than white princess depicted in the press.*

▸**noun COLOUR** ▷ **1 A2** [U] a colour like that of snow, milk, or bone: *In some countries it is traditional for a bride to wear white.* **2 whites** [plural] white clothes, either worn for sports or put together to be washed at the same time: *There was a group of men in* ***cricket*** *whites in the pub.* **3 white of the eye** the part of the eye that is white: *Don't shoot until you see the whites of their eyes (= until the people are very close to you).* **4 egg white/white of an egg** the transparent part of an egg that surrounds the YOLK and becomes white when cooked: *Whisk four egg whites into stiff peaks.* **PERSON** ▷ **5** [C] a person who has skin that is pale in colour: *The neighbourhood is populated mainly by whites.*

W

ˌ**white ˈant** noun [C] a **termite**

whitebait /ˈwaɪt.beɪt/ noun [U] small, young fish of various different types, fried and eaten whole

ˌ**white ˈblood ˌcell** noun [C] (also ˌ**white ˈcorpuscle**) a cell in the blood that has no red colour and is involved in the fight against infection

whiteboard /ˈwaɪt.bɔːd/ (US) /-bɔːrd/ noun [C] **1** a board with a smooth, white surface, often fixed to a wall, on which you can write and draw using special pens **2** a piece of electronic equipment in the shape of a flat, white board connected to a computer that you can write on using a special pen that also controls the computer: *an **interactive** whiteboard*

ˌ**white ˈChristmas** noun [C] a Christmas when it snows: *Do you think we might have a white Christmas this year?*

ˌ**white-ˈcollar** adj [before noun] relating to people who work in offices, doing work that needs mental rather than physical effort: *white-collar workers/unions*

ˌ**white ˈelephant** noun [C usually singular] disapproving something that has cost a lot of money but has no useful purpose

ˌ**white ˈflag** noun [C] a flag that is waved to show that you accept defeat or do not intend to attack: *The soldiers laid down their guns and walked towards the enemy camp, carrying a white flag.*

ˈ**white ˌgoods** noun [plural] specialized large electrical goods for the house, such as cookers and washing machines

Whitehall /ˈwaɪt.hɔːl/ noun [U] the British CIVIL SERVICE (= officials employed to perform the work of the British government)

ˌ**white ˈheat** noun [U] the very high temperature at which metal gives out a white light

ˌ**white ˈhope** noun [S] a person or thing which people hope will be very successful in the near future: *This new car is seen as the **great** white hope of the industry.*

ˌ**white ˈhorses** noun [plural] UK (US **whitecaps**) waves that are white at the top

ˌ**white-ˈhot** adj describes metal that is so hot it is giving out a white light

the ˈWhite ˌHouse noun [S] the official Washington home of the US president, or the American government itself: *The White House is set to announce healthcare reforms.*

ˌ**white ˈknight** noun [C] a person or organization that saves a company from financial difficulties or from a TAKEOVER by putting money into the company or by buying it

ˌ**white-ˈknuckle** adj [before noun] informal describes an experience or activity that makes you feel very frightened and often excited: *a white-knuckle **ride** in a theme park*

ˌ**white ˈlie** noun [C] a lie that is told in order to be polite or to stop someone from being upset by the truth

ˌ**white ˈmagic** noun [U] magic that is used only to do good things

ˈ**white ˌmatter** noun [U] specialized the pale tissue containing nerve FIBRES (= structures like threads) found in the brain and SPINAL CORD → Compare **grey matter**

ˈ**white ˌmeat** noun [U] a meat such as chicken or VEAL that is pale in colour, or the whitest flesh, usually the breast, of a cooked bird

ˌ**white ˈmoney** noun [U] money that is earned legally, or on which the necessary tax is paid → Compare **black money**

whiten /ˈwaɪ.tᵊn/ (US) /-ţᵊn/ verb [I or T] to make or become whiter: *She's had her nicotine-stained teeth whitened.* ◦ *Her hair had whitened over the years.*

whitening /ˈwaɪ.tᵊn.ɪŋ/ (US) /-ţᵊn-/ noun [U] (also **whitener**) a substance that you put on sports shoes to make them whiter and cleaner

ˌ**white ˈnoise** noun [U] a mixture of sounds or electrical signals which consists of all the sounds or signals in a large range

whiteout /ˈwaɪ.taʊt/ (US) /-aʊt/ noun [C] a weather condition in which snow and clouds change the way light is reflected so that only very dark objects can be seen

the ˌWhite ˈPages noun [S] US a book that lists the names, addresses, and phone numbers of people living and businesses operating in a city or area → Compare **the Yellow Pages**

ˌ**White ˈPaper** noun [C] in various countries, a government report on a particular subject giving information and details of future planned laws: *a White Paper on employment* → Compare **Green Paper**

ˌ**white ˈsauce** noun [U] a thick sauce used in cooking, made from flour, butter, and milk

ˌ**white ˈspirit** noun [U] UK (US **turpentine**) a clear alcoholic liquid that is used for making paint thinner and removing paint from brushes and clothes

ˌ**white suˈpremacy** noun [U] the belief that people with pale skin are better than people with darker skin • ˌ**white suˈpremacist** noun [C]

ˌ**white-ˈtie** adj describes a social occasion at which men wear formal clothes including a white BOW TIE: *a white-tie diplomatic reception*

ˈ**white ˌtrash** noun [U] US offensive white people who are poor and badly educated

ˌ**white ˈvan man** noun [C] UK disapproving a man who is thought to be typical of drivers of white VANS by being rude, not well educated, and having very strong, often unpleasant opinions

whitewall /ˈwaɪt.wɔːl/ (US) /-wɑːl/ noun [C] (UK ˌ**whitewall ˈtyre**, US ˌ**whitewall ˈtire**) a tyre with a white stripe around it, or a white side

whitewash /ˈwaɪt.wɒʃ/ (US) /-wɑːʃ/ noun; verb

▸noun **PAINT** ▷ **1** [U] a white liquid that is a mixture of LIME or powdered CHALK and water, used for making walls or ceilings white **ATTEMPT TO HIDE** ▷ **2** [S] disapproving an attempt to stop people finding out the true facts about a situation: *The official report on the killings has been denounced as a whitewash.* **DEFEAT** ▷ **3** [C] UK informal a complete defeat in a game or competition: *a 6–0 whitewash*

▸verb [T] **HIDE** ▷ **1** disapproving to make something bad seem acceptable by hiding the truth: *The government is trying to whitewash the incompetence of the Treasury officials.* **DEFEAT** ▷ **2** UK informal to defeat a player or team completely, especially while preventing them from scoring any points **PAINT** ▷ **3** to paint walls or buildings using whitewash

whitewater /ˈwaɪt.wɔː.təʳ/ (US) /-wɑː.ţɚ/ noun [U] water in a river which flows fast and strongly in an especially narrow CHANNEL: *whitewater rafting*

ˌ**white ˈwedding** noun [C] a traditional Christian marriage in a church, at which the woman who is getting married wears a white dress: *She wants a proper white wedding.*

ˌ**white ˈwine** noun [C or U] wine with a pale yellow colour that is made from green or yellow GRAPES, or from black grapes without their skins: *He poured a glass of white wine.* ◦ *a fruity white wine*

whitey /ˈwaɪ.ti/ (US) /-t̬i/ **noun** [C] offensive a white person

whither /ˈwɪð.əʳ/ (US) /-ɚ/ **adv** old use to where: *Whither are they going?*

whiting /ˈwaɪ.tɪŋ/ (US) /-t̬ɪŋ/ **noun** [C or U] (plural **whiting** or **whitings**) a small, black and silver sea fish, eaten as food

whitish /ˈwaɪ.tɪʃ/ (US) /-t̬ɪʃ/ **adj** almost white in colour: *whitish-grey walls*

Whitsun /ˈwɪt.sᵊn/ **noun** [U] the seventh Sunday after Easter, and the period around it: *We're going to Scotland for a week* ***at*** *Whitsun.*

whittle /ˈwɪt.l̩/ (US) /ˈwɪt̬-/ **verb** [T] to make something from a piece of wood by cutting off small, thin pieces: *An old sailor sat on the dockside, whittling a toy boat.*

PHRASAL VERBS **whittle away at sth** to gradually reduce the size or importance of something: *A series of new laws has gradually whittled away at the powers of the trade unions in this country.* • **whittle sth down** to gradually reduce the size of something or the number of people in a group: *We had 80 applicants for the job, but we've whittled them down* ***to*** *six.*

whizz /wɪz/ **verb; noun**

▸**verb** [I + adv/prep] UK (US usually **whiz**) to move or do something very fast: *A police car whizzed* ***by****, on its way to the accident.* ◦ *We whizzed* ***through*** *the rehearsal, so that we'd be finished by lunchtime.* ◦ *Time just whizzes* ***past*** *when you're enjoying yourself.*

▸**noun** UK **EXPERT** ▷ **1** (US usually **whiz**) [C usually singular] a person with a very high level of skill or knowledge in a particular subject: *a computer whizz* ◦ *He's a whizz* ***at*** *poker.* **DRUG** ▷ **2** [U] slang for AMPHETAMINE (= drug which makes the mind and body more active)

ˈwhizz-kid **noun** [C] informal a young person who is very clever and successful: *They've taken on some financial whizz-kid.*

who /huː/ **pronoun** **QUESTIONS** ▷ **1** (A1) used especially in questions as the subject or object of a verb, when asking which person or people, or when asking what someone's name is: *Who did this?* ◦ *Who's she?* ◦ *Who are all those people?* ◦ *She asked me if I knew who had got the job.* ◦ *Who (also* formal ***whom****) do you want to talk to?* ◦ *I don't know who to ask to the party.* **2** used with verbs that relate to knowing, when you want to say that something is not known: *'Are they going to get married?' 'Who* ***knows****?' (= It is not possible to know at the moment.)* ◦ *Who* ***can tell*** *what will happen now?* **USED TO REFER** ▷ **3** (A2) used as the subject or object of a verb to show which person you are referring to, or to add information about a person just mentioned. It is used for people, not things: *I think it was your Dad who phoned.* ◦ *She's one of those people who love to be the centre of attention.* ◦ *He rang James, who was a good friend as well as the family doctor.* ◦ *The other people who (also* ***that****) live in the house are really friendly.* ◦ *This is Gabriel, who I told you about.*

IDIOM **who's who** **1** the name and position of each person, especially in an organization **2 Who's Who** a book containing information about the world's richest or most famous people: *The guest list reads like a Who's Who of top American businessmen.*

the WHO /ˌdʌb.l̩.juː.eɪtʃˈəʊ/ **noun** [+ sing/pl verb] abbreviation for **the World Health Organization**

whoa /wəʊ/ (US) /woʊ/ **exclamation** **1** used when telling a horse to stop: *'Whoa there, Poppy,' he said to his pony, and pulled up beside the kerb.* **2** informal used when telling a person to stop what they are doing or to do it more slowly: *Yes, carrots please, – whoa! That's plenty.*

who'd /huːd/ short form of **1** who had: *She wondered who'd sent her the mysterious email.* **2** who would: *Well, who'd have thought Joey was going to become so successful?*

whodunnit informal (US **whodunit**) /ˌhuːˈdʌn.ɪt/ **noun** [C] a story about a crime and the attempt to discover who committed it: *It's one of those whodunnits where you don't find out who the murderer is till the very end.*

whoever /huːˈev.əʳ/ (US) /-ɚ/ **pronoun** **PERSON** ▷ **1** (B2) the person who: *Whoever uprooted that tree ought to be ashamed of themselves.* ◦ *Could I speak to whoever is in charge of International Sales please?* **ANYONE** ▷ **2** (B2) any person who: *Can whoever leaves last please lock up?* ◦ *He says he bought the car from Frank, whoever Frank is. (= I do not know who Frank is.)* **SURPRISE** ▷ **3** used in questions as a way of expressing surprise: *Whoever told you that?* ◦ *Whoever could that be phoning at this time?*

whole /həʊl/ (US) /hoʊl/ **adj; adv; noun**

▸**adj** **1** (A2) complete or not divided: *I spent the whole day cleaning.* ◦ *There's still a whole month till my birthday.* ◦ *After my exercise class, my whole body ached.* ◦ *The whole town was destroyed by the earthquake.* ◦ *This whole* ***thing*** *(= situation) is ridiculous.* ◦ *Bill does nothing but moan the whole* ***time*** *(= all the time).* ◦ *You have to stand up in court and promise to tell 'the truth, the whole* ***truth****, and nothing but the truth'.* ◦ *Her dance compositions added a whole (= completely) new dimension to the contemporary dance repertoire.* **2** informal used to emphasize something: *I've got a whole heap of work to do this afternoon.* ◦ *The new computers are* ***a*** *whole* ***lot*** *(= much) faster.*

IDIOMS **go the whole hog** informal to do something as completely as possible: *Having already limited local taxation, why not go the whole hog and abolish it completely?* • **the whole bit** UK (US **the whole enchilada**) informal the whole of something, including everything that is related to it: *He's into jogging, squash, aerobics, the whole exercise bit.* • **a whole lot** **1** informal very much: *Things were about to get a whole lot worse.* ◦ *He didn't like them a whole lot.* **2** informal a large number: *I said no, for a whole lot* ***of*** *reasons.* • **the whole lot** informal all of something, or all of the people or things in a group: *I offered him some chocolate, and he ate the whole lot.* ◦ *She's annoyed with the whole lot* ***of*** *you.*

▸**adv** **IN ONE PIECE** ▷ **1** (C2) as a single object and not in pieces: *The seeds can be eaten whole or milled in a coffee grinder.* **COMPLETELY** ▷ **2** informal completely: *Now he's arrived, it's a whole different situation.*

▸**noun** [C usually singular] **1** a complete thing: *Two halves make a whole.* ◦ *You must consider each problem as an aspect of* ***the*** *whole.* **2 the whole of sth** (B1) all of something: *I'll be on holiday the whole of next week.* ◦ *The whole of his finger was bruised.* ◦ *The whole of the village (= everyone in the village) had come out for the party.*

IDIOMS **as a whole** (B2) when considered as a group and not in parts: *The population as a whole is getting healthier.* • **on the whole** (B1) generally: *We have our bad times but on the whole we're fairly happy.*

wholefood /ˈhəʊl.fuːd/ (US) /ˈhoʊl-/ **noun** [C or U] UK food that has not had any of its natural features taken away or any artificial substances added: *a wholefood shop*

wholegrain /ˈhəʊl.greɪn/ ⓤⓢ /ˈhoʊl-/ **adj** mainly UK (of particular types of food) containing whole seeds: *wholegrain bread ◦ wholegrain mustard ◦ wholegrain breakfast cereal*

wholehearted /ˌhəʊlˈhɑː.tɪd/ ⓤⓢ /ˌhoʊlˈhɑːr.t̬ɪd/ **adj** completely enthusiastic: *The minister has pledged his wholehearted support for the scheme.* • **wholeheartedly** /-li/ **adv**

wholemeal /ˈhəʊl.miːl/ ⓤⓢ /ˈhoʊl-/ **adj** UK (mainly US **wholewheat**) (of flour or food made from flour) containing all the natural features of the grain, with nothing taken away: *wholemeal bread/flour/pastry*

ˌwhole ˈmilk **noun** [U] (UK also **ˌfull-fat ˈmilk**) milk with no fat removed → Compare **skimmed milk, semi-skimmed**

ˈwhole note **noun** [C] US for **semibreve**

ˌwhole ˈnumber **noun** [C] a number, such as 1, 3, or 17, that has no FRACTIONS and no DIGITS after the DECIMAL POINT

wholesale /ˈhəʊl.seɪl/ ⓤⓢ /ˈhoʊl-/ **adj, adv** **SELLING** ▷ **1** of or for the selling of goods in large amounts at low prices to shops and businesses, rather than the selling of goods in shops to customers: *wholesale prices ◦ a wholesale supplier/business ◦ We only sell wholesale, not to the public.* → Compare **retail** **COMPLETE** ▷ **2** often disapproving (especially of something bad or too extreme) complete or affecting a lot of things, people, places, etc.: *wholesale changes ◦ wholesale destruction*

wholesaler /ˈhəʊlˌseɪ.ləʳ/ ⓤⓢ /ˈhoʊlˌseɪ.lɚ/ **noun** [C] someone who buys and sells goods in large amounts to shops and businesses: *a furniture wholesaler*

wholesome /ˈhəʊl.səm/ ⓤⓢ /ˈhoʊl-/ **adj** approving good for you, and likely to improve your life either physically, morally, or emotionally: *wholesome food ◦ good, wholesome family entertainment ◦ He looks like a nice, wholesome, young man.* • **wholesomeness** /-nəs/ **noun** [U]

wholewheat /ˈhəʊl.hwiːt/ ⓤⓢ /ˌhoʊlˈhwiːt/ **adj** mainly US for **wholemeal**

who'll /huːl/ **short form of** who will: *Who'll be at the party tomorrow?*

wholly /ˈhəʊl.li/ ⓤⓢ /ˈhoʊl-/ **adv** **C2** completely: *I wasn't wholly convinced by her explanation. ◦ That's a wholly different matter. ◦ a machine that is wholly British-made*

whom /huːm/ **pronoun** formal **B2** used instead of 'who' as the object of a verb or preposition: *I met a man with whom I used to work. ◦ He took out a photo of his son, whom he adores. ◦ There were 500 passengers, of whom 121 drowned. ◦ To whom do you wish to speak?*

> **!** Usage: **whom or who?**
>
> **Whom** is very formal and most people use **who** instead:
>
> *Who did you invite?*
>
> Although **whom** should be used after a preposition, most people avoid it by putting the preposition towards the end of the sentence and using **who** instead:
>
> *Who did you go out with last night?*
>
> It would be extremely formal and rather unnatural to say **whom**:
>
> *With whom did you go out last night?*

whomever /huːˈmev.əʳ/ ⓤⓢ /-ɚ/ **pronoun** formal **whoever** when used as the object: *Give it to whomever you please.*

whoop /wuːp/ **verb; noun**

▸**verb** [I] to give a loud, excited shout, especially to show your enjoyment of or agreement with something: *The audience was whooping and clapping.* → See also **whooping cough**

IDIOM **whoop it up** informal to enjoy yourself in a noisy and excited way

▸**noun** [C] a loud, excited shout, especially showing your enjoyment of or agreement with something: *When the whoops and cheers had finally died down he started to speak.*

whoop-de-doo /ˌwʊp.diˈduː/ **exclamation** mainly US informal said when you do not think what someone has said or done is important or special: *Well, whoop-de-doo, they're offering us a 0.5 percent pay raise!*

whoopee /ˈwʊp.i/ ⓤⓢ /ˈwuː.pi/ **exclamation** a loud, excited shout of happiness: *Whoopee, it's the holidays!*

IDIOM **make whoopee** US old-fashioned informal to have sex

whooping cough /ˈhuː.pɪŋˌkɒf/ ⓤⓢ /-ˌkɑːf/ **noun** [U] a disease caught especially by children, which causes severe coughing

whoops /wʊps/ **exclamation** (also **oops**) an expression of surprise or feeling sorry about a mistake or slight accident: *Whoops! That's the second time I've spilled coffee today!*

whoosh /wʊʃ/ **noun; verb**

▸**noun** informal **1** [C usually singular] a soft sound made by something moving fast through the air or like that made when air is pushed out of something: *The train sped through the station with a whoosh.* **2** [S] a sudden fast movement of a liquid or air: *I felt a great whoosh of adrenalin.*

▸**verb** [I usually + adv/prep] informal to move along quickly, making a soft sound like the wind: *A fast motorboat whooshed by.*

whop /wɒp/ ⓤⓢ /wɑːp/ **verb** [T] (**-pp-**) mainly US informal to hit or defeat: *She whopped him with her handbag. ◦ The Yankees whopped the Cleveland Indians 17–2.*

whopper /ˈwɒp.əʳ/ ⓤⓢ /ˈwɑː.pɚ/ **noun** [C] **1** humorous informal something that is surprising because it is so much bigger than the usual size: *I mean, my nose is quite big but my Dad's got a whopper.* **2** humorous a big lie: *Amanda's told some whoppers in her time.*

whopping /ˈwɒp.ɪŋ/ ⓤⓢ /ˈwɑː.pɪŋ/ **adj** [before noun] (also **ˌwhopping ˈgreat**) extremely large: *She had a whopping great bruise on her arm. ◦ a whopping 35 percent pay rise ◦ a whopping lie*

who're /ˈhuː.əʳ/ ⓤⓢ /-ɚ/ **short form of** who are: *The film begins with a young couple, who're just about to get married.*

whore /hɔːʳ/ ⓤⓢ /hɔːr/ **noun** [C] **1** old-fashioned a female PROSTITUTE **2** offensive a woman whose behaviour in her sexual relationships is considered IMMORAL

whorehouse /ˈhɔː.haʊs/ ⓤⓢ /ˈhɔːr-/ **noun** [C] mainly US for **brothel**

whorl /wɜːl/ ⓤⓢ /wɝːl/ **noun** [C] literary a circular pattern of lines, with the smallest circle in the middle, surrounded by other circles, each one wider and larger than the previous one

who's /huːz/ **short form of** **1** who has: *Who's been chosen, do you know?* **2** who is: *Who's that talking to Jason?*

whose /huːz/ **pronoun, determiner; determiner**

▸**pronoun, determiner** **B1** used especially in questions when asking about which person owns or is responsible for something: *Whose is this bag? ◦ Whose bag is this?*

▸**determiner** B1 used for adding information about a person or thing just mentioned: *Cohen, whose contract expires next week, is likely to move to play for a European club.* ◦ *There was a picture in the paper of a man whose leg had been blown off.* ◦ *They meet in an old house, whose basement has been converted into a chapel.* ◦ *Fraud detectives are investigating the company, three of whose senior executives have already been arrested.*

whosoever /ˌhuː.səʊˈev.əʳ/ US /-soʊˈev.ɚ/ **pronoun** old use for **whoever**

who've /huːv/ **short form of** who have: *Who've you asked so far?*

why /waɪ/ **adv; exclamation; noun**

▸**adv** A1 for what reason: *'I'm going home.' 'Why?'* ◦ *Why did you choose to live in London?* ◦ *Why wait? Let's leave now.* ◦ *Why should I help him – he never helps me?* ◦ *Why is it that I find chocolate so addictive?* ◦ *The police asked me to explain why I hadn't reported the accident sooner.* ◦ *I don't know why she isn't here.* ◦ *Quite why he isn't here today is a mystery.* ◦ *There is no **reason** why we shouldn't succeed.*

! Common mistake: why

Warning: check your word order!

When **why** is used in a main clause to ask a question, remember to put the verb before the subject:

Why is football such a popular sport?

When **why** is used in a subordinate clause to talk about the reason for something, do not put the verb before the subject:

~~*I can't help wondering why is football so popular.*~~

I can't help wondering why football is so popular.

IDIOMS **why don't you...?** A2 used to make a suggestion: *Why don't you come with us?* • **why not...?** B1 used to make a suggestion or to express agreement: *Why not use my car? You'll fit more in.* ◦ *'Shall we eat Italian tonight?' 'Yes, why not?'*

▸**exclamation** mainly US or old-fashioned used to express surprise or anger: *Why, if it isn't old Georgie Frazer!* ◦ *Why, I've never seen anything like it!*

▸**noun** **the whys and (the) wherefores** the reasons for something: *I know very little about the whys and the wherefores of the situation.*

wick /wɪk/ **noun; verb**

▸**noun** [C] a piece of string in the centre of a candle, or a similar part of a light, that supplies fuel to a flame

IDIOM **get on sb's wick** UK old-fashioned informal to annoy someone

▸**verb** [T] to absorb liquid from something and remove it: *These special fabrics wick moisture from athletes' skin to keep them comfortable.*

wicked /ˈwɪk.ɪd/ **adj; noun**

▸**adj** **BAD** ▷ **1** C2 morally wrong and bad: *It was a wicked thing to do.* ◦ *Of course, in the end, the wicked witch gets killed.* → Compare **evil, naughty** **2** slightly IMMORAL or bad for you, but in an attractive way: *a wicked grin* ◦ *a wicked sense of humour* **EXCELLENT** ▷ **3** informal excellent: *He's got some wicked trainers.*

▸**noun**

IDIOM **there's no rest for the wicked** saying said when you must continue with your work or other activity although you are very tired

wickedness /ˈwɪk.ɪd.nəs/ **noun** [U] the fact of being morally very wrong or bad: *They would be punished for their wickedness.*

wicker /ˈwɪk.əʳ/ US /-ɚ/ **adj** made of very thin pieces of wood twisted together: *a wicker basket/chair*

wickerwork /ˈwɪk.ə.wɜːk/ US /-ɚ.wɜːk/ **noun** [U] furniture or containers made from wicker

wicket /ˈwɪk.ɪt/ **noun** [C] **1** in cricket, a set of three vertical sticks with two small pieces of wood balanced across the top of them, at which the ball is aimed. There are two wickets on a cricket field. **2** in cricket, the length of ground between two sets of wickets

wicketkeeper /ˈwɪk.ɪtˌkiː.pəʳ/ US /-pɚ/ **noun** [C] a cricket player who stands behind the wicket in order to catch the ball

wide /waɪd/ **adj; adv**

▸**adj** **DISTANCE** ▷ **1** A2 having a larger distance from one side to the other than is usual or expected, especially in comparison with the length of something; not narrow: *a wide river/road/gap/foot* ◦ *His eyes were wide (= opened much more than usual)* ***with** surprise.* → See also **width** **2** B1 used when describing how long the distance between the two sides of something is or when asking for this information: *The rectangle is 5 cm long and 1.9 cm wide.* ◦ *How wide are your skis?* **AMOUNT** ▷ **3** B1 describes something that includes a large amount or many different types of thing, or that covers a large range or area: *They sell a wide **range** of skin-care products.* ◦ *She has a wide experience of teaching, in many different schools.* ◦ *The Green Party no longer enjoys wide support (= the support of many people).*

IDIOMS **be wide of the mark** to be wrong: *Yesterday's weather forecast was a little wide of the mark, then.* • **give sth/sb a wide berth** informal to avoid a person or place: *I tend to give the city centre a wide berth on Saturdays because it's so busy.*

▸**adv** **DISTANCE** ▷ **1** B2 farther than usual, or as far as possible: *'**Open** wide,' said the dentist.* ◦ *They moved the goal posts wider **apart**.* **AMOUNT** ▷ **2** C2 completely, or by a large amount: *She left the door wide **open**.* ◦ *It was 3 a.m. and we were still wide **awake**.*

ˌwide-angle ˈlens **noun** [C] (also **ˌwide-ˈangle**) a camera LENS that provides a wider view than usual

ˈwide ˌboy **noun** [C] UK informal disapproving a man who is dishonest or who deceives people in the way he does business: *Some of the younger property developers are real wide boys.*

ˌwide-ˈeyed **adj** **1** having your eyes open much wider than usual **2** too willing to believe and admire what you see or are told: *At that time, I was still a wide-eyed youngster.*

widely /ˈwaɪd.li/ **adv** **1** B2 including a lot of different places, people, subjects, etc.: *They have both travelled widely.* ◦ *His plays are still widely performed in the USA.* ◦ *French used to be widely spoken in Cambodia.* ◦ *His work on DNA was widely **admired**.* ◦ *This theory is no longer widely **accepted**.* **2** **differ/vary widely** B2 to be very different: *Prices vary widely from shop to shop.*

widen /ˈwaɪ.dᵊn/ **verb** [I or T] **DISTANCE** ▷ **1** B2 to become, or to make something greater in width: *As it approaches the sea, the river begins to widen (**out**).* **AMOUNT** ▷ **2** B2 to (cause something to) become larger or to include a larger amount or number: *His eyes/smile widened.* ◦ *Why not widen the discussion to include the Muslim and Jewish points of view?*

ˌwide-ˈranging **adj** covering many subjects: *a wide-ranging discussion*

widescreen /ˈwaɪd.skriːn/ **adj** **1** having a wider than usual screen which shows very clear pictures: *wide-screen televisions* **2** made to be shown on a screen that is wider than usual: *a widescreen version of the movie*

widespread /ˌwaɪdˈspred/ **adj** C1 existing or happening in many places and/or among many people: *There are reports of widespread flooding in northern France.* ◦ *Malnutrition in the region is widespread – affecting up to 78 percent of children under five years old.* ◦ *The campaign has received widespread support.*

widget /ˈwɪdʒ.ɪt/ **noun** [C] **1** informal any small device whose name you have forgotten or do not know **2** an imagined small product made by a company: *Let's assume the company makes ten cents profit on every widget they sell.* **3** a piece of software that is used on a page of a website to give the user changing information of a particular type in a small area of the computer screen: *This new widget will bring fresh content to your website every hour.*

widow /ˈwɪd.əʊ/ US /-oʊ/ **noun; verb**

▸**noun** [C] **1** B2 a woman whose husband or wife has died and who has not married again **2 fishing/football/golf widow** informal humorous a woman whose partner is often not at home because he or she is fishing or playing football or GOLF

▸**verb** [T usually passive] If someone has been widowed, their husband or wife has died: *He was widowed at the age of 52.*

widowed /ˈwɪd.əʊd/ US /-oʊd/ **adj** used to describe a person whose husband or wife has died: *a widowed mother of three*

widower /ˈwɪd.əʊ.əʳ/ US /-oʊ.ɚ/ **noun** [C] a man whose wife or husband has died and who has not married again

widowhood /ˈwɪd.əʊ.hʊd/ US /-oʊ-/ **noun** [U] the state of being a widow or widower

width /wɪtθ/, /wɪdθ/ **noun 1** B2 [C or U] the distance across something from one side to the other: *It is five metres **in** width.* ◦ *The needle is seven times smaller than the width **of** a human hair.* ◦ *The material is available in various widths.* → See also **wide 2** [C] the distance across a swimming pool from one side to the other: *I managed to swim two widths underwater.*

wield /wiːld/ **verb** [T] **1** C2 to hold a weapon or tool and look as if you are going to use it: *She was confronted by a man wielding a knife.* **2 wield influence, power, etc.** C2 to have a lot of influence or power over other people: *He still wields enormous influence within the party.*

wiener /ˈwiː.nəʳ/ US /-nɚ/ **noun** [C] (also **wienie**, **weenie**) US a FRANKFURTER (= thin, red-brown sausage)

wife /waɪf/ **noun** [C] (plural **wives**) A1 the woman that you are married to: *I met Greg's wife for the first time.* ◦ *She's his third wife (= she is the third woman he has been married to).*

wifely /ˈwaɪf.li/ **adj** old-fashioned like a wife or relating to a wife: *wifely duties*

wi-fi /ˈwaɪ.faɪ/ **noun** [U] a system for connecting electronic equipment such as computers and electronic organizers to the internet without using wires

wig /wɪg/ **noun** [C] a covering of artificial hair worn on the head to hide a loss of hair or to cover your own hair: *She was wearing a blonde wig.* ◦ *In Britain, judges wear white wigs in court.* → Compare **toupée**

wiggle /ˈwɪg.l̩/ **verb; noun**

▸**verb** [I or T] informal to (cause to) move up and down and/or from side to side with small, quick movements: *He tried wiggling the control stick but nothing happened.* ◦ *She wiggled her toes in the water.* ◦ *Her hips wiggle as she walks.*

▸**noun** [C] a small, quick movement up and down and/or from side to side: *With a wiggle of her hips, she pulled up the trousers.*

wiggly /ˈwɪg.l̩.i/, /ˈwɪg.li/ **adj** informal shaped like a line with many curves: *a wiggly line* ◦ *a wiggly worm*

wigwam /ˈwɪg.wæm/ **noun** [C] a cone-shaped tent made and lived in, especially in the past, by Native Americans in the eastern US

wiki /ˈwɪ.ki/ **noun** [C] a website which allows users to add, DELETE (= get rid of), and EDIT (= change) the contents, or the program that makes this possible: *Wikipedia is thought to be the world's largest wiki with more than 280,000 articles.*

wild /waɪld/ **adj; noun**

▸**adj NOT CONTROLLED** ▷ **1** B2 uncontrolled, violent, or extreme: *a wild party* ◦ *wild dancing* ◦ *The audience burst into wild applause.* ◦ *When I told him what I'd done, he **went** wild (= became very angry).* ◦ *The children were wild **with** excitement (= were extremely excited).* ◦ *Her eyes were wild/She had a wild look in her eyes (= her eyes were wide open, as if frightened or mentally ill).* ◦ *His hair was wild (= long and untidy) and his clothes full of holes.* ◦ *There have been wild (= extreme) variations in the level of spending.* ◦ *They get some wild weather (= many severe storms) in the north.* ◦ *It was a wild (= stormy or very windy) night, with the wind howling and the rain pouring down.* **2** slang very unusual, often in a way that is attractive or exciting: *Those are wild trousers you're wearing, Fi.* **NATURAL** ▷ **3** A2 refers to plants or animals that live or grow independently of people, in natural conditions and with natural characteristics: *wild flowers/grasses* ◦ *a herd of wild horses* **4** B2 describes land that is not used to grow crops and has few people living in it: *a wild, mountainous region* **NOT THOUGHT ABOUT** ▷ **5 wild accusation/guess/rumour** C2 something that you say that is not based on facts and is probably wrong • **wildness** /ˈwaɪld.nəs/ **noun** [U] *the wildness (= natural and extreme beauty) of the Western Highlands*

IDIOMS **be wild about sth/sb** informal to be very enthusiastic about something or someone: *I'm not wild about Thai food.* • **wild horses wouldn't drag me** If you say wild horses would not drag you somewhere, you mean that nothing could persuade you to go there: *Wild horses wouldn't drag me to a party tonight.*

▸**noun 1 in the wild** in natural conditions, independent of humans: *Animals would produce more young in the wild than they do in the zoo.* **2 in the wilds (of somewhere)** in an area that is far from where people usually live and difficult to get to, and that is not considered easy to live in: *She lives somewhere in the wilds of Borneo.*

ˌwild ˈboar **noun** [C] a large, dangerous pig that is covered in hair and lives wild in forests

ˈwild ˌcard **noun** [C] **COMPUTING** ▷ **1** specialized in computers, a symbol that has no particular meaning of its own so that its space can be filled by any real character that is necessary: *The wild cards are represented here by asterisks.* **COMPETITION** ▷ **2** someone who is allowed to take part in a competition, although they have not achieved this in the usual way, for example by winning games: *Phillips is hoping for a wild card entry to the championships.* **NOT KNOWN** ▷ **3** someone or something whose behaviour is sometimes unexpected: *The wild card in this election is the Green Party – no one knows exactly how much support they will get.*

wildcat /ˈwaɪldˌkæt/ **noun** [C] a small wild animal of the cat family that looks similar to a pet cat and that lives mainly in areas with forests and mountains

ˌwildcat ˈstrike noun [C] (UK also **ˈlightning ˌstrike**) a sudden STRIKE (= act of refusing to work as a protest) without any warning by the workers and often without the official support of the UNIONS

wildebeest /ˈwɪl.də.biːst/ noun [C] (plural **wildebeest** or **wildebeests**) a large African animal with a long tail and horns that curve to the sides that lives in areas covered in grass

wilderness /ˈwɪl.də.nəs/ US /-dɚ-/ noun [C usually singular] **1** C2 an area of land that has not been used to grow crops or had towns and roads built on it, especially because it is difficult to live in as a result of its extremely cold or hot weather or bad earth: *a beautiful mountain wilderness* ◦ *Alaska is the last great wilderness.* ◦ mainly US *It's a wilderness **area**, under the protection of the Parks Department.* **2** an outside area in which plants are left to grow naturally or untidily: *The garden was a wilderness **of** weeds and overgrown bushes.*

IDIOM **in the wilderness** If someone, such as a politician, is in the wilderness, they no longer have a position of authority and are not now in the news: *After five years in the political wilderness, she was recalled to be foreign minister.*

wildfire /ˈwaɪld.faɪəʳ/ US /-faɪr/ noun [C] a fire that is burning strongly and out of control on an area of grass or bushes in the countryside: *Major wildfires have destroyed thousands of acres in Idaho.*

IDIOM **spread like wildfire** If disease or news spreads like wildfire, it quickly affects or becomes known by more and more people: *Once one child in the school has the infection, it spreads like wildfire.*

wildfowl /ˈwaɪld.faʊl/ noun [plural] birds that people shoot for sport, especially ones such as DUCKS that live near water

ˌwild-ˈgoose ˌchase noun [C] informal a search that is completely unsuccessful and a waste of time because the person or thing being searched for does not exist or is somewhere else: *After two hours spent wandering in the snow, I realized we were **on** a wild goose chase.*

wildlife /ˈwaɪld.laɪf/ noun [U] B1 animals and plants that grow independently of people, usually in natural conditions: *a documentary on Peruvian wildlife*

wildly /ˈwaɪld.li/ adv B2 in an uncontrolled or extreme way: *He was dancing wildly.* ◦ *Inflation figures have fluctuated wildly between 0.2 and 25 percent.* ◦ *It was wildly (= very) expensive.* ◦ *I must say I'm not wildly (= very) keen on the idea.*

ˌwild ˈrice noun [U] the black grains of a North American grass that are eaten, often with rice

the ˌWild ˈWest noun [S] the name given to the western part of the US during the time when Europeans were first beginning to live there and when there was fighting between them and the Native Americans

wiles /waɪlz/ noun [plural] formal ways of persuading someone that cleverly trick them into doing something: *She'll have to **use** all her feminine wiles to get him to agree.*

wilful disapproving (US usually **willful**) /ˈwɪl.fᵊl/ adj (of something bad) done intentionally or (of a person) determined to do exactly as you want, even if you know it is wrong: *The present crisis is the result of years of wilful neglect by the council.* ◦ *They eat huge quantities of sweet and fried foods, in wilful disregard of their health.* ◦ *She developed into a wilful, difficult child.* • **wilfully** (US usually **willfully**) /-i/ adv *Some basic safety rules were wilfully ignored.* • **wilfulness** (US usually **willfulness**) /-nəs/ noun [U]

will /wɪl/ modal verb; noun; verb

▸modal verb **FUTURE** ▷ **1** A2 (also **'ll**) used to talk about what is going to happen in the future, especially things that you are certain about or things that are planned: *Clare will be five years old next month.* ◦ *The train leaves at 8.58, so we'll be in Scotland by lunchtime.* ◦ *I'll see him tomorrow./I'll be seeing him tomorrow.* ◦ *Will Susie be there?* ◦ *It won't be easy to find another secretary.* ◦ *There'll be trouble when she finds out.* **ABLE/WILLING** ▷ **2** A1 (also **'ll**) used to talk about what someone or something is able or willing to do: *I'll give you a lift.* ◦ *Ask Ian if he'll take them.* ◦ *I've asked her but she won't come.* ◦ *The car won't start.* ◦ *This quantity of lasagne will feed six people.* **REQUEST** ▷ **3** A2 used to ask someone to do something: *Will you give me her address?* ◦ *Will you give that to Tony when you see him, please?* **4** (also **'ll**) used as a polite way of inviting someone to do something, or of offering someone something: *Will you join us for a drink, Evie?* ◦ *Will you come in for a while?* ◦ *You'll have some cake, won't you, Charles?* **IF** ▷ **5** A2 (also **'ll**) used in CONDITIONAL sentences with 'if': *If he's late again, I'll be very angry.* ◦ *I'll wait with Christopher if his mother isn't here when you go.* **LIKELY** ▷ **6** (also **'ll**) used to refer to what is likely: *That'll be Scott at the door.* ◦ *That'll be his mother with him.* ◦ *As you will all probably already know, election day is next week.* **ORDER** ▷ **7** (also **'ll**) used when angry to tell someone to do something: *Will you stop being such a pain!* ◦ *You'll go upstairs and you'll go straight to bed like your father told you!* **ALWAYS** ▷ **8** (also **'ll**) used when referring to something that always or usually happens: *Accidents will happen.* ◦ *Fruit will keep longer in the fridge.* ◦ *The product with the better-known brand name will always sell better.* ◦ *She's 85 now, but she will insist on doing all her own housework.*

▸noun **MENTAL POWER** ▷ **1** B2 [C or U] the mental power used to control and direct your thoughts and actions, or a determination to do something, despite any difficulties or opposition: *From an early age she had a very strong will.* ◦ [+ to infinitive] *After six months in hospital she began to lose the will **to** live (= the desire and determination to stay alive).* **2** C1 [S] what someone wants to happen: *It was God's will.* ◦ ***Against** their will (= although they did not want to), they were forced to hold a meeting.* ◦ *The government has failed to impose its will **upon** regional communities (= to make them do as it wants).* → See also **free will** **DOCUMENT** ▷ **3** C2 [C] an official statement of what a person has decided should be done with their money and property after their death: *Have you **made** a will yet?* ◦ *She left me some money **in** her will.*

IDIOMS **at will** If you can do something at will, you can do it any time you want: *He can cry at will.* • **where there's a will there's a way** saying used to mean that if you are determined enough, you can find a way to achieve what you want, even if it is very difficult • **with a will** old-fashioned with energy and determination: *They worked with a will and had cleared the path by 10 a.m.*

▸verb **MAKE HAPPEN** ▷ **1** [+ obj + to infinitive] If you will something to happen, you try to make it happen by the power of your thoughts: *She willed her**self to** remember his name.* **2** [I or T] formal to want something: *Stay or go, **as you** will.* **LEAVE** ▷ **3** [T] to arrange to give money or property to others after your death

willful /ˈwɪl.fᵊl/ adj US for **wilful**

willie (also **willy**) /ˈwɪl.i/ noun **1** [C] UK informal or child's word a PENIS **2 the willies** [plural] informal a feeling of nervousness and fear, especially caused by something strange or threatening: *Spending a night in the house alone always* ***gives*** *me the willies.* ◦ *Seeing something in the shadows, I suddenly* ***got*** *the willies and ran.*

willing /ˈwɪl.ɪŋ/ adj **1 be willing (to do sth)** B1 to be happy to do something if it is needed: *If you're willing to fly at night, you can get a much cheaper ticket.* ◦ *You said you needed a volunteer – well, I'm willing.* ◦ *Apparently John and Gabriel are willing* ***for*** *us to use their garden.* **2** approving describes someone who does their work energetically and enthusiastically: *a willing helper* • **willingly** /-li/ adv B2 *I would willingly (= be ready and enthusiastic to) help you if I weren't going away tomorrow.* • **willingness** /-nəs/ noun [S or U] B2 [+ to infinitive] *She shows a willingness* ***to*** *work on her own initiative.*

will-o'-the-wisp /ˌwɪl.ə.ðəˈwɪsp/ noun [C usually singular] something that is impossible to get or achieve: *Full employment is the will-o'-the-wisp that politicians have been chasing for decades.*

willow /ˈwɪl.əʊ/ US /-oʊ-/ noun [C] a tree that grows near water and has long, thin branches that hang down, or wood from this tree

willowy /ˈwɪl.əʊ.i/ US /-oʊ-/ adj approving (especially of a woman) GRACEFUL (= moving smoothly and attractively) and thin: *a willowy blonde*

willpower /ˈwɪl.paʊəʳ/ US /-paʊr/ noun [U] C2 the ability to control your own thoughts and the way in which you behave: *It took a lot of willpower to stay calm.* ◦ *I don't have the willpower to diet.* → Synonym **determination**

willy /ˈwɪl.i/ noun [C] a **willie**

willy-nilly /ˌwɪl.iˈnɪl.i/ adv informal **1** If something happens willy-nilly, it happens even if the people who are involved do not want it to happen: *Both sides were drawn, willy-nilly, into the conflict.* **2** without any order: *She threw her clothes willy-nilly into a drawer.*

wilt /wɪlt/ verb [I] (of a plant) to become weak and begin to bend towards the ground, or (of a person) to become weaker, tired, or less confident: *Cut flowers will soon wilt without water.* ◦ *After only an hour's walking they were beginning to wilt in the heat.*

wily /ˈwaɪ.li/ adj (of a person) clever, having a very good understanding of situations, possibilities, and people, and often willing to use tricks to achieve an aim: *a wily politician* → See also **wiles**

wimp /wɪmp/ noun; verb

▸noun [C] informal disapproving a person who is not strong, brave, or confident: *I'm afraid I'm a bit of a wimp when it comes to climbing up ladders.* • **wimpish** /ˈwɪm.pɪʃ/ adj (also **wimpy**)

▸verb

PHRASAL VERB **wimp out** informal to decide not to do something because you are too frightened: *I was going to do a parachute jump but I wimped out at the last minute.*

W

win /wɪn/ verb; noun

▸verb (present tense **winning**, past tense and past participle **won**) **1** A2 [I or T] to achieve first position and/or get a prize in a competition, election, fight, etc.: *Which year was it that Italy won the World Cup?* ◦ *He won first prize/a bottle of gin in the raffle.* ◦ *Who's winning?* ◦ *This is the third medal she's won this season.* ◦ *Who won the men's finals in the tennis?* ◦ *They won the war, although it cost them millions of lives.* ◦ *If this government win the next election, I'm leaving the country.* ◦ *Everyone likes winning an argument.* ◦ [+ two objects] *It was his goal that won us the match/won the match* ***for*** *us.* ◦ *Her firm have just won (= beaten other companies to get) a cleaning contract worth £3 million.* **2** C2 [T] to receive something positive, such as approval, loyalty, or love because you have earned it: *Her plans have won the support of many local people.* ◦ *This is Jamie, the four-year old who won* ***the hearts*** *of the nation (= made everyone love him and/or feel sympathy for him).* ◦ *She would do anything to win his love.* ◦ *Winning* ***back*** *his trust was the hardest part.*

IDIOMS **sb can't win** informal used to say that nothing someone does in a situation will succeed or please people: *Whatever I do seems to annoy her – I can't win.* • **win hands down** to win very easily • **win the day** to persuade people to support your ideas or opinions • **you can't win 'em all** (also **you win some, you lose some**) something that you say which means it is not possible to succeed at everything you do: *I'd have liked the job but I suppose you can't win 'em all.* • **you win!** something you say to someone who has persuaded you to do something that you did not intend to do, especially when they have used force and you are angry: *Okay, you win – I can't stand it any longer!*

PHRASAL VERBS **win sb over/round** to persuade someone to support you or agree with you, often when they were opposed to you before: *He's not sure about the idea at the moment, but I'm sure we'll win him over in the end.* • **win through** UK to finally succeed after trying hard to achieve something: *Most people are fairly confident that the workers will win through in the end.*

▸noun [C] C1 an occasion when someone wins a game or competition: *It was United's sixth consecutive win this season.* ◦ *Everyone was predicting a Republican win at the last election and look what happened.*

wince /wɪns/ verb [I] to show pain suddenly and for a short time in the face, often moving the head back at the same time: *Did I hurt you? – I thought I saw you wince.* ◦ *It makes me wince even thinking about eye operations.* • **wince noun** [C usually singular] *She* ***gave*** *a wince as the nurse put the needle in.*

winch /wɪntʃ/ noun [C] (also **windlass**) a machine which lifts heavy objects by turning a chain or rope around a tube-shaped device • **winch verb** [T] *Two helicopters winched the passengers to safety from the deck of the ship.*

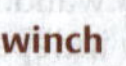

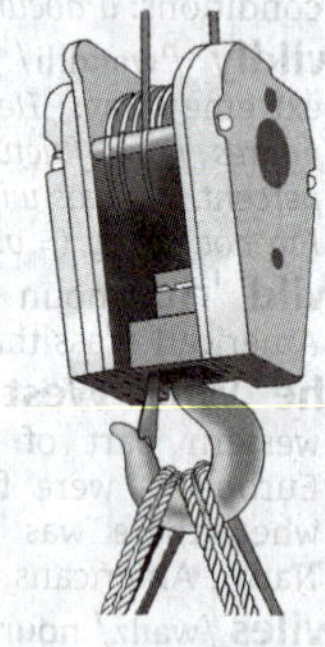

wind¹ /wɪnd/ noun; verb

▸noun CURRENT OF AIR ▷ **1** A1 [C or U] a current of air moving approximately horizontally, especially one strong enough to be felt: *There isn't enough wind to fly a kite.* ◦ *The forecast warned of winds of up to 60 miles an hour today.* ◦ *There was a light wind blowing.* ◦ *Strong/High winds made the crossing very unpleasant.* ◦ *The sails flapped* ***in the*** *wind.* ◦ literary *There wasn't a* ***breath of*** *(= even a slight amount of) wind.* ◦ *A* ***gust*** *of wind suddenly caught her skirt.* ◦ *The wind is beginning to* ***pick up*** *(= get stronger).* ◦ *She ran* ***like the*** *wind (= very fast) to catch up.* BREATH ▷ **2** [U] mainly UK breath or the ability to breathe: *I had to stop halfway up the hill to* ***get my*** *wind (= allow my breathing to return to* *normal).* **3** [U] informal disapproving words that do not mean anything and false statements: *I rarely bother to listen to politicians' speeches – it's all just wind.* **BOWELS** ▷ **4** [U] UK (US **gas**) gas in the bowels or in a baby's stomach, especially that which makes you feel uncomfortable or makes noises: *I like garlic but it gives me terrible wind.*

IDIOMS **get wind of sth** to hear a piece of information that someone else was trying to keep secret: *I don't want my colleagues to get wind of the fact that I'm leaving.* • **put/get the wind up sb** UK to make someone feel worried about their situation: *Tell them your father's a policeman – that'll put the wind up them!* • **take the wind out of sb's sails** to make someone feel less confident or less determined to do something, usually by saying or doing something that they are not expecting: *I was all ready to tell him that the relationship was over when he greeted me with a big bunch of flowers – it rather took the wind out of my sails.*

▸verb [T] (**winded**) **BREATH** ▷ **1** to make it difficult or temporarily impossible for someone to breathe, usually by hitting them in the stomach **BOWELS** ▷ **2** UK (US **burp**) to rub or very gently hit a baby on the back to allow air to come up from the stomach

wind² /waɪnd/ verb (**wound, wound**) **TURN** ▷ **1** [I or T, usually + adv/prep] to turn or cause something to turn: *She wound the handle but nothing happened.* ◦ *Once she'd got into the car, she wound the window* ***down/up*** *(= caused it to open/close by turning a handle).* ◦ UK *Does this camera wind* ***on*** *(= does the film in it move forward) automatically?* ◦ *That noise you can hear is the tape winding* ***back***. → See also **rewind 2** [T] (also **wind up**) If you wind (up) a clock or watch, you cause it to work by turning a key, handle, or other device. **3** B2 [I usually + adv/prep] If a road, path, or river winds, it follows a route that turns repeatedly in different directions: *The river winds through the valley.* **WRAP AROUND** ▷ **4** B2 [T usually + adv/prep] to wrap something around an object several times or twist it repeatedly around itself: *She wound a scarf* ***around*** *her neck.* ◦ *He wound the string* ***into*** *a ball.* ◦ *He wound a small bandage* ***round*** *her finger.* • **winding** /ˈwaɪn.dɪŋ/ **adj** B2 describes a path, road, river, etc. which repeatedly turns in different directions: *There's a very long, winding path leading up to the house.*

PHRASAL VERBS **wind (sth) down 1** to end gradually or in stages, or to cause something to do this: *The government intends to wind the scheme down in early spring.* ◦ *Unfortunately, the party was just winding down as we got there.* **2** If a business or organization winds down, or if someone winds it down, the amount of work it does is gradually reduced until it closes completely: *They're winding down their operations abroad because they're losing money.* • **wind down** to gradually relax after doing something that has made you tired or worried: *When he goes on holiday, it takes him the first couple of days just to wind down.* • **wind sth up** to close a business or organization: *Lawyers were called in to wind up the company.* • **wind up** informal to find yourself in an unexpected and usually unpleasant situation, especially as a result of what you do: *If he carries on like this he's going to wind up in prison!* • **wind (sth) up** to end, or to make an activity end: *I think it's about time we wound this meeting up.* ◦ *We need to wind up now, we've only got five minutes.* • **wind sb up** UK informal **ANNOY** ▷ **1** to annoy or upset someone: *It really winds me up when he goes on about teachers having an easy life.* ◦ *She just knows how to wind me up.* → See also **wound up DECEIVE** ▷ **2** to tell someone something that is not true in order to make a joke: *Are you serious or are you just trying to wind me up?*

windbag /ˈwɪnd.bæɡ/ **noun** [C] informal disapproving a person who talks too much about boring things

windbreak /ˈwɪnd.breɪk/ **noun** [C] something which gives protection from the wind, such as a row of trees, bushes, or a wall

windbreaker /ˈwɪndˌbreɪ.kəʳ/ (US) /-kɚ/ **noun** [C] US (UK old-fashioned **windcheater**) a jacket made from a material which protects you from the wind

windchill /ˈwɪnd.tʃɪl/ **noun** [U] the effect that wind has on how cold the air feels: *It's two degrees outside, but with the windchill* ***factor****, it feels like minus five.*

ˈwind ˌchimes **noun** [plural] an arrangement of shells or small decorative shapes of metal or wood that hang from pieces of wire or string and make a gentle noise when moved by the wind

winded /ˈwɪn.dɪd/ **adj** [after verb] temporarily unable to breathe, either when hit in the stomach or after taking hard physical exercise: *Simon is so unfit – he gets winded just from walking up a flight of stairs.*

winder /ˈwaɪn.dəʳ/ (US) /-dɚ/ **noun** [C] **1** UK (US **stem**) a small KNOB (= round handle) on a watch, which you use for winding it **2** a key or handle for winding a clock

windfall /ˈwɪnd.fɔːl/ (US) /-fɑːl/ **noun** [C] **MONEY** ▷ **1** an amount of money that you win or receive from someone unexpectedly: *Investors each received a windfall of £3,000.* ◦ *The government is hoping to collect a windfall* ***tax*** *(= extra tax on a large unexpected company profit) from British Electric.* **FRUIT** ▷ **2** a piece of fruit blown down from a tree: *I tend to leave the windfalls for the birds to pick at.*

ˈwind ˌfarm **noun** [C] a group of WIND TURBINES (= tall structures with blades that are blown by the wind) that are used for producing electricity

ˈwind ˌgauge **noun** [C] a device for measuring the force of the wind

ˈwind ˌinstrument **noun** [C] a musical instrument whose sound is produced by blowing: *Saxophones and flutes are wind instruments.*

windlass /ˈwɪnd.ləs/ **noun** [C] a **winch**

windmill /ˈwɪnd.mɪl/ **noun** [C] **1** a building or structure with large blades on the outside which, when turned by the force of the wind, provide the power for getting water out of the ground or crushing grain **2** a **wind turbine 3** (US also **pinwheel**) a child's toy which consists of a stick with brightly coloured pieces of plastic at one end which turn around when you blow them or hold the toy in the wind

windmill

window /ˈwɪn.dəʊ/ (US) /-doʊ/ **noun** **GLASS** ▷ **1** A1 [C] a space usually filled with glass in the wall of a building or in a vehicle, to allow light and air in and to allow people inside the building to see out: *Is it all right if I open/close the window?* ◦ *He caught me staring out of the window.* ◦ *I saw a child's face* ***at*** *the window.* ◦ *She's got some wonderful plants* ***in*** *the window (= on a surface at the bottom of the window).* ◦ *I was admiring the cathedral's stained-glass windows.* ◦ *Have* *you paid the window* ***cleaner*** *(= person whose job is to clean the outside of windows)?* ◦ *window frames* ◦ *a window ledge* **2** [S] literary something that makes it possible for you to see and learn about a situation or experience that is different from your own: *The film provides a window* ***on*** *the immigrant experience.* **3** [C] a transparent rectangle on the front of an envelope, through which you can read the address written on the letter inside **4** [C] the decorative arrangement of goods behind the window at the front of a shop, in addition to the window itself: *How much is the jacket* ***in*** *the window?* ◦ *The shop windows are wonderful around Christmas time.* **COMPUTER** ▷ **5** **B1** [C] a separate area on a computer screen that shows information and can be moved around: *to minimize/maximize a window* **OPPORTUNITY** ▷ **6** [C] a period when there is an opportunity to do something: *I'm quite busy this week but there might be a window on Friday.* ◦ *If a window* ***of opportunity*** *(= an opportunity) should present itself, I'd take advantage of it.*

IDIOM **go out (of) the window** If a quality, principle, or idea goes out of the window, it does not exist any more: *Then people start drinking and sense goes out of the window.*

ˈwindow ˌbox noun [C] a box filled with earth, for growing decorative plants in, positioned on an outside WINDOWSILL: *window boxes full of brightly coloured geraniums*

ˈwindow ˌdressing noun [U] **SHOPS** ▷ **1** the skill of decorating shop windows and arranging goods in them so that they look attractive to people going past **DECEIVING** ▷ **2** disapproving things that are of no real importance and are said or done in order to make an attractive effect: *Never mind the extra day's holiday, the free healthcare, and all the other window dressing in the company's offer – the point is, how much more money are we getting?*

ˈwindow ˌledge noun [C] a **windowsill** (= a shelf below a window)

windowpane /ˈwɪn.dəʊ.peɪn/ US /-doʊ-/ noun [C] a single piece of glass in the window of a building

ˈwindow ˌseat noun [C] **1** a seat on a train, aircraft, or other vehicle, especially a public one, that is next to a window **2** a seat in a building that is below a window

ˈwindow ˌshade noun [C] US a BLIND (= a cover for a window)

ˈwindow ˌshopping noun [U] the activity of spending time looking at the goods on sale in shop windows without intending to buy any of them

windowsill /ˈwɪn.dəʊ.sɪl/ US /-doʊ-/ noun [C] (also **ˈwindow ledge**) a shelf below a window, either inside or outside a building: *He's got a few plants in pots on the windowsill.*

windpipe /ˈwɪnd.paɪp/ noun [C] (specialized **trachea**) the tube in the body which carries air that has been breathed in from the upper end of the throat to the lungs

ˈwind ˌpollination noun [U] specialized the process in which the wind carries POLLEN (= powder produced by male part of flower) from one plant to another which is then FERTILIZED

windscreen /ˈwɪnd.skriːn/ noun [C] **1** **B1** UK (US **windshield** /-ʃiːld/) the window at the front of a car, truck, etc. **2** US for **windbreak**

ˈwindscreen ˌwiper noun [C usually plural] UK (US **ˈwindshield ˌwiper**) one of two long metal and rubber parts that move against a windscreen to remove rain

windsock /ˈwɪnd.sɒk/ US /-sɑːk/ noun [C] a tube of cloth fastened at one end to a pole that shows the direction of the wind at an airport

windsurfer /ˈwɪndˌsɜː.fəʳ/ US /-ˌsɝː.fɚ/ noun [C] **1** someone who goes windsurfing **2** (also **sailboard**) a narrow board with a sail fixed to it which you hold, standing up, while the wind blows you along the surface of a sea or lake

windsurfing /ˈwɪndˌsɜː.fɪŋ/ US /-ˌsɝː-/ noun [U] **B1** a sport in which you sail across water by standing on a board and holding onto a large sail: *I* ***went*** *windsurfing most afternoons.* → Compare **surfing** • **windsurf** /-sɜːf/ US /-sɝːf/ verb [I]

windsurfing

windswept /ˈwɪnd.swept/ adj (of places) open to and not protected from strong winds, or (of people) having hair that is untidy because it has been blown in different directions by the wind: *We drove down to the windswept Atlantic coast of Portugal.* ◦ *windswept hair*

ˈwind ˌtunnel noun [C usually singular] a closed passage or room through which currents of air are forced in order to study the effects of moving air on aircraft and other vehicles

ˈwind ˌturbine noun [C] a tall structure with blades that are blown round by the wind and produce power to make electricity

ˈwind-up noun [C usually singular] UK informal something that is not true that you tell someone in order to make a joke: *You can't be serious – is this a wind-up?*

windward /ˈwɪnd.wəd/ US /-wɚd/ adj specialized (on the side of a hill, etc.) facing the wind: *On the windward leg of the race the wind was strong.* → Compare **leeward**

windy /ˈwɪn.di/ adj **A2** with a lot of wind: *It was a windy night.* ◦ *It was wet and windy for most of the week.*

wine /waɪn/ noun; verb

▸noun [C or U] **A1** an alcoholic drink that is usually made from GRAPES, but can also be made from other fruits or flowers. It is made by FERMENTING the fruit with water and sugar: *a wine cellar/connoisseur/cooler/glass* ◦ *red/white/dry/sweet/sparkling/table wine* ◦ *Shall we have a* ***bottle/glass of*** *wine with dinner?* ◦ *I love Australian wines, especially the white wines.* ◦ *Would you like to see the wine* ***list****, sir?*

▸verb **wine and dine sb** to entertain someone by giving them food and drink: *The survey concludes that most women like to be wined and dined on the first few dates.*

ˈwine ˌbar noun [C] UK a bar or small restaurant which serves mainly wines

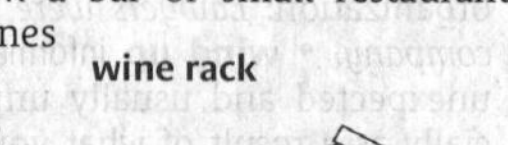

ˈwine ˌrack noun [C] a wooden or metal frame used to store bottles of wine horizontally

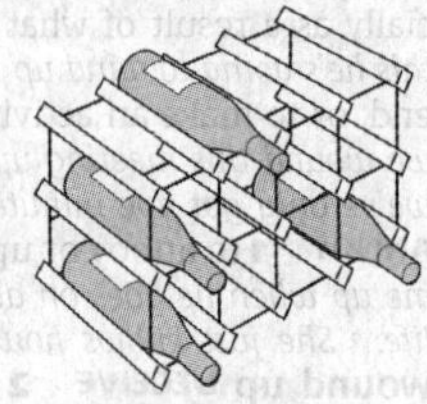

winery /ˈwaɪ.nəʳr.i/ US /-nɚ.i/ noun [C] mainly US a place where wine is made, especially from grapes that are grown there

wing /wɪŋ/ noun; verb
▸noun [C] **FOR FLYING** ▷ **1** B1 the flat part of the body which a bird, insect, or BAT uses for flying, or one of the flat, horizontal structures that stick out from the side of an aircraft and support it when it is flying: *the delicacy of a butterfly's wings* ◦ *I don't like chicken wings – there's not much meat on them.* ◦ *I could see the plane's wing out of my window.* **2 take wing** literary **a** If a bird takes wing, it flies away. **b** to suddenly develop, freely and powerfully: *She walked in the hills, letting her thoughts take wing.* **3 on the wing** literary A bird that is on the wing is flying. **POLITICAL GROUP** ▷ **4** C2 a group within a political party or organization whose beliefs are in some way different from those of the main group: *The president is on the* ***left/right*** *wing of the Democratic party.* **PART OF BUILDING** ▷ **5** a part of a large building which sticks out from the main part, often having been added at a later date: *The maternity ward will be in the new wing of the hospital.* ◦ *The west wing of the house is still lived in by Lord and Lady Carlton, while the rest of the house is open to the public.* **PART OF CAR** ▷ **6** UK (US **fender**) one of the four parts at the side of a car which go over the wheels: *There's a dent in the left wing.* ◦ *Look in your wing* ***mirror***. **SPORTS** ▷ **7** (in various team games, such as football and HOCKEY) either of the two sides of the sports field, or a player whose position is at either of the two sides of the field: *Zinoli passes the ball to Pereira out there on the wing.* ◦ *He played* ***left/right*** *wing for Manchester United.* **THEATRE** ▷ **8 the wings** [plural] the sides of a stage which cannot be seen by the people watching the play: *I was* ***in*** *the wings waiting for my cue to come on stage.*

IDIOMS **on a wing and a prayer** If you do something on a wing and a prayer, you do it hoping that you will succeed, although you are not prepared enough for it: *With scarcely any funding and a staff of six, they were operating on a wing and a prayer.* • **take sb under your wing** If you take someone under your wing, you start to protect and take care of them: *I was a bit lonely and fed up at the time and she took me under her wing.*

▸verb informal **wing it** to perform or speak without having prepared what you are going to do or say: *I hadn't had time to prepare for the talk, so I just had to wing it.*

ˌwing ˈchair noun [C] (also **ˌwing-backed ˈchair**) a chair with a high back from which large side pieces stick out

ˌwing ˈcollar noun [C] the strip of material which goes around the neck on a man's formal shirt and is folded down into the shape of two small triangles at the front

winged /wɪŋd/, /ˈwɪŋ.ɪd/ adj [before noun] **1** having the stated type of wings: *a high-winged plane* **2** with wings: *The winged adult mosquitoes emerge from the pupae.* ◦ *Cupid is usually depicted as a winged boy with a bow and arrow.*

winger /ˈwɪŋ.əʳ/ US /-ɚ/ noun [C] a player whose position is at either of the two sides of the field in a team game such as football or HOCKEY

ˈwing ˌmirror noun [C] UK (US **ˈside ˌmirror**) a mirror on the outside of a car door that allows the driver to see the vehicles that are behind or OVERTAKING

ˈwing ˌnut noun [C] a small, metal fastening device that has two flat pieces on it that you can hold with your fingers while tightening it

wingspan /ˈwɪŋ.spæn/ noun [C] the distance between the ends of the wings of a bird, insect, or aircraft

wink /wɪŋk/ verb; noun
▸verb [I] **1** C2 to close one eye for a short time as a way of greeting someone or showing friendliness, sexual interest, etc., or of showing that you are not serious about something you have said: *She winked* ***at*** *me as he turned his back.* ◦ *For a moment I thought he was being serious, but then he winked* ***at*** *me.* **2** When lights wink, they keep flashing on and off quickly: *Reflected in the water, the lights winked* ***at*** *us from the other side of the lake.* ◦ *The light was winking on the answering machine.*

PHRASAL VERB **wink at sth** to pretend not to notice something bad that is happening because it is more convenient for you

▸noun [C] the action of winking at someone: *He* ***gave*** *me a conspiratorial wink as they left the room.*

IDIOM **not sleep a wink** (also **not get a wink of sleep**) C2 to not sleep at all: *I didn't sleep a wink last night with all that noise.*

winkle /ˈwɪŋ.kl/ noun; verb
▸noun [C] (US usually **periwinkle**) a small sea SNAIL that can be eaten
▸verb

PHRASAL VERB **winkle sth/sb out** mainly UK to get or find something or someone with difficulty: *I managed to winkle the truth out* ***of*** *him eventually.*

Winnebago /ˌwɪn.əˈbeɪ.gəʊ/ US /-goʊ/ noun [C] trademark a large vehicle that is made for you to live in while you are travelling

winner /ˈwɪn.əʳ/ US /-ɚ/ noun [C] **1** A2 someone who wins a game, competition, or election: *There'll be a prize for the winner.* ◦ *The winner of this match will play Pires in the semifinals.* ◦ *And to find out who are the lucky winners of our competition, Samantha is going to draw some names out of the bag.* → See also **breadwinner 2** (US also **ˈgame-ˌwinner**) in sport, a goal or point that causes a player or team to win a game: *Neil Eaves scored the winner in the last minute of the match.* **3** informal something that is extremely successful and popular: *That lemon tart was a winner, wasn't it?* ◦ *I think they're* ***onto*** *a winner with this latest product (= it will succeed).*

winning /ˈwɪn.ɪŋ/ adj [before noun] **1** that has won something: *Have you heard the winning entry in this year's Eurovision Song Contest?* ◦ *It's nice to be on the winning side for a change.* **2** friendly and CHARMING and often making people like you: *a winning smile*

ˈwinning ˌpost noun [C usually singular] UK a post that marks the place where a race ends: *His horse collapsed just 40 yards from the winning post.*

winnings /ˈwɪn.ɪŋz/ noun [plural] an amount of money that has been won: *What are you going to spend your winnings on?*

winnow /ˈwɪn.əʊ/ US /-oʊ/ verb [T] **1** to blow the CHAFF (= the outer coverings) from grain before it can be used as food **2** formal to reduce a large number of people or things to a much smaller number by judging their quality: *A list of 15 candidates has been winnowed* ***down to*** *a shortlist of three.* ◦ *a winnowing process*

wino /ˈwaɪ.nəʊ/ US /-noʊ/ noun [C] (plural **winos**) informal a person, especially a HOMELESS person, who drinks too much wine or other alcoholic drink: *There were the usual bunch of winos outside the station.*

winsome /ˈwɪn.səm/ adj literary approving attractive and pleasing, with simple qualities, sometimes like those a child has: *Maria brought along her eldest* daughter – a winsome lass with brown eyes and a ready smile. • **winsomely** /-li/ adv

winter /ˈwɪn.təʳ/ (US) /-t̬ɚ/ noun; verb

▸noun [C or U] (A1) the season between autumn and spring, lasting from November to March north of the EQUATOR and from May to September south of the equator, when the weather is coldest: *I think you tend to eat more **in** (**the**) winter.* ◦ ***Last** winter we went skiing.* ◦ *It's been a surprisingly mild winter.* ◦ *a winter/winter's day* ◦ *winter weather/snow*

▸verb [I + adv/prep] (especially of a bird) to spend the winter in a particular place: *Birds migrate so that they can winter in a warmer country.* ◦ *Kuwait Bay is one of the world's most important wintering grounds for wading birds.*

ˌwinter ˈsports noun [plural] sports that are done on snow or ice

wintertime /ˈwɪn.tə.taɪm/ (US) /-t̬ɚ-/ noun [U] the season of winter: *Like most seaside resorts **in the** wintertime, it's quite deserted.*

wintry /ˈwɪn.tri/ adj **LIKE WINTER** ▷ **1** typical of winter: *It looks like this wintry weather is here to stay.* ◦ *This afternoon we may see some wintry **showers** (= snow mixed with rain) over higher ground.* **EXPRESSION** ▷ **2** literary unfriendly and disapproving: *She gave a wintry **smile**.*

ˌwin-ˈwin adj [before noun] A win-win situation or result is one that is good for everyone who is involved: *Flexible working hours are a win-win situation for employers and employees.* • **ˌwin-ˈwin noun** [S] a result that is good for everyone who is involved in a situation: *The decision is a win-win for both sides.*

wipe /waɪp/ verb; noun

▸verb [T] (B2) to slide something, especially a piece of cloth, over the surface of something else, in order to remove dirt, food, or liquid: *Have you got a cloth that I can wipe the floor with?* ◦ *I'll just get a sponge and wipe the crumbs off the table.* ◦ *Don't wipe your nose **on** your sleeve!*

IDIOMS **wipe sth off the map** (also **wipe sth off the face of the earth/globe**) to destroy completely: *There are bombs so powerful that whole nations could be wiped off the map by them.* • **wipe the floor with sb** informal to defeat someone very easily: *'I hear Italy beat France in the semifinals last night.' 'Beat them? They wiped the floor with them!'* • **wipe the slate clean** to start a new and better way of behaving, forgetting about any bad experiences in the past: *A new relationship presents you with the opportunity to wipe the slate clean.* • **wipe the smile off sb's face** to make someone feel less happy or confident, especially someone who is annoying you because they think they are very clever: *Tell him you saw Helena at the cinema with another guy – that should wipe the smile off his face!*

PHRASAL VERBS **wipe sth down** to clean the surface of something, such as a table, with a cloth: *Every night we wipe the tables down before we shut the restaurant.* • **wipe sth off sth** to remove something from something: *All their customer information was wiped off the computer by a virus.* ◦ *$8 billion has been wiped off share prices worldwide.* • **wipe sth out** (C2) to destroy something completely: *Whole villages were wiped out in the fighting.* ◦ *One bad harvest could wipe out all of a grower's profits for the previous two years.* • **wipe out** US informal to lose control, especially in a vehicle, and have an accident: *I was going too fast and I wiped out on the bend.* • **wipe sth up** to remove a substance, usually liquid, with a cloth or something similar: *I was just wiping up the soup that you spilled in the kitchen.* ◦ *Have you got something I could wipe up this mess **with**?*

▸noun [C] **1** [C] an act of wiping: *I'd better **give** the floor a quick wipe before someone slips on it.* **2** a piece of soft, wet cloth or paper that you use for wiping: *baby wipes*

ˌwiped ˈout adj [after verb] **TIRED** ▷ **1** informal extremely tired: *After that five-mile run I was completely wiped out.* **DRUNK** ▷ **2** US slang suffering from the effects of drinking alcohol or taking drugs

wiper /ˈwaɪp.əʳ/ (US) /-ɚ/ noun [C] informal for **windscreen wiper**

wire /waɪəʳ/ (US) /waɪr/ noun; verb

▸noun **METAL THREAD** ▷ **1** (B2) [C or U] a piece of thin metal thread that can be bent, used for fastening things and for making particular types of objects that are strong but can bend: *a wire fence* **2** (B2) [C] (a piece of) thin metal thread with a layer of plastic around it, used for carrying electric current: *Someone had cut the phone wires.* ◦ *Don't touch those wires whatever you do.* **3 the wire** the wire fence round a prison or PRISON CAMP: *During the war he spent three years **behind** the wire (= in prison).* **MESSAGE** ▷ **4** [C] US informal a **telegram**

IDIOMS **down to the wire** until the last moment that it is possible to do something: *I think the election will **go** right down to the wire (= be won at the last moment).* • **get your wires crossed** When people get their wires crossed, they have a different understanding of the same situation: *Somehow we got our wires crossed because I'd got the 23rd written down in my diary and Jen had the 16th.* • **under the wire** US If someone does something under the wire, they do it at the last possible moment: *They got in under the wire just before the entry requirements for the training program changed.*

▸verb [T] **METAL THREAD** ▷ **1** to fasten two things together using wire: *She had her jaws wired **together** so that she wouldn't be able to eat.* **2** (also **wire up**) to connect a piece of electrical equipment with wires so that it will work: *The stereo wasn't working because it hadn't been wired up properly.* ◦ *Nearly one home in ten across the country is wired up to receive TV via cable.* **SEND MESSAGE** ▷ **3** to send money using an electrical communication system: *The insurance company wired millions of dollars **to** its accounts to cover the payments.* ◦ [+ two objects] *Luckily my father wired me two hundred bucks.* **4** mainly US in the past, to send someone a TELEGRAM: *Janet wired me to say she'd be here a day later than planned.*

ˌwire ˈbrush noun [C] a brush with pieces of wire fixed into it, used especially for cleaning metal

wired /waɪəd/ (US) /waɪrd/ adj [after verb] (also **ˌwired ˈup**) informal nervous or excited about a future event: *I was totally wired before the interview.*

ˌwired ˈup adj [after verb] UK (US **wired**) secretly provided with an electronic device that records conversations: *The negotiators were wired up when they talked to the kidnappers.*

wireframe /ˈwaɪə.freɪm/ (US) /ˈwaɪr-/ noun [C] a basic plan for a website that shows the type of information that it will contain and how it will be arranged, but does not include design features such as colour or particular details

ˌwire-ˈhaired adj A dog that is wire-haired has stiff, rough hair: *a wire-haired dachshund*

wireless /ˈwaɪə.ləs/ (US) /ˈwaɪr-/ adj; noun

▸adj using a system of radio signals rather than wires

to connect computers, mobile phones, etc. to each other: *a wireless connection*
▸noun [C] mainly UK old-fashioned a radio

ˌwire ˈnetting noun [U] a net made of twisted wire that is often used for fences

ˈwire ˌservice noun [C] mainly US an organization that supplies news to newspapers, radio, and television stations, etc. using an electrical communication system

wiretapping /ˈwaɪəˌtæp.ɪŋ/ ⓤⓢ /ˈwaɪr-/ noun [U] the action of secretly listening to other people's conversations by connecting a listening device to their phone: *If he suspected an employee of dishonesty, he was not above wiretapping.*

ˌwire ˈwool noun [U] UK for **steel wool**

wiring /ˈwaɪə.rɪŋ/ ⓤⓢ /ˈwaɪr.ɪŋ/ noun [U] the system of wires that carry electricity in a building: *The club closed after the fire brigade declared its wiring to be unsafe.*

wiry /ˈwaɪə.ri/ ⓤⓢ /ˈwaɪr.i/ adj **1** (of people and animals) thin but strong, and often able to bend easily: *He has a runner's wiry frame.* **2** describes hair that is strong, thick, and rough to touch

wisdom /ˈwɪz.dəm/ noun [U] B2 the ability to use your knowledge and experience to make good decisions and judgments: *One certainly hopes to gain a little wisdom as one grows older.* ◦ *He's got a weekly radio programme in which he* ***dispenses*** *wisdom (= gives his opinions) on a variety of subjects.* ◦ *I tend to* ***doubt*** *the wisdom of separating a child from its family whatever the circumstances.* ◦ *Did we ever stop to* ***question*** *the wisdom of going to war?* ◦ *Before I went off to university my father gave me a few* ***words of*** *wisdom.* ◦ ***Conventional/Received/Popular*** *wisdom has it (= most people think) that women are more emotional than men, but in my experience it often isn't the case.*

IDIOMS **in his/her/their wisdom** humorous something that you say when you do not understand why someone has done something stupid: *The council, in their wisdom, decided to close the library and now the building stands empty.* • **with the wisdom of hindsight** with the knowledge that experience gives you: *With the wisdom of hindsight we now know that the old-fashioned aerosol sprays were a mistake.*

ˈwisdom ˌtooth noun [C] (plural **wisdom teeth**) one of the four teeth at the back of the JAW that are the last to grow: *She's having her wisdom teeth out.*

wise /waɪz/ adj; verb
▸adj **1** B2 approving having or showing the ability to make good judgments, based on a deep understanding and experience of life: *I think you made a wise choice.* ◦ *'I never drink more than three glasses of wine.' 'How wise.'* ◦ *Looking at the weather, I think we made a wise decision not to go to the coast this weekend.* ◦ *I think it would be wiser* ***to*** *wait and see how much money you've got left before you make any decisions.* ◦ *I never used to save money but now I'm a little* ***older and*** *wiser I can see the sense in it.* ◦ *Was it Thomas More who said that the wise man learns from the experience of others?* **2 wise to sth** informal understanding a dishonest situation or way of doing something: *I used to be scrupulously honest then I got wise to the system.*

IDIOMS **be none the wiser** to still be confused about something even after it has been explained to you: *I've read the instructions twice and I'm still none the wiser.* • **to be wise after the event** mainly UK used to mean that it is easy to understand what you could have done to prevent something bad from happening after it has happened: *In retrospect, we should have insisted on checking his calculations, but it's easy to be wise after the event.*

▸verb

PHRASAL VERB **wise up** mainly US informal to start to understand a situation or fact and believe what you hear about it, even if it is difficult or unpleasant: *Those who think this is a harmless recreational drug should wise up.* ◦ *It's about time employers wised up* ***to*** *the fact that staff who are happy work more efficiently.*

-wise /-waɪz/ suffix **IN THIS WAY** ▷ **1** in this way or in this direction: *clockwise* ◦ *lengthwise* **RELATING TO** ▷ **2** informal relating to a particular thing: *What shall we do food-wise – do you fancy going out to eat?* ◦ *Money-wise, of course, I'm much better off than I used to be.* ◦ *What do we need to take with us clothes-wise?* ◦ *We were very lucky weather-wise yesterday.*

wisecrack /ˈwaɪz.kræk/ noun [C] informal a remark that is intended as a clever joke, especially one that criticizes someone: *He* ***made*** *some wisecrack about my lack of culinary ability.* • **wisecracking** /-ɪŋ/ noun [U], adj [before noun] *Sadly, despite the relentless wisecracking, there's very little plot to carry this film.*

ˈwise guy noun [C] (US offensive ˈ**wise ass**) someone who is always trying to seem more clever than anyone else in a way that is annoying: *Okay, wise guy, if you're so damned smart, you can tell everyone how it's done!* • ˈ**wise-guy** adj [before noun] (US offensive ˈ**wise-ass**) *wise-guy humour*

wisely /ˈwaɪz.li/ adv C1 showing good judgment: *Sian had very wisely left the party before all the trouble started.*

wish /wɪʃ/ verb; noun
▸verb **FEEL SORRY** ▷ **1** B1 [I + (that)] used with the PAST SIMPLE to express that you feel sorry or sad about a state or situation that exists at the moment: *I wish (****that****) I was/were a bit taller.* ◦ *I wish (****that****) you were coming with me, Peter.* **2** B1 [I + (that)] used with the PAST PERFECT to express that you feel sorry or sad about a particular action in the past: *I wish (****that****) I hadn't eaten so much.* ◦ *I bet she wishes (****that****) she'd never got involved in the whole affair.*

> **! Common mistake: wish or hope?**
>
> **Warning:** when **wish** is followed by a verb, the verb should not be in the present or future tense.
> When using a verb to talk about what you want to happen in the future, don't say 'wish', say **hope**:
> ~~*I wish I will pass all my exams.*~~

WANT ▷ **3** B2 [I or T] formal to want to do something: *We could go to the cinema or we could go out for dinner – whatever you wish.* ◦ *'Shall we ask Diana if she'd like to come to the theatre tonight?' 'If/As you wish.'* ◦ [+ to infinitive] *I wish* ***to*** *make a complaint.* ◦ *Passengers wishing* ***to*** *take the Kings Cross train should go to platform 9.* ◦ *I don't wish* ***to*** *worry you but he did say he'd be back by midnight.* ◦ [+ obj + adj] *Sometimes I was so depressed that I wished myself dead.* **4 I wish (that)…** used to express anger at someone's behaviour: *I wish she'd shut up for a moment and let someone else speak.* ◦ *I wish you'd look at me when I'm trying to speak to you!* **HOPE** ▷ **5** B1 [T + two objects] to hope or express hope for another person's success or happiness or pleasure on a particular occasion: *We wish you every success in the future.* ◦ *I didn't even see her to wish her a happy birthday/wish a happy birthday* ***to*** *her.* ◦ *I wished her a safe journey and waved her off.* **6 wish sb well** to hope someone will succeed: *I*

wished him well with his new venture. **MAGIC** ▷ **7** [I or T] to hope that something you want will be made real because of good luck or magical powers: [+ that] *I remember blowing out the candles on my birthday cake and wishing **that** John Lee would be my boyfriend.* ◦ *If I could wish myself anywhere in the world (= go anywhere as a result of making a wish) right now it would be somewhere hot and sunny.* ◦ *He's funny, bright, handsome – everything a girl could wish **for** really.* ◦ *'Your job must be very glamorous.' 'I wish!' (= not at all.)* ◦ *'By the time I'm 40, I'll be rich.' 'You wish!' (= There is no chance of that happening.)* **GREET** ▷ **8** [T] Indian English to welcome someone with particular words or a particular action: *He wishes me every morning.*

IDIOM **I/you wouldn't wish sth on anyone/my/your worst enemy** something you say in order to emphasize that something is extremely unpleasant: *The effects of this disease are horrible. You wouldn't wish them on your worst enemy.*

▸noun [C] **WANT** ▷ **1** (B2) a feeling of wanting something: [+ to infinitive] *Did he express any wish **to** see me?* ◦ *In accordance with his wishes (= what he wanted), he was buried next to his wife.* ◦ *They've deliberately gone against my wishes and sold the apartment.* ◦ [+ that] *It was grandpa's greatest wish **that** one of his grandchildren would become a doctor.* **GREETING** ▷ **2 best wishes** (A2) something you say or write at the end of a letter to show that you hope someone is happy and has good luck: *He ended the letter 'Best wishes, Carlo'.* ◦ *Do **give/send** Patrick my best wishes.* ◦ *Best wishes **for** a speedy recovery.* ◦ ***With** best wishes, Louise Foster.* **MAGIC** ▷ **3** (C2) a hope that is made real with magical powers: [+ that] *If I could have just one wish I suppose it would be **that** all the fighting in the world would stop tomorrow.* ◦ *Close your eyes and **make** a wish.* ◦ *It's that bit in the story where the fairy **grants** the little girl three wishes.* ◦ *May all your wishes come true.*

> Word partners for **wish noun**
>
> ***comply with/honour/ignore/respect*** sb's wishes • ***get*** your wish • a ***fervent/final/heartfelt*** wish • ***according to/against/contrary to*** sb's wishes

wishbone /ˈwɪʃ.bəʊn/ (US) /-boʊn/ **noun** [C] the V-shaped bone between the neck and breast of a cooked bird which traditionally is removed from the bird and pulled apart by two people, allowing the one who gets the longer piece to make a secret wish

ˈwish-fulˌfillment noun [U] the achievement of things you really want in imaginary situations, mainly in dreams, but also in films, literature, and poetry: *Men, in these dramas of female wish-fulfillment, are reduced to the status of playthings.*

wishful thinking /ˌwɪʃ.fəlˈθɪŋ.kɪŋ/ **noun** [U] the imagining or discussion of a very unlikely future event or situation as if it were possible and might one day happen: *'Do you think you might be in line for promotion, then?' 'No, it's just wishful thinking.'*

ˈwish ˌlist noun [C] a list of things you want, often which you know you cannot have: *A new car would be top of my wish list.*

wishy-washy /ˈwɪʃ.iˌwɒʃ.i/ (US) /-ˌwɑː.ʃi/ **adj** informal disapproving having no colour, firm ideas, principles, or noticeable qualities of any type: *Politically they're neither right-wing nor left – just a bunch of wishy-washy pseudo-liberals.* ◦ *Watercolours are a bit wishy-washy for my taste.*

wisp /wɪsp/ **noun** [C] **1 wisp of cloud/smoke/steam** a small, thin line of cloud/smoke/steam: *A blue wisp of cigarette smoke curled in the air.* **2 wisp of hair, grass, etc.** a thin, delicate piece of hair, grass, etc.: *A few wisps of hay still clung to her skirt.* ◦ *soft wisps of baby hair*

wispy /ˈwɪs.pi/ **adj** in the form of a wisp or wisps: *a wispy cloud/fringe*

wisteria /wɪˈstɪə.ri.ə/ (US) /-ˈstɪr.i-/ **noun** [C or U] a climbing plant with groups of small purple, blue, or white flowers hanging from it

wistful /ˈwɪst.fəl/ **adj** sad and thinking about something that is impossible or in the past: *a wistful smile* ◦ *I thought about those days in Spain and grew wistful.* • **wistfully** /-i/ **adv** *'I would love to go back to Venice,' he said wistfully.* • **wistfulness** /-nəs/ **noun** [U]

wit /wɪt/ **noun HUMOUR** ▷ **1** (C1) [S or U] the ability to use words in a clever and humorous way: *a woman of great intelligence and wit* ◦ *Her conversation sparkled with her own subtle blend of wit and charm.* ◦ *He was known for his **dry/ready/sharp** wit.* → See also **witticism 2** [C] a person who is skilled at using words in a clever and humorous way: *Sydney Smith, a notable wit, once remarked that he never read a book before he reviewed it because it might prejudice his opinion of it.* **INTELLIGENCE** ▷ **3 wits** [plural] intelligence and the ability to think quickly: *She learned to survive on her wits.*

IDIOMS **frighten/scare sb out of their wits** (also **frighten/scare the wits out of sb**) to make someone very frightened: *Don't shout like that! You scared me out of my wits.* • **gather your wits** literary to make an effort to become calm and think more clearly: *I spent the five-minute break between games gathering my wits and rethinking my strategy for the second half of the match.* • **have/keep (all) your wits about you** to be ready to think quickly in a situation and react to things that you are not expecting: *Cycling is potentially very dangerous in London – you have to keep your wits about you.* • **not be beyond the wit of man/sb** humorous to be possible to achieve: *It shouldn't be beyond the wit of man to arrange for them both to be there at the same time.* • **to wit** formal used to make clearer or more particular something that you have already said: *Several pieces of major legislation have been introduced in the US over the past few years, to wit: the Americans With Disabilities Act, the Clean Air Act and the Civil Rights Act.*

witch /wɪtʃ/ **noun** [C] **1** (C1) a woman who is believed to have magical powers and who uses them to harm or help other people: *a witch on a broomstick* ◦ *Witches were persecuted all over western Europe from the 15th to the 17th century as it was claimed that they had dealings with the Devil.* **2** informal disapproving an unpleasant and ugly woman

witchcraft /ˈwɪtʃ.krɑːft/ (US) /-kræft/ **noun** [U] the activity of performing magic to help or harm other people

ˈwitch ˌdoctor noun [C] a person in some societies who cures people using traditional magic or medicine → Compare **shaman**

ˈwitch ˌhazel noun [C or U] a small tree that produces flowers, or liquid from this tree, used as a medicine

ˈwitch ˌhunt noun [C] disapproving an attempt to find and punish people whose opinions are unpopular and who are said to be a danger to society: *In America, Senator McCarthy led a witch hunt **against** people suspected of being communists.*

the ˈwitching ˌhour noun [S] the time when WITCHES are said to appear, usually twelve o'clock at night

Wite-Out /ˈwaɪt.aʊt/ (US) /ˈwaɪt̬-/ US trademark (UK

trademark **Tipp-Ex**) a white liquid used for painting over mistakes in a piece of writing

with /wɪð/ preposition **COMPANY** ▷ **1** Ⓐ1 used to say that people or things are in a place together or are doing something together: *I was with Sylvia at the time.* ◦ *He lives with his grandmother.* ◦ *He's impossible to work with.* ◦ *I'm going to France with a couple of friends.* ◦ *Ingrid Bergman starred with Humphrey Bogart in the film 'Casablanca'.* ◦ *I left my coat with the cloakroom attendant.* ◦ *Ice cream with your apple pie?* ◦ *Mix the butter with the sugar and then add the egg.* ◦ *I'll be with you (= I will give you my attention) in a moment.* ◦ *She's staying with her parents (= at their house) for a few months.* ◦ *He's been with the department (= working in it) since 2010.* **METHOD** ▷ **2** Ⓐ2 using something: *He was shot at close range with a pistol.* ◦ *She wiped her lipstick off with a tissue.* ◦ *Fix the two pieces together with glue.* ◦ *Please handle this package with care.* ◦ *They set up a business with the help of a bank loan.* **DESCRIPTION** ▷ **3** Ⓐ1 having or including something: *a tall woman with dark hair* ◦ *He's married with three children.* ◦ *She left school with no qualifications.* ◦ *He spoke with a soft Irish accent.* ◦ *We're an international company with offices in Paris, New York, and Sydney.* ◦ *Two coffees please, one with milk and one without.* ◦ *He arrived in Los Angeles with nothing but the clothes he was wearing.* ◦ *He woke up with a dreadful headache.* ◦ *I was second in the race with a time of 14.2 seconds.* ◦ *With a bit of luck, we should be back in time for dinner.* ◦ *Both their children graduated with degrees in economics.* **4** used at the beginning of various phrases written at the end of a letter: *With best wishes from Charles.* ◦ *With love from Roberta.* **5** including: *With your contribution, that makes a total of £45.* **RELATIONSHIP** ▷ **6** Ⓑ2 relating to or in the case of a person or thing: *How are things with you?* ◦ *Russia has just drawn up a trade agreement with Norway.* ◦ *This hasn't got anything to do with you (= this is not something you should be interested in).* ◦ *The government's policies have not been popular with (= among) the voters.* ◦ *He's very careless with his money.* ◦ *She talked a lot about her relationship with Charlotte.* **CONTAINING/COVERING** ▷ **7** Ⓑ1 used to show what is on or in something: *She'd laid the table with the best china.* ◦ *Her blouse was spattered with blood.* ◦ *The room was littered with toys.* ◦ *The trucks were laden with food and medicine.* ◦ *She filled the jug up with cream.* **CAUSE** ▷ **8** Ⓑ2 because of or caused by someone or something: *He winced with pain.* ◦ *I was trembling with fear.* ◦ *She's been at home with a bad cold for the past week.* ◦ *I can't work with all that noise going on.* ◦ *Hopes were dashed in the war-torn capital with the news that no aid would be arriving that week.* ◦ *With exams approaching, it's a good idea to review your class notes.* ◦ *(**What**) with all the excitement and confusion, I forgot to say goodbye to her.* **OPPOSITION** ▷ **9** against something: *I ended up having an argument with her.* ◦ *She has fought a constant battle with depression throughout her career.* ◦ *The two countries went to war with one another over oil prices.* ◦ *A truck had evidently collided with a car.* **SEPARATION** ▷ **10** used with words showing separation: *I'd rather not part with my cash.* ◦ *He decided to put his failed marriage behind him and make a clean break with the past.* **AND** ▷ **11** and, or followed by: *I'd like a steak and fries with chocolate mousse to follow.* ◦ *$200 is payable immediately with a further $100 payable on delivery.* **COMPARISON** ▷ **12** used in comparisons: *I've got nothing in common with my brother.* ◦ *This cake's very light compared with the last one you made.* **SUPPORT** ▷ **13** supporting someone or something: *If you want to go for a promotion, I'll be with you all the way.* ◦ *You've got to decide where you stand on this issue – you're either with me or against me.* → Opposite **against** **DIRECTION** ▷ **14** in the same direction as something: *The wind was with me on the home stretch and I ran well.* → Opposite **against** **TIME** ▷ **15** at the same rate or time as something: *This wine will improve with age.* ◦ *Stopping distances for cars vary with the speed they are travelling at.* **UNDERSTANDING** ▷ **16 be with sb** informal to understand what someone is saying: *You look puzzled – are you with me?* ◦ *I'm sorry, I'm not with you.* **DESPITE** ▷ **17** despite something: *With all her faults, she's still a really good friend.* **EXPRESSIONS** ▷ **18** used to express a wish or instruction: *Away with you! (= Go away!)* ◦ *Off to bed with you! (= Go to bed!)* ◦ *On with the show! (= Let it continue.)* ◦ *Down with school! (= We don't want/like it.)*

IDIOM **with that** and then, or after doing or saying that: *'I still think you're wrong,' he said and with that he drove off.*

withdraw /wɪðˈdrɔː/ (US) /-ˈdrɑː/ verb (**withdrew**, **withdrawn**) **REMOVE** ▷ **1** Ⓒ1 [I or T] to take or move out or back, or to remove: *This credit card allows you to withdraw up to £200 a day **from** cash dispensers.* ◦ *The UN has withdrawn its troops **from** the country.* ◦ *Eleven million bottles of water had to be withdrawn **from sale** due to a health scare.* ◦ *Once in court, he withdrew the statement he'd made to the police (= he claimed it was false).* ◦ *All charges against them were withdrawn after the prosecution's case collapsed.* ◦ formal *After lunch, we withdrew **into** her office to finish our discussion in private.* ◦ mainly UK *The team captain was forced to withdraw **from** the match due to injury.* ◦ *Following his nervous breakdown, he withdrew **from** public life and refused to give any interviews.* **STOP CONTACT** ▷ **2** [I] to stop talking to other people and start thinking thoughts that are not related to what is happening around you: *As a child, she frequently withdrew **into** her own fantasy world.* ◦ *After the accident, he withdrew **into himself** and refused to talk to family or friends.*

withdrawal /wɪðˈdrɔː.əl/ (US) /-ˈdrɑː-/ noun **TAKING OUT** ▷ **1** Ⓒ2 [C or U] when you take money out of a bank account: *The bank became suspicious after several large withdrawals were made **from** his account in a single week.* **2** [C or U] the process or action of a military force moving out of an area: *The commander-in-chief was given 36 hours to secure a withdrawal of his troops **from** the combat zone.* **NOT AVAILABLE** ▷ **3** Ⓒ2 [U] the act or process of taking something away so that it is no longer available, or of someone stopping being involved in an activity: *Doctors demanded the withdrawal of the drug (**from** the market) after several cases of dangerous side-effects were reported.* ◦ *Her sudden withdrawal **from** the championship caused a lot of press speculation about her health.* **NO CONTACT** ▷ **4** [U] behaviour in which someone prefers to be alone and does not want to talk to other people: *Withdrawal is a classic symptom of depression.*

withˈdrawal ˌsymptoms noun [plural] the unpleasant physical and mental effects that result when you stop doing or taking something, especially a drug, which has become a habit: *He was suffering from all the classic withdrawal symptoms associated with giving up heroin.* ◦ figurative humorous *I haven't seen any TV for over a week and I'm having withdrawal symptoms.*

withdrawn /wɪðˈdrɔːn/ (US) /-ˈdrɑːn/ adj Ⓒ2 shy and quiet and preferring to be alone rather than with other people: *Following her son's death, she became quiet and withdrawn and rarely went out.*

wither /ˈwɪð.əʳ/ (US) /-ɚ/ verb (also **wither away**) **1** [I or T] (to cause) to become weak and dry and decay: *Grass had withered in the fields.* **2** [I] to slowly disappear, lose importance, or become weaker: *This country is in danger of allowing its industrial base to wither away.*

IDIOM **wither on the vine** literary If something withers on the vine, it is destroyed very gradually, usually because no one does anything to help or support it: *There was some debate as to whether the benefit scheme should be withdrawn or simply allowed to wither on the vine.*

withered /ˈwɪð.əd/ (US) /-ɚd/ adj **1** dry and decaying: *withered leaves/flowers* **2** old-fashioned describes an arm or leg that has not grown to its correct size because of disease

withering /ˈwɪð.ər.ɪŋ/ (US) /-ɚ-/ adj **1** A withering look, remark, etc. is one that is intended to make someone feel ashamed: *He said that Lizzie had been drunk at the time and I saw her shoot him a withering glance.* **2** severe and extremely CRITICAL: *He made a withering **attack** on government policy.*

withers /ˈwɪð.əz/ (US) /-ɚz/ noun [plural] specialized the highest part of the back of a horse, above its shoulders

withhold /wɪðˈhəʊld/ (US) /-ˈhoʊld/ verb [T] (**withheld**, **withheld**) to refuse to give something or to keep back something: *to withhold information/support* ◦ *During the trial, the prosecution was accused of withholding crucial **evidence from** the defence.* ◦ *Police are withholding the dead woman's **name** until her relatives have been informed.* ◦ *She withheld her rent until the landlord agreed to have the repairs done.*

withˈholding ˌtax noun [U] US money taken from a person's income and paid directly to the government by their employer

within /wɪˈðɪn/ preposition, adv (B1) inside or not further than an area or period of time: *Two thirds of Californians live within 15 miles of the coast.* ◦ *In 1992 cross-border controls within the EU were dismantled.* ◦ *For orders within the UK, please enclose £2.50 for post and packing.* ◦ *The resort lies within **easy reach** of (= not far from) the ski slopes.* ◦ *We recommend that this wine should be consumed within six months.* ◦ *Within hours of the tragedy happening, an emergency rescue team had been assembled.* ◦ *The tickets should reach you within the week (= before the end of this week).* ◦ *He's very highly regarded within his profession.* ◦ *She managed to complete her last film well within budget.* ◦ *The target was now within range and so she took aim and fired.* ◦ *He could sense that his goal was within **reach** (= it could be reached).* ◦ *The cathedral spire was now within sight (= it could be seen).* ◦ *I was acting within the law (= legally).* ◦ *We came within five points of beating them (= we would have beaten them if we had had five more points).*

IDIOM **from within** by the people who belong to an organization and not by people from outside it: *If things are to change, the company must be reformed from within.*

ˈwith ˌit adj FASHION ▷ **1** old-fashioned informal knowing a lot about new ideas and fashions: *He reads all the style magazines and thinks he's really with it.* **2** informal fashionable MIND ▷ **3 be with it** informal to be able to think or understand quickly: *You're not really with it today, are you?*

without /wɪˈðaʊt/ preposition, adv (A2) not having or doing something, or lacking something: *I've come out without my umbrella.* ◦ *You look nice without make-up.* ◦ *He went without my knowledge.* ◦ *I couldn't have done it without you.* ◦ *She's strong without being bossy.* ◦ *Do start without me.* ◦ formal *He's not without (= he does have some) qualities.* ◦ *This is without a doubt (= certainly) the best Chinese food I've ever had.* ◦ *You shouldn't drive for more than three hours without tak**ing** a break.* ◦ *Without wish**ing** to be rude (= I don't want to be rude, but), don't you think you need a hair cut?* → See also **do without (sth)**, **go without (sth)**

withstand /wɪðˈstænd/ verb [T] (**withstood**, **withstood**) (C2) to bear or not be changed by something, or to oppose a person or thing successfully: *a bridge designed to withstand earthquakes* ◦ *Our toys are designed to withstand the rough treatment of the average five-year-old.* ◦ *The aircraft base is protected with specially designed shelters which are built to withstand ground and air attacks.* ◦ *She is an artist whose work will undoubtedly withstand **the test of time** (= it will still be popular in the future).*

witless /ˈwɪt.ləs/ adj disapproving **1** stupid or showing no intelligence: *The novel centres around a witless father who is continually being conned by his three children.* → See also **wit 2 scare/frighten sb witless** to frighten someone very much

witlof (also **witloof**) /ˈwɪt.luːf/ noun [U] Australian English a vegetable with white leaves that taste bitter and are eaten uncooked in salads → Compare **chicory**

witness /ˈwɪt.nəs/ noun; verb

▸noun [C] SEE ▷ **1** (B2) a person who sees an event happening, especially a crime or an accident: *Police are appealing for witnesses **to** the accident to come forward.* ◦ *According to (**eye**) witnesses, the robbery was carried out by two teenage boys.* **2 be witness to sth** to see something happen: *She was witness to the tragic event.* **3** someone who is asked to be present at a particular event and sign their name in order to prove that things have been done correctly: *He signed the treaty in the presence of two witnesses.* ◦ *They were married a year after they first met, with two friends acting as witnesses.* LAW ▷ **4** a person in a law court who says what they know about a legal case or a particular person: *Ten witnesses are expected to testify at the trial today.* ◦ *The **key** witness **for** the prosecution was offered police protection after she received death threats.* **5 expert witness** a person who is allowed to give their opinion in a law court because of their knowledge or practical experience of a particular subject: *A psychiatrist was called as an expert witness for the defence.*

> **Word partners for witness noun**
>
> be *called as* a witness • *appear as* a witness • a witness *takes the stand/gives evidence/testifies* • a *credible/reliable/unreliable* witness • a *chief/important/key* witness • a witness *account/statement/testimony* • a witness *for the defence/for the prosecution*

IDIOM **bear witness (to sth)** If something bears witness to a fact, it proves that it is true: *The numerous awards on the walls bear witness to his great success.* ◦ *As last week's riots bear witness, the political situation is very unstable.*

▸verb [T] BE PRESENT ▷ **1** (B2) to see something happen, especially an accident or crime: *Did anyone witness the attack?* ◦ *They were staying in the capital at the time of the riots and witnessed several street battles.* ◦ [+ -ing verb] *He arrived home just in time to witness his brother be**ing** taken away by the police.* **2** to be present at an event and to sign your name as proof that it happened or that it was done correctly: *Her will was drawn up by a solicitor and witnessed by two colleagues.* HAPPEN ▷ **3** formal When a place or period witnesses a particular event, the event happens in that place or during that period: *This university has witnessed quite a few changes over the years.* ◦ *The past few years have witnessed momentous changes throughout Eastern Europe.* SHOW ▷ **4** to show or give proof of something: *This year's charity ball was the most successful one ever,* ***as*** *witnessed* ***by*** *the number of tickets sold.* ◦ *The programme aroused strong feelings – witness the number of letters received.*

PHRASAL VERB **witness to sth** UK formal to say publicly, especially in a law court, that something is true or that it happened: *A handwriting expert witnessed to the authenticity of the letter.* ◦ [+ -ing verb] *She witnessed to hav****ing*** *seen the robbery take place.*

ˈwitness ˌbox noun [C usually singular] UK (US **ˈwitness ˌstand**) the place in which a person stands in a law court when they are being asked questions: *He showed no emotion as he walked into the witness box.* ◦ *She was asked to* ***take*** *the witness stand and was then cross-examined.*

witter /ˈwɪt.əʳ/ (US) /ˈwɪt̬.ɚ/ verb [I] UK informal disapproving to talk for a long time about things that are not important: *He'd been wittering* ***on*** *about his neighbours for half the morning.*

witticism /ˈwɪt.ɪ.sɪ.zᵊm/ (US) /ˈwɪt̬-/ noun [C] a remark that is both clever and humorous → See also **wit**

witty /ˈwɪt.i/ (US) /ˈwɪt̬-/ adj (B2) using words in a clever and funny way: *a witty comment/remark* ◦ *He was witty and very charming.* • **wittily** /ˈwɪt.ɪ.li/ (US) /ˈwɪt̬-/ adv

wives /waɪvz/ plural of **wife**

wizard /ˈwɪz.əd/ (US) /-ɚd/ noun [C] **1** a man who is believed to have magical powers and who uses them to harm or help other people **2** (also **wiz**) someone who is an expert at something or who has great ability in a particular subject: *a computer wizard* ◦ *Your mother's a wizard* ***at*** *Scrabble.*

wizardry /ˈwɪz.ə.dri/ (US) /-ɚ-/ noun [U] **1** the skill of a wizard **2** clever or surprising ways of doing things, especially with special machines: *Using their high-tech wizardry, the police were able to locate the owners of the stolen property within hours of it being seized.*

wizened /ˈwɪz.ᵊnd/ adj having dry skin with lines in it, especially because of old age: *He was a wizened* ***old*** *man with yellow skin and deep wrinkles.*

wk written abbreviation for **week**

WMD /ˌdʌb.ᵊl.juːˌemˈdiː/ abbreviation for weapons of mass destruction: weapons, like nuclear bombs, which cause a lot of damage and kill many people

wobble /ˈwɒb.l̩/ (US) /ˈwɑː.bl̩/ verb; noun

▸verb MOVE ▷ **1** [I or T] to (cause something to) shake or move from side to side in a way that shows poor balance: *That bookcase wobbles whenever you put anything on it.* ◦ *Don't wobble the table, please, Dan.* ◦ figurative *The company's shares wobbled with the news of a foreign takeover bid.* NOT CERTAIN ▷ **2** [I] informal to be uncertain what to do or to change repeatedly between two opinions: *The government can't afford to wobble on this issue.*

▸noun [C] MOVEMENT ▷ **1** a movement from side to side which shows poor balance: *I gave the poles a slight wobble and the whole tent collapsed.* ◦ figurative *The closure of the company's German subsidiary caused a sharp wobble in its profits.* NOT CERTAIN ▷ **2** informal a feeling of not being certain about something: *She's having a bit of a wobble about the move to New York.*

wobbly /ˈwɒb.l̩.i/ (US) /ˈwɑː.bl̩-/ adj; noun

▸adj MOVING ▷ **1** likely to wobble: *a wobbly ladder/table* ◦ *I've been in bed with flu and my legs are still feeling all wobbly.* ◦ humorous *I'm trying to tone up my wobbly* ***bits*** *(= fat areas of the body) generally.* NOT CERTAIN ▷ **2** informal uncertain what to do or changing repeatedly between two opinions: *Last week I felt sure I was doing the right thing but I've started to feel a bit wobbly about it.*

▸noun UK informal **throw a wobbly** to become extremely angry and upset: *My parents threw a wobbly when they found out I'd had a party while they were away.*

wodge (also **wadge**) /wɒdʒ/ (US) /wɑːdʒ/ noun [C] mainly UK informal a thick piece or a large amount of something: *She cut herself a* ***great*** *wodge* ***of*** *chocolate cake.* ◦ *He hurried towards the staffroom with a wodge* ***of*** *papers under his arm.*

woe /wəʊ/ (US) /woʊ/ noun **1 woes** [plural] formal great problems or troubles: *The country has been beset by* ***economic*** *woes for the past decade.* ◦ *Unusually poor harvests have* ***added to*** *the country's woes.* **2** [U] literary extreme sadness: *Her face was lined and full of woe.* ◦ *He told me a real* ***tale of*** *woe about how he had lost both his job and his house in the same week.*

IDIOMS **woe betide sb** said when there will be trouble for someone, or they will be punished, if they do a particular thing: *This is the second time he's been sent home from school this week, so woe betide him if it happens again!* • **woe is me** old use or humorous said to express how unhappy you are: *I'm cold and wet and I haven't even got enough money for my bus fare home. Oh woe is me!*

woebegone /ˈwəʊ.bɪ.ɡɒn/ (US) /ˈwoʊ.bɪ.ɡɑːn/ adj literary looking very sad: *When he wants to go for a walk, the dog sits by the door with a woebegone* ***expression.*** ◦ *There's no need to* ***look*** *so woebegone – we can get it fixed.*

woeful /ˈwəʊ.fᵊl/ (US) /ˈwoʊ-/ adj BAD ▷ **1** very bad or (of something very bad or unpleasant) very great or extreme: *The team's woeful* ***record*** *consists of six defeats in seven matches.* ◦ *They displayed woeful* ***ignorance*** *of the safety rules.* SAD ▷ **2** formal extremely sad: *She was looking very woeful, with her eyes red and swollen.*

woefully /ˈwəʊ.fᵊl.i/ (US) /ˈwoʊ-/ adv used to emphasize how bad a situation is: *The safety precautions taken by large resort hotels are often woefully* ***inadequate*** *for the number of people who stay there.* ◦ *The school's text books are woefully out of date.*

wog /wɒɡ/ (US) /wɑːɡ/ noun [C] UK and Australian English offensive a Black person

wok /wɒk/ (US) /wɑːk/ noun [C] a large, bowl-shaped Chinese pan used for frying food quickly in hot oil: *Heat some oil in a wok, then add the vegetables and stir-fry for two minutes.*

wok

woke /wəʊk/ (US) /woʊk/ verb past simple of **wake**

woken /ˈwəʊ.kᵊn/ (US) /ˈwoʊ-/ verb past participle of **wake**

wolf

wolf /wʊlf/ noun; verb

▸noun (plural **wolves**) ANIMAL ▷ (B2) [C] a wild animal of the dog family: *Wolves hunt in groups* *known as packs.* ◦ *We could hear wolves* ***howling*** *in the distance.*

IDIOMS **keep the wolf from the door** to have just enough money to be able to eat and live: *As a student, he took an evening job to keep the wolf from the door.* • **a wolf in sheep's clothing** a person who hides the fact that they are evil, with a pleasant and friendly appearance

▸verb [T] informal to eat a large amount of food very quickly: *The boys wolfed the sandwiches* ***(down)*** *and then started on the cakes.*

wolfhound /ˈwʊlf.haʊnd/ **noun** [C] a type of very large dog: *He specializes in breeding large dogs such as* ***Irish*** *wolfhounds.*

wolfish /ˈwʊl.fɪʃ/ **adj** like a wolf: *wolfish green eyes* ◦ figurative *He gave her a wolfish* ***grin*** *(= smiled at her in a sexually interested way).*

ˈwolf ˌwhistle noun [C] a short, high sound, followed by a longer sound that drops from high to low, that is made when you see a person who you find sexually attractive • **ˈwolf-ˌwhistle verb** [I] *Builders are renowned for wolf-whistling* ***at*** *any woman who walks by.*

wolverine /ˈwʊl.vəʳ.iːn/ Ⓤⓢ /ˌwʊl.vəˈriːn/ **noun** [C] a wild animal with short legs, long fur, and a long tail, found mainly in cold northern areas of Europe and North America

woman /ˈwʊm.ən/ **noun** (plural **women** /ˈwɪmɪn/) **1** Ⓐ1 [C] an adult female human being: *She's a really nice woman.* ◦ *A woman and two men were arrested on the day after the explosion.* ◦ *Women first got the vote in Britain in 1918.* ◦ *She is Ireland's first woman (= female) president.* **2** [C] informal a wife or female sexual partner: *Apparently, Geoff's got a new woman.* **3** [U] women in general: *He is writing a book on the representation of woman in medieval art.* → See also **womankind, womenfolk**

-woman /-wʊm.ən/ **suffix** used to form nouns describing certain types of women or women with certain jobs: *an Englishwoman/Frenchwoman* ◦ *a chairwoman*

womanhood /ˈwʊm.ən.hʊd/ **noun** [U] **1** the state of being a woman, or the period of time when someone is a woman: *The novel deals with a teenage girl's journey towards womanhood.* **2** the qualities that are considered typical of a woman: *Brigitte Bardot was the dominant image of womanhood in French cinema during the 1960s.* **3** formal all women considered as a group: *the womanhood of the nation*

womanize disapproving (UK usually **womanise**) /ˈwʊm.ə.naɪz/ **verb** [I] A man who womanizes often has temporary sexual relationships with women or tries to get women to have sex with him: *He drank, womanized, and wasted money.* • **womanizer** (UK usually **womaniser**) /-naɪ.zəʳ/ Ⓤⓢ /-naɪ.zɚ/ **noun** [C] a man who womanizes: *He was a gambler, a womanizer, and a drunk.* • **womanizing** (UK usually **womanising**) /-naɪ.zɪŋ/ **noun** [U] *Both his first and second wife divorced him on account of his womanizing.*

womankind /ˌwʊm.əŋˈkaɪnd/ **noun** [U] old-fashioned female humans in general: *In her latest book she discusses the menopause, which is a subject that concerns all womankind.* → Compare **mankind, humankind**

womanly /ˈwʊm.ən.li/ **adj** describes qualities, ideas, or physical features which a woman is typically or traditionally thought to have: *She referred in a positive way to the 'traditional womanly goals of marriage and motherhood' several times in her talk.* ◦ *She used her womanly* ***wiles/charms*** *to persuade him to change his mind.* → Compare **manly** • **womanliness** /-nəs/ **noun** [U]

womb /wuːm/ **noun** [C] (specialized **uterus**) the organ in the body of a woman or other female mammal in which a baby develops before birth: *Researchers are looking at how a mother's health can affect the baby in the womb.*

wombat /ˈwɒm.bæt/ Ⓤⓢ /ˈwɑːm-/ **noun** [C] an Australian mammal with strong, short legs that it uses for digging

womenfolk /ˈwɪm.ɪn.fəʊk/ Ⓤⓢ /-foʊk/ **noun** [plural] old-fashioned the women in a family or society: *The communal land is cultivated by the womenfolk in the tribe.* → Compare **menfolk**

women's libber /ˌwɪm.ɪnzˈlɪb.əʳ/ Ⓤⓢ /-ɚ/ **noun** [C] old-fashioned someone who supports efforts to achieve EQUALITY of women and men: *I'm not a women's libber, but I do believe women should be paid the same as men.*

ˌwomen's libeˈration noun [U] (informal **ˌwomen's ˈlib**) the aim of achieving EQUALITY for women in all areas of society: *the women's liberation movement*

ˈwomen's ˌmovement noun [S] those people whose social and political aims are to change women's position in society and increase knowledge about women's condition in society

ˌwomen's ˈrefuge noun [C] UK (US **ˈwomen's ˌshelter**) a house where women whose partners have been violent towards them can go with their children for protection

ˈwomen's ˌstudies noun [plural] a course of studies about women in history, society, and literature: *She's doing a postgraduate course in women's studies.*

womenswear /ˈwɪmɪnz.weəʳ/ Ⓤⓢ /-wer/ **noun** [U] **1** clothes for women **2** the part of a large shop where you find women's clothing

won /wʌn/ **verb** past simple and past participle of **win**

wonder /ˈwʌn.dəʳ/ Ⓤⓢ /-dɚ/ **verb; noun**

▸verb **QUESTION** ▷ **1** Ⓑ1 [I] to ask yourself questions or express a wish to know about something: [+ question word] *Hadn't you better phone home? Your parents will be wondering* ***wh****ere you are.* ◦ *He's starting to wonder* ***wh****ether he did the right thing in accepting this job.* ◦ [+ speech] *Will this turkey be big enough for eight, I wonder?* ◦ *'Have you decided where you're going next summer?' 'I've been wondering* ***about*** *(= considering) going to Florida.'* **2** Ⓑ1 used in phrases, at the beginning of a request, to make it more formal and polite: [+ speech] *I wonder – could you help me carry these books?* ◦ [+ question word] *I* ***wonder whether*** *you could pass me the butter?* ◦ *I* ***wonder if*** *you could give me some information about places to visit in the area?* **SURPRISE** ▷ **3** [I] formal to feel or express great surprise at something: [+ (that)] *He was behaving so badly at school today, I wonder* ***(that)*** *he wasn't sent home.* ◦ *I don't wonder* ***(that)*** *she burst into tears after the way you spoke to her.*

IDIOM **I shouldn't wonder** mainly UK probably: *'Where's Mark been recently?' 'Up to no good, I shouldn't wonder.'*

▸noun **1** [U] a feeling of great surprise and admiration caused by seeing or experiencing something that is strange and new: *The sight of the Grand Canyon stretching out before them* ***filled*** *them* ***with*** *wonder.* ◦ *The boys gazed* ***in wonder*** *at the shiny red Ferrari.* **2** [C usually plural] an object that causes a feeling of great surprise and admiration: *We spent a week visiting the wonders* ***of*** *Ancient Greek civilization.* ◦ *With all the wonders* ***of modern technology****, why has no one come up with a way to make aircraft quieter?*

3 [C] informal an extremely useful or skilful person: *Our new babysitter's an* ***absolute*** *wonder – she'll come at very short notice and the children love her.*

IDIOMS **do/work wonders** informal to have a very good effect: *Doctors have discovered that keeping a pet can do wonders* ***for*** *your health.* • **it's a wonder** it is surprising: *It's a wonder (****that****) he ever reached Paris, because he set off with only £5 in his pocket.* • **little/small wonder** it is not really surprising: *Her car's been broken for the past two months, so* ***it's*** *little wonder (****that****) she hasn't come to visit you recently.* • **no wonder** B2 it is not surprising: *No wonder the children are excited, – this is the first time they've been abroad.* ◦ *'If brutal killers like these two are at work,* ***it is*** *no wonder* ***that*** *so many Kosovans have fled,' he said.* • **wonders never cease** humorous an expression of surprise used when something unusual or unexpected happens: *Lynda actually managed to get up before ten o'clock. Wonders never cease!*

ˈwonder ˌdrug noun [C] informal a very effective new medicine: *It has proved to be a wonder drug for sufferers of epilepsy, reducing seizures by up to 80 percent.*

wonderful /ˈwʌn.də.fəl/ US /-dɚ-/ adj A2 extremely good: *He's a wonderful cook.* ◦ *'Did you know that Daryl's getting married?' 'No, I didn't. How wonderful!'* ◦ *We had a wonderful* ***time*** *in Italy last summer.*

> **! Common mistake: wonderful**
>
> **Warning:** Common word-building error!
> Adjectives which end in the suffix **-ful** have only one 'l'. Don't write 'wonderfull', write **wonderful**.

wonderfully /ˈwʌn.də.fəl.i/ US /-dɚ-/ adv extremely, or extremely well: *This sauce goes wonderfully well with asparagus or new potatoes.* ◦ *As a child I hated my brother, but now we get on wonderfully.*

wonderland /ˈwʌn.dəl.ænd/ US /-dɚ.lænd/ noun [C] a place that is especially attractive or beautiful: *The family emigrated to New Zealand in 1949, which seemed a wonderland in comparison with post-war England.*

wonderment /ˈwʌn.də.mənt/ US /-dɚ-/ noun [U] literary great and pleasant surprise: *He listened* ***with*** *quiet wonderment as his grandfather told him of his life in the circus.*

wondrous /ˈwʌn.drəs/ adj literary extremely and surprisingly good: *a wondrous sight/sound/thing* ◦ *Our new improved face cream has wondrous effects on tired-looking skin.*

wondrously /ˈwʌn.drəs.li/ adv literary extremely, used to emphasize an approving description

wonga /ˈwɒŋ.ɡə/ US /ˈwɑːŋ-/ noun [U] UK slang money

wonk /wɒŋk/ US /wɑːŋk/ noun [C] US informal a person who works or studies too much, especially someone who learns and knows all the details about something: *As the NEC's deputy for domestic policy issues, Sperling has functioned as both* ***policy*** *wonk and political guru.*

wonky /ˈwɒŋ.ki/ US /ˈwɑːŋ-/ adj **1** UK informal weak, unsatisfactory, or not firm: *One of the legs on this chair is a bit wonky.* ◦ *He may have to stop playing cricket because of his wonky knee.* ◦ *The jury system may be a bit wonky but nobody's ever thought of anything better.* **2** informal not straight or level: *wonky teeth* ◦ *a wonky picture* ◦ *I don't enjoy those programmes with wonky camera angles and pop music.*

won't /wəʊnt/ US /woʊnt/ short form of will not: *I won't go without you.* ◦ *Won't it be nice to see Paul again?*

wont /wəʊnt/ US /woʊnt/ noun; adj
▸noun formal **as is someone's wont** in the way that someone usually does: *She arrived an hour late, as is her wont.*
▸adj formal **be wont to do sth** to often do something: *The previous city council was wont to overspend.*

wonted /ˈwəʊn.tɪd/ US /ˈwoʊn.t̬ɪd/ adj [before noun] formal usual: *He replied sharply, and without his wonted courtesy.*

woo /wuː/ verb [T] (present tense **wooing**, past tense and past participle **wooed**) **1** to try to persuade someone to support you or to use your business: *The party has been trying to woo the voters* ***with*** *promises of electoral reform.* ◦ *The airline has been offering discounted tickets to woo passengers* ***away from*** *their competitors.* **2** old-fashioned If a man woos a woman, he gives her a lot of attention in an attempt to persuade her to marry him: *He wooed her for months* ***with*** *flowers and expensive presents.*

wood /wʊd/ noun; adj
▸noun **MATERIAL** ▷ **1** A2 [C or U] a hard substance that forms the branches and TRUNKS of trees and can be used as a building material, for making things, or as a fuel: *He gathered some wood to build a fire.* ◦ *She fixed a couple of* ***planks*** *of wood to the wall for shelves.* ◦ *Mahogany is a* ***hard*** *wood and pine is a* ***soft*** *wood.* ◦ *The room was heated by a wood-****burning*** *stove.* **2** [C] a type of GOLF CLUB (= long, thin stick) with a rounded wooden end, used for hitting the ball over long distances: *He likes to use a number 2 wood to tee off.*
GROUP OF TREES ▷ **3** A2 [C] (also **woods** [plural]) an area of land covered with a thick growth of trees: *an oak wood* ◦ *We went for a walk* ***in the*** *woods after lunch.* → See also **woodland**

IDIOMS **be out of the woods** informal to no longer be in danger or difficulty: *The club has been given funding for another year, but it's not out of the woods yet.* • **not see the wood for the trees** UK (US **not see the forest for the trees**) to be unable to get a general understanding of a situation because you are too worried about the details

▸adj made of wood: *Solid wood furniture is much more sturdy and durable than chipboard furniture.* ◦ *We sanded and polished the wood* ***floor*** *in the living room.* ◦ *Much of the original 18th-century wood* ***panelling*** *was destroyed in the fire.* → See also **wooden**

woodbine /ˈwʊd.baɪn/ noun [U] **1** a climbing plant with pleasant-smelling, yellow flowers **2** US for **Virginia creeper**

woodblock /ˈwʊd.blɒk/ US /-blɑːk/ noun [C] **1** a piece of wood on which a pattern is cut that is used for printing: *She designs her own fabrics using woodblocks and stencils to create patterns on the material.* **2** UK one of a set of small, flat pieces of wood that are used to make a wooden floor: *a woodblock floor* → See also **parquet**

ˌwood-burning ˈstove noun [C] UK (US **ˈwood ˌstove**) a metal container with a CHIMNEY (= pipe for smoke to escape) and usually a glass door, in which you can burn wood to provide heat

woodcarving /ˈwʊdˌkɑː.vɪŋ/ US /-ˌkɑːr-/ noun **1** [U] the process of cutting into the surface of wood to create a decorative shape or pattern: *Some of the finest examples of woodcarving in Europe can be found in medieval churches.* **2** [C] a piece of wood that has been decorated in this way: *Her woodcarvings will be on display at the gallery next month.*

woodchuck /ˈwʊd.tʃʌk/ noun [C] a small animal

W

with short legs and rough, reddish-brown fur that lives in North America

woodcut /ˈwʊd.kʌt/ noun [C] a picture printed from a pattern that has been cut in the surface of a block of wood

wooded /ˈwʊd.ɪd/ adj covered with trees: *wooded hills* ◦ *The police found a vital clue to the girl's disappearance in a wooded* ***area*** *near her home.*

wooden /ˈwʊd.ən/ adj WOOD ▷ **1** A2 made of wood: *The house was surrounded by a tall, wooden* ***fence.*** ◦ *Stir the mixture with a wooden* ***spoon.*** AWKWARD ▷ **2** disapproving describes behaviour that is awkward or shows little expression: *She gave a wooden* ***smile*** *to the camera.* ◦ *I thought the lead actor gave rather a wooden* ***performance.***

woodenly /ˈwʊd.ən.li/ adv disapproving in an awkward way or showing no expression: *She nodded woodenly, her body still numb from the shock.*

the ˌwooden ˈspoon noun [S] UK informal the imaginary prize that a person or team is given if they finish last in a race or competition: *Our college team* ***took*** *the wooden spoon in the inter-collegiate league this season.*

woodland /ˈwʊd.lənd/ noun [C or U] C2 land on which many trees grow, or an area of this: *The Forestry Commission is responsible for preserving over two million acres of woodland.*

woodlouse /ˈwʊd.laʊs/ noun [C] (plural **woodlice**) a small, dark grey creature with a hard outer shell, found under stones or in slightly wet soil

woodpecker /ˈwʊdˌpek.əʳ/ US /-ɚ/ noun [C] a bird which uses its strong beak to make holes in tree TRUNKS in order to find insects to eat

woodpecker

ˈwood ˌpulp noun [U] wood that has been changed into a soft mass that can then be used for making paper

woodshed /ˈwʊd.ʃed/ noun [C] a small building where wood for burning is stored

ˈwood ˌstove noun [C] US (UK **ˌwood-burning ˈstove**) a metal container with a CHIMNEY (= pipe for smoke to escape) and usually a glass door, in which you can burn wood to provide heat

woodwind /ˈwʊd.wɪnd/ adj; noun

▸adj [before noun] belonging or relating to a group of pipe-shaped musical instruments that are played by blowing through one end or across a hole near one end: *The clarinet, flute, saxophone, and bassoon are all woodwind* ***instruments.***

▸noun **the woodwind** [S, + pl verb] the group of woodwind instruments and their players in an ORCHESTRA: *The woodwind were haunting in the slow movement.*

woodwork /ˈwʊd.wɜːk/ US /-wɝːk/ noun [U] STRUCTURE ▷ **1** the wooden parts of a building, especially a house: *There's some rotting woodwork on the outside of the house that we need to replace.* **2** UK informal any part of the wooden or metal frame that forms part of a goal in football: *Liverpool* ***hit the*** *woodwork twice in the first half.* ACTIVITY ▷ **3** mainly UK (US usually **woodworking**) the activity of making objects such as furniture from wood: *woodwork classes/lessons* ◦ *I used to enjoy woodwork at school.*

IDIOM **come/crawl out of the woodwork** mainly disapproving to appear after having been hidden or not active for a long time: *After you've been in a relationship for a while all sorts of little secrets start to come out of the woodwork.*

woodworm /ˈwʊd.wɜːm/ US /-wɝːm/ noun (plural **woodworm**) **1** [C] the young form of particular types of BEETLE which make small holes in wood as they feed on it **2** [U] the damage done to wooden objects when woodworm feed on them: *The roof timbers were riddled with woodworm.*

woody /ˈwʊd.i/ adj MATERIAL ▷ **1** like wood, for example in taste or smell **2** describes plants with hard stems: *The garden was overgrown with woody plants such as hawthorn and bramble.* GROUP OF TREES ▷ **3** having many trees: *They lived in a remote cottage set high on a woody hillside.*

woof /wʊf/ noun [C] used in writing to represent the noise that a dog makes, used especially in children's books • **woof** verb [I]

woofer /ˈwʊf.əʳ/ US /-ɚ/ noun [C] a LOUDSPEAKER designed to produce the low notes in a SOUND SYSTEM → Compare **tweeter**

wool /wʊl/ noun [U] **1** A2 the soft, thick hair which grows on the bodies of sheep and some other animals: *The blankets are made from wool and the sheets from cotton.* **2** thick thread or material that is made from this: *Put on your red wool cardigan – it'll be nice and warm.* ◦ *How many* ***balls of*** *wool did you need to knit that sweater?*

IDIOM **pull the wool over sb's eyes** to deceive someone in order to prevent them from discovering something

woollen (US usually **woolen**) /ˈwʊl.ən/ adj made of wool: *a woollen scarf*

woollens (US usually **woolens**) /ˈwʊl.ənz/ noun [plural] clothes made from wool or sometimes from wool mixed with artificial materials

woolly /ˈwʊl.i/ adj; noun

▸adj (US also **wooly**) OF WOOL ▷ **1** made of wool, or made of something that looks like wool: *a woolly hat/jumper* NOT CLEAR ▷ **2** disapproving Woolly ideas and thinking are confused and not clear, and have not been considered carefully enough: *It's the woolly thinking behind the book that I find so infuriating.* ◦ *I can't stand these woolly-****headed/-minded*** *liberals!* • **woolliness** (US also **wooliness**) /-nəs/ noun [U]

▸noun [C] old-fashioned informal (US also **wooly**) a piece of clothing made from wool, especially a JUMPER

woozy /ˈwuː.zi/ adj informal feeling weak or ill and unable to think clearly: *I was still woozy from the flu/anaesthetic/medication/wine.*

wop /wɒp/ US /wɑːp/ noun [C] offensive a man from southern Europe, especially Italy

word /wɜːd/ US /wɝːd/ noun; verb

▸noun LANGUAGE UNIT ▷ **1** A1 [C] a single unit of language that has meaning and can be spoken or written: *Your essay should be no more than two thousand words long.* ◦ *Some words are more difficult to spell than others.* ◦ *What's the word* ***for*** *bikini in French?* ◦ *It's sometimes difficult to* ***find*** *exactly* ***the right*** *word to express what you want to say.* **2 the F-word, C-word, etc.** used to refer to a word, usually a rude or embarrassing one, by saying only the first letter and not the whole word: *You're still not allowed to say the F-word on TV in the US.* ◦ *So how's the diet going – or would you rather I didn't mention the* d-word? **TALKING** ▷ **3** B2 [S] a short discussion or statement: *The manager wants **a** word.* ◦ *Could I **have a** word (**with** you) about the sales figures?* ◦ *Perhaps you would **have a quiet** word with Simon (= gently explain to him) about the problem.* **4 words** [plural] **a** angry words: *Both competitors **had** words (= argued) after the match.* ◦ *Words **passed between** both competitors (= they argued) after the match.* **b** disapproving discussion, rather than action: *I'm afraid so far there have been more words than action on the matter of childcare provision.* **5 have/exchange words** to talk to each other for a short time: *We exchanged a few words as we were coming out of the meeting.* **6 a good word** a statement of approval and support for someone or something: *If you see the captain could you **put in** a good word **for** me?* ◦ *The critics didn't **have** a good word (**to say**) **for/to say about** the performance.* **NEWS** ▷ **7** [U] news or a message: *Have you **had** word from Paul since he went to New York?* ◦ *We **got** word of their plan from a former colleague.* ◦ *Word **of** the discovery caused a stir among astronomers.* **PROMISE** ▷ **8** [S] a promise: *I said I'd visit him and I shall **keep** my word.* ◦ *You **have** my word – I won't tell a soul.* **ORDER** ▷ **9** [S] an order: *We're waiting for the word from head office before making a statement.* ◦ *The troops will go into action as soon as their commander **gives** the word.* ◦ ***At** a word from their teacher, the children started to tidy away their books.*

IDIOMS **breathe/say a word** to tell other people about something: *Don't say a word **about** the accident to my mother.* ◦ *If you breathe a word **of** this to anyone, I'll be really upset.* • **by word of mouth** in speech but not in writing: *All the orders were given by word of mouth so that no written evidence could be discovered later.* • **from the word go** from the start of something: *The bridge-building project had problems with funding **right** from the word go.* • **give your word** formal C1 to promise: *He **gave** his word that he would marry her and she had no cause to doubt him.* • **have a word in sb's ear** to give someone a piece of advice or information secretly • **in a word** said when you are going to give your opinion about something quickly and directly: *In a word, she's lying.* • **in sb's words** C2 used when you repeat what someone said: *His wife, Mary, was 25 years his junior and, in his words, 'my guiding light'.* • **in your own words** If a person says something in their own words, they speak without copying what someone else has said. • **in words of one syllable** in simple language avoiding long, difficult, or specialized words: *Could you **explain** to me in words of one syllable how an electron microscope works?* • **man/woman of his/her word** someone who keeps their promises: *You can trust him – he's a man of his word.* • **(upon) my word!** old-fashioned used to express surprise: *My word! Isn't that Jenkins on the roof?* • **not get a word in edgeways** UK (US **not get a word in edgewise**) to not be able to say anything because someone else is talking all the time: *Roz was talking so much that nobody else could get a word in edgeways!* • **put in a good word for sb** to say positive things about someone: *I really need a job and I was hoping you might put in a good word for me with your boss.* • **put the word about/around/out/round** to tell people a new piece of news: *So, the new manager has been appointed – should we put the word around?* • **put words in/into sb's mouth** to suggest that someone meant one thing when really they meant another: *Stop putting words in my mouth – I didn't say you looked fat in the red dress – I merely said you looked very slim in the black!* • **take sb at their word** (also **take sb's word for it**) B2 to believe that what someone says is true: *He said he'd give me a job and I just took him at his word.* ◦ *If he says there's $500 in the envelope, then I'll take his word for it.* • **take the words out of sb's mouth** to say something that another person was just about to say or was thinking: *'What a rude and obnoxious man!' 'You took the words **right** out of my mouth!'* • **word for word 1** C2 using exactly the same words: *She listened to everything I said and repeated it word for word to her mum.* → See also **word-for-word** **2** If you TRANSLATE speech or writing word for word, you change one word at a time in the same order rather than in phrases or other larger units of meaning. • **word gets about/around/round** When word gets about/around/round, news spreads fast within a group of people: *'I hear you were having drinks with a tall, dark, handsome man last night.' 'Wow, word gets round fast, doesn't it?'* ◦ *She doesn't want word getting around the office that she's pregnant.* • **word has it** used to refer to something that is generally thought to be true although not official or known to be a fact: *Word has it (**that**) they may separate.* • **(the) word is** used to refer to something that has been reported but not officially stated: *The word is (**that**) more hostages will be released over the next few weeks.* • **your word is your bond** old-fashioned or formal If someone's word is their bond, they always keep their promises: *'But listen, you must promise never to tell anyone.' 'My word is my bond.'* • **(the) word is/gets out** a piece of news is known, especially if it was secret or if it will cause changes: *The word is out **that** superstar Candice is to marry towards the end of this year.* • **words fail me** said to emphasize your surprise or shock, especially at something you have just seen or been told: *'So what did you think of Olive's pink outfit?' 'Words fail me, I've never seen anything quite like it!'*

▸**verb** [T usually + adv/prep] to choose the words you use when you are saying or writing something: *He worded the reply in such a way that he did not admit making the original error.* → See also **reword** • **worded** /ˈwɜː.dɪd/ US /ˈwɝː-/ **adj** *a **carefully/strongly** worded **statement***

ˈword assoc i ˌation noun [U] a method sometimes used in PSYCHOANALYSIS in which the person being treated says the first word they think of when a particular word is said, which may help to discover how parts of the mind work

ˌword-for-ˈword adj using exactly the same words that someone spoke or wrote: *I can give you a word-for-word transcript of what we talked about.* ◦ *a word-for-word copy of a government report*

wording /ˈwɜː.dɪŋ/ US /ˈwɝː-/ **noun** [U] the choice and meaning of the words used when you say or write something: *Norman agreed that the wording **of** the advertisement was unnecessarily offensive and it was changed.* ◦ *We don't yet know the **exact/precise** wording **of** the agreement.*

wordless /ˈwɜːd.ləs/ US /ˈwɝːd-/ **adj** without any words: *We sat in wordless contemplation of the view.* • **wordlessly** /-li/ **adv** *to stare/nod/point wordlessly*

wordlist /ˈwɜːd.lɪst/ US /ˈwɝːd-/ **noun** [C] a list of words, for example words that someone has to learn, or words explained in a dictionary

ˌword-of-ˈmouth adj given or done by people talking about something or telling people about something: *We get most of our work through word-of-mouth recommendations.* ◦ *word-of-mouth publicity*

ˌword-ˈperfect adj UK (US **ˌletter-ˈperfect**) describes words produced without any mistakes, or a person who is able to repeat a particular text from memory without making any mistakes: *His mother rehearsed his lines with him and by the time the play opened he was word-perfect.* ◦ *'Your German was word-perfect,' Franz said.* ◦ *a word-perfect rendition/recitation*

wordplay /ˈwɜːd.pleɪ/ ⓤⓢ /ˈwɝːd-/ **noun** [U] the activity of joking about the meanings of words, especially in a clever way

ˈword ˌprocessing noun [U] the organization of text in electronic form such as on a computer: *a word processing program/package*

ˈword ˌprocessor noun [C] a computer used for preparing documents and letters, or the program that is used for this

wordy /ˈwɜː.di/ ⓤⓢ /ˈwɝː-/ adj disapproving containing too many words: *As usual she gave a reply which was wordy and didn't answer the question.* • **wordiness** /-nəs/ noun [U]

wore /wɔːr/ ⓤⓢ /wɔːr/ verb past simple of **wear**

work /wɜːk/ ⓤⓢ /wɝːk/ noun; verb

▸noun **ACTIVITY** ▷ **1** Ⓐ① [U] an activity, such as a job, that a person uses physical or mental effort to do, usually for money: *I've got so much work to* ***do***. ◦ *Carrying heavy loads around all day is* ***hard*** *work.* ◦ *What time do you* ***start/finish*** *work?* ◦ *Adrian* ***does*** *most of the work around the house.* ◦ *What sort of work are you experienced in?* ◦ *She tends to wear quite smart clothes for work.* ◦ *Roger's work involves a lot of travelling.* **2** Ⓐ② [U] the material used by someone at work, or what they produce: *I'll have to take this work home with me and finish it there.* ◦ *All the furniture is the work of residents here.*

> **!** Common mistake: **work**
>
> **Warning:** Choose the right verb!
>
> Don't say 'make work', say **do work**:
>
> ~~*Francesca always makes her work efficiently and with a smile.*~~
>
> *Francesca always does her work efficiently and with a smile.*

> **!** Common mistake: **work or job?**
>
> **Warning:** Choose the right word!
>
> **Work** is an uncountable noun and refers to the activity that someone does in their job:
>
> *We need to improve the efficiency of our work.*
>
> To talk about a particular piece of work or the regular work that someone does to earn money, don't say 'work', say **job**:
>
> *Sarah is looking for a new job.*

PLACE ▷ **3** Ⓐ① [U] a place where a person goes specially to do their job: *Do you have far to travel* ***to*** *work each day?* ◦ *Thousands of people are seriously injured* ***at*** *work every year.* ◦ *When does she leave* ***for*** *work?* **CREATION** ▷ **4** Ⓑ② [C] something created as a result of effort, especially a painting, book, or piece of music: *The museum has many works* ***by*** *Picasso as well as other modern painters.* **EVERYTHING** ▷ **5 the works** informal everything that you might want or expect to find in a particular situation: *The bridegroom was wearing a morning suit, gloves, top hat – the works.* ◦ mainly US *And let me have two large pizzas* ***with*** *the works* (= with all available types of food on top). **FACTORY** ▷ **6 works** [C, + sing/pl verb] (plural **works**) an industrial building, especially one where a lot of people are employed: *a steel/car works* **MACHINE** ▷ **7 works** [plural] the parts of a machine, especially those that move: *If you take the back off this clock, you can see its/the works.* **PHYSICS** ▷ **8** [U] specialized force multiplied by distance moved

> Word partners for **work noun**
>
> *do* work • *begin/finish/start* work • *look for/seek* work • *find/have* work • *get* work *done* • *excellent/good/poor/shoddy* work • *paid/unpaid/voluntary* work

IDIOMS **be at work 1** to be working: *The labourers were at work in the fields.* **2** literary to be having an effect, usually an obvious or bad effect: *It seems as though forces of destruction are increasingly at work throughout society.* • **be in work/out of work** to have a job, or not to have a job: *He was always in work, right from the day he left school.* ◦ *My father was out of work at the time, so we struggled, obviously.* ◦ *an out-of-work actor/manager* • **get/set to work** to start doing a job or a piece of work: *We'd better get to work* ***on*** *stacking this wood if we want to finish before it gets dark.* • **have your work cut out (for you)** to have something very difficult to do: *She'll really have her work cut out to finish all those reports by the end of the week.*

▸verb **HAVE EFFECT** ▷ **1** Ⓑ① [I usually + adv/prep] to be effective or successful: *Her idea for reorganizing the department will never work* ***in practice***. ◦ *The tablets will start to work* ***in*** *a few minutes.* ◦ *Some people think I'm weird doing meditation, but it works* ***for*** *me and that's all that matters.* ◦ *Arguably, the monarchy worked* ***well*** *for many centuries.* **DO JOB** ▷ **2** Ⓐ① [I or T] to do a job, especially the job you do to earn money, or to make someone do a job: *He works at the local hospital.* ◦ *She worked* ***as*** *a cleaner at the hospital.* ◦ *Mike works* ***for*** *a computer company.* ◦ *It's not unusual for a junior doctor to work a 70 or sometimes an 80-hour week.* ◦ *Have you any experience of working* ***with*** *children who have learning difficulties?* ◦ *The instructors worked us very* ***hard*** *on the survival course.* → See also **work to rule** (**ˌwork-to-ˈrule**) **OPERATE** ▷ **3** Ⓐ② [I or T] If a machine or device works, it operates, especially correctly and without failure, and if you work it, you make it operate: *Our phone isn't working.* ◦ *You need a team of about twelve people to work a furnace this size.* ◦ *The pump works* ***off/on*** (= uses) *wind power.* ◦ *The pump is worked* ***by*** (= uses to operate) *wind power.* ◦ *I can't* ***get*** *the radio* ***to*** *work.* **SUCCEED IN BECOMING** ▷ **4** [I or T, + adv/prep] to succeed gradually in becoming something or cause a person or thing to become something, either by making an effort or by making many small movements: *He started as a technician and worked his* ***way up*** *through the company to become managing director.* ◦ *Eventually she worked her* ***way through*** (= read) *the huge amount of technical papers.* ◦ *Vibration tends to make nuts and screws work them****selves loose***. ◦ *The screws had worked loose over time.* **ARRANGE** ▷ **5** [T] informal to arrange for something to happen, especially by not using official methods and/or by being clever: *I don't know how she worked* ***it***, *but she retired at 50 on a full salary.* ◦ *Can we work* ***things*** (***out***) *so that there's always someone here to answer the phone during office hours?* **SHAPE** ▷ **6** [T] to shape, change, or process a substance: *Working iron requires higher temperatures than bronze.* ◦ *Gently work the butter* ***into*** *the flour until there are no lumps left.*

IDIOMS **work a treat** UK to operate very well: *This new drill works a treat on hard metals.* • **work like a charm** (also **work like magic**) to be very effective, possibly in a surprising way: *Flattery usually works like a charm with him.* • **work wonders/miracles** (UK also **work a treat**) to produce very good effects: *A little bit of oil works wonders on squeaky hinges.* ◦ *Running works*

W

*wonders **for** the metabolism.* • **work your fingers to the bone** to work extremely hard, especially for a long time: *She worked her fingers to the bone to provide a home and food for seven children.* • **work your way around/round to sth** to prepare yourself slowly for doing something: *I think they're both gradually working round to talking to each other again.*

PHRASAL VERBS **work against/for sb** to make it more difficult, or easier, for someone to achieve something: *Inexperience can work against a candidate looking for a job.* • **work at sth** B2 to try hard to achieve something: *Most couples would agree that for a marriage to succeed, both parties have to work at it.* ◦ [+ -ing verb] *You need to work at improv**ing** your writing.* • **work sth off** If you work off an unpleasant feeling, you get rid of it by doing something energetic: *She works off stress by running for at least half an hour every day.* • **work on sth** B2 to spend time repairing or improving something: *His dancing technique is good, but he needs to work on his fitness.* • **work on sb** informal to try to persuade or influence someone: [+ to infinitive] *I'm working on my father **to** get him to take me to the airport.* • **work sth out** CALCULATE ▷ **1** B2 to do a calculation to get an answer to a mathematical question: *We need to work out the total cost of the project.* UNDERSTAND ▷ **2** C2 mainly UK to understand something or to find the answer to something by thinking about it: [+ question word] *There will be a full investigation to work out **what** caused the accident.* ◦ [+ that] *Investigators needed several months to work out **that** a fraud had been committed.* • **work out** EXERCISE ▷ **1** B1 to exercise in order to improve the strength or appearance of your body: *Huw works out in the gym two or three times a week.* RESULT ▷ **2** [L] to be the result of a calculation: *These figures work out differently each time I add them.* ◦ *The safe load for a truck of this size works out **at** nearly 20 tonnes.* ◦ *In fact the trip worked out cheaper than we'd expected.* DEVELOP ▷ **3** to happen or develop in a particular way: *How is the new monitoring procedure working out?* ◦ *Let's hope this new job works out **well** for him.* • **work sb out** to understand the reasons for someone's behaviour: *Why does he behave like that? – I can't work him out at all.* • **work (sth) out** B2 If a problem or difficult situation works out, it gradually becomes better or satisfactory, and if you work it out, you make it better or satisfactory: *Don't worry about anything – it'll **all** work out (for the best) in the end, you'll see.* • **work sb over** slang to attack and injure someone: *Do you want me to get some of the lads to work him over?* • **work up sth** to develop an emotional or physical state that you feel strongly, after a period of effort or time: *We worked up a real **appetite** climbing in the mountains.* ◦ *It's strange, but I can't work up any **enthusiasm** for going on this trip.* • **work sb up** to make yourself or another person feel upset or feel strong emotions: *Try not to work your**self** up **about** the exams.* ◦ *Nationalist speeches worked the crowd up **into a frenzy**.* • **work (yourself) up to sth** to gradually prepare yourself for something difficult: *He's very shy, but he's slowly working (his way/him**self**) up to letting her know what he feels about her.*

-work /-wɜːk/ US /-wɝːk/ **suffix** **1** used to refer to work of a particular type: *homework* ◦ *paperwork* **2** used to refer to a skill or activity using a particular type of material: *Girls and boys study woodwork and metalwork at this school.* **3** used to name things made of a particular material: *stonework* ◦ *ironwork*

workable /ˈwɜː.kə.bl̩/ US /ˈwɝː-/ **adj** HAVING EFFECT ▷ **1** describes a plan or system that can be used effectively: *a workable solution/compromise/proposal* SHAPE ▷ **2** describes a substance that you can shape, change, or process in some way: *The ground is too hard to be workable (= dug).*

workaday /ˈwɜː.kə.deɪ/ US /ˈwɝː-/ **adj** [before noun] ordinary; not unusual: *Compared to the extravagance and glamour of last winter's **clothes**, this season's collection look simple, almost workaday.* ◦ *an escape from the workaday **world***

workaholic /ˌwɜː.kəˈhɒl.ɪk/ US /ˌwɝː.kəˈhɑː.lɪk/ **noun** [C] C2 a person who works a lot of the time and finds it difficult not to work: *A self-confessed workaholic, Tony Richardson can't remember when he last had a holiday.*

workaround /ˈwɜː.kə.raʊnd/ US /ˈwɝː-/ **noun** [C] a way of dealing with a problem or making something work despite the problem, without completely solving it: *The software still has a few glitches but we've come up with a workaround.*

workbasket /ˈwɜːkˌbɑː.skɪt/ US /ˈwɝːkˌbæs.kɪt/ **noun** [C] (mainly UK **workbox**) a small container in which things used for sewing, such as needles, pins, and thread are kept

workbench /ˈwɜːk.bentʃ/ US /ˈwɝːk-/ **noun** [C] a strong table for working on, especially one on which objects such as pieces of wood or metal can be firmly held so that tools can be used on them

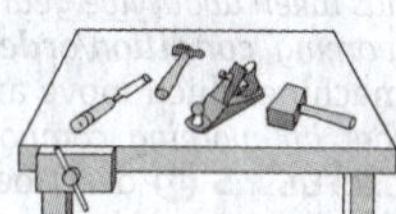
workbench

workbook /ˈwɜːk.bʊk/ US /ˈwɝːk-/ **noun** [C] A2 a book used in school containing text and questions and sometimes having spaces for a student to write answers in: *There's a workbook to accompany the course book.*

workbox /ˈwɜːk.bɒks/ US /ˈwɝːk.bɑːks/ **noun** [C] mainly UK a WORKBASKET

workday /ˈwɜːk.deɪ/ US /ˈwɝːk-/ **noun** [C] mainly US for **working day**

ˌworked ˈup **adj** [after verb] upset or very excited about something: *It's easy to **get** worked up when you're tired and everything seems to be against you.* ◦ *He was very worked up **about** seeing his family again after so many years.*

worker /ˈwɜː.kər/ US /ˈwɝː.kɚ/ **noun** [C] **1** A2 someone who works in a particular job or in a particular way: *factory/social/construction workers* ◦ *a good/tireless/skilled worker* **2** someone who works for a company or organization but does not have a powerful position: *Many companies still treat their management staff better than their workers.* **3** in BEES and some other types of insects, a female that cannot produce young but collects food for the others

ˈwork ˌethic **noun** [S] the belief that work is morally good: *The work ethic was never very strong in Simon.*

ˈwork exˌperience **noun** [U] **1** the experience that a person already has of working: *Please list your educational qualifications and work experience.* **2** a period of time in which a student temporarily works for an employer to get experience: *Many firms understand that giving work experience to students from colleges and schools will benefit everyone in the long term.*

W

workflow /ˈwɜːk.fləʊ/ US /ˈwɝːk.floʊ/ **noun** [C or U] the way that a particular type of work is organized, or the order of the stages in a particular work process: *The right software tools can improve workflow and productivity.*

workforce /ˈwɜːk.fɔːs/ (US) /ˈwɝːk.fɔːrs/ noun [C, + sing/pl verb] C2 the group of people who work in a company, industry, country, etc.: *The majority of factories in the region have a workforce **of** 50 to 100 (people).* ◦ *Much of the workforce in the banking sector is/are affected by the new legislation.*

workhorse /ˈwɜːk.hɔːs/ (US) /ˈwɝːk.hɔːrs/ noun [C] **1** a person who does a lot of work, especially of a type that is necessary but not interesting: *a willing/reliable workhorse* **2** a machine that operates without failing for long periods, although it might not be very interesting or exciting

workhouse /ˈwɜːk.haʊs/ (US) /ˈwɝːk-/ noun [C] a building where very poor people in Britain used to work, in the past, in exchange for food and shelter → Compare **poorhouse**

working /ˈwɜː.kɪŋ/ (US) /ˈwɝː-/ adj [before noun] JOB ▷ **1** B1 relating to work: *a 37-hour working **week*** ◦ *Working **conditions/practices** in the mill have hardly changed over the last 20 years.* ◦ *She has a difficult working **relationship** with many of her staff.* **2** having work: *These tax changes will affect 90 percent of the working population.* MACHINE ▷ **3** operating: *It has taken about five years to restore the aircraft to (**full**) working **condition/order**.* **4** describes the parts of a machine which move and make it work: *It is essential that all working components are properly lubricated.* USEFUL ▷ **5** B2 describes a plan, idea, or knowledge that is not complete but is good enough to be useful: *We have a working **theory/hypothesis** about what caused the crash, which we shall test.* ◦ *She's fluent in French and English and has a working **knowledge** of Spanish.*

ˌworking ˌcapital noun [U] the money belonging to a company that is immediately available for business use, rather than money it has in INVESTMENTS or property

ˌworking ˈclass noun [S, + sing/pl verb] (also **the ˌworking ˈclasses**) a social group that consists of people who earn little money, often being paid only for the hours or days that they work, and who usually do physical work: *The working class usually react/reacts in a predictable way to government policies.* → Compare **lower class, middle class, upper class** • **ˌworking-ˈclass** adj *working-class people/families*

ˌworking ˈday noun [C] (mainly US **workday**) **1** the amount of time a person spends doing their job on a day when they work: *An eight-hour working day is still typical for many people.* **2** a day on which most people go to work: ***On** a working day I tend to get up around seven o'clock.* ◦ *Please allow three full working days for the money to be transferred.*

ˌworking ˌgirl noun [C] old-fashioned informal a female PROSTITUTE

ˌworking ˌgroup noun [C, + sing/pl verb] (UK also **ˈworking ˌparty**) a small group of people, for example one chosen by a government, that studies a particular problem or situation and then reports on what it has discovered and gives suggestions

ˌworking ˈlife noun PERSON ▷ [C] the part of a person's life when they do a job or are at work: *His entire working life was spent with the same firm.*

ˌworking ˈlunch/ˈbreakfast noun [C] a meal in the middle of the day, or at the beginning of the day, during which work is discussed

ˌworking ˈman/ˈwoman/ˈperson noun [C] a man/woman who has a job: *Generally, working people don't have time to shop for food every day.*

ˌworking ˈmother/ˈfather/ˈparent noun [C] a woman/man/parent who has a job and takes care of his or her children: *Little provision is made for working mothers by many large companies.*

ˈworking ˌpapers noun [plural] US official documents which allow someone under 16 years old to be employed

ˈworking ˌparty noun [C, + sing/pl verb] UK for **working group**

workings /ˈwɜː.kɪŋz/ (US) /ˈwɝː-/ noun [plural] UNDERGROUND ▷ **1** the system of holes that has been dug in the ground in order to remove metal, coal, etc.: *disused mine workings* OPERATION ▷ **2 the workings of sth** the way that an organization, machine, or organism operates: *the workings of government* ◦ *I don't know anything about the workings of other departments or about the organization as a whole.*

ˌwork-life ˈbalance noun [S or U] the amount of time you spend doing your job compared with the amount of time you spend with your family and doing things you enjoy: *It can be difficult to get the right work-life balance.*

workload /ˈwɜːk.ləʊd/ (US) /ˈwɝːk.loʊd/ noun [C] the amount of work to be done, especially by a particular person or machine in a period of time: *Teachers are always complaining about their **heavy** workloads.* ◦ *Students do find that their workload **increases** throughout the course.*

workman /ˈwɜːk.mən/ (US) /ˈwɝːk-/ noun [C] (plural **-men** /-mən/) a man who uses physical skill and especially his hands in his job or trade: *We'll have to get a workman in to fix the plumbing/window/roof.*

workmanlike /ˈwɜːk.mən.laɪk/ (US) /ˈwɝːk-/ adj **1** approving skilful: *The Australian side turned in a very workmanlike **performance**.* **2** disapproving showing an acceptable level of skill but no great ability or style: *I had hoped for a little more from the world's greatest tenor, whose performance was workmanlike but hardly inspired.*

workmanship /ˈwɜːk.mən.ʃɪp/ (US) /ˈwɝːk-/ noun [U] the skill with which something was made or done: *shoddy/fine workmanship* ◦ *The workmanship which went into some of these pieces of furniture was truly remarkable.*

workmate /ˈwɜːk.meɪt/ (US) /ˈwɝːk-/ noun [C] informal a person who works in the same place as you, especially one who you are friendly with: *I went out for a drink with a few workmates.*

ˌwork of ˈart noun [C] (plural **works of art**) an object made by an artist of great skill, especially a painting, drawing, or STATUE

workout /ˈwɜː.kaʊt/ (US) /ˈwɝː-/ noun [C] B1 a period of physical exercise: *a light workout*

ˈwork ˌpermit noun [C] an official document which gives permission to someone who is foreign to work in a country

workplace /ˈwɜːk.pleɪs/ (US) /ˈwɝːk-/ noun [C or S] C1 a building or room where people perform their jobs, or these places generally: *The survey asks workers about facilities in their workplace.* ◦ *safety standards in **the** workplace*

ˌwork-reˌlated adj connected with someone's job or with paid work in general: *Many people suffer from work-related stress.*

workroom /ˈwɜːk.rʊm/, /-ruːm/ (US) /ˈwɝːk-/ noun [C] a room in which work is done, especially making things

worksheet /ˈwɜːk.ʃiːt/ (US) /ˈwɝːk-/ noun [C] a piece of paper with questions and exercises for students

workshop /ˈwɜːk.ʃɒp/ (US) /ˈwɝːk.ʃɑːp/ noun [C] ROOM ▷ **1** a room or building where things are

W

made or repaired using machines and/or tools: *a carpenter's/printer's workshop ◦ an engineering workshop* **MEETING** ▷ **2** C1 a meeting of people to discuss and/or perform practical work in a subject or activity: *a drama/poetry/training workshop ◦ The local council* ***runs*** *a stress-management workshop. ◦ a workshop session/production*

ˈwork-shy adj UK disapproving disliking work and trying to avoid it when possible: *Most of the unemployed are not work-shy and genuinely do want jobs.*

workstation /ˈwɜːkˌsteɪ.ʃən/ US /ˈwɝːk-/ noun [C] a keyboard and screen with which a person can use a computer system, or an area in an office, factory, etc. where a single person works

ˈwork ˌsurface noun [C] a **worktop**

worktop /ˈwɜːk.tɒp/ US /ˈwɝːk.tɑːp/ noun [C] UK (US usually **counter**) a flat surface in a kitchen, especially on top of low furniture, on which food can be prepared

ˌwork-to-ˈrule noun; verb

▸noun [C usually singular] a situation in which people carefully obey all the rules and instructions given to them about their jobs, with the intention of reducing the amount of work they do: *A work-to-rule is seen as a way to protest against low pay or bad working conditions.*

▸verb **work to rule** to arrange and perform a work-to-rule: *So far, the dustmen have not resorted to a strike but are working to rule.*

world /wɜːld/ US /wɝːld/ noun **THE EARTH** ▷ **1** A1 [S] the Earth and all the people, places, and things on it: *Different parts of the world have very different climatic conditions. ◦ Which bridge has the longest span in the world? ◦ News of the disaster shocked the (****whole/entire****) world. ◦ We live in a* ***changing*** *world and people must learn to adapt. ◦ She's a world* ***authority*** *on foetal development. ◦ a world* ***record/championship***

> **!** Common mistake: **world**
>
> **Remember:** the most usual preposition to use with 'the world' is **in**:
>
> Don't say 'of the world' or 'on the world', say **in the world**:
>
> ~~*I live in the biggest city of the world.*~~
>
> *I live in the biggest city in the world.*

GROUP/AREA ▷ **2** B1 [C usually singular] a group of things such as countries or animals, or an area of human activity or understanding: *the Muslim world ◦ the modern/industrialized world ◦ the animal world ◦ stars from the rock music world ◦ Unexpected things can happen in* ***the*** *world* ***of*** *subatomic particles.* **PLANET** ▷ **3** [C] a planet or other part of the universe, especially one where life might or does exist: *There was a man on the news last night who reckons we've been visited by beings from other worlds.*

> Word partners for **world**
>
> the *real/whole/wide* world • *travel* the world • *change/rule/save* the world • *across/all over* the world • *in* the world

IDIOMS **at one with the world** happy because you feel that you belong in the world and generally agree with what happens • **be worlds apart** to be completely opposed or different: *They are worlds apart in their political views.* • **do sb the world of good** C2 to make someone feel much healthier or happier: *We had a week away in the sun and it's done us both the world of good.* • **for all the world** exactly: *She sounds for all the world* ***like*** *her mother on the phone.* • **go/come down in the world** UK (US **move down in the world**) to have less money or a worse social position than you had before: *They used to live in a big house with lots of servants, but they've come down in the world since then.* • **go/come up in the world** UK (US **move up in the world**) to have more money or a better social position than you had before: *Roger and Ann have gone up in the world – these days they only ever travel first-class.* • **have the world at your feet** to be extremely successful and admired by a great number of people: *Five years after her debut, the diminutive star of the Royal Ballet has the world at her feet.* • **in a world of your own** (also **in another world**) thinking your own thoughts and ideas and not giving much attention to what is happening around you: *When she was young, she* ***lived in*** *a world of her own and had very few friends.* • **make a world of difference** If something makes a world of difference, it improves something very much: *A little sympathy makes a world of difference to someone who's been badly treated.* • **make the world go around/round** to be extremely important, so that many ordinary events could not happen without it: ***Love/Money*** *makes the world go round.* • **a man/woman of the world** someone who has a lot of experience of life and people, and can deal with most situations • **mean/be (all) the world to sb** to be extremely important to someone: *Her children mean all the world to her.* • **not for (all) the world** never; not in any situation: *If I took that job I'd have to leave the kids and I wouldn't do that for all the world.* • **out of this world** informal C2 extremely good: *What a restaurant – the food was out of this world!* • **the ways of the world** the types of behaviour and ways of doing things that are acceptable: *He's very young and still has a lot to learn about the ways of the world.* • **what, how, why, etc. in the world** informal used to emphasize your surprise when asking a question: *What in the world are you doing in the cupboard?* • **what's the world coming to?** something that you say which means that life is not as pleasant or safe as it was in the past: *What's the world coming to when you can't leave your house for five minutes without someone trying to break in and rob you?* • **the world and his wife** UK a great many people, especially in a particular place at a particular time: *It's going to be quite a party – the world and his wife will be there.* • **the world is sb's oyster** If the world is someone's oyster, they can do what they want to or go where they want to: *You're young and healthy and you have no commitments – the world is your oyster.* • **a world of difference** If there is a world of difference between two people or things, they are very different: *There's a world of difference* ***between*** *the service in the two hotels.*

ˈworld-ˌbeater noun [C] a person or thing that is better than any other of its type: *She has loads of natural talent as a runner and with rigorous training she could be a world-beater.* • **ˈworld-ˌbeating** adj *a world-beating partnership*

ˌworld-ˈclass adj Someone or something world-class is one of the best that there are of that type in the world: *a world-class athlete/performance*

ˌworld-ˈfamous adj known about by many people from most parts of the world: *a world-famous actress/hotel*

the ˌWorld ˈHealth Organiˌzation noun (abbreviation **the WHO**) a department of the United Nations which aims to improve health all over the world and limit the spread of diseases

worldly /ˈwɜːld.li/ (US) /ˈwɝːld-/ **adj** PHYSICAL ▷ **1** [before noun] relating to or consisting of physical things and ordinary life rather than spiritual things: *For many of the refugees, the clothes they are wearing are all the worldly **goods** (= possessions) they have.* ◦ *Her worldly success can hardly be denied.* PRACTICAL ▷ **2** practical and having a lot of experience of life: *She seems to be much more worldly than the other students in her class.* • **worldliness** /-nəs/ **noun** [U]

ˌworldly-ˈwise **adj** experienced in the ways in which people behave and able to deal with most situations: *Tyler is remarkably worldly-wise for such a young girl.*

ˌworld ˈmusic **noun** [U] popular music that has been influenced by the music of traditional cultures

ˌworld ˈpower **noun** [C] a country that has enough economic or political strength to influence events in many other countries

ˈworld-ˌshattering **adj** (also **ˈworld-ˌshaking**) extremely surprising and important, often changing the way you think about something: *world-shattering news*

ˌworld ˈwar **noun** [C usually singular] a war in which large forces from many countries fight

ˌWorld War ˈOne **noun** [S not after the] (written abbreviation **WW1**) → **the First World War**

ˌWorld War ˈTwo **noun** [S not after the] (written abbreviation **WW2**) → **the Second World War**

ˈworld-ˌweary **adj** Someone who is world-weary is not enthusiastic about anything, often because they have had too much experience of a particular way of life: *15 years in the teaching profession had left him world-weary and cynical.* • **ˈworld-ˌweariness** **noun** [U]

worldwide /ˌwɜːldˈwaɪd/ (US) /ˈwɝːld.waɪd/ **adj, adv** B2 existing or happening in all parts of the world: *a worldwide recession* ◦ *An increase in average temperature by only a few degrees could cause environmental problems worldwide.*

the ˌWorld Wide ˈWeb **noun** [S] (abbreviation **www**, also **the Web**) the system of connected documents on the internet, usually with pictures, video, and sound, that can be searched for information about a particular subject

worm /wɜːm/ (US) /wɝːm/ **noun; verb**

▸**noun** **1** B2 [C] a small animal with a long, narrow, soft body without arms, legs, or bones: *The kiwi eats worms, other invertebrates, and berries.* **2** [C] the young of particular types of insect: *It's distressing enough to find a worm in your apple but finding half of one is worse.* → See also **woodworm** **3** [C] a type of worm that lives in an animal's INTESTINE, feeding on the food there, or on an animal's body, feeding off its blood: *a parasitic worm* ◦ *The vet says our dog **has** worms.* → See also **tapeworm** **4** [S] informal an unpleasant person who does not deserve respect: *Don't be such a worm, you don't have to lie to me.*

IDIOM **the worm turns** used to describe when a person or group of people who have been treated badly for a long time suddenly become forceful and stop accepting a difficult situation: *It seems the worm has turned – after years of silence local people are beginning to protest about waste emissions from the factory.*

▸**verb** MOVE ▷ **1** [I or T, + prep] to succeed in moving along in a difficult or crowded situation, by moving your body slowly and carefully: *Because he was so small, he could worm (his **way**) through the crowd.* ◦ *She wormed her**self** under the fence.* ANIMAL ▷ **2** [T] to give an animal, especially a pet dog or cat, medicine to kill any worms which might be living inside it: *Has your dog been wormed?*

PHRASAL VERBS **worm yourself/your way into sth** disapproving to gradually achieve a position of trust, possibly by being dishonest: *He wormed him**self** into her affections without her ever suspecting he only did it for her money.* • **worm sth out of sb** informal to try and get information from someone which they are trying to keep secret: *He wasn't going to tell me, but I managed to worm it out of him.*

ˈworm-ˌeaten **adj** containing small holes which were made by the young of particular types of insect, especially WOODWORM: *a worm-eaten table/beam*

wormery /ˈwɜːm.ə.ri/ (US) /ˈwɝːm-/ **noun** [C] a container into which you put worms and waste food so that the WORMS will make the waste become COMPOST (= a substance you add to earth to improve its quality)

wormhole /ˈwɜːm.həʊl/ (US) /ˈwɝːm.hoʊl/ **noun** [C] SMALL HOLE ▷ **1** a hole made by a worm, sometimes found in furniture, fruit, or the ground PHYSICS ▷ **2** specialized a special type of structure which some scientists think might exist, connecting parts of space and time that are not usually connected

wormy /ˈwɜː.mi/ (US) /ˈwɝː-/ **adj** containing worms, or infected or damaged by worms: *Look at these vegetables – they're all mottled and wormy.*

worn /wɔːn/ (US) /wɔːrn/ **verb** past participle of **wear**

ˌworn ˈout **adj** USED ▷ **1** describes something that can no longer be used because it is so old or because it has been damaged by continued use: [before noun] *worn-out clothes/carpet/equipment* TIRED ▷ **2** extremely tired: *I've been working all night and I'm worn out.*

worried /ˈwʌr.id/ (US) /ˈwɝː-/ **adj** A2 unhappy because you are thinking about problems or unpleasant things that might happen: *She was sitting behind her desk with a worried **expression/look** on her face.* ◦ *They don't seem particularly worried **about** the situation.* ◦ *You **had** me worried (= you made me feel anxious) for a moment back there – I thought you wouldn't be able to stop in time.* ◦ *He was worried **sick** (= extremely worried) when he heard that there had been an accident.* • **worriedly** /-li/ **adv** *He looked back worriedly over his shoulder.*

worrier /ˈwʌr.i.əʳ/ (US) /ˈwɝː.i.ɚ/ **noun** [C] someone who worries a lot: *I can't help being a worrier – some people are just born that way.*

worrisome /ˈwʌr.ɪ.səm/ (US) /ˈwɝː-/ **adj** US formal or old-fashioned worrying: *Alcohol and tobacco consumption by young people is especially worrisome because habits formed early are likely to persist.*

> **! Common mistake: worry**
>
> **Remember**: the most usual preposition to use with **worry** is **about**:
>
> To refer to the thing that is making you worry, don't say 'worry for', say **worry about**:
>
> *There's no need to worry about anything.*

worry /ˈwʌr.i/ (US) /ˈwɝː-/ **verb; noun**

▸**verb** PROBLEM ▷ **1** A2 [I] to think about problems or unpleasant things that might happen in a way that makes you feel unhappy and frightened: *Try not to worry – there's nothing you can do to change the situation.* ◦ ***Don't** worry, she'll be all right.* ◦ *It's silly worrying **about** things which are outside your control.* ◦ [+ (that)] *She's worried (**that**) she might not be able to find another job.* **2** B2 [T] to make someone feel unhappy and frightened because of problems or unpleasant things that might happen: *You worried*

your mother by not writing. ◦ [+ that] *It worries me* ***that*** *he hasn't phoned yet.* ◦ *The continued lack of rain is starting to worry people.*
ANIMAL ▷ **3** [T] If a dog worries another animal, it chases and frightens it and might also bite it: *Any dog caught worrying sheep in these fields will be shot.*

> **Other ways of saying worry**
>
> **Fret** can be used instead of worry:
> *Don't **fret**. I'm sure she'll be OK.*
> If someone is worrying about something, you can say that the person is **concerned** about it:
> *Aren't you **concerned** that she might tell someone?*
> In formal English, you can use **perturbed** to describe someone who is worrying:
> *He didn't seem unduly **perturbed** by the news.*
> **Anxious** or **apprehensive** can be used when someone is worrying about something that might happen in the future:
> *All this waiting is making me **anxious**.*
> *He's a bit **apprehensive** about leaving home.*
> If someone is worrying so much that he or she is very upset and does not know what to do, you could use the word **frantic** or say that the person is **at** *his/her* **wits' end**:
> *Where on earth have you been? I've been **frantic**.*
> *I've been **at my wit's end** wondering where you've been.*
> The phrase **on** *your* **mind** is used when someone is thinking and worrying about something a lot:
> *I've got a lot **on my mind** at the moment.*
> The idiom **lose sleep over** something can also be used to say that someone is worrying about something:
> *It'll be OK. Don't **lose** any more **sleep over** it.*

IDIOM **not to worry** informal said to show that you are not worried or upset because something has gone wrong or something unexpected has happened: *Not to worry – perhaps you'll be able to come next week instead.*

PHRASAL VERB **worry at sth OBJECT** ▷ **1** to shake, pull at or touch something repeatedly: *The dog was worrying away at its bone.* **PROBLEM** ▷ **2** to keep trying to find a way of solving a problem: *She'll worry at those figures until she's sure they've been worked out properly.*

▸**noun 1** B1 [C] a problem that makes you feel unhappy and frightened: *health/financial worries* ◦ *Keeping warm in the winter is a major worry for many old people.* **2** B2 [C or U] a feeling of being unhappy and frightened about something: *Unemployment, bad health – all sorts of things can be a cause of worry.* ◦ *It was clear that Anna had no worries about her husband's attempts to flirt.*

> **Word partners for worry noun**
>
> *have* worries • *allay/calm/dispel/ease* a worry • *express/voice* a worry • a *big/great/huge/real* worry • a *constant/continual/lingering/nagging* worry • a *growing/increasing* worry • a *source of* worry • *beside yourself/out of your mind/sick with* worry • a worry *about/over* sth

worrying /ˈwʌr.i.ɪŋ/ US /ˈwɜː-/ **adj** B2 making you feel unhappy and frightened: *It's a very worrying* ***situation***. • **worryingly** /-li/ **adv** *Worryingly, the gun was never found.*

worrywart /ˈwʌr.i.wɔːt/ US /ˈwɜː.i.wɔːrt/ **noun** [C] US informal a person who often worries, especially about things that are not important: *Don't listen to him – he's just an old worrywart.*

worse /wɜːs/ US /wɜːs/ **adj; noun; adv**
▸**adj 1** A2 comparative of **bad**: more unpleasant, difficult, or severe than before or than something else that is also bad: *The conditions they're living in are worse* ***than*** *we thought.* ◦ *If the rain* ***gets*** *any worse we'll have to stop walking.* ◦ *His manners are* ***even*** *worse than his sister's.* ◦ *The heat is* ***much*** *worse in the daytime.* **2 get worse** B1 to become more ill, or to become a more severe condition: *My cold seems to be getting worse.* ◦ *If he gets* ***any*** *worse I'll take him to the doctor's.*

IDIOMS **make matters worse** B2 to make the situation even more unpleasant or difficult: *Don't say anything – you'll only make matters worse.* • **worse luck** informal said at the end of a statement to show unhappiness or anger about what has been stated: *I've got to work on Saturday, worse luck.*

▸**noun** [U] C1 something that is more unpleasant or difficult: *By the third month of the expedition they had endured many hardships, but worse was to follow.* ◦ *'What about the bride's dress – wasn't it appalling?' 'I don't know, I've* ***seen*** *worse.'* → Compare **better**

IDIOMS **be none the worse** to not be harmed or damaged by something: *They were trapped in the cave for a couple of days but they were none the worse* ***for*** *their experience.* ◦ *He's lost some weight but he's none the worse (= he's better) for that.* • **for the worse** If something changes or happens for the worse, it becomes more unpleasant or difficult: *It looks like the weather is* ***changing*** *for the worse.* • **the worse for wear** tired or in poor condition because of a lot of work or use: *After a month of journeying over rough roads, the drivers and their trucks were looking the worse for wear.*

▸**adv** B1 comparative of **badly**: *He did worse than he was expecting in the exams* ◦ *He was treated much worse than I was.*

worsen /ˈwɜː.sᵊn/ US /ˈwɜː-/ **verb** [I or T] C1 to become worse or to make something become worse: *As the company's financial problems worsened, several directors resigned.* ◦ *The continued supply of arms to the region will only worsen the situation.* • **worsening** /-ɪŋ/ **adj** *the country's worsening political situation* • **worsening noun** [S] *Rather worryingly, the survey shows a worsening of child health.*

ˌworse ˈoff adj [after verb] poorer or in a more difficult situation: *If Rick loses his job we'll be even worse off.*

worship /ˈwɜː.ʃɪp/ US /ˈwɜː-/ **verb; noun**
▸**verb** (**-pp-** or US also **-p-**) **RELIGION** ▷ **1** C1 [T] to have or show a strong feeling of respect and admiration for God or a god: *On the island the people worshipped different gods.* **2** [I] to go to a religious ceremony: *They socialize together and worship in the same mosque.* **ADMIRE** ▷ **3** C1 [T] to love, respect, and admire someone or something very much, often without noticing their bad qualities: *Her parents worship her.* ◦ *As a child, I worshipped my older brother.*

IDIOM **worship the ground sb walks on** to love and admire someone very much

▸**noun RELIGION** ▷ **1** C2 [U] the act of worshipping God or a god, often through praying or singing: *daily* ***acts of*** *worship* ◦ *Christian/Sikh/Muslim worship* ◦ *For Jews, the synagogue is the centre for community worship and study.* ◦ *Local people have complained about improperly dressed tourists entering* ***places of*** *worship (= buildings for religious ceremonies or private prayer).* **ADMIRATION** ▷ **2** [U] disapproving a lot of love or admiration for a particular thing or person, often when this is considered too much: *We're in an era of fitness and health worship.* TITLE ▷ **3 His, Your, etc. Worship** mainly UK formal used as a title of respect when speaking to or about a MAYOR or a MAGISTRATE: *His Worship the Mayor will present the awards.* ◦ [as form of address] *Thank you, Your Worship.*

worshipful /ˈwɜː.ʃɪp.fəl/ (US) /ˈwɝː-/ adj **1** formal giving someone or something great respect or admiration **2 Worshipful** mainly UK formal used in the title of societies of skilled workers or some important officials: *the Worshipful Company of Silversmiths*

worshipper (US usually **worshiper**) /ˈwɜː.ʃɪp.əʳ/ (US) /ˈwɝː.ʃɪp.ɚ/ noun [C] RELIGION ▷ **1** someone who goes to a religious ceremony to worship God: *At 11 a.m. on Sunday morning, worshippers began to stream out of the cathedral.* **2** someone who worships and performs religious ceremonies to a particular god or object: *devil/idol worshippers* ENJOY ▷ **3** informal someone who enjoys or values a particular thing very much or too much: *sun worshippers*

worst /wɜːst/ (US) /wɝːst/ adj; noun; adv; verb

▸adj (A2) superlative of **bad**: of the lowest quality, or the most unpleasant, difficult, or severe: *That was* ***the*** *worst meal I've ever eaten.* ◦ *'It was* ***the*** *worst moment of my life,' she admitted.* ◦ *He is my worst* ***enemy****.*

IDIOM **be your own worst enemy** to cause most of your problems or most of the bad things that happen to you yourself, because of your character: *Carrie is her own worst enemy – she's always falling out with people.*

▸noun [S] (B1) the most unpleasant or difficult thing, person, or situation: *That was* ***the*** *worst I've seen him play in several years.*

IDIOMS **at your worst 1** less active or intelligent than you are at other times: *I'm at my worst first thing in the morning.* **2** showing the most unpleasant side of someone's character: *This problem over late payment has shown him at his worst.* • **at worst 1** used to say what the most unpleasant or difficult situation could possibly be: *At worst, she can only tell you off for being late.* **2** considering someone or something in the most negative or unkind way possible: *She is at worst corrupt, and at best has been knowingly breaking the rules.* • **do your worst** to do the most unpleasant or harmful thing you can: *I'm not frightened of him – let him do his worst.* • **fear the worst** (C2) to think something unpleasant might have happened: *We hoped that they would be found safe and uninjured, but secretly we feared the worst.* • **if the worst comes to the worst** UK (US **if worse/worst comes to worst**) if the situation develops in the most serious or unpleasant way: *We should be in when you arrive, but if the worst comes to the worst, the neighbours have a spare key and will let you into the house.*

▸adv **1** (B2) the most badly: *Small businesses have been worst* ***hit*** *by the recession.* ◦ *Roads in the Tayside region were worst* ***affected*** *by the snow.* ◦ *The students voted him the school's worst-dressed teacher.* **2 worst of all** (B2) used to emphasize what is worst about a situation: *We had no food or light, but worst of all, we had no water.*

▸verb [T] old-fashioned to defeat someone in a fight or argument: *He was challenged to a fight but was severely worsted.*

ˌworst-case sceˈnario noun [S] the most unpleasant or serious thing that could happen in a situation: *The study concludes that* ***in a*** *worst case scenario there might be 80,000 cases of the disease.*

worsted /ˈwʊs.tɪd/ (US) /ˈwɝː.stɪd/ noun [U] a type of cloth made from wool and used to make jackets, trousers, and skirts: *a pale grey worsted suit*

worth /wɜːθ/ (US) /wɝːθ/ adj; noun

▸adj MONEY ▷ **1** (B1) having a particular value, especially in money: *Our house is worth £200,000.* ◦ *Heroin worth about $5 million was seized.* **2** informal having a particular amount of money: *She must be worth at least half a million.* **3 be worth it** to be of reasonable or good value for the price: *Four days' car hire costs £150, which is* ***well*** *worth it for the freedom it gives you.* IMPORTANCE ▷ **4 be worth sth** (B1) to be important or interesting enough to receive a particular action: *I think this matter is worth our attention.* ◦ *When you're in Reykjavík, the National Museum is worth a visit.* **5 be worth having/doing sth** to be important or useful to have or do: *There's nothing worth read****ing*** *in this newspaper.* ◦ *If you are a young, inexperienced driver, it is worth hav****ing*** *comprehensive insurance.* ◦ ***It's*** *worth remember****ing*** *that prices go up on 1 February.* **6 worth it** enjoyable enough or producing enough advantages to make the necessary effort, risk, pain, etc. seem acceptable: *It was a long climb to the top of the hill, but it was worth it for the view from the top.* ◦ *Don't tire yourself out Geri, it's really not worth it.* ◦ *After the plastic surgery I had two black eyes and was very swollen. But I knew it would be worth it.* ◦ *Forget him, love, – he's just not worth it.*

> **!** Common mistake: **be worth doing something**
>
> When **worth** is followed by a verb, that verb cannot be in the infinitive with 'to'.
>
> Do not say 'be worth to do something', say **be worth doing something**:
>
> ~~*Do you think it's worth to ask Patrick first?*~~
>
> *Do you think it's worth asking Patrick first?*

IDIOMS **be worth your/its weight in gold** to be very useful or helpful: *This recipe book is worth its weight in gold – it tells you everything you need to know about cookery.* ◦ *Boys who can sing like that are worth their weight in gold* ***to*** *the choir.* • **be worth your while** (C2) to be an activity or action that you will get an advantage from: *It's worth your while taking out travel insurance before you travel.* • **for all you are worth** informal If you do something for all you are worth, you put a lot of effort into it: *We pushed the car for all we were worth, but we still couldn't get it started.* • **for what it's worth** informal said when you are giving someone a piece of information and you are not certain if that information is useful or important: *For what it's worth, I think he may be right.* ◦ *They are, for what it's worth, the single most successful eastern arts group in the West.* • **make sth/it worth your while** informal to pay you money to do something: *If you can get me the list of names I want, I'll make it worth your while.* • **not worth the paper sth is printed/written on** If a document or agreement is not worth the paper it is written/printed on, it is of very little value. • **what's it worth (to you)?** informal mainly humorous said when you want to know what someone will give you if you give them the piece of information they have asked for: *'Do you know where Dave's living at the moment?' 'What's it worth?'* • **worth your salt** good at your job: ***Any*** *accountant worth their salt should be aware of the latest changes in taxation.*

▸noun MONEY ▷ **1** [U] the amount of money which something can be sold for; value: *The estimated worth of the plastics and petrochemical industry is about $640 billion.* **2 £20, $100, etc. worth of sth** the amount of something that you could buy for £20, $100, etc.: *$4 million worth of souvenirs and gift items have been produced for the event.* IMPORTANCE ▷ **3** [U] the

W

importance or usefulness of something or someone: *He felt as though he had no worth.* ◦ *She has proved her worth on numerous occasions.* ◦ *The study proved that women were paid less than men holding jobs **of** comparable worth.* AMOUNT ▷ **4 a month's, a year's, etc. worth of sth** an amount of something that will last a month, a year, etc. or that takes a month, a year, etc. to do: *a month's worth **of** grocery shopping* ◦ *I've done three hour's worth **of** work this morning.*

IDIOM **get your money's worth** to get good value: *We were determined to get our money's worth from our day tickets and went to every museum in the city.*

worthiness /ˈwɜː.ðɪ.nəs/ (US) /ˈwɝː-/ noun [U] SUITABLE ▷ **1** how suitable someone or something is: *She persuaded the board of her worthiness to run the company.* DESERVING RESPECT ▷ **2** formal the quality of deserving respect or attention: *the worthiness of a project/cause/aim*

worthless /ˈwɜːθ.ləs/ (US) /ˈwɝːθ-/ adj NO MONEY ▷ **1** C2 having no value in money: *The company's shares are now **virtually** worthless shares.* ◦ *He said the jewels were worthless fakes.* NOT IMPORTANT ▷ **2** C1 not important or not useful: *She was criticized so much by her employers that she began to feel worthless.* • **worthlessness** /ˈ-nəs/ noun [U] *People who have been abused as children often experience **feelings/a sense** of worthlessness.*

worthwhile /ˌwɜːθˈwaɪl/ (US) /ˌwɝːθ-/ adj B2 useful, important, or good enough to be a suitable reward for the money or time spent or the effort made: *She considers teaching a worthwhile career.* ◦ *The time and expense involved in keeping up to date with all the changes has been worthwhile.* ◦ *If you need him on this project, you've got to **make** it **financially** worthwhile for him (= you will have to pay him a suitable amount of money for the amount of work involved).*

worthy /ˈwɜː.ði/ (US) /ˈwɝː-/ adj; noun

▸adj DESERVING RESPECT ▷ **1** C1 formal deserving respect, admiration, or support: *He is unlikely to succeed in getting his bill through Congress, however worthy it is.* ◦ *Every year she makes a large donation to a worthy **cause**.* **2 worthy of attention, notice, etc.** C2 formal deserving to be given attention, noticed, etc.: *Two points in this report are especially worthy of notice.* **3** formal describes something that is not very interesting but should be admired for its good and useful qualities: *a worthy book* SUITABLE ▷ **4 worthy of sth** suitable for or characteristic of something: *He threw a party worthy of a millionaire.* • **worthily** /ˈwɜː.ðɪ.li/ (US) /ˈwɝː-/ adv formal

▸noun [C] humorous a person who is important, especially in a small town: *The front row of chairs was reserved for local worthies.*

-worthy /-wɜː.ði/ (US) /-wɝː-/ suffix **1** suitable or deserving to receive a particular thing: *trustworthy* ◦ *creditworthy* ◦ *newsworthy* **2** describes a boat, aircraft, or vehicle that is suitable to be used safely in a particular substance or environment: *seaworthy* ◦ *roadworthy*

wot /wɒt/ (US) /wɑːt/ **pronoun** UK not standard mainly humorous used in writing for what or that: *Wot? No food?* ◦ *It's him wot won it.*

wotcha (also **wotcher**) /ˈwɒt.ʃəʳ/ (US) /ˈwɑː.tʃɚ/ exclamation UK informal used as an informal greeting, especially between friends: *Wotcha, mate!*

would strong /wʊd/ weak /wəd/ /əd/ **modal verb** FUTURE ▷ **1** B1 (also **'d**) used to refer to future time from the point of view of the past: *He said he would see his brother tomorrow.* ◦ *They knew there would be trouble unless the report was finished by the next day.* ◦ *We realized it wouldn't be easy to find another secretary.* **2 would have** used to refer back to a time in the past from a point of view in the future: *We thought they would have got home by five o'clock, but there was no reply when we phoned.*

> **! Common mistake: would**
>
> **Would** is followed by an infinitive verb without 'to'.
>
> Don't say 'would to do something', say **would do something**:
>
> ~~*He promised that he would to come with me.*~~
>
> *He promised that he would come with me.*

> **! Common mistake: would or should?**
>
> **Warning:** Choose the correct verb!
>
> To say what you think is the correct or best thing to do, don't say 'would', say **should**:
>
> ~~*I think the new assistant would be able to speak English.*~~
>
> *I think the new assistant should be able to speak English.*

INTENTION ▷ **3** (also **'d**) used to refer to an intention from the point of view of the past: *He said he would always love her.* ◦ *They promised that they would help.* ◦ *There was nobody left who would (= was willing to) do it.* ◦ *I asked him to move his car but he said he wouldn't (= he refused).* POSSIBLE ▷ **4** B1 (also **'d**) used to refer to a situation that you can imagine happening: *I would hate to miss the show.* ◦ *I'd go myself but I'm too busy.* ◦ *It would **have** been very boring to sit through the whole speech.* **5** B1 (also **'d**) used with if in CONDITIONAL sentences (= sentences which refer to what happens if something else happens): *What would you do if you lost your job?* ◦ *If I'd had time, I would **have** gone to see Graham.* REQUEST ▷ **6** A1 (also **'d**) used in polite requests and offers: *Would you mind sharing a room?* ◦ *Would you like me to come with you?* ◦ *Would you like some cake?* WILLING ▷ **7** B1 past simple of **will**: used to talk about what someone was willing to do or what something was able to do: *The car wouldn't start this morning.* WISH ▷ **8 would rather/sooner** (also **'d**) B1 used to show that you prefer to have or do one thing more than another: *I'd rather have a beer.* ◦ *Which would you sooner do – go swimming or play tennis?* ◦ *Wouldn't you rather finish it tomorrow?* ◦ *He'd rather die than (= he certainly does not want to) let me think he needed help.* **9 would that...** formal used to express a strong wish or DESIRE: *Would that (= if only) she could see her famous son now.* OFTEN ▷ **10** B2 (also **'d**) used to talk about things in the past that happened often or always: *He would always turn and wave at the end of the street.* **11** (also **'d**) used to suggest that what happens is expected because it is typical, especially of a person's behaviour: *'Margot rang to say she's too busy to come.' 'She would – she always has an excuse.'* OPINION ▷ **12** C1 (also **'d**) used to express an opinion in a polite way without being forceful: *I would imagine we need to speak to the headteacher about this first.* ◦ *It's not what we would **have** expected from a professional service.* ADVISE ▷ **13** (also **'d**) **should**: *I wouldn't (= I advise you not to) worry about it, if I were you.* REASON ▷ **14** (also **'d**) **should**: *Why would anyone want to eat something so horrible?* LIKELY ▷ **15** (also **'d**) used to refer to what is quite likely: *'The guy on the phone had an Australian accent.' 'That would be Tom, I expect.'*

ˈwould-be adj [before noun] C2 wanting or trying to be: *a would-be artist/politician*

W

wouldn't /ˈwʊd.ənt/ short form of would not: *I wouldn't do that if I were you.*

wound[1] /wuːnd/ noun; verb

▸noun [C] **INJURY** ▷ **1** B2 a damaged area of the body, such as a cut or hole in the skin or flesh made by a weapon: *a gunshot wound ◦ a chest/leg wound ◦ a **flesh** (= not deep) wound ◦ He died from multiple **stab** wounds **to** the neck and upper body.* **UPSET** ▷ **2** a problem or great unhappiness: *She refuses to talk about the incident, saying it would only **reopen old** wounds (= make her remember unhappy past experiences).*

▸verb [T usually passive] **HURT** ▷ **1** B2 to damage an area of the body, especially by making a cut or hole in the skin: *Flying glass wounded her **in** the face and neck. ◦ The police chief was **badly** wounded in the explosion.* **UPSET** ▷ **2** to make someone feel upset: *He was deeply wounded by her fierce criticism.*

wound[2] /waʊnd/ verb past simple and past participle of **wind** and **wind**

wounded /ˈwuːn.dɪd/ adj; noun

▸adj **UPSET** ▷ **1** offended or upset by what someone has said or done: *a wounded expression ◦ wounded pride* **INJURED** ▷ **2** injured, especially with a cut or hole in the skin: *a wounded soldier*

▸noun [plural] **the wounded** people who are injured: *Ambulances took the wounded to local hospitals.*

ˌwound ˈup adj very worried, nervous, or angry: *She gets quite wound up before a match.*

wove /wəʊv/ US /woʊv/ verb past simple of **weave**

woven /ˈwəʊ.vən/ US /ˈwoʊ-/ verb past participle of **weave**

wow /waʊ/ exclamation; noun; verb

▸exclamation informal A2 used to show surprise and sometimes pleasure: *Wow! Did you make that cake? It looks delicious!*

▸noun [S] informal a person or thing that is very successful, attractive, or pleasant: *He's a real wow **with** the girls in his class.*

▸verb [T] informal to make someone feel great excitement or admiration: *The movie wowed audiences throughout the States with its amazing special effects.*

ˈwow ˌfactor noun [C] informal a quality or feature of something that makes people feel great excitement or admiration: *The wow factor of this house is the amazing kitchen.*

WPC /ˌdʌb.l̩.jʊ.piːˈsiː/ noun [C] UK abbreviation for woman police constable: a female police officer of the lowest rank: *WPC (Andrea) Watson*

WRAC /ræk/, /ˌdʊb.l̩.juː.ɑː.reɪˈsiː/ US /-ɑːr.eɪ-/ noun **1** [+ sing/pl verb] abbreviation for Women's Royal Army Corps **2** [C] abbreviation a member of the Women's Royal Army Corps

wrack → See **rack**

WRAF /ˌdʌb.l̩.juː.ɑː.reɪˈef/ US /-ɑːr.eɪ-/ noun **1** [+ sing/pl verb] abbreviation for Women's Royal Air Force **2** [C] abbreviation a member of the Women's Royal Air Force

wraith /reɪθ/ noun [C] literary a spirit of a dead person, sometimes represented as a pale, transparent image of that person • **wraithlike** /ˈreɪθ.laɪk/ adj literary *a wraithlike (= thin and pale) figure in a grey floating dress*

wrangle /ˈræŋ.gəl/ noun [C] an argument, especially one that continues for a long time: *a lengthy wrangle **about/over** costs ◦ The joint venture ended in a **legal** wrangle between the two companies.* • **wrangle** verb [I] *They had been wrangling **with** the authorities **about/over** parking spaces.* • **wrangling** /-ɪŋ/ noun [U] *political wrangling*

wrap /ræp/ verb; noun

▸verb [T] (-pp-) **1** B1 to cover or surround something with paper, cloth, or other material: *She wrapped the present and tied it with ribbon. ◦ Wrap the chicken **in** foil and cook it for two hours.* **2** B2 to cover someone with a piece of material in order to protect them: *She wrapped the baby **in** a blanket. ◦ He wrapped a towel **around** his shoulders.*

IDIOMS **be wrapped up in sth/sb** informal If you are wrapped up in someone or something, you are very interested in them or it and ignore other people or things: *She's always been completely wrapped up in the children.* • **wrap sb (up) in cotton wool** UK to try to protect someone too carefully: *You can't wrap (up) your children in cotton wool forever.* • **wrap sb around/round your little finger** to persuade someone easily to do what you want them to do: *She could wrap her father round her little finger.*

PHRASAL VERBS **wrap sth around/round sb/sth** UK (US **wrap sth around sb/sth**) to put a piece of clothing or material around someone or something, usually to keep them or it warm: *It was so cold that he wrapped a scarf tightly around his face.* • **wrap sth around/round sth** UK (US **wrap sth around sth**) to put part of your body, such as your fingers or arms, around something tightly: *She wrapped her arms around her knees.* • **wrap (sb) up** to dress in warm clothes, or to dress someone in warm clothes: *Wrap up well – it's cold outside.* • **wrap sth up** **COVER** ▷ **1** B1 to cover or surround something in paper, cloth, or other material: *Have you wrapped up Jenny's present yet?* **FINISH** ▷ **2** informal to complete something successfully: *That just about wraps it up for today.*

▸noun **COVERING** ▷ **1** [C] (US also **wrapper**) a loose piece of clothing that is worn tied around the body: *a beach wrap* **2** [C] a long piece of cloth that a woman wears around her shoulders to keep her warm or for decoration: *a chiffon/silk wrap* **3** [U] material that is used to cover or protect objects: *plastic wrap ◦ gift wrap* **FOOD** ▷ **4** [C] a sandwich made with one piece of very thin bread that is folded around a filling

IDIOMS **it's a wrap** a phrase used in film making to tell actors and CREW that filming of a particular SCENE, film, etc. has finished • **take the wraps off sth** to allow people to know about something • **under wraps** secret: *They tried to **keep** the report under wraps.*

wraparound /ˈræp.ə.raʊnd/ adj, noun [C] (UK also **wrapround**) (a piece of clothing that is) made so that it can be tied around the body: *a wraparound skirt*

wrapped /ræpt/ adj **COVERED** ▷ **1** covered with paper or other material: *individually wrapped chocolates* **HAPPY** ▷ **2** (also **rapt**) Australian English informal extremely happy or excited

wrapper /ˈræp.ər/ US /-ɚ/ noun [C] **COVERING** ▷ **1** a piece of paper, plastic, or other material that covers and protects something: *a sweet (US candy) wrapper* **2** US for WRAP (= a loose piece of clothing) **FINANCE** ▷ **3** a financial product that gives advantages such as reduced tax: *The shares will be held in a tax-free individual savings account wrapper.*

wrapping /ˈræp.ɪŋ/ noun [C or U] paper or plastic which covers or protects something: *cellophane wrapping ◦ The new chairs were covered in protective plastic wrappings.*

ˈwrapping ˌpaper noun [U] decorated paper that is used to cover presents

wrath /rɒθ/ US /rɑːθ/ noun [U] formal or old-fashioned

extreme anger: *The people feared the wrath of God.* • **wrathful** /-fᵊl/ adj • **wrathfully** /-fᵊl.i/ adv

wreak /riːk/ verb [T] formal to cause something to happen in a violent and often uncontrolled way: *The recent storms have wreaked **havoc** on crops.* ◦ *She was determined to wreak **revenge/vengeance** on both him and his family.*

wreath /riːθ/ noun [C] (plural **wreaths** /riːðz/) an arrangement of flowers and leaves in a circular shape, used as a decoration or as a sign of respect and REMEMBRANCE for a person who has died: *a holly/laurel wreath* ◦ *The bride wore a veil with a wreath **of** silk flowers.* ◦ *There were two large wreaths on the coffin.* ◦ *The president ended his visit by **laying** a wreath at the war memorial.*

wreathe /riːð/ verb [T] literary to cover or surround something: *The peak of the mountain is perpetually wreathed **in** cloud.*

IDIOM **be wreathed in smiles** to be smiling and looking extremely happy: *He was wreathed in smiles as he accepted the award.*

wreck /rek/ verb; noun

▸verb [T] **1** Ⓒ to destroy or badly damage something: *The explosion shattered nearby windows and wrecked two cars.* ◦ *Our greenhouse was wrecked in last night's storm.* **2** informal to spoil something completely: *He has been warned that his behaviour might wreck his chances of promotion.*

▸noun [C] **1** Ⓒ a vehicle or ship that has been destroyed or badly damaged: *Divers exploring the wreck managed to salvage some coins and jewellery.* ◦ *The burned-out wrecks **of** two police cars littered the road.* **2** Ⓒ informal someone who is in bad physical or mental condition: *The stress she had been under at work reduced her to a **nervous/quivering** wreck.*

wreckage /ˈrek.ɪdʒ/ noun [U] **1** Ⓒ a badly damaged object or the separated parts of a badly damaged object: *Two children were trapped in the wreckage.* ◦ *The wreckage of the car was scattered over the roadside.* **2** what is left of something that has been spoiled or that has failed: *Kate was still **clinging to** the wreckage of her failed marriage.*

wrecked /rekt/ adj THING ▷ **1** very badly damaged: *Just look at what you've done to my coat – it's wrecked.* PERSON ▷ **2** [after verb] slang very drunk: *He **got** completely wrecked last Saturday night.* **3** [after verb] informal very tired

wrecker /ˈrek.əʳ/ Ⓤⓢ /-ɚ/ noun [C] US for **breakdown truck**

wren /ren/ noun [C] a very small, brown bird

Wren /ren/ noun [C] UK informal a member of the British Women's Royal Naval Service

wrench /rentʃ/ verb; noun

▸verb **1** [T + adv/prep] to pull and twist something suddenly or violently away from a fixed position: *The photographer tripped over a lead, wrenching a microphone **from** its stand.* ◦ *The phone had been wrenched **from/off** the wall.* ◦ *The ball was wrenched **out of** his grasp by another player.* ◦ *His hands were tied but he managed to wrench himself **free**.* **2** [T] to twist part of your body badly, such as your arm or leg, and injure it: *He wrenched his right shoulder during a game of hockey.* **3** [T usually passive] to suddenly take someone from people they love, causing them great unhappiness: *At the age of eight, she was wrenched from her foster parents and sent to live with another family.*

▸noun TOOL ▷ **1** [C] mainly US a SPANNER, usually one that can be made larger or smaller for holding and turning objects of different sizes: *an adjustable wrench* → See also **monkey wrench** PULL ▷ **2** [C usually singular] a sudden, violent twist or pull UNHAPPY FEELING ▷ **3** [S] a feeling of unhappiness when you have to leave a person or place that you love: *She found leaving home a real wrench.*

wrest /rest/ verb [T + adv/prep] **1** formal to get something with effort or difficulty: *The shareholders are planning to wrest **control** of the company (**away**) **from** the current directors.* **2** to violently pull something away from someone: *He wrested the letter from my grasp.*

wrestle /ˈres.l̩/ verb [I or T] to fight with someone (especially as a sport) by holding them and trying to throw them to the ground: *He has wrestled professionally for five years.* ◦ *The police officer tackled the man and wrestled him **to the ground**.*

PHRASAL VERB **wrestle with sth** to try very hard to deal with a problem or to make a difficult decision: *The government is wrestling with difficult economic problems.*

wrestler /ˈres.ləʳ/ Ⓤⓢ /-lɚ/ noun [C] a person who wrestles as a sport

wrestling /ˈres.lɪŋ/ noun [U] a sport where two people fight and try to throw each other to the ground

wretch /retʃ/ noun [C] UNHAPPY PERSON ▷ **1** a person who experiences something unpleasant: *a poor/miserable wretch* BAD PERSON ▷ **2** informal or humorous someone who is unpleasant or annoying: *Who's trampled on my flowers? I bet it was those two little wretches who live next door.* ◦ *You wretch! You promised you'd give me a lift.*

wretched /ˈretʃ.ɪd/ adj **1** Ⓒ unhappy, unpleasant, or of low quality: *a wretched childhood* ◦ *The house was in a wretched state.* **2** used to express anger: *My wretched car's broken down again.* **3** Ⓒ very ill or very unhappy: *I think I must be coming down with flu – I've been feeling wretched all day.* • **wretchedness** /-nəs/ noun [U]

wretchedly /ˈretʃ.ɪd.li/ adv extremely, when referring to something unpleasant or of low quality: *wretchedly inadequate*

wriggle /ˈrɪg.l̩/ verb; noun

▸verb **1** [I or T] to twist your body, or move part of your body, with small, quick movements: *A large worm wriggled in the freshly dug earth.* ◦ *Baby Martha was wriggling her toes in the sand.* **2** [I + adv/prep] to move somewhere using short, quick twisting movements: *The tunnel was low and dark, but she managed to **wriggle through** to the other side.* ◦ *After twisting and turning for a while, he managed to wriggle **free**.*

IDIOM **wriggle off the hook** informal If someone wriggles off the hook, they avoid a responsibility or avoid doing something.

PHRASAL VERB **wriggle out of sth** informal to avoid doing something that you do not want to do: *He promised he'd help me decorate, but now he's trying to wriggle out of it.*

▸noun [C usually singular] an act of wriggling: *With a wriggle, she managed to crawl through the gap.*

wring /rɪŋ/ verb [T] (**wrung**, **wrung**) **1** to hold something tightly with both hands and twist it by turning your hands in opposite directions **2** (also **wring out**) to twist a cloth or piece of clothing with your hands to remove water from it: *She wrung out the shirt and hung it out to dry.* **3** **wring sth's neck** to kill a bird or other animal by twisting and breaking its neck

IDIOMS **I'll wring your/his/her neck!** informal something you say when you are very angry with someone: *I'll wring his neck if he does that again!* • **wring your hands** If you wring your hands, you show that you are worried or unhappy: *Car dealers are wringing their hands* ***over*** *low sales this summer.*

PHRASAL VERB **wring sth from/out of sb** to force or persuade someone to give you something: *They managed to wring a few concessions from the government.*

wringer /ˈrɪŋ.əʳ/ (US) /-ɚ/ noun [C] (UK also **mangle**) a machine used for pressing water out of clothes by putting the clothes between two heavy smooth round bars

IDIOM **put sb through the wringer** informal to ask someone difficult or unpleasant questions, often to find out if they are doing their job in a satisfactory way

wrinkle /ˈrɪŋ.kl̩/ noun; verb
▸noun [C] **LINE** ▷ **1** (C2) a small line in the skin caused by old age: *fine wrinkles around the eyes* ◦ *anti-wrinkle creams* **2** a small line or fold in cloth **PROBLEM** ▷ **3** informal a problem, usually a small one: *There are still a few wrinkles to* ***iron out*** *(= solve) before the agreement can be signed.*
▸verb [I or T] **1** If skin or material wrinkles, or if something wrinkles it, it gets small lines or folds in it: *Sunbathing can prematurely age and wrinkle the skin.* **2 wrinkle your brow** to make folds appear on your face above your eyes to show that you are surprised or confused **3 wrinkle (up) your nose** to show that you dislike something or that you disapprove of something by tightening the muscles in your nose so that small lines appear in the skin: *She wrinkled up her nose* ***at*** *the strange smell coming from the kitchen.* ◦ *Amy wrinkled her nose in disapproval.*

wrinkled /ˈrɪŋ.kl̩d/ adj (C2) with a lot of wrinkles: *a wrinkled face*

wrinkly (also **wrinklie**) /ˈrɪŋ.kli/ noun [C] UK informal an old person

wrist /rɪst/ noun [C] (B2) the part of the body between the hand and the arm: *I sprained my wrist playing squash.*

wristband /ˈrɪst.bænd/ noun [C] **1** a piece of material which goes around the wrist, for example to hold a watch **2** a piece of material that people wear around their wrists to show that they support a particular organization or idea

wristwatch /ˈrɪst.wɒtʃ/ (US) /-wɑːtʃ/ noun [C] a watch that is worn on the wrist

writ /rɪt/ noun; verb
▸noun **DOCUMENT** ▷ **1** [C] legal a legal document from a law court that tells someone that they will be involved in a legal process and explains to them what they must do: *There have been at least seven writs* ***issued against*** *him for late payment of bills.* ◦ *She has* ***served*** *a writ* ***for*** *libel* ***on*** *the newspaper (= she has delivered it to them officially).* **AUTHORITY** ▷ **2** [U] formal the authority to rule or make laws: *holy writ*
▸verb old use past participle of **write**

IDIOMS **be writ large** formal to be very obvious: *Her distress was writ large in her face.* • **writ large** formal If one thing is another thing writ large, it is similar to it but larger or more obvious: *Hollywood is often said to be American society writ large.*

write /raɪt/ verb (**wrote**, **written** or old use **writ**) **1** (A1) [I or T] to make marks which represent letters, words, or numbers on a surface, such as paper or a computer screen, using a pen, pencil, or keyboard, or to use this method to record thoughts, facts, or messages: *When you fill in the form, please write* ***clearly/legibly*** *in black ink.* ◦ [+ speech] *'I hope to see you next Saturday,' she wrote.* ◦ *Why not write (****down****) your ideas on a piece of paper before you start?* **2** (A2) [I or T] to send a letter or message to someone, giving them information or expressing your thoughts or feelings: *She hasn't written* ***to*** *me (US written me) recently.* ◦ [+ two objects] *I wrote my sister a letter.* ◦ [+ to infinitive] *My mother wrote* ***to*** *give me details about the party.* ◦ [+ -ing verb] *The travel company has written giv****ing*** *information about the trip.* **3** [T] (also **write sth out**) to put all the information that is needed on a document: *Please will you write (out) your name and address* ***in full****.* ◦ [+ two objects] *I wrote him a cheque for £50.* **4** (B1) [T] to create and record something, such as a book, poem, song, or computer program, on paper or on a computer: *She writes children's books/poems.* ◦ *Adam designed and wrote the software.* ◦ *He wrote music* ***for*** *films and TV shows.* ◦ *The book is very well written.* **5** (B1) [I] to have the job of creating books, stories, or articles that will be published: *She writes* ***for*** *a national newspaper.* **6** [+ that] to say something in a book, newspaper, magazine, or document: *In the article, he writes* ***that*** *the problems in the refugee camps are getting worse.* **7** [I] specialized to record information in the memory of a computer: *There was a problem writing* ***to*** *the disk in the A drive.*

> **! Common mistake: write**
>
> **Warning:** Check your verb endings!
>
> Many learners make mistakes when using **write** in the past tense. The past participle has 'tt'.
> Don't write 'writen', write **written**. The **-ing** form is **writing**.

> **! Usage: write**
>
> Remember to use the correct grammar after **write**.
>
> **write to** someone:
> *Pamela wrote to me last week.*
>
> **write** someone a letter:
> *Pamela wrote me a letter last week.*
>
> **write** someone (American English):
> *Rachel wrote me last week.*

IDIOMS **nothing to write home about** informal not exciting or special: *Their performance was nothing to write home about.* • **written all over sb's face** If an emotion is written all over someone's face, it is clear what they are feeling: *Guilt was written all over her face.*

PHRASAL VERBS **write back** to reply to someone's letter: *I'll write back and tell her we're coming.* • **write sth down ON PAPER** ▷ **1** (B1) to write something on a piece of paper so that you do not forget it: *Did you write down Jo's phone number?* **FINANCE** ▷ **2** to show in a company's ACCOUNTS (= financial records) that something is worth less than it was before: *The building cost £700,000 to build, but it was written down* ***to*** *£300,000.* • **write in** to write a letter to a newspaper, television company, or other organization, to express an opinion or ask something: [+ to infinitive] *People have written in* ***to*** *complain about the show.* ◦ [+ -ing verb] *Thousands of people wrote in to the BBC ask****ing*** *for an information sheet.* • **write sb in** US to add someone's name to the official list for an election in order to show that you want to vote for them: *a write-in candidate/campaign* • **write sth into sth** [often passive] to add a particular detail or rule to a document: *An agreement to produce five novels a year was written into her contract.* • **write sth off** MONEY ▷ **1** to accept that an amount of money has been lost or that a debt will not be paid: *The World Bank is being urged to write off debts from developing countries.* VEHICLE ▷ **2** UK to damage a vehicle so badly that it cannot be repaired: *His car was completely written off in the accident.* • **write sb/sth off** C2 to decide that a particular person or thing will not be useful, important, or successful: *A lot of companies seem to write people off if they're over 50.* • **write off/away for sth** to write a letter to an organization asking them to send you something: *Did you write off **for** tickets?* • **write sb out of sth** to change the story of a regular television or radio programme so that a particular character is not in it any more • **write sth up** C1 to write something in a complete or final form using notes that you have made: *Have you written up that report yet?* • **write sb up** US to report someone for not obeying a law or rule: *The cop said he'd have to write me up for not stopping at the red light.*

ˈwrite-off noun [C usually singular] VEHICLE ▷ **1** UK a vehicle that is too damaged to be worth repairing: *She wasn't hurt, but the car's a **complete** write-off.* NOTHING ACHIEVED ▷ **2** a period of time during which you fail to achieve anything: *Yesterday was a **complete** write-off as far as work is concerned.*

writer /ˈraɪ.təʳ/ US /-t̬ɚ/ noun [C] B1 a person who writes books or articles to be published: *a travel/sports/fiction/crime writer*

ˌwriter's ˈblock noun [U] the condition of being unable to create a piece of written work because something in your mind prevents you from doing it

ˌwriter's ˈcramp noun [U] a painful stiffness in the hand that people suffer from if they have been writing continuously for a long time

ˈwrite-up noun [C] a report or article which makes a judgment about something, such as a play or film: *The paper didn't give the show a very good write-up.*

writhe /raɪð/ verb [I] **1** to make large twisting movements with the body: *The pain was so unbearable that he was writhing **in** agony.* ◦ *She was writhing **around/about** on the ground.* **2** informal to experience a very difficult or unpleasant situation or emotion, such as extreme embarrassment: *He and four other senators were writhing in the glare of unfavorable publicity.*

writing /ˈraɪ.tɪŋ/ US /-t̬ɪŋ/ noun **1** B1 [U] a person's style of writing with a pen on paper which can be recognized as their own: *Do you recognize the writing on the envelope?* **2** A2 [U] something that has been written or printed **3** B2 [U] the written work, such as stories or poems, of one person or a group of people: *She is studying women's writing at the turn of the century.* **4** B2 [U] the activity of creating pieces of written work, such as stories, poems, or articles: *I did a course in **creative** writing.* **5** A1 [U] the skill or activity of producing words on a surface: *Teachers focus on speaking and writing in the afternoon classes.* **6 in writing** B2 in written form: *All bookings must be confirmed in writing.* **7 writings** [plural] the written works of a person, especially when they have been published as books: *the writings **of** Karl Marx*

IDIOM **the writing is on the wall** (US also **the handwriting is on the wall**) said to mean that there are clear signs that something will fail or no longer exist

ˈwriting ˌdesk noun [C] a desk with drawers

ˈwriting ˌpaper noun [U] (also **notepaper**) paper for writing letters on

written /ˈrɪt.ən/ US /ˈrɪt̬-/ verb; adj
▸verb past participle of **write**
▸adj B1 expressed in writing, or involving writing: *written instructions* ◦ *a written exam*

the ˌwritten ˈword noun [S] formal language in written form: *the communicative power of the written word*

wrong /rɒŋ/ US /rɑːŋ/ adj; adv; noun; verb
▸adj NOT CORRECT ▷ **1** A1 not correct: *Three of your answers were wrong.* ◦ *That clock is wrong – it's 12.30, not 12.15.* ◦ *Some of his facts are questionable, others are **plainly** (= completely) wrong.* → Compare **right** **2** A2 If someone is wrong, they are not correct in their judgment or statement about something: *You were wrong **about** the time – the shop closed at 7.00.* ◦ *He's wrong **in thinking** that we will support the project financially.* **3 prove sb wrong** to show by your actions that someone's judgment of you was not correct: *I thought she couldn't do it, but she proved me wrong.* NOT SUITABLE ▷ **4** C1 not suitable or correct, or not as it should be: *She's the wrong person for the job.* ◦ *We must have taken a wrong turning.* ◦ *I'm sorry, you've got the wrong **number** (= this is not the phone number you wanted).* → Compare **right** **5** describes something that is not considered to be socially acceptable or suitable: *She got in with the wrong crowd (= a group of people who were not considered socially acceptable) at university.* **6** B1 If you ask someone what is wrong, you want to know what is worrying or upsetting them: *You've been quiet all evening. Is there anything wrong?* ◦ *What's wrong with you today?* **7 the wrong way round/around** If something is the wrong way round/around, the part that should be at the front is at the back: *You've got your skirt on the wrong way round.* IMMORAL ▷ **8** B2 not considered morally acceptable by most people: *Children should be taught that violence is wrong.* ◦ ***It** was wrong **of** her to lie to you.* ◦ *What's wrong **with** having a bit of fun?* → Opposite **right** NOT WORKING ▷ **9** B1 [after verb] not working correctly: *Something's wrong **with** the television – the picture's gone fuzzy.* ◦ *The doctors are still trying to **find out** what's wrong.*

> **+ Other ways of saying wrong**
>
> **Incorrect** is an alternative to 'wrong' when information or facts are wrong:
>
> *The information on the website is **incorrect**.*
>
> A formal word which means 'wrong' is **erroneous**:
>
> *No one could explain how the **erroneous** information had gotten into the report.*
>
> If facts are not completely correct or exact, you can use the adjective **inaccurate**:
>
> *Their estimation of the cost was wildly (= extremely) **inaccurate**.*
>
> **False** or **mistaken** can be used when an idea or belief is wrong:
>
> *The title gives a **false** impression of what the movie is about.*
>
> *I went there in the **mistaken** belief that it would help.*
>
> You can also use **mistaken** to describe a person who is wrong about something:
>
> *You're **mistaken** if you believe we've discovered nothing of value.*

IDIOMS **catch sb on the wrong foot** If something catches you on the wrong foot, you are not prepared

for it: *I hadn't expected the question and it caught me on the wrong foot.* • **get the wrong end of the stick** informal to not understand a situation correctly: *Her friend saw us arrive at the party together and got the wrong end of the stick.* • **get/fall into the wrong hands** If something gets/falls into the wrong hands, a dangerous person or enemy starts to control it: *If this sort of information fell into the wrong hands, we could be in serious trouble.* • **go down the wrong way** If food or drink goes down the wrong way, it goes down the wrong tube in your throat and causes you to cough or stop breathing for a short time.

▸adv **1** A2 informal in a way that is not correct: *You've spelled my name wrong.* → See also **wrongly 2 get sth wrong** B1 informal to make a mistake in the way you answer or understand something: *I spent hours doing that calculation and I still got the answer wrong.* ◦ *You've got it all wrong – it was your boss that she was annoyed with and not you!* **3 go wrong a** B2 If a situation or event goes wrong, it becomes unpleasant and is not a success: *Our marriage began to go wrong after we had our first child.* **b** to make a mistake: *These shelves are very easy to put together – you can't go wrong.* **c** B1 If a machine goes wrong, it stops working correctly: *Our TV keeps going wrong.*

IDIOM **don't get me wrong** C2 said when you think someone might not understand what you say, or be upset by it: *Don't get me wrong – I'd love to come but I'm too busy next week.*

▸noun **1** [U] what is considered to be morally unacceptable: *He has no sense of* ***right and*** *wrong.* ◦ *I was brought up to tell the truth and* ***know right from*** *wrong.* ◦ *As far as her parents are concerned, she* ***can do no*** *wrong (= she is perfect in every way).* **2** [C] an unfair action: *He has* ***done*** *us a great wrong.* ◦ *She was trying to* ***right*** *(= do something to make better) the wrongs of the past.* **3 in the wrong** If someone is in the wrong, they have made a mistake or done something that is bad or illegal: *The driver was unquestionably in the wrong.*

IDIOM **two wrongs don't make a right** saying said to emphasize that it is not acceptable to do something bad to someone just because they did something bad to you first

▸verb [T] formal to treat someone in an unfair or unacceptable way: *She felt* ***deeply*** *wronged by his accusations.*

wrongdoer /ˈrɒθˌduː.əʳ/ (US) /ˈrɑːŋˌduː.ɚ/ noun [C] formal a person who does something bad or illegal

wrongdoing /rɒŋˌduː.ɪŋ/ (US) /ˈrɑːŋ-/ noun [C or U] formal a bad or an illegal action: *She has strenuously* ***denied*** *any criminal wrongdoing.*

ˌwrong-ˈfoot verb **1** [T] UK in a sport, to hit or kick the ball so that the other player believes the ball will go in the opposite direction to the one in which it will really go in order to make them move in the wrong direction **2** [T often passive] to cause someone to be in a difficult situation by doing something unexpected: *The company was completely wrong-footed by the dollar's sudden recovery.*

wrongful /ˈrɒŋ.fᵊl/ (US) /ˈrɑːŋ-/ adj describes actions that are unfair or illegal: *She is claiming damages from the company for wrongful* ***dismissal.*** ◦ *wrongful arrest/imprisonment* • **wrongfully** /-i/ adv *wrongfully arrested*

wrongheaded /ˌrɒŋˈhed.ɪd/ (US) /ˌrɑːŋ-/ adj disapproving based on ideas or judgments that are not suitable for a particular situation: *He admitted that the party had followed policies now considered wrongheaded.*

wrongly /ˈrɒŋ.li/ (US) /ˈrɑːŋ-/ adv B2 not correctly: *Several people were wrongly convicted.* ◦ *He even spelled his own client's name wrongly.*

wrote /rəʊt/ (US) /roʊt/ verb past simple of **write**

wrought /rɔːt/ (US) /rɑːt/ verb past simple and past participle of **work**: *Mr Simmonds has wrought (= caused) considerable changes in the company.*

ˌwrought ˈiron noun [U] iron that can be bent into attractive shapes and used to make gates, furniture, etc.: *wrought-iron gates*

wrung /rʌŋ/ verb past simple and past participle of **wring**

wry /raɪ/ adj [before noun] showing that you find a bad or difficult situation slightly funny: *a wry smile/comment* • **wryly** /ˈraɪ.li/ adv

the WSPA /ˌdʌb.l̩.juː.es.piːˈeɪ/ noun abbreviation for the World Society for the Protection of Animals

wt noun [U] written abbreviation for WEIGHT (= the amount that something or someone weighs): *On the card she had written: wt 60 kg, ht 1.64 m.*

wtf offensive slang written abbreviation for what the fuck: used, for example in text messages and on SOCIAL NETWORKING websites, to show that you are surprised or annoyed, or do not care about something

wunderkind /ˈwʊn.də.kɪnd/, /ˈvʊn-/ (US) /-dɚ-/ noun [C] a person who is very clever or good at something and achieves success at a young age

wuss /wʊs/ noun [C] slang a **coward** (= person who is not brave): *Damian, you're such a wuss!*

WW1 noun [S not after the] written abbreviation for **World War One**

WW2 noun [S not after the] written abbreviation for **World War Two**

the WWF /ˌdʌb.l̩.juːˌdʌb.l̩.juːˈef/ noun abbreviation for the Worldwide Fund for Nature

www /ˈdʌb.l̩.juːˌdʌb.l̩.juːˈdʌb.l̩.juː/ noun [S] abbreviation for **the World Wide Web**: *Visit the Cambridge University Press website at www.cambridge.org*

WYSIWYG /ˈwɪz.i.wɪg/ adj specialized abbreviation for what you see is what you get: describes an image on a computer screen that is exactly the same when it is printed

W

X, x /eks/ **noun; adj**
▸**noun** [C or U] (plural **Xs**, **X's** or **x's**) LETTER ▷ **1** the 24th letter of the English alphabet NUMBER ▷ **2** (also **x** (plural **x's**)) the sign used in the Roman system for the number 10 VOTE ▷ **3** used when voting to mark the name of the person that you are choosing
▸**adj** used especially in the past to refer to a film or show that is not suitable for people under 18 years old because it contains violence or sex: *an X-rated film* → See also **18**

x /eks/ **noun; verb**
▸**noun** AMOUNT NOT STATED ▷ **1** [U] used to represent a number, or the name of person or thing that is not known or stated: *If 2x = 8, then x = 4.* ◦ *Witness x stated that she had seen Cooper on repeated occasions.* KISS ▷ **2** [C] (plural **x's**) used at the end of an informal piece of writing to represent a kiss: *Write soon, all my love, Katy xxx* WRONG ▷ **3** [C] (plural **x's**) written on an answer to a question to show that the answer is not correct
▸**verb** [T] (present tense **x's**, present participle **x'ing**, past tense and past participle **x'ed**) US to remove something from a list: *I x'ed **out** all the names of the people I wouldn't be sending cards to.*

X-acto knife /ɪɡˌzækt.əʊˈnaɪf/ Ⓤⓢ /-oʊ-/ **noun** [C] US trademark a sharp knife with a short blade that can be replaced

ˈx-ˌaxis noun [S] (also **horiˈzontal ˌaxis**) the line of FIGURES or COORDINATES that are arranged from left to right along the bottom of a GRAPH or map

ˈX-ˌchromosome noun [C] a sex CHROMOSOME (= structure containing chemical patterns) which exists as a pair in the cells of females and with a Y-CHROMOSOME in the cells of male animals

xenon /ˈzen.ɒn/ Ⓤⓢ /-nɑːn/ **noun** [U] (symbol **Xe**) a chemical element that is a gas with no colour or smell, that does not react with other elements and is used in some types of light BULBS

xenophobe /ˈzen.ə.fəʊb/ Ⓤⓢ /-foʊb/ **noun** [C] a person who strongly dislikes or fears FOREIGNERS, their customs, their religions, etc.

xenophobia /ˌzen.əˈfəʊ.bi.ə/ Ⓤⓢ /-ˈfoʊ-/ **noun** [U] C2 extreme dislike or fear of FOREIGNERS, their customs, their religions, etc. • **xenophobic** /-bɪk/ **adj** *a xenophobic mistrust of everything that isn't British*

xerox /ˈzɪə.rɒks/ Ⓤⓢ /ˈzɪr.ɑːks/ **verb** [T] to make a copy of a document by using a Xerox machine

Xerox /ˈzɪə.rɒks/ Ⓤⓢ /ˈzɪr.ɑːks/ **noun** [C] trademark a copy of a document or other piece of paper with writing or printing on it, made by a machine that uses a photographic process, or the machine itself: *a Xerox of the letter* ◦ *a Xerox machine*

the ˈX ˌfactor noun [S] a quality that you cannot describe which makes someone very special: *He's a singer who has the X factor.*

XHTML /ˌeks.eɪtʃ.tiː.emˈel/ **noun** [U] trademark abbreviation for extensible hypertext markup language: a way of marking text to be shown on computer systems and the internet

xi /saɪ/ **noun** [C] the 14th letter of the Greek alphabet

XL /ˌeksˈel/ abbreviation for extra large: the largest size of clothes

Xmas /ˈkrɪs.məs/, /ˈeks.məs/ abbreviation for **Christmas**: *Happy Xmas to all our customers.*

XML /ˌeks.emˈel/ **noun** [U] trademark abbreviation for extensible mark up language: a way of marking text to be shown in computer systems

ˈX-ray noun [C] **1** a type of RADIATION that can go through many solid substances, allowing hidden objects such as bones and organs in the body to be photographed **2** B2 a photograph of a part of the body made using X-rays: *The X-ray showed a slight irregularity in one lung.* **3** an examination of a part of the body by taking and studying an X-ray photograph: *She **had** an X-ray to see if any of her ribs were broken.* • **ˈX-ray verb** [T] *His hip had to be X-rayed.*

xylem /ˈzaɪ.ləm/ **noun** [U] specialized the type of plant tissue that carries water and minerals from the roots to the leaves and gives support to the stem or TRUNK → Compare **phloem**

xylophone /ˈzaɪ.lə.fəʊn/ Ⓤⓢ /-foʊn/ **noun** [C] a musical instrument consisting of flat wooden bars of different lengths that are hit with sticks

Y, y /waɪ/ **noun** [C or U] (plural **Ys**, **Y's** or **y's**) the 25th letter of the English alphabet

y (also **Y**) /waɪ/ **noun** [U] used to represent the second of two numbers or names that are not known or stated, when the first is represented by 'x': *If 2x = 3y and x = 6, then y = 4.* ◦ *The children on trial were referred to as child X and child Y.*

-y /-i/ **suffix** added to nouns to form adjectives meaning like the stated thing: *cheesy*

yacht /jɒt/ (US) /jɑːt/ **noun** [C] B2 a boat with sails and sometimes an engine, used for either racing or travelling on for pleasure: *a luxury yacht* ◦ *the yacht club*

yachting /ˈjɒt.ɪŋ/ (US) /ˈjɑː.t̬ɪŋ/ **noun** [U] the sport or activity of sailing yachts

yachtsman /ˈjɒt.smən/ (US) /ˈjɑːt-/ **noun** [C] (plural **-men** /-mən/) a man who sails or owns a yacht

yachtswoman /ˈjɒtˌswʊm.ən/ (US) /ˈjɑːt-/ **noun** [C] (plural **-women** /-wɪmɪn/) a woman who sails or owns a yacht

yack /jæk/ **verb** [I] slang to talk continuously, especially informally

yada yada yada /ˌjæd.əˌjæd.əˈjæd.ə/ **exclamation** US informal BLAH BLAH BLAH (= a phrase used to represent boring speech)

yahoo /ˈjɑː.huː/ **noun** [C] (plural **yahoos**) informal a rude, loud, unpleasant person, especially one who has little education

yak /jæk/ **noun** [C] a type of CATTLE with long hair and long horns, found mainly in Tibet

yakka (also **yakker**) /ˈjæk.ə/ **noun** [U] Australian English informal work

Yale lock /ˈjeɪlˌlɒk/ (US) /-ˌlɑːk/ **noun** [C] trademark a type of lock, especially for doors, that is cylinder-shaped and is operated by a flat key: *a Yale key*

y'all /jɔːl/ (US) /jɑːl/ **pronoun** US informal used to address a group of people that you are speaking to: *See y'all later.*

yam /jæm/ **noun** [C or U] **1** a potato-like root from a tropical climbing plant that can be eaten, or the plant it grows from **2** US a **sweet potato**

yammer /ˈjæm.əʳ/ (US) /-ɚ/ **verb** [I] mainly US informal to talk continuously for a long time in a way that is annoying to other people: *She was yammering **on/away** about nothing, as usual.*

yang /jæŋ/ **noun** [U] in Chinese PHILOSOPHY, the male principle of the universe, represented as light and positive

yank /jæŋk/ **verb** **1** [T usually + adv/prep] informal to pull something forcefully with a quick movement: *He tripped over the wire and yanked the plug **out**.* ◦ *She yanked open the cupboard and everything fell out.* **2** [T often passive] mainly US informal to suddenly remove someone or something: *I was yanked **out of** school and forced to seek work.* • **yank noun** [C usually singular] informal ***Give** the door a yank and it should open.*

Yank /jæŋk/ **noun** [C] (also **Yankee**) a person from the US: disapproving *The place was full of yanks.*

Yankee /ˈjæŋ.ki/ **noun** [C] **1** informal a **yank** **2** US an American who comes from the Northern US

yap /jæp/ **verb** (**-pp-**) **1** [I] disapproving If a small dog yaps, it makes short, high sounds: *She's got a horrible little dog that yaps around your ankles.* **2** [I usually + adverb] informal disapproving to talk continuously: *I've just had Ian's mother on the phone, yapping **away** for half an hour!* • **yap noun** [C] • **yappy** /ˈjæp.i/ **adj** *a yappy little dog*

yard /jɑːd/ (US) /jɑːrd/ **noun** [C] **UNIT OF MEASUREMENT** ▷ **1** B1 (written abbreviation **yd**) a unit of measurement equal to three feet or approximately 91.4 centimetres **WORK AREA** ▷ **2** an area of land in which a particular type of work is done, often one from which goods are sold: *a builders' yard* ◦ *a scrap yard* → See also **boatyard, dockyard, junkyard, lumberyard, shipyard, stockyard** **LAND NEXT TO BUILDING** ▷ **3** an area of land next to a building which is covered with concrete or other hard material: *The house has a small yard at the back.* ◦ *the prison yard* → See also **backyard, barnyard, farmyard** **GARDEN** ▷ **4** A2 US (UK **garden**) a piece of land next to a house, usually used for growing flowers, grass, and other plants

Yardie /ˈjɑː.di/ (US) /ˈjɑːr.di/ **noun** [C] a member of a violent criminal organization, involved especially with illegal drugs, that started in Jamaica and now also operates in the UK

yardstick /ˈjɑːd.stɪk/ (US) /ˈjɑːrd-/ **noun** [C] a fact or standard by which you can judge the success or value of something: *Productivity is not the only yardstick **of** success.*

yarmulke /ˈjɑː.mʊl.kə/ (US) /ˈjɑːr-/ **noun** [C] a small, circular cover for the head worn by Jewish men, especially at religious ceremonies

yarn /jɑːn/ (US) /jɑːrn/ **noun** **THREAD** ▷ **1** [C or U] thread used for making cloth or for KNITTING **STORY** ▷ **2** [C] a story, usually a long one with a lot of excitement or interest: *He knew how to **spin** a **good** yarn (= tell a good story).*

yashmak /ˈjæʃ.mæk/ **noun** [C] a piece of cloth worn by some Muslim women to cover parts of the face when they are in public

yaw /jɔː/ (US) /jɑː/ **verb** [I] specialized If an aircraft or ship yaws, it moves slightly to the side of its intended direction. • **yaw noun** [C or U]

yawn /jɔːn/ (US) /jɑːn/ **verb; noun**

▸**verb** [I] B1 to open the mouth wide and take a lot of air into the lungs and slowly send it out, usually when tired or bored: *I can't stop yawning – I must be tired.*

▸**noun** **1** [C] an act of yawning: *Her eyes watered as she tried to **stifle** (= stop) a yawn.* **2** **a yawn** [S] informal something or someone that is very boring: *We have to go to dinner with Simon's boss on Saturday which is a bit of a yawn.*

yawning /ˈjɔː.nɪŋ/ (US) /ˈjɑː-/ **adj** [before noun] **1** describes a difference or amount that is extremely large and difficult to reduce: *There exists nowadays a yawning **gap between** fashion and style.* **2** describes a space or hole that is very wide: *a yawning crevasse*

ˈy-ˌaxis **noun** [S] (also **ˈvertical ˌaxis**) the line of FIGURES or COORDINATES that are arranged from top to bottom at the side of a GRAPH or map

yay /jeɪ/ **exclamation; adv**

▸**exclamation** informal used to show that you are very pleased about something: *'We won.' 'Yay!'*

▸**adv** informal **1** so; to a particular degree: *It was about yay long.* **2** very; much: *a yay good trip*

ˈY-ˌchromosome **noun** [C] a sex CHROMOSOME (= structure containing chemical patterns) that exists only in male cells: *If a Y-chromosome combines with an X-chromosome during fertilization, a male baby will result.*

yd written abbreviation for **yard**

ye /jiː/ **pronoun; determiner**
▸**pronoun** old use a word meaning 'you', used when talking to more than one person
▸**determiner** old use a word meaning 'the', used especially in the names of PUBS to make them seem old: *a pub in the village called Ye Olde Barn*

IDIOM **ye gods!** old-fashioned or humorous used to show surprise: *Ye gods man, what are you doing!*

yea /jeɪ/ **adv** old use yes

IDIOM **yea or nay** yes or no: *They have the power to hire and fire managers and* ***say*** *yea or nay* ***to*** *big investment projects.*

yeah (also **yeh**) /jeə/ **adv** informal A2 yes: *'Do you like your job?' 'Yeah, it's all right I suppose.'* ◦ *'Will you drive?' 'Yeah, sure.'*

IDIOM **yeah, right!** (also **oh yeah.**, also **yeah, yeah**) used when you do not believe what someone has said: *'I always miss you when I go travelling.' 'Yeah, right!'* ◦ *'Anyway, we're just good friends.' 'Yeah, yeah!'* ◦ *'I can run faster than you any day!' 'Oh yeah?'*

year /jɪəʳ/ US /jɪr/ **noun 1** A1 [C] a period of twelve months, especially from 1 January to 31 December: *Annette worked in Italy for two years.* ◦ *1988 was one of the worst years of my life.* ◦ *We went to Egypt on holiday* ***last*** *year.* ◦ *At this* ***time of*** *year the beaches are almost deserted.* ◦ *This species keeps its leaves* ***all*** *(the) year* ***(round)*** (= through the year). **2** [C] a period of twelve months relating to a particular activity: *The* ***financial/tax*** *year begins in April.* **3** A2 [C] the part of the year, in a school or university, during which courses are taught: *the academic/school year* ◦ *She's now* ***in her final/first/second year*** *at Manchester University.* **4** [C, + sing/pl verb] UK a group of students who start school, college, university, or a course together: *Kathy was in the year above me at college.*

> **! Common mistake: year**
> **Remember:** After a number greater than 1, don't say 'year', say **years**:
> ~~*I spent two year in London studying English.*~~
> *I spent two years in London studying English.*

> **Word partners for year**
> *each/every/last/next* year • the *past* year • [3/20] years *old* • [2/5] years *ago*

IDIOMS **for a man/woman/person of his/her years** considering how old someone is: *He dances well for a man of his years.* • **for years 1** B1 for a long time: *Roz and I have been going there for years.* **2** (also **in years**) since a long time ago: *I haven't seen my uncle for/in years.* • **from/since the year dot** UK (US **from/since the year one**) for an extremely long time • **of the year** A thing or person of the year is one that has been chosen as the best in a particular year, especially in a competition: *Young Musician of the Year* • **put years on sb** If something puts years on a person, it makes them appear much older: *Being tired and unhappy puts years on you.* • **take years off sb** If something takes years off a person, it makes them appear or feel much younger: *'Have you seen James without his beard?' 'I know – it takes years off him!'* • **year in, year out** every year, especially in a way that seems boring: *We go to Mike's parents every summer – it's the same thing year in, year out.*

-year /-jɪəʳ/ US /-jɪr/ **suffix** UK used to refer to a student in a particular year group at a school, college, or university: *I like teaching the first-years, but the second-years can be difficult.* ◦ *a first-year student*

yearbook /ˈjɪə.bʊk/ US /ˈjɪr-/ **noun** [C] (US also **annual**) a book published every year by a school or other organization, that gives various facts about the events and achievements of the previous or present year → See also **annual**

ˌyear ˈend noun [singular] (US **ˌyear's ˈend**) the end of the financial year, or the end of December: *Banks have been slow to increase their lending at year end.* ◦ *The year-end results will be published this week.*

yearly /ˈjɪə.li/ US /ˈjɪr-/ **adj, adv** every year or once every year: *We get a yearly pay increase.* ◦ *Interest is paid yearly.*

yearn /jɜːn/ US /jɝːn/ **verb** [I] C2 to wish very strongly, especially for something that you cannot have or something that is very difficult to have: *Despite his great commercial success he still yearns* ***for*** *critical approval.* ◦ [+ to infinitive] *Sometimes I just yearn* ***to*** *be alone.*

yearning /ˈjɜː.nɪŋ/ US /ˈjɝː-/ **noun** [C or U] a strong feeling of wishing for something, especially something that you cannot have or get easily: *I suppose it's because I live in a city that I have this yearning* ***for*** *open spaces.*

ˌyear's ˈend noun [singular] **year end**

yeast /jiːst/ **noun** [C or U] a type of FUNGUS that is used in making alcoholic drinks such as beer and wine, and for making bread swell and become light: *dried/fresh yeast* ◦ *yeast extract* • **yeasty** /ˈjiː.sti/ **adj**

yeh /jeə/ **adv** informal **yeah**

yell /jel/ **verb** [I or T] B2 to shout something or make a loud noise, usually when you are angry, in pain, or excited: *Our neighbours were yelling (obscenities)* ***at*** *each other this morning.* ◦ *The child yelled* ***out*** *in pain.* ◦ [+ speech] *'Just get out of here!' she yelled.* • **yell noun** [C usually singular] B2 *Suddenly there was a* ***loud/great*** *yell from the bathroom.*

yellow /ˈjel.əʊ/ US /-oʊ/ **noun; adj; verb**
▸**noun** [C or U] A1 a colour like that of a lemon or gold or the sun: *It was early autumn and the leaves were turning yellow.* ◦ *You should wear more yellow – it suits you.* • **yellowness** /-nəs/ **noun** [U]
▸**adj** COLOUR ▷ **1** A1 of a colour like that of a lemon or gold or the sun: *a bright yellow flower/T-shirt* PEOPLE ▷ **2** offensive belonging to a race that has pale yellowish-brown skin NOT BRAVE ▷ **3** informal easily frightened and not brave → Synonym **cowardly**
▸**verb** [I or T] to become yellow, or to make something become yellow

ˌyellow ˈcard noun [C usually singular] in football, a small, yellow card that is shown to a player by the REFEREE (= the official who is responsible for making certain the rules are followed) as a warning that the player has not obeyed a rule

ˌyellow ˈfever noun [U] an infectious tropical disease which causes the skin to become yellow and can result in death

yellowish /ˈjel.əʊ.ɪʃ/ US /-oʊ-/ **adj** (also **yellowy**) slightly yellow: *The leaves vary from yellowish-green to dark green.*

ˌyellow ˈline noun [C] in Britain, a line of yellow paint that is put along the sides of particular roads to

Y

show that vehicles cannot be parked there at stated times → See also **double yellow line**

the ˌYellow ˈPages noun [S] trademark a large, yellow book which contains the addresses and phone numbers of businesses and people offering services, listing them in groups according to what type of business they are → Compare **the White Pages**

yelp /jelp/ **verb** [I] to make a sudden, short, high sound, usually when in pain: *I accidentally trod on the dog's foot and it yelped.* • **yelp noun** [C]

yen /jen/ **noun** (plural **yen**) **MONEY** ▷ **1** [C] (symbol ¥) the standard unit of money used in Japan: *She earns 400,000 yen a month as an English teacher in Tokyo.* **2 the yen** [S] the value of the yen, used in comparing the values of different types of money from around the world: *The yen **fell/rose against** (= was worth less/more compared to) the dollar today.* **WISH** ▷ **3** [C usually singular] informal a strong feeling of wanting or wishing for something: *I have a yen **for** travelling.*

yeoman /ˈjəʊ.mən/ (US) /ˈjoʊ-/ **noun** [C] (plural **-men** /-mən/) in the past, a man who was not a servant and owned and CULTIVATED (= grew crops on) an area of land

yep /jep/ **adv** informal yes: *'Do I press this button?' 'Yep, that's right.'*

yer /jəʳ/ (US) /jɚ/ **determiner** informal your: *Get yer hands off me!*

yes /jes/ **adv; noun**

▸**adv** (informal **yeah**, **yep**, **yah**) **1** (A1) used to express willingness or agreement: *'Would you like a glass of wine?' 'Yes please.'* ◦ *'Do you like Thai food?' 'Yes, I love it.'* ◦ *'He's a really nice guy.' 'Yes he is.'* ◦ *'Report to me at nine o'clock tomorrow morning.' 'Yes, sir.'* ◦ *'Have you had enough to eat?' 'Yes, thank you.'* ◦ *If you'd **say** yes (= agree) to the request you'd save a lot of trouble.* **2** (A1) used to show that you are listening to someone, or that you are ready to listen and to give them an answer or information: *'Dad.' 'Yes, what do you want, honey?'* ◦ *Yes, can I help you?* **3** (A2) used when you are disagreeing with a negative statement: *'I'm not a very good cook though.' 'Yes you are – you make wonderful food!'*

IDIOMS **oh yes** (also **oh yeah**) used when you have just remembered something that you were saying: *What was I talking about – oh yes, I was telling you what happened at the party.* • **yes and no** used when you cannot give a particular answer to a question: *'Is the job going okay?' 'Well, yes and no.'*

▸**noun** [C] a vote supporting a particular plan of action or a reply accepting an invitation: *'Have you had any replies yet?' 'Six yeses and two noes so far.'*

ˈyes-man **noun** [C] (plural **-men**) disapproving a person who agrees with everything their employer, leader, etc. says in order to please them

yesterday /ˈjes.tə.deɪ/ (US) /-tɚ-/ **adv; noun**

▸**adv** (A1) on the day before today: *He rang yesterday while you were out.* ◦ *I saw her yesterday afternoon.*

▸**noun 1** [U] the day before today: *'Is that today's paper?' 'No, it's yesterday's.'* **2 the day before yesterday** two days ago: *I rang her the day before yesterday.* **3** [C or U] the recent past: *Nobody's interested in yesterday's pop stars.* ◦ *These songs are a part of **all our** yesterdays.*

yesteryear /ˈjes.tə.jɪəʳ/ (US) /-tɚ.jɪr/ **noun** [U] literary a time in the past: *the Hollywood stars **of** yesteryear*

yet /jet/ **adv; adv, conjunction**

▸**adv UNTIL NOW** ▷ **1** (A2) still; until the present time: *I haven't spoken to her yet.* ◦ *He hasn't finished yet.* ◦ *'Are you ready?' 'Not yet – wait a moment.'* **2 the best, worst, etc. yet** (B2) the best, worst, etc. until now: *Of all the songs I've heard tonight, that's the best yet.* **3 as yet** (C1) formal until and including this time: *We haven't needed extra staff as yet, but may do in the future.* ◦ *No ambulances had as yet managed to get across the river.* **IN THE FUTURE** ▷ **4** (C1) from now and for a particular period of time in the future: *She won't be back for a long time yet.* ◦ *Our holiday isn't for weeks yet.* **5 have yet to** (C2) If you have yet to do something, you have not done it: *They have yet to make a decision.* **EVEN NOW** ▷ **6** (C2) even at this stage or time: *We could yet succeed – you never know.* ◦ *You **might** yet prove me wrong.* ◦ *He **may** win yet.* **MORE** ▷ **7** (B2) used to add emphasis to words such as another and again, especially to show an increase in amount or the number of times something happens: *Rachel bought yet **another** pair of shoes to add to her collection.* ◦ *I'm sorry to bother you yet **again**.* ◦ *He's given us yet **more** work to do.*

▸**adv, conjunction** (B1) (and) despite that; used to add something that seems surprising because of what you have just said: *simple yet effective* ◦ *He's overweight and bald, (**and**) yet somehow, he's attractive.*

yeti /ˈjet.i/ (US) /ˈjet̬-/ **noun** [C] (also **aˌbominable ˈsnowman**) a big creature like a human covered in hair that is believed by some people to live in the Himalayas

yew /juː/ **noun** [C or U] an EVERGREEN tree (= one that never loses its leaves) with flat leaves like needles and small, red CONES, or the wood from this tree: *a yew tree* ◦ *a bowl made from yew*

ˈY-fronts **noun** [plural] UK trademark a piece of underwear for men and boys, covering the area between the waist and the tops of the legs, with an opening at the front in the shape of an upside-down Y

yid /jɪd/ **noun** [C] offensive a Jewish person

Yiddish /ˈjɪd.ɪʃ/ **noun; adj**

▸**noun** [U] a language related to German that is spoken by some Jewish people

▸**adj** in or relating to Yiddish

yield /jiːld/ **verb; noun**

▸**verb PRODUCE** ▷ **1** (C2) [T] to supply or produce something positive such as a profit, an amount of food, or information: *an attempt to yield increased profits* ◦ *The investigation yielded some unexpected results.* ◦ *Favourable weather yielded a good crop.* **GIVE UP** ▷ **2** [I or T] to give up the control of or responsibility for something, often because you have been forced to: *They were forced to yield (**up**) their land **to** the occupying forces.* ◦ *Despite renewed pressure to give up the occupied territory, they will not yield.* **BEND/BREAK** ▷ **3** [I] formal to bend or break under pressure: *His legs began to yield under the sheer weight of his body.*

PHRASAL VERB **yield to sth AGREE** ▷ **1** to agree to do something that you do not want to do or should not do: *It's very easy to yield to temptation and spend too much money.* ◦ *'We will not yield to pressure,' said the president.* **STOP** ▷ **2** (C1) US (UK **give way**) to stop in order to allow other vehicles to go past before you drive onto a bigger road

▸**noun** [C usually plural] an amount of something positive, such as food or profit, that is produced or supplied: ***Crop** yields have risen steadily.* ◦ *Yields on gas and electricity shares are consistently high.*

yielding /ˈjiːl.dɪŋ/ **adj** formal **SOFT** ▷ **1** describes soft substances or qualities that can bend: *a yielding mire of wet leaves* ◦ *yielding flesh/softness* **PERSON** ▷ **2** describes a person who can change the way they normally behave or deal with situations when it is helpful or necessary

Y

yin /jɪn/ **noun** [U] in Chinese PHILOSOPHY, the female principle of the universe, represented as dark and negative

yippee /jɪˈpiː/ US /ˈjɪp.iː/ **exclamation** informal used to express happiness, excitement, or great satisfaction: *No school for five weeks – yippee!*

ymmv written abbreviation for your mileage may vary: used, in emails for example, to warn people that a piece of advice, although it has helped you, might not help them, or to say that different things are attractive to different people: *Their first album is better, but of course YMMV.*

yo /jəʊ/ US /joʊ/ **exclamation** slang used as an informal greeting between people who know each other or as an expression of approval: *'Yo, Mickie! How's things?'*

yob /jɒb/ US /jɑːb/ **noun** [C] (also **yobbo** /jɒb.əʊ/ US /ˈjɑː.boʊ/) UK informal a young man who behaves in a very rude, offensive, and sometimes violent way: *a gang of loud-mouthed yobs*

yodel /ˈjəʊ.dəl/ US /ˈjoʊ-/ **verb; noun**
▸**verb** [I] (-ll- or US usually -l-) to sing by making a series of very fast changes between the natural voice and a much higher voice
▸**noun** [C] a song or a part of a song that is yodelled

yoga /ˈjəʊ.gə/ US /ˈjoʊ-/ **noun** [U] **1** B1 a set of physical and mental exercises, originally from India, intended to give control over the body and mind: *a yoga class* **2** a Hindu system of PHILOSOPHY which aims to unite the SELF with god • **yogic** /-gɪk/ **adj** *yogic exercises*

yogi /ˈjəʊ.gi/ US /ˈjoʊ-/ **noun** [C] a person who has spent a lot of their life doing yoga and studying the PHILOSOPHY of yoga

yogurt (also **yoghurt**, **yoghourt**) /ˈjɒg.ət/ US /ˈjoʊ.gɚt/ **noun** [C or U] A2 a slightly sour, thick liquid made from milk with bacteria added to it, sometimes eaten plain and sometimes with sugar, fruit, etc. added: *natural/plain yogurt ◦ strawberry yogurt ◦ low-fat yogurt ◦ I only had a yogurt (= a container of this) for lunch.*

yoke /jəʊk/ US /joʊk/ **noun; verb**
▸**noun** [C] **WOODEN BAR** ▷ **1** a wooden bar that is fastened over the necks of two animals, especially CATTLE, and connected to the vehicle or LOAD that they are pulling **CLOTHES** ▷ **2** a fitted part of a piece of clothing, especially a strip that goes around the shoulders or waist, to which is sewn a looser piece of material **CONNECTION** ▷ **3** formal something that connects two things or people, usually in a way that unfairly limits freedom: *the yoke of marriage ◦ Both countries had thrown off the communist yoke.*
▸**verb** **WOODEN BAR** ▷ **1** [T] to put a yoke on animals, especially CATTLE, so that they are fastened together and to a connected vehicle or LOAD: *Two oxen yoked **to** a plough walked wearily up and down the field.* **CONNECT** ▷ **2** [T often passive] formal to combine or connect two things: *All these different political elements have somehow been yoked **together** to form a new alliance.*

yokel /ˈjəʊ.kəl/ US /ˈjoʊ-/ **noun** [C] usually humorous a stupid or awkward person who lives in the countryside rather than a town, especially one whose appearance is in some way strange or humorous: *He plays the **country** yokel in the butter ad.*

yolk /jəʊk/ US /joʊk/ **noun** [C or U] the yellow, middle part of an egg: *I like eggs lightly cooked so that the yolk is still runny. ◦ Separate the yolks from the whites.*

Yom Kippur /jɒm.kɪˈpʊəʳ/ US /jɑːmˈkɪp.ɚ/ **noun** [U] (also **the ˌDay of Aˈtonement**) a Jewish holy day in September or October when nothing is eaten all day and people say prayers in the SYNAGOGUE asking God to forgive them for things they have done wrong

yomp /jɒmp/ US /jɑːmp/ **verb** [I] UK (often of soldiers) to walk quickly and energetically, usually while carrying a lot of equipment: *Energetic types can be out before breakfast and yomp about the hills until 10 a.m.* • **yomp noun** [C] *The captain completed a 30-mile yomp across Dartmoor with five minutes to spare.*

yonder /ˈjɒn.dəʳ/ US /ˈjɑːn.dɚ/ **determiner, adv** (also **yon**) in the place or direction shown; over there

yonks /jɒŋks/ US /jɑːŋks/ **noun** [U] UK old-fashioned informal a very long time, usually a number of years: *How is Gareth? I haven't seen him for yonks!*

yoof /juːf/ **adj; noun**
▸**adj** [before noun] UK not standard humorous relating to young people, especially those influenced by the most recent fashions and ideas: *The adverts target yoof culture.*
▸**noun** [U] UK not standard humorous young people: *He's a comedian who claims to be the voice of British yoof.*

yoo-hoo /ˈjuː.huː/ **exclamation** old-fashioned informal used to attract a person's attention: *Yoo-hoo, we're over here!*

yore /jɔːʳ/ US /jɔːr/ **noun** literary **of yore** of a long time ago: *This was once a Roman road **in days** of yore.*

Yorkshire pudding /ˈjɔːk.ʃəˌpʊd.ɪŋ/ US /ˈjɔːrk.ʃɚ-/, /-ʃɪr-/ **noun** [C or U] a type of food from England that is a baked mixture of flour, milk, and eggs, traditionally eaten with ROAST BEEF

you /juː/, /jə/, /jʊ/ **pronoun** **PERSON/PEOPLE ADDRESSED** ▷ **1** A1 used to refer to the person or people being spoken or written to: *You look nice. ◦ I love you. ◦ You said I could go with you. ◦ You're coming tonight, aren't you? ◦ Are you two ready? ◦ You painted that yourself? You clever girl!*

> **! Common mistake: you or your?**
> **Warning:** do not confuse the pronoun **you** with the determiner **your**:
> ~~*I was so pleased to receive you letter.*~~
> *I was so pleased to receive your letter.*

PEOPLE GENERALLY ▷ **2** A2 people in general: *You learn to accept these things as you get older. ◦ You can't get a driving licence till you're 17 in this country. ◦ Too much alcohol is bad for you. ◦ How do you get this thing to start?*

you'd /juːd/ **short form of 1** you had: *It happened just after you'd left the room.* **2** you would: *You'd be much warmer in your black jacket.*

you'll /juːl/ **short form of** you will: *You'll remember to tell her, won't you.*

young /jʌŋ/ **adj; noun**
▸**adj 1** A1 having lived or existed for only a short time and not old: *young adults/children ◦ His girlfriend's very young. ◦ The trees in this part of the forest are still quite young. ◦ Philippa is the youngest person in the family. ◦ Angela is two years younger than Clare.* **2** suitable for young people: *young fashion/ideas ◦ Be honest now – do you think this dress is **a bit/too** young for me (= is more suitable for someone younger)?* **3 look young for your age** to look younger than you really are

IDIOMS **young at heart** thinking and behaving as if you are younger than you really are: *Dad might be nearly 90 but he's still young at heart.* • **young lady/man 1** used when you are speaking angrily to a young person: *Mind your language, young lady!* **2** old-fashioned or humorous someone's GIRLFRIEND or BOY-

Y

FRIEND: *If you'd care to bring your young man along too, we should be delighted to meet him.* • **young love** love between young people

▸**noun** [plural] **1 the young** B2 young people considered together as a group: *I have nothing against miniskirts, but I think they're strictly for the young.* **2** the babies of an animal: *Meanwhile, the mother flies back to the nest to feed her young.*

ˌyoung ˈblood noun [U] young people who have a lot of energy and ideas: *We need to introduce more young blood into the organization.*

ˌyoung ofˈfenders' instiˌtution noun [C] a special place for people who have done bad things and are too young to be sent to prison

youngster /ˈjʌŋ.stəʳ/ US /-stɚ/ noun [C] C1 a young person, usually an older child: *The scheme is for youngsters between the ages of ten and 16.*

your strong /jɔːʳ/ US /jʊr/ weak /jəʳ/ US /jɚ/ determiner PERSON/PEOPLE ADDRESSED ▷ **1** A1 belonging or relating to the person or group of people being spoken or written to: *Is this your bag?* ◦ *It's not your fault.* ◦ *What's your problem?* PEOPLE GENERALLY ▷ **2** B1 belonging or relating to people generally: *Of course you want the best for your children.* ◦ *Garlic is good for your blood.* **3** informal said before a typical example of something is given: *This isn't your usual science-fiction novel, but then Brinkworth isn't exactly your typical author.*

> **!** Common mistake: **your or yours?**
>
> **Warning:** do not confuse the determiner **your** with the pronoun **yours**:
>
> ~~*Your sincerely, M. Henderson.*~~
>
> *Yours sincerely, M. Henderson.*

you're strong /jɔːʳ/ US /jʊr/ weak /jəʳ/ US /jɚ/ short form you are: *You're so nice to me!*

yours /jɔːz/ US /jʊrz/ pronoun PERSON/PEOPLE ADDRESSED ▷ **1** A2 the one(s) belonging to or connected with the person or group of people being spoken or written to: *Is this pen yours?* ◦ *Unfortunately my legs aren't as long as yours.* ◦ *I've got something **of** yours (= that belongs to you).* ◦ *Yours is the room on the top floor, on the left.* **2** B1 used at the beginning of some phrases written at the end of a letter, before giving a name: *Yours, Jack* ◦ UK *Yours **faithfully/sincerely**, K. Maxwell.* PEOPLE GENERALLY ▷ **3** used to show that something belongs to or is connected with people generally: *Other people's children always seem to be better behaved than yours.*

IDIOM **yours truly** informal used to mean the person who is speaking or writing, often when they are talking about something they have done unwillingly: *She didn't have any money, so yours truly ended up having to lend her some.*

yourself strong /jɔːˈself/ US /jʊr-/ weak /jə-/ US /jɚ-/ pronoun (plural **yourselves**) PERSON/PEOPLE ADDRESSED ▷ **1** A2 used when the subject of the verb is 'you' or the person being spoken to, and the object is the same person: *Be careful with that knife or you'll cut yourself!* ◦ *Katie, control yourself!* **2** A2 used for emphasis when the subject is 'you': *Did you make the dress yourself?* ◦ *You can do that yourself.* **3 be yourself** to behave in your usual manner, rather than behaving in a way you think other people might like: *The best thing you can do is to go into the interview and just be yourself.* **4 (all) by yourself** A2 alone or without help from anyone else: *I'm amazed you managed to move those boxes all by yourself.* ◦ *Do you like being by yourself sometimes or do you get lonely?* **5 (all) to yourself** for your use only: *So you've got the whole house to yourself this weekend?* **6 not be/seem/feel yourself** not to be, seem, or feel as happy or healthy as usual: *Why don't you go home early if you're not feeling yourself?* **7 in yourself** UK informal used when asking someone about their state of mind when they are physically ill: *I know you must still be uncomfortable, but how are you in yourself?* PEOPLE GENERALLY ▷ **8** B2 used when both the subject and object of the verb are 'you' and 'you' is also being used to refer to people generally: *You tell yourself everything's all right but you know it's not really.*

Y

youth /juːθ/ noun PERIOD/STATE ▷ **1** B2 [S or U] the period of your life when you are young, or the state of being young: *I was a fairly good football player **in** my youth.* ◦ *The first volume is the author's account of his **misspent** youth in the bars of Dublin.* ◦ *He looks like a man who's found the secret to **eternal** youth (= staying young).* ◦ *You may not have played tennis as often as him, but at least you've got youth on your side (= you are young).* BOY ▷ **2** [C] disapproving a boy or a young man: *Gangs of youths were throwing stones and bottles at the police.* YOUNG PEOPLE ▷ **3** B1 [U, + sing/pl verb] young people, both male and female, considered as a group: *the youth of today* ◦ *the nation's disaffected youth*

ˈyouth ˌclub noun [C] a place where older children can go to meet other children, play sports, and do other social activities

ˈyouth ˌculture noun [U] young people's opinions and the way they live

youthful /ˈjuːθ.fəl/ adj approving **1** having the qualities that are typical of young people: *At the time I admired his youthful enthusiasm.* ◦ *She has very youthful skin.* **2** young: *A youthful president can be good for a country's morale.* • **youthfully** /-i/ adv • **youthfulness** /-nəs/ noun [U]

ˈyouth ˌhostel noun [C] a place where people, especially young people, can stay cheaply for short periods when they are travelling

ˈyouth-ˌhostelling (US usually **ˈyouth-ˌhosteling**) noun [U] the activity of travelling and staying in different youth hostels: *I used to **go** youth-hostelling when I was a student.*

you've strong /juːv/ weak /jəv/ short form of you have: *If you've finished your pasta, then you can have some cake.*

yowl /jaʊl/ verb [I] to make a long, high, unhappy cry, usually when hurt or fighting: *I was woken up by cats yowling outside my window.* • **yowl** noun [C]

ˈyo-yo noun; adj

yo-yo

▸**noun** [C] (plural **yo-yos**) trademark a toy consisting of a circular object that can be made to go up and down a long piece of string to which it is tied

▸**adj** describes something that moves up and down quickly, or something that changes repeatedly between one level and another: *yo-yo **dieting***

yuan /jʊˈɑːn/ noun [C] (plural **yuan**) (symbol ¥) the standard unit of money used in the People's Republic of China → Compare **renminbi**

yucca /ˈjʌk.ə/ noun [C] a plant with long, stiff leaves on a thick stem and sometimes white, bell-shaped flowers

yuck (also **yuk**) /jʌk/ exclamation informal an expression of DISGUST (= disapproval and dislike): *'Yuck, what a revolting smell!'*

yucky (also **yukky**) /ˈjʌk.i/ **adj** informal DISGUSTING or unpleasant: *a yucky green colour*

Yule /juːl/ **noun** [C or U] literary Christmas

ˈyule ˌlog **noun** [C] a cylinder-shaped chocolate cake, eaten at Christmas, that is decorated to look like a LOG (= a thick piece of wood from a tree)

Yuletide /ˈjuːl.taɪd/ **noun** [C or U] old-fashioned or literary the period around Christmas

yum /jʌm/ **exclamation** (also **ˌyum ˈyum**) used to say that food tastes or smells very good

yummy /ˈjʌm.i/ **adj** informal **1** tasting extremely good: *I think I'll have some more of that yummy chocolate cake.* ◦ *There are some yummy-**looking** desserts over there.* **2** sexually attractive: *And tell her to bring along that yummy brother of hers.*

ˌyummy ˈmummy **noun** [C] informal a very attractive woman who is a mother

yuppie (also **yuppy**) /ˈjʌp.i/ **noun** [C] disapproving a young person who lives in a city, earns a lot of money and spends it doing fashionable things and buying expensive possessions

yuppify /ˈjʌp.ɪ.faɪ/ **verb** [T] informal disapproving to change the appearance of a place to suit or attract people who earn and spend a lot of money

yurt /jɜːt/ Ⓤⓢ /jɜːt/ **noun** [C] a type of round tent with a wooden frame, used traditionally as a home by some Central Asian people, and now sometimes used for CAMPING in Western countries

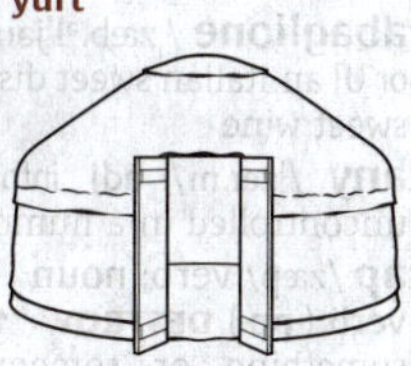

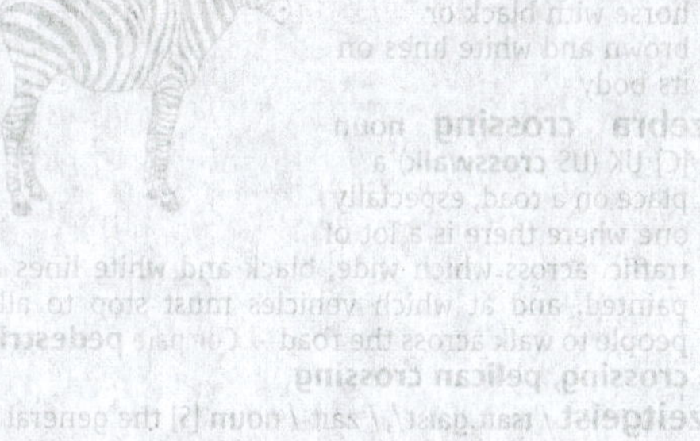

Z

Z, z /zed/ (US) /ziː/ **noun** [C or U] (plural **Zs**, **Z's** or **z's**) the 26th and last letter of the English alphabet

IDIOM **catch/cop/get some z's** US informal to sleep: *All I want to do is go home and catch some z's.*

zabaglione /ˌzæb.əlˈjəʊ.ni/ (US) /ˌzɑː.bəlˈjoʊ-/ **noun** [C or U] an Italian sweet dish made from eggs, sugar, and sweet wine

zany /ˈzeɪ.ni/ **adj** informal strange, surprising, or uncontrolled in a humorous way: *a zany film*

zap /zæp/ **verb; noun**

▸**verb** (-pp-) **DESTROY** ▷ **1** [T] informal to destroy or kill something or someone, especially intentionally: *They've got the kind of weapons that can zap the enemy from thousands of miles away.* ◦ figurative *We're really going to zap the competition with this new product!* **GO QUICKLY** ▷ **2** [I or T, usually + adv/prep] informal to go somewhere or do something quickly: *Have I got time to zap into town and do some shopping?* ◦ *George zapped through his homework and rushed out to play football.* ◦ *There are now over a million American fax machines zapping (= sending quickly) messages from coast to coast.* → See also **zip 3** [I usually + adv/prep] informal to use an electronic device to change television CHANNELS quickly, sometimes to avoid watching advertisements

▸**noun** [U] mainly US informal energy and enthusiasm: *She needs to put a bit more zap into her performance.* • **zappy** /ˈzæp.i/ **adj** *a zappy tune*

zapper /ˈzæp.əʳ/ (US) /-ɚ/ **noun** [C] informal a device for controlling a machine from a distance: *Use the zapper to turn off the TV.*

zeal /ziːl/ **noun** [S or U] great enthusiasm or eagerness: *reforming/missionary/religious zeal* ◦ *a zeal **for** money-making*

zealot /ˈzel.ət/ **noun** [C] a person who has very strong opinions about something, and tries to make other people have them too: *a religious zealot*

zealous /ˈzel.əs/ **adj** enthusiastic and eager: *a zealous supporter of the government's policies* • **zealously** /-li/ **adv** • **zealousness** /-nəs/ **noun** [U]

zebra /ˈzeb.rə/, /ˈziː.brə/ **noun** [C] (plural **zebras** or **zebra**) (B2) an African wild animal that looks like a horse with black or brown and white lines on its body

zebra

ˌzebra ˈcrossing **noun** [C] UK (US **crosswalk**) a place on a road, especially one where there is a lot of traffic, across which wide, black and white lines are painted, and at which vehicles must stop to allow people to walk across the road → Compare **pedestrian crossing, pelican crossing**

zeitgeist /ˈtsaɪt.gaɪst/, /ˈzaɪt-/ **noun** [S] the general set of ideas, beliefs, feelings, etc. that is typical of a particular period in history

zen /zen/ **adj** UK informal relaxed and not worrying about things that you cannot change: *There's nothing you can do to change the situation so you just have to be a bit more zen about it.*

Zen /zen/ **noun** [U] a form of Buddhism originally developed in Japan that emphasizes that religious knowledge is achieved through emptying the mind of thoughts and giving attention to only one thing, rather than by reading religious writings: *Zen Buddhism*

zenith /ˈzen.ɪθ/ **noun** [C usually singular] the best or most successful point or time: *In the 1860s, Tolstoy was **at** the zenith **of** his achievement.* ◦ *His career **reached** its zenith in the 1960s.* → Opposite **nadir**

zephyr /ˈzef.əʳ/ (US) /-ɚ/ **noun** [C] literary a light wind

Zeppelin /ˈzep.əl.ɪn/ **noun** [C] a large AIRSHIP (= an aircraft without wings, containing gas to make it lighter than air, and with an engine)

zero /ˈzɪə.rəʊ/ (US) /ˈzɪr.oʊ/ **number; adj; verb**

▸**number** (plural **zeros**) **1** (A2) [C or U] (the number) 0; nothing: *Five, four, three, two, one, zero.* ◦ *The number one million is written with a one and six zeros.* ◦ *Heavy rain has reduced visibility almost to zero (= its lowest point).* **2** (B1) [U] on a set of numbers for comparing temperature in degrees Celsius, the level of temperature at which water freezes: *The temperature is expected to drop to ten degrees below zero tonight.*

▸**adj** not any or no: *zero growth/inflation* ◦ informal *He said that his chances of getting the job were zero (= he had no chance).*

▸**verb** (present tense **zeroes**)

PHRASAL VERBS **zero in on sth/sb** to aim a weapon directly at something or someone: *Modern military aircraft use computers to help them zero in on their targets.* • **zero in on sth** to direct all your attention towards a particular thing: *We must decide on our target market, then zero in on it.*

ˌzero-ˈcarbon **adj** [before noun] A zero-carbon building, activity, business, etc., is one that does not involve any CARBON DIOXIDE being added to the ATMOSPHERE. → See also **carbon-neutral**

ˈzero ˌhour **noun** [U] **1** the time at which something, especially some type of military activity, is planned to begin **2** Indian English in the Indian parliament, the time during which members of parliament can ask questions without arranging to ask them first

ˌzero-ˈsum **adj** [before noun] describes a situation in which any win by one person always means a loss to another person involved: *The stock market is now a zero-sum **game**, in which one party gains what the other loses.*

ˌzero ˈtolerance **noun** [U] the act of punishing all criminal or unacceptable behaviour severely, even if not very serious: *The police are exercising a new policy of zero tolerance against motoring offenders.*

zest /zest/ **noun** **EXCITEMENT** ▷ **1** [S or U] enthusiasm, eagerness, energy, and interest: *It's wonderful to see the children's zest **for life**.* ◦ *The recording captures the zest **of** this live concert performance.* **FRUIT SKIN** ▷ **2** [U] the skin of an orange, lemon, or LIME, used to add flavour to food: *grated lemon zest*

zestful **adj** full of energy and enthusiasm: *Her zestful performance made the film very successful.* ◦ *They symbolized zestful youth.* • **zestfully** /-i/ **adv**

zhuzh (also **zhoozh, zhoosh**) /ʒʊʒ/ **verb** [T] informal to make something more interesting or attractive: *The stylist said he would zhuzh **up** the outfit with some jewellery.*

zigzag /ˈzɪg.zæg/ **noun; verb**

▸**noun** [C] **LINE** ▷ a line or pattern that looks like a Z or a row of Zs joined together: *a zigzag path/road/coastline* ◦ *a fabric with a zigzag pattern* ◦ *The children ran in zigzags around the playground until they were exhausted.*

zigzag

▸verb [I] (-gg-) **FORM SHAPE** ▷ (also **zig and zag**) to make a movement or shape like a zigzag: *The road zigzags along a rocky coastline.*

zilch /zɪltʃ/ **noun** [U] informal nothing; none; no: *'How many points did you score?' 'Zilch.'*

zillion /ˈzɪl.jən/, /-i.ən/ **noun** [C] informal an extremely large, but not a stated, number: *I've told you **a** zillion times/zillions **of** times not to do that.*

Zimmer frame /ˈzɪm.əˌfreɪm/ (US) /-ɚ-/ **noun** [C] UK trademark (UK also ˈ**walking** ˌ**frame**, US **walker**) a metal frame with four legs which you place in front of you and lean on to help you move forward if you have difficulty in walking, for example when old

zinc /zɪŋk/ **noun** [U] (symbol **Zn**) a chemical element that is a bluish-white metal, used in making other metals or for covering other metals to protect them

zine /ziːn/ **noun** [C] informal a small magazine that is produced cheaply by one person or a small group of people, and is about a subject they are interested in

zing /zɪŋ/ **noun** [U] informal a quality that makes something interesting or exciting; enthusiasm or energy: *We want to **put** more zing **into** our advertising.* ◦ *A bit of lemon juice will **add** zing **to** the sauce.*

zingy /ˈzɪŋ.i/ **adj** informal interesting and exciting

Zionism /ˈzaɪə.nɪ.zᵊm/ **noun** [U] a political movement that had as its original aim the CREATION of a country for Jewish people, and now works to help the development of Israel • **Zionist** /-nɪst/ **adj, noun** [C]

zip /zɪp/ **noun; verb**

▸**noun FASTENER** ▷ **1** B2 [C] UK (US **zipper**) a FASTENER consisting of two rows of metal or plastic teeth-like parts that are brought together by pulling a small sliding piece over them, used for closing openings in clothing, bags, etc.: *to do up/undo a zip* ◦ *I can't open my bag – the zip has **stuck**.* **SPEED** ▷ **2** [U] informal energy or speed: *The new engine has given the car a lot more zip.* **NOTHING** ▷ **3** [U] US informal nothing: *I know zip about computers.* ◦ *The Dolphins are leading the Giants fourteen to zip (= by fourteen points to nothing).*

▸**verb** (-pp-) **FASTEN** ▷ **1** [I or T] to fasten something with a zip: *This bag's too full, I can't zip it shut.* ◦ *This dress zips (**up**) at the back.* ◦ *Zip your coat **up**, it's cold outside.* **GO QUICKLY** ▷ **2** [I or T, usually + adv/prep] informal to move or go somewhere very quickly: *I'm just going to zip **along** to the shops – I won't be long.* ◦ *We were about to cross the road when a car suddenly zipped past.* → See also **zap** **COMPUTING** ▷ **3** [T] to COMPRESS (= reduce the size of) a computer file so that it uses less space, and can be more easily sent or stored: *If you're desperate for disk space you could zip the file (**up**) and stick it on a floppy.*

IDIOM **zip it** slang a rude and angry way of telling someone to stop talking: *Just zip it, mate, I'm fed up with you.*

PHRASAL VERB **zip sth/sb up** to fasten a piece of clothing by using its zip, or to help someone close the zip on a piece of clothing they are wearing: *Could you zip me up, please?* ◦ *Zip up your jacket, it's cold out there.*

ˈ**zip** ˌ**code** **noun** [C] in the US, a series of numbers that forms part of an address, used to help organize post so that it can be DELIVERED more quickly → See also **postcode**

ˈ**Zip** ˌ**drive** **noun** [C] trademark a part of a computer used for copying large documents onto special disks

ˈ**zip** ˌ**file** **noun** [C] a computer file that has been COMPRESSED (= reduced in size) so that it uses up less space

zipper /ˈzɪp.əʳ/ (US) /-ɚ/ **noun** [C] B2 US for **zip**

zippy /ˈzɪp.i/ **adj** informal approving energetic or fast: *a zippy car* ◦ *a zippy performance*

zit /zɪt/ **noun** [C] informal a temporary small spot on the skin

zither /ˈzɪð.əʳ/ (US) /-ɚ/ **noun** [C] a musical instrument shaped like a flat box, which has many strings that you pull at with your fingers or with a small piece of plastic

ˈ**Z-list** **adj** humorous used to describe people who are only slightly famous, or who are famous but not for doing anything special: *They got a few Z-list celebrities to turn up to the party.* → Compare **A-list**

zloty /ˈzlɒt.i/, /ˈzwɒt-/ (US) /ˈzlɑː.t̬i/ /ˈzwɑː.i/ **noun** [C] the standard unit of money used in Poland

zodiac /ˈzəʊ.di.æk/ (US) /ˈzoʊ-/ **noun** **1 the zodiac** [S] (in the study of the planets and their influence on life) an area of the sky through which the sun, moon, and most of the planets appear to move, divided into twelve equal parts, each with a name and symbol, and each connected with an exact time of year: *the signs of the zodiac* **2** [C usually singular] a circular drawing representing the zodiac • **zodiacal** /-ˈdaɪ.ə.kᵊl/ **adj**

zombie /ˈzɒm.bi/ (US) /ˈzɑːm-/ **noun** [C] **1** informal disapproving a person who has no energy, seems to act without thinking and does not notice what is happening around them: *He just sat in front of the TV all day like a zombie.* **2** a dead person who is believed, in some Caribbean religions, to have been brought back to life by magic

zonal /ˈzəʊ.nᵊl/ (US) /ˈzoʊ-/ **adj** specialized relating to or arranged in zones: *zonal boundaries/divisions* • **zonally** /ˈ-i/ **adv**

zone /zəʊn/ (US) /zoʊn/ **noun; verb**

▸**noun** [C] **1** B1 an area, especially one that is different from the areas around it because it has different characteristics or is used for different purposes: *an earthquake zone* ◦ *a nuclear-free zone* ◦ *He was charged with driving 75 mph in a 55 mph zone.* ◦ *This stretch of coast has been **designated** a **danger** zone.* ◦ *The UN Security Council has **established** a **no-fly** zone (= one into which aircraft are not permitted to fly).* **2** specialized one of the five parts the Earth is divided into according to temperature, marked by imaginary lines going around it from east to west: *temperate zones*

▸**verb** [T usually passive] specialized to give a special purpose to a particular area, such as an area in a town: *The former dockyard has been zoned **for** tourist use.*

zoning /ˈzəʊ.nɪŋ/ (US) /ˈzoʊ-/ **noun** [U] specialized the act of deciding, or the decision that has been taken about, what particular use an area should have: *zoning laws*

zonked /zɒŋkt/ (US) /zɑːŋkt/ **adj** [after verb] slang extremely tired: *We were really zonked (**out**) after our long journey.*

zoo /zuː/ **noun** [C] (plural **zoos**) (old-fashioned formal **zoo** ˌ**logical** ˈ**gardens**) A1 an area in which animals,

Z

especially wild animals, are kept so that people can go and look at them or study them

zookeeper /ˈzuːˌkiː.pəʳ/ (US) /ˈzuːˌkiː.pɚ/ **noun** [C] a person who works in a zoo, taking care of the animals

ˌzoological ˈgarden noun [C usually plural] old-fashioned formal for **zoo**

zoologist /zuːˈɒl.ə.dʒɪst/, /zəʊ-/ (US) /zoʊˈɑːlə-/ **noun** [C] a person who scientifically studies animals

zoology /zuːˈɒl.ə.dʒi/, /zəʊ-/ (US) /zoʊˈɑː.lə-/ **noun** [U] the scientific study of animals, especially their structure • **zoological** /ˌzuː.əˈlɒdʒ.ɪ.kəl/, /ˌzəʊ.ə-/ (US) /ˌzoʊ.əˈlɑː.dʒɪ-/ **adj** *zoological research/classification*

zoom /zuːm/ **verb; noun**

▸**verb** informal **1** [I + adv/prep] to move very quickly: *They got into the car and zoomed off.* ◦ *In the last few metres of the race, she suddenly zoomed ahead.* **2** [I] If prices or sales zoom, they increase suddenly and quickly: *House prices suddenly zoomed last year.*

PHRASAL VERBS **zoom in/out** to (cause a camera or computer to) make the image of something or someone appear much larger and nearer, or much smaller and further away: *At the beginning of the film, the camera zooms in to show two people sitting by the side of a river.* ◦ *Click on a photo of any student, and it zooms out to full-size.* ◦ *Television cameras zoomed in on the fans fighting in the stands.* • **zoom in on sth** to notice and give special attention to something: *Henry immediately zoomed in on the weakest part of my argument.*

▸**noun** [C] informal a **zoom lens**

ˈzoom ˌlens noun [C] a device in a camera, or that can be connected to a camera, that can make the thing being photographed appear nearer

zorbing /ˈzɔː.bɪŋ/ (US) /ˈzɔːr-/ **noun** [U] an activity in which someone rolls down a hill in a large transparent plastic ball

Zoroastrianism /ˌzɒr.əʊˈæs.tri.ə.nɪ.zᵊm/ (US) /ˌzɔːr.oʊˈ-/ **noun** [U] a religion which developed in ancient Iran, and is based on the idea that there is a continuous fight between a god who represents good and one who represents evil

zucchini /zʊˈkiː.ni/ (US) /zuː-/ **noun** [C] (plural **zucchini** or **zucchinis**) B2 US for **courgette**

Zulu /ˈzuː.luː/ **noun 1** [C] a member of a race of people who live in South Africa **2** [U] the language spoken by the Zulu people: *He speaks Zulu.* • **Zulu adj** *a Zulu chief*

Zumba /ˈzʊm.bə/ **noun** [U] trademark a type of exercise that uses Latin American music and dance movements

zygote /ˈzaɪ.gəʊt/ (US) /-goʊt/ **noun** [C] specialized the cell that is formed when a female REPRODUCTIVE cell and a male REPRODUCTIVE cell join

zzz /zː/ **exclamation** used in a picture or a piece of writing to represent the noise that people make when they are sleeping

Irregular verbs

This is a list of the English verbs that have an irregular past simple tense and/or an irregular past participle. If more than one form is listed, it may be because each form has a different meaning. Check in the dictionary for more information.

Infinitive	Past simple	Past participle
arise	arose	arisen
awake	awoke (US *also* awaked)	awoken
be	was/were	been
bear	bore	borne
beat	beat	beaten
beget	begot	begotten
become	became	become
befall	befell	befallen
begin	began	begun
behold	beheld	beheld
belie	belied	belied
bend	bent	bent
beseech	beseeched, besought	beseeched, besought
bestrew	bestrewed	bestrewn, bestrewed
bestride	bestrode	bestridden
bet	bet, betted	bet, betted
bid	bid, bade	bid, bidden
bind	bound	bound
bite	bit	bitten
bleed	bled	bled
blow	blew	blown
break	broke	broken
breed	bred	bred
bring	brought	brought
broadcast	broadcast (US *also* broadcasted)	broadcast (US *also* broadcasted)
build	built	built
burn	burnt, burned	burnt, burned
burst	burst	burst
bust	(UK) bust, (US) busted	(UK) bust, (US) busted
buy	bought	bought
cast	cast	cast
catch	caught	caught
choose	chose	chosen
cleave	cleaved (US *also* clove)	cleaved, cloven
cling	clung	clung
come	came	come
cost	cost, costed	cost, costed
creep	crept	crept
cut	cut	cut
deal	dealt	dealt
dig	dug	dug
dive	dived (US *also* dove)	dived
draw	drew	drawn
dream	dreamed, dreamt	dreamed, dreamt
drink	drank	drunk
drive	drove	driven
dwell	dwelt, dwelled	dwelt, dwelled

Infinitive	Past simple	Past participle
eat	ate	eaten
fall	fell	fallen
feed	fed	fed
feel	felt	felt
fight	fought	fought
find	found	found
flee	fled	fled
fling	flung	flung
fly	flew	flown
forbid	forbade, forbad	forbidden
forecast	forecasted, forecast	forecasted, forecast
foresee	foresaw	foreseen
forget	forgot	forgotten
forgive	forgave	forgiven
forgo	forwent	forgone
forsake	forsook	forsaken
forswear	forswore	forsworn
freeze	froze	frozen
gainsay	gainsaid	gainsaid
get	got	got (US *also* gotten)
gird	girded, girt	girded, girt
give	gave	given
go	went	gone
grind	ground	ground
grow	grew	grown
hang	hung, hanged	hung, hanged
have	had	had
hear	heard	heard
hew	hewed	hewed, hewn
hide	hid	hidden
hit	hit	hit
hold	held	held
hurt	hurt	hurt
input	inputted, input	inputted, input
interbreed	interbred	interbred
interweave	interwove	interwoven
keep	kept	kept
kneel	knelt, kneeled	knelt, kneeled
knit	knitted, knit	knitted (US *also* knit)
know	knew	known
lead	led	led
lean	leaned (UK *also* leant)	leaned (UK *also* leant)
leap	leapt, leaped	leapt, leaped
learn	learned (UK *also* learnt)	learned (UK *also* learnt)
leave	left	left
lend	lent	lent
let	let	let
lie	lay, lied	lain, lied
light	lit, lighted	lit, lighted
lip-read	lip-read	lip-read

Infinitive	Past simple	Past participle
lose	lost	lost
make	made	made
mean	meant	meant
meet	met	met
miscast	miscast	miscast
mishear	misheard	misheard
mislay	mislaid	mislaid
mislead	misled	misled
misspell	misspelled (UK *also* misspelt)	misspelled (UK *also* misspelt)
misspend	misspent	misspent
mistake	mistook	mistaken
misunderstand	misunderstood	misunderstood
mow	mowed	mown, mowed
offset	offset	offset
outbid	outbid	outbid, outbidden
outdo	outdid	outdone
outfight	outfought	outfought
outgrow	outgrew	outgrown
outrun	outran	outrun
outsell	outsold	outsold
outshine	outshone	outshone
overbid	overbid	overbid
overcome	overcame	overcome
overdo	overdid	overdone
overdraw	overdrew	overdrawn
overeat	overate	overeaten
overhang	overhung	overhung
overhear	overheard	overheard
overlay	overlaid	overlaid
overpay	overpaid	overpaid
override	overrode	overridden
overrun	overran	overrun
oversee	oversaw	overseen
overshoot	overshot	overshot
oversleep	overslept	overslept
overspend	overspent	overspent
overtake	overtook	overtaken
overthrow	overthrew	overthrown
overwrite	overwrote	overwritten
partake	partook	partaken
pay	paid	paid
plead	pleaded (US *also* pled)	pleaded (US *also* pled)
preset	preset	preset
prove	proved	proved, proven
put	put	put
quit	quit, quitted	quit, quitted
read /ri:d/	read /red/	read /red/
rebuild	rebuilt	rebuilt
recast	recast	recast
remake	remade	remade
rend	rent	rent
repay	repaid	repaid
rerun	reran	rerun
resit	resat	resat
rethink	rethought	rethought
rewrite	rewrote	rewritten
rid	rid	rid
ride	rode	ridden
ring	rang	rung
rise	rose	risen
run	ran	run

Infinitive	Past simple	Past participle
saw	sawed	sawn (US *also* sawed)
say	said	said
see	saw	seen
seek	sought	sought
sell	sold	sold
send	sent	sent
set	set	set
sew	sewed	sewn, sewed
shake	shook	shaken
shear	sheared	sheared, shorn
shed	shed	shed
shine	shone	shone
shit	shit, shat (UK *also* shitted)	shit, shat (UK *also* shitted)
shoe	shod (US *also* shoed)	shod (US *also* shoed)
shoot	shot	shot
show	showed	shown
shrink	shrank	shrunk
shut	shut	shut
sink	sank	sunk
sit	sat	sat
slay	slew, slayed	slain
sleep	slept	slept
slide	slid	slid
sling	slung	slung
slink	slunk	slunk
slit	slit	slit
smell	smelled (UK *also* smelt)	smelled (UK *also* smelt)
smite	smote	smitten
sneak	sneaked (US *also* snuck)	sneaked (US *also* snuck)
sow	sowed	sown, sowed
speak	spoke	spoken
speed	sped, speeded	sped, speeded
spell	spelled (UK *also* spelt)	spelled (UK *also* spelt)
spend	spent	spent
spill	spilled (UK *also* spilt)	spilled (UK *also* spilt)
spin	spun	spun
spit	spat (US *also* spit)	spat (US *also* spit)
split	split	split
spoil	spoiled, spoilt	spoiled, spoilt
spotlight	spotlighted, spotlit	spotlighted, spotlit
spring	sprang	sprung
stand	stood	stood
steal	stole	stolen
stick	stuck	stuck
sting	stung	stung
stink	stank (US *also* stunk)	stunk
strew	strewed	strewn, strewed
stride	strode	strode
strike	struck	struck (US *also* stricken)
string	strung	strung
strive	strove, strived	striven, strived
sublet	sublet	sublet
swear	swore	sworn
sweep	swept	swept
swell	swelled	swollen, swelled

Infinitive	Past simple	Past participle
swim	swam	swum
swing	swung	swung
take	took	taken
teach	taught	taught
tear	tore	torn
tell	told	told
think	thought	thought
thrive	thrived (US *also* throve)	thrived (US *also* thriven)
throw	threw	thrown
thrust	thrust	thrust
tread	trod	trodden (US *also* trod)
typecast	typecast	typecast
unbend	unbent	unbent
undercut	undercut	undercut
undergo	underwent	undergone
underlie	underlay	underlain
underpay	underpaid	underpaid
underwrite	underwrote	underwritten
undersell	undersold	undersold
understand	understood	understood
undertake	undertook	undertaken
undo	undid	undone
unwind	unwound	unwound
uphold	upheld	upheld
upset	upset	upset
wake	woke	woken
waylay	waylaid	waylaid
wear	wore	worn
weave	wove, weaved	woven, weaved
wed	wedded, wed	wedded, wed
weep	wept	wept
wet	wet, wetted	wet, wetted
win	won	won
wind	wound	wound
withdraw	withdrew	withdrawn
withhold	withheld	withheld
withstand	withstood	withstood
wreak	wrought, wreaked	wrought, wreaked
wring	wrung	wrung
write	wrote	written

Geographical names

This list shows the spellings and pronunciations of countries, regions, continents, territories, and oceans. Each name is followed by its related adjective. Most of the time you can use the adjective to refer to a person who comes from each place. For example, a person from Brazil is a **Brazilian**. However, in some cases a different word is used, which is shown after the adjective (for example, **Finn** is the word for a person from Finland). Sometimes the word shown ends in 'man'. This word can only be used to refer to a man; the word for a woman ends in 'woman' (for example **Frenchman**, **Frenchwoman**).

To talk about more than one person from a particular place, add 's', except for:

- **words ending** in 'ese' or 's', which remain the same (**Chinese**, **Swiss**);
- **words ending** in 'man' or 'woman', which change to 'men' and 'women' (**Irishman**, **Irishwoman** become **Irishmen**, **Irishwomen**).

This list is for reference only. Inclusion does not imply or suggest status as a sovereign nation.

Name	Adjective/Person
Afghanistan /æfˈgæn.ɪ.stæn/	Afghan /ˈæf.gæn/
Africa /ˈæf.rɪ.kə/	African /ˈæf.rɪ.kən/
Albania /ælˈbeɪ.ni.ə/	Albanian /ælˈbeɪ.ni.ən/
Algeria /ælˈdʒɪə.ri.ə/ (US) /-ˈdʒɪr.i-/	Algerian /ælˈdʒɪə.ri.ən/ (US) /-ˈdʒɪr.i-/
Andorra /ænˈdɔː.rə/ (US) /-ˈdɔːr.ə/	Andorran /ænˈdɔː.rən/ (US) /-ˈdɔːr.ən/
Angola /æŋˈgəʊ.lə/ (US) /-ˈgoʊ-/	Angolan /æŋˈgəʊ.lən/ (US) /-ˈgoʊ-/
Antarctica /ænˈtɑːk.tɪ.kə/ (US) /-ˈtɑːrk-/	Antarctic /ænˈtɑːk.tɪk/ (US) /-ˈtɑːrk-/
Antigua and Barbuda /ænˌtiː.gə.ᵊnd.bɑːˈbjuː.də/ (US) /-bɑːrˈbuː-/	Antiguan /ænˈtiː.gən/, Barbudan /bɑːˈbjuː.dən/ (US) /bɑːrˈbuː-/
the Arctic Ocean /ˌɑːk.tɪkˈəʊ.ʃᵊn/ (US) /ˌɑːrk.tɪkˈoʊ-/	Arctic /ˈɑːk.tɪk/ (US) /ˈɑːrk-/
Argentina /ˌɑː.dʒᵊnˈtiː.nə/ (US) /ˌɑːr-/	Argentine /ˈɑː.dʒᵊn.taɪn/ (US) /ˈɑːr-/, Argentinian /ˌɑː.dʒᵊnˈtɪn.i.ən/ (US) /ˌɑːr-/
Armenia /ɑːˈmiː.ni.ə/ (US) /ɑːr-/	Armenian /ɑːˈmiː.ni.ən/ (US) /ɑːr-/
Asia /ˈeɪ.ʒə/	Asian /ˈeɪ.ʒᵊn/
the Atlantic /ətˈlæn.tɪk/ (US) /-t̬ɪk/	Atlantic /ətˈlæn.tɪk/ (US) /-t̬ɪk/
Australasia /ˌɒs.trəˈleɪ.ʒə/ (US) /ˌɑː.strə-/	Australasian /ˌɒstrəˈleɪʒᵊn/ (US) /ˌɑː.strə-/
Australia /ɒsˈtreɪ.li.ə/ (US) /ɑːˈstreɪl.jə/	Australian /ɒsˈtreɪ.li.ən/ (US) /ɑːˈstreɪl.jən/
Austria /ˈɒs.tri.ə/ (US) /ˈɑː.stri-/	Austrian /ˈɒs.tri.ən/ (US) /ˈɑː.stri-/
Azerbaijan /ˌæz.ə.baɪˈdʒɑːn/ (US) /ˌɑː.z.ɚ-/	Azerbaijani /ˌæz.ə.baɪˈdʒɑː.ni/ (US) /ˌɑː.z.ɚ-/; *Person*: Azeri /əˈzeə.ri/ (US) /-ˈzer.i/
the Bahamas /bəˈhɑː.məz/	Bahamian /bəˈheɪ.mi.ən/
Bahrain /bɑːˈreɪn/	Bahraini /bɑːˈreɪ.ni/
the Balkans /ˈbɔːl.kənz/ (US) /ˈbɑːl-/	Balkan /ˈbɔːl.kən/ (US) /ˈbɑːl-/
Bangladesh /ˌbæŋ.gləˈdeʃ/	Bangladeshi /ˌbæŋ.gləˈdeʃ.i/
Barbados /bɑːˈbeɪ.dɒs/ (US) /bɑːrˈbeɪ.doʊs/	Barbadian /bɑːˈbeɪ.di.ən/ (US) /bɑːr-/
Belarus /ˌbel.əˈruːs/	Belorussian /ˌbeləˈrʌʃ.ᵊn/
Belgium /ˈbel.dʒəm/	Belgian /ˈbel.dʒən/
Belize /bəˈliːz/	Belizean /bəˈliː.zi.ən/
Benin /benˈiːn/	Beninese /ˌben.ɪˈniːz/
Bermuda /bəˈmjuː.də/ (US) /bɚː-/	Bermudan /bəˈmjuː.dən/ (US) /bɚ-/
Bhutan /buːˈtɑːn/	Bhutanese /ˌbuː.təˈniːz/
Bolivia /bəˈlɪv.i.ə/	Bolivian /bəˈlɪv.i.ən/
Bosnia-Herzegovina /ˌbɒz.ni.əˌhɜːt.səˈgɒv.ɪ.nə/ (US) /ˌbɑːz.ni.əˌhert.sə.goʊˈviː.nə/	Bosnian /ˈbɒz.ni.ən/ (US) /ˌbɑːz-/
Botswana /bɒtˈswɑː.nə/ (US) /bɑːt-/	Botswanan /bɒtˈswɑː.nən/ (US) /bɑːt-/; *Person*: Motswana /mɒtˈswɑː.nə/ (US) /mɑːt-/
Brazil /brəˈzɪl/	Brazilian /brəˈzɪl.i.ən/ (US) /-jən/
Britain /ˈbrɪt.ᵊn/	British /ˈbrɪt.ɪʃ/ (US) /ˈbrɪt̬.ɪʃ/; *Person*: Briton /ˈbrɪt.ᵊn/

Brunei /bruːˈnaɪ/	Bruneian /bruːˈnaɪ.ən/
Bulgaria /bʌlˈgeə.ri.ə/ (US) /-ˈger.i-/	Bulgarian /bʌlˈgeə.ri.ən/ (US) /-ˈger.i-/
Burkina Faso /bɜːˌkiː.nəˈfæseʊ/ (US) /bɚˌkiː.nəˈfɑː.soʊ/	Burkinabe /bɜːˈkiː.nəˌbeɪ/ (US) /bɜː-/
Burma /ˈbɜː.mə/ (US) /ˈbɝː-/	Burmese /bɜːˈmiːz/ (US) /bɝː-/
Burundi /bʊˈrʊn.di/	Burundian /bʊˈrʊn.di.ən/
Cambodia /ˌkæmˈbəʊ.di.ə/ (US) /-ˈboʊ-/	Cambodian /ˌkæmˈbəʊ.di.ən/ (US) /-ˈboʊ-/
Cameroon /ˌkæm.əˈruːn/	Cameroonian /ˌkæm.əˈruː.ni.ən/
Canada /ˈkæn.ə.də/	Canadian /kəˈneɪ.di.ən/
Cape Verde /ˌkeɪpˈvɜːd/ (US) /-ˈvɝːd/	Cape Verdean /ˌkeɪp ˈvɜː.di.ən/ (US) /-ˈvɝː-/
the Caribbean /ˌkær.ɪˈbiː.ən/ (US) /ˌker.ɪˈbiː-/	Caribbean /ˌkær.ɪˈbiː.ən/ (US) /ˌker.ɪˈbiː-/
the Cayman Islands /ˈkeɪ.mənˌaɪ.ləndz/	Cayman /keɪ.mən/; *Person*: Cayman Islander /ˈkeɪ.mənˌaɪ.lən.dəʳ/ (US) /-dɚ/
the Central African Republic /ˌsen.trəlˌæf.rɪ.kən.rɪˈpʌb.lɪk/	Central African /ˌsen.trəlˈæf.rɪ.kən/
Central America /ˌsentrəl.əˈmer.ɪ.kə/	Central American /ˌsentrəl.əˈmer.ɪ.kən/
Chad /tʃæd/	Chadian /ˈtʃæd.i.ən/
Chile /ˈtʃɪl.i/	Chilean /ˈtʃɪl.i.ən/
China /ˈtʃaɪ.nə/	Chinese /tʃaɪˈniːz/
Colombia /kəˈlɒm.bi.ə/	Colombian /kəˈlɒm.bi.ən/
Comoros /ˈkɒm.ə.rəʊz/ (US) /ˈkɑː.mə.roʊz/	Comoran /kəˈmɔː.rən/ (US) /ˈkɑː.mə-/
the Democratic Republic of the Congo /ˌdem.əˌkræt.ɪk.rɪˌpʌb.lɪk.əvˈkɒŋ.gəʊ/ (US) /-kræţ- -ˈkɑː.ŋ.goʊ/	Congolese /ˌkɒŋ.gəˈliːz/ (US) /kɑː.ŋ-/
the Republic of Congo /rɪˌpʌb.lɪk.əv.ðəˈkɒŋ.gəʊ/ (US) /-ˈkɑː.ŋ.goʊ/	Congolese /ˌkɒŋ.gəˈliːz/ (US) /ˌkɑː.ŋ.gəˈliːz/
Costa Rica /ˌkɒs.təˈriː.kə/ (US) /ˌkɑː.stə-/	Costa Rican /ˌkɒs.təˈriː.kən/ (US) /ˌkɑː.stə-/
Côte d'Ivoire /ˌkəʊt.diːˈvwɑːʳ/ (US) /ˌkoʊt.diːˈvwɑːr/	Ivorian /aɪˈvɔː.ri.ən/ (US) /-ˈvɔːr.i.ən/
Croatia /krəʊˈeɪ.ʃə/ (US) /kroʊ-/	Croatian /krəʊˈeɪ.ʃən/ (US) /kroʊ-/; *Person*: Croat /ˈkrəʊ.æt/ (US) /ˈkroʊ-/
Cuba /ˈkjuː.bə/	Cuban /ˈkjuː.bən/
Cyprus /ˈsaɪ.prəs/	Cypriot /ˈsɪp.ri.ət/
the Czech Republic /ˌtʃek.rɪˈpʌb.lɪk/	Czech /tʃek/
Denmark /ˈden.mɑːk/ (US) /-mɑːrk/	Danish /ˈdeɪ.nɪʃ/; *Person*: Dane /deɪn/
Djibouti /dʒɪˈbuː.ti/ (US) /-ţi/	Djiboutian /dʒɪˈbuː.ti.ən/ (US) /-ţi-/
Dominica /dəˈmɪn.ɪ.kə/ (US) /ˌdɑː.mɪˈniː-/	Dominican /dəˈmɪn.ɪ.kən/ (US) /ˌdɑː.mɪˈniː-/
the Dominican Republic /dəˌmɪn.ɪ.kən.rɪˈpʌb.lɪk/	Dominican /dəˈmɪn.ɪ.kən/
East Timor /ˌiːstˈtiː.mɔːʳ/ (US) /-mɔːr/	East Timorese /ˌiːstˌtiː.mɔːˈriːz/ (US) /-məˈiːz/
Ecuador /ˈek.wə.dɔːʳ/ (US) /-dɔːr/	Ecuadorian /ˌek.wəˈdɔː.ri.ən/ (US) /-ˈdɔːr.i.ən/
Egypt /ˈiː.dʒɪpt/	Egyptian /ɪˈdʒɪp.ʃən/
El Salvador /ˌelˈsæl.və.dɔːʳ/ (US) /-dɔːr/	Salvadorean /ˌsæl.vəˈdɔː.ri.ən/ (US) /-ˈdɔːr.i.ən/
England /ˈɪŋ.glənd/	English /ˈɪŋ.glɪʃ/; *Person*: Englishman /ˈɪŋ.glɪʃ.mən/
Equatorial Guinea /ˌek.wəˌtɔː.ri.əlˈgɪn.i/ (US) /-ˌtɔːr.i-/	Equatorial Guinean /ˌek.wəˌtɔː.ri.əlˈgɪn.i.ən/ (US) /-ˌtɔːr.i-/
Eritrea /ˌer.ɪˈtreɪ.ə/ (US) /-ˈtriː-/	Eritrean /ˌer.ɪˈtreɪ.ən/ (US) /-ˈtriː-/
Estonia /esˈtəʊ.ni.ə/ (US) /-ˈtoʊ-/	Estonian /esˈtəʊ.ni.ən/ (US) /-ˈtoʊ-/
Ethiopia /ˌiː.θiˈəʊ.pi.ə/ (US) /-ˈoʊ-/	Ethiopian /ˌiː.θiˈəʊ.pi.ən/ (US) /-ˈoʊ-/
Europe /ˈjʊə.rəp/ (US) /ˈjʊr.əp/	European /ˌjʊə.rəˈpiː.ən/ (US) /ˈjʊr.ə-/
Fiji /ˈfiː.dʒiː/	Fijian /fɪˈdʒiː.ən/
Finland /ˈfɪn.lənd/	Finnish /ˈfɪn.ɪʃ/; *Person*: Finn /fɪn/
France /frɑːns/ (US) /fræns/	French /frentʃ/; *Person*: Frenchman /ˈfrentʃ.mən/
Gabon /gæbˈɒn/ (US) /gæbˈoʊn/	Gabonese /ˌgæb.əˈniːz/
Gambia /ˈgæm.bi.ə/	Gambian /ˈgæm.bi.ən/
Georgia /ˈdʒɔː.dʒə/ (US) /ˈdʒɔːr-/	Georgian /ˈdʒɔː.dʒən/ (US) /ˈdʒɔːr-/
Germany /ˈdʒɜː.mə.ni/ (US) /ˈdʒɝː-/	German /ˈdʒɜː.mən/ (US) /ˈdʒɝː-/
Ghana /ˈgɑː.nə/	Ghanaian /gɑːˈneɪ.ən/
Gibraltar /dʒɪˈbrɔːl.təʳ/ (US) /-ˈbrɑːl.tɚ/	Gibraltarian /ˌdʒɪb.rɔːlˈteə.ri.ən/ (US) /-rɑːlˈter.i-/
Great Britain /ˌgreɪtˈbrɪt.ən/	British /ˈbrɪt.ɪʃ/ (US) /ˈbrɪţ.ɪʃ/; *Person*: Briton /ˈbrɪt.ən/
Greece /griːs/	Greek /griːk/
Greenland /ˈgriːn.lənd/	Greenland /ˈgriːn.lənd/; *Person*: Greenlander /ˈgriːn.lən.dəʳ/ (US) /-dɚ/

Grenada /grəˈneɪ.də/	Grenadian /grəˈneɪ.di.ən/
Guatemala /ˌgwɑː.təˈmɑː.lə/ (US) /-t̬ə-/	Guatemalan /ˌgwɑː.təˈmɑː.lən/ (US) /-t̬ə-/
Guinea /ˈgɪn.i/	Guinean /ˈgɪn.i.ən/
Guinea-Bissau /ˌgɪn.i.bɪˈsaʊ/	Guinea-Bissauan /ˌgɪn.i.bɪˈsaʊ.ən/
Guyana /gaɪˈæn.ə/	Guyanese /ˌgaɪ.əˈniːz/
Haiti /ˈheɪ.ti/ (US) /-t̬i/	Haitian /ˈheɪ.ʃᵊn/
Honduras /hɒnˈdjʊə.rəs/ (US) /hɑːnˈdʊr.əs/	Honduran /hɒnˈdjʊə.rən/ (US) /hɑːnˈdʊr.ən/
Hong Kong /ˌhɒŋˈkɒŋ/ (US) /ˈhɑːŋˌkɑːŋ/	Hong Kong /ˌhɒŋˈkɒŋ/ (US) /ˈhɑːŋˌkɑːŋ/
Hungary /ˈhʌŋ.gᵊr.i/	Hungarian /hʌŋˈgeə.ri.ən/ (US) /-ˈger.i-/
Iceland /ˈaɪs.lənd/	Icelandic /aɪsˈlæn.dɪk/; ***Person***: Icelander /ˈaɪs.lən.dəʳ/ (US) /-dɚ/
India /ˈɪn.di.ə/	Indian /ˈɪn.di.ən/
the Indian Ocean /ˌɪn.di.ənˈəʊ.ʃᵊn/ (US) /-ˈoʊ-/	
Indonesia /ˌɪn.dəˈniː.ʒə/	Indonesian /ˌɪndəˈniː.ʒᵊn/
Iran /ɪˈrɑːn/, /-ˈræn/	Iranian /ɪˈreɪ.ni.ən/
Iraq /ɪˈrɑːk/, /-ˈræk/	Iraqi /ɪˈrɑː.ki/, /-ˈræk.i/
Ireland /ˈaɪə.lənd/ (US) /ˈaɪr-/	Irish /ˈaɪə.rɪʃ/ (US) /ˈaɪ-/; ***Person***: Irishman /ˈaɪə.rɪʃ.mən/ (US) /ˈaɪ-/
Israel /ˈɪz.reɪl/ (US) /-ri.əl/	Israeli /ɪzˈreɪ.li/
Italy /ˈɪt.ᵊl.i/ (US) /ˈɪt̬-/	Italian /ɪˈtæl.i.ən/ (US) /-jən/
Jamaica /dʒəˈmeɪ.kə/	Jamaican /dʒəˈmeɪ.kən/
Japan /dʒəˈpæn/	Japanese /ˌdʒæp.ᵊnˈiːz/
Jordan /ˈdʒɔː.dᵊn/ (US) /ˈdʒɔːr-/	Jordanian /dʒɔːˈdeɪ.ni.ən/ (US) /dʒɔːr-/
Kazakhstan /ˌkæz.ækˈstɑːn/ (US) /ˈkɑː.zɪk.stɑːn/	Kazakh /ˈkæz.æk/ (US) /ˈkɑː.zɑːk/
Kenya /ˈken.jə/	Kenyan /ˈken.jən/
Kiribati /ˌkɪr.əˈbæs/	Kiribati /ˌkɪr.əˈbæs/
North Korea /ˌnɔːθ.kəˈriː.ə/ (US) /ˌnɔːrθ-/	North Korean /ˌnɔːθ.kəˈriː.ən/ (US) /ˌnɔːrθ-/
South Korea /ˌsaʊθ.kəˈriː.ə/	South Korean /ˌsaʊθ.kəˈriː.ən/
Kuwait /kuːˈweɪt/	Kuwaiti /kuːˈweɪ.ti/ (US) /-t̬i/
Kyrgyzstan /ˌkɜː.gɪˈstɑːn/ (US) /kɝː-/	Kyrgyz /ˈkɜː.gɪz/ (US) /kɝː-/
Laos /laʊs/	Laotian /ˈlaʊ.ʃᵊn/
Latvia /ˈlæt.vi.ə/	Latvian /ˈlæt.vi.ən/
Lebanon /ˈleb.ə.nən/ (US) /-nɑːn/	Lebanese /ˌlebəˈniːz/
Lesotho /ləˈsuː.tuː/	Basotho /bəˈsuː.tuː/; ***Person***: Mosotho /məˈsuː.tuː/
Liberia /laɪˈbɪə.ri.ə/ (US) /-ˈbɪr.i-/	Liberian /laɪˈbɪə.ri.ən/ (US) /-ˈbɪr.i-/
Libya /ˈlɪb.i.ə/	Libyan /ˈlɪb.i.ən/
Liechtenstein /ˈlɪk.tᵊn.staɪn/	Liechtenstein /ˈlɪk.tᵊn.staɪn/; ***Person***: Liechtensteiner /ˈlɪk.tᵊn.staɪ.nəʳ/ (US) /-nɚ/
Lithuania /ˌlɪθ.juˈeɪ.ni.ə/ (US) /-u-/	Lithuanian /ˌlɪθ.juˈeɪ.ni.ən/ (US) /-u-/
Luxembourg /ˈlʌk.sᵊm.bɜːg/ (US) /-bɝːg/	Luxembourg /ˈlʌk.sᵊm.bɜːg/ (US) /-bɝːg/; ***Person***: Luxembourger /ˈlʌk.sᵊm.bɜː.gəʳ/ (US) /-bɝː.gɚ/
Macedonia /ˌmæs.əˈdəʊ.ni.ə/ (US) /-ˈdoʊ-/	Macedonian /ˌmæs.əˈdəʊ.ni.ən/ (US) /-ˈdoʊ-/
Madagascar /ˌmæd.əˈgæs.kəʳ/ (US) /-kɚ/	Malagasy /ˌmæl.əˈgæs.i/
Malawi /məˈlɑː.wi/	Malawian /məˈlɑː.wi.ən/
Malaysia /məˈleɪ.zi.ə/ (US) /-ʒə/	Malaysian /məˈleɪ.zi.ən/ (US) /-ʒən/
the Maldives /ˈmɔːl.diːvz/	Maldivian /mɔːlˈdɪv.i.ən/
Mali /ˈmɑː.li/	Malian /ˈmɑː.li.ən/
Malta /ˈmɔːl.tə/	Maltese /mɔːlˈtiːz/
the Marshall Islands /ˈmɑː.ʃᵊlˌaɪ.ləndz/ (US) /ˈmɑːr-/	Marshallese /ˌmɑː.ʃᵊlˈiːz/ (US) /ˌmɑːr-/; ***Person***: Marshall Islander /ˌmɑː.ʃᵊlˈaɪ.lən.dəʳ/ (US) /ˌmɑːr.ʃᵊlˈaɪ.lən.dɚ/
Mauritania /ˌmɒr.ɪˈteɪ.ni.ə/ (US) /ˌmɔːr-/	Mauritanian /ˌmɒr.ɪˈteɪ.ni.ən/ (US) /ˌmɔːr-/
Mauritius /məˈrɪʃ.əs/ (US) /mɔːˈrɪʃ.i.əs/	Mauritian /məˈrɪʃᵊn/ (US) /mɔːˈrɪʃ.i.ən/
Melanesia /ˌmel.əˈniː.zi.ə/ (US) /-ʒə/	Melanesian /ˌmel.əˈniː.zi.ən/ (US) /-ʒᵊn/
Mexico /ˈmek.sɪ.kəʊ/ (US) /-koʊ/	Mexican /ˈmek.sɪ.kᵊn/
Micronesia /ˌmaɪ.krəˈniː.zi.ə/ (US) /-kroʊˈniː.ʒə/	Micronesian /ˌmaɪ.krəˈniː.zi.ən/ (US) /-kroʊˈniː.ʒən/
Moldova /mɒlˈdəʊ.və/ (US) /mɑːlˈdoʊ-/	Moldovan /mɒlˈdəʊ.vən/ (US) /mɑːlˈdoʊ-/
Monaco /ˈmɒn.ə.kəʊ/ (US) /-koʊ/	Monégasque /ˌmɒn.ɪˈgæsk/ (US) /ˌmɑː.neɪ-/
Mongolia /mɒŋˈgəʊ.li.ə/ (US) /mɑːŋˈgoʊ-/	Mongolian /mɒŋˈgəʊ.li.ən/ (US) /mɑːŋˈgoʊ-/
Montenegro /ˌmɒn.tɪˈniː.grəʊ/ (US) /mɑːn.təˈniː.groʊ/	Montenegrin /ˌmɒn.tɪˈniː.grən/ (US) /mɑːn.təˈniː.grən/

Montserrat /ˌmɒnt.səˈræt/ (US) /ˌmɑːnt-/	Montserratian /ˌmɒnt.səˈræt.i.ən/ (US) /ˌmɑːnt-/
Morocco /məˈrɒk.əʊ/ (US) /-ˈrɑː.koʊ/	Moroccan /məˈrɒk.ən/ (US) /-ˈrɑː.kən/
Mozambique /ˌməʊ.zæmˈbiːk/ (US) /ˌmoʊ-/	Mozambican /ˌməʊ.zæmˈbiː.kən/ (US) /ˌmoʊ-/
Myanmar /ˈmjæn.mɑːʳ/ (US) /ˈmjɑːn.mɑːr/	Burmese /bɜːˈmiːz/ (US) /bɝː-/
Namibia /nəˈmɪb.i.ə/	Namibian /nəˈmɪb.i.ən/
Nauru /nɑːˈuː.ruː/	Nauruan /nɑː.uːˈruː.ən/
Nepal /nəˈpɔːl/, /-ˈpɑːl/	Nepalese /ˌnep.əlˈiːz/ (US) /-əˈliːz/
the Netherlands /ˈneð.ə.ləndz/ (US) /-ɚ-/	Dutch /dʌtʃ/; *Person*: Dutchman /ˈdʌtʃ.mən/
New Zealand /ˌnjuːˈziː.lənd/ (US) /ˌnuː-/	New Zealand /ˌnjuːˈziːlənd/ (US) /ˌnuː-/; *Person*: New Zealander /ˌnjuːˈziːlən.dəʳ/ (US) /ˌnuːˈziː.lən.dɚ/
Nicaragua /ˌnɪk.əʳˈæg.ju.ə/ (US) /-ˈrɑː.g.wə/	Nicaraguan /ˌnɪk.əʳˈæg.ju.ən/ (US) /-əˈrɑː.g.wən/
Niger /niːˈʒeəʳ/ (US) /ˈnaɪ.dʒɚ/	Nigerien /niːˈʒeə.ri.ən/ (US) /naɪˈdʒer.i-/
Nigeria /naɪˈdʒɪə.ri.ə/ (US) /-ˈdʒɪr.i-/	Nigerian /naɪˈdʒɪə.ri.ən/ (US) /-ˈdʒɪr.i-/
North America /ˌnɔːθ.əˈmer.ɪ.kə/ (US) /ˌnɔːrθ-/	North American /ˌnɔːθ.əˈmer.ɪ.kən/ (US) /ˌnɔːrθ-/
Northern Ireland /ˌnɔː.ðənˈaɪə.lənd/ (US) /ˌnɔːr.ðɚnˈaɪr-/	Northern Irish /ˌnɔː.ðənˈaɪə.rɪʃ/ (US) /ˌnɔːr.ðɚnˈaɪ-/; *Person*: Northern Irishman /ˌnɔː.ðənˈaɪə.rɪʃ.mən/ (US) /ˌnɔːr.ðɚnˈaɪ-/
Norway /ˈnɔː.weɪ/ (US) /ˈnɔːr-/	Norwegian /nɔːˈwiː.dʒən/ (US) /nɔːr-/
Oman /əʊˈmɑːn/ (US) /oʊ-/	Omani /əʊˈmɑː.ni/ (US) /oʊ-/
the Pacific /pəˈsɪf.ɪk/	Pacific /pəˈsɪf.ɪk/
Pakistan /ˌpɑː.kɪˈstɑːn/ (US) /ˈpæk.ɪ.stæn/	Pakistani /ˌpɑː.kɪˈstɑː.ni/ (US) /ˌpæk.ɪˈstæni/
Palau /pəˈlaʊ/	Palauan /pəˈlaʊ.ən/
Palestine /ˈpæl.ə.staɪn/	Palestinian /ˌpæl.əˈstɪn.i.ən/
Panama /ˈpæn.ə.mɑː/	Panamanian /ˌpæn.əˈmeɪ.ni.ən/
Papua New Guinea /ˌpæp.u.ə.njuːˈgɪn.i/ (US) /-nuː-/	Papua New Guinean /ˌpæp.u.ə.njuːˈgɪn.i.ən/ (US) /-nuː-/
Paraguay /ˈpær.ə.gwaɪ/	Paraguayan /ˌpær.əˈgwaɪ.ən/
Peru /pəˈruː/	Peruvian /pəˈruː.vi.ən/
the Philippines /ˈfɪl.ɪ.piːnz/	Philippine /ˈfɪl.ɪ.piːn/; *Person*: Filipino /ˌfɪl.ɪˈpiː.nəʊ/ (US) /-noʊ/, Filipina /ˌfɪl.ɪˈpiː.nə/
Poland /ˈpəʊ.lənd/ (US) /ˈpoʊ-/	Polish /ˈpəʊ.lɪʃ/ (US) /ˈpoʊ-/; *Person*: Pole /pəʊl/ (US) /poʊl/
Polynesia /ˌpɒl.ɪˈniː.ʒə/ (US) /ˌpɑː.lə-/	Polynesian /ˌpɒl.ɪˈniː.ʒən/ (US) /ˌpɑː.lə-/
Portugal /ˈpɔː.tʃə.gəl/ (US) /ˈpɔːr-/	Portuguese /ˌpɔː.tʃəˈgiːz/ (US) /ˌpɔːr-/
Puerto Rico /ˌpwɜː.təˈriː.kəʊ/ (US) /ˌpwer.t̬əˈriː.koʊ/	Puerto Rican /ˌpwɜː.t̬əˈriː.kən/ (US) /ˌpwer.t̬ə-/
Qatar /ˈkʌt.ɑːʳ/ (US) /ˈkɑː.tɑːr/	Qatari /kʌtˈɑː.ri/ (US) /ˈkɑː.tɑː.ri/
Romania /rʊˈmeɪ.ni.ə/ (US) /roʊ-/	Romanian /rʊˈmeɪ.ni.ən/ (US) /roʊ-/
Russia /ˈrʌʃ.ə/	Russian /ˈrʌʃ.ən/
Rwanda /ruˈæn.də/ (US) /-ˈɑːn-/	Rwandan /ruˈæn.dən/ (US) /-ˈɑːn-/
Samoa /səˈməʊ.ə/ (US) /-ˈmoʊ-/	Samoan /səˈməʊ.ən/ (US) /-ˈmoʊ-/
San Marino /ˌsæn.məˈriː.nəʊ/ (US) /-noʊ/	Sanmarinese /ˌsæn.mær.ɪˈniːz/
São Tomé and Príncipe /ˌsaʊ.təˌmeɪ.əndˈprɪn.sɪ.pəɪ/	São Tomean /ˌsaʊ.təˈmeɪ.ən/
Saudi Arabia /ˌsaʊ.di.əˈreɪ.bi.ə/	Saudi /ˈsaʊ.di/
Scandinavia /ˌskæn.dɪˈneɪ.vi.ə/	Scandinavian /ˌskæn.dɪˈneɪ.vi.ən/
Scotland /ˈskɒt.lənd/ (US) /ˈskɑːt-/	Scottish /ˈskɒt.ɪʃ/ (US) /ˈskɑː.t̬ɪʃ/; *Person*: Scot /skɒt/ (US) /skɑːt/, Scotsman /ˈskɒts.mən/ (US) /skɑːts-/
Senegal /ˌsen.ɪˈgɔːl/	Senegalese /ˌsen.ɪ.gəˈliːz/
Serbia /ˈsɜː.bi.ə/ (US) /ˈsɝː-/	Serbian /ˈsɜː.bi.ən/ (US) /ˈsɝː-/; *Person*: Serb /sɜːb/ (US) /sɝːb/
the Seychelles /seɪˈʃelz/	Seychelles /seɪˈʃelz/; *Person*: Seychellois /seɪ.ʃelˈwɑː/
Sierra Leone /siˌer.ə.liˈəʊn/ (US) /-ˈoʊn/	Sierra Leonean /siˌer.ə.liˈəʊ.ni.ən/ (US) /-ˈoʊ-/
Singapore /ˌsɪŋ.əˈpɔːʳ/ (US) /ˈsɪŋ.ə.pɔːr/	Singaporean /ˌsɪŋ.əˈpɔː.ri.ən/ (US) /-ˈpɔːr.i.ən/
Slovakia /sləˈvæk.i.ə/ (US) /sloʊ-/	Slovak /ˈsləʊ.væk/ (US) /ˈsloʊ-/
Slovenia /sləˈviː.ni.ə/ (US) /sloʊ-/	Slovenian /sləˈviːniən/ (US) /sloʊ-/; *Person*: Slovene /ˈsləʊ.viːn/ (US) /ˈsloʊ-/
the Solomon Islands /ˈsɒl.ə.mənˌaɪ.ləndz/ (US) /ˈsɑːl.ə-/	Solomon Islander /ˈsɒl.ə.mənˌaɪ.lən.dəʳ/ (US) /ˈsɑː.lə.mənˌaɪ.lən.dɚ/
Somalia /səˈmɑː.li.ə/	Somali /səˈmɑː.li/

South Africa /ˌsaʊθˈæf.rɪ.kə/	South African /ˌsaʊθˈæf.rɪ.kən/
South America /ˌsaʊθ.əˈmer.ɪ.kə/	South American /ˌsaʊθ.əˈmer.ɪ.kən/
the Southern Ocean /ˌsʌð.ənˈəʊ.ʃᵊn/ US /ˌsʌð.ɚnˈoʊ-/	
South Sudan /ˌsaʊθ.suːˈdɑːn/ US /-ˈdæn/	South Sudanese /ˌsaʊθˌsuː.dᵊnˈiːz/
Spain /speɪn/	Spanish /ˈspæn.ɪʃ/; *Person*: Spaniard /ˈspæn.jəd/ US /-jɚd/
Sri Lanka /ˌsriːˈlæŋ.kə/	Sri Lankan /ˌsriːˈlæŋ.kən/
St Kitts and Nevis /sᵊntˌkɪts.ᵊndˈniː.vɪs/ US /seɪnt-/	Kittsian /ˈkɪt.si.ən/, Nevisian /niːˈvɪs.i.ən/
St Lucia /sᵊntˈluː.ʃə/ US /seɪnt-/	St Lucian /sᵊntˈluː.ʃᵊn/ US /seɪnt-/
St Vincent and the Grenadines /sᵊntˌvɪn.sᵊnt.ᵊnd.ðəˌgren.əˈdiːnz/ US /seɪnt-/	Vincentian /vɪnˈsɪn.ti.ən/
Sudan /suːˈdɑːn/ US /-ˈdæn/	Sudanese /ˌsuː.dᵊnˈiːz/
Suriname /ˌsʊə.rɪˈnæm/ US /ˌsʊr.ɪˈnɑːm/	Surinamese /ˌsʊə.rɪ.næmˈiːz/ US /ˌsʊr.ɪ.nɑːmˈiːz/
Swaziland /ˈswɑː.zi.lænd/	Swazi /ˈswɑː.zi/
Sweden /ˈswiː.dᵊn/	Swedish /ˈswiː.dɪʃ/; *Person*: Swede /swiːd/
Switzerland /ˈswɪt.sə.lənd/ US /-sɚ-/	Swiss /swɪs/
Syria /ˈsɪr.i.ə/	Syrian /ˈsɪr.i.ən/
Taiwan /ˌtaɪˈwɑːn/	Taiwanese /ˌtaɪ.wəˈniːz/
Tajikistan /tɑːˌdʒiːkɪˈstɑːn/ US /tɑːˈdʒɪk.ɪˌstæn/	Tajik /tɑːˈdʒiːk/
Tanzania /ˌtæn.zəˈniː.ə/	Tanzanian /ˌtæn.zəˈniː.ən/
Thailand /ˈtaɪ.lænd/	Thai /taɪ/
Tibet /tɪˈbet/	Tibetan /tɪˈbetᵊn/
Togo /ˈtəʊ.gəʊ/ US /ˈtoʊ.goʊ/	Togolese /ˌtəʊ.gəˈliːz/ US /ˌtoʊ-/
Tonga /ˈtɒŋ.ə/ US /ˈtɑːŋ-/	Tongan /ˈtɒŋ.ᵊn/ US /ˈtɑːŋ-/
Trinidad and Tobago /ˌtrɪn.ɪ.dæd.ᵊnd.təˈbeɪ.gəʊ/ US /-goʊ/	Trinidadian /ˌtrɪn.ɪˈdæd.i.ən/
Tunisia /tjuːˈnɪz.i.ə/ US /tuːˈniː.ʒə/	Tunisian /tjuːˈnɪz.i.ən/ US /tuːˈniː.ʒən/
Turkey /ˈtɜː.ki/ US /ˈtɝː-/	Turkish /ˈtɜː.kɪʃ/ US /ˈtɝː-/; *Person*: Turk /tɜːk/ US /tɝːk/
Turkmenistan /tɜːkˌmen.ɪˈstɑːn/ US /tɝːkˈmen.ɪ.stæn/	Turkmen /ˈtɜːk.men/ US /ˈtɝːk-/
Tuvalu /tuːˈvɑː.luː/	Tuvaluan /ˌtuː.vɑːˈluː.ən/
Uganda /juːˈgæn.də/	Ugandan /juːˈgæn.dən/
Ukraine /juːˈkreɪn/	Ukrainian /juːˈkreɪ.ni.ən/
the United Arab Emirates /juːˌnaɪ.tɪdˌær.əbˈem.ɪ.rəts/ US /-t̬ɪdˌer.əbˈem.ɚ.əts/	Emirati /emɪˈrɑː.ti/ US /em.əˈrɑː.t̬i/
the United Kingdom /juːˌnaɪ.tɪdˈkɪŋ.dəm/ US /-t̬ɪd-/	British /ˈbrɪt.ɪʃ/ US /ˈbrɪt̬.ɪʃ/; *Person*: Briton /ˈbrɪt.ᵊn/
the United States of America /juːˌnaɪ.tɪdˌsteɪts.əv.əˈmer.ɪ.kə/ US /-t̬ɪd-/	American /əˈmer.ɪ.kən/
Uruguay /ˈjʊə.rə.gwaɪ/ US /ˈjʊr.ə-/	Uruguayan /ˌjʊə.rəˈgwaɪ.ən/ US /ˌjʊr.ə-/
Uzbekistan /ʊzˌbek.ɪˈstɑːn/ US /-ˈstæn/	Uzbek /ˈʊz.bek/
Vanuatu /ˌvæn.uˈɑː.tuː/	Vanuatuan /ˌvæn.u.ɑːˈtuː.ən/
Vatican City /ˌvæt.ɪ.kənˈsɪt.i/ US /ˌvæt̬.ɪ.kənˈsɪt̬-/	Vatican /ˈvæt.ɪ.kən/ US /ˈvæt̬-/
Venezuela /ˌven.ɪˈzweɪ.lə/	Venezuelan /ˌven.ɪˈzweɪ.lən/
Vietnam /ˌvjetˈnæm/	Vietnamese /ˌvjet.nəˈmiːz/
Wales /weɪlz/	Welsh /welʃ/; *Person*: Welshman /ˈwelʃ.mən/
Western Sahara /ˌwes.tən.səˈhɑː.rə/ US /-tɚn.səˈher.ə/	Sahrawian /sɑːˈrɑː.wi.ən/
Yemen /ˈjem.ən/	Yemeni /ˈjem.ə.ni/
Zambia /ˈzæm.bi.ə/	Zambian /ˈzæm.bi.ən/
Zimbabwe /zɪmˈbɑːb.weɪ/	Zimbabwean /zɪmˈbɑːb.wi.ən/

Pronunciation

How we show pronunciation in the dictionary

All the pronunciations use the International Phonetic Alphabet (IPA). All of the symbols are shown in a list on the next page and at the foot of every page in the dictionary. If there are two possible pronunciations, we show both of them separated by a comma.

1. British and American pronunciation

If we only show one pronunciation for a word then it is valid for British and American English. If there is a difference in pronunciation, we show the British first, followed by the American after the symbol ⓤⓢ. We only show the part of the American English pronunciation that is different, like this:

storehouse /ˈstɔː.haʊs/ ⓤⓢ /ˈstɔːr-/

2. Stress

Stress patterns show you which parts of a word you should emphasize when you say the word. We show stress marks in front of the part of the word that should be emphasized.

/ˈ/ primary stress symbol

This symbol shows you the part of a word that you should emphasize most. For example, in **picture** /ˈpɪk.tʃəʳ/ you should emphasize the first part, and in **deny** /dɪˈnaɪ/ you should emphasize the second part.

/ˌ/ secondary stress symbol

This symbol shows you the part of the word that has the second most important emphasis. This is important if you are pronouncing a long word with three or more syllables.

For example, in the word **submarine** /ˌsʌb.məˈriːn/ the main emphasis is on the last part of the word but you should also put a slight emphasis on the first part of the word.

There are some compound words (e.g. **barn dance**, **full-time**) where we do not show a separate pronunciation, because the pronunciations of both of the parts of the word are shown somewhere else in the dictionary. You still need to know about the stress in the phrase. We show this by using stress markers above and below the words in the phrase, like this:

ˈbarn ˌdance, **ˌfull-ˈtime**

3. Syllables

In all of the pronunciations there are marks to show you how many syllables the word has. The syllable mark is like a full stop, and comes before each new syllable. For example, in the word standard /ˈstæn.dəd/ the syllable mark shows you that the word has two syllables. If we show stress marks in a word, these also show when a new syllables starts, so in a word like banana /bəˈnɑː.nə/ the stress mark and syllable mark show that there are three syllables in the word.

4. Strong forms and weak forms

Some very common words (e.g. **and**, **them**, **of**) have strong and weak pronunciations that are different. The weak forms are more common. For example, the word **them** is shown like this in the dictionary:

them strong /ðem/, weak /ðəm/

In a sentence such as 'I saw them leave', the weak form /ðəm/ would be used. If you need to emphasize **them**, you need to use the strong form. For example, in the sentence 'They said they saw me but I didn't see them' the strong form /ðem/ would be used.

Pronunciation Symbols

Vowel sounds

Short vowels		Long vowels		Diphthongs and triphthongs	
ɪ	as in pit	iː	as in see	eɪ	as in day
e	as in wet	ɑː	as in father	aɪ	as in my
æ	as in cat	ɔː	as in saw	ɔɪ	as in boy
ʌ	as in run	uː	as in too	əʊ	as in so (UK)
ʊ	as in put	ɜː	as in bird (UK)	oʊ	as in so (US)
ɒ	as in hot (UK)	ɝː	as in bird (US)	aʊ	as in how
ə	as in ago			ɪə	as in near (UK)
ɚ	as in mother (US)			eə	as in hair (UK)
i	as in happy			ʊə	as in pure (UK)
u	as in situation			aɪə	as in fire
				aʊə	as in sour

Consonant sounds

b	as in bee	m	as in map	z	as in zip
d	as in do	n	as in nose	dʒ	as in job
f	as in fat	p	as in pen	ŋ	as in hang
g	as in go	r	as in red	ð	as in that
h	as in hat	s	as in sun	θ	as in thin
j	as in yet	t	as in ten	ʃ	as in ship
k	as in key	ţ	as in later (US)	ʒ	as in measure
l	as in led	v	as in van	tʃ	as in chin
l̩	as in middle	w	as in wet	x	as in loch

Other symbols used in the pronunciations

/ᵊ/ shows that the /ə/ as in **sudden** /ˈsʌd.ᵊn/ can be pronounced or not. When it is not pronounced, the **n** is pronounced as a syllable.

/ʳ/ shows that the /r/ as in **teacher** /ˈtiː.tʃəʳ/ is pronounced in British English when followed by a vowel sound, but not when followed by a consonant sound. In American English it is always pronounced.

/ˈ/ primary stress (the part of the word you emphasize most), as in **above** /əˈbʌv/

/ˌ/ secondary stress (the part of the word you emphasize as well as but not quite as much as the primary stress), as in **backyard** /ˌbækˈjɑːd/

/˜/ used when a vowel is pronounced with a nasal sound, usually because the word has come from French

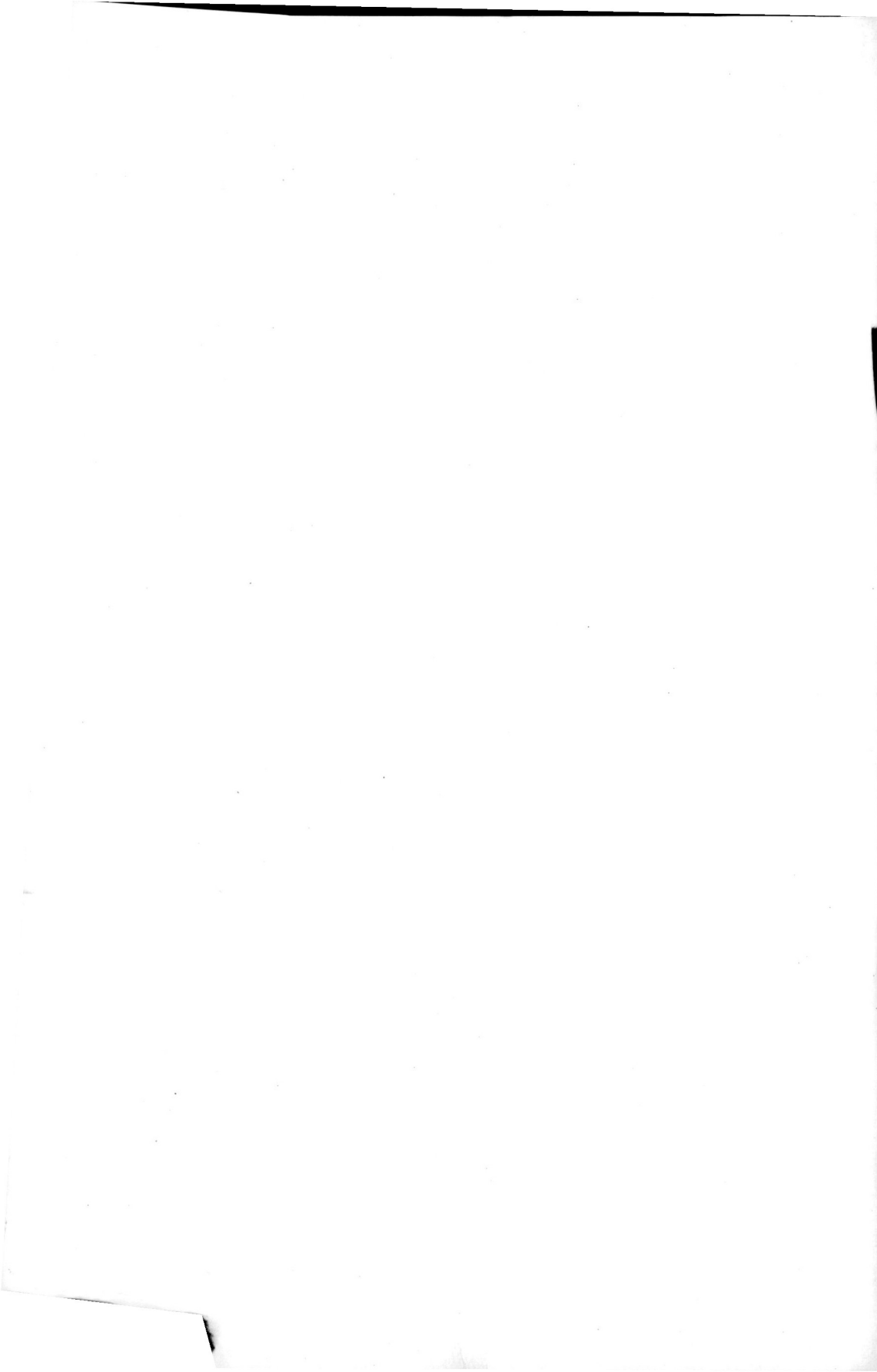